PROFILES OF AMERICA

Volume 3

Second Edition

PROFILES OF AMERICA

Volume 3: Central Region

A UNIVERSAL REFERENCE BOOK

Grey House Publishing

PUBLISHER: Leslie Mackenzie
EDITOR: David Garoogian
EDITORIAL DIRECTOR: Laura Mars-Proietti
EDITORIAL ASSISTANT: Pamela Michaud

PRODUCTION MANAGER: Karen Stevens
PRODUCTION ASSISTANTS: Michael Marturana, Robert Stevens

MARKETING DIRECTOR: Jessica Moody

A Universal Reference Book
Grey House Publishing, Inc.
185 Millerton Road
Millerton, NY 12546
518.789.8700
FAX 518.789.0545
www.greyhouse.com
e-mail: books @greyhouse.com

First edition published in 1995
Second edition published in 2003

Printed in the USA

4-Volume Set ISBN 1-891482-80-7
Volume 1 ISBN 1-59237-013-6
Volume 2 ISBN 1-59237-014-4
Volume 3 ISBN 1-59237-015-2
Volume 4 ISBN 1-59237-016-0

Table of Contents

VOLUME 1: SOUTHERN REGION

VOLUME 2: WESTERN REGION

VOLUME 3: CENTRAL REGION

VOLUME 4: EASTERN REGION

Introduction

This is the second edition of *Profiles of America – Facts, Figures & Statistics for Every Populated Place in the United States.* Originally published in 1995 by Toucan Valley Publications, this award-winning title is now published by Universal Reference Publications, an imprint of Grey House Publishing. These four volumes are a unique compilation of information on more than 42,000 places in the United States, from bustling urban centers to hard-to-find hamlets.

"Best Reference Source of the Year"
■ Library Journal

Profiles of America provides the most comprehensive portrait ever published of the populated places in the United States. These four volumes go beyond Census statistics, beyond metro area coverage, beyond the 100 best places to live. Drawn from official census information, other government statistics and original research (see the Explanation of Data following this Introduction) it pulls together statistical and descriptive information on every populated place in the country. Major fields of information include Geography, Population, Weather, Economy, Industry, Health, Housing, Education, Religion, and Transportation.

The extensive Explanation of Data on the following pages examines, in some detail, each data field in the individual profiles, and provides the source(s) for all elements therein. A review of this section, which we highly recommend before utilizing this work, will show that data is derived as follows: 38% from the 2000 Census and 16% from other Census Bureau data; 24% from government agencies other than the Census Bureau; 22% from non-government sources.

Profiles of America is arranged in four regional volumes: Volume 1: Southern; Volume 2: Western; Volume 3: Central; Volume 4: Eastern. Each volume is organized alphabetically – first by state, then by county, then by place. This edition has over 1,000 more places and nearly 20 more information fields than the previous edition.

Arrangement by State
Each state begins with a state map that defines counties, metropolitan statistical areas (MSA) and major cities. Following the map is an alphabetical index of both counties and communities, with a reference to the county, and the page number of the individual profile. The main body of the state text is arranged alphabetically by county; within each county, places are also arranged alphabetically.

County Profiles
There are 3,141 county profiles. Every county profile starts with a brief Geographical description of the county's location and, in most cases, a Weather Chart – weather statistics from that county's weather stations. Information sectors that follow are Population, Religion, Economy, Income, Taxes, Education,

Housing, Health, Election Results, National and State Parks, and Additional Contact Information -- phone numbers of county offices, plus individual Chambers of Commerce for individual cities. Each county profile is followed by profiles of its communities.

Community Profiles
There are 39,141 community profiles. These are identified as city, town, village, borough, postal area, unincorporated postal area, and CDP (census designated place). Each community profile starts, like the county profiles, with a brief Geographical description. Following this, in many cases, is a brief historical note about the community. This field offers information on its founders, name, economical and industrial origins, famous residents, battles and buildings, and more. Fields that follow are Population, Vital Statistics, Economy, Income, Taxes, Education (School Districts with enrollment figures and phone numbers), Housing, Hospitals, Safety, Newspapers, Airports and Transportation.

New Features
New to both the County and Community profiles in this edition are hard-to-find statistics on **Religion**. You will find the *top religious denominations* (up to five) of each community. Also new is detailed data on **Ancestry** – including the *top ethnic groups* (up to five) of each community. In addition, the following fields, where available, are new to this edition: **Age; Percent foreign born; Martial status; Minority & women business ownership rates; Commuting information; Travel time to work; Retail sales per capita; Median household income; City taxes per capita; Poverty rate; Bankruptcy rate; Homeownership rate; Cancer mortality rate; Air quality**.

More Indexing
Profiles of America has two kinds of indexes. **Individual State Indexes** are located in the front of each state chapter, facing the state map. These indexes are arranged alphabetically, and list every populated place in the state, the type of place (city, town, postal area, etc.), the county it belongs to, and the page on which to find its detailed profile.

A **Master Index** for this new edition includes, in alphabetical order, a complete list of all 42,282 populated places in America. You will see at a glance, for example, how many *Sedgwicks* there are in America, what type of place they are, in what state and county they exist, and what volume in *Profiles of America* to find their profiles on. Especially valuable when you are sure of a place, but not of its state or county, this **Master Index** is located at the back of Volume 4.

Grey House Publishing is pleased to offer this major reference work – the only work of its kind, published every 10 years. We welcome your comments.

Laura Mars
Editorial Director

Explanation of Data

PLACES COVERED

All 3,141 counties and county-equivalents. County-equivalents include census areas and boroughs in Alaska, parishes in Louisiana, the independent cities of Baltimore (MD), Carson City (NV), St. Louis (MO), 41 independent cities in Virginia, and the District of Columbia.

All 19,436 incorporated municipalities. Depending on the state, municipalities are incorporated as either cities, towns, villages, or boroughs. A few municipalities have a form of government combined with another entity (e.g. county) and are listed as "special cities."

All 5,381 census designated places (CDP). The U.S. Bureau of the Census defines a CDP as "a statistical entity, defined for each decennial census according to Census Bureau guidelines, comprising a densely settled concentration of population that is not within an incorporated place, but is locally identified by a name. CDPs are delineated cooperatively by state and local officials and the Census Bureau, following Census Bureau guidelines. Beginning with Census 2000 there are no size limits."

All 8,333 minor civil divisions (called towns, townships, districts, gores, locations, and plantations) for the states where the Census Bureau has determined that they serve as general-purpose governments. Those states are Connecticut, Maine, Massachusetts, Michigan, Minnesota, New Hampshire, New Jersey, New York, Pennsylvania, Rhode Island, Vermont, and Wisconsin. In some states incorporated municipalities are part of minor civil divisions and in some states they are independent of them.

Over 5,991 unincorporated communities. The communities included have both their own zip code and statistics for their ZIP Code Tabulation Area (ZCTA) available from the Census Bureau. They are referred to as "postal areas." A ZCTA is a statistical entity developed by the Census Bureau to approximate the delivery area for a US Postal Service 5-digit or 3-digit ZIP Code in the US and Puerto Rico. A ZCTA is an aggregation of census blocks that have the same predominant ZIP Code associated with the mailing addresses in the Census Bureau's Master Address File. Thus, the Postal Service's delivery areas have been adjusted to encompass whole census blocks so that the Census Bureau can tabulate census data for the ZCTAs. ZCTAs do not include all ZIP Codes used for mail delivery and therefore do not precisely depict the area within which mail deliveries associated with that ZIP Code occur. Additionally, some areas that are known by a unique name, although they are part of a larger incorporated place, are also included as "postal areas."

Notes

- *Profiles of America* uses the term "community" to refer to all places except counties. The term "county" is used to refer to counties and county-equivalents. All places are defined as of the 2000 Census.
- Several states have incorporated municipalities and minor civil divisions in the same county with the same name. Those communities are given separate entries (e.g. South Haven, Michigan, in Van Buren County will be listed under both the city and township of South Haven).
- When a county and city are coextensive (occupying the same geographic area and sharing the same government), they are given a single entry.
- The city of New York (composed of five coextensive counties/boroughs) has a unique format. Statistical information for the individual counties/boroughs is listed under each county as well as each borough (located within the New York City entry). Non-statistical information (e.g. hospitals, newspapers, etc.) is shown in the borough entry only. The five counties/boroughs are: Bronx County and Borough, Kings County and Brooklyn Borough, New York County and Manhattan Borough, Queens County and Borough, and Richmond County and Staten Island Borough.
- Some information (e.g. unemployment rates) is available for both counties and individual communities. Other information is available for just counties (e.g. election results), or just individual communities (e.g. local newspapers). Refer to the "Data Explanation and Sources" section for a complete listing.
- Some statistical information is available only for larger communities. In addition, the larger places are more apt to have services such as newspapers, airports, school districts, etc.
- For the most complete information on any community, you should also check the entry for the county in which the community is located. In addition, more information and services will be listed under the larger places in the county.
- For a more in-depth discussion of geographic areas, please refer to the Census Bureau's Geographic Areas Reference Manual at http://www.census.gov/geo/www/garm.html.

DATA EXPLANATION AND SOURCES

CENSUS 2000

The parts of the data which are from the 2000 Decennial Census are from the following sources: *U.S. Bureau of the Census, Census of Population and Housing, 2000: Summary Files 1 and 3.* Summary File 3 (SF 3) consists of 813 detailed tables of Census 2000 social, economic and housing characteristics compiled from a sample of approximately 19 million housing units (about 1 in 6 households) that received the Census 2000 long-form questionnaire. Summary File 1 (SF 1) contains 286 tables focusing on age, sex, households, families, and housing units. This file presents 100-percent population and housing figures for the total population, for 63 race categories, and for many other race and Hispanic or Latino categories.

Comparing SF 3 Estimates with Corresponding Values in SF 1

As in earlier censuses, the responses from the sample of households reporting on long forms must be weighted to reflect the entire population. Specifically, each responding household represents, on average, six or seven other households who reported using short forms.

One consequence of the weighting procedures is that each estimate based on the long form responses has an associated confidence interval. These confidence intervals are wider (as a percentage of the estimate) for geographic areas with smaller populations and for characteristics that occur less frequently in the area being examined (such as the proportion of people in poverty in a middle-income neighborhood).

In order to release as much useful information as possible, statisticians must balance a number of factors. In particular, for Census 2000, the Bureau of the Census created weighting areas —geographic areas from which about two hundred or more long forms were completed— which are large enough to produce good quality estimates. If smaller weighting areas had been used, the confidence intervals around the estimates would have been significantly wider, rendering many estimates less useful due to their lower reliability.

The disadvantage of using weighting areas this large is that, for smaller geographic areas within them, the estimates of characteristics that are also reported on the short form will not match the counts reported in SF 1. Examples of these characteristics are the total number of people, the number of people reporting specific racial categories, and the number of housing units. The official values for items reported on the short form come from SF 1 and SF 2.

The differences between the long form estimates in SF 3 and values in SF 1 are particularly noticeable for the smallest places, tracts, and block groups. The long form estimates of total population and total housing units in SF 3 will, however, match the SF 1 counts for larger geographic areas such as counties and states, and will be essentially the same for medium and large cities.

SF 1 gives exact numbers even for very small groups and areas, whereas SF 3 gives estimates for small groups and areas such as tracts and small places that are less exact. The goal of SF 3 is to identify large differences among areas or large changes over time. Estimates for small areas and small population groups often do exhibit large changes from one census to the next, so having the capability to measure them is worthwhile.

INFORMATION FOR COMMUNITIES

PHYSICAL CHARACTERISTICS

Place Type: Lists the type of place (city, town, village, borough, special city, CDP, township, plantation, gore, district, grant, location, reservation, or postal area). *Source: U.S. Bureau of the Census, Census of Population and Housing, 2000: Summary File 1 and U.S. Postal Service, City State File.*

Land and Water Area: Land and water area in square miles. *Source: U.S. Bureau of the Census, Census of Population and Housing, 2000: Summary File 1*

Latitude and Longitude: Latitude and longitude in degrees. *Source: U.S. Bureau of the Census, Census of Population and Housing, 2000: Summary File 1*

Elevation: Elevation in feet. *Source: U.S. Geological Survey, Geographic Names Information System (GNIS)*

HISTORY

History: Historical information. *Source: Columbia University Press, The Columbia Gazetteer of North America; Original research.*

POPULATION

Population: 100% count of population. *Source: U.S. Bureau of the Census, Census of Population and Housing, 2000: Summary File 1.*

Population by Race: Includes the U.S. Bureau of the Census categories of White only; Black only; Asian only; American Indian and Alaska Native only; Hispanic of any race; Two or more races. The percentages may not total 100% because of the Census category of "Other."

The data on race, which was asked of all people, were derived from answers to long-form questionnaire Item 6, and short-form questionnaire Item 8. The concept of race, as used by the Census Bureau, reflects self-identification by people according to the race or races with which they most closely identify. These categories are socio-political constructs and should not be interpreted as being scientific or anthropological in nature. Furthermore, the race categories include both racial and national-origin groups.

- **White.** A person having origins in any of the original peoples of Europe, the Middle East, or North Africa. It includes people who indicate their race as "White" or report entries such as Irish, German, Italian, Lebanese, Near Easterner, Arab, or Polish.
- **Black or African American.** A person having origins in any of the Black racial groups of Africa. It includes people who indicate their race as "Black, African American, or Negro," or provide written entries such as African American, Afro-American, Kenyan, Nigerian, or Haitian.
- **American Indian or Alaska Native.** A person having origins in any of the original peoples of North and South America (including Central America) and who maintain tribal affiliation or community attachment.
- **Asian.** A person having origins in any of the original peoples of the Far East, Southeast Asia, or the Indian subcontinent including, for example, Cambodia, China, India, Japan, Korea, Malaysia, Pakistan, the Philippine Islands, Thailand, and Vietnam. It includes "Asian Indian," "Chinese," "Filipino," "Korean," "Japanese," "Vietnamese," and "Other Asian."
- **Hispanic.** The data on the Hispanic or Latino population, which was asked of all people, were derived from answers to long-form questionnaire Item 5, and short-form questionnaire Item 7. The terms "Spanish," "Hispanic origin," and "Latino" are used interchangeably. Some respondents identify with all three terms, while others may identify with only one of these three specific terms. Hispanics or Latinos who identify with the terms "Spanish," "Hispanic," or "Latino" are those who classify themselves in one of the specific Hispanic or Latino categories listed on the questionnaire — "Mexican," "Puerto Rican," or "Cuban" — as well as those who indicate that they are "other Spanish, Hispanic, or Latino." People who do not identify with one of the specific origins listed on the questionnaire but indicate that they are "other Spanish, Hispanic, or Latino" are those whose origins are from Spain, the Spanish-speaking countries of Central or South America, the Dominican Republic, or people identifying themselves generally as Spanish, Spanish-American, Hispanic, Hispano, Latino, and so on. All write-in responses to the "other Spanish/Hispanic/Latino" category were coded. Origin can be viewed as the heritage, nationality group, lineage, or country of birth of the person or the person's parents or ancestors before their arrival in the United States. People who identify their origin as Spanish, Hispanic, or Latino may be of any race.
- Two or more races. People may have chosen to provide two or more races either by checking two or more race response check boxes, by providing multiple write-in responses, or by some combination of check boxes and write-in responses. The race response categories shown on the questionnaire are collapsed into the five minimum races identified by the Office of Management and Budget (OMB), and the Census Bureau "Some other race" category. For data product purposes, "Two or more races" refers to combinations of two or more of the following race categories: White; Black or African American; American Indian and Alaska Native; Asian; Native Hawaiian and Other Pacific Islander; Some other race. There are 57 possible combinations involving the race categories shown above. Thus, according to this approach, a response of "White" and "Asian" was tallied as two or more races, while a response of "Japanese" and "Chinese" was not because "Japanese" and "Chinese' are both Asian responses.

Population Density: 100% count of population divided by the land area in square miles. *Source: U.S. Bureau of the Census, Census of Population and Housing, 2000: Summary File 1.*

Age: Percentage of population under 18 years of age and percentage of population over 64 years of age. *Source: U.S. Bureau of the Census, Census of Population and Housing, 2000: Summary File 3.*

The data on age, which was asked of all people, were derived from answers to the long-form questionnaire Item 4 and short-form questionnaire Item 6. The age classification is based on the age of the person in complete years as of April 1, 2000. The age of the person usually was derived from their date of birth information. Their reported age was used only when date of birth information was unavailable.

Marital Status: Percentage of population never married, now married, widowed, or divorced. *Source: U.S. Bureau of the Census, Census of Population and Housing, 2000: Summary File 3.*

The data on marital status were derived from answers to long-form questionnaire Item 7, "What is this person's marital status," which was asked of a sample of the population. The marital status classification refers to the status at the time of enumeration. Data on marital status are tabulated only for the population 15 years old and over. Each person was asked whether they were "Now married," "Widowed," "Divorced," or "Never married." Couples who live together (for example, people in common-law marriages) were able to report the marital status they considered to be the most appropriate.

- **Never married.** Never married includes all people who have never been married, including people whose only marriage(s) was annulled.
- **Now married.** All people whose current marriage has not ended by widowhood or divorce. This category includes people defined as "separated."
- **Widowed.** This category includes widows and widowers who have not remarried.
- **Divorced.** This category includes people who are legally divorced and who have not remarried.

Foreign Born: Percentage of population who were not U.S. citizens at birth. Foreign-born people are those who indicated they were either a U.S. citizen by naturalization or they were not a citizen of the United States. *Source: U.S. Bureau of the Census, Census of Population and Housing, 2000: Summary File 3.*

The data on place of birth were derived from answers to long-form questionnaire Item 12 which was asked of a sample of the population. Respondents were asked to report the U.S. state, Puerto Rico, U.S. Island Area, or foreign country where they were born. People not reporting a place of birth were assigned the state or country of birth of another family member or their residence 5 years earlier, or were imputed the response of another person with similar characteristics. People born outside the United States were asked to report their place of birth according to current international boundaries. Since numerous changes in boundaries of foreign countries have occurred in the last century, some people may have reported their place of birth in terms of boundaries that existed at the time of their birth or emigration, or in accordance with their own national preference.

Ancestry: Largest ancestry groups reported (up to five). Includes multiple ancestries. *Source: U.S. Bureau of the Census, Census of Population and Housing, 2000: Summary File 3.*

The data on ancestry were derived from answers to long-form questionnaire Item 10, which was asked of a sample of the population. The data represent self-classification by people according to the ancestry group or groups with which they most closely identify. Ancestry refers to a person's ethnic origin or descent, "roots," heritage, or the place of birth of the person, the person's parents, or their ancestors before their arrival in the United States. Some ethnic identities, such as Egyptian or Polish, can be traced to geographic areas outside the United States, while other ethnicities such as Pennsylvania German or Cajun evolved in the United States.

The ancestry question allowed respondents to report one or more ancestry groups, although only the first two were coded. If a response was in terms of a dual ancestry, for example, "Irish English," the person was assigned two codes, in this case one for Irish and another for English. However, in certain cases, multiple responses such as "French Canadian," "Greek Cypriote," and "Scotch Irish" were assigned a single code reflecting their status as unique groups. If a person reported one of these unique groups in addition to another group, for example, "Scotch Irish English," resulting in three terms, that person received one code for the unique group (Scotch-Irish) and another one for the remaining group (English). If a person reported "English Irish French," only English and Irish were coded. Certain combinations of ancestries where the ancestry group is a part of another, such as "German-Bavarian," were coded as a single ancestry using the more specific group (Bavarian). Also, responses such as "Polish-American" or "Italian-American" were coded and tabulated as a single entry (Polish or Italian).

The Census Bureau accepted "American" as a unique ethnicity if it was given alone, with an ambiguous response, or with state names. If the respondent listed any other ethnic identity such as "Italian-American," generally the "American" portion of the response was not coded. However, distinct groups such as "American Indian," "Mexican American," and "African American" were coded and identified separately because they represented groups who considered themselves different from those who reported as "Indian," "Mexican," or "African," respectively.

The data is based on the total number of ancestries reported and coded. Thus, the sum of the counts in this type of presentation is not the total population but the total of all responses.

VITAL STATISTICS

Vital Statistics: Birth rate per 10,000 population. *Source: U.S. Department of Heath and Human Services, Vital Statistics of the United States, Volume I Natality, 1998*

ECONOMY

Unemployment Rate: Includes all civilians age 16 or over who were unemployed and looking for work as of November 2002. *Source: U.S. Department of Labor, Bureau of Labor Statistics, Local Area Unemployment Statistics (http://www.bls.gov/lau/home.htm).*

Total Labor Force: Includes all civilians age 16 or over who were either employed, or unemployed and looking for work as of November 2002. *Source: U.S. Department of Labor, Bureau of Labor Statistics, Local Area Unemployment Statistics (http://www.bls.gov/lau/home.htm).*

Single-Family Building Permits Issued: Building permits issued for new single-family housing units in 2000 and 2001. *Source: U.S. Census Bureau, Manufacturing and Construction Division (MCD) http://www.census.gov/const/www/permitsindex.html*

Multi-Family Building Permits Issued: Building permits issued for new multi-family housing units in 2000 and 2001. *Source: U.S. Census Bureau, Manufacturing and Construction Division (MCD) http://www.census.gov/const/www/permitsindex.html*

Statistics on housing units authorized by building permits include housing units issued in local permit-issuing jurisdictions by a building or zoning permit. Not all areas of the country require a building or zoning permit. The statistics only represent those areas that do require a permit. Current surveys indicate that construction is undertaken for all but a very small percentage of housing units authorized by building permits. A major portion typically get under way during the month of permit issuance and most of the remainder begin within the three following months. Because of this lag, the housing unit authorization statistics do not represent the number of units actually put into construction for the period shown, and should therefore not be directly interpreted as "housing starts."

Statistics are based upon reports submitted by local building permit officials in response to a mail survey. They are obtained using Form C-404 const/www/c404.pdf, "Report of New Privately-Owned Residential Building or Zoning Permits Issued." When a report is not received, missing data are either (1) obtained from the Survey of Use of Permits (SUP) which is used to collect information on housing starts, or (2) imputed based on the assumption that the ratio of current month authorizations to those of a year ago should be the same for reporting and nonreporting places.

Employment by Occupation: Percentage of the employed civilian population 16 years and over in management, professional, service, sales, farming, construction, and production occupations. *Source: U.S. Bureau of the Census, Census of Population and Housing, 2000: Summary File 3.*

- **Management** includes management, business, and financial operations occupations:
  - Management occupations, except farmers and farm managers
  - Farmers and farm managers
  - Business and financial operations occupations:
    - Business operations specialists
    - Financial specialists
- **Professional** includes professional and related occupations:
  - Computer and mathematical occupations
  - Architecture and engineering occupations:
    - Architects, surveyors, cartographers, and engineers
    - Drafters, engineering, and mapping technicians
  - Life, physical, and social science occupations
  - Community and social services occupations
  - Legal occupations
  - Education, training, and library occupations
  - Arts, design, entertainment, sports, and media occupations

Healthcare practitioners and technical occupations:
Health diagnosing and treating practitioners and technical occupations
Health technologists and technicians

- **Service** occupations include:
  Healthcare support occupations
  Protective service occupations:
    Fire fighting, prevention, and law enforcement workers, including supervisors
    Other protective service workers, including supervisors
  Food preparation and serving related occupations
  Building and grounds cleaning and maintenance occupations
  Personal care and service occupations

- **Sales** and office occupations include:
  Sales and related occupations
  Office and administrative support occupations

- **Farming,** fishing, and forestry occupations

- **Construction,** extraction, and maintenance occupations include:
  Construction and extraction occupations:
    Supervisors, construction and extraction workers
    Construction trades workers
    Extraction workers
  Installation, maintenance, and repair occupations

- **Production,** transportation, and material moving occupations include:
  Production occupations
  Transportation and material moving occupations:
    Supervisors, transportation and material moving workers
    Aircraft and traffic control occupations
    Motor vehicle operators
    Rail, water and other transportation occupations
    Material moving workers

INCOME

Per capita income: Per capita income is the mean income computed for every man, woman, and child in a particular group. It is derived by dividing the total income of a particular group by the total population in that group. Per capita income is rounded to the nearest whole dollar. *Source: U.S. Bureau of the Census, Census of Population and Housing, 2000: Summary File 3.*

The data on income in 1999 were derived from answers to long-form questionnaire Items 31 and 32, which were asked of a sample of the population 15 years old and over. "Total income" is the sum of the amounts reported separately for wage or salary income; net self-employment income; interest, dividends, or net rental or royalty income or income from estates and trusts; social security or railroad retirement income; Supplemental Security Income (SSI); public assistance or welfare payments; retirement, survivor, or disability pensions; and all other income.

Receipts from the following sources are not included as income: capital gains, money received from the sale of property (unless the recipient was engaged in the business of selling such property); the value of income "in kind" from food stamps, public housing subsidies, medical care, employer contributions for individuals, etc.; withdrawal of bank deposits; money borrowed; tax refunds; exchange of money between relatives living in the same household; and gifts and lump-sum inheritances, insurance payments, and other types of lump-sum receipts.

The eight types of income reported in the census are defined as follows:

Wage or salary income. Wage or salary income includes total money earnings received for work performed as an employee during the calendar year 1999. It includes wages, salary, armed forces pay, commissions, tips, piece-rate payments, and cash bonuses earned before deductions were made for taxes, bonds, pensions, union dues, etc.

Self-employment income. Self-employment income includes both farm and nonfarm self-employment income. Nonfarm self-employment income includes net money income (gross receipts minus expenses) from one's own business, professional enterprise, or partnership. Gross receipts include the value of all goods sold and services rendered. Expenses include costs of goods purchased, rent, heat, light, power, depreciation charges, wages and salaries paid, business taxes (not personal income taxes), etc. Farm self-employment income includes net money income (gross receipts minus operating expenses) from the operation of a farm by a person on his or her own account, as an owner, renter, or sharecropper. Gross receipts include the value of all products sold, government farm programs, money received from the rental of farm equipment to others, and incidental receipts from the sale of wood, sand, gravel, etc. Operating expenses include cost of feed, fertilizer, seed, and other farming supplies, cash wages paid to farmhands, depreciation charges, cash rent, interest on farm mortgages, farm building repairs, farm taxes (not state and federal personal income taxes), etc. The value of fuel, food, or other farm products used for family living is not included as part of net income.

Interest, dividends, or net rental income. Interest, dividends, or net rental income includes interest on savings or bonds, dividends from stockholdings or membership in associations, net income from rental of property to others and receipts from boarders or lodgers, net royalties, and periodic payments from an estate or trust fund.

Social Security income. Social security income includes social security pensions and survivors benefits, permanent disability insurance payments made by the Social Security Administration prior to deductions for medical insurance, and railroad retirement insurance checks from the U.S. government. Medicare reimbursements are not included.

Supplemental Security Income (SSI). Supplemental Security Income (SSI) is a nationwide U.S. assistance program administered by the Social Security Administration that guarantees a minimum level of income for needy aged, blind, or disabled individuals. The census questionnaire for Puerto Rico asked about the receipt of SSI; however, SSI is not a federally administered program in Puerto Rico. Therefore, it is probably not being interpreted by most respondents as the same as SSI in the United States. The only way a resident of Puerto Rico could have appropriately reported SSI would have been if they lived in the United States at any time during calendar year 1999 and received SSI.

Public assistance income. Public assistance income includes general assistance and Temporary Assistance to Needy Families (TANF). Separate payments received for hospital or other medical care (vendor payments) are excluded. This does not include Supplemental Security Income (SSI).

Retirement income. Retirement income includes: (1) retirement pensions and survivor benefits from a former employer; labor union; or federal, state, or local government; and the U.S. military; (2) income from workers' compensation; disability income from companies or unions; federal, state, or local government; and the U.S. military; (3) periodic receipts from annuities and insurance; and (4) regular income from IRA and KEOGH plans. This does not include social security income.

All other income. All other income includes unemployment compensation, Veterans' Administration (VA) payments, alimony and child support, contributions received periodically from people not living in the household, military family allotments, and other kinds of periodic income other than earnings.

Median Household Income: Includes the income of the householder and all other individuals 15 years old and over in the household, whether they are related to the householder or not. The median divides the income distribution into two equal parts: one-half of the cases falling below the median income and one-half above the median. For households, the median income is based on the distribution of the total number of households including those with no income. Median income for households is computed on the basis of a standard distribution and is rounded to the nearest whole dollar. *Source: U.S. Bureau of the Census, Census of Population and Housing, 2000: Summary File 3.*

Poverty Rate: Percentage of population with income in 1999 below the poverty level. Based on individuals for whom poverty status is determined. Poverty status was determined for all people except institutionalized people, people in military group quarters, people in college dormitories, and unrelated individuals under 15 years old. *Source: U.S. Bureau of the Census, Census of Population and Housing, 2000: Summary File 3.*

The poverty status of families and unrelated individuals in 1999 was determined using 48 thresholds (income cutoffs) arranged in a two dimensional matrix. The matrix consists of family size (from 1 person to 9 or more people) cross-classified by presence and number of family members under 18 years old (from no children present to 8 or more children present). Unrelated individuals and 2-person families were further differentiated by the age of the reference person (RP) (under 65 years old and 65 years old and over).

To determine a person's poverty status, one compares the person's total family income with the poverty threshold appropriate for that person's family size and composition. If the total income of that person's family is less than the threshold appropriate for that family, then the person is considered poor, together with every member of his or her family. If a person is not living with anyone related by birth, marriage, or adoption, then the person's own income is compared with his or her poverty threshold.

TAXES

Total City Taxes Per Capita: Total city taxes collected divided by the population of the city. *Source: U.S. Bureau of the Census, State and Local Government Finances, 2000 (http://www.census.gov/govs/www/estimate.html).*

Taxes include:

- Property Taxes
- Sales and Gross Receipts Taxes
- Federal Customs Duties
- General Sales and Gross Receipts Taxes
- Selective Sales Taxes (alcoholic beverages; amusements; insurance premiums; motor fuels; pari-mutuels; public utilities; tobacco products; other)
- License Taxes (alcoholic beverages; amusements; corporations in general; hunting and fishing; motor vehicles motor vehicle operators; public utilities; occupation and business, NEC; other)
- Income Taxes (individual income; corporation net income; other taxes)
- Death and Gift
- Documentary & Stock Transfer
- Severance
- Taxes, NEC

Total City Property Taxes Per Capita: Total city property taxes collected divided by the population of the city. *Source: U.S. Bureau of the Census, State and Local Government Finances, 2000 (http://www.census.gov/govs/www/estimate.html).*

Property Taxes include general property taxes, relating to property as a whole, taxed at a single rate or at classified rates according to the class of property. Property refers to real property (e.g., land and structures) as well as personal property; personal property can be either tangible (e.g., automobiles and boats) or intangible (e.g., bank accounts and stocks and bonds). Special property taxes, levied on selected types of property (e.g., oil and gas properties, house trailers, motor vehicles, and intangibles) and subject to rates not directly related to general property tax rates. Taxes based on income produced by property as a measure of its value on the assessment date.

EDUCATION

High School Graduation Rate: Percentage of the population age 25 and over who have a high school diploma or higher. This category includes people whose highest degree was a high school diploma or its equivalent, people who attended college but did not receive a degree, and people who received a college, university, or professional degree. People who reported completing the 12th grade but not receiving a diploma are not high school graduates. *Source: U.S. Bureau of the Census, Census of Population and Housing, 2000: Summary File 3.*

College Graduation Rate: Percentage of the population age 25 and over who have a college, university, or professional degree. *Source: U.S. Bureau of the Census, Census of Population and Housing, 2000: Summary File 3.*

Data on educational attainment were derived from answers to long-form questionnaire Item 9, which was asked of a sample of the population. Data on attainment are tabulated for the population 25 years old and over. However, when educational attainment is cross-tabulated by other variables, the universe may change. (e.g. when educational attainment is crossed by disability status, the data are tabulated for the civilian noninstitutionalized population 18 to 34 years old.) People are classified according to the highest degree or level of school completed.

The order in which degrees were listed on the questionnaire suggested that doctorate degrees were "higher" than professional school degrees, which were "higher" than master's degrees. The question included instructions for people currently enrolled in school to report the level of the previous grade attended or the highest degree received. Respondents who did not report educational attainment or enrollment level were assigned the attainment of a person of the same age, race, Hispanic or Latino origin, occupation and sex, where possible, who resided in the same or a nearby area. Respondents who filled more than one box were edited to the highest level or degree reported.

The question included a response category that allowed respondents to report completing the 12th grade without receiving a high school diploma. It allowed people who received either a high school diploma or the equivalent (Test of General Educational Development—G.E.D.) and did not attend college, to be reported as "high school graduate(s)." The category "Associate degree" included people whose highest degree is an associate degree, which generally requires 2 years of college level work and is either in an occupational program that prepares them for a specific occupation, or an academic program primarily in the arts and sciences. The course work may or may not be transferable to a bachelor's degree. Master's degrees include the traditional MA and MS degrees and field-specific degrees, such as MSW, MEd, MBA, MLS, and MEng. Some examples of professional degrees include medicine, dentistry, chiropractic, optometry, osteopathic medicine, pharmacy, podiatry, veterinary medicine, law, and theology. Vocational and technical training such as barber school training; business, trade, technical, and vocational schools; or other training for a specific trade, are specifically excluded.

School Districts: Lists the name of each school district, the grade range (PK=pre-kindergarten; KG=kindergarten), the student enrollment, and the district headquarters' phone number. In cases where a school district serve multiple communities, the entry is listed under the place where the school district headquarters is located. *Source: U.S. Department of Education, National Center for Educational Statistics, Directory of Public Elementary and Secondary Education Agencies, 2000*

Four-year Colleges: Lists the name of each four-year college, the type of institution (private or public; for-profit or non-profit; religious affiliation; historically black college), the student enrollment, the phone number, and the annual tuition (in-state and out-of-state). *Source: U.S. Department of Education, National Center for Educational Statistics, Directory of Postsecondary Institutions.*

Two-year Colleges: Lists the name of each two-year college, the type of institution (private or public; for-profit or non-profit; religious affiliation; historically black college), the student enrollment, the phone number, and the annual tuition (in-state and out-of-state). *Source: U.S. Department of Education, National Center for Educational Statistics, Directory of Postsecondary Institutions.*

HOUSING

Home Ownership Rate: Percentage of housing units that are owner-occupied. *Source: U.S. Bureau of the Census, Census of Population and Housing, 2000: Summary File 3.*

The data on tenure, which was asked at all occupied housing units, were obtained from answers to long-form questionnaire Item 33, and short-form questionnaire Item 2. All occupied housing units are classified as either owner occupied or renter occupied.

A housing unit is owner occupied if the owner or co-owner lives in the unit even if it is mortgaged or not fully paid for. The owner or co-owner must live in the unit and usually is Person 1 on the questionnaire. The unit is "Owned by you or someone in this household with a mortgage or loan" if it is being purchased with a mortgage or some other debt arrangement, such as a deed of trust, trust deed, contract to purchase, land contract, or purchase agreement. The unit is also considered owned with a mortgage if it is built on leased land and there is a mortgage on the unit. Mobile homes occupied by owners with installment loans balances are also included in this category.

Median Home Value: Reported by the owner of specified owner-occupied or specified vacant-for-sale housing units. Specified owner-occupied and specified vacant-for-sale housing units include only 1-family houses on less than 10 acres without a business or medical office on the property. The data for "specified units" exclude mobile homes, houses with a business or medical office, houses on 10 or more acres, and housing units in multi-unit buildings. *Source: U.S. Bureau of the Census, Census of Population and Housing, 2000: Summary File 3.*

The data on value (also referred to as "price asked" for vacant units) were obtained from answers to long-form questionnaire Item 51, which was asked on a sample basis at owner-occupied housing units and units that were being bought, or vacant for sale at the time of enumeration. Value is the respondent's estimate of how much the property (house and lot, mobile home and lot, or condominium unit) would sell for if it were for sale. If the house or mobile home was owned or being bought, but the land on which it sits was not, the respondent was asked to estimate the combined value of the house or mobile home and the land. For vacant units, value was the price asked for the property. Value was tabulated separately for all owner-occupied and vacant-for-sale housing units, owner-occupied and vacant-for-sale mobile homes, and specified owner-occupied and specified vacant-for-sale housing units.

The median divides the value distribution into two equal parts: one-half of the cases falling below the median value of the property (house and lot, mobile home and lot, or condominium unit) and one-half above the median. Median values are computed on the basis of a standard distribution and are rounded to the nearest hundred dollars.

Median Rent: Median monthly contract rent on specified renter-occupied and specified vacant-for-rent units. Specified renter-occupied and specified vacant-for-rent units exclude 1-family houses on 10 acres or more. *Source: U.S. Bureau of the Census, Census of Population and Housing, 2000: Summary File 3.*

The data on contract rent (also referred to as "rent asked" for vacant units) were obtained from answers to long-form questionnaire Item 46, which was asked on a sample basis at occupied housing units that were rented for cash rent and vacant housing units that were for rent at the time of enumeration.

Housing units that are renter occupied without payment of cash rent are shown separately as "No cash rent" in census data products. The unit may be owned by friends or relatives who live elsewhere and who allow occupancy without charge. Rent-free houses or apartments may be provided to compensate caretakers, ministers, tenant farmers, sharecroppers, or others.

Contract rent is the monthly rent agreed to or contracted for, regardless of any furnishings, utilities, fees, meals, or services that may be included. For vacant units, it is the monthly rent asked for the rental unit at the time of enumeration.

If the contract rent includes rent for a business unit or for living quarters occupied by another household, only that part of the rent estimated to be for the respondent's unit was included. Excluded was any rent paid for additional units or for business premises.

If a renter pays rent to the owner of a condominium or cooperative, and the condominium fee or cooperative carrying charge also is paid by the renter to the owner, the condominium fee or carrying charge was included as rent.

If a renter receives payments from lodgers or roomers who are listed as members of the household, the rent without deduction for any payments received from the lodgers or roomers was to be reported. The respondent was to report the rent agreed to or contracted for even if paid by someone else such as friends or relatives living elsewhere, a church or welfare agency, or the government through subsidies or vouchers.

The median divides the rent distribution into two equal parts: one-half of the cases falling below the median contract rent and one-half above the median. Median contract rents are computed on the basis of a standard distribution and are rounded to the nearest whole dollar. Units reported as "No cash rent" are excluded.

Median Age of Housing: Median age of housing was calculated by subtracting median year structure built from 2000 (e.g. if the median year structure built is 1967, the median age of housing in that area is 33 years — 2000 minus 1967). *Source: U.S. Bureau of the Census, Census of Population and Housing, 2000: Summary File 3.*

The data on year structure built were obtained from answers to long-form questionnaire Item 35, which was asked on a sample basis at both occupied and vacant housing units. Year structure built refers to when the building was first constructed, not when it was remodeled, added to, or converted. For housing units under construction that met the housing unit definition—that is, all exterior windows, doors, and final usable floors were in place—the category "1999 or 2000" was used for tabulations. For mobile homes, houseboats, RVs, etc, the manufacturer's model year was assumed to be the year built. The data relate to the number of units built during the specified periods that were still in existence at the time of enumeration.

The median divides the distribution into two equal parts: one-half of the cases falling below the median year structure built and one-half above the median. Median year structure built is computed on the basis of a standard distribution and is rounded to the nearest whole number.

HOSPITALS

Lists the name and the number of licensed beds. *Source: Grey House Publishing, Directory of Hospital Personnel, 2003*

SAFETY

Violent Crime Rate: Number of violent crimes reported per 10,000 population. Violent crimes include murder, forcible rape, robbery, and aggravated assault. *Source: Federal Bureau of Investigation, Uniform Crime Reports 2001 (http://www.fbi.gov/ucr/ucr.htm).*

Property Crime Rate: Number of property crimes reported per 10,000 population. Property crimes include burglary, larceny-theft, and motor vehicle theft. *Source: Federal Bureau of Investigation, Uniform Crime Reports 2001 (http://www.fbi.gov/ucr/ucr.htm).*

NEWSPAPERS

Includes the names of daily and weekly newspapers and their frequency of publication. *Source: Original research.*

TRANSPORTATION

Commute to Work: Percentage of workers 16 years old and over that use the following means of transportation to commute to work: car; public transportation; walk; work from home. *Source: U.S. Bureau of the Census, Census of Population and Housing, 2000: Summary File 3.*

The data on means of transportation to work were derived from answers to long-form questionnaire Item 23a, which was asked of a sample of the population 15 years old and over. This question was asked of people who indicated in Question 21 that they worked at some time during the reference week (the full calendar week, Sunday through Saturday, preceding the date the questionnaire was completed). Means of transportation to work refers to the principal mode of travel or type of conveyance that the worker usually used to get from home to work during the reference week. Data were tabulated for workers 16 years old and over; that is, members of the armed forces and civilians who were at work during the reference week.

People who used different means of transportation on different days of the week were asked to specify the one they used most often, that is, the greatest number of days. People who used more than one means of transportation to get to work each day were asked to report the one used for the longest distance during the work trip. The category "Car, truck, or van — drove alone" includes people who usually drove alone to work, as well as people who were driven to work by someone who then drove back home or to a nonwork destination during the reference week. The category "Car, truck, or van — carpooled" includes workers who reported that two or more people usually rode to work in the vehicle during the reference week. The category "Public transportation" includes workers who usually used a bus or trolley bus, streetcar or trolley car, subway or elevated, railroad, ferryboat, or taxicab during the reference week. The category "Other means" includes workers who used a mode of travel that is not identified separately. The category "Other means" may vary from table to table, depending on the amount of detail shown in a particular distribution.

The means of transportation data for some areas may show workers using modes of public transportation that are not available in those areas (for example, subway or elevated riders in a metropolitan area where there actually is no subway or elevated service). This result is largely due to people who worked during the reference week at a location that was different from their usual place of work (such as people away from home on business in an area where subway service was available) and people who used more than one means of transportation each day but whose principal means was unavailable where they lived (for example, residents of nonmetropolitan areas who drove to the fringe of a metropolitan area and took the commuter railroad most of the distance to work).

Travel Time to Work: Travel time to work for workers 16 years old and over. Reported for the following intervals: less than 15 minutes; 15 to 30 minutes; 30 to 45 minutes; 45 to 60 minutes; 60 minutes or more. *Source: U.S. Bureau of the Census, Census of Population and Housing, 2000: Summary File 3.*

The data on travel time to work were derived from answers to long-form questionnaire Item 24b, which was asked of a sample of the population 15 years old and over. This question was asked of people who indicated in Question 21 that they worked at some time during the reference week (the full calendar week, Sunday through Saturday, preceding the date the questionnaire was completed) and who reported in Question 23a that they worked outside their home. Travel time to work refers to the total number of minutes that it usually took the person to get from home to work each day during the reference week. The elapsed time includes time spent waiting for public transportation, picking up passengers in carpools, and time spent in other activities related to getting to work. Data were tabulated for workers 16 years old and over; that is, members of the armed forces and civilians who were at work during the reference week.

Aggregate travel time to work (minutes) is calculated by adding together all the number of minutes each worker traveled to work (one way) for specified travel times and/or means of transportation. Aggregate travel time to work is zero if the aggregate is zero, is rounded to 4 minutes if the actual aggregate is 1 to 7 minutes, and is rounded to the nearest multiple of 5 minutes for all other values (if the aggregate is not already evenly divisible by 5).

Amtrak: Indicates if Amtrak service is available. Please note that the cities being served continually change. *Source: National Railroad Passenger Corporation, Amtrak National Timetable, 2002.*

AIRPORTS

Lists the local airport(s) along with type of service and hub size. *Source: Federal Aviation Administration, Enplanement Activity at U.S. Airports by State, 2001 (www.faa.gov)*

ADDITIONAL INFORMATION CONTACTS

The following phone numbers are provided as sources of additional information: Chambers of Commerce; Economic Development Agencies; Boards of Realtors; Convention & Visitors Bureaus. Efforts have been made to provide the most recent area codes. However, area code changes may have occurred in listed numbers. *Source: Original research.*

INFORMATION FOR COUNTIES AND COUNTY EQUIVALENTS

PHYSICAL CHARACTERISTICS

Physical Location: Describes the physical location of the county. *Source: Columbia University Press, The Columbia Gazetteer of North America and original research*

Land and Water Area: Land and water area in square miles. *Source: U.S. Bureau of the Census, Census of Population and Housing, 2000: Summary File 1*

Time Zone: Lists the time zone. *Source: Original research*

Year Organized: Year the county government was organized. *Source: National Association of Counties (www.naco.org).*

County Seat: Lists the county seat. If a county has more than one seat, then both are listed. *Source: National Association of Counties (www.naco.org).*

Metropolitan Area: Indicates the metropolitan area the county is located in. Also lists all the component counties of that metropolitan area. *Source: U.S. Bureau of the Census (http://www.census.gov/population/www/estimates/metrodef.html).*

The Office of Management and Budget (OMB) defines metropolitan areas (MAs), including metropolitan statistical areas (MSAs), consolidated metropolitan statistical areas (CMSAs), and primary metropolitan statistical areas (PMSAs). Currently defined MAs are based on application of 1990 standards (which appeared in the Federal Register on March 30, 1990) to 1990 decennial census data and to subsequent Census Bureau population estimates and special census data. Current MA definitions were announced by OMB effective June 30, 1999. Definitions based on the review of 1990 census data became effective June 30, 1993. Annual updates are generally announced by OMB at the end of June.

Except in New England states, where cities and towns are the geographic building blocks, MAs consist of one or more counties. The OMB defines New England County Metropolitan Areas (NECMAs) as a county-based alternative to the city and town-based New England MSAs and CMSAs.

Climate: Includes all weather stations located within the county. Indicates the station name and elevation as well as the monthly average high and low temperatures, average precipitation, and average snowfall. The period of record is generally 1970-1999, however certain weather stations contain averages going back as far as 1900. *Source: Grey House Publishing, Weather America: A Thirty-Year Summary of Statistical Weather Data and Rankings, 2001*

POPULATION

Population: 100% count of population. *Source: U.S. Bureau of the Census, Census of Population and Housing, 2000: Summary File 1.*

Population by Race: Includes the U.S. Bureau of the Census categories of White only; Black only; Asian only; American Indian and Alaska Native only; Hispanic of any race; Two or more races. The percentages may not total 100% because of the Census category of "Other."

The data on race, which was asked of all people, were derived from answers to long-form questionnaire Item 6, and short-form questionnaire Item 8. The concept of race, as used by the Census Bureau, reflects self-identification by people according to the race or races with which they most closely identify. These categories are socio-political constructs and should not be interpreted as being scientific or anthropological in nature. Furthermore, the race categories include both racial and national-origin groups.

- **White.** A person having origins in any of the original peoples of Europe, the Middle East, or North Africa. It includes people who indicate their race as "White" or report entries such as Irish, German, Italian, Lebanese, Near Easterner, Arab, or Polish.

- **Black or African American.** A person having origins in any of the Black racial groups of Africa. It includes people who indicate their race as "Black, African American, or Negro," or provide written entries such as African American, Afro-American, Kenyan, Nigerian, or Haitian.
- **American Indian or Alaska Native.** A person having origins in any of the original peoples of North and South America (including Central America) and who maintain tribal affiliation or community attachment.
- **Asian.** A person having origins in any of the original peoples of the Far East, Southeast Asia, or the Indian subcontinent including, for example, Cambodia, China, India, Japan, Korea, Malaysia, Pakistan, the Philippine Islands, Thailand, and Vietnam. It includes "Asian Indian," "Chinese," "Filipino," "Korean," "Japanese," "Vietnamese," and "Other Asian."
- **Hispanic.** The data on the Hispanic or Latino population, which was asked of all people, were derived from answers to long-form questionnaire Item 5, and short-form questionnaire Item 7. The terms "Spanish," "Hispanic origin," and "Latino" are used interchangeably. Some respondents identify with all three terms, while others may identify with only one of these three specific terms. Hispanics or Latinos who identify with the terms "Spanish," "Hispanic," or "Latino" are those who classify themselves in one of the specific Hispanic or Latino categories listed on the questionnaire — "Mexican," "Puerto Rican," or "Cuban" — as well as those who indicate that they are "other Spanish, Hispanic, or Latino." People who do not identify with one of the specific origins listed on the questionnaire but indicate that they are "other Spanish, Hispanic, or Latino" are those whose origins are from Spain, the Spanish-speaking countries of Central or South America, the Dominican Republic, or people identifying themselves generally as Spanish, Spanish-American, Hispanic, Hispano, Latino, and so on. All write-in responses to the "other Spanish/Hispanic/Latino" category were coded. Origin can be viewed as the heritage, nationality group, lineage, or country of birth of the person or the person's parents or ancestors before their arrival in the United States. People who identify their origin as Spanish, Hispanic, or Latino may be of any race.
- Two or more races. People may have chosen to provide two or more races either by checking two or more race response check boxes, by providing multiple write-in responses, or by some combination of check boxes and write-in responses. The race response categories shown on the questionnaire are collapsed into the five minimum races identified by the OMB, and the Census Bureau "Some other race" category. For data product purposes, "Two or more races" refers to combinations of two or more of the following race categories: White; Black or African American; American Indian and Alaska Native; Asian; Native Hawaiian and Other Pacific Islander; Some other race. There are 57 possible combinations involving the race categories shown above. Thus, according to this approach, a response of "White" and "Asian" was tallied as two or more races, while a response of "Japanese" and "Chinese" was not because "Japanese" and "Chinese' are both Asian responses.

Population Density: 100% count of population divided by the land area in square miles. *Source: U.S. Bureau of the Census, Census of Population and Housing, 2000: Summary File 1.*

Age: Percentage of population under 18 years of age and percentage of population over 64 years of age. *Source: U.S. Bureau of the Census, Census of Population and Housing, 2000: Summary File 3.*

The data on age, which was asked of all people, were derived from answers to the long-form questionnaire Item 4 and short-form questionnaire Item 6. The age classification is based on the age of the person in complete years as of April 1, 2000. The age of the person usually was derived from their date of birth information. Their reported age was used only when date of birth information was unavailable.

RELIGION

Religion: Lists the largest religious groups (up to five) based on the number of adherents divided by the population of the county. Adherents are defined as "all members, including full members, their children and the estimated number of other regular participants who are not considered as communicant, confirmed or full members." The data is based on a study of 149 religious bodies sponsored by the Association of Statisticians of American Religious Bodies. The 149 bodies reported 268,254 congregations and 141,371,963 adherents. *Source: Glenmary Research Center, Religious Congregations & Membership in the United States 2000*

ECONOMY

Unemployment Rate: Includes all civilians age 16 or over who were unemployed and looking for work as of November 2002. *Source: U.S. Department of Labor, Bureau of Labor Statistics, Local Area Unemployment Statistics (http://www.bls.gov/lau/home.htm).*

Total labor force: Includes all civilians age 16 or over who were either employed, or unemployed and looking for work as of November 2002. *Source: U.S. Department of Labor, Bureau of Labor Statistics, Local Area Unemployment Statistics (http://www.bls.gov/lau/home.htm).*

Leading Industries: Lists the three largest industries (excluding government) based on the number of employees. *Source: U.S. Bureau of the Census, County Business Patterns 2000 (http://www.census.gov/epcd/cbp/view/cbpview.html)*

Companies that Employ more than 1,000 persons: The numbers of companies that employ more than 1,000 persons. Includes private employers only. *Source: U.S. Bureau of the Census, County Business Patterns 2000 (http://www.census.gov/epcd/cbp/view/cbpview.html)*

Companies that Employ more than 100 persons: The numbers of companies that employ more than 100 persons. Includes private employers only. *Source: U.S. Bureau of the Census, County Business Patterns 2000 (http://www.census.gov/epcd/cbp/view/cbpview.html)*

Farms: The total number of farms and the total acreage they occupy. Please note that the entry "Farms: 0 totaling 0 acres (1997)" indicates that data was not available. *Source: U.S. Department of Agriculture, National Agricultural Statistics Service, 1997 Census of Agriculture (http://www.nass.usda.gov/census)*

Minority Business Ownership Rate: Percentage of all businesses that are majority-owned by a member of a minority group. *Source: U.S. Bureau of the Census, 1997 Economic Census: Surveys of Minority- and Women-Owned Businesses (http://www.census.gov/csd/mwb/)*

Women Business Ownership Rate: Percentage of all businesses that are majority-owned by a woman. *Source: U.S. Bureau of the Census, 1997 Economic Census: Surveys of Minority- and Women-Owned Businesses (http://www.census.gov/csd/mwb/)*

The Survey of Minority-Owned Business Enterprises (SMOBE) is conducted in conjunction with the Survey of Women-Owned Business Enterprises (SWOBE). The SMOBE and SWOBE provide basic economic data on businesses owned by Blacks, persons of Alaska Native, American Indian, Asian, or Pacific Islander descent, persons of Hispanic or Latin American ancestry, and women. These surveys are based on the entire firm rather than on individual locations of a firm. The published data cover number of firms, gross receipts, number of paid employees, and annual payroll. The data are presented by geographic area, industry, size of firm, and legal form of organization of firm.

The data in this report were compiled by combining data collected on business owners in the 1997 Economic Census Surveys of Minority- and Women-Owned Business Enterprises with data collected on the main economic census and administrative records. Included are all nonfarm businesses filing 1997 tax forms as individual proprietorships, partnerships, and any type of corporation, and with receipts of $1,000 or more.

Minority/women ownership of a business was based on the race/ethnicity/gender of the person(s) owning majority interest in the business. Firms equally male-/female-owned were counted and tabulated as a separate category. The gender of sole proprietors and self-employed persons who were ''single filers'' was taken directly from administrative record data.

Businesses in which ownership was shared among minority and nonminority groups, with no single racial/ethnic group having majority interest, were tabulated as 50-percent minority-/50-percent nonminority-owned and were excluded from the minority business counts.

Businesses with publicly held stock whose ownership was indeterminate relative to gender, race, or ethnicity, and nonprofit, foreign-owned, and mutual companies were tabulated separately and published in the ''other'' category.

Retail Sales per Capita: Total dollar amount of retail sales divided by the population of the county. Please note that a value of $0 indicates that data was suppressed to avoid disclosure of confidential information. *Source: U.S. Bureau of the Census, 1997 Economic Census (http://www.census.gov/epcd/www/econ97.html)*

Single-Family Building Permits Issued: Building permits issued for new single-family housing units in 2000 and 2001. Please note that a value of -1 indicates that data was not available. *Source: U.S. Census Bureau, Manufacturing and Construction Division (MCD) http://www.census.gov/const/www/permitsindex.html*

Multi-Family Building Permits Issued: Building permits issued for new multi-family housing units in 2000 and 2001. Please note that a value of -1 indicates that data was not available. *Source: U.S. Census Bureau, Manufacturing and Construction Division (MCD) http://www.census.gov/const/www/permitsindex.html*

Statistics on housing units authorized by building permits include housing units issued in local permit-issuing jurisdictions by a building or zoning permit. Not all areas of the country require a building or zoning permit. The statistics only represent those areas that do require a permit. Current surveys indicate that construction is undertaken for all but a very small percentage of housing units authorized by building permits. A major portion typically get under way during the month of permit issuance and most of the remainder begin within the three following months. Because of this lag, the housing unit authorization statistics do not represent the number of units actually put into construction for the period shown, and should therefore not be directly interpreted as "housing starts."

Statistics are based upon reports submitted by local building permit officials in response to a mail survey. They are obtained using Form C-404 const/www/c404.pdf, "Report of New Privately-Owned Residential Building or Zoning Permits Issued." When a report is not received, missing data are either (1) obtained from the Survey of Use of Permits (SUP) which is used to collect information on housing starts, or (2) imputed based on the assumption that the ratio of current month authorizations to those of a year ago should be the same for reporting and nonreporting places.

INCOME

Per capita income: Per capita income is the mean income computed for every man, woman, and child in a particular group. It is derived by dividing the total income of a particular group by the total population in that group. Per capita income is rounded to the nearest whole dollar. *Source: U.S. Bureau of the Census, Census of Population and Housing, 2000: Summary File 3.*

The data on income in 1999 were derived from answers to long-form questionnaire Items 31 and 32, which were asked of a sample of the population 15 years old and over. "Total income" is the sum of the amounts reported separately for wage or salary income; net self-employment income; interest, dividends, or net rental or royalty income or income from estates and trusts; social security or railroad retirement income; Supplemental Security Income (SSI); public assistance or welfare payments; retirement, survivor, or disability pensions; and all other income.

Receipts from the following sources are not included as income: capital gains, money received from the sale of property (unless the recipient was engaged in the business of selling such property); the value of income "in kind" from food stamps, public housing subsidies, medical care, employer contributions for individuals, etc.; withdrawal of bank deposits; money borrowed; tax refunds; exchange of money between relatives living in the same household; and gifts and lump-sum inheritances, insurance payments, and other types of lump-sum receipts.

The eight types of income reported in the census are defined as follows:

Wage or salary income. Wage or salary income includes total money earnings received for work performed as an employee during the calendar year 1999. It includes wages, salary, armed forces pay, commissions, tips, piece-rate payments, and cash bonuses earned before deductions were made for taxes, bonds, pensions, union dues, etc.

Self-employment income. Self-employment income includes both farm and nonfarm self-employment income. Nonfarm self-employment income includes net money income (gross receipts minus expenses) from one's own business, professional enterprise, or partnership. Gross receipts include the value of all goods sold and services rendered. Expenses include costs of goods purchased, rent, heat, light, power, depreciation charges, wages and salaries paid, business taxes (not personal income taxes), etc. Farm self-employment income includes net money income (gross receipts minus operating expenses) from the operation of a farm by a person on his or her own account, as an owner, renter, or sharecropper. Gross receipts include the value of all products sold, government farm programs, money received from the rental of farm equipment to others, and incidental receipts from the sale of wood, sand, gravel, etc. Operating expenses include cost of feed, fertilizer, seed, and other farming supplies, cash wages paid to farmhands, depreciation charges, cash rent, interest on farm mortgages, farm building repairs, farm taxes (not state and federal personal income taxes), etc. The value of fuel, food, or other farm products used for family living is not included as part of net income.

Interest, dividends, or net rental income. Interest, dividends, or net rental income includes interest on savings or bonds, dividends from stockholdings or membership in associations, net income from rental of property to others and receipts from boarders or lodgers, net royalties, and periodic payments from an estate or trust fund.

Social Security income. Social security income includes social security pensions and survivors benefits, permanent disability insurance payments made by the Social Security Administration prior to deductions for medical insurance, and railroad retirement insurance checks from the U.S. government. Medicare reimbursements are not included.

Supplemental Security Income (SSI). Supplemental Security Income (SSI) is a nationwide U.S. assistance program administered by the Social Security Administration that guarantees a minimum level of income for needy aged, blind, or disabled individuals. The census questionnaire for Puerto Rico asked about the receipt of SSI; however, SSI is not a federally administered program in

Puerto Rico. Therefore, it is probably not being interpreted by most respondents as the same as SSI in the United States. The only way a resident of Puerto Rico could have appropriately reported SSI would have been if they lived in the United States at any time during calendar year 1999 and received SSI.

Public assistance income. Public assistance income includes general assistance and Temporary Assistance to Needy Families (TANF). Separate payments received for hospital or other medical care (vendor payments) are excluded. This does not include Supplemental Security Income (SSI).

Retirement income. Retirement income includes: (1) retirement pensions and survivor benefits from a former employer; labor union; or federal, state, or local government; and the U.S. military; (2) income from workers' compensation; disability income from companies or unions; federal, state, or local government; and the U.S. military; (3) periodic receipts from annuities and insurance; and (4) regular income from IRA and KEOGH plans. This does not include social security income.

All other income. All other income includes unemployment compensation, Veterans' Administration (VA) payments, alimony and child support, contributions received periodically from people not living in the household, military family allotments, and other kinds of periodic income other than earnings.

Median Household Income: Includes the income of the householder and all other individuals 15 years old and over in the household, whether they are related to the householder or not. The median divides the income distribution into two equal parts: one-half of the cases falling below the median income and one-half above the median. For households, the median income is based on the distribution of the total number of households including those with no income. Median income for households is computed on the basis of a standard distribution and is rounded to the nearest whole dollar. *Source: U.S. Bureau of the Census, Census of Population and Housing, 2000: Summary File 3.*

Poverty Rate: Percentage of population with income in 1999 below the poverty level. Based on individuals for whom poverty status is determined. Poverty status was determined for all people except institutionalized people, people in military group quarters, people in college dormitories, and unrelated individuals under 15 years old. *Source: U.S. Bureau of the Census, Census of Population and Housing, 2000: Summary File 3.*

The poverty status of families and unrelated individuals in 1999 was determined using 48 thresholds (income cutoffs) arranged in a two dimensional matrix. The matrix consists of family size (from 1 person to 9 or more people) cross-classified by presence and number of family members under 18 years old (from no children present to 8 or more children present). Unrelated individuals and 2-person families were further differentiated by the age of the reference person (RP) (under 65 years old and 65 years old and over).

To determine a person's poverty status, one compares the person's total family income with the poverty threshold appropriate for that person's family size and composition. If the total income of that person's family is less than the threshold appropriate for that family, then the person is considered poor, together with every member of his or her family. If a person is not living with anyone related by birth, marriage, or adoption, then the person's own income is compared with his or her poverty threshold.

Bankruptcy Rate: Personal bankruptcy filings include both Chapter 7 (liquidations) and Chapter 13 (reorganizations) based on the county of residence of the filer. The personal bankruptcy filing rate is the number of bankruptcies per thousand residents. *Source: Federal Deposit Insurance Corporation, Regional Economic Conditions 2001 (http://www2.fdic.gov/recon/index.html)*

TAXES

Total County Taxes Per Capita: Total county taxes collected divided by the population of the county. *Source: U.S. Bureau of the Census, State and Local Government Finances, 2000 (http://www.census.gov/govs/www/estimate.html).*

Taxes include:

- Property Taxes
- Sales and Gross Receipts Taxes
- Federal Customs Duties
- General Sales and Gross Receipts Taxes
- Selective Sales Taxes (alcoholic beverages; amusements; insurance premiums; motor fuels; pari-mutuels; public utilities; tobacco products; other)
- License Taxes (alcoholic beverages; amusements; corporations in general; hunting and fishing; motor vehicles motor vehicle operators; public utilities; occupation and business, NEC; other)
- Income Taxes (individual income; corporation net income; other taxes)

- Death and Gift
- Documentary & Stock Transfer
- Severance
- Taxes, NEC

Total County Property Taxes Per Capita: Total county property taxes collected divided by the population of the county. *Source: U.S. Bureau of the Census, State and Local Government Finances, 2000 (http://www.census.gov/govs/www/estimate.html).*

Property Taxes include general property taxes, relating to property as a whole, taxed at a single rate or at classified rates according to the class of property. Property refers to real property (e.g., land and structures) as well as personal property; personal property can be either tangible (e.g., automobiles and boats) or intangible (e.g., bank accounts and stocks and bonds). Special property taxes, levied on selected types of property (e.g., oil and gas properties, house trailers, motor vehicles, and intangibles) and subject to rates not directly related to general property tax rates. Taxes based on income produced by property as a measure of its value on the assessment date.

EDUCATION

High School Graduation Rate: Percentage of the population age 25 and over who have a high school diploma or higher. This category includes people whose highest degree was a high school diploma or its equivalent, people who attended college but did not receive a degree, and people who received a college, university, or professional degree. People who reported completing the 12th grade but not receiving a diploma are not high school graduates. *Source: U.S. Bureau of the Census, Census of Population and Housing, 2000: Summary File 3.*

College Graduation Rate: Percentage of the population age 25 and over who have a college, university, or professional degree. *Source: U.S. Bureau of the Census, Census of Population and Housing, 2000: Summary File 3.*

Data on educational attainment were derived from answers to long-form questionnaire Item 9, which was asked of a sample of the population. Data on attainment are tabulated for the population 25 years old and over. However, when educational attainment is cross-tabulated by other variables, the universe may change. (e.g. when educational attainment is crossed by disability status, the data are tabulated for the civilian noninstitutionalized population 18 to 34 years old.) People are classified according to the highest degree or level of school completed.

The order in which degrees were listed on the questionnaire suggested that doctorate degrees were "higher" than professional school degrees, which were "higher" than master's degrees. The question included instructions for people currently enrolled in school to report the level of the previous grade attended or the highest degree received. Respondents who did not report educational attainment or enrollment level were assigned the attainment of a person of the same age, race, Hispanic or Latino origin, occupation and sex, where possible, who resided in the same or a nearby area. Respondents who filled more than one box were edited to the highest level or degree reported.

The question included a response category that allowed respondents to report completing the 12th grade without receiving a high school diploma. It allowed people who received either a high school diploma or the equivalent (Test of General Educational Development—G.E.D.) and did not attend college, to be reported as "high school graduate(s)." The category "Associate degree" included people whose highest degree is an associate degree, which generally requires 2 years of college level work and is either in an occupational program that prepares them for a specific occupation, or an academic program primarily in the arts and sciences. The course work may or may not be transferable to a bachelor's degree. Master's degrees include the traditional MA and MS degrees and field-specific degrees, such as MSW, MEd, MBA, MLS, and MEng. Some examples of professional degrees include medicine, dentistry, chiropractic, optometry, osteopathic medicine, pharmacy, podiatry, veterinary medicine, law, and theology. Vocational and technical training such as barber school training; business, trade, technical, and vocational schools; or other training for a specific trade, are specifically excluded.

HOUSING

Home Ownership Rate: Percentage of housing units that are owner-occupied. *Source: U.S. Bureau of the Census, Census of Population and Housing, 2000: Summary File 3.*

The data on tenure, which was asked at all occupied housing units, were obtained from answers to long-form questionnaire Item 33, and short-form questionnaire Item 2. All occupied housing units are classified as either owner occupied or renter occupied.

A housing unit is owner occupied if the owner or co-owner lives in the unit even if it is mortgaged or not fully paid for. The owner or co-owner must live in the unit and usually is Person 1 on the questionnaire. The unit is "Owned by you or someone in this household with a mortgage or loan" if it is being purchased with a mortgage or some other debt arrangement, such as a deed of trust, trust deed, contract to purchase, land contract, or purchase agreement. The unit is also considered owned with a mortgage if it is built on leased land and there is a mortgage on the unit. Mobile homes occupied by owners with installment loans balances are also included in this category.

Median Home Value: Reported by the owner of specified owner-occupied or specified vacant-for-sale housing units. Specified owner-occupied and specified vacant-for-sale housing units include only 1-family houses on less than 10 acres without a business or medical office on the property. The data for "specified units" exclude mobile homes, houses with a business or medical office, houses on 10 or more acres, and housing units in multi-unit buildings. *Source: U.S. Bureau of the Census, Census of Population and Housing, 2000: Summary File 3.*

The data on value (also referred to as "price asked" for vacant units) were obtained from answers to long-form questionnaire Item 51, which was asked on a sample basis at owner-occupied housing units and units that were being bought, or vacant for sale at the time of enumeration. Value is the respondent's estimate of how much the property (house and lot, mobile home and lot, or condominium unit) would sell for if it were for sale. If the house or mobile home was owned or being bought, but the land on which it sits was not, the respondent was asked to estimate the combined value of the house or mobile home and the land. For vacant units, value was the price asked for the property. Value was tabulated separately for all owner-occupied and vacant-for-sale housing units, owner-occupied and vacant-for-sale mobile homes, and specified owner-occupied and specified vacant-for-sale housing units.

The median divides the value distribution into two equal parts: one-half of the cases falling below the median value of the property (house and lot, mobile home and lot, or condominium unit) and one-half above the median. Median values are computed on the basis of a standard distribution and are rounded to the nearest hundred dollars.

Median Rent: Median monthly contract rent on specified renter-occupied and specified vacant-for-rent units. Specified renter-occupied and specified vacant-for-rent units exclude 1-family houses on 10 acres or more. *Source: U.S. Bureau of the Census, Census of Population and Housing, 2000: Summary File 3.*

The data on contract rent (also referred to as "rent asked" for vacant units) were obtained from answers to long-form questionnaire Item 46, which was asked on a sample basis at occupied housing units that were rented for cash rent and vacant housing units that were for rent at the time of enumeration.

Housing units that are renter occupied without payment of cash rent are shown separately as "No cash rent" in census data products. The unit may be owned by friends or relatives who live elsewhere and who allow occupancy without charge. Rent-free houses or apartments may be provided to compensate caretakers, ministers, tenant farmers, sharecroppers, or others.

Contract rent is the monthly rent agreed to or contracted for, regardless of any furnishings, utilities, fees, meals, or services that may be included. For vacant units, it is the monthly rent asked for the rental unit at the time of enumeration.

If the contract rent includes rent for a business unit or for living quarters occupied by another household, only that part of the rent estimated to be for the respondent's unit was included. Excluded was any rent paid for additional units or for business premises.

If a renter pays rent to the owner of a condominium or cooperative, and the condominium fee or cooperative carrying charge also is paid by the renter to the owner, the condominium fee or carrying charge was included as rent.

If a renter receives payments from lodgers or roomers who are listed as members of the household, the rent without deduction for any payments received from the lodgers or roomers was to be reported. The respondent was to report the rent agreed to or contracted for even if paid by someone else such as friends or relatives living elsewhere, a church or welfare agency, or the government through subsidies or vouchers.

The median divides the rent distribution into two equal parts: one-half of the cases falling below the median contract rent and one-half above the median. Median contract rents are computed on the basis of a standard distribution and are rounded to the nearest whole dollar. Units reported as "No cash rent" are excluded.

Median Age of Housing: Median age of housing was calculated by subtracting median year structure built from 2000 (e.g. if the median year structure built is 1967, the median age of housing in that area is 33 years — 2000 minus 1967). *Source: U.S. Bureau of the Census, Census of Population and Housing, 2000: Summary File 3.*

The data on year structure built were obtained from answers to long-form questionnaire Item 35, which was asked on a sample basis at both occupied and vacant housing units. Year structure built refers to when the building was first constructed, not when it was remodeled, added to, or converted. For housing units under construction that met the housing unit definition—that is, all exterior windows, doors, and final usable floors were in place—the category "1999 or 2000" was used for tabulations. For mobile homes, houseboats, RVs, etc, the manufacturer's model year was assumed to be the year built. The data relate to the number of units built during the specified periods that were still in existence at the time of enumeration.

The median divides the distribution into two equal parts: one-half of the cases falling below the median year structure built and one-half above the median. Median year structure built is computed on the basis of a standard distribution and is rounded to the nearest whole number.

HEALTH AND VITAL STATISTICS

Birth Rate: Number of births per 10,000 population in 1998. *Source: Centers for Disease Control, CDC Wonder (http://wonder.cdc.gov)*

Age-adjusted Death Rate: Number of age-adjusted deaths per 10,000 population in 1999. *Source: Centers for Disease Control, CDC Wonder (http://wonder.cdc.gov)*

Infant Mortality Rate: Number of infant deaths per 1,000 live births in 1998. Infants are defined as children under 1 year of age. *Source: Centers for Disease Control, CDC Wonder (http://wonder.cdc.gov)*

Age-adjusted Cancer Mortality Rate: Number of age-adjusted deaths from cancer per 100,000 population in 1999. Cancer is defined as International Classification of Disease (ICD) codes C00 - D48.9 Neoplasms. *Source: Centers for Disease Control, CDC Wonder (http://wonder.cdc.gov)*

Age-adjusted death rates are weighted averages of the age-specific death rates, where the weights represent a fixed population by age. They are used because the rates of almost all causes of death vary by age. Age adjustment is a technique for "removing" the effects of age from crude rates, so as to allow meaningful comparisons across populations with different underlying age structures. For example, comparing the crude rate of heart disease in Florida to that of California is misleading, because the relatively older population in Florida will lead to a higher crude death rate, even if the age-specific rates of heart disease in Florida and California are the same. For such a comparison, age-adjusted rates would be preferable. Age-adjusted rates should be viewed as relative indexes rather than as direct or actual measures of mortality risk.

Death rates based on counts of twenty or less (<=20) are flagged as "Unreliable". Death rates based on fewer than three years of data for counties with populations of less than 100,000 in the 1990 Census counts, are also flagged as "Unreliable" if the number of deaths is five or less (<=5).

Air Quality Index: The percentage of days in 2000 the AQI fell into the Good (0-50), Moderate (51-100) and Unhealthy (101+) ranges. *Source: U.S. Environmental Protection Agency, Office of Air and Radiation (http://www.epa.gov/oar)*

The AQI is an index for reporting daily air quality. It tells you how clean or polluted your air is, and what associated health concerns you should be aware of. The AQI focuses on health effects that can happen within a few hours or days after breathing polluted air. EPA uses the AQI for five major air pollutants regulated by the Clean Air Act: ground-level ozone, particulate matter, carbon monoxide, sulfur dioxide, and nitrogen dioxide. For each of these pollutants, EPA has established national air quality standards to protect against harmful health effects.

The AQI runs from 0 to 500. The higher the AQI value, the greater the level of air pollution and the greater the health danger. For example, an AQI value of 50 represents good air quality and little potential to affect public health, while an AQI value over 300 represents hazardous air quality.

An AQI value of 100 generally corresponds to the national air quality standard for the pollutant, which is the level EPA has set to protect public health. So, AQI values below 100 are generally thought of as satisfactory. When AQI values are above 100, air quality is considered to be unhealthy—at first for certain sensitive groups of people, then for everyone as AQI values get higher.

Each category corresponds to a different level of health concern. For example, when the AQI for a pollutant is between 51 and 100, the health concern is "Moderate." Here are the six levels of health concern and what they mean:

"Good" The AQI value for your community is between 0 and 50. Air quality is considered satisfactory and air pollution poses little or no risk.

"Moderate" The AQI for your community is between 51 and 100. Air quality is acceptable; however, for some pollutants there may be a moderate health concern for a very small number of individuals. For example, people who are unusually sensitive to ozone may experience respiratory symptoms.

"Unhealthy for Sensitive Groups" Certain groups of people are particularly sensitive to the harmful effects of certain air pollutants. This means they are likely to be affected at lower levels than the general public. For example, children and adults who are active outdoors and people with respiratory disease are at greater risk from exposure to ozone, while people with heart disease are at greater risk from carbon monoxide. Some people may be sensitive to more than one pollutant. When AQI values are between 101 and 150, members of sensitive groups may experience health effects. The general public is not likely to be affected when the AQI is in this range.

"Unhealthy" AQI values are between 151 and 200. Everyone may begin to experience health effects. Members of sensitive groups may experience more serious health effects.

"Very Unhealthy" AQI values between 201 and 300 trigger a health alert, meaning everyone may experience more serious health effects.

"Hazardous" AQI values over 300 trigger health warnings of emergency conditions. The entire population is more likely to be affected.

Number of Physicians: The number of non-federal physicians per 10,000 population. *Source: Health Resources and Services Administration, Bureau of Health Professions, Area Resource File (ARF) System, (Fairfax, VA: Quality Resource Systems, Inc., February 2002).*

Number of Hospital Beds: The number of hospital beds per 10,000 population. *Source: Health Resources and Services Administration, Bureau of Health Professions, Area Resource File (ARF) System, (Fairfax, VA: Quality Resource Systems, Inc., February 2002).*

ELECTIONS

Elections: 2000 Presidential election results. *Source: Original research*

ADDITIONAL INFORMATION CONTACTS

The following phone numbers are provided as sources of additional information: Chambers of Commerce; Economic Development Agencies; Boards of Realtors; Convention & Visitors Bureaus. Efforts have been made to provide the most recent area codes. However, area code changes may have occurred in listed numbers. *Source: Original research.*

Illinois

The Prairie State

ILLINOIS –Metropolitan Areas, Counties, Independent City, and Central Cities

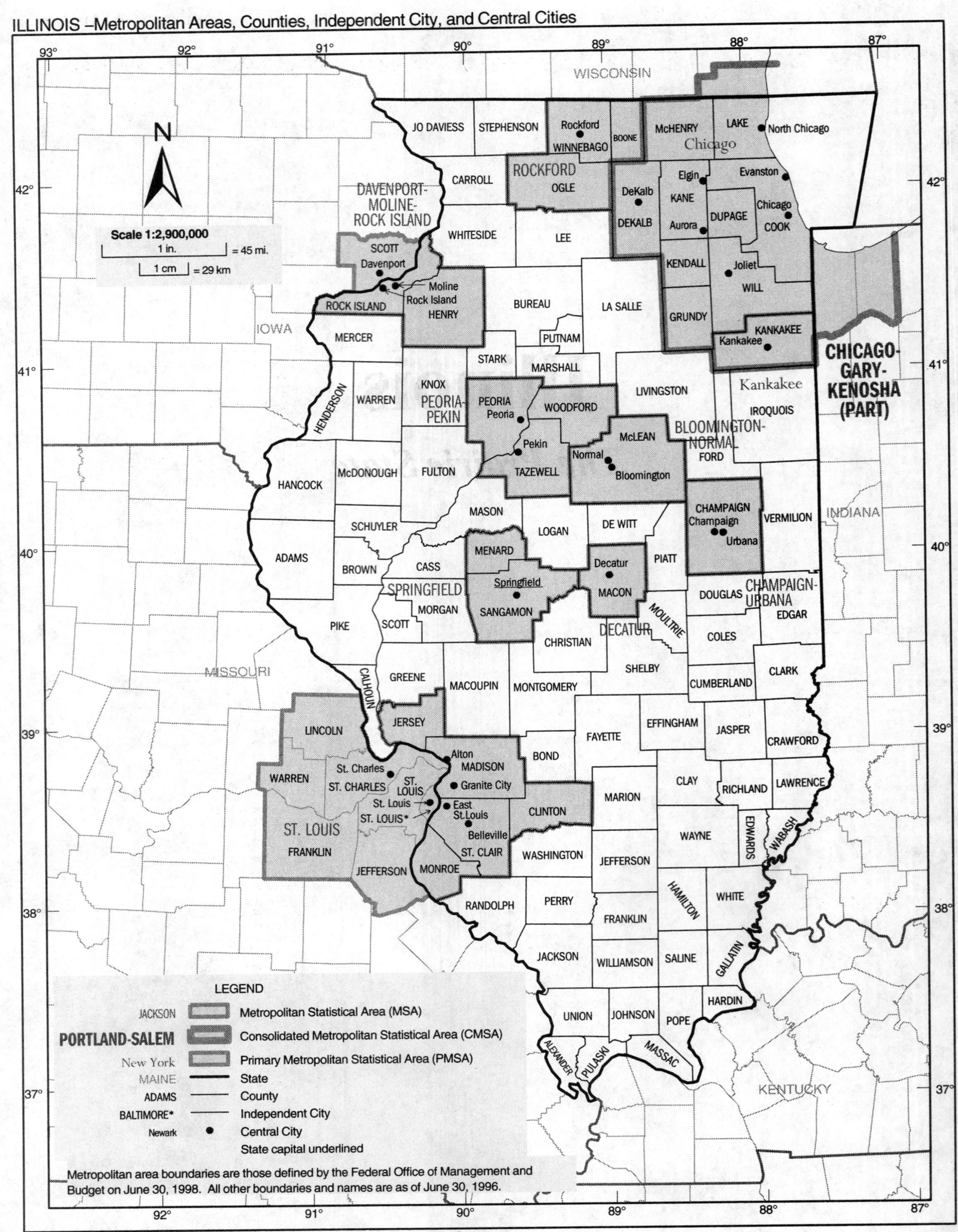

WISCONSIN
IOWA
MISSOURI
INDIANA
KENTUCKY
N
Scale 1:2,900,000
1 in. = 45 mi.
1 cm = 29 km
JO DAVIESS
STEPHENSON
Rockford
WINNEBAGO
BOONE
McHENRY
LAKE
North Chicago
Chicago
ROCKFORD
CARROLL
OGLE
DeKalb
DEKALB
Elgin
KANE
Evanston
Chicago
COOK
Aurora
DUPAGE
DAVENPORT-MOLINE-ROCK ISLAND
SCOTT
Davenport
Moline
Rock Island
ROCK ISLAND
WHITESIDE
LEE
KENDALL
Joliet
WILL
HENRY
BUREAU
LA SALLE
GRUNDY
KANKAKEE
Kankakee
MERCER
PUTNAM
STARK
MARSHALL
CHICAGO-GARY-KENOSHA (PART)
Kankakee
KNOX
WARREN
HENDERSON
PEORIA-PEKIN
PEORIA
Peoria
WOODFORD
LIVINGSTON
IROQUOIS
Pekin
McLEAN
BLOOMINGTON-NORMAL
Normal
Bloomington
FORD
TAZEWELL
HANCOCK
McDONOUGH
FULTON
MASON
CHAMPAIGN
Champaign
Urbana
VERMILION
SCHUYLER
LOGAN
DE WITT
ADAMS
MENARD
BROWN
CASS
Decatur
MACON
PIATT
SPRINGFIELD
Springfield
SANGAMON
MORGAN
DOUGLAS
CHAMPAIGN-URBANA
EDGAR
PIKE
SCOTT
DECATUR
MOULTRIE
COLES
CHRISTIAN
SHELBY
CLARK
CALHOUN
GREENE
MACOUPIN
MONTGOMERY
CUMBERLAND
JERSEY
FAYETTE
EFFINGHAM
JASPER
CRAWFORD
LINCOLN
Alton
MADISON
BOND
St. Charles
WARREN
ST. CHARLES
ST. LOUIS
Granite City
CLAY
RICHLAND
LAWRENCE
St. Louis
East St. Louis
MARION
ST. LOUIS*
CLINTON
ST. LOUIS
Belleville
WAYNE
EDWARDS
WABASH
FRANKLIN
ST. CLAIR
WASHINGTON
JEFFERSON
JEFFERSON
MONROE
HAMILTON
WHITE
RANDOLPH
PERRY
FRANKLIN
JACKSON
WILLIAMSON
SALINE
GALLATIN
HARDIN
UNION
JOHNSON
POPE
ALEXANDER
PULASKI
MASSAC
93°
92°
91°
90°
89°
88°
87°
42°
41°
40°
39°
38°
37°
LEGEND
JACKSON Metropolitan Statistical Area (MSA)
PORTLAND-SALEM Consolidated Metropolitan Statistical Area (CMSA)
New York Primary Metropolitan Statistical Area (PMSA)
MAINE State
ADAMS County
BALTIMORE* Independent City
Newark Central City
State capital underlined
Metropolitan area boundaries are those defined by the Federal Office of Management and Budget on June 30, 1998. All other boundaries and names are as of June 30, 1996.

D

E

F

G

CDP = Census Designated Place

H

I

J

K

L

CDP = Census Designated Place

M

N

CDP = Census Designated Place

T

U

V

W

CDP = Census Designated Place

X

Y

Z

Adams County

Located in western Illinois; bounded on the west by the Mississippi River and the Missouri border. Covers a land area of 856.60 square miles, a water area of 14.60 square miles, and is located in the Central Time Zone. The county government was organized in 1825. County seat is Quincy.

Weather Station: Golden Elevation: 725 feet

	Jan	Feb	Mar	Apr	May	Jun	Jul	Aug	Sep	Oct	Nov	Dec
High	32	38	51	63	74	83	87	85	78	67	50	38
Low	15	20	31	41	52	62	65	63	55	44	32	21
Precip	1.2	1.5	2.7	3.6	5.0	3.7	4.3	3.7	3.9	3.1	3.0	2.1
Snow	6.0	4.9	2.0	0.6	0.0	0.0	0.0	0.0	0.0	tr	1.6	3.9

High and Low temperatures in degrees Fahrenheit; Precipitation and Snow in inches

Weather Station: Quincy Muni Baldwin Field Elevation: 761 feet

	Jan	Feb	Mar	Apr	May	Jun	Jul	Aug	Sep	Oct	Nov	Dec
High	32	38	50	63	73	82	87	84	77	65	50	37
Low	16	22	32	43	53	62	67	64	56	45	33	23
Precip	1.4	1.7	3.1	3.9	5.0	3.6	3.9	3.6	4.1	3.3	3.2	2.4
Snow	7.6	6.0	2.9	0.9	tr	tr	tr	tr	tr	tr	2.2	4.8

High and Low temperatures in degrees Fahrenheit; Precipitation and Snow in inches

Population: 68,277 (2000); Race: 95.1% White, 2.9% Black, 0.3% Asian, 0.2% American Indian and Alaska Native, 0.9% Hispanic of any race, 1.1% two or more races (2000); Density: 79.7 persons per square mile (2000); Age: 25.0% under 18, 17.6% over 64 (2000).
Religion: Five largest groups: 23.3% Catholic Church, 5.4% The United Methodist Church, 4.9% Christian Churches and Churches of Christ, 4.7% United Church of Christ, 4.3% Lutheran Church—Missouri Synod (2000).
Economy: Unemployment rate: 3.9% (11/2002); Total civilian labor force: 35,252 (11/2002); Leading industries: 20.3% manufacturing; 15.9% retail trade; 14.8% health care and social assistance (2000); Companies that employ more than 1,000 persons: 1 (2000); Companies that employ more than 100 persons: 51 (2000); Farms: 1,415 totaling 442,081 acres (1997); Minority business ownership rate: 2.9% (1997); Women business ownership rate: 29.0% (1997); Retail sales per capita: $9,913 (1997). Single-family building permits issued: 81 (2001) / 66 (2000); Multi-family building permits issued: 91 (2001) / 34 (2000).
Income: Per capita income: $17,894 (2000); Median household income: $34,784 (2000); Poverty rate: 10.0% (2000); Bankruptcy rate: 5.11% (2001).
Taxes: Total county taxes per capita: $93 (2000); County property taxes per capita: $64 (2000).
Education: High school graduation rate: 83.7% (2000); College graduation rate: 17.6% (2000).
Housing: Homeownership rate: 73.8% (2000); Median home value: $75,600 (2000); Median rent: $314 per month (2000); Median age of housing: 44 years (2000).
Health: Birth rate: 126.1 per 10,000 population (1998); Age adjusted death rate: 86.5 per 10,000 population (1999); Age adjusted cancer mortality rate: 230.8 deaths per 100,000 population (1999). Air Quality Index: 85% good, 15% moderate, 0% unhealthy (percent of days in 2000). Number of physicians: 20.1 per 10,000 population (1999); Number of hospital beds: 48.8 per 10,000 population (1999).
Elections: 2000 Presidential election results: 40.5% Gore, 57.6% Bush, 1.2% Nader, 0.5% Buchanan
National and State Parks: Sid Simpson State Park; Siloam Springs State Park
Additional Information Contacts
Adams County Government Offices 217-223-6300
Quincy Association of Realtors 217-228-0652
Quincy Chamber of Commerce 217-222-7980

Adams County Communities

CAMP POINT (village). Covers a land area of 0.948 square miles and a water area of 0 square miles. Located at 40.04° N. Lat.; 91.06° W. Long. Elevation is 743 feet.
History: Camp Point was settled about 1870 by people of German ancestry.
Population: 1,244 (2000); Race: 98.6% White, 0.0% Black, 0.0% Asian, 0.2% American Indian and Alaska Native, 1.2% Hispanic of any race, 0.9% two or more races (2000); Density: 1,312.1 persons per square mile (2000); Age: 30.3% under 18, 16.9% over 64 (2000); Marriage status: 24.2% never married, 48.8% now married, 12.7% widowed, 14.3% divorced (2000); Foreign born: 0.0% (2000); Ancestry (includes multiple ancestries): 42.7% German, 13.1% Irish, 10.3% English, 7.5% United States or American, 4.0% Other groups (2000).
Economy: Single-family building permits issued: 0 (2001) / 0 (2000); Multi-family building permits issued: 0 (2001) / 0 (2000); Employment by occupation: 6.2% management, 15.3% professional, 13.4% services, 25.3% sales, 0.7% farming, 9.6% construction, 29.6% production (2000).
Income: Per capita income: $15,211 (2000); Median household income: $31,094 (2000); Poverty rate: 11.7% (2000).
Taxes: Total city taxes per capita: $112 (2000); City property taxes per capita: $80 (2000).
Education: High school graduation rate: 84.3% (2000); College graduation rate: 9.9% (2000).

School District(s)

Camp Point C U School District 3 (PK-12)
2000 Enrollment: 1,042 217-593-7116
Housing: Homeownership rate: 71.4% (2000); Median home value: $57,000 (2000); Median rent: $261 per month (2000); Median age of housing: 46 years (2000).
Newspapers: Mendon Dispatch-Times (1 x week); Golden New Era (1 x week); Camp Point Journal (1 x week); Clayton Enterprise (1 x week)
Transportation: Commute to work: 93.5% car, 0.4% public transportation, 3.9% walk, 1.4% work from home (2000); Travel time to work: 39.9% less than 15 minutes, 20.8% 15 to 30 minutes, 29.9% 30 to 45 minutes, 4.7% 45 to 60 minutes, 4.8% 60 minutes or more (2000)

CLAYTON (village). Covers a land area of 0.874 square miles and a water area of 0.002 square miles. Located at 40.02° N. Lat.; 90.95° W. Long. Elevation is 736 feet.
Population: 904 (2000); Race: 85.5% White, 12.5% Black, 0.0% Asian, 0.0% American Indian and Alaska Native, 2.4% Hispanic of any race, 0.6% two or more races (2000); Density: 1,034.0 persons per square mile (2000); Age: 19.7% under 18, 20.1% over 64 (2000); Marriage status: 17.3% never married, 64.3% now married, 7.7% widowed, 10.7% divorced (2000); Foreign born: 0.0% (2000); Ancestry (includes multiple ancestries): 23.2% German, 16.2% United States or American, 10.5% Irish, 8.6% English, 4.8% French (except Basque) (2000).
Economy: Corn, wheat, soybeans, livestock. Single-family building permits issued: 0 (2001) / 1 (2000); Multi-family building permits issued: 0 (2001) / 0 (2000); Employment by occupation: 8.3% management, 8.0% professional, 19.3% services, 22.7% sales, 0.6% farming, 11.2% construction, 29.9% production (2000).
Income: Per capita income: $13,882 (2000); Median household income: $23,077 (2000); Poverty rate: 14.7% (2000).
Taxes: Total city taxes per capita: $22 (1997); City property taxes per capita: $20 (1997).
Education: High school graduation rate: 59.8% (2000); College graduation rate: 5.1% (2000).
Housing: Homeownership rate: 80.7% (2000); Median home value: $38,000 (2000); Median rent: $200 per month (2000); Median age of housing: 56 years (2000).
Transportation: Commute to work: 85.5% car, 1.5% public transportation, 7.4% walk, 3.1% work from home (2000); Travel time to work: 36.0% less than 15 minutes, 23.9% 15 to 30 minutes, 27.7% 30 to 45 minutes, 5.1% 45 to 60 minutes, 7.3% 60 minutes or more (2000)

COATSBURG (village). Covers a land area of 0.122 square miles and a water area of 0 square miles. Located at 40.03° N. Lat.; 91.16° W. Long. Elevation is 761 feet.
History: Coatsburg was surveyed by R.P. Coates in 1855, and developed as a shipping center for grain and livestock. Coatsburg was incorporated as a village in 1885.
Population: 226 (2000); Race: 100.0% White, 0.0% Black, 0.0% Asian, 0.0% American Indian and Alaska Native, 4.6% Hispanic of any race, 0.0% two or more races (2000); Density: 1,855.7 persons per square mile (2000); Age: 26.9% under 18, 11.1% over 64 (2000); Marriage status: 16.1% never married, 58.9% now married, 10.7% widowed, 14.3% divorced (2000); Foreign born: 0.0% (2000); Ancestry (includes multiple ancestries): 39.4% United States or American, 20.8% German, 6.9% English, 5.1% Other groups, 5.1% Irish (2000).
Economy: Employment by occupation: 9.9% management, 19.8% professional, 24.3% services, 10.8% sales, 2.7% farming, 9.9% construction, 22.5% production (2000).
Income: Per capita income: $15,026 (2000); Median household income: $36,250 (2000); Poverty rate: 9.0% (2000).
Taxes: Total city taxes per capita: $19 (1997); City property taxes per capita: $10 (1997).

Education: High school graduation rate: 74.3% (2000); College graduation rate: 2.9% (2000).
Housing: Homeownership rate: 90.8% (2000); Median home value: $39,000 (2000); Median rent: $325 per month (2000); Median age of housing: 44 years (2000).
Transportation: Commute to work: 95.3% car, 0.0% public transportation, 0.0% walk, 4.7% work from home (2000); Travel time to work: 14.9% less than 15 minutes, 46.5% 15 to 30 minutes, 30.7% 30 to 45 minutes, 4.0% 45 to 60 minutes, 4.0% 60 minutes or more (2000)

COLUMBUS (village). Covers a land area of 0.252 square miles and a water area of 0 square miles. Located at 39.98° N. Lat.; 91.14° W. Long. Elevation is 730 feet.
History: Vigorously competed with Quincy for seat of Adams county in 19th century.
Population: 112 (2000); Race: 95.0% White, 0.0% Black, 0.0% Asian, 0.0% American Indian and Alaska Native, 0.0% Hispanic of any race, 5.0% two or more races (2000); Density: 444.5 persons per square mile (2000); Age: 20.0% under 18, 8.3% over 64 (2000); Marriage status: 16.3% never married, 75.5% now married, 3.1% widowed, 5.1% divorced (2000); Foreign born: 0.0% (2000); Ancestry (includes multiple ancestries): 38.3% German, 15.0% Other groups, 14.2% Irish, 12.5% English, 10.0% Dutch (2000).
Economy: Agriculture: corn, wheat; livestock; dairying. Employment by occupation: 11.8% management, 5.3% professional, 27.6% services, 28.9% sales, 0.0% farming, 9.2% construction, 17.1% production (2000).
Income: Per capita income: $16,429 (2000); Median household income: $38,438 (2000); Poverty rate: 5.8% (2000).
Taxes: Total city taxes per capita: $11 (1997); City property taxes per capita: $11 (1997).
Education: High school graduation rate: 70.9% (2000); College graduation rate: 7.0% (2000).
Housing: Homeownership rate: 90.0% (2000); Median home value: $46,000 (2000); Median rent: $325 per month (2000); Median age of housing: 34 years (2000).
Transportation: Commute to work: 93.4% car, 0.0% public transportation, 0.0% walk, 6.6% work from home (2000); Travel time to work: 9.9% less than 15 minutes, 45.1% 15 to 30 minutes, 33.8% 30 to 45 minutes, 8.5% 45 to 60 minutes, 2.8% 60 minutes or more (2000)

FOWLER (unincorporated postal area, zip code 62338). Covers a land area of 26.247 square miles and a water area of 0.076 square miles. Located at 39.98° N. Lat.; 91.25° W. Long. Elevation is 730 feet.
Population: 1,364 (2000); Race: 98.8% White, 0.0% Black, 0.0% Asian, 0.0% American Indian and Alaska Native, 0.4% Hispanic of any race, 1.2% two or more races (2000); Density: 52.0 persons per square mile (2000); Age: 25.7% under 18, 11.3% over 64 (2000); Marriage status: 19.2% never married, 64.8% now married, 5.9% widowed, 10.1% divorced (2000); Foreign born: 0.1% (2000); Ancestry (includes multiple ancestries): 48.4% German, 17.9% Irish, 5.8% United States or American, 5.5% Other groups, 4.8% English (2000).
Economy: Employment by occupation: 10.9% management, 23.0% professional, 14.1% services, 25.8% sales, 0.7% farming, 9.3% construction, 16.2% production (2000).
Income: Per capita income: $18,181 (2000); Median household income: $45,192 (2000); Poverty rate: 3.3% (2000).
Education: High school graduation rate: 86.9% (2000); College graduation rate: 14.6% (2000).
Housing: Homeownership rate: 94.1% (2000); Median home value: $77,500 (2000); Median rent: $292 per month (2000); Median age of housing: 26 years (2000).
Transportation: Commute to work: 94.3% car, 0.7% public transportation, 0.0% walk, 5.0% work from home (2000); Travel time to work: 24.4% less than 15 minutes, 62.9% 15 to 30 minutes, 11.4% 30 to 45 minutes, 0.9% 45 to 60 minutes, 0.4% 60 minutes or more (2000)

GOLDEN (village). Covers a land area of 0.628 square miles and a water area of 0 square miles. Located at 40.11° N. Lat.; 91.01° W. Long. Elevation is 715 feet.
Population: 629 (2000); Race: 100.0% White, 0.0% Black, 0.0% Asian, 0.0% American Indian and Alaska Native, 0.3% Hispanic of any race, 0.0% two or more races (2000); Density: 1,000.9 persons per square mile (2000); Age: 22.5% under 18, 25.5% over 64 (2000); Marriage status: 15.5% never married, 64.9% now married, 12.5% widowed, 7.1% divorced (2000); Foreign born: 0.0% (2000); Ancestry (includes multiple ancestries): 53.8% German, 8.6% Irish, 7.1% United States or American, 6.1% English, 3.7% Scotch-Irish (2000).
Economy: In agricultural area: corn, wheat, soybeans; livestock; makes seed sowers. Employment by occupation: 13.3% management, 12.3% professional, 17.2% services, 16.3% sales, 1.2% farming, 12.3% construction, 27.4% production (2000).
Income: Per capita income: $16,518 (2000); Median household income: $34,333 (2000); Poverty rate: 3.5% (2000).
Taxes: Total city taxes per capita: $23 (1997); City property taxes per capita: $23 (1997).
Education: High school graduation rate: 79.8% (2000); College graduation rate: 8.2% (2000).
Housing: Homeownership rate: 81.7% (2000); Median home value: $49,300 (2000); Median rent: $286 per month (2000); Median age of housing: 54 years (2000).
Transportation: Commute to work: 87.0% car, 0.0% public transportation, 4.9% walk, 4.9% work from home (2000); Travel time to work: 53.6% less than 15 minutes, 11.0% 15 to 30 minutes, 24.4% 30 to 45 minutes, 9.4% 45 to 60 minutes, 1.6% 60 minutes or more (2000)

LA PRAIRIE (village). Covers a land area of 0.224 square miles and a water area of 0 square miles. Located at 40.14° N. Lat.; 91.00° W. Long. Elevation is 711 feet.
Population: 60 (2000); Race: 100.0% White, 0.0% Black, 0.0% Asian, 0.0% American Indian and Alaska Native, 0.0% Hispanic of any race, 0.0% two or more races (2000); Density: 268.4 persons per square mile (2000); Age: 21.8% under 18, 20.0% over 64 (2000); Marriage status: 15.6% never married, 66.7% now married, 8.9% widowed, 8.9% divorced (2000); Foreign born: 3.6% (2000); Ancestry (includes multiple ancestries): 45.5% United States or American, 30.9% English, 25.5% Other groups, 16.4% German, 3.6% Welsh (2000).
Economy: In agricultural area. Employment by occupation: 9.5% management, 9.5% professional, 52.4% services, 0.0% sales, 0.0% farming, 9.5% construction, 19.0% production (2000).
Income: Per capita income: $8,844 (2000); Median household income: $15,000 (2000); Poverty rate: 50.9% (2000).
Taxes: Total city taxes per capita: $14 (1997); City property taxes per capita: $14 (1997).
Education: High school graduation rate: 60.5% (2000); College graduation rate: 0.0% (2000).
Housing: Homeownership rate: 92.0% (2000); Median home value: $26,300 (2000); Median age of housing: 60+ years (2000).
Transportation: Commute to work: 89.5% car, 0.0% public transportation, 10.5% walk, 0.0% work from home (2000); Travel time to work: 26.3% less than 15 minutes, 10.5% 15 to 30 minutes, 36.8% 30 to 45 minutes, 10.5% 45 to 60 minutes, 15.8% 60 minutes or more (2000)

LIBERTY (village). Covers a land area of 0.374 square miles and a water area of 0 square miles. Located at 39.88° N. Lat.; 91.10° W. Long. Elevation is 757 feet.
Population: 519 (2000); Race: 100.0% White, 0.0% Black, 0.0% Asian, 0.0% American Indian and Alaska Native, 0.4% Hispanic of any race, 0.0% two or more races (2000); Density: 1,386.7 persons per square mile (2000); Age: 21.1% under 18, 10.2% over 64 (2000); Marriage status: 22.9% never married, 62.4% now married, 6.9% widowed, 7.8% divorced (2000); Foreign born: 0.0% (2000); Ancestry (includes multiple ancestries): 38.3% German, 16.2% United States or American, 12.8% Irish, 7.5% English, 4.7% Scottish (2000).
Economy: Employment by occupation: 5.3% management, 16.0% professional, 12.2% services, 28.5% sales, 0.9% farming, 11.9% construction, 25.1% production (2000).
Income: Per capita income: $16,565 (2000); Median household income: $36,417 (2000); Poverty rate: 12.2% (2000).
Taxes: Total city taxes per capita: $23 (1997); City property taxes per capita: $18 (1997).
Education: High school graduation rate: 77.4% (2000); College graduation rate: 10.6% (2000).

School District(s)

Liberty Community Unit School District 2 (PK-12)
2000 Enrollment: 579 217-645-3433

Housing: Homeownership rate: 79.1% (2000); Median home value: $68,300 (2000); Median rent: $275 per month (2000); Median age of housing: 28 years (2000).
Newspapers: The Liberty Bee-Times (1 x week)
Transportation: Commute to work: 93.7% car, 0.0% public transportation, 5.7% walk, 0.0% work from home (2000); Travel time to work: 21.1% less than 15 minutes, 42.5% 15 to 30 minutes, 34.3% 30 to 45 minutes, 0.6% 45 to 60 minutes, 1.6% 60 minutes or more (2000)

LIMA (village). Covers a land area of 0.214 square miles and a water area of 0 square miles. Located at 40.17° N. Lat.; 91.37° W. Long. Elevation is 659 feet.
Population: 159 (2000); Race: 100.0% White, 0.0% Black, 0.0% Asian, 0.0% American Indian and Alaska Native, 1.4% Hispanic of any race, 0.0% two or more races (2000); Density: 741.8 persons per square mile (2000); Age: 25.9% under 18, 19.6% over 64 (2000); Marriage status: 28.0% never married, 55.9% now married, 4.2% widowed, 11.9% divorced (2000); Foreign born: 0.0% (2000); Ancestry (includes multiple ancestries): 23.1% German, 15.4% English, 14.0% Irish, 9.8% United States or American, 2.8% Other groups (2000).
Economy: In agricultural area. Employment by occupation: 6.7% management, 8.3% professional, 13.3% services, 31.7% sales, 0.0% farming, 3.3% construction, 36.7% production (2000).
Income: Per capita income: $13,825 (2000); Median household income: $37,500 (2000); Poverty rate: 0.7% (2000).
Taxes: Total city taxes per capita: $32 (1997); City property taxes per capita: $0 (1997).
Education: High school graduation rate: 78.1% (2000); College graduation rate: 7.3% (2000).
Housing: Homeownership rate: 92.7% (2000); Median home value: $51,000 (2000); Median rent: $225 per month (2000); Median age of housing: 39 years (2000).
Transportation: Commute to work: 95.0% car, 0.0% public transportation, 1.7% walk, 3.3% work from home (2000); Travel time to work: 17.2% less than 15 minutes, 41.4% 15 to 30 minutes, 29.3% 30 to 45 minutes, 3.4% 45 to 60 minutes, 8.6% 60 minutes or more (2000)

LORAINE (village). Covers a land area of 0.846 square miles and a water area of 0 square miles. Located at 40.15° N. Lat.; 91.22° W. Long. Elevation is 642 feet.
Population: 363 (2000); Race: 98.9% White, 0.0% Black, 0.0% Asian, 0.0% American Indian and Alaska Native, 1.1% Hispanic of any race, 1.1% two or more races (2000); Density: 429.0 persons per square mile (2000); Age: 29.8% under 18, 10.3% over 64 (2000); Marriage status: 17.2% never married, 64.6% now married, 7.5% widowed, 10.8% divorced (2000); Foreign born: 0.0% (2000); Ancestry (includes multiple ancestries): 32.6% German, 16.7% Irish, 12.0% United States or American, 10.9% English, 9.5% Other groups (2000).
Economy: In agricultural area. Employment by occupation: 9.1% management, 12.2% professional, 15.9% services, 20.7% sales, 1.2% farming, 11.0% construction, 29.9% production (2000).
Income: Per capita income: $17,333 (2000); Median household income: $41,875 (2000); Poverty rate: 11.7% (2000).
Taxes: Total city taxes per capita: $9 (1997); City property taxes per capita: $9 (1997).
Education: High school graduation rate: 81.9% (2000); College graduation rate: 4.5% (2000).
Housing: Homeownership rate: 87.2% (2000); Median home value: $38,600 (2000); Median rent: $235 per month (2000); Median age of housing: 60+ years (2000).
Transportation: Commute to work: 98.7% car, 0.0% public transportation, 0.0% walk, 1.3% work from home (2000); Travel time to work: 15.9% less than 15 minutes, 38.2% 15 to 30 minutes, 42.7% 30 to 45 minutes, 3.2% 45 to 60 minutes, 0.0% 60 minutes or more (2000)

MENDON (village). Covers a land area of 0.731 square miles and a water area of 0 square miles. Located at 40.08° N. Lat.; 91.28° W. Long. Elevation is 760 feet.
Population: 883 (2000); Race: 99.2% White, 0.0% Black, 0.0% Asian, 0.0% American Indian and Alaska Native, 0.7% Hispanic of any race, 0.3% two or more races (2000); Density: 1,207.5 persons per square mile (2000); Age: 29.5% under 18, 13.3% over 64 (2000); Marriage status: 21.0% never married, 60.7% now married, 10.1% widowed, 8.2% divorced (2000); Foreign born: 0.6% (2000); Ancestry (includes multiple ancestries): 42.7% German, 16.3% Irish, 9.2% English, 6.7% United States or American, 6.6% Other groups (2000).
Economy: In agricultural area: corn, sorghum, soybeans; cattle. Employment by occupation: 8.2% management, 14.3% professional, 22.3% services, 17.1% sales, 1.4% farming, 13.9% construction, 22.7% production (2000).
Income: Per capita income: $15,267 (2000); Median household income: $35,139 (2000); Poverty rate: 8.0% (2000).
Taxes: Total city taxes per capita: $23 (2000); City property taxes per capita: $20 (2000).
Education: High school graduation rate: 80.8% (2000); College graduation rate: 9.8% (2000).

School District(s)

Community Unit School District 4 (PK-12)
2000 Enrollment: 816 217-936-2111
Housing: Homeownership rate: 77.1% (2000); Median home value: $62,600 (2000); Median rent: $245 per month (2000); Median age of housing: 40 years (2000).
Transportation: Commute to work: 96.7% car, 0.4% public transportation, 2.5% walk, 0.4% work from home (2000); Travel time to work: 22.2% less than 15 minutes, 56.3% 15 to 30 minutes, 15.4% 30 to 45 minutes, 2.3% 45 to 60 minutes, 3.9% 60 minutes or more (2000)

PALOMA (unincorporated postal area, zip code 62359). Covers a land area of 10.096 square miles and a water area of 0.003 square miles. Located at 40.02° N. Lat.; 91.21° W. Long. Elevation is 735 feet.
Population: 192 (2000); Race: 100.0% White, 0.0% Black, 0.0% Asian, 0.0% American Indian and Alaska Native, 0.0% Hispanic of any race, 0.0% two or more races (2000); Density: 19.0 persons per square mile (2000); Age: 17.7% under 18, 14.2% over 64 (2000); Marriage status: 8.9% never married, 85.4% now married, 0.0% widowed, 5.7% divorced (2000); Foreign born: 0.0% (2000); Ancestry (includes multiple ancestries): 39.0% United States or American, 21.3% German, 15.6% English, 14.9% Irish, 4.3% Croatian (2000).
Economy: Employment by occupation: 6.7% management, 16.0% professional, 12.0% services, 28.0% sales, 8.0% farming, 0.0% construction, 29.3% production (2000).
Income: Per capita income: $18,310 (2000); Median household income: $43,295 (2000); Poverty rate: 0.0% (2000).
Education: High school graduation rate: 85.0% (2000); College graduation rate: 7.5% (2000).
Housing: Homeownership rate: 85.7% (2000); Median home value: $95,000 (2000); Median rent: $368 per month (2000); Median age of housing: 16 years (2000).
Transportation: Commute to work: 84.0% car, 0.0% public transportation, 0.0% walk, 16.0% work from home (2000); Travel time to work: 12.7% less than 15 minutes, 54.0% 15 to 30 minutes, 25.4% 30 to 45 minutes, 0.0% 45 to 60 minutes, 7.9% 60 minutes or more (2000)

PAYSON (village). Covers a land area of 1.147 square miles and a water area of 0 square miles. Located at 39.81° N. Lat.; 91.24° W. Long. Elevation is 760 feet.
Population: 1,066 (2000); Race: 98.6% White, 0.0% Black, 0.0% Asian, 0.0% American Indian and Alaska Native, 0.6% Hispanic of any race, 1.1% two or more races (2000); Density: 929.4 persons per square mile (2000); Age: 30.8% under 18, 12.5% over 64 (2000); Marriage status: 19.8% never married, 64.0% now married, 6.9% widowed, 9.3% divorced (2000); Foreign born: 0.6% (2000); Ancestry (includes multiple ancestries): 31.1% German, 18.2% United States or American, 10.3% Irish, 8.9% English, 7.0% Other groups (2000).
Economy: In agricultural area; limestone quarries. Employment by occupation: 10.7% management, 12.4% professional, 15.7% services, 25.4% sales, 1.4% farming, 10.9% construction, 23.5% production (2000).
Income: Per capita income: $14,541 (2000); Median household income: $37,321 (2000); Poverty rate: 9.3% (2000).
Taxes: Total city taxes per capita: $10 (1997); City property taxes per capita: $10 (1997).
Education: High school graduation rate: 85.3% (2000); College graduation rate: 9.3% (2000).

School District(s)

Payson Community Unit School District 1 (PK-12)
2000 Enrollment: 640 217-656-3323
Housing: Homeownership rate: 83.3% (2000); Median home value: $58,800 (2000); Median rent: $270 per month (2000); Median age of housing: 28 years (2000).
Transportation: Commute to work: 97.8% car, 0.0% public transportation, 0.4% walk, 1.8% work from home (2000); Travel time to work: 17.8% less than 15 minutes, 59.8% 15 to 30 minutes, 20.1% 30 to 45 minutes, 1.2% 45 to 60 minutes, 1.0% 60 minutes or more (2000)

PLAINVILLE (village). Covers a land area of 0.230 square miles and a water area of 0 square miles. Located at 39.78° N. Lat.; 91.18° W. Long. Elevation is 693 feet.
Population: 248 (2000); Race: 98.3% White, 0.0% Black, 0.0% Asian, 0.0% American Indian and Alaska Native, 0.0% Hispanic of any race, 1.7% two or more races (2000); Density: 1,078.7 persons per square mile (2000); Age:

22.0% under 18, 17.7% over 64 (2000); Marriage status: 12.6% never married, 69.9% now married, 6.6% widowed, 10.9% divorced (2000); Foreign born: 1.7% (2000); Ancestry (includes multiple ancestries): 28.0% United States or American, 23.7% German, 9.1% English, 3.9% Irish, 3.4% Scottish (2000).
Economy: In agricultural area. Employment by occupation: 8.0% management, 18.8% professional, 15.2% services, 21.4% sales, 1.8% farming, 17.9% construction, 17.0% production (2000).
Income: Per capita income: $13,700 (2000); Median household income: $28,438 (2000); Poverty rate: 6.9% (2000).
Taxes: Total city taxes per capita: $7 (1997); City property taxes per capita: $7 (1997).
Education: High school graduation rate: 78.9% (2000); College graduation rate: 9.6% (2000).
Housing: Homeownership rate: 91.2% (2000); Median home value: $43,200 (2000); Median rent: $213 per month (2000); Median age of housing: 60+ years (2000).
Transportation: Commute to work: 94.5% car, 0.0% public transportation, 5.5% walk, 0.0% work from home (2000); Travel time to work: 16.4% less than 15 minutes, 40.9% 15 to 30 minutes, 37.3% 30 to 45 minutes, 0.0% 45 to 60 minutes, 5.5% 60 minutes or more (2000)

QUINCY (city). Covers a land area of 14.619 square miles and a water area of 0.027 square miles. Located at 39.93° N. Lat.; 91.38° W. Long. Elevation is 600 feet.
History: The first settlement at Quincy was called The Bluffs, and centered around the cabin of John Wood. Wood later served as lieutenant governor and governor of Illinois. When Adams County was created in 1825, Quincy was named as the county seat, and the town was platted. In the mid-1800's Quincy was an active shipping center.
Population: 40,366 (2000); Race: 92.9% White, 4.6% Black, 0.4% Asian, 0.2% American Indian and Alaska Native, 0.9% Hispanic of any race, 1.3% two or more races (2000); Density: 2,761.2 persons per square mile (2000); Age: 23.6% under 18, 19.7% over 64 (2000); Marriage status: 24.0% never married, 54.2% now married, 10.6% widowed, 11.2% divorced (2000); Foreign born: 1.0% (2000); Ancestry (includes multiple ancestries): 36.6% German, 12.1% Irish, 9.0% United States or American, 8.8% Other groups, 8.5% English (2000).
Vital Statistics: Birth rate: 135.8 per 10,000 population (1998)
Economy: Unemployment rate: 5.1% (11/2002); Total civilian labor force: 20,541 (11/2002); Single-family building permits issued: 81 (2001) / 65 (2000); Multi-family building permits issued: 91 (2001) / 34 (2000); Employment by occupation: 9.9% management, 17.3% professional, 18.4% services, 28.4% sales, 0.1% farming, 7.5% construction, 18.4% production (2000).
Income: Per capita income: $17,479 (2000); Median household income: $30,956 (2000); Poverty rate: 12.2% (2000).
Taxes: Total city taxes per capita: $230 (2000); City property taxes per capita: $103 (2000).
Education: High school graduation rate: 82.7% (2000); College graduation rate: 19.3% (2000).

School District(s)

Quincy School District 172 (PK-12)
2000 Enrollment: 7,352 217-223-8700

Four-year College(s)

Blessing Rieman College of Nursing (Private, Not-for-profit)
2001 Enrollment: 153 217-228-5520
2001 Tuition: In-state $11,200; Out-of-state $11,200
Quincy University (Private, Not-for-profit, Roman Catholic)
2001 Enrollment: 1,319 217-222-8020
2001 Tuition: In-state $15,010; Out-of-state $15,010

Two-year College(s)

Blessing Hospital School of Radiologic Technology (Private, Not-for-profit)
2001 Enrollment: 18 217-223-8400
Gem City College (Private, For-profit)
2001 Enrollment: 49 217-222-0391
2001 Tuition: In-state $6,300; Out-of-state $6,300
John Wood Community College (Public)
2001 Enrollment: 2,111 217-224-6500
2001 Tuition: In-state $4,650; Out-of-state $4,650

Housing: Homeownership rate: 66.4% (2000); Median home value: $70,600 (2000); Median rent: $323 per month (2000); Median age of housing: 50 years (2000).
Hospitals: Blessing Hospital (426 beds)
Newspapers: The Quincy Herald-Whig (7 x week)
Transportation: Commute to work: 92.3% car, 0.9% public transportation, 3.6% walk, 2.3% work from home (2000); Travel time to work: 68.6% less than 15 minutes, 23.5% 15 to 30 minutes, 4.0% 30 to 45 minutes, 1.8% 45 to 60 minutes, 2.0% 60 minutes or more (2000); Amtrak: Service available.
Airports: Quincy Regional-Baldwin Field (primary service)
Additional Information Contacts
Quincy Association of Realtors 217-228-0652
Quincy Chamber of Commerce 217-222-7980

URSA (village). Covers a land area of 0.682 square miles and a water area of 0 square miles. Located at 40.07° N. Lat.; 91.37° W. Long. Elevation is 600 feet.
Population: 595 (2000); Race: 98.2% White, 0.0% Black, 0.6% Asian, 1.1% American Indian and Alaska Native, 0.5% Hispanic of any race, 0.0% two or more races (2000); Density: 872.9 persons per square mile (2000); Age: 26.6% under 18, 18.9% over 64 (2000); Marriage status: 15.4% never married, 67.9% now married, 9.7% widowed, 7.0% divorced (2000); Foreign born: 0.3% (2000); Ancestry (includes multiple ancestries): 46.6% German, 13.9% Irish, 11.2% United States or American, 8.5% English, 5.8% Other groups (2000).
Economy: Grain, soybeans; livestock; dairying. Manufacturing of plastic products, feeds. Employment by occupation: 8.7% management, 14.2% professional, 14.8% services, 29.4% sales, 0.3% farming, 12.9% construction, 19.7% production (2000).
Income: Per capita income: $16,600 (2000); Median household income: $35,804 (2000); Poverty rate: 10.4% (2000).
Taxes: Total city taxes per capita: $21 (1997); City property taxes per capita: $19 (1997).
Education: High school graduation rate: 84.8% (2000); College graduation rate: 14.5% (2000).
Housing: Homeownership rate: 73.8% (2000); Median home value: $67,400 (2000); Median rent: $269 per month (2000); Median age of housing: 30 years (2000).
Transportation: Commute to work: 85.6% car, 0.0% public transportation, 5.6% walk, 8.2% work from home (2000); Travel time to work: 26.0% less than 15 minutes, 61.2% 15 to 30 minutes, 7.8% 30 to 45 minutes, 0.7% 45 to 60 minutes, 4.3% 60 minutes or more (2000)

Alexander County

Located in southern Illinois; bounded on the west and south by the Mississippi River and the Missouri border, and on the southeast by the Ohio River; includes part of Shawnee National Forest. Covers a land area of 236.40 square miles, a water area of 16.20 square miles, and is located in the Central Time Zone. The county government was organized in 1819. County seat is Cairo.

Weather Station: Cairo WSO City — Elevation: 311 feet

	Jan	Feb	Mar	Apr	May	Jun	Jul	Aug	Sep	Oct	Nov	Dec
High	41	47	57	69	78	86	90	87	81	70	57	46
Low	26	31	40	50	59	67	71	69	61	50	40	31
Precip	3.0	3.5	4.6	5.0	4.8	4.3	4.3	3.8	3.1	3.5	4.3	4.1
Snow	4.0	2.7	1.7	tr	0.0	0.0	0.0	0.0	0.0	0.1	0.2	0.9

High and Low temperatures in degrees Fahrenheit; Precipitation and Snow in inches

Population: 9,590 (2000); Race: 62.6% White, 34.9% Black, 0.5% Asian, 0.1% American Indian and Alaska Native, 1.5% Hispanic of any race, 1.1% two or more races (2000); Density: 40.6 persons per square mile (2000); Age: 25.9% under 18, 16.8% over 64 (2000).
Religion: Five largest groups: 21.4% Southern Baptist Convention, 3.5% American Baptist Churches in the USA, 3.3% Catholic Church, 2.4% The United Methodist Church, 1.5% Assemblies of God (2000).
Economy: Unemployment rate: 8.0% (11/2002); Total civilian labor force: 3,903 (11/2002); Leading industries: 19.5% manufacturing; 18.8% health care and social assistance; 18.0% transportation & warehousing (2000); Companies that employ more than 1,000 persons: 0 (2000); Companies that employ more than 100 persons: 4 (2000); Farms: 166 totaling 71,280 acres (1997); Minority business ownership rate: 0.0% (1997); Women business ownership rate: 23.1% (1997); Retail sales per capita: $2,903 (1997). Single-family building permits issued: 2 (2001) / 2 (2000); Multi-family building permits issued: 0 (2001) / 0 (2000).
Income: Per capita income: $16,084 (2000); Median household income: $26,042 (2000); Poverty rate: 26.1% (2000); Bankruptcy rate: 5.53% (2001).
Taxes: Total county taxes per capita: $82 (1997); County property taxes per capita: $82 (1997).

Education: High school graduation rate: 67.0% (2000); College graduation rate: 6.9% (2000).
Housing: Homeownership rate: 72.0% (2000); Median home value: $33,400 (2000); Median rent: $185 per month (2000); Median age of housing: 39 years (2000).
Health: Birth rate: 146.0 per 10,000 population (1998); Age adjusted death rate: 92.8 per 10,000 population (1999); Age adjusted cancer mortality rate: 276.0 deaths per 100,000 population (1999). Number of physicians: 5.2 per 10,000 population (1999); Number of hospital beds: n/a (1999).
Elections: 2000 Presidential election results: 58.6% Gore, 39.5% Bush, 0.7% Nader, 0.7% Buchanan
National and State Parks: Fort Defiance State Park; Horseshoe Lake State Conservation Area
Additional Information Contacts
Alexander County Government Offices 618-734-0386
Cairo Chamber of Commerce 618-734-2737
Horseshoe Lake Chamber of Commerce 618-776-5198

Alexander County Communities

CAIRO (city). Covers a land area of 7.051 square miles and a water area of 2.081 square miles. Located at 37.01° N. Lat.; 89.18° W. Long. Elevation is 311 feet.
History: John G. Comegys, a St. Louis merchant, in 1818 secured the incorporation of the city of Cairo, named because he thought its site resembled Cairo, Egypt. Comegys died before he could carry out his plans, but the name Cairo remained when the Cairo City and Canal Company was formed in 1837 by Darius B. Holbrook. When the Illinois Central Railroad tracks were laid between Cairo and Chicago, Cairo's economy grew. Cairo was a Union headquarters during the Civil War, and received many thousands of Confederate prisoners.
Population: 3,632 (2000); Race: 36.8% White, 61.3% Black, 1.1% Asian, 0.0% American Indian and Alaska Native, 0.7% Hispanic of any race, 0.8% two or more races (2000); Density: 515.1 persons per square mile (2000); Age: 30.1% under 18, 18.2% over 64 (2000); Marriage status: 29.1% never married, 44.9% now married, 9.7% widowed, 16.2% divorced (2000); Foreign born: 1.4% (2000); Ancestry (includes multiple ancestries): 54.6% Other groups, 6.0% Irish, 6.0% German, 3.9% United States or American, 3.4% English (2000).
Economy: Single-family building permits issued: 2 (2001) / 2 (2000); Multi-family building permits issued: 0 (2001) / 0 (2000); Employment by occupation: 10.9% management, 14.9% professional, 22.7% services, 20.5% sales, 0.0% farming, 9.0% construction, 22.0% production (2000).
Income: Per capita income: $16,220 (2000); Median household income: $21,607 (2000); Poverty rate: 33.5% (2000).
Taxes: Total city taxes per capita: $226 (2000); City property taxes per capita: $105 (2000).
Education: High school graduation rate: 67.3% (2000); College graduation rate: 7.2% (2000).

School District(s)

Cairo Unit School District 1 (PK-12)
2000 Enrollment: 928 618-734-4102
Housing: Homeownership rate: 56.1% (2000); Median home value: $24,900 (2000); Median rent: $176 per month (2000); Median age of housing: 48 years (2000).
Newspapers: The Cairo Citizen (1 x month)
Transportation: Commute to work: 89.9% car, 1.3% public transportation, 7.4% walk, 0.0% work from home (2000); Travel time to work: 61.4% less than 15 minutes, 18.0% 15 to 30 minutes, 10.2% 30 to 45 minutes, 7.2% 45 to 60 minutes, 3.2% 60 minutes or more (2000)
Additional Information Contacts
Cairo Chamber of Commerce 618-734-2737

EAST CAPE GIRARDEAU (village). Covers a land area of 1.969 square miles and a water area of 0.034 square miles. Located at 37.29° N. Lat.; 89.49° W. Long. Elevation is 340 feet.
Population: 437 (2000); Race: 96.7% White, 0.0% Black, 1.2% Asian, 0.0% American Indian and Alaska Native, 1.7% Hispanic of any race, 2.1% two or more races (2000); Density: 222.0 persons per square mile (2000); Age: 25.0% under 18, 13.1% over 64 (2000); Marriage status: 18.2% never married, 61.3% now married, 5.9% widowed, 14.7% divorced (2000); Foreign born: 1.7% (2000); Ancestry (includes multiple ancestries): 25.2% United States or American, 17.6% Other groups, 17.4% German, 14.8% Irish, 3.8% English (2000).
Economy: Wheat. Shawnee National Forest to East. Single-family building permits issued: 0 (2001) / 0 (2000); Multi-family building permits issued: 0 (2001) / 0 (2000); Employment by occupation: 8.1% management, 13.4% professional, 16.1% services, 23.7% sales, 0.0% farming, 7.5% construction, 31.2% production (2000).
Income: Per capita income: $14,420 (2000); Median household income: $29,688 (2000); Poverty rate: 10.5% (2000).
Taxes: Total city taxes per capita: $7 (1997); City property taxes per capita: $7 (1997).
Education: High school graduation rate: 76.4% (2000); College graduation rate: 9.1% (2000).
Housing: Homeownership rate: 80.7% (2000); Median home value: $37,500 (2000); Median rent: $255 per month (2000); Median age of housing: 29 years (2000).
Transportation: Commute to work: 95.1% car, 2.7% public transportation, 0.0% walk, 1.1% work from home (2000); Travel time to work: 42.6% less than 15 minutes, 36.1% 15 to 30 minutes, 11.5% 30 to 45 minutes, 5.5% 45 to 60 minutes, 4.4% 60 minutes or more (2000)

MCCLURE (unincorporated postal area, zip code 62957). Covers a land area of 50.471 square miles and a water area of 0.768 square miles. Located at 37.30° N. Lat.; 89.43° W. Long. Elevation is 343 feet.
Population: 1,174 (2000); Race: 98.8% White, 0.0% Black, 0.4% Asian, 0.0% American Indian and Alaska Native, 0.6% Hispanic of any race, 0.8% two or more races (2000); Density: 23.3 persons per square mile (2000); Age: 26.6% under 18, 17.1% over 64 (2000); Marriage status: 19.6% never married, 61.3% now married, 8.0% widowed, 11.1% divorced (2000); Foreign born: 0.6% (2000); Ancestry (includes multiple ancestries): 24.9% United States or American, 16.3% German, 11.7% Other groups, 11.2% English, 9.0% Irish (2000).
Economy: Employment by occupation: 14.4% management, 9.2% professional, 19.0% services, 17.8% sales, 1.7% farming, 14.4% construction, 23.4% production (2000).
Income: Per capita income: $16,247 (2000); Median household income: $29,766 (2000); Poverty rate: 17.8% (2000).
Education: High school graduation rate: 77.4% (2000); College graduation rate: 9.8% (2000).
Housing: Homeownership rate: 82.8% (2000); Median home value: $45,600 (2000); Median rent: $236 per month (2000); Median age of housing: 30 years (2000).
Transportation: Commute to work: 95.3% car, 1.1% public transportation, 0.0% walk, 3.2% work from home (2000); Travel time to work: 30.5% less than 15 minutes, 38.7% 15 to 30 minutes, 20.4% 30 to 45 minutes, 5.5% 45 to 60 minutes, 4.8% 60 minutes or more (2000)

MILLER CITY (unincorporated postal area, zip code 62962). Covers a land area of 37.441 square miles and a water area of 0.523 square miles. Located at 37.09° N. Lat.; 89.33° W. Long. Elevation is 333 feet.
Population: 93 (2000); Race: 100.0% White, 0.0% Black, 0.0% Asian, 0.0% American Indian and Alaska Native, 0.0% Hispanic of any race, 0.0% two or more races (2000); Density: 2.5 persons per square mile (2000); Age: 0.0% under 18, 14.5% over 64 (2000); Marriage status: 16.4% never married, 61.8% now married, 21.8% widowed, 0.0% divorced (2000); Foreign born: 0.0% (2000); Ancestry (includes multiple ancestries): 43.6% German, 9.1% United States or American, 9.1% Irish (2000).
Economy: Employment by occupation: 47.4% management, 0.0% professional, 0.0% services, 0.0% sales, 26.3% farming, 0.0% construction, 26.3% production (2000).
Income: Per capita income: $18,242 (2000); Median household income: $26,250 (2000); Poverty rate: 50.9% (2000).
Education: High school graduation rate: 58.7% (2000); College graduation rate: 30.4% (2000).
Housing: Homeownership rate: 36.8% (2000); Median home value: $45,000 (2000); Median rent: $150 per month (2000); Median age of housing: 28 years (2000).
Transportation: Commute to work: 100.0% car, 0.0% public transportation, 0.0% walk, 0.0% work from home (2000); Travel time to work: 0.0% less than 15 minutes, 73.7% 15 to 30 minutes, 0.0% 30 to 45 minutes, 0.0% 45 to 60 minutes, 26.3% 60 minutes or more (2000)

OLIVE BRANCH (unincorporated postal area, zip code 62969). Covers a land area of 25.996 square miles and a water area of 2.618 square miles. Located at 37.16° N. Lat.; 89.35° W. Long. Elevation is 340 feet.
Population: 879 (2000); Race: 98.4% White, 0.0% Black, 0.0% Asian, 0.0% American Indian and Alaska Native, 0.0% Hispanic of any race, 1.6% two or more races (2000); Density: 33.8 persons per square mile (2000); Age: 26.0%

under 18, 19.5% over 64 (2000); Marriage status: 13.9% never married, 66.5% now married, 11.0% widowed, 8.6% divorced (2000); Foreign born: 0.7% (2000); Ancestry (includes multiple ancestries): 10.1% Other groups, 10.0% German, 9.9% United States or American, 7.5% Irish, 7.0% English (2000).
Economy: Employment by occupation: 15.5% management, 14.7% professional, 16.6% services, 17.7% sales, 0.0% farming, 22.3% construction, 13.3% production (2000).
Income: Per capita income: $23,970 (2000); Median household income: $30,833 (2000); Poverty rate: 13.5% (2000).
Education: High school graduation rate: 72.6% (2000); College graduation rate: 12.4% (2000).
Housing: Homeownership rate: 88.3% (2000); Median home value: $59,600 (2000); Median rent: $144 per month (2000); Median age of housing: 27 years (2000).
Transportation: Commute to work: 88.3% car, 1.6% public transportation, 4.3% walk, 5.7% work from home (2000); Travel time to work: 18.7% less than 15 minutes, 48.4% 15 to 30 minutes, 20.7% 30 to 45 minutes, 2.0% 45 to 60 minutes, 10.1% 60 minutes or more (2000)
Additional Information Contacts
Horseshoe Lake Chamber of Commerce 618-776-5198

TAMMS (village). Covers a land area of 2.340 square miles and a water area of 0 square miles. Located at 37.24° N. Lat.; 89.26° W. Long. Elevation is 335 feet.
Population: 724 (2000); Race: 73.6% White, 23.4% Black, 0.0% Asian, 0.0% American Indian and Alaska Native, 1.8% Hispanic of any race, 2.9% two or more races (2000); Density: 309.4 persons per square mile (2000); Age: 31.6% under 18, 22.3% over 64 (2000); Marriage status: 20.3% never married, 56.2% now married, 13.1% widowed, 10.5% divorced (2000); Foreign born: 0.0% (2000); Ancestry (includes multiple ancestries): 29.3% Other groups, 12.2% United States or American, 9.6% German, 9.0% Irish, 3.2% French (except Basque) (2000).
Economy: In agricultural area. Employment by occupation: 11.9% management, 11.4% professional, 33.2% services, 15.3% sales, 0.0% farming, 8.4% construction, 19.8% production (2000).
Income: Per capita income: $11,131 (2000); Median household income: $19,511 (2000); Poverty rate: 30.8% (2000).
Taxes: Total city taxes per capita: $8 (1997); City property taxes per capita: $8 (1997).
Education: High school graduation rate: 66.5% (2000); College graduation rate: 1.1% (2000).

School District(s)

Egyptian Community Unit School District 5 (PK-12)
2000 Enrollment: 734 618-776-5306
Housing: Homeownership rate: 81.9% (2000); Median home value: $42,000 (2000); Median rent: $200 per month (2000); Median age of housing: 28 years (2000).
Transportation: Commute to work: 92.0% car, 1.0% public transportation, 3.0% walk, 1.0% work from home (2000); Travel time to work: 29.9% less than 15 minutes, 35.0% 15 to 30 minutes, 17.8% 30 to 45 minutes, 9.6% 45 to 60 minutes, 7.6% 60 minutes or more (2000)

THEBES (village). Covers a land area of 1.800 square miles and a water area of 0.513 square miles. Located at 37.21° N. Lat.; 89.45° W. Long. Elevation is 413 feet.
History: Thebes was laid out in 1844, and once served as the seat of Alexander County. The site was earlier known as Sparhawk's Landing.
Population: 478 (2000); Race: 83.6% White, 16.4% Black, 0.0% Asian, 0.0% American Indian and Alaska Native, 0.0% Hispanic of any race, 0.0% two or more races (2000); Density: 265.6 persons per square mile (2000); Age: 33.8% under 18, 12.0% over 64 (2000); Marriage status: 26.1% never married, 52.8% now married, 10.7% widowed, 10.4% divorced (2000); Foreign born: 0.0% (2000); Ancestry (includes multiple ancestries): 26.9% Other groups, 12.7% German, 9.6% Irish, 7.4% United States or American, 6.1% Scottish (2000).
Economy: Single-family building permits issued: 0 (2001) / 0 (2000); Multi-family building permits issued: 0 (2001) / 0 (2000); Employment by occupation: 5.7% management, 8.6% professional, 22.9% services, 19.3% sales, 2.1% farming, 12.9% construction, 28.6% production (2000).
Income: Per capita income: $11,262 (2000); Median household income: $20,250 (2000); Poverty rate: 31.7% (2000).
Education: High school graduation rate: 59.3% (2000); College graduation rate: 3.7% (2000).
Housing: Homeownership rate: 62.9% (2000); Median home value: $23,200 (2000); Median rent: $213 per month (2000); Median age of housing: 29 years (2000).
Transportation: Commute to work: 97.8% car, 0.0% public transportation, 0.0% walk, 0.0% work from home (2000); Travel time to work: 5.1% less than 15 minutes, 48.6% 15 to 30 minutes, 37.0% 30 to 45 minutes, 2.9% 45 to 60 minutes, 6.5% 60 minutes or more (2000)

Bond County

Located in southwest central Illinois; drained by the Kaskaskia River. Covers a land area of 380.20 square miles, a water area of 2.50 square miles, and is located in the Central Time Zone. The county government was organized in 1817. County seat is Greenville.
Population: 17,633 (2000); Race: 90.7% White, 7.4% Black, 0.1% Asian, 0.6% American Indian and Alaska Native, 1.5% Hispanic of any race, 0.9% two or more races (2000); Density: 46.4 persons per square mile (2000); Age: 21.9% under 18, 14.6% over 64 (2000).
Religion: Five largest groups: 10.6% Christian Churches and Churches of Christ, 10.0% Southern Baptist Convention, 8.2% Catholic Church, 5.1% The United Methodist Church, 3.5% Free Methodist Church of North America (2000).
Economy: Unemployment rate: 5.4% (11/2002); Total civilian labor force: 8,463 (11/2002); Leading industries: 17.1% manufacturing; 13.7% health care and social assistance; 13.1% retail trade (2000); Companies that employ more than 1,000 persons: 0 (2000); Companies that employ more than 100 persons: 7 (2000); Farms: 616 totaling 180,064 acres (1997); Minority business ownership rate: 0.0% (1997); Women business ownership rate: 19.8% (1997); Retail sales per capita: $5,704 (1997). Single-family building permits issued: 60 (2001) / 52 (2000); Multi-family building permits issued: 0 (2001) / 54 (2000).
Income: Per capita income: $17,947 (2000); Median household income: $37,680 (2000); Poverty rate: 9.3% (2000); Bankruptcy rate: 5.14% (2001).
Taxes: Total county taxes per capita: $85 (1997); County property taxes per capita: $70 (1997).
Education: High school graduation rate: 72.8% (2000); College graduation rate: 15.0% (2000).
Housing: Homeownership rate: 79.6% (2000); Median home value: $68,900 (2000); Median rent: $271 per month (2000); Median age of housing: 35 years (2000).
Health: Birth rate: 113.4 per 10,000 population (1998); Age adjusted death rate: 85.4 per 10,000 population (1999); Age adjusted cancer mortality rate: 183.8 deaths per 100,000 population (1999). Number of physicians: 5.7 per 10,000 population (1999); Number of hospital beds: 106.6 per 10,000 population (1999).
Elections: 2000 Presidential election results: 43.5% Gore, 54.1% Bush, 1.6% Nader, 0.4% Buchanan
Additional Information Contacts
Bond County Government Offices. 618-664-1966
Greenville Chamber of Commerce. 618-664-9272

Bond County Communities

GREENVILLE (city). Covers a land area of 5.202 square miles and a water area of 0 square miles. Located at 38.89° N. Lat.; 89.40° W. Long. Elevation is 500 feet.
History: Greenville was settled in 1815, and developed as the seat of Bond County. Early industries were an evaporated milk plant, a glove plant, and a manufacturer of costumes and uniforms.
Population: 6,955 (2000); Race: 82.3% White, 15.9% Black, 0.1% Asian, 0.7% American Indian and Alaska Native, 2.3% Hispanic of any race, 0.6% two or more races (2000); Density: 1,337.0 persons per square mile (2000); Age: 16.0% under 18, 14.9% over 64 (2000); Marriage status: 21.6% never married, 65.4% now married, 7.7% widowed, 5.4% divorced (2000); Foreign born: 1.1% (2000); Ancestry (includes multiple ancestries): 24.5% German, 11.2% English, 8.1% Other groups, 7.4% Irish, 4.9% United States or American (2000).
Economy: Single-family building permits issued: 5 (2001) / 6 (2000); Multi-family building permits issued: 0 (2001) / 54 (2000); Employment by occupation: 9.2% management, 22.8% professional, 20.1% services, 27.1% sales, 0.6% farming, 5.8% construction, 14.3% production (2000).
Income: Per capita income: $17,326 (2000); Median household income: $35,650 (2000); Poverty rate: 11.8% (2000).
Taxes: Total city taxes per capita: $83 (1997); City property taxes per capita: $64 (1997).

Education: High school graduation rate: 64.1% (2000); College graduation rate: 19.2% (2000).

School District(s)

Bond Co C U School District 2 (PK-12)
2000 Enrollment: 1,950 618-664-0170

Four-year College(s)

Greenville College (Private, Not-for-profit, Free Methodist)
2001 Enrollment: 1,160 618-664-2800
2001 Tuition: In-state $13,490; Out-of-state $13,490

Housing: Homeownership rate: 69.6% (2000); Median home value: $68,800 (2000); Median rent: $270 per month (2000); Median age of housing: 43 years (2000).
Hospitals: Edward A. Utlaut Memorial Hospital (50 beds)
Newspapers: The Greenville Advocate (2 x week)
Transportation: Commute to work: 79.7% car, 0.4% public transportation, 14.8% walk, 4.3% work from home (2000); Travel time to work: 68.4% less than 15 minutes, 12.5% 15 to 30 minutes, 9.6% 30 to 45 minutes, 4.4% 45 to 60 minutes, 5.0% 60 minutes or more (2000)
Airports: Greenville
Additional Information Contacts
Greenville Chamber of Commerce. 618-664-9272

MULBERRY GROVE (village). Covers a land area of 0.986 square miles and a water area of 0.009 square miles. Located at 38.92° N. Lat.; 89.26° W. Long. Elevation is 560 feet.
Population: 671 (2000); Race: 97.6% White, 1.9% Black, 0.0% Asian, 0.0% American Indian and Alaska Native, 0.0% Hispanic of any race, 0.4% two or more races (2000); Density: 680.7 persons per square mile (2000); Age: 28.7% under 18, 18.6% over 64 (2000); Marriage status: 19.8% never married, 54.1% now married, 12.5% widowed, 13.5% divorced (2000); Foreign born: 0.3% (2000); Ancestry (includes multiple ancestries): 18.9% German, 12.9% Irish, 12.3% United States or American, 9.9% Other groups, 7.6% English (2000).
Economy: In agricultural area: corn, wheat; livestock; dairy products; ships sand. Employment by occupation: 5.0% management, 9.0% professional, 19.3% services, 21.7% sales, 1.7% farming, 6.3% construction, 37.0% production (2000).
Income: Per capita income: $15,105 (2000); Median household income: $31,094 (2000); Poverty rate: 14.8% (2000).
Taxes: Total city taxes per capita: $49 (1997); City property taxes per capita: $22 (1997).
Education: High school graduation rate: 74.5% (2000); College graduation rate: 5.2% (2000).

School District(s)

Mulberry Grove C U School District 1 (PK-12)
2000 Enrollment: 501 618-326-8812

Housing: Homeownership rate: 75.4% (2000); Median home value: $45,200 (2000); Median rent: $274 per month (2000); Median age of housing: 45 years (2000).
Transportation: Commute to work: 92.4% car, 0.0% public transportation, 1.0% walk, 6.0% work from home (2000); Travel time to work: 30.7% less than 15 minutes, 41.0% 15 to 30 minutes, 9.5% 30 to 45 minutes, 5.7% 45 to 60 minutes, 13.1% 60 minutes or more (2000)

OLD RIPLEY (village). Covers a land area of 0.149 square miles and a water area of 0 square miles. Located at 38.89° N. Lat.; 89.57° W. Long. Elevation is 570 feet.
Population: 127 (2000); Race: 93.5% White, 1.9% Black, 0.0% Asian, 2.8% American Indian and Alaska Native, 0.0% Hispanic of any race, 1.9% two or more races (2000); Density: 851.3 persons per square mile (2000); Age: 24.1% under 18, 13.9% over 64 (2000); Marriage status: 24.1% never married, 65.5% now married, 5.7% widowed, 4.6% divorced (2000); Foreign born: 0.0% (2000); Ancestry (includes multiple ancestries): 22.2% German, 11.1% Irish, 9.3% English, 8.3% Dutch, 8.3% United States or American (2000).
Economy: In agricultural area: corn, wheat; dairy products; livestock. Employment by occupation: 4.1% management, 8.2% professional, 20.4% services, 22.4% sales, 0.0% farming, 28.6% construction, 16.3% production (2000).
Income: Per capita income: $15,363 (2000); Median household income: $35,000 (2000); Poverty rate: 3.7% (2000).
Taxes: Total city taxes per capita: $20 (1997); City property taxes per capita: $10 (1997).
Education: High school graduation rate: 77.9% (2000); College graduation rate: 5.2% (2000).
Housing: Homeownership rate: 97.8% (2000); Median home value: $34,200 (2000); Median age of housing: 49 years (2000).
Transportation: Commute to work: 95.9% car, 0.0% public transportation, 0.0% walk, 4.1% work from home (2000); Travel time to work: 4.3% less than 15 minutes, 42.6% 15 to 30 minutes, 29.8% 30 to 45 minutes, 12.8% 45 to 60 minutes, 10.6% 60 minutes or more (2000)

PIERRON (village). Covers a land area of 0.851 square miles and a water area of 0 square miles. Located at 38.77° N. Lat.; 89.55° W. Long. Elevation is 525 feet.
Population: 653 (2000); Race: 95.6% White, 0.0% Black, 0.0% Asian, 0.3% American Indian and Alaska Native, 5.4% Hispanic of any race, 2.5% two or more races (2000); Density: 767.6 persons per square mile (2000); Age: 28.3% under 18, 11.1% over 64 (2000); Marriage status: 22.1% never married, 55.2% now married, 7.4% widowed, 15.4% divorced (2000); Foreign born: 2.6% (2000); Ancestry (includes multiple ancestries): 41.7% German, 14.4% Other groups, 11.6% Irish, 10.0% United States or American, 9.5% English (2000).
Economy: Employment by occupation: 11.3% management, 7.9% professional, 14.9% services, 16.9% sales, 0.0% farming, 14.9% construction, 34.1% production (2000).
Income: Per capita income: $18,196 (2000); Median household income: $35,595 (2000); Poverty rate: 5.1% (2000).
Taxes: Total city taxes per capita: $18 (1997); City property taxes per capita: $17 (1997).
Education: High school graduation rate: 78.4% (2000); College graduation rate: 8.5% (2000).
Housing: Homeownership rate: 89.3% (2000); Median home value: $65,700 (2000); Median rent: $370 per month (2000); Median age of housing: 22 years (2000).
Transportation: Commute to work: 93.6% car, 0.7% public transportation, 0.0% walk, 5.7% work from home (2000); Travel time to work: 19.0% less than 15 minutes, 47.3% 15 to 30 minutes, 15.1% 30 to 45 minutes, 7.5% 45 to 60 minutes, 11.1% 60 minutes or more (2000)

POCAHONTAS (village). Covers a land area of 0.751 square miles and a water area of 0.021 square miles. Located at 38.82° N. Lat.; 89.54° W. Long. Elevation is 570 feet.
History: Pocahontas, named for the legendary Indian princess, began as a stagecoach stop on the Cumberland Road.
Population: 727 (2000); Race: 98.7% White, 0.3% Black, 0.4% Asian, 0.5% American Indian and Alaska Native, 0.0% Hispanic of any race, 0.1% two or more races (2000); Density: 968.3 persons per square mile (2000); Age: 25.2% under 18, 13.9% over 64 (2000); Marriage status: 30.8% never married, 50.3% now married, 9.8% widowed, 9.0% divorced (2000); Foreign born: 0.0% (2000); Ancestry (includes multiple ancestries): 40.9% German, 13.1% United States or American, 11.7% English, 11.1% Irish, 9.7% Other groups (2000).
Economy: Single-family building permits issued: 1 (2001) / 0 (2000); Multi-family building permits issued: 0 (2001) / 0 (2000); Employment by occupation: 7.4% management, 6.2% professional, 20.5% services, 20.2% sales, 0.0% farming, 11.3% construction, 34.4% production (2000).
Income: Per capita income: $14,562 (2000); Median household income: $28,750 (2000); Poverty rate: 13.8% (2000).
Taxes: Total city taxes per capita: $71 (1997); City property taxes per capita: $64 (1997).
Education: High school graduation rate: 77.9% (2000); College graduation rate: 4.7% (2000).
Housing: Homeownership rate: 81.8% (2000); Median home value: $59,200 (2000); Median rent: $258 per month (2000); Median age of housing: 45 years (2000).
Transportation: Commute to work: 92.8% car, 0.6% public transportation, 5.7% walk, 0.6% work from home (2000); Travel time to work: 20.2% less than 15 minutes, 43.1% 15 to 30 minutes, 11.4% 30 to 45 minutes, 14.2% 45 to 60 minutes, 11.1% 60 minutes or more (2000)

SMITHBORO (village). Covers a land area of 1.182 square miles and a water area of 0 square miles. Located at 38.89° N. Lat.; 89.34° W. Long. Elevation is 550 feet.
Population: 200 (2000); Race: 97.9% White, 0.0% Black, 0.0% Asian, 2.1% American Indian and Alaska Native, 2.1% Hispanic of any race, 0.0% two or more races (2000); Density: 169.1 persons per square mile (2000); Age: 35.9% under 18, 12.8% over 64 (2000); Marriage status: 19.7% never married, 59.1% now married, 8.3% widowed, 12.9% divorced (2000); Foreign born: 1.5% (2000); Ancestry (includes multiple ancestries): 24.1%

German, 20.5% Other groups, 11.3% English, 9.7% Irish, 7.7% Italian (2000).
Economy: Railroad junction. In agricultural area: corn, wheat, barley, sorghum. Single-family building permits issued: 0 (2001) / 0 (2000); Multi-family building permits issued: 0 (2001) / 0 (2000); Employment by occupation: 17.4% management, 2.9% professional, 26.1% services, 13.0% sales, 0.0% farming, 13.0% construction, 27.5% production (2000).
Income: Per capita income: $10,284 (2000); Median household income: $21,250 (2000); Poverty rate: 26.4% (2000).
Taxes: Total city taxes per capita: $30 (1997); City property taxes per capita: $20 (1997).
Education: High school graduation rate: 67.9% (2000); College graduation rate: 5.5% (2000).
Housing: Homeownership rate: 77.3% (2000); Median home value: $44,400 (2000); Median rent: $256 per month (2000); Median age of housing: 36 years (2000).
Transportation: Commute to work: 95.4% car, 0.0% public transportation, 0.0% walk, 0.0% work from home (2000); Travel time to work: 55.4% less than 15 minutes, 6.2% 15 to 30 minutes, 16.9% 30 to 45 minutes, 4.6% 45 to 60 minutes, 16.9% 60 minutes or more (2000)

SORENTO (village). Covers a land area of 0.541 square miles and a water area of 0 square miles. Located at 38.99° N. Lat.; 89.57° W. Long. Elevation is 585 feet.
Population: 601 (2000); Race: 95.0% White, 0.0% Black, 0.5% Asian, 1.5% American Indian and Alaska Native, 2.0% Hispanic of any race, 3.0% two or more races (2000); Density: 1,110.5 persons per square mile (2000); Age: 27.4% under 18, 10.0% over 64 (2000); Marriage status: 22.4% never married, 58.6% now married, 7.6% widowed, 11.5% divorced (2000); Foreign born: 0.5% (2000); Ancestry (includes multiple ancestries): 31.0% German, 16.1% Other groups, 13.5% English, 10.9% Irish, 10.8% United States or American (2000).
Economy: Railroad junction. In agricultural area: corn, wheat, soybeans, sorghum; dairy products. Single-family building permits issued: 1 (2001) / 0 (2000); Multi-family building permits issued: 0 (2001) / 0 (2000); Employment by occupation: 6.6% management, 9.1% professional, 23.7% services, 16.0% sales, 0.0% farming, 14.6% construction, 30.0% production (2000).
Income: Per capita income: $13,167 (2000); Median household income: $31,250 (2000); Poverty rate: 14.2% (2000).
Taxes: Total city taxes per capita: $30 (1997); City property taxes per capita: $28 (1997).
Education: High school graduation rate: 77.0% (2000); College graduation rate: 5.0% (2000).
Housing: Homeownership rate: 85.2% (2000); Median home value: $31,500 (2000); Median rent: $153 per month (2000); Median age of housing: 47 years (2000).
Newspapers: The Sorento News (1 x week)
Transportation: Commute to work: 96.5% car, 0.0% public transportation, 1.4% walk, 1.8% work from home (2000); Travel time to work: 10.0% less than 15 minutes, 30.7% 15 to 30 minutes, 36.8% 30 to 45 minutes, 9.3% 45 to 60 minutes, 13.2% 60 minutes or more (2000)

Boone County

Located in northern Illinois; bounded on the north by Wisconsin. Covers a land area of 281.30 square miles, a water area of 0.70 square miles, and is located in the Central Time Zone. The county government was organized in 1837. County seat is Belvidere.

Boone County is part of the Rockford, IL MSA. The entire metro area includes: Boone County; Ogle County; Winnebago County

Population: 41,786 (2000); Race: 90.3% White, 0.4% Black, 0.3% Asian, 0.2% American Indian and Alaska Native, 12.7% Hispanic of any race, 2.3% two or more races (2000); Density: 148.6 persons per square mile (2000); Age: 29.8% under 18, 10.7% over 64 (2000).
Religion: Five largest groups: 19.0% Catholic Church, 6.0% Lutheran Church—Missouri Synod, 5.1% The United Methodist Church, 2.6% Evangelical Lutheran Church in America, 2.3% Presbyterian Church (U.S.A.) (2000).
Economy: Unemployment rate: 7.2% (11/2002); Total civilian labor force: 21,441 (11/2002); Leading industries: 47.3% manufacturing; 9.7% construction; 9.6% retail trade (2000); Companies that employ more than 1,000 persons: 1 (2000); Companies that employ more than 100 persons: 12 (2000); Farms: 490 totaling 141,426 acres (1997); Minority business ownership rate: 0.0% (1997); Women business ownership rate: 27.3% (1997); Retail sales per capita: $5,239 (1997). Single-family building permits issued: 472 (2001) / 361 (2000); Multi-family building permits issued: 16 (2001) / 4 (2000).
Income: Per capita income: $21,590 (2000); Median household income: $52,397 (2000); Poverty rate: 7.0% (2000); Bankruptcy rate: 6.58% (2001).
Taxes: Total county taxes per capita: $134 (2000); County property taxes per capita: $96 (2000).
Education: High school graduation rate: 80.8% (2000); College graduation rate: 14.5% (2000).
Housing: Homeownership rate: 78.6% (2000); Median home value: $123,600 (2000); Median rent: $455 per month (2000); Median age of housing: 28 years (2000).
Health: Birth rate: 130.9 per 10,000 population (1998); Age adjusted death rate: 89.1 per 10,000 population (1999); Age adjusted cancer mortality rate: 241.4 deaths per 100,000 population (1999). Number of physicians: 13.4 per 10,000 population (1999); Number of hospital beds: 16.5 per 10,000 population (1999).
Elections: 2000 Presidential election results: 41.8% Gore, 55.5% Bush, 2.1% Nader, 0.3% Buchanan
Additional Information Contacts
Boone County Government Offices 815-547-4770
Belvidere Board of Realtors 815-544-2719
Belvidere Chamber of Commerce 815-544-4357

Boone County Communities

BELVIDERE (city). Covers a land area of 9.071 square miles and a water area of 0.053 square miles. Located at 42.25° N. Lat.; 88.84° W. Long. Elevation is 770 feet.
History: Belvidere was founded in 1836 as a stop on the Chicago-Galena stagecoach route. The National Sewing Machine Plant was founded here in 1879.
Population: 20,820 (2000); Race: 85.2% White, 0.4% Black, 0.1% Asian, 0.1% American Indian and Alaska Native, 20.6% Hispanic of any race, 2.7% two or more races (2000); Density: 2,295.3 persons per square mile (2000); Age: 29.5% under 18, 12.2% over 64 (2000); Marriage status: 23.9% never married, 58.6% now married, 6.8% widowed, 10.7% divorced (2000); Foreign born: 11.9% (2000); Ancestry (includes multiple ancestries): 30.6% German, 23.3% Other groups, 13.2% Irish, 9.0% English, 6.9% Swedish (2000).
Vital Statistics: Birth rate: 172.9 per 10,000 population (1998)
Economy: Single-family building permits issued: 232 (2001) / 152 (2000); Multi-family building permits issued: 16 (2001) / 4 (2000); Employment by occupation: 7.9% management, 10.6% professional, 14.9% services, 24.7% sales, 0.8% farming, 10.1% construction, 31.0% production (2000).
Income: Per capita income: $17,804 (2000); Median household income: $42,529 (2000); Poverty rate: 10.0% (2000).
Taxes: Total city taxes per capita: $240 (1997); City property taxes per capita: $233 (1997).
Education: High school graduation rate: 74.6% (2000); College graduation rate: 8.8% (2000).

School District(s)

Belvidere C U School District 100 (PK-12)
2000 Enrollment: 6,626 815-544-0301
Boone County Special Education Coop (PK-12)
2000 Enrollment: 69 815-544-9851

Housing: Homeownership rate: 67.5% (2000); Median home value: $99,600 (2000); Median rent: $451 per month (2000); Median age of housing: 37 years (2000).
Hospitals: Northwest Suburban Community Hospital (27 beds)
Newspapers: Belvidere Daily Republican (6 x week)
Transportation: Commute to work: 95.3% car, 0.4% public transportation, 1.9% walk, 1.9% work from home (2000); Travel time to work: 37.8% less than 15 minutes, 27.0% 15 to 30 minutes, 17.7% 30 to 45 minutes, 7.8% 45 to 60 minutes, 9.7% 60 minutes or more (2000)
Additional Information Contacts
Belvidere Board of Realtors 815-544-2719
Belvidere Chamber of Commerce 815-544-4357

CALEDONIA (village). Aka North Caledonia. Covers a land area of 0.533 square miles and a water area of 0 square miles. Located at 42.36° N. Lat.; 88.89° W. Long. Elevation is 940 feet.

Population: 199 (2000); Race: 100.0% White, 0.0% Black, 0.0% Asian, 0.0% American Indian and Alaska Native, 0.0% Hispanic of any race, 0.0% two or more races (2000); Density: 373.0 persons per square mile (2000); Age: 28.4% under 18, 13.8% over 64 (2000); Marriage status: 18.9% never married, 64.6% now married, 3.7% widowed, 12.8% divorced (2000); Foreign born: 0.9% (2000); Ancestry (includes multiple ancestries): 36.9% German, 16.4% Irish, 13.3% United States or American, 12.4% Norwegian, 9.8% English (2000).
Economy: Employment by occupation: 17.1% management, 15.4% professional, 6.8% services, 17.9% sales, 0.0% farming, 15.4% construction, 27.4% production (2000).
Income: Per capita income: $19,134 (2000); Median household income: $51,250 (2000); Poverty rate: 2.3% (2000).
Education: High school graduation rate: 85.2% (2000); College graduation rate: 11.3% (2000).
Housing: Homeownership rate: 84.8% (2000); Median home value: $96,400 (2000); Median rent: $575 per month (2000); Median age of housing: 60+ years (2000).
Transportation: Commute to work: 100.0% car, 0.0% public transportation, 0.0% walk, 0.0% work from home (2000); Travel time to work: 12.3% less than 15 minutes, 48.2% 15 to 30 minutes, 29.8% 30 to 45 minutes, 3.5% 45 to 60 minutes, 6.1% 60 minutes or more (2000)

CAPRON (village). Covers a land area of 0.728 square miles and a water area of 0 square miles. Located at 42.39° N. Lat.; 88.74° W. Long. Elevation is 910 feet.
Population: 961 (2000); Race: 88.6% White, 1.5% Black, 0.1% Asian, 1.6% American Indian and Alaska Native, 13.8% Hispanic of any race, 2.8% two or more races (2000); Density: 1,319.5 persons per square mile (2000); Age: 33.6% under 18, 11.3% over 64 (2000); Marriage status: 26.8% never married, 59.5% now married, 4.4% widowed, 9.4% divorced (2000); Foreign born: 5.2% (2000); Ancestry (includes multiple ancestries): 35.4% German, 20.8% Other groups, 11.5% Irish, 10.6% Polish, 6.3% Norwegian (2000).
Economy: In agricultural area: corn; dairying. Manufacturing: filters, consumer goods. Single-family building permits issued: 26 (2001) / 0 (2000); Multi-family building permits issued: 0 (2001) / 0 (2000); Employment by occupation: 8.2% management, 6.8% professional, 10.0% services, 25.4% sales, 1.1% farming, 10.0% construction, 38.5% production (2000).
Income: Per capita income: $17,624 (2000); Median household income: $46,786 (2000); Poverty rate: 3.1% (2000).
Taxes: Total city taxes per capita: $82 (1997); City property taxes per capita: $58 (1997).
Education: High school graduation rate: 77.0% (2000); College graduation rate: 7.4% (2000).
Housing: Homeownership rate: 77.8% (2000); Median home value: $106,700 (2000); Median rent: $444 per month (2000); Median age of housing: 45 years (2000).
Transportation: Commute to work: 93.4% car, 0.7% public transportation, 3.2% walk, 2.5% work from home (2000); Travel time to work: 26.8% less than 15 minutes, 27.0% 15 to 30 minutes, 24.0% 30 to 45 minutes, 8.2% 45 to 60 minutes, 14.0% 60 minutes or more (2000)

GARDEN PRAIRIE (unincorporated postal area, zip code 61038). Covers a land area of 43.193 square miles and a water area of 0.010 square miles. Located at 42.25° N. Lat.; 88.74° W. Long. Elevation is 779 feet.
History: Garden Prairie began in 1849 when a station for the Galena & Chicago Union Railroad was built here.
Population: 1,371 (2000); Race: 97.3% White, 0.0% Black, 0.4% Asian, 1.0% American Indian and Alaska Native, 1.3% Hispanic of any race, 1.0% two or more races (2000); Density: 31.7 persons per square mile (2000); Age: 28.4% under 18, 7.4% over 64 (2000); Marriage status: 20.7% never married, 64.7% now married, 3.0% widowed, 11.6% divorced (2000); Foreign born: 1.5% (2000); Ancestry (includes multiple ancestries): 41.7% German, 15.0% Irish, 9.2% Other groups, 8.9% Polish, 7.9% English (2000).
Economy: Employment by occupation: 16.1% management, 9.5% professional, 13.1% services, 15.3% sales, 1.7% farming, 18.3% construction, 26.1% production (2000).
Income: Per capita income: $17,987 (2000); Median household income: $52,833 (2000); Poverty rate: 3.7% (2000).
Education: High school graduation rate: 81.0% (2000); College graduation rate: 8.2% (2000).
Housing: Homeownership rate: 76.6% (2000); Median home value: $134,200 (2000); Median rent: $517 per month (2000); Median age of housing: 51 years (2000).
Transportation: Commute to work: 87.4% car, 0.0% public transportation, 1.7% walk, 7.8% work from home (2000); Travel time to work: 30.2% less than 15 minutes, 30.1% 15 to 30 minutes, 23.2% 30 to 45 minutes, 9.5% 45 to 60 minutes, 7.0% 60 minutes or more (2000)

POPLAR GROVE (village). Covers a land area of 4.495 square miles and a water area of <.001 square miles. Located at 42.35° N. Lat.; 88.83° W. Long. Elevation is 895 feet.
Population: 1,368 (2000); Race: 96.8% White, 0.2% Black, 0.4% Asian, 0.0% American Indian and Alaska Native, 1.4% Hispanic of any race, 1.4% two or more races (2000); Density: 304.4 persons per square mile (2000); Age: 34.1% under 18, 7.8% over 64 (2000); Marriage status: 18.5% never married, 68.3% now married, 4.9% widowed, 8.2% divorced (2000); Foreign born: 1.4% (2000); Ancestry (includes multiple ancestries): 35.6% German, 17.1% Irish, 10.2% Swedish, 9.9% English, 7.1% Other groups (2000).
Economy: In agricultural area. Single-family building permits issued: 38 (2001) / 32 (2000); Multi-family building permits issued: 0 (2001) / 0 (2000); Employment by occupation: 10.6% management, 10.2% professional, 12.0% services, 27.1% sales, 0.7% farming, 11.5% construction, 27.9% production (2000).
Income: Per capita income: $20,493 (2000); Median household income: $56,375 (2000); Poverty rate: 4.2% (2000).
Taxes: Total city taxes per capita: $70 (1997); City property taxes per capita: $46 (1997).
Education: High school graduation rate: 88.3% (2000); College graduation rate: 12.0% (2000).

School District(s)

North Boone C U School District 200 (PK-12)
2000 Enrollment: 1,302 815-765-3322

Housing: Homeownership rate: 84.6% (2000); Median home value: $123,200 (2000); Median rent: $481 per month (2000); Median age of housing: 24 years (2000).
Transportation: Commute to work: 89.8% car, 1.5% public transportation, 1.5% walk, 4.6% work from home (2000); Travel time to work: 16.5% less than 15 minutes, 37.6% 15 to 30 minutes, 21.3% 30 to 45 minutes, 9.8% 45 to 60 minutes, 14.9% 60 minutes or more (2000)

TIMBERLANE (village). Covers a land area of 1.295 square miles and a water area of 0.016 square miles. Located at 42.33° N. Lat.; 88.85° W. Long.
Population: 234 (2000); Race: 99.5% White, 0.0% Black, 0.0% Asian, 0.5% American Indian and Alaska Native, 0.0% Hispanic of any race, 0.0% two or more races (2000); Density: 180.7 persons per square mile (2000); Age: 26.5% under 18, 3.5% over 64 (2000); Marriage status: 20.1% never married, 75.0% now married, 3.7% widowed, 1.2% divorced (2000); Foreign born: 0.0% (2000); Ancestry (includes multiple ancestries): 43.5% German, 13.5% Irish, 13.0% English, 11.0% Swedish, 9.0% Norwegian (2000).
Economy: Employment by occupation: 16.2% management, 28.5% professional, 6.2% services, 27.7% sales, 0.0% farming, 10.0% construction, 11.5% production (2000).
Income: Per capita income: $31,529 (2000); Median household income: $76,851 (2000); Poverty rate: 6.5% (2000).
Education: High school graduation rate: 95.7% (2000); College graduation rate: 33.8% (2000).
Housing: Homeownership rate: 100.0% (2000); Median home value: $169,000 (2000); Median age of housing: 14 years (2000).
Transportation: Commute to work: 95.4% car, 1.5% public transportation, 0.0% walk, 3.1% work from home (2000); Travel time to work: 14.3% less than 15 minutes, 64.3% 15 to 30 minutes, 15.1% 30 to 45 minutes, 0.8% 45 to 60 minutes, 5.6% 60 minutes or more (2000)

Brown County

Located in western Illinois; bounded on the southeast by the Illinois River, and on the northeast by the La Moine River. Covers a land area of 305.60 square miles, a water area of 1.60 square miles, and is located in the Central Time Zone. The county government was organized in 1839. County seat is Mount Sterling.
Population: 6,950 (2000); Race: 80.9% White, 17.9% Black, 0.1% Asian, 0.1% American Indian and Alaska Native, 3.8% Hispanic of any race, 0.2% two or more races (2000); Density: 22.7 persons per square mile (2000); Age: 17.7% under 18, 12.7% over 64 (2000).
Religion: Five largest groups: 11.9% Catholic Church, 9.0% American Baptist Churches in the USA, 4.9% Christian Churches and Churches of Christ, 4.2% Christian Church (Disciples of Christ), 4.1% The United Methodist Church (2000).

Economy: Unemployment rate: 3.5% (11/2002); Total civilian labor force: 2,936 (11/2002); Leading industries: 40.0% wholesale trade; 8.4% health care and social assistance; 6.8% retail trade (2000); Companies that employ more than 1,000 persons: 0 (2000); Companies that employ more than 100 persons: 3 (2000); Farms: 377 totaling 152,160 acres (1997); Minority business ownership rate: 0.0% (1997); Women business ownership rate: 0.0% (1997); Retail sales per capita: $2,438 (1997). Single-family building permits issued: 4 (2001) / 2 (2000); Multi-family building permits issued: 0 (2001) / 15 (2000).
Income: Per capita income: $14,629 (2000); Median household income: $35,445 (2000); Poverty rate: 8.5% (2000); Bankruptcy rate: 3.16% (2001).
Taxes: Total county taxes per capita: $90 (1997); County property taxes per capita: $89 (1997).
Education: High school graduation rate: 63.3% (2000); College graduation rate: 9.2% (2000).
Housing: Homeownership rate: 74.1% (2000); Median home value: $47,400 (2000); Median rent: $225 per month (2000); Median age of housing: 54 years (2000).
Health: Birth rate: 59.0 per 10,000 population (1998); Age adjusted death rate: 72.0 per 10,000 population (1999); Age adjusted cancer mortality rate: 123.7 (Unreliable figure as per CDC) deaths per 100,000 population (1999). Number of physicians: 4.3 per 10,000 population (1999); Number of hospital beds: n/a (1999).
Elections: 2000 Presidential election results: 40.5% Gore, 57.5% Bush, 1.1% Nader, 0.7% Buchanan
Additional Information Contacts
Brown County Government Offices. 217-773-3421

Brown County Communities

MOUND STATION (village). Aka Timewell. Covers a land area of 0.518 square miles and a water area of 0 square miles. Located at 40.00° N. Lat.; 90.87° W. Long.
History: Also called Timewell.
Population: 127 (2000); Race: 95.7% White, 0.0% Black, 0.6% Asian, 0.0% American Indian and Alaska Native, 0.0% Hispanic of any race, 3.7% two or more races (2000); Density: 245.3 persons per square mile (2000); Age: 37.3% under 18, 10.6% over 64 (2000); Marriage status: 18.5% never married, 64.8% now married, 9.3% widowed, 7.4% divorced (2000); Foreign born: 0.6% (2000); Ancestry (includes multiple ancestries): 16.8% German, 13.7% United States or American, 11.8% English, 7.5% Other groups, 7.5% Irish (2000).
Economy: In agricultural area. Employment by occupation: 4.5% management, 10.2% professional, 14.8% services, 33.0% sales, 0.0% farming, 4.5% construction, 33.0% production (2000).
Income: Per capita income: $17,413 (2000); Median household income: $46,250 (2000); Poverty rate: 7.8% (2000).
Taxes: Total city taxes per capita: $33 (1997); City property taxes per capita: $33 (1997).
Education: High school graduation rate: 95.3% (2000); College graduation rate: 3.5% (2000).
Housing: Homeownership rate: 82.5% (2000); Median home value: $28,000 (2000); Median rent: $263 per month (2000); Median age of housing: 60+ years (2000).
Transportation: Commute to work: 91.4% car, 0.0% public transportation, 3.7% walk, 0.0% work from home (2000); Travel time to work: 44.4% less than 15 minutes, 34.6% 15 to 30 minutes, 0.0% 30 to 45 minutes, 11.1% 45 to 60 minutes, 9.9% 60 minutes or more (2000)

MOUNT STERLING (city). Covers a land area of 1.076 square miles and a water area of 0 square miles. Located at 39.98° N. Lat.; 90.76° W. Long. Elevation is 742 feet.
History: Mount Sterling was settled in 1830 by Robert Curry, who named the village for the "sterling" quality of the soil. Mount Sterling developed as the seat of Brown County.
Population: 2,070 (2000); Race: 99.1% White, 0.2% Black, 0.4% Asian, 0.0% American Indian and Alaska Native, 0.5% Hispanic of any race, 0.3% two or more races (2000); Density: 1,923.5 persons per square mile (2000); Age: 24.1% under 18, 20.0% over 64 (2000); Marriage status: 23.5% never married, 54.5% now married, 11.6% widowed, 10.4% divorced (2000); Foreign born: 0.6% (2000); Ancestry (includes multiple ancestries): 26.9% German, 17.2% English, 15.6% United States or American, 14.4% Irish, 4.7% Other groups (2000).
Economy: Single-family building permits issued: 4 (2001) / 2 (2000); Multi-family building permits issued: 0 (2001) / 15 (2000); Employment by occupation: 7.6% management, 14.9% professional, 20.4% services, 27.5% sales, 1.3% farming, 4.0% construction, 24.2% production (2000).
Income: Per capita income: $15,755 (2000); Median household income: $27,434 (2000); Poverty rate: 10.9% (2000).
Taxes: Total city taxes per capita: $253 (1997); City property taxes per capita: $92 (1997).
Education: High school graduation rate: 79.4% (2000); College graduation rate: 13.3% (2000).

School District(s)

Brown County C U School District 1 (PK-12)
2000 Enrollment: 826 217-773-3359
Housing: Homeownership rate: 65.4% (2000); Median home value: $48,600 (2000); Median rent: $211 per month (2000); Median age of housing: 52 years (2000).
Newspapers: The Pennypincher (1 x week); The Democrat Message (1 x week)
Transportation: Commute to work: 91.7% car, 0.0% public transportation, 3.6% walk, 2.7% work from home (2000); Travel time to work: 62.8% less than 15 minutes, 10.6% 15 to 30 minutes, 8.2% 30 to 45 minutes, 11.8% 45 to 60 minutes, 6.6% 60 minutes or more (2000)

RIPLEY (village). Covers a land area of 0.376 square miles and a water area of 0 square miles. Located at 40.02° N. Lat.; 90.63° W. Long. Elevation is 557 feet.
History: Ripley experienced prosperity in the 1830's and 1840's when its pottery kilns were producing.
Population: 103 (2000); Race: 100.0% White, 0.0% Black, 0.0% Asian, 0.0% American Indian and Alaska Native, 0.0% Hispanic of any race, 0.0% two or more races (2000); Density: 274.0 persons per square mile (2000); Age: 24.6% under 18, 19.3% over 64 (2000); Marriage status: 15.9% never married, 73.9% now married, 2.3% widowed, 8.0% divorced (2000); Foreign born: 0.0% (2000); Ancestry (includes multiple ancestries): 33.3% German, 13.2% Irish, 11.4% United States or American, 6.1% Other groups, 4.4% English (2000).
Economy: Employment by occupation: 4.8% management, 2.4% professional, 21.4% services, 38.1% sales, 4.8% farming, 7.1% construction, 21.4% production (2000).
Income: Per capita income: $12,210 (2000); Median household income: $31,250 (2000); Poverty rate: 7.9% (2000).
Taxes: Total city taxes per capita: $18 (1997); City property taxes per capita: $9 (1997).
Education: High school graduation rate: 62.0% (2000); College graduation rate: 3.8% (2000).
Housing: Homeownership rate: 97.7% (2000); Median home value: $18,800 (2000); Median age of housing: 52 years (2000).
Transportation: Commute to work: 95.5% car, 4.5% public transportation, 0.0% walk, 0.0% work from home (2000); Travel time to work: 31.8% less than 15 minutes, 52.3% 15 to 30 minutes, 11.4% 30 to 45 minutes, 0.0% 45 to 60 minutes, 4.5% 60 minutes or more (2000)

TIMEWELL (unincorporated postal area, zip code 62375). Aka Mound Station. Covers a land area of 40.583 square miles and a water area of 0.018 square miles. Located at 40.00° N. Lat.; 90.87° W. Long. Elevation is 753 feet.
Population: 381 (2000); Race: 97.9% White, 0.0% Black, 0.3% Asian, 0.0% American Indian and Alaska Native, 0.0% Hispanic of any race, 1.8% two or more races (2000); Density: 9.4 persons per square mile (2000); Age: 32.5% under 18, 6.9% over 64 (2000); Marriage status: 20.2% never married, 66.4% now married, 6.3% widowed, 7.1% divorced (2000); Foreign born: 2.1% (2000); Ancestry (includes multiple ancestries): 26.0% German, 17.3% United States or American, 14.3% English, 14.0% Irish, 6.6% Scotch-Irish (2000).
Economy: Employment by occupation: 15.1% management, 5.2% professional, 17.4% services, 29.7% sales, 0.0% farming, 10.5% construction, 22.1% production (2000).
Income: Per capita income: $15,507 (2000); Median household income: $42,679 (2000); Poverty rate: 8.3% (2000).
Education: High school graduation rate: 97.0% (2000); College graduation rate: 3.0% (2000).
Housing: Homeownership rate: 78.8% (2000); Median home value: $36,800 (2000); Median rent: $263 per month (2000); Median age of housing: 60+ years (2000).
Transportation: Commute to work: 94.5% car, 0.0% public transportation, 3.0% walk, 0.0% work from home (2000); Travel time to work: 47.3% less than 15 minutes, 39.4% 15 to 30 minutes, 0.0% 30 to 45 minutes, 5.5% 45 to 60 minutes, 7.9% 60 minutes or more (2000)

VERSAILLES (village). Covers a land area of 0.922 square miles and a water area of 0.005 square miles. Located at 39.88° N. Lat.; 90.65° W. Long. Elevation is 640 feet.
Population: 567 (2000); Race: 99.6% White, 0.0% Black, 0.0% Asian, 0.0% American Indian and Alaska Native, 0.0% Hispanic of any race, 0.4% two or more races (2000); Density: 614.7 persons per square mile (2000); Age: 26.5% under 18, 17.3% over 64 (2000); Marriage status: 21.8% never married, 52.1% now married, 13.4% widowed, 12.7% divorced (2000); Foreign born: 0.0% (2000); Ancestry (includes multiple ancestries): 20.4% United States or American, 16.3% German, 8.8% Irish, 7.3% English, 3.1% Other groups (2000).
Economy: In agricultural area. Employment by occupation: 4.8% management, 4.8% professional, 31.2% services, 19.9% sales, 1.7% farming, 8.7% construction, 29.0% production (2000).
Income: Per capita income: $14,876 (2000); Median household income: $32,813 (2000); Poverty rate: 12.5% (2000).
Taxes: Total city taxes per capita: $72 (1997); City property taxes per capita: $42 (1997).
Education: High school graduation rate: 73.4% (2000); College graduation rate: 4.3% (2000).
Housing: Homeownership rate: 78.2% (2000); Median home value: $35,900 (2000); Median rent: $211 per month (2000); Median age of housing: 42 years (2000).
Transportation: Commute to work: 94.3% car, 0.0% public transportation, 3.0% walk, 1.3% work from home (2000); Travel time to work: 37.4% less than 15 minutes, 22.5% 15 to 30 minutes, 27.3% 30 to 45 minutes, 4.8% 45 to 60 minutes, 7.9% 60 minutes or more (2000)

Bureau County

Located in northern Illinois; bounded on the southeast by the Illinois River; includes Lake Depue. Covers a land area of 868.60 square miles, a water area of 4.70 square miles, and is located in the Central Time Zone. The county government was organized in 1837. County seat is Princeton.

Weather Station: Walnut — Elevation: 688 feet

	Jan	Feb	Mar	Apr	May	Jun	Jul	Aug	Sep	Oct	Nov	Dec
High	28	34	46	61	73	82	85	83	76	64	47	34
Low	11	17	28	38	50	59	63	61	52	41	30	18
Precip	1.3	1.3	2.7	3.5	4.4	4.6	3.6	4.4	3.6	2.9	2.6	2.0
Snow	10.8	6.7	4.3	1.3	tr	0.0	0.0	0.0	0.0	0.1	1.9	7.8

High and Low temperatures in degrees Fahrenheit; Precipitation and Snow in inches

Population: 35,503 (2000); Race: 96.5% White, 0.2% Black, 0.5% Asian, 0.3% American Indian and Alaska Native, 4.8% Hispanic of any race, 1.2% two or more races (2000); Density: 40.9 persons per square mile (2000); Age: 24.8% under 18, 17.7% over 64 (2000).
Religion: Five largest groups: 20.9% Catholic Church, 8.5% The United Methodist Church, 8.4% Evangelical Lutheran Church in America, 2.9% United Church of Christ, 2.5% American Baptist Churches in the USA (2000).
Economy: Unemployment rate: 5.5% (11/2002); Total civilian labor force: 18,540 (11/2002); Leading industries: 26.4% manufacturing; 19.5% health care and social assistance; 12.3% retail trade (2000); Companies that employ more than 1,000 persons: 0 (2000); Companies that employ more than 100 persons: 17 (2000); Farms: 1,155 totaling 483,993 acres (1997); Minority business ownership rate: 4.6% (1997); Women business ownership rate: 20.8% (1997); Retail sales per capita: $6,423 (1997). Single-family building permits issued: 57 (2001) / 57 (2000); Multi-family building permits issued: 0 (2001) / 42 (2000).
Income: Per capita income: $19,542 (2000); Median household income: $40,233 (2000); Poverty rate: 7.3% (2000); Bankruptcy rate: 6.20% (2001).
Taxes: Total county taxes per capita: $85 (2000); County property taxes per capita: $82 (2000).
Education: High school graduation rate: 84.1% (2000); College graduation rate: 15.7% (2000).
Housing: Homeownership rate: 76.0% (2000); Median home value: $77,800 (2000); Median rent: $331 per month (2000); Median age of housing: 55 years (2000).
Health: Birth rate: 117.5 per 10,000 population (1998); Age adjusted death rate: 83.8 per 10,000 population (1999); Age adjusted cancer mortality rate: 190.1 deaths per 100,000 population (1999). Number of physicians: 11.3 per 10,000 population (1999); Number of hospital beds: 59.4 per 10,000 population (1999).
Elections: 2000 Presidential election results: 46.1% Gore, 50.7% Bush, 2.2% Nader, 0.7% Buchanan
National and State Parks: Hennepin Canal Parkway State Park; Lake Depue State Fish and Wildlife Area; Miller-Anderson Woods State Nature Preserve
Additional Information Contacts
Bureau County Government Offices 815-875-2014
Princeton Chamber of Commerce 815-875-2616
Spring Valley Business Owners 815-663-1942

Bureau County Communities

ARLINGTON (village). Covers a land area of 0.428 square miles and a water area of 0 square miles. Located at 41.47° N. Lat.; 89.24° W. Long. Elevation is 750 feet.
Population: 211 (2000); Race: 87.8% White, 0.0% Black, 0.0% Asian, 1.4% American Indian and Alaska Native, 13.6% Hispanic of any race, 3.3% two or more races (2000); Density: 493.4 persons per square mile (2000); Age: 37.6% under 18, 8.0% over 64 (2000); Marriage status: 32.9% never married, 53.3% now married, 6.6% widowed, 7.2% divorced (2000); Foreign born: 1.9% (2000); Ancestry (includes multiple ancestries): 31.9% German, 21.1% Other groups, 12.2% Irish, 10.3% Norwegian, 8.5% English (2000).
Economy: In agricultural area: corn, soybeans; cattle, hogs. Employment by occupation: 7.0% management, 9.3% professional, 29.1% services, 17.4% sales, 0.0% farming, 14.0% construction, 23.3% production (2000).
Income: Per capita income: $12,148 (2000); Median household income: $27,292 (2000); Poverty rate: 13.7% (2000).
Taxes: Total city taxes per capita: $114 (1997); City property taxes per capita: $57 (1997).
Education: High school graduation rate: 78.8% (2000); College graduation rate: 5.1% (2000).
Housing: Homeownership rate: 90.7% (2000); Median home value: $49,500 (2000); Median rent: $525 per month (2000); Median age of housing: 60+ years (2000).
Transportation: Commute to work: 91.7% car, 0.0% public transportation, 8.3% walk, 0.0% work from home (2000); Travel time to work: 23.8% less than 15 minutes, 44.0% 15 to 30 minutes, 8.3% 30 to 45 minutes, 13.1% 45 to 60 minutes, 10.7% 60 minutes or more (2000)

BUDA (village). Covers a land area of 1.008 square miles and a water area of 0 square miles. Located at 41.32° N. Lat.; 89.68° W. Long. Elevation is 752 feet.
Population: 592 (2000); Race: 98.3% White, 0.0% Black, 0.0% Asian, 0.0% American Indian and Alaska Native, 3.3% Hispanic of any race, 0.7% two or more races (2000); Density: 587.3 persons per square mile (2000); Age: 29.0% under 18, 15.8% over 64 (2000); Marriage status: 22.1% never married, 59.3% now married, 9.0% widowed, 9.6% divorced (2000); Foreign born: 1.3% (2000); Ancestry (includes multiple ancestries): 27.2% German, 17.2% English, 12.5% United States or American, 11.2% Irish, 5.5% Other groups (2000).
Economy: Grain; livestock. Employment by occupation: 3.6% management, 15.0% professional, 12.4% services, 21.2% sales, 1.5% farming, 9.9% construction, 36.5% production (2000).
Income: Per capita income: $15,320 (2000); Median household income: $34,231 (2000); Poverty rate: 12.5% (2000).
Taxes: Total city taxes per capita: $61 (1997); City property taxes per capita: $60 (1997).
Education: High school graduation rate: 85.1% (2000); College graduation rate: 7.4% (2000).
Housing: Homeownership rate: 88.8% (2000); Median home value: $50,700 (2000); Median rent: $308 per month (2000); Median age of housing: 60+ years (2000).
Transportation: Commute to work: 92.3% car, 0.0% public transportation, 3.3% walk, 4.0% work from home (2000); Travel time to work: 30.4% less than 15 minutes, 43.0% 15 to 30 minutes, 19.0% 30 to 45 minutes, 2.3% 45 to 60 minutes, 5.3% 60 minutes or more (2000)

BUREAU JUNCTION (village). Aka Bureau. Covers a land area of 1.437 square miles and a water area of 0.066 square miles. Located at 41.28° N. Lat.; 89.36° W. Long.
Population: 368 (2000); Race: 98.3% White, 0.0% Black, 0.0% Asian, 0.0% American Indian and Alaska Native, 9.4% Hispanic of any race, 0.0% two or more races (2000); Density: 256.1 persons per square mile (2000); Age: 26.9% under 18, 11.6% over 64 (2000); Marriage status: 29.7% never married, 51.4% now married, 5.6% widowed, 13.3% divorced (2000);

Foreign born: 5.0% (2000); Ancestry (includes multiple ancestries): 25.2% German, 14.7% Irish, 11.9% English, 9.1% French (except Basque), 7.5% Polish (2000).
Economy: Employment by occupation: 4.2% management, 7.9% professional, 26.3% services, 16.3% sales, 0.5% farming, 14.2% construction, 30.5% production (2000).
Income: Per capita income: $15,490 (2000); Median household income: $41,429 (2000); Poverty rate: 5.3% (2000).
Taxes: Total city taxes per capita: $62 (1997); City property taxes per capita: $59 (1997).
Education: High school graduation rate: 83.7% (2000); College graduation rate: 7.4% (2000).
Housing: Homeownership rate: 77.5% (2000); Median home value: $50,600 (2000); Median rent: $217 per month (2000); Median age of housing: 60+ years (2000).
Transportation: Commute to work: 86.5% car, 0.0% public transportation, 8.1% walk, 2.7% work from home (2000); Travel time to work: 25.6% less than 15 minutes, 46.7% 15 to 30 minutes, 19.4% 30 to 45 minutes, 3.9% 45 to 60 minutes, 4.4% 60 minutes or more (2000)

CHERRY (village). Covers a land area of 0.538 square miles and a water area of 0 square miles. Located at 41.42° N. Lat.; 89.21° W. Long. Elevation is 680 feet.
History: Cherry was the scene of a mine fire in 1909 that killed 270 miners.
Population: 509 (2000); Race: 99.4% White, 0.0% Black, 0.0% Asian, 0.0% American Indian and Alaska Native, 1.0% Hispanic of any race, 0.0% two or more races (2000); Density: 946.0 persons per square mile (2000); Age: 22.6% under 18, 14.2% over 64 (2000); Marriage status: 18.2% never married, 64.1% now married, 8.1% widowed, 9.6% divorced (2000); Foreign born: 0.0% (2000); Ancestry (includes multiple ancestries): 32.9% German, 23.2% Italian, 15.2% Irish, 11.9% English, 11.9% Polish (2000).
Economy: Employment by occupation: 6.4% management, 11.1% professional, 11.8% services, 25.0% sales, 0.7% farming, 10.1% construction, 34.8% production (2000).
Income: Per capita income: $19,313 (2000); Median household income: $41,591 (2000); Poverty rate: 1.8% (2000).
Taxes: Total city taxes per capita: $80 (1997); City property taxes per capita: $46 (1997).
Education: High school graduation rate: 80.4% (2000); College graduation rate: 8.0% (2000).

School District(s)

Cherry School District 92 (KG-08)
2000 Enrollment: 91 815-894-2777

Housing: Homeownership rate: 82.1% (2000); Median home value: $66,700 (2000); Median rent: $394 per month (2000); Median age of housing: 60+ years (2000).
Transportation: Commute to work: 95.9% car, 0.0% public transportation, 3.0% walk, 1.0% work from home (2000); Travel time to work: 30.0% less than 15 minutes, 50.2% 15 to 30 minutes, 8.9% 30 to 45 minutes, 1.4% 45 to 60 minutes, 9.6% 60 minutes or more (2000)

DALZELL (village). Covers a land area of 1.270 square miles and a water area of 0.010 square miles. Located at 41.35° N. Lat.; 89.17° W. Long. Elevation is 640 feet.
Population: 717 (2000); Race: 99.0% White, 0.0% Black, 0.0% Asian, 0.0% American Indian and Alaska Native, 1.1% Hispanic of any race, 1.0% two or more races (2000); Density: 564.5 persons per square mile (2000); Age: 24.4% under 18, 15.2% over 64 (2000); Marriage status: 21.0% never married, 65.5% now married, 6.3% widowed, 7.2% divorced (2000); Foreign born: 0.7% (2000); Ancestry (includes multiple ancestries): 35.7% Italian, 23.7% German, 19.1% Polish, 14.9% Irish, 7.6% English (2000).
Economy: Employment by occupation: 5.6% management, 17.0% professional, 13.4% services, 31.3% sales, 0.0% farming, 9.8% construction, 22.9% production (2000).
Income: Per capita income: $20,215 (2000); Median household income: $49,808 (2000); Poverty rate: 3.5% (2000).
Taxes: Total city taxes per capita: $84 (1997); City property taxes per capita: $57 (1997).
Education: High school graduation rate: 85.7% (2000); College graduation rate: 11.7% (2000).

School District(s)

Dalzell School District 98 (KG-08)
2000 Enrollment: 77 815-663-8821

Housing: Homeownership rate: 89.4% (2000); Median home value: $93,200 (2000); Median rent: $410 per month (2000); Median age of housing: 38 years (2000).
Transportation: Commute to work: 98.9% car, 0.0% public transportation, 0.0% walk, 1.1% work from home (2000); Travel time to work: 52.0% less than 15 minutes, 26.3% 15 to 30 minutes, 9.5% 30 to 45 minutes, 2.9% 45 to 60 minutes, 9.2% 60 minutes or more (2000)

DE PUE (village). Aka Depue. Covers a land area of 2.711 square miles and a water area of 0.259 square miles. Located at 41.32° N. Lat.; 89.30° W. Long.
Population: 1,842 (2000); Race: 80.1% White, 0.9% Black, 3.3% Asian, 0.4% American Indian and Alaska Native, 45.4% Hispanic of any race, 4.5% two or more races (2000); Density: 679.4 persons per square mile (2000); Age: 30.0% under 18, 16.5% over 64 (2000); Marriage status: 24.8% never married, 55.9% now married, 9.1% widowed, 10.2% divorced (2000); Foreign born: 20.6% (2000); Ancestry (includes multiple ancestries): 47.3% Other groups, 12.0% German, 7.9% English, 6.8% Irish, 6.8% United States or American (2000).
Economy: Single-family building permits issued: 0 (2001) / 0 (2000); Multi-family building permits issued: 0 (2001) / 0 (2000); Employment by occupation: 3.6% management, 7.5% professional, 11.3% services, 13.3% sales, 10.5% farming, 10.1% construction, 43.7% production (2000).
Income: Per capita income: $15,273 (2000); Median household income: $32,500 (2000); Poverty rate: 13.1% (2000).
Education: High school graduation rate: 60.2% (2000); College graduation rate: 5.0% (2000).
Housing: Homeownership rate: 72.2% (2000); Median home value: $45,300 (2000); Median rent: $315 per month (2000); Median age of housing: 60+ years (2000).
Transportation: Commute to work: 95.5% car, 0.4% public transportation, 2.2% walk, 0.7% work from home (2000); Travel time to work: 29.3% less than 15 minutes, 47.6% 15 to 30 minutes, 11.8% 30 to 45 minutes, 2.0% 45 to 60 minutes, 9.3% 60 minutes or more (2000)

DOVER (village). Covers a land area of 0.268 square miles and a water area of 0 square miles. Located at 41.43° N. Lat.; 89.39° W. Long. Elevation is 750 feet.
Population: 172 (2000); Race: 100.0% White, 0.0% Black, 0.0% Asian, 0.0% American Indian and Alaska Native, 1.9% Hispanic of any race, 0.0% two or more races (2000); Density: 641.6 persons per square mile (2000); Age: 35.4% under 18, 10.8% over 64 (2000); Marriage status: 22.5% never married, 65.8% now married, 4.5% widowed, 7.2% divorced (2000); Foreign born: 0.0% (2000); Ancestry (includes multiple ancestries): 24.7% German, 13.9% United States or American, 11.4% Irish, 7.0% Scottish, 6.3% Lithuanian (2000).
Economy: In agricultural area. Employment by occupation: 1.3% management, 28.9% professional, 21.1% services, 18.4% sales, 0.0% farming, 15.8% construction, 14.5% production (2000).
Income: Per capita income: $14,070 (2000); Median household income: $41,875 (2000); Poverty rate: 5.7% (2000).
Taxes: Total city taxes per capita: $58 (1997); City property taxes per capita: $58 (1997).
Education: High school graduation rate: 90.3% (2000); College graduation rate: 26.9% (2000).
Housing: Homeownership rate: 93.3% (2000); Median home value: $71,800 (2000); Median age of housing: 60+ years (2000).
Transportation: Commute to work: 98.7% car, 0.0% public transportation, 0.0% walk, 0.0% work from home (2000); Travel time to work: 56.6% less than 15 minutes, 27.6% 15 to 30 minutes, 6.6% 30 to 45 minutes, 1.3% 45 to 60 minutes, 7.9% 60 minutes or more (2000)

HOLLOWAYVILLE (village). Covers a land area of 0.049 square miles and a water area of 0 square miles. Located at 41.36° N. Lat.; 89.29° W. Long. Elevation is 660 feet.
Population: 90 (2000); Race: 96.2% White, 0.0% Black, 0.0% Asian, 0.0% American Indian and Alaska Native, 3.8% Hispanic of any race, 0.0% two or more races (2000); Density: 1,836.6 persons per square mile (2000); Age: 40.5% under 18, 2.5% over 64 (2000); Marriage status: 16.0% never married, 74.0% now married, 4.0% widowed, 6.0% divorced (2000); Foreign born: 0.0% (2000); Ancestry (includes multiple ancestries): 54.4% German, 29.1% Italian, 16.5% Irish, 12.7% Other groups, 5.1% English (2000).
Economy: Employment by occupation: 10.8% management, 32.4% professional, 16.2% services, 13.5% sales, 0.0% farming, 13.5% construction, 13.5% production (2000).
Income: Per capita income: $15,825 (2000); Median household income: $52,500 (2000); Poverty rate: 0.0% (2000).
Taxes: Total city taxes per capita: $54 (1997); City property taxes per capita: $54 (1997).

Education: High school graduation rate: 95.2% (2000); College graduation rate: 11.9% (2000).
Housing: Homeownership rate: 82.6% (2000); Median home value: $52,500 (2000); Median rent: $500 per month (2000); Median age of housing: 60+ years (2000).
Transportation: Commute to work: 94.6% car, 0.0% public transportation, 0.0% walk, 0.0% work from home (2000); Travel time to work: 18.9% less than 15 minutes, 59.5% 15 to 30 minutes, 5.4% 30 to 45 minutes, 5.4% 45 to 60 minutes, 10.8% 60 minutes or more (2000)

LA MOILLE (village). Covers a land area of 1.205 square miles and a water area of 0 square miles. Located at 41.52° N. Lat.; 89.28° W. Long. Elevation is 800 feet.
Population: 773 (2000); Race: 98.7% White, 0.1% Black, 0.0% Asian, 0.0% American Indian and Alaska Native, 2.5% Hispanic of any race, 1.2% two or more races (2000); Density: 641.5 persons per square mile (2000); Age: 30.4% under 18, 13.7% over 64 (2000); Marriage status: 19.0% never married, 61.7% now married, 7.8% widowed, 11.5% divorced (2000); Foreign born: 0.3% (2000); Ancestry (includes multiple ancestries): 45.0% German, 11.1% Irish, 10.2% English, 5.9% Other groups, 5.2% Italian (2000).
Economy: In agricultural area. Employment by occupation: 11.3% management, 12.7% professional, 10.3% services, 27.2% sales, 0.8% farming, 11.1% construction, 26.6% production (2000).
Income: Per capita income: $17,008 (2000); Median household income: $37,212 (2000); Poverty rate: 6.5% (2000).
Taxes: Total city taxes per capita: $45 (1997); City property taxes per capita: $42 (1997).
Education: High school graduation rate: 85.9% (2000); College graduation rate: 9.7% (2000).

School District(s)

La Moille C U School District 303 (KG-12)
2000 Enrollment: 341 815-638-2018
Housing: Homeownership rate: 73.3% (2000); Median home value: $73,800 (2000); Median rent: $268 per month (2000); Median age of housing: 56 years (2000).
Transportation: Commute to work: 94.1% car, 0.0% public transportation, 3.2% walk, 1.6% work from home (2000); Travel time to work: 25.3% less than 15 minutes, 56.3% 15 to 30 minutes, 8.0% 30 to 45 minutes, 3.8% 45 to 60 minutes, 6.6% 60 minutes or more (2000)

LADD (village). Covers a land area of 1.193 square miles and a water area of 0 square miles. Located at 41.38° N. Lat.; 89.21° W. Long. Elevation is 650 feet.
History: Incorporated 1890.
Population: 1,313 (2000); Race: 97.3% White, 0.0% Black, 0.6% Asian, 0.0% American Indian and Alaska Native, 4.1% Hispanic of any race, 0.9% two or more races (2000); Density: 1,100.2 persons per square mile (2000); Age: 24.0% under 18, 19.9% over 64 (2000); Marriage status: 18.8% never married, 61.9% now married, 8.7% widowed, 10.6% divorced (2000); Foreign born: 2.0% (2000); Ancestry (includes multiple ancestries): 30.2% German, 25.7% Italian, 17.3% Irish, 9.9% English, 9.4% Other groups (2000).
Economy: In agricultural area. Railroad junction. Single-family building permits issued: 6 (2001) / 3 (2000); Multi-family building permits issued: 0 (2001) / 0 (2000); Employment by occupation: 9.6% management, 19.6% professional, 16.4% services, 25.2% sales, 0.6% farming, 9.6% construction, 19.1% production (2000).
Income: Per capita income: $21,696 (2000); Median household income: $41,029 (2000); Poverty rate: 4.9% (2000).
Taxes: Total city taxes per capita: $142 (1997); City property taxes per capita: $138 (1997).
Education: High school graduation rate: 82.5% (2000); College graduation rate: 13.6% (2000).

School District(s)

Ladd Community Cons School District 94 (KG-08)
2000 Enrollment: 178 815-894-2363
Housing: Homeownership rate: 76.2% (2000); Median home value: $79,100 (2000); Median rent: $351 per month (2000); Median age of housing: 57 years (2000).
Transportation: Commute to work: 93.2% car, 0.0% public transportation, 3.7% walk, 2.6% work from home (2000); Travel time to work: 51.0% less than 15 minutes, 34.2% 15 to 30 minutes, 6.0% 30 to 45 minutes, 2.5% 45 to 60 minutes, 6.3% 60 minutes or more (2000)

MALDEN (village). Covers a land area of 0.274 square miles and a water area of 0 square miles. Located at 41.42° N. Lat.; 89.36° W. Long. Elevation is 700 feet.
Population: 343 (2000); Race: 93.1% White, 1.1% Black, 1.9% Asian, 0.0% American Indian and Alaska Native, 2.2% Hispanic of any race, 3.3% two or more races (2000); Density: 1,253.7 persons per square mile (2000); Age: 34.6% under 18, 8.3% over 64 (2000); Marriage status: 22.2% never married, 53.6% now married, 6.7% widowed, 17.5% divorced (2000); Foreign born: 0.8% (2000); Ancestry (includes multiple ancestries): 42.7% German, 15.5% English, 11.9% Irish, 10.0% Polish, 8.6% Other groups (2000).
Economy: Single-family building permits issued: 0 (2001) / 0 (2000); Multi-family building permits issued: 0 (2001) / 0 (2000); Employment by occupation: 7.9% management, 8.5% professional, 15.2% services, 20.7% sales, 3.7% farming, 15.2% construction, 28.7% production (2000).
Income: Per capita income: $15,820 (2000); Median household income: $41,250 (2000); Poverty rate: 3.1% (2000).
Taxes: Total city taxes per capita: $38 (1997); City property taxes per capita: $35 (1997).
Education: High school graduation rate: 89.3% (2000); College graduation rate: 5.1% (2000).

School District(s)

Malden Community Cons School District 84 (PK-08)
2000 Enrollment: 132 815-643-2436
Housing: Homeownership rate: 88.8% (2000); Median home value: $71,100 (2000); Median rent: $313 per month (2000); Median age of housing: 35 years (2000).
Transportation: Commute to work: 98.8% car, 0.0% public transportation, 0.6% walk, 0.6% work from home (2000); Travel time to work: 44.1% less than 15 minutes, 44.1% 15 to 30 minutes, 4.3% 30 to 45 minutes, 1.9% 45 to 60 minutes, 5.6% 60 minutes or more (2000)

MANLIUS (village). Covers a land area of 0.306 square miles and a water area of 0 square miles. Located at 41.45° N. Lat.; 89.67° W. Long. Elevation is 705 feet.
Population: 355 (2000); Race: 96.9% White, 0.0% Black, 0.0% Asian, 1.2% American Indian and Alaska Native, 2.2% Hispanic of any race, 1.2% two or more races (2000); Density: 1,158.7 persons per square mile (2000); Age: 25.8% under 18, 13.4% over 64 (2000); Marriage status: 23.1% never married, 55.3% now married, 10.6% widowed, 11.0% divorced (2000); Foreign born: 0.9% (2000); Ancestry (includes multiple ancestries): 33.5% German, 18.3% English, 8.1% Swedish, 6.8% Other groups, 6.2% Irish (2000).
Economy: In agricultural area. Employment by occupation: 3.3% management, 14.7% professional, 20.7% services, 21.2% sales, 3.3% farming, 3.8% construction, 33.2% production (2000).
Income: Per capita income: $16,842 (2000); Median household income: $38,214 (2000); Poverty rate: 7.1% (2000).
Taxes: Total city taxes per capita: $55 (1997); City property taxes per capita: $52 (1997).
Education: High school graduation rate: 89.6% (2000); College graduation rate: 6.4% (2000).

School District(s)

Bureau Valley CUSD 340 (PK-12)
2000 Enrollment: 1,451 815-445-3101
Housing: Homeownership rate: 80.3% (2000); Median home value: $60,800 (2000); Median rent: $229 per month (2000); Median age of housing: 60+ years (2000).
Transportation: Commute to work: 89.6% car, 0.0% public transportation, 6.0% walk, 2.7% work from home (2000); Travel time to work: 35.4% less than 15 minutes, 41.0% 15 to 30 minutes, 11.8% 30 to 45 minutes, 8.4% 45 to 60 minutes, 3.4% 60 minutes or more (2000)

MINERAL (village). Covers a land area of 0.308 square miles and a water area of 0 square miles. Located at 41.38° N. Lat.; 89.83° W. Long. Elevation is 640 feet.
Population: 272 (2000); Race: 99.3% White, 0.7% Black, 0.0% Asian, 0.0% American Indian and Alaska Native, 0.0% Hispanic of any race, 0.0% two or more races (2000); Density: 883.4 persons per square mile (2000); Age: 25.3% under 18, 11.4% over 64 (2000); Marriage status: 23.0% never married, 55.8% now married, 10.1% widowed, 11.1% divorced (2000); Foreign born: 0.0% (2000); Ancestry (includes multiple ancestries): 28.2% German, 21.2% Belgian, 11.7% Irish, 10.6% English, 8.1% Swedish (2000).
Economy: In agricultural area. Employment by occupation: 7.4% management, 3.0% professional, 13.3% services, 23.0% sales, 0.0% farming, 17.0% construction, 36.3% production (2000).

Income: Per capita income: $23,017 (2000); Median household income: $38,000 (2000); Poverty rate: 8.4% (2000).
Taxes: Total city taxes per capita: $50 (1997); City property taxes per capita: $50 (1997).
Education: High school graduation rate: 78.5% (2000); College graduation rate: 1.1% (2000).
Housing: Homeownership rate: 79.4% (2000); Median home value: $45,500 (2000); Median rent: $350 per month (2000); Median age of housing: 52 years (2000).
Transportation: Commute to work: 100.0% car, 0.0% public transportation, 0.0% walk, 0.0% work from home (2000); Travel time to work: 27.4% less than 15 minutes, 35.6% 15 to 30 minutes, 30.4% 30 to 45 minutes, 5.9% 45 to 60 minutes, 0.7% 60 minutes or more (2000)

NEPONSET (village). Covers a land area of 1.042 square miles and a water area of 0 square miles. Located at 41.29° N. Lat.; 89.79° W. Long. Elevation is 825 feet.
Population: 519 (2000); Race: 97.6% White, 0.0% Black, 1.8% Asian, 0.0% American Indian and Alaska Native, 0.6% Hispanic of any race, 0.6% two or more races (2000); Density: 498.0 persons per square mile (2000); Age: 20.7% under 18, 18.9% over 64 (2000); Marriage status: 20.8% never married, 62.3% now married, 9.5% widowed, 7.4% divorced (2000); Foreign born: 2.0% (2000); Ancestry (includes multiple ancestries): 30.6% English, 21.7% German, 16.7% Irish, 9.9% United States or American, 4.8% Scottish (2000).
Economy: In agricultural area. Single-family building permits issued: 0 (2001) / 0 (2000); Multi-family building permits issued: 0 (2001) / 0 (2000); Employment by occupation: 9.2% management, 9.6% professional, 19.6% services, 19.6% sales, 0.8% farming, 5.6% construction, 35.6% production (2000).
Income: Per capita income: $19,846 (2000); Median household income: $38,750 (2000); Poverty rate: 11.9% (2000).
Taxes: Total city taxes per capita: $62 (1997); City property taxes per capita: $54 (1997).
Education: High school graduation rate: 81.9% (2000); College graduation rate: 9.6% (2000).

School District(s)

Neponset Com Cons District 307 (PK-08)
2000 Enrollment: 107 309-594-2307

Housing: Homeownership rate: 91.0% (2000); Median home value: $53,600 (2000); Median rent: $289 per month (2000); Median age of housing: 55 years (2000).
Transportation: Commute to work: 86.2% car, 0.4% public transportation, 6.1% walk, 4.5% work from home (2000); Travel time to work: 37.4% less than 15 minutes, 36.6% 15 to 30 minutes, 11.9% 30 to 45 minutes, 4.3% 45 to 60 minutes, 9.8% 60 minutes or more (2000)

NEW BEDFORD (village). Covers a land area of 0.175 square miles and a water area of 0 square miles. Located at 41.51° N. Lat.; 89.71° W. Long. Elevation is 650 feet.
Population: 95 (2000); Race: 89.0% White, 0.0% Black, 3.3% Asian, 0.0% American Indian and Alaska Native, 0.0% Hispanic of any race, 7.7% two or more races (2000); Density: 543.9 persons per square mile (2000); Age: 18.7% under 18, 15.4% over 64 (2000); Marriage status: 14.9% never married, 75.7% now married, 8.1% widowed, 1.4% divorced (2000); Foreign born: 4.4% (2000); Ancestry (includes multiple ancestries): 37.4% German, 18.7% United States or American, 9.9% Danish, 9.9% Irish, 4.4% Scottish (2000).
Economy: Employment by occupation: 4.3% management, 13.0% professional, 28.3% services, 17.4% sales, 0.0% farming, 4.3% construction, 32.6% production (2000).
Income: Per capita income: $14,830 (2000); Median household income: $38,750 (2000); Poverty rate: 3.3% (2000).
Taxes: Total city taxes per capita: $19 (1997); City property taxes per capita: $19 (1997).
Education: High school graduation rate: 76.1% (2000); College graduation rate: 3.0% (2000).
Housing: Homeownership rate: 92.9% (2000); Median home value: $60,700 (2000); Median rent: $175 per month (2000); Median age of housing: 60+ years (2000).
Transportation: Commute to work: 100.0% car, 0.0% public transportation, 0.0% walk, 0.0% work from home (2000); Travel time to work: 0.0% less than 15 minutes, 54.3% 15 to 30 minutes, 28.3% 30 to 45 minutes, 4.3% 45 to 60 minutes, 13.0% 60 minutes or more (2000)

OHIO (village). Covers a land area of 0.753 square miles and a water area of 0 square miles. Located at 41.55° N. Lat.; 89.46° W. Long. Elevation is 900 feet.
Population: 540 (2000); Race: 97.7% White, 0.0% Black, 0.0% Asian, 0.0% American Indian and Alaska Native, 1.5% Hispanic of any race, 2.3% two or more races (2000); Density: 717.3 persons per square mile (2000); Age: 26.3% under 18, 16.9% over 64 (2000); Marriage status: 20.3% never married, 59.3% now married, 11.6% widowed, 8.7% divorced (2000); Foreign born: 0.8% (2000); Ancestry (includes multiple ancestries): 44.0% German, 21.4% Irish, 10.5% Swedish, 6.6% Polish, 6.0% English (2000).
Economy: In agricultural area; dairy products. Employment by occupation: 7.8% management, 13.4% professional, 15.6% services, 23.0% sales, 1.5% farming, 14.5% construction, 24.2% production (2000).
Income: Per capita income: $18,858 (2000); Median household income: $40,179 (2000); Poverty rate: 3.6% (2000).
Taxes: Total city taxes per capita: $170 (1997); City property taxes per capita: $166 (1997).
Education: High school graduation rate: 92.8% (2000); College graduation rate: 13.9% (2000).

School District(s)

Ohio Community Cons School District 17 (KG-08)
2000 Enrollment: 116 815-376-2934
Ohio Community H S District 505 (09-12)
2000 Enrollment: 56 815-376-4414

Housing: Homeownership rate: 79.0% (2000); Median home value: $70,000 (2000); Median rent: $217 per month (2000); Median age of housing: 60+ years (2000).
Transportation: Commute to work: 92.5% car, 0.0% public transportation, 2.6% walk, 3.4% work from home (2000); Travel time to work: 35.8% less than 15 minutes, 34.6% 15 to 30 minutes, 18.7% 30 to 45 minutes, 4.7% 45 to 60 minutes, 6.2% 60 minutes or more (2000)

PRINCETON (city). Covers a land area of 6.730 square miles and a water area of 0 square miles. Located at 41.37° N. Lat.; 89.46° W. Long. Elevation is 720 feet.
History: Princeton was laid out in 1833 by settlers from Massachusetts. The town grew as an orchard and farming center, and as the seat of Bureau County.
Population: 7,501 (2000); Race: 97.4% White, 0.3% Black, 0.4% Asian, 0.3% American Indian and Alaska Native, 1.1% Hispanic of any race, 1.5% two or more races (2000); Density: 1,114.6 persons per square mile (2000); Age: 21.8% under 18, 21.8% over 64 (2000); Marriage status: 20.8% never married, 58.3% now married, 10.0% widowed, 10.9% divorced (2000); Foreign born: 1.8% (2000); Ancestry (includes multiple ancestries): 32.0% German, 14.9% English, 14.4% Irish, 9.6% Swedish, 6.5% United States or American (2000).
Economy: Single-family building permits issued: 12 (2001) / 15 (2000); Multi-family building permits issued: 0 (2001) / 36 (2000); Employment by occupation: 12.9% management, 18.9% professional, 18.6% services, 22.1% sales, 0.5% farming, 7.8% construction, 19.1% production (2000).
Income: Per capita income: $20,632 (2000); Median household income: $39,622 (2000); Poverty rate: 7.2% (2000).
Taxes: Total city taxes per capita: $185 (2000); City property taxes per capita: $144 (2000).
Education: High school graduation rate: 88.9% (2000); College graduation rate: 21.4% (2000).

School District(s)

Princeton Elementary School District 115 (PK-08)
2000 Enrollment: 1,212 815-875-3162
Princeton High School District 500 (09-12)
2000 Enrollment: 701 815-875-3308

Housing: Homeownership rate: 68.7% (2000); Median home value: $91,800 (2000); Median rent: $335 per month (2000); Median age of housing: 47 years (2000).
Hospitals: Perry Memorial Hospital (97 beds)
Newspapers: Illinois Valley Shopping News (1 x week); Bureau County Republican (3 x week)
Transportation: Commute to work: 89.8% car, 0.0% public transportation, 2.7% walk, 4.2% work from home (2000); Travel time to work: 65.9% less than 15 minutes, 17.9% 15 to 30 minutes, 9.0% 30 to 45 minutes, 3.1% 45 to 60 minutes, 4.1% 60 minutes or more (2000); Amtrak: Service available.
Additional Information Contacts
Princeton Chamber of Commerce 815-875-2616

SEATONVILLE (village). Covers a land area of 0.486 square miles and a water area of 0.015 square miles. Located at 41.36° N. Lat.; 89.27° W. Long. Elevation is 600 feet.
Population: 303 (2000); Race: 97.2% White, 0.0% Black, 0.0% Asian, 0.0% American Indian and Alaska Native, 6.0% Hispanic of any race, 0.0% two or more races (2000); Density: 623.5 persons per square mile (2000); Age: 16.9% under 18, 24.1% over 64 (2000); Marriage status: 17.5% never married, 63.3% now married, 12.4% widowed, 6.9% divorced (2000); Foreign born: 1.3% (2000); Ancestry (includes multiple ancestries): 32.9% German, 17.2% Italian, 13.8% Irish, 10.0% English, 9.7% Polish (2000).
Economy: In agricultural area. Single-family building permits issued: 1 (2001) / 1 (2000); Multi-family building permits issued: 0 (2001) / 0 (2000); Employment by occupation: 8.3% management, 6.9% professional, 15.2% services, 28.3% sales, 1.4% farming, 8.3% construction, 31.7% production (2000).
Income: Per capita income: $26,197 (2000); Median household income: $32,656 (2000); Poverty rate: 6.3% (2000).
Taxes: Total city taxes per capita: $46 (2000); City property taxes per capita: $43 (2000).
Education: High school graduation rate: 70.6% (2000); College graduation rate: 6.0% (2000).
Housing: Homeownership rate: 92.7% (2000); Median home value: $68,200 (2000); Median rent: $350 per month (2000); Median age of housing: 60+ years (2000).
Transportation: Commute to work: 93.8% car, 1.4% public transportation, 1.4% walk, 3.4% work from home (2000); Travel time to work: 30.0% less than 15 minutes, 43.6% 15 to 30 minutes, 18.6% 30 to 45 minutes, 1.4% 45 to 60 minutes, 6.4% 60 minutes or more (2000)

SHEFFIELD (village). Covers a land area of 0.749 square miles and a water area of 0 square miles. Located at 41.35° N. Lat.; 89.73° W. Long. Elevation is 764 feet.
Population: 946 (2000); Race: 97.1% White, 0.0% Black, 0.4% Asian, 0.0% American Indian and Alaska Native, 1.0% Hispanic of any race, 0.3% two or more races (2000); Density: 1,263.5 persons per square mile (2000); Age: 23.3% under 18, 23.3% over 64 (2000); Marriage status: 19.0% never married, 62.1% now married, 7.2% widowed, 11.8% divorced (2000); Foreign born: 0.2% (2000); Ancestry (includes multiple ancestries): 22.6% German, 13.4% English, 12.2% Irish, 8.5% Belgian, 6.7% Other groups (2000).
Economy: In agricultural area: corn, soybeans; cattle, hogs. Employment by occupation: 6.0% management, 18.1% professional, 19.0% services, 20.6% sales, 0.7% farming, 10.9% construction, 24.6% production (2000).
Income: Per capita income: $17,723 (2000); Median household income: $36,528 (2000); Poverty rate: 10.6% (2000).
Taxes: Total city taxes per capita: $81 (1997); City property taxes per capita: $78 (1997).
Education: High school graduation rate: 83.3% (2000); College graduation rate: 16.1% (2000).
Housing: Homeownership rate: 83.4% (2000); Median home value: $54,800 (2000); Median rent: $322 per month (2000); Median age of housing: 60+ years (2000).
Transportation: Commute to work: 93.1% car, 0.0% public transportation, 3.2% walk, 3.5% work from home (2000); Travel time to work: 26.6% less than 15 minutes, 39.0% 15 to 30 minutes, 20.8% 30 to 45 minutes, 5.5% 45 to 60 minutes, 8.1% 60 minutes or more (2000)

SPRING VALLEY (city). Covers a land area of 3.886 square miles and a water area of 0.019 square miles. Located at 41.32° N. Lat.; 89.20° W. Long. Elevation is 610 feet.
History: Spring Valley began as a mining operation, but later the economy was based on manufacturing.
Population: 5,398 (2000); Race: 95.7% White, 0.1% Black, 0.2% Asian, 0.6% American Indian and Alaska Native, 6.7% Hispanic of any race, 1.2% two or more races (2000); Density: 1,389.3 persons per square mile (2000); Age: 23.6% under 18, 18.6% over 64 (2000); Marriage status: 22.8% never married, 56.6% now married, 9.3% widowed, 11.3% divorced (2000); Foreign born: 2.9% (2000); Ancestry (includes multiple ancestries): 26.1% German, 22.9% Italian, 18.4% Irish, 12.4% Polish, 10.5% Other groups (2000).
Economy: Single-family building permits issued: 9 (2001) / 11 (2000); Multi-family building permits issued: 0 (2001) / 6 (2000); Employment by occupation: 6.7% management, 16.5% professional, 15.5% services, 28.6% sales, 0.3% farming, 9.5% construction, 22.9% production (2000).
Income: Per capita income: $19,467 (2000); Median household income: $38,775 (2000); Poverty rate: 6.3% (2000).
Taxes: Total city taxes per capita: $110 (1997); City property taxes per capita: $107 (1997).
Education: High school graduation rate: 78.5% (2000); College graduation rate: 17.4% (2000).

School District(s)

Hall High School District 502 (09-12)
2000 Enrollment: 436 815-664-2100
Spring Valley C C School District 99 (PK-08)
2000 Enrollment: 701 815-664-4242

Housing: Homeownership rate: 72.9% (2000); Median home value: $76,100 (2000); Median rent: $385 per month (2000); Median age of housing: 48 years (2000).
Hospitals: Saint Margaret's Hospital (155 beds)
Transportation: Commute to work: 95.7% car, 0.0% public transportation, 2.1% walk, 1.8% work from home (2000); Travel time to work: 42.3% less than 15 minutes, 40.8% 15 to 30 minutes, 7.4% 30 to 45 minutes, 2.1% 45 to 60 minutes, 7.4% 60 minutes or more (2000)
Additional Information Contacts
Spring Valley Business Owners 815-663-1942

TISKILWA (village). Covers a land area of 0.479 square miles and a water area of 0 square miles. Located at 41.29° N. Lat.; 89.50° W. Long. Elevation is 512 feet.
Population: 787 (2000); Race: 96.6% White, 0.1% Black, 0.0% Asian, 0.5% American Indian and Alaska Native, 0.0% Hispanic of any race, 2.8% two or more races (2000); Density: 1,642.7 persons per square mile (2000); Age: 24.9% under 18, 18.6% over 64 (2000); Marriage status: 19.2% never married, 63.6% now married, 8.5% widowed, 8.8% divorced (2000); Foreign born: 0.9% (2000); Ancestry (includes multiple ancestries): 32.5% German, 16.1% English, 12.1% Irish, 9.9% Swedish, 6.6% United States or American (2000).
Economy: In agricultural area. Manufacturing of dairy products. Single-family building permits issued: 0 (2001) / 0 (2000); Multi-family building permits issued: 0 (2001) / 0 (2000); Employment by occupation: 7.5% management, 9.6% professional, 16.0% services, 22.1% sales, 1.6% farming, 10.4% construction, 32.8% production (2000).
Income: Per capita income: $17,625 (2000); Median household income: $35,278 (2000); Poverty rate: 8.0% (2000).
Taxes: Total city taxes per capita: $66 (1997); City property taxes per capita: $66 (1997).
Education: High school graduation rate: 85.2% (2000); College graduation rate: 9.6% (2000).
Housing: Homeownership rate: 83.1% (2000); Median home value: $74,600 (2000); Median rent: $375 per month (2000); Median age of housing: 60+ years (2000).
Newspapers: Bureau Valley Chief (1 x week)
Transportation: Commute to work: 94.9% car, 0.0% public transportation, 1.9% walk, 1.6% work from home (2000); Travel time to work: 34.8% less than 15 minutes, 47.4% 15 to 30 minutes, 8.8% 30 to 45 minutes, 1.9% 45 to 60 minutes, 7.1% 60 minutes or more (2000)

WALNUT (village). Covers a land area of 0.833 square miles and a water area of 0 square miles. Located at 41.55° N. Lat.; 89.59° W. Long. Elevation is 720 feet.
Population: 1,461 (2000); Race: 99.0% White, 0.1% Black, 0.0% Asian, 0.0% American Indian and Alaska Native, 1.0% Hispanic of any race, 0.3% two or more races (2000); Density: 1,754.2 persons per square mile (2000); Age: 26.5% under 18, 20.5% over 64 (2000); Marriage status: 18.9% never married, 67.1% now married, 7.3% widowed, 6.7% divorced (2000); Foreign born: 1.2% (2000); Ancestry (includes multiple ancestries): 38.4% German, 13.5% Irish, 12.1% English, 8.5% Swedish, 7.2% United States or American (2000).
Economy: Dairy products, grain. Single-family building permits issued: 0 (2001) / 0 (2000); Multi-family building permits issued: 0 (2001) / 0 (2000); Employment by occupation: 8.7% management, 15.4% professional, 16.2% services, 25.5% sales, 1.4% farming, 8.4% construction, 24.4% production (2000).
Income: Per capita income: $20,126 (2000); Median household income: $40,227 (2000); Poverty rate: 6.6% (2000).
Taxes: Total city taxes per capita: $127 (1997); City property taxes per capita: $123 (1997).
Education: High school graduation rate: 87.6% (2000); College graduation rate: 14.7% (2000).

Housing: Homeownership rate: 81.5% (2000); Median home value: $67,800 (2000); Median rent: $271 per month (2000); Median age of housing: 49 years (2000).
Newspapers: The Walnut Leader (1 x week)
Transportation: Commute to work: 87.0% car, 0.0% public transportation, 6.6% walk, 5.2% work from home (2000); Travel time to work: 52.4% less than 15 minutes, 20.7% 15 to 30 minutes, 18.9% 30 to 45 minutes, 4.0% 45 to 60 minutes, 4.0% 60 minutes or more (2000)

WYANET (village). Covers a land area of 1.000 square miles and a water area of 0 square miles. Located at 41.36° N. Lat.; 89.58° W. Long. Elevation is 655 feet.
Population: 1,028 (2000); Race: 97.3% White, 0.0% Black, 1.6% Asian, 0.0% American Indian and Alaska Native, 1.0% Hispanic of any race, 1.1% two or more races (2000); Density: 1,028.0 persons per square mile (2000); Age: 27.8% under 18, 13.3% over 64 (2000); Marriage status: 18.6% never married, 60.4% now married, 5.7% widowed, 15.3% divorced (2000); Foreign born: 0.8% (2000); Ancestry (includes multiple ancestries): 23.4% German, 16.6% Irish, 10.2% Swedish, 6.7% United States or American, 6.4% English (2000).
Economy: Railroad junction. Agriculture: corn, soybeans; cattle, hogs; dairying. Fish hatchery nearby. Employment by occupation: 6.6% management, 9.4% professional, 14.8% services, 19.5% sales, 2.1% farming, 8.8% construction, 38.8% production (2000).
Income: Per capita income: $16,888 (2000); Median household income: $38,289 (2000); Poverty rate: 6.4% (2000).
Taxes: Total city taxes per capita: $75 (1997); City property taxes per capita: $65 (1997).
Education: High school graduation rate: 85.0% (2000); College graduation rate: 6.6% (2000).
Housing: Homeownership rate: 78.2% (2000); Median home value: $69,600 (2000); Median rent: $327 per month (2000); Median age of housing: 56 years (2000).
Transportation: Commute to work: 94.6% car, 0.0% public transportation, 1.3% walk, 2.7% work from home (2000); Travel time to work: 35.8% less than 15 minutes, 47.3% 15 to 30 minutes, 8.4% 30 to 45 minutes, 4.1% 45 to 60 minutes, 4.3% 60 minutes or more (2000)

Calhoun County

Located in western Illinois; bounded on the west and south by the Mississippi River and the Missouri border, and on the east by the Illinois River, which joins the Mississippi River at the southeastern tip of the county. Covers a land area of 253.80 square miles, a water area of 29.90 square miles, and is located in the Central Time Zone. The county government was organized in 1825. County seat is Hardin.
Population: 5,084 (2000); Race: 99.0% White, 0.0% Black, 0.2% Asian, 0.4% American Indian and Alaska Native, 0.7% Hispanic of any race, 0.4% two or more races (2000); Density: 20.0 persons per square mile (2000); Age: 23.0% under 18, 19.1% over 64 (2000).
Religion: Five largest groups: 40.9% Catholic Church, 7.5% Lutheran Church—Missouri Synod, 5.3% New Testament Association of Independent Baptist Churches and other Fundamental Baptist Associations, 3.6% Presbyterian Church (U.S.A.), 3.5% Churches
Economy: Unemployment rate: 4.6% (11/2002); Total civilian labor force: 3,172 (11/2002); Leading industries: 17.9% retail trade; 14.8% accommodation & food services; 14.6% construction (2000); Companies that employ more than 1,000 persons: 0 (2000); Companies that employ more than 100 persons: 0 (2000); Farms: 433 totaling 99,483 acres (1997); Minority business ownership rate: 0.0% (1997); Women business ownership rate: 0.0% (1997); Retail sales per capita: $5,365 (1997). Single-family building permits issued: 22 (2001) / 10 (2000); Multi-family building permits issued: 7 (2001) / 3 (2000).
Income: Per capita income: $16,785 (2000); Median household income: $34,375 (2000); Poverty rate: 9.0% (2000); Bankruptcy rate: 1.43% (2001).
Taxes: Total county taxes per capita: $174 (2000); County property taxes per capita: $146 (2000).
Education: High school graduation rate: 79.9% (2000); College graduation rate: 9.4% (2000).
Housing: Homeownership rate: 80.8% (2000); Median home value: $61,600 (2000); Median rent: $242 per month (2000); Median age of housing: 39 years (2000).
Health: Birth rate: 112.1 per 10,000 population (1998); Age adjusted death rate: 99.8 per 10,000 population (1999); Age adjusted cancer mortality rate: 252.3 (Unreliable figure as per CDC) deaths per 100,000 population (1999).
Number of physicians: 5.9 per 10,000 population (1999); Number of hospital beds: n/a (1999).
Elections: 2000 Presidential election results: 50.4% Gore, 47.2% Bush, 1.6% Nader, 0.7% Buchanan
National and State Parks: Batchtown State Fish and Waterfowl Management Area; Diamond-Hurricane Island State Fish and Waterfowl; Fuller Lake State Fish and Waterfowl Management Area; Mark Twain National Wildlife Refuge; Mortland Island State Fish And Waterfowl Man; Reds Landing State Fish And Waterfowl Manage; Rip Rap Landing State Fish and Waterfowl Management Area
Additional Information Contacts
Calhoun County Government Offices 618-576-2351

Calhoun County Communities

BATCHTOWN (village). Covers a land area of 1.881 square miles and a water area of 0 square miles. Located at 39.03° N. Lat.; 90.65° W. Long. Elevation is 580 feet.
Population: 218 (2000); Race: 100.0% White, 0.0% Black, 0.0% Asian, 0.0% American Indian and Alaska Native, 0.0% Hispanic of any race, 0.0% two or more races (2000); Density: 115.9 persons per square mile (2000); Age: 21.0% under 18, 12.3% over 64 (2000); Marriage status: 19.5% never married, 63.6% now married, 8.2% widowed, 8.7% divorced (2000); Foreign born: 0.8% (2000); Ancestry (includes multiple ancestries): 42.0% German, 14.0% English, 7.8% United States or American, 3.7% Irish, 3.3% Czech (2000).
Economy: In apple-growing area. Employment by occupation: 12.2% management, 16.5% professional, 13.9% services, 19.1% sales, 0.0% farming, 20.9% construction, 17.4% production (2000).
Income: Per capita income: $16,013 (2000); Median household income: $42,222 (2000); Poverty rate: 2.5% (2000).
Taxes: Total city taxes per capita: $38 (1997); City property taxes per capita: $28 (1997).
Education: High school graduation rate: 86.0% (2000); College graduation rate: 11.0% (2000).
Housing: Homeownership rate: 89.8% (2000); Median home value: $67,700 (2000); Median rent: $338 per month (2000); Median age of housing: 50 years (2000).
Transportation: Commute to work: 96.4% car, 0.0% public transportation, 0.0% walk, 3.6% work from home (2000); Travel time to work: 13.0% less than 15 minutes, 29.6% 15 to 30 minutes, 13.9% 30 to 45 minutes, 12.0% 45 to 60 minutes, 31.5% 60 minutes or more (2000)

BRUSSELS (village). Covers a land area of 0.607 square miles and a water area of 0 square miles. Located at 38.94° N. Lat.; 90.58° W. Long. Elevation is 520 feet.
Population: 141 (2000); Race: 100.0% White, 0.0% Black, 0.0% Asian, 0.0% American Indian and Alaska Native, 0.0% Hispanic of any race, 0.0% two or more races (2000); Density: 232.4 persons per square mile (2000); Age: 21.4% under 18, 16.4% over 64 (2000); Marriage status: 23.7% never married, 60.2% now married, 6.8% widowed, 9.3% divorced (2000); Foreign born: 0.0% (2000); Ancestry (includes multiple ancestries): 65.0% German, 7.9% United States or American, 2.9% Irish, 1.4% Czech, 1.4% Dutch (2000).
Economy: In apple-growing area. Employment by occupation: 5.8% management, 18.8% professional, 26.1% services, 21.7% sales, 2.9% farming, 17.4% construction, 7.2% production (2000).
Income: Per capita income: $16,281 (2000); Median household income: $40,938 (2000); Poverty rate: 11.4% (2000).
Taxes: Total city taxes per capita: $17 (1997); City property taxes per capita: $9 (1997).
Education: High school graduation rate: 79.4% (2000); College graduation rate: 12.4% (2000).

School District(s)

Brussels Community Unit School District 42 (KG-12)
2000 Enrollment: 148 618-883-2131
Housing: Homeownership rate: 58.3% (2000); Median home value: $57,500 (2000); Median rent: $191 per month (2000); Median age of housing: 60+ years (2000).
Transportation: Commute to work: 92.4% car, 0.0% public transportation, 7.6% walk, 0.0% work from home (2000); Travel time to work: 39.4% less than 15 minutes, 10.6% 15 to 30 minutes, 16.7% 30 to 45 minutes, 19.7% 45 to 60 minutes, 13.6% 60 minutes or more (2000)

GOLDEN EAGLE (unincorporated postal area, zip code 62036). Covers a land area of 27.943 square miles and a water area of 0.008 square miles. Located at 38.91° N. Lat.; 90.57° W. Long. Elevation is 670 feet.
Population: 601 (2000); Race: 98.7% White, 0.0% Black, 0.9% Asian, 0.0% American Indian and Alaska Native, 0.5% Hispanic of any race, 0.4% two or more races (2000); Density: 21.5 persons per square mile (2000); Age: 20.3% under 18, 19.9% over 64 (2000); Marriage status: 20.8% never married, 66.6% now married, 7.1% widowed, 5.5% divorced (2000); Foreign born: 2.0% (2000); Ancestry (includes multiple ancestries): 59.1% German, 10.4% Other groups, 9.9% Irish, 5.4% Dutch, 4.5% United States or American (2000).
Economy: Employment by occupation: 11.5% management, 14.3% professional, 15.5% services, 16.3% sales, 0.0% farming, 27.4% construction, 15.1% production (2000).
Income: Per capita income: $17,641 (2000); Median household income: $36,429 (2000); Poverty rate: 6.1% (2000).
Education: High school graduation rate: 80.1% (2000); College graduation rate: 7.8% (2000).
Housing: Homeownership rate: 83.9% (2000); Median home value: $83,800 (2000); Median rent: $220 per month (2000); Median age of housing: 47 years (2000).
Transportation: Commute to work: 89.8% car, 0.8% public transportation, 2.0% walk, 6.6% work from home (2000); Travel time to work: 24.1% less than 15 minutes, 10.5% 15 to 30 minutes, 14.5% 30 to 45 minutes, 15.8% 45 to 60 minutes, 35.1% 60 minutes or more (2000)

HAMBURG (village). Covers a land area of 0.522 square miles and a water area of 0.134 square miles. Located at 39.23° N. Lat.; 90.71° W. Long. Elevation is 445 feet.
Population: 126 (2000); Race: 97.9% White, 0.0% Black, 0.0% Asian, 0.0% American Indian and Alaska Native, 0.0% Hispanic of any race, 2.1% two or more races (2000); Density: 241.5 persons per square mile (2000); Age: 13.4% under 18, 26.8% over 64 (2000); Marriage status: 11.5% never married, 59.8% now married, 18.4% widowed, 10.3% divorced (2000); Foreign born: 0.0% (2000); Ancestry (includes multiple ancestries): 32.0% German, 18.6% Irish, 9.3% French (except Basque), 7.2% English, 6.2% Italian (2000).
Economy: Apple growing. Employment by occupation: 10.3% management, 28.2% professional, 10.3% services, 5.1% sales, 0.0% farming, 20.5% construction, 25.6% production (2000).
Income: Per capita income: $17,290 (2000); Median household income: $31,250 (2000); Poverty rate: 7.2% (2000).
Taxes: Total city taxes per capita: $36 (1997); City property taxes per capita: $29 (1997).
Education: High school graduation rate: 62.8% (2000); College graduation rate: 17.9% (2000).
Housing: Homeownership rate: 84.3% (2000); Median home value: $34,000 (2000); Median rent: $133 per month (2000); Median age of housing: 52 years (2000).
Transportation: Commute to work: 100.0% car, 0.0% public transportation, 0.0% walk, 0.0% work from home (2000); Travel time to work: 5.1% less than 15 minutes, 64.1% 15 to 30 minutes, 0.0% 30 to 45 minutes, 10.3% 45 to 60 minutes, 20.5% 60 minutes or more (2000)

HARDIN (village). Covers a land area of 2.097 square miles and a water area of 0.182 square miles. Located at 39.15° N. Lat.; 90.61° W. Long. Elevation is 450 feet.
History: Hardin developed as a distribution center for the surrounding apple-growing region, and as the seat of Calhoun County.
Population: 959 (2000); Race: 100.0% White, 0.0% Black, 0.0% Asian, 0.0% American Indian and Alaska Native, 0.7% Hispanic of any race, 0.0% two or more races (2000); Density: 457.2 persons per square mile (2000); Age: 22.9% under 18, 22.8% over 64 (2000); Marriage status: 17.6% never married, 55.3% now married, 17.1% widowed, 9.9% divorced (2000); Foreign born: 0.5% (2000); Ancestry (includes multiple ancestries): 42.4% German, 9.9% Irish, 9.6% French (except Basque), 7.3% United States or American, 6.2% Other groups (2000).
Economy: Employment by occupation: 7.5% management, 21.1% professional, 16.7% services, 23.2% sales, 0.5% farming, 13.6% construction, 17.4% production (2000).
Income: Per capita income: $17,461 (2000); Median household income: $30,972 (2000); Poverty rate: 10.8% (2000).
Taxes: Total city taxes per capita: $31 (1997); City property taxes per capita: $28 (1997).
Education: High school graduation rate: 78.3% (2000); College graduation rate: 10.1% (2000).

School District(s)

Calhoun Community Unit School District 40 (PK-12)
2000 Enrollment: 545 618-576-2722
Housing: Homeownership rate: 69.3% (2000); Median home value: $58,600 (2000); Median rent: $251 per month (2000); Median age of housing: 34 years (2000).
Newspapers: Calhoun News-Herald (1 x week)
Transportation: Commute to work: 93.7% car, 0.0% public transportation, 4.8% walk, 1.0% work from home (2000); Travel time to work: 38.7% less than 15 minutes, 11.7% 15 to 30 minutes, 6.1% 30 to 45 minutes, 13.4% 45 to 60 minutes, 30.2% 60 minutes or more (2000)

KAMPSVILLE (village). Covers a land area of 1.020 square miles and a water area of 0.220 square miles. Located at 39.29° N. Lat.; 90.61° W. Long. Elevation is 438 feet.
Population: 302 (2000); Race: 100.0% White, 0.0% Black, 0.0% Asian, 0.0% American Indian and Alaska Native, 0.0% Hispanic of any race, 0.0% two or more races (2000); Density: 296.2 persons per square mile (2000); Age: 25.0% under 18, 19.6% over 64 (2000); Marriage status: 14.2% never married, 56.9% now married, 8.2% widowed, 20.7% divorced (2000); Foreign born: 0.0% (2000); Ancestry (includes multiple ancestries): 32.4% German, 15.5% Irish, 11.8% Other groups, 9.1% English, 4.4% United States or American (2000).
Economy: Ferry across river. Employment by occupation: 8.2% management, 10.7% professional, 37.7% services, 16.4% sales, 1.6% farming, 15.6% construction, 9.8% production (2000).
Income: Per capita income: $13,158 (2000); Median household income: $26,875 (2000); Poverty rate: 24.5% (2000).
Taxes: Total city taxes per capita: $50 (1997); City property taxes per capita: $11 (1997).
Education: High school graduation rate: 80.3% (2000); College graduation rate: 10.8% (2000).
Housing: Homeownership rate: 67.2% (2000); Median home value: $47,200 (2000); Median rent: $257 per month (2000); Median age of housing: 42 years (2000).
Transportation: Commute to work: 91.7% car, 0.0% public transportation, 8.3% walk, 0.0% work from home (2000); Travel time to work: 29.2% less than 15 minutes, 18.3% 15 to 30 minutes, 13.3% 30 to 45 minutes, 16.7% 45 to 60 minutes, 22.5% 60 minutes or more (2000)

MICHAEL (unincorporated postal area, zip code 62065). Covers a land area of 8.873 square miles and a water area of 0.306 square miles. Located at 39.23° N. Lat.; 90.62° W. Long. Elevation is 441 feet.
Population: 114 (2000); Race: 96.9% White, 0.0% Black, 0.0% Asian, 1.5% American Indian and Alaska Native, 0.0% Hispanic of any race, 1.5% two or more races (2000); Density: 12.8 persons per square mile (2000); Age: 29.8% under 18, 20.6% over 64 (2000); Marriage status: 19.4% never married, 69.4% now married, 6.1% widowed, 5.1% divorced (2000); Foreign born: 6.9% (2000); Ancestry (includes multiple ancestries): 30.5% German, 10.7% United States or American, 6.1% Norwegian, 4.6% French (except Basque), 3.8% English (2000).
Economy: Employment by occupation: 7.4% management, 14.8% professional, 14.8% services, 40.7% sales, 0.0% farming, 7.4% construction, 14.8% production (2000).
Income: Per capita income: $10,806 (2000); Median household income: $24,583 (2000); Poverty rate: 2.3% (2000).
Education: High school graduation rate: 71.1% (2000); College graduation rate: 4.8% (2000).
Housing: Homeownership rate: 87.7% (2000); Median home value: $53,700 (2000); Median rent: $325 per month (2000); Median age of housing: 36 years (2000).
Transportation: Commute to work: 100.0% car, 0.0% public transportation, 0.0% walk, 0.0% work from home (2000); Travel time to work: 44.4% less than 15 minutes, 14.8% 15 to 30 minutes, 11.1% 30 to 45 minutes, 0.0% 45 to 60 minutes, 29.6% 60 minutes or more (2000)

MOZIER (unincorporated postal area, zip code 62070). Aka Baytown. Covers a land area of 10.423 square miles and a water area of 0.258 square miles. Located at 39.32° N. Lat.; 90.76° W. Long. Elevation is 445 feet.
Population: 63 (2000); Race: 100.0% White, 0.0% Black, 0.0% Asian, 0.0% American Indian and Alaska Native, 0.0% Hispanic of any race, 0.0% two or more races (2000); Density: 6.0 persons per square mile (2000); Age: 21.9% under 18, 35.9% over 64 (2000); Marriage status: 4.0% never married, 72.0% now married, 20.0% widowed, 4.0% divorced (2000); Foreign born: 0.0%

(2000); Ancestry (includes multiple ancestries): 39.1% United States or American, 10.9% German, 7.8% English (2000).
Economy: Employment by occupation: 8.3% management, 8.3% professional, 16.7% services, 12.5% sales, 0.0% farming, 16.7% construction, 37.5% production (2000).
Income: Per capita income: $14,966 (2000); Median household income: $33,750 (2000); Poverty rate: 7.8% (2000).
Education: High school graduation rate: 62.0% (2000); College graduation rate: 8.0% (2000).
Housing: Homeownership rate: 96.7% (2000); Median home value: $51,700 (2000); Median age of housing: 42 years (2000).
Transportation: Commute to work: 100.0% car, 0.0% public transportation, 0.0% walk, 0.0% work from home (2000); Travel time to work: 20.8% less than 15 minutes, 37.5% 15 to 30 minutes, 8.3% 30 to 45 minutes, 16.7% 45 to 60 minutes, 16.7% 60 minutes or more (2000)

Carroll County

Located in northwestern Illinois; bounded on the west by the Mississippi River and the Iowa border; drained by the Plum River and Elkhorn Creek. Covers a land area of 444.20 square miles, a water area of 21.60 square miles, and is located in the Central Time Zone. The county government was organized in 1839. County seat is Mount Carroll.

Weather Station: Mount Carroll — Elevation: 639 feet

	Jan	Feb	Mar	Apr	May	Jun	Jul	Aug	Sep	Oct	Nov	Dec
High	28	34	46	60	72	81	85	82	75	63	47	34
Low	7	13	24	35	46	54	59	56	47	36	27	15
Precip	1.4	1.4	2.7	3.7	4.5	4.6	3.7	4.5	3.7	2.8	2.8	2.0
Snow	10.5	6.7	4.3	1.6	tr	0.0	0.0	0.0	tr	0.2	2.6	7.0

High and Low temperatures in degrees Fahrenheit; Precipitation and Snow in inches

Population: 16,674 (2000); Race: 97.0% White, 0.5% Black, 0.3% Asian, 0.2% American Indian and Alaska Native, 1.8% Hispanic of any race, 0.9% two or more races (2000); Density: 37.5 persons per square mile (2000); Age: 24.4% under 18, 19.2% over 64 (2000).
Religion: Five largest groups: 17.2% The United Methodist Church, 14.7% Catholic Church, 8.2% Evangelical Lutheran Church in America, 3.3% Church of the Brethren, 3.0% Churches of God, General Conference (2000).
Economy: Unemployment rate: 6.8% (11/2002); Total civilian labor force: 7,679 (11/2002); Leading industries: 24.7% manufacturing; 13.2% transportation & warehousing; 12.8% retail trade (2000); Companies that employ more than 1,000 persons: 0 (2000); Companies that employ more than 100 persons: 6 (2000); Farms: 625 totaling 243,305 acres (1997); Minority business ownership rate: 0.0% (1997); Women business ownership rate: 15.3% (1997); Retail sales per capita: $4,814 (1997). Single-family building permits issued: 77 (2001) / 66 (2000); Multi-family building permits issued: 0 (2001) / 4 (2000).
Income: Per capita income: $18,688 (2000); Median household income: $37,148 (2000); Poverty rate: 9.6% (2000); Bankruptcy rate: 4.35% (2001).
Taxes: Total county taxes per capita: $72 (1997); County property taxes per capita: $72 (1997).
Education: High school graduation rate: 83.3% (2000); College graduation rate: 13.1% (2000).
Housing: Homeownership rate: 76.7% (2000); Median home value: $68,700 (2000); Median rent: $288 per month (2000); Median age of housing: 52 years (2000).
Health: Birth rate: 111.0 per 10,000 population (1998); Age adjusted death rate: 83.8 per 10,000 population (1999); Age adjusted cancer mortality rate: 215.1 deaths per 100,000 population (1999). Number of physicians: 4.2 per 10,000 population (1999); Number of hospital beds: n/a (1999).
Elections: 2000 Presidential election results: 43.4% Gore, 53.4% Bush, 2.2% Nader, 0.7% Buchanan
National and State Parks: Ayers Sand Prairie State Nature Preserve; Mississippi Palisades State Park
Additional Information Contacts
Carroll County Government Offices 815-244-0221
Savanna Chamber of Commerce 815-273-2722

Carroll County Communities

CHADWICK (village). Covers a land area of 0.317 square miles and a water area of 0 square miles. Located at 42.01° N. Lat.; 89.88° W. Long. Elevation is 790 feet.
Population: 505 (2000); Race: 96.2% White, 0.0% Black, 0.0% Asian, 0.0% American Indian and Alaska Native, 1.6% Hispanic of any race, 2.0% two or more races (2000); Density: 1,595.5 persons per square mile (2000); Age: 27.2% under 18, 17.9% over 64 (2000); Marriage status: 20.6% never married, 60.9% now married, 11.4% widowed, 7.1% divorced (2000); Foreign born: 0.0% (2000); Ancestry (includes multiple ancestries): 46.5% German, 10.1% Irish, 7.0% English, 5.4% Other groups, 5.2% Dutch (2000).
Economy: In rich agricultural area. Employment by occupation: 9.9% management, 8.3% professional, 10.7% services, 26.6% sales, 0.0% farming, 13.5% construction, 31.0% production (2000).
Income: Per capita income: $16,617 (2000); Median household income: $39,583 (2000); Poverty rate: 10.9% (2000).
Taxes: Total city taxes per capita: $50 (1997); City property taxes per capita: $38 (1997).
Education: High school graduation rate: 84.2% (2000); College graduation rate: 9.8% (2000).
Housing: Homeownership rate: 82.1% (2000); Median home value: $62,100 (2000); Median rent: $263 per month (2000); Median age of housing: 60+ years (2000).
Transportation: Commute to work: 90.2% car, 0.0% public transportation, 6.9% walk, 0.8% work from home (2000); Travel time to work: 39.9% less than 15 minutes, 21.0% 15 to 30 minutes, 25.1% 30 to 45 minutes, 9.9% 45 to 60 minutes, 4.1% 60 minutes or more (2000)

LANARK (city). Covers a land area of 1.038 square miles and a water area of 0 square miles. Located at 42.10° N. Lat.; 89.83° W. Long. Elevation is 880 feet.
History: Lanark developed as a trading center and cannery operation for the surrounding farming community.
Population: 1,584 (2000); Race: 98.2% White, 0.1% Black, 0.1% Asian, 0.0% American Indian and Alaska Native, 0.3% Hispanic of any race, 1.3% two or more races (2000); Density: 1,525.7 persons per square mile (2000); Age: 25.8% under 18, 17.5% over 64 (2000); Marriage status: 20.9% never married, 60.2% now married, 8.8% widowed, 10.1% divorced (2000); Foreign born: 0.5% (2000); Ancestry (includes multiple ancestries): 54.1% German, 12.9% Irish, 10.0% English, 4.3% United States or American, 3.7% Other groups (2000).
Economy: Single-family building permits issued: 1 (2001) / 2 (2000); Multi-family building permits issued: 0 (2001) / 0 (2000); Employment by occupation: 11.9% management, 16.2% professional, 12.6% services, 21.5% sales, 1.6% farming, 9.9% construction, 26.4% production (2000).
Income: Per capita income: $17,518 (2000); Median household income: $35,500 (2000); Poverty rate: 8.0% (2000).
Taxes: Total city taxes per capita: $93 (1997); City property taxes per capita: $86 (1997).
Education: High school graduation rate: 85.4% (2000); College graduation rate: 12.1% (2000).

School District(s)
Eastland Community Unit School District 308 (PK-12)
2000 Enrollment: 849 815-493-6301

Housing: Homeownership rate: 81.2% (2000); Median home value: $66,000 (2000); Median rent: $272 per month (2000); Median age of housing: 60+ years (2000).
Transportation: Commute to work: 88.7% car, 0.0% public transportation, 5.1% walk, 5.1% work from home (2000); Travel time to work: 40.8% less than 15 minutes, 24.4% 15 to 30 minutes, 24.8% 30 to 45 minutes, 2.8% 45 to 60 minutes, 7.2% 60 minutes or more (2000)

MILLEDGEVILLE (village). Covers a land area of 0.708 square miles and a water area of 0 square miles. Located at 41.96° N. Lat.; 89.77° W. Long. Elevation is 755 feet.
Population: 1,016 (2000); Race: 96.8% White, 0.5% Black, 0.2% Asian, 0.9% American Indian and Alaska Native, 2.1% Hispanic of any race, 0.4% two or more races (2000); Density: 1,434.2 persons per square mile (2000); Age: 21.6% under 18, 22.9% over 64 (2000); Marriage status: 19.5% never married, 62.9% now married, 11.4% widowed, 6.2% divorced (2000); Foreign born: 1.1% (2000); Ancestry (includes multiple ancestries): 45.6% German, 11.2% Irish, 10.4% English, 7.3% Other groups, 6.6% Dutch (2000).
Economy: Dairying; corn. Manufacturing: fabricated aluminum. Single-family building permits issued: 1 (2001) / 3 (2000); Multi-family building permits issued: 0 (2001) / 0 (2000); Employment by occupation: 7.8% management, 15.8% professional, 9.4% services, 22.5% sales, 1.0% farming, 9.7% construction, 33.8% production (2000).
Income: Per capita income: $19,220 (2000); Median household income: $35,313 (2000); Poverty rate: 5.2% (2000).
Taxes: Total city taxes per capita: $159 (1997); City property taxes per capita: $88 (1997).

Education: High school graduation rate: 88.9% (2000); College graduation rate: 10.8% (2000).

School District(s)

Chadwick-Milledgeville CUSD 399 (PK-12)
2000 Enrollment: 665 815-225-7141

Housing: Homeownership rate: 81.6% (2000); Median home value: $68,900 (2000); Median rent: $283 per month (2000); Median age of housing: 54 years (2000).

Transportation: Commute to work: 90.6% car, 0.0% public transportation, 7.5% walk, 1.2% work from home (2000); Travel time to work: 42.0% less than 15 minutes, 39.1% 15 to 30 minutes, 11.3% 30 to 45 minutes, 1.9% 45 to 60 minutes, 5.6% 60 minutes or more (2000)

MOUNT CARROLL (city). Covers a land area of 1.901 square miles and a water area of 0 square miles. Located at 42.09° N. Lat.; 89.97° W. Long. Elevation is 760 feet.

History: Founded 1843, incorporated 1867.

Population: 1,832 (2000); Race: 99.1% White, 0.0% Black, 0.0% Asian, 0.2% American Indian and Alaska Native, 0.9% Hispanic of any race, 0.6% two or more races (2000); Density: 963.5 persons per square mile (2000); Age: 25.3% under 18, 17.1% over 64 (2000); Marriage status: 18.6% never married, 63.3% now married, 7.6% widowed, 10.6% divorced (2000); Foreign born: 1.4% (2000); Ancestry (includes multiple ancestries): 44.4% German, 10.4% English, 9.5% Irish, 8.8% United States or American, 8.3% Dutch (2000).

Economy: In rich agricultural area: dairy products, grain; livestock, poultry. Single-family building permits issued: 4 (2001) / 2 (2000); Multi-family building permits issued: 0 (2001) / 0 (2000); Employment by occupation: 9.4% management, 12.9% professional, 21.0% services, 18.8% sales, 1.1% farming, 10.5% construction, 26.3% production (2000).

Income: Per capita income: $16,455 (2000); Median household income: $34,861 (2000); Poverty rate: 8.5% (2000).

Taxes: Total city taxes per capita: $103 (1997); City property taxes per capita: $95 (1997).

Education: High school graduation rate: 85.8% (2000); College graduation rate: 12.3% (2000).

School District(s)

Mount Carroll Community Unit District 304 (PK-12)
2000 Enrollment: 517 815-244-2055

Housing: Homeownership rate: 78.2% (2000); Median home value: $70,800 (2000); Median rent: $293 per month (2000); Median age of housing: 60+ years (2000).

Newspapers: Mirror-Democrat (1 x week); Northwestern Illinois Dispatch (1 x week)

Transportation: Commute to work: 91.0% car, 0.0% public transportation, 5.5% walk, 3.2% work from home (2000); Travel time to work: 50.6% less than 15 minutes, 24.5% 15 to 30 minutes, 13.3% 30 to 45 minutes, 5.8% 45 to 60 minutes, 5.8% 60 minutes or more (2000)

SAVANNA (city). Covers a land area of 2.609 square miles and a water area of 0.094 square miles. Located at 42.09° N. Lat.; 90.14° W. Long. Elevation is 606 feet.

History: Savanna was settled in 1828 as a farming center and river port. The coming of the railroad in 1850 made Savanna a trading town and shipping point for livestock and farm produce.

Population: 3,542 (2000); Race: 92.8% White, 2.2% Black, 0.4% Asian, 0.0% American Indian and Alaska Native, 5.2% Hispanic of any race, 0.9% two or more races (2000); Density: 1,357.7 persons per square mile (2000); Age: 24.1% under 18, 21.6% over 64 (2000); Marriage status: 22.2% never married, 50.6% now married, 12.6% widowed, 14.6% divorced (2000); Foreign born: 3.7% (2000); Ancestry (includes multiple ancestries): 29.8% German, 20.2% Irish, 10.7% Other groups, 10.4% United States or American, 9.9% English (2000).

Economy: Single-family building permits issued: 1 (2001) / 4 (2000); Multi-family building permits issued: 0 (2001) / 0 (2000); Employment by occupation: 6.9% management, 14.8% professional, 17.6% services, 17.7% sales, 1.4% farming, 8.5% construction, 33.2% production (2000).

Income: Per capita income: $15,150 (2000); Median household income: $27,180 (2000); Poverty rate: 16.7% (2000).

Taxes: Total city taxes per capita: $270 (1997); City property taxes per capita: $94 (1997).

Education: High school graduation rate: 79.4% (2000); College graduation rate: 11.6% (2000).

School District(s)

Savanna Community Unit District 300 (PK-12)
2000 Enrollment: 794 815-273-3450

Housing: Homeownership rate: 67.4% (2000); Median home value: $48,300 (2000); Median rent: $272 per month (2000); Median age of housing: 57 years (2000).

Newspapers: Savanna Times Journal (1 x week)

Transportation: Commute to work: 91.6% car, 0.9% public transportation, 3.9% walk, 2.3% work from home (2000); Travel time to work: 58.8% less than 15 minutes, 12.7% 15 to 30 minutes, 14.5% 30 to 45 minutes, 4.6% 45 to 60 minutes, 9.3% 60 minutes or more (2000)

Additional Information Contacts

Savanna Chamber of Commerce 815-273-2722

SHANNON (village). Covers a land area of 0.479 square miles and a water area of 0 square miles. Located at 42.15° N. Lat.; 89.74° W. Long. Elevation is 925 feet.

Population: 854 (2000); Race: 95.8% White, 0.0% Black, 3.2% Asian, 0.2% American Indian and Alaska Native, 0.7% Hispanic of any race, 0.8% two or more races (2000); Density: 1,783.4 persons per square mile (2000); Age: 23.2% under 18, 22.0% over 64 (2000); Marriage status: 18.7% never married, 62.5% now married, 9.3% widowed, 9.5% divorced (2000); Foreign born: 2.9% (2000); Ancestry (includes multiple ancestries): 51.9% German, 11.4% Irish, 6.5% English, 6.2% Dutch, 5.9% Other groups (2000).

Economy: In rich agricultural area. Single-family building permits issued: 1 (2001) / 0 (2000); Multi-family building permits issued: 0 (2001) / 0 (2000); Employment by occupation: 10.5% management, 12.4% professional, 15.3% services, 27.7% sales, 1.0% farming, 9.8% construction, 23.4% production (2000).

Income: Per capita income: $21,108 (2000); Median household income: $42,500 (2000); Poverty rate: 7.4% (2000).

Taxes: Total city taxes per capita: $54 (1997); City property taxes per capita: $47 (1997).

Education: High school graduation rate: 87.1% (2000); College graduation rate: 17.7% (2000).

Housing: Homeownership rate: 83.5% (2000); Median home value: $73,500 (2000); Median rent: $325 per month (2000); Median age of housing: 56 years (2000).

Transportation: Commute to work: 84.0% car, 0.0% public transportation, 10.7% walk, 3.6% work from home (2000); Travel time to work: 41.1% less than 15 minutes, 34.9% 15 to 30 minutes, 14.1% 30 to 45 minutes, 4.7% 45 to 60 minutes, 5.2% 60 minutes or more (2000)

THOMSON (village). Covers a land area of 2.208 square miles and a water area of 0 square miles. Located at 41.96° N. Lat.; 90.10° W. Long. Elevation is 600 feet.

Population: 559 (2000); Race: 93.5% White, 0.0% Black, 0.0% Asian, 2.7% American Indian and Alaska Native, 0.5% Hispanic of any race, 3.6% two or more races (2000); Density: 253.2 persons per square mile (2000); Age: 25.8% under 18, 14.0% over 64 (2000); Marriage status: 24.8% never married, 58.0% now married, 6.7% widowed, 10.4% divorced (2000); Foreign born: 0.4% (2000); Ancestry (includes multiple ancestries): 30.0% German, 14.5% Irish, 10.2% English, 9.6% Other groups, 8.4% United States or American (2000).

Economy: In rich agricultural area: corn, soybeans; cattle, hogs; dairying. Single-family building permits issued: 6 (2001) / 2 (2000); Multi-family building permits issued: 0 (2001) / 0 (2000); Employment by occupation: 6.9% management, 12.0% professional, 17.2% services, 18.6% sales, 0.0% farming, 9.5% construction, 35.8% production (2000).

Income: Per capita income: $17,261 (2000); Median household income: $36,667 (2000); Poverty rate: 6.7% (2000).

Taxes: Total city taxes per capita: $36 (1997); City property taxes per capita: $31 (1997).

Education: High school graduation rate: 83.1% (2000); College graduation rate: 10.7% (2000).

School District(s)

Thomson Com Unit District 301 (KG-12)
2000 Enrollment: 301 815-259-2735

Housing: Homeownership rate: 72.1% (2000); Median home value: $72,800 (2000); Median rent: $295 per month (2000); Median age of housing: 50 years (2000).

Newspapers: Carroll County Review (1 x week)

Transportation: Commute to work: 92.2% car, 1.9% public transportation, 3.0% walk, 2.2% work from home (2000); Travel time to work: 32.6% less than 15 minutes, 40.5% 15 to 30 minutes, 13.6% 30 to 45 minutes, 7.2% 45 to 60 minutes, 6.1% 60 minutes or more (2000)

Cass County

Located in west central Illinois; bounded on the north by the Sangamon River, and on the west by the Illinois River. Covers a land area of 375.90 square miles, a water area of 7.80 square miles, and is located in the Central Time Zone. The county government was organized in 1837. County seat is Virginia.

Population: 13,695 (2000); Race: 95.1% White, 0.2% Black, 0.4% Asian, 0.1% American Indian and Alaska Native, 8.8% Hispanic of any race, 0.9% two or more races (2000); Density: 36.4 persons per square mile (2000); Age: 25.3% under 18, 15.6% over 64 (2000).

Religion: Five largest groups: 27.6% Catholic Church, 10.8% The United Methodist Church, 9.4% Lutheran Church—Missouri Synod, 8.6% Evangelical Lutheran Church in America, 5.1% Christian Churches and Churches of Christ (2000).

Economy: Unemployment rate: 5.3% (11/2002); Total civilian labor force: 7,443 (11/2002); Leading industries: 45.5% manufacturing; 11.2% retail trade; 9.3% health care and social assistance (2000); Companies that employ more than 1,000 persons: 1 (2000); Companies that employ more than 100 persons: 4 (2000); Farms: 417 totaling 192,156 acres (1997); Minority business ownership rate: 0.0% (1997); Women business ownership rate: 13.0% (1997); Retail sales per capita: $5,151 (1997). Single-family building permits issued: 12 (2001) / 11 (2000); Multi-family building permits issued: 0 (2001) / 0 (2000).

Income: Per capita income: $16,532 (2000); Median household income: $35,243 (2000); Poverty rate: 12.0% (2000); Bankruptcy rate: 6.52% (2001).

Taxes: Total county taxes per capita: $123 (1997); County property taxes per capita: $107 (1997).

Education: High school graduation rate: 80.0% (2000); College graduation rate: 12.6% (2000).

Housing: Homeownership rate: 75.2% (2000); Median home value: $54,900 (2000); Median rent: $309 per month (2000); Median age of housing: 50 years (2000).

Health: Birth rate: 137.3 per 10,000 population (1998); Age adjusted death rate: 92.4 per 10,000 population (1999); Age adjusted cancer mortality rate: 172.5 deaths per 100,000 population (1999). Number of physicians: 2.2 per 10,000 population (1999); Number of hospital beds: n/a (1999).

Elections: 2000 Presidential election results: 47.3% Gore, 50.3% Bush, 1.6% Nader, 0.6% Buchanan

National and State Parks: Meredosia National Wildlife Refuge; Panther Creek State Conservation Area; Sanganois State Conservation Area; Toppers Hole State Conservation Area

Additional Information Contacts

Cass County Government Offices 217-452-7217
Beardstown Chamber of Commerce 217-323-3271

Cass County Communities

ARENZVILLE (village). Covers a land area of 0.785 square miles and a water area of 0 square miles. Located at 39.87° N. Lat.; 90.37° W. Long. Elevation is 513 feet.

Population: 419 (2000); Race: 99.5% White, 0.0% Black, 0.0% Asian, 0.0% American Indian and Alaska Native, 0.0% Hispanic of any race, 0.5% two or more races (2000); Density: 534.0 persons per square mile (2000); Age: 25.3% under 18, 20.8% over 64 (2000); Marriage status: 15.2% never married, 68.1% now married, 10.7% widowed, 6.0% divorced (2000); Foreign born: 0.0% (2000); Ancestry (includes multiple ancestries): 45.2% German, 10.4% United States or American, 8.7% English, 7.6% Other groups, 6.1% Irish (2000).

Economy: In agricultural area: corn, soybeans, sorghum; cattle, hogs. Corn seed processing, lumber, millwork. Employment by occupation: 12.0% management, 12.4% professional, 17.1% services, 24.0% sales, 4.6% farming, 9.2% construction, 20.7% production (2000).

Income: Per capita income: $19,730 (2000); Median household income: $37,500 (2000); Poverty rate: 2.1% (2000).

Taxes: Total city taxes per capita: $74 (1997); City property taxes per capita: $70 (1997).

Education: High school graduation rate: 86.2% (2000); College graduation rate: 19.9% (2000).

Housing: Homeownership rate: 85.1% (2000); Median home value: $57,400 (2000); Median rent: $225 per month (2000); Median age of housing: 59 years (2000).

Transportation: Commute to work: 83.7% car, 0.0% public transportation, 4.7% walk, 9.8% work from home (2000); Travel time to work: 42.3% less than 15 minutes, 29.9% 15 to 30 minutes, 18.0% 30 to 45 minutes, 3.6% 45 to 60 minutes, 6.2% 60 minutes or more (2000)

ASHLAND (village). Covers a land area of 0.743 square miles and a water area of 0 square miles. Located at 39.88° N. Lat.; 90.00° W. Long. Elevation is 633 feet.

History: Incorporated 1869.

Population: 1,361 (2000); Race: 98.8% White, 0.0% Black, 0.2% Asian, 0.1% American Indian and Alaska Native, 0.1% Hispanic of any race, 0.2% two or more races (2000); Density: 1,832.3 persons per square mile (2000); Age: 26.9% under 18, 13.5% over 64 (2000); Marriage status: 20.2% never married, 62.8% now married, 7.5% widowed, 9.4% divorced (2000); Foreign born: 0.1% (2000); Ancestry (includes multiple ancestries): 29.1% German, 14.5% Irish, 13.7% English, 12.2% United States or American, 5.8% Other groups (2000).

Economy: Ships grain. Agriculture: cattle, hogs; sorghum, corn, soybeans. Single-family building permits issued: 2 (2001) / 0 (2000); Multi-family building permits issued: 0 (2001) / 0 (2000); Employment by occupation: 13.3% management, 14.9% professional, 15.0% services, 28.8% sales, 1.3% farming, 10.4% construction, 16.3% production (2000).

Income: Per capita income: $20,090 (2000); Median household income: $43,125 (2000); Poverty rate: 6.3% (2000).

Taxes: Total city taxes per capita: $49 (1997); City property taxes per capita: $45 (1997).

Education: High school graduation rate: 84.7% (2000); College graduation rate: 17.1% (2000).

School District(s)

A-C Central CUSD 262 (PK-12)
2000 Enrollment: 514 217-476-8112

Housing: Homeownership rate: 81.4% (2000); Median home value: $72,400 (2000); Median rent: $348 per month (2000); Median age of housing: 39 years (2000).

Newspapers: Ashland Sentinel (1 x week)

Transportation: Commute to work: 94.9% car, 0.6% public transportation, 2.5% walk, 1.6% work from home (2000); Travel time to work: 21.6% less than 15 minutes, 19.5% 15 to 30 minutes, 49.6% 30 to 45 minutes, 6.5% 45 to 60 minutes, 2.9% 60 minutes or more (2000)

BEARDSTOWN (city). Covers a land area of 3.408 square miles and a water area of 0.055 square miles. Located at 40.01° N. Lat.; 90.42° W. Long. Elevation is 445 feet.

History: Beardstown, first called Beard's Ferry, was settled in 1819 by Thomas Beard, who operated a ferry across the Illinois River. An early commercial fishing and clam industry gave way to farming and shipping. A 1922 flood covered Beardstown with a lake 18 miles wide, prompting the building of a cement sea wall when the waters receded.

Population: 5,766 (2000); Race: 90.7% White, 0.3% Black, 0.4% Asian, 0.2% American Indian and Alaska Native, 20.2% Hispanic of any race, 1.0% two or more races (2000); Density: 1,692.1 persons per square mile (2000); Age: 26.6% under 18, 15.1% over 64 (2000); Marriage status: 24.5% never married, 53.9% now married, 9.7% widowed, 12.0% divorced (2000); Foreign born: 17.9% (2000); Ancestry (includes multiple ancestries): 24.2% Other groups, 19.7% German, 12.3% United States or American, 10.7% Irish, 6.9% English (2000).

Economy: Single-family building permits issued: 0 (2001) / 0 (2000); Multi-family building permits issued: 0 (2001) / 0 (2000); Employment by occupation: 8.1% management, 12.9% professional, 17.2% services, 15.0% sales, 1.7% farming, 9.8% construction, 35.3% production (2000).

Income: Per capita income: $13,777 (2000); Median household income: $29,104 (2000); Poverty rate: 19.8% (2000).

Taxes: Total city taxes per capita: $470 (1997); City property taxes per capita: $289 (1997).

Education: High school graduation rate: 73.3% (2000); College graduation rate: 8.7% (2000).

School District(s)

Beardstown C U School District 15 (PK-12)
2000 Enrollment: 1,321 217-323-3099

Housing: Homeownership rate: 66.8% (2000); Median home value: $43,800 (2000); Median rent: $311 per month (2000); Median age of housing: 59 years (2000).

Newspapers: Star-Gazette Extra (1 x week)

Transportation: Commute to work: 94.4% car, 0.0% public transportation, 2.6% walk, 2.8% work from home (2000); Travel time to work: 66.4% less than 15 minutes, 15.7% 15 to 30 minutes, 4.9% 30 to 45 minutes, 4.4% 45 to 60 minutes, 8.7% 60 minutes or more (2000)

Additional Information Contacts

Beardstown Chamber of Commerce 217-323-3271

CHANDLERVILLE (village). Covers a land area of 0.861 square miles and a water area of 0 square miles. Located at 40.04° N. Lat.; 90.15° W. Long. Elevation is 464 feet.
History: Chandlerville was named for its founder, Dr. Charles Chandler.
Population: 704 (2000); Race: 98.3% White, 0.0% Black, 0.0% Asian, 0.0% American Indian and Alaska Native, 3.1% Hispanic of any race, 1.4% two or more races (2000); Density: 818.0 persons per square mile (2000); Age: 26.2% under 18, 13.9% over 64 (2000); Marriage status: 20.0% never married, 60.5% now married, 7.3% widowed, 12.2% divorced (2000); Foreign born: 0.4% (2000); Ancestry (includes multiple ancestries): 22.0% English, 21.2% German, 10.7% United States or American, 8.1% Irish, 4.3% Other groups (2000).
Economy: Employment by occupation: 6.9% management, 12.2% professional, 16.1% services, 23.9% sales, 4.5% farming, 10.4% construction, 26.0% production (2000).
Income: Per capita income: $15,812 (2000); Median household income: $33,162 (2000); Poverty rate: 8.4% (2000).
Taxes: Total city taxes per capita: $42 (1997); City property taxes per capita: $41 (1997).
Education: High school graduation rate: 81.6% (2000); College graduation rate: 9.1% (2000).
Housing: Homeownership rate: 79.1% (2000); Median home value: $43,900 (2000); Median rent: $260 per month (2000); Median age of housing: 60+ years (2000).
Transportation: Commute to work: 93.5% car, 0.0% public transportation, 5.4% walk, 1.2% work from home (2000); Travel time to work: 31.0% less than 15 minutes, 27.4% 15 to 30 minutes, 23.2% 30 to 45 minutes, 8.7% 45 to 60 minutes, 9.6% 60 minutes or more (2000)

VIRGINIA (city). Covers a land area of 1.085 square miles and a water area of 0.012 square miles. Located at 39.94° N. Lat.; 90.21° W. Long. Elevation is 622 feet.
History: Virginia was platted in 1836 by Dr. Henry A. Hall, a former surgeon in the British Navy, and was incorporated as a village in 1842. It developed as a city after 1872.
Population: 1,728 (2000); Race: 98.8% White, 0.0% Black, 0.2% Asian, 0.1% American Indian and Alaska Native, 0.4% Hispanic of any race, 0.6% two or more races (2000); Density: 1,593.2 persons per square mile (2000); Age: 22.9% under 18, 22.8% over 64 (2000); Marriage status: 18.4% never married, 57.0% now married, 11.7% widowed, 12.9% divorced (2000); Foreign born: 0.3% (2000); Ancestry (includes multiple ancestries): 24.9% German, 19.5% English, 10.2% United States or American, 9.8% Irish, 5.6% Other groups (2000).
Economy: Single-family building permits issued: 2 (2001) / 2 (2000); Multi-family building permits issued: 0 (2001) / 0 (2000); Employment by occupation: 11.4% management, 12.5% professional, 13.9% services, 27.3% sales, 2.3% farming, 9.0% construction, 23.6% production (2000).
Income: Per capita income: $17,979 (2000); Median household income: $35,741 (2000); Poverty rate: 7.7% (2000).
Taxes: Total city taxes per capita: $115 (1997); City property taxes per capita: $57 (1997).
Education: High school graduation rate: 79.5% (2000); College graduation rate: 14.2% (2000).

School District(s)

Virginia C U School District 64 (PK-12)
2000 Enrollment: 430 217-452-3085
Housing: Homeownership rate: 72.6% (2000); Median home value: $55,300 (2000); Median rent: $311 per month (2000); Median age of housing: 47 years (2000).
Newspapers: Cass County Star-Gazette (1 x week)
Transportation: Commute to work: 94.9% car, 0.0% public transportation, 1.6% walk, 3.0% work from home (2000); Travel time to work: 37.5% less than 15 minutes, 31.9% 15 to 30 minutes, 16.2% 30 to 45 minutes, 9.3% 45 to 60 minutes, 5.0% 60 minutes or more (2000)

Champaign County

Located in eastern Illinois; prairie region, drained by the Sangamon, Kaskaskia, and Embarrass Rivers, and by the South Fork of the Vermilion River. Covers a land area of 996.80 square miles, a water area of 0.70 square miles, and is located in the Central Time Zone. The county government was organized in 1833. County seat is Urbana.

Champaign County is part of the Champaign-Urbana, IL MSA. The entire metro area includes: Champaign County

Weather Station: Rantoul Chanute AFB — Elevation: 754 feet

	Jan	Feb	Mar	Apr	May	Jun	Jul	Aug	Sep	Oct	Nov	Dec
High	32	37	49	62	74	83	87	84	79	66	50	38
Low	14	19	29	39	50	60	64	61	53	41	31	21
Precip	1.7	1.8	3.1	3.9	4.2	3.9	4.5	4.3	3.2	2.9	3.1	2.6
Snow	na	na	1.9	0.4	tr	0.0	0.0	0.0	0.0	tr	0.5	na

High and Low temperatures in degrees Fahrenheit; Precipitation and Snow in inches

Weather Station: Urbana — Elevation: 741 feet

	Jan	Feb	Mar	Apr	May	Jun	Jul	Aug	Sep	Oct	Nov	Dec
High	32	37	49	62	74	83	85	83	78	65	50	37
Low	16	21	31	41	52	61	65	63	55	43	33	23
Precip	1.9	2.0	3.2	3.8	4.7	4.2	4.7	4.4	3.3	2.8	3.4	2.7
Snow	8.5	5.7	3.3	0.6	tr	0.0	0.0	0.0	0.0	0.1	2.1	5.6

High and Low temperatures in degrees Fahrenheit; Precipitation and Snow in inches

Population: 179,669 (2000); Race: 79.0% White, 11.2% Black, 6.5% Asian, 0.2% American Indian and Alaska Native, 2.7% Hispanic of any race, 1.9% two or more races (2000); Density: 180.2 persons per square mile (2000); Age: 21.0% under 18, 9.8% over 64 (2000).
Religion: Five largest groups: 10.8% Catholic Church, 4.8% The United Methodist Church, 4.4% Evangelical Lutheran Church in America, 2.2% Assemblies of God, 2.1% Christian Churches and Churches of Christ (2000).
Economy: Unemployment rate: 2.9% (11/2002); Total civilian labor force: 100,151 (11/2002); Leading industries: 15.3% retail trade; 14.4% manufacturing; 13.7% health care and social assistance (2000); Companies that employ more than 1,000 persons: 6 (2000); Companies that employ more than 100 persons: 117 (2000); Farms: 1,371 totaling 567,697 acres (1997); Minority business ownership rate: 10.0% (1997); Women business ownership rate: 25.2% (1997); Retail sales per capita: $9,131 (1997). Single-family building permits issued: 564 (2001) / 594 (2000); Multi-family building permits issued: 309 (2001) / 455 (2000).
Income: Per capita income: $19,708 (2000); Median household income: $37,780 (2000); Poverty rate: 16.1% (2000); Bankruptcy rate: 4.96% (2001).
Taxes: Total county taxes per capita: $95 (2000); County property taxes per capita: $83 (2000).
Education: High school graduation rate: 91.0% (2000); College graduation rate: 38.0% (2000).
Housing: Homeownership rate: 55.7% (2000); Median home value: $94,700 (2000); Median rent: $455 per month (2000); Median age of housing: 29 years (2000).
Health: Birth rate: 120.4 per 10,000 population (1998); Age adjusted death rate: 75.9 per 10,000 population (1999); Age adjusted cancer mortality rate: 187.1 deaths per 100,000 population (1999). Air Quality Index: 84% good, 16% moderate, 0% unhealthy (percent of days in 2000). Number of physicians: 29.6 per 10,000 population (1999); Number of hospital beds: 39.1 per 10,000 population (1999).
Elections: 2000 Presidential election results: 47.8% Gore, 46.6% Bush, 4.8% Nader, 0.3% Buchanan

Additional Information Contacts

Champaign County Government Offices 217-384-3772
Champaign Chamber of Commerce 217-359-1791
Champaign County Association of Realtors 217-356-1389
Champaign Urbana Convention & Visitors Bureau 217-351-4133
Rantoul Chamber of Commerce 217-893-3323

Champaign County Communities

BONDVILLE (village). Covers a land area of 0.254 square miles and a water area of 0 square miles. Located at 40.11° N. Lat.; 88.36° W. Long. Elevation is 719 feet.
Population: 455 (2000); Race: 96.4% White, 1.3% Black, 0.9% Asian, 0.0% American Indian and Alaska Native, 0.9% Hispanic of any race, 0.9% two or more races (2000); Density: 1,793.2 persons per square mile (2000); Age: 26.7% under 18, 10.5% over 64 (2000); Marriage status: 24.0% never married, 53.5% now married, 1.7% widowed, 20.8% divorced (2000); Foreign born: 0.9% (2000); Ancestry (includes multiple ancestries): 27.4% German, 19.2% Irish, 9.6% English, 6.0% Italian, 6.0% Other groups (2000).
Economy: Corn, soybeans. Single-family building permits issued: 2 (2001) / 2 (2000); Multi-family building permits issued: 0 (2001) / 0 (2000); Employment by occupation: 5.1% management, 13.6% professional, 18.7% services, 33.9% sales, 1.6% farming, 11.3% construction, 16.0% production (2000).

Income: Per capita income: $17,439 (2000); Median household income: $41,250 (2000); Poverty rate: 11.9% (2000).
Taxes: Total city taxes per capita: $24 (1997); City property taxes per capita: $12 (1997).
Education: High school graduation rate: 88.6% (2000); College graduation rate: 6.2% (2000).
Housing: Homeownership rate: 62.6% (2000); Median home value: $73,900 (2000); Median rent: $425 per month (2000); Median age of housing: 40 years (2000).
Transportation: Commute to work: 93.8% car, 0.0% public transportation, 0.0% walk, 6.2% work from home (2000); Travel time to work: 15.4% less than 15 minutes, 52.7% 15 to 30 minutes, 24.5% 30 to 45 minutes, 5.8% 45 to 60 minutes, 1.7% 60 minutes or more (2000)

BROADLANDS (village). Covers a land area of 0.271 square miles and a water area of 0 square miles. Located at 39.90° N. Lat.; 87.99° W. Long. Elevation is 688 feet.
Population: 312 (2000); Race: 95.2% White, 0.6% Black, 0.0% Asian, 0.9% American Indian and Alaska Native, 0.0% Hispanic of any race, 3.3% two or more races (2000); Density: 1,152.7 persons per square mile (2000); Age: 30.7% under 18, 10.8% over 64 (2000); Marriage status: 16.9% never married, 59.5% now married, 13.2% widowed, 10.3% divorced (2000); Foreign born: 0.6% (2000); Ancestry (includes multiple ancestries): 31.0% German, 22.3% Irish, 19.0% United States or American, 6.6% English, 3.0% French (except Basque) (2000).
Economy: In agricultural area. Single-family building permits issued: 1 (2001) / 0 (2000); Multi-family building permits issued: 0 (2001) / 0 (2000); Employment by occupation: 5.3% management, 14.0% professional, 17.3% services, 20.7% sales, 0.0% farming, 14.7% construction, 28.0% production (2000).
Income: Per capita income: $15,366 (2000); Median household income: $36,023 (2000); Poverty rate: 6.3% (2000).
Taxes: Total city taxes per capita: $34 (1997); City property taxes per capita: $31 (1997).
Education: High school graduation rate: 86.4% (2000); College graduation rate: 9.9% (2000).

School District(s)
Heritage Community Unit School District 8 (PK-12)
2000 Enrollment: 562 217-834-3393

Housing: Homeownership rate: 83.6% (2000); Median home value: $53,300 (2000); Median rent: $414 per month (2000); Median age of housing: 49 years (2000).
Transportation: Commute to work: 91.2% car, 0.0% public transportation, 0.0% walk, 8.8% work from home (2000); Travel time to work: 14.8% less than 15 minutes, 20.7% 15 to 30 minutes, 43.0% 30 to 45 minutes, 16.3% 45 to 60 minutes, 5.2% 60 minutes or more (2000)

CHAMPAIGN (city). Covers a land area of 16.987 square miles and a water area of 0.023 square miles. Located at 40.11° N. Lat.; 88.26° W. Long. Elevation is 750 feet.
History: Champaign came into existence as West Urbana in 1854, built around the railroad station when the Illinois Central Railroad chose a route several miles west of the town of Urbana. Resisting a move to be annexed to Urbana, residents of West Urbana incorporated under the name of Champaign in 1860. Rivalry between the two cities was laid aside when they jointly founded a seminary, later to become the University of Illinois, between them.
Population: 67,518 (2000); Race: 73.6% White, 15.5% Black, 6.8% Asian, 0.3% American Indian and Alaska Native, 4.3% Hispanic of any race, 1.9% two or more races (2000); Density: 3,974.6 persons per square mile (2000); Age: 17.9% under 18, 8.8% over 64 (2000); Marriage status: 50.5% never married, 38.4% now married, 3.9% widowed, 7.2% divorced (2000); Foreign born: 9.4% (2000); Ancestry (includes multiple ancestries): 26.1% Other groups, 24.2% German, 13.4% Irish, 10.5% English, 4.6% Polish (2000).
Vital Statistics: Birth rate: 125.3 per 10,000 population (1998)
Economy: Unemployment rate: 3.0% (11/2002); Total civilian labor force: 39,233 (11/2002); Single-family building permits issued: 135 (2001) / 204 (2000); Multi-family building permits issued: 209 (2001) / 171 (2000); Employment by occupation: 11.2% management, 33.9% professional, 16.3% services, 25.7% sales, 0.3% farming, 4.0% construction, 8.7% production (2000).
Income: Per capita income: $18,664 (2000); Median household income: $32,795 (2000); Poverty rate: 22.1% (2000).
Taxes: Total city taxes per capita: $409 (2000); City property taxes per capita: $165 (2000).
Education: High school graduation rate: 91.6% (2000); College graduation rate: 44.3% (2000).

School District(s)
Champaign Community Unit School District 4 (PK-12)
2000 Enrollment: 9,390 217-351-3838

Four-year College(s)
University of Illinois at Urbana-Champaign (Public)
2001 Enrollment: 39,291 217-333-1000
2001 Tuition: In-state $4,410; Out-of-state $12,230

Two-year College(s)
Parkland College (Public)
2001 Enrollment: 8,482 217-351-2200
2001 Tuition: In-state $5,850; Out-of-state $7,050

Housing: Homeownership rate: 47.4% (2000); Median home value: $91,300 (2000); Median rent: $467 per month (2000); Median age of housing: 31 years (2000).
Hospitals: Pavilion Foundation (46 beds)
Newspapers: The Octopus (1 x week); The News-Gazette (7 x week); The Daily Illini (5 x week)
Transportation: Commute to work: 75.3% car, 6.2% public transportation, 12.3% walk, 3.4% work from home (2000); Travel time to work: 57.1% less than 15 minutes, 34.0% 15 to 30 minutes, 5.1% 30 to 45 minutes, 1.7% 45 to 60 minutes, 2.1% 60 minutes or more (2000); Amtrak: Service available.
Airports: University of Illinois-Willard (primary service)
Additional Information Contacts
Champaign Chamber of Commerce 217-359-1791
Champaign Urbana Convention & Visitors Bureau 217-351-4133

DEWEY (unincorporated postal area, zip code 61840). Covers a land area of 33.901 square miles and a water area of 0.039 square miles. Located at 40.31° N. Lat.; 88.30° W. Long. Elevation is 732 feet.
Population: 709 (2000); Race: 97.6% White, 0.0% Black, 1.5% Asian, 0.0% American Indian and Alaska Native, 2.0% Hispanic of any race, 0.8% two or more races (2000); Density: 20.9 persons per square mile (2000); Age: 25.9% under 18, 15.1% over 64 (2000); Marriage status: 16.8% never married, 66.4% now married, 5.6% widowed, 11.2% divorced (2000); Foreign born: 2.1% (2000); Ancestry (includes multiple ancestries): 32.7% German, 14.9% English, 9.8% United States or American, 9.8% Irish, 9.4% Italian (2000).
Economy: Employment by occupation: 21.5% management, 19.6% professional, 12.4% services, 24.0% sales, 1.4% farming, 6.4% construction, 14.6% production (2000).
Income: Per capita income: $24,557 (2000); Median household income: $52,381 (2000); Poverty rate: 1.8% (2000).
Education: High school graduation rate: 96.3% (2000); College graduation rate: 27.7% (2000).
Housing: Homeownership rate: 92.7% (2000); Median home value: $113,900 (2000); Median rent: $400 per month (2000); Median age of housing: 28 years (2000).
Transportation: Commute to work: 93.6% car, 0.0% public transportation, 0.0% walk, 6.4% work from home (2000); Travel time to work: 22.7% less than 15 minutes, 52.2% 15 to 30 minutes, 17.4% 30 to 45 minutes, 3.2% 45 to 60 minutes, 4.4% 60 minutes or more (2000)

FISHER (village). Covers a land area of 0.992 square miles and a water area of 0 square miles. Located at 40.31° N. Lat.; 88.34° W. Long. Elevation is 717 feet.
Population: 1,647 (2000); Race: 98.0% White, 0.0% Black, 0.5% Asian, 0.5% American Indian and Alaska Native, 0.3% Hispanic of any race, 1.1% two or more races (2000); Density: 1,660.4 persons per square mile (2000); Age: 30.0% under 18, 12.5% over 64 (2000); Marriage status: 21.6% never married, 64.4% now married, 6.1% widowed, 8.0% divorced (2000); Foreign born: 1.7% (2000); Ancestry (includes multiple ancestries): 32.1% German, 17.7% English, 11.8% United States or American, 10.2% Irish, 7.0% Other groups (2000).
Economy: In agricultural area. Single-family building permits issued: 5 (2001) / 4 (2000); Multi-family building permits issued: 0 (2001) / 0 (2000); Employment by occupation: 12.0% management, 15.4% professional, 12.8% services, 26.8% sales, 0.2% farming, 11.2% construction, 21.5% production (2000).
Income: Per capita income: $18,262 (2000); Median household income: $41,891 (2000); Poverty rate: 3.6% (2000).
Taxes: Total city taxes per capita: $79 (1997); City property taxes per capita: $37 (1997).
Education: High school graduation rate: 87.7% (2000); College graduation rate: 14.9% (2000).

School District(s)
Fisher C U School District 1 (KG-12)
2000 Enrollment: 579 217-897-6125

Housing: Homeownership rate: 76.6% (2000); Median home value: $79,900 (2000); Median rent: $335 per month (2000); Median age of housing: 34 years (2000).
Newspapers: The Fisher Reporter (1 x week)
Transportation: Commute to work: 93.9% car, 0.0% public transportation, 2.3% walk, 2.9% work from home (2000); Travel time to work: 27.3% less than 15 minutes, 40.7% 15 to 30 minutes, 27.5% 30 to 45 minutes, 1.8% 45 to 60 minutes, 2.8% 60 minutes or more (2000)

FOOSLAND (village). Covers a land area of 0.072 square miles and a water area of 0 square miles. Located at 40.36° N. Lat.; 88.42° W. Long. Elevation is 740 feet.
Population: 90 (2000); Race: 100.0% White, 0.0% Black, 0.0% Asian, 0.0% American Indian and Alaska Native, 0.0% Hispanic of any race, 0.0% two or more races (2000); Density: 1,246.6 persons per square mile (2000); Age: 28.6% under 18, 15.5% over 64 (2000); Marriage status: 24.6% never married, 63.8% now married, 5.8% widowed, 5.8% divorced (2000); Foreign born: 0.0% (2000); Ancestry (includes multiple ancestries): 27.4% German, 22.6% Irish, 22.6% English, 4.8% French (except Basque), 3.6% Scottish (2000).
Economy: Employment by occupation: 7.0% management, 2.3% professional, 7.0% services, 18.6% sales, 4.7% farming, 2.3% construction, 58.1% production (2000).
Income: Per capita income: $20,173 (2000); Median household income: $36,250 (2000); Poverty rate: 15.5% (2000).
Taxes: Total city taxes per capita: $23 (1997); City property taxes per capita: $16 (1997).
Education: High school graduation rate: 72.2% (2000); College graduation rate: 5.6% (2000).
Housing: Homeownership rate: 80.6% (2000); Median home value: $52,500 (2000); Median rent: $292 per month (2000); Median age of housing: 53 years (2000).
Transportation: Commute to work: 88.4% car, 0.0% public transportation, 11.6% walk, 0.0% work from home (2000); Travel time to work: 23.3% less than 15 minutes, 34.9% 15 to 30 minutes, 27.9% 30 to 45 minutes, 0.0% 45 to 60 minutes, 14.0% 60 minutes or more (2000)

GIFFORD (village). Covers a land area of 0.633 square miles and a water area of 0 square miles. Located at 40.30° N. Lat.; 88.02° W. Long. Elevation is 801 feet.
Population: 815 (2000); Race: 97.5% White, 0.9% Black, 0.7% Asian, 0.5% American Indian and Alaska Native, 0.0% Hispanic of any race, 0.4% two or more races (2000); Density: 1,288.2 persons per square mile (2000); Age: 23.0% under 18, 23.3% over 64 (2000); Marriage status: 17.8% never married, 60.1% now married, 15.8% widowed, 6.3% divorced (2000); Foreign born: 1.8% (2000); Ancestry (includes multiple ancestries): 38.0% German, 12.1% Irish, 10.3% English, 6.8% Other groups, 4.8% United States or American (2000).
Economy: Corn, soybeans. Single-family building permits issued: 18 (2001) / 18 (2000); Multi-family building permits issued: 0 (2001) / 0 (2000); Employment by occupation: 13.4% management, 11.7% professional, 9.9% services, 30.5% sales, 0.0% farming, 10.4% construction, 24.1% production (2000).
Income: Per capita income: $22,040 (2000); Median household income: $46,667 (2000); Poverty rate: 1.8% (2000).
Taxes: Total city taxes per capita: $60 (1997); City property taxes per capita: $53 (1997).
Education: High school graduation rate: 79.6% (2000); College graduation rate: 15.7% (2000).

School District(s)

Gifford C C School District 188 (KG-08)
2000 Enrollment: 203 217-568-7733

Housing: Homeownership rate: 87.5% (2000); Median home value: $83,600 (2000); Median rent: $300 per month (2000); Median age of housing: 37 years (2000).
Transportation: Commute to work: 93.7% car, 0.0% public transportation, 4.0% walk, 0.5% work from home (2000); Travel time to work: 33.0% less than 15 minutes, 26.4% 15 to 30 minutes, 26.7% 30 to 45 minutes, 8.8% 45 to 60 minutes, 5.0% 60 minutes or more (2000)

HOMER (village). Covers a land area of 1.026 square miles and a water area of 0 square miles. Located at 40.03° N. Lat.; 87.95° W. Long. Elevation is 672 feet.
History: Village formerly on Salt Creek to North but moved in 19th century to be on railroad.
Population: 1,200 (2000); Race: 99.2% White, 0.0% Black, 0.0% Asian, 0.0% American Indian and Alaska Native, 0.8% Hispanic of any race, 0.6% two or more races (2000); Density: 1,169.3 persons per square mile (2000); Age: 27.5% under 18, 15.7% over 64 (2000); Marriage status: 17.4% never married, 61.6% now married, 8.4% widowed, 12.6% divorced (2000); Foreign born: 0.3% (2000); Ancestry (includes multiple ancestries): 24.2% German, 15.7% English, 15.3% Irish, 14.7% United States or American, 4.9% Other groups (2000).
Economy: In agricultural area; corn, wheat, soybeans, livestock. Single-family building permits issued: 2 (2001) / 2 (2000); Multi-family building permits issued: 0 (2001) / 0 (2000); Employment by occupation: 7.9% management, 15.8% professional, 15.6% services, 27.4% sales, 0.4% farming, 11.1% construction, 21.9% production (2000).
Income: Per capita income: $18,788 (2000); Median household income: $37,429 (2000); Poverty rate: 9.1% (2000).
Taxes: Total city taxes per capita: $91 (1997); City property taxes per capita: $87 (1997).
Education: High school graduation rate: 87.7% (2000); College graduation rate: 11.9% (2000).
Housing: Homeownership rate: 83.9% (2000); Median home value: $63,700 (2000); Median rent: $328 per month (2000); Median age of housing: 48 years (2000).
Transportation: Commute to work: 92.3% car, 0.0% public transportation, 2.9% walk, 3.8% work from home (2000); Travel time to work: 24.2% less than 15 minutes, 30.3% 15 to 30 minutes, 39.4% 30 to 45 minutes, 4.4% 45 to 60 minutes, 1.7% 60 minutes or more (2000)

IVESDALE (village). Covers a land area of 0.749 square miles and a water area of 0 square miles. Located at 39.94° N. Lat.; 88.45° W. Long. Elevation is 688 feet.
Population: 288 (2000); Race: 100.0% White, 0.0% Black, 0.0% Asian, 0.0% American Indian and Alaska Native, 0.0% Hispanic of any race, 0.0% two or more races (2000); Density: 384.4 persons per square mile (2000); Age: 17.9% under 18, 12.6% over 64 (2000); Marriage status: 24.1% never married, 57.7% now married, 5.8% widowed, 12.4% divorced (2000); Foreign born: 1.3% (2000); Ancestry (includes multiple ancestries): 39.6% Irish, 24.8% German, 16.0% United States or American, 9.4% Other groups, 9.1% French (except Basque) (2000).
Economy: In agricultural area: corn, soybeans. Single-family building permits issued: 0 (2001) / 1 (2000); Multi-family building permits issued: 0 (2001) / 0 (2000); Employment by occupation: 9.6% management, 10.2% professional, 11.8% services, 30.5% sales, 0.0% farming, 19.3% construction, 18.7% production (2000).
Income: Per capita income: $18,829 (2000); Median household income: $45,938 (2000); Poverty rate: 3.5% (2000).
Taxes: Total city taxes per capita: $50 (1997); City property taxes per capita: $47 (1997).
Education: High school graduation rate: 89.1% (2000); College graduation rate: 10.9% (2000).
Housing: Homeownership rate: 94.4% (2000); Median home value: $61,900 (2000); Median rent: $335 per month (2000); Median age of housing: 60+ years (2000).
Transportation: Commute to work: 96.1% car, 0.0% public transportation, 0.0% walk, 2.2% work from home (2000); Travel time to work: 25.7% less than 15 minutes, 15.4% 15 to 30 minutes, 49.1% 30 to 45 minutes, 4.0% 45 to 60 minutes, 5.7% 60 minutes or more (2000)

LAKE OF THE WOODS (CDP). Covers a land area of 2.101 square miles and a water area of 0.014 square miles. Located at 40.20° N. Lat.; 88.36° W. Long.
History: Covered bridge.
Population: 3,026 (2000); Race: 97.3% White, 1.5% Black, 0.2% Asian, 0.0% American Indian and Alaska Native, 1.7% Hispanic of any race, 0.8% two or more races (2000); Density: 1,440.0 persons per square mile (2000); Age: 28.5% under 18, 8.5% over 64 (2000); Marriage status: 19.6% never married, 62.6% now married, 4.3% widowed, 13.4% divorced (2000); Foreign born: 0.3% (2000); Ancestry (includes multiple ancestries): 25.8% German, 15.1% United States or American, 14.4% Irish, 14.0% English, 8.6% Other groups (2000).
Economy: Employment by occupation: 10.4% management, 15.5% professional, 19.6% services, 24.4% sales, 1.2% farming, 11.3% construction, 17.6% production (2000).
Income: Per capita income: $19,938 (2000); Median household income: $42,571 (2000); Poverty rate: 8.7% (2000).
Education: High school graduation rate: 92.4% (2000); College graduation rate: 24.9% (2000).

Housing: Homeownership rate: 83.3% (2000); Median home value: $105,700 (2000); Median rent: $486 per month (2000); Median age of housing: 17 years (2000).
Transportation: Commute to work: 97.2% car, 0.0% public transportation, 0.3% walk, 1.6% work from home (2000); Travel time to work: 27.5% less than 15 minutes, 58.1% 15 to 30 minutes, 9.1% 30 to 45 minutes, 1.9% 45 to 60 minutes, 3.4% 60 minutes or more (2000)

LONGVIEW (village). Aka Long View. Covers a land area of 0.251 square miles and a water area of 0 square miles. Located at 39.88° N. Lat.; 88.06° W. Long. Elevation is 684 feet.
Population: 153 (2000); Race: 100.0% White, 0.0% Black, 0.0% Asian, 0.0% American Indian and Alaska Native, 0.0% Hispanic of any race, 0.0% two or more races (2000); Density: 610.6 persons per square mile (2000); Age: 30.9% under 18, 13.3% over 64 (2000); Marriage status: 31.4% never married, 47.1% now married, 8.3% widowed, 13.2% divorced (2000); Foreign born: 0.0% (2000); Ancestry (includes multiple ancestries): 20.0% German, 15.8% United States or American, 13.3% Other groups, 9.7% Italian, 5.5% English (2000).
Economy: In agricultural area. Employment by occupation: 4.5% management, 4.5% professional, 17.9% services, 31.3% sales, 0.0% farming, 25.4% construction, 16.4% production (2000).
Income: Per capita income: $12,116 (2000); Median household income: $31,875 (2000); Poverty rate: 15.2% (2000).
Taxes: Total city taxes per capita: $46 (1997); City property taxes per capita: $46 (1997).
Education: High school graduation rate: 69.9% (2000); College graduation rate: 0.0% (2000).
Housing: Homeownership rate: 82.8% (2000); Median home value: $37,500 (2000); Median rent: $500 per month (2000); Median age of housing: 60+ years (2000).
Transportation: Commute to work: 100.0% car, 0.0% public transportation, 0.0% walk, 0.0% work from home (2000); Travel time to work: 7.5% less than 15 minutes, 20.9% 15 to 30 minutes, 43.3% 30 to 45 minutes, 23.9% 45 to 60 minutes, 4.5% 60 minutes or more (2000)

LUDLOW (village). Covers a land area of 0.348 square miles and a water area of 0 square miles. Located at 40.38° N. Lat.; 88.12° W. Long. Elevation is 769 feet.
Population: 324 (2000); Race: 93.9% White, 0.0% Black, 3.7% Asian, 0.0% American Indian and Alaska Native, 0.0% Hispanic of any race, 2.4% two or more races (2000); Density: 932.2 persons per square mile (2000); Age: 22.9% under 18, 12.8% over 64 (2000); Marriage status: 22.1% never married, 51.2% now married, 10.0% widowed, 16.7% divorced (2000); Foreign born: 1.7% (2000); Ancestry (includes multiple ancestries): 29.6% German, 15.8% Irish, 14.5% Other groups, 8.8% English, 5.7% United States or American (2000).
Economy: In agricultural area. Single-family building permits issued: 2 (2001) / 0 (2000); Multi-family building permits issued: 0 (2001) / 0 (2000); Employment by occupation: 1.2% management, 6.7% professional, 11.0% services, 25.2% sales, 0.0% farming, 14.7% construction, 41.1% production (2000).
Income: Per capita income: $19,507 (2000); Median household income: $35,000 (2000); Poverty rate: 15.0% (2000).
Taxes: Total city taxes per capita: $20 (1997); City property taxes per capita: $20 (1997).
Education: High school graduation rate: 84.8% (2000); College graduation rate: 3.3% (2000).

School District(s)

Ludlow C C School District 142 (KG-08)
2000 Enrollment: 153 217-396-5261

Housing: Homeownership rate: 58.3% (2000); Median home value: $51,700 (2000); Median rent: $262 per month (2000); Median age of housing: 41 years (2000).
Transportation: Commute to work: 94.5% car, 1.2% public transportation, 2.5% walk, 0.0% work from home (2000); Travel time to work: 31.9% less than 15 minutes, 30.1% 15 to 30 minutes, 35.0% 30 to 45 minutes, 0.6% 45 to 60 minutes, 2.5% 60 minutes or more (2000)

MAHOMET (village). Covers a land area of 6.854 square miles and a water area of 0 square miles. Located at 40.19° N. Lat.; 88.40° W. Long. Elevation is 714 feet.
Population: 4,877 (2000); Race: 99.0% White, 0.0% Black, 0.3% Asian, 0.0% American Indian and Alaska Native, 0.7% Hispanic of any race, 0.5% two or more races (2000); Density: 711.6 persons per square mile (2000); Age: 35.2% under 18, 7.6% over 64 (2000); Marriage status: 19.1% never married, 70.5% now married, 3.9% widowed, 6.5% divorced (2000); Foreign born: 0.4% (2000); Ancestry (includes multiple ancestries): 32.3% German, 19.0% English, 11.1% Irish, 7.4% United States or American, 4.2% Other groups (2000).
Economy: In agricultural area. Single-family building permits issued: 73 (2001) / 49 (2000); Multi-family building permits issued: 8 (2001) / 0 (2000); Employment by occupation: 15.5% management, 30.6% professional, 11.7% services, 29.0% sales, 0.0% farming, 7.7% construction, 5.4% production (2000).
Income: Per capita income: $21,990 (2000); Median household income: $57,574 (2000); Poverty rate: 5.1% (2000).
Taxes: Total city taxes per capita: $284 (1997); City property taxes per capita: $112 (1997).
Education: High school graduation rate: 96.5% (2000); College graduation rate: 37.3% (2000).

School District(s)

Mahomet-Seymour C U School District 3 (PK-12)
2000 Enrollment: 2,648 217-586-4995

Housing: Homeownership rate: 81.7% (2000); Median home value: $113,600 (2000); Median rent: $525 per month (2000); Median age of housing: 19 years (2000).
Newspapers: The Mahomet Citizen (1 x week)
Transportation: Commute to work: 92.6% car, 0.5% public transportation, 0.4% walk, 5.4% work from home (2000); Travel time to work: 23.0% less than 15 minutes, 59.3% 15 to 30 minutes, 9.0% 30 to 45 minutes, 3.4% 45 to 60 minutes, 5.3% 60 minutes or more (2000)

OGDEN (village). Covers a land area of 0.567 square miles and a water area of 0 square miles. Located at 40.11° N. Lat.; 87.95° W. Long. Elevation is 670 feet.
Population: 743 (2000); Race: 96.9% White, 0.0% Black, 0.0% Asian, 0.0% American Indian and Alaska Native, 2.0% Hispanic of any race, 2.0% two or more races (2000); Density: 1,311.2 persons per square mile (2000); Age: 33.1% under 18, 11.2% over 64 (2000); Marriage status: 21.3% never married, 59.0% now married, 10.6% widowed, 9.1% divorced (2000); Foreign born: 2.0% (2000); Ancestry (includes multiple ancestries): 37.8% German, 19.3% Irish, 11.8% English, 10.0% Other groups, 6.9% United States or American (2000).
Economy: In agricultural area. Single-family building permits issued: 3 (2001) / 0 (2000); Multi-family building permits issued: 0 (2001) / 3 (2000); Employment by occupation: 7.9% management, 11.8% professional, 18.4% services, 34.7% sales, 0.8% farming, 9.5% construction, 16.8% production (2000).
Income: Per capita income: $19,679 (2000); Median household income: $45,083 (2000); Poverty rate: 3.0% (2000).
Taxes: Total city taxes per capita: $70 (1997); City property taxes per capita: $68 (1997).
Education: High school graduation rate: 90.8% (2000); College graduation rate: 15.1% (2000).

School District(s)

Ogden Community Cons School District 212 (KG-08)
2000 Enrollment: 173 217-582-2725

Housing: Homeownership rate: 88.5% (2000); Median home value: $81,000 (2000); Median rent: $450 per month (2000); Median age of housing: 29 years (2000).
Newspapers: Ogden Leader (1 x week)
Transportation: Commute to work: 93.6% car, 0.0% public transportation, 1.3% walk, 4.3% work from home (2000); Travel time to work: 14.8% less than 15 minutes, 61.6% 15 to 30 minutes, 18.9% 30 to 45 minutes, 3.9% 45 to 60 minutes, 0.8% 60 minutes or more (2000)

PENFIELD (unincorporated postal area, zip code 61862). Covers a land area of 36.908 square miles and a water area of 0 square miles. Located at 40.29° N. Lat.; 87.95° W. Long. Elevation is 710 feet.
Population: 511 (2000); Race: 96.5% White, 0.7% Black, 0.0% Asian, 1.3% American Indian and Alaska Native, 0.9% Hispanic of any race, 1.3% two or more races (2000); Density: 13.8 persons per square mile (2000); Age: 33.2% under 18, 10.4% over 64 (2000); Marriage status: 16.8% never married, 74.6% now married, 2.3% widowed, 6.4% divorced (2000); Foreign born: 0.4% (2000); Ancestry (includes multiple ancestries): 49.8% German, 21.4% Irish, 9.7% English, 7.5% Other groups, 5.5% Swedish (2000).
Economy: Employment by occupation: 10.5% management, 13.9% professional, 22.4% services, 18.4% sales, 1.7% farming, 10.9% construction, 22.1% production (2000).
Income: Per capita income: $18,170 (2000); Median household income: $47,000 (2000); Poverty rate: 3.9% (2000).

Education: High school graduation rate: 92.5% (2000); College graduation rate: 14.6% (2000).
Housing: Homeownership rate: 79.6% (2000); Median home value: $75,600 (2000); Median rent: $278 per month (2000); Median age of housing: 56 years (2000).
Transportation: Commute to work: 86.7% car, 0.7% public transportation, 1.7% walk, 10.9% work from home (2000); Travel time to work: 18.3% less than 15 minutes, 23.3% 15 to 30 minutes, 43.9% 30 to 45 minutes, 10.3% 45 to 60 minutes, 4.2% 60 minutes or more (2000)

PESOTUM (village). Covers a land area of 0.555 square miles and a water area of 0.005 square miles. Located at 39.91° N. Lat.; 88.27° W. Long. Elevation is 720 feet.
History: Pesotum developed as a grain storage and shipping center.
Population: 521 (2000); Race: 99.6% White, 0.0% Black, 0.4% Asian, 0.0% American Indian and Alaska Native, 0.0% Hispanic of any race, 0.0% two or more races (2000); Density: 938.0 persons per square mile (2000); Age: 24.7% under 18, 13.1% over 64 (2000); Marriage status: 19.3% never married, 64.9% now married, 9.5% widowed, 6.3% divorced (2000); Foreign born: 0.4% (2000); Ancestry (includes multiple ancestries): 45.4% German, 19.5% Irish, 18.9% English, 11.2% Other groups, 10.0% United States or American (2000).
Economy: Single-family building permits issued: 1 (2001) / 1 (2000); Multi-family building permits issued: 0 (2001) / 0 (2000); Employment by occupation: 5.5% management, 21.5% professional, 16.1% services, 29.2% sales, 0.0% farming, 13.5% construction, 14.2% production (2000).
Income: Per capita income: $21,191 (2000); Median household income: $49,107 (2000); Poverty rate: 2.8% (2000).
Taxes: Total city taxes per capita: $106 (1997); City property taxes per capita: $35 (1997).
Education: High school graduation rate: 96.0% (2000); College graduation rate: 14.2% (2000).
Housing: Homeownership rate: 90.0% (2000); Median home value: $70,000 (2000); Median rent: $323 per month (2000); Median age of housing: 51 years (2000).
Transportation: Commute to work: 97.4% car, 0.0% public transportation, 2.2% walk, 0.0% work from home (2000); Travel time to work: 15.4% less than 15 minutes, 55.5% 15 to 30 minutes, 25.0% 30 to 45 minutes, 2.2% 45 to 60 minutes, 1.8% 60 minutes or more (2000)

PHILO (village). Covers a land area of 0.762 square miles and a water area of 0 square miles. Located at 40.00° N. Lat.; 88.15° W. Long. Elevation is 737 feet.
Population: 1,314 (2000); Race: 99.5% White, 0.0% Black, 0.2% Asian, 0.0% American Indian and Alaska Native, 0.2% Hispanic of any race, 0.4% two or more races (2000); Density: 1,723.4 persons per square mile (2000); Age: 30.9% under 18, 11.4% over 64 (2000); Marriage status: 21.7% never married, 68.3% now married, 4.7% widowed, 5.2% divorced (2000); Foreign born: 0.5% (2000); Ancestry (includes multiple ancestries): 34.0% German, 24.5% Irish, 14.6% United States or American, 7.9% English, 4.0% Other groups (2000).
Economy: Corn, soybeans; precision sheet metal fabricating. Single-family building permits issued: 20 (2001) / 20 (2000); Multi-family building permits issued: 0 (2001) / 0 (2000); Employment by occupation: 16.1% management, 18.2% professional, 14.1% services, 30.8% sales, 0.0% farming, 12.5% construction, 8.4% production (2000).
Income: Per capita income: $21,502 (2000); Median household income: $56,852 (2000); Poverty rate: 3.4% (2000).
Taxes: Total city taxes per capita: $58 (1997); City property taxes per capita: $56 (1997).
Education: High school graduation rate: 91.7% (2000); College graduation rate: 23.2% (2000).
Housing: Homeownership rate: 93.6% (2000); Median home value: $94,800 (2000); Median rent: $425 per month (2000); Median age of housing: 32 years (2000).
Transportation: Commute to work: 96.8% car, 0.6% public transportation, 0.9% walk, 1.2% work from home (2000); Travel time to work: 19.7% less than 15 minutes, 61.7% 15 to 30 minutes, 11.6% 30 to 45 minutes, 2.1% 45 to 60 minutes, 4.9% 60 minutes or more (2000)

RANTOUL (village). Covers a land area of 7.237 square miles and a water area of 0.113 square miles. Located at 40.30° N. Lat.; 88.15° W. Long. Elevation is 748 feet.
History: Rantoul was named for Robert Rantoul who was a director of the Illinois Central Railroad.
Population: 12,857 (2000); Race: 76.3% White, 17.3% Black, 1.8% Asian, 0.2% American Indian and Alaska Native, 1.5% Hispanic of any race, 3.7% two or more races (2000); Density: 1,776.5 persons per square mile (2000); Age: 28.6% under 18, 11.7% over 64 (2000); Marriage status: 24.9% never married, 53.0% now married, 6.0% widowed, 16.1% divorced (2000); Foreign born: 3.4% (2000); Ancestry (includes multiple ancestries): 23.5% Other groups, 22.2% German, 11.4% Irish, 9.5% United States or American, 7.3% English (2000).
Vital Statistics: Birth rate: 195.2 per 10,000 population (1998)
Economy: Single-family building permits issued: 2 (2001) / 18 (2000); Multi-family building permits issued: 0 (2001) / 48 (2000); Employment by occupation: 9.9% management, 13.3% professional, 14.7% services, 27.7% sales, 0.4% farming, 7.6% construction, 26.5% production (2000).
Income: Per capita income: $17,948 (2000); Median household income: $36,904 (2000); Poverty rate: 10.7% (2000).
Taxes: Total city taxes per capita: $239 (2000); City property taxes per capita: $137 (2000).
Education: High school graduation rate: 88.5% (2000); College graduation rate: 15.9% (2000).

School District(s)

Champaign/Ford Roe (06-12)
2000 Enrollment: 71 217-893-3219
Rantoul City School District 137 (KG-08)
2000 Enrollment: 1,671 217-893-4171
Rantoul Township H S District 193 (09-12)
2000 Enrollment: 812 217-892-2151

Housing: Homeownership rate: 50.7% (2000); Median home value: $74,200 (2000); Median rent: $397 per month (2000); Median age of housing: 38 years (2000).
Newspapers: Rantoul Press (1 x week)
Transportation: Commute to work: 93.6% car, 0.9% public transportation, 1.7% walk, 2.0% work from home (2000); Travel time to work: 51.0% less than 15 minutes, 30.9% 15 to 30 minutes, 13.0% 30 to 45 minutes, 2.0% 45 to 60 minutes, 3.1% 60 minutes or more (2000); Amtrak: Service available.
Airports: Rantoul National Aviation Center-Frank E

Additional Information Contacts
Rantoul Chamber of Commerce. 217-893-3323

ROYAL (village). Covers a land area of 0.225 square miles and a water area of 0 square miles. Located at 40.19° N. Lat.; 87.97° W. Long. Elevation is 680 feet.
Population: 279 (2000); Race: 100.0% White, 0.0% Black, 0.0% Asian, 0.0% American Indian and Alaska Native, 0.0% Hispanic of any race, 0.0% two or more races (2000); Density: 1,239.9 persons per square mile (2000); Age: 25.3% under 18, 16.3% over 64 (2000); Marriage status: 18.1% never married, 67.3% now married, 9.3% widowed, 5.2% divorced (2000); Foreign born: 0.0% (2000); Ancestry (includes multiple ancestries): 62.8% German, 14.1% Irish, 8.8% English, 5.0% Other groups, 4.4% Italian (2000).
Economy: Single-family building permits issued: 1 (2001) / 2 (2000); Multi-family building permits issued: 0 (2001) / 0 (2000); Employment by occupation: 15.7% management, 19.7% professional, 6.2% services, 28.7% sales, 0.0% farming, 13.5% construction, 16.3% production (2000).
Income: Per capita income: $22,019 (2000); Median household income: $47,188 (2000); Poverty rate: 0.6% (2000).
Taxes: Total city taxes per capita: $37 (1997); City property taxes per capita: $32 (1997).
Education: High school graduation rate: 85.6% (2000); College graduation rate: 18.1% (2000).

School District(s)

Prairieview Community Cons District 192 (KG-08)
2000 Enrollment: 142 217-583-3300

Housing: Homeownership rate: 85.2% (2000); Median home value: $84,500 (2000); Median rent: $331 per month (2000); Median age of housing: 39 years (2000).
Transportation: Commute to work: 89.3% car, 0.0% public transportation, 2.8% walk, 7.3% work from home (2000); Travel time to work: 23.0% less than 15 minutes, 46.1% 15 to 30 minutes, 20.0% 30 to 45 minutes, 9.1% 45 to 60 minutes, 1.8% 60 minutes or more (2000)

SADORUS (village). Covers a land area of 0.846 square miles and a water area of 0 square miles. Located at 39.96° N. Lat.; 88.34° W. Long. Elevation is 690 feet.
Population: 426 (2000); Race: 95.0% White, 0.0% Black, 0.0% Asian, 0.0% American Indian and Alaska Native, 0.0% Hispanic of any race, 5.0% two or more races (2000); Density: 503.8 persons per square mile (2000); Age: 23.1% under 18, 9.8% over 64 (2000); Marriage status: 21.5% never married,

63.2% now married, 5.3% widowed, 10.0% divorced (2000); Foreign born: 2.3% (2000); Ancestry (includes multiple ancestries): 34.2% German, 14.6% Irish, 13.1% United States or American, 10.8% English, 3.5% Other groups (2000).
Economy: In agricultural area. Single-family building permits issued: 0 (2001) / 0 (2000); Multi-family building permits issued: 0 (2001) / 0 (2000); Employment by occupation: 12.2% management, 8.7% professional, 16.1% services, 27.0% sales, 0.0% farming, 16.5% construction, 19.6% production (2000).
Income: Per capita income: $18,540 (2000); Median household income: $44,375 (2000); Poverty rate: 3.6% (2000).
Taxes: Total city taxes per capita: $94 (1997); City property taxes per capita: $42 (1997).
Education: High school graduation rate: 81.3% (2000); College graduation rate: 11.0% (2000).
Housing: Homeownership rate: 82.9% (2000); Median home value: $63,300 (2000); Median rent: $375 per month (2000); Median age of housing: 48 years (2000).
Transportation: Commute to work: 93.3% car, 0.0% public transportation, 2.2% walk, 3.6% work from home (2000); Travel time to work: 14.7% less than 15 minutes, 49.8% 15 to 30 minutes, 30.0% 30 to 45 minutes, 2.8% 45 to 60 minutes, 2.8% 60 minutes or more (2000)

SAINT JOSEPH (village). Covers a land area of 1.132 square miles and a water area of 0.004 square miles. Located at 40.11° N. Lat.; 88.03° W. Long. Elevation is 670 feet.
Population: 2,912 (2000); Race: 98.5% White, 0.2% Black, 0.5% Asian, 0.1% American Indian and Alaska Native, 1.4% Hispanic of any race, 0.4% two or more races (2000); Density: 2,572.3 persons per square mile (2000); Age: 28.6% under 18, 10.7% over 64 (2000); Marriage status: 16.9% never married, 69.2% now married, 7.1% widowed, 6.8% divorced (2000); Foreign born: 1.7% (2000); Ancestry (includes multiple ancestries): 36.9% German, 15.8% English, 13.3% Irish, 7.6% United States or American, 5.2% Other groups (2000).
Economy: Single-family building permits issued: 32 (2001) / 32 (2000); Multi-family building permits issued: 0 (2001) / 0 (2000); Employment by occupation: 14.6% management, 19.6% professional, 14.1% services, 29.9% sales, 0.8% farming, 11.0% construction, 9.9% production (2000).
Income: Per capita income: $21,381 (2000); Median household income: $53,424 (2000); Poverty rate: 4.3% (2000).
Education: High school graduation rate: 92.2% (2000); College graduation rate: 26.6% (2000).

School District(s)

Saint Joseph C C School District 169 (KG-08)
2000 Enrollment: 691 217-469-2291
Saint Joseph Ogden C H S District 305 (09-12)
2000 Enrollment: 469 217-469-2586

Housing: Homeownership rate: 81.7% (2000); Median home value: $103,000 (2000); Median rent: $367 per month (2000); Median age of housing: 24 years (2000).
Transportation: Commute to work: 94.5% car, 0.4% public transportation, 1.1% walk, 3.3% work from home (2000); Travel time to work: 23.7% less than 15 minutes, 58.9% 15 to 30 minutes, 12.8% 30 to 45 minutes, 0.3% 45 to 60 minutes, 4.3% 60 minutes or more (2000)

SAVOY (village). Covers a land area of 1.543 square miles and a water area of 0.016 square miles. Located at 40.06° N. Lat.; 88.25° W. Long. Elevation is 738 feet.
Population: 4,476 (2000); Race: 83.5% White, 4.8% Black, 10.6% Asian, 0.0% American Indian and Alaska Native, 1.8% Hispanic of any race, 0.8% two or more races (2000); Density: 2,899.9 persons per square mile (2000); Age: 21.8% under 18, 14.1% over 64 (2000); Marriage status: 24.5% never married, 60.0% now married, 8.2% widowed, 7.3% divorced (2000); Foreign born: 11.5% (2000); Ancestry (includes multiple ancestries): 25.6% German, 15.5% English, 15.1% Other groups, 10.9% Irish, 10.5% United States or American (2000).
Economy: Single-family building permits issued: 30 (2001) / 30 (2000); Multi-family building permits issued: 23 (2001) / 24 (2000); Employment by occupation: 16.1% management, 41.5% professional, 11.2% services, 21.1% sales, 0.2% farming, 5.0% construction, 5.0% production (2000).
Income: Per capita income: $25,949 (2000); Median household income: $48,500 (2000); Poverty rate: 9.1% (2000).
Taxes: Total city taxes per capita: $109 (1997); City property taxes per capita: $106 (1997).
Education: High school graduation rate: 96.3% (2000); College graduation rate: 58.8% (2000).
Housing: Homeownership rate: 43.9% (2000); Median home value: $147,100 (2000); Median rent: $588 per month (2000); Median age of housing: 13 years (2000).
Transportation: Commute to work: 89.2% car, 5.4% public transportation, 0.3% walk, 4.0% work from home (2000); Travel time to work: 44.0% less than 15 minutes, 45.9% 15 to 30 minutes, 4.9% 30 to 45 minutes, 1.9% 45 to 60 minutes, 3.3% 60 minutes or more (2000)

Additional Information Contacts

Champaign County Association of Realtors 217-356-1389

SEYMOUR (unincorporated postal area, zip code 61875). Covers a land area of 30.015 square miles and a water area of 0 square miles. Located at 40.10° N. Lat.; 88.42° W. Long. Elevation is 706 feet.
Population: 795 (2000); Race: 100.0% White, 0.0% Black, 0.0% Asian, 0.0% American Indian and Alaska Native, 0.0% Hispanic of any race, 0.0% two or more races (2000); Density: 26.5 persons per square mile (2000); Age: 30.3% under 18, 6.7% over 64 (2000); Marriage status: 24.0% never married, 68.7% now married, 1.5% widowed, 5.8% divorced (2000); Foreign born: 1.1% (2000); Ancestry (includes multiple ancestries): 31.6% German, 31.2% Irish, 14.1% English, 6.6% Scottish, 5.2% United States or American (2000).
Economy: Employment by occupation: 20.8% management, 13.7% professional, 16.5% services, 20.6% sales, 0.0% farming, 7.3% construction, 21.1% production (2000).
Income: Per capita income: $29,477 (2000); Median household income: $68,750 (2000); Poverty rate: 1.2% (2000).
Education: High school graduation rate: 98.9% (2000); College graduation rate: 30.0% (2000).
Housing: Homeownership rate: 81.7% (2000); Median home value: $118,800 (2000); Median rent: $298 per month (2000); Median age of housing: 39 years (2000).
Transportation: Commute to work: 88.1% car, 3.8% public transportation, 3.1% walk, 5.0% work from home (2000); Travel time to work: 17.8% less than 15 minutes, 50.6% 15 to 30 minutes, 17.8% 30 to 45 minutes, 8.8% 45 to 60 minutes, 5.0% 60 minutes or more (2000)

SIDNEY (village). Covers a land area of 0.532 square miles and a water area of 0 square miles. Located at 40.02° N. Lat.; 88.07° W. Long. Elevation is 672 feet.
Population: 1,062 (2000); Race: 97.7% White, 0.0% Black, 0.0% Asian, 0.0% American Indian and Alaska Native, 0.9% Hispanic of any race, 1.6% two or more races (2000); Density: 1,995.7 persons per square mile (2000); Age: 27.2% under 18, 14.7% over 64 (2000); Marriage status: 18.6% never married, 64.2% now married, 8.0% widowed, 9.1% divorced (2000); Foreign born: 0.0% (2000); Ancestry (includes multiple ancestries): 34.5% German, 15.8% United States or American, 12.2% Irish, 11.8% English, 4.7% Other groups (2000).
Economy: Agriculture includes corn, soybeans, alfalfa. Single-family building permits issued: 5 (2001) / 0 (2000); Multi-family building permits issued: 0 (2001) / 8 (2000); Employment by occupation: 11.2% management, 19.2% professional, 13.7% services, 31.1% sales, 0.0% farming, 11.6% construction, 13.2% production (2000).
Income: Per capita income: $21,425 (2000); Median household income: $51,563 (2000); Poverty rate: 0.9% (2000).
Taxes: Total city taxes per capita: $52 (1997); City property taxes per capita: $46 (1997).
Education: High school graduation rate: 87.2% (2000); College graduation rate: 19.9% (2000).
Housing: Homeownership rate: 82.6% (2000); Median home value: $87,000 (2000); Median rent: $421 per month (2000); Median age of housing: 34 years (2000).
Transportation: Commute to work: 93.3% car, 0.0% public transportation, 0.7% walk, 5.0% work from home (2000); Travel time to work: 9.6% less than 15 minutes, 60.5% 15 to 30 minutes, 22.6% 30 to 45 minutes, 3.3% 45 to 60 minutes, 3.9% 60 minutes or more (2000)

THOMASBORO (village). Covers a land area of 1.035 square miles and a water area of 0 square miles. Located at 40.24° N. Lat.; 88.18° W. Long. Elevation is 732 feet.
Population: 1,233 (2000); Race: 95.2% White, 1.7% Black, 0.8% Asian, 0.0% American Indian and Alaska Native, 1.5% Hispanic of any race, 1.4% two or more races (2000); Density: 1,191.1 persons per square mile (2000); Age: 25.6% under 18, 14.1% over 64 (2000); Marriage status: 18.5% never married, 60.2% now married, 7.1% widowed, 14.2% divorced (2000); Foreign born: 2.6% (2000); Ancestry (includes multiple ancestries): 30.8% German, 10.7% English, 10.2% Irish, 9.8% United States or American, 8.2% Other groups (2000).

Economy: In agricultural area. Single-family building permits issued: 5 (2001) / 5 (2000); Multi-family building permits issued: 0 (2001) / 0 (2000); Employment by occupation: 9.0% management, 9.0% professional, 18.0% services, 25.1% sales, 0.3% farming, 11.6% construction, 27.0% production (2000).
Income: Per capita income: $17,866 (2000); Median household income: $39,667 (2000); Poverty rate: 4.8% (2000).
Taxes: Total city taxes per capita: $58 (1997); City property taxes per capita: $50 (1997).
Education: High school graduation rate: 80.5% (2000); College graduation rate: 8.9% (2000).

School District(s)

Thomasboro C C School District 130 (KG-08)
2000 Enrollment: 219 217-643-3275

Housing: Homeownership rate: 75.2% (2000); Median home value: $72,400 (2000); Median rent: $342 per month (2000); Median age of housing: 29 years (2000).
Transportation: Commute to work: 94.9% car, 0.0% public transportation, 0.7% walk, 1.9% work from home (2000); Travel time to work: 24.0% less than 15 minutes, 57.8% 15 to 30 minutes, 15.9% 30 to 45 minutes, 1.6% 45 to 60 minutes, 0.7% 60 minutes or more (2000)

TOLONO (village). Covers a land area of 1.869 square miles and a water area of 0 square miles. Located at 39.98° N. Lat.; 88.26° W. Long. Elevation is 737 feet.
History: The name of Tolono was made up by J.B. Calhoun of the Illinois Central Railroad.
Population: 2,700 (2000); Race: 99.2% White, 0.1% Black, 0.0% Asian, 0.0% American Indian and Alaska Native, 0.2% Hispanic of any race, 0.4% two or more races (2000); Density: 1,444.4 persons per square mile (2000); Age: 25.6% under 18, 11.0% over 64 (2000); Marriage status: 20.8% never married, 61.7% now married, 6.4% widowed, 11.1% divorced (2000); Foreign born: 0.6% (2000); Ancestry (includes multiple ancestries): 27.6% German, 11.2% English, 10.4% Irish, 8.2% United States or American, 5.4% Other groups (2000).
Economy: Single-family building permits issued: 6 (2001) / 9 (2000); Multi-family building permits issued: 0 (2001) / 0 (2000); Employment by occupation: 11.1% management, 15.5% professional, 19.9% services, 29.4% sales, 0.3% farming, 13.4% construction, 10.4% production (2000).
Income: Per capita income: $19,894 (2000); Median household income: $44,200 (2000); Poverty rate: 5.6% (2000).
Taxes: Total city taxes per capita: $101 (1997); City property taxes per capita: $33 (1997).
Education: High school graduation rate: 89.5% (2000); College graduation rate: 15.7% (2000).

School District(s)

Tolono C U School District 7 (KG-12)
2000 Enrollment: 1,304 217-485-6510

Housing: Homeownership rate: 79.2% (2000); Median home value: $80,600 (2000); Median rent: $358 per month (2000); Median age of housing: 30 years (2000).
Newspapers: County Star (1 x week)
Transportation: Commute to work: 94.2% car, 0.0% public transportation, 1.3% walk, 3.3% work from home (2000); Travel time to work: 22.7% less than 15 minutes, 60.4% 15 to 30 minutes, 11.1% 30 to 45 minutes, 3.8% 45 to 60 minutes, 2.0% 60 minutes or more (2000)

URBANA (city). Covers a land area of 10.494 square miles and a water area of 0.012 square miles. Located at 40.11° N. Lat.; 88.20° W. Long. Elevation is 735 feet.
History: Urbana was settled in 1822 by Willard Tompkins. Although designated as the county seat in 1833, the loss of the railroad to nearby Champaign in 1854 slowed Urbana's development. When the Illinois Industrial College, later to become the University of Illinois, was sited between Urbana and Champaign in 1867, the character of Urbana was determined.
Population: 36,395 (2000); Race: 66.6% White, 14.7% Black, 14.6% Asian, 0.1% American Indian and Alaska Native, 3.1% Hispanic of any race, 2.5% two or more races (2000); Density: 3,468.3 persons per square mile (2000); Age: 14.7% under 18, 9.4% over 64 (2000); Marriage status: 53.6% never married, 35.6% now married, 4.1% widowed, 6.7% divorced (2000); Foreign born: 15.8% (2000); Ancestry (includes multiple ancestries): 32.6% Other groups, 20.5% German, 10.9% Irish, 9.8% English, 4.1% Polish (2000).
Vital Statistics: Birth rate: 123.4 per 10,000 population (1998)
Economy: Unemployment rate: 3.0% (11/2002); Total civilian labor force: 21,605 (11/2002); Single-family building permits issued: 82 (2001) / 49 (2000); Multi-family building permits issued: 59 (2001) / 196 (2000); Employment by occupation: 7.3% management, 45.6% professional, 14.8% services, 21.7% sales, 0.3% farming, 3.6% construction, 6.7% production (2000).
Income: Per capita income: $15,969 (2000); Median household income: $27,819 (2000); Poverty rate: 27.3% (2000).
Taxes: Total city taxes per capita: $352 (2000); City property taxes per capita: $162 (2000).
Education: High school graduation rate: 90.8% (2000); College graduation rate: 53.5% (2000).

School District(s)

Board of Trustees (08-12)
2000 Enrollment: 291 217-333-2870
Urbana School District 116 (PK-12)
2000 Enrollment: 4,617 217-384-3636

Four-year College(s)

Faith School of Theology (Private, Not-for-profit, United Methodist)
2001 Enrollment: n/a 217-344-1983

Housing: Homeownership rate: 36.8% (2000); Median home value: $89,300 (2000); Median rent: $463 per month (2000); Median age of housing: 31 years (2000).
Hospitals: Carle Foundation Hospital (300 beds); Covenant Medical Center (268 beds)
Transportation: Commute to work: 63.8% car, 10.9% public transportation, 17.0% walk, 3.2% work from home (2000); Travel time to work: 57.3% less than 15 minutes, 34.0% 15 to 30 minutes, 5.1% 30 to 45 minutes, 1.7% 45 to 60 minutes, 2.0% 60 minutes or more (2000); Amtrak: Service available.
Airports: University of Illinois-Willard (primary service)

Christian County

Located in central Illinois; bounded on the north by the Sangamon River; drained by the South Fork of the Sangamon River. Covers a land area of 709.10 square miles, a water area of 6.70 square miles, and is located in the Central Time Zone. The county government was organized in 1839. County seat is Taylorville.

Weather Station: Pana 3 E — Elevation: 698 feet

	Jan	Feb	Mar	Apr	May	Jun	Jul	Aug	Sep	Oct	Nov	Dec
High	35	41	53	65	75	84	87	85	79	67	53	40
Low	18	23	33	43	53	62	66	63	56	45	35	24
Precip	2.2	2.2	3.5	4.0	4.0	4.5	3.9	3.0	3.1	2.9	3.8	3.2
Snow	7.4	5.0	4.2	0.9	tr	0.0	0.0	0.0	0.0	0.1	1.8	5.4

High and Low temperatures in degrees Fahrenheit; Precipitation and Snow in inches

Population: 35,372 (2000); Race: 95.9% White, 2.2% Black, 0.6% Asian, 0.2% American Indian and Alaska Native, 0.8% Hispanic of any race, 0.4% two or more races (2000); Density: 49.9 persons per square mile (2000); Age: 24.0% under 18, 17.3% over 64 (2000).
Religion: Five largest groups: 16.5% Catholic Church, 9.0% The United Methodist Church, 5.0% Christian Churches and Churches of Christ, 4.1% Lutheran Church—Missouri Synod, 2.8% American Baptist Churches in the USA (2000).
Economy: Unemployment rate: 6.2% (11/2002); Total civilian labor force: 18,422 (11/2002); Leading industries: 18.3% retail trade; 17.9% health care and social assistance; 16.2% manufacturing (2000); Companies that employ more than 1,000 persons: 1 (2000); Companies that employ more than 100 persons: 12 (2000); Farms: 820 totaling 389,958 acres (1997); Minority business ownership rate: 0.0% (1997); Women business ownership rate: 32.3% (1997); Retail sales per capita: $7,899 (1997). Single-family building permits issued: 81 (2001) / 86 (2000); Multi-family building permits issued: 15 (2001) / 13 (2000).
Income: Per capita income: $17,937 (2000); Median household income: $36,561 (2000); Poverty rate: 9.5% (2000); Bankruptcy rate: 7.41% (2001).
Taxes: Total county taxes per capita: $67 (1997); County property taxes per capita: $67 (1997).
Education: High school graduation rate: 81.0% (2000); College graduation rate: 10.5% (2000).
Housing: Homeownership rate: 76.2% (2000); Median home value: $61,000 (2000); Median rent: $297 per month (2000); Median age of housing: 47 years (2000).
Health: Birth rate: 116.5 per 10,000 population (1998); Age adjusted death rate: 87.3 per 10,000 population (1999); Age adjusted cancer mortality rate: 219.7 deaths per 100,000 population (1999). Number of physicians: 7.1 per 10,000 population (1999); Number of hospital beds: 47.2 per 10,000 population (1999).

Elections: 2000 Presidential election results: 46.0% Gore, 51.0% Bush, 1.8% Nader, 0.9% Buchanan

Additional Information Contacts

Christian County Government Offices. 217-824-4969
Central Illinois Board of Realtors 217-824-4460
East Central Illinois Area Association of Realtors. 217-562-4400
Pana Chamber of Commerce 217-562-4240
Taylorville Chamber of Commerce 217-824-4919

Christian County Communities

ASSUMPTION (city). Covers a land area of 0.880 square miles and a water area of 0 square miles. Located at 39.52° N. Lat.; 89.04° W. Long. Elevation is 647 feet.

History: Incorporated 1902.

Population: 1,261 (2000); Race: 99.6% White, 0.0% Black, 0.2% Asian, 0.0% American Indian and Alaska Native, 0.0% Hispanic of any race, 0.2% two or more races (2000); Density: 1,433.1 persons per square mile (2000); Age: 25.5% under 18, 21.1% over 64 (2000); Marriage status: 18.5% never married, 60.6% now married, 11.4% widowed, 9.5% divorced (2000); Foreign born: 0.7% (2000); Ancestry (includes multiple ancestries): 21.3% German, 14.9% Irish, 10.5% United States or American, 9.3% English, 3.8% French (except Basque) (2000).

Economy: Bituminous coal mining. Agriculture: corn, wheat, soybeans, sorghum; Manufacturing: grain storage structures. Employment by occupation: 10.2% management, 14.9% professional, 16.8% services, 20.5% sales, 1.0% farming, 10.6% construction, 26.0% production (2000).

Income: Per capita income: $16,421 (2000); Median household income: $34,474 (2000); Poverty rate: 9.5% (2000).

Taxes: Total city taxes per capita: $69 (1997); City property taxes per capita: $67 (1997).

Education: High school graduation rate: 84.6% (2000); College graduation rate: 11.3% (2000).

School District(s)

Central A & M C U District #21 (PK-12)
2000 Enrollment: 1,008 217-226-4042

Housing: Homeownership rate: 75.8% (2000); Median home value: $46,600 (2000); Median rent: $269 per month (2000); Median age of housing: 59 years (2000).

Newspapers: Golden Prairie News (1 x week)

Transportation: Commute to work: 95.4% car, 0.7% public transportation, 2.7% walk, 0.5% work from home (2000); Travel time to work: 46.9% less than 15 minutes, 16.2% 15 to 30 minutes, 21.7% 30 to 45 minutes, 5.7% 45 to 60 minutes, 9.6% 60 minutes or more (2000)

BULPITT (village). Covers a land area of 0.071 square miles and a water area of 0 square miles. Located at 39.59° N. Lat.; 89.42° W. Long. Elevation is 600 feet.

Population: 206 (2000); Race: 99.5% White, 0.0% Black, 0.0% Asian, 0.0% American Indian and Alaska Native, 0.5% Hispanic of any race, 0.0% two or more races (2000); Density: 2,908.9 persons per square mile (2000); Age: 17.1% under 18, 24.4% over 64 (2000); Marriage status: 24.6% never married, 42.5% now married, 18.4% widowed, 14.5% divorced (2000); Foreign born: 0.0% (2000); Ancestry (includes multiple ancestries): 24.9% United States or American, 15.1% English, 14.6% Irish, 13.2% German, 5.9% Lithuanian (2000).

Economy: In agricultural area. Bituminous coal. Single-family building permits issued: 1 (2001) / 0 (2000); Multi-family building permits issued: 0 (2001) / 0 (2000); Employment by occupation: 13.8% management, 7.5% professional, 22.5% services, 26.3% sales, 0.0% farming, 22.5% construction, 7.5% production (2000).

Income: Per capita income: $14,807 (2000); Median household income: $29,861 (2000); Poverty rate: 8.3% (2000).

Taxes: Total city taxes per capita: $51 (1997); City property taxes per capita: $10 (1997).

Education: High school graduation rate: 69.1% (2000); College graduation rate: 6.7% (2000).

Housing: Homeownership rate: 91.1% (2000); Median home value: $40,500 (2000); Median rent: $225 per month (2000); Median age of housing: 60+ years (2000).

Transportation: Commute to work: 97.5% car, 0.0% public transportation, 0.0% walk, 2.5% work from home (2000); Travel time to work: 30.8% less than 15 minutes, 21.8% 15 to 30 minutes, 30.8% 30 to 45 minutes, 16.7% 45 to 60 minutes, 0.0% 60 minutes or more (2000)

EDINBURG (village). Covers a land area of 0.581 square miles and a water area of 0 square miles. Located at 39.65° N. Lat.; 89.39° W. Long. Elevation is 580 feet.

Population: 1,135 (2000); Race: 98.7% White, 0.3% Black, 0.7% Asian, 0.0% American Indian and Alaska Native, 0.3% Hispanic of any race, 0.3% two or more races (2000); Density: 1,952.5 persons per square mile (2000); Age: 24.4% under 18, 13.9% over 64 (2000); Marriage status: 16.7% never married, 62.6% now married, 8.7% widowed, 12.0% divorced (2000); Foreign born: 0.8% (2000); Ancestry (includes multiple ancestries): 24.2% German, 13.0% Irish, 12.9% English, 11.7% United States or American, 7.2% Other groups (2000).

Economy: Agriculture: wheat, corn, soybeans. Single-family building permits issued: 4 (2001) / 7 (2000); Multi-family building permits issued: 0 (2001) / 0 (2000); Employment by occupation: 8.4% management, 12.0% professional, 13.9% services, 37.2% sales, 1.0% farming, 10.8% construction, 16.5% production (2000).

Income: Per capita income: $18,243 (2000); Median household income: $37,788 (2000); Poverty rate: 8.5% (2000).

Taxes: Total city taxes per capita: $53 (1997); City property taxes per capita: $47 (1997).

Education: High school graduation rate: 88.2% (2000); College graduation rate: 10.8% (2000).

School District(s)

Edinburg C U School District 4 (PK-12)
2000 Enrollment: 373 217-623-5603

Housing: Homeownership rate: 77.1% (2000); Median home value: $65,300 (2000); Median rent: $348 per month (2000); Median age of housing: 46 years (2000).

Newspapers: The Herald Star (1 x week)

Transportation: Commute to work: 91.4% car, 0.7% public transportation, 2.3% walk, 3.8% work from home (2000); Travel time to work: 14.3% less than 15 minutes, 27.2% 15 to 30 minutes, 47.7% 30 to 45 minutes, 5.6% 45 to 60 minutes, 5.1% 60 minutes or more (2000)

JEISYVILLE (village). Covers a land area of 0.058 square miles and a water area of 0 square miles. Located at 39.57° N. Lat.; 89.40° W. Long. Elevation is 600 feet.

Population: 128 (2000); Race: 100.0% White, 0.0% Black, 0.0% Asian, 0.0% American Indian and Alaska Native, 0.0% Hispanic of any race, 0.0% two or more races (2000); Density: 2,205.5 persons per square mile (2000); Age: 24.4% under 18, 25.6% over 64 (2000); Marriage status: 4.4% never married, 64.7% now married, 23.5% widowed, 7.4% divorced (2000); Foreign born: 0.0% (2000); Ancestry (includes multiple ancestries): 22.2% Irish, 21.1% English, 15.6% Italian, 14.4% United States or American, 13.3% Other groups (2000).

Economy: Employment by occupation: 0.0% management, 15.0% professional, 10.0% services, 40.0% sales, 0.0% farming, 15.0% construction, 20.0% production (2000).

Income: Per capita income: $16,947 (2000); Median household income: $33,750 (2000); Poverty rate: 4.4% (2000).

Taxes: Total city taxes per capita: $8 (1997); City property taxes per capita: $8 (1997).

Education: High school graduation rate: 62.5% (2000); College graduation rate: 7.8% (2000).

Housing: Homeownership rate: 86.4% (2000); Median home value: $35,000 (2000); Median rent: $188 per month (2000); Median age of housing: 60+ years (2000).

Transportation: Commute to work: 100.0% car, 0.0% public transportation, 0.0% walk, 0.0% work from home (2000); Travel time to work: 30.0% less than 15 minutes, 45.0% 15 to 30 minutes, 25.0% 30 to 45 minutes, 0.0% 45 to 60 minutes, 0.0% 60 minutes or more (2000)

KINCAID (village). Covers a land area of 0.624 square miles and a water area of 0 square miles. Located at 39.58° N. Lat.; 89.41° W. Long. Elevation is 600 feet.

History: Incorporated 1915.

Population: 1,441 (2000); Race: 97.6% White, 0.7% Black, 0.0% Asian, 0.7% American Indian and Alaska Native, 1.2% Hispanic of any race, 0.9% two or more races (2000); Density: 2,309.9 persons per square mile (2000); Age: 26.8% under 18, 16.1% over 64 (2000); Marriage status: 17.9% never married, 57.2% now married, 11.5% widowed, 13.4% divorced (2000); Foreign born: 0.5% (2000); Ancestry (includes multiple ancestries): 16.8% German, 13.1% Irish, 11.6% Italian, 11.4% United States or American, 6.9% English (2000).

Economy: In agriculture and bituminous-coal area. Single-family building permits issued: 6 (2001) / 9 (2000); Multi-family building permits issued: 0 (2001) / 0 (2000); Employment by occupation: 9.5% management, 13.6% professional, 17.7% services, 25.5% sales, 1.0% farming, 13.3% construction, 19.4% production (2000).
Income: Per capita income: $16,553 (2000); Median household income: $35,403 (2000); Poverty rate: 10.5% (2000).
Taxes: Total city taxes per capita: $28 (1997); City property taxes per capita: $26 (1997).
Education: High school graduation rate: 78.9% (2000); College graduation rate: 6.0% (2000).

School District(s)

South Fork School District 14 (PK-12)
2000 Enrollment: 402 217-237-4333
Housing: Homeownership rate: 81.0% (2000); Median home value: $48,900 (2000); Median rent: $269 per month (2000); Median age of housing: 54 years (2000).
Transportation: Commute to work: 95.6% car, 0.5% public transportation, 1.8% walk, 1.3% work from home (2000); Travel time to work: 28.6% less than 15 minutes, 22.7% 15 to 30 minutes, 30.6% 30 to 45 minutes, 12.8% 45 to 60 minutes, 5.3% 60 minutes or more (2000)

MORRISONVILLE (village). Covers a land area of 1.031 square miles and a water area of 0 square miles. Located at 39.41° N. Lat.; 89.45° W. Long. Elevation is 630 feet.
History: Incorporated 1872.
Population: 1,068 (2000); Race: 99.3% White, 0.4% Black, 0.0% Asian, 0.0% American Indian and Alaska Native, 0.6% Hispanic of any race, 0.2% two or more races (2000); Density: 1,035.4 persons per square mile (2000); Age: 24.3% under 18, 18.8% over 64 (2000); Marriage status: 17.5% never married, 68.5% now married, 6.3% widowed, 7.7% divorced (2000); Foreign born: 0.8% (2000); Ancestry (includes multiple ancestries): 24.3% German, 19.8% Irish, 12.7% United States or American, 12.6% English, 5.5% Other groups (2000).
Economy: Agriculture: grain; livestock; soybean products. Employment by occupation: 12.3% management, 11.5% professional, 17.6% services, 29.1% sales, 1.2% farming, 13.0% construction, 15.4% production (2000).
Income: Per capita income: $18,324 (2000); Median household income: $35,917 (2000); Poverty rate: 6.2% (2000).
Taxes: Total city taxes per capita: $95 (1997); City property taxes per capita: $91 (1997).
Education: High school graduation rate: 83.1% (2000); College graduation rate: 12.1% (2000).

School District(s)

Morrisonville C U School District 1 (PK-12)
2000 Enrollment: 382 217-526-4431
Housing: Homeownership rate: 83.1% (2000); Median home value: $57,100 (2000); Median rent: $278 per month (2000); Median age of housing: 59 years (2000).
Newspapers: The Morrisonville Times (1 x week)
Transportation: Commute to work: 93.8% car, 0.0% public transportation, 1.0% walk, 4.2% work from home (2000); Travel time to work: 30.8% less than 15 minutes, 23.0% 15 to 30 minutes, 17.6% 30 to 45 minutes, 18.4% 45 to 60 minutes, 10.3% 60 minutes or more (2000)

MOUNT AUBURN (village). Covers a land area of 0.991 square miles and a water area of 0.001 square miles. Located at 39.76° N. Lat.; 89.26° W. Long. Elevation is 628 feet.
Population: 515 (2000); Race: 97.9% White, 0.0% Black, 1.6% Asian, 0.6% American Indian and Alaska Native, 0.0% Hispanic of any race, 0.0% two or more races (2000); Density: 519.7 persons per square mile (2000); Age: 22.1% under 18, 11.7% over 64 (2000); Marriage status: 21.4% never married, 61.4% now married, 6.4% widowed, 10.8% divorced (2000); Foreign born: 1.6% (2000); Ancestry (includes multiple ancestries): 24.4% United States or American, 23.4% German, 11.5% Irish, 6.8% Other groups, 6.4% English (2000).
Economy: Grain; livestock. Single-family building permits issued: 4 (2001) / 4 (2000); Multi-family building permits issued: 0 (2001) / 0 (2000); Employment by occupation: 7.8% management, 10.1% professional, 14.7% services, 30.4% sales, 3.3% farming, 11.1% construction, 22.5% production (2000).
Income: Per capita income: $18,829 (2000); Median household income: $45,417 (2000); Poverty rate: 2.4% (2000).
Taxes: Total city taxes per capita: $40 (1997); City property taxes per capita: $13 (1997).
Education: High school graduation rate: 84.4% (2000); College graduation rate: 6.8% (2000).
Housing: Homeownership rate: 86.0% (2000); Median home value: $49,300 (2000); Median rent: $283 per month (2000); Median age of housing: 36 years (2000).
Transportation: Commute to work: 94.4% car, 0.0% public transportation, 1.3% walk, 3.6% work from home (2000); Travel time to work: 13.4% less than 15 minutes, 29.8% 15 to 30 minutes, 41.8% 30 to 45 minutes, 12.0% 45 to 60 minutes, 3.1% 60 minutes or more (2000)

OWANECO (village). Covers a land area of 0.458 square miles and a water area of 0 square miles. Located at 39.48° N. Lat.; 89.19° W. Long. Elevation is 624 feet.
Population: 256 (2000); Race: 100.0% White, 0.0% Black, 0.0% Asian, 0.0% American Indian and Alaska Native, 0.0% Hispanic of any race, 0.0% two or more races (2000); Density: 559.2 persons per square mile (2000); Age: 25.4% under 18, 13.3% over 64 (2000); Marriage status: 12.8% never married, 72.3% now married, 8.2% widowed, 6.7% divorced (2000); Foreign born: 0.0% (2000); Ancestry (includes multiple ancestries): 33.2% German, 12.9% United States or American, 12.1% Irish, 9.0% English, 8.2% Italian (2000).
Economy: In agricultural area. Near Taylorville Correctional Center. Employment by occupation: 2.5% management, 15.8% professional, 22.5% services, 27.5% sales, 1.7% farming, 10.0% construction, 20.0% production (2000).
Income: Per capita income: $15,171 (2000); Median household income: $31,563 (2000); Poverty rate: 10.2% (2000).
Taxes: Total city taxes per capita: $30 (1997); City property taxes per capita: $30 (1997).
Education: High school graduation rate: 77.5% (2000); College graduation rate: 8.4% (2000).
Housing: Homeownership rate: 82.7% (2000); Median home value: $57,500 (2000); Median rent: $254 per month (2000); Median age of housing: 57 years (2000).
Transportation: Commute to work: 92.5% car, 0.0% public transportation, 2.5% walk, 0.0% work from home (2000); Travel time to work: 22.5% less than 15 minutes, 35.0% 15 to 30 minutes, 10.8% 30 to 45 minutes, 23.3% 45 to 60 minutes, 8.3% 60 minutes or more (2000)

PALMER (village). Covers a land area of 0.998 square miles and a water area of 0 square miles. Located at 39.45° N. Lat.; 89.40° W. Long. Elevation is 620 feet.
Population: 248 (2000); Race: 87.2% White, 0.0% Black, 0.0% Asian, 1.2% American Indian and Alaska Native, 1.6% Hispanic of any race, 9.1% two or more races (2000); Density: 248.5 persons per square mile (2000); Age: 33.3% under 18, 14.0% over 64 (2000); Marriage status: 25.7% never married, 63.9% now married, 7.3% widowed, 3.1% divorced (2000); Foreign born: 0.4% (2000); Ancestry (includes multiple ancestries): 23.9% United States or American, 12.3% Irish, 11.9% Other groups, 6.2% German, 5.8% English (2000).
Economy: In agricultural area. Single-family building permits issued: 0 (2001) / 0 (2000); Multi-family building permits issued: 0 (2001) / 0 (2000); Employment by occupation: 10.7% management, 12.6% professional, 26.2% services, 19.4% sales, 3.9% farming, 10.7% construction, 16.5% production (2000).
Income: Per capita income: $17,615 (2000); Median household income: $35,750 (2000); Poverty rate: 5.3% (2000).
Taxes: Total city taxes per capita: $26 (1997); City property taxes per capita: $22 (1997).
Education: High school graduation rate: 72.3% (2000); College graduation rate: 2.7% (2000).
Housing: Homeownership rate: 89.7% (2000); Median home value: $49,400 (2000); Median rent: $268 per month (2000); Median age of housing: 54 years (2000).
Transportation: Commute to work: 91.3% car, 0.0% public transportation, 1.0% walk, 7.8% work from home (2000); Travel time to work: 37.9% less than 15 minutes, 43.2% 15 to 30 minutes, 5.3% 30 to 45 minutes, 6.3% 45 to 60 minutes, 7.4% 60 minutes or more (2000)

PANA (city). Covers a land area of 2.671 square miles and a water area of 0 square miles. Located at 39.38° N. Lat.; 89.08° W. Long. Elevation is 700 feet.
History: Pana developed as a center for rose cultivation, with acres of greenhouses warmed by steam heat.
Population: 5,614 (2000); Race: 98.7% White, 0.1% Black, 0.6% Asian, 0.2% American Indian and Alaska Native, 0.0% Hispanic of any race, 0.4%

two or more races (2000); Density: 2,101.7 persons per square mile (2000); Age: 24.3% under 18, 22.3% over 64 (2000); Marriage status: 20.5% never married, 59.3% now married, 9.8% widowed, 10.4% divorced (2000); Foreign born: 0.8% (2000); Ancestry (includes multiple ancestries): 23.0% German, 13.1% United States or American, 11.0% Irish, 9.8% English, 7.1% Other groups (2000).
Economy: Single-family building permits issued: 5 (2001) / 8 (2000); Multi-family building permits issued: 0 (2001) / 0 (2000); Employment by occupation: 3.6% management, 14.8% professional, 23.5% services, 19.7% sales, 0.7% farming, 10.2% construction, 27.5% production (2000).
Income: Per capita income: $14,897 (2000); Median household income: $29,611 (2000); Poverty rate: 17.6% (2000).
Taxes: Total city taxes per capita: $106 (1997); City property taxes per capita: $95 (1997).
Education: High school graduation rate: 75.5% (2000); College graduation rate: 7.1% (2000).

School District(s)

Pana Community Unit School District 8 (PK-12)
2000 Enrollment: 1,329 217-562-3976
Housing: Homeownership rate: 70.5% (2000); Median home value: $46,700 (2000); Median rent: $277 per month (2000); Median age of housing: 53 years (2000).
Hospitals: Pana Community Hospital (44 beds)
Newspapers: News-Palladium (2 x week)
Transportation: Commute to work: 92.8% car, 1.9% public transportation, 2.4% walk, 1.1% work from home (2000); Travel time to work: 51.5% less than 15 minutes, 17.9% 15 to 30 minutes, 9.8% 30 to 45 minutes, 10.8% 45 to 60 minutes, 10.0% 60 minutes or more (2000)
Additional Information Contacts
East Central Illinois Area Association of Realtors. 217-562-4400
Pana Chamber of Commerce 217-562-4240

ROSAMOND (unincorporated postal area, zip code 62083). Covers a land area of 22.766 square miles and a water area of 0 square miles. Located at 39.35° N. Lat.; 89.20° W. Long. Elevation is 714 feet.
Population: 317 (2000); Race: 100.0% White, 0.0% Black, 0.0% Asian, 0.0% American Indian and Alaska Native, 0.0% Hispanic of any race, 0.0% two or more races (2000); Density: 13.9 persons per square mile (2000); Age: 32.2% under 18, 12.6% over 64 (2000); Marriage status: 25.7% never married, 37.7% now married, 15.4% widowed, 21.1% divorced (2000); Foreign born: 0.0% (2000); Ancestry (includes multiple ancestries): 54.8% German, 16.7% Irish, 13.0% French (except Basque), 7.5% United States or American, 3.8% Other groups (2000).
Economy: Employment by occupation: 4.3% management, 0.0% professional, 34.0% services, 7.4% sales, 11.7% farming, 19.1% construction, 23.4% production (2000).
Income: Per capita income: $16,027 (2000); Median household income: $27,750 (2000); Poverty rate: 22.5% (2000).
Education: High school graduation rate: 91.9% (2000); College graduation rate: 7.4% (2000).
Housing: Homeownership rate: 93.2% (2000); Median home value: $48,600 (2000); Median age of housing: 51 years (2000).
Transportation: Commute to work: 95.7% car, 0.0% public transportation, 4.3% walk, 0.0% work from home (2000); Travel time to work: 17.0% less than 15 minutes, 31.9% 15 to 30 minutes, 16.0% 30 to 45 minutes, 12.8% 45 to 60 minutes, 22.3% 60 minutes or more (2000)

STONINGTON (village). Covers a land area of 0.454 square miles and a water area of 0 square miles. Located at 39.63° N. Lat.; 89.19° W. Long. Elevation is 615 feet.
History: Incorporated 1885.
Population: 960 (2000); Race: 98.3% White, 0.3% Black, 0.0% Asian, 0.0% American Indian and Alaska Native, 0.4% Hispanic of any race, 0.9% two or more races (2000); Density: 2,114.3 persons per square mile (2000); Age: 28.4% under 18, 19.1% over 64 (2000); Marriage status: 16.2% never married, 64.1% now married, 9.7% widowed, 10.0% divorced (2000); Foreign born: 0.3% (2000); Ancestry (includes multiple ancestries): 19.6% German, 14.9% Irish, 11.8% English, 10.1% United States or American, 6.8% Other groups (2000).
Economy: In agricultural and bituminous-coal-mining area. Single-family building permits issued: 1 (2001) / 0 (2000); Multi-family building permits issued: 0 (2001) / 0 (2000); Employment by occupation: 5.1% management, 13.2% professional, 15.4% services, 31.4% sales, 1.5% farming, 10.4% construction, 23.0% production (2000).
Income: Per capita income: $17,094 (2000); Median household income: $36,413 (2000); Poverty rate: 11.3% (2000).
Taxes: Total city taxes per capita: $46 (1997); City property taxes per capita: $39 (1997).
Education: High school graduation rate: 81.3% (2000); College graduation rate: 11.1% (2000).
Housing: Homeownership rate: 76.0% (2000); Median home value: $55,000 (2000); Median rent: $265 per month (2000); Median age of housing: 60+ years (2000).
Transportation: Commute to work: 95.7% car, 0.5% public transportation, 1.8% walk, 2.0% work from home (2000); Travel time to work: 31.5% less than 15 minutes, 27.3% 15 to 30 minutes, 22.7% 30 to 45 minutes, 14.3% 45 to 60 minutes, 4.2% 60 minutes or more (2000)

TAYLORVILLE (city). Covers a land area of 8.067 square miles and a water area of 1.952 square miles. Located at 39.54° N. Lat.; 89.28° W. Long. Elevation is 634 feet.
History: Incorporated 1881.
Population: 11,427 (2000); Race: 96.8% White, 0.9% Black, 1.2% Asian, 0.1% American Indian and Alaska Native, 0.4% Hispanic of any race, 0.5% two or more races (2000); Density: 1,416.6 persons per square mile (2000); Age: 24.0% under 18, 20.2% over 64 (2000); Marriage status: 19.6% never married, 56.6% now married, 10.9% widowed, 12.9% divorced (2000); Foreign born: 2.0% (2000); Ancestry (includes multiple ancestries): 20.5% German, 12.0% United States or American, 11.5% Irish, 11.2% English, 8.5% Other groups (2000).
Vital Statistics: Birth rate: 143.5 per 10,000 population (1998)
Economy: In a farm, coal, and oil area. Agriculture includes wheat, corn, soybeans, sorghum. Manufacturing: soybean processing, metal products, meatpacking. Single-family building permits issued: 12 (2001) / 12 (2000); Multi-family building permits issued: 15 (2001) / 13 (2000); Employment by occupation: 8.7% management, 18.3% professional, 16.1% services, 27.9% sales, 0.4% farming, 10.6% construction, 17.9% production (2000).
Income: Per capita income: $18,162 (2000); Median household income: $34,235 (2000); Poverty rate: 10.1% (2000).
Taxes: Total city taxes per capita: $91 (1997); City property taxes per capita: $76 (1997).
Education: High school graduation rate: 82.1% (2000); College graduation rate: 13.6% (2000).

School District(s)

Christian/Montgomery Roe (06-09)
2000 Enrollment: 20 217-824-4730
Taylorville C U School District 3 (PK-12)
2000 Enrollment: 2,998 217-824-4951
Housing: Homeownership rate: 69.5% (2000); Median home value: $63,800 (2000); Median rent: $315 per month (2000); Median age of housing: 45 years (2000).
Hospitals: Saint Vincent Memorial Hospital (179 beds)
Newspapers: The Breeze Courier (6 x week)
Transportation: Commute to work: 93.7% car, 0.7% public transportation, 2.5% walk, 2.3% work from home (2000); Travel time to work: 55.9% less than 15 minutes, 9.7% 15 to 30 minutes, 16.5% 30 to 45 minutes, 13.5% 45 to 60 minutes, 4.4% 60 minutes or more (2000)
Additional Information Contacts
Central Illinois Board of Realtors 217-824-4460
Taylorville Chamber of Commerce 217-824-4919

TOVEY (village). Aka Humphrey. Covers a land area of 0.185 square miles and a water area of 0 square miles. Located at 39.58° N. Lat.; 89.44° W. Long. Elevation is 600 feet.
History: Also known as Humphrey.
Population: 516 (2000); Race: 99.1% White, 0.0% Black, 0.0% Asian, 0.2% American Indian and Alaska Native, 0.0% Hispanic of any race, 0.8% two or more races (2000); Density: 2,791.2 persons per square mile (2000); Age: 25.6% under 18, 16.1% over 64 (2000); Marriage status: 21.3% never married, 62.1% now married, 8.0% widowed, 8.7% divorced (2000); Foreign born: 0.4% (2000); Ancestry (includes multiple ancestries): 19.7% Italian, 19.5% Irish, 15.6% German, 14.2% English, 6.1% French (except Basque) (2000).
Economy: Single-family building permits issued: 0 (2001) / 0 (2000); Multi-family building permits issued: 0 (2001) / 0 (2000); Employment by occupation: 6.8% management, 11.3% professional, 11.3% services, 35.3% sales, 3.2% farming, 16.7% construction, 15.4% production (2000).
Income: Per capita income: $14,712 (2000); Median household income: $30,417 (2000); Poverty rate: 11.4% (2000).
Taxes: Total city taxes per capita: $17 (1997); City property taxes per capita: $12 (1997).

Education: High school graduation rate: 75.9% (2000); College graduation rate: 7.1% (2000).
Housing: Homeownership rate: 84.2% (2000); Median home value: $51,800 (2000); Median rent: $263 per month (2000); Median age of housing: 46 years (2000).
Transportation: Commute to work: 94.8% car, 0.0% public transportation, 1.9% walk, 0.9% work from home (2000); Travel time to work: 17.6% less than 15 minutes, 23.3% 15 to 30 minutes, 42.4% 30 to 45 minutes, 9.0% 45 to 60 minutes, 7.6% 60 minutes or more (2000)

Clark County

Located in eastern Illinois; bounded on the southeast by the Wabash River and the Indiana border; drained by the North Fork Embarrass River. Covers a land area of 501.50 square miles, a water area of 3.40 square miles, and is located in the Central Time Zone. The county government was organized in 1819. County seat is Marshall.
Population: 17,008 (2000); Race: 98.8% White, 0.1% Black, 0.1% Asian, 0.1% American Indian and Alaska Native, 0.2% Hispanic of any race, 0.8% two or more races (2000); Density: 33.9 persons per square mile (2000); Age: 24.8% under 18, 17.9% over 64 (2000).
Religion: Five largest groups: 19.8% Southern Baptist Convention, 13.1% The United Methodist Church, 6.2% Christian Churches and Churches of Christ, 4.4% Church of the Nazarene, 3.9% Catholic Church (2000).
Economy: Unemployment rate: 5.8% (11/2002); Total civilian labor force: 9,775 (11/2002); Leading industries: 45.3% manufacturing; 11.7% retail trade; 8.8% accommodation & food services (2000); Companies that employ more than 1,000 persons: 0 (2000); Companies that employ more than 100 persons: 7 (2000); Farms: 603 totaling 268,818 acres (1997); Minority business ownership rate: 0.0% (1997); Women business ownership rate: 18.5% (1997); Retail sales per capita: $6,508 (1997). Single-family building permits issued: 7 (2001) / 12 (2000); Multi-family building permits issued: 2 (2001) / 2 (2000).
Income: Per capita income: $17,655 (2000); Median household income: $35,967 (2000); Poverty rate: 9.2% (2000); Bankruptcy rate: 6.09% (2001).
Taxes: Total county taxes per capita: $108 (2000); County property taxes per capita: $108 (2000).
Education: High school graduation rate: 80.0% (2000); College graduation rate: 13.6% (2000).
Housing: Homeownership rate: 77.5% (2000); Median home value: $63,300 (2000); Median rent: $300 per month (2000); Median age of housing: 42 years (2000).
Health: Birth rate: 123.5 per 10,000 population (1998); Age adjusted death rate: 96.9 per 10,000 population (1999); Age adjusted cancer mortality rate: 195.2 deaths per 100,000 population (1999). Air Quality Index: 73% good, 27% moderate, 0% unhealthy (percent of days in 2000). Number of physicians: 2.9 per 10,000 population (1999); Number of hospital beds: n/a (1999).
Elections: 2000 Presidential election results: 39.0% Gore, 58.6% Bush, 1.7% Nader, 0.4% Buchanan
National and State Parks: Lincoln Trail State Park
Additional Information Contacts
Clark County Government Offices. 217-826-8311
Casey Chamber of Commerce 217-932-2671
Marshall Area Chamber of Commerce 217-826-2034
Martinsville Chamber of Commerce 217-382-4323

Clark County Communities

CASEY (city). Covers a land area of 2.124 square miles and a water area of 0 square miles. Located at 39.30° N. Lat.; 87.99° W. Long. Elevation is 645 feet.
History: Incorporated 1896. Had oil boom in early 20th cent.
Population: 2,942 (2000); Race: 99.8% White, 0.0% Black, 0.0% Asian, 0.0% American Indian and Alaska Native, 0.0% Hispanic of any race, 0.0% two or more races (2000); Density: 1,385.0 persons per square mile (2000); Age: 23.5% under 18, 23.1% over 64 (2000); Marriage status: 20.5% never married, 53.3% now married, 14.8% widowed, 11.4% divorced (2000); Foreign born: 0.5% (2000); Ancestry (includes multiple ancestries): 22.9% United States or American, 15.2% German, 12.8% English, 7.0% Other groups, 5.7% Irish (2000).
Economy: Oil, natural gas. Agriculture: corn, wheat, soybeans, cattle, hogs; dairy products. Manufacturing: circuit boards, toll and machining. Employment by occupation: 9.9% management, 18.7% professional, 18.8% services, 16.3% sales, 0.9% farming, 9.0% construction, 26.4% production (2000).
Income: Per capita income: $16,266 (2000); Median household income: $30,089 (2000); Poverty rate: 15.4% (2000).
Taxes: Total city taxes per capita: $192 (1997); City property taxes per capita: $32 (1997).
Education: High school graduation rate: 73.5% (2000); College graduation rate: 11.5% (2000).

School District(s)
Casey-Westfield C U School District 4c (PK-12)
2000 Enrollment: 1,185 217-932-2184
Housing: Homeownership rate: 72.0% (2000); Median home value: $52,700 (2000); Median rent: $318 per month (2000); Median age of housing: 50 years (2000).
Newspapers: Casey Reporter (2 x week)
Transportation: Commute to work: 93.6% car, 0.4% public transportation, 3.0% walk, 3.0% work from home (2000); Travel time to work: 54.9% less than 15 minutes, 16.7% 15 to 30 minutes, 16.9% 30 to 45 minutes, 7.9% 45 to 60 minutes, 3.5% 60 minutes or more (2000)
Additional Information Contacts
Casey Chamber of Commerce 217-932-2671

DENNISON (unincorporated postal area, zip code 62423). Covers a land area of 26.547 square miles and a water area of 0.016 square miles. Located at 39.45° N. Lat.; 87.57° W. Long. Elevation is 580 feet.
Population: 738 (2000); Race: 98.7% White, 0.0% Black, 1.3% Asian, 0.0% American Indian and Alaska Native, 0.0% Hispanic of any race, 0.0% two or more races (2000); Density: 27.8 persons per square mile (2000); Age: 24.9% under 18, 12.7% over 64 (2000); Marriage status: 18.5% never married, 69.6% now married, 4.1% widowed, 7.8% divorced (2000); Foreign born: 0.0% (2000); Ancestry (includes multiple ancestries): 14.9% English, 14.5% United States or American, 13.2% Irish, 11.3% German, 8.8% Other groups (2000).
Economy: Employment by occupation: 4.7% management, 7.9% professional, 22.9% services, 20.5% sales, 0.0% farming, 14.4% construction, 29.6% production (2000).
Income: Per capita income: $17,058 (2000); Median household income: $34,659 (2000); Poverty rate: 4.5% (2000).
Education: High school graduation rate: 84.7% (2000); College graduation rate: 5.8% (2000).
Housing: Homeownership rate: 85.5% (2000); Median home value: $91,700 (2000); Median rent: $353 per month (2000); Median age of housing: 25 years (2000).
Transportation: Commute to work: 100.0% car, 0.0% public transportation, 0.0% walk, 0.0% work from home (2000); Travel time to work: 13.2% less than 15 minutes, 49.9% 15 to 30 minutes, 18.5% 30 to 45 minutes, 8.8% 45 to 60 minutes, 9.7% 60 minutes or more (2000)

MARSHALL (city). Covers a land area of 3.135 square miles and a water area of 0.010 square miles. Located at 39.39° N. Lat.; 87.69° W. Long. Elevation is 641 feet.
History: Marshall was founded by William B. Archer and named by him for Chief Justice John Marshall. The town developed as the seat of Clark County.
Population: 3,771 (2000); Race: 97.5% White, 0.0% Black, 0.0% Asian, 0.2% American Indian and Alaska Native, 0.0% Hispanic of any race, 2.3% two or more races (2000); Density: 1,202.7 persons per square mile (2000); Age: 23.2% under 18, 23.1% over 64 (2000); Marriage status: 21.2% never married, 52.7% now married, 14.0% widowed, 12.1% divorced (2000); Foreign born: 0.9% (2000); Ancestry (includes multiple ancestries): 22.8% German, 17.0% Irish, 13.1% United States or American, 10.7% English, 6.4% Other groups (2000).
Economy: Single-family building permits issued: 7 (2001) / 12 (2000); Multi-family building permits issued: 2 (2001) / 2 (2000); Employment by occupation: 7.2% management, 16.1% professional, 14.7% services, 29.0% sales, 0.3% farming, 8.1% construction, 24.6% production (2000).
Income: Per capita income: $19,851 (2000); Median household income: $33,413 (2000); Poverty rate: 6.2% (2000).
Taxes: Total city taxes per capita: $174 (1997); City property taxes per capita: $48 (1997).
Education: High school graduation rate: 74.7% (2000); College graduation rate: 14.4% (2000).

School District(s)
Marshall C U School District 2c (PK-12)
2000 Enrollment: 1,453 217-826-5912

Housing: Homeownership rate: 64.2% (2000); Median home value: $68,000 (2000); Median rent: $311 per month (2000); Median age of housing: 39 years (2000).
Newspapers: Independent Choice (3 x week)
Transportation: Commute to work: 92.3% car, 0.4% public transportation, 3.6% walk, 1.9% work from home (2000); Travel time to work: 49.6% less than 15 minutes, 25.6% 15 to 30 minutes, 17.9% 30 to 45 minutes, 2.9% 45 to 60 minutes, 3.9% 60 minutes or more (2000)
Additional Information Contacts
Marshall Area Chamber of Commerce 217-826-2034

MARTINSVILLE (city). Covers a land area of 2.056 square miles and a water area of 0.030 square miles. Located at 39.33° N. Lat.; 87.88° W. Long. Elevation is 610 feet.
History: Martinsville was platted in 1833 by Joseph Martin, and operated as a trading post, stagecoach station, and tavern. A period of growth came in 1904 when oil and gas were discovered, but by 1916 the wells were dry.
Population: 1,225 (2000); Race: 98.3% White, 0.2% Black, 0.0% Asian, 0.2% American Indian and Alaska Native, 0.0% Hispanic of any race, 1.4% two or more races (2000); Density: 596.0 persons per square mile (2000); Age: 25.2% under 18, 18.5% over 64 (2000); Marriage status: 18.5% never married, 62.1% now married, 7.7% widowed, 11.7% divorced (2000); Foreign born: 0.0% (2000); Ancestry (includes multiple ancestries): 20.0% United States or American, 15.8% German, 14.1% English, 10.6% Irish, 5.7% Other groups (2000).
Economy: Employment by occupation: 7.1% management, 11.9% professional, 10.8% services, 25.7% sales, 0.7% farming, 12.9% construction, 30.9% production (2000).
Income: Per capita income: $14,706 (2000); Median household income: $27,961 (2000); Poverty rate: 12.3% (2000).
Taxes: Total city taxes per capita: $27 (1997); City property taxes per capita: $22 (1997).
Education: High school graduation rate: 83.3% (2000); College graduation rate: 9.7% (2000).

School District(s)

Martinsville C U School District 3c (PK-12)
2000 Enrollment: 457 217-382-4321
Housing: Homeownership rate: 74.9% (2000); Median home value: $46,600 (2000); Median rent: $242 per month (2000); Median age of housing: 50 years (2000).
Transportation: Commute to work: 91.3% car, 0.0% public transportation, 4.3% walk, 4.1% work from home (2000); Travel time to work: 49.8% less than 15 minutes, 17.5% 15 to 30 minutes, 13.9% 30 to 45 minutes, 11.6% 45 to 60 minutes, 7.1% 60 minutes or more (2000)
Additional Information Contacts
Martinsville Chamber of Commerce 217-382-4323

WEST UNION (unincorporated postal area, zip code 62477). Aka Hatton. Covers a land area of 64.596 square miles and a water area of 0.113 square miles. Located at 39.23° N. Lat.; 87.66° W. Long. Elevation is 475 feet.
Population: 1,131 (2000); Race: 99.4% White, 0.0% Black, 0.0% Asian, 0.0% American Indian and Alaska Native, 0.0% Hispanic of any race, 0.6% two or more races (2000); Density: 17.5 persons per square mile (2000); Age: 30.0% under 18, 11.6% over 64 (2000); Marriage status: 22.7% never married, 57.1% now married, 6.1% widowed, 14.1% divorced (2000); Foreign born: 0.0% (2000); Ancestry (includes multiple ancestries): 22.8% German, 15.6% United States or American, 13.6% English, 7.9% Irish, 5.2% French (except Basque) (2000).
Economy: Employment by occupation: 13.2% management, 13.0% professional, 9.6% services, 19.3% sales, 1.3% farming, 16.5% construction, 27.0% production (2000).
Income: Per capita income: $14,453 (2000); Median household income: $33,000 (2000); Poverty rate: 14.1% (2000).
Education: High school graduation rate: 85.1% (2000); College graduation rate: 11.8% (2000).
Housing: Homeownership rate: 85.6% (2000); Median home value: $40,800 (2000); Median rent: $253 per month (2000); Median age of housing: 53 years (2000).
Transportation: Commute to work: 89.9% car, 0.0% public transportation, 2.9% walk, 3.7% work from home (2000); Travel time to work: 17.2% less than 15 minutes, 47.8% 15 to 30 minutes, 19.4% 30 to 45 minutes, 8.3% 45 to 60 minutes, 7.3% 60 minutes or more (2000)

WESTFIELD (village). Covers a land area of 1.004 square miles and a water area of 0 square miles. Located at 39.45° N. Lat.; 87.99° W. Long. Elevation is 760 feet.
Population: 678 (2000); Race: 99.4% White, 0.0% Black, 0.0% Asian, 0.6% American Indian and Alaska Native, 0.0% Hispanic of any race, 0.0% two or more races (2000); Density: 675.3 persons per square mile (2000); Age: 29.0% under 18, 14.2% over 64 (2000); Marriage status: 16.7% never married, 68.7% now married, 6.3% widowed, 8.3% divorced (2000); Foreign born: 0.3% (2000); Ancestry (includes multiple ancestries): 19.0% German, 15.7% United States or American, 11.0% Other groups, 7.1% English, 6.7% Irish (2000).
Economy: Agriculture includes corn, wheat, soybeans, sorghum; cattle, hogs, poultry. Employment by occupation: 6.7% management, 15.1% professional, 19.4% services, 18.1% sales, 0.7% farming, 17.4% construction, 22.7% production (2000).
Income: Per capita income: $14,103 (2000); Median household income: $31,953 (2000); Poverty rate: 11.2% (2000).
Taxes: Total city taxes per capita: $91 (1997); City property taxes per capita: $43 (1997).
Education: High school graduation rate: 85.4% (2000); College graduation rate: 7.7% (2000).
Housing: Homeownership rate: 79.6% (2000); Median home value: $43,700 (2000); Median rent: $258 per month (2000); Median age of housing: 60+ years (2000).
Transportation: Commute to work: 93.2% car, 2.0% public transportation, 1.4% walk, 3.4% work from home (2000); Travel time to work: 21.8% less than 15 minutes, 47.0% 15 to 30 minutes, 17.5% 30 to 45 minutes, 11.2% 45 to 60 minutes, 2.5% 60 minutes or more (2000)

Clay County

Located in south central Illinois; drained by the Little Wabash River. Covers a land area of 469.20 square miles, a water area of 0.60 square miles, and is located in the Central Time Zone. The county government was organized in 1824. County seat is Louisville.

Weather Station: Flora 5 NW — Elevation: 498 feet

	Jan	Feb	Mar	Apr	May	Jun	Jul	Aug	Sep	Oct	Nov	Dec
High	38	44	55	67	77	85	89	88	81	70	55	43
Low	21	25	34	43	53	62	65	63	56	45	35	26
Precip	2.6	2.4	4.0	4.3	4.2	4.2	3.8	3.2	3.2	3.0	4.0	3.3
Snow	2.5	2.1	1.2	0.2	tr	0.0	0.0	0.0	0.0	tr	0.8	1.5

High and Low temperatures in degrees Fahrenheit; Precipitation and Snow in inches

Population: 14,560 (2000); Race: 99.1% White, 0.0% Black, 0.5% Asian, 0.1% American Indian and Alaska Native, 0.5% Hispanic of any race, 0.2% two or more races (2000); Density: 31.0 persons per square mile (2000); Age: 23.9% under 18, 19.2% over 64 (2000).
Religion: Five largest groups: 20.6% Christian Churches and Churches of Christ, 16.1% Southern Baptist Convention, 10.4% Catholic Church, 9.2% The United Methodist Church, 2.3% Church of the Nazarene (2000).
Economy: Unemployment rate: 6.8% (11/2002); Total civilian labor force: 7,018 (11/2002); Leading industries: 42.3% manufacturing; 14.3% health care and social assistance; 9.2% retail trade (2000); Companies that employ more than 1,000 persons: 1 (2000); Companies that employ more than 100 persons: 9 (2000); Farms: 627 totaling 238,717 acres (1997); Minority business ownership rate: 0.0% (1997); Women business ownership rate: 25.0% (1997); Retail sales per capita: $6,395 (1997). Single-family building permits issued: 9 (2001) / 11 (2000); Multi-family building permits issued: 0 (2001) / 0 (2000).
Income: Per capita income: $15,771 (2000); Median household income: $30,599 (2000); Poverty rate: 11.8% (2000); Bankruptcy rate: 4.78% (2001).
Taxes: Total county taxes per capita: $135 (1997); County property taxes per capita: $111 (1997).
Education: High school graduation rate: 75.9% (2000); College graduation rate: 9.7% (2000).
Housing: Homeownership rate: 79.8% (2000); Median home value: $51,500 (2000); Median rent: $242 per month (2000); Median age of housing: 37 years (2000).
Health: Birth rate: 125.0 per 10,000 population (1998); Age adjusted death rate: 94.7 per 10,000 population (1999); Age adjusted cancer mortality rate: 212.5 deaths per 100,000 population (1999). Number of physicians: 6.9 per 10,000 population (1999); Number of hospital beds: 15.1 per 10,000 population (1999).

Elections: 2000 Presidential election results: 36.1% Gore, 61.8% Bush, 1.3% Nader, 0.6% Buchanan

Additional Information Contacts

Clay County Government Offices 618-665-3626
Flora Chamber of Commerce 618-662-5646

Clay County Communities

CLAY CITY (village). Covers a land area of 1.782 square miles and a water area of 0 square miles. Located at 38.68° N. Lat.; 88.35° W. Long. Elevation is 433 feet.

History: Clay City developed as a shipping and trading center for the surrounding agricultural area when the railroad arrived here. It was built on the site of the first seat of Clay County, called Maysville. Oil was discovered near Clay City in 1937.

Population: 1,000 (2000); Race: 100.0% White, 0.0% Black, 0.0% Asian, 0.0% American Indian and Alaska Native, 0.7% Hispanic of any race, 0.0% two or more races (2000); Density: 561.0 persons per square mile (2000); Age: 24.8% under 18, 16.6% over 64 (2000); Marriage status: 23.5% never married, 50.3% now married, 11.3% widowed, 15.0% divorced (2000); Foreign born: 0.4% (2000); Ancestry (includes multiple ancestries): 27.6% United States or American, 25.1% German, 11.2% Irish, 7.7% English, 5.1% Other groups (2000).

Economy: Employment by occupation: 6.3% management, 10.9% professional, 16.0% services, 17.4% sales, 2.3% farming, 10.7% construction, 36.4% production (2000).

Income: Per capita income: $13,776 (2000); Median household income: $25,750 (2000); Poverty rate: 16.4% (2000).

Taxes: Total city taxes per capita: $17 (1997); City property taxes per capita: $15 (1997).

Education: High school graduation rate: 80.7% (2000); College graduation rate: 7.1% (2000).

School District(s)

Clay City Community Unit District 10 (PK-12)
2000 Enrollment: 473 618-676-1431

Housing: Homeownership rate: 71.7% (2000); Median home value: $43,900 (2000); Median rent: $224 per month (2000); Median age of housing: 37 years (2000).

Transportation: Commute to work: 95.3% car, 0.0% public transportation, 4.2% walk, 0.5% work from home (2000); Travel time to work: 58.2% less than 15 minutes, 27.4% 15 to 30 minutes, 6.4% 30 to 45 minutes, 2.6% 45 to 60 minutes, 5.4% 60 minutes or more (2000)

FLORA (city). Covers a land area of 4.437 square miles and a water area of <.001 square miles. Located at 38.67° N. Lat.; 88.48° W. Long. Elevation is 485 feet.

History: Flora was named for the daughter of one of its founders. It developed as an industrial center with a diversity of manufacturing.

Population: 5,086 (2000); Race: 98.2% White, 0.0% Black, 1.3% Asian, 0.0% American Indian and Alaska Native, 0.3% Hispanic of any race, 0.3% two or more races (2000); Density: 1,146.2 persons per square mile (2000); Age: 23.3% under 18, 21.9% over 64 (2000); Marriage status: 17.7% never married, 56.9% now married, 11.9% widowed, 13.6% divorced (2000); Foreign born: 1.2% (2000); Ancestry (includes multiple ancestries): 23.7% United States or American, 17.8% German, 11.6% Irish, 8.8% English, 6.6% Other groups (2000).

Economy: Single-family building permits issued: 9 (2001) / 11 (2000); Multi-family building permits issued: 0 (2001) / 0 (2000); Employment by occupation: 7.8% management, 15.7% professional, 16.8% services, 24.3% sales, 0.0% farming, 9.3% construction, 26.2% production (2000).

Income: Per capita income: $15,653 (2000); Median household income: $28,157 (2000); Poverty rate: 11.3% (2000).

Taxes: Total city taxes per capita: $102 (1997); City property taxes per capita: $102 (1997).

Education: High school graduation rate: 76.1% (2000); College graduation rate: 10.6% (2000).

School District(s)

Flora Community Unit School District 35 (PK-12)
2000 Enrollment: 1,540 618-662-2412

Housing: Homeownership rate: 70.9% (2000); Median home value: $52,700 (2000); Median rent: $253 per month (2000); Median age of housing: 41 years (2000).

Hospitals: Clay County Hospital (18 beds)

Newspapers: The Daily Clay County Advocate-Press (5 x week)

Transportation: Commute to work: 92.2% car, 1.0% public transportation, 2.4% walk, 3.6% work from home (2000); Travel time to work: 74.0% less than 15 minutes, 11.2% 15 to 30 minutes, 8.2% 30 to 45 minutes, 3.5% 45 to 60 minutes, 3.1% 60 minutes or more (2000)

Airports: Flora Municipal

Additional Information Contacts

Flora Chamber of Commerce 618-662-5646

INGRAHAM (unincorporated postal area, zip code 62434). Covers a land area of 30.716 square miles and a water area of 0.043 square miles. Located at 38.83° N. Lat.; 88.33° W. Long. Elevation is 490 feet.

Population: 540 (2000); Race: 100.0% White, 0.0% Black, 0.0% Asian, 0.0% American Indian and Alaska Native, 0.0% Hispanic of any race, 0.0% two or more races (2000); Density: 17.6 persons per square mile (2000); Age: 10.0% under 18, 45.0% over 64 (2000); Marriage status: 22.0% never married, 36.2% now married, 28.0% widowed, 13.8% divorced (2000); Foreign born: 0.0% (2000); Ancestry (includes multiple ancestries): 40.5% German, 16.2% United States or American, 10.2% English, 4.9% Other groups, 4.1% Irish (2000).

Economy: Employment by occupation: 11.0% management, 14.4% professional, 9.9% services, 15.5% sales, 5.5% farming, 10.5% construction, 33.1% production (2000).

Income: Per capita income: $15,245 (2000); Median household income: $30,625 (2000); Poverty rate: 8.2% (2000).

Education: High school graduation rate: 58.4% (2000); College graduation rate: 11.8% (2000).

Housing: Homeownership rate: 89.0% (2000); Median home value: $31,300 (2000); Median rent: $375 per month (2000); Median age of housing: 59 years (2000).

Transportation: Commute to work: 97.2% car, 0.0% public transportation, 2.8% walk, 0.0% work from home (2000); Travel time to work: 23.9% less than 15 minutes, 40.3% 15 to 30 minutes, 15.3% 30 to 45 minutes, 15.9% 45 to 60 minutes, 4.5% 60 minutes or more (2000)

IOLA (village). Covers a land area of 0.969 square miles and a water area of 0 square miles. Located at 38.83° N. Lat.; 88.62° W. Long. Elevation is 524 feet.

History: Incorporated 1914.

Population: 171 (2000); Race: 100.0% White, 0.0% Black, 0.0% Asian, 0.0% American Indian and Alaska Native, 0.0% Hispanic of any race, 0.0% two or more races (2000); Density: 176.6 persons per square mile (2000); Age: 35.4% under 18, 14.0% over 64 (2000); Marriage status: 28.8% never married, 59.8% now married, 6.1% widowed, 5.3% divorced (2000); Foreign born: 0.0% (2000); Ancestry (includes multiple ancestries): 39.3% United States or American, 23.0% German, 9.6% Irish, 4.5% Italian, 3.4% English (2000).

Economy: In agricultural area: wheat, corn, soybeans, cattle. Oil and natural-gas area. Employment by occupation: 0.0% management, 26.6% professional, 15.6% services, 14.1% sales, 3.1% farming, 7.8% construction, 32.8% production (2000).

Income: Per capita income: $9,631 (2000); Median household income: $27,500 (2000); Poverty rate: 17.4% (2000).

Taxes: Total city taxes per capita: $18 (1997); City property taxes per capita: $18 (1997).

Education: High school graduation rate: 58.2% (2000); College graduation rate: 2.2% (2000).

Housing: Homeownership rate: 80.3% (2000); Median home value: $31,900 (2000); Median rent: $164 per month (2000); Median age of housing: 47 years (2000).

Transportation: Commute to work: 93.3% car, 0.0% public transportation, 6.7% walk, 0.0% work from home (2000); Travel time to work: 20.0% less than 15 minutes, 20.0% 15 to 30 minutes, 45.0% 30 to 45 minutes, 15.0% 45 to 60 minutes, 0.0% 60 minutes or more (2000)

LOUISVILLE (village). Aka Louis. Covers a land area of 0.692 square miles and a water area of 0 square miles. Located at 38.77° N. Lat.; 88.50° W. Long. Elevation is 478 feet.

Population: 1,242 (2000); Race: 98.8% White, 0.0% Black, 0.2% Asian, 0.8% American Indian and Alaska Native, 0.0% Hispanic of any race, 0.2% two or more races (2000); Density: 1,794.1 persons per square mile (2000); Age: 26.4% under 18, 21.1% over 64 (2000); Marriage status: 22.6% never married, 54.2% now married, 13.0% widowed, 10.2% divorced (2000); Foreign born: 0.3% (2000); Ancestry (includes multiple ancestries): 33.9% United States or American, 15.4% German, 9.1% English, 6.9% Irish, 3.3% Other groups (2000).

Economy: In agricultural, oil, and natural gas area; corn, wheat, fruit; poultry. Employment by occupation: 11.0% management, 17.7%

professional, 14.4% services, 21.3% sales, 0.0% farming, 8.0% construction, 27.6% production (2000).
Income: Per capita income: $13,119 (2000); Median household income: $25,250 (2000); Poverty rate: 18.9% (2000).
Taxes: Total city taxes per capita: $68 (1997); City property taxes per capita: $68 (1997).
Education: High school graduation rate: 70.1% (2000); College graduation rate: 11.1% (2000).

School District(s)

North Clay C U School District 25 (PK-12)
2000 Enrollment: 687 618-665-3358

Housing: Homeownership rate: 72.0% (2000); Median home value: $46,400 (2000); Median rent: $184 per month (2000); Median age of housing: 35 years (2000).
Newspapers: Clay County Republican (1 x week)
Transportation: Commute to work: 92.8% car, 0.2% public transportation, 3.1% walk, 3.1% work from home (2000); Travel time to work: 43.1% less than 15 minutes, 31.8% 15 to 30 minutes, 12.4% 30 to 45 minutes, 9.5% 45 to 60 minutes, 3.2% 60 minutes or more (2000)

SAILOR SPRINGS (village). Covers a land area of 0.254 square miles and a water area of 0 square miles. Located at 38.76° N. Lat.; 88.36° W. Long. Elevation is 460 feet.
Population: 128 (2000); Race: 100.0% White, 0.0% Black, 0.0% Asian, 0.0% American Indian and Alaska Native, 0.0% Hispanic of any race, 0.0% two or more races (2000); Density: 504.1 persons per square mile (2000); Age: 25.4% under 18, 26.2% over 64 (2000); Marriage status: 25.2% never married, 58.9% now married, 13.1% widowed, 2.8% divorced (2000); Foreign born: 0.0% (2000); Ancestry (includes multiple ancestries): 29.2% United States or American, 20.0% German, 18.5% Irish, 10.0% Other groups, 4.6% French (except Basque) (2000).
Economy: In agricultural, oil and natural gas area. Employment by occupation: 0.0% management, 0.0% professional, 22.4% services, 18.4% sales, 0.0% farming, 6.1% construction, 53.1% production (2000).
Income: Per capita income: $12,785 (2000); Median household income: $21,563 (2000); Poverty rate: 22.3% (2000).
Taxes: Total city taxes per capita: $7 (1997); City property taxes per capita: $7 (1997).
Education: High school graduation rate: 62.2% (2000); College graduation rate: 6.7% (2000).
Housing: Homeownership rate: 100.0% (2000); Median home value: $18,800 (2000); Median age of housing: 60+ years (2000).
Transportation: Commute to work: 95.9% car, 0.0% public transportation, 0.0% walk, 4.1% work from home (2000); Travel time to work: 27.7% less than 15 minutes, 34.0% 15 to 30 minutes, 34.0% 30 to 45 minutes, 4.3% 45 to 60 minutes, 0.0% 60 minutes or more (2000)

XENIA (village). Covers a land area of 0.519 square miles and a water area of 0 square miles. Located at 38.63° N. Lat.; 88.63° W. Long. Elevation is 540 feet.
Population: 407 (2000); Race: 98.8% White, 0.0% Black, 0.0% Asian, 0.0% American Indian and Alaska Native, 2.8% Hispanic of any race, 1.3% two or more races (2000); Density: 784.8 persons per square mile (2000); Age: 20.5% under 18, 23.0% over 64 (2000); Marriage status: 16.8% never married, 60.4% now married, 9.1% widowed, 13.7% divorced (2000); Foreign born: 1.8% (2000); Ancestry (includes multiple ancestries): 27.8% German, 19.0% United States or American, 15.3% Irish, 9.5% Other groups, 8.5% English (2000).
Economy: In agricultural, oil and natural-gas area. Employment by occupation: 7.9% management, 13.6% professional, 22.5% services, 13.1% sales, 0.0% farming, 9.9% construction, 33.0% production (2000).
Income: Per capita income: $16,944 (2000); Median household income: $26,944 (2000); Poverty rate: 14.5% (2000).
Taxes: Total city taxes per capita: $28 (1997); City property taxes per capita: $28 (1997).
Education: High school graduation rate: 71.0% (2000); College graduation rate: 10.5% (2000).
Housing: Homeownership rate: 76.4% (2000); Median home value: $44,700 (2000); Median rent: $305 per month (2000); Median age of housing: 47 years (2000).
Transportation: Commute to work: 93.7% car, 1.1% public transportation, 2.1% walk, 1.6% work from home (2000); Travel time to work: 26.9% less than 15 minutes, 48.9% 15 to 30 minutes, 10.8% 30 to 45 minutes, 2.7% 45 to 60 minutes, 10.8% 60 minutes or more (2000)

Clinton County

Located in southern Illinois; bounded on the south by the Kaskaskia River. Covers a land area of 474.20 square miles, a water area of 29.20 square miles, and is located in the Central Time Zone. The county government was organized in 1824. County seat is Carlyle.

Clinton County is part of the St. Louis, MO-IL MSA. The entire metro area includes: Clinton County, IL; Jersey County, IL; Madison County, IL; Monroe County, IL; St. Clair County, IL; Crawford County, MO (pt.)**; Franklin County, MO; Jefferson County, MO; Lincoln County, MO; St. Charles County, MO; St. Louis County, MO; Warren County, MO; St. Louis city, MO

Population: 35,535 (2000); Race: 94.2% White, 4.1% Black, 0.3% Asian, 0.1% American Indian and Alaska Native, 1.6% Hispanic of any race, 0.4% two or more races (2000); Density: 74.9 persons per square mile (2000); Age: 24.9% under 18, 14.5% over 64 (2000).
Religion: Five largest groups: 56.0% Catholic Church, 4.9% Southern Baptist Convention, 4.0% Lutheran Church—Missouri Synod, 3.5% United Church of Christ, 3.5% The United Methodist Church (2000).
Economy: Unemployment rate: 5.2% (11/2002); Total civilian labor force: 16,797 (11/2002); Leading industries: 17.8% health care and social assistance; 16.3% retail trade; 14.2% manufacturing (2000); Companies that employ more than 1,000 persons: 0 (2000); Companies that employ more than 100 persons: 13 (2000); Farms: 860 totaling 233,677 acres (1997); Minority business ownership rate: 0.0% (1997); Women business ownership rate: 32.8% (1997); Retail sales per capita: $6,904 (1997). Single-family building permits issued: 93 (2001) / 81 (2000); Multi-family building permits issued: 4 (2001) / 17 (2000).
Income: Per capita income: $19,109 (2000); Median household income: $44,618 (2000); Poverty rate: 6.4% (2000); Bankruptcy rate: 4.25% (2001).
Taxes: Total county taxes per capita: $86 (2000); County property taxes per capita: $85 (2000).
Education: High school graduation rate: 77.4% (2000); College graduation rate: 13.0% (2000).
Housing: Homeownership rate: 80.3% (2000); Median home value: $83,700 (2000); Median rent: $321 per month (2000); Median age of housing: 31 years (2000).
Health: Birth rate: 103.8 per 10,000 population (1998); Age adjusted death rate: 82.5 per 10,000 population (1999); Age adjusted cancer mortality rate: 212.9 deaths per 100,000 population (1999). Number of physicians: 5.3 per 10,000 population (1999); Number of hospital beds: 16.0 per 10,000 population (1999).
Elections: 2000 Presidential election results: 41.7% Gore, 55.7% Bush, 1.9% Nader, 0.4% Buchanan
National and State Parks: Hazlet State Park; South Shore State Park
Additional Information Contacts
Clinton County Government Offices 618-594-2464
Carlyle Chamber of Commerce 618-594-4015

Clinton County Communities

ALBERS (village). Covers a land area of 0.725 square miles and a water area of 0 square miles. Located at 38.54° N. Lat.; 89.61° W. Long. Elevation is 434 feet.
Population: 878 (2000); Race: 98.2% White, 0.3% Black, 0.0% Asian, 0.0% American Indian and Alaska Native, 2.3% Hispanic of any race, 0.8% two or more races (2000); Density: 1,211.1 persons per square mile (2000); Age: 30.8% under 18, 11.7% over 64 (2000); Marriage status: 26.8% never married, 61.5% now married, 6.9% widowed, 4.8% divorced (2000); Foreign born: 0.6% (2000); Ancestry (includes multiple ancestries): 59.0% German, 8.7% Irish, 6.8% United States or American, 5.0% Other groups, 2.3% French (except Basque) (2000).
Economy: Agricultural area: poultry, dairying. Manufactures wood pallets. Coal-mining region. Single-family building permits issued: 15 (2001) / 13 (2000); Multi-family building permits issued: 0 (2001) / 0 (2000); Employment by occupation: 17.6% management, 14.1% professional, 13.6% services, 23.3% sales, 0.0% farming, 13.9% construction, 17.6% production (2000).
Income: Per capita income: $19,017 (2000); Median household income: $46,964 (2000); Poverty rate: 4.0% (2000).
Taxes: Total city taxes per capita: $42 (1997); City property taxes per capita: $35 (1997).

Education: High school graduation rate: 79.0% (2000); College graduation rate: 13.6% (2000).

School District(s)

Albers School District 63 (PK-08)
2000 Enrollment: 207 618-248-5146

Housing: Homeownership rate: 80.5% (2000); Median home value: $101,200 (2000); Median rent: $377 per month (2000); Median age of housing: 26 years (2000).

Transportation: Commute to work: 93.2% car, 0.5% public transportation, 5.2% walk, 0.5% work from home (2000); Travel time to work: 21.7% less than 15 minutes, 28.1% 15 to 30 minutes, 20.8% 30 to 45 minutes, 19.5% 45 to 60 minutes, 9.8% 60 minutes or more (2000)

AVISTON (village). Covers a land area of 1.103 square miles and a water area of 0 square miles. Located at 38.60° N. Lat.; 89.60° W. Long. Elevation is 473 feet.

Population: 1,231 (2000); Race: 98.6% White, 0.4% Black, 0.2% Asian, 0.0% American Indian and Alaska Native, 0.6% Hispanic of any race, 0.2% two or more races (2000); Density: 1,115.8 persons per square mile (2000); Age: 24.6% under 18, 17.5% over 64 (2000); Marriage status: 22.7% never married, 63.6% now married, 8.0% widowed, 5.7% divorced (2000); Foreign born: 0.5% (2000); Ancestry (includes multiple ancestries): 69.1% German, 5.0% English, 3.6% United States or American, 3.5% Irish, 2.7% Other groups (2000).

Economy: In agricultural and oil-producing area. Single-family building permits issued: 10 (2001) / 6 (2000); Multi-family building permits issued: 0 (2001) / 10 (2000); Employment by occupation: 13.1% management, 21.2% professional, 13.4% services, 25.5% sales, 0.0% farming, 12.8% construction, 14.0% production (2000).

Income: Per capita income: $20,395 (2000); Median household income: $47,917 (2000); Poverty rate: 2.8% (2000).

Taxes: Total city taxes per capita: $39 (1997); City property taxes per capita: $34 (1997).

Education: High school graduation rate: 81.5% (2000); College graduation rate: 18.7% (2000).

School District(s)

Aviston School District 21 (PK-08)
2000 Enrollment: 268 618-228-7245

Housing: Homeownership rate: 77.3% (2000); Median home value: $93,700 (2000); Median rent: $362 per month (2000); Median age of housing: 27 years (2000).

Transportation: Commute to work: 92.1% car, 0.3% public transportation, 3.5% walk, 4.1% work from home (2000); Travel time to work: 31.1% less than 15 minutes, 27.2% 15 to 30 minutes, 19.5% 30 to 45 minutes, 16.2% 45 to 60 minutes, 5.9% 60 minutes or more (2000)

BARTELSO (village). Covers a land area of 0.349 square miles and a water area of 0 square miles. Located at 38.53° N. Lat.; 89.46° W. Long. Elevation is 449 feet.

Population: 593 (2000); Race: 100.0% White, 0.0% Black, 0.0% Asian, 0.0% American Indian and Alaska Native, 0.0% Hispanic of any race, 0.0% two or more races (2000); Density: 1,699.6 persons per square mile (2000); Age: 32.3% under 18, 8.5% over 64 (2000); Marriage status: 28.0% never married, 61.6% now married, 8.6% widowed, 1.8% divorced (2000); Foreign born: 0.0% (2000); Ancestry (includes multiple ancestries): 66.0% German, 8.1% United States or American, 4.4% Irish, 1.6% French (except Basque), 1.6% Polish (2000).

Economy: In agricultural, oil-producing area. Employment by occupation: 13.1% management, 16.1% professional, 14.6% services, 17.9% sales, 0.6% farming, 14.6% construction, 23.2% production (2000).

Income: Per capita income: $16,584 (2000); Median household income: $51,944 (2000); Poverty rate: 1.3% (2000).

Taxes: Total city taxes per capita: $23 (1997); City property taxes per capita: $19 (1997).

Education: High school graduation rate: 77.6% (2000); College graduation rate: 14.1% (2000).

School District(s)

Bartelso School District 57 (KG-08)
2000 Enrollment: 184 618-765-2164

Housing: Homeownership rate: 89.4% (2000); Median home value: $80,300 (2000); Median rent: $320 per month (2000); Median age of housing: 37 years (2000).

Transportation: Commute to work: 93.2% car, 0.6% public transportation, 2.4% walk, 3.8% work from home (2000); Travel time to work: 24.2% less than 15 minutes, 38.8% 15 to 30 minutes, 18.3% 30 to 45 minutes, 10.4% 45 to 60 minutes, 8.3% 60 minutes or more (2000)

BECKEMEYER (village). Covers a land area of 0.492 square miles and a water area of 0 square miles. Located at 38.60° N. Lat.; 89.43° W. Long. Elevation is 455 feet.

Population: 1,043 (2000); Race: 99.1% White, 0.0% Black, 0.5% Asian, 0.3% American Indian and Alaska Native, 1.4% Hispanic of any race, 0.0% two or more races (2000); Density: 2,122.0 persons per square mile (2000); Age: 29.1% under 18, 15.0% over 64 (2000); Marriage status: 27.8% never married, 54.3% now married, 8.0% widowed, 9.9% divorced (2000); Foreign born: 0.5% (2000); Ancestry (includes multiple ancestries): 50.1% German, 13.1% United States or American, 11.6% Other groups, 10.7% Irish, 3.2% French (except Basque) (2000).

Economy: In agricultural area: corn, wheat, sorghum. Manufacturing: metal products, wooden pallets, zinc smelting. Single-family building permits issued: 2 (2001) / 4 (2000); Multi-family building permits issued: 2 (2001) / 0 (2000); Employment by occupation: 7.8% management, 9.7% professional, 21.9% services, 17.6% sales, 0.2% farming, 11.0% construction, 31.8% production (2000).

Income: Per capita income: $17,039 (2000); Median household income: $36,607 (2000); Poverty rate: 8.2% (2000).

Taxes: Total city taxes per capita: $43 (1997); City property taxes per capita: $34 (1997).

Education: High school graduation rate: 77.5% (2000); College graduation rate: 5.4% (2000).

Housing: Homeownership rate: 84.7% (2000); Median home value: $55,600 (2000); Median rent: $266 per month (2000); Median age of housing: 47 years (2000).

Transportation: Commute to work: 96.3% car, 0.2% public transportation, 0.4% walk, 2.0% work from home (2000); Travel time to work: 41.0% less than 15 minutes, 25.5% 15 to 30 minutes, 19.1% 30 to 45 minutes, 6.8% 45 to 60 minutes, 7.6% 60 minutes or more (2000)

BREESE (city). Covers a land area of 2.275 square miles and a water area of 0.025 square miles. Located at 38.61° N. Lat.; 89.52° W. Long. Elevation is 452 feet.

History: Breese was named for Judge Sidney Breese (1800-1876), an Illinois jurist and resident of the city. King Edward VII, then Prince of Wales, visited Breese in 1860.

Population: 4,048 (2000); Race: 99.1% White, 0.0% Black, 0.7% Asian, 0.0% American Indian and Alaska Native, 0.0% Hispanic of any race, 0.1% two or more races (2000); Density: 1,779.1 persons per square mile (2000); Age: 28.8% under 18, 15.2% over 64 (2000); Marriage status: 23.3% never married, 63.0% now married, 8.2% widowed, 5.5% divorced (2000); Foreign born: 1.0% (2000); Ancestry (includes multiple ancestries): 60.8% German, 6.5% United States or American, 5.9% Irish, 4.6% Other groups, 2.3% Dutch (2000).

Economy: Single-family building permits issued: 30 (2001) / 31 (2000); Multi-family building permits issued: 0 (2001) / 0 (2000); Employment by occupation: 11.5% management, 19.4% professional, 15.8% services, 24.3% sales, 0.2% farming, 7.1% construction, 21.6% production (2000).

Income: Per capita income: $20,530 (2000); Median household income: $47,639 (2000); Poverty rate: 3.2% (2000).

Taxes: Total city taxes per capita: $228 (1997); City property taxes per capita: $149 (1997).

Education: High school graduation rate: 82.0% (2000); College graduation rate: 20.0% (2000).

School District(s)

Breese School District 12 (PK-08)
2000 Enrollment: 676 618-526-7128

Central Community H S District 71 (09-12)
2000 Enrollment: 560 618-526-4578

Housing: Homeownership rate: 76.7% (2000); Median home value: $91,600 (2000); Median rent: $353 per month (2000); Median age of housing: 33 years (2000).

Hospitals: Saint Joseph's Hospital (85 beds)

Newspapers: The Breese Journal (1 x week)

Transportation: Commute to work: 94.2% car, 0.5% public transportation, 1.2% walk, 3.5% work from home (2000); Travel time to work: 39.8% less than 15 minutes, 21.5% 15 to 30 minutes, 15.1% 30 to 45 minutes, 7.6% 45 to 60 minutes, 16.0% 60 minutes or more (2000)

CARLYLE (city). Covers a land area of 2.993 square miles and a water area of 0.004 square miles. Located at 38.61° N. Lat.; 89.37° W. Long. Elevation is 462 feet.

History: Carlyle was sited on the location of John Hill's Fort, built in the early 1800's. Carlyle developed as the seat of Clinton County.

Population: 3,406 (2000); Race: 94.5% White, 5.2% Black, 0.2% Asian, 0.0% American Indian and Alaska Native, 1.2% Hispanic of any race, 0.2% two or more races (2000); Density: 1,137.9 persons per square mile (2000); Age: 23.4% under 18, 21.5% over 64 (2000); Marriage status: 24.6% never married, 50.8% now married, 14.9% widowed, 9.8% divorced (2000); Foreign born: 1.7% (2000); Ancestry (includes multiple ancestries): 41.6% German, 12.4% United States or American, 8.9% Other groups, 8.8% Irish, 8.3% English (2000).
Economy: Single-family building permits issued: 13 (2001) / 10 (2000); Multi-family building permits issued: 0 (2001) / 2 (2000); Employment by occupation: 7.4% management, 19.1% professional, 17.0% services, 20.1% sales, 0.6% farming, 11.1% construction, 24.7% production (2000).
Income: Per capita income: $18,744 (2000); Median household income: $36,660 (2000); Poverty rate: 6.7% (2000).
Taxes: Total city taxes per capita: $250 (1997); City property taxes per capita: $58 (1997).
Education: High school graduation rate: 76.7% (2000); College graduation rate: 12.3% (2000).

School District(s)

Carlyle C U School District 1 (PK-12)
2000 Enrollment: 1,375 618-594-8283
Clinton/Marion/Washington Roe (PK-12)
2000 Enrollment: 253 618-594-2432

Housing: Homeownership rate: 71.5% (2000); Median home value: $74,600 (2000); Median rent: $281 per month (2000); Median age of housing: 41 years (2000).
Newspapers: Union Banner (1 x week)
Transportation: Commute to work: 95.0% car, 1.0% public transportation, 1.0% walk, 1.9% work from home (2000); Travel time to work: 40.2% less than 15 minutes, 31.6% 15 to 30 minutes, 12.0% 30 to 45 minutes, 5.7% 45 to 60 minutes, 10.4% 60 minutes or more (2000)
Additional Information Contacts
Carlyle Chamber of Commerce 618-594-4015

DAMIANSVILLE (village). Covers a land area of 0.242 square miles and a water area of 0 square miles. Located at 38.51° N. Lat.; 89.62° W. Long. Elevation is 430 feet.
Population: 368 (2000); Race: 96.9% White, 0.0% Black, 1.9% Asian, 0.6% American Indian and Alaska Native, 1.9% Hispanic of any race, 0.6% two or more races (2000); Density: 1,522.8 persons per square mile (2000); Age: 25.8% under 18, 12.8% over 64 (2000); Marriage status: 22.8% never married, 63.9% now married, 5.6% widowed, 7.7% divorced (2000); Foreign born: 1.9% (2000); Ancestry (includes multiple ancestries): 63.6% German, 8.1% Irish, 8.1% Other groups, 3.3% United States or American, 2.2% Italian (2000).
Economy: Employment by occupation: 14.0% management, 21.5% professional, 14.5% services, 23.7% sales, 0.0% farming, 8.1% construction, 18.3% production (2000).
Income: Per capita income: $18,985 (2000); Median household income: $50,694 (2000); Poverty rate: 5.8% (2000).
Taxes: Total city taxes per capita: $21 (1997); City property taxes per capita: $0 (1997).
Education: High school graduation rate: 83.3% (2000); College graduation rate: 18.9% (2000).

School District(s)

Damiansville School District 62 (KG-08)
2000 Enrollment: 121 618-248-5188

Housing: Homeownership rate: 77.3% (2000); Median home value: $77,900 (2000); Median rent: $279 per month (2000); Median age of housing: 25 years (2000).
Transportation: Commute to work: 94.6% car, 1.1% public transportation, 3.8% walk, 0.5% work from home (2000); Travel time to work: 14.1% less than 15 minutes, 27.0% 15 to 30 minutes, 25.4% 30 to 45 minutes, 11.4% 45 to 60 minutes, 22.2% 60 minutes or more (2000)

GERMANTOWN (village). Covers a land area of 0.794 square miles and a water area of 0 square miles. Located at 38.55° N. Lat.; 89.53° W. Long. Elevation is 432 feet.
Population: 1,118 (2000); Race: 100.0% White, 0.0% Black, 0.0% Asian, 0.0% American Indian and Alaska Native, 1.0% Hispanic of any race, 0.0% two or more races (2000); Density: 1,408.8 persons per square mile (2000); Age: 22.3% under 18, 16.0% over 64 (2000); Marriage status: 27.4% never married, 59.1% now married, 7.4% widowed, 6.1% divorced (2000); Foreign born: 0.6% (2000); Ancestry (includes multiple ancestries): 68.9% German, 7.0% United States or American, 5.1% Irish, 1.9% French (except Basque), 1.8% English (2000).
Economy: In agricultural area. Employment by occupation: 11.3% management, 13.0% professional, 15.2% services, 24.1% sales, 0.3% farming, 14.4% construction, 21.6% production (2000).
Income: Per capita income: $21,851 (2000); Median household income: $47,614 (2000); Poverty rate: 6.0% (2000).
Taxes: Total city taxes per capita: $36 (1997); City property taxes per capita: $19 (1997).
Education: High school graduation rate: 76.8% (2000); College graduation rate: 8.5% (2000).

School District(s)

Germantown School District 60 (PK-08)
2000 Enrollment: 275 618-523-4253

Housing: Homeownership rate: 81.8% (2000); Median home value: $83,300 (2000); Median rent: $366 per month (2000); Median age of housing: 38 years (2000).
Transportation: Commute to work: 93.0% car, 0.3% public transportation, 3.4% walk, 2.8% work from home (2000); Travel time to work: 33.4% less than 15 minutes, 23.0% 15 to 30 minutes, 17.6% 30 to 45 minutes, 13.1% 45 to 60 minutes, 12.8% 60 minutes or more (2000)

HOFFMAN (village). Covers a land area of 0.362 square miles and a water area of 0 square miles. Located at 38.54° N. Lat.; 89.26° W. Long. Elevation is 457 feet.
Population: 460 (2000); Race: 99.3% White, 0.0% Black, 0.0% Asian, 0.7% American Indian and Alaska Native, 0.5% Hispanic of any race, 0.0% two or more races (2000); Density: 1,270.4 persons per square mile (2000); Age: 22.7% under 18, 17.3% over 64 (2000); Marriage status: 19.0% never married, 64.5% now married, 9.1% widowed, 7.4% divorced (2000); Foreign born: 0.2% (2000); Ancestry (includes multiple ancestries): 56.8% German, 7.7% United States or American, 7.7% English, 7.5% Irish, 7.0% Other groups (2000).
Economy: Sorghum, wheat; dairying; coal. Manufacturing of mobile power units, metal stamping. Centralia Correctional Center to East. Single-family building permits issued: 0 (2001) / 0 (2000); Multi-family building permits issued: 0 (2001) / 3 (2000); Employment by occupation: 6.9% management, 13.0% professional, 16.9% services, 30.7% sales, 0.0% farming, 4.8% construction, 27.7% production (2000).
Income: Per capita income: $19,897 (2000); Median household income: $42,115 (2000); Poverty rate: 2.5% (2000).
Taxes: Total city taxes per capita: $20 (1997); City property taxes per capita: $18 (1997).
Education: High school graduation rate: 85.2% (2000); College graduation rate: 8.2% (2000).
Housing: Homeownership rate: 78.8% (2000); Median home value: $59,600 (2000); Median rent: $338 per month (2000); Median age of housing: 28 years (2000).
Transportation: Commute to work: 94.7% car, 0.0% public transportation, 1.8% walk, 1.8% work from home (2000); Travel time to work: 36.2% less than 15 minutes, 40.2% 15 to 30 minutes, 7.1% 30 to 45 minutes, 6.3% 45 to 60 minutes, 10.3% 60 minutes or more (2000)

HUEY (village). Covers a land area of 0.165 square miles and a water area of 0 square miles. Located at 38.60° N. Lat.; 89.29° W. Long. Elevation is 454 feet.
Population: 196 (2000); Race: 100.0% White, 0.0% Black, 0.0% Asian, 0.0% American Indian and Alaska Native, 0.0% Hispanic of any race, 0.0% two or more races (2000); Density: 1,185.3 persons per square mile (2000); Age: 22.7% under 18, 7.1% over 64 (2000); Marriage status: 21.7% never married, 62.7% now married, 2.5% widowed, 13.0% divorced (2000); Foreign born: 0.0% (2000); Ancestry (includes multiple ancestries): 40.4% German, 15.2% United States or American, 13.6% English, 8.1% Other groups, 7.6% Scotch-Irish (2000).
Economy: In agricultural and oil-producing area. Single-family building permits issued: 0 (2001) / 0 (2000); Multi-family building permits issued: 0 (2001) / 0 (2000); Employment by occupation: 7.3% management, 9.7% professional, 10.5% services, 17.7% sales, 0.8% farming, 3.2% construction, 50.8% production (2000).
Income: Per capita income: $17,695 (2000); Median household income: $36,250 (2000); Poverty rate: 7.6% (2000).
Taxes: Total city taxes per capita: $24 (1997); City property taxes per capita: $14 (1997).
Education: High school graduation rate: 78.3% (2000); College graduation rate: 9.8% (2000).
Housing: Homeownership rate: 86.7% (2000); Median home value: $51,300 (2000); Median rent: $238 per month (2000); Median age of housing: 30 years (2000).

Transportation: Commute to work: 96.7% car, 0.0% public transportation, 0.0% walk, 1.7% work from home (2000); Travel time to work: 35.6% less than 15 minutes, 35.6% 15 to 30 minutes, 18.6% 30 to 45 minutes, 6.8% 45 to 60 minutes, 3.4% 60 minutes or more (2000)

KEYESPORT (village). Covers a land area of 0.403 square miles and a water area of 0.017 square miles. Located at 38.74° N. Lat.; 89.27° W. Long. Elevation is 453 feet.

Population: 481 (2000); Race: 99.2% White, 0.0% Black, 0.0% Asian, 0.0% American Indian and Alaska Native, 1.5% Hispanic of any race, 0.8% two or more races (2000); Density: 1,193.7 persons per square mile (2000); Age: 17.5% under 18, 21.8% over 64 (2000); Marriage status: 13.3% never married, 61.4% now married, 12.1% widowed, 13.3% divorced (2000); Foreign born: 0.4% (2000); Ancestry (includes multiple ancestries): 27.2% German, 24.5% United States or American, 11.4% Irish, 7.7% Other groups, 5.8% English (2000).

Economy: Employment by occupation: 11.1% management, 11.1% professional, 17.2% services, 18.7% sales, 0.0% farming, 18.7% construction, 23.2% production (2000).

Income: Per capita income: $14,028 (2000); Median household income: $22,679 (2000); Poverty rate: 17.0% (2000).

Taxes: Total city taxes per capita: $43 (1997); City property taxes per capita: $41 (1997).

Education: High school graduation rate: 62.8% (2000); College graduation rate: 6.3% (2000).

Housing: Homeownership rate: 68.7% (2000); Median home value: $40,000 (2000); Median rent: $275 per month (2000); Median age of housing: 27 years (2000).

Transportation: Commute to work: 88.8% car, 0.0% public transportation, 4.6% walk, 3.6% work from home (2000); Travel time to work: 18.5% less than 15 minutes, 30.2% 15 to 30 minutes, 16.9% 30 to 45 minutes, 15.3% 45 to 60 minutes, 19.0% 60 minutes or more (2000)

NEW BADEN (village). Covers a land area of 1.337 square miles and a water area of 0 square miles. Located at 38.53° N. Lat.; 89.70° W. Long. Elevation is 462 feet.

Population: 3,001 (2000); Race: 96.5% White, 1.2% Black, 0.7% Asian, 0.2% American Indian and Alaska Native, 1.4% Hispanic of any race, 0.8% two or more races (2000); Density: 2,245.4 persons per square mile (2000); Age: 26.5% under 18, 12.9% over 64 (2000); Marriage status: 26.3% never married, 58.5% now married, 7.1% widowed, 8.2% divorced (2000); Foreign born: 1.7% (2000); Ancestry (includes multiple ancestries): 46.7% German, 12.0% Irish, 9.6% United States or American, 9.0% English, 7.9% Other groups (2000).

Economy: Single-family building permits issued: 10 (2001) / 11 (2000); Multi-family building permits issued: 0 (2001) / 0 (2000); Employment by occupation: 11.7% management, 17.5% professional, 18.4% services, 25.8% sales, 1.4% farming, 9.7% construction, 15.5% production (2000).

Income: Per capita income: $19,268 (2000); Median household income: $45,859 (2000); Poverty rate: 5.8% (2000).

Taxes: Total city taxes per capita: $142 (1997); City property taxes per capita: $90 (1997).

Education: High school graduation rate: 81.3% (2000); College graduation rate: 17.8% (2000).

Housing: Homeownership rate: 75.0% (2000); Median home value: $83,700 (2000); Median rent: $364 per month (2000); Median age of housing: 31 years (2000).

Newspapers: Clinton County News (2 x week)

Transportation: Commute to work: 93.2% car, 2.1% public transportation, 2.2% walk, 0.7% work from home (2000); Travel time to work: 23.9% less than 15 minutes, 34.7% 15 to 30 minutes, 24.6% 30 to 45 minutes, 8.9% 45 to 60 minutes, 8.0% 60 minutes or more (2000)

SHATTUC (unincorporated postal area, zip code 62283). Covers a land area of 45.974 square miles and a water area of 0.009 square miles. Located at 38.64° N. Lat.; 89.20° W. Long. Elevation is 477 feet.

Population: 721 (2000); Race: 99.0% White, 0.0% Black, 0.0% Asian, 1.0% American Indian and Alaska Native, 0.0% Hispanic of any race, 0.0% two or more races (2000); Density: 15.7 persons per square mile (2000); Age: 26.8% under 18, 20.2% over 64 (2000); Marriage status: 18.5% never married, 63.3% now married, 6.9% widowed, 11.2% divorced (2000); Foreign born: 0.0% (2000); Ancestry (includes multiple ancestries): 57.0% German, 18.3% United States or American, 11.7% English, 10.0% Italian, 3.2% Irish (2000).

Economy: Employment by occupation: 6.8% management, 15.3% professional, 9.1% services, 26.8% sales, 1.5% farming, 20.6% construction, 19.8% production (2000).

Income: Per capita income: $15,889 (2000); Median household income: $35,694 (2000); Poverty rate: 13.6% (2000).

Education: High school graduation rate: 83.1% (2000); College graduation rate: 8.5% (2000).

Housing: Homeownership rate: 84.2% (2000); Median home value: $63,800 (2000); Median rent: $313 per month (2000); Median age of housing: 39 years (2000).

Transportation: Commute to work: 94.3% car, 0.0% public transportation, 0.0% walk, 5.7% work from home (2000); Travel time to work: 16.4% less than 15 minutes, 36.2% 15 to 30 minutes, 31.9% 30 to 45 minutes, 11.7% 45 to 60 minutes, 3.7% 60 minutes or more (2000)

TRENTON (city). Covers a land area of 0.983 square miles and a water area of 0 square miles. Located at 38.60° N. Lat.; 89.68° W. Long. Elevation is 497 feet.

History: Incorporated 1865.

Population: 2,610 (2000); Race: 99.4% White, 0.0% Black, 0.1% Asian, 0.2% American Indian and Alaska Native, 2.0% Hispanic of any race, 0.2% two or more races (2000); Density: 2,656.1 persons per square mile (2000); Age: 25.0% under 18, 15.7% over 64 (2000); Marriage status: 21.5% never married, 61.4% now married, 9.0% widowed, 8.1% divorced (2000); Foreign born: 1.3% (2000); Ancestry (includes multiple ancestries): 51.6% German, 14.6% Irish, 13.6% English, 7.2% Other groups, 5.6% United States or American (2000).

Economy: In agricultural region: corn, wheat; livestock, poultry. Single-family building permits issued: 13 (2001) / 6 (2000); Multi-family building permits issued: 2 (2001) / 2 (2000); Employment by occupation: 12.0% management, 22.9% professional, 13.3% services, 28.6% sales, 0.4% farming, 7.4% construction, 15.4% production (2000).

Income: Per capita income: $21,393 (2000); Median household income: $48,095 (2000); Poverty rate: 6.2% (2000).

Taxes: Total city taxes per capita: $312 (1997); City property taxes per capita: $72 (1997).

Education: High school graduation rate: 88.7% (2000); College graduation rate: 24.6% (2000).

School District(s)

Wesclin C U School District 3 (PK-12)
2000 Enrollment: 1,388 618-224-7583

Housing: Homeownership rate: 79.3% (2000); Median home value: $89,100 (2000); Median rent: $394 per month (2000); Median age of housing: 38 years (2000).

Newspapers: The Trenton Sun (1 x week)

Transportation: Commute to work: 93.9% car, 0.4% public transportation, 1.5% walk, 3.4% work from home (2000); Travel time to work: 29.0% less than 15 minutes, 27.1% 15 to 30 minutes, 20.3% 30 to 45 minutes, 15.4% 45 to 60 minutes, 8.1% 60 minutes or more (2000)

Coles County

Located in east central Illinois; drained by the Kaskaskia, Embarrass, and Little Wabash Rivers; includes Paradise Lake. Covers a land area of 508.30 square miles, a water area of 1.80 square miles, and is located in the Central Time Zone. The county government was organized in 1830. County seat is Charleston.

Weather Station: Charleston — Elevation: 679 feet

	Jan	Feb	Mar	Apr	May	Jun	Jul	Aug	Sep	Oct	Nov	Dec
High	35	41	52	65	75	83	86	84	78	67	52	40
Low	19	23	33	43	53	62	66	64	57	45	35	25
Precip	2.2	2.4	3.4	4.1	4.2	3.7	4.5	3.3	3.1	3.2	3.8	3.2
Snow	9.3	4.1	2.7	0.2	tr	0.0	0.0	0.0	0.0	tr	1.6	4.2

High and Low temperatures in degrees Fahrenheit; Precipitation and Snow in inches

Weather Station: Mattoon — Elevation: 715 feet

	Jan	Feb	Mar	Apr	May	Jun	Jul	Aug	Sep	Oct	Nov	Dec
High	33	39	51	63	74	83	87	85	79	66	51	39
Low	17	22	32	42	53	62	66	64	56	44	34	23
Precip	2.0	2.0	3.1	4.0	3.9	4.1	4.1	3.1	3.1	3.0	3.7	2.7
Snow	6.9	3.4	1.9	0.1	tr	0.0	0.0	0.0	0.0	tr	1.0	4.4

High and Low temperatures in degrees Fahrenheit; Precipitation and Snow in inches

Population: 53,196 (2000); Race: 95.4% White, 2.5% Black, 0.7% Asian, 0.2% American Indian and Alaska Native, 1.2% Hispanic of any race, 0.9% two or more races (2000); Density: 104.7 persons per square mile (2000); Age: 19.7% under 18, 13.3% over 64 (2000).

Religion: Five largest groups: 6.2% Catholic Church, 5.8% Christian Churches and Churches of Christ, 4.9% The United Methodist Church, 3.8% Lutheran Church—Missouri Synod, 3.7% Southern Baptist Convention (2000).
Economy: Unemployment rate: 5.3% (11/2002); Total civilian labor force: 26,757 (11/2002); Leading industries: 27.3% manufacturing; 14.5% health care and social assistance; 14.2% retail trade (2000); Companies that employ more than 1,000 persons: 2 (2000); Companies that employ more than 100 persons: 34 (2000); Farms: 681 totaling 256,974 acres (1997); Minority business ownership rate: 0.0% (1997); Women business ownership rate: 24.1% (1997); Retail sales per capita: $10,099 (1997). Single-family building permits issued: 39 (2001) / 38 (2000); Multi-family building permits issued: 76 (2001) / 63 (2000).
Income: Per capita income: $17,370 (2000); Median household income: $32,286 (2000); Poverty rate: 17.5% (2000); Bankruptcy rate: 7.68% (2001).
Taxes: Total county taxes per capita: $91 (1997); County property taxes per capita: $90 (1997).
Education: High school graduation rate: 82.9% (2000); College graduation rate: 20.8% (2000).
Housing: Homeownership rate: 61.9% (2000); Median home value: $71,500 (2000); Median rent: $351 per month (2000); Median age of housing: 37 years (2000).
Health: Birth rate: 110.4 per 10,000 population (1998); Age adjusted death rate: 93.8 per 10,000 population (1999); Age adjusted cancer mortality rate: 231.1 deaths per 100,000 population (1999). Number of physicians: 15.6 per 10,000 population (1999); Number of hospital beds: 25.9 per 10,000 population (1999).
Elections: 2000 Presidential election results: 44.3% Gore, 52.2% Bush, 2.5% Nader, 0.6% Buchanan
National and State Parks: Fox Ridge State Park; Lincoln Log Cabin State Historic Site
Additional Information Contacts
Coles County Government Offices 217-348-0501
Charleston Chamber of Commerce 217-345-7041
Mattoon Chamber of Commerce 217-235-5661
Oakland Chamber of Commerce 217-346-2341

Coles County Communities

ASHMORE (village). Covers a land area of 0.834 square miles and a water area of 0 square miles. Located at 39.53° N. Lat.; 88.02° W. Long. Elevation is 696 feet.
Population: 809 (2000); Race: 98.3% White, 0.0% Black, 0.0% Asian, 0.0% American Indian and Alaska Native, 0.6% Hispanic of any race, 0.9% two or more races (2000); Density: 970.4 persons per square mile (2000); Age: 25.2% under 18, 11.3% over 64 (2000); Marriage status: 20.3% never married, 61.9% now married, 7.3% widowed, 10.5% divorced (2000); Foreign born: 0.7% (2000); Ancestry (includes multiple ancestries): 19.3% United States or American, 15.5% German, 13.4% Irish, 8.3% Other groups, 7.9% English (2000).
Economy: In rich agricultural area: corn, soybeans, sorghum; oil. Single-family building permits issued: 0 (2001) / 2 (2000); Multi-family building permits issued: 0 (2001) / 0 (2000); Employment by occupation: 8.1% management, 10.6% professional, 16.6% services, 27.2% sales, 3.3% farming, 10.8% construction, 23.4% production (2000).
Income: Per capita income: $14,886 (2000); Median household income: $38,250 (2000); Poverty rate: 9.4% (2000).
Taxes: Total city taxes per capita: $23 (1997); City property taxes per capita: $14 (1997).
Education: High school graduation rate: 81.2% (2000); College graduation rate: 12.2% (2000).
Housing: Homeownership rate: 80.1% (2000); Median home value: $58,900 (2000); Median rent: $316 per month (2000); Median age of housing: 31 years (2000).
Transportation: Commute to work: 95.1% car, 0.0% public transportation, 2.6% walk, 1.8% work from home (2000); Travel time to work: 29.5% less than 15 minutes, 44.5% 15 to 30 minutes, 20.8% 30 to 45 minutes, 2.6% 45 to 60 minutes, 2.6% 60 minutes or more (2000)

CHARLESTON (city). Covers a land area of 7.993 square miles and a water area of 0.680 square miles. Located at 39.48° N. Lat.; 88.17° W. Long. Elevation is 686 feet.
History: Charleston was the site of the fourth Lincoln-Douglas debate in 1858, when 12,000 people gathered to hear Abraham Lincoln state his views on equality of all people.
Population: 21,039 (2000); Race: 92.7% White, 4.6% Black, 1.0% Asian, 0.3% American Indian and Alaska Native, 1.6% Hispanic of any race, 1.1% two or more races (2000); Density: 2,632.2 persons per square mile (2000); Age: 14.0% under 18, 9.8% over 64 (2000); Marriage status: 55.2% never married, 32.8% now married, 4.9% widowed, 7.0% divorced (2000); Foreign born: 2.2% (2000); Ancestry (includes multiple ancestries): 27.9% German, 17.1% Irish, 11.1% English, 10.3% Other groups, 7.0% United States or American (2000).
Vital Statistics: Birth rate: 87.0 per 10,000 population (1998)
Economy: Single-family building permits issued: 19 (2001) / 16 (2000); Multi-family building permits issued: 76 (2001) / 63 (2000); Employment by occupation: 8.8% management, 24.0% professional, 23.1% services, 27.3% sales, 0.1% farming, 5.7% construction, 10.9% production (2000).
Income: Per capita income: $14,522 (2000); Median household income: $24,140 (2000); Poverty rate: 30.1% (2000).
Taxes: Total city taxes per capita: $185 (1997); City property taxes per capita: $129 (1997).
Education: High school graduation rate: 83.9% (2000); College graduation rate: 33.1% (2000).

School District(s)
Charleston C U School District 1 (PK-12)
2000 Enrollment: 3,017 217-345-2106

Four-year College(s)
Eastern Illinois University (Public)
2001 Enrollment: 10,531 217-581-5000
2001 Tuition: In-state $2,993; Out-of-state $8,978
Housing: Homeownership rate: 45.9% (2000); Median home value: $80,100 (2000); Median rent: $361 per month (2000); Median age of housing: 31 years (2000).
Newspapers: Times-Courier (6 x week); The Daily Eastern News (5 x week)
Transportation: Commute to work: 79.3% car, 0.5% public transportation, 16.2% walk, 2.0% work from home (2000); Travel time to work: 64.5% less than 15 minutes, 25.4% 15 to 30 minutes, 4.9% 30 to 45 minutes, 1.6% 45 to 60 minutes, 3.6% 60 minutes or more (2000)
Airports: Coles County Memorial
Additional Information Contacts
Charleston Chamber of Commerce 217-345-7041

HUMBOLDT (village). Covers a land area of 0.562 square miles and a water area of 0 square miles. Located at 39.60° N. Lat.; 88.32° W. Long. Elevation is 664 feet.
Population: 481 (2000); Race: 98.2% White, 0.0% Black, 0.0% Asian, 0.0% American Indian and Alaska Native, 1.6% Hispanic of any race, 0.4% two or more races (2000); Density: 856.2 persons per square mile (2000); Age: 32.9% under 18, 10.9% over 64 (2000); Marriage status: 20.2% never married, 64.5% now married, 7.4% widowed, 8.0% divorced (2000); Foreign born: 0.8% (2000); Ancestry (includes multiple ancestries): 40.5% United States or American, 15.2% Irish, 11.5% German, 11.5% English, 6.2% Other groups (2000).
Economy: In rich agricultural area. Employment by occupation: 2.2% management, 8.9% professional, 13.3% services, 20.9% sales, 0.0% farming, 9.3% construction, 45.3% production (2000).
Income: Per capita income: $16,244 (2000); Median household income: $39,375 (2000); Poverty rate: 6.7% (2000).
Taxes: Total city taxes per capita: $22 (1997); City property taxes per capita: $15 (1997).
Education: High school graduation rate: 83.8% (2000); College graduation rate: 6.1% (2000).
Housing: Homeownership rate: 87.1% (2000); Median home value: $54,100 (2000); Median rent: $338 per month (2000); Median age of housing: 41 years (2000).
Transportation: Commute to work: 97.7% car, 0.0% public transportation, 0.9% walk, 1.4% work from home (2000); Travel time to work: 27.5% less than 15 minutes, 48.6% 15 to 30 minutes, 20.6% 30 to 45 minutes, 2.3% 45 to 60 minutes, 0.9% 60 minutes or more (2000)

LERNA (village). Covers a land area of 0.117 square miles and a water area of 0 square miles. Located at 39.41° N. Lat.; 88.28° W. Long. Elevation is 754 feet.
Population: 322 (2000); Race: 100.0% White, 0.0% Black, 0.0% Asian, 0.0% American Indian and Alaska Native, 0.0% Hispanic of any race, 0.0% two or more races (2000); Density: 2,761.1 persons per square mile (2000); Age: 22.7% under 18, 10.6% over 64 (2000); Marriage status: 22.3% never married, 54.9% now married, 9.2% widowed, 13.6% divorced (2000); Foreign born: 0.0% (2000); Ancestry (includes multiple ancestries): 32.3%

United States or American, 9.9% English, 9.6% German, 5.9% Irish, 3.1% Other groups (2000).
Economy: In rich agricultural area. Employment by occupation: 9.3% management, 11.0% professional, 9.9% services, 32.6% sales, 0.0% farming, 11.0% construction, 26.2% production (2000).
Income: Per capita income: $19,596 (2000); Median household income: $32,292 (2000); Poverty rate: 2.5% (2000).
Taxes: Total city taxes per capita: $23 (1997); City property taxes per capita: $23 (1997).
Education: High school graduation rate: 73.0% (2000); College graduation rate: 6.0% (2000).
Housing: Homeownership rate: 81.3% (2000); Median home value: $47,500 (2000); Median rent: $238 per month (2000); Median age of housing: 42 years (2000).
Transportation: Commute to work: 98.8% car, 0.0% public transportation, 1.2% walk, 0.0% work from home (2000); Travel time to work: 26.0% less than 15 minutes, 59.8% 15 to 30 minutes, 8.9% 30 to 45 minutes, 0.0% 45 to 60 minutes, 5.3% 60 minutes or more (2000)

MATTOON (city). Covers a land area of 9.309 square miles and a water area of 0.004 square miles. Located at 39.47° N. Lat.; 88.37° W. Long. Elevation is 726 feet.
History: Mattoon was named for William Mattoon of the Illinois Central Railroad. The town was established in the early 1850's as a railroad station and shipping center.
Population: 18,291 (2000); Race: 96.7% White, 1.5% Black, 0.4% Asian, 0.2% American Indian and Alaska Native, 1.0% Hispanic of any race, 0.8% two or more races (2000); Density: 1,964.8 persons per square mile (2000); Age: 22.1% under 18, 18.0% over 64 (2000); Marriage status: 25.8% never married, 52.0% now married, 9.2% widowed, 13.0% divorced (2000); Foreign born: 1.3% (2000); Ancestry (includes multiple ancestries): 20.6% German, 15.9% United States or American, 12.4% Irish, 11.7% English, 8.6% Other groups (2000).
Vital Statistics: Birth rate: 149.8 per 10,000 population (1998)
Economy: Single-family building permits issued: 20 (2001) / 20 (2000); Multi-family building permits issued: 0 (2001) / 0 (2000); Employment by occupation: 7.0% management, 12.4% professional, 17.0% services, 25.6% sales, 0.4% farming, 10.5% construction, 27.0% production (2000).
Income: Per capita income: $18,186 (2000); Median household income: $31,800 (2000); Poverty rate: 13.4% (2000).
Taxes: Total city taxes per capita: $219 (1997); City property taxes per capita: $129 (1997).
Education: High school graduation rate: 80.0% (2000); College graduation rate: 13.3% (2000).

School District(s)

Eastern Ill Area of Special Education (PK-12)
2000 Enrollment: 537 217-235-0551
Mattoon C U School District 2 (PK-12)
2000 Enrollment: 3,493 217-235-5446

Two-year College(s)

Lake Land College (Public)
2001 Enrollment: 6,102 217-234-5253
2001 Tuition: In-state $2,822; Out-of-state $6,675

Housing: Homeownership rate: 62.1% (2000); Median home value: $65,000 (2000); Median rent: $343 per month (2000); Median age of housing: 47 years (2000).
Hospitals: Sarah Bush Lincoln Health Center (202 beds)
Newspapers: Mattoon Journal Gazette (6 x week)
Transportation: Commute to work: 95.1% car, 0.5% public transportation, 1.3% walk, 1.9% work from home (2000); Travel time to work: 60.5% less than 15 minutes, 26.4% 15 to 30 minutes, 8.4% 30 to 45 minutes, 2.2% 45 to 60 minutes, 2.5% 60 minutes or more (2000); Amtrak: Service available.
Airports: Coles County Memorial
Additional Information Contacts
Mattoon Chamber of Commerce 217-235-5661

OAKLAND (city). Covers a land area of 0.819 square miles and a water area of 0.043 square miles. Located at 39.65° N. Lat.; 88.02° W. Long. Elevation is 656 feet.
History: Incorporated 1855.
Population: 996 (2000); Race: 98.5% White, 0.0% Black, 0.3% Asian, 0.2% American Indian and Alaska Native, 0.5% Hispanic of any race, 0.8% two or more races (2000); Density: 1,215.8 persons per square mile (2000); Age: 25.9% under 18, 17.5% over 64 (2000); Marriage status: 16.8% never married, 60.9% now married, 10.0% widowed, 12.3% divorced (2000); Foreign born: 1.5% (2000); Ancestry (includes multiple ancestries): 15.7% German, 14.3% United States or American, 14.2% Irish, 13.6% English, 4.5% Other groups (2000).
Economy: In rich agricultural area: corn, wheat, soybeans; livestock. Single-family building permits issued: 0 (2001) / 0 (2000); Multi-family building permits issued: 0 (2001) / 0 (2000); Employment by occupation: 8.5% management, 13.0% professional, 13.4% services, 21.3% sales, 1.3% farming, 11.1% construction, 31.3% production (2000).
Income: Per capita income: $15,964 (2000); Median household income: $34,038 (2000); Poverty rate: 10.8% (2000).
Taxes: Total city taxes per capita: $70 (1997); City property taxes per capita: $70 (1997).
Education: High school graduation rate: 82.7% (2000); College graduation rate: 15.3% (2000).

School District(s)

Oakland C U School District 5 (KG-12)
2000 Enrollment: 447 217-346-2555

Housing: Homeownership rate: 81.9% (2000); Median home value: $53,800 (2000); Median rent: $279 per month (2000); Median age of housing: 47 years (2000).
Transportation: Commute to work: 97.1% car, 0.0% public transportation, 1.1% walk, 1.8% work from home (2000); Travel time to work: 26.3% less than 15 minutes, 32.8% 15 to 30 minutes, 27.7% 30 to 45 minutes, 7.1% 45 to 60 minutes, 6.0% 60 minutes or more (2000)
Additional Information Contacts
Oakland Chamber of Commerce 217-346-2341

TRILLA (unincorporated postal area, zip code 62469). Covers a land area of 19.320 square miles and a water area of 0.023 square miles. Located at 39.35° N. Lat.; 88.33° W. Long. Elevation is 656 feet.
Population: 322 (2000); Race: 100.0% White, 0.0% Black, 0.0% Asian, 0.0% American Indian and Alaska Native, 0.0% Hispanic of any race, 0.0% two or more races (2000); Density: 16.7 persons per square mile (2000); Age: 28.0% under 18, 20.8% over 64 (2000); Marriage status: 19.0% never married, 66.7% now married, 5.0% widowed, 9.3% divorced (2000); Foreign born: 0.0% (2000); Ancestry (includes multiple ancestries): 36.1% German, 19.1% United States or American, 11.6% Irish, 10.0% Other groups, 7.3% Slovak (2000).
Economy: Employment by occupation: 9.3% management, 16.7% professional, 5.6% services, 34.6% sales, 0.0% farming, 14.8% construction, 19.1% production (2000).
Income: Per capita income: $13,517 (2000); Median household income: $40,375 (2000); Poverty rate: 3.8% (2000).
Education: High school graduation rate: 82.6% (2000); College graduation rate: 14.0% (2000).
Housing: Homeownership rate: 89.4% (2000); Median home value: $81,300 (2000); Median rent: $350 per month (2000); Median age of housing: 39 years (2000).
Transportation: Commute to work: 100.0% car, 0.0% public transportation, 0.0% walk, 0.0% work from home (2000); Travel time to work: 21.0% less than 15 minutes, 69.1% 15 to 30 minutes, 6.2% 30 to 45 minutes, 0.0% 45 to 60 minutes, 3.7% 60 minutes or more (2000)

Cook County

Located in northeastern Illinois; bounded on the east by Lake Michigan and Indiana; crossed by the Chicago and Des Plaines Rivers. Covers a land area of 945.70 square miles, a water area of 689.40 square miles, and is located in the Central Time Zone. The county government was organized in 1831. County seat is Chicago.

Cook County is part of the Chicago, IL PMSA. The entire metro area includes: Cook County; DeKalb County; DuPage County; Grundy County; Kane County; Kendall County; Lake County; McHenry County; Will County

Weather Station: Chicago Midway Airport — Elevation: 610 feet

	Jan	Feb	Mar	Apr	May	Jun	Jul	Aug	Sep	Oct	Nov	Dec
High	30	36	47	59	71	81	85	83	75	63	48	36
Low	16	21	30	40	51	61	66	65	57	45	34	23
Precip	1.9	1.8	2.9	3.9	3.8	4.2	3.8	3.9	3.5	2.9	3.3	2.7
Snow	13.0	10.2	6.6	1.8	tr	0.0	tr	0.0	tr	0.1	2.4	8.7

High and Low temperatures in degrees Fahrenheit; Precipitation and Snow in inches

Weather Station: Chicago O'Hare Int'l Airport — Elevation: 656 feet

	Jan	Feb	Mar	Apr	May	Jun	Jul	Aug	Sep	Oct	Nov	Dec
High	30	35	46	58	70	80	84	82	75	63	48	35
Low	14	19	29	38	48	58	64	63	54	42	32	21
Precip	1.7	1.6	2.7	3.7	3.5	3.7	3.5	4.6	3.4	2.8	3.0	2.4
Snow	11.1	8.1	6.4	1.8	tr	tr	tr	tr	0.0	0.3	1.8	7.8

High and Low temperatures in degrees Fahrenheit; Precipitation and Snow in inches

Weather Station: Chicago University — Elevation: 593 feet

	Jan	Feb	Mar	Apr	May	Jun	Jul	Aug	Sep	Oct	Nov	Dec
High	31	36	47	59	70	80	85	83	76	64	49	37
Low	18	22	32	42	51	61	67	66	58	47	36	24
Precip	1.9	1.7	3.1	3.7	3.5	4.2	3.5	4.1	3.4	2.8	3.5	2.9
Snow	na	na	na	na	na	na	na	na	na	na	na	na

High and Low temperatures in degrees Fahrenheit; Precipitation and Snow in inches

Weather Station: Park Forest — Elevation: 708 feet

	Jan	Feb	Mar	Apr	May	Jun	Jul	Aug	Sep	Oct	Nov	Dec
High	29	35	45	58	70	80	84	82	75	63	48	35
Low	13	18	28	38	49	59	64	62	54	42	32	20
Precip	1.8	1.6	2.8	3.9	4.2	4.6	4.2	3.9	3.3	2.8	3.4	2.5
Snow	10.6	7.6	4.7	1.0	tr	0.0	0.0	0.0	0.0	0.2	1.0	5.7

High and Low temperatures in degrees Fahrenheit; Precipitation and Snow in inches

Population: 5,376,741 (2000); Race: 56.3% White, 26.0% Black, 4.9% Asian, 0.3% American Indian and Alaska Native, 19.9% Hispanic of any race, 2.6% two or more races (2000); Density: 5,685.6 persons per square mile (2000); Age: 25.9% under 18, 11.7% over 64 (2000).

Religion: Five largest groups: 39.9% Catholic Church, 4.3% Jewish estimate, 1.7% Muslim estimate, 1.1% Lutheran Church—Missouri Synod, 1.1% Evangelical Lutheran Church in America (2000).

Economy: Unemployment rate: 7.0% (11/2002); Total civilian labor force: 2,632,464 (11/2002); Leading industries: 13.3% manufacturing; 11.6% health care and social assistance; 9.7% retail trade (2000); Companies that employ more than 1,000 persons: 178 (2000); Companies that employ more than 100 persons: 4,317 (2000); Farms: 237 totaling 39,410 acres (1997); Minority business ownership rate: 20.1% (1997); Women business ownership rate: 26.4% (1997); Retail sales per capita: $8,199 (1997). Single-family building permits issued: 5,339 (2001) / 5,369 (2000); Multi-family building permits issued: 7,754 (2001) / 6,508 (2000).

Income: Per capita income: $23,227 (2000); Median household income: $45,922 (2000); Poverty rate: 13.5% (2000); Bankruptcy rate: 6.50% (2001).

Taxes: Total county taxes per capita: $244 (2000); County property taxes per capita: $146 (2000).

Education: High school graduation rate: 77.7% (2000); College graduation rate: 28.0% (2000).

Housing: Homeownership rate: 57.9% (2000); Median home value: $157,700 (2000); Median rent: $582 per month (2000); Median age of housing: 44 years (2000).

Health: Birth rate: 159.8 per 10,000 population (1998); Age adjusted death rate: 95.4 per 10,000 population (1999); Infant mortality rate: 9.7 per 1,000 live births (1998); Age adjusted cancer mortality rate: 221.3 deaths per 100,000 population (1999). Air Quality Index: 62% good, 38% moderate, <1% unhealthy (percent of days in 2000). Number of physicians: 35.2 per 10,000 population (1999); Number of hospital beds: 38.7 per 10,000 population (1999).

Elections: 2000 Presidential election results: 68.6% Gore, 28.7% Bush, 2.3% Nader, 0.2% Buchanan

National and State Parks: Chicago Portage National Historic Site; Illinois and Michigan Canal State Trail

Additional Information Contacts

Cook County Government Offices........ 312-603-5500
African American Chamber of Commerce 773-238-3840
Alsip Chamber of Commerce........ 708-597-2668
Andersonville Chamber of Commerce........ 773-728-2995
Argo-Summit Chamber of Commerce........ 708-458-3033
Arlington Heights Chamber of Commerce 847-253-1703
Barrington Chamber of Commerce 847-381-2525
Bellwood Chamber of Commerce 708-547-5030
Blue Island Area Chamber of Commerce 708-388-1000
Bridgeview Chamber of Commerce........ 708-598-1700
Broadview Chamber of Commerce 708-345-3011
Brookfield Chamber of Commerce 708-485-1434
Burbank Chamber of Commerce 708-425-4668
Business & Economic Revitalization........ 773-783-2636
Calumet City Chamber of Commerce 708-891-5888
Chicago Area Gay & Lesbian 773-871-4190
Chicago Association of Realtors 312-803-4900
Chicago Avenue Business 312-733-4002
Chicago Chamber of Commerce 312-938-9050
Chicago Convention & Visitors Bureau........ 312-943-5399
Chicago Southland Convention & Visitors Bureau 708-895-8200
Cicero Chamber of Commerce........ 708-652-4990
Cook County Chamber of Commerce 708-531-1117
Des Plaines Chamber of Commerce........ 847-824-4200
Dolton Chamber of Commerce 708-841-4810
Evergreen Park Chamber of Commerce........ 708-423-1118
Forest Park Chamber of Commerce........ 708-366-2543
Franklin Park Chamber of Commerce 847-455-3350
Fullerton Avenue Chamber 773-489-3222
German American Chamber of Commerce 312-644-2662
Glencoe Chamber of Commerce 847-835-3333
Glenview Chamber of Commerce 847-724-0900
Greater North Pulaski Development Corp. 773-384-7074
Greater Palatine Chamber of Commerce 847-359-7200
Greater Woodfield Convention & Visitors Bureau 847-605-1010
Hazel Crest Chamber of Commerce........ 708-335-4699
Hegewisch Chamber of Commerce 773-646-6880
Hickory Hills Chamber of Commerce 708-598-4800
Hillside Chamber of Commerce........ 708-449-2449
Hoffman Estates Chamber of Commerce........ 847-781-9100
Homewood Chamber of Commerce........ 708-957-6950
Italian American Chamber of Commerce 312-553-9137
Lake View East Chamber of Commerce 773-348-8608
Lansing Chamber of Commerce........ 708-474-4170
Latin American Chamber of Commerce 773-252-5211
Lemont Chamber of Commerce........ 630-257-5997
Lincolnwood Chamber of Commerce 847-679-5760
Matteson Chamber of Commerce........ 708-747-6000
Maywood Chamber of Commerce 708-345-7077
Melrose Park Chamber of Commerce 708-338-1007
Midlothian Chamber of Commerce 708-389-0020
Mont Clare-Elmwood Park Chamber........ 708-456-8000
Montrose Kedzie Chamber of Commerce 773-583-1611
Morton Grove Chamber of Commerce 847-965-0330
Mt Prospect Chamber of Commerce 847-398-6616
Near NW Chamber of Chicago 312-850-9013
Niles Chamber of Commerce........ 847-966-7606
North Shore-Barrington Association of Realtors........ 847-480-7177
Northbrook Chamber of Commerce........ 847-498-5555
Northcenter Development Corp. 773-525-1539
Northfield Chamber of Commerce........ 847-441-6113
Northlake Chamber of Commerce 708-562-3110
Northwest Association of Realtors........ 847-956-8440
Oak Forest Chamber of Commerce 708-687-4600
Oak Lawn Chamber of Commerce........ 708-424-8300
Oak Park Board of Realtors 708-386-0150
Oak Park Chamber of Commerce 708-848-8151
Oak Park Visitors Center 708-848-1500
Orland Park Chamber of Commerce 708-349-2972
Park Ridge Chamber of Commerce 847-825-3121
Portgage Park Chamber of Commerce........ 773-777-2020
Prospect Heights Convention Bureau........ 847-577-3666
Puerto Rico Convention Bureau........ 312-840-8090
Riverdale Chamber of Commerce 708-841-3311
Rolling Meadows Chamber of Commerce........ 847-398-3730
Rosemont Chamber of Commerce........ 847-698-1190
Rosemont Convention Bureau 847-823-2100
Schiller Park Chamber of Commerce........ 847-671-3040
Skokie Chamber of Commerce 847-673-0240
South Chicago Chamber of Commerce 773-768-1221
South Shore Chamber Inc. 773-643-1652
Stoney Island Chamber of Commerce 773-734-0626
Streamwood Chamber of Commerce 630-837-5200
Tinley Park Chamber of Commerce........ 708-532-5700
U S Mexico Chamber of Commerce 312-781-7342
West Lawn Chamber of Commerce........ 773-735-7690
West Suburban Chamber of Commerce........ 708-352-0494
West Towns Board of Realtors 708-863-1111
Wilmette Chamber of Commerce........ 847-251-3800
Winnetka Chamber of Commerce 847-446-4451

Cook County Communities

ALSIP (village). Covers a land area of 6.366 square miles and a water area of 0.159 square miles. Located at 41.67° N. Lat.; 87.73° W. Long. Elevation is 600 feet.
Population: 19,725 (2000); Race: 81.9% White, 10.5% Black, 1.5% Asian, 0.3% American Indian and Alaska Native, 8.9% Hispanic of any race, 2.9% two or more races (2000); Density: 3,098.5 persons per square mile (2000); Age: 27.0% under 18, 11.5% over 64 (2000); Marriage status: 30.1% never married, 52.7% now married, 7.6% widowed, 9.6% divorced (2000); Foreign born: 8.9% (2000); Ancestry (includes multiple ancestries): 24.2% Irish, 20.7% German, 20.1% Other groups, 17.3% Polish, 11.8% Italian (2000).
Vital Statistics: Birth rate: 156.7 per 10,000 population (1998)
Economy: Manufactures fixtures, brick presses, metal products, consumer goods, medical equipment. Single-family building permits issued: 2 (2001) / 0 (2000); Multi-family building permits issued: 20 (2001) / 2 (2000); Employment by occupation: 11.0% management, 14.1% professional, 12.9% services, 32.2% sales, 0.1% farming, 13.0% construction, 16.7% production (2000).
Income: Per capita income: $20,498 (2000); Median household income: $47,963 (2000); Poverty rate: 6.6% (2000).
Taxes: Total city taxes per capita: $374 (1997); City property taxes per capita: $167 (1997).
Education: High school graduation rate: 84.2% (2000); College graduation rate: 13.7% (2000).

School District(s)

Alsip-Hazlgrn-Oaklwn S District 126 (PK-08)
2000 Enrollment: 1,739 708-389-1900
Atwood Heights District 125 (PK-08)
2000 Enrollment: 730 708-371-0080

Housing: Homeownership rate: 64.2% (2000); Median home value: $141,200 (2000); Median rent: $601 per month (2000); Median age of housing: 28 years (2000).
Transportation: Commute to work: 89.5% car, 6.7% public transportation, 1.2% walk, 1.7% work from home (2000); Travel time to work: 22.7% less than 15 minutes, 28.2% 15 to 30 minutes, 20.6% 30 to 45 minutes, 13.2% 45 to 60 minutes, 15.2% 60 minutes or more (2000)
Additional Information Contacts
Alsip Chamber of Commerce 708-597-2668

ARLINGTON HEIGHTS (village). Covers a land area of 16.410 square miles and a water area of 0.031 square miles. Located at 42.09° N. Lat.; 87.98° W. Long. Elevation is 700 feet.
History: Arlington Heights was settled in the 1830's. The Arlington Park Race Track opened here in 1929, drawing many visitors from Chicago.
Population: 76,031 (2000); Race: 90.1% White, 1.0% Black, 6.1% Asian, 0.1% American Indian and Alaska Native, 4.3% Hispanic of any race, 1.3% two or more races (2000); Density: 4,633.3 persons per square mile (2000); Age: 23.1% under 18, 15.8% over 64 (2000); Marriage status: 22.0% never married, 62.6% now married, 7.6% widowed, 7.8% divorced (2000); Foreign born: 13.9% (2000); Ancestry (includes multiple ancestries): 27.5% German, 19.2% Irish, 14.5% Polish, 12.0% Other groups, 11.1% Italian (2000).
Vital Statistics: Birth rate: 125.1 per 10,000 population (1998)
Economy: Unemployment rate: 4.3% (11/2002); Total civilian labor force: 44,088 (11/2002); Single-family building permits issued: 33 (2001) / 56 (2000); Multi-family building permits issued: 6 (2001) / 258 (2000); Employment by occupation: 23.5% management, 27.0% professional, 7.5% services, 29.8% sales, 0.0% farming, 4.8% construction, 7.3% production (2000).
Income: Per capita income: $33,544 (2000); Median household income: $67,807 (2000); Poverty rate: 2.5% (2000).
Taxes: Total city taxes per capita: $546 (2000); City property taxes per capita: $410 (2000).
Education: High school graduation rate: 92.7% (2000); College graduation rate: 46.5% (2000).

School District(s)

Arlington Heights School District 25 (PK-08)
2000 Enrollment: 4,899 847-758-4900
Comm Cons School District 59 (PK-08)
2000 Enrollment: 6,501 847-593-4300
Township High School District 214 (09-12)
2000 Enrollment: 11,667 847-718-7600

Housing: Homeownership rate: 76.7% (2000); Median home value: $240,600 (2000); Median rent: $876 per month (2000); Median age of housing: 30 years (2000).
Hospitals: Northwest Community Hospital (400 beds)
Newspapers: Arlington Heights Post (1 x week); Palatine Countryside (1 x week); Daily Herald (7 x week); Elk Grove Times (1 x week); Schaumburg Review (1 x week); Rolling Meadows Review (1 x week); Hoffman Estates Review (1 x week); Lake Zurich Courier (1 x week); Buffalo Grove Countryside (1 x week); Algonquin Countryside (1 x week); Wheeling Countryside (1 x week)
Transportation: Commute to work: 86.3% car, 7.8% public transportation, 1.7% walk, 3.7% work from home (2000); Travel time to work: 22.5% less than 15 minutes, 34.1% 15 to 30 minutes, 22.3% 30 to 45 minutes, 9.4% 45 to 60 minutes, 11.7% 60 minutes or more (2000)
Additional Information Contacts
Arlington Heights Chamber of Commerce 847-253-1703
Northwest Association of Realtors 847-956-8440
Prospect Heights Convention Bureau 847-577-3666

BARRINGTON (village). Covers a land area of 4.597 square miles and a water area of 0.171 square miles. Located at 42.15° N. Lat.; 88.13° W. Long. Elevation is 830 feet.
History: Barrington was founded in the 1850's and developed as an agricultural community.
Population: 10,168 (2000); Race: 94.8% White, 1.1% Black, 1.3% Asian, 0.3% American Indian and Alaska Native, 3.1% Hispanic of any race, 1.7% two or more races (2000); Density: 2,211.7 persons per square mile (2000); Age: 29.9% under 18, 13.7% over 64 (2000); Marriage status: 20.2% never married, 65.6% now married, 6.4% widowed, 7.9% divorced (2000); Foreign born: 6.6% (2000); Ancestry (includes multiple ancestries): 28.5% German, 23.3% Irish, 12.2% English, 8.7% Italian, 8.0% Polish (2000).
Economy: Single-family building permits issued: 13 (2001) / 2 (2000); Multi-family building permits issued: 0 (2001) / 30 (2000); Employment by occupation: 28.8% management, 26.3% professional, 6.6% services, 30.5% sales, 0.0% farming, 3.7% construction, 4.1% production (2000).
Income: Per capita income: $43,942 (2000); Median household income: $83,085 (2000); Poverty rate: 3.1% (2000).
Taxes: Total city taxes per capita: $238 (1997); City property taxes per capita: $219 (1997).
Education: High school graduation rate: 94.5% (2000); College graduation rate: 58.2% (2000).

School District(s)

Barrington C U School District 220 (PK-12)
2000 Enrollment: 8,399 847-381-6300

Housing: Homeownership rate: 78.3% (2000); Median home value: $329,900 (2000); Median rent: $839 per month (2000); Median age of housing: 35 years (2000).
Hospitals: Advocate Good Shephard Hospital (154 beds)
Newspapers: Cary-Grove Countryside (1 x week); Barrington Courier-Review (1 x week)
Transportation: Commute to work: 78.7% car, 9.6% public transportation, 2.4% walk, 8.6% work from home (2000); Travel time to work: 25.6% less than 15 minutes, 26.4% 15 to 30 minutes, 22.7% 30 to 45 minutes, 8.7% 45 to 60 minutes, 16.6% 60 minutes or more (2000)
Additional Information Contacts
Barrington Chamber of Commerce 847-381-2525

BARRINGTON HILLS (village). Covers a land area of 27.879 square miles and a water area of 0.520 square miles. Located at 42.14° N. Lat.; 88.20° W. Long. Elevation is 850 feet.
Population: 3,915 (2000); Race: 96.5% White, 0.5% Black, 0.6% Asian, 0.7% American Indian and Alaska Native, 2.4% Hispanic of any race, 1.2% two or more races (2000); Density: 140.4 persons per square mile (2000); Age: 25.8% under 18, 11.9% over 64 (2000); Marriage status: 18.8% never married, 76.0% now married, 1.8% widowed, 3.4% divorced (2000); Foreign born: 5.1% (2000); Ancestry (includes multiple ancestries): 28.9% German, 20.4% Irish, 17.5% Italian, 14.2% English, 6.5% Other groups (2000).
Economy: Single-family building permits issued: 21 (2001) / 36 (2000); Multi-family building permits issued: 0 (2001) / 0 (2000); Employment by occupation: 34.2% management, 25.5% professional, 6.0% services, 27.3% sales, 0.5% farming, 2.1% construction, 4.4% production (2000).
Income: Per capita income: $73,629 (2000); Median household income: $145,330 (2000); Poverty rate: 3.1% (2000).
Taxes: Total city taxes per capita: $627 (1997); City property taxes per capita: $407 (1997).
Education: High school graduation rate: 96.0% (2000); College graduation rate: 67.8% (2000).

Housing: Homeownership rate: 94.7% (2000); Median home value: $661,500 (2000); Median rent: $1,375 per month (2000); Median age of housing: 31 years (2000).
Transportation: Commute to work: 77.2% car, 9.8% public transportation, 0.3% walk, 11.7% work from home (2000); Travel time to work: 24.8% less than 15 minutes, 28.2% 15 to 30 minutes, 15.0% 30 to 45 minutes, 9.5% 45 to 60 minutes, 22.4% 60 minutes or more (2000)

BEDFORD PARK (village). Covers a land area of 5.965 square miles and a water area of 0.109 square miles. Located at 41.76° N. Lat.; 87.78° W. Long. Elevation is 612 feet.
Population: 574 (2000); Race: 100.0% White, 0.0% Black, 0.0% Asian, 0.0% American Indian and Alaska Native, 5.3% Hispanic of any race, 0.0% two or more races (2000); Density: 96.2 persons per square mile (2000); Age: 19.4% under 18, 13.9% over 64 (2000); Marriage status: 22.9% never married, 62.4% now married, 8.1% widowed, 6.6% divorced (2000); Foreign born: 4.6% (2000); Ancestry (includes multiple ancestries): 26.2% Irish, 24.9% German, 19.6% Polish, 13.5% Italian, 8.4% English (2000).
Economy: Industrial area. Manufacturing: electronic equipment, paper products, fabricated metal, furniture, bookbinding, film processing, lubricants and oils, machinery, chemicals, cosmetics, commercial printing. Single-family building permits issued: 0 (2001) / 0 (2000); Multi-family building permits issued: 0 (2001) / 0 (2000); Employment by occupation: 15.7% management, 15.7% professional, 13.8% services, 26.9% sales, 0.0% farming, 17.9% construction, 9.9% production (2000).
Income: Per capita income: $22,887 (2000); Median household income: $49,722 (2000); Poverty rate: 2.1% (2000).
Taxes: Total city taxes per capita: $24,570 (1997); City property taxes per capita: $22,270 (1997).
Education: High school graduation rate: 83.9% (2000); College graduation rate: 14.4% (2000).
Housing: Homeownership rate: 90.6% (2000); Median home value: $135,400 (2000); Median rent: $444 per month (2000); Median age of housing: 57 years (2000).
Transportation: Commute to work: 90.0% car, 4.2% public transportation, 5.8% walk, 0.0% work from home (2000); Travel time to work: 37.7% less than 15 minutes, 27.1% 15 to 30 minutes, 21.3% 30 to 45 minutes, 5.8% 45 to 60 minutes, 8.1% 60 minutes or more (2000)

BELLWOOD (village). Covers a land area of 2.386 square miles and a water area of 0 square miles. Located at 41.88° N. Lat.; 87.87° W. Long. Elevation is 630 feet.
History: Incorporated 1900.
Population: 20,535 (2000); Race: 11.9% White, 82.0% Black, 0.2% Asian, 0.4% American Indian and Alaska Native, 8.2% Hispanic of any race, 1.6% two or more races (2000); Density: 8,608.0 persons per square mile (2000); Age: 30.4% under 18, 7.8% over 64 (2000); Marriage status: 36.5% never married, 48.1% now married, 6.0% widowed, 9.4% divorced (2000); Foreign born: 6.1% (2000); Ancestry (includes multiple ancestries): 79.6% Other groups, 3.2% German, 1.9% Italian, 1.8% Irish, 1.7% African (2000).
Vital Statistics: Birth rate: 168.0 per 10,000 population (1998)
Economy: Manufacturing includes consumer goods, brass items, printing, paper products, adhesives and concrete products. Single-family building permits issued: 0 (2001) / 2 (2000); Multi-family building permits issued: 0 (2001) / 0 (2000); Employment by occupation: 8.0% management, 12.0% professional, 13.4% services, 34.6% sales, 0.0% farming, 6.0% construction, 26.0% production (2000).
Income: Per capita income: $19,420 (2000); Median household income: $52,856 (2000); Poverty rate: 7.2% (2000).
Taxes: Total city taxes per capita: $369 (1997); City property taxes per capita: $252 (1997).
Education: High school graduation rate: 76.8% (2000); College graduation rate: 11.9% (2000).

School District(s)

Bellwood School District 88 (PK-08)
2000 Enrollment: 3,277 708-344-9344
Housing: Homeownership rate: 76.3% (2000); Median home value: $116,300 (2000); Median rent: $604 per month (2000); Median age of housing: 45 years (2000).
Transportation: Commute to work: 86.8% car, 9.2% public transportation, 1.3% walk, 2.2% work from home (2000); Travel time to work: 17.1% less than 15 minutes, 36.0% 15 to 30 minutes, 27.6% 30 to 45 minutes, 9.7% 45 to 60 minutes, 9.6% 60 minutes or more (2000)
Additional Information Contacts
Bellwood Chamber of Commerce 708-547-5030

BERKELEY (village). Covers a land area of 1.393 square miles and a water area of 0 square miles. Located at 41.88° N. Lat.; 87.91° W. Long. Elevation is 670 feet.
Population: 5,245 (2000); Race: 60.4% White, 27.7% Black, 3.9% Asian, 0.2% American Indian and Alaska Native, 15.8% Hispanic of any race, 1.0% two or more races (2000); Density: 3,765.4 persons per square mile (2000); Age: 25.6% under 18, 14.3% over 64 (2000); Marriage status: 25.7% never married, 58.0% now married, 8.3% widowed, 8.0% divorced (2000); Foreign born: 13.4% (2000); Ancestry (includes multiple ancestries): 45.2% Other groups, 13.9% German, 13.7% Irish, 10.5% Italian, 6.0% English (2000).
Economy: Suburb of Chicago. Single-family building permits issued: 0 (2001) / 0 (2000); Multi-family building permits issued: 0 (2001) / 0 (2000); Employment by occupation: 9.8% management, 17.2% professional, 10.4% services, 33.6% sales, 0.0% farming, 8.0% construction, 21.0% production (2000).
Income: Per capita income: $24,334 (2000); Median household income: $58,984 (2000); Poverty rate: 6.4% (2000).
Taxes: Total city taxes per capita: $478 (1997); City property taxes per capita: $356 (1997).
Education: High school graduation rate: 82.1% (2000); College graduation rate: 19.5% (2000).

School District(s)

Berkeley School District 87 (PK-08)
2000 Enrollment: 2,623 708-547-3050
Housing: Homeownership rate: 85.8% (2000); Median home value: $138,000 (2000); Median rent: $674 per month (2000); Median age of housing: 44 years (2000).
Transportation: Commute to work: 89.4% car, 5.3% public transportation, 2.7% walk, 2.5% work from home (2000); Travel time to work: 22.0% less than 15 minutes, 37.4% 15 to 30 minutes, 20.9% 30 to 45 minutes, 10.1% 45 to 60 minutes, 9.5% 60 minutes or more (2000)

BERWYN (city). Covers a land area of 3.893 square miles and a water area of 0 square miles. Located at 41.84° N. Lat.; 87.79° W. Long. Elevation is 610 feet.
History: Berwyn was organized in 1890 by Charles E. Piper and Wilbur J. Andrews, realtors who felt that a town would be populated if they built it. Berwyn was incorporated as a village in 1891 and chartered as a city in 1908. It grew as a residential suburb, with many of the people employed in neighboring Cicero, where the Western Electric Company had a plant.
Population: 54,016 (2000); Race: 73.8% White, 1.4% Black, 2.4% Asian, 0.4% American Indian and Alaska Native, 38.0% Hispanic of any race, 3.6% two or more races (2000); Density: 13,876.2 persons per square mile (2000); Age: 26.0% under 18, 13.5% over 64 (2000); Marriage status: 31.1% never married, 51.4% now married, 8.1% widowed, 9.4% divorced (2000); Foreign born: 25.1% (2000); Ancestry (includes multiple ancestries): 39.4% Other groups, 12.0% Polish, 11.8% German, 11.1% Irish, 10.4% Italian (2000).
Vital Statistics: Birth rate: 149.2 per 10,000 population (1998)
Economy: Unemployment rate: 7.1% (11/2002); Total civilian labor force: 22,286 (11/2002); Single-family building permits issued: 3 (2001) / 2 (2000); Multi-family building permits issued: 4 (2001) / 46 (2000); Employment by occupation: 10.3% management, 15.9% professional, 14.1% services, 30.0% sales, 0.0% farming, 9.6% construction, 20.1% production (2000).
Income: Per capita income: $19,113 (2000); Median household income: $43,833 (2000); Poverty rate: 7.9% (2000).
Taxes: Total city taxes per capita: $445 (2000); City property taxes per capita: $333 (2000).
Education: High school graduation rate: 74.6% (2000); College graduation rate: 17.2% (2000).

School District(s)

Berwyn North School District 98 (PK-08)
2000 Enrollment: 2,696 708-484-6200
Berwyn South School District 100 (PK-08)
2000 Enrollment: 3,074 708-795-2300
Housing: Homeownership rate: 61.6% (2000); Median home value: $132,900 (2000); Median rent: $545 per month (2000); Median age of housing: 60 years (2000).
Hospitals: MacNeal Hospital (427 beds)
Newspapers: Cicero Life (2 x week); Berwyn-Stickney-Forest View Life (3 x week)
Transportation: Commute to work: 83.7% car, 10.8% public transportation, 3.2% walk, 1.6% work from home (2000); Travel time to work: 17.8% less than 15 minutes, 28.8% 15 to 30 minutes, 27.5% 30 to 45 minutes, 15.3% 45 to 60 minutes, 10.6% 60 minutes or more (2000)

BLUE ISLAND (city). Covers a land area of 4.030 square miles and a water area of 0.095 square miles. Located at 41.65° N. Lat.; 87.67° W. Long. Elevation is 635 feet.
History: Blue Island was named because it looked like an island surrounded by marshes, and a blue haze often hung over its woods. Settlers first came in 1835, and the village was laid out in 1872. Many of the early residents were of German and Italian ancestry.
Population: 23,463 (2000); Race: 53.9% White, 22.3% Black, 0.2% Asian, 0.3% American Indian and Alaska Native, 39.7% Hispanic of any race, 3.4% two or more races (2000); Density: 5,822.4 persons per square mile (2000); Age: 30.3% under 18, 9.7% over 64 (2000); Marriage status: 35.5% never married, 48.5% now married, 6.2% widowed, 9.9% divorced (2000); Foreign born: 22.1% (2000); Ancestry (includes multiple ancestries): 57.4% Other groups, 11.7% German, 10.4% Irish, 6.7% Polish, 6.6% Italian (2000).
Vital Statistics: Birth rate: 191.4 per 10,000 population (1998)
Economy: Single-family building permits issued: 30 (2001) / 11 (2000); Multi-family building permits issued: 0 (2001) / 31 (2000); Employment by occupation: 7.0% management, 12.2% professional, 18.0% services, 27.2% sales, 0.0% farming, 12.5% construction, 23.0% production (2000).
Income: Per capita income: $16,156 (2000); Median household income: $36,520 (2000); Poverty rate: 13.3% (2000).
Taxes: Total city taxes per capita: $225 (1997); City property taxes per capita: $170 (1997).
Education: High school graduation rate: 66.0% (2000); College graduation rate: 11.7% (2000).

School District(s)

Cook County School District 130 (PK-08)
2000 Enrollment: 3,737 708-385-6800

Housing: Homeownership rate: 54.4% (2000); Median home value: $99,400 (2000); Median rent: $521 per month (2000); Median age of housing: 46 years (2000).
Hospitals: Saint Francis Hospital & Health Center (410 beds)
Transportation: Commute to work: 80.8% car, 12.6% public transportation, 4.8% walk, 1.0% work from home (2000); Travel time to work: 23.7% less than 15 minutes, 28.2% 15 to 30 minutes, 18.9% 30 to 45 minutes, 11.9% 45 to 60 minutes, 17.3% 60 minutes or more (2000)

Additional Information Contacts

Blue Island Area Chamber of Commerce 708-388-1000

BRIDGEVIEW (village). Covers a land area of 4.126 square miles and a water area of 0 square miles. Located at 41.74° N. Lat.; 87.80° W. Long. Elevation is 620 feet.
History: Incorporated 1947.
Population: 15,335 (2000); Race: 87.5% White, 0.6% Black, 2.5% Asian, 0.1% American Indian and Alaska Native, 9.5% Hispanic of any race, 5.8% two or more races (2000); Density: 3,716.5 persons per square mile (2000); Age: 24.9% under 18, 14.8% over 64 (2000); Marriage status: 25.1% never married, 54.3% now married, 11.0% widowed, 9.6% divorced (2000); Foreign born: 18.9% (2000); Ancestry (includes multiple ancestries): 25.7% Polish, 17.2% Irish, 15.1% German, 13.2% Other groups, 9.0% Italian (2000).
Vital Statistics: Birth rate: 146.7 per 10,000 population (1998)
Economy: Single-family building permits issued: 16 (2001) / 14 (2000); Multi-family building permits issued: 0 (2001) / 9 (2000); Employment by occupation: 8.2% management, 10.2% professional, 13.5% services, 32.7% sales, 0.1% farming, 13.2% construction, 22.1% production (2000).
Income: Per capita income: $18,802 (2000); Median household income: $42,073 (2000); Poverty rate: 7.2% (2000).
Taxes: Total city taxes per capita: $259 (1997); City property taxes per capita: $234 (1997).
Education: High school graduation rate: 72.8% (2000); College graduation rate: 9.1% (2000).
Housing: Homeownership rate: 75.1% (2000); Median home value: $144,600 (2000); Median rent: $628 per month (2000); Median age of housing: 30 years (2000).
Transportation: Commute to work: 90.4% car, 4.4% public transportation, 2.9% walk, 1.8% work from home (2000); Travel time to work: 26.2% less than 15 minutes, 29.8% 15 to 30 minutes, 22.2% 30 to 45 minutes, 8.6% 45 to 60 minutes, 13.2% 60 minutes or more (2000)

Additional Information Contacts

Bridgeview Chamber of Commerce. 708-598-1700

BROADVIEW (village). Covers a land area of 1.779 square miles and a water area of 0 square miles. Located at 41.85° N. Lat.; 87.85° W. Long. Elevation is 628 feet.
History: Broadview was incorporated as a village in 1910, and developed as a residential community.
Population: 8,264 (2000); Race: 21.7% White, 74.3% Black, 1.1% Asian, 0.0% American Indian and Alaska Native, 2.9% Hispanic of any race, 1.5% two or more races (2000); Density: 4,644.9 persons per square mile (2000); Age: 24.7% under 18, 10.7% over 64 (2000); Marriage status: 30.9% never married, 48.0% now married, 7.8% widowed, 13.3% divorced (2000); Foreign born: 3.9% (2000); Ancestry (includes multiple ancestries): 70.4% Other groups, 6.7% German, 3.8% Irish, 3.5% Polish, 2.7% Italian (2000).
Economy: Single-family building permits issued: 0 (2001) / 0 (2000); Multi-family building permits issued: 0 (2001) / 0 (2000); Employment by occupation: 15.1% management, 15.3% professional, 13.2% services, 34.1% sales, 0.0% farming, 3.8% construction, 18.6% production (2000).
Income: Per capita income: $22,178 (2000); Median household income: $47,651 (2000); Poverty rate: 6.4% (2000).
Taxes: Total city taxes per capita: $969 (1997); City property taxes per capita: $597 (1997).
Education: High school graduation rate: 83.0% (2000); College graduation rate: 16.6% (2000).

School District(s)

Lindop School District 92 (KG-08)
2000 Enrollment: 473 708-345-3110

Housing: Homeownership rate: 69.9% (2000); Median home value: $122,800 (2000); Median rent: $572 per month (2000); Median age of housing: 45 years (2000).
Transportation: Commute to work: 85.8% car, 8.8% public transportation, 2.2% walk, 1.8% work from home (2000); Travel time to work: 17.4% less than 15 minutes, 35.1% 15 to 30 minutes, 27.7% 30 to 45 minutes, 10.6% 45 to 60 minutes, 9.2% 60 minutes or more (2000)

Additional Information Contacts

Broadview Chamber of Commerce 708-345-3011

BROOKFIELD (village). Covers a land area of 3.052 square miles and a water area of 0.004 square miles. Located at 41.82° N. Lat.; 87.84° W. Long. Elevation is 620 feet.
History: Incorporated 1893.
Population: 19,085 (2000); Race: 93.5% White, 1.4% Black, 1.2% Asian, 0.1% American Indian and Alaska Native, 8.4% Hispanic of any race, 1.0% two or more races (2000); Density: 6,252.4 persons per square mile (2000); Age: 23.9% under 18, 15.1% over 64 (2000); Marriage status: 25.4% never married, 55.9% now married, 9.1% widowed, 9.6% divorced (2000); Foreign born: 9.2% (2000); Ancestry (includes multiple ancestries): 23.2% German, 20.1% Irish, 18.0% Polish, 13.0% Italian, 11.1% Other groups (2000).
Vital Statistics: Birth rate: 123.7 per 10,000 population (1998)
Economy: Manufacturing of fabricated metal, especially aluminum products. The noted Chicago Zoological Park (Brookfield Zoo) is here. Single-family building permits issued: 2 (2001) / 3 (2000); Multi-family building permits issued: 0 (2001) / 12 (2000); Employment by occupation: 14.0% management, 22.3% professional, 9.8% services, 33.0% sales, 0.0% farming, 8.7% construction, 12.2% production (2000).
Income: Per capita income: $24,307 (2000); Median household income: $52,636 (2000); Poverty rate: 4.3% (2000).
Taxes: Total city taxes per capita: $296 (1997); City property taxes per capita: $224 (1997).
Education: High school graduation rate: 87.7% (2000); College graduation rate: 26.0% (2000).

School District(s)

Brookfield School District 95 (PK-08)
2000 Enrollment: 958 708-485-0606

Housing: Homeownership rate: 74.6% (2000); Median home value: $151,600 (2000); Median rent: $678 per month (2000); Median age of housing: 50 years (2000).
Transportation: Commute to work: 84.3% car, 9.1% public transportation, 2.3% walk, 3.8% work from home (2000); Travel time to work: 24.9% less than 15 minutes, 31.7% 15 to 30 minutes, 23.0% 30 to 45 minutes, 10.7% 45 to 60 minutes, 9.7% 60 minutes or more (2000)

Additional Information Contacts

Brookfield Chamber of Commerce 708-485-1434

BURBANK (city). Aka South Stickney. Covers a land area of 4.173 square miles and a water area of 0 square miles. Located at 41.74° N. Lat.; 87.77° W. Long. Elevation is 622 feet.
Population: 27,902 (2000); Race: 91.1% White, 0.2% Black, 1.9% Asian, 0.3% American Indian and Alaska Native, 11.3% Hispanic of any race, 2.7% two or more races (2000); Density: 6,686.7 persons per square mile (2000); Age: 24.8% under 18, 14.1% over 64 (2000); Marriage status: 28.4% never

married, 55.1% now married, 9.1% widowed, 7.5% divorced (2000); Foreign born: 21.8% (2000); Ancestry (includes multiple ancestries): 30.3% Polish, 18.7% Irish, 16.1% German, 13.4% Other groups, 9.3% Italian (2000).
Vital Statistics: Birth rate: 115.8 per 10,000 population (1998)
Economy: Manufacturing of packaging control systems; printing. Unemployment rate: 6.0% (11/2002); Total civilian labor force: 14,534 (11/2002); Single-family building permits issued: 54 (2001) / 48 (2000); Multi-family building permits issued: 0 (2001) / 18 (2000); Employment by occupation: 8.5% management, 8.3% professional, 15.1% services, 30.5% sales, 0.0% farming, 12.2% construction, 25.4% production (2000).
Income: Per capita income: $18,923 (2000); Median household income: $49,388 (2000); Poverty rate: 5.1% (2000).
Taxes: Total city taxes per capita: $304 (1997); City property taxes per capita: $197 (1997).
Education: High school graduation rate: 73.6% (2000); College graduation rate: 9.3% (2000).

School District(s)

A E R O Special Education Coop (PK-12)
2000 Enrollment: 193 708-496-3330
Burbank School District 111 (PK-08)
2000 Enrollment: 3,201 708-496-0500
Reavis Township H S District 220 (09-12)
2000 Enrollment: 1,610 708-599-7200
Housing: Homeownership rate: 82.8% (2000); Median home value: $137,800 (2000); Median rent: $629 per month (2000); Median age of housing: 38 years (2000).
Transportation: Commute to work: 90.4% car, 5.6% public transportation, 2.0% walk, 0.9% work from home (2000); Travel time to work: 22.2% less than 15 minutes, 30.4% 15 to 30 minutes, 23.4% 30 to 45 minutes, 11.2% 45 to 60 minutes, 12.8% 60 minutes or more (2000)
Additional Information Contacts
Burbank Chamber of Commerce 708-425-4668

BURNHAM (village). Covers a land area of 1.858 square miles and a water area of 0.093 square miles. Located at 41.63° N. Lat.; 87.55° W. Long. Elevation is 585 feet.
Population: 4,170 (2000); Race: 34.5% White, 53.2% Black, 0.9% Asian, 0.3% American Indian and Alaska Native, 15.2% Hispanic of any race, 2.2% two or more races (2000); Density: 2,244.8 persons per square mile (2000); Age: 27.9% under 18, 11.9% over 64 (2000); Marriage status: 28.0% never married, 50.1% now married, 8.5% widowed, 13.4% divorced (2000); Foreign born: 6.8% (2000); Ancestry (includes multiple ancestries): 66.2% Other groups, 12.8% Polish, 5.7% Irish, 4.5% German, 2.8% Italian (2000).
Economy: Oil refining. Manufacturing of lubrication oils. Single-family building permits issued: 5 (2001) / 7 (2000); Multi-family building permits issued: 0 (2001) / 0 (2000); Employment by occupation: 10.3% management, 13.6% professional, 16.7% services, 30.1% sales, 0.2% farming, 10.4% construction, 18.6% production (2000).
Income: Per capita income: $16,747 (2000); Median household income: $39,053 (2000); Poverty rate: 9.8% (2000).
Taxes: Total city taxes per capita: $455 (1997); City property taxes per capita: $340 (1997).
Education: High school graduation rate: 74.5% (2000); College graduation rate: 12.4% (2000).

School District(s)

Burnham School District 154-5 (PK-08)
2000 Enrollment: 199 708-862-8636
Housing: Homeownership rate: 74.3% (2000); Median home value: $90,400 (2000); Median rent: $554 per month (2000); Median age of housing: 36 years (2000).
Transportation: Commute to work: 86.1% car, 12.8% public transportation, 0.6% walk, 0.1% work from home (2000); Travel time to work: 15.4% less than 15 minutes, 27.9% 15 to 30 minutes, 22.4% 30 to 45 minutes, 11.6% 45 to 60 minutes, 22.8% 60 minutes or more (2000)

CALUMET CITY (city). Covers a land area of 7.265 square miles and a water area of 0.117 square miles. Located at 41.61° N. Lat.; 87.54° W. Long. Elevation is 589 feet.
History: Calumet City was platted in 1833, and developed in the 1920's as a residential outgrowth of Hammond, Indiana. Calumet is the French name for the Indian peace-pipe.
Population: 39,071 (2000); Race: 39.6% White, 52.6% Black, 0.7% Asian, 0.1% American Indian and Alaska Native, 10.9% Hispanic of any race, 1.8% two or more races (2000); Density: 5,378.0 persons per square mile (2000); Age: 28.9% under 18, 12.8% over 64 (2000); Marriage status: 31.7% never married, 47.6% now married, 9.0% widowed, 11.7% divorced (2000); Foreign born: 7.3% (2000); Ancestry (includes multiple ancestries): 58.6% Other groups, 12.7% Polish, 6.5% German, 5.1% Irish, 3.8% Italian (2000).
Vital Statistics: Birth rate: 132.3 per 10,000 population (1998)
Economy: Unemployment rate: 9.2% (11/2002); Total civilian labor force: 18,908 (11/2002); Single-family building permits issued: 40 (2001) / 14 (2000); Multi-family building permits issued: 0 (2001) / 0 (2000); Employment by occupation: 9.5% management, 15.1% professional, 14.0% services, 32.7% sales, 0.1% farming, 8.9% construction, 19.7% production (2000).
Income: Per capita income: $18,123 (2000); Median household income: $38,902 (2000); Poverty rate: 12.2% (2000).
Taxes: Total city taxes per capita: $432 (2000); City property taxes per capita: $246 (2000).
Education: High school graduation rate: 80.7% (2000); College graduation rate: 13.9% (2000).

School District(s)

Calumet City School District 155 (KG-08)
2000 Enrollment: 1,158 708-862-7665
Dolton School District 149 (PK-08)
2000 Enrollment: 3,908 708-868-7861
Hoover-Schrum Memorial SD 157 (PK-08)
2000 Enrollment: 805 708-868-7500
Lincoln Elementary School District 156 (PK-08)
2000 Enrollment: 893 708-862-6625
Thornton Fractional T H S D 215 (09-12)
2000 Enrollment: 2,593 708-585-2309
Housing: Homeownership rate: 63.2% (2000); Median home value: $90,300 (2000); Median rent: $552 per month (2000); Median age of housing: 35 years (2000).
Transportation: Commute to work: 85.1% car, 10.9% public transportation, 2.3% walk, 0.8% work from home (2000); Travel time to work: 18.3% less than 15 minutes, 25.4% 15 to 30 minutes, 23.1% 30 to 45 minutes, 11.8% 45 to 60 minutes, 21.4% 60 minutes or more (2000)
Additional Information Contacts
Calumet City Chamber of Commerce 708-891-5888

CALUMET PARK (village). Covers a land area of 1.107 square miles and a water area of 0.039 square miles. Located at 41.66° N. Lat.; 87.65° W. Long. Elevation is 604 feet.
History: Incorporated 1912; name changed from Burr Oak in 1925.
Population: 8,516 (2000); Race: 10.8% White, 84.0% Black, 0.0% Asian, 0.2% American Indian and Alaska Native, 6.6% Hispanic of any race, 0.8% two or more races (2000); Density: 7,695.4 persons per square mile (2000); Age: 29.5% under 18, 7.9% over 64 (2000); Marriage status: 36.9% never married, 44.9% now married, 6.3% widowed, 11.9% divorced (2000); Foreign born: 4.0% (2000); Ancestry (includes multiple ancestries): 77.9% Other groups, 2.3% Polish, 2.3% African, 2.1% German, 1.1% United States or American (2000).
Economy: Manufacturing: belts, fasteners, rope, metal stampings. Single-family building permits issued: 0 (2001) / 0 (2000); Multi-family building permits issued: 0 (2001) / 0 (2000); Employment by occupation: 10.2% management, 14.9% professional, 14.1% services, 34.4% sales, 0.0% farming, 7.3% construction, 19.2% production (2000).
Income: Per capita income: $18,283 (2000); Median household income: $45,357 (2000); Poverty rate: 11.5% (2000).
Taxes: Total city taxes per capita: $355 (1997); City property taxes per capita: $201 (1997).
Education: High school graduation rate: 79.6% (2000); College graduation rate: 13.4% (2000).

School District(s)

Calumet Public Schools District 132 (PK-08)
2000 Enrollment: 1,217 708-388-8920
Housing: Homeownership rate: 69.0% (2000); Median home value: $91,600 (2000); Median rent: $576 per month (2000); Median age of housing: 39 years (2000).
Transportation: Commute to work: 79.9% car, 16.0% public transportation, 2.3% walk, 0.5% work from home (2000); Travel time to work: 11.5% less than 15 minutes, 27.9% 15 to 30 minutes, 19.8% 30 to 45 minutes, 18.1% 45 to 60 minutes, 22.7% 60 minutes or more (2000)

CHICAGO (city). Covers a land area of 227.133 square miles and a water area of 6.869 square miles. Located at 41.84° N. Lat.; 87.67° W. Long. Elevation is 596 feet.
History: The river here was called Checagou by the Indians, meaning something big, strong, or powerful. In 1803 Captain John Whistler and his men built Fort Dearborn on the site that was to become Chicago, where a few

cabins occupied by Frenchmen and the Sable trading post already existed. John Kinzie, a Scotch-Canadian trader who took over the trading post, was the first English settler in the community that developed around Fort Dearborn. When Chicago was incorporated as a town in 1833, the population numbered under 200. The projected Illinois & Michigan Canal brought speculators; Chicago was incorporated as a city in 1837 and soon became the world's largest grain market and a major slaughterhouse. The completion of the Illinois & Michigan Canal in 1848 increased the commercial importance of Chicago, as did the many railroad lines that soon radiated from it. The quick ramshackle building of Chicago was halted in 1871 when the fire started in Patrick O'Leary's cow barn destroyed 17,450 buildings in 27 hours. Rebuilding was fast and more permanent.

Population: 2,896,016 (2000); Race: 42.0% White, 36.6% Black, 4.4% Asian, 0.3% American Indian and Alaska Native, 26.0% Hispanic of any race, 3.0% two or more races (2000); Density: 12,750.3 persons per square mile (2000); Age: 26.1% under 18, 10.3% over 64 (2000); Marriage status: 40.9% never married, 43.3% now married, 7.0% widowed, 8.8% divorced (2000); Foreign born: 21.7% (2000); Ancestry (includes multiple ancestries): 56.8% Other groups, 7.3% Polish, 6.6% Irish, 6.5% German, 3.5% Italian (2000).

Vital Statistics: Birth rate: 177.8 per 10,000 population (1998)

Economy: Unemployment rate: 8.1% (11/2002); Total civilian labor force: 1,313,387 (11/2002); Single-family building permits issued: 883 (2001) / 1,334 (2000); Multi-family building permits issued: 5,786 (2001) / 5,277 (2000); Employment by occupation: 13.3% management, 20.2% professional, 16.6% services, 27.0% sales, 0.1% farming, 6.6% construction, 16.2% production (2000).

Income: Per capita income: $20,175 (2000); Median household income: $38,625 (2000); Poverty rate: 19.6% (2000).

Taxes: Total city taxes per capita: $660 (2000); City property taxes per capita: $222 (2000).

Education: High school graduation rate: 71.8% (2000); College graduation rate: 25.5% (2000).

School District(s)

Central Stickney School District 110 (PK-08)
2000 Enrollment: 419 708-458-1152

City of Chicago School District 299 (PK-12)
2000 Enrollment: 435,261 773-553-1000

Four-year College(s)

Adler School of Professional Psychology (Private, Not-for-profit)
2001 Enrollment: 408 312-201-5900

American Academy of Art (Private, For-profit)
2001 Enrollment: 360 312-461-0600
2001 Tuition: In-state $15,880; Out-of-state $15,880

American Islamic College (Private, Not-for-profit)
2001 Enrollment: 11 773-281-4700
2001 Tuition: In-state $6,000; Out-of-state $6,000

School of Art Institute of Chicago (Private, Not-for-profit)
2001 Enrollment: 2,675 312-899-5100
2001 Tuition: In-state $21,300; Out-of-state $21,300

Brisk Rabbinical College (Private, Not-for-profit, Jewish)
2001 Enrollment: n/a 312-274-1177

Catholic Theological Union at Chicago (Private, Not-for-profit, Roman Catholic)
2001 Enrollment: n/a 773-324-8000

Chicago National College of Naprapathy (Private, Not-for-profit)
2001 Enrollment: 68 773-282-2686

Chicago School of Professional Psychology (Private, Not-for-profit)
2001 Enrollment: 391 312-786-9443

Chicago State University (Public)
2001 Enrollment: 7,079 312-995-2000
2001 Tuition: In-state $2,484; Out-of-state $7,452

Chicago Theological Seminary (Private, Not-for-profit, United Church of Christ)
2001 Enrollment: 236 773-752-5757

University of Chicago (Private, Not-for-profit)
2001 Enrollment: 12,883 773-702-1234
2001 Tuition: In-state $26,022; Out-of-state $26,022

Columbia College Chicago (Private, Not-for-profit)
2001 Enrollment: 9,416 312-663-1600
2001 Tuition: In-state $12,524; Out-of-state $12,524

DePaul University (Private, Not-for-profit, Roman Catholic)
2001 Enrollment: 21,363 312-362-8000
2001 Tuition: In-state $16,500; Out-of-state $16,500

DeVry Institute of Technology (Private, For-profit)
2001 Enrollment: 4,011 773-929-8500
2001 Tuition: In-state $8,740; Out-of-state $8,740

Dr William Scholl College of Podiatric (Private, Not-for-profit)
2001 Enrollment: 248 312-280-2880

East-West University (Private, Not-for-profit)
2001 Enrollment: 1,076 312-939-0111
2001 Tuition: In-state $8,700; Out-of-state $8,700

Harrington Institute of Interior Design (Private, For-profit)
2001 Enrollment: 782 312-939-4975
2001 Tuition: In-state $12,600; Out-of-state $12,600

University of Illinois at Chicago (Public)
2001 Enrollment: 24,955 312-996-3000
2001 Tuition: In-state $3,830; Out-of-state $10,490

Illinois College of Optometry (Private, Not-for-profit)
2001 Enrollment: 635 312-949-7400

Illinois Institute of Technology (Private, Not-for-profit)
2001 Enrollment: 6,050 312-567-3000
2001 Tuition: In-state $18,600; Out-of-state $18,600

Illinois School of Professional Psychology-Chicago (Private, For-profit)
2001 Enrollment: 576 312-201-0200

Industrial Engineering College (Private, Not-for-profit)
2001 Enrollment: n/a 312-563-1115

Institute for Clinical Social Work (Private, Not-for-profit)
2001 Enrollment: 84 312-726-8480

Institute for Psychoanalysis (Private, Not-for-profit)
2001 Enrollment: n/a 312-922-7474

International Academy of Merchandising and Design (Private, For-profit)
2001 Enrollment: 2,063 312-980-9200
2001 Tuition: In-state $15,700; Out-of-state $15,700

John Marshall Law School (Private, Not-for-profit)
2001 Enrollment: 1,324 312-427-2737

Loyola University Chicago (Private, Not-for-profit, Roman Catholic)
2001 Enrollment: 13,019 312-915-6000
2001 Tuition: In-state $18,814; Out-of-state $18,814

Lutheran School of Theology at Chicago (Private, Not-for-profit, Evangelical Lutheran Church)
2001 Enrollment: 353 773-256-0700

McCormick Theological Seminary (Private, Not-for-profit, Presbyterian Church (USA))
2001 Enrollment: 371 773-947-6300

Meadville-Lombard Theological School (Private, Not-for-profit, Unitarian Universalist)
2001 Enrollment: 81 773-256-3000

Moody Bible Institute (Private, Not-for-profit, Interdenominational)
2001 Enrollment: 1,630 312-329-4000

Native American Educational Services College Inc (Private, Not-for-profit)
2001 Enrollment: n/a 773-761-5000

National-Louis University (Private, Not-for-profit)
2001 Enrollment: 7,879 847-475-1100
2001 Tuition: In-state $14,010; Out-of-state $14,010

North Park University (Private, Not-for-profit, Evangelical Covenant Church of America)
2001 Enrollment: 2,327 773-244-6200
2001 Tuition: In-state $17,790; Out-of-state $17,790

Northeastern Illinois University (Public)
2001 Enrollment: 10,999 773-583-4050
2001 Tuition: In-state $2,424; Out-of-state $7,272

The Illinois Institute of Art (Private, For-profit)
2001 Enrollment: 1,670 312-280-3500
2001 Tuition: In-state $14,470; Out-of-state $14,470

Robert Morris College (Private, Not-for-profit)
2001 Enrollment: 5,319 312-935-6800
2001 Tuition: In-state $12,150; Out-of-state $12,150

Roosevelt University (Private, Not-for-profit)
2001 Enrollment: 7,490 312-341-3500
2001 Tuition: In-state $13,770; Out-of-state $13,770

Rush University (Private, Not-for-profit)
2001 Enrollment: 1,268 312-942-5000
2001 Tuition: In-state $14,725; Out-of-state $14,725

Saint Xavier University (Private, Not-for-profit, Roman Catholic)
2001 Enrollment: 4,916 773-298-3000
2001 Tuition: In-state $15,000; Out-of-state $15,000

Saint Augustine College (Private, Not-for-profit)
2001 Enrollment: 1,814 773-878-8756
2001 Tuition: In-state $6,792; Out-of-state $6,792

Spertus College (Private, Not-for-profit)
2001 Enrollment: 291 312-922-9012
Telshe Yeshiva-Chicago (Private, Not-for-profit, Jewish)
2001 Enrollment: 78 773-463-7738
2001 Tuition: In-state $7,000; Out-of-state $7,000
Vandercook College of Music (Private, Not-for-profit)
2001 Enrollment: 230 312-225-6288
2001 Tuition: In-state $13,440; Out-of-state $13,440
Center for Psychoanalytic Study (Private, Not-for-profit)
2001 Enrollment: 6 847-835-1430
Chicago Baptist Institute (Private, Not-for-profit, Baptist)
2001 Enrollment: n/a 312-268-2250
Erikson Institute-A Graduate School in Child Dev (Private, Not-for-profit)
2001 Enrollment: 147 312-755-2250
Ravenswood Hospital Medical Center-Sch of Anesth (Private, Not-for-profit, Evangelical Lutheran Church)
2001 Enrollment: 47
Keller Graduate School of Management (Private, For-profit)
2001 Enrollment: n/a 773-695-1000
Keller Graduate School of Management (Private, For-profit)
2001 Enrollment: n/a 312-372-4900

Two-year College(s)

The College of Office Technology (Private, For-profit)
2001 Enrollment: 494 773-278-0042
Career Colleges of Chicago (Private, For-profit)
2001 Enrollment: 144 312-895-6300
2001 Tuition: In-state $12,240; Out-of-state $12,240
Chicagoland American Institute of Banking (Private, Not-for-profit)
2001 Enrollment: n/a 312-347-3400
City Colleges of Chicago-Kennedy-King College (Public)
2001 Enrollment: 5,371 773-602-5000
2001 Tuition: In-state $4,987; Out-of-state $7,292
City Colleges of Chicago-Malcolm X College (Public)
2001 Enrollment: 8,519 312-850-7000
2001 Tuition: In-state $4,987; Out-of-state $7,292
City Colleges of Chicago-Olive-Harvey College (Public)
2001 Enrollment: 6,388 773-568-3700
2001 Tuition: In-state $4,987; Out-of-state $7,292
City Colleges of Chicago-Harry S Truman College (Public)
2001 Enrollment: 15,584 773-878-1700
2001 Tuition: In-state $4,987; Out-of-state $7,292
City Colleges of Chicago-Richard J Daley College (Public)
2001 Enrollment: 10,068 773-735-3000
2001 Tuition: In-state $4,987; Out-of-state $7,292
City Colleges of Chicago-Harold Washington College (Public)
2001 Enrollment: 7,946 312-553-5600
2001 Tuition: In-state $4,987; Out-of-state $7,292
City Colleges of Chicago-Wilbur Wright College (Public)
2001 Enrollment: 12,233 773-481-8200
2001 Tuition: In-state $4,987; Out-of-state $7,292
The Cooking and Hospitality Institute of Chicago (Private, For-profit)
2001 Enrollment: 918 312-944-0882
Freemans Fashion Academy (Private, For-profit)
2001 Enrollment: n/a 312-786-2111
Insurance School of Chicago (Private, For-profit)
2001 Enrollment: n/a 312-427-2520
Lexington College (Private, Not-for-profit, Roman Catholic)
2001 Enrollment: 41 773-779-3800
2001 Tuition: In-state $8,850; Out-of-state $8,850
MacCormac College (Private, Not-for-profit)
2001 Enrollment: 514 312-922-1884
2001 Tuition: In-state $9,000; Out-of-state $9,000
Northwestern Business College (Private, For-profit)
2001 Enrollment: 772 773-777-4220
2001 Tuition: In-state $11,520; Out-of-state $11,520
Ravenswood Hosp Med Ctr-Henry J Kutsch School of Nursing (Private, Not-for-profit)
2001 Enrollment: n/a 773-463-9191
2001 Tuition: In-state $2,496; Out-of-state $2,496
Trinity Hospital School of Radiologic Techn (Private, Not-for-profit, United Church of Christ)
2001 Enrollment: 13 773-967-5292
2001 Tuition: In-state $2,000; Out-of-state $2,000
Taylor Business Institute (Private, For-profit)
2001 Enrollment: 108 312-658-5100
2001 Tuition: In-state $9,000; Out-of-state $9,000
Ravenswood Hospital Medical Center-Sch of Rad Tech (Private, Not-for-profit, Evangelical Lutheran Church)
2001 Enrollment: 26 773-878-4300
2001 Tuition: In-state $1,350; Out-of-state $1,350

Housing: Homeownership rate: 43.8% (2000); Median home value: $132,400 (2000); Median rent: $543 per month (2000); Median age of housing: 52 years (2000).

Hospitals: Advocate Bethany Hospital (240 beds); Advocate Illinois Masonic Medical Center (497 beds); Advocate Trinity Hospital; Chicago Lakeshore Hospital (150 beds); Chicago-Read Mental Health Center (200 beds); Children's Memorial Hospital (265 beds); Cook County Hospital (1,018 beds); Grant Hospital (465 beds); Hartgrove Hospital (119 beds); Holy Cross Hospital (331 beds); Jackson Park Hospital & Medical Center (326 beds); Kindred Chicago Lakeshore (103 beds); La Rabida Childrens Hospital (49 beds); Loretto Hospital (212 beds); Louis A. Weiss Memorial Hospital; Mercy Hospital (507 beds); Methodist Hospital of Chicago (245 beds); Michael Reese Hospital (535 beds); Mount Sinai Hospital (431 beds); Northwestern Memorial Hospital (720 beds); Norwegian-American Hospital (220 beds); Our Lady of the Resurrection Medical Center (407 beds); Provident Hospital (243 beds); Ravenswood Hospital Medical Center (306 beds); Rehabilitation Institute of Chicago (155 beds); Resurrection Medical Center (439 beds); Roseland Community Hospital (162 beds); Rush-Presbyterian-Saint Luke's Medical Center (809 beds); Sacred Heart Hospital (119 beds); Saint Anthony Hospital (183 beds); Schwab Rehabilitation Hospital (85 beds); Shriners Hospital for Children (60 beds); Sinai Community Institute; Sinai Medical Group/HealthFirst; South Shore Hospital (170 beds); St Mary of Nazareth Hospital Center (387 beds); Saint Elizabeth's Hospital (276 beds); Saint Joseph Hospital (492 beds); Swedish Covenant Hospital (330 beds); Thorek Hospital and Medical Center (218 beds); University of Chicago Hospitals (662 beds); University of Illinois at Chicago Medical Center (570 beds); Veterans Affairs Lakeside Medical Center (337 beds); Veterans Affairs West Side Medical Center (435 beds)

Safety: Violent crime rate: n/a; Property crime rate: 519.3 per 10,000 population (2001).

Newspapers: Southeast Chicago Observer (1 x month); Chicago Free Press (1 x week); The African-American Times (1 x week); Red Eye (5 x week); Red Streak (5 x week); Dodge Construction News (5 x week); Chicago Daily Law Bulletin (5 x week); Chicago Sun-Times (7 x week); Chicago Tribune (7 x week); Chicago Defender (6 x week); Draugas (5 x week); Polish Daily News (7 x week); Exito (1 x week); Chicago Catolico (1 x month); Bridgeport News (1 x week); Back of the Yards Journal (1 x week); Near North News (1 x week); Chicago Reader (1 x week); La Raza Newspaper (1 x week); Windy City Times (1 x week); Hyde Park Herald (1 x week); The Herald Extra (1 x week); New Metro News (1 x week); La Voz de Chicago (1 x week); South Suburban Citizen (1 x week); South End Citizen (1 x week); Hyde Park Citizen (1 x week); Chicago Weekend (1 x week); Chatham Citizen (1 x week); North Loop News (1 x week); El Heraldo (5 x week); Inside (1 x week); The Greek Star (1 x week); Southwest Shopper (1 x week); Southwest News-Herald (1 x week); Southwest Courier (1 x week); Clear-Ridge Reporter (1 x week); Chicago's Northwest Side Press (1 x week); The Journal (1 x week); Brighton Park Life-McKinley Park Life (1 x week); West Suburban Post (1 x week); Northwest Leader (1 x week); Beverly Review (1 x week); Suburban Leader (1 x week); Independent Bulletin (1 x week); The Extra (1 x week); Metro Extra (1 x week); Chicago Chinese Times (6 x week); Chinese American News (1 x week); New City (1 x week); The Chicago Crusader (1 x week)

Transportation: Commute to work: 64.6% car, 26.1% public transportation, 5.7% walk, 2.4% work from home (2000); Travel time to work: 13.2% less than 15 minutes, 27.9% 15 to 30 minutes, 28.3% 30 to 45 minutes, 14.7% 45 to 60 minutes, 16.0% 60 minutes or more (2000); Amtrak: Service available.

Airports: Chicago O'Hare International (primary service/large hub); Chicago Midway International (primary service/large hub); Merrill C Meigs (commercial service); Dupage (commercial service); Palwaukee Municipal (commercial service); Lewis University (commercial service); Waukegan Regional (commercial service); Aurora Municipal (commercial service); Schaumburg Regional (commercial service); Lake in the Hills (commercial service); Lansing Municipal (commercial service)

Additional Information Contacts

African American Chamber of Commerce 773-238-3840
Andersonville Chamber of Commerce 773-728-2995
Business & Economic Revitalization 773-783-2636
Chicago Area Gay & Lesbian 773-871-4190
Chicago Association of Realtors 312-803-4900
Chicago Avenue Business 312-733-4002
Chicago Chamber of Commerce 312-938-9050
Chicago Convention & Visitors Bureau 312-943-5399

Fullerton Avenue Chamber 773-489-3222
German American Chamber of Commerce 312-644-2662
Greater North Pulaski Development Corp. 773-384-7074
Hegewisch Chamber of Commerce 773-646-6880
Italian American Chamber of Commerce 312-553-9137
Lake View East Chamber of Commerce 773-348-8608
Latin American Chamber of Commerce 773-252-5211
Montrose Kedzie Chamber of Commerce 773-583-1611
Near NW Chamber of Chicago 312-850-9013
Northcenter Development Corp. 773-525-1539
Portgage Park Chamber of Commerce. 773-777-2020
Puerto Rico Convention Bureau. 312-840-8090
South Chicago Chamber of Commerce 773-768-1221
South Shore Chamber Inc. 773-643-1652
Stoney Island Chamber of Commerce 773-734-0626
U S Mexico Chamber of Commerce 312-781-7342
West Lawn Chamber of Commerce. 773-735-7690

CHICAGO HEIGHTS (city). Covers a land area of 9.571 square miles and a water area of 0.011 square miles. Located at 41.51° N. Lat.; 87.64° W. Long. Elevation is 650 feet.

History: Chicago Heights developed at the point where the Hubbard Trail crossed the Sauk Trail, a heavily traveled junction. The first settlement here in the 1830's was called Thorn Grove, but it was renamed Bloom in 1849 by German settlers. In 1890 the Chicago Heights Land Association began encouraging settlers and industry to come here, and the name of the town was changed.

Population: 32,776 (2000); Race: 45.1% White, 37.5% Black, 0.6% Asian, 0.2% American Indian and Alaska Native, 23.6% Hispanic of any race, 3.3% two or more races (2000); Density: 3,424.4 persons per square mile (2000); Age: 31.8% under 18, 11.8% over 64 (2000); Marriage status: 35.2% never married, 48.7% now married, 7.8% widowed, 8.2% divorced (2000); Foreign born: 11.2% (2000); Ancestry (includes multiple ancestries): 55.9% Other groups, 11.4% Italian, 10.2% German, 6.6% Irish, 6.2% Polish (2000).

Vital Statistics: Birth rate: 216.6 per 10,000 population (1998)

Economy: Unemployment rate: 8.9% (11/2002); Total civilian labor force: 14,256 (11/2002); Single-family building permits issued: 5 (2001) / 8 (2000); Multi-family building permits issued: 2 (2001) / 0 (2000); Employment by occupation: 8.1% management, 15.9% professional, 20.0% services, 26.4% sales, 0.1% farming, 7.6% construction, 21.9% production (2000).

Income: Per capita income: $14,963 (2000); Median household income: $36,958 (2000); Poverty rate: 17.5% (2000).

Taxes: Total city taxes per capita: $494 (1997); City property taxes per capita: $377 (1997).

Education: High school graduation rate: 71.7% (2000); College graduation rate: 12.3% (2000).

School District(s)

Bloom Township High School District 206 (09-12)
2000 Enrollment: 2,651 708-755-7010
Chicago Heights School District 170 (PK-08)
2000 Enrollment: 3,408 708-756-4165
Flossmoor School District 161 (PK-08)
2000 Enrollment: 2,508 708-647-7000
Intermediate Service Center 4 (07-12)
2000 Enrollment: 100 708-754-6600
Sandridge School District 172 (PK-08)
2000 Enrollment: 348 708-895-2450
Speed Seja #802 (PK-12)
2000 Enrollment: 410 708-481-6100

Two-year College(s)

Prairie State College (Public)
2001 Enrollment: 4,428 708-709-3500
2001 Tuition: In-state $4,800; Out-of-state $4,968

Housing: Homeownership rate: 63.1% (2000); Median home value: $94,800 (2000); Median rent: $500 per month (2000); Median age of housing: 44 years (2000).

Hospitals: Saint James Hospital and Health Center (587 beds)

Newspapers: South Suburban Standard (1 x week); Chicago Standard News (1 x week)

Transportation: Commute to work: 87.8% car, 6.5% public transportation, 2.7% walk, 1.4% work from home (2000); Travel time to work: 33.9% less than 15 minutes, 33.5% 15 to 30 minutes, 12.9% 30 to 45 minutes, 7.9% 45 to 60 minutes, 11.8% 60 minutes or more (2000)

CHICAGO RIDGE (village). Covers a land area of 2.230 square miles and a water area of 0 square miles. Located at 41.70° N. Lat.; 87.77° W. Long. Elevation is 600 feet.

Population: 14,127 (2000); Race: 88.2% White, 3.3% Black, 1.0% Asian, 0.1% American Indian and Alaska Native, 7.1% Hispanic of any race, 5.1% two or more races (2000); Density: 6,336.3 persons per square mile (2000); Age: 24.6% under 18, 10.9% over 64 (2000); Marriage status: 31.1% never married, 51.8% now married, 7.8% widowed, 9.2% divorced (2000); Foreign born: 13.8% (2000); Ancestry (includes multiple ancestries): 25.5% Irish, 20.3% Polish, 19.1% German, 13.6% Other groups, 11.2% Italian (2000).

Vital Statistics: Birth rate: 194.7 per 10,000 population (1998)

Economy: Suburb of Chicago. Single-family building permits issued: 2 (2001) / 2 (2000); Multi-family building permits issued: 0 (2001) / 0 (2000); Employment by occupation: 11.3% management, 11.4% professional, 11.1% services, 34.3% sales, 0.0% farming, 12.4% construction, 19.5% production (2000).

Income: Per capita income: $20,278 (2000); Median household income: $44,101 (2000); Poverty rate: 10.0% (2000).

Taxes: Total city taxes per capita: $354 (1997); City property taxes per capita: $306 (1997).

Education: High school graduation rate: 81.8% (2000); College graduation rate: 13.8% (2000).

School District(s)

Chicago Ridge School District 127-5 (PK-08)
2000 Enrollment: 1,215 708-636-2000

Housing: Homeownership rate: 51.6% (2000); Median home value: $138,500 (2000); Median rent: $633 per month (2000); Median age of housing: 28 years (2000).

Transportation: Commute to work: 89.6% car, 7.1% public transportation, 1.8% walk, 0.6% work from home (2000); Travel time to work: 22.6% less than 15 minutes, 28.2% 15 to 30 minutes, 21.8% 30 to 45 minutes, 11.0% 45 to 60 minutes, 16.4% 60 minutes or more (2000)

CICERO (town). Covers a land area of 5.846 square miles and a water area of 0 square miles. Located at 41.84° N. Lat.; 87.76° W. Long. Elevation is 606 feet.

History: Cicero was settled in the mid-1800's. The first township election was held in 1857, and Cicero was incorporated as a town in 1867 and as a city in 1869, following an influx of homesteaders during the Civil War. Cicero shrank when parts of it were annexed to Chicago in 1892. During the industrial boom that followed the turn of the century, Al Capone was the proprietor of a row of gambling houses here.

Population: 85,616 (2000); Race: 48.5% White, 1.2% Black, 1.0% Asian, 0.7% American Indian and Alaska Native, 77.3% Hispanic of any race, 3.7% two or more races (2000); Density: 14,645.2 persons per square mile (2000); Age: 34.6% under 18, 7.0% over 64 (2000); Marriage status: 32.5% never married, 56.1% now married, 5.3% widowed, 6.1% divorced (2000); Foreign born: 43.6% (2000); Ancestry (includes multiple ancestries): 72.6% Other groups, 4.7% Polish, 3.7% Irish, 3.7% German, 3.0% Italian (2000).

Vital Statistics: Birth rate: 227.1 per 10,000 population (1998)

Economy: Unemployment rate: 9.0% (11/2002); Total civilian labor force: 32,866 (11/2002); Single-family building permits issued: 1 (2001) / 1 (2000); Multi-family building permits issued: 0 (2001) / 0 (2000); Employment by occupation: 4.9% management, 6.3% professional, 16.6% services, 24.2% sales, 0.5% farming, 12.0% construction, 35.5% production (2000).

Income: Per capita income: $12,489 (2000); Median household income: $38,044 (2000); Poverty rate: 15.5% (2000).

Taxes: Total city taxes per capita: $424 (2000); City property taxes per capita: $273 (2000).

Education: High school graduation rate: 48.2% (2000); College graduation rate: 6.1% (2000).

School District(s)

Cicero School District 99 (PK-08)
2000 Enrollment: 12,577 708-863-4856
J S Morton H S District 201 (09-12)
2000 Enrollment: 6,612 708-222-5700

Two-year College(s)

Morton College (Public)
2001 Enrollment: 4,328 708-656-8000
2001 Tuition: In-state $3,695; Out-of-state $4,704

Housing: Homeownership rate: 55.2% (2000); Median home value: $111,100 (2000); Median rent: $498 per month (2000); Median age of housing: 55 years (2000).

Newspapers: Northside Express (2 x week); Lawndale News/West Side Times (2 x week); El Imparcial (1 x week); El Dia Newspaper (1 x week); Cicero/Berwyn Suburban Edition (2 x week)
Transportation: Commute to work: 83.9% car, 9.7% public transportation, 3.7% walk, 1.1% work from home (2000); Travel time to work: 14.7% less than 15 minutes, 30.7% 15 to 30 minutes, 27.6% 30 to 45 minutes, 13.5% 45 to 60 minutes, 13.5% 60 minutes or more (2000)
Additional Information Contacts
Cicero Chamber of Commerce 708-652-4990
West Towns Board of Realtors 708-863-1111

COUNTRY CLUB HILLS (city). Covers a land area of 4.614 square miles and a water area of 0.024 square miles. Located at 41.56° N. Lat.; 87.72° W. Long. Elevation is 675 feet.
Population: 16,169 (2000); Race: 14.0% White, 83.0% Black, 0.5% Asian, 0.1% American Indian and Alaska Native, 1.8% Hispanic of any race, 1.9% two or more races (2000); Density: 3,504.4 persons per square mile (2000); Age: 30.3% under 18, 7.3% over 64 (2000); Marriage status: 30.7% never married, 51.1% now married, 6.3% widowed, 11.9% divorced (2000); Foreign born: 2.4% (2000); Ancestry (includes multiple ancestries): 74.2% Other groups, 4.0% German, 3.9% Irish, 3.1% African, 2.5% Polish (2000).
Vital Statistics: Birth rate: 139.8 per 10,000 population (1998)
Economy: Single-family building permits issued: 40 (2001) / 56 (2000); Multi-family building permits issued: 0 (2001) / 0 (2000); Employment by occupation: 14.6% management, 19.5% professional, 12.4% services, 33.1% sales, 0.0% farming, 5.2% construction, 15.2% production (2000).
Income: Per capita income: $21,561 (2000); Median household income: $57,701 (2000); Poverty rate: 5.5% (2000).
Taxes: Total city taxes per capita: $270 (1997); City property taxes per capita: $127 (1997).
Education: High school graduation rate: 89.7% (2000); College graduation rate: 22.8% (2000).

School District(s)

Country Club Hills School District 160 (PK-08)
2000 Enrollment: 1,576 708-957-6200
Housing: Homeownership rate: 91.3% (2000); Median home value: $109,400 (2000); Median rent: $799 per month (2000); Median age of housing: 25 years (2000).
Transportation: Commute to work: 86.4% car, 9.8% public transportation, 0.8% walk, 2.1% work from home (2000); Travel time to work: 15.6% less than 15 minutes, 22.8% 15 to 30 minutes, 21.0% 30 to 45 minutes, 16.3% 45 to 60 minutes, 24.2% 60 minutes or more (2000)

COUNTRYSIDE (city). Covers a land area of 2.690 square miles and a water area of 0 square miles. Located at 41.77° N. Lat.; 87.87° W. Long. Elevation is 675 feet.
Population: 5,991 (2000); Race: 91.0% White, 1.4% Black, 2.1% Asian, 0.4% American Indian and Alaska Native, 6.6% Hispanic of any race, 2.1% two or more races (2000); Density: 2,226.7 persons per square mile (2000); Age: 19.1% under 18, 16.7% over 64 (2000); Marriage status: 26.0% never married, 52.2% now married, 8.5% widowed, 13.3% divorced (2000); Foreign born: 16.1% (2000); Ancestry (includes multiple ancestries): 19.4% Polish, 17.9% German, 15.7% Irish, 12.1% Other groups, 10.2% Italian (2000).
Economy: Manufacturing: chemicals, machinery, food. Single-family building permits issued: 4 (2001) / 10 (2000); Multi-family building permits issued: 0 (2001) / 0 (2000); Employment by occupation: 13.4% management, 21.4% professional, 11.6% services, 30.6% sales, 0.0% farming, 9.7% construction, 13.2% production (2000).
Income: Per capita income: $25,449 (2000); Median household income: $45,469 (2000); Poverty rate: 3.7% (2000).
Taxes: Total city taxes per capita: $31 (1997); City property taxes per capita: $6 (1997).
Education: High school graduation rate: 84.3% (2000); College graduation rate: 23.0% (2000).
Housing: Homeownership rate: 72.0% (2000); Median home value: $201,600 (2000); Median rent: $667 per month (2000); Median age of housing: 29 years (2000).
Transportation: Commute to work: 87.1% car, 5.3% public transportation, 2.0% walk, 4.1% work from home (2000); Travel time to work: 25.4% less than 15 minutes, 35.1% 15 to 30 minutes, 21.8% 30 to 45 minutes, 9.7% 45 to 60 minutes, 8.1% 60 minutes or more (2000)

CRESTWOOD (village). Covers a land area of 3.055 square miles and a water area of 0.053 square miles. Located at 41.64° N. Lat.; 87.74° W. Long. Elevation is 600 feet.
Population: 11,251 (2000); Race: 92.5% White, 4.6% Black, 0.5% Asian, 0.0% American Indian and Alaska Native, 4.9% Hispanic of any race, 0.4% two or more races (2000); Density: 3,682.3 persons per square mile (2000); Age: 19.8% under 18, 18.6% over 64 (2000); Marriage status: 28.2% never married, 49.6% now married, 11.4% widowed, 10.8% divorced (2000); Foreign born: 3.4% (2000); Ancestry (includes multiple ancestries): 29.4% Irish, 23.8% German, 19.8% Polish, 12.0% Italian, 9.5% Other groups (2000).
Vital Statistics: Birth rate: 129.8 per 10,000 population (1998)
Economy: Remnant agriculture. Manufacturing: machinery, metal products. Single-family building permits issued: 25 (2001) / 35 (2000); Multi-family building permits issued: 24 (2001) / 0 (2000); Employment by occupation: 8.9% management, 17.6% professional, 11.4% services, 32.2% sales, 0.0% farming, 12.6% construction, 17.4% production (2000).
Income: Per capita income: $21,995 (2000); Median household income: $45,813 (2000); Poverty rate: 4.6% (2000).
Taxes: Total city taxes per capita: $796 (1997); City property taxes per capita: $397 (1997).
Education: High school graduation rate: 84.4% (2000); College graduation rate: 14.9% (2000).
Housing: Homeownership rate: 81.9% (2000); Median home value: $149,000 (2000); Median rent: $606 per month (2000); Median age of housing: 26 years (2000).
Transportation: Commute to work: 90.5% car, 7.1% public transportation, 0.5% walk, 1.2% work from home (2000); Travel time to work: 24.3% less than 15 minutes, 29.8% 15 to 30 minutes, 17.3% 30 to 45 minutes, 14.7% 45 to 60 minutes, 13.9% 60 minutes or more (2000)

DES PLAINES (city). Covers a land area of 14.423 square miles and a water area of 0.111 square miles. Located at 42.03° N. Lat.; 87.90° W. Long. Elevation is 640 feet.
History: When Des Plaines was founded in the 1830's it was known as Rand, for its first settler, Socrates Rand. The name was changed in 1869 to that of the river which transverses the town.
Population: 58,720 (2000); Race: 84.6% White, 0.8% Black, 7.5% Asian, 0.3% American Indian and Alaska Native, 14.4% Hispanic of any race, 2.4% two or more races (2000); Density: 4,071.2 persons per square mile (2000); Age: 21.9% under 18, 17.5% over 64 (2000); Marriage status: 24.9% never married, 58.0% now married, 9.2% widowed, 8.0% divorced (2000); Foreign born: 23.9% (2000); Ancestry (includes multiple ancestries): 22.7% Other groups, 21.5% German, 18.2% Polish, 13.8% Irish, 10.6% Italian (2000).
Vital Statistics: Birth rate: 199.6 per 10,000 population (1998)
Economy: Unemployment rate: 7.2% (11/2002); Total civilian labor force: 33,601 (11/2002); Single-family building permits issued: 32 (2001) / 29 (2000); Multi-family building permits issued: 105 (2001) / 0 (2000); Employment by occupation: 14.3% management, 17.9% professional, 12.3% services, 31.5% sales, 0.1% farming, 9.1% construction, 14.7% production (2000).
Income: Per capita income: $24,146 (2000); Median household income: $53,638 (2000); Poverty rate: 4.6% (2000).
Taxes: Total city taxes per capita: $487 (2000); City property taxes per capita: $281 (2000).
Education: High school graduation rate: 81.9% (2000); College graduation rate: 24.7% (2000).

School District(s)

Comm Consolidated School District 62 (PK-08)
2000 Enrollment: 5,008 847-824-1136
East Maine School District 63 (PK-08)
2000 Enrollment: 3,773 847-299-1900
Intermediate Service Center 1 (09-12)
2000 Enrollment: 65 847-419-5065
Thomas Jefferson Charter School (KG-07)
2000 Enrollment: 57 847-297-9740

Two-year College(s)

Oakton Community College (Public)
2001 Enrollment: 10,792 847-635-1600
2001 Tuition: In-state $4,200; Out-of-state $5,600
Housing: Homeownership rate: 79.7% (2000); Median home value: $184,600 (2000); Median rent: $710 per month (2000); Median age of housing: 37 years (2000).
Hospitals: Holy Family Medical Center (252 beds)
Newspapers: Wheeling Journal & Topics (1 x week); Suburban Journal (1 x week); Rosemont Journal (2 x week); Rolling Meadows Journal & Topics (1 x week); Prospect Heights Journal (2 x week); Park Ridge Journal (1 x week); Palatine Journal & Topics (1 x week); Northwest Journal (1 x week); Mount Prospect Family Journal (2 x week); Elk Grove Journal (1 x week); Des

Plaines Journal (2 x week); Buffalo Grove Journal & Topics (1 x week); Arlington Heights Journal & Topics (1 x week); Niles Journal (1 x week)
Transportation: Commute to work: 88.8% car, 6.7% public transportation, 1.5% walk, 2.5% work from home (2000); Travel time to work: 24.3% less than 15 minutes, 34.9% 15 to 30 minutes, 23.3% 30 to 45 minutes, 8.5% 45 to 60 minutes, 9.0% 60 minutes or more (2000)
Additional Information Contacts
Des Plaines Chamber of Commerce. 847-824-4200

DIXMOOR (village). Covers a land area of 1.243 square miles and a water area of 0 square miles. Located at 41.63° N. Lat.; 87.66° W. Long. Elevation is 600 feet.
History: Incorporated 1922.
Population: 3,934 (2000); Race: 28.7% White, 60.1% Black, 0.0% Asian, 0.0% American Indian and Alaska Native, 17.5% Hispanic of any race, 2.4% two or more races (2000); Density: 3,164.6 persons per square mile (2000); Age: 32.1% under 18, 12.7% over 64 (2000); Marriage status: 34.5% never married, 43.5% now married, 10.0% widowed, 12.0% divorced (2000); Foreign born: 9.2% (2000); Ancestry (includes multiple ancestries): 68.4% Other groups, 6.6% German, 6.0% Irish, 4.8% Polish, 1.7% Dutch (2000).
Economy: Manufacturing: transportation equipment. Single-family building permits issued: 0 (2001) / 1 (2000); Multi-family building permits issued: 0 (2001) / 0 (2000); Employment by occupation: 5.1% management, 10.0% professional, 24.1% services, 28.9% sales, 0.0% farming, 9.0% construction, 23.0% production (2000).
Income: Per capita income: $11,712 (2000); Median household income: $26,677 (2000); Poverty rate: 30.3% (2000).
Taxes: Total city taxes per capita: $326 (1997); City property taxes per capita: $145 (1997).
Education: High school graduation rate: 62.5% (2000); College graduation rate: 7.4% (2000).
Housing: Homeownership rate: 78.4% (2000); Median home value: $57,100 (2000); Median rent: $501 per month (2000); Median age of housing: 32 years (2000).
Transportation: Commute to work: 86.7% car, 9.2% public transportation, 1.2% walk, 1.6% work from home (2000); Travel time to work: 14.8% less than 15 minutes, 36.7% 15 to 30 minutes, 26.2% 30 to 45 minutes, 3.8% 45 to 60 minutes, 18.5% 60 minutes or more (2000)

DOLTON (village). Covers a land area of 4.551 square miles and a water area of 0.116 square miles. Located at 41.62° N. Lat.; 87.59° W. Long. Elevation is 605 feet.
History: Settled 1832, incorporated 1892.
Population: 25,614 (2000); Race: 14.4% White, 82.1% Black, 0.9% Asian, 0.1% American Indian and Alaska Native, 2.6% Hispanic of any race, 1.3% two or more races (2000); Density: 5,627.6 persons per square mile (2000); Age: 31.7% under 18, 9.3% over 64 (2000); Marriage status: 33.4% never married, 49.0% now married, 6.4% widowed, 11.2% divorced (2000); Foreign born: 3.7% (2000); Ancestry (includes multiple ancestries): 74.3% Other groups, 3.6% German, 2.6% Polish, 2.4% Irish, 1.6% African (2000).
Vital Statistics: Birth rate: 136.3 per 10,000 population (1998)
Economy: Manufacturing: steel, aluminum products, glass, chemicals. Unemployment rate: 10.2% (11/2002); Total civilian labor force: 12,802 (11/2002); Single-family building permits issued: 1 (2001) / 3 (2000); Multi-family building permits issued: 0 (2001) / 8 (2000); Employment by occupation: 11.0% management, 16.2% professional, 14.4% services, 33.5% sales, 0.0% farming, 6.2% construction, 18.6% production (2000).
Income: Per capita income: $18,102 (2000); Median household income: $48,020 (2000); Poverty rate: 8.4% (2000).
Taxes: Total city taxes per capita: $334 (1997); City property taxes per capita: $183 (1997).
Education: High school graduation rate: 82.6% (2000); College graduation rate: 15.4% (2000).

School District(s)

Dolton School District 148 (PK-08)
2000 Enrollment: 3,307 708-841-2290
Housing: Homeownership rate: 81.3% (2000); Median home value: $92,800 (2000); Median rent: $623 per month (2000); Median age of housing: 37 years (2000).
Transportation: Commute to work: 81.8% car, 13.0% public transportation, 1.4% walk, 2.6% work from home (2000); Travel time to work: 16.9% less than 15 minutes, 21.0% 15 to 30 minutes, 21.6% 30 to 45 minutes, 16.1% 45 to 60 minutes, 24.4% 60 minutes or more (2000)
Additional Information Contacts
Dolton Chamber of Commerce 708-841-4810

EAST HAZEL CREST (village). Covers a land area of 0.767 square miles and a water area of 0 square miles. Located at 41.57° N. Lat.; 87.65° W. Long. Elevation is 620 feet.
Population: 1,607 (2000); Race: 54.2% White, 37.8% Black, 0.0% Asian, 0.2% American Indian and Alaska Native, 8.0% Hispanic of any race, 4.3% two or more races (2000); Density: 2,094.6 persons per square mile (2000); Age: 26.3% under 18, 11.4% over 64 (2000); Marriage status: 25.7% never married, 51.8% now married, 7.1% widowed, 15.4% divorced (2000); Foreign born: 4.8% (2000); Ancestry (includes multiple ancestries): 45.6% Other groups, 15.6% Irish, 11.3% Polish, 10.9% German, 6.3% Italian (2000).
Economy: Single-family building permits issued: 0 (2001) / 1 (2000); Multi-family building permits issued: 0 (2001) / 0 (2000); Employment by occupation: 9.9% management, 12.5% professional, 14.5% services, 28.3% sales, 0.0% farming, 14.1% construction, 20.8% production (2000).
Income: Per capita income: $18,488 (2000); Median household income: $43,000 (2000); Poverty rate: 8.7% (2000).
Taxes: Total city taxes per capita: $363 (1997); City property taxes per capita: $144 (1997).
Education: High school graduation rate: 81.5% (2000); College graduation rate: 11.2% (2000).
Housing: Homeownership rate: 65.6% (2000); Median home value: $101,200 (2000); Median rent: $605 per month (2000); Median age of housing: 37 years (2000).
Transportation: Commute to work: 82.9% car, 12.1% public transportation, 0.9% walk, 3.0% work from home (2000); Travel time to work: 29.1% less than 15 minutes, 22.1% 15 to 30 minutes, 18.1% 30 to 45 minutes, 15.7% 45 to 60 minutes, 15.1% 60 minutes or more (2000)

ELK GROVE VILLAGE (village). Aka Elk Grove. Covers a land area of 11.039 square miles and a water area of 0.061 square miles. Located at 42.00° N. Lat.; 87.99° W. Long. Elevation is 700 feet.
Population: 34,727 (2000); Race: 85.8% White, 1.1% Black, 9.5% Asian, 0.1% American Indian and Alaska Native, 5.8% Hispanic of any race, 1.4% two or more races (2000); Density: 3,145.8 persons per square mile (2000); Age: 24.7% under 18, 11.9% over 64 (2000); Marriage status: 23.6% never married, 61.2% now married, 6.3% widowed, 8.9% divorced (2000); Foreign born: 14.3% (2000); Ancestry (includes multiple ancestries): 25.5% German, 19.3% Polish, 17.3% Other groups, 17.1% Irish, 14.7% Italian (2000).
Vital Statistics: Birth rate: 131.0 per 10,000 population (1998)
Economy: Unemployment rate: 4.6% (11/2002); Total civilian labor force: 20,932 (11/2002); Single-family building permits issued: 1 (2001) / 60 (2000); Multi-family building permits issued: 77 (2001) / 56 (2000); Employment by occupation: 17.4% management, 19.3% professional, 9.2% services, 34.9% sales, 0.0% farming, 7.4% construction, 11.8% production (2000).
Income: Per capita income: $28,515 (2000); Median household income: $62,132 (2000); Poverty rate: 2.0% (2000).
Taxes: Total city taxes per capita: $518 (2000); City property taxes per capita: $298 (2000).
Education: High school graduation rate: 90.3% (2000); College graduation rate: 31.6% (2000).
Housing: Homeownership rate: 76.6% (2000); Median home value: $189,400 (2000); Median rent: $776 per month (2000); Median age of housing: 27 years (2000).
Hospitals: Alexian Brothers Medical Center (445 beds)
Transportation: Commute to work: 93.0% car, 3.5% public transportation, 0.9% walk, 2.4% work from home (2000); Travel time to work: 28.2% less than 15 minutes, 36.7% 15 to 30 minutes, 18.8% 30 to 45 minutes, 8.0% 45 to 60 minutes, 8.3% 60 minutes or more (2000)

ELMWOOD PARK (village). Covers a land area of 1.906 square miles and a water area of 0 square miles. Located at 41.92° N. Lat.; 87.81° W. Long. Elevation is 635 feet.
Population: 25,405 (2000); Race: 90.8% White, 0.5% Black, 1.8% Asian, 0.9% American Indian and Alaska Native, 10.8% Hispanic of any race, 2.7% two or more races (2000); Density: 13,328.4 persons per square mile (2000); Age: 22.0% under 18, 16.6% over 64 (2000); Marriage status: 27.2% never married, 52.8% now married, 10.1% widowed, 10.0% divorced (2000); Foreign born: 24.3% (2000); Ancestry (includes multiple ancestries): 28.7% Italian, 24.7% Polish, 13.5% Other groups, 12.3% Irish, 12.0% German (2000).
Vital Statistics: Birth rate: 107.1 per 10,000 population (1998)
Economy: Chiefly residential. Single-family building permits issued: 7 (2001) / 1 (2000); Multi-family building permits issued: 9 (2001) / 12 (2000);

Employment by occupation: 13.7% management, 13.4% professional, 12.9% services, 33.3% sales, 0.1% farming, 10.0% construction, 16.4% production (2000).
Income: Per capita income: $22,526 (2000); Median household income: $47,315 (2000); Poverty rate: 5.2% (2000).
Taxes: Total city taxes per capita: $320 (1997); City property taxes per capita: $226 (1997).
Education: High school graduation rate: 80.0% (2000); College graduation rate: 19.5% (2000).

School District(s)

Elmwood Park C U School District 401 (PK-12)
2000 Enrollment: 3,007 708-452-7292

Housing: Homeownership rate: 65.6% (2000); Median home value: $172,400 (2000); Median rent: $625 per month (2000); Median age of housing: 46 years (2000).
Transportation: Commute to work: 86.6% car, 8.8% public transportation, 2.3% walk, 1.5% work from home (2000); Travel time to work: 19.3% less than 15 minutes, 27.8% 15 to 30 minutes, 31.7% 30 to 45 minutes, 12.3% 45 to 60 minutes, 8.9% 60 minutes or more (2000)
Additional Information Contacts
Mont Clare-Elmwood Park Chamber. 708-456-8000

EVANSTON (city). Covers a land area of 7.746 square miles and a water area of 0.023 square miles. Located at 42.04° N. Lat.; 87.69° W. Long. Elevation is 600 feet.
History: Settlement at Evanston began around the harbor formed by the Grosse Pointe bluffs. The town was platted in 1854, and in 1855 Northwestern University was founded by the Methodist Episcopal Church. One of the first professors here was Frances E. Willard, who later founded the Women's Christian Temperance Union. In 1892 Evanston annexed the community of South Evanston and was incorporated as a city. The city was named for John Evans, one of the university founders.
Population: 74,239 (2000); Race: 65.2% White, 22.1% Black, 6.1% Asian, 0.2% American Indian and Alaska Native, 6.2% Hispanic of any race, 3.3% two or more races (2000); Density: 9,584.1 persons per square mile (2000); Age: 20.1% under 18, 10.9% over 64 (2000); Marriage status: 39.2% never married, 47.2% now married, 5.4% widowed, 8.2% divorced (2000); Foreign born: 15.4% (2000); Ancestry (includes multiple ancestries): 29.7% Other groups, 16.2% German, 12.5% Irish, 9.0% English, 5.6% Polish (2000).
Vital Statistics: Birth rate: 144.8 per 10,000 population (1998)
Economy: Unemployment rate: 5.2% (11/2002); Total civilian labor force: 41,502 (11/2002); Single-family building permits issued: 18 (2001) / 2 (2000); Multi-family building permits issued: 100 (2001) / 2 (2000); Employment by occupation: 19.8% management, 40.9% professional, 9.1% services, 22.3% sales, 0.0% farming, 2.8% construction, 5.1% production (2000).
Income: Per capita income: $33,645 (2000); Median household income: $56,335 (2000); Poverty rate: 11.1% (2000).
Taxes: Total city taxes per capita: $685 (2000); City property taxes per capita: $363 (2000).
Education: High school graduation rate: 91.4% (2000); College graduation rate: 62.4% (2000).

School District(s)

Evanston C C School District 65 (PK-12)
2000 Enrollment: 7,188 847-492-5986
Evanston Township H S District 202 (09-12)
2000 Enrollment: 3,033 847-424-7000

Four-year College(s)

Garrett Evangelical Theological Seminary (Private, Not-for-profit, United Methodist)
2001 Enrollment: 326 847-866-3900
Kendall College (Private, Not-for-profit, United Methodist)
2001 Enrollment: 625 847-866-1300
2001 Tuition: In-state $12,840; Out-of-state $12,840
Northwestern University (Private, Not-for-profit)
2001 Enrollment: 17,000 312-491-3741
2001 Tuition: In-state $25,839; Out-of-state $25,839
Seabury-Western Theological Seminary (Private, Not-for-profit, Protestant Episcopal)
2001 Enrollment: 88 847-328-9300

Two-year College(s)

Saint Francis Hospital School of Radiologic Techn (Private, Not-for-profit, Roman Catholic)
2001 Enrollment: n/a 847-316-5810

Housing: Homeownership rate: 52.6% (2000); Median home value: $290,800 (2000); Median rent: $813 per month (2000); Median age of housing: 57 years (2000).
Hospitals: Evanston Hospital; Saint Francis Hospital (445 beds)
Newspapers: Skokie Review (1 x week); Morton Grove Champion (1 x week); Lincolnwood Review (1 x week); Evanston Review (1 x week); The Daily Northwestern (5 x week)
Transportation: Commute to work: 61.7% car, 18.4% public transportation, 11.7% walk, 6.1% work from home (2000); Travel time to work: 26.4% less than 15 minutes, 23.6% 15 to 30 minutes, 22.5% 30 to 45 minutes, 15.6% 45 to 60 minutes, 11.9% 60 minutes or more (2000)

EVERGREEN PARK (village). Covers a land area of 3.174 square miles and a water area of 0 square miles. Located at 41.72° N. Lat.; 87.70° W. Long. Elevation is 625 feet.
History: Incorporated 1893. St. Xavier College nearby.
Population: 20,821 (2000); Race: 88.2% White, 7.8% Black, 1.2% Asian, 0.2% American Indian and Alaska Native, 3.9% Hispanic of any race, 1.8% two or more races (2000); Density: 6,560.0 persons per square mile (2000); Age: 27.6% under 18, 17.5% over 64 (2000); Marriage status: 27.5% never married, 54.6% now married, 10.1% widowed, 7.8% divorced (2000); Foreign born: 4.2% (2000); Ancestry (includes multiple ancestries): 39.6% Irish, 21.4% German, 13.4% Other groups, 13.2% Polish, 10.2% Italian (2000).
Vital Statistics: Birth rate: 122.0 per 10,000 population (1998)
Economy: Manufacturing: advertising novelties. Single-family building permits issued: 3 (2001) / 4 (2000); Multi-family building permits issued: 0 (2001) / 0 (2000); Employment by occupation: 14.6% management, 21.8% professional, 10.8% services, 30.4% sales, 0.1% farming, 10.5% construction, 11.8% production (2000).
Income: Per capita income: $23,038 (2000); Median household income: $53,514 (2000); Poverty rate: 4.2% (2000).
Taxes: Total city taxes per capita: $344 (2000); City property taxes per capita: $231 (2000).
Education: High school graduation rate: 88.3% (2000); College graduation rate: 28.1% (2000).

School District(s)

Evergreen Park Community Hi Sch D 231 (09-12)
2000 Enrollment: 729 708-424-7400
Evergreen Pk Elementary School District 124 (PK-08)
2000 Enrollment: 2,070 708-423-0950

Housing: Homeownership rate: 85.4% (2000); Median home value: $134,900 (2000); Median rent: $567 per month (2000); Median age of housing: 46 years (2000).
Hospitals: Little Company of Mary Hospital & Health Care Centers (477 beds)
Transportation: Commute to work: 82.5% car, 11.7% public transportation, 3.1% walk, 2.3% work from home (2000); Travel time to work: 25.0% less than 15 minutes, 22.0% 15 to 30 minutes, 22.9% 30 to 45 minutes, 14.2% 45 to 60 minutes, 15.8% 60 minutes or more (2000)
Additional Information Contacts
Evergreen Park Chamber of Commerce. 708-423-1118

FLOSSMOOR (village). Covers a land area of 3.553 square miles and a water area of 0 square miles. Located at 41.54° N. Lat.; 87.68° W. Long. Elevation is 674 feet.
History: Incorporated 1924.
Population: 9,301 (2000); Race: 65.4% White, 28.2% Black, 4.8% Asian, 0.0% American Indian and Alaska Native, 1.8% Hispanic of any race, 1.1% two or more races (2000); Density: 2,617.6 persons per square mile (2000); Age: 28.5% under 18, 13.0% over 64 (2000); Marriage status: 20.3% never married, 66.5% now married, 6.3% widowed, 7.0% divorced (2000); Foreign born: 10.0% (2000); Ancestry (includes multiple ancestries): 29.8% Other groups, 13.8% German, 13.8% Irish, 9.7% Italian, 7.6% English (2000).
Economy: Manufacturing. Single-family building permits issued: 28 (2001) / 41 (2000); Multi-family building permits issued: 0 (2001) / 0 (2000); Employment by occupation: 23.4% management, 38.5% professional, 5.2% services, 23.7% sales, 0.0% farming, 4.6% construction, 4.6% production (2000).
Income: Per capita income: $42,820 (2000); Median household income: $94,222 (2000); Poverty rate: 2.8% (2000).
Taxes: Total city taxes per capita: $468 (1997); City property taxes per capita: $344 (1997).
Education: High school graduation rate: 96.9% (2000); College graduation rate: 61.0% (2000).

School District(s)

Homewood Flossmoor C H S D 233 (09-12)
2000 Enrollment: 2,533 708-799-3000

Housing: Homeownership rate: 93.7% (2000); Median home value: $216,200 (2000); Median rent: $890 per month (2000); Median age of housing: 35 years (2000).

Transportation: Commute to work: 80.0% car, 13.7% public transportation, 1.7% walk, 3.9% work from home (2000); Travel time to work: 27.8% less than 15 minutes, 20.9% 15 to 30 minutes, 13.7% 30 to 45 minutes, 18.1% 45 to 60 minutes, 19.5% 60 minutes or more (2000)

FORD HEIGHTS (village). Aka East Chicago Heights. Covers a land area of 1.768 square miles and a water area of 0 square miles. Located at 41.50° N. Lat.; 87.58° W. Long. Elevation is 635 feet.

Population: 3,456 (2000); Race: 2.6% White, 95.3% Black, 0.1% Asian, 0.7% American Indian and Alaska Native, 2.5% Hispanic of any race, 0.7% two or more races (2000); Density: 1,954.9 persons per square mile (2000); Age: 45.3% under 18, 6.3% over 64 (2000); Marriage status: 57.5% never married, 30.7% now married, 5.7% widowed, 6.1% divorced (2000); Foreign born: 0.6% (2000); Ancestry (includes multiple ancestries): 79.6% Other groups, 1.5% United States or American, 0.6% African, 0.3% Irish, 0.2% German (2000).

Economy: Single-family building permits issued: 0 (2001) / 0 (2000); Multi-family building permits issued: 0 (2001) / 0 (2000); Employment by occupation: 4.6% management, 11.6% professional, 29.3% services, 27.7% sales, 0.0% farming, 4.0% construction, 22.9% production (2000).

Income: Per capita income: $8,938 (2000); Median household income: $17,500 (2000); Poverty rate: 49.0% (2000).

Taxes: Total city taxes per capita: $247 (1997); City property taxes per capita: $176 (1997).

Education: High school graduation rate: 69.5% (2000); College graduation rate: 4.3% (2000).

School District(s)

Ford Heights School District 169 (PK-08)
2000 Enrollment: 869 708-758-1370

Housing: Homeownership rate: 35.1% (2000); Median home value: $42,300 (2000); Median rent: $369 per month (2000); Median age of housing: 35 years (2000).

Transportation: Commute to work: 76.2% car, 14.6% public transportation, 5.1% walk, 2.6% work from home (2000); Travel time to work: 26.0% less than 15 minutes, 35.6% 15 to 30 minutes, 22.7% 30 to 45 minutes, 8.0% 45 to 60 minutes, 7.7% 60 minutes or more (2000)

FOREST PARK (village). Covers a land area of 2.421 square miles and a water area of 0 square miles. Located at 41.87° N. Lat.; 87.81° W. Long. Elevation is 625 feet.

Population: 15,688 (2000); Race: 55.9% White, 31.8% Black, 6.7% Asian, 0.1% American Indian and Alaska Native, 7.8% Hispanic of any race, 2.5% two or more races (2000); Density: 6,480.8 persons per square mile (2000); Age: 19.5% under 18, 12.0% over 64 (2000); Marriage status: 36.0% never married, 44.1% now married, 6.8% widowed, 13.1% divorced (2000); Foreign born: 14.8% (2000); Ancestry (includes multiple ancestries): 42.3% Other groups, 15.9% German, 14.6% Irish, 8.1% Italian, 5.9% English (2000).

Vital Statistics: Birth rate: 144.1 per 10,000 population (1998)

Economy: Manufacturing: bronze products, burial vaults, cranes, hoists, power presses. Single-family building permits issued: 14 (2001) / 0 (2000); Multi-family building permits issued: 31 (2001) / 0 (2000); Employment by occupation: 12.8% management, 27.0% professional, 14.0% services, 29.1% sales, 0.0% farming, 6.3% construction, 10.8% production (2000).

Income: Per capita income: $26,045 (2000); Median household income: $44,103 (2000); Poverty rate: 7.0% (2000).

Taxes: Total city taxes per capita: $597 (1997); City property taxes per capita: $333 (1997).

Education: High school graduation rate: 88.3% (2000); College graduation rate: 36.3% (2000).

School District(s)

Forest Park School District 91 (PK-08)
2000 Enrollment: 1,283 708-366-5700

Housing: Homeownership rate: 44.8% (2000); Median home value: $138,300 (2000); Median rent: $621 per month (2000); Median age of housing: 49 years (2000).

Hospitals: Riveredge Hospital (210 beds)

Transportation: Commute to work: 75.5% car, 17.0% public transportation, 5.3% walk, 1.7% work from home (2000); Travel time to work: 20.8% less than 15 minutes, 26.8% 15 to 30 minutes, 28.0% 30 to 45 minutes, 15.7% 45 to 60 minutes, 8.8% 60 minutes or more (2000)

Additional Information Contacts

Forest Park Chamber of Commerce 708-366-2543

FOREST VIEW (village). Covers a land area of 1.037 square miles and a water area of 0.132 square miles. Located at 41.80° N. Lat.; 87.78° W. Long. Elevation is 593 feet.

Population: 778 (2000); Race: 96.6% White, 1.0% Black, 0.0% Asian, 0.0% American Indian and Alaska Native, 6.4% Hispanic of any race, 0.0% two or more races (2000); Density: 749.9 persons per square mile (2000); Age: 20.4% under 18, 20.0% over 64 (2000); Marriage status: 25.9% never married, 55.2% now married, 12.4% widowed, 6.5% divorced (2000); Foreign born: 5.0% (2000); Ancestry (includes multiple ancestries): 25.9% Polish, 16.3% Czech, 15.1% Irish, 14.2% German, 13.4% Italian (2000).

Economy: Single-family building permits issued: 0 (2001) / 0 (2000); Multi-family building permits issued: 0 (2001) / 0 (2000); Employment by occupation: 8.9% management, 11.6% professional, 11.4% services, 38.2% sales, 0.0% farming, 9.9% construction, 20.0% production (2000).

Income: Per capita income: $21,376 (2000); Median household income: $46,000 (2000); Poverty rate: 5.2% (2000).

Taxes: Total city taxes per capita: $857 (1997); City property taxes per capita: $701 (1997).

Education: High school graduation rate: 82.4% (2000); College graduation rate: 8.7% (2000).

Housing: Homeownership rate: 88.4% (2000); Median home value: $139,400 (2000); Median rent: $567 per month (2000); Median age of housing: 45 years (2000).

Transportation: Commute to work: 89.5% car, 7.2% public transportation, 2.8% walk, 0.0% work from home (2000); Travel time to work: 30.8% less than 15 minutes, 30.3% 15 to 30 minutes, 21.8% 30 to 45 minutes, 10.3% 45 to 60 minutes, 6.9% 60 minutes or more (2000)

FRANKLIN PARK (village). Covers a land area of 4.658 square miles and a water area of 0 square miles. Located at 41.93° N. Lat.; 87.87° W. Long. Elevation is 640 feet.

Population: 19,434 (2000); Race: 79.9% White, 0.7% Black, 2.5% Asian, 0.0% American Indian and Alaska Native, 38.0% Hispanic of any race, 2.0% two or more races (2000); Density: 4,172.1 persons per square mile (2000); Age: 26.0% under 18, 13.4% over 64 (2000); Marriage status: 27.4% never married, 56.3% now married, 8.6% widowed, 7.6% divorced (2000); Foreign born: 32.8% (2000); Ancestry (includes multiple ancestries): 38.4% Other groups, 19.6% Polish, 14.4% German, 13.0% Italian, 8.2% Irish (2000).

Vital Statistics: Birth rate: 161.6 per 10,000 population (1998)

Economy: Single-family building permits issued: 2 (2001) / 0 (2000); Multi-family building permits issued: 0 (2001) / 0 (2000); Employment by occupation: 8.7% management, 12.2% professional, 11.3% services, 29.6% sales, 0.1% farming, 9.6% construction, 28.5% production (2000).

Income: Per capita income: $17,550 (2000); Median household income: $46,688 (2000); Poverty rate: 7.1% (2000).

Taxes: Total city taxes per capita: $829 (2000); City property taxes per capita: $468 (2000).

Education: High school graduation rate: 67.2% (2000); College graduation rate: 11.3% (2000).

School District(s)

Franklin Park School District 84 (PK-08)
2000 Enrollment: 1,303 847-455-4230

Leyden Community H S District 212 (09-12)
2000 Enrollment: 3,312 847-451-3000

Mannheim School District 83 (PK-12)
2000 Enrollment: 2,829 847-455-4413

Housing: Homeownership rate: 73.4% (2000); Median home value: $143,900 (2000); Median rent: $536 per month (2000); Median age of housing: 45 years (2000).

Transportation: Commute to work: 90.5% car, 4.9% public transportation, 3.1% walk, 1.0% work from home (2000); Travel time to work: 27.1% less than 15 minutes, 32.6% 15 to 30 minutes, 23.1% 30 to 45 minutes, 10.6% 45 to 60 minutes, 6.5% 60 minutes or more (2000)

Additional Information Contacts

Franklin Park Chamber of Commerce 847-455-3350

GLENCOE (village). Covers a land area of 3.777 square miles and a water area of 0.071 square miles. Located at 42.13° N. Lat.; 87.76° W. Long. Elevation is 670 feet.

History: One of the founders of Glencoe was Walter S. Gurnee, and the "coe" part of the town's name came from his wife's maiden name. Glencoe was incorporated as a village in 1869.
Population: 8,762 (2000); Race: 94.7% White, 1.5% Black, 2.5% Asian, 0.0% American Indian and Alaska Native, 2.1% Hispanic of any race, 0.7% two or more races (2000); Density: 2,319.8 persons per square mile (2000); Age: 31.2% under 18, 15.8% over 64 (2000); Marriage status: 14.7% never married, 75.8% now married, 4.8% widowed, 4.7% divorced (2000); Foreign born: 6.5% (2000); Ancestry (includes multiple ancestries): 16.0% German, 13.6% Irish, 11.8% Russian, 11.6% Other groups, 10.7% English (2000).
Economy: Single-family building permits issued: 44 (2001) / 49 (2000); Multi-family building permits issued: 0 (2001) / 0 (2000); Employment by occupation: 34.7% management, 33.9% professional, 4.4% services, 23.5% sales, 0.0% farming, 2.2% construction, 1.3% production (2000).
Income: Per capita income: $88,059 (2000); Median household income: $164,432 (2000); Poverty rate: 2.3% (2000).
Taxes: Total city taxes per capita: $958 (1997); City property taxes per capita: $744 (1997).
Education: High school graduation rate: 97.8% (2000); College graduation rate: 79.7% (2000).

School District(s)

Glencoe School District 35 (KG-08)
2000 Enrollment: 1,306 847-835-7800
Housing: Homeownership rate: 92.1% (2000); Median home value: $667,000 (2000); Median rent: $983 per month (2000); Median age of housing: 49 years (2000).
Transportation: Commute to work: 64.7% car, 20.2% public transportation, 1.9% walk, 12.4% work from home (2000); Travel time to work: 18.6% less than 15 minutes, 24.1% 15 to 30 minutes, 24.5% 30 to 45 minutes, 16.5% 45 to 60 minutes, 16.3% 60 minutes or more (2000)
Additional Information Contacts
Glencoe Chamber of Commerce 847-835-3333

GLENVIEW (village). Covers a land area of 13.450 square miles and a water area of 0.041 square miles. Located at 42.07° N. Lat.; 87.81° W. Long. Elevation is 650 feet.
History: Settled 1833, incorporated 1899.
Population: 41,847 (2000); Race: 84.6% White, 2.0% Black, 10.1% Asian, 0.1% American Indian and Alaska Native, 4.6% Hispanic of any race, 1.4% two or more races (2000); Density: 3,111.3 persons per square mile (2000); Age: 25.6% under 18, 15.9% over 64 (2000); Marriage status: 19.2% never married, 67.8% now married, 6.3% widowed, 6.8% divorced (2000); Foreign born: 19.5% (2000); Ancestry (includes multiple ancestries): 20.6% German, 18.6% Other groups, 17.0% Irish, 9.3% Polish, 7.5% English (2000).
Vital Statistics: Birth rate: 130.0 per 10,000 population (1998)
Economy: U.S. Coast Guard Air Facility is here, along with varied light industry. Manufacturing: plastic products, machinery, printing and publishing, electronic equipment. Peacock Prairie, a center for important botanical research, is nearby. Unemployment rate: 4.4% (11/2002); Total civilian labor force: 21,721 (11/2002); Single-family building permits issued: 360 (2001) / 190 (2000); Multi-family building permits issued: 338 (2001) / 39 (2000); Employment by occupation: 24.8% management, 28.8% professional, 8.0% services, 28.1% sales, 0.1% farming, 4.0% construction, 6.1% production (2000).
Income: Per capita income: $43,384 (2000); Median household income: $80,730 (2000); Poverty rate: 2.0% (2000).
Taxes: Total city taxes per capita: $381 (2000); City property taxes per capita: $247 (2000).
Education: High school graduation rate: 94.3% (2000); College graduation rate: 55.9% (2000).

School District(s)

Glenview C C School District 34 (PK-08)
2000 Enrollment: 3,864 847-998-5000
Northfield Township High School District 225 (09-12)
2000 Enrollment: 4,454 847-998-6100
Housing: Homeownership rate: 87.3% (2000); Median home value: $336,000 (2000); Median rent: $783 per month (2000); Median age of housing: 33 years (2000).
Hospitals: Glenbrook Hospital (144 beds)
Newspapers: Winnetka Talk (1 x week); Northbrook Star (1 x week); Glenview Announcements (1 x week); Glencoe News (1 x week); Wilmette Life (1 x week)
Transportation: Commute to work: 84.7% car, 8.1% public transportation, 1.5% walk, 5.0% work from home (2000); Travel time to work: 19.9% less than 15 minutes, 33.0% 15 to 30 minutes, 25.6% 30 to 45 minutes, 11.5% 45 to 60 minutes, 10.0% 60 minutes or more (2000); Amtrak: Service available.
Additional Information Contacts
Glenview Chamber of Commerce 847-724-0900

GLENWOOD (village). Covers a land area of 2.687 square miles and a water area of 0 square miles. Located at 41.54° N. Lat.; 87.61° W. Long. Elevation is 620 feet.
Population: 9,000 (2000); Race: 51.8% White, 44.2% Black, 0.5% Asian, 0.0% American Indian and Alaska Native, 4.5% Hispanic of any race, 2.1% two or more races (2000); Density: 3,350.1 persons per square mile (2000); Age: 24.7% under 18, 12.9% over 64 (2000); Marriage status: 27.9% never married, 54.4% now married, 8.1% widowed, 9.6% divorced (2000); Foreign born: 3.5% (2000); Ancestry (includes multiple ancestries): 41.4% Other groups, 14.9% German, 10.0% Irish, 7.6% Polish, 7.4% Italian (2000).
Economy: Light manufacturing. Single-family building permits issued: 2 (2001) / 0 (2000); Multi-family building permits issued: 0 (2001) / 0 (2000); Employment by occupation: 13.7% management, 22.9% professional, 11.3% services, 30.7% sales, 0.0% farming, 7.2% construction, 14.1% production (2000).
Income: Per capita income: $24,356 (2000); Median household income: $53,894 (2000); Poverty rate: 3.7% (2000).
Taxes: Total city taxes per capita: $392 (1997); City property taxes per capita: $221 (1997).
Education: High school graduation rate: 90.9% (2000); College graduation rate: 27.9% (2000).

School District(s)

Brookwood School District 167 (PK-08)
2000 Enrollment: 1,239 708-758-5190
Housing: Homeownership rate: 86.7% (2000); Median home value: $126,800 (2000); Median rent: $657 per month (2000); Median age of housing: 30 years (2000).
Transportation: Commute to work: 89.4% car, 7.3% public transportation, 0.2% walk, 2.3% work from home (2000); Travel time to work: 24.0% less than 15 minutes, 28.4% 15 to 30 minutes, 17.9% 30 to 45 minutes, 13.2% 45 to 60 minutes, 16.5% 60 minutes or more (2000)

GOLF (village). Covers a land area of 0.445 square miles and a water area of 0 square miles. Located at 42.05° N. Lat.; 87.79° W. Long. Elevation is 635 feet.
Population: 451 (2000); Race: 97.1% White, 0.0% Black, 0.0% Asian, 0.0% American Indian and Alaska Native, 0.0% Hispanic of any race, 2.9% two or more races (2000); Density: 1,014.5 persons per square mile (2000); Age: 27.9% under 18, 15.0% over 64 (2000); Marriage status: 20.7% never married, 70.3% now married, 4.3% widowed, 4.6% divorced (2000); Foreign born: 3.8% (2000); Ancestry (includes multiple ancestries): 33.2% Irish, 24.6% English, 22.6% German, 10.8% Italian, 6.4% United States or American (2000).
Economy: Single-family building permits issued: 3 (2001) / 3 (2000); Multi-family building permits issued: 0 (2001) / 0 (2000); Employment by occupation: 27.3% management, 28.7% professional, 6.5% services, 32.4% sales, 0.0% farming, 2.8% construction, 2.3% production (2000).
Income: Per capita income: $69,164 (2000); Median household income: $131,742 (2000); Poverty rate: 0.9% (2000).
Taxes: Total city taxes per capita: $984 (1997); City property taxes per capita: $835 (1997).
Education: High school graduation rate: 100.0% (2000); College graduation rate: 82.3% (2000).
Housing: Homeownership rate: 100.0% (2000); Median home value: $550,000 (2000); Median age of housing: 49 years (2000).
Transportation: Commute to work: 67.6% car, 26.8% public transportation, 0.0% walk, 5.6% work from home (2000); Travel time to work: 21.4% less than 15 minutes, 13.4% 15 to 30 minutes, 42.3% 30 to 45 minutes, 12.9% 45 to 60 minutes, 10.0% 60 minutes or more (2000)

HANOVER PARK (village). Covers a land area of 6.794 square miles and a water area of 0 square miles. Located at 41.97° N. Lat.; 88.14° W. Long.
Population: 38,278 (2000); Race: 69.8% White, 6.3% Black, 11.1% Asian, 0.1% American Indian and Alaska Native, 26.3% Hispanic of any race, 2.9% two or more races (2000); Density: 5,634.4 persons per square mile (2000); Age: 31.2% under 18, 4.0% over 64 (2000); Marriage status: 29.7% never married, 58.9% now married, 3.2% widowed, 8.2% divorced (2000); Foreign born: 28.4% (2000); Ancestry (includes multiple ancestries): 40.7% Other groups, 15.5% German, 12.6% Irish, 11.0% Polish, 8.7% Italian (2000).
Vital Statistics: Birth rate: 176.6 per 10,000 population (1998)
Economy: Unemployment rate: 6.5% (11/2002); Total civilian labor force: 21,275 (11/2002); Single-family building permits issued: 3 (2001) / 1 (2000);

Multi-family building permits issued: 0 (2001) / 0 (2000); Employment by occupation: 12.2% management, 14.1% professional, 13.4% services, 31.5% sales, 0.1% farming, 8.8% construction, 19.9% production (2000).
Income: Per capita income: $19,960 (2000); Median household income: $61,358 (2000); Poverty rate: 6.1% (2000).
Taxes: Total city taxes per capita: $273 (2000); City property taxes per capita: $130 (2000).
Education: High school graduation rate: 78.7% (2000); College graduation rate: 20.2% (2000).

School District(s)

Keeneyville School District 20 (PK-08)
2000 Enrollment: 1,675 630-894-2250

Housing: Homeownership rate: 82.0% (2000); Median home value: $141,500 (2000); Median rent: $696 per month (2000); Median age of housing: 25 years (2000).
Transportation: Commute to work: 92.0% car, 3.7% public transportation, 1.8% walk, 1.5% work from home (2000); Travel time to work: 19.6% less than 15 minutes, 34.5% 15 to 30 minutes, 24.8% 30 to 45 minutes, 11.0% 45 to 60 minutes, 10.1% 60 minutes or more (2000)

HARVEY (city). Covers a land area of 6.196 square miles and a water area of 0 square miles. Located at 41.61° N. Lat.; 87.65° W. Long. Elevation is 603 feet.
History: The site of Harvey was purchased in 1889 by Turlington W. Harvey, a Chicago lumberman, who organized a village that attracted other settlers and industries.
Population: 30,000 (2000); Race: 10.1% White, 79.2% Black, 0.4% Asian, 0.2% American Indian and Alaska Native, 13.6% Hispanic of any race, 2.2% two or more races (2000); Density: 4,842.2 persons per square mile (2000); Age: 35.3% under 18, 8.9% over 64 (2000); Marriage status: 38.8% never married, 44.5% now married, 7.6% widowed, 9.1% divorced (2000); Foreign born: 8.2% (2000); Ancestry (includes multiple ancestries): 77.7% Other groups, 2.5% African, 1.6% Polish, 1.2% German, 1.1% United States or American (2000).
Vital Statistics: Birth rate: 229.3 per 10,000 population (1998)
Economy: Unemployment rate: 11.2% (11/2002); Total civilian labor force: 12,270 (11/2002); Single-family building permits issued: 5 (2001) / 6 (2000); Multi-family building permits issued: 0 (2001) / 0 (2000); Employment by occupation: 5.9% management, 14.1% professional, 21.9% services, 28.5% sales, 0.3% farming, 7.3% construction, 22.0% production (2000).
Income: Per capita income: $12,336 (2000); Median household income: $31,958 (2000); Poverty rate: 21.7% (2000).
Taxes: Total city taxes per capita: $398 (1997); City property taxes per capita: $271 (1997).
Education: High school graduation rate: 69.6% (2000); College graduation rate: 8.2% (2000).

School District(s)

Harvey School District 152 (PK-08)
2000 Enrollment: 3,399 708-333-0300
W Harvey-Dixmoor Pub School District 147 (PK-08)
2000 Enrollment: 1,797 708-339-9500

Four-year College(s)

Ingalls Memorial Hospital (Private, Not-for-profit)
2001 Enrollment: 12 708-915-5723

Housing: Homeownership rate: 56.7% (2000); Median home value: $70,500 (2000); Median rent: $490 per month (2000); Median age of housing: 41 years (2000).
Transportation: Commute to work: 80.6% car, 13.1% public transportation, 3.6% walk, 2.2% work from home (2000); Travel time to work: 19.4% less than 15 minutes, 31.4% 15 to 30 minutes, 20.3% 30 to 45 minutes, 10.8% 45 to 60 minutes, 18.2% 60 minutes or more (2000)

HARWOOD HEIGHTS (village). Covers a land area of 0.822 square miles and a water area of 0 square miles. Located at 41.96° N. Lat.; 87.80° W. Long. Elevation is 653 feet.
Population: 8,297 (2000); Race: 92.7% White, 0.9% Black, 4.4% Asian, 0.3% American Indian and Alaska Native, 4.9% Hispanic of any race, 1.2% two or more races (2000); Density: 10,094.4 persons per square mile (2000); Age: 18.6% under 18, 21.4% over 64 (2000); Marriage status: 25.1% never married, 53.5% now married, 13.8% widowed, 7.7% divorced (2000); Foreign born: 34.1% (2000); Ancestry (includes multiple ancestries): 37.4% Polish, 17.8% Italian, 14.5% German, 12.7% Other groups, 9.8% Irish (2000).
Economy: Manufacturing: fabricated metal products, machinery, tapes and adhesives, tools. Single-family building permits issued: 20 (2001) / 35 (2000); Multi-family building permits issued: 2 (2001) / 0 (2000); Employment by occupation: 11.4% management, 12.9% professional, 13.9% services, 34.3% sales, 0.0% farming, 11.4% construction, 16.2% production (2000).
Income: Per capita income: $22,558 (2000); Median household income: $43,288 (2000); Poverty rate: 4.6% (2000).
Taxes: Total city taxes per capita: $538 (1997); City property taxes per capita: $80 (1997).
Education: High school graduation rate: 77.7% (2000); College graduation rate: 16.7% (2000).

School District(s)

Union Ridge School District 86 (PK-08)
2000 Enrollment: 536 708-867-5822

Housing: Homeownership rate: 61.4% (2000); Median home value: $191,700 (2000); Median rent: $664 per month (2000); Median age of housing: 37 years (2000).
Transportation: Commute to work: 83.6% car, 9.3% public transportation, 3.3% walk, 2.7% work from home (2000); Travel time to work: 21.2% less than 15 minutes, 33.6% 15 to 30 minutes, 25.3% 30 to 45 minutes, 10.3% 45 to 60 minutes, 9.6% 60 minutes or more (2000)

HAZEL CREST (village). Covers a land area of 3.381 square miles and a water area of 0.023 square miles. Located at 41.57° N. Lat.; 87.68° W. Long. Elevation is 648 feet.
Population: 14,816 (2000); Race: 20.0% White, 75.7% Black, 0.3% Asian, 0.0% American Indian and Alaska Native, 3.7% Hispanic of any race, 2.3% two or more races (2000); Density: 4,381.5 persons per square mile (2000); Age: 30.0% under 18, 10.1% over 64 (2000); Marriage status: 32.3% never married, 48.3% now married, 6.9% widowed, 12.5% divorced (2000); Foreign born: 3.4% (2000); Ancestry (includes multiple ancestries): 70.6% Other groups, 4.3% German, 4.0% Irish, 3.1% English, 2.2% Polish (2000).
Vital Statistics: Birth rate: 129.6 per 10,000 population (1998)
Economy: Single-family building permits issued: 23 (2001) / 31 (2000); Multi-family building permits issued: 0 (2001) / 0 (2000); Employment by occupation: 12.8% management, 19.8% professional, 13.9% services, 31.4% sales, 0.0% farming, 6.6% construction, 15.5% production (2000).
Income: Per capita income: $19,908 (2000); Median household income: $50,576 (2000); Poverty rate: 8.4% (2000).
Taxes: Total city taxes per capita: $325 (1997); City property taxes per capita: $208 (1997).
Education: High school graduation rate: 88.2% (2000); College graduation rate: 22.1% (2000).

School District(s)

Hazel Crest School District 152-5 (PK-08)
2000 Enrollment: 1,189 708-335-0790
Prairie-Hills Elementary School District 144 (PK-08)
2000 Enrollment: 2,897 708-210-2888

Housing: Homeownership rate: 81.9% (2000); Median home value: $98,700 (2000); Median rent: $763 per month (2000); Median age of housing: 31 years (2000).
Hospitals: Advocate South Suburban Hospital (291 beds)
Newspapers: Muslim Journal (1 x week)
Transportation: Commute to work: 84.8% car, 9.5% public transportation, 1.2% walk, 2.9% work from home (2000); Travel time to work: 18.1% less than 15 minutes, 24.2% 15 to 30 minutes, 24.2% 30 to 45 minutes, 15.9% 45 to 60 minutes, 17.7% 60 minutes or more (2000)

Additional Information Contacts

Hazel Crest Chamber of Commerce.......................... 708-335-4699

HICKORY HILLS (city). Covers a land area of 2.834 square miles and a water area of 0 square miles. Located at 41.72° N. Lat.; 87.82° W. Long. Elevation is 700 feet.
Population: 13,926 (2000); Race: 88.9% White, 1.0% Black, 2.2% Asian, 0.5% American Indian and Alaska Native, 7.2% Hispanic of any race, 4.8% two or more races (2000); Density: 4,913.0 persons per square mile (2000); Age: 24.4% under 18, 12.5% over 64 (2000); Marriage status: 26.5% never married, 56.8% now married, 8.0% widowed, 8.7% divorced (2000); Foreign born: 16.8% (2000); Ancestry (includes multiple ancestries): 26.9% Polish, 19.9% Irish, 17.2% German, 11.8% Other groups, 10.7% Italian (2000).
Vital Statistics: Birth rate: 142.9 per 10,000 population (1998)
Economy: Manufacturing: fabricated metal products, machinery, electronic goods; sheet metal fabricating, diverse light manufacturing. Single-family building permits issued: 7 (2001) / 1 (2000); Multi-family building permits issued: 0 (2001) / 0 (2000); Employment by occupation: 11.7% management, 17.0% professional, 11.2% services, 31.3% sales, 0.0% farming, 11.8% construction, 16.9% production (2000).

Income: Per capita income: $23,747 (2000); Median household income: $54,779 (2000); Poverty rate: 5.5% (2000).
Taxes: Total city taxes per capita: $278 (2000); City property taxes per capita: $246 (2000).
Education: High school graduation rate: 81.8% (2000); College graduation rate: 21.3% (2000).

School District(s)

North Palos School District 117 (PK-08)
2000 Enrollment: 2,468 708-598-5500

Two-year College(s)

Northwestern Business College-Southwestern Campus (Private, For-profit)
2001 Enrollment: 803 773-777-4220
2001 Tuition: In-state $12,600; Out-of-state $12,600

Housing: Homeownership rate: 73.7% (2000); Median home value: $164,200 (2000); Median rent: $613 per month (2000); Median age of housing: 32 years (2000).
Transportation: Commute to work: 92.0% car, 2.4% public transportation, 2.1% walk, 3.0% work from home (2000); Travel time to work: 18.8% less than 15 minutes, 33.8% 15 to 30 minutes, 21.6% 30 to 45 minutes, 13.1% 45 to 60 minutes, 12.7% 60 minutes or more (2000)
Additional Information Contacts
Hickory Hills Chamber of Commerce 708-598-4800

HILLSIDE (village). Covers a land area of 2.148 square miles and a water area of 0 square miles. Located at 41.87° N. Lat.; 87.90° W. Long. Elevation is 659 feet.
History: Incorporated 1905.
Population: 8,155 (2000); Race: 49.4% White, 37.0% Black, 5.3% Asian, 0.0% American Indian and Alaska Native, 14.1% Hispanic of any race, 2.3% two or more races (2000); Density: 3,797.4 persons per square mile (2000); Age: 23.5% under 18, 16.2% over 64 (2000); Marriage status: 30.5% never married, 52.1% now married, 6.7% widowed, 10.7% divorced (2000); Foreign born: 13.5% (2000); Ancestry (includes multiple ancestries): 46.7% Other groups, 11.4% German, 9.3% Italian, 9.3% Irish, 5.3% Polish (2000).
Economy: Computer services. Single-family building permits issued: 0 (2001) / 0 (2000); Multi-family building permits issued: 0 (2001) / 0 (2000); Employment by occupation: 12.4% management, 20.1% professional, 12.2% services, 27.7% sales, 0.0% farming, 6.0% construction, 21.7% production (2000).
Income: Per capita income: $21,638 (2000); Median household income: $50,776 (2000); Poverty rate: 6.3% (2000).
Taxes: Total city taxes per capita: $968 (2000); City property taxes per capita: $709 (2000).
Education: High school graduation rate: 81.4% (2000); College graduation rate: 20.4% (2000).

School District(s)

Hillside School District 93 (KG-08)
2000 Enrollment: 515 708-449-7280

Housing: Homeownership rate: 69.9% (2000); Median home value: $133,900 (2000); Median rent: $659 per month (2000); Median age of housing: 43 years (2000).
Transportation: Commute to work: 92.0% car, 3.5% public transportation, 2.7% walk, 1.8% work from home (2000); Travel time to work: 19.4% less than 15 minutes, 36.8% 15 to 30 minutes, 22.5% 30 to 45 minutes, 11.2% 45 to 60 minutes, 10.1% 60 minutes or more (2000)
Additional Information Contacts
Hillside Chamber of Commerce 708-449-2449

HODGKINS (village). Covers a land area of 2.572 square miles and a water area of 0.065 square miles. Located at 41.76° N. Lat.; 87.85° W. Long. Elevation is 608 feet.
Population: 2,134 (2000); Race: 79.7% White, 0.0% Black, 0.2% Asian, 1.1% American Indian and Alaska Native, 44.1% Hispanic of any race, 2.3% two or more races (2000); Density: 829.7 persons per square mile (2000); Age: 25.2% under 18, 14.1% over 64 (2000); Marriage status: 26.3% never married, 50.5% now married, 8.8% widowed, 14.4% divorced (2000); Foreign born: 32.9% (2000); Ancestry (includes multiple ancestries): 42.8% Other groups, 12.7% Irish, 12.4% German, 8.0% Polish, 7.0% English (2000).
Economy: On the Sanitary and Ship Canal. Single-family building permits issued: 1 (2001) / 1 (2000); Multi-family building permits issued: 0 (2001) / 0 (2000); Employment by occupation: 7.1% management, 7.3% professional, 31.3% services, 23.5% sales, 0.0% farming, 10.6% construction, 20.2% production (2000).
Income: Per capita income: $17,920 (2000); Median household income: $36,090 (2000); Poverty rate: 15.5% (2000).
Taxes: Total city taxes per capita: $2,108 (1997); City property taxes per capita: $1,778 (1997).
Education: High school graduation rate: 60.2% (2000); College graduation rate: 6.5% (2000).
Housing: Homeownership rate: 66.0% (2000); Median home value: $160,800 (2000); Median rent: $526 per month (2000); Median age of housing: 22 years (2000).
Transportation: Commute to work: 77.8% car, 3.1% public transportation, 9.7% walk, 0.2% work from home (2000); Travel time to work: 34.8% less than 15 minutes, 40.3% 15 to 30 minutes, 12.0% 30 to 45 minutes, 6.4% 45 to 60 minutes, 6.4% 60 minutes or more (2000)

HOFFMAN ESTATES (village). Covers a land area of 19.710 square miles and a water area of 0.158 square miles. Located at 42.06° N. Lat.; 88.11° W. Long. Elevation is 780 feet.
Population: 49,495 (2000); Race: 73.8% White, 4.2% Black, 14.9% Asian, 0.3% American Indian and Alaska Native, 10.4% Hispanic of any race, 2.7% two or more races (2000); Density: 2,511.2 persons per square mile (2000); Age: 28.5% under 18, 6.6% over 64 (2000); Marriage status: 27.6% never married, 59.9% now married, 4.5% widowed, 8.0% divorced (2000); Foreign born: 23.1% (2000); Ancestry (includes multiple ancestries): 29.4% Other groups, 21.9% German, 14.7% Irish, 13.3% Polish, 10.8% Italian (2000).
Economy: Unemployment rate: 4.9% (11/2002); Total civilian labor force: 29,181 (11/2002); Single-family building permits issued: 188 (2001) / 39 (2000); Multi-family building permits issued: 0 (2001) / 0 (2000); Employment by occupation: 18.3% management, 22.8% professional, 9.6% services, 31.2% sales, 0.1% farming, 6.1% construction, 11.9% production (2000).
Income: Per capita income: $26,669 (2000); Median household income: $65,937 (2000); Poverty rate: 4.4% (2000).
Taxes: Total city taxes per capita: $690 (2000); City property taxes per capita: $572 (2000).
Education: High school graduation rate: 89.6% (2000); College graduation rate: 35.9% (2000).
Housing: Homeownership rate: 76.3% (2000); Median home value: $181,700 (2000); Median rent: $845 per month (2000); Median age of housing: 25 years (2000).
Hospitals: Saint Alexius Medical Center (344 beds)
Transportation: Commute to work: 91.8% car, 3.3% public transportation, 1.3% walk, 2.7% work from home (2000); Travel time to work: 18.5% less than 15 minutes, 37.8% 15 to 30 minutes, 24.9% 30 to 45 minutes, 9.8% 45 to 60 minutes, 9.0% 60 minutes or more (2000)
Additional Information Contacts
Hoffman Estates Chamber of Commerce 847-781-9100

HOMETOWN (city). Covers a land area of 0.478 square miles and a water area of 0 square miles. Located at 41.73° N. Lat.; 87.73° W. Long. Elevation is 620 feet.
Population: 4,467 (2000); Race: 97.2% White, 0.2% Black, 0.0% Asian, 0.4% American Indian and Alaska Native, 3.0% Hispanic of any race, 1.0% two or more races (2000); Density: 9,354.6 persons per square mile (2000); Age: 23.1% under 18, 18.9% over 64 (2000); Marriage status: 25.3% never married, 49.8% now married, 14.0% widowed, 10.9% divorced (2000); Foreign born: 2.9% (2000); Ancestry (includes multiple ancestries): 33.6% Irish, 28.7% German, 18.8% Polish, 13.0% Italian, 7.7% Other groups (2000).
Economy: Single-family building permits issued: 0 (2001) / 0 (2000); Multi-family building permits issued: 0 (2001) / 0 (2000); Employment by occupation: 8.9% management, 11.1% professional, 13.9% services, 35.6% sales, 0.0% farming, 16.0% construction, 14.6% production (2000).
Income: Per capita income: $19,149 (2000); Median household income: $39,512 (2000); Poverty rate: 3.0% (2000).
Taxes: Total city taxes per capita: $121 (1997); City property taxes per capita: $75 (1997).
Education: High school graduation rate: 82.1% (2000); College graduation rate: 8.6% (2000).
Housing: Homeownership rate: 77.9% (2000); Median home value: $96,500 (2000); Median rent: $233 per month (2000); Median age of housing: 46 years (2000).
Transportation: Commute to work: 91.3% car, 5.1% public transportation, 1.7% walk, 1.7% work from home (2000); Travel time to work: 26.3% less than 15 minutes, 27.3% 15 to 30 minutes, 25.2% 30 to 45 minutes, 9.5% 45 to 60 minutes, 11.7% 60 minutes or more (2000)

HOMEWOOD (village). Covers a land area of 5.204 square miles and a water area of 0.052 square miles. Located at 41.55° N. Lat.; 87.66° W. Long. Elevation is 650 feet.
History: The site of Homewood was laid out in 1852 by James Hart and was first known as Hartford.
Population: 19,543 (2000); Race: 77.9% White, 18.0% Black, 1.1% Asian, 0.3% American Indian and Alaska Native, 3.1% Hispanic of any race, 1.6% two or more races (2000); Density: 3,755.5 persons per square mile (2000); Age: 27.0% under 18, 16.6% over 64 (2000); Marriage status: 23.7% never married, 59.2% now married, 8.5% widowed, 8.6% divorced (2000); Foreign born: 4.4% (2000); Ancestry (includes multiple ancestries): 22.7% German, 21.7% Other groups, 19.0% Irish, 10.3% Polish, 9.7% Italian (2000).
Vital Statistics: Birth rate: 107.5 per 10,000 population (1998)
Economy: Single-family building permits issued: 36 (2001) / 29 (2000); Multi-family building permits issued: 0 (2001) / 0 (2000); Employment by occupation: 17.0% management, 31.9% professional, 8.9% services, 27.4% sales, 0.0% farming, 7.7% construction, 7.0% production (2000).
Income: Per capita income: $26,074 (2000); Median household income: $57,213 (2000); Poverty rate: 4.3% (2000).
Taxes: Total city taxes per capita: $637 (2000); City property taxes per capita: $592 (2000).
Education: High school graduation rate: 93.3% (2000); College graduation rate: 40.9% (2000).

School District(s)

Homewood School District 153 (PK-08)
2000 Enrollment: 2,288 708-799-5661

Housing: Homeownership rate: 85.4% (2000); Median home value: $137,300 (2000); Median rent: $669 per month (2000); Median age of housing: 38 years (2000).
Transportation: Commute to work: 79.0% car, 15.9% public transportation, 0.9% walk, 3.7% work from home (2000); Travel time to work: 26.4% less than 15 minutes, 25.4% 15 to 30 minutes, 14.1% 30 to 45 minutes, 14.1% 45 to 60 minutes, 20.0% 60 minutes or more (2000); Amtrak: Service available.

Additional Information Contacts

Homewood Chamber of Commerce. 708-957-6950

INDIAN HEAD PARK (village). Covers a land area of 0.842 square miles and a water area of 0 square miles. Located at 41.76° N. Lat.; 87.89° W. Long. Elevation is 700 feet.
Population: 3,685 (2000); Race: 97.3% White, 0.4% Black, 1.3% Asian, 0.2% American Indian and Alaska Native, 2.0% Hispanic of any race, 0.5% two or more races (2000); Density: 4,376.6 persons per square mile (2000); Age: 16.2% under 18, 33.7% over 64 (2000); Marriage status: 17.2% never married, 58.3% now married, 13.3% widowed, 11.2% divorced (2000); Foreign born: 6.6% (2000); Ancestry (includes multiple ancestries): 26.4% German, 22.8% Irish, 14.3% Polish, 8.4% English, 7.7% Italian (2000).
Economy: Single-family building permits issued: 51 (2001) / 5 (2000); Multi-family building permits issued: 0 (2001) / 0 (2000); Employment by occupation: 22.2% management, 22.8% professional, 6.5% services, 37.6% sales, 0.0% farming, 4.8% construction, 6.1% production (2000).
Income: Per capita income: $40,094 (2000); Median household income: $63,250 (2000); Poverty rate: 2.3% (2000).
Taxes: Total city taxes per capita: $395 (1997); City property taxes per capita: $170 (1997).
Education: High school graduation rate: 93.6% (2000); College graduation rate: 37.8% (2000).
Housing: Homeownership rate: 95.3% (2000); Median home value: $230,200 (2000); Median rent: $891 per month (2000); Median age of housing: 22 years (2000).
Transportation: Commute to work: 88.5% car, 6.2% public transportation, 0.0% walk, 5.3% work from home (2000); Travel time to work: 20.8% less than 15 minutes, 32.2% 15 to 30 minutes, 26.2% 30 to 45 minutes, 14.7% 45 to 60 minutes, 6.2% 60 minutes or more (2000)

INVERNESS (village). Covers a land area of 6.318 square miles and a water area of 0.151 square miles. Located at 42.11° N. Lat.; 88.09° W. Long. Elevation is 853 feet.
History: Incorporated 1962.
Population: 6,749 (2000); Race: 92.8% White, 0.6% Black, 2.8% Asian, 0.0% American Indian and Alaska Native, 1.1% Hispanic of any race, 3.1% two or more races (2000); Density: 1,068.3 persons per square mile (2000); Age: 23.7% under 18, 12.5% over 64 (2000); Marriage status: 18.3% never married, 74.2% now married, 4.4% widowed, 3.1% divorced (2000); Foreign born: 11.1% (2000); Ancestry (includes multiple ancestries): 29.1% German, 21.8% Irish, 14.0% Italian, 13.1% Polish, 11.2% English (2000).
Economy: Some remnant agriculture. Single-family building permits issued: 42 (2001) / 29 (2000); Multi-family building permits issued: 0 (2001) / 0 (2000); Employment by occupation: 37.2% management, 18.2% professional, 4.4% services, 31.0% sales, 0.0% farming, 4.2% construction, 5.1% production (2000).
Income: Per capita income: $73,271 (2000); Median household income: $141,672 (2000); Poverty rate: 1.5% (2000).
Taxes: Total city taxes per capita: $206 (1997); City property taxes per capita: $90 (1997).
Education: High school graduation rate: 94.0% (2000); College graduation rate: 53.9% (2000).
Housing: Homeownership rate: 98.2% (2000); Median home value: $469,300 (2000); Median rent: $908 per month (2000); Median age of housing: 20 years (2000).
Transportation: Commute to work: 86.0% car, 7.5% public transportation, 0.5% walk, 5.7% work from home (2000); Travel time to work: 16.4% less than 15 minutes, 34.2% 15 to 30 minutes, 23.8% 30 to 45 minutes, 13.2% 45 to 60 minutes, 12.4% 60 minutes or more (2000)

JUSTICE (village). Covers a land area of 2.912 square miles and a water area of 0.042 square miles. Located at 41.74° N. Lat.; 87.83° W. Long. Elevation is 625 feet.
Population: 12,193 (2000); Race: 71.2% White, 19.5% Black, 2.3% Asian, 0.0% American Indian and Alaska Native, 8.1% Hispanic of any race, 4.0% two or more races (2000); Density: 4,187.5 persons per square mile (2000); Age: 27.2% under 18, 6.6% over 64 (2000); Marriage status: 33.1% never married, 53.3% now married, 4.6% widowed, 9.0% divorced (2000); Foreign born: 19.3% (2000); Ancestry (includes multiple ancestries): 26.7% Other groups, 24.2% Polish, 13.1% German, 11.8% Irish, 5.7% Italian (2000).
Vital Statistics: Birth rate: 195.2 per 10,000 population (1998)
Economy: Single-family building permits issued: 17 (2001) / 5 (2000); Multi-family building permits issued: 30 (2001) / 10 (2000); Employment by occupation: 10.1% management, 12.4% professional, 13.0% services, 29.5% sales, 0.0% farming, 12.2% construction, 22.8% production (2000).
Income: Per capita income: $20,714 (2000); Median household income: $50,254 (2000); Poverty rate: 7.3% (2000).
Taxes: Total city taxes per capita: $129 (1997); City property taxes per capita: $56 (1997).
Education: High school graduation rate: 79.0% (2000); College graduation rate: 12.9% (2000).

School District(s)

Indian Springs School District 109 (PK-08)
2000 Enrollment: 2,877 708-496-8700

Housing: Homeownership rate: 54.1% (2000); Median home value: $143,500 (2000); Median rent: $670 per month (2000); Median age of housing: 28 years (2000).
Transportation: Commute to work: 91.8% car, 5.2% public transportation, 0.9% walk, 0.6% work from home (2000); Travel time to work: 18.5% less than 15 minutes, 30.2% 15 to 30 minutes, 25.8% 30 to 45 minutes, 12.2% 45 to 60 minutes, 13.2% 60 minutes or more (2000)

KENILWORTH (village). Covers a land area of 0.595 square miles and a water area of 0 square miles. Located at 42.08° N. Lat.; 87.71° W. Long. Elevation is 610 feet.
History: Kenilworth was named for the novel by Sir Walter Scott. Many streets in the town are named for places or characters in the book. Kenilworth is the burial place of poet Eugene Field.
Population: 2,494 (2000); Race: 96.2% White, 0.0% Black, 3.5% Asian, 0.0% American Indian and Alaska Native, 2.6% Hispanic of any race, 0.2% two or more races (2000); Density: 4,190.8 persons per square mile (2000); Age: 35.2% under 18, 11.8% over 64 (2000); Marriage status: 18.1% never married, 75.5% now married, 3.8% widowed, 2.5% divorced (2000); Foreign born: 8.5% (2000); Ancestry (includes multiple ancestries): 26.3% Irish, 22.1% English, 20.6% German, 8.9% Italian, 8.0% Other groups (2000).
Economy: Single-family building permits issued: 4 (2001) / 3 (2000); Multi-family building permits issued: 0 (2001) / 0 (2000); Employment by occupation: 39.2% management, 31.8% professional, 4.5% services, 23.4% sales, 0.0% farming, 0.7% construction, 0.3% production (2000).
Income: Per capita income: $100,718 (2000); Median household income: $200,001 (2000); Poverty rate: 1.1% (2000).
Taxes: Total city taxes per capita: $896 (1997); City property taxes per capita: $733 (1997).
Education: High school graduation rate: 99.8% (2000); College graduation rate: 89.4% (2000).

School District(s)
Kenilworth School District 38 (PK-08)
2000 Enrollment: 571 847-256-5006
Housing: Homeownership rate: 95.6% (2000); Median home value: $972,000 (2000); Median rent: $1,031 per month (2000); Median age of housing: 60+ years (2000).
Transportation: Commute to work: 61.8% car, 24.9% public transportation, 1.0% walk, 11.1% work from home (2000); Travel time to work: 14.5% less than 15 minutes, 20.2% 15 to 30 minutes, 23.1% 30 to 45 minutes, 22.2% 45 to 60 minutes, 20.0% 60 minutes or more (2000)

LA GRANGE (village). Covers a land area of 2.509 square miles and a water area of 0 square miles. Located at 41.80° N. Lat.; 87.87° W. Long. Elevation is 640 feet.
History: La Grange was founded by W.D. Cossitt and named for Marquis de Lafayette's home in France. An early settlement along the Chicago, Burlington & Quincy Railroad, La Grange was incorporated in 1879.
Population: 15,608 (2000); Race: 90.8% White, 6.4% Black, 0.6% Asian, 0.0% American Indian and Alaska Native, 3.6% Hispanic of any race, 1.3% two or more races (2000); Density: 6,220.7 persons per square mile (2000); Age: 28.5% under 18, 13.8% over 64 (2000); Marriage status: 22.3% never married, 63.0% now married, 7.4% widowed, 7.3% divorced (2000); Foreign born: 5.6% (2000); Ancestry (includes multiple ancestries): 25.2% Irish, 24.8% German, 10.5% Polish, 10.3% Other groups, 10.2% Italian (2000).
Vital Statistics: Birth rate: 182.6 per 10,000 population (1998)
Economy: Single-family building permits issued: 32 (2001) / 7 (2000); Multi-family building permits issued: 32 (2001) / 0 (2000); Employment by occupation: 28.1% management, 28.0% professional, 6.8% services, 27.7% sales, 0.1% farming, 3.6% construction, 5.8% production (2000).
Income: Per capita income: $34,887 (2000); Median household income: $80,342 (2000); Poverty rate: 4.0% (2000).
Taxes: Total city taxes per capita: $387 (1997); City property taxes per capita: $349 (1997).
Education: High school graduation rate: 92.7% (2000); College graduation rate: 55.0% (2000).

School District(s)
La Grange School District 105 (South) (PK-08)
2000 Enrollment: 1,048 708-482-2700
Lagrange Highlands School District 106 (PK-08)
2000 Enrollment: 898 708-246-3085
Lyons Township H S District 204 (09-12)
2000 Enrollment: 3,283 708-579-6451
Housing: Homeownership rate: 81.6% (2000); Median home value: $271,800 (2000); Median rent: $677 per month (2000); Median age of housing: 50 years (2000).
Hospitals: La Grange Memorial Hospital (274 beds)
Transportation: Commute to work: 74.6% car, 17.6% public transportation, 2.6% walk, 4.6% work from home (2000); Travel time to work: 22.8% less than 15 minutes, 25.3% 15 to 30 minutes, 26.3% 30 to 45 minutes, 13.1% 45 to 60 minutes, 12.5% 60 minutes or more (2000); Amtrak: Service available.
Additional Information Contacts
West Suburban Chamber of Commerce. 708-352-0494

LA GRANGE PARK (village). Covers a land area of 2.253 square miles and a water area of 0 square miles. Located at 41.83° N. Lat.; 87.86° W. Long. Elevation is 625 feet.
History: Incorporated 1892.
Population: 13,295 (2000); Race: 92.2% White, 3.0% Black, 2.2% Asian, 0.4% American Indian and Alaska Native, 2.8% Hispanic of any race, 1.1% two or more races (2000); Density: 5,899.8 persons per square mile (2000); Age: 23.4% under 18, 21.6% over 64 (2000); Marriage status: 22.4% never married, 58.1% now married, 12.7% widowed, 6.8% divorced (2000); Foreign born: 7.1% (2000); Ancestry (includes multiple ancestries): 22.6% Irish, 22.0% German, 16.1% Polish, 11.7% Italian, 9.5% Other groups (2000).
Vital Statistics: Birth rate: 151.9 per 10,000 population (1998)
Economy: Manufacturing: pens. Single-family building permits issued: 13 (2001) / 2 (2000); Multi-family building permits issued: 0 (2001) / 2 (2000); Employment by occupation: 17.8% management, 25.4% professional, 10.1% services, 33.7% sales, 0.3% farming, 5.5% construction, 7.2% production (2000).
Income: Per capita income: $30,247 (2000); Median household income: $58,918 (2000); Poverty rate: 2.6% (2000).
Taxes: Total city taxes per capita: $193 (1997); City property taxes per capita: $106 (1997).
Education: High school graduation rate: 92.3% (2000); College graduation rate: 41.6% (2000).

School District(s)
La Grange School District 102 (PK-08)
2000 Enrollment: 2,578 708-482-2400
Housing: Homeownership rate: 71.5% (2000); Median home value: $205,100 (2000); Median rent: $727 per month (2000); Median age of housing: 46 years (2000).
Transportation: Commute to work: 83.3% car, 9.8% public transportation, 2.2% walk, 4.1% work from home (2000); Travel time to work: 21.3% less than 15 minutes, 29.2% 15 to 30 minutes, 27.4% 30 to 45 minutes, 13.9% 45 to 60 minutes, 8.2% 60 minutes or more (2000); Amtrak: Service available.

LANSING (village). Covers a land area of 6.764 square miles and a water area of 0.064 square miles. Located at 41.56° N. Lat.; 87.54° W. Long. Elevation is 630 feet.
History: Lansing was settled in the 1860's by Dutch and German farmers.
Population: 28,332 (2000); Race: 85.5% White, 10.9% Black, 0.7% Asian, 0.2% American Indian and Alaska Native, 5.6% Hispanic of any race, 1.2% two or more races (2000); Density: 4,188.7 persons per square mile (2000); Age: 24.3% under 18, 15.5% over 64 (2000); Marriage status: 25.7% never married, 56.7% now married, 8.5% widowed, 9.1% divorced (2000); Foreign born: 5.6% (2000); Ancestry (includes multiple ancestries): 20.4% German, 17.2% Other groups, 15.7% Polish, 15.5% Irish, 13.7% Dutch (2000).
Vital Statistics: Birth rate: 127.4 per 10,000 population (1998)
Economy: Unemployment rate: 5.4% (11/2002); Total civilian labor force: 15,537 (11/2002); Single-family building permits issued: 22 (2001) / 6 (2000); Multi-family building permits issued: 0 (2001) / 0 (2000); Employment by occupation: 12.4% management, 17.5% professional, 13.3% services, 29.2% sales, 0.1% farming, 12.6% construction, 15.0% production (2000).
Income: Per capita income: $22,547 (2000); Median household income: $47,554 (2000); Poverty rate: 5.4% (2000).
Taxes: Total city taxes per capita: $153 (1997); City property taxes per capita: $78 (1997).
Education: High school graduation rate: 86.6% (2000); College graduation rate: 18.2% (2000).

School District(s)
Lansing School District 158 (PK-08)
2000 Enrollment: 1,901 708-474-6700
Sunnybrook School District 171 (PK-08)
2000 Enrollment: 1,188 708-895-0750
Housing: Homeownership rate: 75.4% (2000); Median home value: $118,700 (2000); Median rent: $612 per month (2000); Median age of housing: 36 years (2000).
Transportation: Commute to work: 89.2% car, 6.1% public transportation, 2.3% walk, 2.1% work from home (2000); Travel time to work: 29.1% less than 15 minutes, 29.9% 15 to 30 minutes, 16.6% 30 to 45 minutes, 9.7% 45 to 60 minutes, 14.8% 60 minutes or more (2000)
Additional Information Contacts
Chicago Southland Convention & Visitors Bureau 708-895-8200
Lansing Chamber of Commerce. 708-474-4170

LEMONT (village). Covers a land area of 6.453 square miles and a water area of 0.348 square miles. Located at 41.66° N. Lat.; 87.98° W. Long. Elevation is 720 feet.
History: Incorporated 1873.
Population: 13,098 (2000); Race: 97.7% White, 0.4% Black, 0.6% Asian, 0.1% American Indian and Alaska Native, 2.8% Hispanic of any race, 0.5% two or more races (2000); Density: 2,029.9 persons per square mile (2000); Age: 27.5% under 18, 14.5% over 64 (2000); Marriage status: 21.3% never married, 63.9% now married, 9.0% widowed, 5.8% divorced (2000); Foreign born: 9.7% (2000); Ancestry (includes multiple ancestries): 32.8% Polish, 25.5% German, 20.6% Irish, 12.1% Italian, 5.3% Other groups (2000).
Economy: Oil refining. Manufacturing of aluminum products; limestone quarries. Ships petroleum, stone. Argonne National Laboratory for atomic research and Argonne Forest Preserve recreational area are nearby. Single-family building permits issued: 195 (2001) / 142 (2000); Multi-family building permits issued: 0 (2001) / 43 (2000); Employment by occupation: 19.5% management, 24.5% professional, 10.0% services, 26.0% sales, 0.0% farming, 9.0% construction, 11.0% production (2000).
Income: Per capita income: $28,354 (2000); Median household income: $70,563 (2000); Poverty rate: 3.6% (2000).
Taxes: Total city taxes per capita: $215 (1997); City property taxes per capita: $157 (1997).

Education: High school graduation rate: 86.5% (2000); College graduation rate: 32.0% (2000).

School District(s)

Lemont Township H S District 210 (09-12)
2000 Enrollment: 978 630-257-5838
Lemont-Bromberek CSD 113a (PK-08)
2000 Enrollment: 2,316 630-257-2286

Housing: Homeownership rate: 82.3% (2000); Median home value: $225,700 (2000); Median rent: $669 per month (2000); Median age of housing: 17 years (2000).
Newspapers: Romeoville Metropolitan (1 x week); Lemont Metropolitan (1 x week); Bolingbrook Metropolitan (1 x week); Palos Hills-Palos Park Villager (2 x month); New Lenox Villager (2 x month); Tinley Park-Crestwood Villager (2 x month); Oak Forest-Palos Heights Villager (2 x month); Mokena-Frankfort Villager (2 x month)
Transportation: Commute to work: 88.0% car, 6.3% public transportation, 1.0% walk, 3.9% work from home (2000); Travel time to work: 19.2% less than 15 minutes, 23.9% 15 to 30 minutes, 28.8% 30 to 45 minutes, 11.3% 45 to 60 minutes, 16.6% 60 minutes or more (2000)
Additional Information Contacts
Lemont Chamber of Commerce 630-257-5997

LINCOLNWOOD (village). Covers a land area of 2.687 square miles and a water area of 0 square miles. Located at 42.00° N. Lat.; 87.73° W. Long. Elevation is 603 feet.
History: Until 1935 called Tessville.
Population: 12,359 (2000); Race: 74.0% White, 0.0% Black, 21.4% Asian, 0.0% American Indian and Alaska Native, 4.3% Hispanic of any race, 3.0% two or more races (2000); Density: 4,599.7 persons per square mile (2000); Age: 22.7% under 18, 24.2% over 64 (2000); Marriage status: 19.2% never married, 65.5% now married, 11.4% widowed, 3.9% divorced (2000); Foreign born: 34.1% (2000); Ancestry (includes multiple ancestries): 32.8% Other groups, 8.7% Russian, 7.8% Greek, 7.0% Polish, 6.7% German (2000).
Vital Statistics: Birth rate: 89.8 per 10,000 population (1998)
Economy: Manufacturing: machinery, bags, food products, audio visual equipment, computer equipment, lighting systems. Single-family building permits issued: 12 (2001) / 12 (2000); Multi-family building permits issued: 0 (2001) / 0 (2000); Employment by occupation: 20.4% management, 30.7% professional, 7.1% services, 30.3% sales, 0.0% farming, 4.1% construction, 7.3% production (2000).
Income: Per capita income: $35,911 (2000); Median household income: $71,234 (2000); Poverty rate: 2.9% (2000).
Taxes: Total city taxes per capita: $482 (1997); City property taxes per capita: $324 (1997).
Education: High school graduation rate: 89.2% (2000); College graduation rate: 48.2% (2000).

School District(s)

Lincolnwood School District 74 (PK-12)
2000 Enrollment: 1,372 847-675-8234

Housing: Homeownership rate: 91.4% (2000); Median home value: $291,400 (2000); Median rent: $2,000+ per month (2000); Median age of housing: 43 years (2000).
Newspapers: Skyline (1 x week); Skokie Life (1 x week); North Town/Rogers Park/Edgewater/Ravenswood News-Star (1 x week); North Center/Lincoln Belmont/Lakeview Booster (1 x week); Norridge/Harwood Heights/Norwood Park Times (1 x week); Morton Grove/Niles Life (1 x week); Lincolnwood Life (1 x week); Jefferson Park/Portage Park/Belmont/Cragin Times (1 x week); Harlem/Irving Times (1 x week); Harlem/Foster Times (1 x week); Elmwood Park/River Grove Times (1 x week); Weekend Extra (1 x week)
Transportation: Commute to work: 89.0% car, 5.1% public transportation, 1.1% walk, 4.6% work from home (2000); Travel time to work: 23.8% less than 15 minutes, 31.1% 15 to 30 minutes, 27.2% 30 to 45 minutes, 9.7% 45 to 60 minutes, 8.2% 60 minutes or more (2000)
Additional Information Contacts
Lincolnwood Chamber of Commerce 847-679-5760

LYNWOOD (village). Covers a land area of 4.925 square miles and a water area of 0.070 square miles. Located at 41.52° N. Lat.; 87.54° W. Long. Elevation is 615 feet.
Population: 7,377 (2000); Race: 50.9% White, 43.4% Black, 0.7% Asian, 0.0% American Indian and Alaska Native, 5.9% Hispanic of any race, 2.3% two or more races (2000); Density: 1,497.8 persons per square mile (2000); Age: 28.6% under 18, 8.6% over 64 (2000); Marriage status: 28.3% never married, 55.4% now married, 5.4% widowed, 10.9% divorced (2000); Foreign born: 5.1% (2000); Ancestry (includes multiple ancestries): 48.4% Other groups, 12.3% Polish, 10.3% German, 8.8% Irish, 6.1% Italian (2000).
Economy: Manufacturing: screw machine products, light manufacturing. Lansing Municipal Airport to North. Single-family building permits issued: 25 (2001) / 32 (2000); Multi-family building permits issued: 0 (2001) / 0 (2000); Employment by occupation: 13.0% management, 18.0% professional, 13.5% services, 30.8% sales, 0.0% farming, 10.1% construction, 14.5% production (2000).
Income: Per capita income: $22,650 (2000); Median household income: $56,554 (2000); Poverty rate: 5.8% (2000).
Taxes: Total city taxes per capita: $184 (1997); City property taxes per capita: $107 (1997).
Education: High school graduation rate: 89.1% (2000); College graduation rate: 22.2% (2000).
Housing: Homeownership rate: 87.3% (2000); Median home value: $140,800 (2000); Median rent: $598 per month (2000); Median age of housing: 19 years (2000).
Transportation: Commute to work: 88.3% car, 8.3% public transportation, 0.0% walk, 2.4% work from home (2000); Travel time to work: 17.7% less than 15 minutes, 30.4% 15 to 30 minutes, 21.5% 30 to 45 minutes, 10.5% 45 to 60 minutes, 19.8% 60 minutes or more (2000)

LYONS (village). Covers a land area of 2.207 square miles and a water area of 0.048 square miles. Located at 41.81° N. Lat.; 87.82° W. Long. Elevation is 620 feet.
History: Lyons was established near the portage between the Chicago and Des Plaines Rivers, used by Marquette and Jolliet. Lyons developed as a residential community.
Population: 10,255 (2000); Race: 86.8% White, 0.4% Black, 0.9% Asian, 0.2% American Indian and Alaska Native, 16.8% Hispanic of any race, 5.5% two or more races (2000); Density: 4,646.8 persons per square mile (2000); Age: 23.6% under 18, 13.4% over 64 (2000); Marriage status: 26.3% never married, 53.1% now married, 9.1% widowed, 11.5% divorced (2000); Foreign born: 17.7% (2000); Ancestry (includes multiple ancestries): 17.7% Other groups, 15.6% Polish, 15.0% German, 14.0% Irish, 11.3% Italian (2000).
Economy: Single-family building permits issued: 2 (2001) / 3 (2000); Multi-family building permits issued: 120 (2001) / 0 (2000); Employment by occupation: 9.4% management, 13.8% professional, 12.0% services, 32.7% sales, 0.0% farming, 11.0% construction, 21.0% production (2000).
Income: Per capita income: $20,172 (2000); Median household income: $44,306 (2000); Poverty rate: 6.3% (2000).
Taxes: Total city taxes per capita: $281 (1997); City property taxes per capita: $169 (1997).
Education: High school graduation rate: 78.6% (2000); College graduation rate: 14.7% (2000).

School District(s)

Lyons School District 103 (PK-08)
2000 Enrollment: 2,137 708-780-2495

Housing: Homeownership rate: 59.9% (2000); Median home value: $127,900 (2000); Median rent: $605 per month (2000); Median age of housing: 46 years (2000).
Transportation: Commute to work: 90.0% car, 3.7% public transportation, 4.2% walk, 1.4% work from home (2000); Travel time to work: 25.6% less than 15 minutes, 33.4% 15 to 30 minutes, 23.7% 30 to 45 minutes, 8.5% 45 to 60 minutes, 8.9% 60 minutes or more (2000)

MARKHAM (city). Covers a land area of 5.214 square miles and a water area of 0 square miles. Located at 41.59° N. Lat.; 87.69° W. Long. Elevation is 615 feet.
History: Native prairie preserved at Indian Boundaries Prairies. Incorporated 1925.
Population: 12,620 (2000); Race: 17.2% White, 79.4% Black, 1.1% Asian, 0.4% American Indian and Alaska Native, 2.6% Hispanic of any race, 1.1% two or more races (2000); Density: 2,420.6 persons per square mile (2000); Age: 31.6% under 18, 11.9% over 64 (2000); Marriage status: 35.9% never married, 44.7% now married, 9.0% widowed, 10.4% divorced (2000); Foreign born: 2.8% (2000); Ancestry (includes multiple ancestries): 68.5% Other groups, 5.5% Irish, 5.1% German, 3.1% Polish, 1.8% Italian (2000).
Vital Statistics: Birth rate: 160.1 per 10,000 population (1998)
Economy: Manufacturing: building materials, industrial brushes, wood products. Single-family building permits issued: 15 (2001) / 17 (2000); Multi-family building permits issued: 0 (2001) / 0 (2000); Employment by occupation: 7.3% management, 15.8% professional, 18.0% services, 30.0% sales, 0.0% farming, 8.4% construction, 20.4% production (2000).

Income: Per capita income: $14,870 (2000); Median household income: $41,592 (2000); Poverty rate: 16.9% (2000).
Taxes: Total city taxes per capita: $404 (1997); City property taxes per capita: $313 (1997).
Education: High school graduation rate: 77.8% (2000); College graduation rate: 10.6% (2000).
Housing: Homeownership rate: 83.9% (2000); Median home value: $75,200 (2000); Median rent: $633 per month (2000); Median age of housing: 41 years (2000).
Newspapers: Chicago Westside Journal (1 x week)
Transportation: Commute to work: 84.6% car, 9.5% public transportation, 1.6% walk, 2.3% work from home (2000); Travel time to work: 21.5% less than 15 minutes, 31.1% 15 to 30 minutes, 22.8% 30 to 45 minutes, 12.5% 45 to 60 minutes, 12.1% 60 minutes or more (2000)

MATTESON (village). Covers a land area of 7.138 square miles and a water area of 0.069 square miles. Located at 41.51° N. Lat.; 87.73° W. Long. Elevation is 693 feet.
Population: 12,928 (2000); Race: 32.9% White, 61.8% Black, 1.9% Asian, 0.1% American Indian and Alaska Native, 3.3% Hispanic of any race, 1.8% two or more races (2000); Density: 1,811.2 persons per square mile (2000); Age: 27.8% under 18, 10.5% over 64 (2000); Marriage status: 27.8% never married, 57.8% now married, 5.8% widowed, 8.7% divorced (2000); Foreign born: 3.9% (2000); Ancestry (includes multiple ancestries): 60.7% Other groups, 11.2% German, 8.2% Irish, 4.4% Polish, 2.9% English (2000).
Vital Statistics: Birth rate: 131.5 per 10,000 population (1998)
Economy: Lincoln Mall is here. Single-family building permits issued: 177 (2001) / 145 (2000); Multi-family building permits issued: 0 (2001) / 0 (2000); Employment by occupation: 15.8% management, 20.8% professional, 14.0% services, 29.5% sales, 0.0% farming, 6.9% construction, 13.1% production (2000).
Income: Per capita income: $25,024 (2000); Median household income: $59,583 (2000); Poverty rate: 4.4% (2000).
Taxes: Total city taxes per capita: $357 (1997); City property taxes per capita: $305 (1997).
Education: High school graduation rate: 89.4% (2000); College graduation rate: 25.4% (2000).

School District(s)

Elem School District 159 (PK-08)
2000 Enrollment: 1,552 708-720-1300
Matteson Elementary School District 162 (PK-08)
2000 Enrollment: 2,672 708-748-0100

Two-year College(s)

Itt Technical Institute (Private, For-profit)
2001 Enrollment: 331 708-747-2571
2001 Tuition: In-state $10,620; Out-of-state $10,620

Housing: Homeownership rate: 80.8% (2000); Median home value: $135,100 (2000); Median rent: $643 per month (2000); Median age of housing: 23 years (2000).
Transportation: Commute to work: 87.4% car, 9.8% public transportation, 1.1% walk, 1.4% work from home (2000); Travel time to work: 17.9% less than 15 minutes, 27.9% 15 to 30 minutes, 19.1% 30 to 45 minutes, 14.0% 45 to 60 minutes, 21.1% 60 minutes or more (2000)
Additional Information Contacts
Matteson Chamber of Commerce 708-747-6000

MAYWOOD (village). Covers a land area of 2.708 square miles and a water area of 0 square miles. Located at 41.88° N. Lat.; 87.84° W. Long. Elevation is 627 feet.
History: Maywood developed in the 1880's, when industrial growth in the Chicago area created a need for more residential areas.
Population: 26,987 (2000); Race: 9.7% White, 82.8% Black, 0.2% Asian, 0.1% American Indian and Alaska Native, 10.9% Hispanic of any race, 1.4% two or more races (2000); Density: 9,965.7 persons per square mile (2000); Age: 31.7% under 18, 9.7% over 64 (2000); Marriage status: 42.0% never married, 41.4% now married, 7.2% widowed, 9.5% divorced (2000); Foreign born: 7.2% (2000); Ancestry (includes multiple ancestries): 79.1% Other groups, 1.4% German, 1.1% Irish, 1.1% African, 0.8% Italian (2000).
Vital Statistics: Birth rate: 207.1 per 10,000 population (1998)
Economy: Unemployment rate: 10.3% (11/2002); Total civilian labor force: 12,572 (11/2002); Single-family building permits issued: 0 (2001) / 1 (2000); Multi-family building permits issued: 8 (2001) / 22 (2000); Employment by occupation: 7.9% management, 12.8% professional, 17.9% services, 33.2% sales, 0.3% farming, 4.7% construction, 23.3% production (2000).
Income: Per capita income: $14,915 (2000); Median household income: $41,942 (2000); Poverty rate: 13.4% (2000).
Taxes: Total city taxes per capita: $441 (2000); City property taxes per capita: $341 (2000).
Education: High school graduation rate: 74.5% (2000); College graduation rate: 10.3% (2000).

School District(s)

Maywood-Melrose Park-Broadview-89 (PK-08)
2000 Enrollment: 5,941 708-450-2000
Proviso Area Exceptional Child (PK-12)
2000 Enrollment: 367 708-450-2100
Proviso Township H S District 209 (09-12)
2000 Enrollment: 4,482 708-344-7000

Housing: Homeownership rate: 62.9% (2000); Median home value: $105,400 (2000); Median rent: $543 per month (2000); Median age of housing: 54 years (2000).
Hospitals: Loyola University Health System (523 beds)
Transportation: Commute to work: 83.9% car, 9.4% public transportation, 3.2% walk, 1.7% work from home (2000); Travel time to work: 22.7% less than 15 minutes, 30.9% 15 to 30 minutes, 25.5% 30 to 45 minutes, 9.6% 45 to 60 minutes, 11.3% 60 minutes or more (2000)
Additional Information Contacts
Maywood Chamber of Commerce 708-345-7077

MCCOOK (village). Covers a land area of 2.603 square miles and a water area of 0.018 square miles. Located at 41.79° N. Lat.; 87.83° W. Long. Elevation is 615 feet.
Population: 254 (2000); Race: 99.1% White, 0.0% Black, 0.0% Asian, 0.0% American Indian and Alaska Native, 1.8% Hispanic of any race, 0.9% two or more races (2000); Density: 97.6 persons per square mile (2000); Age: 16.7% under 18, 21.6% over 64 (2000); Marriage status: 21.2% never married, 53.4% now married, 12.7% widowed, 12.7% divorced (2000); Foreign born: 0.0% (2000); Ancestry (includes multiple ancestries): 18.9% Polish, 16.3% Irish, 16.3% Croatian, 16.3% Italian, 11.5% German (2000).
Economy: Large locomotive division plant here. Manufacturing: consumer goods, boxes, oils, aluminum products, chemicals, crushed stone. Single-family building permits issued: 0 (2001) / 0 (2000); Multi-family building permits issued: 0 (2001) / 0 (2000); Employment by occupation: 15.1% management, 14.3% professional, 15.1% services, 27.0% sales, 0.0% farming, 9.5% construction, 19.0% production (2000).
Income: Per capita income: $24,996 (2000); Median household income: $43,125 (2000); Poverty rate: 1.8% (2000).
Taxes: Total city taxes per capita: $6,383 (1997); City property taxes per capita: $5,145 (1997).
Education: High school graduation rate: 86.5% (2000); College graduation rate: 11.1% (2000).
Housing: Homeownership rate: 54.9% (2000); Median home value: $156,000 (2000); Median rent: $552 per month (2000); Median age of housing: 46 years (2000).
Transportation: Commute to work: 84.1% car, 6.3% public transportation, 4.8% walk, 4.8% work from home (2000); Travel time to work: 40.8% less than 15 minutes, 24.2% 15 to 30 minutes, 20.8% 30 to 45 minutes, 5.8% 45 to 60 minutes, 8.3% 60 minutes or more (2000)

MELROSE PARK (village). Covers a land area of 4.239 square miles and a water area of 0 square miles. Located at 41.90° N. Lat.; 87.86° W. Long. Elevation is 630 feet.
History: Incorporated 1893.
Population: 23,171 (2000); Race: 71.6% White, 3.0% Black, 1.9% Asian, 0.1% American Indian and Alaska Native, 53.9% Hispanic of any race, 3.1% two or more races (2000); Density: 5,465.7 persons per square mile (2000); Age: 27.5% under 18, 10.8% over 64 (2000); Marriage status: 31.9% never married, 53.9% now married, 6.0% widowed, 8.2% divorced (2000); Foreign born: 35.3% (2000); Ancestry (includes multiple ancestries): 53.2% Other groups, 18.8% Italian, 7.8% German, 5.4% Irish, 4.0% Polish (2000).
Vital Statistics: Birth rate: 234.8 per 10,000 population (1998)
Economy: Has large railroad yards and shops, steel mills, TV manufacturing and factories that make a wide variety of products. Single-family building permits issued: 3 (2001) / 2 (2000); Multi-family building permits issued: 6 (2001) / 12 (2000); Employment by occupation: 8.8% management, 7.9% professional, 15.6% services, 28.0% sales, 0.2% farming, 8.5% construction, 31.0% production (2000).
Income: Per capita income: $16,206 (2000); Median household income: $40,689 (2000); Poverty rate: 10.2% (2000).
Taxes: Total city taxes per capita: $907 (1997); City property taxes per capita: $452 (1997).
Education: High school graduation rate: 60.7% (2000); College graduation rate: 9.6% (2000).

Housing: Homeownership rate: 54.6% (2000); Median home value: $154,600 (2000); Median rent: $549 per month (2000); Median age of housing: 44 years (2000).
Hospitals: Gottlieb Memorial Hospital (247 beds); Westlake Community Hospital (326 beds)
Transportation: Commute to work: 91.7% car, 2.8% public transportation, 3.0% walk, 1.2% work from home (2000); Travel time to work: 30.0% less than 15 minutes, 33.0% 15 to 30 minutes, 22.2% 30 to 45 minutes, 8.9% 45 to 60 minutes, 6.0% 60 minutes or more (2000)
Additional Information Contacts
Melrose Park Chamber of Commerce 708-338-1007

MERRIONETTE PARK (village). Covers a land area of 0.377 square miles and a water area of 0 square miles. Located at 41.68° N. Lat.; 87.69° W. Long. Elevation is 623 feet.
History: Incorporated 1947.
Population: 1,999 (2000); Race: 90.0% White, 6.9% Black, 0.2% Asian, 0.0% American Indian and Alaska Native, 3.6% Hispanic of any race, 1.9% two or more races (2000); Density: 5,309.3 persons per square mile (2000); Age: 19.1% under 18, 19.1% over 64 (2000); Marriage status: 30.2% never married, 44.4% now married, 11.9% widowed, 13.6% divorced (2000); Foreign born: 2.6% (2000); Ancestry (includes multiple ancestries): 34.5% Irish, 23.8% German, 17.2% Polish, 11.4% Other groups, 11.0% Italian (2000).
Economy: Single-family building permits issued: 12 (2001) / 11 (2000); Multi-family building permits issued: 0 (2001) / 0 (2000); Employment by occupation: 10.2% management, 22.0% professional, 9.6% services, 34.4% sales, 0.0% farming, 9.2% construction, 14.5% production (2000).
Income: Per capita income: $22,497 (2000); Median household income: $36,278 (2000); Poverty rate: 7.5% (2000).
Taxes: Total city taxes per capita: $228 (1997); City property taxes per capita: $165 (1997).
Education: High school graduation rate: 86.5% (2000); College graduation rate: 15.7% (2000).
Housing: Homeownership rate: 75.5% (2000); Median home value: $108,900 (2000); Median rent: $555 per month (2000); Median age of housing: 39 years (2000).
Transportation: Commute to work: 86.1% car, 9.2% public transportation, 3.7% walk, 0.0% work from home (2000); Travel time to work: 21.2% less than 15 minutes, 31.8% 15 to 30 minutes, 20.7% 30 to 45 minutes, 12.8% 45 to 60 minutes, 13.4% 60 minutes or more (2000)

MIDLOTHIAN (village). Covers a land area of 2.829 square miles and a water area of 0 square miles. Located at 41.62° N. Lat.; 87.72° W. Long. Elevation is 615 feet.
History: Incorporated 1927.
Population: 14,315 (2000); Race: 88.7% White, 6.4% Black, 1.6% Asian, 0.1% American Indian and Alaska Native, 7.1% Hispanic of any race, 1.1% two or more races (2000); Density: 5,059.5 persons per square mile (2000); Age: 28.4% under 18, 9.4% over 64 (2000); Marriage status: 27.8% never married, 54.2% now married, 7.7% widowed, 10.4% divorced (2000); Foreign born: 3.8% (2000); Ancestry (includes multiple ancestries): 27.5% German, 26.5% Irish, 15.4% Polish, 14.6% Other groups, 10.4% Italian (2000).
Vital Statistics: Birth rate: 155.1 per 10,000 population (1998)
Economy: Manufacturing: sportswear, cleaning compounds, water treatment chemicals. Single-family building permits issued: 16 (2001) / 24 (2000); Multi-family building permits issued: 0 (2001) / 12 (2000); Employment by occupation: 10.4% management, 13.7% professional, 15.3% services, 32.7% sales, 0.0% farming, 13.1% construction, 14.8% production (2000).
Income: Per capita income: $20,150 (2000); Median household income: $50,000 (2000); Poverty rate: 7.0% (2000).
Taxes: Total city taxes per capita: $98 (1997); City property taxes per capita: $20 (1997).
Education: High school graduation rate: 85.4% (2000); College graduation rate: 14.4% (2000).

School District(s)

Bremen Community H S District 228 (09-12)
2000 Enrollment: 4,641 708-389-1175
Midlothian School District 143 (PK-08)
2000 Enrollment: 1,837 708-388-6450

Housing: Homeownership rate: 80.0% (2000); Median home value: $114,800 (2000); Median rent: $559 per month (2000); Median age of housing: 36 years (2000).
Newspapers: Worth Citizen (1 x week); Scottsdale-Ashburn Independent (1 x week); Palos Citizen (1 x week); Orland Township Messenger (1 x week); Oak Lawn Independent (1 x week); Mount Greenwood Express (1 x week); Midlothian/Bremen Messenger (1 x week); Hickory Hills Citizen (1 x week); Evergreen Park Courier (1 x week); Chicago Ridge Citizen (1 x week); Burbank/Stickney Independent (1 x week); Bridgeview Independent (1 x week); Beverly News (1 x week); Alsip Express (1 x week)
Transportation: Commute to work: 88.3% car, 7.2% public transportation, 1.2% walk, 2.2% work from home (2000); Travel time to work: 24.9% less than 15 minutes, 31.7% 15 to 30 minutes, 19.5% 30 to 45 minutes, 9.3% 45 to 60 minutes, 14.6% 60 minutes or more (2000)
Additional Information Contacts
Midlothian Chamber of Commerce 708-389-0020

MORTON GROVE (village). Covers a land area of 5.095 square miles and a water area of 0 square miles. Located at 42.04° N. Lat.; 87.78° W. Long. Elevation is 625 feet.
History: Incorporated 1895.
Population: 22,451 (2000); Race: 74.3% White, 0.5% Black, 22.0% Asian, 0.1% American Indian and Alaska Native, 4.2% Hispanic of any race, 1.9% two or more races (2000); Density: 4,406.4 persons per square mile (2000); Age: 20.3% under 18, 21.8% over 64 (2000); Marriage status: 21.0% never married, 64.7% now married, 9.1% widowed, 5.2% divorced (2000); Foreign born: 33.6% (2000); Ancestry (includes multiple ancestries): 29.2% Other groups, 16.0% German, 11.9% Polish, 8.7% Irish, 5.9% Italian (2000).
Vital Statistics: Birth rate: 86.4 per 10,000 population (1998)
Economy: Has research laboratories and manufacturing plants: pumps, electrical equipment, cosmetics. Single-family building permits issued: 0 (2001) / 2 (2000); Multi-family building permits issued: 88 (2001) / 0 (2000); Employment by occupation: 13.8% management, 25.4% professional, 8.9% services, 34.9% sales, 0.2% farming, 6.2% construction, 10.6% production (2000).
Income: Per capita income: $26,973 (2000); Median household income: $63,511 (2000); Poverty rate: 2.7% (2000).
Taxes: Total city taxes per capita: $350 (1997); City property taxes per capita: $282 (1997).
Education: High school graduation rate: 87.4% (2000); College graduation rate: 34.4% (2000).

School District(s)

Golf Elementary School District 67 (KG-08)
2000 Enrollment: 553 847-966-8200
Morton Grove School District 70 (KG-08)
2000 Enrollment: 779 847-965-6200

Housing: Homeownership rate: 94.5% (2000); Median home value: $217,100 (2000); Median rent: $640 per month (2000); Median age of housing: 42 years (2000).
Transportation: Commute to work: 88.5% car, 6.0% public transportation, 1.5% walk, 3.4% work from home (2000); Travel time to work: 22.5% less than 15 minutes, 33.2% 15 to 30 minutes, 25.7% 30 to 45 minutes, 10.9% 45 to 60 minutes, 7.6% 60 minutes or more (2000)
Additional Information Contacts
Morton Grove Chamber of Commerce 847-965-0330

MOUNT PROSPECT (village). Covers a land area of 10.206 square miles and a water area of 0.036 square miles. Located at 42.06° N. Lat.; 87.93° W. Long. Elevation is 665 feet.
History: Incorporated 1917.
Population: 56,265 (2000); Race: 79.7% White, 2.1% Black, 11.4% Asian, 0.2% American Indian and Alaska Native, 11.7% Hispanic of any race, 2.7% two or more races (2000); Density: 5,513.1 persons per square mile (2000); Age: 22.8% under 18, 14.8% over 64 (2000); Marriage status: 25.4% never married, 61.8% now married, 6.1% widowed, 6.7% divorced (2000); Foreign born: 26.7% (2000); Ancestry (includes multiple ancestries): 25.0% Other groups, 21.1% German, 16.3% Polish, 13.4% Irish, 10.9% Italian (2000).
Vital Statistics: Birth rate: 149.7 per 10,000 population (1998)
Economy: Unemployment rate: 4.7% (11/2002); Total civilian labor force: 32,207 (11/2002); Single-family building permits issued: 8 (2001) / 8 (2000); Multi-family building permits issued: 65 (2001) / 8 (2000); Employment by occupation: 17.5% management, 21.9% professional, 10.4% services, 31.3% sales, 0.1% farming, 5.9% construction, 12.9% production (2000).
Income: Per capita income: $26,464 (2000); Median household income: $57,165 (2000); Poverty rate: 4.6% (2000).
Taxes: Total city taxes per capita: $417 (2000); City property taxes per capita: $197 (2000).
Education: High school graduation rate: 85.7% (2000); College graduation rate: 35.4% (2000).

School District(s)

Mount Prospect School District 57 (PK-08)
2000 Enrollment: 1,917 847-394-7300
Nw Suburban Special Education Org (PK-12)
2000 Enrollment: 801 847-463-8100
River Trails School District 26 (PK-08)
2000 Enrollment: 1,738 847-297-4120

Four-year College(s)

Christian Life College (Private, Not-for-profit, Other Protestant)
2001 Enrollment: 97 847-259-1840
2001 Tuition: In-state $5,250; Out-of-state $5,250
ITT Technical Institute (Private, For-profit)
2001 Enrollment: 447 847-375-8800
2001 Tuition: In-state $10,620; Out-of-state $10,620

Housing: Homeownership rate: 71.3% (2000); Median home value: $217,700 (2000); Median rent: $738 per month (2000); Median age of housing: 32 years (2000).

Transportation: Commute to work: 88.6% car, 6.0% public transportation, 2.1% walk, 2.2% work from home (2000); Travel time to work: 23.4% less than 15 minutes, 35.6% 15 to 30 minutes, 23.6% 30 to 45 minutes, 8.4% 45 to 60 minutes, 8.9% 60 minutes or more (2000)

Additional Information Contacts

Mt Prospect Chamber of Commerce 847-398-6616

NILES (village). Covers a land area of 5.875 square miles and a water area of 0 square miles. Located at 42.03° N. Lat.; 87.81° W. Long. Elevation is 625 feet.

History: Settled 1832, incorporated 1899. The village has a half size replica of the leaning tower of Pisa. Niles College of Loyola University is here.

Population: 30,068 (2000); Race: 83.5% White, 1.0% Black, 11.2% Asian, 0.3% American Indian and Alaska Native, 4.7% Hispanic of any race, 2.0% two or more races (2000); Density: 5,117.9 persons per square mile (2000); Age: 16.9% under 18, 27.0% over 64 (2000); Marriage status: 24.3% never married, 55.5% now married, 13.0% widowed, 7.2% divorced (2000); Foreign born: 33.7% (2000); Ancestry (includes multiple ancestries): 22.8% Polish, 19.3% Other groups, 14.2% German, 9.8% Irish, 8.9% Italian (2000).

Vital Statistics: Birth rate: 79.2 per 10,000 population (1998)

Economy: Unemployment rate: 4.3% (11/2002); Total civilian labor force: 15,783 (11/2002); Single-family building permits issued: 21 (2001) / 9 (2000); Multi-family building permits issued: 68 (2001) / 0 (2000); Employment by occupation: 12.6% management, 18.7% professional, 13.2% services, 32.4% sales, 0.1% farming, 8.2% construction, 14.9% production (2000).

Income: Per capita income: $23,543 (2000); Median household income: $48,627 (2000); Poverty rate: 5.4% (2000).

Taxes: Total city taxes per capita: $460 (2000); City property taxes per capita: $206 (2000).

Education: High school graduation rate: 81.4% (2000); College graduation rate: 24.8% (2000).

School District(s)

Niles Elementary School District 71 (KG-08)
2000 Enrollment: 544 847-966-9280

Housing: Homeownership rate: 76.2% (2000); Median home value: $204,400 (2000); Median rent: $707 per month (2000); Median age of housing: 37 years (2000).

Newspapers: The Bugle (2 x week)

Transportation: Commute to work: 88.9% car, 6.1% public transportation, 2.0% walk, 2.0% work from home (2000); Travel time to work: 20.6% less than 15 minutes, 32.0% 15 to 30 minutes, 26.7% 30 to 45 minutes, 10.5% 45 to 60 minutes, 10.2% 60 minutes or more (2000)

Additional Information Contacts

Niles Chamber of Commerce 847-966-7606

NORRIDGE (village). Covers a land area of 1.820 square miles and a water area of 0 square miles. Located at 41.96° N. Lat.; 87.82° W. Long. Elevation is 645 feet.

History: Incorporated since 1948.

Population: 14,582 (2000); Race: 93.7% White, 0.3% Black, 2.9% Asian, 0.2% American Indian and Alaska Native, 4.1% Hispanic of any race, 1.5% two or more races (2000); Density: 8,013.6 persons per square mile (2000); Age: 16.7% under 18, 28.2% over 64 (2000); Marriage status: 25.5% never married, 56.3% now married, 11.7% widowed, 6.5% divorced (2000); Foreign born: 32.5% (2000); Ancestry (includes multiple ancestries): 31.8% Polish, 25.5% Italian, 13.3% German, 7.9% Other groups, 7.5% Irish (2000).

Vital Statistics: Birth rate: 67.2 per 10,000 population (1998)

Economy: Single-family building permits issued: 6 (2001) / 7 (2000); Multi-family building permits issued: 0 (2001) / 0 (2000); Employment by occupation: 12.7% management, 12.6% professional, 14.2% services, 32.7% sales, 0.1% farming, 11.4% construction, 16.4% production (2000).

Income: Per capita income: $23,431 (2000); Median household income: $47,787 (2000); Poverty rate: 3.9% (2000).

Taxes: Total city taxes per capita: $225 (1997); City property taxes per capita: $210 (1997).

Education: High school graduation rate: 73.8% (2000); College graduation rate: 15.6% (2000).

School District(s)

Norridge School District 80 (KG-08)
2000 Enrollment: 1,008 708-453-4847
Pennoyer School District 79 (PK-08)
2000 Enrollment: 397 708-456-9094
Ridgewood Community H S District 234 (09-12)
2000 Enrollment: 845 708-456-4242

Two-year College(s)

Lincoln Technical Institute (Private, For-profit)
2001 Enrollment: 688 773-625-1535

Housing: Homeownership rate: 84.3% (2000); Median home value: $200,500 (2000); Median rent: $629 per month (2000); Median age of housing: 41 years (2000).

Transportation: Commute to work: 90.7% car, 5.6% public transportation, 1.7% walk, 1.5% work from home (2000); Travel time to work: 24.2% less than 15 minutes, 27.7% 15 to 30 minutes, 27.9% 30 to 45 minutes, 8.9% 45 to 60 minutes, 11.2% 60 minutes or more (2000)

NORTH RIVERSIDE (village). Covers a land area of 1.544 square miles and a water area of 0 square miles. Located at 41.84° N. Lat.; 87.83° W. Long. Elevation is 620 feet.

Population: 6,688 (2000); Race: 91.1% White, 1.3% Black, 3.9% Asian, 0.2% American Indian and Alaska Native, 8.2% Hispanic of any race, 1.2% two or more races (2000); Density: 4,331.2 persons per square mile (2000); Age: 16.4% under 18, 28.4% over 64 (2000); Marriage status: 22.7% never married, 55.8% now married, 11.9% widowed, 9.6% divorced (2000); Foreign born: 14.4% (2000); Ancestry (includes multiple ancestries): 17.7% Polish, 16.2% German, 14.0% Italian, 13.1% Irish, 12.5% Other groups (2000).

Economy: Single-family building permits issued: 1 (2001) / 1 (2000); Multi-family building permits issued: 0 (2001) / 0 (2000); Employment by occupation: 14.0% management, 23.0% professional, 10.8% services, 32.4% sales, 0.0% farming, 7.4% construction, 12.3% production (2000).

Income: Per capita income: $24,034 (2000); Median household income: $43,856 (2000); Poverty rate: 4.7% (2000).

Taxes: Total city taxes per capita: $398 (1997); City property taxes per capita: $199 (1997).

Education: High school graduation rate: 81.4% (2000); College graduation rate: 24.0% (2000).

School District(s)

Komarek School District 94 (KG-08)
2000 Enrollment: 346 708-447-8030

Housing: Homeownership rate: 71.5% (2000); Median home value: $150,000 (2000); Median rent: $601 per month (2000); Median age of housing: 45 years (2000).

Transportation: Commute to work: 89.8% car, 7.5% public transportation, 0.8% walk, 1.8% work from home (2000); Travel time to work: 25.9% less than 15 minutes, 30.8% 15 to 30 minutes, 23.8% 30 to 45 minutes, 9.6% 45 to 60 minutes, 10.0% 60 minutes or more (2000)

NORTHBROOK (village). Covers a land area of 12.919 square miles and a water area of 0.049 square miles. Located at 42.12° N. Lat.; 87.84° W. Long. Elevation is 650 feet.

History: It was incorporated as Shermerville in 1901 and was reincorporated as Northbrook in 1923. Once a farming community, Northbrook developed industry after the coming of a railroad in 1871. Settled 1836.

Population: 33,435 (2000); Race: 89.0% White, 0.7% Black, 8.7% Asian, 0.1% American Indian and Alaska Native, 1.6% Hispanic of any race, 1.4% two or more races (2000); Density: 2,588.1 persons per square mile (2000); Age: 25.1% under 18, 19.1% over 64 (2000); Marriage status: 17.5% never married, 70.1% now married, 6.7% widowed, 5.6% divorced (2000); Foreign born: 15.2% (2000); Ancestry (includes multiple ancestries): 18.3% German, 15.6% Other groups, 12.3% Russian, 12.1% Irish, 10.0% Polish (2000).

Vital Statistics: Birth rate: 114.0 per 10,000 population (1998)

Economy: Has some industry and research laboratories and is an insurance center. Botanical gardens and a forest preserve are just East of the village.

Unemployment rate: 4.1% (11/2002); Total civilian labor force: 18,008 (11/2002); Single-family building permits issued: 171 (2001) / 94 (2000); Multi-family building permits issued: 0 (2001) / 0 (2000); Employment by occupation: 26.4% management, 31.3% professional, 4.7% services, 31.6% sales, 0.0% farming, 2.6% construction, 3.3% production (2000).
Income: Per capita income: $50,765 (2000); Median household income: $95,665 (2000); Poverty rate: 2.3% (2000).
Taxes: Total city taxes per capita: $540 (2000); City property taxes per capita: $285 (2000).
Education: High school graduation rate: 95.6% (2000); College graduation rate: 62.2% (2000).

School District(s)

Northbrook Elementary School District 27 (KG-08)
2000 Enrollment: 1,326 847-498-2610
Northbrook School District 28 (KG-08)
2000 Enrollment: 1,742 847-498-7900
Northbrook/Glenview School District 30 (PK-08)
2000 Enrollment: 1,126 847-498-4190
West Northfield School District 31 (KG-08)
2000 Enrollment: 925 847-272-6880

Four-year College(s)

United States Dental Institute (Private, For-profit)
2001 Enrollment: n/a 847-272-1110

Housing: Homeownership rate: 91.6% (2000); Median home value: $370,800 (2000); Median rent: $1,215 per month (2000); Median age of housing: 31 years (2000).
Transportation: Commute to work: 81.5% car, 9.9% public transportation, 1.3% walk, 6.6% work from home (2000); Travel time to work: 24.2% less than 15 minutes, 29.8% 15 to 30 minutes, 21.9% 30 to 45 minutes, 12.1% 45 to 60 minutes, 12.0% 60 minutes or more (2000)
Additional Information Contacts
North Shore-Barrington Association of Realtors 847-480-7177
Northbrook Chamber of Commerce 847-498-5555

NORTHFIELD (village). Covers a land area of 2.957 square miles and a water area of 0 square miles. Located at 42.10° N. Lat.; 87.77° W. Long. Elevation is 630 feet.
Population: 5,389 (2000); Race: 93.8% White, 0.4% Black, 5.0% Asian, 0.0% American Indian and Alaska Native, 1.0% Hispanic of any race, 0.3% two or more races (2000); Density: 1,822.4 persons per square mile (2000); Age: 24.3% under 18, 21.2% over 64 (2000); Marriage status: 17.0% never married, 68.1% now married, 8.3% widowed, 6.5% divorced (2000); Foreign born: 12.2% (2000); Ancestry (includes multiple ancestries): 21.4% German, 20.0% Irish, 18.8% English, 7.3% Other groups, 6.8% Polish (2000).
Economy: Food processing. Single-family building permits issued: 18 (2001) / 6 (2000); Multi-family building permits issued: 0 (2001) / 13 (2000); Employment by occupation: 21.9% management, 29.9% professional, 8.5% services, 31.3% sales, 0.0% farming, 3.6% construction, 4.9% production (2000).
Income: Per capita income: $63,857 (2000); Median household income: $91,313 (2000); Poverty rate: 1.6% (2000).
Taxes: Total city taxes per capita: $611 (1997); City property taxes per capita: $430 (1997).
Education: High school graduation rate: 96.5% (2000); College graduation rate: 68.1% (2000).

School District(s)

Sunset Ridge School District 29 (KG-08)
2000 Enrollment: 532 847-446-6383

Housing: Homeownership rate: 93.0% (2000); Median home value: $411,200 (2000); Median rent: $917 per month (2000); Median age of housing: 41 years (2000).
Transportation: Commute to work: 85.7% car, 8.2% public transportation, 0.8% walk, 4.9% work from home (2000); Travel time to work: 33.0% less than 15 minutes, 29.9% 15 to 30 minutes, 15.7% 30 to 45 minutes, 8.4% 45 to 60 minutes, 13.1% 60 minutes or more (2000)
Additional Information Contacts
Northfield Chamber of Commerce 847-441-6113

NORTHLAKE (city). Aka North Lake. Covers a land area of 3.015 square miles and a water area of 0 square miles. Located at 41.91° N. Lat.; 87.90° W. Long. Elevation is 650 feet.
History: St. John Vianney Roman Catholic Church, which is shaped like a fish, has the largest mosaic-tile mural in the Western Hemisphere. Incorporated 1949.
Population: 11,878 (2000); Race: 77.4% White, 2.2% Black, 3.4% Asian, 0.2% American Indian and Alaska Native, 33.4% Hispanic of any race, 2.0% two or more races (2000); Density: 3,939.3 persons per square mile (2000); Age: 25.7% under 18, 15.2% over 64 (2000); Marriage status: 26.6% never married, 56.5% now married, 8.4% widowed, 8.4% divorced (2000); Foreign born: 24.6% (2000); Ancestry (includes multiple ancestries): 36.9% Other groups, 17.7% German, 14.2% Irish, 11.9% Italian, 11.8% Polish (2000).
Vital Statistics: Birth rate: 158.3 per 10,000 population (1998)
Economy: Has various manufactures. Single-family building permits issued: 1 (2001) / 0 (2000); Multi-family building permits issued: 0 (2001) / 0 (2000); Employment by occupation: 9.6% management, 6.9% professional, 11.0% services, 33.6% sales, 0.2% farming, 10.0% construction, 28.7% production (2000).
Income: Per capita income: $18,119 (2000); Median household income: $48,406 (2000); Poverty rate: 8.4% (2000).
Taxes: Total city taxes per capita: $325 (1997); City property taxes per capita: $210 (1997).
Education: High school graduation rate: 66.9% (2000); College graduation rate: 7.7% (2000).
Housing: Homeownership rate: 77.3% (2000); Median home value: $136,800 (2000); Median rent: $558 per month (2000); Median age of housing: 44 years (2000).
Hospitals: Vencor Hospital - Northlake (94 beds)
Transportation: Commute to work: 93.5% car, 2.7% public transportation, 1.7% walk, 0.5% work from home (2000); Travel time to work: 28.6% less than 15 minutes, 38.0% 15 to 30 minutes, 21.1% 30 to 45 minutes, 7.0% 45 to 60 minutes, 5.3% 60 minutes or more (2000)
Additional Information Contacts
Northlake Chamber of Commerce 708-562-3110

OAK FOREST (city). Covers a land area of 5.649 square miles and a water area of 0.053 square miles. Located at 41.60° N. Lat.; 87.75° W. Long. Elevation is 672 feet.
History: In 1911 the Oak Forest Infirmary and Tuberculosis Hospital was established in the town of Oak Forest.
Population: 28,051 (2000); Race: 90.9% White, 3.4% Black, 2.7% Asian, 0.0% American Indian and Alaska Native, 5.1% Hispanic of any race, 1.5% two or more races (2000); Density: 4,965.4 persons per square mile (2000); Age: 26.2% under 18, 8.9% over 64 (2000); Marriage status: 26.7% never married, 60.0% now married, 5.6% widowed, 7.6% divorced (2000); Foreign born: 5.8% (2000); Ancestry (includes multiple ancestries): 26.3% Irish, 25.1% German, 18.3% Polish, 13.0% Italian, 11.2% Other groups (2000).
Vital Statistics: Birth rate: 133.0 per 10,000 population (1998)
Economy: Unemployment rate: 4.9% (11/2002); Total civilian labor force: 16,456 (11/2002); Single-family building permits issued: 62 (2001) / 51 (2000); Multi-family building permits issued: 25 (2001) / 24 (2000); Employment by occupation: 12.6% management, 19.6% professional, 11.4% services, 31.6% sales, 0.1% farming, 12.0% construction, 12.8% production (2000).
Income: Per capita income: $23,487 (2000); Median household income: $60,073 (2000); Poverty rate: 3.6% (2000).
Taxes: Total city taxes per capita: $199 (1997); City property taxes per capita: $171 (1997).
Education: High school graduation rate: 89.3% (2000); College graduation rate: 22.5% (2000).

School District(s)

Arbor Park School District 145 (PK-08)
2000 Enrollment: 1,257 708-687-8040
Forest Ridge School District 142 (PK-08)
2000 Enrollment: 1,706 708-687-3334
S W Cook Co Coop Assoc Special Ed (03-12)
2000 Enrollment: 106 708-687-0900

Housing: Homeownership rate: 81.6% (2000); Median home value: $149,200 (2000); Median rent: $629 per month (2000); Median age of housing: 28 years (2000).
Hospitals: Oak Forest Hospital of Cook County (1,103 beds)
Transportation: Commute to work: 87.2% car, 8.8% public transportation, 1.0% walk, 2.4% work from home (2000); Travel time to work: 22.5% less than 15 minutes, 29.2% 15 to 30 minutes, 19.8% 30 to 45 minutes, 11.8% 45 to 60 minutes, 16.7% 60 minutes or more (2000)
Additional Information Contacts
Oak Forest Chamber of Commerce 708-687-4600

OAK LAWN (village). Covers a land area of 8.595 square miles and a water area of <.001 square miles. Located at 41.71° N. Lat.; 87.75° W. Long. Elevation is 615 feet.
History: Incorporated 1909.

Population: 55,245 (2000); Race: 93.4% White, 1.2% Black, 1.8% Asian, 0.1% American Indian and Alaska Native, 5.4% Hispanic of any race, 1.7% two or more races (2000); Density: 6,427.3 persons per square mile (2000); Age: 21.9% under 18, 21.7% over 64 (2000); Marriage status: 24.7% never married, 55.9% now married, 11.6% widowed, 7.8% divorced (2000); Foreign born: 11.5% (2000); Ancestry (includes multiple ancestries): 30.4% Irish, 19.5% German, 19.3% Polish, 9.7% Italian, 8.9% Other groups (2000).
Vital Statistics: Birth rate: 111.5 per 10,000 population (1998)
Economy: Chiefly residential with some light manufacturing industries. Products include metalwork, wood products and school supplies. Unemployment rate: 5.4% (11/2002); Total civilian labor force: 30,053 (11/2002); Single-family building permits issued: 84 (2001) / 68 (2000); Multi-family building permits issued: 18 (2001) / 28 (2000); Employment by occupation: 13.0% management, 18.9% professional, 10.7% services, 31.2% sales, 0.1% farming, 12.0% construction, 14.1% production (2000).
Income: Per capita income: $23,877 (2000); Median household income: $47,585 (2000); Poverty rate: 5.4% (2000).
Taxes: Total city taxes per capita: $237 (2000); City property taxes per capita: $173 (2000).
Education: High school graduation rate: 83.5% (2000); College graduation rate: 20.9% (2000).

School District(s)

Community High School District 218 (09-12)
2000 Enrollment: 4,761 708-424-2000
Oak Lawn Community H S District 229 (09-12)
2000 Enrollment: 1,580 708-424-5200
Oak Lawn-Hometown School District 123 (PK-08)
2000 Enrollment: 2,742 708-423-0150
Ridgeland School District 122 (PK-08)
2000 Enrollment: 2,138 708-599-5550

Two-year College(s)

Fox College Inc (Private, For-profit)
2001 Enrollment: 248 708-636-7700
2001 Tuition: In-state $13,025; Out-of-state $13,025

Housing: Homeownership rate: 82.8% (2000); Median home value: $157,000 (2000); Median rent: $639 per month (2000); Median age of housing: 35 years (2000).
Hospitals: Advocate Christ Medical Center; Advocate Hope Children's Hospital
Transportation: Commute to work: 87.5% car, 8.2% public transportation, 1.8% walk, 2.1% work from home (2000); Travel time to work: 24.5% less than 15 minutes, 26.1% 15 to 30 minutes, 21.5% 30 to 45 minutes, 13.9% 45 to 60 minutes, 14.0% 60 minutes or more (2000)
Additional Information Contacts
Oak Lawn Chamber of Commerce.............................. 708-424-8300

OAK PARK (village). Covers a land area of 4.701 square miles and a water area of 0 square miles. Located at 41.88° N. Lat.; 87.79° W. Long. Elevation is 620 feet.
History: Oak Park was settled in 1833 by Joseph Kettlestrings, who came with his wife from Maryland. They named the village for the oak trees growing there. In the 1890's Oak Park was known as Saints' Rest because of its many churches. This was the site of one of Frank Lloyd Wright's early workshops and examples of his architecture graced the village.
Population: 52,524 (2000); Race: 68.7% White, 22.5% Black, 4.3% Asian, 0.1% American Indian and Alaska Native, 4.0% Hispanic of any race, 3.0% two or more races (2000); Density: 11,173.4 persons per square mile (2000); Age: 24.1% under 18, 9.6% over 64 (2000); Marriage status: 33.5% never married, 51.1% now married, 5.3% widowed, 10.0% divorced (2000); Foreign born: 9.8% (2000); Ancestry (includes multiple ancestries): 29.3% Other groups, 18.0% German, 17.4% Irish, 8.7% English, 7.5% Italian (2000).
Vital Statistics: Birth rate: 140.3 per 10,000 population (1998)
Economy: Unemployment rate: 4.6% (11/2002); Total civilian labor force: 32,458 (11/2002); Single-family building permits issued: 14 (2001) / 6 (2000); Multi-family building permits issued: 0 (2001) / 0 (2000); Employment by occupation: 19.6% management, 40.9% professional, 7.9% services, 23.8% sales, 0.0% farming, 2.8% construction, 5.1% production (2000).
Income: Per capita income: $36,340 (2000); Median household income: $59,183 (2000); Poverty rate: 5.6% (2000).
Taxes: Total city taxes per capita: $523 (2000); City property taxes per capita: $382 (2000).
Education: High school graduation rate: 94.4% (2000); College graduation rate: 62.1% (2000).

School District(s)

Oak Park & River Forest District 200 (09-12)
2000 Enrollment: 2,830 708-383-0700
Oak Park Elementary School District 97 (PK-08)
2000 Enrollment: 5,035 708-524-3000

Four-year College(s)

West Suburban College of Nursing (Private, Not-for-profit)
2001 Enrollment: 67 708-763-6530
2001 Tuition: In-state $15,000; Out-of-state $15,000

Housing: Homeownership rate: 56.3% (2000); Median home value: $231,300 (2000); Median rent: $674 per month (2000); Median age of housing: 60+ years (2000).
Hospitals: Oak Park Hospital (296 beds); West Suburban Health Care
Newspapers: The Chicago Journal (1 x week); Tri-City Journal (1 x week); The Austin Weekly News (1 x week); Westchester Herald (1 x week); Oak Leaves (1 x week); Northlake Herald-Journal (1 x week); Melrose Park Herald (1 x week); Maywood Herald (1 x week); Franklin Park Herald-Journal (1 x week); Forest Leaves (1 x week); Elm Leaves (1 x week); Forest Park Review (1 x week); Wednesday Journal (1 x week); River Grove Messenger (1 x week); West Proviso Herald (1 x week)
Transportation: Commute to work: 68.4% car, 21.8% public transportation, 4.0% walk, 5.1% work from home (2000); Travel time to work: 16.9% less than 15 minutes, 26.4% 15 to 30 minutes, 34.6% 30 to 45 minutes, 14.2% 45 to 60 minutes, 7.8% 60 minutes or more (2000)
Additional Information Contacts
Oak Park Board of Realtors 708-386-0150
Oak Park Chamber of Commerce 708-848-8151
Oak Park Visitors Center 708-848-1500

OLYMPIA FIELDS (village). Covers a land area of 2.842 square miles and a water area of 0.004 square miles. Located at 41.51° N. Lat.; 87.69° W. Long. Elevation is 675 feet.
History: Olympia Fields was developed in 1926 as a residential community centered around the Olympia Fields Country Club and Golf Course.
Population: 4,732 (2000); Race: 40.2% White, 55.1% Black, 3.3% Asian, 0.4% American Indian and Alaska Native, 1.4% Hispanic of any race, 0.6% two or more races (2000); Density: 1,665.3 persons per square mile (2000); Age: 22.5% under 18, 19.3% over 64 (2000); Marriage status: 20.6% never married, 68.2% now married, 6.2% widowed, 5.0% divorced (2000); Foreign born: 8.3% (2000); Ancestry (includes multiple ancestries): 45.2% Other groups, 9.6% German, 7.8% Irish, 6.6% Italian, 4.8% English (2000).
Economy: Single-family building permits issued: 2 (2001) / 16 (2000); Multi-family building permits issued: 2 (2001) / 2 (2000); Employment by occupation: 26.8% management, 31.6% professional, 6.2% services, 27.7% sales, 0.0% farming, 2.9% construction, 4.9% production (2000).
Income: Per capita income: $46,698 (2000); Median household income: $94,827 (2000); Poverty rate: 4.6% (2000).
Taxes: Total city taxes per capita: $310 (1997); City property taxes per capita: $48 (1997).
Education: High school graduation rate: 94.4% (2000); College graduation rate: 56.0% (2000).

School District(s)

Rich Township H S District 227 (09-12)
2000 Enrollment: 3,283 708-747-2600

Housing: Homeownership rate: 97.6% (2000); Median home value: $234,200 (2000); Median rent: $2,000+ per month (2000); Median age of housing: 24 years (2000).
Hospitals: Olympia Fields Osteopathic Hospital & Medical Center (201 beds)
Transportation: Commute to work: 80.6% car, 11.6% public transportation, 1.3% walk, 4.0% work from home (2000); Travel time to work: 19.7% less than 15 minutes, 19.8% 15 to 30 minutes, 22.5% 30 to 45 minutes, 14.1% 45 to 60 minutes, 24.0% 60 minutes or more (2000)

ORLAND HILLS (village). Aka Westhaven. Covers a land area of 1.090 square miles and a water area of 0.008 square miles. Located at 41.58° N. Lat.; 87.84° W. Long. Elevation is 720 feet.
Population: 6,779 (2000); Race: 86.0% White, 4.4% Black, 3.7% Asian, 0.0% American Indian and Alaska Native, 6.3% Hispanic of any race, 4.1% two or more races (2000); Density: 6,217.2 persons per square mile (2000); Age: 34.3% under 18, 3.7% over 64 (2000); Marriage status: 26.5% never married, 62.3% now married, 3.4% widowed, 7.8% divorced (2000); Foreign born: 8.7% (2000); Ancestry (includes multiple ancestries): 22.9% Irish, 21.9% German, 21.7% Polish, 14.1% Other groups, 13.4% Italian (2000).
Economy: Single-family building permits issued: 50 (2001) / 40 (2000); Multi-family building permits issued: 0 (2001) / 0 (2000); Employment by

occupation: 12.3% management, 18.6% professional, 12.3% services, 32.1% sales, 0.0% farming, 13.9% construction, 10.8% production (2000).
Income: Per capita income: $21,415 (2000); Median household income: $61,884 (2000); Poverty rate: 5.3% (2000).
Taxes: Total city taxes per capita: $285 (1997); City property taxes per capita: $66 (1997).
Education: High school graduation rate: 92.2% (2000); College graduation rate: 19.4% (2000).
Housing: Homeownership rate: 77.4% (2000); Median home value: $156,900 (2000); Median rent: $734 per month (2000); Median age of housing: 16 years (2000).
Transportation: Commute to work: 89.6% car, 6.8% public transportation, 0.8% walk, 2.4% work from home (2000); Travel time to work: 19.3% less than 15 minutes, 22.7% 15 to 30 minutes, 22.0% 30 to 45 minutes, 14.7% 45 to 60 minutes, 21.4% 60 minutes or more (2000)

ORLAND PARK (village). Covers a land area of 19.141 square miles and a water area of 0.295 square miles. Located at 41.61° N. Lat.; 87.85° W. Long. Elevation is 700 feet.
Population: 51,077 (2000); Race: 93.2% White, 0.6% Black, 4.2% Asian, 0.1% American Indian and Alaska Native, 3.7% Hispanic of any race, 1.0% two or more races (2000); Density: 2,668.4 persons per square mile (2000); Age: 24.5% under 18, 16.7% over 64 (2000); Marriage status: 22.8% never married, 63.6% now married, 7.6% widowed, 6.1% divorced (2000); Foreign born: 9.4% (2000); Ancestry (includes multiple ancestries): 26.5% Irish, 19.5% German, 18.5% Polish, 14.8% Italian, 9.3% Other groups (2000).
Vital Statistics: Birth rate: 102.4 per 10,000 population (1998)
Economy: Despite urban growth, area still has some agriculture: corn; dairying. Light manufacturing. Unemployment rate: 4.6% (11/2002); Total civilian labor force: 27,574 (11/2002); Single-family building permits issued: 391 (2001) / 357 (2000); Multi-family building permits issued: 36 (2001) / 108 (2000); Employment by occupation: 18.7% management, 21.8% professional, 9.4% services, 32.1% sales, 0.0% farming, 8.1% construction, 9.9% production (2000).
Income: Per capita income: $30,467 (2000); Median household income: $67,574 (2000); Poverty rate: 3.1% (2000).
Taxes: Total city taxes per capita: $147 (1997); City property taxes per capita: $107 (1997).
Education: High school graduation rate: 89.9% (2000); College graduation rate: 31.7% (2000).

School District(s)

Cons High School District 230 (09-12)
2000 Enrollment: 7,567 708-349-5750
Orland School District 135 (PK-08)
2000 Enrollment: 5,653 708-349-5700

Four-year College(s)

Robert Morris College-Orland Park (Private, Not-for-profit)
2001 Enrollment: n/a 708-226-3800
2001 Tuition: In-state $12,150; Out-of-state $12,150
Housing: Homeownership rate: 91.3% (2000); Median home value: $208,300 (2000); Median rent: $710 per month (2000); Median age of housing: 15 years (2000).
Transportation: Commute to work: 89.7% car, 6.5% public transportation, 1.1% walk, 2.1% work from home (2000); Travel time to work: 19.5% less than 15 minutes, 26.0% 15 to 30 minutes, 21.7% 30 to 45 minutes, 12.5% 45 to 60 minutes, 20.3% 60 minutes or more (2000)
Additional Information Contacts
Orland Park Chamber of Commerce 708-349-2972

PALATINE (village). Covers a land area of 12.973 square miles and a water area of 0.134 square miles. Located at 42.11° N. Lat.; 88.04° W. Long. Elevation is 741 feet.
History: William Rainey Harper College is in Palatine. Incorporated 1869.
Population: 65,479 (2000); Race: 82.3% White, 2.1% Black, 8.0% Asian, 0.2% American Indian and Alaska Native, 14.5% Hispanic of any race, 1.8% two or more races (2000); Density: 5,047.2 persons per square mile (2000); Age: 24.4% under 18, 8.8% over 64 (2000); Marriage status: 27.4% never married, 59.2% now married, 5.0% widowed, 8.5% divorced (2000); Foreign born: 21.9% (2000); Ancestry (includes multiple ancestries): 25.2% Other groups, 25.1% German, 14.8% Irish, 12.0% Polish, 9.1% Italian (2000).
Vital Statistics: Birth rate: 163.0 per 10,000 population (1998)
Economy: Primarily residential, the growing village produces a variety of products, such as machine tools and industrial adhesives. Unemployment rate: 6.2% (11/2002); Total civilian labor force: 33,293 (11/2002); Single-family building permits issued: 172 (2001) / 209 (2000); Multi-family building permits issued: 109 (2001) / 36 (2000); Employment by occupation: 19.4% management, 24.4% professional, 10.5% services, 30.0% sales, 0.1% farming, 5.7% construction, 10.0% production (2000).
Income: Per capita income: $30,661 (2000); Median household income: $63,321 (2000); Poverty rate: 4.8% (2000).
Taxes: Total city taxes per capita: $317 (2000); City property taxes per capita: $238 (2000).
Education: High school graduation rate: 89.1% (2000); College graduation rate: 41.4% (2000).

School District(s)

Palatine C C School District 15 (PK-08)
2000 Enrollment: 12,970 847-963-3000
Township H S District 211 (09-12)
2000 Enrollment: 12,585 847-755-6600

Two-year College(s)

William Rainey Harper College (Public)
2001 Enrollment: 14,514 847-925-6000
2001 Tuition: In-state $4,950; Out-of-state $6,655
Housing: Homeownership rate: 69.2% (2000); Median home value: $199,200 (2000); Median rent: $817 per month (2000); Median age of housing: 24 years (2000).
Transportation: Commute to work: 90.3% car, 4.7% public transportation, 1.4% walk, 2.5% work from home (2000); Travel time to work: 21.8% less than 15 minutes, 36.4% 15 to 30 minutes, 24.4% 30 to 45 minutes, 8.5% 45 to 60 minutes, 8.9% 60 minutes or more (2000)
Additional Information Contacts
Greater Palatine Chamber of Commerce 847-359-7200

PALOS HEIGHTS (city). Covers a land area of 3.780 square miles and a water area of 0.086 square miles. Located at 41.66° N. Lat.; 87.79° W. Long. Elevation is 625 feet.
History: Trinity Christian College is here.
Population: 11,260 (2000); Race: 96.2% White, 0.6% Black, 1.8% Asian, 0.1% American Indian and Alaska Native, 1.9% Hispanic of any race, 0.5% two or more races (2000); Density: 2,978.6 persons per square mile (2000); Age: 21.0% under 18, 24.4% over 64 (2000); Marriage status: 19.6% never married, 64.5% now married, 11.2% widowed, 4.7% divorced (2000); Foreign born: 6.4% (2000); Ancestry (includes multiple ancestries): 27.2% Irish, 20.5% German, 14.1% Polish, 10.5% Italian, 9.1% Dutch (2000).
Vital Statistics: Birth rate: 99.5 per 10,000 population (1998)
Economy: Light manufacturing. Single-family building permits issued: 137 (2001) / 98 (2000); Multi-family building permits issued: 55 (2001) / 23 (2000); Employment by occupation: 20.2% management, 25.6% professional, 8.9% services, 27.5% sales, 0.2% farming, 8.7% construction, 8.9% production (2000).
Income: Per capita income: $32,895 (2000); Median household income: $69,907 (2000); Poverty rate: 3.2% (2000).
Taxes: Total city taxes per capita: $387 (1997); City property taxes per capita: $188 (1997).
Education: High school graduation rate: 90.5% (2000); College graduation rate: 38.8% (2000).

School District(s)

Palos Heights School District 128 (PK-08)
2000 Enrollment: 695 708-448-0060

Four-year College(s)

Trinity Christian College (Private, Not-for-profit, Interdenominational)
2001 Enrollment: 973 708-597-3000
2001 Tuition: In-state $13,970; Out-of-state $13,970
Housing: Homeownership rate: 96.9% (2000); Median home value: $219,500 (2000); Median rent: $925 per month (2000); Median age of housing: 29 years (2000).
Hospitals: Palos Community Hospital (369 beds)
Newspapers: The Reporter (1 x week); The Palos Hills/Hickory Hills Reporter (1 x week); The Oak Lawn/Evergreen Park Reporter (1 x week); The Regional News (1 x week)
Transportation: Commute to work: 87.7% car, 5.2% public transportation, 3.2% walk, 3.0% work from home (2000); Travel time to work: 23.2% less than 15 minutes, 31.0% 15 to 30 minutes, 16.2% 30 to 45 minutes, 12.5% 45 to 60 minutes, 17.1% 60 minutes or more (2000)

PALOS HILLS (city). Covers a land area of 4.167 square miles and a water area of 0.070 square miles. Located at 41.69° N. Lat.; 87.82° W. Long. Elevation is 600 feet.
Population: 17,665 (2000); Race: 87.6% White, 5.5% Black, 2.8% Asian, 0.3% American Indian and Alaska Native, 4.3% Hispanic of any race, 1.5% two or more races (2000); Density: 4,239.7 persons per square mile (2000); Age: 19.3% under 18, 16.6% over 64 (2000); Marriage status: 27.4% never

married, 54.4% now married, 8.9% widowed, 9.3% divorced (2000); Foreign born: 16.4% (2000); Ancestry (includes multiple ancestries): 19.1% Irish, 18.9% Polish, 16.3% German, 12.9% Other groups, 10.5% Italian (2000).
Vital Statistics: Birth rate: 105.3 per 10,000 population (1998)
Economy: Light manufacturing. On Calumet Sog Channel. Single-family building permits issued: 19 (2001) / 18 (2000); Multi-family building permits issued: 16 (2001) / 12 (2000); Employment by occupation: 13.8% management, 20.4% professional, 11.9% services, 29.4% sales, 0.0% farming, 10.6% construction, 13.9% production (2000).
Income: Per capita income: $25,331 (2000); Median household income: $52,329 (2000); Poverty rate: 3.4% (2000).
Taxes: Total city taxes per capita: $115 (1997); City property taxes per capita: $83 (1997).
Education: High school graduation rate: 85.2% (2000); College graduation rate: 24.2% (2000).

Two-year College(s)

Moraine Valley Community College (Public)
2001 Enrollment: 14,033 708-974-4300
2001 Tuition: In-state $5,700; Out-of-state $6,600

Housing: Homeownership rate: 77.6% (2000); Median home value: $174,000 (2000); Median rent: $718 per month (2000); Median age of housing: 25 years (2000).
Transportation: Commute to work: 93.6% car, 3.9% public transportation, 0.6% walk, 1.4% work from home (2000); Travel time to work: 18.8% less than 15 minutes, 26.0% 15 to 30 minutes, 26.5% 30 to 45 minutes, 13.1% 45 to 60 minutes, 15.5% 60 minutes or more (2000)

PALOS PARK (village). Covers a land area of 3.776 square miles and a water area of 0.039 square miles. Located at 41.66° N. Lat.; 87.83° W. Long. Elevation is 700 feet.
Population: 4,689 (2000); Race: 97.2% White, 0.0% Black, 2.4% Asian, 0.2% American Indian and Alaska Native, 0.6% Hispanic of any race, 0.3% two or more races (2000); Density: 1,241.8 persons per square mile (2000); Age: 20.4% under 18, 19.7% over 64 (2000); Marriage status: 18.8% never married, 64.2% now married, 9.5% widowed, 7.6% divorced (2000); Foreign born: 8.6% (2000); Ancestry (includes multiple ancestries): 25.0% Irish, 21.7% German, 14.4% Polish, 8.0% Italian, 6.8% English (2000).
Economy: Single-family building permits issued: 7 (2001) / 47 (2000); Multi-family building permits issued: 0 (2001) / 0 (2000); Employment by occupation: 18.9% management, 28.5% professional, 7.9% services, 30.2% sales, 0.6% farming, 7.4% construction, 6.5% production (2000).
Income: Per capita income: $39,861 (2000); Median household income: $78,450 (2000); Poverty rate: 4.5% (2000).
Taxes: Total city taxes per capita: $415 (1997); City property taxes per capita: $132 (1997).
Education: High school graduation rate: 94.3% (2000); College graduation rate: 45.2% (2000).

School District(s)

Palos Community Cons School District 118 (PK-08)
2000 Enrollment: 2,050 708-448-4800

Housing: Homeownership rate: 98.6% (2000); Median home value: $286,800 (2000); Median rent: $607 per month (2000); Median age of housing: 32 years (2000).
Transportation: Commute to work: 88.3% car, 6.6% public transportation, 0.9% walk, 4.2% work from home (2000); Travel time to work: 17.5% less than 15 minutes, 25.9% 15 to 30 minutes, 25.5% 30 to 45 minutes, 13.4% 45 to 60 minutes, 17.7% 60 minutes or more (2000)

PARK FOREST (village). Covers a land area of 4.925 square miles and a water area of 0 square miles. Located at 41.48° N. Lat.; 87.68° W. Long. Elevation is 720 feet.
Population: 23,462 (2000); Race: 55.1% White, 39.7% Black, 1.1% Asian, 0.3% American Indian and Alaska Native, 4.7% Hispanic of any race, 2.4% two or more races (2000); Density: 4,763.6 persons per square mile (2000); Age: 26.7% under 18, 11.6% over 64 (2000); Marriage status: 30.3% never married, 49.7% now married, 7.3% widowed, 12.7% divorced (2000); Foreign born: 3.1% (2000); Ancestry (includes multiple ancestries): 42.0% Other groups, 19.4% German, 11.9% Irish, 8.2% English, 6.7% Italian (2000).
Vital Statistics: Birth rate: 140.2 per 10,000 population (1998)
Economy: Unemployment rate: 7.1% (11/2002); Total civilian labor force: 13,419 (11/2002); Single-family building permits issued: 4 (2001) / 15 (2000); Multi-family building permits issued: 0 (2001) / 95 (2000); Employment by occupation: 12.0% management, 24.1% professional, 14.9% services, 28.8% sales, 0.1% farming, 7.0% construction, 13.1% production (2000).
Income: Per capita income: $21,493 (2000); Median household income: $47,579 (2000); Poverty rate: 6.7% (2000).
Taxes: Total city taxes per capita: $318 (1997); City property taxes per capita: $234 (1997).
Education: High school graduation rate: 88.4% (2000); College graduation rate: 26.9% (2000).

School District(s)

Park Forest School District 163 (PK-08)
2000 Enrollment: 2,161 708-748-7050

Housing: Homeownership rate: 74.5% (2000); Median home value: $84,400 (2000); Median rent: $606 per month (2000); Median age of housing: 44 years (2000).
Transportation: Commute to work: 86.8% car, 10.1% public transportation, 0.8% walk, 1.7% work from home (2000); Travel time to work: 25.2% less than 15 minutes, 29.2% 15 to 30 minutes, 16.4% 30 to 45 minutes, 10.7% 45 to 60 minutes, 18.6% 60 minutes or more (2000)

PARK RIDGE (city). Covers a land area of 7.028 square miles and a water area of 0.042 square miles. Located at 42.01° N. Lat.; 87.84° W. Long. Elevation is 640 feet.
History: Park Ridge began in 1853 when George Penny started a brickyard and lumberyard. Residents called the town Pennyville, but changed it to Brickton when Penny protested. When the clay from which the bricks were produced was gone and the Chicago & North Western Railway had arrived, Brickton became a commuting suburb and changed its name to Park Ridge.
Population: 37,775 (2000); Race: 94.9% White, 0.4% Black, 2.6% Asian, 0.1% American Indian and Alaska Native, 3.1% Hispanic of any race, 1.1% two or more races (2000); Density: 5,374.6 persons per square mile (2000); Age: 24.1% under 18, 19.5% over 64 (2000); Marriage status: 21.9% never married, 63.5% now married, 8.8% widowed, 5.8% divorced (2000); Foreign born: 12.7% (2000); Ancestry (includes multiple ancestries): 24.1% German, 22.4% Irish, 20.8% Polish, 16.3% Italian, 7.1% Other groups (2000).
Vital Statistics: Birth rate: 100.3 per 10,000 population (1998)
Economy: Unemployment rate: 3.7% (11/2002); Total civilian labor force: 20,295 (11/2002); Single-family building permits issued: 82 (2001) / 68 (2000); Multi-family building permits issued: 3 (2001) / 0 (2000); Employment by occupation: 23.0% management, 27.3% professional, 8.3% services, 29.5% sales, 0.0% farming, 5.2% construction, 6.7% production (2000).
Income: Per capita income: $36,046 (2000); Median household income: $73,154 (2000); Poverty rate: 2.4% (2000).
Taxes: Total city taxes per capita: $508 (2000); City property taxes per capita: $276 (2000).
Education: High school graduation rate: 92.4% (2000); College graduation rate: 46.2% (2000).

School District(s)

Maine Township H S District 207 (06-12)
2000 Enrollment: 6,577 847-696-3600
Park Ridge C C School District 64 (PK-08)
2000 Enrollment: 4,212 847-318-4300

Housing: Homeownership rate: 87.9% (2000); Median home value: $295,800 (2000); Median rent: $797 per month (2000); Median age of housing: 44 years (2000).
Hospitals: Advocate Lutheran General Children's Hospital; Advocate Lutheran General Hospital (608 beds)
Newspapers: Mount Prospect Times (1 x week); Edison/Norwood Times Review (1 x week); Edgebrook Times Review (1 x week); Des Plaines Times (1 x week); Park Ridge Herald-Advocate (1 x week); Norridge/Harwood Heights News (1 x week); Niles Herald-Spectator (1 x week)
Transportation: Commute to work: 83.6% car, 10.1% public transportation, 1.8% walk, 4.0% work from home (2000); Travel time to work: 26.3% less than 15 minutes, 29.3% 15 to 30 minutes, 26.6% 30 to 45 minutes, 9.3% 45 to 60 minutes, 8.5% 60 minutes or more (2000)

Additional Information Contacts

Park Ridge Chamber of Commerce 847-825-3121

PHOENIX (village). Covers a land area of 0.451 square miles and a water area of 0 square miles. Located at 41.61° N. Lat.; 87.63° W. Long. Elevation is 600 feet.
History: Phoenix developed as a residential outgrowth of its neighbor, Harvey.
Population: 2,157 (2000); Race: 2.7% White, 93.3% Black, 0.0% Asian, 0.2% American Indian and Alaska Native, 4.5% Hispanic of any race, 2.1% two or more races (2000); Density: 4,785.5 persons per square mile (2000); Age: 30.1% under 18, 15.5% over 64 (2000); Marriage status: 37.6% never married, 36.8% now married, 12.8% widowed, 12.8% divorced (2000);

Foreign born: 2.7% (2000); Ancestry (includes multiple ancestries): 82.6% Other groups, 3.2% African, 1.0% United States or American, 0.7% German, 0.6% Polish (2000).
Economy: Single-family building permits issued: 1 (2001) / 1 (2000); Multi-family building permits issued: 0 (2001) / 0 (2000); Employment by occupation: 7.5% management, 14.6% professional, 25.7% services, 26.5% sales, 0.0% farming, 5.6% construction, 20.2% production (2000).
Income: Per capita income: $14,321 (2000); Median household income: $29,643 (2000); Poverty rate: 22.9% (2000).
Taxes: Total city taxes per capita: $68 (1997); City property taxes per capita: $67 (1997).
Education: High school graduation rate: 69.5% (2000); College graduation rate: 7.0% (2000).
Housing: Homeownership rate: 63.4% (2000); Median home value: $68,100 (2000); Median rent: $423 per month (2000); Median age of housing: 43 years (2000).
Transportation: Commute to work: 87.8% car, 8.8% public transportation, 1.9% walk, 0.0% work from home (2000); Travel time to work: 25.6% less than 15 minutes, 29.2% 15 to 30 minutes, 19.2% 30 to 45 minutes, 11.9% 45 to 60 minutes, 14.2% 60 minutes or more (2000)

POSEN (village). Covers a land area of 1.179 square miles and a water area of 0 square miles. Located at 41.62° N. Lat.; 87.68° W. Long. Elevation is 603 feet.
History: Posen was settled in 1893 when a Chicago realtor sold 12,000 lots, mostly to Polish immigrants. Posen was incorporated in 1901.
Population: 4,730 (2000); Race: 81.1% White, 7.7% Black, 1.3% Asian, 0.1% American Indian and Alaska Native, 18.6% Hispanic of any race, 1.5% two or more races (2000); Density: 4,010.5 persons per square mile (2000); Age: 27.8% under 18, 11.4% over 64 (2000); Marriage status: 29.3% never married, 54.6% now married, 7.4% widowed, 8.8% divorced (2000); Foreign born: 10.7% (2000); Ancestry (includes multiple ancestries): 28.4% Other groups, 25.7% Polish, 22.2% German, 17.4% Irish, 7.8% Italian (2000).
Economy: Single-family building permits issued: 29 (2001) / 18 (2000); Multi-family building permits issued: 0 (2001) / 0 (2000); Employment by occupation: 6.6% management, 10.3% professional, 14.8% services, 30.5% sales, 0.0% farming, 15.9% construction, 21.9% production (2000).
Income: Per capita income: $17,323 (2000); Median household income: $49,470 (2000); Poverty rate: 7.1% (2000).
Taxes: Total city taxes per capita: $205 (1997); City property taxes per capita: $73 (1997).
Education: High school graduation rate: 69.1% (2000); College graduation rate: 8.1% (2000).

School District(s)

Posen-Robbins El School District 143-5 (PK-08)
2000 Enrollment: 1,594 708-388-7200
Housing: Homeownership rate: 79.7% (2000); Median home value: $91,700 (2000); Median rent: $491 per month (2000); Median age of housing: 41 years (2000).
Transportation: Commute to work: 93.9% car, 3.4% public transportation, 0.9% walk, 0.4% work from home (2000); Travel time to work: 28.3% less than 15 minutes, 29.0% 15 to 30 minutes, 20.6% 30 to 45 minutes, 9.5% 45 to 60 minutes, 12.6% 60 minutes or more (2000)

PROSPECT HEIGHTS (city). Covers a land area of 4.258 square miles and a water area of 0.024 square miles. Located at 42.10° N. Lat.; 87.92° W. Long. Elevation is 668 feet.
Population: 17,081 (2000); Race: 78.8% White, 2.5% Black, 3.6% Asian, 0.1% American Indian and Alaska Native, 27.7% Hispanic of any race, 0.7% two or more races (2000); Density: 4,011.1 persons per square mile (2000); Age: 24.4% under 18, 11.5% over 64 (2000); Marriage status: 23.4% never married, 63.6% now married, 6.7% widowed, 6.3% divorced (2000); Foreign born: 36.5% (2000); Ancestry (includes multiple ancestries): 30.6% Other groups, 20.4% Polish, 19.7% German, 8.6% Irish, 6.8% Italian (2000).
Vital Statistics: Birth rate: 165.1 per 10,000 population (1998)
Economy: Palwaukee Airport in East. Diversified light manufacturing. Single-family building permits issued: 5 (2001) / 3 (2000); Multi-family building permits issued: 0 (2001) / 0 (2000); Employment by occupation: 15.6% management, 20.5% professional, 12.2% services, 23.8% sales, 0.0% farming, 9.7% construction, 18.2% production (2000).
Income: Per capita income: $28,200 (2000); Median household income: $55,641 (2000); Poverty rate: 4.3% (2000).
Taxes: Total city taxes per capita: $212 (1997); City property taxes per capita: $9 (1997).
Education: High school graduation rate: 77.4% (2000); College graduation rate: 28.5% (2000).

School District(s)

Prospect Heights School District 23 (PK-08)
2000 Enrollment: 1,623 847-870-3850
Housing: Homeownership rate: 73.0% (2000); Median home value: $243,300 (2000); Median rent: $650 per month (2000); Median age of housing: 27 years (2000).
Transportation: Commute to work: 89.0% car, 4.6% public transportation, 1.3% walk, 2.5% work from home (2000); Travel time to work: 22.1% less than 15 minutes, 38.3% 15 to 30 minutes, 24.4% 30 to 45 minutes, 6.6% 45 to 60 minutes, 8.6% 60 minutes or more (2000)
Airports: Palwaukee Municipal

RICHTON PARK (village). Aka Richton. Covers a land area of 3.374 square miles and a water area of 0.021 square miles. Located at 41.48° N. Lat.; 87.72° W. Long. Elevation is 710 feet.
Population: 12,533 (2000); Race: 35.9% White, 59.0% Black, 2.5% Asian, 0.0% American Indian and Alaska Native, 4.0% Hispanic of any race, 2.1% two or more races (2000); Density: 3,714.7 persons per square mile (2000); Age: 28.3% under 18, 8.1% over 64 (2000); Marriage status: 29.4% never married, 50.5% now married, 5.8% widowed, 14.3% divorced (2000); Foreign born: 4.6% (2000); Ancestry (includes multiple ancestries): 59.0% Other groups, 10.6% German, 7.7% Irish, 4.8% Polish, 4.8% English (2000).
Vital Statistics: Birth rate: 151.6 per 10,000 population (1998)
Economy: Some agriculture. Single-family building permits issued: 81 (2001) / 59 (2000); Multi-family building permits issued: 0 (2001) / 0 (2000); Employment by occupation: 11.9% management, 23.2% professional, 10.7% services, 32.5% sales, 0.0% farming, 9.5% construction, 12.3% production (2000).
Income: Per capita income: $22,626 (2000); Median household income: $48,299 (2000); Poverty rate: 7.0% (2000).
Taxes: Total city taxes per capita: $322 (1997); City property taxes per capita: $211 (1997).
Education: High school graduation rate: 90.4% (2000); College graduation rate: 25.4% (2000).
Housing: Homeownership rate: 65.8% (2000); Median home value: $125,700 (2000); Median rent: $621 per month (2000); Median age of housing: 24 years (2000).
Transportation: Commute to work: 80.9% car, 13.4% public transportation, 1.8% walk, 2.0% work from home (2000); Travel time to work: 19.9% less than 15 minutes, 20.3% 15 to 30 minutes, 16.2% 30 to 45 minutes, 16.2% 45 to 60 minutes, 27.4% 60 minutes or more (2000)

RIVER FOREST (village). Covers a land area of 2.509 square miles and a water area of 0.001 square miles. Located at 41.89° N. Lat.; 87.81° W. Long. Elevation is 627 feet.
History: River Forest was settled in 1836 by the Ashbel Steele family. Another early resident was Daniel Cunningham Thatcher, a Chicago businessman who retired to River Forest in 1854. In 1862 Thatcher persuaded the Chicago & North Western Railway to build a station on his property, which was called Thatcher. For ten years, River Forest was known as Thatcher, but in 1880 the community was organized as the Village of River Forest.
Population: 11,635 (2000); Race: 89.6% White, 5.0% Black, 3.0% Asian, 0.0% American Indian and Alaska Native, 4.1% Hispanic of any race, 1.9% two or more races (2000); Density: 4,638.1 persons per square mile (2000); Age: 25.8% under 18, 14.0% over 64 (2000); Marriage status: 28.6% never married, 58.9% now married, 7.0% widowed, 5.6% divorced (2000); Foreign born: 7.6% (2000); Ancestry (includes multiple ancestries): 30.8% Irish, 24.9% German, 11.8% Other groups, 10.7% English, 10.5% Italian (2000).
Vital Statistics: Birth rate: 107.4 per 10,000 population (1998)
Economy: Single-family building permits issued: 9 (2001) / 6 (2000); Multi-family building permits issued: 64 (2001) / 0 (2000); Employment by occupation: 20.7% management, 39.0% professional, 7.3% services, 25.7% sales, 0.2% farming, 2.3% construction, 4.7% production (2000).
Income: Per capita income: $46,123 (2000); Median household income: $89,284 (2000); Poverty rate: 2.7% (2000).
Taxes: Total city taxes per capita: $469 (1997); City property taxes per capita: $349 (1997).
Education: High school graduation rate: 96.8% (2000); College graduation rate: 69.7% (2000).

School District(s)

River Forest School District 90 (PK-08)
2000 Enrollment: 1,333 708-771-8282

Four-year College(s)

Concordia University (Private, Not-for-profit, Lutheran Church - Missouri Synod)

2001 Enrollment: 1,947 708-771-8300
2001 Tuition: In-state $15,000; Out-of-state $15,000
Dominican University (Private, Not-for-profit, Roman Catholic)
2001 Enrollment: 2,533 708-366-2490
2001 Tuition: In-state $15,600; Out-of-state $15,600

Housing: Homeownership rate: 86.9% (2000); Median home value: $386,600 (2000); Median rent: $665 per month (2000); Median age of housing: 59 years (2000).

Transportation: Commute to work: 68.0% car, 16.3% public transportation, 9.8% walk, 5.4% work from home (2000); Travel time to work: 27.0% less than 15 minutes, 20.8% 15 to 30 minutes, 34.1% 30 to 45 minutes, 12.7% 45 to 60 minutes, 5.4% 60 minutes or more (2000)

RIVER GROVE (village). Covers a land area of 2.386 square miles and a water area of 0 square miles. Located at 41.92° N. Lat.; 87.84° W. Long. Elevation is 630 feet.

History: Triton College. Incorporated 1888.

Population: 10,668 (2000); Race: 91.2% White, 0.8% Black, 2.1% Asian, 0.3% American Indian and Alaska Native, 10.0% Hispanic of any race, 1.5% two or more races (2000); Density: 4,470.4 persons per square mile (2000); Age: 21.3% under 18, 15.7% over 64 (2000); Marriage status: 27.7% never married, 51.6% now married, 10.1% widowed, 10.6% divorced (2000); Foreign born: 25.1% (2000); Ancestry (includes multiple ancestries): 31.8% Polish, 17.6% Italian, 17.1% German, 14.4% Irish, 12.5% Other groups (2000).

Economy: Manufacturing of sports equipment and wire cables. Single-family building permits issued: 2 (2001) / 2 (2000); Multi-family building permits issued: 0 (2001) / 0 (2000); Employment by occupation: 8.3% management, 11.5% professional, 12.4% services, 34.8% sales, 0.0% farming, 12.3% construction, 20.8% production (2000).

Income: Per capita income: $20,390 (2000); Median household income: $40,050 (2000); Poverty rate: 5.9% (2000).

Taxes: Total city taxes per capita: $338 (1997); City property taxes per capita: $175 (1997).

Education: High school graduation rate: 77.3% (2000); College graduation rate: 14.3% (2000).

School District(s)

Rhodes School District 84-5 (PK-08)
2000 Enrollment: 625 708-453-1266
River Grove School District 85-5 (PK-08)
2000 Enrollment: 687 708-453-6172

Two-year College(s)

Triton College (Public)
2001 Enrollment: 14,848 708-456-0300
2001 Tuition: In-state $4,267; Out-of-state $6,480

Housing: Homeownership rate: 58.6% (2000); Median home value: $149,800 (2000); Median rent: $631 per month (2000); Median age of housing: 42 years (2000).

Transportation: Commute to work: 90.2% car, 5.4% public transportation, 3.3% walk, 0.6% work from home (2000); Travel time to work: 21.5% less than 15 minutes, 27.3% 15 to 30 minutes, 27.8% 30 to 45 minutes, 14.3% 45 to 60 minutes, 9.1% 60 minutes or more (2000)

RIVERDALE (village). Covers a land area of 3.638 square miles and a water area of 0.148 square miles. Located at 41.64° N. Lat.; 87.63° W. Long. Elevation is 600 feet.

History: Riverdale began when George Dolton and J.C. Matthews established a ferry across the Little Calumet River in 1836. The town later became a railroad center and a steel manufacturing area.

Population: 15,055 (2000); Race: 11.3% White, 85.5% Black, 0.5% Asian, 0.0% American Indian and Alaska Native, 2.7% Hispanic of any race, 2.0% two or more races (2000); Density: 4,138.6 persons per square mile (2000); Age: 37.0% under 18, 6.6% over 64 (2000); Marriage status: 38.8% never married, 44.9% now married, 5.4% widowed, 10.9% divorced (2000); Foreign born: 3.3% (2000); Ancestry (includes multiple ancestries): 77.8% Other groups, 2.7% German, 2.3% Polish, 1.8% African, 1.5% Irish (2000).

Vital Statistics: Birth rate: 192.0 per 10,000 population (1998)

Economy: Single-family building permits issued: 0 (2001) / 3 (2000); Multi-family building permits issued: 0 (2001) / 0 (2000); Employment by occupation: 8.2% management, 15.0% professional, 20.6% services, 33.4% sales, 0.0% farming, 3.7% construction, 19.0% production (2000).

Income: Per capita income: $14,461 (2000); Median household income: $38,321 (2000); Poverty rate: 18.4% (2000).

Taxes: Total city taxes per capita: $370 (2000); City property taxes per capita: $236 (2000).

Education: High school graduation rate: 82.3% (2000); College graduation rate: 11.7% (2000).

School District(s)

Gen Geo Patton School District 133 (PK-08)
2000 Enrollment: 605 708-841-3955

Housing: Homeownership rate: 57.3% (2000); Median home value: $82,600 (2000); Median rent: $595 per month (2000); Median age of housing: 42 years (2000).

Transportation: Commute to work: 78.0% car, 18.5% public transportation, 1.0% walk, 1.4% work from home (2000); Travel time to work: 9.6% less than 15 minutes, 23.6% 15 to 30 minutes, 25.4% 30 to 45 minutes, 17.8% 45 to 60 minutes, 23.6% 60 minutes or more (2000)

Additional Information Contacts

Riverdale Chamber of Commerce 708-841-3311

RIVERSIDE (village). Covers a land area of 1.973 square miles and a water area of 0.015 square miles. Located at 41.83° N. Lat.; 87.81° W. Long. Elevation is 616 feet.

History: Riverside originated in 1866 with the plan of the Riverside Improvement Company to create an ideal suburb. They commissioned Olmsted and Vaux, New York landscape architects who had designed Central Park. The site for Riverside was selected for its forested terrain, the railroad facilities, and the Des Plaines River whose winding course determined the layout of the town.

Population: 8,895 (2000); Race: 93.0% White, 0.0% Black, 3.3% Asian, 0.1% American Indian and Alaska Native, 5.1% Hispanic of any race, 1.3% two or more races (2000); Density: 4,509.1 persons per square mile (2000); Age: 23.4% under 18, 15.6% over 64 (2000); Marriage status: 24.5% never married, 60.0% now married, 8.3% widowed, 7.2% divorced (2000); Foreign born: 9.0% (2000); Ancestry (includes multiple ancestries): 20.8% Irish, 18.4% Polish, 17.7% German, 13.8% Italian, 8.9% Other groups (2000).

Economy: Manufacturing: trigger pumps. Single-family building permits issued: 1 (2001) / 2 (2000); Multi-family building permits issued: 0 (2001) / 0 (2000); Employment by occupation: 18.9% management, 32.5% professional, 8.3% services, 30.6% sales, 0.3% farming, 3.3% construction, 6.2% production (2000).

Income: Per capita income: $34,712 (2000); Median household income: $64,931 (2000); Poverty rate: 3.0% (2000).

Taxes: Total city taxes per capita: $536 (1997); City property taxes per capita: $434 (1997).

Education: High school graduation rate: 93.6% (2000); College graduation rate: 51.1% (2000).

School District(s)

Riverside Brookfield Township District 208 (09-12)
2000 Enrollment: 1,109 708-442-7500
Riverside School District 96 (PK-08)
2000 Enrollment: 1,130 708-447-5007

Housing: Homeownership rate: 78.8% (2000); Median home value: $264,200 (2000); Median rent: $620 per month (2000); Median age of housing: 60+ years (2000).

Transportation: Commute to work: 80.5% car, 13.5% public transportation, 1.9% walk, 3.7% work from home (2000); Travel time to work: 18.6% less than 15 minutes, 27.2% 15 to 30 minutes, 31.2% 30 to 45 minutes, 13.9% 45 to 60 minutes, 9.1% 60 minutes or more (2000)

ROBBINS (village). Covers a land area of 1.469 square miles and a water area of 0 square miles. Located at 41.64° N. Lat.; 87.70° W. Long. Elevation is 600 feet.

History: Robbins, named for realtor and developer Eugene S. Robbins, was organized as a residential area and incorporated in 1917.

Population: 6,635 (2000); Race: 2.1% White, 97.3% Black, 0.4% Asian, 0.0% American Indian and Alaska Native, 0.8% Hispanic of any race, 0.3% two or more races (2000); Density: 4,516.0 persons per square mile (2000); Age: 31.9% under 18, 12.6% over 64 (2000); Marriage status: 47.2% never married, 32.3% now married, 11.1% widowed, 9.4% divorced (2000); Foreign born: 0.6% (2000); Ancestry (includes multiple ancestries): 82.8% Other groups, 1.3% African, 0.7% United States or American, 0.5% Irish, 0.5% English (2000).

Economy: Single-family building permits issued: 1 (2001) / 0 (2000); Multi-family building permits issued: 0 (2001) / 0 (2000); Employment by occupation: 6.1% management, 12.5% professional, 29.0% services, 25.1% sales, 0.0% farming, 8.5% construction, 18.8% production (2000).

Income: Per capita income: $9,837 (2000); Median household income: $24,145 (2000); Poverty rate: 35.5% (2000).

Taxes: Total city taxes per capita: $24 (1997); City property taxes per capita: $0 (1997).

Education: High school graduation rate: 67.3% (2000); College graduation rate: 8.5% (2000).
Housing: Homeownership rate: 54.9% (2000); Median home value: $56,400 (2000); Median rent: $365 per month (2000); Median age of housing: 39 years (2000).
Transportation: Commute to work: 85.5% car, 4.1% public transportation, 4.9% walk, 2.3% work from home (2000); Travel time to work: 21.2% less than 15 minutes, 33.2% 15 to 30 minutes, 15.4% 30 to 45 minutes, 16.1% 45 to 60 minutes, 14.1% 60 minutes or more (2000)

ROLLING MEADOWS (city). Covers a land area of 5.455 square miles and a water area of 0.005 square miles. Located at 42.07° N. Lat.; 88.02° W. Long. Elevation is 715 feet.
History: Incorporated 1955.
Population: 24,604 (2000); Race: 82.4% White, 2.9% Black, 6.0% Asian, 0.1% American Indian and Alaska Native, 18.7% Hispanic of any race, 2.6% two or more races (2000); Density: 4,510.4 persons per square mile (2000); Age: 24.8% under 18, 10.9% over 64 (2000); Marriage status: 27.2% never married, 60.3% now married, 4.8% widowed, 7.7% divorced (2000); Foreign born: 21.3% (2000); Ancestry (includes multiple ancestries): 27.7% Other groups, 26.5% German, 14.9% Irish, 11.7% Polish, 9.4% Italian (2000).
Vital Statistics: Birth rate: 160.5 per 10,000 population (1998)
Economy: Research and development firms and some light manufacturing: office supplies, printing, electronic components. Some remnant agriculture. Single-family building permits issued: 29 (2001) / 11 (2000); Multi-family building permits issued: 6 (2001) / 8 (2000); Employment by occupation: 17.5% management, 18.2% professional, 14.7% services, 29.9% sales, 0.0% farming, 6.9% construction, 12.8% production (2000).
Income: Per capita income: $26,178 (2000); Median household income: $59,535 (2000); Poverty rate: 5.1% (2000).
Taxes: Total city taxes per capita: $440 (2000); City property taxes per capita: $340 (2000).
Education: High school graduation rate: 83.7% (2000); College graduation rate: 31.0% (2000).

Four-year College(s)

Illinois School of Professional Psychology-Meadows (Private, For-profit)
2001 Enrollment: 201 847-290-7400
Housing: Homeownership rate: 76.8% (2000); Median home value: $176,600 (2000); Median rent: $822 per month (2000); Median age of housing: 31 years (2000).
Transportation: Commute to work: 87.5% car, 4.4% public transportation, 2.7% walk, 3.0% work from home (2000); Travel time to work: 28.8% less than 15 minutes, 37.0% 15 to 30 minutes, 19.8% 30 to 45 minutes, 6.5% 45 to 60 minutes, 7.9% 60 minutes or more (2000)
Additional Information Contacts
Rolling Meadows Chamber of Commerce 847-398-3730

ROSEMONT (village). Covers a land area of 1.743 square miles and a water area of 0 square miles. Located at 41.99° N. Lat.; 87.87° W. Long. Elevation is 635 feet.
Population: 4,224 (2000); Race: 79.1% White, 1.6% Black, 5.8% Asian, 0.3% American Indian and Alaska Native, 32.0% Hispanic of any race, 0.6% two or more races (2000); Density: 2,423.6 persons per square mile (2000); Age: 23.2% under 18, 11.1% over 64 (2000); Marriage status: 29.6% never married, 53.9% now married, 6.9% widowed, 9.5% divorced (2000); Foreign born: 37.3% (2000); Ancestry (includes multiple ancestries): 33.7% Other groups, 15.9% German, 13.4% Polish, 12.5% Italian, 5.8% Irish (2000).
Economy: Manufacturing: electronic ballast, paperboard cartons, aluminum extrusions, printed circuit boards. Major convention center. Single-family building permits issued: 0 (2001) / 0 (2000); Multi-family building permits issued: 0 (2001) / 0 (2000); Employment by occupation: 11.6% management, 10.3% professional, 21.7% services, 27.3% sales, 0.0% farming, 6.5% construction, 22.5% production (2000).
Income: Per capita income: $19,781 (2000); Median household income: $34,663 (2000); Poverty rate: 14.9% (2000).
Taxes: Total city taxes per capita: $2,233 (1997); City property taxes per capita: $857 (1997).
Education: High school graduation rate: 72.9% (2000); College graduation rate: 17.5% (2000).

School District(s)

Rosemont Elementary School District 78 (PK-08)
2000 Enrollment: 283 847-825-0144
Housing: Homeownership rate: 28.9% (2000); Median home value: $259,600 (2000); Median rent: $561 per month (2000); Median age of housing: 33 years (2000).
Transportation: Commute to work: 76.3% car, 10.1% public transportation, 11.5% walk, 1.1% work from home (2000); Travel time to work: 35.6% less than 15 minutes, 31.7% 15 to 30 minutes, 18.9% 30 to 45 minutes, 8.5% 45 to 60 minutes, 5.4% 60 minutes or more (2000)
Additional Information Contacts
Rosemont Chamber of Commerce 847-698-1190
Rosemont Convention Bureau 847-823-2100

SAUK VILLAGE (village). Covers a land area of 3.804 square miles and a water area of 0.044 square miles. Located at 41.48° N. Lat.; 87.56° W. Long. Elevation is 650 feet.
Population: 10,411 (2000); Race: 60.7% White, 31.1% Black, 0.9% Asian, 0.3% American Indian and Alaska Native, 11.7% Hispanic of any race, 3.9% two or more races (2000); Density: 2,737.2 persons per square mile (2000); Age: 33.3% under 18, 7.4% over 64 (2000); Marriage status: 28.9% never married, 56.1% now married, 6.0% widowed, 9.0% divorced (2000); Foreign born: 4.0% (2000); Ancestry (includes multiple ancestries): 43.4% Other groups, 18.1% German, 12.8% Irish, 8.1% Polish, 5.5% English (2000).
Economy: Manufacturing: steel cutting. Single-family building permits issued: 37 (2001) / 21 (2000); Multi-family building permits issued: 0 (2001) / 0 (2000); Employment by occupation: 9.5% management, 10.8% professional, 15.6% services, 27.2% sales, 0.1% farming, 11.1% construction, 25.7% production (2000).
Income: Per capita income: $16,598 (2000); Median household income: $46,718 (2000); Poverty rate: 9.6% (2000).
Taxes: Total city taxes per capita: $318 (1997); City property taxes per capita: $182 (1997).
Education: High school graduation rate: 79.7% (2000); College graduation rate: 8.6% (2000).

School District(s)

Comm Cons School District 168 (PK-08)
2000 Enrollment: 1,636 708-758-1610
Housing: Homeownership rate: 80.9% (2000); Median home value: $77,300 (2000); Median rent: $648 per month (2000); Median age of housing: 30 years (2000).
Transportation: Commute to work: 92.0% car, 3.1% public transportation, 2.2% walk, 1.8% work from home (2000); Travel time to work: 17.8% less than 15 minutes, 32.9% 15 to 30 minutes, 22.8% 30 to 45 minutes, 9.9% 45 to 60 minutes, 16.6% 60 minutes or more (2000)

SCHAUMBURG (village). Aka Schaumburg Center. Covers a land area of 19.003 square miles and a water area of 0.121 square miles. Located at 42.03° N. Lat.; 88.08° W. Long. Elevation is 799 feet.
Population: 75,386 (2000); Race: 79.1% White, 3.4% Black, 13.8% Asian, 0.1% American Indian and Alaska Native, 5.4% Hispanic of any race, 2.3% two or more races (2000); Density: 3,967.1 persons per square mile (2000); Age: 21.7% under 18, 9.4% over 64 (2000); Marriage status: 29.5% never married, 54.9% now married, 6.0% widowed, 9.6% divorced (2000); Foreign born: 19.1% (2000); Ancestry (includes multiple ancestries): 24.8% German, 23.2% Other groups, 15.0% Irish, 14.9% Polish, 12.6% Italian (2000).
Vital Statistics: Birth rate: 132.3 per 10,000 population (1998)
Economy: Manufacturing: plastic molding, food processing, machining, magnesium die casting, metal fabrication, communication systems, rubber printing plates. Headquarters for Motorola. Site of Woodfield, one of the largest shopping centers in the US, as wellas other large shopping malls. Unemployment rate: 4.9% (11/2002); Total civilian labor force: 48,329 (11/2002); Single-family building permits issued: 31 (2001) / 3 (2000); Multi-family building permits issued: 6 (2001) / 0 (2000); Employment by occupation: 19.3% management, 25.0% professional, 8.6% services, 32.2% sales, 0.0% farming, 5.3% construction, 9.6% production (2000).
Income: Per capita income: $30,587 (2000); Median household income: $60,941 (2000); Poverty rate: 3.0% (2000).
Taxes: Total city taxes per capita: $265 (2000); City property taxes per capita: $22 (2000).
Education: High school graduation rate: 91.8% (2000); College graduation rate: 38.9% (2000).

School District(s)

Schaumburg C C School District 54 (PK-08)
2000 Enrollment: 15,575 847-885-6700

Four-year College(s)

The Illinois Institute of Art at Schaumburg (Private, For-profit)
2001 Enrollment: 1,042 847-619-3450
2001 Tuition: In-state $14,496; Out-of-state $14,496
Keller Graduate School of Management (Private, For-profit)
2001 Enrollment: n/a 847-330-0040

Housing: Homeownership rate: 69.4% (2000); Median home value: $178,200 (2000); Median rent: $918 per month (2000); Median age of housing: 22 years (2000).
Transportation: Commute to work: 91.9% car, 4.1% public transportation, 0.9% walk, 2.7% work from home (2000); Travel time to work: 22.1% less than 15 minutes, 33.7% 15 to 30 minutes, 24.0% 30 to 45 minutes, 9.9% 45 to 60 minutes, 10.3% 60 minutes or more (2000)
Airports: Schaumburg Regional
Additional Information Contacts
Greater Woodfield Convention & Visitors Bureau 847-605-1010

SCHILLER PARK (village). Covers a land area of 2.766 square miles and a water area of 0 square miles. Located at 41.95° N. Lat.; 87.87° W. Long. Elevation is 640 feet.
History: Incorporated 1914.
Population: 11,850 (2000); Race: 79.6% White, 1.1% Black, 6.1% Asian, 0.7% American Indian and Alaska Native, 22.3% Hispanic of any race, 3.3% two or more races (2000); Density: 4,283.5 persons per square mile (2000); Age: 23.5% under 18, 11.2% over 64 (2000); Marriage status: 27.7% never married, 58.3% now married, 6.4% widowed, 7.5% divorced (2000); Foreign born: 39.1% (2000); Ancestry (includes multiple ancestries): 29.8% Other groups, 22.2% Polish, 18.7% Italian, 13.0% German, 9.3% Irish (2000).
Vital Statistics: Birth rate: 130.8 per 10,000 population (1998)
Economy: O'Hare International Airport is to the West. Single-family building permits issued: 6 (2001) / 5 (2000); Multi-family building permits issued: 0 (2001) / 0 (2000); Employment by occupation: 10.5% management, 8.7% professional, 16.7% services, 29.4% sales, 0.0% farming, 10.5% construction, 24.2% production (2000).
Income: Per capita income: $17,781 (2000); Median household income: $41,583 (2000); Poverty rate: 9.2% (2000).
Taxes: Total city taxes per capita: $730 (1997); City property taxes per capita: $412 (1997).
Education: High school graduation rate: 72.5% (2000); College graduation rate: 14.4% (2000).

School District(s)
Schiller Park School District 81 (KG-08)
2000 Enrollment: 1,224 847-671-1816

Two-year College(s)
Westwood College of Technology (Private, For-profit)
2001 Enrollment: 217 847-928-0200
2001 Tuition: In-state $9,423; Out-of-state $9,423

Housing: Homeownership rate: 53.5% (2000); Median home value: $161,600 (2000); Median rent: $594 per month (2000); Median age of housing: 36 years (2000).
Transportation: Commute to work: 88.2% car, 4.2% public transportation, 4.8% walk, 1.8% work from home (2000); Travel time to work: 26.7% less than 15 minutes, 34.7% 15 to 30 minutes, 26.4% 30 to 45 minutes, 5.5% 45 to 60 minutes, 6.8% 60 minutes or more (2000)
Additional Information Contacts
Schiller Park Chamber of Commerce.................... 847-671-3040

SKOKIE (village). Aka Niles Center. Covers a land area of 10.041 square miles and a water area of 0 square miles. Located at 42.03° N. Lat.; 87.74° W. Long. Elevation is 607 feet.
History: Hebrew Theological College (1922) was moved here from Chicago in 1958. National Jewish Theater. Incorporated 1888.
Population: 63,348 (2000); Race: 68.8% White, 4.7% Black, 21.0% Asian, 0.2% American Indian and Alaska Native, 5.6% Hispanic of any race, 3.3% two or more races (2000); Density: 6,308.7 persons per square mile (2000); Age: 22.8% under 18, 19.6% over 64 (2000); Marriage status: 24.2% never married, 59.6% now married, 9.7% widowed, 6.5% divorced (2000); Foreign born: 37.0% (2000); Ancestry (includes multiple ancestries): 35.9% Other groups, 9.3% German, 8.9% Russian, 6.7% Polish, 6.1% Irish (2000).
Vital Statistics: Birth rate: 87.6 per 10,000 population (1998)
Economy: Manufacturing includes communications, computer and electrical equipment, rubber products, tools, iron and steel products. Also important are the printing and publishing industries. Site of Old Orchard Shopping Center, one of the largest shopping centers in the U.S. Unemployment rate: 4.8% (11/2002); Total civilian labor force: 31,729 (11/2002); Single-family building permits issued: 17 (2001) / 11 (2000); Multi-family building permits issued: 60 (2001) / 30 (2000); Employment by occupation: 16.1% management, 30.2% professional, 10.5% services, 29.1% sales, 0.0% farming, 4.3% construction, 9.7% production (2000).
Income: Per capita income: $27,136 (2000); Median household income: $57,375 (2000); Poverty rate: 5.4% (2000).
Taxes: Total city taxes per capita: $501 (2000); City property taxes per capita: $362 (2000).
Education: High school graduation rate: 87.4% (2000); College graduation rate: 42.6% (2000).

School District(s)
East Prairie School District 73 (KG-08)
2000 Enrollment: 464 847-673-1141
Fairview School District 72 (KG-08)
2000 Enrollment: 572 847-674-8213
Niles Township Community High School District 219 (09-12)
2000 Enrollment: 4,572 847-568-3950
Skokie School District 68 (KG-08)
2000 Enrollment: 1,816 847-676-9000
Skokie School District 69 (PK-08)
2000 Enrollment: 1,414 847-675-7666
Skokie School District 73-5 (PK-08)
2000 Enrollment: 1,100 847-673-1220

Four-year College(s)
Hebrew Theological College (Private, Not-for-profit, Jewish)
2001 Enrollment: 248 847-982-2500
2001 Tuition: In-state $14,550; Out-of-state $14,550
Knowledge Systems Institute (Private, Not-for-profit)
2001 Enrollment: 50 847-679-3135
Jewish University of America (Private, Not-for-profit, Jewish)
2001 Enrollment: n/a

Two-year College(s)
Chicago School of Violin Making (Private, For-profit)
2001 Enrollment: n/a 847-673-9545

Housing: Homeownership rate: 75.1% (2000); Median home value: $217,500 (2000); Median rent: $748 per month (2000); Median age of housing: 42 years (2000).
Hospitals: Rush North Shore Medical Center (268 beds)
Newspapers: Chicago Jewish Star (2 x month); Chicago Jewish News (1 x week); Eintracht (1 x week)
Transportation: Commute to work: 85.3% car, 8.1% public transportation, 2.2% walk, 3.5% work from home (2000); Travel time to work: 22.8% less than 15 minutes, 30.9% 15 to 30 minutes, 23.3% 30 to 45 minutes, 13.2% 45 to 60 minutes, 9.9% 60 minutes or more (2000)
Additional Information Contacts
Skokie Chamber of Commerce 847-673-0240

SOUTH BARRINGTON (village). Covers a land area of 6.555 square miles and a water area of 0.309 square miles. Located at 42.08° N. Lat.; 88.15° W. Long. Elevation is 858 feet.
Population: 3,760 (2000); Race: 81.4% White, 0.5% Black, 15.8% Asian, 0.0% American Indian and Alaska Native, 2.3% Hispanic of any race, 1.3% two or more races (2000); Density: 573.6 persons per square mile (2000); Age: 27.7% under 18, 5.0% over 64 (2000); Marriage status: 22.6% never married, 73.8% now married, 1.4% widowed, 2.1% divorced (2000); Foreign born: 19.4% (2000); Ancestry (includes multiple ancestries): 22.0% German, 19.3% Other groups, 16.4% Italian, 11.5% Polish, 11.3% Irish (2000).
Economy: Single-family building permits issued: 22 (2001) / 25 (2000); Multi-family building permits issued: 0 (2001) / 0 (2000); Employment by occupation: 32.2% management, 27.3% professional, 3.5% services, 30.4% sales, 0.0% farming, 2.7% construction, 3.9% production (2000).
Income: Per capita income: $76,078 (2000); Median household income: $170,755 (2000); Poverty rate: 2.6% (2000).
Taxes: Total city taxes per capita: $223 (1997); City property taxes per capita: $215 (1997).
Education: High school graduation rate: 97.2% (2000); College graduation rate: 62.6% (2000).
Housing: Homeownership rate: 98.7% (2000); Median home value: $678,800 (2000); Median rent: $2,000+ per month (2000); Median age of housing: 14 years (2000).
Transportation: Commute to work: 86.9% car, 5.2% public transportation, 0.4% walk, 7.0% work from home (2000); Travel time to work: 15.7% less than 15 minutes, 35.8% 15 to 30 minutes, 23.1% 30 to 45 minutes, 11.2% 45 to 60 minutes, 14.2% 60 minutes or more (2000)

SOUTH CHICAGO HEIGHTS (village). Covers a land area of 1.535 square miles and a water area of 0.016 square miles. Located at 41.48° N. Lat.; 87.63° W. Long. Elevation is 717 feet.
History: Incorporated 1907.
Population: 3,970 (2000); Race: 78.7% White, 5.1% Black, 1.0% Asian, 0.0% American Indian and Alaska Native, 18.7% Hispanic of any race, 6.2% two or more races (2000); Density: 2,586.1 persons per square mile (2000);

Age: 21.9% under 18, 17.6% over 64 (2000); Marriage status: 25.8% never married, 54.6% now married, 8.8% widowed, 10.8% divorced (2000); Foreign born: 7.9% (2000); Ancestry (includes multiple ancestries): 30.1% Other groups, 19.4% German, 18.3% Italian, 14.2% Irish, 11.3% Polish (2000).
Economy: In industrial area. Manufacturing: steel fabricating, tool and die, millwork; wood products, food containers. Single-family building permits issued: 9 (2001) / 3 (2000); Multi-family building permits issued: 0 (2001) / 0 (2000); Employment by occupation: 7.3% management, 10.8% professional, 14.4% services, 31.6% sales, 0.4% farming, 12.5% construction, 23.0% production (2000).
Income: Per capita income: $18,179 (2000); Median household income: $39,639 (2000); Poverty rate: 6.7% (2000).
Taxes: Total city taxes per capita: $657 (1997); City property taxes per capita: $276 (1997).
Education: High school graduation rate: 71.6% (2000); College graduation rate: 6.7% (2000).
Housing: Homeownership rate: 70.9% (2000); Median home value: $93,600 (2000); Median rent: $484 per month (2000); Median age of housing: 43 years (2000).
Transportation: Commute to work: 84.9% car, 6.5% public transportation, 6.4% walk, 0.7% work from home (2000); Travel time to work: 35.4% less than 15 minutes, 29.8% 15 to 30 minutes, 12.4% 30 to 45 minutes, 8.7% 45 to 60 minutes, 13.6% 60 minutes or more (2000)

SOUTH HOLLAND (village). Covers a land area of 7.280 square miles and a water area of 0.015 square miles. Located at 41.59° N. Lat.; 87.59° W. Long. Elevation is 600 feet.
History: South Holland was settled in 1840 by immigrants from the Netherlands. An early industry was the raising of onions.
Population: 22,147 (2000); Race: 44.6% White, 50.2% Black, 1.3% Asian, 0.2% American Indian and Alaska Native, 3.7% Hispanic of any race, 1.7% two or more races (2000); Density: 3,042.1 persons per square mile (2000); Age: 25.8% under 18, 17.1% over 64 (2000); Marriage status: 23.1% never married, 61.6% now married, 8.6% widowed, 6.7% divorced (2000); Foreign born: 5.1% (2000); Ancestry (includes multiple ancestries): 48.3% Other groups, 12.2% Dutch, 8.6% German, 6.4% Irish, 6.3% Polish (2000).
Vital Statistics: Birth rate: 113.8 per 10,000 population (1998)
Economy: Single-family building permits issued: 36 (2001) / 32 (2000); Multi-family building permits issued: 0 (2001) / 0 (2000); Employment by occupation: 13.9% management, 22.7% professional, 10.9% services, 30.9% sales, 0.0% farming, 9.1% construction, 12.5% production (2000).
Income: Per capita income: $24,977 (2000); Median household income: $60,246 (2000); Poverty rate: 4.6% (2000).
Taxes: Total city taxes per capita: $457 (2000); City property taxes per capita: $326 (2000).
Education: High school graduation rate: 87.9% (2000); College graduation rate: 25.6% (2000).

School District(s)

Exc Children Have Opportunities (PK-12)
2000 Enrollment: 573 708-333-7880
South Holland School District 150 (PK-08)
2000 Enrollment: 920 708-339-4240
South Holland School District 151 (PK-08)
2000 Enrollment: 1,308 708-339-1516
Thornton Township H S District 205 (09-12)
2000 Enrollment: 6,362 708-225-4000

Two-year College(s)

South Suburban College (Public)
2001 Enrollment: 6,452 708-596-2000
2001 Tuition: In-state $5,280; Out-of-state $5,760

Housing: Homeownership rate: 93.0% (2000); Median home value: $133,600 (2000); Median rent: $539 per month (2000); Median age of housing: 35 years (2000).
Transportation: Commute to work: 85.5% car, 9.4% public transportation, 1.2% walk, 3.1% work from home (2000); Travel time to work: 20.2% less than 15 minutes, 23.6% 15 to 30 minutes, 23.4% 30 to 45 minutes, 13.7% 45 to 60 minutes, 19.1% 60 minutes or more (2000)

STICKNEY (village). Covers a land area of 1.928 square miles and a water area of 0.033 square miles. Located at 41.81° N. Lat.; 87.78° W. Long. Elevation is 604 feet.
History: Incorporated 1913.
Population: 6,148 (2000); Race: 92.8% White, 0.4% Black, 0.9% Asian, 0.0% American Indian and Alaska Native, 21.4% Hispanic of any race, 1.2% two or more races (2000); Density: 3,189.5 persons per square mile (2000); Age: 22.7% under 18, 18.7% over 64 (2000); Marriage status: 25.8% never married, 55.5% now married, 9.2% widowed, 9.5% divorced (2000); Foreign born: 16.2% (2000); Ancestry (includes multiple ancestries): 21.2% Other groups, 19.5% Polish, 14.0% German, 12.9% Czech, 9.2% Italian (2000).
Economy: On Chicago Sanitary and Ship Canal. Single-family building permits issued: 4 (2001) / 1 (2000); Multi-family building permits issued: 0 (2001) / 0 (2000); Employment by occupation: 6.4% management, 11.2% professional, 21.7% services, 33.3% sales, 0.5% farming, 11.9% construction, 14.9% production (2000).
Income: Per capita income: $19,109 (2000); Median household income: $42,772 (2000); Poverty rate: 5.8% (2000).
Taxes: Total city taxes per capita: $16 (1997); City property taxes per capita: $10 (1997).
Education: High school graduation rate: 76.0% (2000); College graduation rate: 8.9% (2000).
Housing: Homeownership rate: 77.4% (2000); Median home value: $136,700 (2000); Median rent: $558 per month (2000); Median age of housing: 45 years (2000).
Transportation: Commute to work: 76.9% car, 6.8% public transportation, 13.0% walk, 2.6% work from home (2000); Travel time to work: 27.3% less than 15 minutes, 28.5% 15 to 30 minutes, 25.5% 30 to 45 minutes, 9.3% 45 to 60 minutes, 9.4% 60 minutes or more (2000)

STONE PARK (village). Covers a land area of 0.333 square miles and a water area of 0 square miles. Located at 41.90° N. Lat.; 87.88° W. Long. Elevation is 640 feet.
History: Incorporated 1939.
Population: 5,127 (2000); Race: 54.0% White, 2.4% Black, 0.7% Asian, 0.0% American Indian and Alaska Native, 79.8% Hispanic of any race, 1.8% two or more races (2000); Density: 15,378.2 persons per square mile (2000); Age: 32.5% under 18, 5.1% over 64 (2000); Marriage status: 34.5% never married, 55.1% now married, 4.0% widowed, 6.4% divorced (2000); Foreign born: 50.3% (2000); Ancestry (includes multiple ancestries): 74.8% Other groups, 3.6% German, 3.0% Italian, 2.9% United States or American, 2.3% Irish (2000).
Economy: Single-family building permits issued: 0 (2001) / 0 (2000); Multi-family building permits issued: 0 (2001) / 0 (2000); Employment by occupation: 0.8% management, 7.9% professional, 11.8% services, 18.9% sales, 0.5% farming, 10.2% construction, 49.9% production (2000).
Income: Per capita income: $12,887 (2000); Median household income: $39,787 (2000); Poverty rate: 15.2% (2000).
Taxes: Total city taxes per capita: $518 (1997); City property taxes per capita: $278 (1997).
Education: High school graduation rate: 43.8% (2000); College graduation rate: 4.1% (2000).
Housing: Homeownership rate: 58.7% (2000); Median home value: $118,900 (2000); Median rent: $583 per month (2000); Median age of housing: 36 years (2000).
Transportation: Commute to work: 91.4% car, 3.3% public transportation, 1.6% walk, 2.1% work from home (2000); Travel time to work: 24.5% less than 15 minutes, 34.3% 15 to 30 minutes, 25.5% 30 to 45 minutes, 9.1% 45 to 60 minutes, 6.6% 60 minutes or more (2000)

STREAMWOOD (village). Covers a land area of 7.297 square miles and a water area of 0.027 square miles. Located at 42.02° N. Lat.; 88.17° W. Long. Elevation is 820 feet.
Population: 36,407 (2000); Race: 76.2% White, 4.7% Black, 9.0% Asian, 0.4% American Indian and Alaska Native, 16.4% Hispanic of any race, 2.1% two or more races (2000); Density: 4,989.0 persons per square mile (2000); Age: 27.9% under 18, 6.0% over 64 (2000); Marriage status: 24.8% never married, 61.6% now married, 4.5% widowed, 9.1% divorced (2000); Foreign born: 19.9% (2000); Ancestry (includes multiple ancestries): 30.3% Other groups, 21.2% German, 14.6% Polish, 13.7% Irish, 10.5% Italian (2000).
Vital Statistics: Birth rate: 196.1 per 10,000 population (1998)
Economy: Manufacturing of plastic products, chemicals, consumer goods; aluminum anodizing, printing. Unemployment rate: 6.4% (11/2002); Total civilian labor force: 21,934 (11/2002); Single-family building permits issued: 82 (2001) / 334 (2000); Multi-family building permits issued: 23 (2001) / 0 (2000); Employment by occupation: 14.7% management, 18.3% professional, 11.3% services, 32.1% sales, 0.1% farming, 9.3% construction, 14.1% production (2000).
Income: Per capita income: $23,961 (2000); Median household income: $65,076 (2000); Poverty rate: 3.0% (2000).
Taxes: Total city taxes per capita: $275 (2000); City property taxes per capita: $139 (2000).

Education: High school graduation rate: 85.3% (2000); College graduation rate: 26.5% (2000).
Housing: Homeownership rate: 89.5% (2000); Median home value: $143,500 (2000); Median rent: $970 per month (2000); Median age of housing: 20 years (2000).
Transportation: Commute to work: 93.0% car, 3.3% public transportation, 0.7% walk, 2.3% work from home (2000); Travel time to work: 14.9% less than 15 minutes, 34.3% 15 to 30 minutes, 26.8% 30 to 45 minutes, 12.6% 45 to 60 minutes, 11.3% 60 minutes or more (2000)
Additional Information Contacts
Streamwood Chamber of Commerce 630-837-5200

SUMMIT (village). Covers a land area of 2.124 square miles and a water area of 0.154 square miles. Located at 41.78° N. Lat.; 87.81° W. Long. Elevation is 610 feet.
History: Summit developed around the Corn Products Company Plant, a corn refinery. It was named for its location at the crest of the watershed between the Great Lakes and the Mississippi drainage systems. Rain falling on the east side of town drains into the Atlantic Ocean; that falling on the west side into the Gulf of Mexico.
Population: 10,637 (2000); Race: 63.0% White, 12.4% Black, 2.4% Asian, 0.2% American Indian and Alaska Native, 48.6% Hispanic of any race, 3.2% two or more races (2000); Density: 5,008.7 persons per square mile (2000); Age: 29.3% under 18, 10.5% over 64 (2000); Marriage status: 33.6% never married, 49.7% now married, 8.7% widowed, 8.0% divorced (2000); Foreign born: 34.1% (2000); Ancestry (includes multiple ancestries): 58.0% Other groups, 11.7% Polish, 5.2% German, 4.4% Irish, 3.0% Italian (2000).
Economy: Single-family building permits issued: 4 (2001) / 9 (2000); Multi-family building permits issued: 6 (2001) / 4 (2000); Employment by occupation: 6.3% management, 10.1% professional, 17.8% services, 24.6% sales, 0.4% farming, 10.4% construction, 30.4% production (2000).
Income: Per capita income: $14,611 (2000); Median household income: $38,132 (2000); Poverty rate: 16.2% (2000).
Taxes: Total city taxes per capita: $297 (1997); City property taxes per capita: $178 (1997).
Education: High school graduation rate: 59.2% (2000); College graduation rate: 7.3% (2000).

School District(s)
Argo Community H S District 217 (09-12)
2000 Enrollment: 1,562 708-728-3200
Summit School District 104 (PK-08)
2000 Enrollment: 1,615 708-458-0505

Housing: Homeownership rate: 52.7% (2000); Median home value: $109,200 (2000); Median rent: $499 per month (2000); Median age of housing: 45 years (2000).
Newspapers: Des Plaines Valley News (1 x week)
Transportation: Commute to work: 85.0% car, 6.3% public transportation, 5.7% walk, 1.0% work from home (2000); Travel time to work: 27.0% less than 15 minutes, 34.2% 15 to 30 minutes, 21.7% 30 to 45 minutes, 9.1% 45 to 60 minutes, 8.0% 60 minutes or more (2000); Amtrak: Service available.
Additional Information Contacts
Argo-Summit Chamber of Commerce 708-458-3033

THORNTON (village). Covers a land area of 2.334 square miles and a water area of 0.044 square miles. Located at 41.57° N. Lat.; 87.61° W. Long. Elevation is 603 feet.
History: Incorporated 1900.
Population: 2,582 (2000); Race: 96.6% White, 1.1% Black, 0.2% Asian, 0.8% American Indian and Alaska Native, 4.2% Hispanic of any race, 0.6% two or more races (2000); Density: 1,106.2 persons per square mile (2000); Age: 23.1% under 18, 16.7% over 64 (2000); Marriage status: 22.0% never married, 58.3% now married, 9.4% widowed, 10.3% divorced (2000); Foreign born: 1.4% (2000); Ancestry (includes multiple ancestries): 26.4% German, 20.3% Irish, 15.7% Polish, 9.5% Italian, 9.1% Dutch (2000).
Economy: Manufacturing includes furniture, packing materials, asphalt paving mixtures, crushed stone. Single-family building permits issued: 0 (2001) / 0 (2000); Multi-family building permits issued: 0 (2001) / 0 (2000); Employment by occupation: 6.0% management, 14.4% professional, 13.7% services, 32.6% sales, 0.0% farming, 16.1% construction, 17.2% production (2000).
Income: Per capita income: $22,899 (2000); Median household income: $46,778 (2000); Poverty rate: 2.9% (2000).
Taxes: Total city taxes per capita: $720 (1997); City property taxes per capita: $547 (1997).
Education: High school graduation rate: 87.1% (2000); College graduation rate: 12.2% (2000).

School District(s)
Thornton School District 154 (PK-08)
2000 Enrollment: 282 708-877-5160

Housing: Homeownership rate: 85.0% (2000); Median home value: $104,900 (2000); Median rent: $548 per month (2000); Median age of housing: 44 years (2000).
Transportation: Commute to work: 90.3% car, 6.6% public transportation, 2.2% walk, 1.0% work from home (2000); Travel time to work: 36.0% less than 15 minutes, 31.1% 15 to 30 minutes, 13.5% 30 to 45 minutes, 6.1% 45 to 60 minutes, 13.4% 60 minutes or more (2000)

TINLEY PARK (village). Covers a land area of 14.953 square miles and a water area of 0.036 square miles. Located at 41.57° N. Lat.; 87.80° W. Long. Elevation is 698 feet.
Population: 48,401 (2000); Race: 93.0% White, 1.9% Black, 2.6% Asian, 0.0% American Indian and Alaska Native, 3.9% Hispanic of any race, 0.9% two or more races (2000); Density: 3,236.9 persons per square mile (2000); Age: 26.4% under 18, 11.0% over 64 (2000); Marriage status: 25.2% never married, 60.3% now married, 7.1% widowed, 7.4% divorced (2000); Foreign born: 5.8% (2000); Ancestry (includes multiple ancestries): 25.4% Irish, 23.1% German, 19.7% Polish, 14.3% Italian, 8.6% Other groups (2000).
Vital Statistics: Birth rate: 135.5 per 10,000 population (1998)
Economy: Unemployment rate: 4.9% (11/2002); Total civilian labor force: 25,602 (11/2002); Single-family building permits issued: 632 (2001) / 577 (2000); Multi-family building permits issued: 56 (2001) / 88 (2000); Employment by occupation: 15.8% management, 20.4% professional, 11.0% services, 30.2% sales, 0.1% farming, 11.4% construction, 11.3% production (2000).
Income: Per capita income: $25,207 (2000); Median household income: $61,648 (2000); Poverty rate: 2.5% (2000).
Taxes: Total city taxes per capita: $221 (2000); City property taxes per capita: $179 (2000).
Education: High school graduation rate: 89.5% (2000); College graduation rate: 24.8% (2000).

School District(s)
Kirby School District 140 (PK-08)
2000 Enrollment: 4,766 708-532-6462
Tinley Park Community Cons Sch Dst 146 (PK-08)
2000 Enrollment: 2,409 708-614-4500

Four-year College(s)
Devry Institute of Technology (Private, For-profit)
2001 Enrollment: 1,662 708-342-3300
2001 Tuition: In-state $8,740; Out-of-state $8,740
Keller Graduate School of Management (Private, For-profit)
2001 Enrollment: n/a 708-342-3750

Housing: Homeownership rate: 84.8% (2000); Median home value: $169,300 (2000); Median rent: $661 per month (2000); Median age of housing: 18 years (2000).
Hospitals: Tinley Park Mental Health Center (150 beds)
Newspapers: The Daily Southtown (7 x week); Worth/Chicago Ridge Star (2 x week); Alsip/Blue Island Star (2 x week); Calumet City Star (2 x week); Chicago Heights Area Star (2 x week); Crete/University Park Star (2 x week); Frankfort Mokena Star (2 x week); Harvey Markham Star (2 x week); Hazel Crest/Country Club Hills Star (2 x week); Homer Township Star (2 x week); Homewood/Flossmoor Star (2 x week); Lansing/Lynwood Star (2 x week); Park Forest Star (2 x week); Palos Area Star (2 x week); Oak Lawn Star (2 x week); Orland Park Star (2 x week); Matteson/Richton Park Star (2 x week); New Lenox/Manhattan Star (2 x week); Oak Forest/Crestwood/Midlothian Star (2 x week); South Holland/Dolton Star (2 x week); Tinley Park Star (2 x week)
Transportation: Commute to work: 86.9% car, 10.2% public transportation, 0.8% walk, 1.7% work from home (2000); Travel time to work: 20.3% less than 15 minutes, 27.7% 15 to 30 minutes, 19.4% 30 to 45 minutes, 14.0% 45 to 60 minutes, 18.5% 60 minutes or more (2000)
Additional Information Contacts
Tinley Park Chamber of Commerce 708-532-5700

WESTCHESTER (village). Covers a land area of 3.195 square miles and a water area of 0 square miles. Located at 41.85° N. Lat.; 87.88° W. Long. Elevation is 645 feet.
Population: 16,824 (2000); Race: 85.8% White, 6.5% Black, 3.5% Asian, 0.3% American Indian and Alaska Native, 5.4% Hispanic of any race, 1.9% two or more races (2000); Density: 5,265.2 persons per square mile (2000); Age: 19.3% under 18, 24.5% over 64 (2000); Marriage status: 20.4% never married, 60.4% now married, 11.9% widowed, 7.4% divorced (2000); Foreign born: 9.5% (2000); Ancestry (includes multiple ancestries): 20.9%

Italian, 19.9% German, 17.1% Irish, 16.0% Other groups, 15.0% Polish (2000).
Vital Statistics: Birth rate: 110.0 per 10,000 population (1998)
Economy: Single-family building permits issued: 2 (2001) / 8 (2000); Multi-family building permits issued: 55 (2001) / 5 (2000); Employment by occupation: 17.3% management, 24.1% professional, 9.3% services, 33.1% sales, 0.1% farming, 5.7% construction, 10.4% production (2000).
Income: Per capita income: $29,634 (2000); Median household income: $58,928 (2000); Poverty rate: 2.5% (2000).
Taxes: Total city taxes per capita: $324 (1997); City property taxes per capita: $248 (1997).
Education: High school graduation rate: 89.0% (2000); College graduation rate: 30.8% (2000).

School District(s)

Westchester School District 92-5 (PK-08)
2000 Enrollment: 1,133 708-450-2700
Housing: Homeownership rate: 93.8% (2000); Median home value: $168,900 (2000); Median rent: $776 per month (2000); Median age of housing: 43 years (2000).
Transportation: Commute to work: 90.1% car, 5.5% public transportation, 1.9% walk, 2.4% work from home (2000); Travel time to work: 23.7% less than 15 minutes, 35.6% 15 to 30 minutes, 25.8% 30 to 45 minutes, 8.2% 45 to 60 minutes, 6.7% 60 minutes or more (2000)
Additional Information Contacts
Cook County Chamber of Commerce 708-531-1117

WESTERN SPRINGS (village). Covers a land area of 2.626 square miles and a water area of 0 square miles. Located at 41.80° N. Lat.; 87.90° W. Long. Elevation is 673 feet.
History: Western Springs was named for the mineral springs, believed to be medicinal when the community was settled by the Quakers in 1866.
Population: 12,493 (2000); Race: 97.7% White, 0.6% Black, 0.7% Asian, 0.1% American Indian and Alaska Native, 1.8% Hispanic of any race, 0.6% two or more races (2000); Density: 4,756.7 persons per square mile (2000); Age: 30.1% under 18, 15.2% over 64 (2000); Marriage status: 17.1% never married, 72.8% now married, 6.1% widowed, 4.0% divorced (2000); Foreign born: 3.8% (2000); Ancestry (includes multiple ancestries): 29.9% Irish, 27.8% German, 13.8% Polish, 13.5% Italian, 9.0% English (2000).
Vital Statistics: Birth rate: 130.5 per 10,000 population (1998)
Economy: Single-family building permits issued: 42 (2001) / 38 (2000); Multi-family building permits issued: 0 (2001) / 0 (2000); Employment by occupation: 27.1% management, 34.9% professional, 4.3% services, 28.0% sales, 0.0% farming, 2.8% construction, 2.9% production (2000).
Income: Per capita income: $43,699 (2000); Median household income: $98,876 (2000); Poverty rate: 0.9% (2000).
Taxes: Total city taxes per capita: $404 (1997); City property taxes per capita: $230 (1997).
Education: High school graduation rate: 97.2% (2000); College graduation rate: 66.4% (2000).

School District(s)

Western Springs School District 101 (PK-08)
2000 Enrollment: 1,340 708-246-3700
Housing: Homeownership rate: 95.9% (2000); Median home value: $323,900 (2000); Median rent: $650 per month (2000); Median age of housing: 46 years (2000).
Transportation: Commute to work: 77.0% car, 16.1% public transportation, 1.2% walk, 5.5% work from home (2000); Travel time to work: 25.3% less than 15 minutes, 23.9% 15 to 30 minutes, 22.2% 30 to 45 minutes, 16.5% 45 to 60 minutes, 12.1% 60 minutes or more (2000)

WHEELING (village). Covers a land area of 8.400 square miles and a water area of 0.036 square miles. Located at 42.13° N. Lat.; 87.93° W. Long. Elevation is 650 feet.
History: The first building in Wheeling was a country store established in 1830 on the Chicago-Milwaukee stage route.
Population: 34,496 (2000); Race: 76.4% White, 2.5% Black, 8.6% Asian, 0.3% American Indian and Alaska Native, 20.9% Hispanic of any race, 2.8% two or more races (2000); Density: 4,106.5 persons per square mile (2000); Age: 23.5% under 18, 10.6% over 64 (2000); Marriage status: 27.6% never married, 57.8% now married, 5.5% widowed, 9.1% divorced (2000); Foreign born: 31.4% (2000); Ancestry (includes multiple ancestries): 33.6% Other groups, 16.7% German, 10.8% Polish, 9.7% Irish, 6.8% Russian (2000).
Vital Statistics: Birth rate: 156.3 per 10,000 population (1998)
Economy: Unemployment rate: 6.2% (11/2002); Total civilian labor force: 19,512 (11/2002); Single-family building permits issued: 12 (2001) / 81 (2000); Multi-family building permits issued: 263 (2001) / 101 (2000); Employment by occupation: 13.4% management, 21.7% professional, 12.4% services, 31.3% sales, 0.1% farming, 6.2% construction, 14.8% production (2000).
Income: Per capita income: $24,989 (2000); Median household income: $55,491 (2000); Poverty rate: 5.3% (2000).
Taxes: Total city taxes per capita: $315 (2000); City property taxes per capita: $209 (2000).
Education: High school graduation rate: 82.6% (2000); College graduation rate: 32.1% (2000).

School District(s)

Wheeling C C School District 21 (PK-08)
2000 Enrollment: 7,264 847-537-8270

Two-year College(s)

Worsham College (Private, For-profit)
2001 Enrollment: 101 847-808-8444
Housing: Homeownership rate: 66.5% (2000); Median home value: $160,900 (2000); Median rent: $824 per month (2000); Median age of housing: 24 years (2000).
Transportation: Commute to work: 92.3% car, 3.3% public transportation, 1.8% walk, 1.9% work from home (2000); Travel time to work: 24.6% less than 15 minutes, 38.5% 15 to 30 minutes, 22.4% 30 to 45 minutes, 6.9% 45 to 60 minutes, 7.5% 60 minutes or more (2000)

WILLOW SPRINGS (village). Covers a land area of 3.868 square miles and a water area of 0.110 square miles. Located at 41.73° N. Lat.; 87.87° W. Long. Elevation is 620 feet.
Population: 5,027 (2000); Race: 95.9% White, 0.2% Black, 0.3% Asian, 0.0% American Indian and Alaska Native, 6.3% Hispanic of any race, 3.6% two or more races (2000); Density: 1,299.8 persons per square mile (2000); Age: 22.7% under 18, 8.1% over 64 (2000); Marriage status: 23.3% never married, 62.0% now married, 6.4% widowed, 8.3% divorced (2000); Foreign born: 13.3% (2000); Ancestry (includes multiple ancestries): 25.3% Polish, 19.6% German, 12.6% Irish, 11.3% Italian, 6.1% Other groups (2000).
Economy: Manufacturing: fabricated metal products, electrical goods, chemicals; remnant agriculture. On Sanitary and Ship Canal. Single-family building permits issued: 124 (2001) / 143 (2000); Multi-family building permits issued: 30 (2001) / 12 (2000); Employment by occupation: 15.0% management, 15.9% professional, 10.3% services, 29.0% sales, 0.0% farming, 12.0% construction, 17.8% production (2000).
Income: Per capita income: $30,394 (2000); Median household income: $58,322 (2000); Poverty rate: 6.2% (2000).
Taxes: Total city taxes per capita: $628 (1997); City property taxes per capita: $259 (1997).
Education: High school graduation rate: 85.1% (2000); College graduation rate: 23.6% (2000).

School District(s)

Willow Springs School District 108 (KG-08)
2000 Enrollment: 420 708-839-6828
Housing: Homeownership rate: 84.7% (2000); Median home value: $215,200 (2000); Median rent: $613 per month (2000); Median age of housing: 27 years (2000).
Transportation: Commute to work: 90.7% car, 3.8% public transportation, 0.8% walk, 3.7% work from home (2000); Travel time to work: 16.3% less than 15 minutes, 26.7% 15 to 30 minutes, 29.3% 30 to 45 minutes, 12.8% 45 to 60 minutes, 14.9% 60 minutes or more (2000)

WILMETTE (village). Covers a land area of 5.384 square miles and a water area of 0.006 square miles. Located at 42.07° N. Lat.; 87.72° W. Long. Elevation is 615 feet.
History: Wilmette was named for Antoine Ouilmette, a French-Canadian who settled here when his wife received the land under a government treaty in 1829.
Population: 27,651 (2000); Race: 89.8% White, 0.4% Black, 8.0% Asian, 0.1% American Indian and Alaska Native, 2.7% Hispanic of any race, 1.1% two or more races (2000); Density: 5,135.8 persons per square mile (2000); Age: 30.2% under 18, 16.5% over 64 (2000); Marriage status: 18.4% never married, 69.5% now married, 6.4% widowed, 5.7% divorced (2000); Foreign born: 13.2% (2000); Ancestry (includes multiple ancestries): 20.2% German, 19.4% Irish, 15.1% Other groups, 11.5% English, 7.2% Polish (2000).
Vital Statistics: Birth rate: 100.9 per 10,000 population (1998)
Economy: Unemployment rate: 3.4% (11/2002); Total civilian labor force: 13,470 (11/2002); Single-family building permits issued: 55 (2001) / 37 (2000); Multi-family building permits issued: 0 (2001) / 0 (2000); Employment by occupation: 27.4% management, 39.5% professional, 4.5% services, 24.6% sales, 0.0% farming, 1.8% construction, 2.1% production (2000).

Income: Per capita income: $55,611 (2000); Median household income: $106,773 (2000); Poverty rate: 2.3% (2000).
Taxes: Total city taxes per capita: $449 (2000); City property taxes per capita: $265 (2000).
Education: High school graduation rate: 96.8% (2000); College graduation rate: 72.6% (2000).

School District(s)

Avoca School District 37 (KG-08)
2000 Enrollment: 692 847-251-3587
Wilmette School District 39 (PK-08)
2000 Enrollment: 3,446 847-256-2450

Housing: Homeownership rate: 86.9% (2000); Median home value: $441,600 (2000); Median rent: $958 per month (2000); Median age of housing: 48 years (2000).
Transportation: Commute to work: 72.1% car, 18.7% public transportation, 1.3% walk, 7.1% work from home (2000); Travel time to work: 21.1% less than 15 minutes, 23.6% 15 to 30 minutes, 21.7% 30 to 45 minutes, 19.9% 45 to 60 minutes, 13.7% 60 minutes or more (2000)
Additional Information Contacts
Wilmette Chamber of Commerce.............................. 847-251-3800

WINNETKA (village). Covers a land area of 3.830 square miles and a water area of 0.086 square miles. Located at 42.10° N. Lat.; 87.73° W. Long. Elevation is 650 feet.
History: Winnetka was incorporated in 1869. The Winnetka public school system, organized in 1919 with Carleton Washburne as superintendent, gained recognition for innovative eucation.
Population: 12,419 (2000); Race: 95.8% White, 0.4% Black, 2.7% Asian, 0.0% American Indian and Alaska Native, 0.9% Hispanic of any race, 1.1% two or more races (2000); Density: 3,242.7 persons per square mile (2000); Age: 34.7% under 18, 13.1% over 64 (2000); Marriage status: 15.1% never married, 75.1% now married, 4.3% widowed, 5.5% divorced (2000); Foreign born: 5.1% (2000); Ancestry (includes multiple ancestries): 23.1% German, 22.4% Irish, 18.3% English, 6.3% Other groups, 5.7% Italian (2000).
Vital Statistics: Birth rate: 132.1 per 10,000 population (1998)
Economy: Single-family building permits issued: 53 (2001) / 41 (2000); Multi-family building permits issued: 0 (2001) / 0 (2000); Employment by occupation: 37.0% management, 32.0% professional, 4.4% services, 24.1% sales, 0.0% farming, 1.5% construction, 0.8% production (2000).
Income: Per capita income: $84,134 (2000); Median household income: $167,458 (2000); Poverty rate: 1.4% (2000).
Taxes: Total city taxes per capita: $787 (2000); City property taxes per capita: $692 (2000).
Education: High school graduation rate: 99.0% (2000); College graduation rate: 84.4% (2000).

School District(s)

New Trier Township H S District 203 (09-12)
2000 Enrollment: 3,606 847-446-7000
Winnetka School District 36 (PK-08)
2000 Enrollment: 1,972 847-446-9400

Housing: Homeownership rate: 89.6% (2000); Median home value: $756,500 (2000); Median rent: $1,018 per month (2000); Median age of housing: 60+ years (2000).
Transportation: Commute to work: 62.5% car, 26.6% public transportation, 2.0% walk, 7.6% work from home (2000); Travel time to work: 19.2% less than 15 minutes, 20.1% 15 to 30 minutes, 24.0% 30 to 45 minutes, 19.8% 45 to 60 minutes, 16.8% 60 minutes or more (2000)
Additional Information Contacts
Winnetka Chamber of Commerce 847-446-4451

WORTH (village). Covers a land area of 2.384 square miles and a water area of 0.022 square miles. Located at 41.68° N. Lat.; 87.79° W. Long. Elevation is 615 feet.
Population: 11,047 (2000); Race: 90.2% White, 1.6% Black, 2.1% Asian, 0.3% American Indian and Alaska Native, 7.4% Hispanic of any race, 3.1% two or more races (2000); Density: 4,634.4 persons per square mile (2000); Age: 23.0% under 18, 15.0% over 64 (2000); Marriage status: 28.7% never married, 49.5% now married, 10.6% widowed, 11.1% divorced (2000); Foreign born: 9.1% (2000); Ancestry (includes multiple ancestries): 23.4% German, 22.7% Irish, 20.3% Polish, 11.9% Other groups, 10.1% Italian (2000).
Vital Statistics: Birth rate: 145.7 per 10,000 population (1998)
Economy: Manufacturing: conveyors, steel processing, packaging materials, furniture. On Calumet Sag Channel. Single-family building permits issued: 3 (2001) / 2 (2000); Multi-family building permits issued: 0 (2001) / 10 (2000); Employment by occupation: 7.7% management, 10.9% professional, 15.3% services, 32.6% sales, 0.0% farming, 15.8% construction, 17.7% production (2000).
Income: Per capita income: $19,449 (2000); Median household income: $42,723 (2000); Poverty rate: 9.3% (2000).
Taxes: Total city taxes per capita: $225 (1997); City property taxes per capita: $193 (1997).
Education: High school graduation rate: 81.3% (2000); College graduation rate: 11.2% (2000).

School District(s)

Eisenhower Cooperative (PK-08)
2000 Enrollment: 149 708-448-0180
Worth School District 127 (PK-08)
2000 Enrollment: 1,193 708-448-2800

Housing: Homeownership rate: 68.8% (2000); Median home value: $141,400 (2000); Median rent: $609 per month (2000); Median age of housing: 37 years (2000).
Transportation: Commute to work: 90.6% car, 5.0% public transportation, 2.0% walk, 1.3% work from home (2000); Travel time to work: 25.1% less than 15 minutes, 31.7% 15 to 30 minutes, 20.1% 30 to 45 minutes, 11.9% 45 to 60 minutes, 11.2% 60 minutes or more (2000)

Crawford County

Located in southeastern Illinois; bounded on the east by the Wabash River and the Indiana border; drained by the Embarrass River. Covers a land area of 443.50 square miles, a water area of 2.20 square miles, and is located in the Central Time Zone. The county government was organized in 1816. County seat is Robinson.

Weather Station: Palestine 2 W — Elevation: 469 feet

	Jan	Feb	Mar	Apr	May	Jun	Jul	Aug	Sep	Oct	Nov	Dec
High	37	43	54	66	76	85	88	86	80	68	54	42
Low	20	25	35	44	54	62	66	65	56	45	36	26
Precip	2.5	2.5	3.8	4.1	4.6	3.8	3.9	3.7	3.3	2.9	3.9	3.1
Snow	6.4	4.5	2.6	0.2	0.0	0.0	0.0	0.0	0.0	tr	1.0	3.8

High and Low temperatures in degrees Fahrenheit; Precipitation and Snow in inches

Population: 20,452 (2000); Race: 93.4% White, 4.5% Black, 0.3% Asian, 0.0% American Indian and Alaska Native, 2.0% Hispanic of any race, 1.2% two or more races (2000); Density: 46.1 persons per square mile (2000); Age: 22.8% under 18, 16.7% over 64 (2000).
Religion: Five largest groups: 10.5% The United Methodist Church, 10.3% Christian Churches and Churches of Christ, 8.8% Southern Baptist Convention, 6.8% Christian Church (Disciples of Christ), 4.1% Catholic Church (2000).
Economy: Unemployment rate: 7.5% (11/2002); Total civilian labor force: 9,788 (11/2002); Leading industries: 34.6% manufacturing; 11.9% retail trade; 11.8% wholesale trade (2000); Companies that employ more than 1,000 persons: 0 (2000); Companies that employ more than 100 persons: 9 (2000); Farms: 473 totaling 208,922 acres (1997); Minority business ownership rate: 0.0% (1997); Women business ownership rate: 18.6% (1997); Retail sales per capita: $6,495 (1997). Single-family building permits issued: 6 (2001) / 5 (2000); Multi-family building permits issued: 0 (2001) / 0 (2000).
Income: Per capita income: $16,869 (2000); Median household income: $32,531 (2000); Poverty rate: 11.2% (2000); Bankruptcy rate: 4.98% (2001).
Taxes: Total county taxes per capita: $85 (1997); County property taxes per capita: $85 (1997).
Education: High school graduation rate: 79.3% (2000); College graduation rate: 10.3% (2000).
Housing: Homeownership rate: 80.2% (2000); Median home value: $54,200 (2000); Median rent: $280 per month (2000); Median age of housing: 44 years (2000).
Health: Birth rate: 114.9 per 10,000 population (1998); Age adjusted death rate: 91.5 per 10,000 population (1999); Age adjusted cancer mortality rate: 206.6 deaths per 100,000 population (1999). Number of physicians: 7.3 per 10,000 population (1999); Number of hospital beds: 45.5 per 10,000 population (1999).
Elections: 2000 Presidential election results: 39.2% Gore, 58.5% Bush, 1.4% Nader, 0.6% Buchanan
National and State Parks: Crawford County State Fish and Wildlife Area
Additional Information Contacts
Crawford County Government Offices 618-546-1212
Palestine Chamber of Commerce.............................. 618-586-2222
Robinson Chamber of Commerce 618-546-1557

Crawford County Communities

ANNAPOLIS (unincorporated postal area, zip code 62413). Covers a land area of 34.895 square miles and a water area of 0.042 square miles. Located at 39.13° N. Lat.; 87.83° W. Long. Elevation is 585 feet.
Population: 441 (2000); Race: 99.3% White, 0.0% Black, 0.0% Asian, 0.0% American Indian and Alaska Native, 2.0% Hispanic of any race, 0.7% two or more races (2000); Density: 12.6 persons per square mile (2000); Age: 26.5% under 18, 14.7% over 64 (2000); Marriage status: 25.9% never married, 65.2% now married, 6.3% widowed, 2.6% divorced (2000); Foreign born: 0.0% (2000); Ancestry (includes multiple ancestries): 12.5% German, 12.5% United States or American, 10.3% Irish, 9.6% English, 8.1% Other groups (2000).
Economy: Employment by occupation: 9.0% management, 8.5% professional, 22.8% services, 17.5% sales, 1.6% farming, 11.6% construction, 29.1% production (2000).
Income: Per capita income: $17,743 (2000); Median household income: $41,827 (2000); Poverty rate: 14.7% (2000).
Education: High school graduation rate: 86.2% (2000); College graduation rate: 7.4% (2000).
Housing: Homeownership rate: 88.4% (2000); Median home value: $34,800 (2000); Median rent: $325 per month (2000); Median age of housing: 41 years (2000).
Transportation: Commute to work: 89.4% car, 0.0% public transportation, 1.6% walk, 9.0% work from home (2000); Travel time to work: 12.2% less than 15 minutes, 63.4% 15 to 30 minutes, 15.1% 30 to 45 minutes, 1.7% 45 to 60 minutes, 7.6% 60 minutes or more (2000)

FLAT ROCK (village). Covers a land area of 0.856 square miles and a water area of 0 square miles. Located at 38.90° N. Lat.; 87.67° W. Long. Elevation is 500 feet.
Population: 415 (2000); Race: 97.8% White, 0.0% Black, 0.5% Asian, 0.0% American Indian and Alaska Native, 0.0% Hispanic of any race, 1.7% two or more races (2000); Density: 485.0 persons per square mile (2000); Age: 21.7% under 18, 22.7% over 64 (2000); Marriage status: 19.1% never married, 61.4% now married, 10.4% widowed, 9.0% divorced (2000); Foreign born: 0.5% (2000); Ancestry (includes multiple ancestries): 27.7% United States or American, 17.1% German, 11.8% English, 6.3% Irish, 3.6% Other groups (2000).
Economy: In agricultural area: corn, wheat; livestock, poultry. Employment by occupation: 3.7% management, 13.9% professional, 16.0% services, 19.8% sales, 0.0% farming, 11.8% construction, 34.8% production (2000).
Income: Per capita income: $16,398 (2000); Median household income: $36,184 (2000); Poverty rate: 12.6% (2000).
Taxes: Total city taxes per capita: $25 (1997); City property taxes per capita: $23 (1997).
Education: High school graduation rate: 81.3% (2000); College graduation rate: 5.2% (2000).
Housing: Homeownership rate: 91.6% (2000); Median home value: $45,200 (2000); Median rent: $188 per month (2000); Median age of housing: 59 years (2000).
Transportation: Commute to work: 94.1% car, 1.6% public transportation, 1.6% walk, 2.7% work from home (2000); Travel time to work: 33.5% less than 15 minutes, 44.5% 15 to 30 minutes, 17.6% 30 to 45 minutes, 1.6% 45 to 60 minutes, 2.7% 60 minutes or more (2000)

HUTSONVILLE (village). Covers a land area of 0.693 square miles and a water area of 0 square miles. Located at 39.10° N. Lat.; 87.65° W. Long. Elevation is 450 feet.
Population: 568 (2000); Race: 98.9% White, 0.0% Black, 0.0% Asian, 0.0% American Indian and Alaska Native, 1.1% Hispanic of any race, 1.1% two or more races (2000); Density: 819.7 persons per square mile (2000); Age: 23.2% under 18, 19.2% over 64 (2000); Marriage status: 22.5% never married, 54.8% now married, 10.4% widowed, 12.3% divorced (2000); Foreign born: 0.4% (2000); Ancestry (includes multiple ancestries): 17.0% German, 13.5% Irish, 9.3% English, 7.6% Other groups, 3.7% United States or American (2000).
Economy: In agricultural area: wheat, corn, livestock, hay. Employment by occupation: 5.4% management, 12.4% professional, 22.0% services, 17.0% sales, 0.8% farming, 8.9% construction, 33.6% production (2000).
Income: Per capita income: $15,774 (2000); Median household income: $33,500 (2000); Poverty rate: 15.6% (2000).
Taxes: Total city taxes per capita: $14 (1997); City property taxes per capita: $14 (1997).
Education: High school graduation rate: 81.5% (2000); College graduation rate: 9.1% (2000).

School District(s)

Hutsonville C U School District 1 (PK-12)
2000 Enrollment: 431 618-563-4912
Housing: Homeownership rate: 75.5% (2000); Median home value: $41,000 (2000); Median rent: $225 per month (2000); Median age of housing: 52 years (2000).
Transportation: Commute to work: 90.1% car, 0.8% public transportation, 7.5% walk, 0.8% work from home (2000); Travel time to work: 43.8% less than 15 minutes, 28.3% 15 to 30 minutes, 11.2% 30 to 45 minutes, 7.6% 45 to 60 minutes, 9.2% 60 minutes or more (2000)

OBLONG (village). Covers a land area of 0.950 square miles and a water area of 0.009 square miles. Located at 39.00° N. Lat.; 87.90° W. Long. Elevation is 524 feet.
History: Incorporated 1883.
Population: 1,580 (2000); Race: 98.7% White, 0.8% Black, 0.0% Asian, 0.1% American Indian and Alaska Native, 0.6% Hispanic of any race, 0.3% two or more races (2000); Density: 1,662.8 persons per square mile (2000); Age: 22.8% under 18, 23.2% over 64 (2000); Marriage status: 17.0% never married, 55.7% now married, 13.4% widowed, 13.8% divorced (2000); Foreign born: 0.4% (2000); Ancestry (includes multiple ancestries): 23.3% United States or American, 14.5% German, 10.1% English, 6.6% Irish, 6.2% Other groups (2000).
Economy: Oil, natural-gas wells. Agriculture: livestock, poultry; corn, wheat, soybeans. Employment by occupation: 5.7% management, 13.3% professional, 18.3% services, 17.9% sales, 1.1% farming, 8.5% construction, 35.2% production (2000).
Income: Per capita income: $14,926 (2000); Median household income: $27,409 (2000); Poverty rate: 9.9% (2000).
Taxes: Total city taxes per capita: $56 (1997); City property taxes per capita: $54 (1997).
Education: High school graduation rate: 77.5% (2000); College graduation rate: 11.8% (2000).

School District(s)

Oblong C U School District 4 (PK-12)
2000 Enrollment: 794 618-592-3933
Housing: Homeownership rate: 76.8% (2000); Median home value: $48,400 (2000); Median rent: $246 per month (2000); Median age of housing: 46 years (2000).
Newspapers: Oblong Gem (1 x week)
Transportation: Commute to work: 93.8% car, 0.2% public transportation, 2.5% walk, 2.8% work from home (2000); Travel time to work: 33.9% less than 15 minutes, 42.8% 15 to 30 minutes, 13.8% 30 to 45 minutes, 4.1% 45 to 60 minutes, 5.4% 60 minutes or more (2000)

PALESTINE (village). Covers a land area of 0.746 square miles and a water area of 0 square miles. Located at 39.00° N. Lat.; 87.61° W. Long. Elevation is 450 feet.
History: Palestine was the location in 1830 of one of the six land offices in Illinois, where settlers came to register their land claims.
Population: 1,366 (2000); Race: 98.5% White, 0.2% Black, 0.1% Asian, 0.0% American Indian and Alaska Native, 1.3% Hispanic of any race, 0.1% two or more races (2000); Density: 1,832.3 persons per square mile (2000); Age: 25.1% under 18, 20.2% over 64 (2000); Marriage status: 16.6% never married, 60.6% now married, 9.9% widowed, 13.0% divorced (2000); Foreign born: 0.7% (2000); Ancestry (includes multiple ancestries): 19.2% United States or American, 14.7% German, 12.9% Irish, 10.2% English, 9.6% Other groups (2000).
Economy: Employment by occupation: 5.0% management, 10.5% professional, 12.5% services, 22.8% sales, 0.0% farming, 12.5% construction, 36.8% production (2000).
Income: Per capita income: $15,185 (2000); Median household income: $28,911 (2000); Poverty rate: 15.8% (2000).
Taxes: Total city taxes per capita: $31 (1997); City property taxes per capita: $25 (1997).
Education: High school graduation rate: 79.1% (2000); College graduation rate: 9.7% (2000).

School District(s)

Palestine C U School District 3 (PK-12)
2000 Enrollment: 456 618-586-2713
Housing: Homeownership rate: 77.4% (2000); Median home value: $43,300 (2000); Median rent: $256 per month (2000); Median age of housing: 53 years (2000).

Transportation: Commute to work: 93.0% car, 0.3% public transportation, 2.7% walk, 3.3% work from home (2000); Travel time to work: 38.9% less than 15 minutes, 43.8% 15 to 30 minutes, 12.5% 30 to 45 minutes, 2.2% 45 to 60 minutes, 2.6% 60 minutes or more (2000)
Additional Information Contacts
Palestine Chamber of Commerce 618-586-2222

ROBINSON (city). Covers a land area of 3.625 square miles and a water area of 0.063 square miles. Located at 39.00° N. Lat.; 87.73° W. Long. Elevation is 540 feet.
History: Lincoln Trail College here. Incorporated 1875.
Population: 6,822 (2000); Race: 96.2% White, 0.7% Black, 0.4% Asian, 0.0% American Indian and Alaska Native, 2.2% Hispanic of any race, 1.7% two or more races (2000); Density: 1,881.9 persons per square mile (2000); Age: 24.0% under 18, 21.4% over 64 (2000); Marriage status: 21.6% never married, 54.8% now married, 11.6% widowed, 11.9% divorced (2000); Foreign born: 0.9% (2000); Ancestry (includes multiple ancestries): 21.8% United States or American, 18.7% German, 10.2% English, 9.4% Irish, 8.6% Other groups (2000).
Economy: Trade and manufacturing center in agricultural and oil-producing area. Manufacturing of pottery, plastic products, fabricated metal products, food. Oil refinery. Poultry, livestock; corn, wheat. Robinson Correctional Center here. Single-family building permits issued: 6 (2001) / 5 (2000); Multi-family building permits issued: 0 (2001) / 0 (2000); Employment by occupation: 8.4% management, 14.8% professional, 18.7% services, 19.9% sales, 0.5% farming, 10.0% construction, 27.7% production (2000).
Income: Per capita income: $16,637 (2000); Median household income: $30,153 (2000); Poverty rate: 11.1% (2000).
Taxes: Total city taxes per capita: $65 (1997); City property taxes per capita: $62 (1997).
Education: High school graduation rate: 82.6% (2000); College graduation rate: 12.8% (2000).

School District(s)

Robinson C U School District 2 (PK-12)
2000 Enrollment: 1,863 618-544-7511

Two-year College(s)

Illinois Eastern Community College-Lincoln Tr College (Public)
2001 Enrollment: 1,100 618-393-2982
2001 Tuition: In-state $5,618; Out-of-state $6,961

Housing: Homeownership rate: 72.0% (2000); Median home value: $54,400 (2000); Median rent: $300 per month (2000); Median age of housing: 46 years (2000).
Hospitals: Crawford Memorial Hospital (93 beds)
Newspapers: The Daily News (6 x week); Robinson Constitution (1 x week); Robinson Argus (1 x week)
Transportation: Commute to work: 93.1% car, 0.4% public transportation, 2.2% walk, 3.3% work from home (2000); Travel time to work: 73.8% less than 15 minutes, 10.2% 15 to 30 minutes, 8.9% 30 to 45 minutes, 3.5% 45 to 60 minutes, 3.8% 60 minutes or more (2000)
Additional Information Contacts
Robinson Chamber of Commerce 618-546-1557

STOY (village). Covers a land area of 0.889 square miles and a water area of 0 square miles. Located at 38.99° N. Lat.; 87.83° W. Long. Elevation is 467 feet.
Population: 119 (2000); Race: 100.0% White, 0.0% Black, 0.0% Asian, 0.0% American Indian and Alaska Native, 0.0% Hispanic of any race, 0.0% two or more races (2000); Density: 133.9 persons per square mile (2000); Age: 13.5% under 18, 13.5% over 64 (2000); Marriage status: 16.5% never married, 70.6% now married, 4.7% widowed, 8.2% divorced (2000); Foreign born: 0.0% (2000); Ancestry (includes multiple ancestries): 33.3% United States or American, 27.1% German, 13.5% Other groups, 6.3% Irish, 5.2% French (except Basque) (2000).
Economy: In oil, natural-gas and agricultural area. Employment by occupation: 4.1% management, 8.2% professional, 12.2% services, 16.3% sales, 0.0% farming, 8.2% construction, 51.0% production (2000).
Income: Per capita income: $14,229 (2000); Median household income: $40,625 (2000); Poverty rate: 1.0% (2000).
Taxes: Total city taxes per capita: $63 (1997); City property taxes per capita: $63 (1997).
Education: High school graduation rate: 83.1% (2000); College graduation rate: 0.0% (2000).
Housing: Homeownership rate: 82.9% (2000); Median home value: $55,700 (2000); Median rent: $213 per month (2000); Median age of housing: 43 years (2000).
Transportation: Commute to work: 100.0% car, 0.0% public transportation, 0.0% walk, 0.0% work from home (2000); Travel time to work: 75.5% less than 15 minutes, 24.5% 15 to 30 minutes, 0.0% 30 to 45 minutes, 0.0% 45 to 60 minutes, 0.0% 60 minutes or more (2000)

WEST YORK (unincorporated postal area, zip code 62478). Covers a land area of 23.200 square miles and a water area of 0.037 square miles. Located at 39.17° N. Lat.; 87.72° W. Long. Elevation is 508 feet.
Population: 414 (2000); Race: 100.0% White, 0.0% Black, 0.0% Asian, 0.0% American Indian and Alaska Native, 4.1% Hispanic of any race, 0.0% two or more races (2000); Density: 17.8 persons per square mile (2000); Age: 23.7% under 18, 12.5% over 64 (2000); Marriage status: 8.0% never married, 80.3% now married, 6.3% widowed, 5.3% divorced (2000); Foreign born: 1.0% (2000); Ancestry (includes multiple ancestries): 18.1% United States or American, 13.5% German, 9.9% English, 5.9% Other groups, 2.3% Norwegian (2000).
Economy: Employment by occupation: 19.6% management, 9.5% professional, 4.8% services, 21.4% sales, 5.4% farming, 8.3% construction, 31.0% production (2000).
Income: Per capita income: $18,541 (2000); Median household income: $32,125 (2000); Poverty rate: 7.9% (2000).
Education: High school graduation rate: 91.2% (2000); College graduation rate: 9.2% (2000).
Housing: Homeownership rate: 82.9% (2000); Median home value: $37,300 (2000); Median rent: $153 per month (2000); Median age of housing: 44 years (2000).
Transportation: Commute to work: 84.4% car, 0.0% public transportation, 3.1% walk, 12.5% work from home (2000); Travel time to work: 21.4% less than 15 minutes, 46.4% 15 to 30 minutes, 10.7% 30 to 45 minutes, 15.7% 45 to 60 minutes, 5.7% 60 minutes or more (2000)

Cumberland County

Located in southeast central Illinois; drained by the Embarrass River. Covers a land area of 346.00 square miles, a water area of 1.00 square miles, and is located in the Central Time Zone. The county government was organized in 1843. County seat is Toledo.
Population: 11,253 (2000); Race: 98.7% White, 0.2% Black, 0.2% Asian, 0.3% American Indian and Alaska Native, 0.6% Hispanic of any race, 0.5% two or more races (2000); Density: 32.5 persons per square mile (2000); Age: 26.6% under 18, 15.9% over 64 (2000).
Religion: Five largest groups: 8.5% Christian Churches and Churches of Christ, 8.2% Catholic Church, 7.4% Southern Baptist Convention, 6.9% The United Methodist Church, 2.0% Churches of God, General Conference (2000).
Economy: Unemployment rate: 6.3% (11/2002); Total civilian labor force: 5,444 (11/2002); Leading industries: 25.7% health care and social assistance; 23.7% manufacturing; 16.2% retail trade (2000); Companies that employ more than 1,000 persons: 0 (2000); Companies that employ more than 100 persons: 2 (2000); Farms: 547 totaling 169,773 acres (1997); Minority business ownership rate: 0.0% (1997); Women business ownership rate: 50.8% (1997); Retail sales per capita: $3,342 (1997). Single-family building permits issued: 9 (2001) / 9 (2000); Multi-family building permits issued: 2 (2001) / 2 (2000).
Income: Per capita income: $16,953 (2000); Median household income: $36,149 (2000); Poverty rate: 9.5% (2000); Bankruptcy rate: 6.55% (2001).
Taxes: Total county taxes per capita: $74 (1997); County property taxes per capita: $74 (1997).
Education: High school graduation rate: 80.2% (2000); College graduation rate: 10.1% (2000).
Housing: Homeownership rate: 82.0% (2000); Median home value: $68,700 (2000); Median rent: $275 per month (2000); Median age of housing: 34 years (2000).
Health: Birth rate: 111.1 per 10,000 population (1998); Age adjusted death rate: 87.0 per 10,000 population (1999); Age adjusted cancer mortality rate: 163.7 deaths per 100,000 population (1999). Number of physicians: 2.7 per 10,000 population (1999); Number of hospital beds: n/a (1999).
Elections: 2000 Presidential election results: 37.6% Gore, 59.6% Bush, 1.5% Nader, 1.1% Buchanan
Additional Information Contacts
Cumberland County Government Offices 217-849-2631

Cumberland County Communities

GREENUP (village). Covers a land area of 1.700 square miles and a water area of 0.002 square miles. Located at 39.24° N. Lat.; 88.16° W. Long. Elevation is 543 feet.
History: Greenup was named for William C. Greenup, the first clerk of the Illinois Territorial Legislature, who donated the townsite. The village was incorporated in 1836, and served for a time as the seat of Cumberland County.
Population: 1,532 (2000); Race: 99.7% White, 0.0% Black, 0.3% Asian, 0.0% American Indian and Alaska Native, 0.1% Hispanic of any race, 0.0% two or more races (2000); Density: 901.1 persons per square mile (2000); Age: 21.4% under 18, 27.9% over 64 (2000); Marriage status: 18.7% never married, 52.9% now married, 15.3% widowed, 13.1% divorced (2000); Foreign born: 1.4% (2000); Ancestry (includes multiple ancestries): 18.4% German, 18.1% United States or American, 9.4% Irish, 9.0% English, 5.0% Other groups (2000).
Economy: Employment by occupation: 8.5% management, 9.3% professional, 15.9% services, 24.9% sales, 0.3% farming, 10.5% construction, 30.6% production (2000).
Income: Per capita income: $18,179 (2000); Median household income: $29,375 (2000); Poverty rate: 13.2% (2000).
Taxes: Total city taxes per capita: $27 (1997); City property taxes per capita: $21 (1997).
Education: High school graduation rate: 74.2% (2000); College graduation rate: 9.5% (2000).
Housing: Homeownership rate: 75.7% (2000); Median home value: $59,800 (2000); Median rent: $272 per month (2000); Median age of housing: 44 years (2000).
Newspapers: Greenup Press (1 x week)
Transportation: Commute to work: 93.4% car, 0.0% public transportation, 1.2% walk, 3.6% work from home (2000); Travel time to work: 44.0% less than 15 minutes, 20.5% 15 to 30 minutes, 25.0% 30 to 45 minutes, 4.9% 45 to 60 minutes, 5.6% 60 minutes or more (2000)

JEWETT (village). Covers a land area of 1.006 square miles and a water area of 0 square miles. Located at 39.20° N. Lat.; 88.24° W. Long. Elevation is 504 feet.
History: The village of Jewett grew from the town of Pleasantville, which had been a stagecoach stop in the mid-1800's.
Population: 232 (2000); Race: 100.0% White, 0.0% Black, 0.0% Asian, 0.0% American Indian and Alaska Native, 0.0% Hispanic of any race, 0.0% two or more races (2000); Density: 230.7 persons per square mile (2000); Age: 28.2% under 18, 13.6% over 64 (2000); Marriage status: 29.2% never married, 51.7% now married, 11.2% widowed, 7.9% divorced (2000); Foreign born: 0.0% (2000); Ancestry (includes multiple ancestries): 21.4% United States or American, 14.5% German, 8.6% Irish, 3.2% English, 2.7% Other groups (2000).
Economy: Employment by occupation: 2.2% management, 4.4% professional, 10.0% services, 23.3% sales, 2.2% farming, 8.9% construction, 48.9% production (2000).
Income: Per capita income: $16,628 (2000); Median household income: $30,313 (2000); Poverty rate: 19.5% (2000).
Taxes: Total city taxes per capita: $49 (1997); City property taxes per capita: $49 (1997).
Education: High school graduation rate: 69.3% (2000); College graduation rate: 4.3% (2000).
Housing: Homeownership rate: 93.5% (2000); Median home value: $41,400 (2000); Median rent: $313 per month (2000); Median age of housing: 37 years (2000).
Transportation: Commute to work: 100.0% car, 0.0% public transportation, 0.0% walk, 0.0% work from home (2000); Travel time to work: 8.9% less than 15 minutes, 33.3% 15 to 30 minutes, 52.2% 30 to 45 minutes, 5.6% 45 to 60 minutes, 0.0% 60 minutes or more (2000)

NEOGA (city). Covers a land area of 1.350 square miles and a water area of 0 square miles. Located at 39.32° N. Lat.; 88.45° W. Long. Elevation is 665 feet.
History: The name of Neoga is of Indian origin, meaning "place of the Deity."
Population: 1,854 (2000); Race: 97.3% White, 0.8% Black, 0.2% Asian, 0.3% American Indian and Alaska Native, 0.6% Hispanic of any race, 0.8% two or more races (2000); Density: 1,372.9 persons per square mile (2000); Age: 29.3% under 18, 11.5% over 64 (2000); Marriage status: 21.7% never married, 61.7% now married, 5.2% widowed, 11.5% divorced (2000); Foreign born: 0.3% (2000); Ancestry (includes multiple ancestries): 25.7% German, 20.5% United States or American, 9.3% Irish, 9.0% English, 8.9% Other groups (2000).
Economy: Single-family building permits issued: 5 (2001) / 4 (2000); Multi-family building permits issued: 2 (2001) / 0 (2000); Employment by occupation: 5.0% management, 13.5% professional, 16.4% services, 25.9% sales, 0.3% farming, 10.6% construction, 28.3% production (2000).
Income: Per capita income: $15,173 (2000); Median household income: $34,500 (2000); Poverty rate: 11.8% (2000).
Taxes: Total city taxes per capita: $117 (1997); City property taxes per capita: $67 (1997).
Education: High school graduation rate: 81.5% (2000); College graduation rate: 12.1% (2000).

School District(s)

Neoga Community Unit School District 3 (PK-12)
2000 Enrollment: 862 217-895-2201

Housing: Homeownership rate: 75.4% (2000); Median home value: $69,300 (2000); Median rent: $281 per month (2000); Median age of housing: 31 years (2000).
Newspapers: Neoga News (1 x week)
Transportation: Commute to work: 94.4% car, 0.5% public transportation, 3.1% walk, 1.7% work from home (2000); Travel time to work: 24.2% less than 15 minutes, 46.4% 15 to 30 minutes, 19.6% 30 to 45 minutes, 4.2% 45 to 60 minutes, 5.6% 60 minutes or more (2000)

TOLEDO (village). Covers a land area of 0.798 square miles and a water area of 0 square miles. Located at 39.27° N. Lat.; 88.24° W. Long. Elevation is 600 feet.
Population: 1,166 (2000); Race: 97.5% White, 0.0% Black, 0.0% Asian, 0.0% American Indian and Alaska Native, 0.3% Hispanic of any race, 2.5% two or more races (2000); Density: 1,461.0 persons per square mile (2000); Age: 28.7% under 18, 18.5% over 64 (2000); Marriage status: 22.6% never married, 46.7% now married, 13.3% widowed, 17.3% divorced (2000); Foreign born: 0.4% (2000); Ancestry (includes multiple ancestries): 28.8% United States or American, 19.4% German, 10.3% Irish, 6.3% English, 5.9% Other groups (2000).
Economy: In agricultural area. Employment by occupation: 6.6% management, 12.8% professional, 19.6% services, 19.5% sales, 1.4% farming, 5.8% construction, 34.2% production (2000).
Income: Per capita income: $14,246 (2000); Median household income: $26,094 (2000); Poverty rate: 16.8% (2000).
Taxes: Total city taxes per capita: $44 (1997); City property taxes per capita: $42 (1997).
Education: High school graduation rate: 76.3% (2000); College graduation rate: 11.5% (2000).

School District(s)

Cumberland C U School District 77 (PK-12)
2000 Enrollment: 1,174 217-923-3132

Housing: Homeownership rate: 68.3% (2000); Median home value: $60,700 (2000); Median rent: $264 per month (2000); Median age of housing: 38 years (2000).
Newspapers: Toledo Democrat (1 x week)
Transportation: Commute to work: 95.1% car, 0.0% public transportation, 1.0% walk, 3.0% work from home (2000); Travel time to work: 32.1% less than 15 minutes, 22.8% 15 to 30 minutes, 31.1% 30 to 45 minutes, 5.7% 45 to 60 minutes, 8.3% 60 minutes or more (2000)

De Witt County

Located in central Illinois; drained by Salt Creek. Covers a land area of 397.60 square miles, a water area of 7.60 square miles, and is located in the Central Time Zone. The county government was organized in 1839. County seat is Clinton.
Population: 16,798 (2000); Race: 98.3% White, 0.2% Black, 0.3% Asian, 0.1% American Indian and Alaska Native, 1.2% Hispanic of any race, 0.9% two or more races (2000); Density: 42.3 persons per square mile (2000); Age: 24.6% under 18, 15.9% over 64 (2000).
Religion: Five largest groups: 19.7% Christian Churches and Churches of Christ, 10.2% Catholic Church, 9.1% The United Methodist Church, 2.0% Assemblies of God, 1.6% New Testament Association of Independent Baptist Churches and other Fundamental Ba
Economy: Unemployment rate: 7.8% (11/2002); Total civilian labor force: 6,840 (11/2002); Leading industries: 18.0% manufacturing; 14.8% retail trade; 8.3% health care and social assistance (2000); Companies that employ more than 1,000 persons: 0 (2000); Companies that employ more than 100 persons: 7 (2000); Farms: 463 totaling 204,896 acres (1997); Minority

business ownership rate: 0.0% (1997); Women business ownership rate: 26.1% (1997); Retail sales per capita: $8,475 (1997). Single-family building permits issued: 42 (2001) / 53 (2000); Multi-family building permits issued: 15 (2001) / 0 (2000).
Income: Per capita income: $20,488 (2000); Median household income: $41,256 (2000); Poverty rate: 8.2% (2000); Bankruptcy rate: 6.49% (2001).
Taxes: Total county taxes per capita: $290 (2000); County property taxes per capita: $290 (2000).
Education: High school graduation rate: 83.5% (2000); College graduation rate: 13.4% (2000).
Housing: Homeownership rate: 74.9% (2000); Median home value: $74,300 (2000); Median rent: $307 per month (2000); Median age of housing: 46 years (2000).
Health: Birth rate: 125.6 per 10,000 population (1998); Age adjusted death rate: 90.3 per 10,000 population (1999); Age adjusted cancer mortality rate: 150.5 deaths per 100,000 population (1999). Number of physicians: 7.1 per 10,000 population (1999); Number of hospital beds: 19.6 per 10,000 population (1999).
Elections: 2000 Presidential election results: 40.7% Gore, 56.3% Bush, 1.9% Nader, 0.8% Buchanan
National and State Parks: Clinton Lake State Recreational Area; Weldon Springs State Park
Additional Information Contacts
De Witt County Government Offices.................... 217-935-2119
Clinton Chamber of Commerce.......................... 217-935-3364
Dewitt County Board of Realtors...................... 217-935-9711

De Witt County Communities

CLINTON (city). Covers a land area of 2.653 square miles and a water area of <.001 square miles. Located at 40.15° N. Lat.; 88.95° W. Long. Elevation is 744 feet.
History: Clinton was the site of Abraham's Lincoln speech in which he gave the oft-quoted lines of "you can fool all the people part of the time and part of the people all of the time, but you cannot fool all the people all the time."
Population: 7,485 (2000); Race: 97.9% White, 0.4% Black, 0.3% Asian, 0.0% American Indian and Alaska Native, 2.2% Hispanic of any race, 1.4% two or more races (2000); Density: 2,821.2 persons per square mile (2000); Age: 25.6% under 18, 15.7% over 64 (2000); Marriage status: 21.1% never married, 58.1% now married, 8.8% widowed, 12.0% divorced (2000); Foreign born: 1.8% (2000); Ancestry (includes multiple ancestries): 17.7% German, 13.0% English, 12.1% United States or American, 11.2% Irish, 9.0% Other groups (2000).
Economy: Single-family building permits issued: 6 (2001) / 12 (2000); Multi-family building permits issued: 15 (2001) / 0 (2000); Employment by occupation: 9.9% management, 13.2% professional, 18.3% services, 27.3% sales, 0.4% farming, 9.9% construction, 21.0% production (2000).
Income: Per capita income: $18,729 (2000); Median household income: $36,279 (2000); Poverty rate: 10.8% (2000).
Taxes: Total city taxes per capita: $71 (1997); City property taxes per capita: $71 (1997).
Education: High school graduation rate: 81.5% (2000); College graduation rate: 11.5% (2000).

School District(s)

Clinton C U School District 15 (PK-12)
2000 Enrollment: 2,259............................ 217-935-8321
Housing: Homeownership rate: 67.1% (2000); Median home value: $69,500 (2000); Median rent: $314 per month (2000); Median age of housing: 50 years (2000).
Hospitals: Dr. John Warner Hospital (43 beds)
Newspapers: Clinton Daily Journal (5 x week)
Transportation: Commute to work: 94.3% car, 0.2% public transportation, 3.9% walk, 1.5% work from home (2000); Travel time to work: 54.1% less than 15 minutes, 14.9% 15 to 30 minutes, 20.9% 30 to 45 minutes, 6.1% 45 to 60 minutes, 4.0% 60 minutes or more (2000)
Additional Information Contacts
Clinton Chamber of Commerce.......................... 217-935-3364
Dewitt County Board of Realtors...................... 217-935-9711

DE WITT (village). Covers a land area of 0.254 square miles and a water area of 0 square miles. Located at 40.18° N. Lat.; 88.78° W. Long. Elevation is 735 feet.
Population: 188 (2000); Race: 97.8% White, 0.0% Black, 0.6% Asian, 1.7% American Indian and Alaska Native, 0.0% Hispanic of any race, 0.0% two or more races (2000); Density: 740.6 persons per square mile (2000); Age: 23.3% under 18, 16.1% over 64 (2000); Marriage status: 14.0% never married, 61.5% now married, 10.5% widowed, 14.0% divorced (2000); Foreign born: 0.0% (2000); Ancestry (includes multiple ancestries): 17.8% United States or American, 11.1% English, 11.1% Irish, 8.9% German, 7.8% Other groups (2000).
Economy: In agricultural area. Employment by occupation: 9.3% management, 6.7% professional, 26.7% services, 16.0% sales, 0.0% farming, 18.7% construction, 22.7% production (2000).
Income: Per capita income: $18,552 (2000); Median household income: $41,250 (2000); Poverty rate: 1.1% (2000).
Taxes: Total city taxes per capita: $63 (1997); City property taxes per capita: $39 (1997).
Education: High school graduation rate: 74.8% (2000); College graduation rate: 3.8% (2000).
Housing: Homeownership rate: 93.3% (2000); Median home value: $58,800 (2000); Median rent: $275 per month (2000); Median age of housing: 60+ years (2000).
Transportation: Commute to work: 98.7% car, 0.0% public transportation, 0.0% walk, 0.0% work from home (2000); Travel time to work: 30.7% less than 15 minutes, 49.3% 15 to 30 minutes, 9.3% 30 to 45 minutes, 8.0% 45 to 60 minutes, 2.7% 60 minutes or more (2000)

DEWITT (unincorporated postal area, zip code 61735). Aka De Witt. Covers a land area of 31.520 square miles and a water area of 0.043 square miles. Located at 40.20° N. Lat.; 88.80° W. Long.
Population: 408 (2000); Race: 97.7% White, 0.0% Black, 0.3% Asian, 0.8% American Indian and Alaska Native, 0.0% Hispanic of any race, 1.3% two or more races (2000); Density: 12.9 persons per square mile (2000); Age: 22.8% under 18, 14.8% over 64 (2000); Marriage status: 11.7% never married, 75.1% now married, 4.9% widowed, 8.4% divorced (2000); Foreign born: 0.0% (2000); Ancestry (includes multiple ancestries): 14.0% German, 10.9% Irish, 9.8% English, 7.8% United States or American, 7.0% Scottish (2000).
Economy: Employment by occupation: 28.4% management, 17.3% professional, 9.6% services, 8.2% sales, 0.0% farming, 13.0% construction, 23.6% production (2000).
Income: Per capita income: $23,504 (2000); Median household income: $45,972 (2000); Poverty rate: 0.5% (2000).
Education: High school graduation rate: 81.2% (2000); College graduation rate: 17.3% (2000).
Housing: Homeownership rate: 87.7% (2000); Median home value: $67,100 (2000); Median rent: $275 per month (2000); Median age of housing: 47 years (2000).
Transportation: Commute to work: 90.9% car, 0.0% public transportation, 1.0% walk, 7.7% work from home (2000); Travel time to work: 26.6% less than 15 minutes, 30.2% 15 to 30 minutes, 29.2% 30 to 45 minutes, 10.4% 45 to 60 minutes, 3.6% 60 minutes or more (2000)

FARMER CITY (city). Covers a land area of 2.302 square miles and a water area of 0.049 square miles. Located at 40.24° N. Lat.; 88.64° W. Long. Elevation is 724 feet.
History: Incorporated 1869.
Population: 2,055 (2000); Race: 99.5% White, 0.0% Black, 0.1% Asian, 0.0% American Indian and Alaska Native, 0.5% Hispanic of any race, 0.3% two or more races (2000); Density: 892.8 persons per square mile (2000); Age: 25.7% under 18, 18.2% over 64 (2000); Marriage status: 21.0% never married, 53.6% now married, 12.2% widowed, 13.1% divorced (2000); Foreign born: 0.3% (2000); Ancestry (includes multiple ancestries): 24.2% German, 12.2% United States or American, 12.1% English, 10.6% Irish, 3.9% Other groups (2000).
Economy: In agricultural area; corn, wheat, soybeans; livestock. Seed-processing plant. Employment by occupation: 9.9% management, 14.0% professional, 15.0% services, 29.2% sales, 0.5% farming, 13.0% construction, 18.5% production (2000).
Income: Per capita income: $19,946 (2000); Median household income: $40,223 (2000); Poverty rate: 8.3% (2000).
Taxes: Total city taxes per capita: $184 (1997); City property taxes per capita: $176 (1997).
Education: High school graduation rate: 82.8% (2000); College graduation rate: 14.2% (2000).

School District(s)

Blue Ridge Community Unit School District 18 (PK-12)
2000 Enrollment: 1,004............................ 309-928-9141
Housing: Homeownership rate: 75.8% (2000); Median home value: $71,600 (2000); Median rent: $293 per month (2000); Median age of housing: 54 years (2000).
Newspapers: The Farmer City Journal (1 x week)

Transportation: Commute to work: 90.9% car, 0.0% public transportation, 5.0% walk, 3.1% work from home (2000); Travel time to work: 41.3% less than 15 minutes, 23.5% 15 to 30 minutes, 28.5% 30 to 45 minutes, 3.9% 45 to 60 minutes, 2.7% 60 minutes or more (2000)

KENNEY (village). Covers a land area of 0.301 square miles and a water area of 0 square miles. Located at 40.09° N. Lat.; 89.08° W. Long. Elevation is 650 feet.
Population: 374 (2000); Race: 99.0% White, 0.5% Black, 0.5% Asian, 0.0% American Indian and Alaska Native, 0.0% Hispanic of any race, 0.0% two or more races (2000); Density: 1,242.7 persons per square mile (2000); Age: 18.8% under 18, 18.5% over 64 (2000); Marriage status: 16.6% never married, 62.5% now married, 11.2% widowed, 9.7% divorced (2000); Foreign born: 0.8% (2000); Ancestry (includes multiple ancestries): 21.4% German, 18.8% English, 15.7% United States or American, 9.1% Irish, 6.8% Other groups (2000).
Economy: In agricultural area. Employment by occupation: 13.0% management, 14.1% professional, 14.1% services, 20.5% sales, 0.5% farming, 14.1% construction, 23.8% production (2000).
Income: Per capita income: $18,553 (2000); Median household income: $34,886 (2000); Poverty rate: 6.5% (2000).
Taxes: Total city taxes per capita: $40 (1997); City property taxes per capita: $35 (1997).
Education: High school graduation rate: 83.7% (2000); College graduation rate: 6.6% (2000).
Housing: Homeownership rate: 84.0% (2000); Median home value: $50,700 (2000); Median rent: $288 per month (2000); Median age of housing: 60+ years (2000).
Transportation: Commute to work: 98.4% car, 0.0% public transportation, 1.6% walk, 0.0% work from home (2000); Travel time to work: 30.1% less than 15 minutes, 37.2% 15 to 30 minutes, 19.1% 30 to 45 minutes, 10.4% 45 to 60 minutes, 3.3% 60 minutes or more (2000)

WAPELLA (village). Covers a land area of 0.545 square miles and a water area of 0 square miles. Located at 40.22° N. Lat.; 88.96° W. Long. Elevation is 748 feet.
Population: 651 (2000); Race: 97.7% White, 0.0% Black, 0.5% Asian, 0.0% American Indian and Alaska Native, 0.3% Hispanic of any race, 1.8% two or more races (2000); Density: 1,193.6 persons per square mile (2000); Age: 28.1% under 18, 11.1% over 64 (2000); Marriage status: 19.3% never married, 64.8% now married, 7.9% widowed, 7.9% divorced (2000); Foreign born: 0.5% (2000); Ancestry (includes multiple ancestries): 16.7% German, 14.4% English, 8.3% Irish, 6.2% United States or American, 6.2% Other groups (2000).
Economy: In agricultural area: corn, soybeans. Single-family building permits issued: 0 (2001) / 0 (2000); Multi-family building permits issued: 0 (2001) / 0 (2000); Employment by occupation: 12.1% management, 10.2% professional, 16.5% services, 24.2% sales, 3.1% farming, 13.0% construction, 20.8% production (2000).
Income: Per capita income: $17,395 (2000); Median household income: $38,000 (2000); Poverty rate: 8.1% (2000).
Taxes: Total city taxes per capita: $61 (1997); City property taxes per capita: $56 (1997).
Education: High school graduation rate: 77.9% (2000); College graduation rate: 4.5% (2000).
Housing: Homeownership rate: 85.6% (2000); Median home value: $65,900 (2000); Median rent: $328 per month (2000); Median age of housing: 37 years (2000).
Transportation: Commute to work: 97.4% car, 0.0% public transportation, 0.6% walk, 1.0% work from home (2000); Travel time to work: 33.9% less than 15 minutes, 31.9% 15 to 30 minutes, 25.2% 30 to 45 minutes, 2.3% 45 to 60 minutes, 6.8% 60 minutes or more (2000)

WAYNESVILLE (village). Covers a land area of 0.322 square miles and a water area of 0 square miles. Located at 40.24° N. Lat.; 89.12° W. Long. Elevation is 735 feet.
Population: 452 (2000); Race: 99.3% White, 0.0% Black, 0.0% Asian, 0.0% American Indian and Alaska Native, 0.0% Hispanic of any race, 0.7% two or more races (2000); Density: 1,404.0 persons per square mile (2000); Age: 26.7% under 18, 13.7% over 64 (2000); Marriage status: 15.3% never married, 62.9% now married, 8.3% widowed, 13.5% divorced (2000); Foreign born: 0.0% (2000); Ancestry (includes multiple ancestries): 28.1% German, 15.6% English, 15.1% Irish, 11.6% United States or American, 4.7% French (except Basque) (2000).
Economy: In agricultural area. Employment by occupation: 9.7% management, 7.2% professional, 17.9% services, 28.2% sales, 2.1% farming, 12.3% construction, 22.6% production (2000).
Income: Per capita income: $16,640 (2000); Median household income: $40,588 (2000); Poverty rate: 7.8% (2000).
Taxes: Total city taxes per capita: $52 (1997); City property taxes per capita: $43 (1997).
Education: High school graduation rate: 76.2% (2000); College graduation rate: 3.6% (2000).
Housing: Homeownership rate: 89.8% (2000); Median home value: $46,100 (2000); Median rent: $245 per month (2000); Median age of housing: 58 years (2000).
Transportation: Commute to work: 94.2% car, 0.0% public transportation, 1.6% walk, 3.7% work from home (2000); Travel time to work: 7.1% less than 15 minutes, 30.4% 15 to 30 minutes, 47.3% 30 to 45 minutes, 9.8% 45 to 60 minutes, 5.4% 60 minutes or more (2000)

WELDON (village). Covers a land area of 0.269 square miles and a water area of 0 square miles. Located at 40.12° N. Lat.; 88.75° W. Long. Elevation is 715 feet.
Population: 440 (2000); Race: 95.9% White, 0.0% Black, 0.0% Asian, 1.1% American Indian and Alaska Native, 0.0% Hispanic of any race, 0.7% two or more races (2000); Density: 1,635.5 persons per square mile (2000); Age: 24.8% under 18, 18.5% over 64 (2000); Marriage status: 19.9% never married, 59.4% now married, 11.8% widowed, 8.9% divorced (2000); Foreign born: 0.5% (2000); Ancestry (includes multiple ancestries): 16.0% English, 13.1% German, 8.8% Irish, 7.4% Other groups, 6.5% United States or American (2000).
Economy: Corn, soybeans. Employment by occupation: 4.7% management, 5.1% professional, 14.0% services, 27.9% sales, 1.9% farming, 19.5% construction, 27.0% production (2000).
Income: Per capita income: $20,851 (2000); Median household income: $39,000 (2000); Poverty rate: 5.7% (2000).
Taxes: Total city taxes per capita: $40 (1997); City property taxes per capita: $40 (1997).
Education: High school graduation rate: 77.9% (2000); College graduation rate: 10.2% (2000).
Housing: Homeownership rate: 84.6% (2000); Median home value: $60,400 (2000); Median rent: $310 per month (2000); Median age of housing: 53 years (2000).
Transportation: Commute to work: 89.0% car, 0.5% public transportation, 5.2% walk, 4.8% work from home (2000); Travel time to work: 24.5% less than 15 minutes, 25.0% 15 to 30 minutes, 37.0% 30 to 45 minutes, 10.5% 45 to 60 minutes, 3.0% 60 minutes or more (2000)

De Kalb County

Located in northern Illinois; drained by branches of the Kishwaukee River. Covers a land area of 634.20 square miles, a water area of 0.80 square miles, and is located in the Central Time Zone. The county government was organized in 1837. County seat is Sycamore.

De Kalb County is part of the Chicago, IL PMSA. The entire metro area includes: Cook County; DeKalb County; DuPage County; Grundy County; Kane County; Kendall County; Lake County; McHenry County; Will County

Weather Station: De Kalb Elevation: 872 feet

	Jan	Feb	Mar	Apr	May	Jun	Jul	Aug	Sep	Oct	Nov	Dec
High	27	33	45	59	72	81	84	82	76	63	46	34
Low	11	17	27	38	48	59	63	61	53	41	30	19
Precip	1.5	1.4	2.5	3.5	4.3	4.5	4.4	4.5	3.7	2.7	2.8	2.2
Snow	9.7	7.1	5.1	1.3	tr	0.0	0.0	0.0	0.0	0.1	2.1	8.6

High and Low temperatures in degrees Fahrenheit; Precipitation and Snow in inches

Population: 88,969 (2000); Race: 88.5% White, 4.5% Black, 2.3% Asian, 0.2% American Indian and Alaska Native, 6.4% Hispanic of any race, 2.0% two or more races (2000); Density: 140.3 persons per square mile (2000); Age: 23.2% under 18, 9.8% over 64 (2000).
Religion: Five largest groups: 19.1% Catholic Church, 6.4% Evangelical Lutheran Church in America, 5.6% The United Methodist Church, 3.4% United Church of Christ, 3.3% Lutheran Church—Missouri Synod (2000).
Economy: Unemployment rate: 5.3% (11/2002); Total civilian labor force: 47,117 (11/2002); Leading industries: 26.8% manufacturing; 15.7% retail trade; 14.9% health care and social assistance (2000); Companies that employ more than 1,000 persons: 0 (2000); Companies that employ more than 100 persons: 47 (2000); Farms: 828 totaling 368,076 acres (1997); Minority

business ownership rate: 4.0% (1997); Women business ownership rate: 38.3% (1997); Retail sales per capita: $7,565 (1997). Single-family building permits issued: 418 (2001) / 319 (2000); Multi-family building permits issued: 282 (2001) / 257 (2000).
Income: Per capita income: $19,462 (2000); Median household income: $45,828 (2000); Poverty rate: 11.4% (2000); Bankruptcy rate: 4.26% (2001).
Taxes: Total county taxes per capita: $127 (2000); County property taxes per capita: $113 (2000).
Education: High school graduation rate: 87.5% (2000); College graduation rate: 26.8% (2000).
Housing: Homeownership rate: 59.6% (2000); Median home value: $135,900 (2000); Median rent: $504 per month (2000); Median age of housing: 32 years (2000).
Health: Birth rate: 121.8 per 10,000 population (1998); Age adjusted death rate: 83.1 per 10,000 population (1999); Age adjusted cancer mortality rate: 212.8 deaths per 100,000 population (1999). Number of physicians: 9.3 per 10,000 population (1999); Number of hospital beds: 19.9 per 10,000 population (1999).
Elections: 2000 Presidential election results: 44.5% Gore, 51.6% Bush, 3.1% Nader, 0.4% Buchanan
National and State Parks: Shabbona Lake State Recreational Area
Additional Information Contacts
De Kalb County Government Offices 815-895-7189
De Kalb Area Association of Realtors 815-899-3301
De Kalb Chamber of Commerce 815-756-6306
De Kalb County Economic Development 815-895-2711
Genoa Chamber of Commerce 815-784-2212
Sandwich Commerce Association 815-786-9075
Sycamore Chamber of Commerce 815-895-3456

De Kalb County Communities

CLARE (unincorporated postal area, zip code 60111). Covers a land area of 23.578 square miles and a water area of 0 square miles. Located at 41.99° N. Lat.; 88.84° W. Long. Elevation is 870 feet.
Population: 305 (2000); Race: 98.9% White, 0.0% Black, 0.0% Asian, 0.0% American Indian and Alaska Native, 0.0% Hispanic of any race, 1.1% two or more races (2000); Density: 12.9 persons per square mile (2000); Age: 30.1% under 18, 13.0% over 64 (2000); Marriage status: 22.5% never married, 67.2% now married, 6.4% widowed, 3.9% divorced (2000); Foreign born: 1.5% (2000); Ancestry (includes multiple ancestries): 31.6% German, 20.1% United States or American, 17.1% English, 14.5% Swedish, 7.4% Irish (2000).
Economy: Employment by occupation: 16.9% management, 19.5% professional, 2.6% services, 26.0% sales, 0.0% farming, 18.8% construction, 16.2% production (2000).
Income: Per capita income: $27,141 (2000); Median household income: $58,750 (2000); Poverty rate: 1.9% (2000).
Education: High school graduation rate: 87.8% (2000); College graduation rate: 27.1% (2000).
Housing: Homeownership rate: 70.4% (2000); Median home value: $146,300 (2000); Median rent: $438 per month (2000); Median age of housing: 60+ years (2000).
Transportation: Commute to work: 90.3% car, 1.9% public transportation, 3.2% walk, 4.5% work from home (2000); Travel time to work: 36.7% less than 15 minutes, 53.1% 15 to 30 minutes, 0.0% 30 to 45 minutes, 7.5% 45 to 60 minutes, 2.7% 60 minutes or more (2000)

CORTLAND (town). Covers a land area of 1.756 square miles and a water area of 0 square miles. Located at 41.92° N. Lat.; 88.69° W. Long. Elevation is 900 feet.
Population: 2,066 (2000); Race: 94.5% White, 1.0% Black, 2.0% Asian, 0.0% American Indian and Alaska Native, 4.0% Hispanic of any race, 2.0% two or more races (2000); Density: 1,176.3 persons per square mile (2000); Age: 36.0% under 18, 4.9% over 64 (2000); Marriage status: 21.2% never married, 67.1% now married, 3.7% widowed, 8.0% divorced (2000); Foreign born: 3.8% (2000); Ancestry (includes multiple ancestries): 31.0% German, 15.3% Irish, 9.2% Other groups, 8.4% English, 7.0% United States or American (2000).
Economy: Single-family building permits issued: 48 (2001) / 14 (2000); Multi-family building permits issued: 0 (2001) / 0 (2000); Employment by occupation: 11.0% management, 17.6% professional, 14.4% services, 25.9% sales, 0.2% farming, 12.0% construction, 19.0% production (2000).
Income: Per capita income: $18,775 (2000); Median household income: $52,750 (2000); Poverty rate: 3.7% (2000).
Taxes: Total city taxes per capita: $131 (1997); City property taxes per capita: $67 (1997).
Education: High school graduation rate: 87.2% (2000); College graduation rate: 22.0% (2000).
Housing: Homeownership rate: 72.3% (2000); Median home value: $134,400 (2000); Median rent: $654 per month (2000); Median age of housing: 9 years (2000).
Transportation: Commute to work: 95.9% car, 0.0% public transportation, 0.7% walk, 2.9% work from home (2000); Travel time to work: 39.6% less than 15 minutes, 27.1% 15 to 30 minutes, 15.7% 30 to 45 minutes, 7.9% 45 to 60 minutes, 9.7% 60 minutes or more (2000)

DE KALB (city). Covers a land area of 12.611 square miles and a water area of 0.008 square miles. Located at 41.93° N. Lat.; 88.75° W. Long. Elevation is 880 feet.
History: De Kalb was named for Baron Johann De Kalb, a major general in the Revolutionary Army. In 1874 Joseph E. Glidden patented an improved barbed wire, and Jacob Haish patented a barbed wire manufacturing process. The two patents overlapped and caused a long legal battle, but until 1938 De Kalb was known as the barbed wire capital of the world.
Population: 39,018 (2000); Race: 79.5% White, 8.7% Black, 4.6% Asian, 0.1% American Indian and Alaska Native, 8.8% Hispanic of any race, 3.0% two or more races (2000); Density: 3,093.9 persons per square mile (2000); Age: 17.3% under 18, 8.1% over 64 (2000); Marriage status: 52.5% never married, 38.2% now married, 3.6% widowed, 5.7% divorced (2000); Foreign born: 9.1% (2000); Ancestry (includes multiple ancestries): 24.5% German, 21.9% Other groups, 14.5% Irish, 7.5% English, 6.1% Polish (2000).
Vital Statistics: Birth rate: 113.8 per 10,000 population (1998)
Economy: Unemployment rate: 4.4% (11/2002); Total civilian labor force: 21,372 (11/2002); Single-family building permits issued: 80 (2001) / 43 (2000); Multi-family building permits issued: 173 (2001) / 227 (2000); Employment by occupation: 10.3% management, 26.7% professional, 18.1% services, 27.5% sales, 0.2% farming, 5.5% construction, 11.7% production (2000).
Income: Per capita income: $16,261 (2000); Median household income: $35,153 (2000); Poverty rate: 21.3% (2000).
Taxes: Total city taxes per capita: $315 (2000); City property taxes per capita: $141 (2000).
Education: High school graduation rate: 87.6% (2000); College graduation rate: 38.0% (2000).

School District(s)
Dekalb Community Unit School District 428 (PK-12)
2000 Enrollment: 5,080 815-754-2350

Four-year College(s)
Northern Illinois University (Public)
2001 Enrollment: 23,783 815-753-1157
2001 Tuition: In-state $3,293; Out-of-state $6,585
Housing: Homeownership rate: 42.0% (2000); Median home value: $130,200 (2000); Median rent: $499 per month (2000); Median age of housing: 29 years (2000).
Hospitals: Kishwaukee Community Hospital (172 beds)
Newspapers: Daily Chronicle (7 x week); The Midweek (1 x week); Northern Star (5 x week)
Transportation: Commute to work: 80.0% car, 2.5% public transportation, 12.8% walk, 2.4% work from home (2000); Travel time to work: 55.9% less than 15 minutes, 18.7% 15 to 30 minutes, 10.5% 30 to 45 minutes, 7.2% 45 to 60 minutes, 7.7% 60 minutes or more (2000)
Additional Information Contacts
De Kalb Chamber of Commerce 815-756-6306

ESMOND (unincorporated postal area, zip code 60129). Covers a land area of 22.108 square miles and a water area of 0 square miles. Located at 42.03° N. Lat.; 88.97° W. Long. Elevation is 825 feet.
Population: 291 (2000); Race: 95.3% White, 0.0% Black, 0.0% Asian, 0.0% American Indian and Alaska Native, 5.7% Hispanic of any race, 4.7% two or more races (2000); Density: 13.2 persons per square mile (2000); Age: 28.3% under 18, 7.7% over 64 (2000); Marriage status: 21.4% never married, 69.4% now married, 3.1% widowed, 6.1% divorced (2000); Foreign born: 3.4% (2000); Ancestry (includes multiple ancestries): 36.7% German, 10.4% Irish, 9.1% English, 7.4% United States or American, 5.4% Dutch (2000).
Economy: Employment by occupation: 14.0% management, 14.5% professional, 12.2% services, 17.4% sales, 1.2% farming, 17.4% construction, 23.3% production (2000).
Income: Per capita income: $17,101 (2000); Median household income: $43,438 (2000); Poverty rate: 4.8% (2000).

Education: High school graduation rate: 85.6% (2000); College graduation rate: 20.3% (2000).
Housing: Homeownership rate: 62.5% (2000); Median home value: $126,100 (2000); Median rent: $392 per month (2000); Median age of housing: 60+ years (2000).
Transportation: Commute to work: 89.5% car, 1.2% public transportation, 0.0% walk, 8.1% work from home (2000); Travel time to work: 9.5% less than 15 minutes, 54.4% 15 to 30 minutes, 20.3% 30 to 45 minutes, 8.9% 45 to 60 minutes, 7.0% 60 minutes or more (2000)

GENOA (city). Covers a land area of 1.913 square miles and a water area of 0 square miles. Located at 42.09° N. Lat.; 88.69° W. Long. Elevation is 840 feet.
Population: 4,169 (2000); Race: 95.2% White, 0.0% Black, 0.0% Asian, 0.0% American Indian and Alaska Native, 11.3% Hispanic of any race, 1.5% two or more races (2000); Density: 2,178.8 persons per square mile (2000); Age: 31.3% under 18, 8.0% over 64 (2000); Marriage status: 19.8% never married, 63.8% now married, 5.6% widowed, 10.8% divorced (2000); Foreign born: 8.1% (2000); Ancestry (includes multiple ancestries): 28.4% German, 15.5% Irish, 15.0% Other groups, 9.7% English, 7.0% Polish (2000).
Economy: Single-family building permits issued: 47 (2001) / 49 (2000); Multi-family building permits issued: 0 (2001) / 8 (2000); Employment by occupation: 9.0% management, 16.3% professional, 12.4% services, 21.1% sales, 0.3% farming, 16.2% construction, 24.7% production (2000).
Income: Per capita income: $19,239 (2000); Median household income: $48,125 (2000); Poverty rate: 3.3% (2000).
Taxes: Total city taxes per capita: $469 (1997); City property taxes per capita: $30 (1997).
Education: High school graduation rate: 79.5% (2000); College graduation rate: 10.2% (2000).

School District(s)

Genoa Kingston C U S District 424 (PK-12)
2000 Enrollment: 1,574 815-784-6222

Housing: Homeownership rate: 70.3% (2000); Median home value: $120,700 (2000); Median rent: $485 per month (2000); Median age of housing: 37 years (2000).
Transportation: Commute to work: 92.2% car, 0.0% public transportation, 3.6% walk, 2.5% work from home (2000); Travel time to work: 28.5% less than 15 minutes, 30.7% 15 to 30 minutes, 22.3% 30 to 45 minutes, 8.6% 45 to 60 minutes, 9.9% 60 minutes or more (2000)

Additional Information Contacts

Genoa Chamber of Commerce 815-784-2212

HINCKLEY (village). Covers a land area of 0.949 square miles and a water area of 0.006 square miles. Located at 41.77° N. Lat.; 88.64° W. Long. Elevation is 750 feet.
Population: 1,994 (2000); Race: 97.9% White, 0.1% Black, 0.1% Asian, 0.4% American Indian and Alaska Native, 4.1% Hispanic of any race, 1.2% two or more races (2000); Density: 2,100.7 persons per square mile (2000); Age: 28.5% under 18, 9.9% over 64 (2000); Marriage status: 18.9% never married, 68.5% now married, 4.1% widowed, 8.5% divorced (2000); Foreign born: 1.1% (2000); Ancestry (includes multiple ancestries): 35.2% German, 15.7% Irish, 10.0% English, 6.9% Norwegian, 6.9% Other groups (2000).
Economy: Single-family building permits issued: 15 (2001) / 0 (2000); Multi-family building permits issued: 2 (2001) / 0 (2000); Employment by occupation: 12.4% management, 17.2% professional, 13.2% services, 27.2% sales, 0.4% farming, 14.3% construction, 15.4% production (2000).
Income: Per capita income: $23,491 (2000); Median household income: $58,043 (2000); Poverty rate: 4.4% (2000).
Taxes: Total city taxes per capita: $114 (1997); City property taxes per capita: $75 (1997).
Education: High school graduation rate: 90.7% (2000); College graduation rate: 20.9% (2000).

School District(s)

Hinckley Big Rock C U S D 429 (PK-12)
2000 Enrollment: 953 815-286-7575

Housing: Homeownership rate: 73.6% (2000); Median home value: $147,100 (2000); Median rent: $577 per month (2000); Median age of housing: 29 years (2000).
Transportation: Commute to work: 92.4% car, 0.5% public transportation, 1.6% walk, 5.0% work from home (2000); Travel time to work: 21.8% less than 15 minutes, 25.5% 15 to 30 minutes, 31.8% 30 to 45 minutes, 11.5% 45 to 60 minutes, 9.3% 60 minutes or more (2000)

KINGSTON (village). Covers a land area of 1.003 square miles and a water area of 0 square miles. Located at 42.10° N. Lat.; 88.76° W. Long. Elevation is 791 feet.
Population: 980 (2000); Race: 96.3% White, 0.2% Black, 0.0% Asian, 0.7% American Indian and Alaska Native, 5.9% Hispanic of any race, 0.9% two or more races (2000); Density: 976.9 persons per square mile (2000); Age: 32.8% under 18, 3.3% over 64 (2000); Marriage status: 26.9% never married, 59.9% now married, 2.7% widowed, 10.4% divorced (2000); Foreign born: 1.6% (2000); Ancestry (includes multiple ancestries): 29.5% German, 15.8% Irish, 13.8% Other groups, 8.0% Italian, 7.4% Polish (2000).
Economy: Employment by occupation: 9.4% management, 9.9% professional, 14.5% services, 18.1% sales, 0.0% farming, 20.3% construction, 27.8% production (2000).
Income: Per capita income: $21,432 (2000); Median household income: $55,179 (2000); Poverty rate: 4.8% (2000).
Taxes: Total city taxes per capita: $127 (1997); City property taxes per capita: $98 (1997).
Education: High school graduation rate: 87.2% (2000); College graduation rate: 17.4% (2000).
Housing: Homeownership rate: 80.5% (2000); Median home value: $127,300 (2000); Median rent: $512 per month (2000); Median age of housing: 29 years (2000).
Transportation: Commute to work: 93.2% car, 0.9% public transportation, 1.7% walk, 3.5% work from home (2000); Travel time to work: 28.0% less than 15 minutes, 30.1% 15 to 30 minutes, 23.8% 30 to 45 minutes, 6.1% 45 to 60 minutes, 12.0% 60 minutes or more (2000)

KIRKLAND (village). Covers a land area of 1.125 square miles and a water area of 0 square miles. Located at 42.09° N. Lat.; 88.85° W. Long. Elevation is 764 feet.
Population: 1,166 (2000); Race: 97.4% White, 0.7% Black, 0.0% Asian, 0.0% American Indian and Alaska Native, 2.4% Hispanic of any race, 1.0% two or more races (2000); Density: 1,036.0 persons per square mile (2000); Age: 29.3% under 18, 11.0% over 64 (2000); Marriage status: 26.2% never married, 57.9% now married, 6.9% widowed, 9.0% divorced (2000); Foreign born: 1.9% (2000); Ancestry (includes multiple ancestries): 35.0% German, 14.2% Irish, 12.9% English, 9.3% Swedish, 7.8% Other groups (2000).
Economy: Single-family building permits issued: 9 (2001) / 4 (2000); Multi-family building permits issued: 0 (2001) / 0 (2000); Employment by occupation: 9.8% management, 14.7% professional, 11.9% services, 21.0% sales, 0.0% farming, 15.5% construction, 27.2% production (2000).
Income: Per capita income: $18,841 (2000); Median household income: $45,938 (2000); Poverty rate: 6.0% (2000).
Taxes: Total city taxes per capita: $79 (1997); City property taxes per capita: $74 (1997).
Education: High school graduation rate: 81.7% (2000); College graduation rate: 15.9% (2000).

School District(s)

Hiawatha C U School District 426 (KG-12)
2000 Enrollment: 497 815-522-6676

Housing: Homeownership rate: 76.7% (2000); Median home value: $111,100 (2000); Median rent: $465 per month (2000); Median age of housing: 46 years (2000).
Transportation: Commute to work: 90.0% car, 0.9% public transportation, 7.1% walk, 2.0% work from home (2000); Travel time to work: 23.2% less than 15 minutes, 36.9% 15 to 30 minutes, 17.6% 30 to 45 minutes, 11.3% 45 to 60 minutes, 10.9% 60 minutes or more (2000)

MALTA (village). Covers a land area of 0.375 square miles and a water area of 0 square miles. Located at 41.92° N. Lat.; 88.86° W. Long. Elevation is 913 feet.
Population: 969 (2000); Race: 97.7% White, 0.2% Black, 0.0% Asian, 0.0% American Indian and Alaska Native, 4.6% Hispanic of any race, 0.6% two or more races (2000); Density: 2,584.0 persons per square mile (2000); Age: 26.2% under 18, 14.3% over 64 (2000); Marriage status: 19.9% never married, 64.0% now married, 6.6% widowed, 9.5% divorced (2000); Foreign born: 0.9% (2000); Ancestry (includes multiple ancestries): 26.6% German, 13.4% English, 12.6% Swedish, 10.9% Irish, 9.1% United States or American (2000).
Economy: Employment by occupation: 11.6% management, 13.3% professional, 17.0% services, 25.8% sales, 0.6% farming, 9.6% construction, 22.2% production (2000).
Income: Per capita income: $20,839 (2000); Median household income: $45,417 (2000); Poverty rate: 6.8% (2000).

Taxes: Total city taxes per capita: $109 (1997); City property taxes per capita: $51 (1997).
Education: High school graduation rate: 87.0% (2000); College graduation rate: 17.2% (2000).

School District(s)

Malta Community Unit School District 433 (N -N)
2000 Enrollment: n/a 815-825-2081

Two-year College(s)

Kishwaukee College (Public)
2001 Enrollment: 3,883 815-825-2086
2001 Tuition: In-state $6,030; Out-of-state $7,200
Housing: Homeownership rate: 73.6% (2000); Median home value: $108,300 (2000); Median rent: $482 per month (2000); Median age of housing: 45 years (2000).
Transportation: Commute to work: 93.3% car, 0.2% public transportation, 1.6% walk, 4.5% work from home (2000); Travel time to work: 25.8% less than 15 minutes, 46.7% 15 to 30 minutes, 8.6% 30 to 45 minutes, 10.2% 45 to 60 minutes, 8.6% 60 minutes or more (2000)

SANDWICH (city). Covers a land area of 3.014 square miles and a water area of 0 square miles. Located at 41.64° N. Lat.; 88.62° W. Long. Elevation is 670 feet.
History: Sandwich was named for Sandwich, Massachusetts. Early industries were the manufacture of plows, reapers, windmills, and cornshellers.
Population: 6,509 (2000); Race: 95.8% White, 0.2% Black, 0.5% Asian, 0.2% American Indian and Alaska Native, 7.9% Hispanic of any race, 0.3% two or more races (2000); Density: 2,159.5 persons per square mile (2000); Age: 27.1% under 18, 13.6% over 64 (2000); Marriage status: 22.1% never married, 57.8% now married, 8.1% widowed, 11.9% divorced (2000); Foreign born: 5.6% (2000); Ancestry (includes multiple ancestries): 31.2% German, 15.7% Irish, 11.6% Other groups, 11.1% English, 9.2% Norwegian (2000).
Economy: Single-family building permits issued: 36 (2001) / 38 (2000); Multi-family building permits issued: 4 (2001) / 2 (2000); Employment by occupation: 9.5% management, 12.0% professional, 12.5% services, 29.6% sales, 0.6% farming, 15.4% construction, 20.5% production (2000).
Income: Per capita income: $19,530 (2000); Median household income: $50,215 (2000); Poverty rate: 5.5% (2000).
Taxes: Total city taxes per capita: $152 (1997); City property taxes per capita: $92 (1997).
Education: High school graduation rate: 78.2% (2000); College graduation rate: 11.2% (2000).

School District(s)

Sandwich C U School District 430 (PK-12)
2000 Enrollment: 2,409 815-786-2187
Housing: Homeownership rate: 69.2% (2000); Median home value: $132,300 (2000); Median rent: $510 per month (2000); Median age of housing: 38 years (2000).
Hospitals: Valley West Community Hospital (84 beds)
Transportation: Commute to work: 90.4% car, 1.3% public transportation, 2.9% walk, 1.9% work from home (2000); Travel time to work: 38.9% less than 15 minutes, 16.6% 15 to 30 minutes, 25.0% 30 to 45 minutes, 10.1% 45 to 60 minutes, 9.4% 60 minutes or more (2000)
Additional Information Contacts
Sandwich Commerce Association 815-786-9075

SHABBONA (village). Covers a land area of 0.742 square miles and a water area of 0 square miles. Located at 41.76° N. Lat.; 88.87° W. Long. Elevation is 900 feet.
Population: 929 (2000); Race: 93.9% White, 0.7% Black, 0.8% Asian, 0.1% American Indian and Alaska Native, 1.9% Hispanic of any race, 3.5% two or more races (2000); Density: 1,252.7 persons per square mile (2000); Age: 29.1% under 18, 18.8% over 64 (2000); Marriage status: 18.8% never married, 54.4% now married, 16.8% widowed, 10.0% divorced (2000); Foreign born: 1.3% (2000); Ancestry (includes multiple ancestries): 29.6% German, 18.6% Irish, 12.3% Norwegian, 11.8% English, 9.2% Other groups (2000).
Economy: Single-family building permits issued: 2 (2001) / 0 (2000); Multi-family building permits issued: 0 (2001) / 0 (2000); Employment by occupation: 11.2% management, 14.0% professional, 12.4% services, 25.5% sales, 2.6% farming, 17.4% construction, 16.9% production (2000).
Income: Per capita income: $20,239 (2000); Median household income: $45,526 (2000); Poverty rate: 5.3% (2000).
Taxes: Total city taxes per capita: $140 (1997); City property taxes per capita: $53 (1997).
Education: High school graduation rate: 85.9% (2000); College graduation rate: 11.6% (2000).

School District(s)

Indian Creek Community Unit District 425 (PK-12)
2000 Enrollment: 950 815-824-2197
Housing: Homeownership rate: 71.8% (2000); Median home value: $110,900 (2000); Median rent: $518 per month (2000); Median age of housing: 47 years (2000).
Transportation: Commute to work: 92.6% car, 0.0% public transportation, 2.7% walk, 3.9% work from home (2000); Travel time to work: 19.7% less than 15 minutes, 32.6% 15 to 30 minutes, 24.9% 30 to 45 minutes, 12.1% 45 to 60 minutes, 10.8% 60 minutes or more (2000)

SOMONAUK (village). Covers a land area of 0.613 square miles and a water area of 0 square miles. Located at 41.63° N. Lat.; 88.68° W. Long. Elevation is 685 feet.
Population: 1,295 (2000); Race: 96.2% White, 0.0% Black, 0.0% Asian, 0.5% American Indian and Alaska Native, 3.5% Hispanic of any race, 1.5% two or more races (2000); Density: 2,113.4 persons per square mile (2000); Age: 27.8% under 18, 13.9% over 64 (2000); Marriage status: 22.3% never married, 62.7% now married, 7.3% widowed, 7.7% divorced (2000); Foreign born: 1.0% (2000); Ancestry (includes multiple ancestries): 31.7% German, 15.0% Irish, 13.3% English, 8.8% French (except Basque), 8.3% United States or American (2000).
Economy: Single-family building permits issued: 19 (2001) / 14 (2000); Multi-family building permits issued: 0 (2001) / 0 (2000); Employment by occupation: 9.9% management, 15.8% professional, 12.8% services, 28.6% sales, 0.3% farming, 14.2% construction, 18.4% production (2000).
Income: Per capita income: $19,110 (2000); Median household income: $45,370 (2000); Poverty rate: 5.4% (2000).
Taxes: Total city taxes per capita: $242 (1997); City property taxes per capita: $133 (1997).
Education: High school graduation rate: 89.9% (2000); College graduation rate: 13.2% (2000).

School District(s)

Somonauk C U School District 432 (KG-12)
2000 Enrollment: 972 815-498-2315
Housing: Homeownership rate: 69.4% (2000); Median home value: $124,800 (2000); Median rent: $568 per month (2000); Median age of housing: 48 years (2000).
Transportation: Commute to work: 94.3% car, 0.3% public transportation, 2.1% walk, 1.7% work from home (2000); Travel time to work: 30.7% less than 15 minutes, 17.9% 15 to 30 minutes, 27.5% 30 to 45 minutes, 15.1% 45 to 60 minutes, 8.7% 60 minutes or more (2000)

SYCAMORE (city). Covers a land area of 5.485 square miles and a water area of 0.018 square miles. Located at 41.98° N. Lat.; 88.69° W. Long. Elevation is 877 feet.
Population: 12,020 (2000); Race: 93.1% White, 3.2% Black, 1.3% Asian, 0.1% American Indian and Alaska Native, 3.8% Hispanic of any race, 1.5% two or more races (2000); Density: 2,191.6 persons per square mile (2000); Age: 28.2% under 18, 10.9% over 64 (2000); Marriage status: 22.7% never married, 60.9% now married, 6.0% widowed, 10.4% divorced (2000); Foreign born: 4.0% (2000); Ancestry (includes multiple ancestries): 30.9% German, 16.0% Irish, 10.4% Other groups, 10.4% English, 8.5% Swedish (2000).
Economy: Single-family building permits issued: 99 (2001) / 106 (2000); Multi-family building permits issued: 103 (2001) / 20 (2000); Employment by occupation: 13.8% management, 20.1% professional, 13.6% services, 24.0% sales, 0.1% farming, 9.1% construction, 19.3% production (2000).
Income: Per capita income: $23,112 (2000); Median household income: $51,921 (2000); Poverty rate: 3.7% (2000).
Taxes: Total city taxes per capita: $205 (1997); City property taxes per capita: $172 (1997).
Education: High school graduation rate: 90.7% (2000); College graduation rate: 28.4% (2000).

School District(s)

Dekalb Roe (07-12)
2000 Enrollment: 29 815-895-3096
Sycamore C U School District 427 (KG-12)
2000 Enrollment: 2,987 815-899-8103
Housing: Homeownership rate: 68.8% (2000); Median home value: $134,700 (2000); Median rent: $529 per month (2000); Median age of housing: 33 years (2000).
Hospitals: Vencor Hospital - Sycamore (77 beds)

Newspapers: Genoa/Kingston/Kirkland News (1 x week); Sycamore News (1 x week); Hampshire Register (1 x week)
Transportation: Commute to work: 94.1% car, 0.1% public transportation, 2.2% walk, 2.3% work from home (2000); Travel time to work: 46.6% less than 15 minutes, 25.2% 15 to 30 minutes, 13.6% 30 to 45 minutes, 7.2% 45 to 60 minutes, 7.4% 60 minutes or more (2000)
Additional Information Contacts
De Kalb Area Association of Realtors 815-899-3301
De Kalb County Economic Development 815-895-2711
Sycamore Chamber of Commerce 815-895-3456

WATERMAN (village). Covers a land area of 1.002 square miles and a water area of 0 square miles. Located at 41.77° N. Lat.; 88.77° W. Long. Elevation is 820 feet.
Population: 1,224 (2000); Race: 97.9% White, 0.9% Black, 0.7% Asian, 0.0% American Indian and Alaska Native, 2.4% Hispanic of any race, 0.2% two or more races (2000); Density: 1,221.5 persons per square mile (2000); Age: 31.3% under 18, 14.6% over 64 (2000); Marriage status: 21.6% never married, 64.3% now married, 6.3% widowed, 7.8% divorced (2000); Foreign born: 1.6% (2000); Ancestry (includes multiple ancestries): 33.2% German, 11.7% English, 10.3% Irish, 10.1% Norwegian, 8.0% Polish (2000).
Economy: Single-family building permits issued: 1 (2001) / 1 (2000); Multi-family building permits issued: 0 (2001) / 0 (2000); Employment by occupation: 14.0% management, 12.6% professional, 15.9% services, 25.4% sales, 1.0% farming, 11.4% construction, 19.6% production (2000).
Income: Per capita income: $18,836 (2000); Median household income: $47,500 (2000); Poverty rate: 6.2% (2000).
Taxes: Total city taxes per capita: $86 (1997); City property taxes per capita: $78 (1997).
Education: High school graduation rate: 90.1% (2000); College graduation rate: 19.3% (2000).
Housing: Homeownership rate: 76.9% (2000); Median home value: $128,600 (2000); Median rent: $500 per month (2000); Median age of housing: 45 years (2000).
Transportation: Commute to work: 90.6% car, 0.0% public transportation, 4.0% walk, 5.1% work from home (2000); Travel time to work: 23.3% less than 15 minutes, 36.0% 15 to 30 minutes, 20.9% 30 to 45 minutes, 6.8% 45 to 60 minutes, 13.0% 60 minutes or more (2000)

Douglas County

Located in east central Illinois; drained by the Embarrass and Kaskaskia Rivers. Covers a land area of 416.90 square miles, a water area of 0.60 square miles, and is located in the Central Time Zone. The county government was organized in 1859. County seat is Tuscola.

Weather Station: Tuscola — Elevation: 652 feet

	Jan	Feb	Mar	Apr	May	Jun	Jul	Aug	Sep	Oct	Nov	Dec
High	34	40	52	66	77	85	88	86	81	68	52	40
Low	17	22	32	42	52	62	65	63	55	44	33	24
Precip	2.1	2.1	3.2	4.0	4.0	4.1	4.7	3.7	3.2	2.9	3.8	3.0
Snow	8.0	4.8	2.5	0.3	tr	0.0	0.0	0.0	0.0	tr	1.7	4.8

High and Low temperatures in degrees Fahrenheit; Precipitation and Snow in inches

Population: 19,922 (2000); Race: 97.2% White, 0.2% Black, 0.4% Asian, 0.2% American Indian and Alaska Native, 3.7% Hispanic of any race, 0.7% two or more races (2000); Density: 47.8 persons per square mile (2000); Age: 27.1% under 18, 16.0% over 64 (2000).
Religion: Five largest groups: 12.3% The United Methodist Church, 11.3% Catholic Church, 8.0% Christian Churches and Churches of Christ, 7.2% Old Order Amish Church, 5.3% Christian Church (Disciples of Christ) (2000).
Economy: Unemployment rate: 4.1% (11/2002); Total civilian labor force: 12,587 (11/2002); Leading industries: 37.7% manufacturing; 20.8% retail trade; 10.1% construction (2000); Companies that employ more than 1,000 persons: 0 (2000); Companies that employ more than 100 persons: 11 (2000); Farms: 630 totaling 249,551 acres (1997); Minority business ownership rate: 0.0% (1997); Women business ownership rate: 14.4% (1997); Retail sales per capita: $9,349 (1997). Single-family building permits issued: 33 (2001) / 32 (2000); Multi-family building permits issued: 2 (2001) / 0 (2000).
Income: Per capita income: $18,474 (2000); Median household income: $39,439 (2000); Poverty rate: 6.4% (2000); Bankruptcy rate: 8.32% (2001).
Taxes: Total county taxes per capita: $125 (1997); County property taxes per capita: $86 (1997).
Education: High school graduation rate: 79.3% (2000); College graduation rate: 13.8% (2000).
Housing: Homeownership rate: 76.9% (2000); Median home value: $70,500 (2000); Median rent: $317 per month (2000); Median age of housing: 42 years (2000).
Health: Birth rate: 138.5 per 10,000 population (1998); Age adjusted death rate: 79.8 per 10,000 population (1999); Age adjusted cancer mortality rate: 161.8 deaths per 100,000 population (1999). Number of physicians: 7.0 per 10,000 population (1999); Number of hospital beds: n/a (1999).
Elections: 2000 Presidential election results: 39.4% Gore, 58.1% Bush, 1.6% Nader, 0.7% Buchanan
National and State Parks: Walnut Point State Park
Additional Information Contacts
Douglas County Government Offices 217-253-2411
Arcola Chamber of Commerce.................. 217-268-4530
Rockome Association of Commerce 217-268-4226
Tuscola Chamber of Commerce.................. 217-253-5013

Douglas County Communities

ARCOLA (city). Covers a land area of 1.368 square miles and a water area of 0.017 square miles. Located at 39.68° N. Lat.; 88.30° W. Long. Elevation is 678 feet.
History: Arcola was laid out in 1855 and named for a town in Italy. Broom corn was grown here, some for the local manufacture of brooms and some for export.
Population: 2,652 (2000); Race: 91.0% White, 0.0% Black, 0.7% Asian, 0.0% American Indian and Alaska Native, 19.0% Hispanic of any race, 1.1% two or more races (2000); Density: 1,938.9 persons per square mile (2000); Age: 26.7% under 18, 14.5% over 64 (2000); Marriage status: 20.9% never married, 63.1% now married, 6.4% widowed, 9.5% divorced (2000); Foreign born: 12.3% (2000); Ancestry (includes multiple ancestries): 20.2% Other groups, 17.4% German, 15.2% United States or American, 9.8% English, 7.3% Irish (2000).
Economy: Single-family building permits issued: 6 (2001) / 4 (2000); Multi-family building permits issued: 0 (2001) / 0 (2000); Employment by occupation: 10.1% management, 10.2% professional, 13.8% services, 24.5% sales, 1.8% farming, 5.5% construction, 34.1% production (2000).
Income: Per capita income: $18,664 (2000); Median household income: $38,125 (2000); Poverty rate: 3.7% (2000).
Taxes: Total city taxes per capita: $211 (1997); City property taxes per capita: $67 (1997).
Education: High school graduation rate: 76.6% (2000); College graduation rate: 13.1% (2000).

School District(s)
Arcola C U School District 306 (KG-12)
2000 Enrollment: 699 217-268-4963
Housing: Homeownership rate: 75.6% (2000); Median home value: $69,500 (2000); Median rent: $322 per month (2000); Median age of housing: 39 years (2000).
Newspapers: Arcola Record-Herald (1 x week)
Transportation: Commute to work: 87.0% car, 0.6% public transportation, 7.7% walk, 4.3% work from home (2000); Travel time to work: 60.4% less than 15 minutes, 24.7% 15 to 30 minutes, 8.8% 30 to 45 minutes, 4.0% 45 to 60 minutes, 2.1% 60 minutes or more (2000)
Additional Information Contacts
Arcola Chamber of Commerce.................. 217-268-4530
Rockome Association of Commerce 217-268-4226

ARTHUR (village). Covers a land area of 1.276 square miles and a water area of 0 square miles. Located at 39.71° N. Lat.; 88.47° W. Long. Elevation is 662 feet.
History: Arthur was settled in 1864 by a group of Amish colonists. The village was platted in 1873 by the Paris & Decatur Railroad Company. An early industry was the production of brooms.
Population: 2,203 (2000); Race: 98.8% White, 0.0% Black, 0.4% Asian, 0.4% American Indian and Alaska Native, 0.2% Hispanic of any race, 0.5% two or more races (2000); Density: 1,726.7 persons per square mile (2000); Age: 23.3% under 18, 22.1% over 64 (2000); Marriage status: 18.9% never married, 66.1% now married, 9.8% widowed, 5.2% divorced (2000); Foreign born: 0.4% (2000); Ancestry (includes multiple ancestries): 29.6% German, 15.0% United States or American, 11.5% English, 8.6% Irish, 4.8% Other groups (2000).
Economy: Single-family building permits issued: 3 (2001) / 3 (2000); Multi-family building permits issued: 0 (2001) / 0 (2000); Employment by occupation: 11.0% management, 11.0% professional, 13.6% services, 29.7% sales, 0.3% farming, 10.8% construction, 23.7% production (2000).

Income: Per capita income: $19,683 (2000); Median household income: $37,438 (2000); Poverty rate: 6.0% (2000).
Taxes: Total city taxes per capita: $119 (1997); City property taxes per capita: $115 (1997).
Education: High school graduation rate: 81.1% (2000); College graduation rate: 16.5% (2000).

School District(s)

Arthur C U School District 305 (PK-12)
2000 Enrollment: 586 217-543-2511

Housing: Homeownership rate: 77.1% (2000); Median home value: $69,200 (2000); Median rent: $326 per month (2000); Median age of housing: 40 years (2000).
Newspapers: Arthur Graphic Clarion (1 x week)
Transportation: Commute to work: 90.1% car, 0.0% public transportation, 4.5% walk, 2.9% work from home (2000); Travel time to work: 68.9% less than 15 minutes, 12.3% 15 to 30 minutes, 11.8% 30 to 45 minutes, 4.5% 45 to 60 minutes, 2.5% 60 minutes or more (2000)

CAMARGO (village). Covers a land area of 1.263 square miles and a water area of 0.013 square miles. Located at 39.79° N. Lat.; 88.16° W. Long. Elevation is 665 feet.
Population: 469 (2000); Race: 98.9% White, 0.0% Black, 0.0% Asian, 0.0% American Indian and Alaska Native, 0.0% Hispanic of any race, 1.1% two or more races (2000); Density: 371.2 persons per square mile (2000); Age: 27.6% under 18, 13.0% over 64 (2000); Marriage status: 19.3% never married, 60.9% now married, 8.5% widowed, 11.3% divorced (2000); Foreign born: 0.0% (2000); Ancestry (includes multiple ancestries): 19.2% United States or American, 17.5% German, 10.9% Irish, 10.9% English, 3.4% French (except Basque) (2000).
Economy: Single-family building permits issued: 6 (2001) / 6 (2000); Multi-family building permits issued: 0 (2001) / 0 (2000); Employment by occupation: 10.0% management, 15.4% professional, 12.9% services, 15.8% sales, 0.0% farming, 14.2% construction, 31.7% production (2000).
Income: Per capita income: $18,369 (2000); Median household income: $39,844 (2000); Poverty rate: 6.9% (2000).
Taxes: Total city taxes per capita: $93 (1997); City property taxes per capita: $33 (1997).
Education: High school graduation rate: 84.5% (2000); College graduation rate: 7.9% (2000).
Housing: Homeownership rate: 84.3% (2000); Median home value: $74,000 (2000); Median rent: $275 per month (2000); Median age of housing: 29 years (2000).
Transportation: Commute to work: 90.8% car, 0.0% public transportation, 3.3% walk, 5.4% work from home (2000); Travel time to work: 37.0% less than 15 minutes, 12.8% 15 to 30 minutes, 39.2% 30 to 45 minutes, 7.5% 45 to 60 minutes, 3.5% 60 minutes or more (2000)

GARRETT (village). Covers a land area of 0.139 square miles and a water area of 0 square miles. Located at 39.79° N. Lat.; 88.42° W. Long. Elevation is 675 feet.
Population: 198 (2000); Race: 100.0% White, 0.0% Black, 0.0% Asian, 0.0% American Indian and Alaska Native, 4.9% Hispanic of any race, 0.0% two or more races (2000); Density: 1,422.9 persons per square mile (2000); Age: 42.4% under 18, 8.4% over 64 (2000); Marriage status: 26.8% never married, 42.8% now married, 7.2% widowed, 23.2% divorced (2000); Foreign born: 0.0% (2000); Ancestry (includes multiple ancestries): 31.5% English, 22.7% German, 18.7% United States or American, 6.9% Other groups, 4.4% Irish (2000).
Economy: Employment by occupation: 1.4% management, 5.6% professional, 22.2% services, 13.9% sales, 2.8% farming, 16.7% construction, 37.5% production (2000).
Income: Per capita income: $10,920 (2000); Median household income: $29,375 (2000); Poverty rate: 14.0% (2000).
Taxes: Total city taxes per capita: $24 (1997); City property taxes per capita: $24 (1997).
Education: High school graduation rate: 81.1% (2000); College graduation rate: 1.9% (2000).
Housing: Homeownership rate: 88.6% (2000); Median home value: $21,300 (2000); Median rent: $240 per month (2000); Median age of housing: 50 years (2000).
Transportation: Commute to work: 100.0% car, 0.0% public transportation, 0.0% walk, 0.0% work from home (2000); Travel time to work: 23.6% less than 15 minutes, 54.2% 15 to 30 minutes, 18.1% 30 to 45 minutes, 1.4% 45 to 60 minutes, 2.8% 60 minutes or more (2000)

HINDSBORO (village). Covers a land area of 0.308 square miles and a water area of 0 square miles. Located at 39.68° N. Lat.; 88.13° W. Long. Elevation is 649 feet.
Population: 361 (2000); Race: 100.0% White, 0.0% Black, 0.0% Asian, 0.0% American Indian and Alaska Native, 0.0% Hispanic of any race, 0.0% two or more races (2000); Density: 1,173.1 persons per square mile (2000); Age: 27.0% under 18, 22.5% over 64 (2000); Marriage status: 20.1% never married, 57.3% now married, 9.9% widowed, 12.8% divorced (2000); Foreign born: 0.8% (2000); Ancestry (includes multiple ancestries): 28.4% German, 17.1% Irish, 15.4% English, 12.1% Other groups, 7.9% United States or American (2000).
Economy: Single-family building permits issued: 0 (2001) / 0 (2000); Multi-family building permits issued: 0 (2001) / 0 (2000); Employment by occupation: 8.4% management, 16.2% professional, 10.4% services, 20.1% sales, 1.3% farming, 7.8% construction, 35.7% production (2000).
Income: Per capita income: $14,014 (2000); Median household income: $32,604 (2000); Poverty rate: 16.0% (2000).
Taxes: Total city taxes per capita: $118 (1997); City property taxes per capita: $63 (1997).
Education: High school graduation rate: 75.4% (2000); College graduation rate: 15.7% (2000).
Housing: Homeownership rate: 87.4% (2000); Median home value: $47,600 (2000); Median rent: $263 per month (2000); Median age of housing: 58 years (2000).
Transportation: Commute to work: 94.1% car, 0.0% public transportation, 3.3% walk, 2.6% work from home (2000); Travel time to work: 35.6% less than 15 minutes, 43.0% 15 to 30 minutes, 16.8% 30 to 45 minutes, 2.0% 45 to 60 minutes, 2.7% 60 minutes or more (2000)

NEWMAN (city). Covers a land area of 0.624 square miles and a water area of 0 square miles. Located at 39.79° N. Lat.; 87.98° W. Long. Elevation is 646 feet.
History: Newman was founded in 1857 and named for B. Newman, son-in-law of the Methodist circuit-rider Peter Cartwright. Early industries included tile factories, and later a corn cannery and dairy products plant.
Population: 956 (2000); Race: 98.4% White, 0.9% Black, 0.0% Asian, 0.0% American Indian and Alaska Native, 0.0% Hispanic of any race, 0.7% two or more races (2000); Density: 1,531.7 persons per square mile (2000); Age: 24.7% under 18, 21.7% over 64 (2000); Marriage status: 19.4% never married, 56.1% now married, 14.3% widowed, 10.2% divorced (2000); Foreign born: 0.5% (2000); Ancestry (includes multiple ancestries): 16.8% German, 15.5% United States or American, 12.7% Irish, 10.9% English, 6.5% Other groups (2000).
Economy: Single-family building permits issued: 1 (2001) / 1 (2000); Multi-family building permits issued: 0 (2001) / 0 (2000); Employment by occupation: 11.1% management, 12.0% professional, 18.9% services, 22.7% sales, 1.8% farming, 9.1% construction, 24.3% production (2000).
Income: Per capita income: $17,971 (2000); Median household income: $30,417 (2000); Poverty rate: 16.7% (2000).
Taxes: Total city taxes per capita: $91 (1997); City property taxes per capita: $33 (1997).
Education: High school graduation rate: 84.6% (2000); College graduation rate: 11.6% (2000).
Housing: Homeownership rate: 73.2% (2000); Median home value: $42,200 (2000); Median rent: $266 per month (2000); Median age of housing: 59 years (2000).
Newspapers: The Newman Independent (1 x week)
Transportation: Commute to work: 93.6% car, 0.7% public transportation, 3.2% walk, 1.6% work from home (2000); Travel time to work: 23.8% less than 15 minutes, 26.3% 15 to 30 minutes, 24.0% 30 to 45 minutes, 21.0% 45 to 60 minutes, 4.8% 60 minutes or more (2000)

TUSCOLA (city). Covers a land area of 2.133 square miles and a water area of 0.007 square miles. Located at 39.79° N. Lat.; 88.28° W. Long. Elevation is 655 feet.
History: The extension of the Illinois Central Railroad across the prairies in 1855 opened the land to cultivation and resulted in the settling of Tuscola in 1857. The name is of Indian origin and means "a level plain."
Population: 4,448 (2000); Race: 97.5% White, 0.0% Black, 0.6% Asian, 0.9% American Indian and Alaska Native, 2.5% Hispanic of any race, 0.6% two or more races (2000); Density: 2,084.9 persons per square mile (2000); Age: 24.8% under 18, 17.5% over 64 (2000); Marriage status: 20.3% never married, 61.9% now married, 7.9% widowed, 9.9% divorced (2000); Foreign born: 1.9% (2000); Ancestry (includes multiple ancestries): 27.9% German,

12.0% English, 11.8% Irish, 11.7% United States or American, 7.6% Other groups (2000).
Economy: Single-family building permits issued: 14 (2001) / 17 (2000); Multi-family building permits issued: 2 (2001) / 0 (2000); Employment by occupation: 13.2% management, 16.5% professional, 16.9% services, 26.5% sales, 0.3% farming, 10.1% construction, 16.5% production (2000).
Income: Per capita income: $19,465 (2000); Median household income: $39,608 (2000); Poverty rate: 4.1% (2000).
Taxes: Total city taxes per capita: $517 (1997); City property taxes per capita: $230 (1997).
Education: High school graduation rate: 89.6% (2000); College graduation rate: 17.6% (2000).

School District(s)

Tuscola C U School District 301 (PK-12)
2000 Enrollment: 1,021 217-253-4241
Housing: Homeownership rate: 72.3% (2000); Median home value: $79,200 (2000); Median rent: $353 per month (2000); Median age of housing: 44 years (2000).
Newspapers: The Tuscola Review (1 x week)
Transportation: Commute to work: 93.5% car, 0.0% public transportation, 1.8% walk, 4.4% work from home (2000); Travel time to work: 53.9% less than 15 minutes, 14.8% 15 to 30 minutes, 25.2% 30 to 45 minutes, 3.9% 45 to 60 minutes, 2.2% 60 minutes or more (2000)
Additional Information Contacts
Tuscola Chamber of Commerce. 217-253-5013

VILLA GROVE (city). Covers a land area of 1.492 square miles and a water area of 0.007 square miles. Located at 39.86° N. Lat.; 88.16° W. Long. Elevation is 655 feet.
Population: 2,553 (2000); Race: 99.1% White, 0.0% Black, 0.5% Asian, 0.0% American Indian and Alaska Native, 0.7% Hispanic of any race, 0.4% two or more races (2000); Density: 1,711.1 persons per square mile (2000); Age: 26.5% under 18, 16.2% over 64 (2000); Marriage status: 20.3% never married, 58.5% now married, 8.3% widowed, 12.9% divorced (2000); Foreign born: 0.8% (2000); Ancestry (includes multiple ancestries): 29.8% German, 15.7% United States or American, 13.2% Irish, 12.5% Other groups, 10.8% English (2000).
Economy: Single-family building permits issued: 3 (2001) / 1 (2000); Multi-family building permits issued: 0 (2001) / 0 (2000); Employment by occupation: 8.9% management, 10.7% professional, 19.7% services, 28.6% sales, 0.7% farming, 8.0% construction, 23.4% production (2000).
Income: Per capita income: $16,504 (2000); Median household income: $35,912 (2000); Poverty rate: 7.1% (2000).
Taxes: Total city taxes per capita: $98 (1997); City property taxes per capita: $48 (1997).
Education: High school graduation rate: 83.9% (2000); College graduation rate: 10.7% (2000).

School District(s)

Villa Grove C U School District 302 (KG-12)
2000 Enrollment: 779 217-832-2261
Housing: Homeownership rate: 76.4% (2000); Median home value: $62,000 (2000); Median rent: $317 per month (2000); Median age of housing: 45 years (2000).
Newspapers: Villa Grove News (1 x week); Southern Champaign County Today (1 x week)
Transportation: Commute to work: 94.8% car, 0.0% public transportation, 3.2% walk, 1.2% work from home (2000); Travel time to work: 22.9% less than 15 minutes, 29.2% 15 to 30 minutes, 37.7% 30 to 45 minutes, 6.7% 45 to 60 minutes, 3.5% 60 minutes or more (2000)

Du Page County

Located in northeastern Illinois; drained by the Du Page River. Covers a land area of 333.60 square miles, a water area of 2.90 square miles, and is located in the Central Time Zone. The county government was organized in 1939. County seat is Wheaton.

Du Page County is part of the Chicago, IL PMSA. The entire metro area includes: Cook County; DeKalb County; DuPage County; Grundy County; Kane County; Kendall County; Lake County; McHenry County; Will County

Weather Station: Wheaton 3 SE — Elevation: 679 feet

	Jan	Feb	Mar	Apr	May	Jun	Jul	Aug	Sep	Oct	Nov	Dec
High	31	37	49	62	74	83	87	85	78	66	49	37
Low	14	18	28	37	47	57	63	61	53	42	31	21
Precip	1.8	1.6	2.7	3.8	4.0	3.9	3.9	4.7	3.5	2.7	3.2	2.4
Snow	11.1	7.8	4.8	0.8	tr	0.0	0.0	0.0	0.0	tr	1.9	6.1

High and Low temperatures in degrees Fahrenheit; Precipitation and Snow in inches

Population: 904,161 (2000); Race: 83.9% White, 3.0% Black, 7.9% Asian, 0.2% American Indian and Alaska Native, 9.0% Hispanic of any race, 1.8% two or more races (2000); Density: 2,710.3 persons per square mile (2000); Age: 26.7% under 18, 9.7% over 64 (2000).
Religion: Five largest groups: 38.6% Catholic Church, 3.0% Lutheran Church—Missouri Synod, 2.9% Evangelical Lutheran Church in America, 2.2% The United Methodist Church, 1.6% Muslim estimate (2000).
Economy: Unemployment rate: 4.9% (11/2002); Total civilian labor force: 517,576 (11/2002); Leading industries: 11.2% manufacturing; 11.2% retail trade; 10.9% administration, support, waste management, remediation services (2000); Companies that employ more than 1,000 persons: 39 (2000); Companies that employ more than 100 persons: 1,113 (2000); Farms: 93 totaling 17,103 acres (1997); Minority business ownership rate: 10.3% (1997); Women business ownership rate: 26.0% (1997); Retail sales per capita: $14,742 (1997). Single-family building permits issued: 2,771 (2001) / 3,292 (2000); Multi-family building permits issued: 1,562 (2001) / 639 (2000).
Income: Per capita income: $31,315 (2000); Median household income: $67,887 (2000); Poverty rate: 3.6% (2000); Bankruptcy rate: 3.16% (2001).
Taxes: Total county taxes per capita: $190 (2000); County property taxes per capita: $158 (2000).
Education: High school graduation rate: 90.0% (2000); College graduation rate: 41.7% (2000).
Housing: Homeownership rate: 76.4% (2000); Median home value: $195,000 (2000); Median rent: $775 per month (2000); Median age of housing: 25 years (2000).
Health: Birth rate: 146.7 per 10,000 population (1998); Age adjusted death rate: 82.4 per 10,000 population (1999); Infant mortality rate: 7.2 per 1,000 live births (1998); Age adjusted cancer mortality rate: 206.5 deaths per 100,000 population (1999). Air Quality Index: 86% good, 14% moderate, 0% unhealthy (percent of days in 2000). Number of physicians: 39.7 per 10,000 population (1999); Number of hospital beds: 22.5 per 10,000 population (1999).
Elections: 2000 Presidential election results: 41.9% Gore, 55.2% Bush, 2.4% Nader, 0.2% Buchanan
Additional Information Contacts
DuPage County Government Offices. 630-682-7467
Bartlett Chamber of Commerce 630-830-0324
Bensenville Chamber of Commerce. 630-350-3040
Bloomingdale Chamber of Commerce. 630-980-9082
Carol Stream Chamber of Commerce 630-665-3325
Clarendon Hills Chamber of Commerce 630-654-3030
Darien Chamber of Commerce. 630-968-0004
Downers Grove Chamber of Commerce 630-968-4050
Elk Grove Village Chamber. 630-350-8503
Elmhurst Chamber of Commerce. 630-834-6060
Glen Ellyn Chamber of Commerce 630-469-0907
Glen Ellyn Economic Development Corp. 630-469-0947
Glendale Heights Chamber of Commerce 630-539-8399
Hinsdale Chamber of Commerce 630-323-3952
Lisle Chamber of Commerce 630-964-0052
Lisle Convention & Visitors Bureau 630-769-1000
Lombard Chamber of Commerce. 630-627-5040
Naperville Chamber of Commerce. 630-355-4141
Northern Illinois Commercial Association of Realtors 630-579-3212
Oak Brook Area Association of Commerce. 630-573-0616
Realtor Association West/South Suburban Chicagoland 630-653-1790
Roselle Chamber of Commerce 630-894-3010
U S Chamber of Commerce 630-684-0387
Villa Park Chamber of Commerce. 630-941-9133
Warrenville Chamber of Commerce 630-393-9080
West Chicago Chamber of Commerce. 630-231-3003
Westmont Chamber of Commerce. 630-960-5553
Wheaton Chamber of Commerce 630-668-6464
Willowbrook-Burr Ridge Chamber 630-654-0909
Winfield Chamber of Commerce. 630-682-3712
Wood Dale Chamber of Commerce. 630-595-0505
Woodridge Area Chamber of Commerce. 630-852-9878

Du Page County Communities

ADDISON (village). Covers a land area of 9.432 square miles and a water area of 0.054 square miles. Located at 41.93° N. Lat.; 88.00° W. Long. Elevation is 691 feet.
History: Addison developed as a community of German Lutherans in the 1840's. It was named for the 18th-century essayist, Joseph Addison.
Population: 35,914 (2000); Race: 74.2% White, 2.7% Black, 8.3% Asian, 0.1% American Indian and Alaska Native, 29.0% Hispanic of any race, 2.5% two or more races (2000); Density: 3,807.6 persons per square mile (2000); Age: 26.7% under 18, 8.3% over 64 (2000); Marriage status: 28.1% never married, 60.0% now married, 4.8% widowed, 7.2% divorced (2000); Foreign born: 34.3% (2000); Ancestry (includes multiple ancestries): 36.9% Other groups, 16.3% Italian, 14.3% German, 13.0% Polish, 8.8% Irish (2000).
Vital Statistics: Birth rate: 168.5 per 10,000 population (1998)
Economy: Unemployment rate: 6.5% (11/2002); Total civilian labor force: 20,239 (11/2002); Single-family building permits issued: 66 (2001) / 59 (2000); Multi-family building permits issued: 36 (2001) / 16 (2000); Employment by occupation: 12.5% management, 14.4% professional, 11.5% services, 29.6% sales, 0.1% farming, 10.2% construction, 21.7% production (2000).
Income: Per capita income: $21,201 (2000); Median household income: $54,090 (2000); Poverty rate: 9.6% (2000).
Taxes: Total city taxes per capita: $324 (2000); City property taxes per capita: $170 (2000).
Education: High school graduation rate: 73.5% (2000); College graduation rate: 19.5% (2000).

School District(s)

Addison School District 4 (PK-08)
2000 Enrollment: 3,854 630-458-2425

Four-year College(s)

DeVry Institute of Technology (Private, For-profit)
2001 Enrollment: 3,543 630-953-1300
2001 Tuition: In-state $8,740; Out-of-state $8,740
Housing: Homeownership rate: 68.3% (2000); Median home value: $173,200 (2000); Median rent: $644 per month (2000); Median age of housing: 29 years (2000).
Transportation: Commute to work: 92.2% car, 2.6% public transportation, 2.4% walk, 1.7% work from home (2000); Travel time to work: 27.4% less than 15 minutes, 38.2% 15 to 30 minutes, 20.5% 30 to 45 minutes, 6.5% 45 to 60 minutes, 7.4% 60 minutes or more (2000)

BARTLETT (village). Covers a land area of 14.814 square miles and a water area of 0.144 square miles. Located at 41.97° N. Lat.; 88.19° W. Long.
Population: 36,706 (2000); Race: 87.8% White, 1.6% Black, 8.0% Asian, 0.0% American Indian and Alaska Native, 5.4% Hispanic of any race, 1.3% two or more races (2000); Density: 2,477.9 persons per square mile (2000); Age: 32.1% under 18, 5.6% over 64 (2000); Marriage status: 19.5% never married, 70.3% now married, 3.2% widowed, 7.1% divorced (2000); Foreign born: 10.9% (2000); Ancestry (includes multiple ancestries): 28.5% German, 17.2% Italian, 16.4% Other groups, 16.3% Irish, 15.3% Polish (2000).
Vital Statistics: Birth rate: 206.5 per 10,000 population (1998)
Economy: Unemployment rate: 5.1% (11/2002); Total civilian labor force: 20,226 (11/2002); Single-family building permits issued: 123 (2001) / 121 (2000); Multi-family building permits issued: 0 (2001) / 0 (2000); Employment by occupation: 23.3% management, 19.9% professional, 7.9% services, 31.9% sales, 0.0% farming, 7.2% construction, 9.8% production (2000).
Income: Per capita income: $29,652 (2000); Median household income: $79,718 (2000); Poverty rate: 1.9% (2000).
Education: High school graduation rate: 92.3% (2000); College graduation rate: 38.3% (2000).
Housing: Homeownership rate: 93.5% (2000); Median home value: $204,700 (2000); Median rent: $691 per month (2000); Median age of housing: 11 years (2000).
Newspapers: Hanover Park Examiner (1 x week); Streamwood Examiner (1 x week); Bartlett Examiner (1 x week); Carol Stream Examiner (1 x week)
Transportation: Commute to work: 90.1% car, 5.4% public transportation, 0.3% walk, 3.4% work from home (2000); Travel time to work: 15.3% less than 15 minutes, 29.3% 15 to 30 minutes, 27.8% 30 to 45 minutes, 12.6% 45 to 60 minutes, 15.0% 60 minutes or more (2000)
Additional Information Contacts
Bartlett Chamber of Commerce 630-830-0324

BENSENVILLE (village). Covers a land area of 6.006 square miles and a water area of 0 square miles. Located at 41.95° N. Lat.; 87.94° W. Long. Elevation is 675 feet.
Population: 20,703 (2000); Race: 69.9% White, 2.5% Black, 6.1% Asian, 0.4% American Indian and Alaska Native, 36.6% Hispanic of any race, 5.0% two or more races (2000); Density: 3,447.2 persons per square mile (2000); Age: 24.6% under 18, 11.8% over 64 (2000); Marriage status: 28.0% never married, 56.9% now married, 6.8% widowed, 8.3% divorced (2000); Foreign born: 31.5% (2000); Ancestry (includes multiple ancestries): 43.8% Other groups, 17.6% German, 10.7% Polish, 9.8% Irish, 9.3% Italian (2000).
Vital Statistics: Birth rate: 188.9 per 10,000 population (1998)
Economy: Single-family building permits issued: 23 (2001) / 46 (2000); Multi-family building permits issued: 0 (2001) / 0 (2000); Employment by occupation: 9.6% management, 13.7% professional, 10.7% services, 30.6% sales, 0.3% farming, 8.1% construction, 26.8% production (2000).
Income: Per capita income: $20,040 (2000); Median household income: $54,662 (2000); Poverty rate: 6.5% (2000).
Taxes: Total city taxes per capita: $437 (1997); City property taxes per capita: $249 (1997).
Education: High school graduation rate: 71.1% (2000); College graduation rate: 19.1% (2000).

School District(s)

Bensenville School District 2 (PK-08)
2000 Enrollment: 2,265 630-766-5940
Fenton Community H S District 100 (09-12)
2000 Enrollment: 1,490 630-860-6257
Housing: Homeownership rate: 55.8% (2000); Median home value: $155,900 (2000); Median rent: $731 per month (2000); Median age of housing: 32 years (2000).
Newspapers: KJT International & Polish News (1 x month)
Transportation: Commute to work: 89.0% car, 4.2% public transportation, 3.2% walk, 2.2% work from home (2000); Travel time to work: 28.6% less than 15 minutes, 39.5% 15 to 30 minutes, 17.4% 30 to 45 minutes, 8.6% 45 to 60 minutes, 6.0% 60 minutes or more (2000)
Additional Information Contacts
Bensenville Chamber of Commerce. 630-350-3040
Elk Grove Village Chamber 630-350-8503

BLOOMINGDALE (village). Covers a land area of 6.765 square miles and a water area of 0.042 square miles. Located at 41.95° N. Lat.; 88.08° W. Long. Elevation is 780 feet.
Population: 21,675 (2000); Race: 85.1% White, 2.7% Black, 9.0% Asian, 0.0% American Indian and Alaska Native, 4.7% Hispanic of any race, 1.9% two or more races (2000); Density: 3,204.1 persons per square mile (2000); Age: 21.7% under 18, 11.6% over 64 (2000); Marriage status: 24.6% never married, 58.0% now married, 8.2% widowed, 9.2% divorced (2000); Foreign born: 13.2% (2000); Ancestry (includes multiple ancestries): 21.0% German, 20.7% Italian, 16.8% Other groups, 15.9% Irish, 12.5% Polish (2000).
Vital Statistics: Birth rate: 111.7 per 10,000 population (1998)
Economy: Single-family building permits issued: 41 (2001) / 71 (2000); Multi-family building permits issued: 0 (2001) / 0 (2000); Employment by occupation: 22.4% management, 19.2% professional, 8.3% services, 33.8% sales, 0.0% farming, 5.8% construction, 10.6% production (2000).
Income: Per capita income: $30,941 (2000); Median household income: $67,365 (2000); Poverty rate: 2.7% (2000).
Taxes: Total city taxes per capita: $309 (2000); City property taxes per capita: $122 (2000).
Education: High school graduation rate: 89.2% (2000); College graduation rate: 34.4% (2000).

School District(s)

Bloomingdale School District 13 (PK-08)
2000 Enrollment: 1,503 630-893-9590
Housing: Homeownership rate: 72.8% (2000); Median home value: $209,200 (2000); Median rent: $912 per month (2000); Median age of housing: 18 years (2000).
Transportation: Commute to work: 90.5% car, 5.4% public transportation, 0.8% walk, 2.7% work from home (2000); Travel time to work: 18.5% less than 15 minutes, 32.9% 15 to 30 minutes, 27.8% 30 to 45 minutes, 8.7% 45 to 60 minutes, 12.0% 60 minutes or more (2000)
Additional Information Contacts
Bloomingdale Chamber of Commerce. 630-980-9082

BURR RIDGE (village). Covers a land area of 6.424 square miles and a water area of 0.112 square miles. Located at 41.75° N. Lat.; 87.92° W. Long. Elevation is 700 feet.

Population: 10,408 (2000); Race: 86.5% White, 1.3% Black, 10.0% Asian, 0.2% American Indian and Alaska Native, 2.0% Hispanic of any race, 1.6% two or more races (2000); Density: 1,620.1 persons per square mile (2000); Age: 27.8% under 18, 13.4% over 64 (2000); Marriage status: 20.2% never married, 69.7% now married, 6.0% widowed, 4.1% divorced (2000); Foreign born: 13.2% (2000); Ancestry (includes multiple ancestries): 21.2% German, 17.4% Irish, 15.0% Other groups, 12.2% Italian, 9.8% Polish (2000).
Economy: Single-family building permits issued: 53 (2001) / 62 (2000); Multi-family building permits issued: 0 (2001) / 0 (2000); Employment by occupation: 28.3% management, 34.0% professional, 5.7% services, 26.8% sales, 0.1% farming, 2.9% construction, 2.1% production (2000).
Income: Per capita income: $58,518 (2000); Median household income: $129,507 (2000); Poverty rate: 2.8% (2000).
Taxes: Total city taxes per capita: $493 (1997); City property taxes per capita: $431 (1997).
Education: High school graduation rate: 95.3% (2000); College graduation rate: 58.2% (2000).

School District(s)

Community Cons School District 180 (PK-08)
2000 Enrollment: 784 630-734-6600
Gower School District 62 (KG-08)
2000 Enrollment: 914 630-986-5383
Pleasantdale School District 107 (PK-08)
2000 Enrollment: 749 708-784-2013

Two-year College(s)

Itt Technical Institute (Private, For-profit)
2001 Enrollment: 270 630-455-6470
2001 Tuition: In-state $10,620; Out-of-state $10,620

Housing: Homeownership rate: 96.5% (2000); Median home value: $477,800 (2000); Median rent: $1,130 per month (2000); Median age of housing: 16 years (2000).
Transportation: Commute to work: 86.2% car, 8.9% public transportation, 0.0% walk, 4.6% work from home (2000); Travel time to work: 16.2% less than 15 minutes, 29.1% 15 to 30 minutes, 25.9% 30 to 45 minutes, 14.9% 45 to 60 minutes, 13.9% 60 minutes or more (2000)

Additional Information Contacts

Willowbrook-Burr Ridge Chamber 630-654-0909

CAROL STREAM (village). Covers a land area of 8.896 square miles and a water area of 0.028 square miles. Located at 41.92° N. Lat.; 88.14° W. Long. Elevation is 750 feet.
Population: 40,438 (2000); Race: 78.9% White, 4.2% Black, 10.2% Asian, 0.3% American Indian and Alaska Native, 10.1% Hispanic of any race, 2.6% two or more races (2000); Density: 4,545.8 persons per square mile (2000); Age: 30.1% under 18, 5.5% over 64 (2000); Marriage status: 25.7% never married, 61.8% now married, 4.9% widowed, 7.5% divorced (2000); Foreign born: 16.8% (2000); Ancestry (includes multiple ancestries): 24.5% Other groups, 24.3% German, 14.3% Irish, 14.2% Italian, 12.7% Polish (2000).
Vital Statistics: Birth rate: 178.1 per 10,000 population (1998)
Economy: Unemployment rate: 5.2% (11/2002); Total civilian labor force: 22,229 (11/2002); Single-family building permits issued: 25 (2001) / 19 (2000); Multi-family building permits issued: 0 (2001) / 0 (2000); Employment by occupation: 17.8% management, 19.9% professional, 9.0% services, 33.4% sales, 0.0% farming, 6.8% construction, 13.1% production (2000).
Income: Per capita income: $25,152 (2000); Median household income: $64,893 (2000); Poverty rate: 3.4% (2000).
Taxes: Total city taxes per capita: $236 (2000); City property taxes per capita: $79 (2000).
Education: High school graduation rate: 89.9% (2000); College graduation rate: 32.0% (2000).

School District(s)

Community Consolidated S D 93 (PK-08)
2000 Enrollment: 5,073 630-462-8900

Housing: Homeownership rate: 70.0% (2000); Median home value: $170,400 (2000); Median rent: $750 per month (2000); Median age of housing: 17 years (2000).
Transportation: Commute to work: 91.9% car, 3.7% public transportation, 0.9% walk, 2.9% work from home (2000); Travel time to work: 24.1% less than 15 minutes, 29.1% 15 to 30 minutes, 25.5% 30 to 45 minutes, 10.0% 45 to 60 minutes, 11.3% 60 minutes or more (2000)

Additional Information Contacts

Carol Stream Chamber of Commerce 630-665-3325

CLARENDON HILLS (village). Covers a land area of 1.739 square miles and a water area of 0.003 square miles. Located at 41.79° N. Lat.; 87.95° W. Long. Elevation is 750 feet.
Population: 7,610 (2000); Race: 94.9% White, 0.2% Black, 4.2% Asian, 0.1% American Indian and Alaska Native, 2.4% Hispanic of any race, 0.3% two or more races (2000); Density: 4,377.1 persons per square mile (2000); Age: 30.4% under 18, 11.1% over 64 (2000); Marriage status: 20.3% never married, 67.0% now married, 5.3% widowed, 7.5% divorced (2000); Foreign born: 8.1% (2000); Ancestry (includes multiple ancestries): 26.9% German, 21.7% Irish, 13.4% Polish, 10.0% Italian, 8.5% English (2000).
Economy: Single-family building permits issued: 55 (2001) / 54 (2000); Multi-family building permits issued: 0 (2001) / 56 (2000); Employment by occupation: 29.2% management, 28.4% professional, 7.2% services, 28.1% sales, 0.0% farming, 2.7% construction, 4.4% production (2000).
Income: Per capita income: $41,859 (2000); Median household income: $84,795 (2000); Poverty rate: 0.6% (2000).
Taxes: Total city taxes per capita: $258 (1997); City property taxes per capita: $250 (1997).
Education: High school graduation rate: 96.2% (2000); College graduation rate: 65.0% (2000).

School District(s)

Maercker School District 60 (PK-08)
2000 Enrollment: 1,253 630-323-2086

Housing: Homeownership rate: 81.2% (2000); Median home value: $307,500 (2000); Median rent: $688 per month (2000); Median age of housing: 41 years (2000).
Transportation: Commute to work: 73.7% car, 18.2% public transportation, 3.5% walk, 3.3% work from home (2000); Travel time to work: 27.4% less than 15 minutes, 24.4% 15 to 30 minutes, 21.8% 30 to 45 minutes, 13.9% 45 to 60 minutes, 12.5% 60 minutes or more (2000)

Additional Information Contacts

Clarendon Hills Chamber of Commerce 630-654-3030

DARIEN (city). Covers a land area of 6.043 square miles and a water area of 0.073 square miles. Located at 41.74° N. Lat.; 87.98° W. Long. Elevation is 756 feet.
Population: 22,860 (2000); Race: 83.7% White, 1.7% Black, 12.7% Asian, 0.0% American Indian and Alaska Native, 2.7% Hispanic of any race, 0.8% two or more races (2000); Density: 3,782.7 persons per square mile (2000); Age: 23.8% under 18, 12.6% over 64 (2000); Marriage status: 21.6% never married, 64.3% now married, 5.8% widowed, 8.3% divorced (2000); Foreign born: 15.2% (2000); Ancestry (includes multiple ancestries): 19.9% German, 19.2% Polish, 19.1% Other groups, 16.1% Irish, 14.8% Italian (2000).
Vital Statistics: Birth rate: 111.1 per 10,000 population (1998)
Economy: Single-family building permits issued: 28 (2001) / 57 (2000); Multi-family building permits issued: 0 (2001) / 0 (2000); Employment by occupation: 23.1% management, 26.1% professional, 8.2% services, 29.9% sales, 0.1% farming, 5.3% construction, 7.4% production (2000).
Income: Per capita income: $34,795 (2000); Median household income: $74,836 (2000); Poverty rate: 2.2% (2000).
Taxes: Total city taxes per capita: $82 (1997); City property taxes per capita: $36 (1997).
Education: High school graduation rate: 93.5% (2000); College graduation rate: 43.5% (2000).

School District(s)

Cass School District 63 (PK-08)
2000 Enrollment: 929 630-985-2000
Darien School District 61 (PK-08)
2000 Enrollment: 1,757 630-968-7505

Housing: Homeownership rate: 85.6% (2000); Median home value: $214,500 (2000); Median rent: $730 per month (2000); Median age of housing: 22 years (2000).
Transportation: Commute to work: 88.6% car, 6.3% public transportation, 1.0% walk, 3.7% work from home (2000); Travel time to work: 19.1% less than 15 minutes, 31.2% 15 to 30 minutes, 23.0% 30 to 45 minutes, 11.7% 45 to 60 minutes, 15.1% 60 minutes or more (2000)

Additional Information Contacts

Darien Chamber of Commerce 630-968-0004

DOWNERS GROVE (village). Covers a land area of 14.246 square miles and a water area of 0.010 square miles. Located at 41.79° N. Lat.; 88.01° W. Long. Elevation is 760 feet.
History: Downers Grove was settled in 1832 by Pierce Downer at the intersection of two trails. The town was incorporated in 1873.

Population: 48,724 (2000); Race: 89.5% White, 1.7% Black, 6.1% Asian, 0.2% American Indian and Alaska Native, 3.7% Hispanic of any race, 1.2% two or more races (2000); Density: 3,420.2 persons per square mile (2000); Age: 24.4% under 18, 14.3% over 64 (2000); Marriage status: 23.1% never married, 62.0% now married, 8.1% widowed, 6.9% divorced (2000); Foreign born: 9.8% (2000); Ancestry (includes multiple ancestries): 25.5% German, 20.3% Irish, 14.9% Polish, 12.4% Other groups, 10.8% Italian (2000).
Vital Statistics: Birth rate: 139.0 per 10,000 population (1998)
Economy: Unemployment rate: 4.4% (11/2002); Total civilian labor force: 29,215 (11/2002); Single-family building permits issued: 62 (2001) / 50 (2000); Multi-family building permits issued: 12 (2001) / 40 (2000); Employment by occupation: 21.5% management, 27.5% professional, 8.1% services, 30.2% sales, 0.0% farming, 5.0% construction, 7.7% production (2000).
Income: Per capita income: $31,580 (2000); Median household income: $65,539 (2000); Poverty rate: 2.3% (2000).
Taxes: Total city taxes per capita: $262 (2000); City property taxes per capita: $140 (2000).
Education: High school graduation rate: 93.0% (2000); College graduation rate: 46.4% (2000).

School District(s)

Center Cass School District 66 (PK-08)
2000 Enrollment: 1,291 630-783-5000
Community High School District 99 (09-12)
2000 Enrollment: 5,329 630-795-7100
Downers Grove Grade School District 58 (PK-08)
2000 Enrollment: 4,934 630-719-5800
Puffer Hefty School District 69 (KG-08)
2000 Enrollment: 403 630-968-0454

Four-year College(s)

Midwestern University (Private, Not-for-profit)
2001 Enrollment: 1,483 630-969-4400
2001 Tuition: In-state $14,650; Out-of-state $16,070

Housing: Homeownership rate: 78.5% (2000); Median home value: $205,900 (2000); Median rent: $718 per month (2000); Median age of housing: 32 years (2000).
Hospitals: Advocate Good Samaritan Hospital (302 beds)
Newspapers: Woodridge Progress (1 x week); Westmont Progress (1 x week); Lemont Reporter (1 x week); Downers Grove Reporter (2 x week); Darien Progress (1 x week); Clarendon Hills Progress (1 x week); Willowbrook Progress (1 x week); Lisle Reporter (1 x week)
Transportation: Commute to work: 82.8% car, 10.7% public transportation, 1.6% walk, 4.3% work from home (2000); Travel time to work: 23.4% less than 15 minutes, 31.6% 15 to 30 minutes, 20.6% 30 to 45 minutes, 11.9% 45 to 60 minutes, 12.5% 60 minutes or more (2000)

Additional Information Contacts

Downers Grove Chamber of Commerce 630-968-4050

ELMHURST (city). Covers a land area of 10.265 square miles and a water area of 0.004 square miles. Located at 41.89° N. Lat.; 87.94° W. Long. Elevation is 685 feet.
History: Elmhurst was first known as Cottage Hill, named for the home built in 1843 by J.L. Hovey. The later name of Elmhurst referred to a double row of elm trees that grew along Cottage Hill Avenue. Poet Carl Sandburg lived in Elmhurst at one time.
Population: 42,762 (2000); Race: 93.4% White, 0.9% Black, 3.3% Asian, 0.1% American Indian and Alaska Native, 3.9% Hispanic of any race, 1.4% two or more races (2000); Density: 4,165.9 persons per square mile (2000); Age: 25.9% under 18, 16.2% over 64 (2000); Marriage status: 22.8% never married, 63.2% now married, 7.6% widowed, 6.4% divorced (2000); Foreign born: 8.0% (2000); Ancestry (includes multiple ancestries): 26.5% German, 21.5% Irish, 14.2% Italian, 13.2% Polish, 9.5% Other groups (2000).
Vital Statistics: Birth rate: 145.2 per 10,000 population (1998)
Economy: Unemployment rate: 4.3% (11/2002); Total civilian labor force: 24,596 (11/2002); Single-family building permits issued: 174 (2001) / 152 (2000); Multi-family building permits issued: 0 (2001) / 24 (2000); Employment by occupation: 20.9% management, 26.5% professional, 7.8% services, 31.6% sales, 0.0% farming, 5.7% construction, 7.5% production (2000).
Income: Per capita income: $32,015 (2000); Median household income: $69,794 (2000); Poverty rate: 2.5% (2000).
Taxes: Total city taxes per capita: $398 (2000); City property taxes per capita: $201 (2000).
Education: High school graduation rate: 91.4% (2000); College graduation rate: 45.1% (2000).

School District(s)

Elmhurst School District 205 (PK-12)
2000 Enrollment: 6,952 630-834-4530

Four-year College(s)

Elmhurst College (Private, Not-for-profit, United Church of Christ)
2001 Enrollment: 2,540 630-279-4100
2001 Tuition: In-state $16,200; Out-of-state $16,200

Housing: Homeownership rate: 82.8% (2000); Median home value: $211,100 (2000); Median rent: $780 per month (2000); Median age of housing: 44 years (2000).
Hospitals: Elmhurst Memorial Hospital (412 beds)
Newspapers: Wood Dale Press (2 x week)
Transportation: Commute to work: 85.3% car, 7.5% public transportation, 3.1% walk, 3.2% work from home (2000); Travel time to work: 27.9% less than 15 minutes, 32.4% 15 to 30 minutes, 21.7% 30 to 45 minutes, 9.2% 45 to 60 minutes, 8.8% 60 minutes or more (2000)

Additional Information Contacts

Elmhurst Chamber of Commerce. 630-834-6060

GLEN ELLYN (village). Covers a land area of 6.616 square miles and a water area of 0.021 square miles. Located at 41.87° N. Lat.; 88.06° W. Long. Elevation is 780 feet.
History: Glen Ellyn was named when the town was platted by Thomas E. Hill for his wife Ellyn. When the Galena & Chicago Union Railroad was constructed south of town in 1849, the residents transplanted their town to the present site, platted in 1851.
Population: 26,999 (2000); Race: 89.5% White, 1.9% Black, 4.9% Asian, 0.1% American Indian and Alaska Native, 4.5% Hispanic of any race, 1.9% two or more races (2000); Density: 4,080.6 persons per square mile (2000); Age: 28.2% under 18, 11.2% over 64 (2000); Marriage status: 22.0% never married, 65.7% now married, 5.6% widowed, 6.8% divorced (2000); Foreign born: 10.7% (2000); Ancestry (includes multiple ancestries): 27.8% German, 22.5% Irish, 13.3% English, 13.0% Other groups, 10.3% Italian (2000).
Vital Statistics: Birth rate: 175.2 per 10,000 population (1998)
Economy: Single-family building permits issued: 60 (2001) / 69 (2000); Multi-family building permits issued: 0 (2001) / 0 (2000); Employment by occupation: 24.3% management, 29.1% professional, 8.0% services, 29.2% sales, 0.0% farming, 3.3% construction, 6.2% production (2000).
Income: Per capita income: $39,783 (2000); Median household income: $74,846 (2000); Poverty rate: 2.8% (2000).
Taxes: Total city taxes per capita: $305 (2000); City property taxes per capita: $159 (2000).
Education: High school graduation rate: 94.5% (2000); College graduation rate: 58.8% (2000).

School District(s)

Coop Assoc for Special Education (KG-12)
2000 Enrollment: 85 630-942-5600
Glen Ellyn C C School District 89 (PK-08)
2000 Enrollment: 2,530 630-469-8900
Glen Ellyn School District 41 (PK-08)
2000 Enrollment: 3,384 630-790-6400
Glenbard Township H S District 87 (09-12)
2000 Enrollment: 8,567 630-469-9100
Phillip J Rock Center and School (PK-12)
2000 Enrollment: 19 630-790-2474

Two-year College(s)

College of Dupage (Public)
2001 Enrollment: 29,423 630-942-2800
2001 Tuition: In-state $5,760; Out-of-state $7,824

Housing: Homeownership rate: 78.0% (2000); Median home value: $274,800 (2000); Median rent: $687 per month (2000); Median age of housing: 35 years (2000).
Newspapers: The Wheaton Leader (1 x week); The Glen Ellyn News (2 x week); Warrenville Post (1 x week)
Transportation: Commute to work: 78.6% car, 11.7% public transportation, 2.8% walk, 5.7% work from home (2000); Travel time to work: 25.3% less than 15 minutes, 31.3% 15 to 30 minutes, 17.0% 30 to 45 minutes, 10.3% 45 to 60 minutes, 16.2% 60 minutes or more (2000)

Additional Information Contacts

Glen Ellyn Chamber of Commerce 630-469-0907
Glen Ellyn Economic Development Corp. 630-469-0947

GLENDALE HEIGHTS (village). Covers a land area of 5.404 square miles and a water area of 0.003 square miles. Located at 41.92° N. Lat.; 88.07° W. Long. Elevation is 762 feet.

Population: 31,765 (2000); Race: 64.7% White, 4.6% Black, 19.9% Asian, 0.3% American Indian and Alaska Native, 18.0% Hispanic of any race, 3.1% two or more races (2000); Density: 5,877.8 persons per square mile (2000); Age: 26.9% under 18, 4.8% over 64 (2000); Marriage status: 31.0% never married, 56.8% now married, 3.6% widowed, 8.6% divorced (2000); Foreign born: 30.3% (2000); Ancestry (includes multiple ancestries): 40.0% Other groups, 16.8% German, 11.4% Polish, 10.1% Italian, 9.5% Irish (2000).
Vital Statistics: Birth rate: 170.3 per 10,000 population (1998)
Economy: Unemployment rate: 6.2% (11/2002); Total civilian labor force: 18,727 (11/2002); Single-family building permits issued: 192 (2001) / 194 (2000); Multi-family building permits issued: 36 (2001) / 0 (2000); Employment by occupation: 13.3% management, 17.4% professional, 10.1% services, 31.8% sales, 0.1% farming, 8.0% construction, 19.3% production (2000).
Income: Per capita income: $21,911 (2000); Median household income: $56,285 (2000); Poverty rate: 6.1% (2000).
Taxes: Total city taxes per capita: $293 (2000); City property taxes per capita: $142 (2000).
Education: High school graduation rate: 81.5% (2000); College graduation rate: 26.7% (2000).

School District(s)

Marquardt School District 15 (PK-08)
2000 Enrollment: 2,661 630-295-5450
Queen Bee School District 16 (PK-08)
2000 Enrollment: 2,151 630-260-6100

Two-year College(s)

Universal Technical Institute Inc (Private, For-profit)
2001 Enrollment: 1,153 630-529-2662
Housing: Homeownership rate: 70.0% (2000); Median home value: $142,800 (2000); Median rent: $764 per month (2000); Median age of housing: 23 years (2000).
Hospitals: GlenOaks Hospital (186 beds)
Transportation: Commute to work: 93.9% car, 2.6% public transportation, 1.1% walk, 1.5% work from home (2000); Travel time to work: 23.0% less than 15 minutes, 33.9% 15 to 30 minutes, 25.7% 30 to 45 minutes, 8.4% 45 to 60 minutes, 9.0% 60 minutes or more (2000)
Additional Information Contacts
Glendale Heights Chamber of Commerce 630-539-8399

HINSDALE (village). Covers a land area of 4.636 square miles and a water area of 0.005 square miles. Located at 41.80° N. Lat.; 87.92° W. Long. Elevation is 725 feet.
History: Hinsdale developed along the route of the Chicago, Burlington & Quincy Railroad, and was named for railroad director H.W. Hinsdale. In 1923 Hinsdale annexed nearby Fullersburg, which had been settled in 1835 by Jacob Fuller and his family.
Population: 17,349 (2000); Race: 93.0% White, 1.0% Black, 5.0% Asian, 0.1% American Indian and Alaska Native, 1.9% Hispanic of any race, 0.8% two or more races (2000); Density: 3,742.3 persons per square mile (2000); Age: 32.5% under 18, 11.9% over 64 (2000); Marriage status: 18.4% never married, 70.6% now married, 5.7% widowed, 5.4% divorced (2000); Foreign born: 9.0% (2000); Ancestry (includes multiple ancestries): 24.5% German, 23.5% Irish, 13.9% English, 9.9% Italian, 9.3% Other groups (2000).
Vital Statistics: Birth rate: 163.7 per 10,000 population (1998)
Economy: Single-family building permits issued: 105 (2001) / 95 (2000); Multi-family building permits issued: 0 (2001) / 0 (2000); Employment by occupation: 32.0% management, 29.9% professional, 4.9% services, 26.8% sales, 0.0% farming, 2.6% construction, 3.9% production (2000).
Income: Per capita income: $63,765 (2000); Median household income: $104,551 (2000); Poverty rate: 3.2% (2000).
Taxes: Total city taxes per capita: $399 (1997); City property taxes per capita: $304 (1997).
Education: High school graduation rate: 97.3% (2000); College graduation rate: 68.6% (2000).

School District(s)

Hinsdale C C School District 181 (PK-08)
2000 Enrollment: 3,695 630-887-1070
Hinsdale Township H S District 86 (09-12)
2000 Enrollment: 3,930 630-655-6100
Housing: Homeownership rate: 83.7% (2000); Median home value: $520,100 (2000); Median rent: $765 per month (2000); Median age of housing: 40 years (2000).
Hospitals: Hinsdale Hospital (426 beds)
Newspapers: The La Grange Doings (1 x week); The Elmhurst Doings (1 x week); The Western Springs Doings with News of Indian Head Park (1 x week); The Oak Brook Doings (1 x week); The Doings - Hinsdale Edition (1 x week); The Doings - Clarendon Hills Edition (1 x week); The Weekly Doings - Burr Ridge/Willowbrook/Darien Edition (1 x week)
Transportation: Commute to work: 71.3% car, 18.3% public transportation, 3.1% walk, 6.1% work from home (2000); Travel time to work: 29.6% less than 15 minutes, 20.8% 15 to 30 minutes, 25.0% 30 to 45 minutes, 13.6% 45 to 60 minutes, 10.9% 60 minutes or more (2000)
Additional Information Contacts
Hinsdale Chamber of Commerce 630-323-3952

ITASCA (village). Covers a land area of 4.916 square miles and a water area of 0.069 square miles. Located at 41.97° N. Lat.; 88.01° W. Long. Elevation is 700 feet.
Population: 8,302 (2000); Race: 87.7% White, 1.7% Black, 5.6% Asian, 0.2% American Indian and Alaska Native, 6.8% Hispanic of any race, 2.6% two or more races (2000); Density: 1,688.8 persons per square mile (2000); Age: 23.6% under 18, 11.1% over 64 (2000); Marriage status: 26.9% never married, 59.6% now married, 7.2% widowed, 6.4% divorced (2000); Foreign born: 18.8% (2000); Ancestry (includes multiple ancestries): 24.9% German, 17.7% Polish, 17.1% Italian, 16.3% Other groups, 15.5% Irish (2000).
Economy: Single-family building permits issued: 18 (2001) / 12 (2000); Multi-family building permits issued: 0 (2001) / 20 (2000); Employment by occupation: 18.9% management, 20.4% professional, 8.8% services, 32.1% sales, 0.0% farming, 7.0% construction, 12.8% production (2000).
Income: Per capita income: $34,117 (2000); Median household income: $70,156 (2000); Poverty rate: 4.7% (2000).
Taxes: Total city taxes per capita: $663 (2000); City property taxes per capita: $403 (2000).
Education: High school graduation rate: 88.0% (2000); College graduation rate: 32.8% (2000).

School District(s)

Itasca School District 10 (PK-08)
2000 Enrollment: 815 630-773-1232
Housing: Homeownership rate: 74.4% (2000); Median home value: $208,300 (2000); Median rent: $827 per month (2000); Median age of housing: 26 years (2000).
Transportation: Commute to work: 88.6% car, 5.1% public transportation, 1.9% walk, 4.1% work from home (2000); Travel time to work: 22.8% less than 15 minutes, 39.1% 15 to 30 minutes, 23.8% 30 to 45 minutes, 6.6% 45 to 60 minutes, 7.8% 60 minutes or more (2000)

LISLE (village). Covers a land area of 6.373 square miles and a water area of 0.045 square miles. Located at 41.79° N. Lat.; 88.08° W. Long. Elevation is 680 feet.
Population: 21,182 (2000); Race: 81.9% White, 3.5% Black, 10.3% Asian, 0.6% American Indian and Alaska Native, 5.5% Hispanic of any race, 1.7% two or more races (2000); Density: 3,323.7 persons per square mile (2000); Age: 24.7% under 18, 7.3% over 64 (2000); Marriage status: 28.8% never married, 57.0% now married, 5.2% widowed, 9.0% divorced (2000); Foreign born: 13.1% (2000); Ancestry (includes multiple ancestries): 22.3% German, 20.2% Other groups, 16.0% Irish, 12.8% Polish, 10.3% Italian (2000).
Vital Statistics: Birth rate: 162.4 per 10,000 population (1998)
Economy: Single-family building permits issued: 144 (2001) / 137 (2000); Multi-family building permits issued: 0 (2001) / 0 (2000); Employment by occupation: 23.4% management, 28.2% professional, 8.7% services, 27.1% sales, 0.0% farming, 5.1% construction, 7.5% production (2000).
Income: Per capita income: $35,693 (2000); Median household income: $65,821 (2000); Poverty rate: 3.6% (2000).
Taxes: Total city taxes per capita: $271 (2000); City property taxes per capita: $125 (2000).
Education: High school graduation rate: 95.4% (2000); College graduation rate: 50.0% (2000).

School District(s)

Lisle C U School District 202 (PK-12)
2000 Enrollment: 1,881 630-493-8000

Four-year College(s)

Benedictine University (Private, Not-for-profit, Roman Catholic)
2001 Enrollment: 2,700 630-829-6090
2001 Tuition: In-state $15,200; Out-of-state $15,200
Keller Graduate School of Management (Private, For-profit)
2001 Enrollment: n/a 630-969-6624
Housing: Homeownership rate: 56.8% (2000); Median home value: $219,200 (2000); Median rent: $832 per month (2000); Median age of housing: 21 years (2000).
Transportation: Commute to work: 84.8% car, 9.8% public transportation, 1.6% walk, 3.4% work from home (2000); Travel time to work: 25.0% less

than 15 minutes, 31.2% 15 to 30 minutes, 19.7% 30 to 45 minutes, 10.5% 45 to 60 minutes, 13.6% 60 minutes or more (2000)

Additional Information Contacts

Lisle Chamber of Commerce 630-964-0052
Lisle Convention & Visitors Bureau 630-769-1000

LOMBARD (village). Covers a land area of 9.685 square miles and a water area of 0.014 square miles. Located at 41.87° N. Lat.; 88.01° W. Long. Elevation is 720 feet.

History: Lombard was settled in 1834 by Winslow Churchill. The town was platted in 1868 by Joseph Lombard of Chicago, for whom it was named. Lombard has been known for its many varieties of lilacs, displayed in Lilacia Park, the gift of Colonel William Plum who collected lilacs from around the world.

Population: 42,322 (2000); Race: 87.1% White, 2.6% Black, 7.0% Asian, 0.2% American Indian and Alaska Native, 4.7% Hispanic of any race, 1.8% two or more races (2000); Density: 4,369.8 persons per square mile (2000); Age: 22.4% under 18, 14.9% over 64 (2000); Marriage status: 26.1% never married, 58.0% now married, 7.5% widowed, 8.5% divorced (2000); Foreign born: 11.6% (2000); Ancestry (includes multiple ancestries): 27.1% German, 19.7% Irish, 15.3% Other groups, 14.4% Italian, 11.0% Polish (2000).

Vital Statistics: Birth rate: 151.2 per 10,000 population (1998)

Economy: Unemployment rate: 5.6% (11/2002); Total civilian labor force: 25,291 (11/2002); Single-family building permits issued: 39 (2001) / 38 (2000); Multi-family building permits issued: 304 (2001) / 82 (2000); Employment by occupation: 17.0% management, 22.9% professional, 8.0% services, 35.4% sales, 0.0% farming, 7.4% construction, 9.2% production (2000).

Income: Per capita income: $27,667 (2000); Median household income: $60,015 (2000); Poverty rate: 3.8% (2000).

Taxes: Total city taxes per capita: $264 (1997); City property taxes per capita: $97 (1997).

Education: High school graduation rate: 90.4% (2000); College graduation rate: 36.0% (2000).

School District(s)

Lombard School District 44 (PK-08)
2000 Enrollment: 3,213 630-620-3700

Four-year College(s)

National University of Health Sciences (Private, Not-for-profit)
2001 Enrollment: 649 630-629-2000
2001 Tuition: In-state $12,829; Out-of-state $12,829
Northern Baptist Theological Seminary (Private, Not-for-profit, Baptist)
2001 Enrollment: 257 630-620-2128

Housing: Homeownership rate: 75.0% (2000); Median home value: $168,500 (2000); Median rent: $845 per month (2000); Median age of housing: 33 years (2000).

Newspapers: Villa Park Review (1 x week); Lombardian (1 x week)

Transportation: Commute to work: 88.7% car, 6.4% public transportation, 1.6% walk, 2.7% work from home (2000); Travel time to work: 24.4% less than 15 minutes, 32.5% 15 to 30 minutes, 23.4% 30 to 45 minutes, 9.3% 45 to 60 minutes, 10.4% 60 minutes or more (2000)

Additional Information Contacts

Lombard Chamber of Commerce. 630-627-5040

MEDINAH (unincorporated postal area, zip code 60157). Covers a land area of 1.467 square miles and a water area of 0.007 square miles. Located at 41.84° N. Lat.; 88.08° W. Long. Elevation is 740 feet.

Population: 2,111 (2000); Race: 91.2% White, 0.5% Black, 5.8% Asian, 0.6% American Indian and Alaska Native, 4.5% Hispanic of any race, 0.4% two or more races (2000); Density: 1,439.0 persons per square mile (2000); Age: 20.0% under 18, 17.7% over 64 (2000); Marriage status: 16.4% never married, 73.3% now married, 8.0% widowed, 2.3% divorced (2000); Foreign born: 13.8% (2000); Ancestry (includes multiple ancestries): 35.7% German, 19.8% Polish, 18.6% Italian, 12.3% Irish, 11.5% Other groups (2000).

Economy: Employment by occupation: 25.6% management, 15.2% professional, 3.1% services, 31.6% sales, 0.0% farming, 13.3% construction, 11.1% production (2000).

Income: Per capita income: $36,250 (2000); Median household income: $81,251 (2000); Poverty rate: 3.6% (2000).

Education: High school graduation rate: 91.8% (2000); College graduation rate: 35.3% (2000).

Housing: Homeownership rate: 98.1% (2000); Median home value: $254,100 (2000); Median rent: $544 per month (2000); Median age of housing: 38 years (2000).

Transportation: Commute to work: 90.5% car, 8.1% public transportation, 0.0% walk, 0.7% work from home (2000); Travel time to work: 18.4% less than 15 minutes, 39.5% 15 to 30 minutes, 20.3% 30 to 45 minutes, 14.7% 45 to 60 minutes, 7.0% 60 minutes or more (2000)

NAPERVILLE (city). Covers a land area of 35.377 square miles and a water area of 0.145 square miles. Located at 41.75° N. Lat.; 88.15° W. Long. Elevation is 700 feet.

History: The first settlement at Naperville was Fort Payne, built in 1832. That same year, Joseph Naper built a saw mill and platted the town site. From 1839 to 1868 Naperville was the seat of DuPage County.

Population: 128,358 (2000); Race: 85.7% White, 2.8% Black, 9.1% Asian, 0.2% American Indian and Alaska Native, 3.5% Hispanic of any race, 1.4% two or more races (2000); Density: 3,628.3 persons per square mile (2000); Age: 32.0% under 18, 6.2% over 64 (2000); Marriage status: 22.2% never married, 68.4% now married, 3.5% widowed, 6.0% divorced (2000); Foreign born: 11.7% (2000); Ancestry (includes multiple ancestries): 27.0% German, 18.5% Irish, 16.8% Other groups, 10.9% Polish, 10.6% Italian (2000).

Vital Statistics: Birth rate: 153.4 per 10,000 population (1998)

Economy: Unemployment rate: 5.4% (11/2002); Total civilian labor force: 69,206 (11/2002); Single-family building permits issued: 764 (2001) / 1,107 (2000); Multi-family building permits issued: 298 (2001) / 22 (2000); Employment by occupation: 26.9% management, 29.1% professional, 7.5% services, 28.2% sales, 0.0% farming, 3.6% construction, 4.7% production (2000).

Income: Per capita income: $35,551 (2000); Median household income: $88,771 (2000); Poverty rate: 2.2% (2000).

Taxes: Total city taxes per capita: $366 (2000); City property taxes per capita: $215 (2000).

Education: High school graduation rate: 96.3% (2000); College graduation rate: 60.6% (2000).

School District(s)

Indian Prairie C U School District 204 (PK-12)
2000 Enrollment: 23,173 630-375-3000
Naperville C U District 203 (PK-12)
2000 Enrollment: 18,762 630-420-6300
Sch Assoc Special Education Dupage Sased (02-12)
2000 Enrollment: 148 630-778-4500

Four-year College(s)

North Central College (Private, Not-for-profit, United Methodist)
2001 Enrollment: 2,605 630-637-5100
2001 Tuition: In-state $16,995; Out-of-state $16,995
Robert Morris College-Naperville (Private, Not-for-profit)
2001 Enrollment: n/a 630-577-8700
2001 Tuition: In-state $12,150; Out-of-state $12,150

Housing: Homeownership rate: 80.0% (2000); Median home value: $254,200 (2000); Median rent: $865 per month (2000); Median age of housing: 14 years (2000).

Hospitals: Edward Hospital (179 beds)

Safety: Violent crime rate: n/a; Property crime rate: 184.9 per 10,000 population (2001).

Newspapers: Lisle Sun (1 x week); Cover Story (1 x week); Naperville Sun (3 x week); Bolingbrook/Romeoville Sun (1 x week); The Wheaton Sun (1 x week)

Transportation: Commute to work: 83.4% car, 9.0% public transportation, 1.4% walk, 5.6% work from home (2000); Travel time to work: 21.3% less than 15 minutes, 29.8% 15 to 30 minutes, 19.0% 30 to 45 minutes, 11.8% 45 to 60 minutes, 17.9% 60 minutes or more (2000); Amtrak: Service available.

Additional Information Contacts

Naperville Chamber of Commerce. 630-355-4141
Northern Illinois Commercial Association of Realtors 630-579-3212

OAK BROOK (village). Covers a land area of 8.161 square miles and a water area of 0.097 square miles. Located at 41.84° N. Lat.; 87.95° W. Long. Elevation is 660 feet.

Population: 8,702 (2000); Race: 73.7% White, 1.0% Black, 21.9% Asian, 0.0% American Indian and Alaska Native, 1.3% Hispanic of any race, 3.0% two or more races (2000); Density: 1,066.4 persons per square mile (2000); Age: 18.7% under 18, 20.7% over 64 (2000); Marriage status: 20.3% never married, 69.5% now married, 6.9% widowed, 3.3% divorced (2000); Foreign born: 22.2% (2000); Ancestry (includes multiple ancestries): 25.7% Other groups, 16.8% German, 13.0% Irish, 12.6% Italian, 5.9% Polish (2000).

Economy: Single-family building permits issued: 33 (2001) / 37 (2000); Multi-family building permits issued: 0 (2001) / 0 (2000); Employment by occupation: 26.8% management, 35.9% professional, 6.6% services, 25.9% sales, 0.0% farming, 2.6% construction, 2.2% production (2000).

Income: Per capita income: $76,668 (2000); Median household income: $146,537 (2000); Poverty rate: 2.1% (2000).

Taxes: Total city taxes per capita: $370 (2000); City property taxes per capita: $11 (2000).
Education: High school graduation rate: 96.0% (2000); College graduation rate: 60.7% (2000).

School District(s)

Butler School District 53 (KG-08)
2000 Enrollment: 506 630-573-2887

Housing: Homeownership rate: 97.2% (2000); Median home value: $635,400 (2000); Median rent: $894 per month (2000); Median age of housing: 23 years (2000).
Newspapers: North Aurora Herald (1 x week); Suburban Life Citizen (2 x week); Westchester News (1 x week); West Cook County Press (1 x week); Villa Park Argus (2 x week); Roselle Press (1 x week); The Press-Oakbrook Terrace (2 x week); Lombard Spectator (2 x week); La Grange Press (1 x week); La Grange Park Press (1 x week); Itasca Press (1 x week); Glendale Heights Press (1 x week); Glen Ellyn Press (1 x week); Elmhurst Express (1 x week); Elmhurst Press (2 x week); Countryside Press (1 x week); Carol Stream Press (1 x week); Bloomingdale Press (1 x week); Bensenville Press (2 x week); Addison Press (2 x week); Suburban Life - Lombard, Oakbrook Terrace, Villa Park (1 x week); Suburban Life - Du Page (2 x week)
Transportation: Commute to work: 91.1% car, 4.0% public transportation, 0.9% walk, 3.9% work from home (2000); Travel time to work: 21.4% less than 15 minutes, 27.5% 15 to 30 minutes, 28.3% 30 to 45 minutes, 15.3% 45 to 60 minutes, 7.5% 60 minutes or more (2000)

Additional Information Contacts

U S Chamber of Commerce 630-684-0387

OAKBROOK TERRACE (city). Covers a land area of 1.393 square miles and a water area of 0 square miles. Located at 41.85° N. Lat.; 87.96° W. Long. Elevation is 675 feet.
Population: 2,300 (2000); Race: 80.5% White, 5.5% Black, 9.7% Asian, 0.0% American Indian and Alaska Native, 0.9% Hispanic of any race, 3.5% two or more races (2000); Density: 1,651.2 persons per square mile (2000); Age: 13.2% under 18, 20.7% over 64 (2000); Marriage status: 19.9% never married, 58.6% now married, 11.8% widowed, 9.7% divorced (2000); Foreign born: 14.9% (2000); Ancestry (includes multiple ancestries): 20.9% German, 20.5% Other groups, 19.9% Italian, 13.8% Irish, 13.2% Polish (2000).
Economy: Single-family building permits issued: 3 (2001) / 1 (2000); Multi-family building permits issued: 0 (2001) / 0 (2000); Employment by occupation: 23.3% management, 38.6% professional, 3.3% services, 24.1% sales, 0.0% farming, 6.2% construction, 4.5% production (2000).
Income: Per capita income: $44,345 (2000); Median household income: $59,148 (2000); Poverty rate: 3.3% (2000).
Taxes: Total city taxes per capita: $1,187 (1997); City property taxes per capita: $174 (1997).
Education: High school graduation rate: 91.6% (2000); College graduation rate: 44.5% (2000).

Four-year College(s)

Keller Graduate School of Management Inc (Private, For-profit)
2001 Enrollment: 3,121 630-571-1818

Housing: Homeownership rate: 40.3% (2000); Median home value: $170,700 (2000); Median rent: $943 per month (2000); Median age of housing: 26 years (2000).
Transportation: Commute to work: 90.0% car, 4.7% public transportation, 2.1% walk, 1.8% work from home (2000); Travel time to work: 25.7% less than 15 minutes, 27.8% 15 to 30 minutes, 23.7% 30 to 45 minutes, 16.3% 45 to 60 minutes, 6.5% 60 minutes or more (2000)

ROSELLE (village). Covers a land area of 5.374 square miles and a water area of 0.017 square miles. Located at 41.98° N. Lat.; 88.08° W. Long. Elevation is 770 feet.
Population: 23,115 (2000); Race: 87.7% White, 1.2% Black, 7.8% Asian, 0.2% American Indian and Alaska Native, 6.1% Hispanic of any race, 1.3% two or more races (2000); Density: 4,301.1 persons per square mile (2000); Age: 26.0% under 18, 7.7% over 64 (2000); Marriage status: 24.9% never married, 62.2% now married, 4.7% widowed, 8.2% divorced (2000); Foreign born: 15.1% (2000); Ancestry (includes multiple ancestries): 28.3% German, 17.1% Polish, 17.0% Irish, 16.1% Other groups, 16.0% Italian (2000).
Vital Statistics: Birth rate: 152.3 per 10,000 population (1998)
Economy: Single-family building permits issued: 21 (2001) / 22 (2000); Multi-family building permits issued: 52 (2001) / 37 (2000); Employment by occupation: 19.4% management, 20.2% professional, 9.8% services, 33.9% sales, 0.0% farming, 6.2% construction, 10.5% production (2000).
Income: Per capita income: $28,501 (2000); Median household income: $65,254 (2000); Poverty rate: 2.0% (2000).
Taxes: Total city taxes per capita: $305 (2000); City property taxes per capita: $160 (2000).
Education: High school graduation rate: 91.0% (2000); College graduation rate: 34.0% (2000).

School District(s)

Lake Park Community H S District 108 (09-12)
2000 Enrollment: 2,789 630-295-5410
Medinah School District 11 (KG-08)
2000 Enrollment: 702 630-893-3737
North Dupage Special Education Cooperative (PK-12)
2000 Enrollment: 65 630-894-0490
Roselle School District 12 (KG-08)
2000 Enrollment: 708 630-529-2091

Housing: Homeownership rate: 81.3% (2000); Median home value: $169,900 (2000); Median rent: $842 per month (2000); Median age of housing: 23 years (2000).
Transportation: Commute to work: 89.0% car, 6.1% public transportation, 1.1% walk, 3.4% work from home (2000); Travel time to work: 18.5% less than 15 minutes, 33.9% 15 to 30 minutes, 25.0% 30 to 45 minutes, 11.4% 45 to 60 minutes, 11.1% 60 minutes or more (2000)

Additional Information Contacts

Roselle Chamber of Commerce 630-894-3010

VILLA PARK (village). Covers a land area of 4.702 square miles and a water area of 0.004 square miles. Located at 41.88° N. Lat.; 87.97° W. Long. Elevation is 700 feet.
Population: 22,075 (2000); Race: 88.9% White, 1.5% Black, 4.0% Asian, 0.1% American Indian and Alaska Native, 13.0% Hispanic of any race, 2.0% two or more races (2000); Density: 4,695.2 persons per square mile (2000); Age: 27.3% under 18, 11.5% over 64 (2000); Marriage status: 26.4% never married, 59.7% now married, 5.6% widowed, 8.3% divorced (2000); Foreign born: 14.4% (2000); Ancestry (includes multiple ancestries): 27.2% German, 19.2% Irish, 18.3% Other groups, 12.9% Italian, 11.8% Polish (2000).
Vital Statistics: Birth rate: 165.8 per 10,000 population (1998)
Economy: Single-family building permits issued: 7 (2001) / 11 (2000); Multi-family building permits issued: 0 (2001) / 340 (2000); Employment by occupation: 12.6% management, 15.8% professional, 14.1% services, 31.5% sales, 0.0% farming, 11.1% construction, 14.9% production (2000).
Income: Per capita income: $22,354 (2000); Median household income: $55,706 (2000); Poverty rate: 4.8% (2000).
Taxes: Total city taxes per capita: $270 (1997); City property taxes per capita: $152 (1997).
Education: High school graduation rate: 86.0% (2000); College graduation rate: 23.7% (2000).

School District(s)

Du Page High School District 88 (09-12)
2000 Enrollment: 3,783 630-530-3980
East Dupage Special Education District Edsed (07-12)
2000 Enrollment: 47 630-617-2647
Salt Creek School District 48 (PK-08)
2000 Enrollment: 638 630-279-8400
School District 45 (PK-08)
2000 Enrollment: 3,876 630-530-6200

Housing: Homeownership rate: 76.7% (2000); Median home value: $155,900 (2000); Median rent: $664 per month (2000); Median age of housing: 44 years (2000).
Transportation: Commute to work: 89.0% car, 4.3% public transportation, 2.8% walk, 2.4% work from home (2000); Travel time to work: 27.6% less than 15 minutes, 34.6% 15 to 30 minutes, 21.7% 30 to 45 minutes, 8.0% 45 to 60 minutes, 8.1% 60 minutes or more (2000)

Additional Information Contacts

Oak Brook Area Association of Commerce 630-573-0616
Villa Park Chamber of Commerce 630-941-9133

WARRENVILLE (city). Covers a land area of 5.498 square miles and a water area of 0.119 square miles. Located at 41.82° N. Lat.; 88.18° W. Long. Elevation is 700 feet.
History: Warrenville was settled in the 1830's around a tannery and gristmill.
Population: 13,363 (2000); Race: 90.0% White, 2.2% Black, 3.9% Asian, 0.1% American Indian and Alaska Native, 9.5% Hispanic of any race, 0.8% two or more races (2000); Density: 2,430.6 persons per square mile (2000); Age: 28.7% under 18, 5.7% over 64 (2000); Marriage status: 26.3% never married, 60.4% now married, 2.6% widowed, 10.7% divorced (2000); Foreign born: 9.4% (2000); Ancestry (includes multiple ancestries): 27.3% German, 16.8% Irish, 16.1% Other groups, 10.1% English, 9.7% Italian (2000).

Vital Statistics: Birth rate: 144.4 per 10,000 population (1998)
Economy: Single-family building permits issued: 18 (2001) / 10 (2000); Multi-family building permits issued: 0 (2001) / 0 (2000); Employment by occupation: 15.1% management, 27.7% professional, 10.4% services, 28.1% sales, 0.0% farming, 9.4% construction, 9.2% production (2000).
Income: Per capita income: $28,922 (2000); Median household income: $62,430 (2000); Poverty rate: 1.6% (2000).
Taxes: Total city taxes per capita: $424 (2000); City property taxes per capita: $323 (2000).
Education: High school graduation rate: 92.8% (2000); College graduation rate: 39.8% (2000).
Housing: Homeownership rate: 82.8% (2000); Median home value: $148,900 (2000); Median rent: $934 per month (2000); Median age of housing: 22 years (2000).
Transportation: Commute to work: 88.8% car, 4.1% public transportation, 1.1% walk, 5.2% work from home (2000); Travel time to work: 24.8% less than 15 minutes, 35.9% 15 to 30 minutes, 20.7% 30 to 45 minutes, 8.0% 45 to 60 minutes, 10.6% 60 minutes or more (2000)
Additional Information Contacts
Warrenville Chamber of Commerce 630-393-9080

WEST CHICAGO (city). Covers a land area of 13.839 square miles and a water area of 0.004 square miles. Located at 41.88° N. Lat.; 88.21° W. Long. Elevation is 784 feet.
Population: 23,469 (2000); Race: 77.9% White, 2.0% Black, 2.3% Asian, 0.2% American Indian and Alaska Native, 47.9% Hispanic of any race, 2.7% two or more races (2000); Density: 1,695.9 persons per square mile (2000); Age: 31.5% under 18, 4.2% over 64 (2000); Marriage status: 29.7% never married, 61.8% now married, 2.8% widowed, 5.8% divorced (2000); Foreign born: 34.1% (2000); Ancestry (includes multiple ancestries): 45.3% Other groups, 17.2% German, 9.7% Irish, 6.4% Italian, 6.4% Polish (2000).
Vital Statistics: Birth rate: 245.9 per 10,000 population (1998)
Economy: Single-family building permits issued: 177 (2001) / 288 (2000); Multi-family building permits issued: 0 (2001) / 0 (2000); Employment by occupation: 11.3% management, 14.4% professional, 17.6% services, 23.3% sales, 0.5% farming, 10.5% construction, 22.5% production (2000).
Income: Per capita income: $19,287 (2000); Median household income: $63,424 (2000); Poverty rate: 9.3% (2000).
Taxes: Total city taxes per capita: $269 (2000); City property taxes per capita: $132 (2000).
Education: High school graduation rate: 67.0% (2000); College graduation rate: 21.9% (2000).

School District(s)

Benjamin School District 25 (PK-08)
2000 Enrollment: 1,096 630-231-3852
Community High School Districtrict 94 (09-12)
2000 Enrollment: 1,965 630-876-6200
West Chicago Elementary School District 33 (PK-08)
2000 Enrollment: 3,878 630-293-6000
Housing: Homeownership rate: 67.4% (2000); Median home value: $160,000 (2000); Median rent: $715 per month (2000); Median age of housing: 27 years (2000).
Newspapers: The West Chicago Press (1 x week)
Transportation: Commute to work: 89.7% car, 3.1% public transportation, 3.0% walk, 2.0% work from home (2000); Travel time to work: 30.0% less than 15 minutes, 37.8% 15 to 30 minutes, 17.0% 30 to 45 minutes, 7.1% 45 to 60 minutes, 8.1% 60 minutes or more (2000)
Airports: Dupage
Additional Information Contacts
West Chicago Chamber of Commerce. 630-231-3003

WESTMONT (village). Covers a land area of 4.897 square miles and a water area of 0.010 square miles. Located at 41.79° N. Lat.; 87.97° W. Long. Elevation is 755 feet.
Population: 24,554 (2000); Race: 78.2% White, 5.5% Black, 11.9% Asian, 0.1% American Indian and Alaska Native, 7.5% Hispanic of any race, 1.9% two or more races (2000); Density: 5,014.4 persons per square mile (2000); Age: 21.7% under 18, 15.9% over 64 (2000); Marriage status: 26.0% never married, 55.9% now married, 8.2% widowed, 9.9% divorced (2000); Foreign born: 19.7% (2000); Ancestry (includes multiple ancestries): 25.3% Other groups, 17.6% German, 15.3% Irish, 13.7% Polish, 8.7% Italian (2000).
Vital Statistics: Birth rate: 159.7 per 10,000 population (1998)
Economy: Single-family building permits issued: 53 (2001) / 57 (2000); Multi-family building permits issued: 24 (2001) / 2 (2000); Employment by occupation: 15.9% management, 22.4% professional, 13.7% services, 30.7% sales, 0.1% farming, 7.0% construction, 10.2% production (2000).
Income: Per capita income: $26,394 (2000); Median household income: $51,422 (2000); Poverty rate: 5.8% (2000).
Taxes: Total city taxes per capita: $316 (2000); City property taxes per capita: $158 (2000).
Education: High school graduation rate: 86.6% (2000); College graduation rate: 35.0% (2000).

School District(s)

Westmont C U School District 201 (PK-12)
2000 Enrollment: 1,714 630-969-7741
Housing: Homeownership rate: 54.7% (2000); Median home value: $180,200 (2000); Median rent: $711 per month (2000); Median age of housing: 26 years (2000).
Transportation: Commute to work: 86.2% car, 7.6% public transportation, 1.9% walk, 2.7% work from home (2000); Travel time to work: 24.8% less than 15 minutes, 31.6% 15 to 30 minutes, 21.2% 30 to 45 minutes, 9.9% 45 to 60 minutes, 12.6% 60 minutes or more (2000)
Additional Information Contacts
Westmont Chamber of Commerce 630-960-5553

WHEATON (city). Covers a land area of 11.221 square miles and a water area of 0.045 square miles. Located at 41.86° N. Lat.; 88.10° W. Long. Elevation is 753 feet.
History: Wheaton was settled in 1838 by Warren and Jesse Wheaton, who were instrumental in bringing to the town the railroad, a college, and the county courthouse. In 1853, Warren Wheaton donated the land for the Illinois Institute, which seven years later became Wheaton College. In 1867 the seat of DuPage County was moved from Naperville to Wheaton, and the courthouse was built on land donated by Warren Wheaton.
Population: 55,416 (2000); Race: 89.7% White, 2.5% Black, 4.9% Asian, 0.1% American Indian and Alaska Native, 3.9% Hispanic of any race, 1.2% two or more races (2000); Density: 4,938.5 persons per square mile (2000); Age: 26.2% under 18, 11.2% over 64 (2000); Marriage status: 26.9% never married, 61.3% now married, 4.9% widowed, 6.8% divorced (2000); Foreign born: 9.5% (2000); Ancestry (includes multiple ancestries): 28.1% German, 18.4% Irish, 12.9% English, 12.0% Other groups, 9.4% Italian (2000).
Vital Statistics: Birth rate: 133.9 per 10,000 population (1998)
Economy: Unemployment rate: 4.0% (11/2002); Total civilian labor force: 31,351 (11/2002); Single-family building permits issued: 45 (2001) / 57 (2000); Multi-family building permits issued: 0 (2001) / 0 (2000); Employment by occupation: 22.7% management, 31.1% professional, 8.8% services, 28.0% sales, 0.0% farming, 4.2% construction, 5.2% production (2000).
Income: Per capita income: $34,147 (2000); Median household income: $73,385 (2000); Poverty rate: 3.6% (2000).
Taxes: Total city taxes per capita: $255 (2000); City property taxes per capita: $171 (2000).
Education: High school graduation rate: 94.4% (2000); College graduation rate: 57.3% (2000).

School District(s)

Community Unit School District 200 (PK-12)
2000 Enrollment: 14,308 630-682-2000
Dupage Roe (07-12)
2000 Enrollment: 35 630-682-7150

Four-year College(s)

Wheaton College (Private, Not-for-profit, Undenominational)
2001 Enrollment: 2,844 630-752-5000
2001 Tuition: In-state $16,390; Out-of-state $16,390
Housing: Homeownership rate: 74.1% (2000); Median home value: $222,100 (2000); Median rent: $834 per month (2000); Median age of housing: 27 years (2000).
Hospitals: Marianjoy Rehabilitation Hospital (110 beds)
Transportation: Commute to work: 81.7% car, 8.5% public transportation, 4.2% walk, 4.5% work from home (2000); Travel time to work: 32.6% less than 15 minutes, 28.1% 15 to 30 minutes, 17.2% 30 to 45 minutes, 8.5% 45 to 60 minutes, 13.7% 60 minutes or more (2000)
Additional Information Contacts
Realtor Association West/South Suburban Chicagoland 630-653-1790
Wheaton Chamber of Commerce 630-668-6464

WILLOWBROOK (village). Covers a land area of 2.601 square miles and a water area of 0.025 square miles. Located at 41.76° N. Lat.; 87.94° W. Long. Elevation is 710 feet.
Population: 8,967 (2000); Race: 85.0% White, 2.2% Black, 9.1% Asian, 0.4% American Indian and Alaska Native, 5.6% Hispanic of any race, 1.8% two or more races (2000); Density: 3,447.8 persons per square mile (2000); Age: 18.2% under 18, 21.1% over 64 (2000); Marriage status: 27.3% never

married, 54.4% now married, 9.4% widowed, 8.8% divorced (2000); Foreign born: 16.8% (2000); Ancestry (includes multiple ancestries): 19.9% German, 17.5% Irish, 17.2% Other groups, 12.7% Italian, 11.4% Polish (2000).
Economy: Single-family building permits issued: 20 (2001) / 27 (2000); Multi-family building permits issued: 0 (2001) / 0 (2000); Employment by occupation: 20.1% management, 30.5% professional, 9.1% services, 28.8% sales, 0.0% farming, 3.8% construction, 7.7% production (2000).
Income: Per capita income: $37,715 (2000); Median household income: $56,725 (2000); Poverty rate: 2.0% (2000).
Taxes: Total city taxes per capita: $106 (1997); City property taxes per capita: $15 (1997).
Education: High school graduation rate: 92.3% (2000); College graduation rate: 44.0% (2000).
Housing: Homeownership rate: 78.7% (2000); Median home value: $245,800 (2000); Median rent: $890 per month (2000); Median age of housing: 22 years (2000).
Transportation: Commute to work: 88.0% car, 6.1% public transportation, 2.2% walk, 3.4% work from home (2000); Travel time to work: 18.8% less than 15 minutes, 29.7% 15 to 30 minutes, 26.7% 30 to 45 minutes, 13.0% 45 to 60 minutes, 11.8% 60 minutes or more (2000)

WINFIELD (village). Covers a land area of 2.700 square miles and a water area of 0.006 square miles. Located at 41.87° N. Lat.; 88.15° W. Long. Elevation is 720 feet.
Population: 8,718 (2000); Race: 92.0% White, 1.5% Black, 3.7% Asian, 0.5% American Indian and Alaska Native, 2.9% Hispanic of any race, 1.2% two or more races (2000); Density: 3,228.3 persons per square mile (2000); Age: 31.2% under 18, 7.2% over 64 (2000); Marriage status: 18.8% never married, 71.4% now married, 3.7% widowed, 6.1% divorced (2000); Foreign born: 6.3% (2000); Ancestry (includes multiple ancestries): 28.5% German, 18.4% Irish, 13.7% English, 12.7% Italian, 11.7% Polish (2000).
Economy: Single-family building permits issued: 87 (2001) / 84 (2000); Multi-family building permits issued: 0 (2001) / 0 (2000); Employment by occupation: 22.8% management, 26.7% professional, 7.6% services, 28.1% sales, 0.0% farming, 7.4% construction, 7.4% production (2000).
Income: Per capita income: $35,482 (2000); Median household income: $89,060 (2000); Poverty rate: 3.0% (2000).
Taxes: Total city taxes per capita: $255 (1997); City property taxes per capita: $142 (1997).
Education: High school graduation rate: 91.6% (2000); College graduation rate: 45.9% (2000).

School District(s)

Winfield School District 34 (PK-08)
2000 Enrollment: 449 630-260-2380
Housing: Homeownership rate: 96.2% (2000); Median home value: $210,400 (2000); Median rent: $837 per month (2000); Median age of housing: 17 years (2000).
Hospitals: Behavioral Health Service (52 beds)
Transportation: Commute to work: 84.7% car, 10.8% public transportation, 0.5% walk, 3.5% work from home (2000); Travel time to work: 23.7% less than 15 minutes, 27.8% 15 to 30 minutes, 21.2% 30 to 45 minutes, 11.7% 45 to 60 minutes, 15.7% 60 minutes or more (2000)
Additional Information Contacts
Winfield Chamber of Commerce 630-682-3712

WOOD DALE (city). Covers a land area of 4.671 square miles and a water area of 0 square miles. Located at 41.96° N. Lat.; 87.97° W. Long. Elevation is 696 feet.
Population: 13,535 (2000); Race: 88.1% White, 0.4% Black, 3.5% Asian, 0.3% American Indian and Alaska Native, 14.1% Hispanic of any race, 2.1% two or more races (2000); Density: 2,897.8 persons per square mile (2000); Age: 22.5% under 18, 14.7% over 64 (2000); Marriage status: 23.6% never married, 60.3% now married, 7.8% widowed, 8.4% divorced (2000); Foreign born: 21.2% (2000); Ancestry (includes multiple ancestries): 20.6% Polish, 19.3% German, 18.8% Italian, 18.5% Other groups, 12.0% Irish (2000).
Vital Statistics: Birth rate: 113.8 per 10,000 population (1998)
Economy: Single-family building permits issued: 16 (2001) / 18 (2000); Multi-family building permits issued: 0 (2001) / 0 (2000); Employment by occupation: 16.4% management, 17.3% professional, 10.2% services, 28.7% sales, 0.1% farming, 10.4% construction, 16.9% production (2000).
Income: Per capita income: $25,507 (2000); Median household income: $57,509 (2000); Poverty rate: 4.1% (2000).
Taxes: Total city taxes per capita: $395 (1997); City property taxes per capita: $223 (1997).
Education: High school graduation rate: 82.9% (2000); College graduation rate: 19.6% (2000).

School District(s)

Wood Dale School District 7 (PK-08)
2000 Enrollment: 1,174 630-595-9510
Housing: Homeownership rate: 84.9% (2000); Median home value: $171,800 (2000); Median rent: $801 per month (2000); Median age of housing: 28 years (2000).
Transportation: Commute to work: 92.4% car, 3.3% public transportation, 1.4% walk, 2.4% work from home (2000); Travel time to work: 24.7% less than 15 minutes, 39.1% 15 to 30 minutes, 20.9% 30 to 45 minutes, 7.3% 45 to 60 minutes, 8.1% 60 minutes or more (2000)
Additional Information Contacts
Wood Dale Chamber of Commerce 630-595-0505

WOODRIDGE (village). Covers a land area of 8.323 square miles and a water area of 0.023 square miles. Located at 41.74° N. Lat.; 88.04° W. Long. Elevation is 750 feet.
Population: 30,934 (2000); Race: 75.5% White, 8.2% Black, 11.3% Asian, 0.4% American Indian and Alaska Native, 8.9% Hispanic of any race, 1.7% two or more races (2000); Density: 3,716.7 persons per square mile (2000); Age: 26.7% under 18, 5.8% over 64 (2000); Marriage status: 28.2% never married, 59.3% now married, 3.6% widowed, 8.8% divorced (2000); Foreign born: 17.3% (2000); Ancestry (includes multiple ancestries): 27.4% Other groups, 21.6% German, 17.4% Irish, 12.0% Polish, 10.0% Italian (2000).
Vital Statistics: Birth rate: 148.4 per 10,000 population (1998)
Economy: Unemployment rate: 5.2% (11/2002); Total civilian labor force: 18,653 (11/2002); Single-family building permits issued: 134 (2001) / 164 (2000); Multi-family building permits issued: 800 (2001) / 0 (2000); Employment by occupation: 18.4% management, 24.8% professional, 10.3% services, 29.6% sales, 0.0% farming, 6.9% construction, 10.0% production (2000).
Income: Per capita income: $27,851 (2000); Median household income: $61,944 (2000); Poverty rate: 3.8% (2000).
Taxes: Total city taxes per capita: $181 (1997); City property taxes per capita: $80 (1997).
Education: High school graduation rate: 90.0% (2000); College graduation rate: 39.0% (2000).

School District(s)

Woodridge School District 68 (PK-08)
2000 Enrollment: 3,276 630-985-7925
Housing: Homeownership rate: 67.2% (2000); Median home value: $168,400 (2000); Median rent: $719 per month (2000); Median age of housing: 24 years (2000).
Transportation: Commute to work: 88.2% car, 7.0% public transportation, 1.4% walk, 2.7% work from home (2000); Travel time to work: 18.5% less than 15 minutes, 35.2% 15 to 30 minutes, 23.1% 30 to 45 minutes, 10.1% 45 to 60 minutes, 13.0% 60 minutes or more (2000)
Additional Information Contacts
Woodridge Area Chamber of Commerce 630-852-9878

Edgar County

Located in eastern Illinois; bounded on the east by Indiana; drained by tributaries of the Wabash River. Covers a land area of 623.60 square miles, a water area of 0.60 square miles, and is located in the Central Time Zone. The county government was organized in 1823. County seat is Paris.

Weather Station: Paris Waterworks — Elevation: 679 feet

	Jan	Feb	Mar	Apr	May	Jun	Jul	Aug	Sep	Oct	Nov	Dec
High	34	40	51	64	75	83	86	84	79	66	52	40
Low	18	23	33	43	53	62	66	64	57	45	35	24
Precip	2.2	2.2	3.3	4.1	4.2	4.1	4.4	4.4	3.0	2.8	3.6	3.1
Snow	10.4	6.6	3.6	0.3	0.0	0.0	0.0	0.0	0.0	0.1	1.3	5.9

High and Low temperatures in degrees Fahrenheit; Precipitation and Snow in inches

Population: 19,704 (2000); Race: 97.6% White, 1.3% Black, 0.1% Asian, 0.3% American Indian and Alaska Native, 0.7% Hispanic of any race, 0.6% two or more races (2000); Density: 31.6 persons per square mile (2000); Age: 23.8% under 18, 17.8% over 64 (2000).
Religion: Five largest groups: 15.0% Christian Churches and Churches of Christ, 10.9% The United Methodist Church, 7.1% Catholic Church, 4.3% Christian Church (Disciples of Christ), 2.7% New Testament Association of Independent Baptist Churches and
Economy: Unemployment rate: 6.0% (11/2002); Total civilian labor force: 10,534 (11/2002); Leading industries: 34.3% manufacturing; 14.4% health care and social assistance; 14.2% retail trade (2000); Companies that employ more than 1,000 persons: 0 (2000); Companies that employ more than 100

persons: 11 (2000); Farms: 766 totaling 352,401 acres (1997); Minority business ownership rate: 0.0% (1997); Women business ownership rate: 21.1% (1997); Retail sales per capita: $5,451 (1997). Single-family building permits issued: 14 (2001) / 22 (2000); Multi-family building permits issued: 7 (2001) / 46 (2000).
Income: Per capita income: $17,857 (2000); Median household income: $35,203 (2000); Poverty rate: 10.5% (2000); Bankruptcy rate: 6.66% (2001).
Taxes: Total county taxes per capita: $98 (1997); County property taxes per capita: $95 (1997).
Education: High school graduation rate: 81.4% (2000); College graduation rate: 13.3% (2000).
Housing: Homeownership rate: 74.6% (2000); Median home value: $54,300 (2000); Median rent: $282 per month (2000); Median age of housing: 49 years (2000).
Health: Birth rate: 111.7 per 10,000 population (1998); Age adjusted death rate: 95.4 per 10,000 population (1999); Age adjusted cancer mortality rate: 212.8 deaths per 100,000 population (1999). Number of physicians: 5.1 per 10,000 population (1999); Number of hospital beds: 22.8 per 10,000 population (1999).
Elections: 2000 Presidential election results: 39.1% Gore, 58.7% Bush, 1.4% Nader, 0.6% Buchanan
Additional Information Contacts
Edgar County Government Offices 217-466-7433
Paris Chamber of Commerce 217-465-4179

Edgar County Communities

BROCTON (village). Covers a land area of 0.579 square miles and a water area of 0 square miles. Located at 39.71° N. Lat.; 87.93° W. Long. Elevation is 669 feet.
Population: 322 (2000); Race: 99.4% White, 0.0% Black, 0.0% Asian, 0.0% American Indian and Alaska Native, 0.6% Hispanic of any race, 0.6% two or more races (2000); Density: 556.5 persons per square mile (2000); Age: 27.2% under 18, 11.5% over 64 (2000); Marriage status: 14.3% never married, 57.9% now married, 10.0% widowed, 17.8% divorced (2000); Foreign born: 0.0% (2000); Ancestry (includes multiple ancestries): 25.4% United States or American, 11.5% German, 6.5% Other groups, 6.2% Irish, 3.8% English (2000).
Economy: Agriculture: corn, soybeans, sorghum; cattle, hogs. Single-family building permits issued: 0 (2001) / 0 (2000); Multi-family building permits issued: 0 (2001) / 0 (2000); Employment by occupation: 5.4% management, 4.0% professional, 12.8% services, 20.1% sales, 3.4% farming, 4.7% construction, 49.7% production (2000).
Income: Per capita income: $20,960 (2000); Median household income: $30,250 (2000); Poverty rate: 16.5% (2000).
Taxes: Total city taxes per capita: $16 (1997); City property taxes per capita: $13 (1997).
Education: High school graduation rate: 74.2% (2000); College graduation rate: 5.2% (2000).
Housing: Homeownership rate: 78.2% (2000); Median home value: $29,600 (2000); Median rent: $208 per month (2000); Median age of housing: 60+ years (2000).
Transportation: Commute to work: 93.2% car, 0.0% public transportation, 4.8% walk, 0.0% work from home (2000); Travel time to work: 12.3% less than 15 minutes, 37.0% 15 to 30 minutes, 26.7% 30 to 45 minutes, 11.0% 45 to 60 minutes, 13.0% 60 minutes or more (2000)

CHRISMAN (city). Covers a land area of 0.732 square miles and a water area of 0 square miles. Located at 39.80° N. Lat.; 87.67° W. Long. Elevation is 645 feet.
History: Chrisman was platted in 1872 by Matthias Chrisman, and grew as a trading center and shipping point.
Population: 1,318 (2000); Race: 99.1% White, 0.0% Black, 0.0% Asian, 0.1% American Indian and Alaska Native, 0.0% Hispanic of any race, 0.8% two or more races (2000); Density: 1,801.6 persons per square mile (2000); Age: 21.1% under 18, 27.5% over 64 (2000); Marriage status: 19.1% never married, 54.7% now married, 17.5% widowed, 8.7% divorced (2000); Foreign born: 0.6% (2000); Ancestry (includes multiple ancestries): 26.3% United States or American, 16.3% German, 12.1% English, 11.1% Irish, 4.4% Other groups (2000).
Economy: Single-family building permits issued: 2 (2001) / 0 (2000); Multi-family building permits issued: 7 (2001) / 0 (2000); Employment by occupation: 10.2% management, 17.6% professional, 20.8% services, 21.3% sales, 3.7% farming, 5.7% construction, 20.7% production (2000).
Income: Per capita income: $16,651 (2000); Median household income: $33,167 (2000); Poverty rate: 10.7% (2000).
Taxes: Total city taxes per capita: $30 (1997); City property taxes per capita: $30 (1997).
Education: High school graduation rate: 80.8% (2000); College graduation rate: 14.5% (2000).
School District(s)
Edgar County C U District 6 (KG-12)
2000 Enrollment: 412 217-269-2513
Housing: Homeownership rate: 72.3% (2000); Median home value: $55,500 (2000); Median rent: $247 per month (2000); Median age of housing: 48 years (2000).
Newspapers: Chrisman Leader (1 x week)
Transportation: Commute to work: 93.8% car, 0.5% public transportation, 1.8% walk, 3.3% work from home (2000); Travel time to work: 32.3% less than 15 minutes, 29.7% 15 to 30 minutes, 25.0% 30 to 45 minutes, 8.4% 45 to 60 minutes, 4.5% 60 minutes or more (2000)

HUME (village). Covers a land area of 0.514 square miles and a water area of 0 square miles. Located at 39.79° N. Lat.; 87.86° W. Long. Elevation is 653 feet.
Population: 382 (2000); Race: 99.3% White, 0.0% Black, 0.0% Asian, 0.0% American Indian and Alaska Native, 0.7% Hispanic of any race, 0.5% two or more races (2000); Density: 743.1 persons per square mile (2000); Age: 22.2% under 18, 24.9% over 64 (2000); Marriage status: 16.4% never married, 58.4% now married, 12.8% widowed, 12.5% divorced (2000); Foreign born: 0.0% (2000); Ancestry (includes multiple ancestries): 19.5% United States or American, 17.2% German, 12.3% Irish, 9.4% English, 5.4% Other groups (2000).
Economy: In agricultural area; ships grain. Employment by occupation: 6.1% management, 12.2% professional, 14.9% services, 31.5% sales, 2.8% farming, 10.5% construction, 22.1% production (2000).
Income: Per capita income: $14,970 (2000); Median household income: $27,404 (2000); Poverty rate: 10.9% (2000).
Taxes: Total city taxes per capita: $15 (1997); City property taxes per capita: $10 (1997).
Education: High school graduation rate: 81.9% (2000); College graduation rate: 9.4% (2000).
School District(s)
Shiloh Community Unit School District 1 (PK-12)
2000 Enrollment: 547 217-887-2364
Housing: Homeownership rate: 81.9% (2000); Median home value: $40,400 (2000); Median rent: $220 per month (2000); Median age of housing: 52 years (2000).
Transportation: Commute to work: 96.7% car, 0.0% public transportation, 1.7% walk, 1.7% work from home (2000); Travel time to work: 21.3% less than 15 minutes, 24.7% 15 to 30 minutes, 25.3% 30 to 45 minutes, 14.0% 45 to 60 minutes, 14.6% 60 minutes or more (2000)

KANSAS (village). Covers a land area of 1.028 square miles and a water area of 0 square miles. Located at 39.55° N. Lat.; 87.93° W. Long. Elevation is 710 feet.
Population: 842 (2000); Race: 97.9% White, 0.0% Black, 0.0% Asian, 1.1% American Indian and Alaska Native, 0.7% Hispanic of any race, 0.8% two or more races (2000); Density: 818.9 persons per square mile (2000); Age: 28.3% under 18, 16.7% over 64 (2000); Marriage status: 19.8% never married, 61.0% now married, 8.6% widowed, 10.7% divorced (2000); Foreign born: 1.4% (2000); Ancestry (includes multiple ancestries): 21.1% German, 19.7% United States or American, 10.7% Irish, 9.4% Other groups, 9.2% English (2000).
Economy: Livestock, grain. Employment by occupation: 10.6% management, 10.3% professional, 15.7% services, 21.5% sales, 2.7% farming, 11.5% construction, 27.8% production (2000).
Income: Per capita income: $14,590 (2000); Median household income: $27,688 (2000); Poverty rate: 15.4% (2000).
Taxes: Total city taxes per capita: $27 (1997); City property taxes per capita: $2 (1997).
Education: High school graduation rate: 87.4% (2000); College graduation rate: 13.3% (2000).
School District(s)
Kansas Community Unit School District 3 (PK-12)
2000 Enrollment: 299 217-948-5174
Housing: Homeownership rate: 72.5% (2000); Median home value: $49,300 (2000); Median rent: $256 per month (2000); Median age of housing: 49 years (2000).

Transportation: Commute to work: 92.1% car, 0.6% public transportation, 2.4% walk, 3.3% work from home (2000); Travel time to work: 28.5% less than 15 minutes, 41.4% 15 to 30 minutes, 21.9% 30 to 45 minutes, 3.4% 45 to 60 minutes, 4.7% 60 minutes or more (2000)

METCALF (village). Covers a land area of 0.552 square miles and a water area of 0 square miles. Located at 39.80° N. Lat.; 87.80° W. Long. Elevation is 668 feet.
Population: 213 (2000); Race: 99.0% White, 0.0% Black, 0.0% Asian, 0.0% American Indian and Alaska Native, 0.0% Hispanic of any race, 1.0% two or more races (2000); Density: 385.8 persons per square mile (2000); Age: 20.1% under 18, 11.9% over 64 (2000); Marriage status: 24.7% never married, 56.0% now married, 9.0% widowed, 10.2% divorced (2000); Foreign born: 0.0% (2000); Ancestry (includes multiple ancestries): 33.0% United States or American, 10.8% English, 9.8% Other groups, 9.3% German, 6.2% Irish (2000).
Economy: In agricultural area. Employment by occupation: 8.7% management, 9.8% professional, 18.5% services, 20.7% sales, 8.7% farming, 9.8% construction, 23.9% production (2000).
Income: Per capita income: $15,568 (2000); Median household income: $29,861 (2000); Poverty rate: 15.5% (2000).
Taxes: Total city taxes per capita: $13 (1997); City property taxes per capita: $9 (1997).
Education: High school graduation rate: 65.4% (2000); College graduation rate: 3.1% (2000).
Housing: Homeownership rate: 79.7% (2000); Median home value: $15,200 (2000); Median rent: $245 per month (2000); Median age of housing: 57 years (2000).
Transportation: Commute to work: 97.8% car, 0.0% public transportation, 0.0% walk, 2.2% work from home (2000); Travel time to work: 26.1% less than 15 minutes, 23.9% 15 to 30 minutes, 12.5% 30 to 45 minutes, 22.7% 45 to 60 minutes, 14.8% 60 minutes or more (2000)

PARIS (city). Covers a land area of 4.815 square miles and a water area of 0.396 square miles. Located at 39.61° N. Lat.; 87.69° W. Long. Elevation is 726 feet.
History: Paris was the site of several speeches by Abraham Lincoln. The town was platted in 1853 and grew as the seat of Edgar County.
Population: 9,077 (2000); Race: 98.6% White, 0.1% Black, 0.1% Asian, 0.3% American Indian and Alaska Native, 0.6% Hispanic of any race, 0.8% two or more races (2000); Density: 1,885.3 persons per square mile (2000); Age: 23.7% under 18, 19.7% over 64 (2000); Marriage status: 19.0% never married, 56.4% now married, 11.9% widowed, 12.8% divorced (2000); Foreign born: 0.7% (2000); Ancestry (includes multiple ancestries): 21.6% United States or American, 16.9% German, 12.5% Irish, 10.2% English, 6.9% Other groups (2000).
Economy: Single-family building permits issued: 12 (2001) / 22 (2000); Multi-family building permits issued: 0 (2001) / 46 (2000); Employment by occupation: 7.5% management, 14.7% professional, 16.3% services, 19.4% sales, 0.4% farming, 8.2% construction, 33.5% production (2000).
Income: Per capita income: $17,750 (2000); Median household income: $30,902 (2000); Poverty rate: 12.7% (2000).
Taxes: Total city taxes per capita: $135 (1997); City property taxes per capita: $74 (1997).
Education: High school graduation rate: 79.5% (2000); College graduation rate: 11.1% (2000).

School District(s)

Paris Community Unit School District 4 (PK-08)
2000 Enrollment: 607 217-465-5391
Paris-Union School District 95 (PK-12)
2000 Enrollment: 1,775 217-465-8448

Housing: Homeownership rate: 70.0% (2000); Median home value: $50,900 (2000); Median rent: $290 per month (2000); Median age of housing: 51 years (2000).
Hospitals: Paris Community Hospital (49 beds)
Newspapers: The Paris Daily Beacon News (6 x week)
Transportation: Commute to work: 95.3% car, 0.0% public transportation, 2.1% walk, 1.9% work from home (2000); Travel time to work: 66.8% less than 15 minutes, 12.4% 15 to 30 minutes, 11.3% 30 to 45 minutes, 4.2% 45 to 60 minutes, 5.3% 60 minutes or more (2000)
Additional Information Contacts
Paris Chamber of Commerce 217-465-4179

REDMON (village). Covers a land area of 0.148 square miles and a water area of 0 square miles. Located at 39.64° N. Lat.; 87.86° W. Long. Elevation is 690 feet.
Population: 199 (2000); Race: 100.0% White, 0.0% Black, 0.0% Asian, 0.0% American Indian and Alaska Native, 0.0% Hispanic of any race, 0.0% two or more races (2000); Density: 1,346.8 persons per square mile (2000); Age: 17.1% under 18, 14.4% over 64 (2000); Marriage status: 19.5% never married, 57.9% now married, 6.1% widowed, 16.5% divorced (2000); Foreign born: 0.0% (2000); Ancestry (includes multiple ancestries): 12.3% United States or American, 10.2% German, 8.6% Other groups, 8.0% English, 4.3% Irish (2000).
Economy: In agricultural area. Employment by occupation: 4.0% management, 18.2% professional, 9.1% services, 21.2% sales, 2.0% farming, 5.1% construction, 40.4% production (2000).
Income: Per capita income: $17,020 (2000); Median household income: $29,375 (2000); Poverty rate: 19.4% (2000).
Taxes: Total city taxes per capita: $5 (1997); City property taxes per capita: $5 (1997).
Education: High school graduation rate: 80.8% (2000); College graduation rate: 8.9% (2000).
Housing: Homeownership rate: 72.0% (2000); Median home value: $46,100 (2000); Median rent: $305 per month (2000); Median age of housing: 58 years (2000).
Transportation: Commute to work: 96.0% car, 2.0% public transportation, 0.0% walk, 2.0% work from home (2000); Travel time to work: 17.5% less than 15 minutes, 48.5% 15 to 30 minutes, 15.5% 30 to 45 minutes, 14.4% 45 to 60 minutes, 4.1% 60 minutes or more (2000)

VERMILION (village). Covers a land area of 0.762 square miles and a water area of 0 square miles. Located at 39.58° N. Lat.; 87.58° W. Long. Elevation is 675 feet.
History: Formerly Vermillion.
Population: 239 (2000); Race: 100.0% White, 0.0% Black, 0.0% Asian, 0.0% American Indian and Alaska Native, 0.0% Hispanic of any race, 0.0% two or more races (2000); Density: 313.6 persons per square mile (2000); Age: 33.3% under 18, 7.4% over 64 (2000); Marriage status: 22.0% never married, 57.8% now married, 7.5% widowed, 12.7% divorced (2000); Foreign born: 0.0% (2000); Ancestry (includes multiple ancestries): 30.9% United States or American, 14.4% German, 11.1% English, 6.2% Other groups, 3.7% Scottish (2000).
Economy: In agricultural area. Single-family building permits issued: 0 (2001) / 0 (2000); Multi-family building permits issued: 0 (2001) / 0 (2000); Employment by occupation: 1.8% management, 10.0% professional, 8.2% services, 22.7% sales, 0.0% farming, 12.7% construction, 44.5% production (2000).
Income: Per capita income: $13,157 (2000); Median household income: $33,750 (2000); Poverty rate: 17.3% (2000).
Taxes: Total city taxes per capita: $7 (1997); City property taxes per capita: $7 (1997).
Education: High school graduation rate: 79.3% (2000); College graduation rate: 8.6% (2000).
Housing: Homeownership rate: 71.0% (2000); Median home value: $37,500 (2000); Median rent: $317 per month (2000); Median age of housing: 59 years (2000).
Transportation: Commute to work: 96.4% car, 0.0% public transportation, 0.9% walk, 2.7% work from home (2000); Travel time to work: 14.0% less than 15 minutes, 64.5% 15 to 30 minutes, 11.2% 30 to 45 minutes, 4.7% 45 to 60 minutes, 5.6% 60 minutes or more (2000)

Edwards County

Located in southeastern Illinois; drained by the Little Wabash River. Covers a land area of 222.30 square miles, a water area of 0.30 square miles, and is located in the Central Time Zone. The county government was organized in 1814. County seat is Albion.

Weather Station: Albion Elevation: 528 feet

	Jan	Feb	Mar	Apr	May	Jun	Jul	Aug	Sep	Oct	Nov	Dec
High	39	45	56	67	77	86	90	88	82	71	55	44
Low	23	27	36	45	55	64	68	66	59	47	37	27
Precip	2.6	2.8	4.2	5.3	4.7	4.2	3.8	3.1	3.0	3.5	4.3	3.3
Snow	2.7	2.7	2.0	0.1	0.0	0.0	0.0	0.0	0.0	0.1	0.2	2.5

High and Low temperatures in degrees Fahrenheit; Precipitation and Snow in inches

Population: 6,971 (2000); Race: 98.4% White, 0.1% Black, 0.6% Asian, 0.2% American Indian and Alaska Native, 0.2% Hispanic of any race, 0.5% two or more races (2000); Density: 31.4 persons per square mile (2000); Age: 23.1% under 18, 18.5% over 64 (2000).

Religion: Five largest groups: 23.2% Christian Churches and Churches of Christ, 14.4% Southern Baptist Convention, 14.1% The United Methodist Church, 9.6% Independent, Non-Charismatic Churches, 4.4% Christian Church (Disciples of Christ) (2000).
Economy: Unemployment rate: 5.0% (11/2002); Total civilian labor force: 3,473 (11/2002); Leading industries: 6.5% wholesale trade; 5.3% retail trade; 2.1% construction (2000); Companies that employ more than 1,000 persons: 1 (2000); Companies that employ more than 100 persons: 2 (2000); Farms: 329 totaling 112,917 acres (1997); Minority business ownership rate: 0.0% (1997); Women business ownership rate: 24.0% (1997); Retail sales per capita: $4,038 (1997). Single-family building permits issued: -1 (2001) / -1 (2000); Multi-family building permits issued: -1 (2001) / -1 (2000).
Income: Per capita income: $16,187 (2000); Median household income: $31,816 (2000); Poverty rate: 9.8% (2000); Bankruptcy rate: 3.33% (2001).
Taxes: Total county taxes per capita: $61 (1997); County property taxes per capita: $61 (1997).
Education: High school graduation rate: 82.3% (2000); College graduation rate: 9.8% (2000).
Housing: Homeownership rate: 81.2% (2000); Median home value: $46,700 (2000); Median rent: $210 per month (2000); Median age of housing: 40 years (2000).
Health: Birth rate: 99.0 per 10,000 population (1998); Age adjusted death rate: 80.5 per 10,000 population (1999); Age adjusted cancer mortality rate: 206.2 deaths per 100,000 population (1999). Number of physicians: n/a (1999); Number of hospital beds: n/a (1999).
Elections: 2000 Presidential election results: 30.0% Gore, 67.9% Bush, 1.3% Nader, 0.8% Buchanan

Additional Information Contacts

Edwards County Government Offices 618-445-2115
Albion Chamber of Commerce 618-445-2303

Edwards County Communities

ALBION (city). Covers a land area of 2.139 square miles and a water area of 0.049 square miles. Located at 38.37° N. Lat.; 88.06° W. Long. Elevation is 478 feet.
History: In 1818 Morris Birkbeck and George Flower came from England to find a place that would provide a better life for the English working class. They settled on this section of prairie and led many English colonists here, who named the town Albion, remembering their former homeland.
Population: 1,933 (2000); Race: 98.0% White, 0.3% Black, 0.3% Asian, 0.3% American Indian and Alaska Native, 0.4% Hispanic of any race, 0.4% two or more races (2000); Density: 903.8 persons per square mile (2000); Age: 22.4% under 18, 23.7% over 64 (2000); Marriage status: 15.6% never married, 61.0% now married, 11.9% widowed, 11.5% divorced (2000); Foreign born: 0.5% (2000); Ancestry (includes multiple ancestries): 25.0% English, 23.5% United States or American, 18.5% German, 9.0% Irish, 4.8% Other groups (2000).
Economy: Employment by occupation: 5.6% management, 13.0% professional, 13.8% services, 23.9% sales, 0.2% farming, 10.5% construction, 32.9% production (2000).
Income: Per capita income: $14,747 (2000); Median household income: $29,476 (2000); Poverty rate: 12.2% (2000).
Taxes: Total city taxes per capita: $67 (1997); City property taxes per capita: $63 (1997).
Education: High school graduation rate: 78.8% (2000); College graduation rate: 9.3% (2000).

School District(s)

Edwards County C U School District 1 (PK-12)
2000 Enrollment: 1,038 618-445-2814

Housing: Homeownership rate: 74.5% (2000); Median home value: $46,000 (2000); Median rent: $210 per month (2000); Median age of housing: 42 years (2000).
Newspapers: The Prairie Post (1 x week); Navigator & Journal-Register (1 x week)
Transportation: Commute to work: 89.9% car, 0.0% public transportation, 5.2% walk, 4.7% work from home (2000); Travel time to work: 54.7% less than 15 minutes, 18.3% 15 to 30 minutes, 11.5% 30 to 45 minutes, 7.1% 45 to 60 minutes, 8.4% 60 minutes or more (2000)

Additional Information Contacts

Albion Chamber of Commerce 618-445-2303

BONE GAP (village). Covers a land area of 0.604 square miles and a water area of 0 square miles. Located at 38.44° N. Lat.; 87.99° W. Long. Elevation is 462 feet.
Population: 272 (2000); Race: 98.5% White, 0.8% Black, 0.0% Asian, 0.0% American Indian and Alaska Native, 0.0% Hispanic of any race, 0.8% two or more races (2000); Density: 450.5 persons per square mile (2000); Age: 23.6% under 18, 15.1% over 64 (2000); Marriage status: 24.8% never married, 57.5% now married, 8.9% widowed, 8.9% divorced (2000); Foreign born: 0.0% (2000); Ancestry (includes multiple ancestries): 23.9% German, 17.8% English, 13.1% United States or American, 8.5% Other groups, 4.6% Polish (2000).
Economy: In agricultural area. Employment by occupation: 13.1% management, 1.9% professional, 15.0% services, 26.2% sales, 0.9% farming, 8.4% construction, 34.6% production (2000).
Income: Per capita income: $10,804 (2000); Median household income: $27,813 (2000); Poverty rate: 25.1% (2000).
Taxes: Total city taxes per capita: $42 (1997); City property taxes per capita: $42 (1997).
Education: High school graduation rate: 82.9% (2000); College graduation rate: 4.1% (2000).
Housing: Homeownership rate: 79.8% (2000); Median home value: $30,700 (2000); Median rent: $235 per month (2000); Median age of housing: 38 years (2000).
Transportation: Commute to work: 90.3% car, 0.0% public transportation, 1.9% walk, 7.8% work from home (2000); Travel time to work: 26.3% less than 15 minutes, 41.1% 15 to 30 minutes, 7.4% 30 to 45 minutes, 11.6% 45 to 60 minutes, 13.7% 60 minutes or more (2000)

BROWNS (village). Covers a land area of 0.292 square miles and a water area of 0 square miles. Located at 38.37° N. Lat.; 87.98° W. Long. Elevation is 400 feet.
Population: 175 (2000); Race: 99.4% White, 0.0% Black, 0.6% Asian, 0.0% American Indian and Alaska Native, 0.0% Hispanic of any race, 0.0% two or more races (2000); Density: 599.5 persons per square mile (2000); Age: 26.8% under 18, 8.3% over 64 (2000); Marriage status: 24.2% never married, 64.4% now married, 5.3% widowed, 6.1% divorced (2000); Foreign born: 0.6% (2000); Ancestry (includes multiple ancestries): 23.2% English, 19.0% German, 13.7% French (except Basque), 11.3% Irish, 7.7% United States or American (2000).
Economy: Railroad junction. Agriculture: oil. Employment by occupation: 0.0% management, 5.5% professional, 21.9% services, 30.1% sales, 1.4% farming, 2.7% construction, 38.4% production (2000).
Income: Per capita income: $10,922 (2000); Median household income: $23,214 (2000); Poverty rate: 6.5% (2000).
Taxes: Total city taxes per capita: $54 (1997); City property taxes per capita: $40 (1997).
Education: High school graduation rate: 75.0% (2000); College graduation rate: 5.6% (2000).
Housing: Homeownership rate: 96.9% (2000); Median home value: $18,300 (2000); Median rent: $175 per month (2000); Median age of housing: 57 years (2000).
Transportation: Commute to work: 98.6% car, 0.0% public transportation, 1.4% walk, 0.0% work from home (2000); Travel time to work: 56.2% less than 15 minutes, 15.1% 15 to 30 minutes, 11.0% 30 to 45 minutes, 9.6% 45 to 60 minutes, 8.2% 60 minutes or more (2000)

ELLERY (unincorporated postal area, zip code 62833). Covers a land area of 49.474 square miles and a water area of 0.244 square miles. Located at 38.36° N. Lat.; 88.16° W. Long.
Population: 376 (2000); Race: 96.5% White, 0.0% Black, 0.0% Asian, 1.9% American Indian and Alaska Native, 0.0% Hispanic of any race, 1.6% two or more races (2000); Density: 7.6 persons per square mile (2000); Age: 22.1% under 18, 17.1% over 64 (2000); Marriage status: 13.7% never married, 76.3% now married, 3.0% widowed, 7.0% divorced (2000); Foreign born: 0.0% (2000); Ancestry (includes multiple ancestries): 32.8% English, 16.8% United States or American, 10.4% German, 8.0% Irish, 6.4% Other groups (2000).
Economy: Employment by occupation: 18.1% management, 4.8% professional, 22.9% services, 24.1% sales, 2.4% farming, 4.8% construction, 22.9% production (2000).
Income: Per capita income: $12,419 (2000); Median household income: $32,885 (2000); Poverty rate: 7.5% (2000).
Education: High school graduation rate: 75.1% (2000); College graduation rate: 7.1% (2000).
Housing: Homeownership rate: 91.7% (2000); Median home value: $54,700 (2000); Median rent: <$100 per month (2000); Median age of housing: 41 years (2000).
Transportation: Commute to work: 92.8% car, 0.0% public transportation, 6.0% walk, 1.2% work from home (2000); Travel time to work: 32.3% less

than 15 minutes, 46.3% 15 to 30 minutes, 9.8% 30 to 45 minutes, 5.5% 45 to 60 minutes, 6.1% 60 minutes or more (2000)

WEST SALEM (village). Covers a land area of 1.559 square miles and a water area of <.001 square miles. Located at 38.52° N. Lat.; 88.00° W. Long. Elevation is 530 feet.
History: West Salem was settled in 1838 by German Moravians from North Carolina.
Population: 1,001 (2000); Race: 99.4% White, 0.0% Black, 0.0% Asian, 0.1% American Indian and Alaska Native, 0.0% Hispanic of any race, 0.5% two or more races (2000); Density: 642.2 persons per square mile (2000); Age: 23.8% under 18, 23.8% over 64 (2000); Marriage status: 16.1% never married, 63.2% now married, 7.3% widowed, 13.4% divorced (2000); Foreign born: 0.4% (2000); Ancestry (includes multiple ancestries): 23.7% German, 15.1% English, 14.9% United States or American, 8.7% Irish, 6.1% Other groups (2000).
Economy: Employment by occupation: 5.0% management, 12.3% professional, 9.5% services, 19.9% sales, 0.4% farming, 9.5% construction, 43.3% production (2000).
Income: Per capita income: $15,179 (2000); Median household income: $27,031 (2000); Poverty rate: 11.2% (2000).
Taxes: Total city taxes per capita: $84 (1997); City property taxes per capita: $82 (1997).
Education: High school graduation rate: 84.2% (2000); College graduation rate: 9.5% (2000).
Housing: Homeownership rate: 80.1% (2000); Median home value: $43,900 (2000); Median rent: $238 per month (2000); Median age of housing: 51 years (2000).
Newspapers: Edwards County Times Advocate (1 x week); Times Advocate Shopping Messenger (1 x week)
Transportation: Commute to work: 90.2% car, 0.0% public transportation, 7.2% walk, 2.2% work from home (2000); Travel time to work: 45.9% less than 15 minutes, 35.6% 15 to 30 minutes, 8.9% 30 to 45 minutes, 3.6% 45 to 60 minutes, 6.0% 60 minutes or more (2000)

Effingham County

Located in southeast central Illinois; drained by the Little Wabash River. Covers a land area of 478.70 square miles, a water area of 1.20 square miles, and is located in the Central Time Zone. The county government was organized in 1831. County seat is Effingham.

Weather Station: Effingham — Elevation: 606 feet

	Jan	Feb	Mar	Apr	May	Jun	Jul	Aug	Sep	Oct	Nov	Dec
High	34	40	52	64	74	83	87	85	79	67	53	40
Low	17	21	32	42	52	61	66	63	55	43	34	23
Precip	2.1	2.4	3.7	4.0	4.2	4.2	4.3	2.9	3.2	3.0	4.0	3.4
Snow	7.3	5.2	2.9	0.2	0.0	0.0	0.0	0.0	0.0	tr	1.3	3.8

High and Low temperatures in degrees Fahrenheit; Precipitation and Snow in inches

Population: 34,264 (2000); Race: 98.5% White, 0.2% Black, 0.4% Asian, 0.2% American Indian and Alaska Native, 0.9% Hispanic of any race, 0.3% two or more races (2000); Density: 71.6 persons per square mile (2000); Age: 28.6% under 18, 13.9% over 64 (2000).
Religion: Five largest groups: 37.0% Catholic Church, 11.1% Lutheran Church—Missouri Synod, 9.3% Southern Baptist Convention, 6.5% The United Methodist Church, 4.0% Christian Churches and Churches of Christ (2000).
Economy: Unemployment rate: 5.9% (11/2002); Total civilian labor force: 17,804 (11/2002); Leading industries: 26.6% manufacturing; 14.8% retail trade; 13.2% health care and social assistance (2000); Companies that employ more than 1,000 persons: 1 (2000); Companies that employ more than 100 persons: 31 (2000); Farms: 1,035 totaling 256,786 acres (1997); Minority business ownership rate: 0.0% (1997); Women business ownership rate: 15.3% (1997); Retail sales per capita: $16,814 (1997). Single-family building permits issued: 41 (2001) / 49 (2000); Multi-family building permits issued: 8 (2001) / 8 (2000).
Income: Per capita income: $18,301 (2000); Median household income: $39,379 (2000); Poverty rate: 8.1% (2000); Bankruptcy rate: 6.09% (2001).
Taxes: Total county taxes per capita: $93 (1997); County property taxes per capita: $93 (1997).
Education: High school graduation rate: 83.4% (2000); College graduation rate: 15.1% (2000).
Housing: Homeownership rate: 76.0% (2000); Median home value: $85,400 (2000); Median rent: $348 per month (2000); Median age of housing: 28 years (2000).
Health: Birth rate: 140.4 per 10,000 population (1998); Age adjusted death rate: 87.9 per 10,000 population (1999); Age adjusted cancer mortality rate: 203.7 deaths per 100,000 population (1999). Air Quality Index: 68% good, 32% moderate, 0% unhealthy (percent of days in 2000). Number of physicians: 19.8 per 10,000 population (1999); Number of hospital beds: 42.6 per 10,000 population (1999).
Elections: 2000 Presidential election results: 29.2% Gore, 68.0% Bush, 1.5% Nader, 1.0% Buchanan
Additional Information Contacts
Effingham County Government Offices 217-342-4990
Altamont Chamber of Commerce 618-483-5714
Effingham Chamber of Commerce 217-342-4147

Effingham County Communities

ALTAMONT (city). Covers a land area of 1.303 square miles and a water area of 0 square miles. Located at 39.06° N. Lat.; 88.74° W. Long. Elevation is 619 feet.
History: Altamont was organized in 1872 along the Pennsylvania and Baltimore & Ohio Railroads. Named for a nearby hill, Altamont developed as a wheat shipping center.
Population: 2,283 (2000); Race: 98.6% White, 0.0% Black, 0.0% Asian, 0.1% American Indian and Alaska Native, 0.7% Hispanic of any race, 1.1% two or more races (2000); Density: 1,751.6 persons per square mile (2000); Age: 24.6% under 18, 20.7% over 64 (2000); Marriage status: 20.3% never married, 59.2% now married, 10.5% widowed, 10.0% divorced (2000); Foreign born: 0.4% (2000); Ancestry (includes multiple ancestries): 34.2% German, 13.1% United States or American, 11.7% Irish, 7.8% English, 7.0% Other groups (2000).
Economy: Single-family building permits issued: 3 (2001) / 9 (2000); Multi-family building permits issued: 0 (2001) / 0 (2000); Employment by occupation: 9.0% management, 15.0% professional, 17.6% services, 26.4% sales, 0.1% farming, 9.1% construction, 22.8% production (2000).
Income: Per capita income: $15,478 (2000); Median household income: $33,186 (2000); Poverty rate: 6.9% (2000).
Taxes: Total city taxes per capita: $75 (1997); City property taxes per capita: $67 (1997).
Education: High school graduation rate: 77.0% (2000); College graduation rate: 12.6% (2000).

School District(s)
Altamont Community Unit School District 10 (PK-12)
2000 Enrollment: 841 618-483-6195

Housing: Homeownership rate: 77.0% (2000); Median home value: $64,100 (2000); Median rent: $358 per month (2000); Median age of housing: 38 years (2000).
Newspapers: The Altamont Independent (1 x week); The Altamont News (1 x week)
Transportation: Commute to work: 93.1% car, 0.0% public transportation, 2.0% walk, 3.9% work from home (2000); Travel time to work: 35.1% less than 15 minutes, 54.7% 15 to 30 minutes, 5.9% 30 to 45 minutes, 1.7% 45 to 60 minutes, 2.6% 60 minutes or more (2000)
Additional Information Contacts
Altamont Chamber of Commerce 618-483-5714

BEECHER CITY (village). Covers a land area of 0.905 square miles and a water area of 0 square miles. Located at 39.18° N. Lat.; 88.78° W. Long. Elevation is 617 feet.
Population: 493 (2000); Race: 97.1% White, 0.0% Black, 0.0% Asian, 0.0% American Indian and Alaska Native, 0.6% Hispanic of any race, 2.5% two or more races (2000); Density: 544.9 persons per square mile (2000); Age: 31.5% under 18, 12.5% over 64 (2000); Marriage status: 21.0% never married, 56.6% now married, 10.4% widowed, 12.0% divorced (2000); Foreign born: 0.6% (2000); Ancestry (includes multiple ancestries): 23.5% German, 14.0% English, 10.2% United States or American, 10.0% Irish, 4.4% Other groups (2000).
Economy: Agriculture: wheat, soybeans; cattle, hogs. Employment by occupation: 4.2% management, 8.9% professional, 8.4% services, 20.4% sales, 1.0% farming, 14.1% construction, 42.9% production (2000).
Income: Per capita income: $12,779 (2000); Median household income: $27,500 (2000); Poverty rate: 18.4% (2000).
Taxes: Total city taxes per capita: $42 (1997); City property taxes per capita: $42 (1997).
Education: High school graduation rate: 77.2% (2000); College graduation rate: 9.3% (2000).

School District(s)

Beecher City C U School District 20 (PK-12)
2000 Enrollment: 524 618-487-5100

Housing: Homeownership rate: 67.4% (2000); Median home value: $46,400 (2000); Median rent: $308 per month (2000); Median age of housing: 44 years (2000).

Newspapers: Beecher City Journal (1 x week)

Transportation: Commute to work: 92.4% car, 0.0% public transportation, 4.9% walk, 1.1% work from home (2000); Travel time to work: 20.3% less than 15 minutes, 56.0% 15 to 30 minutes, 12.1% 30 to 45 minutes, 1.6% 45 to 60 minutes, 9.9% 60 minutes or more (2000)

DIETERICH (village). Covers a land area of 1.185 square miles and a water area of 0 square miles. Located at 39.06° N. Lat.; 88.37° W. Long. Elevation is 591 feet.

Population: 591 (2000); Race: 100.0% White, 0.0% Black, 0.0% Asian, 0.0% American Indian and Alaska Native, 0.0% Hispanic of any race, 0.0% two or more races (2000); Density: 498.6 persons per square mile (2000); Age: 29.4% under 18, 14.6% over 64 (2000); Marriage status: 17.5% never married, 66.4% now married, 6.1% widowed, 10.0% divorced (2000); Foreign born: 0.7% (2000); Ancestry (includes multiple ancestries): 41.8% German, 20.2% United States or American, 8.1% Irish, 6.5% English, 3.3% Other groups (2000).

Economy: Redtop seed-cleaning plant. Agriculture: corn, wheat; dairying; livestock; lumber. Employment by occupation: 8.4% management, 12.9% professional, 14.1% services, 22.8% sales, 1.5% farming, 11.1% construction, 29.1% production (2000).

Income: Per capita income: $16,652 (2000); Median household income: $45,972 (2000); Poverty rate: 7.5% (2000).

Taxes: Total city taxes per capita: $56 (1997); City property taxes per capita: $51 (1997).

Education: High school graduation rate: 83.3% (2000); College graduation rate: 11.8% (2000).

School District(s)

Dieterich Community Unit School District 30 (PK-12)
2000 Enrollment: 558 217-925-5247

Housing: Homeownership rate: 87.8% (2000); Median home value: $65,700 (2000); Median rent: $325 per month (2000); Median age of housing: 42 years (2000).

Transportation: Commute to work: 92.4% car, 0.9% public transportation, 1.8% walk, 4.3% work from home (2000); Travel time to work: 33.7% less than 15 minutes, 57.1% 15 to 30 minutes, 6.3% 30 to 45 minutes, 1.9% 45 to 60 minutes, 1.0% 60 minutes or more (2000)

EDGEWOOD (village). Covers a land area of 1.003 square miles and a water area of 0.011 square miles. Located at 38.92° N. Lat.; 88.66° W. Long. Elevation is 579 feet.

Population: 527 (2000); Race: 100.0% White, 0.0% Black, 0.0% Asian, 0.0% American Indian and Alaska Native, 1.0% Hispanic of any race, 0.0% two or more races (2000); Density: 525.3 persons per square mile (2000); Age: 29.2% under 18, 12.4% over 64 (2000); Marriage status: 22.2% never married, 53.8% now married, 10.5% widowed, 13.5% divorced (2000); Foreign born: 0.8% (2000); Ancestry (includes multiple ancestries): 27.5% German, 10.6% United States or American, 10.4% Irish, 5.2% Other groups, 4.1% English (2000).

Economy: In agricultural area: corn, soybeans, wheat. Rail junction nearby. Employment by occupation: 4.7% management, 4.3% professional, 15.1% services, 16.8% sales, 2.2% farming, 10.3% construction, 46.6% production (2000).

Income: Per capita income: $12,338 (2000); Median household income: $20,987 (2000); Poverty rate: 16.7% (2000).

Taxes: Total city taxes per capita: $87 (1997); City property taxes per capita: $40 (1997).

Education: High school graduation rate: 65.2% (2000); College graduation rate: 2.9% (2000).

Housing: Homeownership rate: 69.9% (2000); Median home value: $32,500 (2000); Median rent: $232 per month (2000); Median age of housing: 42 years (2000).

Transportation: Commute to work: 96.1% car, 0.9% public transportation, 0.4% walk, 2.6% work from home (2000); Travel time to work: 15.2% less than 15 minutes, 59.2% 15 to 30 minutes, 15.2% 30 to 45 minutes, 0.9% 45 to 60 minutes, 9.4% 60 minutes or more (2000)

EFFINGHAM (city). Covers a land area of 8.667 square miles and a water area of 0.058 square miles. Located at 39.12° N. Lat.; 88.54° W. Long. Elevation is 592 feet.

History: Effingham was settled by German immigrants, and was incorporated as a village in 1861.

Population: 12,384 (2000); Race: 97.7% White, 0.2% Black, 0.7% Asian, 0.3% American Indian and Alaska Native, 1.5% Hispanic of any race, 0.3% two or more races (2000); Density: 1,428.9 persons per square mile (2000); Age: 24.9% under 18, 18.4% over 64 (2000); Marriage status: 22.2% never married, 55.2% now married, 11.6% widowed, 11.0% divorced (2000); Foreign born: 1.7% (2000); Ancestry (includes multiple ancestries): 37.3% German, 10.3% Irish, 10.2% English, 9.0% United States or American, 6.2% Other groups (2000).

Vital Statistics: Birth rate: 162.3 per 10,000 population (1998)

Economy: Single-family building permits issued: 31 (2001) / 28 (2000); Multi-family building permits issued: 8 (2001) / 8 (2000); Employment by occupation: 10.4% management, 17.4% professional, 18.1% services, 26.4% sales, 0.5% farming, 5.5% construction, 21.7% production (2000).

Income: Per capita income: $19,132 (2000); Median household income: $34,761 (2000); Poverty rate: 9.6% (2000).

Taxes: Total city taxes per capita: $358 (2000); City property taxes per capita: $276 (2000).

Education: High school graduation rate: 81.6% (2000); College graduation rate: 17.0% (2000).

School District(s)

Effingham Community Unit School District 40 (PK-12)
2000 Enrollment: 3,030 217-342-7700

Housing: Homeownership rate: 63.1% (2000); Median home value: $86,900 (2000); Median rent: $358 per month (2000); Median age of housing: 30 years (2000).

Hospitals: Saint Anthony's Memorial Hospital (146 beds)

Newspapers: Effingham Daily News (6 x week)

Transportation: Commute to work: 93.0% car, 0.6% public transportation, 2.2% walk, 2.7% work from home (2000); Travel time to work: 70.4% less than 15 minutes, 19.8% 15 to 30 minutes, 5.0% 30 to 45 minutes, 1.4% 45 to 60 minutes, 3.4% 60 minutes or more (2000); Amtrak: Service available.

Airports: Effingham County Memorial

Additional Information Contacts

Effingham Chamber of Commerce 217-342-4147

MASON (town). Covers a land area of 1.137 square miles and a water area of 0.005 square miles. Located at 38.95° N. Lat.; 88.62° W. Long. Elevation is 594 feet.

Population: 396 (2000); Race: 95.8% White, 0.0% Black, 0.0% Asian, 0.0% American Indian and Alaska Native, 0.5% Hispanic of any race, 2.6% two or more races (2000); Density: 348.3 persons per square mile (2000); Age: 28.4% under 18, 9.6% over 64 (2000); Marriage status: 19.6% never married, 59.2% now married, 6.4% widowed, 14.7% divorced (2000); Foreign born: 0.0% (2000); Ancestry (includes multiple ancestries): 31.9% German, 12.7% English, 9.2% Other groups, 5.9% United States or American, 4.5% Irish (2000).

Economy: Agriculture: cattle, hogs; wheat, soybeans, sorghum. Employment by occupation: 2.5% management, 7.5% professional, 13.5% services, 21.5% sales, 0.0% farming, 13.0% construction, 42.0% production (2000).

Income: Per capita income: $13,392 (2000); Median household income: $40,441 (2000); Poverty rate: 6.1% (2000).

Taxes: Total city taxes per capita: $37 (1997); City property taxes per capita: $37 (1997).

Education: High school graduation rate: 70.9% (2000); College graduation rate: 4.5% (2000).

Housing: Homeownership rate: 88.7% (2000); Median home value: $39,000 (2000); Median rent: $275 per month (2000); Median age of housing: 45 years (2000).

Transportation: Commute to work: 96.5% car, 2.5% public transportation, 1.0% walk, 0.0% work from home (2000); Travel time to work: 10.1% less than 15 minutes, 70.7% 15 to 30 minutes, 12.6% 30 to 45 minutes, 1.5% 45 to 60 minutes, 5.1% 60 minutes or more (2000)

MONTROSE (village). Covers a land area of 0.710 square miles and a water area of 0 square miles. Located at 39.16° N. Lat.; 88.37° W. Long. Elevation is 600 feet.

Population: 257 (2000); Race: 100.0% White, 0.0% Black, 0.0% Asian, 0.0% American Indian and Alaska Native, 0.0% Hispanic of any race, 0.0% two or more races (2000); Density: 361.9 persons per square mile (2000); Age: 23.2% under 18, 13.7% over 64 (2000); Marriage status: 28.9% never married, 46.3% now married, 14.2% widowed, 10.5% divorced (2000); Foreign born: 0.0% (2000); Ancestry (includes multiple ancestries): 34.3% German, 18.0% Irish, 7.3% United States or American, 6.0% English, 5.6% Other groups (2000).

Economy: In agricultural area. Employment by occupation: 1.8% management, 6.2% professional, 17.7% services, 20.4% sales, 1.8% farming, 13.3% construction, 38.9% production (2000).
Income: Per capita income: $14,443 (2000); Median household income: $26,250 (2000); Poverty rate: 16.7% (2000).
Taxes: Total city taxes per capita: $74 (1997); City property taxes per capita: $65 (1997).
Education: High school graduation rate: 62.9% (2000); College graduation rate: 5.3% (2000).
Housing: Homeownership rate: 77.7% (2000); Median home value: $51,700 (2000); Median rent: $265 per month (2000); Median age of housing: 40 years (2000).
Transportation: Commute to work: 95.6% car, 0.0% public transportation, 0.0% walk, 2.7% work from home (2000); Travel time to work: 38.2% less than 15 minutes, 50.0% 15 to 30 minutes, 4.5% 30 to 45 minutes, 0.9% 45 to 60 minutes, 6.4% 60 minutes or more (2000)

SHUMWAY (village). Covers a land area of 0.312 square miles and a water area of 0 square miles. Located at 39.18° N. Lat.; 88.65° W. Long. Elevation is 655 feet.
Population: 217 (2000); Race: 99.2% White, 0.0% Black, 0.0% Asian, 0.0% American Indian and Alaska Native, 0.0% Hispanic of any race, 0.8% two or more races (2000); Density: 696.1 persons per square mile (2000); Age: 30.1% under 18, 10.4% over 64 (2000); Marriage status: 27.9% never married, 48.9% now married, 9.5% widowed, 13.7% divorced (2000); Foreign born: 0.8% (2000); Ancestry (includes multiple ancestries): 21.7% German, 14.1% Italian, 9.6% English, 6.0% United States or American, 6.0% Irish (2000).
Economy: In agricultural area. Employment by occupation: 4.9% management, 6.8% professional, 25.2% services, 20.4% sales, 2.9% farming, 4.9% construction, 35.0% production (2000).
Income: Per capita income: $16,032 (2000); Median household income: $43,125 (2000); Poverty rate: 8.0% (2000).
Taxes: Total city taxes per capita: $28 (1997); City property taxes per capita: $20 (1997).
Education: High school graduation rate: 84.8% (2000); College graduation rate: 9.3% (2000).
Housing: Homeownership rate: 92.0% (2000); Median home value: $50,800 (2000); Median rent: $275 per month (2000); Median age of housing: 45 years (2000).
Transportation: Commute to work: 89.3% car, 0.0% public transportation, 0.0% walk, 10.7% work from home (2000); Travel time to work: 14.1% less than 15 minutes, 82.6% 15 to 30 minutes, 1.1% 30 to 45 minutes, 2.2% 45 to 60 minutes, 0.0% 60 minutes or more (2000)

TEUTOPOLIS (village). Covers a land area of 1.580 square miles and a water area of 0 square miles. Located at 39.13° N. Lat.; 88.47° W. Long. Elevation is 604 feet.
History: Teutopolis was established in 1839 by a group of German Catholics from Cincinnati, Ohio.
Population: 1,559 (2000); Race: 99.5% White, 0.1% Black, 0.1% Asian, 0.0% American Indian and Alaska Native, 0.0% Hispanic of any race, 0.3% two or more races (2000); Density: 986.8 persons per square mile (2000); Age: 33.4% under 18, 11.3% over 64 (2000); Marriage status: 26.7% never married, 60.6% now married, 6.1% widowed, 6.7% divorced (2000); Foreign born: 0.3% (2000); Ancestry (includes multiple ancestries): 71.1% German, 8.3% Irish, 6.5% United States or American, 2.8% English, 1.9% Other groups (2000).
Economy: Single-family building permits issued: 7 (2001) / 12 (2000); Multi-family building permits issued: 0 (2001) / 0 (2000); Employment by occupation: 12.2% management, 16.8% professional, 11.0% services, 28.4% sales, 0.0% farming, 13.8% construction, 17.8% production (2000).
Income: Per capita income: $21,280 (2000); Median household income: $47,450 (2000); Poverty rate: 4.8% (2000).
Taxes: Total city taxes per capita: $60 (1997); City property taxes per capita: $55 (1997).
Education: High school graduation rate: 88.9% (2000); College graduation rate: 21.7% (2000).

School District(s)

Teutopolis C U School District 50 (PK-12)
2000 Enrollment: 1,487 217-857-3535

Housing: Homeownership rate: 78.4% (2000); Median home value: $96,100 (2000); Median rent: $384 per month (2000); Median age of housing: 32 years (2000).
Newspapers: Teutopolis Press-Dieterich Special Gazette (1 x week)
Transportation: Commute to work: 94.0% car, 0.0% public transportation, 1.6% walk, 1.7% work from home (2000); Travel time to work: 72.3% less than 15 minutes, 18.9% 15 to 30 minutes, 3.3% 30 to 45 minutes, 2.8% 45 to 60 minutes, 2.7% 60 minutes or more (2000)

WATSON (village). Covers a land area of 0.977 square miles and a water area of 0 square miles. Located at 39.02° N. Lat.; 88.56° W. Long. Elevation is 561 feet.
Population: 729 (2000); Race: 97.3% White, 0.0% Black, 0.0% Asian, 0.9% American Indian and Alaska Native, 3.1% Hispanic of any race, 0.0% two or more races (2000); Density: 746.0 persons per square mile (2000); Age: 36.7% under 18, 5.5% over 64 (2000); Marriage status: 22.2% never married, 61.1% now married, 5.3% widowed, 11.5% divorced (2000); Foreign born: 1.2% (2000); Ancestry (includes multiple ancestries): 31.7% German, 18.1% Irish, 12.9% United States or American, 12.5% Other groups, 4.8% English (2000).
Economy: In agricultural area: wheat, soybeans; cattle, hogs. Employment by occupation: 5.9% management, 7.7% professional, 22.7% services, 19.7% sales, 0.3% farming, 9.9% construction, 33.9% production (2000).
Income: Per capita income: $13,000 (2000); Median household income: $39,028 (2000); Poverty rate: 9.5% (2000).
Taxes: Total city taxes per capita: $35 (1997); City property taxes per capita: $35 (1997).
Education: High school graduation rate: 81.6% (2000); College graduation rate: 5.3% (2000).
Housing: Homeownership rate: 85.7% (2000); Median home value: $61,900 (2000); Median rent: $300 per month (2000); Median age of housing: 21 years (2000).
Transportation: Commute to work: 94.4% car, 0.0% public transportation, 2.1% walk, 3.5% work from home (2000); Travel time to work: 27.5% less than 15 minutes, 56.7% 15 to 30 minutes, 7.5% 30 to 45 minutes, 5.3% 45 to 60 minutes, 3.1% 60 minutes or more (2000)

Fayette County

Located in south central Illinois; drained by the Kaskaskia River. Covers a land area of 716.50 square miles, a water area of 8.90 square miles, and is located in the Central Time Zone. The county government was organized in 1821. County seat is Vandalia.
Population: 21,802 (2000); Race: 94.3% White, 5.1% Black, 0.1% Asian, 0.2% American Indian and Alaska Native, 0.8% Hispanic of any race, 0.3% two or more races (2000); Density: 30.4 persons per square mile (2000); Age: 23.7% under 18, 15.9% over 64 (2000).
Religion: Five largest groups: 19.4% Southern Baptist Convention, 7.8% Lutheran Church—Missouri Synod, 7.5% The United Methodist Church, 4.8% Christian Churches and Churches of Christ, 3.8% Catholic Church (2000).
Economy: Unemployment rate: 7.5% (11/2002); Total civilian labor force: 10,190 (11/2002); Leading industries: 24.6% manufacturing; 19.2% retail trade; 16.3% health care and social assistance (2000); Companies that employ more than 1,000 persons: 0 (2000); Companies that employ more than 100 persons: 6 (2000); Farms: 1,119 totaling 333,232 acres (1997); Minority business ownership rate: 0.0% (1997); Women business ownership rate: 44.5% (1997); Retail sales per capita: $6,938 (1997). Single-family building permits issued: 6 (2001) / 11 (2000); Multi-family building permits issued: 2 (2001) / 0 (2000).
Income: Per capita income: $15,357 (2000); Median household income: $31,873 (2000); Poverty rate: 12.2% (2000); Bankruptcy rate: 5.28% (2001).
Taxes: Total county taxes per capita: $67 (1997); County property taxes per capita: $67 (1997).
Education: High school graduation rate: 72.2% (2000); College graduation rate: 9.0% (2000).
Housing: Homeownership rate: 79.7% (2000); Median home value: $59,500 (2000); Median rent: $266 per month (2000); Median age of housing: 38 years (2000).
Health: Birth rate: 117.4 per 10,000 population (1998); Age adjusted death rate: 85.2 per 10,000 population (1999); Age adjusted cancer mortality rate: 163.0 deaths per 100,000 population (1999). Number of physicians: 5.0 per 10,000 population (1999); Number of hospital beds: 66.5 per 10,000 population (1999).
Elections: 2000 Presidential election results: 41.6% Gore, 55.7% Bush, 1.3% Nader, 1.0% Buchanan
National and State Parks: Carlyle Lake State Wildlife Management Area; Ramsey Lake State Park; Vandalia State House Historic Site
Additional Information Contacts

Fayette County Government Offices 618-283-5000
Vandalia Chamber of Commerce 618-283-2728

Fayette County Communities

BINGHAM (village). Covers a land area of 0.272 square miles and a water area of 0 square miles. Located at 39.11° N. Lat.; 89.21° W. Long. Elevation is 600 feet.
Population: 117 (2000); Race: 94.8% White, 0.0% Black, 0.0% Asian, 0.0% American Indian and Alaska Native, 0.0% Hispanic of any race, 5.2% two or more races (2000); Density: 429.6 persons per square mile (2000); Age: 37.1% under 18, 12.4% over 64 (2000); Marriage status: 24.6% never married, 40.0% now married, 4.6% widowed, 30.8% divorced (2000); Foreign born: 0.0% (2000); Ancestry (includes multiple ancestries): 36.1% German, 29.9% Other groups, 7.2% English, 7.2% Irish, 5.2% Scottish (2000).
Economy: In agricultural area. Employment by occupation: 5.7% management, 20.0% professional, 0.0% services, 22.9% sales, 11.4% farming, 11.4% construction, 28.6% production (2000).
Income: Per capita income: $9,780 (2000); Median household income: $20,938 (2000); Poverty rate: 39.2% (2000).
Taxes: Total city taxes per capita: $21 (1997); City property taxes per capita: $0 (1997).
Education: High school graduation rate: 64.3% (2000); College graduation rate: 7.1% (2000).
Housing: Homeownership rate: 65.9% (2000); Median home value: $23,500 (2000); Median rent: $175 per month (2000); Median age of housing: 42 years (2000).
Transportation: Commute to work: 93.5% car, 0.0% public transportation, 0.0% walk, 6.5% work from home (2000); Travel time to work: 6.9% less than 15 minutes, 24.1% 15 to 30 minutes, 62.1% 30 to 45 minutes, 0.0% 45 to 60 minutes, 6.9% 60 minutes or more (2000)

BROWNSTOWN (village). Covers a land area of 0.628 square miles and a water area of 0 square miles. Located at 38.99° N. Lat.; 88.95° W. Long. Elevation is 586 feet.
Population: 705 (2000); Race: 98.4% White, 0.0% Black, 0.0% Asian, 0.6% American Indian and Alaska Native, 0.0% Hispanic of any race, 0.3% two or more races (2000); Density: 1,123.0 persons per square mile (2000); Age: 22.3% under 18, 17.5% over 64 (2000); Marriage status: 24.6% never married, 49.3% now married, 11.9% widowed, 14.3% divorced (2000); Foreign born: 0.3% (2000); Ancestry (includes multiple ancestries): 24.3% German, 16.9% United States or American, 13.9% English, 9.3% Irish, 5.6% Other groups (2000).
Economy: In agricultural area: corn, wheat, sorghum, soybeans; cattle; dairying. Oil-producing area. Employment by occupation: 4.0% management, 13.1% professional, 26.4% services, 21.3% sales, 2.7% farming, 9.7% construction, 22.8% production (2000).
Income: Per capita income: $15,239 (2000); Median household income: $28,839 (2000); Poverty rate: 14.8% (2000).
Taxes: Total city taxes per capita: $33 (1997); City property taxes per capita: $29 (1997).
Education: High school graduation rate: 84.3% (2000); College graduation rate: 9.2% (2000).

School District(s)

Brownstown C U School District 201 (PK-12)
2000 Enrollment: 449 618-427-3355
Housing: Homeownership rate: 80.5% (2000); Median home value: $47,800 (2000); Median rent: $237 per month (2000); Median age of housing: 47 years (2000).
Transportation: Commute to work: 88.5% car, 0.0% public transportation, 4.1% walk, 6.7% work from home (2000); Travel time to work: 43.3% less than 15 minutes, 29.7% 15 to 30 minutes, 15.0% 30 to 45 minutes, 2.4% 45 to 60 minutes, 9.6% 60 minutes or more (2000)

FARINA (village). Covers a land area of 1.440 square miles and a water area of 0.007 square miles. Located at 38.83° N. Lat.; 88.77° W. Long. Elevation is 585 feet.
Population: 558 (2000); Race: 99.6% White, 0.0% Black, 0.0% Asian, 0.0% American Indian and Alaska Native, 0.5% Hispanic of any race, 0.4% two or more races (2000); Density: 387.6 persons per square mile (2000); Age: 21.8% under 18, 20.9% over 64 (2000); Marriage status: 21.7% never married, 55.2% now married, 10.0% widowed, 13.0% divorced (2000); Foreign born: 0.2% (2000); Ancestry (includes multiple ancestries): 35.5% German, 11.0% Irish, 10.1% United States or American, 7.6% English, 6.7% Other groups (2000).
Economy: In agricultural area. Employment by occupation: 10.9% management, 7.4% professional, 21.0% services, 20.2% sales, 1.9% farming, 8.6% construction, 30.0% production (2000).
Income: Per capita income: $17,068 (2000); Median household income: $31,406 (2000); Poverty rate: 10.8% (2000).
Taxes: Total city taxes per capita: $61 (1997); City property taxes per capita: $61 (1997).
Education: High school graduation rate: 77.8% (2000); College graduation rate: 8.4% (2000).
Housing: Homeownership rate: 85.7% (2000); Median home value: $37,900 (2000); Median rent: $230 per month (2000); Median age of housing: 45 years (2000).
Newspapers: The Farina News (1 x week)
Transportation: Commute to work: 88.2% car, 0.0% public transportation, 4.3% walk, 4.7% work from home (2000); Travel time to work: 44.4% less than 15 minutes, 14.4% 15 to 30 minutes, 33.3% 30 to 45 minutes, 3.7% 45 to 60 minutes, 4.1% 60 minutes or more (2000)

RAMSEY (village). Covers a land area of 1.007 square miles and a water area of 0 square miles. Located at 39.14° N. Lat.; 89.11° W. Long. Elevation is 610 feet.
Population: 1,056 (2000); Race: 99.2% White, 0.0% Black, 0.2% Asian, 0.6% American Indian and Alaska Native, 0.3% Hispanic of any race, 0.0% two or more races (2000); Density: 1,048.7 persons per square mile (2000); Age: 27.0% under 18, 20.4% over 64 (2000); Marriage status: 21.7% never married, 55.3% now married, 12.2% widowed, 10.8% divorced (2000); Foreign born: 0.7% (2000); Ancestry (includes multiple ancestries): 22.4% German, 10.5% English, 7.9% United States or American, 7.9% Irish, 5.6% Other groups (2000).
Economy: Corn, wheat; dairy products; poultry, livestock. Employment by occupation: 3.4% management, 11.0% professional, 22.3% services, 21.6% sales, 2.5% farming, 6.9% construction, 32.2% production (2000).
Income: Per capita income: $13,878 (2000); Median household income: $29,792 (2000); Poverty rate: 13.0% (2000).
Taxes: Total city taxes per capita: $41 (1997); City property taxes per capita: $37 (1997).
Education: High school graduation rate: 73.9% (2000); College graduation rate: 6.9% (2000).

School District(s)

Ramsey Community Unit School District 204 (PK-12)
2000 Enrollment: 509 618-423-2335
Housing: Homeownership rate: 74.9% (2000); Median home value: $43,000 (2000); Median rent: $235 per month (2000); Median age of housing: 32 years (2000).
Newspapers: Ramsey News-Journal (1 x week)
Transportation: Commute to work: 94.3% car, 0.5% public transportation, 2.4% walk, 2.8% work from home (2000); Travel time to work: 28.5% less than 15 minutes, 41.2% 15 to 30 minutes, 14.4% 30 to 45 minutes, 6.6% 45 to 60 minutes, 9.3% 60 minutes or more (2000)

SAINT ELMO (city). Covers a land area of 0.957 square miles and a water area of 0.024 square miles. Located at 39.02° N. Lat.; 88.85° W. Long. Elevation is 619 feet.
History: St. Elmo was settled in 1830 by a group of Kentucky Catholics, and developed as a railroad and brick manufacturing town. Later, oil was discovered and the economy boomed.
Population: 1,456 (2000); Race: 98.8% White, 0.1% Black, 0.0% Asian, 0.1% American Indian and Alaska Native, 0.0% Hispanic of any race, 1.0% two or more races (2000); Density: 1,521.6 persons per square mile (2000); Age: 28.2% under 18, 19.5% over 64 (2000); Marriage status: 17.1% never married, 65.1% now married, 9.3% widowed, 8.5% divorced (2000); Foreign born: 0.1% (2000); Ancestry (includes multiple ancestries): 18.3% German, 17.5% United States or American, 11.2% Irish, 9.2% English, 7.5% Other groups (2000).
Economy: Single-family building permits issued: 0 (2001) / 0 (2000); Multi-family building permits issued: 0 (2001) / 0 (2000); Employment by occupation: 6.2% management, 9.0% professional, 21.9% services, 20.1% sales, 3.7% farming, 8.0% construction, 31.1% production (2000).
Income: Per capita income: $14,048 (2000); Median household income: $30,750 (2000); Poverty rate: 12.7% (2000).
Education: High school graduation rate: 76.2% (2000); College graduation rate: 8.5% (2000).

School District(s)

Saint Elmo C U School District 202 (KG-12)
2000 Enrollment: 498 618-829-3264

Housing: Homeownership rate: 79.9% (2000); Median home value: $47,400 (2000); Median rent: $260 per month (2000); Median age of housing: 46 years (2000).
Newspapers: Saint Elmo Banner (1 x week)
Transportation: Commute to work: 91.2% car, 0.0% public transportation, 4.8% walk, 3.7% work from home (2000); Travel time to work: 31.6% less than 15 minutes, 37.9% 15 to 30 minutes, 24.5% 30 to 45 minutes, 2.5% 45 to 60 minutes, 3.5% 60 minutes or more (2000)

SAINT PETER (village). Covers a land area of 0.535 square miles and a water area of 0 square miles. Located at 38.86° N. Lat.; 88.85° W. Long. Elevation is 591 feet.
Population: 386 (2000); Race: 100.0% White, 0.0% Black, 0.0% Asian, 0.0% American Indian and Alaska Native, 0.8% Hispanic of any race, 0.0% two or more races (2000); Density: 721.4 persons per square mile (2000); Age: 27.4% under 18, 18.6% over 64 (2000); Marriage status: 26.7% never married, 51.4% now married, 13.9% widowed, 8.1% divorced (2000); Foreign born: 0.0% (2000); Ancestry (includes multiple ancestries): 43.7% German, 10.9% United States or American, 7.5% Irish, 6.7% English, 3.4% Other groups (2000).
Economy: Employment by occupation: 10.5% management, 9.4% professional, 27.1% services, 24.9% sales, 0.0% farming, 12.2% construction, 16.0% production (2000).
Income: Per capita income: $15,192 (2000); Median household income: $31,406 (2000); Poverty rate: 12.7% (2000).
Education: High school graduation rate: 74.5% (2000); College graduation rate: 8.2% (2000).
Housing: Homeownership rate: 87.9% (2000); Median home value: $51,300 (2000); Median rent: $206 per month (2000); Median age of housing: 46 years (2000).
Transportation: Commute to work: 87.4% car, 1.1% public transportation, 10.3% walk, 1.1% work from home (2000); Travel time to work: 41.3% less than 15 minutes, 18.0% 15 to 30 minutes, 30.8% 30 to 45 minutes, 5.2% 45 to 60 minutes, 4.7% 60 minutes or more (2000)

SHOBONIER (unincorporated postal area, zip code 62885). Covers a land area of 56.052 square miles and a water area of 0.065 square miles. Located at 38.86° N. Lat.; 89.05° W. Long. Elevation is 516 feet.
Population: 837 (2000); Race: 100.0% White, 0.0% Black, 0.0% Asian, 0.0% American Indian and Alaska Native, 3.8% Hispanic of any race, 0.0% two or more races (2000); Density: 14.9 persons per square mile (2000); Age: 27.5% under 18, 14.8% over 64 (2000); Marriage status: 19.5% never married, 62.4% now married, 8.5% widowed, 9.5% divorced (2000); Foreign born: 0.0% (2000); Ancestry (includes multiple ancestries): 31.1% German, 13.4% Other groups, 12.7% United States or American, 5.5% English, 5.3% Scotch-Irish (2000).
Economy: Employment by occupation: 17.4% management, 7.1% professional, 24.0% services, 15.5% sales, 2.5% farming, 10.6% construction, 22.9% production (2000).
Income: Per capita income: $14,896 (2000); Median household income: $32,188 (2000); Poverty rate: 16.7% (2000).
Education: High school graduation rate: 65.7% (2000); College graduation rate: 1.6% (2000).
Housing: Homeownership rate: 80.1% (2000); Median home value: $60,600 (2000); Median rent: $225 per month (2000); Median age of housing: 43 years (2000).
Transportation: Commute to work: 89.4% car, 0.0% public transportation, 3.0% walk, 7.6% work from home (2000); Travel time to work: 32.4% less than 15 minutes, 39.5% 15 to 30 minutes, 18.3% 30 to 45 minutes, 3.8% 45 to 60 minutes, 5.9% 60 minutes or more (2000)

VANDALIA (city). Covers a land area of 5.665 square miles and a water area of 0.016 square miles. Located at 38.96° N. Lat.; 89.10° W. Long. Elevation is 515 feet.
History: Vandalia was laid out in 1819 at the direction of the Illinois State Legislature, and served until 1839 as the capital. Three capitol buildings were erected in Vandalia during its 20 years as the state capital.
Population: 6,975 (2000); Race: 83.8% White, 15.6% Black, 0.2% Asian, 0.3% American Indian and Alaska Native, 1.5% Hispanic of any race, 0.1% two or more races (2000); Density: 1,231.3 persons per square mile (2000); Age: 18.3% under 18, 17.2% over 64 (2000); Marriage status: 19.2% never married, 58.6% now married, 7.7% widowed, 14.5% divorced (2000); Foreign born: 0.7% (2000); Ancestry (includes multiple ancestries): 21.4% German, 10.3% United States or American, 9.9% English, 7.4% Irish, 5.4% Other groups (2000).
Economy: Single-family building permits issued: 6 (2001) / 11 (2000); Multi-family building permits issued: 2 (2001) / 0 (2000); Employment by occupation: 7.1% management, 13.7% professional, 23.3% services, 23.1% sales, 1.0% farming, 8.8% construction, 23.2% production (2000).
Income: Per capita income: $14,918 (2000); Median household income: $30,857 (2000); Poverty rate: 15.6% (2000).
Taxes: Total city taxes per capita: $80 (1997); City property taxes per capita: $68 (1997).
Education: High school graduation rate: 60.6% (2000); College graduation rate: 9.9% (2000).

School District(s)

Bond/Effingham/Fayette Roe (06-12)
2000 Enrollment: 36 618-283-5011
Vandalia C U School District 203 (PK-12)
2000 Enrollment: 1,829 618-283-4525

Housing: Homeownership rate: 68.5% (2000); Median home value: $60,300 (2000); Median rent: $282 per month (2000); Median age of housing: 47 years (2000).
Hospitals: Fayette County Hospital (160 beds)
Newspapers: Vandalia Leader Union (2 x week)
Transportation: Commute to work: 95.5% car, 0.0% public transportation, 1.9% walk, 1.4% work from home (2000); Travel time to work: 75.9% less than 15 minutes, 9.1% 15 to 30 minutes, 7.0% 30 to 45 minutes, 3.2% 45 to 60 minutes, 4.8% 60 minutes or more (2000)
Additional Information Contacts
Vandalia Chamber of Commerce 618-283-2728

Ford County

Located in east central Illinois; drained by the Mackinaw River. Covers a land area of 485.90 square miles, a water area of 0.50 square miles, and is located in the Central Time Zone. The county government was organized in 1859. County seat is Paxton.

Weather Station: Piper City — Elevation: 669 feet

	Jan	Feb	Mar	Apr	May	Jun	Jul	Aug	Sep	Oct	Nov	Dec
High	31	37	49	63	75	84	86	84	78	66	49	37
Low	14	19	29	38	50	59	63	60	52	41	31	21
Precip	1.8	1.7	2.8	3.4	4.2	3.7	4.2	3.9	3.0	2.6	2.9	2.5
Snow	9.4	6.2	3.4	1.1	tr	0.0	0.0	0.0	0.0	0.2	2.0	5.8

High and Low temperatures in degrees Fahrenheit; Precipitation and Snow in inches

Population: 14,241 (2000); Race: 98.2% White, 0.6% Black, 0.4% Asian, 0.0% American Indian and Alaska Native, 1.2% Hispanic of any race, 0.7% two or more races (2000); Density: 29.3 persons per square mile (2000); Age: 25.9% under 18, 19.4% over 64 (2000).
Religion: Five largest groups: 18.0% The United Methodist Church, 12.7% Evangelical Lutheran Church in America, 11.1% Catholic Church, 3.9% New Testament Association of Independent Baptist Churches and other Fundamental Baptist Associations, 3.5% S
Economy: Unemployment rate: 3.9% (11/2002); Total civilian labor force: 6,698 (11/2002); Leading industries: 19.9% manufacturing; 17.5% health care and social assistance; 16.8% retail trade (2000); Companies that employ more than 1,000 persons: 0 (2000); Companies that employ more than 100 persons: 7 (2000); Farms: 550 totaling 314,806 acres (1997); Minority business ownership rate: 0.0% (1997); Women business ownership rate: 22.5% (1997); Retail sales per capita: $8,502 (1997). Single-family building permits issued: 27 (2001) / 31 (2000); Multi-family building permits issued: 12 (2001) / 6 (2000).
Income: Per capita income: $18,860 (2000); Median household income: $38,073 (2000); Poverty rate: 7.0% (2000); Bankruptcy rate: 6.82% (2001).
Taxes: Total county taxes per capita: $155 (1997); County property taxes per capita: $120 (1997).
Education: High school graduation rate: 86.0% (2000); College graduation rate: 13.9% (2000).
Housing: Homeownership rate: 76.0% (2000); Median home value: $70,600 (2000); Median rent: $317 per month (2000); Median age of housing: 50 years (2000).
Health: Birth rate: 120.1 per 10,000 population (1998); Age adjusted death rate: 92.1 per 10,000 population (1999); Age adjusted cancer mortality rate: 222.0 deaths per 100,000 population (1999). Number of physicians: 9.8 per 10,000 population (1999); Number of hospital beds: 57.6 per 10,000 population (1999).

Elections: 2000 Presidential election results: 34.0% Gore, 63.2% Bush, 1.9% Nader, 0.6% Buchanan

Additional Information Contacts

Ford County Government Offices 217-686-2361
Gibson City Chamber of Commerce 217-784-5217
Paxton Chamber of Commerce 217-379-4655

Ford County Communities

CABERY (village). Covers a land area of 0.350 square miles and a water area of 0 square miles. Located at 40.99° N. Lat.; 88.20° W. Long. Elevation is 698 feet.

Population: 263 (2000); Race: 99.2% White, 0.0% Black, 0.0% Asian, 0.0% American Indian and Alaska Native, 0.8% Hispanic of any race, 0.8% two or more races (2000); Density: 751.1 persons per square mile (2000); Age: 32.8% under 18, 11.1% over 64 (2000); Marriage status: 28.4% never married, 55.2% now married, 8.8% widowed, 7.7% divorced (2000); Foreign born: 0.8% (2000); Ancestry (includes multiple ancestries): 38.9% German, 13.4% English, 12.2% French (except Basque), 11.8% United States or American, 8.8% Irish (2000).

Economy: Employment by occupation: 19.1% management, 12.7% professional, 17.3% services, 17.3% sales, 0.0% farming, 5.5% construction, 28.2% production (2000).

Income: Per capita income: $14,839 (2000); Median household income: $37,000 (2000); Poverty rate: 11.6% (2000).

Taxes: Total city taxes per capita: $37 (1997); City property taxes per capita: $22 (1997).

Education: High school graduation rate: 81.1% (2000); College graduation rate: 11.3% (2000).

Housing: Homeownership rate: 80.8% (2000); Median home value: $59,600 (2000); Median rent: $400 per month (2000); Median age of housing: 60+ years (2000).

Transportation: Commute to work: 85.0% car, 0.0% public transportation, 10.3% walk, 4.7% work from home (2000); Travel time to work: 23.5% less than 15 minutes, 23.5% 15 to 30 minutes, 22.5% 30 to 45 minutes, 21.6% 45 to 60 minutes, 8.8% 60 minutes or more (2000)

ELLIOTT (village). Covers a land area of 0.484 square miles and a water area of 0 square miles. Located at 40.46° N. Lat.; 88.27° W. Long. Elevation is 781 feet.

Population: 341 (2000); Race: 98.8% White, 0.0% Black, 0.0% Asian, 0.0% American Indian and Alaska Native, 0.0% Hispanic of any race, 1.2% two or more races (2000); Density: 704.2 persons per square mile (2000); Age: 26.8% under 18, 10.5% over 64 (2000); Marriage status: 20.4% never married, 70.3% now married, 2.6% widowed, 6.7% divorced (2000); Foreign born: 0.0% (2000); Ancestry (includes multiple ancestries): 34.4% German, 20.1% Irish, 6.7% French (except Basque), 5.2% Norwegian, 5.2% English (2000).

Economy: In rich agricultural area. Employment by occupation: 10.4% management, 11.4% professional, 12.8% services, 29.4% sales, 0.9% farming, 20.4% construction, 14.7% production (2000).

Income: Per capita income: $18,203 (2000); Median household income: $41,000 (2000); Poverty rate: 8.5% (2000).

Taxes: Total city taxes per capita: $43 (1997); City property taxes per capita: $43 (1997).

Education: High school graduation rate: 88.6% (2000); College graduation rate: 12.3% (2000).

Housing: Homeownership rate: 90.5% (2000); Median home value: $61,600 (2000); Median rent: $333 per month (2000); Median age of housing: 60+ years (2000).

Transportation: Commute to work: 91.3% car, 0.0% public transportation, 1.5% walk, 7.3% work from home (2000); Travel time to work: 45.5% less than 15 minutes, 17.3% 15 to 30 minutes, 29.8% 30 to 45 minutes, 7.3% 45 to 60 minutes, 0.0% 60 minutes or more (2000)

GIBSON (city). Aka Gibson City. Covers a land area of 2.103 square miles and a water area of 0.021 square miles. Located at 40.46° N. Lat.; 88.37° W. Long.

Population: 3,373 (2000); Race: 98.4% White, 1.1% Black, 0.0% Asian, 0.0% American Indian and Alaska Native, 0.4% Hispanic of any race, 0.5% two or more races (2000); Density: 1,604.0 persons per square mile (2000); Age: 22.9% under 18, 23.2% over 64 (2000); Marriage status: 17.7% never married, 60.9% now married, 11.7% widowed, 9.7% divorced (2000); Foreign born: 0.3% (2000); Ancestry (includes multiple ancestries): 32.0% German, 11.8% Irish, 11.0% English, 9.4% United States or American, 5.6% Other groups (2000).

Economy: Single-family building permits issued: 1 (2001) / 1 (2000); Multi-family building permits issued: 0 (2001) / 4 (2000); Employment by occupation: 12.8% management, 14.1% professional, 16.0% services, 21.2% sales, 0.8% farming, 13.1% construction, 22.0% production (2000).

Income: Per capita income: $18,926 (2000); Median household income: $33,638 (2000); Poverty rate: 9.4% (2000).

Taxes: Total city taxes per capita: $156 (1997); City property taxes per capita: $112 (1997).

Education: High school graduation rate: 80.1% (2000); College graduation rate: 14.3% (2000).

School District(s)

Gibson City-Melvin-Sibley CUSD 5 (PK-12)
2000 Enrollment: 1,035 217-784-8296

Housing: Homeownership rate: 68.1% (2000); Median home value: $68,700 (2000); Median rent: $309 per month (2000); Median age of housing: 49 years (2000).

Hospitals: Gibson Area Hospital & Health Services (82 beds)

Newspapers: Target (1 x week); Gibson City Courier (1 x week)

Transportation: Commute to work: 88.9% car, 0.0% public transportation, 6.4% walk, 3.7% work from home (2000); Travel time to work: 59.9% less than 15 minutes, 13.4% 15 to 30 minutes, 15.8% 30 to 45 minutes, 9.4% 45 to 60 minutes, 1.6% 60 minutes or more (2000)

Additional Information Contacts

Gibson City Chamber of Commerce 217-784-5217

KEMPTON (village). Covers a land area of 0.212 square miles and a water area of 0 square miles. Located at 40.93° N. Lat.; 88.23° W. Long. Elevation is 738 feet.

Population: 235 (2000); Race: 97.0% White, 0.8% Black, 0.0% Asian, 0.0% American Indian and Alaska Native, 3.4% Hispanic of any race, 2.3% two or more races (2000); Density: 1,111.1 persons per square mile (2000); Age: 49.1% under 18, 4.5% over 64 (2000); Marriage status: 30.4% never married, 56.8% now married, 7.4% widowed, 5.4% divorced (2000); Foreign born: 0.4% (2000); Ancestry (includes multiple ancestries): 46.4% German, 24.2% Irish, 11.7% United States or American, 7.2% Italian, 7.2% English (2000).

Economy: In rich agricultural area: corn, soybeans, livestock. Employment by occupation: 19.2% management, 8.7% professional, 10.6% services, 24.0% sales, 2.9% farming, 11.5% construction, 23.1% production (2000).

Income: Per capita income: $12,641 (2000); Median household income: $41,667 (2000); Poverty rate: 18.9% (2000).

Taxes: Total city taxes per capita: $46 (1997); City property taxes per capita: $46 (1997).

Education: High school graduation rate: 90.1% (2000); College graduation rate: 8.3% (2000).

School District(s)

Tri Point C U School District 6-J (PK-12)
2000 Enrollment: 659 815-253-6299

Housing: Homeownership rate: 82.8% (2000); Median home value: $62,900 (2000); Median rent: $367 per month (2000); Median age of housing: 60+ years (2000).

Transportation: Commute to work: 84.0% car, 0.0% public transportation, 13.0% walk, 3.0% work from home (2000); Travel time to work: 20.6% less than 15 minutes, 14.4% 15 to 30 minutes, 45.4% 30 to 45 minutes, 11.3% 45 to 60 minutes, 8.2% 60 minutes or more (2000)

MELVIN (village). Covers a land area of 0.339 square miles and a water area of 0 square miles. Located at 40.56° N. Lat.; 88.24° W. Long. Elevation is 810 feet.

Population: 465 (2000); Race: 98.9% White, 0.0% Black, 0.0% Asian, 0.0% American Indian and Alaska Native, 2.1% Hispanic of any race, 1.1% two or more races (2000); Density: 1,372.2 persons per square mile (2000); Age: 33.6% under 18, 18.4% over 64 (2000); Marriage status: 18.4% never married, 60.3% now married, 10.8% widowed, 10.5% divorced (2000); Foreign born: 1.5% (2000); Ancestry (includes multiple ancestries): 37.2% German, 12.1% English, 9.5% Irish, 9.1% Other groups, 8.0% United States or American (2000).

Economy: Agriculture: grain; livestock; feed milling. Employment by occupation: 7.4% management, 15.7% professional, 20.3% services, 17.5% sales, 0.0% farming, 15.7% construction, 23.5% production (2000).

Income: Per capita income: $16,383 (2000); Median household income: $37,500 (2000); Poverty rate: 7.0% (2000).

Taxes: Total city taxes per capita: $93 (1997); City property taxes per capita: $32 (1997).

Education: High school graduation rate: 87.1% (2000); College graduation rate: 15.0% (2000).
Housing: Homeownership rate: 85.0% (2000); Median home value: $45,600 (2000); Median rent: $270 per month (2000); Median age of housing: 60+ years (2000).
Newspapers: Ford County Press (1 x week)
Transportation: Commute to work: 92.1% car, 0.0% public transportation, 2.8% walk, 4.2% work from home (2000); Travel time to work: 32.9% less than 15 minutes, 33.3% 15 to 30 minutes, 13.5% 30 to 45 minutes, 12.1% 45 to 60 minutes, 8.2% 60 minutes or more (2000)

PAXTON (city). Covers a land area of 2.228 square miles and a water area of 0 square miles. Located at 40.45° N. Lat.; 88.09° W. Long. Elevation is 800 feet.
History: Paxton was settled in the 1850's by immigrants from Sweden.
Population: 4,525 (2000); Race: 98.2% White, 0.5% Black, 0.1% Asian, 0.0% American Indian and Alaska Native, 2.2% Hispanic of any race, 1.0% two or more races (2000); Density: 2,031.4 persons per square mile (2000); Age: 26.1% under 18, 19.0% over 64 (2000); Marriage status: 20.1% never married, 61.2% now married, 8.1% widowed, 10.6% divorced (2000); Foreign born: 1.2% (2000); Ancestry (includes multiple ancestries): 35.9% German, 13.1% Irish, 12.4% English, 9.7% Swedish, 7.0% Other groups (2000).
Economy: Single-family building permits issued: 9 (2001) / 11 (2000); Multi-family building permits issued: 12 (2001) / 2 (2000); Employment by occupation: 8.7% management, 11.8% professional, 15.9% services, 25.9% sales, 0.6% farming, 9.6% construction, 27.5% production (2000).
Income: Per capita income: $18,617 (2000); Median household income: $37,804 (2000); Poverty rate: 4.8% (2000).
Taxes: Total city taxes per capita: $277 (1997); City property taxes per capita: $95 (1997).
Education: High school graduation rate: 88.0% (2000); College graduation rate: 13.4% (2000).

School District(s)

Paxton-Buckley-Loda CU District 10 (PK-12)
2000 Enrollment: 1,450 217-379-3314
Housing: Homeownership rate: 78.0% (2000); Median home value: $69,000 (2000); Median rent: $330 per month (2000); Median age of housing: 49 years (2000).
Newspapers: Paxton Daily Record (5 x week); The Record (1 x week); Loda Times (1 x week)
Transportation: Commute to work: 95.0% car, 0.4% public transportation, 1.2% walk, 1.6% work from home (2000); Travel time to work: 46.6% less than 15 minutes, 21.8% 15 to 30 minutes, 22.3% 30 to 45 minutes, 5.0% 45 to 60 minutes, 4.3% 60 minutes or more (2000)

Additional Information Contacts

Paxton Chamber of Commerce 217-379-4655

PIPER CITY (village). Covers a land area of 0.554 square miles and a water area of 0 square miles. Located at 40.75° N. Lat.; 88.19° W. Long. Elevation is 668 feet.
Population: 781 (2000); Race: 94.1% White, 0.0% Black, 2.6% Asian, 0.0% American Indian and Alaska Native, 3.3% Hispanic of any race, 1.3% two or more races (2000); Density: 1,409.2 persons per square mile (2000); Age: 27.1% under 18, 20.7% over 64 (2000); Marriage status: 21.2% never married, 57.3% now married, 15.5% widowed, 6.1% divorced (2000); Foreign born: 2.6% (2000); Ancestry (includes multiple ancestries): 36.8% German, 27.4% Irish, 13.1% English, 10.7% French (except Basque), 9.0% Other groups (2000).
Economy: In agricultural area: corn, soybeans; livestock; light manufacturing. Single-family building permits issued: 0 (2001) / 0 (2000); Multi-family building permits issued: 0 (2001) / 0 (2000); Employment by occupation: 14.1% management, 14.1% professional, 20.6% services, 20.6% sales, 1.4% farming, 12.2% construction, 17.1% production (2000).
Income: Per capita income: $19,393 (2000); Median household income: $36,250 (2000); Poverty rate: 10.0% (2000).
Taxes: Total city taxes per capita: $85 (1997); City property taxes per capita: $46 (1997).
Education: High school graduation rate: 80.8% (2000); College graduation rate: 12.9% (2000).
Housing: Homeownership rate: 79.0% (2000); Median home value: $72,900 (2000); Median rent: $340 per month (2000); Median age of housing: 54 years (2000).
Transportation: Commute to work: 92.8% car, 0.0% public transportation, 1.4% walk, 5.8% work from home (2000); Travel time to work: 35.2% less than 15 minutes, 20.7% 15 to 30 minutes, 15.7% 30 to 45 minutes, 13.0% 45 to 60 minutes, 15.4% 60 minutes or more (2000)

ROBERTS (village). Covers a land area of 0.518 square miles and a water area of 0 square miles. Located at 40.61° N. Lat.; 88.18° W. Long. Elevation is 788 feet.
Population: 387 (2000); Race: 99.0% White, 0.0% Black, 0.0% Asian, 0.5% American Indian and Alaska Native, 2.6% Hispanic of any race, 0.5% two or more races (2000); Density: 746.9 persons per square mile (2000); Age: 20.6% under 18, 21.6% over 64 (2000); Marriage status: 21.2% never married, 52.6% now married, 14.6% widowed, 11.5% divorced (2000); Foreign born: 0.8% (2000); Ancestry (includes multiple ancestries): 44.0% German, 19.0% English, 12.1% Irish, 9.0% Other groups, 8.5% French (except Basque) (2000).
Economy: Grain, hay; livestock, poultry; some manufacturing. Employment by occupation: 10.4% management, 10.9% professional, 13.3% services, 29.9% sales, 0.9% farming, 12.3% construction, 22.3% production (2000).
Income: Per capita income: $17,926 (2000); Median household income: $32,321 (2000); Poverty rate: 7.5% (2000).
Taxes: Total city taxes per capita: $20 (1997); City property taxes per capita: $18 (1997).
Education: High school graduation rate: 89.8% (2000); College graduation rate: 8.7% (2000).
Housing: Homeownership rate: 93.6% (2000); Median home value: $59,100 (2000); Median rent: $213 per month (2000); Median age of housing: 58 years (2000).
Transportation: Commute to work: 92.8% car, 0.0% public transportation, 7.2% walk, 0.0% work from home (2000); Travel time to work: 43.0% less than 15 minutes, 33.3% 15 to 30 minutes, 9.7% 30 to 45 minutes, 10.6% 45 to 60 minutes, 3.4% 60 minutes or more (2000)

SIBLEY (village). Covers a land area of 0.538 square miles and a water area of 0.013 square miles. Located at 40.58° N. Lat.; 88.38° W. Long. Elevation is 813 feet.
Population: 329 (2000); Race: 98.1% White, 0.0% Black, 0.0% Asian, 0.0% American Indian and Alaska Native, 0.0% Hispanic of any race, 1.9% two or more races (2000); Density: 611.6 persons per square mile (2000); Age: 19.6% under 18, 26.4% over 64 (2000); Marriage status: 19.1% never married, 64.8% now married, 10.5% widowed, 5.6% divorced (2000); Foreign born: 0.6% (2000); Ancestry (includes multiple ancestries): 39.5% German, 11.3% English, 8.4% United States or American, 5.8% French (except Basque), 4.8% Swedish (2000).
Economy: In rich agricultural area. Employment by occupation: 9.1% management, 7.0% professional, 21.0% services, 21.0% sales, 2.8% farming, 14.7% construction, 24.5% production (2000).
Income: Per capita income: $21,317 (2000); Median household income: $31,667 (2000); Poverty rate: 7.4% (2000).
Taxes: Total city taxes per capita: $36 (1997); City property taxes per capita: $34 (1997).
Education: High school graduation rate: 76.9% (2000); College graduation rate: 6.0% (2000).
Housing: Homeownership rate: 83.2% (2000); Median home value: $37,900 (2000); Median rent: $304 per month (2000); Median age of housing: 60+ years (2000).
Transportation: Commute to work: 89.2% car, 2.2% public transportation, 3.6% walk, 2.9% work from home (2000); Travel time to work: 17.8% less than 15 minutes, 33.3% 15 to 30 minutes, 13.3% 30 to 45 minutes, 21.5% 45 to 60 minutes, 14.1% 60 minutes or more (2000)

Franklin County

Located in southern Illinois; bounded on the northwest by the Little Muddy River; drained by the Big Muddy River. Covers a land area of 412.10 square miles, a water area of 19.30 square miles, and is located in the Central Time Zone. The county government was organized in 1818. County seat is Benton.
Population: 39,018 (2000); Race: 98.4% White, 0.1% Black, 0.1% Asian, 0.3% American Indian and Alaska Native, 0.9% Hispanic of any race, 0.9% two or more races (2000); Density: 94.7 persons per square mile (2000); Age: 23.1% under 18, 18.6% over 64 (2000).
Religion: Five largest groups: 30.8% Southern Baptist Convention, 5.8% Christian Churches and Churches of Christ, 3.8% Catholic Church, 3.6% Church of God (Cleveland, Tennessee), 3.5% The United Methodist Church (2000).
Economy: Unemployment rate: 8.4% (11/2002); Total civilian labor force: 17,296 (11/2002); Leading industries: 21.2% manufacturing; 19.4% retail

trade; 16.2% health care and social assistance (2000); Companies that employ more than 1,000 persons: 0 (2000); Companies that employ more than 100 persons: 10 (2000); Farms: 658 totaling 179,588 acres (1997); Minority business ownership rate: 0.0% (1997); Women business ownership rate: 44.8% (1997); Retail sales per capita: $6,826 (1997). Single-family building permits issued: 38 (2001) / 27 (2000); Multi-family building permits issued: 2 (2001) / 2 (2000).
Income: Per capita income: $15,407 (2000); Median household income: $28,411 (2000); Poverty rate: 16.2% (2000); Bankruptcy rate: 8.69% (2001).
Taxes: Total county taxes per capita: $51 (2000); County property taxes per capita: $51 (2000).
Education: High school graduation rate: 76.7% (2000); College graduation rate: 11.3% (2000).
Housing: Homeownership rate: 77.7% (2000); Median home value: $45,100 (2000); Median rent: $264 per month (2000); Median age of housing: 45 years (2000).
Health: Birth rate: 103.5 per 10,000 population (1998); Age adjusted death rate: 102.8 per 10,000 population (1999); Age adjusted cancer mortality rate: 243.2 deaths per 100,000 population (1999). Number of physicians: 6.9 per 10,000 population (1999); Number of hospital beds: 32.0 per 10,000 population (1999).
Elections: 2000 Presidential election results: 53.1% Gore, 44.2% Bush, 1.8% Nader, 0.7% Buchanan
National and State Parks: Wayne Fitzgerrell State Park
Additional Information Contacts
Franklin County Government Offices 618-438-3221
Benton Chamber of Commerce 618-438-2121
West Frankfort Chamber of Commerce 618-932-2181

Franklin County Communities

BENTON (city). Covers a land area of 5.349 square miles and a water area of 0.141 square miles. Located at 38.00° N. Lat.; 88.91° W. Long. Elevation is 470 feet.
History: Incorporated 1841.
Population: 6,880 (2000); Race: 98.5% White, 0.4% Black, 0.2% Asian, 0.1% American Indian and Alaska Native, 0.9% Hispanic of any race, 0.5% two or more races (2000); Density: 1,286.2 persons per square mile (2000); Age: 22.0% under 18, 22.3% over 64 (2000); Marriage status: 18.2% never married, 59.9% now married, 10.8% widowed, 11.0% divorced (2000); Foreign born: 0.8% (2000); Ancestry (includes multiple ancestries): 16.4% German, 15.1% English, 15.0% United States or American, 12.6% Irish, 6.7% Other groups (2000).
Economy: Trade center for coal-mining, oil, and natural gas. Agricultural area. Manufacturing: chemicals, consumer goods. Livestock, poultry; dairy products; sorghum. Single-family building permits issued: 6 (2001) / 6 (2000); Multi-family building permits issued: 0 (2001) / 0 (2000); Employment by occupation: 6.9% management, 16.8% professional, 20.2% services, 29.4% sales, 0.3% farming, 8.4% construction, 18.0% production (2000).
Income: Per capita income: $15,787 (2000); Median household income: $27,177 (2000); Poverty rate: 17.5% (2000).
Taxes: Total city taxes per capita: $142 (1997); City property taxes per capita: $137 (1997).
Education: High school graduation rate: 76.1% (2000); College graduation rate: 13.3% (2000).

School District(s)

Benton Community Cons School District 47 (PK-08)
2000 Enrollment: 1,126 618-439-3136
Benton Cons High School District 103 (09-12)
2000 Enrollment: 633 618-439-6415
Franklin-Jefferson Co Special Education District (05-12)
2000 Enrollment: 21 618-439-7231
Franklin/Williamson Roe (07-12)
2000 Enrollment: 80 618-438-9711
Housing: Homeownership rate: 70.0% (2000); Median home value: $48,000 (2000); Median rent: $287 per month (2000); Median age of housing: 46 years (2000).
Hospitals: Franklin Hospital (25 beds)
Newspapers: The Benton Evening News (6 x week); The Benton Standard (1 x week)
Transportation: Commute to work: 93.2% car, 0.0% public transportation, 3.5% walk, 2.9% work from home (2000); Travel time to work: 49.8% less than 15 minutes, 23.4% 15 to 30 minutes, 17.1% 30 to 45 minutes, 4.7% 45 to 60 minutes, 4.9% 60 minutes or more (2000)
Additional Information Contacts
Benton Chamber of Commerce 618-438-2121

BUCKNER (village). Covers a land area of 0.887 square miles and a water area of 0.013 square miles. Located at 37.98° N. Lat.; 89.01° W. Long. Elevation is 410 feet.
Population: 479 (2000); Race: 96.7% White, 0.4% Black, 0.0% Asian, 0.8% American Indian and Alaska Native, 0.8% Hispanic of any race, 1.7% two or more races (2000); Density: 540.3 persons per square mile (2000); Age: 23.8% under 18, 14.0% over 64 (2000); Marriage status: 23.3% never married, 46.4% now married, 9.0% widowed, 21.2% divorced (2000); Foreign born: 1.0% (2000); Ancestry (includes multiple ancestries): 14.2% Irish, 13.4% United States or American, 10.0% German, 8.8% Other groups, 7.7% English (2000).
Economy: In bituminous-coal-mining and agricultural area. Employment by occupation: 2.6% management, 5.7% professional, 21.4% services, 25.0% sales, 0.0% farming, 10.4% construction, 34.9% production (2000).
Income: Per capita income: $12,260 (2000); Median household income: $25,119 (2000); Poverty rate: 23.3% (2000).
Taxes: Total city taxes per capita: $30 (1997); City property taxes per capita: $12 (1997).
Education: High school graduation rate: 71.4% (2000); College graduation rate: 4.4% (2000).
Housing: Homeownership rate: 83.0% (2000); Median home value: $24,600 (2000); Median rent: $272 per month (2000); Median age of housing: 60+ years (2000).
Transportation: Commute to work: 98.9% car, 0.0% public transportation, 1.1% walk, 0.0% work from home (2000); Travel time to work: 33.2% less than 15 minutes, 31.5% 15 to 30 minutes, 16.8% 30 to 45 minutes, 9.2% 45 to 60 minutes, 9.2% 60 minutes or more (2000)

CHRISTOPHER (city). Covers a land area of 1.410 square miles and a water area of 0 square miles. Located at 37.97° N. Lat.; 89.05° W. Long. Elevation is 443 feet.
History: Incorporated 1903.
Population: 2,836 (2000); Race: 98.8% White, 0.0% Black, 0.0% Asian, 0.0% American Indian and Alaska Native, 2.4% Hispanic of any race, 1.1% two or more races (2000); Density: 2,011.0 persons per square mile (2000); Age: 19.9% under 18, 22.0% over 64 (2000); Marriage status: 18.4% never married, 57.2% now married, 12.3% widowed, 12.1% divorced (2000); Foreign born: 0.3% (2000); Ancestry (includes multiple ancestries): 17.0% German, 13.5% English, 12.6% Irish, 11.6% Other groups, 9.5% United States or American (2000).
Economy: Railroad junction. In bituminous-coal-mining, oil, and agricultural area. Agriculture: grain and livestock. Manufacturing: boat trailers, mining equipment. Single-family building permits issued: 2 (2001) / 1 (2000); Multi-family building permits issued: 0 (2001) / 0 (2000); Employment by occupation: 4.3% management, 16.4% professional, 19.9% services, 28.2% sales, 0.0% farming, 10.3% construction, 20.9% production (2000).
Income: Per capita income: $15,141 (2000); Median household income: $25,045 (2000); Poverty rate: 19.8% (2000).
Taxes: Total city taxes per capita: $110 (1997); City property taxes per capita: $48 (1997).
Education: High school graduation rate: 73.0% (2000); College graduation rate: 10.9% (2000).

School District(s)

Christopher Unit 99 (PK-12)
2000 Enrollment: 793 618-724-9461
Housing: Homeownership rate: 73.0% (2000); Median home value: $36,000 (2000); Median rent: $228 per month (2000); Median age of housing: 52 years (2000).
Newspapers: The Progress (1 x week)
Transportation: Commute to work: 95.2% car, 0.0% public transportation, 0.7% walk, 3.3% work from home (2000); Travel time to work: 36.2% less than 15 minutes, 29.6% 15 to 30 minutes, 21.8% 30 to 45 minutes, 5.2% 45 to 60 minutes, 7.2% 60 minutes or more (2000)

EWING (village). Covers a land area of 1.014 square miles and a water area of 0 square miles. Located at 38.09° N. Lat.; 88.85° W. Long. Elevation is 471 feet.
Population: 310 (2000); Race: 99.3% White, 0.0% Black, 0.0% Asian, 0.0% American Indian and Alaska Native, 5.3% Hispanic of any race, 0.0% two or more races (2000); Density: 305.8 persons per square mile (2000); Age: 26.6% under 18, 11.6% over 64 (2000); Marriage status: 12.5% never married, 69.4% now married, 8.6% widowed, 9.5% divorced (2000); Foreign born: 0.7% (2000); Ancestry (includes multiple ancestries): 22.3% German,

17.3% United States or American, 16.9% English, 14.6% Irish, 8.6% Other groups (2000).
Economy: In bituminous-coal-mining, oil, and agricultural area.
Employment by occupation: 0.0% management, 8.2% professional, 17.2% services, 32.0% sales, 0.0% farming, 13.9% construction, 28.7% production (2000).
Income: Per capita income: $14,917 (2000); Median household income: $31,000 (2000); Poverty rate: 9.3% (2000).
Taxes: Total city taxes per capita: $31 (1997); City property taxes per capita: $27 (1997).
Education: High school graduation rate: 81.8% (2000); College graduation rate: 8.1% (2000).

School District(s)

Ewing Northern C C District 115 (PK-08)
2000 Enrollment: 202 618-629-2181

Housing: Homeownership rate: 83.2% (2000); Median home value: $45,000 (2000); Median rent: $275 per month (2000); Median age of housing: 29 years (2000).
Transportation: Commute to work: 92.5% car, 0.0% public transportation, 2.5% walk, 5.0% work from home (2000); Travel time to work: 18.4% less than 15 minutes, 46.5% 15 to 30 minutes, 32.5% 30 to 45 minutes, 1.8% 45 to 60 minutes, 0.9% 60 minutes or more (2000)

FREEMAN SPUR (village). Aka Freemanspur. Covers a land area of 0.404 square miles and a water area of 0 square miles. Located at 37.86° N. Lat.; 89.00° W. Long.
Population: 273 (2000); Race: 91.6% White, 1.5% Black, 0.0% Asian, 0.8% American Indian and Alaska Native, 4.6% Hispanic of any race, 6.1% two or more races (2000); Density: 676.0 persons per square mile (2000); Age: 32.1% under 18, 13.4% over 64 (2000); Marriage status: 26.3% never married, 46.0% now married, 10.1% widowed, 17.7% divorced (2000); Foreign born: 0.0% (2000); Ancestry (includes multiple ancestries): 21.8% Other groups, 18.7% Irish, 12.2% German, 10.3% Italian, 8.4% United States or American (2000).
Economy: Employment by occupation: 0.0% management, 7.1% professional, 29.3% services, 20.2% sales, 2.0% farming, 14.1% construction, 27.3% production (2000).
Income: Per capita income: $11,416 (2000); Median household income: $24,219 (2000); Poverty rate: 22.1% (2000).
Education: High school graduation rate: 68.1% (2000); College graduation rate: 6.1% (2000).
Housing: Homeownership rate: 75.5% (2000); Median home value: $30,500 (2000); Median rent: $289 per month (2000); Median age of housing: 53 years (2000).
Transportation: Commute to work: 94.9% car, 0.0% public transportation, 0.0% walk, 5.1% work from home (2000); Travel time to work: 22.3% less than 15 minutes, 38.3% 15 to 30 minutes, 30.9% 30 to 45 minutes, 3.2% 45 to 60 minutes, 5.3% 60 minutes or more (2000)

HANAFORD (village). Aka Logan. Covers a land area of 1.022 square miles and a water area of 0 square miles. Located at 37.95° N. Lat.; 88.83° W. Long. Elevation is 480 feet.
History: Also called Logan.
Population: 55 (2000); Race: 100.0% White, 0.0% Black, 0.0% Asian, 0.0% American Indian and Alaska Native, 0.0% Hispanic of any race, 0.0% two or more races (2000); Density: 53.8 persons per square mile (2000); Age: 0.0% under 18, 0.0% over 64 (2000); Marriage status: 0.0% never married, 0.0% now married, 100.0% widowed, 0.0% divorced (2000); Foreign born: 0.0% (2000); Ancestry (includes multiple ancestries): 100.0% German, 100.0% English (2000).
Economy: In bituminous-coal and agricultural area. Employment by occupation: 0.0% management, 0.0% professional, 0.0% services, 100.0% sales, 0.0% farming, 0.0% construction, 0.0% production (2000).
Income: Per capita income: $46,500 (2000); Median household income: $46,250 (2000); Poverty rate: 0.0% (2000).
Taxes: Total city taxes per capita: $22 (1997); City property taxes per capita: $2 (1997).
Education: High school graduation rate: 100.0% (2000); College graduation rate: 0.0% (2000).
Housing: Homeownership rate: 100.0% (2000); Median home value: $85,000 (2000); Median age of housing: 16 years (2000).
Transportation: Commute to work: 100.0% car, 0.0% public transportation, 0.0% walk, 0.0% work from home (2000); Travel time to work: 0.0% less than 15 minutes, 100.0% 15 to 30 minutes, 0.0% 30 to 45 minutes, 0.0% 45 to 60 minutes, 0.0% 60 minutes or more (2000)

MULKEYTOWN (unincorporated postal area, zip code 62865). Covers a land area of 50.295 square miles and a water area of 0.441 square miles. Located at 37.96° N. Lat.; 89.06° W. Long. Elevation is 451 feet.
Population: 1,879 (2000); Race: 96.5% White, 0.0% Black, 0.0% Asian, 0.9% American Indian and Alaska Native, 2.5% Hispanic of any race, 2.6% two or more races (2000); Density: 37.4 persons per square mile (2000); Age: 25.5% under 18, 13.5% over 64 (2000); Marriage status: 18.5% never married, 67.0% now married, 6.4% widowed, 8.1% divorced (2000); Foreign born: 0.1% (2000); Ancestry (includes multiple ancestries): 16.4% English, 15.0% German, 12.4% Irish, 11.7% United States or American, 9.1% Other groups (2000).
Economy: Employment by occupation: 11.0% management, 17.8% professional, 20.6% services, 26.1% sales, 0.0% farming, 12.7% construction, 11.8% production (2000).
Income: Per capita income: $17,037 (2000); Median household income: $38,200 (2000); Poverty rate: 12.7% (2000).
Education: High school graduation rate: 80.1% (2000); College graduation rate: 12.4% (2000).
Housing: Homeownership rate: 91.3% (2000); Median home value: $54,000 (2000); Median rent: $181 per month (2000); Median age of housing: 27 years (2000).
Transportation: Commute to work: 95.1% car, 0.7% public transportation, 0.2% walk, 4.0% work from home (2000); Travel time to work: 25.4% less than 15 minutes, 38.8% 15 to 30 minutes, 27.8% 30 to 45 minutes, 5.4% 45 to 60 minutes, 2.6% 60 minutes or more (2000)

NORTH CITY (village). Aka Coello. Covers a land area of 2.193 square miles and a water area of 0.040 square miles. Located at 37.99° N. Lat.; 89.06° W. Long.
Population: 630 (2000); Race: 97.8% White, 0.6% Black, 0.5% Asian, 0.0% American Indian and Alaska Native, 0.0% Hispanic of any race, 1.1% two or more races (2000); Density: 287.3 persons per square mile (2000); Age: 21.6% under 18, 18.7% over 64 (2000); Marriage status: 21.5% never married, 60.9% now married, 5.8% widowed, 11.7% divorced (2000); Foreign born: 1.9% (2000); Ancestry (includes multiple ancestries): 16.8% English, 13.5% German, 12.6% Irish, 12.1% Italian, 11.0% Other groups (2000).
Economy: In bituminous-coal and agricultural area. Employment by occupation: 9.3% management, 11.5% professional, 18.5% services, 19.6% sales, 1.1% farming, 15.9% construction, 24.1% production (2000).
Income: Per capita income: $13,360 (2000); Median household income: $27,381 (2000); Poverty rate: 19.6% (2000).
Taxes: Total city taxes per capita: $11 (1997); City property taxes per capita: $6 (1997).
Education: High school graduation rate: 75.1% (2000); College graduation rate: 6.2% (2000).
Housing: Homeownership rate: 81.6% (2000); Median home value: $36,600 (2000); Median rent: $213 per month (2000); Median age of housing: 44 years (2000).
Transportation: Commute to work: 95.4% car, 0.0% public transportation, 2.3% walk, 2.3% work from home (2000); Travel time to work: 27.0% less than 15 minutes, 27.7% 15 to 30 minutes, 24.2% 30 to 45 minutes, 13.3% 45 to 60 minutes, 7.8% 60 minutes or more (2000)

ORIENT (city). Covers a land area of 0.750 square miles and a water area of 0.006 square miles. Located at 37.91° N. Lat.; 88.97° W. Long. Elevation is 480 feet.
Population: 296 (2000); Race: 100.0% White, 0.0% Black, 0.0% Asian, 0.0% American Indian and Alaska Native, 0.0% Hispanic of any race, 0.0% two or more races (2000); Density: 394.7 persons per square mile (2000); Age: 31.9% under 18, 8.5% over 64 (2000); Marriage status: 16.6% never married, 54.4% now married, 14.7% widowed, 14.3% divorced (2000); Foreign born: 0.0% (2000); Ancestry (includes multiple ancestries): 30.2% United States or American, 19.9% Other groups, 19.7% Irish, 6.0% German, 5.7% Italian (2000).
Economy: In bituminous coal-mining and agricultural area. Employment by occupation: 6.9% management, 5.4% professional, 29.2% services, 12.3% sales, 0.0% farming, 10.8% construction, 35.4% production (2000).
Income: Per capita income: $8,713 (2000); Median household income: $21,250 (2000); Poverty rate: 19.0% (2000).
Taxes: Total city taxes per capita: $34 (1997); City property taxes per capita: $7 (1997).
Education: High school graduation rate: 59.4% (2000); College graduation rate: 4.5% (2000).

Housing: Homeownership rate: 92.6% (2000); Median home value: $25,600 (2000); Median rent: $225 per month (2000); Median age of housing: 60+ years (2000).
Transportation: Commute to work: 97.6% car, 0.0% public transportation, 0.0% walk, 2.4% work from home (2000); Travel time to work: 23.1% less than 15 minutes, 45.5% 15 to 30 minutes, 25.6% 30 to 45 minutes, 0.0% 45 to 60 minutes, 5.8% 60 minutes or more (2000)

ROYALTON (village). Covers a land area of 1.131 square miles and a water area of 0.001 square miles. Located at 37.88° N. Lat.; 89.11° W. Long. Elevation is 391 feet.
History: Incorporated 1907.
Population: 1,130 (2000); Race: 99.8% White, 0.0% Black, 0.0% Asian, 0.0% American Indian and Alaska Native, 0.5% Hispanic of any race, 0.2% two or more races (2000); Density: 999.2 persons per square mile (2000); Age: 24.0% under 18, 19.0% over 64 (2000); Marriage status: 19.2% never married, 53.1% now married, 12.2% widowed, 15.4% divorced (2000); Foreign born: 0.4% (2000); Ancestry (includes multiple ancestries): 19.5% United States or American, 14.3% German, 11.4% Irish, 10.6% Other groups, 9.8% English (2000).
Economy: In agricultural and bituminous-coal-mining area. Employment by occupation: 10.6% management, 14.9% professional, 17.2% services, 18.1% sales, 0.5% farming, 11.9% construction, 26.8% production (2000).
Income: Per capita income: $15,778 (2000); Median household income: $23,947 (2000); Poverty rate: 20.3% (2000).
Taxes: Total city taxes per capita: $108 (1997); City property taxes per capita: $25 (1997).
Education: High school graduation rate: 76.4% (2000); College graduation rate: 7.6% (2000).
Housing: Homeownership rate: 76.7% (2000); Median home value: $35,400 (2000); Median rent: $238 per month (2000); Median age of housing: 52 years (2000).
Transportation: Commute to work: 93.2% car, 0.7% public transportation, 1.4% walk, 4.0% work from home (2000); Travel time to work: 17.6% less than 15 minutes, 51.0% 15 to 30 minutes, 21.0% 30 to 45 minutes, 4.4% 45 to 60 minutes, 6.1% 60 minutes or more (2000)

SESSER (city). Covers a land area of 1.021 square miles and a water area of 0 square miles. Located at 38.09° N. Lat.; 89.05° W. Long. Elevation is 480 feet.
History: Incorporated 1906.
Population: 2,128 (2000); Race: 97.5% White, 0.0% Black, 0.0% Asian, 0.7% American Indian and Alaska Native, 1.3% Hispanic of any race, 0.6% two or more races (2000); Density: 2,084.9 persons per square mile (2000); Age: 24.5% under 18, 18.2% over 64 (2000); Marriage status: 19.3% never married, 56.1% now married, 11.6% widowed, 12.9% divorced (2000); Foreign born: 0.5% (2000); Ancestry (includes multiple ancestries): 14.9% United States or American, 11.3% German, 9.8% English, 7.6% Irish, 6.6% Other groups (2000).
Economy: Livestock, dairy products, corn, wheat. Single-family building permits issued: 3 (2001) / 2 (2000); Multi-family building permits issued: 0 (2001) / 0 (2000); Employment by occupation: 6.2% management, 14.7% professional, 19.9% services, 23.7% sales, 0.0% farming, 17.6% construction, 17.9% production (2000).
Income: Per capita income: $15,378 (2000); Median household income: $25,714 (2000); Poverty rate: 20.4% (2000).
Taxes: Total city taxes per capita: $76 (1997); City property taxes per capita: $60 (1997).
Education: High school graduation rate: 74.0% (2000); College graduation rate: 8.7% (2000).

School District(s)

Sesser-Valier Community Unit S D 196 (PK-12)
2000 Enrollment: 732 618-625-5105

Housing: Homeownership rate: 78.3% (2000); Median home value: $44,600 (2000); Median rent: $259 per month (2000); Median age of housing: 44 years (2000).
Transportation: Commute to work: 95.4% car, 0.0% public transportation, 1.3% walk, 2.8% work from home (2000); Travel time to work: 24.9% less than 15 minutes, 39.2% 15 to 30 minutes, 25.7% 30 to 45 minutes, 6.4% 45 to 60 minutes, 3.8% 60 minutes or more (2000)

THOMPSONVILLE (village). Covers a land area of 2.050 square miles and a water area of 0.013 square miles. Located at 37.91° N. Lat.; 88.76° W. Long. Elevation is 507 feet.
Population: 571 (2000); Race: 99.0% White, 0.0% Black, 0.0% Asian, 0.3% American Indian and Alaska Native, 1.5% Hispanic of any race, 0.7% two or more races (2000); Density: 278.6 persons per square mile (2000); Age: 25.0% under 18, 12.4% over 64 (2000); Marriage status: 22.3% never married, 60.7% now married, 9.2% widowed, 7.8% divorced (2000); Foreign born: 0.5% (2000); Ancestry (includes multiple ancestries): 19.5% United States or American, 14.9% Irish, 13.5% English, 13.0% German, 5.9% French (except Basque) (2000).
Economy: In bituminous coal, agricultural area. Employment by occupation: 7.7% management, 15.3% professional, 13.2% services, 19.1% sales, 4.3% farming, 12.3% construction, 28.1% production (2000).
Income: Per capita income: $13,327 (2000); Median household income: $30,500 (2000); Poverty rate: 17.8% (2000).
Taxes: Total city taxes per capita: $14 (1997); City property taxes per capita: $14 (1997).
Education: High school graduation rate: 83.9% (2000); College graduation rate: 8.4% (2000).

School District(s)

Thompsonville Community H S District 112 (09-12)
2000 Enrollment: 90 618-627-2446
Thompsonville School District 62 (KG-08)
2000 Enrollment: 202 618-627-2446

Housing: Homeownership rate: 72.8% (2000); Median home value: $39,600 (2000); Median rent: $198 per month (2000); Median age of housing: 35 years (2000).
Transportation: Commute to work: 91.3% car, 0.0% public transportation, 0.0% walk, 7.4% work from home (2000); Travel time to work: 11.3% less than 15 minutes, 41.0% 15 to 30 minutes, 26.4% 30 to 45 minutes, 16.0% 45 to 60 minutes, 5.2% 60 minutes or more (2000)

VALIER (village). Covers a land area of 1.128 square miles and a water area of 0 square miles. Located at 38.01° N. Lat.; 89.04° W. Long. Elevation is 460 feet.
Population: 662 (2000); Race: 95.4% White, 0.0% Black, 0.5% Asian, 1.1% American Indian and Alaska Native, 1.8% Hispanic of any race, 3.0% two or more races (2000); Density: 587.0 persons per square mile (2000); Age: 21.3% under 18, 19.2% over 64 (2000); Marriage status: 25.1% never married, 56.3% now married, 7.0% widowed, 11.6% divorced (2000); Foreign born: 0.9% (2000); Ancestry (includes multiple ancestries): 15.7% United States or American, 12.8% Irish, 12.8% German, 9.6% English, 5.2% French (except Basque) (2000).
Economy: In bituminous-coal-mining, oil and agricultural area. Single-family building permits issued: 1 (2001) / 0 (2000); Multi-family building permits issued: 0 (2001) / 0 (2000); Employment by occupation: 5.1% management, 15.9% professional, 15.2% services, 34.7% sales, 0.0% farming, 11.9% construction, 17.3% production (2000).
Income: Per capita income: $16,366 (2000); Median household income: $31,397 (2000); Poverty rate: 7.3% (2000).
Taxes: Total city taxes per capita: $85 (1997); City property taxes per capita: $34 (1997).
Education: High school graduation rate: 85.0% (2000); College graduation rate: 9.3% (2000).
Housing: Homeownership rate: 87.6% (2000); Median home value: $40,300 (2000); Median rent: $261 per month (2000); Median age of housing: 54 years (2000).
Transportation: Commute to work: 98.2% car, 0.0% public transportation, 0.0% walk, 0.7% work from home (2000); Travel time to work: 21.1% less than 15 minutes, 41.5% 15 to 30 minutes, 21.1% 30 to 45 minutes, 12.2% 45 to 60 minutes, 4.1% 60 minutes or more (2000)

WEST CITY (village). Covers a land area of 1.614 square miles and a water area of 0 square miles. Located at 37.99° N. Lat.; 88.94° W. Long. Elevation is 440 feet.
History: Incorporated 1911
Population: 716 (2000); Race: 95.6% White, 1.0% Black, 1.4% Asian, 0.0% American Indian and Alaska Native, 0.0% Hispanic of any race, 2.0% two or more races (2000); Density: 443.7 persons per square mile (2000); Age: 20.1% under 18, 18.8% over 64 (2000); Marriage status: 19.9% never married, 51.6% now married, 13.9% widowed, 14.6% divorced (2000); Foreign born: 0.0% (2000); Ancestry (includes multiple ancestries): 14.4% United States or American, 13.9% Irish, 12.3% German, 8.6% English, 7.6% Other groups (2000).
Economy: In bituminous-coal-mining, oil and agricultural area. Single-family building permits issued: 3 (2001) / 1 (2000); Multi-family building permits issued: 0 (2001) / 0 (2000); Employment by occupation: 5.9% management, 9.2% professional, 28.6% services, 29.7% sales, 1.1% farming, 8.8% construction, 16.8% production (2000).

Income: Per capita income: $12,328 (2000); Median household income: $21,250 (2000); Poverty rate: 22.1% (2000).
Taxes: Total city taxes per capita: $66 (1997); City property taxes per capita: $48 (1997).
Education: High school graduation rate: 68.5% (2000); College graduation rate: 5.5% (2000).
Housing: Homeownership rate: 66.1% (2000); Median home value: $38,700 (2000); Median rent: $222 per month (2000); Median age of housing: 46 years (2000).
Transportation: Commute to work: 92.9% car, 0.0% public transportation, 3.0% walk, 3.0% work from home (2000); Travel time to work: 41.4% less than 15 minutes, 26.1% 15 to 30 minutes, 14.2% 30 to 45 minutes, 7.7% 45 to 60 minutes, 10.7% 60 minutes or more (2000)

WEST FRANKFORT (city). Covers a land area of 4.746 square miles and a water area of 0.013 square miles. Located at 37.89° N. Lat.; 88.92° W. Long. Elevation is 401 feet.
History: Incorporated 1901; annexed Frankfort Heights in 1923.
Population: 8,196 (2000); Race: 98.8% White, 0.0% Black, 0.0% Asian, 0.3% American Indian and Alaska Native, 1.0% Hispanic of any race, 0.7% two or more races (2000); Density: 1,726.8 persons per square mile (2000); Age: 22.5% under 18, 21.4% over 64 (2000); Marriage status: 19.8% never married, 54.1% now married, 10.4% widowed, 15.7% divorced (2000); Foreign born: 0.9% (2000); Ancestry (includes multiple ancestries): 20.6% United States or American, 13.3% German, 10.9% Irish, 10.7% English, 9.5% Other groups (2000).
Economy: Trade center in bituminous-coal, oil and agricultural area. Large shaft mine. Livestock; produce; poultry; fruit. Single-family building permits issued: 11 (2001) / 17 (2000); Multi-family building permits issued: 2 (2001) / 2 (2000); Employment by occupation: 8.1% management, 11.7% professional, 22.6% services, 25.8% sales, 0.0% farming, 8.7% construction, 23.0% production (2000).
Income: Per capita income: $14,671 (2000); Median household income: $25,358 (2000); Poverty rate: 18.6% (2000).
Taxes: Total city taxes per capita: $105 (1997); City property taxes per capita: $95 (1997).
Education: High school graduation rate: 75.2% (2000); College graduation rate: 11.5% (2000).

School District(s)

Frankfort Community Unit School District 168 (PK-12)
2000 Enrollment: 1,797 618-937-2421
Housing: Homeownership rate: 67.4% (2000); Median home value: $41,500 (2000); Median rent: $271 per month (2000); Median age of housing: 52 years (2000).
Newspapers: The Daily American (6 x week); Southern Illinois Trader (1 x week); Central Illinois Trader (1 x week)
Transportation: Commute to work: 94.0% car, 0.0% public transportation, 1.9% walk, 2.3% work from home (2000); Travel time to work: 42.8% less than 15 minutes, 33.1% 15 to 30 minutes, 12.2% 30 to 45 minutes, 7.0% 45 to 60 minutes, 4.9% 60 minutes or more (2000)
Additional Information Contacts
West Frankfort Chamber of Commerce 618-932-2181

WHITTINGTON (unincorporated postal area, zip code 62897). Covers a land area of 14.931 square miles and a water area of 0.050 square miles. Located at 38.08° N. Lat.; 88.92° W. Long. Elevation is 445 feet.
Population: 335 (2000); Race: 100.0% White, 0.0% Black, 0.0% Asian, 0.0% American Indian and Alaska Native, 0.0% Hispanic of any race, 0.0% two or more races (2000); Density: 22.4 persons per square mile (2000); Age: 26.3% under 18, 12.5% over 64 (2000); Marriage status: 16.5% never married, 62.6% now married, 7.1% widowed, 13.8% divorced (2000); Foreign born: 0.0% (2000); Ancestry (includes multiple ancestries): 19.9% English, 16.5% United States or American, 12.8% German, 9.8% Irish, 4.9% Other groups (2000).
Economy: Employment by occupation: 11.4% management, 8.3% professional, 20.5% services, 31.1% sales, 0.0% farming, 6.8% construction, 22.0% production (2000).
Income: Per capita income: $14,399 (2000); Median household income: $27,708 (2000); Poverty rate: 14.3% (2000).
Education: High school graduation rate: 79.5% (2000); College graduation rate: 10.5% (2000).
Housing: Homeownership rate: 88.0% (2000); Median home value: $63,100 (2000); Median rent: $325 per month (2000); Median age of housing: 34 years (2000).
Transportation: Commute to work: 80.8% car, 0.0% public transportation, 6.2% walk, 13.1% work from home (2000); Travel time to work: 46.0% less than 15 minutes, 23.9% 15 to 30 minutes, 11.5% 30 to 45 minutes, 15.0% 45 to 60 minutes, 3.5% 60 minutes or more (2000)

ZEIGLER (city). Covers a land area of 0.860 square miles and a water area of 0 square miles. Located at 37.90° N. Lat.; 89.05° W. Long. Elevation is 400 feet.
Population: 1,669 (2000); Race: 99.0% White, 0.0% Black, 0.0% Asian, 0.0% American Indian and Alaska Native, 0.5% Hispanic of any race, 1.0% two or more races (2000); Density: 1,940.8 persons per square mile (2000); Age: 21.0% under 18, 19.6% over 64 (2000); Marriage status: 20.2% never married, 55.4% now married, 12.1% widowed, 12.3% divorced (2000); Foreign born: 1.0% (2000); Ancestry (includes multiple ancestries): 21.3% United States or American, 14.4% German, 10.5% Irish, 9.4% English, 7.2% Other groups (2000).
Economy: Bituminous-coal mines; oil; agriculture includes fruit, grain, livestock; dairy products. Single-family building permits issued: 12 (2001) / 0 (2000); Multi-family building permits issued: 0 (2001) / 0 (2000); Employment by occupation: 6.1% management, 14.3% professional, 18.0% services, 22.1% sales, 0.0% farming, 15.1% construction, 24.4% production (2000).
Income: Per capita income: $13,781 (2000); Median household income: $22,344 (2000); Poverty rate: 17.5% (2000).
Taxes: Total city taxes per capita: $100 (1997); City property taxes per capita: $49 (1997).
Education: High school graduation rate: 73.7% (2000); College graduation rate: 8.5% (2000).

School District(s)

Zeigler-Royalton C U S District 188 (PK-12)
2000 Enrollment: 643 618-596-5841
Housing: Homeownership rate: 77.4% (2000); Median home value: $30,700 (2000); Median rent: $210 per month (2000); Median age of housing: 60+ years (2000).
Transportation: Commute to work: 94.0% car, 0.0% public transportation, 3.6% walk, 1.7% work from home (2000); Travel time to work: 26.7% less than 15 minutes, 41.5% 15 to 30 minutes, 19.7% 30 to 45 minutes, 4.6% 45 to 60 minutes, 7.5% 60 minutes or more (2000)

Fulton County

Located in west central Illinois; bounded on the southeast by the Illinois River; drained by the Spoon River. Covers a land area of 865.60 square miles, a water area of 17.00 square miles, and is located in the Central Time Zone. The county government was organized in 1823. County seat is Lewistown.
Population: 38,250 (2000); Race: 95.2% White, 3.7% Black, 0.1% Asian, 0.1% American Indian and Alaska Native, 1.2% Hispanic of any race, 0.6% two or more races (2000); Density: 44.2 persons per square mile (2000); Age: 22.0% under 18, 18.3% over 64 (2000).
Religion: Five largest groups: 10.1% The United Methodist Church, 5.1% Catholic Church, 4.3% Christian Church (Disciples of Christ), 2.9% Christian Churches and Churches of Christ, 2.2% Church of the Nazarene (2000).
Economy: Unemployment rate: 9.1% (11/2002); Total civilian labor force: 13,706 (11/2002); Leading industries: 25.3% health care and social assistance; 24.3% retail trade; 11.4% accommodation & food services (2000); Companies that employ more than 1,000 persons: 0 (2000); Companies that employ more than 100 persons: 11 (2000); Farms: 1,101 totaling 424,942 acres (1997); Minority business ownership rate: 0.0% (1997); Women business ownership rate: 20.9% (1997); Retail sales per capita: $6,398 (1997). Single-family building permits issued: 71 (2001) / 73 (2000); Multi-family building permits issued: 0 (2001) / 0 (2000).
Income: Per capita income: $17,373 (2000); Median household income: $33,952 (2000); Poverty rate: 9.9% (2000); Bankruptcy rate: 8.16% (2001).
Taxes: Total county taxes per capita: $79 (1997); County property taxes per capita: $79 (1997).
Education: High school graduation rate: 78.3% (2000); College graduation rate: 11.4% (2000).
Housing: Homeownership rate: 76.3% (2000); Median home value: $58,100 (2000); Median rent: $282 per month (2000); Median age of housing: 51 years (2000).
Health: Birth rate: 103.5 per 10,000 population (1998); Age adjusted death rate: 88.3 per 10,000 population (1999); Age adjusted cancer mortality rate: 213.3 deaths per 100,000 population (1999). Number of physicians: 7.6 per 10,000 population (1999); Number of hospital beds: 32.4 per 10,000 population (1999).
Elections: 2000 Presidential election results: 54.9% Gore, 42.6% Bush, 1.7% Nader, 0.6% Buchanan

National and State Parks: Anderson Lake State Conservation Area; Dickson Mounds State Park; Rice Lake State Conservation Area

Additional Information Contacts

Fulton County Government Offices 309-547-3041
Canton Chamber of Commerce 309-647-2677
Lewistown Chamber of Commerce 309-547-4300

Fulton County Communities

ASTORIA (village). Covers a land area of 0.590 square miles and a water area of 0 square miles. Located at 40.22° N. Lat.; 90.35° W. Long. Elevation is 712 feet.

History: The villages of Washington, laid out in 1836, and Vienna, platted in 1837, were later combined and named Astoria, for John Jacob Astor who owned land in the area. Astoria was a station on the stagecoach line between Peoria and Quincy.

Population: 1,193 (2000); Race: 98.2% White, 0.0% Black, 0.0% Asian, 0.4% American Indian and Alaska Native, 0.0% Hispanic of any race, 1.4% two or more races (2000); Density: 2,020.8 persons per square mile (2000); Age: 26.9% under 18, 22.5% over 64 (2000); Marriage status: 18.1% never married, 63.4% now married, 10.5% widowed, 8.0% divorced (2000); Foreign born: 0.2% (2000); Ancestry (includes multiple ancestries): 24.5% German, 16.0% United States or American, 12.5% English, 5.9% Irish, 5.6% Other groups (2000).

Economy: Single-family building permits issued: 1 (2001) / 1 (2000); Multi-family building permits issued: 0 (2001) / 0 (2000); Employment by occupation: 8.3% management, 14.5% professional, 21.6% services, 15.6% sales, 3.0% farming, 8.1% construction, 28.9% production (2000).

Income: Per capita income: $12,758 (2000); Median household income: $26,694 (2000); Poverty rate: 11.3% (2000).

Taxes: Total city taxes per capita: $32 (1997); City property taxes per capita: $32 (1997).

Education: High school graduation rate: 79.1% (2000); College graduation rate: 9.6% (2000).

School District(s)

Astoria Community Unit School District 1 (PK-12)
2000 Enrollment: 409 309-329-2111

Housing: Homeownership rate: 74.9% (2000); Median home value: $34,400 (2000); Median rent: $226 per month (2000); Median age of housing: 60+ years (2000).

Newspapers: The South Fulton Argus (1 x week)

Transportation: Commute to work: 90.7% car, 0.0% public transportation, 4.9% walk, 3.9% work from home (2000); Travel time to work: 38.4% less than 15 minutes, 17.4% 15 to 30 minutes, 15.9% 30 to 45 minutes, 14.4% 45 to 60 minutes, 13.9% 60 minutes or more (2000)

AVON (village). Covers a land area of 0.443 square miles and a water area of 0 square miles. Located at 40.66° N. Lat.; 90.43° W. Long. Elevation is 635 feet.

Population: 915 (2000); Race: 97.8% White, 0.0% Black, 0.0% Asian, 0.3% American Indian and Alaska Native, 1.1% Hispanic of any race, 1.7% two or more races (2000); Density: 2,065.3 persons per square mile (2000); Age: 24.1% under 18, 20.7% over 64 (2000); Marriage status: 20.1% never married, 57.8% now married, 8.3% widowed, 13.8% divorced (2000); Foreign born: 0.8% (2000); Ancestry (includes multiple ancestries): 20.9% German, 12.3% Irish, 10.1% English, 9.9% United States or American, 5.3% Swedish (2000).

Economy: Grain; dairy products; livestock. Single-family building permits issued: 0 (2001) / 0 (2000); Multi-family building permits issued: 0 (2001) / 0 (2000); Employment by occupation: 8.0% management, 12.7% professional, 22.4% services, 15.3% sales, 1.0% farming, 9.7% construction, 30.9% production (2000).

Income: Per capita income: $16,257 (2000); Median household income: $33,417 (2000); Poverty rate: 11.7% (2000).

Taxes: Total city taxes per capita: $48 (1997); City property taxes per capita: $43 (1997).

Education: High school graduation rate: 80.7% (2000); College graduation rate: 9.5% (2000).

School District(s)

Avon Community Unit School District 176 (PK-12)
2000 Enrollment: 331 309-465-3708

Housing: Homeownership rate: 76.0% (2000); Median home value: $45,700 (2000); Median rent: $202 per month (2000); Median age of housing: 48 years (2000).

Newspapers: Avon Sentinel (1 x week)

Transportation: Commute to work: 92.9% car, 0.0% public transportation, 3.9% walk, 2.0% work from home (2000); Travel time to work: 28.1% less than 15 minutes, 27.9% 15 to 30 minutes, 34.7% 30 to 45 minutes, 3.5% 45 to 60 minutes, 5.8% 60 minutes or more (2000)

BANNER (village). Covers a land area of 0.336 square miles and a water area of 0 square miles. Located at 40.51° N. Lat.; 89.91° W. Long. Elevation is 475 feet.

Population: 149 (2000); Race: 100.0% White, 0.0% Black, 0.0% Asian, 0.0% American Indian and Alaska Native, 0.0% Hispanic of any race, 0.0% two or more races (2000); Density: 443.6 persons per square mile (2000); Age: 30.5% under 18, 17.7% over 64 (2000); Marriage status: 30.0% never married, 53.6% now married, 7.3% widowed, 9.1% divorced (2000); Foreign born: 0.0% (2000); Ancestry (includes multiple ancestries): 26.2% United States or American, 20.6% German, 19.1% English, 5.7% Other groups, 5.0% Irish (2000).

Economy: In agriculture and bituminous coal area. Employment by occupation: 14.8% management, 9.3% professional, 25.9% services, 11.1% sales, 0.0% farming, 16.7% construction, 22.2% production (2000).

Income: Per capita income: $13,101 (2000); Median household income: $31,250 (2000); Poverty rate: 19.1% (2000).

Taxes: Total city taxes per capita: $12 (1997); City property taxes per capita: $0 (1997).

Education: High school graduation rate: 77.7% (2000); College graduation rate: 3.2% (2000).

Housing: Homeownership rate: 70.2% (2000); Median home value: $45,300 (2000); Median rent: $317 per month (2000); Median age of housing: 43 years (2000).

Transportation: Commute to work: 90.4% car, 0.0% public transportation, 0.0% walk, 9.6% work from home (2000); Travel time to work: 0.0% less than 15 minutes, 25.5% 15 to 30 minutes, 51.1% 30 to 45 minutes, 19.1% 45 to 60 minutes, 4.3% 60 minutes or more (2000)

BRYANT (village). Covers a land area of 0.256 square miles and a water area of 0 square miles. Located at 40.46° N. Lat.; 90.09° W. Long. Elevation is 610 feet.

Population: 255 (2000); Race: 100.0% White, 0.0% Black, 0.0% Asian, 0.0% American Indian and Alaska Native, 0.0% Hispanic of any race, 0.0% two or more races (2000); Density: 994.6 persons per square mile (2000); Age: 26.9% under 18, 11.2% over 64 (2000); Marriage status: 26.1% never married, 58.4% now married, 9.3% widowed, 6.2% divorced (2000); Foreign born: 0.0% (2000); Ancestry (includes multiple ancestries): 22.4% German, 17.7% Irish, 11.9% Other groups, 10.2% English, 9.5% United States or American (2000).

Economy: In agricultural area. Bituminous coal. Employment by occupation: 8.8% management, 11.6% professional, 18.4% services, 29.3% sales, 3.4% farming, 3.4% construction, 25.2% production (2000).

Income: Per capita income: $13,740 (2000); Median household income: $28,636 (2000); Poverty rate: 14.3% (2000).

Taxes: Total city taxes per capita: $11 (1997); City property taxes per capita: $7 (1997).

Education: High school graduation rate: 78.2% (2000); College graduation rate: 7.9% (2000).

Housing: Homeownership rate: 84.8% (2000); Median home value: $37,100 (2000); Median rent: $267 per month (2000); Median age of housing: 49 years (2000).

Transportation: Commute to work: 100.0% car, 0.0% public transportation, 0.0% walk, 0.0% work from home (2000); Travel time to work: 23.1% less than 15 minutes, 39.2% 15 to 30 minutes, 9.8% 30 to 45 minutes, 14.0% 45 to 60 minutes, 14.0% 60 minutes or more (2000)

CANTON (city). Covers a land area of 7.849 square miles and a water area of 0.163 square miles. Located at 40.55° N. Lat.; 90.03° W. Long. Elevation is 660 feet.

History: Canton was founded in 1825 by Isaac Swan of New York. He selected the name for the town in the belief that the city of Canton in China was located directly opposite on the globe.

Population: 15,288 (2000); Race: 89.6% White, 8.8% Black, 0.2% Asian, 0.2% American Indian and Alaska Native, 2.1% Hispanic of any race, 0.7% two or more races (2000); Density: 1,947.8 persons per square mile (2000); Age: 20.3% under 18, 18.3% over 64 (2000); Marriage status: 17.2% never married, 56.7% now married, 9.0% widowed, 17.1% divorced (2000); Foreign born: 1.2% (2000); Ancestry (includes multiple ancestries): 17.4% German, 11.4% United States or American, 10.5% English, 7.7% Irish, 5.7% Other groups (2000).

Vital Statistics: Birth rate: 107.3 per 10,000 population (1998)

Economy: Single-family building permits issued: 14 (2001) / 10 (2000); Multi-family building permits issued: 0 (2001) / 0 (2000); Employment by occupation: 7.3% management, 20.1% professional, 21.0% services, 27.6% sales, 0.6% farming, 10.3% construction, 13.1% production (2000).
Income: Per capita income: $17,012 (2000); Median household income: $31,011 (2000); Poverty rate: 13.4% (2000).
Taxes: Total city taxes per capita: $137 (1997); City property taxes per capita: $90 (1997).
Education: High school graduation rate: 72.5% (2000); College graduation rate: 11.9% (2000).

School District(s)

Canton Union School District 66 (PK-12)
2000 Enrollment: 2,707 309-647-9411

Two-year College(s)

Graham Hospital School of Nursing (Private, Not-for-profit)
2001 Enrollment: 50 309-647-4086
2001 Tuition: In-state $5,600; Out-of-state $5,600
Spoon River College (Public)
2001 Enrollment: 1,909 309-647-4645
2001 Tuition: In-state $2,250; Out-of-state $3,750

Housing: Homeownership rate: 69.2% (2000); Median home value: $61,500 (2000); Median rent: $317 per month (2000); Median age of housing: 48 years (2000).
Hospitals: Graham Hospital (124 beds)
Newspapers: Daily Ledger (6 x week)
Transportation: Commute to work: 94.2% car, 0.3% public transportation, 2.0% walk, 2.1% work from home (2000); Travel time to work: 52.0% less than 15 minutes, 13.1% 15 to 30 minutes, 12.4% 30 to 45 minutes, 16.5% 45 to 60 minutes, 5.9% 60 minutes or more (2000)
Airports: Ingersoll
Additional Information Contacts
Canton Chamber of Commerce 309-647-2677

CUBA (city). Covers a land area of 0.542 square miles and a water area of 0 square miles. Located at 40.49° N. Lat.; 90.19° W. Long. Elevation is 690 feet.
History: Incorporated 1853.
Population: 1,418 (2000); Race: 98.6% White, 0.2% Black, 0.0% Asian, 0.0% American Indian and Alaska Native, 1.1% Hispanic of any race, 0.5% two or more races (2000); Density: 2,616.7 persons per square mile (2000); Age: 22.0% under 18, 22.2% over 64 (2000); Marriage status: 21.3% never married, 55.5% now married, 11.5% widowed, 11.7% divorced (2000); Foreign born: 0.8% (2000); Ancestry (includes multiple ancestries): 16.9% German, 14.2% United States or American, 12.7% English, 7.2% Irish, 4.6% Other groups (2000).
Economy: In agricultural and bituminous coal-mining area. Single-family building permits issued: 1 (2001) / 2 (2000); Multi-family building permits issued: 0 (2001) / 0 (2000); Employment by occupation: 6.0% management, 13.6% professional, 23.4% services, 28.0% sales, 0.4% farming, 10.2% construction, 18.4% production (2000).
Income: Per capita income: $16,608 (2000); Median household income: $30,682 (2000); Poverty rate: 9.8% (2000).
Taxes: Total city taxes per capita: $30 (2000); City property taxes per capita: $28 (2000).
Education: High school graduation rate: 78.5% (2000); College graduation rate: 9.0% (2000).

School District(s)

Comm Unit School District 3 Fulton Cty (PK-12)
2000 Enrollment: 615 309-785-5021

Housing: Homeownership rate: 80.4% (2000); Median home value: $46,200 (2000); Median rent: $286 per month (2000); Median age of housing: 58 years (2000).
Transportation: Commute to work: 93.7% car, 0.0% public transportation, 4.3% walk, 1.2% work from home (2000); Travel time to work: 39.2% less than 15 minutes, 21.2% 15 to 30 minutes, 14.0% 30 to 45 minutes, 11.0% 45 to 60 minutes, 14.6% 60 minutes or more (2000)

DUNFERMLINE (village). Covers a land area of 0.131 square miles and a water area of 0 square miles. Located at 40.49° N. Lat.; 90.03° W. Long. Elevation is 635 feet.
Population: 262 (2000); Race: 98.4% White, 0.0% Black, 0.0% Asian, 0.0% American Indian and Alaska Native, 0.0% Hispanic of any race, 1.6% two or more races (2000); Density: 1,999.9 persons per square mile (2000); Age: 21.8% under 18, 16.7% over 64 (2000); Marriage status: 17.6% never married, 64.3% now married, 5.7% widowed, 12.4% divorced (2000); Foreign born: 0.0% (2000); Ancestry (includes multiple ancestries): 18.3% United States or American, 15.6% English, 11.7% German, 4.3% Croatian, 3.9% Other groups (2000).
Economy: Corn, wheat, soybeans; cattle. Bituminous coal. Single-family building permits issued: 4 (2001) / 1 (2000); Multi-family building permits issued: 0 (2001) / 0 (2000); Employment by occupation: 5.0% management, 12.5% professional, 20.8% services, 24.2% sales, 0.0% farming, 20.0% construction, 17.5% production (2000).
Income: Per capita income: $16,152 (2000); Median household income: $35,357 (2000); Poverty rate: 9.5% (2000).
Taxes: Total city taxes per capita: $109 (1997); City property taxes per capita: $93 (1997).
Education: High school graduation rate: 81.8% (2000); College graduation rate: 1.1% (2000).
Housing: Homeownership rate: 80.4% (2000); Median home value: $48,000 (2000); Median rent: $260 per month (2000); Median age of housing: 46 years (2000).
Transportation: Commute to work: 96.6% car, 0.0% public transportation, 0.0% walk, 3.4% work from home (2000); Travel time to work: 36.0% less than 15 minutes, 26.3% 15 to 30 minutes, 12.3% 30 to 45 minutes, 16.7% 45 to 60 minutes, 8.8% 60 minutes or more (2000)

ELLISVILLE (village). Covers a land area of 0.271 square miles and a water area of 0 square miles. Located at 40.62° N. Lat.; 90.30° W. Long. Elevation is 550 feet.
Population: 87 (2000); Race: 100.0% White, 0.0% Black, 0.0% Asian, 0.0% American Indian and Alaska Native, 0.0% Hispanic of any race, 0.0% two or more races (2000); Density: 320.6 persons per square mile (2000); Age: 17.6% under 18, 15.7% over 64 (2000); Marriage status: 23.1% never married, 58.2% now married, 14.3% widowed, 4.4% divorced (2000); Foreign born: 0.0% (2000); Ancestry (includes multiple ancestries): 17.6% German, 11.1% Irish, 8.3% United States or American, 7.4% English, 4.6% Other groups (2000).
Economy: In agricultural and bituminous-coal area. Employment by occupation: 3.3% management, 6.7% professional, 15.0% services, 25.0% sales, 0.0% farming, 23.3% construction, 26.7% production (2000).
Income: Per capita income: $16,225 (2000); Median household income: $35,250 (2000); Poverty rate: 3.7% (2000).
Taxes: Total city taxes per capita: $9 (1997); City property taxes per capita: $9 (1997).
Education: High school graduation rate: 80.2% (2000); College graduation rate: 0.0% (2000).
Housing: Homeownership rate: 84.0% (2000); Median home value: $24,600 (2000); Median rent: $225 per month (2000); Median age of housing: 60+ years (2000).
Transportation: Commute to work: 91.2% car, 0.0% public transportation, 8.8% walk, 0.0% work from home (2000); Travel time to work: 12.3% less than 15 minutes, 64.9% 15 to 30 minutes, 12.3% 30 to 45 minutes, 0.0% 45 to 60 minutes, 10.5% 60 minutes or more (2000)

FAIRVIEW (village). Covers a land area of 4.162 square miles and a water area of 0.074 square miles. Located at 40.63° N. Lat.; 90.16° W. Long. Elevation is 735 feet.
Population: 493 (2000); Race: 99.4% White, 0.0% Black, 0.0% Asian, 0.6% American Indian and Alaska Native, 0.4% Hispanic of any race, 0.0% two or more races (2000); Density: 118.4 persons per square mile (2000); Age: 19.0% under 18, 22.6% over 64 (2000); Marriage status: 27.1% never married, 53.7% now married, 9.7% widowed, 9.5% divorced (2000); Foreign born: 0.4% (2000); Ancestry (includes multiple ancestries): 32.5% German, 17.7% English, 15.0% Irish, 8.1% Other groups, 4.7% United States or American (2000).
Economy: In agricultural area: corn, wheat, sorghum, soybeans; cattle. Bituminous coal-mining area. Ships grain. Single-family building permits issued: 0 (2001) / 2 (2000); Multi-family building permits issued: 0 (2001) / 0 (2000); Employment by occupation: 7.4% management, 20.3% professional, 14.7% services, 14.7% sales, 0.9% farming, 11.5% construction, 30.4% production (2000).
Income: Per capita income: $18,677 (2000); Median household income: $32,750 (2000); Poverty rate: 10.9% (2000).
Taxes: Total city taxes per capita: $28 (1997); City property taxes per capita: $28 (1997).
Education: High school graduation rate: 88.0% (2000); College graduation rate: 15.5% (2000).
Housing: Homeownership rate: 84.1% (2000); Median home value: $56,100 (2000); Median rent: $367 per month (2000); Median age of housing: 60+ years (2000).

Transportation: Commute to work: 93.9% car, 0.0% public transportation, 4.2% walk, 1.9% work from home (2000); Travel time to work: 22.4% less than 15 minutes, 27.6% 15 to 30 minutes, 20.0% 30 to 45 minutes, 20.0% 45 to 60 minutes, 10.0% 60 minutes or more (2000)

FARMINGTON (city). Covers a land area of 1.241 square miles and a water area of 0 square miles. Located at 40.69° N. Lat.; 90.00° W. Long. Elevation is 752 feet.

History: Farmington was laid out in 1834, and grew as a mining town. In 1856 Farmington was the scene of a "whiskey war" when a group of women marched on the saloons, breaking windows and smashing bottles.

Population: 2,601 (2000); Race: 99.5% White, 0.2% Black, 0.0% Asian, 0.2% American Indian and Alaska Native, 0.4% Hispanic of any race, 0.2% two or more races (2000); Density: 2,095.1 persons per square mile (2000); Age: 23.6% under 18, 21.2% over 64 (2000); Marriage status: 20.8% never married, 59.8% now married, 11.7% widowed, 7.7% divorced (2000); Foreign born: 0.7% (2000); Ancestry (includes multiple ancestries): 27.5% German, 14.7% Irish, 14.1% English, 13.3% United States or American, 5.2% Italian (2000).

Economy: Single-family building permits issued: 0 (2001) / 0 (2000); Multi-family building permits issued: 0 (2001) / 0 (2000); Employment by occupation: 10.1% management, 13.8% professional, 20.5% services, 21.0% sales, 0.0% farming, 10.2% construction, 24.3% production (2000).

Income: Per capita income: $19,336 (2000); Median household income: $35,893 (2000); Poverty rate: 7.0% (2000).

Taxes: Total city taxes per capita: $71 (1997); City property taxes per capita: $61 (1997).

Education: High school graduation rate: 84.7% (2000); College graduation rate: 11.9% (2000).

Housing: Homeownership rate: 79.8% (2000); Median home value: $65,800 (2000); Median rent: $263 per month (2000); Median age of housing: 60 years (2000).

Transportation: Commute to work: 97.0% car, 0.0% public transportation, 2.0% walk, 1.0% work from home (2000); Travel time to work: 37.7% less than 15 minutes, 15.9% 15 to 30 minutes, 27.5% 30 to 45 minutes, 13.8% 45 to 60 minutes, 5.0% 60 minutes or more (2000)

IPAVA (village). Covers a land area of 0.270 square miles and a water area of 0 square miles. Located at 40.35° N. Lat.; 90.32° W. Long. Elevation is 655 feet.

History: Vestiges of Camp Ellis, a World War II prisoner-of-war camp, nearby.

Population: 506 (2000); Race: 97.9% White, 0.0% Black, 0.0% Asian, 1.0% American Indian and Alaska Native, 0.8% Hispanic of any race, 0.8% two or more races (2000); Density: 1,877.0 persons per square mile (2000); Age: 22.2% under 18, 25.1% over 64 (2000); Marriage status: 15.8% never married, 61.5% now married, 12.1% widowed, 10.6% divorced (2000); Foreign born: 1.0% (2000); Ancestry (includes multiple ancestries): 23.7% United States or American, 20.8% German, 9.3% English, 7.2% Other groups, 7.2% Irish (2000).

Economy: In agricultural area: corn, wheat, sorghum, soybeans, cattle. Bituminous-coal-mining area. Ships grain. Single-family building permits issued: 0 (2001) / 0 (2000); Multi-family building permits issued: 0 (2001) / 0 (2000); Employment by occupation: 9.5% management, 11.3% professional, 13.5% services, 27.9% sales, 1.4% farming, 13.1% construction, 23.4% production (2000).

Income: Per capita income: $16,007 (2000); Median household income: $31,250 (2000); Poverty rate: 10.1% (2000).

Taxes: Total city taxes per capita: $21 (1997); City property taxes per capita: $15 (1997).

Education: High school graduation rate: 75.9% (2000); College graduation rate: 6.7% (2000).

Housing: Homeownership rate: 85.0% (2000); Median home value: $37,600 (2000); Median rent: $227 per month (2000); Median age of housing: 60+ years (2000).

Transportation: Commute to work: 94.0% car, 0.0% public transportation, 2.3% walk, 2.3% work from home (2000); Travel time to work: 17.5% less than 15 minutes, 25.6% 15 to 30 minutes, 40.3% 30 to 45 minutes, 5.7% 45 to 60 minutes, 10.9% 60 minutes or more (2000)

LEWISTOWN (city). Covers a land area of 1.838 square miles and a water area of 0 square miles. Located at 40.39° N. Lat.; 90.15° W. Long. Elevation is 590 feet.

History: Lewiston was founded in 1821 by Major Ossian M. Ross, who had received the land for his service in the War of 1812. The town was named for the Major's son, Lewis. In 1823 Ross organized Fulton County and had Lewiston named as the seat, with the courthouse built on land he donated.

Population: 2,522 (2000); Race: 98.6% White, 1.0% Black, 0.1% Asian, 0.0% American Indian and Alaska Native, 0.0% Hispanic of any race, 0.3% two or more races (2000); Density: 1,372.2 persons per square mile (2000); Age: 22.3% under 18, 24.0% over 64 (2000); Marriage status: 18.7% never married, 57.9% now married, 12.1% widowed, 11.4% divorced (2000); Foreign born: 0.5% (2000); Ancestry (includes multiple ancestries): 14.9% United States or American, 14.7% German, 10.5% English, 10.0% Irish, 6.0% Other groups (2000).

Economy: Single-family building permits issued: 2 (2001) / 1 (2000); Multi-family building permits issued: 0 (2001) / 0 (2000); Employment by occupation: 9.4% management, 16.4% professional, 21.6% services, 23.4% sales, 0.7% farming, 8.2% construction, 20.4% production (2000).

Income: Per capita income: $15,620 (2000); Median household income: $30,943 (2000); Poverty rate: 7.1% (2000).

Taxes: Total city taxes per capita: $208 (1997); City property taxes per capita: $84 (1997).

Education: High school graduation rate: 80.1% (2000); College graduation rate: 11.7% (2000).

School District(s)

Fulton/Schuyler Roe (08-12)
2000 Enrollment: 20 309-547-3041

Housing: Homeownership rate: 66.9% (2000); Median home value: $55,100 (2000); Median rent: $215 per month (2000); Median age of housing: 51 years (2000).

Newspapers: The Fulton Democrat (1 x week)

Transportation: Commute to work: 88.3% car, 0.7% public transportation, 6.3% walk, 2.7% work from home (2000); Travel time to work: 41.7% less than 15 minutes, 24.3% 15 to 30 minutes, 13.9% 30 to 45 minutes, 9.7% 45 to 60 minutes, 10.5% 60 minutes or more (2000)

Additional Information Contacts

Lewistown Chamber of Commerce 309-547-4300

LIVERPOOL (village). Covers a land area of 0.081 square miles and a water area of 0.001 square miles. Located at 40.39° N. Lat.; 90.00° W. Long. Elevation is 445 feet.

History: Liverpool, named for the town in England, began as a river town and shipping center. Commercial fishing developed later.

Population: 119 (2000); Race: 100.0% White, 0.0% Black, 0.0% Asian, 0.0% American Indian and Alaska Native, 0.0% Hispanic of any race, 0.0% two or more races (2000); Density: 1,475.7 persons per square mile (2000); Age: 42.1% under 18, 6.3% over 64 (2000); Marriage status: 37.5% never married, 46.9% now married, 9.4% widowed, 6.3% divorced (2000); Foreign born: 0.0% (2000); Ancestry (includes multiple ancestries): 38.9% United States or American, 10.5% British, 9.5% Other groups, 4.2% English, 3.2% Austrian (2000).

Economy: Employment by occupation: 6.7% management, 0.0% professional, 30.0% services, 6.7% sales, 6.7% farming, 36.7% construction, 13.3% production (2000).

Income: Per capita income: $11,848 (2000); Median household income: $33,333 (2000); Poverty rate: 2.1% (2000).

Taxes: Total city taxes per capita: $176 (1997); City property taxes per capita: $140 (1997).

Education: High school graduation rate: 59.6% (2000); College graduation rate: 0.0% (2000).

Housing: Homeownership rate: 67.7% (2000); Median home value: $31,800 (2000); Median rent: $375 per month (2000); Median age of housing: 47 years (2000).

Transportation: Commute to work: 100.0% car, 0.0% public transportation, 0.0% walk, 0.0% work from home (2000); Travel time to work: 6.7% less than 15 minutes, 56.7% 15 to 30 minutes, 16.7% 30 to 45 minutes, 6.7% 45 to 60 minutes, 13.3% 60 minutes or more (2000)

LONDON MILLS (village). Covers a land area of 0.694 square miles and a water area of 0 square miles. Located at 40.71° N. Lat.; 90.26° W. Long. Elevation is 533 feet.

Population: 447 (2000); Race: 100.0% White, 0.0% Black, 0.0% Asian, 0.0% American Indian and Alaska Native, 0.0% Hispanic of any race, 0.0% two or more races (2000); Density: 644.5 persons per square mile (2000); Age: 33.2% under 18, 12.4% over 64 (2000); Marriage status: 18.0% never married, 65.5% now married, 2.2% widowed, 14.2% divorced (2000); Foreign born: 0.0% (2000); Ancestry (includes multiple ancestries): 23.6% German, 13.8% Irish, 8.4% Swedish, 6.3% English, 5.8% Other groups (2000).

Economy: In agricultural area: corn, wheat, sorghum; cattle. Bituminous-coal-mining area. Feed milling. Employment by occupation: 10.9% management, 12.2% professional, 17.9% services, 14.1% sales, 3.2% farming, 13.5% construction, 28.2% production (2000).
Income: Per capita income: $16,453 (2000); Median household income: $38,125 (2000); Poverty rate: 9.3% (2000).
Taxes: Total city taxes per capita: $20 (1997); City property taxes per capita: $20 (1997).
Education: High school graduation rate: 80.7% (2000); College graduation rate: 12.1% (2000).

School District(s)

Spoon River Valley C U S District 4 (PK-12)
2000 Enrollment: 465 309-778-2204

Housing: Homeownership rate: 90.4% (2000); Median home value: $42,500 (2000); Median rent: $234 per month (2000); Median age of housing: 60+ years (2000).
Transportation: Commute to work: 95.3% car, 0.0% public transportation, 2.0% walk, 2.7% work from home (2000); Travel time to work: 20.5% less than 15 minutes, 22.6% 15 to 30 minutes, 34.2% 30 to 45 minutes, 8.9% 45 to 60 minutes, 13.7% 60 minutes or more (2000)

MARIETTA (village). Covers a land area of 0.269 square miles and a water area of 0 square miles. Located at 40.50° N. Lat.; 90.39° W. Long. Elevation is 650 feet.
Population: 150 (2000); Race: 98.6% White, 0.0% Black, 0.0% Asian, 0.0% American Indian and Alaska Native, 0.0% Hispanic of any race, 1.4% two or more races (2000); Density: 557.0 persons per square mile (2000); Age: 19.9% under 18, 10.3% over 64 (2000); Marriage status: 18.5% never married, 66.4% now married, 1.7% widowed, 13.4% divorced (2000); Foreign born: 0.0% (2000); Ancestry (includes multiple ancestries): 21.9% German, 17.8% United States or American, 14.4% Irish, 13.7% Other groups, 6.2% English (2000).
Economy: In agricultural and bituminous-coal area. Employment by occupation: 7.5% management, 6.3% professional, 15.0% services, 7.5% sales, 0.0% farming, 12.5% construction, 51.2% production (2000).
Income: Per capita income: $15,662 (2000); Median household income: $40,000 (2000); Poverty rate: 2.7% (2000).
Taxes: Total city taxes per capita: $20 (1997); City property taxes per capita: $7 (1997).
Education: High school graduation rate: 79.3% (2000); College graduation rate: 4.3% (2000).
Housing: Homeownership rate: 82.5% (2000); Median home value: $23,900 (2000); Median rent: $300 per month (2000); Median age of housing: 58 years (2000).
Transportation: Commute to work: 93.6% car, 0.0% public transportation, 3.8% walk, 2.6% work from home (2000); Travel time to work: 13.2% less than 15 minutes, 43.4% 15 to 30 minutes, 15.8% 30 to 45 minutes, 2.6% 45 to 60 minutes, 25.0% 60 minutes or more (2000)

NORRIS (village). Covers a land area of 0.281 square miles and a water area of 0 square miles. Located at 40.62° N. Lat.; 90.03° W. Long. Elevation is 730 feet.
Population: 194 (2000); Race: 100.0% White, 0.0% Black, 0.0% Asian, 0.0% American Indian and Alaska Native, 0.0% Hispanic of any race, 0.0% two or more races (2000); Density: 689.8 persons per square mile (2000); Age: 18.6% under 18, 18.6% over 64 (2000); Marriage status: 22.7% never married, 64.3% now married, 6.5% widowed, 6.5% divorced (2000); Foreign born: 0.0% (2000); Ancestry (includes multiple ancestries): 20.5% German, 14.5% Other groups, 13.2% English, 9.1% Polish, 9.1% United States or American (2000).
Economy: In agricultural and bituminous-coal area. Employment by occupation: 6.6% management, 15.1% professional, 16.0% services, 26.4% sales, 0.0% farming, 13.2% construction, 22.6% production (2000).
Income: Per capita income: $16,205 (2000); Median household income: $27,000 (2000); Poverty rate: 4.6% (2000).
Taxes: Total city taxes per capita: $19 (1997); City property taxes per capita: $14 (1997).
Education: High school graduation rate: 74.7% (2000); College graduation rate: 5.8% (2000).
Housing: Homeownership rate: 83.7% (2000); Median home value: $43,800 (2000); Median rent: $263 per month (2000); Median age of housing: 60+ years (2000).
Transportation: Commute to work: 95.3% car, 0.0% public transportation, 4.7% walk, 0.0% work from home (2000); Travel time to work: 36.8% less than 15 minutes, 32.1% 15 to 30 minutes, 17.9% 30 to 45 minutes, 13.2% 45 to 60 minutes, 0.0% 60 minutes or more (2000)

SAINT DAVID (village). Covers a land area of 0.296 square miles and a water area of 0 square miles. Located at 40.49° N. Lat.; 90.05° W. Long. Elevation is 630 feet.
Population: 587 (2000); Race: 99.5% White, 0.0% Black, 0.0% Asian, 0.0% American Indian and Alaska Native, 0.0% Hispanic of any race, 0.5% two or more races (2000); Density: 1,982.1 persons per square mile (2000); Age: 25.3% under 18, 20.0% over 64 (2000); Marriage status: 17.2% never married, 64.0% now married, 8.3% widowed, 10.6% divorced (2000); Foreign born: 0.7% (2000); Ancestry (includes multiple ancestries): 22.0% United States or American, 12.6% English, 12.4% German, 7.9% Irish, 7.1% Italian (2000).
Economy: Single-family building permits issued: 0 (2001) / 0 (2000); Multi-family building permits issued: 0 (2001) / 0 (2000); Employment by occupation: 8.6% management, 14.4% professional, 14.0% services, 25.5% sales, 0.8% farming, 14.0% construction, 22.6% production (2000).
Income: Per capita income: $14,292 (2000); Median household income: $30,625 (2000); Poverty rate: 11.1% (2000).
Education: High school graduation rate: 78.9% (2000); College graduation rate: 4.1% (2000).
Housing: Homeownership rate: 84.8% (2000); Median home value: $40,800 (2000); Median rent: $300 per month (2000); Median age of housing: 59 years (2000).
Transportation: Commute to work: 93.7% car, 0.0% public transportation, 1.7% walk, 1.7% work from home (2000); Travel time to work: 39.3% less than 15 minutes, 21.4% 15 to 30 minutes, 12.4% 30 to 45 minutes, 12.0% 45 to 60 minutes, 15.0% 60 minutes or more (2000)

SMITHFIELD (village). Covers a land area of 0.476 square miles and a water area of 0 square miles. Located at 40.47° N. Lat.; 90.29° W. Long. Elevation is 645 feet.
Population: 214 (2000); Race: 100.0% White, 0.0% Black, 0.0% Asian, 0.0% American Indian and Alaska Native, 0.0% Hispanic of any race, 0.0% two or more races (2000); Density: 450.0 persons per square mile (2000); Age: 19.6% under 18, 18.2% over 64 (2000); Marriage status: 21.2% never married, 56.4% now married, 12.8% widowed, 9.5% divorced (2000); Foreign born: 1.0% (2000); Ancestry (includes multiple ancestries): 16.3% United States or American, 12.0% German, 9.6% Irish, 8.6% English, 7.2% Eastern European (2000).
Economy: In agricultural and bituminous-coal area. Employment by occupation: 7.1% management, 15.2% professional, 17.2% services, 17.2% sales, 0.0% farming, 18.2% construction, 25.3% production (2000).
Income: Per capita income: $16,661 (2000); Median household income: $32,031 (2000); Poverty rate: 3.8% (2000).
Taxes: Total city taxes per capita: $18 (1997); City property taxes per capita: $18 (1997).
Education: High school graduation rate: 87.6% (2000); College graduation rate: 4.6% (2000).
Housing: Homeownership rate: 84.9% (2000); Median home value: $33,800 (2000); Median rent: $233 per month (2000); Median age of housing: 60+ years (2000).
Transportation: Commute to work: 86.9% car, 5.1% public transportation, 2.0% walk, 2.0% work from home (2000); Travel time to work: 19.6% less than 15 minutes, 37.1% 15 to 30 minutes, 16.5% 30 to 45 minutes, 17.5% 45 to 60 minutes, 9.3% 60 minutes or more (2000)

TABLE GROVE (village). Covers a land area of 0.280 square miles and a water area of 0 square miles. Located at 40.36° N. Lat.; 90.42° W. Long. Elevation is 734 feet.
Population: 396 (2000); Race: 100.0% White, 0.0% Black, 0.0% Asian, 0.0% American Indian and Alaska Native, 0.0% Hispanic of any race, 0.0% two or more races (2000); Density: 1,413.8 persons per square mile (2000); Age: 22.1% under 18, 21.3% over 64 (2000); Marriage status: 17.0% never married, 62.5% now married, 10.5% widowed, 9.9% divorced (2000); Foreign born: 0.0% (2000); Ancestry (includes multiple ancestries): 21.1% English, 20.1% German, 9.4% Irish, 6.0% United States or American, 4.7% Scottish (2000).
Economy: In agricultural and bituminous-coal-mining area. Employment by occupation: 8.8% management, 16.1% professional, 9.3% services, 23.9% sales, 2.0% farming, 13.2% construction, 26.8% production (2000).
Income: Per capita income: $17,877 (2000); Median household income: $37,750 (2000); Poverty rate: 12.7% (2000).
Taxes: Total city taxes per capita: $46 (1997); City property taxes per capita: $41 (1997).
Education: High school graduation rate: 85.0% (2000); College graduation rate: 11.1% (2000).

School District(s)

V I T Community Unit School Districtrict 2 (PK-12)
2000 Enrollment: 441 309-758-5138

Housing: Homeownership rate: 90.7% (2000); Median home value: $34,800 (2000); Median rent: $208 per month (2000); Median age of housing: 60+ years (2000).

Transportation: Commute to work: 96.0% car, 0.0% public transportation, 3.0% walk, 1.0% work from home (2000); Travel time to work: 29.1% less than 15 minutes, 39.2% 15 to 30 minutes, 15.6% 30 to 45 minutes, 3.0% 45 to 60 minutes, 13.1% 60 minutes or more (2000)

VERMONT (village). Covers a land area of 1.263 square miles and a water area of 0 square miles. Located at 40.29° N. Lat.; 90.42° W. Long. Elevation is 697 feet.

Population: 792 (2000); Race: 98.4% White, 0.0% Black, 0.0% Asian, 0.0% American Indian and Alaska Native, 1.5% Hispanic of any race, 0.6% two or more races (2000); Density: 627.2 persons per square mile (2000); Age: 27.8% under 18, 14.3% over 64 (2000); Marriage status: 23.0% never married, 61.9% now married, 4.9% widowed, 10.2% divorced (2000); Foreign born: 0.6% (2000); Ancestry (includes multiple ancestries): 17.6% German, 14.4% United States or American, 8.2% English, 7.9% Irish, 5.3% Other groups (2000).

Economy: In agricultural and bituminous-coal area. Railroad junction. Employment by occupation: 6.9% management, 14.1% professional, 16.2% services, 17.7% sales, 2.1% farming, 7.8% construction, 35.3% production (2000).

Income: Per capita income: $13,333 (2000); Median household income: $29,375 (2000); Poverty rate: 14.2% (2000).

Taxes: Total city taxes per capita: $105 (1997); City property taxes per capita: $61 (1997).

Education: High school graduation rate: 79.2% (2000); College graduation rate: 6.5% (2000).

Housing: Homeownership rate: 82.7% (2000); Median home value: $34,300 (2000); Median rent: $196 per month (2000); Median age of housing: 60+ years (2000).

Transportation: Commute to work: 90.5% car, 0.0% public transportation, 5.5% walk, 1.8% work from home (2000); Travel time to work: 30.4% less than 15 minutes, 21.7% 15 to 30 minutes, 30.4% 30 to 45 minutes, 6.2% 45 to 60 minutes, 11.2% 60 minutes or more (2000)

Gallatin County

Located in southeastern Illinois, partly in the Ozarks; bounded on the northeast by the Wabash River and the Indiana border, and on the southeast by the Ohio River and the Kentucky border; includes part of Shawnee National Forest. Covers a land area of 323.70 square miles, a water area of 4.70 square miles, and is located in the Central Time Zone. The county government was organized in 1812. County seat is Shawneetown.

Population: 6,445 (2000); Race: 98.1% White, 0.2% Black, 0.2% Asian, 0.8% American Indian and Alaska Native, 1.2% Hispanic of any race, 0.4% two or more races (2000); Density: 19.9 persons per square mile (2000); Age: 22.2% under 18, 18.0% over 64 (2000).

Religion: Five largest groups: 17.6% Catholic Church, 14.0% Southern Baptist Convention, 3.6% The United Methodist Church, 3.0% The Church of Jesus Christ of Latter-day Saints, 2.1% Presbyterian Church (U.S.A.) (2000).

Economy: Unemployment rate: 7.3% (11/2002); Total civilian labor force: 2,647 (11/2002); Leading industries: 34.3% mining; 12.3% wholesale trade; 11.6% retail trade (2000); Companies that employ more than 1,000 persons: 0 (2000); Companies that employ more than 100 persons: 2 (2000); Farms: 238 totaling 191,113 acres (1997); Minority business ownership rate: 0.0% (1997); Women business ownership rate: 51.0% (1997); Retail sales per capita: $3,522 (1997). Single-family building permits issued: 0 (2001) / 0 (2000); Multi-family building permits issued: 0 (2001) / 0 (2000).

Income: Per capita income: $15,575 (2000); Median household income: $26,118 (2000); Poverty rate: 20.7% (2000); Bankruptcy rate: 4.71% (2001).

Taxes: Total county taxes per capita: $77 (1997); County property taxes per capita: $77 (1997).

Education: High school graduation rate: 73.6% (2000); College graduation rate: 7.7% (2000).

Housing: Homeownership rate: 81.1% (2000); Median home value: $46,300 (2000); Median rent: $191 per month (2000); Median age of housing: 33 years (2000).

Health: Birth rate: 74.5 per 10,000 population (1998); Age adjusted death rate: 77.4 per 10,000 population (1999); Age adjusted cancer mortality rate: 229.6 (Unreliable figure as per CDC) deaths per 100,000 population (1999). Number of physicians: 4.7 per 10,000 population (1999); Number of hospital beds: n/a (1999).

Elections: 2000 Presidential election results: 52.8% Gore, 44.7% Bush, 1.1% Nader, 1.1% Buchanan

Additional Information Contacts

Gallatin County Government Offices..................... 618-269-3025

Gallatin County Communities

EQUALITY (village). Covers a land area of 0.901 square miles and a water area of 0 square miles. Located at 37.73° N. Lat.; 88.34° W. Long. Elevation is 420 feet.

History: Formerly county seat and site of salt works.

Population: 721 (2000); Race: 98.8% White, 0.0% Black, 0.3% Asian, 0.0% American Indian and Alaska Native, 0.0% Hispanic of any race, 0.5% two or more races (2000); Density: 800.3 persons per square mile (2000); Age: 25.7% under 18, 17.4% over 64 (2000); Marriage status: 15.8% never married, 60.5% now married, 11.9% widowed, 11.9% divorced (2000); Foreign born: 0.3% (2000); Ancestry (includes multiple ancestries): 31.0% United States or American, 11.9% Irish, 11.5% German, 6.8% Other groups, 4.9% English (2000).

Economy: In agricultural area. Employment by occupation: 5.6% management, 14.7% professional, 18.3% services, 28.2% sales, 0.8% farming, 14.3% construction, 18.3% production (2000).

Income: Per capita income: $12,961 (2000); Median household income: $22,171 (2000); Poverty rate: 20.7% (2000).

Taxes: Total city taxes per capita: $50 (2000); City property taxes per capita: $6 (2000).

Education: High school graduation rate: 77.0% (2000); College graduation rate: 6.0% (2000).

Housing: Homeownership rate: 80.3% (2000); Median home value: $35,600 (2000); Median rent: $188 per month (2000); Median age of housing: 40 years (2000).

Transportation: Commute to work: 95.2% car, 0.0% public transportation, 0.0% walk, 4.8% work from home (2000); Travel time to work: 34.6% less than 15 minutes, 41.3% 15 to 30 minutes, 9.6% 30 to 45 minutes, 4.2% 45 to 60 minutes, 10.4% 60 minutes or more (2000)

JUNCTION (village). Covers a land area of 0.887 square miles and a water area of 0 square miles. Located at 37.72° N. Lat.; 88.23° W. Long. Elevation is 363 feet.

Population: 139 (2000); Race: 85.8% White, 1.9% Black, 4.9% Asian, 7.4% American Indian and Alaska Native, 8.0% Hispanic of any race, 0.0% two or more races (2000); Density: 156.7 persons per square mile (2000); Age: 18.5% under 18, 17.9% over 64 (2000); Marriage status: 22.1% never married, 54.3% now married, 16.4% widowed, 7.1% divorced (2000); Foreign born: 3.1% (2000); Ancestry (includes multiple ancestries): 29.0% United States or American, 11.7% Italian, 11.1% Irish, 8.6% Other groups, 7.4% English (2000).

Economy: In agricultural area. Employment by occupation: 7.2% management, 29.0% professional, 10.1% services, 15.9% sales, 0.0% farming, 2.9% construction, 34.8% production (2000).

Income: Per capita income: $16,256 (2000); Median household income: $33,750 (2000); Poverty rate: 11.1% (2000).

Taxes: Total city taxes per capita: $34 (1997); City property taxes per capita: $17 (1997).

Education: High school graduation rate: 66.1% (2000); College graduation rate: 10.2% (2000).

School District(s)

Gallatin C U School District 7 (PK-12)
2000 Enrollment: 1,020 618-272-3821

Housing: Homeownership rate: 90.3% (2000); Median home value: $19,400 (2000); Median rent: $175 per month (2000); Median age of housing: 32 years (2000).

Transportation: Commute to work: 100.0% car, 0.0% public transportation, 0.0% walk, 0.0% work from home (2000); Travel time to work: 40.6% less than 15 minutes, 7.2% 15 to 30 minutes, 17.4% 30 to 45 minutes, 2.9% 45 to 60 minutes, 31.9% 60 minutes or more (2000)

NEW HAVEN (village). Covers a land area of 1.205 square miles and a water area of 0.028 square miles. Located at 37.90° N. Lat.; 88.12° W. Long. Elevation is 370 feet.

Population: 477 (2000); Race: 98.9% White, 0.7% Black, 0.0% Asian, 0.0% American Indian and Alaska Native, 2.5% Hispanic of any race, 0.5% two or

more races (2000); Density: 395.7 persons per square mile (2000); Age: 23.0% under 18, 16.2% over 64 (2000); Marriage status: 16.2% never married, 64.2% now married, 8.2% widowed, 11.4% divorced (2000); Foreign born: 0.5% (2000); Ancestry (includes multiple ancestries): 16.4% English, 13.2% Irish, 10.9% United States or American, 10.3% Other groups, 9.3% German (2000).
Economy: In agricultural area. Employment by occupation: 5.7% management, 17.1% professional, 20.0% services, 12.0% sales, 3.4% farming, 16.0% construction, 25.7% production (2000).
Income: Per capita income: $12,367 (2000); Median household income: $27,083 (2000); Poverty rate: 22.6% (2000).
Taxes: Total city taxes per capita: $38 (1997); City property taxes per capita: $4 (1997).
Education: High school graduation rate: 72.8% (2000); College graduation rate: 0.7% (2000).
Housing: Homeownership rate: 85.0% (2000); Median home value: $42,600 (2000); Median rent: $158 per month (2000); Median age of housing: 34 years (2000).
Transportation: Commute to work: 95.3% car, 1.2% public transportation, 3.5% walk, 0.0% work from home (2000); Travel time to work: 17.0% less than 15 minutes, 30.4% 15 to 30 minutes, 18.1% 30 to 45 minutes, 12.3% 45 to 60 minutes, 22.2% 60 minutes or more (2000)

OLD SHAWNEETOWN (village). Covers a land area of 0.523 square miles and a water area of 0 square miles. Located at 37.69° N. Lat.; 88.13° W. Long. Elevation is 370 feet.
Population: 278 (2000); Race: 99.3% White, 0.0% Black, 0.0% Asian, 0.0% American Indian and Alaska Native, 0.0% Hispanic of any race, 0.7% two or more races (2000); Density: 531.7 persons per square mile (2000); Age: 26.4% under 18, 7.8% over 64 (2000); Marriage status: 22.5% never married, 46.9% now married, 4.7% widowed, 25.8% divorced (2000); Foreign born: 0.0% (2000); Ancestry (includes multiple ancestries): 37.9% Other groups, 10.8% United States or American, 8.9% English, 7.4% German, 6.7% Irish (2000).
Economy: Employment by occupation: 0.0% management, 8.3% professional, 25.0% services, 7.1% sales, 0.0% farming, 7.1% construction, 52.4% production (2000).
Income: Per capita income: $9,379 (2000); Median household income: $18,214 (2000); Poverty rate: 39.4% (2000).
Taxes: Total city taxes per capita: $45 (1997); City property taxes per capita: $27 (1997).
Education: High school graduation rate: 48.1% (2000); College graduation rate: 0.0% (2000).
Housing: Homeownership rate: 82.9% (2000); Median home value: $17,500 (2000); Median rent: $225 per month (2000); Median age of housing: 25 years (2000).
Transportation: Commute to work: 97.6% car, 0.0% public transportation, 2.4% walk, 0.0% work from home (2000); Travel time to work: 25.6% less than 15 minutes, 28.0% 15 to 30 minutes, 4.9% 30 to 45 minutes, 18.3% 45 to 60 minutes, 23.2% 60 minutes or more (2000)

OMAHA (village). Covers a land area of 0.830 square miles and a water area of 0 square miles. Located at 37.89° N. Lat.; 88.30° W. Long. Elevation is 370 feet.
Population: 263 (2000); Race: 100.0% White, 0.0% Black, 0.0% Asian, 0.0% American Indian and Alaska Native, 0.0% Hispanic of any race, 0.0% two or more races (2000); Density: 316.7 persons per square mile (2000); Age: 26.8% under 18, 18.4% over 64 (2000); Marriage status: 17.4% never married, 57.0% now married, 12.1% widowed, 13.5% divorced (2000); Foreign born: 0.0% (2000); Ancestry (includes multiple ancestries): 17.6% Irish, 16.2% English, 16.2% United States or American, 10.7% French (except Basque), 9.6% German (2000).
Economy: In agricultural area. Employment by occupation: 1.6% management, 15.3% professional, 16.1% services, 25.8% sales, 2.4% farming, 9.7% construction, 29.0% production (2000).
Income: Per capita income: $12,766 (2000); Median household income: $23,750 (2000); Poverty rate: 18.8% (2000).
Taxes: Total city taxes per capita: $11 (1997); City property taxes per capita: $11 (1997).
Education: High school graduation rate: 76.9% (2000); College graduation rate: 11.8% (2000).
Housing: Homeownership rate: 79.2% (2000); Median home value: $32,700 (2000); Median rent: $182 per month (2000); Median age of housing: 32 years (2000).
Transportation: Commute to work: 93.2% car, 3.4% public transportation, 0.0% walk, 1.7% work from home (2000); Travel time to work: 19.0% less than 15 minutes, 27.6% 15 to 30 minutes, 35.3% 30 to 45 minutes, 8.6% 45 to 60 minutes, 9.5% 60 minutes or more (2000)

RIDGWAY (village). Covers a land area of 0.900 square miles and a water area of 0 square miles. Located at 37.79° N. Lat.; 88.26° W. Long. Elevation is 380 feet.
History: Incorporated 1886.
Population: 928 (2000); Race: 98.9% White, 0.4% Black, 0.0% Asian, 0.0% American Indian and Alaska Native, 0.6% Hispanic of any race, 0.4% two or more races (2000); Density: 1,030.6 persons per square mile (2000); Age: 18.4% under 18, 21.7% over 64 (2000); Marriage status: 19.4% never married, 58.5% now married, 11.7% widowed, 10.4% divorced (2000); Foreign born: 0.0% (2000); Ancestry (includes multiple ancestries): 22.0% German, 13.9% Irish, 12.3% United States or American, 10.4% French (except Basque), 8.1% English (2000).
Economy: Agriculture: corn, soybeans. Coal, oil and natural gas. Manufacturing of popcorn. Employment by occupation: 9.4% management, 19.9% professional, 19.4% services, 18.0% sales, 2.1% farming, 11.7% construction, 19.4% production (2000).
Income: Per capita income: $16,959 (2000); Median household income: $27,670 (2000); Poverty rate: 18.0% (2000).
Taxes: Total city taxes per capita: $119 (1997); City property taxes per capita: $49 (1997).
Education: High school graduation rate: 78.8% (2000); College graduation rate: 11.5% (2000).
Housing: Homeownership rate: 79.1% (2000); Median home value: $47,300 (2000); Median rent: $206 per month (2000); Median age of housing: 34 years (2000).
Transportation: Commute to work: 95.0% car, 0.0% public transportation, 1.9% walk, 2.6% work from home (2000); Travel time to work: 35.5% less than 15 minutes, 26.9% 15 to 30 minutes, 19.8% 30 to 45 minutes, 4.2% 45 to 60 minutes, 13.7% 60 minutes or more (2000)

SHAWNEETOWN (city). Aka New Shawneetown. Covers a land area of 1.193 square miles and a water area of 0.037 square miles. Located at 37.71° N. Lat.; 88.18° W. Long. Elevation is 400 feet.
History: Shawneetown, settled in the early 1800's, developed as a port on the Ohio River and as a financial center when Chicago was still a small village. Salt was an important export for the growing town, through which travelers and merchandise passed on the river.
Population: 1,410 (2000); Race: 96.5% White, 0.4% Black, 0.1% Asian, 2.1% American Indian and Alaska Native, 2.4% Hispanic of any race, 0.0% two or more races (2000); Density: 1,181.8 persons per square mile (2000); Age: 18.6% under 18, 21.3% over 64 (2000); Marriage status: 17.5% never married, 56.9% now married, 12.9% widowed, 12.7% divorced (2000); Foreign born: 1.0% (2000); Ancestry (includes multiple ancestries): 13.0% German, 11.3% United States or American, 9.7% Irish, 9.1% Other groups, 7.4% English (2000).
Economy: Highway bridge to Kentucky. Shawnee National Forest to Southwest. Employment by occupation: 8.8% management, 13.7% professional, 24.3% services, 18.7% sales, 2.8% farming, 13.5% construction, 18.1% production (2000).
Income: Per capita income: $17,834 (2000); Median household income: $20,789 (2000); Poverty rate: 27.8% (2000).
Taxes: Total city taxes per capita: $164 (1997); City property taxes per capita: $31 (1997).
Education: High school graduation rate: 64.1% (2000); College graduation rate: 4.1% (2000).
Housing: Homeownership rate: 73.5% (2000); Median home value: $43,300 (2000); Median rent: $172 per month (2000); Median age of housing: 36 years (2000).
Newspapers: The Ridgway News (1 x week); Gallatin Democrat (1 x week)
Transportation: Commute to work: 91.9% car, 0.4% public transportation, 1.6% walk, 6.1% work from home (2000); Travel time to work: 37.8% less than 15 minutes, 16.8% 15 to 30 minutes, 15.9% 30 to 45 minutes, 11.0% 45 to 60 minutes, 18.5% 60 minutes or more (2000)

Greene County

Located in southwest central Illinois; bounded on the west by the Illinois River; drained by Macoupin and Apple Creeks. Covers a land area of 543.10 square miles, a water area of 3.30 square miles, and is located in the Central Time Zone. The county government was organized in 1821. County seat is Carrollton.

Weather Station: White Hall 1 E Elevation: 577 feet

	Jan	Feb	Mar	Apr	May	Jun	Jul	Aug	Sep	Oct	Nov	Dec
High	35	41	52	65	75	83	87	85	79	68	53	40
Low	17	21	31	42	52	61	65	63	55	44	33	23
Precip	1.6	1.7	3.3	3.8	4.5	3.6	3.3	3.0	3.1	2.6	3.2	2.5
Snow	na	na	2.0	0.5	0.0	0.0	0.0	0.0	0.0	tr	0.7	2.9

High and Low temperatures in degrees Fahrenheit; Precipitation and Snow in inches

Population: 14,761 (2000); Race: 98.1% White, 0.8% Black, 0.1% Asian, 0.3% American Indian and Alaska Native, 0.5% Hispanic of any race, 0.5% two or more races (2000); Density: 27.2 persons per square mile (2000); Age: 25.4% under 18, 17.5% over 64 (2000).
Religion: Five largest groups: 20.7% Southern Baptist Convention, 17.6% American Baptist Churches in the USA, 13.7% Catholic Church, 6.0% The United Methodist Church, 1.7% Lutheran Church—Missouri Synod (2000).
Economy: Unemployment rate: 5.8% (11/2002); Total civilian labor force: 7,135 (11/2002); Leading industries: 25.3% retail trade; 16.2% health care and social assistance; 12.5% manufacturing (2000); Companies that employ more than 1,000 persons: 0 (2000); Companies that employ more than 100 persons: 1 (2000); Farms: 720 totaling 327,590 acres (1997); Minority business ownership rate: 0.0% (1997); Women business ownership rate: 35.9% (1997); Retail sales per capita: $4,527 (1997). Single-family building permits issued: 4 (2001) / 6 (2000); Multi-family building permits issued: 3 (2001) / 0 (2000).
Income: Per capita income: $15,246 (2000); Median household income: $31,754 (2000); Poverty rate: 12.4% (2000); Bankruptcy rate: 4.62% (2001).
Taxes: Total county taxes per capita: $72 (1997); County property taxes per capita: $72 (1997).
Education: High school graduation rate: 78.9% (2000); College graduation rate: 10.1% (2000).
Housing: Homeownership rate: 76.4% (2000); Median home value: $47,900 (2000); Median rent: $257 per month (2000); Median age of housing: 56 years (2000).
Health: Birth rate: 112.5 per 10,000 population (1998); Age adjusted death rate: 89.1 per 10,000 population (1999); Age adjusted cancer mortality rate: 236.6 deaths per 100,000 population (1999). Number of physicians: 6.1 per 10,000 population (1999); Number of hospital beds: 40.6 per 10,000 population (1999).
Elections: 2000 Presidential election results: 43.2% Gore, 54.3% Bush, 1.6% Nader, 0.7% Buchanan
Additional Information Contacts
Greene County Government Offices 217-942-5443

Greene County Communities

CARROLLTON (city). Covers a land area of 1.669 square miles and a water area of 0.002 square miles. Located at 39.29° N. Lat.; 90.40° W. Long. Elevation is 610 feet.
History: Carrollton was settled in 1818 and developed as the seat of Green County.
Population: 2,605 (2000); Race: 98.8% White, 0.0% Black, 0.0% Asian, 0.5% American Indian and Alaska Native, 0.0% Hispanic of any race, 0.7% two or more races (2000); Density: 1,561.2 persons per square mile (2000); Age: 23.4% under 18, 21.5% over 64 (2000); Marriage status: 19.1% never married, 59.0% now married, 12.9% widowed, 9.0% divorced (2000); Foreign born: 0.2% (2000); Ancestry (includes multiple ancestries): 31.0% German, 17.3% United States or American, 11.5% English, 11.1% Irish, 4.9% Other groups (2000).
Economy: Single-family building permits issued: 1 (2001) / 4 (2000); Multi-family building permits issued: 3 (2001) / 0 (2000); Employment by occupation: 8.8% management, 17.9% professional, 18.7% services, 25.0% sales, 0.0% farming, 8.3% construction, 21.3% production (2000).
Income: Per capita income: $16,340 (2000); Median household income: $30,154 (2000); Poverty rate: 9.0% (2000).
Taxes: Total city taxes per capita: $110 (1997); City property taxes per capita: $99 (1997).
Education: High school graduation rate: 81.2% (2000); College graduation rate: 15.8% (2000).

School District(s)
Carrollton C U School District 1 (PK-12)
2000 Enrollment: 732 217-942-5314
Housing: Homeownership rate: 75.3% (2000); Median home value: $62,300 (2000); Median rent: $269 per month (2000); Median age of housing: 56 years (2000).
Hospitals: Thomas H. Boyd Memorial Hospital (65 beds)
Newspapers: Greene County Shopper (1 x week); Jersey County Shopper (1 x week); Gazette Patriot (1 x week)
Transportation: Commute to work: 90.9% car, 0.0% public transportation, 3.6% walk, 4.4% work from home (2000); Travel time to work: 49.0% less than 15 minutes, 16.0% 15 to 30 minutes, 5.9% 30 to 45 minutes, 14.2% 45 to 60 minutes, 15.0% 60 minutes or more (2000)

ELDRED (village). Covers a land area of 0.135 square miles and a water area of 0 square miles. Located at 39.28° N. Lat.; 90.55° W. Long. Elevation is 454 feet.
Population: 211 (2000); Race: 98.6% White, 0.0% Black, 1.4% Asian, 0.0% American Indian and Alaska Native, 0.0% Hispanic of any race, 0.0% two or more races (2000); Density: 1,567.6 persons per square mile (2000); Age: 26.9% under 18, 14.2% over 64 (2000); Marriage status: 33.0% never married, 36.9% now married, 8.0% widowed, 22.2% divorced (2000); Foreign born: 1.4% (2000); Ancestry (includes multiple ancestries): 49.8% United States or American, 25.1% German, 10.5% English, 6.4% Irish, 4.1% Other groups (2000).
Economy: In agricultural area: corn, wheat, soybeans, sorghum, cattle, hogs; dairying. Employment by occupation: 3.8% management, 10.4% professional, 23.6% services, 21.7% sales, 0.0% farming, 19.8% construction, 20.8% production (2000).
Income: Per capita income: $13,772 (2000); Median household income: $26,250 (2000); Poverty rate: 37.2% (2000).
Taxes: Total city taxes per capita: $11 (1997); City property taxes per capita: $8 (1997).
Education: High school graduation rate: 75.2% (2000); College graduation rate: 5.0% (2000).
Housing: Homeownership rate: 73.0% (2000); Median home value: $43,500 (2000); Median rent: $233 per month (2000); Median age of housing: 60+ years (2000).
Transportation: Commute to work: 93.4% car, 0.0% public transportation, 4.7% walk, 0.0% work from home (2000); Travel time to work: 34.0% less than 15 minutes, 33.0% 15 to 30 minutes, 11.3% 30 to 45 minutes, 2.8% 45 to 60 minutes, 18.9% 60 minutes or more (2000)

GREENFIELD (city). Covers a land area of 1.716 square miles and a water area of 0.063 square miles. Located at 39.34° N. Lat.; 90.21° W. Long. Elevation is 594 feet.
History: Incorporated 1837.
Population: 1,179 (2000); Race: 98.7% White, 0.0% Black, 0.0% Asian, 0.0% American Indian and Alaska Native, 1.2% Hispanic of any race, 0.6% two or more races (2000); Density: 687.2 persons per square mile (2000); Age: 24.4% under 18, 21.2% over 64 (2000); Marriage status: 24.9% never married, 50.6% now married, 14.1% widowed, 10.4% divorced (2000); Foreign born: 0.5% (2000); Ancestry (includes multiple ancestries): 19.4% German, 12.6% United States or American, 11.0% Irish, 10.1% English, 5.0% Other groups (2000).
Economy: In agricultural area: corn, wheat, oats, soybeans; cattle, hogs. Single-family building permits issued: 3 (2001) / 2 (2000); Multi-family building permits issued: 0 (2001) / 0 (2000); Employment by occupation: 9.2% management, 17.8% professional, 22.2% services, 16.4% sales, 3.0% farming, 9.2% construction, 22.4% production (2000).
Income: Per capita income: $16,386 (2000); Median household income: $30,833 (2000); Poverty rate: 10.2% (2000).
Taxes: Total city taxes per capita: $46 (1997); City property taxes per capita: $46 (1997).
Education: High school graduation rate: 83.9% (2000); College graduation rate: 6.3% (2000).

School District(s)
Greenfield C U School District 10 (KG-12)
2000 Enrollment: 556 217-368-2447
Housing: Homeownership rate: 74.8% (2000); Median home value: $48,500 (2000); Median rent: $256 per month (2000); Median age of housing: 47 years (2000).
Transportation: Commute to work: 93.2% car, 0.0% public transportation, 2.1% walk, 4.6% work from home (2000); Travel time to work: 30.3% less than 15 minutes, 6.9% 15 to 30 minutes, 30.7% 30 to 45 minutes, 18.5% 45 to 60 minutes, 13.6% 60 minutes or more (2000)

HILLVIEW (village). Covers a land area of 0.848 square miles and a water area of 0 square miles. Located at 39.45° N. Lat.; 90.53° W. Long. Elevation is 447 feet.
Population: 179 (2000); Race: 99.4% White, 0.0% Black, 0.0% Asian, 0.0% American Indian and Alaska Native, 0.0% Hispanic of any race, 0.6% two or more races (2000); Density: 211.2 persons per square mile (2000); Age:

29.0% under 18, 16.0% over 64 (2000); Marriage status: 23.1% never married, 66.9% now married, 5.8% widowed, 4.1% divorced (2000); Foreign born: 0.0% (2000); Ancestry (includes multiple ancestries): 16.0% United States or American, 14.8% Other groups, 11.7% Irish, 10.5% Swedish, 7.4% German (2000).
Economy: In agricultural area. Employment by occupation: 2.1% management, 12.8% professional, 21.3% services, 19.1% sales, 4.3% farming, 0.0% construction, 40.4% production (2000).
Income: Per capita income: $9,157 (2000); Median household income: $24,167 (2000); Poverty rate: 25.3% (2000).
Taxes: Total city taxes per capita: $25 (1997); City property taxes per capita: $22 (1997).
Education: High school graduation rate: 57.4% (2000); College graduation rate: 0.0% (2000).
Housing: Homeownership rate: 88.9% (2000); Median home value: $22,000 (2000); Median rent: $238 per month (2000); Median age of housing: 60+ years (2000).
Transportation: Commute to work: 91.5% car, 0.0% public transportation, 0.0% walk, 6.4% work from home (2000); Travel time to work: 15.9% less than 15 minutes, 36.4% 15 to 30 minutes, 11.4% 30 to 45 minutes, 18.2% 45 to 60 minutes, 18.2% 60 minutes or more (2000)

KANE (village). Covers a land area of 0.541 square miles and a water area of 0 square miles. Located at 39.19° N. Lat.; 90.35° W. Long. Elevation is 561 feet.
Population: 459 (2000); Race: 99.5% White, 0.0% Black, 0.0% Asian, 0.5% American Indian and Alaska Native, 0.0% Hispanic of any race, 0.0% two or more races (2000); Density: 847.8 persons per square mile (2000); Age: 28.7% under 18, 15.4% over 64 (2000); Marriage status: 18.8% never married, 58.2% now married, 8.5% widowed, 14.5% divorced (2000); Foreign born: 0.7% (2000); Ancestry (includes multiple ancestries): 18.1% German, 12.7% United States or American, 5.9% English, 5.9% Other groups, 4.3% Irish (2000).
Economy: In agricultural area: corn, soybeans. Employment by occupation: 6.7% management, 13.5% professional, 27.0% services, 20.2% sales, 2.2% farming, 14.6% construction, 15.7% production (2000).
Income: Per capita income: $11,325 (2000); Median household income: $28,125 (2000); Poverty rate: 11.8% (2000).
Taxes: Total city taxes per capita: $21 (1997); City property taxes per capita: $21 (1997).
Education: High school graduation rate: 72.0% (2000); College graduation rate: 3.5% (2000).
Housing: Homeownership rate: 76.6% (2000); Median home value: $44,500 (2000); Median rent: $244 per month (2000); Median age of housing: 56 years (2000).
Transportation: Commute to work: 97.7% car, 0.0% public transportation, 2.3% walk, 0.0% work from home (2000); Travel time to work: 26.1% less than 15 minutes, 30.7% 15 to 30 minutes, 16.5% 30 to 45 minutes, 11.9% 45 to 60 minutes, 14.8% 60 minutes or more (2000)

ROCKBRIDGE (village). Covers a land area of 0.739 square miles and a water area of 0 square miles. Located at 39.27° N. Lat.; 90.20° W. Long. Elevation is 542 feet.
Population: 189 (2000); Race: 98.9% White, 0.0% Black, 0.0% Asian, 0.0% American Indian and Alaska Native, 1.7% Hispanic of any race, 1.1% two or more races (2000); Density: 255.7 persons per square mile (2000); Age: 14.4% under 18, 26.1% over 64 (2000); Marriage status: 13.8% never married, 70.4% now married, 11.3% widowed, 4.4% divorced (2000); Foreign born: 0.0% (2000); Ancestry (includes multiple ancestries): 22.2% German, 16.1% United States or American, 9.4% Irish, 7.8% English, 7.2% Other groups (2000).
Economy: In agricultural area: corn, wheat, soybeans, sorghum; cattle, hogs. Employment by occupation: 9.5% management, 9.5% professional, 13.7% services, 27.4% sales, 2.1% farming, 3.2% construction, 34.7% production (2000).
Income: Per capita income: $16,243 (2000); Median household income: $31,667 (2000); Poverty rate: 7.2% (2000).
Taxes: Total city taxes per capita: $18 (1997); City property taxes per capita: $13 (1997).
Education: High school graduation rate: 73.4% (2000); College graduation rate: 3.6% (2000).
Housing: Homeownership rate: 83.3% (2000); Median home value: $29,400 (2000); Median rent: $271 per month (2000); Median age of housing: 49 years (2000).
Transportation: Commute to work: 95.7% car, 0.0% public transportation, 2.2% walk, 2.2% work from home (2000); Travel time to work: 29.7% less than 15 minutes, 12.1% 15 to 30 minutes, 30.8% 30 to 45 minutes, 14.3% 45 to 60 minutes, 13.2% 60 minutes or more (2000)

ROODHOUSE (city). Covers a land area of 1.132 square miles and a water area of 0 square miles. Located at 39.48° N. Lat.; 90.37° W. Long. Elevation is 655 feet.
History: Roodhouse was laid out by an early settler, John Roodhouse, and developed as a railroad center.
Population: 2,214 (2000); Race: 93.6% White, 5.0% Black, 0.1% Asian, 0.0% American Indian and Alaska Native, 0.7% Hispanic of any race, 0.4% two or more races (2000); Density: 1,955.6 persons per square mile (2000); Age: 25.9% under 18, 14.4% over 64 (2000); Marriage status: 20.5% never married, 56.9% now married, 9.5% widowed, 13.1% divorced (2000); Foreign born: 0.8% (2000); Ancestry (includes multiple ancestries): 15.8% United States or American, 13.3% English, 11.2% German, 10.3% Irish, 7.3% Other groups (2000).
Economy: Employment by occupation: 4.4% management, 10.4% professional, 17.3% services, 23.8% sales, 1.3% farming, 9.7% construction, 33.1% production (2000).
Income: Per capita income: $12,281 (2000); Median household income: $28,109 (2000); Poverty rate: 16.8% (2000).
Taxes: Total city taxes per capita: $107 (1997); City property taxes per capita: $56 (1997).
Education: High school graduation rate: 73.8% (2000); College graduation rate: 6.8% (2000).
Housing: Homeownership rate: 75.4% (2000); Median home value: $39,100 (2000); Median rent: $260 per month (2000); Median age of housing: 54 years (2000).
Transportation: Commute to work: 93.8% car, 0.4% public transportation, 2.8% walk, 1.8% work from home (2000); Travel time to work: 36.9% less than 15 minutes, 15.2% 15 to 30 minutes, 33.8% 30 to 45 minutes, 4.6% 45 to 60 minutes, 9.5% 60 minutes or more (2000)

WHITE HALL (city). Aka Whitehall. Covers a land area of 2.579 square miles and a water area of 0.057 square miles. Located at 39.43° N. Lat.; 90.39° W. Long. Elevation is 575 feet.
History: White Hall was founded in 1820 and developed around the manufacture of pottery from local clay.
Population: 2,629 (2000); Race: 98.9% White, 0.0% Black, 0.2% Asian, 0.8% American Indian and Alaska Native, 0.5% Hispanic of any race, 0.0% two or more races (2000); Density: 1,019.3 persons per square mile (2000); Age: 22.9% under 18, 22.6% over 64 (2000); Marriage status: 17.8% never married, 57.7% now married, 12.2% widowed, 12.3% divorced (2000); Foreign born: 0.3% (2000); Ancestry (includes multiple ancestries): 16.4% German, 15.4% United States or American, 13.6% English, 11.8% Irish, 7.8% Other groups (2000).
Economy: Employment by occupation: 7.6% management, 16.3% professional, 19.1% services, 18.7% sales, 2.2% farming, 14.8% construction, 21.3% production (2000).
Income: Per capita income: $14,982 (2000); Median household income: $26,552 (2000); Poverty rate: 18.8% (2000).
Taxes: Total city taxes per capita: $102 (1997); City property taxes per capita: $37 (1997).
Education: High school graduation rate: 72.6% (2000); College graduation rate: 8.9% (2000).

School District(s)

North Greene Unit District 3 (PK-12)
2000 Enrollment: 1,196 217-374-2842
Housing: Homeownership rate: 73.7% (2000); Median home value: $39,900 (2000); Median rent: $237 per month (2000); Median age of housing: 60 years (2000).
Newspapers: Greene Prairie Press (1 x week)
Transportation: Commute to work: 88.8% car, 0.0% public transportation, 4.6% walk, 5.1% work from home (2000); Travel time to work: 41.5% less than 15 minutes, 8.2% 15 to 30 minutes, 29.1% 30 to 45 minutes, 9.2% 45 to 60 minutes, 12.0% 60 minutes or more (2000)

WILMINGTON (village). Aka Patterson. Covers a land area of 0.792 square miles and a water area of 0 square miles. Located at 39.48° N. Lat.; 90.49° W. Long.
Population: 120 (2000); Race: 100.0% White, 0.0% Black, 0.0% Asian, 0.0% American Indian and Alaska Native, 0.0% Hispanic of any race, 0.0% two or more races (2000); Density: 151.5 persons per square mile (2000); Age: 37.5% under 18, 8.0% over 64 (2000); Marriage status: 18.5% never married, 66.7% now married, 6.2% widowed, 8.6% divorced (2000); Foreign born: 0.0% (2000); Ancestry (includes multiple ancestries): 23.2% Dutch,

22.3% Irish, 19.6% German, 17.0% United States or American, 13.4% English (2000).
Economy: Employment by occupation: 1.9% management, 15.1% professional, 32.1% services, 9.4% sales, 3.8% farming, 22.6% construction, 15.1% production (2000).
Income: Per capita income: $14,670 (2000); Median household income: $33,750 (2000); Poverty rate: 2.7% (2000).
Taxes: Total city taxes per capita: $44 (1997); City property taxes per capita: $30 (1997).
Education: High school graduation rate: 84.8% (2000); College graduation rate: 6.1% (2000).
Housing: Homeownership rate: 100.0% (2000); Median home value: $24,000 (2000); Median age of housing: 50 years (2000).
Transportation: Commute to work: 81.1% car, 0.0% public transportation, 1.9% walk, 0.0% work from home (2000); Travel time to work: 28.3% less than 15 minutes, 35.8% 15 to 30 minutes, 20.8% 30 to 45 minutes, 1.9% 45 to 60 minutes, 13.2% 60 minutes or more (2000)

Grundy County

Located in northeastern Illinois; drained by the Illinois, Des Plaines, and Kankakee Rivers. Covers a land area of 419.90 square miles, a water area of 10.50 square miles, and is located in the Central Time Zone. The county government was organized in 1841. County seat is Morris.

Grundy County is part of the Chicago, IL PMSA. The entire metro area includes: Cook County; DeKalb County; DuPage County; Grundy County; Kane County; Kendall County; Lake County; McHenry County; Will County

Population: 37,535 (2000); Race: 96.8% White, 0.2% Black, 0.3% Asian, 0.2% American Indian and Alaska Native, 4.8% Hispanic of any race, 1.0% two or more races (2000); Density: 89.4 persons per square mile (2000); Age: 26.8% under 18, 12.2% over 64 (2000).
Religion: Five largest groups: 26.6% Catholic Church, 6.5% The United Methodist Church, 4.1% Christian Churches and Churches of Christ, 4.1% Evangelical Lutheran Church in America, 2.4% Presbyterian Church (U.S.A.) (2000).
Economy: Unemployment rate: 7.0% (11/2002); Total civilian labor force: 18,641 (11/2002); Leading industries: 17.2% retail trade; 14.1% manufacturing; 12.2% accommodation & food services (2000); Companies that employ more than 1,000 persons: 0 (2000); Companies that employ more than 100 persons: 12 (2000); Farms: 463 totaling 201,452 acres (1997); Minority business ownership rate: 0.0% (1997); Women business ownership rate: 22.5% (1997); Retail sales per capita: $7,949 (1997). Single-family building permits issued: 199 (2001) / 170 (2000); Multi-family building permits issued: 80 (2001) / 57 (2000).
Income: Per capita income: $22,591 (2000); Median household income: $51,719 (2000); Poverty rate: 4.8% (2000); Bankruptcy rate: 7.19% (2001).
Taxes: Total county taxes per capita: $137 (2000); County property taxes per capita: $126 (2000).
Education: High school graduation rate: 86.9% (2000); College graduation rate: 15.2% (2000).
Housing: Homeownership rate: 72.3% (2000); Median home value: $128,600 (2000); Median rent: $508 per month (2000); Median age of housing: 29 years (2000).
Health: Birth rate: 120.7 per 10,000 population (1998); Age adjusted death rate: 89.2 per 10,000 population (1999); Age adjusted cancer mortality rate: 270.6 deaths per 100,000 population (1999). Number of physicians: 8.3 per 10,000 population (1999); Number of hospital beds: 21.8 per 10,000 population (1999).
Elections: 2000 Presidential election results: 45.3% Gore, 52.5% Bush, 1.6% Nader, 0.4% Buchanan
National and State Parks: Gebhard Woods State Park; Goose Lake Prairie State Park; Heidecke State Fish and Wildlife Area; Mazonia State Fish and Wildlife Area; William Stratton State Access Area
Additional Information Contacts
Grundy County Government Offices 815-941-3400
Grundy County Association of Commerce 815-942-0113

Grundy County Communities

BRACEVILLE (village). Covers a land area of 1.316 square miles and a water area of 0.011 square miles. Located at 41.22° N. Lat.; 88.26° W. Long. Elevation is 582 feet.
History: Braceville boomed as a coal-mining town in the late 1800's, but declined when the mines closed.
Population: 792 (2000); Race: 98.0% White, 0.0% Black, 0.0% Asian, 0.0% American Indian and Alaska Native, 2.3% Hispanic of any race, 1.7% two or more races (2000); Density: 601.8 persons per square mile (2000); Age: 28.3% under 18, 8.7% over 64 (2000); Marriage status: 24.2% never married, 60.0% now married, 3.5% widowed, 12.3% divorced (2000); Foreign born: 0.2% (2000); Ancestry (includes multiple ancestries): 33.4% German, 18.8% Irish, 11.3% Other groups, 9.7% English, 8.2% Italian (2000).
Economy: Employment by occupation: 6.0% management, 10.5% professional, 18.4% services, 22.6% sales, 0.0% farming, 20.2% construction, 22.3% production (2000).
Income: Per capita income: $17,586 (2000); Median household income: $47,059 (2000); Poverty rate: 4.3% (2000).
Taxes: Total city taxes per capita: $73 (1997); City property taxes per capita: $46 (1997).
Education: High school graduation rate: 82.2% (2000); College graduation rate: 6.6% (2000).

School District(s)
Braceville School District 75 (KG-08)
2000 Enrollment: 183 815-237-8040
Housing: Homeownership rate: 85.8% (2000); Median home value: $100,000 (2000); Median rent: $565 per month (2000); Median age of housing: 41 years (2000).
Transportation: Commute to work: 95.8% car, 0.5% public transportation, 1.3% walk, 1.9% work from home (2000); Travel time to work: 21.4% less than 15 minutes, 24.3% 15 to 30 minutes, 29.5% 30 to 45 minutes, 10.3% 45 to 60 minutes, 14.6% 60 minutes or more (2000)

CARBON HILL (village). Covers a land area of 0.176 square miles and a water area of 0 square miles. Located at 41.29° N. Lat.; 88.30° W. Long. Elevation is 560 feet.
Population: 392 (2000); Race: 95.3% White, 0.0% Black, 0.5% Asian, 0.0% American Indian and Alaska Native, 3.7% Hispanic of any race, 0.5% two or more races (2000); Density: 2,226.9 persons per square mile (2000); Age: 21.1% under 18, 10.0% over 64 (2000); Marriage status: 23.1% never married, 56.0% now married, 5.5% widowed, 15.3% divorced (2000); Foreign born: 1.8% (2000); Ancestry (includes multiple ancestries): 25.0% Irish, 24.7% German, 18.2% Italian, 12.1% Other groups, 7.4% English (2000).
Economy: In agricultural (corn, soybeans; dairying) and bituminous-coal area. Single-family building permits issued: 0 (2001) / 2 (2000); Multi-family building permits issued: 0 (2001) / 0 (2000); Employment by occupation: 8.2% management, 10.9% professional, 10.4% services, 27.9% sales, 0.0% farming, 24.6% construction, 18.0% production (2000).
Income: Per capita income: $22,228 (2000); Median household income: $53,750 (2000); Poverty rate: 3.0% (2000).
Taxes: Total city taxes per capita: $30 (1997); City property taxes per capita: $23 (1997).
Education: High school graduation rate: 78.7% (2000); College graduation rate: 6.3% (2000).
Housing: Homeownership rate: 75.0% (2000); Median home value: $110,800 (2000); Median rent: $482 per month (2000); Median age of housing: 28 years (2000).
Transportation: Commute to work: 95.1% car, 0.0% public transportation, 0.5% walk, 4.4% work from home (2000); Travel time to work: 24.0% less than 15 minutes, 28.0% 15 to 30 minutes, 23.4% 30 to 45 minutes, 8.0% 45 to 60 minutes, 16.6% 60 minutes or more (2000)

COAL CITY (village). Covers a land area of 2.423 square miles and a water area of 0 square miles. Located at 41.28° N. Lat.; 88.28° W. Long. Elevation is 565 feet.
History: Coal City began when shaft mines were opened here in 1875. The shaft mines were followed by strip mining.
Population: 4,797 (2000); Race: 99.3% White, 0.0% Black, 0.2% Asian, 0.0% American Indian and Alaska Native, 2.6% Hispanic of any race, 0.5% two or more races (2000); Density: 1,980.1 persons per square mile (2000); Age: 27.9% under 18, 12.8% over 64 (2000); Marriage status: 23.2% never married, 59.8% now married, 8.3% widowed, 8.7% divorced (2000); Foreign born: 1.1% (2000); Ancestry (includes multiple ancestries): 27.5% German, 21.2% Irish, 19.6% Italian, 14.4% English, 5.3% Other groups (2000).
Economy: Single-family building permits issued: 18 (2001) / 15 (2000); Multi-family building permits issued: 0 (2001) / 0 (2000); Employment by occupation: 7.4% management, 18.0% professional, 14.7% services, 20.2% sales, 0.2% farming, 18.9% construction, 20.6% production (2000).

Income: Per capita income: $23,662 (2000); Median household income: $51,921 (2000); Poverty rate: 3.1% (2000).
Taxes: Total city taxes per capita: $245 (1997); City property taxes per capita: $98 (1997).
Education: High school graduation rate: 90.4% (2000); College graduation rate: 13.8% (2000).

School District(s)

Coal City C U School District 1 (PK-12)
2000 Enrollment: 1,857 815-634-2287

Housing: Homeownership rate: 73.9% (2000); Median home value: $114,700 (2000); Median rent: $501 per month (2000); Median age of housing: 33 years (2000).
Newspapers: The Coal City Courant (1 x week)
Transportation: Commute to work: 97.0% car, 0.0% public transportation, 1.3% walk, 1.0% work from home (2000); Travel time to work: 28.0% less than 15 minutes, 35.7% 15 to 30 minutes, 20.8% 30 to 45 minutes, 7.0% 45 to 60 minutes, 8.5% 60 minutes or more (2000)

DIAMOND (village). Covers a land area of 1.582 square miles and a water area of 0 square miles. Located at 41.28° N. Lat.; 88.25° W. Long. Elevation is 563 feet.
Population: 1,393 (2000); Race: 97.7% White, 0.0% Black, 0.0% Asian, 0.6% American Indian and Alaska Native, 3.7% Hispanic of any race, 0.8% two or more races (2000); Density: 880.3 persons per square mile (2000); Age: 28.0% under 18, 9.9% over 64 (2000); Marriage status: 23.2% never married, 55.2% now married, 5.5% widowed, 16.0% divorced (2000); Foreign born: 0.4% (2000); Ancestry (includes multiple ancestries): 24.6% German, 19.2% Italian, 17.5% Irish, 13.8% English, 7.7% Polish (2000).
Economy: In agricultural area: corn, soybeans. Single-family building permits issued: 32 (2001) / 9 (2000); Multi-family building permits issued: 13 (2001) / 16 (2000); Employment by occupation: 9.8% management, 11.1% professional, 14.5% services, 28.4% sales, 0.0% farming, 16.0% construction, 20.3% production (2000).
Income: Per capita income: $20,223 (2000); Median household income: $43,750 (2000); Poverty rate: 8.6% (2000).
Taxes: Total city taxes per capita: $42 (1997); City property taxes per capita: $38 (1997).
Education: High school graduation rate: 84.8% (2000); College graduation rate: 9.0% (2000).
Housing: Homeownership rate: 74.6% (2000); Median home value: $132,000 (2000); Median rent: $596 per month (2000); Median age of housing: 22 years (2000).
Transportation: Commute to work: 95.7% car, 0.6% public transportation, 1.7% walk, 1.2% work from home (2000); Travel time to work: 20.8% less than 15 minutes, 33.0% 15 to 30 minutes, 23.5% 30 to 45 minutes, 8.9% 45 to 60 minutes, 13.8% 60 minutes or more (2000)

EAST BROOKLYN (village). Covers a land area of 0.052 square miles and a water area of 0 square miles. Located at 41.17° N. Lat.; 88.26° W. Long. Elevation is 587 feet.
Population: 123 (2000); Race: 92.2% White, 0.0% Black, 0.0% Asian, 2.0% American Indian and Alaska Native, 7.8% Hispanic of any race, 5.9% two or more races (2000); Density: 2,369.4 persons per square mile (2000); Age: 33.3% under 18, 10.8% over 64 (2000); Marriage status: 35.4% never married, 54.9% now married, 6.1% widowed, 3.7% divorced (2000); Foreign born: 0.0% (2000); Ancestry (includes multiple ancestries): 54.9% Italian, 16.7% German, 12.7% Irish, 9.8% Czech, 9.8% Norwegian (2000).
Economy: In agricultural area. Single-family building permits issued: 0 (2001) / 0 (2000); Multi-family building permits issued: 0 (2001) / 0 (2000); Employment by occupation: 6.3% management, 27.1% professional, 6.3% services, 8.3% sales, 0.0% farming, 29.2% construction, 22.9% production (2000).
Income: Per capita income: $21,470 (2000); Median household income: $40,000 (2000); Poverty rate: 12.7% (2000).
Taxes: Total city taxes per capita: $53 (1997); City property taxes per capita: $32 (1997).
Education: High school graduation rate: 80.3% (2000); College graduation rate: 9.1% (2000).
Housing: Homeownership rate: 87.5% (2000); Median home value: $99,400 (2000); Median rent: $275 per month (2000); Median age of housing: 41 years (2000).
Transportation: Commute to work: 100.0% car, 0.0% public transportation, 0.0% walk, 0.0% work from home (2000); Travel time to work: 16.7% less than 15 minutes, 35.4% 15 to 30 minutes, 37.5% 30 to 45 minutes, 0.0% 45 to 60 minutes, 10.4% 60 minutes or more (2000)

GARDNER (village). Covers a land area of 1.040 square miles and a water area of 0.014 square miles. Located at 41.18° N. Lat.; 88.31° W. Long. Elevation is 590 feet.
Population: 1,406 (2000); Race: 97.7% White, 0.1% Black, 0.0% Asian, 0.4% American Indian and Alaska Native, 4.8% Hispanic of any race, 0.8% two or more races (2000); Density: 1,351.4 persons per square mile (2000); Age: 28.5% under 18, 10.6% over 64 (2000); Marriage status: 20.4% never married, 60.5% now married, 6.9% widowed, 12.2% divorced (2000); Foreign born: 2.5% (2000); Ancestry (includes multiple ancestries): 22.3% German, 18.5% Irish, 17.1% Italian, 11.5% English, 7.3% Norwegian (2000).
Economy: In agricultural area. Bituminous coal in area. Single-family building permits issued: 4 (2001) / 3 (2000); Multi-family building permits issued: 0 (2001) / 0 (2000); Employment by occupation: 4.5% management, 18.0% professional, 14.5% services, 21.6% sales, 0.6% farming, 17.8% construction, 23.0% production (2000).
Income: Per capita income: $18,995 (2000); Median household income: $42,500 (2000); Poverty rate: 6.8% (2000).
Taxes: Total city taxes per capita: $401 (1997); City property taxes per capita: $379 (1997).
Education: High school graduation rate: 83.5% (2000); College graduation rate: 9.1% (2000).

School District(s)

Gardner Community Cons School District 72c (KG-08)
2000 Enrollment: 234 815-237-2313
Gardner S Wilmington Ths District 73 (09-12)
2000 Enrollment: 190 815-237-2176

Housing: Homeownership rate: 73.0% (2000); Median home value: $96,600 (2000); Median rent: $435 per month (2000); Median age of housing: 47 years (2000).
Transportation: Commute to work: 95.0% car, 0.0% public transportation, 2.6% walk, 1.1% work from home (2000); Travel time to work: 25.3% less than 15 minutes, 23.9% 15 to 30 minutes, 26.1% 30 to 45 minutes, 12.8% 45 to 60 minutes, 11.9% 60 minutes or more (2000)

KINSMAN (village). Covers a land area of 0.067 square miles and a water area of 0 square miles. Located at 41.19° N. Lat.; 88.57° W. Long. Elevation is 660 feet.
Population: 109 (2000); Race: 98.4% White, 0.0% Black, 0.0% Asian, 0.0% American Indian and Alaska Native, 1.6% Hispanic of any race, 0.0% two or more races (2000); Density: 1,638.0 persons per square mile (2000); Age: 22.1% under 18, 17.2% over 64 (2000); Marriage status: 16.0% never married, 72.0% now married, 10.0% widowed, 2.0% divorced (2000); Foreign born: 4.1% (2000); Ancestry (includes multiple ancestries): 29.5% German, 22.1% United States or American, 21.3% Irish, 7.4% Norwegian, 6.6% Danish (2000).
Economy: In agricultural area. Single-family building permits issued: 0 (2001) / 0 (2000); Multi-family building permits issued: 0 (2001) / 0 (2000); Employment by occupation: 6.5% management, 4.8% professional, 3.2% services, 38.7% sales, 0.0% farming, 9.7% construction, 37.1% production (2000).
Income: Per capita income: $20,011 (2000); Median household income: $42,083 (2000); Poverty rate: 0.0% (2000).
Taxes: Total city taxes per capita: $74 (1997); City property taxes per capita: $46 (1997).
Education: High school graduation rate: 77.3% (2000); College graduation rate: 9.1% (2000).
Housing: Homeownership rate: 95.8% (2000); Median home value: $70,000 (2000); Median rent: $425 per month (2000); Median age of housing: 56 years (2000).
Transportation: Commute to work: 88.7% car, 0.0% public transportation, 3.2% walk, 4.8% work from home (2000); Travel time to work: 16.9% less than 15 minutes, 37.3% 15 to 30 minutes, 18.6% 30 to 45 minutes, 18.6% 45 to 60 minutes, 8.5% 60 minutes or more (2000)

MAZON (village). Covers a land area of 0.598 square miles and a water area of 0 square miles. Located at 41.24° N. Lat.; 88.42° W. Long. Elevation is 586 feet.
History: Near the Mazon River, a classic source of fossils from a middle Pennsylvanian formation.
Population: 904 (2000); Race: 93.6% White, 0.4% Black, 0.4% Asian, 1.3% American Indian and Alaska Native, 4.2% Hispanic of any race, 2.0% two or more races (2000); Density: 1,510.7 persons per square mile (2000); Age: 25.9% under 18, 14.3% over 64 (2000); Marriage status: 16.7% never married, 69.5% now married, 5.3% widowed, 8.4% divorced (2000); Foreign

born: 1.6% (2000); Ancestry (includes multiple ancestries): 22.3% German, 20.8% English, 19.1% Irish, 12.0% Other groups, 10.4% Norwegian (2000).
Economy: In agricultural area. Single-family building permits issued: 1 (2001) / 2 (2000); Multi-family building permits issued: 0 (2001) / 0 (2000); Employment by occupation: 10.8% management, 18.0% professional, 12.2% services, 19.0% sales, 0.9% farming, 16.6% construction, 22.5% production (2000).
Income: Per capita income: $21,890 (2000); Median household income: $55,250 (2000); Poverty rate: 3.4% (2000).
Taxes: Total city taxes per capita: $79 (1997); City property taxes per capita: $66 (1997).
Education: High school graduation rate: 90.5% (2000); College graduation rate: 15.3% (2000).

School District(s)

Mazon-Verona-Kinsman ESD 2c (KG-08)
2000 Enrollment: 327 815-448-2200

Housing: Homeownership rate: 78.4% (2000); Median home value: $105,900 (2000); Median rent: $504 per month (2000); Median age of housing: 41 years (2000).
Transportation: Commute to work: 94.3% car, 0.5% public transportation, 2.2% walk, 2.9% work from home (2000); Travel time to work: 30.5% less than 15 minutes, 27.8% 15 to 30 minutes, 20.7% 30 to 45 minutes, 13.5% 45 to 60 minutes, 7.4% 60 minutes or more (2000)

MINOOKA (village). Covers a land area of 4.263 square miles and a water area of 0.071 square miles. Located at 41.45° N. Lat.; 88.26° W. Long. Elevation is 610 feet.
Population: 3,971 (2000); Race: 97.3% White, 0.5% Black, 0.0% Asian, 0.1% American Indian and Alaska Native, 3.7% Hispanic of any race, 0.8% two or more races (2000); Density: 931.5 persons per square mile (2000); Age: 31.6% under 18, 5.0% over 64 (2000); Marriage status: 23.7% never married, 65.9% now married, 2.9% widowed, 7.5% divorced (2000); Foreign born: 1.9% (2000); Ancestry (includes multiple ancestries): 34.2% German, 22.6% Irish, 11.0% Italian, 10.0% English, 7.8% Polish (2000).
Economy: In agricultural area. Single-family building permits issued: 42 (2001) / 44 (2000); Multi-family building permits issued: 14 (2001) / 18 (2000); Employment by occupation: 14.7% management, 23.1% professional, 12.0% services, 23.1% sales, 0.6% farming, 12.5% construction, 14.0% production (2000).
Income: Per capita income: $26,054 (2000); Median household income: $75,249 (2000); Poverty rate: 2.2% (2000).
Taxes: Total city taxes per capita: $357 (1997); City property taxes per capita: $103 (1997).
Education: High school graduation rate: 95.0% (2000); College graduation rate: 28.6% (2000).

School District(s)

Minooka Community Cons S District 201 (PK-08)
2000 Enrollment: 1,299 815-467-6121
Minooka Community H S District 111 (09-12)
2000 Enrollment: 1,316 815-467-2140

Housing: Homeownership rate: 86.1% (2000); Median home value: $176,400 (2000); Median rent: $557 per month (2000); Median age of housing: 14 years (2000).
Transportation: Commute to work: 96.0% car, 0.7% public transportation, 1.3% walk, 2.0% work from home (2000); Travel time to work: 27.2% less than 15 minutes, 38.9% 15 to 30 minutes, 17.8% 30 to 45 minutes, 7.1% 45 to 60 minutes, 9.1% 60 minutes or more (2000)

MORRIS (city). Covers a land area of 6.879 square miles and a water area of 0.281 square miles. Located at 41.36° N. Lat.; 88.42° W. Long. Elevation is 519 feet.
History: Morris was platted in 1842 and named for Isaac N. Morris, an Illinois & Michigan Canal commissioner, who negotiated to have the village named as the county seat. Morris grew as a shipping and paper manufacturing center.
Population: 11,928 (2000); Race: 95.2% White, 0.3% Black, 0.3% Asian, 0.2% American Indian and Alaska Native, 7.3% Hispanic of any race, 1.3% two or more races (2000); Density: 1,734.0 persons per square mile (2000); Age: 25.2% under 18, 16.3% over 64 (2000); Marriage status: 24.0% never married, 56.2% now married, 9.6% widowed, 10.2% divorced (2000); Foreign born: 3.9% (2000); Ancestry (includes multiple ancestries): 21.6% German, 20.1% Irish, 13.4% Norwegian, 12.3% Other groups, 8.9% English (2000).
Vital Statistics: Birth rate: 137.5 per 10,000 population (1998)
Economy: Single-family building permits issued: 44 (2001) / 34 (2000); Multi-family building permits issued: 53 (2001) / 23 (2000); Employment by occupation: 9.8% management, 15.3% professional, 17.6% services, 26.7% sales, 0.0% farming, 11.3% construction, 19.3% production (2000).
Income: Per capita income: $22,256 (2000); Median household income: $44,739 (2000); Poverty rate: 6.6% (2000).
Taxes: Total city taxes per capita: $274 (1997); City property taxes per capita: $214 (1997).
Education: High school graduation rate: 84.4% (2000); College graduation rate: 19.0% (2000).

School District(s)

Grundy/Kendall Roe (07-12)
2000 Enrollment: 134 815-941-3247
Morris Community High School District 101 (09-12)
2000 Enrollment: 977 815-941-5327
Morris School District 54 (PK-08)
2000 Enrollment: 1,297 815-942-0056
Nettle Creek C C School District 24c (KG-08)
2000 Enrollment: 72 815-942-0511
Saratoga Community Cons S District 60c (PK-08)
2000 Enrollment: 532 815-942-2128

Housing: Homeownership rate: 57.0% (2000); Median home value: $127,700 (2000); Median rent: $500 per month (2000); Median age of housing: 32 years (2000).
Hospitals: Morris Hospital (82 beds)
Newspapers: Morris Daily Herald (5 x week)
Transportation: Commute to work: 93.3% car, 1.1% public transportation, 2.4% walk, 2.5% work from home (2000); Travel time to work: 47.4% less than 15 minutes, 20.7% 15 to 30 minutes, 18.2% 30 to 45 minutes, 5.0% 45 to 60 minutes, 8.7% 60 minutes or more (2000)
Airports: Morris Municipal - James R. Washburn Fie
Additional Information Contacts
Grundy County Association of Commerce 815-942-0113

SOUTH WILMINGTON (village). Covers a land area of 0.570 square miles and a water area of 0 square miles. Located at 41.17° N. Lat.; 88.27° W. Long. Elevation is 587 feet.
Population: 621 (2000); Race: 100.0% White, 0.0% Black, 0.0% Asian, 0.0% American Indian and Alaska Native, 2.0% Hispanic of any race, 0.0% two or more races (2000); Density: 1,089.8 persons per square mile (2000); Age: 25.1% under 18, 19.5% over 64 (2000); Marriage status: 25.8% never married, 55.4% now married, 9.6% widowed, 9.2% divorced (2000); Foreign born: 0.0% (2000); Ancestry (includes multiple ancestries): 38.2% Italian, 19.7% Irish, 17.8% German, 14.9% English, 7.4% Polish (2000).
Economy: In agricultural area: corn, soybeans; dairying. Single-family building permits issued: 1 (2001) / 2 (2000); Multi-family building permits issued: 0 (2001) / 0 (2000); Employment by occupation: 6.2% management, 14.1% professional, 12.4% services, 19.9% sales, 1.0% farming, 23.9% construction, 22.5% production (2000).
Income: Per capita income: $19,078 (2000); Median household income: $39,688 (2000); Poverty rate: 7.9% (2000).
Taxes: Total city taxes per capita: $34 (1997); City property taxes per capita: $30 (1997).
Education: High school graduation rate: 83.1% (2000); College graduation rate: 6.6% (2000).

School District(s)

South Wilmington Cons School District 74 (KG-08)
2000 Enrollment: 98 815-237-2281

Housing: Homeownership rate: 84.1% (2000); Median home value: $89,600 (2000); Median rent: $500 per month (2000); Median age of housing: 55 years (2000).
Transportation: Commute to work: 96.0% car, 0.0% public transportation, 2.7% walk, 0.7% work from home (2000); Travel time to work: 20.7% less than 15 minutes, 25.4% 15 to 30 minutes, 36.8% 30 to 45 minutes, 8.7% 45 to 60 minutes, 8.4% 60 minutes or more (2000)

VERONA (village). Covers a land area of 0.146 square miles and a water area of 0 square miles. Located at 41.21° N. Lat.; 88.50° W. Long. Elevation is 640 feet.
Population: 257 (2000); Race: 92.0% White, 2.4% Black, 0.0% Asian, 0.0% American Indian and Alaska Native, 10.0% Hispanic of any race, 0.0% two or more races (2000); Density: 1,762.7 persons per square mile (2000); Age: 32.7% under 18, 12.7% over 64 (2000); Marriage status: 19.7% never married, 63.7% now married, 12.4% widowed, 4.1% divorced (2000); Foreign born: 4.0% (2000); Ancestry (includes multiple ancestries): 19.5% Irish, 16.3% Other groups, 16.3% German, 8.0% United States or American, 7.2% Italian (2000).

Economy: In agricultural area. Single-family building permits issued: 0 (2001) / 0 (2000); Multi-family building permits issued: 0 (2001) / 0 (2000); Employment by occupation: 1.9% management, 8.7% professional, 18.3% services, 27.9% sales, 0.0% farming, 12.5% construction, 30.8% production (2000).
Income: Per capita income: $16,387 (2000); Median household income: $46,094 (2000); Poverty rate: 5.2% (2000).
Taxes: Total city taxes per capita: $20 (1997); City property taxes per capita: $20 (1997).
Education: High school graduation rate: 70.8% (2000); College graduation rate: 4.3% (2000).
Housing: Homeownership rate: 87.8% (2000); Median home value: $67,000 (2000); Median rent: $381 per month (2000); Median age of housing: 59 years (2000).
Transportation: Commute to work: 91.8% car, 0.0% public transportation, 0.0% walk, 8.2% work from home (2000); Travel time to work: 11.1% less than 15 minutes, 42.2% 15 to 30 minutes, 26.7% 30 to 45 minutes, 0.0% 45 to 60 minutes, 20.0% 60 minutes or more (2000)

Hamilton County

Located in southeastern Illinois; drained by the North Fork of the Saline River. Covers a land area of 435.20 square miles, a water area of 0.70 square miles, and is located in the Central Time Zone. The county government was organized in 1821. County seat is McLeansboro.

Weather Station: McLeansboro 2 ENE — Elevation: 479 feet

	Jan	Feb	Mar	Apr	May	Jun	Jul	Aug	Sep	Oct	Nov	Dec
High	38	44	54	66	76	85	89	88	81	69	55	44
Low	20	24	34	44	53	62	66	63	55	43	35	25
Precip	3.1	2.7	4.5	4.7	4.6	3.8	3.5	3.0	2.9	3.1	4.5	3.6
Snow	5.0	4.4	2.5	0.4	0.0	0.0	0.0	0.0	0.0	0.2	0.7	3.1

High and Low temperatures in degrees Fahrenheit; Precipitation and Snow in inches

Population: 8,621 (2000); Race: 97.7% White, 0.2% Black, 0.2% Asian, 0.8% American Indian and Alaska Native, 0.3% Hispanic of any race, 0.9% two or more races (2000); Density: 19.8 persons per square mile (2000); Age: 24.0% under 18, 19.2% over 64 (2000).
Religion: Five largest groups: 33.2% Southern Baptist Convention, 11.8% Catholic Church, 4.9% The United Methodist Church, 3.7% Christian Churches and Churches of Christ, 1.3% Church of God (Cleveland, Tennessee) (2000).
Economy: Unemployment rate: 6.2% (11/2002); Total civilian labor force: 3,737 (11/2002); Leading industries: 30.7% health care and social assistance; 16.6% retail trade; except pub other services (2000); Companies that employ more than 1,000 persons: 0 (2000); Companies that employ more than 100 persons: 1 (2000); Farms: 563 totaling 214,780 acres (1997); Minority business ownership rate: 0.0% (1997); Women business ownership rate: 19.9% (1997); Retail sales per capita: $4,385 (1997). Single-family building permits issued: -1 (2001) / -1 (2000); Multi-family building permits issued: -1 (2001) / -1 (2000).
Income: Per capita income: $16,262 (2000); Median household income: $30,496 (2000); Poverty rate: 12.9% (2000); Bankruptcy rate: 3.25% (2001).
Taxes: Total county taxes per capita: $72 (1997); County property taxes per capita: $50 (1997).
Education: High school graduation rate: 74.3% (2000); College graduation rate: 10.5% (2000).
Housing: Homeownership rate: 81.5% (2000); Median home value: $47,800 (2000); Median rent: $164 per month (2000); Median age of housing: 39 years (2000).
Health: Birth rate: 98.6 per 10,000 population (1998); Age adjusted death rate: 85.0 per 10,000 population (1999); Age adjusted cancer mortality rate: 216.9 deaths per 100,000 population (1999). Air Quality Index: 72% good, 28% moderate, 0% unhealthy (percent of days in 2000). Number of physicians: 8.1 per 10,000 population (1999); Number of hospital beds: 105.6 per 10,000 population (1999).
Elections: 2000 Presidential election results: 42.4% Gore, 54.9% Bush, 1.6% Nader, 0.8% Buchanan
National and State Parks: Hamilton County State Conservation Area
Additional Information Contacts
Hamilton County Government Offices 618-643-2721
Mc Leansboro Chamber of Commerce 618-643-3531

Hamilton County Communities

BELLE PRAIRIE CITY (town). Aka Belle Prairie. Covers a land area of 0.449 square miles and a water area of 0 square miles. Located at 38.22° N. Lat.; 88.55° W. Long. Elevation is 477 feet.
Population: 60 (2000); Race: 100.0% White, 0.0% Black, 0.0% Asian, 0.0% American Indian and Alaska Native, 0.0% Hispanic of any race, 0.0% two or more races (2000); Density: 133.6 persons per square mile (2000); Age: 24.1% under 18, 19.0% over 64 (2000); Marriage status: 13.6% never married, 70.5% now married, 13.6% widowed, 2.3% divorced (2000); Foreign born: 0.0% (2000); Ancestry (includes multiple ancestries): 17.2% German, 15.5% Italian, 15.5% English, 12.1% Irish, 5.2% Other groups (2000).
Economy: In rich agricultural area. Employment by occupation: 19.2% management, 26.9% professional, 19.2% services, 19.2% sales, 0.0% farming, 7.7% construction, 7.7% production (2000).
Income: Per capita income: $19,528 (2000); Median household income: $37,031 (2000); Poverty rate: 0.0% (2000).
Education: High school graduation rate: 84.2% (2000); College graduation rate: 13.2% (2000).
Housing: Homeownership rate: 100.0% (2000); Median home value: $65,000 (2000); Median age of housing: 48 years (2000).
Transportation: Commute to work: 100.0% car, 0.0% public transportation, 0.0% walk, 0.0% work from home (2000); Travel time to work: 11.5% less than 15 minutes, 30.8% 15 to 30 minutes, 38.5% 30 to 45 minutes, 3.8% 45 to 60 minutes, 15.4% 60 minutes or more (2000)

BROUGHTON (village). Covers a land area of 1.918 square miles and a water area of 0 square miles. Located at 37.93° N. Lat.; 88.46° W. Long. Elevation is 378 feet.
Population: 193 (2000); Race: 99.0% White, 0.0% Black, 0.0% Asian, 0.0% American Indian and Alaska Native, 0.0% Hispanic of any race, 1.0% two or more races (2000); Density: 100.6 persons per square mile (2000); Age: 21.8% under 18, 18.3% over 64 (2000); Marriage status: 13.8% never married, 56.9% now married, 10.6% widowed, 18.8% divorced (2000); Foreign born: 0.5% (2000); Ancestry (includes multiple ancestries): 18.8% United States or American, 17.3% English, 8.9% German, 7.9% Irish, 5.4% Other groups (2000).
Economy: In agricultural area. Employment by occupation: 9.3% management, 13.3% professional, 24.0% services, 24.0% sales, 8.0% farming, 14.7% construction, 6.7% production (2000).
Income: Per capita income: $11,926 (2000); Median household income: $19,500 (2000); Poverty rate: 27.2% (2000).
Taxes: Total city taxes per capita: $23 (1997); City property taxes per capita: $23 (1997).
Education: High school graduation rate: 71.3% (2000); College graduation rate: 4.2% (2000).
Housing: Homeownership rate: 90.7% (2000); Median home value: $27,100 (2000); Median rent: $125 per month (2000); Median age of housing: 44 years (2000).
Transportation: Commute to work: 92.0% car, 0.0% public transportation, 8.0% walk, 0.0% work from home (2000); Travel time to work: 26.7% less than 15 minutes, 29.3% 15 to 30 minutes, 24.0% 30 to 45 minutes, 9.3% 45 to 60 minutes, 10.7% 60 minutes or more (2000)

DAHLGREN (village). Covers a land area of 1.004 square miles and a water area of 0 square miles. Located at 38.19° N. Lat.; 88.68° W. Long. Elevation is 510 feet.
Population: 514 (2000); Race: 100.0% White, 0.0% Black, 0.0% Asian, 0.0% American Indian and Alaska Native, 1.0% Hispanic of any race, 0.0% two or more races (2000); Density: 512.1 persons per square mile (2000); Age: 18.9% under 18, 25.3% over 64 (2000); Marriage status: 23.6% never married, 57.1% now married, 11.0% widowed, 8.3% divorced (2000); Foreign born: 0.6% (2000); Ancestry (includes multiple ancestries): 23.4% German, 18.5% United States or American, 17.2% English, 14.4% Irish, 7.8% Other groups (2000).
Economy: In agricultural area. Employment by occupation: 6.5% management, 8.9% professional, 23.8% services, 29.0% sales, 4.2% farming, 4.2% construction, 23.4% production (2000).
Income: Per capita income: $13,862 (2000); Median household income: $26,944 (2000); Poverty rate: 13.5% (2000).
Taxes: Total city taxes per capita: $17 (1997); City property taxes per capita: $16 (1997).
Education: High school graduation rate: 78.7% (2000); College graduation rate: 6.0% (2000).

Housing: Homeownership rate: 86.3% (2000); Median home value: $31,400 (2000); Median rent: $178 per month (2000); Median age of housing: 54 years (2000).
Transportation: Commute to work: 94.8% car, 0.0% public transportation, 0.5% walk, 2.8% work from home (2000); Travel time to work: 14.0% less than 15 minutes, 57.0% 15 to 30 minutes, 20.3% 30 to 45 minutes, 5.3% 45 to 60 minutes, 3.4% 60 minutes or more (2000)

DALE (unincorporated postal area, zip code 62829). Aka Dales. Covers a land area of 6.561 square miles and a water area of 0 square miles. Located at 38.00° N. Lat.; 88.50° W. Long. Elevation is 400 feet.
Population: 157 (2000); Race: 100.0% White, 0.0% Black, 0.0% Asian, 0.0% American Indian and Alaska Native, 3.5% Hispanic of any race, 0.0% two or more races (2000); Density: 23.9 persons per square mile (2000); Age: 22.9% under 18, 5.3% over 64 (2000); Marriage status: 15.7% never married, 75.7% now married, 0.0% widowed, 8.6% divorced (2000); Foreign born: 1.8% (2000); Ancestry (includes multiple ancestries): 17.1% German, 11.2% United States or American, 11.2% Irish, 8.2% European, 4.7% Danish (2000).
Economy: Employment by occupation: 0.0% management, 28.0% professional, 22.6% services, 15.1% sales, 9.7% farming, 8.6% construction, 16.1% production (2000).
Income: Per capita income: $16,996 (2000); Median household income: $50,417 (2000); Poverty rate: 0.0% (2000).
Education: High school graduation rate: 83.9% (2000); College graduation rate: 11.9% (2000).
Housing: Homeownership rate: 90.2% (2000); Median home value: $58,600 (2000); Median age of housing: 43 years (2000).
Transportation: Commute to work: 93.5% car, 0.0% public transportation, 0.0% walk, 6.5% work from home (2000); Travel time to work: 21.8% less than 15 minutes, 40.2% 15 to 30 minutes, 19.5% 30 to 45 minutes, 8.0% 45 to 60 minutes, 10.3% 60 minutes or more (2000)

MACEDONIA (village). Covers a land area of 0.271 square miles and a water area of 0 square miles. Located at 38.05° N. Lat.; 88.70° W. Long.
Population: 51 (2000); Race: 100.0% White, 0.0% Black, 0.0% Asian, 0.0% American Indian and Alaska Native, 0.0% Hispanic of any race, 0.0% two or more races (2000); Density: 188.4 persons per square mile (2000); Age: 29.1% under 18, 5.5% over 64 (2000); Marriage status: 31.7% never married, 61.0% now married, 4.9% widowed, 2.4% divorced (2000); Foreign born: 0.0% (2000); Ancestry (includes multiple ancestries): 18.2% United States or American, 7.3% German, 7.3% English, 3.6% Dutch, 3.6% Irish (2000).
Economy: In agricultural area. Employment by occupation: 10.3% management, 6.9% professional, 20.7% services, 34.5% sales, 0.0% farming, 0.0% construction, 27.6% production (2000).
Income: Per capita income: $11,465 (2000); Median household income: $24,375 (2000); Poverty rate: 23.6% (2000).
Taxes: Total city taxes per capita: $49 (1997); City property taxes per capita: $49 (1997).
Education: High school graduation rate: 71.9% (2000); College graduation rate: 6.3% (2000).
Housing: Homeownership rate: 83.3% (2000); Median home value: $50,000 (2000); Median rent: $313 per month (2000); Median age of housing: 32 years (2000).
Transportation: Commute to work: 82.8% car, 0.0% public transportation, 0.0% walk, 17.2% work from home (2000); Travel time to work: 8.3% less than 15 minutes, 41.7% 15 to 30 minutes, 16.7% 30 to 45 minutes, 20.8% 45 to 60 minutes, 12.5% 60 minutes or more (2000)

MCLEANSBORO (city). Covers a land area of 2.290 square miles and a water area of 0 square miles. Located at 38.09° N. Lat.; 88.53° W. Long. Elevation is 495 feet.
History: Incorporated 1840.
Population: 2,945 (2000); Race: 97.6% White, 0.0% Black, 0.2% Asian, 0.0% American Indian and Alaska Native, 0.0% Hispanic of any race, 2.2% two or more races (2000); Density: 1,286.3 persons per square mile (2000); Age: 22.8% under 18, 24.1% over 64 (2000); Marriage status: 23.3% never married, 54.4% now married, 13.1% widowed, 9.2% divorced (2000); Foreign born: 0.2% (2000); Ancestry (includes multiple ancestries): 13.7% United States or American, 13.4% German, 11.0% English, 7.9% Irish, 6.0% Other groups (2000).
Economy: In agricultural area; corn, wheat; livestock. Employment by occupation: 7.6% management, 18.9% professional, 23.2% services, 22.9% sales, 0.8% farming, 11.2% construction, 15.4% production (2000).
Income: Per capita income: $15,354 (2000); Median household income: $22,183 (2000); Poverty rate: 19.7% (2000).
Taxes: Total city taxes per capita: $254 (1997); City property taxes per capita: $67 (1997).
Education: High school graduation rate: 68.4% (2000); College graduation rate: 11.7% (2000).

School District(s)

Hamilton Co C U School District 10 (PK-12)
2000 Enrollment: 1,388 618-643-2328

Housing: Homeownership rate: 68.5% (2000); Median home value: $45,100 (2000); Median rent: $146 per month (2000); Median age of housing: 37 years (2000).
Newspapers: The Times Leader (1 x week)
Transportation: Commute to work: 96.1% car, 1.1% public transportation, 2.0% walk, 0.8% work from home (2000); Travel time to work: 43.8% less than 15 minutes, 11.8% 15 to 30 minutes, 30.1% 30 to 45 minutes, 8.6% 45 to 60 minutes, 5.7% 60 minutes or more (2000)
Additional Information Contacts
Mc Leansboro Chamber of Commerce 618-643-3531

Hancock County

Located in western Illinois; bounded on the west by Lake Keokuk (on the Mississippi River) and the Iowa and Missouri borders; drained by the La Moine River and Bear Creek. Covers a land area of 794.60 square miles, a water area of 19.90 square miles, and is located in the Central Time Zone. The county government was organized in 1825. County seat is Carthage.

Weather Station: La Harpe — Elevation: 698 feet

	Jan	Feb	Mar	Apr	May	Jun	Jul	Aug	Sep	Oct	Nov	Dec
High	32	38	50	63	74	83	87	85	78	66	50	37
Low	13	18	29	39	50	59	63	61	52	41	30	19
Precip	1.4	1.6	2.9	3.9	4.6	4.2	4.5	3.9	4.3	2.9	3.1	2.3
Snow	7.8	5.1	3.7	1.1	0.0	0.0	0.0	0.0	0.0	tr	1.9	5.5

High and Low temperatures in degrees Fahrenheit; Precipitation and Snow in inches

Population: 20,121 (2000); Race: 99.0% White, 0.1% Black, 0.1% Asian, 0.2% American Indian and Alaska Native, 0.3% Hispanic of any race, 0.5% two or more races (2000); Density: 25.3 persons per square mile (2000); Age: 24.6% under 18, 18.2% over 64 (2000).
Religion: Five largest groups: 12.9% Catholic Church, 9.9% The United Methodist Church, 6.3% Christian Churches and Churches of Christ, 5.7% Evangelical Lutheran Church in America, 3.4% Presbyterian Church (U.S.A.) (2000).
Economy: Unemployment rate: 4.7% (11/2002); Total civilian labor force: 11,781 (11/2002); Leading industries: 37.6% manufacturing; 14.3% retail trade; 12.0% health care and social assistance (2000); Companies that employ more than 1,000 persons: 1 (2000); Companies that employ more than 100 persons: 3 (2000); Farms: 1,137 totaling 438,342 acres (1997); Minority business ownership rate: 0.0% (1997); Women business ownership rate: 25.1% (1997); Retail sales per capita: $4,800 (1997). Single-family building permits issued: 44 (2001) / 20 (2000); Multi-family building permits issued: 40 (2001) / 2 (2000).
Income: Per capita income: $17,478 (2000); Median household income: $36,654 (2000); Poverty rate: 8.3% (2000); Bankruptcy rate: 5.30% (2001).
Taxes: Total county taxes per capita: $79 (1997); County property taxes per capita: $79 (1997).
Education: High school graduation rate: 85.7% (2000); College graduation rate: 15.6% (2000).
Housing: Homeownership rate: 80.3% (2000); Median home value: $58,200 (2000); Median rent: $260 per month (2000); Median age of housing: 49 years (2000).
Health: Birth rate: 105.4 per 10,000 population (1998); Age adjusted death rate: 73.5 per 10,000 population (1999); Age adjusted cancer mortality rate: 190.5 deaths per 100,000 population (1999). Number of physicians: 7.0 per 10,000 population (1999); Number of hospital beds: 23.9 per 10,000 population (1999).
Elections: 2000 Presidential election results: 43.9% Gore, 53.0% Bush, 1.7% Nader, 0.9% Buchanan
National and State Parks: Montebello State Park; Nauvoo State Park
Additional Information Contacts
Hancock County Government Offices 217-357-3911
Carthage Chamber of Commerce 217-357-3024
Nauvoo Chamber of Commerce 217-453-6648
Warsaw Chamber of Commerce 217-256-4235

Hancock County Communities

AUGUSTA (village). Covers a land area of 0.713 square miles and a water area of 0 square miles. Located at 40.23° N. Lat.; 90.95° W. Long. Elevation is 668 feet.
Population: 657 (2000); Race: 100.0% White, 0.0% Black, 0.0% Asian, 0.0% American Indian and Alaska Native, 1.3% Hispanic of any race, 0.0% two or more races (2000); Density: 921.1 persons per square mile (2000); Age: 19.1% under 18, 22.5% over 64 (2000); Marriage status: 20.3% never married, 55.8% now married, 12.7% widowed, 11.1% divorced (2000); Foreign born: 0.0% (2000); Ancestry (includes multiple ancestries): 23.6% United States or American, 20.7% German, 13.4% English, 7.0% Irish, 4.8% Other groups (2000).
Economy: Agriculture: cattle, hogs; corn, wheat, soybeans, sorghum. Employment by occupation: 8.7% management, 16.5% professional, 15.2% services, 21.4% sales, 0.6% farming, 11.5% construction, 26.1% production (2000).
Income: Per capita income: $15,237 (2000); Median household income: $29,167 (2000); Poverty rate: 9.7% (2000).
Taxes: Total city taxes per capita: $51 (1997); City property taxes per capita: $42 (1997).
Education: High school graduation rate: 81.5% (2000); College graduation rate: 12.5% (2000).
Housing: Homeownership rate: 83.8% (2000); Median home value: $32,500 (2000); Median rent: $213 per month (2000); Median age of housing: 60+ years (2000).
Newspapers: Eagle-Scribe (1 x week)
Transportation: Commute to work: 89.7% car, 0.9% public transportation, 5.0% walk, 3.1% work from home (2000); Travel time to work: 38.6% less than 15 minutes, 17.0% 15 to 30 minutes, 20.9% 30 to 45 minutes, 14.5% 45 to 60 minutes, 9.0% 60 minutes or more (2000)

BASCO (village). Covers a land area of 0.227 square miles and a water area of 0 square miles. Located at 40.32° N. Lat.; 91.19° W. Long. Elevation is 640 feet.
Population: 107 (2000); Race: 100.0% White, 0.0% Black, 0.0% Asian, 0.0% American Indian and Alaska Native, 0.0% Hispanic of any race, 0.0% two or more races (2000); Density: 471.7 persons per square mile (2000); Age: 30.3% under 18, 14.8% over 64 (2000); Marriage status: 27.8% never married, 47.4% now married, 13.4% widowed, 11.3% divorced (2000); Foreign born: 0.0% (2000); Ancestry (includes multiple ancestries): 41.0% German, 18.0% United States or American, 13.1% Irish, 10.7% English, 4.9% French (except Basque) (2000).
Economy: In agricultural area: corn, wheat, soybeans; cattle, hogs; limestone processing. Employment by occupation: 8.3% management, 9.7% professional, 22.2% services, 23.6% sales, 0.0% farming, 12.5% construction, 23.6% production (2000).
Income: Per capita income: $16,746 (2000); Median household income: $29,306 (2000); Poverty rate: 9.2% (2000).
Taxes: Total city taxes per capita: $28 (2000); City property taxes per capita: $9 (2000).
Education: High school graduation rate: 84.8% (2000); College graduation rate: 19.0% (2000).
Housing: Homeownership rate: 88.5% (2000); Median home value: $41,500 (2000); Median rent: $188 per month (2000); Median age of housing: 60+ years (2000).
Transportation: Commute to work: 88.9% car, 0.0% public transportation, 8.3% walk, 2.8% work from home (2000); Travel time to work: 22.9% less than 15 minutes, 51.4% 15 to 30 minutes, 18.6% 30 to 45 minutes, 7.1% 45 to 60 minutes, 0.0% 60 minutes or more (2000)

BENTLEY (town). Aka Bently. Covers a land area of 0.142 square miles and a water area of 0 square miles. Located at 40.34° N. Lat.; 91.11° W. Long. Elevation is 675 feet.
Population: 43 (2000); Race: 100.0% White, 0.0% Black, 0.0% Asian, 0.0% American Indian and Alaska Native, 0.0% Hispanic of any race, 0.0% two or more races (2000); Density: 301.8 persons per square mile (2000); Age: 30.8% under 18, 17.9% over 64 (2000); Marriage status: 30.0% never married, 63.3% now married, 0.0% widowed, 6.7% divorced (2000); Foreign born: 0.0% (2000); Ancestry (includes multiple ancestries): 38.5% United States or American, 33.3% Irish, 23.1% German, 23.1% English, 7.7% Other groups (2000).
Economy: In agricultural area: corn, wheat, soybeans. Employment by occupation: 15.0% management, 35.0% professional, 15.0% services, 15.0% sales, 0.0% farming, 10.0% construction, 10.0% production (2000).
Income: Per capita income: $9,269 (2000); Median household income: $23,125 (2000); Poverty rate: 15.4% (2000).
Education: High school graduation rate: 84.6% (2000); College graduation rate: 34.6% (2000).
Housing: Homeownership rate: 100.0% (2000); Median home value: $18,800 (2000); Median age of housing: 57 years (2000).
Transportation: Commute to work: 90.0% car, 0.0% public transportation, 10.0% walk, 0.0% work from home (2000); Travel time to work: 30.0% less than 15 minutes, 20.0% 15 to 30 minutes, 30.0% 30 to 45 minutes, 20.0% 45 to 60 minutes, 0.0% 60 minutes or more (2000)

BOWEN (village). Covers a land area of 0.431 square miles and a water area of 0 square miles. Located at 40.23° N. Lat.; 91.06° W. Long. Elevation is 685 feet.
Population: 535 (2000); Race: 99.5% White, 0.0% Black, 0.0% Asian, 0.0% American Indian and Alaska Native, 0.4% Hispanic of any race, 0.5% two or more races (2000); Density: 1,241.6 persons per square mile (2000); Age: 26.9% under 18, 18.1% over 64 (2000); Marriage status: 21.2% never married, 58.7% now married, 7.2% widowed, 12.8% divorced (2000); Foreign born: 0.4% (2000); Ancestry (includes multiple ancestries): 36.4% German, 12.1% United States or American, 11.7% English, 11.4% Irish, 6.8% Other groups (2000).
Economy: In agricultural area. Employment by occupation: 4.3% management, 12.8% professional, 9.3% services, 25.7% sales, 1.2% farming, 12.5% construction, 34.2% production (2000).
Income: Per capita income: $13,241 (2000); Median household income: $29,091 (2000); Poverty rate: 16.3% (2000).
Taxes: Total city taxes per capita: $21 (1997); City property taxes per capita: $21 (1997).
Education: High school graduation rate: 83.8% (2000); College graduation rate: 12.4% (2000).

School District(s)

Southeastern C U School District 337 (PK-12)
2000 Enrollment: 631 217-842-5236
Housing: Homeownership rate: 75.1% (2000); Median home value: $41,700 (2000); Median rent: $272 per month (2000); Median age of housing: 60+ years (2000).
Transportation: Commute to work: 93.1% car, 0.0% public transportation, 2.8% walk, 4.0% work from home (2000); Travel time to work: 20.7% less than 15 minutes, 38.0% 15 to 30 minutes, 18.6% 30 to 45 minutes, 13.1% 45 to 60 minutes, 9.7% 60 minutes or more (2000)

BURNSIDE (unincorporated postal area, zip code 62318). Covers a land area of 40.074 square miles and a water area of 0 square miles. Located at 40.51° N. Lat.; 91.12° W. Long. Elevation is 647 feet.
Population: 358 (2000); Race: 100.0% White, 0.0% Black, 0.0% Asian, 0.0% American Indian and Alaska Native, 0.0% Hispanic of any race, 0.0% two or more races (2000); Density: 8.9 persons per square mile (2000); Age: 22.6% under 18, 15.8% over 64 (2000); Marriage status: 25.5% never married, 58.2% now married, 5.6% widowed, 10.8% divorced (2000); Foreign born: 0.0% (2000); Ancestry (includes multiple ancestries): 24.2% English, 23.9% German, 13.9% United States or American, 8.4% Irish, 2.4% Scottish (2000).
Economy: Employment by occupation: 17.8% management, 22.3% professional, 8.1% services, 21.3% sales, 3.0% farming, 6.1% construction, 21.3% production (2000).
Income: Per capita income: $17,642 (2000); Median household income: $44,063 (2000); Poverty rate: 12.8% (2000).
Education: High school graduation rate: 83.1% (2000); College graduation rate: 14.1% (2000).
Housing: Homeownership rate: 71.4% (2000); Median home value: $48,500 (2000); Median rent: $225 per month (2000); Median age of housing: 60+ years (2000).
Transportation: Commute to work: 91.9% car, 0.0% public transportation, 1.0% walk, 7.1% work from home (2000); Travel time to work: 35.5% less than 15 minutes, 38.3% 15 to 30 minutes, 2.7% 30 to 45 minutes, 18.6% 45 to 60 minutes, 4.9% 60 minutes or more (2000)

CARTHAGE (city). Covers a land area of 1.605 square miles and a water area of 0 square miles. Located at 40.41° N. Lat.; 91.13° W. Long. Elevation is 676 feet.
History: Incorporated 1837. In 1844, Joseph Smith, Mormon leader, and his brother were killed in the city jail by a mob; the old jail is now property of the Mormon Church.
Population: 2,725 (2000); Race: 98.4% White, 0.4% Black, 0.3% Asian, 1.0% American Indian and Alaska Native, 0.3% Hispanic of any race, 0.0%

two or more races (2000); Density: 1,698.0 persons per square mile (2000); Age: 23.9% under 18, 21.4% over 64 (2000); Marriage status: 18.9% never married, 58.9% now married, 9.9% widowed, 12.3% divorced (2000); Foreign born: 0.9% (2000); Ancestry (includes multiple ancestries): 28.6% German, 14.7% United States or American, 13.6% English, 10.7% Irish, 6.0% Other groups (2000).
Economy: Trade center in agricultural area: corn, wheat, soybeans, cattle, hogs; dairy products. Manufacturing: cigars, electronic switches. Single-family building permits issued: 5 (2001) / 4 (2000); Multi-family building permits issued: 2 (2001) / 2 (2000); Employment by occupation: 9.9% management, 19.5% professional, 17.6% services, 22.0% sales, 1.8% farming, 7.0% construction, 22.2% production (2000).
Income: Per capita income: $18,269 (2000); Median household income: $34,677 (2000); Poverty rate: 8.4% (2000).
Taxes: Total city taxes per capita: $71 (1997); City property taxes per capita: $64 (1997).
Education: High school graduation rate: 85.7% (2000); College graduation rate: 19.9% (2000).

School District(s)

Carthage Community Unit School District #338 (PK-12)
2000 Enrollment: 888 217-357-3922
Housing: Homeownership rate: 69.7% (2000); Median home value: $66,000 (2000); Median rent: $278 per month (2000); Median age of housing: 46 years (2000).
Hospitals: Memorial Hospital (67 beds)
Newspapers: Hancock County Journal Pilot (1 x week)
Transportation: Commute to work: 94.0% car, 1.0% public transportation, 1.5% walk, 3.2% work from home (2000); Travel time to work: 63.4% less than 15 minutes, 14.9% 15 to 30 minutes, 14.1% 30 to 45 minutes, 3.7% 45 to 60 minutes, 3.9% 60 minutes or more (2000)
Additional Information Contacts
Carthage Chamber of Commerce. 217-357-3024

DALLAS CITY (city). Covers a land area of 2.375 square miles and a water area of 0.905 square miles. Located at 40.63° N. Lat.; 91.16° W. Long. Elevation is 537 feet.
Population: 1,055 (2000); Race: 99.6% White, 0.0% Black, 0.0% Asian, 0.0% American Indian and Alaska Native, 0.2% Hispanic of any race, 0.4% two or more races (2000); Density: 444.2 persons per square mile (2000); Age: 19.3% under 18, 24.6% over 64 (2000); Marriage status: 14.9% never married, 64.2% now married, 11.6% widowed, 9.3% divorced (2000); Foreign born: 0.0% (2000); Ancestry (includes multiple ancestries): 22.6% German, 16.7% United States or American, 13.0% English, 9.4% Irish, 5.0% Other groups (2000).
Economy: Employment by occupation: 5.5% management, 16.8% professional, 16.1% services, 22.5% sales, 1.4% farming, 12.0% construction, 25.7% production (2000).
Income: Per capita income: $16,188 (2000); Median household income: $31,731 (2000); Poverty rate: 13.4% (2000).
Taxes: Total city taxes per capita: $36 (1997); City property taxes per capita: $26 (1997).
Education: High school graduation rate: 80.0% (2000); College graduation rate: 8.8% (2000).

School District(s)

Dallas City C U School District 336 (PK-12)
2000 Enrollment: 313 217-852-3203
Housing: Homeownership rate: 74.9% (2000); Median home value: $53,700 (2000); Median rent: $230 per month (2000); Median age of housing: 50 years (2000).
Transportation: Commute to work: 88.5% car, 0.0% public transportation, 6.7% walk, 4.4% work from home (2000); Travel time to work: 34.5% less than 15 minutes, 34.9% 15 to 30 minutes, 17.1% 30 to 45 minutes, 2.7% 45 to 60 minutes, 10.8% 60 minutes or more (2000)

ELVASTON (village). Covers a land area of 0.797 square miles and a water area of 0 square miles. Located at 40.39° N. Lat.; 91.25° W. Long. Elevation is 660 feet.
Population: 152 (2000); Race: 95.6% White, 0.0% Black, 0.0% Asian, 0.0% American Indian and Alaska Native, 0.0% Hispanic of any race, 1.3% two or more races (2000); Density: 190.8 persons per square mile (2000); Age: 24.7% under 18, 14.6% over 64 (2000); Marriage status: 7.1% never married, 63.5% now married, 12.7% widowed, 16.7% divorced (2000); Foreign born: 0.0% (2000); Ancestry (includes multiple ancestries): 30.4% German, 13.9% Irish, 8.2% Dutch, 7.0% French (except Basque), 5.1% Scotch-Irish (2000).
Economy: In agricultural area. Employment by occupation: 5.4% management, 6.5% professional, 19.6% services, 17.4% sales, 5.4% farming, 14.1% construction, 31.5% production (2000).
Income: Per capita income: $27,947 (2000); Median household income: $34,792 (2000); Poverty rate: 12.7% (2000).
Taxes: Total city taxes per capita: $15 (1997); City property taxes per capita: $15 (1997).
Education: High school graduation rate: 85.0% (2000); College graduation rate: 2.7% (2000).
Housing: Homeownership rate: 91.0% (2000); Median home value: $37,500 (2000); Median rent: $275 per month (2000); Median age of housing: 60+ years (2000).
Transportation: Commute to work: 100.0% car, 0.0% public transportation, 0.0% walk, 0.0% work from home (2000); Travel time to work: 63.6% less than 15 minutes, 27.3% 15 to 30 minutes, 6.8% 30 to 45 minutes, 2.3% 45 to 60 minutes, 0.0% 60 minutes or more (2000)

FERRIS (village). Covers a land area of 1.957 square miles and a water area of 0 square miles. Located at 40.46° N. Lat.; 91.16° W. Long. Elevation is 688 feet.
Population: 168 (2000); Race: 100.0% White, 0.0% Black, 0.0% Asian, 0.0% American Indian and Alaska Native, 0.0% Hispanic of any race, 0.0% two or more races (2000); Density: 85.8 persons per square mile (2000); Age: 19.7% under 18, 16.9% over 64 (2000); Marriage status: 17.8% never married, 61.2% now married, 15.1% widowed, 5.9% divorced (2000); Foreign born: 0.0% (2000); Ancestry (includes multiple ancestries): 35.0% German, 20.2% English, 10.9% Irish, 6.6% United States or American, 5.5% Scottish (2000).
Economy: In agricultural area. Employment by occupation: 15.9% management, 11.4% professional, 15.9% services, 20.5% sales, 0.0% farming, 18.2% construction, 18.2% production (2000).
Income: Per capita income: $16,341 (2000); Median household income: $41,667 (2000); Poverty rate: 2.7% (2000).
Taxes: Total city taxes per capita: $28 (1997); City property taxes per capita: $28 (1997).
Education: High school graduation rate: 87.4% (2000); College graduation rate: 10.4% (2000).
Housing: Homeownership rate: 77.9% (2000); Median home value: $41,600 (2000); Median rent: $292 per month (2000); Median age of housing: 56 years (2000).
Transportation: Commute to work: 93.0% car, 0.0% public transportation, 0.0% walk, 3.5% work from home (2000); Travel time to work: 39.8% less than 15 minutes, 27.7% 15 to 30 minutes, 16.9% 30 to 45 minutes, 9.6% 45 to 60 minutes, 6.0% 60 minutes or more (2000)

HAMILTON (city). Covers a land area of 3.748 square miles and a water area of 1.611 square miles. Located at 40.39° N. Lat.; 91.34° W. Long. Elevation is 637 feet.
History: Incorporated 1859.
Population: 3,029 (2000); Race: 99.0% White, 0.0% Black, 0.0% Asian, 0.2% American Indian and Alaska Native, 0.3% Hispanic of any race, 0.8% two or more races (2000); Density: 808.3 persons per square mile (2000); Age: 23.5% under 18, 16.6% over 64 (2000); Marriage status: 17.4% never married, 61.0% now married, 8.8% widowed, 12.9% divorced (2000); Foreign born: 1.0% (2000); Ancestry (includes multiple ancestries): 27.9% German, 16.3% United States or American, 12.0% Irish, 11.9% English, 4.7% Other groups (2000).
Economy: Trade and shipping center in agricultural area: corn, wheat, soybeans; livestock. Stone quarry. Nearby is Lake Keokuk, with recreational and resort facilities. Single-family building permits issued: 8 (2001) / 8 (2000); Multi-family building permits issued: 0 (2001) / 0 (2000); Employment by occupation: 11.0% management, 12.1% professional, 13.2% services, 23.1% sales, 0.9% farming, 11.8% construction, 27.9% production (2000).
Income: Per capita income: $18,775 (2000); Median household income: $40,179 (2000); Poverty rate: 7.1% (2000).
Taxes: Total city taxes per capita: $340 (1997); City property taxes per capita: $247 (1997).
Education: High school graduation rate: 85.6% (2000); College graduation rate: 14.4% (2000).

School District(s)

Hamilton C C School District 328 (PK-12)
2000 Enrollment: 758 217-847-3315
Housing: Homeownership rate: 81.7% (2000); Median home value: $65,800 (2000); Median rent: $352 per month (2000); Median age of housing: 34 years (2000).

Transportation: Commute to work: 93.6% car, 0.0% public transportation, 1.9% walk, 3.5% work from home (2000); Travel time to work: 52.7% less than 15 minutes, 35.0% 15 to 30 minutes, 8.7% 30 to 45 minutes, 2.1% 45 to 60 minutes, 1.5% 60 minutes or more (2000)

LA HARPE (city). Covers a land area of 1.355 square miles and a water area of 0 square miles. Located at 40.58° N. Lat.; 90.96° W. Long. Elevation is 697 feet.
History: Incorporated 1859.
Population: 1,385 (2000); Race: 99.0% White, 0.4% Black, 0.0% Asian, 0.0% American Indian and Alaska Native, 0.2% Hispanic of any race, 0.4% two or more races (2000); Density: 1,021.8 persons per square mile (2000); Age: 24.2% under 18, 23.1% over 64 (2000); Marriage status: 20.4% never married, 61.9% now married, 10.4% widowed, 7.2% divorced (2000); Foreign born: 0.1% (2000); Ancestry (includes multiple ancestries): 18.1% German, 15.2% United States or American, 14.0% English, 9.2% Irish, 4.2% Other groups (2000).
Economy: In agricultural area: corn, soybeans, livestock; dairy products. Railroad junction. Employment by occupation: 7.0% management, 14.5% professional, 21.5% services, 18.2% sales, 0.2% farming, 11.5% construction, 27.2% production (2000).
Income: Per capita income: $15,586 (2000); Median household income: $32,589 (2000); Poverty rate: 7.4% (2000).
Taxes: Total city taxes per capita: $55 (1997); City property taxes per capita: $49 (1997).
Education: High school graduation rate: 83.4% (2000); College graduation rate: 12.8% (2000).

School District(s)

Laharpe Community Unit School District 335 (PK-12)
2000 Enrollment: 496 217-659-7739
Housing: Homeownership rate: 85.4% (2000); Median home value: $54,100 (2000); Median rent: $244 per month (2000); Median age of housing: 43 years (2000).
Newspapers: Hancock County Quill (1 x week)
Transportation: Commute to work: 89.9% car, 0.0% public transportation, 5.9% walk, 3.5% work from home (2000); Travel time to work: 42.8% less than 15 minutes, 17.9% 15 to 30 minutes, 29.0% 30 to 45 minutes, 4.6% 45 to 60 minutes, 5.7% 60 minutes or more (2000)

NAUVOO (city). Covers a land area of 3.382 square miles and a water area of 1.441 square miles. Located at 40.54° N. Lat.; 91.38° W. Long. Elevation is 670 feet.
History: Joseph Smith built the city of Nauvoo in 1839 as the headquarters for the Mormon church, on the site of a small settlement called Commerce. The charter for Nauvoo gave it a measure of autonomy such as maintaining its own militia and courts. Internal discord and outside opposition troubled the church, and in 1845 the Nauvoo charter was repealed and Brigham Young soon led the members westward. In 1849 the deserted city became the scene of the Icarian colony attempt at a Utopian communistic society, which crumbled in 1856. The resettlement of Nauvoo, mostly by German immigrants, began in the 1860's. Joseph Smith and his brother Hyrum were buried in Nauvoo.
Population: 1,063 (2000); Race: 98.6% White, 0.0% Black, 1.0% Asian, 0.0% American Indian and Alaska Native, 0.5% Hispanic of any race, 0.4% two or more races (2000); Density: 314.4 persons per square mile (2000); Age: 24.6% under 18, 21.9% over 64 (2000); Marriage status: 23.2% never married, 63.4% now married, 8.0% widowed, 5.5% divorced (2000); Foreign born: 1.2% (2000); Ancestry (includes multiple ancestries): 40.0% German, 21.2% Irish, 17.0% English, 7.5% French (except Basque), 5.4% Other groups (2000).
Economy: Single-family building permits issued: 31 (2001) / 5 (2000); Multi-family building permits issued: 38 (2001) / 0 (2000); Employment by occupation: 11.2% management, 13.2% professional, 18.6% services, 23.2% sales, 0.4% farming, 10.8% construction, 22.6% production (2000).
Income: Per capita income: $18,150 (2000); Median household income: $39,519 (2000); Poverty rate: 12.8% (2000).
Taxes: Total city taxes per capita: $83 (1997); City property taxes per capita: $62 (1997).
Education: High school graduation rate: 92.3% (2000); College graduation rate: 23.2% (2000).

School District(s)

Nauvoo-Colusa C U S District 325 (PK-12)
2000 Enrollment: 290 217-453-6639
Housing: Homeownership rate: 81.0% (2000); Median home value: $78,400 (2000); Median rent: $236 per month (2000); Median age of housing: 37 years (2000).
Newspapers: The New Independent (1 x week)
Transportation: Commute to work: 86.8% car, 1.0% public transportation, 8.7% walk, 2.7% work from home (2000); Travel time to work: 45.9% less than 15 minutes, 28.8% 15 to 30 minutes, 20.1% 30 to 45 minutes, 1.0% 45 to 60 minutes, 4.2% 60 minutes or more (2000)
Additional Information Contacts
Nauvoo Chamber of Commerce 217-453-6648

NIOTA (unincorporated postal area, zip code 62358). Covers a land area of 40.663 square miles and a water area of 0.018 square miles. Located at 40.58° N. Lat.; 91.26° W. Long. Elevation is 525 feet.
Population: 646 (2000); Race: 96.6% White, 0.0% Black, 0.6% Asian, 1.5% American Indian and Alaska Native, 0.6% Hispanic of any race, 1.3% two or more races (2000); Density: 15.9 persons per square mile (2000); Age: 22.2% under 18, 17.3% over 64 (2000); Marriage status: 21.2% never married, 62.0% now married, 8.2% widowed, 8.6% divorced (2000); Foreign born: 1.0% (2000); Ancestry (includes multiple ancestries): 30.8% German, 18.2% Irish, 8.9% English, 7.7% United States or American, 5.1% Other groups (2000).
Economy: Employment by occupation: 16.6% management, 7.5% professional, 19.8% services, 15.8% sales, 2.4% farming, 8.8% construction, 29.1% production (2000).
Income: Per capita income: $16,672 (2000); Median household income: $41,630 (2000); Poverty rate: 5.2% (2000).
Education: High school graduation rate: 87.2% (2000); College graduation rate: 13.1% (2000).
Housing: Homeownership rate: 89.2% (2000); Median home value: $47,300 (2000); Median rent: $219 per month (2000); Median age of housing: 46 years (2000).
Transportation: Commute to work: 88.7% car, 1.9% public transportation, 2.5% walk, 5.8% work from home (2000); Travel time to work: 27.2% less than 15 minutes, 42.7% 15 to 30 minutes, 24.0% 30 to 45 minutes, 4.1% 45 to 60 minutes, 2.0% 60 minutes or more (2000)

PLYMOUTH (village). Covers a land area of 0.589 square miles and a water area of 0 square miles. Located at 40.29° N. Lat.; 90.91° W. Long. Elevation is 656 feet.
Population: 562 (2000); Race: 99.6% White, 0.0% Black, 0.0% Asian, 0.0% American Indian and Alaska Native, 0.9% Hispanic of any race, 0.0% two or more races (2000); Density: 953.8 persons per square mile (2000); Age: 32.3% under 18, 16.4% over 64 (2000); Marriage status: 18.0% never married, 59.1% now married, 11.0% widowed, 11.8% divorced (2000); Foreign born: 0.4% (2000); Ancestry (includes multiple ancestries): 32.7% United States or American, 17.5% German, 15.2% Irish, 6.3% Dutch, 5.6% Other groups (2000).
Economy: In agricultural area: grain; dairy products; livestock. Oil refinery. Employment by occupation: 6.6% management, 4.3% professional, 24.2% services, 12.3% sales, 8.1% farming, 11.4% construction, 33.2% production (2000).
Income: Per capita income: $12,150 (2000); Median household income: $24,500 (2000); Poverty rate: 18.8% (2000).
Taxes: Total city taxes per capita: $24 (1997); City property taxes per capita: $23 (1997).
Education: High school graduation rate: 77.3% (2000); College graduation rate: 6.0% (2000).
Housing: Homeownership rate: 72.5% (2000); Median home value: $20,900 (2000); Median rent: $220 per month (2000); Median age of housing: 60+ years (2000).
Newspapers: Tri-County Scribe (1 x week)
Transportation: Commute to work: 93.3% car, 0.0% public transportation, 3.3% walk, 1.9% work from home (2000); Travel time to work: 31.7% less than 15 minutes, 26.3% 15 to 30 minutes, 27.8% 30 to 45 minutes, 6.8% 45 to 60 minutes, 7.3% 60 minutes or more (2000)

PONTOOSUC (village). Covers a land area of 1.409 square miles and a water area of 0.667 square miles. Located at 40.63° N. Lat.; 91.21° W. Long. Elevation is 535 feet.
Population: 171 (2000); Race: 99.4% White, 0.0% Black, 0.0% Asian, 0.0% American Indian and Alaska Native, 0.0% Hispanic of any race, 0.6% two or more races (2000); Density: 121.3 persons per square mile (2000); Age: 18.6% under 18, 19.3% over 64 (2000); Marriage status: 25.4% never married, 52.8% now married, 7.7% widowed, 14.1% divorced (2000); Foreign born: 0.0% (2000); Ancestry (includes multiple ancestries): 21.7% United States or American, 19.9% German, 15.5% Irish, 10.6% English, 6.2% Other groups (2000).

Economy: In agricultural area: corn, wheat, soybeans; cattle, hogs. Employment by occupation: 10.5% management, 6.6% professional, 26.3% services, 9.2% sales, 2.6% farming, 6.6% construction, 38.2% production (2000).
Income: Per capita income: $14,453 (2000); Median household income: $27,813 (2000); Poverty rate: 16.8% (2000).
Taxes: Total city taxes per capita: $11 (1997); City property taxes per capita: $11 (1997).
Education: High school graduation rate: 70.8% (2000); College graduation rate: 4.2% (2000).
Housing: Homeownership rate: 81.8% (2000); Median home value: $45,000 (2000); Median rent: $182 per month (2000); Median age of housing: 29 years (2000).
Transportation: Commute to work: 92.1% car, 0.0% public transportation, 0.0% walk, 2.6% work from home (2000); Travel time to work: 24.3% less than 15 minutes, 31.1% 15 to 30 minutes, 23.0% 30 to 45 minutes, 2.7% 45 to 60 minutes, 18.9% 60 minutes or more (2000)

SUTTER (unincorporated postal area, zip code 62373). Covers a land area of 52.216 square miles and a water area of 0.210 square miles. Located at 40.24° N. Lat.; 91.35° W. Long. Elevation is 655 feet.
Population: 415 (2000); Race: 100.0% White, 0.0% Black, 0.0% Asian, 0.0% American Indian and Alaska Native, 0.0% Hispanic of any race, 0.0% two or more races (2000); Density: 7.9 persons per square mile (2000); Age: 34.4% under 18, 12.4% over 64 (2000); Marriage status: 18.5% never married, 75.5% now married, 2.4% widowed, 3.6% divorced (2000); Foreign born: 0.0% (2000); Ancestry (includes multiple ancestries): 28.5% German, 11.5% Irish, 8.5% United States or American, 4.8% English, 4.8% Other groups (2000).
Economy: Employment by occupation: 31.8% management, 18.9% professional, 7.0% services, 14.4% sales, 7.5% farming, 4.0% construction, 16.4% production (2000).
Income: Per capita income: $15,697 (2000); Median household income: $46,250 (2000); Poverty rate: 2.4% (2000).
Education: High school graduation rate: 88.5% (2000); College graduation rate: 24.1% (2000).
Housing: Homeownership rate: 75.9% (2000); Median home value: $91,600 (2000); Median rent: $192 per month (2000); Median age of housing: 60+ years (2000).
Transportation: Commute to work: 72.6% car, 0.0% public transportation, 5.5% walk, 21.9% work from home (2000); Travel time to work: 34.4% less than 15 minutes, 22.3% 15 to 30 minutes, 40.8% 30 to 45 minutes, 0.0% 45 to 60 minutes, 2.5% 60 minutes or more (2000)

WARSAW (city). Covers a land area of 6.617 square miles and a water area of 0.871 square miles. Located at 40.35° N. Lat.; 91.43° W. Long. Elevation is 577 feet.
History: Laid out 1834, incorporated 1837. Two forts were established here in 1814.
Population: 1,793 (2000); Race: 99.2% White, 0.0% Black, 0.0% Asian, 0.2% American Indian and Alaska Native, 0.4% Hispanic of any race, 0.6% two or more races (2000); Density: 271.0 persons per square mile (2000); Age: 25.0% under 18, 16.3% over 64 (2000); Marriage status: 20.6% never married, 62.5% now married, 8.9% widowed, 8.0% divorced (2000); Foreign born: 0.3% (2000); Ancestry (includes multiple ancestries): 30.8% German, 13.8% United States or American, 12.0% Irish, 10.6% English, 5.5% Other groups (2000).
Economy: In agricultural area: corn, wheat, soybeans; cattle, hogs; dairy products. Manufacturing. Limestone quarries. Single-family building permits issued: 0 (2001) / 3 (2000); Multi-family building permits issued: 0 (2001) / 0 (2000); Employment by occupation: 7.3% management, 16.3% professional, 13.1% services, 21.2% sales, 0.9% farming, 9.0% construction, 32.3% production (2000).
Income: Per capita income: $18,279 (2000); Median household income: $35,000 (2000); Poverty rate: 8.0% (2000).
Taxes: Total city taxes per capita: $57 (1997); City property taxes per capita: $55 (1997).
Education: High school graduation rate: 83.5% (2000); College graduation rate: 13.8% (2000).

School District(s)
Warsaw Community Unit School Districtrict 316 (KG-12)
2000 Enrollment: 568 217-256-4282
Housing: Homeownership rate: 81.7% (2000); Median home value: $58,600 (2000); Median rent: $251 per month (2000); Median age of housing: 60+ years (2000).
Transportation: Commute to work: 93.6% car, 0.2% public transportation, 2.6% walk, 3.1% work from home (2000); Travel time to work: 29.5% less than 15 minutes, 44.4% 15 to 30 minutes, 16.7% 30 to 45 minutes, 5.4% 45 to 60 minutes, 3.9% 60 minutes or more (2000)
Additional Information Contacts
Warsaw Chamber of Commerce 217-256-4235

WEST POINT (village). Covers a land area of 0.168 square miles and a water area of 0 square miles. Located at 40.25° N. Lat.; 91.18° W. Long. Elevation is 670 feet.
Population: 195 (2000); Race: 95.9% White, 0.0% Black, 0.0% Asian, 0.0% American Indian and Alaska Native, 0.0% Hispanic of any race, 4.1% two or more races (2000); Density: 1,158.0 persons per square mile (2000); Age: 28.1% under 18, 10.7% over 64 (2000); Marriage status: 30.5% never married, 50.0% now married, 6.5% widowed, 13.0% divorced (2000); Foreign born: 1.5% (2000); Ancestry (includes multiple ancestries): 33.2% United States or American, 25.5% German, 15.8% Other groups, 15.3% English, 13.8% Irish (2000).
Economy: In agricultural and bituminous-coal area. Employment by occupation: 2.3% management, 14.8% professional, 12.5% services, 11.4% sales, 3.4% farming, 18.2% construction, 37.5% production (2000).
Income: Per capita income: $13,631 (2000); Median household income: $29,500 (2000); Poverty rate: 16.3% (2000).
Taxes: Total city taxes per capita: $19 (1997); City property taxes per capita: $19 (1997).
Education: High school graduation rate: 75.8% (2000); College graduation rate: 7.8% (2000).
Housing: Homeownership rate: 96.0% (2000); Median home value: $18,200 (2000); Median rent: $325 per month (2000); Median age of housing: 60+ years (2000).
Transportation: Commute to work: 96.6% car, 0.0% public transportation, 0.0% walk, 3.4% work from home (2000); Travel time to work: 1.2% less than 15 minutes, 41.2% 15 to 30 minutes, 31.8% 30 to 45 minutes, 16.5% 45 to 60 minutes, 9.4% 60 minutes or more (2000)

Hardin County

Located in southeastern Illinois; bounded on the south and east by the Ohio River and the Kentucky border; drained by Big Creek; includes part of Shawnee National Forest. Covers a land area of 178.30 square miles, a water area of 3.20 square miles, and is located in the Central Time Zone. The county government was organized in 1839. County seat is Elizabethtown.

Weather Station: Rosiclare 5 NW — Elevation: 396 feet

	Jan	Feb	Mar	Apr	May	Jun	Jul	Aug	Sep	Oct	Nov	Dec
High	42	48	58	69	77	84	88	87	81	70	58	47
Low	22	26	35	43	53	61	66	64	56	44	36	27
Precip	3.3	3.6	4.8	5.0	5.0	4.3	4.2	3.5	3.2	3.4	4.3	4.3
Snow	4.3	3.3	1.4	0.1	0.0	0.0	0.0	0.0	0.0	0.2	0.1	1.3

High and Low temperatures in degrees Fahrenheit; Precipitation and Snow in inches

Population: 4,800 (2000); Race: 94.7% White, 2.8% Black, 0.6% Asian, 0.0% American Indian and Alaska Native, 1.3% Hispanic of any race, 1.1% two or more races (2000); Density: 26.9 persons per square mile (2000); Age: 20.5% under 18, 18.6% over 64 (2000).
Religion: Five largest groups: 15.2% Southern Baptist Convention, 4.3% Christian Churches and Churches of Christ, 3.2% Catholic Church, 2.9% Churches of Christ, 2.6% The United Methodist Church (2000).
Economy: Unemployment rate: 6.1% (11/2002); Total civilian labor force: 1,729 (11/2002); Leading industries: 44.0% health care and social assistance; 18.3% mining; 10.8% transportation & warehousing (2000); Companies that employ more than 1,000 persons: 0 (2000); Companies that employ more than 100 persons: 2 (2000); Farms: 172 totaling 39,264 acres (1997); Minority business ownership rate: 0.0% (1997); Women business ownership rate: 0.0% (1997); Retail sales per capita: $1,732 (1997). Single-family building permits issued: 0 (2001) / 0 (2000); Multi-family building permits issued: 0 (2001) / 0 (2000).
Income: Per capita income: $15,984 (2000); Median household income: $27,693 (2000); Poverty rate: 18.6% (2000); Bankruptcy rate: 4.45% (2001).
Taxes: Total county taxes per capita: $72 (1997); County property taxes per capita: $72 (1997).
Education: High school graduation rate: 68.1% (2000); College graduation rate: 9.6% (2000).
Housing: Homeownership rate: 80.5% (2000); Median home value: $40,800 (2000); Median rent: $185 per month (2000); Median age of housing: 39 years (2000).

Health: Birth rate: 93.8 per 10,000 population (1998); Age adjusted death rate: 113.5 per 10,000 population (1999); Age adjusted cancer mortality rate: 268.9 (Unreliable figure as per CDC) deaths per 100,000 population (1999). Number of physicians: 6.3 per 10,000 population (1999); Number of hospital beds: 100.0 per 10,000 population (1999).
Elections: 2000 Presidential election results: 44.9% Gore, 51.8% Bush, 1.6% Nader, 1.4% Buchanan
National and State Parks: Cave-In-Rock State Park
Additional Information Contacts
Hardin County Government Offices 618-287-2251

Hardin County Communities

CAVE-IN-ROCK (village). Covers a land area of 0.396 square miles and a water area of 0.029 square miles. Located at 37.47° N. Lat.; 88.16° W. Long.
History: Cave-in-Rock was named for a natural cave above the water line in the Ohio River bluff, a landmark for boatmen. The cave served as a pirate's den for a number of thieves beginning with Samuel Mason, who in 1797 lured victims there by promises of liquor and entertainment, and then robbed them.
Population: 346 (2000); Race: 97.8% White, 0.0% Black, 0.0% Asian, 0.0% American Indian and Alaska Native, 1.9% Hispanic of any race, 0.6% two or more races (2000); Density: 874.6 persons per square mile (2000); Age: 26.2% under 18, 25.2% over 64 (2000); Marriage status: 14.5% never married, 49.0% now married, 23.7% widowed, 12.9% divorced (2000); Foreign born: 0.0% (2000); Ancestry (includes multiple ancestries): 23.6% Other groups, 12.8% United States or American, 12.8% English, 9.6% German, 8.3% Irish (2000).
Economy: Single-family building permits issued: 0 (2001) / 0 (2000); Multi-family building permits issued: 0 (2001) / 0 (2000); Employment by occupation: 2.8% management, 27.4% professional, 29.2% services, 12.3% sales, 1.9% farming, 7.5% construction, 18.9% production (2000).
Income: Per capita income: $12,050 (2000); Median household income: $20,694 (2000); Poverty rate: 28.6% (2000).
Education: High school graduation rate: 68.7% (2000); College graduation rate: 8.9% (2000).
Housing: Homeownership rate: 60.8% (2000); Median home value: $31,800 (2000); Median rent: $190 per month (2000); Median age of housing: 37 years (2000).
Transportation: Commute to work: 85.8% car, 0.0% public transportation, 10.4% walk, 0.9% work from home (2000); Travel time to work: 51.4% less than 15 minutes, 26.7% 15 to 30 minutes, 11.4% 30 to 45 minutes, 7.6% 45 to 60 minutes, 2.9% 60 minutes or more (2000)

ELIZABETHTOWN (village). Covers a land area of 0.702 square miles and a water area of 0 square miles. Located at 37.44° N. Lat.; 88.30° W. Long. Elevation is 400 feet.
Population: 348 (2000); Race: 97.8% White, 1.4% Black, 0.0% Asian, 0.0% American Indian and Alaska Native, 0.5% Hispanic of any race, 0.8% two or more races (2000); Density: 495.6 persons per square mile (2000); Age: 16.5% under 18, 28.8% over 64 (2000); Marriage status: 16.8% never married, 50.2% now married, 15.9% widowed, 17.1% divorced (2000); Foreign born: 0.0% (2000); Ancestry (includes multiple ancestries): 18.7% German, 17.0% Irish, 13.5% English, 10.4% Other groups, 10.2% United States or American (2000).
Economy: Farming: wheat, corn; livestock. Shawnee National Forest nearby. Single-family building permits issued: 0 (2001) / 0 (2000); Multi-family building permits issued: 0 (2001) / 0 (2000); Employment by occupation: 5.1% management, 28.3% professional, 21.0% services, 19.6% sales, 0.0% farming, 10.9% construction, 15.2% production (2000).
Income: Per capita income: $17,567 (2000); Median household income: $17,750 (2000); Poverty rate: 22.5% (2000).
Taxes: Total city taxes per capita: $57 (1997); City property taxes per capita: $10 (1997).
Education: High school graduation rate: 76.2% (2000); College graduation rate: 10.3% (2000).

School District(s)
Hardin Co Community Unit District 1 (PK-12)
2000 Enrollment: 671 618-287-2411
Housing: Homeownership rate: 60.1% (2000); Median home value: $40,000 (2000); Median rent: $174 per month (2000); Median age of housing: 37 years (2000).
Newspapers: Hardin County Independent (1 x week)
Transportation: Commute to work: 93.5% car, 2.2% public transportation, 0.0% walk, 2.9% work from home (2000); Travel time to work: 45.5% less than 15 minutes, 26.9% 15 to 30 minutes, 9.0% 30 to 45 minutes, 9.7% 45 to 60 minutes, 9.0% 60 minutes or more (2000)

ROSICLARE (city). Covers a land area of 2.168 square miles and a water area of 0.116 square miles. Located at 37.42° N. Lat.; 88.34° W. Long. Elevation is 420 feet.
History: Incorporated as village 1874, as city 1932.
Population: 1,213 (2000); Race: 95.7% White, 0.6% Black, 1.2% Asian, 0.0% American Indian and Alaska Native, 1.1% Hispanic of any race, 1.9% two or more races (2000); Density: 559.6 persons per square mile (2000); Age: 20.6% under 18, 23.5% over 64 (2000); Marriage status: 18.3% never married, 58.2% now married, 12.9% widowed, 10.6% divorced (2000); Foreign born: 0.3% (2000); Ancestry (includes multiple ancestries): 12.9% Other groups, 12.3% Irish, 11.2% German, 8.8% United States or American, 8.6% English (2000).
Economy: Agriculture: sorghum, corn. Manufacturing: fluorspar processing. Single-family building permits issued: 0 (2001) / 0 (2000); Multi-family building permits issued: 0 (2001) / 0 (2000); Employment by occupation: 6.4% management, 17.8% professional, 26.3% services, 17.3% sales, 0.0% farming, 13.9% construction, 18.2% production (2000).
Income: Per capita income: $15,398 (2000); Median household income: $22,600 (2000); Poverty rate: 22.5% (2000).
Taxes: Total city taxes per capita: $42 (1997); City property taxes per capita: $39 (1997).
Education: High school graduation rate: 67.8% (2000); College graduation rate: 9.6% (2000).
Housing: Homeownership rate: 74.5% (2000); Median home value: $35,500 (2000); Median rent: $177 per month (2000); Median age of housing: 49 years (2000).
Hospitals: Hardin County General Hospital (48 beds)
Transportation: Commute to work: 91.6% car, 1.8% public transportation, 4.9% walk, 0.4% work from home (2000); Travel time to work: 47.2% less than 15 minutes, 23.2% 15 to 30 minutes, 9.8% 30 to 45 minutes, 9.8% 45 to 60 minutes, 10.0% 60 minutes or more (2000)

Henderson County

Located in western Illinois; bounded on the west by the Mississippi River and the Iowa border; drained by Henderson Creek. Covers a land area of 378.80 square miles, a water area of 16.30 square miles, and is located in the Central Time Zone. The county government was organized in 1841. County seat is Oquawka.
Population: 8,213 (2000); Race: 98.0% White, 0.5% Black, 0.1% Asian, 0.3% American Indian and Alaska Native, 0.6% Hispanic of any race, 0.8% two or more races (2000); Density: 21.7 persons per square mile (2000); Age: 23.3% under 18, 16.7% over 64 (2000).
Religion: Five largest groups: 11.1% The United Methodist Church, 4.3% Catholic Church, 4.0% Presbyterian Church (U.S.A.), 3.6% Christian Churches and Churches of Christ, 2.7% American Baptist Churches in the USA (2000).
Economy: Unemployment rate: 5.2% (11/2002); Total civilian labor force: 5,465 (11/2002); Leading industries: 23.2% retail trade; 16.1% health care and social assistance; 12.6% finance & insurance (2000); Companies that employ more than 1,000 persons: 0 (2000); Companies that employ more than 100 persons: 0 (2000); Farms: 414 totaling 202,186 acres (1997); Minority business ownership rate: 0.0% (1997); Women business ownership rate: 19.0% (1997); Retail sales per capita: $2,426 (1997). Single-family building permits issued: 26 (2001) / 18 (2000); Multi-family building permits issued: 0 (2001) / 0 (2000).
Income: Per capita income: $17,456 (2000); Median household income: $36,405 (2000); Poverty rate: 9.5% (2000); Bankruptcy rate: 6.34% (2001).
Taxes: Total county taxes per capita: $100 (1997); County property taxes per capita: $100 (1997).
Education: High school graduation rate: 82.4% (2000); College graduation rate: 10.0% (2000).
Housing: Homeownership rate: 78.9% (2000); Median home value: $57,300 (2000); Median rent: $262 per month (2000); Median age of housing: 37 years (2000).
Health: Birth rate: 98.6 per 10,000 population (1998); Age adjusted death rate: 70.0 per 10,000 population (1999); Age adjusted cancer mortality rate: 135.2 (Unreliable figure as per CDC) deaths per 100,000 population (1999). Number of physicians: 7.3 per 10,000 population (1999); Number of hospital beds: n/a (1999).

Elections: 2000 Presidential election results: 52.5% Gore, 44.2% Bush, 1.9% Nader, 1.0% Buchanan
National and State Parks: Big River State Forest; Delabar State Park; Oquawka State Wildlife Refuge
Additional Information Contacts
Henderson County Government Offices 309-867-2911

Henderson County Communities

BIGGSVILLE (village). Covers a land area of 0.332 square miles and a water area of 0 square miles. Located at 40.85° N. Lat.; 90.86° W. Long. Elevation is 650 feet.
Population: 343 (2000); Race: 99.4% White, 0.0% Black, 0.6% Asian, 0.0% American Indian and Alaska Native, 2.0% Hispanic of any race, 0.0% two or more races (2000); Density: 1,032.0 persons per square mile (2000); Age: 27.2% under 18, 18.8% over 64 (2000); Marriage status: 26.8% never married, 56.4% now married, 7.5% widowed, 9.3% divorced (2000); Foreign born: 1.7% (2000); Ancestry (includes multiple ancestries): 24.9% German, 18.8% Irish, 14.7% United States or American, 10.1% English, 7.8% Dutch (2000).
Economy: In agricultural area. Single-family building permits issued: 2 (2001) / 0 (2000); Multi-family building permits issued: 0 (2001) / 0 (2000); Employment by occupation: 5.4% management, 6.0% professional, 16.7% services, 25.6% sales, 1.2% farming, 17.3% construction, 28.0% production (2000).
Income: Per capita income: $17,215 (2000); Median household income: $35,714 (2000); Poverty rate: 7.5% (2000).
Taxes: Total city taxes per capita: $33 (1997); City property taxes per capita: $14 (1997).
Education: High school graduation rate: 85.3% (2000); College graduation rate: 10.6% (2000).

School District(s)
Union Community Unit School District 115 (PK-12)
2000 Enrollment: 713 309-627-2371
Housing: Homeownership rate: 79.6% (2000); Median home value: $45,200 (2000); Median rent: $284 per month (2000); Median age of housing: 50 years (2000).
Transportation: Commute to work: 94.0% car, 0.0% public transportation, 4.8% walk, 1.2% work from home (2000); Travel time to work: 26.2% less than 15 minutes, 49.4% 15 to 30 minutes, 15.2% 30 to 45 minutes, 6.7% 45 to 60 minutes, 2.4% 60 minutes or more (2000)

CARMAN (unincorporated postal area, zip code 61425). Covers a land area of 41.606 square miles and a water area of 1.316 square miles. Located at 40.77° N. Lat.; 91.05° W. Long. Elevation is 530 feet.
Population: 743 (2000); Race: 98.7% White, 0.0% Black, 1.0% Asian, 0.3% American Indian and Alaska Native, 0.3% Hispanic of any race, 0.0% two or more races (2000); Density: 17.9 persons per square mile (2000); Age: 19.7% under 18, 11.6% over 64 (2000); Marriage status: 19.9% never married, 64.1% now married, 6.1% widowed, 9.9% divorced (2000); Foreign born: 1.0% (2000); Ancestry (includes multiple ancestries): 18.4% German, 13.0% Irish, 10.6% United States or American, 9.3% English, 5.0% Other groups (2000).
Economy: Employment by occupation: 10.2% management, 6.9% professional, 20.6% services, 19.1% sales, 0.0% farming, 12.7% construction, 30.5% production (2000).
Income: Per capita income: $20,071 (2000); Median household income: $42,639 (2000); Poverty rate: 7.2% (2000).
Education: High school graduation rate: 84.2% (2000); College graduation rate: 8.5% (2000).
Housing: Homeownership rate: 86.1% (2000); Median home value: $64,100 (2000); Median rent: $305 per month (2000); Median age of housing: 26 years (2000).
Transportation: Commute to work: 95.0% car, 0.0% public transportation, 0.8% walk, 2.6% work from home (2000); Travel time to work: 42.2% less than 15 minutes, 44.9% 15 to 30 minutes, 5.4% 30 to 45 minutes, 5.7% 45 to 60 minutes, 1.9% 60 minutes or more (2000)

GLADSTONE (village). Covers a land area of 0.393 square miles and a water area of 0 square miles. Located at 40.86° N. Lat.; 90.95° W. Long. Elevation is 548 feet.
History: Gladstone was platted in 1856 and settled by Irish, Swedish, and German immigrants. The town developed around the quarrying of limestone on nearby Henderson Creek.
Population: 284 (2000); Race: 98.9% White, 1.1% Black, 0.0% Asian, 0.0% American Indian and Alaska Native, 0.0% Hispanic of any race, 0.0% two or more races (2000); Density: 722.1 persons per square mile (2000); Age: 21.1% under 18, 19.5% over 64 (2000); Marriage status: 18.8% never married, 55.2% now married, 9.9% widowed, 16.1% divorced (2000); Foreign born: 0.0% (2000); Ancestry (includes multiple ancestries): 24.8% United States or American, 13.5% German, 10.9% Irish, 6.0% Swedish, 3.4% English (2000).
Economy: Single-family building permits issued: 1 (2001) / 2 (2000); Multi-family building permits issued: 0 (2001) / 0 (2000); Employment by occupation: 5.9% management, 13.6% professional, 20.3% services, 11.9% sales, 0.0% farming, 15.3% construction, 33.1% production (2000).
Income: Per capita income: $16,245 (2000); Median household income: $30,694 (2000); Poverty rate: 10.5% (2000).
Taxes: Total city taxes per capita: $38 (1997); City property taxes per capita: $34 (1997).
Education: High school graduation rate: 78.6% (2000); College graduation rate: 3.0% (2000).
Housing: Homeownership rate: 79.7% (2000); Median home value: $45,400 (2000); Median rent: $220 per month (2000); Median age of housing: 44 years (2000).
Transportation: Commute to work: 91.5% car, 0.0% public transportation, 0.0% walk, 6.8% work from home (2000); Travel time to work: 20.0% less than 15 minutes, 52.7% 15 to 30 minutes, 9.1% 30 to 45 minutes, 7.3% 45 to 60 minutes, 10.9% 60 minutes or more (2000)

GULF PORT (village). Aka Gulfport. Covers a land area of 1.505 square miles and a water area of 0.921 square miles. Located at 40.80° N. Lat.; 91.08° W. Long.
Population: 207 (2000); Race: 99.0% White, 0.0% Black, 0.0% Asian, 1.0% American Indian and Alaska Native, 1.0% Hispanic of any race, 0.0% two or more races (2000); Density: 137.5 persons per square mile (2000); Age: 21.0% under 18, 8.3% over 64 (2000); Marriage status: 17.8% never married, 64.9% now married, 2.9% widowed, 14.4% divorced (2000); Foreign born: 0.0% (2000); Ancestry (includes multiple ancestries): 17.6% German, 14.6% English, 11.7% Irish, 11.2% United States or American, 9.8% Other groups (2000).
Economy: Single-family building permits issued: 2 (2001) / 3 (2000); Multi-family building permits issued: 0 (2001) / 0 (2000); Employment by occupation: 4.5% management, 0.0% professional, 29.5% services, 18.8% sales, 0.0% farming, 8.9% construction, 38.4% production (2000).
Income: Per capita income: $16,918 (2000); Median household income: $36,167 (2000); Poverty rate: 5.4% (2000).
Education: High school graduation rate: 83.6% (2000); College graduation rate: 2.1% (2000).
Housing: Homeownership rate: 78.9% (2000); Median home value: $55,000 (2000); Median rent: $232 per month (2000); Median age of housing: 28 years (2000).
Transportation: Commute to work: 94.0% car, 0.0% public transportation, 3.0% walk, 0.0% work from home (2000); Travel time to work: 66.0% less than 15 minutes, 19.0% 15 to 30 minutes, 5.0% 30 to 45 minutes, 7.0% 45 to 60 minutes, 3.0% 60 minutes or more (2000)

LOMAX (village). Covers a land area of 1.043 square miles and a water area of 0 square miles. Located at 40.68° N. Lat.; 91.07° W. Long. Elevation is 548 feet.
Population: 477 (2000); Race: 98.1% White, 0.0% Black, 0.0% Asian, 0.0% American Indian and Alaska Native, 1.5% Hispanic of any race, 1.5% two or more races (2000); Density: 457.3 persons per square mile (2000); Age: 24.0% under 18, 12.9% over 64 (2000); Marriage status: 21.6% never married, 53.6% now married, 8.3% widowed, 16.5% divorced (2000); Foreign born: 0.4% (2000); Ancestry (includes multiple ancestries): 26.9% German, 18.6% United States or American, 11.3% Irish, 10.9% English, 4.0% Other groups (2000).
Economy: Grain; livestock. Single-family building permits issued: 0 (2001) / 0 (2000); Multi-family building permits issued: 0 (2001) / 0 (2000); Employment by occupation: 10.0% management, 12.8% professional, 13.7% services, 17.8% sales, 0.0% farming, 10.5% construction, 35.2% production (2000).
Income: Per capita income: $14,066 (2000); Median household income: $29,609 (2000); Poverty rate: 11.4% (2000).
Taxes: Total city taxes per capita: $26 (1997); City property taxes per capita: $10 (1997).
Education: High school graduation rate: 71.8% (2000); College graduation rate: 8.7% (2000).

Housing: Homeownership rate: 79.5% (2000); Median home value: $38,800 (2000); Median rent: $263 per month (2000); Median age of housing: 41 years (2000).
Transportation: Commute to work: 95.8% car, 0.0% public transportation, 2.3% walk, 1.9% work from home (2000); Travel time to work: 10.0% less than 15 minutes, 63.0% 15 to 30 minutes, 15.2% 30 to 45 minutes, 4.3% 45 to 60 minutes, 7.6% 60 minutes or more (2000)

MEDIA (village). Covers a land area of 1.698 square miles and a water area of 0 square miles. Located at 40.77° N. Lat.; 90.83° W. Long. Elevation is 710 feet.
Population: 130 (2000); Race: 100.0% White, 0.0% Black, 0.0% Asian, 0.0% American Indian and Alaska Native, 0.0% Hispanic of any race, 0.0% two or more races (2000); Density: 76.5 persons per square mile (2000); Age: 15.8% under 18, 19.3% over 64 (2000); Marriage status: 25.0% never married, 52.9% now married, 6.7% widowed, 15.4% divorced (2000); Foreign born: 0.0% (2000); Ancestry (includes multiple ancestries): 29.8% United States or American, 14.0% Dutch, 11.4% Irish, 7.9% German, 7.0% Swedish (2000).
Economy: In agricultural area. Single-family building permits issued: 0 (2001) / 0 (2000); Multi-family building permits issued: 0 (2001) / 0 (2000); Employment by occupation: 15.4% management, 16.9% professional, 10.8% services, 23.1% sales, 0.0% farming, 13.8% construction, 20.0% production (2000).
Income: Per capita income: $20,149 (2000); Median household income: $35,125 (2000); Poverty rate: 12.4% (2000).
Taxes: Total city taxes per capita: $7 (1997); City property taxes per capita: $7 (1997).
Education: High school graduation rate: 91.4% (2000); College graduation rate: 6.2% (2000).
Housing: Homeownership rate: 63.3% (2000); Median home value: $55,600 (2000); Median rent: $265 per month (2000); Median age of housing: 47 years (2000).
Transportation: Commute to work: 96.9% car, 0.0% public transportation, 0.0% walk, 0.0% work from home (2000); Travel time to work: 27.7% less than 15 minutes, 47.7% 15 to 30 minutes, 18.5% 30 to 45 minutes, 6.2% 45 to 60 minutes, 0.0% 60 minutes or more (2000)

OQUAWKA (village). Covers a land area of 1.463 square miles and a water area of 0.389 square miles. Located at 40.93° N. Lat.; 90.94° W. Long. Elevation is 562 feet.
History: Oquawka began as a trading post built in 1827 by the Phelps brothers. The name is of Indian origin, a variation of Ozaukee meaning "yellow banks." An early industry was the manufacture of pearl button blanks from mussel shells.
Population: 1,539 (2000); Race: 98.4% White, 0.0% Black, 0.0% Asian, 0.0% American Indian and Alaska Native, 0.7% Hispanic of any race, 1.6% two or more races (2000); Density: 1,051.8 persons per square mile (2000); Age: 23.8% under 18, 17.4% over 64 (2000); Marriage status: 21.5% never married, 56.5% now married, 9.2% widowed, 12.8% divorced (2000); Foreign born: 0.0% (2000); Ancestry (includes multiple ancestries): 20.3% German, 16.0% United States or American, 12.9% English, 11.2% Irish, 7.2% Other groups (2000).
Economy: Single-family building permits issued: 1 (2001) / 0 (2000); Multi-family building permits issued: 0 (2001) / 0 (2000); Employment by occupation: 4.9% management, 9.9% professional, 14.5% services, 21.6% sales, 0.4% farming, 12.8% construction, 35.8% production (2000).
Income: Per capita income: $15,254 (2000); Median household income: $32,500 (2000); Poverty rate: 12.8% (2000).
Taxes: Total city taxes per capita: $70 (1997); City property taxes per capita: $41 (1997).
Education: High school graduation rate: 73.1% (2000); College graduation rate: 4.8% (2000).
Housing: Homeownership rate: 76.7% (2000); Median home value: $57,500 (2000); Median rent: $250 per month (2000); Median age of housing: 33 years (2000).
Newspapers: Oquawka Current (1 x week)
Transportation: Commute to work: 97.4% car, 0.0% public transportation, 0.3% walk, 2.0% work from home (2000); Travel time to work: 17.5% less than 15 minutes, 47.3% 15 to 30 minutes, 21.4% 30 to 45 minutes, 7.2% 45 to 60 minutes, 6.6% 60 minutes or more (2000)

RARITAN (village). Covers a land area of 0.099 square miles and a water area of 0 square miles. Located at 40.69° N. Lat.; 90.82° W. Long. Elevation is 760 feet.
Population: 140 (2000); Race: 98.1% White, 0.0% Black, 0.0% Asian, 0.0% American Indian and Alaska Native, 0.0% Hispanic of any race, 1.9% two or more races (2000); Density: 1,411.7 persons per square mile (2000); Age: 29.9% under 18, 13.4% over 64 (2000); Marriage status: 11.2% never married, 82.8% now married, 4.3% widowed, 1.7% divorced (2000); Foreign born: 0.0% (2000); Ancestry (includes multiple ancestries): 22.9% United States or American, 19.7% German, 13.4% Other groups, 12.7% Irish, 11.5% English (2000).
Economy: Single-family building permits issued: 0 (2001) / 0 (2000); Multi-family building permits issued: 0 (2001) / 0 (2000); Employment by occupation: 3.5% management, 10.6% professional, 10.6% services, 32.9% sales, 0.0% farming, 11.8% construction, 30.6% production (2000).
Income: Per capita income: $14,484 (2000); Median household income: $27,917 (2000); Poverty rate: 0.0% (2000).
Taxes: Total city taxes per capita: $59 (1997); City property taxes per capita: $26 (1997).
Education: High school graduation rate: 90.2% (2000); College graduation rate: 13.7% (2000).
Housing: Homeownership rate: 75.0% (2000); Median home value: $37,500 (2000); Median rent: $222 per month (2000); Median age of housing: 54 years (2000).
Transportation: Commute to work: 89.2% car, 0.0% public transportation, 8.4% walk, 0.0% work from home (2000); Travel time to work: 21.7% less than 15 minutes, 44.6% 15 to 30 minutes, 20.5% 30 to 45 minutes, 1.2% 45 to 60 minutes, 12.0% 60 minutes or more (2000)

STRONGHURST (village). Covers a land area of 0.887 square miles and a water area of 0 square miles. Located at 40.74° N. Lat.; 90.90° W. Long. Elevation is 680 feet.
Population: 896 (2000); Race: 98.9% White, 0.0% Black, 0.0% Asian, 0.0% American Indian and Alaska Native, 0.2% Hispanic of any race, 1.1% two or more races (2000); Density: 1,009.8 persons per square mile (2000); Age: 26.5% under 18, 24.9% over 64 (2000); Marriage status: 18.3% never married, 59.0% now married, 11.6% widowed, 11.1% divorced (2000); Foreign born: 0.4% (2000); Ancestry (includes multiple ancestries): 26.4% German, 14.8% Irish, 12.6% English, 9.8% United States or American, 8.4% Swedish (2000).
Economy: Corn, soybeans; livestock. Single-family building permits issued: 1 (2001) / 0 (2000); Multi-family building permits issued: 0 (2001) / 0 (2000); Employment by occupation: 9.6% management, 15.4% professional, 12.8% services, 29.7% sales, 1.8% farming, 9.6% construction, 21.1% production (2000).
Income: Per capita income: $17,269 (2000); Median household income: $32,054 (2000); Poverty rate: 6.9% (2000).
Taxes: Total city taxes per capita: $34 (1997); City property taxes per capita: $34 (1997).
Education: High school graduation rate: 85.8% (2000); College graduation rate: 12.6% (2000).

School District(s)

Southern C U School District 120 (PK-12)
2000 Enrollment: 471 309-924-1461

Housing: Homeownership rate: 73.4% (2000); Median home value: $52,400 (2000); Median rent: $308 per month (2000); Median age of housing: 54 years (2000).
Newspapers: The Henderson County Quill (1 x week)
Transportation: Commute to work: 88.7% car, 0.0% public transportation, 7.1% walk, 4.2% work from home (2000); Travel time to work: 35.2% less than 15 minutes, 34.2% 15 to 30 minutes, 21.0% 30 to 45 minutes, 3.8% 45 to 60 minutes, 5.7% 60 minutes or more (2000)

Henry County

Located in northwestern Illinois; bounded on the northwest by the Rock River; drained by the Green and Edwards Rivers. Covers a land area of 823.20 square miles, a water area of 2.40 square miles, and is located in the Central Time Zone. The county government was organized in 1825. County seat is Cambridge.

Henry County is part of the Davenport-Moline-Rock Island, IA-IL MSA. The entire metro area includes: Henry County, IL; Rock Island County, IL; Scott County, IA

Weather Station: Galva Elevation: 807 feet

	Jan	Feb	Mar	Apr	May	Jun	Jul	Aug	Sep	Oct	Nov	Dec
High	28	34	46	60	72	81	85	83	76	63	47	34
Low	12	17	27	39	50	60	64	62	53	41	30	18
Precip	1.5	1.5	2.8	3.9	4.2	4.5	4.0	4.4	3.7	2.8	2.9	2.3
Snow	8.2	6.2	4.2	1.7	0.0	0.0	0.0	0.0	0.0	0.4	2.2	5.7

High and Low temperatures in degrees Fahrenheit; Precipitation and Snow in inches

Weather Station: Geneseo Elevation: 636 feet

	Jan	Feb	Mar	Apr	May	Jun	Jul	Aug	Sep	Oct	Nov	Dec
High	28	34	47	61	73	82	86	83	76	63	47	34
Low	12	18	29	40	51	61	65	62	54	42	30	19
Precip	1.5	1.5	2.7	3.8	4.4	4.2	4.0	4.3	3.2	3.0	2.9	2.2
Snow	7.8	5.1	3.7	1.7	0.0	0.0	0.0	0.0	0.0	tr	2.2	6.6

High and Low temperatures in degrees Fahrenheit; Precipitation and Snow in inches

Population: 51,020 (2000); Race: 95.8% White, 1.0% Black, 0.2% Asian, 0.1% American Indian and Alaska Native, 2.7% Hispanic of any race, 1.6% two or more races (2000); Density: 62.0 persons per square mile (2000); Age: 25.3% under 18, 16.4% over 64 (2000).
Religion: Five largest groups: 19.2% Catholic Church, 11.1% The United Methodist Church, 10.3% Evangelical Lutheran Church in America, 3.8% American Baptist Churches in the USA, 2.9% Lutheran Church—Missouri Synod (2000).
Economy: Unemployment rate: 4.8% (11/2002); Total civilian labor force: 26,016 (11/2002); Leading industries: 33.5% manufacturing; 16.8% retail trade; 9.1% accommodation & food services (2000); Companies that employ more than 1,000 persons: 1 (2000); Companies that employ more than 100 persons: 14 (2000); Farms: 1,344 totaling 456,596 acres (1997); Minority business ownership rate: 0.0% (1997); Women business ownership rate: 30.8% (1997); Retail sales per capita: $7,222 (1997). Single-family building permits issued: 79 (2001) / 94 (2000); Multi-family building permits issued: 58 (2001) / 13 (2000).
Income: Per capita income: $18,716 (2000); Median household income: $39,854 (2000); Poverty rate: 8.0% (2000); Bankruptcy rate: 5.84% (2001).
Taxes: Total county taxes per capita: $75 (2000); County property taxes per capita: $73 (2000).
Education: High school graduation rate: 84.5% (2000); College graduation rate: 15.7% (2000).
Housing: Homeownership rate: 78.8% (2000); Median home value: $77,700 (2000); Median rent: $322 per month (2000); Median age of housing: 48 years (2000).
Health: Birth rate: 109.8 per 10,000 population (1998); Age adjusted death rate: 81.4 per 10,000 population (1999); Age adjusted cancer mortality rate: 178.9 deaths per 100,000 population (1999). Number of physicians: 6.1 per 10,000 population (1999); Number of hospital beds: 32.7 per 10,000 population (1999).
Elections: 2000 Presidential election results: 50.8% Gore, 46.4% Bush, 1.8% Nader, 0.8% Buchanan
National and State Parks: Johnson Sauk Trail State Park
Additional Information Contacts
Henry County Government Offices 309-937-5192
Cambridge Chamber of Commerce 309-937-5474
Geneseo Chamber of Commerce 309-944-2686
Kewanee Chamber of Commerce 309-852-2175
Mid Valley Association of Realtors 309-852-5002

Henry County Communities

ALPHA (village). Covers a land area of 0.322 square miles and a water area of 0 square miles. Located at 41.19° N. Lat.; 90.38° W. Long. Elevation is 803 feet.
Population: 726 (2000); Race: 98.7% White, 0.0% Black, 0.1% Asian, 0.0% American Indian and Alaska Native, 0.0% Hispanic of any race, 1.1% two or more races (2000); Density: 2,254.7 persons per square mile (2000); Age: 25.2% under 18, 18.4% over 64 (2000); Marriage status: 18.4% never married, 59.5% now married, 8.9% widowed, 13.2% divorced (2000); Foreign born: 0.8% (2000); Ancestry (includes multiple ancestries): 21.7% German, 19.6% Swedish, 12.3% English, 9.7% Irish, 8.5% United States or American (2000).
Economy: In agricultural area: corn, oats, soybeans; cattle, hogs; dairying. Manufactures feed. Single-family building permits issued: 0 (2001) / 1 (2000); Multi-family building permits issued: 0 (2001) / 0 (2000); Employment by occupation: 9.6% management, 11.5% professional, 16.9% services, 28.5% sales, 1.7% farming, 10.1% construction, 21.7% production (2000).
Income: Per capita income: $17,407 (2000); Median household income: $36,250 (2000); Poverty rate: 5.8% (2000).
Taxes: Total city taxes per capita: $30 (1997); City property taxes per capita: $27 (1997).
Education: High school graduation rate: 86.9% (2000); College graduation rate: 11.1% (2000).
Housing: Homeownership rate: 86.6% (2000); Median home value: $64,200 (2000); Median rent: $306 per month (2000); Median age of housing: 50 years (2000).
Transportation: Commute to work: 91.5% car, 0.0% public transportation, 5.1% walk, 3.4% work from home (2000); Travel time to work: 34.7% less than 15 minutes, 31.8% 15 to 30 minutes, 24.8% 30 to 45 minutes, 4.7% 45 to 60 minutes, 4.1% 60 minutes or more (2000)

ANDOVER (village). Covers a land area of 0.999 square miles and a water area of 0 square miles. Located at 41.29° N. Lat.; 90.29° W. Long. Elevation is 776 feet.
Population: 594 (2000); Race: 98.3% White, 0.0% Black, 0.2% Asian, 0.0% American Indian and Alaska Native, 0.0% Hispanic of any race, 1.5% two or more races (2000); Density: 594.8 persons per square mile (2000); Age: 25.9% under 18, 12.3% over 64 (2000); Marriage status: 18.1% never married, 69.9% now married, 4.0% widowed, 8.0% divorced (2000); Foreign born: 0.8% (2000); Ancestry (includes multiple ancestries): 26.8% German, 20.5% Swedish, 15.8% Irish, 10.4% English, 5.2% Other groups (2000).
Economy: In agricultural area: corn, soybeans, oats; cattle, hogs; dairying. Single-family building permits issued: 1 (2001) / 1 (2000); Multi-family building permits issued: 0 (2001) / 0 (2000); Employment by occupation: 5.3% management, 13.5% professional, 14.5% services, 25.7% sales, 0.0% farming, 15.2% construction, 25.7% production (2000).
Income: Per capita income: $18,439 (2000); Median household income: $46,944 (2000); Poverty rate: 5.9% (2000).
Taxes: Total city taxes per capita: $54 (1997); City property taxes per capita: $24 (1997).
Education: High school graduation rate: 86.8% (2000); College graduation rate: 12.7% (2000).
Housing: Homeownership rate: 84.9% (2000); Median home value: $77,500 (2000); Median rent: $325 per month (2000); Median age of housing: 32 years (2000).
Transportation: Commute to work: 94.6% car, 0.0% public transportation, 1.0% walk, 2.4% work from home (2000); Travel time to work: 11.1% less than 15 minutes, 24.6% 15 to 30 minutes, 49.5% 30 to 45 minutes, 8.3% 45 to 60 minutes, 6.6% 60 minutes or more (2000)

ANNAWAN (town). Covers a land area of 0.682 square miles and a water area of 0 square miles. Located at 41.39° N. Lat.; 89.90° W. Long. Elevation is 625 feet.
History: Annawan developed as the center of a stock farming and coal mining region.
Population: 868 (2000); Race: 99.4% White, 0.0% Black, 0.3% Asian, 0.0% American Indian and Alaska Native, 0.2% Hispanic of any race, 0.2% two or more races (2000); Density: 1,273.6 persons per square mile (2000); Age: 34.3% under 18, 12.6% over 64 (2000); Marriage status: 26.7% never married, 60.0% now married, 5.8% widowed, 7.4% divorced (2000); Foreign born: 0.2% (2000); Ancestry (includes multiple ancestries): 33.6% Belgian, 27.7% German, 8.8% Irish, 7.9% English, 6.8% Swedish (2000).
Economy: Single-family building permits issued: 6 (2001) / 3 (2000); Multi-family building permits issued: 0 (2001) / 0 (2000); Employment by occupation: 7.3% management, 17.4% professional, 13.0% services, 30.5% sales, 1.8% farming, 10.7% construction, 19.3% production (2000).
Income: Per capita income: $15,839 (2000); Median household income: $38,571 (2000); Poverty rate: 9.7% (2000).
Taxes: Total city taxes per capita: $54 (1997); City property taxes per capita: $45 (1997).
Education: High school graduation rate: 86.5% (2000); College graduation rate: 13.1% (2000).

School District(s)

Annawan Community Unit School District 226 (PK-12)
2000 Enrollment: 460 309-935-6781
Housing: Homeownership rate: 76.6% (2000); Median home value: $75,700 (2000); Median rent: $294 per month (2000); Median age of housing: 48 years (2000).
Transportation: Commute to work: 93.9% car, 0.0% public transportation, 3.9% walk, 1.3% work from home (2000); Travel time to work: 36.8% less than 15 minutes, 31.5% 15 to 30 minutes, 15.7% 30 to 45 minutes, 10.1% 45 to 60 minutes, 5.9% 60 minutes or more (2000)

ATKINSON (town). Covers a land area of 1.509 square miles and a water area of 0.004 square miles. Located at 41.41° N. Lat.; 90.01° W. Long. Elevation is 661 feet.
Population: 1,001 (2000); Race: 99.2% White, 0.0% Black, 0.3% Asian, 0.0% American Indian and Alaska Native, 2.0% Hispanic of any race, 0.5% two or more races (2000); Density: 663.2 persons per square mile (2000); Age: 23.9% under 18, 17.9% over 64 (2000); Marriage status: 25.3% never married, 57.0% now married, 10.1% widowed, 7.7% divorced (2000); Foreign born: 0.3% (2000); Ancestry (includes multiple ancestries): 33.9% Belgian, 26.0% German, 11.9% Irish, 9.6% Swedish, 8.5% English (2000).
Economy: In agricultural area. Single-family building permits issued: 0 (2001) / 1 (2000); Multi-family building permits issued: 0 (2001) / 0 (2000); Employment by occupation: 8.1% management, 12.6% professional, 16.4% services, 28.9% sales, 2.2% farming, 16.4% construction, 15.5% production (2000).
Income: Per capita income: $17,732 (2000); Median household income: $35,750 (2000); Poverty rate: 10.0% (2000).
Taxes: Total city taxes per capita: $46 (1997); City property taxes per capita: $38 (1997).
Education: High school graduation rate: 81.2% (2000); College graduation rate: 13.2% (2000).
Housing: Homeownership rate: 79.2% (2000); Median home value: $66,800 (2000); Median rent: $320 per month (2000); Median age of housing: 55 years (2000).
Transportation: Commute to work: 94.6% car, 0.0% public transportation, 3.4% walk, 1.6% work from home (2000); Travel time to work: 43.7% less than 15 minutes, 27.2% 15 to 30 minutes, 21.1% 30 to 45 minutes, 5.3% 45 to 60 minutes, 2.7% 60 minutes or more (2000)

BISHOP HILL (village). Covers a land area of 0.539 square miles and a water area of 0 square miles. Located at 41.20° N. Lat.; 90.11° W. Long. Elevation is 775 feet.
History: Bishop Hill was settled in 1846 by a group of Swedish emigrants led by Erik Jansson, who envisioned a communistic society based on religion. Jansson's leadership lasted only a few years, and by 1861 the communal property had been divided among individuals.
Population: 125 (2000); Race: 100.0% White, 0.0% Black, 0.0% Asian, 0.0% American Indian and Alaska Native, 1.5% Hispanic of any race, 0.0% two or more races (2000); Density: 232.0 persons per square mile (2000); Age: 20.4% under 18, 14.6% over 64 (2000); Marriage status: 8.0% never married, 77.9% now married, 7.1% widowed, 7.1% divorced (2000); Foreign born: 4.4% (2000); Ancestry (includes multiple ancestries): 26.3% Swedish, 22.6% German, 13.9% English, 13.1% United States or American, 6.6% Italian (2000).
Economy: Single-family building permits issued: 0 (2001) / 0 (2000); Multi-family building permits issued: 0 (2001) / 0 (2000); Employment by occupation: 15.9% management, 20.6% professional, 14.3% services, 30.2% sales, 0.0% farming, 4.8% construction, 14.3% production (2000).
Income: Per capita income: $26,145 (2000); Median household income: $47,083 (2000); Poverty rate: 0.0% (2000).
Taxes: Total city taxes per capita: $39 (1997); City property taxes per capita: $24 (1997).
Education: High school graduation rate: 96.2% (2000); College graduation rate: 34.9% (2000).
Housing: Homeownership rate: 93.2% (2000); Median home value: $75,800 (2000); Median rent: $325 per month (2000); Median age of housing: 60+ years (2000).
Transportation: Commute to work: 76.2% car, 0.0% public transportation, 11.1% walk, 12.7% work from home (2000); Travel time to work: 41.8% less than 15 minutes, 16.4% 15 to 30 minutes, 18.2% 30 to 45 minutes, 10.9% 45 to 60 minutes, 12.7% 60 minutes or more (2000)

CAMBRIDGE (village). Covers a land area of 1.415 square miles and a water area of 0.013 square miles. Located at 41.30° N. Lat.; 90.19° W. Long. Elevation is 810 feet.
History: Incorporated 1861.
Population: 2,180 (2000); Race: 97.3% White, 0.0% Black, 1.2% Asian, 0.9% American Indian and Alaska Native, 0.9% Hispanic of any race, 0.6% two or more races (2000); Density: 1,540.2 persons per square mile (2000); Age: 26.6% under 18, 15.8% over 64 (2000); Marriage status: 20.0% never married, 62.3% now married, 8.8% widowed, 8.9% divorced (2000); Foreign born: 0.9% (2000); Ancestry (includes multiple ancestries): 24.0% German, 20.5% Swedish, 15.2% English, 11.9% United States or American, 10.3% Irish (2000).
Economy: In agricultural and bituminous-coal area. Single-family building permits issued: 0 (2001) / 0 (2000); Multi-family building permits issued: 0 (2001) / 0 (2000); Employment by occupation: 13.1% management, 16.6% professional, 18.4% services, 21.9% sales, 1.0% farming, 13.9% construction, 15.1% production (2000).
Income: Per capita income: $17,842 (2000); Median household income: $38,636 (2000); Poverty rate: 10.3% (2000).
Taxes: Total city taxes per capita: $86 (1997); City property taxes per capita: $50 (1997).
Education: High school graduation rate: 83.2% (2000); College graduation rate: 14.3% (2000).

School District(s)

Cambridge C U School District 227 (PK-12)
2000 Enrollment: 582 309-937-2144
Housing: Homeownership rate: 79.5% (2000); Median home value: $74,000 (2000); Median rent: $306 per month (2000); Median age of housing: 48 years (2000).
Newspapers: Cambridge Chronicle (1 x week)
Transportation: Commute to work: 91.7% car, 0.0% public transportation, 4.4% walk, 1.8% work from home (2000); Travel time to work: 42.3% less than 15 minutes, 24.9% 15 to 30 minutes, 18.5% 30 to 45 minutes, 11.9% 45 to 60 minutes, 2.5% 60 minutes or more (2000)
Additional Information Contacts
Cambridge Chamber of Commerce 309-937-5474

CLEVELAND (village). Covers a land area of 0.361 square miles and a water area of 0.003 square miles. Located at 41.50° N. Lat.; 90.31° W. Long. Elevation is 576 feet.
Population: 253 (2000); Race: 100.0% White, 0.0% Black, 0.0% Asian, 0.0% American Indian and Alaska Native, 6.8% Hispanic of any race, 0.0% two or more races (2000); Density: 700.1 persons per square mile (2000); Age: 23.5% under 18, 11.6% over 64 (2000); Marriage status: 16.2% never married, 66.2% now married, 8.1% widowed, 9.6% divorced (2000); Foreign born: 0.0% (2000); Ancestry (includes multiple ancestries): 20.7% German, 13.9% Other groups, 13.5% Irish, 11.2% Swedish, 10.0% English (2000).
Economy: Agriculture: corn, soybeans, cattle, hogs; dairying. Single-family building permits issued: 0 (2001) / 0 (2000); Multi-family building permits issued: 0 (2001) / 0 (2000); Employment by occupation: 5.6% management, 16.1% professional, 7.0% services, 39.2% sales, 0.0% farming, 11.2% construction, 21.0% production (2000).
Income: Per capita income: $19,990 (2000); Median household income: $46,339 (2000); Poverty rate: 6.4% (2000).
Taxes: Total city taxes per capita: $25 (1997); City property taxes per capita: $21 (1997).
Education: High school graduation rate: 80.1% (2000); College graduation rate: 8.5% (2000).
Housing: Homeownership rate: 83.5% (2000); Median home value: $78,100 (2000); Median rent: $392 per month (2000); Median age of housing: 36 years (2000).
Transportation: Commute to work: 89.4% car, 0.0% public transportation, 2.1% walk, 3.5% work from home (2000); Travel time to work: 22.8% less than 15 minutes, 58.8% 15 to 30 minutes, 10.3% 30 to 45 minutes, 4.4% 45 to 60 minutes, 3.7% 60 minutes or more (2000)

COLONA (city). Covers a land area of 3.497 square miles and a water area of 0.061 square miles. Located at 41.47° N. Lat.; 90.34° W. Long. Elevation is 580 feet.
Population: 5,173 (2000); Race: 93.8% White, 1.5% Black, 0.3% Asian, 0.0% American Indian and Alaska Native, 4.2% Hispanic of any race, 1.0% two or more races (2000); Density: 1,479.1 persons per square mile (2000); Age: 27.4% under 18, 8.7% over 64 (2000); Marriage status: 23.3% never married, 62.9% now married, 4.2% widowed, 9.6% divorced (2000); Foreign born: 1.8% (2000); Ancestry (includes multiple ancestries): 22.6% German, 15.8% Irish, 11.8% Other groups, 8.8% United States or American, 7.5% English (2000).
Economy: In agricultural area: cattle, hogs; corn, soybeans. Single-family building permits issued: 7 (2001) / 12 (2000); Multi-family building permits issued: 4 (2001) / 0 (2000); Employment by occupation: 7.9% management, 12.3% professional, 19.9% services, 26.6% sales, 0.3% farming, 10.3% construction, 22.7% production (2000).
Income: Per capita income: $17,265 (2000); Median household income: $41,476 (2000); Poverty rate: 7.6% (2000).
Taxes: Total city taxes per capita: $29 (1997); City property taxes per capita: $0 (1997).
Education: High school graduation rate: 76.8% (2000); College graduation rate: 8.5% (2000).

School District(s)

Colona School District 190 (PK-08)
2000 Enrollment: 568 309-792-1232

Housing: Homeownership rate: 83.0% (2000); Median home value: $76,300 (2000); Median rent: $355 per month (2000); Median age of housing: 33 years (2000).

Transportation: Commute to work: 95.7% car, 0.0% public transportation, 2.1% walk, 1.9% work from home (2000); Travel time to work: 21.1% less than 15 minutes, 50.8% 15 to 30 minutes, 22.4% 30 to 45 minutes, 1.8% 45 to 60 minutes, 3.8% 60 minutes or more (2000)

GALVA (city). Covers a land area of 1.714 square miles and a water area of 0 square miles. Located at 41.16° N. Lat.; 90.04° W. Long. Elevation is 845 feet.

History: Galva was founded in 1854 by a group of Swedish settlers, who named it for their home in Sweden, Gefle. These first residents had been members of the religious colony at Bishop Hill.

Population: 2,758 (2000); Race: 97.3% White, 0.2% Black, 0.2% Asian, 0.1% American Indian and Alaska Native, 2.1% Hispanic of any race, 1.4% two or more races (2000); Density: 1,609.5 persons per square mile (2000); Age: 24.6% under 18, 17.8% over 64 (2000); Marriage status: 19.9% never married, 58.8% now married, 10.8% widowed, 10.4% divorced (2000); Foreign born: 1.4% (2000); Ancestry (includes multiple ancestries): 21.5% German, 18.3% Swedish, 15.5% English, 11.1% Irish, 10.6% United States or American (2000).

Economy: Single-family building permits issued: 6 (2001) / 6 (2000); Multi-family building permits issued: 0 (2001) / 0 (2000); Employment by occupation: 12.1% management, 15.6% professional, 16.0% services, 26.7% sales, 1.2% farming, 9.7% construction, 18.6% production (2000).

Income: Per capita income: $17,165 (2000); Median household income: $35,071 (2000); Poverty rate: 7.2% (2000).

Taxes: Total city taxes per capita: $274 (1997); City property taxes per capita: $178 (1997).

Education: High school graduation rate: 86.2% (2000); College graduation rate: 16.4% (2000).

School District(s)

Galva Community Unit School District 224 (PK-12)
2000 Enrollment: 716 309-932-2108

Housing: Homeownership rate: 77.1% (2000); Median home value: $58,500 (2000); Median rent: $298 per month (2000); Median age of housing: 59 years (2000).

Newspapers: The Wrova Shopper (1 x week); The Galva News (1 x week)

Transportation: Commute to work: 92.6% car, 0.0% public transportation, 3.5% walk, 2.4% work from home (2000); Travel time to work: 50.3% less than 15 minutes, 24.0% 15 to 30 minutes, 11.5% 30 to 45 minutes, 9.3% 45 to 60 minutes, 5.0% 60 minutes or more (2000)

GENESEO (city). Covers a land area of 4.032 square miles and a water area of 0.008 square miles. Located at 41.45° N. Lat.; 90.15° W. Long. Elevation is 643 feet.

History: Geneseo was settled in 1836 by people from New York, and named for Geneseo in that state. Early industries were a corn and pea cannery, and a bandage factory.

Population: 6,480 (2000); Race: 99.2% White, 0.1% Black, 0.1% Asian, 0.2% American Indian and Alaska Native, 0.2% Hispanic of any race, 0.2% two or more races (2000); Density: 1,607.0 persons per square mile (2000); Age: 24.5% under 18, 21.4% over 64 (2000); Marriage status: 20.6% never married, 60.8% now married, 11.5% widowed, 7.1% divorced (2000); Foreign born: 1.1% (2000); Ancestry (includes multiple ancestries): 31.9% German, 13.5% English, 13.4% Irish, 12.8% Swedish, 9.7% Belgian (2000).

Economy: Single-family building permits issued: 17 (2001) / 13 (2000); Multi-family building permits issued: 4 (2001) / 7 (2000); Employment by occupation: 14.9% management, 19.8% professional, 13.7% services, 26.0% sales, 0.8% farming, 10.1% construction, 14.7% production (2000).

Income: Per capita income: $20,115 (2000); Median household income: $40,760 (2000); Poverty rate: 5.3% (2000).

Taxes: Total city taxes per capita: $82 (1997); City property taxes per capita: $72 (1997).

Education: High school graduation rate: 88.8% (2000); College graduation rate: 23.9% (2000).

School District(s)

Geneseo Community Unit School District 228 (PK-12)
2000 Enrollment: 2,998 309-945-0450

Housing: Homeownership rate: 76.3% (2000); Median home value: $99,700 (2000); Median rent: $380 per month (2000); Median age of housing: 45 years (2000).

Hospitals: Hammond-Henry Hospital (105 beds)

Newspapers: Henry County Advertiser and Shopper (1 x week); Henry County Advertizer Shopper (1 x week); Geneseo Republic (1 x week)

Transportation: Commute to work: 91.8% car, 0.0% public transportation, 4.0% walk, 2.5% work from home (2000); Travel time to work: 54.9% less than 15 minutes, 18.4% 15 to 30 minutes, 19.2% 30 to 45 minutes, 3.6% 45 to 60 minutes, 4.0% 60 minutes or more (2000)

Additional Information Contacts

Geneseo Chamber of Commerce 309-944-2686

HOOPPOLE (village). Covers a land area of 0.347 square miles and a water area of 0 square miles. Located at 41.52° N. Lat.; 89.91° W. Long. Elevation is 625 feet.

History: In a grove of hickory trees near Hooppole, coopers cut bands to use in the crafting of their barrels, and from this the town was named.

Population: 162 (2000); Race: 100.0% White, 0.0% Black, 0.0% Asian, 0.0% American Indian and Alaska Native, 0.0% Hispanic of any race, 0.0% two or more races (2000); Density: 466.7 persons per square mile (2000); Age: 17.2% under 18, 19.6% over 64 (2000); Marriage status: 9.6% never married, 69.6% now married, 6.7% widowed, 14.1% divorced (2000); Foreign born: 0.0% (2000); Ancestry (includes multiple ancestries): 33.1% German, 20.9% Swedish, 14.1% Irish, 9.2% Belgian, 8.6% English (2000).

Economy: Single-family building permits issued: 0 (2001) / 0 (2000); Multi-family building permits issued: 0 (2001) / 0 (2000); Employment by occupation: 3.3% management, 13.3% professional, 27.8% services, 22.2% sales, 0.0% farming, 12.2% construction, 21.1% production (2000).

Income: Per capita income: $16,638 (2000); Median household income: $32,188 (2000); Poverty rate: 4.3% (2000).

Taxes: Total city taxes per capita: $42 (1997); City property taxes per capita: $42 (1997).

Education: High school graduation rate: 82.9% (2000); College graduation rate: 8.9% (2000).

Housing: Homeownership rate: 91.8% (2000); Median home value: $44,400 (2000); Median rent: $175 per month (2000); Median age of housing: 60+ years (2000).

Transportation: Commute to work: 88.9% car, 0.0% public transportation, 2.2% walk, 3.3% work from home (2000); Travel time to work: 8.0% less than 15 minutes, 46.0% 15 to 30 minutes, 13.8% 30 to 45 minutes, 18.4% 45 to 60 minutes, 13.8% 60 minutes or more (2000)

KEWANEE (city). Covers a land area of 6.277 square miles and a water area of 0.013 square miles. Located at 41.24° N. Lat.; 89.92° W. Long. Elevation is 820 feet.

History: Kewanee was established in 1836 by the Connecticut Association to promote Protestantism in Illinois. The town was first called Wethersfield after the town in Connecticut. When the railroad line was laid a mile north, a settlement developed around the depot. By 1857 the new settlement, named Kewanee, had surpassed the older Wethersfield, which was incorporated with Kewanee in 1924.

Population: 12,944 (2000); Race: 89.6% White, 3.0% Black, 0.2% Asian, 0.0% American Indian and Alaska Native, 5.9% Hispanic of any race, 4.2% two or more races (2000); Density: 2,062.1 persons per square mile (2000); Age: 24.9% under 18, 20.6% over 64 (2000); Marriage status: 21.3% never married, 53.1% now married, 12.9% widowed, 12.7% divorced (2000); Foreign born: 2.9% (2000); Ancestry (includes multiple ancestries): 23.2% German, 12.9% Other groups, 11.7% Irish, 10.9% English, 10.4% United States or American (2000).

Vital Statistics: Birth rate: 146.0 per 10,000 population (1998)

Economy: Single-family building permits issued: 4 (2001) / 10 (2000); Multi-family building permits issued: 50 (2001) / 4 (2000); Employment by occupation: 8.6% management, 13.2% professional, 18.9% services, 26.2% sales, 0.5% farming, 9.8% construction, 22.9% production (2000).

Income: Per capita income: $15,746 (2000); Median household income: $29,895 (2000); Poverty rate: 13.9% (2000).

Taxes: Total city taxes per capita: $153 (2000); City property taxes per capita: $105 (2000).

Education: High school graduation rate: 77.8% (2000); College graduation rate: 10.3% (2000).

School District(s)

Kewanee Community Unit School District 229 (PK-12)
2000 Enrollment: 1,776 309-853-3341

Wethersfield C U School District 230 (PK-12)
2000 Enrollment: 658 309-853-4860

Housing: Homeownership rate: 74.4% (2000); Median home value: $48,200 (2000); Median rent: $291 per month (2000); Median age of housing: 60+ years (2000).

Hospitals: Kewanee Hospital (82 beds)
Newspapers: Star-Courier (6 x week)
Transportation: Commute to work: 93.9% car, 0.3% public transportation, 2.5% walk, 1.6% work from home (2000); Travel time to work: 67.5% less than 15 minutes, 14.5% 15 to 30 minutes, 6.2% 30 to 45 minutes, 5.4% 45 to 60 minutes, 6.5% 60 minutes or more (2000); Amtrak: Service available.
Additional Information Contacts
Kewanee Chamber of Commerce. 309-852-2175
Mid Valley Association of Realtors 309-852-5002

LYNN CENTER (unincorporated postal area, zip code 61262). Covers a land area of 44.229 square miles and a water area of 0.029 square miles. Located at 41.28° N. Lat.; 90.36° W. Long. Elevation is 756 feet.
Population: 878 (2000); Race: 100.0% White, 0.0% Black, 0.0% Asian, 0.0% American Indian and Alaska Native, 0.0% Hispanic of any race, 0.0% two or more races (2000); Density: 19.9 persons per square mile (2000); Age: 22.8% under 18, 13.3% over 64 (2000); Marriage status: 16.1% never married, 72.9% now married, 3.9% widowed, 7.1% divorced (2000); Foreign born: 0.2% (2000); Ancestry (includes multiple ancestries): 25.7% German, 25.0% Swedish, 14.7% English, 10.6% Irish, 8.5% Belgian (2000).
Economy: Employment by occupation: 16.1% management, 14.9% professional, 8.3% services, 20.9% sales, 0.2% farming, 14.9% construction, 24.8% production (2000).
Income: Per capita income: $20,088 (2000); Median household income: $51,518 (2000); Poverty rate: 1.1% (2000).
Education: High school graduation rate: 90.8% (2000); College graduation rate: 9.6% (2000).
Housing: Homeownership rate: 80.8% (2000); Median home value: $93,500 (2000); Median rent: $243 per month (2000); Median age of housing: 39 years (2000).
Transportation: Commute to work: 92.7% car, 0.0% public transportation, 3.8% walk, 3.5% work from home (2000); Travel time to work: 12.7% less than 15 minutes, 28.9% 15 to 30 minutes, 52.1% 30 to 45 minutes, 4.6% 45 to 60 minutes, 1.7% 60 minutes or more (2000)

OPHEIM (unincorporated postal area, zip code 61468). Covers a land area of 7.229 square miles and a water area of 0 square miles. Located at 41.25° N. Lat.; 90.40° W. Long.
Population: 143 (2000); Race: 92.5% White, 7.5% Black, 0.0% Asian, 0.0% American Indian and Alaska Native, 0.0% Hispanic of any race, 0.0% two or more races (2000); Density: 19.8 persons per square mile (2000); Age: 48.5% under 18, 6.7% over 64 (2000); Marriage status: 31.7% never married, 51.2% now married, 6.1% widowed, 11.0% divorced (2000); Foreign born: 0.0% (2000); Ancestry (includes multiple ancestries): 19.4% Swedish, 14.2% United States or American, 11.9% Irish, 6.0% Other groups, 4.5% German (2000).
Economy: Employment by occupation: 3.4% management, 6.8% professional, 16.9% services, 23.7% sales, 0.0% farming, 15.3% construction, 33.9% production (2000).
Income: Per capita income: $10,793 (2000); Median household income: $40,750 (2000); Poverty rate: 5.3% (2000).
Education: High school graduation rate: 88.1% (2000); College graduation rate: 11.9% (2000).
Housing: Homeownership rate: 83.3% (2000); Median home value: $53,300 (2000); Median rent: $275 per month (2000); Median age of housing: 60+ years (2000).
Transportation: Commute to work: 100.0% car, 0.0% public transportation, 0.0% walk, 0.0% work from home (2000); Travel time to work: 7.8% less than 15 minutes, 9.8% 15 to 30 minutes, 62.7% 30 to 45 minutes, 19.6% 45 to 60 minutes, 0.0% 60 minutes or more (2000)

ORION (village). Covers a land area of 0.861 square miles and a water area of 0 square miles. Located at 41.35° N. Lat.; 90.37° W. Long. Elevation is 784 feet.
Population: 1,713 (2000); Race: 99.2% White, 0.0% Black, 0.1% Asian, 0.1% American Indian and Alaska Native, 1.6% Hispanic of any race, 0.4% two or more races (2000); Density: 1,989.1 persons per square mile (2000); Age: 25.5% under 18, 17.5% over 64 (2000); Marriage status: 20.2% never married, 64.3% now married, 8.6% widowed, 6.9% divorced (2000); Foreign born: 0.7% (2000); Ancestry (includes multiple ancestries): 31.8% German, 22.5% Swedish, 14.7% Irish, 12.0% English, 7.8% United States or American (2000).
Economy: In agricultural area. Single-family building permits issued: 1 (2001) / 6 (2000); Multi-family building permits issued: 0 (2001) / 0 (2000); Employment by occupation: 10.6% management, 17.1% professional, 12.8% services, 31.8% sales, 0.5% farming, 9.9% construction, 17.4% production (2000).
Income: Per capita income: $21,043 (2000); Median household income: $48,147 (2000); Poverty rate: 3.8% (2000).
Taxes: Total city taxes per capita: $64 (1997); City property taxes per capita: $54 (1997).
Education: High school graduation rate: 90.2% (2000); College graduation rate: 17.7% (2000).

School District(s)

Orion Community Unit School District 223 (PK-12)
2000 Enrollment: 1,151 309-526-3388
Housing: Homeownership rate: 83.3% (2000); Median home value: $94,800 (2000); Median rent: $365 per month (2000); Median age of housing: 39 years (2000).
Newspapers: Orion Gazette (1 x week)
Transportation: Commute to work: 95.6% car, 0.0% public transportation, 2.1% walk, 2.2% work from home (2000); Travel time to work: 23.0% less than 15 minutes, 46.6% 15 to 30 minutes, 25.9% 30 to 45 minutes, 2.3% 45 to 60 minutes, 2.2% 60 minutes or more (2000)

OSCO (unincorporated postal area, zip code 61274). Covers a land area of 24.924 square miles and a water area of 0 square miles. Located at 41.37° N. Lat.; 90.27° W. Long. Elevation is 772 feet.
Population: 404 (2000); Race: 97.8% White, 0.0% Black, 0.0% Asian, 0.0% American Indian and Alaska Native, 0.0% Hispanic of any race, 2.2% two or more races (2000); Density: 16.2 persons per square mile (2000); Age: 27.1% under 18, 10.4% over 64 (2000); Marriage status: 20.4% never married, 72.3% now married, 3.4% widowed, 3.9% divorced (2000); Foreign born: 0.0% (2000); Ancestry (includes multiple ancestries): 29.9% German, 29.3% Swedish, 19.1% English, 9.3% United States or American, 8.0% Belgian (2000).
Economy: Employment by occupation: 28.7% management, 0.0% professional, 15.0% services, 24.3% sales, 2.4% farming, 16.6% construction, 13.0% production (2000).
Income: Per capita income: $16,351 (2000); Median household income: $39,808 (2000); Poverty rate: 5.1% (2000).
Education: High school graduation rate: 93.6% (2000); College graduation rate: 0.0% (2000).
Housing: Homeownership rate: 74.5% (2000); Median home value: $85,800 (2000); Median rent: $325 per month (2000); Median age of housing: 60+ years (2000).
Transportation: Commute to work: 63.2% car, 0.0% public transportation, 9.3% walk, 27.5% work from home (2000); Travel time to work: 41.9% less than 15 minutes, 27.4% 15 to 30 minutes, 22.9% 30 to 45 minutes, 4.5% 45 to 60 minutes, 3.4% 60 minutes or more (2000)

WOODHULL (village). Covers a land area of 0.825 square miles and a water area of 0 square miles. Located at 41.17° N. Lat.; 90.31° W. Long. Elevation is 815 feet.
Population: 809 (2000); Race: 98.5% White, 0.0% Black, 0.4% Asian, 0.0% American Indian and Alaska Native, 0.7% Hispanic of any race, 1.1% two or more races (2000); Density: 980.6 persons per square mile (2000); Age: 20.6% under 18, 20.7% over 64 (2000); Marriage status: 16.1% never married, 63.8% now married, 11.0% widowed, 9.1% divorced (2000); Foreign born: 0.6% (2000); Ancestry (includes multiple ancestries): 28.7% Swedish, 16.9% German, 13.1% Irish, 10.4% English, 9.3% United States or American (2000).
Economy: In agricultural area; ships grain. Site of commercial seed-processing plant. Single-family building permits issued: 6 (2001) / 0 (2000); Multi-family building permits issued: 0 (2001) / 2 (2000); Employment by occupation: 6.9% management, 14.8% professional, 14.6% services, 25.9% sales, 0.8% farming, 13.0% construction, 24.1% production (2000).
Income: Per capita income: $18,738 (2000); Median household income: $35,288 (2000); Poverty rate: 9.1% (2000).
Taxes: Total city taxes per capita: $52 (1997); City property taxes per capita: $42 (1997).
Education: High school graduation rate: 86.5% (2000); College graduation rate: 10.7% (2000).

School District(s)

Alwood Community Unit School District 225 (PK-12)
2000 Enrollment: 540 309-334-2719
Housing: Homeownership rate: 76.0% (2000); Median home value: $66,700 (2000); Median rent: $272 per month (2000); Median age of housing: 58 years (2000).

Transportation: Commute to work: 91.3% car, 0.0% public transportation, 4.2% walk, 4.5% work from home (2000); Travel time to work: 29.1% less than 15 minutes, 25.5% 15 to 30 minutes, 28.0% 30 to 45 minutes, 10.5% 45 to 60 minutes, 6.9% 60 minutes or more (2000)

Iroquois County

Located in eastern Illinois; bounded on the east by Indiana; drained by the Iroquois River and Sugar Creek. Covers a land area of 1,116.40 square miles, a water area of 1.60 square miles, and is located in the Central Time Zone. The county government was organized in 1833. County seat is Watseka.

Weather Station: Watseka 2 NW — Elevation: 620 feet

	Jan	Feb	Mar	Apr	May	Jun	Jul	Aug	Sep	Oct	Nov	Dec
High	30	36	48	60	72	82	85	83	77	64	49	36
Low	14	18	29	38	49	59	62	60	52	40	31	21
Precip	1.7	1.6	3.5	4.1	4.2	4.7	4.2	3.8	3.6	2.8	3.3	2.6
Snow	6.9	4.6	2.5	0.9	0.0	0.0	0.0	0.0	0.0	tr	1.3	5.2

High and Low temperatures in degrees Fahrenheit; Precipitation and Snow in inches

Population: 31,334 (2000); Race: 95.5% White, 0.9% Black, 0.4% Asian, 0.1% American Indian and Alaska Native, 3.3% Hispanic of any race, 1.1% two or more races (2000); Density: 28.1 persons per square mile (2000); Age: 25.5% under 18, 18.1% over 64 (2000).
Religion: Five largest groups: 12.9% Catholic Church, 11.3% Lutheran Church—Missouri Synod, 9.7% The United Methodist Church, 6.9% Evangelical Lutheran Church in America, 5.0% Christian Churches and Churches of Christ (2000).
Economy: Unemployment rate: 5.5% (11/2002); Total civilian labor force: 14,993 (11/2002); Leading industries: 19.5% health care and social assistance; 19.5% manufacturing; 14.5% retail trade (2000); Companies that employ more than 1,000 persons: 0 (2000); Companies that employ more than 100 persons: 11 (2000); Farms: 1,393 totaling 667,134 acres (1997); Minority business ownership rate: 9.4% (1997); Women business ownership rate: 26.8% (1997); Retail sales per capita: $5,606 (1997). Single-family building permits issued: 69 (2001) / 65 (2000). Multi-family building permits issued: 8 (2001) / 4 (2000).
Income: Per capita income: $18,435 (2000); Median household income: $38,071 (2000); Poverty rate: 8.7% (2000); Bankruptcy rate: 6.65% (2001).
Taxes: Total county taxes per capita: $98 (1997); County property taxes per capita: $95 (1997).
Education: High school graduation rate: 80.3% (2000); College graduation rate: 11.8% (2000).
Housing: Homeownership rate: 76.4% (2000); Median home value: $77,900 (2000); Median rent: $329 per month (2000); Median age of housing: 47 years (2000).
Health: Birth rate: 114.3 per 10,000 population (1998); Age adjusted death rate: 86.8 per 10,000 population (1999); Age adjusted cancer mortality rate: 194.8 deaths per 100,000 population (1999). Number of physicians: 8.3 per 10,000 population (1999); Number of hospital beds: 35.7 per 10,000 population (1999).
Elections: 2000 Presidential election results: 32.8% Gore, 64.7% Bush, 1.7% Nader, 0.6% Buchanan
National and State Parks: Iroquois County State Conservation Area
Additional Information Contacts
Iroquois County Government Offices 815-432-6960
Gilman Chamber of Commerce 815-265-4818
Watseka Chamber of Commerce 815-432-2416

Iroquois County Communities

ASHKUM (village). Covers a land area of 0.820 square miles and a water area of 0 square miles. Located at 40.88° N. Lat.; 87.95° W. Long. Elevation is 671 feet.
Population: 724 (2000); Race: 98.0% White, 0.0% Black, 0.0% Asian, 0.0% American Indian and Alaska Native, 1.5% Hispanic of any race, 1.4% two or more races (2000); Density: 883.2 persons per square mile (2000); Age: 28.9% under 18, 19.0% over 64 (2000); Marriage status: 22.3% never married, 61.1% now married, 8.9% widowed, 7.7% divorced (2000); Foreign born: 0.0% (2000); Ancestry (includes multiple ancestries): 35.1% German, 21.3% French (except Basque), 18.0% Irish, 9.8% English, 5.6% United States or American (2000).
Economy: In rich agricultural area. Single-family building permits issued: 1 (2001) / 3 (2000); Multi-family building permits issued: 0 (2001) / 0 (2000); Employment by occupation: 7.0% management, 17.1% professional, 20.0% services, 23.2% sales, 1.2% farming, 10.4% construction, 21.2% production (2000).
Income: Per capita income: $20,806 (2000); Median household income: $40,313 (2000); Poverty rate: 3.8% (2000).
Taxes: Total city taxes per capita: $73 (1997); City property taxes per capita: $56 (1997).
Education: High school graduation rate: 85.8% (2000); College graduation rate: 11.9% (2000).
Housing: Homeownership rate: 79.5% (2000); Median home value: $90,000 (2000); Median rent: $381 per month (2000); Median age of housing: 44 years (2000).
Transportation: Commute to work: 93.6% car, 0.0% public transportation, 2.0% walk, 4.4% work from home (2000); Travel time to work: 38.0% less than 15 minutes, 26.7% 15 to 30 minutes, 19.8% 30 to 45 minutes, 5.5% 45 to 60 minutes, 10.0% 60 minutes or more (2000)

BEAVERVILLE (village). Covers a land area of 0.262 square miles and a water area of 0.004 square miles. Located at 40.95° N. Lat.; 87.65° W. Long. Elevation is 675 feet.
Population: 391 (2000); Race: 99.5% White, 0.0% Black, 0.0% Asian, 0.0% American Indian and Alaska Native, 0.0% Hispanic of any race, 0.5% two or more races (2000); Density: 1,491.4 persons per square mile (2000); Age: 27.4% under 18, 21.7% over 64 (2000); Marriage status: 23.2% never married, 55.0% now married, 14.9% widowed, 7.0% divorced (2000); Foreign born: 0.0% (2000); Ancestry (includes multiple ancestries): 20.6% French (except Basque), 19.3% German, 12.0% French Canadian, 9.9% Irish, 8.9% United States or American (2000).
Economy: In rich agricultural area: corn, soybeans; cattle, hogs. Single-family building permits issued: 1 (2001) / 1 (2000); Multi-family building permits issued: 0 (2001) / 0 (2000); Employment by occupation: 7.3% management, 6.0% professional, 18.0% services, 23.3% sales, 0.0% farming, 14.0% construction, 31.3% production (2000).
Income: Per capita income: $13,707 (2000); Median household income: $30,833 (2000); Poverty rate: 9.7% (2000).
Taxes: Total city taxes per capita: $36 (1997); City property taxes per capita: $32 (1997).
Education: High school graduation rate: 74.6% (2000); College graduation rate: 2.4% (2000).
Housing: Homeownership rate: 76.6% (2000); Median home value: $68,500 (2000); Median rent: $338 per month (2000); Median age of housing: 60+ years (2000).
Transportation: Commute to work: 89.8% car, 0.0% public transportation, 8.2% walk, 0.0% work from home (2000); Travel time to work: 23.8% less than 15 minutes, 29.9% 15 to 30 minutes, 36.1% 30 to 45 minutes, 4.1% 45 to 60 minutes, 6.1% 60 minutes or more (2000)

BUCKLEY (village). Covers a land area of 0.345 square miles and a water area of 0.006 square miles. Located at 40.59° N. Lat.; 88.03° W. Long. Elevation is 699 feet.
Population: 593 (2000); Race: 95.0% White, 0.0% Black, 1.1% Asian, 0.0% American Indian and Alaska Native, 3.5% Hispanic of any race, 1.3% two or more races (2000); Density: 1,721.1 persons per square mile (2000); Age: 22.1% under 18, 23.0% over 64 (2000); Marriage status: 19.3% never married, 66.5% now married, 8.6% widowed, 5.6% divorced (2000); Foreign born: 3.7% (2000); Ancestry (includes multiple ancestries): 50.9% German, 11.4% United States or American, 7.7% Other groups, 7.7% Irish, 6.3% English (2000).
Economy: In agricultural area. Single-family building permits issued: 3 (2001) / 1 (2000); Multi-family building permits issued: 0 (2001) / 0 (2000); Employment by occupation: 14.2% management, 13.5% professional, 13.5% services, 18.1% sales, 0.6% farming, 20.0% construction, 20.0% production (2000).
Income: Per capita income: $21,251 (2000); Median household income: $35,781 (2000); Poverty rate: 5.3% (2000).
Taxes: Total city taxes per capita: $75 (1997); City property taxes per capita: $45 (1997).
Education: High school graduation rate: 81.3% (2000); College graduation rate: 11.2% (2000).
Housing: Homeownership rate: 76.0% (2000); Median home value: $66,700 (2000); Median rent: $345 per month (2000); Median age of housing: 46 years (2000).
Transportation: Commute to work: 93.5% car, 0.0% public transportation, 3.9% walk, 1.3% work from home (2000); Travel time to work: 38.2% less than 15 minutes, 28.8% 15 to 30 minutes, 19.9% 30 to 45 minutes, 8.2% 45 to 60 minutes, 4.9% 60 minutes or more (2000)

CHEBANSE (village). Covers a land area of 0.437 square miles and a water area of 0 square miles. Located at 41.00° N. Lat.; 87.91° W. Long.
History: Chebanse developed as an agricultural community, settled by many people of German descent.
Population: 1,148 (2000); Race: 96.4% White, 0.2% Black, 0.6% Asian, 0.8% American Indian and Alaska Native, 0.3% Hispanic of any race, 1.8% two or more races (2000); Density: 2,625.4 persons per square mile (2000); Age: 25.8% under 18, 12.9% over 64 (2000); Marriage status: 19.4% never married, 66.1% now married, 6.8% widowed, 7.7% divorced (2000); Foreign born: 1.0% (2000); Ancestry (includes multiple ancestries): 37.6% German, 17.3% French (except Basque), 15.2% Irish, 8.5% United States or American, 7.3% Other groups (2000).
Economy: Single-family building permits issued: 0 (2001) / 0 (2000); Multi-family building permits issued: 0 (2001) / 0 (2000); Employment by occupation: 6.6% management, 14.3% professional, 18.2% services, 29.2% sales, 0.7% farming, 13.9% construction, 17.2% production (2000).
Income: Per capita income: $19,290 (2000); Median household income: $50,066 (2000); Poverty rate: 3.2% (2000).
Taxes: Total city taxes per capita: $85 (1997); City property taxes per capita: $65 (1997).
Education: High school graduation rate: 91.1% (2000); College graduation rate: 10.3% (2000).
Housing: Homeownership rate: 77.5% (2000); Median home value: $96,900 (2000); Median rent: $425 per month (2000); Median age of housing: 43 years (2000).
Transportation: Commute to work: 96.2% car, 0.0% public transportation, 2.7% walk, 0.8% work from home (2000); Travel time to work: 26.0% less than 15 minutes, 49.0% 15 to 30 minutes, 13.6% 30 to 45 minutes, 1.8% 45 to 60 minutes, 9.6% 60 minutes or more (2000)

CISSNA PARK (village). Covers a land area of 0.719 square miles and a water area of 0 square miles. Located at 40.56° N. Lat.; 87.89° W. Long. Elevation is 666 feet.
History: Cissna Park developed as the center of a community of members of the Apostolic Church, known as New Amish, led by Samuel Frolich of Switzerland.
Population: 811 (2000); Race: 99.9% White, 0.0% Black, 0.1% Asian, 0.0% American Indian and Alaska Native, 0.5% Hispanic of any race, 0.0% two or more races (2000); Density: 1,128.5 persons per square mile (2000); Age: 20.2% under 18, 26.1% over 64 (2000); Marriage status: 23.6% never married, 54.5% now married, 14.1% widowed, 7.8% divorced (2000); Foreign born: 0.4% (2000); Ancestry (includes multiple ancestries): 53.0% German, 10.9% English, 7.1% Irish, 6.9% United States or American, 5.9% Swiss (2000).
Economy: Single-family building permits issued: 0 (2001) / 1 (2000); Multi-family building permits issued: 0 (2001) / 0 (2000); Employment by occupation: 8.3% management, 15.0% professional, 19.4% services, 32.5% sales, 0.0% farming, 11.1% construction, 13.8% production (2000).
Income: Per capita income: $18,285 (2000); Median household income: $35,592 (2000); Poverty rate: 7.4% (2000).
Taxes: Total city taxes per capita: $101 (1997); City property taxes per capita: $96 (1997).
Education: High school graduation rate: 76.2% (2000); College graduation rate: 14.8% (2000).

School District(s)

Cissna Park Community Unit School District 6 (KG-12)
2000 Enrollment: 391 815-457-2171

Housing: Homeownership rate: 79.2% (2000); Median home value: $70,700 (2000); Median rent: $252 per month (2000); Median age of housing: 46 years (2000).
Newspapers: The Rankin Independent (1 x week); The Cissna Park News (1 x week)
Transportation: Commute to work: 84.2% car, 1.7% public transportation, 8.3% walk, 5.0% work from home (2000); Travel time to work: 48.1% less than 15 minutes, 16.9% 15 to 30 minutes, 21.8% 30 to 45 minutes, 7.9% 45 to 60 minutes, 5.2% 60 minutes or more (2000)

CLIFTON (village). Covers a land area of 0.887 square miles and a water area of 0 square miles. Located at 40.93° N. Lat.; 87.93° W. Long. Elevation is 661 feet.
Population: 1,317 (2000); Race: 99.1% White, 0.0% Black, 0.2% Asian, 0.0% American Indian and Alaska Native, 1.4% Hispanic of any race, 0.3% two or more races (2000); Density: 1,485.1 persons per square mile (2000); Age: 28.7% under 18, 15.2% over 64 (2000); Marriage status: 20.9% never married, 65.1% now married, 8.2% widowed, 5.8% divorced (2000); Foreign born: 1.0% (2000); Ancestry (includes multiple ancestries): 34.6% German, 17.2% French (except Basque), 14.3% United States or American, 11.6% Irish, 9.4% English (2000).
Economy: In agricultural area: corn, soybeans, sorghum; cattle, hogs. Single-family building permits issued: 2 (2001) / 2 (2000); Multi-family building permits issued: 0 (2001) / 0 (2000); Employment by occupation: 13.2% management, 15.7% professional, 13.5% services, 30.5% sales, 0.7% farming, 10.7% construction, 15.7% production (2000).
Income: Per capita income: $20,618 (2000); Median household income: $47,216 (2000); Poverty rate: 4.5% (2000).
Taxes: Total city taxes per capita: $55 (1997); City property taxes per capita: $53 (1997).
Education: High school graduation rate: 86.5% (2000); College graduation rate: 13.9% (2000).

School District(s)

Central Community Unit School District 4 (PK-12)
2000 Enrollment: 1,385 815-694-2231

Housing: Homeownership rate: 77.7% (2000); Median home value: $92,800 (2000); Median rent: $349 per month (2000); Median age of housing: 43 years (2000).
Newspapers: Advocate (1 x week)
Transportation: Commute to work: 90.2% car, 1.5% public transportation, 3.8% walk, 4.3% work from home (2000); Travel time to work: 27.7% less than 15 minutes, 40.2% 15 to 30 minutes, 17.5% 30 to 45 minutes, 3.2% 45 to 60 minutes, 11.4% 60 minutes or more (2000)

CRESCENT CITY (village). Aka Crescent. Covers a land area of 0.503 square miles and a water area of 0 square miles. Located at 40.77° N. Lat.; 87.85° W. Long. Elevation is 636 feet.
Population: 631 (2000); Race: 98.4% White, 0.6% Black, 0.0% Asian, 0.0% American Indian and Alaska Native, 1.4% Hispanic of any race, 0.0% two or more races (2000); Density: 1,253.7 persons per square mile (2000); Age: 27.1% under 18, 20.2% over 64 (2000); Marriage status: 16.1% never married, 66.5% now married, 9.4% widowed, 7.9% divorced (2000); Foreign born: 0.0% (2000); Ancestry (includes multiple ancestries): 44.9% German, 9.6% English, 8.0% United States or American, 8.0% Irish, 7.2% Other groups (2000).
Economy: In rich agricultural area. Single-family building permits issued: 1 (2001) / 0 (2000); Multi-family building permits issued: 0 (2001) / 0 (2000); Employment by occupation: 9.9% management, 17.7% professional, 17.0% services, 23.0% sales, 1.4% farming, 10.3% construction, 20.6% production (2000).
Income: Per capita income: $17,308 (2000); Median household income: $38,500 (2000); Poverty rate: 1.9% (2000).
Taxes: Total city taxes per capita: $74 (1997); City property taxes per capita: $71 (1997).
Education: High school graduation rate: 82.6% (2000); College graduation rate: 9.7% (2000).

School District(s)

Crescent City C C School District 275 (KG-08)
2000 Enrollment: 140 815-683-2141
Crescent Iroquois Community District 252 (09-12)
2000 Enrollment: 60 815-683-2161

Housing: Homeownership rate: 79.9% (2000); Median home value: $83,400 (2000); Median rent: $372 per month (2000); Median age of housing: 36 years (2000).
Transportation: Commute to work: 90.4% car, 0.0% public transportation, 3.2% walk, 6.4% work from home (2000); Travel time to work: 41.2% less than 15 minutes, 32.4% 15 to 30 minutes, 19.5% 30 to 45 minutes, 4.2% 45 to 60 minutes, 2.7% 60 minutes or more (2000)

DANFORTH (village). Covers a land area of 0.477 square miles and a water area of 0 square miles. Located at 40.82° N. Lat.; 87.97° W. Long. Elevation is 653 feet.
History: Danforth was settled by immigrants from the Netherlands, on land purchased in the 1850's by A.H. and George Danforth. The swampy land was ditched and drained by the Dutch, who built windmills and established farms.
Population: 587 (2000); Race: 97.1% White, 0.0% Black, 0.0% Asian, 0.0% American Indian and Alaska Native, 2.6% Hispanic of any race, 1.2% two or more races (2000); Density: 1,230.8 persons per square mile (2000); Age: 21.3% under 18, 32.2% over 64 (2000); Marriage status: 15.4% never married, 67.1% now married, 9.4% widowed, 8.1% divorced (2000); Foreign born: 0.3% (2000); Ancestry (includes multiple ancestries): 39.0% German, 14.4% Other groups, 8.7% French (except Basque), 6.8% English, 6.1% Dutch (2000).

Economy: Single-family building permits issued: 2 (2001) / 0 (2000); Multi-family building permits issued: 0 (2001) / 0 (2000); Employment by occupation: 8.1% management, 13.8% professional, 18.8% services, 27.3% sales, 2.7% farming, 12.7% construction, 16.5% production (2000).
Income: Per capita income: $17,754 (2000); Median household income: $35,341 (2000); Poverty rate: 1.3% (2000).
Taxes: Total city taxes per capita: $55 (1997); City property taxes per capita: $31 (1997).
Education: High school graduation rate: 73.5% (2000); College graduation rate: 15.2% (2000).
Housing: Homeownership rate: 83.7% (2000); Median home value: $77,300 (2000); Median rent: $341 per month (2000); Median age of housing: 59 years (2000).
Transportation: Commute to work: 90.7% car, 0.0% public transportation, 2.3% walk, 5.8% work from home (2000); Travel time to work: 38.4% less than 15 minutes, 21.5% 15 to 30 minutes, 25.6% 30 to 45 minutes, 9.5% 45 to 60 minutes, 5.0% 60 minutes or more (2000)

DONOVAN (village). Covers a land area of 0.311 square miles and a water area of 0 square miles. Located at 40.88° N. Lat.; 87.61° W. Long. Elevation is 673 feet.
History: Donovan was settled by Swedish immigrants after the railroad was built here, and named for the operator of the Buckhorn Tavern.
Population: 351 (2000); Race: 99.5% White, 0.5% Black, 0.0% Asian, 0.0% American Indian and Alaska Native, 0.5% Hispanic of any race, 0.0% two or more races (2000); Density: 1,127.4 persons per square mile (2000); Age: 37.5% under 18, 14.2% over 64 (2000); Marriage status: 20.2% never married, 62.5% now married, 10.5% widowed, 6.9% divorced (2000); Foreign born: 0.0% (2000); Ancestry (includes multiple ancestries): 26.6% German, 18.5% French (except Basque), 13.2% Swedish, 10.6% English, 10.1% United States or American (2000).
Economy: Single-family building permits issued: 0 (2001) / 0 (2000); Multi-family building permits issued: 0 (2001) / 0 (2000); Employment by occupation: 8.4% management, 13.5% professional, 23.2% services, 13.5% sales, 0.0% farming, 8.4% construction, 32.9% production (2000).
Income: Per capita income: $22,215 (2000); Median household income: $42,083 (2000); Poverty rate: 4.1% (2000).
Taxes: Total city taxes per capita: $25 (1997); City property taxes per capita: $14 (1997).
Education: High school graduation rate: 85.0% (2000); College graduation rate: 14.6% (2000).

School District(s)

Donovan Community Unit School District 3 (KG-12)
2000 Enrollment: 525 815-486-7395
Housing: Homeownership rate: 78.1% (2000); Median home value: $59,200 (2000); Median rent: $305 per month (2000); Median age of housing: 60+ years (2000).
Transportation: Commute to work: 87.7% car, 0.0% public transportation, 3.2% walk, 5.2% work from home (2000); Travel time to work: 22.4% less than 15 minutes, 34.7% 15 to 30 minutes, 21.8% 30 to 45 minutes, 10.9% 45 to 60 minutes, 10.2% 60 minutes or more (2000)

GILMAN (city). Covers a land area of 2.114 square miles and a water area of 0.020 square miles. Located at 40.76° N. Lat.; 87.99° W. Long. Elevation is 646 feet.
History: Incorporated 1867.
Population: 1,793 (2000); Race: 92.6% White, 0.7% Black, 0.2% Asian, 0.1% American Indian and Alaska Native, 9.3% Hispanic of any race, 1.8% two or more races (2000); Density: 848.0 persons per square mile (2000); Age: 23.1% under 18, 19.6% over 64 (2000); Marriage status: 22.2% never married, 56.1% now married, 11.3% widowed, 10.3% divorced (2000); Foreign born: 4.5% (2000); Ancestry (includes multiple ancestries): 34.2% German, 13.3% Other groups, 11.2% Irish, 10.2% United States or American, 9.7% English (2000).
Economy: Railroad junction. In agricultural area: corn, wheat, soybeans, livestock; dairy products. Single-family building permits issued: 4 (2001) / 4 (2000); Multi-family building permits issued: 0 (2001) / 0 (2000); Employment by occupation: 7.9% management, 17.3% professional, 24.3% services, 18.1% sales, 0.7% farming, 10.7% construction, 21.0% production (2000).
Income: Per capita income: $17,396 (2000); Median household income: $36,450 (2000); Poverty rate: 9.9% (2000).
Taxes: Total city taxes per capita: $111 (1997); City property taxes per capita: $97 (1997).
Education: High school graduation rate: 74.0% (2000); College graduation rate: 9.5% (2000).

School District(s)

Ford-Iroquois Co Special Education Assoc (PK-12)
2000 Enrollment: 108 815-265-8601
Iroquois West C U S District 10 (PK-12)
2000 Enrollment: 954 815-265-4642
Housing: Homeownership rate: 71.3% (2000); Median home value: $73,600 (2000); Median rent: $329 per month (2000); Median age of housing: 51 years (2000).
Newspapers: The Gilman Star (1 x week)
Transportation: Commute to work: 95.4% car, 0.2% public transportation, 1.1% walk, 1.9% work from home (2000); Travel time to work: 52.1% less than 15 minutes, 19.8% 15 to 30 minutes, 15.2% 30 to 45 minutes, 7.5% 45 to 60 minutes, 5.4% 60 minutes or more (2000); Amtrak: Service available.
Additional Information Contacts
Gilman Chamber of Commerce 815-265-4818

IROQUOIS (village). Covers a land area of 0.598 square miles and a water area of 0 square miles. Located at 40.82° N. Lat.; 87.58° W. Long. Elevation is 660 feet.
History: Iroquois was the name given by the Big Four Railroad in 1871 to its station on the Iroquois River. In 1875 the town of Concord, on the other side of the river, was incorporated under the Iroquois name.
Population: 207 (2000); Race: 98.4% White, 0.0% Black, 0.0% Asian, 0.0% American Indian and Alaska Native, 0.0% Hispanic of any race, 1.6% two or more races (2000); Density: 346.1 persons per square mile (2000); Age: 20.4% under 18, 15.6% over 64 (2000); Marriage status: 19.9% never married, 67.9% now married, 2.6% widowed, 9.6% divorced (2000); Foreign born: 1.6% (2000); Ancestry (includes multiple ancestries): 35.5% German, 13.4% French (except Basque), 12.4% Irish, 11.8% United States or American, 10.8% English (2000).
Economy: Single-family building permits issued: 0 (2001) / 0 (2000); Multi-family building permits issued: 0 (2001) / 0 (2000); Employment by occupation: 6.4% management, 9.6% professional, 14.9% services, 19.1% sales, 2.1% farming, 8.5% construction, 39.4% production (2000).
Income: Per capita income: $16,624 (2000); Median household income: $35,781 (2000); Poverty rate: 1.6% (2000).
Taxes: Total city taxes per capita: $55 (1997); City property taxes per capita: $25 (1997).
Education: High school graduation rate: 74.6% (2000); College graduation rate: 10.4% (2000).
Housing: Homeownership rate: 86.4% (2000); Median home value: $48,600 (2000); Median rent: $263 per month (2000); Median age of housing: 60+ years (2000).
Transportation: Commute to work: 91.5% car, 0.0% public transportation, 6.4% walk, 2.1% work from home (2000); Travel time to work: 22.8% less than 15 minutes, 44.6% 15 to 30 minutes, 10.9% 30 to 45 minutes, 13.0% 45 to 60 minutes, 8.7% 60 minutes or more (2000)

LODA (village). Covers a land area of 1.448 square miles and a water area of 0.008 square miles. Located at 40.51° N. Lat.; 88.07° W. Long. Elevation is 781 feet.
Population: 419 (2000); Race: 94.3% White, 5.0% Black, 0.2% Asian, 0.0% American Indian and Alaska Native, 1.7% Hispanic of any race, 0.0% two or more races (2000); Density: 289.4 persons per square mile (2000); Age: 23.3% under 18, 16.7% over 64 (2000); Marriage status: 19.8% never married, 57.8% now married, 11.3% widowed, 11.0% divorced (2000); Foreign born: 2.4% (2000); Ancestry (includes multiple ancestries): 26.4% German, 14.4% United States or American, 11.3% Irish, 11.1% Other groups, 9.0% English (2000).
Economy: Corn, soybeans; cattle, hogs; egg and poultry processing; fertilizer. Single-family building permits issued: 0 (2001) / 3 (2000); Multi-family building permits issued: 0 (2001) / 0 (2000); Employment by occupation: 15.3% management, 7.7% professional, 18.4% services, 13.8% sales, 0.0% farming, 12.2% construction, 32.7% production (2000).
Income: Per capita income: $18,877 (2000); Median household income: $36,625 (2000); Poverty rate: 16.0% (2000).
Taxes: Total city taxes per capita: $79 (1997); City property taxes per capita: $28 (1997).
Education: High school graduation rate: 81.1% (2000); College graduation rate: 9.3% (2000).
Housing: Homeownership rate: 76.2% (2000); Median home value: $60,000 (2000); Median rent: $275 per month (2000); Median age of housing: 52 years (2000).
Transportation: Commute to work: 94.2% car, 0.0% public transportation, 2.6% walk, 3.2% work from home (2000); Travel time to work: 38.6% less

than 15 minutes, 28.3% 15 to 30 minutes, 16.8% 30 to 45 minutes, 15.2% 45 to 60 minutes, 1.1% 60 minutes or more (2000)

MARTINTON (village). Covers a land area of 0.251 square miles and a water area of 0 square miles. Located at 40.91° N. Lat.; 87.72° W. Long. Elevation is 627 feet.

History: Martinton was founded in 1871 as a station on the Chicago & Eastern Illinois Railway, and named for Porter Martin, an early resident.

Population: 375 (2000); Race: 100.0% White, 0.0% Black, 0.0% Asian, 0.0% American Indian and Alaska Native, 0.0% Hispanic of any race, 0.0% two or more races (2000); Density: 1,492.8 persons per square mile (2000); Age: 33.8% under 18, 10.3% over 64 (2000); Marriage status: 14.9% never married, 74.3% now married, 4.1% widowed, 6.7% divorced (2000); Foreign born: 0.0% (2000); Ancestry (includes multiple ancestries): 16.9% German, 14.6% French (except Basque), 14.1% Irish, 10.8% United States or American, 8.7% French Canadian (2000).

Economy: Single-family building permits issued: 3 (2001) / 3 (2000); Multi-family building permits issued: 0 (2001) / 0 (2000); Employment by occupation: 5.4% management, 10.8% professional, 10.8% services, 24.7% sales, 2.2% farming, 11.8% construction, 34.4% production (2000).

Income: Per capita income: $16,208 (2000); Median household income: $44,583 (2000); Poverty rate: 4.6% (2000).

Taxes: Total city taxes per capita: $38 (1997); City property taxes per capita: $26 (1997).

Education: High school graduation rate: 79.7% (2000); College graduation rate: 2.5% (2000).

Housing: Homeownership rate: 83.2% (2000); Median home value: $75,800 (2000); Median rent: $331 per month (2000); Median age of housing: 53 years (2000).

Transportation: Commute to work: 98.4% car, 0.0% public transportation, 0.0% walk, 1.6% work from home (2000); Travel time to work: 17.1% less than 15 minutes, 43.6% 15 to 30 minutes, 30.4% 30 to 45 minutes, 5.5% 45 to 60 minutes, 3.3% 60 minutes or more (2000)

MILFORD (village). Covers a land area of 0.632 square miles and a water area of 0 square miles. Located at 40.62° N. Lat.; 87.69° W. Long. Elevation is 660 feet.

History: Milford, incorporated as a village in 1874, was first laid out in 1836 by William Pickerel who operated a mill near a ford on Sugar Creek.

Population: 1,369 (2000); Race: 98.7% White, 0.0% Black, 0.0% Asian, 0.0% American Indian and Alaska Native, 1.9% Hispanic of any race, 0.3% two or more races (2000); Density: 2,166.8 persons per square mile (2000); Age: 19.5% under 18, 25.3% over 64 (2000); Marriage status: 18.8% never married, 58.3% now married, 12.0% widowed, 11.0% divorced (2000); Foreign born: 0.7% (2000); Ancestry (includes multiple ancestries): 25.2% German, 9.2% English, 8.9% United States or American, 7.6% Irish, 5.1% Other groups (2000).

Economy: Single-family building permits issued: 0 (2001) / 3 (2000); Multi-family building permits issued: 0 (2001) / 0 (2000); Employment by occupation: 7.9% management, 12.1% professional, 17.9% services, 23.0% sales, 0.6% farming, 9.5% construction, 28.9% production (2000).

Income: Per capita income: $19,078 (2000); Median household income: $30,109 (2000); Poverty rate: 7.2% (2000).

Taxes: Total city taxes per capita: $79 (1997); City property taxes per capita: $76 (1997).

Education: High school graduation rate: 74.5% (2000); College graduation rate: 7.8% (2000).

School District(s)

Milford Community Cons School District 280 (PK-08)
2000 Enrollment: 254 815-889-4174

Milford Township High School District 233 (09-12)
2000 Enrollment: 165 815-889-4184

Housing: Homeownership rate: 73.9% (2000); Median home value: $51,100 (2000); Median rent: $311 per month (2000); Median age of housing: 53 years (2000).

Newspapers: Milford Herald-News (1 x week)

Transportation: Commute to work: 93.5% car, 0.8% public transportation, 2.3% walk, 1.8% work from home (2000); Travel time to work: 39.4% less than 15 minutes, 38.3% 15 to 30 minutes, 9.4% 30 to 45 minutes, 5.0% 45 to 60 minutes, 7.9% 60 minutes or more (2000)

ONARGA (village). Covers a land area of 1.310 square miles and a water area of 0 square miles. Located at 40.71° N. Lat.; 88.00° W. Long. Elevation is 667 feet.

History: Benjamin Hardy, the composer of the song "Darling Nellie Gray," lived in Onarga.

Population: 1,438 (2000); Race: 64.8% White, 2.3% Black, 0.4% Asian, 0.6% American Indian and Alaska Native, 38.7% Hispanic of any race, 1.9% two or more races (2000); Density: 1,097.9 persons per square mile (2000); Age: 33.4% under 18, 11.1% over 64 (2000); Marriage status: 25.7% never married, 58.4% now married, 8.1% widowed, 7.7% divorced (2000); Foreign born: 19.7% (2000); Ancestry (includes multiple ancestries): 44.3% Other groups, 18.6% German, 8.9% Irish, 8.3% English, 6.9% United States or American (2000).

Economy: Single-family building permits issued: 2 (2001) / 0 (2000); Multi-family building permits issued: 4 (2001) / 0 (2000); Employment by occupation: 8.1% management, 10.6% professional, 17.9% services, 15.3% sales, 7.6% farming, 9.8% construction, 30.6% production (2000).

Income: Per capita income: $13,623 (2000); Median household income: $35,852 (2000); Poverty rate: 10.9% (2000).

Taxes: Total city taxes per capita: $66 (1997); City property taxes per capita: $59 (1997).

Education: High school graduation rate: 64.4% (2000); College graduation rate: 4.3% (2000).

Housing: Homeownership rate: 80.3% (2000); Median home value: $69,000 (2000); Median rent: $345 per month (2000); Median age of housing: 60+ years (2000).

Transportation: Commute to work: 90.5% car, 0.0% public transportation, 5.4% walk, 2.9% work from home (2000); Travel time to work: 48.5% less than 15 minutes, 21.2% 15 to 30 minutes, 20.0% 30 to 45 minutes, 5.4% 45 to 60 minutes, 4.9% 60 minutes or more (2000)

PAPINEAU (village). Covers a land area of 0.226 square miles and a water area of 0 square miles. Located at 40.96° N. Lat.; 87.71° W. Long. Elevation is 630 feet.

Population: 196 (2000); Race: 96.2% White, 0.0% Black, 0.0% Asian, 0.0% American Indian and Alaska Native, 0.0% Hispanic of any race, 1.6% two or more races (2000); Density: 867.7 persons per square mile (2000); Age: 29.5% under 18, 3.8% over 64 (2000); Marriage status: 11.8% never married, 80.1% now married, 5.1% widowed, 2.9% divorced (2000); Foreign born: 2.7% (2000); Ancestry (includes multiple ancestries): 36.1% German, 18.0% United States or American, 13.1% Polish, 11.5% French (except Basque), 7.7% Irish (2000).

Economy: In agricultural area. Single-family building permits issued: 1 (2001) / 1 (2000); Multi-family building permits issued: 0 (2001) / 0 (2000); Employment by occupation: 8.4% management, 13.7% professional, 13.7% services, 30.5% sales, 2.1% farming, 9.5% construction, 22.1% production (2000).

Income: Per capita income: $16,730 (2000); Median household income: $47,750 (2000); Poverty rate: 1.6% (2000).

Taxes: Total city taxes per capita: $64 (1997); City property taxes per capita: $64 (1997).

Education: High school graduation rate: 81.8% (2000); College graduation rate: 10.0% (2000).

Housing: Homeownership rate: 91.2% (2000); Median home value: $42,500 (2000); Median rent: $250 per month (2000); Median age of housing: 60+ years (2000).

Transportation: Commute to work: 97.9% car, 0.0% public transportation, 1.1% walk, 1.1% work from home (2000); Travel time to work: 26.6% less than 15 minutes, 37.2% 15 to 30 minutes, 20.2% 30 to 45 minutes, 6.4% 45 to 60 minutes, 9.6% 60 minutes or more (2000)

SHELDON (village). Covers a land area of 0.753 square miles and a water area of 0 square miles. Located at 40.77° N. Lat.; 87.56° W. Long. Elevation is 687 feet.

History: Sheldon was established in 1860 by the Toledo, Peoria & Western Railroad as a switching point, and named for a railroad director. The town was a grain shipping center.

Population: 1,232 (2000); Race: 98.6% White, 0.0% Black, 0.0% Asian, 0.3% American Indian and Alaska Native, 2.2% Hispanic of any race, 0.7% two or more races (2000); Density: 1,635.3 persons per square mile (2000); Age: 24.9% under 18, 18.6% over 64 (2000); Marriage status: 21.5% never married, 56.1% now married, 9.9% widowed, 12.5% divorced (2000); Foreign born: 1.1% (2000); Ancestry (includes multiple ancestries): 24.8% German, 11.9% Irish, 10.1% English, 5.6% Other groups, 4.6% United States or American (2000).

Economy: Single-family building permits issued: 1 (2001) / 1 (2000); Multi-family building permits issued: 0 (2001) / 0 (2000); Employment by occupation: 6.7% management, 12.2% professional, 16.5% services, 15.8% sales, 1.0% farming, 8.4% construction, 39.5% production (2000).

Income: Per capita income: $15,627 (2000); Median household income: $35,463 (2000); Poverty rate: 10.7% (2000).

Taxes: Total city taxes per capita: $55 (1997); City property taxes per capita: $50 (1997).
Education: High school graduation rate: 74.2% (2000); College graduation rate: 8.4% (2000).

School District(s)

Sheldon Community Unit School District 5 (PK-12)
2000 Enrollment: 288 815-429-3317

Housing: Homeownership rate: 76.3% (2000); Median home value: $66,800 (2000); Median rent: $333 per month (2000); Median age of housing: 60 years (2000).
Transportation: Commute to work: 95.7% car, 0.0% public transportation, 1.2% walk, 2.1% work from home (2000); Travel time to work: 39.2% less than 15 minutes, 39.0% 15 to 30 minutes, 6.8% 30 to 45 minutes, 7.6% 45 to 60 minutes, 7.4% 60 minutes or more (2000)

THAWVILLE (village). Covers a land area of 0.324 square miles and a water area of 0 square miles. Located at 40.67° N. Lat.; 88.11° W. Long. Elevation is 695 feet.
Population: 258 (2000); Race: 98.3% White, 0.0% Black, 0.0% Asian, 0.0% American Indian and Alaska Native, 0.0% Hispanic of any race, 1.7% two or more races (2000); Density: 797.4 persons per square mile (2000); Age: 22.1% under 18, 18.7% over 64 (2000); Marriage status: 16.8% never married, 65.3% now married, 8.2% widowed, 9.7% divorced (2000); Foreign born: 0.0% (2000); Ancestry (includes multiple ancestries): 32.8% German, 11.5% Irish, 11.1% English, 9.8% Other groups, 5.5% French (except Basque) (2000).
Economy: In rich agricultural area. Single-family building permits issued: 0 (2001) / 0 (2000); Multi-family building permits issued: 4 (2001) / 4 (2000); Employment by occupation: 11.5% management, 21.2% professional, 15.9% services, 20.4% sales, 3.5% farming, 8.8% construction, 18.6% production (2000).
Income: Per capita income: $18,149 (2000); Median household income: $39,659 (2000); Poverty rate: 2.6% (2000).
Taxes: Total city taxes per capita: $43 (1997); City property taxes per capita: $43 (1997).
Education: High school graduation rate: 80.1% (2000); College graduation rate: 11.4% (2000).
Housing: Homeownership rate: 94.5% (2000); Median home value: $56,700 (2000); Median rent: $375 per month (2000); Median age of housing: 60+ years (2000).
Transportation: Commute to work: 92.9% car, 0.0% public transportation, 0.0% walk, 7.1% work from home (2000); Travel time to work: 23.8% less than 15 minutes, 41.0% 15 to 30 minutes, 22.9% 30 to 45 minutes, 7.6% 45 to 60 minutes, 4.8% 60 minutes or more (2000)

WATSEKA (city). Covers a land area of 2.618 square miles and a water area of 0 square miles. Located at 40.77° N. Lat.; 87.73° W. Long. Elevation is 637 feet.
History: Watseka was first called South Middleport when it was laid out in 1860. The name was changed in 1865 to honor the Potawatomi wife (Watch-e-kee) of Gurdon Hubbard of the American Fur Company. Watseka developed as the seat of Iroquois County.
Population: 5,670 (2000); Race: 96.1% White, 1.6% Black, 0.9% Asian, 0.1% American Indian and Alaska Native, 0.6% Hispanic of any race, 1.4% two or more races (2000); Density: 2,165.4 persons per square mile (2000); Age: 23.9% under 18, 22.3% over 64 (2000); Marriage status: 24.0% never married, 56.0% now married, 10.0% widowed, 10.1% divorced (2000); Foreign born: 2.2% (2000); Ancestry (includes multiple ancestries): 24.1% German, 10.8% United States or American, 10.2% Irish, 9.1% Other groups, 9.0% English (2000).
Economy: Single-family building permits issued: 12 (2001) / 12 (2000); Multi-family building permits issued: 0 (2001) / 0 (2000); Employment by occupation: 8.5% management, 11.8% professional, 19.4% services, 24.7% sales, 0.4% farming, 8.4% construction, 26.8% production (2000).
Income: Per capita income: $16,638 (2000); Median household income: $30,440 (2000); Poverty rate: 15.4% (2000).
Taxes: Total city taxes per capita: $258 (1997); City property taxes per capita: $250 (1997).
Education: High school graduation rate: 74.6% (2000); College graduation rate: 12.5% (2000).

School District(s)

Iroquois Co C U School District 9 (PK-12)
2000 Enrollment: 1,226 815-432-4931

Housing: Homeownership rate: 67.0% (2000); Median home value: $71,200 (2000); Median rent: $336 per month (2000); Median age of housing: 44 years (2000).
Hospitals: Iroquois Memorial Hospital & Resident Home (94 beds)
Newspapers: Times-Republic (5 x week)
Transportation: Commute to work: 89.7% car, 0.4% public transportation, 6.4% walk, 2.7% work from home (2000); Travel time to work: 67.3% less than 15 minutes, 12.8% 15 to 30 minutes, 8.2% 30 to 45 minutes, 5.3% 45 to 60 minutes, 6.4% 60 minutes or more (2000)
Additional Information Contacts
Watseka Chamber of Commerce 815-432-2416

WELLINGTON (village). Covers a land area of 0.277 square miles and a water area of 0 square miles. Located at 40.54° N. Lat.; 87.68° W. Long. Elevation is 700 feet.
Population: 264 (2000); Race: 98.9% White, 0.0% Black, 0.0% Asian, 0.0% American Indian and Alaska Native, 0.0% Hispanic of any race, 1.1% two or more races (2000); Density: 954.0 persons per square mile (2000); Age: 24.4% under 18, 14.1% over 64 (2000); Marriage status: 9.8% never married, 71.2% now married, 4.9% widowed, 14.1% divorced (2000); Foreign born: 1.9% (2000); Ancestry (includes multiple ancestries): 25.6% German, 13.0% United States or American, 12.6% Irish, 10.7% English, 6.1% Other groups (2000).
Economy: In rich agricultural area. Single-family building permits issued: 1 (2001) / 0 (2000); Multi-family building permits issued: 0 (2001) / 0 (2000); Employment by occupation: 11.1% management, 9.5% professional, 4.8% services, 17.5% sales, 0.0% farming, 25.4% construction, 31.7% production (2000).
Income: Per capita income: $17,324 (2000); Median household income: $32,083 (2000); Poverty rate: 3.9% (2000).
Taxes: Total city taxes per capita: $30 (1997); City property taxes per capita: $27 (1997).
Education: High school graduation rate: 82.6% (2000); College graduation rate: 5.4% (2000).
Housing: Homeownership rate: 86.4% (2000); Median home value: $44,700 (2000); Median rent: $256 per month (2000); Median age of housing: 60+ years (2000).
Transportation: Commute to work: 84.4% car, 0.0% public transportation, 10.7% walk, 0.0% work from home (2000); Travel time to work: 50.8% less than 15 minutes, 22.1% 15 to 30 minutes, 9.8% 30 to 45 minutes, 10.7% 45 to 60 minutes, 6.6% 60 minutes or more (2000)

WOODLAND (village). Covers a land area of 0.449 square miles and a water area of 0 square miles. Located at 40.71° N. Lat.; 87.73° W. Long. Elevation is 635 feet.
Population: 319 (2000); Race: 94.8% White, 1.5% Black, 0.0% Asian, 0.0% American Indian and Alaska Native, 0.0% Hispanic of any race, 3.7% two or more races (2000); Density: 709.7 persons per square mile (2000); Age: 28.9% under 18, 12.0% over 64 (2000); Marriage status: 20.7% never married, 59.4% now married, 8.0% widowed, 12.0% divorced (2000); Foreign born: 1.5% (2000); Ancestry (includes multiple ancestries): 31.4% German, 11.7% Irish, 10.2% Other groups, 10.2% French (except Basque), 8.9% English (2000).
Economy: In rich agricultural area. Single-family building permits issued: 0 (2001) / 1 (2000); Multi-family building permits issued: 0 (2001) / 0 (2000); Employment by occupation: 4.9% management, 7.0% professional, 18.2% services, 24.5% sales, 0.0% farming, 15.4% construction, 30.1% production (2000).
Income: Per capita income: $14,707 (2000); Median household income: $32,115 (2000); Poverty rate: 21.2% (2000).
Taxes: Total city taxes per capita: $99 (1997); City property taxes per capita: $81 (1997).
Education: High school graduation rate: 75.6% (2000); College graduation rate: 4.7% (2000).
Housing: Homeownership rate: 78.0% (2000); Median home value: $56,400 (2000); Median rent: $402 per month (2000); Median age of housing: 38 years (2000).
Transportation: Commute to work: 96.5% car, 0.0% public transportation, 3.5% walk, 0.0% work from home (2000); Travel time to work: 39.2% less than 15 minutes, 35.7% 15 to 30 minutes, 6.3% 30 to 45 minutes, 2.8% 45 to 60 minutes, 16.1% 60 minutes or more (2000)

Jackson County

Located in southwestern Illinois; bounded on the southwest by the Mississippi River and the Missouri border; drained by the Big Muddy and Little Muddy Rivers; includes part of Shawnee National Forest. Covers a land area of 588.10 square miles, a water area of 14.40 square miles, and is located in the Central Time Zone. The county government was organized in 1816. County seat is Murphysboro.

Weather Station: Carbondale Sewage Plant Elevation: 387 feet

	Jan	Feb	Mar	Apr	May	Jun	Jul	Aug	Sep	Oct	Nov	Dec
High	40	46	55	67	76	85	89	88	81	70	56	45
Low	21	24	34	44	53	62	66	63	55	42	35	26
Precip	3.0	2.8	4.4	4.6	4.7	4.5	3.3	4.0	3.1	2.8	4.5	3.7
Snow	4.9	3.8	2.0	0.3	0.0	0.0	0.0	0.0	0.0	0.1	0.5	2.2

High and Low temperatures in degrees Fahrenheit; Precipitation and Snow in inches

Population: 59,612 (2000); Race: 80.9% White, 12.4% Black, 3.2% Asian, 0.3% American Indian and Alaska Native, 2.3% Hispanic of any race, 2.1% two or more races (2000); Density: 101.4 persons per square mile (2000); Age: 19.2% under 18, 11.1% over 64 (2000).
Religion: Five largest groups: 10.9% Southern Baptist Convention, 4.6% Catholic Church, 3.9% The United Methodist Church, 3.8% American Baptist Churches in the USA, 3.6% Lutheran Church—Missouri Synod (2000).
Economy: Unemployment rate: 3.9% (11/2002); Total civilian labor force: 30,723 (11/2002); Leading industries: 20.6% retail trade; 19.2% health care and social assistance; 13.9% accommodation & food services (2000); Companies that employ more than 1,000 persons: 0 (2000); Companies that employ more than 100 persons: 27 (2000); Farms: 680 totaling 202,558 acres (1997); Minority business ownership rate: 12.0% (1997); Women business ownership rate: 24.0% (1997); Retail sales per capita: $9,029 (1997). Single-family building permits issued: 30 (2001) / 45 (2000); Multi-family building permits issued: 76 (2001) / 67 (2000).
Income: Per capita income: $15,755 (2000); Median household income: $24,946 (2000); Poverty rate: 25.2% (2000); Bankruptcy rate: 4.71% (2001).
Taxes: Total county taxes per capita: $78 (2000); County property taxes per capita: $78 (2000).
Education: High school graduation rate: 85.2% (2000); College graduation rate: 32.0% (2000).
Housing: Homeownership rate: 53.3% (2000); Median home value: $68,200 (2000); Median rent: $332 per month (2000); Median age of housing: 29 years (2000).
Health: Birth rate: 108.0 per 10,000 population (1998); Age adjusted death rate: 95.9 per 10,000 population (1999); Age adjusted cancer mortality rate: 244.6 deaths per 100,000 population (1999). Air Quality Index: 100% good, 0% moderate, 0% unhealthy (percent of days in 2000). Number of physicians: 32.2 per 10,000 population (1999); Number of hospital beds: 28.9 per 10,000 population (1999).
Elections: 2000 Presidential election results: 51.0% Gore, 42.5% Bush, 5.3% Nader, 0.6% Buchanan
National and State Parks: Giant City State Park; Lake Murphysboro State Park
Additional Information Contacts
Jackson County Government Offices. 618-687-7360
Carbondale Chamber of Commerce 618-549-2146
Carbondale Convention & Tour. 618-529-4451
Murphysboro Chamber of Commerce 618-684-6421

Jackson County Communities

AVA (city). Covers a land area of 1.064 square miles and a water area of 0.006 square miles. Located at 37.88° N. Lat.; 89.49° W. Long. Elevation is 605 feet.
Population: 662 (2000); Race: 98.6% White, 0.0% Black, 0.0% Asian, 0.0% American Indian and Alaska Native, 0.0% Hispanic of any race, 0.6% two or more races (2000); Density: 622.0 persons per square mile (2000); Age: 23.1% under 18, 21.7% over 64 (2000); Marriage status: 20.8% never married, 56.0% now married, 15.3% widowed, 7.9% divorced (2000); Foreign born: 0.3% (2000); Ancestry (includes multiple ancestries): 30.8% German, 18.0% Irish, 11.2% English, 8.9% United States or American, 7.4% Other groups (2000).
Economy: In bituminous coal mining and agricultural region: wheat, sorghum; cattle; dairying. Employment by occupation: 2.8% management, 16.0% professional, 14.8% services, 26.8% sales, 0.0% farming, 17.6% construction, 22.0% production (2000).
Income: Per capita income: $16,324 (2000); Median household income: $24,750 (2000); Poverty rate: 14.4% (2000).
Education: High school graduation rate: 70.5% (2000); College graduation rate: 9.2% (2000).
Housing: Homeownership rate: 76.4% (2000); Median home value: $51,500 (2000); Median rent: $183 per month (2000); Median age of housing: 45 years (2000).
Transportation: Commute to work: 92.9% car, 0.0% public transportation, 1.7% walk, 4.6% work from home (2000); Travel time to work: 25.2% less than 15 minutes, 33.5% 15 to 30 minutes, 30.0% 30 to 45 minutes, 5.2% 45 to 60 minutes, 6.1% 60 minutes or more (2000)

CAMPBELL HILL (village). Covers a land area of 0.408 square miles and a water area of 0 square miles. Located at 37.92° N. Lat.; 89.55° W. Long. Elevation is 570 feet.
Population: 333 (2000); Race: 97.1% White, 0.0% Black, 2.9% Asian, 0.0% American Indian and Alaska Native, 0.0% Hispanic of any race, 0.0% two or more races (2000); Density: 815.3 persons per square mile (2000); Age: 22.1% under 18, 22.8% over 64 (2000); Marriage status: 29.8% never married, 45.8% now married, 19.5% widowed, 5.0% divorced (2000); Foreign born: 2.9% (2000); Ancestry (includes multiple ancestries): 51.8% German, 6.8% Polish, 6.5% Irish, 4.9% Other groups, 4.6% Dutch (2000).
Economy: In agricultural region. Single-family building permits issued: 0 (2001) / 0 (2000); Multi-family building permits issued: 0 (2001) / 0 (2000); Employment by occupation: 13.8% management, 10.8% professional, 7.7% services, 28.5% sales, 0.0% farming, 16.2% construction, 23.1% production (2000).
Income: Per capita income: $17,009 (2000); Median household income: $33,929 (2000); Poverty rate: 5.5% (2000).
Taxes: Total city taxes per capita: $54 (1997); City property taxes per capita: $14 (1997).
Education: High school graduation rate: 69.2% (2000); College graduation rate: 14.9% (2000).

School District(s)

Trico Community Unit School Districtrict 176 (PK-12)
2000 Enrollment: 1,017 618-426-1111
Housing: Homeownership rate: 86.4% (2000); Median home value: $47,100 (2000); Median rent: $292 per month (2000); Median age of housing: 35 years (2000).
Transportation: Commute to work: 96.0% car, 0.0% public transportation, 4.0% walk, 0.0% work from home (2000); Travel time to work: 27.0% less than 15 minutes, 30.2% 15 to 30 minutes, 34.9% 30 to 45 minutes, 1.6% 45 to 60 minutes, 6.3% 60 minutes or more (2000)

CARBONDALE (city). Covers a land area of 11.895 square miles and a water area of 0.249 square miles. Located at 37.72° N. Lat.; 89.22° W. Long. Elevation is 415 feet.
History: Carbondale developed as a coal mining center and a division point on the Illinois Central Railroad. In 1874 the Southern Illinois State Normal University was founded here.
Population: 20,681 (2000); Race: 65.5% White, 23.1% Black, 6.9% Asian, 0.3% American Indian and Alaska Native, 3.2% Hispanic of any race, 3.0% two or more races (2000); Density: 1,738.7 persons per square mile (2000); Age: 16.0% under 18, 9.3% over 64 (2000); Marriage status: 58.8% never married, 28.5% now married, 5.0% widowed, 7.7% divorced (2000); Foreign born: 10.6% (2000); Ancestry (includes multiple ancestries): 32.7% Other groups, 18.4% German, 11.4% Irish, 9.1% English, 4.6% United States or American (2000).
Vital Statistics: Birth rate: 129.6 per 10,000 population (1998)
Economy: Unemployment rate: 3.8% (11/2002); Total civilian labor force: 12,861 (11/2002); Single-family building permits issued: 16 (2001) / 37 (2000); Multi-family building permits issued: 76 (2001) / 67 (2000); Employment by occupation: 6.8% management, 34.3% professional, 21.1% services, 27.3% sales, 0.6% farming, 2.7% construction, 7.1% production (2000).
Income: Per capita income: $13,346 (2000); Median household income: $15,882 (2000); Poverty rate: 41.4% (2000).
Taxes: Total city taxes per capita: $304 (2000); City property taxes per capita: $56 (2000).
Education: High school graduation rate: 90.7% (2000); College graduation rate: 47.8% (2000).

School District(s)

Carbondale Community H S District 165 (09-12)
2000 Enrollment: 1,238 618-457-4722
Carbondale Elementary School District 95 (PK-08)
2000 Enrollment: 1,462 618-457-3591
Giant City C C School District 130 (KG-08)
2000 Enrollment: 257 618-457-5391
Unity Point C C School District 140 (PK-08)
2000 Enrollment: 736 618-529-4151

Four-year College(s)

Southern Illinois University-Carbondale (Public)
2001 Enrollment: 21,598 618-453-2121
2001 Tuition: In-state $2,482; Out-of-state $4,963

Housing: Homeownership rate: 28.4% (2000); Median home value: $73,400 (2000); Median rent: $341 per month (2000); Median age of housing: 29 years (2000).

Hospitals: Memorial Hospital Carbondale (150 beds)

Newspapers: Southern Illinoisan (7 x week); Daily Egyptian (5 x week)

Transportation: Commute to work: 81.0% car, 3.1% public transportation, 10.6% walk, 2.4% work from home (2000); Travel time to work: 67.7% less than 15 minutes, 22.1% 15 to 30 minutes, 5.1% 30 to 45 minutes, 2.1% 45 to 60 minutes, 3.0% 60 minutes or more (2000); Amtrak: Service available.

Airports: Southern Illinois

Additional Information Contacts

Carbondale Chamber of Commerce 618-549-2146
Carbondale Convention & Tour 618-529-4451

DE SOTO (village). Covers a land area of 0.943 square miles and a water area of 0 square miles. Located at 37.81° N. Lat.; 89.22° W. Long. Elevation is 395 feet.

Population: 1,653 (2000); Race: 98.2% White, 0.2% Black, 0.3% Asian, 0.2% American Indian and Alaska Native, 2.9% Hispanic of any race, 1.1% two or more races (2000); Density: 1,752.4 persons per square mile (2000); Age: 25.9% under 18, 11.6% over 64 (2000); Marriage status: 27.4% never married, 55.0% now married, 6.3% widowed, 11.3% divorced (2000); Foreign born: 1.3% (2000); Ancestry (includes multiple ancestries): 21.3% German, 14.9% Irish, 11.9% United States or American, 11.5% Other groups, 9.1% English (2000).

Economy: Railroad junction. In bituminous-coal mining and agricultural area: livestock, wheat, sorghum; dairying. Single-family building permits issued: 4 (2001) / 0 (2000); Multi-family building permits issued: 0 (2001) / 0 (2000); Employment by occupation: 8.2% management, 18.2% professional, 22.5% services, 28.2% sales, 0.7% farming, 7.6% construction, 14.6% production (2000).

Income: Per capita income: $15,526 (2000); Median household income: $31,563 (2000); Poverty rate: 14.3% (2000).

Education: High school graduation rate: 83.3% (2000); College graduation rate: 17.7% (2000).

School District(s)

Desoto Cons School District 86 (KG-08)
2000 Enrollment: 232 618-867-2317

Housing: Homeownership rate: 68.1% (2000); Median home value: $55,800 (2000); Median rent: $321 per month (2000); Median age of housing: 27 years (2000).

Transportation: Commute to work: 94.9% car, 0.4% public transportation, 2.1% walk, 0.7% work from home (2000); Travel time to work: 32.1% less than 15 minutes, 49.4% 15 to 30 minutes, 10.6% 30 to 45 minutes, 2.2% 45 to 60 minutes, 5.6% 60 minutes or more (2000)

DOWELL (village). Covers a land area of 0.371 square miles and a water area of 0 square miles. Located at 37.94° N. Lat.; 89.24° W. Long. Elevation is 400 feet.

History: Dowell grew around the Kathleen Coal Company Mine in 1916, and was named for George Dowell, legal advisor for the Progressive Miners of America.

Population: 441 (2000); Race: 96.8% White, 0.0% Black, 0.4% Asian, 0.9% American Indian and Alaska Native, 0.9% Hispanic of any race, 1.9% two or more races (2000); Density: 1,188.0 persons per square mile (2000); Age: 24.7% under 18, 20.2% over 64 (2000); Marriage status: 24.9% never married, 50.7% now married, 11.3% widowed, 13.1% divorced (2000); Foreign born: 0.4% (2000); Ancestry (includes multiple ancestries): 13.9% Other groups, 12.7% German, 8.6% English, 7.9% United States or American, 7.7% Irish (2000).

Economy: Employment by occupation: 6.6% management, 12.2% professional, 13.7% services, 22.8% sales, 1.0% farming, 11.7% construction, 32.0% production (2000).

Income: Per capita income: $12,464 (2000); Median household income: $24,750 (2000); Poverty rate: 13.3% (2000).

Taxes: Total city taxes per capita: $65 (1997); City property taxes per capita: $26 (1997).

Education: High school graduation rate: 65.5% (2000); College graduation rate: 4.7% (2000).

Housing: Homeownership rate: 78.4% (2000); Median home value: $28,800 (2000); Median rent: $313 per month (2000); Median age of housing: 51 years (2000).

Transportation: Commute to work: 98.4% car, 0.0% public transportation, 0.5% walk, 1.1% work from home (2000); Travel time to work: 31.7% less than 15 minutes, 30.6% 15 to 30 minutes, 24.7% 30 to 45 minutes, 4.8% 45 to 60 minutes, 8.1% 60 minutes or more (2000)

ELKVILLE (village). Covers a land area of 0.767 square miles and a water area of 0 square miles. Located at 37.91° N. Lat.; 89.23° W. Long. Elevation is 401 feet.

Population: 1,001 (2000); Race: 94.5% White, 3.0% Black, 0.0% Asian, 0.6% American Indian and Alaska Native, 0.8% Hispanic of any race, 1.6% two or more races (2000); Density: 1,305.6 persons per square mile (2000); Age: 27.1% under 18, 13.6% over 64 (2000); Marriage status: 21.7% never married, 65.2% now married, 5.5% widowed, 7.6% divorced (2000); Foreign born: 0.0% (2000); Ancestry (includes multiple ancestries): 21.3% German, 13.7% Other groups, 10.6% Irish, 8.6% United States or American, 8.5% English (2000).

Economy: Bituminous-coal mining. Agriculture: grain, fruit, vegetables. Single-family building permits issued: 0 (2001) / 0 (2000); Multi-family building permits issued: 0 (2001) / 0 (2000); Employment by occupation: 4.0% management, 8.7% professional, 18.6% services, 24.4% sales, 0.0% farming, 13.2% construction, 31.1% production (2000).

Income: Per capita income: $12,475 (2000); Median household income: $27,969 (2000); Poverty rate: 21.2% (2000).

Taxes: Total city taxes per capita: $86 (1997); City property taxes per capita: $30 (1997).

Education: High school graduation rate: 77.5% (2000); College graduation rate: 9.2% (2000).

School District(s)

Elverado C U School District 196 (PK-12)
2000 Enrollment: 526 618-568-1321

Housing: Homeownership rate: 70.6% (2000); Median home value: $44,400 (2000); Median rent: $266 per month (2000); Median age of housing: 40 years (2000).

Transportation: Commute to work: 93.6% car, 0.0% public transportation, 3.3% walk, 1.4% work from home (2000); Travel time to work: 27.0% less than 15 minutes, 40.1% 15 to 30 minutes, 20.5% 30 to 45 minutes, 5.0% 45 to 60 minutes, 7.4% 60 minutes or more (2000)

GORHAM (village). Covers a land area of 1.218 square miles and a water area of 0.011 square miles. Located at 37.71° N. Lat.; 89.48° W. Long. Elevation is 364 feet.

Population: 256 (2000); Race: 99.2% White, 0.0% Black, 0.0% Asian, 0.0% American Indian and Alaska Native, 0.8% Hispanic of any race, 0.0% two or more races (2000); Density: 210.2 persons per square mile (2000); Age: 30.7% under 18, 15.6% over 64 (2000); Marriage status: 19.7% never married, 58.1% now married, 14.6% widowed, 7.6% divorced (2000); Foreign born: 0.0% (2000); Ancestry (includes multiple ancestries): 19.5% United States or American, 16.3% German, 12.1% Other groups, 11.3% Irish, 7.8% French (except Basque) (2000).

Economy: In agricultural region. Railroad junction. Near Shawnee National Forest. Employment by occupation: 2.1% management, 8.5% professional, 18.1% services, 28.7% sales, 2.1% farming, 10.6% construction, 29.8% production (2000).

Income: Per capita income: $11,739 (2000); Median household income: $22,750 (2000); Poverty rate: 26.8% (2000).

Taxes: Total city taxes per capita: $34 (1997); City property taxes per capita: $34 (1997).

Education: High school graduation rate: 68.8% (2000); College graduation rate: 2.5% (2000).

Housing: Homeownership rate: 84.2% (2000); Median home value: $21,800 (2000); Median rent: $225 per month (2000); Median age of housing: 51 years (2000).

Transportation: Commute to work: 100.0% car, 0.0% public transportation, 0.0% walk, 0.0% work from home (2000); Travel time to work: 14.1% less than 15 minutes, 35.9% 15 to 30 minutes, 21.7% 30 to 45 minutes, 15.2% 45 to 60 minutes, 13.0% 60 minutes or more (2000)

GRAND TOWER (city). Covers a land area of 1.258 square miles and a water area of 0.002 square miles. Located at 37.63° N. Lat.; 89.50° W. Long. Elevation is 361 feet.

History: Grand Tower was named for the 60-foot-high Tower Rock in the middle of the Mississippi River.

Population: 624 (2000); Race: 98.9% White, 0.0% Black, 0.0% Asian, 0.2% American Indian and Alaska Native, 1.4% Hispanic of any race, 0.9% two or more races (2000); Density: 496.0 persons per square mile (2000); Age: 27.9% under 18, 17.4% over 64 (2000); Marriage status: 17.2% never

married, 65.1% now married, 6.1% widowed, 11.7% divorced (2000); Foreign born: 0.3% (2000); Ancestry (includes multiple ancestries): 15.7% Irish, 15.1% United States or American, 10.9% English, 10.4% Other groups, 7.3% German (2000).
Economy: Single-family building permits issued: 0 (2001) / 0 (2000); Multi-family building permits issued: 0 (2001) / 0 (2000); Employment by occupation: 9.4% management, 16.3% professional, 13.1% services, 15.5% sales, 0.4% farming, 18.8% construction, 26.5% production (2000).
Income: Per capita income: $14,525 (2000); Median household income: $27,135 (2000); Poverty rate: 20.9% (2000).
Taxes: Total city taxes per capita: $59 (1997); City property taxes per capita: $27 (1997).
Education: High school graduation rate: 70.9% (2000); College graduation rate: 8.9% (2000).
Housing: Homeownership rate: 75.6% (2000); Median home value: $33,300 (2000); Median rent: $170 per month (2000); Median age of housing: 40 years (2000).
Transportation: Commute to work: 87.4% car, 0.0% public transportation, 3.5% walk, 2.6% work from home (2000); Travel time to work: 25.8% less than 15 minutes, 28.9% 15 to 30 minutes, 30.2% 30 to 45 minutes, 7.6% 45 to 60 minutes, 7.6% 60 minutes or more (2000)

JACOB (unincorporated postal area, zip code 62950). Covers a land area of 28.982 square miles and a water area of 0.074 square miles. Located at 37.75° N. Lat.; 89.56° W. Long. Elevation is 360 feet.
Population: 232 (2000); Race: 100.0% White, 0.0% Black, 0.0% Asian, 0.0% American Indian and Alaska Native, 4.7% Hispanic of any race, 0.0% two or more races (2000); Density: 8.0 persons per square mile (2000); Age: 14.1% under 18, 32.3% over 64 (2000); Marriage status: 9.7% never married, 80.6% now married, 9.7% widowed, 0.0% divorced (2000); Foreign born: 4.7% (2000); Ancestry (includes multiple ancestries): 60.4% German, 6.3% Other groups, 4.7% Italian, 4.7% Lebanese, 3.1% Dutch (2000).
Economy: Employment by occupation: 26.4% management, 14.5% professional, 22.7% services, 24.5% sales, 0.0% farming, 5.5% construction, 6.4% production (2000).
Income: Per capita income: $20,713 (2000); Median household income: $23,750 (2000); Poverty rate: 14.1% (2000).
Education: High school graduation rate: 65.5% (2000); College graduation rate: 10.3% (2000).
Housing: Homeownership rate: 78.6% (2000); Median home value: $32,900 (2000); Median rent: $321 per month (2000); Median age of housing: 51 years (2000).
Transportation: Commute to work: 87.3% car, 0.0% public transportation, 0.0% walk, 6.4% work from home (2000); Travel time to work: 35.9% less than 15 minutes, 23.3% 15 to 30 minutes, 34.0% 30 to 45 minutes, 0.0% 45 to 60 minutes, 6.8% 60 minutes or more (2000)

MAKANDA (village). Covers a land area of 4.332 square miles and a water area of 0 square miles. Located at 37.61° N. Lat.; 89.23° W. Long. Elevation is 437 feet.
Population: 419 (2000); Race: 94.1% White, 4.4% Black, 0.2% Asian, 0.7% American Indian and Alaska Native, 0.0% Hispanic of any race, 0.0% two or more races (2000); Density: 96.7 persons per square mile (2000); Age: 18.2% under 18, 10.8% over 64 (2000); Marriage status: 23.6% never married, 61.1% now married, 4.3% widowed, 11.0% divorced (2000); Foreign born: 7.9% (2000); Ancestry (includes multiple ancestries): 25.1% German, 22.9% Irish, 9.6% English, 9.6% Other groups, 8.4% United States or American (2000).
Economy: In agricultural region. Employment by occupation: 10.4% management, 29.0% professional, 13.4% services, 22.9% sales, 1.3% farming, 10.4% construction, 12.6% production (2000).
Income: Per capita income: $20,937 (2000); Median household income: $41,607 (2000); Poverty rate: 10.8% (2000).
Taxes: Total city taxes per capita: $52 (1997); City property taxes per capita: $52 (1997).
Education: High school graduation rate: 91.2% (2000); College graduation rate: 39.7% (2000).
Housing: Homeownership rate: 83.1% (2000); Median home value: $66,800 (2000); Median rent: $275 per month (2000); Median age of housing: 28 years (2000).
Transportation: Commute to work: 94.4% car, 0.0% public transportation, 1.3% walk, 4.3% work from home (2000); Travel time to work: 18.6% less than 15 minutes, 57.5% 15 to 30 minutes, 17.6% 30 to 45 minutes, 0.0% 45 to 60 minutes, 6.3% 60 minutes or more (2000)

MURPHYSBORO (city). Covers a land area of 4.832 square miles and a water area of 0.008 square miles. Located at 37.76° N. Lat.; 89.33° W. Long. Elevation is 421 feet.
History: A memorial to John A. Logan is in the city. Incorporated 1867.
Population: 13,295 (2000); Race: 79.7% White, 15.5% Black, 1.6% Asian, 0.1% American Indian and Alaska Native, 2.5% Hispanic of any race, 1.9% two or more races (2000); Density: 2,751.3 persons per square mile (2000); Age: 15.1% under 18, 12.5% over 64 (2000); Marriage status: 46.7% never married, 38.7% now married, 7.5% widowed, 7.2% divorced (2000); Foreign born: 2.8% (2000); Ancestry (includes multiple ancestries): 22.0% German, 21.2% Other groups, 13.3% Irish, 7.1% English, 4.9% Italian (2000).
Economy: It is a trade and distributing center for a fertile farm area. Shoes, feed, and fertilizer are made there. Nearby is a national forest. Single-family building permits issued: 10 (2001) / 8 (2000); Multi-family building permits issued: 0 (2001) / 0 (2000); Employment by occupation: 7.6% management, 22.5% professional, 23.2% services, 28.7% sales, 0.0% farming, 8.2% construction, 9.7% production (2000).
Income: Per capita income: $13,527 (2000); Median household income: $25,551 (2000); Poverty rate: 21.3% (2000).
Taxes: Total city taxes per capita: $68 (1997); City property taxes per capita: $61 (1997).
Education: High school graduation rate: 76.2% (2000); College graduation rate: 18.5% (2000).

School District(s)

Jackson/Perry Roe (07-09)
2000 Enrollment: 7 618-687-7290
Murphysboro C U School District 186 (PK-12)
2000 Enrollment: 2,386 618-684-3781
Tri-County Special Education Jnt Agreement (PK-12)
2000 Enrollment: 169 618-684-2109

Housing: Homeownership rate: 59.3% (2000); Median home value: $50,100 (2000); Median rent: $325 per month (2000); Median age of housing: 44 years (2000).
Hospitals: Saint Joseph Memorial Hospital (59 beds)
Newspapers: Murphysboro American (2 x week)
Transportation: Commute to work: 75.4% car, 0.3% public transportation, 17.9% walk, 3.0% work from home (2000); Travel time to work: 53.9% less than 15 minutes, 31.0% 15 to 30 minutes, 8.4% 30 to 45 minutes, 3.5% 45 to 60 minutes, 3.2% 60 minutes or more (2000)
Airports: Southern Illinois
Additional Information Contacts
Murphysboro Chamber of Commerce 618-684-6421

POMONA (unincorporated postal area, zip code 62975). Covers a land area of 20.400 square miles and a water area of 0 square miles. Located at 37.61° N. Lat.; 89.36° W. Long. Elevation is 410 feet.
Population: 240 (2000); Race: 100.0% White, 0.0% Black, 0.0% Asian, 0.0% American Indian and Alaska Native, 0.0% Hispanic of any race, 0.0% two or more races (2000); Density: 11.8 persons per square mile (2000); Age: 29.6% under 18, 5.2% over 64 (2000); Marriage status: 33.1% never married, 55.8% now married, 7.0% widowed, 4.1% divorced (2000); Foreign born: 0.0% (2000); Ancestry (includes multiple ancestries): 20.4% German, 17.0% Irish, 9.1% United States or American, 7.0% Polish, 6.5% Other groups (2000).
Economy: Employment by occupation: 21.1% management, 3.7% professional, 15.6% services, 23.9% sales, 0.0% farming, 22.0% construction, 13.8% production (2000).
Income: Per capita income: $19,845 (2000); Median household income: $41,250 (2000); Poverty rate: 16.1% (2000).
Education: High school graduation rate: 60.9% (2000); College graduation rate: 8.7% (2000).
Housing: Homeownership rate: 83.1% (2000); Median home value: $17,500 (2000); Median rent: $275 per month (2000); Median age of housing: 17 years (2000).
Transportation: Commute to work: 94.2% car, 0.0% public transportation, 0.0% walk, 0.0% work from home (2000); Travel time to work: 0.0% less than 15 minutes, 27.2% 15 to 30 minutes, 45.6% 30 to 45 minutes, 8.7% 45 to 60 minutes, 18.4% 60 minutes or more (2000)

VERGENNES (village). Covers a land area of 0.362 square miles and a water area of 0 square miles. Located at 37.90° N. Lat.; 89.34° W. Long. Elevation is 400 feet.
Population: 491 (2000); Race: 73.0% White, 23.2% Black, 0.0% Asian, 0.0% American Indian and Alaska Native, 3.9% Hispanic of any race, 3.9% two or more races (2000); Density: 1,357.6 persons per square mile (2000);

Age: 52.0% under 18, 7.8% over 64 (2000); Marriage status: 42.4% never married, 47.3% now married, 4.7% widowed, 5.6% divorced (2000); Foreign born: 0.0% (2000); Ancestry (includes multiple ancestries): 16.6% German, 9.2% Other groups, 8.0% United States or American, 5.7% English, 3.1% Irish (2000).
Economy: In agricultural region: wheat, soybeans, sorghum, corn. Employment by occupation: 9.9% management, 11.1% professional, 17.5% services, 36.8% sales, 0.0% farming, 7.6% construction, 17.0% production (2000).
Income: Per capita income: $8,574 (2000); Median household income: $36,458 (2000); Poverty rate: 19.1% (2000).
Taxes: Total city taxes per capita: $22 (1997); City property taxes per capita: $22 (1997).
Education: High school graduation rate: 80.6% (2000); College graduation rate: 5.7% (2000).
Housing: Homeownership rate: 86.6% (2000); Median home value: $48,400 (2000); Median rent: $260 per month (2000); Median age of housing: 37 years (2000).
Transportation: Commute to work: 90.6% car, 0.0% public transportation, 2.3% walk, 7.0% work from home (2000); Travel time to work: 17.0% less than 15 minutes, 47.8% 15 to 30 minutes, 24.5% 30 to 45 minutes, 3.1% 45 to 60 minutes, 7.5% 60 minutes or more (2000)

Jasper County

Located in southeast central Illinois; drained by the Embarrass River. Covers a land area of 494.40 square miles, a water area of 3.60 square miles, and is located in the Central Time Zone. The county government was organized in 1831. County seat is Newton.

Weather Station: Newton 6 SSE — Elevation: 508 feet

	Jan	Feb	Mar	Apr	May	Jun	Jul	Aug	Sep	Oct	Nov	Dec
High	35	41	52	63	74	83	87	85	79	67	53	41
Low	18	22	33	42	52	62	65	62	54	43	34	24
Precip	2.4	2.3	3.8	3.9	4.4	3.7	4.2	3.3	3.2	2.8	3.9	2.9
Snow	4.9	3.2	2.2	0.1	tr	0.0	0.0	0.0	0.0	0.1	0.9	3.4

High and Low temperatures in degrees Fahrenheit; Precipitation and Snow in inches

Population: 10,117 (2000); Race: 99.2% White, 0.0% Black, 0.1% Asian, 0.0% American Indian and Alaska Native, 0.1% Hispanic of any race, 0.6% two or more races (2000); Density: 20.5 persons per square mile (2000); Age: 25.9% under 18, 16.5% over 64 (2000).
Religion: Five largest groups: 22.1% Catholic Church, 10.1% Christian Churches and Churches of Christ, 8.2% The United Methodist Church, 5.0% Southern Baptist Convention, 4.9% American Baptist Churches in the USA (2000).
Economy: Unemployment rate: 9.2% (11/2002); Total civilian labor force: 3,831 (11/2002); Leading industries: 17.1% manufacturing; 15.8% transportation & warehousing; 14.3% retail trade (2000); Companies that employ more than 1,000 persons: 0 (2000); Companies that employ more than 100 persons: 3 (2000); Farms: 729 totaling 252,272 acres (1997); Minority business ownership rate: 0.0% (1997); Women business ownership rate: 14.7% (1997); Retail sales per capita: $7,395 (1997). Single-family building permits issued: 1 (2001) / 2 (2000); Multi-family building permits issued: 0 (2001) / 0 (2000).
Income: Per capita income: $16,649 (2000); Median household income: $34,721 (2000); Poverty rate: 9.9% (2000); Bankruptcy rate: 3.67% (2001).
Taxes: Total county taxes per capita: $150 (1997); County property taxes per capita: $150 (1997).
Education: High school graduation rate: 82.6% (2000); College graduation rate: 11.2% (2000).
Housing: Homeownership rate: 83.2% (2000); Median home value: $65,000 (2000); Median rent: $256 per month (2000); Median age of housing: 35 years (2000).
Health: Birth rate: 113.7 per 10,000 population (1998); Age adjusted death rate: 78.3 per 10,000 population (1999); Age adjusted cancer mortality rate: 128.8 (Unreliable figure as per CDC) deaths per 100,000 population (1999). Number of physicians: 1.0 per 10,000 population (1999); Number of hospital beds: n/a (1999).
Elections: 2000 Presidential election results: 36.2% Gore, 62.1% Bush, 1.0% Nader, 0.6% Buchanan
National and State Parks: Newton Lake State Fish and Wildlife Area; Sam Parr State Park
Additional Information Contacts
Jasper County Government Offices 618-783-3124
Newton Chamber of Commerce 618-783-3399

Jasper County Communities

HIDALGO (village). Covers a land area of 0.343 square miles and a water area of 0 square miles. Located at 39.15° N. Lat.; 88.15° W. Long. Elevation is 583 feet.
Population: 123 (2000); Race: 100.0% White, 0.0% Black, 0.0% Asian, 0.0% American Indian and Alaska Native, 0.0% Hispanic of any race, 0.0% two or more races (2000); Density: 358.2 persons per square mile (2000); Age: 24.6% under 18, 19.0% over 64 (2000); Marriage status: 36.1% never married, 50.0% now married, 4.6% widowed, 9.3% divorced (2000); Foreign born: 0.0% (2000); Ancestry (includes multiple ancestries): 12.7% Irish, 12.7% German, 9.5% English, 8.7% Other groups, 4.0% Dutch (2000).
Economy: In agricultural area. Employment by occupation: 7.4% management, 11.1% professional, 25.9% services, 25.9% sales, 0.0% farming, 13.0% construction, 16.7% production (2000).
Income: Per capita income: $13,167 (2000); Median household income: $25,972 (2000); Poverty rate: 6.3% (2000).
Taxes: Total city taxes per capita: $17 (1997); City property taxes per capita: $0 (1997).
Education: High school graduation rate: 69.3% (2000); College graduation rate: 5.7% (2000).
Housing: Homeownership rate: 80.0% (2000); Median home value: $48,600 (2000); Median rent: $213 per month (2000); Median age of housing: 39 years (2000).
Transportation: Commute to work: 88.7% car, 0.0% public transportation, 3.8% walk, 3.8% work from home (2000); Travel time to work: 3.9% less than 15 minutes, 27.5% 15 to 30 minutes, 27.5% 30 to 45 minutes, 37.3% 45 to 60 minutes, 3.9% 60 minutes or more (2000)

NEWTON (city). Covers a land area of 1.863 square miles and a water area of 0 square miles. Located at 38.98° N. Lat.; 88.16° W. Long. Elevation is 535 feet.
History: Settled 1828, incorporated 1831.
Population: 3,069 (2000); Race: 99.3% White, 0.0% Black, 0.0% Asian, 0.0% American Indian and Alaska Native, 0.2% Hispanic of any race, 0.5% two or more races (2000); Density: 1,647.3 persons per square mile (2000); Age: 24.1% under 18, 21.0% over 64 (2000); Marriage status: 23.2% never married, 57.2% now married, 9.6% widowed, 10.0% divorced (2000); Foreign born: 0.2% (2000); Ancestry (includes multiple ancestries): 34.8% German, 10.4% Irish, 9.9% United States or American, 8.3% English, 5.2% Other groups (2000).
Economy: In agricultural area; livestock; corn, wheat; dairy products. Employment by occupation: 9.1% management, 9.7% professional, 19.1% services, 29.1% sales, 0.0% farming, 8.4% construction, 24.7% production (2000).
Income: Per capita income: $16,363 (2000); Median household income: $30,280 (2000); Poverty rate: 11.7% (2000).
Taxes: Total city taxes per capita: $323 (1997); City property taxes per capita: $70 (1997).
Education: High school graduation rate: 80.2% (2000); College graduation rate: 12.6% (2000).

School District(s)
Jasper County Community Unit District 1 (PK-12)
2000 Enrollment: 1,690 618-783-8459
Housing: Homeownership rate: 73.8% (2000); Median home value: $59,200 (2000); Median rent: $255 per month (2000); Median age of housing: 41 years (2000).
Newspapers: Newton Press-Mentor (1 x week)
Transportation: Commute to work: 89.7% car, 0.0% public transportation, 7.0% walk, 1.6% work from home (2000); Travel time to work: 66.4% less than 15 minutes, 12.2% 15 to 30 minutes, 17.9% 30 to 45 minutes, 2.0% 45 to 60 minutes, 1.5% 60 minutes or more (2000)
Additional Information Contacts
Newton Chamber of Commerce 618-783-3399

ROSE HILL (village). Covers a land area of 0.633 square miles and a water area of 0 square miles. Located at 39.10° N. Lat.; 88.14° W. Long. Elevation is 565 feet.
Population: 79 (2000); Race: 100.0% White, 0.0% Black, 0.0% Asian, 0.0% American Indian and Alaska Native, 0.0% Hispanic of any race, 0.0% two or more races (2000); Density: 124.8 persons per square mile (2000); Age: 18.7% under 18, 22.0% over 64 (2000); Marriage status: 29.5% never married, 50.0% now married, 15.4% widowed, 5.1% divorced (2000); Foreign born: 0.0% (2000); Ancestry (includes multiple ancestries): 17.6%

English, 17.6% German, 15.4% Irish, 13.2% United States or American, 4.4% Scottish (2000).
Economy: In agricultural area: wheat, corn, soybeans; cattle; dairying. Employment by occupation: 0.0% management, 27.8% professional, 0.0% services, 27.8% sales, 0.0% farming, 11.1% construction, 33.3% production (2000).
Income: Per capita income: $17,510 (2000); Median household income: $30,938 (2000); Poverty rate: 2.2% (2000).
Education: High school graduation rate: 74.6% (2000); College graduation rate: 8.5% (2000).
Housing: Homeownership rate: 87.8% (2000); Median home value: $30,000 (2000); Median rent: $175 per month (2000); Median age of housing: 40 years (2000).
Transportation: Commute to work: 94.4% car, 0.0% public transportation, 0.0% walk, 5.6% work from home (2000); Travel time to work: 8.8% less than 15 minutes, 23.5% 15 to 30 minutes, 38.2% 30 to 45 minutes, 5.9% 45 to 60 minutes, 23.5% 60 minutes or more (2000)

SAINTE MARIE (village). Aka Saint Marie. Covers a land area of 1.112 square miles and a water area of 0 square miles. Located at 38.93° N. Lat.; 88.02° W. Long. Elevation is 482 feet.
Population: 261 (2000); Race: 98.8% White, 0.0% Black, 1.2% Asian, 0.0% American Indian and Alaska Native, 0.0% Hispanic of any race, 0.0% two or more races (2000); Density: 234.7 persons per square mile (2000); Age: 20.7% under 18, 31.1% over 64 (2000); Marriage status: 17.2% never married, 65.6% now married, 13.4% widowed, 3.8% divorced (2000); Foreign born: 0.0% (2000); Ancestry (includes multiple ancestries): 49.0% German, 9.6% Irish, 7.6% French (except Basque), 5.6% Other groups, 5.2% Dutch (2000).
Economy: Single-family building permits issued: 1 (2001) / 2 (2000); Multi-family building permits issued: 0 (2001) / 0 (2000); Employment by occupation: 16.2% management, 12.1% professional, 20.2% services, 18.2% sales, 3.0% farming, 8.1% construction, 22.2% production (2000).
Income: Per capita income: $14,479 (2000); Median household income: $32,500 (2000); Poverty rate: 6.8% (2000).
Education: High school graduation rate: 76.9% (2000); College graduation rate: 11.0% (2000).
Housing: Homeownership rate: 86.8% (2000); Median home value: $46,900 (2000); Median rent: $131 per month (2000); Median age of housing: 44 years (2000).
Transportation: Commute to work: 83.8% car, 0.0% public transportation, 3.0% walk, 10.1% work from home (2000); Travel time to work: 39.3% less than 15 minutes, 40.4% 15 to 30 minutes, 13.5% 30 to 45 minutes, 4.5% 45 to 60 minutes, 2.2% 60 minutes or more (2000)

WEST LIBERTY (unincorporated postal area, zip code 62475). Covers a land area of 28.531 square miles and a water area of 0.057 square miles. Located at 38.86° N. Lat.; 88.05° W. Long. Elevation is 481 feet.
Population: 416 (2000); Race: 100.0% White, 0.0% Black, 0.0% Asian, 0.0% American Indian and Alaska Native, 0.0% Hispanic of any race, 0.0% two or more races (2000); Density: 14.6 persons per square mile (2000); Age: 29.1% under 18, 11.9% over 64 (2000); Marriage status: 26.3% never married, 72.5% now married, 1.2% widowed, 0.0% divorced (2000); Foreign born: 0.0% (2000); Ancestry (includes multiple ancestries): 55.5% German, 12.6% English, 8.3% Swiss, 7.6% United States or American, 6.7% Other groups (2000).
Economy: Employment by occupation: 24.9% management, 1.9% professional, 15.0% services, 36.6% sales, 4.2% farming, 0.0% construction, 17.4% production (2000).
Income: Per capita income: $14,590 (2000); Median household income: $40,179 (2000); Poverty rate: 8.9% (2000).
Education: High school graduation rate: 89.2% (2000); College graduation rate: 12.2% (2000).
Housing: Homeownership rate: 100.0% (2000); Median home value: $56,900 (2000); Median age of housing: 50 years (2000).
Transportation: Commute to work: 83.6% car, 0.0% public transportation, 8.5% walk, 5.2% work from home (2000); Travel time to work: 37.1% less than 15 minutes, 52.5% 15 to 30 minutes, 9.4% 30 to 45 minutes, 1.0% 45 to 60 minutes, 0.0% 60 minutes or more (2000)

WHEELER (village). Covers a land area of 0.576 square miles and a water area of 0 square miles. Located at 39.04° N. Lat.; 88.31° W. Long. Elevation is 573 feet.
Population: 119 (2000); Race: 100.0% White, 0.0% Black, 0.0% Asian, 0.0% American Indian and Alaska Native, 0.0% Hispanic of any race, 0.0% two or more races (2000); Density: 206.5 persons per square mile (2000); Age: 28.3% under 18, 14.2% over 64 (2000); Marriage status: 28.9% never married, 50.6% now married, 6.0% widowed, 14.5% divorced (2000); Foreign born: 0.0% (2000); Ancestry (includes multiple ancestries): 32.7% German, 12.4% English, 8.0% Irish, 7.1% United States or American, 5.3% Dutch (2000).
Economy: In agricultural area: grain; cattle. Manufacturing of wood products. Employment by occupation: 0.0% management, 4.5% professional, 27.3% services, 22.7% sales, 0.0% farming, 9.1% construction, 36.4% production (2000).
Income: Per capita income: $9,425 (2000); Median household income: $24,250 (2000); Poverty rate: 27.4% (2000).
Taxes: Total city taxes per capita: $36 (1997); City property taxes per capita: $36 (1997).
Education: High school graduation rate: 55.0% (2000); College graduation rate: 3.3% (2000).
Housing: Homeownership rate: 65.1% (2000); Median home value: $37,500 (2000); Median rent: $275 per month (2000); Median age of housing: 41 years (2000).
Transportation: Commute to work: 100.0% car, 0.0% public transportation, 0.0% walk, 0.0% work from home (2000); Travel time to work: 9.1% less than 15 minutes, 34.1% 15 to 30 minutes, 40.9% 30 to 45 minutes, 15.9% 45 to 60 minutes, 0.0% 60 minutes or more (2000)

WILLOW HILL (village). Covers a land area of 1.038 square miles and a water area of 0 square miles. Located at 38.99° N. Lat.; 88.02° W. Long. Elevation is 502 feet.
Population: 250 (2000); Race: 96.9% White, 0.0% Black, 0.0% Asian, 0.0% American Indian and Alaska Native, 0.8% Hispanic of any race, 3.1% two or more races (2000); Density: 240.9 persons per square mile (2000); Age: 33.6% under 18, 10.7% over 64 (2000); Marriage status: 21.5% never married, 56.9% now married, 4.1% widowed, 17.4% divorced (2000); Foreign born: 0.4% (2000); Ancestry (includes multiple ancestries): 18.3% German, 13.0% United States or American, 8.0% Other groups, 6.5% Irish, 4.2% English (2000).
Economy: Grain; livestock; oil. Employment by occupation: 4.0% management, 5.6% professional, 16.7% services, 6.3% sales, 0.0% farming, 7.9% construction, 59.5% production (2000).
Income: Per capita income: $10,926 (2000); Median household income: $26,429 (2000); Poverty rate: 24.0% (2000).
Taxes: Total city taxes per capita: $33 (1997); City property taxes per capita: $33 (1997).
Education: High school graduation rate: 76.8% (2000); College graduation rate: 0.0% (2000).
Housing: Homeownership rate: 83.1% (2000); Median home value: $29,600 (2000); Median rent: $220 per month (2000); Median age of housing: 51 years (2000).
Transportation: Commute to work: 97.6% car, 0.0% public transportation, 2.4% walk, 0.0% work from home (2000); Travel time to work: 20.6% less than 15 minutes, 46.0% 15 to 30 minutes, 19.0% 30 to 45 minutes, 11.1% 45 to 60 minutes, 3.2% 60 minutes or more (2000)

YALE (village). Covers a land area of 0.575 square miles and a water area of 0 square miles. Located at 39.12° N. Lat.; 88.02° W. Long. Elevation is 555 feet.
Population: 97 (2000); Race: 94.2% White, 0.0% Black, 0.0% Asian, 2.3% American Indian and Alaska Native, 0.0% Hispanic of any race, 3.5% two or more races (2000); Density: 168.7 persons per square mile (2000); Age: 36.0% under 18, 16.3% over 64 (2000); Marriage status: 17.7% never married, 62.9% now married, 9.7% widowed, 9.7% divorced (2000); Foreign born: 0.0% (2000); Ancestry (includes multiple ancestries): 20.9% United States or American, 20.9% Other groups, 16.3% German, 11.6% Irish, 4.7% English (2000).
Economy: In agricultural area: grain; cattle. Employment by occupation: 0.0% management, 0.0% professional, 3.6% services, 32.1% sales, 7.1% farming, 7.1% construction, 50.0% production (2000).
Income: Per capita income: $18,199 (2000); Median household income: $21,136 (2000); Poverty rate: 29.1% (2000).
Taxes: Total city taxes per capita: $247 (1997); City property taxes per capita: $237 (1997).
Education: High school graduation rate: 53.8% (2000); College graduation rate: 3.8% (2000).
Housing: Homeownership rate: 81.3% (2000); Median home value: $32,500 (2000); Median rent: $200 per month (2000); Median age of housing: 60+ years (2000).
Transportation: Commute to work: 82.1% car, 0.0% public transportation, 10.7% walk, 3.6% work from home (2000); Travel time to work: 29.6% less

than 15 minutes, 37.0% 15 to 30 minutes, 7.4% 30 to 45 minutes, 22.2% 45 to 60 minutes, 3.7% 60 minutes or more (2000)

Jefferson County

Located in southern Illinois; drained by the Big Muddy River. Covers a land area of 571.00 square miles, a water area of 12.80 square miles, and is located in the Central Time Zone. The county government was organized in 1819. County seat is Mount Vernon.

Weather Station: Mount Vernon-Outland Airport — Elevation: 465 feet

	Jan	Feb	Mar	Apr	May	Jun	Jul	Aug	Sep	Oct	Nov	Dec
High	37	43	54	65	75	84	88	87	80	68	54	43
Low	20	24	34	44	53	62	67	64	56	44	35	25
Precip	2.5	2.6	4.0	4.4	4.5	3.5	3.5	3.2	3.2	3.0	4.3	3.2
Snow	6.4	4.8	1.9	0.4	0.0	0.0	0.0	0.0	0.0	0.2	0.7	2.9

High and Low temperatures in degrees Fahrenheit; Precipitation and Snow in inches

Population: 40,045 (2000); Race: 89.6% White, 8.1% Black, 0.3% Asian, 0.2% American Indian and Alaska Native, 1.5% Hispanic of any race, 1.4% two or more races (2000); Density: 70.1 persons per square mile (2000); Age: 24.3% under 18, 15.3% over 64 (2000).
Religion: Five largest groups: 25.8% Southern Baptist Convention, 7.5% Christian Churches and Churches of Christ, 6.0% Catholic Church, 5.0% The United Methodist Church, 1.8% National Association of Free Will Baptists (2000).
Economy: Unemployment rate: 6.3% (11/2002); Total civilian labor force: 19,118 (11/2002); Leading industries: 18.3% manufacturing; 17.4% health care and social assistance; 16.4% retail trade (2000); Companies that employ more than 1,000 persons: 1 (2000); Companies that employ more than 100 persons: 19 (2000); Farms: 962 totaling 229,512 acres (1997); Minority business ownership rate: 0.0% (1997); Women business ownership rate: 22.7% (1997); Retail sales per capita: $9,862 (1997). Single-family building permits issued: 57 (2001) / 29 (2000); Multi-family building permits issued: 8 (2001) / 58 (2000).
Income: Per capita income: $16,644 (2000); Median household income: $33,555 (2000); Poverty rate: 12.3% (2000); Bankruptcy rate: 6.10% (2001).
Taxes: Total county taxes per capita: $48 (2000); County property taxes per capita: $42 (2000).
Education: High school graduation rate: 77.0% (2000); College graduation rate: 13.7% (2000).
Housing: Homeownership rate: 74.4% (2000); Median home value: $63,800 (2000); Median rent: $288 per month (2000); Median age of housing: 31 years (2000).
Health: Birth rate: 113.4 per 10,000 population (1998); Age adjusted death rate: 88.8 per 10,000 population (1999); Age adjusted cancer mortality rate: 212.9 deaths per 100,000 population (1999). Number of physicians: 15.5 per 10,000 population (1999); Number of hospital beds: 44.4 per 10,000 population (1999).
Elections: 2000 Presidential election results: 43.5% Gore, 54.4% Bush, 1.4% Nader, 0.5% Buchanan
National and State Parks: Mount Vernon State Game Farm; Rend Lake State Waterfowl Management Area
Additional Information Contacts
Jefferson County Government Offices.................. 618-244-8000
Egyptian Board of Realtors.................. 618-244-3301
Jefferson County Chamber of Commerce.................. 618-242-5725

Jefferson County Communities

BELLE RIVE (village). Covers a land area of 1.026 square miles and a water area of 0 square miles. Located at 38.23° N. Lat.; 88.74° W. Long. Elevation is 478 feet.
Population: 371 (2000); Race: 94.4% White, 0.0% Black, 0.8% Asian, 0.0% American Indian and Alaska Native, 0.5% Hispanic of any race, 4.3% two or more races (2000); Density: 361.5 persons per square mile (2000); Age: 20.7% under 18, 17.8% over 64 (2000); Marriage status: 19.6% never married, 68.5% now married, 7.7% widowed, 4.2% divorced (2000); Foreign born: 1.3% (2000); Ancestry (includes multiple ancestries): 17.3% German, 10.9% Other groups, 10.6% English, 10.4% Irish, 8.0% United States or American (2000).
Economy: In agricultural area: wheat, sorghum, cattle. Manufacturing. Employment by occupation: 3.4% management, 11.7% professional, 12.8% services, 30.7% sales, 1.1% farming, 11.7% construction, 28.5% production (2000).
Income: Per capita income: $15,221 (2000); Median household income: $37,292 (2000); Poverty rate: 13.8% (2000).
Taxes: Total city taxes per capita: $17 (1997); City property taxes per capita: $17 (1997).
Education: High school graduation rate: 78.5% (2000); College graduation rate: 2.8% (2000).
Housing: Homeownership rate: 75.3% (2000); Median home value: $52,100 (2000); Median rent: $281 per month (2000); Median age of housing: 32 years (2000).
Transportation: Commute to work: 92.4% car, 0.0% public transportation, 1.2% walk, 2.3% work from home (2000); Travel time to work: 24.4% less than 15 minutes, 57.1% 15 to 30 minutes, 13.7% 30 to 45 minutes, 1.2% 45 to 60 minutes, 3.6% 60 minutes or more (2000)

BLUFORD (village). Covers a land area of 1.456 square miles and a water area of 0.008 square miles. Located at 38.32° N. Lat.; 88.73° W. Long. Elevation is 520 feet.
Population: 785 (2000); Race: 98.7% White, 1.2% Black, 0.0% Asian, 0.0% American Indian and Alaska Native, 0.0% Hispanic of any race, 0.1% two or more races (2000); Density: 539.1 persons per square mile (2000); Age: 29.2% under 18, 14.4% over 64 (2000); Marriage status: 21.4% never married, 64.6% now married, 4.4% widowed, 9.5% divorced (2000); Foreign born: 0.3% (2000); Ancestry (includes multiple ancestries): 12.3% Irish, 11.8% German, 9.9% United States or American, 9.3% English, 8.3% Other groups (2000).
Economy: In agricultural area. Single-family building permits issued: 0 (2001) / 0 (2000); Multi-family building permits issued: 0 (2001) / 0 (2000); Employment by occupation: 7.4% management, 5.0% professional, 18.9% services, 28.2% sales, 0.0% farming, 10.5% construction, 30.0% production (2000).
Income: Per capita income: $15,537 (2000); Median household income: $38,250 (2000); Poverty rate: 7.9% (2000).
Taxes: Total city taxes per capita: $16 (1997); City property taxes per capita: $12 (1997).
Education: High school graduation rate: 78.8% (2000); College graduation rate: 5.2% (2000).

School District(s)
Bluford C C School District 114 (PK-08)
2000 Enrollment: 350 618-732-8242
Farrington C C School District 99 (KG-08)
2000 Enrollment: 71 618-755-4414
Webber Township H S District 204 (09-12)
2000 Enrollment: 184 618-732-6121

Housing: Homeownership rate: 84.7% (2000); Median home value: $49,400 (2000); Median rent: $320 per month (2000); Median age of housing: 30 years (2000).
Transportation: Commute to work: 96.5% car, 1.3% public transportation, 0.0% walk, 0.0% work from home (2000); Travel time to work: 11.6% less than 15 minutes, 57.9% 15 to 30 minutes, 18.2% 30 to 45 minutes, 9.4% 45 to 60 minutes, 2.8% 60 minutes or more (2000)

BONNIE (village). Covers a land area of 1.233 square miles and a water area of <.001 square miles. Located at 38.20° N. Lat.; 88.90° W. Long. Elevation is 432 feet.
Population: 424 (2000); Race: 94.6% White, 2.3% Black, 0.0% Asian, 3.1% American Indian and Alaska Native, 1.6% Hispanic of any race, 0.0% two or more races (2000); Density: 343.8 persons per square mile (2000); Age: 20.9% under 18, 16.0% over 64 (2000); Marriage status: 19.5% never married, 59.3% now married, 10.9% widowed, 10.3% divorced (2000); Foreign born: 0.9% (2000); Ancestry (includes multiple ancestries): 20.7% German, 18.1% Other groups, 13.8% United States or American, 13.4% Irish, 10.6% English (2000).
Economy: In agricultural area: wheat, corn, soybeans; cattle. Employment by occupation: 7.4% management, 18.3% professional, 18.3% services, 23.8% sales, 0.0% farming, 11.9% construction, 20.3% production (2000).
Income: Per capita income: $13,998 (2000); Median household income: $27,768 (2000); Poverty rate: 9.7% (2000).
Taxes: Total city taxes per capita: $17 (1997); City property taxes per capita: $17 (1997).
Education: High school graduation rate: 73.6% (2000); College graduation rate: 5.1% (2000).
Housing: Homeownership rate: 80.6% (2000); Median home value: $43,500 (2000); Median rent: $244 per month (2000); Median age of housing: 28 years (2000).
Transportation: Commute to work: 99.0% car, 0.0% public transportation, 0.0% walk, 0.0% work from home (2000); Travel time to work: 27.8% less

than 15 minutes, 50.0% 15 to 30 minutes, 10.6% 30 to 45 minutes, 4.0% 45 to 60 minutes, 7.6% 60 minutes or more (2000)

DIX (village). Aka Rome. Covers a land area of 2.094 square miles and a water area of 0.009 square miles. Located at 38.44° N. Lat.; 88.94° W. Long. Elevation is 580 feet.
Population: 494 (2000); Race: 98.6% White, 0.4% Black, 0.0% Asian, 0.0% American Indian and Alaska Native, 0.6% Hispanic of any race, 0.4% two or more races (2000); Density: 235.9 persons per square mile (2000); Age: 20.5% under 18, 33.1% over 64 (2000); Marriage status: 13.9% never married, 45.5% now married, 18.7% widowed, 22.0% divorced (2000); Foreign born: 0.2% (2000); Ancestry (includes multiple ancestries): 23.3% German, 19.9% United States or American, 16.3% English, 11.4% Irish, 3.2% Other groups (2000).
Economy: Wheat, sorghum; cattle; lumber; oil and coal-producing region. Employment by occupation: 11.2% management, 12.2% professional, 22.8% services, 23.4% sales, 3.0% farming, 9.6% construction, 17.8% production (2000).
Income: Per capita income: $12,463 (2000); Median household income: $12,222 (2000); Poverty rate: 22.0% (2000).
Education: High school graduation rate: 71.0% (2000); College graduation rate: 8.6% (2000).

School District(s)

Rome Community Cons School District 2 (KG-08)
2000 Enrollment: 334 618-266-7214
Housing: Homeownership rate: 38.6% (2000); Median home value: $63,900 (2000); Median rent: $144 per month (2000); Median age of housing: 20 years (2000).
Transportation: Commute to work: 85.6% car, 3.6% public transportation, 7.2% walk, 3.6% work from home (2000); Travel time to work: 27.1% less than 15 minutes, 62.8% 15 to 30 minutes, 2.1% 30 to 45 minutes, 1.6% 45 to 60 minutes, 6.4% 60 minutes or more (2000)

INA (village). Covers a land area of 2.405 square miles and a water area of 0 square miles. Located at 38.15° N. Lat.; 88.90° W. Long. Elevation is 430 feet.
Population: 2,455 (2000); Race: 55.4% White, 41.8% Black, 0.0% Asian, 0.4% American Indian and Alaska Native, 6.2% Hispanic of any race, 0.4% two or more races (2000); Density: 1,020.6 persons per square mile (2000); Age: 5.4% under 18, 4.4% over 64 (2000); Marriage status: 4.2% never married, 74.0% now married, 3.3% widowed, 18.6% divorced (2000); Foreign born: 1.8% (2000); Ancestry (includes multiple ancestries): 3.6% German, 2.6% Irish, 2.3% United States or American, 1.6% English, 1.6% Other groups (2000).
Economy: Agriculture. Big Muddy River Correctional Center nearby. Single-family building permits issued: 5 (2001) / 0 (2000); Multi-family building permits issued: 0 (2001) / 0 (2000); Employment by occupation: 8.3% management, 7.8% professional, 22.5% services, 25.5% sales, 0.0% farming, 10.8% construction, 25.0% production (2000).
Income: Per capita income: $8,596 (2000); Median household income: $24,453 (2000); Poverty rate: 19.2% (2000).
Education: High school graduation rate: 33.3% (2000); College graduation rate: 1.4% (2000).

School District(s)

Ina Community Cons School District 8 (PK-08)
2000 Enrollment: 147 618-437-5361

Two-year College(s)

Rend Lake College (Public)
2001 Enrollment: 2,950 618-437-5321
2001 Tuition: In-state $2,240; Out-of-state $4,800
Housing: Homeownership rate: 70.7% (2000); Median home value: $41,400 (2000); Median rent: $188 per month (2000); Median age of housing: 38 years (2000).
Transportation: Commute to work: 93.5% car, 0.0% public transportation, 3.0% walk, 3.0% work from home (2000); Travel time to work: 31.3% less than 15 minutes, 48.2% 15 to 30 minutes, 9.7% 30 to 45 minutes, 2.1% 45 to 60 minutes, 8.7% 60 minutes or more (2000)

MOUNT VERNON (city). Covers a land area of 11.521 square miles and a water area of 0.099 square miles. Located at 38.31° N. Lat.; 88.90° W. Long. Elevation is 510 feet.
History: Mount Vernon was settled by people from the southern states. It grew slowly as the seat of Jefferson County after 1819.
Population: 16,269 (2000); Race: 84.2% White, 12.2% Black, 0.4% Asian, 0.3% American Indian and Alaska Native, 1.4% Hispanic of any race, 2.3% two or more races (2000); Density: 1,412.1 persons per square mile (2000); Age: 24.5% under 18, 19.2% over 64 (2000); Marriage status: 21.9% never married, 53.7% now married, 11.3% widowed, 13.0% divorced (2000); Foreign born: 1.1% (2000); Ancestry (includes multiple ancestries): 16.6% German, 16.3% Other groups, 16.0% United States or American, 10.8% English, 9.1% Irish (2000).
Vital Statistics: Birth rate: 154.9 per 10,000 population (1998)
Economy: Single-family building permits issued: 52 (2001) / 29 (2000); Multi-family building permits issued: 8 (2001) / 58 (2000); Employment by occupation: 9.7% management, 19.7% professional, 18.4% services, 27.9% sales, 0.3% farming, 8.2% construction, 15.7% production (2000).
Income: Per capita income: $16,268 (2000); Median household income: $28,145 (2000); Poverty rate: 17.1% (2000).
Taxes: Total city taxes per capita: $508 (1997); City property taxes per capita: $124 (1997).
Education: High school graduation rate: 77.6% (2000); College graduation rate: 17.1% (2000).

School District(s)

Dodds Community Cons School District 7 (PK-08)
2000 Enrollment: 175 618-244-8070
Hamilton/Jefferson Roe (06-12)
2000 Enrollment: 41 618-244-8040
Mcclellan C C School District 12 (KG-08)
2000 Enrollment: 86 618-244-8072
Mount Vernon School District 80 (PK-08)
2000 Enrollment: 1,944 618-244-8080
Mount Vernon Township H S District 201 (09-12)
2000 Enrollment: 1,488 618-244-3700
Summersville School District 79 (KG-08)
2000 Enrollment: 243 618-244-8079
Housing: Homeownership rate: 60.6% (2000); Median home value: $57,700 (2000); Median rent: $303 per month (2000); Median age of housing: 40 years (2000).
Hospitals: Crossroads Community Hospital (55 beds); Good Samaritan Regional Health Center (175 beds)
Newspapers: Register News (6 x week)
Transportation: Commute to work: 92.1% car, 1.4% public transportation, 2.7% walk, 2.4% work from home (2000); Travel time to work: 60.7% less than 15 minutes, 24.4% 15 to 30 minutes, 8.8% 30 to 45 minutes, 1.7% 45 to 60 minutes, 4.5% 60 minutes or more (2000)
Airports: Mount Vernon
Additional Information Contacts
Egyptian Board of Realtors 618-244-3301
Jefferson County Chamber of Commerce 618-242-5725

NASON (city). Covers a land area of 0.903 square miles and a water area of 0 square miles. Located at 38.17° N. Lat.; 88.96° W. Long. Elevation is 433 feet.
Population: 234 (2000); Race: 100.0% White, 0.0% Black, 0.0% Asian, 0.0% American Indian and Alaska Native, 0.0% Hispanic of any race, 0.0% two or more races (2000); Density: 259.0 persons per square mile (2000); Age: 13.6% under 18, 12.1% over 64 (2000); Marriage status: 20.1% never married, 51.7% now married, 8.6% widowed, 19.5% divorced (2000); Foreign born: 0.0% (2000); Ancestry (includes multiple ancestries): 26.8% Irish, 25.8% German, 9.6% United States or American, 9.6% English, 5.1% Other groups (2000).
Economy: In agricultural area: wheat, sorghum; cattle. Employment by occupation: 3.6% management, 6.3% professional, 27.7% services, 23.2% sales, 0.0% farming, 17.9% construction, 21.4% production (2000).
Income: Per capita income: $15,866 (2000); Median household income: $33,125 (2000); Poverty rate: 4.6% (2000).
Taxes: Total city taxes per capita: $20 (1997); City property taxes per capita: $8 (1997).
Education: High school graduation rate: 77.6% (2000); College graduation rate: 6.4% (2000).
Housing: Homeownership rate: 90.8% (2000); Median home value: $36,700 (2000); Median rent: $200 per month (2000); Median age of housing: 39 years (2000).
Transportation: Commute to work: 100.0% car, 0.0% public transportation, 0.0% walk, 0.0% work from home (2000); Travel time to work: 11.8% less than 15 minutes, 54.5% 15 to 30 minutes, 10.9% 30 to 45 minutes, 12.7% 45 to 60 minutes, 10.0% 60 minutes or more (2000)

OPDYKE (unincorporated postal area, zip code 62872). Covers a land area of 27.292 square miles and a water area of 0.033 square miles. Located at 38.28° N. Lat.; 88.79° W. Long. Elevation is 515 feet.

Population: 1,327 (2000); Race: 98.9% White, 0.2% Black, 0.1% Asian, 0.0% American Indian and Alaska Native, 3.3% Hispanic of any race, 0.4% two or more races (2000); Density: 48.6 persons per square mile (2000); Age: 33.5% under 18, 8.7% over 64 (2000); Marriage status: 18.3% never married, 69.1% now married, 5.1% widowed, 7.5% divorced (2000); Foreign born: 0.3% (2000); Ancestry (includes multiple ancestries): 20.9% German, 15.4% United States or American, 10.4% Irish, 8.3% English, 7.6% Other groups (2000).
Economy: Employment by occupation: 10.8% management, 11.5% professional, 16.7% services, 22.3% sales, 0.7% farming, 12.5% construction, 25.6% production (2000).
Income: Per capita income: $14,881 (2000); Median household income: $38,854 (2000); Poverty rate: 12.7% (2000).
Education: High school graduation rate: 76.8% (2000); College graduation rate: 8.0% (2000).

School District(s)

Opdyke-Belle-Rive Cc School District 5 (KG-08)
2000 Enrollment: 200 618-756-2492

Housing: Homeownership rate: 92.0% (2000); Median home value: $68,700 (2000); Median rent: $241 per month (2000); Median age of housing: 25 years (2000).
Transportation: Commute to work: 93.1% car, 0.7% public transportation, 2.0% walk, 2.9% work from home (2000); Travel time to work: 23.6% less than 15 minutes, 57.8% 15 to 30 minutes, 10.8% 30 to 45 minutes, 3.0% 45 to 60 minutes, 4.9% 60 minutes or more (2000)

SCHELLER (unincorporated postal area, zip code 62883). Covers a land area of 38.171 square miles and a water area of 0.082 square miles. Located at 38.16° N. Lat.; 89.11° W. Long. Elevation is 519 feet.
Population: 607 (2000); Race: 100.0% White, 0.0% Black, 0.0% Asian, 0.0% American Indian and Alaska Native, 0.5% Hispanic of any race, 0.0% two or more races (2000); Density: 15.9 persons per square mile (2000); Age: 17.0% under 18, 20.5% over 64 (2000); Marriage status: 21.2% never married, 61.6% now married, 8.9% widowed, 8.3% divorced (2000); Foreign born: 0.0% (2000); Ancestry (includes multiple ancestries): 43.0% Polish, 24.3% German, 9.6% Irish, 8.9% United States or American, 8.4% English (2000).
Economy: Employment by occupation: 11.5% management, 17.5% professional, 10.5% services, 15.4% sales, 2.1% farming, 10.8% construction, 32.2% production (2000).
Income: Per capita income: $21,207 (2000); Median household income: $43,021 (2000); Poverty rate: 1.4% (2000).
Education: High school graduation rate: 80.9% (2000); College graduation rate: 5.9% (2000).
Housing: Homeownership rate: 86.0% (2000); Median home value: $68,700 (2000); Median rent: $186 per month (2000); Median age of housing: 28 years (2000).
Transportation: Commute to work: 88.8% car, 0.0% public transportation, 4.0% walk, 5.8% work from home (2000); Travel time to work: 27.5% less than 15 minutes, 24.8% 15 to 30 minutes, 28.6% 30 to 45 minutes, 14.5% 45 to 60 minutes, 4.6% 60 minutes or more (2000)

TEXICO (unincorporated postal area, zip code 62889). Covers a land area of 34.835 square miles and a water area of 0.062 square miles. Located at 38.45° N. Lat.; 88.82° W. Long. Elevation is 510 feet.
Population: 943 (2000); Race: 97.1% White, 1.8% Black, 0.0% Asian, 0.0% American Indian and Alaska Native, 0.0% Hispanic of any race, 1.1% two or more races (2000); Density: 27.1 persons per square mile (2000); Age: 25.9% under 18, 13.4% over 64 (2000); Marriage status: 19.6% never married, 66.4% now married, 6.4% widowed, 7.7% divorced (2000); Foreign born: 0.4% (2000); Ancestry (includes multiple ancestries): 20.4% United States or American, 16.9% English, 12.3% Other groups, 10.7% German, 8.6% Irish (2000).
Economy: Employment by occupation: 8.9% management, 10.2% professional, 14.9% services, 23.1% sales, 0.0% farming, 12.2% construction, 30.7% production (2000).
Income: Per capita income: $17,291 (2000); Median household income: $38,452 (2000); Poverty rate: 16.0% (2000).
Education: High school graduation rate: 83.3% (2000); College graduation rate: 8.1% (2000).

School District(s)

Field Community Cons School District 3 (PK-08)
2000 Enrollment: 313 618-755-4611

Housing: Homeownership rate: 89.7% (2000); Median home value: $43,200 (2000); Median rent: $341 per month (2000); Median age of housing: 28 years (2000).
Transportation: Commute to work: 94.4% car, 1.8% public transportation, 0.4% walk, 2.0% work from home (2000); Travel time to work: 9.1% less than 15 minutes, 58.1% 15 to 30 minutes, 15.9% 30 to 45 minutes, 4.6% 45 to 60 minutes, 12.3% 60 minutes or more (2000)

WALTONVILLE (village). Covers a land area of 0.958 square miles and a water area of 0.026 square miles. Located at 38.21° N. Lat.; 89.04° W. Long. Elevation is 460 feet.
Population: 422 (2000); Race: 98.5% White, 0.0% Black, 0.7% Asian, 0.0% American Indian and Alaska Native, 2.4% Hispanic of any race, 0.7% two or more races (2000); Density: 440.6 persons per square mile (2000); Age: 27.4% under 18, 20.3% over 64 (2000); Marriage status: 6.9% never married, 75.3% now married, 7.2% widowed, 10.5% divorced (2000); Foreign born: 0.7% (2000); Ancestry (includes multiple ancestries): 17.1% German, 15.4% Irish, 12.7% United States or American, 8.3% English, 6.6% Other groups (2000).
Economy: In agricultural area. Employment by occupation: 12.2% management, 16.0% professional, 4.6% services, 22.9% sales, 0.0% farming, 14.5% construction, 29.8% production (2000).
Income: Per capita income: $12,233 (2000); Median household income: $24,318 (2000); Poverty rate: 16.6% (2000).
Taxes: Total city taxes per capita: $12 (1997); City property taxes per capita: $12 (1997).
Education: High school graduation rate: 72.3% (2000); College graduation rate: 6.7% (2000).

School District(s)

Waltonville C U School District 1 (PK-12)
2000 Enrollment: 356 618-279-7211

Housing: Homeownership rate: 73.7% (2000); Median home value: $48,800 (2000); Median rent: $218 per month (2000); Median age of housing: 52 years (2000).
Transportation: Commute to work: 89.9% car, 0.0% public transportation, 6.2% walk, 3.9% work from home (2000); Travel time to work: 25.0% less than 15 minutes, 46.0% 15 to 30 minutes, 16.1% 30 to 45 minutes, 4.8% 45 to 60 minutes, 8.1% 60 minutes or more (2000)

WOODLAWN (village). Covers a land area of 0.714 square miles and a water area of 0 square miles. Located at 38.33° N. Lat.; 89.03° W. Long. Elevation is 495 feet.
Population: 630 (2000); Race: 98.6% White, 0.0% Black, 0.6% Asian, 0.0% American Indian and Alaska Native, 0.0% Hispanic of any race, 0.8% two or more races (2000); Density: 882.3 persons per square mile (2000); Age: 33.7% under 18, 12.7% over 64 (2000); Marriage status: 14.6% never married, 66.9% now married, 8.2% widowed, 10.4% divorced (2000); Foreign born: 0.6% (2000); Ancestry (includes multiple ancestries): 19.4% German, 13.6% United States or American, 9.1% English, 8.3% Polish, 8.0% Irish (2000).
Economy: In agricultural area. Employment by occupation: 8.4% management, 16.8% professional, 14.2% services, 28.1% sales, 0.0% farming, 8.0% construction, 24.5% production (2000).
Income: Per capita income: $16,013 (2000); Median household income: $40,000 (2000); Poverty rate: 11.4% (2000).
Taxes: Total city taxes per capita: $8 (1997); City property taxes per capita: $8 (1997).
Education: High school graduation rate: 90.7% (2000); College graduation rate: 13.9% (2000).

School District(s)

Woodlawn Community Cons School District 4 (KG-08)
2000 Enrollment: 367 618-735-2661
Woodlawn Community H S District 205 (09-12)
2000 Enrollment: 196 618-735-2631

Housing: Homeownership rate: 80.6% (2000); Median home value: $63,900 (2000); Median rent: $148 per month (2000); Median age of housing: 20 years (2000).
Transportation: Commute to work: 93.0% car, 0.0% public transportation, 4.4% walk, 1.8% work from home (2000); Travel time to work: 41.4% less than 15 minutes, 39.5% 15 to 30 minutes, 15.8% 30 to 45 minutes, 1.9% 45 to 60 minutes, 1.5% 60 minutes or more (2000)

Jersey County

Located in western Illinois; bounded on the south by the Mississippi River and the Missouri border, and on the west by the Illinois River. Covers a land area of 369.20 square miles, a water area of 7.90 square miles, and is located in the Central Time Zone. The county government was organized in 1839. County seat is Jerseyville.

Jersey County is part of the St. Louis, MO-IL MSA. The entire metro area includes: Clinton County, IL; Jersey County, IL; Madison County, IL; Monroe County, IL; St. Clair County, IL; Crawford County, MO (pt.)**; Franklin County, MO; Jefferson County, MO; Lincoln County, MO; St. Charles County, MO; St. Louis County, MO; Warren County, MO; St. Louis city, MO

Weather Station: Jerseyville 2 SW Elevation: 629 feet

	Jan	Feb	Mar	Apr	May	Jun	Jul	Aug	Sep	Oct	Nov	Dec
High	35	41	53	65	75	83	88	86	79	68	53	41
Low	17	22	32	42	52	61	65	63	54	43	33	23
Precip	1.9	2.0	3.5	4.3	3.9	3.7	3.4	2.9	3.4	2.9	3.7	2.8
Snow	5.1	3.7	2.8	0.5	0.0	0.0	0.0	0.0	0.0	tr	1.2	3.5

High and Low temperatures in degrees Fahrenheit; Precipitation and Snow in inches

Population: 21,668 (2000); Race: 97.8% White, 0.7% Black, 0.5% Asian, 0.4% American Indian and Alaska Native, 0.4% Hispanic of any race, 0.6% two or more races (2000); Density: 58.7 persons per square mile (2000); Age: 25.5% under 18, 14.4% over 64 (2000).
Religion: Five largest groups: 20.0% Catholic Church, 6.8% American Baptist Churches in the USA, 6.2% Southern Baptist Convention, 4.9% Assemblies of God, 3.6% The United Methodist Church (2000).
Economy: Unemployment rate: 5.9% (11/2002); Total civilian labor force: 10,280 (11/2002); Leading industries: 20.6% retail trade; 17.8% health care and social assistance; 16.3% accommodation & food services (2000); Companies that employ more than 1,000 persons: 0 (2000); Companies that employ more than 100 persons: 4 (2000); Farms: 481 totaling 164,164 acres (1997); Minority business ownership rate: 0.0% (1997); Women business ownership rate: 15.6% (1997); Retail sales per capita: $8,037 (1997). Single-family building permits issued: 101 (2001) / 103 (2000); Multi-family building permits issued: 10 (2001) / 0 (2000).
Income: Per capita income: $19,581 (2000); Median household income: $42,065 (2000); Poverty rate: 7.1% (2000); Bankruptcy rate: 6.01% (2001).
Taxes: Total county taxes per capita: $58 (2000); County property taxes per capita: $53 (2000).
Education: High school graduation rate: 82.5% (2000); College graduation rate: 12.6% (2000).
Housing: Homeownership rate: 77.7% (2000); Median home value: $82,800 (2000); Median rent: $319 per month (2000); Median age of housing: 32 years (2000).
Health: Birth rate: 113.1 per 10,000 population (1998); Age adjusted death rate: 107.4 per 10,000 population (1999); Age adjusted cancer mortality rate: 159.8 deaths per 100,000 population (1999). Air Quality Index: 58% good, 42% moderate, 1% unhealthy (percent of days in 2000). Number of physicians: 7.4 per 10,000 population (1999); Number of hospital beds: 30.9 per 10,000 population (1999).
Elections: 2000 Presidential election results: 46.3% Gore, 49.9% Bush, 2.5% Nader, 1.1% Buchanan
National and State Parks: Pere Marquette State Park; Stump Lake State Fish And Waterfowl Manageme; The Glades State Fish And Waterfowl Manageme
Additional Information Contacts
Jersey County Government Offices 618-498-5571
Jersey County Chamber of Commerce 618-498-5506

Jersey County Communities

DOW (unincorporated postal area, zip code 62022). Covers a land area of 17.512 square miles and a water area of 0.001 square miles. Located at 38.99° N. Lat.; 90.34° W. Long. Elevation is 669 feet.
Population: 962 (2000); Race: 97.8% White, 0.7% Black, 0.5% Asian, 0.0% American Indian and Alaska Native, 0.0% Hispanic of any race, 1.1% two or more races (2000); Density: 54.9 persons per square mile (2000); Age: 16.5% under 18, 14.9% over 64 (2000); Marriage status: 15.9% never married, 68.1% now married, 4.4% widowed, 11.6% divorced (2000); Foreign born: 2.0% (2000); Ancestry (includes multiple ancestries): 32.9% German, 14.1% United States or American, 13.1% Irish, 8.0% English, 5.8% Other groups (2000).
Economy: Employment by occupation: 11.9% management, 22.2% professional, 15.9% services, 23.6% sales, 0.0% farming, 14.5% construction, 11.9% production (2000).
Income: Per capita income: $24,943 (2000); Median household income: $48,750 (2000); Poverty rate: 3.3% (2000).
Education: High school graduation rate: 85.0% (2000); College graduation rate: 11.5% (2000).
Housing: Homeownership rate: 94.0% (2000); Median home value: $81,500 (2000); Median rent: $425 per month (2000); Median age of housing: 33 years (2000).
Transportation: Commute to work: 90.2% car, 1.2% public transportation, 0.0% walk, 8.6% work from home (2000); Travel time to work: 9.4% less than 15 minutes, 37.9% 15 to 30 minutes, 30.3% 30 to 45 minutes, 14.6% 45 to 60 minutes, 7.8% 60 minutes or more (2000)

ELSAH (village). Covers a land area of 1.062 square miles and a water area of 0 square miles. Located at 38.95° N. Lat.; 90.35° W. Long. Elevation is 450 feet.
History: The first settler in Elsah was Addision Greene in 1847, who chopped wood for the steamboats that came along the Mississippi River. The settlement of Jersey Landing developed and was purchased in 1853 by General James Semple, who changed its name to Elsah and built a distillery and two grist mills.
Population: 635 (2000); Race: 86.6% White, 7.5% Black, 2.2% Asian, 1.0% American Indian and Alaska Native, 2.6% Hispanic of any race, 1.1% two or more races (2000); Density: 598.1 persons per square mile (2000); Age: 5.4% under 18, 4.5% over 64 (2000); Marriage status: 62.2% never married, 34.3% now married, 2.5% widowed, 1.0% divorced (2000); Foreign born: 13.3% (2000); Ancestry (includes multiple ancestries): 31.2% German, 19.7% English, 13.0% Other groups, 9.3% Scottish, 7.0% Irish (2000).
Economy: Single-family building permits issued: 0 (2001) / 1 (2000); Multi-family building permits issued: 0 (2001) / 0 (2000); Employment by occupation: 9.3% management, 24.0% professional, 16.9% services, 43.3% sales, 0.0% farming, 2.0% construction, 4.6% production (2000).
Income: Per capita income: $13,154 (2000); Median household income: $57,083 (2000); Poverty rate: 0.0% (2000).
Taxes: Total city taxes per capita: $23 (1997); City property taxes per capita: $13 (1997).
Education: High school graduation rate: 98.3% (2000); College graduation rate: 66.4% (2000).

Four-year College(s)

Principia College (Private, Not-for-profit)
2001 Enrollment: 554 618-374-2131
2001 Tuition: In-state $16,570; Out-of-state $16,570
Housing: Homeownership rate: 61.6% (2000); Median home value: $129,700 (2000); Median rent: $380 per month (2000); Median age of housing: 60+ years (2000).
Transportation: Commute to work: 15.9% car, 0.5% public transportation, 71.6% walk, 3.7% work from home (2000); Travel time to work: 87.3% less than 15 minutes, 2.0% 15 to 30 minutes, 2.0% 30 to 45 minutes, 4.8% 45 to 60 minutes, 3.8% 60 minutes or more (2000)

FIDELITY (village). Covers a land area of 0.112 square miles and a water area of 0 square miles. Located at 39.15° N. Lat.; 90.16° W. Long. Elevation is 630 feet.
Population: 105 (2000); Race: 100.0% White, 0.0% Black, 0.0% Asian, 0.0% American Indian and Alaska Native, 0.0% Hispanic of any race, 0.0% two or more races (2000); Density: 941.2 persons per square mile (2000); Age: 31.1% under 18, 14.6% over 64 (2000); Marriage status: 15.2% never married, 65.8% now married, 6.3% widowed, 12.7% divorced (2000); Foreign born: 0.0% (2000); Ancestry (includes multiple ancestries): 35.9% Other groups, 10.7% United States or American, 9.7% German, 6.8% French (except Basque), 5.8% Irish (2000).
Economy: Apples. Employment by occupation: 7.1% management, 0.0% professional, 25.0% services, 17.9% sales, 0.0% farming, 28.6% construction, 21.4% production (2000).
Income: Per capita income: $7,798 (2000); Median household income: $17,500 (2000); Poverty rate: 28.2% (2000).
Taxes: Total city taxes per capita: $7 (1997); City property taxes per capita: $7 (1997).
Education: High school graduation rate: 70.6% (2000); College graduation rate: 4.4% (2000).
Housing: Homeownership rate: 61.0% (2000); Median home value: $14,500 (2000); Median rent: $283 per month (2000); Median age of housing: 40 years (2000).
Transportation: Commute to work: 100.0% car, 0.0% public transportation, 0.0% walk, 0.0% work from home (2000); Travel time to work: 15.4% less than 15 minutes, 26.9% 15 to 30 minutes, 30.8% 30 to 45 minutes, 0.0% 45 to 60 minutes, 26.9% 60 minutes or more (2000)

FIELDON (village). Covers a land area of 0.199 square miles and a water area of 0 square miles. Located at 39.10° N. Lat.; 90.50° W. Long. Elevation is 700 feet.
Population: 271 (2000); Race: 100.0% White, 0.0% Black, 0.0% Asian, 0.0% American Indian and Alaska Native, 0.0% Hispanic of any race, 0.0% two or more races (2000); Density: 1,362.1 persons per square mile (2000); Age: 27.4% under 18, 12.4% over 64 (2000); Marriage status: 18.8% never married, 70.8% now married, 5.4% widowed, 5.0% divorced (2000); Foreign born: 0.0% (2000); Ancestry (includes multiple ancestries): 41.7% German, 9.3% Irish, 6.2% Dutch, 3.5% United States or American, 2.7% French (except Basque) (2000).
Economy: In apple-growing area. Employment by occupation: 4.8% management, 14.4% professional, 22.1% services, 13.5% sales, 1.0% farming, 15.4% construction, 28.8% production (2000).
Income: Per capita income: $14,811 (2000); Median household income: $38,393 (2000); Poverty rate: 0.8% (2000).
Taxes: Total city taxes per capita: $38 (1997); City property taxes per capita: $10 (1997).
Education: High school graduation rate: 78.9% (2000); College graduation rate: 6.4% (2000).
Housing: Homeownership rate: 82.0% (2000); Median home value: $49,700 (2000); Median rent: $363 per month (2000); Median age of housing: 47 years (2000).
Transportation: Commute to work: 94.2% car, 0.0% public transportation, 1.9% walk, 3.9% work from home (2000); Travel time to work: 12.1% less than 15 minutes, 52.5% 15 to 30 minutes, 11.1% 30 to 45 minutes, 11.1% 45 to 60 minutes, 13.1% 60 minutes or more (2000)

GRAFTON (city). Covers a land area of 4.056 square miles and a water area of 0 square miles. Located at 38.97° N. Lat.; 90.43° W. Long. Elevation is 435 feet.
History: City suffered greatly during a devastating flood (1993). Incorporated 1837.
Population: 609 (2000); Race: 99.2% White, 0.2% Black, 0.0% Asian, 0.0% American Indian and Alaska Native, 0.0% Hispanic of any race, 0.7% two or more races (2000); Density: 150.2 persons per square mile (2000); Age: 20.0% under 18, 18.4% over 64 (2000); Marriage status: 21.3% never married, 53.6% now married, 9.3% widowed, 15.9% divorced (2000); Foreign born: 1.1% (2000); Ancestry (includes multiple ancestries): 25.2% German, 17.9% English, 13.2% Irish, 12.2% United States or American, 5.4% Other groups (2000).
Economy: In agricultural area. Single-family building permits issued: 6 (2001) / 5 (2000); Multi-family building permits issued: 0 (2001) / 0 (2000); Employment by occupation: 15.8% management, 8.8% professional, 24.2% services, 16.9% sales, 0.8% farming, 9.2% construction, 24.2% production (2000).
Income: Per capita income: $21,989 (2000); Median household income: $34,706 (2000); Poverty rate: 14.0% (2000).
Taxes: Total city taxes per capita: $136 (1997); City property taxes per capita: $38 (1997).
Education: High school graduation rate: 79.4% (2000); College graduation rate: 11.8% (2000).
Housing: Homeownership rate: 63.5% (2000); Median home value: $88,300 (2000); Median rent: $282 per month (2000); Median age of housing: 32 years (2000).
Transportation: Commute to work: 93.1% car, 0.8% public transportation, 6.2% walk, 0.0% work from home (2000); Travel time to work: 36.2% less than 15 minutes, 17.7% 15 to 30 minutes, 20.4% 30 to 45 minutes, 12.7% 45 to 60 minutes, 13.1% 60 minutes or more (2000)

JERSEYVILLE (city). Covers a land area of 4.392 square miles and a water area of 0 square miles. Located at 39.12° N. Lat.; 90.32° W. Long. Elevation is 663 feet.
History: Plotted 1834, incorporated 1855.
Population: 7,984 (2000); Race: 99.1% White, 0.3% Black, 0.1% Asian, 0.1% American Indian and Alaska Native, 0.1% Hispanic of any race, 0.5% two or more races (2000); Density: 1,817.9 persons per square mile (2000); Age: 23.7% under 18, 21.8% over 64 (2000); Marriage status: 19.9% never married, 55.6% now married, 11.4% widowed, 13.0% divorced (2000); Foreign born: 0.2% (2000); Ancestry (includes multiple ancestries): 32.6% German, 12.2% Irish, 11.9% English, 11.1% United States or American, 6.0% Other groups (2000).
Economy: Trade and shipping center in agricultural area: apples, corn, wheat; livestock. Single-family building permits issued: 20 (2001) / 25 (2000); Multi-family building permits issued: 10 (2001) / 0 (2000); Employment by occupation: 9.3% management, 18.2% professional, 18.1% services, 27.3% sales, 0.0% farming, 11.7% construction, 15.3% production (2000).
Income: Per capita income: $20,178 (2000); Median household income: $35,556 (2000); Poverty rate: 7.3% (2000).
Taxes: Total city taxes per capita: $134 (1997); City property taxes per capita: $62 (1997).
Education: High school graduation rate: 76.5% (2000); College graduation rate: 11.0% (2000).

School District(s)

Jersey C U School District 100 (PK-12)
2000 Enrollment: 3,129 618-498-5561
Housing: Homeownership rate: 66.1% (2000); Median home value: $74,700 (2000); Median rent: $309 per month (2000); Median age of housing: 42 years (2000).
Hospitals: Jersey Community Hospital (67 beds)
Newspapers: Jersey County Star (1 x week); Quad County Edition of the Telegraph (2 x week)
Transportation: Commute to work: 93.6% car, 0.3% public transportation, 2.1% walk, 2.9% work from home (2000); Travel time to work: 46.1% less than 15 minutes, 15.6% 15 to 30 minutes, 18.5% 30 to 45 minutes, 8.3% 45 to 60 minutes, 11.4% 60 minutes or more (2000)
Additional Information Contacts
Jersey County Chamber of Commerce. 618-498-5506

OTTERVILLE (town). Covers a land area of 1.002 square miles and a water area of 0 square miles. Located at 39.05° N. Lat.; 90.39° W. Long. Elevation is 610 feet.
Population: 120 (2000); Race: 97.9% White, 0.0% Black, 0.0% Asian, 2.1% American Indian and Alaska Native, 1.4% Hispanic of any race, 0.0% two or more races (2000); Density: 119.8 persons per square mile (2000); Age: 43.1% under 18, 6.9% over 64 (2000); Marriage status: 28.6% never married, 59.2% now married, 2.0% widowed, 10.2% divorced (2000); Foreign born: 0.0% (2000); Ancestry (includes multiple ancestries): 50.7% German, 27.8% Other groups, 25.7% Irish, 13.2% United States or American, 4.2% Scottish (2000).
Economy: In apple-growing area. Employment by occupation: 5.6% management, 5.6% professional, 11.1% services, 42.6% sales, 0.0% farming, 7.4% construction, 27.8% production (2000).
Income: Per capita income: $10,588 (2000); Median household income: $34,063 (2000); Poverty rate: 14.6% (2000).
Taxes: Total city taxes per capita: $16 (1997); City property taxes per capita: $16 (1997).
Education: High school graduation rate: 70.7% (2000); College graduation rate: 1.3% (2000).
Housing: Homeownership rate: 90.7% (2000); Median home value: $55,000 (2000); Median rent: $175 per month (2000); Median age of housing: 35 years (2000).
Transportation: Commute to work: 82.7% car, 0.0% public transportation, 9.6% walk, 7.7% work from home (2000); Travel time to work: 18.8% less than 15 minutes, 41.7% 15 to 30 minutes, 14.6% 30 to 45 minutes, 8.3% 45 to 60 minutes, 16.7% 60 minutes or more (2000)

Jo Daviess County

Located in northwestern Illinois; bounded on the north by Wisconsin, and on the west by the Mississippi River and the Iowa border; drained by the Apple, Plum, and Galena Rivers; includes Charles Mound, highest point in the state (1,241 ft). Covers a land area of 601.10 square miles, a water area of 17.60 square miles, and is located in the Central Time Zone. The county government was organized in 1827. County seat is Galena.

Weather Station: Stockton 3 NNE — Elevation: 967 feet

	Jan	Feb	Mar	Apr	May	Jun	Jul	Aug	Sep	Oct	Nov	Dec
High	26	31	43	58	70	79	82	80	72	61	44	31
Low	9	15	25	37	48	57	62	59	51	40	28	16
Precip	1.2	1.3	2.4	3.5	3.8	4.6	3.2	4.3	3.9	2.8	2.7	1.6
Snow	8.8	6.5	4.8	2.0	tr	0.0	0.0	0.0	0.0	0.3	2.6	7.4

High and Low temperatures in degrees Fahrenheit; Precipitation and Snow in inches

Population: 22,289 (2000); Race: 98.7% White, 0.1% Black, 0.1% Asian, 0.2% American Indian and Alaska Native, 1.1% Hispanic of any race, 0.7% two or more races (2000); Density: 37.1 persons per square mile (2000); Age: 23.1% under 18, 17.9% over 64 (2000).
Religion: Five largest groups: 50.0% Catholic Church, 10.5% The United Methodist Church, 10.5% Evangelical Lutheran Church in America, 2.7%

Presbyterian Church (U.S.A.), 1.3% Lutheran Church—Missouri Synod (2000).
Economy: Unemployment rate: 4.0% (11/2002); Total civilian labor force: 12,484 (11/2002); Leading industries: 25.0% accommodation & food services; 21.4% manufacturing; 11.5% retail trade (2000); Companies that employ more than 1,000 persons: 0 (2000); Companies that employ more than 100 persons: 12 (2000); Farms: 941 totaling 275,750 acres (1997); Minority business ownership rate: 0.0% (1997); Women business ownership rate: 23.4% (1997); Retail sales per capita: $6,931 (1997). Single-family building permits issued: 137 (2001) / 134 (2000); Multi-family building permits issued: 0 (2001) / 0 (2000).
Income: Per capita income: $21,497 (2000); Median household income: $40,411 (2000); Poverty rate: 6.7% (2000); Bankruptcy rate: 3.27% (2001).
Taxes: Total county taxes per capita: $137 (1997); County property taxes per capita: $78 (1997).
Education: High school graduation rate: 83.6% (2000); College graduation rate: 15.2% (2000).
Housing: Homeownership rate: 77.3% (2000); Median home value: $89,100 (2000); Median rent: $307 per month (2000); Median age of housing: 34 years (2000).
Health: Birth rate: 104.5 per 10,000 population (1998); Age adjusted death rate: 74.8 per 10,000 population (1999); Age adjusted cancer mortality rate: 210.2 deaths per 100,000 population (1999). Number of physicians: 5.8 per 10,000 population (1999); Number of hospital beds: 36.8 per 10,000 population (1999).
Elections: 2000 Presidential election results: 44.4% Gore, 51.4% Bush, 3.0% Nader, 0.9% Buchanan
National and State Parks: Apple River Canyon State Park
Additional Information Contacts
Jo Daviess County Government Offices 815-777-0161
Jo Daviess County Convention & Visitors Bureau 815-777-3557

Jo Daviess County Communities

APPLE RIVER (village). Covers a land area of 0.790 square miles and a water area of 0 square miles. Located at 42.50° N. Lat.; 90.09° W. Long. Elevation is 995 feet.
Population: 379 (2000); Race: 98.3% White, 0.7% Black, 0.0% Asian, 0.0% American Indian and Alaska Native, 0.0% Hispanic of any race, 1.0% two or more races (2000); Density: 479.6 persons per square mile (2000); Age: 30.6% under 18, 14.9% over 64 (2000); Marriage status: 24.2% never married, 53.7% now married, 10.4% widowed, 11.7% divorced (2000); Foreign born: 0.0% (2000); Ancestry (includes multiple ancestries): 38.8% German, 11.4% Irish, 9.7% English, 8.2% Belgian, 7.7% United States or American (2000).
Economy: In agricultural area. Employment by occupation: 6.6% management, 8.1% professional, 16.2% services, 20.7% sales, 4.5% farming, 16.7% construction, 27.3% production (2000).
Income: Per capita income: $18,267 (2000); Median household income: $40,250 (2000); Poverty rate: 10.2% (2000).
Taxes: Total city taxes per capita: $57 (1997); City property taxes per capita: $51 (1997).
Education: High school graduation rate: 74.6% (2000); College graduation rate: 5.9% (2000).
Housing: Homeownership rate: 72.0% (2000); Median home value: $51,300 (2000); Median rent: $275 per month (2000); Median age of housing: 60+ years (2000).
Transportation: Commute to work: 86.4% car, 0.0% public transportation, 9.1% walk, 4.5% work from home (2000); Travel time to work: 35.4% less than 15 minutes, 22.8% 15 to 30 minutes, 13.8% 30 to 45 minutes, 9.5% 45 to 60 minutes, 18.5% 60 minutes or more (2000)

EAST DUBUQUE (city). Covers a land area of 2.062 square miles and a water area of 0.081 square miles. Located at 42.49° N. Lat.; 90.64° W. Long. Elevation is 610 feet.
History: Incorporated 1857.
Population: 1,995 (2000); Race: 99.5% White, 0.0% Black, 0.2% Asian, 0.0% American Indian and Alaska Native, 0.5% Hispanic of any race, 0.0% two or more races (2000); Density: 967.4 persons per square mile (2000); Age: 21.0% under 18, 17.4% over 64 (2000); Marriage status: 23.0% never married, 55.6% now married, 8.6% widowed, 12.8% divorced (2000); Foreign born: 0.4% (2000); Ancestry (includes multiple ancestries): 51.8% German, 18.7% Irish, 7.7% United States or American, 5.3% English, 5.0% French (except Basque) (2000).
Economy: In agricultural area: cattle, hogs, sheep; dairy products. Manufacturing: iron castings, ammonia solutions. Popular ski resort. A national wildlife refuge is nearby. Single-family building permits issued: 1 (2001) / 0 (2000); Multi-family building permits issued: 0 (2001) / 0 (2000); Employment by occupation: 5.9% management, 12.8% professional, 20.7% services, 27.7% sales, 0.4% farming, 7.9% construction, 24.5% production (2000).
Income: Per capita income: $20,984 (2000); Median household income: $35,099 (2000); Poverty rate: 4.3% (2000).
Taxes: Total city taxes per capita: $282 (1997); City property taxes per capita: $57 (1997).
Education: High school graduation rate: 78.2% (2000); College graduation rate: 8.2% (2000).

School District(s)
East Dubuque Unit School District 119 (PK-12)
2000 Enrollment: 607 815-747-3188
Housing: Homeownership rate: 66.3% (2000); Median home value: $79,500 (2000); Median rent: $328 per month (2000); Median age of housing: 52 years (2000).
Newspapers: East Dubuque Register (1 x week)
Transportation: Commute to work: 94.7% car, 0.6% public transportation, 2.3% walk, 1.9% work from home (2000); Travel time to work: 51.9% less than 15 minutes, 36.6% 15 to 30 minutes, 1.8% 30 to 45 minutes, 2.5% 45 to 60 minutes, 7.2% 60 minutes or more (2000)

ELIZABETH (village). Covers a land area of 0.439 square miles and a water area of 0 square miles. Located at 42.31° N. Lat.; 90.22° W. Long. Elevation is 800 feet.
History: Elizabeth was built on the site of the Apple River Fort, established during the Black Hawk War.
Population: 682 (2000); Race: 99.3% White, 0.0% Black, 0.0% Asian, 0.0% American Indian and Alaska Native, 0.3% Hispanic of any race, 0.7% two or more races (2000); Density: 1,554.8 persons per square mile (2000); Age: 17.3% under 18, 31.4% over 64 (2000); Marriage status: 21.5% never married, 48.8% now married, 17.6% widowed, 12.2% divorced (2000); Foreign born: 2.2% (2000); Ancestry (includes multiple ancestries): 50.1% German, 13.2% Irish, 13.1% English, 2.6% Dutch, 2.0% United States or American (2000).
Economy: Employment by occupation: 6.7% management, 13.7% professional, 22.5% services, 24.6% sales, 0.6% farming, 18.7% construction, 13.2% production (2000).
Income: Per capita income: $17,235 (2000); Median household income: $33,587 (2000); Poverty rate: 8.2% (2000).
Taxes: Total city taxes per capita: $64 (1997); City property taxes per capita: $56 (1997).
Education: High school graduation rate: 78.7% (2000); College graduation rate: 10.3% (2000).

School District(s)
River Ridge C U School District 210 (PK-12)
2000 Enrollment: 533 815-858-2300
Housing: Homeownership rate: 71.1% (2000); Median home value: $71,700 (2000); Median rent: $354 per month (2000); Median age of housing: 60+ years (2000).
Transportation: Commute to work: 83.6% car, 0.0% public transportation, 11.1% walk, 4.7% work from home (2000); Travel time to work: 43.3% less than 15 minutes, 31.0% 15 to 30 minutes, 11.0% 30 to 45 minutes, 9.8% 45 to 60 minutes, 4.9% 60 minutes or more (2000)

GALENA (city). Covers a land area of 3.735 square miles and a water area of <.001 square miles. Located at 42.41° N. Lat.; 90.43° W. Long. Elevation is 700 feet.
History: The lead deposits in the Galena area interested French explorers in the 1700's. The town of Galena was laid out in 1826 and named for the mineral galena, the principal ore of lead. By this time the government was controlling the mineral lands and issuing leases. Smelter operations were responsible for Galena's early growth, and traffic on the old Fever River made it a trading center until the middle of the 1800's, when the lead veins were exhausted and the river silted in. Ulysses S. Grant was a resident of Galena when he was chosen to lead the Federal troops in the Civil War.
Population: 3,460 (2000); Race: 96.5% White, 0.2% Black, 0.2% Asian, 0.6% American Indian and Alaska Native, 3.9% Hispanic of any race, 1.6% two or more races (2000); Density: 926.4 persons per square mile (2000); Age: 20.0% under 18, 23.2% over 64 (2000); Marriage status: 22.8% never married, 54.0% now married, 10.2% widowed, 13.1% divorced (2000); Foreign born: 4.0% (2000); Ancestry (includes multiple ancestries): 40.9%

German, 16.8% Irish, 11.7% English, 8.1% United States or American, 7.4% Other groups (2000).
Economy: Single-family building permits issued: 12 (2001) / 5 (2000); Multi-family building permits issued: 0 (2001) / 0 (2000); Employment by occupation: 13.0% management, 16.1% professional, 27.5% services, 20.3% sales, 1.2% farming, 9.0% construction, 13.1% production (2000).
Income: Per capita income: $19,773 (2000); Median household income: $36,103 (2000); Poverty rate: 9.9% (2000).
Taxes: Total city taxes per capita: $502 (1997); City property taxes per capita: $380 (1997).
Education: High school graduation rate: 78.7% (2000); College graduation rate: 16.8% (2000).

School District(s)

Galena Unit School District 120 (PK-12)
2000 Enrollment: 873 815-777-3086
Housing: Homeownership rate: 65.9% (2000); Median home value: $91,900 (2000); Median rent: $352 per month (2000); Median age of housing: 60+ years (2000).
Newspapers: Galena Gazette (1 x week)
Transportation: Commute to work: 80.2% car, 0.5% public transportation, 12.2% walk, 7.1% work from home (2000); Travel time to work: 54.5% less than 15 minutes, 30.0% 15 to 30 minutes, 10.7% 30 to 45 minutes, 2.0% 45 to 60 minutes, 2.8% 60 minutes or more (2000)
Additional Information Contacts
Jo Daviess County Convention & Visitors Bureau 815-777-3557

HANOVER (village). Covers a land area of 0.592 square miles and a water area of 0 square miles. Located at 42.25° N. Lat.; 90.28° W. Long. Elevation is 630 feet.
History: Hanover's early development depended on mining. When this declined, the town built a dam across the Apple River and established a grist mill. When a woolen mill was added in 1864, the town became a textile center.
Population: 836 (2000); Race: 97.0% White, 0.4% Black, 0.0% Asian, 0.0% American Indian and Alaska Native, 1.5% Hispanic of any race, 2.1% two or more races (2000); Density: 1,411.2 persons per square mile (2000); Age: 19.3% under 18, 24.5% over 64 (2000); Marriage status: 24.3% never married, 45.9% now married, 15.1% widowed, 14.8% divorced (2000); Foreign born: 0.8% (2000); Ancestry (includes multiple ancestries): 40.5% German, 20.1% Irish, 13.7% English, 6.4% French (except Basque), 6.3% Norwegian (2000).
Economy: Employment by occupation: 6.5% management, 11.6% professional, 21.2% services, 23.7% sales, 2.3% farming, 14.1% construction, 20.6% production (2000).
Income: Per capita income: $17,535 (2000); Median household income: $29,236 (2000); Poverty rate: 14.4% (2000).
Taxes: Total city taxes per capita: $47 (1997); City property taxes per capita: $44 (1997).
Education: High school graduation rate: 81.6% (2000); College graduation rate: 9.0% (2000).
Housing: Homeownership rate: 63.2% (2000); Median home value: $56,000 (2000); Median rent: $234 per month (2000); Median age of housing: 58 years (2000).
Transportation: Commute to work: 87.2% car, 0.0% public transportation, 9.0% walk, 2.3% work from home (2000); Travel time to work: 44.2% less than 15 minutes, 28.1% 15 to 30 minutes, 9.0% 30 to 45 minutes, 11.3% 45 to 60 minutes, 7.5% 60 minutes or more (2000)

MENOMINEE (village). Covers a land area of 1.925 square miles and a water area of 0 square miles. Located at 42.47° N. Lat.; 90.54° W. Long. Elevation is 760 feet.
Population: 237 (2000); Race: 99.2% White, 0.8% Black, 0.0% Asian, 0.0% American Indian and Alaska Native, 9.1% Hispanic of any race, 0.0% two or more races (2000); Density: 123.1 persons per square mile (2000); Age: 35.1% under 18, 10.7% over 64 (2000); Marriage status: 33.7% never married, 57.5% now married, 5.5% widowed, 3.3% divorced (2000); Foreign born: 9.1% (2000); Ancestry (includes multiple ancestries): 38.4% German, 17.8% Irish, 10.7% United States or American, 5.8% European, 5.0% Italian (2000).
Economy: Employment by occupation: 6.7% management, 13.3% professional, 22.5% services, 18.3% sales, 1.7% farming, 11.7% construction, 25.8% production (2000).
Income: Per capita income: $14,518 (2000); Median household income: $45,972 (2000); Poverty rate: 18.2% (2000).
Taxes: Total city taxes per capita: $15 (1997); City property taxes per capita: $10 (1997).
Education: High school graduation rate: 71.4% (2000); College graduation rate: 15.0% (2000).
Housing: Homeownership rate: 75.9% (2000); Median home value: $100,000 (2000); Median rent: $263 per month (2000); Median age of housing: 42 years (2000).
Transportation: Commute to work: 98.3% car, 0.0% public transportation, 0.0% walk, 1.7% work from home (2000); Travel time to work: 24.1% less than 15 minutes, 57.8% 15 to 30 minutes, 16.4% 30 to 45 minutes, 1.7% 45 to 60 minutes, 0.0% 60 minutes or more (2000)

NORA (village). Covers a land area of 0.906 square miles and a water area of 0 square miles. Located at 42.45° N. Lat.; 89.94° W. Long. Elevation is 1,010 feet.
Population: 118 (2000); Race: 100.0% White, 0.0% Black, 0.0% Asian, 0.0% American Indian and Alaska Native, 0.0% Hispanic of any race, 0.0% two or more races (2000); Density: 130.2 persons per square mile (2000); Age: 18.0% under 18, 24.0% over 64 (2000); Marriage status: 17.9% never married, 44.0% now married, 11.9% widowed, 26.2% divorced (2000); Foreign born: 0.0% (2000); Ancestry (includes multiple ancestries): 36.0% German, 17.0% United States or American, 14.0% English, 8.0% Dutch, 7.0% French (except Basque) (2000).
Economy: In agricultural area. Employment by occupation: 10.2% management, 4.1% professional, 6.1% services, 6.1% sales, 4.1% farming, 8.2% construction, 61.2% production (2000).
Income: Per capita income: $17,608 (2000); Median household income: $28,125 (2000); Poverty rate: 11.0% (2000).
Taxes: Total city taxes per capita: $42 (1997); City property taxes per capita: $21 (1997).
Education: High school graduation rate: 78.7% (2000); College graduation rate: 2.7% (2000).
Housing: Homeownership rate: 77.8% (2000); Median home value: $53,300 (2000); Median rent: $260 per month (2000); Median age of housing: 28 years (2000).
Transportation: Commute to work: 85.7% car, 0.0% public transportation, 0.0% walk, 12.2% work from home (2000); Travel time to work: 23.3% less than 15 minutes, 39.5% 15 to 30 minutes, 27.9% 30 to 45 minutes, 4.7% 45 to 60 minutes, 4.7% 60 minutes or more (2000)

SCALES MOUND (village). Covers a land area of 0.235 square miles and a water area of 0 square miles. Located at 42.47° N. Lat.; 90.25° W. Long. Elevation is 950 feet.
Population: 401 (2000); Race: 100.0% White, 0.0% Black, 0.0% Asian, 0.0% American Indian and Alaska Native, 0.7% Hispanic of any race, 0.0% two or more races (2000); Density: 1,709.5 persons per square mile (2000); Age: 27.1% under 18, 16.0% over 64 (2000); Marriage status: 28.4% never married, 47.4% now married, 12.2% widowed, 11.9% divorced (2000); Foreign born: 0.4% (2000); Ancestry (includes multiple ancestries): 57.3% German, 18.2% English, 12.7% Irish, 7.6% United States or American, 4.9% Other groups (2000).
Economy: In agricultural area. Employment by occupation: 9.1% management, 14.4% professional, 18.9% services, 15.2% sales, 3.3% farming, 13.2% construction, 25.9% production (2000).
Income: Per capita income: $15,992 (2000); Median household income: $35,294 (2000); Poverty rate: 7.8% (2000).
Taxes: Total city taxes per capita: $44 (1997); City property taxes per capita: $39 (1997).
Education: High school graduation rate: 81.9% (2000); College graduation rate: 8.7% (2000).

School District(s)

Scales Mound C U School Districtict 211 (PK-12)
2000 Enrollment: 273 815-845-2215
Housing: Homeownership rate: 79.3% (2000); Median home value: $76,600 (2000); Median rent: $419 per month (2000); Median age of housing: 60+ years (2000).
Transportation: Commute to work: 81.9% car, 0.8% public transportation, 11.9% walk, 3.3% work from home (2000); Travel time to work: 31.1% less than 15 minutes, 40.0% 15 to 30 minutes, 13.6% 30 to 45 minutes, 10.2% 45 to 60 minutes, 5.1% 60 minutes or more (2000)

STOCKTON (village). Aka Plum River. Covers a land area of 0.852 square miles and a water area of 0 square miles. Located at 42.35° N. Lat.; 90.00° W. Long. Elevation is 1,000 feet.
History: Stockton was named by Alanson Parker, an early settler, who saw the prospects of this becoming a stock raising center, which it did near the end of the 1800's. Before the cattle came, Stockton was the home of lead smelters.

Population: 1,926 (2000); Race: 99.0% White, 0.0% Black, 0.1% Asian, 0.0% American Indian and Alaska Native, 0.4% Hispanic of any race, 0.9% two or more races (2000); Density: 2,260.2 persons per square mile (2000); Age: 24.5% under 18, 21.9% over 64 (2000); Marriage status: 20.6% never married, 56.8% now married, 11.3% widowed, 11.3% divorced (2000); Foreign born: 0.9% (2000); Ancestry (includes multiple ancestries): 47.8% German, 13.7% Irish, 10.5% English, 8.3% United States or American, 4.6% Dutch (2000).
Economy: Single-family building permits issued: 1 (2001) / 1 (2000); Multi-family building permits issued: 0 (2001) / 0 (2000); Employment by occupation: 6.8% management, 10.9% professional, 14.6% services, 22.0% sales, 1.7% farming, 13.7% construction, 30.3% production (2000).
Income: Per capita income: $17,728 (2000); Median household income: $35,921 (2000); Poverty rate: 8.2% (2000).
Taxes: Total city taxes per capita: $94 (1997); City property taxes per capita: $84 (1997).
Education: High school graduation rate: 81.9% (2000); College graduation rate: 9.2% (2000).

School District(s)

Carroll/Jo Daviess/Stephenson Roe (07-12)
2000 Enrollment: 30 815-947-3810
Stockton C U School District 206 (PK-12)
2000 Enrollment: 679 815-947-3391

Housing: Homeownership rate: 74.1% (2000); Median home value: $74,900 (2000); Median rent: $315 per month (2000); Median age of housing: 52 years (2000).
Transportation: Commute to work: 88.3% car, 0.4% public transportation, 7.4% walk, 3.4% work from home (2000); Travel time to work: 54.0% less than 15 minutes, 13.5% 15 to 30 minutes, 21.3% 30 to 45 minutes, 4.3% 45 to 60 minutes, 6.9% 60 minutes or more (2000)

WARREN (village). Covers a land area of 0.964 square miles and a water area of 0 square miles. Located at 42.49° N. Lat.; 89.99° W. Long. Elevation is 1,012 feet.
History: Warren began in 1850 with the name of Courtland, but was renamed in 1853 to honor the son of Alexander Burnett, who had founded the town in 1843. Warren was located at the crossing of the Old Sucker Trail with the Chicago-Galena Stagecoach Road, and later became a station on the railroad line between Galena and Chicago.
Population: 1,496 (2000); Race: 98.8% White, 0.4% Black, 0.0% Asian, 0.7% American Indian and Alaska Native, 0.9% Hispanic of any race, 0.1% two or more races (2000); Density: 1,551.1 persons per square mile (2000); Age: 24.1% under 18, 20.3% over 64 (2000); Marriage status: 23.1% never married, 58.2% now married, 9.3% widowed, 9.4% divorced (2000); Foreign born: 1.4% (2000); Ancestry (includes multiple ancestries): 48.1% German, 13.7% Irish, 13.5% English, 11.4% United States or American, 5.0% Norwegian (2000).
Economy: Single-family building permits issued: 3 (2001) / 4 (2000); Multi-family building permits issued: 0 (2001) / 0 (2000); Employment by occupation: 6.1% management, 12.4% professional, 12.0% services, 21.8% sales, 2.0% farming, 10.3% construction, 35.3% production (2000).
Income: Per capita income: $19,611 (2000); Median household income: $37,083 (2000); Poverty rate: 6.4% (2000).
Taxes: Total city taxes per capita: $133 (1997); City property taxes per capita: $63 (1997).
Education: High school graduation rate: 82.5% (2000); College graduation rate: 10.8% (2000).

School District(s)

Warren Community Unit School District 205 (PK-12)
2000 Enrollment: 564 815-745-2653

Housing: Homeownership rate: 81.5% (2000); Median home value: $72,900 (2000); Median rent: $257 per month (2000); Median age of housing: 60+ years (2000).
Transportation: Commute to work: 89.7% car, 0.3% public transportation, 7.0% walk, 2.6% work from home (2000); Travel time to work: 40.0% less than 15 minutes, 17.6% 15 to 30 minutes, 27.8% 30 to 45 minutes, 8.6% 45 to 60 minutes, 6.0% 60 minutes or more (2000)

Johnson County

Located in southern Illinois, in the Ozarks; drained by the Cache River; includes part of Shawnee National Forest. Covers a land area of 344.60 square miles, a water area of 4.20 square miles, and is located in the Central Time Zone. The county government was organized in 1812. County seat is Vienna.

Population: 12,878 (2000); Race: 84.4% White, 13.9% Black, 0.1% Asian, 0.2% American Indian and Alaska Native, 2.2% Hispanic of any race, 0.7% two or more races (2000); Density: 37.4 persons per square mile (2000); Age: 18.6% under 18, 13.5% over 64 (2000).
Religion: Five largest groups: 21.4% Southern Baptist Convention, 5.2% The United Methodist Church, 1.4% Catholic Church, 1.1% Cumberland Presbyterian Church, 1.0% Churches of Christ (2000).
Economy: Unemployment rate: 5.0% (11/2002); Total civilian labor force: 5,081 (11/2002); Leading industries: 25.2% retail trade; 15.4% accommodation & food services; 10.9% health care and social assistance (2000); Companies that employ more than 1,000 persons: 0 (2000); Companies that employ more than 100 persons: 0 (2000); Farms: 515 totaling 104,321 acres (1997); Minority business ownership rate: 0.0% (1997); Women business ownership rate: 13.0% (1997); Retail sales per capita: $3,251 (1997). Single-family building permits issued: -1 (2001) / -1 (2000); Multi-family building permits issued: -1 (2001) / -1 (2000).
Income: Per capita income: $17,990 (2000); Median household income: $33,326 (2000); Poverty rate: 11.3% (2000); Bankruptcy rate: 4.58% (2001).
Taxes: Total county taxes per capita: $57 (1997); County property taxes per capita: $57 (1997).
Education: High school graduation rate: 67.1% (2000); College graduation rate: 11.7% (2000).
Housing: Homeownership rate: 84.9% (2000); Median home value: $64,700 (2000); Median rent: $241 per month (2000); Median age of housing: 26 years (2000).
Health: Birth rate: 91.6 per 10,000 population (1998); Age adjusted death rate: 72.9 per 10,000 population (1999); Age adjusted cancer mortality rate: 162.0 deaths per 100,000 population (1999). Number of physicians: 2.3 per 10,000 population (1999); Number of hospital beds: n/a (1999).
Elections: 2000 Presidential election results: 36.0% Gore, 61.3% Bush, 1.6% Nader, 1.0% Buchanan
National and State Parks: Cache River State Natural Area; Ferne Clyffe State Park

Additional Information Contacts

Johnson County Government Offices 618-658-3611
Johnson County Chamber of Commerce 618-658-2063

Johnson County Communities

BELKNAP (village). Covers a land area of 1.035 square miles and a water area of 0 square miles. Located at 37.32° N. Lat.; 88.94° W. Long. Elevation is 341 feet.
Population: 133 (2000); Race: 94.2% White, 0.0% Black, 0.0% Asian, 0.0% American Indian and Alaska Native, 0.0% Hispanic of any race, 5.8% two or more races (2000); Density: 128.6 persons per square mile (2000); Age: 27.3% under 18, 18.2% over 64 (2000); Marriage status: 26.3% never married, 56.8% now married, 6.3% widowed, 10.5% divorced (2000); Foreign born: 0.0% (2000); Ancestry (includes multiple ancestries): 26.4% German, 20.7% English, 16.5% United States or American, 14.0% Irish, 10.7% Other groups (2000).
Economy: Employment by occupation: 3.8% management, 11.5% professional, 34.6% services, 38.5% sales, 0.0% farming, 7.7% construction, 3.8% production (2000).
Income: Per capita income: $13,319 (2000); Median household income: $25,625 (2000); Poverty rate: 13.2% (2000).
Taxes: Total city taxes per capita: $8 (1997); City property taxes per capita: $8 (1997).
Education: High school graduation rate: 74.7% (2000); College graduation rate: 3.6% (2000).
Housing: Homeownership rate: 96.2% (2000); Median home value: $22,500 (2000); Median age of housing: 55 years (2000).
Transportation: Commute to work: 100.0% car, 0.0% public transportation, 0.0% walk, 0.0% work from home (2000); Travel time to work: 3.8% less than 15 minutes, 40.4% 15 to 30 minutes, 46.2% 30 to 45 minutes, 3.8% 45 to 60 minutes, 5.8% 60 minutes or more (2000)

BUNCOMBE (village). Covers a land area of 1.209 square miles and a water area of 0 square miles. Located at 37.47° N. Lat.; 88.97° W. Long. Elevation is 510 feet.
Population: 186 (2000); Race: 100.0% White, 0.0% Black, 0.0% Asian, 0.0% American Indian and Alaska Native, 0.5% Hispanic of any race, 0.0% two or more races (2000); Density: 153.9 persons per square mile (2000); Age: 24.1% under 18, 19.2% over 64 (2000); Marriage status: 16.3% never married, 69.3% now married, 5.4% widowed, 9.0% divorced (2000); Foreign born: 0.0% (2000); Ancestry (includes multiple ancestries): 26.1% Other

groups, 17.7% Irish, 12.8% German, 9.4% English, 5.9% United States or American (2000).
Economy: In agricultural area. Employment by occupation: 12.5% management, 5.7% professional, 23.9% services, 27.3% sales, 0.0% farming, 19.3% construction, 11.4% production (2000).
Income: Per capita income: $14,975 (2000); Median household income: $31,500 (2000); Poverty rate: 8.5% (2000).
Taxes: Total city taxes per capita: $9 (1997); City property taxes per capita: $9 (1997).
Education: High school graduation rate: 73.4% (2000); College graduation rate: 6.5% (2000).

School District(s)

Buncombe Cons School District 43 (KG-08)
2000 Enrollment: 55 618-658-8830
Lick Creek C C School Districtict 16 (PK-08)
2000 Enrollment: 138 618-833-2545
Housing: Homeownership rate: 86.6% (2000); Median home value: $39,200 (2000); Median rent: $125 per month (2000); Median age of housing: 51 years (2000).
Transportation: Commute to work: 93.2% car, 0.0% public transportation, 2.3% walk, 1.1% work from home (2000); Travel time to work: 29.9% less than 15 minutes, 23.0% 15 to 30 minutes, 29.9% 30 to 45 minutes, 8.0% 45 to 60 minutes, 9.2% 60 minutes or more (2000)

CYPRESS (village). Aka Whitehill. Covers a land area of 0.747 square miles and a water area of 0 square miles. Located at 37.36° N. Lat.; 89.01° W. Long. Elevation is 432 feet.
Population: 271 (2000); Race: 97.9% White, 0.0% Black, 0.0% Asian, 0.0% American Indian and Alaska Native, 0.0% Hispanic of any race, 2.1% two or more races (2000); Density: 362.7 persons per square mile (2000); Age: 17.6% under 18, 12.6% over 64 (2000); Marriage status: 17.7% never married, 57.6% now married, 7.6% widowed, 17.2% divorced (2000); Foreign born: 0.0% (2000); Ancestry (includes multiple ancestries): 21.4% German, 16.0% English, 15.1% Irish, 13.9% Other groups, 12.6% Dutch (2000).
Economy: In rich agricultural area. Employment by occupation: 6.4% management, 9.1% professional, 20.0% services, 15.5% sales, 0.0% farming, 10.0% construction, 39.1% production (2000).
Income: Per capita income: $13,849 (2000); Median household income: $30,208 (2000); Poverty rate: 7.6% (2000).
Taxes: Total city taxes per capita: $10 (1997); City property taxes per capita: $7 (1997).
Education: High school graduation rate: 83.1% (2000); College graduation rate: 1.9% (2000).

School District(s)

Cypress School District 64 (KG-08)
2000 Enrollment: 104 618-657-2525
Housing: Homeownership rate: 88.8% (2000); Median home value: $25,200 (2000); Median rent: $163 per month (2000); Median age of housing: 50 years (2000).
Transportation: Commute to work: 95.5% car, 2.7% public transportation, 1.8% walk, 0.0% work from home (2000); Travel time to work: 24.5% less than 15 minutes, 31.8% 15 to 30 minutes, 21.8% 30 to 45 minutes, 6.4% 45 to 60 minutes, 15.5% 60 minutes or more (2000)

GOREVILLE (village). Covers a land area of 1.630 square miles and a water area of 0.011 square miles. Located at 37.55° N. Lat.; 88.97° W. Long. Elevation is 770 feet.
Population: 938 (2000); Race: 98.9% White, 0.0% Black, 0.2% Asian, 0.4% American Indian and Alaska Native, 0.0% Hispanic of any race, 0.5% two or more races (2000); Density: 575.3 persons per square mile (2000); Age: 19.9% under 18, 19.9% over 64 (2000); Marriage status: 15.6% never married, 62.8% now married, 10.4% widowed, 11.2% divorced (2000); Foreign born: 0.4% (2000); Ancestry (includes multiple ancestries): 20.5% United States or American, 12.6% English, 12.1% German, 10.9% Irish, 6.8% Other groups (2000).
Economy: In fruitgrowing region. In Shawnee National Forest. Employment by occupation: 8.2% management, 16.7% professional, 23.3% services, 23.3% sales, 1.6% farming, 11.7% construction, 15.2% production (2000).
Income: Per capita income: $16,491 (2000); Median household income: $33,750 (2000); Poverty rate: 12.2% (2000).
Taxes: Total city taxes per capita: $37 (1997); City property taxes per capita: $37 (1997).
Education: High school graduation rate: 80.9% (2000); College graduation rate: 10.5% (2000).

School District(s)

Goreville Community Unit District 1 (PK-12)
2000 Enrollment: 586 618-995-9831
Housing: Homeownership rate: 77.2% (2000); Median home value: $63,600 (2000); Median rent: $250 per month (2000); Median age of housing: 32 years (2000).
Newspapers: Goreville Gazette (1 x week)
Transportation: Commute to work: 94.8% car, 0.0% public transportation, 2.3% walk, 2.9% work from home (2000); Travel time to work: 22.5% less than 15 minutes, 39.6% 15 to 30 minutes, 22.3% 30 to 45 minutes, 6.2% 45 to 60 minutes, 9.4% 60 minutes or more (2000)

GRANTSBURG (unincorporated postal area, zip code 62943). Covers a land area of 32.210 square miles and a water area of 0.135 square miles. Located at 37.34° N. Lat.; 88.73° W. Long. Elevation is 365 feet.
Population: 547 (2000); Race: 98.0% White, 0.0% Black, 0.0% Asian, 0.0% American Indian and Alaska Native, 0.0% Hispanic of any race, 2.0% two or more races (2000); Density: 17.0 persons per square mile (2000); Age: 28.2% under 18, 21.0% over 64 (2000); Marriage status: 9.3% never married, 72.4% now married, 6.3% widowed, 12.0% divorced (2000); Foreign born: 0.9% (2000); Ancestry (includes multiple ancestries): 21.0% Other groups, 19.0% German, 17.3% Irish, 13.1% United States or American, 5.5% Dutch (2000).
Economy: Employment by occupation: 18.3% management, 16.7% professional, 30.4% services, 17.5% sales, 2.1% farming, 7.1% construction, 7.9% production (2000).
Income: Per capita income: $15,316 (2000); Median household income: $29,539 (2000); Poverty rate: 16.0% (2000).
Education: High school graduation rate: 76.2% (2000); College graduation rate: 8.4% (2000).
Housing: Homeownership rate: 91.6% (2000); Median home value: $53,900 (2000); Median rent: $288 per month (2000); Median age of housing: 38 years (2000).
Transportation: Commute to work: 86.1% car, 0.0% public transportation, 0.0% walk, 6.1% work from home (2000); Travel time to work: 22.7% less than 15 minutes, 38.0% 15 to 30 minutes, 15.7% 30 to 45 minutes, 21.4% 45 to 60 minutes, 2.2% 60 minutes or more (2000)

NEW BURNSIDE (village). Covers a land area of 1.055 square miles and a water area of 0 square miles. Located at 37.57° N. Lat.; 88.77° W. Long. Elevation is 550 feet.
History: New Burnside was founded in 1872 and named for Major General Ambrose E. Burnside, president of the Big Four Railroad. Fruit growing was an important industry.
Population: 242 (2000); Race: 100.0% White, 0.0% Black, 0.0% Asian, 0.0% American Indian and Alaska Native, 0.0% Hispanic of any race, 0.0% two or more races (2000); Density: 229.4 persons per square mile (2000); Age: 27.5% under 18, 9.9% over 64 (2000); Marriage status: 17.7% never married, 68.7% now married, 8.6% widowed, 5.1% divorced (2000); Foreign born: 1.9% (2000); Ancestry (includes multiple ancestries): 13.0% United States or American, 5.0% German, 4.6% Other groups, 4.6% Irish, 3.4% Dutch (2000).
Economy: Employment by occupation: 8.6% management, 17.3% professional, 27.2% services, 21.0% sales, 0.0% farming, 2.5% construction, 23.5% production (2000).
Income: Per capita income: $12,709 (2000); Median household income: $31,591 (2000); Poverty rate: 15.4% (2000).
Education: High school graduation rate: 74.8% (2000); College graduation rate: 9.4% (2000).
Housing: Homeownership rate: 86.6% (2000); Median home value: $30,700 (2000); Median rent: $190 per month (2000); Median age of housing: 28 years (2000).
Transportation: Commute to work: 92.3% car, 0.0% public transportation, 1.3% walk, 6.4% work from home (2000); Travel time to work: 15.1% less than 15 minutes, 35.6% 15 to 30 minutes, 35.6% 30 to 45 minutes, 13.7% 45 to 60 minutes, 0.0% 60 minutes or more (2000)

OZARK (unincorporated postal area, zip code 62972). Covers a land area of 19.848 square miles and a water area of 0.112 square miles. Located at 37.54° N. Lat.; 88.74° W. Long. Elevation is 696 feet.
Population: 408 (2000); Race: 98.3% White, 0.0% Black, 0.0% Asian, 0.0% American Indian and Alaska Native, 1.7% Hispanic of any race, 0.0% two or more races (2000); Density: 20.6 persons per square mile (2000); Age: 33.5% under 18, 7.4% over 64 (2000); Marriage status: 24.5% never married, 62.8% now married, 6.3% widowed, 6.3% divorced (2000); Foreign born: 1.7% (2000); Ancestry (includes multiple ancestries): 21.6% English, 19.5%

German, 12.5% Other groups, 9.5% United States or American, 7.2% Irish (2000).
Economy: Employment by occupation: 7.7% management, 6.5% professional, 10.7% services, 29.0% sales, 0.0% farming, 19.5% construction, 26.6% production (2000).
Income: Per capita income: $11,309 (2000); Median household income: $28,558 (2000); Poverty rate: 11.5% (2000).
Education: High school graduation rate: 80.3% (2000); College graduation rate: 3.9% (2000).
Housing: Homeownership rate: 91.6% (2000); Median home value: $52,900 (2000); Median rent: $265 per month (2000); Median age of housing: 25 years (2000).
Transportation: Commute to work: 95.1% car, 0.0% public transportation, 0.0% walk, 1.2% work from home (2000); Travel time to work: 11.7% less than 15 minutes, 27.2% 15 to 30 minutes, 10.5% 30 to 45 minutes, 19.1% 45 to 60 minutes, 31.5% 60 minutes or more (2000)

SIMPSON (village). Covers a land area of 0.522 square miles and a water area of 0 square miles. Located at 37.46° N. Lat.; 88.75° W. Long. Elevation is 405 feet.
Population: 54 (2000); Race: 100.0% White, 0.0% Black, 0.0% Asian, 0.0% American Indian and Alaska Native, 0.0% Hispanic of any race, 0.0% two or more races (2000); Density: 103.4 persons per square mile (2000); Age: 28.1% under 18, 15.8% over 64 (2000); Marriage status: 28.3% never married, 60.9% now married, 10.9% widowed, 0.0% divorced (2000); Foreign born: 0.0% (2000); Ancestry (includes multiple ancestries): 38.6% English, 17.5% German, 15.8% Irish, 10.5% Other groups, 10.5% Scottish (2000).
Economy: In fruit-growing region. Next to Shawnee National Forest. Employment by occupation: 0.0% management, 10.0% professional, 15.0% services, 40.0% sales, 0.0% farming, 5.0% construction, 30.0% production (2000).
Income: Per capita income: $13,325 (2000); Median household income: $23,125 (2000); Poverty rate: 7.0% (2000).
Education: High school graduation rate: 85.7% (2000); College graduation rate: 11.4% (2000).
Housing: Homeownership rate: 91.7% (2000); Median home value: $38,800 (2000); Median rent: $225 per month (2000); Median age of housing: 30 years (2000).
Transportation: Commute to work: 90.0% car, 0.0% public transportation, 10.0% walk, 0.0% work from home (2000); Travel time to work: 20.0% less than 15 minutes, 5.0% 15 to 30 minutes, 25.0% 30 to 45 minutes, 20.0% 45 to 60 minutes, 30.0% 60 minutes or more (2000)

TUNNEL HILL (unincorporated postal area, zip code 62991). Covers a land area of 34.134 square miles and a water area of 0.038 square miles. Located at 37.54° N. Lat.; 88.86° W. Long. Elevation is 650 feet.
Population: 685 (2000); Race: 100.0% White, 0.0% Black, 0.0% Asian, 0.0% American Indian and Alaska Native, 0.4% Hispanic of any race, 0.0% two or more races (2000); Density: 20.1 persons per square mile (2000); Age: 22.0% under 18, 10.2% over 64 (2000); Marriage status: 16.9% never married, 66.9% now married, 8.1% widowed, 8.1% divorced (2000); Foreign born: 0.0% (2000); Ancestry (includes multiple ancestries): 26.6% Irish, 21.3% German, 13.3% English, 13.0% Other groups, 10.3% United States or American (2000).
Economy: Employment by occupation: 13.6% management, 25.2% professional, 27.8% services, 17.7% sales, 1.0% farming, 7.0% construction, 7.7% production (2000).
Income: Per capita income: $20,884 (2000); Median household income: $40,893 (2000); Poverty rate: 11.2% (2000).
Education: High school graduation rate: 84.6% (2000); College graduation rate: 18.1% (2000).

School District(s)

New Simpson Hill Cons District 32 (KG-08)
2000 Enrollment: 264 618-658-9066
Housing: Homeownership rate: 94.1% (2000); Median home value: $96,700 (2000); Median rent: $318 per month (2000); Median age of housing: 12 years (2000).
Transportation: Commute to work: 94.4% car, 1.2% public transportation, 0.0% walk, 3.6% work from home (2000); Travel time to work: 16.3% less than 15 minutes, 43.7% 15 to 30 minutes, 24.1% 30 to 45 minutes, 12.1% 45 to 60 minutes, 3.8% 60 minutes or more (2000)

VIENNA (city). Covers a land area of 2.240 square miles and a water area of 0.011 square miles. Located at 37.41° N. Lat.; 88.89° W. Long. Elevation is 404 feet.
History: Incorporated 1837.
Population: 1,234 (2000); Race: 97.4% White, 0.0% Black, 0.0% Asian, 0.2% American Indian and Alaska Native, 1.4% Hispanic of any race, 2.4% two or more races (2000); Density: 550.8 persons per square mile (2000); Age: 21.6% under 18, 22.2% over 64 (2000); Marriage status: 23.2% never married, 47.6% now married, 16.1% widowed, 13.1% divorced (2000); Foreign born: 0.3% (2000); Ancestry (includes multiple ancestries): 26.4% United States or American, 20.9% Other groups, 11.5% German, 8.9% English, 8.9% Irish (2000).
Economy: In fruitgrowing region; wheat, corn; livestock; dairy products. Employment by occupation: 6.9% management, 16.3% professional, 33.9% services, 25.0% sales, 0.6% farming, 7.5% construction, 9.9% production (2000).
Income: Per capita income: $13,662 (2000); Median household income: $21,702 (2000); Poverty rate: 20.0% (2000).
Taxes: Total city taxes per capita: $54 (1997); City property taxes per capita: $52 (1997).
Education: High school graduation rate: 67.9% (2000); College graduation rate: 8.8% (2000).

School District(s)

Vienna H S District 133 (09-12)
2000 Enrollment: 344 618-658-4461
Vienna School District 55 (PK-08)
2000 Enrollment: 416 618-658-8286
Housing: Homeownership rate: 61.4% (2000); Median home value: $51,000 (2000); Median rent: $197 per month (2000); Median age of housing: 33 years (2000).
Newspapers: The Vienna Times (1 x week)
Transportation: Commute to work: 92.1% car, 1.0% public transportation, 4.4% walk, 0.8% work from home (2000); Travel time to work: 46.3% less than 15 minutes, 18.2% 15 to 30 minutes, 25.8% 30 to 45 minutes, 6.1% 45 to 60 minutes, 3.6% 60 minutes or more (2000)
Additional Information Contacts
Johnson County Chamber of Commerce 618-658-2063

Kane County

Located in northeastern Illinois; drained by the Fox River and Mill Creek. Covers a land area of 520.40 square miles, a water area of 3.60 square miles, and is located in the Central Time Zone. The county government was organized in 1836. County seat is Geneva.

Kane County is part of the Chicago, IL PMSA. The entire metro area includes: Cook County; DeKalb County; DuPage County; Grundy County; Kane County; Kendall County; Lake County; McHenry County; Will County

Weather Station: Aurora — Elevation: 639 feet

	Jan	Feb	Mar	Apr	May	Jun	Jul	Aug	Sep	Oct	Nov	Dec
High	29	35	47	60	72	81	85	83	75	63	48	35
Low	11	17	27	38	48	57	62	60	52	40	30	18
Precip	1.6	1.5	2.6	4.0	4.0	4.4	4.3	4.4	3.6	2.7	3.2	2.4
Snow	9.9	6.9	3.8	0.9	0.0	0.0	0.0	0.0	0.0	tr	1.5	6.7

High and Low temperatures in degrees Fahrenheit; Precipitation and Snow in inches

Population: 404,119 (2000); Race: 79.1% White, 5.7% Black, 1.7% Asian, 0.3% American Indian and Alaska Native, 23.7% Hispanic of any race, 2.4% two or more races (2000); Density: 776.5 persons per square mile (2000); Age: 30.3% under 18, 8.3% over 64 (2000).
Religion: Five largest groups: 34.3% Catholic Church, 3.6% Lutheran Church—Missouri Synod, 3.5% Evangelical Lutheran Church in America, 3.3% The United Methodist Church, 1.8% United Church of Christ (2000).
Economy: Unemployment rate: 6.6% (11/2002); Total civilian labor force: 217,703 (11/2002); Leading industries: 22.4% manufacturing; 12.1% retail trade; 10.7% administration, support, waste management, remediation services (2000); Companies that employ more than 1,000 persons: 14 (2000); Companies that employ more than 100 persons: 303 (2000); Farms: 650 totaling 209,941 acres (1997); Minority business ownership rate: 10.3% (1997); Women business ownership rate: 27.1% (1997); Retail sales per capita: $8,163 (1997). Single-family building permits issued: 4,705 (2001) / 4,351 (2000); Multi-family building permits issued: 1,087 (2001) / 1,433 (2000).
Income: Per capita income: $24,315 (2000); Median household income: $59,351 (2000); Poverty rate: 6.7% (2000); Bankruptcy rate: 4.70% (2001).
Taxes: Total county taxes per capita: $110 (2000); County property taxes per capita: $106 (2000).

Education: High school graduation rate: 80.2% (2000); College graduation rate: 27.7% (2000).
Housing: Homeownership rate: 76.0% (2000); Median home value: $160,400 (2000); Median rent: $615 per month (2000); Median age of housing: 29 years (2000).
Health: Birth rate: 177.8 per 10,000 population (1998); Age adjusted death rate: 81.3 per 10,000 population (1999); Infant mortality rate: 6.1 per 1,000 live births (1998); Age adjusted cancer mortality rate: 196.4 deaths per 100,000 population (1999). Air Quality Index: 85% good, 15% moderate, 0% unhealthy (percent of days in 2000). Number of physicians: 13.1 per 10,000 population (1999); Number of hospital beds: 29.8 per 10,000 population (1999).
Elections: 2000 Presidential election results: 42.5% Gore, 54.5% Bush, 2.3% Nader, 0.4% Buchanan
Additional Information Contacts
Kane County Government Offices 630-232-3400
Aurora Chamber of Commerce 630-897-9214
Aurora Hispanic Chamber of Commerce. 630-264-2422
Aurora Tri-County Association of Realtors 630-859-1300
Cardunal Area Chamber of Commerce 847-426-8565
Elgin Area Convention Visitors Bureau. 847-695-7540
Elgin Chamber of Commerce. 847-741-5660
Geneva Chamber of Commerce 630-232-6060
Realtor Association of The Fox Valley 630-232-2360
St. Charles Chamber of Commerce 630-584-8384
St. Charles Convention & Visitors Bureau 630-377-6161
Sugar Grove Chamber of Commerce 630-466-7895

Kane County Communities

AURORA (city). Covers a land area of 38.526 square miles and a water area of 0.893 square miles. Located at 41.76° N. Lat.; 88.29° W. Long. Elevation is 676 feet.
History: Joseph McCarty of Elmira, New York, came to Illinois in 1834 and chose the site on the Fox River as superior to Chicago as a place to settle. The community of Aurora was platted in 1836 and a post office was soon established. Development along both sides of the river resulted in separate towns of East Aurora and West Aurora until 1857, when the two were joined in incorporation. Meanwhile, the Chicago, Burlington & Quincy Railroad had arrived with its tracks and shops, and with it a period of growth. Aurora, in 1881, was one of the first towns in the U.S. to have electric street lights.
Population: 142,990 (2000); Race: 68.0% White, 10.9% Black, 3.1% Asian, 0.3% American Indian and Alaska Native, 32.9% Hispanic of any race, 2.9% two or more races (2000); Density: 3,711.5 persons per square mile (2000); Age: 31.8% under 18, 5.9% over 64 (2000); Marriage status: 29.0% never married, 58.9% now married, 4.0% widowed, 8.2% divorced (2000); Foreign born: 21.5% (2000); Ancestry (includes multiple ancestries): 44.4% Other groups, 17.5% German, 9.7% Irish, 5.6% English, 4.7% Italian (2000).
Vital Statistics: Birth rate: 215.5 per 10,000 population (1998)
Economy: Unemployment rate: 8.5% (11/2002); Total civilian labor force: 69,727 (11/2002); Single-family building permits issued: 1,156 (2001) / 1,030 (2000); Multi-family building permits issued: 879 (2001) / 937 (2000); Employment by occupation: 15.0% management, 18.3% professional, 12.4% services, 25.9% sales, 0.3% farming, 7.6% construction, 20.5% production (2000).
Income: Per capita income: $22,131 (2000); Median household income: $54,861 (2000); Poverty rate: 8.5% (2000).
Taxes: Total city taxes per capita: $424 (2000); City property taxes per capita: $230 (2000).
Education: High school graduation rate: 75.6% (2000); College graduation rate: 29.9% (2000).

School District(s)

Aurora East Unit School District 131 (PK-12)
2000 Enrollment: 10,861 630-844-5550
Aurora West Unit School District 129 (PK-12)
2000 Enrollment: 10,569 630-844-4400
Il Mathematics & Science Academy (10-12)
2000 Enrollment: 640 630-907-5053

Four-year College(s)

Aurora University (Private, Not-for-profit)
2001 Enrollment: 2,801 630-892-6431
2001 Tuition: In-state $13,368; Out-of-state $13,368
Housing: Homeownership rate: 70.0% (2000); Median home value: $135,500 (2000); Median rent: $609 per month (2000); Median age of housing: 25 years (2000).
Hospitals: Provena Mercy Center (356 beds); Rush-Copley Medical Center (142 beds)
Safety: Violent crime rate: n/a; Property crime rate: 354.3 per 10,000 population (2001).
Newspapers: The Beacon-News (7 x week)
Transportation: Commute to work: 88.9% car, 5.5% public transportation, 1.6% walk, 2.7% work from home (2000); Travel time to work: 23.5% less than 15 minutes, 35.6% 15 to 30 minutes, 19.5% 30 to 45 minutes, 9.3% 45 to 60 minutes, 12.1% 60 minutes or more (2000)
Airports: Aurora Municipal
Additional Information Contacts
Aurora Chamber of Commerce 630-897-9214
Aurora Hispanic Chamber of Commerce. 630-264-2422
Aurora Tri-County Association of Realtors 630-859-1300

BATAVIA (city). Covers a land area of 9.046 square miles and a water area of 0.140 square miles. Located at 41.84° N. Lat.; 88.30° W. Long. Elevation is 716 feet.
History: Batavia was settled in 1832 by people from New York, who chose the site for its water power, fertile soil, and surface limestone. They named the new town for their home in New York. Early Batavia had the nickname of Quarry City.
Population: 23,866 (2000); Race: 93.2% White, 2.7% Black, 1.1% Asian, 0.0% American Indian and Alaska Native, 5.8% Hispanic of any race, 1.1% two or more races (2000); Density: 2,638.4 persons per square mile (2000); Age: 31.9% under 18, 9.5% over 64 (2000); Marriage status: 21.4% never married, 64.8% now married, 5.7% widowed, 8.0% divorced (2000); Foreign born: 5.2% (2000); Ancestry (includes multiple ancestries): 31.6% German, 18.1% Irish, 11.5% English, 10.8% Other groups, 8.8% Italian (2000).
Vital Statistics: Birth rate: 142.0 per 10,000 population (1998)
Economy: Single-family building permits issued: 135 (2001) / 215 (2000); Multi-family building permits issued: 0 (2001) / 0 (2000); Employment by occupation: 20.5% management, 23.8% professional, 10.8% services, 28.0% sales, 0.0% farming, 7.1% construction, 9.7% production (2000).
Income: Per capita income: $27,783 (2000); Median household income: $68,656 (2000); Poverty rate: 3.6% (2000).
Taxes: Total city taxes per capita: $201 (2000); City property taxes per capita: $145 (2000).
Education: High school graduation rate: 93.6% (2000); College graduation rate: 42.6% (2000).

School District(s)

Batavia Unit School District 101 (PK-12)
2000 Enrollment: 5,585 630-879-4600
Housing: Homeownership rate: 77.6% (2000); Median home value: $202,700 (2000); Median rent: $702 per month (2000); Median age of housing: 22 years (2000).
Transportation: Commute to work: 90.2% car, 2.3% public transportation, 1.6% walk, 4.4% work from home (2000); Travel time to work: 31.9% less than 15 minutes, 31.3% 15 to 30 minutes, 18.1% 30 to 45 minutes, 7.9% 45 to 60 minutes, 10.8% 60 minutes or more (2000)

BIG ROCK (unincorporated postal area, zip code 60511). Covers a land area of 29.145 square miles and a water area of 0 square miles. Located at 41.75° N. Lat.; 88.54° W. Long. Elevation is 710 feet.
Population: 1,862 (2000); Race: 99.3% White, 0.0% Black, 0.0% Asian, 0.7% American Indian and Alaska Native, 1.8% Hispanic of any race, 0.0% two or more races (2000); Density: 63.9 persons per square mile (2000); Age: 23.7% under 18, 9.5% over 64 (2000); Marriage status: 21.1% never married, 74.6% now married, 3.0% widowed, 1.3% divorced (2000); Foreign born: 0.8% (2000); Ancestry (includes multiple ancestries): 28.9% German, 13.5% Irish, 12.4% English, 8.5% United States or American, 6.7% French (except Basque) (2000).
Economy: Employment by occupation: 13.7% management, 9.9% professional, 11.9% services, 32.4% sales, 0.0% farming, 14.8% construction, 17.3% production (2000).
Income: Per capita income: $30,689 (2000); Median household income: $72,622 (2000); Poverty rate: 4.5% (2000).
Education: High school graduation rate: 92.7% (2000); College graduation rate: 20.2% (2000).
Housing: Homeownership rate: 87.3% (2000); Median home value: $188,100 (2000); Median rent: $547 per month (2000); Median age of housing: 29 years (2000).
Transportation: Commute to work: 94.1% car, 0.0% public transportation, 0.0% walk, 5.9% work from home (2000); Travel time to work: 15.4% less than 15 minutes, 37.4% 15 to 30 minutes, 29.6% 30 to 45 minutes, 11.4% 45 to 60 minutes, 6.2% 60 minutes or more (2000)

BURLINGTON (village). Covers a land area of 0.354 square miles and a water area of 0 square miles. Located at 42.05° N. Lat.; 88.54° W. Long. Elevation is 930 feet.
Population: 452 (2000); Race: 95.4% White, 0.0% Black, 3.0% Asian, 0.0% American Indian and Alaska Native, 0.0% Hispanic of any race, 1.5% two or more races (2000); Density: 1,277.2 persons per square mile (2000); Age: 31.7% under 18, 8.5% over 64 (2000); Marriage status: 24.5% never married, 59.2% now married, 4.2% widowed, 12.1% divorced (2000); Foreign born: 6.1% (2000); Ancestry (includes multiple ancestries): 41.4% German, 14.8% Irish, 14.3% Polish, 8.0% Other groups, 6.9% English (2000).
Economy: In dairying and livestock area. Employment by occupation: 8.5% management, 18.4% professional, 11.1% services, 23.1% sales, 0.0% farming, 14.5% construction, 24.4% production (2000).
Income: Per capita income: $25,349 (2000); Median household income: $53,438 (2000); Poverty rate: 5.7% (2000).
Taxes: Total city taxes per capita: $137 (1997); City property taxes per capita: $127 (1997).
Education: High school graduation rate: 93.5% (2000); College graduation rate: 18.8% (2000).

School District(s)
Central Community Unit School District 301 (PK-12)
2000 Enrollment: 2,262 847-464-6005
Housing: Homeownership rate: 69.5% (2000); Median home value: $145,400 (2000); Median rent: $610 per month (2000); Median age of housing: 43 years (2000).
Transportation: Commute to work: 92.1% car, 0.0% public transportation, 4.8% walk, 0.9% work from home (2000); Travel time to work: 21.1% less than 15 minutes, 38.3% 15 to 30 minutes, 23.8% 30 to 45 minutes, 8.4% 45 to 60 minutes, 8.4% 60 minutes or more (2000)

CARPENTERSVILLE (village). Covers a land area of 7.450 square miles and a water area of 0.148 square miles. Located at 42.12° N. Lat.; 88.27° W. Long. Elevation is 800 feet.
History: Carpentersville was settled in 1834 by Angelo Carpenter of Massachusetts and his father and uncle. Carpenter built several mills and a store, and in 1851 he platted the town. An early industry was the Illinois Iron and Bolt Company.
Population: 30,586 (2000); Race: 67.9% White, 3.8% Black, 2.0% Asian, 0.4% American Indian and Alaska Native, 41.3% Hispanic of any race, 4.4% two or more races (2000); Density: 4,105.4 persons per square mile (2000); Age: 33.0% under 18, 5.4% over 64 (2000); Marriage status: 28.2% never married, 60.4% now married, 3.8% widowed, 7.5% divorced (2000); Foreign born: 26.4% (2000); Ancestry (includes multiple ancestries): 43.0% Other groups, 17.9% German, 9.6% Irish, 7.7% Polish, 5.2% Italian (2000).
Vital Statistics: Birth rate: 216.4 per 10,000 population (1998)
Economy: Unemployment rate: 8.6% (11/2002); Total civilian labor force: 14,933 (11/2002); Single-family building permits issued: 332 (2001) / 475 (2000); Multi-family building permits issued: 0 (2001) / 0 (2000); Employment by occupation: 9.2% management, 10.5% professional, 14.6% services, 29.4% sales, 0.4% farming, 11.1% construction, 24.7% production (2000).
Income: Per capita income: $17,424 (2000); Median household income: $54,526 (2000); Poverty rate: 8.5% (2000).
Taxes: Total city taxes per capita: $264 (1997); City property taxes per capita: $115 (1997).
Education: High school graduation rate: 66.7% (2000); College graduation rate: 12.2% (2000).

School District(s)
Comm Unit School District 300 (PK-12)
2000 Enrollment: 16,711 847-426-1300
Housing: Homeownership rate: 80.2% (2000); Median home value: $116,300 (2000); Median rent: $618 per month (2000); Median age of housing: 34 years (2000).
Transportation: Commute to work: 94.6% car, 1.1% public transportation, 1.1% walk, 1.4% work from home (2000); Travel time to work: 20.6% less than 15 minutes, 31.2% 15 to 30 minutes, 23.1% 30 to 45 minutes, 13.6% 45 to 60 minutes, 11.5% 60 minutes or more (2000)

DUNDEE (unincorporated postal area, zip code 60118). Aka West Dundee. Covers a land area of 22.307 square miles and a water area of 0.373 square miles. Located at 42.02° N. Lat.; 88.41° W. Long.
Population: 14,739 (2000); Race: 95.1% White, 0.6% Black, 1.0% Asian, 0.0% American Indian and Alaska Native, 3.2% Hispanic of any race, 1.9% two or more races (2000); Density: 660.7 persons per square mile (2000); Age: 26.0% under 18, 9.3% over 64 (2000); Marriage status: 20.8% never married, 65.7% now married, 4.1% widowed, 9.4% divorced (2000); Foreign born: 7.9% (2000); Ancestry (includes multiple ancestries): 35.3% German, 15.8% Irish, 13.0% Polish, 9.7% Italian, 9.1% English (2000).
Economy: Employment by occupation: 22.8% management, 20.2% professional, 8.1% services, 30.9% sales, 0.3% farming, 8.5% construction, 9.2% production (2000).
Income: Per capita income: $31,260 (2000); Median household income: $72,500 (2000); Poverty rate: 3.0% (2000).
Education: High school graduation rate: 91.4% (2000); College graduation rate: 37.0% (2000).
Housing: Homeownership rate: 82.4% (2000); Median home value: $214,000 (2000); Median rent: $679 per month (2000); Median age of housing: 29 years (2000).
Transportation: Commute to work: 90.4% car, 2.3% public transportation, 1.5% walk, 5.4% work from home (2000); Travel time to work: 25.5% less than 15 minutes, 27.5% 15 to 30 minutes, 23.9% 30 to 45 minutes, 12.6% 45 to 60 minutes, 10.6% 60 minutes or more (2000)

Additional Information Contacts
Cardunal Area Chamber of Commerce 847-426-8565

EAST DUNDEE (village). Covers a land area of 2.679 square miles and a water area of 0.235 square miles. Located at 42.10° N. Lat.; 88.27° W. Long. Elevation is 840 feet.
History: East Dundee was settled mainly by German immigrants who left their home country during the 1848 Revolution.
Population: 2,955 (2000); Race: 97.3% White, 0.2% Black, 0.0% Asian, 0.0% American Indian and Alaska Native, 3.5% Hispanic of any race, 0.6% two or more races (2000); Density: 1,103.1 persons per square mile (2000); Age: 20.6% under 18, 14.7% over 64 (2000); Marriage status: 21.5% never married, 62.5% now married, 5.1% widowed, 10.9% divorced (2000); Foreign born: 6.9% (2000); Ancestry (includes multiple ancestries): 37.9% German, 13.8% Irish, 11.5% English, 8.6% Italian, 7.4% Polish (2000).
Economy: Single-family building permits issued: 0 (2001) / 1 (2000); Multi-family building permits issued: 0 (2001) / 51 (2000); Employment by occupation: 17.7% management, 18.8% professional, 12.1% services, 29.4% sales, 0.0% farming, 11.2% construction, 10.8% production (2000).
Income: Per capita income: $31,695 (2000); Median household income: $61,219 (2000); Poverty rate: 4.8% (2000).
Taxes: Total city taxes per capita: $510 (1997); City property taxes per capita: $101 (1997).
Education: High school graduation rate: 90.6% (2000); College graduation rate: 32.3% (2000).
Housing: Homeownership rate: 85.3% (2000); Median home value: $162,700 (2000); Median rent: $660 per month (2000); Median age of housing: 41 years (2000).
Transportation: Commute to work: 91.5% car, 1.2% public transportation, 2.3% walk, 4.4% work from home (2000); Travel time to work: 26.6% less than 15 minutes, 34.3% 15 to 30 minutes, 22.6% 30 to 45 minutes, 8.1% 45 to 60 minutes, 8.4% 60 minutes or more (2000)

ELBURN (village). Covers a land area of 2.727 square miles and a water area of 0 square miles. Located at 41.89° N. Lat.; 88.46° W. Long. Elevation is 850 feet.
History: Elburn began in 1854 when the Galena & Chicago Union Railroad line was laid, and developed as a farming center. It is said that when Lincoln visited Elburn in 1858, he was greeted by a group calling itself the Lincoln True Hearts, pledging support.
Population: 2,756 (2000); Race: 98.7% White, 0.0% Black, 0.5% Asian, 0.4% American Indian and Alaska Native, 2.2% Hispanic of any race, 0.4% two or more races (2000); Density: 1,010.5 persons per square mile (2000); Age: 29.0% under 18, 9.7% over 64 (2000); Marriage status: 18.2% never married, 64.9% now married, 7.8% widowed, 9.0% divorced (2000); Foreign born: 3.5% (2000); Ancestry (includes multiple ancestries): 31.7% German, 18.0% Irish, 11.8% Swedish, 11.1% Italian, 8.6% English (2000).
Economy: Single-family building permits issued: 51 (2001) / 49 (2000); Multi-family building permits issued: 10 (2001) / 41 (2000); Employment by occupation: 17.4% management, 20.0% professional, 12.4% services, 32.0% sales, 0.0% farming, 8.8% construction, 9.3% production (2000).
Income: Per capita income: $26,781 (2000); Median household income: $67,788 (2000); Poverty rate: 4.1% (2000).
Taxes: Total city taxes per capita: $295 (1997); City property taxes per capita: $172 (1997).
Education: High school graduation rate: 92.1% (2000); College graduation rate: 34.4% (2000).

Housing: Homeownership rate: 79.7% (2000); Median home value: $183,200 (2000); Median rent: $621 per month (2000); Median age of housing: 8 years (2000).
Newspapers: The Elburn Herald (1 x week)
Transportation: Commute to work: 89.7% car, 1.1% public transportation, 3.6% walk, 4.4% work from home (2000); Travel time to work: 29.3% less than 15 minutes, 34.6% 15 to 30 minutes, 18.8% 30 to 45 minutes, 8.2% 45 to 60 minutes, 9.0% 60 minutes or more (2000)

ELGIN (city). Covers a land area of 25.003 square miles and a water area of 0.386 square miles. Located at 42.03° N. Lat.; 88.28° W. Long. Elevation is 745 feet.
History: Elgin was settled in 1835 by James and Hezekiah Gifford from New York, who dammed the river and built a sawmill and a gristmill. It was incorporated as a village in 1847 and as a town in 1854. An early industry here was the production of condensed milk, a process developed by Gail Borden. The Elgin watch industry, which made the name of Elgin known around the world, began in 1866, followed by the Elgin Watchmakers College which opened in the 1920's.
Population: 94,487 (2000); Race: 70.8% White, 6.8% Black, 3.5% Asian, 0.5% American Indian and Alaska Native, 34.0% Hispanic of any race, 3.7% two or more races (2000); Density: 3,779.1 persons per square mile (2000); Age: 28.8% under 18, 8.8% over 64 (2000); Marriage status: 28.6% never married, 57.5% now married, 5.0% widowed, 8.9% divorced (2000); Foreign born: 23.7% (2000); Ancestry (includes multiple ancestries): 41.2% Other groups, 22.0% German, 9.8% Irish, 6.3% Polish, 5.6% English (2000).
Vital Statistics: Birth rate: 217.1 per 10,000 population (1998)
Economy: Unemployment rate: 8.6% (11/2002); Total civilian labor force: 49,588 (11/2002); Single-family building permits issued: 126 (2001) / 194 (2000); Multi-family building permits issued: 64 (2001) / 0 (2000); Employment by occupation: 12.3% management, 15.6% professional, 15.0% services, 25.5% sales, 0.3% farming, 8.6% construction, 22.6% production (2000).
Income: Per capita income: $21,112 (2000); Median household income: $52,605 (2000); Poverty rate: 8.1% (2000).
Taxes: Total city taxes per capita: $317 (2000); City property taxes per capita: $250 (2000).
Education: High school graduation rate: 73.8% (2000); College graduation rate: 20.5% (2000).

School District(s)

School District 46 (PK-12)
2000 Enrollment: 36,767 847-888-5000

Four-year College(s)

Judson College (Private, Not-for-profit, American Baptist)
2001 Enrollment: 1,085 847-695-2500
2001 Tuition: In-state $13,872; Out-of-state $13,872
Keller Graduate School of Management (Private, For-profit)
2001 Enrollment: n/a 847-622-1135

Two-year College(s)

Elgin Community College (Public)
2001 Enrollment: 9,636 847-888-7373
2001 Tuition: In-state $5,526; Out-of-state $6,689

Housing: Homeownership rate: 70.3% (2000); Median home value: $141,400 (2000); Median rent: $611 per month (2000); Median age of housing: 31 years (2000).
Hospitals: Provena Saint Joseph Hospital (260 beds); Sherman Hospital (353 beds)
Newspapers: Courier-News (7 x week)
Transportation: Commute to work: 92.6% car, 2.7% public transportation, 1.9% walk, 2.1% work from home (2000); Travel time to work: 29.5% less than 15 minutes, 32.7% 15 to 30 minutes, 19.8% 30 to 45 minutes, 9.3% 45 to 60 minutes, 8.6% 60 minutes or more (2000)
Additional Information Contacts
Elgin Area Convention Visitors Bureau. 847-695-7540
Elgin Chamber of Commerce 847-741-5660

GENEVA (city). Covers a land area of 8.407 square miles and a water area of 0.176 square miles. Located at 41.88° N. Lat.; 88.31° W. Long. Elevation is 725 feet.
History: Geneva was settled about 1832 by soldiers returning from the Black Hawk War and by pioneers heading west.
Population: 19,515 (2000); Race: 96.3% White, 1.3% Black, 1.4% Asian, 0.1% American Indian and Alaska Native, 2.4% Hispanic of any race, 0.6% two or more races (2000); Density: 2,321.4 persons per square mile (2000); Age: 31.4% under 18, 9.3% over 64 (2000); Marriage status: 20.4% never married, 67.0% now married, 5.2% widowed, 7.4% divorced (2000); Foreign born: 4.5% (2000); Ancestry (includes multiple ancestries): 29.7% German, 23.9% Irish, 11.0% Polish, 10.3% English, 9.8% Italian (2000).
Vital Statistics: Birth rate: 135.3 per 10,000 population (1998)
Economy: Single-family building permits issued: 290 (2001) / 240 (2000); Multi-family building permits issued: 18 (2001) / 4 (2000); Employment by occupation: 24.5% management, 27.4% professional, 8.8% services, 27.7% sales, 0.3% farming, 4.5% construction, 6.8% production (2000).
Income: Per capita income: $33,026 (2000); Median household income: $77,299 (2000); Poverty rate: 2.2% (2000).
Taxes: Total city taxes per capita: $296 (2000); City property taxes per capita: $179 (2000).
Education: High school graduation rate: 95.4% (2000); College graduation rate: 53.2% (2000).

School District(s)

Geneva Community Unit School District 304 (PK-12)
2000 Enrollment: 4,836 630-463-3000
Kane Roe (08-12)
2000 Enrollment: 23 630-232-5955

Housing: Homeownership rate: 84.1% (2000); Median home value: $217,900 (2000); Median rent: $810 per month (2000); Median age of housing: 20 years (2000).
Hospitals: Delnor-Community Hospital (118 beds)
Newspapers: Kane County Chronicle (6 x week)
Transportation: Commute to work: 87.9% car, 5.8% public transportation, 2.0% walk, 4.0% work from home (2000); Travel time to work: 32.7% less than 15 minutes, 26.7% 15 to 30 minutes, 16.4% 30 to 45 minutes, 9.1% 45 to 60 minutes, 15.1% 60 minutes or more (2000)
Additional Information Contacts
Geneva Chamber of Commerce. 630-232-6060
Realtor Association of The Fox Valley 630-232-2360

GILBERTS (village). Covers a land area of 3.214 square miles and a water area of 0.004 square miles. Located at 42.10° N. Lat.; 88.36° W. Long. Elevation is 895 feet.
Population: 1,279 (2000); Race: 97.5% White, 0.0% Black, 0.0% Asian, 0.3% American Indian and Alaska Native, 3.0% Hispanic of any race, 1.6% two or more races (2000); Density: 398.0 persons per square mile (2000); Age: 28.7% under 18, 3.1% over 64 (2000); Marriage status: 21.5% never married, 70.8% now married, 3.5% widowed, 4.2% divorced (2000); Foreign born: 2.4% (2000); Ancestry (includes multiple ancestries): 38.6% German, 16.5% Irish, 14.7% Polish, 13.2% Italian, 9.0% English (2000).
Economy: Single-family building permits issued: 24 (2001) / 1 (2000); Multi-family building permits issued: 0 (2001) / 0 (2000); Employment by occupation: 16.8% management, 20.1% professional, 9.9% services, 30.5% sales, 0.0% farming, 14.0% construction, 8.7% production (2000).
Income: Per capita income: $31,898 (2000); Median household income: $87,847 (2000); Poverty rate: 0.6% (2000).
Taxes: Total city taxes per capita: $255 (1997); City property taxes per capita: $140 (1997).
Education: High school graduation rate: 93.4% (2000); College graduation rate: 25.4% (2000).
Housing: Homeownership rate: 95.2% (2000); Median home value: $210,600 (2000); Median rent: $688 per month (2000); Median age of housing: 16 years (2000).
Transportation: Commute to work: 92.9% car, 1.7% public transportation, 0.8% walk, 3.8% work from home (2000); Travel time to work: 22.4% less than 15 minutes, 30.1% 15 to 30 minutes, 22.0% 30 to 45 minutes, 14.2% 45 to 60 minutes, 11.3% 60 minutes or more (2000)

HAMPSHIRE (village). Covers a land area of 4.877 square miles and a water area of 0 square miles. Located at 42.09° N. Lat.; 88.52° W. Long. Elevation is 900 feet.
Population: 2,900 (2000); Race: 95.0% White, 0.1% Black, 1.2% Asian, 1.0% American Indian and Alaska Native, 0.8% Hispanic of any race, 2.7% two or more races (2000); Density: 594.7 persons per square mile (2000); Age: 29.8% under 18, 11.3% over 64 (2000); Marriage status: 23.5% never married, 62.0% now married, 6.4% widowed, 8.1% divorced (2000); Foreign born: 2.0% (2000); Ancestry (includes multiple ancestries): 45.8% German, 18.1% Irish, 11.2% Italian, 9.9% Polish, 9.1% English (2000).
Economy: In agricultural area: dairy products; livestock; grain. Employment by occupation: 13.6% management, 17.5% professional, 12.7% services, 27.2% sales, 0.3% farming, 12.7% construction, 16.1% production (2000).
Income: Per capita income: $22,143 (2000); Median household income: $58,519 (2000); Poverty rate: 2.9% (2000).
Taxes: Total city taxes per capita: $190 (1997); City property taxes per capita: $182 (1997).

Education: High school graduation rate: 87.1% (2000); College graduation rate: 18.8% (2000).
Housing: Homeownership rate: 81.9% (2000); Median home value: $157,700 (2000); Median rent: $633 per month (2000); Median age of housing: 24 years (2000).
Transportation: Commute to work: 90.6% car, 1.3% public transportation, 3.0% walk, 3.6% work from home (2000); Travel time to work: 29.5% less than 15 minutes, 30.3% 15 to 30 minutes, 22.9% 30 to 45 minutes, 7.4% 45 to 60 minutes, 9.9% 60 minutes or more (2000)

LILY LAKE (village). Covers a land area of 2.246 square miles and a water area of <.001 square miles. Located at 41.94° N. Lat.; 88.47° W. Long. Elevation is 962 feet.
Population: 825 (2000); Race: 95.4% White, 2.2% Black, 0.7% Asian, 0.0% American Indian and Alaska Native, 0.7% Hispanic of any race, 1.7% two or more races (2000); Density: 367.3 persons per square mile (2000); Age: 33.3% under 18, 5.6% over 64 (2000); Marriage status: 21.0% never married, 72.4% now married, 3.1% widowed, 3.5% divorced (2000); Foreign born: 3.5% (2000); Ancestry (includes multiple ancestries): 31.6% German, 14.6% Irish, 13.4% Polish, 9.2% Swedish, 7.4% Italian (2000).
Economy: Employment by occupation: 17.3% management, 20.7% professional, 6.1% services, 35.1% sales, 0.0% farming, 10.8% construction, 9.9% production (2000).
Income: Per capita income: $29,611 (2000); Median household income: $77,139 (2000); Poverty rate: 0.6% (2000).
Taxes: Total city taxes per capita: $57 (1997); City property taxes per capita: $26 (1997).
Education: High school graduation rate: 95.0% (2000); College graduation rate: 27.9% (2000).
Housing: Homeownership rate: 92.3% (2000); Median home value: $195,800 (2000); Median rent: $675 per month (2000); Median age of housing: 22 years (2000).
Transportation: Commute to work: 91.6% car, 2.9% public transportation, 1.1% walk, 4.1% work from home (2000); Travel time to work: 13.7% less than 15 minutes, 36.1% 15 to 30 minutes, 25.2% 30 to 45 minutes, 11.6% 45 to 60 minutes, 13.4% 60 minutes or more (2000)

MAPLE PARK (village). Covers a land area of 0.594 square miles and a water area of 0 square miles. Located at 41.90° N. Lat.; 88.59° W. Long. Elevation is 865 feet.
Population: 765 (2000); Race: 96.6% White, 0.9% Black, 0.0% Asian, 0.3% American Indian and Alaska Native, 2.4% Hispanic of any race, 1.7% two or more races (2000); Density: 1,288.1 persons per square mile (2000); Age: 31.6% under 18, 8.2% over 64 (2000); Marriage status: 29.0% never married, 54.6% now married, 7.7% widowed, 8.7% divorced (2000); Foreign born: 0.4% (2000); Ancestry (includes multiple ancestries): 37.1% German, 13.2% Irish, 12.0% Norwegian, 11.8% United States or American, 9.4% English (2000).
Economy: In agricultural area: dairy products; livestock. Single-family building permits issued: 26 (2001) / 17 (2000); Multi-family building permits issued: 0 (2001) / 7 (2000); Employment by occupation: 10.0% management, 13.7% professional, 8.9% services, 28.3% sales, 1.9% farming, 15.9% construction, 21.3% production (2000).
Income: Per capita income: $21,932 (2000); Median household income: $49,583 (2000); Poverty rate: 5.8% (2000).
Taxes: Total city taxes per capita: $220 (1997); City property taxes per capita: $76 (1997).
Education: High school graduation rate: 91.1% (2000); College graduation rate: 15.6% (2000).

School District(s)

Kaneland C U School District 302 (PK-12)
2000 Enrollment: 2,747 630-365-5100
Housing: Homeownership rate: 76.1% (2000); Median home value: $129,300 (2000); Median rent: $522 per month (2000); Median age of housing: 43 years (2000).
Transportation: Commute to work: 93.3% car, 1.1% public transportation, 1.1% walk, 4.6% work from home (2000); Travel time to work: 16.7% less than 15 minutes, 45.2% 15 to 30 minutes, 23.2% 30 to 45 minutes, 9.0% 45 to 60 minutes, 5.9% 60 minutes or more (2000)

MONTGOMERY (village). Covers a land area of 6.415 square miles and a water area of 0.196 square miles. Located at 41.72° N. Lat.; 88.32° W. Long. Elevation is 642 feet.
Population: 5,471 (2000); Race: 90.3% White, 2.1% Black, 0.8% Asian, 0.0% American Indian and Alaska Native, 12.2% Hispanic of any race, 1.7% two or more races (2000); Density: 852.9 persons per square mile (2000); Age: 25.8% under 18, 14.9% over 64 (2000); Marriage status: 21.5% never married, 62.7% now married, 8.1% widowed, 7.7% divorced (2000); Foreign born: 5.8% (2000); Ancestry (includes multiple ancestries): 30.6% German, 14.9% Other groups, 12.1% Irish, 10.6% English, 6.0% Polish (2000).
Economy: In agricultural area: dairy products; corn, soybeans. Manufacturing. Single-family building permits issued: 524 (2001) / 20 (2000); Multi-family building permits issued: 12 (2001) / 0 (2000); Employment by occupation: 14.2% management, 12.6% professional, 11.4% services, 32.5% sales, 0.2% farming, 11.9% construction, 17.1% production (2000).
Income: Per capita income: $23,395 (2000); Median household income: $51,028 (2000); Poverty rate: 3.7% (2000).
Taxes: Total city taxes per capita: $174 (1997); City property taxes per capita: $94 (1997).
Education: High school graduation rate: 82.2% (2000); College graduation rate: 19.6% (2000).
Housing: Homeownership rate: 77.1% (2000); Median home value: $135,200 (2000); Median rent: $578 per month (2000); Median age of housing: 32 years (2000).
Transportation: Commute to work: 94.2% car, 1.9% public transportation, 0.4% walk, 3.2% work from home (2000); Travel time to work: 27.6% less than 15 minutes, 35.4% 15 to 30 minutes, 18.0% 30 to 45 minutes, 8.7% 45 to 60 minutes, 10.4% 60 minutes or more (2000)

NORTH AURORA (village). Covers a land area of 5.159 square miles and a water area of 0.147 square miles. Located at 41.80° N. Lat.; 88.32° W. Long. Elevation is 730 feet.
Population: 10,585 (2000); Race: 87.7% White, 3.2% Black, 4.1% Asian, 0.3% American Indian and Alaska Native, 7.9% Hispanic of any race, 1.9% two or more races (2000); Density: 2,051.8 persons per square mile (2000); Age: 26.4% under 18, 10.4% over 64 (2000); Marriage status: 22.0% never married, 64.4% now married, 5.8% widowed, 7.9% divorced (2000); Foreign born: 8.0% (2000); Ancestry (includes multiple ancestries): 32.8% German, 17.9% Other groups, 17.2% Irish, 9.1% Polish, 7.9% English (2000).
Economy: Single-family building permits issued: 239 (2001) / 418 (2000); Multi-family building permits issued: 0 (2001) / 0 (2000); Employment by occupation: 14.2% management, 19.4% professional, 10.5% services, 34.9% sales, 0.1% farming, 8.3% construction, 12.5% production (2000).
Income: Per capita income: $25,552 (2000); Median household income: $58,557 (2000); Poverty rate: 3.0% (2000).
Taxes: Total city taxes per capita: $366 (1997); City property taxes per capita: $323 (1997).
Education: High school graduation rate: 87.7% (2000); College graduation rate: 30.7% (2000).
Housing: Homeownership rate: 80.0% (2000); Median home value: $149,400 (2000); Median rent: $662 per month (2000); Median age of housing: 19 years (2000).
Transportation: Commute to work: 94.5% car, 1.3% public transportation, 0.7% walk, 2.6% work from home (2000); Travel time to work: 24.7% less than 15 minutes, 39.3% 15 to 30 minutes, 18.7% 30 to 45 minutes, 9.2% 45 to 60 minutes, 8.1% 60 minutes or more (2000)

PINGREE GROVE (village). Covers a land area of 0.616 square miles and a water area of 0 square miles. Located at 42.06° N. Lat.; 88.41° W. Long. Elevation is 912 feet.
Population: 124 (2000); Race: 100.0% White, 0.0% Black, 0.0% Asian, 0.0% American Indian and Alaska Native, 9.8% Hispanic of any race, 0.0% two or more races (2000); Density: 201.3 persons per square mile (2000); Age: 7.6% under 18, 30.4% over 64 (2000); Marriage status: 9.4% never married, 65.9% now married, 15.3% widowed, 9.4% divorced (2000); Foreign born: 0.0% (2000); Ancestry (includes multiple ancestries): 52.2% German, 13.0% French (except Basque), 9.8% Other groups, 7.6% English, 6.5% Irish (2000).
Economy: In agricultural area: dairy products; corn, soybeans. Employment by occupation: 6.7% management, 24.4% professional, 13.3% services, 35.6% sales, 0.0% farming, 8.9% construction, 11.1% production (2000).
Income: Per capita income: $23,396 (2000); Median household income: $45,313 (2000); Poverty rate: 0.0% (2000).
Taxes: Total city taxes per capita: $44 (1997); City property taxes per capita: $15 (1997).
Education: High school graduation rate: 67.5% (2000); College graduation rate: 5.2% (2000).
Housing: Homeownership rate: 89.6% (2000); Median home value: $106,800 (2000); Median rent: $425 per month (2000); Median age of housing: 59 years (2000).

Transportation: Commute to work: 93.3% car, 0.0% public transportation, 6.7% walk, 0.0% work from home (2000); Travel time to work: 20.0% less than 15 minutes, 55.6% 15 to 30 minutes, 8.9% 30 to 45 minutes, 15.6% 45 to 60 minutes, 0.0% 60 minutes or more (2000)

SAINT CHARLES (city). Covers a land area of 13.990 square miles and a water area of 0.158 square miles. Located at 41.91° N. Lat.; 88.31° W. Long. Elevation is 735 feet.
History: The community of St. Charles developed around a mill in the mid-1800's, and became a residential area for people moving out from Chicago.
Population: 27,896 (2000); Race: 93.9% White, 1.8% Black, 1.4% Asian, 0.3% American Indian and Alaska Native, 5.5% Hispanic of any race, 0.9% two or more races (2000); Density: 1,993.9 persons per square mile (2000); Age: 27.8% under 18, 10.0% over 64 (2000); Marriage status: 24.3% never married, 61.6% now married, 5.4% widowed, 8.8% divorced (2000); Foreign born: 6.6% (2000); Ancestry (includes multiple ancestries): 29.7% German, 17.9% Irish, 12.2% English, 10.6% Polish, 9.6% Italian (2000).
Vital Statistics: Birth rate: 135.9 per 10,000 population (1998)
Economy: Unemployment rate: 7.4% (11/2002); Total civilian labor force: 16,293 (11/2002); Single-family building permits issued: 425 (2001) / 431 (2000); Multi-family building permits issued: 104 (2001) / 10 (2000); Employment by occupation: 20.1% management, 22.7% professional, 9.8% services, 31.8% sales, 0.1% farming, 6.5% construction, 8.9% production (2000).
Income: Per capita income: $33,969 (2000); Median household income: $69,424 (2000); Poverty rate: 3.4% (2000).
Education: High school graduation rate: 91.6% (2000); College graduation rate: 42.9% (2000).

School District(s)

Mid-Valley Special Education Coop (05-12)
2000 Enrollment: 93 630-377-4848
Saint Charles C U School District 303 (PK-12)
2000 Enrollment: 11,093 630-513-3030

Housing: Homeownership rate: 73.8% (2000); Median home value: $196,200 (2000); Median rent: $748 per month (2000); Median age of housing: 22 years (2000).
Newspapers: The Winfield Press (1 x week); Geneva Republican (1 x week); Batavia Republican (1 x week); The Saint Charles Republican (1 x week)
Transportation: Commute to work: 90.9% car, 3.2% public transportation, 1.6% walk, 3.8% work from home (2000); Travel time to work: 37.2% less than 15 minutes, 26.1% 15 to 30 minutes, 19.2% 30 to 45 minutes, 8.2% 45 to 60 minutes, 9.4% 60 minutes or more (2000)
Additional Information Contacts
St. Charles Chamber of Commerce 630-584-8384
St. Charles Convention & Visitors Bureau 630-377-6161

SLEEPY HOLLOW (village). Covers a land area of 2.011 square miles and a water area of 0.015 square miles. Located at 42.09° N. Lat.; 88.31° W. Long. Elevation is 802 feet.
Population: 3,553 (2000); Race: 92.8% White, 0.9% Black, 1.7% Asian, 0.0% American Indian and Alaska Native, 4.5% Hispanic of any race, 2.1% two or more races (2000); Density: 1,766.3 persons per square mile (2000); Age: 30.3% under 18, 7.5% over 64 (2000); Marriage status: 17.4% never married, 74.7% now married, 2.2% widowed, 5.7% divorced (2000); Foreign born: 8.8% (2000); Ancestry (includes multiple ancestries): 33.6% German, 17.5% Polish, 14.8% Irish, 12.0% Italian, 10.3% English (2000).
Economy: Agriculture to West. Single-family building permits issued: 8 (2001) / 9 (2000); Multi-family building permits issued: 0 (2001) / 0 (2000); Employment by occupation: 28.6% management, 20.6% professional, 5.6% services, 29.3% sales, 0.0% farming, 7.7% construction, 8.1% production (2000).
Income: Per capita income: $31,005 (2000); Median household income: $91,279 (2000); Poverty rate: 1.8% (2000).
Taxes: Total city taxes per capita: $178 (1997); City property taxes per capita: $98 (1997).
Education: High school graduation rate: 94.3% (2000); College graduation rate: 41.5% (2000).
Housing: Homeownership rate: 90.1% (2000); Median home value: $246,400 (2000); Median rent: $752 per month (2000); Median age of housing: 24 years (2000).
Transportation: Commute to work: 91.5% car, 2.2% public transportation, 0.4% walk, 5.1% work from home (2000); Travel time to work: 24.2% less than 15 minutes, 22.7% 15 to 30 minutes, 27.7% 30 to 45 minutes, 13.7% 45 to 60 minutes, 11.7% 60 minutes or more (2000)

SOUTH ELGIN (village). Covers a land area of 6.288 square miles and a water area of 0.123 square miles. Located at 41.99° N. Lat.; 88.30° W. Long. Elevation is 743 feet.
Population: 16,100 (2000); Race: 85.4% White, 2.9% Black, 5.4% Asian, 0.3% American Indian and Alaska Native, 12.5% Hispanic of any race, 2.1% two or more races (2000); Density: 2,560.5 persons per square mile (2000); Age: 29.5% under 18, 5.8% over 64 (2000); Marriage status: 21.2% never married, 64.5% now married, 4.5% widowed, 9.8% divorced (2000); Foreign born: 9.1% (2000); Ancestry (includes multiple ancestries): 29.6% German, 22.0% Other groups, 14.2% Irish, 11.8% Italian, 10.8% Polish (2000).
Economy: Single-family building permits issued: 490 (2001) / 509 (2000); Multi-family building permits issued: 0 (2001) / 31 (2000); Employment by occupation: 16.4% management, 16.3% professional, 11.8% services, 30.2% sales, 0.1% farming, 9.3% construction, 15.9% production (2000).
Income: Per capita income: $25,676 (2000); Median household income: $67,323 (2000); Poverty rate: 3.0% (2000).
Taxes: Total city taxes per capita: $158 (1997); City property taxes per capita: $90 (1997).
Education: High school graduation rate: 90.4% (2000); College graduation rate: 25.3% (2000).
Housing: Homeownership rate: 88.9% (2000); Median home value: $154,000 (2000); Median rent: $675 per month (2000); Median age of housing: 8 years (2000).
Newspapers: El Conquistador (2 x month)
Transportation: Commute to work: 92.2% car, 2.6% public transportation, 0.8% walk, 4.1% work from home (2000); Travel time to work: 21.5% less than 15 minutes, 30.8% 15 to 30 minutes, 22.5% 30 to 45 minutes, 11.0% 45 to 60 minutes, 14.2% 60 minutes or more (2000)

SUGAR GROVE (village). Covers a land area of 6.449 square miles and a water area of 0.015 square miles. Located at 41.77° N. Lat.; 88.44° W. Long. Elevation is 726 feet.
Population: 3,909 (2000); Race: 95.4% White, 3.0% Black, 0.0% Asian, 0.0% American Indian and Alaska Native, 7.1% Hispanic of any race, 0.2% two or more races (2000); Density: 606.1 persons per square mile (2000); Age: 33.7% under 18, 5.0% over 64 (2000); Marriage status: 17.3% never married, 70.6% now married, 3.0% widowed, 9.1% divorced (2000); Foreign born: 1.7% (2000); Ancestry (includes multiple ancestries): 30.5% German, 15.9% Irish, 11.8% Other groups, 11.7% Italian, 9.2% English (2000).
Economy: In agricultural area: grain; dairying. Manufacturing. Aurora Municipal Airport to West. Single-family building permits issued: 304 (2001) / 140 (2000); Multi-family building permits issued: 0 (2001) / 0 (2000); Employment by occupation: 22.2% management, 20.3% professional, 6.1% services, 29.3% sales, 0.0% farming, 9.5% construction, 12.7% production (2000).
Income: Per capita income: $30,299 (2000); Median household income: $75,856 (2000); Poverty rate: 1.8% (2000).
Taxes: Total city taxes per capita: $390 (1997); City property taxes per capita: $183 (1997).
Education: High school graduation rate: 97.3% (2000); College graduation rate: 33.3% (2000).

Two-year College(s)

Waubonsee Community College (Public)
2001 Enrollment: 7,890 630-466-7900
2001 Tuition: In-state $4,752; Out-of-state $5,688

Housing: Homeownership rate: 88.6% (2000); Median home value: $184,000 (2000); Median rent: $694 per month (2000); Median age of housing: 12 years (2000).
Transportation: Commute to work: 91.8% car, 1.8% public transportation, 0.3% walk, 5.3% work from home (2000); Travel time to work: 18.6% less than 15 minutes, 34.4% 15 to 30 minutes, 25.6% 30 to 45 minutes, 12.9% 45 to 60 minutes, 8.5% 60 minutes or more (2000)
Additional Information Contacts
Sugar Grove Chamber of Commerce 630-466-7895

VIRGIL (village). Covers a land area of 1.882 square miles and a water area of 0 square miles. Located at 41.95° N. Lat.; 88.52° W. Long. Elevation is 870 feet.
Population: 266 (2000); Race: 92.5% White, 4.1% Black, 0.0% Asian, 0.0% American Indian and Alaska Native, 3.3% Hispanic of any race, 3.3% two or more races (2000); Density: 141.3 persons per square mile (2000); Age: 33.6% under 18, 2.5% over 64 (2000); Marriage status: 18.1% never married, 66.7% now married, 3.4% widowed, 11.9% divorced (2000); Foreign born: 0.0% (2000); Ancestry (includes multiple ancestries): 32.0% German, 19.9% Irish, 14.1% English, 11.2% Italian, 10.8% Other groups (2000).

Economy: Employment by occupation: 16.5% management, 12.8% professional, 15.8% services, 22.6% sales, 0.8% farming, 11.3% construction, 20.3% production (2000).
Income: Per capita income: $26,881 (2000); Median household income: $78,252 (2000); Poverty rate: 0.4% (2000).
Taxes: Total city taxes per capita: $26 (2000); City property taxes per capita: $0 (2000).
Education: High school graduation rate: 85.0% (2000); College graduation rate: 10.2% (2000).
Housing: Homeownership rate: 90.4% (2000); Median home value: $153,100 (2000); Median rent: $575 per month (2000); Median age of housing: 28 years (2000).
Transportation: Commute to work: 91.0% car, 3.0% public transportation, 3.8% walk, 2.3% work from home (2000); Travel time to work: 20.8% less than 15 minutes, 20.8% 15 to 30 minutes, 32.3% 30 to 45 minutes, 10.0% 45 to 60 minutes, 16.2% 60 minutes or more (2000)

WAYNE (village). Covers a land area of 5.816 square miles and a water area of 0 square miles. Located at 41.95° N. Lat.; 88.25° W. Long. Elevation is 744 feet.
Population: 2,137 (2000); Race: 98.1% White, 0.0% Black, 1.6% Asian, 0.2% American Indian and Alaska Native, 5.2% Hispanic of any race, 0.0% two or more races (2000); Density: 367.4 persons per square mile (2000); Age: 28.7% under 18, 6.0% over 64 (2000); Marriage status: 17.3% never married, 71.7% now married, 4.7% widowed, 6.3% divorced (2000); Foreign born: 5.0% (2000); Ancestry (includes multiple ancestries): 20.2% German, 18.6% Irish, 17.6% Italian, 15.2% Polish, 9.3% English (2000).
Economy: Single-family building permits issued: 20 (2001) / 26 (2000); Multi-family building permits issued: 0 (2001) / 0 (2000); Employment by occupation: 29.7% management, 18.2% professional, 6.5% services, 33.2% sales, 1.0% farming, 7.2% construction, 4.2% production (2000).
Income: Per capita income: $54,990 (2000); Median household income: $115,338 (2000); Poverty rate: 0.6% (2000).
Education: High school graduation rate: 95.5% (2000); College graduation rate: 53.8% (2000).
Housing: Homeownership rate: 98.3% (2000); Median home value: $442,500 (2000); Median rent: $550 per month (2000); Median age of housing: 20 years (2000).
Transportation: Commute to work: 90.2% car, 4.4% public transportation, 0.4% walk, 5.0% work from home (2000); Travel time to work: 13.8% less than 15 minutes, 30.7% 15 to 30 minutes, 20.1% 30 to 45 minutes, 18.3% 45 to 60 minutes, 17.1% 60 minutes or more (2000)

WEST DUNDEE (village). Aka Dundee. Covers a land area of 2.660 square miles and a water area of 0.078 square miles. Located at 42.09° N. Lat.; 88.28° W. Long. Elevation is 750 feet.
History: West Dundee was settled by Scots and English in the 1830's, and named for Dundee, Scotland. Allan Pinkerton (1819-1884) operated a coopers trade in West Dundee, but found a second career as a detective when his evidence resulted in the capture of some counterfeiters.
Population: 5,428 (2000); Race: 94.1% White, 0.9% Black, 1.5% Asian, 0.0% American Indian and Alaska Native, 3.1% Hispanic of any race, 2.8% two or more races (2000); Density: 2,040.5 persons per square mile (2000); Age: 26.5% under 18, 7.3% over 64 (2000); Marriage status: 21.3% never married, 60.4% now married, 6.0% widowed, 12.2% divorced (2000); Foreign born: 6.9% (2000); Ancestry (includes multiple ancestries): 35.9% German, 19.7% Irish, 11.2% Polish, 8.3% English, 7.9% Italian (2000).
Economy: Single-family building permits issued: 21 (2001) / 3 (2000); Multi-family building permits issued: 0 (2001) / 352 (2000); Employment by occupation: 23.3% management, 21.4% professional, 7.0% services, 32.3% sales, 0.0% farming, 6.4% construction, 9.7% production (2000).
Income: Per capita income: $30,674 (2000); Median household income: $62,540 (2000); Poverty rate: 3.7% (2000).
Taxes: Total city taxes per capita: $1,443 (1997); City property taxes per capita: $161 (1997).
Education: High school graduation rate: 91.1% (2000); College graduation rate: 36.8% (2000).
Housing: Homeownership rate: 70.5% (2000); Median home value: $209,900 (2000); Median rent: $669 per month (2000); Median age of housing: 32 years (2000).
Transportation: Commute to work: 91.5% car, 2.8% public transportation, 1.0% walk, 4.8% work from home (2000); Travel time to work: 27.9% less than 15 minutes, 28.9% 15 to 30 minutes, 21.6% 30 to 45 minutes, 12.6% 45 to 60 minutes, 9.0% 60 minutes or more (2000)

Kankakee County

Located in northeastern Illinois; bounded on the east by Indiana; drained by the Kankakee and Iroquois Rivers. Covers a land area of 676.70 square miles, a water area of 4.70 square miles, and is located in the Central Time Zone. The county government was organized in 1853. County seat is Kankakee.

Kankakee County is part of the Kankakee, IL PMSA. The entire metro area includes: Kankakee County

Weather Station: Kankakee Metro Wastewater — Elevation: 639 feet

	Jan	Feb	Mar	Apr	May	Jun	Jul	Aug	Sep	Oct	Nov	Dec
High	31	36	48	60	72	82	86	83	77	65	50	36
Low	13	18	28	38	49	59	63	61	52	40	31	20
Precip	1.9	1.7	2.8	3.8	4.6	4.4	4.3	3.2	3.3	2.7	3.4	2.5
Snow	8.9	6.4	2.9	1.0	tr	0.0	0.0	0.0	0.0	tr	1.0	5.6

High and Low temperatures in degrees Fahrenheit; Precipitation and Snow in inches

Population: 103,833 (2000); Race: 79.8% White, 15.2% Black, 0.7% Asian, 0.3% American Indian and Alaska Native, 4.8% Hispanic of any race, 1.5% two or more races (2000); Density: 153.4 persons per square mile (2000); Age: 27.0% under 18, 13.1% over 64 (2000).
Religion: Five largest groups: 21.3% Catholic Church, 5.2% Church of the Nazarene, 4.6% The United Methodist Church, 4.5% Lutheran Church—Missouri Synod, 1.3% Southern Baptist Convention (2000).
Economy: Unemployment rate: 7.0% (11/2002); Total civilian labor force: 51,973 (11/2002); Leading industries: 11.0% manufacturing; 10.2% retail trade; 10.1% health care and social assistance (2000); Companies that employ more than 1,000 persons: 2 (2000); Companies that employ more than 100 persons: 67 (2000); Farms: 831 totaling 351,567 acres (1997); Minority business ownership rate: 4.1% (1997); Women business ownership rate: 31.5% (1997); Retail sales per capita: $8,878 (1997). Single-family building permits issued: 405 (2001) / 313 (2000); Multi-family building permits issued: 48 (2001) / 76 (2000).
Income: Per capita income: $19,055 (2000); Median household income: $41,532 (2000); Poverty rate: 11.4% (2000); Bankruptcy rate: 7.80% (2001).
Taxes: Total county taxes per capita: $90 (2000); County property taxes per capita: $88 (2000).
Education: High school graduation rate: 79.8% (2000); College graduation rate: 15.0% (2000).
Housing: Homeownership rate: 69.4% (2000); Median home value: $99,200 (2000); Median rent: $443 per month (2000); Median age of housing: 36 years (2000).
Health: Birth rate: 144.4 per 10,000 population (1998); Age adjusted death rate: 100.6 per 10,000 population (1999); Age adjusted cancer mortality rate: 231.8 deaths per 100,000 population (1999). Number of physicians: 14.1 per 10,000 population (1999); Number of hospital beds: 58.5 per 10,000 population (1999).
Elections: 2000 Presidential election results: 47.7% Gore, 49.9% Bush, 1.8% Nader, 0.4% Buchanan

Additional Information Contacts

Kankakee County Government Offices 815-937-2990
Bradley Bourbonnais Chamber 815-932-2222
Kankakee County Association of Realtors. 815-937-5551
Kankakee River Valley Chamber. 815-933-7721
Manteno Chamber of Commerce 815-468-3720
Momence Chamber of Commerce 815-472-4620

Kankakee County Communities

AROMA PARK (village). Covers a land area of 1.200 square miles and a water area of 0.185 square miles. Located at 41.07° N. Lat.; 87.80° W. Long. Elevation is 615 feet.
Population: 821 (2000); Race: 95.4% White, 0.9% Black, 0.0% Asian, 0.2% American Indian and Alaska Native, 8.2% Hispanic of any race, 0.7% two or more races (2000); Density: 684.1 persons per square mile (2000); Age: 25.1% under 18, 14.0% over 64 (2000); Marriage status: 21.6% never married, 60.1% now married, 5.3% widowed, 13.0% divorced (2000); Foreign born: 4.5% (2000); Ancestry (includes multiple ancestries): 31.1% German, 15.7% Other groups, 14.4% French (except Basque), 10.3% Irish, 8.0% English (2000).
Economy: In agricultural area. Single-family building permits issued: 1 (2001) / 1 (2000); Multi-family building permits issued: 0 (2001) / 0 (2000); Employment by occupation: 9.3% management, 12.5% professional, 16.2% services, 25.8% sales, 0.5% farming, 16.0% construction, 19.7% production (2000).

Income: Per capita income: $17,806 (2000); Median household income: $41,375 (2000); Poverty rate: 6.9% (2000).
Taxes: Total city taxes per capita: $49 (1997); City property taxes per capita: $38 (1997).
Education: High school graduation rate: 82.2% (2000); College graduation rate: 10.1% (2000).
Housing: Homeownership rate: 75.5% (2000); Median home value: $83,900 (2000); Median rent: $389 per month (2000); Median age of housing: 44 years (2000).
Transportation: Commute to work: 92.7% car, 1.1% public transportation, 1.1% walk, 4.6% work from home (2000); Travel time to work: 29.8% less than 15 minutes, 47.4% 15 to 30 minutes, 11.9% 30 to 45 minutes, 5.1% 45 to 60 minutes, 5.7% 60 minutes or more (2000)

BONFIELD (village). Covers a land area of 0.274 square miles and a water area of 0 square miles. Located at 41.14° N. Lat.; 88.05° W. Long. Elevation is 630 feet.
Population: 364 (2000); Race: 98.7% White, 0.0% Black, 0.8% Asian, 0.0% American Indian and Alaska Native, 0.0% Hispanic of any race, 0.5% two or more races (2000); Density: 1,328.9 persons per square mile (2000); Age: 29.6% under 18, 8.2% over 64 (2000); Marriage status: 17.8% never married, 76.3% now married, 4.1% widowed, 1.9% divorced (2000); Foreign born: 0.3% (2000); Ancestry (includes multiple ancestries): 36.8% German, 13.0% Irish, 11.6% French (except Basque), 9.5% United States or American, 9.0% Polish (2000).
Economy: In agricultural area. Single-family building permits issued: 2 (2001) / 2 (2000); Multi-family building permits issued: 0 (2001) / 0 (2000); Employment by occupation: 7.3% management, 16.3% professional, 10.1% services, 26.4% sales, 1.7% farming, 21.3% construction, 16.9% production (2000).
Income: Per capita income: $18,531 (2000); Median household income: $49,722 (2000); Poverty rate: 2.6% (2000).
Taxes: Total city taxes per capita: $39 (1997); City property taxes per capita: $6 (1997).
Education: High school graduation rate: 91.0% (2000); College graduation rate: 10.7% (2000).
Housing: Homeownership rate: 82.3% (2000); Median home value: $121,900 (2000); Median rent: $425 per month (2000); Median age of housing: 34 years (2000).
Transportation: Commute to work: 87.6% car, 0.0% public transportation, 5.6% walk, 5.1% work from home (2000); Travel time to work: 17.9% less than 15 minutes, 42.3% 15 to 30 minutes, 20.8% 30 to 45 minutes, 11.3% 45 to 60 minutes, 7.7% 60 minutes or more (2000)

BOURBONNAIS (village). Covers a land area of 4.620 square miles and a water area of 0 square miles. Located at 41.16° N. Lat.; 87.87° W. Long. Elevation is 663 feet.
History: Fur trader Noel La Vasseur established a trading post here in 1832, which drew French-Canadian settlers to the community named for Francois Bourbonnais. Bourbonnais was the first settlement on the Kankakee River.
Population: 15,256 (2000); Race: 90.5% White, 3.9% Black, 2.4% Asian, 0.4% American Indian and Alaska Native, 2.6% Hispanic of any race, 1.8% two or more races (2000); Density: 3,302.1 persons per square mile (2000); Age: 24.8% under 18, 9.7% over 64 (2000); Marriage status: 29.1% never married, 58.1% now married, 5.3% widowed, 7.4% divorced (2000); Foreign born: 4.0% (2000); Ancestry (includes multiple ancestries): 25.4% German, 14.7% Irish, 13.1% Other groups, 12.1% French (except Basque), 8.2% English (2000).
Vital Statistics: Birth rate: 184.2 per 10,000 population (1998)
Economy: Single-family building permits issued: 74 (2001) / 39 (2000); Multi-family building permits issued: 0 (2001) / 0 (2000); Employment by occupation: 11.8% management, 22.5% professional, 14.7% services, 29.5% sales, 0.0% farming, 7.5% construction, 14.0% production (2000).
Income: Per capita income: $22,476 (2000); Median household income: $49,329 (2000); Poverty rate: 6.5% (2000).
Taxes: Total city taxes per capita: $170 (1997); City property taxes per capita: $102 (1997).
Education: High school graduation rate: 88.9% (2000); College graduation rate: 26.7% (2000).

School District(s)

Bourbonnais School District 53 (PK-08)
2000 Enrollment: 2,372 815-939-2574
Saint George C C School District 258 (PK-08)
2000 Enrollment: 195 815-933-1503

Four-year College(s)

Olivet Nazarene University (Private, Not-for-profit, Church of the Nazarene)
2001 Enrollment: 3,350 815-939-5011
2001 Tuition: In-state $12,644; Out-of-state $12,644

Housing: Homeownership rate: 63.5% (2000); Median home value: $120,300 (2000); Median rent: $526 per month (2000); Median age of housing: 24 years (2000).
Newspapers: The Herald (1 x week)
Transportation: Commute to work: 91.0% car, 1.0% public transportation, 4.9% walk, 2.9% work from home (2000); Travel time to work: 52.8% less than 15 minutes, 25.4% 15 to 30 minutes, 8.0% 30 to 45 minutes, 4.6% 45 to 60 minutes, 9.2% 60 minutes or more (2000)
Additional Information Contacts
Bradley Bourbonnais Chamber 815-932-2222

BRADLEY (village). Covers a land area of 3.781 square miles and a water area of 0.005 square miles. Located at 41.14° N. Lat.; 87.85° W. Long. Elevation is 632 feet.
History: Bradley was known as North Kankakee when it was organized in 1892, but soon was renamed for resident and factory-owner David Bradley.
Population: 12,784 (2000); Race: 95.0% White, 1.0% Black, 0.7% Asian, 0.6% American Indian and Alaska Native, 3.6% Hispanic of any race, 1.6% two or more races (2000); Density: 3,381.3 persons per square mile (2000); Age: 26.7% under 18, 13.5% over 64 (2000); Marriage status: 23.6% never married, 54.9% now married, 8.1% widowed, 13.4% divorced (2000); Foreign born: 1.8% (2000); Ancestry (includes multiple ancestries): 27.0% German, 16.4% Irish, 13.5% French (except Basque), 9.2% English, 8.9% Other groups (2000).
Vital Statistics: Birth rate: 138.5 per 10,000 population (1998)
Economy: Single-family building permits issued: 93 (2001) / 36 (2000); Multi-family building permits issued: 16 (2001) / 24 (2000); Employment by occupation: 9.2% management, 13.5% professional, 14.2% services, 31.6% sales, 0.3% farming, 12.2% construction, 19.1% production (2000).
Income: Per capita income: $19,035 (2000); Median household income: $41,757 (2000); Poverty rate: 6.8% (2000).
Taxes: Total city taxes per capita: $333 (1997); City property taxes per capita: $244 (1997).
Education: High school graduation rate: 83.0% (2000); College graduation rate: 11.7% (2000).

School District(s)

Bradley Bourbonnais CHSD 307 (09-12)
2000 Enrollment: 1,611 815-937-3715
Bradley School District 61 (PK-08)
2000 Enrollment: 1,423 815-933-3371

Housing: Homeownership rate: 67.3% (2000); Median home value: $91,500 (2000); Median rent: $487 per month (2000); Median age of housing: 38 years (2000).
Transportation: Commute to work: 95.3% car, 1.0% public transportation, 1.7% walk, 1.1% work from home (2000); Travel time to work: 55.8% less than 15 minutes, 26.0% 15 to 30 minutes, 7.0% 30 to 45 minutes, 5.1% 45 to 60 minutes, 6.2% 60 minutes or more (2000)

BUCKINGHAM (village). Covers a land area of 0.276 square miles and a water area of 0 square miles. Located at 41.04° N. Lat.; 88.17° W. Long. Elevation is 655 feet.
Population: 237 (2000); Race: 98.3% White, 0.0% Black, 0.0% Asian, 0.0% American Indian and Alaska Native, 0.0% Hispanic of any race, 1.7% two or more races (2000); Density: 859.4 persons per square mile (2000); Age: 31.0% under 18, 5.6% over 64 (2000); Marriage status: 24.3% never married, 64.4% now married, 4.0% widowed, 7.3% divorced (2000); Foreign born: 0.0% (2000); Ancestry (includes multiple ancestries): 27.2% German, 17.2% Irish, 17.2% Other groups, 14.2% French (except Basque), 9.5% United States or American (2000).
Economy: In agricultural area. Single-family building permits issued: 1 (2001) / 0 (2000); Multi-family building permits issued: 0 (2001) / 0 (2000); Employment by occupation: 1.7% management, 12.6% professional, 21.0% services, 17.6% sales, 0.0% farming, 13.4% construction, 33.6% production (2000).
Income: Per capita income: $19,816 (2000); Median household income: $53,542 (2000); Poverty rate: 8.3% (2000).
Taxes: Total city taxes per capita: $35 (1997); City property taxes per capita: $35 (1997).
Education: High school graduation rate: 82.8% (2000); College graduation rate: 10.4% (2000).

Housing: Homeownership rate: 92.9% (2000); Median home value: $77,300 (2000); Median rent: $363 per month (2000); Median age of housing: 42 years (2000).
Transportation: Commute to work: 95.3% car, 0.0% public transportation, 0.0% walk, 4.7% work from home (2000); Travel time to work: 14.7% less than 15 minutes, 33.3% 15 to 30 minutes, 39.2% 30 to 45 minutes, 7.8% 45 to 60 minutes, 4.9% 60 minutes or more (2000)

ESSEX (village). Covers a land area of 2.030 square miles and a water area of 0.024 square miles. Located at 41.17° N. Lat.; 88.19° W. Long. Elevation is 590 feet.
Population: 554 (2000); Race: 100.0% White, 0.0% Black, 0.0% Asian, 0.0% American Indian and Alaska Native, 0.0% Hispanic of any race, 0.0% two or more races (2000); Density: 272.9 persons per square mile (2000); Age: 25.9% under 18, 10.6% over 64 (2000); Marriage status: 21.2% never married, 67.1% now married, 5.5% widowed, 6.2% divorced (2000); Foreign born: 0.5% (2000); Ancestry (includes multiple ancestries): 26.9% German, 17.4% Irish, 11.1% Italian, 9.5% English, 8.0% Polish (2000).
Economy: In agricultural area: grain. Single-family building permits issued: 16 (2001) / 14 (2000); Multi-family building permits issued: 0 (2001) / 0 (2000); Employment by occupation: 5.1% management, 14.9% professional, 19.9% services, 18.8% sales, 0.0% farming, 19.2% construction, 22.1% production (2000).
Income: Per capita income: $18,686 (2000); Median household income: $50,238 (2000); Poverty rate: 5.8% (2000).
Taxes: Total city taxes per capita: $42 (1997); City property taxes per capita: $26 (1997).
Education: High school graduation rate: 87.1% (2000); College graduation rate: 6.6% (2000).
Housing: Homeownership rate: 89.7% (2000); Median home value: $106,700 (2000); Median rent: $500 per month (2000); Median age of housing: 29 years (2000).
Transportation: Commute to work: 98.1% car, 0.0% public transportation, 0.0% walk, 1.1% work from home (2000); Travel time to work: 21.9% less than 15 minutes, 23.5% 15 to 30 minutes, 26.5% 30 to 45 minutes, 13.1% 45 to 60 minutes, 15.0% 60 minutes or more (2000)

GRANT PARK (village). Covers a land area of 0.618 square miles and a water area of 0.026 square miles. Located at 41.24° N. Lat.; 87.64° W. Long. Elevation is 695 feet.
Population: 1,358 (2000); Race: 97.2% White, 0.0% Black, 0.1% Asian, 0.0% American Indian and Alaska Native, 3.3% Hispanic of any race, 1.2% two or more races (2000); Density: 2,196.2 persons per square mile (2000); Age: 28.2% under 18, 12.6% over 64 (2000); Marriage status: 20.7% never married, 65.3% now married, 7.6% widowed, 6.5% divorced (2000); Foreign born: 1.7% (2000); Ancestry (includes multiple ancestries): 37.7% German, 19.4% Irish, 13.5% Polish, 8.2% Italian, 8.1% Other groups (2000).
Economy: In agricultural area. Single-family building permits issued: 5 (2001) / 5 (2000); Multi-family building permits issued: 12 (2001) / 6 (2000); Employment by occupation: 12.1% management, 9.6% professional, 9.7% services, 27.5% sales, 0.6% farming, 14.6% construction, 25.8% production (2000).
Income: Per capita income: $22,403 (2000); Median household income: $52,153 (2000); Poverty rate: 4.4% (2000).
Taxes: Total city taxes per capita: $152 (1997); City property taxes per capita: $128 (1997).
Education: High school graduation rate: 85.1% (2000); College graduation rate: 9.3% (2000).

School District(s)

Grant Park C U School District 6 (KG-12)
2000 Enrollment: 565 815-465-6013
Housing: Homeownership rate: 72.5% (2000); Median home value: $124,900 (2000); Median rent: $460 per month (2000); Median age of housing: 37 years (2000).
Transportation: Commute to work: 90.3% car, 1.2% public transportation, 5.0% walk, 2.7% work from home (2000); Travel time to work: 25.5% less than 15 minutes, 23.1% 15 to 30 minutes, 23.4% 30 to 45 minutes, 13.8% 45 to 60 minutes, 14.1% 60 minutes or more (2000)

HERSCHER (village). Covers a land area of 1.725 square miles and a water area of 0 square miles. Located at 41.05° N. Lat.; 88.09° W. Long. Elevation is 660 feet.
Population: 1,523 (2000); Race: 97.7% White, 0.0% Black, 0.0% Asian, 0.7% American Indian and Alaska Native, 1.1% Hispanic of any race, 1.6% two or more races (2000); Density: 883.1 persons per square mile (2000); Age: 31.2% under 18, 14.9% over 64 (2000); Marriage status: 26.2% never married, 60.8% now married, 6.0% widowed, 7.0% divorced (2000); Foreign born: 0.7% (2000); Ancestry (includes multiple ancestries): 36.6% German, 18.2% Irish, 13.5% English, 10.9% French (except Basque), 9.4% United States or American (2000).
Economy: In agricultural area. Single-family building permits issued: 1 (2001) / 8 (2000); Multi-family building permits issued: 0 (2001) / 12 (2000); Employment by occupation: 13.2% management, 25.2% professional, 11.7% services, 24.5% sales, 0.3% farming, 8.2% construction, 16.7% production (2000).
Income: Per capita income: $18,522 (2000); Median household income: $48,250 (2000); Poverty rate: 7.7% (2000).
Taxes: Total city taxes per capita: $31 (1997); City property taxes per capita: $31 (1997).
Education: High school graduation rate: 91.9% (2000); College graduation rate: 25.6% (2000).

School District(s)

Herscher Community Unit School District 2 (PK-12)
2000 Enrollment: 2,255 815-426-2162
Housing: Homeownership rate: 76.9% (2000); Median home value: $108,100 (2000); Median rent: $431 per month (2000); Median age of housing: 34 years (2000).
Newspapers: Herscher Pilot (1 x week)
Transportation: Commute to work: 92.7% car, 0.0% public transportation, 4.4% walk, 3.0% work from home (2000); Travel time to work: 28.2% less than 15 minutes, 35.0% 15 to 30 minutes, 21.9% 30 to 45 minutes, 5.7% 45 to 60 minutes, 9.2% 60 minutes or more (2000)

HOPKINS PARK (village). Aka Pembroke. Covers a land area of 3.661 square miles and a water area of 0 square miles. Located at 41.07° N. Lat.; 87.60° W. Long. Elevation is 675 feet.
Population: 711 (2000); Race: 3.6% White, 95.4% Black, 0.0% Asian, 0.0% American Indian and Alaska Native, 0.8% Hispanic of any race, 0.0% two or more races (2000); Density: 194.2 persons per square mile (2000); Age: 32.3% under 18, 13.6% over 64 (2000); Marriage status: 42.6% never married, 30.8% now married, 13.1% widowed, 13.5% divorced (2000); Foreign born: 0.3% (2000); Ancestry (includes multiple ancestries): 68.5% Other groups, 2.0% United States or American, 1.9% African, 0.5% English, 0.4% Polish (2000).
Economy: Corn, soybeans. Manufacturing: liquid food supplements. Single-family building permits issued: 40 (2001) / 0 (2000); Multi-family building permits issued: 0 (2001) / 0 (2000); Employment by occupation: 4.6% management, 29.1% professional, 22.9% services, 14.9% sales, 0.0% farming, 0.6% construction, 28.0% production (2000).
Income: Per capita income: $8,788 (2000); Median household income: $17,778 (2000); Poverty rate: 44.2% (2000).
Taxes: Total city taxes per capita: $40 (1997); City property taxes per capita: $11 (1997).
Education: High school graduation rate: 54.9% (2000); College graduation rate: 2.8% (2000).

School District(s)

Pembroke C C School District 259 (PK-08)
2000 Enrollment: 549 815-944-8168
Housing: Homeownership rate: 75.1% (2000); Median home value: $63,400 (2000); Median rent: $350 per month (2000); Median age of housing: 28 years (2000).
Transportation: Commute to work: 93.4% car, 2.4% public transportation, 0.0% walk, 4.2% work from home (2000); Travel time to work: 18.1% less than 15 minutes, 28.7% 15 to 30 minutes, 35.6% 30 to 45 minutes, 12.5% 45 to 60 minutes, 5.0% 60 minutes or more (2000)

IRWIN (village). Covers a land area of 0.068 square miles and a water area of 0 square miles. Located at 41.05° N. Lat.; 87.98° W. Long. Elevation is 662 feet.
Population: 92 (2000); Race: 100.0% White, 0.0% Black, 0.0% Asian, 0.0% American Indian and Alaska Native, 0.0% Hispanic of any race, 0.0% two or more races (2000); Density: 1,355.1 persons per square mile (2000); Age: 9.5% under 18, 28.6% over 64 (2000); Marriage status: 25.4% never married, 46.0% now married, 17.5% widowed, 11.1% divorced (2000); Foreign born: 0.0% (2000); Ancestry (includes multiple ancestries): 38.1% German, 20.6% Irish, 19.0% French (except Basque), 11.1% English, 6.3% Scotch-Irish (2000).
Economy: In agricultural area: corn, soybeans; dairying. Single-family building permits issued: 0 (2001) / 0 (2000); Multi-family building permits issued: 0 (2001) / 0 (2000); Employment by occupation: 0.0% management, 16.7% professional, 50.0% services, 8.3% sales, 12.5% farming, 12.5% construction, 0.0% production (2000).

Income: Per capita income: $19,027 (2000); Median household income: $35,417 (2000); Poverty rate: 0.0% (2000).
Taxes: Total city taxes per capita: $47 (1997); City property taxes per capita: $47 (1997).
Education: High school graduation rate: 72.7% (2000); College graduation rate: 23.6% (2000).
Housing: Homeownership rate: 94.1% (2000); Median home value: $88,000 (2000); Median rent: $325 per month (2000); Median age of housing: 42 years (2000).
Transportation: Commute to work: 83.3% car, 0.0% public transportation, 16.7% walk, 0.0% work from home (2000); Travel time to work: 50.0% less than 15 minutes, 41.7% 15 to 30 minutes, 8.3% 30 to 45 minutes, 0.0% 45 to 60 minutes, 0.0% 60 minutes or more (2000)

KANKAKEE (city). Covers a land area of 12.274 square miles and a water area of 0.476 square miles. Located at 41.11° N. Lat.; 87.86° W. Long. Elevation is 663 feet.
History: Kankakee developed around the Illinois Central Railroad depot, and was incorporated in 1855.
Population: 27,491 (2000); Race: 51.1% White, 40.4% Black, 0.6% Asian, 0.3% American Indian and Alaska Native, 9.1% Hispanic of any race, 2.0% two or more races (2000); Density: 2,239.8 persons per square mile (2000); Age: 29.8% under 18, 13.3% over 64 (2000); Marriage status: 33.8% never married, 44.6% now married, 9.4% widowed, 12.2% divorced (2000); Foreign born: 6.7% (2000); Ancestry (includes multiple ancestries): 45.3% Other groups, 14.0% German, 7.7% Irish, 6.5% French (except Basque), 4.2% English (2000).
Vital Statistics: Birth rate: 211.7 per 10,000 population (1998)
Economy: Unemployment rate: 12.6% (11/2002); Total civilian labor force: 12,215 (11/2002); Single-family building permits issued: 6 (2001) / 11 (2000); Multi-family building permits issued: 0 (2001) / 0 (2000); Employment by occupation: 6.9% management, 15.6% professional, 21.5% services, 22.1% sales, 0.8% farming, 7.8% construction, 25.4% production (2000).
Income: Per capita income: $15,479 (2000); Median household income: $30,469 (2000); Poverty rate: 21.4% (2000).
Taxes: Total city taxes per capita: $360 (2000); City property taxes per capita: $184 (2000).
Education: High school graduation rate: 68.3% (2000); College graduation rate: 13.2% (2000).

School District(s)

Iroquois/Kankakee Roe (08-12)
2000 Enrollment: 22 815-937-2950
Kankakee Area Special Education Coop (01-12)
2000 Enrollment: 78 815-939-3651
Kankakee School District 111 (PK-12)
2000 Enrollment: 5,944 815-933-0700

Two-year College(s)

Kankakee Community College (Public)
2001 Enrollment: 3,164 815-933-0345
2001 Tuition: In-state $4,309; Out-of-state $9,740

Housing: Homeownership rate: 53.1% (2000); Median home value: $73,400 (2000); Median rent: $401 per month (2000); Median age of housing: 48 years (2000).
Hospitals: Riverside Medical Center (336 beds); Saint Mary's Hospital of Kankakee (210 beds)
Newspapers: The Daily Journal (6 x week)
Transportation: Commute to work: 90.9% car, 1.4% public transportation, 3.0% walk, 2.0% work from home (2000); Travel time to work: 45.3% less than 15 minutes, 30.9% 15 to 30 minutes, 11.1% 30 to 45 minutes, 3.8% 45 to 60 minutes, 8.9% 60 minutes or more (2000); Amtrak: Service available.
Airports: Greater Kankakee
Additional Information Contacts
Kankakee County Association of Realtors. 815-937-5551
Kankakee River Valley Chamber. 815-933-7721

MANTENO (village). Covers a land area of 2.993 square miles and a water area of 0.032 square miles. Located at 41.25° N. Lat.; 87.83° W. Long. Elevation is 685 feet.
History: Incorporated 1878.
Population: 6,414 (2000); Race: 97.2% White, 0.4% Black, 0.6% Asian, 0.1% American Indian and Alaska Native, 2.2% Hispanic of any race, 0.5% two or more races (2000); Density: 2,143.0 persons per square mile (2000); Age: 25.5% under 18, 15.5% over 64 (2000); Marriage status: 19.5% never married, 64.2% now married, 7.6% widowed, 8.7% divorced (2000); Foreign born: 2.0% (2000); Ancestry (includes multiple ancestries): 32.6% German, 19.8% Irish, 9.6% English, 9.0% French (except Basque), 8.5% Polish (2000).
Economy: In agricultural area. Single-family building permits issued: 46 (2001) / 65 (2000); Multi-family building permits issued: 20 (2001) / 34 (2000); Employment by occupation: 12.3% management, 14.2% professional, 15.9% services, 27.2% sales, 0.2% farming, 9.7% construction, 20.5% production (2000).
Income: Per capita income: $22,826 (2000); Median household income: $48,599 (2000); Poverty rate: 5.3% (2000).
Taxes: Total city taxes per capita: $339 (1997); City property taxes per capita: $277 (1997).
Education: High school graduation rate: 85.5% (2000); College graduation rate: 17.0% (2000).

School District(s)

Manteno Community Unit School District 5 (KG-12)
2000 Enrollment: 1,676 815-928-7000

Housing: Homeownership rate: 68.8% (2000); Median home value: $138,300 (2000); Median rent: $526 per month (2000); Median age of housing: 16 years (2000).
Newspapers: Manteno News (1 x week)
Transportation: Commute to work: 94.1% car, 1.9% public transportation, 1.1% walk, 2.8% work from home (2000); Travel time to work: 29.1% less than 15 minutes, 29.8% 15 to 30 minutes, 18.8% 30 to 45 minutes, 10.2% 45 to 60 minutes, 12.2% 60 minutes or more (2000)
Additional Information Contacts
Manteno Chamber of Commerce 815-468-3720

MOMENCE (city). Covers a land area of 1.369 square miles and a water area of 0.077 square miles. Located at 41.16° N. Lat.; 87.66° W. Long. Elevation is 626 feet.
History: Momence, named for Isadore Momence, was laid out in 1844 on the Kankakee River. This was a camping place for travelers on the Hubbard Trail, who forded the Kankakee here.
Population: 3,171 (2000); Race: 90.3% White, 4.4% Black, 0.0% Asian, 0.4% American Indian and Alaska Native, 12.2% Hispanic of any race, 1.1% two or more races (2000); Density: 2,316.3 persons per square mile (2000); Age: 26.7% under 18, 18.1% over 64 (2000); Marriage status: 22.7% never married, 55.9% now married, 11.9% widowed, 9.5% divorced (2000); Foreign born: 6.4% (2000); Ancestry (includes multiple ancestries): 26.7% German, 15.4% Other groups, 14.2% Irish, 11.1% English, 10.1% French (except Basque) (2000).
Economy: Single-family building permits issued: 0 (2001) / 0 (2000); Multi-family building permits issued: 0 (2001) / 0 (2000); Employment by occupation: 7.0% management, 14.6% professional, 10.9% services, 24.8% sales, 2.2% farming, 12.7% construction, 27.7% production (2000).
Income: Per capita income: $17,836 (2000); Median household income: $37,898 (2000); Poverty rate: 9.2% (2000).
Taxes: Total city taxes per capita: $228 (1997); City property taxes per capita: $89 (1997).
Education: High school graduation rate: 73.2% (2000); College graduation rate: 11.6% (2000).

School District(s)

Momence Community Unit School District 1 (PK-12)
2000 Enrollment: 1,351 815-472-3500

Housing: Homeownership rate: 67.4% (2000); Median home value: $94,900 (2000); Median rent: $399 per month (2000); Median age of housing: 59 years (2000).
Newspapers: Momence Progress-Reporter (1 x week)
Transportation: Commute to work: 87.7% car, 0.6% public transportation, 8.7% walk, 1.6% work from home (2000); Travel time to work: 48.0% less than 15 minutes, 31.2% 15 to 30 minutes, 8.5% 30 to 45 minutes, 3.8% 45 to 60 minutes, 8.4% 60 minutes or more (2000)
Additional Information Contacts
Momence Chamber of Commerce 815-472-4620

REDDICK (village). Covers a land area of 0.234 square miles and a water area of 0 square miles. Located at 41.09° N. Lat.; 88.24° W. Long.
Population: 219 (2000); Race: 99.2% White, 0.0% Black, 0.0% Asian, 0.0% American Indian and Alaska Native, 0.0% Hispanic of any race, 0.8% two or more races (2000); Density: 936.3 persons per square mile (2000); Age: 22.7% under 18, 11.3% over 64 (2000); Marriage status: 34.8% never married, 58.0% now married, 4.8% widowed, 2.4% divorced (2000); Foreign born: 0.8% (2000); Ancestry (includes multiple ancestries): 40.2% German, 16.0% Irish, 14.5% French (except Basque), 10.5% Italian, 5.9% English (2000).

Economy: Employment by occupation: 8.1% management, 18.4% professional, 16.2% services, 20.6% sales, 0.0% farming, 14.0% construction, 22.8% production (2000).
Income: Per capita income: $21,207 (2000); Median household income: $61,250 (2000); Poverty rate: 8.7% (2000).
Taxes: Total city taxes per capita: $28 (1997); City property taxes per capita: $19 (1997).
Education: High school graduation rate: 93.2% (2000); College graduation rate: 12.3% (2000).
Housing: Homeownership rate: 90.9% (2000); Median home value: $87,900 (2000); Median rent: $675 per month (2000); Median age of housing: 46 years (2000).
Transportation: Commute to work: 94.0% car, 2.2% public transportation, 0.0% walk, 2.2% work from home (2000); Travel time to work: 10.7% less than 15 minutes, 35.1% 15 to 30 minutes, 27.5% 30 to 45 minutes, 17.6% 45 to 60 minutes, 9.2% 60 minutes or more (2000)

SAINT ANNE (village). Covers a land area of 0.508 square miles and a water area of 0.007 square miles. Located at 41.02° N. Lat.; 87.71° W. Long. Elevation is 675 feet.
History: In 1852 Father Charles Chiniquy and many of his French-Canadian parishioners immigrated here from Bourbonnais and founded the town of St. Anne.
Population: 1,212 (2000); Race: 86.6% White, 0.8% Black, 0.2% Asian, 0.2% American Indian and Alaska Native, 13.9% Hispanic of any race, 1.7% two or more races (2000); Density: 2,385.3 persons per square mile (2000); Age: 28.0% under 18, 11.7% over 64 (2000); Marriage status: 23.9% never married, 59.7% now married, 5.2% widowed, 11.2% divorced (2000); Foreign born: 4.7% (2000); Ancestry (includes multiple ancestries): 23.7% German, 19.8% French (except Basque), 17.3% Other groups, 10.0% Irish, 9.5% United States or American (2000).
Economy: Single-family building permits issued: 1 (2001) / 1 (2000); Multi-family building permits issued: 0 (2001) / 0 (2000); Employment by occupation: 7.0% management, 12.4% professional, 15.2% services, 26.1% sales, 2.3% farming, 10.9% construction, 26.1% production (2000).
Income: Per capita income: $16,702 (2000); Median household income: $39,306 (2000); Poverty rate: 13.4% (2000).
Education: High school graduation rate: 80.8% (2000); College graduation rate: 12.0% (2000).

School District(s)

Saint Anne C C School District 256 (PK-08)
2000 Enrollment: 469 815-427-8190
Saint Anne Community H S District 302 (09-12)
2000 Enrollment: 258 815-427-8214

Housing: Homeownership rate: 67.7% (2000); Median home value: $78,100 (2000); Median rent: $347 per month (2000); Median age of housing: 56 years (2000).
Newspapers: Record (1 x week)
Transportation: Commute to work: 92.0% car, 0.0% public transportation, 4.5% walk, 2.9% work from home (2000); Travel time to work: 25.5% less than 15 minutes, 43.5% 15 to 30 minutes, 18.9% 30 to 45 minutes, 3.7% 45 to 60 minutes, 8.4% 60 minutes or more (2000)

SUN RIVER TERRACE (village). Covers a land area of 0.454 square miles and a water area of 0.025 square miles. Located at 41.12° N. Lat.; 87.73° W. Long. Elevation is 625 feet.
Population: 383 (2000); Race: 2.4% White, 93.2% Black, 0.0% Asian, 0.0% American Indian and Alaska Native, 0.7% Hispanic of any race, 1.9% two or more races (2000); Density: 843.2 persons per square mile (2000); Age: 33.9% under 18, 13.6% over 64 (2000); Marriage status: 31.6% never married, 46.4% now married, 10.5% widowed, 11.5% divorced (2000); Foreign born: 1.2% (2000); Ancestry (includes multiple ancestries): 80.1% Other groups, 1.0% United States or American, 0.7% African, 0.5% Jamaican, 0.5% Italian (2000).
Economy: Single-family building permits issued: 0 (2001) / 1 (2000); Multi-family building permits issued: 0 (2001) / 0 (2000); Employment by occupation: 0.0% management, 17.3% professional, 25.2% services, 26.8% sales, 0.0% farming, 3.9% construction, 26.8% production (2000).
Income: Per capita income: $11,692 (2000); Median household income: $26,875 (2000); Poverty rate: 17.5% (2000).
Taxes: Total city taxes per capita: $60 (1997); City property taxes per capita: $35 (1997).
Education: High school graduation rate: 57.7% (2000); College graduation rate: 5.3% (2000).
Housing: Homeownership rate: 65.5% (2000); Median home value: $65,000 (2000); Median rent: $194 per month (2000); Median age of housing: 33 years (2000).
Transportation: Commute to work: 99.2% car, 0.0% public transportation, 0.8% walk, 0.0% work from home (2000); Travel time to work: 13.1% less than 15 minutes, 70.5% 15 to 30 minutes, 6.6% 30 to 45 minutes, 4.1% 45 to 60 minutes, 5.7% 60 minutes or more (2000)

UNION HILL (village). Covers a land area of 0.047 square miles and a water area of 0 square miles. Located at 41.10° N. Lat.; 88.14° W. Long. Elevation is 617 feet.
Population: 66 (2000); Race: 100.0% White, 0.0% Black, 0.0% Asian, 0.0% American Indian and Alaska Native, 0.0% Hispanic of any race, 0.0% two or more races (2000); Density: 1,417.9 persons per square mile (2000); Age: 12.5% under 18, 20.8% over 64 (2000); Marriage status: 38.1% never married, 38.1% now married, 9.5% widowed, 14.3% divorced (2000); Foreign born: 0.0% (2000); Ancestry (includes multiple ancestries): 62.5% German, 8.3% French (except Basque), 8.3% Polish, 8.3% Irish (2000).
Economy: Agriculture: corn, soybeans; dairying. Lumber processing. Single-family building permits issued: 0 (2001) / 0 (2000); Multi-family building permits issued: 0 (2001) / 0 (2000); Employment by occupation: 0.0% management, 0.0% professional, 12.5% services, 31.3% sales, 0.0% farming, 0.0% construction, 56.3% production (2000).
Income: Per capita income: $21,371 (2000); Median household income: $28,125 (2000); Poverty rate: 0.0% (2000).
Taxes: Total city taxes per capita: $60 (1997); City property taxes per capita: $0 (1997).
Education: High school graduation rate: 100.0% (2000); College graduation rate: 0.0% (2000).
Housing: Homeownership rate: 90.0% (2000); Median home value: $85,000 (2000); Median age of housing: 60+ years (2000).
Transportation: Commute to work: 81.3% car, 0.0% public transportation, 18.8% walk, 0.0% work from home (2000); Travel time to work: 18.8% less than 15 minutes, 43.8% 15 to 30 minutes, 37.5% 30 to 45 minutes, 0.0% 45 to 60 minutes, 0.0% 60 minutes or more (2000)

Kendall County

Located in northeastern Illinois; drained by the Fox River. Covers a land area of 320.60 square miles, a water area of 2.10 square miles, and is located in the Central Time Zone. The county government was organized in 1841. County seat is Yorkville.

Kendall County is part of the Chicago, IL PMSA. The entire metro area includes: Cook County; DeKalb County; DuPage County; Grundy County; Kane County; Kendall County; Lake County; McHenry County; Will County

Population: 54,544 (2000); Race: 91.9% White, 1.1% Black, 1.2% Asian, 0.3% American Indian and Alaska Native, 7.5% Hispanic of any race, 1.8% two or more races (2000); Density: 170.1 persons per square mile (2000); Age: 29.5% under 18, 8.4% over 64 (2000).
Religion: Five largest groups: 17.8% Catholic Church, 4.2% The United Methodist Church, 3.5% Lutheran Church—Missouri Synod, 2.9% The Association of Free Lutheran Congregations, 2.2% Evangelical Lutheran Church in America (2000).
Economy: Unemployment rate: 5.9% (11/2002); Total civilian labor force: 29,905 (11/2002); Leading industries: 21.4% manufacturing; 18.3% retail trade; 11.5% construction (2000); Companies that employ more than 1,000 persons: 0 (2000); Companies that employ more than 100 persons: 21 (2000); Farms: 441 totaling 167,486 acres (1997); Minority business ownership rate: 0.0% (1997); Women business ownership rate: 27.0% (1997); Retail sales per capita: $7,441 (1997). Single-family building permits issued: 751 (2001) / 767 (2000); Multi-family building permits issued: 238 (2001) / 96 (2000).
Income: Per capita income: $25,188 (2000); Median household income: $64,625 (2000); Poverty rate: 3.0% (2000); Bankruptcy rate: 4.48% (2001).
Taxes: Total county taxes per capita: $189 (2000); County property taxes per capita: $146 (2000).
Education: High school graduation rate: 89.9% (2000); College graduation rate: 25.3% (2000).
Housing: Homeownership rate: 84.1% (2000); Median home value: $154,900 (2000); Median rent: $638 per month (2000); Median age of housing: 24 years (2000).
Health: Birth rate: 142.6 per 10,000 population (1998); Age adjusted death rate: 76.7 per 10,000 population (1999); Age adjusted cancer mortality rate:

192.0 deaths per 100,000 population (1999). Number of physicians: 5.0 per 10,000 population (1999); Number of hospital beds: n/a (1999).
Elections: 2000 Presidential election results: 37.1% Gore, 60.1% Bush, 2.1% Nader, 0.4% Buchanan
National and State Parks: Silver Springs State Park
Additional Information Contacts
Kendall County Government Offices 630-553-4143
Oswego Chamber of Commerce 630-554-3505
Plano Commerce Association 630-552-7272
Yorkville Area Chamber Commrc 630-553-2808
Yorkville Chamber of Commerce 630-553-6853

Kendall County Communities

BOULDER HILL (CDP). Covers a land area of 1.458 square miles and a water area of 0.009 square miles. Located at 41.71° N. Lat.; 88.33° W. Long.
Population: 8,169 (2000); Race: 89.5% White, 2.1% Black, 0.4% Asian, 0.3% American Indian and Alaska Native, 9.9% Hispanic of any race, 3.2% two or more races (2000); Density: 5,604.3 persons per square mile (2000); Age: 30.3% under 18, 8.4% over 64 (2000); Marriage status: 22.6% never married, 63.6% now married, 4.7% widowed, 9.0% divorced (2000); Foreign born: 4.1% (2000); Ancestry (includes multiple ancestries): 34.5% German, 15.7% Irish, 15.6% Other groups, 10.4% English, 6.0% Italian (2000).
Economy: Railroad junction. Employment by occupation: 9.4% management, 17.3% professional, 13.5% services, 34.5% sales, 0.2% farming, 10.1% construction, 15.0% production (2000).
Income: Per capita income: $21,536 (2000); Median household income: $60,016 (2000); Poverty rate: 1.8% (2000).
Education: High school graduation rate: 89.9% (2000); College graduation rate: 21.7% (2000).
Housing: Homeownership rate: 86.2% (2000); Median home value: $119,900 (2000); Median rent: $765 per month (2000); Median age of housing: 29 years (2000).
Transportation: Commute to work: 94.4% car, 1.4% public transportation, 1.3% walk, 2.9% work from home (2000); Travel time to work: 28.6% less than 15 minutes, 35.4% 15 to 30 minutes, 20.9% 30 to 45 minutes, 7.4% 45 to 60 minutes, 7.7% 60 minutes or more (2000)

BRISTOL (unincorporated postal area, zip code 60512). Aka Bristol Station. Covers a land area of 10.460 square miles and a water area of 0 square miles. Located at 41.70° N. Lat.; 88.41° W. Long. Elevation is 640 feet.
Population: 892 (2000); Race: 94.0% White, 0.0% Black, 4.5% Asian, 0.0% American Indian and Alaska Native, 2.5% Hispanic of any race, 0.6% two or more races (2000); Density: 85.3 persons per square mile (2000); Age: 16.8% under 18, 17.5% over 64 (2000); Marriage status: 22.3% never married, 68.9% now married, 4.1% widowed, 4.7% divorced (2000); Foreign born: 9.2% (2000); Ancestry (includes multiple ancestries): 37.9% German, 18.3% Irish, 9.8% English, 8.4% Other groups, 6.2% Swedish (2000).
Economy: In agricultural area. Employment by occupation: 12.0% management, 22.3% professional, 5.6% services, 26.3% sales, 0.0% farming, 18.2% construction, 15.6% production (2000).
Income: Per capita income: $28,669 (2000); Median household income: $65,625 (2000); Poverty rate: 1.5% (2000).
Education: High school graduation rate: 88.0% (2000); College graduation rate: 20.7% (2000).
Housing: Homeownership rate: 92.9% (2000); Median home value: $176,700 (2000); Median rent: $442 per month (2000); Median age of housing: 30 years (2000).
Transportation: Commute to work: 93.9% car, 2.6% public transportation, 2.3% walk, 1.3% work from home (2000); Travel time to work: 12.2% less than 15 minutes, 46.1% 15 to 30 minutes, 10.6% 30 to 45 minutes, 4.4% 45 to 60 minutes, 26.7% 60 minutes or more (2000)

LISBON (village). Covers a land area of 0.310 square miles and a water area of 0 square miles. Located at 41.48° N. Lat.; 88.48° W. Long. Elevation is 665 feet.
Population: 248 (2000); Race: 95.5% White, 0.0% Black, 0.0% Asian, 0.0% American Indian and Alaska Native, 5.7% Hispanic of any race, 0.8% two or more races (2000); Density: 801.0 persons per square mile (2000); Age: 25.6% under 18, 17.9% over 64 (2000); Marriage status: 22.4% never married, 58.2% now married, 10.7% widowed, 8.7% divorced (2000); Foreign born: 0.8% (2000); Ancestry (includes multiple ancestries): 35.4% German, 26.8% Norwegian, 17.5% Irish, 10.6% Other groups, 10.2% Italian (2000).
Economy: In rich agricultural area. Single-family building permits issued: 0 (2001) / 2 (2000); Multi-family building permits issued: 0 (2001) / 0 (2000); Employment by occupation: 6.1% management, 19.1% professional, 16.8% services, 16.0% sales, 0.0% farming, 17.6% construction, 24.4% production (2000).
Income: Per capita income: $21,456 (2000); Median household income: $51,042 (2000); Poverty rate: 0.8% (2000).
Taxes: Total city taxes per capita: $34 (1997); City property taxes per capita: $26 (1997).
Education: High school graduation rate: 82.5% (2000); College graduation rate: 11.3% (2000).
Housing: Homeownership rate: 86.8% (2000); Median home value: $112,500 (2000); Median rent: $430 per month (2000); Median age of housing: 49 years (2000).
Transportation: Commute to work: 94.6% car, 0.0% public transportation, 0.0% walk, 5.4% work from home (2000); Travel time to work: 13.9% less than 15 minutes, 23.0% 15 to 30 minutes, 37.7% 30 to 45 minutes, 13.9% 45 to 60 minutes, 11.5% 60 minutes or more (2000)

MILLINGTON (village). Covers a land area of 0.557 square miles and a water area of 0.052 square miles. Located at 41.56° N. Lat.; 88.60° W. Long. Elevation is 560 feet.
Population: 458 (2000); Race: 97.3% White, 0.0% Black, 0.0% Asian, 0.0% American Indian and Alaska Native, 5.3% Hispanic of any race, 0.8% two or more races (2000); Density: 822.8 persons per square mile (2000); Age: 35.9% under 18, 10.6% over 64 (2000); Marriage status: 20.7% never married, 70.3% now married, 3.6% widowed, 5.4% divorced (2000); Foreign born: 0.6% (2000); Ancestry (includes multiple ancestries): 38.1% German, 15.2% Irish, 9.7% English, 8.7% Norwegian, 8.0% Swedish (2000).
Economy: Employment by occupation: 10.4% management, 5.2% professional, 19.0% services, 32.0% sales, 0.4% farming, 12.1% construction, 20.8% production (2000).
Income: Per capita income: $13,898 (2000); Median household income: $43,583 (2000); Poverty rate: 10.4% (2000).
Taxes: Total city taxes per capita: $29 (1997); City property taxes per capita: $21 (1997).
Education: High school graduation rate: 74.3% (2000); College graduation rate: 3.4% (2000).
Housing: Homeownership rate: 81.1% (2000); Median home value: $105,900 (2000); Median rent: $525 per month (2000); Median age of housing: 42 years (2000).
Transportation: Commute to work: 98.7% car, 0.0% public transportation, 1.3% walk, 0.0% work from home (2000); Travel time to work: 18.9% less than 15 minutes, 23.7% 15 to 30 minutes, 26.3% 30 to 45 minutes, 14.5% 45 to 60 minutes, 16.7% 60 minutes or more (2000)

NEWARK (village). Covers a land area of 1.133 square miles and a water area of <.001 square miles. Located at 41.53° N. Lat.; 88.58° W. Long. Elevation is 680 feet.
Population: 887 (2000); Race: 98.1% White, 0.0% Black, 0.0% Asian, 0.0% American Indian and Alaska Native, 2.4% Hispanic of any race, 1.0% two or more races (2000); Density: 782.8 persons per square mile (2000); Age: 27.3% under 18, 12.1% over 64 (2000); Marriage status: 25.5% never married, 63.0% now married, 8.0% widowed, 3.4% divorced (2000); Foreign born: 2.3% (2000); Ancestry (includes multiple ancestries): 34.1% Norwegian, 27.3% German, 12.3% Irish, 11.9% English, 7.8% Italian (2000).
Economy: In rich agricultural area. Single-family building permits issued: 7 (2001) / 5 (2000); Multi-family building permits issued: 0 (2001) / 0 (2000); Employment by occupation: 10.8% management, 14.9% professional, 18.5% services, 23.2% sales, 0.8% farming, 14.1% construction, 17.7% production (2000).
Income: Per capita income: $22,078 (2000); Median household income: $59,904 (2000); Poverty rate: 3.7% (2000).
Taxes: Total city taxes per capita: $115 (1997); City property taxes per capita: $36 (1997).
Education: High school graduation rate: 91.5% (2000); College graduation rate: 15.5% (2000).

School District(s)
Lisbon Community Cons School District 90 (KG-08)
2000 Enrollment: 107 815-736-6324
Newark Community Cons School District 66 (PK-08)
2000 Enrollment: 250 815-695-5143
Newark Community H S District 18 (09-12)
2000 Enrollment: 203 815-695-5164

Housing: Homeownership rate: 83.4% (2000); Median home value: $131,000 (2000); Median rent: $525 per month (2000); Median age of housing: 44 years (2000).
Transportation: Commute to work: 89.5% car, 1.2% public transportation, 2.7% walk, 6.6% work from home (2000); Travel time to work: 20.5% less than 15 minutes, 31.1% 15 to 30 minutes, 20.7% 30 to 45 minutes, 12.6% 45 to 60 minutes, 15.2% 60 minutes or more (2000)

OSWEGO (village). Covers a land area of 6.582 square miles and a water area of 0.097 square miles. Located at 41.69° N. Lat.; 88.34° W. Long. Elevation is 646 feet.
Population: 13,326 (2000); Race: 91.6% White, 1.7% Black, 1.7% Asian, 0.6% American Indian and Alaska Native, 5.5% Hispanic of any race, 1.5% two or more races (2000); Density: 2,024.5 persons per square mile (2000); Age: 30.8% under 18, 7.8% over 64 (2000); Marriage status: 18.0% never married, 71.3% now married, 5.1% widowed, 5.7% divorced (2000); Foreign born: 4.7% (2000); Ancestry (includes multiple ancestries): 33.9% German, 20.0% Irish, 13.2% Other groups, 11.3% Polish, 11.3% English (2000).
Economy: Initial stages of urban growth occurring here. Dairying. Manufacturing: consumer goods, water softeners, telecommunications equipment. Single-family building permits issued: 439 (2001) / 513 (2000); Multi-family building permits issued: 184 (2001) / 80 (2000); Employment by occupation: 17.2% management, 24.6% professional, 8.9% services, 31.9% sales, 0.2% farming, 7.5% construction, 9.7% production (2000).
Income: Per capita income: $27,204 (2000); Median household income: $71,502 (2000); Poverty rate: 2.8% (2000).
Taxes: Total city taxes per capita: $43 (1997); City property taxes per capita: $20 (1997).
Education: High school graduation rate: 93.5% (2000); College graduation rate: 33.5% (2000).

School District(s)

Oswego Community Unit School District 308 (PK-12)
2000 Enrollment: 6,846 630-554-3447

Housing: Homeownership rate: 92.3% (2000); Median home value: $171,200 (2000); Median rent: $657 per month (2000); Median age of housing: 5 years (2000).
Newspapers: Ledger-Sentinel (1 x week)
Transportation: Commute to work: 89.7% car, 3.7% public transportation, 0.5% walk, 5.7% work from home (2000); Travel time to work: 19.3% less than 15 minutes, 29.0% 15 to 30 minutes, 22.4% 30 to 45 minutes, 13.7% 45 to 60 minutes, 15.6% 60 minutes or more (2000)
Additional Information Contacts
Oswego Chamber of Commerce 630-554-3505

PLANO (city). Covers a land area of 3.513 square miles and a water area of 0.042 square miles. Located at 41.66° N. Lat.; 88.53° W. Long. Elevation is 650 feet.
History: Plano was settled by a group of Norwegian Quakers led by Kleng Peerson in 1835.
Population: 5,633 (2000); Race: 79.9% White, 0.4% Black, 1.4% Asian, 0.3% American Indian and Alaska Native, 28.1% Hispanic of any race, 3.1% two or more races (2000); Density: 1,603.3 persons per square mile (2000); Age: 31.7% under 18, 9.0% over 64 (2000); Marriage status: 25.5% never married, 56.4% now married, 6.1% widowed, 12.0% divorced (2000); Foreign born: 17.0% (2000); Ancestry (includes multiple ancestries): 32.5% Other groups, 21.5% German, 10.7% Irish, 7.2% English, 5.0% Norwegian (2000).
Economy: Single-family building permits issued: 11 (2001) / 10 (2000); Multi-family building permits issued: 0 (2001) / 0 (2000); Employment by occupation: 10.1% management, 7.6% professional, 11.1% services, 24.6% sales, 0.0% farming, 9.7% construction, 36.8% production (2000).
Income: Per capita income: $17,837 (2000); Median household income: $46,526 (2000); Poverty rate: 5.4% (2000).
Taxes: Total city taxes per capita: $131 (1997); City property taxes per capita: $129 (1997).
Education: High school graduation rate: 75.4% (2000); College graduation rate: 10.2% (2000).

School District(s)

Plano Community Unit School District 88 (PK-12)
2000 Enrollment: 1,376 630-552-8978

Housing: Homeownership rate: 70.9% (2000); Median home value: $114,600 (2000); Median rent: $527 per month (2000); Median age of housing: 37 years (2000).
Transportation: Commute to work: 92.0% car, 0.0% public transportation, 3.4% walk, 4.3% work from home (2000); Travel time to work: 38.2% less than 15 minutes, 26.5% 15 to 30 minutes, 21.2% 30 to 45 minutes, 7.7% 45 to 60 minutes, 6.5% 60 minutes or more (2000); Amtrak: Service available.
Additional Information Contacts
Plano Commerce Association 630-552-7272

YORKVILLE (city). Covers a land area of 7.043 square miles and a water area of 0.111 square miles. Located at 41.64° N. Lat.; 88.44° W. Long. Elevation is 630 feet.
Population: 6,189 (2000); Race: 96.3% White, 0.1% Black, 0.0% Asian, 0.3% American Indian and Alaska Native, 3.7% Hispanic of any race, 2.0% two or more races (2000); Density: 878.8 persons per square mile (2000); Age: 31.4% under 18, 9.9% over 64 (2000); Marriage status: 18.9% never married, 66.9% now married, 6.5% widowed, 7.7% divorced (2000); Foreign born: 3.6% (2000); Ancestry (includes multiple ancestries): 34.0% German, 15.5% Irish, 8.8% English, 8.4% Polish, 6.7% Other groups (2000).
Economy: Dairying. Manufacturing: confections, toolboxes, circuit boards, seasonings. Single-family building permits issued: 198 (2001) / 127 (2000); Multi-family building permits issued: 54 (2001) / 16 (2000); Employment by occupation: 18.2% management, 16.9% professional, 12.8% services, 26.4% sales, 0.0% farming, 9.2% construction, 16.4% production (2000).
Income: Per capita income: $24,514 (2000); Median household income: $60,391 (2000); Poverty rate: 1.4% (2000).
Taxes: Total city taxes per capita: $304 (1997); City property taxes per capita: $103 (1997).
Education: High school graduation rate: 90.6% (2000); College graduation rate: 24.6% (2000).

School District(s)

Kendall Co Special Education Coop (03-12)
2000 Enrollment: 53 630-553-5833
Yorkville Community Unit School District 115 (PK-12)
2000 Enrollment: 2,253 630-553-4382

Housing: Homeownership rate: 74.5% (2000); Median home value: $157,700 (2000); Median rent: $652 per month (2000); Median age of housing: 21 years (2000).
Newspapers: Sandwich Record (1 x week); Plano Record (1 x week); Kendall County Record (1 x week)
Transportation: Commute to work: 95.3% car, 1.6% public transportation, 0.6% walk, 2.6% work from home (2000); Travel time to work: 22.3% less than 15 minutes, 31.3% 15 to 30 minutes, 23.5% 30 to 45 minutes, 12.6% 45 to 60 minutes, 10.3% 60 minutes or more (2000)
Additional Information Contacts
Yorkville Area Chamber Commrc 630-553-2808
Yorkville Chamber of Commerce 630-553-6853

Knox County

Located in northwest central Illinois; drained by the Spoon River and Pope and Henderson Creeks. Covers a land area of 716.30 square miles, a water area of 3.40 square miles, and is located in the Central Time Zone. The county government was organized in 1825. County seat is Galesburg.

Weather Station: Galesburg — Elevation: 770 feet

	Jan	Feb	Mar	Apr	May	Jun	Jul	Aug	Sep	Oct	Nov	Dec
High	29	35	48	61	72	82	85	82	75	63	48	35
Low	13	19	29	40	51	61	65	63	55	43	31	20
Precip	1.4	1.5	2.8	3.9	4.0	4.2	4.4	4.2	3.7	2.5	2.7	2.3
Snow	8.2	5.4	3.0	1.8	tr	0.0	0.0	0.0	0.0	tr	1.8	5.1

High and Low temperatures in degrees Fahrenheit; Precipitation and Snow in inches

Population: 55,836 (2000); Race: 89.8% White, 6.3% Black, 0.8% Asian, 0.2% American Indian and Alaska Native, 3.4% Hispanic of any race, 1.3% two or more races (2000); Density: 78.0 persons per square mile (2000); Age: 21.9% under 18, 17.5% over 64 (2000).
Religion: Five largest groups: 10.3% Catholic Church, 6.9% The United Methodist Church, 5.6% Evangelical Lutheran Church in America, 3.0% Christian Church (Disciples of Christ), 2.5% Presbyterian Church (U.S.A.) (2000).
Economy: Unemployment rate: 7.1% (11/2002); Total civilian labor force: 28,446 (11/2002); Leading industries: 24.1% manufacturing; 21.0% health care and social assistance; 16.5% retail trade (2000); Companies that employ more than 1,000 persons: 1 (2000); Companies that employ more than 100 persons: 30 (2000); Farms: 928 totaling 389,776 acres (1997); Minority business ownership rate: 0.0% (1997); Women business ownership rate: 22.6% (1997); Retail sales per capita: $8,804 (1997). Single-family building permits issued: 74 (2001) / 110 (2000); Multi-family building permits issued: 152 (2001) / 0 (2000).

Income: Per capita income: $17,985 (2000); Median household income: $35,407 (2000); Poverty rate: 11.1% (2000); Bankruptcy rate: 8.37% (2001).
Taxes: Total county taxes per capita: $97 (2000); County property taxes per capita: $73 (2000).
Education: High school graduation rate: 81.8% (2000); College graduation rate: 14.6% (2000).
Housing: Homeownership rate: 71.6% (2000); Median home value: $63,500 (2000); Median rent: $315 per month (2000); Median age of housing: 48 years (2000).
Health: Birth rate: 118.9 per 10,000 population (1998); Age adjusted death rate: 89.2 per 10,000 population (1999); Age adjusted cancer mortality rate: 208.5 deaths per 100,000 population (1999). Number of physicians: 17.7 per 10,000 population (1999); Number of hospital beds: 52.1 per 10,000 population (1999).
Elections: 2000 Presidential election results: 54.3% Gore, 42.8% Bush, 2.0% Nader, 0.7% Buchanan
National and State Parks: Snakeden Hollow State Fish and Wildlife Area
Additional Information Contacts
Knox County Government Offices 309-343-3121
Galesburg Association of Realtors 309-342-1050
Galesburg Chamber of Commerce 309-343-1194
Galesburg Convention Information Bureau 309-343-2485

Knox County Communities

ABINGDON (city). Covers a land area of 1.459 square miles and a water area of 0 square miles. Located at 40.80° N. Lat.; 90.40° W. Long. Elevation is 753 feet.
History: Incorporated 1857.
Population: 3,612 (2000); Race: 96.5% White, 0.7% Black, 0.5% Asian, 0.0% American Indian and Alaska Native, 2.2% Hispanic of any race, 1.2% two or more races (2000); Density: 2,475.1 persons per square mile (2000); Age: 25.4% under 18, 14.9% over 64 (2000); Marriage status: 20.5% never married, 57.4% now married, 9.4% widowed, 12.8% divorced (2000); Foreign born: 0.3% (2000); Ancestry (includes multiple ancestries): 18.2% German, 14.6% Irish, 11.9% Other groups, 9.8% English, 9.3% United States or American (2000).
Economy: Trade and shipping center in agricultural area. Cattle, hogs, poultry, corn, oats, barley, fruit, soybeans and dairy products. Manufactures fabricated metal products and consumer goods. Single-family building permits issued: 2 (2001) / 1 (2000); Multi-family building permits issued: 0 (2001) / 0 (2000); Employment by occupation: 7.1% management, 13.3% professional, 17.4% services, 21.1% sales, 0.6% farming, 9.0% construction, 31.5% production (2000).
Income: Per capita income: $15,711 (2000); Median household income: $35,642 (2000); Poverty rate: 9.9% (2000).
Taxes: Total city taxes per capita: $164 (1997); City property taxes per capita: $113 (1997).
Education: High school graduation rate: 81.5% (2000); College graduation rate: 8.6% (2000).

School District(s)

Abingdon C U School District 217 (PK-12)
2000 Enrollment: 880 309-462-2301
Housing: Homeownership rate: 80.1% (2000); Median home value: $51,400 (2000); Median rent: $279 per month (2000); Median age of housing: 44 years (2000).
Newspapers: Abingdon Argus (1 x week)
Transportation: Commute to work: 95.1% car, 0.0% public transportation, 2.4% walk, 1.7% work from home (2000); Travel time to work: 28.5% less than 15 minutes, 47.9% 15 to 30 minutes, 12.9% 30 to 45 minutes, 1.2% 45 to 60 minutes, 9.6% 60 minutes or more (2000)

ALTONA (village). Covers a land area of 1.016 square miles and a water area of 0 square miles. Located at 41.11° N. Lat.; 90.16° W. Long. Elevation is 760 feet.
Population: 570 (2000); Race: 98.6% White, 0.0% Black, 0.0% Asian, 0.7% American Indian and Alaska Native, 0.0% Hispanic of any race, 0.7% two or more races (2000); Density: 560.8 persons per square mile (2000); Age: 24.6% under 18, 15.2% over 64 (2000); Marriage status: 18.1% never married, 68.8% now married, 7.0% widowed, 6.1% divorced (2000); Foreign born: 0.0% (2000); Ancestry (includes multiple ancestries): 31.9% Swedish, 22.3% German, 12.7% English, 11.8% Irish, 6.3% Other groups (2000).
Economy: In agricultural area: corn, wheat; dairying. Employment by occupation: 8.3% management, 9.3% professional, 18.0% services, 22.5% sales, 6.6% farming, 10.7% construction, 24.6% production (2000).
Income: Per capita income: $15,805 (2000); Median household income: $35,729 (2000); Poverty rate: 6.2% (2000).
Taxes: Total city taxes per capita: $32 (1997); City property taxes per capita: $27 (1997).
Education: High school graduation rate: 86.7% (2000); College graduation rate: 10.2% (2000).
Housing: Homeownership rate: 89.6% (2000); Median home value: $49,300 (2000); Median rent: $269 per month (2000); Median age of housing: 49 years (2000).
Transportation: Commute to work: 97.2% car, 0.0% public transportation, 0.0% walk, 2.8% work from home (2000); Travel time to work: 30.2% less than 15 minutes, 43.2% 15 to 30 minutes, 18.7% 30 to 45 minutes, 1.8% 45 to 60 minutes, 6.1% 60 minutes or more (2000)

DAHINDA (unincorporated postal area, zip code 61428). Covers a land area of 33.362 square miles and a water area of 0.953 square miles. Located at 40.95° N. Lat.; 90.12° W. Long. Elevation is 596 feet.
Population: 954 (2000); Race: 97.2% White, 0.0% Black, 0.0% Asian, 0.0% American Indian and Alaska Native, 1.8% Hispanic of any race, 2.0% two or more races (2000); Density: 28.6 persons per square mile (2000); Age: 17.1% under 18, 21.7% over 64 (2000); Marriage status: 15.6% never married, 75.3% now married, 3.8% widowed, 5.3% divorced (2000); Foreign born: 2.2% (2000); Ancestry (includes multiple ancestries): 24.4% English, 19.5% German, 16.9% Irish, 13.5% United States or American, 7.1% Swedish (2000).
Economy: Employment by occupation: 12.1% management, 17.5% professional, 8.8% services, 26.5% sales, 0.0% farming, 16.3% construction, 18.8% production (2000).
Income: Per capita income: $23,532 (2000); Median household income: $46,188 (2000); Poverty rate: 5.2% (2000).
Education: High school graduation rate: 89.8% (2000); College graduation rate: 17.8% (2000).
Housing: Homeownership rate: 89.8% (2000); Median home value: $92,900 (2000); Median rent: $355 per month (2000); Median age of housing: 22 years (2000).
Transportation: Commute to work: 96.7% car, 0.0% public transportation, 1.5% walk, 1.9% work from home (2000); Travel time to work: 12.8% less than 15 minutes, 36.6% 15 to 30 minutes, 31.1% 30 to 45 minutes, 8.9% 45 to 60 minutes, 10.6% 60 minutes or more (2000)

EAST GALESBURG (village). Covers a land area of 1.460 square miles and a water area of 0.051 square miles. Located at 40.94° N. Lat.; 90.31° W. Long. Elevation is 770 feet.
Population: 839 (2000); Race: 96.1% White, 1.1% Black, 1.3% Asian, 0.0% American Indian and Alaska Native, 2.8% Hispanic of any race, 1.2% two or more races (2000); Density: 574.7 persons per square mile (2000); Age: 22.6% under 18, 11.7% over 64 (2000); Marriage status: 15.9% never married, 66.2% now married, 5.7% widowed, 12.2% divorced (2000); Foreign born: 1.1% (2000); Ancestry (includes multiple ancestries): 19.6% German, 13.4% Irish, 13.2% English, 9.4% United States or American, 7.6% Swedish (2000).
Economy: Single-family building permits issued: 2 (2001) / 2 (2000); Multi-family building permits issued: 0 (2001) / 0 (2000); Employment by occupation: 9.9% management, 23.1% professional, 12.0% services, 20.5% sales, 0.5% farming, 8.5% construction, 25.5% production (2000).
Income: Per capita income: $21,532 (2000); Median household income: $41,324 (2000); Poverty rate: 6.3% (2000).
Taxes: Total city taxes per capita: $88 (1997); City property taxes per capita: $44 (1997).
Education: High school graduation rate: 80.9% (2000); College graduation rate: 19.6% (2000).
Housing: Homeownership rate: 84.1% (2000); Median home value: $63,100 (2000); Median rent: $378 per month (2000); Median age of housing: 33 years (2000).
Transportation: Commute to work: 97.6% car, 0.2% public transportation, 0.0% walk, 1.7% work from home (2000); Travel time to work: 50.4% less than 15 minutes, 36.0% 15 to 30 minutes, 4.1% 30 to 45 minutes, 4.1% 45 to 60 minutes, 5.4% 60 minutes or more (2000)

GALESBURG (city). Covers a land area of 16.896 square miles and a water area of 0.178 square miles. Located at 40.95° N. Lat.; 90.36° W. Long. Elevation is 773 feet.
History: Galesburg was settled in 1836 on a site selected by an advance guard sent by Reverend George Washington Gale, a Presbyterian minister from New York who planned a town where morality and industry would rule.

Among the early residents was the Ferris family, one of whom invented the ferris wheel, first shown at the Columbian Exposition in Chicago in 1893.
Population: 33,706 (2000); Race: 84.4% White, 10.1% Black, 1.1% Asian, 0.3% American Indian and Alaska Native, 4.9% Hispanic of any race, 1.8% two or more races (2000); Density: 1,994.9 persons per square mile (2000); Age: 21.1% under 18, 17.9% over 64 (2000); Marriage status: 24.2% never married, 51.6% now married, 9.3% widowed, 14.9% divorced (2000); Foreign born: 2.2% (2000); Ancestry (includes multiple ancestries): 18.0% German, 14.2% Other groups, 12.3% Irish, 10.0% English, 10.0% Swedish (2000).
Vital Statistics: Birth rate: 125.2 per 10,000 population (1998)
Economy: Unemployment rate: 8.1% (11/2002); Total civilian labor force: 16,138 (11/2002); Single-family building permits issued: 20 (2001) / 30 (2000); Multi-family building permits issued: 152 (2001) / 0 (2000); Employment by occupation: 8.2% management, 18.5% professional, 19.8% services, 23.0% sales, 0.5% farming, 8.0% construction, 22.0% production (2000).
Income: Per capita income: $17,214 (2000); Median household income: $31,987 (2000); Poverty rate: 14.7% (2000).
Taxes: Total city taxes per capita: $275 (2000); City property taxes per capita: $136 (2000).
Education: High school graduation rate: 79.2% (2000); College graduation rate: 14.9% (2000).

School District(s)

Galesburg C U School District 205 (PK-12)
2000 Enrollment: 5,012 309-343-1151
Knox Roe (06-11)
2000 Enrollment: 24 309-345-3832
Knox-Warren Special Education District (07-12)
2000 Enrollment: 13 309-343-2143

Four-year College(s)

Knox College (Private, Not-for-profit)
2001 Enrollment: 1,143 309-341-7000
2001 Tuition: In-state $22,380; Out-of-state $22,380

Two-year College(s)

Carl Sandburg College (Public)
2001 Enrollment: 3,341 309-344-2518
2001 Tuition: In-state $5,430; Out-of-state $9,390

Housing: Homeownership rate: 64.1% (2000); Median home value: $60,900 (2000); Median rent: $322 per month (2000); Median age of housing: 51 years (2000).
Hospitals: Galesburg Cottage Hospital (182 beds); OSF St Mary Medical Center (156 beds)
Newspapers: The Zephyr (1 x week); The Register-Mail (7 x week); The Extra (1 x week)
Transportation: Commute to work: 89.4% car, 1.6% public transportation, 5.8% walk, 1.8% work from home (2000); Travel time to work: 69.2% less than 15 minutes, 20.7% 15 to 30 minutes, 3.4% 30 to 45 minutes, 2.8% 45 to 60 minutes, 3.8% 60 minutes or more (2000); Amtrak: Service available.
Airports: Galesburg Municipal
Additional Information Contacts
Galesburg Association of Realtors 309-342-1050
Galesburg Chamber of Commerce 309-343-1194
Galesburg Convention Information Bureau 309-343-2485

GILSON (unincorporated postal area, zip code 61436). Covers a land area of 64.363 square miles and a water area of 0.015 square miles. Located at 40.86° N. Lat.; 90.22° W. Long. Elevation is 685 feet.
Population: 1,021 (2000); Race: 99.2% White, 0.0% Black, 0.8% Asian, 0.0% American Indian and Alaska Native, 0.0% Hispanic of any race, 0.0% two or more races (2000); Density: 15.9 persons per square mile (2000); Age: 23.4% under 18, 12.6% over 64 (2000); Marriage status: 14.5% never married, 74.9% now married, 3.8% widowed, 6.8% divorced (2000); Foreign born: 0.8% (2000); Ancestry (includes multiple ancestries): 27.4% German, 17.5% United States or American, 17.3% English, 15.6% Swedish, 9.3% Irish (2000).
Economy: Employment by occupation: 12.9% management, 5.1% professional, 11.6% services, 21.3% sales, 5.3% farming, 5.1% construction, 38.7% production (2000).
Income: Per capita income: $19,092 (2000); Median household income: $44,000 (2000); Poverty rate: 1.5% (2000).
Education: High school graduation rate: 88.3% (2000); College graduation rate: 8.7% (2000).
Housing: Homeownership rate: 87.1% (2000); Median home value: $68,400 (2000); Median rent: $211 per month (2000); Median age of housing: 60+ years (2000).
Transportation: Commute to work: 89.2% car, 0.0% public transportation, 0.0% walk, 9.7% work from home (2000); Travel time to work: 19.1% less than 15 minutes, 57.1% 15 to 30 minutes, 15.1% 30 to 45 minutes, 4.0% 45 to 60 minutes, 4.6% 60 minutes or more (2000)

HENDERSON (village). Aka Soperville. Covers a land area of 0.272 square miles and a water area of 0 square miles. Located at 41.02° N. Lat.; 90.35° W. Long. Elevation is 815 feet.
Population: 319 (2000); Race: 97.7% White, 0.0% Black, 1.4% Asian, 0.0% American Indian and Alaska Native, 0.0% Hispanic of any race, 0.8% two or more races (2000); Density: 1,172.3 persons per square mile (2000); Age: 16.4% under 18, 16.9% over 64 (2000); Marriage status: 17.0% never married, 68.6% now married, 2.5% widowed, 11.9% divorced (2000); Foreign born: 3.4% (2000); Ancestry (includes multiple ancestries): 19.5% Irish, 19.5% German, 13.6% Swedish, 6.8% Other groups, 6.5% United States or American (2000).
Economy: In agricultural area: cattle, hogs; corn, soybeans, sorghum; dairying. Employment by occupation: 6.4% management, 24.0% professional, 15.2% services, 20.5% sales, 0.0% farming, 14.6% construction, 19.3% production (2000).
Income: Per capita income: $17,114 (2000); Median household income: $33,636 (2000); Poverty rate: 7.9% (2000).
Taxes: Total city taxes per capita: $44 (1997); City property taxes per capita: $44 (1997).
Education: High school graduation rate: 82.3% (2000); College graduation rate: 10.7% (2000).
Housing: Homeownership rate: 89.5% (2000); Median home value: $62,700 (2000); Median rent: $221 per month (2000); Median age of housing: 38 years (2000).
Transportation: Commute to work: 97.1% car, 0.0% public transportation, 0.0% walk, 2.9% work from home (2000); Travel time to work: 52.4% less than 15 minutes, 39.2% 15 to 30 minutes, 3.0% 30 to 45 minutes, 1.2% 45 to 60 minutes, 4.2% 60 minutes or more (2000)

KNOXVILLE (city). Covers a land area of 2.198 square miles and a water area of 0 square miles. Located at 40.90° N. Lat.; 90.28° W. Long. Elevation is 775 feet.
History: Incorporated 1832. Formerly the county seat.
Population: 3,183 (2000); Race: 99.2% White, 0.2% Black, 0.2% Asian, 0.1% American Indian and Alaska Native, 0.8% Hispanic of any race, 0.1% two or more races (2000); Density: 1,448.0 persons per square mile (2000); Age: 23.0% under 18, 22.2% over 64 (2000); Marriage status: 16.4% never married, 68.3% now married, 6.5% widowed, 8.7% divorced (2000); Foreign born: 0.6% (2000); Ancestry (includes multiple ancestries): 19.1% German, 17.9% English, 11.3% Swedish, 9.5% United States or American, 8.9% Irish (2000).
Economy: In agricultural area; dairy products. Single-family building permits issued: 1 (2001) / 2 (2000); Multi-family building permits issued: 0 (2001) / 0 (2000); Employment by occupation: 11.0% management, 17.6% professional, 16.6% services, 24.9% sales, 0.0% farming, 6.5% construction, 23.4% production (2000).
Income: Per capita income: $18,643 (2000); Median household income: $43,438 (2000); Poverty rate: 3.1% (2000).
Taxes: Total city taxes per capita: $201 (1997); City property taxes per capita: $72 (1997).
Education: High school graduation rate: 81.6% (2000); College graduation rate: 13.9% (2000).

School District(s)

Knoxville C U School District 202 (PK-12)
2000 Enrollment: 1,112 309-289-2328

Housing: Homeownership rate: 80.6% (2000); Median home value: $71,900 (2000); Median rent: $253 per month (2000); Median age of housing: 47 years (2000).
Transportation: Commute to work: 93.4% car, 0.0% public transportation, 2.1% walk, 4.0% work from home (2000); Travel time to work: 44.9% less than 15 minutes, 43.8% 15 to 30 minutes, 4.2% 30 to 45 minutes, 3.1% 45 to 60 minutes, 3.9% 60 minutes or more (2000)

MAQUON (village). Covers a land area of 0.161 square miles and a water area of 0 square miles. Located at 40.79° N. Lat.; 90.16° W. Long. Elevation is 630 feet.
Population: 318 (2000); Race: 99.4% White, 0.0% Black, 0.0% Asian, 0.0% American Indian and Alaska Native, 2.4% Hispanic of any race, 0.0% two or more races (2000); Density: 1,971.4 persons per square mile (2000); Age: 28.4% under 18, 16.5% over 64 (2000); Marriage status: 21.3% never married, 55.3% now married, 9.9% widowed, 13.4% divorced (2000);

Foreign born: 0.0% (2000); Ancestry (includes multiple ancestries): 34.6% United States or American, 10.1% English, 9.5% Irish, 8.9% Swedish, 7.0% German (2000).
Economy: In agricultural area. Single-family building permits issued: 0 (2001) / 0 (2000); Multi-family building permits issued: 0 (2001) / 0 (2000); Employment by occupation: 7.2% management, 9.2% professional, 19.0% services, 15.7% sales, 3.3% farming, 11.1% construction, 34.6% production (2000).
Income: Per capita income: $15,199 (2000); Median household income: $32,917 (2000); Poverty rate: 10.3% (2000).
Taxes: Total city taxes per capita: $29 (1997); City property taxes per capita: $29 (1997).
Education: High school graduation rate: 81.8% (2000); College graduation rate: 5.5% (2000).
Housing: Homeownership rate: 79.6% (2000); Median home value: $41,200 (2000); Median rent: $319 per month (2000); Median age of housing: 60+ years (2000).
Transportation: Commute to work: 89.6% car, 0.0% public transportation, 6.5% walk, 1.3% work from home (2000); Travel time to work: 11.8% less than 15 minutes, 33.6% 15 to 30 minutes, 25.7% 30 to 45 minutes, 11.2% 45 to 60 minutes, 17.8% 60 minutes or more (2000)

ONEIDA (city). Covers a land area of 0.726 square miles and a water area of 0 square miles. Located at 41.07° N. Lat.; 90.22° W. Long. Elevation is 810 feet.
Population: 752 (2000); Race: 98.4% White, 0.0% Black, 1.3% Asian, 0.0% American Indian and Alaska Native, 0.9% Hispanic of any race, 0.3% two or more races (2000); Density: 1,035.9 persons per square mile (2000); Age: 25.9% under 18, 17.4% over 64 (2000); Marriage status: 20.0% never married, 61.8% now married, 8.8% widowed, 9.3% divorced (2000); Foreign born: 0.0% (2000); Ancestry (includes multiple ancestries): 22.6% Swedish, 20.1% German, 18.0% Irish, 15.2% English, 6.7% Other groups (2000).
Economy: In agricultural area. Employment by occupation: 12.4% management, 14.7% professional, 7.9% services, 23.2% sales, 0.8% farming, 15.8% construction, 25.1% production (2000).
Income: Per capita income: $16,991 (2000); Median household income: $39,712 (2000); Poverty rate: 5.3% (2000).
Taxes: Total city taxes per capita: $27 (1997); City property taxes per capita: $27 (1997).
Education: High school graduation rate: 90.8% (2000); College graduation rate: 15.7% (2000).

School District(s)

R O W V A Community Unit School District 208 (PK-12)
2000 Enrollment: 837 309-483-3711
Housing: Homeownership rate: 76.8% (2000); Median home value: $62,100 (2000); Median rent: $353 per month (2000); Median age of housing: 60 years (2000).
Transportation: Commute to work: 94.6% car, 0.0% public transportation, 2.3% walk, 3.1% work from home (2000); Travel time to work: 22.4% less than 15 minutes, 54.6% 15 to 30 minutes, 9.1% 30 to 45 minutes, 3.8% 45 to 60 minutes, 10.0% 60 minutes or more (2000)

RIO (village). Covers a land area of 0.325 square miles and a water area of 0 square miles. Located at 41.11° N. Lat.; 90.39° W. Long. Elevation is 778 feet.
Population: 240 (2000); Race: 98.8% White, 0.0% Black, 0.4% Asian, 0.8% American Indian and Alaska Native, 0.0% Hispanic of any race, 0.0% two or more races (2000); Density: 737.6 persons per square mile (2000); Age: 26.8% under 18, 19.2% over 64 (2000); Marriage status: 19.7% never married, 67.2% now married, 7.6% widowed, 5.6% divorced (2000); Foreign born: 0.4% (2000); Ancestry (includes multiple ancestries): 40.4% Swedish, 20.4% German, 12.0% Irish, 6.0% United States or American, 5.2% Italian (2000).
Economy: Hogs, cattle; dairying; soybeans, corn. Employment by occupation: 6.0% management, 13.7% professional, 17.9% services, 18.8% sales, 5.1% farming, 11.1% construction, 27.4% production (2000).
Income: Per capita income: $17,181 (2000); Median household income: $37,750 (2000); Poverty rate: 2.0% (2000).
Education: High school graduation rate: 84.7% (2000); College graduation rate: 12.4% (2000).
Housing: Homeownership rate: 88.2% (2000); Median home value: $70,000 (2000); Median rent: $313 per month (2000); Median age of housing: 42 years (2000).
Transportation: Commute to work: 86.0% car, 0.0% public transportation, 5.6% walk, 8.4% work from home (2000); Travel time to work: 22.4% less than 15 minutes, 52.0% 15 to 30 minutes, 18.4% 30 to 45 minutes, 4.1% 45 to 60 minutes, 3.1% 60 minutes or more (2000)

SAINT AUGUSTINE (village). Covers a land area of 0.615 square miles and a water area of 0 square miles. Located at 40.72° N. Lat.; 90.41° W. Long. Elevation is 650 feet.
Population: 152 (2000); Race: 100.0% White, 0.0% Black, 0.0% Asian, 0.0% American Indian and Alaska Native, 0.0% Hispanic of any race, 0.0% two or more races (2000); Density: 247.2 persons per square mile (2000); Age: 16.3% under 18, 24.4% over 64 (2000); Marriage status: 23.4% never married, 54.5% now married, 8.3% widowed, 13.8% divorced (2000); Foreign born: 0.6% (2000); Ancestry (includes multiple ancestries): 20.6% German, 13.1% Irish, 11.9% United States or American, 5.6% Swedish, 3.1% English (2000).
Economy: Single-family building permits issued: 0 (2001) / 0 (2000); Multi-family building permits issued: 0 (2001) / 0 (2000); Employment by occupation: 4.8% management, 7.2% professional, 34.9% services, 19.3% sales, 0.0% farming, 2.4% construction, 31.3% production (2000).
Income: Per capita income: $15,549 (2000); Median household income: $34,375 (2000); Poverty rate: 5.6% (2000).
Education: High school graduation rate: 81.8% (2000); College graduation rate: 7.4% (2000).
Housing: Homeownership rate: 91.5% (2000); Median home value: $38,800 (2000); Median rent: $238 per month (2000); Median age of housing: 52 years (2000).
Transportation: Commute to work: 87.5% car, 0.0% public transportation, 10.0% walk, 2.5% work from home (2000); Travel time to work: 30.8% less than 15 minutes, 43.6% 15 to 30 minutes, 17.9% 30 to 45 minutes, 2.6% 45 to 60 minutes, 5.1% 60 minutes or more (2000)

VICTORIA (village). Covers a land area of 0.663 square miles and a water area of 0 square miles. Located at 41.03° N. Lat.; 90.09° W. Long. Elevation is 834 feet.
Population: 323 (2000); Race: 100.0% White, 0.0% Black, 0.0% Asian, 0.0% American Indian and Alaska Native, 0.0% Hispanic of any race, 0.0% two or more races (2000); Density: 486.9 persons per square mile (2000); Age: 26.0% under 18, 19.3% over 64 (2000); Marriage status: 20.0% never married, 61.7% now married, 12.3% widowed, 6.0% divorced (2000); Foreign born: 0.0% (2000); Ancestry (includes multiple ancestries): 20.7% German, 15.7% English, 14.7% United States or American, 12.0% Swedish, 11.0% Irish (2000).
Economy: In agricultural area; bituminous-coal area. Single-family building permits issued: 0 (2001) / 0 (2000); Multi-family building permits issued: 0 (2001) / 0 (2000); Employment by occupation: 9.8% management, 9.8% professional, 14.3% services, 24.1% sales, 0.0% farming, 8.0% construction, 33.9% production (2000).
Income: Per capita income: $13,446 (2000); Median household income: $30,000 (2000); Poverty rate: 7.3% (2000).
Taxes: Total city taxes per capita: $42 (1997); City property taxes per capita: $42 (1997).
Education: High school graduation rate: 81.2% (2000); College graduation rate: 3.0% (2000).
Housing: Homeownership rate: 89.0% (2000); Median home value: $37,200 (2000); Median rent: $179 per month (2000); Median age of housing: 60+ years (2000).
Transportation: Commute to work: 91.1% car, 0.0% public transportation, 8.0% walk, 0.0% work from home (2000); Travel time to work: 9.8% less than 15 minutes, 56.3% 15 to 30 minutes, 26.8% 30 to 45 minutes, 6.3% 45 to 60 minutes, 0.9% 60 minutes or more (2000)

WATAGA (village). Covers a land area of 0.866 square miles and a water area of 0 square miles. Located at 41.02° N. Lat.; 90.27° W. Long. Elevation is 830 feet.
Population: 857 (2000); Race: 97.9% White, 0.0% Black, 0.0% Asian, 0.3% American Indian and Alaska Native, 1.6% Hispanic of any race, 1.7% two or more races (2000); Density: 989.5 persons per square mile (2000); Age: 29.6% under 18, 9.7% over 64 (2000); Marriage status: 21.4% never married, 61.2% now married, 4.0% widowed, 13.4% divorced (2000); Foreign born: 0.2% (2000); Ancestry (includes multiple ancestries): 24.5% German, 13.3% Swedish, 12.1% Irish, 11.3% United States or American, 10.6% English (2000).
Economy: In agricultural area: corn, soybeans; cattle, hogs; dairying. Single-family building permits issued: 1 (2001) / 1 (2000); Multi-family building permits issued: 0 (2001) / 0 (2000); Employment by occupation: 8.8% management, 14.1% professional, 14.5% services, 25.6% sales, 1.2% farming, 12.9% construction, 22.9% production (2000).

Income: Per capita income: $15,553 (2000); Median household income: $39,205 (2000); Poverty rate: 11.2% (2000).
Taxes: Total city taxes per capita: $29 (1997); City property taxes per capita: $23 (1997).
Education: High school graduation rate: 83.2% (2000); College graduation rate: 10.3% (2000).
Housing: Homeownership rate: 80.1% (2000); Median home value: $60,300 (2000); Median rent: $328 per month (2000); Median age of housing: 37 years (2000).
Transportation: Commute to work: 94.5% car, 0.0% public transportation, 0.7% walk, 1.9% work from home (2000); Travel time to work: 30.0% less than 15 minutes, 52.2% 15 to 30 minutes, 6.8% 30 to 45 minutes, 5.3% 45 to 60 minutes, 5.8% 60 minutes or more (2000)

WILLIAMSFIELD (village). Covers a land area of 1.271 square miles and a water area of 0 square miles. Located at 40.92° N. Lat.; 90.01° W. Long. Elevation is 711 feet.
Population: 620 (2000); Race: 98.4% White, 1.1% Black, 0.0% Asian, 0.0% American Indian and Alaska Native, 0.7% Hispanic of any race, 0.5% two or more races (2000); Density: 487.9 persons per square mile (2000); Age: 24.1% under 18, 16.5% over 64 (2000); Marriage status: 24.5% never married, 56.7% now married, 11.4% widowed, 7.3% divorced (2000); Foreign born: 0.3% (2000); Ancestry (includes multiple ancestries): 21.9% German, 19.3% English, 14.7% Irish, 12.8% Swedish, 10.1% United States or American (2000).
Economy: Agriculture includes corn, soybeans; cattle, hogs; dairying. Employment by occupation: 7.6% management, 13.7% professional, 18.2% services, 24.2% sales, 0.0% farming, 8.0% construction, 28.3% production (2000).
Income: Per capita income: $17,941 (2000); Median household income: $38,854 (2000); Poverty rate: 5.3% (2000).
Taxes: Total city taxes per capita: $33 (1997); City property taxes per capita: $28 (1997).
Education: High school graduation rate: 89.4% (2000); College graduation rate: 15.8% (2000).

School District(s)

Williamsfield C U S District 210 (PK-12)
2000 Enrollment: 280 309-639-2219

Housing: Homeownership rate: 80.3% (2000); Median home value: $56,400 (2000); Median rent: $275 per month (2000); Median age of housing: 45 years (2000).
Transportation: Commute to work: 94.9% car, 0.0% public transportation, 1.6% walk, 2.9% work from home (2000); Travel time to work: 22.0% less than 15 minutes, 22.4% 15 to 30 minutes, 45.1% 30 to 45 minutes, 10.2% 45 to 60 minutes, 0.3% 60 minutes or more (2000)

YATES CITY (village). Covers a land area of 0.587 square miles and a water area of 0 square miles. Located at 40.77° N. Lat.; 90.01° W. Long. Elevation is 673 feet.
Population: 725 (2000); Race: 97.8% White, 0.1% Black, 0.0% Asian, 0.3% American Indian and Alaska Native, 0.0% Hispanic of any race, 1.2% two or more races (2000); Density: 1,235.2 persons per square mile (2000); Age: 24.1% under 18, 19.9% over 64 (2000); Marriage status: 14.9% never married, 65.4% now married, 10.8% widowed, 8.9% divorced (2000); Foreign born: 0.0% (2000); Ancestry (includes multiple ancestries): 21.9% German, 17.7% English, 13.3% United States or American, 12.1% Irish, 9.2% Other groups (2000).
Economy: Railroad junction; corn, soybeans; livestock; dairying. Employment by occupation: 4.5% management, 11.9% professional, 15.0% services, 26.9% sales, 2.5% farming, 11.0% construction, 28.0% production (2000).
Income: Per capita income: $18,036 (2000); Median household income: $37,344 (2000); Poverty rate: 8.5% (2000).
Taxes: Total city taxes per capita: $77 (1997); City property taxes per capita: $37 (1997).
Education: High school graduation rate: 87.9% (2000); College graduation rate: 9.6% (2000).
Housing: Homeownership rate: 82.1% (2000); Median home value: $65,100 (2000); Median rent: $316 per month (2000); Median age of housing: 55 years (2000).
Transportation: Commute to work: 96.5% car, 0.0% public transportation, 0.6% walk, 2.0% work from home (2000); Travel time to work: 16.2% less than 15 minutes, 12.1% 15 to 30 minutes, 52.4% 30 to 45 minutes, 15.6% 45 to 60 minutes, 3.8% 60 minutes or more (2000)

La Salle County

Located in northern Illinois; drained by the Illinois, Fox, Vermilion, and Little Vermilion Rivers. Covers a land area of 1,134.90 square miles, a water area of 13.10 square miles, and is located in the Central Time Zone. The county government was organized in 1831. County seat is Ottawa.

Weather Station: Ottawa 5 SW — Elevation: 524 feet

	Jan	Feb	Mar	Apr	May	Jun	Jul	Aug	Sep	Oct	Nov	Dec
High	31	37	49	63	74	82	85	84	77	66	50	37
Low	14	19	30	40	51	60	65	62	54	42	32	21
Precip	1.5	1.3	2.6	3.5	4.1	4.2	3.7	3.8	3.7	2.6	2.9	2.3
Snow	8.6	5.0	3.2	0.8	0.0	0.0	0.0	0.0	0.0	tr	1.0	5.4

High and Low temperatures in degrees Fahrenheit; Precipitation and Snow in inches

Weather Station: Peru — Elevation: 620 feet

	Jan	Feb	Mar	Apr	May	Jun	Jul	Aug	Sep	Oct	Nov	Dec
High	29	35	47	61	73	83	86	84	77	65	49	36
Low	12	18	28	38	49	59	63	61	52	41	31	20
Precip	1.4	1.4	2.8	3.8	4.8	4.2	4.1	4.3	3.8	3.1	2.8	2.3
Snow	8.0	4.5	3.6	0.6	tr	0.0	0.0	0.0	0.0	0.1	1.3	5.6

High and Low temperatures in degrees Fahrenheit; Precipitation and Snow in inches

Population: 111,509 (2000); Race: 94.9% White, 1.7% Black, 0.5% Asian, 0.2% American Indian and Alaska Native, 5.2% Hispanic of any race, 1.0% two or more races (2000); Density: 98.3 persons per square mile (2000); Age: 25.1% under 18, 16.5% over 64 (2000).
Religion: Five largest groups: 40.1% Catholic Church, 6.1% The United Methodist Church, 4.9% Evangelical Lutheran Church in America, 1.4% Presbyterian Church (U.S.A.), 1.3% Church of the Nazarene (2000).
Economy: Unemployment rate: 8.0% (11/2002); Total civilian labor force: 56,168 (11/2002); Leading industries: 18.4% retail trade; 16.6% manufacturing; 13.7% health care and social assistance (2000); Companies that employ more than 1,000 persons: 0 (2000); Companies that employ more than 100 persons: 61 (2000); Farms: 1,581 totaling 587,676 acres (1997); Minority business ownership rate: 2.5% (1997); Women business ownership rate: 24.4% (1997); Retail sales per capita: $9,529 (1997). Single-family building permits issued: 280 (2001) / 324 (2000); Multi-family building permits issued: 72 (2001) / 170 (2000).
Income: Per capita income: $19,185 (2000); Median household income: $40,308 (2000); Poverty rate: 9.1% (2000); Bankruptcy rate: 6.65% (2001).
Taxes: Total county taxes per capita: $99 (2000); County property taxes per capita: $99 (2000).
Education: High school graduation rate: 81.4% (2000); College graduation rate: 13.3% (2000).
Housing: Homeownership rate: 75.1% (2000); Median home value: $87,000 (2000); Median rent: $379 per month (2000); Median age of housing: 47 years (2000).
Health: Birth rate: 127.7 per 10,000 population (1998); Age adjusted death rate: 85.3 per 10,000 population (1999); Age adjusted cancer mortality rate: 217.0 deaths per 100,000 population (1999). Air Quality Index: 95% good, 5% moderate, 0% unhealthy (percent of days in 2000). Number of physicians: 10.0 per 10,000 population (1999); Number of hospital beds: 39.5 per 10,000 population (1999).
Elections: 2000 Presidential election results: 50.8% Gore, 46.3% Bush, 2.2% Nader, 0.5% Buchanan
National and State Parks: Buffalo Rock State Park; Illini State Park; La Salle Lake State Fish and Wildlife Area; Marseilles State Fish and Wildlife Area; Matthiessen State Park; Norwegian Settlers State Memorial; Starved Rock State Park

Additional Information Contacts

La Salle County Government Offices 815-434-8200
Illini Valley Association of Realtors 815-224-1868
Illinois Valley Chamber of Commerce 815-223-0227
Marseilles Chamber of Commerce. 815-795-2323
Mendota Chamber of Commerce 815-539-6507
Ottawa Area Chamber of Commerce. 815-433-0084
Streator Chamber of Commerce. 815-672-2921

La Salle County Communities

CEDAR POINT (village). Covers a land area of 1.022 square miles and a water area of 0 square miles. Located at 41.26° N. Lat.; 89.12° W. Long. Elevation is 660 feet.
Population: 262 (2000); Race: 96.7% White, 2.2% Black, 0.0% Asian, 0.0% American Indian and Alaska Native, 3.0% Hispanic of any race, 1.1% two or

more races (2000); Density: 256.3 persons per square mile (2000); Age: 22.1% under 18, 18.8% over 64 (2000); Marriage status: 21.8% never married, 55.1% now married, 10.6% widowed, 12.5% divorced (2000); Foreign born: 0.7% (2000); Ancestry (includes multiple ancestries): 33.9% Italian, 15.9% German, 14.4% Irish, 10.0% Other groups, 10.0% English (2000).

Economy: In agricultural area. Single-family building permits issued: 0 (2001) / 0 (2000); Multi-family building permits issued: 0 (2001) / 0 (2000); Employment by occupation: 4.7% management, 7.1% professional, 15.0% services, 31.5% sales, 0.0% farming, 11.0% construction, 30.7% production (2000).

Income: Per capita income: $18,988 (2000); Median household income: $41,875 (2000); Poverty rate: 3.0% (2000).

Taxes: Total city taxes per capita: $49 (1997); City property taxes per capita: $45 (1997).

Education: High school graduation rate: 83.7% (2000); College graduation rate: 3.2% (2000).

Housing: Homeownership rate: 81.7% (2000); Median home value: $62,900 (2000); Median rent: $331 per month (2000); Median age of housing: 60+ years (2000).

Transportation: Commute to work: 96.8% car, 0.0% public transportation, 1.6% walk, 1.6% work from home (2000); Travel time to work: 40.7% less than 15 minutes, 39.8% 15 to 30 minutes, 9.8% 30 to 45 minutes, 0.8% 45 to 60 minutes, 8.9% 60 minutes or more (2000)

DANA (village). Covers a land area of 0.220 square miles and a water area of 0 square miles. Located at 40.95° N. Lat.; 88.95° W. Long. Elevation is 671 feet.

Population: 171 (2000); Race: 96.0% White, 0.0% Black, 1.1% Asian, 0.0% American Indian and Alaska Native, 6.8% Hispanic of any race, 2.8% two or more races (2000); Density: 778.4 persons per square mile (2000); Age: 31.8% under 18, 17.6% over 64 (2000); Marriage status: 20.1% never married, 59.0% now married, 8.2% widowed, 12.7% divorced (2000); Foreign born: 1.1% (2000); Ancestry (includes multiple ancestries): 22.7% German, 14.8% English, 13.1% Other groups, 11.9% Irish, 8.5% United States or American (2000).

Economy: In agricultural area. Employment by occupation: 6.9% management, 3.4% professional, 27.6% services, 22.4% sales, 0.0% farming, 8.6% construction, 31.0% production (2000).

Income: Per capita income: $13,349 (2000); Median household income: $35,000 (2000); Poverty rate: 26.7% (2000).

Taxes: Total city taxes per capita: $24 (1997); City property taxes per capita: $18 (1997).

Education: High school graduation rate: 75.5% (2000); College graduation rate: 0.0% (2000).

Housing: Homeownership rate: 78.9% (2000); Median home value: $37,500 (2000); Median rent: $225 per month (2000); Median age of housing: 54 years (2000).

Transportation: Commute to work: 100.0% car, 0.0% public transportation, 0.0% walk, 0.0% work from home (2000); Travel time to work: 6.9% less than 15 minutes, 34.5% 15 to 30 minutes, 31.0% 30 to 45 minutes, 19.0% 45 to 60 minutes, 8.6% 60 minutes or more (2000)

EARLVILLE (city). Covers a land area of 1.164 square miles and a water area of 0 square miles. Located at 41.58° N. Lat.; 88.92° W. Long. Elevation is 705 feet.

History: Founded c.1854, incorporated 1869.

Population: 1,778 (2000); Race: 97.2% White, 0.3% Black, 0.1% Asian, 0.3% American Indian and Alaska Native, 3.4% Hispanic of any race, 1.4% two or more races (2000); Density: 1,527.4 persons per square mile (2000); Age: 28.4% under 18, 14.8% over 64 (2000); Marriage status: 17.6% never married, 64.3% now married, 7.3% widowed, 10.7% divorced (2000); Foreign born: 0.8% (2000); Ancestry (includes multiple ancestries): 30.2% German, 17.0% Irish, 11.2% English, 8.6% Other groups, 7.5% Norwegian (2000).

Economy: In agricultural area; Railroad junction. Food processing; corn, soybeans, livestock. Single-family building permits issued: 4 (2001) / 4 (2000); Multi-family building permits issued: 0 (2001) / 2 (2000); Employment by occupation: 7.3% management, 11.0% professional, 17.3% services, 24.0% sales, 0.5% farming, 13.8% construction, 26.2% production (2000).

Income: Per capita income: $16,722 (2000); Median household income: $39,286 (2000); Poverty rate: 7.5% (2000).

Taxes: Total city taxes per capita: $152 (1997); City property taxes per capita: $122 (1997).

Education: High school graduation rate: 81.7% (2000); College graduation rate: 10.4% (2000).

School District(s)

Earlville Community Unit School District 9 (PK-12)
2000 Enrollment: 537 815-246-8371

Housing: Homeownership rate: 73.2% (2000); Median home value: $89,700 (2000); Median rent: $339 per month (2000); Median age of housing: 52 years (2000).

Newspapers: The Earlville Leader (1 x week)

Transportation: Commute to work: 91.8% car, 0.0% public transportation, 3.3% walk, 3.5% work from home (2000); Travel time to work: 23.5% less than 15 minutes, 25.0% 15 to 30 minutes, 19.1% 30 to 45 minutes, 15.4% 45 to 60 minutes, 16.9% 60 minutes or more (2000)

GRAND RIDGE (village). Covers a land area of 0.474 square miles and a water area of 0 square miles. Located at 41.23° N. Lat.; 88.83° W. Long. Elevation is 645 feet.

Population: 546 (2000); Race: 99.7% White, 0.0% Black, 0.0% Asian, 0.3% American Indian and Alaska Native, 10.4% Hispanic of any race, 0.0% two or more races (2000); Density: 1,152.5 persons per square mile (2000); Age: 27.4% under 18, 14.6% over 64 (2000); Marriage status: 19.3% never married, 68.5% now married, 7.2% widowed, 4.9% divorced (2000); Foreign born: 11.1% (2000); Ancestry (includes multiple ancestries): 24.6% German, 16.6% Irish, 12.8% English, 9.5% Other groups, 6.1% United States or American (2000).

Economy: In agricultural and bituminous coal area. Single-family building permits issued: 0 (2001) / 0 (2000); Multi-family building permits issued: 0 (2001) / 0 (2000); Employment by occupation: 10.2% management, 20.1% professional, 15.7% services, 17.3% sales, 2.0% farming, 15.7% construction, 18.9% production (2000).

Income: Per capita income: $18,287 (2000); Median household income: $45,000 (2000); Poverty rate: 5.6% (2000).

Taxes: Total city taxes per capita: $76 (1997); City property taxes per capita: $32 (1997).

Education: High school graduation rate: 86.9% (2000); College graduation rate: 12.8% (2000).

School District(s)

Grand Ridge C C School District 95 (PK-08)
2000 Enrollment: 373 815-249-6225

Housing: Homeownership rate: 83.4% (2000); Median home value: $77,000 (2000); Median rent: $392 per month (2000); Median age of housing: 60 years (2000).

Transportation: Commute to work: 88.3% car, 0.8% public transportation, 7.7% walk, 1.2% work from home (2000); Travel time to work: 30.6% less than 15 minutes, 50.2% 15 to 30 minutes, 7.8% 30 to 45 minutes, 3.3% 45 to 60 minutes, 8.2% 60 minutes or more (2000)

KANGLEY (village). Covers a land area of 0.338 square miles and a water area of 0 square miles. Located at 41.14° N. Lat.; 88.87° W. Long. Elevation is 634 feet.

Population: 287 (2000); Race: 97.3% White, 0.0% Black, 0.0% Asian, 0.0% American Indian and Alaska Native, 2.0% Hispanic of any race, 0.7% two or more races (2000); Density: 849.5 persons per square mile (2000); Age: 30.5% under 18, 8.7% over 64 (2000); Marriage status: 29.9% never married, 52.8% now married, 5.2% widowed, 12.1% divorced (2000); Foreign born: 2.0% (2000); Ancestry (includes multiple ancestries): 14.1% Irish, 13.8% German, 13.1% English, 6.4% Other groups, 6.0% Polish (2000).

Economy: Agriculture: dairying; corn, wheat, soybeans. Single-family building permits issued: 0 (2001) / 0 (2000); Multi-family building permits issued: 0 (2001) / 0 (2000); Employment by occupation: 4.0% management, 8.0% professional, 18.4% services, 23.2% sales, 0.0% farming, 17.6% construction, 28.8% production (2000).

Income: Per capita income: $15,505 (2000); Median household income: $32,500 (2000); Poverty rate: 14.8% (2000).

Taxes: Total city taxes per capita: $53 (1997); City property taxes per capita: $11 (1997).

Education: High school graduation rate: 76.4% (2000); College graduation rate: 6.3% (2000).

Housing: Homeownership rate: 90.7% (2000); Median home value: $53,000 (2000); Median rent: $292 per month (2000); Median age of housing: 54 years (2000).

Transportation: Commute to work: 96.7% car, 0.0% public transportation, 2.4% walk, 0.8% work from home (2000); Travel time to work: 39.3% less than 15 minutes, 16.4% 15 to 30 minutes, 16.4% 30 to 45 minutes, 12.3% 45 to 60 minutes, 15.6% 60 minutes or more (2000)

LA SALLE (city). Aka La Salle-Peru. Covers a land area of 6.346 square miles and a water area of 0.093 square miles. Located at 41.34° N. Lat.; 89.09° W. Long. Elevation is 640 feet.
History: La Salle was organized in 1827, and prospered with the opening of the Illinois & Michigan Canal in 1848. When the railroads replaced canal traffic, mining became an important industry for La Salle. The Matthiessen & Hegeler Zinc Company plant was established here in 1858. The town was named for La Salle, the French explorer of North America, who crossed this area in 1679.
Population: 9,796 (2000); Race: 93.1% White, 1.5% Black, 0.4% Asian, 0.6% American Indian and Alaska Native, 7.9% Hispanic of any race, 1.9% two or more races (2000); Density: 1,543.6 persons per square mile (2000); Age: 23.1% under 18, 18.9% over 64 (2000); Marriage status: 28.5% never married, 50.9% now married, 9.0% widowed, 11.7% divorced (2000); Foreign born: 3.3% (2000); Ancestry (includes multiple ancestries): 27.9% German, 19.6% Polish, 15.4% Irish, 11.8% Italian, 10.8% Other groups (2000).
Economy: Single-family building permits issued: 13 (2001) / 10 (2000); Multi-family building permits issued: 4 (2001) / 4 (2000); Employment by occupation: 7.4% management, 13.6% professional, 16.1% services, 27.6% sales, 0.9% farming, 13.5% construction, 21.0% production (2000).
Income: Per capita income: $19,099 (2000); Median household income: $32,491 (2000); Poverty rate: 15.7% (2000).
Taxes: Total city taxes per capita: $315 (2000); City property taxes per capita: $171 (2000).
Education: High school graduation rate: 79.3% (2000); College graduation rate: 12.5% (2000).

School District(s)

Dimmick C C School District 175 (PK-08)
2000 Enrollment: 123 815-223-2933
La Salle-Peru Township H S D 120 (09-12)
2000 Enrollment: 1,293 815-223-1721
Lasalle Elementary School District 122 (PK-08)
2000 Enrollment: 798 815-223-0786

Housing: Homeownership rate: 65.5% (2000); Median home value: $72,300 (2000); Median rent: $339 per month (2000); Median age of housing: 58 years (2000).
Newspapers: Daily News Tribune (6 x week)
Transportation: Commute to work: 91.6% car, 0.4% public transportation, 4.9% walk, 1.9% work from home (2000); Travel time to work: 60.6% less than 15 minutes, 23.4% 15 to 30 minutes, 6.4% 30 to 45 minutes, 3.0% 45 to 60 minutes, 6.6% 60 minutes or more (2000)

Additional Information Contacts

Illinois Valley Chamber of Commerce 815-223-0227

LELAND (village). Covers a land area of 0.542 square miles and a water area of 0 square miles. Located at 41.61° N. Lat.; 88.79° W. Long. Elevation is 695 feet.
Population: 970 (2000); Race: 98.0% White, 0.0% Black, 0.3% Asian, 0.0% American Indian and Alaska Native, 3.3% Hispanic of any race, 1.5% two or more races (2000); Density: 1,788.1 persons per square mile (2000); Age: 29.9% under 18, 10.9% over 64 (2000); Marriage status: 21.3% never married, 62.0% now married, 7.7% widowed, 9.0% divorced (2000); Foreign born: 1.6% (2000); Ancestry (includes multiple ancestries): 29.7% German, 18.2% Irish, 13.6% Norwegian, 10.1% Other groups, 7.7% English (2000).
Economy: In agricultural area. Single-family building permits issued: 2 (2001) / 1 (2000); Multi-family building permits issued: 0 (2001) / 0 (2000); Employment by occupation: 6.4% management, 12.2% professional, 15.7% services, 26.4% sales, 0.9% farming, 14.6% construction, 23.7% production (2000).
Income: Per capita income: $17,142 (2000); Median household income: $45,417 (2000); Poverty rate: 6.4% (2000).
Taxes: Total city taxes per capita: $97 (1997); City property taxes per capita: $77 (1997).
Education: High school graduation rate: 85.7% (2000); College graduation rate: 15.2% (2000).

School District(s)

Leland Community Unit School District 1 (KG-12)
2000 Enrollment: 351 815-495-3821

Housing: Homeownership rate: 74.7% (2000); Median home value: $106,700 (2000); Median rent: $464 per month (2000); Median age of housing: 52 years (2000).
Transportation: Commute to work: 93.9% car, 0.0% public transportation, 5.6% walk, 0.4% work from home (2000); Travel time to work: 15.8% less than 15 minutes, 26.4% 15 to 30 minutes, 18.9% 30 to 45 minutes, 19.8% 45 to 60 minutes, 19.1% 60 minutes or more (2000)

LEONORE (village). Covers a land area of 0.086 square miles and a water area of 0 square miles. Located at 41.18° N. Lat.; 88.98° W. Long. Elevation is 682 feet.
Population: 110 (2000); Race: 100.0% White, 0.0% Black, 0.0% Asian, 0.0% American Indian and Alaska Native, 3.6% Hispanic of any race, 0.0% two or more races (2000); Density: 1,279.8 persons per square mile (2000); Age: 15.5% under 18, 28.2% over 64 (2000); Marriage status: 14.0% never married, 61.3% now married, 10.8% widowed, 14.0% divorced (2000); Foreign born: 1.8% (2000); Ancestry (includes multiple ancestries): 48.2% German, 14.5% Irish, 10.9% Italian, 8.2% United States or American, 8.2% English (2000).
Economy: In agricultural area. Employment by occupation: 12.0% management, 2.0% professional, 10.0% services, 24.0% sales, 0.0% farming, 8.0% construction, 44.0% production (2000).
Income: Per capita income: $19,465 (2000); Median household income: $36,250 (2000); Poverty rate: 1.8% (2000).
Taxes: Total city taxes per capita: $14 (1997); City property taxes per capita: $7 (1997).
Education: High school graduation rate: 70.2% (2000); College graduation rate: 6.0% (2000).
Housing: Homeownership rate: 92.7% (2000); Median home value: $51,900 (2000); Median rent: $300 per month (2000); Median age of housing: 60+ years (2000).
Transportation: Commute to work: 84.0% car, 0.0% public transportation, 16.0% walk, 0.0% work from home (2000); Travel time to work: 26.0% less than 15 minutes, 58.0% 15 to 30 minutes, 0.0% 30 to 45 minutes, 14.0% 45 to 60 minutes, 2.0% 60 minutes or more (2000)

LOSTANT (village). Covers a land area of 0.386 square miles and a water area of 0 square miles. Located at 41.14° N. Lat.; 89.06° W. Long. Elevation is 703 feet.
Population: 486 (2000); Race: 99.8% White, 0.0% Black, 0.2% Asian, 0.0% American Indian and Alaska Native, 0.6% Hispanic of any race, 0.0% two or more races (2000); Density: 1,259.7 persons per square mile (2000); Age: 26.6% under 18, 14.8% over 64 (2000); Marriage status: 22.7% never married, 62.0% now married, 8.3% widowed, 7.0% divorced (2000); Foreign born: 1.4% (2000); Ancestry (includes multiple ancestries): 44.5% German, 10.0% Italian, 9.1% Polish, 8.3% Irish, 6.7% English (2000).
Economy: In agricultural area. Single-family building permits issued: 0 (2001) / 2 (2000); Multi-family building permits issued: 0 (2001) / 0 (2000); Employment by occupation: 13.5% management, 13.9% professional, 14.7% services, 19.5% sales, 0.0% farming, 7.1% construction, 31.2% production (2000).
Income: Per capita income: $18,782 (2000); Median household income: $41,964 (2000); Poverty rate: 4.3% (2000).
Taxes: Total city taxes per capita: $58 (2000); City property taxes per capita: $53 (2000).
Education: High school graduation rate: 87.0% (2000); College graduation rate: 14.2% (2000).

School District(s)

Lostant Community Unit School District 425 (PK-08)
2000 Enrollment: 110 815-368-3392

Housing: Homeownership rate: 86.1% (2000); Median home value: $70,000 (2000); Median rent: $283 per month (2000); Median age of housing: 50 years (2000).
Transportation: Commute to work: 92.4% car, 0.0% public transportation, 5.3% walk, 2.3% work from home (2000); Travel time to work: 37.4% less than 15 minutes, 31.5% 15 to 30 minutes, 17.1% 30 to 45 minutes, 7.4% 45 to 60 minutes, 6.6% 60 minutes or more (2000)

MARSEILLES (city). Covers a land area of 8.311 square miles and a water area of 0.387 square miles. Located at 41.32° N. Lat.; 88.70° W. Long. Elevation is 504 feet.
History: Marseilles developed along a stretch of rapids on the Illinois River, providing water power for its early industries which included a paper mill.
Population: 4,655 (2000); Race: 98.5% White, 0.0% Black, 0.3% Asian, 0.3% American Indian and Alaska Native, 0.8% Hispanic of any race, 0.6% two or more races (2000); Density: 560.1 persons per square mile (2000); Age: 23.7% under 18, 17.9% over 64 (2000); Marriage status: 18.2% never married, 58.2% now married, 10.9% widowed, 12.7% divorced (2000); Foreign born: 1.2% (2000); Ancestry (includes multiple ancestries): 24.0% German, 20.3% Irish, 12.5% English, 11.2% Italian, 8.5% Norwegian (2000).

Economy: Single-family building permits issued: 23 (2001) / 45 (2000); Multi-family building permits issued: 0 (2001) / 20 (2000); Employment by occupation: 7.3% management, 12.7% professional, 19.1% services, 26.1% sales, 0.7% farming, 14.4% construction, 19.7% production (2000).
Income: Per capita income: $17,793 (2000); Median household income: $38,432 (2000); Poverty rate: 8.7% (2000).
Taxes: Total city taxes per capita: $108 (1997); City property taxes per capita: $106 (1997).
Education: High school graduation rate: 81.5% (2000); College graduation rate: 8.1% (2000).

School District(s)

Marseilles Elementary School District 150 (PK-08)
2000 Enrollment: 621 815-795-2162
Miller Township Cc School District 210 (KG-08)
2000 Enrollment: 202 815-357-8151

Housing: Homeownership rate: 75.5% (2000); Median home value: $79,000 (2000); Median rent: $370 per month (2000); Median age of housing: 50 years (2000).
Transportation: Commute to work: 91.9% car, 0.8% public transportation, 2.4% walk, 3.7% work from home (2000); Travel time to work: 34.6% less than 15 minutes, 32.8% 15 to 30 minutes, 12.9% 30 to 45 minutes, 10.4% 45 to 60 minutes, 9.4% 60 minutes or more (2000)
Additional Information Contacts
Marseilles Chamber of Commerce........................ 815-795-2323

MENDOTA (city). Covers a land area of 3.779 square miles and a water area of 0.096 square miles. Located at 41.54° N. Lat.; 89.11° W. Long. Elevation is 740 feet.
History: Mendota developed as a trading and processing center for the produce of an agricultural area.
Population: 7,272 (2000); Race: 89.7% White, 0.2% Black, 0.0% Asian, 0.2% American Indian and Alaska Native, 18.9% Hispanic of any race, 0.6% two or more races (2000); Density: 1,924.3 persons per square mile (2000); Age: 25.7% under 18, 19.0% over 64 (2000); Marriage status: 21.2% never married, 59.9% now married, 10.0% widowed, 8.9% divorced (2000); Foreign born: 8.7% (2000); Ancestry (includes multiple ancestries): 31.2% German, 20.4% Other groups, 14.2% Irish, 7.8% English, 6.0% United States or American (2000).
Economy: Single-family building permits issued: 4 (2001) / 18 (2000); Multi-family building permits issued: 0 (2001) / 4 (2000); Employment by occupation: 9.5% management, 13.8% professional, 17.4% services, 18.4% sales, 1.4% farming, 9.3% construction, 30.2% production (2000).
Income: Per capita income: $17,731 (2000); Median household income: $39,354 (2000); Poverty rate: 11.2% (2000).
Taxes: Total city taxes per capita: $202 (1997); City property taxes per capita: $186 (1997).
Education: High school graduation rate: 76.3% (2000); College graduation rate: 13.2% (2000).

School District(s)

Mendota C C School District 289 (PK-08)
2000 Enrollment: 1,203.............................. 815-539-7631
Mendota Township H S District 280 (09-12)
2000 Enrollment: 584 815-539-7446

Housing: Homeownership rate: 74.2% (2000); Median home value: $87,800 (2000); Median rent: $368 per month (2000); Median age of housing: 50 years (2000).
Hospitals: Mendota Community Hospital (68 beds)
Newspapers: Mendota Reporter (1 x week)
Transportation: Commute to work: 90.7% car, 0.2% public transportation, 5.0% walk, 2.7% work from home (2000); Travel time to work: 64.3% less than 15 minutes, 14.0% 15 to 30 minutes, 12.2% 30 to 45 minutes, 5.0% 45 to 60 minutes, 4.4% 60 minutes or more (2000); Amtrak: Service available.
Additional Information Contacts
Mendota Chamber of Commerce.......................... 815-539-6507

NAPLATE (village). Covers a land area of 0.112 square miles and a water area of 0 square miles. Located at 41.33° N. Lat.; 88.87° W. Long. Elevation is 480 feet.
Population: 523 (2000); Race: 95.4% White, 0.0% Black, 1.1% Asian, 0.0% American Indian and Alaska Native, 5.3% Hispanic of any race, 2.3% two or more races (2000); Density: 4,671.6 persons per square mile (2000); Age: 23.3% under 18, 22.6% over 64 (2000); Marriage status: 25.0% never married, 49.8% now married, 10.6% widowed, 14.7% divorced (2000); Foreign born: 3.2% (2000); Ancestry (includes multiple ancestries): 18.8% Irish, 17.1% German, 15.2% Italian, 11.6% Polish, 9.7% Other groups (2000).
Economy: Employment by occupation: 5.2% management, 10.9% professional, 22.6% services, 23.9% sales, 0.0% farming, 14.3% construction, 23.0% production (2000).
Income: Per capita income: $16,459 (2000); Median household income: $31,083 (2000); Poverty rate: 9.7% (2000).
Taxes: Total city taxes per capita: $50 (1997); City property taxes per capita: $15 (1997).
Education: High school graduation rate: 73.3% (2000); College graduation rate: 7.2% (2000).
Housing: Homeownership rate: 76.2% (2000); Median home value: $69,400 (2000); Median rent: $386 per month (2000); Median age of housing: 60+ years (2000).
Transportation: Commute to work: 94.2% car, 0.0% public transportation, 2.2% walk, 3.5% work from home (2000); Travel time to work: 61.9% less than 15 minutes, 24.8% 15 to 30 minutes, 6.9% 30 to 45 minutes, 0.9% 45 to 60 minutes, 5.5% 60 minutes or more (2000)

NORTH UTICA (village). Aka Utica. Covers a land area of 1.506 square miles and a water area of 0 square miles. Located at 41.34° N. Lat.; 89.01° W. Long.
Population: 977 (2000); Race: 97.3% White, 0.2% Black, 0.0% Asian, 0.0% American Indian and Alaska Native, 2.1% Hispanic of any race, 2.3% two or more races (2000); Density: 648.6 persons per square mile (2000); Age: 21.4% under 18, 13.8% over 64 (2000); Marriage status: 18.5% never married, 62.0% now married, 8.1% widowed, 11.5% divorced (2000); Foreign born: 1.2% (2000); Ancestry (includes multiple ancestries): 31.2% German, 15.5% Irish, 14.8% English, 14.0% Polish, 13.3% Italian (2000).
Economy: Single-family building permits issued: 7 (2001) / 8 (2000); Multi-family building permits issued: 0 (2001) / 0 (2000); Employment by occupation: 10.7% management, 10.1% professional, 18.2% services, 32.4% sales, 0.0% farming, 12.8% construction, 15.8% production (2000).
Income: Per capita income: $23,061 (2000); Median household income: $43,182 (2000); Poverty rate: 7.2% (2000).
Taxes: Total city taxes per capita: $212 (1997); City property taxes per capita: $115 (1997).
Education: High school graduation rate: 86.4% (2000); College graduation rate: 11.9% (2000).
Housing: Homeownership rate: 79.2% (2000); Median home value: $90,800 (2000); Median rent: $461 per month (2000); Median age of housing: 40 years (2000).
Transportation: Commute to work: 95.8% car, 0.8% public transportation, 1.5% walk, 1.5% work from home (2000); Travel time to work: 39.4% less than 15 minutes, 41.9% 15 to 30 minutes, 7.0% 30 to 45 minutes, 1.7% 45 to 60 minutes, 10.0% 60 minutes or more (2000)

OGLESBY (city). Covers a land area of 4.001 square miles and a water area of 0 square miles. Located at 41.29° N. Lat.; 89.06° W. Long. Elevation is 636 feet.
History: Oglesby developed as an industrial town, producing cement from the nearby limestone deposits. The town was named for Governor Richard J. Oglesby.
Population: 3,647 (2000); Race: 99.1% White, 0.0% Black, 0.4% Asian, 0.2% American Indian and Alaska Native, 3.7% Hispanic of any race, 0.2% two or more races (2000); Density: 911.6 persons per square mile (2000); Age: 22.6% under 18, 21.3% over 64 (2000); Marriage status: 21.4% never married, 59.2% now married, 9.4% widowed, 9.9% divorced (2000); Foreign born: 1.8% (2000); Ancestry (includes multiple ancestries): 29.6% German, 25.2% Italian, 18.3% Polish, 11.5% Irish, 10.0% English (2000).
Economy: Single-family building permits issued: 9 (2001) / 4 (2000); Multi-family building permits issued: 0 (2001) / 10 (2000); Employment by occupation: 13.1% management, 15.2% professional, 18.4% services, 21.7% sales, 0.1% farming, 10.4% construction, 21.1% production (2000).
Income: Per capita income: $18,674 (2000); Median household income: $35,000 (2000); Poverty rate: 10.1% (2000).
Taxes: Total city taxes per capita: $198 (1997); City property taxes per capita: $116 (1997).
Education: High school graduation rate: 79.9% (2000); College graduation rate: 10.9% (2000).

School District(s)

Oglesby Elementary School District 125 (PK-08)
2000 Enrollment: 483 815-883-8932

Two-year College(s)

Illinois Valley Community College (Public)
2001 Enrollment: 3,673.............................. 815-224-2720
2001 Tuition: In-state $5,412; Out-of-state $6,691

Housing: Homeownership rate: 79.0% (2000); Median home value: $76,300 (2000); Median rent: $329 per month (2000); Median age of housing: 52 years (2000).
Transportation: Commute to work: 94.2% car, 0.5% public transportation, 0.8% walk, 1.9% work from home (2000); Travel time to work: 52.8% less than 15 minutes, 32.4% 15 to 30 minutes, 7.6% 30 to 45 minutes, 2.9% 45 to 60 minutes, 4.3% 60 minutes or more (2000)

OTTAWA (city). Covers a land area of 7.329 square miles and a water area of 0.334 square miles. Located at 41.34° N. Lat.; 88.84° W. Long. Elevation is 480 feet.
History: Ottawa was laid out in 1830 by the Illinois & Michigan Canal commissioners. A settlement soon grew as the town was on the travel route between Chicago and the Illinois Valley. In 1858 Abraham Lincoln and Stephen Douglas held their first, highly-publicized debate in Ottawa.
Population: 18,307 (2000); Race: 96.3% White, 1.9% Black, 0.6% Asian, 0.2% American Indian and Alaska Native, 4.6% Hispanic of any race, 0.6% two or more races (2000); Density: 2,497.9 persons per square mile (2000); Age: 25.2% under 18, 18.2% over 64 (2000); Marriage status: 24.2% never married, 54.7% now married, 10.2% widowed, 10.9% divorced (2000); Foreign born: 2.0% (2000); Ancestry (includes multiple ancestries): 27.4% German, 20.8% Irish, 9.7% Other groups, 9.0% English, 8.4% Italian (2000).
Vital Statistics: Birth rate: 133.8 per 10,000 population (1998)
Economy: Single-family building permits issued: 71 (2001) / 73 (2000); Multi-family building permits issued: 40 (2001) / 38 (2000); Employment by occupation: 8.3% management, 18.1% professional, 17.1% services, 27.1% sales, 0.3% farming, 9.9% construction, 19.2% production (2000).
Income: Per capita income: $19,426 (2000); Median household income: $36,513 (2000); Poverty rate: 11.3% (2000).
Taxes: Total city taxes per capita: $156 (1997); City property taxes per capita: $103 (1997).
Education: High school graduation rate: 82.5% (2000); College graduation rate: 16.3% (2000).

School District(s)

Deer Park C C School District 82 (PK-08)
2000 Enrollment: 99 815-434-6930
Lasalle Putnam Alliance (04-12)
2000 Enrollment: 41 815-433-6433
Lasalle Roe (06-12)
2000 Enrollment: 43 815-434-0780
Ottawa Elementary School District 141 (PK-08)
2000 Enrollment: 2,147 815-433-1133
Ottawa Township H S District 140 (09-12)
2000 Enrollment: 1,571 815-433-1323
Rutland C C School District 230 (KG-08)
2000 Enrollment: 119 815-433-2949
Wallace C C School District 195 (KG-08)
2000 Enrollment: 316 815-433-2986

Housing: Homeownership rate: 67.9% (2000); Median home value: $87,500 (2000); Median rent: $413 per month (2000); Median age of housing: 49 years (2000).
Hospitals: Community Hospital of Ottawa (124 beds)
Newspapers: The Daily Times (6 x week); Town & Country (1 x week); Illinois Valley Thrif-T-Nikel (1 x week)
Transportation: Commute to work: 93.6% car, 0.9% public transportation, 2.2% walk, 2.1% work from home (2000); Travel time to work: 53.5% less than 15 minutes, 24.2% 15 to 30 minutes, 9.4% 30 to 45 minutes, 4.5% 45 to 60 minutes, 8.3% 60 minutes or more (2000)
Additional Information Contacts
Ottawa Area Chamber of Commerce 815-433-0084

PERU (city). Covers a land area of 5.941 square miles and a water area of 0.108 square miles. Located at 41.33° N. Lat.; 89.12° W. Long. Elevation is 610 feet.
History: Peru's name is of Indian origin, meaning "plenty of everything." The town was founded in 1835 on the Illinois River, and became the terminus of the Illinois & Michigan Canal. River traffic influenced the development of Peru's early industries, which included the Peru Wheel Company and the Star Union Products Company.
Population: 9,835 (2000); Race: 96.5% White, 0.8% Black, 0.6% Asian, 0.2% American Indian and Alaska Native, 4.2% Hispanic of any race, 0.6% two or more races (2000); Density: 1,655.5 persons per square mile (2000); Age: 21.6% under 18, 21.6% over 64 (2000); Marriage status: 21.7% never married, 60.0% now married, 9.4% widowed, 8.9% divorced (2000); Foreign born: 3.4% (2000); Ancestry (includes multiple ancestries): 31.1% German, 21.5% Polish, 17.4% Italian, 15.4% Irish, 9.5% English (2000).
Economy: Single-family building permits issued: 16 (2001) / 29 (2000); Multi-family building permits issued: 6 (2001) / 12 (2000); Employment by occupation: 8.6% management, 19.1% professional, 17.0% services, 28.2% sales, 0.5% farming, 8.6% construction, 18.0% production (2000).
Income: Per capita income: $20,658 (2000); Median household income: $37,060 (2000); Poverty rate: 7.5% (2000).
Taxes: Total city taxes per capita: $123 (1997); City property taxes per capita: $61 (1997).
Education: High school graduation rate: 81.3% (2000); College graduation rate: 16.8% (2000).

School District(s)

Peru Elementary School District 124 (PK-08)
2000 Enrollment: 922 815-223-0486

Housing: Homeownership rate: 75.1% (2000); Median home value: $85,700 (2000); Median rent: $410 per month (2000); Median age of housing: 49 years (2000).
Hospitals: Illinois Valley Community Hospital
Transportation: Commute to work: 94.8% car, 0.5% public transportation, 1.3% walk, 2.8% work from home (2000); Travel time to work: 62.4% less than 15 minutes, 22.7% 15 to 30 minutes, 7.0% 30 to 45 minutes, 1.8% 45 to 60 minutes, 6.1% 60 minutes or more (2000)
Airports: Illinois Valley Regional-Walter A Duncan
Additional Information Contacts
Illini Valley Association of Realtors 815-224-1868

RANSOM (village). Covers a land area of 0.991 square miles and a water area of 0 square miles. Located at 41.15° N. Lat.; 88.65° W. Long. Elevation is 720 feet.
Population: 409 (2000); Race: 97.2% White, 0.0% Black, 0.0% Asian, 0.4% American Indian and Alaska Native, 2.2% Hispanic of any race, 2.4% two or more races (2000); Density: 412.6 persons per square mile (2000); Age: 33.3% under 18, 7.6% over 64 (2000); Marriage status: 18.9% never married, 64.6% now married, 8.7% widowed, 7.8% divorced (2000); Foreign born: 0.0% (2000); Ancestry (includes multiple ancestries): 39.8% German, 26.2% Irish, 8.9% United States or American, 6.3% Other groups, 4.8% Norwegian (2000).
Economy: In agricultural area. Single-family building permits issued: 0 (2001) / 0 (2000); Multi-family building permits issued: 0 (2001) / 0 (2000); Employment by occupation: 7.9% management, 9.7% professional, 23.8% services, 25.1% sales, 0.0% farming, 9.7% construction, 23.8% production (2000).
Income: Per capita income: $17,524 (2000); Median household income: $53,333 (2000); Poverty rate: 1.9% (2000).
Taxes: Total city taxes per capita: $61 (2000); City property taxes per capita: $56 (2000).
Education: High school graduation rate: 88.4% (2000); College graduation rate: 9.5% (2000).

School District(s)

Allen Township C C School District 65 (KG-08)
2000 Enrollment: 105 815-586-4611

Housing: Homeownership rate: 80.0% (2000); Median home value: $67,900 (2000); Median rent: $438 per month (2000); Median age of housing: 58 years (2000).
Transportation: Commute to work: 96.8% car, 0.0% public transportation, 0.9% walk, 0.9% work from home (2000); Travel time to work: 32.7% less than 15 minutes, 38.6% 15 to 30 minutes, 16.4% 30 to 45 minutes, 4.1% 45 to 60 minutes, 8.2% 60 minutes or more (2000)

RUTLAND (village). Covers a land area of 0.820 square miles and a water area of 0 square miles. Located at 40.98° N. Lat.; 89.04° W. Long. Elevation is 710 feet.
Population: 354 (2000); Race: 96.2% White, 0.0% Black, 0.0% Asian, 0.6% American Indian and Alaska Native, 0.0% Hispanic of any race, 0.9% two or more races (2000); Density: 431.5 persons per square mile (2000); Age: 20.9% under 18, 20.6% over 64 (2000); Marriage status: 17.8% never married, 61.6% now married, 8.2% widowed, 12.3% divorced (2000); Foreign born: 0.9% (2000); Ancestry (includes multiple ancestries): 31.3% German, 13.3% Irish, 9.6% Polish, 7.8% United States or American, 7.5% Italian (2000).
Economy: In agricultural area. Employment by occupation: 7.4% management, 7.4% professional, 25.3% services, 14.8% sales, 0.0% farming, 11.7% construction, 33.3% production (2000).
Income: Per capita income: $16,892 (2000); Median household income: $31,500 (2000); Poverty rate: 4.3% (2000).
Taxes: Total city taxes per capita: $40 (1997); City property taxes per capita: $37 (1997).

Education: High school graduation rate: 77.3% (2000); College graduation rate: 5.4% (2000).
Housing: Homeownership rate: 85.1% (2000); Median home value: $44,600 (2000); Median rent: $267 per month (2000); Median age of housing: 43 years (2000).
Transportation: Commute to work: 98.8% car, 0.0% public transportation, 0.0% walk, 0.0% work from home (2000); Travel time to work: 48.8% less than 15 minutes, 14.2% 15 to 30 minutes, 23.5% 30 to 45 minutes, 11.1% 45 to 60 minutes, 2.5% 60 minutes or more (2000)

SENECA (village). Aka Crotty. Covers a land area of 3.307 square miles and a water area of 0.258 square miles. Located at 41.30° N. Lat.; 88.60° W. Long. Elevation is 510 feet.
History: Seneca was built along the Illinois & Michigan Canal, and developed as a sawmill town.
Population: 2,053 (2000); Race: 97.5% White, 0.1% Black, 0.2% Asian, 0.0% American Indian and Alaska Native, 1.3% Hispanic of any race, 1.7% two or more races (2000); Density: 620.7 persons per square mile (2000); Age: 33.3% under 18, 10.7% over 64 (2000); Marriage status: 22.2% never married, 63.9% now married, 6.3% widowed, 7.5% divorced (2000); Foreign born: 1.2% (2000); Ancestry (includes multiple ancestries): 27.4% German, 23.6% Irish, 14.5% English, 11.4% Norwegian, 8.1% Italian (2000).
Economy: Single-family building permits issued: 4 (2001) / 8 (2000); Multi-family building permits issued: 0 (2001) / 0 (2000); Employment by occupation: 8.5% management, 18.1% professional, 14.9% services, 26.4% sales, 0.2% farming, 14.5% construction, 17.5% production (2000).
Income: Per capita income: $19,273 (2000); Median household income: $52,188 (2000); Poverty rate: 7.3% (2000).
Taxes: Total city taxes per capita: $239 (1997); City property taxes per capita: $173 (1997).
Education: High school graduation rate: 86.4% (2000); College graduation rate: 12.9% (2000).

School District(s)

Seneca Community Cons School District 170 (PK-08)
2000 Enrollment: 612 815-357-8744
Seneca Township H S District 160 (09-12)
2000 Enrollment: 490 815-357-8761

Housing: Homeownership rate: 80.0% (2000); Median home value: $107,000 (2000); Median rent: $391 per month (2000); Median age of housing: 41 years (2000).
Transportation: Commute to work: 92.5% car, 0.0% public transportation, 3.3% walk, 3.0% work from home (2000); Travel time to work: 36.2% less than 15 minutes, 28.3% 15 to 30 minutes, 16.8% 30 to 45 minutes, 7.9% 45 to 60 minutes, 10.8% 60 minutes or more (2000)

SERENA (unincorporated postal area, zip code 60549). Covers a land area of 24.144 square miles and a water area of 0 square miles. Located at 41.49° N. Lat.; 88.75° W. Long. Elevation is 633 feet.
Population: 594 (2000); Race: 100.0% White, 0.0% Black, 0.0% Asian, 0.0% American Indian and Alaska Native, 5.2% Hispanic of any race, 0.0% two or more races (2000); Density: 24.6 persons per square mile (2000); Age: 23.0% under 18, 10.6% over 64 (2000); Marriage status: 15.7% never married, 70.6% now married, 1.1% widowed, 12.5% divorced (2000); Foreign born: 0.0% (2000); Ancestry (includes multiple ancestries): 30.3% Norwegian, 22.8% Irish, 21.7% German, 18.5% English, 9.9% Italian (2000).
Economy: Employment by occupation: 25.0% management, 22.7% professional, 10.5% services, 18.4% sales, 0.0% farming, 16.1% construction, 7.2% production (2000).
Income: Per capita income: $20,022 (2000); Median household income: $52,000 (2000); Poverty rate: 6.5% (2000).
Education: High school graduation rate: 93.7% (2000); College graduation rate: 13.2% (2000).

School District(s)

Community Unit School District 2 (KG-12)
2000 Enrollment: 894 815-496-2850

Housing: Homeownership rate: 79.5% (2000); Median home value: $126,400 (2000); Median rent: $443 per month (2000); Median age of housing: 38 years (2000).
Transportation: Commute to work: 95.1% car, 0.0% public transportation, 0.0% walk, 4.9% work from home (2000); Travel time to work: 15.6% less than 15 minutes, 49.8% 15 to 30 minutes, 23.9% 30 to 45 minutes, 10.7% 45 to 60 minutes, 0.0% 60 minutes or more (2000)

SHERIDAN (village). Covers a land area of 1.405 square miles and a water area of 0.040 square miles. Located at 41.52° N. Lat.; 88.68° W. Long. Elevation is 592 feet.
Population: 2,411 (2000); Race: 53.8% White, 37.3% Black, 0.0% Asian, 0.2% American Indian and Alaska Native, 8.3% Hispanic of any race, 0.4% two or more races (2000); Density: 1,715.5 persons per square mile (2000); Age: 10.8% under 18, 3.9% over 64 (2000); Marriage status: 6.7% never married, 76.1% now married, 8.1% widowed, 9.1% divorced (2000); Foreign born: 2.9% (2000); Ancestry (includes multiple ancestries): 10.4% German, 6.8% Irish, 6.1% English, 4.0% Norwegian, 2.4% Other groups (2000).
Economy: In agricultural area. Sheridan Correctional Center here. Single-family building permits issued: 11 (2001) / 4 (2000); Multi-family building permits issued: 0 (2001) / 0 (2000); Employment by occupation: 5.0% management, 9.4% professional, 17.0% services, 26.6% sales, 0.0% farming, 20.6% construction, 21.3% production (2000).
Income: Per capita income: $11,352 (2000); Median household income: $45,000 (2000); Poverty rate: 3.3% (2000).
Taxes: Total city taxes per capita: $19 (1997); City property taxes per capita: $10 (1997).
Education: High school graduation rate: 50.6% (2000); College graduation rate: 3.5% (2000).
Housing: Homeownership rate: 73.1% (2000); Median home value: $96,700 (2000); Median rent: $473 per month (2000); Median age of housing: 54 years (2000).
Transportation: Commute to work: 96.1% car, 0.0% public transportation, 3.2% walk, 0.7% work from home (2000); Travel time to work: 17.6% less than 15 minutes, 29.7% 15 to 30 minutes, 23.0% 30 to 45 minutes, 17.6% 45 to 60 minutes, 12.1% 60 minutes or more (2000)

STREATOR (city). Covers a land area of 5.767 square miles and a water area of 0.013 square miles. Located at 41.12° N. Lat.; 88.83° W. Long. Elevation is 626 feet.
History: Coal mining began in Streator in 1872, and the name of the town was changed from Unionville to Streator to honor the president of the coal company. Streator was sited near deposits of shale, clay, and sand which led to the manufacturing of glass.
Population: 14,190 (2000); Race: 93.7% White, 2.6% Black, 0.5% Asian, 0.1% American Indian and Alaska Native, 6.3% Hispanic of any race, 1.7% two or more races (2000); Density: 2,460.6 persons per square mile (2000); Age: 25.7% under 18, 19.6% over 64 (2000); Marriage status: 23.6% never married, 53.0% now married, 11.9% widowed, 11.5% divorced (2000); Foreign born: 3.2% (2000); Ancestry (includes multiple ancestries): 22.0% German, 14.8% Irish, 11.7% Slovak, 10.8% Other groups, 10.2% United States or American (2000).
Vital Statistics: Birth rate: 187.5 per 10,000 population (1998)
Economy: Single-family building permits issued: 9 (2001) / 9 (2000); Multi-family building permits issued: 6 (2001) / 58 (2000); Employment by occupation: 7.1% management, 12.8% professional, 18.9% services, 21.7% sales, 0.7% farming, 7.7% construction, 31.3% production (2000).
Income: Per capita income: $16,650 (2000); Median household income: $33,868 (2000); Poverty rate: 11.3% (2000).
Taxes: Total city taxes per capita: $97 (1997); City property taxes per capita: $87 (1997).
Education: High school graduation rate: 74.0% (2000); College graduation rate: 9.0% (2000).

School District(s)

Otter Creek-Hyatt School District 56 (KG-08)
2000 Enrollment: 30 815-672-9113
Streator Elementary School District 44 (PK-08)
2000 Enrollment: 1,900 815-672-2926
Streator Township H S District 40 (09-12)
2000 Enrollment: 967 815-672-0545
Woodland C U S District 5 (PK-12)
2000 Enrollment: 581 815-672-5974

Housing: Homeownership rate: 70.8% (2000); Median home value: $56,800 (2000); Median rent: $359 per month (2000); Median age of housing: 55 years (2000).
Hospitals: Saint Mary's Hospital Home (251 beds)
Newspapers: The Times-Press (3 x week)
Transportation: Commute to work: 94.0% car, 0.1% public transportation, 3.4% walk, 1.0% work from home (2000); Travel time to work: 58.4% less than 15 minutes, 15.9% 15 to 30 minutes, 15.0% 30 to 45 minutes, 4.8% 45 to 60 minutes, 6.0% 60 minutes or more (2000)
Additional Information Contacts
Streator Chamber of Commerce.............................. 815-672-2921

TONICA (village). Covers a land area of 1.355 square miles and a water area of 0 square miles. Located at 41.21° N. Lat.; 89.06° W. Long. Elevation is 660 feet.

Population: 685 (2000); Race: 99.1% White, 0.0% Black, 0.0% Asian, 0.0% American Indian and Alaska Native, 2.9% Hispanic of any race, 0.0% two or more races (2000); Density: 505.5 persons per square mile (2000); Age: 24.2% under 18, 22.9% over 64 (2000); Marriage status: 15.7% never married, 61.7% now married, 10.4% widowed, 12.2% divorced (2000); Foreign born: 3.7% (2000); Ancestry (includes multiple ancestries): 40.6% German, 15.1% Irish, 11.6% English, 11.3% Polish, 8.5% Italian (2000).
Economy: Dairy products; cattle, hogs; corn, soybeans, wheat; charcoal briquettes. Single-family building permits issued: 2 (2001) / 5 (2000); Multi-family building permits issued: 0 (2001) / 0 (2000); Employment by occupation: 6.6% management, 13.2% professional, 14.1% services, 25.8% sales, 1.8% farming, 15.6% construction, 22.8% production (2000).
Income: Per capita income: $22,484 (2000); Median household income: $38,333 (2000); Poverty rate: 5.3% (2000).
Taxes: Total city taxes per capita: $74 (1997); City property taxes per capita: $71 (1997).
Education: High school graduation rate: 81.9% (2000); College graduation rate: 11.8% (2000).

School District(s)

Tonica Community Cons School District 79 (KG-08)
2000 Enrollment: 147 815-442-3420

Housing: Homeownership rate: 77.7% (2000); Median home value: $77,900 (2000); Median rent: $297 per month (2000); Median age of housing: 60+ years (2000).
Newspapers: The Tonica News (1 x week)
Transportation: Commute to work: 90.5% car, 0.0% public transportation, 5.4% walk, 3.2% work from home (2000); Travel time to work: 36.1% less than 15 minutes, 38.4% 15 to 30 minutes, 16.7% 30 to 45 minutes, 4.3% 45 to 60 minutes, 4.6% 60 minutes or more (2000)

TROY GROVE (village). Covers a land area of 0.687 square miles and a water area of 0 square miles. Located at 41.46° N. Lat.; 89.08° W. Long. Elevation is 660 feet.
History: Troy Grove is the birthplace and boyhood home of James Butler "Wild Bill" Hickok (1837-1876), who toured with Buffalo Bill Cody in 1872-1873.
Population: 305 (2000); Race: 93.2% White, 1.0% Black, 0.0% Asian, 0.0% American Indian and Alaska Native, 6.5% Hispanic of any race, 2.9% two or more races (2000); Density: 444.2 persons per square mile (2000); Age: 33.5% under 18, 8.7% over 64 (2000); Marriage status: 26.1% never married, 60.6% now married, 4.0% widowed, 9.3% divorced (2000); Foreign born: 1.6% (2000); Ancestry (includes multiple ancestries): 32.6% German, 15.8% Irish, 10.6% Other groups, 10.3% United States or American, 8.7% Polish (2000).
Economy: Employment by occupation: 7.7% management, 12.3% professional, 14.2% services, 34.8% sales, 0.0% farming, 12.9% construction, 18.1% production (2000).
Income: Per capita income: $16,595 (2000); Median household income: $55,682 (2000); Poverty rate: 4.5% (2000).
Taxes: Total city taxes per capita: $41 (1997); City property taxes per capita: $30 (1997).
Education: High school graduation rate: 84.8% (2000); College graduation rate: 11.6% (2000).
Housing: Homeownership rate: 91.1% (2000); Median home value: $80,900 (2000); Median rent: $300 per month (2000); Median age of housing: 43 years (2000).
Transportation: Commute to work: 88.7% car, 3.3% public transportation, 4.0% walk, 4.0% work from home (2000); Travel time to work: 45.1% less than 15 minutes, 34.7% 15 to 30 minutes, 4.9% 30 to 45 minutes, 4.2% 45 to 60 minutes, 11.1% 60 minutes or more (2000)

UTICA (unincorporated postal area, zip code 61373). Aka North Utica. Covers a land area of 48.603 square miles and a water area of 0.177 square miles. Located at 41.41° N. Lat.; 89.00° W. Long. Elevation is 470 feet.
Population: 1,998 (2000); Race: 97.5% White, 0.1% Black, 0.6% Asian, 0.0% American Indian and Alaska Native, 1.1% Hispanic of any race, 1.7% two or more races (2000); Density: 41.1 persons per square mile (2000); Age: 26.8% under 18, 11.3% over 64 (2000); Marriage status: 19.6% never married, 66.9% now married, 5.8% widowed, 7.6% divorced (2000); Foreign born: 1.1% (2000); Ancestry (includes multiple ancestries): 32.8% German, 19.0% Irish, 12.5% English, 11.6% Polish, 10.9% Italian (2000).
Economy: Employment by occupation: 15.0% management, 14.4% professional, 13.0% services, 30.3% sales, 0.6% farming, 12.7% construction, 14.0% production (2000).
Income: Per capita income: $22,970 (2000); Median household income: $49,688 (2000); Poverty rate: 4.9% (2000).
Education: High school graduation rate: 89.5% (2000); College graduation rate: 16.5% (2000).

School District(s)

Utica Elementary School District 135 (KG-08)
2000 Enrollment: 65 815-667-4790
Waltham C C School District 185 (KG-08)
2000 Enrollment: 181 815-667-4417

Housing: Homeownership rate: 82.0% (2000); Median home value: $120,900 (2000); Median rent: $448 per month (2000); Median age of housing: 32 years (2000).
Transportation: Commute to work: 92.0% car, 0.4% public transportation, 2.1% walk, 5.0% work from home (2000); Travel time to work: 37.3% less than 15 minutes, 43.6% 15 to 30 minutes, 7.9% 30 to 45 minutes, 2.2% 45 to 60 minutes, 9.0% 60 minutes or more (2000)

Lake County

Located in northeastern Illinois; bounded on the east by Lake Michigan, and on the north by Wisconsin; drained by the Fox and Des Plaines Rivers; includes many lakes. Covers a land area of 447.60 square miles, a water area of 920.40 square miles, and is located in the Central Time Zone. The county government was organized in 1839. County seat is Waukegan.

Lake County is part of the Chicago, IL PMSA. The entire metro area includes: Cook County; DeKalb County; DuPage County; Grundy County; Kane County; Kendall County; Lake County; McHenry County; Will County

Weather Station: Waukegan Elevation: 698 feet

	Jan	Feb	Mar	Apr	May	Jun	Jul	Aug	Sep	Oct	Nov	Dec
High	28	33	42	54	67	77	81	80	72	61	47	34
Low	12	16	26	36	46	55	61	60	52	41	30	19
Precip	1.6	1.3	2.2	3.7	3.4	3.6	3.4	4.2	3.5	2.5	2.7	2.1
Snow	12.0	9.2	5.7	1.7	tr	0.0	0.0	0.0	0.0	0.1	1.9	7.3

High and Low temperatures in degrees Fahrenheit; Precipitation and Snow in inches

Population: 644,356 (2000); Race: 80.1% White, 6.8% Black, 3.9% Asian, 0.2% American Indian and Alaska Native, 14.4% Hispanic of any race, 2.1% two or more races (2000); Density: 1,439.7 persons per square mile (2000); Age: 29.3% under 18, 8.5% over 64 (2000).
Religion: Five largest groups: 39.2% Catholic Church, 3.8% Jewish estimate, 2.7% Independent, Non-Charismatic Churches, 2.5% Evangelical Lutheran Church in America, 1.6% Presbyterian Church (U.S.A.) (2000).
Economy: Unemployment rate: 5.5% (11/2002); Total civilian labor force: 325,585 (11/2002); Leading industries: 17.0% manufacturing; 13.7% retail trade; 8.6% health care and social assistance (2000); Companies that employ more than 1,000 persons: 21 (2000); Companies that employ more than 100 persons: 474 (2000); Farms: 335 totaling 50,901 acres (1997); Minority business ownership rate: 8.7% (1997); Women business ownership rate: 29.4% (1997); Retail sales per capita: $14,316 (1997). Single-family building permits issued: 3,366 (2001) / 3,168 (2000); Multi-family building permits issued: 837 (2001) / 966 (2000).
Income: Per capita income: $32,102 (2000); Median household income: $66,973 (2000); Poverty rate: 5.7% (2000); Bankruptcy rate: 3.86% (2001).
Taxes: Total county taxes per capita: $170 (2000); County property taxes per capita: $167 (2000).
Education: High school graduation rate: 86.6% (2000); College graduation rate: 38.6% (2000).
Housing: Homeownership rate: 77.8% (2000); Median home value: $198,200 (2000); Median rent: $669 per month (2000); Median age of housing: 25 years (2000).
Health: Birth rate: 162.5 per 10,000 population (1998); Age adjusted death rate: 83.4 per 10,000 population (1999); Infant mortality rate: 5.0 per 1,000 live births (1998); Age adjusted cancer mortality rate: 212.1 deaths per 100,000 population (1999). Air Quality Index: 81% good, 19% moderate, 0% unhealthy (percent of days in 2000). Number of physicians: 29.4 per 10,000 population (1999); Number of hospital beds: 29.5 per 10,000 population (1999).
Elections: 2000 Presidential election results: 47.5% Gore, 50.0% Bush, 2.0% Nader, 0.2% Buchanan
National and State Parks: Chain O'Lakes State Park; Illinois Beach State Park; Volo Bog State Nature Preserve
Additional Information Contacts
Lake County Government Offices 847-360-6336
Antioch Chamber of Commerce.............................. 847-395-2233
Buffalo Grove Chamber of Commerce 847-541-7799
Deerfield Chamber of Commerce 847-945-4660

Fox Lake Area Chamber of Commerce 847-587-7474
Grayslake Chamber of Commerce 847-223-6888
Gurnee Chamber of Commerce 847-249-3800
Highland Park Chamber of Commerce 847-432-0284
Highwood Chamber of Commerce 847-433-2100
Lake Forest Chamber of Commerce 847-604-4522
Lake Zurich Chamber of Commerce 847-438-5572
Lindenhurst Lake Villa Chamber 847-356-8446
North Chicago Chamber of Commerce 847-785-1912
Round Lake Chamber of Commerce 847-546-2002
St. Louis Convention & Visitors Bureau 847-735-0218
Wauconda Chamber of Commerce 847-526-5580
Winthrop Harbor Chamber of Commerce 847-872-7723
Zion Chamber of Commerce 847-872-5405

Lake County Communities

ANTIOCH (village). Covers a land area of 7.383 square miles and a water area of 0.262 square miles. Located at 42.47° N. Lat.; 88.09° W. Long. Elevation is 770 feet.
History: Settled 1836, incorporated 1857.
Population: 8,788 (2000); Race: 96.9% White, 0.1% Black, 1.2% Asian, 0.1% American Indian and Alaska Native, 3.5% Hispanic of any race, 0.8% two or more races (2000); Density: 1,190.4 persons per square mile (2000); Age: 30.1% under 18, 8.6% over 64 (2000); Marriage status: 25.6% never married, 59.6% now married, 5.4% widowed, 9.3% divorced (2000); Foreign born: 3.3% (2000); Ancestry (includes multiple ancestries): 33.4% German, 20.3% Irish, 12.2% Polish, 10.3% Italian, 9.2% English (2000).
Economy: In farming and lake-resort area; food processing. Single-family building permits issued: 180 (2001) / 129 (2000); Multi-family building permits issued: 0 (2001) / 40 (2000); Employment by occupation: 15.8% management, 21.1% professional, 10.0% services, 31.4% sales, 0.2% farming, 10.1% construction, 11.4% production (2000).
Income: Per capita income: $25,711 (2000); Median household income: $56,481 (2000); Poverty rate: 3.9% (2000).
Taxes: Total city taxes per capita: $160 (1997); City property taxes per capita: $131 (1997).
Education: High school graduation rate: 89.5% (2000); College graduation rate: 26.7% (2000).

School District(s)

Antioch C C School District 34 (PK-08)
2000 Enrollment: 2,152 847-838-8400
Antioch Community High School District 117 (04-12)
2000 Enrollment: 2,142 847-395-1421
Emmons School District 33 (KG-08)
2000 Enrollment: 351 847-395-1105
Grass Lake School District 36 (PK-08)
2000 Enrollment: 286 847-395-1550

Housing: Homeownership rate: 67.3% (2000); Median home value: $166,400 (2000); Median rent: $631 per month (2000); Median age of housing: 21 years (2000).
Transportation: Commute to work: 92.3% car, 1.6% public transportation, 3.1% walk, 2.4% work from home (2000); Travel time to work: 23.9% less than 15 minutes, 21.0% 15 to 30 minutes, 27.9% 30 to 45 minutes, 15.5% 45 to 60 minutes, 11.6% 60 minutes or more (2000)
Additional Information Contacts
Antioch Chamber of Commerce 847-395-2233

BANNOCKBURN (village). Covers a land area of 2.024 square miles and a water area of 0.008 square miles. Located at 42.19° N. Lat.; 87.86° W. Long. Elevation is 685 feet.
Population: 1,429 (2000); Race: 91.4% White, 1.9% Black, 6.5% Asian, 0.0% American Indian and Alaska Native, 4.8% Hispanic of any race, 0.1% two or more races (2000); Density: 706.1 persons per square mile (2000); Age: 14.1% under 18, 6.1% over 64 (2000); Marriage status: 62.2% never married, 34.9% now married, 1.7% widowed, 1.2% divorced (2000); Foreign born: 13.0% (2000); Ancestry (includes multiple ancestries): 21.2% German, 12.1% Other groups, 7.3% Swedish, 7.0% Italian, 6.7% Irish (2000).
Economy: Agriculture: dairying to West. Manufacturing: metal fabrication, machinery. Single-family building permits issued: 3 (2001) / 4 (2000); Multi-family building permits issued: 0 (2001) / 0 (2000); Employment by occupation: 12.4% management, 31.7% professional, 17.6% services, 35.7% sales, 0.0% farming, 2.2% construction, 0.6% production (2000).
Income: Per capita income: $39,303 (2000); Median household income: $150,415 (2000); Poverty rate: 3.0% (2000).
Taxes: Total city taxes per capita: $1,531 (1997); City property taxes per capita: $555 (1997).
Education: High school graduation rate: 97.8% (2000); College graduation rate: 76.9% (2000).
Housing: Homeownership rate: 82.3% (2000); Median home value: $933,500 (2000); Median rent: $634 per month (2000); Median age of housing: 28 years (2000).
Transportation: Commute to work: 79.8% car, 4.1% public transportation, 7.1% walk, 3.6% work from home (2000); Travel time to work: 56.1% less than 15 minutes, 20.5% 15 to 30 minutes, 13.7% 30 to 45 minutes, 4.1% 45 to 60 minutes, 5.6% 60 minutes or more (2000)

BEACH PARK (village). Covers a land area of 6.419 square miles and a water area of 0 square miles. Located at 42.42° N. Lat.; 87.84° W. Long. Elevation is 690 feet.
Population: 10,072 (2000); Race: 84.4% White, 3.9% Black, 1.2% Asian, 0.0% American Indian and Alaska Native, 13.0% Hispanic of any race, 4.8% two or more races (2000); Density: 1,569.0 persons per square mile (2000); Age: 25.3% under 18, 11.2% over 64 (2000); Marriage status: 22.1% never married, 60.7% now married, 6.6% widowed, 10.6% divorced (2000); Foreign born: 7.5% (2000); Ancestry (includes multiple ancestries): 27.4% German, 20.0% Other groups, 16.1% Irish, 9.4% English, 8.7% Polish (2000).
Economy: Residential suburb of downtown Chicago. Single-family building permits issued: 21 (2001) / 21 (2000); Multi-family building permits issued: 0 (2001) / 0 (2000); Employment by occupation: 10.1% management, 16.0% professional, 12.7% services, 29.3% sales, 0.2% farming, 16.7% construction, 15.1% production (2000).
Income: Per capita income: $23,803 (2000); Median household income: $56,553 (2000); Poverty rate: 3.7% (2000).
Taxes: Total city taxes per capita: $61 (1997); City property taxes per capita: $6 (1997).
Education: High school graduation rate: 84.1% (2000); College graduation rate: 14.9% (2000).
Housing: Homeownership rate: 89.2% (2000); Median home value: $144,300 (2000); Median rent: $623 per month (2000); Median age of housing: 25 years (2000).
Transportation: Commute to work: 94.8% car, 1.6% public transportation, 0.2% walk, 2.4% work from home (2000); Travel time to work: 24.4% less than 15 minutes, 34.0% 15 to 30 minutes, 21.3% 30 to 45 minutes, 9.8% 45 to 60 minutes, 10.5% 60 minutes or more (2000)

BUFFALO GROVE (village). Covers a land area of 9.194 square miles and a water area of 0.020 square miles. Located at 42.16° N. Lat.; 87.96° W. Long.
Population: 42,909 (2000); Race: 87.9% White, 0.7% Black, 8.7% Asian, 0.1% American Indian and Alaska Native, 3.6% Hispanic of any race, 1.4% two or more races (2000); Density: 4,666.9 persons per square mile (2000); Age: 28.6% under 18, 9.1% over 64 (2000); Marriage status: 20.7% never married, 67.7% now married, 4.4% widowed, 7.2% divorced (2000); Foreign born: 20.4% (2000); Ancestry (includes multiple ancestries): 19.1% Other groups, 16.1% German, 15.4% Russian, 12.7% Polish, 9.7% Irish (2000).
Vital Statistics: Birth rate: 130.7 per 10,000 population (1998)
Economy: Unemployment rate: 4.6% (11/2002); Total civilian labor force: 25,578 (11/2002); Single-family building permits issued: 27 (2001) / 18 (2000); Multi-family building permits issued: 0 (2001) / 32 (2000); Employment by occupation: 24.7% management, 30.2% professional, 6.2% services, 29.3% sales, 0.0% farming, 4.0% construction, 5.6% production (2000).
Income: Per capita income: $36,696 (2000); Median household income: $80,525 (2000); Poverty rate: 2.3% (2000).
Education: High school graduation rate: 95.3% (2000); College graduation rate: 55.9% (2000).

School District(s)

Aptakisic-Tripp C C S District 102 (PK-08)
2000 Enrollment: 2,613 847-353-5650
Kildeer Countryside C C S District 96 (PK-08)
2000 Enrollment: 3,536 847-459-4260

Housing: Homeownership rate: 87.1% (2000); Median home value: $236,200 (2000); Median rent: $994 per month (2000); Median age of housing: 18 years (2000).
Transportation: Commute to work: 89.0% car, 5.5% public transportation, 0.9% walk, 4.1% work from home (2000); Travel time to work: 20.5% less than 15 minutes, 30.7% 15 to 30 minutes, 27.0% 30 to 45 minutes, 10.5% 45 to 60 minutes, 11.2% 60 minutes or more (2000)
Additional Information Contacts

Buffalo Grove Chamber of Commerce 847-541-7799

CHANNEL LAKE (CDP). Covers a land area of 1.949 square miles and a water area of 0.338 square miles. Located at 42.47° N. Lat.; 88.14° W. Long. Elevation is 745 feet.
Population: 1,785 (2000); Race: 96.0% White, 0.0% Black, 0.0% Asian, 0.3% American Indian and Alaska Native, 0.3% Hispanic of any race, 2.2% two or more races (2000); Density: 916.1 persons per square mile (2000); Age: 27.5% under 18, 9.4% over 64 (2000); Marriage status: 25.6% never married, 54.7% now married, 5.4% widowed, 14.3% divorced (2000); Foreign born: 3.9% (2000); Ancestry (includes multiple ancestries): 35.0% German, 16.9% Polish, 14.7% Irish, 8.6% English, 5.7% Italian (2000).
Economy: Suburb of downtown Chicago. Employment by occupation: 7.3% management, 16.9% professional, 9.9% services, 26.2% sales, 1.9% farming, 20.5% construction, 17.4% production (2000).
Income: Per capita income: $27,772 (2000); Median household income: $51,384 (2000); Poverty rate: 9.9% (2000).
Education: High school graduation rate: 82.5% (2000); College graduation rate: 19.0% (2000).
Housing: Homeownership rate: 81.0% (2000); Median home value: $136,600 (2000); Median rent: $599 per month (2000); Median age of housing: 44 years (2000).
Transportation: Commute to work: 88.4% car, 0.9% public transportation, 0.9% walk, 7.7% work from home (2000); Travel time to work: 6.5% less than 15 minutes, 18.9% 15 to 30 minutes, 27.5% 30 to 45 minutes, 19.9% 45 to 60 minutes, 27.2% 60 minutes or more (2000)

DEER PARK (village). Covers a land area of 3.646 square miles and a water area of 0.061 square miles. Located at 42.16° N. Lat.; 88.08° W. Long. Elevation is 850 feet.
Population: 3,102 (2000); Race: 96.0% White, 1.1% Black, 1.7% Asian, 0.0% American Indian and Alaska Native, 2.1% Hispanic of any race, 1.3% two or more races (2000); Density: 850.7 persons per square mile (2000); Age: 32.4% under 18, 4.9% over 64 (2000); Marriage status: 17.8% never married, 76.4% now married, 2.5% widowed, 3.3% divorced (2000); Foreign born: 8.4% (2000); Ancestry (includes multiple ancestries): 29.1% German, 19.0% Irish, 14.6% Italian, 14.2% Polish, 8.0% English (2000).
Economy: Residential suburb of downtown Chicago. Single-family building permits issued: 4 (2001) / 5 (2000); Multi-family building permits issued: 0 (2001) / 0 (2000); Employment by occupation: 40.2% management, 21.0% professional, 5.3% services, 26.8% sales, 0.0% farming, 2.3% construction, 4.5% production (2000).
Income: Per capita income: $61,429 (2000); Median household income: $149,233 (2000); Poverty rate: 0.6% (2000).
Taxes: Total city taxes per capita: $112 (2000); City property taxes per capita: $0 (2000).
Education: High school graduation rate: 96.8% (2000); College graduation rate: 61.7% (2000).
Housing: Homeownership rate: 97.9% (2000); Median home value: $449,600 (2000); Median rent: $642 per month (2000); Median age of housing: 16 years (2000).
Transportation: Commute to work: 85.3% car, 7.0% public transportation, 0.0% walk, 6.9% work from home (2000); Travel time to work: 12.6% less than 15 minutes, 35.9% 15 to 30 minutes, 31.6% 30 to 45 minutes, 8.2% 45 to 60 minutes, 11.7% 60 minutes or more (2000)

DEERFIELD (village). Covers a land area of 5.483 square miles and a water area of 0.035 square miles. Located at 42.16° N. Lat.; 87.85° W. Long. Elevation is 675 feet.
History: Incorporated 1903.
Population: 18,420 (2000); Race: 96.0% White, 0.1% Black, 2.8% Asian, 0.0% American Indian and Alaska Native, 1.6% Hispanic of any race, 0.4% two or more races (2000); Density: 3,359.4 persons per square mile (2000); Age: 30.1% under 18, 12.7% over 64 (2000); Marriage status: 15.4% never married, 72.4% now married, 5.5% widowed, 6.6% divorced (2000); Foreign born: 8.8% (2000); Ancestry (includes multiple ancestries): 17.6% German, 13.4% Russian, 11.2% Irish, 10.4% Other groups, 9.0% Polish (2000).
Vital Statistics: Birth rate: 154.2 per 10,000 population (1998)
Economy: The huge Sara Lee Bakery is its major industry; other light manufacturing. Single-family building permits issued: 22 (2001) / 79 (2000); Multi-family building permits issued: 0 (2001) / 61 (2000); Employment by occupation: 25.2% management, 34.3% professional, 5.2% services, 29.2% sales, 0.0% farming, 2.1% construction, 4.0% production (2000).
Income: Per capita income: $50,664 (2000); Median household income: $107,194 (2000); Poverty rate: 1.6% (2000).
Taxes: Total city taxes per capita: $757 (1997); City property taxes per capita: $621 (1997).
Education: High school graduation rate: 95.9% (2000); College graduation rate: 68.5% (2000).

School District(s)

Bannockburn School District 106 (KG-08)
2000 Enrollment: 189 847-945-5900
Deerfield School District 109 (PK-08)
2000 Enrollment: 3,171 847-945-1844

Four-year College(s)

Trinity International University (Private, Not-for-profit, Evangelical Free Church of America)
2001 Enrollment: 2,054 847-945-8800
2001 Tuition: In-state $15,100; Out-of-state $15,100

Housing: Homeownership rate: 90.1% (2000); Median home value: $342,900 (2000); Median rent: $963 per month (2000); Median age of housing: 37 years (2000).
Transportation: Commute to work: 79.2% car, 11.3% public transportation, 0.9% walk, 7.9% work from home (2000); Travel time to work: 25.4% less than 15 minutes, 31.2% 15 to 30 minutes, 17.3% 30 to 45 minutes, 10.6% 45 to 60 minutes, 15.4% 60 minutes or more (2000)
Additional Information Contacts
Deerfield Chamber of Commerce 847-945-4660

FOREST LAKE (CDP). Covers a land area of 0.632 square miles and a water area of 0.062 square miles. Located at 42.20° N. Lat.; 88.05° W. Long. Elevation is 810 feet.
Population: 1,530 (2000); Race: 95.0% White, 0.0% Black, 0.0% Asian, 0.0% American Indian and Alaska Native, 6.9% Hispanic of any race, 3.0% two or more races (2000); Density: 2,421.6 persons per square mile (2000); Age: 28.6% under 18, 7.2% over 64 (2000); Marriage status: 24.8% never married, 63.2% now married, 3.7% widowed, 8.4% divorced (2000); Foreign born: 10.1% (2000); Ancestry (includes multiple ancestries): 28.8% Irish, 24.6% German, 18.4% Polish, 11.0% English, 8.7% Other groups (2000).
Economy: Employment by occupation: 13.8% management, 20.7% professional, 8.4% services, 30.3% sales, 1.4% farming, 13.2% construction, 12.2% production (2000).
Income: Per capita income: $28,737 (2000); Median household income: $78,428 (2000); Poverty rate: 3.0% (2000).
Education: High school graduation rate: 94.3% (2000); College graduation rate: 40.6% (2000).
Housing: Homeownership rate: 91.9% (2000); Median home value: $189,200 (2000); Median rent: $984 per month (2000); Median age of housing: 30 years (2000).
Transportation: Commute to work: 84.7% car, 1.7% public transportation, 0.0% walk, 7.8% work from home (2000); Travel time to work: 15.0% less than 15 minutes, 32.3% 15 to 30 minutes, 30.0% 30 to 45 minutes, 15.1% 45 to 60 minutes, 7.6% 60 minutes or more (2000)

FORT SHERIDAN (unincorporated postal area, zip code 60037). Covers a land area of 0.450 square miles and a water area of 0 square miles. Located at 42.25° N. Lat.; 87.81° W. Long.
Population: 901 (2000); Race: 82.5% White, 14.7% Black, 0.0% Asian, 0.0% American Indian and Alaska Native, 3.8% Hispanic of any race, 1.3% two or more races (2000); Density: 2,002.2 persons per square mile (2000); Age: 47.0% under 18, 0.0% over 64 (2000); Marriage status: 7.1% never married, 89.8% now married, 0.0% widowed, 3.1% divorced (2000); Foreign born: 1.7% (2000); Ancestry (includes multiple ancestries): 26.1% German, 24.3% Other groups, 10.0% United States or American, 9.8% Irish, 9.5% English (2000).
Economy: Employment by occupation: 9.2% management, 34.1% professional, 9.6% services, 36.0% sales, 0.0% farming, 5.4% construction, 5.7% production (2000).
Income: Per capita income: $16,727 (2000); Median household income: $46,750 (2000); Poverty rate: 0.0% (2000).
Education: High school graduation rate: 98.7% (2000); College graduation rate: 36.8% (2000).
Housing: Homeownership rate: 4.6% (2000); Median home value: $700,000 (2000); Median rent: $779 per month (2000); Median age of housing: 39 years (2000).
Transportation: Commute to work: 92.8% car, 0.0% public transportation, 1.9% walk, 3.9% work from home (2000); Travel time to work: 21.8% less than 15 minutes, 55.1% 15 to 30 minutes, 17.8% 30 to 45 minutes, 1.5% 45 to 60 minutes, 3.8% 60 minutes or more (2000)

FOX LAKE (village). Covers a land area of 7.348 square miles and a water area of 1.632 square miles. Located at 42.40° N. Lat.; 88.17° W. Long. Elevation is 740 feet.
History: Fox Lake developed as a resort community for vacationers who enjoyed the numerous lakes in the area.
Population: 9,178 (2000); Race: 95.1% White, 0.4% Black, 1.2% Asian, 0.0% American Indian and Alaska Native, 6.0% Hispanic of any race, 1.0% two or more races (2000); Density: 1,249.1 persons per square mile (2000); Age: 22.1% under 18, 14.0% over 64 (2000); Marriage status: 24.9% never married, 53.9% now married, 7.2% widowed, 13.9% divorced (2000); Foreign born: 6.7% (2000); Ancestry (includes multiple ancestries): 29.7% German, 17.5% Irish, 12.5% Polish, 10.3% Other groups, 10.0% Italian (2000).
Economy: Single-family building permits issued: 110 (2001) / 56 (2000); Multi-family building permits issued: 21 (2001) / 0 (2000); Employment by occupation: 11.9% management, 14.2% professional, 11.5% services, 34.4% sales, 0.5% farming, 12.8% construction, 14.7% production (2000).
Income: Per capita income: $24,350 (2000); Median household income: $46,548 (2000); Poverty rate: 6.4% (2000).
Taxes: Total city taxes per capita: $383 (1997); City property taxes per capita: $324 (1997).
Education: High school graduation rate: 84.5% (2000); College graduation rate: 15.4% (2000).

School District(s)

Fox Lake Grade School District 114 (PK-08)
2000 Enrollment: 901 847-973-4000
Grant Community H S District 124 (09-12)
2000 Enrollment: 1,129 847-587-2561

Housing: Homeownership rate: 68.0% (2000); Median home value: $137,600 (2000); Median rent: $631 per month (2000); Median age of housing: 28 years (2000).
Transportation: Commute to work: 92.1% car, 3.8% public transportation, 2.4% walk, 1.6% work from home (2000); Travel time to work: 19.0% less than 15 minutes, 24.7% 15 to 30 minutes, 16.0% 30 to 45 minutes, 16.7% 45 to 60 minutes, 23.5% 60 minutes or more (2000)

Additional Information Contacts

Fox Lake Area Chamber of Commerce 847-587-7474

FOX LAKE HILLS (CDP). Covers a land area of 1.328 square miles and a water area of 0.456 square miles. Located at 42.40° N. Lat.; 88.12° W. Long. Elevation is 750 feet.
Population: 2,561 (2000); Race: 94.8% White, 3.3% Black, 0.0% Asian, 0.2% American Indian and Alaska Native, 3.5% Hispanic of any race, 1.1% two or more races (2000); Density: 1,928.7 persons per square mile (2000); Age: 24.8% under 18, 10.8% over 64 (2000); Marriage status: 16.3% never married, 69.4% now married, 5.5% widowed, 8.8% divorced (2000); Foreign born: 2.9% (2000); Ancestry (includes multiple ancestries): 27.2% German, 18.4% Irish, 13.8% Polish, 9.4% Other groups, 9.2% English (2000).
Economy: Recreation. Employment by occupation: 14.2% management, 22.4% professional, 8.8% services, 27.8% sales, 0.0% farming, 11.2% construction, 15.6% production (2000).
Income: Per capita income: $27,343 (2000); Median household income: $69,545 (2000); Poverty rate: 3.0% (2000).
Education: High school graduation rate: 88.3% (2000); College graduation rate: 24.2% (2000).
Housing: Homeownership rate: 92.6% (2000); Median home value: $137,500 (2000); Median rent: $733 per month (2000); Median age of housing: 29 years (2000).
Transportation: Commute to work: 93.9% car, 2.5% public transportation, 0.0% walk, 3.5% work from home (2000); Travel time to work: 12.7% less than 15 minutes, 23.1% 15 to 30 minutes, 24.7% 30 to 45 minutes, 17.9% 45 to 60 minutes, 21.7% 60 minutes or more (2000)

GAGES LAKE (CDP). Covers a land area of 3.087 square miles and a water area of 0.219 square miles. Located at 42.35° N. Lat.; 87.98° W. Long.
Population: 10,415 (2000); Race: 91.3% White, 2.4% Black, 3.9% Asian, 0.4% American Indian and Alaska Native, 4.4% Hispanic of any race, 1.4% two or more races (2000); Density: 3,374.0 persons per square mile (2000); Age: 30.1% under 18, 7.2% over 64 (2000); Marriage status: 21.7% never married, 65.0% now married, 3.8% widowed, 9.5% divorced (2000); Foreign born: 8.3% (2000); Ancestry (includes multiple ancestries): 35.1% German, 17.4% Irish, 12.1% Other groups, 11.4% Polish, 10.0% English (2000).
Economy: Manufacturing. Employment by occupation: 20.1% management, 21.9% professional, 11.4% services, 31.3% sales, 0.0% farming, 6.8% construction, 8.4% production (2000).
Income: Per capita income: $28,391 (2000); Median household income: $71,750 (2000); Poverty rate: 3.0% (2000).
Education: High school graduation rate: 92.7% (2000); College graduation rate: 37.5% (2000).

School District(s)

Spec Education District Lake County/Sedol (PK-12)
2000 Enrollment: 485 847-548-8470
Woodland C C School District 50 (PK-08)
2000 Enrollment: 6,552 847-856-3601

Housing: Homeownership rate: 86.7% (2000); Median home value: $161,800 (2000); Median rent: $778 per month (2000); Median age of housing: 20 years (2000).
Transportation: Commute to work: 93.8% car, 2.2% public transportation, 0.5% walk, 3.4% work from home (2000); Travel time to work: 21.7% less than 15 minutes, 33.3% 15 to 30 minutes, 22.4% 30 to 45 minutes, 11.8% 45 to 60 minutes, 10.8% 60 minutes or more (2000)

GRANDWOOD PARK (CDP). Covers a land area of 1.616 square miles and a water area of 0.015 square miles. Located at 42.39° N. Lat.; 87.98° W. Long.
Population: 4,521 (2000); Race: 86.2% White, 4.6% Black, 4.3% Asian, 0.4% American Indian and Alaska Native, 5.4% Hispanic of any race, 2.5% two or more races (2000); Density: 2,798.3 persons per square mile (2000); Age: 32.3% under 18, 5.3% over 64 (2000); Marriage status: 19.7% never married, 65.7% now married, 4.2% widowed, 10.4% divorced (2000); Foreign born: 9.2% (2000); Ancestry (includes multiple ancestries): 26.7% German, 17.8% Other groups, 17.4% Irish, 11.6% Polish, 8.5% Italian (2000).
Economy: Employment by occupation: 25.2% management, 17.9% professional, 11.0% services, 26.0% sales, 0.0% farming, 8.5% construction, 11.4% production (2000).
Income: Per capita income: $30,912 (2000); Median household income: $71,674 (2000); Poverty rate: 3.2% (2000).
Education: High school graduation rate: 91.8% (2000); College graduation rate: 43.1% (2000).
Housing: Homeownership rate: 86.1% (2000); Median home value: $165,500 (2000); Median rent: $938 per month (2000); Median age of housing: 10 years (2000).
Transportation: Commute to work: 92.9% car, 2.1% public transportation, 0.7% walk, 3.2% work from home (2000); Travel time to work: 17.3% less than 15 minutes, 30.4% 15 to 30 minutes, 27.9% 30 to 45 minutes, 12.0% 45 to 60 minutes, 12.4% 60 minutes or more (2000)

GRAYSLAKE (village). Aka Grays Lake. Covers a land area of 9.398 square miles and a water area of 0.157 square miles. Located at 42.34° N. Lat.; 88.03° W. Long. Elevation is 780 feet.
History: College of Lake County here. Incorporated 1895.
Population: 18,506 (2000); Race: 90.4% White, 1.1% Black, 4.9% Asian, 0.2% American Indian and Alaska Native, 4.5% Hispanic of any race, 1.9% two or more races (2000); Density: 1,969.2 persons per square mile (2000); Age: 33.0% under 18, 4.5% over 64 (2000); Marriage status: 18.9% never married, 70.4% now married, 2.7% widowed, 7.9% divorced (2000); Foreign born: 8.4% (2000); Ancestry (includes multiple ancestries): 31.4% German, 16.9% Irish, 13.9% Other groups, 10.8% Polish, 10.2% Italian (2000).
Economy: In dairying, agricultural and lake-resort area. Manufacturing: cement and wood products. Single-family building permits issued: 327 (2001) / 237 (2000); Multi-family building permits issued: 0 (2001) / 148 (2000); Employment by occupation: 24.8% management, 27.2% professional, 7.7% services, 26.9% sales, 0.1% farming, 7.0% construction, 6.4% production (2000).
Income: Per capita income: $28,898 (2000); Median household income: $73,143 (2000); Poverty rate: 3.0% (2000).
Taxes: Total city taxes per capita: $72 (1997); City property taxes per capita: $54 (1997).
Education: High school graduation rate: 94.6% (2000); College graduation rate: 50.8% (2000).

School District(s)

Comm Consolidated School Districtrict 46 (PK-08)
2000 Enrollment: 3,379 847-223-3650
Grayslake Community High School District 127 (09-12)
2000 Enrollment: 1,661 847-223-8621
Lake Roe (06-12)
2000 Enrollment: 22 847-543-7833
Prairie Crossing Charter School (KG-03)
2000 Enrollment: 120 847-543-9722

Two-year College(s)

College of Lake County (Public)
2001 Enrollment: 12,917 847-223-6601
2001 Tuition: In-state $5,310; Out-of-state $7,440

Housing: Homeownership rate: 78.4% (2000); Median home value: $192,900 (2000); Median rent: $754 per month (2000); Median age of housing: 9 years (2000).

Newspapers: Wauconda Leader (1 x week); Wadsworth News (1 x week); Round Lake News (1 x week); Mundelein News (1 x week); Market/Journal VIII (1 x week); Market/Journal VII (1 x week); Market/Journal VI (1 x week); Market/Journal V (1 x week); Market/Journal III (1 x week); Market/Journal II (1 x week); Market Journal (1 x week); Lindenhurst News (1 x week); Libertyville News (1 x week); Lake Villa Record (1 x week); Gurnee Press (1 x week); Great Lakes Bulletin (1 x week); Grayslake Times (1 x week); Fox Lake Press (1 x week); Antioch News Reporter (1 x week)

Transportation: Commute to work: 88.9% car, 6.2% public transportation, 0.8% walk, 3.8% work from home (2000); Travel time to work: 16.7% less than 15 minutes, 24.0% 15 to 30 minutes, 25.2% 30 to 45 minutes, 17.4% 45 to 60 minutes, 16.7% 60 minutes or more (2000)

Additional Information Contacts

Grayslake Chamber of Commerce 847-223-6888

GREAT LAKES (unincorporated postal area, zip code 60088). Covers a land area of 2.362 square miles and a water area of 0 square miles. Located at 42.30° N. Lat.; 87.85° W. Long.

Population: 13,319 (2000); Race: 63.7% White, 20.7% Black, 5.0% Asian, 0.9% American Indian and Alaska Native, 10.6% Hispanic of any race, 6.2% two or more races (2000); Density: 5,638.9 persons per square mile (2000); Age: 23.9% under 18, 0.1% over 64 (2000); Marriage status: 53.9% never married, 42.8% now married, 0.1% widowed, 3.3% divorced (2000); Foreign born: 6.8% (2000); Ancestry (includes multiple ancestries): 40.1% Other groups, 15.5% German, 12.2% Irish, 6.2% English, 6.1% United States or American (2000).

Economy: Employment by occupation: 14.3% management, 24.0% professional, 22.2% services, 29.0% sales, 0.0% farming, 1.9% construction, 8.6% production (2000).

Income: Per capita income: $12,340 (2000); Median household income: $39,299 (2000); Poverty rate: 6.5% (2000).

Education: High school graduation rate: 95.0% (2000); College graduation rate: 17.6% (2000).

Housing: Homeownership rate: 4.6% (2000); Median home value: $112,500 (2000); Median rent: $818 per month (2000); Median age of housing: 32 years (2000).

Hospitals: Naval Hospital-Great Lakes (186 beds)

Transportation: Commute to work: 39.6% car, 0.5% public transportation, 55.9% walk, 1.7% work from home (2000); Travel time to work: 76.1% less than 15 minutes, 16.0% 15 to 30 minutes, 3.2% 30 to 45 minutes, 2.4% 45 to 60 minutes, 2.2% 60 minutes or more (2000)

GREEN OAKS (village). Aka Oak Grove. Covers a land area of 4.004 square miles and a water area of 0.056 square miles. Located at 42.28° N. Lat.; 87.91° W. Long. Elevation is 690 feet.

Population: 3,572 (2000); Race: 91.4% White, 2.6% Black, 5.1% Asian, 0.4% American Indian and Alaska Native, 1.7% Hispanic of any race, 0.4% two or more races (2000); Density: 892.0 persons per square mile (2000); Age: 34.2% under 18, 7.5% over 64 (2000); Marriage status: 14.9% never married, 80.2% now married, 2.3% widowed, 2.6% divorced (2000); Foreign born: 9.6% (2000); Ancestry (includes multiple ancestries): 30.9% German, 16.3% Irish, 10.8% Other groups, 10.5% Italian, 9.3% Polish (2000).

Economy: Single-family building permits issued: 9 (2001) / 42 (2000); Multi-family building permits issued: 0 (2001) / 0 (2000); Employment by occupation: 36.7% management, 26.5% professional, 5.3% services, 23.4% sales, 0.0% farming, 3.3% construction, 4.8% production (2000).

Income: Per capita income: $51,066 (2000); Median household income: $127,905 (2000); Poverty rate: 1.7% (2000).

Taxes: Total city taxes per capita: $218 (1997); City property taxes per capita: $40 (1997).

Education: High school graduation rate: 95.0% (2000); College graduation rate: 59.2% (2000).

School District(s)

Oak Grove School District 68 (KG-08)
2000 Enrollment: 979 847-367-4120

Housing: Homeownership rate: 97.4% (2000); Median home value: $406,000 (2000); Median rent: $1,222 per month (2000); Median age of housing: 15 years (2000).

Transportation: Commute to work: 87.6% car, 6.1% public transportation, 0.7% walk, 5.6% work from home (2000); Travel time to work: 27.3% less than 15 minutes, 28.1% 15 to 30 minutes, 25.1% 30 to 45 minutes, 8.8% 45 to 60 minutes, 10.8% 60 minutes or more (2000)

GURNEE (village). Covers a land area of 13.401 square miles and a water area of 0.014 square miles. Located at 42.37° N. Lat.; 87.93° W. Long. Elevation is 680 feet.

Population: 28,834 (2000); Race: 82.5% White, 4.3% Black, 8.3% Asian, 0.1% American Indian and Alaska Native, 6.2% Hispanic of any race, 2.2% two or more races (2000); Density: 2,151.6 persons per square mile (2000); Age: 30.7% under 18, 7.0% over 64 (2000); Marriage status: 20.9% never married, 67.0% now married, 3.8% widowed, 8.3% divorced (2000); Foreign born: 11.7% (2000); Ancestry (includes multiple ancestries): 27.3% German, 20.9% Other groups, 14.5% Irish, 9.2% Polish, 8.6% Italian (2000).

Vital Statistics: Birth rate: 208.1 per 10,000 population (1998)

Economy: Remnant agriculture. Manufacturing of medical equipment, pharmaceuticals, digital controls, inks, lighting fixtures, lubricants, emulsifiers, pumps and compressors, packaging and video games. Site of Gurnee Mills, one of the largest shopping centersin U.S., major amusement park (Six Flags Great America) and outlet mall. Unemployment rate: 4.9% (11/2002); Total civilian labor force: 15,833 (11/2002); Single-family building permits issued: 135 (2001) / 150 (2000); Multi-family building permits issued: 60 (2001) / 9 (2000); Employment by occupation: 24.0% management, 26.4% professional, 7.6% services, 28.6% sales, 0.1% farming, 5.6% construction, 7.6% production (2000).

Income: Per capita income: $31,517 (2000); Median household income: $75,742 (2000); Poverty rate: 3.0% (2000).

Taxes: Total city taxes per capita: $169 (1997); City property taxes per capita: $47 (1997).

Education: High school graduation rate: 94.1% (2000); College graduation rate: 47.8% (2000).

School District(s)

Gurnee School District 56 (PK-08)
2000 Enrollment: 1,942 847-336-0800
Warren Township High School District 121 (09-12)
2000 Enrollment: 2,998 847-662-1400

Housing: Homeownership rate: 78.1% (2000); Median home value: $199,000 (2000); Median rent: $733 per month (2000); Median age of housing: 10 years (2000).

Transportation: Commute to work: 93.4% car, 2.7% public transportation, 0.6% walk, 3.0% work from home (2000); Travel time to work: 20.1% less than 15 minutes, 34.0% 15 to 30 minutes, 21.5% 30 to 45 minutes, 11.9% 45 to 60 minutes, 12.4% 60 minutes or more (2000)

Additional Information Contacts

Gurnee Chamber of Commerce 847-249-3800

HAINESVILLE (village). Covers a land area of 1.743 square miles and a water area of 0.034 square miles. Located at 42.34° N. Lat.; 88.06° W. Long. Elevation is 802 feet.

Population: 2,129 (2000); Race: 79.0% White, 1.5% Black, 7.9% Asian, 0.4% American Indian and Alaska Native, 10.8% Hispanic of any race, 2.8% two or more races (2000); Density: 1,221.2 persons per square mile (2000); Age: 37.1% under 18, 2.8% over 64 (2000); Marriage status: 12.2% never married, 81.0% now married, 1.5% widowed, 5.4% divorced (2000); Foreign born: 13.9% (2000); Ancestry (includes multiple ancestries): 27.0% German, 21.8% Polish, 21.5% Other groups, 14.5% Irish, 8.9% Italian (2000).

Economy: Single-family building permits issued: 38 (2001) / 73 (2000); Multi-family building permits issued: 67 (2001) / 31 (2000); Employment by occupation: 22.5% management, 24.0% professional, 11.5% services, 22.2% sales, 0.0% farming, 8.0% construction, 11.9% production (2000).

Income: Per capita income: $22,250 (2000); Median household income: $69,938 (2000); Poverty rate: 3.9% (2000).

Taxes: Total city taxes per capita: $1,496 (1997); City property taxes per capita: $90 (1997).

Education: High school graduation rate: 89.3% (2000); College graduation rate: 36.6% (2000).

Housing: Homeownership rate: 92.2% (2000); Median home value: $180,600 (2000); Median rent: $665 per month (2000); Median age of housing: 3 years (2000).

Transportation: Commute to work: 90.5% car, 5.8% public transportation, 0.0% walk, 3.7% work from home (2000); Travel time to work: 11.3% less than 15 minutes, 20.4% 15 to 30 minutes, 26.7% 30 to 45 minutes, 20.3% 45 to 60 minutes, 21.4% 60 minutes or more (2000)

HAWTHORN WOODS (village). Covers a land area of 5.359 square miles and a water area of 0.056 square miles. Located at 42.22° N. Lat.; 88.05° W. Long. Elevation is 790 feet.
Population: 6,002 (2000); Race: 94.8% White, 0.9% Black, 2.0% Asian, 0.0% American Indian and Alaska Native, 1.9% Hispanic of any race, 1.4% two or more races (2000); Density: 1,119.9 persons per square mile (2000); Age: 35.7% under 18, 4.0% over 64 (2000); Marriage status: 16.0% never married, 79.8% now married, 1.3% widowed, 2.8% divorced (2000); Foreign born: 7.1% (2000); Ancestry (includes multiple ancestries): 31.3% German, 16.1% Irish, 13.2% Italian, 10.6% Polish, 7.5% Other groups (2000).
Economy: Single-family building permits issued: 48 (2001) / 48 (2000); Multi-family building permits issued: 0 (2001) / 0 (2000); Employment by occupation: 34.3% management, 25.6% professional, 5.4% services, 28.1% sales, 0.0% farming, 2.7% construction, 3.9% production (2000).
Income: Per capita income: $49,346 (2000); Median household income: $132,720 (2000); Poverty rate: 1.9% (2000).
Taxes: Total city taxes per capita: $166 (1997); City property taxes per capita: $136 (1997).
Education: High school graduation rate: 97.2% (2000); College graduation rate: 60.2% (2000).
Housing: Homeownership rate: 97.8% (2000); Median home value: $395,300 (2000); Median rent: $2,000+ per month (2000); Median age of housing: 14 years (2000).
Transportation: Commute to work: 87.4% car, 5.9% public transportation, 0.0% walk, 6.0% work from home (2000); Travel time to work: 14.7% less than 15 minutes, 28.7% 15 to 30 minutes, 28.7% 30 to 45 minutes, 14.2% 45 to 60 minutes, 13.6% 60 minutes or more (2000)

HIGHLAND PARK (city). Covers a land area of 12.360 square miles and a water area of 0.006 square miles. Located at 42.18° N. Lat.; 87.80° W. Long. Elevation is 675 feet.
History: The Green Bay House tavern was opened in 1834 on the Chicago-Milwaukee post road, where the city of Highland Park later developed. The name was given by the railroad company to their station here, and the town was incorporated under that name in 1867.
Population: 31,365 (2000); Race: 91.4% White, 1.2% Black, 2.6% Asian, 0.2% American Indian and Alaska Native, 9.4% Hispanic of any race, 1.2% two or more races (2000); Density: 2,537.5 persons per square mile (2000); Age: 27.2% under 18, 15.0% over 64 (2000); Marriage status: 17.1% never married, 71.9% now married, 5.6% widowed, 5.3% divorced (2000); Foreign born: 15.3% (2000); Ancestry (includes multiple ancestries): 17.5% Other groups, 16.4% Russian, 12.6% German, 8.8% United States or American, 8.7% Polish (2000).
Vital Statistics: Birth rate: 123.7 per 10,000 population (1998)
Economy: Unemployment rate: 3.4% (11/2002); Total civilian labor force: 16,846 (11/2002); Single-family building permits issued: 56 (2001) / 54 (2000); Multi-family building permits issued: 20 (2001) / 10 (2000); Employment by occupation: 25.0% management, 30.6% professional, 10.4% services, 27.3% sales, 0.0% farming, 3.2% construction, 3.5% production (2000).
Income: Per capita income: $55,331 (2000); Median household income: $100,967 (2000); Poverty rate: 3.8% (2000).
Taxes: Total city taxes per capita: $705 (2000); City property taxes per capita: $367 (2000).
Education: High school graduation rate: 91.7% (2000); College graduation rate: 61.6% (2000).

School District(s)

North Shore SD 112 (PK-08)
2000 Enrollment: 4,420 847-681-6700
Northern Suburban Special Education District (01-12)
2000 Enrollment: 117 847-831-5100
Township High School District 113 (09-12)
2000 Enrollment: 3,119 847-926-9327

Housing: Homeownership rate: 81.9% (2000); Median home value: $380,000 (2000); Median rent: $852 per month (2000); Median age of housing: 41 years (2000).
Transportation: Commute to work: 78.2% car, 12.3% public transportation, 2.2% walk, 6.3% work from home (2000); Travel time to work: 26.1% less than 15 minutes, 27.6% 15 to 30 minutes, 20.3% 30 to 45 minutes, 10.8% 45 to 60 minutes, 15.1% 60 minutes or more (2000)
Additional Information Contacts
Highland Park Chamber of Commerce 847-432-0284

HIGHWOOD (city). Covers a land area of 0.632 square miles and a water area of 0 square miles. Located at 42.20° N. Lat.; 87.81° W. Long. Elevation is 675 feet.
History: Fort Sheridan decommissioned in 1990s. Incorporated 1886.
Population: 4,143 (2000); Race: 73.8% White, 3.0% Black, 3.2% Asian, 0.0% American Indian and Alaska Native, 37.0% Hispanic of any race, 6.0% two or more races (2000); Density: 6,552.1 persons per square mile (2000); Age: 22.4% under 18, 15.1% over 64 (2000); Marriage status: 32.8% never married, 50.6% now married, 7.2% widowed, 9.3% divorced (2000); Foreign born: 38.6% (2000); Ancestry (includes multiple ancestries): 37.9% Other groups, 22.6% Italian, 10.0% Irish, 9.3% German, 3.5% English (2000).
Economy: Site of Sheridan U.S. Army Reserve Center. Single-family building permits issued: 3 (2001) / 0 (2000); Multi-family building permits issued: 0 (2001) / 2 (2000); Employment by occupation: 12.4% management, 16.3% professional, 26.6% services, 26.2% sales, 0.0% farming, 9.6% construction, 8.9% production (2000).
Income: Per capita income: $24,138 (2000); Median household income: $42,993 (2000); Poverty rate: 7.0% (2000).
Taxes: Total city taxes per capita: $214 (1997); City property taxes per capita: $51 (1997).
Education: High school graduation rate: 70.8% (2000); College graduation rate: 27.1% (2000).
Housing: Homeownership rate: 43.4% (2000); Median home value: $229,200 (2000); Median rent: $723 per month (2000); Median age of housing: 48 years (2000).
Transportation: Commute to work: 83.4% car, 7.8% public transportation, 5.3% walk, 3.3% work from home (2000); Travel time to work: 36.0% less than 15 minutes, 38.8% 15 to 30 minutes, 11.2% 30 to 45 minutes, 4.4% 45 to 60 minutes, 9.5% 60 minutes or more (2000)
Additional Information Contacts
Highwood Chamber of Commerce. 847-433-2100

INDIAN CREEK (village). Covers a land area of 0.267 square miles and a water area of 0 square miles. Located at 42.22° N. Lat.; 87.97° W. Long. Elevation is 741 feet.
Population: 194 (2000); Race: 93.4% White, 0.0% Black, 1.4% Asian, 0.0% American Indian and Alaska Native, 1.9% Hispanic of any race, 1.4% two or more races (2000); Density: 726.5 persons per square mile (2000); Age: 32.2% under 18, 7.1% over 64 (2000); Marriage status: 15.5% never married, 76.8% now married, 6.5% widowed, 1.3% divorced (2000); Foreign born: 2.4% (2000); Ancestry (includes multiple ancestries): 42.2% German, 12.8% Polish, 10.9% Norwegian, 9.5% Irish, 8.5% English (2000).
Economy: Single-family building permits issued: 4 (2001) / 0 (2000); Multi-family building permits issued: 0 (2001) / 0 (2000); Employment by occupation: 34.5% management, 28.3% professional, 4.4% services, 27.4% sales, 0.0% farming, 4.4% construction, 0.9% production (2000).
Income: Per capita income: $33,515 (2000); Median household income: $88,206 (2000); Poverty rate: 0.9% (2000).
Taxes: Total city taxes per capita: $4 (1997); City property taxes per capita: $4 (1997).
Education: High school graduation rate: 94.4% (2000); College graduation rate: 51.4% (2000).
Housing: Homeownership rate: 94.0% (2000); Median home value: $236,500 (2000); Median age of housing: 34 years (2000).
Transportation: Commute to work: 87.6% car, 0.0% public transportation, 2.7% walk, 9.7% work from home (2000); Travel time to work: 33.3% less than 15 minutes, 30.4% 15 to 30 minutes, 19.6% 30 to 45 minutes, 10.8% 45 to 60 minutes, 5.9% 60 minutes or more (2000)

INGLESIDE (unincorporated postal area, zip code 60041). Part of the Village of Fox Lake. Covers a land area of 11.437 square miles and a water area of 0.538 square miles. Located at 42.37° N. Lat.; 88.15° W. Long. Elevation is 770 feet.
Population: 9,286 (2000); Race: 96.8% White, 0.9% Black, 0.3% Asian, 0.2% American Indian and Alaska Native, 1.7% Hispanic of any race, 1.1% two or more races (2000); Density: 811.9 persons per square mile (2000); Age: 26.5% under 18, 8.0% over 64 (2000); Marriage status: 23.8% never married, 62.3% now married, 4.8% widowed, 9.1% divorced (2000); Foreign born: 4.0% (2000); Ancestry (includes multiple ancestries): 36.1% German, 15.9% Polish, 15.1% Irish, 8.2% Italian, 7.6% Other groups (2000).
Economy: Employment by occupation: 10.9% management, 15.9% professional, 13.4% services, 30.8% sales, 0.0% farming, 14.7% construction, 14.2% production (2000).
Income: Per capita income: $24,726 (2000); Median household income: $59,874 (2000); Poverty rate: 3.8% (2000).

Education: High school graduation rate: 88.8% (2000); College graduation rate: 18.6% (2000).

School District(s)

Big Hollow School District 38 (KG-08)
2000 Enrollment: 625 847-587-2632

Gavin School District 37 (PK-08)
2000 Enrollment: 1,096 847-973-2370

Housing: Homeownership rate: 82.0% (2000); Median home value: $153,800 (2000); Median rent: $692 per month (2000); Median age of housing: 39 years (2000).

Transportation: Commute to work: 92.9% car, 2.0% public transportation, 0.9% walk, 4.1% work from home (2000); Travel time to work: 21.2% less than 15 minutes, 24.5% 15 to 30 minutes, 21.9% 30 to 45 minutes, 17.8% 45 to 60 minutes, 14.6% 60 minutes or more (2000)

KILDEER (village). Covers a land area of 3.472 square miles and a water area of 0.046 square miles. Located at 42.18° N. Lat.; 88.05° W. Long. Elevation is 790 feet.

Population: 3,460 (2000); Race: 95.0% White, 0.3% Black, 3.6% Asian, 0.0% American Indian and Alaska Native, 3.1% Hispanic of any race, 0.5% two or more races (2000); Density: 996.6 persons per square mile (2000); Age: 33.9% under 18, 5.9% over 64 (2000); Marriage status: 15.5% never married, 79.4% now married, 1.7% widowed, 3.4% divorced (2000); Foreign born: 8.3% (2000); Ancestry (includes multiple ancestries): 27.4% German, 19.3% Irish, 15.1% Polish, 14.2% Italian, 12.7% English (2000).

Economy: Single-family building permits issued: 38 (2001) / 42 (2000); Multi-family building permits issued: 0 (2001) / 0 (2000); Employment by occupation: 36.1% management, 21.0% professional, 6.4% services, 31.6% sales, 0.2% farming, 2.1% construction, 2.4% production (2000).

Income: Per capita income: $51,973 (2000); Median household income: $137,498 (2000); Poverty rate: 0.5% (2000).

Taxes: Total city taxes per capita: $198 (1997); City property taxes per capita: $129 (1997).

Education: High school graduation rate: 97.4% (2000); College graduation rate: 64.9% (2000).

Housing: Homeownership rate: 99.2% (2000); Median home value: $459,600 (2000); Median rent: $575 per month (2000); Median age of housing: 18 years (2000).

Transportation: Commute to work: 81.3% car, 6.5% public transportation, 0.2% walk, 11.4% work from home (2000); Travel time to work: 14.2% less than 15 minutes, 29.8% 15 to 30 minutes, 28.0% 30 to 45 minutes, 12.3% 45 to 60 minutes, 15.7% 60 minutes or more (2000)

LAKE BARRINGTON (village). Covers a land area of 5.336 square miles and a water area of 0.232 square miles. Located at 42.21° N. Lat.; 88.16° W. Long. Elevation is 800 feet.

Population: 4,757 (2000); Race: 97.8% White, 1.0% Black, 0.4% Asian, 0.0% American Indian and Alaska Native, 0.6% Hispanic of any race, 0.4% two or more races (2000); Density: 891.6 persons per square mile (2000); Age: 19.5% under 18, 17.0% over 64 (2000); Marriage status: 17.4% never married, 68.7% now married, 5.9% widowed, 8.0% divorced (2000); Foreign born: 5.1% (2000); Ancestry (includes multiple ancestries): 29.7% German, 18.7% Irish, 14.0% English, 11.6% Italian, 11.4% Polish (2000).

Economy: Manufacturing: printing equipment. Single-family building permits issued: 60 (2001) / 25 (2000); Multi-family building permits issued: 0 (2001) / 0 (2000); Employment by occupation: 41.0% management, 18.8% professional, 5.8% services, 28.3% sales, 0.0% farming, 2.5% construction, 3.7% production (2000).

Income: Per capita income: $63,158 (2000); Median household income: $106,951 (2000); Poverty rate: 2.0% (2000).

Taxes: Total city taxes per capita: $89 (1997); City property taxes per capita: $42 (1997).

Education: High school graduation rate: 97.7% (2000); College graduation rate: 56.4% (2000).

Housing: Homeownership rate: 96.1% (2000); Median home value: $343,900 (2000); Median rent: $1,406 per month (2000); Median age of housing: 18 years (2000).

Transportation: Commute to work: 82.8% car, 7.6% public transportation, 0.3% walk, 8.1% work from home (2000); Travel time to work: 15.4% less than 15 minutes, 19.1% 15 to 30 minutes, 20.7% 30 to 45 minutes, 20.6% 45 to 60 minutes, 24.1% 60 minutes or more (2000)

LAKE BLUFF (village). Covers a land area of 4.059 square miles and a water area of 0.003 square miles. Located at 42.28° N. Lat.; 87.84° W. Long. Elevation is 670 feet.

History: Lake Bluff began in 1874 as a Methodist camp-meeting ground.

Population: 6,056 (2000); Race: 95.2% White, 1.2% Black, 2.9% Asian, 0.1% American Indian and Alaska Native, 1.9% Hispanic of any race, 0.2% two or more races (2000); Density: 1,492.0 persons per square mile (2000); Age: 33.0% under 18, 12.9% over 64 (2000); Marriage status: 14.9% never married, 74.3% now married, 4.6% widowed, 6.1% divorced (2000); Foreign born: 7.4% (2000); Ancestry (includes multiple ancestries): 28.4% German, 22.7% Irish, 18.2% English, 7.0% Other groups, 6.7% Italian (2000).

Economy: Single-family building permits issued: 12 (2001) / 12 (2000); Multi-family building permits issued: 0 (2001) / 0 (2000); Employment by occupation: 31.2% management, 29.5% professional, 5.8% services, 28.9% sales, 0.0% farming, 1.8% construction, 2.6% production (2000).

Income: Per capita income: $54,824 (2000); Median household income: $114,521 (2000); Poverty rate: 1.1% (2000).

Taxes: Total city taxes per capita: $629 (1997); City property taxes per capita: $406 (1997).

Education: High school graduation rate: 98.8% (2000); College graduation rate: 72.9% (2000).

School District(s)

Lake Bluff Elementary School District 65 (KG-08)
2000 Enrollment: 1,119 847-234-9400

Housing: Homeownership rate: 91.1% (2000); Median home value: $439,600 (2000); Median rent: $782 per month (2000); Median age of housing: 34 years (2000).

Transportation: Commute to work: 79.5% car, 9.6% public transportation, 1.1% walk, 9.8% work from home (2000); Travel time to work: 29.4% less than 15 minutes, 23.5% 15 to 30 minutes, 20.2% 30 to 45 minutes, 7.1% 45 to 60 minutes, 19.9% 60 minutes or more (2000)

LAKE CATHERINE (CDP). Covers a land area of 1.064 square miles and a water area of 0.484 square miles. Located at 42.48° N. Lat.; 88.12° W. Long. Elevation is 750 feet.

Population: 1,490 (2000); Race: 95.5% White, 2.9% Black, 0.3% Asian, 0.0% American Indian and Alaska Native, 0.0% Hispanic of any race, 1.3% two or more races (2000); Density: 1,400.3 persons per square mile (2000); Age: 22.1% under 18, 10.9% over 64 (2000); Marriage status: 20.4% never married, 64.3% now married, 6.3% widowed, 9.0% divorced (2000); Foreign born: 7.4% (2000); Ancestry (includes multiple ancestries): 28.1% German, 20.8% Irish, 10.9% English, 7.8% Other groups, 6.0% Italian (2000).

Economy: Employment by occupation: 15.5% management, 12.3% professional, 15.2% services, 27.6% sales, 0.0% farming, 17.3% construction, 12.1% production (2000).

Income: Per capita income: $23,401 (2000); Median household income: $56,970 (2000); Poverty rate: 8.5% (2000).

Education: High school graduation rate: 86.5% (2000); College graduation rate: 14.6% (2000).

Housing: Homeownership rate: 81.6% (2000); Median home value: $139,500 (2000); Median rent: $744 per month (2000); Median age of housing: 45 years (2000).

Transportation: Commute to work: 90.5% car, 3.5% public transportation, 0.0% walk, 5.9% work from home (2000); Travel time to work: 22.6% less than 15 minutes, 21.4% 15 to 30 minutes, 19.7% 30 to 45 minutes, 12.9% 45 to 60 minutes, 23.4% 60 minutes or more (2000)

LAKE FOREST (city). Covers a land area of 16.865 square miles and a water area of 0.048 square miles. Located at 42.23° N. Lat.; 87.85° W. Long. Elevation is 700 feet.

History: Lake Forest was laid out in 1856 by David Hotchkiss, a St. Louis landscape architect, for a company of Chicago businessmen who had purchased land here. The town grew around Lake Forest College, opened in 1857.

Population: 20,059 (2000); Race: 93.7% White, 1.2% Black, 3.5% Asian, 0.0% American Indian and Alaska Native, 1.7% Hispanic of any race, 1.0% two or more races (2000); Density: 1,189.4 persons per square mile (2000); Age: 27.8% under 18, 14.7% over 64 (2000); Marriage status: 20.6% never married, 69.4% now married, 5.1% widowed, 5.0% divorced (2000); Foreign born: 6.5% (2000); Ancestry (includes multiple ancestries): 22.3% German, 20.0% Irish, 16.4% English, 8.4% Italian, 8.0% Other groups (2000).

Vital Statistics: Birth rate: 90.2 per 10,000 population (1998)

Economy: Single-family building permits issued: 76 (2001) / 113 (2000); Multi-family building permits issued: 0 (2001) / 0 (2000); Employment by occupation: 35.8% management, 25.5% professional, 6.2% services, 28.8% sales, 0.1% farming, 2.0% construction, 1.5% production (2000).

Income: Per capita income: $77,092 (2000); Median household income: $136,462 (2000); Poverty rate: 2.1% (2000).

Taxes: Total city taxes per capita: $1,002 (1997); City property taxes per capita: $757 (1997).

Education: High school graduation rate: 97.2% (2000); College graduation rate: 73.8% (2000).

School District(s)

Lake Forest Community H S District 115 (09-12)
2000 Enrollment: 1,628 847-234-3600
Lake Forest School District 67 (PK-08)
2000 Enrollment: 2,187 847-604-7401
Rondout School District 72 (KG-08)
2000 Enrollment: 121 847-362-2021

Four-year College(s)

Barat College (Private, Not-for-profit, Roman Catholic)
2001 Enrollment: 652 847-234-3000
2001 Tuition: In-state $16,500; Out-of-state $16,500
Lake Forest College (Private, Not-for-profit, Presbyterian Church (USA))
2001 Enrollment: 1,277 847-735-6010
2001 Tuition: In-state $21,896; Out-of-state $21,896
Lake Forest Graduate School of Management (Private, Not-for-profit)
2001 Enrollment: 771 847-295-3656

Housing: Homeownership rate: 87.2% (2000); Median home value: $662,400 (2000); Median rent: $908 per month (2000); Median age of housing: 32 years (2000).
Hospitals: Lake Forest Hospital (261 beds)
Transportation: Commute to work: 72.4% car, 12.0% public transportation, 4.9% walk, 9.9% work from home (2000); Travel time to work: 25.2% less than 15 minutes, 30.8% 15 to 30 minutes, 17.2% 30 to 45 minutes, 9.7% 45 to 60 minutes, 17.1% 60 minutes or more (2000)
Additional Information Contacts
Lake Forest Chamber of Commerce 847-604-4522

LAKE VILLA (village). Covers a land area of 5.724 square miles and a water area of 0.754 square miles. Located at 42.41° N. Lat.; 88.08° W. Long. Elevation is 795 feet.
History: Lake Villa grew around a railroad station and the resort trade. It was the site of the Allendale Farm School, an experimental community founded in 1897 as a home for neglected boys.
Population: 5,864 (2000); Race: 91.2% White, 3.4% Black, 1.6% Asian, 0.2% American Indian and Alaska Native, 3.4% Hispanic of any race, 2.2% two or more races (2000); Density: 1,024.4 persons per square mile (2000); Age: 32.5% under 18, 6.1% over 64 (2000); Marriage status: 23.4% never married, 65.8% now married, 5.1% widowed, 5.7% divorced (2000); Foreign born: 4.6% (2000); Ancestry (includes multiple ancestries): 32.6% German, 17.9% Irish, 11.4% Polish, 10.8% Italian, 10.1% Other groups (2000).
Economy: Single-family building permits issued: 185 (2001) / 220 (2000); Multi-family building permits issued: 0 (2001) / 171 (2000); Employment by occupation: 24.5% management, 21.6% professional, 11.1% services, 26.7% sales, 0.0% farming, 8.7% construction, 7.4% production (2000).
Income: Per capita income: $26,238 (2000); Median household income: $65,078 (2000); Poverty rate: 3.7% (2000).
Taxes: Total city taxes per capita: $481 (1997); City property taxes per capita: $129 (1997).
Education: High school graduation rate: 93.1% (2000); College graduation rate: 36.9% (2000).

School District(s)

Lake Villa C C School District 41 (PK-08)
2000 Enrollment: 2,854 847-356-2385

Housing: Homeownership rate: 76.0% (2000); Median home value: $207,200 (2000); Median rent: $750 per month (2000); Median age of housing: 10 years (2000).
Transportation: Commute to work: 94.0% car, 2.2% public transportation, 1.6% walk, 2.2% work from home (2000); Travel time to work: 16.4% less than 15 minutes, 24.2% 15 to 30 minutes, 27.5% 30 to 45 minutes, 15.9% 45 to 60 minutes, 16.0% 60 minutes or more (2000)

LAKE ZURICH (village). Covers a land area of 6.484 square miles and a water area of 0.359 square miles. Located at 42.19° N. Lat.; 88.08° W. Long. Elevation is 880 feet.
Population: 18,104 (2000); Race: 92.5% White, 0.7% Black, 3.8% Asian, 0.0% American Indian and Alaska Native, 5.8% Hispanic of any race, 0.6% two or more races (2000); Density: 2,792.3 persons per square mile (2000); Age: 34.5% under 18, 5.4% over 64 (2000); Marriage status: 19.9% never married, 71.1% now married, 2.4% widowed, 6.6% divorced (2000); Foreign born: 8.8% (2000); Ancestry (includes multiple ancestries): 31.0% German, 16.5% Polish, 16.5% Irish, 12.8% Other groups, 10.6% Italian (2000).
Vital Statistics: Birth rate: 174.0 per 10,000 population (1998)
Economy: Urban growth area; remnant agriculture; manufacturing: fabricated metal products, appliances, textiles, food processing and equipment, aluminum die, water treatment products. Single-family building permits issued: 111 (2001) / 34 (2000); Multi-family building permits issued: 26 (2001) / 0 (2000); Employment by occupation: 23.9% management, 21.2% professional, 9.3% services, 31.8% sales, 0.1% farming, 6.3% construction, 7.3% production (2000).
Income: Per capita income: $30,287 (2000); Median household income: $84,125 (2000); Poverty rate: 2.5% (2000).
Taxes: Total city taxes per capita: $304 (1997); City property taxes per capita: $267 (1997).
Education: High school graduation rate: 93.8% (2000); College graduation rate: 43.8% (2000).

School District(s)

Lake Zurich C U School District 95 (KG-12)
2000 Enrollment: 6,156 847-438-2831

Housing: Homeownership rate: 91.2% (2000); Median home value: $225,100 (2000); Median rent: $725 per month (2000); Median age of housing: 19 years (2000).
Transportation: Commute to work: 90.7% car, 3.1% public transportation, 1.5% walk, 4.4% work from home (2000); Travel time to work: 18.9% less than 15 minutes, 25.6% 15 to 30 minutes, 30.9% 30 to 45 minutes, 13.8% 45 to 60 minutes, 10.8% 60 minutes or more (2000)
Additional Information Contacts
Lake Zurich Chamber of Commerce 847-438-5572

LIBERTYVILLE (village). Covers a land area of 8.772 square miles and a water area of 0.291 square miles. Located at 42.28° N. Lat.; 87.96° W. Long. Elevation is 700 feet.
History: Daniel Webster (1782-1852) was one of the first purchasers of land in Independence Grove, which changed its name to Libertyville in 1837 when the post office was established. Settlers and vacationists were attracted by the mineral springs in the area.
Population: 20,742 (2000); Race: 93.0% White, 0.4% Black, 4.8% Asian, 0.1% American Indian and Alaska Native, 3.5% Hispanic of any race, 0.6% two or more races (2000); Density: 2,364.5 persons per square mile (2000); Age: 28.4% under 18, 11.3% over 64 (2000); Marriage status: 21.4% never married, 65.6% now married, 5.8% widowed, 7.2% divorced (2000); Foreign born: 10.3% (2000); Ancestry (includes multiple ancestries): 27.1% German, 18.3% Irish, 12.5% English, 10.0% Other groups, 9.5% Italian (2000).
Vital Statistics: Birth rate: 121.0 per 10,000 population (1998)
Economy: Single-family building permits issued: 19 (2001) / 25 (2000); Multi-family building permits issued: 28 (2001) / 3 (2000); Employment by occupation: 25.7% management, 29.3% professional, 7.7% services, 27.5% sales, 0.0% farming, 3.5% construction, 6.3% production (2000).
Income: Per capita income: $40,426 (2000); Median household income: $88,828 (2000); Poverty rate: 3.5% (2000).
Taxes: Total city taxes per capita: $538 (1997); City property taxes per capita: $185 (1997).
Education: High school graduation rate: 94.2% (2000); College graduation rate: 56.1% (2000).

School District(s)

Community High School District 128 (09-12)
2000 Enrollment: 2,658 847-367-3159
Libertyville School District 70 (PK-08)
2000 Enrollment: 2,652 847-362-8393

Four-year College(s)

Saint Sava Serbian Orthodox School of Theology (Private, Not-for-profit, Seventh Day Adventists)
2001 Enrollment: n/a 847-367-0698

Housing: Homeownership rate: 81.0% (2000); Median home value: $263,700 (2000); Median rent: $771 per month (2000); Median age of housing: 27 years (2000).
Hospitals: Condell Medical Center (191 beds)
Transportation: Commute to work: 87.7% car, 5.7% public transportation, 1.7% walk, 4.4% work from home (2000); Travel time to work: 29.0% less than 15 minutes, 34.8% 15 to 30 minutes, 16.7% 30 to 45 minutes, 8.6% 45 to 60 minutes, 10.8% 60 minutes or more (2000)

LINCOLNSHIRE (village). Covers a land area of 4.406 square miles and a water area of 0.029 square miles. Located at 42.19° N. Lat.; 87.91° W. Long. Elevation is 670 feet.
Population: 6,108 (2000); Race: 95.5% White, 0.3% Black, 3.7% Asian, 0.0% American Indian and Alaska Native, 2.5% Hispanic of any race, 0.3% two or more races (2000); Density: 1,386.2 persons per square mile (2000); Age: 26.9% under 18, 16.2% over 64 (2000); Marriage status: 14.7% never married, 77.7% now married, 4.8% widowed, 2.9% divorced (2000); Foreign

born: 10.6% (2000); Ancestry (includes multiple ancestries): 21.4% German, 13.5% Irish, 10.3% Polish, 8.8% Other groups, 8.7% English (2000).
Economy: Manufacturing: construction and mining equipment, educational aids, toxic-gas-monitoring equipment, storage tanks. Single-family building permits issued: 6 (2001) / 13 (2000); Multi-family building permits issued: 52 (2001) / 0 (2000); Employment by occupation: 36.4% management, 22.5% professional, 3.7% services, 32.6% sales, 0.1% farming, 1.0% construction, 3.8% production (2000).
Income: Per capita income: $60,115 (2000); Median household income: $134,259 (2000); Poverty rate: 1.6% (2000).
Taxes: Total city taxes per capita: $769 (1997); City property taxes per capita: $63 (1997).
Education: High school graduation rate: 96.4% (2000); College graduation rate: 66.4% (2000).

School District(s)

Adlai E Stevenson District 125 (09-12)
2000 Enrollment: 3,925 847-634-4000
Lincolnshire-Prairieview S D 103 (KG-08)
2000 Enrollment: 1,725 847-295-4030

Four-year College(s)

Keller Graduate School of Management (Private, For-profit)
2001 Enrollment: n/a 847-940-7768

Housing: Homeownership rate: 97.1% (2000); Median home value: $442,400 (2000); Median rent: $1,058 per month (2000); Median age of housing: 23 years (2000).
Transportation: Commute to work: 85.7% car, 7.9% public transportation, 1.0% walk, 4.9% work from home (2000); Travel time to work: 20.7% less than 15 minutes, 34.1% 15 to 30 minutes, 22.5% 30 to 45 minutes, 10.8% 45 to 60 minutes, 12.0% 60 minutes or more (2000)

LINDENHURST (village). Covers a land area of 3.721 square miles and a water area of 0.361 square miles. Located at 42.41° N. Lat.; 88.02° W. Long. Elevation is 780 feet.
Population: 12,539 (2000); Race: 92.2% White, 1.6% Black, 2.8% Asian, 0.1% American Indian and Alaska Native, 4.3% Hispanic of any race, 1.2% two or more races (2000); Density: 3,369.5 persons per square mile (2000); Age: 29.9% under 18, 7.3% over 64 (2000); Marriage status: 19.4% never married, 71.7% now married, 3.1% widowed, 5.8% divorced (2000); Foreign born: 5.3% (2000); Ancestry (includes multiple ancestries): 30.4% German, 18.0% Irish, 13.7% Polish, 9.5% Other groups, 9.1% English (2000).
Economy: Recreation. Single-family building permits issued: 85 (2001) / 125 (2000); Multi-family building permits issued: 70 (2001) / 130 (2000); Employment by occupation: 20.2% management, 22.6% professional, 8.3% services, 31.0% sales, 0.0% farming, 8.4% construction, 9.5% production (2000).
Income: Per capita income: $27,534 (2000); Median household income: $74,841 (2000); Poverty rate: 1.6% (2000).
Taxes: Total city taxes per capita: $150 (1997); City property taxes per capita: $52 (1997).
Education: High school graduation rate: 93.8% (2000); College graduation rate: 37.8% (2000).
Housing: Homeownership rate: 90.8% (2000); Median home value: $167,700 (2000); Median rent: $862 per month (2000); Median age of housing: 16 years (2000).
Transportation: Commute to work: 94.0% car, 1.1% public transportation, 0.5% walk, 3.9% work from home (2000); Travel time to work: 14.5% less than 15 minutes, 27.2% 15 to 30 minutes, 27.6% 30 to 45 minutes, 15.4% 45 to 60 minutes, 15.4% 60 minutes or more (2000)
Additional Information Contacts
Lindenhurst Lake Villa Chamber 847-356-8446

LONG GROVE (village). Aka Longgrove. Covers a land area of 12.275 square miles and a water area of 0.155 square miles. Located at 42.20° N. Lat.; 88.00° W. Long. Elevation is 730 feet.
Population: 6,735 (2000); Race: 91.5% White, 1.0% Black, 5.5% Asian, 1.1% American Indian and Alaska Native, 2.0% Hispanic of any race, 0.7% two or more races (2000); Density: 548.7 persons per square mile (2000); Age: 30.1% under 18, 8.5% over 64 (2000); Marriage status: 19.6% never married, 75.1% now married, 2.7% widowed, 2.5% divorced (2000); Foreign born: 8.3% (2000); Ancestry (includes multiple ancestries): 21.8% German, 13.3% Irish, 11.8% Other groups, 10.5% Polish, 9.6% Italian (2000).
Economy: Single-family building permits issued: 82 (2001) / 80 (2000); Multi-family building permits issued: 0 (2001) / 0 (2000); Employment by occupation: 34.2% management, 23.6% professional, 4.4% services, 30.5% sales, 0.0% farming, 3.1% construction, 4.1% production (2000).
Income: Per capita income: $62,185 (2000); Median household income: $148,150 (2000); Poverty rate: 2.6% (2000).
Taxes: Total city taxes per capita: $56 (1997); City property taxes per capita: $0 (1997).
Education: High school graduation rate: 97.2% (2000); College graduation rate: 57.1% (2000).
Housing: Homeownership rate: 97.0% (2000); Median home value: $555,400 (2000); Median rent: $635 per month (2000); Median age of housing: 15 years (2000).
Transportation: Commute to work: 85.9% car, 5.8% public transportation, 0.0% walk, 8.0% work from home (2000); Travel time to work: 13.4% less than 15 minutes, 33.4% 15 to 30 minutes, 27.9% 30 to 45 minutes, 10.3% 45 to 60 minutes, 15.0% 60 minutes or more (2000)

LONG LAKE (CDP). Covers a land area of 1.051 square miles and a water area of 0.606 square miles. Located at 42.37° N. Lat.; 88.12° W. Long. Elevation is 750 feet.
Population: 3,356 (2000); Race: 92.4% White, 2.4% Black, 0.0% Asian, 0.6% American Indian and Alaska Native, 9.2% Hispanic of any race, 0.7% two or more races (2000); Density: 3,193.3 persons per square mile (2000); Age: 31.5% under 18, 6.8% over 64 (2000); Marriage status: 25.7% never married, 59.4% now married, 4.4% widowed, 10.5% divorced (2000); Foreign born: 6.4% (2000); Ancestry (includes multiple ancestries): 34.1% German, 15.8% Irish, 14.8% Polish, 14.3% Other groups, 9.4% United States or American (2000).
Economy: In agricultural area. Employment by occupation: 11.7% management, 14.8% professional, 11.5% services, 22.1% sales, 0.0% farming, 21.2% construction, 18.7% production (2000).
Income: Per capita income: $21,034 (2000); Median household income: $57,179 (2000); Poverty rate: 3.8% (2000).
Education: High school graduation rate: 79.5% (2000); College graduation rate: 12.1% (2000).
Housing: Homeownership rate: 76.9% (2000); Median home value: $128,500 (2000); Median rent: $698 per month (2000); Median age of housing: 47 years (2000).
Transportation: Commute to work: 96.2% car, 1.5% public transportation, 0.0% walk, 2.2% work from home (2000); Travel time to work: 16.3% less than 15 minutes, 22.8% 15 to 30 minutes, 24.1% 30 to 45 minutes, 20.0% 45 to 60 minutes, 16.8% 60 minutes or more (2000)

METTAWA (village). Covers a land area of 5.467 square miles and a water area of 0.026 square miles. Located at 42.24° N. Lat.; 87.91° W. Long. Elevation is 680 feet.
Population: 367 (2000); Race: 93.5% White, 0.0% Black, 1.2% Asian, 0.0% American Indian and Alaska Native, 11.4% Hispanic of any race, 0.6% two or more races (2000); Density: 67.1 persons per square mile (2000); Age: 21.6% under 18, 13.0% over 64 (2000); Marriage status: 19.2% never married, 70.3% now married, 4.9% widowed, 5.6% divorced (2000); Foreign born: 20.7% (2000); Ancestry (includes multiple ancestries): 27.2% German, 16.0% Other groups, 13.6% Irish, 7.7% Italian, 7.7% Scottish (2000).
Economy: Single-family building permits issued: 12 (2001) / 9 (2000); Multi-family building permits issued: 0 (2001) / 0 (2000); Employment by occupation: 28.8% management, 25.4% professional, 13.0% services, 22.0% sales, 0.0% farming, 0.6% construction, 10.2% production (2000).
Income: Per capita income: $89,104 (2000); Median household income: $127,388 (2000); Poverty rate: 4.6% (2000).
Taxes: Total city taxes per capita: $48 (1997); City property taxes per capita: $43 (1997).
Education: High school graduation rate: 93.5% (2000); College graduation rate: 56.9% (2000).
Housing: Homeownership rate: 87.9% (2000); Median home value: $823,300 (2000); Median rent: $925 per month (2000); Median age of housing: 20 years (2000).
Transportation: Commute to work: 75.1% car, 9.2% public transportation, 6.4% walk, 8.7% work from home (2000); Travel time to work: 25.3% less than 15 minutes, 37.3% 15 to 30 minutes, 19.6% 30 to 45 minutes, 6.3% 45 to 60 minutes, 11.4% 60 minutes or more (2000)

MUNDELEIN (village). Covers a land area of 8.623 square miles and a water area of 0.323 square miles. Located at 42.26° N. Lat.; 88.00° W. Long. Elevation is 754 feet.
History: The community here developed around the Sheldon School of Business Administration and was called Area, a reflection of the school's motto of "Ability, Reliability, Endurance, and Action." When this school was replaced by a Catholic seminary, the town name was changed to Mundelein for George Cardinal Mundelein, Archbishop of Chicago.

Population: 30,935 (2000); Race: 79.7% White, 0.7% Black, 6.7% Asian, 0.5% American Indian and Alaska Native, 24.2% Hispanic of any race, 2.5% two or more races (2000); Density: 3,587.5 persons per square mile (2000); Age: 31.1% under 18, 6.5% over 64 (2000); Marriage status: 25.3% never married, 64.9% now married, 3.1% widowed, 6.7% divorced (2000); Foreign born: 23.8% (2000); Ancestry (includes multiple ancestries): 31.6% Other groups, 22.8% German, 13.9% Irish, 10.7% Polish, 7.5% Italian (2000).
Vital Statistics: Birth rate: 218.9 per 10,000 population (1998)
Economy: Unemployment rate: 6.5% (11/2002); Total civilian labor force: 17,166 (11/2002); Single-family building permits issued: 118 (2001) / 111 (2000); Multi-family building permits issued: 0 (2001) / 0 (2000); Employment by occupation: 18.8% management, 22.4% professional, 12.8% services, 25.0% sales, 0.3% farming, 7.9% construction, 12.8% production (2000).
Income: Per capita income: $26,280 (2000); Median household income: $69,651 (2000); Poverty rate: 4.6% (2000).
Taxes: Total city taxes per capita: $286 (2000); City property taxes per capita: $225 (2000).
Education: High school graduation rate: 83.5% (2000); College graduation rate: 39.9% (2000).

School District(s)

Diamond Lake School District 76 (PK-08)
2000 Enrollment: 1,228 847-566-9221
Fremont School District 79 (KG-08)
2000 Enrollment: 1,535 847-566-0169
Mundelein Cons High School District 120 (09-12)
2000 Enrollment: 2,003 847-949-2200
Mundelein Elementary School District 75 (PK-08)
2000 Enrollment: 2,307 847-949-2700

Four-year College(s)

University of Saint Mary of the Lake (Private, Not-for-profit, Roman Catholic)
2001 Enrollment: 254 847-566-6401

Housing: Homeownership rate: 79.9% (2000); Median home value: $164,300 (2000); Median rent: $726 per month (2000); Median age of housing: 21 years (2000).
Transportation: Commute to work: 90.5% car, 4.1% public transportation, 0.8% walk, 3.3% work from home (2000); Travel time to work: 24.6% less than 15 minutes, 31.4% 15 to 30 minutes, 23.0% 30 to 45 minutes, 11.3% 45 to 60 minutes, 9.6% 60 minutes or more (2000)

NORTH BARRINGTON (village). Covers a land area of 4.389 square miles and a water area of 0.197 square miles. Located at 42.20° N. Lat.; 88.13° W. Long. Elevation is 800 feet.
Population: 2,918 (2000); Race: 96.3% White, 0.1% Black, 2.2% Asian, 0.0% American Indian and Alaska Native, 2.3% Hispanic of any race, 0.7% two or more races (2000); Density: 664.9 persons per square mile (2000); Age: 29.2% under 18, 8.7% over 64 (2000); Marriage status: 13.8% never married, 81.1% now married, 2.0% widowed, 3.1% divorced (2000); Foreign born: 6.9% (2000); Ancestry (includes multiple ancestries): 26.3% German, 21.7% Irish, 12.3% Italian, 12.0% English, 10.1% Polish (2000).
Economy: Manufacturing of greeting cards. Single-family building permits issued: 21 (2001) / 42 (2000); Multi-family building permits issued: 0 (2001) / 0 (2000); Employment by occupation: 37.1% management, 26.8% professional, 2.7% services, 27.4% sales, 0.0% farming, 3.0% construction, 2.9% production (2000).
Income: Per capita income: $81,243 (2000); Median household income: $146,251 (2000); Poverty rate: 2.8% (2000).
Taxes: Total city taxes per capita: $277 (1997); City property taxes per capita: $186 (1997).
Education: High school graduation rate: 98.5% (2000); College graduation rate: 62.6% (2000).
Housing: Homeownership rate: 98.6% (2000); Median home value: $528,600 (2000); Median rent: $1,563 per month (2000); Median age of housing: 19 years (2000).
Transportation: Commute to work: 79.0% car, 10.6% public transportation, 0.0% walk, 9.5% work from home (2000); Travel time to work: 15.0% less than 15 minutes, 23.8% 15 to 30 minutes, 26.1% 30 to 45 minutes, 13.3% 45 to 60 minutes, 21.8% 60 minutes or more (2000)

NORTH CHICAGO (city). Covers a land area of 7.832 square miles and a water area of 0.013 square miles. Located at 42.32° N. Lat.; 87.85° W. Long. Elevation is 670 feet.
History: A sit-down strike at a steel plant here in 1937 led to a U.S. Supreme Court decision (1939) ruling sit-down strikes illegal. Incorporated 1895.
Population: 35,918 (2000); Race: 48.0% White, 36.2% Black, 3.1% Asian, 0.7% American Indian and Alaska Native, 18.2% Hispanic of any race, 3.7% two or more races (2000); Density: 4,586.3 persons per square mile (2000); Age: 24.1% under 18, 4.2% over 64 (2000); Marriage status: 51.3% never married, 39.5% now married, 2.8% widowed, 6.4% divorced (2000); Foreign born: 12.9% (2000); Ancestry (includes multiple ancestries): 51.9% Other groups, 10.0% German, 7.7% Irish, 4.0% English, 3.5% United States or American (2000).
Vital Statistics: Birth rate: 88.3 per 10,000 population (1998)
Economy: Industrial city. Its economy is closely intertwined with the neighboring city of Waukegan, which has a harbor on Lake Michigan. Pharmaceuticals, medical diagnostic testing equipment, chemicals, steel and automobile parts are among the many manufactures. Unemployment rate: 11.2% (11/2002); Total civilian labor force: 8,826 (11/2002); Single-family building permits issued: 24 (2001) / 39 (2000); Multi-family building permits issued: 2 (2001) / 7 (2000); Employment by occupation: 10.9% management, 14.3% professional, 22.3% services, 26.8% sales, 0.4% farming, 5.3% construction, 20.1% production (2000).
Income: Per capita income: $14,564 (2000); Median household income: $38,180 (2000); Poverty rate: 15.1% (2000).
Taxes: Total city taxes per capita: $155 (2000); City property taxes per capita: $59 (2000).
Education: High school graduation rate: 76.3% (2000); College graduation rate: 14.8% (2000).

School District(s)

North Chicago School District 187 (PK-12)
2000 Enrollment: 4,718 847-689-8150

Four-year College(s)

Finch University of Health Science-Chicago Med Sch (Private, Not-for-profit)
2001 Enrollment: 1,349 847-578-3000
2001 Tuition: In-state $13,689; Out-of-state $13,689

Housing: Homeownership rate: 36.0% (2000); Median home value: $100,400 (2000); Median rent: $595 per month (2000); Median age of housing: 34 years (2000).
Hospitals: North Chicago Veterans Affairs Medical Center (1,101 beds)
Transportation: Commute to work: 48.6% car, 1.4% public transportation, 27.2% walk, 6.6% work from home (2000); Travel time to work: 61.3% less than 15 minutes, 22.1% 15 to 30 minutes, 9.0% 30 to 45 minutes, 3.9% 45 to 60 minutes, 3.6% 60 minutes or more (2000)

Additional Information Contacts

North Chicago Chamber of Commerce 847-785-1912

OLD MILL CREEK (village). Aka Mill Creek. Covers a land area of 10.113 square miles and a water area of 0.119 square miles. Located at 42.42° N. Lat.; 87.98° W. Long. Elevation is 709 feet.
Population: 251 (2000); Race: 83.2% White, 2.0% Black, 11.2% Asian, 0.0% American Indian and Alaska Native, 1.0% Hispanic of any race, 3.0% two or more races (2000); Density: 24.8 persons per square mile (2000); Age: 25.4% under 18, 5.0% over 64 (2000); Marriage status: 30.3% never married, 56.4% now married, 5.1% widowed, 8.1% divorced (2000); Foreign born: 12.2% (2000); Ancestry (includes multiple ancestries): 22.8% Irish, 22.4% German, 16.8% Other groups, 11.6% English, 11.2% French (except Basque) (2000).
Economy: Single-family building permits issued: 1 (2001) / 0 (2000); Multi-family building permits issued: 0 (2001) / 0 (2000); Employment by occupation: 25.4% management, 22.5% professional, 13.3% services, 24.3% sales, 4.0% farming, 7.5% construction, 2.9% production (2000).
Income: Per capita income: $43,314 (2000); Median household income: $82,426 (2000); Poverty rate: 2.7% (2000).
Taxes: Total city taxes per capita: $958 (1997); City property taxes per capita: $521 (1997).
Education: High school graduation rate: 95.5% (2000); College graduation rate: 44.0% (2000).
Housing: Homeownership rate: 55.0% (2000); Median home value: $254,500 (2000); Median rent: $933 per month (2000); Median age of housing: 48 years (2000).
Transportation: Commute to work: 85.9% car, 6.5% public transportation, 2.4% walk, 5.3% work from home (2000); Travel time to work: 27.3% less than 15 minutes, 26.7% 15 to 30 minutes, 17.4% 30 to 45 minutes, 5.6% 45 to 60 minutes, 23.0% 60 minutes or more (2000)

PARK CITY (city). Covers a land area of 1.150 square miles and a water area of 0 square miles. Located at 42.35° N. Lat.; 87.88° W. Long. Elevation is 710 feet.

Population: 6,637 (2000); Race: 63.0% White, 7.7% Black, 9.5% Asian, 0.5% American Indian and Alaska Native, 36.1% Hispanic of any race, 5.1% two or more races (2000); Density: 5,773.0 persons per square mile (2000); Age: 25.7% under 18, 7.6% over 64 (2000); Marriage status: 32.0% never married, 50.1% now married, 3.8% widowed, 14.0% divorced (2000); Foreign born: 30.7% (2000); Ancestry (includes multiple ancestries): 47.4% Other groups, 12.3% German, 7.4% Irish, 5.6% Polish, 3.9% United States or American (2000).
Economy: Manufacturing of wood products. Single-family building permits issued: 7 (2001) / 0 (2000); Multi-family building permits issued: 0 (2001) / 0 (2000); Employment by occupation: 10.2% management, 12.8% professional, 19.4% services, 25.6% sales, 0.2% farming, 9.7% construction, 22.0% production (2000).
Income: Per capita income: $18,595 (2000); Median household income: $36,508 (2000); Poverty rate: 8.0% (2000).
Taxes: Total city taxes per capita: $37 (1997); City property taxes per capita: $10 (1997).
Education: High school graduation rate: 69.6% (2000); College graduation rate: 16.0% (2000).
Housing: Homeownership rate: 61.5% (2000); Median home value: $139,000 (2000); Median rent: $612 per month (2000); Median age of housing: 16 years (2000).
Transportation: Commute to work: 94.5% car, 1.8% public transportation, 2.8% walk, 0.2% work from home (2000); Travel time to work: 25.8% less than 15 minutes, 37.6% 15 to 30 minutes, 22.0% 30 to 45 minutes, 4.9% 45 to 60 minutes, 9.7% 60 minutes or more (2000)

RIVERWOODS (village). Covers a land area of 3.989 square miles and a water area of 0.011 square miles. Located at 42.17° N. Lat.; 87.89° W. Long. Elevation is 656 feet.
Population: 3,843 (2000); Race: 94.0% White, 0.4% Black, 4.9% Asian, 0.0% American Indian and Alaska Native, 2.5% Hispanic of any race, 0.6% two or more races (2000); Density: 963.3 persons per square mile (2000); Age: 30.0% under 18, 12.6% over 64 (2000); Marriage status: 13.5% never married, 80.6% now married, 3.4% widowed, 2.5% divorced (2000); Foreign born: 13.8% (2000); Ancestry (includes multiple ancestries): 17.4% German, 11.9% Russian, 11.9% Irish, 11.6% Other groups, 10.6% United States or American (2000).
Economy: Law report printing. Single-family building permits issued: 40 (2001) / 11 (2000); Multi-family building permits issued: 0 (2001) / 0 (2000); Employment by occupation: 29.1% management, 32.9% professional, 3.6% services, 29.0% sales, 0.0% farming, 2.5% construction, 2.9% production (2000).
Income: Per capita income: $67,878 (2000); Median household income: $158,990 (2000); Poverty rate: 3.2% (2000).
Taxes: Total city taxes per capita: $205 (1997); City property taxes per capita: $73 (1997).
Education: High school graduation rate: 94.4% (2000); College graduation rate: 65.6% (2000).
Housing: Homeownership rate: 97.1% (2000); Median home value: $522,200 (2000); Median rent: $539 per month (2000); Median age of housing: 22 years (2000).
Transportation: Commute to work: 80.5% car, 8.8% public transportation, 0.2% walk, 10.5% work from home (2000); Travel time to work: 15.7% less than 15 minutes, 32.8% 15 to 30 minutes, 24.6% 30 to 45 minutes, 14.2% 45 to 60 minutes, 12.7% 60 minutes or more (2000)

ROUND LAKE (village). Covers a land area of 3.520 square miles and a water area of 0.064 square miles. Located at 42.35° N. Lat.; 88.10° W. Long. Elevation is 785 feet.
Population: 5,842 (2000); Race: 78.4% White, 1.6% Black, 2.2% Asian, 0.6% American Indian and Alaska Native, 25.6% Hispanic of any race, 2.9% two or more races (2000); Density: 1,659.8 persons per square mile (2000); Age: 28.7% under 18, 6.5% over 64 (2000); Marriage status: 23.2% never married, 60.2% now married, 5.8% widowed, 10.8% divorced (2000); Foreign born: 21.0% (2000); Ancestry (includes multiple ancestries): 32.3% Other groups, 25.6% German, 12.6% Irish, 12.3% Polish, 6.7% English (2000).
Economy: Railroad junction. In agricultural area: grain; dairying. Manufacturing: signs, hospital equipment, industrial ovens and furnaces. Single-family building permits issued: 368 (2001) / 194 (2000); Multi-family building permits issued: 0 (2001) / 0 (2000); Employment by occupation: 14.5% management, 14.3% professional, 14.9% services, 31.3% sales, 0.0% farming, 10.0% construction, 15.0% production (2000).
Income: Per capita income: $21,585 (2000); Median household income: $58,051 (2000); Poverty rate: 6.8% (2000).
Taxes: Total city taxes per capita: $408 (1997); City property taxes per capita: $134 (1997).
Education: High school graduation rate: 73.8% (2000); College graduation rate: 21.3% (2000).

School District(s)

Round Lake Area Schs - District 116 (KG-12)
2000 Enrollment: 5,855 847-270-9000
Housing: Homeownership rate: 78.1% (2000); Median home value: $150,900 (2000); Median rent: $531 per month (2000); Median age of housing: 20 years (2000).
Transportation: Commute to work: 90.1% car, 4.7% public transportation, 2.2% walk, 2.7% work from home (2000); Travel time to work: 17.2% less than 15 minutes, 21.8% 15 to 30 minutes, 27.0% 30 to 45 minutes, 17.8% 45 to 60 minutes, 16.2% 60 minutes or more (2000)
Additional Information Contacts
Round Lake Chamber of Commerce 847-546-2002

ROUND LAKE BEACH (village). Covers a land area of 4.996 square miles and a water area of 0.100 square miles. Located at 42.37° N. Lat.; 88.08° W. Long. Elevation is 740 feet.
History: Incorporated 1937.
Population: 25,859 (2000); Race: 74.3% White, 2.8% Black, 2.2% Asian, 0.3% American Indian and Alaska Native, 31.4% Hispanic of any race, 3.6% two or more races (2000); Density: 5,176.4 persons per square mile (2000); Age: 35.1% under 18, 4.6% over 64 (2000); Marriage status: 24.1% never married, 64.0% now married, 3.5% widowed, 8.4% divorced (2000); Foreign born: 21.5% (2000); Ancestry (includes multiple ancestries): 36.9% Other groups, 23.7% German, 13.8% Irish, 10.2% Polish, 6.2% English (2000).
Vital Statistics: Birth rate: 202.6 per 10,000 population (1998)
Economy: Remnant agriculture. Manufacturing: circuit boards, forklift equipment. Single-family building permits issued: 126 (2001) / 200 (2000); Multi-family building permits issued: 75 (2001) / 99 (2000); Employment by occupation: 11.9% management, 11.4% professional, 15.3% services, 30.4% sales, 0.3% farming, 11.4% construction, 19.3% production (2000).
Income: Per capita income: $18,113 (2000); Median household income: $59,359 (2000); Poverty rate: 5.1% (2000).
Taxes: Total city taxes per capita: $127 (2000); City property taxes per capita: $59 (2000).
Education: High school graduation rate: 75.0% (2000); College graduation rate: 16.1% (2000).
Housing: Homeownership rate: 85.7% (2000); Median home value: $123,000 (2000); Median rent: $696 per month (2000); Median age of housing: 20 years (2000).
Transportation: Commute to work: 92.6% car, 3.0% public transportation, 0.9% walk, 2.4% work from home (2000); Travel time to work: 15.3% less than 15 minutes, 25.1% 15 to 30 minutes, 26.8% 30 to 45 minutes, 16.4% 45 to 60 minutes, 16.4% 60 minutes or more (2000)

ROUND LAKE HEIGHTS (village). Aka Indian Hills. Covers a land area of 0.612 square miles and a water area of 0 square miles. Located at 42.38° N. Lat.; 88.10° W. Long. Elevation is 785 feet.
Population: 1,347 (2000); Race: 84.0% White, 2.5% Black, 0.6% Asian, 0.3% American Indian and Alaska Native, 17.7% Hispanic of any race, 4.9% two or more races (2000); Density: 2,200.7 persons per square mile (2000); Age: 35.4% under 18, 5.1% over 64 (2000); Marriage status: 27.8% never married, 58.8% now married, 4.9% widowed, 8.6% divorced (2000); Foreign born: 11.4% (2000); Ancestry (includes multiple ancestries): 28.0% German, 25.7% Other groups, 17.5% Irish, 10.5% Polish, 7.6% Italian (2000).
Economy: Single-family building permits issued: 150 (2001) / 33 (2000); Multi-family building permits issued: 0 (2001) / 0 (2000); Employment by occupation: 8.4% management, 12.3% professional, 13.3% services, 33.3% sales, 0.0% farming, 13.9% construction, 18.7% production (2000).
Income: Per capita income: $17,868 (2000); Median household income: $54,706 (2000); Poverty rate: 5.9% (2000).
Taxes: Total city taxes per capita: $106 (1997); City property taxes per capita: $52 (1997).
Education: High school graduation rate: 78.9% (2000); College graduation rate: 12.9% (2000).
Housing: Homeownership rate: 79.1% (2000); Median home value: $101,000 (2000); Median rent: $709 per month (2000); Median age of housing: 41 years (2000).
Transportation: Commute to work: 92.8% car, 2.4% public transportation, 1.9% walk, 2.8% work from home (2000); Travel time to work: 22.3% less than 15 minutes, 23.4% 15 to 30 minutes, 22.3% 30 to 45 minutes, 14.9% 45 to 60 minutes, 16.9% 60 minutes or more (2000)

ROUND LAKE PARK (village). Covers a land area of 2.990 square miles and a water area of 0.055 square miles. Located at 42.34° N. Lat.; 88.07° W. Long. Elevation is 800 feet.
History: Incorporated 1947.
Population: 6,038 (2000); Race: 83.8% White, 0.4% Black, 0.6% Asian, 1.2% American Indian and Alaska Native, 24.2% Hispanic of any race, 2.2% two or more races (2000); Density: 2,019.4 persons per square mile (2000); Age: 26.8% under 18, 18.1% over 64 (2000); Marriage status: 21.8% never married, 61.3% now married, 7.1% widowed, 9.8% divorced (2000); Foreign born: 15.4% (2000); Ancestry (includes multiple ancestries): 25.3% Other groups, 25.1% German, 15.4% Irish, 10.9% Polish, 7.0% English (2000).
Economy: Manufacturing: metal fabrication. Remnant agriculture. Campbell's Airport here. Single-family building permits issued: 7 (2001) / 5 (2000); Multi-family building permits issued: 0 (2001) / 0 (2000); Employment by occupation: 7.8% management, 9.5% professional, 15.5% services, 30.2% sales, 0.4% farming, 15.0% construction, 21.6% production (2000).
Income: Per capita income: $18,279 (2000); Median household income: $44,896 (2000); Poverty rate: 10.0% (2000).
Taxes: Total city taxes per capita: $116 (1997); City property taxes per capita: $93 (1997).
Education: High school graduation rate: 75.9% (2000); College graduation rate: 11.2% (2000).
Housing: Homeownership rate: 83.5% (2000); Median home value: $115,600 (2000); Median rent: $677 per month (2000); Median age of housing: 20 years (2000).
Transportation: Commute to work: 94.9% car, 2.7% public transportation, 0.4% walk, 1.3% work from home (2000); Travel time to work: 21.3% less than 15 minutes, 24.2% 15 to 30 minutes, 31.4% 30 to 45 minutes, 10.9% 45 to 60 minutes, 12.1% 60 minutes or more (2000)

THIRD LAKE (village). Covers a land area of 0.548 square miles and a water area of 0.252 square miles. Located at 42.36° N. Lat.; 88.00° W. Long. Elevation is 770 feet.
Population: 1,355 (2000); Race: 95.5% White, 1.5% Black, 1.6% Asian, 0.1% American Indian and Alaska Native, 0.3% Hispanic of any race, 1.3% two or more races (2000); Density: 2,474.7 persons per square mile (2000); Age: 30.9% under 18, 3.9% over 64 (2000); Marriage status: 22.3% never married, 70.1% now married, 3.2% widowed, 4.5% divorced (2000); Foreign born: 5.2% (2000); Ancestry (includes multiple ancestries): 34.7% German, 25.3% Irish, 13.3% Polish, 10.8% English, 5.7% United States or American (2000).
Economy: Employment by occupation: 23.2% management, 33.1% professional, 7.4% services, 25.3% sales, 0.3% farming, 4.2% construction, 6.5% production (2000).
Income: Per capita income: $34,921 (2000); Median household income: $96,719 (2000); Poverty rate: 2.7% (2000).
Taxes: Total city taxes per capita: $38 (1997); City property taxes per capita: $29 (1997).
Education: High school graduation rate: 97.4% (2000); College graduation rate: 54.9% (2000).
Housing: Homeownership rate: 95.7% (2000); Median home value: $213,100 (2000); Median rent: $1,054 per month (2000); Median age of housing: 16 years (2000).
Transportation: Commute to work: 87.6% car, 4.0% public transportation, 3.8% walk, 4.0% work from home (2000); Travel time to work: 17.4% less than 15 minutes, 30.9% 15 to 30 minutes, 26.6% 30 to 45 minutes, 13.7% 45 to 60 minutes, 11.4% 60 minutes or more (2000)

TOWER LAKES (village). Covers a land area of 0.947 square miles and a water area of 0.120 square miles. Located at 42.23° N. Lat.; 88.15° W. Long.
Population: 1,310 (2000); Race: 98.0% White, 0.2% Black, 0.7% Asian, 0.2% American Indian and Alaska Native, 0.9% Hispanic of any race, 0.8% two or more races (2000); Density: 1,383.2 persons per square mile (2000); Age: 29.2% under 18, 7.2% over 64 (2000); Marriage status: 18.8% never married, 74.8% now married, 3.2% widowed, 3.3% divorced (2000); Foreign born: 7.5% (2000); Ancestry (includes multiple ancestries): 32.9% German, 18.7% Irish, 14.3% English, 13.7% Italian, 11.3% Polish (2000).
Economy: Single-family building permits issued: 1 (2001) / 2 (2000); Multi-family building permits issued: 0 (2001) / 0 (2000); Employment by occupation: 30.8% management, 28.9% professional, 5.6% services, 28.9% sales, 0.0% farming, 2.7% construction, 3.0% production (2000).
Income: Per capita income: $52,025 (2000); Median household income: $130,388 (2000); Poverty rate: 2.1% (2000).
Taxes: Total city taxes per capita: $368 (1997); City property taxes per capita: $350 (1997).
Education: High school graduation rate: 98.7% (2000); College graduation rate: 64.5% (2000).
Housing: Homeownership rate: 99.1% (2000); Median home value: $356,100 (2000); Median rent: $1,125 per month (2000); Median age of housing: 32 years (2000).
Transportation: Commute to work: 78.8% car, 11.4% public transportation, 1.3% walk, 8.0% work from home (2000); Travel time to work: 13.8% less than 15 minutes, 20.1% 15 to 30 minutes, 22.2% 30 to 45 minutes, 17.6% 45 to 60 minutes, 26.4% 60 minutes or more (2000)

VENETIAN VILLAGE (CDP). Covers a land area of 2.418 square miles and a water area of 0.696 square miles. Located at 42.39° N. Lat.; 88.04° W. Long. Elevation is 755 feet.
Population: 3,082 (2000); Race: 95.9% White, 0.4% Black, 0.4% Asian, 0.0% American Indian and Alaska Native, 4.0% Hispanic of any race, 2.3% two or more races (2000); Density: 1,274.6 persons per square mile (2000); Age: 27.9% under 18, 7.6% over 64 (2000); Marriage status: 21.9% never married, 66.3% now married, 4.2% widowed, 7.5% divorced (2000); Foreign born: 4.1% (2000); Ancestry (includes multiple ancestries): 37.3% German, 19.0% Irish, 12.9% Polish, 9.8% Swedish, 9.3% English (2000).
Economy: Employment by occupation: 10.6% management, 15.1% professional, 11.9% services, 30.4% sales, 0.0% farming, 17.7% construction, 14.3% production (2000).
Income: Per capita income: $23,504 (2000); Median household income: $57,829 (2000); Poverty rate: 3.0% (2000).
Education: High school graduation rate: 90.5% (2000); College graduation rate: 18.7% (2000).
Housing: Homeownership rate: 90.0% (2000); Median home value: $135,100 (2000); Median rent: $738 per month (2000); Median age of housing: 35 years (2000).
Transportation: Commute to work: 96.0% car, 1.1% public transportation, 0.2% walk, 2.3% work from home (2000); Travel time to work: 23.6% less than 15 minutes, 24.8% 15 to 30 minutes, 22.6% 30 to 45 minutes, 13.9% 45 to 60 minutes, 15.1% 60 minutes or more (2000)

VERNON HILLS (village). Covers a land area of 7.429 square miles and a water area of 0.190 square miles. Located at 42.23° N. Lat.; 87.96° W. Long. Elevation is 745 feet.
Population: 20,120 (2000); Race: 82.1% White, 1.7% Black, 11.2% Asian, 0.1% American Indian and Alaska Native, 8.2% Hispanic of any race, 1.7% two or more races (2000); Density: 2,708.3 persons per square mile (2000); Age: 29.3% under 18, 5.8% over 64 (2000); Marriage status: 24.8% never married, 62.0% now married, 4.3% widowed, 8.9% divorced (2000); Foreign born: 21.2% (2000); Ancestry (includes multiple ancestries): 24.5% Other groups, 18.8% German, 13.9% Irish, 10.1% Polish, 9.2% Italian (2000).
Vital Statistics: Birth rate: 145.6 per 10,000 population (1998)
Economy: Railroad junction. Manufacturing: tool and die, transmissions, bar-coding machines. Single-family building permits issued: 218 (2001) / 296 (2000); Multi-family building permits issued: 0 (2001) / 0 (2000); Employment by occupation: 23.4% management, 28.1% professional, 7.8% services, 29.7% sales, 0.0% farming, 4.1% construction, 6.9% production (2000).
Income: Per capita income: $32,246 (2000); Median household income: $71,297 (2000); Poverty rate: 2.9% (2000).
Taxes: Total city taxes per capita: $172 (2000); City property taxes per capita: $0 (2000).
Education: High school graduation rate: 94.0% (2000); College graduation rate: 54.3% (2000).

School District(s)

Hawthorn C C School District 73 (PK-08)
2000 Enrollment: 3,517 847-367-3226

Housing: Homeownership rate: 79.8% (2000); Median home value: $223,300 (2000); Median rent: $825 per month (2000); Median age of housing: 17 years (2000).
Newspapers: Lincolnshire Review (1 x week); Antioch Review (1 x week); Vernon Hills Review (1 x week); Review of Lake Villa/Lindenhurst (1 x week); Mundelein Review (1 x week); Libertyville Review (1 x week); Lake Forester (1 x week); Highland Park News (1 x week); Gurnee Review (1 x week); Grayslake Review (1 x week); Deerfield Review (1 x week)
Transportation: Commute to work: 91.5% car, 3.8% public transportation, 0.6% walk, 3.5% work from home (2000); Travel time to work: 23.0% less than 15 minutes, 31.2% 15 to 30 minutes, 24.8% 30 to 45 minutes, 10.0% 45 tc 60 minutes, 10.9% 60 minutes or more (2000)

VOLO (village). Covers a land area of 2.791 square miles and a water area of 0.012 square miles. Located at 42.33° N. Lat.; 88.16° W. Long. Elevation is 790 feet.
Population: 180 (2000); Race: 68.9% White, 0.0% Black, 0.5% Asian, 0.0% American Indian and Alaska Native, 49.8% Hispanic of any race, 30.6% two or more races (2000); Density: 64.5 persons per square mile (2000); Age: 26.3% under 18, 11.5% over 64 (2000); Marriage status: 28.6% never married, 52.8% now married, 11.8% widowed, 6.8% divorced (2000); Foreign born: 29.7% (2000); Ancestry (includes multiple ancestries): 30.1% Other groups, 19.6% German, 12.0% Polish, 7.7% English, 3.8% Irish (2000).
Economy: Employment by occupation: 12.7% management, 9.5% professional, 20.6% services, 23.8% sales, 0.0% farming, 9.5% construction, 23.8% production (2000).
Income: Per capita income: $22,791 (2000); Median household income: $45,833 (2000); Poverty rate: 33.0% (2000).
Taxes: Total city taxes per capita: $70 (1997); City property taxes per capita: $0 (1997).
Education: High school graduation rate: 64.4% (2000); College graduation rate: 5.9% (2000).
Housing: Homeownership rate: 59.6% (2000); Median home value: $271,900 (2000); Median rent: $642 per month (2000); Median age of housing: 47 years (2000).
Transportation: Commute to work: 58.7% car, 0.0% public transportation, 22.2% walk, 12.7% work from home (2000); Travel time to work: 34.5% less than 15 minutes, 34.5% 15 to 30 minutes, 9.1% 30 to 45 minutes, 3.6% 45 to 60 minutes, 18.2% 60 minutes or more (2000)

WADSWORTH (village). Covers a land area of 8.773 square miles and a water area of 0.037 square miles. Located at 42.43° N. Lat.; 87.92° W. Long. Elevation is 670 feet.
Population: 3,083 (2000); Race: 93.4% White, 0.7% Black, 2.0% Asian, 0.0% American Indian and Alaska Native, 4.4% Hispanic of any race, 3.8% two or more races (2000); Density: 351.4 persons per square mile (2000); Age: 26.3% under 18, 9.3% over 64 (2000); Marriage status: 18.8% never married, 71.6% now married, 3.9% widowed, 5.7% divorced (2000); Foreign born: 5.1% (2000); Ancestry (includes multiple ancestries): 32.1% German, 15.2% Irish, 14.4% English, 13.0% Polish, 8.7% Italian (2000).
Economy: Manufacturing of transformer cores. Single-family building permits issued: 32 (2001) / 24 (2000); Multi-family building permits issued: 0 (2001) / 0 (2000); Employment by occupation: 25.3% management, 20.5% professional, 8.3% services, 29.1% sales, 0.0% farming, 7.9% construction, 8.9% production (2000).
Income: Per capita income: $35,171 (2000); Median household income: $86,867 (2000); Poverty rate: 2.2% (2000).
Taxes: Total city taxes per capita: $63 (2000); City property taxes per capita: $20 (2000).
Education: High school graduation rate: 95.4% (2000); College graduation rate: 38.1% (2000).

School District(s)

Millburn C C School District 24 (PK-08)
2000 Enrollment: 1,030 847-356-8331
Housing: Homeownership rate: 92.3% (2000); Median home value: $249,600 (2000); Median rent: $640 per month (2000); Median age of housing: 20 years (2000).
Transportation: Commute to work: 94.8% car, 0.8% public transportation, 0.4% walk, 2.8% work from home (2000); Travel time to work: 18.3% less than 15 minutes, 49.5% 15 to 30 minutes, 16.8% 30 to 45 minutes, 6.6% 45 to 60 minutes, 8.8% 60 minutes or more (2000)

WAUCONDA (village). Covers a land area of 3.864 square miles and a water area of 0.419 square miles. Located at 42.26° N. Lat.; 88.14° W. Long. Elevation is 800 feet.
History: Wauconda was settled in 1836 by Justus Bangs. The name he gave the village probably came from a favorite book of his, and was Indian in origin.
Population: 9,448 (2000); Race: 91.0% White, 0.3% Black, 1.7% Asian, 0.1% American Indian and Alaska Native, 11.0% Hispanic of any race, 0.9% two or more races (2000); Density: 2,445.0 persons per square mile (2000); Age: 24.6% under 18, 11.7% over 64 (2000); Marriage status: 21.4% never married, 61.0% now married, 5.7% widowed, 11.9% divorced (2000); Foreign born: 11.9% (2000); Ancestry (includes multiple ancestries): 28.2% German, 14.5% Other groups, 12.3% Irish, 11.4% Polish, 9.1% Italian (2000).
Economy: Single-family building permits issued: 38 (2001) / 47 (2000); Multi-family building permits issued: 17 (2001) / 12 (2000); Employment by occupation: 12.8% management, 16.0% professional, 13.0% services, 31.0% sales, 0.0% farming, 13.3% construction, 13.9% production (2000).
Income: Per capita income: $26,355 (2000); Median household income: $57,805 (2000); Poverty rate: 4.0% (2000).
Taxes: Total city taxes per capita: $350 (1997); City property taxes per capita: $172 (1997).
Education: High school graduation rate: 86.6% (2000); College graduation rate: 24.0% (2000).

School District(s)

Wauconda Community Unit S District 118 (PK-12)
2000 Enrollment: 3,829 847-526-7690
Housing: Homeownership rate: 79.7% (2000); Median home value: $161,000 (2000); Median rent: $720 per month (2000); Median age of housing: 24 years (2000).
Transportation: Commute to work: 93.2% car, 1.3% public transportation, 1.5% walk, 2.6% work from home (2000); Travel time to work: 26.3% less than 15 minutes, 23.7% 15 to 30 minutes, 26.7% 30 to 45 minutes, 11.4% 45 to 60 minutes, 11.9% 60 minutes or more (2000)
Additional Information Contacts
Wauconda Chamber of Commerce 847-526-5580

WAUKEGAN (city). Covers a land area of 23.012 square miles and a water area of 0.079 square miles. Located at 42.37° N. Lat.; 87.86° W. Long. Elevation is 660 feet.
History: Waukegan began with the founding of Little Fort by the French in the 1700's, the present name being of Indian origin meaning "fort or trading post." Settlers came to Little Fort in 1835, and in 1846 it was designated as a U.S. port of entry. Waukegan was incorporated as a village in 1849, and as a city in 1859.
Population: 87,901 (2000); Race: 50.1% White, 18.7% Black, 3.5% Asian, 0.3% American Indian and Alaska Native, 45.1% Hispanic of any race, 3.4% two or more races (2000); Density: 3,819.8 persons per square mile (2000); Age: 30.5% under 18, 7.8% over 64 (2000); Marriage status: 31.6% never married, 55.0% now married, 4.8% widowed, 8.5% divorced (2000); Foreign born: 30.2% (2000); Ancestry (includes multiple ancestries): 59.6% Other groups, 8.6% German, 5.1% Irish, 3.3% English, 3.2% Polish (2000).
Vital Statistics: Birth rate: 214.8 per 10,000 population (1998)
Economy: Unemployment rate: 7.8% (11/2002); Total civilian labor force: 39,622 (11/2002); Single-family building permits issued: 121 (2001) / 162 (2000); Multi-family building permits issued: 365 (2001) / 211 (2000); Employment by occupation: 9.2% management, 13.5% professional, 17.9% services, 24.6% sales, 0.3% farming, 9.7% construction, 25.0% production (2000).
Income: Per capita income: $17,368 (2000); Median household income: $42,335 (2000); Poverty rate: 13.9% (2000).
Taxes: Total city taxes per capita: $266 (2000); City property taxes per capita: $137 (2000).
Education: High school graduation rate: 66.5% (2000); College graduation rate: 16.3% (2000).

School District(s)

Waukegan C U School District 60 (PK-12)
2000 Enrollment: 15,510 847-336-3100

Four-year College(s)

Shimer College (Private, Not-for-profit)
2001 Enrollment: 105 847-623-8400
2001 Tuition: In-state $14,950; Out-of-state $14,950
Housing: Homeownership rate: 56.7% (2000); Median home value: $118,200 (2000); Median rent: $586 per month (2000); Median age of housing: 38 years (2000).
Hospitals: Victory Memorial Hospital (299 beds); Vista Health - Saint Therese Medical Center (388 beds)
Newspapers: The News Sun (6 x week)
Transportation: Commute to work: 91.3% car, 3.6% public transportation, 2.0% walk, 1.6% work from home (2000); Travel time to work: 23.4% less than 15 minutes, 37.9% 15 to 30 minutes, 21.8% 30 to 45 minutes, 9.5% 45 to 60 minutes, 7.4% 60 minutes or more (2000)
Airports: Waukegan Regional

WINTHROP HARBOR (village). Covers a land area of 4.309 square miles and a water area of 0.069 square miles. Located at 42.48° N. Lat.; 87.82° W. Long. Elevation is 650 feet.
History: The Winthrop Harbor and Dock Company purchased land here in 1892, but plans to develop the harbor and town were abandoned. The community that grew here depended on dairying.

Population: 6,670 (2000); Race: 95.1% White, 0.3% Black, 1.2% Asian, 0.3% American Indian and Alaska Native, 5.1% Hispanic of any race, 1.7% two or more races (2000); Density: 1,548.0 persons per square mile (2000); Age: 27.8% under 18, 8.6% over 64 (2000); Marriage status: 20.7% never married, 67.4% now married, 3.6% widowed, 8.3% divorced (2000); Foreign born: 3.0% (2000); Ancestry (includes multiple ancestries): 25.7% German, 16.0% Irish, 11.5% English, 11.0% Other groups, 7.2% United States or American (2000).
Economy: Single-family building permits issued: 16 (2001) / 19 (2000); Multi-family building permits issued: 0 (2001) / 0 (2000); Employment by occupation: 15.8% management, 13.0% professional, 11.0% services, 30.4% sales, 0.5% farming, 11.6% construction, 17.6% production (2000).
Income: Per capita income: $24,256 (2000); Median household income: $62,795 (2000); Poverty rate: 3.1% (2000).
Taxes: Total city taxes per capita: $233 (2000); City property taxes per capita: $163 (2000).
Education: High school graduation rate: 89.9% (2000); College graduation rate: 18.2% (2000).

School District(s)

Winthrop Harbor School District 1 (PK-08)
2000 Enrollment: 857 847-731-3085

Housing: Homeownership rate: 83.2% (2000); Median home value: $143,900 (2000); Median rent: $646 per month (2000); Median age of housing: 28 years (2000).
Transportation: Commute to work: 96.7% car, 0.7% public transportation, 0.7% walk, 1.7% work from home (2000); Travel time to work: 25.4% less than 15 minutes, 34.2% 15 to 30 minutes, 23.3% 30 to 45 minutes, 8.2% 45 to 60 minutes, 8.9% 60 minutes or more (2000)

Additional Information Contacts

Winthrop Harbor Chamber of Commerce 847-872-7723

ZION (city). Covers a land area of 8.197 square miles and a water area of 0 square miles. Located at 42.45° N. Lat.; 87.84° W. Long. Elevation is 660 feet.
History: Zion began as the dream of John Alexander Dowie (1847-1907), the Scottish founder of the Christian Catholic Apostolic Church, who planned Zion as a city where the tenets of the church would govern. In 1899 Dowie's followers began to settle here. Dowie was succeeded by Wilbur Glenn Voliva, who attempted to industrialize Zion, but the church owned all industries and commercial establishments. In 1939, after several bankruptcies, titles were transferred to individuals.
Population: 22,866 (2000); Race: 58.1% White, 27.9% Black, 1.6% Asian, 0.4% American Indian and Alaska Native, 15.1% Hispanic of any race, 3.5% two or more races (2000); Density: 2,789.5 persons per square mile (2000); Age: 33.2% under 18, 8.2% over 64 (2000); Marriage status: 28.2% never married, 54.9% now married, 5.0% widowed, 11.9% divorced (2000); Foreign born: 8.8% (2000); Ancestry (includes multiple ancestries): 40.5% Other groups, 16.0% German, 7.9% Irish, 6.7% English, 4.6% United States or American (2000).
Vital Statistics: Birth rate: 195.5 per 10,000 population (1998)
Economy: Single-family building permits issued: 98 (2001) / 89 (2000); Multi-family building permits issued: 14 (2001) / 0 (2000); Employment by occupation: 8.5% management, 15.1% professional, 16.4% services, 30.4% sales, 0.0% farming, 10.5% construction, 19.1% production (2000).
Income: Per capita income: $17,730 (2000); Median household income: $45,723 (2000); Poverty rate: 11.9% (2000).
Taxes: Total city taxes per capita: $304 (1997); City property taxes per capita: $234 (1997).
Education: High school graduation rate: 77.8% (2000); College graduation rate: 15.7% (2000).

School District(s)

Beach Park C C School District 3 (PK-08)
2000 Enrollment: 2,061 847-599-5070
Zion Elementary School District 6 (PK-08)
2000 Enrollment: 2,987 847-872-5455
Zion-Benton Township H S District 126 (09-12)
2000 Enrollment: 2,132 847-746-1202

Housing: Homeownership rate: 59.2% (2000); Median home value: $115,700 (2000); Median rent: $595 per month (2000); Median age of housing: 32 years (2000).
Hospitals: Midwestern Regional Medical Center (95 beds)
Newspapers: Zion-Benton News (1 x week)
Transportation: Commute to work: 92.4% car, 3.5% public transportation, 1.3% walk, 1.9% work from home (2000); Travel time to work: 17.7% less than 15 minutes, 34.9% 15 to 30 minutes, 24.4% 30 to 45 minutes, 12.2% 45 to 60 minutes, 10.8% 60 minutes or more (2000)

Additional Information Contacts

Zion Chamber of Commerce 847-872-5405

Lawrence County

Located in southeastern Illinois; bounded on the east by the Wabash River and the Indiana border; drained by the Embarrass River. Covers a land area of 372.00 square miles, a water area of 2.00 square miles, and is located in the Central Time Zone. The county government was organized in 1821. County seat is Lawrenceville.
Population: 15,452 (2000); Race: 98.3% White, 0.9% Black, 0.1% Asian, 0.0% American Indian and Alaska Native, 0.6% Hispanic of any race, 0.5% two or more races (2000); Density: 41.5 persons per square mile (2000); Age: 22.6% under 18, 20.2% over 64 (2000).
Religion: Five largest groups: 15.2% The United Methodist Church, 10.2% Christian Churches and Churches of Christ, 5.2% Catholic Church, 5.1% Southern Baptist Convention, 2.4% The Wesleyan Church (2000).
Economy: Unemployment rate: 5.4% (11/2002); Total civilian labor force: 7,252 (11/2002); Leading industries: 30.3% health care and social assistance; 12.3% retail trade; 8.1% wholesale trade (2000); Companies that employ more than 1,000 persons: 0 (2000); Companies that employ more than 100 persons: 7 (2000); Farms: 376 totaling 182,511 acres (1997); Minority business ownership rate: 0.0% (1997); Women business ownership rate: 20.5% (1997); Retail sales per capita: $4,624 (1997). Single-family building permits issued: 1 (2001) / 3 (2000); Multi-family building permits issued: 0 (2001) / 0 (2000).
Income: Per capita income: $17,070 (2000); Median household income: $30,361 (2000); Poverty rate: 13.7% (2000); Bankruptcy rate: 3.96% (2001).
Taxes: Total county taxes per capita: $88 (1997); County property taxes per capita: $78 (1997).
Education: High school graduation rate: 81.3% (2000); College graduation rate: 9.7% (2000).
Housing: Homeownership rate: 77.0% (2000); Median home value: $45,800 (2000); Median rent: $253 per month (2000); Median age of housing: 45 years (2000).
Health: Birth rate: 110.7 per 10,000 population (1998); Age adjusted death rate: 94.8 per 10,000 population (1999); Age adjusted cancer mortality rate: 181.6 deaths per 100,000 population (1999). Number of physicians: 6.5 per 10,000 population (1999); Number of hospital beds: 37.5 per 10,000 population (1999).
Elections: 2000 Presidential election results: 42.9% Gore, 54.6% Bush, 1.5% Nader, 0.6% Buchanan
National and State Parks: Lincoln Trail State Memorial; Red Hills State Park

Additional Information Contacts

Lawrence County Government Offices 618-943-2346
Lawrenceville Chamber of Commerce 618-943-3516

Lawrence County Communities

BIRDS (village). Covers a land area of 0.216 square miles and a water area of 0 square miles. Located at 38.83° N. Lat.; 87.66° W. Long. Elevation is 435 feet.
Population: 51 (2000); Race: 100.0% White, 0.0% Black, 0.0% Asian, 0.0% American Indian and Alaska Native, 0.0% Hispanic of any race, 0.0% two or more races (2000); Density: 235.6 persons per square mile (2000); Age: 34.0% under 18, 4.0% over 64 (2000); Marriage status: 24.3% never married, 35.1% now married, 10.8% widowed, 29.7% divorced (2000); Foreign born: 0.0% (2000); Ancestry (includes multiple ancestries): 12.0% Irish, 8.0% German, 4.0% Scotch-Irish, 4.0% United States or American (2000).
Economy: In agricultural area. Employment by occupation: 0.0% management, 5.0% professional, 20.0% services, 20.0% sales, 0.0% farming, 10.0% construction, 45.0% production (2000).
Income: Per capita income: $9,216 (2000); Median household income: $23,438 (2000); Poverty rate: 20.0% (2000).
Taxes: Total city taxes per capita: $12 (1997); City property taxes per capita: $6 (1997).
Education: High school graduation rate: 100.0% (2000); College graduation rate: 12.0% (2000).
Housing: Homeownership rate: 60.0% (2000); Median home value: $22,500 (2000); Median rent: $213 per month (2000); Median age of housing: 35 years (2000).
Transportation: Commute to work: 85.0% car, 0.0% public transportation, 10.0% walk, 5.0% work from home (2000); Travel time to work: 26.3% less

than 15 minutes, 42.1% 15 to 30 minutes, 10.5% 30 to 45 minutes, 21.1% 45 to 60 minutes, 0.0% 60 minutes or more (2000)

BRIDGEPORT (city). Covers a land area of 1.071 square miles and a water area of 0.025 square miles. Located at 38.71° N. Lat.; 87.75° W. Long. Elevation is 446 feet.
History: Bridgeport was the center of an early oil boom, when a company built a pumping station and supply yards here.
Population: 2,168 (2000); Race: 99.3% White, 0.3% Black, 0.0% Asian, 0.0% American Indian and Alaska Native, 0.0% Hispanic of any race, 0.4% two or more races (2000); Density: 2,024.0 persons per square mile (2000); Age: 27.7% under 18, 17.4% over 64 (2000); Marriage status: 23.0% never married, 52.8% now married, 9.8% widowed, 14.4% divorced (2000); Foreign born: 0.0% (2000); Ancestry (includes multiple ancestries): 19.9% United States or American, 13.3% English, 11.6% German, 8.7% Irish, 6.2% Other groups (2000).
Economy: Employment by occupation: 4.8% management, 9.8% professional, 25.4% services, 21.6% sales, 0.0% farming, 12.6% construction, 25.8% production (2000).
Income: Per capita income: $12,960 (2000); Median household income: $27,635 (2000); Poverty rate: 17.3% (2000).
Taxes: Total city taxes per capita: $13 (1997); City property taxes per capita: $7 (1997).
Education: High school graduation rate: 75.7% (2000); College graduation rate: 5.0% (2000).

School District(s)

Red Hill C U School District 10 (KG-12)
2000 Enrollment: 1,150 618-945-2061
Housing: Homeownership rate: 72.2% (2000); Median home value: $43,300 (2000); Median rent: $263 per month (2000); Median age of housing: 45 years (2000).
Newspapers: Bridgeport Leader (1 x week)
Transportation: Commute to work: 91.6% car, 0.0% public transportation, 2.9% walk, 4.0% work from home (2000); Travel time to work: 48.2% less than 15 minutes, 27.9% 15 to 30 minutes, 16.6% 30 to 45 minutes, 4.9% 45 to 60 minutes, 2.3% 60 minutes or more (2000)

LAWRENCEVILLE (city). Covers a land area of 2.022 square miles and a water area of 0 square miles. Located at 38.72° N. Lat.; 87.68° W. Long. Elevation is 460 feet.
History: The first settler here was Captain Toussaint Dubois, veteran of the American Revolution, who came about 1780 and planted an orchard. Jessie K. Dubois, the captain's son, was a friend of Abraham Lincoln and one of the pall bearers at his funeral. Lawrenceville was organized in 1821 and named for Captain James Lawrence, commander of the "Chesapeake" in the War of 1812, who said, "Don't give up the ship." Lawrenceville developed as an oil town in the early 1900's, and as the seat of Lawrence County.
Population: 4,745 (2000); Race: 98.0% White, 1.6% Black, 0.0% Asian, 0.0% American Indian and Alaska Native, 1.5% Hispanic of any race, 0.1% two or more races (2000); Density: 2,346.8 persons per square mile (2000); Age: 19.8% under 18, 28.7% over 64 (2000); Marriage status: 16.7% never married, 56.5% now married, 15.5% widowed, 11.3% divorced (2000); Foreign born: 1.1% (2000); Ancestry (includes multiple ancestries): 20.4% German, 13.6% United States or American, 13.1% English, 10.7% Irish, 8.5% Other groups (2000).
Economy: Single-family building permits issued: 1 (2001) / 3 (2000); Multi-family building permits issued: 0 (2001) / 0 (2000); Employment by occupation: 8.7% management, 18.8% professional, 20.3% services, 25.4% sales, 0.0% farming, 9.6% construction, 17.2% production (2000).
Income: Per capita income: $16,717 (2000); Median household income: $24,951 (2000); Poverty rate: 16.9% (2000).
Taxes: Total city taxes per capita: $130 (1997); City property taxes per capita: $115 (1997).
Education: High school graduation rate: 79.1% (2000); College graduation rate: 12.5% (2000).

School District(s)

Lawrence Co C U District 20 (PK-12)
2000 Enrollment: 1,265 618-943-2326
Housing: Homeownership rate: 66.1% (2000); Median home value: $39,800 (2000); Median rent: $230 per month (2000); Median age of housing: 52 years (2000).
Hospitals: Lawrence County Memorial Hospital (58 beds)
Newspapers: Daily Record (5 x week); Lawrence County News (1 x week)
Transportation: Commute to work: 93.5% car, 0.0% public transportation, 4.7% walk, 1.3% work from home (2000); Travel time to work: 55.7% less than 15 minutes, 25.9% 15 to 30 minutes, 11.0% 30 to 45 minutes, 1.7% 45 to 60 minutes, 5.6% 60 minutes or more (2000)
Additional Information Contacts
Lawrenceville Chamber of Commerce. 618-943-3516

RUSSELLVILLE (village). Covers a land area of 0.459 square miles and a water area of 0 square miles. Located at 38.82° N. Lat.; 87.53° W. Long. Elevation is 425 feet.
History: Russellville grew around a ferry that crossed the Wabash River here.
Population: 119 (2000); Race: 100.0% White, 0.0% Black, 0.0% Asian, 0.0% American Indian and Alaska Native, 0.0% Hispanic of any race, 0.0% two or more races (2000); Density: 259.5 persons per square mile (2000); Age: 40.8% under 18, 16.7% over 64 (2000); Marriage status: 11.8% never married, 60.5% now married, 10.5% widowed, 17.1% divorced (2000); Foreign born: 0.0% (2000); Ancestry (includes multiple ancestries): 8.3% Other groups, 5.0% Irish, 3.3% English, 1.7% Polish, 1.7% German (2000).
Economy: Employment by occupation: 0.0% management, 9.8% professional, 14.6% services, 29.3% sales, 0.0% farming, 31.7% construction, 14.6% production (2000).
Income: Per capita income: $11,843 (2000); Median household income: $23,750 (2000); Poverty rate: 42.5% (2000).
Taxes: Total city taxes per capita: $7 (1997); City property taxes per capita: $0 (1997).
Education: High school graduation rate: 74.2% (2000); College graduation rate: 0.0% (2000).
Housing: Homeownership rate: 77.6% (2000); Median home value: $21,300 (2000); Median rent: $317 per month (2000); Median age of housing: 36 years (2000).
Transportation: Commute to work: 89.7% car, 0.0% public transportation, 10.3% walk, 0.0% work from home (2000); Travel time to work: 20.5% less than 15 minutes, 66.7% 15 to 30 minutes, 5.1% 30 to 45 minutes, 7.7% 45 to 60 minutes, 0.0% 60 minutes or more (2000)

SAINT FRANCISVILLE (city). Covers a land area of 0.746 square miles and a water area of 0.034 square miles. Located at 38.59° N. Lat.; 87.64° W. Long. Elevation is 451 feet.
Population: 759 (2000); Race: 99.0% White, 0.0% Black, 0.0% Asian, 0.0% American Indian and Alaska Native, 0.8% Hispanic of any race, 0.5% two or more races (2000); Density: 1,017.3 persons per square mile (2000); Age: 24.6% under 18, 16.2% over 64 (2000); Marriage status: 28.3% never married, 49.4% now married, 9.9% widowed, 12.4% divorced (2000); Foreign born: 0.1% (2000); Ancestry (includes multiple ancestries): 20.3% German, 12.8% United States or American, 11.3% Irish, 6.8% English, 5.0% French (except Basque) (2000).
Economy: Employment by occupation: 4.5% management, 15.0% professional, 18.4% services, 23.8% sales, 1.1% farming, 16.1% construction, 21.0% production (2000).
Income: Per capita income: $12,955 (2000); Median household income: $25,543 (2000); Poverty rate: 21.1% (2000).
Education: High school graduation rate: 75.5% (2000); College graduation rate: 6.6% (2000).
Housing: Homeownership rate: 83.1% (2000); Median home value: $32,300 (2000); Median rent: $216 per month (2000); Median age of housing: 54 years (2000).
Transportation: Commute to work: 96.5% car, 0.0% public transportation, 2.0% walk, 0.6% work from home (2000); Travel time to work: 17.4% less than 15 minutes, 53.2% 15 to 30 minutes, 20.0% 30 to 45 minutes, 8.2% 45 to 60 minutes, 1.2% 60 minutes or more (2000)

SUMNER (city). Covers a land area of 1.031 square miles and a water area of 0 square miles. Located at 38.71° N. Lat.; 87.86° W. Long. Elevation is 455 feet.
History: Incorporated 1887.
Population: 1,022 (2000); Race: 95.4% White, 2.3% Black, 0.5% Asian, 0.0% American Indian and Alaska Native, 0.7% Hispanic of any race, 1.3% two or more races (2000); Density: 991.0 persons per square mile (2000); Age: 20.4% under 18, 18.8% over 64 (2000); Marriage status: 27.5% never married, 53.8% now married, 7.5% widowed, 11.2% divorced (2000); Foreign born: 0.5% (2000); Ancestry (includes multiple ancestries): 18.9% German, 18.2% English, 9.8% United States or American, 9.5% Irish, 4.5% Other groups (2000).
Economy: In oil, natural gas, and agricultural area. Single-family building permits issued: 0 (2001) / 0 (2000); Multi-family building permits issued: 0 (2001) / 0 (2000); Employment by occupation: 4.7% management, 15.5%

professional, 14.3% services, 23.8% sales, 0.4% farming, 13.0% construction, 28.3% production (2000).
Income: Per capita income: $14,808 (2000); Median household income: $25,489 (2000); Poverty rate: 16.9% (2000).
Taxes: Total city taxes per capita: $17 (1997); City property taxes per capita: $15 (1997).
Education: High school graduation rate: 64.4% (2000); College graduation rate: 3.9% (2000).
Housing: Homeownership rate: 74.2% (2000); Median home value: $36,700 (2000); Median rent: $255 per month (2000); Median age of housing: 56 years (2000).
Newspapers: The Sumner Press (1 x week)
Transportation: Commute to work: 86.8% car, 8.5% public transportation, 2.4% walk, 0.9% work from home (2000); Travel time to work: 33.0% less than 15 minutes, 43.8% 15 to 30 minutes, 13.3% 30 to 45 minutes, 4.8% 45 to 60 minutes, 5.0% 60 minutes or more (2000)

Lee County

Located in northern Illinois; drained by the Rock, Green, and Kyte Rivers. Covers a land area of 725.40 square miles, a water area of 3.90 square miles, and is located in the Central Time Zone. The county government was organized in 1839. County seat is Dixon.

Weather Station: Dixon 1 NW — Elevation: 698 feet

	Jan	Feb	Mar	Apr	May	Jun	Jul	Aug	Sep	Oct	Nov	Dec
High	28	33	46	60	72	81	84	82	75	63	47	33
Low	10	15	27	38	49	58	62	60	51	40	29	17
Precip	1.6	1.4	2.6	3.6	4.4	4.8	3.4	4.4	3.5	2.8	2.8	2.1
Snow	11.1	6.8	4.6	1.2	0.0	0.0	0.0	0.0	0.0	tr	2.1	8.4

High and Low temperatures in degrees Fahrenheit; Precipitation and Snow in inches

Weather Station: Paw Paw 2 NW — Elevation: 948 feet

	Jan	Feb	Mar	Apr	May	Jun	Jul	Aug	Sep	Oct	Nov	Dec
High	26	31	43	58	70	80	83	80	74	62	45	32
Low	10	15	25	36	48	57	62	59	51	39	28	17
Precip	1.4	1.2	2.3	3.5	4.3	4.5	3.6	4.2	4.2	2.7	3.0	2.2
Snow	9.0	5.8	4.2	1.0	tr	0.0	0.0	0.0	0.0	0.2	2.6	7.4

High and Low temperatures in degrees Fahrenheit; Precipitation and Snow in inches

Population: 36,062 (2000); Race: 92.5% White, 5.0% Black, 0.7% Asian, 0.1% American Indian and Alaska Native, 3.1% Hispanic of any race, 1.0% two or more races (2000); Density: 49.7 persons per square mile (2000); Age: 24.2% under 18, 14.7% over 64 (2000).
Religion: Five largest groups: 33.2% Catholic Church, 10.4% Evangelical Lutheran Church in America, 8.5% The United Methodist Church, 1.6% Southern Baptist Convention, 1.5% New Testament Association of Independent Baptist Churches and other Fundame
Economy: Unemployment rate: 5.4% (11/2002); Total civilian labor force: 18,019 (11/2002); Leading industries: 34.3% manufacturing; 17.3% health care and social assistance; 11.7% retail trade (2000); Companies that employ more than 1,000 persons: 0 (2000); Companies that employ more than 100 persons: 22 (2000); Farms: 904 totaling 393,043 acres (1997); Minority business ownership rate: 0.0% (1997); Women business ownership rate: 23.8% (1997); Retail sales per capita: $6,525 (1997). Single-family building permits issued: 83 (2001) / 90 (2000); Multi-family building permits issued: 37 (2001) / 28 (2000).
Income: Per capita income: $18,650 (2000); Median household income: $40,967 (2000); Poverty rate: 7.7% (2000); Bankruptcy rate: 5.93% (2001).
Taxes: Total county taxes per capita: $132 (2000); County property taxes per capita: $106 (2000).
Education: High school graduation rate: 80.2% (2000); College graduation rate: 13.2% (2000).
Housing: Homeownership rate: 73.9% (2000); Median home value: $83,400 (2000); Median rent: $374 per month (2000); Median age of housing: 47 years (2000).
Health: Birth rate: 104.3 per 10,000 population (1998); Age adjusted death rate: 94.0 per 10,000 population (1999); Age adjusted cancer mortality rate: 242.8 deaths per 100,000 population (1999). Number of physicians: 10.5 per 10,000 population (1999); Number of hospital beds: 27.7 per 10,000 population (1999).
Elections: 2000 Presidential election results: 41.8% Gore, 55.2% Bush, 2.2% Nader, 0.5% Buchanan
National and State Parks: Franklin Creek State Park; Green River State Wildlife Management Area; Hennepin Canal Parkway State Park
Additional Information Contacts

Lee County Government Offices 815-288-3309
Dixon Chamber of Commerce 815-284-3361
Lee County Area Association of Realtors 815-284-3044

Lee County Communities

AMBOY (city). Covers a land area of 1.258 square miles and a water area of 0 square miles. Located at 41.71° N. Lat.; 89.33° W. Long. Elevation is 743 feet.
History: In Amboy in 1854, Scotch-Irish immigrants Samuel Carson and John T. Pirie opened a small grocery store which later became the firm of Carson Pirie Scott & Company.
Population: 2,561 (2000); Race: 97.4% White, 0.6% Black, 0.0% Asian, 0.2% American Indian and Alaska Native, 2.4% Hispanic of any race, 1.7% two or more races (2000); Density: 2,035.5 persons per square mile (2000); Age: 26.9% under 18, 17.9% over 64 (2000); Marriage status: 22.4% never married, 59.1% now married, 7.0% widowed, 11.4% divorced (2000); Foreign born: 1.5% (2000); Ancestry (includes multiple ancestries): 35.8% German, 24.2% Irish, 10.0% English, 6.5% United States or American, 6.2% Other groups (2000).
Economy: Single-family building permits issued: 8 (2001) / 5 (2000); Multi-family building permits issued: 0 (2001) / 0 (2000); Employment by occupation: 8.9% management, 12.5% professional, 18.0% services, 20.5% sales, 0.0% farming, 10.7% construction, 29.4% production (2000).
Income: Per capita income: $18,183 (2000); Median household income: $36,250 (2000); Poverty rate: 8.3% (2000).
Taxes: Total city taxes per capita: $74 (1997); City property taxes per capita: $65 (1997).
Education: High school graduation rate: 79.7% (2000); College graduation rate: 8.4% (2000).

School District(s)

Amboy Community Unit School District 272 (PK-12)
2000 Enrollment: 1,114 815-857-2164
Housing: Homeownership rate: 70.2% (2000); Median home value: $75,500 (2000); Median rent: $358 per month (2000); Median age of housing: 52 years (2000).
Newspapers: The Amboy News (1 x week)
Transportation: Commute to work: 90.9% car, 0.0% public transportation, 4.8% walk, 2.8% work from home (2000); Travel time to work: 31.5% less than 15 minutes, 32.7% 15 to 30 minutes, 23.2% 30 to 45 minutes, 5.0% 45 to 60 minutes, 7.6% 60 minutes or more (2000)

ASHTON (village). Covers a land area of 0.661 square miles and a water area of 0 square miles. Located at 41.86° N. Lat.; 89.22° W. Long. Elevation is 825 feet.
Population: 1,142 (2000); Race: 97.7% White, 1.6% Black, 0.0% Asian, 0.1% American Indian and Alaska Native, 3.0% Hispanic of any race, 0.4% two or more races (2000); Density: 1,727.6 persons per square mile (2000); Age: 27.9% under 18, 14.4% over 64 (2000); Marriage status: 24.1% never married, 53.1% now married, 7.4% widowed, 15.4% divorced (2000); Foreign born: 1.5% (2000); Ancestry (includes multiple ancestries): 36.0% German, 12.4% Irish, 8.9% United States or American, 7.9% Other groups, 7.6% English (2000).
Economy: In rich agricultural area: corn, oats, soybeans; cattle; ice cream and dairy products. Single-family building permits issued: 2 (2001) / 2 (2000); Multi-family building permits issued: 19 (2001) / 14 (2000); Employment by occupation: 6.8% management, 14.8% professional, 12.2% services, 20.3% sales, 0.4% farming, 13.2% construction, 32.4% production (2000).
Income: Per capita income: $21,200 (2000); Median household income: $39,896 (2000); Poverty rate: 6.2% (2000).
Taxes: Total city taxes per capita: $100 (1997); City property taxes per capita: $62 (1997).
Education: High school graduation rate: 81.4% (2000); College graduation rate: 11.7% (2000).

School District(s)

Ashton Community Unit School District 275 (KG-12)
2000 Enrollment: 355 815-453-7463
Housing: Homeownership rate: 71.6% (2000); Median home value: $79,400 (2000); Median rent: $330 per month (2000); Median age of housing: 60+ years (2000).
Newspapers: The Ashton Gazette (1 x week)
Transportation: Commute to work: 89.1% car, 0.0% public transportation, 7.0% walk, 2.5% work from home (2000); Travel time to work: 42.4% less than 15 minutes, 31.1% 15 to 30 minutes, 9.3% 30 to 45 minutes, 11.6% 45 to 60 minutes, 5.6% 60 minutes or more (2000)

COMPTON (village). Covers a land area of 0.166 square miles and a water area of 0 square miles. Located at 41.69° N. Lat.; 89.08° W. Long. Elevation is 970 feet.

Population: 347 (2000); Race: 97.3% White, 0.0% Black, 2.1% Asian, 0.0% American Indian and Alaska Native, 1.5% Hispanic of any race, 0.0% two or more races (2000); Density: 2,092.1 persons per square mile (2000); Age: 36.4% under 18, 7.1% over 64 (2000); Marriage status: 15.0% never married, 62.4% now married, 6.2% widowed, 16.4% divorced (2000); Foreign born: 1.8% (2000); Ancestry (includes multiple ancestries): 32.0% Irish, 31.7% German, 12.4% English, 8.6% Other groups, 5.0% French (except Basque) (2000).

Economy: In rich agricultural area: corn, soybeans; cattle. Employment by occupation: 6.5% management, 9.4% professional, 17.4% services, 18.1% sales, 0.0% farming, 15.9% construction, 32.6% production (2000).

Income: Per capita income: $13,205 (2000); Median household income: $34,167 (2000); Poverty rate: 4.8% (2000).

Taxes: Total city taxes per capita: $14 (1997); City property taxes per capita: $0 (1997).

Education: High school graduation rate: 76.1% (2000); College graduation rate: 7.6% (2000).

Housing: Homeownership rate: 93.0% (2000); Median home value: $75,900 (2000); Median rent: $388 per month (2000); Median age of housing: 60+ years (2000).

Transportation: Commute to work: 81.9% car, 2.2% public transportation, 4.3% walk, 7.2% work from home (2000); Travel time to work: 14.1% less than 15 minutes, 37.5% 15 to 30 minutes, 12.5% 30 to 45 minutes, 7.8% 45 to 60 minutes, 28.1% 60 minutes or more (2000)

DIXON (city). Covers a land area of 6.326 square miles and a water area of 0.421 square miles. Located at 41.84° N. Lat.; 89.48° W. Long. Elevation is 659 feet.

History: Dixon was settled in 1830 by John Dixon, who operated a trading post and tavern. Industry soon came to Dixon because of the water power available from the Rock River.

Population: 15,941 (2000); Race: 85.8% White, 10.8% Black, 1.0% Asian, 0.1% American Indian and Alaska Native, 4.3% Hispanic of any race, 1.1% two or more races (2000); Density: 2,519.8 persons per square mile (2000); Age: 21.5% under 18, 15.2% over 64 (2000); Marriage status: 21.1% never married, 55.4% now married, 8.2% widowed, 15.4% divorced (2000); Foreign born: 2.6% (2000); Ancestry (includes multiple ancestries): 27.3% German, 15.7% Irish, 9.3% Other groups, 8.7% English, 5.8% United States or American (2000).

Vital Statistics: Birth rate: 104.8 per 10,000 population (1998)

Economy: Single-family building permits issued: 13 (2001) / 12 (2000); Multi-family building permits issued: 16 (2001) / 12 (2000); Employment by occupation: 8.2% management, 15.8% professional, 18.5% services, 22.8% sales, 0.3% farming, 9.2% construction, 25.2% production (2000).

Income: Per capita income: $16,630 (2000); Median household income: $35,720 (2000); Poverty rate: 10.1% (2000).

Taxes: Total city taxes per capita: $143 (1997); City property taxes per capita: $131 (1997).

Education: High school graduation rate: 73.8% (2000); College graduation rate: 12.7% (2000).

School District(s)

Dixon Unit School District 170 (PK-12)
2000 Enrollment: 3,104 815-284-7722

Two-year College(s)

Sauk Valley Community College (Public)
2001 Enrollment: 2,688 815-288-5511
2001 Tuition: In-state $6,360; Out-of-state $7,980

Housing: Homeownership rate: 66.4% (2000); Median home value: $75,100 (2000); Median rent: $371 per month (2000); Median age of housing: 50 years (2000).

Hospitals: Katherine Shaw Bethea Hospital (101 beds)

Newspapers: Telegraph (7 x week)

Transportation: Commute to work: 91.6% car, 1.4% public transportation, 3.6% walk, 2.3% work from home (2000); Travel time to work: 60.9% less than 15 minutes, 23.9% 15 to 30 minutes, 6.9% 30 to 45 minutes, 2.1% 45 to 60 minutes, 6.1% 60 minutes or more (2000)

Airports: Dixon Municipal-Charles R. Walgreen Fiel

Additional Information Contacts

Dixon Chamber of Commerce 815-284-3361
Lee County Area Association of Realtors 815-284-3044

FRANKLIN GROVE (village). Covers a land area of 0.371 square miles and a water area of 0 square miles. Located at 41.84° N. Lat.; 89.30° W. Long. Elevation is 806 feet.

Population: 1,052 (2000); Race: 99.3% White, 0.0% Black, 0.0% Asian, 0.0% American Indian and Alaska Native, 0.8% Hispanic of any race, 0.7% two or more races (2000); Density: 2,835.5 persons per square mile (2000); Age: 24.9% under 18, 26.5% over 64 (2000); Marriage status: 18.5% never married, 61.8% now married, 10.9% widowed, 8.9% divorced (2000); Foreign born: 0.2% (2000); Ancestry (includes multiple ancestries): 27.1% German, 14.2% English, 13.9% Irish, 9.2% United States or American, 5.9% Other groups (2000).

Economy: In rich agricultural area. Single-family building permits issued: 0 (2001) / 0 (2000); Multi-family building permits issued: 0 (2001) / 0 (2000); Employment by occupation: 6.7% management, 11.6% professional, 20.8% services, 23.9% sales, 0.0% farming, 10.7% construction, 26.2% production (2000).

Income: Per capita income: $15,427 (2000); Median household income: $41,181 (2000); Poverty rate: 7.7% (2000).

Taxes: Total city taxes per capita: $28 (1997); City property taxes per capita: $24 (1997).

Education: High school graduation rate: 82.7% (2000); College graduation rate: 13.7% (2000).

Housing: Homeownership rate: 67.0% (2000); Median home value: $79,000 (2000); Median rent: $443 per month (2000); Median age of housing: 58 years (2000).

Transportation: Commute to work: 93.2% car, 0.0% public transportation, 4.3% walk, 1.1% work from home (2000); Travel time to work: 28.5% less than 15 minutes, 46.0% 15 to 30 minutes, 11.3% 30 to 45 minutes, 4.6% 45 to 60 minutes, 9.7% 60 minutes or more (2000)

HARMON (village). Covers a land area of 0.142 square miles and a water area of 0 square miles. Located at 41.72° N. Lat.; 89.55° W. Long. Elevation is 675 feet.

Population: 149 (2000); Race: 100.0% White, 0.0% Black, 0.0% Asian, 0.0% American Indian and Alaska Native, 7.0% Hispanic of any race, 0.0% two or more races (2000); Density: 1,049.7 persons per square mile (2000); Age: 33.8% under 18, 6.4% over 64 (2000); Marriage status: 40.4% never married, 52.9% now married, 2.9% widowed, 3.7% divorced (2000); Foreign born: 0.0% (2000); Ancestry (includes multiple ancestries): 64.3% German, 46.5% Irish, 8.9% United States or American, 6.4% Swedish, 6.4% French (except Basque) (2000).

Economy: In rich agricultural area. Employment by occupation: 6.7% management, 14.7% professional, 8.0% services, 33.3% sales, 0.0% farming, 8.0% construction, 29.3% production (2000).

Income: Per capita income: $14,697 (2000); Median household income: $58,750 (2000); Poverty rate: 3.2% (2000).

Taxes: Total city taxes per capita: $56 (1997); City property taxes per capita: $15 (1997).

Education: High school graduation rate: 82.9% (2000); College graduation rate: 2.4% (2000).

Housing: Homeownership rate: 95.0% (2000); Median home value: $52,900 (2000); Median rent: $725 per month (2000); Median age of housing: 60+ years (2000).

Transportation: Commute to work: 98.7% car, 0.0% public transportation, 1.3% walk, 0.0% work from home (2000); Travel time to work: 2.7% less than 15 minutes, 80.0% 15 to 30 minutes, 2.7% 30 to 45 minutes, 10.7% 45 to 60 minutes, 4.0% 60 minutes or more (2000)

LEE (village). Covers a land area of 0.223 square miles and a water area of 0 square miles. Located at 41.79° N. Lat.; 88.94° W. Long. Elevation is 940 feet.

Population: 313 (2000); Race: 97.4% White, 0.0% Black, 0.0% Asian, 1.5% American Indian and Alaska Native, 1.1% Hispanic of any race, 0.0% two or more races (2000); Density: 1,404.2 persons per square mile (2000); Age: 25.0% under 18, 9.2% over 64 (2000); Marriage status: 27.8% never married, 55.5% now married, 9.1% widowed, 7.7% divorced (2000); Foreign born: 0.7% (2000); Ancestry (includes multiple ancestries): 32.4% German, 17.3% Irish, 16.9% English, 16.5% Norwegian, 8.1% Other groups (2000).

Economy: Single-family building permits issued: 2 (2001) / 1 (2000); Multi-family building permits issued: 0 (2001) / 0 (2000); Employment by occupation: 8.7% management, 20.3% professional, 16.7% services, 31.2% sales, 1.4% farming, 12.3% construction, 9.4% production (2000).

Income: Per capita income: $19,709 (2000); Median household income: $42,813 (2000); Poverty rate: 11.5% (2000).

Education: High school graduation rate: 92.1% (2000); College graduation rate: 18.1% (2000).
Housing: Homeownership rate: 71.7% (2000); Median home value: $99,700 (2000); Median rent: $503 per month (2000); Median age of housing: 60+ years (2000).
Transportation: Commute to work: 92.6% car, 0.0% public transportation, 3.7% walk, 3.7% work from home (2000); Travel time to work: 11.5% less than 15 minutes, 16.0% 15 to 30 minutes, 47.3% 30 to 45 minutes, 19.8% 45 to 60 minutes, 5.3% 60 minutes or more (2000)

NELSON (village). Covers a land area of 0.227 square miles and a water area of 0.005 square miles. Located at 41.79° N. Lat.; 89.60° W. Long. Elevation is 656 feet.
Population: 163 (2000); Race: 100.0% White, 0.0% Black, 0.0% Asian, 0.0% American Indian and Alaska Native, 2.7% Hispanic of any race, 0.0% two or more races (2000); Density: 719.0 persons per square mile (2000); Age: 30.0% under 18, 14.7% over 64 (2000); Marriage status: 22.0% never married, 64.4% now married, 5.1% widowed, 8.5% divorced (2000); Foreign born: 1.3% (2000); Ancestry (includes multiple ancestries): 39.3% German, 8.0% Danish, 7.3% English, 6.0% Irish, 4.0% United States or American (2000).
Economy: In rich agricultural area. Employment by occupation: 5.6% management, 3.7% professional, 11.1% services, 13.0% sales, 0.0% farming, 29.6% construction, 37.0% production (2000).
Income: Per capita income: $15,043 (2000); Median household income: $35,833 (2000); Poverty rate: 30.0% (2000).
Taxes: Total city taxes per capita: $37 (2000); City property taxes per capita: $25 (2000).
Education: High school graduation rate: 60.6% (2000); College graduation rate: 0.0% (2000).
Housing: Homeownership rate: 94.1% (2000); Median home value: $52,400 (2000); Median rent: $313 per month (2000); Median age of housing: 60+ years (2000).
Transportation: Commute to work: 90.7% car, 0.0% public transportation, 5.6% walk, 0.0% work from home (2000); Travel time to work: 25.9% less than 15 minutes, 51.9% 15 to 30 minutes, 11.1% 30 to 45 minutes, 1.9% 45 to 60 minutes, 9.3% 60 minutes or more (2000)

PAW PAW (village). Aka Pawpaw. Covers a land area of 0.566 square miles and a water area of 0 square miles. Located at 41.68° N. Lat.; 88.98° W. Long. Elevation is 930 feet.
Population: 852 (2000); Race: 98.5% White, 0.0% Black, 0.0% Asian, 0.2% American Indian and Alaska Native, 0.7% Hispanic of any race, 1.1% two or more races (2000); Density: 1,506.2 persons per square mile (2000); Age: 25.8% under 18, 15.9% over 64 (2000); Marriage status: 23.0% never married, 59.4% now married, 10.3% widowed, 7.4% divorced (2000); Foreign born: 0.2% (2000); Ancestry (includes multiple ancestries): 30.5% German, 13.5% Irish, 11.8% English, 5.7% Swedish, 5.3% United States or American (2000).
Economy: In rich agricultural area. Single-family building permits issued: 2 (2001) / 2 (2000); Multi-family building permits issued: 0 (2001) / 0 (2000); Employment by occupation: 9.1% management, 7.4% professional, 17.5% services, 26.2% sales, 1.7% farming, 14.1% construction, 24.0% production (2000).
Income: Per capita income: $17,461 (2000); Median household income: $37,563 (2000); Poverty rate: 5.9% (2000).
Taxes: Total city taxes per capita: $76 (1997); City property taxes per capita: $68 (1997).
Education: High school graduation rate: 85.1% (2000); College graduation rate: 8.8% (2000).

School District(s)

Lee Center C U School District 271 (KG-12)
2000 Enrollment: 694 815-627-2841
Housing: Homeownership rate: 80.1% (2000); Median home value: $89,900 (2000); Median rent: $439 per month (2000); Median age of housing: 56 years (2000).
Transportation: Commute to work: 91.5% car, 1.3% public transportation, 5.0% walk, 2.3% work from home (2000); Travel time to work: 20.2% less than 15 minutes, 21.2% 15 to 30 minutes, 22.8% 30 to 45 minutes, 16.4% 45 to 60 minutes, 19.4% 60 minutes or more (2000)

STEWARD (village). Covers a land area of 0.124 square miles and a water area of 0 square miles. Located at 41.84° N. Lat.; 89.02° W. Long. Elevation is 820 feet.
Population: 271 (2000); Race: 98.9% White, 0.0% Black, 0.0% Asian, 0.0% American Indian and Alaska Native, 5.5% Hispanic of any race, 1.1% two or more races (2000); Density: 2,180.9 persons per square mile (2000); Age: 32.5% under 18, 8.0% over 64 (2000); Marriage status: 16.0% never married, 71.6% now married, 3.6% widowed, 8.8% divorced (2000); Foreign born: 0.0% (2000); Ancestry (includes multiple ancestries): 29.9% German, 17.2% Irish, 14.6% English, 12.4% French (except Basque), 11.3% Norwegian (2000).
Economy: In rich agricultural area. Employment by occupation: 8.1% management, 22.6% professional, 12.9% services, 24.2% sales, 0.0% farming, 4.0% construction, 28.2% production (2000).
Income: Per capita income: $16,270 (2000); Median household income: $46,071 (2000); Poverty rate: 4.5% (2000).
Taxes: Total city taxes per capita: $17 (1997); City property taxes per capita: $14 (1997).
Education: High school graduation rate: 84.2% (2000); College graduation rate: 18.1% (2000).

School District(s)

Steward Elementary School District 220 (KG-08)
2000 Enrollment: 97 815-396-2413
Housing: Homeownership rate: 80.4% (2000); Median home value: $92,600 (2000); Median rent: $375 per month (2000); Median age of housing: 60+ years (2000).
Transportation: Commute to work: 94.4% car, 0.0% public transportation, 2.4% walk, 3.2% work from home (2000); Travel time to work: 14.2% less than 15 minutes, 41.7% 15 to 30 minutes, 28.3% 30 to 45 minutes, 10.0% 45 to 60 minutes, 5.8% 60 minutes or more (2000)

SUBLETTE (village). Covers a land area of 0.350 square miles and a water area of 0 square miles. Located at 41.64° N. Lat.; 89.23° W. Long. Elevation is 927 feet.
Population: 456 (2000); Race: 98.2% White, 0.0% Black, 0.0% Asian, 0.0% American Indian and Alaska Native, 10.2% Hispanic of any race, 0.0% two or more races (2000); Density: 1,303.5 persons per square mile (2000); Age: 23.4% under 18, 15.8% over 64 (2000); Marriage status: 25.1% never married, 61.6% now married, 8.1% widowed, 5.3% divorced (2000); Foreign born: 4.9% (2000); Ancestry (includes multiple ancestries): 41.2% German, 20.3% Irish, 10.0% Other groups, 7.8% English, 7.3% Dutch (2000).
Economy: In rich agricultural area. Employment by occupation: 11.3% management, 12.2% professional, 13.5% services, 32.4% sales, 0.0% farming, 8.1% construction, 22.5% production (2000).
Income: Per capita income: $22,982 (2000); Median household income: $43,393 (2000); Poverty rate: 4.0% (2000).
Taxes: Total city taxes per capita: $49 (1997); City property taxes per capita: $44 (1997).
Education: High school graduation rate: 82.3% (2000); College graduation rate: 6.0% (2000).
Housing: Homeownership rate: 80.4% (2000); Median home value: $81,800 (2000); Median rent: $300 per month (2000); Median age of housing: 29 years (2000).
Transportation: Commute to work: 95.9% car, 0.0% public transportation, 3.2% walk, 0.9% work from home (2000); Travel time to work: 45.9% less than 15 minutes, 17.3% 15 to 30 minutes, 25.5% 30 to 45 minutes, 2.7% 45 to 60 minutes, 8.6% 60 minutes or more (2000)

WEST BROOKLYN (village). Covers a land area of 0.107 square miles and a water area of 0 square miles. Located at 41.69° N. Lat.; 89.14° W. Long. Elevation is 940 feet.
Population: 174 (2000); Race: 96.1% White, 0.0% Black, 0.0% Asian, 2.8% American Indian and Alaska Native, 2.8% Hispanic of any race, 0.0% two or more races (2000); Density: 1,629.0 persons per square mile (2000); Age: 36.9% under 18, 7.8% over 64 (2000); Marriage status: 13.8% never married, 77.6% now married, 4.3% widowed, 4.3% divorced (2000); Foreign born: 1.1% (2000); Ancestry (includes multiple ancestries): 39.7% German, 17.9% French (except Basque), 15.1% Other groups, 12.3% Irish, 7.8% English (2000).
Economy: In agricultural area. Employment by occupation: 7.2% management, 12.0% professional, 13.3% services, 30.1% sales, 0.0% farming, 18.1% construction, 19.3% production (2000).
Income: Per capita income: $16,102 (2000); Median household income: $34,375 (2000); Poverty rate: 1.7% (2000).
Taxes: Total city taxes per capita: $52 (1997); City property taxes per capita: $47 (1997).
Education: High school graduation rate: 83.0% (2000); College graduation rate: 5.7% (2000).
Housing: Homeownership rate: 85.2% (2000); Median home value: $74,000 (2000); Median rent: $238 per month (2000); Median age of housing: 60+ years (2000).

Transportation: Commute to work: 95.1% car, 0.0% public transportation, 4.9% walk, 0.0% work from home (2000); Travel time to work: 12.3% less than 15 minutes, 59.3% 15 to 30 minutes, 7.4% 30 to 45 minutes, 12.3% 45 to 60 minutes, 8.6% 60 minutes or more (2000)

Livingston County

Located in east central Illinois; drained by the Vermilion River. Covers a land area of 1,043.80 square miles, a water area of 1.70 square miles, and is located in the Central Time Zone. The county government was organized in 1837. County seat is Pontiac.

Weather Station: Pontiac Elevation: 649 feet

	Jan	Feb	Mar	Apr	May	Jun	Jul	Aug	Sep	Oct	Nov	Dec
High	30	36	48	62	73	82	85	83	77	65	49	36
Low	14	19	29	40	51	61	64	62	54	42	32	21
Precip	1.6	1.4	2.8	3.5	4.0	4.1	4.1	3.6	3.2	2.7	2.9	2.5
Snow	8.9	5.7	3.3	1.0	0.0	0.0	0.0	0.0	0.0	tr	1.7	5.2

High and Low temperatures in degrees Fahrenheit; Precipitation and Snow in inches

Population: 39,678 (2000); Race: 92.0% White, 5.2% Black, 0.2% Asian, 0.2% American Indian and Alaska Native, 2.8% Hispanic of any race, 1.1% two or more races (2000); Density: 38.0 persons per square mile (2000); Age: 25.0% under 18, 15.2% over 64 (2000).
Religion: Five largest groups: 17.7% Catholic Church, 12.6% Evangelical Lutheran Church in America, 11.0% The United Methodist Church, 3.9% American Baptist Churches in the USA, 3.5% Apostolic Christian Church of America, Inc. (2000).
Economy: Unemployment rate: 5.1% (11/2002); Total civilian labor force: 20,321 (11/2002); Leading industries: 37.2% manufacturing; 15.2% retail trade; 12.6% health care and social assistance (2000); Companies that employ more than 1,000 persons: 1 (2000); Companies that employ more than 100 persons: 16 (2000); Farms: 1,380 totaling 613,645 acres (1997); Minority business ownership rate: 0.0% (1997); Women business ownership rate: 30.0% (1997); Retail sales per capita: $8,451 (1997). Single-family building permits issued: 69 (2001) / 83 (2000); Multi-family building permits issued: 0 (2001) / 12 (2000).
Income: Per capita income: $18,347 (2000); Median household income: $41,342 (2000); Poverty rate: 8.8% (2000); Bankruptcy rate: 5.28% (2001).
Taxes: Total county taxes per capita: $79 (1997); County property taxes per capita: $79 (1997).
Education: High school graduation rate: 78.1% (2000); College graduation rate: 12.6% (2000).
Housing: Homeownership rate: 74.2% (2000); Median home value: $79,700 (2000); Median rent: $364 per month (2000); Median age of housing: 45 years (2000).
Health: Birth rate: 111.7 per 10,000 population (1998); Age adjusted death rate: 81.2 per 10,000 population (1999); Age adjusted cancer mortality rate: 191.5 deaths per 100,000 population (1999). Number of physicians: 7.3 per 10,000 population (1999); Number of hospital beds: 20.4 per 10,000 population (1999).
Elections: 2000 Presidential election results: 37.8% Gore, 59.6% Bush, 1.9% Nader, 0.5% Buchanan
Additional Information Contacts
Livingston County Government Offices 815-844-2006
Dwight Area Chamber of Commerce.......... 815-584-2091
Livingston County Board of Realtors 815-842-4123
Pontiac Chamber of Commerce.......... 815-844-5131

Livingston County Communities

ANCONA (unincorporated postal area, zip code 61311). Covers a land area of 28.939 square miles and a water area of 0 square miles. Located at 41.04° N. Lat.; 88.86° W. Long. Elevation is 630 feet.
Population: 353 (2000); Race: 96.8% White, 0.0% Black, 0.0% Asian, 0.0% American Indian and Alaska Native, 7.6% Hispanic of any race, 1.5% two or more races (2000); Density: 12.2 persons per square mile (2000); Age: 28.9% under 18, 15.2% over 64 (2000); Marriage status: 20.3% never married, 69.0% now married, 4.6% widowed, 6.1% divorced (2000); Foreign born: 0.0% (2000); Ancestry (includes multiple ancestries): 29.8% German, 9.4% Irish, 8.5% English, 7.0% Norwegian, 6.7% Slovak (2000).
Economy: Employment by occupation: 18.5% management, 22.2% professional, 8.6% services, 11.1% sales, 1.2% farming, 16.7% construction, 21.6% production (2000).
Income: Per capita income: $23,007 (2000); Median household income: $55,500 (2000); Poverty rate: 11.7% (2000).
Education: High school graduation rate: 80.5% (2000); College graduation rate: 20.3% (2000).
Housing: Homeownership rate: 88.4% (2000); Median home value: $90,300 (2000); Median age of housing: 60+ years (2000).
Transportation: Commute to work: 80.9% car, 0.0% public transportation, 0.0% walk, 19.1% work from home (2000); Travel time to work: 35.1% less than 15 minutes, 35.1% 15 to 30 minutes, 22.1% 30 to 45 minutes, 0.0% 45 to 60 minutes, 7.6% 60 minutes or more (2000)

BLACKSTONE (unincorporated postal area, zip code 61313). Covers a land area of 44.936 square miles and a water area of 0 square miles. Located at 41.06° N. Lat.; 88.66° W. Long. Elevation is 743 feet.
Population: 316 (2000); Race: 95.8% White, 4.2% Black, 0.0% Asian, 0.0% American Indian and Alaska Native, 0.0% Hispanic of any race, 0.0% two or more races (2000); Density: 7.0 persons per square mile (2000); Age: 27.6% under 18, 12.0% over 64 (2000); Marriage status: 20.7% never married, 70.0% now married, 2.1% widowed, 7.1% divorced (2000); Foreign born: 0.3% (2000); Ancestry (includes multiple ancestries): 33.4% German, 12.0% United States or American, 10.3% Irish, 8.4% English, 7.8% Other groups (2000).
Economy: Employment by occupation: 20.9% management, 18.6% professional, 21.9% services, 6.0% sales, 0.5% farming, 10.7% construction, 21.4% production (2000).
Income: Per capita income: $22,553 (2000); Median household income: $59,583 (2000); Poverty rate: 3.3% (2000).
Education: High school graduation rate: 90.9% (2000); College graduation rate: 19.0% (2000).
Housing: Homeownership rate: 81.3% (2000); Median home value: $86,300 (2000); Median rent: $392 per month (2000); Median age of housing: 59 years (2000).
Transportation: Commute to work: 88.2% car, 0.0% public transportation, 3.8% walk, 6.6% work from home (2000); Travel time to work: 23.9% less than 15 minutes, 58.9% 15 to 30 minutes, 8.6% 30 to 45 minutes, 2.5% 45 to 60 minutes, 6.1% 60 minutes or more (2000)

CAMPUS (village). Covers a land area of 0.099 square miles and a water area of 0 square miles. Located at 41.02° N. Lat.; 88.30° W. Long. Elevation is 658 feet.
Population: 145 (2000); Race: 100.0% White, 0.0% Black, 0.0% Asian, 0.0% American Indian and Alaska Native, 0.0% Hispanic of any race, 0.0% two or more races (2000); Density: 1,459.1 persons per square mile (2000); Age: 33.6% under 18, 9.2% over 64 (2000); Marriage status: 29.9% never married, 51.7% now married, 5.7% widowed, 12.6% divorced (2000); Foreign born: 2.5% (2000); Ancestry (includes multiple ancestries): 52.1% United States or American, 20.2% French (except Basque), 17.6% German, 6.7% Irish, 6.7% Polish (2000).
Economy: In agricultural area. Employment by occupation: 1.8% management, 10.7% professional, 21.4% services, 19.6% sales, 0.0% farming, 3.6% construction, 42.9% production (2000).
Income: Per capita income: $19,005 (2000); Median household income: $47,750 (2000); Poverty rate: 3.4% (2000).
Taxes: Total city taxes per capita: $29 (1997); City property taxes per capita: $22 (1997).
Education: High school graduation rate: 83.1% (2000); College graduation rate: 4.2% (2000).
Housing: Homeownership rate: 70.7% (2000); Median home value: $59,400 (2000); Median rent: $350 per month (2000); Median age of housing: 60 years (2000).
Transportation: Commute to work: 91.1% car, 0.0% public transportation, 8.9% walk, 0.0% work from home (2000); Travel time to work: 12.5% less than 15 minutes, 33.9% 15 to 30 minutes, 44.6% 30 to 45 minutes, 8.9% 45 to 60 minutes, 0.0% 60 minutes or more (2000)

CHATSWORTH (town). Covers a land area of 0.895 square miles and a water area of 0 square miles. Located at 40.75° N. Lat.; 88.29° W. Long. Elevation is 735 feet.
History: Chatsworth was laid out in 1858, and devloped as a farming community and manufacturer of tiles and bricks from local clay.
Population: 1,265 (2000); Race: 96.8% White, 0.8% Black, 0.0% Asian, 0.5% American Indian and Alaska Native, 1.0% Hispanic of any race, 1.6% two or more races (2000); Density: 1,412.8 persons per square mile (2000); Age: 26.8% under 18, 18.4% over 64 (2000); Marriage status: 20.7% never married, 53.8% now married, 11.3% widowed, 14.2% divorced (2000); Foreign born: 0.7% (2000); Ancestry (includes multiple ancestries): 39.0% German, 15.7% Irish, 12.4% United States or American, 6.9% Italian, 6.2% Other groups (2000).

Economy: Single-family building permits issued: 0 (2001) / 0 (2000); Multi-family building permits issued: 0 (2001) / 0 (2000); Employment by occupation: 5.8% management, 8.0% professional, 16.7% services, 20.6% sales, 2.0% farming, 11.1% construction, 35.7% production (2000).
Income: Per capita income: $15,241 (2000); Median household income: $32,159 (2000); Poverty rate: 14.1% (2000).
Taxes: Total city taxes per capita: $53 (1997); City property taxes per capita: $52 (1997).
Education: High school graduation rate: 79.9% (2000); College graduation rate: 8.7% (2000).
Housing: Homeownership rate: 72.1% (2000); Median home value: $59,500 (2000); Median rent: $263 per month (2000); Median age of housing: 57 years (2000).
Transportation: Commute to work: 94.1% car, 0.0% public transportation, 2.4% walk, 1.4% work from home (2000); Travel time to work: 49.8% less than 15 minutes, 14.7% 15 to 30 minutes, 16.1% 30 to 45 minutes, 10.8% 45 to 60 minutes, 8.6% 60 minutes or more (2000)

CORNELL (village). Covers a land area of 0.636 square miles and a water area of 0 square miles. Located at 40.99° N. Lat.; 88.73° W. Long. Elevation is 638 feet.
Population: 511 (2000); Race: 98.2% White, 0.0% Black, 0.0% Asian, 0.0% American Indian and Alaska Native, 3.6% Hispanic of any race, 0.0% two or more races (2000); Density: 803.8 persons per square mile (2000); Age: 26.9% under 18, 12.4% over 64 (2000); Marriage status: 24.5% never married, 60.7% now married, 6.1% widowed, 8.8% divorced (2000); Foreign born: 0.7% (2000); Ancestry (includes multiple ancestries): 38.0% German, 10.4% United States or American, 9.9% English, 9.3% Other groups, 9.1% Irish (2000).
Economy: In agricultural area. Single-family building permits issued: 0 (2001) / 3 (2000); Multi-family building permits issued: 0 (2001) / 0 (2000); Employment by occupation: 3.4% management, 10.1% professional, 18.5% services, 22.2% sales, 1.7% farming, 10.1% construction, 34.0% production (2000).
Income: Per capita income: $18,655 (2000); Median household income: $45,313 (2000); Poverty rate: 8.8% (2000).
Taxes: Total city taxes per capita: $56 (1997); City property taxes per capita: $34 (1997).
Education: High school graduation rate: 83.8% (2000); College graduation rate: 8.4% (2000).

School District(s)

Cornell C C School District 426 (KG-08)
2000 Enrollment: 153 815-358-2216
Housing: Homeownership rate: 77.0% (2000); Median home value: $59,800 (2000); Median rent: $306 per month (2000); Median age of housing: 41 years (2000).
Transportation: Commute to work: 91.0% car, 1.4% public transportation, 6.6% walk, 0.7% work from home (2000); Travel time to work: 21.5% less than 15 minutes, 57.6% 15 to 30 minutes, 4.9% 30 to 45 minutes, 7.3% 45 to 60 minutes, 8.7% 60 minutes or more (2000)

CULLOM (village). Covers a land area of 0.308 square miles and a water area of 0 square miles. Located at 40.87° N. Lat.; 88.26° W. Long. Elevation is 689 feet.
Population: 563 (2000); Race: 99.6% White, 0.0% Black, 0.0% Asian, 0.0% American Indian and Alaska Native, 0.4% Hispanic of any race, 0.4% two or more races (2000); Density: 1,827.0 persons per square mile (2000); Age: 26.9% under 18, 23.4% over 64 (2000); Marriage status: 18.0% never married, 63.2% now married, 10.0% widowed, 8.7% divorced (2000); Foreign born: 0.4% (2000); Ancestry (includes multiple ancestries): 34.2% German, 13.7% Irish, 13.0% English, 10.7% United States or American, 4.8% Other groups (2000).
Economy: In agricultural area. Single-family building permits issued: 0 (2001) / 0 (2000); Multi-family building permits issued: 0 (2001) / 0 (2000); Employment by occupation: 6.8% management, 11.0% professional, 18.6% services, 27.0% sales, 1.1% farming, 12.5% construction, 22.8% production (2000).
Income: Per capita income: $17,207 (2000); Median household income: $31,042 (2000); Poverty rate: 5.3% (2000).
Taxes: Total city taxes per capita: $57 (2000); City property taxes per capita: $53 (2000).
Education: High school graduation rate: 84.6% (2000); College graduation rate: 9.1% (2000).
Housing: Homeownership rate: 80.2% (2000); Median home value: $69,300 (2000); Median rent: $275 per month (2000); Median age of housing: 55 years (2000).
Transportation: Commute to work: 85.9% car, 0.0% public transportation, 9.4% walk, 3.9% work from home (2000); Travel time to work: 43.5% less than 15 minutes, 17.5% 15 to 30 minutes, 20.3% 30 to 45 minutes, 11.0% 45 to 60 minutes, 7.7% 60 minutes or more (2000)

DWIGHT (village). Covers a land area of 2.574 square miles and a water area of 0.008 square miles. Located at 41.09° N. Lat.; 88.42° W. Long. Elevation is 640 feet.
History: In Dwight, Dr. Leslie Keeley, a Civil War surgeon, established the Keeley Institute for the treatment of alcoholism and drug addiction, and achieved much success and acclaim.
Population: 4,363 (2000); Race: 95.4% White, 0.7% Black, 0.6% Asian, 0.2% American Indian and Alaska Native, 3.5% Hispanic of any race, 1.8% two or more races (2000); Density: 1,694.8 persons per square mile (2000); Age: 26.6% under 18, 15.2% over 64 (2000); Marriage status: 23.0% never married, 58.8% now married, 7.8% widowed, 10.5% divorced (2000); Foreign born: 1.9% (2000); Ancestry (includes multiple ancestries): 30.8% German, 19.4% Irish, 8.3% United States or American, 7.2% Danish, 6.8% English (2000).
Economy: Single-family building permits issued: 8 (2001) / 20 (2000); Multi-family building permits issued: 0 (2001) / 0 (2000); Employment by occupation: 8.1% management, 16.2% professional, 17.5% services, 21.7% sales, 0.0% farming, 12.4% construction, 24.1% production (2000).
Income: Per capita income: $20,928 (2000); Median household income: $40,071 (2000); Poverty rate: 10.8% (2000).
Taxes: Total city taxes per capita: $126 (1997); City property taxes per capita: $54 (1997).
Education: High school graduation rate: 80.3% (2000); College graduation rate: 11.0% (2000).

School District(s)

Dwight Common School District 232 (PK-08)
2000 Enrollment: 729 815-584-2950
Dwight Township H S District 230 (09-12)
2000 Enrollment: 308 815-584-2950
Housing: Homeownership rate: 71.6% (2000); Median home value: $94,100 (2000); Median rent: $409 per month (2000); Median age of housing: 43 years (2000).
Newspapers: Star Regional (1 x week); Courier-Press (1 x week); Gardner Chronicle (1 x week); Dwight Star & Herald (1 x week)
Transportation: Commute to work: 93.4% car, 1.1% public transportation, 4.3% walk, 1.3% work from home (2000); Travel time to work: 55.9% less than 15 minutes, 12.7% 15 to 30 minutes, 15.6% 30 to 45 minutes, 6.4% 45 to 60 minutes, 9.4% 60 minutes or more (2000); Amtrak: Service available.
Additional Information Contacts
Dwight Area Chamber of Commerce. 815-584-2091

EMINGTON (village). Covers a land area of 0.101 square miles and a water area of 0 square miles. Located at 40.97° N. Lat.; 88.35° W. Long. Elevation is 717 feet.
Population: 120 (2000); Race: 100.0% White, 0.0% Black, 0.0% Asian, 0.0% American Indian and Alaska Native, 0.0% Hispanic of any race, 0.0% two or more races (2000); Density: 1,184.7 persons per square mile (2000); Age: 38.3% under 18, 10.2% over 64 (2000); Marriage status: 21.6% never married, 56.8% now married, 10.2% widowed, 11.4% divorced (2000); Foreign born: 0.0% (2000); Ancestry (includes multiple ancestries): 43.8% United States or American, 19.5% German, 8.6% Irish, 8.6% Other groups, 6.3% English (2000).
Economy: In agricultural area. Single-family building permits issued: 0 (2001) / 0 (2000); Multi-family building permits issued: 0 (2001) / 0 (2000); Employment by occupation: 0.0% management, 19.1% professional, 8.5% services, 21.3% sales, 0.0% farming, 25.5% construction, 25.5% production (2000).
Income: Per capita income: $12,183 (2000); Median household income: $30,417 (2000); Poverty rate: 12.5% (2000).
Taxes: Total city taxes per capita: $39 (1997); City property taxes per capita: $39 (1997).
Education: High school graduation rate: 80.0% (2000); College graduation rate: 3.1% (2000).
Housing: Homeownership rate: 79.5% (2000); Median home value: $57,200 (2000); Median rent: $400 per month (2000); Median age of housing: 60+ years (2000).
Transportation: Commute to work: 93.6% car, 0.0% public transportation, 0.0% walk, 6.4% work from home (2000); Travel time to work: 0.0% less than 15 minutes, 34.1% 15 to 30 minutes, 25.0% 30 to 45 minutes, 6.8% 45 to 60 minutes, 34.1% 60 minutes or more (2000)

FAIRBURY (city). Covers a land area of 1.297 square miles and a water area of 0 square miles. Located at 40.74° N. Lat.; 88.51° W. Long. Elevation is 689 feet.
History: Incorporated 1890.
Population: 3,968 (2000); Race: 96.3% White, 0.0% Black, 0.0% Asian, 0.1% American Indian and Alaska Native, 4.2% Hispanic of any race, 0.9% two or more races (2000); Density: 3,060.1 persons per square mile (2000); Age: 26.0% under 18, 22.0% over 64 (2000); Marriage status: 20.4% never married, 66.3% now married, 7.4% widowed, 6.0% divorced (2000); Foreign born: 1.1% (2000); Ancestry (includes multiple ancestries): 36.4% German, 17.6% United States or American, 14.0% Irish, 9.3% English, 7.8% Other groups (2000).
Economy: In agricultural area; corn, wheat, soybeans, livestock, poultry; dairy products. Manufacturing: clothing. Gravel pits. Single-family building permits issued: 4 (2001) / 6 (2000); Multi-family building permits issued: 0 (2001) / 2 (2000); Employment by occupation: 11.0% management, 17.5% professional, 18.6% services, 18.6% sales, 1.1% farming, 9.2% construction, 23.9% production (2000).
Income: Per capita income: $19,145 (2000); Median household income: $41,298 (2000); Poverty rate: 4.9% (2000).
Taxes: Total city taxes per capita: $82 (1997); City property taxes per capita: $79 (1997).
Education: High school graduation rate: 78.2% (2000); College graduation rate: 15.4% (2000).
Housing: Homeownership rate: 69.6% (2000); Median home value: $85,700 (2000); Median rent: $383 per month (2000); Median age of housing: 41 years (2000).
Newspapers: The Blade (1 x week)
Transportation: Commute to work: 91.2% car, 0.8% public transportation, 4.4% walk, 3.3% work from home (2000); Travel time to work: 46.4% less than 15 minutes, 25.2% 15 to 30 minutes, 11.6% 30 to 45 minutes, 11.8% 45 to 60 minutes, 5.0% 60 minutes or more (2000)

FLANAGAN (village). Covers a land area of 0.534 square miles and a water area of 0 square miles. Located at 40.87° N. Lat.; 88.85° W. Long. Elevation is 666 feet.
Population: 1,083 (2000); Race: 97.9% White, 0.1% Black, 0.7% Asian, 0.0% American Indian and Alaska Native, 0.6% Hispanic of any race, 0.8% two or more races (2000); Density: 2,028.8 persons per square mile (2000); Age: 21.7% under 18, 25.5% over 64 (2000); Marriage status: 14.9% never married, 65.0% now married, 12.8% widowed, 7.3% divorced (2000); Foreign born: 1.4% (2000); Ancestry (includes multiple ancestries): 39.9% German, 11.2% English, 10.5% Irish, 9.5% United States or American, 3.8% Dutch (2000).
Economy: In agricultural area; grain, dairy products, poultry. Single-family building permits issued: 1 (2001) / 3 (2000); Multi-family building permits issued: 0 (2001) / 0 (2000); Employment by occupation: 10.0% management, 17.4% professional, 19.2% services, 26.7% sales, 1.3% farming, 6.4% construction, 19.1% production (2000).
Income: Per capita income: $19,767 (2000); Median household income: $39,479 (2000); Poverty rate: 4.9% (2000).
Taxes: Total city taxes per capita: $23 (1997); City property taxes per capita: $22 (1997).
Education: High school graduation rate: 87.9% (2000); College graduation rate: 19.7% (2000).

School District(s)

Flanagan C U School District 4 (PK-12)
2000 Enrollment: 464 815-796-2233
Housing: Homeownership rate: 75.7% (2000); Median home value: $79,500 (2000); Median rent: $406 per month (2000); Median age of housing: 45 years (2000).
Transportation: Commute to work: 91.5% car, 0.6% public transportation, 4.8% walk, 1.9% work from home (2000); Travel time to work: 40.3% less than 15 minutes, 43.1% 15 to 30 minutes, 7.2% 30 to 45 minutes, 6.4% 45 to 60 minutes, 3.0% 60 minutes or more (2000)

FORREST (village). Covers a land area of 0.626 square miles and a water area of 0 square miles. Located at 40.75° N. Lat.; 88.41° W. Long. Elevation is 688 feet.
History: Forrest was settled in 1836, but grew in the 1860's when German-Amish immigrants arrived.
Population: 1,225 (2000); Race: 95.3% White, 1.4% Black, 0.2% Asian, 1.0% American Indian and Alaska Native, 4.1% Hispanic of any race, 0.9% two or more races (2000); Density: 1,956.4 persons per square mile (2000); Age: 30.4% under 18, 16.5% over 64 (2000); Marriage status: 20.6% never married, 61.7% now married, 8.9% widowed, 8.9% divorced (2000); Foreign born: 2.6% (2000); Ancestry (includes multiple ancestries): 29.7% German, 13.6% Irish, 9.4% English, 8.7% Other groups, 8.3% United States or American (2000).
Economy: Single-family building permits issued: 2 (2001) / 1 (2000); Multi-family building permits issued: 0 (2001) / 0 (2000); Employment by occupation: 10.5% management, 16.2% professional, 15.5% services, 22.4% sales, 0.9% farming, 9.8% construction, 24.8% production (2000).
Income: Per capita income: $17,707 (2000); Median household income: $40,677 (2000); Poverty rate: 8.9% (2000).
Taxes: Total city taxes per capita: $154 (1997); City property taxes per capita: $128 (1997).
Education: High school graduation rate: 78.5% (2000); College graduation rate: 14.8% (2000).

School District(s)

Prairie Central C U School District 8 (PK-12)
2000 Enrollment: 2,077 815-657-8237
Housing: Homeownership rate: 73.8% (2000); Median home value: $71,600 (2000); Median rent: $344 per month (2000); Median age of housing: 52 years (2000).
Transportation: Commute to work: 95.1% car, 0.0% public transportation, 2.3% walk, 1.4% work from home (2000); Travel time to work: 51.8% less than 15 minutes, 19.0% 15 to 30 minutes, 11.2% 30 to 45 minutes, 10.0% 45 to 60 minutes, 8.0% 60 minutes or more (2000)

GRAYMONT (unincorporated postal area, zip code 61743). Covers a land area of 15.916 square miles and a water area of 0 square miles. Located at 40.87° N. Lat.; 88.77° W. Long. Elevation is 661 feet.
Population: 270 (2000); Race: 100.0% White, 0.0% Black, 0.0% Asian, 0.0% American Indian and Alaska Native, 0.0% Hispanic of any race, 0.0% two or more races (2000); Density: 17.0 persons per square mile (2000); Age: 32.2% under 18, 11.4% over 64 (2000); Marriage status: 21.7% never married, 59.3% now married, 5.8% widowed, 13.2% divorced (2000); Foreign born: 0.0% (2000); Ancestry (includes multiple ancestries): 44.7% German, 15.7% English, 14.1% United States or American, 9.4% Irish, 3.9% Scotch-Irish (2000).
Economy: Employment by occupation: 13.1% management, 12.4% professional, 25.5% services, 19.0% sales, 0.0% farming, 13.1% construction, 16.8% production (2000).
Income: Per capita income: $16,810 (2000); Median household income: $41,250 (2000); Poverty rate: 9.9% (2000).
Education: High school graduation rate: 90.0% (2000); College graduation rate: 14.7% (2000).

School District(s)

Rooks Creek C C School District 425 (KG-08)
2000 Enrollment: 60 815-743-5346
Housing: Homeownership rate: 71.0% (2000); Median home value: $49,200 (2000); Median rent: $332 per month (2000); Median age of housing: 60+ years (2000).
Transportation: Commute to work: 82.8% car, 0.0% public transportation, 6.7% walk, 9.7% work from home (2000); Travel time to work: 50.4% less than 15 minutes, 25.6% 15 to 30 minutes, 9.9% 30 to 45 minutes, 9.1% 45 to 60 minutes, 5.0% 60 minutes or more (2000)

LONG POINT (village). Covers a land area of 0.188 square miles and a water area of 0 square miles. Located at 41.00° N. Lat.; 88.89° W. Long. Elevation is 643 feet.
Population: 247 (2000); Race: 96.1% White, 0.0% Black, 0.0% Asian, 3.9% American Indian and Alaska Native, 0.0% Hispanic of any race, 0.0% two or more races (2000); Density: 1,313.8 persons per square mile (2000); Age: 29.6% under 18, 14.4% over 64 (2000); Marriage status: 26.9% never married, 59.6% now married, 5.3% widowed, 8.2% divorced (2000); Foreign born: 0.8% (2000); Ancestry (includes multiple ancestries): 39.7% German, 14.4% English, 14.0% Other groups, 8.6% United States or American, 8.2% Irish (2000).
Economy: In agricultural area. Employment by occupation: 14.6% management, 7.7% professional, 20.0% services, 17.7% sales, 0.0% farming, 16.9% construction, 23.1% production (2000).
Income: Per capita income: $16,416 (2000); Median household income: $45,625 (2000); Poverty rate: 6.6% (2000).
Taxes: Total city taxes per capita: $23 (1997); City property taxes per capita: $19 (1997).
Education: High school graduation rate: 82.2% (2000); College graduation rate: 6.1% (2000).

Housing: Homeownership rate: 90.5% (2000); Median home value: $51,700 (2000); Median rent: $263 per month (2000); Median age of housing: 60+ years (2000).
Transportation: Commute to work: 91.8% car, 0.0% public transportation, 2.5% walk, 5.7% work from home (2000); Travel time to work: 16.5% less than 15 minutes, 67.0% 15 to 30 minutes, 7.0% 30 to 45 minutes, 1.7% 45 to 60 minutes, 7.8% 60 minutes or more (2000)

ODELL (village). Covers a land area of 1.115 square miles and a water area of 0.014 square miles. Located at 41.00° N. Lat.; 88.52° W. Long. Elevation is 720 feet.
Population: 1,014 (2000); Race: 96.6% White, 1.7% Black, 0.0% Asian, 0.0% American Indian and Alaska Native, 2.1% Hispanic of any race, 1.1% two or more races (2000); Density: 909.0 persons per square mile (2000); Age: 29.7% under 18, 13.9% over 64 (2000); Marriage status: 21.0% never married, 61.3% now married, 5.1% widowed, 12.6% divorced (2000); Foreign born: 0.9% (2000); Ancestry (includes multiple ancestries): 36.2% German, 24.3% Irish, 12.2% English, 7.7% United States or American, 6.3% French (except Basque) (2000).
Economy: In agricultural area. Manufacturing of clothing. Single-family building permits issued: 1 (2001) / 1 (2000); Multi-family building permits issued: 0 (2001) / 0 (2000); Employment by occupation: 7.6% management, 18.0% professional, 17.3% services, 22.0% sales, 1.0% farming, 11.6% construction, 22.4% production (2000).
Income: Per capita income: $18,538 (2000); Median household income: $41,346 (2000); Poverty rate: 8.9% (2000).
Taxes: Total city taxes per capita: $40 (1997); City property taxes per capita: $39 (1997).
Education: High school graduation rate: 86.3% (2000); College graduation rate: 11.8% (2000).

School District(s)

Odell Community Cons School District 435 (PK-08)
2000 Enrollment: 143 815-998-2272

Housing: Homeownership rate: 79.7% (2000); Median home value: $82,600 (2000); Median rent: $402 per month (2000); Median age of housing: 49 years (2000).
Transportation: Commute to work: 97.1% car, 0.0% public transportation, 1.3% walk, 1.3% work from home (2000); Travel time to work: 31.8% less than 15 minutes, 45.6% 15 to 30 minutes, 5.7% 30 to 45 minutes, 8.9% 45 to 60 minutes, 8.1% 60 minutes or more (2000)

PONTIAC (city). Covers a land area of 5.243 square miles and a water area of 0.010 square miles. Located at 40.88° N. Lat.; 88.63° W. Long. Elevation is 642 feet.
History: Pontiac was founded in 1837 and named for the Ottawa Chief Pontiac. Jesse W. Fell was a leader in the development of Pontiac, and chose the name for the town. Pontiac developed as the seat of Livingston County.
Population: 11,864 (2000); Race: 85.2% White, 10.7% Black, 0.2% Asian, 0.2% American Indian and Alaska Native, 3.6% Hispanic of any race, 1.5% two or more races (2000); Density: 2,263.0 persons per square mile (2000); Age: 22.9% under 18, 13.4% over 64 (2000); Marriage status: 18.3% never married, 60.5% now married, 6.8% widowed, 14.4% divorced (2000); Foreign born: 2.3% (2000); Ancestry (includes multiple ancestries): 26.1% German, 14.7% Irish, 10.1% United States or American, 9.7% English, 7.0% Other groups (2000).
Vital Statistics: Birth rate: 129.0 per 10,000 population (1998)
Economy: Single-family building permits issued: 13 (2001) / 17 (2000); Multi-family building permits issued: 0 (2001) / 10 (2000); Employment by occupation: 7.6% management, 14.9% professional, 21.5% services, 23.3% sales, 0.3% farming, 7.7% construction, 24.7% production (2000).
Income: Per capita income: $16,863 (2000); Median household income: $37,593 (2000); Poverty rate: 11.7% (2000).
Taxes: Total city taxes per capita: $178 (1997); City property taxes per capita: $174 (1997).
Education: High school graduation rate: 74.7% (2000); College graduation rate: 13.8% (2000).

School District(s)

Livingston Co Special Services Unit (01-11)
2000 Enrollment: 39 815-844-7115
Pontiac C C School District 429 (PK-08)
2000 Enrollment: 1,447 815-844-5632
Pontiac Township H S District 90 (09-12)
2000 Enrollment: 814 815-844-6113

Housing: Homeownership rate: 66.7% (2000); Median home value: $73,800 (2000); Median rent: $360 per month (2000); Median age of housing: 40 years (2000).
Hospitals: Saint James Hospital (89 beds)
Newspapers: The Daily Leader (6 x week)
Transportation: Commute to work: 89.4% car, 1.7% public transportation, 4.7% walk, 3.4% work from home (2000); Travel time to work: 71.4% less than 15 minutes, 12.6% 15 to 30 minutes, 7.8% 30 to 45 minutes, 4.1% 45 to 60 minutes, 4.1% 60 minutes or more (2000); Amtrak: Service available.
Airports: Pontiac Municipal
Additional Information Contacts
Livingston County Board of Realtors 815-842-4123
Pontiac Chamber of Commerce 815-844-5131

SAUNEMIN (village). Covers a land area of 0.223 square miles and a water area of 0 square miles. Located at 40.89° N. Lat.; 88.40° W. Long. Elevation is 690 feet.
Population: 456 (2000); Race: 98.8% White, 0.2% Black, 0.0% Asian, 0.0% American Indian and Alaska Native, 1.2% Hispanic of any race, 1.0% two or more races (2000); Density: 2,045.9 persons per square mile (2000); Age: 36.2% under 18, 8.3% over 64 (2000); Marriage status: 27.5% never married, 55.6% now married, 3.8% widowed, 13.0% divorced (2000); Foreign born: 0.2% (2000); Ancestry (includes multiple ancestries): 32.9% German, 14.5% English, 12.7% United States or American, 12.3% Irish, 4.6% French (except Basque) (2000).
Economy: In agricultural area. Employment by occupation: 8.5% management, 4.0% professional, 23.6% services, 19.6% sales, 0.0% farming, 10.1% construction, 34.2% production (2000).
Income: Per capita income: $15,439 (2000); Median household income: $45,536 (2000); Poverty rate: 6.5% (2000).
Taxes: Total city taxes per capita: $82 (1997); City property taxes per capita: $30 (1997).
Education: High school graduation rate: 86.1% (2000); College graduation rate: 8.0% (2000).

School District(s)

Saunemin C Consol School District 438 (PK-08)
2000 Enrollment: 187 815-832-4421

Housing: Homeownership rate: 81.2% (2000); Median home value: $62,400 (2000); Median rent: $315 per month (2000); Median age of housing: 60+ years (2000).
Transportation: Commute to work: 95.9% car, 0.0% public transportation, 1.0% walk, 3.1% work from home (2000); Travel time to work: 9.5% less than 15 minutes, 67.4% 15 to 30 minutes, 5.3% 30 to 45 minutes, 6.8% 45 to 60 minutes, 11.1% 60 minutes or more (2000)

STRAWN (village). Covers a land area of 0.142 square miles and a water area of 0 square miles. Located at 40.65° N. Lat.; 88.39° W. Long. Elevation is 767 feet.
Population: 104 (2000); Race: 99.1% White, 0.0% Black, 0.0% Asian, 0.0% American Indian and Alaska Native, 0.0% Hispanic of any race, 0.9% two or more races (2000); Density: 732.5 persons per square mile (2000); Age: 34.8% under 18, 7.8% over 64 (2000); Marriage status: 19.5% never married, 61.0% now married, 8.5% widowed, 11.0% divorced (2000); Foreign born: 0.0% (2000); Ancestry (includes multiple ancestries): 32.2% United States or American, 21.7% Irish, 13.0% German, 13.0% Dutch, 2.6% English (2000).
Economy: In agricultural area. Employment by occupation: 1.6% management, 6.6% professional, 26.2% services, 19.7% sales, 3.3% farming, 14.8% construction, 27.9% production (2000).
Income: Per capita income: $14,424 (2000); Median household income: $35,625 (2000); Poverty rate: 2.6% (2000).
Taxes: Total city taxes per capita: $53 (1997); City property taxes per capita: $38 (1997).
Education: High school graduation rate: 84.7% (2000); College graduation rate: 3.4% (2000).
Housing: Homeownership rate: 89.1% (2000); Median home value: $37,300 (2000); Median rent: $275 per month (2000); Median age of housing: 60+ years (2000).
Transportation: Commute to work: 83.3% car, 0.0% public transportation, 0.0% walk, 13.3% work from home (2000); Travel time to work: 0.0% less than 15 minutes, 53.8% 15 to 30 minutes, 23.1% 30 to 45 minutes, 23.1% 45 to 60 minutes, 0.0% 60 minutes or more (2000)

Logan County

Located in central Illinois; drained by Salt and Kickapoo Creeks. Covers a land area of 618.10 square miles, a water area of 0.90 square miles, and is located in the Central Time Zone. The county government was organized in 1839. County seat is Lincoln.

Weather Station: Lincoln Elevation: 580 feet

	Jan	Feb	Mar	Apr	May	Jun	Jul	Aug	Sep	Oct	Nov	Dec
High	32	39	51	64	75	83	86	84	78	67	51	39
Low	15	21	31	41	52	61	65	63	54	42	32	22
Precip	1.7	1.5	3.1	3.8	4.6	4.0	4.2	4.0	3.2	2.9	3.0	2.6
Snow	6.6	4.8	2.1	0.6	0.0	0.0	0.0	0.0	0.0	tr	1.2	4.6

High and Low temperatures in degrees Fahrenheit; Precipitation and Snow in inches

Population: 31,183 (2000); Race: 92.3% White, 6.1% Black, 0.6% Asian, 0.1% American Indian and Alaska Native, 1.6% Hispanic of any race, 0.5% two or more races (2000); Density: 50.4 persons per square mile (2000); Age: 21.9% under 18, 14.9% over 64 (2000).
Religion: Five largest groups: 15.4% Christian Churches and Churches of Christ, 12.4% Catholic Church, 7.5% The United Methodist Church, 7.1% Lutheran Church—Missouri Synod, 6.1% Evangelical Lutheran Church in America (2000).
Economy: Unemployment rate: 6.9% (11/2002); Total civilian labor force: 12,739 (11/2002); Leading industries: 17.2% manufacturing; 15.8% health care and social assistance; 14.0% retail trade (2000); Companies that employ more than 1,000 persons: 0 (2000); Companies that employ more than 100 persons: 17 (2000); Farms: 739 totaling 380,921 acres (1997); Minority business ownership rate: 0.0% (1997); Women business ownership rate: 35.0% (1997); Retail sales per capita: $7,574 (1997). Single-family building permits issued: 35 (2001) / 25 (2000); Multi-family building permits issued: 3 (2001) / 2 (2000).
Income: Per capita income: $17,953 (2000); Median household income: $39,389 (2000); Poverty rate: 8.1% (2000); Bankruptcy rate: 6.38% (2001).
Taxes: Total county taxes per capita: $85 (1997); County property taxes per capita: $83 (1997).
Education: High school graduation rate: 80.4% (2000); College graduation rate: 14.2% (2000).
Housing: Homeownership rate: 71.3% (2000); Median home value: $75,700 (2000); Median rent: $345 per month (2000); Median age of housing: 45 years (2000).
Health: Birth rate: 114.5 per 10,000 population (1998); Age adjusted death rate: 88.3 per 10,000 population (1999); Age adjusted cancer mortality rate: 219.8 deaths per 100,000 population (1999). Number of physicians: 7.7 per 10,000 population (1999); Number of hospital beds: 163.6 per 10,000 population (1999).
Elections: 2000 Presidential election results: 35.2% Gore, 62.3% Bush, 1.6% Nader, 0.6% Buchanan
National and State Parks: Railsplitter State Park
Additional Information Contacts
Logan County Government Offices 217-732-6400
Lincoln Chamber of Commerce 217-735-2385
Logan County Board of Realtors 217-732-8172

Logan County Communities

ATLANTA (city). Covers a land area of 1.258 square miles and a water area of 0.008 square miles. Located at 40.26° N. Lat.; 89.23° W. Long. Elevation is 720 feet.
History: Atlanta came into existence when the Chicago & Mississippi Railroad placed its tracks a mile away from the village of Newcastle, and the village moved to the railroad. The railroad station had been named Zenia, but town and railroad adopted the name of Atlanta in 1855.
Population: 1,649 (2000); Race: 99.1% White, 0.2% Black, 0.0% Asian, 0.1% American Indian and Alaska Native, 1.0% Hispanic of any race, 0.4% two or more races (2000); Density: 1,310.5 persons per square mile (2000); Age: 24.2% under 18, 14.8% over 64 (2000); Marriage status: 20.5% never married, 62.1% now married, 7.6% widowed, 9.9% divorced (2000); Foreign born: 0.1% (2000); Ancestry (includes multiple ancestries): 28.9% German, 12.3% Irish, 12.3% United States or American, 11.2% English, 5.6% Other groups (2000).
Economy: Single-family building permits issued: 11 (2001) / 5 (2000); Multi-family building permits issued: 3 (2001) / 2 (2000); Employment by occupation: 9.7% management, 12.6% professional, 15.5% services, 25.1% sales, 1.2% farming, 12.6% construction, 23.4% production (2000).
Income: Per capita income: $20,460 (2000); Median household income: $43,194 (2000); Poverty rate: 4.4% (2000).
Taxes: Total city taxes per capita: $99 (1997); City property taxes per capita: $41 (1997).
Education: High school graduation rate: 84.5% (2000); College graduation rate: 14.4% (2000).
Housing: Homeownership rate: 79.9% (2000); Median home value: $79,300 (2000); Median rent: $371 per month (2000); Median age of housing: 43 years (2000).
Transportation: Commute to work: 96.0% car, 0.4% public transportation, 0.5% walk, 2.7% work from home (2000); Travel time to work: 24.0% less than 15 minutes, 33.1% 15 to 30 minutes, 30.0% 30 to 45 minutes, 6.2% 45 to 60 minutes, 6.7% 60 minutes or more (2000)

BEASON (unincorporated postal area, zip code 62512). Covers a land area of 43.004 square miles and a water area of 0.004 square miles. Located at 40.13° N. Lat.; 89.20° W. Long. Elevation is 640 feet.
Population: 552 (2000); Race: 100.0% White, 0.0% Black, 0.0% Asian, 0.0% American Indian and Alaska Native, 0.9% Hispanic of any race, 0.0% two or more races (2000); Density: 12.8 persons per square mile (2000); Age: 28.7% under 18, 13.0% over 64 (2000); Marriage status: 18.6% never married, 71.6% now married, 4.4% widowed, 5.3% divorced (2000); Foreign born: 0.0% (2000); Ancestry (includes multiple ancestries): 37.8% German, 21.8% Irish, 17.3% United States or American, 13.4% Other groups, 10.6% English (2000).
Economy: Employment by occupation: 2.8% management, 21.2% professional, 14.2% services, 12.2% sales, 7.6% farming, 2.4% construction, 39.6% production (2000).
Income: Per capita income: $19,329 (2000); Median household income: $57,875 (2000); Poverty rate: 1.7% (2000).
Education: High school graduation rate: 91.6% (2000); College graduation rate: 12.8% (2000).
Housing: Homeownership rate: 83.5% (2000); Median home value: $77,100 (2000); Median rent: $198 per month (2000); Median age of housing: 59 years (2000).
Transportation: Commute to work: 98.6% car, 0.0% public transportation, 0.0% walk, 1.4% work from home (2000); Travel time to work: 11.3% less than 15 minutes, 38.7% 15 to 30 minutes, 12.7% 30 to 45 minutes, 16.1% 45 to 60 minutes, 21.2% 60 minutes or more (2000)

BROADWELL (village). Covers a land area of 0.191 square miles and a water area of 0 square miles. Located at 40.06° N. Lat.; 89.44° W. Long. Elevation is 585 feet.
Population: 169 (2000); Race: 95.8% White, 2.4% Black, 0.0% Asian, 0.0% American Indian and Alaska Native, 1.8% Hispanic of any race, 0.0% two or more races (2000); Density: 884.2 persons per square mile (2000); Age: 25.0% under 18, 10.1% over 64 (2000); Marriage status: 27.8% never married, 58.7% now married, 8.7% widowed, 4.8% divorced (2000); Foreign born: 0.0% (2000); Ancestry (includes multiple ancestries): 33.3% German, 30.4% United States or American, 10.7% Irish, 8.9% French (except Basque), 4.8% Other groups (2000).
Economy: In agricultural area: corn, soybeans; cattle, hogs; bituminous coal. Single-family building permits issued: 1 (2001) / 0 (2000); Multi-family building permits issued: 0 (2001) / 0 (2000); Employment by occupation: 6.8% management, 19.3% professional, 30.7% services, 17.0% sales, 0.0% farming, 8.0% construction, 18.2% production (2000).
Income: Per capita income: $19,911 (2000); Median household income: $40,000 (2000); Poverty rate: 8.5% (2000).
Education: High school graduation rate: 93.1% (2000); College graduation rate: 13.7% (2000).
Housing: Homeownership rate: 81.9% (2000); Median home value: $57,500 (2000); Median rent: $318 per month (2000); Median age of housing: 60+ years (2000).
Transportation: Commute to work: 92.0% car, 0.0% public transportation, 1.1% walk, 6.8% work from home (2000); Travel time to work: 47.6% less than 15 minutes, 26.8% 15 to 30 minutes, 17.1% 30 to 45 minutes, 4.9% 45 to 60 minutes, 3.7% 60 minutes or more (2000)

CHESTNUT (unincorporated postal area, zip code 62518). Covers a land area of 24.895 square miles and a water area of 0.025 square miles. Located at 40.05° N. Lat.; 89.18° W. Long. Elevation is 620 feet.
Population: 468 (2000); Race: 100.0% White, 0.0% Black, 0.0% Asian, 0.0% American Indian and Alaska Native, 0.0% Hispanic of any race, 0.0% two or more races (2000); Density: 18.8 persons per square mile (2000); Age: 21.2% under 18, 14.5% over 64 (2000); Marriage status: 21.5% never married, 71.0% now married, 3.5% widowed, 4.0% divorced (2000); Foreign born: 1.1% (2000); Ancestry (includes multiple ancestries): 37.8% German, 22.5% Irish, 12.3% Other groups, 7.6% English, 6.0% Dutch (2000).
Economy: Employment by occupation: 13.8% management, 16.3% professional, 21.1% services, 27.6% sales, 5.3% farming, 8.5% construction, 7.3% production (2000).

Income: Per capita income: $17,836 (2000); Median household income: $45,288 (2000); Poverty rate: 0.0% (2000).
Education: High school graduation rate: 87.8% (2000); College graduation rate: 23.1% (2000).
Housing: Homeownership rate: 85.6% (2000); Median home value: $62,500 (2000); Median rent: $359 per month (2000); Median age of housing: 60+ years (2000).
Transportation: Commute to work: 100.0% car, 0.0% public transportation, 0.0% walk, 0.0% work from home (2000); Travel time to work: 23.2% less than 15 minutes, 29.9% 15 to 30 minutes, 24.5% 30 to 45 minutes, 12.4% 45 to 60 minutes, 10.0% 60 minutes or more (2000)

ELKHART (village). Aka Elk Hart City. Covers a land area of 1.458 square miles and a water area of 0.008 square miles. Located at 40.02° N. Lat.; 89.48° W. Long. Elevation is 592 feet.
History: Elkhart was the home of Richard J. Oglesby (1824-1899), a man of many occupations (farmer, carpenter, ropemaker, lawyer, miner, soldier) who served three times as the governor of Illinois, and as a U.S. senator.
Population: 443 (2000); Race: 100.0% White, 0.0% Black, 0.0% Asian, 0.0% American Indian and Alaska Native, 0.0% Hispanic of any race, 0.0% two or more races (2000); Density: 303.9 persons per square mile (2000); Age: 30.5% under 18, 11.4% over 64 (2000); Marriage status: 26.6% never married, 58.4% now married, 6.8% widowed, 8.2% divorced (2000); Foreign born: 0.0% (2000); Ancestry (includes multiple ancestries): 37.0% German, 14.9% English, 12.9% Irish, 9.8% United States or American, 5.3% Swedish (2000).
Economy: Single-family building permits issued: 0 (2001) / 0 (2000); Multi-family building permits issued: 0 (2001) / 0 (2000); Employment by occupation: 12.8% management, 16.2% professional, 20.0% services, 31.9% sales, 3.0% farming, 6.8% construction, 9.4% production (2000).
Income: Per capita income: $19,958 (2000); Median household income: $41,838 (2000); Poverty rate: 4.2% (2000).
Taxes: Total city taxes per capita: $49 (1997); City property taxes per capita: $44 (1997).
Education: High school graduation rate: 90.5% (2000); College graduation rate: 24.2% (2000).
Housing: Homeownership rate: 77.2% (2000); Median home value: $68,300 (2000); Median rent: $350 per month (2000); Median age of housing: 51 years (2000).
Transportation: Commute to work: 97.0% car, 0.0% public transportation, 0.0% walk, 3.0% work from home (2000); Travel time to work: 30.5% less than 15 minutes, 44.7% 15 to 30 minutes, 17.7% 30 to 45 minutes, 4.0% 45 to 60 minutes, 3.1% 60 minutes or more (2000)

EMDEN (village). Covers a land area of 0.226 square miles and a water area of 0 square miles. Located at 40.29° N. Lat.; 89.48° W. Long. Elevation is 590 feet.
Population: 515 (2000); Race: 100.0% White, 0.0% Black, 0.0% Asian, 0.0% American Indian and Alaska Native, 0.3% Hispanic of any race, 0.0% two or more races (2000); Density: 2,278.9 persons per square mile (2000); Age: 31.2% under 18, 19.9% over 64 (2000); Marriage status: 19.9% never married, 65.2% now married, 9.1% widowed, 5.8% divorced (2000); Foreign born: 0.6% (2000); Ancestry (includes multiple ancestries): 54.7% German, 13.7% Irish, 11.8% United States or American, 7.8% English, 7.4% Other groups (2000).
Economy: In agricultural area. Single-family building permits issued: 0 (2001) / 0 (2000); Multi-family building permits issued: 0 (2001) / 0 (2000); Employment by occupation: 11.2% management, 11.5% professional, 18.2% services, 28.2% sales, 0.0% farming, 14.8% construction, 16.1% production (2000).
Income: Per capita income: $17,082 (2000); Median household income: $36,776 (2000); Poverty rate: 6.1% (2000).
Taxes: Total city taxes per capita: $20 (1997); City property taxes per capita: $15 (1997).
Education: High school graduation rate: 92.0% (2000); College graduation rate: 15.1% (2000).
Housing: Homeownership rate: 79.2% (2000); Median home value: $68,000 (2000); Median rent: $375 per month (2000); Median age of housing: 56 years (2000).
Transportation: Commute to work: 92.6% car, 0.0% public transportation, 3.8% walk, 2.6% work from home (2000); Travel time to work: 36.5% less than 15 minutes, 35.9% 15 to 30 minutes, 20.1% 30 to 45 minutes, 4.9% 45 to 60 minutes, 2.6% 60 minutes or more (2000)

HARTSBURG (village). Covers a land area of 0.145 square miles and a water area of 0 square miles. Located at 40.25° N. Lat.; 89.44° W. Long. Elevation is 600 feet.
Population: 358 (2000); Race: 100.0% White, 0.0% Black, 0.0% Asian, 0.0% American Indian and Alaska Native, 0.0% Hispanic of any race, 0.0% two or more races (2000); Density: 2,465.6 persons per square mile (2000); Age: 30.4% under 18, 14.0% over 64 (2000); Marriage status: 26.1% never married, 58.0% now married, 7.1% widowed, 8.8% divorced (2000); Foreign born: 0.0% (2000); Ancestry (includes multiple ancestries): 37.3% German, 9.5% Irish, 7.4% Other groups, 5.3% English, 2.6% French (except Basque) (2000).
Economy: In agricultural area: cattle, hogs; corn, soybeans. Single-family building permits issued: 0 (2001) / 0 (2000); Multi-family building permits issued: 0 (2001) / 0 (2000); Employment by occupation: 7.1% management, 11.2% professional, 27.0% services, 24.5% sales, 4.1% farming, 7.1% construction, 18.9% production (2000).
Income: Per capita income: $17,057 (2000); Median household income: $39,000 (2000); Poverty rate: 8.5% (2000).
Taxes: Total city taxes per capita: $10 (1997); City property taxes per capita: $7 (1997).
Education: High school graduation rate: 86.6% (2000); College graduation rate: 12.1% (2000).

School District(s)

Hartsburg Emden C U S District 21 (PK-12)
2000 Enrollment: 274 217-642-5244
Housing: Homeownership rate: 72.0% (2000); Median home value: $63,500 (2000); Median rent: $335 per month (2000); Median age of housing: 59 years (2000).
Transportation: Commute to work: 93.9% car, 0.0% public transportation, 6.1% walk, 0.0% work from home (2000); Travel time to work: 46.9% less than 15 minutes, 30.6% 15 to 30 minutes, 10.2% 30 to 45 minutes, 9.7% 45 to 60 minutes, 2.6% 60 minutes or more (2000)

LATHAM (village). Covers a land area of 0.278 square miles and a water area of 0 square miles. Located at 39.96° N. Lat.; 89.16° W. Long. Elevation is 615 feet.
Population: 371 (2000); Race: 100.0% White, 0.0% Black, 0.0% Asian, 0.0% American Indian and Alaska Native, 0.0% Hispanic of any race, 0.0% two or more races (2000); Density: 1,333.7 persons per square mile (2000); Age: 31.2% under 18, 6.9% over 64 (2000); Marriage status: 17.7% never married, 63.3% now married, 4.6% widowed, 14.5% divorced (2000); Foreign born: 1.0% (2000); Ancestry (includes multiple ancestries): 25.1% German, 19.9% United States or American, 16.1% Irish, 12.5% English, 3.1% Other groups (2000).
Economy: In agricultural area. Single-family building permits issued: 0 (2001) / 0 (2000); Multi-family building permits issued: 0 (2001) / 0 (2000); Employment by occupation: 7.2% management, 18.6% professional, 10.8% services, 18.6% sales, 1.5% farming, 8.8% construction, 34.5% production (2000).
Income: Per capita income: $16,917 (2000); Median household income: $43,750 (2000); Poverty rate: 12.9% (2000).
Taxes: Total city taxes per capita: $47 (1997); City property taxes per capita: $47 (1997).
Education: High school graduation rate: 93.4% (2000); College graduation rate: 11.6% (2000).
Housing: Homeownership rate: 72.0% (2000); Median home value: $60,500 (2000); Median rent: $259 per month (2000); Median age of housing: 57 years (2000).
Transportation: Commute to work: 92.2% car, 0.0% public transportation, 2.6% walk, 3.6% work from home (2000); Travel time to work: 15.7% less than 15 minutes, 48.1% 15 to 30 minutes, 27.6% 30 to 45 minutes, 2.7% 45 to 60 minutes, 5.9% 60 minutes or more (2000)

LINCOLN (city). Covers a land area of 5.919 square miles and a water area of 0 square miles. Located at 40.15° N. Lat.; 89.36° W. Long. Elevation is 591 feet.
History: Lincoln was settled in 1853 on land owned by promoter Colonel Latham, who hired Springfield lawyer Abraham Lincoln to draw up the documents for the town lots and decided to name the town Lincoln. The seat of Logan County was changed from Mount Pulaski to Lincoln, which is the only town named for Lincoln with his knowledge and consent.
Population: 15,369 (2000); Race: 95.6% White, 2.0% Black, 1.0% Asian, 0.2% American Indian and Alaska Native, 1.3% Hispanic of any race, 0.8% two or more races (2000); Density: 2,596.6 persons per square mile (2000); Age: 22.0% under 18, 16.5% over 64 (2000); Marriage status: 23.0% never

married, 56.5% now married, 7.7% widowed, 12.7% divorced (2000); Foreign born: 1.5% (2000); Ancestry (includes multiple ancestries): 28.6% German, 12.4% United States or American, 11.8% Irish, 10.0% English, 7.8% Other groups (2000).
Vital Statistics: Birth rate: 134.0 per 10,000 population (1998)
Economy: Single-family building permits issued: 6 (2001) / 5 (2000); Multi-family building permits issued: 0 (2001) / 0 (2000); Employment by occupation: 8.7% management, 14.7% professional, 24.6% services, 24.1% sales, 0.3% farming, 9.2% construction, 18.4% production (2000).
Income: Per capita income: $17,207 (2000); Median household income: $34,435 (2000); Poverty rate: 10.7% (2000).
Taxes: Total city taxes per capita: $100 (1997); City property taxes per capita: $97 (1997).
Education: High school graduation rate: 82.4% (2000); College graduation rate: 13.7% (2000).

School District(s)

Chester-East Lincoln Ccs District 61 (PK-08)
2000 Enrollment: 325 217-732-4136
Lincoln Community H S District 404 (09-12)
2000 Enrollment: 980 217-732-4131
Lincoln Elementary School District 27 (PK-08)
2000 Enrollment: 1,254 217-732-2522
Logan-Mason-Menard Pub Sch Prog (05-12)
2000 Enrollment: 12 217-732-8388
Logan/Mason/Menard Roe (07-12)
2000 Enrollment: 43 217-732-8388
West Lincoln-Broadwell E S D #92 (KG-08)
2000 Enrollment: 201 217-732-2630

Four-year College(s)

Lincoln Christian College and Seminary (Private, Not-for-profit, Christian Churches and Churches of Christ)
2001 Enrollment: 909 217-732-3168
2001 Tuition: In-state $7,008; Out-of-state $7,008

Two-year College(s)

Lincoln College (Private, Not-for-profit)
2001 Enrollment: 1,124 217-732-3155
2001 Tuition: In-state $11,000; Out-of-state $11,000

Housing: Homeownership rate: 64.5% (2000); Median home value: $73,700 (2000); Median rent: $351 per month (2000); Median age of housing: 43 years (2000).
Hospitals: Abraham Lincoln Memorial Hospital (66 beds)
Newspapers: Lincoln Courier (6 x week)
Transportation: Commute to work: 92.3% car, 1.0% public transportation, 2.8% walk, 2.3% work from home (2000); Travel time to work: 64.3% less than 15 minutes, 13.6% 15 to 30 minutes, 10.2% 30 to 45 minutes, 8.9% 45 to 60 minutes, 3.1% 60 minutes or more (2000); Amtrak: Service available.
Additional Information Contacts
Lincoln Chamber of Commerce 217-735-2385
Logan County Board of Realtors 217-732-8172

MIDDLETOWN (village). Covers a land area of 0.240 square miles and a water area of 0 square miles. Located at 40.10° N. Lat.; 89.59° W. Long. Elevation is 584 feet.
Population: 434 (2000); Race: 98.5% White, 1.0% Black, 0.0% Asian, 0.5% American Indian and Alaska Native, 2.4% Hispanic of any race, 0.0% two or more races (2000); Density: 1,809.5 persons per square mile (2000); Age: 29.6% under 18, 10.3% over 64 (2000); Marriage status: 26.1% never married, 55.7% now married, 6.7% widowed, 11.5% divorced (2000); Foreign born: 0.0% (2000); Ancestry (includes multiple ancestries): 25.2% German, 17.6% Irish, 11.0% United States or American, 9.3% Other groups, 9.0% English (2000).
Economy: Agriculture includes corn, soybeans; cattle, hogs. Employment by occupation: 7.7% management, 12.0% professional, 16.4% services, 26.2% sales, 0.0% farming, 16.9% construction, 20.8% production (2000).
Income: Per capita income: $14,478 (2000); Median household income: $33,929 (2000); Poverty rate: 16.1% (2000).
Taxes: Total city taxes per capita: $15 (1997); City property taxes per capita: $6 (1997).
Education: High school graduation rate: 79.1% (2000); College graduation rate: 10.2% (2000).

School District(s)

New Holland-Middletown E District 88 (KG-08)
2000 Enrollment: 144 217-445-2421

Housing: Homeownership rate: 77.4% (2000); Median home value: $48,000 (2000); Median rent: $263 per month (2000); Median age of housing: 55 years (2000).
Transportation: Commute to work: 97.8% car, 0.0% public transportation, 0.0% walk, 1.1% work from home (2000); Travel time to work: 10.6% less than 15 minutes, 47.2% 15 to 30 minutes, 22.2% 30 to 45 minutes, 11.7% 45 to 60 minutes, 8.3% 60 minutes or more (2000)

MOUNT PULASKI (city). Covers a land area of 1.139 square miles and a water area of 0 square miles. Located at 40.01° N. Lat.; 89.28° W. Long. Elevation is 695 feet.
History: Mount Pulaski served as the seat of Logan County from 1847 to 1853.
Population: 1,701 (2000); Race: 98.3% White, 0.4% Black, 0.2% Asian, 0.2% American Indian and Alaska Native, 0.1% Hispanic of any race, 0.9% two or more races (2000); Density: 1,494.1 persons per square mile (2000); Age: 22.2% under 18, 26.6% over 64 (2000); Marriage status: 17.4% never married, 64.0% now married, 11.0% widowed, 7.6% divorced (2000); Foreign born: 0.4% (2000); Ancestry (includes multiple ancestries): 30.2% German, 15.4% United States or American, 13.6% Irish, 11.4% English, 3.6% French (except Basque) (2000).
Economy: Single-family building permits issued: 0 (2001) / 0 (2000); Multi-family building permits issued: 0 (2001) / 0 (2000); Employment by occupation: 13.7% management, 17.0% professional, 19.7% services, 20.7% sales, 0.8% farming, 10.5% construction, 17.7% production (2000).
Income: Per capita income: $18,616 (2000); Median household income: $38,750 (2000); Poverty rate: 5.6% (2000).
Taxes: Total city taxes per capita: $96 (1997); City property taxes per capita: $87 (1997).
Education: High school graduation rate: 82.8% (2000); College graduation rate: 16.1% (2000).

School District(s)

Mount Pulaski Community Unit District 23 (PK-12)
2000 Enrollment: 657 217-792-7222

Housing: Homeownership rate: 79.5% (2000); Median home value: $73,400 (2000); Median rent: $317 per month (2000); Median age of housing: 53 years (2000).
Newspapers: Mount Pulaski Weekly News (1 x week)
Transportation: Commute to work: 95.4% car, 0.0% public transportation, 0.9% walk, 2.8% work from home (2000); Travel time to work: 35.7% less than 15 minutes, 30.3% 15 to 30 minutes, 23.7% 30 to 45 minutes, 6.9% 45 to 60 minutes, 3.5% 60 minutes or more (2000)

NEW HOLLAND (village). Covers a land area of 0.287 square miles and a water area of 0 square miles. Located at 40.18° N. Lat.; 89.58° W. Long. Elevation is 560 feet.
Population: 318 (2000); Race: 99.4% White, 0.0% Black, 0.0% Asian, 0.0% American Indian and Alaska Native, 0.0% Hispanic of any race, 0.6% two or more races (2000); Density: 1,107.8 persons per square mile (2000); Age: 23.7% under 18, 20.9% over 64 (2000); Marriage status: 18.5% never married, 65.0% now married, 10.2% widowed, 6.3% divorced (2000); Foreign born: 0.0% (2000); Ancestry (includes multiple ancestries): 39.2% German, 19.3% United States or American, 13.6% Irish, 9.8% English, 3.5% Dutch (2000).
Economy: In agricultural and bituminous coal area. Employment by occupation: 11.7% management, 17.9% professional, 19.3% services, 26.2% sales, 0.0% farming, 13.1% construction, 11.7% production (2000).
Income: Per capita income: $19,241 (2000); Median household income: $40,278 (2000); Poverty rate: 10.8% (2000).
Taxes: Total city taxes per capita: $27 (1997); City property taxes per capita: $24 (1997).
Education: High school graduation rate: 86.0% (2000); College graduation rate: 16.4% (2000).
Housing: Homeownership rate: 85.2% (2000); Median home value: $55,900 (2000); Median rent: $300 per month (2000); Median age of housing: 60+ years (2000).
Transportation: Commute to work: 89.2% car, 0.0% public transportation, 0.0% walk, 10.8% work from home (2000); Travel time to work: 7.6% less than 15 minutes, 55.3% 15 to 30 minutes, 15.2% 30 to 45 minutes, 14.4% 45 to 60 minutes, 7.6% 60 minutes or more (2000)

Macon County

Located in central Illinois; drained by the Sangamon River. Covers a land area of 580.50 square miles, a water area of 4.90 square miles, and is located in the Central Time Zone. The county government was organized in 1829. County seat is Decatur.

Macon County is part of the Decatur, IL MSA. The entire metro area includes: Macon County

Weather Station: Decatur Elevation: 620 feet

	Jan	Feb	Mar	Apr	May	Jun	Jul	Aug	Sep	Oct	Nov	Dec
High	34	40	52	65	76	85	88	86	80	68	52	40
Low	17	22	32	42	51	60	64	63	55	44	33	23
Precip	2.1	1.9	3.3	3.8	4.6	3.9	4.4	4.0	3.0	2.8	3.1	2.8
Snow	7.8	5.1	2.7	0.4	tr	0.0	0.0	0.0	0.0	tr	1.1	5.4

High and Low temperatures in degrees Fahrenheit; Precipitation and Snow in inches

Population: 114,706 (2000); Race: 83.5% White, 13.9% Black, 0.6% Asian, 0.1% American Indian and Alaska Native, 0.9% Hispanic of any race, 1.5% two or more races (2000); Density: 197.6 persons per square mile (2000); Age: 24.5% under 18, 15.3% over 64 (2000).
Religion: Five largest groups: 9.2% Catholic Church, 6.8% The United Methodist Church, 5.7% Lutheran Church—Missouri Synod, 4.8% Southern Baptist Convention, 4.2% Christian Church (Disciples of Christ) (2000).
Economy: Unemployment rate: 7.6% (11/2002); Total civilian labor force: 55,149 (11/2002); Leading industries: 19.1% manufacturing; 12.5% retail trade; 11.9% health care and social assistance (2000); Companies that employ more than 1,000 persons: 8 (2000); Companies that employ more than 100 persons: 76 (2000); Farms: 665 totaling 322,875 acres (1997); Minority business ownership rate: 8.9% (1997); Women business ownership rate: 32.0% (1997); Retail sales per capita: $9,895 (1997). Single-family building permits issued: 215 (2001) / 241 (2000); Multi-family building permits issued: 10 (2001) / 120 (2000).
Income: Per capita income: $20,067 (2000); Median household income: $37,859 (2000); Poverty rate: 12.9% (2000); Bankruptcy rate: 8.60% (2001).
Taxes: Total county taxes per capita: $134 (2000); County property taxes per capita: $132 (2000).
Education: High school graduation rate: 83.2% (2000); College graduation rate: 16.9% (2000).
Housing: Homeownership rate: 71.7% (2000); Median home value: $69,800 (2000); Median rent: $349 per month (2000); Median age of housing: 41 years (2000).
Health: Birth rate: 134.3 per 10,000 population (1998); Age adjusted death rate: 87.5 per 10,000 population (1999); Age adjusted cancer mortality rate: 235.1 deaths per 100,000 population (1999). Air Quality Index: 84% good, 16% moderate, 0% unhealthy (percent of days in 2000). Number of physicians: 19.3 per 10,000 population (1999); Number of hospital beds: 35.2 per 10,000 population (1999).
Elections: 2000 Presidential election results: 49.0% Gore, 48.1% Bush, 2.0% Nader, 0.6% Buchanan
National and State Parks: Lincoln Trail Homestead State Park; Spitler Woods State Park
Additional Information Contacts
Macon County Government Offices 217-424-1470
Decatur Association of Realtors 217-428-4321

Macon County Communities

ARGENTA (village). Covers a land area of 0.560 square miles and a water area of 0 square miles. Located at 39.98° N. Lat.; 88.82° W. Long. Elevation is 610 feet.
Population: 921 (2000); Race: 98.4% White, 0.6% Black, 0.2% Asian, 0.2% American Indian and Alaska Native, 0.7% Hispanic of any race, 0.0% two or more races (2000); Density: 1,643.8 persons per square mile (2000); Age: 27.5% under 18, 11.2% over 64 (2000); Marriage status: 18.8% never married, 62.9% now married, 7.8% widowed, 10.4% divorced (2000); Foreign born: 0.6% (2000); Ancestry (includes multiple ancestries): 24.1% German, 11.1% United States or American, 10.5% English, 9.5% Irish, 6.8% Other groups (2000).
Economy: Corn, wheat, soybeans. Single-family building permits issued: 0 (2001) / 0 (2000); Multi-family building permits issued: 0 (2001) / 0 (2000); Employment by occupation: 8.2% management, 11.4% professional, 12.8% services, 26.9% sales, 0.9% farming, 14.1% construction, 25.7% production (2000).
Income: Per capita income: $18,154 (2000); Median household income: $42,315 (2000); Poverty rate: 3.7% (2000).
Taxes: Total city taxes per capita: $58 (1997); City property taxes per capita: $57 (1997).
Education: High school graduation rate: 89.9% (2000); College graduation rate: 8.0% (2000).

School District(s)
Argenta-Oreana Community Unit Sch D 1 (PK-12)
2000 Enrollment: 1,084 217-795-2313
Housing: Homeownership rate: 85.3% (2000); Median home value: $67,800 (2000); Median rent: $300 per month (2000); Median age of housing: 47 years (2000).
Transportation: Commute to work: 94.8% car, 0.0% public transportation, 2.5% walk, 1.8% work from home (2000); Travel time to work: 26.7% less than 15 minutes, 47.8% 15 to 30 minutes, 16.2% 30 to 45 minutes, 4.2% 45 to 60 minutes, 5.1% 60 minutes or more (2000)

BLUE MOUND (village). Covers a land area of 0.595 square miles and a water area of 0 square miles. Located at 39.70° N. Lat.; 89.12° W. Long. Elevation is 625 feet.
Population: 1,129 (2000); Race: 98.8% White, 0.4% Black, 0.0% Asian, 0.3% American Indian and Alaska Native, 0.4% Hispanic of any race, 0.2% two or more races (2000); Density: 1,898.9 persons per square mile (2000); Age: 24.0% under 18, 15.5% over 64 (2000); Marriage status: 20.4% never married, 58.5% now married, 9.5% widowed, 11.6% divorced (2000); Foreign born: 0.4% (2000); Ancestry (includes multiple ancestries): 23.3% United States or American, 21.4% German, 11.2% Irish, 9.0% English, 6.3% Other groups (2000).
Economy: Wheat, corn, soybeans. Single-family building permits issued: 2 (2001) / 1 (2000); Multi-family building permits issued: 0 (2001) / 0 (2000); Employment by occupation: 4.9% management, 14.5% professional, 13.1% services, 32.8% sales, 1.0% farming, 9.4% construction, 24.2% production (2000).
Income: Per capita income: $20,039 (2000); Median household income: $44,018 (2000); Poverty rate: 4.2% (2000).
Taxes: Total city taxes per capita: $74 (1997); City property taxes per capita: $72 (1997).
Education: High school graduation rate: 87.8% (2000); College graduation rate: 11.5% (2000).

School District(s)
Meridian Community Unit School District 15 (PK-12)
2000 Enrollment: 1,111 217-692-2599
Housing: Homeownership rate: 78.4% (2000); Median home value: $64,700 (2000); Median rent: $312 per month (2000); Median age of housing: 46 years (2000).
Newspapers: Blue Mound Leader (1 x week)
Transportation: Commute to work: 96.6% car, 0.0% public transportation, 1.9% walk, 0.3% work from home (2000); Travel time to work: 24.8% less than 15 minutes, 26.7% 15 to 30 minutes, 39.1% 30 to 45 minutes, 6.5% 45 to 60 minutes, 2.9% 60 minutes or more (2000)

BOODY (unincorporated postal area, zip code 62514). Covers a land area of 4.047 square miles and a water area of 0 square miles. Located at 39.76° N. Lat.; 89.05° W. Long. Elevation is 685 feet.
Population: 340 (2000); Race: 100.0% White, 0.0% Black, 0.0% Asian, 0.0% American Indian and Alaska Native, 0.0% Hispanic of any race, 0.0% two or more races (2000); Density: 84.0 persons per square mile (2000); Age: 19.8% under 18, 9.7% over 64 (2000); Marriage status: 21.8% never married, 64.3% now married, 4.8% widowed, 9.1% divorced (2000); Foreign born: 0.0% (2000); Ancestry (includes multiple ancestries): 28.5% German, 28.2% English, 19.5% Irish, 19.1% United States or American, 8.1% French (except Basque) (2000).
Economy: Employment by occupation: 3.8% management, 18.9% professional, 29.6% services, 18.9% sales, 0.0% farming, 25.8% construction, 3.1% production (2000).
Income: Per capita income: $17,957 (2000); Median household income: $39,875 (2000); Poverty rate: 2.0% (2000).
Education: High school graduation rate: 96.3% (2000); College graduation rate: 2.3% (2000).
Housing: Homeownership rate: 85.0% (2000); Median home value: $36,500 (2000); Median rent: <$100 per month (2000); Median age of housing: 60+ years (2000).
Transportation: Commute to work: 91.2% car, 0.0% public transportation, 1.9% walk, 6.9% work from home (2000); Travel time to work: 2.0% less than 15 minutes, 75.0% 15 to 30 minutes, 18.9% 30 to 45 minutes, 4.1% 45 to 60 minutes, 0.0% 60 minutes or more (2000)

DECATUR (city). Covers a land area of 41.560 square miles and a water area of 4.317 square miles. Located at 39.85° N. Lat.; 88.94° W. Long. Elevation is 670 feet.
History: Decatur was named and designated the seat of Macon County in 1829, though there was no settlement here at the time. In 1830 Abraham

Lincoln and his family settled nearby, and in 1836 Richard J. Oglesby, who was to become a senator, three times governor of the state, and a friend of Lincoln's. First an agricultural center, manufacturing began in Decatur with the arrival of the railroad in 1854. Coal was discovered under the city in 1874.
Population: 81,860 (2000); Race: 77.8% White, 19.2% Black, 0.7% Asian, 0.1% American Indian and Alaska Native, 1.1% Hispanic of any race, 1.8% two or more races (2000); Density: 1,969.7 persons per square mile (2000); Age: 24.0% under 18, 16.5% over 64 (2000); Marriage status: 26.3% never married, 52.1% now married, 8.2% widowed, 13.3% divorced (2000); Foreign born: 1.6% (2000); Ancestry (includes multiple ancestries): 22.2% Other groups, 19.3% German, 11.2% Irish, 10.3% United States or American, 9.3% English (2000).
Vital Statistics: Birth rate: 152.7 per 10,000 population (1998)
Economy: Unemployment rate: 9.3% (11/2002); Total civilian labor force: 38,497 (11/2002); Single-family building permits issued: 68 (2001) / 68 (2000); Multi-family building permits issued: 0 (2001) / 120 (2000); Employment by occupation: 9.9% management, 17.5% professional, 16.9% services, 26.5% sales, 0.3% farming, 8.9% construction, 20.1% production (2000).
Income: Per capita income: $19,009 (2000); Median household income: $33,111 (2000); Poverty rate: 16.5% (2000).
Taxes: Total city taxes per capita: $242 (2000); City property taxes per capita: $97 (2000).
Education: High school graduation rate: 80.8% (2000); College graduation rate: 17.0% (2000).

School District(s)

Decatur School District 61 (PK-12)
2000 Enrollment: 10,825 217-424-3011
Macon-Piatt Special Education Jnt Agr (PK-12)
2000 Enrollment: 142 217-424-3025
Macon/Piatt Roe (03-12)
2000 Enrollment: 320 217-872-3721

Four-year College(s)

Millikin University (Private, Not-for-profit, Presbyterian Church (USA))
2001 Enrollment: 2,412 217-424-6211
2001 Tuition: In-state $17,084; Out-of-state $17,084

Two-year College(s)

Mr John's School of Cosmetology Esthetics and Nails (Private, For-profit)
2001 Enrollment: 93 217-423-8173
Richland Community College (Public)
2001 Enrollment: 3,260 217-875-7200
2001 Tuition: In-state $4,900; Out-of-state $8,500

Housing: Homeownership rate: 66.5% (2000); Median home value: $63,200 (2000); Median rent: $350 per month (2000); Median age of housing: 43 years (2000).
Hospitals: Decatur Memorial Hospital (401 beds); Saint Mary's Hospital (371 beds)
Newspapers: Herald & Review (7 x week); Decatur Tribune (1 x week); The Voice (1 x week); Prairie Shopper (1 x week)
Transportation: Commute to work: 93.1% car, 1.3% public transportation, 2.7% walk, 2.0% work from home (2000); Travel time to work: 53.3% less than 15 minutes, 34.9% 15 to 30 minutes, 4.5% 30 to 45 minutes, 3.8% 45 to 60 minutes, 3.5% 60 minutes or more (2000)
Airports: Decatur (primary service)
Additional Information Contacts
Decatur Association of Realtors 217-428-4321

FORSYTH (village). Covers a land area of 2.104 square miles and a water area of 0 square miles. Located at 39.92° N. Lat.; 88.95° W. Long. Elevation is 678 feet.
Population: 2,434 (2000); Race: 96.0% White, 1.8% Black, 1.5% Asian, 0.4% American Indian and Alaska Native, 0.4% Hispanic of any race, 0.3% two or more races (2000); Density: 1,156.6 persons per square mile (2000); Age: 27.5% under 18, 13.3% over 64 (2000); Marriage status: 15.0% never married, 75.4% now married, 5.6% widowed, 4.0% divorced (2000); Foreign born: 2.3% (2000); Ancestry (includes multiple ancestries): 26.0% German, 16.5% English, 13.9% Irish, 8.4% United States or American, 6.7% Other groups (2000).
Economy: Corn, soybeans; manufacturing: farm chemicals. Single-family building permits issued: 26 (2001) / 44 (2000); Multi-family building permits issued: 0 (2001) / 0 (2000); Employment by occupation: 25.6% management, 23.3% professional, 6.1% services, 28.8% sales, 0.0% farming, 5.6% construction, 10.7% production (2000).
Income: Per capita income: $34,010 (2000); Median household income: $69,000 (2000); Poverty rate: 1.9% (2000).
Taxes: Total city taxes per capita: $250 (1997); City property taxes per capita: $170 (1997).
Education: High school graduation rate: 94.2% (2000); College graduation rate: 36.6% (2000).
Housing: Homeownership rate: 93.9% (2000); Median home value: $145,400 (2000); Median rent: $383 per month (2000); Median age of housing: 21 years (2000).
Transportation: Commute to work: 95.6% car, 0.0% public transportation, 1.0% walk, 3.2% work from home (2000); Travel time to work: 36.0% less than 15 minutes, 52.1% 15 to 30 minutes, 5.2% 30 to 45 minutes, 3.9% 45 to 60 minutes, 2.9% 60 minutes or more (2000)

HARRISTOWN (village). Covers a land area of 1.856 square miles and a water area of 0 square miles. Located at 39.84° N. Lat.; 89.06° W. Long. Elevation is 675 feet.
Population: 1,338 (2000); Race: 97.5% White, 0.2% Black, 0.2% Asian, 0.0% American Indian and Alaska Native, 0.9% Hispanic of any race, 2.1% two or more races (2000); Density: 720.9 persons per square mile (2000); Age: 25.1% under 18, 12.9% over 64 (2000); Marriage status: 16.0% never married, 69.1% now married, 5.1% widowed, 9.8% divorced (2000); Foreign born: 0.5% (2000); Ancestry (includes multiple ancestries): 20.4% German, 16.7% United States or American, 14.4% Irish, 13.8% English, 6.8% Other groups (2000).
Economy: Wheat, corn, soybeans. Single-family building permits issued: 4 (2001) / 1 (2000); Multi-family building permits issued: 0 (2001) / 0 (2000); Employment by occupation: 8.4% management, 12.0% professional, 14.3% services, 26.7% sales, 0.0% farming, 16.5% construction, 22.1% production (2000).
Income: Per capita income: $18,689 (2000); Median household income: $42,946 (2000); Poverty rate: 5.0% (2000).
Taxes: Total city taxes per capita: $11 (1997); City property taxes per capita: $9 (1997).
Education: High school graduation rate: 84.7% (2000); College graduation rate: 10.6% (2000).
Housing: Homeownership rate: 89.2% (2000); Median home value: $67,200 (2000); Median rent: $328 per month (2000); Median age of housing: 43 years (2000).
Transportation: Commute to work: 95.3% car, 0.0% public transportation, 1.0% walk, 3.3% work from home (2000); Travel time to work: 19.2% less than 15 minutes, 58.7% 15 to 30 minutes, 12.9% 30 to 45 minutes, 4.0% 45 to 60 minutes, 5.2% 60 minutes or more (2000)

LONG CREEK (village). Covers a land area of 2.658 square miles and a water area of 0 square miles. Located at 39.80° N. Lat.; 88.85° W. Long. Elevation is 675 feet.
Population: 1,364 (2000); Race: 99.2% White, 0.3% Black, 0.4% Asian, 0.0% American Indian and Alaska Native, 0.0% Hispanic of any race, 0.1% two or more races (2000); Density: 513.2 persons per square mile (2000); Age: 27.7% under 18, 6.8% over 64 (2000); Marriage status: 17.2% never married, 72.4% now married, 3.0% widowed, 7.5% divorced (2000); Foreign born: 0.7% (2000); Ancestry (includes multiple ancestries): 26.9% German, 12.6% English, 11.5% United States or American, 11.3% Irish, 3.6% Other groups (2000).
Economy: Corn, soybeans. Single-family building permits issued: 5 (2001) / 5 (2000); Multi-family building permits issued: 0 (2001) / 0 (2000); Employment by occupation: 10.0% management, 12.1% professional, 10.8% services, 29.2% sales, 0.0% farming, 15.1% construction, 22.8% production (2000).
Income: Per capita income: $23,141 (2000); Median household income: $56,083 (2000); Poverty rate: 5.1% (2000).
Taxes: Total city taxes per capita: $8 (1997); City property taxes per capita: $6 (1997).
Education: High school graduation rate: 87.3% (2000); College graduation rate: 14.8% (2000).
Housing: Homeownership rate: 93.6% (2000); Median home value: $85,200 (2000); Median rent: $450 per month (2000); Median age of housing: 31 years (2000).
Transportation: Commute to work: 97.5% car, 0.0% public transportation, 0.0% walk, 2.1% work from home (2000); Travel time to work: 24.6% less than 15 minutes, 59.5% 15 to 30 minutes, 7.4% 30 to 45 minutes, 3.1% 45 to 60 minutes, 5.4% 60 minutes or more (2000)

MACON (city). Covers a land area of 0.881 square miles and a water area of 0 square miles. Located at 39.70° N. Lat.; 89.00° W. Long. Elevation is 714 feet.

Population: 1,213 (2000); Race: 99.3% White, 0.0% Black, 0.2% Asian, 0.0% American Indian and Alaska Native, 0.7% Hispanic of any race, 0.4% two or more races (2000); Density: 1,376.2 persons per square mile (2000); Age: 24.1% under 18, 18.3% over 64 (2000); Marriage status: 16.7% never married, 59.5% now married, 11.6% widowed, 12.1% divorced (2000); Foreign born: 0.2% (2000); Ancestry (includes multiple ancestries): 21.9% German, 11.8% United States or American, 11.8% English, 9.0% Irish, 7.6% Other groups (2000).
Economy: In agricultural area: corn, soybeans, oats. Bituminous-coal area. Single-family building permits issued: 3 (2001) / 1 (2000); Multi-family building permits issued: 0 (2001) / 0 (2000); Employment by occupation: 7.3% management, 12.5% professional, 16.0% services, 26.3% sales, 0.0% farming, 14.2% construction, 23.7% production (2000).
Income: Per capita income: $18,029 (2000); Median household income: $40,917 (2000); Poverty rate: 5.8% (2000).
Taxes: Total city taxes per capita: $44 (1997); City property taxes per capita: $35 (1997).
Education: High school graduation rate: 90.4% (2000); College graduation rate: 7.7% (2000).
Housing: Homeownership rate: 77.2% (2000); Median home value: $61,200 (2000); Median rent: $343 per month (2000); Median age of housing: 47 years (2000).
Transportation: Commute to work: 96.9% car, 0.0% public transportation, 1.6% walk, 1.6% work from home (2000); Travel time to work: 24.9% less than 15 minutes, 49.6% 15 to 30 minutes, 15.8% 30 to 45 minutes, 5.1% 45 to 60 minutes, 4.7% 60 minutes or more (2000)

MAROA (city). Covers a land area of 0.673 square miles and a water area of 0 square miles. Located at 40.03° N. Lat.; 88.95° W. Long. Elevation is 721 feet.
Population: 1,654 (2000); Race: 98.9% White, 0.0% Black, 0.2% Asian, 0.3% American Indian and Alaska Native, 0.7% Hispanic of any race, 0.6% two or more races (2000); Density: 2,456.2 persons per square mile (2000); Age: 27.7% under 18, 14.1% over 64 (2000); Marriage status: 19.7% never married, 59.4% now married, 7.5% widowed, 13.4% divorced (2000); Foreign born: 1.0% (2000); Ancestry (includes multiple ancestries): 26.7% German, 13.9% Irish, 13.8% English, 9.9% United States or American, 6.7% Other groups (2000).
Economy: In agricultural area: corn, soybeans. Single-family building permits issued: 5 (2001) / 2 (2000); Multi-family building permits issued: 0 (2001) / 0 (2000); Employment by occupation: 6.7% management, 9.6% professional, 17.8% services, 28.5% sales, 0.4% farming, 12.0% construction, 25.2% production (2000).
Income: Per capita income: $18,308 (2000); Median household income: $41,615 (2000); Poverty rate: 4.4% (2000).
Taxes: Total city taxes per capita: $105 (1997); City property taxes per capita: $71 (1997).
Education: High school graduation rate: 86.4% (2000); College graduation rate: 10.5% (2000).

School District(s)

Maroa Forsyth C U School District 2 (PK-12)
2000 Enrollment: 1,022 217-794-3488
Housing: Homeownership rate: 77.3% (2000); Median home value: $64,400 (2000); Median rent: $332 per month (2000); Median age of housing: 43 years (2000).
Transportation: Commute to work: 96.4% car, 0.0% public transportation, 1.9% walk, 1.6% work from home (2000); Travel time to work: 21.3% less than 15 minutes, 51.4% 15 to 30 minutes, 15.0% 30 to 45 minutes, 9.4% 45 to 60 minutes, 3.0% 60 minutes or more (2000)

MOUNT ZION (village). Covers a land area of 3.768 square miles and a water area of <.001 square miles. Located at 39.77° N. Lat.; 88.87° W. Long. Elevation is 690 feet.
Population: 4,845 (2000); Race: 96.4% White, 0.5% Black, 0.8% Asian, 0.4% American Indian and Alaska Native, 0.0% Hispanic of any race, 1.9% two or more races (2000); Density: 1,285.7 persons per square mile (2000); Age: 30.8% under 18, 9.3% over 64 (2000); Marriage status: 20.4% never married, 70.0% now married, 4.0% widowed, 5.5% divorced (2000); Foreign born: 0.7% (2000); Ancestry (includes multiple ancestries): 27.1% German, 13.7% United States or American, 13.4% Irish, 13.3% English, 5.2% Other groups (2000).
Economy: In agricultural area. Single-family building permits issued: 27 (2001) / 38 (2000); Multi-family building permits issued: 0 (2001) / 0 (2000); Employment by occupation: 14.9% management, 23.9% professional, 12.9% services, 24.6% sales, 0.0% farming, 6.4% construction, 17.2% production (2000).
Income: Per capita income: $22,784 (2000); Median household income: $54,936 (2000); Poverty rate: 5.0% (2000).
Taxes: Total city taxes per capita: $207 (1997); City property taxes per capita: $68 (1997).
Education: High school graduation rate: 90.2% (2000); College graduation rate: 23.9% (2000).

School District(s)

Mount Zion Community Unit School District 3 (KG-12)
2000 Enrollment: 2,395 217-864-2366
Housing: Homeownership rate: 76.6% (2000); Median home value: $90,100 (2000); Median rent: $353 per month (2000); Median age of housing: 27 years (2000).
Newspapers: The Mount Zion Region News (1 x week)
Transportation: Commute to work: 96.7% car, 0.0% public transportation, 0.7% walk, 2.3% work from home (2000); Travel time to work: 27.3% less than 15 minutes, 60.8% 15 to 30 minutes, 4.9% 30 to 45 minutes, 2.5% 45 to 60 minutes, 4.6% 60 minutes or more (2000)

NIANTIC (village). Covers a land area of 1.075 square miles and a water area of 0 square miles. Located at 39.85° N. Lat.; 89.16° W. Long. Elevation is 602 feet.
Population: 738 (2000); Race: 99.2% White, 0.5% Black, 0.3% Asian, 0.0% American Indian and Alaska Native, 0.9% Hispanic of any race, 0.0% two or more races (2000); Density: 686.7 persons per square mile (2000); Age: 30.5% under 18, 13.2% over 64 (2000); Marriage status: 20.3% never married, 67.9% now married, 6.0% widowed, 5.8% divorced (2000); Foreign born: 0.3% (2000); Ancestry (includes multiple ancestries): 21.9% German, 17.3% United States or American, 15.5% English, 13.7% Irish, 6.9% Other groups (2000).
Economy: Grain; livestock; dairy products. Single-family building permits issued: 0 (2001) / 2 (2000); Multi-family building permits issued: 0 (2001) / 0 (2000); Employment by occupation: 6.7% management, 11.6% professional, 15.2% services, 25.8% sales, 3.0% farming, 15.2% construction, 22.5% production (2000).
Income: Per capita income: $19,448 (2000); Median household income: $41,184 (2000); Poverty rate: 7.8% (2000).
Taxes: Total city taxes per capita: $42 (1997); City property taxes per capita: $39 (1997).
Education: High school graduation rate: 90.3% (2000); College graduation rate: 11.7% (2000).

School District(s)

Niantic-Harristown C U S D 6 (KG-12)
2000 Enrollment: 507 217-668-2338
Housing: Homeownership rate: 86.0% (2000); Median home value: $69,000 (2000); Median rent: $305 per month (2000); Median age of housing: 47 years (2000).
Transportation: Commute to work: 94.4% car, 0.9% public transportation, 1.2% walk, 1.6% work from home (2000); Travel time to work: 14.6% less than 15 minutes, 44.6% 15 to 30 minutes, 26.6% 30 to 45 minutes, 7.9% 45 to 60 minutes, 6.3% 60 minutes or more (2000)

OAKLEY (unincorporated postal area, zip code 62552). Covers a land area of 38.230 square miles and a water area of 0.004 square miles. Located at 39.87° N. Lat.; 88.81° W. Long. Elevation is 686 feet.
Population: 1,063 (2000); Race: 100.0% White, 0.0% Black, 0.0% Asian, 0.0% American Indian and Alaska Native, 0.0% Hispanic of any race, 0.0% two or more races (2000); Density: 27.8 persons per square mile (2000); Age: 19.7% under 18, 13.8% over 64 (2000); Marriage status: 13.9% never married, 75.1% now married, 2.7% widowed, 8.3% divorced (2000); Foreign born: 0.0% (2000); Ancestry (includes multiple ancestries): 22.4% German, 16.9% English, 10.9% United States or American, 5.1% Irish, 4.3% Other groups (2000).
Economy: Employment by occupation: 7.5% management, 15.7% professional, 16.1% services, 25.7% sales, 1.4% farming, 17.3% construction, 16.3% production (2000).
Income: Per capita income: $19,102 (2000); Median household income: $49,228 (2000); Poverty rate: 3.3% (2000).
Education: High school graduation rate: 82.6% (2000); College graduation rate: 5.3% (2000).
Housing: Homeownership rate: 85.2% (2000); Median home value: $80,600 (2000); Median rent: $373 per month (2000); Median age of housing: 35 years (2000).
Transportation: Commute to work: 96.9% car, 0.0% public transportation, 1.2% walk, 2.0% work from home (2000); Travel time to work: 16.8% less than 15 minutes, 59.1% 15 to 30 minutes, 11.2% 30 to 45 minutes, 3.2% 45 to 60 minutes, 9.6% 60 minutes or more (2000)

OREANA (village). Covers a land area of 0.500 square miles and a water area of 0 square miles. Located at 39.93° N. Lat.; 88.86° W. Long. Elevation is 688 feet.
Population: 892 (2000); Race: 99.4% White, 0.0% Black, 0.0% Asian, 0.3% American Indian and Alaska Native, 0.4% Hispanic of any race, 0.2% two or more races (2000); Density: 1,785.3 persons per square mile (2000); Age: 27.2% under 18, 12.5% over 64 (2000); Marriage status: 17.8% never married, 68.7% now married, 6.2% widowed, 7.3% divorced (2000); Foreign born: 0.2% (2000); Ancestry (includes multiple ancestries): 23.5% German, 15.4% Irish, 13.6% English, 11.2% United States or American, 3.2% Other groups (2000).
Economy: Agricultural area; light manufacturing. Single-family building permits issued: 3 (2001) / 6 (2000); Multi-family building permits issued: 8 (2001) / 0 (2000); Employment by occupation: 5.2% management, 13.4% professional, 18.3% services, 26.1% sales, 0.4% farming, 14.0% construction, 22.6% production (2000).
Income: Per capita income: $20,133 (2000); Median household income: $51,339 (2000); Poverty rate: 2.8% (2000).
Taxes: Total city taxes per capita: $59 (1997); City property taxes per capita: $49 (1997).
Education: High school graduation rate: 91.4% (2000); College graduation rate: 11.4% (2000).
Housing: Homeownership rate: 90.2% (2000); Median home value: $74,100 (2000); Median rent: $280 per month (2000); Median age of housing: 36 years (2000).
Transportation: Commute to work: 96.3% car, 0.0% public transportation, 0.9% walk, 2.4% work from home (2000); Travel time to work: 29.8% less than 15 minutes, 56.4% 15 to 30 minutes, 7.0% 30 to 45 minutes, 2.3% 45 to 60 minutes, 4.5% 60 minutes or more (2000)

WARRENSBURG (village). Covers a land area of 0.678 square miles and a water area of 0 square miles. Located at 39.93° N. Lat.; 89.06° W. Long. Elevation is 710 feet.
Population: 1,289 (2000); Race: 96.7% White, 0.5% Black, 0.3% Asian, 0.3% American Indian and Alaska Native, 0.9% Hispanic of any race, 2.2% two or more races (2000); Density: 1,900.6 persons per square mile (2000); Age: 29.3% under 18, 6.9% over 64 (2000); Marriage status: 22.7% never married, 59.8% now married, 5.1% widowed, 12.5% divorced (2000); Foreign born: 0.9% (2000); Ancestry (includes multiple ancestries): 29.5% German, 17.2% Irish, 15.1% English, 9.0% Other groups, 6.5% United States or American (2000).
Economy: Agriculture includes corn, wheat, soybeans; livestock. Manufacturing of aerosol cans. Single-family building permits issued: 0 (2001) / 6 (2000); Multi-family building permits issued: 0 (2001) / 0 (2000); Employment by occupation: 9.3% management, 19.3% professional, 17.1% services, 24.0% sales, 0.0% farming, 10.5% construction, 19.8% production (2000).
Income: Per capita income: $19,041 (2000); Median household income: $45,708 (2000); Poverty rate: 3.7% (2000).
Taxes: Total city taxes per capita: $73 (1997); City property taxes per capita: $67 (1997).
Education: High school graduation rate: 88.9% (2000); College graduation rate: 15.3% (2000).

School District(s)

Warrensburg-Latham C U District 11 (PK-12)
2000 Enrollment: 1,165 217-672-3514
Housing: Homeownership rate: 74.6% (2000); Median home value: $74,900 (2000); Median rent: $323 per month (2000); Median age of housing: 30 years (2000).
Transportation: Commute to work: 96.1% car, 0.0% public transportation, 1.0% walk, 2.5% work from home (2000); Travel time to work: 27.6% less than 15 minutes, 56.2% 15 to 30 minutes, 8.0% 30 to 45 minutes, 4.3% 45 to 60 minutes, 3.9% 60 minutes or more (2000)

Macoupin County

Located in southwest central Illinois; drained by Macoupin, Cahokia, and Otter Creeks. Covers a land area of 863.60 square miles, a water area of 4.00 square miles, and is located in the Central Time Zone. The county government was organized in 1829. County seat is Carlinville.

Weather Station: Carlinville — Elevation: 629 feet

	Jan	Feb	Mar	Apr	May	Jun	Jul	Aug	Sep	Oct	Nov	Dec
High	35	42	53	66	76	84	88	86	80	68	53	41
Low	18	24	33	43	53	62	66	64	56	45	35	25
Precip	2.0	1.9	3.5	4.2	4.3	3.8	3.6	3.4	3.1	2.7	3.6	2.9
Snow	6.8	4.4	3.3	0.7	tr	0.0	0.0	0.0	0.0	tr	1.4	3.6

High and Low temperatures in degrees Fahrenheit; Precipitation and Snow in inches

Weather Station: Virden — Elevation: 672 feet

	Jan	Feb	Mar	Apr	May	Jun	Jul	Aug	Sep	Oct	Nov	Dec
High	35	40	52	66	76	84	88	86	80	68	52	40
Low	18	23	33	44	54	62	66	63	56	45	34	24
Precip	1.8	2.0	3.3	3.8	4.4	3.9	3.5	3.1	3.0	2.5	3.3	2.5
Snow	6.5	6.5	3.9	0.7	0.0	0.0	0.0	0.0	0.0	tr	1.5	4.7

High and Low temperatures in degrees Fahrenheit; Precipitation and Snow in inches

Population: 49,019 (2000); Race: 98.2% White, 0.7% Black, 0.3% Asian, 0.2% American Indian and Alaska Native, 0.8% Hispanic of any race, 0.5% two or more races (2000); Density: 56.8 persons per square mile (2000); Age: 24.7% under 18, 17.5% over 64 (2000).
Religion: Five largest groups: 14.4% Catholic Church, 9.3% Southern Baptist Convention, 6.4% Lutheran Church—Missouri Synod, 6.2% The United Methodist Church, 2.5% United Church of Christ (2000).
Economy: Unemployment rate: 5.9% (11/2002); Total civilian labor force: 23,587 (11/2002); Leading industries: 15.7% retail trade; 14.7% health care and social assistance; 8.2% manufacturing (2000); Companies that employ more than 1,000 persons: 0 (2000); Companies that employ more than 100 persons: 15 (2000); Farms: 1,206 totaling 395,696 acres (1997); Minority business ownership rate: 0.0% (1997); Women business ownership rate: 29.9% (1997); Retail sales per capita: $6,331 (1997). Single-family building permits issued: 44 (2001) / 47 (2000); Multi-family building permits issued: 2 (2001) / 12 (2000).
Income: Per capita income: $17,298 (2000); Median household income: $36,190 (2000); Poverty rate: 9.4% (2000); Bankruptcy rate: 4.39% (2001).
Taxes: Total county taxes per capita: $144 (1997); County property taxes per capita: $52 (1997).
Education: High school graduation rate: 82.1% (2000); College graduation rate: 11.8% (2000).
Housing: Homeownership rate: 79.0% (2000); Median home value: $66,700 (2000); Median rent: $299 per month (2000); Median age of housing: 42 years (2000).
Health: Birth rate: 107.1 per 10,000 population (1998); Age adjusted death rate: 98.5 per 10,000 population (1999); Age adjusted cancer mortality rate: 211.6 deaths per 100,000 population (1999). Air Quality Index: 73% good, 27% moderate, 0% unhealthy (percent of days in 2000). Number of physicians: 3.9 per 10,000 population (1999); Number of hospital beds: 15.7 per 10,000 population (1999).
Elections: 2000 Presidential election results: 51.5% Gore, 45.6% Bush, 2.0% Nader, 0.7% Buchanan
National and State Parks: Beaver Dam State Park
Additional Information Contacts
Macoupin County Government Offices 217-854-3214
Carlinville Chamber of Commerce 217-854-2141
Coal Country Chamber of Commerce 217-839-4888
Staunton Chamber of Commerce 618-635-8356

Macoupin County Communities

ATWATER (unincorporated postal area, zip code 62511). Covers a land area of 12.205 square miles and a water area of 0 square miles. Located at 39.34° N. Lat.; 89.73° W. Long. Elevation is 640 feet.
Population: 176 (2000); Race: 100.0% White, 0.0% Black, 0.0% Asian, 0.0% American Indian and Alaska Native, 0.0% Hispanic of any race, 0.0% two or more races (2000); Density: 14.4 persons per square mile (2000); Age: 16.9% under 18, 13.6% over 64 (2000); Marriage status: 14.2% never married, 66.5% now married, 11.6% widowed, 7.7% divorced (2000); Foreign born: 0.0% (2000); Ancestry (includes multiple ancestries): 37.3% German, 19.8% Irish, 14.1% Scotch-Irish, 9.6% English, 7.9% United States or American (2000).
Economy: Employment by occupation: 16.5% management, 3.5% professional, 10.4% services, 37.4% sales, 0.0% farming, 10.4% construction, 21.7% production (2000).
Income: Per capita income: $19,332 (2000); Median household income: $33,958 (2000); Poverty rate: 0.0% (2000).
Education: High school graduation rate: 82.1% (2000); College graduation rate: 3.7% (2000).

Housing: Homeownership rate: 80.7% (2000); Median home value: $125,000 (2000); Median age of housing: 27 years (2000).
Transportation: Commute to work: 88.7% car, 0.0% public transportation, 0.0% walk, 11.3% work from home (2000); Travel time to work: 18.6% less than 15 minutes, 49.0% 15 to 30 minutes, 18.6% 30 to 45 minutes, 9.8% 45 to 60 minutes, 3.9% 60 minutes or more (2000)

BENLD (city). Covers a land area of 1.058 square miles and a water area of 0 square miles. Located at 39.09° N. Lat.; 89.80° W. Long. Elevation is 640 feet.
History: Incorporated 1904; reincorporated 1930 as city.
Population: 1,541 (2000); Race: 99.3% White, 0.3% Black, 0.0% Asian, 0.0% American Indian and Alaska Native, 0.9% Hispanic of any race, 0.3% two or more races (2000); Density: 1,455.9 persons per square mile (2000); Age: 23.8% under 18, 21.4% over 64 (2000); Marriage status: 21.1% never married, 53.7% now married, 11.1% widowed, 14.2% divorced (2000); Foreign born: 0.5% (2000); Ancestry (includes multiple ancestries): 22.2% German, 19.2% Italian, 13.3% Irish, 11.3% United States or American, 6.5% Other groups (2000).
Economy: In agricultural and bituminous-coal-mining area. Manufacturing: tool and die. Employment by occupation: 8.4% management, 16.9% professional, 20.6% services, 22.8% sales, 0.3% farming, 11.2% construction, 19.6% production (2000).
Income: Per capita income: $15,521 (2000); Median household income: $30,395 (2000); Poverty rate: 14.3% (2000).
Taxes: Total city taxes per capita: $99 (1997); City property taxes per capita: $40 (1997).
Education: High school graduation rate: 77.1% (2000); College graduation rate: 9.8% (2000).
Housing: Homeownership rate: 79.8% (2000); Median home value: $45,400 (2000); Median rent: $315 per month (2000); Median age of housing: 60+ years (2000).
Newspapers: Enterprise (1 x week)
Transportation: Commute to work: 96.6% car, 0.3% public transportation, 0.3% walk, 2.0% work from home (2000); Travel time to work: 37.4% less than 15 minutes, 25.4% 15 to 30 minutes, 11.3% 30 to 45 minutes, 11.1% 45 to 60 minutes, 14.8% 60 minutes or more (2000)

BRIGHTON (village). Covers a land area of 1.610 square miles and a water area of 0.030 square miles. Located at 39.03° N. Lat.; 90.14° W. Long. Elevation is 653 feet.
Population: 2,196 (2000); Race: 98.2% White, 0.0% Black, 0.7% Asian, 0.0% American Indian and Alaska Native, 0.9% Hispanic of any race, 0.9% two or more races (2000); Density: 1,364.2 persons per square mile (2000); Age: 26.6% under 18, 14.4% over 64 (2000); Marriage status: 19.6% never married, 60.7% now married, 9.3% widowed, 10.5% divorced (2000); Foreign born: 0.6% (2000); Ancestry (includes multiple ancestries): 26.5% German, 13.9% English, 11.4% Irish, 10.9% Other groups, 9.5% United States or American (2000).
Economy: Agriculture, bituminous-coal mining. Single-family building permits issued: 21 (2001) / 23 (2000); Multi-family building permits issued: 0 (2001) / 0 (2000); Employment by occupation: 8.2% management, 13.9% professional, 19.1% services, 26.7% sales, 0.3% farming, 11.8% construction, 19.9% production (2000).
Income: Per capita income: $16,453 (2000); Median household income: $38,750 (2000); Poverty rate: 6.5% (2000).
Taxes: Total city taxes per capita: $66 (1997); City property taxes per capita: $63 (1997).
Education: High school graduation rate: 85.3% (2000); College graduation rate: 12.0% (2000).
Housing: Homeownership rate: 81.9% (2000); Median home value: $74,100 (2000); Median rent: $341 per month (2000); Median age of housing: 34 years (2000).
Newspapers: Southwestern Shoppers Guide (1 x week); The Southwestern Journal (1 x week)
Transportation: Commute to work: 98.2% car, 0.2% public transportation, 0.7% walk, 0.7% work from home (2000); Travel time to work: 16.7% less than 15 minutes, 35.6% 15 to 30 minutes, 18.6% 30 to 45 minutes, 10.9% 45 to 60 minutes, 18.2% 60 minutes or more (2000)

BUNKER HILL (city). Covers a land area of 1.180 square miles and a water area of 0.023 square miles. Located at 39.04° N. Lat.; 89.95° W. Long. Elevation is 668 feet.
History: Incorporated 1857.
Population: 1,801 (2000); Race: 97.1% White, 1.3% Black, 0.1% Asian, 0.0% American Indian and Alaska Native, 0.8% Hispanic of any race, 1.3% two or more races (2000); Density: 1,526.9 persons per square mile (2000); Age: 26.6% under 18, 17.0% over 64 (2000); Marriage status: 19.6% never married, 62.8% now married, 9.3% widowed, 8.3% divorced (2000); Foreign born: 0.4% (2000); Ancestry (includes multiple ancestries): 31.3% German, 14.1% English, 13.6% Irish, 8.4% Other groups, 7.5% United States or American (2000).
Economy: In agricultural area; bituminous coal mining; ships grain; food processing. Employment by occupation: 7.5% management, 14.8% professional, 14.4% services, 26.3% sales, 0.5% farming, 16.1% construction, 20.4% production (2000).
Income: Per capita income: $16,798 (2000); Median household income: $37,156 (2000); Poverty rate: 10.3% (2000).
Taxes: Total city taxes per capita: $85 (1997); City property taxes per capita: $80 (1997).
Education: High school graduation rate: 80.8% (2000); College graduation rate: 11.8% (2000).

School District(s)

Bunker Hill C U School District 8 (PK-12)
2000 Enrollment: 760 618-585-3116

Housing: Homeownership rate: 74.9% (2000); Median home value: $64,100 (2000); Median rent: $288 per month (2000); Median age of housing: 41 years (2000).
Newspapers: The Bunker Hill Gazette-News (1 x week); The Advertiser (1 x week)
Transportation: Commute to work: 94.9% car, 0.0% public transportation, 3.2% walk, 1.5% work from home (2000); Travel time to work: 26.2% less than 15 minutes, 20.7% 15 to 30 minutes, 30.3% 30 to 45 minutes, 8.6% 45 to 60 minutes, 14.1% 60 minutes or more (2000)

CARLINVILLE (city). Covers a land area of 2.379 square miles and a water area of 0 square miles. Located at 39.28° N. Lat.; 89.88° W. Long. Elevation is 626 feet.
History: Carlinville was the site of the "million-dollar courthouse" of Macoupin County, completed in 1870 at a cost of $1,380,500, and opposed by the taxpayers. Built of limestone, the courthouse was designed as two rectangles crossing at the center under a dome that rose 191 feet.
Population: 5,685 (2000); Race: 98.8% White, 0.3% Black, 0.2% Asian, 0.0% American Indian and Alaska Native, 1.5% Hispanic of any race, 0.7% two or more races (2000); Density: 2,389.9 persons per square mile (2000); Age: 24.5% under 18, 18.3% over 64 (2000); Marriage status: 24.8% never married, 56.6% now married, 7.3% widowed, 11.3% divorced (2000); Foreign born: 0.1% (2000); Ancestry (includes multiple ancestries): 34.8% German, 15.4% English, 12.4% Irish, 7.9% Other groups, 7.1% United States or American (2000).
Economy: Employment by occupation: 10.9% management, 18.2% professional, 21.0% services, 25.6% sales, 0.0% farming, 10.7% construction, 13.7% production (2000).
Income: Per capita income: $16,663 (2000); Median household income: $34,259 (2000); Poverty rate: 12.5% (2000).
Taxes: Total city taxes per capita: $73 (1997); City property taxes per capita: $70 (1997).
Education: High school graduation rate: 79.5% (2000); College graduation rate: 16.5% (2000).

School District(s)

Calhoun/Greene/Jersey/Macoupn Roe (06-12)
2000 Enrollment: 40 217-854-4016
Carlinville C U School District 1 (PK-12)
2000 Enrollment: 1,690 217-854-9823

Four-year College(s)

Blackburn College (Private, Not-for-profit, Presbyterian Church (USA))
2001 Enrollment: 571 217-854-3231
2001 Tuition: In-state $8,600; Out-of-state $8,600

Housing: Homeownership rate: 70.0% (2000); Median home value: $66,800 (2000); Median rent: $305 per month (2000); Median age of housing: 54 years (2000).
Hospitals: Carlinville Area Hospital (33 beds)
Newspapers: Macoupin County Enquirer (1 x week); Carlinville Democrat (1 x week)
Transportation: Commute to work: 86.6% car, 0.4% public transportation, 8.3% walk, 4.2% work from home (2000); Travel time to work: 63.1% less than 15 minutes, 14.2% 15 to 30 minutes, 3.7% 30 to 45 minutes, 7.1% 45 to 60 minutes, 11.9% 60 minutes or more (2000); Amtrak: Service available.
Additional Information Contacts
Carlinville Chamber of Commerce 217-854-2141

CHESTERFIELD (village). Covers a land area of 0.541 square miles and a water area of 0 square miles. Located at 39.25° N. Lat.; 90.06° W. Long. Elevation is 585 feet.
Population: 223 (2000); Race: 98.8% White, 0.0% Black, 0.0% Asian, 0.0% American Indian and Alaska Native, 0.0% Hispanic of any race, 1.2% two or more races (2000); Density: 412.2 persons per square mile (2000); Age: 29.3% under 18, 14.0% over 64 (2000); Marriage status: 30.1% never married, 56.6% now married, 7.7% widowed, 5.6% divorced (2000); Foreign born: 1.2% (2000); Ancestry (includes multiple ancestries): 19.0% English, 14.0% German, 13.6% Irish, 13.2% Italian, 8.7% French (except Basque) (2000).
Economy: In agricultural and bituminous-coal area. Employment by occupation: 5.9% management, 12.6% professional, 16.8% services, 16.0% sales, 1.7% farming, 12.6% construction, 34.5% production (2000).
Income: Per capita income: $18,555 (2000); Median household income: $33,125 (2000); Poverty rate: 12.1% (2000).
Taxes: Total city taxes per capita: $37 (1997); City property taxes per capita: $29 (1997).
Education: High school graduation rate: 79.1% (2000); College graduation rate: 7.9% (2000).
Housing: Homeownership rate: 80.9% (2000); Median home value: $43,200 (2000); Median rent: $308 per month (2000); Median age of housing: 48 years (2000).
Transportation: Commute to work: 93.0% car, 0.0% public transportation, 1.8% walk, 5.3% work from home (2000); Travel time to work: 14.8% less than 15 minutes, 41.7% 15 to 30 minutes, 18.5% 30 to 45 minutes, 13.0% 45 to 60 minutes, 12.0% 60 minutes or more (2000)

DORCHESTER (village). Covers a land area of 0.715 square miles and a water area of 0 square miles. Located at 39.08° N. Lat.; 89.88° W. Long. Elevation is 660 feet.
Population: 142 (2000); Race: 100.0% White, 0.0% Black, 0.0% Asian, 0.0% American Indian and Alaska Native, 1.2% Hispanic of any race, 0.0% two or more races (2000); Density: 198.5 persons per square mile (2000); Age: 21.1% under 18, 8.1% over 64 (2000); Marriage status: 22.1% never married, 58.8% now married, 7.4% widowed, 11.8% divorced (2000); Foreign born: 0.0% (2000); Ancestry (includes multiple ancestries): 36.6% German, 16.1% United States or American, 15.5% Italian, 9.9% Scottish, 8.7% Irish (2000).
Economy: In agricultural and bituminous coal area. Single-family building permits issued: 1 (2001) / 0 (2000); Multi-family building permits issued: 0 (2001) / 0 (2000); Employment by occupation: 18.4% management, 8.2% professional, 25.5% services, 15.3% sales, 3.1% farming, 15.3% construction, 14.3% production (2000).
Income: Per capita income: $17,753 (2000); Median household income: $37,500 (2000); Poverty rate: 5.6% (2000).
Taxes: Total city taxes per capita: $15 (1997); City property taxes per capita: $8 (1997).
Education: High school graduation rate: 89.0% (2000); College graduation rate: 3.7% (2000).
Housing: Homeownership rate: 95.2% (2000); Median home value: $50,600 (2000); Median rent: $275 per month (2000); Median age of housing: 51 years (2000).
Transportation: Commute to work: 95.9% car, 0.0% public transportation, 0.0% walk, 4.1% work from home (2000); Travel time to work: 8.5% less than 15 minutes, 44.7% 15 to 30 minutes, 30.9% 30 to 45 minutes, 11.7% 45 to 60 minutes, 4.3% 60 minutes or more (2000)

EAGARVILLE (village). Aka Eagerville. Covers a land area of 0.931 square miles and a water area of 0.002 square miles. Located at 39.11° N. Lat.; 89.78° W. Long. Elevation is 643 feet.
Population: 128 (2000); Race: 100.0% White, 0.0% Black, 0.0% Asian, 0.0% American Indian and Alaska Native, 0.0% Hispanic of any race, 0.0% two or more races (2000); Density: 137.5 persons per square mile (2000); Age: 31.7% under 18, 12.5% over 64 (2000); Marriage status: 14.3% never married, 73.6% now married, 6.6% widowed, 5.5% divorced (2000); Foreign born: 0.0% (2000); Ancestry (includes multiple ancestries): 20.0% Italian, 18.3% German, 12.5% Other groups, 10.8% Irish, 10.0% United States or American (2000).
Economy: Employment by occupation: 5.5% management, 10.9% professional, 25.5% services, 30.9% sales, 0.0% farming, 9.1% construction, 18.2% production (2000).
Income: Per capita income: $18,605 (2000); Median household income: $31,667 (2000); Poverty rate: 4.2% (2000).
Taxes: Total city taxes per capita: $8 (1997); City property taxes per capita: $8 (1997).
Education: High school graduation rate: 85.3% (2000); College graduation rate: 13.3% (2000).
Housing: Homeownership rate: 86.0% (2000); Median home value: $47,500 (2000); Median rent: $425 per month (2000); Median age of housing: 44 years (2000).
Transportation: Commute to work: 85.5% car, 7.3% public transportation, 0.0% walk, 0.0% work from home (2000); Travel time to work: 20.0% less than 15 minutes, 18.2% 15 to 30 minutes, 32.7% 30 to 45 minutes, 5.5% 45 to 60 minutes, 23.6% 60 minutes or more (2000)

EAST GILLESPIE (village). Covers a land area of 0.318 square miles and a water area of 0 square miles. Located at 39.13° N. Lat.; 89.81° W. Long. Elevation is 660 feet.
Population: 234 (2000); Race: 93.8% White, 1.3% Black, 0.0% Asian, 0.0% American Indian and Alaska Native, 3.1% Hispanic of any race, 4.0% two or more races (2000); Density: 735.9 persons per square mile (2000); Age: 21.1% under 18, 19.8% over 64 (2000); Marriage status: 29.8% never married, 55.5% now married, 7.9% widowed, 6.8% divorced (2000); Foreign born: 0.9% (2000); Ancestry (includes multiple ancestries): 31.3% German, 13.7% Italian, 13.7% Other groups, 8.4% English, 7.5% Irish (2000).
Economy: Employment by occupation: 8.0% management, 4.0% professional, 20.0% services, 10.0% sales, 0.0% farming, 6.0% construction, 52.0% production (2000).
Income: Per capita income: $20,628 (2000); Median household income: $35,000 (2000); Poverty rate: 5.3% (2000).
Taxes: Total city taxes per capita: $14 (1997); City property taxes per capita: $9 (1997).
Education: High school graduation rate: 81.5% (2000); College graduation rate: 5.6% (2000).
Housing: Homeownership rate: 84.9% (2000); Median home value: $48,000 (2000); Median rent: $300 per month (2000); Median age of housing: 53 years (2000).
Transportation: Commute to work: 82.7% car, 0.0% public transportation, 4.1% walk, 5.1% work from home (2000); Travel time to work: 36.6% less than 15 minutes, 26.9% 15 to 30 minutes, 10.8% 30 to 45 minutes, 4.3% 45 to 60 minutes, 21.5% 60 minutes or more (2000)

GILLESPIE (city). Covers a land area of 1.452 square miles and a water area of 0 square miles. Located at 39.12° N. Lat.; 89.81° W. Long. Elevation is 663 feet.
Population: 3,412 (2000); Race: 98.9% White, 0.0% Black, 0.2% Asian, 0.2% American Indian and Alaska Native, 1.6% Hispanic of any race, 0.7% two or more races (2000); Density: 2,349.3 persons per square mile (2000); Age: 23.1% under 18, 17.3% over 64 (2000); Marriage status: 21.9% never married, 56.7% now married, 10.1% widowed, 11.3% divorced (2000); Foreign born: 0.7% (2000); Ancestry (includes multiple ancestries): 28.9% German, 16.3% Italian, 12.1% Irish, 10.0% English, 7.1% Scottish (2000).
Economy: In agricultural and bituminous-coal area. Single-family building permits issued: 2 (2001) / 4 (2000); Multi-family building permits issued: 0 (2001) / 0 (2000); Employment by occupation: 7.8% management, 12.3% professional, 18.6% services, 26.1% sales, 1.1% farming, 10.4% construction, 23.7% production (2000).
Income: Per capita income: $19,042 (2000); Median household income: $33,168 (2000); Poverty rate: 12.4% (2000).
Taxes: Total city taxes per capita: $53 (1997); City property taxes per capita: $51 (1997).
Education: High school graduation rate: 84.8% (2000); College graduation rate: 7.6% (2000).

School District(s)

Gillespie Community Unit School District 7 (PK-12)
2000 Enrollment: 1,370 217-839-2464

Housing: Homeownership rate: 76.4% (2000); Median home value: $55,700 (2000); Median rent: $316 per month (2000); Median age of housing: 55 years (2000).
Newspapers: Gillespie Area News (1 x week)
Transportation: Commute to work: 95.0% car, 0.8% public transportation, 1.2% walk, 2.3% work from home (2000); Travel time to work: 37.6% less than 15 minutes, 23.0% 15 to 30 minutes, 10.3% 30 to 45 minutes, 10.1% 45 to 60 minutes, 19.0% 60 minutes or more (2000)

Additional Information Contacts

Coal Country Chamber of Commerce 217-839-4888

GIRARD (city). Covers a land area of 0.936 square miles and a water area of 0 square miles. Located at 39.44° N. Lat.; 89.78° W. Long. Elevation is 670 feet.
History: Incorporated 1855.
Population: 2,245 (2000); Race: 98.8% White, 0.0% Black, 0.7% Asian, 0.3% American Indian and Alaska Native, 0.4% Hispanic of any race, 0.2% two or more races (2000); Density: 2,398.9 persons per square mile (2000); Age: 23.9% under 18, 16.9% over 64 (2000); Marriage status: 23.2% never married, 53.9% now married, 10.9% widowed, 12.0% divorced (2000); Foreign born: 0.5% (2000); Ancestry (includes multiple ancestries): 22.6% German, 15.1% English, 13.8% Irish, 13.0% United States or American, 9.6% Other groups (2000).
Economy: In agricultural and bituminous coal area; ships grain. Railroad junction. Employment by occupation: 11.4% management, 14.5% professional, 19.0% services, 21.8% sales, 0.8% farming, 11.4% construction, 21.1% production (2000).
Income: Per capita income: $15,090 (2000); Median household income: $31,806 (2000); Poverty rate: 13.2% (2000).
Taxes: Total city taxes per capita: $28 (1997); City property taxes per capita: $26 (1997).
Education: High school graduation rate: 79.4% (2000); College graduation rate: 9.9% (2000).

School District(s)

Girard Community Unit School District 3 (PK-12)
2000 Enrollment: 693 217-627-2915
Housing: Homeownership rate: 69.8% (2000); Median home value: $62,900 (2000); Median rent: $282 per month (2000); Median age of housing: 47 years (2000).
Newspapers: The Girard Gazette (1 x week)
Transportation: Commute to work: 92.1% car, 0.0% public transportation, 3.9% walk, 2.6% work from home (2000); Travel time to work: 37.7% less than 15 minutes, 22.6% 15 to 30 minutes, 21.3% 30 to 45 minutes, 12.9% 45 to 60 minutes, 5.5% 60 minutes or more (2000)

HETTICK (village). Covers a land area of 0.332 square miles and a water area of 0 square miles. Located at 39.35° N. Lat.; 90.03° W. Long. Elevation is 598 feet.
Population: 182 (2000); Race: 100.0% White, 0.0% Black, 0.0% Asian, 0.0% American Indian and Alaska Native, 0.0% Hispanic of any race, 0.0% two or more races (2000); Density: 548.9 persons per square mile (2000); Age: 26.8% under 18, 20.5% over 64 (2000); Marriage status: 14.4% never married, 66.4% now married, 7.5% widowed, 11.6% divorced (2000); Foreign born: 0.0% (2000); Ancestry (includes multiple ancestries): 21.6% German, 12.1% Irish, 11.1% English, 5.3% United States or American, 2.6% Italian (2000).
Economy: In agricultural and bituminous-coal area. Employment by occupation: 5.1% management, 16.7% professional, 6.4% services, 24.4% sales, 6.4% farming, 17.9% construction, 23.1% production (2000).
Income: Per capita income: $14,117 (2000); Median household income: $30,417 (2000); Poverty rate: 10.5% (2000).
Taxes: Total city taxes per capita: $9 (1997); City property taxes per capita: $9 (1997).
Education: High school graduation rate: 71.9% (2000); College graduation rate: 8.6% (2000).
Housing: Homeownership rate: 77.1% (2000); Median home value: $42,200 (2000); Median rent: $188 per month (2000); Median age of housing: 48 years (2000).
Transportation: Commute to work: 100.0% car, 0.0% public transportation, 0.0% walk, 0.0% work from home (2000); Travel time to work: 32.1% less than 15 minutes, 39.7% 15 to 30 minutes, 7.7% 30 to 45 minutes, 15.4% 45 to 60 minutes, 5.1% 60 minutes or more (2000)

MEDORA (village). Covers a land area of 0.313 square miles and a water area of 0 square miles. Located at 39.17° N. Lat.; 90.14° W. Long. Elevation is 613 feet.
Population: 501 (2000); Race: 98.0% White, 0.0% Black, 0.0% Asian, 0.4% American Indian and Alaska Native, 0.0% Hispanic of any race, 1.6% two or more races (2000); Density: 1,598.7 persons per square mile (2000); Age: 34.8% under 18, 8.5% over 64 (2000); Marriage status: 29.3% never married, 55.9% now married, 6.8% widowed, 7.9% divorced (2000); Foreign born: 0.0% (2000); Ancestry (includes multiple ancestries): 24.1% German, 13.6% English, 11.7% United States or American, 10.9% Irish, 8.5% Other groups (2000).
Economy: In agricultural and bituminous-coal area. Employment by occupation: 5.9% management, 7.0% professional, 18.3% services, 19.9% sales, 1.6% farming, 17.2% construction, 30.1% production (2000).
Income: Per capita income: $11,052 (2000); Median household income: $26,583 (2000); Poverty rate: 12.4% (2000).
Taxes: Total city taxes per capita: $18 (1997); City property taxes per capita: $18 (1997).
Education: High school graduation rate: 78.4% (2000); College graduation rate: 3.2% (2000).
Housing: Homeownership rate: 81.0% (2000); Median home value: $44,600 (2000); Median rent: $250 per month (2000); Median age of housing: 56 years (2000).
Transportation: Commute to work: 95.1% car, 0.0% public transportation, 2.7% walk, 2.2% work from home (2000); Travel time to work: 23.9% less than 15 minutes, 25.0% 15 to 30 minutes, 28.9% 30 to 45 minutes, 8.9% 45 to 60 minutes, 13.3% 60 minutes or more (2000)

MODESTO (village). Covers a land area of 0.561 square miles and a water area of 0 square miles. Located at 39.47° N. Lat.; 89.98° W. Long. Elevation is 685 feet.
Population: 252 (2000); Race: 100.0% White, 0.0% Black, 0.0% Asian, 0.0% American Indian and Alaska Native, 0.0% Hispanic of any race, 0.0% two or more races (2000); Density: 449.2 persons per square mile (2000); Age: 27.1% under 18, 20.5% over 64 (2000); Marriage status: 23.7% never married, 58.8% now married, 10.4% widowed, 7.1% divorced (2000); Foreign born: 0.0% (2000); Ancestry (includes multiple ancestries): 15.1% United States or American, 13.6% German, 12.4% English, 5.8% Irish, 2.3% Other groups (2000).
Economy: In agricultural area: cattle, hogs; corn, wheat, sorghum, soybeans. Bituminous-coal area. Employment by occupation: 20.3% management, 6.3% professional, 16.4% services, 23.4% sales, 2.3% farming, 8.6% construction, 22.7% production (2000).
Income: Per capita income: $14,356 (2000); Median household income: $33,393 (2000); Poverty rate: 12.4% (2000).
Taxes: Total city taxes per capita: $16 (1997); City property taxes per capita: $16 (1997).
Education: High school graduation rate: 81.5% (2000); College graduation rate: 10.1% (2000).
Housing: Homeownership rate: 69.2% (2000); Median home value: $56,700 (2000); Median rent: $250 per month (2000); Median age of housing: 47 years (2000).
Transportation: Commute to work: 89.1% car, 0.0% public transportation, 7.0% walk, 0.0% work from home (2000); Travel time to work: 39.1% less than 15 minutes, 15.6% 15 to 30 minutes, 21.1% 30 to 45 minutes, 10.9% 45 to 60 minutes, 13.3% 60 minutes or more (2000)

MOUNT CLARE (village). Covers a land area of 1.516 square miles and a water area of 0.036 square miles. Located at 39.10° N. Lat.; 89.82° W. Long. Elevation is 650 feet.
Population: 433 (2000); Race: 95.6% White, 3.9% Black, 0.0% Asian, 0.0% American Indian and Alaska Native, 0.0% Hispanic of any race, 0.5% two or more races (2000); Density: 285.5 persons per square mile (2000); Age: 15.4% under 18, 42.3% over 64 (2000); Marriage status: 17.9% never married, 40.8% now married, 33.7% widowed, 7.6% divorced (2000); Foreign born: 0.2% (2000); Ancestry (includes multiple ancestries): 27.6% Italian, 26.7% German, 13.0% Irish, 9.5% Scottish, 7.8% United States or American (2000).
Economy: Employment by occupation: 11.8% management, 11.8% professional, 17.4% services, 18.6% sales, 0.0% farming, 13.7% construction, 26.7% production (2000).
Income: Per capita income: $13,451 (2000); Median household income: $37,000 (2000); Poverty rate: 6.0% (2000).
Taxes: Total city taxes per capita: $19 (1997); City property taxes per capita: $13 (1997).
Education: High school graduation rate: 60.4% (2000); College graduation rate: 5.4% (2000).
Housing: Homeownership rate: 90.1% (2000); Median home value: $46,000 (2000); Median rent: $296 per month (2000); Median age of housing: 48 years (2000).
Transportation: Commute to work: 92.5% car, 1.9% public transportation, 1.3% walk, 4.4% work from home (2000); Travel time to work: 28.3% less than 15 minutes, 32.2% 15 to 30 minutes, 13.8% 30 to 45 minutes, 13.8% 45 to 60 minutes, 11.8% 60 minutes or more (2000)

MOUNT OLIVE (city). Covers a land area of 1.104 square miles and a water area of 0 square miles. Located at 39.07° N. Lat.; 89.72° W. Long. Elevation is 684 feet.
History: Mount Olive, an early coal-mining town, was connected with two labor organizers. Alexander Bradley (1866-1918) was a leader in union organization. "Mother" Jones (1830-1930), born Mary Harris in Ireland, was buried in Mount Olive.
Population: 2,150 (2000); Race: 98.3% White, 0.0% Black, 0.0% Asian, 0.8% American Indian and Alaska Native, 0.6% Hispanic of any race, 0.2% two or more races (2000); Density: 1,948.2 persons per square mile (2000); Age: 24.1% under 18, 18.8% over 64 (2000); Marriage status: 21.1% never married, 59.6% now married, 10.2% widowed, 9.1% divorced (2000); Foreign born: 1.1% (2000); Ancestry (includes multiple ancestries): 36.8% German, 14.9% United States or American, 6.9% Irish, 5.7% English, 5.5% Other groups (2000).
Economy: Employment by occupation: 8.3% management, 16.9% professional, 13.5% services, 23.0% sales, 0.2% farming, 9.7% construction, 28.4% production (2000).
Income: Per capita income: $17,172 (2000); Median household income: $35,065 (2000); Poverty rate: 6.1% (2000).
Taxes: Total city taxes per capita: $150 (1997); City property taxes per capita: $60 (1997).
Education: High school graduation rate: 80.3% (2000); College graduation rate: 8.4% (2000).

School District(s)

Mount Olive C U School District 5 (PK-12)
2000 Enrollment: 614 217-999-7831
Housing: Homeownership rate: 83.2% (2000); Median home value: $48,500 (2000); Median rent: $257 per month (2000); Median age of housing: 60+ years (2000).
Newspapers: Mount Olive Herald (1 x week)
Transportation: Commute to work: 95.4% car, 0.0% public transportation, 1.9% walk, 1.5% work from home (2000); Travel time to work: 39.8% less than 15 minutes, 22.4% 15 to 30 minutes, 12.1% 30 to 45 minutes, 6.7% 45 to 60 minutes, 19.0% 60 minutes or more (2000)

NILWOOD (town). Covers a land area of 0.465 square miles and a water area of 0 square miles. Located at 39.39° N. Lat.; 89.80° W. Long. Elevation is 670 feet.
Population: 284 (2000); Race: 99.3% White, 0.0% Black, 0.0% Asian, 0.0% American Indian and Alaska Native, 2.5% Hispanic of any race, 0.7% two or more races (2000); Density: 610.4 persons per square mile (2000); Age: 31.4% under 18, 14.8% over 64 (2000); Marriage status: 19.5% never married, 64.9% now married, 6.3% widowed, 9.3% divorced (2000); Foreign born: 0.0% (2000); Ancestry (includes multiple ancestries): 23.0% German, 15.2% Irish, 14.1% English, 10.6% Other groups, 9.5% United States or American (2000).
Economy: In agricultural and bituminous-coal area. Employment by occupation: 6.9% management, 2.6% professional, 17.2% services, 28.4% sales, 0.0% farming, 21.6% construction, 23.3% production (2000).
Income: Per capita income: $12,365 (2000); Median household income: $32,386 (2000); Poverty rate: 16.7% (2000).
Taxes: Total city taxes per capita: $16 (1997); City property taxes per capita: $12 (1997).
Education: High school graduation rate: 70.1% (2000); College graduation rate: 5.1% (2000).
Housing: Homeownership rate: 94.3% (2000); Median home value: $52,200 (2000); Median rent: $225 per month (2000); Median age of housing: 47 years (2000).
Transportation: Commute to work: 96.5% car, 0.0% public transportation, 0.0% walk, 3.5% work from home (2000); Travel time to work: 20.9% less than 15 minutes, 35.5% 15 to 30 minutes, 18.2% 30 to 45 minutes, 12.7% 45 to 60 minutes, 12.7% 60 minutes or more (2000)

PALMYRA (village). Covers a land area of 1.000 square miles and a water area of 0 square miles. Located at 39.43° N. Lat.; 89.99° W. Long. Elevation is 680 feet.
Population: 733 (2000); Race: 98.9% White, 0.8% Black, 0.0% Asian, 0.0% American Indian and Alaska Native, 1.1% Hispanic of any race, 0.3% two or more races (2000); Density: 732.9 persons per square mile (2000); Age: 20.8% under 18, 24.6% over 64 (2000); Marriage status: 21.9% never married, 54.9% now married, 12.2% widowed, 11.0% divorced (2000); Foreign born: 0.0% (2000); Ancestry (includes multiple ancestries): 20.0% German, 15.0% Irish, 14.6% English, 8.5% United States or American, 6.3% Other groups (2000).
Economy: In agricultural and coal area. Employment by occupation: 8.3% management, 8.0% professional, 17.7% services, 31.0% sales, 0.6% farming, 17.7% construction, 16.8% production (2000).
Income: Per capita income: $14,801 (2000); Median household income: $27,188 (2000); Poverty rate: 14.7% (2000).
Taxes: Total city taxes per capita: $24 (1997); City property taxes per capita: $21 (1997).
Education: High school graduation rate: 73.7% (2000); College graduation rate: 6.0% (2000).

School District(s)

Northwestern C U School District 2 (PK-12)
2000 Enrollment: 427 217-436-2442
Housing: Homeownership rate: 71.6% (2000); Median home value: $41,900 (2000); Median rent: $264 per month (2000); Median age of housing: 52 years (2000).
Transportation: Commute to work: 94.0% car, 0.0% public transportation, 3.6% walk, 1.5% work from home (2000); Travel time to work: 24.8% less than 15 minutes, 26.4% 15 to 30 minutes, 23.0% 30 to 45 minutes, 10.1% 45 to 60 minutes, 15.6% 60 minutes or more (2000)

PIASA (unincorporated postal area, zip code 62079). Covers a land area of 6.456 square miles and a water area of 0.031 square miles. Located at 39.11° N. Lat.; 90.13° W. Long. Elevation is 600 feet.
Population: 180 (2000); Race: 100.0% White, 0.0% Black, 0.0% Asian, 0.0% American Indian and Alaska Native, 0.0% Hispanic of any race, 0.0% two or more races (2000); Density: 27.9 persons per square mile (2000); Age: 27.5% under 18, 11.3% over 64 (2000); Marriage status: 12.0% never married, 75.2% now married, 4.8% widowed, 8.0% divorced (2000); Foreign born: 0.0% (2000); Ancestry (includes multiple ancestries): 42.5% German, 20.6% United States or American, 8.8% English, 3.8% Irish, 3.8% Other groups (2000).
Economy: Employment by occupation: 27.6% management, 5.3% professional, 11.8% services, 39.5% sales, 0.0% farming, 0.0% construction, 15.8% production (2000).
Income: Per capita income: $25,089 (2000); Median household income: $66,000 (2000); Poverty rate: 3.8% (2000).
Education: High school graduation rate: 79.3% (2000); College graduation rate: 23.3% (2000).

School District(s)

Southwestern C U School District 9 (PK-12)
2000 Enrollment: 1,946 618-729-3221
Housing: Homeownership rate: 73.0% (2000); Median home value: $98,600 (2000); Median rent: $225 per month (2000); Median age of housing: 24 years (2000).
Transportation: Commute to work: 100.0% car, 0.0% public transportation, 0.0% walk, 0.0% work from home (2000); Travel time to work: 35.5% less than 15 minutes, 40.8% 15 to 30 minutes, 6.6% 30 to 45 minutes, 17.1% 45 to 60 minutes, 0.0% 60 minutes or more (2000)

ROYAL LAKES (village). Aka Royal Lake. Covers a land area of 0.466 square miles and a water area of 0.046 square miles. Located at 39.11° N. Lat.; 89.96° W. Long.
Population: 190 (2000); Race: 8.0% White, 90.3% Black, 0.0% Asian, 0.0% American Indian and Alaska Native, 1.7% Hispanic of any race, 0.0% two or more races (2000); Density: 408.1 persons per square mile (2000); Age: 29.5% under 18, 20.5% over 64 (2000); Marriage status: 22.7% never married, 53.8% now married, 13.6% widowed, 9.8% divorced (2000); Foreign born: 0.0% (2000); Ancestry (includes multiple ancestries): 39.2% Other groups, 4.5% German, 1.1% West Indian, 1.1% African (2000).
Economy: In agricultural and coal-mining region. Employment by occupation: 0.0% management, 3.4% professional, 33.9% services, 8.5% sales, 0.0% farming, 16.9% construction, 37.3% production (2000).
Income: Per capita income: $10,049 (2000); Median household income: $17,708 (2000); Poverty rate: 27.3% (2000).
Taxes: Total city taxes per capita: $37 (2000); City property taxes per capita: $37 (2000).
Education: High school graduation rate: 52.9% (2000); College graduation rate: 1.7% (2000).
Housing: Homeownership rate: 79.7% (2000); Median home value: $50,600 (2000); Median rent: $255 per month (2000); Median age of housing: 32 years (2000).
Transportation: Commute to work: 90.9% car, 0.0% public transportation, 9.1% walk, 0.0% work from home (2000); Travel time to work: 23.6% less than 15 minutes, 21.8% 15 to 30 minutes, 21.8% 30 to 45 minutes, 14.5% 45 to 60 minutes, 18.2% 60 minutes or more (2000)

SAWYERVILLE (village). Covers a land area of 1.013 square miles and a water area of 0 square miles. Located at 39.07° N. Lat.; 89.80° W. Long. Elevation is 630 feet.
Population: 295 (2000); Race: 97.8% White, 0.9% Black, 0.0% Asian, 0.0% American Indian and Alaska Native, 0.0% Hispanic of any race, 1.3% two or more races (2000); Density: 291.1 persons per square mile (2000); Age: 24.5% under 18, 16.7% over 64 (2000); Marriage status: 26.7% never married, 55.3% now married, 8.0% widowed, 9.9% divorced (2000); Foreign born: 0.0% (2000); Ancestry (includes multiple ancestries): 25.2% German, 12.6% Italian, 10.1% Irish, 8.8% English, 8.2% United States or American (2000).
Economy: Employment by occupation: 9.0% management, 9.0% professional, 26.9% services, 20.9% sales, 0.7% farming, 9.0% construction, 24.6% production (2000).
Income: Per capita income: $13,415 (2000); Median household income: $28,571 (2000); Poverty rate: 15.4% (2000).
Taxes: Total city taxes per capita: $15 (1997); City property taxes per capita: $15 (1997).
Education: High school graduation rate: 70.0% (2000); College graduation rate: 10.8% (2000).
Housing: Homeownership rate: 82.4% (2000); Median home value: $48,800 (2000); Median rent: $217 per month (2000); Median age of housing: 53 years (2000).
Transportation: Commute to work: 94.7% car, 0.0% public transportation, 0.0% walk, 5.3% work from home (2000); Travel time to work: 35.2% less than 15 minutes, 28.8% 15 to 30 minutes, 16.8% 30 to 45 minutes, 8.8% 45 to 60 minutes, 10.4% 60 minutes or more (2000)

SCOTTVILLE (village). Aka Scottsville. Covers a land area of 1.001 square miles and a water area of 0 square miles. Located at 39.47° N. Lat.; 90.10° W. Long. Elevation is 660 feet.
Population: 140 (2000); Race: 100.0% White, 0.0% Black, 0.0% Asian, 0.0% American Indian and Alaska Native, 1.4% Hispanic of any race, 0.0% two or more races (2000); Density: 139.9 persons per square mile (2000); Age: 24.5% under 18, 7.0% over 64 (2000); Marriage status: 21.7% never married, 57.4% now married, 6.1% widowed, 14.8% divorced (2000); Foreign born: 0.0% (2000); Ancestry (includes multiple ancestries): 15.4% United States or American, 15.4% Irish, 14.0% Other groups, 9.8% English, 8.4% German (2000).
Economy: In agricultural area: cattle, hogs, corn, wheat, sorghum, soybeans. Bituminous coal area. Employment by occupation: 12.0% management, 13.3% professional, 9.3% services, 16.0% sales, 5.3% farming, 8.0% construction, 36.0% production (2000).
Income: Per capita income: $14,362 (2000); Median household income: $31,875 (2000); Poverty rate: 17.5% (2000).
Taxes: Total city taxes per capita: $6 (1997); City property taxes per capita: $0 (1997).
Education: High school graduation rate: 76.0% (2000); College graduation rate: 4.0% (2000).
Housing: Homeownership rate: 91.4% (2000); Median home value: $42,500 (2000); Median rent: $142 per month (2000); Median age of housing: 60+ years (2000).
Transportation: Commute to work: 88.4% car, 0.0% public transportation, 2.9% walk, 5.8% work from home (2000); Travel time to work: 15.4% less than 15 minutes, 16.9% 15 to 30 minutes, 29.2% 30 to 45 minutes, 12.3% 45 to 60 minutes, 26.2% 60 minutes or more (2000)

SHIPMAN (town). Covers a land area of 1.321 square miles and a water area of 0.013 square miles. Located at 39.11° N. Lat.; 90.04° W. Long. Elevation is 630 feet.
Population: 655 (2000); Race: 97.0% White, 0.6% Black, 0.3% Asian, 0.0% American Indian and Alaska Native, 0.3% Hispanic of any race, 2.1% two or more races (2000); Density: 495.8 persons per square mile (2000); Age: 26.8% under 18, 14.5% over 64 (2000); Marriage status: 20.5% never married, 64.4% now married, 5.6% widowed, 9.5% divorced (2000); Foreign born: 0.3% (2000); Ancestry (includes multiple ancestries): 20.2% German, 16.7% Irish, 14.9% United States or American, 10.8% English, 7.5% Other groups (2000).
Economy: Agriculture: cattle, hogs; corn, wheat, soybeans, sorghum. Bituminous coal. Employment by occupation: 7.2% management, 12.1% professional, 14.1% services, 23.8% sales, 2.1% farming, 15.2% construction, 25.5% production (2000).
Income: Per capita income: $15,139 (2000); Median household income: $34,318 (2000); Poverty rate: 14.6% (2000).
Taxes: Total city taxes per capita: $111 (1997); City property taxes per capita: $111 (1997).
Education: High school graduation rate: 83.2% (2000); College graduation rate: 7.1% (2000).
Housing: Homeownership rate: 80.7% (2000); Median home value: $55,000 (2000); Median rent: $273 per month (2000); Median age of housing: 32 years (2000).
Transportation: Commute to work: 90.0% car, 0.0% public transportation, 5.9% walk, 3.1% work from home (2000); Travel time to work: 22.1% less than 15 minutes, 25.4% 15 to 30 minutes, 33.9% 30 to 45 minutes, 6.8% 45 to 60 minutes, 11.8% 60 minutes or more (2000)

STANDARD CITY (village). Aka South Standard. Covers a land area of 0.637 square miles and a water area of 0.003 square miles. Located at 39.35° N. Lat.; 89.78° W. Long. Elevation is 635 feet.
Population: 138 (2000); Race: 98.6% White, 0.0% Black, 0.0% Asian, 0.0% American Indian and Alaska Native, 1.4% Hispanic of any race, 0.0% two or more races (2000); Density: 216.7 persons per square mile (2000); Age: 22.5% under 18, 8.0% over 64 (2000); Marriage status: 26.3% never married, 48.2% now married, 9.6% widowed, 15.8% divorced (2000); Foreign born: 0.0% (2000); Ancestry (includes multiple ancestries): 29.0% German, 15.9% United States or American, 13.8% English, 12.3% Italian, 10.9% Other groups (2000).
Economy: In agricultural and bituminous-coal area. Employment by occupation: 2.8% management, 8.3% professional, 33.3% services, 19.4% sales, 6.9% farming, 9.7% construction, 19.4% production (2000).
Income: Per capita income: $22,852 (2000); Median household income: $19,688 (2000); Poverty rate: 22.5% (2000).
Taxes: Total city taxes per capita: $22 (1997); City property taxes per capita: $15 (1997).
Education: High school graduation rate: 72.6% (2000); College graduation rate: 3.6% (2000).
Housing: Homeownership rate: 89.7% (2000); Median home value: $40,600 (2000); Median rent: $275 per month (2000); Median age of housing: 40 years (2000).
Transportation: Commute to work: 84.3% car, 0.0% public transportation, 2.9% walk, 2.9% work from home (2000); Travel time to work: 11.8% less than 15 minutes, 45.6% 15 to 30 minutes, 20.6% 30 to 45 minutes, 22.1% 45 to 60 minutes, 0.0% 60 minutes or more (2000)

STAUNTON (city). Covers a land area of 2.282 square miles and a water area of 0.027 square miles. Located at 39.01° N. Lat.; 89.78° W. Long. Elevation is 622 feet.
History: Staunton was settled in 1817 by John Wood of Virginia, and a village was laid out in 1835. Staunton was named for one of its founders, and operated as a trading point for settlers. Later, coal mining was an important industry.
Population: 5,030 (2000); Race: 98.5% White, 0.2% Black, 0.4% Asian, 0.1% American Indian and Alaska Native, 0.8% Hispanic of any race, 0.5% two or more races (2000); Density: 2,204.6 persons per square mile (2000); Age: 25.8% under 18, 18.4% over 64 (2000); Marriage status: 18.9% never married, 62.8% now married, 7.9% widowed, 10.3% divorced (2000); Foreign born: 0.6% (2000); Ancestry (includes multiple ancestries): 36.2% German, 13.6% Irish, 12.8% Italian, 7.9% English, 7.8% Other groups (2000).
Economy: Single-family building permits issued: 20 (2001) / 20 (2000); Multi-family building permits issued: 2 (2001) / 12 (2000); Employment by occupation: 8.5% management, 15.1% professional, 14.8% services, 29.9% sales, 0.0% farming, 14.6% construction, 17.2% production (2000).
Income: Per capita income: $16,905 (2000); Median household income: $35,893 (2000); Poverty rate: 6.6% (2000).
Taxes: Total city taxes per capita: $59 (1997); City property taxes per capita: $55 (1997).
Education: High school graduation rate: 82.9% (2000); College graduation rate: 12.9% (2000).

School District(s)

Staunton Community Unit School District 6 (PK-12)
2000 Enrollment: 1,240 618-635-2962

Housing: Homeownership rate: 75.4% (2000); Median home value: $69,500 (2000); Median rent: $315 per month (2000); Median age of housing: 51 years (2000).
Hospitals: Community Memorial Hospital (49 beds)
Newspapers: Staunton Star-Times (1 x week)
Transportation: Commute to work: 95.3% car, 0.0% public transportation, 1.6% walk, 2.0% work from home (2000); Travel time to work: 40.1% less

than 15 minutes, 16.7% 15 to 30 minutes, 21.6% 30 to 45 minutes, 14.3% 45 to 60 minutes, 7.3% 60 minutes or more (2000)
Additional Information Contacts
Staunton Chamber of Commerce 618-635-8356

VIRDEN (city). Covers a land area of 1.716 square miles and a water area of 0 square miles. Located at 39.50° N. Lat.; 89.76° W. Long. Elevation is 675 feet.
History: Virden was a coal mining town and the location of the Virden riot in 1898 when mine operators refused to pay the rates established by the Illinois Coal Operators Association.
Population: 3,488 (2000); Race: 98.7% White, 0.4% Black, 0.2% Asian, 0.2% American Indian and Alaska Native, 0.4% Hispanic of any race, 0.3% two or more races (2000); Density: 2,032.6 persons per square mile (2000); Age: 23.5% under 18, 20.7% over 64 (2000); Marriage status: 17.8% never married, 61.4% now married, 9.5% widowed, 11.2% divorced (2000); Foreign born: 0.3% (2000); Ancestry (includes multiple ancestries): 22.9% German, 16.8% English, 13.5% Irish, 11.5% United States or American, 5.4% Other groups (2000).
Economy: Employment by occupation: 9.1% management, 20.3% professional, 13.9% services, 27.7% sales, 0.7% farming, 10.2% construction, 18.2% production (2000).
Income: Per capita income: $16,541 (2000); Median household income: $31,905 (2000); Poverty rate: 10.7% (2000).
Taxes: Total city taxes per capita: $56 (1997); City property taxes per capita: $50 (1997).
Education: High school graduation rate: 82.1% (2000); College graduation rate: 9.5% (2000).

School District(s)

Virden Community Unit School District 4 (PK-12)
2000 Enrollment: 978 217-965-4226
Housing: Homeownership rate: 74.0% (2000); Median home value: $66,900 (2000); Median rent: $299 per month (2000); Median age of housing: 48 years (2000).
Newspapers: The Virden Recorder (1 x week); Northwestern News (1 x week)
Transportation: Commute to work: 93.8% car, 0.0% public transportation, 1.5% walk, 4.3% work from home (2000); Travel time to work: 33.0% less than 15 minutes, 18.8% 15 to 30 minutes, 33.0% 30 to 45 minutes, 11.5% 45 to 60 minutes, 3.7% 60 minutes or more (2000)

WHITE CITY (village). Covers a land area of 1.215 square miles and a water area of 0 square miles. Located at 39.07° N. Lat.; 89.76° W. Long. Elevation is 652 feet.
Population: 221 (2000); Race: 99.0% White, 0.0% Black, 0.0% Asian, 0.0% American Indian and Alaska Native, 0.0% Hispanic of any race, 1.0% two or more races (2000); Density: 181.9 persons per square mile (2000); Age: 27.9% under 18, 14.2% over 64 (2000); Marriage status: 20.6% never married, 42.6% now married, 12.9% widowed, 23.9% divorced (2000); Foreign born: 0.0% (2000); Ancestry (includes multiple ancestries): 43.7% German, 12.7% Other groups, 12.7% English, 12.2% Irish, 11.7% United States or American (2000).
Economy: In agricultural and bituminous-coal area: cattle, hogs; corn, wheat, soybeans, sorghum. Employment by occupation: 9.7% management, 6.9% professional, 20.8% services, 27.8% sales, 0.0% farming, 16.7% construction, 18.1% production (2000).
Income: Per capita income: $14,826 (2000); Median household income: $26,000 (2000); Poverty rate: 19.3% (2000).
Taxes: Total city taxes per capita: $58 (1997); City property taxes per capita: $4 (1997).
Education: High school graduation rate: 83.2% (2000); College graduation rate: 3.1% (2000).
Housing: Homeownership rate: 94.5% (2000); Median home value: $60,600 (2000); Median rent: $225 per month (2000); Median age of housing: 32 years (2000).
Transportation: Commute to work: 97.1% car, 0.0% public transportation, 0.0% walk, 2.9% work from home (2000); Travel time to work: 25.8% less than 15 minutes, 33.3% 15 to 30 minutes, 18.2% 30 to 45 minutes, 13.6% 45 to 60 minutes, 9.1% 60 minutes or more (2000)

WILSONVILLE (village). Covers a land area of 0.954 square miles and a water area of 0.024 square miles. Located at 39.07° N. Lat.; 89.85° W. Long. Elevation is 640 feet.
Population: 604 (2000); Race: 97.1% White, 1.3% Black, 0.0% Asian, 0.8% American Indian and Alaska Native, 0.0% Hispanic of any race, 0.8% two or more races (2000); Density: 633.4 persons per square mile (2000); Age: 25.6% under 18, 19.5% over 64 (2000); Marriage status: 25.2% never married, 55.7% now married, 10.4% widowed, 8.7% divorced (2000); Foreign born: 1.0% (2000); Ancestry (includes multiple ancestries): 20.8% Italian, 16.9% United States or American, 15.1% Other groups, 14.7% German, 9.8% English (2000).
Economy: Employment by occupation: 5.7% management, 11.7% professional, 10.0% services, 21.3% sales, 0.0% farming, 13.5% construction, 37.8% production (2000).
Income: Per capita income: $15,089 (2000); Median household income: $27,917 (2000); Poverty rate: 9.8% (2000).
Taxes: Total city taxes per capita: $22 (1997); City property taxes per capita: $17 (1997).
Education: High school graduation rate: 74.7% (2000); College graduation rate: 5.1% (2000).
Housing: Homeownership rate: 86.8% (2000); Median home value: $39,400 (2000); Median rent: $336 per month (2000); Median age of housing: 60+ years (2000).
Transportation: Commute to work: 93.7% car, 0.0% public transportation, 0.0% walk, 3.2% work from home (2000); Travel time to work: 12.6% less than 15 minutes, 23.7% 15 to 30 minutes, 20.0% 30 to 45 minutes, 18.6% 45 to 60 minutes, 25.1% 60 minutes or more (2000)

Madison County

Located in southwestern Illinois; bounded on the west by the Mississippi River and the Missouri border; drained by Cahokia and Silver Creeks. Covers a land area of 725.00 square miles, a water area of 15.30 square miles, and is located in the Central Time Zone. The county government was organized in 1812. County seat is Edwardsville.

Madison County is part of the St. Louis, MO-IL MSA. The entire metro area includes: Clinton County, IL; Jersey County, IL; Madison County, IL; Monroe County, IL; St. Clair County, IL; Crawford County, MO (pt.)**; Franklin County, MO; Jefferson County, MO; Lincoln County, MO; St. Charles County, MO; St. Louis County, MO; Warren County, MO; St. Louis city, MO

Weather Station: Alton Melvin Price Lock & Dam — Elevation: 429 feet

	Jan	Feb	Mar	Apr	May	Jun	Jul	Aug	Sep	Oct	Nov	Dec
High	35	41	52	64	75	84	88	86	79	67	53	41
Low	19	23	33	45	55	64	69	66	58	46	35	25
Precip	2.0	2.1	3.5	4.4	4.3	3.2	3.5	3.1	3.1	2.7	3.8	3.0
Snow	na	na	2.1	0.4	0.0	0.0	0.0	0.0	0.0	tr	0.3	0.4

High and Low temperatures in degrees Fahrenheit; Precipitation and Snow in inches

Population: 258,941 (2000); Race: 90.2% White, 7.2% Black, 0.5% Asian, 0.3% American Indian and Alaska Native, 1.7% Hispanic of any race, 1.3% two or more races (2000); Density: 357.2 persons per square mile (2000); Age: 24.9% under 18, 14.3% over 64 (2000).
Religion: Five largest groups: 16.4% Catholic Church, 8.4% Southern Baptist Convention, 5.3% Lutheran Church—Missouri Synod, 4.2% United Church of Christ, 3.5% The United Methodist Church (2000).
Economy: Unemployment rate: 6.0% (11/2002); Total civilian labor force: 126,208 (11/2002); Leading industries: 21.2% manufacturing; 15.2% health care and social assistance; 14.1% retail trade (2000); Companies that employ more than 1,000 persons: 5 (2000); Companies that employ more than 100 persons: 116 (2000); Farms: 1,195 totaling 283,608 acres (1997); Minority business ownership rate: 4.7% (1997); Women business ownership rate: 30.0% (1997); Retail sales per capita: $7,945 (1997). Single-family building permits issued: 971 (2001) / 910 (2000); Multi-family building permits issued: 297 (2001) / 255 (2000).
Income: Per capita income: $20,509 (2000); Median household income: $41,541 (2000); Poverty rate: 9.8% (2000); Bankruptcy rate: 7.64% (2001).
Taxes: Total county taxes per capita: $78 (2000); County property taxes per capita: $76 (2000).
Education: High school graduation rate: 84.3% (2000); College graduation rate: 19.2% (2000).
Housing: Homeownership rate: 73.8% (2000); Median home value: $77,200 (2000); Median rent: $383 per month (2000); Median age of housing: 38 years (2000).
Health: Birth rate: 130.2 per 10,000 population (1998); Age adjusted death rate: 95.1 per 10,000 population (1999); Age adjusted cancer mortality rate: 213.9 deaths per 100,000 population (1999). Air Quality Index: 50% good, 49% moderate, 1% unhealthy (percent of days in 2000). Number of physicians: 11.6 per 10,000 population (1999); Number of hospital beds: 45.1 per 10,000 population (1999).

Elections: 2000 Presidential election results: 53.2% Gore, 43.9% Bush, 2.1% Nader, 0.4% Buchanan
National and State Parks: Horseshoe Lake State Park; Lovejoy State Memorial
Additional Information Contacts
Madison County Government Offices 618-692-6290
Collinsville Chamber of Commerce...................... 618-344-2884
Edwardsville Chamber of Commerce 618-656-7600
Godfrey Chamber of Commerce 618-467-2280
Greater Gateway Association of Realtors 618-692-8300
Highland Chamber of Commerce.......................... 618-654-3721
Tri-Cities Area Chamber of Commerce.................. 618-876-6400
Troy Chamber of Commerce 618-667-8769

Madison County Communities

ALHAMBRA (village). Covers a land area of 0.755 square miles and a water area of 0.006 square miles. Located at 38.88° N. Lat.; 89.73° W. Long. Elevation is 570 feet.
Population: 630 (2000); Race: 98.6% White, 0.0% Black, 0.0% Asian, 0.0% American Indian and Alaska Native, 0.0% Hispanic of any race, 1.4% two or more races (2000); Density: 834.4 persons per square mile (2000); Age: 18.8% under 18, 33.4% over 64 (2000); Marriage status: 15.5% never married, 62.8% now married, 14.9% widowed, 6.9% divorced (2000); Foreign born: 0.0% (2000); Ancestry (includes multiple ancestries): 46.9% German, 13.2% Irish, 9.6% English, 7.6% United States or American, 7.5% Other groups (2000).
Economy: In agricultural area: wheat, corn, soybeans; cattle; dairy. Single-family building permits issued: 0 (2001) / 4 (2000); Multi-family building permits issued: 0 (2001) / 0 (2000); Employment by occupation: 10.3% management, 6.5% professional, 14.5% services, 29.4% sales, 0.0% farming, 17.6% construction, 21.8% production (2000).
Income: Per capita income: $16,124 (2000); Median household income: $36,818 (2000); Poverty rate: 4.7% (2000).
Taxes: Total city taxes per capita: $51 (1997); City property taxes per capita: $50 (1997).
Education: High school graduation rate: 69.6% (2000); College graduation rate: 8.5% (2000).
Housing: Homeownership rate: 81.1% (2000); Median home value: $70,200 (2000); Median rent: $317 per month (2000); Median age of housing: 39 years (2000).
Transportation: Commute to work: 85.7% car, 0.0% public transportation, 5.8% walk, 7.7% work from home (2000); Travel time to work: 24.3% less than 15 minutes, 32.2% 15 to 30 minutes, 24.3% 30 to 45 minutes, 10.0% 45 to 60 minutes, 9.2% 60 minutes or more (2000)

ALTON (city). Covers a land area of 15.645 square miles and a water area of 0.961 square miles. Located at 38.90° N. Lat.; 90.16° W. Long. Elevation is 520 feet.
History: Alton's first known settler arrived about 1783, but significant settlement began between 1816 and 1818, when three towns were founded at this advantageous river location. One of these, planned by Colonel Rufus Easton and named for one of his sons, Alton, absorbed the other towns and was incorporated as a city in 1837. Alton was the site of the Lincoln-Shields duel in 1842, and the last Lincoln-Douglas debate in 1858.
Population: 30,496 (2000); Race: 72.5% White, 23.5% Black, 0.2% Asian, 0.4% American Indian and Alaska Native, 1.8% Hispanic of any race, 2.5% two or more races (2000); Density: 1,949.3 persons per square mile (2000); Age: 25.7% under 18, 16.1% over 64 (2000); Marriage status: 29.0% never married, 47.9% now married, 9.7% widowed, 13.4% divorced (2000); Foreign born: 0.9% (2000); Ancestry (includes multiple ancestries): 27.4% Other groups, 22.1% German, 12.2% Irish, 8.2% United States or American, 7.9% English (2000).
Vital Statistics: Birth rate: 169.2 per 10,000 population (1998)
Economy: Unemployment rate: 9.3% (11/2002); Total civilian labor force: 13,598 (11/2002); Single-family building permits issued: 10 (2001) / 12 (2000); Multi-family building permits issued: 16 (2001) / 62 (2000); Employment by occupation: 7.4% management, 18.1% professional, 22.3% services, 26.2% sales, 0.2% farming, 7.5% construction, 18.4% production (2000).
Income: Per capita income: $16,817 (2000); Median household income: $31,213 (2000); Poverty rate: 18.7% (2000).
Taxes: Total city taxes per capita: $243 (2000); City property taxes per capita: $112 (2000).
Education: High school graduation rate: 81.2% (2000); College graduation rate: 16.1% (2000).

School District(s)
Alton Community Unit School District 11 (PK-12)
2000 Enrollment: 7,025 618-474-2600
Housing: Homeownership rate: 65.4% (2000); Median home value: $56,500 (2000); Median rent: $330 per month (2000); Median age of housing: 51 years (2000).
Hospitals: Alton Memorial Hospital (222 beds); Saint Anthony's Hospital (292 beds)
Newspapers: The Telegraph (7 x week); The Cover Story (1 x week)
Transportation: Commute to work: 92.9% car, 2.6% public transportation, 2.1% walk, 1.5% work from home (2000); Travel time to work: 39.5% less than 15 minutes, 26.7% 15 to 30 minutes, 17.5% 30 to 45 minutes, 11.6% 45 to 60 minutes, 4.6% 60 minutes or more (2000); Amtrak: Service available.
Airports: St Louis Regional

BETHALTO (village). Covers a land area of 6.578 square miles and a water area of 0 square miles. Located at 38.90° N. Lat.; 90.04° W. Long. Elevation is 521 feet.
History: Incorporated 1869.
Population: 9,454 (2000); Race: 97.0% White, 0.5% Black, 0.4% Asian, 0.6% American Indian and Alaska Native, 1.1% Hispanic of any race, 0.9% two or more races (2000); Density: 1,437.3 persons per square mile (2000); Age: 26.8% under 18, 13.9% over 64 (2000); Marriage status: 22.4% never married, 58.7% now married, 8.1% widowed, 10.9% divorced (2000); Foreign born: 1.2% (2000); Ancestry (includes multiple ancestries): 25.4% German, 14.8% Irish, 13.1% United States or American, 12.4% English, 7.3% Other groups (2000).
Economy: In agricultural area: corn, wheat; poultry, livestock; dairy products. Single-family building permits issued: 16 (2001) / 15 (2000); Multi-family building permits issued: 22 (2001) / 22 (2000); Employment by occupation: 8.0% management, 17.8% professional, 18.2% services, 24.7% sales, 0.0% farming, 12.3% construction, 18.9% production (2000).
Income: Per capita income: $18,697 (2000); Median household income: $42,201 (2000); Poverty rate: 9.2% (2000).
Taxes: Total city taxes per capita: $188 (1997); City property taxes per capita: $102 (1997).
Education: High school graduation rate: 85.9% (2000); College graduation rate: 13.9% (2000).

School District(s)
Bethalto C U School District 8 (PK-12)
2000 Enrollment: 2,880 618-377-7200
Housing: Homeownership rate: 72.0% (2000); Median home value: $78,900 (2000); Median rent: $422 per month (2000); Median age of housing: 31 years (2000).
Transportation: Commute to work: 96.3% car, 0.2% public transportation, 1.7% walk, 1.2% work from home (2000); Travel time to work: 35.6% less than 15 minutes, 37.8% 15 to 30 minutes, 14.2% 30 to 45 minutes, 8.9% 45 to 60 minutes, 3.5% 60 minutes or more (2000)

COLLINSVILLE (city). Covers a land area of 13.594 square miles and a water area of 0.014 square miles. Located at 38.67° N. Lat.; 89.99° W. Long. Elevation is 565 feet.
History: Collinsville was settled in 1817 by William Collins and his brothers from Connecticut. Between the five brothers they operated a store, blacksmith shop, shoe shop, wagon shop, sawmill, tannery, distillery, and a church. Collinsville was incorporated as a village in 1856, and as a city in 1859. The arrival of the railroad in 1869 led to mining of a coal seam and building of an ore-smelting furnace.
Population: 24,707 (2000); Race: 91.2% White, 6.4% Black, 0.7% Asian, 0.3% American Indian and Alaska Native, 1.6% Hispanic of any race, 1.1% two or more races (2000); Density: 1,817.4 persons per square mile (2000); Age: 22.3% under 18, 15.4% over 64 (2000); Marriage status: 25.1% never married, 54.1% now married, 8.8% widowed, 12.0% divorced (2000); Foreign born: 1.7% (2000); Ancestry (includes multiple ancestries): 32.5% German, 16.3% Irish, 12.8% Other groups, 12.1% English, 9.3% Italian (2000).
Vital Statistics: Birth rate: 159.5 per 10,000 population (1998)
Economy: Single-family building permits issued: 61 (2001) / 67 (2000); Multi-family building permits issued: 72 (2001) / 42 (2000); Employment by occupation: 12.6% management, 20.3% professional, 13.8% services, 30.0% sales, 0.3% farming, 9.2% construction, 13.7% production (2000).
Income: Per capita income: $22,048 (2000); Median household income: $42,353 (2000); Poverty rate: 7.2% (2000).

Taxes: Total city taxes per capita: $160 (2000); City property taxes per capita: $98 (2000).
Education: High school graduation rate: 85.4% (2000); College graduation rate: 21.4% (2000).

School District(s)

Collinsville C U School District 10 (PK-12)
2000 Enrollment: 5,900 618-346-6350
Housing: Homeownership rate: 67.2% (2000); Median home value: $83,500 (2000); Median rent: $415 per month (2000); Median age of housing: 35 years (2000).
Newspapers: Collinsville Journal (2 x week); Collinsville Herald (1 x week); Edwardsville Journal (1 x week); East St. Louis News Journal (1 x week); Cahokia-Dupo Journal (2 x week)
Transportation: Commute to work: 95.1% car, 1.5% public transportation, 1.1% walk, 1.6% work from home (2000); Travel time to work: 27.0% less than 15 minutes, 35.5% 15 to 30 minutes, 25.0% 30 to 45 minutes, 8.4% 45 to 60 minutes, 4.3% 60 minutes or more (2000)
Additional Information Contacts
Collinsville Chamber of Commerce. 618-344-2884

COTTAGE HILLS (unincorporated postal area, zip code 62018). Covers a land area of 3.618 square miles and a water area of 0 square miles. Located at 38.90° N. Lat.; 90.08° W. Long. Elevation is 530 feet.
Population: 4,387 (2000); Race: 94.4% White, 2.5% Black, 0.0% Asian, 0.2% American Indian and Alaska Native, 0.6% Hispanic of any race, 2.9% two or more races (2000); Density: 1,212.5 persons per square mile (2000); Age: 27.2% under 18, 10.8% over 64 (2000); Marriage status: 28.0% never married, 52.3% now married, 6.1% widowed, 13.6% divorced (2000); Foreign born: 0.6% (2000); Ancestry (includes multiple ancestries): 23.9% German, 23.4% United States or American, 12.5% Other groups, 8.0% Irish, 4.4% French (except Basque) (2000).
Economy: Residential suburb of St. Louis. Employment by occupation: 5.3% management, 9.5% professional, 24.8% services, 25.8% sales, 0.0% farming, 14.9% construction, 19.7% production (2000).
Income: Per capita income: $13,242 (2000); Median household income: $29,898 (2000); Poverty rate: 17.3% (2000).
Education: High school graduation rate: 75.0% (2000); College graduation rate: 3.2% (2000).
Housing: Homeownership rate: 73.3% (2000); Median home value: $52,300 (2000); Median rent: $326 per month (2000); Median age of housing: 38 years (2000).
Transportation: Commute to work: 96.8% car, 0.0% public transportation, 2.1% walk, 0.7% work from home (2000); Travel time to work: 32.0% less than 15 minutes, 35.8% 15 to 30 minutes, 17.0% 30 to 45 minutes, 9.9% 45 to 60 minutes, 5.4% 60 minutes or more (2000)

DORSEY (unincorporated postal area, zip code 62021). Aka Dorsey's. Covers a land area of 20.799 square miles and a water area of 0.041 square miles. Located at 38.97° N. Lat.; 89.97° W. Long. Elevation is 585 feet.
Population: 965 (2000); Race: 100.0% White, 0.0% Black, 0.0% Asian, 0.0% American Indian and Alaska Native, 0.0% Hispanic of any race, 0.0% two or more races (2000); Density: 46.4 persons per square mile (2000); Age: 24.5% under 18, 10.4% over 64 (2000); Marriage status: 17.6% never married, 70.9% now married, 3.7% widowed, 7.8% divorced (2000); Foreign born: 0.5% (2000); Ancestry (includes multiple ancestries): 41.5% German, 14.2% United States or American, 12.1% Irish, 7.4% English, 5.7% Italian (2000).
Economy: Employment by occupation: 13.6% management, 14.5% professional, 10.9% services, 26.4% sales, 0.9% farming, 14.5% construction, 19.2% production (2000).
Income: Per capita income: $21,055 (2000); Median household income: $40,000 (2000); Poverty rate: 0.0% (2000).
Education: High school graduation rate: 89.7% (2000); College graduation rate: 17.5% (2000).
Housing: Homeownership rate: 95.1% (2000); Median home value: $85,700 (2000); Median rent: $375 per month (2000); Median age of housing: 32 years (2000).
Transportation: Commute to work: 96.8% car, 0.0% public transportation, 0.0% walk, 3.2% work from home (2000); Travel time to work: 20.0% less than 15 minutes, 46.5% 15 to 30 minutes, 22.7% 30 to 45 minutes, 9.3% 45 to 60 minutes, 1.5% 60 minutes or more (2000)

EAST ALTON (village). Covers a land area of 5.502 square miles and a water area of 0.131 square miles. Located at 38.88° N. Lat.; 90.10° W. Long. Elevation is 440 feet.
History: In 1893 the Western Cartridge Company established a powder mill in East Alton and began the manufacture of ammunition.
Population: 6,830 (2000); Race: 96.2% White, 1.4% Black, 0.2% Asian, 0.1% American Indian and Alaska Native, 1.7% Hispanic of any race, 1.4% two or more races (2000); Density: 1,241.3 persons per square mile (2000); Age: 24.0% under 18, 17.6% over 64 (2000); Marriage status: 22.2% never married, 51.4% now married, 10.8% widowed, 15.7% divorced (2000); Foreign born: 0.5% (2000); Ancestry (includes multiple ancestries): 23.6% German, 13.4% Irish, 12.0% Other groups, 11.9% English, 10.7% United States or American (2000).
Economy: Single-family building permits issued: 4 (2001) / 3 (2000); Multi-family building permits issued: 0 (2001) / 0 (2000); Employment by occupation: 6.6% management, 11.3% professional, 19.9% services, 31.0% sales, 0.3% farming, 12.1% construction, 18.9% production (2000).
Income: Per capita income: $15,572 (2000); Median household income: $28,404 (2000); Poverty rate: 13.3% (2000).
Taxes: Total city taxes per capita: $190 (1997); City property taxes per capita: $176 (1997).
Education: High school graduation rate: 73.6% (2000); College graduation rate: 7.7% (2000).

School District(s)

East Alton School District 13 (PK-08)
2000 Enrollment: 1,032 618-433-2051
Housing: Homeownership rate: 58.6% (2000); Median home value: $55,600 (2000); Median rent: $317 per month (2000); Median age of housing: 51 years (2000).
Transportation: Commute to work: 94.8% car, 0.8% public transportation, 1.6% walk, 1.8% work from home (2000); Travel time to work: 40.5% less than 15 minutes, 26.6% 15 to 30 minutes, 18.7% 30 to 45 minutes, 9.1% 45 to 60 minutes, 5.1% 60 minutes or more (2000)

EDWARDSVILLE (city). Covers a land area of 13.872 square miles and a water area of 0.218 square miles. Located at 38.80° N. Lat.; 89.95° W. Long. Elevation is 540 feet.
History: Edwardsville was settled by James Gillham of Kentucky in 1800. Some of his friends followed and a town was platted in 1813, named for Ninian Edwards, governor of Illinois Territory from 1809-1818. Edwardsville was incorporated in 1837.
Population: 21,491 (2000); Race: 87.8% White, 8.0% Black, 1.6% Asian, 0.5% American Indian and Alaska Native, 1.0% Hispanic of any race, 1.9% two or more races (2000); Density: 1,549.2 persons per square mile (2000); Age: 22.9% under 18, 11.8% over 64 (2000); Marriage status: 28.8% never married, 56.0% now married, 5.7% widowed, 9.4% divorced (2000); Foreign born: 3.1% (2000); Ancestry (includes multiple ancestries): 33.9% German, 15.8% Other groups, 12.9% Irish, 11.6% English, 5.3% Italian (2000).
Vital Statistics: Birth rate: 141.0 per 10,000 population (1998)
Economy: Single-family building permits issued: 131 (2001) / 139 (2000); Multi-family building permits issued: 50 (2001) / 52 (2000); Employment by occupation: 16.5% management, 30.4% professional, 14.4% services, 24.5% sales, 0.1% farming, 5.3% construction, 8.7% production (2000).
Income: Per capita income: $26,510 (2000); Median household income: $50,921 (2000); Poverty rate: 8.6% (2000).
Taxes: Total city taxes per capita: $211 (2000); City property taxes per capita: $177 (2000).
Education: High school graduation rate: 92.6% (2000); College graduation rate: 41.9% (2000).

School District(s)

Edwardsville C U School District 7 (PK-12)
2000 Enrollment: 6,501 618-656-1182
Madison Co Education Therapy Center (05-12)
2000 Enrollment: 39 618-692-6200
Madison Roe (08-12)
2000 Enrollment: 7 618-692-6200

Four-year College(s)

Southern Illinois University-Edwardsville (Public)
2001 Enrollment: 12,442 618-650-2000
2001 Tuition: In-state $2,574; Out-of-state $5,148
Housing: Homeownership rate: 70.8% (2000); Median home value: $99,200 (2000); Median rent: $473 per month (2000); Median age of housing: 33 years (2000).
Newspapers: Edwardsville Intelligencer (6 x week)
Transportation: Commute to work: 91.9% car, 2.0% public transportation, 2.8% walk, 2.5% work from home (2000); Travel time to work: 35.4% less than 15 minutes, 25.6% 15 to 30 minutes, 23.1% 30 to 45 minutes, 11.3% 45 to 60 minutes, 4.7% 60 minutes or more (2000)
Additional Information Contacts

Edwardsville Chamber of Commerce 618-656-7600

GLEN CARBON (village). Covers a land area of 7.417 square miles and a water area of 0.043 square miles. Located at 38.76° N. Lat.; 89.96° W. Long. Elevation is 530 feet.
History: Incorporated 1892.
Population: 10,425 (2000); Race: 90.3% White, 6.5% Black, 1.2% Asian, 0.3% American Indian and Alaska Native, 2.5% Hispanic of any race, 0.9% two or more races (2000); Density: 1,405.5 persons per square mile (2000); Age: 25.5% under 18, 11.4% over 64 (2000); Marriage status: 24.3% never married, 64.0% now married, 5.6% widowed, 6.1% divorced (2000); Foreign born: 2.4% (2000); Ancestry (includes multiple ancestries): 32.7% German, 15.1% Irish, 13.7% Other groups, 12.0% English, 4.9% United States or American (2000).
Economy: In agricultural area: corn, wheat, cattle. Single-family building permits issued: 73 (2001) / 83 (2000); Multi-family building permits issued: 59 (2001) / 8 (2000); Employment by occupation: 19.5% management, 30.0% professional, 10.1% services, 24.9% sales, 0.0% farming, 5.0% construction, 10.5% production (2000).
Income: Per capita income: $26,374 (2000); Median household income: $55,841 (2000); Poverty rate: 5.8% (2000).
Taxes: Total city taxes per capita: $163 (1997); City property taxes per capita: $119 (1997).
Education: High school graduation rate: 90.4% (2000); College graduation rate: 42.5% (2000).
Housing: Homeownership rate: 74.2% (2000); Median home value: $125,700 (2000); Median rent: $494 per month (2000); Median age of housing: 16 years (2000).
Transportation: Commute to work: 94.4% car, 1.2% public transportation, 0.7% walk, 3.5% work from home (2000); Travel time to work: 25.3% less than 15 minutes, 30.9% 15 to 30 minutes, 29.4% 30 to 45 minutes, 10.4% 45 to 60 minutes, 4.1% 60 minutes or more (2000)
Additional Information Contacts
Greater Gateway Association of Realtors 618-692-8300

GODFREY (village). Covers a land area of 34.481 square miles and a water area of 1.686 square miles. Located at 38.94° N. Lat.; 90.20° W. Long. Elevation is 610 feet.
History: Godfrey grew around the Monticello College and Preparatory School for Girls, founded in 1835 by a retired Cape Cod sea captain, Benjamin Godfrey.
Population: 16,286 (2000); Race: 94.2% White, 3.4% Black, 0.9% Asian, 0.3% American Indian and Alaska Native, 1.6% Hispanic of any race, 1.0% two or more races (2000); Density: 472.3 persons per square mile (2000); Age: 22.5% under 18, 17.4% over 64 (2000); Marriage status: 20.4% never married, 63.3% now married, 8.1% widowed, 8.2% divorced (2000); Foreign born: 1.8% (2000); Ancestry (includes multiple ancestries): 34.2% German, 14.2% Irish, 13.6% English, 9.9% Other groups, 8.4% United States or American (2000).
Economy: Single-family building permits issued: 74 (2001) / 61 (2000); Multi-family building permits issued: 2 (2001) / 0 (2000); Employment by occupation: 13.2% management, 24.4% professional, 13.2% services, 25.6% sales, 0.2% farming, 8.7% construction, 14.8% production (2000).
Income: Per capita income: $25,292 (2000); Median household income: $50,342 (2000); Poverty rate: 5.9% (2000).
Taxes: Total city taxes per capita: $5 (1997); City property taxes per capita: $0 (1997).
Education: High school graduation rate: 87.8% (2000); College graduation rate: 25.0% (2000).

Two-year College(s)
Lewis and Clark Community College (Public)
2001 Enrollment: 6,985 618-466-3411
2001 Tuition: In-state $5,811; Out-of-state $8,921
Housing: Homeownership rate: 85.1% (2000); Median home value: $89,400 (2000); Median rent: $436 per month (2000); Median age of housing: 32 years (2000).
Transportation: Commute to work: 96.0% car, 0.7% public transportation, 0.6% walk, 2.1% work from home (2000); Travel time to work: 31.7% less than 15 minutes, 35.1% 15 to 30 minutes, 14.2% 30 to 45 minutes, 11.5% 45 to 60 minutes, 7.6% 60 minutes or more (2000)
Additional Information Contacts
Godfrey Chamber of Commerce 618-467-2280

GRANITE CITY (city). Covers a land area of 16.683 square miles and a water area of 0.487 square miles. Located at 38.71° N. Lat.; 90.13° W. Long. Elevation is 425 feet.
History: Farmers settled here in the early 1800's, but Granite City began when William F. Niedringhaus purchased land here for his National Enameling and Stamping Company plant. The American Steel Foundry followed, and in 1896 Granite City was incorporated, named for the granite ware produced there.
Population: 31,301 (2000); Race: 94.9% White, 2.1% Black, 0.3% Asian, 0.3% American Indian and Alaska Native, 2.9% Hispanic of any race, 1.2% two or more races (2000); Density: 1,876.2 persons per square mile (2000); Age: 24.9% under 18, 16.1% over 64 (2000); Marriage status: 25.2% never married, 51.7% now married, 9.6% widowed, 13.6% divorced (2000); Foreign born: 1.1% (2000); Ancestry (includes multiple ancestries): 20.6% German, 16.8% Irish, 14.0% Other groups, 10.3% United States or American, 9.7% English (2000).
Vital Statistics: Birth rate: 188.5 per 10,000 population (1998)
Economy: Unemployment rate: 8.2% (11/2002); Total civilian labor force: 14,487 (11/2002); Single-family building permits issued: 18 (2001) / 15 (2000); Multi-family building permits issued: 40 (2001) / 4 (2000); Employment by occupation: 9.0% management, 12.9% professional, 17.2% services, 27.5% sales, 0.2% farming, 9.3% construction, 24.0% production (2000).
Income: Per capita income: $17,691 (2000); Median household income: $35,615 (2000); Poverty rate: 11.3% (2000).
Taxes: Total city taxes per capita: $259 (2000); City property taxes per capita: $105 (2000).
Education: High school graduation rate: 77.8% (2000); College graduation rate: 9.8% (2000).

School District(s)
Granite City C U School District 9 (PK-12)
2000 Enrollment: 7,780 618-451-5800
Housing: Homeownership rate: 70.4% (2000); Median home value: $57,200 (2000); Median rent: $341 per month (2000); Median age of housing: 46 years (2000).
Hospitals: Saint Elizabeth Medical Center (393 beds)
Newspapers: Granite City Press Record (1 x week); Granite City Journal (2 x week)
Transportation: Commute to work: 93.8% car, 2.1% public transportation, 1.9% walk, 1.2% work from home (2000); Travel time to work: 38.4% less than 15 minutes, 31.2% 15 to 30 minutes, 18.6% 30 to 45 minutes, 8.2% 45 to 60 minutes, 3.6% 60 minutes or more (2000)
Additional Information Contacts
Tri-Cities Area Chamber of Commerce 618-876-6400

GRANTFORK (village). Covers a land area of 0.228 square miles and a water area of 0 square miles. Located at 38.83° N. Lat.; 89.66° W. Long. Elevation is 535 feet.
Population: 254 (2000); Race: 97.2% White, 0.0% Black, 0.0% Asian, 0.8% American Indian and Alaska Native, 0.8% Hispanic of any race, 2.0% two or more races (2000); Density: 1,112.1 persons per square mile (2000); Age: 29.2% under 18, 10.3% over 64 (2000); Marriage status: 29.6% never married, 50.5% now married, 11.2% widowed, 8.7% divorced (2000); Foreign born: 0.0% (2000); Ancestry (includes multiple ancestries): 41.5% German, 10.7% English, 8.7% United States or American, 8.3% Other groups, 5.1% Irish (2000).
Economy: In agricultural area. Single-family building permits issued: 0 (2001) / 1 (2000); Multi-family building permits issued: 0 (2001) / 0 (2000); Employment by occupation: 11.0% management, 5.1% professional, 30.1% services, 21.3% sales, 0.0% farming, 12.5% construction, 19.9% production (2000).
Income: Per capita income: $17,415 (2000); Median household income: $42,917 (2000); Poverty rate: 4.4% (2000).
Taxes: Total city taxes per capita: $29 (1997); City property taxes per capita: $22 (1997).
Education: High school graduation rate: 82.1% (2000); College graduation rate: 9.3% (2000).
Housing: Homeownership rate: 83.9% (2000); Median home value: $60,000 (2000); Median rent: $368 per month (2000); Median age of housing: 28 years (2000).
Transportation: Commute to work: 93.4% car, 0.0% public transportation, 2.2% walk, 4.4% work from home (2000); Travel time to work: 41.5% less than 15 minutes, 26.9% 15 to 30 minutes, 15.4% 30 to 45 minutes, 10.0% 45 to 60 minutes, 6.2% 60 minutes or more (2000)

HAMEL (village). Covers a land area of 1.160 square miles and a water area of 0 square miles. Located at 38.88° N. Lat.; 89.84° W. Long. Elevation is 545 feet.

Population: 570 (2000); Race: 98.8% White, 0.0% Black, 0.0% Asian, 0.0% American Indian and Alaska Native, 1.2% Hispanic of any race, 0.3% two or more races (2000); Density: 491.3 persons per square mile (2000); Age: 26.6% under 18, 15.7% over 64 (2000); Marriage status: 16.2% never married, 72.1% now married, 5.6% widowed, 6.1% divorced (2000); Foreign born: 0.7% (2000); Ancestry (includes multiple ancestries): 48.6% German, 12.5% Other groups, 10.6% English, 6.9% Irish, 6.7% United States or American (2000).
Economy: Corn, soybeans. Manufacturing: concrete, metal tools. Single-family building permits issued: 4 (2001) / 6 (2000); Multi-family building permits issued: 0 (2001) / 0 (2000); Employment by occupation: 12.2% management, 14.2% professional, 19.8% services, 25.0% sales, 0.3% farming, 9.4% construction, 19.1% production (2000).
Income: Per capita income: $19,062 (2000); Median household income: $45,750 (2000); Poverty rate: 3.6% (2000).
Taxes: Total city taxes per capita: $73 (1997); City property taxes per capita: $0 (1997).
Education: High school graduation rate: 85.3% (2000); College graduation rate: 14.2% (2000).
Housing: Homeownership rate: 77.7% (2000); Median home value: $84,100 (2000); Median rent: $419 per month (2000); Median age of housing: 29 years (2000).
Transportation: Commute to work: 92.7% car, 0.7% public transportation, 4.2% walk, 2.4% work from home (2000); Travel time to work: 26.3% less than 15 minutes, 32.4% 15 to 30 minutes, 21.4% 30 to 45 minutes, 13.2% 45 to 60 minutes, 6.8% 60 minutes or more (2000)

HARTFORD (village). Covers a land area of 3.898 square miles and a water area of 0.014 square miles. Located at 38.82° N. Lat.; 90.09° W. Long. Elevation is 430 feet.
History: In 1915 the International Shoe Company established a tannery in Hartford, and the town developed around it.
Population: 1,545 (2000); Race: 99.0% White, 0.0% Black, 0.0% Asian, 0.0% American Indian and Alaska Native, 1.3% Hispanic of any race, 0.5% two or more races (2000); Density: 396.4 persons per square mile (2000); Age: 23.8% under 18, 16.6% over 64 (2000); Marriage status: 18.4% never married, 59.2% now married, 9.0% widowed, 13.4% divorced (2000); Foreign born: 1.0% (2000); Ancestry (includes multiple ancestries): 20.5% German, 14.2% United States or American, 12.9% Irish, 10.7% English, 10.5% Other groups (2000).
Economy: Single-family building permits issued: 0 (2001) / 0 (2000); Multi-family building permits issued: 0 (2001) / 0 (2000); Employment by occupation: 7.6% management, 8.0% professional, 21.9% services, 24.2% sales, 0.0% farming, 16.5% construction, 21.9% production (2000).
Income: Per capita income: $16,160 (2000); Median household income: $33,828 (2000); Poverty rate: 13.0% (2000).
Taxes: Total city taxes per capita: $350 (1997); City property taxes per capita: $254 (1997).
Education: High school graduation rate: 77.4% (2000); College graduation rate: 3.2% (2000).
Housing: Homeownership rate: 75.4% (2000); Median home value: $44,400 (2000); Median rent: $318 per month (2000); Median age of housing: 52 years (2000).
Transportation: Commute to work: 95.6% car, 0.4% public transportation, 1.0% walk, 1.6% work from home (2000); Travel time to work: 39.5% less than 15 minutes, 33.8% 15 to 30 minutes, 13.4% 30 to 45 minutes, 6.8% 45 to 60 minutes, 6.6% 60 minutes or more (2000)

HIGHLAND (city). Covers a land area of 5.405 square miles and a water area of 1.018 square miles. Located at 38.74° N. Lat.; 89.67° W. Long. Elevation is 540 feet.
History: Highland was settled about 1804 by families from Kentucky and North Carolina. In 1831 a group of Swiss colonists led by Dr. Caspar Koepfli located in Highland, and the community became a dairy producer. A leading firm here in the early 1900's was the Wicks Organ Company.
Population: 8,438 (2000); Race: 98.9% White, 0.0% Black, 0.3% Asian, 0.2% American Indian and Alaska Native, 1.3% Hispanic of any race, 0.4% two or more races (2000); Density: 1,561.1 persons per square mile (2000); Age: 25.5% under 18, 18.2% over 64 (2000); Marriage status: 20.9% never married, 58.0% now married, 10.9% widowed, 10.2% divorced (2000); Foreign born: 1.0% (2000); Ancestry (includes multiple ancestries): 48.2% German, 9.0% United States or American, 9.0% Irish, 7.5% English, 6.5% Swiss (2000).
Economy: Single-family building permits issued: 23 (2001) / 27 (2000); Multi-family building permits issued: 12 (2001) / 58 (2000); Employment by occupation: 10.8% management, 18.3% professional, 15.3% services, 30.9% sales, 0.0% farming, 8.0% construction, 16.8% production (2000).
Income: Per capita income: $21,101 (2000); Median household income: $39,524 (2000); Poverty rate: 6.8% (2000).
Taxes: Total city taxes per capita: $190 (1997); City property taxes per capita: $184 (1997).
Education: High school graduation rate: 85.2% (2000); College graduation rate: 21.8% (2000).

School District(s)

Highland Community Unit School District 5 (PK-12)
2000 Enrollment: 2,873 618-654-2106
Housing: Homeownership rate: 68.7% (2000); Median home value: $90,400 (2000); Median rent: $386 per month (2000); Median age of housing: 31 years (2000).
Hospitals: Saint Joseph's Hospital (106 beds)
Newspapers: Highland News Leader (2 x week)
Transportation: Commute to work: 94.1% car, 1.3% public transportation, 2.9% walk, 1.6% work from home (2000); Travel time to work: 49.4% less than 15 minutes, 15.6% 15 to 30 minutes, 14.0% 30 to 45 minutes, 14.5% 45 to 60 minutes, 6.5% 60 minutes or more (2000)
Additional Information Contacts
Highland Chamber of Commerce. 618-654-3721

LIVINGSTON (village). Covers a land area of 1.061 square miles and a water area of 0.008 square miles. Located at 38.96° N. Lat.; 89.76° W. Long. Elevation is 590 feet.
History: Incorporated 1905.
Population: 825 (2000); Race: 98.8% White, 0.0% Black, 0.8% Asian, 0.0% American Indian and Alaska Native, 0.0% Hispanic of any race, 0.4% two or more races (2000); Density: 777.5 persons per square mile (2000); Age: 25.7% under 18, 17.3% over 64 (2000); Marriage status: 25.8% never married, 53.0% now married, 9.9% widowed, 11.4% divorced (2000); Foreign born: 2.2% (2000); Ancestry (includes multiple ancestries): 42.5% German, 12.7% Italian, 10.8% Other groups, 8.8% Irish, 7.8% United States or American (2000).
Economy: In agricultural area. Single-family building permits issued: 0 (2001) / 0 (2000); Multi-family building permits issued: 0 (2001) / 0 (2000); Employment by occupation: 4.8% management, 14.5% professional, 21.3% services, 17.8% sales, 0.0% farming, 15.5% construction, 26.1% production (2000).
Income: Per capita income: $16,291 (2000); Median household income: $37,083 (2000); Poverty rate: 9.1% (2000).
Taxes: Total city taxes per capita: $53 (1997); City property taxes per capita: $13 (1997).
Education: High school graduation rate: 78.9% (2000); College graduation rate: 5.9% (2000).

School District(s)

Livingston C C School District 4 (PK-12)
2000 Enrollment: 251 618-637-2131
Housing: Homeownership rate: 80.2% (2000); Median home value: $51,900 (2000); Median rent: $283 per month (2000); Median age of housing: 48 years (2000).
Transportation: Commute to work: 96.1% car, 0.0% public transportation, 1.8% walk, 1.3% work from home (2000); Travel time to work: 19.5% less than 15 minutes, 32.0% 15 to 30 minutes, 25.6% 30 to 45 minutes, 10.7% 45 to 60 minutes, 12.3% 60 minutes or more (2000)

MADISON (city). Covers a land area of 7.011 square miles and a water area of 0.266 square miles. Located at 38.68° N. Lat.; 90.15° W. Long. Elevation is 410 feet.
History: The Madison Land Syndicate was formed in 1887 by a group of St. Louis businessmen who promoted the construction of Merchants Bridge over the Mississippi River. An American Car and Foundry plant was built near the new bridge, and the town of Madison was incorporated in 1891 by the Land Syndicate.
Population: 4,545 (2000); Race: 57.4% White, 40.7% Black, 0.2% Asian, 0.0% American Indian and Alaska Native, 1.1% Hispanic of any race, 1.7% two or more races (2000); Density: 648.3 persons per square mile (2000); Age: 27.9% under 18, 16.2% over 64 (2000); Marriage status: 33.0% never married, 37.4% now married, 10.3% widowed, 19.3% divorced (2000); Foreign born: 0.7% (2000); Ancestry (includes multiple ancestries): 36.8% Other groups, 11.9% German, 6.7% Irish, 5.1% Polish, 4.4% English (2000).
Economy: Single-family building permits issued: 1 (2001) / 4 (2000); Multi-family building permits issued: 0 (2001) / 0 (2000); Employment by occupation: 9.3% management, 9.6% professional, 25.6% services, 20.0% sales, 0.0% farming, 10.5% construction, 25.0% production (2000).

Income: Per capita income: $13,090 (2000); Median household income: $24,828 (2000); Poverty rate: 24.0% (2000).
Taxes: Total city taxes per capita: $125 (1997); City property taxes per capita: $53 (1997).
Education: High school graduation rate: 66.9% (2000); College graduation rate: 5.2% (2000).

School District(s)

Madison Community Unit School District 12 (PK-12)
2000 Enrollment: 1,111 618-877-1712
Housing: Homeownership rate: 61.5% (2000); Median home value: $38,000 (2000); Median rent: $295 per month (2000); Median age of housing: 50 years (2000).
Transportation: Commute to work: 88.2% car, 6.4% public transportation, 2.9% walk, 2.5% work from home (2000); Travel time to work: 31.6% less than 15 minutes, 38.2% 15 to 30 minutes, 19.7% 30 to 45 minutes, 3.4% 45 to 60 minutes, 7.2% 60 minutes or more (2000)

MARINE (village). Covers a land area of 0.761 square miles and a water area of 0.019 square miles. Located at 38.78° N. Lat.; 89.77° W. Long. Elevation is 520 feet.
Population: 910 (2000); Race: 98.2% White, 0.0% Black, 0.3% Asian, 0.0% American Indian and Alaska Native, 0.6% Hispanic of any race, 1.5% two or more races (2000); Density: 1,196.3 persons per square mile (2000); Age: 28.1% under 18, 12.0% over 64 (2000); Marriage status: 23.0% never married, 59.9% now married, 7.2% widowed, 9.8% divorced (2000); Foreign born: 0.0% (2000); Ancestry (includes multiple ancestries): 38.4% German, 13.7% Irish, 12.9% English, 8.3% United States or American, 4.8% Other groups (2000).
Economy: In agricultural area: wheat; dairy products; poultry, cattle. Single-family building permits issued: 7 (2001) / 4 (2000); Multi-family building permits issued: 0 (2001) / 0 (2000); Employment by occupation: 14.6% management, 13.5% professional, 17.8% services, 27.5% sales, 0.0% farming, 12.6% construction, 14.0% production (2000).
Income: Per capita income: $18,133 (2000); Median household income: $37,361 (2000); Poverty rate: 6.2% (2000).
Taxes: Total city taxes per capita: $51 (1997); City property taxes per capita: $39 (1997).
Education: High school graduation rate: 83.7% (2000); College graduation rate: 12.3% (2000).
Housing: Homeownership rate: 73.1% (2000); Median home value: $77,700 (2000); Median rent: $354 per month (2000); Median age of housing: 44 years (2000).
Transportation: Commute to work: 92.8% car, 0.2% public transportation, 2.7% walk, 4.1% work from home (2000); Travel time to work: 19.3% less than 15 minutes, 44.0% 15 to 30 minutes, 19.8% 30 to 45 minutes, 11.6% 45 to 60 minutes, 5.3% 60 minutes or more (2000)

MARYVILLE (village). Covers a land area of 4.667 square miles and a water area of 0.032 square miles. Located at 38.72° N. Lat.; 89.95° W. Long. Elevation is 583 feet.
Population: 4,651 (2000); Race: 95.3% White, 2.3% Black, 0.1% Asian, 0.1% American Indian and Alaska Native, 2.7% Hispanic of any race, 1.6% two or more races (2000); Density: 996.5 persons per square mile (2000); Age: 24.9% under 18, 11.2% over 64 (2000); Marriage status: 20.3% never married, 66.6% now married, 4.1% widowed, 9.0% divorced (2000); Foreign born: 1.5% (2000); Ancestry (includes multiple ancestries): 31.6% German, 12.4% Irish, 12.1% English, 8.4% Other groups, 7.8% Italian (2000).
Economy: Agriculture: corn, wheat; cattle. Manufacturing: marble products. Single-family building permits issued: 49 (2001) / 31 (2000); Multi-family building permits issued: 8 (2001) / 0 (2000); Employment by occupation: 12.5% management, 28.2% professional, 9.9% services, 32.7% sales, 0.0% farming, 6.1% construction, 10.5% production (2000).
Income: Per capita income: $27,634 (2000); Median household income: $60,135 (2000); Poverty rate: 4.1% (2000).
Taxes: Total city taxes per capita: $324 (1997); City property taxes per capita: $183 (1997).
Education: High school graduation rate: 87.9% (2000); College graduation rate: 27.9% (2000).
Housing: Homeownership rate: 78.2% (2000); Median home value: $116,400 (2000); Median rent: $369 per month (2000); Median age of housing: 16 years (2000).
Hospitals: Anderson Hospital (130 beds)
Transportation: Commute to work: 94.6% car, 0.3% public transportation, 0.0% walk, 5.1% work from home (2000); Travel time to work: 19.5% less than 15 minutes, 37.2% 15 to 30 minutes, 30.3% 30 to 45 minutes, 9.1% 45 to 60 minutes, 4.0% 60 minutes or more (2000)

MORO (unincorporated postal area, zip code 62067). Covers a land area of 16.810 square miles and a water area of 0.046 square miles. Located at 38.92° N. Lat.; 90.01° W. Long. Elevation is 530 feet.
Population: 2,089 (2000); Race: 98.9% White, 0.0% Black, 0.0% Asian, 1.1% American Indian and Alaska Native, 0.3% Hispanic of any race, 0.0% two or more races (2000); Density: 124.3 persons per square mile (2000); Age: 23.6% under 18, 15.6% over 64 (2000); Marriage status: 21.5% never married, 66.0% now married, 6.1% widowed, 6.4% divorced (2000); Foreign born: 1.0% (2000); Ancestry (includes multiple ancestries): 36.8% German, 14.2% English, 13.9% United States or American, 6.3% Irish, 5.4% French (except Basque) (2000).
Economy: Employment by occupation: 17.8% management, 11.8% professional, 16.7% services, 21.2% sales, 0.8% farming, 13.3% construction, 18.3% production (2000).
Income: Per capita income: $18,510 (2000); Median household income: $38,491 (2000); Poverty rate: 9.3% (2000).
Education: High school graduation rate: 81.3% (2000); College graduation rate: 15.5% (2000).
Housing: Homeownership rate: 85.4% (2000); Median home value: $78,200 (2000); Median rent: $334 per month (2000); Median age of housing: 30 years (2000).
Transportation: Commute to work: 91.1% car, 0.7% public transportation, 0.8% walk, 7.4% work from home (2000); Travel time to work: 21.1% less than 15 minutes, 47.6% 15 to 30 minutes, 20.8% 30 to 45 minutes, 5.1% 45 to 60 minutes, 5.4% 60 minutes or more (2000)

NEW DOUGLAS (village). Covers a land area of 1.068 square miles and a water area of 0 square miles. Located at 38.97° N. Lat.; 89.66° W. Long. Elevation is 619 feet.
Population: 369 (2000); Race: 97.9% White, 0.0% Black, 0.5% Asian, 0.0% American Indian and Alaska Native, 3.4% Hispanic of any race, 1.6% two or more races (2000); Density: 345.6 persons per square mile (2000); Age: 25.5% under 18, 15.8% over 64 (2000); Marriage status: 23.7% never married, 62.3% now married, 6.7% widowed, 7.3% divorced (2000); Foreign born: 2.1% (2000); Ancestry (includes multiple ancestries): 33.0% German, 16.4% Other groups, 14.8% Irish, 11.9% United States or American, 5.5% English (2000).
Economy: In agricultural area: corn, wheat; dairy products; poultry, livestock. Single-family building permits issued: 3 (2001) / 0 (2000); Multi-family building permits issued: 0 (2001) / 0 (2000); Employment by occupation: 8.7% management, 11.2% professional, 12.4% services, 26.1% sales, 1.2% farming, 23.6% construction, 16.8% production (2000).
Income: Per capita income: $14,617 (2000); Median household income: $30,417 (2000); Poverty rate: 9.7% (2000).
Taxes: Total city taxes per capita: $30 (1997); City property taxes per capita: $13 (1997).
Education: High school graduation rate: 77.7% (2000); College graduation rate: 10.5% (2000).
Housing: Homeownership rate: 80.8% (2000); Median home value: $58,200 (2000); Median rent: $260 per month (2000); Median age of housing: 52 years (2000).
Transportation: Commute to work: 85.7% car, 0.0% public transportation, 1.9% walk, 12.4% work from home (2000); Travel time to work: 17.0% less than 15 minutes, 23.4% 15 to 30 minutes, 20.6% 30 to 45 minutes, 14.9% 45 to 60 minutes, 24.1% 60 minutes or more (2000)

PONTOON BEACH (village). Covers a land area of 8.182 square miles and a water area of 0.279 square miles. Located at 38.72° N. Lat.; 90.06° W. Long. Elevation is 420 feet.
Population: 5,620 (2000); Race: 85.4% White, 11.1% Black, 0.8% Asian, 0.5% American Indian and Alaska Native, 2.5% Hispanic of any race, 0.6% two or more races (2000); Density: 686.9 persons per square mile (2000); Age: 31.1% under 18, 8.8% over 64 (2000); Marriage status: 26.3% never married, 56.6% now married, 5.7% widowed, 11.5% divorced (2000); Foreign born: 1.5% (2000); Ancestry (includes multiple ancestries): 19.6% Other groups, 18.3% German, 12.2% United States or American, 11.8% Irish, 6.2% English (2000).
Economy: Single-family building permits issued: 33 (2001) / 37 (2000); Multi-family building permits issued: 0 (2001) / 0 (2000); Employment by occupation: 10.3% management, 12.0% professional, 15.0% services, 32.9% sales, 0.7% farming, 9.2% construction, 19.8% production (2000).
Income: Per capita income: $15,960 (2000); Median household income: $38,348 (2000); Poverty rate: 10.6% (2000).
Taxes: Total city taxes per capita: $160 (2000); City property taxes per capita: $70 (2000).

Education: High school graduation rate: 83.0% (2000); College graduation rate: 9.8% (2000).
Housing: Homeownership rate: 66.6% (2000); Median home value: $74,600 (2000); Median rent: $428 per month (2000); Median age of housing: 22 years (2000).
Transportation: Commute to work: 93.7% car, 2.4% public transportation, 2.3% walk, 1.3% work from home (2000); Travel time to work: 25.5% less than 15 minutes, 41.9% 15 to 30 minutes, 19.7% 30 to 45 minutes, 9.1% 45 to 60 minutes, 3.8% 60 minutes or more (2000)

ROSEWOOD HEIGHTS (CDP). Covers a land area of 2.144 square miles and a water area of 0 square miles. Located at 38.89° N. Lat.; 90.07° W. Long. Elevation is 510 feet.
Population: 4,262 (2000); Race: 98.9% White, 0.2% Black, 0.0% Asian, 0.0% American Indian and Alaska Native, 0.9% Hispanic of any race, 0.7% two or more races (2000); Density: 1,988.0 persons per square mile (2000); Age: 22.5% under 18, 15.5% over 64 (2000); Marriage status: 19.5% never married, 62.0% now married, 7.8% widowed, 10.8% divorced (2000); Foreign born: 0.2% (2000); Ancestry (includes multiple ancestries): 26.6% German, 13.5% United States or American, 12.3% English, 9.4% Irish, 6.8% Other groups (2000).
Economy: St. Louis Regional Airport to East. Employment by occupation: 8.1% management, 22.4% professional, 12.6% services, 25.2% sales, 0.0% farming, 14.2% construction, 17.4% production (2000).
Income: Per capita income: $20,527 (2000); Median household income: $46,701 (2000); Poverty rate: 7.8% (2000).
Education: High school graduation rate: 89.1% (2000); College graduation rate: 15.3% (2000).
Housing: Homeownership rate: 89.6% (2000); Median home value: $76,500 (2000); Median rent: $293 per month (2000); Median age of housing: 42 years (2000).
Transportation: Commute to work: 97.6% car, 0.0% public transportation, 0.4% walk, 1.6% work from home (2000); Travel time to work: 42.6% less than 15 minutes, 27.5% 15 to 30 minutes, 16.2% 30 to 45 minutes, 8.0% 45 to 60 minutes, 5.8% 60 minutes or more (2000)

ROXANA (village). Covers a land area of 6.801 square miles and a water area of 0.022 square miles. Located at 38.83° N. Lat.; 90.06° W. Long. Elevation is 449 feet.
History: Incorporated 1921.
Population: 1,547 (2000); Race: 96.9% White, 0.3% Black, 0.0% Asian, 0.0% American Indian and Alaska Native, 0.8% Hispanic of any race, 1.8% two or more races (2000); Density: 227.5 persons per square mile (2000); Age: 21.2% under 18, 16.7% over 64 (2000); Marriage status: 19.0% never married, 62.3% now married, 8.6% widowed, 10.2% divorced (2000); Foreign born: 0.0% (2000); Ancestry (includes multiple ancestries): 23.4% German, 14.4% Other groups, 12.2% English, 10.6% Irish, 9.6% United States or American (2000).
Economy: Agricultural area to East: wheat; cattle. Large oil refinery and storage. Single-family building permits issued: 0 (2001) / 0 (2000); Multi-family building permits issued: 0 (2001) / 0 (2000); Employment by occupation: 14.3% management, 10.4% professional, 18.3% services, 22.2% sales, 0.1% farming, 10.4% construction, 24.3% production (2000).
Income: Per capita income: $20,511 (2000); Median household income: $38,800 (2000); Poverty rate: 3.8% (2000).
Taxes: Total city taxes per capita: $650 (1997); City property taxes per capita: $641 (1997).
Education: High school graduation rate: 86.2% (2000); College graduation rate: 10.2% (2000).

School District(s)

Roxana Community Unit School District 1 (PK-12)
2000 Enrollment: 1,922 618-254-7544
Housing: Homeownership rate: 75.6% (2000); Median home value: $54,800 (2000); Median rent: $401 per month (2000); Median age of housing: 51 years (2000).
Transportation: Commute to work: 94.6% car, 1.1% public transportation, 2.3% walk, 2.0% work from home (2000); Travel time to work: 31.6% less than 15 minutes, 26.4% 15 to 30 minutes, 20.0% 30 to 45 minutes, 15.7% 45 to 60 minutes, 6.4% 60 minutes or more (2000)

SAINT JACOB (village). Covers a land area of 0.559 square miles and a water area of 0 square miles. Located at 38.71° N. Lat.; 89.76° W. Long. Elevation is 518 feet.
History: St. Jacob was built near the site of Fort Chilton, established in 1812.
Population: 801 (2000); Race: 98.6% White, 0.0% Black, 0.4% Asian, 1.0% American Indian and Alaska Native, 2.0% Hispanic of any race, 0.0% two or more races (2000); Density: 1,433.1 persons per square mile (2000); Age: 28.3% under 18, 9.7% over 64 (2000); Marriage status: 22.7% never married, 61.1% now married, 3.6% widowed, 12.5% divorced (2000); Foreign born: 0.4% (2000); Ancestry (includes multiple ancestries): 48.5% German, 11.0% Other groups, 10.2% Irish, 7.0% United States or American, 6.1% French (except Basque) (2000).
Economy: Single-family building permits issued: 20 (2001) / 12 (2000); Multi-family building permits issued: 0 (2001) / 0 (2000); Employment by occupation: 13.8% management, 8.0% professional, 12.8% services, 26.6% sales, 0.0% farming, 15.3% construction, 23.5% production (2000).
Income: Per capita income: $20,340 (2000); Median household income: $47,917 (2000); Poverty rate: 9.7% (2000).
Education: High school graduation rate: 84.1% (2000); College graduation rate: 10.8% (2000).
Housing: Homeownership rate: 78.2% (2000); Median home value: $78,600 (2000); Median rent: $309 per month (2000); Median age of housing: 38 years (2000).
Transportation: Commute to work: 89.6% car, 2.0% public transportation, 5.2% walk, 3.2% work from home (2000); Travel time to work: 31.1% less than 15 minutes, 23.1% 15 to 30 minutes, 28.0% 30 to 45 minutes, 12.6% 45 to 60 minutes, 5.1% 60 minutes or more (2000)

SOUTH ROXANA (village). Covers a land area of 1.587 square miles and a water area of 0 square miles. Located at 38.82° N. Lat.; 90.05° W. Long. Elevation is 440 feet.
Population: 1,888 (2000); Race: 96.5% White, 0.6% Black, 0.7% Asian, 0.3% American Indian and Alaska Native, 0.7% Hispanic of any race, 1.7% two or more races (2000); Density: 1,190.0 persons per square mile (2000); Age: 28.6% under 18, 10.0% over 64 (2000); Marriage status: 23.0% never married, 56.4% now married, 6.9% widowed, 13.7% divorced (2000); Foreign born: 1.0% (2000); Ancestry (includes multiple ancestries): 20.3% German, 18.1% Irish, 13.2% Other groups, 12.9% United States or American, 11.8% English (2000).
Economy: In oil-refining area. Manufacturing of air compressors. Single-family building permits issued: 0 (2001) / 1 (2000); Multi-family building permits issued: 0 (2001) / 0 (2000); Employment by occupation: 7.2% management, 8.5% professional, 19.9% services, 20.2% sales, 0.2% farming, 14.8% construction, 29.1% production (2000).
Income: Per capita income: $14,938 (2000); Median household income: $33,295 (2000); Poverty rate: 19.8% (2000).
Taxes: Total city taxes per capita: $118 (1997); City property taxes per capita: $58 (1997).
Education: High school graduation rate: 73.6% (2000); College graduation rate: 3.5% (2000).
Housing: Homeownership rate: 74.5% (2000); Median home value: $45,800 (2000); Median rent: $351 per month (2000); Median age of housing: 40 years (2000).
Transportation: Commute to work: 91.6% car, 0.5% public transportation, 2.0% walk, 3.2% work from home (2000); Travel time to work: 28.2% less than 15 minutes, 38.9% 15 to 30 minutes, 16.8% 30 to 45 minutes, 8.9% 45 to 60 minutes, 7.1% 60 minutes or more (2000)

TROY (city). Covers a land area of 4.183 square miles and a water area of 0 square miles. Located at 38.72° N. Lat.; 89.89° W. Long. Elevation is 550 feet.
History: Troy began as the community of Columbia, with a grist mill and tavern built by John G. Jarvis about 1814. When the property was purchased in 1819 by land speculators, it was renamed Troy, for the New York town. In 1857 Mechanicsburg, which had been platted in 1836, merged with Troy, and in 1891 Brookside did the same. Troy was incorporated as a city in 1892.
Population: 8,524 (2000); Race: 93.6% White, 2.5% Black, 0.6% Asian, 0.2% American Indian and Alaska Native, 1.2% Hispanic of any race, 2.5% two or more races (2000); Density: 2,037.6 persons per square mile (2000); Age: 29.6% under 18, 7.4% over 64 (2000); Marriage status: 22.4% never married, 62.3% now married, 5.6% widowed, 9.7% divorced (2000); Foreign born: 0.6% (2000); Ancestry (includes multiple ancestries): 36.0% German, 16.4% Irish, 11.9% Other groups, 10.2% English, 8.2% United States or American (2000).
Economy: Single-family building permits issued: 66 (2001) / 60 (2000); Multi-family building permits issued: 14 (2001) / 5 (2000); Employment by occupation: 13.8% management, 18.5% professional, 16.8% services, 26.8% sales, 0.0% farming, 8.4% construction, 15.8% production (2000).
Income: Per capita income: $21,174 (2000); Median household income: $53,720 (2000); Poverty rate: 3.4% (2000).
Taxes: Total city taxes per capita: $114 (1997); City property taxes per capita: $50 (1997).

Education: High school graduation rate: 90.0% (2000); College graduation rate: 24.3% (2000).

School District(s)

Triad Community Unit School District 2 (PK-12)
2000 Enrollment: 3,582 618-667-8851

Housing: Homeownership rate: 73.3% (2000); Median home value: $102,900 (2000); Median rent: $459 per month (2000); Median age of housing: 17 years (2000).

Newspapers: Times Tribune (1 x week)

Transportation: Commute to work: 93.3% car, 1.5% public transportation, 0.9% walk, 3.1% work from home (2000); Travel time to work: 25.2% less than 15 minutes, 36.2% 15 to 30 minutes, 27.6% 30 to 45 minutes, 6.0% 45 to 60 minutes, 5.0% 60 minutes or more (2000)

Additional Information Contacts

Troy Chamber of Commerce 618-667-8769

VENICE (city). Covers a land area of 1.875 square miles and a water area of 0 square miles. Located at 38.67° N. Lat.; 90.16° W. Long. Elevation is 410 feet.

History: Before the construction of levees, Venice experienced frequent flooding of its streets, which led to its being named after the Italian city of waterways. A ferry landing was established here in 1804. The town was platted in 1841 and incorporated in 1873.

Population: 2,528 (2000); Race: 5.5% White, 93.4% Black, 0.1% Asian, 0.1% American Indian and Alaska Native, 0.9% Hispanic of any race, 0.8% two or more races (2000); Density: 1,348.5 persons per square mile (2000); Age: 33.6% under 18, 12.1% over 64 (2000); Marriage status: 49.7% never married, 31.0% now married, 8.6% widowed, 10.7% divorced (2000); Foreign born: 0.2% (2000); Ancestry (includes multiple ancestries): 75.7% Other groups, 1.5% African, 1.4% German, 0.9% Irish, 0.8% United States or American (2000).

Economy: Single-family building permits issued: 0 (2001) / 2 (2000); Multi-family building permits issued: 0 (2001) / 0 (2000); Employment by occupation: 6.7% management, 10.5% professional, 24.1% services, 29.8% sales, 0.4% farming, 8.6% construction, 20.0% production (2000).

Income: Per capita income: $11,483 (2000); Median household income: $19,853 (2000); Poverty rate: 39.6% (2000).

Taxes: Total city taxes per capita: $371 (1997); City property taxes per capita: $225 (1997).

Education: High school graduation rate: 67.6% (2000); College graduation rate: 5.4% (2000).

School District(s)

Venice Community Unit School District 3 (PK-12)
2000 Enrollment: 308 618-451-7953

Housing: Homeownership rate: 45.7% (2000); Median home value: $31,900 (2000); Median rent: $277 per month (2000); Median age of housing: 47 years (2000).

Transportation: Commute to work: 81.9% car, 9.3% public transportation, 4.5% walk, 3.0% work from home (2000); Travel time to work: 30.8% less than 15 minutes, 40.6% 15 to 30 minutes, 18.3% 30 to 45 minutes, 4.1% 45 to 60 minutes, 6.2% 60 minutes or more (2000)

WILLIAMSON (village). Covers a land area of 1.518 square miles and a water area of 0.043 square miles. Located at 38.98° N. Lat.; 89.76° W. Long. Elevation is 600 feet.

Population: 251 (2000); Race: 93.5% White, 0.0% Black, 0.0% Asian, 6.5% American Indian and Alaska Native, 0.0% Hispanic of any race, 0.0% two or more races (2000); Density: 165.4 persons per square mile (2000); Age: 25.6% under 18, 14.9% over 64 (2000); Marriage status: 21.1% never married, 53.8% now married, 11.7% widowed, 13.5% divorced (2000); Foreign born: 0.0% (2000); Ancestry (includes multiple ancestries): 18.1% German, 14.9% Italian, 12.1% Irish, 11.6% English, 9.3% United States or American (2000).

Economy: Single-family building permits issued: 0 (2001) / 0 (2000); Multi-family building permits issued: 0 (2001) / 0 (2000); Employment by occupation: 3.0% management, 13.0% professional, 30.0% services, 17.0% sales, 0.0% farming, 17.0% construction, 20.0% production (2000).

Income: Per capita income: $12,988 (2000); Median household income: $23,750 (2000); Poverty rate: 14.4% (2000).

Taxes: Total city taxes per capita: $38 (1997); City property taxes per capita: $30 (1997).

Education: High school graduation rate: 80.4% (2000); College graduation rate: 7.7% (2000).

Housing: Homeownership rate: 89.4% (2000); Median home value: $33,400 (2000); Median rent: $317 per month (2000); Median age of housing: 59 years (2000).

Transportation: Commute to work: 98.0% car, 0.0% public transportation, 2.0% walk, 0.0% work from home (2000); Travel time to work: 20.4% less than 15 minutes, 27.6% 15 to 30 minutes, 28.6% 30 to 45 minutes, 17.3% 45 to 60 minutes, 6.1% 60 minutes or more (2000)

WOOD RIVER (city). Covers a land area of 6.056 square miles and a water area of 0.025 square miles. Located at 38.86° N. Lat.; 90.08° W. Long. Elevation is 440 feet.

History: Wood River was selected by the Standard Oil Company in 1907 as the site of its refinery because of the rail and river transportation available here.

Population: 11,296 (2000); Race: 97.8% White, 0.4% Black, 0.0% Asian, 0.2% American Indian and Alaska Native, 1.2% Hispanic of any race, 1.1% two or more races (2000); Density: 1,865.2 persons per square mile (2000); Age: 24.6% under 18, 18.4% over 64 (2000); Marriage status: 21.8% never married, 55.5% now married, 9.1% widowed, 13.6% divorced (2000); Foreign born: 0.6% (2000); Ancestry (includes multiple ancestries): 21.5% German, 13.5% Irish, 12.7% United States or American, 10.3% English, 9.7% Other groups (2000).

Vital Statistics: Birth rate: 143.4 per 10,000 population (1998)

Economy: Single-family building permits issued: 7 (2001) / 2 (2000); Multi-family building permits issued: 2 (2001) / 0 (2000); Employment by occupation: 10.5% management, 14.5% professional, 19.4% services, 27.9% sales, 0.0% farming, 8.3% construction, 19.4% production (2000).

Income: Per capita income: $18,098 (2000); Median household income: $33,875 (2000); Poverty rate: 14.8% (2000).

Taxes: Total city taxes per capita: $302 (1997); City property taxes per capita: $80 (1997).

Education: High school graduation rate: 83.6% (2000); College graduation rate: 11.2% (2000).

School District(s)

East Alton-Wood River C H S D 14 (09-12)
2000 Enrollment: 725 618-254-3151

Wood River-Hartford Elementary S D 15 (PK-08)
2000 Enrollment: 882 618-254-0607

Housing: Homeownership rate: 65.2% (2000); Median home value: $59,600 (2000); Median rent: $375 per month (2000); Median age of housing: 47 years (2000).

Transportation: Commute to work: 93.8% car, 1.2% public transportation, 1.6% walk, 2.7% work from home (2000); Travel time to work: 34.6% less than 15 minutes, 31.5% 15 to 30 minutes, 21.1% 30 to 45 minutes, 9.5% 45 to 60 minutes, 3.2% 60 minutes or more (2000)

WORDEN (village). Covers a land area of 0.660 square miles and a water area of 0 square miles. Located at 38.93° N. Lat.; 89.84° W. Long. Elevation is 570 feet.

History: Incorporated 1877.

Population: 905 (2000); Race: 99.1% White, 0.0% Black, 0.0% Asian, 0.0% American Indian and Alaska Native, 1.6% Hispanic of any race, 0.7% two or more races (2000); Density: 1,370.3 persons per square mile (2000); Age: 24.5% under 18, 14.4% over 64 (2000); Marriage status: 21.3% never married, 58.9% now married, 10.4% widowed, 9.4% divorced (2000); Foreign born: 0.2% (2000); Ancestry (includes multiple ancestries): 41.8% German, 16.8% Irish, 9.8% English, 7.2% Other groups, 5.1% United States or American (2000).

Economy: Railroad junction. In agricultural area: wheat, corn, sorghum, cattle. Oil area. Single-family building permits issued: 15 (2001) / 8 (2000); Multi-family building permits issued: 0 (2001) / 0 (2000); Employment by occupation: 6.6% management, 14.9% professional, 15.9% services, 21.6% sales, 0.9% farming, 14.5% construction, 25.6% production (2000).

Income: Per capita income: $18,485 (2000); Median household income: $36,100 (2000); Poverty rate: 12.0% (2000).

Taxes: Total city taxes per capita: $96 (1997); City property taxes per capita: $54 (1997).

Education: High school graduation rate: 80.1% (2000); College graduation rate: 7.9% (2000).

Housing: Homeownership rate: 79.2% (2000); Median home value: $52,900 (2000); Median rent: $263 per month (2000); Median age of housing: 55 years (2000).

Newspapers: The Madison County Chronicle (1 x week)

Transportation: Commute to work: 93.5% car, 0.0% public transportation, 4.1% walk, 1.9% work from home (2000); Travel time to work: 21.8% less than 15 minutes, 22.8% 15 to 30 minutes, 33.3% 30 to 45 minutes, 13.0% 45 to 60 minutes, 9.1% 60 minutes or more (2000)

Marion County

Located in south central Illinois; drained by Skillet Fork, Crooked Creek, and a headstream of Kaskaskia River. Covers a land area of 572.30 square miles, a water area of 3.40 square miles, and is located in the Central Time Zone. The county government was organized in 1823. County seat is Salem.

Weather Station: Salem Leckrone Airport Elevation: 567 feet

	Jan	Feb	Mar	Apr	May	Jun	Jul	Aug	Sep	Oct	Nov	Dec
High	38	44	55	67	77	85	89	87	81	69	55	43
Low	21	25	34	44	54	63	67	65	57	45	36	26
Precip	2.4	2.5	4.0	4.2	4.3	4.2	3.8	3.3	3.2	3.1	4.0	3.2
Snow	5.4	3.5	1.1	0.3	0.0	0.0	0.0	0.0	0.0	tr	0.7	2.7

High and Low temperatures in degrees Fahrenheit; Precipitation and Snow in inches

Population: 41,691 (2000); Race: 94.3% White, 3.9% Black, 0.5% Asian, 0.2% American Indian and Alaska Native, 0.9% Hispanic of any race, 0.9% two or more races (2000); Density: 72.9 persons per square mile (2000); Age: 25.5% under 18, 16.6% over 64 (2000).
Religion: Five largest groups: 17.2% Southern Baptist Convention, 10.9% Christian Churches and Churches of Christ, 8.5% Catholic Church, 6.4% The United Methodist Church, 5.2% Lutheran Church—Missouri Synod (2000).
Economy: Unemployment rate: 9.6% (11/2002); Total civilian labor force: 18,376 (11/2002); Leading industries: 38.3% manufacturing; 18.4% health care and social assistance; 12.3% retail trade (2000); Companies that employ more than 1,000 persons: 1 (2000); Companies that employ more than 100 persons: 23 (2000); Farms: 882 totaling 249,395 acres (1997); Minority business ownership rate: 5.7% (1997); Women business ownership rate: 30.3% (1997); Retail sales per capita: $7,352 (1997). Single-family building permits issued: 27 (2001) / 15 (2000); Multi-family building permits issued: 17 (2001) / 2 (2000).
Income: Per capita income: $17,235 (2000); Median household income: $35,227 (2000); Poverty rate: 11.3% (2000); Bankruptcy rate: 7.64% (2001).
Taxes: Total county taxes per capita: $86 (1997); County property taxes per capita: $54 (1997).
Education: High school graduation rate: 79.1% (2000); College graduation rate: 12.1% (2000).
Housing: Homeownership rate: 76.6% (2000); Median home value: $53,700 (2000); Median rent: $266 per month (2000); Median age of housing: 37 years (2000).
Health: Birth rate: 123.3 per 10,000 population (1998); Age adjusted death rate: 97.5 per 10,000 population (1999); Age adjusted cancer mortality rate: 197.3 deaths per 100,000 population (1999). Number of physicians: 14.2 per 10,000 population (1999); Number of hospital beds: 48.0 per 10,000 population (1999).
Elections: 2000 Presidential election results: 48.4% Gore, 49.5% Bush, 1.4% Nader, 0.4% Buchanan
National and State Parks: Stephen A Forbes State Park
Additional Information Contacts
Marion County Government Offices 618-548-3400
Centralia Chamber of Commerce 618-532-6789
Salem Chamber of Commerce 618-548-3010

Marion County Communities

ALMA (village). Covers a land area of 1.080 square miles and a water area of 0 square miles. Located at 38.72° N. Lat.; 88.91° W. Long. Elevation is 630 feet.
Population: 386 (2000); Race: 98.2% White, 0.0% Black, 0.0% Asian, 0.0% American Indian and Alaska Native, 0.0% Hispanic of any race, 1.8% two or more races (2000); Density: 357.5 persons per square mile (2000); Age: 31.2% under 18, 9.1% over 64 (2000); Marriage status: 27.9% never married, 44.9% now married, 8.2% widowed, 19.0% divorced (2000); Foreign born: 0.8% (2000); Ancestry (includes multiple ancestries): 39.8% United States or American, 15.6% German, 9.1% Irish, 7.8% English, 3.0% Other groups (2000).
Economy: In agricultural region: wheat, soybeans, sorghum; cattle; dairying. Oil-producing area. Employment by occupation: 4.9% management, 9.8% professional, 24.5% services, 15.3% sales, 0.0% farming, 14.7% construction, 30.7% production (2000).
Income: Per capita income: $12,693 (2000); Median household income: $27,083 (2000); Poverty rate: 24.9% (2000).
Taxes: Total city taxes per capita: $30 (1997); City property taxes per capita: $30 (1997).
Education: High school graduation rate: 73.4% (2000); College graduation rate: 5.7% (2000).
Housing: Homeownership rate: 74.4% (2000); Median home value: $30,300 (2000); Median rent: $125 per month (2000); Median age of housing: 39 years (2000).
Transportation: Commute to work: 95.8% car, 0.0% public transportation, 4.2% walk, 0.0% work from home (2000); Travel time to work: 28.1% less than 15 minutes, 52.1% 15 to 30 minutes, 14.4% 30 to 45 minutes, 2.4% 45 to 60 minutes, 3.0% 60 minutes or more (2000)

CENTRAL CITY (village). Covers a land area of 0.580 square miles and a water area of 0 square miles. Located at 38.54° N. Lat.; 89.12° W. Long. Elevation is 485 feet.
History: Central City was settled by German immigrants, and incorporated in 1857.
Population: 1,371 (2000); Race: 93.4% White, 2.3% Black, 0.2% Asian, 0.2% American Indian and Alaska Native, 2.7% Hispanic of any race, 2.8% two or more races (2000); Density: 2,365.5 persons per square mile (2000); Age: 33.9% under 18, 9.2% over 64 (2000); Marriage status: 28.2% never married, 53.8% now married, 6.1% widowed, 11.9% divorced (2000); Foreign born: 0.5% (2000); Ancestry (includes multiple ancestries): 26.8% German, 13.5% Other groups, 13.4% Irish, 12.2% United States or American, 10.0% English (2000).
Economy: Employment by occupation: 7.1% management, 13.8% professional, 19.7% services, 17.4% sales, 0.0% farming, 13.6% construction, 28.4% production (2000).
Income: Per capita income: $13,151 (2000); Median household income: $31,136 (2000); Poverty rate: 15.1% (2000).
Taxes: Total city taxes per capita: $46 (1997); City property taxes per capita: $1 (1997).
Education: High school graduation rate: 75.9% (2000); College graduation rate: 6.3% (2000).

School District(s)

Grand Prairie C C School District 6 (KG-08)
2000 Enrollment: 101 618-249-6289
North Wamac School District 186 (KG-08)
2000 Enrollment: 142 618-532-1826
Willow Grove School District 46 (PK-08)
2000 Enrollment: 215 618-532-3313
Central City School District 133 (PK-08)
2000 Enrollment: 275 618-532-9521
Centralia H S District 200 (09-12)
2000 Enrollment: 1,107 618-532-7391
Centralia School District 135 (PK-08)
2000 Enrollment: 1,570 618-532-1907
Kaskaskia Special Education District (01-12)
2000 Enrollment: 127 618-532-4721
Raccoon Cons School District 1 (KG-08)
2000 Enrollment: 282 618-532-7329

Housing: Homeownership rate: 77.5% (2000); Median home value: $42,000 (2000); Median rent: $281 per month (2000); Median age of housing: 32 years (2000).
Transportation: Commute to work: 92.7% car, 0.0% public transportation, 2.6% walk, 3.9% work from home (2000); Travel time to work: 58.8% less than 15 minutes, 26.4% 15 to 30 minutes, 7.1% 30 to 45 minutes, 3.4% 45 to 60 minutes, 4.4% 60 minutes or more (2000)

CENTRALIA (city). Covers a land area of 7.502 square miles and a water area of 0.137 square miles. Located at 38.52° N. Lat.; 89.13° W. Long. Elevation is 500 feet.
History: Centralia was laid out by the Illinois Central Railroad in 1853, and named for the company. Many early residents were of German descent. Since Centralia was located in a fruit-producing area, the railroad company was interested in refrigerated cars for shipping the fruit, and in 1868 the first such train began operation between Centralia and Chicago.
Population: 14,136 (2000); Race: 86.5% White, 10.7% Black, 1.0% Asian, 0.1% American Indian and Alaska Native, 1.4% Hispanic of any race, 1.2% two or more races (2000); Density: 1,884.4 persons per square mile (2000); Age: 24.0% under 18, 20.0% over 64 (2000); Marriage status: 21.4% never married, 53.4% now married, 10.9% widowed, 14.2% divorced (2000); Foreign born: 1.3% (2000); Ancestry (includes multiple ancestries): 23.4% German, 14.6% Other groups, 11.1% United States or American, 10.0% Irish, 9.9% English (2000).
Vital Statistics: Birth rate: 162.0 per 10,000 population (1998)
Economy: Single-family building permits issued: 10 (2001) / 7 (2000); Multi-family building permits issued: 5 (2001) / 0 (2000); Employment by occupation: 7.0% management, 16.8% professional, 20.2% services, 20.7% sales, 0.6% farming, 6.3% construction, 28.5% production (2000).

Income: Per capita income: $17,174 (2000); Median household income: $31,905 (2000); Poverty rate: 14.6% (2000).
Taxes: Total city taxes per capita: $296 (1997); City property taxes per capita: $291 (1997).
Education: High school graduation rate: 74.9% (2000); College graduation rate: 14.2% (2000).

School District(s)

Central City School District 133 (PK-08)
2000 Enrollment: 275 618-532-9521
Centralia H S District 200 (09-12)
2000 Enrollment: 1,107 618-532-7391
Centralia School District 135 (PK-08)
2000 Enrollment: 1,570 618-532-1907
Kaskaskia Special Education District (01-12)
2000 Enrollment: 127 618-532-4721
Raccoon Cons School District 1 (KG-08)
2000 Enrollment: 282 618-532-7329

Two-year College(s)

Kaskaskia College (Public)
2001 Enrollment: 3,097 618-545-3000
2001 Tuition: In-state $4,224; Out-of-state $7,232
Housing: Homeownership rate: 69.3% (2000); Median home value: $50,000 (2000); Median rent: $277 per month (2000); Median age of housing: 45 years (2000).
Hospitals: Saint Mary's Good Samaritan (276 beds)
Newspapers: Centralia Sentinel (7 x week)
Transportation: Commute to work: 92.7% car, 0.7% public transportation, 3.4% walk, 2.5% work from home (2000); Travel time to work: 65.6% less than 15 minutes, 19.4% 15 to 30 minutes, 8.4% 30 to 45 minutes, 2.3% 45 to 60 minutes, 4.3% 60 minutes or more (2000); Amtrak: Service available.
Additional Information Contacts
Centralia Chamber of Commerce........................ 618-532-6789

IUKA (village). Covers a land area of 0.792 square miles and a water area of 0.002 square miles. Located at 38.61° N. Lat.; 88.78° W. Long. Elevation is 518 feet.
Population: 598 (2000); Race: 99.3% White, 0.0% Black, 0.3% Asian, 0.0% American Indian and Alaska Native, 1.8% Hispanic of any race, 0.3% two or more races (2000); Density: 754.7 persons per square mile (2000); Age: 35.2% under 18, 13.9% over 64 (2000); Marriage status: 15.5% never married, 62.8% now married, 9.2% widowed, 12.5% divorced (2000); Foreign born: 0.3% (2000); Ancestry (includes multiple ancestries): 15.7% German, 12.6% Irish, 11.7% United States or American, 9.3% Other groups, 8.9% English (2000).
Economy: In agricultural area: grain, cattle. Oil area. Employment by occupation: 2.4% management, 15.9% professional, 16.7% services, 15.5% sales, 0.0% farming, 8.6% construction, 40.8% production (2000).
Income: Per capita income: $11,520 (2000); Median household income: $27,375 (2000); Poverty rate: 16.7% (2000).
Taxes: Total city taxes per capita: $20 (1997); City property taxes per capita: $15 (1997).
Education: High school graduation rate: 72.7% (2000); College graduation rate: 5.7% (2000).

School District(s)

Iuka Community Cons School District 7 (PK-08)
2000 Enrollment: 299 618-323-6233
Housing: Homeownership rate: 83.2% (2000); Median home value: $47,700 (2000); Median rent: $217 per month (2000); Median age of housing: 40 years (2000).
Transportation: Commute to work: 96.5% car, 0.0% public transportation, 0.9% walk, 0.0% work from home (2000); Travel time to work: 19.9% less than 15 minutes, 41.2% 15 to 30 minutes, 14.2% 30 to 45 minutes, 9.3% 45 to 60 minutes, 15.5% 60 minutes or more (2000)

JUNCTION CITY (village). Aka Glenridge. Covers a land area of 0.675 square miles and a water area of 0.018 square miles. Located at 38.58° N. Lat.; 89.12° W. Long. Elevation is 493 feet.
Population: 559 (2000); Race: 99.6% White, 0.0% Black, 0.0% Asian, 0.4% American Indian and Alaska Native, 2.6% Hispanic of any race, 0.0% two or more races (2000); Density: 827.9 persons per square mile (2000); Age: 26.7% under 18, 13.1% over 64 (2000); Marriage status: 16.3% never married, 67.4% now married, 7.3% widowed, 9.0% divorced (2000); Foreign born: 0.6% (2000); Ancestry (includes multiple ancestries): 18.7% German, 18.5% United States or American, 13.1% Irish, 10.8% Other groups, 5.8% English (2000).
Economy: Employment by occupation: 0.0% management, 7.2% professional, 19.6% services, 11.9% sales, 0.0% farming, 11.5% construction, 49.8% production (2000).
Income: Per capita income: $14,114 (2000); Median household income: $33,500 (2000); Poverty rate: 9.9% (2000).
Taxes: Total city taxes per capita: $14 (1997); City property taxes per capita: $9 (1997).
Education: High school graduation rate: 58.1% (2000); College graduation rate: 4.1% (2000).
Housing: Homeownership rate: 90.7% (2000); Median home value: $46,400 (2000); Median rent: $219 per month (2000); Median age of housing: 24 years (2000).
Transportation: Commute to work: 91.6% car, 1.3% public transportation, 0.0% walk, 3.6% work from home (2000); Travel time to work: 20.7% less than 15 minutes, 56.2% 15 to 30 minutes, 8.3% 30 to 45 minutes, 4.1% 45 to 60 minutes, 10.6% 60 minutes or more (2000)

KELL (village). Covers a land area of 1.010 square miles and a water area of 0 square miles. Located at 38.49° N. Lat.; 88.90° W. Long. Elevation is 615 feet.
Population: 231 (2000); Race: 100.0% White, 0.0% Black, 0.0% Asian, 0.0% American Indian and Alaska Native, 0.0% Hispanic of any race, 0.0% two or more races (2000); Density: 228.7 persons per square mile (2000); Age: 16.8% under 18, 15.6% over 64 (2000); Marriage status: 15.9% never married, 72.8% now married, 6.0% widowed, 5.3% divorced (2000); Foreign born: 0.0% (2000); Ancestry (includes multiple ancestries): 24.9% United States or American, 19.7% German, 14.5% Irish, 8.1% English, 5.8% Other groups (2000).
Economy: In agricultural and oil area. Employment by occupation: 6.3% management, 22.9% professional, 8.3% services, 20.8% sales, 0.0% farming, 15.6% construction, 26.0% production (2000).
Income: Per capita income: $17,002 (2000); Median household income: $40,909 (2000); Poverty rate: 0.0% (2000).
Taxes: Total city taxes per capita: $36 (1997); City property taxes per capita: $32 (1997).
Education: High school graduation rate: 76.5% (2000); College graduation rate: 11.4% (2000).

School District(s)

Kell Consolidated School District 2 (PK-08)
2000 Enrollment: 128 618-822-6234
Housing: Homeownership rate: 89.0% (2000); Median home value: $40,700 (2000); Median rent: $175 per month (2000); Median age of housing: 49 years (2000).
Transportation: Commute to work: 95.8% car, 0.0% public transportation, 4.2% walk, 0.0% work from home (2000); Travel time to work: 13.5% less than 15 minutes, 53.1% 15 to 30 minutes, 18.8% 30 to 45 minutes, 3.1% 45 to 60 minutes, 11.5% 60 minutes or more (2000)

KINMUNDY (city). Covers a land area of 1.031 square miles and a water area of 0 square miles. Located at 38.77° N. Lat.; 88.85° W. Long. Elevation is 619 feet.
Population: 892 (2000); Race: 97.6% White, 0.0% Black, 0.0% Asian, 0.0% American Indian and Alaska Native, 0.7% Hispanic of any race, 1.7% two or more races (2000); Density: 865.2 persons per square mile (2000); Age: 27.7% under 18, 15.4% over 64 (2000); Marriage status: 19.6% never married, 56.7% now married, 12.1% widowed, 11.5% divorced (2000); Foreign born: 0.2% (2000); Ancestry (includes multiple ancestries): 22.7% United States or American, 12.5% German, 8.2% Irish, 6.9% Other groups, 5.2% English (2000).
Economy: In oil-producing area; food processing. Agriculture: corn, wheat, livestock. Employment by occupation: 9.3% management, 16.6% professional, 18.5% services, 18.0% sales, 3.0% farming, 9.3% construction, 25.3% production (2000).
Income: Per capita income: $15,279 (2000); Median household income: $28,500 (2000); Poverty rate: 12.8% (2000).
Taxes: Total city taxes per capita: $33 (1997); City property taxes per capita: $27 (1997).
Education: High school graduation rate: 75.5% (2000); College graduation rate: 8.5% (2000).

School District(s)

South Central Community Unit District 401 (PK-12)
2000 Enrollment: 795 618-547-3414
Housing: Homeownership rate: 73.0% (2000); Median home value: $39,500 (2000); Median rent: $206 per month (2000); Median age of housing: 37 years (2000).
Newspapers: Kinmundy Express (1 x week)

Transportation: Commute to work: 90.7% car, 0.0% public transportation, 3.6% walk, 3.3% work from home (2000); Travel time to work: 24.4% less than 15 minutes, 47.6% 15 to 30 minutes, 13.9% 30 to 45 minutes, 8.8% 45 to 60 minutes, 5.4% 60 minutes or more (2000)

ODIN (village). Covers a land area of 1.010 square miles and a water area of 0 square miles. Located at 38.61° N. Lat.; 89.05° W. Long. Elevation is 526 feet.
History: Odin developed as a mining and agricultural center along the Illinois Central Railroad.
Population: 1,122 (2000); Race: 98.7% White, 0.2% Black, 0.0% Asian, 0.3% American Indian and Alaska Native, 0.5% Hispanic of any race, 0.5% two or more races (2000); Density: 1,110.8 persons per square mile (2000); Age: 26.1% under 18, 18.2% over 64 (2000); Marriage status: 17.5% never married, 60.7% now married, 5.5% widowed, 16.2% divorced (2000); Foreign born: 0.3% (2000); Ancestry (includes multiple ancestries): 22.5% United States or American, 16.8% German, 15.8% Irish, 7.1% Other groups, 6.5% English (2000).
Economy: Employment by occupation: 6.3% management, 16.0% professional, 18.1% services, 21.9% sales, 0.0% farming, 8.7% construction, 29.0% production (2000).
Income: Per capita income: $14,814 (2000); Median household income: $32,019 (2000); Poverty rate: 11.7% (2000).
Taxes: Total city taxes per capita: $32 (1997); City property taxes per capita: $32 (1997).
Education: High school graduation rate: 76.8% (2000); College graduation rate: 7.0% (2000).

School District(s)

Odin Community H S District 700 (09-12)
2000 Enrollment: 95 618-775-8266
Odin School District 122 (PK-08)
2000 Enrollment: 295 618-775-8266

Housing: Homeownership rate: 75.5% (2000); Median home value: $39,300 (2000); Median rent: $265 per month (2000); Median age of housing: 35 years (2000).
Transportation: Commute to work: 95.4% car, 0.0% public transportation, 2.2% walk, 1.6% work from home (2000); Travel time to work: 47.3% less than 15 minutes, 32.0% 15 to 30 minutes, 11.7% 30 to 45 minutes, 2.9% 45 to 60 minutes, 6.1% 60 minutes or more (2000)

PATOKA (village). Covers a land area of 1.100 square miles and a water area of 0 square miles. Located at 38.75° N. Lat.; 89.09° W. Long. Elevation is 507 feet.
History: Patoka was named for an Indian chief. Oil was discovered in Patoka in 1937, bringing new growth to the town.
Population: 633 (2000); Race: 100.0% White, 0.0% Black, 0.0% Asian, 0.0% American Indian and Alaska Native, 0.0% Hispanic of any race, 0.0% two or more races (2000); Density: 575.5 persons per square mile (2000); Age: 24.4% under 18, 17.3% over 64 (2000); Marriage status: 20.5% never married, 55.5% now married, 12.4% widowed, 11.6% divorced (2000); Foreign born: 0.0% (2000); Ancestry (includes multiple ancestries): 24.3% German, 12.5% Irish, 11.8% English, 10.7% United States or American, 7.8% Other groups (2000).
Economy: Employment by occupation: 6.9% management, 14.5% professional, 23.3% services, 16.7% sales, 0.7% farming, 9.1% construction, 28.7% production (2000).
Income: Per capita income: $15,382 (2000); Median household income: $28,571 (2000); Poverty rate: 13.3% (2000).
Taxes: Total city taxes per capita: $41 (1997); City property taxes per capita: $41 (1997).
Education: High school graduation rate: 74.8% (2000); College graduation rate: 4.8% (2000).

School District(s)

Patoka Community Unit School District 100 (KG-12)
2000 Enrollment: 306 618-432-5440

Housing: Homeownership rate: 82.1% (2000); Median home value: $47,600 (2000); Median rent: $188 per month (2000); Median age of housing: 41 years (2000).
Transportation: Commute to work: 93.0% car, 0.4% public transportation, 5.2% walk, 1.1% work from home (2000); Travel time to work: 25.8% less than 15 minutes, 38.2% 15 to 30 minutes, 26.6% 30 to 45 minutes, 2.2% 45 to 60 minutes, 7.1% 60 minutes or more (2000)

SALEM (city). Covers a land area of 6.100 square miles and a water area of 0.157 square miles. Located at 38.62° N. Lat.; 88.94° W. Long. Elevation is 544 feet.
History: Salem was laid out in 1813 on the St. Louis-Vincennes stagecoach route, and incorporated in 1837. William Jennings Bryan (1860-1925) was born and grew up in Salem. Oil was discovered in Salem in 1939.
Population: 7,909 (2000); Race: 97.3% White, 1.1% Black, 0.5% Asian, 0.8% American Indian and Alaska Native, 0.7% Hispanic of any race, 0.4% two or more races (2000); Density: 1,296.5 persons per square mile (2000); Age: 23.9% under 18, 19.4% over 64 (2000); Marriage status: 21.6% never married, 56.7% now married, 9.4% widowed, 12.2% divorced (2000); Foreign born: 0.8% (2000); Ancestry (includes multiple ancestries): 18.8% German, 10.6% English, 10.5% Irish, 10.2% United States or American, 7.7% Other groups (2000).
Economy: Single-family building permits issued: 14 (2001) / 5 (2000); Multi-family building permits issued: 12 (2001) / 2 (2000); Employment by occupation: 9.0% management, 19.9% professional, 15.8% services, 21.5% sales, 0.0% farming, 5.5% construction, 28.4% production (2000).
Income: Per capita income: $16,954 (2000); Median household income: $34,339 (2000); Poverty rate: 9.2% (2000).
Taxes: Total city taxes per capita: $138 (2000); City property taxes per capita: $131 (2000).
Education: High school graduation rate: 77.2% (2000); College graduation rate: 13.3% (2000).

School District(s)

Salem Community H S District 600 (09-12)
2000 Enrollment: 837 618-548-0727
Salem School District 111 (PK-08)
2000 Enrollment: 1,033 618-548-7700
Selmaville C C School District 10 (PK-08)
2000 Enrollment: 259 618-548-2416

Housing: Homeownership rate: 69.9% (2000); Median home value: $58,200 (2000); Median rent: $277 per month (2000); Median age of housing: 35 years (2000).
Hospitals: Salem Township Hospital (46 beds)
Newspapers: Salem Times-Commoner (3 x week)
Transportation: Commute to work: 94.6% car, 0.0% public transportation, 2.9% walk, 1.9% work from home (2000); Travel time to work: 63.2% less than 15 minutes, 17.8% 15 to 30 minutes, 11.4% 30 to 45 minutes, 3.7% 45 to 60 minutes, 3.9% 60 minutes or more (2000)
Additional Information Contacts
Salem Chamber of Commerce 618-548-3010

SANDOVAL (village). Covers a land area of 0.960 square miles and a water area of 0 square miles. Located at 38.61° N. Lat.; 89.12° W. Long. Elevation is 505 feet.
History: Incorporated 1859.
Population: 1,434 (2000); Race: 97.3% White, 0.0% Black, 0.0% Asian, 0.4% American Indian and Alaska Native, 0.6% Hispanic of any race, 2.1% two or more races (2000); Density: 1,494.0 persons per square mile (2000); Age: 31.7% under 18, 9.4% over 64 (2000); Marriage status: 22.2% never married, 58.1% now married, 4.0% widowed, 15.7% divorced (2000); Foreign born: 0.7% (2000); Ancestry (includes multiple ancestries): 22.5% United States or American, 16.2% German, 11.9% Other groups, 8.0% Irish, 6.5% English (2000).
Economy: In oil- and natural-gas-producing, and agricultural area. Single-family building permits issued: 3 (2001) / 3 (2000); Multi-family building permits issued: 0 (2001) / 0 (2000); Employment by occupation: 3.8% management, 11.0% professional, 21.8% services, 18.2% sales, 1.4% farming, 11.5% construction, 32.2% production (2000).
Income: Per capita income: $14,739 (2000); Median household income: $30,000 (2000); Poverty rate: 21.1% (2000).
Taxes: Total city taxes per capita: $21 (1997); City property taxes per capita: $21 (1997).
Education: High school graduation rate: 73.4% (2000); College graduation rate: 5.9% (2000).

School District(s)

Sandoval C U School District 501 (PK-12)
2000 Enrollment: 590 618-247-3233

Housing: Homeownership rate: 68.9% (2000); Median home value: $39,100 (2000); Median rent: $219 per month (2000); Median age of housing: 32 years (2000).
Transportation: Commute to work: 94.0% car, 0.0% public transportation, 0.8% walk, 3.7% work from home (2000); Travel time to work: 30.4% less than 15 minutes, 49.2% 15 to 30 minutes, 9.6% 30 to 45 minutes, 3.4% 45 to 60 minutes, 7.6% 60 minutes or more (2000)

VERNON (village). Covers a land area of 0.911 square miles and a water area of 0 square miles. Located at 38.80° N. Lat.; 89.08° W. Long. Elevation is 515 feet.
History: Vernon developed as the center of a peach and pear growing area.
Population: 178 (2000); Race: 97.0% White, 1.0% Black, 0.0% Asian, 0.0% American Indian and Alaska Native, 2.0% Hispanic of any race, 2.0% two or more races (2000); Density: 195.5 persons per square mile (2000); Age: 25.4% under 18, 11.4% over 64 (2000); Marriage status: 19.5% never married, 58.5% now married, 10.7% widowed, 11.3% divorced (2000); Foreign born: 0.0% (2000); Ancestry (includes multiple ancestries): 26.4% United States or American, 18.9% Other groups, 15.9% Irish, 15.9% German, 7.5% English (2000).
Economy: Employment by occupation: 5.1% management, 3.8% professional, 23.1% services, 12.8% sales, 2.6% farming, 16.7% construction, 35.9% production (2000).
Income: Per capita income: $9,686 (2000); Median household income: $21,667 (2000); Poverty rate: 27.4% (2000).
Taxes: Total city taxes per capita: $9 (1997); City property taxes per capita: $9 (1997).
Education: High school graduation rate: 70.7% (2000); College graduation rate: 2.1% (2000).
Housing: Homeownership rate: 90.4% (2000); Median home value: $32,100 (2000); Median rent: $188 per month (2000); Median age of housing: 43 years (2000).
Transportation: Commute to work: 89.7% car, 0.0% public transportation, 0.0% walk, 3.8% work from home (2000); Travel time to work: 26.7% less than 15 minutes, 57.3% 15 to 30 minutes, 8.0% 30 to 45 minutes, 0.0% 45 to 60 minutes, 8.0% 60 minutes or more (2000)

WALNUT HILL (village). Covers a land area of 0.371 square miles and a water area of 0 square miles. Located at 38.47° N. Lat.; 89.04° W. Long. Elevation is 570 feet.
Population: 109 (2000); Race: 100.0% White, 0.0% Black, 0.0% Asian, 0.0% American Indian and Alaska Native, 0.0% Hispanic of any race, 0.0% two or more races (2000); Density: 294.2 persons per square mile (2000); Age: 35.3% under 18, 14.7% over 64 (2000); Marriage status: 14.7% never married, 60.3% now married, 17.6% widowed, 7.4% divorced (2000); Foreign born: 0.0% (2000); Ancestry (includes multiple ancestries): 15.7% Other groups, 13.7% United States or American, 9.8% Irish, 8.8% German, 6.9% Italian (2000).
Economy: Agricultural and oil area. Employment by occupation: 0.0% management, 10.0% professional, 18.0% services, 18.0% sales, 0.0% farming, 0.0% construction, 54.0% production (2000).
Income: Per capita income: $9,025 (2000); Median household income: $21,250 (2000); Poverty rate: 3.9% (2000).
Taxes: Total city taxes per capita: $14 (1997); City property taxes per capita: $14 (1997).
Education: High school graduation rate: 73.1% (2000); College graduation rate: 0.0% (2000).
Housing: Homeownership rate: 86.4% (2000); Median home value: $45,700 (2000); Median rent: $225 per month (2000); Median age of housing: 35 years (2000).
Transportation: Commute to work: 100.0% car, 0.0% public transportation, 0.0% walk, 0.0% work from home (2000); Travel time to work: 19.1% less than 15 minutes, 44.7% 15 to 30 minutes, 23.4% 30 to 45 minutes, 0.0% 45 to 60 minutes, 12.8% 60 minutes or more (2000)

WAMAC (city). Covers a land area of 1.508 square miles and a water area of 0 square miles. Located at 38.50° N. Lat.; 89.14° W. Long.
History: Wamac was incorporated as a city in 1913. Its name was made from the first letters of the counties in which the town was situated—Washington, Marion, and Clinton.
Population: 1,378 (2000); Race: 99.2% White, 0.3% Black, 0.1% Asian, 0.0% American Indian and Alaska Native, 1.0% Hispanic of any race, 0.4% two or more races (2000); Density: 913.6 persons per square mile (2000); Age: 28.5% under 18, 11.1% over 64 (2000); Marriage status: 22.6% never married, 51.1% now married, 8.2% widowed, 18.1% divorced (2000); Foreign born: 0.4% (2000); Ancestry (includes multiple ancestries): 19.0% German, 17.6% United States or American, 9.7% Irish, 8.8% Other groups, 7.6% English (2000).
Economy: Single-family building permits issued: 0 (2001) / 0 (2000); Multi-family building permits issued: 0 (2001) / 0 (2000); Employment by occupation: 2.6% management, 7.5% professional, 24.3% services, 16.1% sales, 0.3% farming, 10.6% construction, 38.5% production (2000).
Income: Per capita income: $13,781 (2000); Median household income: $26,149 (2000); Poverty rate: 27.3% (2000).
Taxes: Total city taxes per capita: $142 (1997); City property taxes per capita: $43 (1997).
Education: High school graduation rate: 69.1% (2000); College graduation rate: 2.6% (2000).
Housing: Homeownership rate: 65.1% (2000); Median home value: $32,600 (2000); Median rent: $261 per month (2000); Median age of housing: 36 years (2000).
Transportation: Commute to work: 88.7% car, 0.0% public transportation, 7.4% walk, 1.6% work from home (2000); Travel time to work: 66.5% less than 15 minutes, 18.4% 15 to 30 minutes, 9.1% 30 to 45 minutes, 2.7% 45 to 60 minutes, 3.2% 60 minutes or more (2000)

Marshall County

Located in north central Illinois; drained by the Illinois River and Sandy Creek. Covers a land area of 386.10 square miles, a water area of 12.50 square miles, and is located in the Central Time Zone. The county government was organized in 1839. County seat is Lacon.

Weather Station: Lacon 1 N — Elevation: 459 feet

	Jan	Feb	Mar	Apr	May	Jun	Jul	Aug	Sep	Oct	Nov	Dec
High	31	38	50	64	75	84	87	85	78	66	51	38
Low	15	20	30	41	51	60	64	62	54	43	32	22
Precip	1.6	1.6	3.2	4.1	4.4	4.3	4.2	3.7	3.7	3.1	3.0	2.3
Snow	7.3	4.6	2.8	0.8	tr	0.0	0.0	0.0	0.0	tr	1.7	5.4

High and Low temperatures in degrees Fahrenheit; Precipitation and Snow in inches

Population: 13,180 (2000); Race: 98.4% White, 0.5% Black, 0.3% Asian, 0.1% American Indian and Alaska Native, 0.8% Hispanic of any race, 0.6% two or more races (2000); Density: 34.1 persons per square mile (2000); Age: 23.4% under 18, 18.8% over 64 (2000).
Religion: Five largest groups: 26.7% Catholic Church, 7.0% Evangelical Lutheran Church in America, 6.9% The United Methodist Church, 4.9% Christian Church (Disciples of Christ), 3.8% Lutheran Church—Missouri Synod (2000).
Economy: Unemployment rate: 5.5% (11/2002); Total civilian labor force: 6,600 (11/2002); Leading industries: 30.1% manufacturing; 14.5% retail trade; 13.5% accommodation & food services (2000); Companies that employ more than 1,000 persons: 0 (2000); Companies that employ more than 100 persons: 5 (2000); Farms: 494 totaling 227,521 acres (1997); Minority business ownership rate: 0.0% (1997); Women business ownership rate: 25.9% (1997); Retail sales per capita: $5,350 (1997). Single-family building permits issued: 17 (2001) / 17 (2000); Multi-family building permits issued: 28 (2001) / 0 (2000).
Income: Per capita income: $19,065 (2000); Median household income: $41,576 (2000); Poverty rate: 5.6% (2000); Bankruptcy rate: 6.75% (2001).
Taxes: Total county taxes per capita: $136 (2000); County property taxes per capita: $109 (2000).
Education: High school graduation rate: 85.0% (2000); College graduation rate: 14.5% (2000).
Housing: Homeownership rate: 80.2% (2000); Median home value: $75,900 (2000); Median rent: $303 per month (2000); Median age of housing: 46 years (2000).
Health: Birth rate: 109.3 per 10,000 population (1998); Age adjusted death rate: 82.0 per 10,000 population (1999); Age adjusted cancer mortality rate: 204.7 deaths per 100,000 population (1999). Number of physicians: 6.1 per 10,000 population (1999); Number of hospital beds: n/a (1999).
Elections: 2000 Presidential election results: 43.5% Gore, 53.2% Bush, 2.3% Nader, 0.7% Buchanan
National and State Parks: Cameron National Wildlife Refuge; Marshall County State Conservation Areas; Sparland State Conservation Area
Additional Information Contacts
Marshall County Government Offices 309-246-6325
Lacon Area Chamber of Commerce. 309-246-5222

Marshall County Communities

HENRY (city). Covers a land area of 1.395 square miles and a water area of 0.069 square miles. Located at 41.11° N. Lat.; 89.36° W. Long. Elevation is 495 feet.
History: Founded in early 1840s; incorporated 1854.
Population: 2,540 (2000); Race: 95.8% White, 1.3% Black, 0.8% Asian, 0.0% American Indian and Alaska Native, 0.7% Hispanic of any race, 1.9% two or more races (2000); Density: 1,821.3 persons per square mile (2000);

Age: 24.1% under 18, 22.0% over 64 (2000); Marriage status: 18.2% never married, 65.2% now married, 8.2% widowed, 8.3% divorced (2000); Foreign born: 1.6% (2000); Ancestry (includes multiple ancestries): 34.5% German, 16.5% Irish, 13.3% English, 6.7% Other groups, 6.0% Swedish (2000).
Economy: In agricultural area: corn, soybeans, fruit; cattle; ships grain. Manufacturing: chemicals. Nurseries. Single-family building permits issued: 3 (2001) / 1 (2000); Multi-family building permits issued: 28 (2001) / 0 (2000); Employment by occupation: 6.0% management, 16.7% professional, 21.3% services, 21.3% sales, 0.2% farming, 10.3% construction, 24.1% production (2000).
Income: Per capita income: $18,473 (2000); Median household income: $40,236 (2000); Poverty rate: 5.6% (2000).
Taxes: Total city taxes per capita: $83 (1997); City property taxes per capita: $74 (1997).
Education: High school graduation rate: 81.5% (2000); College graduation rate: 17.2% (2000).

School District(s)

Henry-Senachwine CUSD 5 (KG-12)
2000 Enrollment: 657 309-364-3614

Housing: Homeownership rate: 78.6% (2000); Median home value: $71,200 (2000); Median rent: $350 per month (2000); Median age of housing: 53 years (2000).
Newspapers: Wenona Index (1 x week); Henry News Republican (1 x week)
Transportation: Commute to work: 94.2% car, 0.3% public transportation, 2.4% walk, 2.0% work from home (2000); Travel time to work: 46.9% less than 15 minutes, 19.2% 15 to 30 minutes, 17.6% 30 to 45 minutes, 10.1% 45 to 60 minutes, 6.2% 60 minutes or more (2000)

HOPEWELL (village). Covers a land area of 1.125 square miles and a water area of 0 square miles. Located at 40.98° N. Lat.; 89.45° W. Long. Elevation is 476 feet.
Population: 396 (2000); Race: 97.5% White, 1.9% Black, 0.0% Asian, 0.0% American Indian and Alaska Native, 0.5% Hispanic of any race, 0.5% two or more races (2000); Density: 352.0 persons per square mile (2000); Age: 23.6% under 18, 7.4% over 64 (2000); Marriage status: 14.3% never married, 73.5% now married, 0.0% widowed, 12.2% divorced (2000); Foreign born: 1.1% (2000); Ancestry (includes multiple ancestries): 30.8% German, 14.3% English, 11.8% Irish, 5.5% Swedish, 4.7% Italian (2000).
Economy: Corn, soybeans. Single-family building permits issued: 5 (2001) / 5 (2000); Multi-family building permits issued: 0 (2001) / 0 (2000); Employment by occupation: 9.5% management, 36.7% professional, 7.7% services, 24.9% sales, 0.9% farming, 7.7% construction, 12.7% production (2000).
Income: Per capita income: $25,143 (2000); Median household income: $63,250 (2000); Poverty rate: 0.0% (2000).
Taxes: Total city taxes per capita: $98 (1997); City property taxes per capita: $80 (1997).
Education: High school graduation rate: 97.4% (2000); College graduation rate: 24.4% (2000).
Housing: Homeownership rate: 97.2% (2000); Median home value: $123,400 (2000); Median rent: $175 per month (2000); Median age of housing: 21 years (2000).
Transportation: Commute to work: 100.0% car, 0.0% public transportation, 0.0% walk, 0.0% work from home (2000); Travel time to work: 23.0% less than 15 minutes, 35.9% 15 to 30 minutes, 30.4% 30 to 45 minutes, 6.5% 45 to 60 minutes, 4.1% 60 minutes or more (2000)

LA ROSE (village). Covers a land area of 0.220 square miles and a water area of 0 square miles. Located at 40.98° N. Lat.; 89.23° W. Long. Elevation is 685 feet.
Population: 159 (2000); Race: 100.0% White, 0.0% Black, 0.0% Asian, 0.0% American Indian and Alaska Native, 0.0% Hispanic of any race, 0.0% two or more races (2000); Density: 722.5 persons per square mile (2000); Age: 20.6% under 18, 12.2% over 64 (2000); Marriage status: 24.0% never married, 63.3% now married, 5.3% widowed, 7.3% divorced (2000); Foreign born: 1.1% (2000); Ancestry (includes multiple ancestries): 42.9% German, 13.8% English, 11.6% Swedish, 10.1% United States or American, 10.1% Irish (2000).
Economy: In agricultural area. Single-family building permits issued: 0 (2001) / 0 (2000); Multi-family building permits issued: 0 (2001) / 0 (2000); Employment by occupation: 8.8% management, 5.9% professional, 21.6% services, 23.5% sales, 0.0% farming, 6.9% construction, 33.3% production (2000).
Income: Per capita income: $17,480 (2000); Median household income: $46,667 (2000); Poverty rate: 10.1% (2000).
Taxes: Total city taxes per capita: $73 (1997); City property taxes per capita: $65 (1997).
Education: High school graduation rate: 84.7% (2000); College graduation rate: 6.9% (2000).
Housing: Homeownership rate: 89.6% (2000); Median home value: $46,000 (2000); Median rent: $231 per month (2000); Median age of housing: 60+ years (2000).
Transportation: Commute to work: 97.0% car, 0.0% public transportation, 3.0% walk, 0.0% work from home (2000); Travel time to work: 34.3% less than 15 minutes, 29.3% 15 to 30 minutes, 22.2% 30 to 45 minutes, 7.1% 45 to 60 minutes, 7.1% 60 minutes or more (2000)

LACON (city). Covers a land area of 1.604 square miles and a water area of 0.044 square miles. Located at 41.02° N. Lat.; 89.40° W. Long. Elevation is 495 feet.
History: Laid out as Columbia in 1826; incorporated 1839.
Population: 1,979 (2000); Race: 100.0% White, 0.0% Black, 0.0% Asian, 0.0% American Indian and Alaska Native, 0.5% Hispanic of any race, 0.0% two or more races (2000); Density: 1,233.9 persons per square mile (2000); Age: 22.3% under 18, 24.0% over 64 (2000); Marriage status: 20.2% never married, 57.4% now married, 12.4% widowed, 10.0% divorced (2000); Foreign born: 0.5% (2000); Ancestry (includes multiple ancestries): 28.8% German, 15.1% Irish, 12.0% English, 7.3% Swedish, 6.3% United States or American (2000).
Economy: In agricultural area; grain elevator, textiles. Single-family building permits issued: 2 (2001) / 4 (2000); Multi-family building permits issued: 0 (2001) / 0 (2000); Employment by occupation: 7.0% management, 15.6% professional, 19.9% services, 22.2% sales, 0.0% farming, 10.5% construction, 24.8% production (2000).
Income: Per capita income: $18,309 (2000); Median household income: $40,203 (2000); Poverty rate: 5.0% (2000).
Taxes: Total city taxes per capita: $100 (1997); City property taxes per capita: $96 (1997).
Education: High school graduation rate: 82.3% (2000); College graduation rate: 12.8% (2000).

School District(s)

Midland Community Unit District 7 (PK-12)
2000 Enrollment: 949 309-246-2310

Housing: Homeownership rate: 77.1% (2000); Median home value: $69,500 (2000); Median rent: $306 per month (2000); Median age of housing: 52 years (2000).
Newspapers: Lacon Home Journal (1 x week); Illinois Valley Peach (1 x week)
Transportation: Commute to work: 89.5% car, 2.2% public transportation, 5.5% walk, 1.6% work from home (2000); Travel time to work: 36.7% less than 15 minutes, 19.6% 15 to 30 minutes, 26.2% 30 to 45 minutes, 12.0% 45 to 60 minutes, 5.5% 60 minutes or more (2000)

Additional Information Contacts

Lacon Area Chamber of Commerce. 309-246-5222

SPARLAND (village). Covers a land area of 0.582 square miles and a water area of 0 square miles. Located at 41.03° N. Lat.; 89.43° W. Long. Elevation is 500 feet.
Population: 504 (2000); Race: 98.4% White, 1.0% Black, 0.0% Asian, 0.0% American Indian and Alaska Native, 6.4% Hispanic of any race, 0.0% two or more races (2000); Density: 865.3 persons per square mile (2000); Age: 30.1% under 18, 16.4% over 64 (2000); Marriage status: 16.6% never married, 69.6% now married, 5.3% widowed, 8.4% divorced (2000); Foreign born: 1.2% (2000); Ancestry (includes multiple ancestries): 24.4% German, 16.3% Irish, 14.9% United States or American, 10.9% English, 10.7% Other groups (2000).
Economy: In agricultural area. Employment by occupation: 3.8% management, 8.0% professional, 17.6% services, 24.4% sales, 0.0% farming, 17.6% construction, 28.6% production (2000).
Income: Per capita income: $13,924 (2000); Median household income: $32,019 (2000); Poverty rate: 5.8% (2000).
Taxes: Total city taxes per capita: $29 (1997); City property taxes per capita: $27 (1997).
Education: High school graduation rate: 74.4% (2000); College graduation rate: 3.1% (2000).
Housing: Homeownership rate: 75.9% (2000); Median home value: $66,300 (2000); Median rent: $248 per month (2000); Median age of housing: 59 years (2000).
Transportation: Commute to work: 97.3% car, 0.0% public transportation, 1.5% walk, 1.2% work from home (2000); Travel time to work: 34.4% less

than 15 minutes, 16.0% 15 to 30 minutes, 37.9% 30 to 45 minutes, 5.9% 45 to 60 minutes, 5.9% 60 minutes or more (2000)

TOLUCA (city). Covers a land area of 1.062 square miles and a water area of 0 square miles. Located at 41.00° N. Lat.; 89.13° W. Long. Elevation is 695 feet.

History: Incorporated 1894.

Population: 1,339 (2000); Race: 98.1% White, 0.0% Black, 0.2% Asian, 0.2% American Indian and Alaska Native, 1.5% Hispanic of any race, 0.3% two or more races (2000); Density: 1,260.9 persons per square mile (2000); Age: 19.9% under 18, 27.0% over 64 (2000); Marriage status: 17.9% never married, 59.3% now married, 11.9% widowed, 11.0% divorced (2000); Foreign born: 1.9% (2000); Ancestry (includes multiple ancestries): 42.5% German, 16.0% Italian, 8.7% Irish, 7.8% English, 7.4% Polish (2000).

Economy: In agricultural area. Single-family building permits issued: 4 (2001) / 4 (2000); Multi-family building permits issued: 0 (2001) / 0 (2000); Employment by occupation: 12.2% management, 12.4% professional, 16.0% services, 18.9% sales, 0.5% farming, 7.7% construction, 32.3% production (2000).

Income: Per capita income: $20,243 (2000); Median household income: $37,072 (2000); Poverty rate: 6.5% (2000).

Taxes: Total city taxes per capita: $80 (1997); City property taxes per capita: $78 (1997).

Education: High school graduation rate: 80.2% (2000); College graduation rate: 12.2% (2000).

Housing: Homeownership rate: 79.3% (2000); Median home value: $60,000 (2000); Median rent: $265 per month (2000); Median age of housing: 51 years (2000).

Transportation: Commute to work: 88.4% car, 0.0% public transportation, 8.2% walk, 2.8% work from home (2000); Travel time to work: 62.1% less than 15 minutes, 11.7% 15 to 30 minutes, 13.2% 30 to 45 minutes, 10.3% 45 to 60 minutes, 2.7% 60 minutes or more (2000)

VARNA (village). Covers a land area of 0.293 square miles and a water area of 0 square miles. Located at 41.03° N. Lat.; 89.22° W. Long. Elevation is 729 feet.

Population: 436 (2000); Race: 96.0% White, 0.0% Black, 2.1% Asian, 0.2% American Indian and Alaska Native, 0.5% Hispanic of any race, 1.7% two or more races (2000); Density: 1,488.2 persons per square mile (2000); Age: 22.7% under 18, 22.5% over 64 (2000); Marriage status: 16.5% never married, 69.1% now married, 7.2% widowed, 7.2% divorced (2000); Foreign born: 1.2% (2000); Ancestry (includes multiple ancestries): 45.0% German, 14.2% Irish, 12.3% English, 10.0% Other groups, 7.6% Italian (2000).

Economy: In agricultural area: corn, soybeans; cattle. Employment by occupation: 5.2% management, 7.3% professional, 27.1% services, 20.3% sales, 0.0% farming, 5.7% construction, 34.4% production (2000).

Income: Per capita income: $15,948 (2000); Median household income: $32,308 (2000); Poverty rate: 8.1% (2000).

Taxes: Total city taxes per capita: $97 (1997); City property taxes per capita: $30 (1997).

Education: High school graduation rate: 84.5% (2000); College graduation rate: 4.3% (2000).

Housing: Homeownership rate: 85.9% (2000); Median home value: $63,400 (2000); Median rent: $314 per month (2000); Median age of housing: 60+ years (2000).

Transportation: Commute to work: 85.9% car, 0.0% public transportation, 4.7% walk, 6.3% work from home (2000); Travel time to work: 34.4% less than 15 minutes, 30.6% 15 to 30 minutes, 17.8% 30 to 45 minutes, 7.2% 45 to 60 minutes, 10.0% 60 minutes or more (2000)

WENONA (city). Covers a land area of 0.672 square miles and a water area of 0 square miles. Located at 41.05° N. Lat.; 89.05° W. Long. Elevation is 699 feet.

History: Wenona's early economy was based on soy beans and corn.

Population: 1,065 (2000); Race: 98.6% White, 0.0% Black, 0.2% Asian, 0.4% American Indian and Alaska Native, 2.1% Hispanic of any race, 0.8% two or more races (2000); Density: 1,583.9 persons per square mile (2000); Age: 26.0% under 18, 20.7% over 64 (2000); Marriage status: 24.3% never married, 57.0% now married, 10.1% widowed, 8.6% divorced (2000); Foreign born: 0.7% (2000); Ancestry (includes multiple ancestries): 41.4% German, 17.6% Irish, 12.2% Italian, 9.5% Swedish, 8.0% English (2000).

Economy: Single-family building permits issued: 3 (2001) / 3 (2000); Multi-family building permits issued: 0 (2001) / 0 (2000); Employment by occupation: 8.3% management, 15.4% professional, 22.4% services, 23.9% sales, 0.4% farming, 9.6% construction, 20.0% production (2000).

Income: Per capita income: $17,951 (2000); Median household income: $36,711 (2000); Poverty rate: 7.8% (2000).

Taxes: Total city taxes per capita: $137 (1997); City property taxes per capita: $126 (1997).

Education: High school graduation rate: 86.0% (2000); College graduation rate: 12.2% (2000).

Housing: Homeownership rate: 76.7% (2000); Median home value: $65,600 (2000); Median rent: $258 per month (2000); Median age of housing: 58 years (2000).

Transportation: Commute to work: 93.5% car, 0.4% public transportation, 2.9% walk, 2.5% work from home (2000); Travel time to work: 39.1% less than 15 minutes, 28.2% 15 to 30 minutes, 11.2% 30 to 45 minutes, 15.9% 45 to 60 minutes, 5.7% 60 minutes or more (2000)

Mason County

Located in central Illinois; bounded on the west by the Illinois River, and on the south by the Sangamon River and Salt Creek. Covers a land area of 538.90 square miles, a water area of 24.40 square miles, and is located in the Central Time Zone. The county government was organized in 1841. County seat is Havana.

Weather Station: Havana 4 NNE — Elevation: 459 feet

	Jan	Feb	Mar	Apr	May	Jun	Jul	Aug	Sep	Oct	Nov	Dec
High	32	38	51	64	74	84	88	86	79	67	51	38
Low	15	20	30	41	51	61	65	62	54	42	32	21
Precip	1.8	1.9	3.0	3.5	4.5	3.7	3.8	3.6	3.5	2.9	3.2	2.6
Snow	9.9	7.7	3.8	1.1	0.0	0.0	0.0	0.0	0.0	tr	1.5	6.1

High and Low temperatures in degrees Fahrenheit; Precipitation and Snow in inches

Weather Station: Mason City 1 W — Elevation: 583 feet

	Jan	Feb	Mar	Apr	May	Jun	Jul	Aug	Sep	Oct	Nov	Dec
High	33	39	51	65	75	84	87	85	79	67	51	38
Low	16	21	31	42	52	61	65	63	55	44	33	22
Precip	1.5	1.5	2.8	3.5	4.3	3.6	3.9	3.5	3.2	2.8	2.9	2.4
Snow	6.0	4.9	2.4	0.6	tr	0.0	0.0	0.0	0.0	tr	1.3	4.6

High and Low temperatures in degrees Fahrenheit; Precipitation and Snow in inches

Population: 16,038 (2000); Race: 98.3% White, 0.3% Black, 0.2% Asian, 0.4% American Indian and Alaska Native, 0.3% Hispanic of any race, 0.6% two or more races (2000); Density: 29.8 persons per square mile (2000); Age: 24.3% under 18, 17.2% over 64 (2000).

Religion: Five largest groups: 13.8% Lutheran Church—Missouri Synod, 9.1% The United Methodist Church, 6.6% Catholic Church, 4.7% American Baptist Churches in the USA, 4.1% Christian Churches and Churches of Christ (2000).

Economy: Unemployment rate: 7.4% (11/2002); Total civilian labor force: 8,494 (11/2002); Leading industries: 19.5% retail trade; 16.2% health care and social assistance; 15.3% manufacturing (2000); Companies that employ more than 1,000 persons: 0 (2000); Companies that employ more than 100 persons: 3 (2000); Farms: 486 totaling 291,579 acres (1997); Minority business ownership rate: 0.0% (1997); Women business ownership rate: 28.1% (1997); Retail sales per capita: $5,838 (1997). Single-family building permits issued: 28 (2001) / 15 (2000); Multi-family building permits issued: 2 (2001) / 0 (2000).

Income: Per capita income: $17,357 (2000); Median household income: $35,985 (2000); Poverty rate: 9.7% (2000); Bankruptcy rate: 6.69% (2001).

Taxes: Total county taxes per capita: $99 (1997); County property taxes per capita: $97 (1997).

Education: High school graduation rate: 79.9% (2000); College graduation rate: 11.2% (2000).

Housing: Homeownership rate: 76.7% (2000); Median home value: $61,200 (2000); Median rent: $289 per month (2000); Median age of housing: 46 years (2000).

Health: Birth rate: 119.1 per 10,000 population (1998); Age adjusted death rate: 88.3 per 10,000 population (1999); Age adjusted cancer mortality rate: 232.6 deaths per 100,000 population (1999). Number of physicians: 6.9 per 10,000 population (1999); Number of hospital beds: 15.6 per 10,000 population (1999).

Elections: 2000 Presidential election results: 47.1% Gore, 50.4% Bush, 1.7% Nader, 0.5% Buchanan

National and State Parks: Chautauqua National Wildlife Refuge; Chautauqua National Migratory Waterfowl Refuge; Mason County State Wildlife Refuge and Recreation; Sand Ridge State Forest

Additional Information Contacts

Mason County Government Offices. 309-543-6661

Havana Chamber of Commerce 309-543-3528

Mason County Communities

BATH (village). Covers a land area of 0.365 square miles and a water area of <.001 square miles. Located at 40.19° N. Lat.; 90.14° W. Long. Elevation is 462 feet.
History: Bath was surveyed in 1836 by Abraham Lincoln, who was then the Deputy Surveyor of Sangamon County. Bath served as the county seat from 1843 to 1851.
Population: 310 (2000); Race: 97.8% White, 0.6% Black, 0.6% Asian, 0.6% American Indian and Alaska Native, 0.0% Hispanic of any race, 0.3% two or more races (2000); Density: 848.9 persons per square mile (2000); Age: 36.3% under 18, 9.8% over 64 (2000); Marriage status: 22.7% never married, 63.2% now married, 5.9% widowed, 8.2% divorced (2000); Foreign born: 0.6% (2000); Ancestry (includes multiple ancestries): 18.3% United States or American, 17.4% German, 11.4% Irish, 6.9% English, 5.0% Other groups (2000).
Economy: Single-family building permits issued: 1 (2001) / 0 (2000); Multi-family building permits issued: 0 (2001) / 0 (2000); Employment by occupation: 6.0% management, 3.4% professional, 16.4% services, 23.3% sales, 4.3% farming, 19.8% construction, 26.7% production (2000).
Income: Per capita income: $10,262 (2000); Median household income: $30,208 (2000); Poverty rate: 24.7% (2000).
Taxes: Total city taxes per capita: $22 (1997); City property taxes per capita: $10 (1997).
Education: High school graduation rate: 81.9% (2000); College graduation rate: 2.2% (2000).
Housing: Homeownership rate: 82.0% (2000); Median home value: $41,600 (2000); Median rent: $288 per month (2000); Median age of housing: 37 years (2000).
Transportation: Commute to work: 94.0% car, 0.0% public transportation, 1.7% walk, 2.6% work from home (2000); Travel time to work: 26.5% less than 15 minutes, 31.0% 15 to 30 minutes, 21.2% 30 to 45 minutes, 7.1% 45 to 60 minutes, 14.2% 60 minutes or more (2000)

EASTON (village). Covers a land area of 0.233 square miles and a water area of 0 square miles. Located at 40.23° N. Lat.; 89.84° W. Long. Elevation is 510 feet.
Population: 373 (2000); Race: 100.0% White, 0.0% Black, 0.0% Asian, 0.0% American Indian and Alaska Native, 0.0% Hispanic of any race, 0.0% two or more races (2000); Density: 1,599.5 persons per square mile (2000); Age: 26.8% under 18, 15.9% over 64 (2000); Marriage status: 21.7% never married, 68.0% now married, 7.0% widowed, 3.3% divorced (2000); Foreign born: 0.0% (2000); Ancestry (includes multiple ancestries): 36.2% German, 20.6% English, 13.5% Irish, 4.7% Other groups, 3.1% French (except Basque) (2000).
Economy: In agricultural area: corn, wheat, soybeans. Manufacturing: feed, fertilizer. Single-family building permits issued: 1 (2001) / 0 (2000); Multi-family building permits issued: 0 (2001) / 0 (2000); Employment by occupation: 8.2% management, 9.9% professional, 25.7% services, 14.0% sales, 9.9% farming, 13.5% construction, 18.7% production (2000).
Income: Per capita income: $14,745 (2000); Median household income: $32,045 (2000); Poverty rate: 1.0% (2000).
Taxes: Total city taxes per capita: $57 (1997); City property taxes per capita: $32 (1997).
Education: High school graduation rate: 87.0% (2000); College graduation rate: 16.7% (2000).
Housing: Homeownership rate: 82.2% (2000); Median home value: $50,000 (2000); Median rent: $320 per month (2000); Median age of housing: 54 years (2000).
Transportation: Commute to work: 95.3% car, 0.0% public transportation, 3.0% walk, 0.0% work from home (2000); Travel time to work: 29.0% less than 15 minutes, 26.6% 15 to 30 minutes, 10.7% 30 to 45 minutes, 20.7% 45 to 60 minutes, 13.0% 60 minutes or more (2000)

FOREST CITY (village). Covers a land area of 0.524 square miles and a water area of 0 square miles. Located at 40.37° N. Lat.; 89.82° W. Long. Elevation is 496 feet.
Population: 287 (2000); Race: 99.4% White, 0.0% Black, 0.0% Asian, 0.0% American Indian and Alaska Native, 0.0% Hispanic of any race, 0.6% two or more races (2000); Density: 547.8 persons per square mile (2000); Age: 28.3% under 18, 13.3% over 64 (2000); Marriage status: 17.3% never married, 67.1% now married, 2.4% widowed, 13.3% divorced (2000); Foreign born: 0.0% (2000); Ancestry (includes multiple ancestries): 17.7% United States or American, 15.3% German, 11.8% Other groups, 9.7% Irish, 4.7% Scottish (2000).
Economy: In agricultural area: corn, wheat, soybeans. Employment by occupation: 10.3% management, 0.0% professional, 19.0% services, 24.6% sales, 4.8% farming, 11.9% construction, 29.4% production (2000).
Income: Per capita income: $13,855 (2000); Median household income: $36,250 (2000); Poverty rate: 8.0% (2000).
Taxes: Total city taxes per capita: $39 (1997); City property taxes per capita: $27 (1997).
Education: High school graduation rate: 72.5% (2000); College graduation rate: 4.1% (2000).
Housing: Homeownership rate: 83.5% (2000); Median home value: $40,800 (2000); Median rent: $363 per month (2000); Median age of housing: 54 years (2000).
Transportation: Commute to work: 96.8% car, 0.0% public transportation, 1.6% walk, 1.6% work from home (2000); Travel time to work: 16.9% less than 15 minutes, 17.7% 15 to 30 minutes, 37.1% 30 to 45 minutes, 16.1% 45 to 60 minutes, 12.1% 60 minutes or more (2000)

HAVANA (city). Covers a land area of 2.628 square miles and a water area of 0.151 square miles. Located at 40.29° N. Lat.; 90.06° W. Long. Elevation is 470 feet.
History: Havana grew up around the ferry across the Spoon River, established in 1824 by Major Ossian M. Ross. Havana shared in the prosperity brought by steamboat travel on the Illinois River, shipping grain and produce to market. Commercial fishing was important here in the early 1900's.
Population: 3,577 (2000); Race: 97.5% White, 1.2% Black, 0.5% Asian, 0.3% American Indian and Alaska Native, 0.2% Hispanic of any race, 0.4% two or more races (2000); Density: 1,361.0 persons per square mile (2000); Age: 23.6% under 18, 21.9% over 64 (2000); Marriage status: 21.4% never married, 57.2% now married, 11.2% widowed, 10.3% divorced (2000); Foreign born: 0.9% (2000); Ancestry (includes multiple ancestries): 23.1% German, 14.0% English, 11.8% United States or American, 10.1% Irish, 6.3% French (except Basque) (2000).
Economy: Single-family building permits issued: 3 (2001) / 4 (2000); Multi-family building permits issued: 0 (2001) / 0 (2000); Employment by occupation: 9.7% management, 10.6% professional, 25.1% services, 30.6% sales, 2.6% farming, 7.6% construction, 13.7% production (2000).
Income: Per capita income: $16,781 (2000); Median household income: $30,316 (2000); Poverty rate: 12.0% (2000).
Taxes: Total city taxes per capita: $364 (1997); City property taxes per capita: $146 (1997).
Education: High school graduation rate: 77.6% (2000); College graduation rate: 11.9% (2000).

School District(s)

Havana Community Unit School District 126 (PK-12)
2000 Enrollment: 1,252 309-543-3384

Housing: Homeownership rate: 67.8% (2000); Median home value: $52,900 (2000); Median rent: $291 per month (2000); Median age of housing: 57 years (2000).
Hospitals: Mason District Hospital (48 beds)
Newspapers: The Market Place (1 x week); Mason County Democrat (1 x week)
Transportation: Commute to work: 90.7% car, 0.7% public transportation, 3.4% walk, 3.1% work from home (2000); Travel time to work: 56.7% less than 15 minutes, 8.3% 15 to 30 minutes, 13.0% 30 to 45 minutes, 8.9% 45 to 60 minutes, 13.1% 60 minutes or more (2000)

Additional Information Contacts

Havana Chamber of Commerce 309-543-3528

KILBOURNE (village). Covers a land area of 1.062 square miles and a water area of 0 square miles. Located at 40.15° N. Lat.; 90.01° W. Long. Elevation is 500 feet.
Population: 375 (2000); Race: 95.6% White, 0.0% Black, 0.0% Asian, 4.4% American Indian and Alaska Native, 0.0% Hispanic of any race, 0.0% two or more races (2000); Density: 353.2 persons per square mile (2000); Age: 37.9% under 18, 8.7% over 64 (2000); Marriage status: 15.8% never married, 63.8% now married, 6.8% widowed, 13.6% divorced (2000); Foreign born: 0.0% (2000); Ancestry (includes multiple ancestries): 18.2% English, 16.9% German, 8.5% Other groups, 6.4% Irish, 4.4% United States or American (2000).
Economy: In agricultural area. Employment by occupation: 4.9% management, 7.3% professional, 28.5% services, 27.6% sales, 4.9% farming, 12.2% construction, 14.6% production (2000).

Income: Per capita income: $10,710 (2000); Median household income: $26,000 (2000); Poverty rate: 22.1% (2000).
Education: High school graduation rate: 76.6% (2000); College graduation rate: 3.6% (2000).
Housing: Homeownership rate: 79.5% (2000); Median home value: $37,800 (2000); Median rent: $267 per month (2000); Median age of housing: 47 years (2000).
Transportation: Commute to work: 93.5% car, 0.0% public transportation, 0.0% walk, 6.5% work from home (2000); Travel time to work: 29.6% less than 15 minutes, 32.2% 15 to 30 minutes, 7.0% 30 to 45 minutes, 19.1% 45 to 60 minutes, 12.2% 60 minutes or more (2000)

MANITO (village). Covers a land area of 1.539 square miles and a water area of 0 square miles. Located at 40.42° N. Lat.; 89.78° W. Long. Elevation is 500 feet.
Population: 1,733 (2000); Race: 99.6% White, 0.0% Black, 0.0% Asian, 0.0% American Indian and Alaska Native, 0.3% Hispanic of any race, 0.4% two or more races (2000); Density: 1,126.0 persons per square mile (2000); Age: 25.1% under 18, 13.1% over 64 (2000); Marriage status: 19.2% never married, 65.3% now married, 5.8% widowed, 9.6% divorced (2000); Foreign born: 0.0% (2000); Ancestry (includes multiple ancestries): 30.0% German, 14.6% Irish, 10.5% English, 9.8% Other groups, 8.4% United States or American (2000).
Economy: Corn, wheat, watermelons, vegetables. Single-family building permits issued: 2 (2001) / 0 (2000); Multi-family building permits issued: 0 (2001) / 0 (2000); Employment by occupation: 5.2% management, 16.1% professional, 13.2% services, 23.3% sales, 2.3% farming, 14.6% construction, 25.4% production (2000).
Income: Per capita income: $18,345 (2000); Median household income: $41,767 (2000); Poverty rate: 8.2% (2000).
Taxes: Total city taxes per capita: $55 (1997); City property taxes per capita: $51 (1997).
Education: High school graduation rate: 82.1% (2000); College graduation rate: 10.4% (2000).

School District(s)

Midwest Central CUSD 191 (PK-12)
2000 Enrollment: 1,269 309-968-6868
Spring Lake C C School District 606 (KG-06)
2000 Enrollment: 63 309-545-2241

Housing: Homeownership rate: 75.3% (2000); Median home value: $74,000 (2000); Median rent: $282 per month (2000); Median age of housing: 37 years (2000).
Newspapers: Manito Review (1 x week)
Transportation: Commute to work: 96.8% car, 0.4% public transportation, 1.1% walk, 1.6% work from home (2000); Travel time to work: 28.4% less than 15 minutes, 22.6% 15 to 30 minutes, 24.8% 30 to 45 minutes, 15.9% 45 to 60 minutes, 8.4% 60 minutes or more (2000)

MASON CITY (city). Covers a land area of 0.984 square miles and a water area of 0 square miles. Located at 40.20° N. Lat.; 89.69° W. Long. Elevation is 575 feet.
History: Incorporated 1869.
Population: 2,558 (2000); Race: 99.4% White, 0.3% Black, 0.0% Asian, 0.0% American Indian and Alaska Native, 0.0% Hispanic of any race, 0.3% two or more races (2000); Density: 2,599.1 persons per square mile (2000); Age: 24.7% under 18, 22.6% over 64 (2000); Marriage status: 22.3% never married, 56.8% now married, 12.6% widowed, 8.3% divorced (2000); Foreign born: 0.5% (2000); Ancestry (includes multiple ancestries): 30.8% German, 13.5% United States or American, 12.4% English, 11.1% Irish, 9.1% Other groups (2000).
Economy: In clay and agricultural area: corn, wheat, soybeans. Manufacturing: edible oils. Single-family building permits issued: 3 (2001) / 1 (2000); Multi-family building permits issued: 2 (2001) / 0 (2000); Employment by occupation: 8.8% management, 15.1% professional, 15.8% services, 29.2% sales, 0.6% farming, 8.9% construction, 21.6% production (2000).
Income: Per capita income: $18,411 (2000); Median household income: $35,615 (2000); Poverty rate: 9.3% (2000).
Taxes: Total city taxes per capita: $191 (1997); City property taxes per capita: $77 (1997).
Education: High school graduation rate: 80.6% (2000); College graduation rate: 11.2% (2000).

School District(s)

Illini Central C U School District 189 (PK-12)
2000 Enrollment: 1,007 217-482-5180

Housing: Homeownership rate: 76.8% (2000); Median home value: $60,000 (2000); Median rent: $259 per month (2000); Median age of housing: 47 years (2000).
Newspapers: Wham (1 x week); Mason City Banner Times (1 x week)
Transportation: Commute to work: 96.5% car, 0.0% public transportation, 1.1% walk, 2.4% work from home (2000); Travel time to work: 32.8% less than 15 minutes, 18.2% 15 to 30 minutes, 21.2% 30 to 45 minutes, 18.9% 45 to 60 minutes, 9.0% 60 minutes or more (2000)

SAN JOSE (village). Covers a land area of 0.511 square miles and a water area of 0 square miles. Located at 40.30° N. Lat.; 89.60° W. Long.
Population: 696 (2000); Race: 99.2% White, 0.0% Black, 0.0% Asian, 0.8% American Indian and Alaska Native, 1.3% Hispanic of any race, 0.0% two or more races (2000); Density: 1,361.3 persons per square mile (2000); Age: 22.5% under 18, 15.8% over 64 (2000); Marriage status: 22.5% never married, 63.7% now married, 4.3% widowed, 9.5% divorced (2000); Foreign born: 0.3% (2000); Ancestry (includes multiple ancestries): 36.3% German, 10.9% Other groups, 10.3% English, 9.5% United States or American, 7.3% Irish (2000).
Economy: Single-family building permits issued: 0 (2001) / 0 (2000); Multi-family building permits issued: 0 (2001) / 0 (2000); Employment by occupation: 10.2% management, 11.1% professional, 12.7% services, 29.8% sales, 1.3% farming, 11.1% construction, 23.8% production (2000).
Income: Per capita income: $18,110 (2000); Median household income: $39,028 (2000); Poverty rate: 2.9% (2000).
Education: High school graduation rate: 87.7% (2000); College graduation rate: 11.0% (2000).
Housing: Homeownership rate: 74.2% (2000); Median home value: $55,800 (2000); Median rent: $305 per month (2000); Median age of housing: 52 years (2000).
Transportation: Commute to work: 94.0% car, 0.0% public transportation, 0.9% walk, 3.4% work from home (2000); Travel time to work: 19.2% less than 15 minutes, 24.0% 15 to 30 minutes, 26.0% 30 to 45 minutes, 18.2% 45 to 60 minutes, 12.7% 60 minutes or more (2000)

TOPEKA (village). Covers a land area of 0.139 square miles and a water area of 0 square miles. Located at 40.33° N. Lat.; 89.93° W. Long. Elevation is 485 feet.
Population: 90 (2000); Race: 100.0% White, 0.0% Black, 0.0% Asian, 0.0% American Indian and Alaska Native, 0.0% Hispanic of any race, 0.0% two or more races (2000); Density: 648.1 persons per square mile (2000); Age: 38.4% under 18, 5.5% over 64 (2000); Marriage status: 8.2% never married, 73.5% now married, 0.0% widowed, 18.4% divorced (2000); Foreign born: 0.0% (2000); Ancestry (includes multiple ancestries): 42.5% German, 26.0% Irish, 13.7% Portuguese, 9.6% Other groups, 6.8% Dutch (2000).
Economy: In agricultural area: corn, wheat, soybeans. Popcorn processing. Employment by occupation: 0.0% management, 48.6% professional, 8.1% services, 10.8% sales, 8.1% farming, 0.0% construction, 24.3% production (2000).
Income: Per capita income: $39,651 (2000); Median household income: $41,750 (2000); Poverty rate: 0.0% (2000).
Education: High school graduation rate: 88.9% (2000); College graduation rate: 0.0% (2000).
Housing: Homeownership rate: 84.4% (2000); Median home value: $42,500 (2000); Median age of housing: 29 years (2000).
Transportation: Commute to work: 100.0% car, 0.0% public transportation, 0.0% walk, 0.0% work from home (2000); Travel time to work: 35.1% less than 15 minutes, 35.1% 15 to 30 minutes, 29.7% 30 to 45 minutes, 0.0% 45 to 60 minutes, 0.0% 60 minutes or more (2000)

Massac County

Located in southern Illinois; bounded on the south and east by the Ohio River and the Kentucky border, and on the northwest by the Cache River; includes part of Shawnee National Forest. Covers a land area of 239.10 square miles, a water area of 3.10 square miles, and is located in the Central Time Zone. The county government was organized in 1843. County seat is Metropolis.

Weather Station: Brookport Dam 52 Elevation: 328 feet

	Jan	Feb	Mar	Apr	May	Jun	Jul	Aug	Sep	Oct	Nov	Dec
High	42	48	58	69	78	86	90	88	82	71	58	47
Low	25	29	37	47	56	64	68	66	59	47	38	29
Precip	3.4	3.8	4.5	4.9	4.7	4.1	4.2	3.0	3.2	3.4	4.4	4.5
Snow	3.3	3.0	1.3	tr	0.0	0.0	0.0	0.0	0.0	0.0	tr	1.0

High and Low temperatures in degrees Fahrenheit; Precipitation and Snow in inches

Population: 15,161 (2000); Race: 92.9% White, 5.1% Black, 0.3% Asian, 0.1% American Indian and Alaska Native, 1.1% Hispanic of any race, 1.3% two or more races (2000); Density: 63.4 persons per square mile (2000); Age: 22.9% under 18, 17.8% over 64 (2000).
Religion: Five largest groups: 37.9% Southern Baptist Convention, 5.8% The United Methodist Church, 5.1% Evangelical Lutheran Church in America, 3.5% Churches of Christ, 2.5% United Church of Christ (2000).
Economy: Unemployment rate: 5.1% (11/2002); Total civilian labor force: 7,789 (11/2002); Leading industries: 27.5% accommodation & food services; 15.9% transportation & warehousing; 15.3% health care and social assistance (2000); Companies that employ more than 1,000 persons: 0 (2000); Companies that employ more than 100 persons: 8 (2000); Farms: 400 totaling 103,769 acres (1997); Minority business ownership rate: 0.0% (1997); Women business ownership rate: 29.2% (1997); Retail sales per capita: $5,143 (1997). Single-family building permits issued: 5 (2001) / 5 (2000); Multi-family building permits issued: 0 (2001) / 0 (2000).
Income: Per capita income: $16,334 (2000); Median household income: $31,498 (2000); Poverty rate: 13.5% (2000); Bankruptcy rate: 7.21% (2001).
Taxes: Total county taxes per capita: $110 (1997); County property taxes per capita: $110 (1997).
Education: High school graduation rate: 76.5% (2000); College graduation rate: 10.7% (2000).
Housing: Homeownership rate: 78.6% (2000); Median home value: $63,300 (2000); Median rent: $263 per month (2000); Median age of housing: 35 years (2000).
Health: Birth rate: 133.9 per 10,000 population (1998); Age adjusted death rate: 114.0 per 10,000 population (1999); Age adjusted cancer mortality rate: 203.0 deaths per 100,000 population (1999). Number of physicians: 5.9 per 10,000 population (1999); Number of hospital beds: 25.1 per 10,000 population (1999).
Elections: 2000 Presidential election results: 43.2% Gore, 54.5% Bush, 1.2% Nader, 0.8% Buchanan
National and State Parks: Fort Massac State Park; Mermet Lake State Conservation Area

Additional Information Contacts
Massac County Government Offices 618-524-5213
Metropolis Area Chamber of Commerce 618-524-2714

Massac County Communities

BROOKPORT (city). Covers a land area of 0.797 square miles and a water area of 0 square miles. Located at 37.12° N. Lat.; 88.62° W. Long. Elevation is 340 feet.
History: Brookport developed as an agricultural trading center on the Ohio River. The flooding of the river in 1937 damaged much of Brookport.
Population: 1,054 (2000); Race: 91.8% White, 7.7% Black, 0.0% Asian, 0.0% American Indian and Alaska Native, 3.5% Hispanic of any race, 0.5% two or more races (2000); Density: 1,321.8 persons per square mile (2000); Age: 29.6% under 18, 13.5% over 64 (2000); Marriage status: 21.7% never married, 54.2% now married, 7.8% widowed, 16.4% divorced (2000); Foreign born: 0.3% (2000); Ancestry (includes multiple ancestries): 25.7% Other groups, 15.3% German, 12.9% United States or American, 11.8% Irish, 7.4% English (2000).
Economy: Employment by occupation: 6.9% management, 7.6% professional, 27.5% services, 25.9% sales, 0.7% farming, 9.2% construction, 22.3% production (2000).
Income: Per capita income: $11,751 (2000); Median household income: $24,438 (2000); Poverty rate: 19.8% (2000).
Taxes: Total city taxes per capita: $30 (1997); City property taxes per capita: $20 (1997).
Education: High school graduation rate: 67.2% (2000); College graduation rate: 3.8% (2000).
Housing: Homeownership rate: 74.5% (2000); Median home value: $41,600 (2000); Median rent: $216 per month (2000); Median age of housing: 32 years (2000).
Transportation: Commute to work: 98.6% car, 0.0% public transportation, 1.2% walk, 0.0% work from home (2000); Travel time to work: 28.8% less than 15 minutes, 53.1% 15 to 30 minutes, 7.9% 30 to 45 minutes, 5.6% 45 to 60 minutes, 4.6% 60 minutes or more (2000)

JOPPA (village). Covers a land area of 0.488 square miles and a water area of 0.008 square miles. Located at 37.20° N. Lat.; 88.84° W. Long. Elevation is 350 feet.
Population: 409 (2000); Race: 89.8% White, 7.8% Black, 0.0% Asian, 0.0% American Indian and Alaska Native, 2.3% Hispanic of any race, 2.3% two or more races (2000); Density: 838.2 persons per square mile (2000); Age: 28.5% under 18, 17.0% over 64 (2000); Marriage status: 20.1% never married, 52.0% now married, 10.9% widowed, 17.0% divorced (2000); Foreign born: 0.0% (2000); Ancestry (includes multiple ancestries): 17.2% Other groups, 11.0% United States or American, 8.1% Irish, 7.6% German, 2.6% English (2000).
Economy: Steam power plant here for Atomic Energy Commission plant near Paducah, Kentucky. Employment by occupation: 4.2% management, 10.1% professional, 28.6% services, 16.0% sales, 0.0% farming, 16.0% construction, 25.2% production (2000).
Income: Per capita income: $8,890 (2000); Median household income: $17,813 (2000); Poverty rate: 44.6% (2000).
Taxes: Total city taxes per capita: $31 (1997); City property taxes per capita: $31 (1997).
Education: High school graduation rate: 60.7% (2000); College graduation rate: 6.7% (2000).

School District(s)
Joppa-Maple Grove Unit District 38 (PK-12)
2000 Enrollment: 267 618-543-9023
Housing: Homeownership rate: 68.6% (2000); Median home value: $29,400 (2000); Median rent: $169 per month (2000); Median age of housing: 47 years (2000).
Transportation: Commute to work: 92.1% car, 3.5% public transportation, 0.0% walk, 3.5% work from home (2000); Travel time to work: 23.6% less than 15 minutes, 41.8% 15 to 30 minutes, 21.8% 30 to 45 minutes, 3.6% 45 to 60 minutes, 9.1% 60 minutes or more (2000)

METROPOLIS (city). Covers a land area of 5.005 square miles and a water area of 0.064 square miles. Located at 37.15° N. Lat.; 88.72° W. Long. Elevation is 350 feet.
History: The first settlement in Metropolis was in 1796. This was platted in 1836 as the City of Massac. Metropolis City was platted in 1839 by William A. McBane and James H.G. Wilcox, who dreamed that their community would be a metropolis. Metropolis City was incorporated in 1845, and in 1892 the two communities united.
Population: 6,482 (2000); Race: 91.9% White, 6.8% Black, 0.0% Asian, 0.0% American Indian and Alaska Native, 0.5% Hispanic of any race, 0.9% two or more races (2000); Density: 1,295.1 persons per square mile (2000); Age: 18.0% under 18, 25.7% over 64 (2000); Marriage status: 17.5% never married, 54.9% now married, 13.0% widowed, 14.6% divorced (2000); Foreign born: 0.1% (2000); Ancestry (includes multiple ancestries): 18.3% Other groups, 18.1% German, 13.4% English, 10.9% Irish, 10.2% United States or American (2000).
Economy: Single-family building permits issued: 5 (2001) / 5 (2000); Multi-family building permits issued: 0 (2001) / 0 (2000); Employment by occupation: 7.5% management, 14.2% professional, 23.9% services, 26.3% sales, 0.0% farming, 9.5% construction, 18.5% production (2000).
Income: Per capita income: $15,967 (2000); Median household income: $25,371 (2000); Poverty rate: 17.2% (2000).
Taxes: Total city taxes per capita: $138 (1997); City property taxes per capita: $85 (1997).
Education: High school graduation rate: 73.6% (2000); College graduation rate: 9.8% (2000).

School District(s)
Massac Unit District #1 (PK-12)
2000 Enrollment: 2,320 618-524-9376
Housing: Homeownership rate: 70.2% (2000); Median home value: $54,800 (2000); Median rent: $279 per month (2000); Median age of housing: 45 years (2000).
Hospitals: Massac Memorial Hospital (57 beds)
Newspapers: The Metropolis Planet (1 x week); The Southern Scene (1 x week)
Transportation: Commute to work: 93.9% car, 0.3% public transportation, 3.4% walk, 1.3% work from home (2000); Travel time to work: 53.8% less than 15 minutes, 26.7% 15 to 30 minutes, 12.4% 30 to 45 minutes, 2.6% 45 to 60 minutes, 4.5% 60 minutes or more (2000)

Additional Information Contacts
Metropolis Area Chamber of Commerce 618-524-2714

McDonough County

Located in western Illinois; drained by the La Moine River. Covers a land area of 589.30 square miles, a water area of 0.80 square miles, and is located in the Central Time Zone. The county government was organized in 1826. County seat is Macomb.

Population: 32,913 (2000); Race: 93.5% White, 3.2% Black, 1.9% Asian, 0.1% American Indian and Alaska Native, 1.6% Hispanic of any race, 0.9% two or more races (2000); Density: 55.9 persons per square mile (2000); Age: 17.7% under 18, 14.1% over 64 (2000).
Religion: Five largest groups: 7.7% The United Methodist Church, 6.7% Catholic Church, 3.8% Presbyterian Church (U.S.A.), 3.6% Christian Churches and Churches of Christ, 2.8% Assemblies of God (2000).
Economy: Unemployment rate: 2.7% (11/2002); Total civilian labor force: 18,729 (11/2002); Leading industries: 20.1% manufacturing; 17.5% retail trade; 15.6% accommodation & food services (2000); Companies that employ more than 1,000 persons: 0 (2000); Companies that employ more than 100 persons: 15 (2000); Farms: 824 totaling 340,071 acres (1997); Minority business ownership rate: 0.0% (1997); Women business ownership rate: 19.0% (1997); Retail sales per capita: $6,966 (1997). Single-family building permits issued: 12 (2001) / 19 (2000); Multi-family building permits issued: 92 (2001) / 133 (2000).
Income: Per capita income: $15,890 (2000); Median household income: $32,141 (2000); Poverty rate: 19.8% (2000); Bankruptcy rate: 4.13% (2001).
Taxes: Total county taxes per capita: $106 (2000); County property taxes per capita: $104 (2000).
Education: High school graduation rate: 86.9% (2000); College graduation rate: 26.9% (2000).
Housing: Homeownership rate: 63.1% (2000); Median home value: $61,200 (2000); Median rent: $321 per month (2000); Median age of housing: 40 years (2000).
Health: Birth rate: 86.9 per 10,000 population (1998); Age adjusted death rate: 68.1 per 10,000 population (1999); Age adjusted cancer mortality rate: 209.7 deaths per 100,000 population (1999). Number of physicians: 14.9 per 10,000 population (1999); Number of hospital beds: 34.3 per 10,000 population (1999).
Elections: 2000 Presidential election results: 46.7% Gore, 49.7% Bush, 2.8% Nader, 0.5% Buchanan
National and State Parks: Argyle Lake State Park
Additional Information Contacts
McDonough County Government Offices 309-837-2308
Lamoine Valley Board of Realtors 309-837-2546
Macomb Area Convention & Visitors Bureau 309-833-1315
Macomb Chamber of Commerce 309-837-4855

McDonough County Communities

ADAIR (unincorporated postal area, zip code 61411). Covers a land area of 38.024 square miles and a water area of 0.016 square miles. Located at 40.40° N. Lat.; 90.50° W. Long. Elevation is 652 feet.
Population: 419 (2000); Race: 100.0% White, 0.0% Black, 0.0% Asian, 0.0% American Indian and Alaska Native, 0.0% Hispanic of any race, 0.0% two or more races (2000); Density: 11.0 persons per square mile (2000); Age: 14.4% under 18, 22.2% over 64 (2000); Marriage status: 22.0% never married, 58.8% now married, 10.4% widowed, 8.8% divorced (2000); Foreign born: 0.0% (2000); Ancestry (includes multiple ancestries): 21.0% English, 17.4% United States or American, 15.4% German, 5.6% Other groups, 4.5% Swedish (2000).
Economy: Employment by occupation: 19.4% management, 21.0% professional, 9.7% services, 20.6% sales, 5.6% farming, 5.6% construction, 18.1% production (2000).
Income: Per capita income: $20,915 (2000); Median household income: $40,893 (2000); Poverty rate: 3.8% (2000).
Education: High school graduation rate: 84.5% (2000); College graduation rate: 13.8% (2000).
Housing: Homeownership rate: 72.2% (2000); Median home value: $49,700 (2000); Median rent: $218 per month (2000); Median age of housing: 57 years (2000).
Transportation: Commute to work: 91.1% car, 0.0% public transportation, 0.0% walk, 0.8% work from home (2000); Travel time to work: 26.8% less than 15 minutes, 53.3% 15 to 30 minutes, 12.2% 30 to 45 minutes, 7.7% 45 to 60 minutes, 0.0% 60 minutes or more (2000)

BARDOLPH (village). Covers a land area of 0.595 square miles and a water area of 0 square miles. Located at 40.49° N. Lat.; 90.56° W. Long. Elevation is 675 feet.
Population: 253 (2000); Race: 97.3% White, 0.0% Black, 0.0% Asian, 0.0% American Indian and Alaska Native, 0.0% Hispanic of any race, 2.7% two or more races (2000); Density: 425.4 persons per square mile (2000); Age: 35.0% under 18, 11.1% over 64 (2000); Marriage status: 24.3% never married, 60.5% now married, 4.6% widowed, 10.5% divorced (2000); Foreign born: 0.0% (2000); Ancestry (includes multiple ancestries): 21.2% United States or American, 11.9% German, 10.2% Other groups, 8.4% Irish, 6.6% English (2000).
Economy: In agricultural area: corn, sorghum; cattle, hogs. Employment by occupation: 4.2% management, 16.8% professional, 21.1% services, 21.1% sales, 0.0% farming, 12.6% construction, 24.2% production (2000).
Income: Per capita income: $11,361 (2000); Median household income: $25,833 (2000); Poverty rate: 28.8% (2000).
Taxes: Total city taxes per capita: $28 (1997); City property taxes per capita: $25 (1997).
Education: High school graduation rate: 73.4% (2000); College graduation rate: 13.7% (2000).
Housing: Homeownership rate: 63.2% (2000); Median home value: $36,300 (2000); Median rent: $316 per month (2000); Median age of housing: 35 years (2000).
Transportation: Commute to work: 95.7% car, 2.2% public transportation, 0.0% walk, 0.0% work from home (2000); Travel time to work: 33.3% less than 15 minutes, 41.9% 15 to 30 minutes, 12.9% 30 to 45 minutes, 4.3% 45 to 60 minutes, 7.5% 60 minutes or more (2000)

BLANDINSVILLE (village). Covers a land area of 0.885 square miles and a water area of 0 square miles. Located at 40.55° N. Lat.; 90.86° W. Long. Elevation is 729 feet.
Population: 777 (2000); Race: 100.0% White, 0.0% Black, 0.0% Asian, 0.0% American Indian and Alaska Native, 0.9% Hispanic of any race, 0.0% two or more races (2000); Density: 878.2 persons per square mile (2000); Age: 20.7% under 18, 17.6% over 64 (2000); Marriage status: 21.9% never married, 57.5% now married, 12.3% widowed, 8.4% divorced (2000); Foreign born: 0.3% (2000); Ancestry (includes multiple ancestries): 21.3% German, 14.0% English, 12.8% United States or American, 8.0% Other groups, 6.0% Irish (2000).
Economy: Corn, wheat; livestock. Employment by occupation: 12.0% management, 11.5% professional, 15.8% services, 31.2% sales, 1.0% farming, 6.0% construction, 22.5% production (2000).
Income: Per capita income: $15,203 (2000); Median household income: $30,272 (2000); Poverty rate: 8.8% (2000).
Taxes: Total city taxes per capita: $35 (1997); City property taxes per capita: $31 (1997).
Education: High school graduation rate: 85.0% (2000); College graduation rate: 11.4% (2000).
Housing: Homeownership rate: 77.8% (2000); Median home value: $50,100 (2000); Median rent: $264 per month (2000); Median age of housing: 60+ years (2000).
Transportation: Commute to work: 95.4% car, 1.2% public transportation, 2.4% walk, 1.0% work from home (2000); Travel time to work: 24.2% less than 15 minutes, 48.9% 15 to 30 minutes, 13.4% 30 to 45 minutes, 7.3% 45 to 60 minutes, 6.1% 60 minutes or more (2000)

BUSHNELL (city). Covers a land area of 2.047 square miles and a water area of 0.008 square miles. Located at 40.55° N. Lat.; 90.50° W. Long. Elevation is 661 feet.
History: Incorporated 1865.
Population: 3,221 (2000); Race: 100.0% White, 0.0% Black, 0.0% Asian, 0.0% American Indian and Alaska Native, 0.2% Hispanic of any race, 0.0% two or more races (2000); Density: 1,573.9 persons per square mile (2000); Age: 25.1% under 18, 17.6% over 64 (2000); Marriage status: 21.8% never married, 58.5% now married, 9.5% widowed, 10.1% divorced (2000); Foreign born: 0.2% (2000); Ancestry (includes multiple ancestries): 15.7% United States or American, 15.2% German, 13.3% Irish, 10.4% English, 4.7% Other groups (2000).
Economy: Railroad and industrial center in agricultural area; corn, wheat; livestock; stockyards. Manufacturing: food products, handtools. Employment by occupation: 5.1% management, 13.7% professional, 19.5% services, 23.7% sales, 0.4% farming, 13.0% construction, 24.5% production (2000).
Income: Per capita income: $17,263 (2000); Median household income: $30,482 (2000); Poverty rate: 17.0% (2000).
Taxes: Total city taxes per capita: $71 (1997); City property taxes per capita: $64 (1997).
Education: High school graduation rate: 82.7% (2000); College graduation rate: 9.9% (2000).

School District(s)
Bushnell Prairie City Cus D 170 (PK-12)
2000 Enrollment: 871 309-772-9461
Housing: Homeownership rate: 74.8% (2000); Median home value: $42,200 (2000); Median rent: $247 per month (2000); Median age of housing: 48 years (2000).

Newspapers: McDonough Democrat (1 x week)
Transportation: Commute to work: 86.4% car, 0.0% public transportation, 7.9% walk, 3.4% work from home (2000); Travel time to work: 51.4% less than 15 minutes, 30.6% 15 to 30 minutes, 9.8% 30 to 45 minutes, 3.0% 45 to 60 minutes, 5.2% 60 minutes or more (2000)

COLCHESTER (city). Covers a land area of 0.995 square miles and a water area of 0 square miles. Located at 40.42° N. Lat.; 90.79° W. Long. Elevation is 697 feet.
History: Incorporated 1867.
Population: 1,493 (2000); Race: 99.3% White, 0.0% Black, 0.0% Asian, 0.0% American Indian and Alaska Native, 0.3% Hispanic of any race, 0.4% two or more races (2000); Density: 1,500.7 persons per square mile (2000); Age: 23.2% under 18, 16.6% over 64 (2000); Marriage status: 19.0% never married, 58.8% now married, 11.1% widowed, 11.1% divorced (2000); Foreign born: 0.8% (2000); Ancestry (includes multiple ancestries): 21.2% English, 19.6% German, 9.2% Irish, 9.1% United States or American, 6.9% Other groups (2000).
Economy: Clay pits. Agriculture: corn, wheat, hay; livestock. Manufacturing: agricultural implements. Employment by occupation: 5.9% management, 14.8% professional, 23.9% services, 23.0% sales, 1.0% farming, 9.6% construction, 21.8% production (2000).
Income: Per capita income: $15,354 (2000); Median household income: $31,283 (2000); Poverty rate: 7.3% (2000).
Taxes: Total city taxes per capita: $58 (1997); City property taxes per capita: $50 (1997).
Education: High school graduation rate: 84.2% (2000); College graduation rate: 10.3% (2000).

School District(s)

Colchester C U School District 180 (PK-12)
2000 Enrollment: 482 309-776-3180
Housing: Homeownership rate: 72.6% (2000); Median home value: $45,800 (2000); Median rent: $256 per month (2000); Median age of housing: 46 years (2000).
Transportation: Commute to work: 91.4% car, 0.3% public transportation, 3.5% walk, 2.7% work from home (2000); Travel time to work: 33.7% less than 15 minutes, 51.0% 15 to 30 minutes, 6.9% 30 to 45 minutes, 1.9% 45 to 60 minutes, 6.6% 60 minutes or more (2000)

GOOD HOPE (village). Covers a land area of 0.295 square miles and a water area of 0 square miles. Located at 40.55° N. Lat.; 90.67° W. Long. Elevation is 714 feet.
History: When Good Hope was platted in 1866, it was called Sheridan by its founder, J.E. Morris. The town of Milan was laid out next to Sheridan the following year. Since both were served by the post office which was called Good Hope, that is the name that survived.
Population: 415 (2000); Race: 98.8% White, 0.0% Black, 1.2% Asian, 0.0% American Indian and Alaska Native, 0.0% Hispanic of any race, 0.0% two or more races (2000); Density: 1,408.0 persons per square mile (2000); Age: 29.0% under 18, 16.0% over 64 (2000); Marriage status: 20.2% never married, 65.7% now married, 7.1% widowed, 7.1% divorced (2000); Foreign born: 1.2% (2000); Ancestry (includes multiple ancestries): 25.1% German, 23.8% English, 8.1% United States or American, 8.1% Irish, 6.9% Scottish (2000).
Economy: Employment by occupation: 8.9% management, 15.6% professional, 25.0% services, 21.4% sales, 3.1% farming, 16.1% construction, 9.9% production (2000).
Income: Per capita income: $14,555 (2000); Median household income: $37,386 (2000); Poverty rate: 9.8% (2000).
Taxes: Total city taxes per capita: $25 (1997); City property taxes per capita: $21 (1997).
Education: High school graduation rate: 91.1% (2000); College graduation rate: 18.3% (2000).

School District(s)

Northwest C U School Districtict 175 (PK-12)
2000 Enrollment: 398 309-456-3500
Housing: Homeownership rate: 77.0% (2000); Median home value: $60,300 (2000); Median rent: $275 per month (2000); Median age of housing: 52 years (2000).
Transportation: Commute to work: 96.9% car, 0.0% public transportation, 1.6% walk, 1.6% work from home (2000); Travel time to work: 41.8% less than 15 minutes, 46.6% 15 to 30 minutes, 5.3% 30 to 45 minutes, 3.2% 45 to 60 minutes, 3.2% 60 minutes or more (2000)

INDUSTRY (village). Covers a land area of 0.471 square miles and a water area of <.001 square miles. Located at 40.32° N. Lat.; 90.60° W. Long. Elevation is 660 feet.
History: The first settler in Industry was William Carter who came in 1826. The village was organized in the 1840's.
Population: 540 (2000); Race: 99.4% White, 0.0% Black, 0.0% Asian, 0.0% American Indian and Alaska Native, 0.2% Hispanic of any race, 0.6% two or more races (2000); Density: 1,146.2 persons per square mile (2000); Age: 28.5% under 18, 15.8% over 64 (2000); Marriage status: 18.9% never married, 67.4% now married, 7.2% widowed, 6.5% divorced (2000); Foreign born: 0.0% (2000); Ancestry (includes multiple ancestries): 18.6% German, 12.3% English, 11.5% United States or American, 6.7% Dutch, 4.5% Other groups (2000).
Economy: Employment by occupation: 8.8% management, 19.2% professional, 16.0% services, 23.6% sales, 1.2% farming, 13.6% construction, 17.6% production (2000).
Income: Per capita income: $14,411 (2000); Median household income: $35,455 (2000); Poverty rate: 13.8% (2000).
Taxes: Total city taxes per capita: $20 (1997); City property taxes per capita: $18 (1997).
Education: High school graduation rate: 83.8% (2000); College graduation rate: 17.9% (2000).

School District(s)

Industry C U School District 165 (PK-12)
2000 Enrollment: 236 309-254-3560
Housing: Homeownership rate: 84.8% (2000); Median home value: $42,300 (2000); Median rent: $208 per month (2000); Median age of housing: 50 years (2000).
Transportation: Commute to work: 89.8% car, 0.0% public transportation, 6.9% walk, 2.8% work from home (2000); Travel time to work: 33.5% less than 15 minutes, 54.8% 15 to 30 minutes, 6.7% 30 to 45 minutes, 3.8% 45 to 60 minutes, 1.3% 60 minutes or more (2000)

MACOMB (city). Covers a land area of 9.849 square miles and a water area of 0.401 square miles. Located at 40.46° N. Lat.; 90.67° W. Long. Elevation is 705 feet.
History: Macomb was settled in 1830, incorporated as a village in 1841, and as a city in 1856. Many of the early settlers were from New England, and they named the town for Alexander Macomb, Commander-in-Chief of the U.S. Army from 1828 to 1841.
Population: 18,558 (2000); Race: 89.2% White, 5.4% Black, 2.8% Asian, 0.2% American Indian and Alaska Native, 2.5% Hispanic of any race, 1.4% two or more races (2000); Density: 1,884.2 persons per square mile (2000); Age: 12.6% under 18, 12.3% over 64 (2000); Marriage status: 49.3% never married, 39.2% now married, 5.6% widowed, 5.9% divorced (2000); Foreign born: 4.1% (2000); Ancestry (includes multiple ancestries): 26.5% German, 15.7% Irish, 12.8% Other groups, 11.7% English, 6.5% United States or American (2000).
Vital Statistics: Birth rate: 67.9 per 10,000 population (1998)
Economy: Single-family building permits issued: 12 (2001) / 19 (2000); Multi-family building permits issued: 92 (2001) / 133 (2000); Employment by occupation: 7.0% management, 27.4% professional, 23.4% services, 26.4% sales, 1.3% farming, 5.3% construction, 9.2% production (2000).
Income: Per capita income: $13,470 (2000); Median household income: $25,994 (2000); Poverty rate: 29.1% (2000).
Taxes: Total city taxes per capita: $91 (1997); City property taxes per capita: $76 (1997).
Education: High school graduation rate: 88.0% (2000); College graduation rate: 35.3% (2000).

School District(s)

Hancock/Mc Donough Roe (07-12)
2000 Enrollment: 68 309-837-4821
Macomb Community Unit School District 185 (PK-12)
2000 Enrollment: 1,993 309-833-4161
West Central Illinois Special Education Coop (07-12)
2000 Enrollment: 89 309-837-3911

Four-year College(s)

Western Illinois University (Public)
2001 Enrollment: 13,206 309-295-1414
2001 Tuition: In-state $2,982; Out-of-state $5,964

Two-year College(s)

McDonough District Hospital (Public)
2001 Enrollment: n/a 309-833-4101
Housing: Homeownership rate: 48.4% (2000); Median home value: $69,600 (2000); Median rent: $340 per month (2000); Median age of housing: 37 years (2000).

Hospitals: McDonough District Hospital (113 beds)
Newspapers: Macomb Eagle (1 x week); Macomb Journal (6 x week)
Transportation: Commute to work: 77.3% car, 2.3% public transportation, 15.5% walk, 2.9% work from home (2000); Travel time to work: 76.8% less than 15 minutes, 14.1% 15 to 30 minutes, 4.6% 30 to 45 minutes, 1.2% 45 to 60 minutes, 3.4% 60 minutes or more (2000); Amtrak: Service available.
Airports: Macomb Municipal
Additional Information Contacts
Lamoine Valley Board of Realtors 309-837-2546
Macomb Area Convention & Visitors Bureau 309-833-1315
Macomb Chamber of Commerce 309-837-4855

PRAIRIE CITY (village). Covers a land area of 1.013 square miles and a water area of 0 square miles. Located at 40.62° N. Lat.; 90.46° W. Long. Elevation is 667 feet.
Population: 461 (2000); Race: 100.0% White, 0.0% Black, 0.0% Asian, 0.0% American Indian and Alaska Native, 0.0% Hispanic of any race, 0.0% two or more races (2000); Density: 455.2 persons per square mile (2000); Age: 30.7% under 18, 17.8% over 64 (2000); Marriage status: 26.0% never married, 52.8% now married, 14.1% widowed, 7.1% divorced (2000); Foreign born: 0.2% (2000); Ancestry (includes multiple ancestries): 14.8% German, 12.2% United States or American, 5.8% English, 5.6% Welsh, 5.2% Irish (2000).
Economy: In agricultural and bituminous-coal area. Employment by occupation: 8.9% management, 8.4% professional, 14.0% services, 21.2% sales, 0.0% farming, 8.9% construction, 38.5% production (2000).
Income: Per capita income: $12,269 (2000); Median household income: $36,875 (2000); Poverty rate: 22.6% (2000).
Taxes: Total city taxes per capita: $25 (1997); City property taxes per capita: $23 (1997).
Education: High school graduation rate: 82.0% (2000); College graduation rate: 6.7% (2000).
Housing: Homeownership rate: 87.2% (2000); Median home value: $26,900 (2000); Median rent: $219 per month (2000); Median age of housing: 60+ years (2000).
Transportation: Commute to work: 93.4% car, 0.0% public transportation, 3.8% walk, 0.0% work from home (2000); Travel time to work: 44.5% less than 15 minutes, 21.4% 15 to 30 minutes, 22.0% 30 to 45 minutes, 2.7% 45 to 60 minutes, 9.3% 60 minutes or more (2000)

SCIOTA (village). Covers a land area of 0.317 square miles and a water area of 0 square miles. Located at 40.56° N. Lat.; 90.75° W. Long. Elevation is 753 feet.
Population: 58 (2000); Race: 100.0% White, 0.0% Black, 0.0% Asian, 0.0% American Indian and Alaska Native, 0.0% Hispanic of any race, 0.0% two or more races (2000); Density: 182.7 persons per square mile (2000); Age: 26.7% under 18, 15.6% over 64 (2000); Marriage status: 19.4% never married, 44.4% now married, 16.7% widowed, 19.4% divorced (2000); Foreign born: 0.0% (2000); Ancestry (includes multiple ancestries): 11.1% Swedish, 11.1% English, 6.7% United States or American, 6.7% German, 6.7% Danish (2000).
Economy: In agricultural and bituminous coal area. Employment by occupation: 22.7% management, 9.1% professional, 18.2% services, 13.6% sales, 0.0% farming, 27.3% construction, 9.1% production (2000).
Income: Per capita income: $15,280 (2000); Median household income: $28,750 (2000); Poverty rate: 4.4% (2000).
Taxes: Total city taxes per capita: $14 (1997); City property taxes per capita: $14 (1997).
Education: High school graduation rate: 93.1% (2000); College graduation rate: 13.8% (2000).
Housing: Homeownership rate: 75.0% (2000); Median home value: $14,400 (2000); Median rent: $225 per month (2000); Median age of housing: 60+ years (2000).
Transportation: Commute to work: 90.9% car, 0.0% public transportation, 9.1% walk, 0.0% work from home (2000); Travel time to work: 27.3% less than 15 minutes, 59.1% 15 to 30 minutes, 13.6% 30 to 45 minutes, 0.0% 45 to 60 minutes, 0.0% 60 minutes or more (2000)

TENNESSEE (village). Covers a land area of 0.425 square miles and a water area of 0 square miles. Located at 40.41° N. Lat.; 90.83° W. Long. Elevation is 687 feet.
Population: 144 (2000); Race: 98.6% White, 0.0% Black, 0.0% Asian, 0.0% American Indian and Alaska Native, 0.0% Hispanic of any race, 1.4% two or more races (2000); Density: 339.2 persons per square mile (2000); Age: 18.7% under 18, 26.6% over 64 (2000); Marriage status: 10.3% never married, 65.0% now married, 14.5% widowed, 10.3% divorced (2000); Foreign born: 0.0% (2000); Ancestry (includes multiple ancestries): 22.3% German, 12.9% Other groups, 11.5% United States or American, 7.2% English, 5.0% Irish (2000).
Economy: In agricultural area. Employment by occupation: 5.9% management, 5.9% professional, 17.6% services, 17.6% sales, 2.0% farming, 13.7% construction, 37.3% production (2000).
Income: Per capita income: $13,311 (2000); Median household income: $27,188 (2000); Poverty rate: 22.3% (2000).
Taxes: Total city taxes per capita: $22 (1997); City property taxes per capita: $15 (1997).
Education: High school graduation rate: 75.2% (2000); College graduation rate: 1.9% (2000).
Housing: Homeownership rate: 94.0% (2000); Median home value: $36,600 (2000); Median rent: $275 per month (2000); Median age of housing: 41 years (2000).
Transportation: Commute to work: 91.8% car, 0.0% public transportation, 0.0% walk, 8.2% work from home (2000); Travel time to work: 37.8% less than 15 minutes, 57.8% 15 to 30 minutes, 0.0% 30 to 45 minutes, 0.0% 45 to 60 minutes, 4.4% 60 minutes or more (2000)

McHenry County

Located in northeastern Illinois; bounded on the north by Wisconsin; drained by the Fox and Kishwaukee Rivers; includes many lakes. Covers a land area of 603.50 square miles, a water area of 7.60 square miles, and is located in the Central Time Zone. The county government was organized in 1836. County seat is Woodstock.

McHenry County is part of the Chicago, IL PMSA. The entire metro area includes: Cook County; DeKalb County; DuPage County; Grundy County; Kane County; Kendall County; Lake County; McHenry County; Will County

Weather Station: Marengo — Elevation: 816 feet

	Jan	Feb	Mar	Apr	May	Jun	Jul	Aug	Sep	Oct	Nov	Dec
High	28	33	45	59	72	82	85	82	75	63	47	33
Low	10	14	25	36	46	56	61	59	50	38	28	16
Precip	1.4	1.2	2.4	3.6	3.9	4.4	3.9	4.4	3.6	2.7	2.7	2.0
Snow	11.7	7.7	4.8	1.7	0.1	0.0	0.0	0.0	0.0	tr	2.5	8.4

High and Low temperatures in degrees Fahrenheit; Precipitation and Snow in inches

Population: 260,077 (2000); Race: 94.0% White, 0.6% Black, 1.3% Asian, 0.2% American Indian and Alaska Native, 7.5% Hispanic of any race, 1.2% two or more races (2000); Density: 430.9 persons per square mile (2000); Age: 30.2% under 18, 8.0% over 64 (2000).
Religion: Five largest groups: 29.3% Catholic Church, 4.9% Evangelical Lutheran Church in America, 4.0% Lutheran Church—Missouri Synod, 2.6% The United Methodist Church, 2.1% United Church of Christ (2000).
Economy: Unemployment rate: 5.8% (11/2002); Total civilian labor force: 136,430 (11/2002); Leading industries: 30.3% manufacturing; 13.6% retail trade; 8.9% construction (2000); Companies that employ more than 1,000 persons: 1 (2000); Companies that employ more than 100 persons: 149 (2000); Farms: 921 totaling 242,484 acres (1997); Minority business ownership rate: 4.9% (1997); Women business ownership rate: 27.6% (1997); Retail sales per capita: $8,620 (1997). Single-family building permits issued: 3,627 (2001) / 3,269 (2000); Multi-family building permits issued: 174 (2001) / 253 (2000).
Income: Per capita income: $26,476 (2000); Median household income: $64,826 (2000); Poverty rate: 3.7% (2000); Bankruptcy rate: 4.03% (2001).
Taxes: Total county taxes per capita: $130 (2000); County property taxes per capita: $111 (2000).
Education: High school graduation rate: 89.2% (2000); College graduation rate: 27.7% (2000).
Housing: Homeownership rate: 83.1% (2000); Median home value: $168,100 (2000); Median rent: $677 per month (2000); Median age of housing: 22 years (2000).
Health: Birth rate: 147.1 per 10,000 population (1998); Age adjusted death rate: 86.0 per 10,000 population (1999); Age adjusted cancer mortality rate: 219.0 deaths per 100,000 population (1999). Air Quality Index: 81% good, 19% moderate, 0% unhealthy (percent of days in 2000). Number of physicians: 11.0 per 10,000 population (1999); Number of hospital beds: 13.2 per 10,000 population (1999).
Elections: 2000 Presidential election results: 38.3% Gore, 58.5% Bush, 2.6% Nader, 0.3% Buchanan
National and State Parks: Moraine Hills State Park
Additional Information Contacts
McHenry County Government Offices 815-338-2040

Algonquin Chamber of Commerce 847-658-5300
Cary Chamber of Commerce 847-639-2800
Crystal Lake Chamber of Commerce 815-459-1300
Harvard Chamber of Commerce 815-943-4404
Huntley Chamber of Commerce 847-669-0166
Marengo-Union Chamber of Commerce 815-568-6680
Mc Henry Chamber of Commerce 815-385-4300
Mchenry County Association of Realtors 815-338-3660
Richmond/Spring Grove Chamber 815-678-7742
Wonder Lake Chamber of Commerce 815-728-0682
Woodstock Chamber of Commerce 815-338-2436

McHenry County Communities

ALGONQUIN (village). Covers a land area of 9.832 square miles and a water area of 0.164 square miles. Located at 42.16° N. Lat.; 88.30° W. Long. Elevation is 800 feet.
Population: 23,276 (2000); Race: 94.1% White, 0.8% Black, 2.1% Asian, 0.1% American Indian and Alaska Native, 3.9% Hispanic of any race, 1.3% two or more races (2000); Density: 2,367.4 persons per square mile (2000); Age: 33.5% under 18, 5.3% over 64 (2000); Marriage status: 18.5% never married, 71.4% now married, 3.3% widowed, 6.7% divorced (2000); Foreign born: 6.3% (2000); Ancestry (includes multiple ancestries): 33.1% German, 18.6% Polish, 17.0% Irish, 12.1% Italian, 9.1% English (2000).
Vital Statistics: Birth rate: 188.2 per 10,000 population (1998)
Economy: In dairying area; corn, oats. Manufactures fabricated metal and plastic products, dental instruments. Single-family building permits issued: 594 (2001) / 387 (2000); Multi-family building permits issued: 0 (2001) / 11 (2000); Employment by occupation: 20.9% management, 22.1% professional, 8.6% services, 30.9% sales, 0.0% farming, 7.4% construction, 10.0% production (2000).
Income: Per capita income: $29,820 (2000); Median household income: $79,730 (2000); Poverty rate: 1.7% (2000).
Taxes: Total city taxes per capita: $243 (1997); City property taxes per capita: $98 (1997).
Education: High school graduation rate: 95.0% (2000); College graduation rate: 38.7% (2000).
Housing: Homeownership rate: 93.2% (2000); Median home value: $195,100 (2000); Median rent: $711 per month (2000); Median age of housing: 10 years (2000).
Transportation: Commute to work: 91.5% car, 2.5% public transportation, 1.0% walk, 4.1% work from home (2000); Travel time to work: 16.2% less than 15 minutes, 24.9% 15 to 30 minutes, 27.7% 30 to 45 minutes, 16.2% 45 to 60 minutes, 15.0% 60 minutes or more (2000)
Additional Information Contacts
Algonquin Chamber of Commerce 847-658-5300

BULL VALLEY (village). Covers a land area of 5.609 square miles and a water area of 0 square miles. Located at 42.31° N. Lat.; 88.36° W. Long. Elevation is 855 feet.
Population: 726 (2000); Race: 98.6% White, 0.0% Black, 0.7% Asian, 0.0% American Indian and Alaska Native, 5.5% Hispanic of any race, 0.4% two or more races (2000); Density: 129.4 persons per square mile (2000); Age: 22.9% under 18, 17.6% over 64 (2000); Marriage status: 14.5% never married, 76.7% now married, 5.7% widowed, 3.1% divorced (2000); Foreign born: 4.2% (2000); Ancestry (includes multiple ancestries): 34.6% German, 18.0% Irish, 13.3% English, 9.7% Italian, 8.1% Other groups (2000).
Economy: Residential suburb of Woodstock. Single-family building permits issued: 1 (2001) / 3 (2000); Multi-family building permits issued: 0 (2001) / 0 (2000); Employment by occupation: 33.5% management, 26.9% professional, 2.5% services, 28.8% sales, 0.3% farming, 3.5% construction, 4.4% production (2000).
Income: Per capita income: $54,022 (2000); Median household income: $92,693 (2000); Poverty rate: 2.3% (2000).
Taxes: Total city taxes per capita: $244 (1997); City property taxes per capita: $154 (1997).
Education: High school graduation rate: 96.8% (2000); College graduation rate: 52.7% (2000).
Housing: Homeownership rate: 97.3% (2000); Median home value: $352,700 (2000); Median rent: $1,542 per month (2000); Median age of housing: 26 years (2000).
Transportation: Commute to work: 78.8% car, 9.1% public transportation, 1.6% walk, 9.8% work from home (2000); Travel time to work: 29.6% less than 15 minutes, 26.0% 15 to 30 minutes, 14.8% 30 to 45 minutes, 5.1% 45 to 60 minutes, 24.5% 60 minutes or more (2000)

CARY (village). Covers a land area of 5.253 square miles and a water area of 0.058 square miles. Located at 42.21° N. Lat.; 88.24° W. Long. Elevation is 825 feet.
Population: 15,531 (2000); Race: 96.2% White, 0.3% Black, 0.5% Asian, 0.2% American Indian and Alaska Native, 5.4% Hispanic of any race, 0.7% two or more races (2000); Density: 2,956.3 persons per square mile (2000); Age: 35.0% under 18, 5.1% over 64 (2000); Marriage status: 20.2% never married, 69.8% now married, 2.9% widowed, 7.0% divorced (2000); Foreign born: 4.4% (2000); Ancestry (includes multiple ancestries): 33.9% German, 24.0% Irish, 13.7% Polish, 12.2% Italian, 10.3% English (2000).
Vital Statistics: Birth rate: 192.5 per 10,000 population (1998)
Economy: Manufacturing: saws, circuit boards, heaters, seals, drill bits, valves, stripping machines. Single-family building permits issued: 462 (2001) / 14 (2000); Multi-family building permits issued: 20 (2001) / 0 (2000); Employment by occupation: 20.3% management, 22.0% professional, 10.3% services, 31.1% sales, 0.0% farming, 6.6% construction, 9.7% production (2000).
Income: Per capita income: $26,903 (2000); Median household income: $76,801 (2000); Poverty rate: 1.3% (2000).
Taxes: Total city taxes per capita: $107 (1997); City property taxes per capita: $86 (1997).
Education: High school graduation rate: 94.0% (2000); College graduation rate: 40.9% (2000).

School District(s)

Cary C C School District 26 (PK-08)
2000 Enrollment: 3,589 847-639-7788

Housing: Homeownership rate: 91.0% (2000); Median home value: $184,100 (2000); Median rent: $746 per month (2000); Median age of housing: 17 years (2000).
Transportation: Commute to work: 87.6% car, 6.6% public transportation, 0.4% walk, 4.2% work from home (2000); Travel time to work: 24.3% less than 15 minutes, 18.0% 15 to 30 minutes, 20.2% 30 to 45 minutes, 16.4% 45 to 60 minutes, 21.1% 60 minutes or more (2000)
Additional Information Contacts
Cary Chamber of Commerce 847-639-2800

CRYSTAL LAKE (city). Covers a land area of 16.243 square miles and a water area of 0.560 square miles. Located at 42.22° N. Lat.; 88.33° W. Long. Elevation is 934 feet.
History: Crystal Lake was settled in 1825 when the Erie Canal opened, and grew when the Chicago & North Western Railroad arrived.
Population: 38,000 (2000); Race: 93.9% White, 0.8% Black, 1.4% Asian, 0.1% American Indian and Alaska Native, 6.8% Hispanic of any race, 1.1% two or more races (2000); Density: 2,339.5 persons per square mile (2000); Age: 32.0% under 18, 8.8% over 64 (2000); Marriage status: 21.3% never married, 65.2% now married, 5.4% widowed, 8.1% divorced (2000); Foreign born: 7.4% (2000); Ancestry (includes multiple ancestries): 34.5% German, 21.1% Irish, 11.9% Polish, 10.0% English, 9.3% Other groups (2000).
Vital Statistics: Birth rate: 164.0 per 10,000 population (1998)
Economy: Unemployment rate: 7.0% (11/2002); Total civilian labor force: 19,550 (11/2002); Single-family building permits issued: 271 (2001) / 252 (2000); Multi-family building permits issued: 7 (2001) / 58 (2000); Employment by occupation: 19.5% management, 21.2% professional, 10.4% services, 29.7% sales, 0.1% farming, 7.2% construction, 11.9% production (2000).
Income: Per capita income: $26,146 (2000); Median household income: $66,872 (2000); Poverty rate: 3.5% (2000).
Taxes: Total city taxes per capita: $218 (2000); City property taxes per capita: $170 (2000).
Education: High school graduation rate: 91.5% (2000); College graduation rate: 36.2% (2000).

School District(s)

Community High School District 155 (09-12)
2000 Enrollment: 5,428 815-455-8500
Crystal Lake C C School District 47 (PK-08)
2000 Enrollment: 8,426 815-459-6070
Prairie Grove C School District 46 (KG-08)
2000 Enrollment: 1,002 815-459-3023

Two-year College(s)

McHenry County College (Public)
2001 Enrollment: 5,747 815-455-3700
2001 Tuition: In-state $6,841; Out-of-state $8,085

Housing: Homeownership rate: 79.2% (2000); Median home value: $170,100 (2000); Median rent: $773 per month (2000); Median age of housing: 19 years (2000).

Newspapers: Northwest Herald (7 x week)
Transportation: Commute to work: 90.3% car, 4.3% public transportation, 1.3% walk, 3.3% work from home (2000); Travel time to work: 29.6% less than 15 minutes, 23.9% 15 to 30 minutes, 16.9% 30 to 45 minutes, 12.5% 45 to 60 minutes, 17.1% 60 minutes or more (2000)
Additional Information Contacts
Crystal Lake Chamber of Commerce.................... 815-459-1300

FOX RIVER GROVE (village). Covers a land area of 1.660 square miles and a water area of 0.104 square miles. Located at 42.19° N. Lat.; 88.21° W. Long. Elevation is 760 feet.
History: Fox River Grove developed as a summer resort town.
Population: 4,862 (2000); Race: 95.8% White, 0.7% Black, 0.4% Asian, 0.4% American Indian and Alaska Native, 3.7% Hispanic of any race, 1.1% two or more races (2000); Density: 2,929.6 persons per square mile (2000); Age: 31.4% under 18, 6.2% over 64 (2000); Marriage status: 20.8% never married, 66.9% now married, 1.8% widowed, 10.4% divorced (2000); Foreign born: 4.4% (2000); Ancestry (includes multiple ancestries): 32.3% German, 22.4% Irish, 13.9% Polish, 11.5% Italian, 7.9% English (2000).
Economy: Single-family building permits issued: 18 (2001) / 53 (2000); Multi-family building permits issued: 0 (2001) / 0 (2000); Employment by occupation: 16.4% management, 18.9% professional, 10.1% services, 31.8% sales, 0.0% farming, 11.0% construction, 11.8% production (2000).
Income: Per capita income: $28,870 (2000); Median household income: $66,469 (2000); Poverty rate: 7.1% (2000).
Taxes: Total city taxes per capita: $201 (1997); City property taxes per capita: $100 (1997).
Education: High school graduation rate: 92.7% (2000); College graduation rate: 33.3% (2000).

School District(s)
Fox River Grove Cons S D 3 (KG-08)
2000 Enrollment: 667 847-516-5100
Housing: Homeownership rate: 83.5% (2000); Median home value: $175,300 (2000); Median rent: $720 per month (2000); Median age of housing: 24 years (2000).
Transportation: Commute to work: 86.0% car, 6.5% public transportation, 1.2% walk, 6.0% work from home (2000); Travel time to work: 21.2% less than 15 minutes, 21.7% 15 to 30 minutes, 20.6% 30 to 45 minutes, 13.4% 45 to 60 minutes, 23.0% 60 minutes or more (2000)

FOX RIVER VALLEY GARDENS (village). Covers a land area of 0.979 square miles and a water area of 0.096 square miles. Located at 42.24° N. Lat.; 88.19° W. Long. Elevation is 738 feet.
Population: 788 (2000); Race: 94.6% White, 0.1% Black, 3.6% Asian, 0.0% American Indian and Alaska Native, 5.0% Hispanic of any race, 1.7% two or more races (2000); Density: 805.0 persons per square mile (2000); Age: 30.8% under 18, 5.5% over 64 (2000); Marriage status: 16.5% never married, 73.5% now married, 3.1% widowed, 6.9% divorced (2000); Foreign born: 8.6% (2000); Ancestry (includes multiple ancestries): 37.6% German, 25.0% Irish, 12.9% Other groups, 12.4% Italian, 8.8% English (2000).
Economy: Single-family building permits issued: 47 (2001) / 56 (2000); Multi-family building permits issued: 0 (2001) / 0 (2000); Employment by occupation: 23.1% management, 16.4% professional, 8.6% services, 30.5% sales, 0.0% farming, 10.8% construction, 10.6% production (2000).
Income: Per capita income: $41,284 (2000); Median household income: $83,508 (2000); Poverty rate: 2.5% (2000).
Taxes: Total city taxes per capita: $143 (1997); City property taxes per capita: $47 (1997).
Education: High school graduation rate: 91.9% (2000); College graduation rate: 32.2% (2000).
Housing: Homeownership rate: 93.2% (2000); Median home value: $207,600 (2000); Median rent: $756 per month (2000); Median age of housing: 19 years (2000).
Transportation: Commute to work: 90.2% car, 3.9% public transportation, 0.0% walk, 5.0% work from home (2000); Travel time to work: 7.9% less than 15 minutes, 17.3% 15 to 30 minutes, 22.6% 30 to 45 minutes, 20.2% 45 to 60 minutes, 32.0% 60 minutes or more (2000)

GREENWOOD (village). Covers a land area of 1.559 square miles and a water area of 0 square miles. Located at 42.39° N. Lat.; 88.38° W. Long. Elevation is 838 feet.
Population: 244 (2000); Race: 100.0% White, 0.0% Black, 0.0% Asian, 0.0% American Indian and Alaska Native, 0.0% Hispanic of any race, 0.0% two or more races (2000); Density: 156.6 persons per square mile (2000); Age: 35.8% under 18, 7.5% over 64 (2000); Marriage status: 20.9% never married, 67.0% now married, 3.3% widowed, 8.8% divorced (2000); Foreign born: 0.0% (2000); Ancestry (includes multiple ancestries): 46.4% German, 15.1% English, 14.0% United States or American, 12.8% Polish, 10.6% Irish (2000).
Economy: Employment by occupation: 14.8% management, 24.2% professional, 17.2% services, 13.3% sales, 0.0% farming, 18.0% construction, 12.5% production (2000).
Income: Per capita income: $19,216 (2000); Median household income: $56,250 (2000); Poverty rate: 7.2% (2000).
Taxes: Total city taxes per capita: $15 (1997); City property taxes per capita: $15 (1997).
Education: High school graduation rate: 93.4% (2000); College graduation rate: 23.2% (2000).
Housing: Homeownership rate: 84.1% (2000); Median home value: $181,800 (2000); Median rent: $850 per month (2000); Median age of housing: 60+ years (2000).
Transportation: Commute to work: 96.0% car, 0.8% public transportation, 0.0% walk, 3.2% work from home (2000); Travel time to work: 18.0% less than 15 minutes, 50.8% 15 to 30 minutes, 16.4% 30 to 45 minutes, 9.0% 45 to 60 minutes, 5.7% 60 minutes or more (2000)

HARVARD (city). Covers a land area of 5.337 square miles and a water area of 0 square miles. Located at 42.42° N. Lat.; 88.61° W. Long. Elevation is 966 feet.
History: Incorporated 1867.
Population: 7,996 (2000); Race: 77.8% White, 0.7% Black, 1.4% Asian, 0.7% American Indian and Alaska Native, 38.7% Hispanic of any race, 3.0% two or more races (2000); Density: 1,498.2 persons per square mile (2000); Age: 29.5% under 18, 9.3% over 64 (2000); Marriage status: 28.0% never married, 59.4% now married, 6.2% widowed, 6.4% divorced (2000); Foreign born: 26.8% (2000); Ancestry (includes multiple ancestries): 37.4% Other groups, 23.1% German, 10.5% Irish, 6.1% English, 3.2% Norwegian (2000).
Economy: Railroad town with repair shops; trade center in dairying and resort area. Manufacturing of dairy products, hardware, telecommunications. Single-family building permits issued: 52 (2001) / 40 (2000); Multi-family building permits issued: 9 (2001) / 50 (2000); Employment by occupation: 6.0% management, 13.6% professional, 16.4% services, 19.5% sales, 1.7% farming, 11.8% construction, 31.0% production (2000).
Income: Per capita income: $17,253 (2000); Median household income: $44,363 (2000); Poverty rate: 9.1% (2000).
Taxes: Total city taxes per capita: $186 (1997); City property taxes per capita: $131 (1997).
Education: High school graduation rate: 69.7% (2000); College graduation rate: 15.2% (2000).

School District(s)
Harvard C U School District 50 (PK-12)
2000 Enrollment: 2,258 815-943-4022
Housing: Homeownership rate: 54.3% (2000); Median home value: $114,700 (2000); Median rent: $582 per month (2000); Median age of housing: 37 years (2000).
Hospitals: Harvard Memorial Hospital (77 beds)
Transportation: Commute to work: 90.1% car, 1.5% public transportation, 5.2% walk, 2.1% work from home (2000); Travel time to work: 35.7% less than 15 minutes, 30.6% 15 to 30 minutes, 20.7% 30 to 45 minutes, 3.7% 45 to 60 minutes, 9.2% 60 minutes or more (2000)
Additional Information Contacts
Harvard Chamber of Commerce 815-943-4404

HEBRON (village). Covers a land area of 0.685 square miles and a water area of 0 square miles. Located at 42.47° N. Lat.; 88.43° W. Long. Elevation is 930 feet.
Population: 1,038 (2000); Race: 97.1% White, 0.9% Black, 0.0% Asian, 0.0% American Indian and Alaska Native, 2.5% Hispanic of any race, 0.4% two or more races (2000); Density: 1,515.9 persons per square mile (2000); Age: 31.0% under 18, 9.8% over 64 (2000); Marriage status: 26.8% never married, 54.6% now married, 5.2% widowed, 13.4% divorced (2000); Foreign born: 1.4% (2000); Ancestry (includes multiple ancestries): 43.7% German, 19.9% Irish, 9.7% English, 9.1% Polish, 7.6% Italian (2000).
Economy: In agricultural area: corn; dairying. Manufacturing: plastic products, garden tools. Single-family building permits issued: 6 (2001) / 7 (2000); Multi-family building permits issued: 0 (2001) / 4 (2000); Employment by occupation: 2.2% management, 10.4% professional, 10.7% services, 31.4% sales, 0.9% farming, 21.8% construction, 22.6% production (2000).
Income: Per capita income: $18,829 (2000); Median household income: $46,607 (2000); Poverty rate: 5.1% (2000).

Taxes: Total city taxes per capita: $195 (1997); City property taxes per capita: $109 (1997).
Education: High school graduation rate: 87.5% (2000); College graduation rate: 9.1% (2000).

School District(s)

Alden Hebron School District 19 (PK-12)
2000 Enrollment: 501 815-648-2886

Housing: Homeownership rate: 65.3% (2000); Median home value: $127,700 (2000); Median rent: $507 per month (2000); Median age of housing: 60+ years (2000).
Transportation: Commute to work: 93.7% car, 0.7% public transportation, 3.5% walk, 1.3% work from home (2000); Travel time to work: 24.4% less than 15 minutes, 39.5% 15 to 30 minutes, 20.5% 30 to 45 minutes, 7.7% 45 to 60 minutes, 7.9% 60 minutes or more (2000)

HOLIDAY HILLS (village). Covers a land area of 0.947 square miles and a water area of 0.037 square miles. Located at 42.29° N. Lat.; 88.22° W. Long. Elevation is 740 feet.
Population: 831 (2000); Race: 95.8% White, 0.0% Black, 0.0% Asian, 0.6% American Indian and Alaska Native, 6.3% Hispanic of any race, 0.9% two or more races (2000); Density: 877.7 persons per square mile (2000); Age: 29.8% under 18, 5.8% over 64 (2000); Marriage status: 25.6% never married, 63.7% now married, 3.1% widowed, 7.6% divorced (2000); Foreign born: 3.3% (2000); Ancestry (includes multiple ancestries): 33.9% German, 17.4% Polish, 17.1% Irish, 12.1% Italian, 10.2% Other groups (2000).
Economy: Single-family building permits issued: 0 (2001) / 0 (2000); Multi-family building permits issued: 0 (2001) / 0 (2000); Employment by occupation: 11.0% management, 11.9% professional, 12.6% services, 34.0% sales, 0.0% farming, 14.5% construction, 16.0% production (2000).
Income: Per capita income: $20,883 (2000); Median household income: $57,857 (2000); Poverty rate: 0.0% (2000).
Taxes: Total city taxes per capita: $25 (1997); City property taxes per capita: $13 (1997).
Education: High school graduation rate: 84.8% (2000); College graduation rate: 14.4% (2000).
Housing: Homeownership rate: 91.1% (2000); Median home value: $129,400 (2000); Median rent: $775 per month (2000); Median age of housing: 38 years (2000).
Transportation: Commute to work: 96.0% car, 0.4% public transportation, 0.0% walk, 3.1% work from home (2000); Travel time to work: 15.1% less than 15 minutes, 33.9% 15 to 30 minutes, 23.8% 30 to 45 minutes, 11.7% 45 to 60 minutes, 15.6% 60 minutes or more (2000)

HUNTLEY (village). Covers a land area of 11.716 square miles and a water area of 0.032 square miles. Located at 42.16° N. Lat.; 88.42° W. Long. Elevation is 900 feet.
Population: 5,730 (2000); Race: 94.6% White, 0.8% Black, 2.2% Asian, 0.0% American Indian and Alaska Native, 3.9% Hispanic of any race, 1.7% two or more races (2000); Density: 489.1 persons per square mile (2000); Age: 21.1% under 18, 18.5% over 64 (2000); Marriage status: 13.9% never married, 71.7% now married, 6.2% widowed, 8.2% divorced (2000); Foreign born: 5.6% (2000); Ancestry (includes multiple ancestries): 40.3% German, 14.9% Irish, 13.7% Polish, 10.9% Italian, 10.5% English (2000).
Economy: Single-family building permits issued: 828 (2001) / 803 (2000); Multi-family building permits issued: 32 (2001) / 0 (2000); Employment by occupation: 14.2% management, 17.3% professional, 11.9% services, 33.7% sales, 0.7% farming, 8.3% construction, 13.8% production (2000).
Income: Per capita income: $27,451 (2000); Median household income: $60,456 (2000); Poverty rate: 2.8% (2000).
Taxes: Total city taxes per capita: $558 (1997); City property taxes per capita: $254 (1997).
Education: High school graduation rate: 90.0% (2000); College graduation rate: 22.6% (2000).

School District(s)

Huntley Cons School District 158 (PK-12)
2000 Enrollment: 3,188 847-659-6158

Housing: Homeownership rate: 79.4% (2000); Median home value: $191,600 (2000); Median rent: $714 per month (2000); Median age of housing: 4 years (2000).
Newspapers: The Huntley Farmside/Marengo Press (1 x week)
Transportation: Commute to work: 90.7% car, 2.5% public transportation, 3.3% walk, 2.6% work from home (2000); Travel time to work: 28.0% less than 15 minutes, 27.1% 15 to 30 minutes, 19.0% 30 to 45 minutes, 9.1% 45 to 60 minutes, 16.7% 60 minutes or more (2000)
Additional Information Contacts
Huntley Chamber of Commerce. 847-669-0166

ISLAND LAKE (village). Covers a land area of 2.854 square miles and a water area of 0.208 square miles. Located at 42.27° N. Lat.; 88.20° W. Long.
Population: 8,153 (2000); Race: 95.4% White, 0.9% Black, 0.7% Asian, 0.2% American Indian and Alaska Native, 8.0% Hispanic of any race, 1.5% two or more races (2000); Density: 2,856.3 persons per square mile (2000); Age: 32.4% under 18, 4.3% over 64 (2000); Marriage status: 20.2% never married, 65.9% now married, 4.2% widowed, 9.7% divorced (2000); Foreign born: 5.7% (2000); Ancestry (includes multiple ancestries): 34.9% German, 17.3% Irish, 14.9% Polish, 12.0% Other groups, 11.3% Italian (2000).
Economy: Single-family building permits issued: 36 (2001) / 6 (2000); Multi-family building permits issued: 0 (2001) / 40 (2000); Employment by occupation: 14.4% management, 17.9% professional, 8.8% services, 30.7% sales, 0.0% farming, 15.0% construction, 13.2% production (2000).
Income: Per capita income: $24,206 (2000); Median household income: $63,455 (2000); Poverty rate: 2.6% (2000).
Education: High school graduation rate: 89.6% (2000); College graduation rate: 23.6% (2000).
Housing: Homeownership rate: 90.1% (2000); Median home value: $144,300 (2000); Median rent: $839 per month (2000); Median age of housing: 12 years (2000).
Transportation: Commute to work: 93.7% car, 0.9% public transportation, 0.5% walk, 4.4% work from home (2000); Travel time to work: 14.2% less than 15 minutes, 24.2% 15 to 30 minutes, 22.9% 30 to 45 minutes, 22.1% 45 to 60 minutes, 16.7% 60 minutes or more (2000)

JOHNSBURG (village). Aka Sunnyside. Covers a land area of 5.537 square miles and a water area of 0.576 square miles. Located at 42.38° N. Lat.; 88.23° W. Long. Elevation is 750 feet.
Population: 5,391 (2000); Race: 98.5% White, 0.0% Black, 0.0% Asian, 0.3% American Indian and Alaska Native, 1.5% Hispanic of any race, 0.6% two or more races (2000); Density: 973.7 persons per square mile (2000); Age: 31.6% under 18, 7.4% over 64 (2000); Marriage status: 23.1% never married, 64.3% now married, 3.5% widowed, 9.1% divorced (2000); Foreign born: 0.8% (2000); Ancestry (includes multiple ancestries): 40.9% German, 19.7% Irish, 13.7% Polish, 8.8% Italian, 7.6% English (2000).
Economy: Single-family building permits issued: 79 (2001) / 54 (2000); Multi-family building permits issued: 0 (2001) / 0 (2000); Employment by occupation: 18.5% management, 16.3% professional, 10.3% services, 26.9% sales, 0.2% farming, 16.7% construction, 11.1% production (2000).
Income: Per capita income: $27,582 (2000); Median household income: $69,864 (2000); Poverty rate: 1.3% (2000).
Taxes: Total city taxes per capita: $305 (1997); City property taxes per capita: $216 (1997).
Education: High school graduation rate: 91.7% (2000); College graduation rate: 27.3% (2000).

School District(s)

Johnsburg C U School District 12 (PK-12)
2000 Enrollment: 2,497 815-385-6916

Housing: Homeownership rate: 90.8% (2000); Median home value: $190,900 (2000); Median rent: $807 per month (2000); Median age of housing: 28 years (2000).
Transportation: Commute to work: 91.4% car, 2.9% public transportation, 0.6% walk, 3.6% work from home (2000); Travel time to work: 29.3% less than 15 minutes, 27.3% 15 to 30 minutes, 13.1% 30 to 45 minutes, 12.9% 45 to 60 minutes, 17.5% 60 minutes or more (2000)

LAKE IN THE HILLS (village). Covers a land area of 9.404 square miles and a water area of 0.232 square miles. Located at 42.18° N. Lat.; 88.34° W. Long. Elevation is 870 feet.
Population: 23,152 (2000); Race: 92.6% White, 1.3% Black, 3.1% Asian, 0.1% American Indian and Alaska Native, 6.9% Hispanic of any race, 1.2% two or more races (2000); Density: 2,461.9 persons per square mile (2000); Age: 34.0% under 18, 2.7% over 64 (2000); Marriage status: 17.6% never married, 74.0% now married, 2.1% widowed, 6.3% divorced (2000); Foreign born: 8.5% (2000); Ancestry (includes multiple ancestries): 30.8% German, 18.3% Irish, 17.8% Italian, 16.6% Polish, 13.1% Other groups (2000).
Economy: Lake in the Hills Airport. Manufacturing: protective clothing, warning signs. Single-family building permits issued: 306 (2001) / 620 (2000); Multi-family building permits issued: 0 (2001) / 0 (2000); Employment by occupation: 20.6% management, 21.4% professional, 9.4% services, 28.3% sales, 0.1% farming, 8.7% construction, 11.6% production (2000).
Income: Per capita income: $26,239 (2000); Median household income: $73,313 (2000); Poverty rate: 2.1% (2000).

Taxes: Total city taxes per capita: $108 (1997); City property taxes per capita: $55 (1997).
Education: High school graduation rate: 93.2% (2000); College graduation rate: 32.5% (2000).
Housing: Homeownership rate: 93.5% (2000); Median home value: $168,700 (2000); Median rent: $872 per month (2000); Median age of housing: 5 years (2000).
Transportation: Commute to work: 94.2% car, 2.3% public transportation, 0.2% walk, 3.1% work from home (2000); Travel time to work: 14.3% less than 15 minutes, 25.2% 15 to 30 minutes, 23.1% 30 to 45 minutes, 18.7% 45 to 60 minutes, 18.7% 60 minutes or more (2000)

LAKEMOOR (village). Covers a land area of 4.280 square miles and a water area of 0.221 square miles. Located at 42.33° N. Lat.; 88.20° W. Long. Elevation is 760 feet.
Population: 2,788 (2000); Race: 95.1% White, 2.2% Black, 1.0% Asian, 0.1% American Indian and Alaska Native, 3.4% Hispanic of any race, 1.4% two or more races (2000); Density: 651.4 persons per square mile (2000); Age: 31.4% under 18, 4.8% over 64 (2000); Marriage status: 19.7% never married, 66.3% now married, 2.5% widowed, 11.6% divorced (2000); Foreign born: 4.0% (2000); Ancestry (includes multiple ancestries): 37.7% German, 15.4% Irish, 14.2% Polish, 8.1% Other groups, 7.1% Italian (2000).
Economy: Single-family building permits issued: 56 (2001) / 129 (2000); Multi-family building permits issued: 0 (2001) / 0 (2000); Employment by occupation: 12.4% management, 17.3% professional, 13.0% services, 29.6% sales, 0.0% farming, 16.1% construction, 11.6% production (2000).
Income: Per capita income: $22,499 (2000); Median household income: $56,217 (2000); Poverty rate: 8.7% (2000).
Taxes: Total city taxes per capita: $129 (1997); City property taxes per capita: $97 (1997).
Education: High school graduation rate: 84.7% (2000); College graduation rate: 16.6% (2000).
Housing: Homeownership rate: 75.7% (2000); Median home value: $147,200 (2000); Median rent: $846 per month (2000); Median age of housing: 7 years (2000).
Transportation: Commute to work: 95.3% car, 2.3% public transportation, 0.6% walk, 1.2% work from home (2000); Travel time to work: 17.4% less than 15 minutes, 23.0% 15 to 30 minutes, 27.0% 30 to 45 minutes, 17.0% 45 to 60 minutes, 15.6% 60 minutes or more (2000)

LAKEWOOD (village). Covers a land area of 3.091 square miles and a water area of 0.294 square miles. Located at 42.22° N. Lat.; 88.37° W. Long. Elevation is 894 feet.
Population: 2,337 (2000); Race: 96.0% White, 0.4% Black, 0.6% Asian, 0.0% American Indian and Alaska Native, 0.7% Hispanic of any race, 0.3% two or more races (2000); Density: 756.0 persons per square mile (2000); Age: 28.2% under 18, 8.6% over 64 (2000); Marriage status: 16.2% never married, 76.1% now married, 3.1% widowed, 4.6% divorced (2000); Foreign born: 4.9% (2000); Ancestry (includes multiple ancestries): 32.0% German, 24.8% Irish, 11.4% English, 9.9% Italian, 9.8% Polish (2000).
Economy: In agricultural area: dairying; corn. Employment by occupation: 29.9% management, 25.3% professional, 5.6% services, 28.0% sales, 0.3% farming, 5.6% construction, 5.3% production (2000).
Income: Per capita income: $44,579 (2000); Median household income: $111,172 (2000); Poverty rate: 1.7% (2000).
Taxes: Total city taxes per capita: $560 (1997); City property taxes per capita: $412 (1997).
Education: High school graduation rate: 95.7% (2000); College graduation rate: 55.3% (2000).
Housing: Homeownership rate: 98.4% (2000); Median home value: $284,900 (2000); Median rent: $775 per month (2000); Median age of housing: 16 years (2000).
Transportation: Commute to work: 86.7% car, 6.3% public transportation, 0.0% walk, 6.6% work from home (2000); Travel time to work: 19.1% less than 15 minutes, 31.7% 15 to 30 minutes, 14.2% 30 to 45 minutes, 11.8% 45 to 60 minutes, 23.2% 60 minutes or more (2000)

MARENGO (city). Covers a land area of 3.975 square miles and a water area of 0 square miles. Located at 42.25° N. Lat.; 88.60° W. Long. Elevation is 837 feet.
History: Marengo was the birthplace of Egbert Van Alstyne who composed the songs "In the Shade of the Old Apple Tree," and "Pony Boy." An early industry here was the McGill Metal Products Plant, a manufacturer of mousetraps.
Population: 6,355 (2000); Race: 91.6% White, 0.1% Black, 1.0% Asian, 0.0% American Indian and Alaska Native, 11.4% Hispanic of any race, 1.0% two or more races (2000); Density: 1,598.5 persons per square mile (2000); Age: 29.8% under 18, 12.6% over 64 (2000); Marriage status: 19.7% never married, 63.2% now married, 6.2% widowed, 11.0% divorced (2000); Foreign born: 7.1% (2000); Ancestry (includes multiple ancestries): 38.6% German, 14.4% Other groups, 12.7% Irish, 12.1% Polish, 9.0% Italian (2000).
Economy: Single-family building permits issued: 58 (2001) / 35 (2000); Multi-family building permits issued: 4 (2001) / 2 (2000); Employment by occupation: 9.3% management, 14.5% professional, 12.2% services, 26.4% sales, 0.2% farming, 14.6% construction, 22.8% production (2000).
Income: Per capita income: $22,225 (2000); Median household income: $50,214 (2000); Poverty rate: 4.4% (2000).
Taxes: Total city taxes per capita: $340 (1997); City property taxes per capita: $138 (1997).
Education: High school graduation rate: 85.7% (2000); College graduation rate: 14.0% (2000).

School District(s)

Marengo Community HS District 154 (09-12)
2000 Enrollment: 672 815-568-6511
Marengo-Union Elementary Cons District 165 (PK-08)
2000 Enrollment: 1,176 815-568-8323
Riley C C School District 18 (KG-08)
2000 Enrollment: 328 815-568-8637

Housing: Homeownership rate: 65.7% (2000); Median home value: $140,400 (2000); Median rent: $551 per month (2000); Median age of housing: 35 years (2000).
Transportation: Commute to work: 90.9% car, 2.2% public transportation, 3.2% walk, 2.6% work from home (2000); Travel time to work: 36.5% less than 15 minutes, 23.1% 15 to 30 minutes, 19.6% 30 to 45 minutes, 5.9% 45 to 60 minutes, 14.9% 60 minutes or more (2000)

Additional Information Contacts

Marengo-Union Chamber of Commerce 815-568-6680

MCCULLOM LAKE (village). Covers a land area of 0.280 square miles and a water area of 0 square miles. Located at 42.37° N. Lat.; 88.29° W. Long. Elevation is 800 feet.
Population: 1,038 (2000); Race: 94.5% White, 1.0% Black, 0.7% Asian, 0.0% American Indian and Alaska Native, 5.1% Hispanic of any race, 2.4% two or more races (2000); Density: 3,708.2 persons per square mile (2000); Age: 26.2% under 18, 10.8% over 64 (2000); Marriage status: 25.8% never married, 62.2% now married, 6.1% widowed, 6.0% divorced (2000); Foreign born: 2.6% (2000); Ancestry (includes multiple ancestries): 37.3% German, 20.6% Irish, 13.9% Polish, 10.4% Italian, 9.4% Other groups (2000).
Economy: Single-family building permits issued: 1 (2001) / 1 (2000); Multi-family building permits issued: 0 (2001) / 0 (2000); Employment by occupation: 8.6% management, 11.4% professional, 17.2% services, 24.9% sales, 0.4% farming, 18.7% construction, 18.9% production (2000).
Income: Per capita income: $20,350 (2000); Median household income: $54,500 (2000); Poverty rate: 5.5% (2000).
Taxes: Total city taxes per capita: $67 (1997); City property taxes per capita: $40 (1997).
Education: High school graduation rate: 81.3% (2000); College graduation rate: 6.4% (2000).
Housing: Homeownership rate: 81.0% (2000); Median home value: $116,300 (2000); Median rent: $703 per month (2000); Median age of housing: 50 years (2000).
Transportation: Commute to work: 94.6% car, 0.9% public transportation, 0.8% walk, 3.2% work from home (2000); Travel time to work: 33.5% less than 15 minutes, 31.2% 15 to 30 minutes, 15.3% 30 to 45 minutes, 6.2% 45 to 60 minutes, 13.8% 60 minutes or more (2000)

MCHENRY (city). Covers a land area of 11.621 square miles and a water area of 0.491 square miles. Located at 42.33° N. Lat.; 88.28° W. Long. Elevation is 761 feet.
History: McHenry began in 1836 when Dr. Christy C. Wheeler became the first postmaster and storekeeper. McHenry was located on the Chicago Pike route and entertained many travelers. Later the economy depended on butter, cheese, and pickle production.
Population: 21,501 (2000); Race: 94.6% White, 0.5% Black, 1.1% Asian, 0.0% American Indian and Alaska Native, 6.9% Hispanic of any race, 0.9% two or more races (2000); Density: 1,850.2 persons per square mile (2000); Age: 29.2% under 18, 10.5% over 64 (2000); Marriage status: 22.3% never married, 61.0% now married, 6.6% widowed, 10.1% divorced (2000); Foreign born: 6.2% (2000); Ancestry (includes multiple ancestries): 36.6% German, 20.9% Irish, 13.1% Polish, 9.4% Other groups, 8.7% Italian (2000).
Vital Statistics: Birth rate: 194.9 per 10,000 population (1998)

Economy: Single-family building permits issued: 209 (2001) / 162 (2000); Multi-family building permits issued: 22 (2001) / 38 (2000); Employment by occupation: 14.0% management, 17.4% professional, 11.9% services, 29.4% sales, 0.1% farming, 11.3% construction, 16.0% production (2000).
Income: Per capita income: $23,272 (2000); Median household income: $55,759 (2000); Poverty rate: 4.6% (2000).
Taxes: Total city taxes per capita: $210 (1997); City property taxes per capita: $126 (1997).
Education: High school graduation rate: 87.2% (2000); College graduation rate: 22.1% (2000).

School District(s)

Mchenry C C School District 15 (PK-08)
2000 Enrollment: 4,586 815-385-7210
Mchenry Community H S District 156 (09-12)
2000 Enrollment: 2,123 815-385-7900

Housing: Homeownership rate: 76.6% (2000); Median home value: $150,000 (2000); Median rent: $645 per month (2000); Median age of housing: 22 years (2000).
Hospitals: Northern Illinois Medical Center (196 beds)
Transportation: Commute to work: 94.2% car, 1.7% public transportation, 1.4% walk, 2.0% work from home (2000); Travel time to work: 30.8% less than 15 minutes, 29.5% 15 to 30 minutes, 14.0% 30 to 45 minutes, 11.4% 45 to 60 minutes, 14.4% 60 minutes or more (2000)

Additional Information Contacts

Mc Henry Chamber of Commerce 815-385-4300

OAKWOOD HILLS (village). Covers a land area of 1.129 square miles and a water area of 0.079 square miles. Located at 42.24° N. Lat.; 88.24° W. Long. Elevation is 820 feet.
Population: 2,194 (2000); Race: 97.5% White, 0.5% Black, 0.0% Asian, 0.0% American Indian and Alaska Native, 5.0% Hispanic of any race, 0.9% two or more races (2000); Density: 1,943.9 persons per square mile (2000); Age: 32.0% under 18, 3.1% over 64 (2000); Marriage status: 21.6% never married, 67.6% now married, 2.3% widowed, 8.5% divorced (2000); Foreign born: 5.4% (2000); Ancestry (includes multiple ancestries): 38.6% German, 22.4% Irish, 16.0% Polish, 11.8% Italian, 9.9% English (2000).
Economy: Single-family building permits issued: 13 (2001) / 15 (2000); Multi-family building permits issued: 0 (2001) / 0 (2000); Employment by occupation: 15.3% management, 17.8% professional, 10.3% services, 31.5% sales, 0.3% farming, 11.3% construction, 13.5% production (2000).
Income: Per capita income: $26,397 (2000); Median household income: $68,182 (2000); Poverty rate: 5.0% (2000).
Taxes: Total city taxes per capita: $122 (1997); City property taxes per capita: $76 (1997).
Education: High school graduation rate: 92.2% (2000); College graduation rate: 30.3% (2000).
Housing: Homeownership rate: 94.5% (2000); Median home value: $166,000 (2000); Median rent: $850 per month (2000); Median age of housing: 21 years (2000).
Transportation: Commute to work: 90.4% car, 5.1% public transportation, 0.0% walk, 4.5% work from home (2000); Travel time to work: 20.7% less than 15 minutes, 26.7% 15 to 30 minutes, 20.7% 30 to 45 minutes, 14.8% 45 to 60 minutes, 17.1% 60 minutes or more (2000)

PISTAKEE HIGHLANDS (CDP). Aka Pistakee. Covers a land area of 1.437 square miles and a water area of 0.329 square miles. Located at 42.40° N. Lat.; 88.21° W. Long. Elevation is 755 feet.
Population: 3,812 (2000); Race: 97.9% White, 0.0% Black, 0.7% Asian, 0.7% American Indian and Alaska Native, 3.5% Hispanic of any race, 0.1% two or more races (2000); Density: 2,653.0 persons per square mile (2000); Age: 28.9% under 18, 8.3% over 64 (2000); Marriage status: 25.2% never married, 62.8% now married, 3.4% widowed, 8.5% divorced (2000); Foreign born: 2.1% (2000); Ancestry (includes multiple ancestries): 36.7% German, 14.4% Polish, 14.0% Irish, 6.0% Other groups, 5.3% English (2000).
Economy: Recreation area. Employment by occupation: 11.0% management, 16.3% professional, 10.4% services, 26.6% sales, 0.5% farming, 12.9% construction, 22.3% production (2000).
Income: Per capita income: $21,852 (2000); Median household income: $54,943 (2000); Poverty rate: 4.4% (2000).
Education: High school graduation rate: 84.9% (2000); College graduation rate: 11.3% (2000).
Housing: Homeownership rate: 91.8% (2000); Median home value: $127,700 (2000); Median rent: $820 per month (2000); Median age of housing: 30 years (2000).
Transportation: Commute to work: 92.7% car, 5.5% public transportation, 0.0% walk, 1.8% work from home (2000); Travel time to work: 25.4% less than 15 minutes, 19.8% 15 to 30 minutes, 20.7% 30 to 45 minutes, 15.4% 45 to 60 minutes, 18.7% 60 minutes or more (2000)

PRAIRIE GROVE (village). Covers a land area of 4.633 square miles and a water area of 0.139 square miles. Located at 42.27° N. Lat.; 88.26° W. Long. Elevation is 760 feet.
Population: 960 (2000); Race: 98.2% White, 0.4% Black, 0.3% Asian, 0.4% American Indian and Alaska Native, 2.5% Hispanic of any race, 0.0% two or more races (2000); Density: 207.2 persons per square mile (2000); Age: 33.8% under 18, 6.2% over 64 (2000); Marriage status: 22.3% never married, 65.4% now married, 4.2% widowed, 8.1% divorced (2000); Foreign born: 3.7% (2000); Ancestry (includes multiple ancestries): 30.7% German, 17.0% Irish, 11.4% Polish, 8.2% Italian, 7.5% English (2000).
Economy: Light manufacturing. Single-family building permits issued: 49 (2001) / 42 (2000); Multi-family building permits issued: 0 (2001) / 0 (2000); Employment by occupation: 22.3% management, 21.2% professional, 14.0% services, 21.1% sales, 0.4% farming, 10.9% construction, 10.2% production (2000).
Income: Per capita income: $36,234 (2000); Median household income: $93,361 (2000); Poverty rate: 1.3% (2000).
Taxes: Total city taxes per capita: $240 (1997); City property taxes per capita: $164 (1997).
Education: High school graduation rate: 91.0% (2000); College graduation rate: 38.1% (2000).
Housing: Homeownership rate: 88.9% (2000); Median home value: $285,800 (2000); Median rent: $675 per month (2000); Median age of housing: 22 years (2000).
Transportation: Commute to work: 94.7% car, 2.0% public transportation, 0.0% walk, 3.3% work from home (2000); Travel time to work: 25.2% less than 15 minutes, 25.8% 15 to 30 minutes, 21.8% 30 to 45 minutes, 10.7% 45 to 60 minutes, 16.5% 60 minutes or more (2000)

RICHMOND (village). Covers a land area of 1.360 square miles and a water area of 0 square miles. Located at 42.47° N. Lat.; 88.30° W. Long. Elevation is 820 feet.
History: Richmond was settled in 1837, and developed around a grist mill.
Population: 1,091 (2000); Race: 97.8% White, 0.0% Black, 0.0% Asian, 0.5% American Indian and Alaska Native, 5.6% Hispanic of any race, 0.4% two or more races (2000); Density: 802.2 persons per square mile (2000); Age: 31.7% under 18, 12.4% over 64 (2000); Marriage status: 27.8% never married, 56.1% now married, 6.3% widowed, 9.8% divorced (2000); Foreign born: 3.4% (2000); Ancestry (includes multiple ancestries): 36.9% German, 20.5% Irish, 11.3% Polish, 9.6% English, 9.1% Italian (2000).
Economy: Single-family building permits issued: 0 (2001) / 6 (2000); Multi-family building permits issued: 0 (2001) / 0 (2000); Employment by occupation: 12.2% management, 14.9% professional, 15.1% services, 20.7% sales, 0.0% farming, 14.9% construction, 22.3% production (2000).
Income: Per capita income: $22,332 (2000); Median household income: $52,361 (2000); Poverty rate: 6.5% (2000).
Taxes: Total city taxes per capita: $360 (1997); City property taxes per capita: $179 (1997).
Education: High school graduation rate: 88.8% (2000); College graduation rate: 21.0% (2000).

School District(s)

Nippersink School District 2 (KG-08)
2000 Enrollment: 1,524 815-678-7129
Richmond Cons School District 13 (N -N)
2000 Enrollment: n/a 815-678-4717
Richmond-Burton Community H Sc D 157 (09-12)
2000 Enrollment: 556 815-678-4525

Housing: Homeownership rate: 72.3% (2000); Median home value: $140,100 (2000); Median rent: $581 per month (2000); Median age of housing: 45 years (2000).
Transportation: Commute to work: 84.2% car, 1.8% public transportation, 9.0% walk, 4.6% work from home (2000); Travel time to work: 42.2% less than 15 minutes, 22.5% 15 to 30 minutes, 17.1% 30 to 45 minutes, 7.9% 45 to 60 minutes, 10.2% 60 minutes or more (2000)

Additional Information Contacts

Richmond/Spring Grove Chamber 815-678-7742

RINGWOOD (village). Covers a land area of 2.338 square miles and a water area of 0 square miles. Located at 42.39° N. Lat.; 88.30° W. Long. Elevation is 840 feet.
Population: 471 (2000); Race: 98.0% White, 0.9% Black, 1.1% Asian, 0.0% American Indian and Alaska Native, 0.0% Hispanic of any race, 0.0% two or more races (2000); Density: 201.5 persons per square mile (2000); Age:

19.6% under 18, 15.3% over 64 (2000); Marriage status: 19.5% never married, 70.1% now married, 5.7% widowed, 4.7% divorced (2000); Foreign born: 7.0% (2000); Ancestry (includes multiple ancestries): 42.1% German, 14.9% Irish, 11.3% English, 9.2% Polish, 7.2% Italian (2000).
Economy: Employment by occupation: 14.8% management, 16.9% professional, 7.8% services, 28.0% sales, 1.6% farming, 16.9% construction, 14.0% production (2000).
Income: Per capita income: $27,137 (2000); Median household income: $71,250 (2000); Poverty rate: 0.9% (2000).
Taxes: Total city taxes per capita: $65 (1997); City property taxes per capita: $27 (1997).
Education: High school graduation rate: 85.9% (2000); College graduation rate: 20.6% (2000).
Housing: Homeownership rate: 88.4% (2000); Median home value: $200,700 (2000); Median rent: $566 per month (2000); Median age of housing: 29 years (2000).
Transportation: Commute to work: 86.3% car, 2.9% public transportation, 5.4% walk, 5.4% work from home (2000); Travel time to work: 34.4% less than 15 minutes, 27.3% 15 to 30 minutes, 16.7% 30 to 45 minutes, 5.3% 45 to 60 minutes, 16.3% 60 minutes or more (2000)

SPRING GROVE (village). Covers a land area of 6.211 square miles and a water area of 0.025 square miles. Located at 42.45° N. Lat.; 88.24° W. Long. Elevation is 800 feet.
Population: 3,880 (2000); Race: 97.0% White, 0.2% Black, 0.9% Asian, 0.1% American Indian and Alaska Native, 1.9% Hispanic of any race, 0.7% two or more races (2000); Density: 624.7 persons per square mile (2000); Age: 36.3% under 18, 4.4% over 64 (2000); Marriage status: 18.1% never married, 76.1% now married, 2.4% widowed, 3.4% divorced (2000); Foreign born: 2.1% (2000); Ancestry (includes multiple ancestries): 37.7% German, 18.9% Irish, 18.6% Polish, 7.7% Italian, 7.6% English (2000).
Economy: In agricultural and lake-resort area. Single-family building permits issued: 76 (2001) / 81 (2000); Multi-family building permits issued: 0 (2001) / 0 (2000); Employment by occupation: 19.8% management, 19.3% professional, 10.2% services, 26.1% sales, 0.2% farming, 12.7% construction, 11.7% production (2000).
Income: Per capita income: $25,506 (2000); Median household income: $80,542 (2000); Poverty rate: 2.4% (2000).
Taxes: Total city taxes per capita: $251 (1997); City property taxes per capita: $41 (1997).
Education: High school graduation rate: 94.1% (2000); College graduation rate: 28.7% (2000).

School District(s)

Spring Grove School District 11 (N -N)
2000 Enrollment: n/a 815-675-2342

Housing: Homeownership rate: 95.8% (2000); Median home value: $241,000 (2000); Median rent: $538 per month (2000); Median age of housing: 7 years (2000).
Transportation: Commute to work: 90.6% car, 3.7% public transportation, 1.9% walk, 3.8% work from home (2000); Travel time to work: 19.4% less than 15 minutes, 23.9% 15 to 30 minutes, 17.6% 30 to 45 minutes, 16.4% 45 to 60 minutes, 22.8% 60 minutes or more (2000)

TROUT VALLEY (village). Covers a land area of 0.428 square miles and a water area of <.001 square miles. Located at 42.19° N. Lat.; 88.25° W. Long.
Population: 599 (2000); Race: 94.6% White, 1.3% Black, 1.7% Asian, 0.0% American Indian and Alaska Native, 0.7% Hispanic of any race, 1.7% two or more races (2000); Density: 1,399.7 persons per square mile (2000); Age: 31.3% under 18, 10.3% over 64 (2000); Marriage status: 16.4% never married, 75.1% now married, 2.8% widowed, 5.8% divorced (2000); Foreign born: 4.2% (2000); Ancestry (includes multiple ancestries): 28.5% German, 24.6% Irish, 17.0% Italian, 10.6% English, 7.9% Polish (2000).
Economy: Employment by occupation: 30.8% management, 23.7% professional, 2.3% services, 33.5% sales, 0.0% farming, 4.5% construction, 5.3% production (2000).
Income: Per capita income: $58,013 (2000); Median household income: $99,297 (2000); Poverty rate: 3.4% (2000).
Education: High school graduation rate: 96.4% (2000); College graduation rate: 60.6% (2000).
Housing: Homeownership rate: 97.9% (2000); Median home value: $297,200 (2000); Median rent: $850 per month (2000); Median age of housing: 35 years (2000).
Transportation: Commute to work: 77.8% car, 13.5% public transportation, 1.9% walk, 6.0% work from home (2000); Travel time to work: 24.8% less than 15 minutes, 14.0% 15 to 30 minutes, 14.8% 30 to 45 minutes, 16.8% 45 to 60 minutes, 29.6% 60 minutes or more (2000)

UNION (village). Covers a land area of 0.606 square miles and a water area of 0 square miles. Located at 42.23° N. Lat.; 88.54° W. Long. Elevation is 840 feet.
History: Illinois Railroad Museum here.
Population: 576 (2000); Race: 99.3% White, 0.3% Black, 0.0% Asian, 0.0% American Indian and Alaska Native, 3.4% Hispanic of any race, 0.0% two or more races (2000); Density: 950.4 persons per square mile (2000); Age: 25.7% under 18, 9.3% over 64 (2000); Marriage status: 25.5% never married, 62.3% now married, 4.0% widowed, 8.1% divorced (2000); Foreign born: 2.1% (2000); Ancestry (includes multiple ancestries): 53.8% German, 11.9% Irish, 6.7% Polish, 5.9% English, 4.7% Other groups (2000).
Economy: In agricultural area: corn; dairying. Manufacturing of consumer goods, transportation equipment, fabricated metal products. Single-family building permits issued: 1 (2001) / 2 (2000); Multi-family building permits issued: 0 (2001) / 0 (2000); Employment by occupation: 11.0% management, 14.6% professional, 14.0% services, 23.0% sales, 0.6% farming, 15.7% construction, 21.1% production (2000).
Income: Per capita income: $21,218 (2000); Median household income: $56,528 (2000); Poverty rate: 5.2% (2000).
Taxes: Total city taxes per capita: $275 (1997); City property taxes per capita: $77 (1997).
Education: High school graduation rate: 84.1% (2000); College graduation rate: 13.7% (2000).
Housing: Homeownership rate: 82.6% (2000); Median home value: $133,200 (2000); Median rent: $571 per month (2000); Median age of housing: 53 years (2000).
Transportation: Commute to work: 92.6% car, 1.5% public transportation, 1.8% walk, 4.2% work from home (2000); Travel time to work: 31.4% less than 15 minutes, 36.0% 15 to 30 minutes, 13.0% 30 to 45 minutes, 11.2% 45 to 60 minutes, 8.4% 60 minutes or more (2000)

WONDER LAKE (CDP). Aka Wonder Center. Covers a land area of 6.247 square miles and a water area of 0.965 square miles. Located at 42.38° N. Lat.; 88.35° W. Long. Elevation is 850 feet.
Population: 7,463 (2000); Race: 95.4% White, 0.0% Black, 0.4% Asian, 0.0% American Indian and Alaska Native, 5.0% Hispanic of any race, 1.1% two or more races (2000); Density: 1,194.6 persons per square mile (2000); Age: 27.8% under 18, 8.2% over 64 (2000); Marriage status: 22.3% never married, 64.1% now married, 5.4% widowed, 8.3% divorced (2000); Foreign born: 4.5% (2000); Ancestry (includes multiple ancestries): 35.1% German, 18.4% Irish, 13.6% Polish, 13.3% Italian, 8.2% English (2000).
Economy: Employment by occupation: 7.6% management, 11.2% professional, 13.1% services, 26.8% sales, 0.1% farming, 16.8% construction, 24.4% production (2000).
Income: Per capita income: $21,352 (2000); Median household income: $51,698 (2000); Poverty rate: 3.4% (2000).
Education: High school graduation rate: 85.3% (2000); College graduation rate: 10.0% (2000).

School District(s)

Harrison School District 36 (PK-08)
2000 Enrollment: 485 815-653-2311

Housing: Homeownership rate: 85.9% (2000); Median home value: $120,400 (2000); Median rent: $763 per month (2000); Median age of housing: 40 years (2000).
Transportation: Commute to work: 96.2% car, 1.1% public transportation, 1.1% walk, 1.4% work from home (2000); Travel time to work: 18.5% less than 15 minutes, 37.1% 15 to 30 minutes, 21.3% 30 to 45 minutes, 9.2% 45 to 60 minutes, 14.0% 60 minutes or more (2000)

Additional Information Contacts

Wonder Lake Chamber of Commerce 815-728-0682

WONDER LAKE (village). Aka Wonder Center. Covers a land area of 0.811 square miles and a water area of 0.005 square miles. Located at 42.38° N. Lat.; 88.36° W. Long. Elevation is 850 feet.
Population: 1,345 (2000); Race: 96.5% White, 0.1% Black, 0.0% Asian, 0.1% American Indian and Alaska Native, 5.3% Hispanic of any race, 1.7% two or more races (2000); Density: 1,657.4 persons per square mile (2000); Age: 34.5% under 18, 7.2% over 64 (2000); Marriage status: 21.2% never married, 66.0% now married, 3.7% widowed, 9.1% divorced (2000); Foreign born: 2.1% (2000); Ancestry (includes multiple ancestries): 37.0% German, 20.0% Irish, 14.8% Polish, 10.6% Italian, 8.3% Other groups (2000).
Economy: Agricultural area. Galt Wonder Lake Airport to North. Single-family building permits issued: 39 (2001) / 22 (2000); Multi-family

building permits issued: 0 (2001) / 0 (2000); Employment by occupation: 12.8% management, 13.0% professional, 14.1% services, 27.9% sales, 0.0% farming, 19.1% construction, 13.1% production (2000).
Income: Per capita income: $21,428 (2000); Median household income: $59,712 (2000); Poverty rate: 2.7% (2000).
Taxes: Total city taxes per capita: $80 (1997); City property taxes per capita: $64 (1997).
Education: High school graduation rate: 89.8% (2000); College graduation rate: 15.5% (2000).
Housing: Homeownership rate: 93.8% (2000); Median home value: $144,600 (2000); Median rent: $821 per month (2000); Median age of housing: 23 years (2000).
Transportation: Commute to work: 95.8% car, 2.1% public transportation, 0.0% walk, 1.7% work from home (2000); Travel time to work: 13.0% less than 15 minutes, 35.9% 15 to 30 minutes, 20.5% 30 to 45 minutes, 10.0% 45 to 60 minutes, 20.5% 60 minutes or more (2000)

WOODSTOCK (city). Covers a land area of 10.656 square miles and a water area of 0 square miles. Located at 42.31° N. Lat.; 88.44° W. Long. Elevation is 942 feet.
History: Woodstock was settled in the 1830's and 1840's by people from Vermont, who named it for the Vermont town. After 1844, Woodstock grew as the seat of McHenry County.
Population: 20,151 (2000); Race: 88.2% White, 0.5% Black, 2.0% Asian, 0.2% American Indian and Alaska Native, 19.0% Hispanic of any race, 1.7% two or more races (2000); Density: 1,891.1 persons per square mile (2000); Age: 27.9% under 18, 10.1% over 64 (2000); Marriage status: 24.4% never married, 58.4% now married, 6.1% widowed, 11.1% divorced (2000); Foreign born: 16.8% (2000); Ancestry (includes multiple ancestries): 31.3% German, 22.9% Other groups, 13.7% Irish, 8.4% English, 6.7% Polish (2000).
Vital Statistics: Birth rate: 162.3 per 10,000 population (1998)
Economy: Single-family building permits issued: 72 (2001) / 108 (2000); Multi-family building permits issued: 54 (2001) / 40 (2000); Employment by occupation: 12.5% management, 16.8% professional, 13.1% services, 24.1% sales, 0.7% farming, 9.7% construction, 23.0% production (2000).
Income: Per capita income: $23,210 (2000); Median household income: $47,871 (2000); Poverty rate: 7.2% (2000).
Taxes: Total city taxes per capita: $207 (1997); City property taxes per capita: $191 (1997).
Education: High school graduation rate: 80.1% (2000); College graduation rate: 22.9% (2000).

School District(s)

Mchenry Roe (08-10)
2000 Enrollment: 11 815-334-4475
Spec Education District of Mchenry Co-Sedom (PK-12)
2000 Enrollment: 157 815-338-3622
Woodstock C U School District 200 (PK-12)
2000 Enrollment: 5,435 815-337-5406

Housing: Homeownership rate: 61.1% (2000); Median home value: $145,400 (2000); Median rent: $633 per month (2000); Median age of housing: 27 years (2000).
Hospitals: Memorial Medical Center (154 beds)
Newspapers: The Woodstock Independent (1 x week)
Transportation: Commute to work: 91.2% car, 3.7% public transportation, 1.9% walk, 2.1% work from home (2000); Travel time to work: 35.8% less than 15 minutes, 31.0% 15 to 30 minutes, 15.1% 30 to 45 minutes, 5.9% 45 to 60 minutes, 12.1% 60 minutes or more (2000)
Additional Information Contacts
Mchenry County Association of Realtors 815-338-3660
Woodstock Chamber of Commerce 815-338-2436

McLean County

Located in central Illinois; drained by the Sangamon and Mackinaw Rivers; includes Lake Bloomington. Covers a land area of 1,183.50 square miles, a water area of 2.80 square miles, and is located in the Central Time Zone. The county government was organized in 1830. County seat is Bloomington.

McLean County is part of the Bloomington-Normal, IL MSA. The entire metro area includes: McLean County

Weather Station: Chenoa — Elevation: 711 feet

	Jan	Feb	Mar	Apr	May	Jun	Jul	Aug	Sep	Oct	Nov	Dec
High	31	37	49	63	74	83	86	84	78	65	50	37
Low	15	20	30	40	50	60	64	61	54	43	32	21
Precip	1.6	1.4	3.0	3.4	3.9	4.1	3.4	3.3	3.1	2.7	2.6	2.5
Snow	7.0	5.4	2.8	1.1	tr	0.0	0.0	0.0	0.0	tr	1.6	4.8

High and Low temperatures in degrees Fahrenheit; Precipitation and Snow in inches

Population: 150,433 (2000); Race: 89.2% White, 6.0% Black, 2.1% Asian, 0.2% American Indian and Alaska Native, 2.4% Hispanic of any race, 1.5% two or more races (2000); Density: 127.1 persons per square mile (2000); Age: 23.4% under 18, 9.8% over 64 (2000).
Religion: Five largest groups: 12.6% Catholic Church, 6.5% The United Methodist Church, 3.7% Lutheran Church—Missouri Synod, 3.7% Christian Churches and Churches of Christ, 2.9% Evangelical Lutheran Church in America (2000).
Economy: Unemployment rate: 2.5% (11/2002); Total civilian labor force: 91,591 (11/2002); Leading industries: 26.2% finance & insurance; 11.9% retail trade; 9.5% administration, support, waste management, remediation services (2000); Companies that employ more than 1,000 persons: 7 (2000); Companies that employ more than 100 persons: 106 (2000); Farms: 1,475 totaling 696,575 acres (1997); Minority business ownership rate: 6.5% (1997); Women business ownership rate: 30.9% (1997); Retail sales per capita: $10,406 (1997). Single-family building permits issued: 990 (2001) / 650 (2000); Multi-family building permits issued: 560 (2001) / 259 (2000).
Income: Per capita income: $22,227 (2000); Median household income: $47,021 (2000); Poverty rate: 9.7% (2000); Bankruptcy rate: 4.64% (2001).
Taxes: Total county taxes per capita: $156 (2000); County property taxes per capita: $133 (2000).
Education: High school graduation rate: 90.7% (2000); College graduation rate: 36.2% (2000).
Housing: Homeownership rate: 66.4% (2000); Median home value: $114,800 (2000); Median rent: $461 per month (2000); Median age of housing: 27 years (2000).
Health: Birth rate: 128.2 per 10,000 population (1998); Age adjusted death rate: 80.7 per 10,000 population (1999); Age adjusted cancer mortality rate: 203.1 deaths per 100,000 population (1999). Air Quality Index: 69% good, 31% moderate, 0% unhealthy (percent of days in 2000). Number of physicians: 18.3 per 10,000 population (1999); Number of hospital beds: 27.2 per 10,000 population (1999).
Elections: 2000 Presidential election results: 41.0% Gore, 55.8% Bush, 2.5% Nader, 0.4% Buchanan
National and State Parks: Moraine View State Park
Additional Information Contacts
McLean County Government Offices 309-888-5110
Bloomington Chamber of Commerce 309-829-6344
Bloomington Normal Association of Realtors 309-829-3341

McLean County Communities

ANCHOR (village). Covers a land area of 0.193 square miles and a water area of 0 square miles. Located at 40.56° N. Lat.; 88.53° W. Long. Elevation is 778 feet.
Population: 175 (2000); Race: 99.4% White, 0.0% Black, 0.0% Asian, 0.6% American Indian and Alaska Native, 0.0% Hispanic of any race, 0.0% two or more races (2000); Density: 904.5 persons per square mile (2000); Age: 30.1% under 18, 25.8% over 64 (2000); Marriage status: 16.0% never married, 66.4% now married, 8.8% widowed, 8.8% divorced (2000); Foreign born: 0.0% (2000); Ancestry (includes multiple ancestries): 38.7% German, 32.5% Irish, 12.9% English, 11.7% Other groups, 6.1% Norwegian (2000).
Economy: Single-family building permits issued: 0 (2001) / 1 (2000); Multi-family building permits issued: 0 (2001) / 0 (2000); Employment by occupation: 1.4% management, 13.7% professional, 11.0% services, 37.0% sales, 0.0% farming, 17.8% construction, 19.2% production (2000).
Income: Per capita income: $17,642 (2000); Median household income: $50,250 (2000); Poverty rate: 1.9% (2000).
Taxes: Total city taxes per capita: $48 (1997); City property taxes per capita: $48 (1997).
Education: High school graduation rate: 86.4% (2000); College graduation rate: 10.0% (2000).
Housing: Homeownership rate: 92.2% (2000); Median home value: $55,000 (2000); Median rent: $342 per month (2000); Median age of housing: 50 years (2000).
Transportation: Commute to work: 97.3% car, 0.0% public transportation, 0.0% walk, 2.7% work from home (2000); Travel time to work: 21.1% less

than 15 minutes, 14.1% 15 to 30 minutes, 50.7% 30 to 45 minutes, 7.0% 45 to 60 minutes, 7.0% 60 minutes or more (2000)

ARROWSMITH (village). Covers a land area of 0.203 square miles and a water area of 0 square miles. Located at 40.44° N. Lat.; 88.63° W. Long. Elevation is 881 feet.

Population: 298 (2000); Race: 97.4% White, 0.0% Black, 1.0% Asian, 0.0% American Indian and Alaska Native, 0.0% Hispanic of any race, 1.6% two or more races (2000); Density: 1,464.4 persons per square mile (2000); Age: 27.9% under 18, 10.1% over 64 (2000); Marriage status: 15.1% never married, 72.7% now married, 4.2% widowed, 8.0% divorced (2000); Foreign born: 1.0% (2000); Ancestry (includes multiple ancestries): 24.7% German, 11.0% Irish, 9.7% Other groups, 7.5% United States or American, 6.8% English (2000).

Economy: In grain-growing area. Single-family building permits issued: 0 (2001) / 1 (2000); Multi-family building permits issued: 0 (2001) / 0 (2000); Employment by occupation: 8.7% management, 17.4% professional, 14.0% services, 27.3% sales, 1.7% farming, 15.7% construction, 15.1% production (2000).

Income: Per capita income: $17,261 (2000); Median household income: $49,375 (2000); Poverty rate: 3.3% (2000).

Taxes: Total city taxes per capita: $34 (1997); City property taxes per capita: $27 (1997).

Education: High school graduation rate: 94.2% (2000); College graduation rate: 16.9% (2000).

Housing: Homeownership rate: 90.9% (2000); Median home value: $77,900 (2000); Median rent: $517 per month (2000); Median age of housing: 56 years (2000).

Transportation: Commute to work: 94.7% car, 0.0% public transportation, 4.1% walk, 1.2% work from home (2000); Travel time to work: 11.4% less than 15 minutes, 40.7% 15 to 30 minutes, 37.7% 30 to 45 minutes, 6.6% 45 to 60 minutes, 3.6% 60 minutes or more (2000)

BELLFLOWER (village). Covers a land area of 0.365 square miles and a water area of 0 square miles. Located at 40.34° N. Lat.; 88.52° W. Long. Elevation is 797 feet.

Population: 408 (2000); Race: 100.0% White, 0.0% Black, 0.0% Asian, 0.0% American Indian and Alaska Native, 0.0% Hispanic of any race, 0.0% two or more races (2000); Density: 1,118.1 persons per square mile (2000); Age: 36.1% under 18, 12.8% over 64 (2000); Marriage status: 19.6% never married, 61.5% now married, 8.2% widowed, 10.7% divorced (2000); Foreign born: 0.0% (2000); Ancestry (includes multiple ancestries): 25.8% German, 13.3% English, 8.6% Other groups, 8.4% Irish, 5.4% United States or American (2000).

Economy: Single-family building permits issued: 0 (2001) / 0 (2000); Multi-family building permits issued: 0 (2001) / 0 (2000); Employment by occupation: 11.3% management, 9.9% professional, 13.7% services, 31.1% sales, 1.4% farming, 10.8% construction, 21.7% production (2000).

Income: Per capita income: $16,200 (2000); Median household income: $41,442 (2000); Poverty rate: 0.5% (2000).

Education: High school graduation rate: 85.5% (2000); College graduation rate: 12.0% (2000).

Housing: Homeownership rate: 83.1% (2000); Median home value: $65,200 (2000); Median rent: $315 per month (2000); Median age of housing: 60 years (2000).

Transportation: Commute to work: 92.8% car, 0.0% public transportation, 1.4% walk, 3.4% work from home (2000); Travel time to work: 14.9% less than 15 minutes, 23.9% 15 to 30 minutes, 52.2% 30 to 45 minutes, 5.0% 45 to 60 minutes, 4.0% 60 minutes or more (2000)

BLOOMINGTON (city). Covers a land area of 22.500 square miles and a water area of 0 square miles. Located at 40.47° N. Lat.; 88.98° W. Long. Elevation is 829 feet.

History: Bloomington was laid out in 1831 on land belonging to James Allin, adjoining the settlement called Blooming Grove. Allin also donated land for the county courthouse. Bloomington's growth was given impetus by the founding in 1853 of Illinois Wesleyan University, and the arrival in 1854 of both the Illinois Central and the Chicago & Mississippi Railroads. Adlai Stevenson (1835-1914) practiced law in Bloomington before serving in Congress and as vice-president, and returned to Bloomington in 1900.

Population: 64,808 (2000); Race: 85.0% White, 8.4% Black, 2.9% Asian, 0.2% American Indian and Alaska Native, 3.3% Hispanic of any race, 2.2% two or more races (2000); Density: 2,880.3 persons per square mile (2000); Age: 24.7% under 18, 10.1% over 64 (2000); Marriage status: 29.7% never married, 54.1% now married, 5.3% widowed, 10.9% divorced (2000); Foreign born: 4.5% (2000); Ancestry (includes multiple ancestries): 28.0% German, 17.0% Other groups, 14.1% Irish, 10.8% English, 7.1% United States or American (2000).

Vital Statistics: Birth rate: 147.1 per 10,000 population (1998)

Economy: Unemployment rate: 2.9% (11/2002); Total civilian labor force: 39,432 (11/2002); Single-family building permits issued: 501 (2001) / 363 (2000); Multi-family building permits issued: 343 (2001) / 107 (2000); Employment by occupation: 16.9% management, 23.9% professional, 13.9% services, 28.1% sales, 0.2% farming, 6.7% construction, 10.4% production (2000).

Income: Per capita income: $24,751 (2000); Median household income: $46,496 (2000); Poverty rate: 7.8% (2000).

Taxes: Total city taxes per capita: $300 (2000); City property taxes per capita: $168 (2000).

Education: High school graduation rate: 89.8% (2000); College graduation rate: 39.7% (2000).

School District(s)

Bloomington School District 87 (PK-12)
2000 Enrollment: 5,731 309-827-6031

Four-year College(s)

Illinois Wesleyan University (Private, Not-for-profit, United Methodist)
2001 Enrollment: 2,064 309-556-1000
2001 Tuition: In-state $21,504; Out-of-state $21,504

Housing: Homeownership rate: 63.4% (2000); Median home value: $116,500 (2000); Median rent: $461 per month (2000); Median age of housing: 27 years (2000).

Hospitals: BroMenn Healthcare (247 beds); Saint Joseph Medical Center (182 beds)

Newspapers: The Pantagraph (7 x week); Twin City Community News (1 x week)

Transportation: Commute to work: 91.6% car, 1.4% public transportation, 3.5% walk, 2.7% work from home (2000); Travel time to work: 58.8% less than 15 minutes, 31.1% 15 to 30 minutes, 4.0% 30 to 45 minutes, 2.9% 45 to 60 minutes, 3.0% 60 minutes or more (2000); Amtrak: Service available.

Airports: Central IL Regional Airport at Bloomingt (primary service)

Additional Information Contacts

Bloomington Chamber of Commerce 309-829-6344
Bloomington Normal Association of Realtors 309-829-3341

CARLOCK (village). Covers a land area of 0.244 square miles and a water area of 0 square miles. Located at 40.58° N. Lat.; 89.13° W. Long. Elevation is 770 feet.

Population: 456 (2000); Race: 97.4% White, 1.1% Black, 1.1% Asian, 0.0% American Indian and Alaska Native, 0.2% Hispanic of any race, 0.4% two or more races (2000); Density: 1,871.8 persons per square mile (2000); Age: 23.2% under 18, 13.9% over 64 (2000); Marriage status: 22.3% never married, 68.8% now married, 1.9% widowed, 7.1% divorced (2000); Foreign born: 1.5% (2000); Ancestry (includes multiple ancestries): 44.2% German, 13.5% Irish, 9.9% Other groups, 7.7% English, 5.7% French (except Basque) (2000).

Economy: Agriculture: corn, soybeans; cattle. Single-family building permits issued: 1 (2001) / 0 (2000); Multi-family building permits issued: 0 (2001) / 0 (2000); Employment by occupation: 12.2% management, 16.8% professional, 20.2% services, 22.3% sales, 0.0% farming, 12.2% construction, 16.4% production (2000).

Income: Per capita income: $20,227 (2000); Median household income: $50,000 (2000); Poverty rate: 5.3% (2000).

Taxes: Total city taxes per capita: $23 (1997); City property taxes per capita: $23 (1997).

Education: High school graduation rate: 86.9% (2000); College graduation rate: 22.6% (2000).

Housing: Homeownership rate: 76.5% (2000); Median home value: $83,700 (2000); Median rent: $413 per month (2000); Median age of housing: 52 years (2000).

Transportation: Commute to work: 98.7% car, 0.0% public transportation, 0.8% walk, 0.4% work from home (2000); Travel time to work: 23.3% less than 15 minutes, 60.2% 15 to 30 minutes, 11.9% 30 to 45 minutes, 2.5% 45 to 60 minutes, 2.1% 60 minutes or more (2000)

CHENOA (city). Covers a land area of 1.253 square miles and a water area of 0.037 square miles. Located at 40.74° N. Lat.; 88.72° W. Long. Elevation is 717 feet.

History: Chenoa was laid out in 1856 by Matthew T. Scott, and grew up around the junction of the Peoria & Oquawka and the Chicago & Mississippi Railroads. Chenoa is of Indian origin and means "white dove."

Population: 1,845 (2000); Race: 98.8% White, 0.0% Black, 0.0% Asian, 0.0% American Indian and Alaska Native, 4.4% Hispanic of any race, 0.2%

two or more races (2000); Density: 1,472.2 persons per square mile (2000); Age: 26.8% under 18, 14.6% over 64 (2000); Marriage status: 14.6% never married, 68.8% now married, 7.3% widowed, 9.3% divorced (2000); Foreign born: 1.1% (2000); Ancestry (includes multiple ancestries): 31.5% German, 12.8% Irish, 12.8% English, 11.1% United States or American, 9.0% Other groups (2000).
Economy: Single-family building permits issued: 8 (2001) / 4 (2000); Multi-family building permits issued: 0 (2001) / 0 (2000); Employment by occupation: 8.2% management, 10.6% professional, 20.3% services, 25.9% sales, 0.4% farming, 10.3% construction, 24.3% production (2000).
Income: Per capita income: $19,559 (2000); Median household income: $44,420 (2000); Poverty rate: 5.7% (2000).
Taxes: Total city taxes per capita: $50 (1997); City property taxes per capita: $43 (1997).
Education: High school graduation rate: 83.0% (2000); College graduation rate: 15.1% (2000).

School District(s)

Chenoa C U School District 9 (PK-12)
2000 Enrollment: 484 815-945-7214
Housing: Homeownership rate: 81.8% (2000); Median home value: $74,800 (2000); Median rent: $369 per month (2000); Median age of housing: 45 years (2000).
Transportation: Commute to work: 92.2% car, 0.0% public transportation, 3.7% walk, 3.5% work from home (2000); Travel time to work: 38.6% less than 15 minutes, 31.0% 15 to 30 minutes, 24.7% 30 to 45 minutes, 2.8% 45 to 60 minutes, 2.9% 60 minutes or more (2000)

COLFAX (village). Covers a land area of 0.541 square miles and a water area of 0 square miles. Located at 40.56° N. Lat.; 88.61° W. Long. Elevation is 759 feet.
History: Site of defunct coal mine.
Population: 989 (2000); Race: 97.6% White, 0.0% Black, 0.0% Asian, 0.6% American Indian and Alaska Native, 1.6% Hispanic of any race, 1.3% two or more races (2000); Density: 1,829.4 persons per square mile (2000); Age: 25.6% under 18, 22.4% over 64 (2000); Marriage status: 15.1% never married, 64.4% now married, 10.1% widowed, 10.4% divorced (2000); Foreign born: 0.3% (2000); Ancestry (includes multiple ancestries): 37.7% German, 15.6% English, 11.7% United States or American, 11.5% Irish, 5.1% Other groups (2000).
Economy: In rich agricultural area: corn, soybeans; cattle. Single-family building permits issued: 6 (2001) / 6 (2000); Multi-family building permits issued: 0 (2001) / 0 (2000); Employment by occupation: 9.8% management, 15.9% professional, 14.8% services, 29.4% sales, 0.8% farming, 11.1% construction, 18.2% production (2000).
Income: Per capita income: $17,993 (2000); Median household income: $41,544 (2000); Poverty rate: 3.1% (2000).
Taxes: Total city taxes per capita: $146 (1997); City property taxes per capita: $65 (1997).
Education: High school graduation rate: 81.2% (2000); College graduation rate: 15.3% (2000).

School District(s)

Ridgeview Community Unit School District 19 (PK-12)
2000 Enrollment: 738 309-723-5111
Housing: Homeownership rate: 80.0% (2000); Median home value: $74,000 (2000); Median rent: $299 per month (2000); Median age of housing: 52 years (2000).
Transportation: Commute to work: 90.6% car, 0.8% public transportation, 4.2% walk, 3.4% work from home (2000); Travel time to work: 30.6% less than 15 minutes, 14.1% 15 to 30 minutes, 44.3% 30 to 45 minutes, 3.9% 45 to 60 minutes, 7.2% 60 minutes or more (2000)

COOKSVILLE (village). Covers a land area of 0.232 square miles and a water area of 0 square miles. Located at 40.54° N. Lat.; 88.71° W. Long. Elevation is 775 feet.
Population: 213 (2000); Race: 100.0% White, 0.0% Black, 0.0% Asian, 0.0% American Indian and Alaska Native, 0.0% Hispanic of any race, 0.0% two or more races (2000); Density: 917.9 persons per square mile (2000); Age: 29.8% under 18, 6.7% over 64 (2000); Marriage status: 13.1% never married, 72.6% now married, 4.6% widowed, 9.7% divorced (2000); Foreign born: 0.0% (2000); Ancestry (includes multiple ancestries): 23.1% German, 16.8% Irish, 8.0% Polish, 7.1% United States or American, 5.5% Scottish (2000).
Economy: In rich agricultural area. Single-family building permits issued: 0 (2001) / 0 (2000); Multi-family building permits issued: 0 (2001) / 0 (2000); Employment by occupation: 11.6% management, 6.2% professional, 12.4% services, 34.9% sales, 1.6% farming, 11.6% construction, 21.7% production (2000).
Income: Per capita income: $16,984 (2000); Median household income: $41,094 (2000); Poverty rate: 0.8% (2000).
Taxes: Total city taxes per capita: $75 (1997); City property taxes per capita: $70 (1997).
Education: High school graduation rate: 95.7% (2000); College graduation rate: 9.9% (2000).
Housing: Homeownership rate: 87.9% (2000); Median home value: $81,700 (2000); Median rent: $508 per month (2000); Median age of housing: 60+ years (2000).
Transportation: Commute to work: 96.9% car, 0.0% public transportation, 0.0% walk, 3.1% work from home (2000); Travel time to work: 16.8% less than 15 minutes, 63.2% 15 to 30 minutes, 14.4% 30 to 45 minutes, 4.0% 45 to 60 minutes, 1.6% 60 minutes or more (2000)

CROPSEY (unincorporated postal area, zip code 61731). Covers a land area of 19.941 square miles and a water area of 0 square miles. Located at 40.60° N. Lat.; 88.49° W. Long. Elevation is 798 feet.
Population: 254 (2000); Race: 100.0% White, 0.0% Black, 0.0% Asian, 0.0% American Indian and Alaska Native, 0.0% Hispanic of any race, 0.0% two or more races (2000); Density: 12.7 persons per square mile (2000); Age: 37.1% under 18, 12.9% over 64 (2000); Marriage status: 20.8% never married, 66.9% now married, 12.3% widowed, 0.0% divorced (2000); Foreign born: 0.0% (2000); Ancestry (includes multiple ancestries): 48.7% German, 8.5% English, 7.1% European, 6.3% Irish, 5.8% Other groups (2000).
Economy: Employment by occupation: 18.9% management, 6.6% professional, 0.0% services, 0.0% sales, 11.3% farming, 19.8% construction, 43.4% production (2000).
Income: Per capita income: $14,385 (2000); Median household income: $42,625 (2000); Poverty rate: 37.9% (2000).
Education: High school graduation rate: 72.4% (2000); College graduation rate: 8.2% (2000).
Housing: Homeownership rate: 72.2% (2000); Median home value: $62,400 (2000); Median rent: $325 per month (2000); Median age of housing: 60+ years (2000).
Transportation: Commute to work: 86.8% car, 0.0% public transportation, 0.0% walk, 13.2% work from home (2000); Travel time to work: 18.5% less than 15 minutes, 35.9% 15 to 30 minutes, 9.8% 30 to 45 minutes, 35.9% 45 to 60 minutes, 0.0% 60 minutes or more (2000)

DANVERS (village). Covers a land area of 0.864 square miles and a water area of 0 square miles. Located at 40.52° N. Lat.; 89.17° W. Long. Elevation is 810 feet.
Population: 1,183 (2000); Race: 97.8% White, 0.7% Black, 0.0% Asian, 0.3% American Indian and Alaska Native, 1.3% Hispanic of any race, 1.0% two or more races (2000); Density: 1,368.6 persons per square mile (2000); Age: 32.9% under 18, 7.5% over 64 (2000); Marriage status: 21.6% never married, 63.7% now married, 5.1% widowed, 9.7% divorced (2000); Foreign born: 1.5% (2000); Ancestry (includes multiple ancestries): 35.5% German, 10.4% Irish, 8.0% English, 5.0% Other groups, 5.0% United States or American (2000).
Economy: In rich agricultural area: corn, wheat, soybeans; cattle; dairying. Single-family building permits issued: 2 (2001) / 0 (2000); Multi-family building permits issued: 0 (2001) / 0 (2000); Employment by occupation: 13.3% management, 14.0% professional, 11.2% services, 26.8% sales, 0.3% farming, 13.8% construction, 20.5% production (2000).
Income: Per capita income: $19,598 (2000); Median household income: $52,647 (2000); Poverty rate: 6.5% (2000).
Taxes: Total city taxes per capita: $93 (1997); City property taxes per capita: $84 (1997).
Education: High school graduation rate: 94.3% (2000); College graduation rate: 21.7% (2000).
Housing: Homeownership rate: 85.3% (2000); Median home value: $93,200 (2000); Median rent: $377 per month (2000); Median age of housing: 42 years (2000).
Transportation: Commute to work: 95.1% car, 0.0% public transportation, 1.8% walk, 3.1% work from home (2000); Travel time to work: 15.3% less than 15 minutes, 64.1% 15 to 30 minutes, 18.6% 30 to 45 minutes, 0.7% 45 to 60 minutes, 1.4% 60 minutes or more (2000)

DOWNS (village). Covers a land area of 2.706 square miles and a water area of 0 square miles. Located at 40.39° N. Lat.; 88.88° W. Long. Elevation is 795 feet.

Population: 776 (2000); Race: 98.4% White, 0.9% Black, 0.0% Asian, 0.0% American Indian and Alaska Native, 1.2% Hispanic of any race, 0.4% two or more races (2000); Density: 286.8 persons per square mile (2000); Age: 29.8% under 18, 4.7% over 64 (2000); Marriage status: 19.8% never married, 64.8% now married, 4.6% widowed, 10.9% divorced (2000); Foreign born: 0.9% (2000); Ancestry (includes multiple ancestries): 33.5% German, 13.5% United States or American, 11.4% Irish, 11.3% English, 6.0% Other groups (2000).
Economy: In rich agricultural area: corn, wheat, soybeans, sorghum, cattle. Subdivisions encroaching from Northwest. Single-family building permits issued: 1 (2001) / 1 (2000); Multi-family building permits issued: 0 (2001) / 0 (2000); Employment by occupation: 12.9% management, 12.9% professional, 11.2% services, 33.3% sales, 0.9% farming, 8.7% construction, 20.1% production (2000).
Income: Per capita income: $22,468 (2000); Median household income: $53,750 (2000); Poverty rate: 4.3% (2000).
Taxes: Total city taxes per capita: $55 (1997); City property taxes per capita: $55 (1997).
Education: High school graduation rate: 87.5% (2000); College graduation rate: 21.1% (2000).

School District(s)

Tri Valley C U School District 3 (PK-12)
2000 Enrollment: 992 309-378-2351

Housing: Homeownership rate: 84.4% (2000); Median home value: $89,700 (2000); Median rent: $430 per month (2000); Median age of housing: 37 years (2000).
Transportation: Commute to work: 94.3% car, 0.0% public transportation, 1.0% walk, 3.8% work from home (2000); Travel time to work: 32.9% less than 15 minutes, 57.4% 15 to 30 minutes, 5.4% 30 to 45 minutes, 3.5% 45 to 60 minutes, 0.7% 60 minutes or more (2000)

ELLSWORTH (village). Covers a land area of 0.237 square miles and a water area of 0 square miles. Located at 40.44° N. Lat.; 88.71° W. Long. Elevation is 874 feet.
Population: 271 (2000); Race: 93.0% White, 0.0% Black, 0.0% Asian, 2.6% American Indian and Alaska Native, 1.1% Hispanic of any race, 2.6% two or more races (2000); Density: 1,145.7 persons per square mile (2000); Age: 33.0% under 18, 5.6% over 64 (2000); Marriage status: 21.6% never married, 69.8% now married, 3.5% widowed, 5.0% divorced (2000); Foreign born: 0.0% (2000); Ancestry (includes multiple ancestries): 39.3% German, 16.3% Irish, 13.7% Other groups, 11.9% United States or American, 8.5% English (2000).
Economy: In rich agricultural area. Single-family building permits issued: 0 (2001) / 1 (2000); Multi-family building permits issued: 0 (2001) / 0 (2000); Employment by occupation: 11.7% management, 12.4% professional, 13.1% services, 32.4% sales, 0.7% farming, 9.7% construction, 20.0% production (2000).
Income: Per capita income: $18,439 (2000); Median household income: $45,714 (2000); Poverty rate: 1.5% (2000).
Taxes: Total city taxes per capita: $42 (1997); City property taxes per capita: $42 (1997).
Education: High school graduation rate: 88.3% (2000); College graduation rate: 16.7% (2000).
Housing: Homeownership rate: 75.8% (2000); Median home value: $79,700 (2000); Median rent: $375 per month (2000); Median age of housing: 60+ years (2000).
Transportation: Commute to work: 90.8% car, 0.0% public transportation, 1.4% walk, 4.3% work from home (2000); Travel time to work: 11.9% less than 15 minutes, 40.0% 15 to 30 minutes, 40.7% 30 to 45 minutes, 5.9% 45 to 60 minutes, 1.5% 60 minutes or more (2000)

GRIDLEY (village). Covers a land area of 1.161 square miles and a water area of 0 square miles. Located at 40.74° N. Lat.; 88.88° W. Long. Elevation is 752 feet.
History: Gridley was named for Asahel Gridley (1810-1881), a New Yorker who came to Illinois in 1831 and served in the Civil War as a brigadier general.
Population: 1,411 (2000); Race: 98.5% White, 0.0% Black, 0.6% Asian, 0.1% American Indian and Alaska Native, 0.4% Hispanic of any race, 0.7% two or more races (2000); Density: 1,215.6 persons per square mile (2000); Age: 26.7% under 18, 16.7% over 64 (2000); Marriage status: 23.8% never married, 59.8% now married, 9.0% widowed, 7.3% divorced (2000); Foreign born: 0.6% (2000); Ancestry (includes multiple ancestries): 43.4% German, 10.1% Irish, 9.4% English, 7.8% United States or American, 6.7% Swiss (2000).
Economy: Single-family building permits issued: 6 (2001) / 5 (2000); Multi-family building permits issued: 0 (2001) / 0 (2000); Employment by occupation: 11.0% management, 18.4% professional, 15.5% services, 26.3% sales, 0.6% farming, 13.1% construction, 15.2% production (2000).
Income: Per capita income: $19,752 (2000); Median household income: $46,458 (2000); Poverty rate: 6.4% (2000).
Taxes: Total city taxes per capita: $68 (1997); City property taxes per capita: $67 (1997).
Education: High school graduation rate: 87.2% (2000); College graduation rate: 21.8% (2000).

School District(s)

Gridley C U School District 10 (PK-12)
2000 Enrollment: 382 309-747-3057

Housing: Homeownership rate: 79.7% (2000); Median home value: $87,400 (2000); Median rent: $408 per month (2000); Median age of housing: 37 years (2000).
Transportation: Commute to work: 93.4% car, 0.5% public transportation, 2.6% walk, 3.3% work from home (2000); Travel time to work: 30.6% less than 15 minutes, 28.1% 15 to 30 minutes, 33.1% 30 to 45 minutes, 5.8% 45 to 60 minutes, 2.5% 60 minutes or more (2000)

HEYWORTH (village). Covers a land area of 1.545 square miles and a water area of 0 square miles. Located at 40.31° N. Lat.; 88.97° W. Long. Elevation is 749 feet.
Population: 2,431 (2000); Race: 96.8% White, 0.3% Black, 0.4% Asian, 0.1% American Indian and Alaska Native, 0.7% Hispanic of any race, 2.1% two or more races (2000); Density: 1,573.6 persons per square mile (2000); Age: 31.1% under 18, 10.3% over 64 (2000); Marriage status: 17.1% never married, 67.8% now married, 5.6% widowed, 9.5% divorced (2000); Foreign born: 0.9% (2000); Ancestry (includes multiple ancestries): 25.3% German, 12.0% Irish, 11.8% United States or American, 9.3% Other groups, 8.9% English (2000).
Economy: Trade center in agricultural area: corn, soybeans; livestock. Single-family building permits issued: 16 (2001) / 13 (2000); Multi-family building permits issued: 0 (2001) / 0 (2000); Employment by occupation: 10.5% management, 15.7% professional, 12.4% services, 32.5% sales, 0.5% farming, 12.1% construction, 16.3% production (2000).
Income: Per capita income: $20,655 (2000); Median household income: $53,043 (2000); Poverty rate: 3.1% (2000).
Taxes: Total city taxes per capita: $179 (1997); City property taxes per capita: $130 (1997).
Education: High school graduation rate: 86.9% (2000); College graduation rate: 18.9% (2000).

School District(s)

Heyworth C U School District 4 (PK-12)
2000 Enrollment: 850 309-473-3727

Housing: Homeownership rate: 82.2% (2000); Median home value: $97,800 (2000); Median rent: $388 per month (2000); Median age of housing: 28 years (2000).
Newspapers: Heyworth Star (1 x week)
Transportation: Commute to work: 94.6% car, 0.2% public transportation, 0.8% walk, 3.8% work from home (2000); Travel time to work: 15.4% less than 15 minutes, 61.6% 15 to 30 minutes, 17.5% 30 to 45 minutes, 1.5% 45 to 60 minutes, 4.0% 60 minutes or more (2000)

HUDSON (village). Covers a land area of 0.665 square miles and a water area of 0 square miles. Located at 40.60° N. Lat.; 88.98° W. Long. Elevation is 765 feet.
History: Hudson was settled in 1836 by a group of New Yorkers called the Hudson Colony.
Population: 1,510 (2000); Race: 98.3% White, 0.0% Black, 0.9% Asian, 0.0% American Indian and Alaska Native, 0.4% Hispanic of any race, 0.7% two or more races (2000); Density: 2,272.1 persons per square mile (2000); Age: 33.3% under 18, 6.4% over 64 (2000); Marriage status: 16.7% never married, 74.8% now married, 2.8% widowed, 5.8% divorced (2000); Foreign born: 1.1% (2000); Ancestry (includes multiple ancestries): 38.8% German, 16.3% Irish, 10.9% English, 6.6% Other groups, 6.2% United States or American (2000).
Economy: Single-family building permits issued: 12 (2001) / 10 (2000); Multi-family building permits issued: 0 (2001) / 0 (2000); Employment by occupation: 11.9% management, 22.1% professional, 16.2% services, 27.4% sales, 0.6% farming, 8.6% construction, 13.3% production (2000).
Income: Per capita income: $22,141 (2000); Median household income: $62,632 (2000); Poverty rate: 1.2% (2000).
Taxes: Total city taxes per capita: $43 (1997); City property taxes per capita: $32 (1997).

Education: High school graduation rate: 92.5% (2000); College graduation rate: 30.4% (2000).
Housing: Homeownership rate: 92.3% (2000); Median home value: $118,500 (2000); Median rent: $505 per month (2000); Median age of housing: 24 years (2000).
Transportation: Commute to work: 96.4% car, 0.0% public transportation, 0.4% walk, 3.0% work from home (2000); Travel time to work: 21.7% less than 15 minutes, 67.3% 15 to 30 minutes, 7.0% 30 to 45 minutes, 2.7% 45 to 60 minutes, 1.2% 60 minutes or more (2000)

LE ROY (city). Aka Leroy. Covers a land area of 2.221 square miles and a water area of 0.016 square miles. Located at 40.34° N. Lat.; 88.76° W. Long. Elevation is 796 feet.
History: Incorporated 1857.
Population: 3,332 (2000); Race: 99.7% White, 0.3% Black, 0.0% Asian, 0.0% American Indian and Alaska Native, 0.1% Hispanic of any race, 0.0% two or more races (2000); Density: 1,500.3 persons per square mile (2000); Age: 25.7% under 18, 15.0% over 64 (2000); Marriage status: 19.6% never married, 64.4% now married, 7.4% widowed, 8.6% divorced (2000); Foreign born: 0.4% (2000); Ancestry (includes multiple ancestries): 23.9% German, 14.7% United States or American, 13.4% English, 12.4% Irish, 5.3% Other groups (2000).
Economy: Trade and processing center in rich agricultural area; food processing. Single-family building permits issued: 13 (2001) / 15 (2000); Multi-family building permits issued: 0 (2001) / 0 (2000); Employment by occupation: 9.9% management, 15.0% professional, 18.0% services, 28.2% sales, 0.9% farming, 10.6% construction, 17.4% production (2000).
Income: Per capita income: $20,743 (2000); Median household income: $45,781 (2000); Poverty rate: 1.9% (2000).
Taxes: Total city taxes per capita: $192 (1997); City property taxes per capita: $184 (1997).
Education: High school graduation rate: 87.7% (2000); College graduation rate: 16.7% (2000).

School District(s)

Leroy Community Unit School District 2 (PK-12)
2000 Enrollment: 834 309-962-4211

Housing: Homeownership rate: 78.2% (2000); Median home value: $95,300 (2000); Median rent: $401 per month (2000); Median age of housing: 36 years (2000).
Newspapers: The Le Roy Journal (1 x week)
Transportation: Commute to work: 93.3% car, 0.0% public transportation, 2.9% walk, 3.8% work from home (2000); Travel time to work: 24.9% less than 15 minutes, 48.3% 15 to 30 minutes, 20.7% 30 to 45 minutes, 3.6% 45 to 60 minutes, 2.5% 60 minutes or more (2000)

LEXINGTON (city). Covers a land area of 1.050 square miles and a water area of 0 square miles. Located at 40.64° N. Lat.; 88.78° W. Long. Elevation is 754 feet.
History: Lexington was settled in 1828 and named for the battlefield in Massachusetts. The town developed along the Chicago & Mississippi Railroad as a produce center.
Population: 1,912 (2000); Race: 98.6% White, 0.0% Black, 0.2% Asian, 0.4% American Indian and Alaska Native, 0.5% Hispanic of any race, 0.8% two or more races (2000); Density: 1,820.3 persons per square mile (2000); Age: 27.9% under 18, 13.3% over 64 (2000); Marriage status: 23.1% never married, 61.4% now married, 8.1% widowed, 7.4% divorced (2000); Foreign born: 0.5% (2000); Ancestry (includes multiple ancestries): 34.3% German, 16.6% Irish, 13.8% United States or American, 13.2% English, 5.4% Other groups (2000).
Economy: Single-family building permits issued: 5 (2001) / 8 (2000); Multi-family building permits issued: 0 (2001) / 0 (2000); Employment by occupation: 12.0% management, 18.4% professional, 13.1% services, 24.7% sales, 0.3% farming, 12.8% construction, 18.6% production (2000).
Income: Per capita income: $20,898 (2000); Median household income: $46,146 (2000); Poverty rate: 4.4% (2000).
Taxes: Total city taxes per capita: $120 (2000); City property taxes per capita: $112 (2000).
Education: High school graduation rate: 89.4% (2000); College graduation rate: 19.5% (2000).

School District(s)

Lexington C U School District 7 (PK-12)
2000 Enrollment: 577 309-365-4141

Housing: Homeownership rate: 83.6% (2000); Median home value: $100,100 (2000); Median rent: $358 per month (2000); Median age of housing: 41 years (2000).
Newspapers: The Lexingtonian (1 x week)
Transportation: Commute to work: 91.5% car, 0.2% public transportation, 3.0% walk, 4.9% work from home (2000); Travel time to work: 29.4% less than 15 minutes, 42.8% 15 to 30 minutes, 20.9% 30 to 45 minutes, 2.8% 45 to 60 minutes, 4.1% 60 minutes or more (2000)

MCLEAN (village). Covers a land area of 0.431 square miles and a water area of 0 square miles. Located at 40.31° N. Lat.; 89.17° W. Long. Elevation is 710 feet.
Population: 808 (2000); Race: 96.7% White, 0.0% Black, 2.1% Asian, 0.0% American Indian and Alaska Native, 0.0% Hispanic of any race, 1.2% two or more races (2000); Density: 1,874.1 persons per square mile (2000); Age: 26.2% under 18, 13.9% over 64 (2000); Marriage status: 15.3% never married, 70.0% now married, 4.7% widowed, 10.1% divorced (2000); Foreign born: 1.5% (2000); Ancestry (includes multiple ancestries): 26.7% German, 17.6% United States or American, 12.0% Irish, 8.1% English, 8.0% Other groups (2000).
Economy: In rich agricultural area: corn, soybeans; cattle. Single-family building permits issued: 0 (2001) / 0 (2000); Multi-family building permits issued: 0 (2001) / 0 (2000); Employment by occupation: 13.4% management, 13.2% professional, 14.5% services, 28.6% sales, 0.4% farming, 12.3% construction, 17.6% production (2000).
Income: Per capita income: $19,200 (2000); Median household income: $47,337 (2000); Poverty rate: 0.7% (2000).
Taxes: Total city taxes per capita: $29 (1997); City property taxes per capita: $28 (1997).
Education: High school graduation rate: 84.1% (2000); College graduation rate: 10.0% (2000).
Housing: Homeownership rate: 90.3% (2000); Median home value: $77,000 (2000); Median rent: $416 per month (2000); Median age of housing: 48 years (2000).
Transportation: Commute to work: 95.0% car, 0.0% public transportation, 1.6% walk, 2.3% work from home (2000); Travel time to work: 13.6% less than 15 minutes, 45.5% 15 to 30 minutes, 33.5% 30 to 45 minutes, 3.5% 45 to 60 minutes, 3.9% 60 minutes or more (2000)

NORMAL (town). Covers a land area of 13.619 square miles and a water area of 0.062 square miles. Located at 40.51° N. Lat.; 88.98° W. Long. Elevation is 800 feet.
History: Normal began as North Bloomington, but soon changed its name to Normal when the Illinois State Normal University was founded here in 1857.
Population: 45,386 (2000); Race: 87.3% White, 7.6% Black, 2.4% Asian, 0.2% American Indian and Alaska Native, 2.3% Hispanic of any race, 1.4% two or more races (2000); Density: 3,332.6 persons per square mile (2000); Age: 17.3% under 18, 7.7% over 64 (2000); Marriage status: 47.9% never married, 42.9% now married, 3.4% widowed, 5.9% divorced (2000); Foreign born: 3.6% (2000); Ancestry (includes multiple ancestries): 31.3% German, 15.1% Irish, 12.6% Other groups, 9.9% English, 5.1% Italian (2000).
Vital Statistics: Birth rate: 100.5 per 10,000 population (1998)
Economy: Unemployment rate: 2.2% (11/2002); Total civilian labor force: 28,834 (11/2002); Single-family building permits issued: 341 (2001) / 140 (2000); Multi-family building permits issued: 217 (2001) / 152 (2000); Employment by occupation: 13.3% management, 22.2% professional, 19.5% services, 32.4% sales, 0.1% farming, 4.8% construction, 7.6% production (2000).
Income: Per capita income: $17,775 (2000); Median household income: $40,379 (2000); Poverty rate: 19.3% (2000).
Taxes: Total city taxes per capita: $297 (2000); City property taxes per capita: $86 (2000).
Education: High school graduation rate: 93.9% (2000); College graduation rate: 42.4% (2000).

School District(s)

De Witt Livingston Mclean Roe (07-12)
2000 Enrollment: 162 309-888-5120
Isu Laboratory Schools (PK-12)
2000 Enrollment: 1,073 309-438-8542
Mclean County Unit District No 5 (PK-12)
2000 Enrollment: 10,128 309-452-4476

Four-year College(s)

Illinois State University (Public)
2001 Enrollment: 21,240 309-438-2111
2001 Tuition: In-state $3,332; Out-of-state $7,275

Two-year College(s)

Bloomington Normal School of Radiography (Private, Not-for-profit)
2001 Enrollment: n/a 309-452-2834

Heartland Community College (Public)
2001 Enrollment: 4,558 309-268-8000
2001 Tuition: In-state $203; Out-of-state $203
Housing: Homeownership rate: 54.9% (2000); Median home value: $120,400 (2000); Median rent: $480 per month (2000); Median age of housing: 23 years (2000).
Newspapers: Normalite (1 x week); Daily Vidette (5 x week)
Transportation: Commute to work: 83.8% car, 1.5% public transportation, 11.0% walk, 2.5% work from home (2000); Travel time to work: 55.9% less than 15 minutes, 35.4% 15 to 30 minutes, 4.3% 30 to 45 minutes, 2.2% 45 to 60 minutes, 2.3% 60 minutes or more (2000); Amtrak: Service available.
Airports: Central IL Regional Airport at Bloomingt (primary service)

SAYBROOK (village). Covers a land area of 0.792 square miles and a water area of 0.027 square miles. Located at 40.42° N. Lat.; 88.52° W. Long. Elevation is 790 feet.
Population: 764 (2000); Race: 96.7% White, 1.4% Black, 1.0% Asian, 0.0% American Indian and Alaska Native, 0.0% Hispanic of any race, 0.8% two or more races (2000); Density: 964.3 persons per square mile (2000); Age: 25.6% under 18, 14.8% over 64 (2000); Marriage status: 22.4% never married, 59.9% now married, 6.4% widowed, 11.3% divorced (2000); Foreign born: 0.7% (2000); Ancestry (includes multiple ancestries): 24.9% German, 8.9% United States or American, 8.9% Irish, 8.6% English, 4.3% Other groups (2000).
Economy: Grain, livestock, poultry. Single-family building permits issued: 1 (2001) / 1 (2000); Multi-family building permits issued: 0 (2001) / 0 (2000); Employment by occupation: 8.0% management, 7.6% professional, 21.0% services, 25.1% sales, 0.7% farming, 8.0% construction, 29.5% production (2000).
Income: Per capita income: $16,671 (2000); Median household income: $37,778 (2000); Poverty rate: 8.6% (2000).
Taxes: Total city taxes per capita: $33 (1997); City property taxes per capita: $5 (1997).
Education: High school graduation rate: 87.6% (2000); College graduation rate: 7.0% (2000).
Housing: Homeownership rate: 75.6% (2000); Median home value: $66,900 (2000); Median rent: $280 per month (2000); Median age of housing: 60+ years (2000).
Transportation: Commute to work: 93.7% car, 0.0% public transportation, 2.7% walk, 3.2% work from home (2000); Travel time to work: 16.6% less than 15 minutes, 21.7% 15 to 30 minutes, 36.8% 30 to 45 minutes, 19.6% 45 to 60 minutes, 5.3% 60 minutes or more (2000)

SHIRLEY (unincorporated postal area, zip code 61772). Covers a land area of 24.352 square miles and a water area of 0 square miles. Located at 40.40° N. Lat.; 89.06° W. Long. Elevation is 764 feet.
Population: 388 (2000); Race: 94.9% White, 0.0% Black, 2.0% Asian, 3.1% American Indian and Alaska Native, 3.1% Hispanic of any race, 0.0% two or more races (2000); Density: 15.9 persons per square mile (2000); Age: 14.8% under 18, 14.5% over 64 (2000); Marriage status: 18.4% never married, 60.5% now married, 8.2% widowed, 12.8% divorced (2000); Foreign born: 2.0% (2000); Ancestry (includes multiple ancestries): 30.7% German, 23.6% United States or American, 11.1% English, 8.0% Other groups, 6.3% Italian (2000).
Economy: Employment by occupation: 4.7% management, 16.8% professional, 23.7% services, 16.8% sales, 0.0% farming, 13.2% construction, 24.7% production (2000).
Income: Per capita income: $28,002 (2000); Median household income: $67,917 (2000); Poverty rate: 4.8% (2000).
Education: High school graduation rate: 93.0% (2000); College graduation rate: 22.4% (2000).
Housing: Homeownership rate: 85.2% (2000); Median home value: $80,800 (2000); Median rent: $425 per month (2000); Median age of housing: 39 years (2000).
Transportation: Commute to work: 97.4% car, 0.0% public transportation, 2.6% walk, 0.0% work from home (2000); Travel time to work: 11.1% less than 15 minutes, 75.8% 15 to 30 minutes, 3.2% 30 to 45 minutes, 10.0% 45 to 60 minutes, 0.0% 60 minutes or more (2000)

STANFORD (village). Covers a land area of 0.383 square miles and a water area of 0 square miles. Located at 40.43° N. Lat.; 89.22° W. Long. Elevation is 680 feet.
Population: 670 (2000); Race: 95.7% White, 0.0% Black, 0.0% Asian, 2.2% American Indian and Alaska Native, 3.3% Hispanic of any race, 2.1% two or more races (2000); Density: 1,749.8 persons per square mile (2000); Age: 29.8% under 18, 7.0% over 64 (2000); Marriage status: 27.5% never married, 58.2% now married, 6.8% widowed, 7.6% divorced (2000); Foreign born: 0.0% (2000); Ancestry (includes multiple ancestries): 25.9% German, 15.9% Irish, 10.7% United States or American, 9.7% Other groups, 6.4% Dutch (2000).
Economy: In rich agricultural area. Single-family building permits issued: 0 (2001) / 4 (2000); Multi-family building permits issued: 0 (2001) / 0 (2000); Employment by occupation: 8.0% management, 17.3% professional, 16.9% services, 24.0% sales, 0.0% farming, 11.2% construction, 22.7% production (2000).
Income: Per capita income: $18,687 (2000); Median household income: $49,375 (2000); Poverty rate: 3.7% (2000).
Taxes: Total city taxes per capita: $130 (1997); City property taxes per capita: $61 (1997).
Education: High school graduation rate: 85.7% (2000); College graduation rate: 12.5% (2000).

School District(s)

Olympia C U School District 16 (PK-12)
2000 Enrollment: 2,391 309-379-6011
Housing: Homeownership rate: 84.7% (2000); Median home value: $76,700 (2000); Median rent: $334 per month (2000); Median age of housing: 52 years (2000).
Transportation: Commute to work: 92.6% car, 0.0% public transportation, 2.6% walk, 2.9% work from home (2000); Travel time to work: 15.0% less than 15 minutes, 37.7% 15 to 30 minutes, 37.0% 30 to 45 minutes, 7.0% 45 to 60 minutes, 3.3% 60 minutes or more (2000)

TOWANDA (village). Covers a land area of 0.695 square miles and a water area of 0 square miles. Located at 40.56° N. Lat.; 88.89° W. Long. Elevation is 776 feet.
History: The first settler in Towanda was John Smith, who built a home in 1826 at Smith's Grove. The town of Towanda was laid out in 1854 when the railroad reached the community. The name is of Indian origin and means "where we bury our dead."
Population: 493 (2000); Race: 99.0% White, 0.4% Black, 0.0% Asian, 0.0% American Indian and Alaska Native, 0.6% Hispanic of any race, 0.0% two or more races (2000); Density: 709.0 persons per square mile (2000); Age: 24.6% under 18, 11.7% over 64 (2000); Marriage status: 18.0% never married, 66.8% now married, 7.0% widowed, 8.3% divorced (2000); Foreign born: 0.4% (2000); Ancestry (includes multiple ancestries): 33.3% German, 14.7% Irish, 14.5% English, 8.9% United States or American, 5.7% Italian (2000).
Economy: Single-family building permits issued: 0 (2001) / 3 (2000); Multi-family building permits issued: 0 (2001) / 0 (2000); Employment by occupation: 11.1% management, 12.8% professional, 12.8% services, 30.2% sales, 0.0% farming, 13.9% construction, 19.1% production (2000).
Income: Per capita income: $18,702 (2000); Median household income: $41,705 (2000); Poverty rate: 5.3% (2000).
Taxes: Total city taxes per capita: $140 (1997); City property taxes per capita: $56 (1997).
Education: High school graduation rate: 89.5% (2000); College graduation rate: 18.3% (2000).
Housing: Homeownership rate: 79.0% (2000); Median home value: $85,300 (2000); Median rent: $433 per month (2000); Median age of housing: 41 years (2000).
Transportation: Commute to work: 98.3% car, 0.0% public transportation, 0.0% walk, 1.7% work from home (2000); Travel time to work: 32.9% less than 15 minutes, 50.2% 15 to 30 minutes, 10.2% 30 to 45 minutes, 2.5% 45 to 60 minutes, 4.2% 60 minutes or more (2000)

Menard County

Located in central Illinois; drained by the Sangamon River and Salt Creek. Covers a land area of 314.20 square miles, a water area of 1.10 square miles, and is located in the Central Time Zone. The county government was organized in 1839. County seat is Petersburg.

Menard County is part of the Springfield, IL MSA. The entire metro area includes: Menard County; Sangamon County

Population: 12,486 (2000); Race: 98.1% White, 0.5% Black, 0.2% Asian, 0.3% American Indian and Alaska Native, 0.8% Hispanic of any race, 0.8% two or more races (2000); Density: 39.7 persons per square mile (2000); Age: 26.6% under 18, 13.3% over 64 (2000).

Religion: Five largest groups: 11.4% Catholic Church, 10.7% Christian Churches and Churches of Christ, 8.4% Southern Baptist Convention, 6.2% Presbyterian Church (U.S.A.), 6.1% The United Methodist Church (2000).
Economy: Unemployment rate: 4.4% (11/2002); Total civilian labor force: 6,155 (11/2002); Leading industries: 24.1% retail trade; 10.6% construction; 10.1% health care and social assistance (2000); Companies that employ more than 1,000 persons: 0 (2000); Companies that employ more than 100 persons: 0 (2000); Farms: 352 totaling 170,231 acres (1997); Minority business ownership rate: 0.0% (1997); Women business ownership rate: 24.7% (1997); Retail sales per capita: $4,681 (1997). Single-family building permits issued: 79 (2001) / 79 (2000); Multi-family building permits issued: 0 (2001) /.0 (2000).
Income: Per capita income: $21,584 (2000); Median household income: $46,596 (2000); Poverty rate: 8.2% (2000); Bankruptcy rate: 4.76% (2001).
Taxes: Total county taxes per capita: $173 (2000); County property taxes per capita: $173 (2000).
Education: High school graduation rate: 88.3% (2000); College graduation rate: 20.5% (2000).
Housing: Homeownership rate: 78.9% (2000); Median home value: $93,600 (2000); Median rent: $335 per month (2000); Median age of housing: 31 years (2000).
Health: Birth rate: 103.3 per 10,000 population (1998); Age adjusted death rate: 81.3 per 10,000 population (1999); Age adjusted cancer mortality rate: 204.7 deaths per 100,000 population (1999). Number of physicians: 8.0 per 10,000 population (1999); Number of hospital beds: n/a (1999).
Elections: 2000 Presidential election results: 34.9% Gore, 62.3% Bush, 2.2% Nader, 0.5% Buchanan
National and State Parks: Lincolns New Salem State Park
Additional Information Contacts
Menard County Government Offices 217-632-2415
Petersburg Chamber of Commerce 217-632-7363

Menard County Communities

ATHENS (city). Covers a land area of 1.468 square miles and a water area of 0 square miles. Located at 39.96° N. Lat.; 89.72° W. Long. Elevation is 606 feet.
History: Incorporated 1892.
Population: 1,726 (2000); Race: 97.1% White, 1.0% Black, 0.5% Asian, 0.0% American Indian and Alaska Native, 1.0% Hispanic of any race, 1.1% two or more races (2000); Density: 1,175.4 persons per square mile (2000); Age: 30.4% under 18, 10.7% over 64 (2000); Marriage status: 24.2% never married, 54.1% now married, 8.9% widowed, 12.8% divorced (2000); Foreign born: 0.6% (2000); Ancestry (includes multiple ancestries): 29.1% German, 13.2% Irish, 10.0% United States or American, 9.9% English, 7.0% Other groups (2000).
Economy: Ships grain. Agriculture: wheat, soybeans. Manufacturing: storage tanks. Single-family building permits issued: 20 (2001) / 18 (2000); Multi-family building permits issued: 0 (2001) / 0 (2000); Employment by occupation: 10.5% management, 15.5% professional, 14.1% services, 34.7% sales, 1.3% farming, 11.1% construction, 12.8% production (2000).
Income: Per capita income: $17,981 (2000); Median household income: $41,208 (2000); Poverty rate: 6.9% (2000).
Taxes: Total city taxes per capita: $47 (1997); City property taxes per capita: $32 (1997).
Education: High school graduation rate: 87.0% (2000); College graduation rate: 17.1% (2000).

School District(s)

Athens Community Unit School District 213 (PK-12)
2000 Enrollment: 1,036 217-636-8761
Housing: Homeownership rate: 77.0% (2000); Median home value: $85,000 (2000); Median rent: $369 per month (2000); Median age of housing: 30 years (2000).
Transportation: Commute to work: 95.7% car, 0.1% public transportation, 1.3% walk, 2.8% work from home (2000); Travel time to work: 11.5% less than 15 minutes, 46.1% 15 to 30 minutes, 34.9% 30 to 45 minutes, 4.2% 45 to 60 minutes, 3.2% 60 minutes or more (2000)

GREENVIEW (village). Covers a land area of 0.850 square miles and a water area of 0 square miles. Located at 40.08° N. Lat.; 89.74° W. Long. Elevation is 540 feet.
Population: 862 (2000); Race: 98.2% White, 1.3% Black, 0.0% Asian, 0.3% American Indian and Alaska Native, 0.0% Hispanic of any race, 0.2% two or more races (2000); Density: 1,014.2 persons per square mile (2000); Age: 24.7% under 18, 17.5% over 64 (2000); Marriage status: 22.9% never married, 57.9% now married, 8.5% widowed, 10.7% divorced (2000); Foreign born: 0.5% (2000); Ancestry (includes multiple ancestries): 33.2% German, 17.0% United States or American, 10.8% English, 9.3% Irish, 4.8% Other groups (2000).
Economy: Grain; livestock. Single-family building permits issued: 0 (2001) / 1 (2000); Multi-family building permits issued: 0 (2001) / 0 (2000); Employment by occupation: 10.4% management, 13.9% professional, 19.8% services, 26.3% sales, 2.4% farming, 13.9% construction, 13.3% production (2000).
Income: Per capita income: $21,050 (2000); Median household income: $39,196 (2000); Poverty rate: 7.5% (2000).
Taxes: Total city taxes per capita: $31 (1997); City property taxes per capita: $27 (1997).
Education: High school graduation rate: 82.5% (2000); College graduation rate: 17.3% (2000).

School District(s)

Greenview C U School District 200 (KG-12)
2000 Enrollment: 305 217-968-2295
Housing: Homeownership rate: 75.2% (2000); Median home value: $69,100 (2000); Median rent: $293 per month (2000); Median age of housing: 60+ years (2000).
Transportation: Commute to work: 88.6% car, 0.0% public transportation, 5.0% walk, 6.4% work from home (2000); Travel time to work: 27.6% less than 15 minutes, 22.0% 15 to 30 minutes, 39.1% 30 to 45 minutes, 8.2% 45 to 60 minutes, 3.0% 60 minutes or more (2000)

OAKFORD (village). Covers a land area of 0.247 square miles and a water area of 0 square miles. Located at 40.10° N. Lat.; 89.96° W. Long. Elevation is 495 feet.
Population: 309 (2000); Race: 100.0% White, 0.0% Black, 0.0% Asian, 0.0% American Indian and Alaska Native, 0.0% Hispanic of any race, 0.0% two or more races (2000); Density: 1,249.3 persons per square mile (2000); Age: 31.7% under 18, 16.8% over 64 (2000); Marriage status: 21.8% never married, 59.3% now married, 9.5% widowed, 9.5% divorced (2000); Foreign born: 0.0% (2000); Ancestry (includes multiple ancestries): 15.5% German, 13.7% United States or American, 12.8% English, 6.4% Irish, 4.9% Other groups (2000).
Economy: In agricultural area. Employment by occupation: 13.2% management, 10.3% professional, 16.9% services, 25.0% sales, 6.6% farming, 5.1% construction, 22.8% production (2000).
Income: Per capita income: $21,309 (2000); Median household income: $37,857 (2000); Poverty rate: 13.7% (2000).
Taxes: Total city taxes per capita: $32 (1997); City property taxes per capita: $18 (1997).
Education: High school graduation rate: 90.9% (2000); College graduation rate: 14.1% (2000).
Housing: Homeownership rate: 79.9% (2000); Median home value: $47,100 (2000); Median rent: $185 per month (2000); Median age of housing: 45 years (2000).
Transportation: Commute to work: 97.0% car, 0.0% public transportation, 3.0% walk, 0.0% work from home (2000); Travel time to work: 26.1% less than 15 minutes, 20.1% 15 to 30 minutes, 17.2% 30 to 45 minutes, 29.1% 45 to 60 minutes, 7.5% 60 minutes or more (2000)

PETERSBURG (city). Covers a land area of 1.348 square miles and a water area of 0 square miles. Located at 40.01° N. Lat.; 89.85° W. Long. Elevation is 524 feet.
History: Founded c.1836, incorporated 1841. Ann Rutledge's grave is here. Lincoln's New Salem (State Historic Site) is South.
Population: 2,299 (2000); Race: 97.7% White, 1.2% Black, 0.0% Asian, 0.8% American Indian and Alaska Native, 1.5% Hispanic of any race, 0.0% two or more races (2000); Density: 1,705.7 persons per square mile (2000); Age: 24.7% under 18, 21.4% over 64 (2000); Marriage status: 23.9% never married, 50.9% now married, 12.9% widowed, 12.3% divorced (2000); Foreign born: 0.5% (2000); Ancestry (includes multiple ancestries): 25.8% German, 13.2% English, 11.5% United States or American, 10.9% Irish, 7.1% Other groups (2000).
Economy: Agricultural area: corn, wheat, soybeans; livestock. Manufacturing. Single-family building permits issued: 6 (2001) / 9 (2000); Multi-family building permits issued: 0 (2001) / 0 (2000); Employment by occupation: 12.2% management, 25.7% professional, 23.8% services, 22.9% sales, 0.1% farming, 6.7% construction, 8.5% production (2000).
Income: Per capita income: $18,718 (2000); Median household income: $34,688 (2000); Poverty rate: 16.0% (2000).
Taxes: Total city taxes per capita: $107 (1997); City property taxes per capita: $91 (1997).

Education: High school graduation rate: 84.5% (2000); College graduation rate: 18.5% (2000).

School District(s)

Porta Community Unit School District 202 (PK-12)
2000 Enrollment: 1,469 217-632-3803

Housing: Homeownership rate: 60.9% (2000); Median home value: $81,400 (2000); Median rent: $303 per month (2000); Median age of housing: 43 years (2000).

Newspapers: Menard County Review (1 x week); The Petersburg Observer (1 x week)

Transportation: Commute to work: 94.8% car, 0.0% public transportation, 2.3% walk, 2.9% work from home (2000); Travel time to work: 36.8% less than 15 minutes, 9.2% 15 to 30 minutes, 40.6% 30 to 45 minutes, 11.2% 45 to 60 minutes, 2.1% 60 minutes or more (2000)

Additional Information Contacts

Petersburg Chamber of Commerce 217-632-7363

TALLULA (village). Covers a land area of 0.528 square miles and a water area of 0 square miles. Located at 39.94° N. Lat.; 89.93° W. Long. Elevation is 620 feet.

Population: 638 (2000); Race: 95.1% White, 0.3% Black, 0.0% Asian, 0.0% American Indian and Alaska Native, 0.5% Hispanic of any race, 4.1% two or more races (2000); Density: 1,207.4 persons per square mile (2000); Age: 27.6% under 18, 12.9% over 64 (2000); Marriage status: 22.0% never married, 66.1% now married, 6.1% widowed, 5.7% divorced (2000); Foreign born: 0.0% (2000); Ancestry (includes multiple ancestries): 18.4% German, 14.9% United States or American, 13.4% English, 12.7% Irish, 8.6% Other groups (2000).

Economy: In agricultural area. Employment by occupation: 8.1% management, 12.1% professional, 18.9% services, 18.9% sales, 2.7% farming, 21.9% construction, 17.5% production (2000).

Income: Per capita income: $16,088 (2000); Median household income: $38,269 (2000); Poverty rate: 18.9% (2000).

Taxes: Total city taxes per capita: $16 (1997); City property taxes per capita: $16 (1997).

Education: High school graduation rate: 73.3% (2000); College graduation rate: 7.1% (2000).

Housing: Homeownership rate: 82.5% (2000); Median home value: $53,100 (2000); Median rent: $354 per month (2000); Median age of housing: 57 years (2000).

Transportation: Commute to work: 96.6% car, 0.0% public transportation, 0.7% walk, 2.7% work from home (2000); Travel time to work: 11.4% less than 15 minutes, 25.9% 15 to 30 minutes, 33.4% 30 to 45 minutes, 23.8% 45 to 60 minutes, 5.5% 60 minutes or more (2000)

Mercer County

Located in northwestern Illinois; bounded on the west by the Mississippi River and the Iowa border; drained by the Edwards River. Covers a land area of 561.00 square miles, a water area of 7.90 square miles, and is located in the Central Time Zone. The county government was organized in 1825. County seat is Aledo.

Weather Station: Aledo — Elevation: 718 feet

	Jan	Feb	Mar	Apr	May	Jun	Jul	Aug	Sep	Oct	Nov	Dec
High	30	36	48	62	74	82	86	84	76	64	48	35
Low	13	19	29	40	51	60	64	62	53	42	31	19
Precip	1.3	1.3	2.5	3.6	4.0	4.4	4.1	4.4	3.4	2.8	2.5	2.0
Snow	8.7	6.1	4.0	1.1	tr	0.0	0.0	0.0	0.0	0.2	2.2	5.8

High and Low temperatures in degrees Fahrenheit; Precipitation and Snow in inches

Population: 16,957 (2000); Race: 98.7% White, 0.4% Black, 0.3% Asian, 0.1% American Indian and Alaska Native, 0.7% Hispanic of any race, 0.4% two or more races (2000); Density: 30.2 persons per square mile (2000); Age: 24.7% under 18, 16.0% over 64 (2000).

Religion: Five largest groups: 15.2% Catholic Church, 9.5% The United Methodist Church, 8.3% Evangelical Lutheran Church in America, 6.9% Presbyterian Church (U.S.A.), 3.4% American Baptist Churches in the USA (2000).

Economy: Unemployment rate: 6.0% (11/2002); Total civilian labor force: 8,685 (11/2002); Leading industries: 26.0% retail trade; 16.5% health care and social assistance; 14.1% manufacturing (2000); Companies that employ more than 1,000 persons: 0 (2000); Companies that employ more than 100 persons: 2 (2000); Farms: 754 totaling 309,591 acres (1997); Minority business ownership rate: 0.0% (1997); Women business ownership rate: 0.0% (1997); Retail sales per capita: $5,036 (1997). Single-family building permits issued: 25 (2001) / 39 (2000); Multi-family building permits issued: 0 (2001) / 2 (2000).

Income: Per capita income: $18,645 (2000); Median household income: $40,893 (2000); Poverty rate: 7.8% (2000); Bankruptcy rate: 5.23% (2001).

Taxes: Total county taxes per capita: $119 (2000); County property taxes per capita: $119 (2000).

Education: High school graduation rate: 84.9% (2000); College graduation rate: 12.6% (2000).

Housing: Homeownership rate: 79.7% (2000); Median home value: $68,500 (2000); Median rent: $292 per month (2000); Median age of housing: 48 years (2000).

Health: Birth rate: 106.2 per 10,000 population (1998); Age adjusted death rate: 77.7 per 10,000 population (1999); Age adjusted cancer mortality rate: 164.9 deaths per 100,000 population (1999). Number of physicians: 4.1 per 10,000 population (1999); Number of hospital beds: 26.5 per 10,000 population (1999).

Elections: 2000 Presidential election results: 52.9% Gore, 44.3% Bush, 1.9% Nader, 0.7% Buchanan

National and State Parks: Mark Twain National Wildlife Refuge

Additional Information Contacts

Mercer County Government Offices 309-582-7021
Aledo Chamber of Commerce 309-582-5373

Mercer County Communities

ALEDO (city). Covers a land area of 2.242 square miles and a water area of 0.014 square miles. Located at 41.20° N. Lat.; 90.75° W. Long. Elevation is 731 feet.

History: Aledo developed as a trading center, and as the seat of Mercer County.

Population: 3,613 (2000); Race: 98.3% White, 1.3% Black, 0.0% Asian, 0.0% American Indian and Alaska Native, 0.0% Hispanic of any race, 0.4% two or more races (2000); Density: 1,611.2 persons per square mile (2000); Age: 23.1% under 18, 21.0% over 64 (2000); Marriage status: 18.6% never married, 59.7% now married, 11.0% widowed, 10.8% divorced (2000); Foreign born: 0.0% (2000); Ancestry (includes multiple ancestries): 22.2% German, 14.1% English, 12.5% Irish, 12.3% United States or American, 9.3% Swedish (2000).

Economy: Single-family building permits issued: 1 (2001) / 0 (2000); Multi-family building permits issued: 0 (2001) / 2 (2000); Employment by occupation: 8.8% management, 19.8% professional, 18.5% services, 24.5% sales, 0.4% farming, 11.4% construction, 16.6% production (2000).

Income: Per capita income: $18,498 (2000); Median household income: $33,449 (2000); Poverty rate: 8.1% (2000).

Taxes: Total city taxes per capita: $56 (1997); City property taxes per capita: $56 (1997).

Education: High school graduation rate: 81.5% (2000); College graduation rate: 17.9% (2000).

School District(s)

Aledo Community Unit School District 201 (PK-12)
2000 Enrollment: 1,035 309-582-2238

Housing: Homeownership rate: 70.8% (2000); Median home value: $67,800 (2000); Median rent: $322 per month (2000); Median age of housing: 49 years (2000).

Newspapers: The Times Record (1 x week)

Transportation: Commute to work: 94.8% car, 0.0% public transportation, 2.3% walk, 1.3% work from home (2000); Travel time to work: 50.9% less than 15 minutes, 7.8% 15 to 30 minutes, 21.9% 30 to 45 minutes, 12.5% 45 to 60 minutes, 6.9% 60 minutes or more (2000)

Additional Information Contacts

Aledo Chamber of Commerce 309-582-5373

JOY (village). Covers a land area of 0.420 square miles and a water area of 0 square miles. Located at 41.19° N. Lat.; 90.88° W. Long. Elevation is 688 feet.

Population: 373 (2000); Race: 100.0% White, 0.0% Black, 0.0% Asian, 0.0% American Indian and Alaska Native, 0.2% Hispanic of any race, 0.0% two or more races (2000); Density: 888.3 persons per square mile (2000); Age: 32.3% under 18, 11.2% over 64 (2000); Marriage status: 17.6% never married, 64.0% now married, 7.6% widowed, 10.7% divorced (2000); Foreign born: 0.0% (2000); Ancestry (includes multiple ancestries): 28.3% German, 19.5% United States or American, 12.6% Irish, 10.2% English, 10.0% Swedish (2000).

Economy: In agricultural area. Single-family building permits issued: 1 (2001) / 0 (2000); Multi-family building permits issued: 0 (2001) / 0 (2000);

Employment by occupation: 3.6% management, 10.7% professional, 20.8% services, 15.5% sales, 0.6% farming, 17.9% construction, 31.0% production (2000).
Income: Per capita income: $14,201 (2000); Median household income: $36,625 (2000); Poverty rate: 18.6% (2000).
Education: High school graduation rate: 84.4% (2000); College graduation rate: 4.5% (2000).

School District(s)

Westmer Community Unit School District 203 (PK-12)
2000 Enrollment: 648 309-584-4173

Housing: Homeownership rate: 87.3% (2000); Median home value: $41,900 (2000); Median rent: $363 per month (2000); Median age of housing: 60+ years (2000).
Transportation: Commute to work: 91.5% car, 0.0% public transportation, 1.2% walk, 6.7% work from home (2000); Travel time to work: 41.8% less than 15 minutes, 13.1% 15 to 30 minutes, 19.0% 30 to 45 minutes, 18.3% 45 to 60 minutes, 7.8% 60 minutes or more (2000)

KEITHSBURG (city). Covers a land area of 2.579 square miles and a water area of 0.599 square miles. Located at 41.10° N. Lat.; 90.93° W. Long. Elevation is 549 feet.
History: Incorporated 1857.
Population: 714 (2000); Race: 95.9% White, 0.0% Black, 0.0% Asian, 1.2% American Indian and Alaska Native, 0.0% Hispanic of any race, 2.9% two or more races (2000); Density: 276.9 persons per square mile (2000); Age: 29.6% under 18, 12.0% over 64 (2000); Marriage status: 21.1% never married, 62.2% now married, 7.0% widowed, 9.7% divorced (2000); Foreign born: 0.0% (2000); Ancestry (includes multiple ancestries): 22.5% German, 9.7% Other groups, 9.7% Irish, 8.0% United States or American, 5.9% Swedish (2000).
Economy: In agricultural area. Mark Twain National Wildlife Refuge nearby. Single-family building permits issued: 2 (2001) / 1 (2000); Multi-family building permits issued: 0 (2001) / 0 (2000); Employment by occupation: 4.7% management, 9.0% professional, 20.1% services, 15.8% sales, 1.8% farming, 14.0% construction, 34.8% production (2000).
Income: Per capita income: $14,008 (2000); Median household income: $32,500 (2000); Poverty rate: 14.0% (2000).
Taxes: Total city taxes per capita: $99 (1997); City property taxes per capita: $27 (1997).
Education: High school graduation rate: 72.5% (2000); College graduation rate: 7.3% (2000).
Housing: Homeownership rate: 81.8% (2000); Median home value: $41,100 (2000); Median rent: $272 per month (2000); Median age of housing: 30 years (2000).
Transportation: Commute to work: 96.4% car, 0.0% public transportation, 2.2% walk, 1.4% work from home (2000); Travel time to work: 24.5% less than 15 minutes, 23.1% 15 to 30 minutes, 15.4% 30 to 45 minutes, 17.2% 45 to 60 minutes, 19.8% 60 minutes or more (2000)

MATHERVILLE (village). Covers a land area of 0.392 square miles and a water area of 0.007 square miles. Located at 41.26° N. Lat.; 90.60° W. Long. Elevation is 750 feet.
Population: 772 (2000); Race: 96.8% White, 0.0% Black, 0.6% Asian, 0.0% American Indian and Alaska Native, 1.2% Hispanic of any race, 1.4% two or more races (2000); Density: 1,968.7 persons per square mile (2000); Age: 34.8% under 18, 13.0% over 64 (2000); Marriage status: 21.4% never married, 55.6% now married, 6.7% widowed, 16.3% divorced (2000); Foreign born: 0.6% (2000); Ancestry (includes multiple ancestries): 17.8% Irish, 16.7% German, 14.1% United States or American, 10.6% English, 5.7% Dutch (2000).
Economy: In agricultural area. Single-family building permits issued: 3 (2001) / 3 (2000); Multi-family building permits issued: 0 (2001) / 0 (2000); Employment by occupation: 9.8% management, 5.0% professional, 17.7% services, 27.8% sales, 0.0% farming, 13.2% construction, 26.5% production (2000).
Income: Per capita income: $14,956 (2000); Median household income: $33,438 (2000); Poverty rate: 15.8% (2000).
Taxes: Total city taxes per capita: $75 (1997); City property taxes per capita: $74 (1997).
Education: High school graduation rate: 85.6% (2000); College graduation rate: 4.0% (2000).
Housing: Homeownership rate: 81.7% (2000); Median home value: $56,000 (2000); Median rent: $156 per month (2000); Median age of housing: 55 years (2000).
Transportation: Commute to work: 95.8% car, 0.0% public transportation, 0.0% walk, 2.9% work from home (2000); Travel time to work: 14.9% less than 15 minutes, 34.4% 15 to 30 minutes, 36.4% 30 to 45 minutes, 9.9% 45 to 60 minutes, 4.3% 60 minutes or more (2000)

NEW BOSTON (city). Covers a land area of 0.940 square miles and a water area of 0.453 square miles. Located at 41.17° N. Lat.; 90.99° W. Long. Elevation is 560 feet.
Population: 632 (2000); Race: 99.4% White, 0.0% Black, 0.0% Asian, 0.0% American Indian and Alaska Native, 1.0% Hispanic of any race, 0.6% two or more races (2000); Density: 672.6 persons per square mile (2000); Age: 22.4% under 18, 17.8% over 64 (2000); Marriage status: 16.7% never married, 61.5% now married, 8.8% widowed, 13.0% divorced (2000); Foreign born: 0.3% (2000); Ancestry (includes multiple ancestries): 17.8% German, 10.4% United States or American, 10.3% English, 6.6% Other groups, 6.4% Irish (2000).
Economy: In agricultural area. Employment by occupation: 5.2% management, 2.4% professional, 26.3% services, 22.3% sales, 2.0% farming, 15.9% construction, 25.9% production (2000).
Income: Per capita income: $15,593 (2000); Median household income: $29,231 (2000); Poverty rate: 11.2% (2000).
Taxes: Total city taxes per capita: $79 (2000); City property taxes per capita: $63 (2000).
Education: High school graduation rate: 70.1% (2000); College graduation rate: 2.3% (2000).
Housing: Homeownership rate: 83.8% (2000); Median home value: $51,100 (2000); Median rent: $225 per month (2000); Median age of housing: 47 years (2000).
Transportation: Commute to work: 89.5% car, 0.0% public transportation, 6.1% walk, 4.0% work from home (2000); Travel time to work: 26.6% less than 15 minutes, 26.2% 15 to 30 minutes, 21.5% 30 to 45 minutes, 12.2% 45 to 60 minutes, 13.5% 60 minutes or more (2000)

NEW WINDSOR (unincorporated postal area, zip code 61465). Aka Windsor. Covers a land area of 36.425 square miles and a water area of 0.017 square miles. Located at 41.17° N. Lat.; 90.68° W. Long. Elevation is 615 feet.
Population: 1,144 (2000); Race: 97.9% White, 0.0% Black, 0.5% Asian, 0.6% American Indian and Alaska Native, 2.0% Hispanic of any race, 0.9% two or more races (2000); Density: 31.4 persons per square mile (2000); Age: 23.0% under 18, 19.9% over 64 (2000); Marriage status: 16.2% never married, 63.7% now married, 10.2% widowed, 10.0% divorced (2000); Foreign born: 0.5% (2000); Ancestry (includes multiple ancestries): 20.0% German, 18.0% Swedish, 14.9% Irish, 10.6% English, 9.3% Other groups (2000).
Economy: Employment by occupation: 10.2% management, 13.3% professional, 14.5% services, 22.7% sales, 2.8% farming, 11.4% construction, 25.1% production (2000).
Income: Per capita income: $19,286 (2000); Median household income: $40,069 (2000); Poverty rate: 12.0% (2000).
Education: High school graduation rate: 86.8% (2000); College graduation rate: 11.1% (2000).
Housing: Homeownership rate: 80.9% (2000); Median home value: $64,200 (2000); Median rent: $228 per month (2000); Median age of housing: 52 years (2000).
Transportation: Commute to work: 94.4% car, 0.0% public transportation, 0.6% walk, 2.8% work from home (2000); Travel time to work: 26.1% less than 15 minutes, 20.6% 15 to 30 minutes, 23.0% 30 to 45 minutes, 24.1% 45 to 60 minutes, 6.2% 60 minutes or more (2000)

NORTH HENDERSON (village). Covers a land area of 0.225 square miles and a water area of 0 square miles. Located at 41.09° N. Lat.; 90.47° W. Long. Elevation is 774 feet.
Population: 187 (2000); Race: 97.5% White, 1.0% Black, 0.0% Asian, 1.5% American Indian and Alaska Native, 1.0% Hispanic of any race, 0.0% two or more races (2000); Density: 832.3 persons per square mile (2000); Age: 24.7% under 18, 16.2% over 64 (2000); Marriage status: 22.8% never married, 64.6% now married, 7.6% widowed, 5.1% divorced (2000); Foreign born: 0.0% (2000); Ancestry (includes multiple ancestries): 29.8% Irish, 20.2% English, 19.2% German, 15.2% Swedish, 3.0% Swiss (2000).
Economy: Employment by occupation: 8.2% management, 9.3% professional, 10.3% services, 32.0% sales, 0.0% farming, 7.2% construction, 33.0% production (2000).
Income: Per capita income: $16,292 (2000); Median household income: $35,500 (2000); Poverty rate: 8.7% (2000).
Taxes: Total city taxes per capita: $31 (1997); City property taxes per capita: $10 (1997).

Education: High school graduation rate: 85.3% (2000); College graduation rate: 5.9% (2000).
Housing: Homeownership rate: 91.8% (2000); Median home value: $36,500 (2000); Median rent: $250 per month (2000); Median age of housing: 60+ years (2000).
Transportation: Commute to work: 91.6% car, 0.0% public transportation, 0.0% walk, 4.2% work from home (2000); Travel time to work: 14.3% less than 15 minutes, 52.7% 15 to 30 minutes, 19.8% 30 to 45 minutes, 0.0% 45 to 60 minutes, 13.2% 60 minutes or more (2000)

SEATON (village). Covers a land area of 1.568 square miles and a water area of 0 square miles. Located at 41.10° N. Lat.; 90.80° W. Long. Elevation is 615 feet.
Population: 242 (2000); Race: 100.0% White, 0.0% Black, 0.0% Asian, 0.0% American Indian and Alaska Native, 0.0% Hispanic of any race, 0.0% two or more races (2000); Density: 154.3 persons per square mile (2000); Age: 26.5% under 18, 24.8% over 64 (2000); Marriage status: 20.2% never married, 66.1% now married, 4.4% widowed, 9.3% divorced (2000); Foreign born: 0.0% (2000); Ancestry (includes multiple ancestries): 15.9% English, 15.5% United States or American, 14.2% Irish, 11.1% Other groups, 9.3% German (2000).
Economy: In agricultural area: cattle, hogs, corn, soybeans. Single-family building permits issued: 0 (2001) / 0 (2000); Multi-family building permits issued: 0 (2001) / 0 (2000); Employment by occupation: 15.8% management, 15.8% professional, 28.4% services, 11.6% sales, 3.2% farming, 2.1% construction, 23.2% production (2000).
Income: Per capita income: $35,832 (2000); Median household income: $45,694 (2000); Poverty rate: 2.7% (2000).
Taxes: Total city taxes per capita: $19 (1997); City property taxes per capita: $19 (1997).
Education: High school graduation rate: 86.2% (2000); College graduation rate: 11.2% (2000).
Housing: Homeownership rate: 87.9% (2000); Median home value: $46,200 (2000); Median rent: $294 per month (2000); Median age of housing: 60+ years (2000).
Transportation: Commute to work: 89.5% car, 0.0% public transportation, 2.1% walk, 0.0% work from home (2000); Travel time to work: 43.2% less than 15 minutes, 36.8% 15 to 30 minutes, 7.4% 30 to 45 minutes, 3.2% 45 to 60 minutes, 9.5% 60 minutes or more (2000)

SHERRARD (village). Covers a land area of 0.419 square miles and a water area of 0 square miles. Located at 41.31° N. Lat.; 90.50° W. Long. Elevation is 800 feet.
Population: 694 (2000); Race: 98.0% White, 0.3% Black, 0.4% Asian, 0.0% American Indian and Alaska Native, 1.0% Hispanic of any race, 0.9% two or more races (2000); Density: 1,658.2 persons per square mile (2000); Age: 23.7% under 18, 10.3% over 64 (2000); Marriage status: 20.4% never married, 62.7% now married, 6.9% widowed, 10.0% divorced (2000); Foreign born: 0.0% (2000); Ancestry (includes multiple ancestries): 26.3% German, 19.0% Swedish, 10.2% Irish, 9.4% Belgian, 9.4% English (2000).
Economy: In agricultural area. Single-family building permits issued: 0 (2001) / 0 (2000); Multi-family building permits issued: 0 (2001) / 0 (2000); Employment by occupation: 7.6% management, 15.7% professional, 13.7% services, 27.9% sales, 0.0% farming, 15.5% construction, 19.5% production (2000).
Income: Per capita income: $18,967 (2000); Median household income: $47,171 (2000); Poverty rate: 5.0% (2000).
Taxes: Total city taxes per capita: $33 (1997); City property taxes per capita: $27 (1997).
Education: High school graduation rate: 91.5% (2000); College graduation rate: 10.6% (2000).
Housing: Homeownership rate: 77.4% (2000); Median home value: $71,700 (2000); Median rent: $319 per month (2000); Median age of housing: 44 years (2000).
Transportation: Commute to work: 97.4% car, 0.0% public transportation, 1.5% walk, 0.8% work from home (2000); Travel time to work: 12.6% less than 15 minutes, 42.0% 15 to 30 minutes, 36.9% 30 to 45 minutes, 4.4% 45 to 60 minutes, 4.1% 60 minutes or more (2000)

VIOLA (village). Covers a land area of 0.827 square miles and a water area of 0 square miles. Located at 41.20° N. Lat.; 90.58° W. Long. Elevation is 795 feet.
History: Viola developed as a coal mining town.
Population: 956 (2000); Race: 98.9% White, 0.0% Black, 0.0% Asian, 0.0% American Indian and Alaska Native, 1.4% Hispanic of any race, 0.6% two or more races (2000); Density: 1,155.8 persons per square mile (2000); Age: 25.6% under 18, 15.8% over 64 (2000); Marriage status: 17.5% never married, 66.7% now married, 7.1% widowed, 8.7% divorced (2000); Foreign born: 1.3% (2000); Ancestry (includes multiple ancestries): 22.5% German, 15.8% Irish, 15.0% Swedish, 13.2% United States or American, 10.3% English (2000).
Economy: Single-family building permits issued: 0 (2001) / 0 (2000); Multi-family building permits issued: 0 (2001) / 0 (2000); Employment by occupation: 7.6% management, 13.2% professional, 17.9% services, 27.5% sales, 1.6% farming, 10.1% construction, 22.1% production (2000).
Income: Per capita income: $18,127 (2000); Median household income: $41,161 (2000); Poverty rate: 8.5% (2000).
Taxes: Total city taxes per capita: $26 (1997); City property taxes per capita: $19 (1997).
Education: High school graduation rate: 83.1% (2000); College graduation rate: 11.9% (2000).

School District(s)

Sherrard Community Unit School District 200 (PK-12)
2000 Enrollment: 1,802 309-596-2974

Housing: Homeownership rate: 80.2% (2000); Median home value: $62,200 (2000); Median rent: $323 per month (2000); Median age of housing: 47 years (2000).
Transportation: Commute to work: 91.1% car, 0.0% public transportation, 3.0% walk, 4.3% work from home (2000); Travel time to work: 26.2% less than 15 minutes, 23.1% 15 to 30 minutes, 35.5% 30 to 45 minutes, 12.1% 45 to 60 minutes, 3.1% 60 minutes or more (2000)

WINDSOR (village). Aka New Windsor. Covers a land area of 0.442 square miles and a water area of 0 square miles. Located at 41.20° N. Lat.; 90.44° W. Long.
Population: 720 (2000); Race: 96.8% White, 0.0% Black, 0.8% Asian, 1.0% American Indian and Alaska Native, 3.0% Hispanic of any race, 1.4% two or more races (2000); Density: 1,628.5 persons per square mile (2000); Age: 23.3% under 18, 20.0% over 64 (2000); Marriage status: 16.0% never married, 63.9% now married, 8.5% widowed, 11.6% divorced (2000); Foreign born: 0.8% (2000); Ancestry (includes multiple ancestries): 20.8% German, 20.0% Swedish, 14.0% Irish, 13.1% English, 12.8% Other groups (2000).
Economy: Single-family building permits issued: 2 (2001) / 0 (2000); Multi-family building permits issued: 0 (2001) / 0 (2000); Employment by occupation: 6.1% management, 17.7% professional, 15.3% services, 24.5% sales, 0.9% farming, 11.9% construction, 23.5% production (2000).
Income: Per capita income: $19,811 (2000); Median household income: $37,500 (2000); Poverty rate: 7.8% (2000).
Taxes: Total city taxes per capita: $33 (1997); City property taxes per capita: $20 (1997).
Education: High school graduation rate: 88.0% (2000); College graduation rate: 9.4% (2000).
Housing: Homeownership rate: 79.7% (2000); Median home value: $59,500 (2000); Median rent: $225 per month (2000); Median age of housing: 48 years (2000).
Transportation: Commute to work: 91.4% car, 0.0% public transportation, 0.9% walk, 4.3% work from home (2000); Travel time to work: 25.1% less than 15 minutes, 19.0% 15 to 30 minutes, 26.4% 30 to 45 minutes, 22.2% 45 to 60 minutes, 7.4% 60 minutes or more (2000)

Monroe County

Located in southwestern Illinois; bounded on the west by the Mississippi River and the Missouri border; drained by the Kaskaskia River. Covers a land area of 388.30 square miles, a water area of 9.40 square miles, and is located in the Central Time Zone. The county government was organized in 1816. County seat is Waterloo.

Monroe County is part of the St. Louis, MO-IL MSA. The entire metro area includes: Clinton County, IL; Jersey County, IL; Madison County, IL; Monroe County, IL; St. Clair County, IL; Crawford County, MO (pt.)**; Franklin County, MO; Jefferson County, MO; Lincoln County, MO; St. Charles County, MO; St. Louis County, MO; Warren County, MO; St. Louis city, MO

Weather Station: Waterloo Elevation: 649 feet

	Jan	Feb	Mar	Apr	May	Jun	Jul	Aug	Sep	Oct	Nov	Dec
High	38	44	55	67	76	85	89	87	80	69	55	43
Low	21	26	35	45	55	64	68	66	58	47	37	26
Precip	2.3	2.4	3.8	4.2	4.0	3.8	4.0	3.1	3.3	3.1	4.0	3.4
Snow	4.5	3.2	2.0	0.7	0.0	0.0	0.0	0.0	0.0	0.0	1.2	3.0

High and Low temperatures in degrees Fahrenheit; Precipitation and Snow in inches

Population: 27,619 (2000); Race: 98.9% White, 0.1% Black, 0.3% Asian, 0.2% American Indian and Alaska Native, 0.5% Hispanic of any race, 0.5% two or more races (2000); Density: 71.1 persons per square mile (2000); Age: 26.5% under 18, 13.3% over 64 (2000).
Religion: Five largest groups: 35.4% Catholic Church, 18.3% United Church of Christ, 8.3% Lutheran Church—Missouri Synod, 6.2% Southern Baptist Convention, 0.6% The United Methodist Church (2000).
Economy: Unemployment rate: 4.1% (11/2002); Total civilian labor force: 13,901 (11/2002); Leading industries: 17.9% retail trade; 15.1% construction; 10.6% health care and social assistance (2000); Companies that employ more than 1,000 persons: 0 (2000); Companies that employ more than 100 persons: 9 (2000); Farms: 556 totaling 186,781 acres (1997); Minority business ownership rate: 0.0% (1997); Women business ownership rate: 42.3% (1997); Retail sales per capita: $6,771 (1997). Single-family building permits issued: 253 (2001) / 252 (2000); Multi-family building permits issued: 14 (2001) / 16 (2000).
Income: Per capita income: $22,954 (2000); Median household income: $55,320 (2000); Poverty rate: 3.4% (2000); Bankruptcy rate: 3.03% (2001).
Taxes: Total county taxes per capita: $155 (2000); County property taxes per capita: $132 (2000).
Education: High school graduation rate: 87.2% (2000); College graduation rate: 20.4% (2000).
Housing: Homeownership rate: 80.2% (2000); Median home value: $125,500 (2000); Median rent: $449 per month (2000); Median age of housing: 26 years (2000).
Health: Birth rate: 111.2 per 10,000 population (1998); Age adjusted death rate: 74.5 per 10,000 population (1999); Age adjusted cancer mortality rate: 198.0 deaths per 100,000 population (1999). Number of physicians: 6.9 per 10,000 population (1999); Number of hospital beds: n/a (1999).
Elections: 2000 Presidential election results: 42.0% Gore, 55.3% Bush, 1.9% Nader, 0.5% Buchanan
National and State Parks: Illinois Caverns State Natural Area
Additional Information Contacts
Monroe County Government Offices.................... 618-939-8681
Columbia Chamber of Commerce 618-281-7144
Waterloo Chamber of Commerce.................... 618-939-5300

Monroe County Communities

COLUMBIA (city). Covers a land area of 9.414 square miles and a water area of 0.021 square miles. Located at 38.44° N. Lat.; 90.20° W. Long. Elevation is 500 feet.
History: Columbia was established as a stop on the Kaskaskia-Cahokia trail. Many early residents were of German descent. The quarrying of Keokuk limestone began here in 1840.
Population: 7,922 (2000); Race: 99.4% White, 0.0% Black, 0.0% Asian, 0.1% American Indian and Alaska Native, 0.4% Hispanic of any race, 0.5% two or more races (2000); Density: 841.5 persons per square mile (2000); Age: 25.0% under 18, 16.2% over 64 (2000); Marriage status: 18.1% never married, 66.3% now married, 6.4% widowed, 9.2% divorced (2000); Foreign born: 1.0% (2000); Ancestry (includes multiple ancestries): 49.7% German, 16.0% Irish, 10.0% English, 6.9% French (except Basque), 5.6% Other groups (2000).
Economy: Single-family building permits issued: 81 (2001) / 74 (2000); Multi-family building permits issued: 0 (2001) / 0 (2000); Employment by occupation: 17.1% management, 26.5% professional, 8.7% services, 26.3% sales, 0.6% farming, 9.8% construction, 11.0% production (2000).
Income: Per capita income: $26,767 (2000); Median household income: $58,003 (2000); Poverty rate: 2.5% (2000).
Taxes: Total city taxes per capita: $255 (1997); City property taxes per capita: $169 (1997).
Education: High school graduation rate: 89.9% (2000); College graduation rate: 28.5% (2000).

School District(s)

Columbia Community Unit School District 4 (PK-12)
2000 Enrollment: 1,590 618-281-4772

Housing: Homeownership rate: 76.4% (2000); Median home value: $127,600 (2000); Median rent: $520 per month (2000); Median age of housing: 27 years (2000).
Newspapers: Clarion Journal (3 x week); Enterprise Journal (1 x week)
Transportation: Commute to work: 94.4% car, 0.3% public transportation, 1.0% walk, 3.4% work from home (2000); Travel time to work: 25.2% less than 15 minutes, 31.9% 15 to 30 minutes, 29.7% 30 to 45 minutes, 11.0% 45 to 60 minutes, 2.1% 60 minutes or more (2000)
Additional Information Contacts
Columbia Chamber of Commerce 618-281-7144

FULTS (village). Covers a land area of 0.068 square miles and a water area of 0 square miles. Located at 38.16° N. Lat.; 90.21° W. Long. Elevation is 395 feet.
History: Heavily damaged in floods of 1993.
Population: 28 (2000); Race: 100.0% White, 0.0% Black, 0.0% Asian, 0.0% American Indian and Alaska Native, 0.0% Hispanic of any race, 0.0% two or more races (2000); Density: 411.2 persons per square mile (2000); Age: 42.1% under 18, 2.6% over 64 (2000); Marriage status: 27.3% never married, 72.7% now married, 0.0% widowed, 0.0% divorced (2000); Foreign born: 0.0% (2000); Ancestry (includes multiple ancestries): 100.0% German, 5.3% Italian (2000).
Economy: In agricultural area: wheat, corn, soybeans, sorghum. Employment by occupation: 25.0% management, 12.5% professional, 12.5% services, 0.0% sales, 0.0% farming, 37.5% construction, 12.5% production (2000).
Income: Per capita income: $11,389 (2000); Median household income: $47,813 (2000); Poverty rate: 0.0% (2000).
Taxes: Total city taxes per capita: $13 (1997); City property taxes per capita: $13 (1997).
Education: High school graduation rate: 100.0% (2000); College graduation rate: 0.0% (2000).
Housing: Homeownership rate: 100.0% (2000); Median home value: $49,200 (2000); Median age of housing: 60+ years (2000).
Transportation: Commute to work: 87.5% car, 0.0% public transportation, 12.5% walk, 0.0% work from home (2000); Travel time to work: 25.0% less than 15 minutes, 37.5% 15 to 30 minutes, 0.0% 30 to 45 minutes, 0.0% 45 to 60 minutes, 37.5% 60 minutes or more (2000)

HECKER (village). Covers a land area of 0.238 square miles and a water area of 0 square miles. Located at 38.30° N. Lat.; 89.99° W. Long. Elevation is 465 feet.
Population: 475 (2000); Race: 99.6% White, 0.0% Black, 0.0% Asian, 0.0% American Indian and Alaska Native, 0.4% Hispanic of any race, 0.4% two or more races (2000); Density: 1,993.8 persons per square mile (2000); Age: 25.6% under 18, 14.2% over 64 (2000); Marriage status: 21.9% never married, 62.8% now married, 6.8% widowed, 8.5% divorced (2000); Foreign born: 0.6% (2000); Ancestry (includes multiple ancestries): 46.9% German, 10.8% French (except Basque), 9.1% Irish, 8.9% English, 8.9% United States or American (2000).
Economy: In agricultural area. Employment by occupation: 10.5% management, 10.1% professional, 15.6% services, 31.1% sales, 1.2% farming, 13.6% construction, 17.9% production (2000).
Income: Per capita income: $18,423 (2000); Median household income: $43,333 (2000); Poverty rate: 4.7% (2000).
Taxes: Total city taxes per capita: $74 (1997); City property taxes per capita: $24 (1997).
Education: High school graduation rate: 82.5% (2000); College graduation rate: 6.1% (2000).
Housing: Homeownership rate: 80.4% (2000); Median home value: $93,300 (2000); Median rent: $352 per month (2000); Median age of housing: 30 years (2000).
Transportation: Commute to work: 92.5% car, 0.4% public transportation, 0.4% walk, 5.6% work from home (2000); Travel time to work: 14.3% less than 15 minutes, 37.4% 15 to 30 minutes, 21.4% 30 to 45 minutes, 16.4% 45 to 60 minutes, 10.5% 60 minutes or more (2000)

MAEYSTOWN (village). Covers a land area of 0.304 square miles and a water area of 0 square miles. Located at 38.22° N. Lat.; 90.23° W. Long. Elevation is 500 feet.
Population: 148 (2000); Race: 98.6% White, 0.0% Black, 0.0% Asian, 0.0% American Indian and Alaska Native, 2.1% Hispanic of any race, 0.0% two or more races (2000); Density: 487.3 persons per square mile (2000); Age: 32.4% under 18, 12.4% over 64 (2000); Marriage status: 21.4% never married, 73.8% now married, 4.9% widowed, 0.0% divorced (2000); Foreign born: 1.4% (2000); Ancestry (includes multiple ancestries): 49.0% German,

8.3% Irish, 7.6% United States or American, 7.6% English, 6.9% Other groups (2000).
Economy: Employment by occupation: 5.8% management, 13.0% professional, 13.0% services, 23.2% sales, 0.0% farming, 30.4% construction, 14.5% production (2000).
Income: Per capita income: $14,432 (2000); Median household income: $40,417 (2000); Poverty rate: 4.1% (2000).
Taxes: Total city taxes per capita: $56 (1997); City property taxes per capita: $56 (1997).
Education: High school graduation rate: 89.8% (2000); College graduation rate: 12.5% (2000).
Housing: Homeownership rate: 88.9% (2000); Median home value: $68,800 (2000); Median rent: $425 per month (2000); Median age of housing: 60+ years (2000).
Transportation: Commute to work: 86.4% car, 0.0% public transportation, 3.0% walk, 9.1% work from home (2000); Travel time to work: 15.0% less than 15 minutes, 53.3% 15 to 30 minutes, 10.0% 30 to 45 minutes, 10.0% 45 to 60 minutes, 11.7% 60 minutes or more (2000)

VALMEYER (village). Aka Maeys. Covers a land area of 3.328 square miles and a water area of 0.026 square miles. Located at 38.30° N. Lat.; 90.30° W. Long. Elevation is 401 feet.
History: Town established by Swiss farmers at the end of the 19th century on rich Mississippi bottom land. Town flooded twice in September and October of 1993, with 90% of the homes beyond repair. A new town was constructed two miles east of the old Valmeyeron 500 acres of former dairy lands.
Population: 608 (2000); Race: 99.1% White, 0.5% Black, 0.5% Asian, 0.0% American Indian and Alaska Native, 1.4% Hispanic of any race, 0.0% two or more races (2000); Density: 182.7 persons per square mile (2000); Age: 25.1% under 18, 13.4% over 64 (2000); Marriage status: 20.8% never married, 65.2% now married, 8.3% widowed, 5.7% divorced (2000); Foreign born: 0.8% (2000); Ancestry (includes multiple ancestries): 46.4% German, 11.9% United States or American, 11.2% English, 9.9% Irish, 6.2% Other groups (2000).
Economy: In agricultural area: wheat, barley, sorghum and dairying. Manufacturing includes wood products and commercial printing. Employment by occupation: 8.7% management, 16.3% professional, 21.3% services, 23.6% sales, 0.0% farming, 8.2% construction, 21.9% production (2000).
Income: Per capita income: $20,420 (2000); Median household income: $53,214 (2000); Poverty rate: 3.0% (2000).
Taxes: Total city taxes per capita: $22 (1997); City property taxes per capita: $15 (1997).
Education: High school graduation rate: 79.7% (2000); College graduation rate: 12.9% (2000).

School District(s)

Valmeyer Community Unit School District 3 (PK-12)
2000 Enrollment: 458 618-935-2100

Housing: Homeownership rate: 83.5% (2000); Median home value: $126,900 (2000); Median rent: $164 per month (2000); Median age of housing: 3 years (2000).
Transportation: Commute to work: 99.1% car, 0.0% public transportation, 0.0% walk, 0.9% work from home (2000); Travel time to work: 20.8% less than 15 minutes, 25.8% 15 to 30 minutes, 29.4% 30 to 45 minutes, 18.4% 45 to 60 minutes, 5.6% 60 minutes or more (2000)

WATERLOO (city). Covers a land area of 5.567 square miles and a water area of 0.051 square miles. Located at 38.33° N. Lat.; 90.15° W. Long. Elevation is 717 feet.
History: Waterloo was established on the trail from Fort Chartresto Cahokia, and developed as the seat of Monroe County. For a time it had a reputation as a place for quick marriages.
Population: 7,614 (2000); Race: 98.8% White, 0.1% Black, 0.4% Asian, 0.0% American Indian and Alaska Native, 0.8% Hispanic of any race, 0.7% two or more races (2000); Density: 1,367.8 persons per square mile (2000); Age: 26.2% under 18, 16.7% over 64 (2000); Marriage status: 20.2% never married, 63.0% now married, 8.3% widowed, 8.6% divorced (2000); Foreign born: 0.9% (2000); Ancestry (includes multiple ancestries): 56.9% German, 15.2% Irish, 7.4% French (except Basque), 7.3% English, 5.2% Other groups (2000).
Economy: Single-family building permits issued: 77 (2001) / 81 (2000); Multi-family building permits issued: 14 (2001) / 16 (2000); Employment by occupation: 13.3% management, 16.9% professional, 16.8% services, 32.6% sales, 0.0% farming, 10.1% construction, 10.3% production (2000).
Income: Per capita income: $21,081 (2000); Median household income: $46,938 (2000); Poverty rate: 3.8% (2000).
Taxes: Total city taxes per capita: $137 (1997); City property taxes per capita: $62 (1997).
Education: High school graduation rate: 85.4% (2000); College graduation rate: 19.3% (2000).

School District(s)

Monroe-Randolph Orphan Act Prog (09-12)
2000 Enrollment: 16 618-939-5650
Monroe/Randolph Roe (06-12)
2000 Enrollment: 140 618-939-5650
Waterloo Community Unit School District 5 (PK-12)
2000 Enrollment: 2,427 618-939-3453

Housing: Homeownership rate: 71.2% (2000); Median home value: $119,600 (2000); Median rent: $424 per month (2000); Median age of housing: 29 years (2000).
Newspapers: Waterloo Republic-Times Shopper (1 x week); The Waterloo Republic-Times (1 x week)
Transportation: Commute to work: 94.9% car, 2.0% public transportation, 0.7% walk, 1.9% work from home (2000); Travel time to work: 33.9% less than 15 minutes, 15.0% 15 to 30 minutes, 28.2% 30 to 45 minutes, 16.0% 45 to 60 minutes, 7.0% 60 minutes or more (2000)
Additional Information Contacts
Waterloo Chamber of Commerce. 618-939-5300

Montgomery County

Located in south central Illinois; drained by Shoal and Macoupin Creeks. Covers a land area of 703.80 square miles, a water area of 6.00 square miles, and is located in the Central Time Zone. The county government was organized in 1821. County seat is Hillsboro.

Weather Station: Hillsboro — Elevation: 629 feet

	Jan	Feb	Mar	Apr	May	Jun	Jul	Aug	Sep	Oct	Nov	Dec
High	36	43	55	67	77	86	90	87	81	69	54	42
Low	19	24	33	44	53	62	66	64	56	45	35	25
Precip	2.1	2.0	3.5	4.4	4.3	4.0	3.5	3.4	3.2	2.9	3.7	3.0
Snow	5.8	4.2	3.2	0.5	tr	0.0	0.0	0.0	0.0	tr	1.0	3.9

High and Low temperatures in degrees Fahrenheit; Precipitation and Snow in inches

Population: 30,652 (2000); Race: 95.3% White, 3.7% Black, 0.2% Asian, 0.2% American Indian and Alaska Native, 1.1% Hispanic of any race, 0.3% two or more races (2000); Density: 43.6 persons per square mile (2000); Age: 23.6% under 18, 16.9% over 64 (2000).
Religion: Five largest groups: 12.6% Southern Baptist Convention, 10.9% Catholic Church, 6.8% Lutheran Church—Missouri Synod, 5.0% The United Methodist Church, 4.3% Evangelical Lutheran Church in America (2000).
Economy: Unemployment rate: 7.7% (11/2002); Total civilian labor force: 15,047 (11/2002); Leading industries: 17.7% manufacturing; 17.2% retail trade; 16.0% health care and social assistance (2000); Companies that employ more than 1,000 persons: 0 (2000); Companies that employ more than 100 persons: 10 (2000); Farms: 980 totaling 361,022 acres (1997); Minority business ownership rate: 0.0% (1997); Women business ownership rate: 19.1% (1997); Retail sales per capita: $7,532 (1997). Single-family building permits issued: 27 (2001) / 17 (2000); Multi-family building permits issued: 8 (2001) / 0 (2000).
Income: Per capita income: $16,272 (2000); Median household income: $33,123 (2000); Poverty rate: 13.4% (2000); Bankruptcy rate: 5.36% (2001).
Taxes: Total county taxes per capita: $86 (1997); County property taxes per capita: $18 (1997).
Education: High school graduation rate: 77.1% (2000); College graduation rate: 11.2% (2000).
Housing: Homeownership rate: 78.4% (2000); Median home value: $54,800 (2000); Median rent: $275 per month (2000); Median age of housing: 48 years (2000).
Health: Birth rate: 110.9 per 10,000 population (1998); Age adjusted death rate: 94.5 per 10,000 population (1999); Age adjusted cancer mortality rate: 256.2 deaths per 100,000 population (1999). Number of physicians: 6.5 per 10,000 population (1999); Number of hospital beds: 64.3 per 10,000 population (1999).
Elections: 2000 Presidential election results: 50.0% Gore, 47.6% Bush, 1.5% Nader, 0.6% Buchanan
National and State Parks: Coffeen Lake State Fish and Wildlife Area
Additional Information Contacts
Montgomery County Government Offices. 217-532-9530
Hillsboro Chamber of Commerce 217-532-3711
Litchfield Chamber of Commerce 217-324-2533

Montgomery County Communities

BUTLER (village). Covers a land area of 0.570 square miles and a water area of 0 square miles. Located at 39.19° N. Lat.; 89.53° W. Long. Elevation is 630 feet.
Population: 197 (2000); Race: 99.1% White, 0.0% Black, 0.9% Asian, 0.0% American Indian and Alaska Native, 0.0% Hispanic of any race, 0.0% two or more races (2000); Density: 345.7 persons per square mile (2000); Age: 25.9% under 18, 22.2% over 64 (2000); Marriage status: 15.7% never married, 65.1% now married, 10.5% widowed, 8.7% divorced (2000); Foreign born: 0.9% (2000); Ancestry (includes multiple ancestries): 29.6% German, 19.0% United States or American, 12.5% English, 9.7% Irish, 3.7% Italian (2000).
Economy: In agricultural and bituminous-coal-mining area. Employment by occupation: 4.8% management, 0.0% professional, 22.6% services, 27.4% sales, 0.0% farming, 19.0% construction, 26.2% production (2000).
Income: Per capita income: $11,081 (2000); Median household income: $31,364 (2000); Poverty rate: 17.5% (2000).
Taxes: Total city taxes per capita: $30 (1997); City property taxes per capita: $30 (1997).
Education: High school graduation rate: 76.4% (2000); College graduation rate: 0.0% (2000).
Housing: Homeownership rate: 92.5% (2000); Median home value: $33,800 (2000); Median age of housing: 60+ years (2000).
Transportation: Commute to work: 86.9% car, 0.0% public transportation, 8.3% walk, 4.8% work from home (2000); Travel time to work: 12.5% less than 15 minutes, 56.3% 15 to 30 minutes, 8.8% 30 to 45 minutes, 5.0% 45 to 60 minutes, 17.5% 60 minutes or more (2000)

COALTON (village). Covers a land area of 0.519 square miles and a water area of 0 square miles. Located at 39.28° N. Lat.; 89.30° W. Long. Elevation is 660 feet.
Population: 307 (2000); Race: 95.6% White, 2.3% Black, 1.0% Asian, 0.0% American Indian and Alaska Native, 0.0% Hispanic of any race, 1.0% two or more races (2000); Density: 592.1 persons per square mile (2000); Age: 32.9% under 18, 16.4% over 64 (2000); Marriage status: 18.6% never married, 66.2% now married, 7.6% widowed, 7.6% divorced (2000); Foreign born: 2.7% (2000); Ancestry (includes multiple ancestries): 19.5% German, 9.4% Other groups, 8.1% Irish, 7.0% United States or American, 5.4% English (2000).
Economy: In agricultural and bituminous-coal area. Employment by occupation: 9.9% management, 17.4% professional, 12.4% services, 21.5% sales, 0.0% farming, 18.2% construction, 20.7% production (2000).
Income: Per capita income: $21,901 (2000); Median household income: $37,500 (2000); Poverty rate: 22.6% (2000).
Taxes: Total city taxes per capita: $16 (1997); City property taxes per capita: $13 (1997).
Education: High school graduation rate: 79.3% (2000); College graduation rate: 9.8% (2000).
Housing: Homeownership rate: 91.7% (2000); Median home value: $41,000 (2000); Median rent: $413 per month (2000); Median age of housing: 60+ years (2000).
Transportation: Commute to work: 87.6% car, 0.0% public transportation, 0.0% walk, 9.9% work from home (2000); Travel time to work: 43.1% less than 15 minutes, 18.3% 15 to 30 minutes, 20.2% 30 to 45 minutes, 7.3% 45 to 60 minutes, 11.0% 60 minutes or more (2000)

COFFEEN (city). Covers a land area of 1.032 square miles and a water area of 0 square miles. Located at 39.09° N. Lat.; 89.39° W. Long. Elevation is 632 feet.
Population: 709 (2000); Race: 99.5% White, 0.0% Black, 0.5% Asian, 0.0% American Indian and Alaska Native, 0.0% Hispanic of any race, 0.0% two or more races (2000); Density: 687.2 persons per square mile (2000); Age: 25.4% under 18, 19.6% over 64 (2000); Marriage status: 18.5% never married, 60.6% now married, 10.7% widowed, 10.2% divorced (2000); Foreign born: 0.8% (2000); Ancestry (includes multiple ancestries): 25.4% United States or American, 18.4% German, 9.4% Irish, 7.3% English, 5.0% Other groups (2000).
Economy: In agricultural and bituminous-coal area. Employment by occupation: 7.6% management, 10.9% professional, 33.7% services, 22.5% sales, 0.0% farming, 12.3% construction, 13.0% production (2000).
Income: Per capita income: $13,755 (2000); Median household income: $29,375 (2000); Poverty rate: 20.6% (2000).
Taxes: Total city taxes per capita: $45 (1997); City property taxes per capita: $24 (1997).
Education: High school graduation rate: 78.1% (2000); College graduation rate: 5.5% (2000).
Housing: Homeownership rate: 77.9% (2000); Median home value: $34,100 (2000); Median rent: $217 per month (2000); Median age of housing: 37 years (2000).
Transportation: Commute to work: 94.4% car, 0.0% public transportation, 2.2% walk, 3.4% work from home (2000); Travel time to work: 31.4% less than 15 minutes, 44.6% 15 to 30 minutes, 9.7% 30 to 45 minutes, 4.7% 45 to 60 minutes, 9.7% 60 minutes or more (2000)

DONNELLSON (village). Covers a land area of 0.238 square miles and a water area of 0 square miles. Located at 39.03° N. Lat.; 89.47° W. Long. Elevation is 611 feet.
Population: 243 (2000); Race: 98.2% White, 0.0% Black, 0.0% Asian, 1.8% American Indian and Alaska Native, 0.0% Hispanic of any race, 0.0% two or more races (2000); Density: 1,021.2 persons per square mile (2000); Age: 27.2% under 18, 16.5% over 64 (2000); Marriage status: 23.7% never married, 58.8% now married, 8.5% widowed, 9.0% divorced (2000); Foreign born: 0.0% (2000); Ancestry (includes multiple ancestries): 32.1% German, 22.8% Irish, 17.0% English, 12.9% Other groups, 10.7% United States or American (2000).
Economy: In agricultural area: corn, wheat; dairy products; livestock. Employment by occupation: 7.1% management, 9.4% professional, 22.4% services, 22.4% sales, 0.0% farming, 16.5% construction, 22.4% production (2000).
Income: Per capita income: $13,665 (2000); Median household income: $28,365 (2000); Poverty rate: 13.4% (2000).
Taxes: Total city taxes per capita: $34 (1997); City property taxes per capita: $34 (1997).
Education: High school graduation rate: 66.9% (2000); College graduation rate: 6.8% (2000).
Housing: Homeownership rate: 87.6% (2000); Median home value: $40,700 (2000); Median rent: $192 per month (2000); Median age of housing: 45 years (2000).
Transportation: Commute to work: 91.0% car, 0.0% public transportation, 2.6% walk, 3.8% work from home (2000); Travel time to work: 14.7% less than 15 minutes, 44.0% 15 to 30 minutes, 25.3% 30 to 45 minutes, 5.3% 45 to 60 minutes, 10.7% 60 minutes or more (2000)

FARMERSVILLE (village). Covers a land area of 0.988 square miles and a water area of 0.008 square miles. Located at 39.44° N. Lat.; 89.65° W. Long. Elevation is 643 feet.
Population: 768 (2000); Race: 98.4% White, 0.0% Black, 0.0% Asian, 0.5% American Indian and Alaska Native, 0.0% Hispanic of any race, 1.1% two or more races (2000); Density: 777.7 persons per square mile (2000); Age: 24.6% under 18, 11.6% over 64 (2000); Marriage status: 23.3% never married, 59.3% now married, 6.8% widowed, 10.6% divorced (2000); Foreign born: 0.0% (2000); Ancestry (includes multiple ancestries): 28.0% German, 18.0% Irish, 8.8% Other groups, 8.1% United States or American, 6.1% English (2000).
Economy: In agricultural and bituminous-coal area. Employment by occupation: 6.4% management, 15.7% professional, 25.3% services, 24.0% sales, 0.0% farming, 14.2% construction, 14.4% production (2000).
Income: Per capita income: $16,606 (2000); Median household income: $35,893 (2000); Poverty rate: 8.2% (2000).
Taxes: Total city taxes per capita: $29 (1997); City property taxes per capita: $25 (1997).
Education: High school graduation rate: 82.7% (2000); College graduation rate: 11.7% (2000).
Housing: Homeownership rate: 83.9% (2000); Median home value: $65,400 (2000); Median rent: $293 per month (2000); Median age of housing: 29 years (2000).
Transportation: Commute to work: 88.8% car, 0.0% public transportation, 1.8% walk, 4.7% work from home (2000); Travel time to work: 26.0% less than 15 minutes, 27.0% 15 to 30 minutes, 33.1% 30 to 45 minutes, 8.5% 45 to 60 minutes, 5.5% 60 minutes or more (2000)

FILLMORE (village). Covers a land area of 0.774 square miles and a water area of 0 square miles. Located at 39.11° N. Lat.; 89.27° W. Long. Elevation is 635 feet.
Population: 362 (2000); Race: 100.0% White, 0.0% Black, 0.0% Asian, 0.0% American Indian and Alaska Native, 0.0% Hispanic of any race, 0.0% two or more races (2000); Density: 467.5 persons per square mile (2000); Age: 29.6% under 18, 16.3% over 64 (2000); Marriage status: 19.3% never married, 62.2% now married, 11.3% widowed, 7.3% divorced (2000); Foreign born: 0.0% (2000); Ancestry (includes multiple ancestries): 23.8%

German, 12.7% Irish, 10.5% United States or American, 8.9% Other groups, 4.7% English (2000).
Economy: In agricultural and bituminous-coal area. Employment by occupation: 5.8% management, 3.2% professional, 33.1% services, 25.3% sales, 1.3% farming, 13.0% construction, 18.2% production (2000).
Income: Per capita income: $14,363 (2000); Median household income: $30,313 (2000); Poverty rate: 21.6% (2000).
Taxes: Total city taxes per capita: $29 (1997); City property taxes per capita: $29 (1997).
Education: High school graduation rate: 75.7% (2000); College graduation rate: 3.2% (2000).
Housing: Homeownership rate: 83.1% (2000); Median home value: $37,600 (2000); Median rent: $242 per month (2000); Median age of housing: 48 years (2000).
Transportation: Commute to work: 89.4% car, 0.0% public transportation, 5.3% walk, 4.0% work from home (2000); Travel time to work: 22.1% less than 15 minutes, 51.7% 15 to 30 minutes, 8.3% 30 to 45 minutes, 0.0% 45 to 60 minutes, 17.9% 60 minutes or more (2000)

HARVEL (village). Covers a land area of 0.727 square miles and a water area of 0 square miles. Located at 39.35° N. Lat.; 89.53° W. Long.
Population: 235 (2000); Race: 99.1% White, 0.0% Black, 0.0% Asian, 0.0% American Indian and Alaska Native, 0.0% Hispanic of any race, 0.0% two or more races (2000); Density: 323.2 persons per square mile (2000); Age: 24.3% under 18, 17.4% over 64 (2000); Marriage status: 20.4% never married, 57.1% now married, 9.9% widowed, 12.6% divorced (2000); Foreign born: 1.7% (2000); Ancestry (includes multiple ancestries): 27.2% German, 23.0% United States or American, 6.8% Irish, 6.8% Other groups, 5.1% French (except Basque) (2000).
Economy: Employment by occupation: 14.3% management, 14.3% professional, 21.4% services, 21.4% sales, 1.8% farming, 12.5% construction, 14.3% production (2000).
Income: Per capita income: $15,740 (2000); Median household income: $31,625 (2000); Poverty rate: 14.9% (2000).
Taxes: Total city taxes per capita: $63 (1997); City property taxes per capita: $41 (1997).
Education: High school graduation rate: 80.2% (2000); College graduation rate: 6.8% (2000).
Housing: Homeownership rate: 85.1% (2000); Median home value: $37,800 (2000); Median rent: $269 per month (2000); Median age of housing: 55 years (2000).
Transportation: Commute to work: 86.1% car, 0.0% public transportation, 0.9% walk, 10.2% work from home (2000); Travel time to work: 18.6% less than 15 minutes, 13.4% 15 to 30 minutes, 47.4% 30 to 45 minutes, 14.4% 45 to 60 minutes, 6.2% 60 minutes or more (2000)

HILLSBORO (city). Covers a land area of 3.588 square miles and a water area of 1.742 square miles. Located at 39.16° N. Lat.; 89.48° W. Long. Elevation is 630 feet.
History: Incorporated 1855.
Population: 4,359 (2000); Race: 97.8% White, 1.6% Black, 0.0% Asian, 0.0% American Indian and Alaska Native, 1.5% Hispanic of any race, 0.1% two or more races (2000); Density: 1,214.9 persons per square mile (2000); Age: 25.4% under 18, 18.0% over 64 (2000); Marriage status: 20.9% never married, 57.3% now married, 10.0% widowed, 11.8% divorced (2000); Foreign born: 1.0% (2000); Ancestry (includes multiple ancestries): 26.8% German, 11.6% English, 10.6% Irish, 7.7% Other groups, 6.3% United States or American (2000).
Economy: In agricultural area: soybeans, corn, wheat, hay; cattle. Manufacturing: zinc oxide, glass products. Several recreational reservoirs in area. Single-family building permits issued: 8 (2001) / 5 (2000); Multi-family building permits issued: 0 (2001) / 0 (2000); Employment by occupation: 13.2% management, 16.5% professional, 22.1% services, 26.1% sales, 0.5% farming, 10.2% construction, 11.4% production (2000).
Income: Per capita income: $17,458 (2000); Median household income: $33,075 (2000); Poverty rate: 17.2% (2000).
Taxes: Total city taxes per capita: $149 (1997); City property taxes per capita: $131 (1997).
Education: High school graduation rate: 82.6% (2000); College graduation rate: 15.4% (2000).

School District(s)

Hillsboro Community Unit School District 3 (PK-12)
2000 Enrollment: 2,194 217-532-2942
Housing: Homeownership rate: 68.7% (2000); Median home value: $62,400 (2000); Median rent: $293 per month (2000); Median age of housing: 49 years (2000).
Hospitals: Hillsboro Area Hospital (100 beds)
Newspapers: Macoupin County Shopper (2 x week); M & M Journal (1 x week); Hillsboro Journal (2 x week); The Montgomery County News (3 x week)
Transportation: Commute to work: 95.9% car, 0.0% public transportation, 2.1% walk, 2.0% work from home (2000); Travel time to work: 50.6% less than 15 minutes, 25.0% 15 to 30 minutes, 7.6% 30 to 45 minutes, 5.1% 45 to 60 minutes, 11.7% 60 minutes or more (2000)
Additional Information Contacts
Hillsboro Chamber of Commerce 217-532-3711

IRVING (village). Covers a land area of 0.818 square miles and a water area of 0 square miles. Located at 39.20° N. Lat.; 89.40° W. Long. Elevation is 655 feet.
Population: 2,484 (2000); Race: 57.3% White, 40.6% Black, 0.0% Asian, 0.9% American Indian and Alaska Native, 6.6% Hispanic of any race, 0.1% two or more races (2000); Density: 3,038.1 persons per square mile (2000); Age: 5.3% under 18, 3.7% over 64 (2000); Marriage status: 29.1% never married, 43.3% now married, 2.6% widowed, 25.1% divorced (2000); Foreign born: 2.6% (2000); Ancestry (includes multiple ancestries): 4.3% United States or American, 3.2% German, 1.9% English, 1.6% Other groups, 1.0% Irish (2000).
Economy: In agricultural and bituminous coal area. Employment by occupation: 9.4% management, 6.7% professional, 21.1% services, 23.9% sales, 2.8% farming, 12.8% construction, 23.3% production (2000).
Income: Per capita income: $12,144 (2000); Median household income: $24,583 (2000); Poverty rate: 29.2% (2000).
Taxes: Total city taxes per capita: $24 (1997); City property taxes per capita: $20 (1997).
Education: High school graduation rate: 45.7% (2000); College graduation rate: 0.3% (2000).
Housing: Homeownership rate: 77.8% (2000); Median home value: $31,600 (2000); Median rent: $257 per month (2000); Median age of housing: 57 years (2000).
Transportation: Commute to work: 88.8% car, 0.0% public transportation, 7.3% walk, 2.2% work from home (2000); Travel time to work: 27.6% less than 15 minutes, 38.5% 15 to 30 minutes, 14.9% 30 to 45 minutes, 10.9% 45 to 60 minutes, 8.0% 60 minutes or more (2000)

LITCHFIELD (city). Covers a land area of 5.091 square miles and a water area of 0.003 square miles. Located at 39.17° N. Lat.; 89.65° W. Long. Elevation is 696 feet.
History: Litchfield was incorporated in 1859 and developed around a coal field. An early employer was the International Stove Company.
Population: 6,815 (2000); Race: 98.0% White, 0.6% Black, 0.1% Asian, 0.1% American Indian and Alaska Native, 0.7% Hispanic of any race, 0.5% two or more races (2000); Density: 1,338.5 persons per square mile (2000); Age: 26.0% under 18, 19.8% over 64 (2000); Marriage status: 20.1% never married, 54.2% now married, 11.4% widowed, 14.2% divorced (2000); Foreign born: 1.0% (2000); Ancestry (includes multiple ancestries): 26.5% German, 13.0% United States or American, 12.4% English, 10.4% Irish, 8.8% Other groups (2000).
Economy: Single-family building permits issued: 14 (2001) / 6 (2000); Multi-family building permits issued: 8 (2001) / 0 (2000); Employment by occupation: 8.5% management, 13.1% professional, 20.7% services, 28.2% sales, 0.4% farming, 9.4% construction, 19.8% production (2000).
Income: Per capita income: $14,612 (2000); Median household income: $28,717 (2000); Poverty rate: 16.6% (2000).
Taxes: Total city taxes per capita: $114 (2000); City property taxes per capita: $102 (2000).
Education: High school graduation rate: 73.6% (2000); College graduation rate: 10.7% (2000).

School District(s)

Litchfield C U School District 12 (PK-12)
2000 Enrollment: 1,753 217-324-2157
Housing: Homeownership rate: 72.1% (2000); Median home value: $55,100 (2000); Median rent: $267 per month (2000); Median age of housing: 50 years (2000).
Hospitals: Saint Francis Hospital (138 beds)
Newspapers: News-Herald (5 x week)
Transportation: Commute to work: 93.3% car, 0.6% public transportation, 2.7% walk, 1.7% work from home (2000); Travel time to work: 65.3% less than 15 minutes, 12.6% 15 to 30 minutes, 6.2% 30 to 45 minutes, 6.8% 45 to 60 minutes, 9.1% 60 minutes or more (2000)
Airports: Litchfield Municipal
Additional Information Contacts

Litchfield Chamber of Commerce 217-324-2533

NOKOMIS (city). Covers a land area of 1.300 square miles and a water area of 0 square miles. Located at 39.30° N. Lat.; 89.28° W. Long. Elevation is 670 feet.
History: Incorporated 1867.
Population: 2,389 (2000); Race: 99.5% White, 0.0% Black, 0.5% Asian, 0.0% American Indian and Alaska Native, 0.3% Hispanic of any race, 0.0% two or more races (2000); Density: 1,837.3 persons per square mile (2000); Age: 22.3% under 18, 24.1% over 64 (2000); Marriage status: 21.9% never married, 58.2% now married, 8.9% widowed, 10.9% divorced (2000); Foreign born: 1.0% (2000); Ancestry (includes multiple ancestries): 27.6% German, 11.1% United States or American, 10.4% Irish, 10.0% English, 5.9% Italian (2000).
Economy: In agricultural area; dairy products. Single-family building permits issued: 2 (2001) / 2 (2000); Multi-family building permits issued: 0 (2001) / 0 (2000); Employment by occupation: 9.6% management, 15.2% professional, 19.2% services, 21.2% sales, 1.9% farming, 11.7% construction, 21.1% production (2000).
Income: Per capita income: $16,328 (2000); Median household income: $29,612 (2000); Poverty rate: 14.3% (2000).
Taxes: Total city taxes per capita: $155 (1997); City property taxes per capita: $62 (1997).
Education: High school graduation rate: 79.4% (2000); College graduation rate: 10.5% (2000).

School District(s)

Nokomis Community Unit School District 22 (PK-12)
2000 Enrollment: 842 217-563-7311
Housing: Homeownership rate: 79.9% (2000); Median home value: $46,900 (2000); Median rent: $262 per month (2000); Median age of housing: 59 years (2000).
Newspapers: Free Press-Progress (1 x week)
Transportation: Commute to work: 87.3% car, 0.0% public transportation, 2.1% walk, 6.3% work from home (2000); Travel time to work: 34.8% less than 15 minutes, 19.4% 15 to 30 minutes, 17.8% 30 to 45 minutes, 5.9% 45 to 60 minutes, 22.1% 60 minutes or more (2000)

PANAMA (village). Covers a land area of 0.337 square miles and a water area of <.001 square miles. Located at 39.03° N. Lat.; 89.52° W. Long.
Population: 323 (2000); Race: 93.6% White, 2.1% Black, 0.0% Asian, 0.0% American Indian and Alaska Native, 0.0% Hispanic of any race, 4.2% two or more races (2000); Density: 958.3 persons per square mile (2000); Age: 21.8% under 18, 14.5% over 64 (2000); Marriage status: 21.3% never married, 56.3% now married, 8.2% widowed, 14.2% divorced (2000); Foreign born: 0.6% (2000); Ancestry (includes multiple ancestries): 29.7% German, 20.3% Irish, 16.1% English, 8.2% Other groups, 6.7% Italian (2000).
Economy: Employment by occupation: 1.4% management, 8.0% professional, 20.3% services, 26.8% sales, 0.0% farming, 10.9% construction, 32.6% production (2000).
Income: Per capita income: $21,634 (2000); Median household income: $28,889 (2000); Poverty rate: 14.0% (2000).
Taxes: Total city taxes per capita: $17 (1997); City property taxes per capita: $11 (1997).
Education: High school graduation rate: 72.3% (2000); College graduation rate: 1.3% (2000).
Housing: Homeownership rate: 89.1% (2000); Median home value: $28,100 (2000); Median rent: $238 per month (2000); Median age of housing: 60+ years (2000).
Transportation: Commute to work: 95.6% car, 0.0% public transportation, 0.0% walk, 4.4% work from home (2000); Travel time to work: 4.6% less than 15 minutes, 47.3% 15 to 30 minutes, 22.9% 30 to 45 minutes, 8.4% 45 to 60 minutes, 16.8% 60 minutes or more (2000)

RAYMOND (village). Covers a land area of 1.255 square miles and a water area of 0 square miles. Located at 39.32° N. Lat.; 89.57° W. Long. Elevation is 640 feet.
Population: 927 (2000); Race: 98.7% White, 0.5% Black, 0.2% Asian, 0.2% American Indian and Alaska Native, 0.0% Hispanic of any race, 0.3% two or more races (2000); Density: 738.6 persons per square mile (2000); Age: 22.6% under 18, 22.4% over 64 (2000); Marriage status: 17.2% never married, 65.3% now married, 8.2% widowed, 9.4% divorced (2000); Foreign born: 0.2% (2000); Ancestry (includes multiple ancestries): 41.5% German, 11.9% Irish, 10.7% English, 8.3% United States or American, 5.2% Other groups (2000).
Economy: In agricultural area: corn, wheat, hay, soybeans, sorghum; cattle; dairy products. Single-family building permits issued: 3 (2001) / 4 (2000); Multi-family building permits issued: 0 (2001) / 0 (2000); Employment by occupation: 13.7% management, 15.6% professional, 12.7% services, 30.8% sales, 0.6% farming, 12.7% construction, 13.9% production (2000).
Income: Per capita income: $18,231 (2000); Median household income: $37,500 (2000); Poverty rate: 8.4% (2000).
Taxes: Total city taxes per capita: $59 (1997); City property taxes per capita: $58 (1997).
Education: High school graduation rate: 81.7% (2000); College graduation rate: 15.6% (2000).

School District(s)

Panhandle Community Unit School District 2 (PK-12)
2000 Enrollment: 583 217-229-4215
Housing: Homeownership rate: 77.9% (2000); Median home value: $59,800 (2000); Median rent: $309 per month (2000); Median age of housing: 43 years (2000).
Newspapers: The Panhandle Press (1 x week); The Raymond News (1 x week)
Transportation: Commute to work: 94.0% car, 0.6% public transportation, 1.9% walk, 2.6% work from home (2000); Travel time to work: 34.7% less than 15 minutes, 24.5% 15 to 30 minutes, 17.9% 30 to 45 minutes, 15.9% 45 to 60 minutes, 7.0% 60 minutes or more (2000)

SCHRAM CITY (village). Covers a land area of 0.733 square miles and a water area of 0 square miles. Located at 39.16° N. Lat.; 89.46° W. Long. Elevation is 600 feet.
Population: 653 (2000); Race: 99.7% White, 0.2% Black, 0.0% Asian, 0.2% American Indian and Alaska Native, 0.3% Hispanic of any race, 0.0% two or more races (2000); Density: 891.1 persons per square mile (2000); Age: 24.4% under 18, 18.9% over 64 (2000); Marriage status: 24.0% never married, 51.3% now married, 12.5% widowed, 12.2% divorced (2000); Foreign born: 0.6% (2000); Ancestry (includes multiple ancestries): 21.1% United States or American, 20.8% German, 12.4% Irish, 9.2% Italian, 8.2% English (2000).
Economy: In agricultural area. Single-family building permits issued: 0 (2001) / 0 (2000); Multi-family building permits issued: 0 (2001) / 0 (2000); Employment by occupation: 8.4% management, 8.1% professional, 17.6% services, 24.0% sales, 0.7% farming, 11.1% construction, 30.1% production (2000).
Income: Per capita income: $16,994 (2000); Median household income: $33,750 (2000); Poverty rate: 7.9% (2000).
Taxes: Total city taxes per capita: $32 (1997); City property taxes per capita: $24 (1997).
Education: High school graduation rate: 74.4% (2000); College graduation rate: 4.8% (2000).
Housing: Homeownership rate: 82.6% (2000); Median home value: $47,400 (2000); Median rent: $298 per month (2000); Median age of housing: 57 years (2000).
Transportation: Commute to work: 95.5% car, 0.0% public transportation, 1.7% walk, 1.7% work from home (2000); Travel time to work: 35.1% less than 15 minutes, 36.1% 15 to 30 minutes, 6.0% 30 to 45 minutes, 3.5% 45 to 60 minutes, 19.3% 60 minutes or more (2000)

TAYLOR SPRINGS (village). Covers a land area of 0.861 square miles and a water area of 0.033 square miles. Located at 39.13° N. Lat.; 89.49° W. Long. Elevation is 620 feet.
Population: 583 (2000); Race: 97.9% White, 0.0% Black, 0.0% Asian, 1.2% American Indian and Alaska Native, 1.5% Hispanic of any race, 0.5% two or more races (2000); Density: 677.1 persons per square mile (2000); Age: 26.8% under 18, 15.3% over 64 (2000); Marriage status: 23.7% never married, 55.8% now married, 7.8% widowed, 12.8% divorced (2000); Foreign born: 1.2% (2000); Ancestry (includes multiple ancestries): 20.7% German, 15.5% Irish, 15.3% United States or American, 12.7% Other groups, 8.9% English (2000).
Economy: In agricultural and bituminous coal-mining area. Employment by occupation: 6.7% management, 12.8% professional, 25.9% services, 17.7% sales, 0.0% farming, 16.0% construction, 20.9% production (2000).
Income: Per capita income: $14,279 (2000); Median household income: $29,773 (2000); Poverty rate: 9.1% (2000).
Taxes: Total city taxes per capita: $34 (1997); City property taxes per capita: $26 (1997).
Education: High school graduation rate: 76.9% (2000); College graduation rate: 5.5% (2000).

Housing: Homeownership rate: 79.7% (2000); Median home value: $45,000 (2000); Median rent: $280 per month (2000); Median age of housing: 45 years (2000).
Transportation: Commute to work: 96.4% car, 0.0% public transportation, 0.0% walk, 2.9% work from home (2000); Travel time to work: 53.1% less than 15 minutes, 26.6% 15 to 30 minutes, 7.0% 30 to 45 minutes, 1.8% 45 to 60 minutes, 11.4% 60 minutes or more (2000)

WAGGONER (village). Covers a land area of 0.264 square miles and a water area of 0 square miles. Located at 39.37° N. Lat.; 89.65° W. Long. Elevation is 642 feet.
Population: 245 (2000); Race: 100.0% White, 0.0% Black, 0.0% Asian, 0.0% American Indian and Alaska Native, 0.0% Hispanic of any race, 0.0% two or more races (2000); Density: 929.8 persons per square mile (2000); Age: 27.7% under 18, 12.0% over 64 (2000); Marriage status: 22.6% never married, 54.8% now married, 11.8% widowed, 10.9% divorced (2000); Foreign born: 0.0% (2000); Ancestry (includes multiple ancestries): 24.7% English, 18.7% German, 9.3% Irish, 7.0% United States or American, 4.3% French (except Basque) (2000).
Economy: Employment by occupation: 8.3% management, 5.3% professional, 30.3% services, 20.5% sales, 0.0% farming, 12.1% construction, 23.5% production (2000).
Income: Per capita income: $12,534 (2000); Median household income: $30,938 (2000); Poverty rate: 12.3% (2000).
Taxes: Total city taxes per capita: $17 (1997); City property taxes per capita: $17 (1997).
Education: High school graduation rate: 67.9% (2000); College graduation rate: 3.8% (2000).
Housing: Homeownership rate: 87.6% (2000); Median home value: $36,600 (2000); Median rent: $308 per month (2000); Median age of housing: 32 years (2000).
Transportation: Commute to work: 86.2% car, 0.0% public transportation, 0.0% walk, 13.8% work from home (2000); Travel time to work: 10.4% less than 15 minutes, 20.8% 15 to 30 minutes, 65.1% 30 to 45 minutes, 3.8% 45 to 60 minutes, 0.0% 60 minutes or more (2000)

WALSHVILLE (village). Covers a land area of 0.256 square miles and a water area of 0 square miles. Located at 39.07° N. Lat.; 89.61° W. Long. Elevation is 620 feet.
Population: 89 (2000); Race: 100.0% White, 0.0% Black, 0.0% Asian, 0.0% American Indian and Alaska Native, 0.0% Hispanic of any race, 0.0% two or more races (2000); Density: 348.1 persons per square mile (2000); Age: 34.1% under 18, 9.4% over 64 (2000); Marriage status: 19.0% never married, 52.4% now married, 6.3% widowed, 22.2% divorced (2000); Foreign born: 0.0% (2000); Ancestry (includes multiple ancestries): 32.9% United States or American, 12.9% English, 9.4% German, 4.7% Scotch-Irish, 4.7% British (2000).
Economy: In agricultural and coal area. Employment by occupation: 6.5% management, 6.5% professional, 12.9% services, 29.0% sales, 0.0% farming, 22.6% construction, 22.6% production (2000).
Income: Per capita income: $11,080 (2000); Median household income: $19,219 (2000); Poverty rate: 40.0% (2000).
Taxes: Total city taxes per capita: $40 (1997); City property taxes per capita: $40 (1997).
Education: High school graduation rate: 63.0% (2000); College graduation rate: 7.4% (2000).
Housing: Homeownership rate: 75.9% (2000); Median home value: $40,000 (2000); Median rent: $325 per month (2000); Median age of housing: 30 years (2000).
Transportation: Commute to work: 93.5% car, 0.0% public transportation, 0.0% walk, 6.5% work from home (2000); Travel time to work: 20.7% less than 15 minutes, 48.3% 15 to 30 minutes, 10.3% 30 to 45 minutes, 20.7% 45 to 60 minutes, 0.0% 60 minutes or more (2000)

WENONAH (village). Covers a land area of 1.509 square miles and a water area of 0 square miles. Located at 39.32° N. Lat.; 89.28° W. Long. Elevation is 675 feet.
Population: 44 (2000); Race: 100.0% White, 0.0% Black, 0.0% Asian, 0.0% American Indian and Alaska Native, 0.0% Hispanic of any race, 0.0% two or more races (2000); Density: 29.2 persons per square mile (2000); Age: 6.5% under 18, 29.0% over 64 (2000); Marriage status: 10.3% never married, 79.3% now married, 0.0% widowed, 10.3% divorced (2000); Foreign born: 0.0% (2000); Ancestry (includes multiple ancestries): 35.5% German, 19.4% Irish, 16.1% Scotch-Irish, 9.7% Italian, 6.5% English (2000).
Economy: In agricultural and bituminous-coal area. Employment by occupation: 0.0% management, 0.0% professional, 54.5% services, 0.0% sales, 0.0% farming, 0.0% construction, 45.5% production (2000).
Income: Per capita income: $19,890 (2000); Median household income: $34,375 (2000); Poverty rate: 0.0% (2000).
Taxes: Total city taxes per capita: $25 (1997); City property taxes per capita: $0 (1997).
Education: High school graduation rate: 81.5% (2000); College graduation rate: 0.0% (2000).
Housing: Homeownership rate: 100.0% (2000); Median home value: $46,100 (2000); Median age of housing: 47 years (2000).
Transportation: Commute to work: 100.0% car, 0.0% public transportation, 0.0% walk, 0.0% work from home (2000); Travel time to work: 20.0% less than 15 minutes, 10.0% 15 to 30 minutes, 40.0% 30 to 45 minutes, 0.0% 45 to 60 minutes, 30.0% 60 minutes or more (2000)

WITT (city). Covers a land area of 1.394 square miles and a water area of 0 square miles. Located at 39.25° N. Lat.; 89.35° W. Long. Elevation is 666 feet.
Population: 991 (2000); Race: 99.3% White, 0.2% Black, 0.3% Asian, 0.0% American Indian and Alaska Native, 0.0% Hispanic of any race, 0.2% two or more races (2000); Density: 710.9 persons per square mile (2000); Age: 26.3% under 18, 16.1% over 64 (2000); Marriage status: 19.7% never married, 53.6% now married, 11.1% widowed, 15.5% divorced (2000); Foreign born: 0.0% (2000); Ancestry (includes multiple ancestries): 23.7% German, 18.7% United States or American, 13.4% English, 10.3% Other groups, 9.5% Irish (2000).
Economy: Grain; cattle; dairying. Employment by occupation: 6.0% management, 10.2% professional, 21.4% services, 24.2% sales, 0.5% farming, 7.7% construction, 29.9% production (2000).
Income: Per capita income: $14,817 (2000); Median household income: $25,329 (2000); Poverty rate: 21.4% (2000).
Taxes: Total city taxes per capita: $31 (1997); City property taxes per capita: $24 (1997).
Education: High school graduation rate: 74.3% (2000); College graduation rate: 7.4% (2000).
Housing: Homeownership rate: 78.7% (2000); Median home value: $34,900 (2000); Median rent: $192 per month (2000); Median age of housing: 55 years (2000).
Transportation: Commute to work: 91.9% car, 0.5% public transportation, 4.3% walk, 1.5% work from home (2000); Travel time to work: 22.8% less than 15 minutes, 30.8% 15 to 30 minutes, 18.5% 30 to 45 minutes, 11.5% 45 to 60 minutes, 16.4% 60 minutes or more (2000)

Morgan County

Located in west central Illinois; bounded on the west by the Illinois River; includes part of Lake Meredosia. Covers a land area of 568.80 square miles, a water area of 3.50 square miles, and is located in the Central Time Zone. The county government was organized in 1823. County seat is Jacksonville.

Weather Station: Jacksonville 2 E — Elevation: 606 feet

	Jan	Feb	Mar	Apr	May	Jun	Jul	Aug	Sep	Oct	Nov	Dec
High	33	39	51	63	74	83	86	84	79	67	52	39
Low	15	20	29	40	50	60	64	61	53	42	32	21
Precip	1.4	1.7	3.2	3.9	5.0	4.3	3.8	3.4	3.6	2.7	3.4	2.6
Snow	7.3	5.6	3.1	0.5	0.0	0.0	0.0	0.0	0.0	tr	1.4	5.0

High and Low temperatures in degrees Fahrenheit; Precipitation and Snow in inches

Population: 36,616 (2000); Race: 92.4% White, 5.3% Black, 0.4% Asian, 0.2% American Indian and Alaska Native, 1.2% Hispanic of any race, 0.8% two or more races (2000); Density: 64.4 persons per square mile (2000); Age: 22.7% under 18, 15.7% over 64 (2000).
Religion: Five largest groups: 11.2% Catholic Church, 7.2% The United Methodist Church, 6.2% Christian Church (Disciples of Christ), 5.4% Southern Baptist Convention, 5.2% Lutheran Church—Missouri Synod (2000).
Economy: Unemployment rate: 4.5% (11/2002); Total civilian labor force: 17,904 (11/2002); Leading industries: 24.8% manufacturing; 16.8% health care and social assistance; 13.7% retail trade (2000); Companies that employ more than 1,000 persons: 0 (2000); Companies that employ more than 100 persons: 27 (2000); Farms: 780 totaling 305,585 acres (1997); Minority business ownership rate: 0.0% (1997); Women business ownership rate: 21.6% (1997); Retail sales per capita: $9,628 (1997). Single-family building permits issued: 20 (2001) / 14 (2000); Multi-family building permits issued: 2 (2001) / 8 (2000).

Income: Per capita income: $18,205 (2000); Median household income: $36,933 (2000); Poverty rate: 9.7% (2000); Bankruptcy rate: 6.07% (2001).
Taxes: Total county taxes per capita: $117 (1997); County property taxes per capita: $79 (1997).
Education: High school graduation rate: 79.9% (2000); College graduation rate: 19.9% (2000).
Housing: Homeownership rate: 70.3% (2000); Median home value: $75,800 (2000); Median rent: $322 per month (2000); Median age of housing: 40 years (2000).
Health: Birth rate: 116.3 per 10,000 population (1998); Age adjusted death rate: 89.0 per 10,000 population (1999); Age adjusted cancer mortality rate: 211.8 deaths per 100,000 population (1999). Number of physicians: 12.8 per 10,000 population (1999); Number of hospital beds: 31.1 per 10,000 population (1999).
Elections: 2000 Presidential election results: 41.2% Gore, 56.2% Bush, 1.8% Nader, 0.7% Buchanan

Additional Information Contacts
Morgan County Government Offices. 217-245-4619
Jacksonville Area Association of Realtors. 217-243-2611
Jacksonville Area Economic Development 217-479-4627
Jacksonville Chamber of Commerce 217-245-2174

Morgan County Communities

ALEXANDER (unincorporated postal area, zip code 62601). Covers a land area of 55.344 square miles and a water area of 0 square miles. Located at 39.75° N. Lat.; 90.02° W. Long. Elevation is 660 feet.
Population: 512 (2000); Race: 97.7% White, 1.3% Black, 0.0% Asian, 0.6% American Indian and Alaska Native, 0.0% Hispanic of any race, 0.0% two or more races (2000); Density: 9.3 persons per square mile (2000); Age: 25.0% under 18, 11.4% over 64 (2000); Marriage status: 20.1% never married, 63.8% now married, 4.6% widowed, 11.4% divorced (2000); Foreign born: 0.0% (2000); Ancestry (includes multiple ancestries): 23.3% German, 20.3% English, 10.9% Irish, 7.7% United States or American, 3.8% Swedish (2000).
Economy: Employment by occupation: 22.6% management, 7.7% professional, 13.1% services, 26.2% sales, 4.5% farming, 12.8% construction, 13.1% production (2000).
Income: Per capita income: $19,414 (2000); Median household income: $46,932 (2000); Poverty rate: 6.2% (2000).
Education: High school graduation rate: 86.3% (2000); College graduation rate: 12.9% (2000).

School District(s)
Franklin C U School District 1 (PK-12)
2000 Enrollment: 446 217-478-3011
Housing: Homeownership rate: 73.1% (2000); Median home value: $75,700 (2000); Median rent: $352 per month (2000); Median age of housing: 55 years (2000).
Transportation: Commute to work: 90.1% car, 0.0% public transportation, 1.8% walk, 8.1% work from home (2000); Travel time to work: 29.3% less than 15 minutes, 40.1% 15 to 30 minutes, 20.2% 30 to 45 minutes, 8.8% 45 to 60 minutes, 1.6% 60 minutes or more (2000)

CHAPIN (village). Covers a land area of 0.975 square miles and a water area of 0 square miles. Located at 39.76° N. Lat.; 90.40° W. Long. Elevation is 628 feet.
Population: 592 (2000); Race: 100.0% White, 0.0% Black, 0.0% Asian, 0.0% American Indian and Alaska Native, 0.0% Hispanic of any race, 0.0% two or more races (2000); Density: 607.1 persons per square mile (2000); Age: 31.2% under 18, 11.2% over 64 (2000); Marriage status: 16.7% never married, 65.2% now married, 6.9% widowed, 11.2% divorced (2000); Foreign born: 0.0% (2000); Ancestry (includes multiple ancestries): 28.7% German, 14.5% Irish, 11.3% English, 10.1% Other groups, 8.9% United States or American (2000).
Economy: In agricultural area: corn, wheat, sorghum, soybeans; cattle, hogs. Employment by occupation: 9.0% management, 10.9% professional, 13.2% services, 28.9% sales, 0.0% farming, 9.0% construction, 28.9% production (2000).
Income: Per capita income: $16,972 (2000); Median household income: $42,143 (2000); Poverty rate: 8.9% (2000).
Taxes: Total city taxes per capita: $52 (1997); City property taxes per capita: $47 (1997).
Education: High school graduation rate: 86.3% (2000); College graduation rate: 8.9% (2000).
Housing: Homeownership rate: 91.6% (2000); Median home value: $60,400 (2000); Median rent: $271 per month (2000); Median age of housing: 58 years (2000).
Transportation: Commute to work: 98.5% car, 0.0% public transportation, 1.5% walk, 0.0% work from home (2000); Travel time to work: 32.3% less than 15 minutes, 54.1% 15 to 30 minutes, 4.9% 30 to 45 minutes, 1.9% 45 to 60 minutes, 6.8% 60 minutes or more (2000)

CONCORD (village). Covers a land area of 0.263 square miles and a water area of 0 square miles. Located at 39.81° N. Lat.; 90.37° W. Long. Elevation is 595 feet.
Population: 176 (2000); Race: 96.7% White, 0.0% Black, 0.0% Asian, 1.1% American Indian and Alaska Native, 2.2% Hispanic of any race, 2.2% two or more races (2000); Density: 670.2 persons per square mile (2000); Age: 23.0% under 18, 19.1% over 64 (2000); Marriage status: 13.5% never married, 70.3% now married, 3.4% widowed, 12.8% divorced (2000); Foreign born: 1.1% (2000); Ancestry (includes multiple ancestries): 25.1% German, 21.3% Irish, 19.1% English, 14.2% United States or American, 12.0% Other groups (2000).
Economy: In agricultural area: corn, wheat, sorghum; cattle, hogs. Employment by occupation: 0.0% management, 15.3% professional, 17.6% services, 23.5% sales, 0.0% farming, 15.3% construction, 28.2% production (2000).
Income: Per capita income: $13,212 (2000); Median household income: $30,000 (2000); Poverty rate: 18.6% (2000).
Taxes: Total city taxes per capita: $47 (1997); City property taxes per capita: $47 (1997).
Education: High school graduation rate: 72.0% (2000); College graduation rate: 6.8% (2000).

School District(s)
Triopia C U School District 27 (PK-12)
2000 Enrollment: 504 217-457-2283
Housing: Homeownership rate: 91.5% (2000); Median home value: $45,900 (2000); Median rent: $250 per month (2000); Median age of housing: 60+ years (2000).
Transportation: Commute to work: 98.8% car, 0.0% public transportation, 0.0% walk, 1.2% work from home (2000); Travel time to work: 15.5% less than 15 minutes, 58.3% 15 to 30 minutes, 9.5% 30 to 45 minutes, 11.9% 45 to 60 minutes, 4.8% 60 minutes or more (2000)

FRANKLIN (village). Covers a land area of 0.731 square miles and a water area of 0 square miles. Located at 39.62° N. Lat.; 90.04° W. Long. Elevation is 693 feet.
Population: 586 (2000); Race: 97.3% White, 0.7% Black, 0.0% Asian, 1.0% American Indian and Alaska Native, 1.0% Hispanic of any race, 0.7% two or more races (2000); Density: 801.3 persons per square mile (2000); Age: 30.9% under 18, 9.6% over 64 (2000); Marriage status: 15.9% never married, 69.1% now married, 5.2% widowed, 9.9% divorced (2000); Foreign born: 0.3% (2000); Ancestry (includes multiple ancestries): 19.3% Irish, 16.4% German, 13.5% Other groups, 12.6% English, 9.1% United States or American (2000).
Economy: Agriculture: corn, soybeans. Employment by occupation: 8.8% management, 17.8% professional, 18.5% services, 20.5% sales, 1.0% farming, 11.8% construction, 21.5% production (2000).
Income: Per capita income: $16,327 (2000); Median household income: $39,375 (2000); Poverty rate: 8.6% (2000).
Taxes: Total city taxes per capita: $33 (1997); City property taxes per capita: $31 (1997).
Education: High school graduation rate: 89.0% (2000); College graduation rate: 14.4% (2000).
Housing: Homeownership rate: 77.9% (2000); Median home value: $62,500 (2000); Median rent: $371 per month (2000); Median age of housing: 39 years (2000).
Newspapers: Murrayville Gazette (1 x week); Franklin Times (1 x week)
Transportation: Commute to work: 87.3% car, 0.0% public transportation, 7.2% walk, 3.1% work from home (2000); Travel time to work: 25.1% less than 15 minutes, 42.4% 15 to 30 minutes, 15.5% 30 to 45 minutes, 13.4% 45 to 60 minutes, 3.5% 60 minutes or more (2000)

JACKSONVILLE (city). Covers a land area of 10.133 square miles and a water area of 0.193 square miles. Located at 39.73° N. Lat.; 90.23° W. Long. Elevation is 613 feet.
History: Jacksonville was founded in 1825, and named for Andrew Jackson. The first settlers were southerners, but they were followed by people from New England. Abolitionist sentiment was strong, and Jacksonville served as a station on the Underground Railroad. Both William Jennings Bryan (1883)

and Stephen A. Douglas (1834) began their law practices in Jacksonville, and Abraham Lincoln was a frequent speaker here.
Population: 18,940 (2000); Race: 90.9% White, 6.6% Black, 0.6% Asian, 0.2% American Indian and Alaska Native, 1.4% Hispanic of any race, 1.2% two or more races (2000); Density: 1,869.1 persons per square mile (2000); Age: 21.8% under 18, 17.1% over 64 (2000); Marriage status: 25.0% never married, 56.2% now married, 8.1% widowed, 10.8% divorced (2000); Foreign born: 1.4% (2000); Ancestry (includes multiple ancestries): 19.6% German, 13.8% English, 11.2% Other groups, 10.5% United States or American, 10.0% Irish (2000).
Vital Statistics: Birth rate: 164.2 per 10,000 population (1998)
Economy: Single-family building permits issued: 16 (2001) / 12 (2000); Multi-family building permits issued: 2 (2001) / 6 (2000); Employment by occupation: 9.3% management, 21.2% professional, 19.8% services, 24.0% sales, 0.8% farming, 6.6% construction, 18.2% production (2000).
Income: Per capita income: $17,482 (2000); Median household income: $33,117 (2000); Poverty rate: 12.4% (2000).
Taxes: Total city taxes per capita: $175 (1997); City property taxes per capita: $138 (1997).
Education: High school graduation rate: 79.6% (2000); College graduation rate: 23.2% (2000).

School District(s)

Brown/Cass/Morgan/Scott Roe (05-12)
2000 Enrollment: 81 217-243-1804
Four Rivers Special Education District (02-12)
2000 Enrollment: 62 217-245-7174
Jacksonville School District 117 (PK-12)
2000 Enrollment: 3,715 217-243-9411

Four-year College(s)

Illinois College (Private, Not-for-profit, Presbyterian Church (USA))
2001 Enrollment: 874 217-245-3000
2001 Tuition: In-state $11,272; Out-of-state $11,272
MacMurray College (Private, Not-for-profit, United Methodist)
2001 Enrollment: 655 217-479-7000
2001 Tuition: In-state $14,000; Out-of-state $14,000

Housing: Homeownership rate: 61.4% (2000); Median home value: $75,200 (2000); Median rent: $324 per month (2000); Median age of housing: 43 years (2000).
Hospitals: Passavant Memorial Area Hospital (173 beds)
Newspapers: Jacksonville Journal-Courier (7 x week); Shoppers Guide (1 x week)
Transportation: Commute to work: 88.0% car, 0.9% public transportation, 6.4% walk, 2.7% work from home (2000); Travel time to work: 68.9% less than 15 minutes, 14.9% 15 to 30 minutes, 6.3% 30 to 45 minutes, 6.2% 45 to 60 minutes, 3.6% 60 minutes or more (2000)

Additional Information Contacts

Jacksonville Area Association of Realtors 217-243-2611
Jacksonville Area Economic Development 217-479-4627
Jacksonville Chamber of Commerce 217-245-2174

LYNNVILLE (village). Covers a land area of 0.079 square miles and a water area of 0 square miles. Located at 39.68° N. Lat.; 90.34° W. Long. Elevation is 618 feet.
Population: 137 (2000); Race: 100.0% White, 0.0% Black, 0.0% Asian, 0.0% American Indian and Alaska Native, 0.0% Hispanic of any race, 0.0% two or more races (2000); Density: 1,737.1 persons per square mile (2000); Age: 27.6% under 18, 7.6% over 64 (2000); Marriage status: 20.5% never married, 65.2% now married, 6.3% widowed, 8.0% divorced (2000); Foreign born: 0.0% (2000); Ancestry (includes multiple ancestries): 22.1% United States or American, 13.1% English, 10.3% German, 6.9% Irish, 6.2% Dutch (2000).
Economy: In agricultural area. Employment by occupation: 2.8% management, 9.9% professional, 22.5% services, 21.1% sales, 2.8% farming, 14.1% construction, 26.8% production (2000).
Income: Per capita income: $14,919 (2000); Median household income: $38,000 (2000); Poverty rate: 1.4% (2000).
Taxes: Total city taxes per capita: $16 (1997); City property taxes per capita: $16 (1997).
Education: High school graduation rate: 71.1% (2000); College graduation rate: 9.6% (2000).
Housing: Homeownership rate: 83.9% (2000); Median home value: $58,800 (2000); Median rent: $363 per month (2000); Median age of housing: 20 years (2000).
Transportation: Commute to work: 95.8% car, 0.0% public transportation, 0.0% walk, 4.2% work from home (2000); Travel time to work: 33.8% less than 15 minutes, 63.2% 15 to 30 minutes, 0.0% 30 to 45 minutes, 0.0% 45 to 60 minutes, 2.9% 60 minutes or more (2000)

MEREDOSIA (village). Covers a land area of 0.921 square miles and a water area of 0.078 square miles. Located at 39.83° N. Lat.; 90.55° W. Long. Elevation is 448 feet.
History: The name of Meredosia is from the French "marais d'osier" meaning "swamp of the basket reeds." The town was located at the mouth of Meredosia Lake. The railroad connecting with the Illinois & Michigan Canal was constructed here in 1838, but the Canal continued to hold supremacy over the railroad until 1878.
Population: 1,041 (2000); Race: 99.5% White, 0.0% Black, 0.0% Asian, 0.0% American Indian and Alaska Native, 0.0% Hispanic of any race, 0.5% two or more races (2000); Density: 1,130.3 persons per square mile (2000); Age: 24.3% under 18, 18.7% over 64 (2000); Marriage status: 17.0% never married, 61.6% now married, 10.9% widowed, 10.5% divorced (2000); Foreign born: 0.2% (2000); Ancestry (includes multiple ancestries): 22.8% German, 12.6% English, 8.7% United States or American, 8.7% Irish, 5.0% Other groups (2000).
Economy: Single-family building permits issued: 2 (2001) / 0 (2000); Multi-family building permits issued: 0 (2001) / 0 (2000); Employment by occupation: 4.9% management, 10.8% professional, 18.1% services, 21.6% sales, 0.0% farming, 7.9% construction, 36.6% production (2000).
Income: Per capita income: $19,391 (2000); Median household income: $32,961 (2000); Poverty rate: 9.2% (2000).
Taxes: Total city taxes per capita: $52 (1997); City property taxes per capita: $44 (1997).
Education: High school graduation rate: 76.3% (2000); College graduation rate: 5.2% (2000).

School District(s)

Meredosia-Chambersburg CUSD 11 (PK-12)
2000 Enrollment: 345 217-584-1744

Housing: Homeownership rate: 81.6% (2000); Median home value: $50,800 (2000); Median rent: $279 per month (2000); Median age of housing: 37 years (2000).
Transportation: Commute to work: 94.0% car, 0.0% public transportation, 3.1% walk, 0.9% work from home (2000); Travel time to work: 38.7% less than 15 minutes, 28.6% 15 to 30 minutes, 20.7% 30 to 45 minutes, 4.7% 45 to 60 minutes, 7.2% 60 minutes or more (2000)

MURRAYVILLE (village). Covers a land area of 0.498 square miles and a water area of 0 square miles. Located at 39.58° N. Lat.; 90.25° W. Long. Elevation is 687 feet.
Population: 644 (2000); Race: 99.7% White, 0.0% Black, 0.0% Asian, 0.2% American Indian and Alaska Native, 0.0% Hispanic of any race, 0.2% two or more races (2000); Density: 1,292.4 persons per square mile (2000); Age: 30.5% under 18, 9.0% over 64 (2000); Marriage status: 21.0% never married, 64.2% now married, 7.3% widowed, 7.5% divorced (2000); Foreign born: 0.0% (2000); Ancestry (includes multiple ancestries): 25.5% German, 20.4% United States or American, 16.0% English, 11.6% Irish, 3.9% Other groups (2000).
Economy: In agricultural area: corn, wheat, soybeans, cattle, hogs. Employment by occupation: 4.8% management, 8.4% professional, 13.6% services, 30.1% sales, 0.6% farming, 15.1% construction, 27.4% production (2000).
Income: Per capita income: $15,353 (2000); Median household income: $42,917 (2000); Poverty rate: 11.2% (2000).
Taxes: Total city taxes per capita: $40 (1997); City property taxes per capita: $40 (1997).
Education: High school graduation rate: 82.5% (2000); College graduation rate: 8.6% (2000).
Housing: Homeownership rate: 82.9% (2000); Median home value: $61,100 (2000); Median rent: $321 per month (2000); Median age of housing: 49 years (2000).
Transportation: Commute to work: 95.2% car, 0.0% public transportation, 2.4% walk, 2.4% work from home (2000); Travel time to work: 16.0% less than 15 minutes, 58.6% 15 to 30 minutes, 14.5% 30 to 45 minutes, 6.5% 45 to 60 minutes, 4.3% 60 minutes or more (2000)

SOUTH JACKSONVILLE (village). Covers a land area of 1.653 square miles and a water area of 0.058 square miles. Located at 39.71° N. Lat.; 90.23° W. Long. Elevation is 621 feet.
Population: 3,475 (2000); Race: 97.5% White, 0.7% Black, 1.0% Asian, 0.5% American Indian and Alaska Native, 0.0% Hispanic of any race, 0.3% two or more races (2000); Density: 2,102.3 persons per square mile (2000); Age: 19.9% under 18, 21.3% over 64 (2000); Marriage status: 21.0% never

married, 57.6% now married, 10.4% widowed, 11.1% divorced (2000); Foreign born: 1.1% (2000); Ancestry (includes multiple ancestries): 26.1% German, 16.2% English, 12.3% United States or American, 11.3% Irish, 6.3% Other groups (2000).
Economy: Single-family building permits issued: 2 (2001) / 2 (2000); Multi-family building permits issued: 0 (2001) / 2 (2000); Employment by occupation: 13.1% management, 23.6% professional, 16.8% services, 27.6% sales, 0.0% farming, 5.8% construction, 13.0% production (2000).
Income: Per capita income: $20,973 (2000); Median household income: $37,548 (2000); Poverty rate: 6.5% (2000).
Taxes: Total city taxes per capita: $94 (1997); City property taxes per capita: $77 (1997).
Education: High school graduation rate: 84.2% (2000); College graduation rate: 26.1% (2000).
Housing: Homeownership rate: 70.6% (2000); Median home value: $82,500 (2000); Median rent: $309 per month (2000); Median age of housing: 38 years (2000).
Transportation: Commute to work: 94.7% car, 0.0% public transportation, 0.2% walk, 3.7% work from home (2000); Travel time to work: 59.5% less than 15 minutes, 19.1% 15 to 30 minutes, 12.6% 30 to 45 minutes, 6.5% 45 to 60 minutes, 2.4% 60 minutes or more (2000)

WAVERLY (city). Covers a land area of 1.032 square miles and a water area of 0 square miles. Located at 39.59° N. Lat.; 89.95° W. Long. Elevation is 685 feet.
History: Incorporated 1867.
Population: 1,346 (2000); Race: 98.7% White, 0.0% Black, 0.1% Asian, 0.0% American Indian and Alaska Native, 0.7% Hispanic of any race, 1.0% two or more races (2000); Density: 1,303.9 persons per square mile (2000); Age: 25.2% under 18, 19.6% over 64 (2000); Marriage status: 21.5% never married, 58.7% now married, 10.6% widowed, 9.2% divorced (2000); Foreign born: 0.7% (2000); Ancestry (includes multiple ancestries): 20.9% German, 18.2% English, 12.9% Irish, 12.8% United States or American, 7.8% Other groups (2000).
Economy: In agricultural area: corn, wheat, soybeans; cattle, hogs. Single-family building permits issued: 0 (2001) / 0 (2000); Multi-family building permits issued: 0 (2001) / 0 (2000); Employment by occupation: 13.3% management, 9.8% professional, 12.3% services, 32.1% sales, 0.3% farming, 9.5% construction, 22.6% production (2000).
Income: Per capita income: $18,205 (2000); Median household income: $36,111 (2000); Poverty rate: 8.0% (2000).
Taxes: Total city taxes per capita: $41 (1997); City property taxes per capita: $35 (1997).
Education: High school graduation rate: 82.6% (2000); College graduation rate: 12.8% (2000).

School District(s)

Waverly C U School District 6 (PK-12)
2000 Enrollment: 410 217-435-8121

Housing: Homeownership rate: 83.5% (2000); Median home value: $56,400 (2000); Median rent: $308 per month (2000); Median age of housing: 56 years (2000).
Newspapers: Waverly Journal (1 x week)
Transportation: Commute to work: 90.8% car, 0.3% public transportation, 2.5% walk, 4.9% work from home (2000); Travel time to work: 23.4% less than 15 minutes, 21.2% 15 to 30 minutes, 34.6% 30 to 45 minutes, 16.9% 45 to 60 minutes, 3.8% 60 minutes or more (2000)

WOODSON (village). Covers a land area of 0.387 square miles and a water area of 0 square miles. Located at 39.62° N. Lat.; 90.22° W. Long. Elevation is 677 feet.
Population: 559 (2000); Race: 95.3% White, 0.5% Black, 0.4% Asian, 1.2% American Indian and Alaska Native, 2.1% Hispanic of any race, 1.8% two or more races (2000); Density: 1,442.6 persons per square mile (2000); Age: 29.0% under 18, 10.9% over 64 (2000); Marriage status: 24.2% never married, 60.8% now married, 6.2% widowed, 8.9% divorced (2000); Foreign born: 0.4% (2000); Ancestry (includes multiple ancestries): 22.3% German, 16.2% United States or American, 12.1% English, 12.0% Irish, 5.8% Other groups (2000).
Economy: In agricultural area: corn, wheat, soybeans; cattle, hogs. Employment by occupation: 12.1% management, 15.7% professional, 20.3% services, 23.6% sales, 0.0% farming, 11.5% construction, 16.7% production (2000).
Income: Per capita income: $17,175 (2000); Median household income: $41,500 (2000); Poverty rate: 6.2% (2000).
Taxes: Total city taxes per capita: $49 (1997); City property taxes per capita: $45 (1997).
Education: High school graduation rate: 83.5% (2000); College graduation rate: 15.3% (2000).
Housing: Homeownership rate: 87.3% (2000); Median home value: $75,000 (2000); Median rent: $369 per month (2000); Median age of housing: 26 years (2000).
Transportation: Commute to work: 97.3% car, 0.0% public transportation, 0.0% walk, 1.0% work from home (2000); Travel time to work: 26.6% less than 15 minutes, 51.2% 15 to 30 minutes, 9.4% 30 to 45 minutes, 7.4% 45 to 60 minutes, 5.4% 60 minutes or more (2000)

Moultrie County

Located in central Illinois; drained by the Kaskaskia River. Covers a land area of 335.60 square miles, a water area of 8.90 square miles, and is located in the Central Time Zone. The county government was organized in 1843. County seat is Sullivan.
Population: 14,287 (2000); Race: 98.8% White, 0.3% Black, 0.2% Asian, 0.2% American Indian and Alaska Native, 0.6% Hispanic of any race, 0.5% two or more races (2000); Density: 42.6 persons per square mile (2000); Age: 25.5% under 18, 17.7% over 64 (2000).
Religion: Five largest groups: 10.0% Christian Church (Disciples of Christ), 7.4% The United Methodist Church, 5.9% Southern Baptist Convention, 4.2% Catholic Church, 3.1% Lutheran Church—Missouri Synod (2000).
Economy: Unemployment rate: 4.5% (11/2002); Total civilian labor force: 8,339 (11/2002); Leading industries: 25.3% manufacturing; 21.0% health care and social assistance; 11.1% retail trade (2000); Companies that employ more than 1,000 persons: 0 (2000); Companies that employ more than 100 persons: 6 (2000); Farms: 464 totaling 172,657 acres (1997); Minority business ownership rate: 0.0% (1997); Women business ownership rate: 14.7% (1997); Retail sales per capita: $2,940 (1997). Single-family building permits issued: 55 (2001) / 45 (2000); Multi-family building permits issued: 0 (2001) / 2 (2000).
Income: Per capita income: $18,562 (2000); Median household income: $40,084 (2000); Poverty rate: 7.8% (2000); Bankruptcy rate: 5.45% (2001).
Taxes: Total county taxes per capita: $58 (1997); County property taxes per capita: $58 (1997).
Education: High school graduation rate: 78.8% (2000); College graduation rate: 14.7% (2000).
Housing: Homeownership rate: 78.4% (2000); Median home value: $72,800 (2000); Median rent: $331 per month (2000); Median age of housing: 41 years (2000).
Health: Birth rate: 113.4 per 10,000 population (1998); Age adjusted death rate: 93.4 per 10,000 population (1999); Age adjusted cancer mortality rate: 208.1 deaths per 100,000 population (1999). Number of physicians: 6.3 per 10,000 population (1999); Number of hospital beds: n/a (1999).
Elections: 2000 Presidential election results: 44.2% Gore, 53.4% Bush, 1.4% Nader, 0.7% Buchanan
National and State Parks: Kaskaskia River State Fish and Wildlife Management; West Okaw River State Fish and Wildlife Management
Additional Information Contacts
Moultrie County Government Offices 217-728-4389
Sullivan Chamber of Commerce 217-728-4223

Moultrie County Communities

ALLENVILLE (village). Covers a land area of 0.582 square miles and a water area of 0 square miles. Located at 39.55° N. Lat.; 88.53° W. Long. Elevation is 650 feet.
Population: 154 (2000); Race: 100.0% White, 0.0% Black, 0.0% Asian, 0.0% American Indian and Alaska Native, 0.0% Hispanic of any race, 0.0% two or more races (2000); Density: 264.4 persons per square mile (2000); Age: 11.2% under 18, 7.7% over 64 (2000); Marriage status: 27.6% never married, 59.2% now married, 4.6% widowed, 8.6% divorced (2000); Foreign born: 1.2% (2000); Ancestry (includes multiple ancestries): 31.4% United States or American, 18.3% German, 10.7% Irish, 10.1% Other groups, 4.1% English (2000).
Economy: In agricultural area. Single-family building permits issued: 0 (2001) / 0 (2000); Multi-family building permits issued: 0 (2001) / 0 (2000); Employment by occupation: 12.1% management, 3.7% professional, 15.9% services, 26.2% sales, 0.0% farming, 6.5% construction, 35.5% production (2000).
Income: Per capita income: $16,586 (2000); Median household income: $46,146 (2000); Poverty rate: 7.7% (2000).
Taxes: Total city taxes per capita: $12 (1997); City property taxes per capita: $6 (1997).

Education: High school graduation rate: 76.0% (2000); College graduation rate: 6.2% (2000).
Housing: Homeownership rate: 93.5% (2000); Median home value: $47,500 (2000); Median rent: $275 per month (2000); Median age of housing: 29 years (2000).
Transportation: Commute to work: 95.1% car, 0.0% public transportation, 2.0% walk, 2.9% work from home (2000); Travel time to work: 17.2% less than 15 minutes, 59.6% 15 to 30 minutes, 12.1% 30 to 45 minutes, 6.1% 45 to 60 minutes, 5.1% 60 minutes or more (2000)

BETHANY (village). Covers a land area of 0.972 square miles and a water area of 0.004 square miles. Located at 39.64° N. Lat.; 88.73° W. Long. Elevation is 661 feet.
Population: 1,287 (2000); Race: 99.1% White, 0.2% Black, 0.5% Asian, 0.0% American Indian and Alaska Native, 0.5% Hispanic of any race, 0.2% two or more races (2000); Density: 1,323.6 persons per square mile (2000); Age: 22.4% under 18, 19.8% over 64 (2000); Marriage status: 16.8% never married, 63.8% now married, 12.1% widowed, 7.3% divorced (2000); Foreign born: 1.1% (2000); Ancestry (includes multiple ancestries): 23.0% German, 17.8% United States or American, 12.0% English, 12.0% Irish, 6.4% Other groups (2000).
Economy: Corn, wheat, soybeans; livestock, poultry; dairy products. Single-family building permits issued: 2 (2001) / 1 (2000); Multi-family building permits issued: 0 (2001) / 0 (2000); Employment by occupation: 9.9% management, 9.6% professional, 13.8% services, 21.9% sales, 0.8% farming, 9.4% construction, 34.5% production (2000).
Income: Per capita income: $16,888 (2000); Median household income: $34,091 (2000); Poverty rate: 7.4% (2000).
Taxes: Total city taxes per capita: $41 (1997); City property taxes per capita: $35 (1997).
Education: High school graduation rate: 85.3% (2000); College graduation rate: 7.6% (2000).

School District(s)

Bethany C U School District 301 (PK-12)
2000 Enrollment: 391 217-665-3232
Housing: Homeownership rate: 85.5% (2000); Median home value: $61,600 (2000); Median rent: $256 per month (2000); Median age of housing: 43 years (2000).
Transportation: Commute to work: 91.8% car, 0.0% public transportation, 6.1% walk, 1.4% work from home (2000); Travel time to work: 33.6% less than 15 minutes, 30.2% 15 to 30 minutes, 26.5% 30 to 45 minutes, 5.3% 45 to 60 minutes, 4.4% 60 minutes or more (2000)

DALTON CITY (village). Covers a land area of 0.617 square miles and a water area of 0.003 square miles. Located at 39.71° N. Lat.; 88.80° W. Long. Elevation is 693 feet.
Population: 581 (2000); Race: 98.2% White, 0.0% Black, 0.0% Asian, 0.5% American Indian and Alaska Native, 2.0% Hispanic of any race, 0.8% two or more races (2000); Density: 941.7 persons per square mile (2000); Age: 31.0% under 18, 8.2% over 64 (2000); Marriage status: 18.0% never married, 72.9% now married, 3.6% widowed, 5.6% divorced (2000); Foreign born: 0.8% (2000); Ancestry (includes multiple ancestries): 26.8% German, 17.8% Irish, 12.4% English, 8.5% United States or American, 6.5% Other groups (2000).
Economy: In agricultural area. Single-family building permits issued: 0 (2001) / 0 (2000); Multi-family building permits issued: 0 (2001) / 0 (2000); Employment by occupation: 6.9% management, 11.6% professional, 14.8% services, 25.5% sales, 1.3% farming, 18.6% construction, 21.4% production (2000).
Income: Per capita income: $16,946 (2000); Median household income: $48,958 (2000); Poverty rate: 4.1% (2000).
Taxes: Total city taxes per capita: $63 (1997); City property taxes per capita: $39 (1997).
Education: High school graduation rate: 89.0% (2000); College graduation rate: 8.1% (2000).
Housing: Homeownership rate: 78.7% (2000); Median home value: $71,200 (2000); Median rent: $360 per month (2000); Median age of housing: 40 years (2000).
Transportation: Commute to work: 95.8% car, 0.0% public transportation, 1.6% walk, 1.3% work from home (2000); Travel time to work: 17.9% less than 15 minutes, 56.0% 15 to 30 minutes, 17.5% 30 to 45 minutes, 0.7% 45 to 60 minutes, 7.9% 60 minutes or more (2000)

GAYS (village). Covers a land area of 0.409 square miles and a water area of 0 square miles. Located at 39.45° N. Lat.; 88.49° W. Long. Elevation is 755 feet.
Population: 259 (2000); Race: 98.4% White, 0.0% Black, 0.0% Asian, 0.0% American Indian and Alaska Native, 0.0% Hispanic of any race, 1.6% two or more races (2000); Density: 633.5 persons per square mile (2000); Age: 28.5% under 18, 10.3% over 64 (2000); Marriage status: 17.4% never married, 72.6% now married, 1.1% widowed, 8.9% divorced (2000); Foreign born: 0.4% (2000); Ancestry (includes multiple ancestries): 22.5% United States or American, 14.6% German, 7.9% Other groups, 5.1% English, 4.7% Irish (2000).
Economy: In agricultural area. Single-family building permits issued: 0 (2001) / 3 (2000); Multi-family building permits issued: 0 (2001) / 0 (2000); Employment by occupation: 7.8% management, 15.7% professional, 15.7% services, 26.1% sales, 0.0% farming, 7.8% construction, 27.0% production (2000).
Income: Per capita income: $19,131 (2000); Median household income: $42,500 (2000); Poverty rate: 3.6% (2000).
Taxes: Total city taxes per capita: $8 (1997); City property taxes per capita: $0 (1997).
Education: High school graduation rate: 92.4% (2000); College graduation rate: 12.4% (2000).
Housing: Homeownership rate: 89.8% (2000); Median home value: $55,000 (2000); Median rent: $425 per month (2000); Median age of housing: 55 years (2000).
Transportation: Commute to work: 97.5% car, 0.0% public transportation, 0.0% walk, 2.5% work from home (2000); Travel time to work: 19.0% less than 15 minutes, 57.8% 15 to 30 minutes, 14.7% 30 to 45 minutes, 1.7% 45 to 60 minutes, 6.9% 60 minutes or more (2000)

LOVINGTON (village). Covers a land area of 0.805 square miles and a water area of 0 square miles. Located at 39.71° N. Lat.; 88.63° W. Long. Elevation is 679 feet.
History: Incorporated 1873.
Population: 1,222 (2000); Race: 97.6% White, 0.4% Black, 0.0% Asian, 1.0% American Indian and Alaska Native, 0.0% Hispanic of any race, 1.0% two or more races (2000); Density: 1,518.4 persons per square mile (2000); Age: 24.9% under 18, 17.1% over 64 (2000); Marriage status: 23.7% never married, 59.0% now married, 9.2% widowed, 8.1% divorced (2000); Foreign born: 0.2% (2000); Ancestry (includes multiple ancestries): 21.1% German, 17.3% United States or American, 12.9% Irish, 12.3% English, 7.2% Other groups (2000).
Economy: Corn, wheat, soybeans; livestock; dairy products. Single-family building permits issued: 5 (2001) / 1 (2000); Multi-family building permits issued: 0 (2001) / 0 (2000); Employment by occupation: 12.1% management, 10.2% professional, 17.3% services, 18.8% sales, 0.5% farming, 8.3% construction, 32.8% production (2000).
Income: Per capita income: $17,311 (2000); Median household income: $34,115 (2000); Poverty rate: 8.7% (2000).
Taxes: Total city taxes per capita: $91 (1997); City property taxes per capita: $85 (1997).
Education: High school graduation rate: 82.3% (2000); College graduation rate: 8.5% (2000).

School District(s)

Lovington C U School District 303 (PK-12)
2000 Enrollment: 374 217-873-4310
Housing: Homeownership rate: 73.8% (2000); Median home value: $55,400 (2000); Median rent: $288 per month (2000); Median age of housing: 50 years (2000).
Transportation: Commute to work: 93.9% car, 0.9% public transportation, 0.9% walk, 2.8% work from home (2000); Travel time to work: 27.2% less than 15 minutes, 36.9% 15 to 30 minutes, 29.1% 30 to 45 minutes, 4.0% 45 to 60 minutes, 2.9% 60 minutes or more (2000)

SULLIVAN (city). Covers a land area of 2.039 square miles and a water area of 0.004 square miles. Located at 39.59° N. Lat.; 88.61° W. Long. Elevation is 680 feet.
History: Incorporated 1869.
Population: 4,326 (2000); Race: 98.8% White, 0.6% Black, 0.4% Asian, 0.0% American Indian and Alaska Native, 0.7% Hispanic of any race, 0.0% two or more races (2000); Density: 2,121.5 persons per square mile (2000); Age: 22.5% under 18, 21.5% over 64 (2000); Marriage status: 17.3% never married, 57.9% now married, 13.3% widowed, 11.5% divorced (2000); Foreign born: 0.5% (2000); Ancestry (includes multiple ancestries): 23.9% United States or American, 18.5% German, 10.8% Irish, 7.9% English, 4.7% Other groups (2000).
Economy: In agricultural area: corn, soybeans; livestock. Manufacturing: wood products, dairy products. Single-family building permits issued: 11 (2001) / 9 (2000); Multi-family building permits issued: 0 (2001) / 2 (2000);

Employment by occupation: 9.1% management, 16.6% professional, 18.0% services, 20.1% sales, 0.4% farming, 7.9% construction, 28.0% production (2000).
Income: Per capita income: $17,693 (2000); Median household income: $33,197 (2000); Poverty rate: 8.8% (2000).
Taxes: Total city taxes per capita: $166 (1997); City property taxes per capita: $166 (1997).
Education: High school graduation rate: 78.4% (2000); College graduation rate: 16.3% (2000).

School District(s)

Sullivan C U School District 300 (PK-12)
2000 Enrollment: 1,146 217-728-8341
Housing: Homeownership rate: 71.8% (2000); Median home value: $69,800 (2000); Median rent: $355 per month (2000); Median age of housing: 42 years (2000).
Newspapers: News-Progress (1 x week)
Transportation: Commute to work: 95.2% car, 0.2% public transportation, 2.7% walk, 1.3% work from home (2000); Travel time to work: 53.0% less than 15 minutes, 20.5% 15 to 30 minutes, 16.1% 30 to 45 minutes, 5.5% 45 to 60 minutes, 4.8% 60 minutes or more (2000)
Additional Information Contacts
Sullivan Chamber of Commerce 217-728-4223

Ogle County

Located in northern Illinois; drained by the Rock, Leaf, and Kyte Rivers. Covers a land area of 758.80 square miles, a water area of 4.40 square miles, and is located in the Central Time Zone. The county government was organized in 1836. County seat is Oregon.

Ogle County is part of the Rockford, IL MSA. The entire metro area includes: Boone County; Ogle County; Winnebago County

Population: 51,032 (2000); Race: 95.5% White, 0.3% Black, 0.4% Asian, 0.5% American Indian and Alaska Native, 6.1% Hispanic of any race, 1.1% two or more races (2000); Density: 67.3 persons per square mile (2000); Age: 27.4% under 18, 13.4% over 64 (2000).
Religion: Five largest groups: 16.3% Catholic Church, 7.7% Evangelical Lutheran Church in America, 7.5% The United Methodist Church, 3.1% Presbyterian Church (U.S.A.), 2.5% Lutheran Church—Missouri Synod (2000).
Economy: Unemployment rate: 5.7% (11/2002); Total civilian labor force: 26,933 (11/2002); Leading industries: 37.5% manufacturing; 9.9% retail trade; 7.9% wholesale trade (2000); Companies that employ more than 1,000 persons: 1 (2000); Companies that employ more than 100 persons: 22 (2000); Farms: 1,099 totaling 379,419 acres (1997); Minority business ownership rate: 4.5% (1997); Women business ownership rate: 24.5% (1997); Retail sales per capita: $5,344 (1997). Single-family building permits issued: 235 (2001) / 207 (2000); Multi-family building permits issued: 2 (2001) / 0 (2000).
Income: Per capita income: $20,515 (2000); Median household income: $45,448 (2000); Poverty rate: 7.1% (2000); Bankruptcy rate: 4.95% (2001).
Taxes: Total county taxes per capita: $158 (2000); County property taxes per capita: $138 (2000).
Education: High school graduation rate: 83.1% (2000); College graduation rate: 17.0% (2000).
Housing: Homeownership rate: 74.5% (2000); Median home value: $102,700 (2000); Median rent: $401 per month (2000); Median age of housing: 39 years (2000).
Health: Birth rate: 122.1 per 10,000 population (1998); Age adjusted death rate: 81.6 per 10,000 population (1999); Age adjusted cancer mortality rate: 226.2 deaths per 100,000 population (1999). Number of physicians: 8.2 per 10,000 population (1999); Number of hospital beds: 10.6 per 10,000 population (1999).
Elections: 2000 Presidential election results: 37.3% Gore, 59.8% Bush, 2.3% Nader, 0.4% Buchanan
National and State Parks: Lowden State Park; White Pines Forest State Park
Additional Information Contacts
Ogle County Government Offices 815-732-3201
Byron Chamber of Commerce 815-234-5500
Mt Morris Chamber of Commerce 815-734-7423
Oregon Chamber of Commerce 815-732-2100
Polo Chamber of Commerce 815-946-3131
Rochelle Chamber of Commerce 815-562-4189

Ogle County Communities

ADELINE (village). Covers a land area of 0.269 square miles and a water area of 0 square miles. Located at 42.14° N. Lat.; 89.49° W. Long. Elevation is 796 feet.
Population: 139 (2000); Race: 95.7% White, 0.0% Black, 0.0% Asian, 0.0% American Indian and Alaska Native, 5.0% Hispanic of any race, 0.0% two or more races (2000); Density: 517.1 persons per square mile (2000); Age: 31.9% under 18, 4.3% over 64 (2000); Marriage status: 21.4% never married, 64.1% now married, 9.7% widowed, 4.9% divorced (2000); Foreign born: 0.0% (2000); Ancestry (includes multiple ancestries): 35.5% German, 12.1% Dutch, 7.1% Other groups, 6.4% English, 5.0% Scotch-Irish (2000).
Economy: In rich agricultural area: corn, oats, soybeans, hay; cattle, hogs; dairying. Employment by occupation: 11.9% management, 3.4% professional, 5.1% services, 5.1% sales, 0.0% farming, 18.6% construction, 55.9% production (2000).
Income: Per capita income: $20,301 (2000); Median household income: $59,583 (2000); Poverty rate: 2.8% (2000).
Taxes: Total city taxes per capita: $25 (1997); City property taxes per capita: $19 (1997).
Education: High school graduation rate: 82.0% (2000); College graduation rate: 5.6% (2000).
Housing: Homeownership rate: 88.9% (2000); Median home value: $79,200 (2000); Median rent: $375 per month (2000); Median age of housing: 60+ years (2000).
Transportation: Commute to work: 96.6% car, 0.0% public transportation, 0.0% walk, 0.0% work from home (2000); Travel time to work: 11.9% less than 15 minutes, 45.8% 15 to 30 minutes, 27.1% 30 to 45 minutes, 0.0% 45 to 60 minutes, 15.3% 60 minutes or more (2000)

BAILEYVILLE (unincorporated postal area, zip code 61007). Covers a land area of 24.962 square miles and a water area of 0 square miles. Located at 42.19° N. Lat.; 89.59° W. Long. Elevation is 940 feet.
Population: 548 (2000); Race: 100.0% White, 0.0% Black, 0.0% Asian, 0.0% American Indian and Alaska Native, 0.0% Hispanic of any race, 0.0% two or more races (2000); Density: 22.0 persons per square mile (2000); Age: 22.0% under 18, 13.1% over 64 (2000); Marriage status: 12.9% never married, 79.6% now married, 2.4% widowed, 5.2% divorced (2000); Foreign born: 0.0% (2000); Ancestry (includes multiple ancestries): 52.1% German, 10.7% United States or American, 7.5% Irish, 6.3% Polish, 5.9% Norwegian (2000).
Economy: Employment by occupation: 15.5% management, 12.6% professional, 9.1% services, 14.2% sales, 4.5% farming, 14.9% construction, 29.1% production (2000).
Income: Per capita income: $17,301 (2000); Median household income: $49,375 (2000); Poverty rate: 3.7% (2000).
Education: High school graduation rate: 79.6% (2000); College graduation rate: 11.9% (2000).
Housing: Homeownership rate: 84.7% (2000); Median home value: $96,300 (2000); Median rent: $419 per month (2000); Median age of housing: 60+ years (2000).
Transportation: Commute to work: 84.0% car, 0.0% public transportation, 0.0% walk, 16.0% work from home (2000); Travel time to work: 50.0% less than 15 minutes, 33.5% 15 to 30 minutes, 7.0% 30 to 45 minutes, 1.7% 45 to 60 minutes, 7.9% 60 minutes or more (2000)

BYRON (city). Covers a land area of 2.474 square miles and a water area of <.001 square miles. Located at 42.12° N. Lat.; 89.26° W. Long. Elevation is 729 feet.
History: Byron was founded in 1835 by settlers from New England, and named for the English poet Lord Byron. Many houses in Byron were stations on the Underground Railroad, offering escape for slaves from the south.
Population: 2,917 (2000); Race: 97.8% White, 0.6% Black, 0.6% Asian, 0.0% American Indian and Alaska Native, 2.2% Hispanic of any race, 0.5% two or more races (2000); Density: 1,179.2 persons per square mile (2000); Age: 30.7% under 18, 15.6% over 64 (2000); Marriage status: 22.4% never married, 58.0% now married, 7.0% widowed, 12.6% divorced (2000); Foreign born: 2.0% (2000); Ancestry (includes multiple ancestries): 29.8% German, 18.7% Irish, 10.0% English, 6.7% Other groups, 6.2% Italian (2000).
Economy: Single-family building permits issued: 46 (2001) / 45 (2000); Multi-family building permits issued: 2 (2001) / 0 (2000); Employment by occupation: 10.0% management, 17.8% professional, 17.8% services, 24.3% sales, 0.2% farming, 11.4% construction, 18.4% production (2000).

Income: Per capita income: $17,164 (2000); Median household income: $37,027 (2000); Poverty rate: 7.8% (2000).
Taxes: Total city taxes per capita: $114 (1997); City property taxes per capita: $76 (1997).
Education: High school graduation rate: 87.4% (2000); College graduation rate: 13.2% (2000).

School District(s)

Byron Community Unit School District 226 (PK-12)
2000 Enrollment: 1,836 815-234-5491
Ogle Co Education Cooperative (PK-11)
2000 Enrollment: 61 815-234-2722

Housing: Homeownership rate: 59.7% (2000); Median home value: $103,200 (2000); Median rent: $461 per month (2000); Median age of housing: 28 years (2000).
Transportation: Commute to work: 92.6% car, 0.3% public transportation, 2.8% walk, 3.8% work from home (2000); Travel time to work: 30.3% less than 15 minutes, 40.5% 15 to 30 minutes, 21.9% 30 to 45 minutes, 3.0% 45 to 60 minutes, 4.3% 60 minutes or more (2000)
Additional Information Contacts
Byron Chamber of Commerce 815-234-5500

CHANA (unincorporated postal area, zip code 61015). Covers a land area of 40.799 square miles and a water area of 0.057 square miles. Located at 41.98° N. Lat.; 89.21° W. Long. Elevation is 780 feet.
Population: 993 (2000); Race: 99.0% White, 0.3% Black, 0.0% Asian, 0.0% American Indian and Alaska Native, 1.8% Hispanic of any race, 0.7% two or more races (2000); Density: 24.3 persons per square mile (2000); Age: 21.5% under 18, 11.2% over 64 (2000); Marriage status: 21.4% never married, 66.5% now married, 5.5% widowed, 6.6% divorced (2000); Foreign born: 0.2% (2000); Ancestry (includes multiple ancestries): 39.5% German, 12.1% English, 7.6% Irish, 5.6% Polish, 5.1% Norwegian (2000).
Economy: Employment by occupation: 12.4% management, 7.4% professional, 12.7% services, 23.3% sales, 0.0% farming, 20.5% construction, 23.7% production (2000).
Income: Per capita income: $20,508 (2000); Median household income: $49,000 (2000); Poverty rate: 0.7% (2000).
Education: High school graduation rate: 86.7% (2000); College graduation rate: 15.9% (2000).
Housing: Homeownership rate: 80.3% (2000); Median home value: $114,400 (2000); Median rent: $342 per month (2000); Median age of housing: 47 years (2000).
Transportation: Commute to work: 97.8% car, 0.0% public transportation, 1.8% walk, 0.4% work from home (2000); Travel time to work: 8.5% less than 15 minutes, 40.0% 15 to 30 minutes, 28.9% 30 to 45 minutes, 11.4% 45 to 60 minutes, 11.2% 60 minutes or more (2000)

CRESTON (village). Covers a land area of 0.418 square miles and a water area of 0 square miles. Located at 41.93° N. Lat.; 88.96° W. Long. Elevation is 900 feet.
Population: 543 (2000); Race: 96.3% White, 2.0% Black, 0.0% Asian, 0.0% American Indian and Alaska Native, 3.7% Hispanic of any race, 1.1% two or more races (2000); Density: 1,299.3 persons per square mile (2000); Age: 25.8% under 18, 12.7% over 64 (2000); Marriage status: 22.4% never married, 58.4% now married, 9.3% widowed, 9.8% divorced (2000); Foreign born: 0.4% (2000); Ancestry (includes multiple ancestries): 26.2% German, 12.0% English, 10.7% United States or American, 9.6% Irish, 7.2% Norwegian (2000).
Economy: In rich agricultural area. Single-family building permits issued: 1 (2001) / 1 (2000); Multi-family building permits issued: 0 (2001) / 0 (2000); Employment by occupation: 8.2% management, 15.7% professional, 9.3% services, 23.6% sales, 2.1% farming, 9.6% construction, 31.4% production (2000).
Income: Per capita income: $18,927 (2000); Median household income: $40,000 (2000); Poverty rate: 5.2% (2000).
Taxes: Total city taxes per capita: $31 (1997); City property taxes per capita: $18 (1997).
Education: High school graduation rate: 80.9% (2000); College graduation rate: 14.2% (2000).

School District(s)

Creston Community Cons School District 161 (KG-08)
2000 Enrollment: 112 815-384-3920

Housing: Homeownership rate: 70.9% (2000); Median home value: $93,600 (2000); Median rent: $481 per month (2000); Median age of housing: 40 years (2000).
Transportation: Commute to work: 94.3% car, 0.0% public transportation, 3.9% walk, 1.8% work from home (2000); Travel time to work: 27.6% less than 15 minutes, 42.2% 15 to 30 minutes, 16.0% 30 to 45 minutes, 5.1% 45 to 60 minutes, 9.1% 60 minutes or more (2000)

DAVIS JUNCTION (village). Covers a land area of 3.790 square miles and a water area of 0 square miles. Located at 42.10° N. Lat.; 89.09° W. Long. Elevation is 789 feet.
Population: 491 (2000); Race: 94.7% White, 0.0% Black, 0.0% Asian, 0.0% American Indian and Alaska Native, 5.9% Hispanic of any race, 3.7% two or more races (2000); Density: 129.6 persons per square mile (2000); Age: 32.1% under 18, 11.4% over 64 (2000); Marriage status: 13.8% never married, 63.3% now married, 11.9% widowed, 11.0% divorced (2000); Foreign born: 2.4% (2000); Ancestry (includes multiple ancestries): 29.0% German, 13.4% United States or American, 12.7% Other groups, 12.1% Irish, 6.8% Swedish (2000).
Economy: Railroad junction. Grain; livestock, dairying. Manufacturing: leather. Single-family building permits issued: 0 (2001) / 0 (2000); Multi-family building permits issued: 0 (2001) / 0 (2000); Employment by occupation: 9.6% management, 11.8% professional, 8.0% services, 35.8% sales, 0.0% farming, 11.8% construction, 23.0% production (2000).
Income: Per capita income: $16,915 (2000); Median household income: $47,375 (2000); Poverty rate: 2.6% (2000).
Taxes: Total city taxes per capita: $66 (1997); City property taxes per capita: $25 (1997).
Education: High school graduation rate: 81.9% (2000); College graduation rate: 9.9% (2000).
Housing: Homeownership rate: 92.8% (2000); Median home value: $112,900 (2000); Median rent: $838 per month (2000); Median age of housing: 7 years (2000).
Transportation: Commute to work: 97.3% car, 0.0% public transportation, 0.5% walk, 2.2% work from home (2000); Travel time to work: 8.2% less than 15 minutes, 61.5% 15 to 30 minutes, 20.9% 30 to 45 minutes, 6.0% 45 to 60 minutes, 3.3% 60 minutes or more (2000)

FORRESTON (village). Covers a land area of 0.831 square miles and a water area of 0 square miles. Located at 42.12° N. Lat.; 89.58° W. Long. Elevation is 937 feet.
History: The first sauerkraut festival was held in Forreston in 1913.
Population: 1,469 (2000); Race: 98.8% White, 0.0% Black, 0.0% Asian, 0.5% American Indian and Alaska Native, 1.8% Hispanic of any race, 0.5% two or more races (2000); Density: 1,767.4 persons per square mile (2000); Age: 28.2% under 18, 17.7% over 64 (2000); Marriage status: 17.8% never married, 62.7% now married, 10.8% widowed, 8.7% divorced (2000); Foreign born: 1.4% (2000); Ancestry (includes multiple ancestries): 46.3% German, 12.9% Irish, 8.6% English, 7.6% United States or American, 3.7% Other groups (2000).
Economy: Single-family building permits issued: 6 (2001) / 2 (2000); Multi-family building permits issued: 0 (2001) / 0 (2000); Employment by occupation: 8.6% management, 13.8% professional, 12.4% services, 22.5% sales, 1.5% farming, 8.8% construction, 32.4% production (2000).
Income: Per capita income: $16,958 (2000); Median household income: $36,554 (2000); Poverty rate: 9.6% (2000).
Taxes: Total city taxes per capita: $100 (1997); City property taxes per capita: $86 (1997).
Education: High school graduation rate: 81.2% (2000); College graduation rate: 15.4% (2000).

School District(s)

Forrestville Valley C U S D 221 (PK-12)
2000 Enrollment: 1,105 815-938-2036

Housing: Homeownership rate: 76.4% (2000); Median home value: $80,700 (2000); Median rent: $312 per month (2000); Median age of housing: 47 years (2000).
Newspapers: Forreston Journal (1 x week)
Transportation: Commute to work: 88.2% car, 0.0% public transportation, 7.5% walk, 3.2% work from home (2000); Travel time to work: 32.9% less than 15 minutes, 45.6% 15 to 30 minutes, 11.1% 30 to 45 minutes, 5.9% 45 to 60 minutes, 4.5% 60 minutes or more (2000)

HILLCREST (village). Covers a land area of 0.557 square miles and a water area of 0 square miles. Located at 41.95° N. Lat.; 89.06° W. Long. Elevation is 830 feet.
Population: 1,158 (2000); Race: 85.8% White, 0.8% Black, 0.0% Asian, 1.8% American Indian and Alaska Native, 20.1% Hispanic of any race, 1.6% two or more races (2000); Density: 2,080.8 persons per square mile (2000); Age: 36.8% under 18, 4.4% over 64 (2000); Marriage status: 23.4% never married, 66.5% now married, 3.4% widowed, 6.6% divorced (2000); Foreign born: 9.4% (2000); Ancestry (includes multiple ancestries): 27.4% Other

groups, 23.8% German, 12.1% Irish, 8.4% United States or American, 5.6% English (2000).
Economy: Agricultural area. Single-family building permits issued: 10 (2001) / 10 (2000); Multi-family building permits issued: 0 (2001) / 0 (2000); Employment by occupation: 7.8% management, 8.9% professional, 16.1% services, 21.5% sales, 1.1% farming, 8.7% construction, 36.0% production (2000).
Income: Per capita income: $15,340 (2000); Median household income: $49,821 (2000); Poverty rate: 6.1% (2000).
Taxes: Total city taxes per capita: $53 (1997); City property taxes per capita: $20 (1997).
Education: High school graduation rate: 71.9% (2000); College graduation rate: 7.7% (2000).
Housing: Homeownership rate: 86.4% (2000); Median home value: $92,800 (2000); Median rent: $493 per month (2000); Median age of housing: 25 years (2000).
Transportation: Commute to work: 95.8% car, 0.4% public transportation, 0.6% walk, 2.4% work from home (2000); Travel time to work: 48.1% less than 15 minutes, 21.5% 15 to 30 minutes, 17.7% 30 to 45 minutes, 4.9% 45 to 60 minutes, 7.7% 60 minutes or more (2000)

LEAF RIVER (village). Covers a land area of 0.857 square miles and a water area of 0 square miles. Located at 42.12° N. Lat.; 89.40° W. Long. Elevation is 709 feet.
Population: 555 (2000); Race: 99.3% White, 0.0% Black, 0.0% Asian, 0.0% American Indian and Alaska Native, 0.0% Hispanic of any race, 0.7% two or more races (2000); Density: 647.6 persons per square mile (2000); Age: 23.8% under 18, 14.1% over 64 (2000); Marriage status: 20.1% never married, 61.6% now married, 5.9% widowed, 12.4% divorced (2000); Foreign born: 0.5% (2000); Ancestry (includes multiple ancestries): 36.8% German, 12.9% English, 11.6% Irish, 7.0% United States or American, 5.9% Swedish (2000).
Economy: In rich agricultural area. Single-family building permits issued: 0 (2001) / 0 (2000); Multi-family building permits issued: 0 (2001) / 0 (2000); Employment by occupation: 2.0% management, 11.4% professional, 11.8% services, 31.7% sales, 0.4% farming, 8.9% construction, 33.7% production (2000).
Income: Per capita income: $15,620 (2000); Median household income: $36,528 (2000); Poverty rate: 5.7% (2000).
Taxes: Total city taxes per capita: $97 (1997); City property taxes per capita: $22 (1997).
Education: High school graduation rate: 81.5% (2000); College graduation rate: 7.1% (2000).
Housing: Homeownership rate: 74.4% (2000); Median home value: $76,700 (2000); Median rent: $353 per month (2000); Median age of housing: 60+ years (2000).
Transportation: Commute to work: 93.3% car, 0.0% public transportation, 2.9% walk, 2.5% work from home (2000); Travel time to work: 33.3% less than 15 minutes, 28.6% 15 to 30 minutes, 19.2% 30 to 45 minutes, 12.8% 45 to 60 minutes, 6.0% 60 minutes or more (2000)

LINDENWOOD (unincorporated postal area, zip code 61049). Covers a land area of 17.773 square miles and a water area of 0 square miles. Located at 42.05° N. Lat.; 89.02° W. Long. Elevation is 770 feet.
Population: 505 (2000); Race: 96.6% White, 0.4% Black, 0.2% Asian, 0.0% American Indian and Alaska Native, 1.9% Hispanic of any race, 1.3% two or more races (2000); Density: 28.4 persons per square mile (2000); Age: 24.5% under 18, 14.8% over 64 (2000); Marriage status: 21.0% never married, 65.3% now married, 4.0% widowed, 9.7% divorced (2000); Foreign born: 1.9% (2000); Ancestry (includes multiple ancestries): 40.1% German, 11.0% Norwegian, 10.5% Irish, 10.3% English, 8.6% United States or American (2000).
Economy: Employment by occupation: 9.4% management, 13.5% professional, 8.8% services, 31.6% sales, 3.0% farming, 12.1% construction, 21.5% production (2000).
Income: Per capita income: $22,639 (2000); Median household income: $47,625 (2000); Poverty rate: 3.6% (2000).
Education: High school graduation rate: 88.1% (2000); College graduation rate: 14.6% (2000).

School District(s)

Eswood C C District 269 (KG-08)
2000 Enrollment: 127 815-393-4477

Housing: Homeownership rate: 79.7% (2000); Median home value: $108,200 (2000); Median rent: $439 per month (2000); Median age of housing: 60+ years (2000).
Transportation: Commute to work: 84.2% car, 4.1% public transportation, 3.8% walk, 7.2% work from home (2000); Travel time to work: 18.1% less than 15 minutes, 37.0% 15 to 30 minutes, 28.9% 30 to 45 minutes, 5.9% 45 to 60 minutes, 10.0% 60 minutes or more (2000)

MONROE CENTER (unincorporated postal area, zip code 61052). Covers a land area of 26.156 square miles and a water area of 0 square miles. Located at 42.11° N. Lat.; 89.00° W. Long. Elevation is 870 feet.
Population: 1,238 (2000); Race: 98.9% White, 0.0% Black, 0.0% Asian, 0.0% American Indian and Alaska Native, 3.0% Hispanic of any race, 1.1% two or more races (2000); Density: 47.3 persons per square mile (2000); Age: 30.8% under 18, 6.9% over 64 (2000); Marriage status: 25.1% never married, 61.6% now married, 4.0% widowed, 9.3% divorced (2000); Foreign born: 1.5% (2000); Ancestry (includes multiple ancestries): 37.1% German, 12.3% English, 10.2% Irish, 8.0% Norwegian, 7.1% Swedish (2000).
Economy: Employment by occupation: 7.8% management, 17.4% professional, 9.5% services, 34.6% sales, 2.4% farming, 12.3% construction, 16.1% production (2000).
Income: Per capita income: $23,232 (2000); Median household income: $59,309 (2000); Poverty rate: 3.9% (2000).
Education: High school graduation rate: 90.3% (2000); College graduation rate: 17.8% (2000).
Housing: Homeownership rate: 82.5% (2000); Median home value: $127,900 (2000); Median rent: $475 per month (2000); Median age of housing: 35 years (2000).
Transportation: Commute to work: 95.2% car, 0.0% public transportation, 0.0% walk, 3.5% work from home (2000); Travel time to work: 12.6% less than 15 minutes, 58.9% 15 to 30 minutes, 17.6% 30 to 45 minutes, 1.1% 45 to 60 minutes, 9.8% 60 minutes or more (2000)

MOUNT MORRIS (village). Covers a land area of 1.166 square miles and a water area of 0 square miles. Located at 42.04° N. Lat.; 89.43° W. Long. Elevation is 916 feet.
History: Mount Morris was settled in 1838 by a group from Maryland. The railroad bypassed Mount Morris, but the town continued to grow. An early industry was the Kable Brothers printing company founded in 1898.
Population: 3,013 (2000); Race: 97.7% White, 0.0% Black, 0.2% Asian, 0.0% American Indian and Alaska Native, 2.5% Hispanic of any race, 0.7% two or more races (2000); Density: 2,585.1 persons per square mile (2000); Age: 24.7% under 18, 21.3% over 64 (2000); Marriage status: 21.3% never married, 56.7% now married, 10.3% widowed, 11.7% divorced (2000); Foreign born: 1.9% (2000); Ancestry (includes multiple ancestries): 32.2% German, 15.3% Irish, 11.6% English, 11.3% United States or American, 6.9% Other groups (2000).
Economy: Single-family building permits issued: 2 (2001) / 1 (2000); Multi-family building permits issued: 0 (2001) / 0 (2000); Employment by occupation: 6.0% management, 16.9% professional, 12.3% services, 26.7% sales, 0.0% farming, 10.6% construction, 27.5% production (2000).
Income: Per capita income: $20,326 (2000); Median household income: $41,333 (2000); Poverty rate: 6.9% (2000).
Taxes: Total city taxes per capita: $127 (1997); City property taxes per capita: $77 (1997).
Education: High school graduation rate: 85.5% (2000); College graduation rate: 17.8% (2000).
Housing: Homeownership rate: 70.3% (2000); Median home value: $83,300 (2000); Median rent: $318 per month (2000); Median age of housing: 49 years (2000).
Transportation: Commute to work: 92.1% car, 0.8% public transportation, 6.4% walk, 0.4% work from home (2000); Travel time to work: 54.2% less than 15 minutes, 24.1% 15 to 30 minutes, 9.8% 30 to 45 minutes, 6.3% 45 to 60 minutes, 5.5% 60 minutes or more (2000)

Additional Information Contacts

Mt Morris Chamber of Commerce 815-734-7423

OREGON (city). Covers a land area of 2.031 square miles and a water area of 0.079 square miles. Located at 42.01° N. Lat.; 89.33° W. Long. Elevation is 695 feet.
History: Oregon developed as a trading center and industrial town, and as the seat of Ogle County. It was also known as an artistic community, with the Eagle's Nest Art Colony established nearby in 1898.
Population: 4,060 (2000); Race: 95.4% White, 0.4% Black, 0.2% Asian, 0.3% American Indian and Alaska Native, 3.0% Hispanic of any race, 1.8% two or more races (2000); Density: 1,998.5 persons per square mile (2000); Age: 23.9% under 18, 17.5% over 64 (2000); Marriage status: 25.4% never married, 55.6% now married, 8.8% widowed, 10.2% divorced (2000); Foreign born: 4.2% (2000); Ancestry (includes multiple ancestries): 32.1%

German, 14.2% Irish, 12.4% English, 8.2% United States or American, 7.8% Other groups (2000).
Economy: Single-family building permits issued: 15 (2001) / 7 (2000); Multi-family building permits issued: 0 (2001) / 0 (2000); Employment by occupation: 10.1% management, 21.0% professional, 20.8% services, 21.6% sales, 0.4% farming, 6.3% construction, 19.7% production (2000).
Income: Per capita income: $19,019 (2000); Median household income: $34,842 (2000); Poverty rate: 15.9% (2000).
Taxes: Total city taxes per capita: $143 (1997); City property taxes per capita: $95 (1997).
Education: High school graduation rate: 79.2% (2000); College graduation rate: 17.0% (2000).

School District(s)

Oregon C U School Dist-220 (PK-12)
2000 Enrollment: 1,955 815-732-2186
Housing: Homeownership rate: 64.7% (2000); Median home value: $88,500 (2000); Median rent: $381 per month (2000); Median age of housing: 49 years (2000).
Newspapers: Oregon Republican Reporter (1 x week); Ogle County News (1 x week); The Ogle County Life (1 x week); Mount Morris Times (1 x week)
Transportation: Commute to work: 88.2% car, 0.0% public transportation, 7.7% walk, 3.7% work from home (2000); Travel time to work: 53.8% less than 15 minutes, 21.8% 15 to 30 minutes, 11.4% 30 to 45 minutes, 6.8% 45 to 60 minutes, 6.2% 60 minutes or more (2000)
Additional Information Contacts
Oregon Chamber of Commerce 815-732-2100

POLO (city). Covers a land area of 1.313 square miles and a water area of 0 square miles. Located at 41.98° N. Lat.; 89.57° W. Long. Elevation is 874 feet.
History: The city of Polo was named for Venetian traveler Marco Polo, and developed as a trading center for a stock raising area.
Population: 2,477 (2000); Race: 99.3% White, 0.0% Black, 0.6% Asian, 0.2% American Indian and Alaska Native, 0.8% Hispanic of any race, 0.0% two or more races (2000); Density: 1,886.2 persons per square mile (2000); Age: 23.6% under 18, 19.5% over 64 (2000); Marriage status: 21.2% never married, 55.9% now married, 9.8% widowed, 13.1% divorced (2000); Foreign born: 0.8% (2000); Ancestry (includes multiple ancestries): 40.9% German, 18.2% Irish, 12.4% English, 6.5% Other groups, 5.0% Dutch (2000).
Economy: Single-family building permits issued: 4 (2001) / 2 (2000); Multi-family building permits issued: 0 (2001) / 0 (2000); Employment by occupation: 9.8% management, 19.2% professional, 11.0% services, 23.8% sales, 0.7% farming, 10.4% construction, 25.1% production (2000).
Income: Per capita income: $18,604 (2000); Median household income: $38,833 (2000); Poverty rate: 9.2% (2000).
Taxes: Total city taxes per capita: $84 (1997); City property taxes per capita: $36 (1997).
Education: High school graduation rate: 82.4% (2000); College graduation rate: 12.7% (2000).

School District(s)

Polo Community Unit School District 222 (PK-12)
2000 Enrollment: 826 815-946-3815
Housing: Homeownership rate: 74.1% (2000); Median home value: $79,300 (2000); Median rent: $331 per month (2000); Median age of housing: 56 years (2000).
Newspapers: Tri-County Press (1 x week)
Transportation: Commute to work: 92.1% car, 1.0% public transportation, 4.9% walk, 1.6% work from home (2000); Travel time to work: 33.4% less than 15 minutes, 41.5% 15 to 30 minutes, 12.7% 30 to 45 minutes, 5.9% 45 to 60 minutes, 6.6% 60 minutes or more (2000)
Additional Information Contacts
Polo Chamber of Commerce 815-946-3131

ROCHELLE (city). Covers a land area of 7.474 square miles and a water area of 0.023 square miles. Located at 41.92° N. Lat.; 89.06° W. Long. Elevation is 821 feet.
History: Rochelle developed as an agricultural center and the home of the Del Monte cannery. Charles Butterfield, composer of "When You and I Were Young, Maggie," and Francis Rose, who wrote "Just Before the Battle, Mother," both lived in Rochelle.
Population: 9,424 (2000); Race: 88.6% White, 0.3% Black, 1.0% Asian, 0.8% American Indian and Alaska Native, 18.5% Hispanic of any race, 2.5% two or more races (2000); Density: 1,260.9 persons per square mile (2000); Age: 26.5% under 18, 14.5% over 64 (2000); Marriage status: 23.7% never married, 56.8% now married, 7.5% widowed, 12.0% divorced (2000); Foreign born: 13.1% (2000); Ancestry (includes multiple ancestries): 21.9% German, 20.7% Other groups, 10.6% Irish, 9.5% United States or American, 7.9% English (2000).
Economy: Single-family building permits issued: 12 (2001) / 11 (2000); Multi-family building permits issued: 0 (2001) / 0 (2000); Employment by occupation: 8.7% management, 14.1% professional, 17.1% services, 22.5% sales, 0.3% farming, 10.1% construction, 27.2% production (2000).
Income: Per capita income: $18,139 (2000); Median household income: $37,984 (2000); Poverty rate: 10.4% (2000).
Taxes: Total city taxes per capita: $157 (2000); City property taxes per capita: $106 (2000).
Education: High school graduation rate: 72.7% (2000); College graduation rate: 15.7% (2000).

School District(s)

Rochelle Community Cons District 231 (PK-08)
2000 Enrollment: 1,814 815-562-6363
Rochelle Township High School District 212 (09-12)
2000 Enrollment: 982 815-562-4161
Housing: Homeownership rate: 57.8% (2000); Median home value: $96,200 (2000); Median rent: $403 per month (2000); Median age of housing: 38 years (2000).
Hospitals: Rochelle Community Hospital (42 beds)
Newspapers: Rochelle Shoppers Special (1 x week); Rochelle News Leader (3 x week)
Transportation: Commute to work: 90.0% car, 0.5% public transportation, 5.0% walk, 2.2% work from home (2000); Travel time to work: 59.8% less than 15 minutes, 13.4% 15 to 30 minutes, 16.5% 30 to 45 minutes, 5.3% 45 to 60 minutes, 5.0% 60 minutes or more (2000)
Additional Information Contacts
Rochelle Chamber of Commerce 815-562-4189

STILLMAN VALLEY (village). Covers a land area of 0.548 square miles and a water area of 0 square miles. Located at 42.10° N. Lat.; 89.18° W. Long. Elevation is 720 feet.
History: The Battle of Stillman's Run took place here in 1832, where a monument was placed to mark the dead.
Population: 1,048 (2000); Race: 97.7% White, 0.4% Black, 0.2% Asian, 1.2% American Indian and Alaska Native, 0.2% Hispanic of any race, 0.4% two or more races (2000); Density: 1,912.8 persons per square mile (2000); Age: 30.7% under 18, 10.3% over 64 (2000); Marriage status: 22.9% never married, 63.3% now married, 3.6% widowed, 10.2% divorced (2000); Foreign born: 0.8% (2000); Ancestry (includes multiple ancestries): 45.4% German, 14.1% Swedish, 10.5% Irish, 9.1% English, 7.1% Other groups (2000).
Economy: Single-family building permits issued: 4 (2001) / 3 (2000); Multi-family building permits issued: 0 (2001) / 0 (2000); Employment by occupation: 12.2% management, 17.5% professional, 13.3% services, 18.6% sales, 0.4% farming, 9.8% construction, 28.2% production (2000).
Income: Per capita income: $21,036 (2000); Median household income: $46,845 (2000); Poverty rate: 4.6% (2000).
Taxes: Total city taxes per capita: $66 (1997); City property taxes per capita: $61 (1997).
Education: High school graduation rate: 87.6% (2000); College graduation rate: 17.1% (2000).

School District(s)

Meridian C U School District 223 (PK-12)
2000 Enrollment: 1,567 815-645-2606
Housing: Homeownership rate: 73.1% (2000); Median home value: $108,000 (2000); Median rent: $479 per month (2000); Median age of housing: 36 years (2000).
Transportation: Commute to work: 95.0% car, 0.0% public transportation, 2.6% walk, 2.4% work from home (2000); Travel time to work: 27.5% less than 15 minutes, 42.8% 15 to 30 minutes, 20.1% 30 to 45 minutes, 7.1% 45 to 60 minutes, 2.5% 60 minutes or more (2000)

Peoria County

Located in central Illinois; bounded on the east and south by the Illinois River and Lake Peorio; drained by the Spoon River and Kickapoo Creek. Covers a land area of 619.50 square miles, a water area of 11.40 square miles, and is located in the Central Time Zone. The county government was organized in 1825. County seat is Peoria.

Peoria County is part of the Peoria-Pekin, IL MSA. The entire metro area includes: Peoria County; Tazewell County; Woodford County

Weather Station: Greater Peoria Airport Elevation: 649 feet

	Jan	Feb	Mar	Apr	May	Jun	Jul	Aug	Sep	Oct	Nov	Dec
High	30	36	49	62	73	82	86	83	77	64	49	36
Low	14	20	30	41	51	60	65	63	55	43	32	21
Precip	1.5	1.6	2.8	3.7	4.2	3.8	4.1	3.2	3.4	2.9	2.9	2.4
Snow	8.0	5.8	3.5	1.1	tr	0.0	tr	0.0	tr	tr	2.1	6.3

High and Low temperatures in degrees Fahrenheit; Precipitation and Snow in inches

Weather Station: Princeville Elevation: 734 feet

	Jan	Feb	Mar	Apr	May	Jun	Jul	Aug	Sep	Oct	Nov	Dec
High	30	36	49	62	73	81	85	83	76	65	49	36
Low	11	17	27	37	48	57	61	59	51	40	29	18
Precip	1.7	1.7	3.1	3.9	4.7	3.9	4.0	3.7	3.7	2.9	3.0	2.5
Snow	6.4	5.6	2.9	0.7	tr	0.0	0.0	0.0	0.0	0.1	2.1	5.5

High and Low temperatures in degrees Fahrenheit; Precipitation and Snow in inches

Population: 183,433 (2000); Race: 79.4% White, 15.9% Black, 1.7% Asian, 0.2% American Indian and Alaska Native, 2.1% Hispanic of any race, 1.8% two or more races (2000); Density: 296.1 persons per square mile (2000); Age: 25.1% under 18, 14.1% over 64 (2000).
Religion: Five largest groups: 19.3% Catholic Church, 5.4% The United Methodist Church, 3.4% Evangelical Lutheran Church in America, 3.1% Lutheran Church—Missouri Synod, 1.9% Southern Baptist Convention (2000).
Economy: Unemployment rate: 6.1% (11/2002); Total civilian labor force: 92,632 (11/2002); Leading industries: 16.3% health care and social assistance; 14.2% manufacturing; 10.6% management of companies & enterprises (2000); Companies that employ more than 1,000 persons: 7 (2000); Companies that employ more than 100 persons: 163 (2000); Farms: 924 totaling 267,283 acres (1997); Minority business ownership rate: 8.3% (1997); Women business ownership rate: 27.3% (1997); Retail sales per capita: $10,138 (1997). Single-family building permits issued: 473 (2001) / 604 (2000); Multi-family building permits issued: 12 (2001) / 334 (2000).
Income: Per capita income: $21,219 (2000); Median household income: $39,978 (2000); Poverty rate: 13.7% (2000); Bankruptcy rate: 8.47% (2001).
Taxes: Total county taxes per capita: $78 (2000); County property taxes per capita: $75 (2000).
Education: High school graduation rate: 83.8% (2000); College graduation rate: 23.3% (2000).
Housing: Homeownership rate: 67.8% (2000); Median home value: $85,800 (2000); Median rent: $400 per month (2000); Median age of housing: 41 years (2000).
Health: Birth rate: 148.2 per 10,000 population (1998); Age adjusted death rate: 89.8 per 10,000 population (1999); Age adjusted cancer mortality rate: 225.1 deaths per 100,000 population (1999). Air Quality Index: 77% good, 23% moderate, 0% unhealthy (percent of days in 2000). Number of physicians: 40.3 per 10,000 population (1999); Number of hospital beds: 63.9 per 10,000 population (1999).
Elections: 2000 Presidential election results: 50.3% Gore, 47.4% Bush, 1.7% Nader, 0.4% Buchanan
National and State Parks: Jubilee College State Park; Spring Branch State Conservation Area; Spring Lake State Park
Additional Information Contacts
Peoria County Government Offices 309-672-6059
Chillicothe Chamber of Commerce 309-274-4556
Fulton County Board of Realtors 309-688-8591
Limestone Chamber of Commerce. 309-697-1031
Peoria Area Association of Realtors 309-688-8591
Peoria Chamber of Commerce 309-676-0755
Peoria Heights Chamber of Commerce 309-685-4812

Peoria County Communities

BARTONVILLE (village). Covers a land area of 8.026 square miles and a water area of 0.424 square miles. Located at 40.64° N. Lat.; 89.66° W. Long. Elevation is 550 feet.
History: Bartonville developed as a coal mining community, with factories that manufactured steel wire and fence.
Population: 6,310 (2000); Race: 98.1% White, 0.5% Black, 0.7% Asian, 0.1% American Indian and Alaska Native, 0.9% Hispanic of any race, 0.4% two or more races (2000); Density: 786.2 persons per square mile (2000); Age: 22.6% under 18, 17.2% over 64 (2000); Marriage status: 20.8% never married, 60.5% now married, 5.8% widowed, 12.9% divorced (2000); Foreign born: 0.9% (2000); Ancestry (includes multiple ancestries): 31.2% German, 11.9% Irish, 11.5% English, 10.5% United States or American, 7.2% Other groups (2000).
Economy: Single-family building permits issued: 12 (2001) / 16 (2000); Multi-family building permits issued: 0 (2001) / 12 (2000); Employment by occupation: 9.4% management, 14.3% professional, 14.5% services, 31.6% sales, 0.4% farming, 11.2% construction, 18.6% production (2000).
Income: Per capita income: $20,580 (2000); Median household income: $40,766 (2000); Poverty rate: 7.0% (2000).
Taxes: Total city taxes per capita: $104 (1997); City property taxes per capita: $43 (1997).
Education: High school graduation rate: 81.1% (2000); College graduation rate: 10.0% (2000).

School District(s)
Bartonville School District 66 (PK-08)
2000 Enrollment: 294 309-697-3253
Limestone Community High School District 310 (09-12)
2000 Enrollment: 1,069 309-697-6271
Monroe School District 70 (KG-08)
2000 Enrollment: 296 309-697-3120
Oak Grove School District 68 (KG-08)
2000 Enrollment: 467 309-697-3367
Housing: Homeownership rate: 80.2% (2000); Median home value: $73,400 (2000); Median rent: $396 per month (2000); Median age of housing: 46 years (2000).
Newspapers: Limestone Independent News (1 x week)
Transportation: Commute to work: 95.0% car, 0.3% public transportation, 1.6% walk, 2.2% work from home (2000); Travel time to work: 29.8% less than 15 minutes, 55.0% 15 to 30 minutes, 9.2% 30 to 45 minutes, 2.9% 45 to 60 minutes, 3.1% 60 minutes or more (2000)
Additional Information Contacts
Limestone Chamber of Commerce. 309-697-1031

BELLEVUE (village). Covers a land area of 1.678 square miles and a water area of 0 square miles. Located at 40.68° N. Lat.; 89.66° W. Long. Elevation is 680 feet.
History: Incorporated 1941.
Population: 1,887 (2000); Race: 97.1% White, 0.2% Black, 1.7% Asian, 0.0% American Indian and Alaska Native, 1.5% Hispanic of any race, 0.5% two or more races (2000); Density: 1,124.3 persons per square mile (2000); Age: 30.0% under 18, 11.6% over 64 (2000); Marriage status: 21.2% never married, 60.8% now married, 5.5% widowed, 12.5% divorced (2000); Foreign born: 0.2% (2000); Ancestry (includes multiple ancestries): 24.1% German, 15.1% United States or American, 11.4% Irish, 9.6% English, 9.0% Other groups (2000).
Economy: Agriculture: corn, oats, vegetables; cattle. Single-family building permits issued: 0 (2001) / 0 (2000); Multi-family building permits issued: 0 (2001) / 0 (2000); Employment by occupation: 3.6% management, 11.8% professional, 20.9% services, 26.0% sales, 0.0% farming, 14.2% construction, 23.6% production (2000).
Income: Per capita income: $14,228 (2000); Median household income: $31,098 (2000); Poverty rate: 10.9% (2000).
Taxes: Total city taxes per capita: $38 (1997); City property taxes per capita: $35 (1997).
Education: High school graduation rate: 69.3% (2000); College graduation rate: 5.8% (2000).
Housing: Homeownership rate: 78.7% (2000); Median home value: $59,900 (2000); Median rent: $386 per month (2000); Median age of housing: 35 years (2000).
Transportation: Commute to work: 97.9% car, 0.5% public transportation, 1.0% walk, 0.6% work from home (2000); Travel time to work: 32.5% less than 15 minutes, 54.1% 15 to 30 minutes, 7.9% 30 to 45 minutes, 1.4% 45 to 60 minutes, 4.0% 60 minutes or more (2000)

BRIMFIELD (village). Covers a land area of 0.753 square miles and a water area of 0.005 square miles. Located at 40.83° N. Lat.; 89.88° W. Long. Elevation is 707 feet.
Population: 933 (2000); Race: 98.4% White, 0.8% Black, 0.6% Asian, 0.0% American Indian and Alaska Native, 0.7% Hispanic of any race, 0.0% two or more races (2000); Density: 1,238.7 persons per square mile (2000); Age: 31.0% under 18, 11.6% over 64 (2000); Marriage status: 25.0% never married, 58.5% now married, 6.7% widowed, 9.8% divorced (2000); Foreign born: 0.1% (2000); Ancestry (includes multiple ancestries): 32.8% German, 18.4% English, 16.1% Irish, 9.1% United States or American, 6.6% Other groups (2000).
Economy: In agricultural and bituminous-coal area. Single-family building permits issued: 2 (2001) / 2 (2000); Multi-family building permits issued: 0 (2001) / 0 (2000); Employment by occupation: 10.7% management, 17.9%

professional, 19.4% services, 22.0% sales, 0.0% farming, 11.7% construction, 18.3% production (2000).
Income: Per capita income: $16,090 (2000); Median household income: $38,542 (2000); Poverty rate: 8.5% (2000).
Taxes: Total city taxes per capita: $45 (1997); City property taxes per capita: $39 (1997).
Education: High school graduation rate: 87.5% (2000); College graduation rate: 13.1% (2000).

School District(s)

Brimfield C U School District 309 (PK-12)
2000 Enrollment: 671 309-446-3378
Housing: Homeownership rate: 83.9% (2000); Median home value: $77,100 (2000); Median rent: $314 per month (2000); Median age of housing: 39 years (2000).
Transportation: Commute to work: 92.5% car, 0.4% public transportation, 2.4% walk, 3.0% work from home (2000); Travel time to work: 21.1% less than 15 minutes, 44.2% 15 to 30 minutes, 29.6% 30 to 45 minutes, 1.6% 45 to 60 minutes, 3.6% 60 minutes or more (2000)

CHILLICOTHE (city). Covers a land area of 4.940 square miles and a water area of 0.283 square miles. Located at 40.92° N. Lat.; 89.49° W. Long. Elevation is 500 feet.
History: Incorporated 1861.
Population: 5,996 (2000); Race: 98.5% White, 0.0% Black, 0.0% Asian, 0.3% American Indian and Alaska Native, 3.5% Hispanic of any race, 0.6% two or more races (2000); Density: 1,213.8 persons per square mile (2000); Age: 25.3% under 18, 16.8% over 64 (2000); Marriage status: 21.3% never married, 60.5% now married, 9.6% widowed, 8.5% divorced (2000); Foreign born: 1.2% (2000); Ancestry (includes multiple ancestries): 30.1% German, 17.9% Irish, 12.5% English, 7.8% United States or American, 7.4% Other groups (2000).
Economy: In agricultural and bituminous-coal area; sand, gravel pits. Manufacturing: clothing, concrete products. Single-family building permits issued: 14 (2001) / 3 (2000); Multi-family building permits issued: 0 (2001) / 0 (2000); Employment by occupation: 7.1% management, 19.7% professional, 16.8% services, 28.8% sales, 0.0% farming, 10.6% construction, 17.0% production (2000).
Income: Per capita income: $22,118 (2000); Median household income: $40,697 (2000); Poverty rate: 6.2% (2000).
Taxes: Total city taxes per capita: $175 (1997); City property taxes per capita: $52 (1997).
Education: High school graduation rate: 86.7% (2000); College graduation rate: 12.6% (2000).

School District(s)

Il Valley Central Unit District 321 (PK-12)
2000 Enrollment: 2,192 309-274-5418
Housing: Homeownership rate: 74.6% (2000); Median home value: $78,900 (2000); Median rent: $347 per month (2000); Median age of housing: 42 years (2000).
Transportation: Commute to work: 94.5% car, 0.6% public transportation, 1.5% walk, 2.2% work from home (2000); Travel time to work: 39.5% less than 15 minutes, 31.4% 15 to 30 minutes, 24.3% 30 to 45 minutes, 3.2% 45 to 60 minutes, 1.7% 60 minutes or more (2000)
Additional Information Contacts
Chillicothe Chamber of Commerce 309-274-4556

DUNLAP (village). Covers a land area of 0.373 square miles and a water area of 0 square miles. Located at 40.86° N. Lat.; 89.67° W. Long. Elevation is 730 feet.
Population: 926 (2000); Race: 96.1% White, 0.2% Black, 3.0% Asian, 0.0% American Indian and Alaska Native, 2.4% Hispanic of any race, 0.4% two or more races (2000); Density: 2,482.3 persons per square mile (2000); Age: 28.9% under 18, 10.6% over 64 (2000); Marriage status: 25.8% never married, 62.4% now married, 4.7% widowed, 7.1% divorced (2000); Foreign born: 4.5% (2000); Ancestry (includes multiple ancestries): 30.0% German, 12.4% Irish, 10.0% English, 8.1% Other groups, 7.1% United States or American (2000).
Economy: Corn, soybeans; light manufacturing. Employment by occupation: 12.7% management, 24.0% professional, 15.3% services, 28.2% sales, 0.0% farming, 7.9% construction, 12.0% production (2000).
Income: Per capita income: $20,407 (2000); Median household income: $56,364 (2000); Poverty rate: 6.3% (2000).
Taxes: Total city taxes per capita: $44 (1997); City property taxes per capita: $36 (1997).
Education: High school graduation rate: 90.3% (2000); College graduation rate: 29.7% (2000).

School District(s)

Dunlap C U School District 323 (PK-12)
2000 Enrollment: 2,253 309-243-7716
Housing: Homeownership rate: 76.1% (2000); Median home value: $106,400 (2000); Median rent: $396 per month (2000); Median age of housing: 30 years (2000).
Transportation: Commute to work: 96.0% car, 0.7% public transportation, 0.4% walk, 1.1% work from home (2000); Travel time to work: 28.9% less than 15 minutes, 50.4% 15 to 30 minutes, 15.9% 30 to 45 minutes, 1.3% 45 to 60 minutes, 3.4% 60 minutes or more (2000)

EDELSTEIN (unincorporated postal area, zip code 61526). Covers a land area of 33.664 square miles and a water area of 0.009 square miles. Located at 40.93° N. Lat.; 89.62° W. Long. Elevation is 780 feet.
Population: 1,173 (2000); Race: 97.9% White, 0.0% Black, 0.0% Asian, 0.0% American Indian and Alaska Native, 0.0% Hispanic of any race, 2.1% two or more races (2000); Density: 34.8 persons per square mile (2000); Age: 28.2% under 18, 12.1% over 64 (2000); Marriage status: 14.6% never married, 77.3% now married, 4.1% widowed, 4.0% divorced (2000); Foreign born: 0.5% (2000); Ancestry (includes multiple ancestries): 41.3% German, 18.8% English, 12.6% Irish, 5.7% United States or American, 3.8% Swedish (2000).
Economy: Employment by occupation: 11.7% management, 20.8% professional, 9.2% services, 29.2% sales, 0.0% farming, 14.1% construction, 15.1% production (2000).
Income: Per capita income: $24,575 (2000); Median household income: $65,217 (2000); Poverty rate: 0.8% (2000).
Education: High school graduation rate: 84.1% (2000); College graduation rate: 17.0% (2000).
Housing: Homeownership rate: 96.1% (2000); Median home value: $123,600 (2000); Median rent: $275 per month (2000); Median age of housing: 28 years (2000).
Transportation: Commute to work: 94.8% car, 0.0% public transportation, 1.0% walk, 4.2% work from home (2000); Travel time to work: 24.7% less than 15 minutes, 46.6% 15 to 30 minutes, 19.8% 30 to 45 minutes, 5.2% 45 to 60 minutes, 3.7% 60 minutes or more (2000)

EDWARDS (unincorporated postal area, zip code 61528). Covers a land area of 17.631 square miles and a water area of 0 square miles. Located at 40.77° N. Lat.; 89.74° W. Long. Elevation is 510 feet.
Population: 1,608 (2000); Race: 97.8% White, 0.2% Black, 0.4% Asian, 0.0% American Indian and Alaska Native, 1.3% Hispanic of any race, 1.2% two or more races (2000); Density: 91.2 persons per square mile (2000); Age: 25.7% under 18, 12.3% over 64 (2000); Marriage status: 21.0% never married, 67.6% now married, 5.2% widowed, 6.2% divorced (2000); Foreign born: 1.3% (2000); Ancestry (includes multiple ancestries): 35.3% German, 17.4% Irish, 17.1% English, 10.0% United States or American, 6.0% French (except Basque) (2000).
Economy: Employment by occupation: 16.6% management, 21.9% professional, 15.4% services, 23.2% sales, 0.0% farming, 8.4% construction, 14.5% production (2000).
Income: Per capita income: $28,248 (2000); Median household income: $63,867 (2000); Poverty rate: 3.6% (2000).
Education: High school graduation rate: 85.8% (2000); College graduation rate: 29.5% (2000).
Housing: Homeownership rate: 92.4% (2000); Median home value: $136,800 (2000); Median rent: $328 per month (2000); Median age of housing: 28 years (2000).
Transportation: Commute to work: 95.2% car, 0.0% public transportation, 0.9% walk, 3.9% work from home (2000); Travel time to work: 18.3% less than 15 minutes, 63.8% 15 to 30 minutes, 13.0% 30 to 45 minutes, 2.6% 45 to 60 minutes, 2.3% 60 minutes or more (2000)

ELMWOOD (city). Covers a land area of 1.233 square miles and a water area of 0 square miles. Located at 40.77° N. Lat.; 89.96° W. Long. Elevation is 643 feet.
History: Incorporated 1867. Lorado Taft born here; his statue *Pioneers of the Prairies* (1928) is in city park.
Population: 1,945 (2000); Race: 97.6% White, 0.4% Black, 0.1% Asian, 0.6% American Indian and Alaska Native, 1.2% Hispanic of any race, 0.8% two or more races (2000); Density: 1,577.1 persons per square mile (2000); Age: 27.5% under 18, 14.6% over 64 (2000); Marriage status: 18.0% never married, 67.6% now married, 7.3% widowed, 7.1% divorced (2000); Foreign born: 1.0% (2000); Ancestry (includes multiple ancestries): 32.3% German, 21.1% English, 11.0% Irish, 8.4% United States or American, 4.8% Other groups (2000).

Economy: In agricultural, bituminous-coal mining, and timber area. Employment by occupation: 11.0% management, 22.6% professional, 11.2% services, 28.1% sales, 0.2% farming, 9.7% construction, 17.3% production (2000).
Income: Per capita income: $19,797 (2000); Median household income: $44,500 (2000); Poverty rate: 2.8% (2000).
Taxes: Total city taxes per capita: $78 (1997); City property taxes per capita: $69 (1997).
Education: High school graduation rate: 87.9% (2000); College graduation rate: 16.3% (2000).

School District(s)

Elmwood C U School District 322 (PK-12)
2000 Enrollment: 663 309-742-8464
Housing: Homeownership rate: 82.4% (2000); Median home value: $76,700 (2000); Median rent: $364 per month (2000); Median age of housing: 51 years (2000).
Newspapers: Tri County News-Yates City Banner Edition (1 x week); Tri-County News-Williamsfield Times Edition (1 x week); Tri-County News-The Princeville Telephone Edition (1 x week); Home Shopper (1 x week); Tri-County News-Farmington Bugle Edition (1 x week); Tri County News-Elmwood Gazette Edition (1 x week); The Advertiser (1 x week)
Transportation: Commute to work: 94.2% car, 0.0% public transportation, 4.0% walk, 1.0% work from home (2000); Travel time to work: 32.4% less than 15 minutes, 15.0% 15 to 30 minutes, 39.2% 30 to 45 minutes, 8.1% 45 to 60 minutes, 5.3% 60 minutes or more (2000)

GLASFORD (village). Covers a land area of 0.883 square miles and a water area of 0 square miles. Located at 40.57° N. Lat.; 89.81° W. Long. Elevation is 610 feet.
Population: 1,076 (2000); Race: 99.1% White, 0.0% Black, 0.0% Asian, 0.0% American Indian and Alaska Native, 1.4% Hispanic of any race, 0.6% two or more races (2000); Density: 1,218.4 persons per square mile (2000); Age: 26.6% under 18, 10.5% over 64 (2000); Marriage status: 23.4% never married, 61.7% now married, 6.3% widowed, 8.6% divorced (2000); Foreign born: 0.5% (2000); Ancestry (includes multiple ancestries): 28.7% German, 14.9% United States or American, 13.4% English, 11.0% Irish, 6.0% Other groups (2000).
Economy: Agriculture: corn, cattle; dairying; bituminous coal-mining; wood products. Single-family building permits issued: 0 (2001) / 2 (2000); Multi-family building permits issued: 0 (2001) / 0 (2000); Employment by occupation: 6.6% management, 13.8% professional, 16.5% services, 28.7% sales, 0.0% farming, 10.2% construction, 24.1% production (2000).
Income: Per capita income: $16,754 (2000); Median household income: $37,019 (2000); Poverty rate: 7.1% (2000).
Taxes: Total city taxes per capita: $52 (1997); City property taxes per capita: $50 (1997).
Education: High school graduation rate: 86.7% (2000); College graduation rate: 11.4% (2000).

School District(s)

Illini Bluffs Cu School District 327 (PK-12)
2000 Enrollment: 934 309-389-2231
Housing: Homeownership rate: 80.2% (2000); Median home value: $67,600 (2000); Median rent: $323 per month (2000); Median age of housing: 46 years (2000).
Newspapers: The Glasford Gazette (1 x week)
Transportation: Commute to work: 93.7% car, 0.0% public transportation, 4.3% walk, 0.6% work from home (2000); Travel time to work: 25.4% less than 15 minutes, 30.8% 15 to 30 minutes, 35.0% 30 to 45 minutes, 4.7% 45 to 60 minutes, 4.1% 60 minutes or more (2000)

HANNA CITY (village). Aka Hanna. Covers a land area of 0.477 square miles and a water area of 0 square miles. Located at 40.69° N. Lat.; 89.79° W. Long. Elevation is 725 feet.
Population: 1,013 (2000); Race: 97.6% White, 0.4% Black, 1.1% Asian, 0.0% American Indian and Alaska Native, 0.0% Hispanic of any race, 0.3% two or more races (2000); Density: 2,123.8 persons per square mile (2000); Age: 23.8% under 18, 16.6% over 64 (2000); Marriage status: 22.1% never married, 62.1% now married, 7.9% widowed, 7.9% divorced (2000); Foreign born: 1.5% (2000); Ancestry (includes multiple ancestries): 26.1% German, 11.6% English, 10.7% Irish, 8.7% United States or American, 5.9% Other groups (2000).
Economy: In agricultural area: corn, soybeans; cattle. Bituminous coal-mining area. Employment by occupation: 10.5% management, 12.5% professional, 16.6% services, 32.9% sales, 0.0% farming, 10.5% construction, 17.0% production (2000).
Income: Per capita income: $20,710 (2000); Median household income: $42,639 (2000); Poverty rate: 7.2% (2000).
Taxes: Total city taxes per capita: $29 (1997); City property taxes per capita: $26 (1997).
Education: High school graduation rate: 83.2% (2000); College graduation rate: 9.2% (2000).
Housing: Homeownership rate: 80.5% (2000); Median home value: $74,700 (2000); Median rent: $398 per month (2000); Median age of housing: 41 years (2000).
Transportation: Commute to work: 93.2% car, 1.4% public transportation, 4.0% walk, 1.4% work from home (2000); Travel time to work: 17.9% less than 15 minutes, 52.1% 15 to 30 minutes, 20.8% 30 to 45 minutes, 4.1% 45 to 60 minutes, 5.1% 60 minutes or more (2000)

KINGSTON MINES (village). Covers a land area of 1.340 square miles and a water area of 0.103 square miles. Located at 40.55° N. Lat.; 89.77° W. Long.
Population: 259 (2000); Race: 95.2% White, 0.0% Black, 0.0% Asian, 0.0% American Indian and Alaska Native, 4.0% Hispanic of any race, 4.8% two or more races (2000); Density: 193.2 persons per square mile (2000); Age: 20.6% under 18, 15.7% over 64 (2000); Marriage status: 29.6% never married, 49.3% now married, 11.3% widowed, 9.9% divorced (2000); Foreign born: 0.0% (2000); Ancestry (includes multiple ancestries): 24.2% United States or American, 18.1% German, 14.5% Irish, 9.3% Other groups, 7.7% English (2000).
Economy: In agricultural and bituminous-coal-mining area; gravel pits. Single-family building permits issued: 0 (2001) / 0 (2000); Multi-family building permits issued: 0 (2001) / 0 (2000); Employment by occupation: 1.8% management, 8.3% professional, 17.4% services, 22.0% sales, 0.0% farming, 11.0% construction, 39.4% production (2000).
Income: Per capita income: $14,908 (2000); Median household income: $31,250 (2000); Poverty rate: 5.2% (2000).
Taxes: Total city taxes per capita: $34 (1997); City property taxes per capita: $31 (1997).
Education: High school graduation rate: 77.3% (2000); College graduation rate: 3.1% (2000).
Housing: Homeownership rate: 80.4% (2000); Median home value: $52,100 (2000); Median rent: $275 per month (2000); Median age of housing: 55 years (2000).
Transportation: Commute to work: 98.1% car, 0.0% public transportation, 0.0% walk, 1.9% work from home (2000); Travel time to work: 21.2% less than 15 minutes, 32.7% 15 to 30 minutes, 32.7% 30 to 45 minutes, 3.8% 45 to 60 minutes, 9.6% 60 minutes or more (2000)

LAURA (unincorporated postal area, zip code 61451). Covers a land area of 22.326 square miles and a water area of 0.106 square miles. Located at 40.95° N. Lat.; 89.94° W. Long. Elevation is 729 feet.
Population: 383 (2000); Race: 98.9% White, 0.0% Black, 0.0% Asian, 0.0% American Indian and Alaska Native, 0.0% Hispanic of any race, 1.1% two or more races (2000); Density: 17.2 persons per square mile (2000); Age: 23.9% under 18, 8.8% over 64 (2000); Marriage status: 17.8% never married, 60.1% now married, 8.7% widowed, 13.4% divorced (2000); Foreign born: 0.0% (2000); Ancestry (includes multiple ancestries): 22.1% German, 15.2% English, 10.9% Irish, 7.7% French (except Basque), 7.7% Swedish (2000).
Economy: Employment by occupation: 9.7% management, 2.2% professional, 14.0% services, 15.6% sales, 1.6% farming, 23.1% construction, 33.9% production (2000).
Income: Per capita income: $18,145 (2000); Median household income: $45,000 (2000); Poverty rate: 0.0% (2000).
Education: High school graduation rate: 92.0% (2000); College graduation rate: 12.5% (2000).
Housing: Homeownership rate: 82.2% (2000); Median home value: $49,200 (2000); Median rent: $200 per month (2000); Median age of housing: 58 years (2000).
Transportation: Commute to work: 93.0% car, 0.0% public transportation, 0.0% walk, 7.0% work from home (2000); Travel time to work: 14.5% less than 15 minutes, 26.6% 15 to 30 minutes, 46.2% 30 to 45 minutes, 8.7% 45 to 60 minutes, 4.0% 60 minutes or more (2000)

MAPLETON (village). Covers a land area of 0.718 square miles and a water area of 0 square miles. Located at 40.57° N. Lat.; 89.72° W. Long. Elevation is 490 feet.
Population: 227 (2000); Race: 94.2% White, 0.0% Black, 5.8% Asian, 0.0% American Indian and Alaska Native, 0.9% Hispanic of any race, 0.0% two or more races (2000); Density: 316.1 persons per square mile (2000); Age: 15.0% under 18, 16.8% over 64 (2000); Marriage status: 13.4% never

married, 54.1% now married, 10.3% widowed, 22.2% divorced (2000); Foreign born: 5.3% (2000); Ancestry (includes multiple ancestries): 35.4% United States or American, 14.6% German, 9.7% Other groups, 8.8% Irish, 4.9% English (2000).
Economy: Single-family building permits issued: 0 (2001) / 0 (2000); Multi-family building permits issued: 0 (2001) / 0 (2000); Employment by occupation: 4.1% management, 21.5% professional, 10.7% services, 23.1% sales, 0.0% farming, 9.9% construction, 30.6% production (2000).
Income: Per capita income: $22,728 (2000); Median household income: $45,357 (2000); Poverty rate: 6.6% (2000).
Taxes: Total city taxes per capita: $29 (1997); City property taxes per capita: $19 (1997).
Education: High school graduation rate: 74.7% (2000); College graduation rate: 13.2% (2000).
Housing: Homeownership rate: 74.5% (2000); Median home value: $63,800 (2000); Median rent: $248 per month (2000); Median age of housing: 43 years (2000).
Transportation: Commute to work: 98.3% car, 0.0% public transportation, 1.7% walk, 0.0% work from home (2000); Travel time to work: 24.0% less than 15 minutes, 33.9% 15 to 30 minutes, 32.2% 30 to 45 minutes, 3.3% 45 to 60 minutes, 6.6% 60 minutes or more (2000)

NORWOOD (village). Aka Norwood Park. Covers a land area of 0.264 square miles and a water area of 0 square miles. Located at 40.70° N. Lat.; 89.70° W. Long. Elevation is 690 feet.
Population: 473 (2000); Race: 99.1% White, 0.0% Black, 0.0% Asian, 0.4% American Indian and Alaska Native, 1.1% Hispanic of any race, 0.4% two or more races (2000); Density: 1,788.9 persons per square mile (2000); Age: 28.3% under 18, 13.2% over 64 (2000); Marriage status: 20.3% never married, 61.8% now married, 4.8% widowed, 13.1% divorced (2000); Foreign born: 0.0% (2000); Ancestry (includes multiple ancestries): 27.9% German, 10.3% Other groups, 7.6% English, 7.1% Italian, 6.3% Irish (2000).
Economy: Greater Peoria Airport to South. Employment by occupation: 9.8% management, 16.4% professional, 10.4% services, 31.7% sales, 0.0% farming, 14.2% construction, 17.5% production (2000).
Income: Per capita income: $16,089 (2000); Median household income: $40,156 (2000); Poverty rate: 7.5% (2000).
Taxes: Total city taxes per capita: $19 (1997); City property taxes per capita: $18 (1997).
Education: High school graduation rate: 76.3% (2000); College graduation rate: 5.5% (2000).
Housing: Homeownership rate: 95.5% (2000); Median home value: $67,400 (2000); Median rent: $525 per month (2000); Median age of housing: 43 years (2000).
Transportation: Commute to work: 95.0% car, 0.0% public transportation, 0.0% walk, 2.2% work from home (2000); Travel time to work: 16.0% less than 15 minutes, 68.6% 15 to 30 minutes, 10.9% 30 to 45 minutes, 1.1% 45 to 60 minutes, 3.4% 60 minutes or more (2000)

PEORIA (city). Covers a land area of 44.404 square miles and a water area of 2.230 square miles. Located at 40.72° N. Lat.; 89.60° W. Long. Elevation is 600 feet.
History: Peoria began with the establishment by the French of Fort Pimiteoui on Lake Peoria in 1691. This trading post thrived for over a century, and the village which grew around it was at times called Au Pe, Le Pe, Opa, Au Pay, and Piorias. The American Fort Clark was erected here in 1813 and settlers from New England moved in. When Peoria County was created in 1825, the French-Indian name of Peoria was given to the community at Fort Clark, which became the county seat. Peoria was incorporated as a town in 1835, and received a city charter in 1845. In a speech in Peoria in 1854, following a talk by Stephen Douglas that lasted all afternoon, Abraham Lincoln first publicly denounced slavery.
Population: 112,936 (2000); Race: 69.2% White, 24.4% Black, 2.4% Asian, 0.2% American Indian and Alaska Native, 2.5% Hispanic of any race, 2.3% two or more races (2000); Density: 2,543.4 persons per square mile (2000); Age: 25.7% under 18, 14.1% over 64 (2000); Marriage status: 32.3% never married, 49.1% now married, 7.6% widowed, 11.0% divorced (2000); Foreign born: 4.4% (2000); Ancestry (includes multiple ancestries): 29.4% Other groups, 21.9% German, 12.2% Irish, 8.8% English, 5.6% United States or American (2000).
Vital Statistics: Birth rate: 177.8 per 10,000 population (1998)
Economy: Unemployment rate: 6.6% (11/2002); Total civilian labor force: 55,322 (11/2002); Single-family building permits issued: 296 (2001) / 401 (2000); Multi-family building permits issued: 8 (2001) / 288 (2000); Employment by occupation: 11.6% management, 26.8% professional, 17.7% services, 26.4% sales, 0.1% farming, 5.7% construction, 11.8% production (2000).
Income: Per capita income: $20,512 (2000); Median household income: $36,397 (2000); Poverty rate: 18.8% (2000).
Taxes: Total city taxes per capita: $376 (2000); City property taxes per capita: $117 (2000).
Education: High school graduation rate: 82.8% (2000); College graduation rate: 28.0% (2000).

School District(s)

Hollis Cons School District 328 (KG-08)
2000 Enrollment: 115 309-697-1325
Limestone Walters C C S District 316 (KG-08)
2000 Enrollment: 191 309-697-3035
Norwood Elementary School District 63 (PK-08)
2000 Enrollment: 520 309-676-3523
Peoria School District 150 (PK-12)
2000 Enrollment: 15,724 309-672-6768
Pleasant Hill School District 69 (PK-08)
2000 Enrollment: 247 309-637-6829
Pleasant Valley School District 62 (PK-08)
2000 Enrollment: 533 309-673-2494

Four-year College(s)

Bradley University (Private, Not-for-profit)
2001 Enrollment: 5,996 309-676-7611
2001 Tuition: In-state $15,230; Out-of-state $15,230
Midstate College (Private, For-profit)
2001 Enrollment: 303 309-692-4092
2001 Tuition: In-state $8,100; Out-of-state $8,100
Saint Francis Medical Center College of Nursing (Private, Not-for-profit, Roman Catholic)
2001 Enrollment: 159 309-655-2086
2001 Tuition: In-state $9,048; Out-of-state $9,048

Two-year College(s)

Methodist Medical Center of Illinois-School of Nursing (Private, Not-for-profit, Other Protestant)
2001 Enrollment: 92 309-672-5512
2001 Tuition: In-state $5,133; Out-of-state $5,133

Housing: Homeownership rate: 59.9% (2000); Median home value: $85,400 (2000); Median rent: $406 per month (2000); Median age of housing: 41 years (2000).
Hospitals: Methodist Medical Center of Illinois (342 beds); Saint Francis Medical Center (731 beds)
Safety: Violent crime rate: n/a; Property crime rate: 741.9 per 10,000 population (2001).
Newspapers: Journal Star (7 x week); Chillicothe Times-Bulletin (1 x week); The Catholic Post (1 x week); PeoriaTimes-Observer (1 x week); Washington Times Reporter (1 x week); Morton Times-News (1 x week); East Peoria Times-Courier (1 x week); El Paso Times - Journal (1 x week)
Transportation: Commute to work: 90.5% car, 3.2% public transportation, 3.8% walk, 2.0% work from home (2000); Travel time to work: 45.2% less than 15 minutes, 42.9% 15 to 30 minutes, 7.1% 30 to 45 minutes, 2.1% 45 to 60 minutes, 2.7% 60 minutes or more (2000); Amtrak: Service available.
Airports: Greater Peoria Regional (primary service); Mount Hawley Auxiliary (primary service)
Additional Information Contacts
Fulton County Board of Realtors 309-688-8591
Peoria Area Association of Realtors 309-688-8591
Peoria Chamber of Commerce 309-676-0755

PEORIA HEIGHTS (village). Covers a land area of 2.644 square miles and a water area of 4.268 square miles. Located at 40.74° N. Lat.; 89.57° W. Long. Elevation is 789 feet.
History: Incorporated 1898.
Population: 6,635 (2000); Race: 93.3% White, 2.2% Black, 1.3% Asian, 0.0% American Indian and Alaska Native, 2.7% Hispanic of any race, 1.4% two or more races (2000); Density: 2,509.0 persons per square mile (2000); Age: 20.0% under 18, 15.8% over 64 (2000); Marriage status: 28.2% never married, 47.8% now married, 8.6% widowed, 15.4% divorced (2000); Foreign born: 2.1% (2000); Ancestry (includes multiple ancestries): 25.9% German, 18.7% Irish, 13.4% Other groups, 13.2% English, 10.3% United States or American (2000).
Economy: Single-family building permits issued: 2 (2001) / 2 (2000); Multi-family building permits issued: 2 (2001) / 0 (2000); Employment by occupation: 11.4% management, 20.0% professional, 17.6% services, 28.2% sales, 0.0% farming, 9.5% construction, 13.3% production (2000).

Income: Per capita income: $20,999 (2000); Median household income: $32,161 (2000); Poverty rate: 8.8% (2000).
Taxes: Total city taxes per capita: $178 (1997); City property taxes per capita: $32 (1997).
Education: High school graduation rate: 84.9% (2000); College graduation rate: 15.6% (2000).

School District(s)

Peoria Hghts C U School District 325 (PK-12)
2000 Enrollment: 801 309-686-8800

Housing: Homeownership rate: 60.5% (2000); Median home value: $61,600 (2000); Median rent: $393 per month (2000); Median age of housing: 46 years (2000).
Transportation: Commute to work: 97.0% car, 0.5% public transportation, 0.6% walk, 1.5% work from home (2000); Travel time to work: 43.3% less than 15 minutes, 44.1% 15 to 30 minutes, 7.6% 30 to 45 minutes, 2.0% 45 to 60 minutes, 3.1% 60 minutes or more (2000)

Additional Information Contacts

Peoria Heights Chamber of Commerce 309-685-4812

PRINCEVILLE (village). Covers a land area of 1.308 square miles and a water area of 0 square miles. Located at 40.93° N. Lat.; 89.75° W. Long. Elevation is 740 feet.
Population: 1,621 (2000); Race: 95.0% White, 0.0% Black, 0.3% Asian, 1.0% American Indian and Alaska Native, 4.2% Hispanic of any race, 1.9% two or more races (2000); Density: 1,239.4 persons per square mile (2000); Age: 23.7% under 18, 18.4% over 64 (2000); Marriage status: 24.3% never married, 59.1% now married, 8.4% widowed, 8.2% divorced (2000); Foreign born: 1.5% (2000); Ancestry (includes multiple ancestries): 32.9% German, 15.7% English, 12.9% Irish, 9.9% Other groups, 8.4% United States or American (2000).
Economy: In agricultural area. Single-family building permits issued: 2 (2001) / 1 (2000); Multi-family building permits issued: 0 (2001) / 0 (2000); Employment by occupation: 10.8% management, 15.8% professional, 12.7% services, 27.1% sales, 1.3% farming, 8.5% construction, 23.7% production (2000).
Income: Per capita income: $19,137 (2000); Median household income: $40,060 (2000); Poverty rate: 6.7% (2000).
Taxes: Total city taxes per capita: $77 (1997); City property taxes per capita: $67 (1997).
Education: High school graduation rate: 87.0% (2000); College graduation rate: 14.0% (2000).

School District(s)

Princeville C U School District 326 (PK-12)
2000 Enrollment: 807 309-385-2213

Housing: Homeownership rate: 75.5% (2000); Median home value: $78,800 (2000); Median rent: $364 per month (2000); Median age of housing: 39 years (2000).
Transportation: Commute to work: 91.2% car, 0.0% public transportation, 6.1% walk, 2.1% work from home (2000); Travel time to work: 38.9% less than 15 minutes, 28.1% 15 to 30 minutes, 24.1% 30 to 45 minutes, 4.2% 45 to 60 minutes, 4.6% 60 minutes or more (2000)

ROME (CDP). Covers a land area of 1.905 square miles and a water area of 0 square miles. Located at 40.87° N. Lat.; 89.50° W. Long. Elevation is 465 feet.
Population: 1,776 (2000); Race: 98.3% White, 0.0% Black, 0.7% Asian, 0.0% American Indian and Alaska Native, 0.5% Hispanic of any race, 0.5% two or more races (2000); Density: 932.5 persons per square mile (2000); Age: 23.3% under 18, 12.3% over 64 (2000); Marriage status: 20.3% never married, 62.3% now married, 5.6% widowed, 11.8% divorced (2000); Foreign born: 1.8% (2000); Ancestry (includes multiple ancestries): 24.5% German, 20.1% Irish, 15.9% English, 6.3% United States or American, 5.9% Italian (2000).
Economy: Employment by occupation: 4.8% management, 18.9% professional, 19.3% services, 26.5% sales, 0.0% farming, 11.0% construction, 19.5% production (2000).
Income: Per capita income: $18,345 (2000); Median household income: $40,962 (2000); Poverty rate: 4.4% (2000).
Education: High school graduation rate: 85.8% (2000); College graduation rate: 16.1% (2000).
Housing: Homeownership rate: 85.7% (2000); Median home value: $80,500 (2000); Median rent: $388 per month (2000); Median age of housing: 38 years (2000).
Transportation: Commute to work: 97.4% car, 0.0% public transportation, 0.0% walk, 1.8% work from home (2000); Travel time to work: 34.1% less than 15 minutes, 44.6% 15 to 30 minutes, 15.4% 30 to 45 minutes, 1.2% 45 to 60 minutes, 4.8% 60 minutes or more (2000)

TRIVOLI (unincorporated postal area, zip code 61569). Covers a land area of 38.577 square miles and a water area of 0.317 square miles. Located at 40.69° N. Lat.; 89.89° W. Long. Elevation is 752 feet.
Population: 1,215 (2000); Race: 100.0% White, 0.0% Black, 0.0% Asian, 0.0% American Indian and Alaska Native, 0.0% Hispanic of any race, 0.0% two or more races (2000); Density: 31.5 persons per square mile (2000); Age: 18.9% under 18, 21.2% over 64 (2000); Marriage status: 15.1% never married, 75.4% now married, 4.6% widowed, 4.8% divorced (2000); Foreign born: 0.0% (2000); Ancestry (includes multiple ancestries): 29.2% German, 16.9% English, 16.9% Irish, 7.8% United States or American, 7.4% French (except Basque) (2000).
Economy: Employment by occupation: 16.6% management, 10.9% professional, 16.1% services, 26.0% sales, 0.0% farming, 14.9% construction, 15.6% production (2000).
Income: Per capita income: $24,636 (2000); Median household income: $53,542 (2000); Poverty rate: 3.9% (2000).
Education: High school graduation rate: 92.5% (2000); College graduation rate: 16.4% (2000).

School District(s)

Farmington Central C U S D 265 (PK-12)
2000 Enrollment: 1,372 309-362-2424

Housing: Homeownership rate: 93.4% (2000); Median home value: $102,700 (2000); Median rent: $415 per month (2000); Median age of housing: 37 years (2000).
Transportation: Commute to work: 93.7% car, 0.0% public transportation, 1.9% walk, 4.4% work from home (2000); Travel time to work: 21.6% less than 15 minutes, 39.5% 15 to 30 minutes, 29.2% 30 to 45 minutes, 6.4% 45 to 60 minutes, 3.4% 60 minutes or more (2000)

WEST PEORIA (city). Covers a land area of 1.286 square miles and a water area of 0 square miles. Located at 40.69° N. Lat.; 89.63° W. Long. Elevation is 595 feet.
History: Bradley University to East.
Population: 4,762 (2000); Race: 89.4% White, 8.5% Black, 0.4% Asian, 0.1% American Indian and Alaska Native, 1.4% Hispanic of any race, 1.5% two or more races (2000); Density: 3,703.7 persons per square mile (2000); Age: 21.5% under 18, 19.5% over 64 (2000); Marriage status: 26.2% never married, 52.4% now married, 9.4% widowed, 11.9% divorced (2000); Foreign born: 0.6% (2000); Ancestry (includes multiple ancestries): 35.2% German, 17.7% Irish, 11.9% Other groups, 11.1% United States or American, 10.1% English (2000).
Economy: Employment by occupation: 13.4% management, 18.4% professional, 15.2% services, 31.8% sales, 0.3% farming, 7.1% construction, 13.9% production (2000).
Income: Per capita income: $22,247 (2000); Median household income: $41,148 (2000); Poverty rate: 8.1% (2000).
Taxes: Total city taxes per capita: $56 (1997); City property taxes per capita: $41 (1997).
Education: High school graduation rate: 83.7% (2000); College graduation rate: 21.7% (2000).
Housing: Homeownership rate: 78.6% (2000); Median home value: $74,800 (2000); Median rent: $388 per month (2000); Median age of housing: 53 years (2000).
Transportation: Commute to work: 95.9% car, 0.9% public transportation, 1.0% walk, 2.2% work from home (2000); Travel time to work: 43.5% less than 15 minutes, 45.5% 15 to 30 minutes, 3.8% 30 to 45 minutes, 4.5% 45 to 60 minutes, 2.8% 60 minutes or more (2000)

Perry County

Located in southwestern Illinois; bounded partly on the east by the Little Muddy River; drained by Beaucoup and Galum Creeks. Covers a land area of 441.00 square miles, a water area of 5.90 square miles, and is located in the Central Time Zone. The county government was organized in 1827. County seat is Pinckneyville.

Weather Station: Du Quoin 4 SE — Elevation: 419 feet

	Jan	Feb	Mar	Apr	May	Jun	Jul	Aug	Sep	Oct	Nov	Dec
High	39	46	56	68	77	85	90	88	81	70	56	44
Low	21	26	35	45	55	63	67	64	57	45	36	27
Precip	2.7	2.6	4.3	4.3	4.8	4.1	3.5	3.2	3.3	3.3	4.4	3.4
Snow	5.1	3.4	1.2	0.5	0.0	0.0	0.0	0.0	0.0	0.2	0.8	2.5

High and Low temperatures in degrees Fahrenheit; Precipitation and Snow in inches

Population: 23,094 (2000); Race: 89.6% White, 8.0% Black, 0.3% Asian, 0.2% American Indian and Alaska Native, 1.6% Hispanic of any race, 0.7% two or more races (2000); Density: 52.4 persons per square mile (2000); Age: 21.9% under 18, 16.1% over 64 (2000).
Religion: Five largest groups: 26.1% Southern Baptist Convention, 14.7% Catholic Church, 4.3% The United Methodist Church, 3.0% United Church of Christ, 2.4% Christian Church (Disciples of Christ) (2000).
Economy: Unemployment rate: 9.3% (11/2002); Total civilian labor force: 8,936 (11/2002); Leading industries: 34.8% manufacturing; 15.5% health care and social assistance; 14.5% retail trade (2000); Companies that employ more than 1,000 persons: 0 (2000); Companies that employ more than 100 persons: 10 (2000); Farms: 551 totaling 172,013 acres (1997); Minority business ownership rate: 0.0% (1997); Women business ownership rate: 15.7% (1997); Retail sales per capita: $5,329 (1997). Single-family building permits issued: -1 (2001) / -1 (2000); Multi-family building permits issued: -1 (2001) / -1 (2000).
Income: Per capita income: $15,935 (2000); Median household income: $33,281 (2000); Poverty rate: 13.2% (2000); Bankruptcy rate: 5.35% (2001).
Taxes: Total county taxes per capita: $86 (2000); County property taxes per capita: $72 (2000).
Education: High school graduation rate: 72.3% (2000); College graduation rate: 10.1% (2000).
Housing: Homeownership rate: 78.6% (2000); Median home value: $55,000 (2000); Median rent: $257 per month (2000); Median age of housing: 39 years (2000).
Health: Birth rate: 108.7 per 10,000 population (1998); Age adjusted death rate: 78.6 per 10,000 population (1999); Age adjusted cancer mortality rate: 205.3 deaths per 100,000 population (1999). Number of physicians: 7.8 per 10,000 population (1999); Number of hospital beds: 42.4 per 10,000 population (1999).
Elections: 2000 Presidential election results: 48.9% Gore, 48.3% Bush, 1.7% Nader, 0.8% Buchanan
National and State Parks: Pyramid State Park
Additional Information Contacts
Perry County Government Offices 618-357-5116
Du Quoin Chamber of Commerce 618-542-9570
Pinckneyville Chamber of Commerce 618-357-3243

Perry County Communities

CUTLER (village). Covers a land area of 0.474 square miles and a water area of 0 square miles. Located at 38.03° N. Lat.; 89.56° W. Long. Elevation is 500 feet.
Population: 543 (2000); Race: 99.4% White, 0.4% Black, 0.2% Asian, 0.0% American Indian and Alaska Native, 0.7% Hispanic of any race, 0.0% two or more races (2000); Density: 1,146.4 persons per square mile (2000); Age: 33.8% under 18, 9.8% over 64 (2000); Marriage status: 24.0% never married, 53.2% now married, 8.6% widowed, 14.2% divorced (2000); Foreign born: 0.0% (2000); Ancestry (includes multiple ancestries): 23.4% German, 18.6% United States or American, 15.4% Other groups, 11.1% Irish, 3.5% Dutch (2000).
Economy: In agricultural and bituminous coal-mining area. Employment by occupation: 3.1% management, 7.3% professional, 28.1% services, 16.7% sales, 0.0% farming, 9.4% construction, 35.4% production (2000).
Income: Per capita income: $13,678 (2000); Median household income: $30,417 (2000); Poverty rate: 29.2% (2000).
Taxes: Total city taxes per capita: $88 (1997); City property taxes per capita: $48 (1997).
Education: High school graduation rate: 57.8% (2000); College graduation rate: 3.6% (2000).
Housing: Homeownership rate: 77.2% (2000); Median home value: $38,300 (2000); Median rent: $228 per month (2000); Median age of housing: 40 years (2000).
Transportation: Commute to work: 92.5% car, 0.0% public transportation, 1.6% walk, 3.7% work from home (2000); Travel time to work: 18.9% less than 15 minutes, 29.4% 15 to 30 minutes, 21.1% 30 to 45 minutes, 16.1% 45 to 60 minutes, 14.4% 60 minutes or more (2000)

DU QUOIN (city). Covers a land area of 6.865 square miles and a water area of 0.067 square miles. Located at 38.00° N. Lat.; 89.23° W. Long. Elevation is 446 feet.
History: Du Quoin developed as a coal mining town. It was named for Jean Baptiste Du Quoigne, chief of the Kaskaskia tribe.
Population: 6,448 (2000); Race: 90.8% White, 7.3% Black, 0.0% Asian, 0.0% American Indian and Alaska Native, 0.6% Hispanic of any race, 1.5% two or more races (2000); Density: 939.3 persons per square mile (2000); Age: 23.4% under 18, 21.5% over 64 (2000); Marriage status: 18.0% never married, 56.2% now married, 12.7% widowed, 13.1% divorced (2000); Foreign born: 0.6% (2000); Ancestry (includes multiple ancestries): 20.7% German, 11.9% Other groups, 10.0% Irish, 10.0% English, 9.0% United States or American (2000).
Economy: Employment by occupation: 8.2% management, 14.8% professional, 17.1% services, 27.9% sales, 0.4% farming, 8.3% construction, 23.2% production (2000).
Income: Per capita income: $14,883 (2000); Median household income: $29,124 (2000); Poverty rate: 18.1% (2000).
Taxes: Total city taxes per capita: $74 (1997); City property taxes per capita: $63 (1997).
Education: High school graduation rate: 74.3% (2000); College graduation rate: 13.1% (2000).

School District(s)
Du Quoin C U School District 300 (PK-12)
2000 Enrollment: 1,572 618-542-3856
Housing: Homeownership rate: 71.6% (2000); Median home value: $48,600 (2000); Median rent: $261 per month (2000); Median age of housing: 50 years (2000).
Hospitals: Marshall Browning Hospital (33 beds)
Newspapers: Du Quoin Evening Call (6 x week); Ashley News (1 x week)
Transportation: Commute to work: 92.0% car, 0.3% public transportation, 4.5% walk, 1.9% work from home (2000); Travel time to work: 52.0% less than 15 minutes, 18.8% 15 to 30 minutes, 15.3% 30 to 45 minutes, 8.7% 45 to 60 minutes, 5.2% 60 minutes or more (2000); Amtrak: Service available.
Additional Information Contacts
Du Quoin Chamber of Commerce 618-542-9570

PINCKNEYVILLE (city). Covers a land area of 3.161 square miles and a water area of 0.002 square miles. Located at 38.07° N. Lat.; 89.38° W. Long. Elevation is 439 feet.
History: Pyramid State Park to South, created from reclaimed coal strip mines. Incorporated 1861.
Population: 5,464 (2000); Race: 71.1% White, 24.2% Black, 0.5% Asian, 0.3% American Indian and Alaska Native, 4.1% Hispanic of any race, 0.3% two or more races (2000); Density: 1,728.5 persons per square mile (2000); Age: 14.4% under 18, 14.1% over 64 (2000); Marriage status: 15.5% never married, 64.7% now married, 5.0% widowed, 14.8% divorced (2000); Foreign born: 1.3% (2000); Ancestry (includes multiple ancestries): 14.1% German, 10.7% United States or American, 9.0% Irish, 8.7% Other groups, 4.2% English (2000).
Economy: Railroad junction. In bituminous coal (large strip mine) and agricultural area: sorghum, wheat, corn, soybeans; dairying. Manufacturing: construction materials, compact discs. Employment by occupation: 9.9% management, 15.6% professional, 22.2% services, 18.3% sales, 0.8% farming, 8.3% construction, 24.9% production (2000).
Income: Per capita income: $15,601 (2000); Median household income: $30,391 (2000); Poverty rate: 11.0% (2000).
Taxes: Total city taxes per capita: $201 (1997); City property taxes per capita: $78 (1997).
Education: High school graduation rate: 58.5% (2000); College graduation rate: 7.4% (2000).

School District(s)
Community Cons School District 204 (PK-08)
2000 Enrollment: 201 618-357-2419
Pinckneyville Community H S District 101 (09-12)
2000 Enrollment: 482 618-357-5013
Pinckneyville School District 50 (KG-08)
2000 Enrollment: 664 618-357-5161
Housing: Homeownership rate: 70.5% (2000); Median home value: $57,300 (2000); Median rent: $261 per month (2000); Median age of housing: 46 years (2000).
Hospitals: Pinckneyville Community Hospital (85 beds)
Newspapers: Pinckneyville Democrat (1 x week)
Transportation: Commute to work: 90.1% car, 0.7% public transportation, 3.1% walk, 5.4% work from home (2000); Travel time to work: 49.3% less than 15 minutes, 17.8% 15 to 30 minutes, 17.4% 30 to 45 minutes, 11.7% 45 to 60 minutes, 3.8% 60 minutes or more (2000)
Airports: Pinckneyville-Du Quoin
Additional Information Contacts
Pinckneyville Chamber of Commerce 618-357-3243

SAINT JOHNS (village). Covers a land area of 0.703 square miles and a water area of 0.045 square miles. Located at 38.03° N. Lat.; 89.24° W. Long. Elevation is 460 feet.
Population: 218 (2000); Race: 88.7% White, 7.4% Black, 3.9% Asian, 0.0% American Indian and Alaska Native, 0.0% Hispanic of any race, 0.0% two or more races (2000); Density: 310.0 persons per square mile (2000); Age: 17.7% under 18, 6.5% over 64 (2000); Marriage status: 30.7% never married, 46.3% now married, 9.8% widowed, 13.2% divorced (2000); Foreign born: 1.7% (2000); Ancestry (includes multiple ancestries): 36.4% German, 22.5% Other groups, 13.0% Irish, 10.4% English, 5.6% Swedish (2000).
Economy: Employment by occupation: 5.9% management, 11.0% professional, 18.4% services, 17.6% sales, 0.0% farming, 11.0% construction, 36.0% production (2000).
Income: Per capita income: $15,802 (2000); Median household income: $35,455 (2000); Poverty rate: 11.4% (2000).
Education: High school graduation rate: 80.2% (2000); College graduation rate: 9.9% (2000).
Housing: Homeownership rate: 60.2% (2000); Median home value: $42,500 (2000); Median rent: $246 per month (2000); Median age of housing: 29 years (2000).
Transportation: Commute to work: 97.0% car, 0.0% public transportation, 1.5% walk, 1.5% work from home (2000); Travel time to work: 43.9% less than 15 minutes, 13.6% 15 to 30 minutes, 19.7% 30 to 45 minutes, 10.6% 45 to 60 minutes, 12.1% 60 minutes or more (2000)

TAMAROA (village). Covers a land area of 0.983 square miles and a water area of 0 square miles. Located at 38.13° N. Lat.; 89.22° W. Long. Elevation is 505 feet.
History: Tamaroa was named for the Tamaroa Indians that lived in this area.
Population: 740 (2000); Race: 96.9% White, 0.0% Black, 0.8% Asian, 1.5% American Indian and Alaska Native, 0.0% Hispanic of any race, 0.8% two or more races (2000); Density: 753.0 persons per square mile (2000); Age: 22.1% under 18, 16.4% over 64 (2000); Marriage status: 27.0% never married, 50.8% now married, 10.0% widowed, 12.3% divorced (2000); Foreign born: 0.8% (2000); Ancestry (includes multiple ancestries): 23.7% German, 15.2% Irish, 10.3% Other groups, 9.5% Polish, 6.5% English (2000).
Economy: Employment by occupation: 1.9% management, 14.6% professional, 23.2% services, 17.5% sales, 0.6% farming, 6.7% construction, 35.4% production (2000).
Income: Per capita income: $14,573 (2000); Median household income: $25,682 (2000); Poverty rate: 17.3% (2000).
Taxes: Total city taxes per capita: $38 (1997); City property taxes per capita: $22 (1997).
Education: High school graduation rate: 68.3% (2000); College graduation rate: 4.8% (2000).

School District(s)

Tamaroa School District 5 (KG-08)
2000 Enrollment: 119 618-496-5513
Housing: Homeownership rate: 79.1% (2000); Median home value: $38,900 (2000); Median rent: $219 per month (2000); Median age of housing: 47 years (2000).
Transportation: Commute to work: 93.5% car, 0.0% public transportation, 3.6% walk, 2.3% work from home (2000); Travel time to work: 20.9% less than 15 minutes, 38.5% 15 to 30 minutes, 19.3% 30 to 45 minutes, 7.6% 45 to 60 minutes, 13.6% 60 minutes or more (2000)

WILLISVILLE (village). Covers a land area of 0.377 square miles and a water area of 0 square miles. Located at 37.98° N. Lat.; 89.59° W. Long. Elevation is 500 feet.
Population: 694 (2000); Race: 97.0% White, 1.7% Black, 0.0% Asian, 0.0% American Indian and Alaska Native, 0.6% Hispanic of any race, 1.3% two or more races (2000); Density: 1,840.4 persons per square mile (2000); Age: 29.6% under 18, 14.9% over 64 (2000); Marriage status: 21.2% never married, 59.1% now married, 7.9% widowed, 11.8% divorced (2000); Foreign born: 0.3% (2000); Ancestry (includes multiple ancestries): 33.6% German, 14.4% Irish, 13.0% United States or American, 11.9% Other groups, 6.9% French (except Basque) (2000).
Economy: In agricultural and bituminous-coal-mining area. Employment by occupation: 2.6% management, 9.0% professional, 20.6% services, 13.9% sales, 1.0% farming, 14.8% construction, 38.1% production (2000).
Income: Per capita income: $12,832 (2000); Median household income: $31,000 (2000); Poverty rate: 17.8% (2000).
Taxes: Total city taxes per capita: $91 (1997); City property taxes per capita: $40 (1997).
Education: High school graduation rate: 67.0% (2000); College graduation rate: 2.1% (2000).
Housing: Homeownership rate: 81.5% (2000); Median home value: $39,300 (2000); Median rent: $250 per month (2000); Median age of housing: 41 years (2000).
Transportation: Commute to work: 92.9% car, 0.0% public transportation, 2.4% walk, 4.1% work from home (2000); Travel time to work: 32.3% less than 15 minutes, 30.5% 15 to 30 minutes, 19.5% 30 to 45 minutes, 7.4% 45 to 60 minutes, 10.3% 60 minutes or more (2000)

Piatt County

Located in central Illinois; drained by the Sangamon River. Covers a land area of 440.00 square miles, a water area of 0.30 square miles, and is located in the Central Time Zone. The county government was organized in 1841. County seat is Monticello.
Population: 16,365 (2000); Race: 98.3% White, 0.4% Black, 0.4% Asian, 0.2% American Indian and Alaska Native, 0.7% Hispanic of any race, 0.6% two or more races (2000); Density: 37.2 persons per square mile (2000); Age: 25.2% under 18, 15.4% over 64 (2000).
Religion: Five largest groups: 17.2% The United Methodist Church, 6.0% Southern Baptist Convention, 5.8% Christian Churches and Churches of Christ, 5.7% Catholic Church, 3.9% United Church of Christ (2000).
Economy: Unemployment rate: 5.1% (11/2002); Total civilian labor force: 8,455 (11/2002); Leading industries: 19.7% retail trade; 15.6% manufacturing; 13.1% health care and social assistance (2000); Companies that employ more than 1,000 persons: 0 (2000); Companies that employ more than 100 persons: 4 (2000); Farms: 448 totaling 253,317 acres (1997); Minority business ownership rate: 0.0% (1997); Women business ownership rate: 23.1% (1997); Retail sales per capita: $6,031 (1997). Single-family building permits issued: 72 (2001) / 69 (2000); Multi-family building permits issued: 4 (2001) / 0 (2000).
Income: Per capita income: $21,075 (2000); Median household income: $45,752 (2000); Poverty rate: 5.0% (2000); Bankruptcy rate: 4.56% (2001).
Taxes: Total county taxes per capita: $153 (2000); County property taxes per capita: $152 (2000).
Education: High school graduation rate: 88.7% (2000); College graduation rate: 21.0% (2000).
Housing: Homeownership rate: 80.3% (2000); Median home value: $82,600 (2000); Median rent: $346 per month (2000); Median age of housing: 40 years (2000).
Health: Birth rate: 109.4 per 10,000 population (1998); Age adjusted death rate: 79.3 per 10,000 population (1999); Age adjusted cancer mortality rate: 243.1 deaths per 100,000 population (1999). Number of physicians: 7.9 per 10,000 population (1999); Number of hospital beds: 9.8 per 10,000 population (1999).
Elections: 2000 Presidential election results: 41.6% Gore, 55.1% Bush, 2.6% Nader, 0.5% Buchanan
Additional Information Contacts
Piatt County Government Offices 217-762-9487
Monticello Chamber of Commerce 217-762-9318

Piatt County Communities

ATWOOD (village). Covers a land area of 0.569 square miles and a water area of 0 square miles. Located at 39.80° N. Lat.; 88.46° W. Long.
Population: 1,290 (2000); Race: 99.0% White, 0.0% Black, 0.2% Asian, 0.0% American Indian and Alaska Native, 2.0% Hispanic of any race, 0.4% two or more races (2000); Density: 2,265.8 persons per square mile (2000); Age: 26.3% under 18, 16.6% over 64 (2000); Marriage status: 17.7% never married, 61.7% now married, 9.6% widowed, 11.0% divorced (2000); Foreign born: 1.3% (2000); Ancestry (includes multiple ancestries): 20.7% German, 18.8% United States or American, 9.5% English, 8.1% Irish, 5.3% Other groups (2000).
Economy: Single-family building permits issued: 2 (2001) / 2 (2000); Multi-family building permits issued: 0 (2001) / 0 (2000); Employment by occupation: 10.1% management, 10.3% professional, 13.9% services, 24.3% sales, 1.2% farming, 13.6% construction, 26.7% production (2000).
Income: Per capita income: $18,028 (2000); Median household income: $36,806 (2000); Poverty rate: 12.0% (2000).
Taxes: Total city taxes per capita: $63 (1997); City property taxes per capita: $60 (1997).
Education: High school graduation rate: 83.8% (2000); College graduation rate: 9.2% (2000).

School District(s)
Atwood Hammond C U School District 39 (KG-12)
2000 Enrollment: 488 217-578-3111
Housing: Homeownership rate: 77.1% (2000); Median home value: $60,000 (2000); Median rent: $300 per month (2000); Median age of housing: 39 years (2000).
Newspapers: The Atwood Herald (1 x week)
Transportation: Commute to work: 91.8% car, 0.0% public transportation, 3.6% walk, 3.3% work from home (2000); Travel time to work: 39.8% less than 15 minutes, 25.6% 15 to 30 minutes, 15.6% 30 to 45 minutes, 14.6% 45 to 60 minutes, 4.4% 60 minutes or more (2000)

BEMENT (village). Covers a land area of 0.812 square miles and a water area of 0 square miles. Located at 39.92° N. Lat.; 88.57° W. Long. Elevation is 690 feet.
History: Incorporated 1874. Bryant Cottage State Historical Site.
Population: 1,784 (2000); Race: 98.2% White, 0.4% Black, 0.6% Asian, 0.0% American Indian and Alaska Native, 0.5% Hispanic of any race, 0.7% two or more races (2000); Density: 2,197.1 persons per square mile (2000); Age: 23.0% under 18, 15.9% over 64 (2000); Marriage status: 23.5% never married, 55.3% now married, 9.6% widowed, 11.6% divorced (2000); Foreign born: 0.7% (2000); Ancestry (includes multiple ancestries): 21.0% German, 15.2% United States or American, 10.1% English, 9.6% Irish, 5.2% Other groups (2000).
Economy: In corn and soybean area. Manufacturing: wood cabinets. Single-family building permits issued: 2 (2001) / 1 (2000); Multi-family building permits issued: 0 (2001) / 0 (2000); Employment by occupation: 9.2% management, 11.2% professional, 19.9% services, 22.4% sales, 0.0% farming, 9.6% construction, 27.8% production (2000).
Income: Per capita income: $17,995 (2000); Median household income: $40,163 (2000); Poverty rate: 6.2% (2000).
Taxes: Total city taxes per capita: $55 (1997); City property taxes per capita: $46 (1997).
Education: High school graduation rate: 84.6% (2000); College graduation rate: 12.2% (2000).

School District(s)
Bement Community Unit School District 5 (PK-12)
2000 Enrollment: 454 217-678-2111
Housing: Homeownership rate: 79.9% (2000); Median home value: $64,000 (2000); Median rent: $330 per month (2000); Median age of housing: 46 years (2000).
Transportation: Commute to work: 89.4% car, 0.8% public transportation, 5.9% walk, 3.2% work from home (2000); Travel time to work: 33.9% less than 15 minutes, 18.8% 15 to 30 minutes, 30.6% 30 to 45 minutes, 13.3% 45 to 60 minutes, 3.4% 60 minutes or more (2000)

CERRO GORDO (village). Covers a land area of 0.741 square miles and a water area of 0 square miles. Located at 39.89° N. Lat.; 88.73° W. Long. Elevation is 742 feet.
History: Incorporated 1873.
Population: 1,436 (2000); Race: 98.8% White, 0.1% Black, 0.0% Asian, 0.0% American Indian and Alaska Native, 0.1% Hispanic of any race, 1.0% two or more races (2000); Density: 1,938.0 persons per square mile (2000); Age: 28.5% under 18, 13.4% over 64 (2000); Marriage status: 19.7% never married, 60.1% now married, 8.0% widowed, 12.2% divorced (2000); Foreign born: 0.0% (2000); Ancestry (includes multiple ancestries): 28.4% German, 12.4% English, 10.2% Irish, 7.3% United States or American, 5.6% Other groups (2000).
Economy: In rich agricultural area; ships grain. Single-family building permits issued: 0 (2001) / 1 (2000); Multi-family building permits issued: 0 (2001) / 0 (2000); Employment by occupation: 6.4% management, 15.6% professional, 15.0% services, 27.0% sales, 1.4% farming, 9.9% construction, 24.7% production (2000).
Income: Per capita income: $16,635 (2000); Median household income: $40,529 (2000); Poverty rate: 7.1% (2000).
Taxes: Total city taxes per capita: $54 (1997); City property taxes per capita: $47 (1997).
Education: High school graduation rate: 89.2% (2000); College graduation rate: 10.5% (2000).

School District(s)
Cerro Gordo C U School District 100 (PK-12)
2000 Enrollment: 654 217-763-5221
Housing: Homeownership rate: 80.2% (2000); Median home value: $69,100 (2000); Median rent: $324 per month (2000); Median age of housing: 43 years (2000).
Transportation: Commute to work: 94.8% car, 0.0% public transportation, 2.4% walk, 2.0% work from home (2000); Travel time to work: 19.3% less than 15 minutes, 51.8% 15 to 30 minutes, 19.7% 30 to 45 minutes, 3.3% 45 to 60 minutes, 5.9% 60 minutes or more (2000)

CISCO (village). Covers a land area of 0.381 square miles and a water area of 0 square miles. Located at 40.01° N. Lat.; 88.72° W. Long. Elevation is 690 feet.
Population: 264 (2000); Race: 99.3% White, 0.0% Black, 0.7% Asian, 0.0% American Indian and Alaska Native, 0.0% Hispanic of any race, 0.0% two or more races (2000); Density: 692.7 persons per square mile (2000); Age: 18.1% under 18, 17.4% over 64 (2000); Marriage status: 15.7% never married, 69.4% now married, 10.2% widowed, 4.7% divorced (2000); Foreign born: 1.1% (2000); Ancestry (includes multiple ancestries): 16.3% German, 13.0% Irish, 11.2% Other groups, 8.3% English, 5.8% Dutch (2000).
Economy: In rich agricultural area. Employment by occupation: 11.1% management, 17.0% professional, 22.9% services, 15.0% sales, 1.3% farming, 17.0% construction, 15.7% production (2000).
Income: Per capita income: $17,722 (2000); Median household income: $40,625 (2000); Poverty rate: 8.3% (2000).
Taxes: Total city taxes per capita: $30 (1997); City property taxes per capita: $30 (1997).
Education: High school graduation rate: 91.0% (2000); College graduation rate: 9.0% (2000).
Housing: Homeownership rate: 86.7% (2000); Median home value: $68,000 (2000); Median rent: $375 per month (2000); Median age of housing: 60+ years (2000).
Transportation: Commute to work: 92.0% car, 0.0% public transportation, 4.0% walk, 4.0% work from home (2000); Travel time to work: 21.5% less than 15 minutes, 38.2% 15 to 30 minutes, 28.5% 30 to 45 minutes, 4.9% 45 to 60 minutes, 6.9% 60 minutes or more (2000)

DE LAND (village). Aka Deland. Covers a land area of 0.396 square miles and a water area of 0 square miles. Located at 40.12° N. Lat.; 88.64° W. Long. Elevation is 706 feet.
Population: 475 (2000); Race: 97.9% White, 0.0% Black, 0.0% Asian, 0.0% American Indian and Alaska Native, 0.4% Hispanic of any race, 2.1% two or more races (2000); Density: 1,198.1 persons per square mile (2000); Age: 22.3% under 18, 20.0% over 64 (2000); Marriage status: 21.5% never married, 63.7% now married, 7.3% widowed, 7.5% divorced (2000); Foreign born: 0.8% (2000); Ancestry (includes multiple ancestries): 18.9% German, 16.4% English, 13.0% Irish, 12.2% United States or American, 9.7% Other groups (2000).
Economy: In corn, soybeans, and livestock area. Single-family building permits issued: 1 (2001) / 1 (2000); Multi-family building permits issued: 0 (2001) / 0 (2000); Employment by occupation: 9.1% management, 11.6% professional, 21.1% services, 22.4% sales, 2.6% farming, 11.6% construction, 21.6% production (2000).
Income: Per capita income: $17,377 (2000); Median household income: $40,982 (2000); Poverty rate: 4.6% (2000).
Taxes: Total city taxes per capita: $67 (1997); City property taxes per capita: $67 (1997).
Education: High school graduation rate: 82.7% (2000); College graduation rate: 7.4% (2000).

School District(s)
Deland-Weldon C U School District 57 (KG-12)
2000 Enrollment: 195 217-736-2311
Housing: Homeownership rate: 75.8% (2000); Median home value: $64,100 (2000); Median rent: $267 per month (2000); Median age of housing: 47 years (2000).
Transportation: Commute to work: 90.9% car, 0.9% public transportation, 1.7% walk, 4.3% work from home (2000); Travel time to work: 27.1% less than 15 minutes, 28.5% 15 to 30 minutes, 38.0% 30 to 45 minutes, 4.5% 45 to 60 minutes, 1.8% 60 minutes or more (2000)

HAMMOND (village). Covers a land area of 0.762 square miles and a water area of 0.006 square miles. Located at 39.79° N. Lat.; 88.59° W. Long. Elevation is 678 feet.
Population: 518 (2000); Race: 96.1% White, 0.4% Black, 2.1% Asian, 0.0% American Indian and Alaska Native, 0.0% Hispanic of any race, 0.0% two or more races (2000); Density: 679.8 persons per square mile (2000); Age: 23.7% under 18, 15.6% over 64 (2000); Marriage status: 17.3% never married, 62.4% now married, 7.7% widowed, 12.5% divorced (2000); Foreign born: 1.2% (2000); Ancestry (includes multiple ancestries): 28.3%

German, 15.4% English, 14.5% United States or American, 12.7% Irish, 8.5% Other groups (2000).
Economy: In grain area. Single-family building permits issued: 0 (2001) / 6 (2000); Multi-family building permits issued: 0 (2001) / 0 (2000); Employment by occupation: 7.5% management, 8.3% professional, 8.3% services, 18.1% sales, 0.8% farming, 17.7% construction, 39.4% production (2000).
Income: Per capita income: $19,313 (2000); Median household income: $45,833 (2000); Poverty rate: 7.1% (2000).
Taxes: Total city taxes per capita: $62 (1997); City property taxes per capita: $52 (1997).
Education: High school graduation rate: 85.3% (2000); College graduation rate: 7.9% (2000).
Housing: Homeownership rate: 78.9% (2000); Median home value: $66,300 (2000); Median rent: $231 per month (2000); Median age of housing: 40 years (2000).
Transportation: Commute to work: 96.7% car, 0.4% public transportation, 2.0% walk, 0.8% work from home (2000); Travel time to work: 16.4% less than 15 minutes, 29.5% 15 to 30 minutes, 39.3% 30 to 45 minutes, 6.1% 45 to 60 minutes, 8.6% 60 minutes or more (2000)

MANSFIELD (village). Covers a land area of 0.511 square miles and a water area of 0.025 square miles. Located at 40.21° N. Lat.; 88.50° W. Long. Elevation is 730 feet.
Population: 949 (2000); Race: 98.9% White, 0.7% Black, 0.0% Asian, 0.0% American Indian and Alaska Native, 1.5% Hispanic of any race, 0.0% two or more races (2000); Density: 1,856.3 persons per square mile (2000); Age: 23.2% under 18, 13.3% over 64 (2000); Marriage status: 17.2% never married, 68.8% now married, 6.1% widowed, 7.8% divorced (2000); Foreign born: 0.2% (2000); Ancestry (includes multiple ancestries): 29.9% German, 15.4% United States or American, 13.1% Irish, 11.0% English, 4.6% Other groups (2000).
Economy: In grain-growing area. Single-family building permits issued: 0 (2001) / 5 (2000); Multi-family building permits issued: 0 (2001) / 0 (2000); Employment by occupation: 9.1% management, 14.3% professional, 15.8% services, 31.6% sales, 0.4% farming, 13.5% construction, 15.4% production (2000).
Income: Per capita income: $20,947 (2000); Median household income: $43,942 (2000); Poverty rate: 3.9% (2000).
Taxes: Total city taxes per capita: $47 (1997); City property taxes per capita: $22 (1997).
Education: High school graduation rate: 87.6% (2000); College graduation rate: 14.6% (2000).
Housing: Homeownership rate: 79.1% (2000); Median home value: $73,900 (2000); Median rent: $384 per month (2000); Median age of housing: 44 years (2000).
Transportation: Commute to work: 95.5% car, 0.0% public transportation, 2.7% walk, 1.4% work from home (2000); Travel time to work: 26.2% less than 15 minutes, 50.1% 15 to 30 minutes, 16.5% 30 to 45 minutes, 5.2% 45 to 60 minutes, 2.0% 60 minutes or more (2000)

MILMINE (unincorporated postal area, zip code 61855). Covers a land area of 5.535 square miles and a water area of 0 square miles. Located at 39.92° N. Lat.; 88.67° W. Long. Elevation is 710 feet.
Population: 74 (2000); Race: 100.0% White, 0.0% Black, 0.0% Asian, 0.0% American Indian and Alaska Native, 0.0% Hispanic of any race, 0.0% two or more races (2000); Density: 13.4 persons per square mile (2000); Age: 19.6% under 18, 16.1% over 64 (2000); Marriage status: 6.7% never married, 86.7% now married, 6.7% widowed, 0.0% divorced (2000); Foreign born: 0.0% (2000); Ancestry (includes multiple ancestries): 10.7% English, 10.7% United States or American, 8.9% Other groups, 7.1% Norwegian, 7.1% French (except Basque) (2000).
Economy: Employment by occupation: 0.0% management, 13.0% professional, 17.4% services, 13.0% sales, 0.0% farming, 21.7% construction, 34.8% production (2000).
Income: Per capita income: $18,811 (2000); Median household income: $34,531 (2000); Poverty rate: 0.0% (2000).
Education: High school graduation rate: 70.7% (2000); College graduation rate: 0.0% (2000).
Housing: Homeownership rate: 77.8% (2000); Median home value: $58,100 (2000); Median rent: $225 per month (2000); Median age of housing: 60+ years (2000).
Transportation: Commute to work: 100.0% car, 0.0% public transportation, 0.0% walk, 0.0% work from home (2000); Travel time to work: 0.0% less than 15 minutes, 47.8% 15 to 30 minutes, 30.4% 30 to 45 minutes, 21.7% 45 to 60 minutes, 0.0% 60 minutes or more (2000)

MONTICELLO (city). Covers a land area of 2.979 square miles and a water area of 0 square miles. Located at 40.02° N. Lat.; 88.57° W. Long. Elevation is 675 feet.
History: Incorporated 1841.
Population: 5,138 (2000); Race: 97.3% White, 0.7% Black, 0.8% Asian, 0.7% American Indian and Alaska Native, 1.4% Hispanic of any race, 0.6% two or more races (2000); Density: 1,724.7 persons per square mile (2000); Age: 23.4% under 18, 19.3% over 64 (2000); Marriage status: 18.5% never married, 62.1% now married, 8.0% widowed, 11.3% divorced (2000); Foreign born: 1.2% (2000); Ancestry (includes multiple ancestries): 26.2% German, 13.5% Irish, 12.4% English, 6.9% Other groups, 6.1% United States or American (2000).
Economy: In rich agricultural area; manufacturing of drugs, food products; corn, soybeans, wheat, livestock, dairy products. Single-family building permits issued: 28 (2001) / 25 (2000); Multi-family building permits issued: 4 (2001) / 0 (2000); Employment by occupation: 15.5% management, 26.4% professional, 14.1% services, 24.9% sales, 0.5% farming, 6.3% construction, 12.3% production (2000).
Income: Per capita income: $23,257 (2000); Median household income: $45,754 (2000); Poverty rate: 3.8% (2000).
Taxes: Total city taxes per capita: $107 (1997); City property taxes per capita: $51 (1997).
Education: High school graduation rate: 88.4% (2000); College graduation rate: 30.7% (2000).

School District(s)

Monticello C U School District 25 (PK-12)
2000 Enrollment: 1,615 217-762-8511
Housing: Homeownership rate: 78.8% (2000); Median home value: $100,700 (2000); Median rent: $404 per month (2000); Median age of housing: 37 years (2000).
Hospitals: John & Mary Kirby Hospital (17 beds)
Newspapers: Piatt County Journal-Republican (1 x week)
Transportation: Commute to work: 90.2% car, 0.3% public transportation, 5.0% walk, 3.3% work from home (2000); Travel time to work: 43.9% less than 15 minutes, 22.2% 15 to 30 minutes, 28.9% 30 to 45 minutes, 2.3% 45 to 60 minutes, 2.8% 60 minutes or more (2000)
Additional Information Contacts
Monticello Chamber of Commerce 217-762-9318

WHITE HEATH (unincorporated postal area, zip code 61884). Covers a land area of 25.358 square miles and a water area of 0.081 square miles. Located at 40.10° N. Lat.; 88.49° W. Long. Elevation is 705 feet.
Population: 1,172 (2000); Race: 100.0% White, 0.0% Black, 0.0% Asian, 0.0% American Indian and Alaska Native, 0.0% Hispanic of any race, 0.0% two or more races (2000); Density: 46.2 persons per square mile (2000); Age: 32.7% under 18, 10.6% over 64 (2000); Marriage status: 23.3% never married, 70.5% now married, 2.4% widowed, 3.9% divorced (2000); Foreign born: 0.0% (2000); Ancestry (includes multiple ancestries): 18.5% German, 17.9% Irish, 15.5% United States or American, 12.0% English, 3.7% Italian (2000).
Economy: Employment by occupation: 8.9% management, 19.7% professional, 12.2% services, 27.4% sales, 3.5% farming, 8.2% construction, 20.1% production (2000).
Income: Per capita income: $23,131 (2000); Median household income: $53,819 (2000); Poverty rate: 0.5% (2000).
Education: High school graduation rate: 92.4% (2000); College graduation rate: 28.1% (2000).
Housing: Homeownership rate: 87.7% (2000); Median home value: $128,800 (2000); Median rent: $360 per month (2000); Median age of housing: 27 years (2000).
Transportation: Commute to work: 93.8% car, 0.0% public transportation, 0.0% walk, 5.1% work from home (2000); Travel time to work: 18.4% less than 15 minutes, 47.8% 15 to 30 minutes, 19.5% 30 to 45 minutes, 3.3% 45 to 60 minutes, 11.0% 60 minutes or more (2000)

Pike County

Located in western Illinois; bounded on the west and southwest by the Mississippi River and the Missouri border, and on the east by the Illinois River. Covers a land area of 830.30 square miles, a water area of 18.60 square miles, and is located in the Central Time Zone. The county government was organized in 1821. County seat is Pittsfield.
Population: 17,384 (2000); Race: 97.6% White, 1.4% Black, 0.4% Asian, 0.1% American Indian and Alaska Native, 0.6% Hispanic of any race, 0.5%

two or more races (2000); Density: 20.9 persons per square mile (2000); Age: 24.1% under 18, 19.3% over 64 (2000).
Religion: Five largest groups: 11.7% The United Methodist Church, 9.1% Christian Churches and Churches of Christ, 7.0% Southern Baptist Convention, 5.3% Christian Church (Disciples of Christ), 3.4% Assemblies of God (2000).
Economy: Unemployment rate: 5.2% (11/2002); Total civilian labor force: 8,694 (11/2002); Leading industries: 23.1% retail trade; 20.5% health care and social assistance; 13.2% accommodation & food services (2000); Companies that employ more than 1,000 persons: 0 (2000); Companies that employ more than 100 persons: 2 (2000); Farms: 1,028 totaling 461,360 acres (1997); Minority business ownership rate: 0.0% (1997); Women business ownership rate: 31.8% (1997); Retail sales per capita: $6,938 (1997). Single-family building permits issued: 30 (2001) / 46 (2000); Multi-family building permits issued: 0 (2001) / 0 (2000).
Income: Per capita income: $15,946 (2000); Median household income: $31,127 (2000); Poverty rate: 12.4% (2000); Bankruptcy rate: 5.24% (2001).
Taxes: Total county taxes per capita: $107 (1997); County property taxes per capita: $101 (1997).
Education: High school graduation rate: 79.6% (2000); College graduation rate: 9.9% (2000).
Housing: Homeownership rate: 77.2% (2000); Median home value: $54,000 (2000); Median rent: $235 per month (2000); Median age of housing: 47 years (2000).
Health: Birth rate: 114.5 per 10,000 population (1998); Age adjusted death rate: 88.1 per 10,000 population (1999); Age adjusted cancer mortality rate: 268.5 deaths per 100,000 population (1999). Number of physicians: 6.3 per 10,000 population (1999); Number of hospital beds: 17.3 per 10,000 population (1999).
Elections: 2000 Presidential election results: 39.4% Gore, 58.0% Bush, 1.4% Nader, 0.8% Buchanan
Additional Information Contacts
Pike County Government Offices 217-285-6812

Pike County Communities

BARRY (city). Covers a land area of 1.142 square miles and a water area of 0 square miles. Located at 39.69° N. Lat.; 91.04° W. Long. Elevation is 730 feet.
History: Barry developed as a trading center for a dairying and agricultural area.
Population: 1,368 (2000); Race: 97.7% White, 0.2% Black, 0.0% Asian, 0.0% American Indian and Alaska Native, 1.0% Hispanic of any race, 2.1% two or more races (2000); Density: 1,198.0 persons per square mile (2000); Age: 23.0% under 18, 24.1% over 64 (2000); Marriage status: 17.4% never married, 58.5% now married, 15.0% widowed, 9.1% divorced (2000); Foreign born: 0.7% (2000); Ancestry (includes multiple ancestries): 24.2% United States or American, 14.7% German, 10.2% English, 9.8% Irish, 7.6% Other groups (2000).
Economy: Single-family building permits issued: 2 (2001) / 0 (2000); Multi-family building permits issued: 0 (2001) / 0 (2000); Employment by occupation: 6.8% management, 14.9% professional, 22.2% services, 23.0% sales, 2.0% farming, 8.1% construction, 23.0% production (2000).
Income: Per capita income: $18,097 (2000); Median household income: $27,635 (2000); Poverty rate: 11.5% (2000).
Taxes: Total city taxes per capita: $43 (1997); City property taxes per capita: $32 (1997).
Education: High school graduation rate: 73.7% (2000); College graduation rate: 8.2% (2000).

School District(s)

Barry Community Unit School District 1 (PK-12)
2000 Enrollment: 407 217-335-2323
Housing: Homeownership rate: 77.0% (2000); Median home value: $48,600 (2000); Median rent: $216 per month (2000); Median age of housing: 60+ years (2000).
Newspapers: The Paper (1 x week); Pike County Express (1 x week)
Transportation: Commute to work: 93.0% car, 0.0% public transportation, 3.9% walk, 2.2% work from home (2000); Travel time to work: 47.6% less than 15 minutes, 14.5% 15 to 30 minutes, 21.9% 30 to 45 minutes, 11.6% 45 to 60 minutes, 4.4% 60 minutes or more (2000)

BAYLIS (village). Covers a land area of 0.479 square miles and a water area of 0 square miles. Located at 39.72° N. Lat.; 90.90° W. Long. Elevation is 865 feet.
Population: 265 (2000); Race: 99.0% White, 0.0% Black, 0.0% Asian, 1.0% American Indian and Alaska Native, 0.0% Hispanic of any race, 0.0% two or more races (2000); Density: 552.8 persons per square mile (2000); Age: 40.5% under 18, 8.4% over 64 (2000); Marriage status: 20.2% never married, 63.1% now married, 5.9% widowed, 10.8% divorced (2000); Foreign born: 0.0% (2000); Ancestry (includes multiple ancestries): 10.0% United States or American, 8.0% English, 5.5% Irish, 5.1% German, 5.1% Other groups (2000).
Economy: Grain; livestock. Employment by occupation: 7.0% management, 11.4% professional, 8.8% services, 12.3% sales, 0.0% farming, 7.9% construction, 52.6% production (2000).
Income: Per capita income: $11,251 (2000); Median household income: $32,344 (2000); Poverty rate: 15.8% (2000).
Taxes: Total city taxes per capita: $4 (1997); City property taxes per capita: $4 (1997).
Education: High school graduation rate: 74.1% (2000); College graduation rate: 3.5% (2000).
Housing: Homeownership rate: 77.2% (2000); Median home value: $23,800 (2000); Median rent: $258 per month (2000); Median age of housing: 60+ years (2000).
Transportation: Commute to work: 100.0% car, 0.0% public transportation, 0.0% walk, 0.0% work from home (2000); Travel time to work: 1.9% less than 15 minutes, 39.8% 15 to 30 minutes, 4.9% 30 to 45 minutes, 37.9% 45 to 60 minutes, 15.5% 60 minutes or more (2000)

CHAMBERSBURG (unincorporated postal area, zip code 62323). Covers a land area of 42.802 square miles and a water area of 0.058 square miles. Located at 39.81° N. Lat.; 90.66° W. Long. Elevation is 460 feet.
Population: 294 (2000); Race: 99.1% White, 0.0% Black, 0.0% Asian, 0.0% American Indian and Alaska Native, 0.0% Hispanic of any race, 0.9% two or more races (2000); Density: 6.9 persons per square mile (2000); Age: 23.5% under 18, 17.4% over 64 (2000); Marriage status: 18.0% never married, 73.9% now married, 3.2% widowed, 4.9% divorced (2000); Foreign born: 0.0% (2000); Ancestry (includes multiple ancestries): 47.7% German, 16.9% English, 14.0% Irish, 12.8% Other groups, 7.8% United States or American (2000).
Economy: Employment by occupation: 19.2% management, 16.8% professional, 11.4% services, 13.8% sales, 1.8% farming, 9.6% construction, 27.5% production (2000).
Income: Per capita income: $18,810 (2000); Median household income: $31,875 (2000); Poverty rate: 3.8% (2000).
Education: High school graduation rate: 91.1% (2000); College graduation rate: 12.2% (2000).
Housing: Homeownership rate: 75.2% (2000); Median home value: $57,500 (2000); Median rent: $265 per month (2000); Median age of housing: 49 years (2000).
Transportation: Commute to work: 96.2% car, 0.0% public transportation, 1.3% walk, 2.5% work from home (2000); Travel time to work: 43.2% less than 15 minutes, 20.0% 15 to 30 minutes, 17.4% 30 to 45 minutes, 10.3% 45 to 60 minutes, 9.0% 60 minutes or more (2000)

DETROIT (village). Covers a land area of 0.239 square miles and a water area of 0 square miles. Located at 39.62° N. Lat.; 90.67° W. Long. Elevation is 639 feet.
Population: 93 (2000); Race: 98.2% White, 0.0% Black, 0.0% Asian, 0.0% American Indian and Alaska Native, 0.0% Hispanic of any race, 1.8% two or more races (2000); Density: 388.7 persons per square mile (2000); Age: 36.3% under 18, 9.7% over 64 (2000); Marriage status: 15.0% never married, 62.5% now married, 10.0% widowed, 12.5% divorced (2000); Foreign born: 0.0% (2000); Ancestry (includes multiple ancestries): 8.8% Irish, 7.1% Other groups, 6.2% United States or American, 5.3% English, 4.4% Dutch (2000).
Economy: In agricultural area: corn, wheat, soybeans, sorghum, cattle, hogs. Employment by occupation: 5.4% management, 8.1% professional, 35.1% services, 10.8% sales, 8.1% farming, 5.4% construction, 27.0% production (2000).
Income: Per capita income: $11,127 (2000); Median household income: $21,875 (2000); Poverty rate: 13.1% (2000).
Education: High school graduation rate: 84.4% (2000); College graduation rate: 4.7% (2000).
Housing: Homeownership rate: 79.1% (2000); Median home value: $32,500 (2000); Median rent: $185 per month (2000); Median age of housing: 43 years (2000).
Transportation: Commute to work: 91.4% car, 0.0% public transportation, 0.0% walk, 2.9% work from home (2000); Travel time to work: 41.2% less than 15 minutes, 35.3% 15 to 30 minutes, 8.8% 30 to 45 minutes, 0.0% 45 to 60 minutes, 14.7% 60 minutes or more (2000)

EL DARA (village). Covers a land area of 0.967 square miles and a water area of 0 square miles. Located at 39.62° N. Lat.; 90.99° W. Long. Elevation is 741 feet.
Population: 89 (2000); Race: 100.0% White, 0.0% Black, 0.0% Asian, 0.0% American Indian and Alaska Native, 0.0% Hispanic of any race, 0.0% two or more races (2000); Density: 92.0 persons per square mile (2000); Age: 43.0% under 18, 10.5% over 64 (2000); Marriage status: 18.7% never married, 66.7% now married, 10.7% widowed, 4.0% divorced (2000); Foreign born: 1.8% (2000); Ancestry (includes multiple ancestries): 21.1% United States or American, 15.8% German, 2.6% Irish, 1.8% French (except Basque), 1.8% Welsh (2000).
Economy: In agricultural area. Employment by occupation: 11.4% management, 20.5% professional, 25.0% services, 15.9% sales, 4.5% farming, 0.0% construction, 22.7% production (2000).
Income: Per capita income: $11,422 (2000); Median household income: $36,250 (2000); Poverty rate: 9.6% (2000).
Taxes: Total city taxes per capita: $11 (1997); City property taxes per capita: $11 (1997).
Education: High school graduation rate: 85.2% (2000); College graduation rate: 3.3% (2000).
Housing: Homeownership rate: 100.0% (2000); Median home value: $37,500 (2000); Median age of housing: 60+ years (2000).
Transportation: Commute to work: 100.0% car, 0.0% public transportation, 0.0% walk, 0.0% work from home (2000); Travel time to work: 22.7% less than 15 minutes, 34.1% 15 to 30 minutes, 22.7% 30 to 45 minutes, 4.5% 45 to 60 minutes, 15.9% 60 minutes or more (2000)

FLORENCE (village). Covers a land area of 0.203 square miles and a water area of 0 square miles. Located at 39.62° N. Lat.; 90.61° W. Long. Elevation is 450 feet.
Population: 71 (2000); Race: 100.0% White, 0.0% Black, 0.0% Asian, 0.0% American Indian and Alaska Native, 0.0% Hispanic of any race, 0.0% two or more races (2000); Density: 350.4 persons per square mile (2000); Age: 15.3% under 18, 33.9% over 64 (2000); Marriage status: 18.0% never married, 56.0% now married, 16.0% widowed, 10.0% divorced (2000); Foreign born: 0.0% (2000); Ancestry (includes multiple ancestries): 30.5% English, 8.5% German, 3.4% Dutch, 3.4% Irish, 3.4% Other groups (2000).
Economy: In agricultural area: corn, wheat, soybeans; cattle, hogs. Employment by occupation: 0.0% management, 0.0% professional, 77.8% services, 11.1% sales, 0.0% farming, 11.1% construction, 0.0% production (2000).
Income: Per capita income: $9,878 (2000); Median household income: $20,000 (2000); Poverty rate: 15.1% (2000).
Taxes: Total city taxes per capita: $87 (1997); City property taxes per capita: $43 (1997).
Education: High school graduation rate: 43.5% (2000); College graduation rate: 0.0% (2000).
Housing: Homeownership rate: 65.4% (2000); Median home value: $19,600 (2000); Median rent: $225 per month (2000); Median age of housing: 45 years (2000).
Transportation: Commute to work: 77.8% car, 0.0% public transportation, 11.1% walk, 0.0% work from home (2000); Travel time to work: 33.3% less than 15 minutes, 22.2% 15 to 30 minutes, 22.2% 30 to 45 minutes, 0.0% 45 to 60 minutes, 22.2% 60 minutes or more (2000)

GRIGGSVILLE (city). Covers a land area of 1.035 square miles and a water area of 0 square miles. Located at 39.70° N. Lat.; 90.72° W. Long. Elevation is 715 feet.
History: Incorporated 1878.
Population: 1,258 (2000); Race: 99.4% White, 0.0% Black, 0.6% Asian, 0.0% American Indian and Alaska Native, 0.0% Hispanic of any race, 0.0% two or more races (2000); Density: 1,215.0 persons per square mile (2000); Age: 29.1% under 18, 16.2% over 64 (2000); Marriage status: 17.6% never married, 63.3% now married, 8.7% widowed, 10.4% divorced (2000); Foreign born: 0.3% (2000); Ancestry (includes multiple ancestries): 21.7% German, 14.9% United States or American, 14.5% English, 10.2% Irish, 3.3% Other groups (2000).
Economy: In agricultural area: corn, wheat, cattle, hogs, poultry; dairy products; light manufacturing. Single-family building permits issued: 1 (2001) / 2 (2000); Multi-family building permits issued: 0 (2001) / 0 (2000); Employment by occupation: 12.9% management, 11.5% professional, 19.1% services, 18.4% sales, 2.7% farming, 11.2% construction, 24.1% production (2000).
Income: Per capita income: $14,578 (2000); Median household income: $31,875 (2000); Poverty rate: 12.3% (2000).
Taxes: Total city taxes per capita: $64 (1997); City property taxes per capita: $46 (1997).
Education: High school graduation rate: 82.3% (2000); College graduation rate: 9.4% (2000).

School District(s)

Griggsville-Perry C U School District 4 (PK-12)
2000 Enrollment: 512 217-833-2352
Housing: Homeownership rate: 76.3% (2000); Median home value: $50,900 (2000); Median rent: $258 per month (2000); Median age of housing: 45 years (2000).
Transportation: Commute to work: 91.5% car, 0.4% public transportation, 3.1% walk, 3.1% work from home (2000); Travel time to work: 41.0% less than 15 minutes, 26.7% 15 to 30 minutes, 17.7% 30 to 45 minutes, 11.9% 45 to 60 minutes, 2.6% 60 minutes or more (2000)

HULL (village). Aka Hulls. Covers a land area of 1.836 square miles and a water area of 0.010 square miles. Located at 39.70° N. Lat.; 91.20° W. Long. Elevation is 468 feet.
Population: 474 (2000); Race: 99.0% White, 0.0% Black, 0.0% Asian, 0.0% American Indian and Alaska Native, 0.0% Hispanic of any race, 1.0% two or more races (2000); Density: 258.2 persons per square mile (2000); Age: 26.5% under 18, 14.9% over 64 (2000); Marriage status: 21.1% never married, 58.0% now married, 7.8% widowed, 13.1% divorced (2000); Foreign born: 0.0% (2000); Ancestry (includes multiple ancestries): 29.5% German, 18.5% United States or American, 15.5% Irish, 14.5% English, 6.4% Dutch (2000).
Economy: Single-family building permits issued: 0 (2001) / 0 (2000); Multi-family building permits issued: 0 (2001) / 0 (2000); Employment by occupation: 11.0% management, 9.0% professional, 14.5% services, 27.8% sales, 2.4% farming, 13.3% construction, 22.0% production (2000).
Income: Per capita income: $13,821 (2000); Median household income: $28,281 (2000); Poverty rate: 16.4% (2000).
Taxes: Total city taxes per capita: $16 (1997); City property taxes per capita: $16 (1997).
Education: High school graduation rate: 74.1% (2000); College graduation rate: 14.8% (2000).
Housing: Homeownership rate: 79.6% (2000); Median home value: $46,800 (2000); Median rent: $291 per month (2000); Median age of housing: 48 years (2000).
Transportation: Commute to work: 92.4% car, 0.8% public transportation, 4.0% walk, 1.2% work from home (2000); Travel time to work: 20.6% less than 15 minutes, 36.7% 15 to 30 minutes, 31.0% 30 to 45 minutes, 6.0% 45 to 60 minutes, 5.6% 60 minutes or more (2000)

KINDERHOOK (village). Covers a land area of 0.884 square miles and a water area of 0 square miles. Located at 39.70° N. Lat.; 91.15° W. Long. Elevation is 478 feet.
Population: 249 (2000); Race: 100.0% White, 0.0% Black, 0.0% Asian, 0.0% American Indian and Alaska Native, 0.0% Hispanic of any race, 0.0% two or more races (2000); Density: 281.7 persons per square mile (2000); Age: 27.5% under 18, 9.7% over 64 (2000); Marriage status: 19.5% never married, 65.4% now married, 4.9% widowed, 10.2% divorced (2000); Foreign born: 0.8% (2000); Ancestry (includes multiple ancestries): 29.5% United States or American, 16.7% German, 16.7% English, 7.4% Irish, 5.4% Other groups (2000).
Economy: In agricultural area. Employment by occupation: 5.4% management, 16.2% professional, 17.6% services, 20.9% sales, 0.0% farming, 9.5% construction, 30.4% production (2000).
Income: Per capita income: $16,328 (2000); Median household income: $38,438 (2000); Poverty rate: 6.3% (2000).
Taxes: Total city taxes per capita: $4 (1997); City property taxes per capita: $4 (1997).
Education: High school graduation rate: 86.3% (2000); College graduation rate: 6.0% (2000).

School District(s)

West Pike Community Unit School District 2 (PK-12)
2000 Enrollment: 330 217-432-8324
Housing: Homeownership rate: 82.2% (2000); Median home value: $37,000 (2000); Median rent: $254 per month (2000); Median age of housing: 46 years (2000).
Transportation: Commute to work: 95.9% car, 0.0% public transportation, 2.7% walk, 1.4% work from home (2000); Travel time to work: 15.1% less than 15 minutes, 19.9% 15 to 30 minutes, 50.7% 30 to 45 minutes, 5.5% 45 to 60 minutes, 8.9% 60 minutes or more (2000)

MILTON (village). Covers a land area of 0.375 square miles and a water area of 0 square miles. Located at 39.56° N. Lat.; 90.64° W. Long. Elevation is 660 feet.

Population: 274 (2000); Race: 100.0% White, 0.0% Black, 0.0% Asian, 0.0% American Indian and Alaska Native, 0.7% Hispanic of any race, 0.0% two or more races (2000); Density: 731.0 persons per square mile (2000); Age: 29.2% under 18, 23.2% over 64 (2000); Marriage status: 17.9% never married, 57.2% now married, 19.4% widowed, 5.5% divorced (2000); Foreign born: 0.0% (2000); Ancestry (includes multiple ancestries): 16.2% United States or American, 15.5% English, 10.0% French (except Basque), 9.2% Irish, 6.6% German (2000).

Economy: In agricultural area. Employment by occupation: 2.9% management, 11.8% professional, 17.6% services, 19.6% sales, 2.9% farming, 17.6% construction, 27.5% production (2000).

Income: Per capita income: $11,847 (2000); Median household income: $26,591 (2000); Poverty rate: 10.0% (2000).

Taxes: Total city taxes per capita: $7 (1997); City property taxes per capita: $7 (1997).

Education: High school graduation rate: 72.2% (2000); College graduation rate: 4.0% (2000).

Housing: Homeownership rate: 86.1% (2000); Median home value: $37,500 (2000); Median rent: $142 per month (2000); Median age of housing: 45 years (2000).

Transportation: Commute to work: 86.7% car, 0.0% public transportation, 3.1% walk, 7.1% work from home (2000); Travel time to work: 20.9% less than 15 minutes, 36.3% 15 to 30 minutes, 7.7% 30 to 45 minutes, 15.4% 45 to 60 minutes, 19.8% 60 minutes or more (2000)

NEBO (village). Covers a land area of 0.423 square miles and a water area of 0.006 square miles. Located at 39.44° N. Lat.; 90.78° W. Long. Elevation is 483 feet.

Population: 408 (2000); Race: 95.9% White, 0.0% Black, 0.0% Asian, 1.8% American Indian and Alaska Native, 2.3% Hispanic of any race, 2.3% two or more races (2000); Density: 964.9 persons per square mile (2000); Age: 30.8% under 18, 10.4% over 64 (2000); Marriage status: 23.4% never married, 50.5% now married, 10.0% widowed, 16.1% divorced (2000); Foreign born: 1.3% (2000); Ancestry (includes multiple ancestries): 18.8% United States or American, 18.3% German, 12.2% Other groups, 9.7% Irish, 6.1% Dutch (2000).

Economy: Grain, fruit; livestock. Employment by occupation: 1.9% management, 8.1% professional, 18.1% services, 12.5% sales, 3.8% farming, 22.5% construction, 33.1% production (2000).

Income: Per capita income: $12,468 (2000); Median household income: $29,000 (2000); Poverty rate: 20.1% (2000).

Taxes: Total city taxes per capita: $33 (1997); City property taxes per capita: $30 (1997).

Education: High school graduation rate: 71.1% (2000); College graduation rate: 5.4% (2000).

Housing: Homeownership rate: 87.0% (2000); Median home value: $30,500 (2000); Median rent: $144 per month (2000); Median age of housing: 49 years (2000).

Transportation: Commute to work: 93.1% car, 1.3% public transportation, 1.9% walk, 1.9% work from home (2000); Travel time to work: 10.2% less than 15 minutes, 35.7% 15 to 30 minutes, 20.4% 30 to 45 minutes, 10.2% 45 to 60 minutes, 23.6% 60 minutes or more (2000)

NEW CANTON (town). Covers a land area of 0.778 square miles and a water area of 0 square miles. Located at 39.63° N. Lat.; 91.09° W. Long. Elevation is 477 feet.

Population: 417 (2000); Race: 100.0% White, 0.0% Black, 0.0% Asian, 0.0% American Indian and Alaska Native, 0.0% Hispanic of any race, 0.0% two or more races (2000); Density: 535.8 persons per square mile (2000); Age: 29.1% under 18, 17.2% over 64 (2000); Marriage status: 16.2% never married, 58.6% now married, 11.4% widowed, 13.8% divorced (2000); Foreign born: 0.7% (2000); Ancestry (includes multiple ancestries): 22.4% German, 14.3% United States or American, 12.3% Irish, 10.7% English, 8.5% Other groups (2000).

Economy: In agricultural area. Employment by occupation: 5.9% management, 10.7% professional, 17.2% services, 18.3% sales, 3.6% farming, 16.6% construction, 27.8% production (2000).

Income: Per capita income: $11,571 (2000); Median household income: $24,583 (2000); Poverty rate: 19.9% (2000).

Taxes: Total city taxes per capita: $15 (1997); City property taxes per capita: $13 (1997).

Education: High school graduation rate: 79.0% (2000); College graduation rate: 5.9% (2000).

Housing: Homeownership rate: 78.1% (2000); Median home value: $34,700 (2000); Median rent: $218 per month (2000); Median age of housing: 56 years (2000).

Transportation: Commute to work: 97.0% car, 0.0% public transportation, 0.6% walk, 2.4% work from home (2000); Travel time to work: 23.9% less than 15 minutes, 21.5% 15 to 30 minutes, 34.4% 30 to 45 minutes, 15.3% 45 to 60 minutes, 4.9% 60 minutes or more (2000)

NEW SALEM (village). Covers a land area of 1.043 square miles and a water area of 0 square miles. Located at 39.70° N. Lat.; 90.84° W. Long. Elevation is 800 feet.

Population: 136 (2000); Race: 98.7% White, 0.0% Black, 0.0% Asian, 0.0% American Indian and Alaska Native, 2.0% Hispanic of any race, 0.0% two or more races (2000); Density: 130.4 persons per square mile (2000); Age: 34.0% under 18, 16.0% over 64 (2000); Marriage status: 18.0% never married, 70.0% now married, 9.0% widowed, 3.0% divorced (2000); Foreign born: 0.0% (2000); Ancestry (includes multiple ancestries): 24.0% United States or American, 23.3% German, 18.7% Irish, 11.3% English, 6.0% British (2000).

Economy: In agricultural area: corn, wheat, soybeans; cattle, hogs. Employment by occupation: 22.7% management, 15.9% professional, 31.8% services, 9.1% sales, 0.0% farming, 6.8% construction, 13.6% production (2000).

Income: Per capita income: $19,351 (2000); Median household income: $27,917 (2000); Poverty rate: 24.7% (2000).

Taxes: Total city taxes per capita: $7 (1997); City property taxes per capita: $7 (1997).

Education: High school graduation rate: 74.0% (2000); College graduation rate: 14.3% (2000).

Housing: Homeownership rate: 64.4% (2000); Median home value: $32,500 (2000); Median rent: $288 per month (2000); Median age of housing: 60+ years (2000).

Transportation: Commute to work: 81.8% car, 0.0% public transportation, 4.5% walk, 13.6% work from home (2000); Travel time to work: 26.3% less than 15 minutes, 34.2% 15 to 30 minutes, 5.3% 30 to 45 minutes, 23.7% 45 to 60 minutes, 10.5% 60 minutes or more (2000)

PEARL (village). Covers a land area of 1.507 square miles and a water area of 0.087 square miles. Located at 39.45° N. Lat.; 90.62° W. Long. Elevation is 446 feet.

Population: 187 (2000); Race: 100.0% White, 0.0% Black, 0.0% Asian, 0.0% American Indian and Alaska Native, 0.0% Hispanic of any race, 0.0% two or more races (2000); Density: 124.1 persons per square mile (2000); Age: 34.0% under 18, 16.5% over 64 (2000); Marriage status: 20.0% never married, 49.2% now married, 15.4% widowed, 15.4% divorced (2000); Foreign born: 0.0% (2000); Ancestry (includes multiple ancestries): 26.1% Irish, 21.8% German, 17.0% United States or American, 11.7% English, 3.7% Italian (2000).

Economy: In agricultural area. Employment by occupation: 5.4% management, 7.1% professional, 25.0% services, 28.6% sales, 0.0% farming, 19.6% construction, 14.3% production (2000).

Income: Per capita income: $9,524 (2000); Median household income: $15,500 (2000); Poverty rate: 29.8% (2000).

Taxes: Total city taxes per capita: $34 (1997); City property taxes per capita: $29 (1997).

Education: High school graduation rate: 65.5% (2000); College graduation rate: 0.0% (2000).

Housing: Homeownership rate: 88.0% (2000); Median home value: $15,900 (2000); Median rent: $133 per month (2000); Median age of housing: 60+ years (2000).

Transportation: Commute to work: 80.4% car, 0.0% public transportation, 7.1% walk, 12.5% work from home (2000); Travel time to work: 22.4% less than 15 minutes, 16.3% 15 to 30 minutes, 28.6% 30 to 45 minutes, 14.3% 45 to 60 minutes, 18.4% 60 minutes or more (2000)

PERRY (village). Covers a land area of 0.382 square miles and a water area of 0 square miles. Located at 39.78° N. Lat.; 90.74° W. Long. Elevation is 590 feet.

Population: 437 (2000); Race: 99.2% White, 0.0% Black, 0.0% Asian, 0.0% American Indian and Alaska Native, 0.0% Hispanic of any race, 0.8% two or more races (2000); Density: 1,143.5 persons per square mile (2000); Age: 23.1% under 18, 24.6% over 64 (2000); Marriage status: 14.7% never married, 59.1% now married, 16.9% widowed, 9.3% divorced (2000); Foreign born: 0.0% (2000); Ancestry (includes multiple ancestries): 23.3%

German, 19.2% English, 11.7% United States or American, 6.0% Irish, 5.7% Other groups (2000).
Economy: In agricultural area. Single-family building permits issued: 0 (2001) / 0 (2000); Multi-family building permits issued: 0 (2001) / 0 (2000); Employment by occupation: 13.1% management, 11.0% professional, 25.5% services, 19.3% sales, 4.8% farming, 10.3% construction, 15.9% production (2000).
Income: Per capita income: $20,383 (2000); Median household income: $26,458 (2000); Poverty rate: 24.4% (2000).
Taxes: Total city taxes per capita: $34 (1997); City property taxes per capita: $17 (1997).
Education: High school graduation rate: 81.1% (2000); College graduation rate: 7.5% (2000).
Housing: Homeownership rate: 76.3% (2000); Median home value: $41,200 (2000); Median rent: $137 per month (2000); Median age of housing: 37 years (2000).
Transportation: Commute to work: 84.1% car, 0.0% public transportation, 6.2% walk, 6.9% work from home (2000); Travel time to work: 35.6% less than 15 minutes, 33.3% 15 to 30 minutes, 20.0% 30 to 45 minutes, 7.4% 45 to 60 minutes, 3.7% 60 minutes or more (2000)

PITTSFIELD (city). Covers a land area of 3.574 square miles and a water area of 0.045 square miles. Located at 39.61° N. Lat.; 90.80° W. Long. Elevation is 740 feet.
History: Pittsfield was founded in 1833 by settlers from Pittsfield, Massachusetts. The town developed as the seat of Pike County, and as a pork-packing center, using barrels made of white oak that grew around the town. John Hay (1838-1905), Secretary of State under Presidents McKinley and Theodore Roosevelt, was a resident of Pittsfield for several years.
Population: 4,211 (2000); Race: 99.3% White, 0.3% Black, 0.4% Asian, 0.0% American Indian and Alaska Native, 0.8% Hispanic of any race, 0.0% two or more races (2000); Density: 1,178.2 persons per square mile (2000); Age: 21.7% under 18, 26.0% over 64 (2000); Marriage status: 19.2% never married, 56.1% now married, 13.5% widowed, 11.2% divorced (2000); Foreign born: 2.0% (2000); Ancestry (includes multiple ancestries): 20.1% German, 16.3% United States or American, 15.8% English, 10.6% Irish, 9.2% Other groups (2000).
Economy: Single-family building permits issued: 13 (2001) / 13 (2000); Multi-family building permits issued: 0 (2001) / 0 (2000); Employment by occupation: 6.8% management, 19.2% professional, 20.5% services, 26.2% sales, 2.3% farming, 8.0% construction, 17.0% production (2000).
Income: Per capita income: $16,628 (2000); Median household income: $29,129 (2000); Poverty rate: 12.3% (2000).
Taxes: Total city taxes per capita: $197 (1997); City property taxes per capita: $38 (1997).
Education: High school graduation rate: 82.3% (2000); College graduation rate: 13.7% (2000).

School District(s)

Pikeland C U School District 10 (PK-12)
2000 Enrollment: 1,496 217-285-2147
Housing: Homeownership rate: 72.1% (2000); Median home value: $66,500 (2000); Median rent: $280 per month (2000); Median age of housing: 44 years (2000).
Hospitals: Illinois Community Hospital (37 beds)
Newspapers: Pike Press (1 x week)
Transportation: Commute to work: 92.2% car, 0.2% public transportation, 4.6% walk, 2.9% work from home (2000); Travel time to work: 68.4% less than 15 minutes, 9.5% 15 to 30 minutes, 7.4% 30 to 45 minutes, 9.8% 45 to 60 minutes, 4.9% 60 minutes or more (2000)
Airports: Pittsfield Penstone Municipal

PLEASANT HILL (village). Covers a land area of 0.763 square miles and a water area of 0.023 square miles. Located at 39.44° N. Lat.; 90.87° W. Long. Elevation is 495 feet.
Population: 1,047 (2000); Race: 99.3% White, 0.0% Black, 0.5% Asian, 0.0% American Indian and Alaska Native, 0.1% Hispanic of any race, 0.1% two or more races (2000); Density: 1,372.8 persons per square mile (2000); Age: 25.1% under 18, 23.9% over 64 (2000); Marriage status: 16.6% never married, 61.4% now married, 14.1% widowed, 7.9% divorced (2000); Foreign born: 1.3% (2000); Ancestry (includes multiple ancestries): 18.0% United States or American, 15.2% German, 10.0% English, 9.6% Irish, 5.4% Other groups (2000).
Economy: In agricultural area. Employment by occupation: 9.8% management, 13.8% professional, 17.6% services, 26.9% sales, 5.2% farming, 8.6% construction, 18.1% production (2000).
Income: Per capita income: $12,682 (2000); Median household income: $25,156 (2000); Poverty rate: 17.0% (2000).
Taxes: Total city taxes per capita: $26 (1997); City property taxes per capita: $26 (1997).
Education: High school graduation rate: 72.1% (2000); College graduation rate: 9.6% (2000).

School District(s)

Pleasant Hill C U School District 3 (PK-12)
2000 Enrollment: 403 217-734-2311
Housing: Homeownership rate: 77.7% (2000); Median home value: $46,300 (2000); Median rent: $207 per month (2000); Median age of housing: 45 years (2000).
Newspapers: The Weekly Messenger (1 x week)
Transportation: Commute to work: 93.9% car, 0.0% public transportation, 1.7% walk, 3.6% work from home (2000); Travel time to work: 38.1% less than 15 minutes, 37.9% 15 to 30 minutes, 15.7% 30 to 45 minutes, 2.0% 45 to 60 minutes, 6.3% 60 minutes or more (2000)

ROCKPORT (unincorporated postal area, zip code 62370). Covers a land area of 55.630 square miles and a water area of 0.377 square miles. Located at 39.51° N. Lat.; 90.99° W. Long. Elevation is 480 feet.
Population: 641 (2000); Race: 100.0% White, 0.0% Black, 0.0% Asian, 0.0% American Indian and Alaska Native, 0.0% Hispanic of any race, 0.0% two or more races (2000); Density: 11.5 persons per square mile (2000); Age: 29.7% under 18, 8.3% over 64 (2000); Marriage status: 25.4% never married, 60.1% now married, 5.4% widowed, 9.1% divorced (2000); Foreign born: 0.9% (2000); Ancestry (includes multiple ancestries): 28.6% United States or American, 16.3% German, 7.1% English, 6.9% Other groups, 6.3% Irish (2000).
Economy: Employment by occupation: 13.7% management, 8.5% professional, 18.6% services, 22.9% sales, 7.3% farming, 7.6% construction, 21.3% production (2000).
Income: Per capita income: $14,348 (2000); Median household income: $33,036 (2000); Poverty rate: 10.4% (2000).
Education: High school graduation rate: 83.3% (2000); College graduation rate: 2.5% (2000).
Housing: Homeownership rate: 81.7% (2000); Median home value: $51,700 (2000); Median rent: $225 per month (2000); Median age of housing: 46 years (2000).
Transportation: Commute to work: 95.0% car, 0.0% public transportation, 0.0% walk, 4.3% work from home (2000); Travel time to work: 18.2% less than 15 minutes, 41.6% 15 to 30 minutes, 14.9% 30 to 45 minutes, 9.1% 45 to 60 minutes, 16.2% 60 minutes or more (2000)

TIME (village). Covers a land area of 0.436 square miles and a water area of 0 square miles. Located at 39.56° N. Lat.; 90.72° W. Long. Elevation is 692 feet.
Population: 29 (2000); Race: 100.0% White, 0.0% Black, 0.0% Asian, 0.0% American Indian and Alaska Native, 0.0% Hispanic of any race, 0.0% two or more races (2000); Density: 66.5 persons per square mile (2000); Age: 5.3% under 18, 36.8% over 64 (2000); Marriage status: 22.2% never married, 22.2% now married, 38.9% widowed, 16.7% divorced (2000); Foreign born: 0.0% (2000); Ancestry (includes multiple ancestries): 52.6% German, 21.1% Irish, 5.3% English (2000).
Economy: In agricultural area: corn, wheat, sorghum, soybeans; cattle, hogs. Employment by occupation: 0.0% management, 0.0% professional, 0.0% services, 0.0% sales, 0.0% farming, 100.0% construction, 0.0% production (2000).
Income: Per capita income: $12,253 (2000); Median household income: $14,375 (2000); Poverty rate: 5.3% (2000).
Taxes: Total city taxes per capita: $27 (1997); City property taxes per capita: $27 (1997).
Education: High school graduation rate: 20.0% (2000); College graduation rate: 0.0% (2000).
Housing: Homeownership rate: 50.0% (2000); Median home value: $22,500 (2000); Median rent: $225 per month (2000); Median age of housing: 55 years (2000).
Transportation: Commute to work: 100.0% car, 0.0% public transportation, 0.0% walk, 0.0% work from home (2000); Travel time to work: 0.0% less than 15 minutes, 0.0% 15 to 30 minutes, 0.0% 30 to 45 minutes, 100.0% 45 to 60 minutes, 0.0% 60 minutes or more (2000)

VALLEY CITY (village). Covers a land area of 0.196 square miles and a water area of 0.013 square miles. Located at 39.70° N. Lat.; 90.65° W. Long. Elevation is 450 feet.

Population: 14 (2000); Race: 100.0% White, 0.0% Black, 0.0% Asian, 0.0% American Indian and Alaska Native, 0.0% Hispanic of any race, 0.0% two or more races (2000); Density: 71.5 persons per square mile (2000); Age: 16.7% under 18, 0.0% over 64 (2000); Marriage status: 40.0% never married, 40.0% now married, 0.0% widowed, 20.0% divorced (2000); Foreign born: 0.0% (2000); Ancestry (includes multiple ancestries): 100.0% United States or American (2000).
Economy: Employment by occupation: 0.0% management, 0.0% professional, 0.0% services, 0.0% sales, 0.0% farming, 0.0% construction, 100.0% production (2000).
Income: Per capita income: $6,833 (2000); Median household income: $41,250 (2000); Poverty rate: 0.0% (2000).
Taxes: Total city taxes per capita: $136 (1997); City property taxes per capita: $45 (1997).
Education: High school graduation rate: 0.0% (2000); College graduation rate: 0.0% (2000).
Housing: Homeownership rate: 100.0% (2000); Median age of housing: 35 years (2000).
Transportation: Commute to work: 100.0% car, 0.0% public transportation, 0.0% walk, 0.0% work from home (2000); Travel time to work: 0.0% less than 15 minutes, 0.0% 15 to 30 minutes, 0.0% 30 to 45 minutes, 0.0% 45 to 60 minutes, 100.0% 60 minutes or more (2000)

Pope County

Located in southeastern Illinois, partly in the Ozarks; bounded on the east by the Ohio River and the Kentucky border; drained by tributaries of the Ohio River; includes part of Shawnee National Forest. Covers a land area of 370.90 square miles, a water area of 3.80 square miles, and is located in the Central Time Zone. The county government was organized in 1816. County seat is Golconda.

Weather Station: Dixon Springs Agr. Center — Elevation: 538 feet

	Jan	Feb	Mar	Apr	May	Jun	Jul	Aug	Sep	Oct	Nov	Dec
High	42	48	59	69	78	85	89	88	82	72	58	47
Low	24	28	38	47	55	63	67	65	58	47	39	30
Precip	3.2	3.3	4.7	4.9	5.2	4.1	3.7	3.6	3.2	3.3	4.6	4.3
Snow	3.8	3.3	1.5	0.1	0.0	0.0	0.0	0.0	0.0	0.2	tr	0.8

High and Low temperatures in degrees Fahrenheit; Precipitation and Snow in inches

Population: 4,413 (2000); Race: 93.2% White, 4.0% Black, 0.0% Asian, 0.7% American Indian and Alaska Native, 0.7% Hispanic of any race, 1.5% two or more races (2000); Density: 11.9 persons per square mile (2000); Age: 21.5% under 18, 17.7% over 64 (2000).
Religion: Five largest groups: 33.6% Southern Baptist Convention, 4.4% The United Methodist Church, 2.6% Lutheran Church—Missouri Synod, 2.6% Church of God (Cleveland, Tennessee), 0.8% Presbyterian Church (U.S.A.) (2000).
Economy: Unemployment rate: 8.2% (11/2002); Total civilian labor force: 1,680 (11/2002); Leading industries: Companies that employ more than 1,000 persons: 0 (2000); Companies that employ more than 100 persons: 1 (2000); Farms: 282 totaling 72,233 acres (1997); Minority business ownership rate: 0.0% (1997); Women business ownership rate: 0.0% (1997); Retail sales per capita: $1,585 (1997). Single-family building permits issued: 0 (2001) / 2 (2000); Multi-family building permits issued: 0 (2001) / 0 (2000).
Income: Per capita income: $16,440 (2000); Median household income: $30,048 (2000); Poverty rate: 18.2% (2000); Bankruptcy rate: 3.53% (2001).
Taxes: Total county taxes per capita: $108 (1997); County property taxes per capita: $90 (1997).
Education: High school graduation rate: 75.8% (2000); College graduation rate: 10.5% (2000).
Housing: Homeownership rate: 82.1% (2000); Median home value: $50,600 (2000); Median rent: $169 per month (2000); Median age of housing: 29 years (2000).
Health: Birth rate: 104.2 per 10,000 population (1998); Age adjusted death rate: 63.4 per 10,000 population (1999); Age adjusted cancer mortality rate: 216.3 (Unreliable figure as per CDC) deaths per 100,000 population (1999). Number of physicians: n/a (1999); Number of hospital beds: n/a (1999).
Elections: 2000 Presidential election results: 39.8% Gore, 57.8% Bush, 1.3% Nader, 0.9% Buchanan
National and State Parks: Dixon Springs State Park; Dog Island State Wetlands; Millstone Bluff National Register Site; Shawnee National Forest
Additional Information Contacts
Pope County Government Offices 618-683-4466
Golconda Pope County Chamber 618-683-9702

Pope County Communities

EDDYVILLE (village). Covers a land area of 0.287 square miles and a water area of 0 square miles. Located at 37.50° N. Lat.; 88.58° W. Long. Elevation is 662 feet.
Population: 153 (2000); Race: 100.0% White, 0.0% Black, 0.0% Asian, 0.0% American Indian and Alaska Native, 0.0% Hispanic of any race, 0.0% two or more races (2000); Density: 533.1 persons per square mile (2000); Age: 26.1% under 18, 28.6% over 64 (2000); Marriage status: 16.8% never married, 58.9% now married, 16.8% widowed, 7.4% divorced (2000); Foreign born: 0.0% (2000); Ancestry (includes multiple ancestries): 24.4% German, 20.2% Irish, 8.4% United States or American, 7.6% English, 5.0% Other groups (2000).
Economy: Agriculture: cattle; timber. In Shawnee National Forest. Employment by occupation: 4.9% management, 9.8% professional, 24.4% services, 22.0% sales, 0.0% farming, 14.6% construction, 24.4% production (2000).
Income: Per capita income: $13,084 (2000); Median household income: $22,083 (2000); Poverty rate: 16.8% (2000).
Taxes: Total city taxes per capita: $31 (1997); City property taxes per capita: $12 (1997).
Education: High school graduation rate: 66.7% (2000); College graduation rate: 1.2% (2000).
Housing: Homeownership rate: 77.6% (2000); Median home value: $42,900 (2000); Median rent: $142 per month (2000); Median age of housing: 34 years (2000).
Transportation: Commute to work: 97.4% car, 0.0% public transportation, 0.0% walk, 0.0% work from home (2000); Travel time to work: 0.0% less than 15 minutes, 48.7% 15 to 30 minutes, 33.3% 30 to 45 minutes, 5.1% 45 to 60 minutes, 12.8% 60 minutes or more (2000)

GOLCONDA (city). Covers a land area of 0.564 square miles and a water area of 0.026 square miles. Located at 37.36° N. Lat.; 88.48° W. Long. Elevation is 352 feet.
History: Incorporated 1845.
Population: 726 (2000); Race: 94.0% White, 2.1% Black, 0.3% Asian, 0.5% American Indian and Alaska Native, 0.0% Hispanic of any race, 2.9% two or more races (2000); Density: 1,287.0 persons per square mile (2000); Age: 16.8% under 18, 29.9% over 64 (2000); Marriage status: 21.9% never married, 43.2% now married, 21.2% widowed, 13.7% divorced (2000); Foreign born: 0.5% (2000); Ancestry (includes multiple ancestries): 25.6% German, 13.7% Irish, 13.3% English, 7.7% Other groups, 7.4% United States or American (2000).
Economy: In rich agricultural area: corn, wheat; livestock. Site of Ohio River lock and dam. Single-family building permits issued: 0 (2001) / 2 (2000); Multi-family building permits issued: 0 (2001) / 0 (2000); Employment by occupation: 6.3% management, 11.4% professional, 24.8% services, 29.5% sales, 0.0% farming, 8.3% construction, 19.7% production (2000).
Income: Per capita income: $14,698 (2000); Median household income: $19,000 (2000); Poverty rate: 25.0% (2000).
Taxes: Total city taxes per capita: $45 (1997); City property taxes per capita: $37 (1997).
Education: High school graduation rate: 65.5% (2000); College graduation rate: 9.2% (2000).

School District(s)
Pope Co Community Unit District 1 (PK-12)
2000 Enrollment: 641 618-683-2301
Housing: Homeownership rate: 53.9% (2000); Median home value: $45,500 (2000); Median rent: $153 per month (2000); Median age of housing: 40 years (2000).
Newspapers: Herald-Enterprise (1 x week)
Transportation: Commute to work: 78.9% car, 1.2% public transportation, 11.8% walk, 6.9% work from home (2000); Travel time to work: 48.9% less than 15 minutes, 9.2% 15 to 30 minutes, 15.3% 30 to 45 minutes, 16.6% 45 to 60 minutes, 10.0% 60 minutes or more (2000)
Additional Information Contacts
Golconda Pope County Chamber 618-683-9702

HEROD (unincorporated postal area, zip code 62947). Covers a land area of 68.806 square miles and a water area of 0.144 square miles. Located at 37.56° N. Lat.; 88.39° W. Long. Elevation is 430 feet.
Population: 597 (2000); Race: 98.8% White, 0.0% Black, 0.0% Asian, 0.0% American Indian and Alaska Native, 0.0% Hispanic of any race, 1.2% two or more races (2000); Density: 8.7 persons per square mile (2000); Age: 23.2% under 18, 6.6% over 64 (2000); Marriage status: 28.7% never married, 54.9%

now married, 2.8% widowed, 13.6% divorced (2000); Foreign born: 8.1% (2000); Ancestry (includes multiple ancestries): 14.0% United States or American, 10.7% German, 10.5% Irish, 8.1% Swiss, 7.6% Other groups (2000).
Economy: Employment by occupation: 13.1% management, 13.1% professional, 12.7% services, 15.0% sales, 0.0% farming, 28.1% construction, 18.0% production (2000).
Income: Per capita income: $18,727 (2000); Median household income: $35,769 (2000); Poverty rate: 7.4% (2000).
Education: High school graduation rate: 91.0% (2000); College graduation rate: 19.3% (2000).
Housing: Homeownership rate: 90.2% (2000); Median home value: $36,400 (2000); Median rent: $275 per month (2000); Median age of housing: 29 years (2000).
Transportation: Commute to work: 95.7% car, 0.0% public transportation, 0.0% walk, 2.3% work from home (2000); Travel time to work: 7.9% less than 15 minutes, 54.5% 15 to 30 minutes, 15.4% 30 to 45 minutes, 13.7% 45 to 60 minutes, 8.6% 60 minutes or more (2000)

Pulaski County

Located in southern Illinois; bounded on the south by the Ohio River and the Kentucky border; drained by the Cache River. Covers a land area of 200.80 square miles, a water area of 2.50 square miles, and is located in the Central Time Zone. The county government was organized in 1843. County seat is Mound City.
Population: 7,348 (2000); Race: 66.8% White, 30.4% Black, 1.1% Asian, 0.1% American Indian and Alaska Native, 1.5% Hispanic of any race, 1.3% two or more races (2000); Density: 36.6 persons per square mile (2000); Age: 27.4% under 18, 17.4% over 64 (2000).
Religion: Five largest groups: 30.4% Southern Baptist Convention, 8.4% Catholic Church, 6.8% The United Methodist Church, 3.0% Conservative Congregational Christian Conference, 2.8% Churches of Christ (2000).
Economy: Unemployment rate: 9.7% (11/2002); Total civilian labor force: 2,946 (11/2002); Leading industries: 21.2% health care and social assistance; 10.6% retail trade; 6.8% wholesale trade (2000); Companies that employ more than 1,000 persons: 0 (2000); Companies that employ more than 100 persons: 2 (2000); Farms: 239 totaling 83,127 acres (1997); Minority business ownership rate: 0.0% (1997); Women business ownership rate: 30.5% (1997); Retail sales per capita: $2,150 (1997). Single-family building permits issued: 3 (2001) / 3 (2000); Multi-family building permits issued: 0 (2001) / 0 (2000).
Income: Per capita income: $13,325 (2000); Median household income: $25,361 (2000); Poverty rate: 24.7% (2000); Bankruptcy rate: 5.31% (2001).
Taxes: Total county taxes per capita: $153 (1997); County property taxes per capita: $153 (1997).
Education: High school graduation rate: 70.7% (2000); College graduation rate: 7.1% (2000).
Housing: Homeownership rate: 75.7% (2000); Median home value: $33,300 (2000); Median rent: $201 per month (2000); Median age of housing: 36 years (2000).
Health: Birth rate: 115.7 per 10,000 population (1998); Age adjusted death rate: 110.6 per 10,000 population (1999); Age adjusted cancer mortality rate: 208.0 deaths per 100,000 population (1999). Number of physicians: n/a (1999); Number of hospital beds: n/a (1999).
Elections: 2000 Presidential election results: 50.3% Gore, 47.4% Bush, 1.0% Nader, 0.9% Buchanan
Additional Information Contacts
Pulaski County Government Offices 618-748-9360

Pulaski County Communities

GRAND CHAIN (unincorporated postal area, zip code 62941). Aka New Grand Chain. Covers a land area of 35.579 square miles and a water area of 0.817 square miles. Located at 37.24° N. Lat.; 88.99° W. Long. Elevation is 412 feet.
Population: 890 (2000); Race: 90.7% White, 6.0% Black, 0.0% Asian, 0.0% American Indian and Alaska Native, 0.0% Hispanic of any race, 3.3% two or more races (2000); Density: 25.0 persons per square mile (2000); Age: 24.1% under 18, 16.9% over 64 (2000); Marriage status: 13.9% never married, 66.7% now married, 8.7% widowed, 10.7% divorced (2000); Foreign born: 0.4% (2000); Ancestry (includes multiple ancestries): 27.6% German, 18.3% Other groups, 16.6% Irish, 14.6% English, 6.3% United States or American (2000).
Economy: Employment by occupation: 10.9% management, 15.6% professional, 20.3% services, 17.4% sales, 1.0% farming, 16.6% construction, 18.1% production (2000).
Income: Per capita income: $19,028 (2000); Median household income: $38,173 (2000); Poverty rate: 14.6% (2000).
Education: High school graduation rate: 82.8% (2000); College graduation rate: 8.1% (2000).
Housing: Homeownership rate: 84.7% (2000); Median home value: $51,500 (2000); Median rent: $244 per month (2000); Median age of housing: 32 years (2000).
Transportation: Commute to work: 91.6% car, 1.5% public transportation, 1.3% walk, 4.3% work from home (2000); Travel time to work: 23.8% less than 15 minutes, 29.1% 15 to 30 minutes, 24.1% 30 to 45 minutes, 13.1% 45 to 60 minutes, 9.9% 60 minutes or more (2000)

KARNAK (village). Covers a land area of 1.813 square miles and a water area of 0 square miles. Located at 37.29° N. Lat.; 88.97° W. Long. Elevation is 340 feet.
History: Karnak was established as a company town for a logging and milling industry.
Population: 619 (2000); Race: 92.8% White, 5.2% Black, 0.0% Asian, 0.0% American Indian and Alaska Native, 6.0% Hispanic of any race, 1.0% two or more races (2000); Density: 341.4 persons per square mile (2000); Age: 27.9% under 18, 20.7% over 64 (2000); Marriage status: 19.6% never married, 60.0% now married, 11.7% widowed, 8.7% divorced (2000); Foreign born: 2.4% (2000); Ancestry (includes multiple ancestries): 19.7% United States or American, 14.4% Other groups, 13.2% German, 6.2% English, 6.0% Irish (2000).
Economy: Employment by occupation: 6.7% management, 12.2% professional, 29.8% services, 13.0% sales, 0.0% farming, 14.7% construction, 23.5% production (2000).
Income: Per capita income: $13,346 (2000); Median household income: $28,125 (2000); Poverty rate: 20.0% (2000).
Taxes: Total city taxes per capita: $9 (1997); City property taxes per capita: $9 (1997).
Education: High school graduation rate: 74.2% (2000); College graduation rate: 7.1% (2000).
Housing: Homeownership rate: 77.2% (2000); Median home value: $33,300 (2000); Median rent: $248 per month (2000); Median age of housing: 37 years (2000).
Transportation: Commute to work: 91.5% car, 0.0% public transportation, 2.6% walk, 3.8% work from home (2000); Travel time to work: 34.7% less than 15 minutes, 27.6% 15 to 30 minutes, 23.1% 30 to 45 minutes, 8.0% 45 to 60 minutes, 6.7% 60 minutes or more (2000)

MOUND CITY (city). Covers a land area of 0.711 square miles and a water area of 0.050 square miles. Located at 37.08° N. Lat.; 89.16° W. Long. Elevation is 320 feet.
History: Important Union naval base in Civil War. National cemetery is nearby. City severely damaged in 1937 flood. Incorporated 1857.
Population: 692 (2000); Race: 52.1% White, 47.3% Black, 0.0% Asian, 0.0% American Indian and Alaska Native, 0.0% Hispanic of any race, 0.6% two or more races (2000); Density: 973.5 persons per square mile (2000); Age: 35.8% under 18, 11.3% over 64 (2000); Marriage status: 32.6% never married, 43.3% now married, 11.1% widowed, 13.0% divorced (2000); Foreign born: 0.3% (2000); Ancestry (includes multiple ancestries): 38.9% Other groups, 25.0% United States or American, 6.3% German, 2.1% Irish, 1.5% English (2000).
Economy: Manufacturing of mineral products. Agriculture: grains, vegetables; livestock. Single-family building permits issued: 3 (2001) / 3 (2000); Multi-family building permits issued: 0 (2001) / 0 (2000); Employment by occupation: 3.2% management, 9.9% professional, 30.2% services, 26.1% sales, 0.0% farming, 8.6% construction, 22.1% production (2000).
Income: Per capita income: $10,020 (2000); Median household income: $16,607 (2000); Poverty rate: 39.3% (2000).
Taxes: Total city taxes per capita: $134 (1997); City property taxes per capita: $36 (1997).
Education: High school graduation rate: 65.7% (2000); College graduation rate: 5.8% (2000).
Housing: Homeownership rate: 54.1% (2000); Median home value: $29,100 (2000); Median rent: $138 per month (2000); Median age of housing: 30 years (2000).
Transportation: Commute to work: 91.2% car, 0.9% public transportation, 3.2% walk, 2.3% work from home (2000); Travel time to work: 43.1% less

than 15 minutes, 40.3% 15 to 30 minutes, 1.4% 30 to 45 minutes, 7.6% 45 to 60 minutes, 7.6% 60 minutes or more (2000)

MOUNDS (city). Covers a land area of 1.216 square miles and a water area of 0 square miles. Located at 37.11° N. Lat.; 89.19° W. Long. Elevation is 325 feet.
History: Incorporated 1904.
Population: 1,117 (2000); Race: 33.7% White, 64.0% Black, 0.0% Asian, 0.0% American Indian and Alaska Native, 0.0% Hispanic of any race, 1.5% two or more races (2000); Density: 918.9 persons per square mile (2000); Age: 32.7% under 18, 19.1% over 64 (2000); Marriage status: 30.2% never married, 41.2% now married, 15.1% widowed, 13.5% divorced (2000); Foreign born: 0.0% (2000); Ancestry (includes multiple ancestries): 41.7% Other groups, 20.2% United States or American, 6.5% English, 5.5% German, 4.1% Irish (2000).
Economy: In agricultural area: corn. Single-family building permits issued: 0 (2001) / 0 (2000); Multi-family building permits issued: 0 (2001) / 0 (2000); Employment by occupation: 5.2% management, 11.3% professional, 32.6% services, 14.5% sales, 0.0% farming, 9.0% construction, 27.3% production (2000).
Income: Per capita income: $11,035 (2000); Median household income: $17,727 (2000); Poverty rate: 42.8% (2000).
Taxes: Total city taxes per capita: $58 (1997); City property taxes per capita: $6 (1997).
Education: High school graduation rate: 65.6% (2000); College graduation rate: 6.0% (2000).

School District(s)

Meridian C U School Districtrict 101 (PK-12)
2000 Enrollment: 852 618-342-6776
Housing: Homeownership rate: 67.1% (2000); Median home value: $20,800 (2000); Median rent: $188 per month (2000); Median age of housing: 53 years (2000).
Transportation: Commute to work: 81.2% car, 3.8% public transportation, 9.1% walk, 2.4% work from home (2000); Travel time to work: 39.5% less than 15 minutes, 36.7% 15 to 30 minutes, 4.2% 30 to 45 minutes, 11.1% 45 to 60 minutes, 8.4% 60 minutes or more (2000)

NEW GRAND CHAIN (village). Aka Grand Chain. Covers a land area of 1.058 square miles and a water area of 0 square miles. Located at 37.25° N. Lat.; 89.02° W. Long. Elevation is 404 feet.
History: New Grand Chain was named for a row of rocks in the Ohio River, where the town was first located. It was moved in 1872 to be on the new railroad line.
Population: 233 (2000); Race: 86.4% White, 12.7% Black, 0.0% Asian, 0.0% American Indian and Alaska Native, 0.0% Hispanic of any race, 0.9% two or more races (2000); Density: 220.2 persons per square mile (2000); Age: 31.1% under 18, 17.5% over 64 (2000); Marriage status: 19.0% never married, 57.7% now married, 7.1% widowed, 16.1% divorced (2000); Foreign born: 0.0% (2000); Ancestry (includes multiple ancestries): 16.2% German, 15.4% Other groups, 12.3% Irish, 7.9% English, 7.9% United States or American (2000).
Economy: Employment by occupation: 7.8% management, 16.7% professional, 22.5% services, 16.7% sales, 3.9% farming, 14.7% construction, 17.6% production (2000).
Income: Per capita income: $14,617 (2000); Median household income: $29,688 (2000); Poverty rate: 21.5% (2000).
Taxes: Total city taxes per capita: $7 (1997); City property taxes per capita: $7 (1997).
Education: High school graduation rate: 84.9% (2000); College graduation rate: 11.6% (2000).
Housing: Homeownership rate: 76.8% (2000); Median home value: $43,100 (2000); Median rent: $250 per month (2000); Median age of housing: 49 years (2000).
Transportation: Commute to work: 93.9% car, 2.0% public transportation, 3.1% walk, 1.0% work from home (2000); Travel time to work: 33.0% less than 15 minutes, 24.7% 15 to 30 minutes, 17.5% 30 to 45 minutes, 9.3% 45 to 60 minutes, 15.5% 60 minutes or more (2000)

OLMSTED (village). Covers a land area of 1.680 square miles and a water area of 0.045 square miles. Located at 37.18° N. Lat.; 89.08° W. Long. Elevation is 370 feet.
Population: 299 (2000); Race: 79.7% White, 18.0% Black, 0.0% Asian, 1.7% American Indian and Alaska Native, 0.7% Hispanic of any race, 0.0% two or more races (2000); Density: 178.0 persons per square mile (2000); Age: 21.3% under 18, 23.7% over 64 (2000); Marriage status: 18.3% never married, 54.8% now married, 19.4% widowed, 7.5% divorced (2000); Foreign born: 0.0% (2000); Ancestry (includes multiple ancestries): 33.3% Other groups, 20.3% United States or American, 17.3% German, 10.7% Irish, 6.3% Dutch (2000).
Economy: In agricultural area. Near Lock and Dam 53 on Ohio River. Single-family building permits issued: 0 (2001) / 0 (2000); Multi-family building permits issued: 0 (2001) / 0 (2000); Employment by occupation: 11.8% management, 11.8% professional, 22.7% services, 18.2% sales, 1.8% farming, 11.8% construction, 21.8% production (2000).
Income: Per capita income: $13,615 (2000); Median household income: $19,833 (2000); Poverty rate: 21.7% (2000).
Taxes: Total city taxes per capita: $163 (1997); City property taxes per capita: $12 (1997).
Education: High school graduation rate: 64.9% (2000); College graduation rate: 4.3% (2000).
Housing: Homeownership rate: 66.2% (2000); Median home value: $36,700 (2000); Median rent: $196 per month (2000); Median age of housing: 36 years (2000).
Transportation: Commute to work: 95.5% car, 0.0% public transportation, 0.0% walk, 4.5% work from home (2000); Travel time to work: 32.4% less than 15 minutes, 29.5% 15 to 30 minutes, 30.5% 30 to 45 minutes, 4.8% 45 to 60 minutes, 2.9% 60 minutes or more (2000)

PULASKI (village). Covers a land area of 1.275 square miles and a water area of 0 square miles. Located at 37.21° N. Lat.; 89.20° W. Long. Elevation is 343 feet.
Population: 274 (2000); Race: 18.8% White, 80.8% Black, 0.0% Asian, 0.3% American Indian and Alaska Native, 0.0% Hispanic of any race, 0.0% two or more races (2000); Density: 214.9 persons per square mile (2000); Age: 24.0% under 18, 19.5% over 64 (2000); Marriage status: 31.1% never married, 43.3% now married, 18.1% widowed, 7.6% divorced (2000); Foreign born: 0.0% (2000); Ancestry (includes multiple ancestries): 41.1% United States or American, 34.6% Other groups, 5.1% African, 2.1% Irish, 1.0% English (2000).
Economy: In agricultural area. Single-family building permits issued: 0 (2001) / 0 (2000); Multi-family building permits issued: 0 (2001) / 0 (2000); Employment by occupation: 6.0% management, 9.5% professional, 28.6% services, 17.9% sales, 0.0% farming, 7.1% construction, 31.0% production (2000).
Income: Per capita income: $12,946 (2000); Median household income: $16,786 (2000); Poverty rate: 32.9% (2000).
Taxes: Total city taxes per capita: $12 (1997); City property taxes per capita: $6 (1997).
Education: High school graduation rate: 61.5% (2000); College graduation rate: 5.9% (2000).
Housing: Homeownership rate: 79.0% (2000); Median home value: $24,100 (2000); Median rent: $190 per month (2000); Median age of housing: 28 years (2000).
Transportation: Commute to work: 92.9% car, 0.0% public transportation, 6.0% walk, 1.2% work from home (2000); Travel time to work: 36.1% less than 15 minutes, 27.7% 15 to 30 minutes, 8.4% 30 to 45 minutes, 18.1% 45 to 60 minutes, 9.6% 60 minutes or more (2000)

ULLIN (village). Covers a land area of 2.863 square miles and a water area of 0 square miles. Located at 37.27° N. Lat.; 89.18° W. Long. Elevation is 340 feet.
Population: 779 (2000); Race: 66.9% White, 23.9% Black, 8.4% Asian, 0.0% American Indian and Alaska Native, 7.0% Hispanic of any race, 0.8% two or more races (2000); Density: 272.1 persons per square mile (2000); Age: 23.1% under 18, 16.1% over 64 (2000); Marriage status: 21.8% never married, 56.0% now married, 11.9% widowed, 10.3% divorced (2000); Foreign born: 0.3% (2000); Ancestry (includes multiple ancestries): 24.9% Other groups, 13.9% United States or American, 8.7% German, 6.3% Irish, 2.9% English (2000).
Economy: In agricultural area. Single-family building permits issued: 0 (2001) / 0 (2000); Multi-family building permits issued: 0 (2001) / 0 (2000); Employment by occupation: 5.6% management, 20.6% professional, 34.6% services, 14.5% sales, 2.3% farming, 7.0% construction, 15.4% production (2000).
Income: Per capita income: $12,789 (2000); Median household income: $20,000 (2000); Poverty rate: 16.8% (2000).
Taxes: Total city taxes per capita: $20 (1997); City property taxes per capita: $13 (1997).
Education: High school graduation rate: 75.5% (2000); College graduation rate: 6.7% (2000).

School District(s)

Alxndr/John/Masc/Pulski/Union Roe (02-12)

2000 Enrollment: 107 618-634-2292

Century Community Unit School District 100 (PK-12)

2000 Enrollment: 551 618-845-3518

Two-year College(s)

Shawnee Community College (Public)

2001 Enrollment: 1,887 618-634-3200

2001 Tuition: In-state $4,408; Out-of-state $9,120

Housing: Homeownership rate: 64.9% (2000); Median home value: $35,300 (2000); Median rent: $292 per month (2000); Median age of housing: 26 years (2000).

Transportation: Commute to work: 88.6% car, 2.8% public transportation, 3.8% walk, 2.8% work from home (2000); Travel time to work: 27.3% less than 15 minutes, 30.2% 15 to 30 minutes, 19.5% 30 to 45 minutes, 7.8% 45 to 60 minutes, 15.1% 60 minutes or more (2000)

VILLA RIDGE (unincorporated postal area, zip code 62996). Covers a land area of 26.870 square miles and a water area of 0.031 square miles. Located at 37.15° N. Lat.; 89.16° W. Long. Elevation is 398 feet.

Population: 759 (2000); Race: 70.9% White, 25.7% Black, 1.1% Asian, 0.0% American Indian and Alaska Native, 0.9% Hispanic of any race, 2.3% two or more races (2000); Density: 28.2 persons per square mile (2000); Age: 26.0% under 18, 9.3% over 64 (2000); Marriage status: 17.3% never married, 71.5% now married, 3.9% widowed, 7.3% divorced (2000); Foreign born: 2.0% (2000); Ancestry (includes multiple ancestries): 26.7% Other groups, 24.5% United States or American, 12.8% Irish, 10.9% German, 8.6% English (2000).

Economy: Employment by occupation: 13.7% management, 8.1% professional, 16.3% services, 32.8% sales, 1.5% farming, 10.7% construction, 16.8% production (2000).

Income: Per capita income: $13,995 (2000); Median household income: $26,513 (2000); Poverty rate: 12.9% (2000).

Education: High school graduation rate: 70.3% (2000); College graduation rate: 3.7% (2000).

Housing: Homeownership rate: 89.1% (2000); Median home value: $48,000 (2000); Median rent: $232 per month (2000); Median age of housing: 30 years (2000).

Transportation: Commute to work: 93.5% car, 0.0% public transportation, 0.0% walk, 6.5% work from home (2000); Travel time to work: 31.5% less than 15 minutes, 41.6% 15 to 30 minutes, 18.2% 30 to 45 minutes, 6.4% 45 to 60 minutes, 2.3% 60 minutes or more (2000)

Putnam County

Located in north central Illinois; bounded on the north and west by the Illinois River. Covers a land area of 159.80 square miles, a water area of 12.40 square miles, and is located in the Central Time Zone. The county government was organized in 1825. County seat is Hennepin.

Weather Station: Hennepin Power Plant — Elevation: 459 feet

	Jan	Feb	Mar	Apr	May	Jun	Jul	Aug	Sep	Oct	Nov	Dec
High	30	36	48	62	74	83	86	84	78	65	49	36
Low	11	16	28	38	48	58	62	60	52	40	29	18
Precip	1.1	1.1	2.2	3.3	3.8	4.3	3.9	4.5	3.9	2.7	2.5	2.2
Snow	na	na	na	0.4	0.0	0.0	0.0	0.0	0.0	tr	0.8	na

High and Low temperatures in degrees Fahrenheit; Precipitation and Snow in inches

Population: 6,086 (2000); Race: 97.6% White, 0.6% Black, 0.1% Asian, 0.2% American Indian and Alaska Native, 3.3% Hispanic of any race, 0.7% two or more races (2000); Density: 38.1 persons per square mile (2000); Age: 25.1% under 18, 16.0% over 64 (2000).

Religion: Five largest groups: 27.1% Catholic Church, 6.7% United Church of Christ, 5.2% The United Methodist Church, 4.6% Evangelical Lutheran Church in America, 1.1% Friends (Quakers) (2000).

Economy: Unemployment rate: 7.4% (11/2002); Total civilian labor force: 3,183 (11/2002); Leading industries: 57.7% manufacturing; 8.6% retail trade; 7.9% construction (2000); Companies that employ more than 1,000 persons: 0 (2000); Companies that employ more than 100 persons: 3 (2000); Farms: 190 totaling 76,950 acres (1997); Minority business ownership rate: 0.0% (1997); Women business ownership rate: 0.0% (1997); Retail sales per capita: $4,032 (1997). Single-family building permits issued: 40 (2001) / 40 (2000); Multi-family building permits issued: 2 (2001) / 0 (2000).

Income: Per capita income: $19,792 (2000); Median household income: $45,492 (2000); Poverty rate: 5.5% (2000); Bankruptcy rate: 6.15% (2001).

Taxes: Total county taxes per capita: $82 (1997); County property taxes per capita: $82 (1997).

Education: High school graduation rate: 83.8% (2000); College graduation rate: 12.1% (2000).

Housing: Homeownership rate: 82.3% (2000); Median home value: $89,100 (2000); Median rent: $340 per month (2000); Median age of housing: 33 years (2000).

Health: Birth rate: 105.2 per 10,000 population (1998); Age adjusted death rate: 94.6 per 10,000 population (1999); Age adjusted cancer mortality rate: 199.6 (Unreliable figure as per CDC) deaths per 100,000 population (1999). Number of physicians: 1.6 per 10,000 population (1999); Number of hospital beds: n/a (1999).

Elections: 2000 Presidential election results: 52.1% Gore, 45.2% Bush, 1.8% Nader, 0.7% Buchanan

National and State Parks: Donnelley State Fish and Wildlife Area; Fox Run State Conservation Area

Additional Information Contacts

Putnam County Government Offices 815-925-7129

Putnam County Communities

GRANVILLE (village). Covers a land area of 0.957 square miles and a water area of 0 square miles. Located at 41.26° N. Lat.; 89.22° W. Long. Elevation is 690 feet.

History: Incorporated 1861.

Population: 1,414 (2000); Race: 97.3% White, 1.3% Black, 0.0% Asian, 0.0% American Indian and Alaska Native, 3.8% Hispanic of any race, 0.8% two or more races (2000); Density: 1,476.8 persons per square mile (2000); Age: 23.5% under 18, 18.0% over 64 (2000); Marriage status: 17.6% never married, 62.3% now married, 9.6% widowed, 10.5% divorced (2000); Foreign born: 3.5% (2000); Ancestry (includes multiple ancestries): 35.2% German, 19.3% Italian, 11.3% Irish, 11.0% English, 8.6% Polish (2000).

Economy: Corn, soybeans, wheat; poultry, livestock; dairy products. Single-family building permits issued: 5 (2001) / 7 (2000); Multi-family building permits issued: 2 (2001) / 0 (2000); Employment by occupation: 6.9% management, 13.2% professional, 12.5% services, 29.5% sales, 0.4% farming, 15.3% construction, 22.2% production (2000).

Income: Per capita income: $20,074 (2000); Median household income: $41,548 (2000); Poverty rate: 4.1% (2000).

Taxes: Total city taxes per capita: $62 (1997); City property taxes per capita: $48 (1997).

Education: High school graduation rate: 83.2% (2000); College graduation rate: 10.6% (2000).

School District(s)

Putnam Co C U School District 535 (PK-12)

2000 Enrollment: 1,016 815-339-2238

Housing: Homeownership rate: 77.7% (2000); Median home value: $84,700 (2000); Median rent: $330 per month (2000); Median age of housing: 39 years (2000).

Newspapers: Putnam County Record (1 x week)

Transportation: Commute to work: 94.9% car, 0.0% public transportation, 2.6% walk, 1.8% work from home (2000); Travel time to work: 45.0% less than 15 minutes, 36.2% 15 to 30 minutes, 9.5% 30 to 45 minutes, 1.9% 45 to 60 minutes, 7.3% 60 minutes or more (2000)

HENNEPIN (village). Covers a land area of 5.223 square miles and a water area of 0.360 square miles. Located at 41.25° N. Lat.; 89.33° W. Long. Elevation is 505 feet.

History: Hennepin was named for Father Louis Hennepin, an early missionary pilot who guided explorers on the waterways.

Population: 707 (2000); Race: 95.2% White, 0.6% Black, 0.4% Asian, 0.0% American Indian and Alaska Native, 5.8% Hispanic of any race, 0.6% two or more races (2000); Density: 135.4 persons per square mile (2000); Age: 23.5% under 18, 19.9% over 64 (2000); Marriage status: 18.0% never married, 59.4% now married, 10.0% widowed, 12.6% divorced (2000); Foreign born: 2.7% (2000); Ancestry (includes multiple ancestries): 34.7% German, 16.6% Irish, 13.8% Italian, 13.5% English, 8.8% Other groups (2000).

Economy: Single-family building permits issued: 5 (2001) / 5 (2000); Multi-family building permits issued: 0 (2001) / 0 (2000); Employment by occupation: 14.3% management, 12.8% professional, 16.2% services, 23.8% sales, 0.9% farming, 11.0% construction, 21.0% production (2000).

Income: Per capita income: $23,981 (2000); Median household income: $46,827 (2000); Poverty rate: 2.9% (2000).

Taxes: Total city taxes per capita: $45 (1997); City property taxes per capita: $43 (1997).
Education: High school graduation rate: 81.5% (2000); College graduation rate: 12.3% (2000).
Housing: Homeownership rate: 79.5% (2000); Median home value: $93,700 (2000); Median rent: $351 per month (2000); Median age of housing: 32 years (2000).
Transportation: Commute to work: 89.0% car, 0.6% public transportation, 5.0% walk, 4.7% work from home (2000); Travel time to work: 57.1% less than 15 minutes, 26.7% 15 to 30 minutes, 9.2% 30 to 45 minutes, 2.3% 45 to 60 minutes, 4.6% 60 minutes or more (2000)

MAGNOLIA (village). Covers a land area of 0.298 square miles and a water area of 0 square miles. Located at 41.11° N. Lat.; 89.19° W. Long. Elevation is 673 feet.
Population: 279 (2000); Race: 95.0% White, 0.0% Black, 1.6% Asian, 1.6% American Indian and Alaska Native, 5.3% Hispanic of any race, 1.9% two or more races (2000); Density: 936.9 persons per square mile (2000); Age: 35.1% under 18, 13.5% over 64 (2000); Marriage status: 23.3% never married, 54.7% now married, 9.4% widowed, 12.6% divorced (2000); Foreign born: 2.5% (2000); Ancestry (includes multiple ancestries): 33.9% German, 14.7% Other groups, 14.4% Swedish, 9.4% English, 8.8% French (except Basque) (2000).
Economy: In agricultural area. Single-family building permits issued: 1 (2001) / 1 (2000); Multi-family building permits issued: 0 (2001) / 0 (2000); Employment by occupation: 4.7% management, 6.1% professional, 20.3% services, 25.0% sales, 5.4% farming, 7.4% construction, 31.1% production (2000).
Income: Per capita income: $13,909 (2000); Median household income: $38,125 (2000); Poverty rate: 11.1% (2000).
Taxes: Total city taxes per capita: $39 (1997); City property taxes per capita: $16 (1997).
Education: High school graduation rate: 73.7% (2000); College graduation rate: 7.4% (2000).
Housing: Homeownership rate: 87.4% (2000); Median home value: $55,600 (2000); Median rent: $320 per month (2000); Median age of housing: 60+ years (2000).
Transportation: Commute to work: 97.9% car, 0.0% public transportation, 2.1% walk, 0.0% work from home (2000); Travel time to work: 15.8% less than 15 minutes, 46.6% 15 to 30 minutes, 24.0% 30 to 45 minutes, 8.9% 45 to 60 minutes, 4.8% 60 minutes or more (2000)

MARK (village). Covers a land area of 0.812 square miles and a water area of 0 square miles. Located at 41.26° N. Lat.; 89.24° W. Long. Elevation is 690 feet.
Population: 491 (2000); Race: 98.0% White, 0.0% Black, 0.0% Asian, 2.0% American Indian and Alaska Native, 4.9% Hispanic of any race, 0.0% two or more races (2000); Density: 604.9 persons per square mile (2000); Age: 25.2% under 18, 13.3% over 64 (2000); Marriage status: 24.6% never married, 59.1% now married, 7.7% widowed, 8.7% divorced (2000); Foreign born: 0.8% (2000); Ancestry (includes multiple ancestries): 27.6% Italian, 27.4% German, 13.9% Polish, 12.5% Irish, 10.6% Other groups (2000).
Economy: In agricultural area: corn, wheat, barley; cattle; mushroom processing. Single-family building permits issued: 1 (2001) / 1 (2000); Multi-family building permits issued: 0 (2001) / 0 (2000); Employment by occupation: 7.9% management, 16.5% professional, 14.3% services, 27.4% sales, 0.4% farming, 10.9% construction, 22.6% production (2000).
Income: Per capita income: $18,912 (2000); Median household income: $45,208 (2000); Poverty rate: 10.3% (2000).
Taxes: Total city taxes per capita: $83 (1997); City property taxes per capita: $29 (1997).
Education: High school graduation rate: 83.5% (2000); College graduation rate: 10.9% (2000).
Housing: Homeownership rate: 90.4% (2000); Median home value: $71,800 (2000); Median rent: $375 per month (2000); Median age of housing: 47 years (2000).
Transportation: Commute to work: 93.2% car, 0.0% public transportation, 2.6% walk, 4.1% work from home (2000); Travel time to work: 31.8% less than 15 minutes, 48.6% 15 to 30 minutes, 8.6% 30 to 45 minutes, 3.1% 45 to 60 minutes, 7.8% 60 minutes or more (2000)

MCNABB (village). Covers a land area of 0.199 square miles and a water area of 0 square miles. Located at 41.17° N. Lat.; 89.20° W. Long. Elevation is 686 feet.
Population: 310 (2000); Race: 100.0% White, 0.0% Black, 0.0% Asian, 0.0% American Indian and Alaska Native, 0.0% Hispanic of any race, 0.0% two or more races (2000); Density: 1,555.4 persons per square mile (2000); Age: 25.4% under 18, 11.8% over 64 (2000); Marriage status: 18.3% never married, 67.8% now married, 5.7% widowed, 8.3% divorced (2000); Foreign born: 0.0% (2000); Ancestry (includes multiple ancestries): 40.8% German, 17.8% English, 11.5% Irish, 10.1% Italian, 8.7% Swedish (2000).
Economy: Corn, soybeans. Single-family building permits issued: 0 (2001) / 0 (2000); Multi-family building permits issued: 0 (2001) / 0 (2000); Employment by occupation: 5.1% management, 17.7% professional, 19.0% services, 19.6% sales, 0.0% farming, 11.4% construction, 27.2% production (2000).
Income: Per capita income: $20,374 (2000); Median household income: $51,389 (2000); Poverty rate: 5.6% (2000).
Taxes: Total city taxes per capita: $30 (1997); City property taxes per capita: $27 (1997).
Education: High school graduation rate: 89.0% (2000); College graduation rate: 18.3% (2000).
Housing: Homeownership rate: 83.5% (2000); Median home value: $86,300 (2000); Median rent: $307 per month (2000); Median age of housing: 43 years (2000).
Transportation: Commute to work: 95.4% car, 0.0% public transportation, 0.0% walk, 4.6% work from home (2000); Travel time to work: 18.6% less than 15 minutes, 51.0% 15 to 30 minutes, 13.8% 30 to 45 minutes, 4.1% 45 to 60 minutes, 12.4% 60 minutes or more (2000)

PUTNAM (unincorporated postal area, zip code 61560). Covers a land area of 33.771 square miles and a water area of 0.505 square miles. Located at 41.19° N. Lat.; 89.43° W. Long. Elevation is 515 feet.
Population: 705 (2000); Race: 98.9% White, 0.3% Black, 0.0% Asian, 0.0% American Indian and Alaska Native, 1.6% Hispanic of any race, 0.8% two or more races (2000); Density: 20.9 persons per square mile (2000); Age: 15.9% under 18, 19.8% over 64 (2000); Marriage status: 19.6% never married, 71.3% now married, 5.6% widowed, 3.6% divorced (2000); Foreign born: 0.5% (2000); Ancestry (includes multiple ancestries): 36.0% German, 15.6% Irish, 12.4% Polish, 12.0% English, 7.1% Swedish (2000).
Economy: Employment by occupation: 16.0% management, 15.7% professional, 7.1% services, 16.3% sales, 1.3% farming, 15.7% construction, 27.9% production (2000).
Income: Per capita income: $21,515 (2000); Median household income: $46,917 (2000); Poverty rate: 5.0% (2000).
Education: High school graduation rate: 93.3% (2000); College graduation rate: 20.3% (2000).
Housing: Homeownership rate: 90.3% (2000); Median home value: $118,200 (2000); Median rent: $275 per month (2000); Median age of housing: 18 years (2000).
Transportation: Commute to work: 88.3% car, 2.0% public transportation, 4.0% walk, 5.7% work from home (2000); Travel time to work: 24.2% less than 15 minutes, 40.9% 15 to 30 minutes, 7.5% 30 to 45 minutes, 12.1% 45 to 60 minutes, 15.3% 60 minutes or more (2000)

STANDARD (village). Covers a land area of 0.565 square miles and a water area of 0 square miles. Located at 41.25° N. Lat.; 89.17° W. Long. Elevation is 680 feet.
Population: 256 (2000); Race: 97.3% White, 0.0% Black, 0.0% Asian, 0.0% American Indian and Alaska Native, 3.9% Hispanic of any race, 2.7% two or more races (2000); Density: 453.2 persons per square mile (2000); Age: 24.4% under 18, 21.7% over 64 (2000); Marriage status: 26.9% never married, 50.0% now married, 14.6% widowed, 8.5% divorced (2000); Foreign born: 3.9% (2000); Ancestry (includes multiple ancestries): 44.2% Italian, 25.6% German, 13.6% Irish, 8.9% English, 7.4% Other groups (2000).
Economy: Single-family building permits issued: 2 (2001) / 0 (2000); Multi-family building permits issued: 0 (2001) / 0 (2000); Employment by occupation: 11.5% management, 17.2% professional, 12.3% services, 22.1% sales, 1.6% farming, 11.5% construction, 23.8% production (2000).
Income: Per capita income: $17,453 (2000); Median household income: $35,972 (2000); Poverty rate: 5.8% (2000).
Taxes: Total city taxes per capita: $53 (1997); City property taxes per capita: $45 (1997).
Education: High school graduation rate: 77.5% (2000); College graduation rate: 9.1% (2000).
Housing: Homeownership rate: 81.9% (2000); Median home value: $58,100 (2000); Median rent: $269 per month (2000); Median age of housing: 60+ years (2000).
Transportation: Commute to work: 97.5% car, 0.0% public transportation, 1.6% walk, 0.8% work from home (2000); Travel time to work: 21.5% less

than 15 minutes, 65.3% 15 to 30 minutes, 7.4% 30 to 45 minutes, 0.0% 45 to 60 minutes, 5.8% 60 minutes or more (2000)

Randolph County

Located in southwestern Illinois; bounded on the west and south by the Mississippi River and the Missouri border; drained by the Kaskaskia River. Covers a land area of 578.40 square miles, a water area of 18.80 square miles, and is located in the Central Time Zone. The county government was organized in 1795. County seat is Chester.

Weather Station: Sparta 1 W Elevation: 534 feet

	Jan	Feb	Mar	Apr	May	Jun	Jul	Aug	Sep	Oct	Nov	Dec
High	39	46	57	68	77	86	90	88	81	70	56	44
Low	22	27	36	45	54	64	67	65	58	46	37	27
Precip	2.4	2.5	4.2	4.1	4.5	3.7	3.9	3.3	2.9	3.4	4.1	3.3
Snow	5.1	3.5	2.0	0.5	0.0	0.0	0.0	0.0	0.0	tr	1.0	2.7

High and Low temperatures in degrees Fahrenheit; Precipitation and Snow in inches

Population: 33,893 (2000); Race: 88.6% White, 9.6% Black, 0.3% Asian, 0.1% American Indian and Alaska Native, 1.2% Hispanic of any race, 0.6% two or more races (2000); Density: 58.6 persons per square mile (2000); Age: 22.2% under 18, 15.5% over 64 (2000).
Religion: Five largest groups: 18.7% Catholic Church, 18.5% Lutheran Church—Missouri Synod, 7.8% Southern Baptist Convention, 5.4% Evangelical Lutheran Church in America, 4.1% The United Methodist Church (2000).
Economy: Unemployment rate: 5.4% (11/2002); Total civilian labor force: 14,025 (11/2002); Leading industries: 26.4% manufacturing; 19.1% health care and social assistance; 14.6% retail trade (2000); Companies that employ more than 1,000 persons: 0 (2000); Companies that employ more than 100 persons: 16 (2000); Farms: 843 totaling 262,464 acres (1997); Minority business ownership rate: 9.8% (1997); Women business ownership rate: 35.0% (1997); Retail sales per capita: $7,743 (1997). Single-family building permits issued: 53 (2001) / 51 (2000); Multi-family building permits issued: 6 (2001) / 13 (2000).
Income: Per capita income: $17,696 (2000); Median household income: $37,013 (2000); Poverty rate: 10.0% (2000); Bankruptcy rate: 5.69% (2001).
Taxes: Total county taxes per capita: $93 (2000); County property taxes per capita: $92 (2000).
Education: High school graduation rate: 71.3% (2000); College graduation rate: 8.6% (2000).
Housing: Homeownership rate: 79.4% (2000); Median home value: $65,700 (2000); Median rent: $286 per month (2000); Median age of housing: 38 years (2000).
Health: Birth rate: 116.0 per 10,000 population (1998); Age adjusted death rate: 91.9 per 10,000 population (1999); Age adjusted cancer mortality rate: 220.4 deaths per 100,000 population (1999). Air Quality Index: 77% good, 23% moderate, 0% unhealthy (percent of days in 2000). Number of physicians: 8.6 per 10,000 population (1999); Number of hospital beds: 162.0 per 10,000 population (1999).
Elections: 2000 Presidential election results: 47.6% Gore, 49.9% Bush, 1.6% Nader, 0.7% Buchanan
National and State Parks: Baldwin Lake State Fish and Wildlife Area; Fort Chartres State Park; Fort Kaskaskia State Park; Modoc Rock Shelter National Historic Site; Randolph County State Conservation Area
Additional Information Contacts
Randolph County Government Offices 618-826-2510
Chester Chamber of Commerce 618-826-2721
Red Bud Chamber of Commerce 618-282-3505

Randolph County Communities

BALDWIN (village). Covers a land area of 0.669 square miles and a water area of 0 square miles. Located at 38.18° N. Lat.; 89.84° W. Long. Elevation is 468 feet.
Population: 3,627 (2000); Race: 35.1% White, 58.5% Black, 0.0% Asian, 0.0% American Indian and Alaska Native, 7.9% Hispanic of any race, 0.3% two or more races (2000); Density: 5,421.7 persons per square mile (2000); Age: 3.6% under 18, 1.8% over 64 (2000); Marriage status: 2.3% never married, 91.3% now married, 1.5% widowed, 4.9% divorced (2000); Foreign born: 2.2% (2000); Ancestry (includes multiple ancestries): 5.8% German, 1.6% Irish, 1.5% Other groups, 1.3% English, 0.6% French (except Basque) (2000).
Economy: In agricultural and bituminous coal mining area. Site of nuclear plant. Single-family building permits issued: 0 (2001) / 0 (2000); Multi-family building permits issued: 0 (2001) / 0 (2000); Employment by occupation: 2.7% management, 15.1% professional, 12.4% services, 23.2% sales, 0.0% farming, 9.2% construction, 37.3% production (2000).
Income: Per capita income: $13,009 (2000); Median household income: $32,083 (2000); Poverty rate: 9.3% (2000).
Taxes: Total city taxes per capita: $92 (1997); City property taxes per capita: $38 (1997).
Education: High school graduation rate: 28.3% (2000); College graduation rate: 1.0% (2000).
Housing: Homeownership rate: 82.9% (2000); Median home value: $46,100 (2000); Median rent: $263 per month (2000); Median age of housing: 46 years (2000).
Transportation: Commute to work: 96.7% car, 0.0% public transportation, 2.2% walk, 1.1% work from home (2000); Travel time to work: 30.7% less than 15 minutes, 27.4% 15 to 30 minutes, 20.7% 30 to 45 minutes, 16.2% 45 to 60 minutes, 5.0% 60 minutes or more (2000)

CHESTER (city). Covers a land area of 5.893 square miles and a water area of 0.012 square miles. Located at 37.91° N. Lat.; 89.82° W. Long. Elevation is 670 feet.
History: Chester was established in 1819 as a commercial rival for Kaskaskia by a land company from Cincinnati.
Population: 5,185 (2000); Race: 95.2% White, 3.8% Black, 0.2% Asian, 0.2% American Indian and Alaska Native, 0.9% Hispanic of any race, 0.6% two or more races (2000); Density: 879.9 persons per square mile (2000); Age: 22.1% under 18, 19.1% over 64 (2000); Marriage status: 24.8% never married, 53.1% now married, 9.2% widowed, 12.9% divorced (2000); Foreign born: 0.7% (2000); Ancestry (includes multiple ancestries): 33.8% German, 12.3% Irish, 8.7% United States or American, 8.7% Other groups, 7.2% English (2000).
Economy: Single-family building permits issued: 4 (2001) / 9 (2000); Multi-family building permits issued: 0 (2001) / 7 (2000); Employment by occupation: 11.1% management, 17.8% professional, 21.1% services, 19.7% sales, 0.5% farming, 8.4% construction, 21.4% production (2000).
Income: Per capita income: $22,190 (2000); Median household income: $39,079 (2000); Poverty rate: 9.7% (2000).
Taxes: Total city taxes per capita: $82 (1997); City property taxes per capita: $44 (1997).
Education: High school graduation rate: 72.5% (2000); College graduation rate: 11.2% (2000).

School District(s)

Chester Community Unit School District 139 (PK-12)
2000 Enrollment: 1,077 618-826-4509
Housing: Homeownership rate: 74.6% (2000); Median home value: $60,900 (2000); Median rent: $284 per month (2000); Median age of housing: 46 years (2000).
Hospitals: Chester Mental Health Center (288 beds); Memorial Hospital (61 beds)
Newspapers: Randolph Herald Tribune (1 x week)
Transportation: Commute to work: 94.9% car, 0.0% public transportation, 3.1% walk, 1.7% work from home (2000); Travel time to work: 66.8% less than 15 minutes, 18.0% 15 to 30 minutes, 8.3% 30 to 45 minutes, 2.0% 45 to 60 minutes, 4.9% 60 minutes or more (2000)
Additional Information Contacts
Chester Chamber of Commerce 618-826-2721

COULTERVILLE (village). Covers a land area of 0.566 square miles and a water area of 0 square miles. Located at 38.18° N. Lat.; 89.60° W. Long. Elevation is 550 feet.
History: Incorporated 1874.
Population: 1,230 (2000); Race: 95.5% White, 2.1% Black, 0.0% Asian, 0.0% American Indian and Alaska Native, 0.0% Hispanic of any race, 2.3% two or more races (2000); Density: 2,174.4 persons per square mile (2000); Age: 22.3% under 18, 16.7% over 64 (2000); Marriage status: 21.4% never married, 55.6% now married, 8.3% widowed, 14.6% divorced (2000); Foreign born: 0.4% (2000); Ancestry (includes multiple ancestries): 25.7% German, 15.7% United States or American, 12.5% Irish, 9.7% English, 8.0% Other groups (2000).
Economy: Railroad junction. Corn, wheat; cattle; dairy products; bituminous-coal mines. Single-family building permits issued: 0 (2001) / 1 (2000); Multi-family building permits issued: 0 (2001) / 0 (2000); Employment by occupation: 7.0% management, 6.8% professional, 19.9% services, 17.5% sales, 0.0% farming, 15.0% construction, 33.7% production (2000).
Income: Per capita income: $17,994 (2000); Median household income: $26,776 (2000); Poverty rate: 18.6% (2000).

Taxes: Total city taxes per capita: $96 (1997); City property taxes per capita: $45 (1997).
Education: High school graduation rate: 72.2% (2000); College graduation rate: 4.9% (2000).

School District(s)

Coulterville Unit School District 1 (KG-12)
2000 Enrollment: 272 618-758-2338

Housing: Homeownership rate: 82.8% (2000); Median home value: $45,000 (2000); Median rent: $264 per month (2000); Median age of housing: 44 years (2000).
Transportation: Commute to work: 95.3% car, 0.0% public transportation, 1.5% walk, 0.8% work from home (2000); Travel time to work: 32.5% less than 15 minutes, 39.8% 15 to 30 minutes, 15.4% 30 to 45 minutes, 2.3% 45 to 60 minutes, 10.1% 60 minutes or more (2000)

ELLIS GROVE (village). Aka Ellisgrove. Covers a land area of 0.465 square miles and a water area of 0 square miles. Located at 38.01° N. Lat.; 89.90° W. Long. Elevation is 555 feet.
History: Fort Kaskaskia State Historical Site nearby.
Population: 381 (2000); Race: 100.0% White, 0.0% Black, 0.0% Asian, 0.0% American Indian and Alaska Native, 0.0% Hispanic of any race, 0.0% two or more races (2000); Density: 819.4 persons per square mile (2000); Age: 28.7% under 18, 18.1% over 64 (2000); Marriage status: 17.4% never married, 62.1% now married, 8.4% widowed, 12.1% divorced (2000); Foreign born: 0.0% (2000); Ancestry (includes multiple ancestries): 38.8% German, 16.5% Irish, 14.0% United States or American, 12.9% French (except Basque), 12.1% Other groups (2000).
Economy: In agricultural area. Employment by occupation: 3.7% management, 11.2% professional, 29.2% services, 21.1% sales, 3.7% farming, 8.7% construction, 22.4% production (2000).
Income: Per capita income: $14,527 (2000); Median household income: $33,250 (2000); Poverty rate: 8.3% (2000).
Taxes: Total city taxes per capita: $26 (1997); City property taxes per capita: $23 (1997).
Education: High school graduation rate: 63.1% (2000); College graduation rate: 5.4% (2000).
Housing: Homeownership rate: 74.5% (2000); Median home value: $56,800 (2000); Median rent: $288 per month (2000); Median age of housing: 33 years (2000).
Transportation: Commute to work: 98.7% car, 0.0% public transportation, 1.3% walk, 0.0% work from home (2000); Travel time to work: 30.2% less than 15 minutes, 26.4% 15 to 30 minutes, 20.8% 30 to 45 minutes, 5.7% 45 to 60 minutes, 17.0% 60 minutes or more (2000)

EVANSVILLE (village). Covers a land area of 0.741 square miles and a water area of 0.018 square miles. Located at 38.09° N. Lat.; 89.93° W. Long. Elevation is 420 feet.
Population: 724 (2000); Race: 96.2% White, 0.6% Black, 0.0% Asian, 0.0% American Indian and Alaska Native, 1.4% Hispanic of any race, 2.1% two or more races (2000); Density: 976.9 persons per square mile (2000); Age: 24.9% under 18, 13.2% over 64 (2000); Marriage status: 21.6% never married, 57.6% now married, 10.2% widowed, 10.6% divorced (2000); Foreign born: 0.0% (2000); Ancestry (includes multiple ancestries): 43.3% German, 10.1% French (except Basque), 5.8% Other groups, 5.7% Irish, 5.5% United States or American (2000).
Economy: In agricultural and bituminous coal area. Single-family building permits issued: 0 (2001) / 0 (2000); Multi-family building permits issued: 0 (2001) / 0 (2000); Employment by occupation: 6.2% management, 11.1% professional, 18.6% services, 15.5% sales, 0.0% farming, 17.6% construction, 31.0% production (2000).
Income: Per capita income: $20,194 (2000); Median household income: $32,292 (2000); Poverty rate: 14.0% (2000).
Taxes: Total city taxes per capita: $106 (1997); City property taxes per capita: $51 (1997).
Education: High school graduation rate: 75.6% (2000); College graduation rate: 4.2% (2000).
Housing: Homeownership rate: 78.5% (2000); Median home value: $52,400 (2000); Median rent: $263 per month (2000); Median age of housing: 49 years (2000).
Transportation: Commute to work: 93.4% car, 2.5% public transportation, 0.9% walk, 0.0% work from home (2000); Travel time to work: 19.1% less than 15 minutes, 32.2% 15 to 30 minutes, 16.6% 30 to 45 minutes, 5.9% 45 to 60 minutes, 26.3% 60 minutes or more (2000)

MODOC (unincorporated postal area, zip code 62261). Covers a land area of 31.259 square miles and a water area of 0.032 square miles. Located at 37.98° N. Lat.; 90.00° W. Long. Elevation is 395 feet.
Population: 221 (2000); Race: 100.0% White, 0.0% Black, 0.0% Asian, 0.0% American Indian and Alaska Native, 0.0% Hispanic of any race, 0.0% two or more races (2000); Density: 7.1 persons per square mile (2000); Age: 32.8% under 18, 11.2% over 64 (2000); Marriage status: 20.8% never married, 58.9% now married, 7.1% widowed, 13.1% divorced (2000); Foreign born: 0.0% (2000); Ancestry (includes multiple ancestries): 37.6% German, 24.0% United States or American, 11.6% French (except Basque), 3.6% Scottish, 3.2% Other groups (2000).
Economy: Employment by occupation: 7.3% management, 16.5% professional, 14.7% services, 14.7% sales, 0.0% farming, 14.7% construction, 32.1% production (2000).
Income: Per capita income: $15,081 (2000); Median household income: $34,286 (2000); Poverty rate: 2.9% (2000).
Education: High school graduation rate: 77.6% (2000); College graduation rate: 12.2% (2000).
Housing: Homeownership rate: 91.6% (2000); Median home value: $43,300 (2000); Median rent: $2,000+ per month (2000); Median age of housing: 33 years (2000).
Transportation: Commute to work: 93.6% car, 0.0% public transportation, 0.0% walk, 6.4% work from home (2000); Travel time to work: 25.5% less than 15 minutes, 30.4% 15 to 30 minutes, 31.4% 30 to 45 minutes, 0.0% 45 to 60 minutes, 12.7% 60 minutes or more (2000)

PERCY (village). Covers a land area of 0.880 square miles and a water area of 0 square miles. Located at 38.01° N. Lat.; 89.61° W. Long. Elevation is 490 feet.
Population: 942 (2000); Race: 98.8% White, 0.2% Black, 0.2% Asian, 0.0% American Indian and Alaska Native, 2.7% Hispanic of any race, 0.2% two or more races (2000); Density: 1,070.6 persons per square mile (2000); Age: 20.6% under 18, 19.9% over 64 (2000); Marriage status: 17.2% never married, 63.5% now married, 9.3% widowed, 10.0% divorced (2000); Foreign born: 2.1% (2000); Ancestry (includes multiple ancestries): 34.2% German, 13.6% Irish, 9.9% Other groups, 8.3% United States or American, 6.2% English (2000).
Economy: In agricultural and coal area. Single-family building permits issued: 0 (2001) / 0 (2000); Multi-family building permits issued: 0 (2001) / 0 (2000); Employment by occupation: 3.3% management, 11.5% professional, 18.4% services, 17.2% sales, 1.2% farming, 12.0% construction, 36.5% production (2000).
Income: Per capita income: $15,524 (2000); Median household income: $31,333 (2000); Poverty rate: 11.3% (2000).
Taxes: Total city taxes per capita: $48 (1997); City property taxes per capita: $42 (1997).
Education: High school graduation rate: 71.2% (2000); College graduation rate: 6.1% (2000).
Housing: Homeownership rate: 72.5% (2000); Median home value: $42,100 (2000); Median rent: $246 per month (2000); Median age of housing: 42 years (2000).
Newspapers: County Journal (1 x week)
Transportation: Commute to work: 91.3% car, 0.0% public transportation, 2.2% walk, 3.4% work from home (2000); Travel time to work: 41.1% less than 15 minutes, 27.4% 15 to 30 minutes, 13.5% 30 to 45 minutes, 9.2% 45 to 60 minutes, 8.7% 60 minutes or more (2000)

PRAIRIE DU ROCHER (village). Aka Prairie Du Rocher. Covers a land area of 0.570 square miles and a water area of 0 square miles. Located at 38.08° N. Lat.; 90.09° W. Long. Elevation is 396 feet.
History: Prairie du Rocher was founded in the early 1700's by people brought to the area by John Law, a Scotch promoter who organized a company and was granted a charter for the Louisiana Territory.
Population: 613 (2000); Race: 97.9% White, 0.0% Black, 0.0% Asian, 0.0% American Indian and Alaska Native, 0.0% Hispanic of any race, 0.0% two or more races (2000); Density: 1,076.2 persons per square mile (2000); Age: 31.0% under 18, 11.3% over 64 (2000); Marriage status: 22.8% never married, 58.5% now married, 7.3% widowed, 11.4% divorced (2000); Foreign born: 0.0% (2000); Ancestry (includes multiple ancestries): 36.0% German, 31.0% French (except Basque), 13.3% Irish, 11.8% Other groups, 7.0% United States or American (2000).
Economy: Single-family building permits issued: 0 (2001) / 0 (2000); Multi-family building permits issued: 0 (2001) / 0 (2000); Employment by occupation: 7.5% management, 10.4% professional, 20.4% services, 21.4% sales, 0.7% farming, 13.2% construction, 26.4% production (2000).

Income: Per capita income: $14,771 (2000); Median household income: $35,795 (2000); Poverty rate: 8.3% (2000).
Taxes: Total city taxes per capita: $59 (1997); City property taxes per capita: $14 (1997).
Education: High school graduation rate: 73.5% (2000); College graduation rate: 8.3% (2000).

School District(s)

Prairie Du Rocher C C S D 134 (PK-08)
2000 Enrollment: 158 618-284-3530
Housing: Homeownership rate: 76.5% (2000); Median home value: $59,900 (2000); Median rent: $325 per month (2000); Median age of housing: 42 years (2000).
Transportation: Commute to work: 90.9% car, 1.5% public transportation, 5.1% walk, 2.2% work from home (2000); Travel time to work: 20.1% less than 15 minutes, 23.5% 15 to 30 minutes, 22.8% 30 to 45 minutes, 9.3% 45 to 60 minutes, 24.3% 60 minutes or more (2000)

RED BUD (city). Covers a land area of 2.104 square miles and a water area of 0.007 square miles. Located at 38.21° N. Lat.; 89.99° W. Long. Elevation is 479 feet.
History: Red Bud was named for the red-bud trees that once covered the town site.
Population: 3,422 (2000); Race: 98.4% White, 0.0% Black, 0.6% Asian, 0.1% American Indian and Alaska Native, 0.4% Hispanic of any race, 0.7% two or more races (2000); Density: 1,626.3 persons per square mile (2000); Age: 22.6% under 18, 18.3% over 64 (2000); Marriage status: 20.6% never married, 63.5% now married, 9.2% widowed, 6.7% divorced (2000); Foreign born: 1.8% (2000); Ancestry (includes multiple ancestries): 45.6% German, 11.6% French (except Basque), 8.4% Irish, 7.7% English, 6.6% Other groups (2000).
Economy: Single-family building permits issued: 16 (2001) / 15 (2000); Multi-family building permits issued: 6 (2001) / 6 (2000); Employment by occupation: 10.0% management, 21.3% professional, 16.5% services, 23.1% sales, 0.4% farming, 12.9% construction, 15.7% production (2000).
Income: Per capita income: $19,967 (2000); Median household income: $40,300 (2000); Poverty rate: 9.4% (2000).
Taxes: Total city taxes per capita: $230 (1997); City property taxes per capita: $76 (1997).
Education: High school graduation rate: 77.4% (2000); College graduation rate: 14.4% (2000).

School District(s)

Red Bud C U School District 132 (PK-12)
2000 Enrollment: 1,057 618-282-3507
Housing: Homeownership rate: 76.9% (2000); Median home value: $90,900 (2000); Median rent: $311 per month (2000); Median age of housing: 32 years (2000).
Hospitals: Saint Clement Health Services (202 beds)
Newspapers: North County News (1 x week)
Transportation: Commute to work: 88.7% car, 0.4% public transportation, 4.2% walk, 4.3% work from home (2000); Travel time to work: 43.1% less than 15 minutes, 21.3% 15 to 30 minutes, 14.6% 30 to 45 minutes, 14.7% 45 to 60 minutes, 6.3% 60 minutes or more (2000)
Additional Information Contacts
Red Bud Chamber of Commerce 618-282-3505

ROCKWOOD (village). Covers a land area of 0.211 square miles and a water area of 0 square miles. Located at 37.83° N. Lat.; 89.69° W. Long. Elevation is 380 feet.
History: Early settlers in Rockwood provided river steamers with wood for fuel, and built flatboats for transporting cargo.
Population: 41 (2000); Race: 100.0% White, 0.0% Black, 0.0% Asian, 0.0% American Indian and Alaska Native, 0.0% Hispanic of any race, 0.0% two or more races (2000); Density: 193.9 persons per square mile (2000); Age: 55.3% under 18, 0.0% over 64 (2000); Marriage status: 45.2% never married, 48.4% now married, 0.0% widowed, 6.5% divorced (2000); Foreign born: 0.0% (2000); Ancestry (includes multiple ancestries): 80.9% United States or American, 10.6% German, 4.3% French (except Basque) (2000).
Economy: Employment by occupation: 18.8% management, 0.0% professional, 43.8% services, 0.0% sales, 0.0% farming, 12.5% construction, 25.0% production (2000).
Income: Per capita income: $9,387 (2000); Median household income: $61,250 (2000); Poverty rate: 0.0% (2000).
Taxes: Total city taxes per capita: $47 (1997); City property taxes per capita: $47 (1997).
Education: High school graduation rate: 52.4% (2000); College graduation rate: 14.3% (2000).
Housing: Homeownership rate: 66.7% (2000); Median home value: $32,500 (2000); Median rent: $225 per month (2000); Median age of housing: 32 years (2000).
Transportation: Commute to work: 100.0% car, 0.0% public transportation, 0.0% walk, 0.0% work from home (2000); Travel time to work: 0.0% less than 15 minutes, 100.0% 15 to 30 minutes, 0.0% 30 to 45 minutes, 0.0% 45 to 60 minutes, 0.0% 60 minutes or more (2000)

RUMA (village). Covers a land area of 0.410 square miles and a water area of 0 square miles. Located at 38.13° N. Lat.; 89.99° W. Long. Elevation is 442 feet.
Population: 260 (2000); Race: 95.8% White, 0.0% Black, 4.2% Asian, 0.0% American Indian and Alaska Native, 0.0% Hispanic of any race, 0.0% two or more races (2000); Density: 634.0 persons per square mile (2000); Age: 28.4% under 18, 8.7% over 64 (2000); Marriage status: 20.6% never married, 60.3% now married, 4.8% widowed, 14.4% divorced (2000); Foreign born: 3.0% (2000); Ancestry (includes multiple ancestries): 47.7% German, 16.3% French (except Basque), 14.0% Irish, 9.8% Other groups, 8.3% English (2000).
Economy: In agricultural area. Single-family building permits issued: 1 (2001) / 1 (2000); Multi-family building permits issued: 0 (2001) / 0 (2000); Employment by occupation: 4.0% management, 10.4% professional, 20.8% services, 23.2% sales, 0.0% farming, 13.6% construction, 28.0% production (2000).
Income: Per capita income: $16,176 (2000); Median household income: $33,929 (2000); Poverty rate: 13.6% (2000).
Taxes: Total city taxes per capita: $31 (1997); City property taxes per capita: $12 (1997).
Education: High school graduation rate: 79.9% (2000); College graduation rate: 7.3% (2000).
Housing: Homeownership rate: 87.8% (2000); Median home value: $91,400 (2000); Median rent: $363 per month (2000); Median age of housing: 23 years (2000).
Transportation: Commute to work: 96.7% car, 0.0% public transportation, 3.3% walk, 0.0% work from home (2000); Travel time to work: 29.5% less than 15 minutes, 25.4% 15 to 30 minutes, 27.9% 30 to 45 minutes, 4.9% 45 to 60 minutes, 12.3% 60 minutes or more (2000)

SPARTA (city). Covers a land area of 9.033 square miles and a water area of 0.150 square miles. Located at 38.12° N. Lat.; 89.70° W. Long. Elevation is 560 feet.
History: Incorporated 1847.
Population: 4,486 (2000); Race: 80.9% White, 16.8% Black, 0.8% Asian, 0.0% American Indian and Alaska Native, 0.4% Hispanic of any race, 1.0% two or more races (2000); Density: 496.6 persons per square mile (2000); Age: 25.9% under 18, 18.4% over 64 (2000); Marriage status: 23.1% never married, 57.8% now married, 9.5% widowed, 9.6% divorced (2000); Foreign born: 0.7% (2000); Ancestry (includes multiple ancestries): 26.2% German, 16.1% Other groups, 12.2% Irish, 9.0% English, 6.3% United States or American (2000).
Economy: Manufacturing of clothing; railroad shops. Agriculture: corn, wheat; dairy products; livestock, poultry. Bituminous coal mines. Single-family building permits issued: 1 (2001) / 1 (2000); Multi-family building permits issued: 0 (2001) / 0 (2000); Employment by occupation: 6.8% management, 18.1% professional, 16.3% services, 25.7% sales, 0.3% farming, 9.8% construction, 23.1% production (2000).
Income: Per capita income: $16,343 (2000); Median household income: $34,139 (2000); Poverty rate: 16.0% (2000).
Taxes: Total city taxes per capita: $433 (1997); City property taxes per capita: $132 (1997).
Education: High school graduation rate: 82.5% (2000); College graduation rate: 12.4% (2000).

School District(s)

Sparta C U School District 140 (PK-12)
2000 Enrollment: 1,676 618-443-5331
Housing: Homeownership rate: 73.2% (2000); Median home value: $57,300 (2000); Median rent: $306 per month (2000); Median age of housing: 40 years (2000).
Hospitals: Sparta Community Hospital (39 beds)
Newspapers: Sparta News-Plaindealer (1 x week)
Transportation: Commute to work: 93.2% car, 1.3% public transportation, 1.7% walk, 3.0% work from home (2000); Travel time to work: 62.2% less than 15 minutes, 16.0% 15 to 30 minutes, 9.4% 30 to 45 minutes, 5.4% 45 to 60 minutes, 7.0% 60 minutes or more (2000)

STEELEVILLE (village). Covers a land area of 1.304 square miles and a water area of 0.008 square miles. Located at 38.00° N. Lat.; 89.65° W. Long. Elevation is 430 feet.
History: Incorporated 1851.
Population: 2,077 (2000); Race: 98.4% White, 0.0% Black, 1.4% Asian, 0.0% American Indian and Alaska Native, 0.0% Hispanic of any race, 0.2% two or more races (2000); Density: 1,593.0 persons per square mile (2000); Age: 23.9% under 18, 20.1% over 64 (2000); Marriage status: 19.6% never married, 57.2% now married, 11.8% widowed, 11.4% divorced (2000); Foreign born: 0.9% (2000); Ancestry (includes multiple ancestries): 45.9% German, 10.9% Irish, 7.1% Other groups, 6.8% English, 6.8% United States or American (2000).
Economy: Agriculture includes grain; poultry; dairying. Bituminous-coal mines. Manufacturing of fabricated metal products, food products. Single-family building permits issued: 1 (2001) / 1 (2000); Multi-family building permits issued: 0 (2001) / 0 (2000); Employment by occupation: 8.1% management, 18.2% professional, 18.9% services, 22.5% sales, 0.5% farming, 9.4% construction, 22.4% production (2000).
Income: Per capita income: $19,124 (2000); Median household income: $34,679 (2000); Poverty rate: 7.9% (2000).
Taxes: Total city taxes per capita: $152 (1997); City property taxes per capita: $40 (1997).
Education: High school graduation rate: 76.3% (2000); College graduation rate: 10.1% (2000).

School District(s)

Steeleville C U School District 138 (KG-12)
2000 Enrollment: 434 618-965-3432
Housing: Homeownership rate: 79.8% (2000); Median home value: $67,300 (2000); Median rent: $304 per month (2000); Median age of housing: 41 years (2000).
Newspapers: Steeleville Ledger (1 x week)
Transportation: Commute to work: 89.0% car, 0.0% public transportation, 8.6% walk, 2.4% work from home (2000); Travel time to work: 50.7% less than 15 minutes, 30.9% 15 to 30 minutes, 7.4% 30 to 45 minutes, 2.7% 45 to 60 minutes, 8.2% 60 minutes or more (2000)

TILDEN (village). Covers a land area of 0.965 square miles and a water area of 0.010 square miles. Located at 38.21° N. Lat.; 89.68° W. Long. Elevation is 522 feet.
Population: 922 (2000); Race: 98.6% White, 0.0% Black, 0.0% Asian, 0.0% American Indian and Alaska Native, 0.4% Hispanic of any race, 1.4% two or more races (2000); Density: 955.2 persons per square mile (2000); Age: 25.1% under 18, 14.9% over 64 (2000); Marriage status: 22.5% never married, 53.8% now married, 9.2% widowed, 14.5% divorced (2000); Foreign born: 0.0% (2000); Ancestry (includes multiple ancestries): 27.9% German, 19.4% Irish, 18.9% Other groups, 10.4% United States or American, 6.0% French (except Basque) (2000).
Economy: In agricultural and bituminous coal-mining area. Employment by occupation: 4.1% management, 13.4% professional, 20.5% services, 12.9% sales, 1.1% farming, 14.0% construction, 34.0% production (2000).
Income: Per capita income: $14,738 (2000); Median household income: $34,115 (2000); Poverty rate: 14.7% (2000).
Taxes: Total city taxes per capita: $38 (1997); City property taxes per capita: $33 (1997).
Education: High school graduation rate: 75.1% (2000); College graduation rate: 4.1% (2000).
Housing: Homeownership rate: 76.0% (2000); Median home value: $42,400 (2000); Median rent: $255 per month (2000); Median age of housing: 28 years (2000).
Transportation: Commute to work: 98.0% car, 0.0% public transportation, 2.0% walk, 0.0% work from home (2000); Travel time to work: 28.1% less than 15 minutes, 26.4% 15 to 30 minutes, 18.1% 30 to 45 minutes, 12.9% 45 to 60 minutes, 14.6% 60 minutes or more (2000)

WALSH (unincorporated postal area, zip code 62297). Covers a land area of 22.664 square miles and a water area of 0.064 square miles. Located at 38.05° N. Lat.; 89.80° W. Long. Elevation is 480 feet.
Population: 411 (2000); Race: 100.0% White, 0.0% Black, 0.0% Asian, 0.0% American Indian and Alaska Native, 0.0% Hispanic of any race, 0.0% two or more races (2000); Density: 18.1 persons per square mile (2000); Age: 21.0% under 18, 20.5% over 64 (2000); Marriage status: 18.8% never married, 76.1% now married, 5.2% widowed, 0.0% divorced (2000); Foreign born: 0.0% (2000); Ancestry (includes multiple ancestries): 51.7% German, 13.8% Irish, 8.8% Italian, 7.5% United States or American, 7.0% Scotch-Irish (2000).
Economy: Employment by occupation: 2.5% management, 8.7% professional, 10.6% services, 23.0% sales, 0.0% farming, 20.5% construction, 34.8% production (2000).
Income: Per capita income: $17,737 (2000); Median household income: $50,197 (2000); Poverty rate: 2.8% (2000).
Education: High school graduation rate: 77.8% (2000); College graduation rate: 6.6% (2000).
Housing: Homeownership rate: 96.2% (2000); Median home value: $68,600 (2000); Median age of housing: 53 years (2000).
Transportation: Commute to work: 94.4% car, 0.0% public transportation, 5.6% walk, 0.0% work from home (2000); Travel time to work: 8.1% less than 15 minutes, 47.8% 15 to 30 minutes, 21.1% 30 to 45 minutes, 4.3% 45 to 60 minutes, 18.6% 60 minutes or more (2000)

Richland County

Located in southeastern Illinois; bounded partly on the west by the Little Wabash River; drained by the Fox River and Bonpas Creek. Covers a land area of 360.10 square miles, a water area of 1.90 square miles, and is located in the Central Time Zone. The county government was organized in 1841. County seat is Olney.

Weather Station: Olney 2 S — Elevation: 479 feet

	Jan	Feb	Mar	Apr	May	Jun	Jul	Aug	Sep	Oct	Nov	Dec
High	37	43	54	66	76	85	88	87	81	69	55	43
Low	21	25	35	44	53	62	66	64	57	45	36	26
Precip	2.8	2.6	4.3	4.6	4.6	4.0	3.9	3.3	3.1	3.3	4.4	3.6
Snow	4.2	3.3	1.9	0.2	0.0	0.0	0.0	0.0	0.0	tr	0.8	2.9

High and Low temperatures in degrees Fahrenheit; Precipitation and Snow in inches

Population: 16,149 (2000); Race: 98.6% White, 0.1% Black, 0.3% Asian, 0.0% American Indian and Alaska Native, 0.7% Hispanic of any race, 0.6% two or more races (2000); Density: 44.8 persons per square mile (2000); Age: 24.5% under 18, 17.6% over 64 (2000).
Religion: Five largest groups: 14.8% Catholic Church, 13.5% Christian Churches and Churches of Christ, 10.1% The United Methodist Church, 4.6% Southern Baptist Convention, 3.9% Evangelical Lutheran Church in America (2000).
Economy: Unemployment rate: 5.2% (11/2002); Total civilian labor force: 7,933 (11/2002); Leading industries: 16.4% health care and social assistance; 15.5% retail trade; 9.6% administration, support, waste management, remediation services (2000); Companies that employ more than 1,000 persons: 0 (2000); Companies that employ more than 100 persons: 9 (2000); Farms: 495 totaling 197,224 acres (1997); Minority business ownership rate: 10.0% (1997); Women business ownership rate: 11.7% (1997); Retail sales per capita: $8,834 (1997). Single-family building permits issued: 19 (2001) / 15 (2000); Multi-family building permits issued: 42 (2001) / 30 (2000).
Income: Per capita income: $16,847 (2000); Median household income: $31,185 (2000); Poverty rate: 12.9% (2000); Bankruptcy rate: 4.42% (2001).
Taxes: Total county taxes per capita: $64 (2000); County property taxes per capita: $63 (2000).
Education: High school graduation rate: 83.4% (2000); College graduation rate: 15.2% (2000).
Housing: Homeownership rate: 76.4% (2000); Median home value: $62,500 (2000); Median rent: $288 per month (2000); Median age of housing: 38 years (2000).
Health: Birth rate: 130.7 per 10,000 population (1998); Age adjusted death rate: 84.9 per 10,000 population (1999); Age adjusted cancer mortality rate: 226.0 deaths per 100,000 population (1999). Number of physicians: 25.4 per 10,000 population (1999); Number of hospital beds: 55.7 per 10,000 population (1999).
Elections: 2000 Presidential election results: 33.5% Gore, 63.5% Bush, 1.8% Nader, 0.7% Buchanan

Additional Information Contacts

Richland County Government Offices 618-392-3111
Olney Chamber of Commerce 618-392-2241

Richland County Communities

CALHOUN (village). Covers a land area of 1.047 square miles and a water area of 0 square miles. Located at 38.65° N. Lat.; 88.04° W. Long. Elevation is 540 feet.
Population: 222 (2000); Race: 95.7% White, 0.0% Black, 0.0% Asian, 0.0% American Indian and Alaska Native, 0.0% Hispanic of any race, 4.3% two or more races (2000); Density: 211.9 persons per square mile (2000); Age: 26.4% under 18, 12.8% over 64 (2000); Marriage status: 21.2% never

married, 51.3% now married, 9.5% widowed, 18.0% divorced (2000); Foreign born: 0.0% (2000); Ancestry (includes multiple ancestries): 23.4% German, 20.0% English, 9.4% Other groups, 8.5% Irish, 6.8% United States or American (2000).
Economy: Agriculture: sorghum, apples; dairying; oil. Employment by occupation: 6.9% management, 8.0% professional, 25.3% services, 11.5% sales, 0.0% farming, 12.6% construction, 35.6% production (2000).
Income: Per capita income: $14,679 (2000); Median household income: $25,809 (2000); Poverty rate: 27.2% (2000).
Taxes: Total city taxes per capita: $21 (1997); City property taxes per capita: $13 (1997).
Education: High school graduation rate: 75.2% (2000); College graduation rate: 9.0% (2000).
Housing: Homeownership rate: 80.0% (2000); Median home value: $35,600 (2000); Median rent: $188 per month (2000); Median age of housing: 34 years (2000).
Transportation: Commute to work: 96.5% car, 0.0% public transportation, 0.0% walk, 3.5% work from home (2000); Travel time to work: 11.0% less than 15 minutes, 67.1% 15 to 30 minutes, 18.3% 30 to 45 minutes, 0.0% 45 to 60 minutes, 3.7% 60 minutes or more (2000)

CLAREMONT (village). Covers a land area of 1.135 square miles and a water area of 0 square miles. Located at 38.72° N. Lat.; 87.97° W. Long. Elevation is 510 feet.
Population: 212 (2000); Race: 100.0% White, 0.0% Black, 0.0% Asian, 0.0% American Indian and Alaska Native, 0.0% Hispanic of any race, 0.0% two or more races (2000); Density: 186.7 persons per square mile (2000); Age: 21.4% under 18, 17.5% over 64 (2000); Marriage status: 10.8% never married, 77.2% now married, 4.2% widowed, 7.8% divorced (2000); Foreign born: 1.5% (2000); Ancestry (includes multiple ancestries): 22.3% United States or American, 16.0% German, 12.1% Irish, 8.7% Other groups, 6.3% English (2000).
Economy: In agricultural area: grain and livestock. manufacturing: agricultural machines. Employment by occupation: 16.9% management, 19.1% professional, 5.6% services, 15.7% sales, 0.0% farming, 16.9% construction, 25.8% production (2000).
Income: Per capita income: $15,606 (2000); Median household income: $31,667 (2000); Poverty rate: 2.5% (2000).
Taxes: Total city taxes per capita: $22 (1997); City property taxes per capita: $11 (1997).
Education: High school graduation rate: 73.7% (2000); College graduation rate: 11.2% (2000).
Housing: Homeownership rate: 83.0% (2000); Median home value: $36,300 (2000); Median rent: $296 per month (2000); Median age of housing: 44 years (2000).
Transportation: Commute to work: 100.0% car, 0.0% public transportation, 0.0% walk, 0.0% work from home (2000); Travel time to work: 31.5% less than 15 minutes, 37.1% 15 to 30 minutes, 25.8% 30 to 45 minutes, 4.5% 45 to 60 minutes, 1.1% 60 minutes or more (2000)

DUNDAS (unincorporated postal area, zip code 62425). Covers a land area of 43.742 square miles and a water area of 0.009 square miles. Located at 38.83° N. Lat.; 88.09° W. Long. Elevation is 478 feet.
Population: 716 (2000); Race: 100.0% White, 0.0% Black, 0.0% Asian, 0.0% American Indian and Alaska Native, 2.0% Hispanic of any race, 0.0% two or more races (2000); Density: 16.4 persons per square mile (2000); Age: 32.8% under 18, 24.4% over 64 (2000); Marriage status: 17.0% never married, 69.7% now married, 9.8% widowed, 3.4% divorced (2000); Foreign born: 0.0% (2000); Ancestry (includes multiple ancestries): 36.3% German, 16.0% United States or American, 13.6% English, 10.3% Irish, 3.0% Other groups (2000).
Economy: Employment by occupation: 15.1% management, 18.3% professional, 12.3% services, 25.4% sales, 4.6% farming, 10.9% construction, 13.4% production (2000).
Income: Per capita income: $14,419 (2000); Median household income: $32,222 (2000); Poverty rate: 6.0% (2000).
Education: High school graduation rate: 80.6% (2000); College graduation rate: 9.3% (2000).
Housing: Homeownership rate: 91.2% (2000); Median home value: $55,700 (2000); Median rent: $253 per month (2000); Median age of housing: 37 years (2000).
Transportation: Commute to work: 90.1% car, 0.0% public transportation, 0.0% walk, 9.9% work from home (2000); Travel time to work: 43.8% less than 15 minutes, 35.2% 15 to 30 minutes, 14.8% 30 to 45 minutes, 3.1% 45 to 60 minutes, 3.1% 60 minutes or more (2000)

NOBLE (village). Covers a land area of 1.024 square miles and a water area of 0.005 square miles. Located at 38.69° N. Lat.; 88.22° W. Long. Elevation is 478 feet.
Population: 746 (2000); Race: 98.4% White, 0.0% Black, 0.4% Asian, 0.3% American Indian and Alaska Native, 2.1% Hispanic of any race, 0.9% two or more races (2000); Density: 728.7 persons per square mile (2000); Age: 28.4% under 18, 12.9% over 64 (2000); Marriage status: 16.2% never married, 58.9% now married, 9.1% widowed, 15.8% divorced (2000); Foreign born: 0.4% (2000); Ancestry (includes multiple ancestries): 17.5% German, 13.3% United States or American, 8.2% English, 8.0% Irish, 6.6% Other groups (2000).
Economy: In agricultural area: corn, wheat, apples; livestock. Employment by occupation: 7.1% management, 9.2% professional, 16.4% services, 24.1% sales, 0.6% farming, 5.7% construction, 36.9% production (2000).
Income: Per capita income: $14,290 (2000); Median household income: $28,828 (2000); Poverty rate: 18.6% (2000).
Taxes: Total city taxes per capita: $46 (1997); City property taxes per capita: $32 (1997).
Education: High school graduation rate: 80.3% (2000); College graduation rate: 12.3% (2000).

School District(s)

West Richland C U School Districtict 2 (PK-12)
2000 Enrollment: 498 618-723-2334

Housing: Homeownership rate: 73.2% (2000); Median home value: $44,200 (2000); Median rent: $269 per month (2000); Median age of housing: 41 years (2000).
Newspapers: The County Commoner (1 x week)
Transportation: Commute to work: 91.0% car, 0.0% public transportation, 3.1% walk, 2.8% work from home (2000); Travel time to work: 36.9% less than 15 minutes, 40.8% 15 to 30 minutes, 16.6% 30 to 45 minutes, 1.6% 45 to 60 minutes, 4.1% 60 minutes or more (2000)

OLNEY (city). Covers a land area of 5.760 square miles and a water area of <.001 square miles. Located at 38.73° N. Lat.; 88.08° W. Long. Elevation is 490 feet.
History: Olney was named for John Olney, lawyer and officer in the Civil War. It developed as a shipping and trading center, and as the seat of Richland County. In 1902 a naturalist brought a pair of albino squirrels to Olney and set them loose. Soon Olney became known as "the home of white squirrels," as thousands of these squirrels took up residence in the parks and gardens.
Population: 8,631 (2000); Race: 98.0% White, 0.2% Black, 0.4% Asian, 0.0% American Indian and Alaska Native, 0.9% Hispanic of any race, 0.7% two or more races (2000); Density: 1,498.4 persons per square mile (2000); Age: 23.8% under 18, 20.5% over 64 (2000); Marriage status: 23.1% never married, 51.6% now married, 11.3% widowed, 14.0% divorced (2000); Foreign born: 0.9% (2000); Ancestry (includes multiple ancestries): 24.9% German, 19.1% United States or American, 9.2% English, 7.7% Irish, 6.8% Other groups (2000).
Economy: Single-family building permits issued: 19 (2001) / 15 (2000); Multi-family building permits issued: 42 (2001) / 30 (2000); Employment by occupation: 13.0% management, 17.5% professional, 21.0% services, 24.2% sales, 0.2% farming, 8.4% construction, 15.6% production (2000).
Income: Per capita income: $16,218 (2000); Median household income: $28,084 (2000); Poverty rate: 17.0% (2000).
Taxes: Total city taxes per capita: $104 (1997); City property taxes per capita: $93 (1997).
Education: High school graduation rate: 83.1% (2000); College graduation rate: 16.3% (2000).

School District(s)

Clay/Cwford/Jsper/Lwrnce/Rhland (06-12)
2000 Enrollment: 61 618-392-4631
East Richland C U School District 1 (PK-12)
2000 Enrollment: 2,208 618-395-2324

Two-year College(s)

Illinois Eastern Community Colleges-Olney Central College (Public)
2001 Enrollment: 1,617 618-393-2982
2001 Tuition: In-state $5,618; Out-of-state $6,961

Housing: Homeownership rate: 69.0% (2000); Median home value: $57,600 (2000); Median rent: $295 per month (2000); Median age of housing: 42 years (2000).
Hospitals: Richland Memorial Hospital (137 beds)
Newspapers: Olney Daily Mail (6 x week)
Transportation: Commute to work: 94.3% car, 0.2% public transportation, 2.2% walk, 2.6% work from home (2000); Travel time to work: 71.8% less

than 15 minutes, 14.8% 15 to 30 minutes, 8.0% 30 to 45 minutes, 2.9% 45 to 60 minutes, 2.5% 60 minutes or more (2000)
Airports: Olney-Noble
Additional Information Contacts
Olney Chamber of Commerce 618-392-2241

PARKERSBURG (village). Covers a land area of 0.746 square miles and a water area of 0 square miles. Located at 38.59° N. Lat.; 88.05° W. Long. Elevation is 480 feet.
Population: 234 (2000); Race: 98.0% White, 0.0% Black, 0.0% Asian, 0.0% American Indian and Alaska Native, 0.0% Hispanic of any race, 2.0% two or more races (2000); Density: 313.6 persons per square mile (2000); Age: 19.1% under 18, 19.1% over 64 (2000); Marriage status: 17.6% never married, 58.0% now married, 10.8% widowed, 13.6% divorced (2000); Foreign born: 0.0% (2000); Ancestry (includes multiple ancestries): 15.7% United States or American, 13.2% German, 6.4% English, 4.9% Irish, 4.9% Dutch (2000).
Economy: In agricultural area: corn, wheat, apples; livestock. Employment by occupation: 4.5% management, 7.9% professional, 4.5% services, 22.5% sales, 0.0% farming, 9.0% construction, 51.7% production (2000).
Income: Per capita income: $14,581 (2000); Median household income: $23,250 (2000); Poverty rate: 18.6% (2000).
Taxes: Total city taxes per capita: $9 (1997); City property taxes per capita: $9 (1997).
Education: High school graduation rate: 70.9% (2000); College graduation rate: 0.0% (2000).
Housing: Homeownership rate: 86.0% (2000); Median home value: $34,600 (2000); Median rent: $186 per month (2000); Median age of housing: 46 years (2000).
Transportation: Commute to work: 95.4% car, 0.0% public transportation, 2.3% walk, 2.3% work from home (2000); Travel time to work: 43.5% less than 15 minutes, 48.2% 15 to 30 minutes, 5.9% 30 to 45 minutes, 2.4% 45 to 60 minutes, 0.0% 60 minutes or more (2000)

Rock Island County

Located in northwestern Illinois; bounded on the north and west by the Mississippi River and the Iowa border, and partly on the east by the Rock River. Covers a land area of 426.80 square miles, a water area of 24.40 square miles, and is located in the Central Time Zone. The county government was organized in 1831. County seat is Rock Island.

Rock Island County is part of the Davenport-Moline-Rock Island, IA-IL MSA. The entire metro area includes: Henry County, IL; Rock Island County, IL; Scott County, IA

Weather Station: Moline Quad City Airport Elevation: 590 feet

	Jan	Feb	Mar	Apr	May	Jun	Jul	Aug	Sep	Oct	Nov	Dec
High	29	35	48	61	73	83	86	84	76	64	48	35
Low	12	18	29	39	50	60	65	62	53	41	30	19
Precip	1.6	1.4	3.0	3.8	4.5	4.5	4.1	4.5	3.5	2.8	2.7	2.2
Snow	9.8	6.7	5.2	1.6	tr	tr	tr	0.0	tr	0.2	3.0	7.3

High and Low temperatures in degrees Fahrenheit; Precipitation and Snow in inches

Population: 149,374 (2000); Race: 85.5% White, 7.1% Black, 1.0% Asian, 0.4% American Indian and Alaska Native, 8.7% Hispanic of any race, 2.0% two or more races (2000); Density: 350.0 persons per square mile (2000); Age: 23.8% under 18, 15.0% over 64 (2000).
Religion: Five largest groups: 18.6% Catholic Church, 4.5% Evangelical Lutheran Church in America, 3.8% The United Methodist Church, 3.5% Lutheran Church—Missouri Synod, 2.3% International Church of the Foursquare Gospel (2000).
Economy: Unemployment rate: 5.1% (11/2002); Total civilian labor force: 72,772 (11/2002); Leading industries: 13.6% manufacturing; 12.5% retail trade; 12.1% health care and social assistance (2000); Companies that employ more than 1,000 persons: 5 (2000); Companies that employ more than 100 persons: 110 (2000); Farms: 618 totaling 170,072 acres (1997); Minority business ownership rate: 7.2% (1997); Women business ownership rate: 26.5% (1997); Retail sales per capita: $9,640 (1997). Single-family building permits issued: 222 (2001) / 206 (2000); Multi-family building permits issued: 10 (2001) / 14 (2000).
Income: Per capita income: $20,164 (2000); Median household income: $38,608 (2000); Poverty rate: 10.7% (2000); Bankruptcy rate: 6.03% (2001).
Taxes: Total county taxes per capita: $70 (2000); County property taxes per capita: $68 (2000).
Education: High school graduation rate: 82.6% (2000); College graduation rate: 17.1% (2000).
Housing: Homeownership rate: 69.7% (2000); Median home value: $78,900 (2000); Median rent: $376 per month (2000); Median age of housing: 43 years (2000).
Health: Birth rate: 131.1 per 10,000 population (1998); Age adjusted death rate: 90.9 per 10,000 population (1999); Age adjusted cancer mortality rate: 227.3 deaths per 100,000 population (1999). Air Quality Index: 83% good, 17% moderate, 0% unhealthy (percent of days in 2000). Number of physicians: 17.2 per 10,000 population (1999); Number of hospital beds: 29.9 per 10,000 population (1999).
Elections: 2000 Presidential election results: 58.3% Gore, 38.7% Bush, 2.1% Nader, 0.6% Buchanan
National and State Parks: Black Hawk State Historical Site; Campbells Island State Park
Additional Information Contacts
Rock Island County Government Offices 309-786-4451
Illinois Quad City Area Realtor Association 309-797-4158
Illinois Quad City Chamber 309-757-5416
Milan Chamber of Commerce 309-787-3144
Quad Cities Convention Bureau. 309-788-7800

Rock Island County Communities

ANDALUSIA (village). Covers a land area of 0.717 square miles and a water area of 0.004 square miles. Located at 41.44° N. Lat.; 90.72° W. Long. Elevation is 565 feet.
History: Andalusia was the location on the Mississippi River of Clark's Ferry which gave passage to Buffalo, Iowa, to thousands of settlers in the 1830's.
Population: 1,050 (2000); Race: 97.4% White, 1.0% Black, 0.0% Asian, 0.0% American Indian and Alaska Native, 1.0% Hispanic of any race, 1.4% two or more races (2000); Density: 1,463.4 persons per square mile (2000); Age: 24.5% under 18, 9.4% over 64 (2000); Marriage status: 21.8% never married, 60.2% now married, 6.9% widowed, 11.1% divorced (2000); Foreign born: 1.4% (2000); Ancestry (includes multiple ancestries): 32.8% German, 16.4% Irish, 12.4% United States or American, 11.0% English, 5.5% Swedish (2000).
Economy: Single-family building permits issued: 3 (2001) / 2 (2000); Multi-family building permits issued: 0 (2001) / 0 (2000); Employment by occupation: 11.2% management, 14.2% professional, 13.4% services, 29.0% sales, 0.5% farming, 9.5% construction, 22.2% production (2000).
Income: Per capita income: $20,626 (2000); Median household income: $46,552 (2000); Poverty rate: 2.9% (2000).
Taxes: Total city taxes per capita: $194 (1997); City property taxes per capita: $127 (1997).
Education: High school graduation rate: 90.3% (2000); College graduation rate: 13.0% (2000).
Housing: Homeownership rate: 85.0% (2000); Median home value: $83,000 (2000); Median rent: $383 per month (2000); Median age of housing: 33 years (2000).
Transportation: Commute to work: 96.2% car, 0.2% public transportation, 0.7% walk, 2.0% work from home (2000); Travel time to work: 16.6% less than 15 minutes, 48.6% 15 to 30 minutes, 28.7% 30 to 45 minutes, 3.9% 45 to 60 minutes, 2.2% 60 minutes or more (2000)

CARBON CLIFF (village). Covers a land area of 2.041 square miles and a water area of 0 square miles. Located at 41.49° N. Lat.; 90.39° W. Long. Elevation is 590 feet.
Population: 1,689 (2000); Race: 89.8% White, 5.4% Black, 0.7% Asian, 0.7% American Indian and Alaska Native, 4.8% Hispanic of any race, 2.7% two or more races (2000); Density: 827.4 persons per square mile (2000); Age: 26.7% under 18, 10.2% over 64 (2000); Marriage status: 24.4% never married, 56.0% now married, 4.3% widowed, 15.3% divorced (2000); Foreign born: 2.1% (2000); Ancestry (includes multiple ancestries): 24.7% German, 14.4% Other groups, 14.1% Irish, 13.4% United States or American, 8.6% Swedish (2000).
Economy: Agriculture: cattle, corn, soybeans; dairying. Single-family building permits issued: 1 (2001) / 8 (2000); Multi-family building permits issued: 0 (2001) / 0 (2000); Employment by occupation: 8.9% management, 11.1% professional, 18.7% services, 28.9% sales, 0.0% farming, 10.7% construction, 21.6% production (2000).
Income: Per capita income: $16,998 (2000); Median household income: $35,921 (2000); Poverty rate: 12.0% (2000).

Taxes: Total city taxes per capita: $194 (1997); City property taxes per capita: $133 (1997).
Education: High school graduation rate: 81.4% (2000); College graduation rate: 11.0% (2000).
Housing: Homeownership rate: 68.5% (2000); Median home value: $68,100 (2000); Median rent: $462 per month (2000); Median age of housing: 38 years (2000).
Transportation: Commute to work: 93.4% car, 0.6% public transportation, 2.2% walk, 2.1% work from home (2000); Travel time to work: 36.3% less than 15 minutes, 41.6% 15 to 30 minutes, 16.3% 30 to 45 minutes, 1.3% 45 to 60 minutes, 4.6% 60 minutes or more (2000)

COAL VALLEY (village). Covers a land area of 2.861 square miles and a water area of 0 square miles. Located at 41.44° N. Lat.; 90.45° W. Long. Elevation is 700 feet.
Population: 3,606 (2000); Race: 98.0% White, 0.5% Black, 0.4% Asian, 0.1% American Indian and Alaska Native, 2.5% Hispanic of any race, 0.5% two or more races (2000); Density: 1,260.5 persons per square mile (2000); Age: 24.7% under 18, 9.2% over 64 (2000); Marriage status: 20.8% never married, 62.7% now married, 3.6% widowed, 12.9% divorced (2000); Foreign born: 1.5% (2000); Ancestry (includes multiple ancestries): 26.1% German, 14.4% Irish, 11.6% English, 9.6% Swedish, 9.5% United States or American (2000).
Economy: In agricultural area. Single-family building permits issued: 31 (2001) / 36 (2000); Multi-family building permits issued: 0 (2001) / 0 (2000); Employment by occupation: 9.1% management, 18.6% professional, 15.0% services, 29.9% sales, 0.0% farming, 12.2% construction, 15.1% production (2000).
Income: Per capita income: $20,996 (2000); Median household income: $49,228 (2000); Poverty rate: 7.4% (2000).
Taxes: Total city taxes per capita: $114 (1997); City property taxes per capita: $39 (1997).
Education: High school graduation rate: 85.2% (2000); College graduation rate: 17.6% (2000).
Housing: Homeownership rate: 91.7% (2000); Median home value: $99,000 (2000); Median rent: $379 per month (2000); Median age of housing: 28 years (2000).
Transportation: Commute to work: 96.2% car, 0.3% public transportation, 0.8% walk, 2.4% work from home (2000); Travel time to work: 24.9% less than 15 minutes, 62.0% 15 to 30 minutes, 9.8% 30 to 45 minutes, 1.3% 45 to 60 minutes, 2.1% 60 minutes or more (2000)

CORDOVA (village). Covers a land area of 0.562 square miles and a water area of 0.005 square miles. Located at 41.67° N. Lat.; 90.32° W. Long. Elevation is 600 feet.
Population: 633 (2000); Race: 95.7% White, 0.8% Black, 0.0% Asian, 0.0% American Indian and Alaska Native, 3.8% Hispanic of any race, 2.1% two or more races (2000); Density: 1,125.9 persons per square mile (2000); Age: 24.3% under 18, 11.7% over 64 (2000); Marriage status: 19.4% never married, 57.9% now married, 8.4% widowed, 14.4% divorced (2000); Foreign born: 1.0% (2000); Ancestry (includes multiple ancestries): 23.8% German, 19.2% Irish, 14.5% English, 7.3% Other groups, 6.2% Belgian (2000).
Economy: Single-family building permits issued: 15 (2001) / 2 (2000); Multi-family building permits issued: 0 (2001) / 0 (2000); Employment by occupation: 10.3% management, 12.2% professional, 19.1% services, 21.0% sales, 0.6% farming, 21.3% construction, 15.4% production (2000).
Income: Per capita income: $21,442 (2000); Median household income: $50,000 (2000); Poverty rate: 6.2% (2000).
Taxes: Total city taxes per capita: $53 (1997); City property taxes per capita: $27 (1997).
Education: High school graduation rate: 86.8% (2000); College graduation rate: 13.4% (2000).
Housing: Homeownership rate: 82.9% (2000); Median home value: $84,700 (2000); Median rent: $315 per month (2000); Median age of housing: 40 years (2000).
Transportation: Commute to work: 94.6% car, 0.6% public transportation, 3.2% walk, 1.6% work from home (2000); Travel time to work: 23.4% less than 15 minutes, 31.4% 15 to 30 minutes, 30.4% 30 to 45 minutes, 8.7% 45 to 60 minutes, 6.1% 60 minutes or more (2000)

COYNE CENTER (CDP). Covers a land area of 1.793 square miles and a water area of 0 square miles. Located at 41.40° N. Lat.; 90.56° W. Long. Elevation is 745 feet.
Population: 906 (2000); Race: 97.8% White, 1.0% Black, 0.0% Asian, 0.5% American Indian and Alaska Native, 0.3% Hispanic of any race, 0.4% two or more races (2000); Density: 505.4 persons per square mile (2000); Age: 20.9% under 18, 16.3% over 64 (2000); Marriage status: 15.4% never married, 66.2% now married, 8.2% widowed, 10.2% divorced (2000); Foreign born: 1.7% (2000); Ancestry (includes multiple ancestries): 30.4% German, 16.6% Irish, 13.0% English, 11.0% United States or American, 7.7% Other groups (2000).
Economy: Employment by occupation: 10.3% management, 13.0% professional, 10.1% services, 26.2% sales, 0.0% farming, 18.8% construction, 21.6% production (2000).
Income: Per capita income: $19,093 (2000); Median household income: $50,000 (2000); Poverty rate: 4.3% (2000).
Education: High school graduation rate: 85.5% (2000); College graduation rate: 9.8% (2000).
Housing: Homeownership rate: 93.7% (2000); Median home value: $80,900 (2000); Median rent: $375 per month (2000); Median age of housing: 39 years (2000).
Transportation: Commute to work: 96.4% car, 0.0% public transportation, 0.6% walk, 2.9% work from home (2000); Travel time to work: 17.1% less than 15 minutes, 63.0% 15 to 30 minutes, 15.6% 30 to 45 minutes, 0.0% 45 to 60 minutes, 4.3% 60 minutes or more (2000)

EAST MOLINE (city). Covers a land area of 9.017 square miles and a water area of 0 square miles. Located at 41.51° N. Lat.; 90.43° W. Long. Elevation is 700 feet.
History: East Moline was incorporated as a city in 1907, and developed as an industrial center for nearby Moline and Rock Island. An International Harvester plant was a major employer.
Population: 20,333 (2000); Race: 80.1% White, 6.7% Black, 2.4% Asian, 0.7% American Indian and Alaska Native, 15.3% Hispanic of any race, 2.5% two or more races (2000); Density: 2,254.9 persons per square mile (2000); Age: 24.8% under 18, 16.8% over 64 (2000); Marriage status: 25.1% never married, 52.8% now married, 9.4% widowed, 12.7% divorced (2000); Foreign born: 8.2% (2000); Ancestry (includes multiple ancestries): 24.9% Other groups, 22.3% German, 11.0% Irish, 9.0% English, 7.3% Belgian (2000).
Vital Statistics: Birth rate: 147.5 per 10,000 population (1998)
Economy: Single-family building permits issued: 20 (2001) / 11 (2000); Multi-family building permits issued: 0 (2001) / 4 (2000); Employment by occupation: 10.3% management, 17.7% professional, 19.0% services, 24.2% sales, 0.0% farming, 8.4% construction, 20.4% production (2000).
Income: Per capita income: $18,245 (2000); Median household income: $35,836 (2000); Poverty rate: 13.9% (2000).
Taxes: Total city taxes per capita: $239 (1997); City property taxes per capita: $163 (1997).
Education: High school graduation rate: 80.8% (2000); College graduation rate: 15.5% (2000).

School District(s)

Black Hawk Area Special Education District (07-12)
2000 Enrollment: 37 309-796-2500
East Moline School District 37 (PK-08)
2000 Enrollment: 2,500 309-755-4533
United Township HS District 30 (09-12)
2000 Enrollment: 1,868 309-752-1633

Housing: Homeownership rate: 64.9% (2000); Median home value: $78,100 (2000); Median rent: $353 per month (2000); Median age of housing: 37 years (2000).
Newspapers: Thrifty Nickel (1 x week)
Transportation: Commute to work: 94.6% car, 1.1% public transportation, 1.4% walk, 2.0% work from home (2000); Travel time to work: 39.5% less than 15 minutes, 47.1% 15 to 30 minutes, 10.5% 30 to 45 minutes, 1.0% 45 to 60 minutes, 1.9% 60 minutes or more (2000)

HAMPTON (village). Covers a land area of 1.580 square miles and a water area of 0 square miles. Located at 41.55° N. Lat.; 90.40° W. Long. Elevation is 580 feet.
Population: 1,626 (2000); Race: 96.1% White, 0.0% Black, 1.1% Asian, 0.6% American Indian and Alaska Native, 3.6% Hispanic of any race, 1.4% two or more races (2000); Density: 1,028.8 persons per square mile (2000); Age: 23.3% under 18, 15.5% over 64 (2000); Marriage status: 19.5% never married, 62.2% now married, 6.7% widowed, 11.5% divorced (2000); Foreign born: 5.1% (2000); Ancestry (includes multiple ancestries): 28.3% German, 15.1% Irish, 13.3% English, 10.9% Swedish, 10.5% Other groups (2000).
Economy: Metal electroplating. Single-family building permits issued: 5 (2001) / 7 (2000); Multi-family building permits issued: 0 (2001) / 0 (2000); Employment by occupation: 11.7% management, 15.7% professional, 14.6%

services, 32.0% sales, 0.0% farming, 7.8% construction, 18.1% production (2000).
Income: Per capita income: $22,492 (2000); Median household income: $48,438 (2000); Poverty rate: 7.3% (2000).
Taxes: Total city taxes per capita: $147 (1997); City property taxes per capita: $97 (1997).
Education: High school graduation rate: 85.3% (2000); College graduation rate: 14.1% (2000).

School District(s)

Hampton School District 29 (KG-08)
2000 Enrollment: 190 309-755-0693
Housing: Homeownership rate: 87.3% (2000); Median home value: $85,900 (2000); Median rent: $456 per month (2000); Median age of housing: 34 years (2000).
Transportation: Commute to work: 95.9% car, 1.6% public transportation, 0.7% walk, 1.8% work from home (2000); Travel time to work: 24.2% less than 15 minutes, 51.2% 15 to 30 minutes, 18.0% 30 to 45 minutes, 0.6% 45 to 60 minutes, 6.0% 60 minutes or more (2000)

HILLSDALE (village). Covers a land area of 0.754 square miles and a water area of 0.025 square miles. Located at 41.61° N. Lat.; 90.17° W. Long. Elevation is 580 feet.
Population: 588 (2000); Race: 95.4% White, 0.0% Black, 1.3% Asian, 1.1% American Indian and Alaska Native, 2.7% Hispanic of any race, 0.0% two or more races (2000); Density: 780.2 persons per square mile (2000); Age: 25.7% under 18, 9.1% over 64 (2000); Marriage status: 22.1% never married, 51.4% now married, 6.5% widowed, 20.0% divorced (2000); Foreign born: 0.0% (2000); Ancestry (includes multiple ancestries): 30.2% German, 12.0% Irish, 8.9% English, 7.9% Other groups, 7.5% Dutch (2000).
Economy: Corn, soybeans; cattle, hogs; dairying. Manufacturing: firearms, wood products, meatpacking. Single-family building permits issued: 0 (2001) / 0 (2000); Multi-family building permits issued: 0 (2001) / 0 (2000); Employment by occupation: 6.0% management, 9.7% professional, 23.3% services, 18.2% sales, 0.0% farming, 11.6% construction, 31.1% production (2000).
Income: Per capita income: $21,772 (2000); Median household income: $46,964 (2000); Poverty rate: 11.0% (2000).
Taxes: Total city taxes per capita: $91 (1997); City property taxes per capita: $31 (1997).
Education: High school graduation rate: 81.5% (2000); College graduation rate: 5.5% (2000).
Housing: Homeownership rate: 76.1% (2000); Median home value: $71,800 (2000); Median rent: $371 per month (2000); Median age of housing: 39 years (2000).
Transportation: Commute to work: 91.8% car, 0.0% public transportation, 3.2% walk, 3.2% work from home (2000); Travel time to work: 20.3% less than 15 minutes, 35.6% 15 to 30 minutes, 30.7% 30 to 45 minutes, 8.8% 45 to 60 minutes, 4.6% 60 minutes or more (2000)

ILLINOIS CITY (unincorporated postal area, zip code 61259). Covers a land area of 61.147 square miles and a water area of 0.376 square miles. Located at 41.36° N. Lat.; 90.92° W. Long. Elevation is 768 feet.
Population: 1,209 (2000); Race: 95.5% White, 0.0% Black, 0.5% Asian, 0.4% American Indian and Alaska Native, 3.1% Hispanic of any race, 1.6% two or more races (2000); Density: 19.8 persons per square mile (2000); Age: 21.0% under 18, 15.1% over 64 (2000); Marriage status: 18.7% never married, 74.0% now married, 3.4% widowed, 4.0% divorced (2000); Foreign born: 0.9% (2000); Ancestry (includes multiple ancestries): 26.9% German, 12.9% English, 9.8% Irish, 7.0% Swedish, 6.0% Other groups (2000).
Economy: Employment by occupation: 10.1% management, 15.3% professional, 11.5% services, 26.8% sales, 1.9% farming, 11.2% construction, 23.3% production (2000).
Income: Per capita income: $21,311 (2000); Median household income: $46,741 (2000); Poverty rate: 3.8% (2000).
Education: High school graduation rate: 78.3% (2000); College graduation rate: 15.7% (2000).
Housing: Homeownership rate: 83.4% (2000); Median home value: $107,400 (2000); Median rent: $438 per month (2000); Median age of housing: 45 years (2000).
Transportation: Commute to work: 95.9% car, 0.0% public transportation, 0.6% walk, 3.5% work from home (2000); Travel time to work: 9.5% less than 15 minutes, 56.6% 15 to 30 minutes, 26.1% 30 to 45 minutes, 5.9% 45 to 60 minutes, 2.0% 60 minutes or more (2000)

MILAN (village). Covers a land area of 5.537 square miles and a water area of 0.514 square miles. Located at 41.44° N. Lat.; 90.56° W. Long. Elevation is 565 feet.
History: Incorporated 1865.
Population: 5,348 (2000); Race: 91.1% White, 3.8% Black, 0.1% Asian, 0.5% American Indian and Alaska Native, 3.8% Hispanic of any race, 2.0% two or more races (2000); Density: 965.9 persons per square mile (2000); Age: 23.3% under 18, 15.9% over 64 (2000); Marriage status: 22.7% never married, 52.9% now married, 9.4% widowed, 15.1% divorced (2000); Foreign born: 1.1% (2000); Ancestry (includes multiple ancestries): 25.1% German, 14.2% Irish, 14.0% Other groups, 9.4% United States or American, 8.5% English (2000).
Economy: In agricultural area: corn, soybeans; cattle, hogs; dairying. Bituminous-coal-mining area. Manufacturing: forklift components, printing, packaging and assembly, lighting fixtures. Quad Cities Airport to East. Single-family building permits issued: 0 (2001) / 3 (2000); Multi-family building permits issued: 0 (2001) / 0 (2000); Employment by occupation: 8.6% management, 12.1% professional, 21.1% services, 30.5% sales, 0.4% farming, 8.9% construction, 18.5% production (2000).
Income: Per capita income: $17,608 (2000); Median household income: $34,556 (2000); Poverty rate: 10.7% (2000).
Taxes: Total city taxes per capita: $199 (1997); City property taxes per capita: $184 (1997).
Education: High school graduation rate: 79.5% (2000); College graduation rate: 8.1% (2000).
Housing: Homeownership rate: 68.5% (2000); Median home value: $70,700 (2000); Median rent: $287 per month (2000); Median age of housing: 34 years (2000).
Transportation: Commute to work: 95.0% car, 0.2% public transportation, 3.0% walk, 1.5% work from home (2000); Travel time to work: 35.7% less than 15 minutes, 49.2% 15 to 30 minutes, 11.8% 30 to 45 minutes, 1.6% 45 to 60 minutes, 1.7% 60 minutes or more (2000)
Additional Information Contacts
Milan Chamber of Commerce 309-787-3144

MOLINE (city). Covers a land area of 15.599 square miles and a water area of 0.222 square miles. Located at 41.49° N. Lat.; 90.50° W. Long. Elevation is 600 feet.
History: Moline was laid out in 1843. An early resident was John Deere, who had been producing plows in Grand Detour, but moved to Moline for the availability of steel for his machinery. The John Deere plants founded here soon became a major employer. Moline was incorporated as a town in 1848, and as a city in 1872.
Population: 43,768 (2000); Race: 88.5% White, 2.8% Black, 1.2% Asian, 0.3% American Indian and Alaska Native, 12.1% Hispanic of any race, 2.0% two or more races (2000); Density: 2,805.7 persons per square mile (2000); Age: 23.9% under 18, 15.3% over 64 (2000); Marriage status: 24.8% never married, 55.2% now married, 7.6% widowed, 12.4% divorced (2000); Foreign born: 7.1% (2000); Ancestry (includes multiple ancestries): 24.1% German, 18.2% Other groups, 13.9% Irish, 10.0% English, 9.3% Swedish (2000).
Vital Statistics: Birth rate: 142.3 per 10,000 population (1998)
Economy: Unemployment rate: 4.6% (11/2002); Total civilian labor force: 21,531 (11/2002); Single-family building permits issued: 34 (2001) / 37 (2000); Multi-family building permits issued: 0 (2001) / 8 (2000); Employment by occupation: 11.0% management, 18.2% professional, 17.5% services, 27.3% sales, 0.1% farming, 7.4% construction, 18.4% production (2000).
Income: Per capita income: $21,557 (2000); Median household income: $39,363 (2000); Poverty rate: 9.5% (2000).
Taxes: Total city taxes per capita: $384 (2000); City property taxes per capita: $233 (2000).
Education: High school graduation rate: 84.1% (2000); College graduation rate: 20.8% (2000).

School District(s)

Moline Unit School District 40 (PK-12)
2000 Enrollment: 7,960 309-736-2100

Four-year College(s)

Trinity College of Nursing (Private, Not-for-profit)
2001 Enrollment: n/a 309-779-7700
2001 Tuition: In-state $3,874; Out-of-state $3,874

Two-year College(s)

Black Hawk College (Public)
2001 Enrollment: 6,248 309-796-1311
2001 Tuition: In-state $4,200; Out-of-state $7,770

Trinity School of Radiography (Private, Not-for-profit)
2001 Enrollment: n/a 309-779-7700
2001 Tuition: In-state $3,355; Out-of-state $3,355

Housing: Homeownership rate: 67.3% (2000); Median home value: $80,500 (2000); Median rent: $405 per month (2000); Median age of housing: 48 years (2000).
Newspapers: The Dispatch (7 x week)
Transportation: Commute to work: 93.6% car, 1.9% public transportation, 1.6% walk, 2.1% work from home (2000); Travel time to work: 43.5% less than 15 minutes, 45.6% 15 to 30 minutes, 6.2% 30 to 45 minutes, 1.7% 45 to 60 minutes, 2.9% 60 minutes or more (2000); Amtrak: Service available.
Airports: Quad City International (primary service/small hub)
Additional Information Contacts
Illinois Quad City Area Realtor Association 309-797-4158
Illinois Quad City Chamber 309-757-5416
Quad Cities Convention Bureau 309-788-7800

OAK GROVE (village). Aka Oak Grove Park. Covers a land area of 0.631 square miles and a water area of 0 square miles. Located at 41.41° N. Lat.; 90.57° W. Long. Elevation is 721 feet.
Population: 1,318 (2000); Race: 32.1% White, 57.8% Black, 0.4% Asian, 0.8% American Indian and Alaska Native, 10.5% Hispanic of any race, 0.0% two or more races (2000); Density: 2,088.2 persons per square mile (2000); Age: 1.8% under 18, 3.4% over 64 (2000); Marriage status: 22.5% never married, 43.4% now married, 0.5% widowed, 33.5% divorced (2000); Foreign born: 1.2% (2000); Ancestry (includes multiple ancestries): 3.9% German, 2.1% Irish, 1.7% Other groups, 1.0% Swedish, 0.7% English (2000).
Economy: Residential suburb in agricultural area: corn, soybeans; livestock. Single-family building permits issued: 0 (2001) / 0 (2000); Multi-family building permits issued: 0 (2001) / 0 (2000); Employment by occupation: 7.8% management, 7.0% professional, 21.7% services, 21.7% sales, 0.0% farming, 14.0% construction, 27.9% production (2000).
Income: Per capita income: $15,045 (2000); Median household income: $30,833 (2000); Poverty rate: 13.3% (2000).
Taxes: Total city taxes per capita: $19 (1997); City property taxes per capita: $0 (1997).
Education: High school graduation rate: 34.5% (2000); College graduation rate: 1.1% (2000).
Housing: Homeownership rate: 45.4% (2000); Median home value: $100,000 (2000); Median rent: $263 per month (2000); Median age of housing: 34 years (2000).
Transportation: Commute to work: 96.1% car, 0.8% public transportation, 0.0% walk, 1.6% work from home (2000); Travel time to work: 18.9% less than 15 minutes, 67.7% 15 to 30 minutes, 4.7% 30 to 45 minutes, 4.7% 45 to 60 minutes, 3.9% 60 minutes or more (2000)

PORT BYRON (village). Covers a land area of 2.311 square miles and a water area of 0 square miles. Located at 41.61° N. Lat.; 90.33° W. Long. Elevation is 590 feet.
Population: 1,535 (2000); Race: 98.8% White, 0.2% Black, 0.0% Asian, 0.2% American Indian and Alaska Native, 0.7% Hispanic of any race, 0.7% two or more races (2000); Density: 664.3 persons per square mile (2000); Age: 25.3% under 18, 14.6% over 64 (2000); Marriage status: 20.0% never married, 63.2% now married, 6.7% widowed, 10.1% divorced (2000); Foreign born: 1.4% (2000); Ancestry (includes multiple ancestries): 32.1% German, 15.7% Irish, 12.1% English, 8.2% Swedish, 5.6% Belgian (2000).
Economy: In agricultural area. Single-family building permits issued: 12 (2001) / 6 (2000); Multi-family building permits issued: 0 (2001) / 2 (2000); Employment by occupation: 15.2% management, 15.1% professional, 11.0% services, 27.1% sales, 0.5% farming, 14.3% construction, 16.8% production (2000).
Income: Per capita income: $24,363 (2000); Median household income: $47,768 (2000); Poverty rate: 4.0% (2000).
Taxes: Total city taxes per capita: $163 (1997); City property taxes per capita: $112 (1997).
Education: High school graduation rate: 91.9% (2000); College graduation rate: 19.9% (2000).

School District(s)

Riverdale C U School District 100 (KG-12)
2000 Enrollment: 1,287 309-523-3184

Housing: Homeownership rate: 75.6% (2000); Median home value: $97,600 (2000); Median rent: $289 per month (2000); Median age of housing: 35 years (2000).
Transportation: Commute to work: 95.0% car, 0.0% public transportation, 2.1% walk, 2.6% work from home (2000); Travel time to work: 23.6% less than 15 minutes, 44.5% 15 to 30 minutes, 25.5% 30 to 45 minutes, 2.8% 45 to 60 minutes, 3.5% 60 minutes or more (2000)

RAPIDS CITY (village). Covers a land area of 1.530 square miles and a water area of 0 square miles. Located at 41.58° N. Lat.; 90.34° W. Long. Elevation is 590 feet.
Population: 953 (2000); Race: 98.7% White, 0.0% Black, 0.0% Asian, 0.0% American Indian and Alaska Native, 1.9% Hispanic of any race, 1.3% two or more races (2000); Density: 623.0 persons per square mile (2000); Age: 23.4% under 18, 11.7% over 64 (2000); Marriage status: 18.1% never married, 65.0% now married, 6.0% widowed, 10.9% divorced (2000); Foreign born: 0.0% (2000); Ancestry (includes multiple ancestries): 27.2% German, 11.1% Irish, 9.7% English, 7.4% Belgian, 6.8% United States or American (2000).
Economy: In agricultural area. Single-family building permits issued: 4 (2001) / 3 (2000); Multi-family building permits issued: 0 (2001) / 0 (2000); Employment by occupation: 15.8% management, 19.1% professional, 11.0% services, 21.6% sales, 0.0% farming, 12.2% construction, 20.3% production (2000).
Income: Per capita income: $24,499 (2000); Median household income: $44,474 (2000); Poverty rate: 3.0% (2000).
Taxes: Total city taxes per capita: $73 (1997); City property taxes per capita: $39 (1997).
Education: High school graduation rate: 87.7% (2000); College graduation rate: 18.0% (2000).
Housing: Homeownership rate: 90.7% (2000); Median home value: $88,500 (2000); Median rent: $393 per month (2000); Median age of housing: 33 years (2000).
Transportation: Commute to work: 96.4% car, 0.7% public transportation, 1.4% walk, 1.6% work from home (2000); Travel time to work: 15.2% less than 15 minutes, 56.6% 15 to 30 minutes, 26.2% 30 to 45 minutes, 0.7% 45 to 60 minutes, 1.4% 60 minutes or more (2000)

REYNOLDS (village). Covers a land area of 0.369 square miles and a water area of 0 square miles. Located at 41.33° N. Lat.; 90.67° W. Long. Elevation is 800 feet.
Population: 508 (2000); Race: 100.0% White, 0.0% Black, 0.0% Asian, 0.0% American Indian and Alaska Native, 1.0% Hispanic of any race, 0.0% two or more races (2000); Density: 1,377.6 persons per square mile (2000); Age: 24.4% under 18, 15.6% over 64 (2000); Marriage status: 16.5% never married, 60.7% now married, 6.2% widowed, 16.5% divorced (2000); Foreign born: 0.0% (2000); Ancestry (includes multiple ancestries): 24.2% German, 22.2% Irish, 18.6% English, 9.4% Other groups, 8.2% Swedish (2000).
Economy: In agricultural area. Single-family building permits issued: 0 (2001) / 0 (2000); Multi-family building permits issued: 0 (2001) / 0 (2000); Employment by occupation: 7.3% management, 12.2% professional, 12.2% services, 35.0% sales, 0.8% farming, 11.8% construction, 20.7% production (2000).
Income: Per capita income: $21,804 (2000); Median household income: $42,917 (2000); Poverty rate: 10.2% (2000).
Taxes: Total city taxes per capita: $130 (1997); City property taxes per capita: $127 (1997).
Education: High school graduation rate: 91.7% (2000); College graduation rate: 13.6% (2000).
Housing: Homeownership rate: 80.4% (2000); Median home value: $79,300 (2000); Median rent: $346 per month (2000); Median age of housing: 57 years (2000).
Transportation: Commute to work: 92.2% car, 0.0% public transportation, 2.9% walk, 4.9% work from home (2000); Travel time to work: 14.7% less than 15 minutes, 35.1% 15 to 30 minutes, 39.8% 30 to 45 minutes, 7.4% 45 to 60 minutes, 3.0% 60 minutes or more (2000)

ROCK ISLAND (city). Aka Quad Cities. Covers a land area of 15.924 square miles and a water area of 1.223 square miles. Located at 41.48° N. Lat.; 90.57° W. Long. Elevation is 580 feet.
History: Rock Island developed from a community called Stephenson, whose name was changed in 1841. Rock Island was a steamboat port until the Rock Island Railroad Company completed a bridge across the Mississippi in 1855 and rail began to replace water as the means of transportation of goods. The Farmall Works of the International Harvester Company was established in Rock Island. The limestone island that became the location of the Rock Island Arsenal first served as a prison for Confederate soldiers, with more than 12,000 at a time confined here.
Population: 39,684 (2000); Race: 77.7% White, 16.2% Black, 0.6% Asian, 0.6% American Indian and Alaska Native, 6.2% Hispanic of any race, 2.4%

two or more races (2000); Density: 2,492.0 persons per square mile (2000); Age: 23.1% under 18, 16.2% over 64 (2000); Marriage status: 30.9% never married, 48.4% now married, 9.2% widowed, 11.5% divorced (2000); Foreign born: 3.2% (2000); Ancestry (includes multiple ancestries): 24.0% Other groups, 23.4% German, 13.2% Irish, 8.2% English, 6.8% United States or American (2000).
Vital Statistics: Birth rate: 138.9 per 10,000 population (1998)
Economy: Unemployment rate: 5.5% (11/2002); Total civilian labor force: 17,954 (11/2002); Single-family building permits issued: 17 (2001) / 17 (2000); Multi-family building permits issued: 0 (2001) / 0 (2000); Employment by occupation: 9.0% management, 18.4% professional, 18.5% services, 28.5% sales, 0.4% farming, 7.6% construction, 17.8% production (2000).
Income: Per capita income: $19,202 (2000); Median household income: $34,729 (2000); Poverty rate: 14.5% (2000).
Taxes: Total city taxes per capita: $311 (2000); City property taxes per capita: $221 (2000).
Education: High school graduation rate: 82.9% (2000); College graduation rate: 18.7% (2000).

School District(s)

Rock Island School District 41 (PK-12)
2000 Enrollment: 6,745 309-793-5900

Four-year College(s)

Augustana College (Private, Not-for-profit, Evangelical Lutheran Church)
2001 Enrollment: 2,232 309-794-7000
2001 Tuition: In-state $18,330; Out-of-state $18,330
Bible Missionary Institute (Private, Not-for-profit, Missionary Church Inc)
2001 Enrollment: n/a 309-788-0491
Housing: Homeownership rate: 65.1% (2000); Median home value: $70,600 (2000); Median rent: $361 per month (2000); Median age of housing: 51 years (2000).
Hospitals: Trinity Medical Center; Trinity Medical Center (349 beds)
Newspapers: The Rock Island Argus (7 x week); The Leader (1 x week)
Transportation: Commute to work: 89.2% car, 2.3% public transportation, 5.7% walk, 1.7% work from home (2000); Travel time to work: 46.8% less than 15 minutes, 40.5% 15 to 30 minutes, 6.9% 30 to 45 minutes, 2.4% 45 to 60 minutes, 3.4% 60 minutes or more (2000)

ROCK ISLAND ARSENAL (CDP). Covers a land area of 1.595 square miles and a water area of 0.968 square miles. Located at 41.51° N. Lat.; 90.53° W. Long.
Population: 145 (2000); Race: 67.7% White, 15.8% Black, 0.0% Asian, 0.0% American Indian and Alaska Native, 16.5% Hispanic of any race, 0.0% two or more races (2000); Density: 90.9 persons per square mile (2000); Age: 42.1% under 18, 0.0% over 64 (2000); Marriage status: 26.1% never married, 73.9% now married, 0.0% widowed, 0.0% divorced (2000); Foreign born: 8.3% (2000); Ancestry (includes multiple ancestries): 28.6% Other groups, 18.0% German, 7.5% Scottish, 4.5% English, 3.0% Irish (2000).
Economy: Employment by occupation: 10.9% management, 0.0% professional, 18.2% services, 49.1% sales, 0.0% farming, 10.9% construction, 10.9% production (2000).
Income: Per capita income: $15,710 (2000); Median household income: $45,417 (2000); Poverty rate: 0.0% (2000).
Education: High school graduation rate: 73.4% (2000); College graduation rate: 7.8% (2000).
Housing: Homeownership rate: 0.0% (2000); Median rent: $350 per month (2000); Median age of housing: 36 years (2000).
Transportation: Commute to work: 93.0% car, 0.0% public transportation, 0.0% walk, 7.0% work from home (2000); Travel time to work: 83.3% less than 15 minutes, 16.7% 15 to 30 minutes, 0.0% 30 to 45 minutes, 0.0% 45 to 60 minutes, 0.0% 60 minutes or more (2000)

SILVIS (city). Covers a land area of 3.646 square miles and a water area of 0 square miles. Located at 41.50° N. Lat.; 90.41° W. Long. Elevation is 670 feet.
History: Incorporated 1906.
Population: 7,269 (2000); Race: 84.9% White, 3.1% Black, 1.1% Asian, 0.0% American Indian and Alaska Native, 14.6% Hispanic of any race, 2.9% two or more races (2000); Density: 1,993.8 persons per square mile (2000); Age: 25.7% under 18, 16.8% over 64 (2000); Marriage status: 18.7% never married, 57.2% now married, 9.6% widowed, 14.5% divorced (2000); Foreign born: 4.1% (2000); Ancestry (includes multiple ancestries): 20.9% Other groups, 19.4% German, 13.4% Irish, 6.8% United States or American, 6.5% Belgian (2000).
Economy: Manufacturing: rebuilt locomotives and parts. Agriculture in area: corn, soybeans; cattle. Single-family building permits issued: 23 (2001) / 13 (2000); Multi-family building permits issued: 10 (2001) / 0 (2000); Employment by occupation: 9.6% management, 9.1% professional, 19.1% services, 26.9% sales, 0.2% farming, 10.4% construction, 24.6% production (2000).
Income: Per capita income: $16,764 (2000); Median household income: $35,047 (2000); Poverty rate: 9.5% (2000).
Taxes: Total city taxes per capita: $141 (1997); City property taxes per capita: $85 (1997).
Education: High school graduation rate: 75.6% (2000); College graduation rate: 9.1% (2000).

School District(s)

Silvis School District 34 (PK-08)
2000 Enrollment: 688 309-792-9325
Housing: Homeownership rate: 61.7% (2000); Median home value: $71,800 (2000); Median rent: $381 per month (2000); Median age of housing: 37 years (2000).
Hospitals: INI Hospital (150 beds)
Transportation: Commute to work: 92.1% car, 0.6% public transportation, 2.5% walk, 2.4% work from home (2000); Travel time to work: 37.9% less than 15 minutes, 42.9% 15 to 30 minutes, 15.3% 30 to 45 minutes, 0.9% 45 to 60 minutes, 3.0% 60 minutes or more (2000)

TAYLOR RIDGE (unincorporated postal area, zip code 61284). Covers a land area of 56.358 square miles and a water area of 0.198 square miles. Located at 41.40° N. Lat.; 90.73° W. Long. Elevation is 775 feet.
Population: 3,439 (2000); Race: 98.6% White, 0.9% Black, 0.0% Asian, 0.0% American Indian and Alaska Native, 0.7% Hispanic of any race, 0.5% two or more races (2000); Density: 61.0 persons per square mile (2000); Age: 26.9% under 18, 10.6% over 64 (2000); Marriage status: 18.4% never married, 69.0% now married, 5.9% widowed, 6.7% divorced (2000); Foreign born: 0.1% (2000); Ancestry (includes multiple ancestries): 34.4% German, 12.5% Irish, 9.3% English, 7.5% United States or American, 6.1% Belgian (2000).
Economy: Employment by occupation: 16.2% management, 19.3% professional, 8.8% services, 28.1% sales, 0.2% farming, 8.6% construction, 18.8% production (2000).
Income: Per capita income: $26,077 (2000); Median household income: $62,882 (2000); Poverty rate: 5.0% (2000).
Education: High school graduation rate: 88.9% (2000); College graduation rate: 19.1% (2000).

School District(s)

Rockridge C U School District 300 (PK-12)
2000 Enrollment: 1,395 309-795-1167
Housing: Homeownership rate: 91.8% (2000); Median home value: $109,800 (2000); Median rent: $378 per month (2000); Median age of housing: 31 years (2000).
Transportation: Commute to work: 94.8% car, 0.1% public transportation, 0.8% walk, 4.1% work from home (2000); Travel time to work: 12.8% less than 15 minutes, 54.4% 15 to 30 minutes, 26.8% 30 to 45 minutes, 2.7% 45 to 60 minutes, 3.3% 60 minutes or more (2000)

Saint Clair County

Located in southwestern Illinois; bounded on the northwest by the Mississippi River and the Missouri border; also drained by the Kaskaskia River and Silver Creek. Covers a land area of 663.80 square miles, a water area of 10.10 square miles, and is located in the Central Time Zone. The county government was organized in 1790. County seat is Belleville.

Saint Clair County is part of the St. Louis, MO-IL MSA. The entire metro area includes: Clinton County, IL; Jersey County, IL; Madison County, IL; Monroe County, IL; St. Clair County, IL; Crawford County, MO (pt.)**; Franklin County, MO; Jefferson County, MO; Lincoln County, MO; St. Charles County, MO; St. Louis County, MO; Warren County, MO; St. Louis city, MO

Weather Station: Belleville Scott AFB — Elevation: 442 feet

	Jan	Feb	Mar	Apr	May	Jun	Jul	Aug	Sep	Oct	Nov	Dec
High	39	46	57	68	77	86	90	88	82	71	56	44
Low	22	26	35	45	54	62	66	63	56	45	36	27
Precip	2.0	2.2	3.6	4.0	4.2	3.8	3.3	3.3	3.1	2.9	3.8	3.0
Snow	6.5	3.2	2.1	0.8	0.0	0.0	0.0	0.0	0.0	0.0	0.9	2.6

High and Low temperatures in degrees Fahrenheit; Precipitation and Snow in inches

Population: 256,082 (2000); Race: 68.0% White, 28.6% Black, 0.9% Asian, 0.3% American Indian and Alaska Native, 2.2% Hispanic of any race, 1.4%

two or more races (2000); Density: 385.8 persons per square mile (2000); Age: 27.7% under 18, 13.1% over 64 (2000).
Religion: Five largest groups: 20.5% Catholic Church, 6.6% Southern Baptist Convention, 4.3% United Church of Christ, 2.7% The United Methodist Church, 1.9% Lutheran Church—Missouri Synod (2000).
Economy: Unemployment rate: 7.1% (11/2002); Total civilian labor force: 113,238 (11/2002); Leading industries: 17.6% retail trade; 17.1% health care and social assistance; 11.4% accommodation & food services (2000); Companies that employ more than 1,000 persons: 3 (2000); Companies that employ more than 100 persons: 97 (2000); Farms: 844 totaling 264,507 acres (1997); Minority business ownership rate: 11.1% (1997); Women business ownership rate: 32.1% (1997); Retail sales per capita: $7,768 (1997). Single-family building permits issued: 1,061 (2001) / 909 (2000); Multi-family building permits issued: 121 (2001) / 193 (2000).
Income: Per capita income: $18,932 (2000); Median household income: $39,148 (2000); Poverty rate: 14.5% (2000); Bankruptcy rate: 7.69% (2001).
Taxes: Total county taxes per capita: $82 (2000); County property taxes per capita: $80 (2000).
Education: High school graduation rate: 80.9% (2000); College graduation rate: 19.3% (2000).
Housing: Homeownership rate: 67.0% (2000); Median home value: $77,700 (2000); Median rent: $379 per month (2000); Median age of housing: 36 years (2000).
Health: Birth rate: 148.5 per 10,000 population (1998); Age adjusted death rate: 98.0 per 10,000 population (1999); Infant mortality rate: 11.3 per 1,000 live births (1998); Age adjusted cancer mortality rate: 224.6 deaths per 100,000 population (1999). Air Quality Index: 70% good, 30% moderate, 0% unhealthy (percent of days in 2000). Number of physicians: 16.9 per 10,000 population (1999); Number of hospital beds: 38.5 per 10,000 population (1999).
Elections: 2000 Presidential election results: 55.7% Gore, 42.1% Bush, 1.6% Nader, 0.3% Buchanan
National and State Parks: Cahokia Mounds State Park; Holten State Park
Additional Information Contacts
St. Clair County Government Offices 618-277-6600
Belleville Area Association of Realtors 618-277-1980
Belleville Chamber of Commerce 618-233-2015
Belleville Economic Progress 618-233-2015
Cahokia Chamber of Commerce 618-332-1900
East St. Louis Chamber of Commerce 618-271-2855
Fairview Heights Chamber of Commerce 618-397-3127
O Fallon Chamber of Commerce 618-632-3377

Saint Clair County Communities

ALORTON (village). Covers a land area of 1.779 square miles and a water area of 0 square miles. Located at 38.58° N. Lat.; 90.11° W. Long. Elevation is 418 feet.
History: Incorporated 1944.
Population: 2,749 (2000); Race: 0.1% White, 98.2% Black, 0.3% Asian, 0.0% American Indian and Alaska Native, 0.4% Hispanic of any race, 0.7% two or more races (2000); Density: 1,545.3 persons per square mile (2000); Age: 38.8% under 18, 8.3% over 64 (2000); Marriage status: 45.7% never married, 35.8% now married, 7.7% widowed, 10.7% divorced (2000); Foreign born: 1.1% (2000); Ancestry (includes multiple ancestries): 76.3% Other groups, 1.1% African, 0.4% Belizean, 0.2% United States or American, 0.1% Jordanian (2000).
Economy: Agriculture nearby: soybeans; dairying. Employment by occupation: 2.3% management, 8.2% professional, 37.5% services, 26.7% sales, 0.0% farming, 6.8% construction, 18.6% production (2000).
Income: Per capita income: $8,777 (2000); Median household income: $17,860 (2000); Poverty rate: 47.3% (2000).
Taxes: Total city taxes per capita: $52 (1997); City property taxes per capita: $45 (1997).
Education: High school graduation rate: 57.9% (2000); College graduation rate: 3.4% (2000).
Housing: Homeownership rate: 44.7% (2000); Median home value: $31,700 (2000); Median rent: $274 per month (2000); Median age of housing: 35 years (2000).
Transportation: Commute to work: 75.9% car, 15.6% public transportation, 4.4% walk, 4.1% work from home (2000); Travel time to work: 16.4% less than 15 minutes, 44.1% 15 to 30 minutes, 26.0% 30 to 45 minutes, 9.3% 45 to 60 minutes, 4.1% 60 minutes or more (2000)

BELLEVILLE (city). Covers a land area of 18.854 square miles and a water area of 0.128 square miles. Located at 38.52° N. Lat.; 89.99° W. Long. Elevation is 529 feet.
History: Settlers came to Belleville early in the 1800's, and in 1814 the settlement became the seat of St. Clair County, succeeding Cahokia. The town was incorporated in 1819. The discovery of coal in 1828 brought many German immigrants to Belleville, which came to be known as Dutch Town.
Population: 41,410 (2000); Race: 81.7% White, 15.2% Black, 0.7% Asian, 0.2% American Indian and Alaska Native, 2.3% Hispanic of any race, 1.6% two or more races (2000); Density: 2,196.4 persons per square mile (2000); Age: 23.5% under 18, 17.0% over 64 (2000); Marriage status: 26.3% never married, 50.9% now married, 9.4% widowed, 13.5% divorced (2000); Foreign born: 1.9% (2000); Ancestry (includes multiple ancestries): 33.2% German, 19.7% Other groups, 11.5% Irish, 8.4% English, 6.0% United States or American (2000).
Vital Statistics: Birth rate: 179.9 per 10,000 population (1998)
Economy: Unemployment rate: 10.5% (11/2002); Total civilian labor force: 20,053 (11/2002); Single-family building permits issued: 94 (2001) / 100 (2000); Multi-family building permits issued: 29 (2001) / 49 (2000); Employment by occupation: 9.8% management, 18.9% professional, 19.3% services, 29.7% sales, 0.0% farming, 8.3% construction, 14.0% production (2000).
Income: Per capita income: $18,990 (2000); Median household income: $35,979 (2000); Poverty rate: 11.7% (2000).
Taxes: Total city taxes per capita: $371 (1997); City property taxes per capita: $167 (1997).
Education: High school graduation rate: 83.8% (2000); College graduation rate: 17.6% (2000).

School District(s)

Belle Valley School District 119 (PK-08)
2000 Enrollment: 952 618-234-3445
Belleville Area Special Services (03-12)
2000 Enrollment: 69 618-355-4700
Belleville School District 118 (PK-08)
2000 Enrollment: 3,818 618-233-2830
Belleville Township Hs District 201 (09-12)
2000 Enrollment: 4,710 618-233-5070
Harmony Emge School District 175 (PK-08)
2000 Enrollment: 876 618-397-8444
Saint Clair Roe (06-12)
2000 Enrollment: 22 618-397-8930
Signal Hill School District 181 (PK-08)
2000 Enrollment: 403 618-397-0325
Whiteside School District 115 (PK-08)
2000 Enrollment: 1,048 618-233-7917

Two-year College(s)

Southwestern Illinois College (Public)
2001 Enrollment: 13,307 618-235-2700
2001 Tuition: In-state $3,444; Out-of-state $5,852
Housing: Homeownership rate: 60.6% (2000); Median home value: $70,500 (2000); Median rent: $380 per month (2000); Median age of housing: 44 years (2000).
Hospitals: 375th Medical Group Hospital (161 beds); Memorial Hospital (391 beds); Saint Elizabeth's Hospital (498 beds)
Newspapers: Belleville News-Democrat (7 x week); Messenger (1 x week); O'Fallon Journal (2 x week); Fairview Heights Journal (2 x week); Belleville Journal (2 x week)
Transportation: Commute to work: 92.4% car, 2.8% public transportation, 2.1% walk, 2.2% work from home (2000); Travel time to work: 34.7% less than 15 minutes, 32.5% 15 to 30 minutes, 18.4% 30 to 45 minutes, 9.2% 45 to 60 minutes, 5.3% 60 minutes or more (2000)
Airports: Scott AFB/Midamerica (primary service)
Additional Information Contacts
Belleville Area Association of Realtors 618-277-1980
Belleville Chamber of Commerce 618-233-2015
Belleville Economic Progress 618-233-2015

BROOKLYN (village). Aka Lovejoy. Covers a land area of 0.843 square miles and a water area of 0 square miles. Located at 38.65° N. Lat.; 90.16° W. Long. Elevation is 410 feet.
History: When it was incorporated in 1874 Brooklyn was called Lovejoy, in honor of Abolitionist editor Elijah P. Lovejoy.
Population: 676 (2000); Race: 6.7% White, 93.3% Black, 0.0% Asian, 0.0% American Indian and Alaska Native, 0.0% Hispanic of any race, 0.0% two or more races (2000); Density: 801.9 persons per square mile (2000); Age:

23.6% under 18, 22.8% over 64 (2000); Marriage status: 43.2% never married, 18.4% now married, 14.8% widowed, 23.7% divorced (2000); Foreign born: 0.0% (2000); Ancestry (includes multiple ancestries): 59.3% Other groups, 4.6% English, 4.6% Lithuanian (2000).
Economy: Employment by occupation: 7.0% management, 37.3% professional, 19.6% services, 20.9% sales, 0.0% farming, 0.0% construction, 15.2% production (2000).
Income: Per capita income: $7,944 (2000); Median household income: $16,630 (2000); Poverty rate: 48.5% (2000).
Taxes: Total city taxes per capita: $240 (1997); City property taxes per capita: $24 (1997).
Education: High school graduation rate: 59.0% (2000); College graduation rate: 3.1% (2000).
Housing: Homeownership rate: 53.5% (2000); Median home value: $31,000 (2000); Median rent: $193 per month (2000); Median age of housing: 29 years (2000).
Transportation: Commute to work: 50.3% car, 23.4% public transportation, 21.8% walk, 4.4% work from home (2000); Travel time to work: 38.4% less than 15 minutes, 12.6% 15 to 30 minutes, 19.2% 30 to 45 minutes, 25.8% 45 to 60 minutes, 4.0% 60 minutes or more (2000)

CAHOKIA (village). Aka Maplewood Park. Covers a land area of 9.609 square miles and a water area of 0.367 square miles. Located at 38.56° N. Lat.; 90.17° W. Long. Elevation is 411 feet.
History: Cahokia began with a mission established in 1699 by Jean Francois Buisson de St. Cosme of the Seminary of Foreign Missions, and a trading post developed around the mission. In 1809 county lines were redrawn so that Cahokia served as the seat of a territory that later was divided into 80 northern counties.
Population: 16,391 (2000); Race: 58.6% White, 38.0% Black, 0.2% Asian, 1.2% American Indian and Alaska Native, 1.5% Hispanic of any race, 1.0% two or more races (2000); Density: 1,705.8 persons per square mile (2000); Age: 33.8% under 18, 11.3% over 64 (2000); Marriage status: 32.0% never married, 48.3% now married, 8.3% widowed, 11.4% divorced (2000); Foreign born: 0.7% (2000); Ancestry (includes multiple ancestries): 35.7% Other groups, 14.0% German, 9.0% Irish, 7.8% United States or American, 5.2% English (2000).
Vital Statistics: Birth rate: 205.6 per 10,000 population (1998)
Economy: Single-family building permits issued: 3 (2001) / 0 (2000); Multi-family building permits issued: 0 (2001) / 0 (2000); Employment by occupation: 6.9% management, 10.1% professional, 21.2% services, 28.2% sales, 0.2% farming, 10.6% construction, 23.0% production (2000).
Income: Per capita income: $14,545 (2000); Median household income: $31,001 (2000); Poverty rate: 24.9% (2000).
Taxes: Total city taxes per capita: $242 (1997); City property taxes per capita: $90 (1997).
Education: High school graduation rate: 70.7% (2000); College graduation rate: 5.6% (2000).

School District(s)

Cahokia Community Unit School District 187 (PK-12)
2000 Enrollment: 5,207 618-332-3700
Housing: Homeownership rate: 66.3% (2000); Median home value: $39,500 (2000); Median rent: $419 per month (2000); Median age of housing: 40 years (2000).
Newspapers: Cahokia-Dupo Herald (1 x week)
Transportation: Commute to work: 93.0% car, 2.3% public transportation, 1.5% walk, 1.8% work from home (2000); Travel time to work: 25.7% less than 15 minutes, 41.4% 15 to 30 minutes, 21.5% 30 to 45 minutes, 4.6% 45 to 60 minutes, 6.8% 60 minutes or more (2000)
Airports: St Louis Downtown
Additional Information Contacts
Cahokia Chamber of Commerce 618-332-1900

CASEYVILLE (village). Covers a land area of 6.211 square miles and a water area of 0 square miles. Located at 38.63° N. Lat.; 90.03° W. Long. Elevation is 425 feet.
Population: 4,310 (2000); Race: 89.6% White, 7.3% Black, 0.6% Asian, 0.2% American Indian and Alaska Native, 2.6% Hispanic of any race, 0.6% two or more races (2000); Density: 694.0 persons per square mile (2000); Age: 21.0% under 18, 19.8% over 64 (2000); Marriage status: 24.1% never married, 53.2% now married, 10.8% widowed, 11.9% divorced (2000); Foreign born: 1.4% (2000); Ancestry (includes multiple ancestries): 25.4% German, 15.4% Other groups, 14.5% Irish, 7.0% English, 5.8% United States or American (2000).
Economy: Some agriculture. Single-family building permits issued: 6 (2001) / 46 (2000); Multi-family building permits issued: 0 (2001) / 0 (2000); Employment by occupation: 4.8% management, 11.8% professional, 19.8% services, 31.1% sales, 1.2% farming, 15.7% construction, 15.6% production (2000).
Income: Per capita income: $15,467 (2000); Median household income: $31,512 (2000); Poverty rate: 9.8% (2000).
Taxes: Total city taxes per capita: $141 (1997); City property taxes per capita: $64 (1997).
Education: High school graduation rate: 71.6% (2000); College graduation rate: 8.0% (2000).
Housing: Homeownership rate: 79.4% (2000); Median home value: $62,200 (2000); Median rent: $384 per month (2000); Median age of housing: 42 years (2000).
Transportation: Commute to work: 96.2% car, 0.0% public transportation, 0.8% walk, 1.6% work from home (2000); Travel time to work: 19.0% less than 15 minutes, 53.7% 15 to 30 minutes, 18.4% 30 to 45 minutes, 6.2% 45 to 60 minutes, 2.8% 60 minutes or more (2000)

CENTREVILLE (city). Covers a land area of 4.333 square miles and a water area of 0 square miles. Located at 38.58° N. Lat.; 90.10° W. Long. Elevation is 415 feet.
Population: 5,951 (2000); Race: 3.0% White, 94.9% Black, 0.2% Asian, 0.0% American Indian and Alaska Native, 1.4% Hispanic of any race, 1.7% two or more races (2000); Density: 1,373.3 persons per square mile (2000); Age: 33.6% under 18, 13.2% over 64 (2000); Marriage status: 41.1% never married, 35.7% now married, 12.5% widowed, 10.8% divorced (2000); Foreign born: 0.4% (2000); Ancestry (includes multiple ancestries): 77.0% Other groups, 1.8% African, 0.8% United States or American, 0.7% Irish, 0.5% Greek (2000).
Economy: Railroad yards. Single-family building permits issued: 0 (2001) / 3 (2000); Multi-family building permits issued: 0 (2001) / 0 (2000); Employment by occupation: 4.3% management, 12.5% professional, 30.0% services, 26.3% sales, 0.0% farming, 6.0% construction, 20.9% production (2000).
Income: Per capita income: $11,150 (2000); Median household income: $23,500 (2000); Poverty rate: 34.4% (2000).
Taxes: Total city taxes per capita: $137 (1997); City property taxes per capita: $71 (1997).
Education: High school graduation rate: 67.0% (2000); College graduation rate: 9.5% (2000).
Housing: Homeownership rate: 59.1% (2000); Median home value: $43,800 (2000); Median rent: $246 per month (2000); Median age of housing: 38 years (2000).
Hospitals: Tochette Regional Hospital (114 beds)
Transportation: Commute to work: 85.1% car, 11.5% public transportation, 0.5% walk, 2.7% work from home (2000); Travel time to work: 23.0% less than 15 minutes, 44.6% 15 to 30 minutes, 15.9% 30 to 45 minutes, 7.4% 45 to 60 minutes, 9.0% 60 minutes or more (2000)

DUPO (village). Aka Sugar Loaf Heights. Covers a land area of 4.426 square miles and a water area of 0 square miles. Located at 38.51° N. Lat.; 90.20° W. Long. Elevation is 415 feet.
History: The name of Dupo is a shortened form of Prairie du Pont, which is a French term meaning "meadow of the bridge." Oil was discovered near Dupo in 1928 and a brief period of fast growth ensued.
Population: 3,933 (2000); Race: 95.7% White, 1.7% Black, 0.2% Asian, 1.3% American Indian and Alaska Native, 1.3% Hispanic of any race, 0.4% two or more races (2000); Density: 888.6 persons per square mile (2000); Age: 25.9% under 18, 12.8% over 64 (2000); Marriage status: 21.3% never married, 60.2% now married, 8.1% widowed, 10.3% divorced (2000); Foreign born: 0.9% (2000); Ancestry (includes multiple ancestries): 25.4% German, 11.6% Other groups, 11.5% Irish, 10.6% United States or American, 9.0% French (except Basque) (2000).
Economy: Single-family building permits issued: 3 (2001) / 13 (2000); Multi-family building permits issued: 0 (2001) / 8 (2000); Employment by occupation: 8.1% management, 14.3% professional, 17.3% services, 33.7% sales, 0.0% farming, 8.9% construction, 17.8% production (2000).
Income: Per capita income: $18,505 (2000); Median household income: $43,036 (2000); Poverty rate: 4.3% (2000).
Taxes: Total city taxes per capita: $60 (1997); City property taxes per capita: $53 (1997).
Education: High school graduation rate: 75.1% (2000); College graduation rate: 10.3% (2000).

School District(s)

Dupo Community Unit School Districtrict 196 (PK-12)
2000 Enrollment: 1,337 618-286-3812

Housing: Homeownership rate: 72.4% (2000); Median home value: $71,900 (2000); Median rent: $374 per month (2000); Median age of housing: 43 years (2000).
Transportation: Commute to work: 98.0% car, 0.0% public transportation, 0.0% walk, 2.0% work from home (2000); Travel time to work: 18.9% less than 15 minutes, 42.1% 15 to 30 minutes, 30.4% 30 to 45 minutes, 6.3% 45 to 60 minutes, 2.3% 60 minutes or more (2000)

EAST CARONDELET (village). Covers a land area of 1.251 square miles and a water area of 0.412 square miles. Located at 38.54° N. Lat.; 90.23° W. Long. Elevation is 405 feet.
History: Damaged in floods of 1993.
Population: 267 (2000); Race: 97.1% White, 2.9% Black, 0.0% Asian, 0.0% American Indian and Alaska Native, 0.0% Hispanic of any race, 0.0% two or more races (2000); Density: 213.5 persons per square mile (2000); Age: 31.4% under 18, 11.6% over 64 (2000); Marriage status: 32.5% never married, 54.6% now married, 2.5% widowed, 10.4% divorced (2000); Foreign born: 0.0% (2000); Ancestry (includes multiple ancestries): 18.8% German, 15.0% Irish, 10.1% United States or American, 7.2% Other groups, 6.3% Italian (2000).
Economy: Agriculture: soybeans, hogs. Manufacturing: paints. Single-family building permits issued: 0 (2001) / 2 (2000); Multi-family building permits issued: 0 (2001) / 0 (2000); Employment by occupation: 6.9% management, 2.3% professional, 17.2% services, 19.5% sales, 0.0% farming, 19.5% construction, 34.5% production (2000).
Income: Per capita income: $13,402 (2000); Median household income: $36,071 (2000); Poverty rate: 2.9% (2000).
Taxes: Total city taxes per capita: $37 (1997); City property taxes per capita: $18 (1997).
Education: High school graduation rate: 68.2% (2000); College graduation rate: 0.0% (2000).
Housing: Homeownership rate: 71.2% (2000); Median home value: $67,500 (2000); Median rent: $313 per month (2000); Median age of housing: 41 years (2000).
Transportation: Commute to work: 95.5% car, 2.2% public transportation, 2.2% walk, 0.0% work from home (2000); Travel time to work: 22.5% less than 15 minutes, 40.4% 15 to 30 minutes, 32.6% 30 to 45 minutes, 2.2% 45 to 60 minutes, 2.2% 60 minutes or more (2000)

EAST SAINT LOUIS (city). Covers a land area of 14.063 square miles and a water area of 0.367 square miles. Located at 38.61° N. Lat.; 90.12° W. Long. Elevation is 405 feet.
History: Settlement across the Mississippi River from St. Louis, Missouri, was achieved by Captain James Piggott who established ferry service here in 1795. A village called Illinoistown was platted near the ferry dock in 1816. When Illinoistown was incorporated in 1859, a town called East St. Louis had been established nearby. In 1861 the charter of Illinoistown was extended to include the new town, and the name was changed to East St. Louis. Near the end of the 19th century, East St. Louis changed from a river town to an industrial center.
Population: 31,542 (2000); Race: 1.5% White, 97.7% Black, 0.1% Asian, 0.0% American Indian and Alaska Native, 0.4% Hispanic of any race, 0.5% two or more races (2000); Density: 2,242.9 persons per square mile (2000); Age: 33.0% under 18, 12.6% over 64 (2000); Marriage status: 45.3% never married, 30.7% now married, 10.9% widowed, 13.2% divorced (2000); Foreign born: 0.3% (2000); Ancestry (includes multiple ancestries): 77.5% Other groups, 1.1% African, 0.6% United States or American, 0.4% German, 0.4% Irish (2000).
Vital Statistics: Birth rate: 226.1 per 10,000 population (1998)
Economy: Unemployment rate: 12.0% (11/2002); Total civilian labor force: 11,104 (11/2002); Single-family building permits issued: 9 (2001) / 27 (2000); Multi-family building permits issued: 0 (2001) / 0 (2000); Employment by occupation: 5.5% management, 16.4% professional, 30.8% services, 23.6% sales, 0.1% farming, 5.2% construction, 18.4% production (2000).
Income: Per capita income: $11,169 (2000); Median household income: $21,324 (2000); Poverty rate: 35.1% (2000).
Taxes: Total city taxes per capita: $324 (2000); City property taxes per capita: $155 (2000).
Education: High school graduation rate: 66.3% (2000); College graduation rate: 9.1% (2000).

School District(s)

East Saint Louis School District 189 (PK-12)
2000 Enrollment: 11,009 618-583-8200

Housing: Homeownership rate: 53.0% (2000); Median home value: $41,800 (2000); Median rent: $265 per month (2000); Median age of housing: 47 years (2000).
Hospitals: Saint Mary's Hospital (169 beds)
Newspapers: East Saint Louis Monitor (1 x week)
Transportation: Commute to work: 79.6% car, 14.6% public transportation, 2.4% walk, 2.6% work from home (2000); Travel time to work: 23.0% less than 15 minutes, 40.0% 15 to 30 minutes, 21.4% 30 to 45 minutes, 6.6% 45 to 60 minutes, 9.0% 60 minutes or more (2000)
Additional Information Contacts
East St. Louis Chamber of Commerce 618-271-2855

FAIRMONT CITY (village). Covers a land area of 2.405 square miles and a water area of 0 square miles. Located at 38.65° N. Lat.; 90.10° W. Long. Elevation is 420 feet.
History: Fairmont City came into being in 1910 when the Pennsylvania Railroad built a roundhouse here. First called Willow Town, the name was changed to Fairmont City when it was incorporated in 1914.
Population: 2,436 (2000); Race: 66.1% White, 1.3% Black, 0.5% Asian, 0.4% American Indian and Alaska Native, 55.0% Hispanic of any race, 5.2% two or more races (2000); Density: 1,013.1 persons per square mile (2000); Age: 26.8% under 18, 14.3% over 64 (2000); Marriage status: 25.7% never married, 56.3% now married, 9.0% widowed, 9.0% divorced (2000); Foreign born: 34.9% (2000); Ancestry (includes multiple ancestries): 55.3% Other groups, 9.6% German, 5.6% Polish, 5.5% Irish, 3.1% United States or American (2000).
Economy: Employment by occupation: 7.5% management, 5.9% professional, 21.0% services, 21.3% sales, 5.3% farming, 15.5% construction, 23.4% production (2000).
Income: Per capita income: $12,203 (2000); Median household income: $27,070 (2000); Poverty rate: 18.4% (2000).
Taxes: Total city taxes per capita: $848 (1997); City property taxes per capita: $56 (1997).
Education: High school graduation rate: 46.5% (2000); College graduation rate: 5.5% (2000).
Housing: Homeownership rate: 72.9% (2000); Median home value: $45,000 (2000); Median rent: $295 per month (2000); Median age of housing: 41 years (2000).
Transportation: Commute to work: 93.8% car, 0.8% public transportation, 2.8% walk, 0.0% work from home (2000); Travel time to work: 27.8% less than 15 minutes, 36.2% 15 to 30 minutes, 23.1% 30 to 45 minutes, 4.6% 45 to 60 minutes, 8.4% 60 minutes or more (2000)

FAIRVIEW HEIGHTS (city). Aka Fairview. Covers a land area of 11.148 square miles and a water area of 0.065 square miles. Located at 38.59° N. Lat.; 89.99° W. Long. Elevation is 593 feet.
History: Also known as Fairview. Formerly called Lincoln Heights.
Population: 15,034 (2000); Race: 79.4% White, 15.7% Black, 2.1% Asian, 0.2% American Indian and Alaska Native, 1.9% Hispanic of any race, 1.9% two or more races (2000); Density: 1,348.6 persons per square mile (2000); Age: 24.1% under 18, 16.5% over 64 (2000); Marriage status: 22.6% never married, 59.4% now married, 7.1% widowed, 11.0% divorced (2000); Foreign born: 3.3% (2000); Ancestry (includes multiple ancestries): 28.7% German, 21.8% Other groups, 14.3% Irish, 9.7% English, 5.3% French (except Basque) (2000).
Vital Statistics: Birth rate: 105.1 per 10,000 population (1998)
Economy: Commercial and office center of East metro area. Manufacturing: electric products. Single-family building permits issued: 105 (2001) / 54 (2000); Multi-family building permits issued: 0 (2001) / 0 (2000); Employment by occupation: 13.2% management, 23.3% professional, 13.7% services, 27.9% sales, 0.0% farming, 8.4% construction, 13.6% production (2000).
Income: Per capita income: $22,614 (2000); Median household income: $49,131 (2000); Poverty rate: 5.9% (2000).
Education: High school graduation rate: 84.7% (2000); College graduation rate: 26.3% (2000).

School District(s)

Grant Community Cons School District 110 (PK-08)
2000 Enrollment: 772 618-398-5577
Pontiac-W Holliday School District 105 (PK-08)
2000 Enrollment: 568 618-233-2320

Housing: Homeownership rate: 76.6% (2000); Median home value: $84,800 (2000); Median rent: $503 per month (2000); Median age of housing: 33 years (2000).
Transportation: Commute to work: 94.0% car, 1.0% public transportation, 1.6% walk, 2.8% work from home (2000); Travel time to work: 23.5% less

than 15 minutes, 38.5% 15 to 30 minutes, 25.4% 30 to 45 minutes, 8.4% 45 to 60 minutes, 4.3% 60 minutes or more (2000)

Additional Information Contacts

Fairview Heights Chamber of Commerce 618-397-3127

FAYETTEVILLE (village). Covers a land area of 0.255 square miles and a water area of 0 square miles. Located at 38.37° N. Lat.; 89.79° W. Long. Elevation is 411 feet.

Population: 384 (2000); Race: 99.2% White, 0.0% Black, 0.3% Asian, 0.0% American Indian and Alaska Native, 2.6% Hispanic of any race, 0.5% two or more races (2000); Density: 1,503.7 persons per square mile (2000); Age: 37.2% under 18, 4.7% over 64 (2000); Marriage status: 25.2% never married, 59.4% now married, 3.5% widowed, 11.8% divorced (2000); Foreign born: 1.8% (2000); Ancestry (includes multiple ancestries): 53.9% German, 11.7% Other groups, 9.6% Polish, 9.6% Irish, 8.9% English (2000).

Economy: In bituminous-coal and agricultural area. Single-family building permits issued: 2 (2001) / 4 (2000); Multi-family building permits issued: 0 (2001) / 0 (2000); Employment by occupation: 1.8% management, 9.6% professional, 13.8% services, 25.1% sales, 1.2% farming, 17.4% construction, 31.1% production (2000).

Income: Per capita income: $12,163 (2000); Median household income: $35,417 (2000); Poverty rate: 21.0% (2000).

Taxes: Total city taxes per capita: $83 (1997); City property taxes per capita: $43 (1997).

Education: High school graduation rate: 84.3% (2000); College graduation rate: 3.6% (2000).

Housing: Homeownership rate: 77.2% (2000); Median home value: $51,300 (2000); Median rent: $392 per month (2000); Median age of housing: 38 years (2000).

Transportation: Commute to work: 94.6% car, 0.0% public transportation, 3.6% walk, 1.8% work from home (2000); Travel time to work: 26.7% less than 15 minutes, 28.5% 15 to 30 minutes, 23.0% 30 to 45 minutes, 12.1% 45 to 60 minutes, 9.7% 60 minutes or more (2000)

FREEBURG (village). Covers a land area of 3.187 square miles and a water area of 0.051 square miles. Located at 38.42° N. Lat.; 89.91° W. Long. Elevation is 518 feet.

History: Incorporated 1859.

Population: 3,872 (2000); Race: 97.7% White, 0.0% Black, 0.7% Asian, 0.0% American Indian and Alaska Native, 1.1% Hispanic of any race, 1.2% two or more races (2000); Density: 1,215.1 persons per square mile (2000); Age: 27.1% under 18, 14.7% over 64 (2000); Marriage status: 20.2% never married, 60.3% now married, 8.9% widowed, 10.5% divorced (2000); Foreign born: 0.9% (2000); Ancestry (includes multiple ancestries): 51.9% German, 16.2% Irish, 13.5% English, 5.4% French (except Basque), 5.4% Other groups (2000).

Economy: Bituminous coal mines; corn, wheat, dairy products, livestock, vegetables. Single-family building permits issued: 26 (2001) / 20 (2000); Multi-family building permits issued: 0 (2001) / 0 (2000); Employment by occupation: 13.1% management, 24.2% professional, 11.4% services, 25.2% sales, 0.0% farming, 13.8% construction, 12.3% production (2000).

Income: Per capita income: $19,851 (2000); Median household income: $51,434 (2000); Poverty rate: 5.7% (2000).

Taxes: Total city taxes per capita: $35 (1997); City property taxes per capita: $32 (1997).

Education: High school graduation rate: 88.3% (2000); College graduation rate: 17.6% (2000).

School District(s)

Freeburg C C School District 70 (PK-08)
2000 Enrollment: 881 618-539-3188

Freeburg Community H S District 77 (09-12)
2000 Enrollment: 658 618-539-5533

Housing: Homeownership rate: 79.7% (2000); Median home value: $106,900 (2000); Median rent: $460 per month (2000); Median age of housing: 29 years (2000).

Newspapers: Freeburg Tribune (1 x week)

Transportation: Commute to work: 94.9% car, 0.0% public transportation, 2.8% walk, 2.1% work from home (2000); Travel time to work: 26.4% less than 15 minutes, 41.1% 15 to 30 minutes, 20.9% 30 to 45 minutes, 6.1% 45 to 60 minutes, 5.5% 60 minutes or more (2000)

LEBANON (city). Covers a land area of 2.146 square miles and a water area of 0.002 square miles. Located at 38.60° N. Lat.; 89.81° W. Long. Elevation is 515 feet.

History: Lebanon was platted in the early 1800's. It grew as the site of McKendree College, organized in 1818 by the Methodist Church. Both Abraham Lincoln and Charles Dickens were guests at the Mermaid Inn, built in 1830 in Lebanon.

Population: 3,523 (2000); Race: 79.7% White, 15.5% Black, 0.4% Asian, 0.0% American Indian and Alaska Native, 4.1% Hispanic of any race, 2.4% two or more races (2000); Density: 1,641.4 persons per square mile (2000); Age: 21.5% under 18, 18.9% over 64 (2000); Marriage status: 31.5% never married, 49.3% now married, 11.2% widowed, 7.9% divorced (2000); Foreign born: 3.3% (2000); Ancestry (includes multiple ancestries): 36.3% German, 24.4% Other groups, 9.3% English, 8.4% Irish, 4.7% French (except Basque) (2000).

Economy: Single-family building permits issued: 22 (2001) / 1 (2000); Multi-family building permits issued: 0 (2001) / 0 (2000); Employment by occupation: 11.3% management, 24.7% professional, 19.0% services, 27.6% sales, 0.0% farming, 7.6% construction, 9.8% production (2000).

Income: Per capita income: $17,125 (2000); Median household income: $37,042 (2000); Poverty rate: 13.4% (2000).

Taxes: Total city taxes per capita: $167 (1997); City property taxes per capita: $42 (1997).

Education: High school graduation rate: 81.2% (2000); College graduation rate: 26.5% (2000).

School District(s)

Lebanon Community Unit School District 9 (PK-12)
2000 Enrollment: 829 618-537-4611

Four-year College(s)

McKendree College (Private, Not-for-profit, United Methodist)
2001 Enrollment: 2,107 618-537-4481
2001 Tuition: In-state $13,350; Out-of-state $13,350

Housing: Homeownership rate: 64.3% (2000); Median home value: $83,100 (2000); Median rent: $345 per month (2000); Median age of housing: 41 years (2000).

Newspapers: Lebanon Advertiser (1 x week)

Transportation: Commute to work: 86.8% car, 0.6% public transportation, 10.3% walk, 1.7% work from home (2000); Travel time to work: 36.6% less than 15 minutes, 37.0% 15 to 30 minutes, 13.5% 30 to 45 minutes, 7.7% 45 to 60 minutes, 5.2% 60 minutes or more (2000)

LENZBURG (village). Covers a land area of 1.235 square miles and a water area of 0.059 square miles. Located at 38.28° N. Lat.; 89.81° W. Long. Elevation is 443 feet.

Population: 577 (2000); Race: 92.7% White, 1.9% Black, 0.7% Asian, 0.0% American Indian and Alaska Native, 1.6% Hispanic of any race, 4.7% two or more races (2000); Density: 467.2 persons per square mile (2000); Age: 33.3% under 18, 14.6% over 64 (2000); Marriage status: 19.4% never married, 57.0% now married, 7.1% widowed, 16.5% divorced (2000); Foreign born: 0.7% (2000); Ancestry (includes multiple ancestries): 43.7% German, 16.5% Other groups, 14.6% Irish, 8.8% French (except Basque), 7.5% United States or American (2000).

Economy: In bituminous-coal and agricultural area. Employment by occupation: 12.9% management, 6.2% professional, 19.5% services, 17.6% sales, 0.0% farming, 14.8% construction, 29.0% production (2000).

Income: Per capita income: $13,505 (2000); Median household income: $30,417 (2000); Poverty rate: 12.7% (2000).

Taxes: Total city taxes per capita: $75 (1997); City property taxes per capita: $12 (1997).

Education: High school graduation rate: 75.0% (2000); College graduation rate: 5.6% (2000).

Housing: Homeownership rate: 74.3% (2000); Median home value: $55,200 (2000); Median rent: $225 per month (2000); Median age of housing: 38 years (2000).

Transportation: Commute to work: 95.8% car, 0.0% public transportation, 0.9% walk, 3.3% work from home (2000); Travel time to work: 21.0% less than 15 minutes, 16.6% 15 to 30 minutes, 37.1% 30 to 45 minutes, 17.1% 45 to 60 minutes, 8.3% 60 minutes or more (2000)

MARISSA (village). Covers a land area of 3.717 square miles and a water area of 0.195 square miles. Located at 38.24° N. Lat.; 89.75° W. Long. Elevation is 460 feet.

History: Incorporated 1882.

Population: 2,141 (2000); Race: 98.5% White, 0.3% Black, 0.0% Asian, 0.0% American Indian and Alaska Native, 0.7% Hispanic of any race, 0.9% two or more races (2000); Density: 576.1 persons per square mile (2000); Age: 23.4% under 18, 16.8% over 64 (2000); Marriage status: 21.4% never married, 58.2% now married, 8.2% widowed, 12.2% divorced (2000); Foreign born: 0.9% (2000); Ancestry (includes multiple ancestries): 30.8% German, 15.0% Irish, 12.2% United States or American, 10.7% English, 5.2% Other groups (2000).

Economy: Stone and wood products; bituminous-coal mines. Agriculture: corn, wheat; dairy products; poultry, livestock. Single-family building permits issued: 1 (2001) / 3 (2000); Multi-family building permits issued: 0 (2001) / 0 (2000); Employment by occupation: 7.9% management, 16.6% professional, 16.0% services, 20.6% sales, 0.7% farming, 13.1% construction, 25.2% production (2000).
Income: Per capita income: $15,930 (2000); Median household income: $31,684 (2000); Poverty rate: 9.5% (2000).
Taxes: Total city taxes per capita: $62 (1997); City property taxes per capita: $17 (1997).
Education: High school graduation rate: 77.5% (2000); College graduation rate: 10.9% (2000).

School District(s)

Marissa C U School District 40 (PK-12)
2000 Enrollment: 672 618-295-2313
Housing: Homeownership rate: 75.0% (2000); Median home value: $48,300 (2000); Median rent: $275 per month (2000); Median age of housing: 44 years (2000).
Newspapers: Journal-Messenger (1 x week)
Transportation: Commute to work: 92.2% car, 0.8% public transportation, 3.9% walk, 2.5% work from home (2000); Travel time to work: 32.0% less than 15 minutes, 18.8% 15 to 30 minutes, 27.5% 30 to 45 minutes, 10.5% 45 to 60 minutes, 11.3% 60 minutes or more (2000)

MASCOUTAH (city). Covers a land area of 8.638 square miles and a water area of 0.061 square miles. Located at 38.49° N. Lat.; 89.80° W. Long. Elevation is 424 feet.
History: Incorporated 1839.
Population: 5,659 (2000); Race: 92.2% White, 3.2% Black, 0.2% Asian, 0.3% American Indian and Alaska Native, 2.8% Hispanic of any race, 2.2% two or more races (2000); Density: 655.1 persons per square mile (2000); Age: 26.4% under 18, 13.6% over 64 (2000); Marriage status: 24.0% never married, 60.8% now married, 6.2% widowed, 9.0% divorced (2000); Foreign born: 2.0% (2000); Ancestry (includes multiple ancestries): 46.3% German, 12.2% Other groups, 8.9% Irish, 8.6% English, 5.5% United States or American (2000).
Economy: Bituminous coal mines. Agriculture: wheat, soybeans, corn, apples, poultry, hogs; dairy products. Single-family building permits issued: 14 (2001) / 7 (2000); Multi-family building permits issued: 16 (2001) / 0 (2000); Employment by occupation: 10.1% management, 18.7% professional, 21.9% services, 28.2% sales, 0.0% farming, 8.4% construction, 12.6% production (2000).
Income: Per capita income: $21,569 (2000); Median household income: $46,451 (2000); Poverty rate: 7.8% (2000).
Taxes: Total city taxes per capita: $209 (1997); City property taxes per capita: $82 (1997).
Education: High school graduation rate: 86.7% (2000); College graduation rate: 19.3% (2000).

School District(s)

Mascoutah C U District 19 (PK-12)
2000 Enrollment: 3,029 618-566-7414
Housing: Homeownership rate: 71.7% (2000); Median home value: $81,800 (2000); Median rent: $406 per month (2000); Median age of housing: 36 years (2000).
Newspapers: Mascoutah Herald (2 x week); Herald Scott Flier (2 x week); Fairview Heights Tribune (1 x week); Command Post (2 x week); Lebanon Herald (2 x week)
Transportation: Commute to work: 93.7% car, 0.3% public transportation, 2.5% walk, 3.3% work from home (2000); Travel time to work: 34.8% less than 15 minutes, 37.9% 15 to 30 minutes, 13.9% 30 to 45 minutes, 6.5% 45 to 60 minutes, 6.9% 60 minutes or more (2000)

MILLSTADT (village). Covers a land area of 1.112 square miles and a water area of 0 square miles. Located at 38.45° N. Lat.; 90.09° W. Long. Elevation is 620 feet.
History: Incorporated 1878.
Population: 2,794 (2000); Race: 98.5% White, 0.0% Black, 0.7% Asian, 0.2% American Indian and Alaska Native, 0.1% Hispanic of any race, 0.6% two or more races (2000); Density: 2,511.9 persons per square mile (2000); Age: 24.6% under 18, 15.6% over 64 (2000); Marriage status: 20.2% never married, 64.4% now married, 7.0% widowed, 8.4% divorced (2000); Foreign born: 0.8% (2000); Ancestry (includes multiple ancestries): 50.0% German, 16.9% Irish, 9.4% French (except Basque), 8.4% English, 6.4% Other groups (2000).
Economy: Flour milling. Manufacturing: food processing systems. Bituminous-coal mines. Agriculture: wheat, apples; dairy products; hogs, poultry. Single-family building permits issued: 14 (2001) / 27 (2000); Multi-family building permits issued: 0 (2001) / 2 (2000); Employment by occupation: 13.5% management, 19.6% professional, 13.3% services, 26.1% sales, 0.0% farming, 10.3% construction, 17.2% production (2000).
Income: Per capita income: $21,914 (2000); Median household income: $47,824 (2000); Poverty rate: 4.0% (2000).
Taxes: Total city taxes per capita: $163 (1997); City property taxes per capita: $87 (1997).
Education: High school graduation rate: 84.3% (2000); College graduation rate: 18.5% (2000).

School District(s)

Millstadt C C School District 160 (PK-08)
2000 Enrollment: 746 618-476-1803
Housing: Homeownership rate: 73.3% (2000); Median home value: $102,000 (2000); Median rent: $411 per month (2000); Median age of housing: 32 years (2000).
Transportation: Commute to work: 96.2% car, 0.0% public transportation, 2.3% walk, 0.9% work from home (2000); Travel time to work: 22.9% less than 15 minutes, 40.2% 15 to 30 minutes, 21.0% 30 to 45 minutes, 12.6% 45 to 60 minutes, 3.2% 60 minutes or more (2000)

NEW ATHENS (village). Covers a land area of 1.725 square miles and a water area of 0.111 square miles. Located at 38.32° N. Lat.; 89.87° W. Long. Elevation is 429 feet.
History: Incorporated 1869.
Population: 1,981 (2000); Race: 97.3% White, 0.5% Black, 0.2% Asian, 0.4% American Indian and Alaska Native, 0.6% Hispanic of any race, 1.7% two or more races (2000); Density: 1,148.3 persons per square mile (2000); Age: 26.1% under 18, 16.9% over 64 (2000); Marriage status: 21.5% never married, 59.2% now married, 10.2% widowed, 9.0% divorced (2000); Foreign born: 0.5% (2000); Ancestry (includes multiple ancestries): 49.5% German, 13.0% Irish, 8.9% English, 8.9% United States or American, 4.6% French (except Basque) (2000).
Economy: Manufacturing: stoves, enamelware. Bituminous coal mines. Agriculture: corn, wheat, fruit; dairy products, livestock. Single-family building permits issued: 12 (2001) / 9 (2000); Multi-family building permits issued: 0 (2001) / 0 (2000); Employment by occupation: 8.8% management, 15.0% professional, 15.2% services, 24.2% sales, 0.2% farming, 14.4% construction, 22.1% production (2000).
Income: Per capita income: $17,627 (2000); Median household income: $39,625 (2000); Poverty rate: 8.4% (2000).
Taxes: Total city taxes per capita: $68 (1997); City property taxes per capita: $20 (1997).
Education: High school graduation rate: 79.7% (2000); College graduation rate: 11.6% (2000).

School District(s)

New Athens C U School District 60 (PK-12)
2000 Enrollment: 677 618-475-2174
Housing: Homeownership rate: 78.9% (2000); Median home value: $72,200 (2000); Median rent: $292 per month (2000); Median age of housing: 50 years (2000).
Transportation: Commute to work: 93.0% car, 0.0% public transportation, 2.8% walk, 3.5% work from home (2000); Travel time to work: 29.4% less than 15 minutes, 19.4% 15 to 30 minutes, 26.4% 30 to 45 minutes, 13.8% 45 to 60 minutes, 11.0% 60 minutes or more (2000)

O'FALLON (city). Covers a land area of 10.913 square miles and a water area of 0.012 square miles. Located at 38.59° N. Lat.; 89.91° W. Long. Elevation is 550 feet.
History: O'Fallon developed in 1854 along the railroad route. Named for the owner of the land on which the town was sited, it grew as a residential community.
Population: 21,910 (2000); Race: 82.9% White, 11.9% Black, 2.2% Asian, 0.3% American Indian and Alaska Native, 2.5% Hispanic of any race, 2.1% two or more races (2000); Density: 2,007.6 persons per square mile (2000); Age: 28.7% under 18, 8.3% over 64 (2000); Marriage status: 23.3% never married, 63.5% now married, 4.0% widowed, 9.2% divorced (2000); Foreign born: 3.7% (2000); Ancestry (includes multiple ancestries): 30.8% German, 19.2% Other groups, 12.6% Irish, 11.1% English, 6.1% United States or American (2000).
Vital Statistics: Birth rate: 115.0 per 10,000 population (1998)
Economy: Single-family building permits issued: 240 (2001) / 224 (2000); Multi-family building permits issued: 40 (2001) / 24 (2000); Employment by occupation: 16.3% management, 26.1% professional, 13.4% services, 27.6% sales, 0.3% farming, 6.2% construction, 10.1% production (2000).

Income: Per capita income: $24,821 (2000); Median household income: $55,927 (2000); Poverty rate: 5.0% (2000).
Education: High school graduation rate: 92.3% (2000); College graduation rate: 38.7% (2000).

School District(s)

O Fallon C C School District 90 (PK-08)
2000 Enrollment: 2,899 618-632-3666
O Fallon Township High School District 203 (09-12)
2000 Enrollment: 2,010 618-632-3507

Housing: Homeownership rate: 68.6% (2000); Median home value: $121,400 (2000); Median rent: $541 per month (2000); Median age of housing: 17 years (2000).
Newspapers: Smart Shopper (1 x week); O'Fallon Progress (1 x week); Base News (1 x week)
Transportation: Commute to work: 95.2% car, 0.9% public transportation, 1.2% walk, 2.2% work from home (2000); Travel time to work: 29.5% less than 15 minutes, 41.1% 15 to 30 minutes, 16.5% 30 to 45 minutes, 8.2% 45 to 60 minutes, 4.7% 60 minutes or more (2000)
Additional Information Contacts
O Fallon Chamber of Commerce 618-632-3377

SAINT LIBORY (village). Covers a land area of 0.943 square miles and a water area of 0 square miles. Located at 38.36° N. Lat.; 89.71° W. Long. Elevation is 420 feet.
Population: 583 (2000); Race: 100.0% White, 0.0% Black, 0.0% Asian, 0.0% American Indian and Alaska Native, 0.0% Hispanic of any race, 0.0% two or more races (2000); Density: 618.1 persons per square mile (2000); Age: 24.0% under 18, 18.2% over 64 (2000); Marriage status: 19.3% never married, 60.0% now married, 8.7% widowed, 12.0% divorced (2000); Foreign born: 0.5% (2000); Ancestry (includes multiple ancestries): 67.2% German, 10.2% Irish, 7.7% Polish, 5.3% United States or American, 4.8% French (except Basque) (2000).
Economy: Single-family building permits issued: 2 (2001) / 3 (2000); Multi-family building permits issued: 0 (2001) / 0 (2000); Employment by occupation: 17.5% management, 8.0% professional, 14.0% services, 26.8% sales, 0.6% farming, 10.8% construction, 22.3% production (2000).
Income: Per capita income: $20,024 (2000); Median household income: $50,625 (2000); Poverty rate: 6.0% (2000).
Education: High school graduation rate: 78.6% (2000); College graduation rate: 7.7% (2000).

School District(s)

Saint Libory Cons School District 30 (PK-08)
2000 Enrollment: 126 618-768-4923

Housing: Homeownership rate: 80.1% (2000); Median home value: $87,300 (2000); Median rent: $269 per month (2000); Median age of housing: 29 years (2000).
Transportation: Commute to work: 93.6% car, 0.7% public transportation, 1.3% walk, 4.3% work from home (2000); Travel time to work: 17.5% less than 15 minutes, 25.2% 15 to 30 minutes, 26.6% 30 to 45 minutes, 17.8% 45 to 60 minutes, 12.9% 60 minutes or more (2000)

SAUGET (village). Aka Monsanto. Covers a land area of 4.130 square miles and a water area of 0.319 square miles. Located at 38.58° N. Lat.; 90.16° W. Long. Elevation is 410 feet.
History: Formerly called Monsanto.
Population: 249 (2000); Race: 84.4% White, 15.6% Black, 0.0% Asian, 0.0% American Indian and Alaska Native, 0.0% Hispanic of any race, 0.0% two or more races (2000); Density: 60.3 persons per square mile (2000); Age: 19.4% under 18, 14.5% over 64 (2000); Marriage status: 23.4% never married, 51.3% now married, 13.3% widowed, 12.0% divorced (2000); Foreign born: 0.0% (2000); Ancestry (includes multiple ancestries): 24.2% German, 17.2% Irish, 10.2% Other groups, 9.1% United States or American, 9.1% English (2000).
Economy: Zinc and copper processing, manufacturing, chemicals, petroleum additives; steel foundry. Popular night club area. Employment by occupation: 11.9% management, 7.1% professional, 28.6% services, 20.2% sales, 0.0% farming, 13.1% construction, 19.0% production (2000).
Income: Per capita income: $19,330 (2000); Median household income: $35,833 (2000); Poverty rate: 17.3% (2000).
Taxes: Total city taxes per capita: $20,823 (2000); City property taxes per capita: $20,779 (2000).
Education: High school graduation rate: 79.1% (2000); College graduation rate: 7.5% (2000).
Housing: Homeownership rate: 66.3% (2000); Median home value: $50,800 (2000); Median rent: $333 per month (2000); Median age of housing: 40 years (2000).
Transportation: Commute to work: 100.0% car, 0.0% public transportation, 0.0% walk, 0.0% work from home (2000); Travel time to work: 58.8% less than 15 minutes, 31.3% 15 to 30 minutes, 6.3% 30 to 45 minutes, 0.0% 45 to 60 minutes, 3.8% 60 minutes or more (2000)

SCOTT AFB (CDP). Covers a land area of 3.755 square miles and a water area of 0 square miles. Located at 38.54° N. Lat.; 89.85° W. Long.
Population: 2,707 (2000); Race: 77.0% White, 16.6% Black, 4.0% Asian, 0.0% American Indian and Alaska Native, 1.8% Hispanic of any race, 2.3% two or more races (2000); Density: 721.0 persons per square mile (2000); Age: 44.7% under 18, 0.5% over 64 (2000); Marriage status: 19.1% never married, 75.4% now married, 0.8% widowed, 4.8% divorced (2000); Foreign born: 4.3% (2000); Ancestry (includes multiple ancestries): 20.7% Other groups, 17.6% German, 12.0% United States or American, 6.3% Irish, 5.9% English (2000).
Economy: Employment by occupation: 11.8% management, 21.9% professional, 17.8% services, 39.9% sales, 0.0% farming, 0.9% construction, 7.7% production (2000).
Income: Per capita income: $15,421 (2000); Median household income: $51,290 (2000); Poverty rate: 1.5% (2000).
Education: High school graduation rate: 98.9% (2000); College graduation rate: 45.0% (2000).
Housing: Homeownership rate: 11.1% (2000); Median rent: $742 per month (2000); Median age of housing: 34 years (2000).
Transportation: Commute to work: 87.3% car, 0.8% public transportation, 9.7% walk, 1.5% work from home (2000); Travel time to work: 73.8% less than 15 minutes, 16.5% 15 to 30 minutes, 5.0% 30 to 45 minutes, 4.1% 45 to 60 minutes, 0.7% 60 minutes or more (2000)

SHILOH (village). Covers a land area of 10.054 square miles and a water area of 0.033 square miles. Located at 38.55° N. Lat.; 89.91° W. Long. Elevation is 660 feet.
Population: 7,643 (2000); Race: 79.5% White, 17.1% Black, 1.6% Asian, 0.3% American Indian and Alaska Native, 2.0% Hispanic of any race, 1.6% two or more races (2000); Density: 760.2 persons per square mile (2000); Age: 28.4% under 18, 6.5% over 64 (2000); Marriage status: 23.5% never married, 64.2% now married, 4.1% widowed, 8.2% divorced (2000); Foreign born: 2.3% (2000); Ancestry (includes multiple ancestries): 28.3% German, 23.5% Other groups, 15.8% Irish, 7.0% United States or American, 6.7% English (2000).
Economy: In agricultural area: soybeans, wheat, sorghum, hogs; dairying. Bituminous coal in area. Single-family building permits issued: 204 (2001) / 149 (2000); Multi-family building permits issued: 6 (2001) / 8 (2000); Employment by occupation: 14.9% management, 23.3% professional, 12.0% services, 29.5% sales, 0.0% farming, 7.6% construction, 12.7% production (2000).
Income: Per capita income: $25,550 (2000); Median household income: $57,692 (2000); Poverty rate: 7.7% (2000).
Taxes: Total city taxes per capita: $37 (1997); City property taxes per capita: $19 (1997).
Education: High school graduation rate: 91.6% (2000); College graduation rate: 32.7% (2000).
Housing: Homeownership rate: 69.3% (2000); Median home value: $136,100 (2000); Median rent: $431 per month (2000); Median age of housing: 11 years (2000).
Transportation: Commute to work: 94.3% car, 0.7% public transportation, 2.2% walk, 2.5% work from home (2000); Travel time to work: 29.2% less than 15 minutes, 34.9% 15 to 30 minutes, 21.0% 30 to 45 minutes, 10.2% 45 to 60 minutes, 4.7% 60 minutes or more (2000)

SMITHTON (village). Covers a land area of 1.672 square miles and a water area of 0.006 square miles. Located at 38.40° N. Lat.; 89.99° W. Long. Elevation is 478 feet.
Population: 2,248 (2000); Race: 96.4% White, 0.5% Black, 0.0% Asian, 0.5% American Indian and Alaska Native, 0.2% Hispanic of any race, 2.6% two or more races (2000); Density: 1,344.5 persons per square mile (2000); Age: 28.4% under 18, 11.6% over 64 (2000); Marriage status: 22.1% never married, 59.6% now married, 6.1% widowed, 12.1% divorced (2000); Foreign born: 0.6% (2000); Ancestry (includes multiple ancestries): 42.4% German, 11.4% Irish, 9.1% United States or American, 7.0% Other groups, 5.1% English (2000).
Economy: In bituminous-coal and agricultural area. Single-family building permits issued: 53 (2001) / 32 (2000); Multi-family building permits issued: 0 (2001) / 0 (2000); Employment by occupation: 10.6% management, 17.0% professional, 12.9% services, 32.8% sales, 0.0% farming, 10.8% construction, 15.9% production (2000).

Income: Per capita income: $19,695 (2000); Median household income: $51,806 (2000); Poverty rate: 9.3% (2000).
Taxes: Total city taxes per capita: $145 (1997); City property taxes per capita: $74 (1997).
Education: High school graduation rate: 85.0% (2000); College graduation rate: 16.4% (2000).

School District(s)

Smithton C C School District 130 (KG-08)
2000 Enrollment: 375 618-233-6863

Housing: Homeownership rate: 88.9% (2000); Median home value: $105,700 (2000); Median rent: $369 per month (2000); Median age of housing: 17 years (2000).
Transportation: Commute to work: 94.4% car, 0.0% public transportation, 1.3% walk, 3.6% work from home (2000); Travel time to work: 14.1% less than 15 minutes, 37.7% 15 to 30 minutes, 30.7% 30 to 45 minutes, 12.6% 45 to 60 minutes, 4.8% 60 minutes or more (2000)

SUMMERFIELD (village). Covers a land area of 0.420 square miles and a water area of 0 square miles. Located at 38.59° N. Lat.; 89.75° W. Long. Elevation is 478 feet.
Population: 472 (2000); Race: 97.3% White, 1.4% Black, 0.6% Asian, 0.0% American Indian and Alaska Native, 1.2% Hispanic of any race, 0.6% two or more races (2000); Density: 1,122.6 persons per square mile (2000); Age: 32.8% under 18, 9.2% over 64 (2000); Marriage status: 24.0% never married, 60.0% now married, 6.3% widowed, 9.7% divorced (2000); Foreign born: 1.0% (2000); Ancestry (includes multiple ancestries): 21.9% Other groups, 20.5% Irish, 14.5% German, 13.7% French (except Basque), 7.2% English (2000).
Economy: In agricultural area: dairying; soybeans, wheat, sorghum; hogs. Single-family building permits issued: 7 (2001) / 3 (2000); Multi-family building permits issued: 0 (2001) / 0 (2000); Employment by occupation: 7.6% management, 12.1% professional, 21.5% services, 13.9% sales, 0.9% farming, 21.5% construction, 22.4% production (2000).
Income: Per capita income: $13,283 (2000); Median household income: $42,031 (2000); Poverty rate: 6.7% (2000).
Taxes: Total city taxes per capita: $37 (1997); City property taxes per capita: $29 (1997).
Education: High school graduation rate: 66.4% (2000); College graduation rate: 11.7% (2000).
Housing: Homeownership rate: 78.9% (2000); Median home value: $62,200 (2000); Median rent: $327 per month (2000); Median age of housing: 39 years (2000).
Transportation: Commute to work: 93.8% car, 0.0% public transportation, 5.7% walk, 0.5% work from home (2000); Travel time to work: 21.9% less than 15 minutes, 44.3% 15 to 30 minutes, 18.1% 30 to 45 minutes, 11.9% 45 to 60 minutes, 3.8% 60 minutes or more (2000)

SWANSEA (village). Covers a land area of 5.073 square miles and a water area of 0.020 square miles. Located at 38.54° N. Lat.; 89.98° W. Long. Elevation is 547 feet.
History: Incorporated 1895.
Population: 10,579 (2000); Race: 89.7% White, 8.1% Black, 0.9% Asian, 0.2% American Indian and Alaska Native, 1.3% Hispanic of any race, 0.8% two or more races (2000); Density: 2,085.6 persons per square mile (2000); Age: 25.7% under 18, 14.6% over 64 (2000); Marriage status: 23.0% never married, 58.7% now married, 6.8% widowed, 11.4% divorced (2000); Foreign born: 1.4% (2000); Ancestry (includes multiple ancestries): 39.3% German, 14.1% Irish, 13.3% Other groups, 10.5% English, 6.4% United States or American (2000).
Economy: Single-family building permits issued: 79 (2001) / 50 (2000); Multi-family building permits issued: 12 (2001) / 92 (2000); Employment by occupation: 13.7% management, 22.4% professional, 13.2% services, 31.9% sales, 0.2% farming, 9.0% construction, 9.6% production (2000).
Income: Per capita income: $25,634 (2000); Median household income: $49,851 (2000); Poverty rate: 6.7% (2000).
Taxes: Total city taxes per capita: $43 (1997); City property taxes per capita: $39 (1997).
Education: High school graduation rate: 84.7% (2000); College graduation rate: 27.4% (2000).

School District(s)

High Mount School District 116 (PK-08)
2000 Enrollment: 455 618-233-1054
Wolf Branch School District 113 (KG-08)
2000 Enrollment: 897 618-277-2100

Housing: Homeownership rate: 77.0% (2000); Median home value: $115,300 (2000); Median rent: $408 per month (2000); Median age of housing: 22 years (2000).
Transportation: Commute to work: 95.2% car, 1.7% public transportation, 0.6% walk, 2.4% work from home (2000); Travel time to work: 35.6% less than 15 minutes, 32.8% 15 to 30 minutes, 15.9% 30 to 45 minutes, 11.5% 45 to 60 minutes, 4.2% 60 minutes or more (2000)

WASHINGTON PARK (village). Covers a land area of 2.451 square miles and a water area of 0 square miles. Located at 38.63° N. Lat.; 90.09° W. Long. Elevation is 415 feet.
History: Incorporated 1917.
Population: 5,345 (2000); Race: 5.3% White, 93.9% Black, 0.0% Asian, 0.0% American Indian and Alaska Native, 0.5% Hispanic of any race, 0.1% two or more races (2000); Density: 2,180.4 persons per square mile (2000); Age: 36.6% under 18, 5.8% over 64 (2000); Marriage status: 45.5% never married, 38.1% now married, 6.3% widowed, 10.2% divorced (2000); Foreign born: 1.0% (2000); Ancestry (includes multiple ancestries): 74.0% Other groups, 1.7% African, 1.3% United States or American, 1.2% Polish, 0.6% German (2000).
Economy: Some agriculture to East: wheat, soybeans; cattle. Manufacturing of gas heating stoves, barbecue grills. Single-family building permits issued: 8 (2001) / 2 (2000); Multi-family building permits issued: 0 (2001) / 0 (2000); Employment by occupation: 5.3% management, 7.4% professional, 34.0% services, 19.4% sales, 0.0% farming, 6.3% construction, 27.6% production (2000).
Income: Per capita income: $8,495 (2000); Median household income: $21,132 (2000); Poverty rate: 44.8% (2000).
Taxes: Total city taxes per capita: $135 (1997); City property taxes per capita: $71 (1997).
Education: High school graduation rate: 62.6% (2000); College graduation rate: 3.8% (2000).
Housing: Homeownership rate: 57.0% (2000); Median home value: $33,700 (2000); Median rent: $337 per month (2000); Median age of housing: 43 years (2000).
Transportation: Commute to work: 81.7% car, 14.5% public transportation, 0.5% walk, 2.0% work from home (2000); Travel time to work: 15.8% less than 15 minutes, 39.5% 15 to 30 minutes, 28.2% 30 to 45 minutes, 4.8% 45 to 60 minutes, 11.7% 60 minutes or more (2000)

Saline County

Located in southeastern Illinois, partly in the Ozarks; drained by the Saline River; includes part of Shawnee National Forest. Covers a land area of 383.30 square miles, a water area of 3.70 square miles, and is located in the Central Time Zone. The county government was organized in 1847. County seat is Harrisburg.

Weather Station: Harrisburg — Elevation: 364 feet

	Jan	Feb	Mar	Apr	May	Jun	Jul	Aug	Sep	Oct	Nov	Dec
High	40	47	57	69	78	86	90	89	82	71	57	46
Low	23	27	36	46	55	64	67	65	58	45	37	29
Precip	3.0	2.7	4.5	4.8	4.8	4.4	4.0	3.2	3.1	3.1	4.1	4.0
Snow	4.8	3.8	2.3	0.4	0.0	0.0	0.0	0.0	0.0	tr	0.6	1.7

High and Low temperatures in degrees Fahrenheit; Precipitation and Snow in inches

Population: 26,733 (2000); Race: 94.4% White, 4.1% Black, 0.2% Asian, 0.3% American Indian and Alaska Native, 0.7% Hispanic of any race, 0.8% two or more races (2000); Density: 69.7 persons per square mile (2000); Age: 24.0% under 18, 18.9% over 64 (2000).
Religion: Five largest groups: 41.1% Southern Baptist Convention, 4.3% The United Methodist Church, 4.3% Catholic Church, 1.5% Church of God (Cleveland, Tennessee), 1.4% Christian Churches and Churches of Christ (2000).
Economy: Unemployment rate: 7.7% (11/2002); Total civilian labor force: 9,863 (11/2002); Leading industries: 28.3% health care and social assistance; 16.7% retail trade; 11.0% mining (2000); Companies that employ more than 1,000 persons: 0 (2000); Companies that employ more than 100 persons: 10 (2000); Farms: 441 totaling 130,680 acres (1997); Minority business ownership rate: 0.0% (1997); Women business ownership rate: 15.6% (1997); Retail sales per capita: $8,868 (1997). Single-family building permits issued: 0 (2001) / 0 (2000); Multi-family building permits issued: 0 (2001) / 0 (2000).
Income: Per capita income: $15,590 (2000); Median household income: $28,768 (2000); Poverty rate: 14.2% (2000); Bankruptcy rate: 6.63% (2001).

Taxes: Total county taxes per capita: $98 (1997); County property taxes per capita: $95 (1997).
Education: High school graduation rate: 76.1% (2000); College graduation rate: 12.1% (2000).
Housing: Homeownership rate: 76.5% (2000); Median home value: $48,300 (2000); Median rent: $226 per month (2000); Median age of housing: 39 years (2000).
Health: Birth rate: 120.1 per 10,000 population (1998); Age adjusted death rate: 110.8 per 10,000 population (1999); Age adjusted cancer mortality rate: 248.3 deaths per 100,000 population (1999). Number of physicians: 10.1 per 10,000 population (1999); Number of hospital beds: 43.4 per 10,000 population (1999).
Elections: 2000 Presidential election results: 46.6% Gore, 50.9% Bush, 1.6% Nader, 0.8% Buchanan
National and State Parks: Saline County State Conservation Area
Additional Information Contacts
Saline County Government Offices 618-252-6905
Eldorado Chamber of Commerce. 618-273-3119
Harrisburg Chamber of Commerce 618-252-4192

Saline County Communities

CARRIER MILLS (village). Aka Carriers Mills. Covers a land area of 1.238 square miles and a water area of 0.005 square miles. Located at 37.68° N. Lat.; 88.62° W. Long. Elevation is 391 feet.
History: Carriers (or Carrier) Mills was named for William H. Carrier who built a sawmill here in 1870. The town developed around the mining industry.
Population: 1,886 (2000); Race: 85.0% White, 14.0% Black, 0.0% Asian, 0.2% American Indian and Alaska Native, 0.4% Hispanic of any race, 0.4% two or more races (2000); Density: 1,522.9 persons per square mile (2000); Age: 22.6% under 18, 23.5% over 64 (2000); Marriage status: 11.7% never married, 65.6% now married, 12.5% widowed, 10.1% divorced (2000); Foreign born: 0.0% (2000); Ancestry (includes multiple ancestries): 16.6% United States or American, 15.6% Other groups, 11.2% English, 10.2% Irish, 9.0% German (2000).
Economy: Employment by occupation: 8.5% management, 17.4% professional, 14.9% services, 25.1% sales, 0.6% farming, 19.0% construction, 14.6% production (2000).
Income: Per capita income: $14,314 (2000); Median household income: $25,493 (2000); Poverty rate: 17.7% (2000).
Taxes: Total city taxes per capita: $26 (1997); City property taxes per capita: $18 (1997).
Education: High school graduation rate: 72.0% (2000); College graduation rate: 8.6% (2000).

School District(s)
Carrier Mills-Stonefort CUSD 2 (PK-12)
2000 Enrollment: 482 618-994-2392
Housing: Homeownership rate: 72.8% (2000); Median home value: $42,000 (2000); Median rent: $224 per month (2000); Median age of housing: 36 years (2000).
Transportation: Commute to work: 92.1% car, 0.6% public transportation, 2.8% walk, 0.7% work from home (2000); Travel time to work: 33.8% less than 15 minutes, 29.9% 15 to 30 minutes, 17.6% 30 to 45 minutes, 7.5% 45 to 60 minutes, 11.2% 60 minutes or more (2000)

ELDORADO (city). Covers a land area of 2.304 square miles and a water area of 0.032 square miles. Located at 37.81° N. Lat.; 88.44° W. Long. Elevation is 389 feet.
History: Incorporated 1873.
Population: 4,534 (2000); Race: 98.2% White, 0.4% Black, 0.0% Asian, 0.0% American Indian and Alaska Native, 0.0% Hispanic of any race, 0.9% two or more races (2000); Density: 1,967.8 persons per square mile (2000); Age: 24.0% under 18, 23.9% over 64 (2000); Marriage status: 20.3% never married, 53.6% now married, 13.9% widowed, 12.2% divorced (2000); Foreign born: 0.1% (2000); Ancestry (includes multiple ancestries): 15.6% Irish, 14.0% United States or American, 13.8% German, 8.8% English, 7.7% Other groups (2000).
Economy: Trade center of bituminous-coal-mining and agricultural area; corn, wheat, oats; poultry. Employment by occupation: 5.3% management, 14.7% professional, 27.9% services, 18.8% sales, 1.1% farming, 16.3% construction, 15.9% production (2000).
Income: Per capita income: $12,980 (2000); Median household income: $22,500 (2000); Poverty rate: 23.1% (2000).
Taxes: Total city taxes per capita: $47 (1997); City property taxes per capita: $41 (1997).
Education: High school graduation rate: 66.9% (2000); College graduation rate: 8.5% (2000).

School District(s)
Eldorado Community Unit District 4 (PK-12)
2000 Enrollment: 1,301 618-273-6394
Housing: Homeownership rate: 69.3% (2000); Median home value: $36,700 (2000); Median rent: $203 per month (2000); Median age of housing: 48 years (2000).
Hospitals: Ferrell Hospital (51 beds)
Newspapers: Eldorado Daily Journal (6 x week)
Transportation: Commute to work: 93.7% car, 0.5% public transportation, 3.1% walk, 2.0% work from home (2000); Travel time to work: 46.3% less than 15 minutes, 25.2% 15 to 30 minutes, 12.1% 30 to 45 minutes, 9.9% 45 to 60 minutes, 6.5% 60 minutes or more (2000)
Additional Information Contacts
Eldorado Chamber of Commerce. 618-273-3119

GALATIA (village). Covers a land area of 1.961 square miles and a water area of 0.016 square miles. Located at 37.84° N. Lat.; 88.61° W. Long. Elevation is 397 feet.
Population: 1,013 (2000); Race: 98.7% White, 0.0% Black, 0.0% Asian, 0.0% American Indian and Alaska Native, 0.6% Hispanic of any race, 1.3% two or more races (2000); Density: 516.5 persons per square mile (2000); Age: 22.5% under 18, 26.3% over 64 (2000); Marriage status: 20.9% never married, 53.9% now married, 14.8% widowed, 10.4% divorced (2000); Foreign born: 0.3% (2000); Ancestry (includes multiple ancestries): 19.0% Irish, 18.0% German, 16.0% United States or American, 11.8% English, 4.8% French (except Basque) (2000).
Economy: In bituminous coal-mining and agricultural region. Employment by occupation: 3.7% management, 18.6% professional, 24.6% services, 25.7% sales, 0.6% farming, 11.7% construction, 15.1% production (2000).
Income: Per capita income: $12,810 (2000); Median household income: $23,750 (2000); Poverty rate: 16.7% (2000).
Taxes: Total city taxes per capita: $19 (1997); City property taxes per capita: $19 (1997).
Education: High school graduation rate: 72.0% (2000); College graduation rate: 6.5% (2000).

School District(s)
Galatia C U School District 1 (KG-12)
2000 Enrollment: 393 618-268-6371
Housing: Homeownership rate: 78.1% (2000); Median home value: $45,500 (2000); Median rent: $192 per month (2000); Median age of housing: 39 years (2000).
Transportation: Commute to work: 87.9% car, 0.0% public transportation, 5.9% walk, 5.9% work from home (2000); Travel time to work: 35.7% less than 15 minutes, 41.4% 15 to 30 minutes, 7.5% 30 to 45 minutes, 6.6% 45 to 60 minutes, 8.8% 60 minutes or more (2000)

HARRISBURG (city). Covers a land area of 6.239 square miles and a water area of 0.141 square miles. Located at 37.73° N. Lat.; 88.54° W. Long. Elevation is 403 feet.
History: Harrisburg was platted in 1853 and developed as an industrial center with planing, flour, and woolen mills founded in the late 1800's. Coal mining began in 1905.
Population: 9,860 (2000); Race: 90.5% White, 7.3% Black, 0.4% Asian, 0.4% American Indian and Alaska Native, 1.0% Hispanic of any race, 1.3% two or more races (2000); Density: 1,580.3 persons per square mile (2000); Age: 24.0% under 18, 19.1% over 64 (2000); Marriage status: 23.0% never married, 50.2% now married, 12.0% widowed, 14.8% divorced (2000); Foreign born: 1.4% (2000); Ancestry (includes multiple ancestries): 14.8% United States or American, 12.7% German, 12.0% Irish, 11.0% English, 10.0% Other groups (2000).
Economy: Employment by occupation: 8.9% management, 18.7% professional, 21.7% services, 24.9% sales, 0.0% farming, 11.8% construction, 14.0% production (2000).
Income: Per capita income: $15,005 (2000); Median household income: $26,507 (2000); Poverty rate: 13.2% (2000).
Taxes: Total city taxes per capita: $16 (1997); City property taxes per capita: $9 (1997).
Education: High school graduation rate: 75.2% (2000); College graduation rate: 12.8% (2000).

School District(s)
Edwd/Gltn/Hdin/Pop/Slne/Wbh/Wn/Wh (07-12)
2000 Enrollment: 64 618-253-5581
Harrisburg C U School District 3 (PK-12)
2000 Enrollment: 2,207 618-253-7637

Two-year College(s)

Southeastern Illinois College (Public)
2001 Enrollment: 2,704 618-252-5400
2001 Tuition: In-state $6,336; Out-of-state $7,968

Housing: Homeownership rate: 70.6% (2000); Median home value: $43,600 (2000); Median rent: $253 per month (2000); Median age of housing: 44 years (2000).
Hospitals: Harrisburg Medical Center (80 beds)
Newspapers: The Daily Register (6 x week)
Transportation: Commute to work: 91.1% car, 1.6% public transportation, 2.9% walk, 3.6% work from home (2000); Travel time to work: 57.7% less than 15 minutes, 21.1% 15 to 30 minutes, 9.7% 30 to 45 minutes, 4.7% 45 to 60 minutes, 6.8% 60 minutes or more (2000)
Additional Information Contacts
Harrisburg Chamber of Commerce 618-252-4192

MUDDY (village). Covers a land area of 0.263 square miles and a water area of 0 square miles. Located at 37.76° N. Lat.; 88.51° W. Long. Elevation is 372 feet.
Population: 78 (2000); Race: 87.9% White, 0.0% Black, 0.0% Asian, 4.4% American Indian and Alaska Native, 7.7% Hispanic of any race, 0.0% two or more races (2000); Density: 296.9 persons per square mile (2000); Age: 18.7% under 18, 15.4% over 64 (2000); Marriage status: 13.0% never married, 66.2% now married, 0.0% widowed, 20.8% divorced (2000); Foreign born: 0.0% (2000); Ancestry (includes multiple ancestries): 27.5% German, 15.4% Italian, 14.3% United States or American, 12.1% Irish, 9.9% Dutch (2000).
Economy: Single-family building permits issued: 0 (2001) / 0 (2000); Multi-family building permits issued: 0 (2001) / 0 (2000); Employment by occupation: 16.7% management, 9.5% professional, 19.0% services, 11.9% sales, 0.0% farming, 7.1% construction, 35.7% production (2000).
Income: Per capita income: $13,384 (2000); Median household income: $24,375 (2000); Poverty rate: 7.7% (2000).
Taxes: Total city taxes per capita: $273 (1997); City property taxes per capita: $65 (1997).
Education: High school graduation rate: 77.2% (2000); College graduation rate: 7.0% (2000).
Housing: Homeownership rate: 28.6% (2000); Median home value: $55,000 (2000); Median rent: $180 per month (2000); Median age of housing: 54 years (2000).
Transportation: Commute to work: 95.2% car, 0.0% public transportation, 0.0% walk, 4.8% work from home (2000); Travel time to work: 67.5% less than 15 minutes, 17.5% 15 to 30 minutes, 0.0% 30 to 45 minutes, 5.0% 45 to 60 minutes, 10.0% 60 minutes or more (2000)

RALEIGH (village). Covers a land area of 1.974 square miles and a water area of 0 square miles. Located at 37.82° N. Lat.; 88.53° W. Long. Elevation is 415 feet.
Population: 330 (2000); Race: 98.3% White, 0.0% Black, 1.1% Asian, 0.0% American Indian and Alaska Native, 0.6% Hispanic of any race, 0.6% two or more races (2000); Density: 167.1 persons per square mile (2000); Age: 28.0% under 18, 12.1% over 64 (2000); Marriage status: 15.1% never married, 65.3% now married, 6.3% widowed, 13.3% divorced (2000); Foreign born: 1.1% (2000); Ancestry (includes multiple ancestries): 25.1% United States or American, 12.4% Irish, 6.2% German, 5.9% Other groups, 5.1% English (2000).
Economy: In bituminous-coal-mining and agricultural area. Employment by occupation: 6.2% management, 18.6% professional, 15.9% services, 17.9% sales, 0.0% farming, 18.6% construction, 22.8% production (2000).
Income: Per capita income: $13,054 (2000); Median household income: $25,000 (2000); Poverty rate: 29.4% (2000).
Taxes: Total city taxes per capita: $11 (1997); City property taxes per capita: $11 (1997).
Education: High school graduation rate: 82.3% (2000); College graduation rate: 11.6% (2000).
Housing: Homeownership rate: 81.8% (2000); Median home value: $48,100 (2000); Median rent: $197 per month (2000); Median age of housing: 39 years (2000).
Transportation: Commute to work: 93.7% car, 0.0% public transportation, 0.0% walk, 4.2% work from home (2000); Travel time to work: 30.7% less than 15 minutes, 33.6% 15 to 30 minutes, 9.5% 30 to 45 minutes, 8.8% 45 to 60 minutes, 17.5% 60 minutes or more (2000)

Sangamon County

Located in central Illinois; drained by the Sangamon River and its South Fork; includes Lake Springfield. Covers a land area of 868.20 square miles, a water area of 8.80 square miles, and is located in the Central Time Zone. The county government was organized in 1821. County seat is Springfield.

Sangamon County is part of the Springfield, IL MSA. The entire metro area includes: Menard County; Sangamon County

Weather Station: Springfield Capital Airport — Elevation: 583 feet

	Jan	Feb	Mar	Apr	May	Jun	Jul	Aug	Sep	Oct	Nov	Dec
High	33	39	51	64	75	84	87	85	79	67	51	39
Low	17	22	32	42	53	62	66	64	56	44	34	23
Precip	1.6	1.8	3.1	3.6	4.1	3.7	3.5	3.4	3.0	2.6	2.8	2.6
Snow	7.4	5.9	3.4	0.8	tr	0.0	tr	0.0	0.0	tr	1.6	5.0

High and Low temperatures in degrees Fahrenheit; Precipitation and Snow in inches

Population: 188,951 (2000); Race: 87.6% White, 9.4% Black, 1.1% Asian, 0.2% American Indian and Alaska Native, 0.9% Hispanic of any race, 1.5% two or more races (2000); Density: 217.6 persons per square mile (2000); Age: 24.9% under 18, 13.7% over 64 (2000).
Religion: Five largest groups: 19.4% Catholic Church, 7.9% Assemblies of God, 6.0% The United Methodist Church, 4.3% Lutheran Church—Missouri Synod, 3.9% Christian Churches and Churches of Christ (2000).
Economy: Unemployment rate: 4.7% (11/2002); Total civilian labor force: 99,201 (11/2002); Leading industries: 21.2% health care and social assistance; 14.6% retail trade; 10.2% accommodation & food services (2000); Companies that employ more than 1,000 persons: 5 (2000); Companies that employ more than 100 persons: 125 (2000); Farms: 993 totaling 466,956 acres (1997); Minority business ownership rate: 7.4% (1997); Women business ownership rate: 28.8% (1997); Retail sales per capita: $10,404 (1997). Single-family building permits issued: 727 (2001) / 680 (2000); Multi-family building permits issued: 113 (2001) / 170 (2000).
Income: Per capita income: $23,173 (2000); Median household income: $42,957 (2000); Poverty rate: 9.3% (2000); Bankruptcy rate: 6.20% (2001).
Taxes: Total county taxes per capita: $111 (2000); County property taxes per capita: $97 (2000).
Education: High school graduation rate: 88.1% (2000); College graduation rate: 28.6% (2000).
Housing: Homeownership rate: 70.0% (2000); Median home value: $91,200 (2000); Median rent: $424 per month (2000); Median age of housing: 32 years (2000).
Health: Birth rate: 134.3 per 10,000 population (1998); Age adjusted death rate: 85.8 per 10,000 population (1999); Age adjusted cancer mortality rate: 217.9 deaths per 100,000 population (1999). Air Quality Index: 81% good, 19% moderate, 0% unhealthy (percent of days in 2000). Number of physicians: 45.5 per 10,000 population (1999); Number of hospital beds: 66.1 per 10,000 population (1999).
Elections: 2000 Presidential election results: 42.0% Gore, 55.1% Bush, 2.2% Nader, 0.5% Buchanan
National and State Parks: Lincoln Home National Historic Site; Lincolns Tomb State Historic Site; Sangchris Lake State Park
Additional Information Contacts
Sangamon County Government Offices 217-753-6600
Capital Area Association of Realtors 217-698-7000
Chatham Chamber of Commerce 217-483-6450
Illinois Association of Realtors 217-529-2600
Illinois State Chamber of Commerce 217-522-5512
Springfield Chamber of Commerce 217-525-1173
Springfield Convention & Visitors Bureau 217-789-2360

Sangamon County Communities

AUBURN (city). Covers a land area of 3.156 square miles and a water area of 0 square miles. Located at 39.58° N. Lat.; 89.74° W. Long. Elevation is 626 feet.
History: Incorporated 1865.
Population: 4,317 (2000); Race: 99.2% White, 0.0% Black, 0.2% Asian, 0.0% American Indian and Alaska Native, 1.0% Hispanic of any race, 0.5% two or more races (2000); Density: 1,368.0 persons per square mile (2000); Age: 30.9% under 18, 12.3% over 64 (2000); Marriage status: 16.7% never married, 66.1% now married, 5.7% widowed, 11.5% divorced (2000); Foreign born: 1.0% (2000); Ancestry (includes multiple ancestries): 32.3% German, 15.6% Irish, 12.0% English, 7.3% United States or American, 6.9% Italian (2000).

Economy: Agriculture: corn, sorghum; cattle, hogs. Manufacturing: agricultural machinery, sewer pipe. Single-family building permits issued: 19 (2001) / 13 (2000); Multi-family building permits issued: 0 (2001) / 2 (2000); Employment by occupation: 12.5% management, 22.1% professional, 17.4% services, 26.9% sales, 1.2% farming, 11.4% construction, 8.5% production (2000).
Income: Per capita income: $18,368 (2000); Median household income: $43,250 (2000); Poverty rate: 5.5% (2000).
Taxes: Total city taxes per capita: $32 (1997); City property taxes per capita: $16 (1997).
Education: High school graduation rate: 88.0% (2000); College graduation rate: 19.8% (2000).

School District(s)

Auburn Community Unit School District 10 (PK-12)
2000 Enrollment: 1,157 217-438-6164
Housing: Homeownership rate: 75.1% (2000); Median home value: $81,900 (2000); Median rent: $357 per month (2000); Median age of housing: 33 years (2000).
Newspapers: The Pawnee Post (1 x week); The Divernon News (1 x week); The Auburn Citizen (1 x week)
Transportation: Commute to work: 94.1% car, 0.5% public transportation, 2.0% walk, 2.5% work from home (2000); Travel time to work: 24.1% less than 15 minutes, 26.2% 15 to 30 minutes, 39.9% 30 to 45 minutes, 3.6% 45 to 60 minutes, 6.2% 60 minutes or more (2000)

BERLIN (village). Covers a land area of 0.996 square miles and a water area of 0 square miles. Located at 39.75° N. Lat.; 89.90° W. Long. Elevation is 640 feet.
Population: 140 (2000); Race: 90.8% White, 5.3% Black, 0.0% Asian, 0.0% American Indian and Alaska Native, 0.0% Hispanic of any race, 3.8% two or more races (2000); Density: 140.6 persons per square mile (2000); Age: 24.4% under 18, 19.8% over 64 (2000); Marriage status: 13.7% never married, 54.9% now married, 7.8% widowed, 23.5% divorced (2000); Foreign born: 0.0% (2000); Ancestry (includes multiple ancestries): 15.3% German, 13.7% United States or American, 11.5% Other groups, 4.6% Scottish, 3.8% Irish (2000).
Economy: In agricultural area. Employment by occupation: 5.2% management, 5.2% professional, 13.8% services, 39.7% sales, 0.0% farming, 19.0% construction, 17.2% production (2000).
Income: Per capita income: $15,079 (2000); Median household income: $38,125 (2000); Poverty rate: 21.1% (2000).
Taxes: Total city taxes per capita: $15 (1997); City property taxes per capita: $5 (1997).
Education: High school graduation rate: 78.7% (2000); College graduation rate: 4.3% (2000).
Housing: Homeownership rate: 75.4% (2000); Median home value: $83,800 (2000); Median rent: $425 per month (2000); Median age of housing: 32 years (2000).
Transportation: Commute to work: 87.9% car, 0.0% public transportation, 1.7% walk, 6.9% work from home (2000); Travel time to work: 22.2% less than 15 minutes, 44.4% 15 to 30 minutes, 33.3% 30 to 45 minutes, 0.0% 45 to 60 minutes, 0.0% 60 minutes or more (2000)

BUFFALO (village). Covers a land area of 0.369 square miles and a water area of 0 square miles. Located at 39.85° N. Lat.; 89.40° W. Long. Elevation is 611 feet.
Population: 491 (2000); Race: 95.9% White, 0.0% Black, 1.3% Asian, 0.0% American Indian and Alaska Native, 1.1% Hispanic of any race, 1.3% two or more races (2000); Density: 1,332.2 persons per square mile (2000); Age: 22.9% under 18, 14.3% over 64 (2000); Marriage status: 24.3% never married, 52.8% now married, 11.1% widowed, 11.9% divorced (2000); Foreign born: 2.4% (2000); Ancestry (includes multiple ancestries): 16.9% German, 13.9% English, 12.6% Irish, 7.3% Other groups, 4.9% United States or American (2000).
Economy: In agricultural area. Single-family building permits issued: 0 (2001) / 0 (2000); Multi-family building permits issued: 0 (2001) / 0 (2000); Employment by occupation: 11.8% management, 11.8% professional, 15.3% services, 34.5% sales, 0.0% farming, 12.5% construction, 14.1% production (2000).
Income: Per capita income: $19,637 (2000); Median household income: $36,250 (2000); Poverty rate: 10.8% (2000).
Taxes: Total city taxes per capita: $78 (1997); City property taxes per capita: $36 (1997).
Education: High school graduation rate: 85.9% (2000); College graduation rate: 12.2% (2000).

School District(s)

Tri City Community Unit School District 1 (PK-12)
2000 Enrollment: 632 217-364-4811
Housing: Homeownership rate: 74.5% (2000); Median home value: $72,700 (2000); Median rent: $216 per month (2000); Median age of housing: 40 years (2000).
Transportation: Commute to work: 90.8% car, 0.0% public transportation, 6.0% walk, 3.2% work from home (2000); Travel time to work: 13.6% less than 15 minutes, 43.8% 15 to 30 minutes, 33.9% 30 to 45 minutes, 3.3% 45 to 60 minutes, 5.4% 60 minutes or more (2000)

CANTRALL (village). Covers a land area of 0.255 square miles and a water area of 0 square miles. Located at 39.93° N. Lat.; 89.67° W. Long. Elevation is 595 feet.
Population: 139 (2000); Race: 97.1% White, 0.0% Black, 0.0% Asian, 0.0% American Indian and Alaska Native, 0.0% Hispanic of any race, 2.9% two or more races (2000); Density: 545.3 persons per square mile (2000); Age: 23.2% under 18, 20.3% over 64 (2000); Marriage status: 15.7% never married, 73.0% now married, 6.1% widowed, 5.2% divorced (2000); Foreign born: 0.0% (2000); Ancestry (includes multiple ancestries): 40.6% German, 21.0% English, 8.7% Italian, 8.7% Dutch, 5.1% Irish (2000).
Economy: Agriculture: corn, soybeans; cattle, hogs. Employment by occupation: 8.3% management, 16.7% professional, 33.3% services, 19.4% sales, 0.0% farming, 16.7% construction, 5.6% production (2000).
Income: Per capita income: $21,610 (2000); Median household income: $45,000 (2000); Poverty rate: 1.4% (2000).
Taxes: Total city taxes per capita: $8 (1997); City property taxes per capita: $8 (1997).
Education: High school graduation rate: 92.2% (2000); College graduation rate: 20.4% (2000).
Housing: Homeownership rate: 90.2% (2000); Median home value: $80,000 (2000); Median rent: $358 per month (2000); Median age of housing: 43 years (2000).
Transportation: Commute to work: 100.0% car, 0.0% public transportation, 0.0% walk, 0.0% work from home (2000); Travel time to work: 19.4% less than 15 minutes, 70.8% 15 to 30 minutes, 5.6% 30 to 45 minutes, 1.4% 45 to 60 minutes, 2.8% 60 minutes or more (2000)

CHATHAM (village). Covers a land area of 4.965 square miles and a water area of 0.003 square miles. Located at 39.67° N. Lat.; 89.69° W. Long. Elevation is 606 feet.
Population: 8,583 (2000); Race: 98.1% White, 0.6% Black, 0.1% Asian, 0.5% American Indian and Alaska Native, 0.2% Hispanic of any race, 0.7% two or more races (2000); Density: 1,728.7 persons per square mile (2000); Age: 31.3% under 18, 7.6% over 64 (2000); Marriage status: 19.8% never married, 65.6% now married, 3.6% widowed, 11.0% divorced (2000); Foreign born: 1.2% (2000); Ancestry (includes multiple ancestries): 35.7% German, 19.1% Irish, 14.5% English, 6.4% Italian, 6.2% United States or American (2000).
Economy: In agricultural area. Single-family building permits issued: 99 (2001) / 96 (2000); Multi-family building permits issued: 4 (2001) / 6 (2000); Employment by occupation: 20.2% management, 26.9% professional, 12.2% services, 29.1% sales, 0.0% farming, 6.5% construction, 5.1% production (2000).
Income: Per capita income: $23,167 (2000); Median household income: $60,350 (2000); Poverty rate: 4.7% (2000).
Taxes: Total city taxes per capita: $132 (1997); City property taxes per capita: $44 (1997).
Education: High school graduation rate: 94.8% (2000); College graduation rate: 37.0% (2000).

School District(s)

Ball Chatham C U School District 5 (PK-12)
2000 Enrollment: 3,930 217-483-2416
Housing: Homeownership rate: 86.0% (2000); Median home value: $110,300 (2000); Median rent: $493 per month (2000); Median age of housing: 21 years (2000).
Newspapers: The Chatham Clarion (1 x week)
Transportation: Commute to work: 93.7% car, 0.2% public transportation, 1.4% walk, 4.7% work from home (2000); Travel time to work: 21.5% less than 15 minutes, 56.6% 15 to 30 minutes, 17.9% 30 to 45 minutes, 1.5% 45 to 60 minutes, 2.4% 60 minutes or more (2000)

Additional Information Contacts

Chatham Chamber of Commerce 217-483-6450

CLEAR LAKE (village). Covers a land area of 0.093 square miles and a water area of 0 square miles. Located at 39.81° N. Lat.; 89.56° W. Long. Elevation is 580 feet.
Population: 267 (2000); Race: 96.6% White, 0.0% Black, 0.0% Asian, 0.0% American Indian and Alaska Native, 4.1% Hispanic of any race, 1.4% two or more races (2000); Density: 2,871.8 persons per square mile (2000); Age: 24.7% under 18, 11.9% over 64 (2000); Marriage status: 25.6% never married, 42.0% now married, 7.6% widowed, 24.8% divorced (2000); Foreign born: 0.0% (2000); Ancestry (includes multiple ancestries): 13.9% United States or American, 7.5% English, 7.5% German, 6.8% Irish, 6.4% Italian (2000).
Economy: Employment by occupation: 10.0% management, 12.5% professional, 4.2% services, 22.5% sales, 0.0% farming, 8.3% construction, 42.5% production (2000).
Income: Per capita income: $15,284 (2000); Median household income: $37,708 (2000); Poverty rate: 14.1% (2000).
Taxes: Total city taxes per capita: $5 (1997); City property taxes per capita: $5 (1997).
Education: High school graduation rate: 68.0% (2000); College graduation rate: 8.6% (2000).
Housing: Homeownership rate: 83.6% (2000); Median home value: $60,300 (2000); Median rent: $325 per month (2000); Median age of housing: 32 years (2000).
Transportation: Commute to work: 100.0% car, 0.0% public transportation, 0.0% walk, 0.0% work from home (2000); Travel time to work: 28.6% less than 15 minutes, 43.8% 15 to 30 minutes, 21.4% 30 to 45 minutes, 4.5% 45 to 60 minutes, 1.8% 60 minutes or more (2000)

DAWSON (village). Covers a land area of 0.871 square miles and a water area of 0 square miles. Located at 39.85° N. Lat.; 89.46° W. Long. Elevation is 599 feet.
Population: 466 (2000); Race: 96.2% White, 0.0% Black, 0.0% Asian, 3.0% American Indian and Alaska Native, 1.3% Hispanic of any race, 0.8% two or more races (2000); Density: 535.0 persons per square mile (2000); Age: 20.1% under 18, 9.9% over 64 (2000); Marriage status: 25.9% never married, 56.7% now married, 5.7% widowed, 11.8% divorced (2000); Foreign born: 0.0% (2000); Ancestry (includes multiple ancestries): 22.0% English, 22.0% German, 11.0% United States or American, 9.1% Irish, 3.4% Other groups (2000).
Economy: In agricultural area: corn, sorghum, cattle, hogs; dairying; oil and natural gas. Single-family building permits issued: 2 (2001) / 2 (2000); Multi-family building permits issued: 0 (2001) / 0 (2000); Employment by occupation: 8.7% management, 17.4% professional, 10.1% services, 35.8% sales, 0.0% farming, 15.6% construction, 12.5% production (2000).
Income: Per capita income: $19,686 (2000); Median household income: $51,250 (2000); Poverty rate: 5.9% (2000).
Taxes: Total city taxes per capita: $70 (1997); City property taxes per capita: $15 (1997).
Education: High school graduation rate: 88.8% (2000); College graduation rate: 14.2% (2000).
Housing: Homeownership rate: 87.3% (2000); Median home value: $78,800 (2000); Median rent: $378 per month (2000); Median age of housing: 34 years (2000).
Transportation: Commute to work: 96.9% car, 0.0% public transportation, 2.1% walk, 1.0% work from home (2000); Travel time to work: 18.9% less than 15 minutes, 55.8% 15 to 30 minutes, 23.9% 30 to 45 minutes, 1.4% 45 to 60 minutes, 0.0% 60 minutes or more (2000)

DIVERNON (village). Covers a land area of 0.797 square miles and a water area of 0.002 square miles. Located at 39.56° N. Lat.; 89.65° W. Long. Elevation is 617 feet.
History: Incorporated 1900.
Population: 1,201 (2000); Race: 99.2% White, 0.0% Black, 0.0% Asian, 0.8% American Indian and Alaska Native, 1.0% Hispanic of any race, 0.1% two or more races (2000); Density: 1,507.3 persons per square mile (2000); Age: 27.8% under 18, 11.0% over 64 (2000); Marriage status: 26.1% never married, 57.9% now married, 5.3% widowed, 10.7% divorced (2000); Foreign born: 0.4% (2000); Ancestry (includes multiple ancestries): 28.0% German, 13.1% English, 10.5% Irish, 8.9% Italian, 6.5% United States or American (2000).
Economy: In agricultural area. Oil wells. Single-family building permits issued: 2 (2001) / 2 (2000); Multi-family building permits issued: 0 (2001) / 0 (2000); Employment by occupation: 13.2% management, 12.2% professional, 13.8% services, 37.4% sales, 0.0% farming, 11.0% construction, 12.4% production (2000).
Income: Per capita income: $18,670 (2000); Median household income: $43,750 (2000); Poverty rate: 7.2% (2000).
Taxes: Total city taxes per capita: $29 (1997); City property taxes per capita: $21 (1997).
Education: High school graduation rate: 91.4% (2000); College graduation rate: 14.9% (2000).

School District(s)

Divernon C U School District 13 (PK-12)
2000 Enrollment: 315 217-628-3414
Housing: Homeownership rate: 75.9% (2000); Median home value: $78,500 (2000); Median rent: $413 per month (2000); Median age of housing: 37 years (2000).
Transportation: Commute to work: 93.9% car, 0.0% public transportation, 2.2% walk, 2.9% work from home (2000); Travel time to work: 15.5% less than 15 minutes, 44.6% 15 to 30 minutes, 33.3% 30 to 45 minutes, 3.6% 45 to 60 minutes, 2.9% 60 minutes or more (2000)

GLENARM (unincorporated postal area, zip code 62536). Covers a land area of 7.817 square miles and a water area of 0.066 square miles. Located at 39.64° N. Lat.; 89.65° W. Long. Elevation is 600 feet.
Population: 942 (2000); Race: 100.0% White, 0.0% Black, 0.0% Asian, 0.0% American Indian and Alaska Native, 0.0% Hispanic of any race, 0.0% two or more races (2000); Density: 120.5 persons per square mile (2000); Age: 22.2% under 18, 7.5% over 64 (2000); Marriage status: 13.4% never married, 76.0% now married, 3.3% widowed, 7.3% divorced (2000); Foreign born: 1.1% (2000); Ancestry (includes multiple ancestries): 35.2% German, 24.4% Irish, 19.7% English, 8.0% United States or American, 7.7% Dutch (2000).
Economy: Employment by occupation: 16.6% management, 31.0% professional, 4.9% services, 27.9% sales, 1.9% farming, 12.7% construction, 5.0% production (2000).
Income: Per capita income: $27,618 (2000); Median household income: $62,382 (2000); Poverty rate: 0.8% (2000).
Education: High school graduation rate: 94.0% (2000); College graduation rate: 32.4% (2000).
Housing: Homeownership rate: 89.0% (2000); Median home value: $118,500 (2000); Median rent: $668 per month (2000); Median age of housing: 18 years (2000).
Transportation: Commute to work: 93.2% car, 0.0% public transportation, 0.0% walk, 6.8% work from home (2000); Travel time to work: 16.2% less than 15 minutes, 59.5% 15 to 30 minutes, 18.0% 30 to 45 minutes, 6.3% 45 to 60 minutes, 0.0% 60 minutes or more (2000)

GRANDVIEW (village). Covers a land area of 0.341 square miles and a water area of 0 square miles. Located at 39.81° N. Lat.; 89.62° W. Long. Elevation is 595 feet.
History: Incorporated 1939.
Population: 1,537 (2000); Race: 93.0% White, 5.2% Black, 0.3% Asian, 0.2% American Indian and Alaska Native, 0.7% Hispanic of any race, 1.3% two or more races (2000); Density: 4,501.4 persons per square mile (2000); Age: 24.8% under 18, 16.0% over 64 (2000); Marriage status: 26.2% never married, 52.1% now married, 7.7% widowed, 14.0% divorced (2000); Foreign born: 1.2% (2000); Ancestry (includes multiple ancestries): 21.6% German, 14.4% United States or American, 13.9% Irish, 11.9% English, 11.3% Other groups (2000).
Economy: In agricultural area. Single-family building permits issued: 0 (2001) / 1 (2000); Multi-family building permits issued: 0 (2001) / 0 (2000); Employment by occupation: 6.6% management, 12.5% professional, 18.3% services, 36.7% sales, 0.5% farming, 13.6% construction, 11.8% production (2000).
Income: Per capita income: $17,499 (2000); Median household income: $36,349 (2000); Poverty rate: 12.3% (2000).
Taxes: Total city taxes per capita: $31 (1997); City property taxes per capita: $22 (1997).
Education: High school graduation rate: 77.8% (2000); College graduation rate: 8.4% (2000).
Housing: Homeownership rate: 79.6% (2000); Median home value: $57,300 (2000); Median rent: $455 per month (2000); Median age of housing: 47 years (2000).
Transportation: Commute to work: 94.8% car, 1.2% public transportation, 0.3% walk, 2.4% work from home (2000); Travel time to work: 32.6% less than 15 minutes, 52.8% 15 to 30 minutes, 10.6% 30 to 45 minutes, 2.6% 45 to 60 minutes, 1.5% 60 minutes or more (2000)

ILLIOPOLIS (village). Covers a land area of 0.452 square miles and a water area of 0 square miles. Located at 39.85° N. Lat.; 89.24° W. Long. Elevation is 602 feet.
Population: 916 (2000); Race: 98.4% White, 0.0% Black, 0.3% Asian, 0.0% American Indian and Alaska Native, 0.6% Hispanic of any race, 1.2% two or more races (2000); Density: 2,027.0 persons per square mile (2000); Age: 25.1% under 18, 12.2% over 64 (2000); Marriage status: 23.4% never married, 62.4% now married, 5.9% widowed, 8.3% divorced (2000); Foreign born: 0.3% (2000); Ancestry (includes multiple ancestries): 26.8% German, 13.0% English, 12.9% Irish, 11.6% United States or American, 4.6% Other groups (2000).
Economy: In agricultural area; ships grain. Single-family building permits issued: 3 (2001) / 1 (2000); Multi-family building permits issued: 0 (2001) / 0 (2000); Employment by occupation: 11.2% management, 15.0% professional, 13.3% services, 23.9% sales, 2.1% farming, 11.4% construction, 23.0% production (2000).
Income: Per capita income: $19,473 (2000); Median household income: $46,442 (2000); Poverty rate: 3.0% (2000).
Taxes: Total city taxes per capita: $23 (1997); City property taxes per capita: $16 (1997).
Education: High school graduation rate: 88.9% (2000); College graduation rate: 12.4% (2000).

School District(s)

Illiopolis C U School District 12 (PK-12)
2000 Enrollment: 311 217-486-2241
Housing: Homeownership rate: 77.2% (2000); Median home value: $64,800 (2000); Median rent: $325 per month (2000); Median age of housing: 49 years (2000).
Newspapers: Illiopolis Sentinel (1 x week); County Line Observer (1 x week)
Transportation: Commute to work: 95.7% car, 0.0% public transportation, 2.6% walk, 1.3% work from home (2000); Travel time to work: 34.0% less than 15 minutes, 20.6% 15 to 30 minutes, 32.0% 30 to 45 minutes, 9.1% 45 to 60 minutes, 4.3% 60 minutes or more (2000)

JEROME (village). Covers a land area of 0.371 square miles and a water area of 0 square miles. Located at 39.76° N. Lat.; 89.67° W. Long. Elevation is 600 feet.
Population: 1,414 (2000); Race: 95.3% White, 1.2% Black, 1.5% Asian, 0.0% American Indian and Alaska Native, 1.6% Hispanic of any race, 2.0% two or more races (2000); Density: 3,806.8 persons per square mile (2000); Age: 19.3% under 18, 25.0% over 64 (2000); Marriage status: 21.0% never married, 53.6% now married, 10.0% widowed, 15.4% divorced (2000); Foreign born: 1.5% (2000); Ancestry (includes multiple ancestries): 31.8% German, 16.4% Irish, 16.1% English, 8.7% United States or American, 8.4% Other groups (2000).
Economy: In agricultural and oil area. Single-family building permits issued: 0 (2001) / 0 (2000); Multi-family building permits issued: 0 (2001) / 0 (2000); Employment by occupation: 18.5% management, 20.5% professional, 12.5% services, 34.7% sales, 0.3% farming, 6.5% construction, 7.0% production (2000).
Income: Per capita income: $23,350 (2000); Median household income: $41,974 (2000); Poverty rate: 3.5% (2000).
Taxes: Total city taxes per capita: $20 (1997); City property taxes per capita: $18 (1997).
Education: High school graduation rate: 92.7% (2000); College graduation rate: 25.9% (2000).
Housing: Homeownership rate: 81.7% (2000); Median home value: $80,500 (2000); Median rent: $498 per month (2000); Median age of housing: 46 years (2000).
Transportation: Commute to work: 94.0% car, 1.7% public transportation, 1.0% walk, 2.4% work from home (2000); Travel time to work: 40.4% less than 15 minutes, 49.0% 15 to 30 minutes, 6.2% 30 to 45 minutes, 1.0% 45 to 60 minutes, 3.4% 60 minutes or more (2000)

LELAND GROVE (city). Covers a land area of 0.627 square miles and a water area of 0 square miles. Located at 39.77° N. Lat.; 89.68° W. Long. Elevation is 600 feet.
Population: 1,592 (2000); Race: 98.5% White, 0.3% Black, 0.7% Asian, 0.0% American Indian and Alaska Native, 0.0% Hispanic of any race, 0.4% two or more races (2000); Density: 2,540.3 persons per square mile (2000); Age: 19.8% under 18, 25.3% over 64 (2000); Marriage status: 17.5% never married, 66.4% now married, 7.6% widowed, 8.5% divorced (2000); Foreign born: 2.3% (2000); Ancestry (includes multiple ancestries): 31.1% German, 20.8% English, 18.0% Irish, 6.1% Italian, 4.7% Scottish (2000).
Economy: Single-family building permits issued: 0 (2001) / 0 (2000); Multi-family building permits issued: 0 (2001) / 0 (2000); Employment by occupation: 28.6% management, 44.5% professional, 4.4% services, 18.6% sales, 0.0% farming, 2.3% construction, 1.6% production (2000).
Income: Per capita income: $51,714 (2000); Median household income: $75,437 (2000); Poverty rate: 2.7% (2000).
Taxes: Total city taxes per capita: $184 (1997); City property taxes per capita: $158 (1997).
Education: High school graduation rate: 98.0% (2000); College graduation rate: 65.9% (2000).
Housing: Homeownership rate: 92.9% (2000); Median home value: $166,000 (2000); Median rent: $488 per month (2000); Median age of housing: 49 years (2000).
Transportation: Commute to work: 93.3% car, 0.7% public transportation, 0.6% walk, 5.4% work from home (2000); Travel time to work: 60.8% less than 15 minutes, 30.3% 15 to 30 minutes, 4.1% 30 to 45 minutes, 1.2% 45 to 60 minutes, 3.5% 60 minutes or more (2000)

LOAMI (village). Covers a land area of 0.977 square miles and a water area of 0.004 square miles. Located at 39.67° N. Lat.; 89.84° W. Long. Elevation is 638 feet.
Population: 804 (2000); Race: 97.2% White, 2.1% Black, 0.0% Asian, 0.0% American Indian and Alaska Native, 2.2% Hispanic of any race, 0.7% two or more races (2000); Density: 822.5 persons per square mile (2000); Age: 30.4% under 18, 5.9% over 64 (2000); Marriage status: 30.2% never married, 56.8% now married, 2.7% widowed, 10.2% divorced (2000); Foreign born: 0.0% (2000); Ancestry (includes multiple ancestries): 31.1% German, 13.7% Irish, 13.5% English, 12.1% Other groups, 8.8% United States or American (2000).
Economy: In agricultural area. Single-family building permits issued: 2 (2001) / 1 (2000); Multi-family building permits issued: 0 (2001) / 0 (2000); Employment by occupation: 11.6% management, 15.6% professional, 16.3% services, 35.3% sales, 0.2% farming, 10.5% construction, 10.5% production (2000).
Income: Per capita income: $17,661 (2000); Median household income: $46,591 (2000); Poverty rate: 10.0% (2000).
Taxes: Total city taxes per capita: $64 (1997); City property taxes per capita: $25 (1997).
Education: High school graduation rate: 87.6% (2000); College graduation rate: 13.5% (2000).
Housing: Homeownership rate: 90.1% (2000); Median home value: $68,700 (2000); Median rent: $410 per month (2000); Median age of housing: 29 years (2000).
Transportation: Commute to work: 95.2% car, 0.0% public transportation, 1.1% walk, 3.2% work from home (2000); Travel time to work: 4.5% less than 15 minutes, 54.1% 15 to 30 minutes, 35.7% 30 to 45 minutes, 4.5% 45 to 60 minutes, 1.2% 60 minutes or more (2000)

MECHANICSBURG (village). Covers a land area of 0.379 square miles and a water area of 0 square miles. Located at 39.80° N. Lat.; 89.39° W. Long. Elevation is 590 feet.
Population: 456 (2000); Race: 100.0% White, 0.0% Black, 0.0% Asian, 0.0% American Indian and Alaska Native, 0.0% Hispanic of any race, 0.0% two or more races (2000); Density: 1,203.2 persons per square mile (2000); Age: 25.7% under 18, 11.9% over 64 (2000); Marriage status: 25.2% never married, 53.6% now married, 8.0% widowed, 13.2% divorced (2000); Foreign born: 0.0% (2000); Ancestry (includes multiple ancestries): 32.9% German, 18.8% Irish, 12.3% United States or American, 8.9% English, 5.6% French (except Basque) (2000).
Economy: In agricultural area. Single-family building permits issued: 1 (2001) / 2 (2000); Multi-family building permits issued: 0 (2001) / 0 (2000); Employment by occupation: 10.1% management, 10.9% professional, 26.5% services, 22.3% sales, 0.0% farming, 16.8% construction, 13.4% production (2000).
Income: Per capita income: $16,906 (2000); Median household income: $36,250 (2000); Poverty rate: 3.2% (2000).
Taxes: Total city taxes per capita: $22 (1997); City property taxes per capita: $13 (1997).
Education: High school graduation rate: 71.2% (2000); College graduation rate: 2.8% (2000).
Housing: Homeownership rate: 77.9% (2000); Median home value: $59,800 (2000); Median rent: $391 per month (2000); Median age of housing: 39 years (2000).
Transportation: Commute to work: 92.0% car, 1.7% public transportation, 0.8% walk, 2.5% work from home (2000); Travel time to work: 9.1% less

than 15 minutes, 41.8% 15 to 30 minutes, 38.4% 30 to 45 minutes, 6.0% 45 to 60 minutes, 4.7% 60 minutes or more (2000)

NEW BERLIN (village). Covers a land area of 1.108 square miles and a water area of 0 square miles. Located at 39.72° N. Lat.; 89.91° W. Long. Elevation is 654 feet.

Population: 1,030 (2000); Race: 97.6% White, 0.0% Black, 0.9% Asian, 0.0% American Indian and Alaska Native, 0.4% Hispanic of any race, 0.6% two or more races (2000); Density: 929.3 persons per square mile (2000); Age: 25.3% under 18, 15.4% over 64 (2000); Marriage status: 18.6% never married, 65.7% now married, 6.6% widowed, 9.2% divorced (2000); Foreign born: 1.1% (2000); Ancestry (includes multiple ancestries): 33.3% German, 18.8% Irish, 14.1% English, 8.9% United States or American, 4.3% Other groups (2000).

Economy: Bituminous-coal mining. Agriculture: corn, wheat, soybeans. Single-family building permits issued: 5 (2001) / 20 (2000); Multi-family building permits issued: 4 (2001) / 0 (2000); Employment by occupation: 15.1% management, 21.4% professional, 12.2% services, 33.6% sales, 1.8% farming, 8.2% construction, 7.7% production (2000).

Income: Per capita income: $19,313 (2000); Median household income: $41,635 (2000); Poverty rate: 5.8% (2000).

Taxes: Total city taxes per capita: $72 (1997); City property taxes per capita: $64 (1997).

Education: High school graduation rate: 87.4% (2000); College graduation rate: 22.0% (2000).

School District(s)

Community Unit School District 16 (PK-12)
2000 Enrollment: 624 217-488-6111

Housing: Homeownership rate: 80.9% (2000); Median home value: $84,100 (2000); Median rent: $414 per month (2000); Median age of housing: 29 years (2000).

Newspapers: The County Tribune (1 x week)

Transportation: Commute to work: 94.0% car, 0.0% public transportation, 1.9% walk, 4.1% work from home (2000); Travel time to work: 24.8% less than 15 minutes, 40.5% 15 to 30 minutes, 30.0% 30 to 45 minutes, 1.2% 45 to 60 minutes, 3.5% 60 minutes or more (2000)

PAWNEE (village). Covers a land area of 1.192 square miles and a water area of 0 square miles. Located at 39.59° N. Lat.; 89.58° W. Long. Elevation is 600 feet.

History: Incorporated 1891.

Population: 2,647 (2000); Race: 99.2% White, 0.2% Black, 0.3% Asian, 0.0% American Indian and Alaska Native, 0.5% Hispanic of any race, 0.3% two or more races (2000); Density: 2,221.0 persons per square mile (2000); Age: 27.4% under 18, 11.1% over 64 (2000); Marriage status: 18.8% never married, 63.5% now married, 7.6% widowed, 10.1% divorced (2000); Foreign born: 0.1% (2000); Ancestry (includes multiple ancestries): 31.7% German, 13.9% Irish, 12.8% English, 6.9% United States or American, 5.2% Italian (2000).

Economy: In agricultural and bituminous-coal area; grain; livestock. Single-family building permits issued: 5 (2001) / 4 (2000); Multi-family building permits issued: 0 (2001) / 0 (2000); Employment by occupation: 13.3% management, 21.1% professional, 16.2% services, 29.5% sales, 0.0% farming, 10.7% construction, 9.1% production (2000).

Income: Per capita income: $21,599 (2000); Median household income: $50,787 (2000); Poverty rate: 6.3% (2000).

Taxes: Total city taxes per capita: $100 (1997); City property taxes per capita: $66 (1997).

Education: High school graduation rate: 88.6% (2000); College graduation rate: 19.6% (2000).

School District(s)

Pawnee Community Unit School District 11 (PK-12)
2000 Enrollment: 734 217-625-2471

Housing: Homeownership rate: 83.1% (2000); Median home value: $80,400 (2000); Median rent: $417 per month (2000); Median age of housing: 34 years (2000).

Transportation: Commute to work: 95.0% car, 0.0% public transportation, 2.0% walk, 2.2% work from home (2000); Travel time to work: 20.3% less than 15 minutes, 33.2% 15 to 30 minutes, 41.3% 30 to 45 minutes, 3.3% 45 to 60 minutes, 1.9% 60 minutes or more (2000)

PLEASANT PLAINS (village). Covers a land area of 1.241 square miles and a water area of 0 square miles. Located at 39.87° N. Lat.; 89.92° W. Long. Elevation is 615 feet.

Population: 777 (2000); Race: 100.0% White, 0.0% Black, 0.0% Asian, 0.0% American Indian and Alaska Native, 1.0% Hispanic of any race, 0.0% two or more races (2000); Density: 626.0 persons per square mile (2000); Age: 30.4% under 18, 15.1% over 64 (2000); Marriage status: 22.7% never married, 63.8% now married, 3.2% widowed, 10.4% divorced (2000); Foreign born: 0.0% (2000); Ancestry (includes multiple ancestries): 37.6% German, 14.0% English, 11.3% Irish, 7.7% United States or American, 2.7% Polish (2000).

Economy: Agriculture. Bituminous-coal mines; ships grain. Single-family building permits issued: 1 (2001) / 1 (2000); Multi-family building permits issued: 0 (2001) / 0 (2000); Employment by occupation: 11.7% management, 15.9% professional, 15.6% services, 33.6% sales, 0.8% farming, 9.6% construction, 12.8% production (2000).

Income: Per capita income: $18,714 (2000); Median household income: $46,053 (2000); Poverty rate: 2.9% (2000).

Taxes: Total city taxes per capita: $70 (1997); City property taxes per capita: $49 (1997).

Education: High school graduation rate: 88.1% (2000); College graduation rate: 15.3% (2000).

School District(s)

Pleasant Plains C U School District 8 (PK-12)
2000 Enrollment: 1,239 217-626-1041

Housing: Homeownership rate: 87.8% (2000); Median home value: $85,100 (2000); Median rent: $404 per month (2000); Median age of housing: 33 years (2000).

Newspapers: The Pleasant Plains Press (1 x week); New Berlin Bee (1 x week)

Transportation: Commute to work: 97.6% car, 0.0% public transportation, 0.5% walk, 1.9% work from home (2000); Travel time to work: 20.7% less than 15 minutes, 41.6% 15 to 30 minutes, 33.9% 30 to 45 minutes, 0.6% 45 to 60 minutes, 3.3% 60 minutes or more (2000)

RIVERTON (village). Covers a land area of 2.036 square miles and a water area of 0.035 square miles. Located at 39.84° N. Lat.; 89.54° W. Long. Elevation is 552 feet.

History: Incorporated 1873.

Population: 3,048 (2000); Race: 98.8% White, 0.1% Black, 0.1% Asian, 0.3% American Indian and Alaska Native, 0.3% Hispanic of any race, 0.7% two or more races (2000); Density: 1,497.4 persons per square mile (2000); Age: 27.9% under 18, 10.7% over 64 (2000); Marriage status: 24.3% never married, 58.6% now married, 6.9% widowed, 10.2% divorced (2000); Foreign born: 0.2% (2000); Ancestry (includes multiple ancestries): 26.1% German, 15.0% Irish, 14.3% English, 13.3% Italian, 6.4% United States or American (2000).

Economy: In agricultural and bituminous coal area. Single-family building permits issued: 29 (2001) / 29 (2000); Multi-family building permits issued: 0 (2001) / 0 (2000); Employment by occupation: 9.7% management, 19.2% professional, 13.6% services, 31.7% sales, 0.0% farming, 13.1% construction, 12.7% production (2000).

Income: Per capita income: $20,678 (2000); Median household income: $45,531 (2000); Poverty rate: 6.8% (2000).

Taxes: Total city taxes per capita: $111 (1997); City property taxes per capita: $45 (1997).

Education: High school graduation rate: 89.7% (2000); College graduation rate: 19.9% (2000).

School District(s)

Riverton C U School District 14 (PK-12)
2000 Enrollment: 1,439 217-629-6009

Housing: Homeownership rate: 76.4% (2000); Median home value: $85,300 (2000); Median rent: $381 per month (2000); Median age of housing: 26 years (2000).

Newspapers: Williamsville Sun (1 x week); Tri-City Register (1 x week); Riverton Register (1 x week)

Transportation: Commute to work: 97.5% car, 0.2% public transportation, 1.2% walk, 0.6% work from home (2000); Travel time to work: 20.6% less than 15 minutes, 64.9% 15 to 30 minutes, 9.4% 30 to 45 minutes, 4.6% 45 to 60 minutes, 0.5% 60 minutes or more (2000)

ROCHESTER (village). Covers a land area of 2.107 square miles and a water area of 0.011 square miles. Located at 39.75° N. Lat.; 89.54° W. Long. Elevation is 577 feet.

Population: 2,893 (2000); Race: 97.7% White, 0.8% Black, 0.3% Asian, 0.2% American Indian and Alaska Native, 1.0% Hispanic of any race, 1.0% two or more races (2000); Density: 1,372.9 persons per square mile (2000); Age: 27.1% under 18, 11.4% over 64 (2000); Marriage status: 20.3% never married, 67.2% now married, 4.8% widowed, 7.8% divorced (2000); Foreign born: 0.7% (2000); Ancestry (includes multiple ancestries): 33.9% German, 17.5% English, 17.4% Irish, 7.5% Italian, 4.9% Other groups (2000).

Economy: In agricultural and bituminous coal area. Single-family building permits issued: 15 (2001) / 12 (2000); Multi-family building permits issued: 0 (2001) / 0 (2000); Employment by occupation: 17.0% management, 32.7% professional, 9.8% services, 31.8% sales, 0.0% farming, 4.0% construction, 4.7% production (2000).
Income: Per capita income: $26,881 (2000); Median household income: $62,891 (2000); Poverty rate: 1.2% (2000).
Taxes: Total city taxes per capita: $112 (1997); City property taxes per capita: $42 (1997).
Education: High school graduation rate: 92.9% (2000); College graduation rate: 44.3% (2000).

School District(s)

Rochester Community Unit School District 3a (PK-12)
2000 Enrollment: 1,844 217-498-6210

Housing: Homeownership rate: 91.6% (2000); Median home value: $115,300 (2000); Median rent: $422 per month (2000); Median age of housing: 26 years (2000).
Transportation: Commute to work: 94.8% car, 0.2% public transportation, 1.1% walk, 3.5% work from home (2000); Travel time to work: 20.3% less than 15 minutes, 65.6% 15 to 30 minutes, 11.0% 30 to 45 minutes, 2.0% 45 to 60 minutes, 1.2% 60 minutes or more (2000)

SHERMAN (village). Covers a land area of 3.076 square miles and a water area of 0.050 square miles. Located at 39.89° N. Lat.; 89.60° W. Long. Elevation is 580 feet.
Population: 2,871 (2000); Race: 97.7% White, 0.0% Black, 1.5% Asian, 0.2% American Indian and Alaska Native, 0.3% Hispanic of any race, 0.5% two or more races (2000); Density: 933.5 persons per square mile (2000); Age: 25.7% under 18, 15.9% over 64 (2000); Marriage status: 21.2% never married, 59.4% now married, 10.3% widowed, 9.1% divorced (2000); Foreign born: 1.5% (2000); Ancestry (includes multiple ancestries): 31.9% German, 18.9% Irish, 13.1% English, 8.7% Italian, 4.5% Other groups (2000).
Economy: Agricultural area; light manufacturing. Single-family building permits issued: 57 (2001) / 33 (2000); Multi-family building permits issued: 4 (2001) / 12 (2000); Employment by occupation: 19.4% management, 30.5% professional, 9.4% services, 29.3% sales, 0.0% farming, 6.2% construction, 5.2% production (2000).
Income: Per capita income: $27,491 (2000); Median household income: $71,393 (2000); Poverty rate: 3.0% (2000).
Taxes: Total city taxes per capita: $134 (1997); City property taxes per capita: $127 (1997).
Education: High school graduation rate: 90.2% (2000); College graduation rate: 34.1% (2000).
Housing: Homeownership rate: 82.6% (2000); Median home value: $127,600 (2000); Median rent: $497 per month (2000); Median age of housing: 20 years (2000).
Transportation: Commute to work: 97.8% car, 0.2% public transportation, 0.0% walk, 2.0% work from home (2000); Travel time to work: 16.4% less than 15 minutes, 65.3% 15 to 30 minutes, 11.1% 30 to 45 minutes, 2.3% 45 to 60 minutes, 5.0% 60 minutes or more (2000)

SOUTHERN VIEW (village). Covers a land area of 0.527 square miles and a water area of 0 square miles. Located at 39.75° N. Lat.; 89.65° W. Long. Elevation is 610 feet.
Population: 1,695 (2000); Race: 95.5% White, 2.1% Black, 0.0% Asian, 0.4% American Indian and Alaska Native, 1.1% Hispanic of any race, 1.2% two or more races (2000); Density: 3,218.4 persons per square mile (2000); Age: 19.3% under 18, 18.9% over 64 (2000); Marriage status: 24.2% never married, 52.7% now married, 9.1% widowed, 14.0% divorced (2000); Foreign born: 1.3% (2000); Ancestry (includes multiple ancestries): 27.6% German, 18.9% Irish, 11.1% English, 7.3% United States or American, 6.9% Other groups (2000).
Economy: Railroad junction. In agricultural and bituminous-coal area. Single-family building permits issued: 0 (2001) / 2 (2000); Multi-family building permits issued: 0 (2001) / 0 (2000); Employment by occupation: 11.5% management, 16.5% professional, 16.0% services, 38.9% sales, 0.0% farming, 8.9% construction, 8.2% production (2000).
Income: Per capita income: $18,633 (2000); Median household income: $37,964 (2000); Poverty rate: 7.6% (2000).
Taxes: Total city taxes per capita: $66 (1997); City property taxes per capita: $20 (1997).
Education: High school graduation rate: 87.1% (2000); College graduation rate: 14.1% (2000).
Housing: Homeownership rate: 75.1% (2000); Median home value: $68,000 (2000); Median rent: $476 per month (2000); Median age of housing: 47 years (2000).
Transportation: Commute to work: 96.3% car, 0.5% public transportation, 2.0% walk, 1.3% work from home (2000); Travel time to work: 41.5% less than 15 minutes, 47.5% 15 to 30 minutes, 6.1% 30 to 45 minutes, 2.4% 45 to 60 minutes, 2.6% 60 minutes or more (2000)

SPAULDING (village). Covers a land area of 0.777 square miles and a water area of 0.002 square miles. Located at 39.86° N. Lat.; 89.54° W. Long. Elevation is 578 feet.
Population: 559 (2000); Race: 97.8% White, 0.0% Black, 0.0% Asian, 0.0% American Indian and Alaska Native, 3.6% Hispanic of any race, 2.2% two or more races (2000); Density: 719.4 persons per square mile (2000); Age: 34.9% under 18, 3.2% over 64 (2000); Marriage status: 20.8% never married, 69.4% now married, 1.8% widowed, 8.1% divorced (2000); Foreign born: 0.0% (2000); Ancestry (includes multiple ancestries): 25.3% German, 16.7% Irish, 16.5% English, 12.0% Other groups, 9.3% Italian (2000).
Economy: Single-family building permits issued: 16 (2001) / 16 (2000); Multi-family building permits issued: 0 (2001) / 0 (2000); Employment by occupation: 22.4% management, 19.7% professional, 9.9% services, 28.9% sales, 0.0% farming, 13.2% construction, 5.9% production (2000).
Income: Per capita income: $21,168 (2000); Median household income: $67,083 (2000); Poverty rate: 5.1% (2000).
Taxes: Total city taxes per capita: $29 (1997); City property taxes per capita: $29 (1997).
Education: High school graduation rate: 92.2% (2000); College graduation rate: 16.3% (2000).
Housing: Homeownership rate: 80.2% (2000); Median home value: $119,300 (2000); Median rent: $525 per month (2000); Median age of housing: 20 years (2000).
Transportation: Commute to work: 96.7% car, 1.3% public transportation, 0.0% walk, 2.0% work from home (2000); Travel time to work: 21.7% less than 15 minutes, 51.5% 15 to 30 minutes, 19.0% 30 to 45 minutes, 2.7% 45 to 60 minutes, 5.1% 60 minutes or more (2000)

SPRINGFIELD (city). Aka Southlawn. Covers a land area of 54.001 square miles and a water area of 6.307 square miles. Located at 39.78° N. Lat.; 89.65° W. Long. Elevation is 600 feet.
History: Springfield's history is closely linked with Abraham Lincoln, who practiced law here from 1837 to 1861. The first settlers here were Elisha Kelly and his brothers, and in 1821 Springfield received its name, from nearby Spring Creek, and became the seat of the new Sangamon County, with the courthouse built in John Kelly's field. Due to Lincoln's leadership, Springfield was chosen for the state capital in 1837, and was incorporated as a city in 1840. Coal mining became an important industry after 1867.
Population: 111,454 (2000); Race: 81.2% White, 15.1% Black, 1.4% Asian, 0.2% American Indian and Alaska Native, 1.0% Hispanic of any race, 1.8% two or more races (2000); Density: 2,063.9 persons per square mile (2000); Age: 24.0% under 18, 14.5% over 64 (2000); Marriage status: 29.1% never married, 49.8% now married, 8.0% widowed, 13.1% divorced (2000); Foreign born: 2.3% (2000); Ancestry (includes multiple ancestries): 24.4% German, 17.0% Other groups, 15.6% Irish, 11.8% English, 7.1% United States or American (2000).
Vital Statistics: Birth rate: 166.2 per 10,000 population (1998)
Economy: Unemployment rate: 5.7% (11/2002); Total civilian labor force: 61,005 (11/2002); Single-family building permits issued: 304 (2001) / 336 (2000); Multi-family building permits issued: 101 (2001) / 150 (2000); Employment by occupation: 16.0% management, 24.3% professional, 15.6% services, 29.9% sales, 0.1% farming, 6.4% construction, 7.7% production (2000).
Income: Per capita income: $23,324 (2000); Median household income: $39,388 (2000); Poverty rate: 11.7% (2000).
Taxes: Total city taxes per capita: $333 (2000); City property taxes per capita: $158 (2000).
Education: High school graduation rate: 87.4% (2000); College graduation rate: 30.6% (2000).

School District(s)

Corrections School District 428 Dept Of (07-12)
2000 Enrollment: 12,555 217-522-2666
Dept of Human Services (PK-12)
2000 Enrollment: 297 217-782-2004
Sangamon Area Special Education District (KG-12)
2000 Enrollment: 66 217-786-3250
Sangamon Roe (08-12)
2000 Enrollment: 58 217-753-6620

Springfield School District 186 (PK-12)
2000 Enrollment: 15,387 217-525-3002

Four-year College(s)

Saint John's College (Private, Not-for-profit, Roman Catholic)
2001 Enrollment: n/a 217-544-6464
2001 Tuition: In-state $8,282; Out-of-state $8,282
University of Illinois at Springfield (Public)
2001 Enrollment: 4,288 217-206-6600
2001 Tuition: In-state $2,985; Out-of-state $8,955
Saint John's Hospital School of Clinical Lab Science (Private, Not-for-profit, Roman Catholic)
2001 Enrollment: n/a 217-757-6788
2001 Tuition: In-state $800; Out-of-state $800
Saint John's Hospital School of Dietetics (Private, Not-for-profit, Roman Catholic)
2001 Enrollment: 6 217-544-6464
Robert Morris College-Springfield (Private, Not-for-profit)
2001 Enrollment: n/a 217-793-2500
2001 Tuition: In-state $12,150; Out-of-state $12,150

Two-year College(s)

Lincoln Land Community College (Public)
2001 Enrollment: 6,883 217-786-2200
2001 Tuition: In-state $2,765; Out-of-state $6,043
Springfield School of Court Reporting (Private, For-profit)
2001 Enrollment: n/a 217-546-0883
Springfield College in Illinois (Private, Not-for-profit, Roman Catholic)
2001 Enrollment: 380 217-525-1420
2001 Tuition: In-state $6,480; Out-of-state $6,480

Housing: Homeownership rate: 62.8% (2000); Median home value: $88,600 (2000); Median rent: $427 per month (2000); Median age of housing: 33 years (2000).
Hospitals: Andrew McFarland Mental Health Center (122 beds); Doctors Hospital (177 beds); Memorial Medical Center (562 beds); Saint John's Hospital (742 beds)
Safety: Violent crime rate: n/a; Property crime rate: 679.7 per 10,000 population (2001).
Newspapers: Pure News USA (1 x month); The State Journal-Register (7 x week); Illinois Times (1 x week); Catholic Times (1 x week)
Transportation: Commute to work: 91.8% car, 2.5% public transportation, 2.6% walk, 2.1% work from home (2000); Travel time to work: 41.6% less than 15 minutes, 47.6% 15 to 30 minutes, 6.1% 30 to 45 minutes, 1.7% 45 to 60 minutes, 3.0% 60 minutes or more (2000); Amtrak: Service available.
Airports: Capital (primary service)

Additional Information Contacts

Capital Area Association of Realtors 217-698-7000
Illinois Association of Realtors 217-529-2600
Illinois State Chamber of Commerce 217-522-5512
Springfield Chamber of Commerce 217-525-1173
Springfield Convention & Visitors Bureau 217-789-2360

THAYER (village). Covers a land area of 0.601 square miles and a water area of 0 square miles. Located at 39.53° N. Lat.; 89.76° W. Long. Elevation is 645 feet.
Population: 750 (2000); Race: 99.1% White, 0.0% Black, 0.6% Asian, 0.0% American Indian and Alaska Native, 0.3% Hispanic of any race, 0.3% two or more races (2000); Density: 1,248.4 persons per square mile (2000); Age: 27.8% under 18, 13.8% over 64 (2000); Marriage status: 18.7% never married, 62.7% now married, 7.4% widowed, 11.2% divorced (2000); Foreign born: 0.6% (2000); Ancestry (includes multiple ancestries): 17.7% German, 16.8% English, 13.7% United States or American, 9.7% Irish, 8.8% Italian (2000).
Economy: In agricultural and bituminous coal area. Single-family building permits issued: 0 (2001) / 0 (2000); Multi-family building permits issued: 0 (2001) / 0 (2000); Employment by occupation: 16.5% management, 18.4% professional, 10.8% services, 26.3% sales, 0.0% farming, 14.1% construction, 13.8% production (2000).
Income: Per capita income: $20,933 (2000); Median household income: $42,031 (2000); Poverty rate: 5.1% (2000).
Taxes: Total city taxes per capita: $12 (1997); City property taxes per capita: $9 (1997).
Education: High school graduation rate: 80.2% (2000); College graduation rate: 11.4% (2000).
Housing: Homeownership rate: 87.4% (2000); Median home value: $61,900 (2000); Median rent: $404 per month (2000); Median age of housing: 48 years (2000).
Transportation: Commute to work: 96.0% car, 0.0% public transportation, 0.8% walk, 3.2% work from home (2000); Travel time to work: 23.4% less than 15 minutes, 18.4% 15 to 30 minutes, 44.8% 30 to 45 minutes, 9.5% 45 to 60 minutes, 3.9% 60 minutes or more (2000)

WILLIAMSVILLE (village). Covers a land area of 1.242 square miles and a water area of 0 square miles. Located at 39.95° N. Lat.; 89.55° W. Long. Elevation is 600 feet.
Population: 1,439 (2000); Race: 98.6% White, 0.3% Black, 0.1% Asian, 0.0% American Indian and Alaska Native, 0.7% Hispanic of any race, 0.3% two or more races (2000); Density: 1,159.0 persons per square mile (2000); Age: 28.7% under 18, 14.4% over 64 (2000); Marriage status: 19.1% never married, 69.7% now married, 5.6% widowed, 5.7% divorced (2000); Foreign born: 1.3% (2000); Ancestry (includes multiple ancestries): 29.1% German, 16.3% English, 16.0% Irish, 8.2% Italian, 7.9% United States or American (2000).
Economy: Grain; dairy products; livestock. Single-family building permits issued: 2 (2001) / 2 (2000); Multi-family building permits issued: 0 (2001) / 0 (2000); Employment by occupation: 15.7% management, 22.4% professional, 11.7% services, 30.5% sales, 0.6% farming, 11.0% construction, 8.1% production (2000).
Income: Per capita income: $20,201 (2000); Median household income: $50,238 (2000); Poverty rate: 3.1% (2000).
Taxes: Total city taxes per capita: $36 (1997); City property taxes per capita: $29 (1997).
Education: High school graduation rate: 87.8% (2000); College graduation rate: 23.6% (2000).

School District(s)

Williamsville C U School District 15 (PK-12)
2000 Enrollment: 1,248 217-566-2014

Housing: Homeownership rate: 78.8% (2000); Median home value: $101,800 (2000); Median rent: $394 per month (2000); Median age of housing: 28 years (2000).
Transportation: Commute to work: 94.7% car, 0.0% public transportation, 2.2% walk, 2.4% work from home (2000); Travel time to work: 19.8% less than 15 minutes, 56.0% 15 to 30 minutes, 18.2% 30 to 45 minutes, 3.0% 45 to 60 minutes, 3.0% 60 minutes or more (2000)

Schuyler County

Located in western Illinois; bounded on the southeast by the Illinois River; drained by the La Moine River. Covers a land area of 437.30 square miles, a water area of 4.10 square miles, and is located in the Central Time Zone. The county government was organized in 1825. County seat is Rushville.

Weather Station: Rushville — Elevation: 659 feet

	Jan	Feb	Mar	Apr	May	Jun	Jul	Aug	Sep	Oct	Nov	Dec
High	33	39	51	64	74	83	87	85	78	66	51	38
Low	15	21	31	42	52	61	65	63	55	43	32	22
Precip	1.5	1.8	3.1	4.0	5.2	4.0	3.8	3.7	4.0	3.3	3.1	2.5
Snow	5.6	4.6	2.3	0.7	0.0	0.0	0.0	0.0	0.0	tr	1.0	3.7

High and Low temperatures in degrees Fahrenheit; Precipitation and Snow in inches

Population: 7,189 (2000); Race: 98.7% White, 0.2% Black, 0.2% Asian, 0.3% American Indian and Alaska Native, 0.7% Hispanic of any race, 0.4% two or more races (2000); Density: 16.4 persons per square mile (2000); Age: 23.2% under 18, 19.3% over 64 (2000).
Religion: Five largest groups: 15.9% The United Methodist Church, 8.9% Christian Churches and Churches of Christ, 6.5% Christian Church (Disciples of Christ), 5.8% Southern Baptist Convention, 4.1% Catholic Church (2000).
Economy: Unemployment rate: 4.0% (11/2002); Total civilian labor force: 4,202 (11/2002); Leading industries: 22.0% health care and social assistance; 19.4% retail trade; 12.2% accommodation & food services (2000); Companies that employ more than 1,000 persons: 0 (2000); Companies that employ more than 100 persons: 1 (2000); Farms: 477 totaling 208,935 acres (1997); Minority business ownership rate: 0.0% (1997); Women business ownership rate: 30.1% (1997); Retail sales per capita: $5,937 (1997). Single-family building permits issued: -1 (2001) / -1 (2000); Multi-family building permits issued: -1 (2001) / -1 (2000).
Income: Per capita income: $17,158 (2000); Median household income: $35,233 (2000); Poverty rate: 10.1% (2000); Bankruptcy rate: 4.77% (2001).
Taxes: Total county taxes per capita: $118 (2000); County property taxes per capita: $118 (2000).
Education: High school graduation rate: 83.6% (2000); College graduation rate: 11.7% (2000).

Housing: Homeownership rate: 79.0% (2000); Median home value: $54,000 (2000); Median rent: $253 per month (2000); Median age of housing: 41 years (2000).
Health: Birth rate: 114.1 per 10,000 population (1998); Age adjusted death rate: 84.2 per 10,000 population (1999); Age adjusted cancer mortality rate: 157.9 (Unreliable figure as per CDC) deaths per 100,000 population (1999). Number of physicians: 5.6 per 10,000 population (1999); Number of hospital beds: 80.7 per 10,000 population (1999).
Elections: 2000 Presidential election results: 42.1% Gore, 55.1% Bush, 1.9% Nader, 0.7% Buchanan
National and State Parks: Weinborg-King State Park
Additional Information Contacts
Schuyler County Government Offices 217-322-4734
Rushville Area Chamber of Commerce 217-322-3689

Schuyler County Communities

BROWNING (village). Covers a land area of 0.310 square miles and a water area of 0 square miles. Located at 40.12° N. Lat.; 90.37° W. Long. Elevation is 460 feet.
Population: 130 (2000); Race: 98.5% White, 0.0% Black, 0.0% Asian, 1.5% American Indian and Alaska Native, 0.0% Hispanic of any race, 0.0% two or more races (2000); Density: 419.0 persons per square mile (2000); Age: 11.8% under 18, 28.7% over 64 (2000); Marriage status: 8.8% never married, 64.8% now married, 6.4% widowed, 20.0% divorced (2000); Foreign born: 0.0% (2000); Ancestry (includes multiple ancestries): 27.9% United States or American, 19.9% German, 13.2% Irish, 6.6% English, 3.7% Other groups (2000).
Economy: In agricultural area. Employment by occupation: 10.4% management, 0.0% professional, 23.9% services, 26.9% sales, 0.0% farming, 22.4% construction, 16.4% production (2000).
Income: Per capita income: $18,109 (2000); Median household income: $44,107 (2000); Poverty rate: 3.7% (2000).
Taxes: Total city taxes per capita: $36 (1997); City property taxes per capita: $36 (1997).
Education: High school graduation rate: 73.7% (2000); College graduation rate: 0.0% (2000).
Housing: Homeownership rate: 100.0% (2000); Median home value: $28,500 (2000); Median age of housing: 55 years (2000).
Transportation: Commute to work: 100.0% car, 0.0% public transportation, 0.0% walk, 0.0% work from home (2000); Travel time to work: 40.3% less than 15 minutes, 19.4% 15 to 30 minutes, 25.4% 30 to 45 minutes, 14.9% 45 to 60 minutes, 0.0% 60 minutes or more (2000)

CAMDEN (village). Covers a land area of 0.762 square miles and a water area of 0 square miles. Located at 40.15° N. Lat.; 90.77° W. Long. Elevation is 600 feet.
Population: 97 (2000); Race: 100.0% White, 0.0% Black, 0.0% Asian, 0.0% American Indian and Alaska Native, 0.0% Hispanic of any race, 0.0% two or more races (2000); Density: 127.3 persons per square mile (2000); Age: 28.1% under 18, 9.4% over 64 (2000); Marriage status: 11.1% never married, 75.0% now married, 8.3% widowed, 5.6% divorced (2000); Foreign born: 0.0% (2000); Ancestry (includes multiple ancestries): 21.9% German, 14.6% United States or American, 11.5% Irish, 6.3% Scottish, 4.2% Scotch-Irish (2000).
Economy: In agricultural area. Employment by occupation: 13.5% management, 0.0% professional, 2.7% services, 35.1% sales, 0.0% farming, 8.1% construction, 40.5% production (2000).
Income: Per capita income: $9,981 (2000); Median household income: $26,250 (2000); Poverty rate: 33.3% (2000).
Taxes: Total city taxes per capita: $9 (1997); City property taxes per capita: $9 (1997).
Education: High school graduation rate: 72.4% (2000); College graduation rate: 0.0% (2000).
Housing: Homeownership rate: 88.6% (2000); Median home value: $21,300 (2000); Median rent: <$100 per month (2000); Median age of housing: 32 years (2000).
Transportation: Commute to work: 89.2% car, 0.0% public transportation, 8.1% walk, 2.7% work from home (2000); Travel time to work: 13.9% less than 15 minutes, 30.6% 15 to 30 minutes, 50.0% 30 to 45 minutes, 5.6% 45 to 60 minutes, 0.0% 60 minutes or more (2000)

FREDERICK (unincorporated postal area, zip code 62639). Covers a land area of 34.538 square miles and a water area of 1.058 square miles. Located at 40.04° N. Lat.; 90.46° W. Long. Elevation is 445 feet.
Population: 341 (2000); Race: 97.4% White, 0.0% Black, 0.0% Asian, 0.0% American Indian and Alaska Native, 2.6% Hispanic of any race, 0.0% two or more races (2000); Density: 9.9 persons per square mile (2000); Age: 24.9% under 18, 14.9% over 64 (2000); Marriage status: 27.4% never married, 61.4% now married, 3.2% widowed, 8.1% divorced (2000); Foreign born: 0.0% (2000); Ancestry (includes multiple ancestries): 24.1% German, 10.6% English, 9.7% Irish, 8.3% Italian, 6.6% British (2000).
Economy: Employment by occupation: 11.6% management, 16.3% professional, 21.8% services, 25.2% sales, 0.0% farming, 3.4% construction, 21.8% production (2000).
Income: Per capita income: $16,011 (2000); Median household income: $38,125 (2000); Poverty rate: 20.3% (2000).
Education: High school graduation rate: 90.1% (2000); College graduation rate: 8.3% (2000).
Housing: Homeownership rate: 92.6% (2000); Median home value: $43,700 (2000); Median age of housing: 49 years (2000).
Transportation: Commute to work: 95.0% car, 0.0% public transportation, 0.0% walk, 0.0% work from home (2000); Travel time to work: 37.1% less than 15 minutes, 42.1% 15 to 30 minutes, 5.0% 30 to 45 minutes, 0.0% 45 to 60 minutes, 15.7% 60 minutes or more (2000)

HUNTSVILLE (unincorporated postal area, zip code 62344). Covers a land area of 37.078 square miles and a water area of 0 square miles. Located at 40.18° N. Lat.; 90.81° W. Long. Elevation is 654 feet.
Population: 185 (2000); Race: 100.0% White, 0.0% Black, 0.0% Asian, 0.0% American Indian and Alaska Native, 0.0% Hispanic of any race, 0.0% two or more races (2000); Density: 5.0 persons per square mile (2000); Age: 29.3% under 18, 2.4% over 64 (2000); Marriage status: 23.6% never married, 61.5% now married, 3.1% widowed, 11.8% divorced (2000); Foreign born: 0.0% (2000); Ancestry (includes multiple ancestries): 39.9% English, 32.2% German, 21.2% United States or American, 10.6% Irish, 5.3% Dutch (2000).
Economy: Employment by occupation: 26.4% management, 21.8% professional, 16.4% services, 14.5% sales, 4.5% farming, 4.5% construction, 11.8% production (2000).
Income: Per capita income: $10,976 (2000); Median household income: $38,542 (2000); Poverty rate: 4.8% (2000).
Education: High school graduation rate: 79.3% (2000); College graduation rate: 12.4% (2000).
Housing: Homeownership rate: 69.1% (2000); Median home value: $58,000 (2000); Median rent: $125 per month (2000); Median age of housing: 52 years (2000).
Transportation: Commute to work: 100.0% car, 0.0% public transportation, 0.0% walk, 0.0% work from home (2000); Travel time to work: 20.0% less than 15 minutes, 25.5% 15 to 30 minutes, 20.0% 30 to 45 minutes, 6.4% 45 to 60 minutes, 28.2% 60 minutes or more (2000)

LITTLETON (village). Covers a land area of 1.163 square miles and a water area of 0 square miles. Located at 40.23° N. Lat.; 90.61° W. Long. Elevation is 690 feet.
Population: 197 (2000); Race: 94.0% White, 6.0% Black, 0.0% Asian, 0.0% American Indian and Alaska Native, 4.0% Hispanic of any race, 0.0% two or more races (2000); Density: 169.3 persons per square mile (2000); Age: 31.8% under 18, 6.5% over 64 (2000); Marriage status: 25.5% never married, 61.4% now married, 5.5% widowed, 7.6% divorced (2000); Foreign born: 0.0% (2000); Ancestry (includes multiple ancestries): 20.4% German, 15.9% Other groups, 12.4% United States or American, 9.5% English, 7.5% Irish (2000).
Economy: In agricultural area. Employment by occupation: 5.8% management, 13.6% professional, 24.3% services, 14.6% sales, 0.0% farming, 6.8% construction, 35.0% production (2000).
Income: Per capita income: $14,670 (2000); Median household income: $43,750 (2000); Poverty rate: 0.5% (2000).
Taxes: Total city taxes per capita: $11 (1997); City property taxes per capita: $0 (1997).
Education: High school graduation rate: 85.8% (2000); College graduation rate: 8.3% (2000).
Housing: Homeownership rate: 86.4% (2000); Median home value: $34,500 (2000); Median rent: $163 per month (2000); Median age of housing: 60+ years (2000).
Transportation: Commute to work: 90.3% car, 0.0% public transportation, 5.8% walk, 0.0% work from home (2000); Travel time to work: 16.5% less than 15 minutes, 31.1% 15 to 30 minutes, 41.7% 30 to 45 minutes, 1.9% 45 to 60 minutes, 8.7% 60 minutes or more (2000)

RUSHVILLE (city). Covers a land area of 1.572 square miles and a water area of 0 square miles. Located at 40.12° N. Lat.; 90.56° W. Long. Elevation is 676 feet.
History: Rushville was founded in 1825 as Rushton. Both names honor Dr. William Rush, a Philadelphia physician.
Population: 3,212 (2000); Race: 99.1% White, 0.0% Black, 0.2% Asian, 0.1% American Indian and Alaska Native, 0.3% Hispanic of any race, 0.5% two or more races (2000); Density: 2,043.7 persons per square mile (2000); Age: 21.9% under 18, 24.1% over 64 (2000); Marriage status: 14.5% never married, 63.1% now married, 13.8% widowed, 8.6% divorced (2000); Foreign born: 0.7% (2000); Ancestry (includes multiple ancestries): 21.1% United States or American, 15.3% German, 12.4% Irish, 10.8% English, 3.8% Dutch (2000).
Economy: Employment by occupation: 6.7% management, 15.2% professional, 24.0% services, 22.1% sales, 0.5% farming, 7.7% construction, 23.9% production (2000).
Income: Per capita income: $16,180 (2000); Median household income: $30,450 (2000); Poverty rate: 10.8% (2000).
Taxes: Total city taxes per capita: $145 (1997); City property taxes per capita: $33 (1997).
Education: High school graduation rate: 83.3% (2000); College graduation rate: 12.4% (2000).

School District(s)

Schuyler Co C U School District 1 (PK-12)
2000 Enrollment: 1,161 217-322-4311
Housing: Homeownership rate: 74.1% (2000); Median home value: $54,100 (2000); Median rent: $264 per month (2000); Median age of housing: 46 years (2000).
Hospitals: Culbertson Memorial Hospital (64 beds)
Newspapers: The Rushville Times (1 x week)
Transportation: Commute to work: 89.8% car, 0.0% public transportation, 3.5% walk, 4.8% work from home (2000); Travel time to work: 53.9% less than 15 minutes, 26.4% 15 to 30 minutes, 9.8% 30 to 45 minutes, 3.8% 45 to 60 minutes, 6.0% 60 minutes or more (2000)
Additional Information Contacts
Rushville Area Chamber of Commerce 217-322-3689

Scott County

Located in west central Illinois; bounded on the west by the Illinois River; drained by Sandy and Mauvaise Terre Creeks. Covers a land area of 250.90 square miles, a water area of 1.80 square miles, and is located in the Central Time Zone. The county government was organized in 1839. County seat is Winchester.
Population: 5,537 (2000); Race: 99.3% White, 0.1% Black, 0.1% Asian, 0.2% American Indian and Alaska Native, 0.2% Hispanic of any race, 0.2% two or more races (2000); Density: 22.1 persons per square mile (2000); Age: 24.9% under 18, 16.5% over 64 (2000).
Religion: Five largest groups: 17.9% American Baptist Churches in the USA, 17.1% Southern Baptist Convention, 9.5% Lutheran Church—Missouri Synod, 8.6% Catholic Church, 8.0% The United Methodist Church (2000).
Economy: Unemployment rate: 4.7% (11/2002); Total civilian labor force: 2,740 (11/2002); Leading industries: 44.5% construction; 12.0% wholesale trade; 9.6% retail trade (2000); Companies that employ more than 1,000 persons: 0 (2000); Companies that employ more than 100 persons: 1 (2000); Farms: 327 totaling 145,529 acres (1997); Minority business ownership rate: 0.0% (1997); Women business ownership rate: 0.0% (1997); Retail sales per capita: $3,652 (1997). Single-family building permits issued: 0 (2001) / 0 (2000); Multi-family building permits issued: 0 (2001) / 0 (2000).
Income: Per capita income: $16,998 (2000); Median household income: $36,566 (2000); Poverty rate: 9.7% (2000); Bankruptcy rate: 3.20% (2001).
Taxes: Total county taxes per capita: $109 (1997); County property taxes per capita: $103 (1997).
Education: High school graduation rate: 83.1% (2000); College graduation rate: 12.1% (2000).
Housing: Homeownership rate: 77.6% (2000); Median home value: $57,800 (2000); Median rent: $221 per month (2000); Median age of housing: 46 years (2000).
Health: Birth rate: 106.6 per 10,000 population (1998); Age adjusted death rate: 78.5 per 10,000 population (1999); Age adjusted cancer mortality rate: 144.9 (Unreliable figure as per CDC) deaths per 100,000 population (1999). Number of physicians: 3.6 per 10,000 population (1999); Number of hospital beds: n/a (1999).
Elections: 2000 Presidential election results: 38.6% Gore, 59.1% Bush, 1.3% Nader, 0.9% Buchanan

Additional Information Contacts
Scott County Government Offices 217-742-3178

Scott County Communities

ALSEY (village). Covers a land area of 0.557 square miles and a water area of 0.010 square miles. Located at 39.56° N. Lat.; 90.43° W. Long. Elevation is 633 feet.
Population: 246 (2000); Race: 100.0% White, 0.0% Black, 0.0% Asian, 0.0% American Indian and Alaska Native, 0.0% Hispanic of any race, 0.0% two or more races (2000); Density: 441.7 persons per square mile (2000); Age: 23.2% under 18, 19.1% over 64 (2000); Marriage status: 15.1% never married, 60.3% now married, 16.6% widowed, 8.0% divorced (2000); Foreign born: 0.8% (2000); Ancestry (includes multiple ancestries): 16.7% United States or American, 16.3% Other groups, 12.2% English, 11.8% German, 6.5% Irish (2000).
Economy: In agricultural area. Employment by occupation: 5.2% management, 8.7% professional, 13.9% services, 28.7% sales, 0.0% farming, 9.6% construction, 33.9% production (2000).
Income: Per capita income: $15,652 (2000); Median household income: $33,750 (2000); Poverty rate: 8.1% (2000).
Taxes: Total city taxes per capita: $12 (1997); City property taxes per capita: $4 (1997).
Education: High school graduation rate: 71.6% (2000); College graduation rate: 4.5% (2000).
Housing: Homeownership rate: 82.2% (2000); Median home value: $38,800 (2000); Median rent: $238 per month (2000); Median age of housing: 48 years (2000).
Transportation: Commute to work: 96.5% car, 0.0% public transportation, 3.5% walk, 0.0% work from home (2000); Travel time to work: 11.3% less than 15 minutes, 20.9% 15 to 30 minutes, 53.0% 30 to 45 minutes, 7.8% 45 to 60 minutes, 7.0% 60 minutes or more (2000)

BLUFFS (village). Covers a land area of 1.015 square miles and a water area of 0 square miles. Located at 39.74° N. Lat.; 90.53° W. Long. Elevation is 474 feet.
Population: 748 (2000); Race: 99.2% White, 0.0% Black, 0.5% Asian, 0.0% American Indian and Alaska Native, 0.0% Hispanic of any race, 0.0% two or more races (2000); Density: 736.9 persons per square mile (2000); Age: 28.8% under 18, 13.6% over 64 (2000); Marriage status: 23.7% never married, 57.0% now married, 9.9% widowed, 9.4% divorced (2000); Foreign born: 0.5% (2000); Ancestry (includes multiple ancestries): 32.4% German, 17.4% English, 10.2% United States or American, 8.8% Other groups, 7.1% Irish (2000).
Economy: In agricultural area: corn, soybeans, sorghum; cattle, hogs. Single-family building permits issued: 0 (2001) / 0 (2000); Multi-family building permits issued: 0 (2001) / 0 (2000); Employment by occupation: 10.9% management, 17.9% professional, 11.7% services, 29.3% sales, 2.0% farming, 11.5% construction, 16.8% production (2000).
Income: Per capita income: $16,705 (2000); Median household income: $34,531 (2000); Poverty rate: 11.8% (2000).
Taxes: Total city taxes per capita: $91 (1997); City property taxes per capita: $22 (1997).
Education: High school graduation rate: 82.7% (2000); College graduation rate: 13.4% (2000).

School District(s)

Scott-Morgan C U School District 2 (PK-12)
2000 Enrollment: 301 217-754-3351
Housing: Homeownership rate: 78.1% (2000); Median home value: $47,600 (2000); Median rent: $115 per month (2000); Median age of housing: 60 years (2000).
Newspapers: Triopia Tribune (1 x week); Meredosia Budget (1 x week); Bluffs Times (1 x week)
Transportation: Commute to work: 97.5% car, 0.0% public transportation, 1.4% walk, 0.6% work from home (2000); Travel time to work: 33.3% less than 15 minutes, 32.5% 15 to 30 minutes, 25.1% 30 to 45 minutes, 2.3% 45 to 60 minutes, 6.8% 60 minutes or more (2000)

EXETER (village). Covers a land area of 0.690 square miles and a water area of 0 square miles. Located at 39.71° N. Lat.; 90.49° W. Long. Elevation is 570 feet.
Population: 70 (2000); Race: 97.5% White, 0.0% Black, 0.0% Asian, 2.5% American Indian and Alaska Native, 0.0% Hispanic of any race, 0.0% two or more races (2000); Density: 101.5 persons per square mile (2000); Age: 21.3% under 18, 5.0% over 64 (2000); Marriage status: 42.0% never married,

42.0% now married, 10.1% widowed, 5.8% divorced (2000); Foreign born: 0.0% (2000); Ancestry (includes multiple ancestries): 23.8% English, 13.8% Irish, 12.5% United States or American, 7.5% German, 3.8% Swiss (2000).
Economy: In agricultural area. Employment by occupation: 22.0% management, 14.0% professional, 20.0% services, 6.0% sales, 4.0% farming, 8.0% construction, 26.0% production (2000).
Income: Per capita income: $18,968 (2000); Median household income: $46,875 (2000); Poverty rate: 0.0% (2000).
Education: High school graduation rate: 72.5% (2000); College graduation rate: 15.0% (2000).
Housing: Homeownership rate: 88.5% (2000); Median home value: $70,800 (2000); Median rent: $275 per month (2000); Median age of housing: 60+ years (2000).
Transportation: Commute to work: 86.0% car, 0.0% public transportation, 14.0% walk, 0.0% work from home (2000); Travel time to work: 24.0% less than 15 minutes, 60.0% 15 to 30 minutes, 16.0% 30 to 45 minutes, 0.0% 45 to 60 minutes, 0.0% 60 minutes or more (2000)

GLASGOW (village). Covers a land area of 1.011 square miles and a water area of 0 square miles. Located at 39.55° N. Lat.; 90.48° W. Long. Elevation is 587 feet.
Population: 170 (2000); Race: 100.0% White, 0.0% Black, 0.0% Asian, 0.0% American Indian and Alaska Native, 0.0% Hispanic of any race, 0.0% two or more races (2000); Density: 168.1 persons per square mile (2000); Age: 29.4% under 18, 16.6% over 64 (2000); Marriage status: 7.7% never married, 82.1% now married, 3.4% widowed, 6.8% divorced (2000); Foreign born: 1.2% (2000); Ancestry (includes multiple ancestries): 13.5% United States or American, 11.0% English, 10.4% German, 9.2% Irish, 9.2% Other groups (2000).
Economy: In agricultural area: cattle, hogs, corn, soybeans, sorghum. Employment by occupation: 4.8% management, 4.8% professional, 31.7% services, 17.5% sales, 3.2% farming, 23.8% construction, 14.3% production (2000).
Income: Per capita income: $11,172 (2000); Median household income: $25,000 (2000); Poverty rate: 20.2% (2000).
Taxes: Total city taxes per capita: $6 (1997); City property taxes per capita: $6 (1997).
Education: High school graduation rate: 88.2% (2000); College graduation rate: 2.7% (2000).
Housing: Homeownership rate: 85.5% (2000); Median home value: $36,500 (2000); Median rent: $250 per month (2000); Median age of housing: 31 years (2000).
Transportation: Commute to work: 93.3% car, 0.0% public transportation, 3.3% walk, 3.3% work from home (2000); Travel time to work: 34.5% less than 15 minutes, 13.8% 15 to 30 minutes, 31.0% 30 to 45 minutes, 8.6% 45 to 60 minutes, 12.1% 60 minutes or more (2000)

MANCHESTER (village). Covers a land area of 1.036 square miles and a water area of 0 square miles. Located at 39.54° N. Lat.; 90.32° W. Long. Elevation is 691 feet.
Population: 354 (2000); Race: 97.8% White, 0.0% Black, 0.0% Asian, 2.2% American Indian and Alaska Native, 0.0% Hispanic of any race, 0.0% two or more races (2000); Density: 341.8 persons per square mile (2000); Age: 26.3% under 18, 15.6% over 64 (2000); Marriage status: 16.4% never married, 68.2% now married, 2.6% widowed, 12.8% divorced (2000); Foreign born: 0.0% (2000); Ancestry (includes multiple ancestries): 26.5% English, 20.4% German, 14.2% Irish, 7.0% United States or American, 6.7% Other groups (2000).
Economy: In agricultural area. Employment by occupation: 7.0% management, 12.9% professional, 15.1% services, 30.1% sales, 1.1% farming, 9.1% construction, 24.7% production (2000).
Income: Per capita income: $13,728 (2000); Median household income: $31,875 (2000); Poverty rate: 10.7% (2000).
Taxes: Total city taxes per capita: $23 (1997); City property taxes per capita: $23 (1997).
Education: High school graduation rate: 84.8% (2000); College graduation rate: 10.9% (2000).
Housing: Homeownership rate: 84.8% (2000); Median home value: $50,500 (2000); Median rent: $256 per month (2000); Median age of housing: 40 years (2000).
Transportation: Commute to work: 89.4% car, 0.0% public transportation, 3.9% walk, 5.6% work from home (2000); Travel time to work: 13.6% less than 15 minutes, 49.7% 15 to 30 minutes, 27.2% 30 to 45 minutes, 4.1% 45 to 60 minutes, 5.3% 60 minutes or more (2000)

NAPLES (town). Covers a land area of 0.605 square miles and a water area of 0 square miles. Located at 39.75° N. Lat.; 90.60° W. Long. Elevation is 440 feet.
History: It was in Naples that the steamboat "Olitippa" was built on the Illinois River, before regular steamboat service began.
Population: 134 (2000); Race: 89.7% White, 0.0% Black, 0.0% Asian, 2.6% American Indian and Alaska Native, 6.9% Hispanic of any race, 0.9% two or more races (2000); Density: 221.6 persons per square mile (2000); Age: 31.9% under 18, 1.7% over 64 (2000); Marriage status: 27.6% never married, 44.8% now married, 9.2% widowed, 18.4% divorced (2000); Foreign born: 9.5% (2000); Ancestry (includes multiple ancestries): 24.1% German, 15.5% United States or American, 12.9% Other groups, 12.9% Irish, 12.9% Polish (2000).
Economy: Employment by occupation: 0.0% management, 0.0% professional, 30.9% services, 30.9% sales, 0.0% farming, 7.3% construction, 30.9% production (2000).
Income: Per capita income: $10,719 (2000); Median household income: $27,083 (2000); Poverty rate: 29.3% (2000).
Taxes: Total city taxes per capita: $70 (1997); City property taxes per capita: $61 (1997).
Education: High school graduation rate: 67.2% (2000); College graduation rate: 3.1% (2000).
Housing: Homeownership rate: 82.9% (2000); Median home value: $33,300 (2000); Median rent: $217 per month (2000); Median age of housing: 31 years (2000).
Transportation: Commute to work: 100.0% car, 0.0% public transportation, 0.0% walk, 0.0% work from home (2000); Travel time to work: 21.8% less than 15 minutes, 9.1% 15 to 30 minutes, 61.8% 30 to 45 minutes, 0.0% 45 to 60 minutes, 7.3% 60 minutes or more (2000)

WINCHESTER (city). Covers a land area of 1.064 square miles and a water area of 0 square miles. Located at 39.63° N. Lat.; 90.45° W. Long. Elevation is 546 feet.
History: A grist mill was operating in Winchester in 1824. When the town was platted in 1830, so the story is told, the surveyor allowed a resident from Kentucky to name the townsite in exchange for a jug of whiskey. Stephen A. Douglas taught school and began his legal career here in 1833. Winchester developed as the seat of Scott County.
Population: 1,650 (2000); Race: 99.8% White, 0.2% Black, 0.0% Asian, 0.0% American Indian and Alaska Native, 0.2% Hispanic of any race, 0.0% two or more races (2000); Density: 1,551.3 persons per square mile (2000); Age: 25.1% under 18, 20.9% over 64 (2000); Marriage status: 20.0% never married, 56.7% now married, 12.7% widowed, 10.7% divorced (2000); Foreign born: 0.2% (2000); Ancestry (includes multiple ancestries): 19.6% German, 18.0% English, 13.9% United States or American, 11.1% Irish, 4.5% Other groups (2000).
Economy: Employment by occupation: 10.3% management, 16.5% professional, 18.2% services, 26.1% sales, 0.8% farming, 8.6% construction, 19.5% production (2000).
Income: Per capita income: $17,354 (2000); Median household income: $30,938 (2000); Poverty rate: 10.4% (2000).
Taxes: Total city taxes per capita: $75 (1997); City property taxes per capita: $70 (1997).
Education: High school graduation rate: 81.5% (2000); College graduation rate: 14.1% (2000).

School District(s)

Winchester C U School District 1 (PK-12)
2000 Enrollment: 718 217-742-3175
Housing: Homeownership rate: 72.2% (2000); Median home value: $59,900 (2000); Median rent: $199 per month (2000); Median age of housing: 55 years (2000).
Newspapers: Scott County Times (1 x week)
Transportation: Commute to work: 90.9% car, 0.0% public transportation, 4.3% walk, 4.3% work from home (2000); Travel time to work: 35.9% less than 15 minutes, 33.6% 15 to 30 minutes, 20.1% 30 to 45 minutes, 3.0% 45 to 60 minutes, 7.5% 60 minutes or more (2000)

Shelby County

Located in central Illinois; drained by the South Fork of the Sangamon River, and by the Kaskaskia and Little Wabash Rivers. Covers a land area of 758.50 square miles, a water area of 9.50 square miles, and is located in the Central Time Zone. The county government was organized in 1827. County seat is Shelbyville.

Weather Station: Moweaqua Elevation: 613 feet

	Jan	Feb	Mar	Apr	May	Jun	Jul	Aug	Sep	Oct	Nov	Dec
High	34	40	52	65	75	84	87	85	80	68	52	40
Low	17	21	31	41	52	61	64	62	54	43	33	23
Precip	1.7	1.9	2.9	3.9	4.2	4.2	4.0	3.3	3.0	2.8	3.6	2.2
Snow	na	na	0.9	0.2	tr	0.0	0.0	0.0	0.0	tr	0.5	na

High and Low temperatures in degrees Fahrenheit; Precipitation and Snow in inches

Weather Station: Windsor Elevation: 688 feet

	Jan	Feb	Mar	Apr	May	Jun	Jul	Aug	Sep	Oct	Nov	Dec
High	35	41	52	65	75	84	87	85	80	68	52	40
Low	19	23	33	43	53	62	66	63	56	45	35	25
Precip	2.0	1.9	3.3	3.9	4.0	3.9	4.0	3.1	3.0	3.0	3.7	3.0
Snow	7.9	4.3	3.0	0.3	0.0	0.0	0.0	0.0	0.0	tr	1.3	5.0

High and Low temperatures in degrees Fahrenheit; Precipitation and Snow in inches

Population: 22,893 (2000); Race: 99.0% White, 0.1% Black, 0.3% Asian, 0.1% American Indian and Alaska Native, 0.3% Hispanic of any race, 0.3% two or more races (2000); Density: 30.2 persons per square mile (2000); Age: 24.9% under 18, 17.7% over 64 (2000).
Religion: Five largest groups: 13.3% Christian Churches and Churches of Christ, 11.7% The United Methodist Church, 7.6% Lutheran Church—Missouri Synod, 7.5% Catholic Church, 3.9% Southern Baptist Convention (2000).
Economy: Unemployment rate: 7.2% (11/2002); Total civilian labor force: 11,121 (11/2002); Leading industries: 28.5% manufacturing; 14.8% health care and social assistance; 11.3% retail trade (2000); Companies that employ more than 1,000 persons: 1 (2000); Companies that employ more than 100 persons: 6 (2000); Farms: 1,250 totaling 418,688 acres (1997); Minority business ownership rate: 0.0% (1997); Women business ownership rate: 29.0% (1997); Retail sales per capita: $5,465 (1997). Single-family building permits issued: 48 (2001) / 51 (2000); Multi-family building permits issued: 0 (2001) / 9 (2000).
Income: Per capita income: $17,313 (2000); Median household income: $37,313 (2000); Poverty rate: 9.1% (2000); Bankruptcy rate: 5.12% (2001).
Taxes: Total county taxes per capita: $100 (2000); County property taxes per capita: $96 (2000).
Education: High school graduation rate: 82.9% (2000); College graduation rate: 11.5% (2000).
Housing: Homeownership rate: 81.0% (2000); Median home value: $66,600 (2000); Median rent: $301 per month (2000); Median age of housing: 39 years (2000).
Health: Birth rate: 110.5 per 10,000 population (1998); Age adjusted death rate: 74.3 per 10,000 population (1999); Age adjusted cancer mortality rate: 156.1 deaths per 100,000 population (1999). Number of physicians: 4.8 per 10,000 population (1999); Number of hospital beds: 22.7 per 10,000 population (1999).
Elections: 2000 Presidential election results: 39.5% Gore, 57.6% Bush, 1.6% Nader, 1.1% Buchanan
National and State Parks: Eagle Creek State Park; Hidden Springs State Forest; Wolf Creek State Park
Additional Information Contacts
Shelby County Government Offices 217-774-4421
Shelbyville Chamber of Commerce 217-774-2221

Shelby County Communities

COWDEN (village). Covers a land area of 0.401 square miles and a water area of 0 square miles. Located at 39.24° N. Lat.; 88.86° W. Long. Elevation is 604 feet.
Population: 612 (2000); Race: 95.3% White, 2.6% Black, 0.0% Asian, 1.3% American Indian and Alaska Native, 0.3% Hispanic of any race, 0.8% two or more races (2000); Density: 1,526.3 persons per square mile (2000); Age: 31.9% under 18, 13.3% over 64 (2000); Marriage status: 20.8% never married, 59.4% now married, 8.3% widowed, 11.4% divorced (2000); Foreign born: 0.0% (2000); Ancestry (includes multiple ancestries): 20.9% German, 17.8% Irish, 17.0% United States or American, 13.3% Other groups, 5.5% English (2000).
Economy: Agriculture: corn, wheat, soybeans, sorghum; cattle; dairying. Single-family building permits issued: 0 (2001) / 4 (2000); Multi-family building permits issued: 0 (2001) / 0 (2000); Employment by occupation: 5.0% management, 10.4% professional, 11.8% services, 21.3% sales, 0.0% farming, 10.9% construction, 40.7% production (2000).
Income: Per capita income: $12,583 (2000); Median household income: $25,938 (2000); Poverty rate: 19.8% (2000).
Taxes: Total city taxes per capita: $25 (1997); City property taxes per capita: $25 (1997).
Education: High school graduation rate: 77.6% (2000); College graduation rate: 6.9% (2000).

School District(s)

Cowden-Herrick CUSD 3a (KG-12)
2000 Enrollment: 512 217-783-2126

Housing: Homeownership rate: 80.6% (2000); Median home value: $35,000 (2000); Median rent: $294 per month (2000); Median age of housing: 35 years (2000).
Transportation: Commute to work: 99.5% car, 0.0% public transportation, 0.5% walk, 0.0% work from home (2000); Travel time to work: 18.1% less than 15 minutes, 40.3% 15 to 30 minutes, 21.8% 30 to 45 minutes, 4.6% 45 to 60 minutes, 15.3% 60 minutes or more (2000)

FINDLAY (village). Covers a land area of 0.919 square miles and a water area of 0 square miles. Located at 39.52° N. Lat.; 88.75° W. Long. Elevation is 695 feet.
Population: 723 (2000); Race: 98.8% White, 1.0% Black, 0.0% Asian, 0.3% American Indian and Alaska Native, 0.0% Hispanic of any race, 0.0% two or more races (2000); Density: 786.7 persons per square mile (2000); Age: 23.2% under 18, 16.2% over 64 (2000); Marriage status: 19.7% never married, 63.6% now married, 10.0% widowed, 6.6% divorced (2000); Foreign born: 0.0% (2000); Ancestry (includes multiple ancestries): 19.7% German, 10.1% United States or American, 9.9% Irish, 9.2% English, 5.0% Other groups (2000).
Economy: In agricultural area; ships grain. Single-family building permits issued: 2 (2001) / 0 (2000); Multi-family building permits issued: 0 (2001) / 0 (2000); Employment by occupation: 8.2% management, 20.7% professional, 16.4% services, 16.7% sales, 0.8% farming, 8.8% construction, 28.3% production (2000).
Income: Per capita income: $15,990 (2000); Median household income: $30,962 (2000); Poverty rate: 12.6% (2000).
Taxes: Total city taxes per capita: $44 (1997); City property taxes per capita: $38 (1997).
Education: High school graduation rate: 82.8% (2000); College graduation rate: 12.6% (2000).

School District(s)

Findlay Community Unit School District 2 (KG-12)
2000 Enrollment: 207 217-756-8522

Housing: Homeownership rate: 74.4% (2000); Median home value: $52,500 (2000); Median rent: $293 per month (2000); Median age of housing: 52 years (2000).
Transportation: Commute to work: 91.4% car, 0.6% public transportation, 3.2% walk, 2.0% work from home (2000); Travel time to work: 24.0% less than 15 minutes, 35.1% 15 to 30 minutes, 22.2% 30 to 45 minutes, 13.7% 45 to 60 minutes, 5.0% 60 minutes or more (2000)

HERRICK (village). Covers a land area of 0.363 square miles and a water area of 0 square miles. Located at 39.21° N. Lat.; 88.98° W. Long. Elevation is 605 feet.
Population: 524 (2000); Race: 99.1% White, 0.0% Black, 0.0% Asian, 0.0% American Indian and Alaska Native, 0.0% Hispanic of any race, 0.9% two or more races (2000); Density: 1,442.8 persons per square mile (2000); Age: 27.2% under 18, 22.4% over 64 (2000); Marriage status: 20.5% never married, 59.8% now married, 11.6% widowed, 8.1% divorced (2000); Foreign born: 0.0% (2000); Ancestry (includes multiple ancestries): 20.9% German, 15.7% United States or American, 10.6% Other groups, 7.4% Irish, 5.0% English (2000).
Economy: In agricultural area. Employment by occupation: 8.9% management, 8.3% professional, 17.3% services, 24.4% sales, 1.8% farming, 14.9% construction, 24.4% production (2000).
Income: Per capita income: $11,243 (2000); Median household income: $24,722 (2000); Poverty rate: 22.0% (2000).
Taxes: Total city taxes per capita: $30 (1997); City property taxes per capita: $30 (1997).
Education: High school graduation rate: 53.5% (2000); College graduation rate: 1.5% (2000).
Housing: Homeownership rate: 82.0% (2000); Median home value: $38,400 (2000); Median rent: $238 per month (2000); Median age of housing: 28 years (2000).
Transportation: Commute to work: 94.0% car, 2.4% public transportation, 3.0% walk, 0.0% work from home (2000); Travel time to work: 21.1% less than 15 minutes, 4.8% 15 to 30 minutes, 36.7% 30 to 45 minutes, 15.7% 45 to 60 minutes, 21.7% 60 minutes or more (2000)

LAKEWOOD (unincorporated postal area, zip code 62438). Covers a land area of 26.118 square miles and a water area of 0 square miles. Located at 39.31° N. Lat.; 88.87° W. Long. Elevation is 630 feet.
Population: 404 (2000); Race: 100.0% White, 0.0% Black, 0.0% Asian, 0.0% American Indian and Alaska Native, 1.1% Hispanic of any race, 0.0% two or more races (2000); Density: 15.5 persons per square mile (2000); Age: 28.9% under 18, 12.8% over 64 (2000); Marriage status: 20.5% never married, 71.8% now married, 0.0% widowed, 7.8% divorced (2000); Foreign born: 0.0% (2000); Ancestry (includes multiple ancestries): 12.6% United States or American, 10.5% German, 8.5% English, 3.6% Irish, 2.9% European (2000).
Economy: Employment by occupation: 17.0% management, 4.8% professional, 6.1% services, 15.7% sales, 4.3% farming, 13.0% construction, 39.1% production (2000).
Income: Per capita income: $16,951 (2000); Median household income: $38,750 (2000); Poverty rate: 7.6% (2000).
Education: High school graduation rate: 90.3% (2000); College graduation rate: 5.9% (2000).
Housing: Homeownership rate: 82.5% (2000); Median home value: $46,000 (2000); Median rent: $320 per month (2000); Median age of housing: 45 years (2000).
Transportation: Commute to work: 93.0% car, 0.0% public transportation, 0.0% walk, 7.0% work from home (2000); Travel time to work: 16.6% less than 15 minutes, 49.3% 15 to 30 minutes, 13.3% 30 to 45 minutes, 10.0% 45 to 60 minutes, 10.9% 60 minutes or more (2000)

MODE (unincorporated postal area, zip code 62444). Covers a land area of 20.301 square miles and a water area of 0 square miles. Located at 39.43° N. Lat.; 88.80° W. Long. Elevation is 625 feet.
Population: 339 (2000); Race: 100.0% White, 0.0% Black, 0.0% Asian, 0.0% American Indian and Alaska Native, 0.0% Hispanic of any race, 0.0% two or more races (2000); Density: 16.7 persons per square mile (2000); Age: 15.8% under 18, 16.1% over 64 (2000); Marriage status: 8.2% never married, 66.3% now married, 5.8% widowed, 19.6% divorced (2000); Foreign born: 0.0% (2000); Ancestry (includes multiple ancestries): 21.4% United States or American, 16.7% German, 12.0% Irish, 11.4% English, 5.6% Other groups (2000).
Economy: Employment by occupation: 9.6% management, 9.0% professional, 15.4% services, 9.6% sales, 10.3% farming, 9.0% construction, 37.2% production (2000).
Income: Per capita income: $18,500 (2000); Median household income: $32,083 (2000); Poverty rate: 16.1% (2000).
Education: High school graduation rate: 61.8% (2000); College graduation rate: 8.1% (2000).
Housing: Homeownership rate: 86.6% (2000); Median home value: $56,700 (2000); Median rent: $205 per month (2000); Median age of housing: 36 years (2000).
Transportation: Commute to work: 100.0% car, 0.0% public transportation, 0.0% walk, 0.0% work from home (2000); Travel time to work: 11.5% less than 15 minutes, 20.5% 15 to 30 minutes, 48.7% 30 to 45 minutes, 4.5% 45 to 60 minutes, 14.7% 60 minutes or more (2000)

MOWEAQUA (village). Covers a land area of 1.118 square miles and a water area of 0 square miles. Located at 39.62° N. Lat.; 89.01° W. Long. Elevation is 629 feet.
History: Incorporated 1877.
Population: 1,923 (2000); Race: 97.7% White, 0.3% Black, 0.9% Asian, 0.0% American Indian and Alaska Native, 1.1% Hispanic of any race, 0.3% two or more races (2000); Density: 1,720.0 persons per square mile (2000); Age: 24.2% under 18, 22.0% over 64 (2000); Marriage status: 14.8% never married, 65.7% now married, 11.2% widowed, 8.3% divorced (2000); Foreign born: 0.9% (2000); Ancestry (includes multiple ancestries): 25.7% German, 14.3% English, 13.6% Irish, 12.0% United States or American, 8.8% Other groups (2000).
Economy: Agriculture: corn, wheat, soybeans; dairy products; livestock. Single-family building permits issued: 0 (2001) / 4 (2000); Multi-family building permits issued: 0 (2001) / 0 (2000); Employment by occupation: 11.2% management, 20.8% professional, 13.2% services, 21.4% sales, 0.8% farming, 8.4% construction, 24.2% production (2000).
Income: Per capita income: $18,195 (2000); Median household income: $40,114 (2000); Poverty rate: 11.9% (2000).
Taxes: Total city taxes per capita: $92 (1997); City property taxes per capita: $49 (1997).
Education: High school graduation rate: 80.2% (2000); College graduation rate: 14.8% (2000).
Housing: Homeownership rate: 77.9% (2000); Median home value: $71,800 (2000); Median rent: $334 per month (2000); Median age of housing: 47 years (2000).
Transportation: Commute to work: 94.8% car, 0.6% public transportation, 1.0% walk, 3.2% work from home (2000); Travel time to work: 27.4% less than 15 minutes, 31.6% 15 to 30 minutes, 33.2% 30 to 45 minutes, 5.4% 45 to 60 minutes, 2.4% 60 minutes or more (2000)

OCONEE (village). Covers a land area of 0.360 square miles and a water area of 0 square miles. Located at 39.28° N. Lat.; 89.10° W. Long. Elevation is 680 feet.
Population: 202 (2000); Race: 99.5% White, 0.0% Black, 0.0% Asian, 0.0% American Indian and Alaska Native, 0.0% Hispanic of any race, 0.5% two or more races (2000); Density: 560.8 persons per square mile (2000); Age: 23.1% under 18, 29.7% over 64 (2000); Marriage status: 12.9% never married, 79.1% now married, 6.7% widowed, 1.2% divorced (2000); Foreign born: 0.0% (2000); Ancestry (includes multiple ancestries): 25.6% United States or American, 12.8% German, 11.3% Irish, 6.7% Other groups, 4.1% French (except Basque) (2000).
Economy: In agricultural area. Single-family building permits issued: 0 (2001) / 0 (2000); Multi-family building permits issued: 0 (2001) / 0 (2000); Employment by occupation: 8.0% management, 12.5% professional, 19.3% services, 20.5% sales, 2.3% farming, 18.2% construction, 19.3% production (2000).
Income: Per capita income: $14,068 (2000); Median household income: $38,750 (2000); Poverty rate: 3.6% (2000).
Taxes: Total city taxes per capita: $26 (1997); City property taxes per capita: $26 (1997).
Education: High school graduation rate: 75.8% (2000); College graduation rate: 3.1% (2000).
Housing: Homeownership rate: 93.3% (2000); Median home value: $35,000 (2000); Median rent: $300 per month (2000); Median age of housing: 51 years (2000).
Transportation: Commute to work: 100.0% car, 0.0% public transportation, 0.0% walk, 0.0% work from home (2000); Travel time to work: 37.6% less than 15 minutes, 24.7% 15 to 30 minutes, 25.9% 30 to 45 minutes, 5.9% 45 to 60 minutes, 5.9% 60 minutes or more (2000)

SHELBYVILLE (city). Covers a land area of 3.696 square miles and a water area of 0.185 square miles. Located at 39.40° N. Lat.; 88.80° W. Long. Elevation is 650 feet.
History: Incorporated 1839.
Population: 4,971 (2000); Race: 99.4% White, 0.0% Black, 0.0% Asian, 0.2% American Indian and Alaska Native, 0.6% Hispanic of any race, 0.3% two or more races (2000); Density: 1,345.0 persons per square mile (2000); Age: 21.8% under 18, 23.3% over 64 (2000); Marriage status: 21.1% never married, 53.6% now married, 14.3% widowed, 11.0% divorced (2000); Foreign born: 0.1% (2000); Ancestry (includes multiple ancestries): 21.3% German, 14.4% United States or American, 9.1% English, 8.7% Irish, 5.0% Other groups (2000).
Economy: Manufacturing: machinery, metal products. Agriculture: soybeans, corn, wheat, hay; livestock; dairy products. Single-family building permits issued: 5 (2001) / 2 (2000); Multi-family building permits issued: 0 (2001) / 3 (2000); Employment by occupation: 9.7% management, 13.0% professional, 19.2% services, 21.8% sales, 0.7% farming, 10.4% construction, 25.2% production (2000).
Income: Per capita income: $17,596 (2000); Median household income: $32,458 (2000); Poverty rate: 9.9% (2000).
Taxes: Total city taxes per capita: $471 (1997); City property taxes per capita: $256 (1997).
Education: High school graduation rate: 82.2% (2000); College graduation rate: 12.7% (2000).

School District(s)

Shelbyville C U School District 4 (PK-12)
2000 Enrollment: 1,327 217-774-4626

Two-year College(s)

Sparks College (Private, For-profit)
2001 Enrollment: 38 217-774-5112
2001 Tuition: In-state $4,500; Out-of-state $4,500

Housing: Homeownership rate: 69.8% (2000); Median home value: $64,400 (2000); Median rent: $303 per month (2000); Median age of housing: 48 years (2000).
Hospitals: Shelby Memorial Hospital (54 beds)
Newspapers: Shelbyville Daily Union (5 x week)
Transportation: Commute to work: 89.5% car, 0.0% public transportation, 3.4% walk, 6.3% work from home (2000); Travel time to work: 61.9% less

than 15 minutes, 6.4% 15 to 30 minutes, 11.8% 30 to 45 minutes, 9.7% 45 to 60 minutes, 10.2% 60 minutes or more (2000)

Additional Information Contacts

Shelbyville Chamber of Commerce 217-774-2221

SIGEL (town). Covers a land area of 0.273 square miles and a water area of 0.008 square miles. Located at 39.22° N. Lat.; 88.49° W. Long. Elevation is 640 feet.

Population: 386 (2000); Race: 100.0% White, 0.0% Black, 0.0% Asian, 0.0% American Indian and Alaska Native, 0.0% Hispanic of any race, 0.0% two or more races (2000); Density: 1,411.6 persons per square mile (2000); Age: 30.0% under 18, 10.6% over 64 (2000); Marriage status: 35.8% never married, 47.5% now married, 9.0% widowed, 7.7% divorced (2000); Foreign born: 0.0% (2000); Ancestry (includes multiple ancestries): 69.8% German, 12.4% Irish, 11.4% United States or American, 5.4% English, 1.3% Other groups (2000).

Economy: Grain, soybeans; livestock; dairy products. Single-family building permits issued: 4 (2001) / 4 (2000); Multi-family building permits issued: 0 (2001) / 0 (2000); Employment by occupation: 11.8% management, 9.6% professional, 14.6% services, 24.7% sales, 5.1% farming, 12.9% construction, 21.3% production (2000).

Income: Per capita income: $15,933 (2000); Median household income: $36,607 (2000); Poverty rate: 3.9% (2000).

Taxes: Total city taxes per capita: $34 (1997); City property taxes per capita: $31 (1997).

Education: High school graduation rate: 85.8% (2000); College graduation rate: 10.4% (2000).

Housing: Homeownership rate: 78.0% (2000); Median home value: $70,000 (2000); Median rent: $314 per month (2000); Median age of housing: 42 years (2000).

Transportation: Commute to work: 92.4% car, 0.0% public transportation, 5.3% walk, 1.2% work from home (2000); Travel time to work: 37.3% less than 15 minutes, 44.4% 15 to 30 minutes, 10.7% 30 to 45 minutes, 3.6% 45 to 60 minutes, 4.1% 60 minutes or more (2000)

STEWARDSON (village). Covers a land area of 0.605 square miles and a water area of 0 square miles. Located at 39.26° N. Lat.; 88.62° W. Long. Elevation is 640 feet.

Population: 747 (2000); Race: 96.9% White, 0.0% Black, 0.8% Asian, 0.0% American Indian and Alaska Native, 0.5% Hispanic of any race, 1.7% two or more races (2000); Density: 1,235.0 persons per square mile (2000); Age: 23.6% under 18, 19.5% over 64 (2000); Marriage status: 25.2% never married, 55.8% now married, 10.8% widowed, 8.1% divorced (2000); Foreign born: 1.5% (2000); Ancestry (includes multiple ancestries): 28.7% German, 13.9% United States or American, 6.4% Irish, 5.7% Other groups, 3.2% English (2000).

Economy: Grain. Single-family building permits issued: 1 (2001) / 3 (2000); Multi-family building permits issued: 0 (2001) / 2 (2000); Employment by occupation: 10.3% management, 9.0% professional, 22.0% services, 21.2% sales, 1.0% farming, 8.5% construction, 27.9% production (2000).

Income: Per capita income: $15,586 (2000); Median household income: $31,923 (2000); Poverty rate: 11.6% (2000).

Taxes: Total city taxes per capita: $22 (1997); City property taxes per capita: $22 (1997).

Education: High school graduation rate: 83.5% (2000); College graduation rate: 8.4% (2000).

Housing: Homeownership rate: 76.6% (2000); Median home value: $58,000 (2000); Median rent: $279 per month (2000); Median age of housing: 38 years (2000).

Transportation: Commute to work: 86.1% car, 2.7% public transportation, 3.3% walk, 3.0% work from home (2000); Travel time to work: 23.9% less than 15 minutes, 48.9% 15 to 30 minutes, 17.7% 30 to 45 minutes, 6.5% 45 to 60 minutes, 3.1% 60 minutes or more (2000)

STRASBURG (village). Covers a land area of 0.528 square miles and a water area of 0 square miles. Located at 39.35° N. Lat.; 88.61° W. Long. Elevation is 642 feet.

Population: 603 (2000); Race: 100.0% White, 0.0% Black, 0.0% Asian, 0.0% American Indian and Alaska Native, 0.0% Hispanic of any race, 0.0% two or more races (2000); Density: 1,141.9 persons per square mile (2000); Age: 20.3% under 18, 34.0% over 64 (2000); Marriage status: 11.2% never married, 64.4% now married, 16.3% widowed, 8.1% divorced (2000); Foreign born: 0.0% (2000); Ancestry (includes multiple ancestries): 30.9% German, 16.2% United States or American, 7.8% Irish, 6.2% English, 2.1% Dutch (2000).

Economy: In agricultural area. Employment by occupation: 6.1% management, 16.8% professional, 12.3% services, 23.8% sales, 2.0% farming, 10.7% construction, 28.3% production (2000).

Income: Per capita income: $16,102 (2000); Median household income: $40,673 (2000); Poverty rate: 6.0% (2000).

Taxes: Total city taxes per capita: $35 (1997); City property taxes per capita: $18 (1997).

Education: High school graduation rate: 84.6% (2000); College graduation rate: 14.5% (2000).

School District(s)

Stewardson-Strasburg Cu District 5a (PK-12)
2000 Enrollment: 469 217-682-3355

Housing: Homeownership rate: 92.9% (2000); Median home value: $65,200 (2000); Median rent: $313 per month (2000); Median age of housing: 45 years (2000).

Transportation: Commute to work: 98.0% car, 0.0% public transportation, 1.2% walk, 0.8% work from home (2000); Travel time to work: 24.0% less than 15 minutes, 27.7% 15 to 30 minutes, 33.1% 30 to 45 minutes, 6.2% 45 to 60 minutes, 9.1% 60 minutes or more (2000)

TOWER HILL (village). Covers a land area of 1.003 square miles and a water area of 0 square miles. Located at 39.38° N. Lat.; 88.96° W. Long. Elevation is 658 feet.

Population: 609 (2000); Race: 99.3% White, 0.0% Black, 0.0% Asian, 0.7% American Indian and Alaska Native, 0.7% Hispanic of any race, 0.0% two or more races (2000); Density: 607.1 persons per square mile (2000); Age: 25.9% under 18, 13.3% over 64 (2000); Marriage status: 24.8% never married, 51.5% now married, 8.1% widowed, 15.7% divorced (2000); Foreign born: 0.3% (2000); Ancestry (includes multiple ancestries): 16.4% German, 13.3% United States or American, 11.0% Irish, 6.2% English, 3.9% Dutch (2000).

Economy: In farm area; grain milling. Employment by occupation: 2.5% management, 8.3% professional, 20.2% services, 20.9% sales, 3.2% farming, 10.8% construction, 33.9% production (2000).

Income: Per capita income: $14,208 (2000); Median household income: $30,909 (2000); Poverty rate: 16.7% (2000).

Taxes: Total city taxes per capita: $34 (1997); City property taxes per capita: $32 (1997).

Education: High school graduation rate: 78.4% (2000); College graduation rate: 7.3% (2000).

School District(s)

Tower Hill CUSD 6 (KG-12)
2000 Enrollment: 218 217-567-3161

Housing: Homeownership rate: 78.4% (2000); Median home value: $33,100 (2000); Median rent: $296 per month (2000); Median age of housing: 60+ years (2000).

Transportation: Commute to work: 92.8% car, 0.0% public transportation, 2.2% walk, 4.3% work from home (2000); Travel time to work: 26.0% less than 15 minutes, 38.5% 15 to 30 minutes, 9.4% 30 to 45 minutes, 12.1% 45 to 60 minutes, 14.0% 60 minutes or more (2000)

WINDSOR (city). Covers a land area of 0.618 square miles and a water area of 0 square miles. Located at 39.43° N. Lat.; 88.59° W. Long. Elevation is 711 feet.

History: Incorporated 1869.

Population: 1,125 (2000); Race: 98.8% White, 0.0% Black, 0.0% Asian, 0.0% American Indian and Alaska Native, 0.4% Hispanic of any race, 0.9% two or more races (2000); Density: 1,820.3 persons per square mile (2000); Age: 27.5% under 18, 16.2% over 64 (2000); Marriage status: 15.3% never married, 62.3% now married, 8.7% widowed, 13.7% divorced (2000); Foreign born: 0.6% (2000); Ancestry (includes multiple ancestries): 22.6% German, 14.3% United States or American, 10.3% Irish, 7.0% Other groups, 6.7% English (2000).

Economy: In agricultural area; dairy products; corn, soybeans. Single-family building permits issued: 0 (2001) / 0 (2000); Multi-family building permits issued: 0 (2001) / 0 (2000); Employment by occupation: 6.6% management, 9.2% professional, 15.9% services, 24.7% sales, 0.8% farming, 9.4% construction, 33.5% production (2000).

Income: Per capita income: $16,002 (2000); Median household income: $33,095 (2000); Poverty rate: 8.4% (2000).

Taxes: Total city taxes per capita: $33 (1997); City property taxes per capita: $26 (1997).

Education: High school graduation rate: 79.7% (2000); College graduation rate: 7.7% (2000).

School District(s)
Windsor Community Unit School District 1 (PK-12)
2000 Enrollment: 507 217-459-2636

Housing: Homeownership rate: 81.5% (2000); Median home value: $53,800 (2000); Median rent: $320 per month (2000); Median age of housing: 40 years (2000).

Newspapers: Shelby County News-Gazette (1 x week)

Transportation: Commute to work: 95.1% car, 0.4% public transportation, 2.3% walk, 2.3% work from home (2000); Travel time to work: 24.2% less than 15 minutes, 45.7% 15 to 30 minutes, 22.5% 30 to 45 minutes, 1.7% 45 to 60 minutes, 5.9% 60 minutes or more (2000)

Stark County

Located in north central Illinois; drained by the Spoon River and Indian Creek. Covers a land area of 287.90 square miles, a water area of 0.30 square miles, and is located in the Central Time Zone. The county government was organized in 1839. County seat is Toulon.

Population: 6,332 (2000); Race: 98.4% White, 0.1% Black, 0.2% Asian, 0.1% American Indian and Alaska Native, 1.2% Hispanic of any race, 1.0% two or more races (2000); Density: 22.0 persons per square mile (2000); Age: 25.1% under 18, 19.1% over 64 (2000).

Religion: Five largest groups: 14.5% Apostolic Christian Church of America, Inc., 14.2% The United Methodist Church, 13.5% Catholic Church, 4.3% New Testament Association of Independent Baptist Churches and other Fundamental Baptist Associations, 3

Economy: Unemployment rate: 7.9% (11/2002); Total civilian labor force: 2,908 (11/2002); Leading industries: 24.8% health care and social assistance; 20.2% manufacturing; 12.5% retail trade (2000); Companies that employ more than 1,000 persons: 0 (2000); Companies that employ more than 100 persons: 1 (2000); Farms: 354 totaling 179,711 acres (1997); Minority business ownership rate: 0.0% (1997); Women business ownership rate: 32.0% (1997); Retail sales per capita: $4,326 (1997). Single-family building permits issued: 10 (2001) / 17 (2000); Multi-family building permits issued: 0 (2001) / 0 (2000).

Income: Per capita income: $16,767 (2000); Median household income: $35,826 (2000); Poverty rate: 8.6% (2000); Bankruptcy rate: 5.71% (2001).

Taxes: Total county taxes per capita: $112 (1997); County property taxes per capita: $96 (1997).

Education: High school graduation rate: 83.4% (2000); College graduation rate: 13.4% (2000).

Housing: Homeownership rate: 77.4% (2000); Median home value: $61,800 (2000); Median rent: $280 per month (2000); Median age of housing: 2000 years (2000).

Health: Birth rate: 129.5 per 10,000 population (1998); Age adjusted death rate: 88.9 per 10,000 population (1999); Age adjusted cancer mortality rate: 215.4 deaths per 100,000 population (1999). Number of physicians: 9.5 per 10,000 population (1999); Number of hospital beds: n/a (1999).

Elections: 2000 Presidential election results: 40.5% Gore, 56.7% Bush, 1.8% Nader, 0.7% Buchanan

Additional Information Contacts
Stark County Government Offices 309-286-5911

Stark County Communities

BRADFORD (village). Covers a land area of 0.397 square miles and a water area of 0 square miles. Located at 41.17° N. Lat.; 89.65° W. Long. Elevation is 810 feet.

Population: 787 (2000); Race: 98.0% White, 0.0% Black, 0.3% Asian, 0.3% American Indian and Alaska Native, 2.7% Hispanic of any race, 0.0% two or more races (2000); Density: 1,984.8 persons per square mile (2000); Age: 25.7% under 18, 21.4% over 64 (2000); Marriage status: 14.3% never married, 64.6% now married, 11.4% widowed, 9.6% divorced (2000); Foreign born: 0.7% (2000); Ancestry (includes multiple ancestries): 23.9% German, 18.3% Irish, 17.1% English, 6.5% United States or American, 5.1% Other groups (2000).

Economy: In agricultural and bituminous-coal area. Employment by occupation: 5.8% management, 17.1% professional, 18.7% services, 20.0% sales, 1.9% farming, 11.0% construction, 25.5% production (2000).

Income: Per capita income: $16,279 (2000); Median household income: $33,750 (2000); Poverty rate: 9.8% (2000).

Taxes: Total city taxes per capita: $95 (1997); City property taxes per capita: $95 (1997).

Education: High school graduation rate: 78.8% (2000); College graduation rate: 9.1% (2000).

School District(s)
Bradford Community Unit School District 1 (PK-12)
2000 Enrollment: 275 309-897-4611

Housing: Homeownership rate: 83.2% (2000); Median home value: $50,800 (2000); Median rent: $275 per month (2000); Median age of housing: 60+ years (2000).

Transportation: Commute to work: 92.2% car, 0.0% public transportation, 2.6% walk, 4.2% work from home (2000); Travel time to work: 23.1% less than 15 minutes, 23.7% 15 to 30 minutes, 35.3% 30 to 45 minutes, 14.2% 45 to 60 minutes, 3.7% 60 minutes or more (2000)

LA FAYETTE (village). Aka Lafayette. Covers a land area of 0.184 square miles and a water area of 0 square miles. Located at 41.11° N. Lat.; 89.97° W. Long.

Population: 227 (2000); Race: 97.8% White, 0.0% Black, 0.9% Asian, 0.0% American Indian and Alaska Native, 0.0% Hispanic of any race, 1.3% two or more races (2000); Density: 1,235.2 persons per square mile (2000); Age: 23.3% under 18, 20.3% over 64 (2000); Marriage status: 17.4% never married, 64.2% now married, 3.7% widowed, 14.7% divorced (2000); Foreign born: 0.9% (2000); Ancestry (includes multiple ancestries): 18.9% English, 11.9% Irish, 8.4% German, 7.0% Other groups, 4.8% Scottish (2000).

Economy: In agricultural and bituminous-coal area. Employment by occupation: 26.0% management, 2.7% professional, 13.7% services, 32.9% sales, 0.0% farming, 9.6% construction, 15.1% production (2000).

Income: Per capita income: $15,002 (2000); Median household income: $26,563 (2000); Poverty rate: 13.2% (2000).

Taxes: Total city taxes per capita: $44 (1997); City property taxes per capita: $44 (1997).

Education: High school graduation rate: 79.4% (2000); College graduation rate: 6.1% (2000).

Housing: Homeownership rate: 76.3% (2000); Median home value: $40,000 (2000); Median rent: $236 per month (2000); Median age of housing: 60+ years (2000).

Newspapers: Prairie Shopper (1 x week)

Transportation: Commute to work: 87.7% car, 0.0% public transportation, 2.7% walk, 9.6% work from home (2000); Travel time to work: 36.4% less than 15 minutes, 33.3% 15 to 30 minutes, 12.1% 30 to 45 minutes, 6.1% 45 to 60 minutes, 12.1% 60 minutes or more (2000)

SPEER (unincorporated postal area, zip code 61479). Covers a land area of 13.178 square miles and a water area of 0 square miles. Located at 40.99° N. Lat.; 89.65° W. Long. Elevation is 748 feet.

Population: 169 (2000); Race: 100.0% White, 0.0% Black, 0.0% Asian, 0.0% American Indian and Alaska Native, 0.0% Hispanic of any race, 0.0% two or more races (2000); Density: 12.8 persons per square mile (2000); Age: 16.5% under 18, 12.0% over 64 (2000); Marriage status: 12.5% never married, 79.2% now married, 8.3% widowed, 0.0% divorced (2000); Foreign born: 0.0% (2000); Ancestry (includes multiple ancestries): 42.4% German, 19.6% French (except Basque), 19.6% Irish, 13.3% Scottish, 12.0% English (2000).

Economy: Employment by occupation: 7.2% management, 7.2% professional, 15.9% services, 34.8% sales, 0.0% farming, 0.0% construction, 34.8% production (2000).

Income: Per capita income: $19,389 (2000); Median household income: $35,455 (2000); Poverty rate: 0.0% (2000).

Education: High school graduation rate: 85.7% (2000); College graduation rate: 4.0% (2000).

Housing: Homeownership rate: 78.9% (2000); Median home value: $70,800 (2000); Median rent: $397 per month (2000); Median age of housing: 60+ years (2000).

Transportation: Commute to work: 89.9% car, 0.0% public transportation, 10.1% walk, 0.0% work from home (2000); Travel time to work: 33.3% less than 15 minutes, 58.0% 15 to 30 minutes, 8.7% 30 to 45 minutes, 0.0% 45 to 60 minutes, 0.0% 60 minutes or more (2000)

TOULON (city). Covers a land area of 0.889 square miles and a water area of 0 square miles. Located at 41.09° N. Lat.; 89.86° W. Long. Elevation is 740 feet.

History: Incorporated 1859.

Population: 1,400 (2000); Race: 98.3% White, 0.4% Black, 0.1% Asian, 0.2% American Indian and Alaska Native, 0.0% Hispanic of any race, 1.0% two or more races (2000); Density: 1,575.4 persons per square mile (2000); Age: 23.6% under 18, 26.7% over 64 (2000); Marriage status: 17.7% never married, 64.9% now married, 8.9% widowed, 8.5% divorced (2000); Foreign born: 0.3% (2000); Ancestry (includes multiple ancestries): 19.4% German,

16.5% English, 13.1% Irish, 9.1% Other groups, 5.7% United States or American (2000).
Economy: In agricultural area: corn, soybeans, wheat; livestock, poultry. Bituminous-coal area. Employment by occupation: 9.5% management, 17.2% professional, 14.4% services, 25.4% sales, 1.8% farming, 9.7% construction, 22.1% production (2000).
Income: Per capita income: $16,219 (2000); Median household income: $31,792 (2000); Poverty rate: 7.4% (2000).
Taxes: Total city taxes per capita: $80 (1997); City property taxes per capita: $64 (1997).
Education: High school graduation rate: 81.7% (2000); College graduation rate: 13.1% (2000).

School District(s)

Stark County C U School District 100 (PK-12)
2000 Enrollment: 940 309-286-7171
Housing: Homeownership rate: 73.4% (2000); Median home value: $58,000 (2000); Median rent: $270 per month (2000); Median age of housing: 57 years (2000).
Transportation: Commute to work: 91.2% car, 0.0% public transportation, 6.0% walk, 2.0% work from home (2000); Travel time to work: 37.4% less than 15 minutes, 24.5% 15 to 30 minutes, 12.9% 30 to 45 minutes, 20.7% 45 to 60 minutes, 4.5% 60 minutes or more (2000)

WYOMING (city). Covers a land area of 0.742 square miles and a water area of 0 square miles. Located at 41.06° N. Lat.; 89.77° W. Long. Elevation is 707 feet.
History: Incorporated 1865.
Population: 1,424 (2000); Race: 98.9% White, 0.0% Black, 0.4% Asian, 0.0% American Indian and Alaska Native, 0.7% Hispanic of any race, 0.7% two or more races (2000); Density: 1,918.1 persons per square mile (2000); Age: 21.3% under 18, 19.5% over 64 (2000); Marriage status: 21.7% never married, 57.8% now married, 10.9% widowed, 9.7% divorced (2000); Foreign born: 0.4% (2000); Ancestry (includes multiple ancestries): 19.9% German, 15.1% Irish, 14.4% English, 11.6% United States or American, 6.4% Other groups (2000).
Economy: Agriculture: corn, oats, wheat. Employment by occupation: 7.6% management, 14.5% professional, 15.9% services, 26.7% sales, 0.9% farming, 9.2% construction, 25.3% production (2000).
Income: Per capita income: $16,574 (2000); Median household income: $30,463 (2000); Poverty rate: 10.6% (2000).
Taxes: Total city taxes per capita: $91 (1997); City property taxes per capita: $88 (1997).
Education: High school graduation rate: 81.9% (2000); College graduation rate: 13.0% (2000).
Housing: Homeownership rate: 74.1% (2000); Median home value: $64,600 (2000); Median rent: $292 per month (2000); Median age of housing: 49 years (2000).
Transportation: Commute to work: 90.4% car, 0.3% public transportation, 3.7% walk, 4.0% work from home (2000); Travel time to work: 40.8% less than 15 minutes, 14.0% 15 to 30 minutes, 28.1% 30 to 45 minutes, 13.8% 45 to 60 minutes, 3.2% 60 minutes or more (2000)

Stephenson County

Located in northern Illinois; bounded on the north by Wisconsin; drained by the Pecatonica River. Covers a land area of 564.20 square miles, a water area of 0.50 square miles, and is located in the Central Time Zone. The county government was organized in 1837. County seat is Freeport.

Weather Station: Freeport Waste Water Plant — Elevation: 748 feet

	Jan	Feb	Mar	Apr	May	Jun	Jul	Aug	Sep	Oct	Nov	Dec
High	26	32	44	58	71	80	84	81	74	62	46	32
Low	9	14	25	36	48	57	62	59	50	38	28	16
Precip	1.3	1.3	2.2	3.2	4.0	4.3	3.6	4.1	3.7	2.6	2.7	1.7
Snow	9.6	6.5	4.4	1.7	tr	0.0	0.0	0.0	0.0	tr	2.5	7.3

High and Low temperatures in degrees Fahrenheit; Precipitation and Snow in inches

Population: 48,979 (2000); Race: 89.3% White, 7.6% Black, 0.4% Asian, 0.3% American Indian and Alaska Native, 1.5% Hispanic of any race, 1.7% two or more races (2000); Density: 86.8 persons per square mile (2000); Age: 25.2% under 18, 16.3% over 64 (2000).
Religion: Five largest groups: 17.0% Catholic Church, 11.5% The United Methodist Church, 5.2% Evangelical Lutheran Church in America, 4.7% United Church of Christ, 4.0% Lutheran Church—Missouri Synod (2000).
Economy: Unemployment rate: 7.0% (11/2002); Total civilian labor force: 23,424 (11/2002); Leading industries: 34.3% manufacturing; 12.4% health care and social assistance; 12.4% retail trade (2000); Companies that employ more than 1,000 persons: 3 (2000); Companies that employ more than 100 persons: 29 (2000); Farms: 1,081 totaling 308,574 acres (1997); Minority business ownership rate: 4.8% (1997); Women business ownership rate: 21.9% (1997); Retail sales per capita: $8,451 (1997). Single-family building permits issued: 83 (2001) / 81 (2000); Multi-family building permits issued: 51 (2001) / 60 (2000).
Income: Per capita income: $19,794 (2000); Median household income: $40,366 (2000); Poverty rate: 9.0% (2000); Bankruptcy rate: 5.30% (2001).
Taxes: Total county taxes per capita: $87 (2000); County property taxes per capita: $87 (2000).
Education: High school graduation rate: 84.1% (2000); College graduation rate: 15.6% (2000).
Housing: Homeownership rate: 74.8% (2000); Median home value: $81,400 (2000); Median rent: $331 per month (2000); Median age of housing: 46 years (2000).
Health: Birth rate: 130.1 per 10,000 population (1998); Age adjusted death rate: 87.3 per 10,000 population (1999); Age adjusted cancer mortality rate: 199.5 deaths per 100,000 population (1999). Number of physicians: 12.3 per 10,000 population (1999); Number of hospital beds: 35.9 per 10,000 population (1999).
Elections: 2000 Presidential election results: 41.6% Gore, 55.3% Bush, 2.5% Nader, 0.3% Buchanan
National and State Parks: Lake Le-Aqua-Na State Park
Additional Information Contacts
Stephenson County Government Offices 815-235-8289
Freeport Chamber of Commerce 815-233-1350
Freeport Galena Area Association of Realtors 815-235-3068

Stephenson County Communities

CEDARVILLE (village). Covers a land area of 0.449 square miles and a water area of 0 square miles. Located at 42.37° N. Lat.; 89.63° W. Long. Elevation is 870 feet.
History: Cedarville was the birthplace and burial place of Jane Addams (1860-1935), whose parents built a house here in 1850 and raised their family on the homestead. John Addams operated a mill.
Population: 719 (2000); Race: 97.4% White, 0.3% Black, 0.8% Asian, 0.0% American Indian and Alaska Native, 1.1% Hispanic of any race, 1.3% two or more races (2000); Density: 1,599.8 persons per square mile (2000); Age: 23.0% under 18, 14.5% over 64 (2000); Marriage status: 17.2% never married, 71.9% now married, 5.2% widowed, 5.7% divorced (2000); Foreign born: 0.6% (2000); Ancestry (includes multiple ancestries): 45.1% German, 12.4% Irish, 11.8% English, 6.4% United States or American, 4.0% Swiss (2000).
Economy: Single-family building permits issued: 1 (2001) / 1 (2000); Multi-family building permits issued: 0 (2001) / 0 (2000); Employment by occupation: 6.9% management, 17.3% professional, 9.6% services, 26.9% sales, 0.5% farming, 14.9% construction, 23.9% production (2000).
Income: Per capita income: $20,076 (2000); Median household income: $44,609 (2000); Poverty rate: 2.6% (2000).
Taxes: Total city taxes per capita: $68 (1997); City property taxes per capita: $62 (1997).
Education: High school graduation rate: 90.0% (2000); College graduation rate: 18.1% (2000).
Housing: Homeownership rate: 90.9% (2000); Median home value: $77,000 (2000); Median rent: $500 per month (2000); Median age of housing: 39 years (2000).
Transportation: Commute to work: 95.1% car, 0.0% public transportation, 1.4% walk, 3.5% work from home (2000); Travel time to work: 36.1% less than 15 minutes, 43.9% 15 to 30 minutes, 8.7% 30 to 45 minutes, 5.1% 45 to 60 minutes, 6.2% 60 minutes or more (2000)

DAKOTA (village). Covers a land area of 0.288 square miles and a water area of 0 square miles. Located at 42.38° N. Lat.; 89.52° W. Long. Elevation is 940 feet.
Population: 499 (2000); Race: 99.2% White, 0.0% Black, 0.2% Asian, 0.0% American Indian and Alaska Native, 0.0% Hispanic of any race, 0.6% two or more races (2000); Density: 1,731.9 persons per square mile (2000); Age: 23.5% under 18, 13.8% over 64 (2000); Marriage status: 25.5% never married, 56.9% now married, 8.2% widowed, 9.4% divorced (2000); Foreign born: 0.8% (2000); Ancestry (includes multiple ancestries): 46.8% German, 9.1% Irish, 8.3% English, 7.9% United States or American, 5.3% Swiss (2000).

Economy: In agricultural area: dairying. Single-family building permits issued: 0 (2001) / 1 (2000); Multi-family building permits issued: 0 (2001) / 0 (2000); Employment by occupation: 5.7% management, 13.4% professional, 16.4% services, 19.1% sales, 1.7% farming, 9.4% construction, 34.2% production (2000).
Income: Per capita income: $18,440 (2000); Median household income: $43,942 (2000); Poverty rate: 3.9% (2000).
Taxes: Total city taxes per capita: $13 (1997); City property taxes per capita: $13 (1997).
Education: High school graduation rate: 87.0% (2000); College graduation rate: 6.7% (2000).

School District(s)

Dakota Community Unit School District 201 (PK-12)
2000 Enrollment: 976 815-449-2832

Housing: Homeownership rate: 78.8% (2000); Median home value: $76,700 (2000); Median rent: $321 per month (2000); Median age of housing: 57 years (2000).
Transportation: Commute to work: 91.2% car, 0.7% public transportation, 4.7% walk, 3.0% work from home (2000); Travel time to work: 28.5% less than 15 minutes, 50.3% 15 to 30 minutes, 10.8% 30 to 45 minutes, 5.9% 45 to 60 minutes, 4.5% 60 minutes or more (2000)

DAVIS (village). Covers a land area of 0.428 square miles and a water area of 0 square miles. Located at 42.42° N. Lat.; 89.41° W. Long. Elevation is 900 feet.
Population: 662 (2000); Race: 99.1% White, 0.6% Black, 0.0% Asian, 0.0% American Indian and Alaska Native, 0.0% Hispanic of any race, 0.3% two or more races (2000); Density: 1,546.7 persons per square mile (2000); Age: 27.2% under 18, 11.1% over 64 (2000); Marriage status: 18.4% never married, 65.5% now married, 7.1% widowed, 8.9% divorced (2000); Foreign born: 0.3% (2000); Ancestry (includes multiple ancestries): 42.0% German, 8.9% Irish, 6.8% Swiss, 6.3% United States or American, 4.9% Norwegian (2000).
Economy: In agricultural area: corn; cattle, hogs; dairying; cheese factories. Single-family building permits issued: 0 (2001) / 0 (2000); Multi-family building permits issued: 0 (2001) / 0 (2000); Employment by occupation: 10.8% management, 10.5% professional, 12.0% services, 27.9% sales, 2.6% farming, 17.1% construction, 19.1% production (2000).
Income: Per capita income: $18,595 (2000); Median household income: $45,385 (2000); Poverty rate: 7.1% (2000).
Taxes: Total city taxes per capita: $210 (1997); City property taxes per capita: $208 (1997).
Education: High school graduation rate: 80.9% (2000); College graduation rate: 11.5% (2000).
Housing: Homeownership rate: 86.9% (2000); Median home value: $88,500 (2000); Median rent: $288 per month (2000); Median age of housing: 50 years (2000).
Transportation: Commute to work: 94.0% car, 0.6% public transportation, 1.1% walk, 4.3% work from home (2000); Travel time to work: 22.8% less than 15 minutes, 26.6% 15 to 30 minutes, 31.4% 30 to 45 minutes, 11.4% 45 to 60 minutes, 7.8% 60 minutes or more (2000)

FREEPORT (city). Covers a land area of 11.413 square miles and a water area of 0.010 square miles. Located at 42.29° N. Lat.; 89.63° W. Long. Elevation is 800 feet.
History: Freeport was settled in 1835 by William "Tutty" Baker and his wife. The name reportedly came from Baker's generosity in sharing his food with anyone who came along. Miners returning from the Galena lead mines joined the Bakers, and Freeport became the seat of Stephenson County. It was here that the second Lincoln-Douglas debate took place in 1858.
Population: 26,443 (2000); Race: 81.5% White, 13.8% Black, 0.5% Asian, 0.5% American Indian and Alaska Native, 2.1% Hispanic of any race, 2.5% two or more races (2000); Density: 2,316.9 persons per square mile (2000); Age: 24.4% under 18, 18.1% over 64 (2000); Marriage status: 26.2% never married, 53.2% now married, 8.9% widowed, 11.6% divorced (2000); Foreign born: 2.7% (2000); Ancestry (includes multiple ancestries): 36.3% German, 18.8% Other groups, 11.0% Irish, 8.1% English, 5.2% United States or American (2000).
Vital Statistics: Birth rate: 156.2 per 10,000 population (1998)
Economy: Unemployment rate: 9.6% (11/2002); Total civilian labor force: 12,288 (11/2002); Single-family building permits issued: 15 (2001) / 11 (2000); Multi-family building permits issued: 51 (2001) / 60 (2000); Employment by occupation: 10.3% management, 17.8% professional, 14.7% services, 26.1% sales, 0.1% farming, 7.8% construction, 23.2% production (2000).
Income: Per capita income: $18,680 (2000); Median household income: $35,399 (2000); Poverty rate: 13.1% (2000).
Taxes: Total city taxes per capita: $119 (1997); City property taxes per capita: $81 (1997).
Education: High school graduation rate: 82.2% (2000); College graduation rate: 17.1% (2000).

School District(s)

Freeport School District 145 (PK-12)
2000 Enrollment: 4,717 815-232-0300

Two-year College(s)

Highland Community College (Public)
2001 Enrollment: 2,541 815-235-6121
2001 Tuition: In-state $4,807; Out-of-state $6,096

Housing: Homeownership rate: 68.2% (2000); Median home value: $71,600 (2000); Median rent: $328 per month (2000); Median age of housing: 48 years (2000).
Newspapers: Freeport Journal-Standard (7 x week)
Transportation: Commute to work: 94.0% car, 1.2% public transportation, 2.7% walk, 1.8% work from home (2000); Travel time to work: 66.2% less than 15 minutes, 17.2% 15 to 30 minutes, 8.3% 30 to 45 minutes, 4.5% 45 to 60 minutes, 3.9% 60 minutes or more (2000)
Airports: Albertus
Additional Information Contacts
Freeport Chamber of Commerce 815-233-1350
Freeport Galena Area Association of Realtors. 815-235-3068

GERMAN VALLEY (village). Covers a land area of 0.487 square miles and a water area of 0 square miles. Located at 42.21° N. Lat.; 89.47° W. Long. Elevation is 841 feet.
Population: 481 (2000); Race: 97.1% White, 0.0% Black, 0.4% Asian, 0.0% American Indian and Alaska Native, 1.0% Hispanic of any race, 2.5% two or more races (2000); Density: 987.8 persons per square mile (2000); Age: 27.2% under 18, 11.0% over 64 (2000); Marriage status: 21.1% never married, 60.8% now married, 6.8% widowed, 11.3% divorced (2000); Foreign born: 1.4% (2000); Ancestry (includes multiple ancestries): 59.5% German, 10.0% Irish, 8.0% Norwegian, 7.0% English, 5.5% Other groups (2000).
Economy: In agricultural area; nursery. Single-family building permits issued: 0 (2001) / 0 (2000); Multi-family building permits issued: 0 (2001) / 0 (2000); Employment by occupation: 9.8% management, 20.1% professional, 16.3% services, 23.5% sales, 0.0% farming, 9.8% construction, 20.5% production (2000).
Income: Per capita income: $18,564 (2000); Median household income: $42,500 (2000); Poverty rate: 6.2% (2000).
Taxes: Total city taxes per capita: $60 (1997); City property taxes per capita: $60 (1997).
Education: High school graduation rate: 92.0% (2000); College graduation rate: 12.1% (2000).
Housing: Homeownership rate: 82.4% (2000); Median home value: $77,000 (2000); Median rent: $375 per month (2000); Median age of housing: 44 years (2000).
Transportation: Commute to work: 91.5% car, 0.8% public transportation, 3.5% walk, 3.5% work from home (2000); Travel time to work: 15.5% less than 15 minutes, 51.0% 15 to 30 minutes, 24.7% 30 to 45 minutes, 7.2% 45 to 60 minutes, 1.6% 60 minutes or more (2000)

KENT (unincorporated postal area, zip code 61044). Covers a land area of 14.493 square miles and a water area of 0 square miles. Located at 42.32° N. Lat.; 89.91° W. Long. Elevation is 900 feet.
Population: 234 (2000); Race: 100.0% White, 0.0% Black, 0.0% Asian, 0.0% American Indian and Alaska Native, 0.0% Hispanic of any race, 0.0% two or more races (2000); Density: 16.1 persons per square mile (2000); Age: 19.2% under 18, 5.3% over 64 (2000); Marriage status: 17.3% never married, 77.2% now married, 3.1% widowed, 2.4% divorced (2000); Foreign born: 0.0% (2000); Ancestry (includes multiple ancestries): 76.8% German, 16.6% Dutch, 15.9% English, 10.6% Irish, 4.6% Swedish (2000).
Economy: Employment by occupation: 28.7% management, 4.3% professional, 7.0% services, 24.3% sales, 0.0% farming, 8.7% construction, 27.0% production (2000).
Income: Per capita income: $24,019 (2000); Median household income: $44,000 (2000); Poverty rate: 0.0% (2000).
Education: High school graduation rate: 90.9% (2000); College graduation rate: 6.4% (2000).
Housing: Homeownership rate: 89.8% (2000); Median home value: $65,000 (2000); Median age of housing: 60+ years (2000).

Transportation: Commute to work: 82.7% car, 0.0% public transportation, 4.5% walk, 12.7% work from home (2000); Travel time to work: 38.5% less than 15 minutes, 28.1% 15 to 30 minutes, 30.2% 30 to 45 minutes, 0.0% 45 to 60 minutes, 3.1% 60 minutes or more (2000)

LENA (village). Covers a land area of 2.139 square miles and a water area of 0 square miles. Located at 42.37° N. Lat.; 89.82° W. Long. Elevation is 960 feet.
History: Lena was known as one of the first places in the United States where Camembert and Brie cheeses were made.
Population: 2,887 (2000); Race: 99.1% White, 0.0% Black, 0.0% Asian, 0.0% American Indian and Alaska Native, 1.4% Hispanic of any race, 0.2% two or more races (2000); Density: 1,350.0 persons per square mile (2000); Age: 24.8% under 18, 22.8% over 64 (2000); Marriage status: 17.5% never married, 64.9% now married, 10.3% widowed, 7.3% divorced (2000); Foreign born: 1.1% (2000); Ancestry (includes multiple ancestries): 46.0% German, 12.4% Irish, 11.2% English, 7.0% United States or American, 6.7% Dutch (2000).
Economy: Single-family building permits issued: 2 (2001) / 3 (2000); Multi-family building permits issued: 0 (2001) / 0 (2000); Employment by occupation: 8.1% management, 18.2% professional, 11.6% services, 28.5% sales, 2.9% farming, 8.4% construction, 22.3% production (2000).
Income: Per capita income: $18,613 (2000); Median household income: $39,947 (2000); Poverty rate: 4.7% (2000).
Taxes: Total city taxes per capita: $95 (1997); City property taxes per capita: $73 (1997).
Education: High school graduation rate: 84.0% (2000); College graduation rate: 14.1% (2000).

School District(s)

Lena Winslow C U School District 202 (PK-12)
2000 Enrollment: 1,185 815-369-3100

Housing: Homeownership rate: 76.5% (2000); Median home value: $88,000 (2000); Median rent: $336 per month (2000); Median age of housing: 32 years (2000).
Transportation: Commute to work: 95.7% car, 0.0% public transportation, 1.1% walk, 2.9% work from home (2000); Travel time to work: 37.8% less than 15 minutes, 39.5% 15 to 30 minutes, 13.3% 30 to 45 minutes, 3.2% 45 to 60 minutes, 6.1% 60 minutes or more (2000)

MCCONNELL (unincorporated postal area, zip code 61050). Covers a land area of 13.223 square miles and a water area of 0 square miles. Located at 42.44° N. Lat.; 89.72° W. Long. Elevation is 777 feet.
Population: 447 (2000); Race: 100.0% White, 0.0% Black, 0.0% Asian, 0.0% American Indian and Alaska Native, 0.0% Hispanic of any race, 0.0% two or more races (2000); Density: 33.8 persons per square mile (2000); Age: 20.2% under 18, 18.0% over 64 (2000); Marriage status: 16.1% never married, 67.4% now married, 4.9% widowed, 11.7% divorced (2000); Foreign born: 2.8% (2000); Ancestry (includes multiple ancestries): 50.6% German, 13.7% Irish, 10.7% English, 9.9% Swiss, 9.4% United States or American (2000).
Economy: Employment by occupation: 23.5% management, 11.3% professional, 9.0% services, 21.3% sales, 1.8% farming, 12.2% construction, 20.8% production (2000).
Income: Per capita income: $16,634 (2000); Median household income: $32,143 (2000); Poverty rate: 11.8% (2000).
Education: High school graduation rate: 85.0% (2000); College graduation rate: 2.2% (2000).
Housing: Homeownership rate: 83.5% (2000); Median home value: $65,000 (2000); Median rent: $325 per month (2000); Median age of housing: 60+ years (2000).
Transportation: Commute to work: 84.7% car, 0.0% public transportation, 0.0% walk, 15.3% work from home (2000); Travel time to work: 26.9% less than 15 minutes, 34.6% 15 to 30 minutes, 25.3% 30 to 45 minutes, 7.1% 45 to 60 minutes, 6.0% 60 minutes or more (2000)

ORANGEVILLE (village). Covers a land area of 0.642 square miles and a water area of 0 square miles. Located at 42.46° N. Lat.; 89.64° W. Long. Elevation is 830 feet.
Population: 751 (2000); Race: 98.9% White, 0.1% Black, 0.0% Asian, 0.0% American Indian and Alaska Native, 1.6% Hispanic of any race, 0.0% two or more races (2000); Density: 1,168.9 persons per square mile (2000); Age: 31.9% under 18, 10.3% over 64 (2000); Marriage status: 18.4% never married, 66.4% now married, 6.3% widowed, 8.8% divorced (2000); Foreign born: 1.1% (2000); Ancestry (includes multiple ancestries): 55.0% German, 13.2% Irish, 9.1% Swiss, 5.8% English, 5.0% United States or American (2000).
Economy: In agricultural area: dairying; corn, oats; cattle, hogs. Single-family building permits issued: 4 (2001) / 5 (2000); Multi-family building permits issued: 0 (2001) / 0 (2000); Employment by occupation: 4.4% management, 10.9% professional, 11.1% services, 23.8% sales, 3.1% farming, 7.8% construction, 38.9% production (2000).
Income: Per capita income: $17,437 (2000); Median household income: $39,875 (2000); Poverty rate: 3.3% (2000).
Taxes: Total city taxes per capita: $136 (1997); City property taxes per capita: $133 (1997).
Education: High school graduation rate: 87.8% (2000); College graduation rate: 11.3% (2000).

School District(s)

Orangeville C U School District 203 (PK-12)
2000 Enrollment: 529 815-789-4450

Housing: Homeownership rate: 75.9% (2000); Median home value: $80,000 (2000); Median rent: $308 per month (2000); Median age of housing: 46 years (2000).
Transportation: Commute to work: 89.3% car, 0.0% public transportation, 5.2% walk, 4.7% work from home (2000); Travel time to work: 21.9% less than 15 minutes, 56.6% 15 to 30 minutes, 12.0% 30 to 45 minutes, 4.9% 45 to 60 minutes, 4.6% 60 minutes or more (2000)

PEARL CITY (village). Covers a land area of 0.567 square miles and a water area of 0.009 square miles. Located at 42.26° N. Lat.; 89.82° W. Long. Elevation is 830 feet.
Population: 780 (2000); Race: 99.6% White, 0.0% Black, 0.1% Asian, 0.3% American Indian and Alaska Native, 0.9% Hispanic of any race, 0.0% two or more races (2000); Density: 1,376.7 persons per square mile (2000); Age: 26.3% under 18, 12.5% over 64 (2000); Marriage status: 24.0% never married, 59.6% now married, 8.1% widowed, 8.4% divorced (2000); Foreign born: 0.9% (2000); Ancestry (includes multiple ancestries): 58.0% German, 10.3% English, 10.2% Irish, 5.3% United States or American, 4.5% Norwegian (2000).
Economy: In agricultural area: corn, oats; cattle, hogs. Dairy products. Single-family building permits issued: 3 (2001) / 3 (2000); Multi-family building permits issued: 0 (2001) / 0 (2000); Employment by occupation: 10.6% management, 14.2% professional, 17.7% services, 24.1% sales, 3.4% farming, 11.7% construction, 18.3% production (2000).
Income: Per capita income: $19,256 (2000); Median household income: $43,929 (2000); Poverty rate: 4.6% (2000).
Taxes: Total city taxes per capita: $94 (1997); City property taxes per capita: $87 (1997).
Education: High school graduation rate: 90.8% (2000); College graduation rate: 14.5% (2000).

School District(s)

Pearl City C U School District 200 (PK-12)
2000 Enrollment: 521 815-443-2715

Housing: Homeownership rate: 80.1% (2000); Median home value: $78,800 (2000); Median rent: $331 per month (2000); Median age of housing: 46 years (2000).
Transportation: Commute to work: 91.5% car, 0.0% public transportation, 4.6% walk, 3.0% work from home (2000); Travel time to work: 28.1% less than 15 minutes, 54.1% 15 to 30 minutes, 10.6% 30 to 45 minutes, 1.2% 45 to 60 minutes, 5.9% 60 minutes or more (2000)

RIDOTT (village). Covers a land area of 0.105 square miles and a water area of 0 square miles. Located at 42.29° N. Lat.; 89.47° W. Long. Elevation is 770 feet.
Population: 159 (2000); Race: 100.0% White, 0.0% Black, 0.0% Asian, 0.0% American Indian and Alaska Native, 0.0% Hispanic of any race, 0.0% two or more races (2000); Density: 1,518.9 persons per square mile (2000); Age: 16.9% under 18, 22.8% over 64 (2000); Marriage status: 10.0% never married, 82.5% now married, 5.0% widowed, 2.5% divorced (2000); Foreign born: 2.2% (2000); Ancestry (includes multiple ancestries): 25.0% German, 11.8% Swedish, 7.4% Irish, 6.6% Other groups, 6.6% Swiss (2000).
Economy: In agricultural area. Single-family building permits issued: 0 (2001) / 0 (2000); Multi-family building permits issued: 0 (2001) / 0 (2000); Employment by occupation: 2.6% management, 6.6% professional, 18.4% services, 32.9% sales, 2.6% farming, 14.5% construction, 22.4% production (2000).
Income: Per capita income: $16,846 (2000); Median household income: $41,875 (2000); Poverty rate: 2.9% (2000).
Taxes: Total city taxes per capita: $82 (2000); City property taxes per capita: $75 (2000).
Education: High school graduation rate: 69.2% (2000); College graduation rate: 1.9% (2000).

Housing: Homeownership rate: 91.4% (2000); Median home value: $58,100 (2000); Median rent: $342 per month (2000); Median age of housing: 60+ years (2000).
Transportation: Commute to work: 97.1% car, 0.0% public transportation, 0.0% walk, 2.9% work from home (2000); Travel time to work: 3.0% less than 15 minutes, 69.7% 15 to 30 minutes, 16.7% 30 to 45 minutes, 6.1% 45 to 60 minutes, 4.5% 60 minutes or more (2000)

ROCK CITY (village). Covers a land area of 0.143 square miles and a water area of 0 square miles. Located at 42.41° N. Lat.; 89.46° W. Long. Elevation is 910 feet.
Population: 313 (2000); Race: 100.0% White, 0.0% Black, 0.0% Asian, 0.0% American Indian and Alaska Native, 0.0% Hispanic of any race, 0.0% two or more races (2000); Density: 2,195.8 persons per square mile (2000); Age: 30.3% under 18, 23.4% over 64 (2000); Marriage status: 18.3% never married, 55.7% now married, 16.0% widowed, 9.9% divorced (2000); Foreign born: 0.0% (2000); Ancestry (includes multiple ancestries): 41.5% German, 11.9% Swedish, 7.7% Irish, 6.8% Swiss, 5.9% United States or American (2000).
Economy: In agricultural area. Single-family building permits issued: 2 (2001) / 1 (2000); Multi-family building permits issued: 0 (2001) / 0 (2000); Employment by occupation: 7.5% management, 16.3% professional, 10.2% services, 25.2% sales, 1.4% farming, 6.1% construction, 33.3% production (2000).
Income: Per capita income: $20,920 (2000); Median household income: $46,250 (2000); Poverty rate: 4.7% (2000).
Taxes: Total city taxes per capita: $21 (1997); City property taxes per capita: $18 (1997).
Education: High school graduation rate: 79.9% (2000); College graduation rate: 6.5% (2000).
Housing: Homeownership rate: 89.8% (2000); Median home value: $81,000 (2000); Median rent: $200 per month (2000); Median age of housing: 47 years (2000).
Transportation: Commute to work: 81.8% car, 0.0% public transportation, 2.1% walk, 14.7% work from home (2000); Travel time to work: 32.8% less than 15 minutes, 29.5% 15 to 30 minutes, 24.6% 30 to 45 minutes, 11.5% 45 to 60 minutes, 1.6% 60 minutes or more (2000)

WINSLOW (village). Covers a land area of 0.446 square miles and a water area of 0 square miles. Located at 42.49° N. Lat.; 89.79° W. Long. Elevation is 780 feet.
Population: 345 (2000); Race: 95.7% White, 0.0% Black, 0.0% Asian, 2.6% American Indian and Alaska Native, 3.7% Hispanic of any race, 1.7% two or more races (2000); Density: 773.1 persons per square mile (2000); Age: 29.6% under 18, 12.1% over 64 (2000); Marriage status: 35.2% never married, 53.0% now married, 5.9% widowed, 5.9% divorced (2000); Foreign born: 0.0% (2000); Ancestry (includes multiple ancestries): 50.3% German, 16.1% Irish, 7.5% English, 6.9% Swiss, 6.9% Other groups (2000).
Economy: In agricultural area: corn, barley, oats, cattle, hogs; dairying. Manufacturing of stereo equipment. Single-family building permits issued: 0 (2001) / 0 (2000); Multi-family building permits issued: 0 (2001) / 0 (2000); Employment by occupation: 3.8% management, 7.6% professional, 15.2% services, 22.3% sales, 10.3% farming, 9.8% construction, 31.0% production (2000).
Income: Per capita income: $15,595 (2000); Median household income: $42,679 (2000); Poverty rate: 5.5% (2000).
Taxes: Total city taxes per capita: $90 (1997); City property taxes per capita: $83 (1997).
Education: High school graduation rate: 82.5% (2000); College graduation rate: 7.3% (2000).
Housing: Homeownership rate: 69.6% (2000); Median home value: $60,000 (2000); Median rent: $285 per month (2000); Median age of housing: 60+ years (2000).
Transportation: Commute to work: 90.8% car, 0.0% public transportation, 3.3% walk, 3.8% work from home (2000); Travel time to work: 27.1% less than 15 minutes, 40.1% 15 to 30 minutes, 18.6% 30 to 45 minutes, 8.5% 45 to 60 minutes, 5.6% 60 minutes or more (2000)

Tazewell County

Located in central Illinois; bounded on the northwest by the Illinois River; drained by the Mackinaw River. Covers a land area of 648.90 square miles, a water area of 9.00 square miles, and is located in the Central Time Zone. The county government was organized in 1827. County seat is Pekin.

Tazewell County is part of the Peoria-Pekin, IL MSA. The entire metro area includes: Peoria County; Tazewell County; Woodford County

Population: 128,485 (2000); Race: 97.4% White, 0.9% Black, 0.4% Asian, 0.2% American Indian and Alaska Native, 1.0% Hispanic of any race, 0.7% two or more races (2000); Density: 198.0 persons per square mile (2000); Age: 24.3% under 18, 14.9% over 64 (2000).
Religion: Five largest groups: 10.9% Catholic Church, 5.8% The United Methodist Church, 5.1% Lutheran Church—Missouri Synod, 3.0% Southern Baptist Convention, 2.1% Christian Churches and Churches of Christ (2000).
Economy: Unemployment rate: 4.9% (11/2002); Total civilian labor force: 68,624 (11/2002); Leading industries: 16.7% retail trade; 16.4% manufacturing; 12.7% accommodation & food services (2000); Companies that employ more than 1,000 persons: 3 (2000); Companies that employ more than 100 persons: 65 (2000); Farms: 909 totaling 328,289 acres (1997); Minority business ownership rate: 1.4% (1997); Women business ownership rate: 27.5% (1997); Retail sales per capita: $9,896 (1997). Single-family building permits issued: 383 (2001) / 394 (2000); Multi-family building permits issued: 46 (2001) / 51 (2000).
Income: Per capita income: $21,511 (2000); Median household income: $45,250 (2000); Poverty rate: 6.3% (2000); Bankruptcy rate: 7.04% (2001).
Taxes: Total county taxes per capita: $58 (2000); County property taxes per capita: $57 (2000).
Education: High school graduation rate: 85.0% (2000); College graduation rate: 18.1% (2000).
Housing: Homeownership rate: 76.1% (2000); Median home value: $89,200 (2000); Median rent: $378 per month (2000); Median age of housing: 37 years (2000).
Health: Birth rate: 121.9 per 10,000 population (1998); Age adjusted death rate: 78.1 per 10,000 population (1999); Age adjusted cancer mortality rate: 198.4 deaths per 100,000 population (1999). Air Quality Index: 97% good, 3% moderate, 0% unhealthy (percent of days in 2000). Number of physicians: 9.9 per 10,000 population (1999); Number of hospital beds: 18.0 per 10,000 population (1999).
Elections: 2000 Presidential election results: 43.5% Gore, 54.1% Bush, 1.8% Nader, 0.4% Buchanan
National and State Parks: Fort Creve Coeur State Park
Additional Information Contacts
Tazewell County Government Offices.................... 309-477-2272
East Peoria Chamber of Commerce........................ 309-699-6212
Morton Chamber of Commerce............................ 309-263-2491
Pekin Area Association of Realtors..................... 309-346-4020
Pekin Chamber of Commerce............................. 309-346-2106
Washington Chamber of Commerce........................ 309-444-9921

Tazewell County Communities

ARMINGTON (village). Covers a land area of 0.287 square miles and a water area of 0 square miles. Located at 40.33° N. Lat.; 89.31° W. Long. Elevation is 630 feet.
Population: 368 (2000); Race: 97.9% White, 0.0% Black, 1.2% Asian, 0.0% American Indian and Alaska Native, 0.0% Hispanic of any race, 0.9% two or more races (2000); Density: 1,283.7 persons per square mile (2000); Age: 29.1% under 18, 11.2% over 64 (2000); Marriage status: 12.9% never married, 72.2% now married, 5.5% widowed, 9.4% divorced (2000); Foreign born: 1.2% (2000); Ancestry (includes multiple ancestries): 31.5% German, 14.7% English, 10.3% Irish, 8.2% United States or American, 7.9% Other groups (2000).
Economy: In agricultural area: corn, oats, soybeans; cattle, hogs. Single-family building permits issued: 0 (2001) / 1 (2000); Multi-family building permits issued: 0 (2001) / 0 (2000); Employment by occupation: 7.7% management, 18.7% professional, 12.3% services, 23.9% sales, 1.3% farming, 15.5% construction, 20.6% production (2000).
Income: Per capita income: $17,866 (2000); Median household income: $39,583 (2000); Poverty rate: 8.0% (2000).
Taxes: Total city taxes per capita: $96 (1997); City property taxes per capita: $49 (1997).
Education: High school graduation rate: 84.6% (2000); College graduation rate: 15.4% (2000).
Housing: Homeownership rate: 91.7% (2000); Median home value: $59,000 (2000); Median rent: $263 per month (2000); Median age of housing: 60+ years (2000).
Transportation: Commute to work: 88.9% car, 1.3% public transportation, 2.0% walk, 3.9% work from home (2000); Travel time to work: 25.9% less

than 15 minutes, 9.5% 15 to 30 minutes, 47.6% 30 to 45 minutes, 12.9% 45 to 60 minutes, 4.1% 60 minutes or more (2000)

CREVE COEUR (village). Covers a land area of 4.059 square miles and a water area of 0.376 square miles. Located at 40.64° N. Lat.; 89.59° W. Long. Elevation is 700 feet.

History: Incorporated 1921. Nearby is site of old Fort Creve Coeur, built 1680 by La Salle.

Population: 5,448 (2000); Race: 97.2% White, 0.0% Black, 0.9% Asian, 0.4% American Indian and Alaska Native, 1.9% Hispanic of any race, 0.0% two or more races (2000); Density: 1,342.2 persons per square mile (2000); Age: 24.7% under 18, 13.3% over 64 (2000); Marriage status: 21.8% never married, 56.8% now married, 8.5% widowed, 12.9% divorced (2000); Foreign born: 1.2% (2000); Ancestry (includes multiple ancestries): 22.9% German, 16.1% United States or American, 10.7% Irish, 9.4% Other groups, 8.5% English (2000).

Economy: In agricultural area. Manufacturing: locomotives. Single-family building permits issued: 2 (2001) / 2 (2000); Multi-family building permits issued: 0 (2001) / 0 (2000); Employment by occupation: 5.7% management, 8.6% professional, 20.0% services, 30.4% sales, 0.3% farming, 9.2% construction, 25.9% production (2000).

Income: Per capita income: $16,712 (2000); Median household income: $36,138 (2000); Poverty rate: 7.3% (2000).

Taxes: Total city taxes per capita: $117 (1997); City property taxes per capita: $66 (1997).

Education: High school graduation rate: 79.7% (2000); College graduation rate: 5.2% (2000).

School District(s)

Creve Coeur School District 76 (PK-08)
2000 Enrollment: 762 309-698-3600

Housing: Homeownership rate: 74.9% (2000); Median home value: $62,100 (2000); Median rent: $345 per month (2000); Median age of housing: 45 years (2000).

Transportation: Commute to work: 94.2% car, 0.9% public transportation, 1.6% walk, 2.1% work from home (2000); Travel time to work: 32.1% less than 15 minutes, 53.8% 15 to 30 minutes, 9.2% 30 to 45 minutes, 1.5% 45 to 60 minutes, 3.4% 60 minutes or more (2000)

DEER CREEK (village). Covers a land area of 0.314 square miles and a water area of 0 square miles. Located at 40.62° N. Lat.; 89.33° W. Long. Elevation is 755 feet.

Population: 605 (2000); Race: 96.8% White, 0.3% Black, 2.6% Asian, 0.0% American Indian and Alaska Native, 0.0% Hispanic of any race, 0.0% two or more races (2000); Density: 1,924.2 persons per square mile (2000); Age: 27.4% under 18, 12.3% over 64 (2000); Marriage status: 23.6% never married, 60.3% now married, 4.4% widowed, 11.7% divorced (2000); Foreign born: 2.1% (2000); Ancestry (includes multiple ancestries): 45.9% German, 19.2% Irish, 12.8% Other groups, 9.3% English, 8.1% United States or American (2000).

Economy: In agricultural area. Single-family building permits issued: 3 (2001) / 2 (2000); Multi-family building permits issued: 0 (2001) / 0 (2000); Employment by occupation: 6.4% management, 13.4% professional, 17.3% services, 21.2% sales, 0.7% farming, 17.0% construction, 24.0% production (2000).

Income: Per capita income: $17,578 (2000); Median household income: $38,542 (2000); Poverty rate: 5.5% (2000).

Taxes: Total city taxes per capita: $93 (1997); City property taxes per capita: $49 (1997).

Education: High school graduation rate: 87.3% (2000); College graduation rate: 8.9% (2000).

Housing: Homeownership rate: 78.5% (2000); Median home value: $87,400 (2000); Median rent: $402 per month (2000); Median age of housing: 44 years (2000).

Transportation: Commute to work: 95.3% car, 0.0% public transportation, 1.4% walk, 3.2% work from home (2000); Travel time to work: 34.8% less than 15 minutes, 33.7% 15 to 30 minutes, 17.0% 30 to 45 minutes, 6.3% 45 to 60 minutes, 8.1% 60 minutes or more (2000)

DELAVAN (city). Covers a land area of 0.711 square miles and a water area of 0 square miles. Located at 40.37° N. Lat.; 89.54° W. Long. Elevation is 609 feet.

History: Founded 1837, incorporated 1888.

Population: 1,825 (2000); Race: 98.7% White, 0.7% Black, 0.0% Asian, 0.5% American Indian and Alaska Native, 0.5% Hispanic of any race, 0.1% two or more races (2000); Density: 2,567.4 persons per square mile (2000); Age: 27.4% under 18, 15.1% over 64 (2000); Marriage status: 20.0% never married, 63.5% now married, 8.6% widowed, 7.9% divorced (2000); Foreign born: 0.5% (2000); Ancestry (includes multiple ancestries): 34.4% German, 15.8% Irish, 11.0% United States or American, 7.5% English, 6.3% Other groups (2000).

Economy: In agricultural area. Single-family building permits issued: 0 (2001) / 1 (2000); Multi-family building permits issued: 0 (2001) / 8 (2000); Employment by occupation: 6.0% management, 13.5% professional, 17.4% services, 27.3% sales, 1.3% farming, 14.1% construction, 20.4% production (2000).

Income: Per capita income: $18,734 (2000); Median household income: $39,063 (2000); Poverty rate: 5.7% (2000).

Taxes: Total city taxes per capita: $114 (1997); City property taxes per capita: $69 (1997).

Education: High school graduation rate: 86.1% (2000); College graduation rate: 11.6% (2000).

School District(s)

Delavan Community Unit District 703 (PK-12)
2000 Enrollment: 522 309-244-8283

Housing: Homeownership rate: 78.9% (2000); Median home value: $71,300 (2000); Median rent: $291 per month (2000); Median age of housing: 48 years (2000).

Newspapers: The Delavan Times (1 x week)

Transportation: Commute to work: 93.2% car, 0.0% public transportation, 4.7% walk, 1.8% work from home (2000); Travel time to work: 24.1% less than 15 minutes, 25.9% 15 to 30 minutes, 31.1% 30 to 45 minutes, 13.2% 45 to 60 minutes, 5.7% 60 minutes or more (2000)

EAST PEORIA (city). Covers a land area of 18.812 square miles and a water area of 2.215 square miles. Located at 40.66° N. Lat.; 89.54° W. Long. Elevation is 450 feet.

History: East Peoria developed as an industrial and residential neighbor of Peoria. The Caterpillar Tractor Company plant was a major industry.

Population: 22,638 (2000); Race: 97.4% White, 0.4% Black, 0.8% Asian, 0.0% American Indian and Alaska Native, 0.9% Hispanic of any race, 1.1% two or more races (2000); Density: 1,203.4 persons per square mile (2000); Age: 22.5% under 18, 17.7% over 64 (2000); Marriage status: 20.7% never married, 59.7% now married, 7.4% widowed, 12.3% divorced (2000); Foreign born: 1.2% (2000); Ancestry (includes multiple ancestries): 29.8% German, 14.2% Irish, 13.2% English, 12.2% United States or American, 7.8% Other groups (2000).

Vital Statistics: Birth rate: 104.7 per 10,000 population (1998)

Economy: Single-family building permits issued: 54 (2001) / 55 (2000); Multi-family building permits issued: 0 (2001) / 0 (2000); Employment by occupation: 9.9% management, 16.0% professional, 15.6% services, 31.0% sales, 0.1% farming, 10.0% construction, 17.4% production (2000).

Income: Per capita income: $20,147 (2000); Median household income: $41,538 (2000); Poverty rate: 7.2% (2000).

Taxes: Total city taxes per capita: $355 (1997); City property taxes per capita: $137 (1997).

Education: High school graduation rate: 81.9% (2000); College graduation rate: 14.9% (2000).

School District(s)

East Peoria Community H S District 309 (09-12)
2000 Enrollment: 1,155 309-694-8300

East Peoria School District 86 (PK-08)
2000 Enrollment: 1,933 309-699-7228

Riverview C C School District 2 (PK-08)
2000 Enrollment: 320 309-822-8550

Robein School District 85 (KG-08)
2000 Enrollment: 217 309-694-1409

Two-year College(s)

Illinois Central College (Public)
2001 Enrollment: 11,083 309-694-5011
2001 Tuition: In-state $3,300; Out-of-state $3,300

Housing: Homeownership rate: 73.1% (2000); Median home value: $89,900 (2000); Median rent: $364 per month (2000); Median age of housing: 38 years (2000).

Transportation: Commute to work: 95.1% car, 1.0% public transportation, 0.9% walk, 1.9% work from home (2000); Travel time to work: 36.8% less than 15 minutes, 49.6% 15 to 30 minutes, 9.0% 30 to 45 minutes, 2.0% 45 to 60 minutes, 2.5% 60 minutes or more (2000)

Additional Information Contacts

East Peoria Chamber of Commerce 309-699-6212

GREEN VALLEY (village). Covers a land area of 0.308 square miles and a water area of 0 square miles. Located at 40.40° N. Lat.; 89.64° W. Long. Elevation is 537 feet.

Population: 728 (2000); Race: 97.8% White, 1.5% Black, 0.0% Asian, 0.3% American Indian and Alaska Native, 0.0% Hispanic of any race, 0.3% two or more races (2000); Density: 2,360.6 persons per square mile (2000); Age: 26.1% under 18, 14.2% over 64 (2000); Marriage status: 17.4% never married, 66.3% now married, 8.2% widowed, 8.1% divorced (2000); Foreign born: 0.0% (2000); Ancestry (includes multiple ancestries): 28.8% German, 12.6% Irish, 11.5% United States or American, 7.4% Other groups, 6.5% English (2000).

Economy: In agricultural area. Single-family building permits issued: 0 (2001) / 0 (2000); Multi-family building permits issued: 0 (2001) / 0 (2000); Employment by occupation: 7.0% management, 9.8% professional, 17.4% services, 26.8% sales, 1.5% farming, 10.7% construction, 26.8% production (2000).

Income: Per capita income: $17,830 (2000); Median household income: $40,833 (2000); Poverty rate: 7.5% (2000).

Taxes: Total city taxes per capita: $28 (1997); City property taxes per capita: $26 (1997).

Education: High school graduation rate: 82.6% (2000); College graduation rate: 9.9% (2000).

Housing: Homeownership rate: 76.9% (2000); Median home value: $72,300 (2000); Median rent: $320 per month (2000); Median age of housing: 45 years (2000).

Transportation: Commute to work: 95.4% car, 0.6% public transportation, 0.0% walk, 2.2% work from home (2000); Travel time to work: 16.8% less than 15 minutes, 43.0% 15 to 30 minutes, 21.5% 30 to 45 minutes, 13.9% 45 to 60 minutes, 4.7% 60 minutes or more (2000)

GROVELAND (unincorporated postal area, zip code 61535). Covers a land area of 8.063 square miles and a water area of 0.077 square miles. Located at 40.60° N. Lat.; 89.55° W. Long. Elevation is 779 feet.

Population: 1,398 (2000); Race: 97.9% White, 0.0% Black, 0.0% Asian, 2.1% American Indian and Alaska Native, 0.0% Hispanic of any race, 0.0% two or more races (2000); Density: 173.4 persons per square mile (2000); Age: 29.1% under 18, 7.0% over 64 (2000); Marriage status: 16.9% never married, 74.7% now married, 4.4% widowed, 4.0% divorced (2000); Foreign born: 0.0% (2000); Ancestry (includes multiple ancestries): 45.9% German, 13.3% Irish, 12.8% English, 6.8% Italian, 4.5% United States or American (2000).

Economy: Employment by occupation: 14.1% management, 38.7% professional, 10.1% services, 27.2% sales, 0.0% farming, 4.7% construction, 5.3% production (2000).

Income: Per capita income: $28,588 (2000); Median household income: $61,359 (2000); Poverty rate: 2.1% (2000).

Education: High school graduation rate: 96.2% (2000); College graduation rate: 32.3% (2000).

Housing: Homeownership rate: 92.5% (2000); Median home value: $141,100 (2000); Median rent: $478 per month (2000); Median age of housing: 27 years (2000).

Transportation: Commute to work: 95.6% car, 1.8% public transportation, 1.7% walk, 0.9% work from home (2000); Travel time to work: 29.1% less than 15 minutes, 54.2% 15 to 30 minutes, 8.5% 30 to 45 minutes, 5.8% 45 to 60 minutes, 2.4% 60 minutes or more (2000)

HOPEDALE (village). Covers a land area of 0.537 square miles and a water area of 0.004 square miles. Located at 40.42° N. Lat.; 89.41° W. Long. Elevation is 640 feet.

Population: 929 (2000); Race: 99.3% White, 0.0% Black, 0.0% Asian, 0.0% American Indian and Alaska Native, 0.2% Hispanic of any race, 0.5% two or more races (2000); Density: 1,729.8 persons per square mile (2000); Age: 19.5% under 18, 31.1% over 64 (2000); Marriage status: 19.5% never married, 62.2% now married, 10.8% widowed, 7.5% divorced (2000); Foreign born: 4.2% (2000); Ancestry (includes multiple ancestries): 38.2% German, 15.4% Irish, 12.9% United States or American, 12.8% English, 5.6% Other groups (2000).

Economy: In agricultural area. Single-family building permits issued: 2 (2001) / 2 (2000); Multi-family building permits issued: 0 (2001) / 0 (2000); Employment by occupation: 9.0% management, 16.4% professional, 17.6% services, 21.2% sales, 3.6% farming, 13.0% construction, 19.2% production (2000).

Income: Per capita income: $17,784 (2000); Median household income: $37,596 (2000); Poverty rate: 6.4% (2000).

Taxes: Total city taxes per capita: $145 (1997); City property taxes per capita: $89 (1997).

Education: High school graduation rate: 79.5% (2000); College graduation rate: 12.6% (2000).

Housing: Homeownership rate: 71.0% (2000); Median home value: $76,700 (2000); Median rent: $334 per month (2000); Median age of housing: 42 years (2000).

Transportation: Commute to work: 91.6% car, 0.0% public transportation, 4.2% walk, 3.7% work from home (2000); Travel time to work: 37.0% less than 15 minutes, 20.1% 15 to 30 minutes, 28.8% 30 to 45 minutes, 6.0% 45 to 60 minutes, 8.2% 60 minutes or more (2000)

MACKINAW (village). Covers a land area of 1.255 square miles and a water area of 0.030 square miles. Located at 40.53° N. Lat.; 89.35° W. Long. Elevation is 730 feet.

Population: 1,452 (2000); Race: 96.9% White, 1.2% Black, 0.5% Asian, 0.0% American Indian and Alaska Native, 1.0% Hispanic of any race, 1.3% two or more races (2000); Density: 1,157.2 persons per square mile (2000); Age: 25.7% under 18, 17.2% over 64 (2000); Marriage status: 20.8% never married, 60.9% now married, 10.0% widowed, 8.3% divorced (2000); Foreign born: 1.3% (2000); Ancestry (includes multiple ancestries): 23.6% German, 12.8% Irish, 10.8% United States or American, 9.6% English, 6.6% Other groups (2000).

Economy: In agricultural area; sand, gravel pits. Single-family building permits issued: 9 (2001) / 5 (2000); Multi-family building permits issued: 2 (2001) / 0 (2000); Employment by occupation: 9.4% management, 13.9% professional, 18.5% services, 26.6% sales, 0.3% farming, 11.7% construction, 19.6% production (2000).

Income: Per capita income: $19,279 (2000); Median household income: $40,766 (2000); Poverty rate: 3.1% (2000).

Taxes: Total city taxes per capita: $129 (1997); City property taxes per capita: $58 (1997).

Education: High school graduation rate: 85.1% (2000); College graduation rate: 12.0% (2000).

School District(s)

Deer Creek-Mackinaw CUSD 701 (PK-12)
2000 Enrollment: 969 309-359-8965

Housing: Homeownership rate: 73.3% (2000); Median home value: $84,100 (2000); Median rent: $399 per month (2000); Median age of housing: 44 years (2000).

Transportation: Commute to work: 90.9% car, 0.0% public transportation, 5.4% walk, 3.7% work from home (2000); Travel time to work: 29.1% less than 15 minutes, 38.8% 15 to 30 minutes, 23.1% 30 to 45 minutes, 5.3% 45 to 60 minutes, 3.7% 60 minutes or more (2000)

MARQUETTE HEIGHTS (city). Covers a land area of 1.641 square miles and a water area of 0 square miles. Located at 40.61° N. Lat.; 89.60° W. Long. Elevation is 600 feet.

Population: 2,794 (2000); Race: 96.7% White, 0.3% Black, 0.5% Asian, 0.0% American Indian and Alaska Native, 2.0% Hispanic of any race, 1.5% two or more races (2000); Density: 1,702.7 persons per square mile (2000); Age: 28.5% under 18, 7.8% over 64 (2000); Marriage status: 22.5% never married, 64.7% now married, 5.2% widowed, 7.6% divorced (2000); Foreign born: 1.4% (2000); Ancestry (includes multiple ancestries): 33.8% German, 16.9% Irish, 12.9% English, 8.7% United States or American, 6.2% Other groups (2000).

Economy: Single-family building permits issued: 12 (2001) / 12 (2000); Multi-family building permits issued: 0 (2001) / 0 (2000); Employment by occupation: 7.4% management, 11.5% professional, 16.2% services, 31.2% sales, 0.2% farming, 12.0% construction, 21.5% production (2000).

Income: Per capita income: $17,935 (2000); Median household income: $47,073 (2000); Poverty rate: 2.9% (2000).

Taxes: Total city taxes per capita: $77 (1997); City property taxes per capita: $34 (1997).

Education: High school graduation rate: 87.2% (2000); College graduation rate: 9.5% (2000).

Housing: Homeownership rate: 90.9% (2000); Median home value: $71,300 (2000); Median rent: $470 per month (2000); Median age of housing: 42 years (2000).

Transportation: Commute to work: 96.6% car, 0.0% public transportation, 0.6% walk, 2.0% work from home (2000); Travel time to work: 20.5% less than 15 minutes, 63.7% 15 to 30 minutes, 10.8% 30 to 45 minutes, 2.8% 45 to 60 minutes, 2.2% 60 minutes or more (2000)

MINIER (village). Covers a land area of 0.625 square miles and a water area of 0 square miles. Located at 40.43° N. Lat.; 89.31° W. Long. Elevation is 635 feet.
Population: 1,244 (2000); Race: 97.8% White, 0.2% Black, 0.6% Asian, 0.0% American Indian and Alaska Native, 1.3% Hispanic of any race, 0.8% two or more races (2000); Density: 1,991.2 persons per square mile (2000); Age: 23.7% under 18, 15.1% over 64 (2000); Marriage status: 18.9% never married, 62.5% now married, 8.5% widowed, 10.1% divorced (2000); Foreign born: 1.1% (2000); Ancestry (includes multiple ancestries): 33.0% German, 13.6% Irish, 11.7% United States or American, 11.3% English, 8.3% Other groups (2000).
Economy: In agricultural area. Single-family building permits issued: 8 (2001) / 9 (2000); Multi-family building permits issued: 0 (2001) / 2 (2000); Employment by occupation: 7.9% management, 13.4% professional, 13.6% services, 32.6% sales, 1.1% farming, 7.9% construction, 23.6% production (2000).
Income: Per capita income: $19,478 (2000); Median household income: $41,900 (2000); Poverty rate: 7.9% (2000).
Taxes: Total city taxes per capita: $169 (1997); City property taxes per capita: $105 (1997).
Education: High school graduation rate: 85.8% (2000); College graduation rate: 14.0% (2000).
Housing: Homeownership rate: 78.5% (2000); Median home value: $85,700 (2000); Median rent: $402 per month (2000); Median age of housing: 39 years (2000).
Newspapers: Olympia Review (1 x week)
Transportation: Commute to work: 96.2% car, 0.3% public transportation, 1.3% walk, 1.5% work from home (2000); Travel time to work: 35.1% less than 15 minutes, 21.8% 15 to 30 minutes, 38.0% 30 to 45 minutes, 3.2% 45 to 60 minutes, 1.8% 60 minutes or more (2000)

MORTON (village). Covers a land area of 12.182 square miles and a water area of 0.044 square miles. Located at 40.61° N. Lat.; 89.46° W. Long. Elevation is 720 feet.
History: Incorporated 1877.
Population: 15,198 (2000); Race: 98.4% White, 0.1% Black, 0.7% Asian, 0.3% American Indian and Alaska Native, 1.0% Hispanic of any race, 0.5% two or more races (2000); Density: 1,247.6 persons per square mile (2000); Age: 23.4% under 18, 18.9% over 64 (2000); Marriage status: 21.5% never married, 64.6% now married, 7.2% widowed, 6.7% divorced (2000); Foreign born: 2.1% (2000); Ancestry (includes multiple ancestries): 40.2% German, 13.4% Irish, 13.2% English, 5.8% United States or American, 4.0% Other groups (2000).
Vital Statistics: Birth rate: 104.0 per 10,000 population (1998)
Economy: In a grain-farming and livestock area. Manufacturing: food processing, tractor parts, washing machines, pottery. Single-family building permits issued: 41 (2001) / 47 (2000); Multi-family building permits issued: 18 (2001) / 29 (2000); Employment by occupation: 18.0% management, 25.8% professional, 11.2% services, 26.6% sales, 0.1% farming, 7.2% construction, 11.1% production (2000).
Income: Per capita income: $26,531 (2000); Median household income: $53,869 (2000); Poverty rate: 5.0% (2000).
Taxes: Total city taxes per capita: $82 (1997); City property taxes per capita: $42 (1997).
Education: High school graduation rate: 90.0% (2000); College graduation rate: 34.3% (2000).

School District(s)

Morton C U School District 709 (PK-12)
2000 Enrollment: 2,763 309-263-2581

Housing: Homeownership rate: 76.7% (2000); Median home value: $131,000 (2000); Median rent: $475 per month (2000); Median age of housing: 30 years (2000).
Newspapers: Morton Courier (1 x week)
Transportation: Commute to work: 95.1% car, 0.5% public transportation, 1.2% walk, 2.5% work from home (2000); Travel time to work: 40.6% less than 15 minutes, 44.0% 15 to 30 minutes, 11.6% 30 to 45 minutes, 2.0% 45 to 60 minutes, 1.7% 60 minutes or more (2000)
Additional Information Contacts
Morton Chamber of Commerce 309-263-2491

NORTH PEKIN (village). Covers a land area of 1.157 square miles and a water area of 0.028 square miles. Located at 40.61° N. Lat.; 89.62° W. Long. Elevation is 480 feet.
Population: 1,574 (2000); Race: 97.6% White, 0.6% Black, 1.0% Asian, 0.0% American Indian and Alaska Native, 0.0% Hispanic of any race, 0.7% two or more races (2000); Density: 1,359.9 persons per square mile (2000); Age: 25.2% under 18, 12.5% over 64 (2000); Marriage status: 17.3% never married, 66.2% now married, 5.0% widowed, 11.5% divorced (2000); Foreign born: 1.3% (2000); Ancestry (includes multiple ancestries): 30.9% German, 17.2% United States or American, 12.9% Irish, 11.1% Other groups, 7.1% English (2000).
Economy: Single-family building permits issued: 6 (2001) / 1 (2000); Multi-family building permits issued: 0 (2001) / 0 (2000); Employment by occupation: 3.6% management, 7.9% professional, 22.0% services, 29.2% sales, 0.0% farming, 17.1% construction, 20.2% production (2000).
Income: Per capita income: $18,072 (2000); Median household income: $41,375 (2000); Poverty rate: 8.4% (2000).
Taxes: Total city taxes per capita: $83 (1997); City property taxes per capita: $78 (1997).
Education: High school graduation rate: 82.0% (2000); College graduation rate: 2.8% (2000).
Housing: Homeownership rate: 85.2% (2000); Median home value: $63,600 (2000); Median rent: $381 per month (2000); Median age of housing: 45 years (2000).
Transportation: Commute to work: 95.4% car, 0.0% public transportation, 0.7% walk, 3.0% work from home (2000); Travel time to work: 29.9% less than 15 minutes, 48.8% 15 to 30 minutes, 12.0% 30 to 45 minutes, 6.5% 45 to 60 minutes, 2.8% 60 minutes or more (2000)

PEKIN (city). Covers a land area of 13.150 square miles and a water area of 0.596 square miles. Located at 40.56° N. Lat.; 89.63° W. Long. Elevation is 500 feet.
History: Pekin was settled by pioneers of English descent who came from Virginia, Kentucky, and Tennessee. Abraham Lincoln argued many of his legal cases in the courthouse at Pekin.
Population: 33,857 (2000); Race: 95.5% White, 2.8% Black, 0.2% Asian, 0.4% American Indian and Alaska Native, 1.4% Hispanic of any race, 0.8% two or more races (2000); Density: 2,574.8 persons per square mile (2000); Age: 23.3% under 18, 15.6% over 64 (2000); Marriage status: 20.5% never married, 59.3% now married, 8.2% widowed, 12.0% divorced (2000); Foreign born: 0.8% (2000); Ancestry (includes multiple ancestries): 28.4% German, 11.5% Irish, 11.3% English, 10.2% United States or American, 7.8% Other groups (2000).
Vital Statistics: Birth rate: 143.0 per 10,000 population (1998)
Economy: In agricultural area. Manufacturing: grinding wheels, machinery. Unemployment rate: 6.8% (11/2002); Total civilian labor force: 16,581 (11/2002); Single-family building permits issued: 62 (2001) / 56 (2000); Multi-family building permits issued: 0 (2001) / 0 (2000); Employment by occupation: 9.5% management, 15.3% professional, 17.4% services, 29.7% sales, 0.1% farming, 8.1% construction, 20.0% production (2000).
Income: Per capita income: $19,616 (2000); Median household income: $37,972 (2000); Poverty rate: 9.4% (2000).
Taxes: Total city taxes per capita: $158 (1997); City property taxes per capita: $141 (1997).
Education: High school graduation rate: 81.6% (2000); College graduation rate: 13.4% (2000).

School District(s)

N Pekin & Marquette Hght S D 102 (PK-08)
2000 Enrollment: 645 309-382-2172
Pekin Community H S District 303 (09-12)
2000 Enrollment: 2,158 309-477-4222
Pekin Public School District 108 (PK-12)
2000 Enrollment: 3,883 309-346-3151
Rankin Community School District 98 (PK-08)
2000 Enrollment: 203 309-346-3182
Tazewell Roe (09-12)
2000 Enrollment: 65 309-477-2290
Tazewell-Mason Cntys Special Education Assoc (PK-12)
2000 Enrollment: 32 309-347-5164

Housing: Homeownership rate: 67.2% (2000); Median home value: $75,900 (2000); Median rent: $349 per month (2000); Median age of housing: 41 years (2000).
Hospitals: Pekin Hospital (132 beds)
Newspapers: Pekin Daily Times (6 x week)
Transportation: Commute to work: 95.7% car, 0.6% public transportation, 1.5% walk, 1.6% work from home (2000); Travel time to work: 43.4% less than 15 minutes, 35.1% 15 to 30 minutes, 14.5% 30 to 45 minutes, 3.5% 45 to 60 minutes, 3.5% 60 minutes or more (2000)
Airports: Pekin Municipal
Additional Information Contacts
Pekin Area Association of Realtors 309-346-4020

Pekin Chamber of Commerce 309-346-2106

SOUTH PEKIN (village). Covers a land area of 0.429 square miles and a water area of 0 square miles. Located at 40.49° N. Lat.; 89.65° W. Long. Elevation is 514 feet.
History: Incorporated 1917.
Population: 1,162 (2000); Race: 98.7% White, 0.2% Black, 0.0% Asian, 0.2% American Indian and Alaska Native, 0.7% Hispanic of any race, 0.9% two or more races (2000); Density: 2,708.2 persons per square mile (2000); Age: 31.0% under 18, 9.4% over 64 (2000); Marriage status: 23.2% never married, 62.4% now married, 5.6% widowed, 8.8% divorced (2000); Foreign born: 0.7% (2000); Ancestry (includes multiple ancestries): 26.8% German, 12.4% Irish, 11.7% English, 9.9% Other groups, 6.3% United States or American (2000).
Economy: Agriculture: corn, soybeans; cattle, hogs; dairying. Single-family building permits issued: 0 (2001) / 1 (2000); Multi-family building permits issued: 0 (2001) / 0 (2000); Employment by occupation: 4.3% management, 9.0% professional, 23.4% services, 25.6% sales, 0.0% farming, 13.9% construction, 23.7% production (2000).
Income: Per capita income: $15,717 (2000); Median household income: $40,455 (2000); Poverty rate: 7.1% (2000).
Taxes: Total city taxes per capita: $113 (1997); City property taxes per capita: $68 (1997).
Education: High school graduation rate: 77.2% (2000); College graduation rate: 2.7% (2000).

School District(s)

South Pekin School District 137 (PK-08)
2000 Enrollment: 294 309-348-3695
Housing: Homeownership rate: 82.1% (2000); Median home value: $59,800 (2000); Median rent: $363 per month (2000); Median age of housing: 44 years (2000).
Transportation: Commute to work: 94.9% car, 0.7% public transportation, 0.9% walk, 1.2% work from home (2000); Travel time to work: 29.5% less than 15 minutes, 42.5% 15 to 30 minutes, 20.5% 30 to 45 minutes, 5.0% 45 to 60 minutes, 2.5% 60 minutes or more (2000)

TREMONT (village). Covers a land area of 0.953 square miles and a water area of 0 square miles. Located at 40.52° N. Lat.; 89.49° W. Long. Elevation is 650 feet.
Population: 2,029 (2000); Race: 98.7% White, 0.2% Black, 0.3% Asian, 0.1% American Indian and Alaska Native, 0.3% Hispanic of any race, 0.5% two or more races (2000); Density: 2,128.8 persons per square mile (2000); Age: 24.7% under 18, 15.0% over 64 (2000); Marriage status: 18.0% never married, 68.7% now married, 5.9% widowed, 7.4% divorced (2000); Foreign born: 0.5% (2000); Ancestry (includes multiple ancestries): 41.6% German, 11.3% English, 10.7% Irish, 7.5% United States or American, 3.9% Other groups (2000).
Economy: In agricultural area. Single-family building permits issued: 2 (2001) / 0 (2000); Multi-family building permits issued: 10 (2001) / 0 (2000); Employment by occupation: 12.6% management, 19.7% professional, 12.7% services, 24.8% sales, 0.2% farming, 11.5% construction, 18.4% production (2000).
Income: Per capita income: $21,888 (2000); Median household income: $47,137 (2000); Poverty rate: 2.5% (2000).
Taxes: Total city taxes per capita: $72 (1997); City property taxes per capita: $65 (1997).
Education: High school graduation rate: 91.1% (2000); College graduation rate: 20.0% (2000).

School District(s)

Tremont Community Unit District 702 (PK-12)
2000 Enrollment: 1,000 309-925-3461
Housing: Homeownership rate: 75.4% (2000); Median home value: $95,100 (2000); Median rent: $380 per month (2000); Median age of housing: 40 years (2000).
Transportation: Commute to work: 94.3% car, 0.0% public transportation, 2.0% walk, 3.3% work from home (2000); Travel time to work: 35.6% less than 15 minutes, 36.6% 15 to 30 minutes, 19.4% 30 to 45 minutes, 5.2% 45 to 60 minutes, 3.2% 60 minutes or more (2000)

WASHINGTON (city). Covers a land area of 7.476 square miles and a water area of 0.012 square miles. Located at 40.70° N. Lat.; 89.42° W. Long. Elevation is 710 feet.
History: Incorporated 1857.
Population: 10,841 (2000); Race: 98.6% White, 0.0% Black, 0.2% Asian, 0.1% American Indian and Alaska Native, 0.4% Hispanic of any race, 0.9% two or more races (2000); Density: 1,450.0 persons per square mile (2000); Age: 26.2% under 18, 12.4% over 64 (2000); Marriage status: 18.1% never married, 66.3% now married, 6.9% widowed, 8.7% divorced (2000); Foreign born: 1.1% (2000); Ancestry (includes multiple ancestries): 39.8% German, 15.7% English, 14.8% Irish, 7.2% United States or American, 5.8% Other groups (2000).
Vital Statistics: Birth rate: 186.3 per 10,000 population (1998)
Economy: Trade center in agricultural area: corn, hay, barley, soybeans; dairying. Manufacturing: railroad wheels, transportation equipment, machining, transformers. Single-family building permits issued: 81 (2001) / 82 (2000); Multi-family building permits issued: 16 (2001) / 8 (2000); Employment by occupation: 11.6% management, 26.6% professional, 13.3% services, 27.5% sales, 0.1% farming, 8.1% construction, 12.8% production (2000).
Income: Per capita income: $24,231 (2000); Median household income: $52,210 (2000); Poverty rate: 4.1% (2000).
Taxes: Total city taxes per capita: $249 (1997); City property taxes per capita: $96 (1997).
Education: High school graduation rate: 91.7% (2000); College graduation rate: 30.6% (2000).

School District(s)

Central School District 51 (PK-08)
2000 Enrollment: 620 309-444-3943
District 50 Schools (PK-08)
2000 Enrollment: 784 309-745-8914
Washington Community H S District 308 (09-12)
2000 Enrollment: 1,057 309-444-7704
Washington School District 52 (KG-08)
2000 Enrollment: 823 309-444-4182

Four-year College(s)

Illinois Baptist College (Private, Not-for-profit, Baptist)
2001 Enrollment: 26 309-745-9229
Housing: Homeownership rate: 79.1% (2000); Median home value: $97,600 (2000); Median rent: $460 per month (2000); Median age of housing: 37 years (2000).
Newspapers: Courier (1 x week)
Transportation: Commute to work: 94.6% car, 0.0% public transportation, 1.5% walk, 3.5% work from home (2000); Travel time to work: 28.5% less than 15 minutes, 49.4% 15 to 30 minutes, 16.4% 30 to 45 minutes, 2.6% 45 to 60 minutes, 3.1% 60 minutes or more (2000)
Additional Information Contacts
Washington Chamber of Commerce 309-444-9921

Union County

Located in southern Illinois; bounded on the west by the Mississippi River and the Missouri border; drained by the Cache River; includes part of Shawnee National Forest. Covers a land area of 416.20 square miles, a water area of 6.00 square miles, and is located in the Central Time Zone. The county government was organized in 1818. County seat is Jonesboro.

Weather Station: Anna 2 NNE — Elevation: 597 feet

	Jan	Feb	Mar	Apr	May	Jun	Jul	Aug	Sep	Oct	Nov	Dec
High	41	47	58	68	77	85	89	88	81	70	57	46
Low	23	28	36	46	55	63	68	66	58	47	37	28
Precip	3.5	3.3	4.8	4.9	5.2	4.3	3.2	3.6	3.1	3.5	4.6	4.3
Snow	4.9	4.5	2.3	0.1	0.0	0.0	0.0	0.0	0.0	0.1	0.5	2.3

High and Low temperatures in degrees Fahrenheit; Precipitation and Snow in inches

Population: 18,293 (2000); Race: 95.9% White, 0.7% Black, 0.5% Asian, 0.4% American Indian and Alaska Native, 2.7% Hispanic of any race, 1.1% two or more races (2000); Density: 44.0 persons per square mile (2000); Age: 23.2% under 18, 17.5% over 64 (2000).
Religion: Five largest groups: 43.8% Southern Baptist Convention, 7.6% Catholic Church, 5.0% Evangelical Lutheran Church in America, 1.9% Christian Churches and Churches of Christ, 1.9% The United Methodist Church (2000).
Economy: Unemployment rate: 6.0% (11/2002); Total civilian labor force: 8,502 (11/2002); Leading industries: 43.7% health care and social assistance; 15.2% retail trade; 11.3% manufacturing (2000); Companies that employ more than 1,000 persons: 0 (2000); Companies that employ more than 100 persons: 7 (2000); Farms: 591 totaling 136,060 acres (1997); Minority business ownership rate: 0.0% (1997); Women business ownership rate: 32.9% (1997); Retail sales per capita: $5,354 (1997). Single-family building permits issued: 48 (2001) / 48 (2000); Multi-family building permits issued: 0 (2001) / 0 (2000).

Income: Per capita income: $16,450 (2000); Median household income: $30,994 (2000); Poverty rate: 16.5% (2000); Bankruptcy rate: 4.40% (2001).
Taxes: Total county taxes per capita: $93 (1997); County property taxes per capita: $93 (1997).
Education: High school graduation rate: 74.8% (2000); College graduation rate: 15.8% (2000).
Housing: Homeownership rate: 75.4% (2000); Median home value: $59,900 (2000); Median rent: $257 per month (2000); Median age of housing: 37 years (2000).
Health: Birth rate: 118.6 per 10,000 population (1998); Age adjusted death rate: 102.5 per 10,000 population (1999); Age adjusted cancer mortality rate: 246.4 deaths per 100,000 population (1999). Number of physicians: 14.8 per 10,000 population (1999); Number of hospital beds: 85.8 per 10,000 population (1999).
Elections: 2000 Presidential election results: 46.0% Gore, 50.8% Bush, 2.2% Nader, 0.8% Buchanan
National and State Parks: Larue-Pine Hills National Natural Landmark; Trail of Tears State Forest; Union County State Conservation Area; Union County State Forest
Additional Information Contacts
Union County Government Offices 618-833-5711

Union County Communities

ALTO PASS (village). Covers a land area of 2.150 square miles and a water area of 0.025 square miles. Located at 37.57° N. Lat.; 89.31° W. Long. Elevation is 757 feet.
Population: 388 (2000); Race: 85.7% White, 0.0% Black, 0.0% Asian, 1.0% American Indian and Alaska Native, 23.4% Hispanic of any race, 2.3% two or more races (2000); Density: 180.5 persons per square mile (2000); Age: 29.4% under 18, 11.3% over 64 (2000); Marriage status: 14.5% never married, 69.3% now married, 9.1% widowed, 7.1% divorced (2000); Foreign born: 17.1% (2000); Ancestry (includes multiple ancestries): 25.9% Other groups, 17.6% United States or American, 10.1% German, 9.0% English, 3.0% Irish (2000).
Economy: Agriculture: cattle; sorghum, wheat; dairy products. Manufacturing: wine, jewelry. Employment by occupation: 5.8% management, 25.4% professional, 15.0% services, 9.2% sales, 9.8% farming, 9.8% construction, 24.9% production (2000).
Income: Per capita income: $17,288 (2000); Median household income: $33,500 (2000); Poverty rate: 15.3% (2000).
Taxes: Total city taxes per capita: $36 (1997); City property taxes per capita: $11 (1997).
Education: High school graduation rate: 70.0% (2000); College graduation rate: 14.2% (2000).
Housing: Homeownership rate: 84.1% (2000); Median home value: $34,400 (2000); Median rent: $219 per month (2000); Median age of housing: 30 years (2000).
Transportation: Commute to work: 89.2% car, 0.0% public transportation, 2.4% walk, 6.6% work from home (2000); Travel time to work: 14.8% less than 15 minutes, 49.0% 15 to 30 minutes, 9.7% 30 to 45 minutes, 16.1% 45 to 60 minutes, 10.3% 60 minutes or more (2000)

ANNA (city). Covers a land area of 3.380 square miles and a water area of 0.009 square miles. Located at 37.46° N. Lat.; 89.24° W. Long. Elevation is 631 feet.
History: Incorporated 1865.
Population: 5,136 (2000); Race: 95.4% White, 1.6% Black, 0.0% Asian, 0.4% American Indian and Alaska Native, 1.4% Hispanic of any race, 2.0% two or more races (2000); Density: 1,519.3 persons per square mile (2000); Age: 19.1% under 18, 25.0% over 64 (2000); Marriage status: 21.5% never married, 51.4% now married, 14.0% widowed, 13.2% divorced (2000); Foreign born: 0.0% (2000); Ancestry (includes multiple ancestries): 16.8% German, 13.1% Irish, 11.5% Other groups, 11.2% United States or American, 8.4% English (2000).
Economy: Agriculture: fruit, vegetables, sorghum, wheat; dairying. Manufacturing: shoes, construction materials, transportation equipment. Single-family building permits issued: 19 (2001) / 13 (2000); Multi-family building permits issued: 0 (2001) / 0 (2000); Employment by occupation: 8.1% management, 23.8% professional, 23.6% services, 25.0% sales, 0.5% farming, 8.3% construction, 10.7% production (2000).
Income: Per capita income: $16,714 (2000); Median household income: $24,663 (2000); Poverty rate: 23.6% (2000).
Taxes: Total city taxes per capita: $52 (1997); City property taxes per capita: $45 (1997).
Education: High school graduation rate: 68.6% (2000); College graduation rate: 14.7% (2000).

School District(s)

Anna C C School District 37 (KG-08)
2000 Enrollment: 750 618-833-6812
Anna Jonesboro Community H S District 81 (09-12)
2000 Enrollment: 496 618-833-8421

Housing: Homeownership rate: 57.8% (2000); Median home value: $57,300 (2000); Median rent: $261 per month (2000); Median age of housing: 45 years (2000).
Hospitals: Union County Hospital District (58 beds)
Newspapers: Monday's Pub (1 x week); The Gazette-Democrat (1 x week)
Transportation: Commute to work: 88.3% car, 3.2% public transportation, 3.7% walk, 3.7% work from home (2000); Travel time to work: 60.6% less than 15 minutes, 13.2% 15 to 30 minutes, 19.4% 30 to 45 minutes, 4.0% 45 to 60 minutes, 2.8% 60 minutes or more (2000)

COBDEN (village). Covers a land area of 1.228 square miles and a water area of 0 square miles. Located at 37.53° N. Lat.; 89.25° W. Long. Elevation is 616 feet.
History: Cobden was named for an English director of the railroad. The town grew as a fruit shipping station on the Illinois Central Railroad.
Population: 1,116 (2000); Race: 87.8% White, 1.9% Black, 0.0% Asian, 0.7% American Indian and Alaska Native, 16.0% Hispanic of any race, 1.1% two or more races (2000); Density: 908.6 persons per square mile (2000); Age: 24.7% under 18, 18.8% over 64 (2000); Marriage status: 29.3% never married, 47.3% now married, 12.5% widowed, 10.8% divorced (2000); Foreign born: 11.5% (2000); Ancestry (includes multiple ancestries): 19.1% German, 18.4% Other groups, 9.5% United States or American, 9.1% Irish, 4.9% English (2000).
Economy: Single-family building permits issued: 1 (2001) / 2 (2000); Multi-family building permits issued: 0 (2001) / 0 (2000); Employment by occupation: 8.9% management, 17.4% professional, 26.6% services, 20.7% sales, 3.1% farming, 9.6% construction, 13.6% production (2000).
Income: Per capita income: $13,978 (2000); Median household income: $26,364 (2000); Poverty rate: 22.1% (2000).
Taxes: Total city taxes per capita: $79 (1997); City property taxes per capita: $26 (1997).
Education: High school graduation rate: 67.4% (2000); College graduation rate: 16.9% (2000).

School District(s)

Cobden Sch Unit District 17 (PK-12)
2000 Enrollment: 698 618-893-2313

Housing: Homeownership rate: 79.3% (2000); Median home value: $50,600 (2000); Median rent: $243 per month (2000); Median age of housing: 42 years (2000).
Transportation: Commute to work: 95.5% car, 0.0% public transportation, 1.2% walk, 3.3% work from home (2000); Travel time to work: 37.6% less than 15 minutes, 34.4% 15 to 30 minutes, 15.8% 30 to 45 minutes, 4.2% 45 to 60 minutes, 7.9% 60 minutes or more (2000)

DONGOLA (village). Covers a land area of 1.106 square miles and a water area of 0.030 square miles. Located at 37.36° N. Lat.; 89.16° W. Long. Elevation is 400 feet.
Population: 806 (2000); Race: 96.6% White, 0.0% Black, 0.0% Asian, 0.9% American Indian and Alaska Native, 0.0% Hispanic of any race, 2.5% two or more races (2000); Density: 728.8 persons per square mile (2000); Age: 25.9% under 18, 15.1% over 64 (2000); Marriage status: 24.1% never married, 55.1% now married, 8.7% widowed, 12.1% divorced (2000); Foreign born: 0.2% (2000); Ancestry (includes multiple ancestries): 18.1% German, 11.6% Other groups, 10.8% United States or American, 10.5% English, 9.9% Irish (2000).
Economy: Fruit, sweet potatoes, vegetables. Employment by occupation: 3.3% management, 22.3% professional, 23.3% services, 19.3% sales, 0.0% farming, 12.1% construction, 19.7% production (2000).
Income: Per capita income: $11,917 (2000); Median household income: $24,539 (2000); Poverty rate: 21.5% (2000).
Taxes: Total city taxes per capita: $38 (1997); City property taxes per capita: $37 (1997).
Education: High school graduation rate: 72.3% (2000); College graduation rate: 8.8% (2000).

School District(s)

Dongola Sch Unit District 66 (PK-12)
2000 Enrollment: 342 618-827-3841

Housing: Homeownership rate: 70.5% (2000); Median home value: $39,900 (2000); Median rent: $205 per month (2000); Median age of housing: 45 years (2000).
Newspapers: Dongola Tri-County Record (1 x week)
Transportation: Commute to work: 97.0% car, 0.0% public transportation, 0.0% walk, 3.0% work from home (2000); Travel time to work: 25.0% less than 15 minutes, 42.4% 15 to 30 minutes, 14.2% 30 to 45 minutes, 10.8% 45 to 60 minutes, 7.6% 60 minutes or more (2000)

JONESBORO (city). Covers a land area of 1.914 square miles and a water area of 0 square miles. Located at 37.45° N. Lat.; 89.26° W. Long. Elevation is 568 feet.
History: Jonesboro was platted in 1816 and named for a physician who was a resident there.
Population: 1,853 (2000); Race: 98.7% White, 0.2% Black, 0.1% Asian, 0.3% American Indian and Alaska Native, 0.7% Hispanic of any race, 0.5% two or more races (2000); Density: 968.0 persons per square mile (2000); Age: 23.4% under 18, 18.8% over 64 (2000); Marriage status: 20.6% never married, 56.4% now married, 11.7% widowed, 11.3% divorced (2000); Foreign born: 1.4% (2000); Ancestry (includes multiple ancestries): 17.1% German, 10.9% United States or American, 9.8% Irish, 9.6% Other groups, 9.2% English (2000).
Economy: Single-family building permits issued: 6 (2001) / 5 (2000); Multi-family building permits issued: 0 (2001) / 0 (2000); Employment by occupation: 9.4% management, 21.3% professional, 21.7% services, 24.8% sales, 0.5% farming, 7.9% construction, 14.4% production (2000).
Income: Per capita income: $15,372 (2000); Median household income: $30,441 (2000); Poverty rate: 17.1% (2000).
Taxes: Total city taxes per capita: $30 (1997); City property taxes per capita: $26 (1997).
Education: High school graduation rate: 76.8% (2000); College graduation rate: 13.9% (2000).

School District(s)

Jonesboro C C School District 43 (PK-08)
2000 Enrollment: 459 618-833-6651
Housing: Homeownership rate: 73.9% (2000); Median home value: $54,400 (2000); Median rent: $221 per month (2000); Median age of housing: 42 years (2000).
Transportation: Commute to work: 94.0% car, 0.0% public transportation, 1.2% walk, 3.6% work from home (2000); Travel time to work: 50.6% less than 15 minutes, 21.1% 15 to 30 minutes, 18.6% 30 to 45 minutes, 7.2% 45 to 60 minutes, 2.5% 60 minutes or more (2000)

MILL CREEK (village). Aka Millcreek. Covers a land area of 0.366 square miles and a water area of 0.009 square miles. Located at 37.34° N. Lat.; 89.25° W. Long. Elevation is 374 feet.
Population: 76 (2000); Race: 100.0% White, 0.0% Black, 0.0% Asian, 0.0% American Indian and Alaska Native, 0.0% Hispanic of any race, 0.0% two or more races (2000); Density: 207.7 persons per square mile (2000); Age: 35.7% under 18, 9.5% over 64 (2000); Marriage status: 21.3% never married, 67.2% now married, 6.6% widowed, 4.9% divorced (2000); Foreign born: 0.0% (2000); Ancestry (includes multiple ancestries): 20.2% German, 13.1% United States or American, 13.1% Other groups, 2.4% Scottish, 2.4% Scotch-Irish (2000).
Economy: Employment by occupation: 0.0% management, 12.0% professional, 32.0% services, 12.0% sales, 0.0% farming, 16.0% construction, 28.0% production (2000).
Income: Per capita income: $8,317 (2000); Median household income: $16,563 (2000); Poverty rate: 36.9% (2000).
Education: High school graduation rate: 63.0% (2000); College graduation rate: 6.5% (2000).
Housing: Homeownership rate: 100.0% (2000); Median home value: $25,000 (2000); Median age of housing: 55 years (2000).
Transportation: Commute to work: 91.3% car, 0.0% public transportation, 0.0% walk, 8.7% work from home (2000); Travel time to work: 0.0% less than 15 minutes, 52.4% 15 to 30 minutes, 23.8% 30 to 45 minutes, 23.8% 45 to 60 minutes, 0.0% 60 minutes or more (2000)

WOLF LAKE (unincorporated postal area, zip code 62998). Covers a land area of 41.246 square miles and a water area of 0.528 square miles. Located at 37.50° N. Lat.; 89.44° W. Long. Elevation is 353 feet.
Population: 491 (2000); Race: 100.0% White, 0.0% Black, 0.0% Asian, 0.0% American Indian and Alaska Native, 0.0% Hispanic of any race, 0.0% two or more races (2000); Density: 11.9 persons per square mile (2000); Age: 23.6% under 18, 8.1% over 64 (2000); Marriage status: 30.6% never married, 51.7% now married, 6.6% widowed, 11.0% divorced (2000); Foreign born: 0.0% (2000); Ancestry (includes multiple ancestries): 21.0% United States or American, 16.9% German, 7.9% English, 7.2% Irish, 4.2% Scotch-Irish (2000).
Economy: Employment by occupation: 4.9% management, 3.3% professional, 24.6% services, 20.2% sales, 3.8% farming, 18.0% construction, 25.1% production (2000).
Income: Per capita income: $17,343 (2000); Median household income: $32,833 (2000); Poverty rate: 19.4% (2000).
Education: High school graduation rate: 78.4% (2000); College graduation rate: 17.3% (2000).

School District(s)

Shawnee C U School District 84 (KG-12)
2000 Enrollment: 521 618-833-5709
Housing: Homeownership rate: 80.4% (2000); Median home value: $50,000 (2000); Median rent: $250 per month (2000); Median age of housing: 37 years (2000).
Transportation: Commute to work: 100.0% car, 0.0% public transportation, 0.0% walk, 0.0% work from home (2000); Travel time to work: 37.6% less than 15 minutes, 34.4% 15 to 30 minutes, 0.0% 30 to 45 minutes, 8.9% 45 to 60 minutes, 19.1% 60 minutes or more (2000)

Vermilion County

Located in eastern Illinois; bounded on the east by Indiana; drained by the Vermilion and Little Vermilion Rivers; includes Lake Vermilion. Covers a land area of 899.10 square miles, a water area of 3.10 square miles, and is located in the Central Time Zone. The county government was organized in 1826. County seat is Danville.

Weather Station: Danville — Elevation: 557 feet

	Jan	Feb	Mar	Apr	May	Jun	Jul	Aug	Sep	Oct	Nov	Dec
High	34	40	51	65	75	84	86	84	78	67	52	39
Low	17	22	31	41	51	60	64	63	55	43	34	24
Precip	2.0	1.9	3.2	4.1	4.5	4.5	4.5	4.0	3.0	3.1	3.5	2.8
Snow	6.2	4.1	3.1	0.3	tr	0.0	0.0	0.0	0.0	0.2	1.2	4.7

High and Low temperatures in degrees Fahrenheit; Precipitation and Snow in inches

Weather Station: Hoopeston 1 NE — Elevation: 708 feet

	Jan	Feb	Mar	Apr	May	Jun	Jul	Aug	Sep	Oct	Nov	Dec
High	32	37	49	62	74	83	85	83	77	65	50	37
Low	17	21	31	41	51	61	65	62	55	44	34	23
Precip	1.5	1.6	3.0	3.7	4.2	4.0	4.1	3.8	2.9	3.1	2.9	2.4
Snow	5.4	4.1	2.2	0.6	tr	0.0	0.0	0.0	0.0	0.1	1.2	4.2

High and Low temperatures in degrees Fahrenheit; Precipitation and Snow in inches

Population: 83,919 (2000); Race: 85.9% White, 10.4% Black, 0.6% Asian, 0.2% American Indian and Alaska Native, 3.0% Hispanic of any race, 1.6% two or more races (2000); Density: 93.3 persons per square mile (2000); Age: 25.0% under 18, 16.0% over 64 (2000).
Religion: Five largest groups: 7.5% Christian Churches and Churches of Christ, 7.0% Catholic Church, 6.1% The United Methodist Church, 2.6% Church of the Nazarene, 2.5% Lutheran Church—Missouri Synod (2000).
Economy: Unemployment rate: 7.7% (11/2002); Total civilian labor force: 37,042 (11/2002); Leading industries: 23.3% manufacturing; 15.0% health care and social assistance; 14.3% retail trade (2000); Companies that employ more than 1,000 persons: 3 (2000); Companies that employ more than 100 persons: 46 (2000); Farms: 984 totaling 484,846 acres (1997); Minority business ownership rate: 6.4% (1997); Women business ownership rate: 25.8% (1997); Retail sales per capita: $7,540 (1997). Single-family building permits issued: 58 (2001) / 64 (2000); Multi-family building permits issued: 2 (2001) / 6 (2000).
Income: Per capita income: $16,787 (2000); Median household income: $34,071 (2000); Poverty rate: 13.3% (2000); Bankruptcy rate: 8.98% (2001).
Taxes: Total county taxes per capita: $85 (2000); County property taxes per capita: $82 (2000).
Education: High school graduation rate: 78.7% (2000); College graduation rate: 12.5% (2000).
Housing: Homeownership rate: 71.8% (2000); Median home value: $56,000 (2000); Median rent: $312 per month (2000); Median age of housing: 45 years (2000).
Health: Birth rate: 140.7 per 10,000 population (1998); Age adjusted death rate: 96.6 per 10,000 population (1999); Age adjusted cancer mortality rate: 251.4 deaths per 100,000 population (1999). Number of physicians: 13.0 per 10,000 population (1999); Number of hospital beds: 95.9 per 10,000 population (1999).

Elections: 2000 Presidential election results: 48.0% Gore, 49.2% Bush, 1.9% Nader, 0.6% Buchanan
National and State Parks: Kickapoo State Park; Middle Fork State Fish and Wildlife Areas
Additional Information Contacts
Danville Area Board of Realtors 217-443-2170
Danville Area Chamber of Commerce 217-442-1887
Danville Area Economic Development 217-442-6201
Small Business Development Center 217-442-7232

Vermilion County Communities

ALLERTON (village). Covers a land area of 0.645 square miles and a water area of 0 square miles. Located at 39.91° N. Lat.; 87.93° W. Long.
Population: 293 (2000); Race: 97.1% White, 0.0% Black, 0.0% Asian, 0.0% American Indian and Alaska Native, 4.4% Hispanic of any race, 2.9% two or more races (2000); Density: 454.4 persons per square mile (2000); Age: 29.1% under 18, 12.7% over 64 (2000); Marriage status: 19.1% never married, 58.6% now married, 10.9% widowed, 11.4% divorced (2000); Foreign born: 3.3% (2000); Ancestry (includes multiple ancestries): 30.2% United States or American, 22.2% German, 14.9% Other groups, 12.0% English, 10.9% Irish (2000).
Economy: In agricultural and bituminous-coal area. Single-family building permits issued: 0 (2001) / 0 (2000); Multi-family building permits issued: 0 (2001) / 0 (2000); Employment by occupation: 7.0% management, 10.6% professional, 19.0% services, 33.8% sales, 2.1% farming, 12.0% construction, 15.5% production (2000).
Income: Per capita income: $17,512 (2000); Median household income: $42,250 (2000); Poverty rate: 4.5% (2000).
Taxes: Total city taxes per capita: $8 (1997); City property taxes per capita: $8 (1997).
Education: High school graduation rate: 84.7% (2000); College graduation rate: 7.1% (2000).
Housing: Homeownership rate: 86.7% (2000); Median home value: $46,300 (2000); Median rent: $240 per month (2000); Median age of housing: 60+ years (2000).
Transportation: Commute to work: 100.0% car, 0.0% public transportation, 0.0% walk, 0.0% work from home (2000); Travel time to work: 32.4% less than 15 minutes, 7.2% 15 to 30 minutes, 46.0% 30 to 45 minutes, 12.9% 45 to 60 minutes, 1.4% 60 minutes or more (2000)

ALVIN (village). Aka Alvan. Covers a land area of 0.795 square miles and a water area of 0 square miles. Located at 40.30° N. Lat.; 87.60° W. Long. Elevation is 660 feet.
History: Alvin was platted in 1876. The village developed around a grain elevator.
Population: 316 (2000); Race: 97.6% White, 0.0% Black, 0.0% Asian, 1.0% American Indian and Alaska Native, 0.0% Hispanic of any race, 1.4% two or more races (2000); Density: 397.2 persons per square mile (2000); Age: 33.6% under 18, 6.5% over 64 (2000); Marriage status: 21.2% never married, 63.1% now married, 5.5% widowed, 10.1% divorced (2000); Foreign born: 0.0% (2000); Ancestry (includes multiple ancestries): 17.5% English, 13.4% Other groups, 13.0% German, 10.3% Irish, 7.9% United States or American (2000).
Economy: Employment by occupation: 6.8% management, 6.8% professional, 11.9% services, 24.6% sales, 1.7% farming, 11.0% construction, 37.3% production (2000).
Income: Per capita income: $13,773 (2000); Median household income: $36,000 (2000); Poverty rate: 8.2% (2000).
Taxes: Total city taxes per capita: $6 (1997); City property taxes per capita: $6 (1997).
Education: High school graduation rate: 77.1% (2000); College graduation rate: 4.7% (2000).
Housing: Homeownership rate: 75.3% (2000); Median home value: $40,800 (2000); Median rent: $350 per month (2000); Median age of housing: 39 years (2000).
Transportation: Commute to work: 87.0% car, 0.0% public transportation, 8.7% walk, 4.3% work from home (2000); Travel time to work: 13.6% less than 15 minutes, 55.5% 15 to 30 minutes, 18.2% 30 to 45 minutes, 7.3% 45 to 60 minutes, 5.5% 60 minutes or more (2000)

ARMSTRONG (unincorporated postal area, zip code 61812). Covers a land area of 27.238 square miles and a water area of 0 square miles. Located at 40.27° N. Lat.; 87.88° W. Long. Elevation is 696 feet.
Population: 420 (2000); Race: 96.8% White, 3.0% Black, 0.0% Asian, 0.2% American Indian and Alaska Native, 0.7% Hispanic of any race, 0.0% two or more races (2000); Density: 15.4 persons per square mile (2000); Age: 25.3% under 18, 16.4% over 64 (2000); Marriage status: 17.3% never married, 63.0% now married, 9.9% widowed, 9.9% divorced (2000); Foreign born: 1.0% (2000); Ancestry (includes multiple ancestries): 20.6% German, 11.2% English, 6.9% Other groups, 6.7% United States or American, 4.2% Irish (2000).
Economy: Employment by occupation: 14.4% management, 14.4% professional, 10.8% services, 14.9% sales, 2.1% farming, 13.9% construction, 29.4% production (2000).
Income: Per capita income: $17,395 (2000); Median household income: $34,091 (2000); Poverty rate: 4.0% (2000).
Education: High school graduation rate: 90.7% (2000); College graduation rate: 11.7% (2000).

School District(s)
Armstrong Township Hs District 225 (09-12)
2000 Enrollment: 169 217-569-2122
Armstrong-Ellis Cons School District 61 (KG-08)
2000 Enrollment: 140 217-569-2115
Housing: Homeownership rate: 82.4% (2000); Median home value: $55,400 (2000); Median rent: $313 per month (2000); Median age of housing: 43 years (2000).
Transportation: Commute to work: 86.8% car, 0.0% public transportation, 0.5% walk, 11.6% work from home (2000); Travel time to work: 11.9% less than 15 minutes, 26.2% 15 to 30 minutes, 40.5% 30 to 45 minutes, 14.3% 45 to 60 minutes, 7.1% 60 minutes or more (2000)

BELGIUM (village). Covers a land area of 0.423 square miles and a water area of 0 square miles. Located at 40.06° N. Lat.; 87.63° W. Long. Elevation is 652 feet.
History: Many of the early residents of Belgium were from the country of Belgium. The village was incorporated in 1909, with coal mining as the major industry.
Population: 466 (2000); Race: 99.1% White, 0.0% Black, 0.5% Asian, 0.0% American Indian and Alaska Native, 0.5% Hispanic of any race, 0.5% two or more races (2000); Density: 1,101.2 persons per square mile (2000); Age: 25.9% under 18, 12.2% over 64 (2000); Marriage status: 27.9% never married, 50.0% now married, 6.2% widowed, 15.9% divorced (2000); Foreign born: 0.9% (2000); Ancestry (includes multiple ancestries): 29.2% United States or American, 9.9% English, 7.5% French (except Basque), 6.4% German, 4.7% Irish (2000).
Economy: Single-family building permits issued: 3 (2001) / 3 (2000); Multi-family building permits issued: 0 (2001) / 0 (2000); Employment by occupation: 4.9% management, 10.3% professional, 17.4% services, 31.5% sales, 0.0% farming, 9.8% construction, 26.1% production (2000).
Income: Per capita income: $16,038 (2000); Median household income: $32,500 (2000); Poverty rate: 13.1% (2000).
Taxes: Total city taxes per capita: $18 (1997); City property taxes per capita: $8 (1997).
Education: High school graduation rate: 71.9% (2000); College graduation rate: 5.1% (2000).
Housing: Homeownership rate: 74.6% (2000); Median home value: $42,400 (2000); Median rent: $310 per month (2000); Median age of housing: 40 years (2000).
Transportation: Commute to work: 98.9% car, 0.0% public transportation, 0.0% walk, 1.1% work from home (2000); Travel time to work: 28.3% less than 15 minutes, 53.3% 15 to 30 minutes, 7.8% 30 to 45 minutes, 6.1% 45 to 60 minutes, 4.4% 60 minutes or more (2000)

BISMARCK (village). Covers a land area of 0.679 square miles and a water area of 0 square miles. Located at 40.26° N. Lat.; 87.61° W. Long. Elevation is 665 feet.
Population: 542 (2000); Race: 98.9% White, 0.0% Black, 0.0% Asian, 0.0% American Indian and Alaska Native, 0.0% Hispanic of any race, 1.1% two or more races (2000); Density: 797.8 persons per square mile (2000); Age: 32.9% under 18, 9.3% over 64 (2000); Marriage status: 22.7% never married, 63.2% now married, 5.5% widowed, 8.6% divorced (2000); Foreign born: 0.0% (2000); Ancestry (includes multiple ancestries): 27.5% German, 14.0% English, 11.0% Irish, 8.1% United States or American, 6.0% Other groups (2000).
Economy: Employment by occupation: 11.2% management, 10.9% professional, 13.2% services, 32.6% sales, 0.0% farming, 9.3% construction, 22.9% production (2000).
Income: Per capita income: $15,255 (2000); Median household income: $41,731 (2000); Poverty rate: 4.2% (2000).

Education: High school graduation rate: 84.3% (2000); College graduation rate: 15.4% (2000).

School District(s)

Bismarck Henning C U School District (KG-12)
2000 Enrollment: 833 217-759-7261

Housing: Homeownership rate: 76.5% (2000); Median home value: $62,500 (2000); Median rent: $381 per month (2000); Median age of housing: 45 years (2000).

Transportation: Commute to work: 96.0% car, 0.0% public transportation, 1.2% walk, 2.8% work from home (2000); Travel time to work: 23.8% less than 15 minutes, 60.2% 15 to 30 minutes, 9.0% 30 to 45 minutes, 4.1% 45 to 60 minutes, 2.9% 60 minutes or more (2000)

CATLIN (village). Covers a land area of 0.785 square miles and a water area of 0.004 square miles. Located at 40.06° N. Lat.; 87.70° W. Long. Elevation is 657 feet.

Population: 2,087 (2000); Race: 99.4% White, 0.2% Black, 0.0% Asian, 0.0% American Indian and Alaska Native, 0.2% Hispanic of any race, 0.4% two or more races (2000); Density: 2,657.1 persons per square mile (2000); Age: 25.8% under 18, 14.1% over 64 (2000); Marriage status: 17.8% never married, 66.4% now married, 5.9% widowed, 9.9% divorced (2000); Foreign born: 0.2% (2000); Ancestry (includes multiple ancestries): 22.5% German, 16.6% United States or American, 13.1% English, 13.1% Irish, 5.2% Other groups (2000).

Economy: Single-family building permits issued: 1 (2001) / 3 (2000); Multi-family building permits issued: 0 (2001) / 0 (2000); Employment by occupation: 9.6% management, 20.1% professional, 14.8% services, 29.3% sales, 0.0% farming, 8.1% construction, 18.1% production (2000).

Income: Per capita income: $19,164 (2000); Median household income: $46,210 (2000); Poverty rate: 4.0% (2000).

Taxes: Total city taxes per capita: $43 (1997); City property taxes per capita: $39 (1997).

Education: High school graduation rate: 89.4% (2000); College graduation rate: 18.5% (2000).

School District(s)

Catlin C U School District 5 (PK-12)
2000 Enrollment: 579 217-427-2116

Housing: Homeownership rate: 79.8% (2000); Median home value: $70,200 (2000); Median rent: $382 per month (2000); Median age of housing: 37 years (2000).

Transportation: Commute to work: 96.2% car, 0.5% public transportation, 0.5% walk, 1.9% work from home (2000); Travel time to work: 29.2% less than 15 minutes, 54.5% 15 to 30 minutes, 8.6% 30 to 45 minutes, 4.8% 45 to 60 minutes, 3.0% 60 minutes or more (2000)

COLLISON (unincorporated postal area, zip code 61831). Covers a land area of 11.691 square miles and a water area of 0 square miles. Located at 40.21° N. Lat.; 87.78° W. Long. Elevation is 677 feet.

Population: 180 (2000); Race: 100.0% White, 0.0% Black, 0.0% Asian, 0.0% American Indian and Alaska Native, 0.0% Hispanic of any race, 0.0% two or more races (2000); Density: 15.4 persons per square mile (2000); Age: 24.5% under 18, 10.9% over 64 (2000); Marriage status: 15.8% never married, 65.0% now married, 7.5% widowed, 11.7% divorced (2000); Foreign born: 0.0% (2000); Ancestry (includes multiple ancestries): 19.7% United States or American, 17.7% Irish, 17.0% German, 12.2% Other groups, 8.2% English (2000).

Economy: Employment by occupation: 5.1% management, 10.3% professional, 7.7% services, 41.0% sales, 2.6% farming, 9.0% construction, 24.4% production (2000).

Income: Per capita income: $16,937 (2000); Median household income: $42,750 (2000); Poverty rate: 8.8% (2000).

Education: High school graduation rate: 82.7% (2000); College graduation rate: 11.5% (2000).

Housing: Homeownership rate: 87.9% (2000); Median home value: $63,000 (2000); Median rent: $263 per month (2000); Median age of housing: 50 years (2000).

Transportation: Commute to work: 96.2% car, 0.0% public transportation, 0.0% walk, 3.8% work from home (2000); Travel time to work: 12.0% less than 15 minutes, 36.0% 15 to 30 minutes, 44.0% 30 to 45 minutes, 5.3% 45 to 60 minutes, 2.7% 60 minutes or more (2000)

DANVILLE (city). Covers a land area of 17.003 square miles and a water area of 0.095 square miles. Located at 40.13° N. Lat.; 87.62° W. Long. Elevation is 597 feet.

History: Danville had its beginning when a salt works was established in 1824. The town was laid out nearby in 1827 by Dan Beckwith, on land donated by him and Guy W. Smith, and the town was named for Beckwith.

Population: 33,904 (2000); Race: 70.6% White, 24.0% Black, 1.2% Asian, 0.1% American Indian and Alaska Native, 4.7% Hispanic of any race, 2.1% two or more races (2000); Density: 1,994.0 persons per square mile (2000); Age: 24.7% under 18, 16.6% over 64 (2000); Marriage status: 25.8% never married, 52.7% now married, 8.6% widowed, 12.9% divorced (2000); Foreign born: 2.9% (2000); Ancestry (includes multiple ancestries): 26.0% Other groups, 15.7% German, 9.6% Irish, 8.9% United States or American, 7.8% English (2000).

Vital Statistics: Birth rate: 190.0 per 10,000 population (1998)

Economy: Unemployment rate: 10.7% (11/2002); Total civilian labor force: 14,402 (11/2002); Single-family building permits issued: 33 (2001) / 30 (2000); Multi-family building permits issued: 0 (2001) / 0 (2000); Employment by occupation: 8.6% management, 18.5% professional, 18.3% services, 24.8% sales, 0.4% farming, 7.5% construction, 21.8% production (2000).

Income: Per capita income: $16,476 (2000); Median household income: $30,431 (2000); Poverty rate: 18.1% (2000).

Taxes: Total city taxes per capita: $210 (1997); City property taxes per capita: $193 (1997).

Education: High school graduation rate: 75.2% (2000); College graduation rate: 15.7% (2000).

School District(s)

Danville C C School District 118 (PK-12)
2000 Enrollment: 6,117 217-444-1004

Vermillion Roe (09-09)
2000 Enrollment: 2 217-431-2668

Four-year College(s)

Lakeview College of Nursing (Private, Not-for-profit)
2001 Enrollment: 56 217-443-5238
2001 Tuition: In-state $7,500; Out-of-state $7,500

Two-year College(s)

Danville Area Community College (Public)
2001 Enrollment: 2,585 217-443-3222
2001 Tuition: In-state $6,000; Out-of-state $6,000

Provena United Samaritans Med Ctr School of Rad Techn (Private, Not-for-profit, Roman Catholic)
2001 Enrollment: n/a 217-443-5000
2001 Tuition: In-state $2,500; Out-of-state $2,500

Housing: Homeownership rate: 62.0% (2000); Median home value: $52,500 (2000); Median rent: $317 per month (2000); Median age of housing: 49 years (2000).

Hospitals: Danville Veterans Affairs Medical Center; Provena United Samaritans Medical Center (308 beds)

Newspapers: The Commercial News (7 x week)

Transportation: Commute to work: 93.1% car, 1.2% public transportation, 2.4% walk, 2.4% work from home (2000); Travel time to work: 60.0% less than 15 minutes, 27.9% 15 to 30 minutes, 5.3% 30 to 45 minutes, 4.0% 45 to 60 minutes, 2.8% 60 minutes or more (2000); Amtrak: Service available.

Airports: Vermilion County

Additional Information Contacts

Danville Area Board of Realtors 217-443-2170
Danville Area Chamber of Commerce 217-442-1887
Danville Area Economic Development 217-442-6201
Small Business Development Center 217-442-7232

FAIRMOUNT (village). Covers a land area of 0.311 square miles and a water area of 0 square miles. Located at 40.04° N. Lat.; 87.83° W. Long. Elevation is 665 feet.

Population: 640 (2000); Race: 99.2% White, 0.0% Black, 0.0% Asian, 0.0% American Indian and Alaska Native, 0.8% Hispanic of any race, 0.0% two or more races (2000); Density: 2,055.4 persons per square mile (2000); Age: 27.0% under 18, 14.6% over 64 (2000); Marriage status: 19.0% never married, 62.3% now married, 11.0% widowed, 7.6% divorced (2000); Foreign born: 0.5% (2000); Ancestry (includes multiple ancestries): 32.3% United States or American, 14.9% German, 9.2% English, 9.1% Irish, 8.2% Other groups (2000).

Economy: In bituminous-coal and agricultural area: corn, soybeans, cattle. Employment by occupation: 5.7% management, 8.7% professional, 15.3% services, 29.0% sales, 1.3% farming, 18.7% construction, 21.3% production (2000).

Income: Per capita income: $16,691 (2000); Median household income: $39,712 (2000); Poverty rate: 9.5% (2000).

Taxes: Total city taxes per capita: $33 (1997); City property taxes per capita: $26 (1997).
Education: High school graduation rate: 77.2% (2000); College graduation rate: 4.9% (2000).
Housing: Homeownership rate: 84.5% (2000); Median home value: $53,600 (2000); Median rent: $308 per month (2000); Median age of housing: 47 years (2000).
Transportation: Commute to work: 89.1% car, 0.0% public transportation, 5.4% walk, 4.4% work from home (2000); Travel time to work: 22.8% less than 15 minutes, 34.2% 15 to 30 minutes, 30.2% 30 to 45 minutes, 7.5% 45 to 60 minutes, 5.3% 60 minutes or more (2000)

FITHIAN (village). Covers a land area of 0.387 square miles and a water area of 0 square miles. Located at 40.11° N. Lat.; 87.87° W. Long. Elevation is 659 feet.
Population: 506 (2000); Race: 99.2% White, 0.0% Black, 0.0% Asian, 0.0% American Indian and Alaska Native, 0.0% Hispanic of any race, 0.8% two or more races (2000); Density: 1,308.9 persons per square mile (2000); Age: 22.9% under 18, 8.5% over 64 (2000); Marriage status: 16.5% never married, 71.5% now married, 6.1% widowed, 5.9% divorced (2000); Foreign born: 0.0% (2000); Ancestry (includes multiple ancestries): 23.1% German, 14.6% English, 12.0% United States or American, 9.1% Irish, 8.9% Other groups (2000).
Economy: In agricultural and bituminous-coal area. Single-family building permits issued: 2 (2001) / 2 (2000); Multi-family building permits issued: 0 (2001) / 0 (2000); Employment by occupation: 3.8% management, 13.2% professional, 11.7% services, 30.9% sales, 1.5% farming, 10.2% construction, 28.7% production (2000).
Income: Per capita income: $19,856 (2000); Median household income: $47,344 (2000); Poverty rate: 4.9% (2000).
Taxes: Total city taxes per capita: $56 (1997); City property taxes per capita: $14 (1997).
Education: High school graduation rate: 89.2% (2000); College graduation rate: 8.0% (2000).

School District(s)

Oakwood Community Unit District #76 (PK-12)
2000 Enrollment: 1,076 217-354-4355
Housing: Homeownership rate: 73.3% (2000); Median home value: $59,700 (2000); Median rent: $408 per month (2000); Median age of housing: 45 years (2000).
Transportation: Commute to work: 94.0% car, 0.0% public transportation, 0.8% walk, 4.5% work from home (2000); Travel time to work: 9.5% less than 15 minutes, 48.6% 15 to 30 minutes, 34.8% 30 to 45 minutes, 3.6% 45 to 60 minutes, 3.6% 60 minutes or more (2000)

GEORGETOWN (city). Covers a land area of 1.612 square miles and a water area of 0 square miles. Located at 39.97° N. Lat.; 87.63° W. Long. Elevation is 660 feet.
History: Georgetown was settled by Quakers from Tennessee and North Carolina. The town was laid out in 1827.
Population: 3,628 (2000); Race: 94.6% White, 3.4% Black, 0.2% Asian, 0.2% American Indian and Alaska Native, 1.0% Hispanic of any race, 1.4% two or more races (2000); Density: 2,250.6 persons per square mile (2000); Age: 29.0% under 18, 16.6% over 64 (2000); Marriage status: 22.6% never married, 53.9% now married, 8.2% widowed, 15.3% divorced (2000); Foreign born: 0.5% (2000); Ancestry (includes multiple ancestries): 23.6% United States or American, 17.8% German, 9.0% English, 8.7% Irish, 7.9% Other groups (2000).
Economy: Single-family building permits issued: 5 (2001) / 5 (2000); Multi-family building permits issued: 0 (2001) / 0 (2000); Employment by occupation: 8.1% management, 12.8% professional, 16.3% services, 25.5% sales, 1.0% farming, 13.4% construction, 23.0% production (2000).
Income: Per capita income: $14,275 (2000); Median household income: $33,852 (2000); Poverty rate: 13.9% (2000).
Taxes: Total city taxes per capita: $33 (1997); City property taxes per capita: $28 (1997).
Education: High school graduation rate: 76.2% (2000); College graduation rate: 5.9% (2000).

School District(s)

Georgetown-Ridge Farm C U D 4 (PK-12)
2000 Enrollment: 1,335 217-662-8488
Housing: Homeownership rate: 72.4% (2000); Median home value: $45,600 (2000); Median rent: $283 per month (2000); Median age of housing: 41 years (2000).
Newspapers: Independent News (1 x week)

Transportation: Commute to work: 95.8% car, 0.3% public transportation, 1.9% walk, 1.1% work from home (2000); Travel time to work: 17.3% less than 15 minutes, 44.2% 15 to 30 minutes, 26.3% 30 to 45 minutes, 7.0% 45 to 60 minutes, 5.2% 60 minutes or more (2000)

HENNING (village). Covers a land area of 1.524 square miles and a water area of 0 square miles. Located at 40.30° N. Lat.; 87.70° W. Long. Elevation is 685 feet.
Population: 241 (2000); Race: 93.9% White, 0.0% Black, 0.0% Asian, 1.2% American Indian and Alaska Native, 1.2% Hispanic of any race, 4.9% two or more races (2000); Density: 158.1 persons per square mile (2000); Age: 22.5% under 18, 11.5% over 64 (2000); Marriage status: 23.2% never married, 53.6% now married, 16.5% widowed, 6.7% divorced (2000); Foreign born: 0.0% (2000); Ancestry (includes multiple ancestries): 18.4% German, 16.8% United States or American, 16.8% Irish, 16.8% Other groups, 11.1% English (2000).
Economy: In agricultural and bituminous-coal area. Employment by occupation: 6.1% management, 3.8% professional, 13.0% services, 20.6% sales, 0.0% farming, 13.7% construction, 42.7% production (2000).
Income: Per capita income: $18,974 (2000); Median household income: $40,250 (2000); Poverty rate: 4.5% (2000).
Taxes: Total city taxes per capita: $15 (1997); City property taxes per capita: $15 (1997).
Education: High school graduation rate: 79.2% (2000); College graduation rate: 5.0% (2000).
Housing: Homeownership rate: 84.2% (2000); Median home value: $40,300 (2000); Median rent: $229 per month (2000); Median age of housing: 46 years (2000).
Transportation: Commute to work: 93.8% car, 0.0% public transportation, 3.1% walk, 2.3% work from home (2000); Travel time to work: 11.2% less than 15 minutes, 52.8% 15 to 30 minutes, 23.2% 30 to 45 minutes, 7.2% 45 to 60 minutes, 5.6% 60 minutes or more (2000)

HOOPESTON (city). Covers a land area of 3.117 square miles and a water area of 0 square miles. Located at 40.46° N. Lat.; 87.67° W. Long. Elevation is 718 feet.
History: Townsites were laid out on the Hoope farm, near the intersection of two railway lines, in 1871. Hoopeston grew rapidly as a canning center.
Population: 5,965 (2000); Race: 92.9% White, 0.4% Black, 0.0% Asian, 0.1% American Indian and Alaska Native, 7.9% Hispanic of any race, 0.8% two or more races (2000); Density: 1,913.8 persons per square mile (2000); Age: 25.2% under 18, 20.2% over 64 (2000); Marriage status: 22.7% never married, 60.7% now married, 7.3% widowed, 9.2% divorced (2000); Foreign born: 2.0% (2000); Ancestry (includes multiple ancestries): 16.3% Other groups, 14.2% German, 13.9% United States or American, 12.3% English, 7.4% Irish (2000).
Economy: Single-family building permits issued: 5 (2001) / 6 (2000); Multi-family building permits issued: 0 (2001) / 2 (2000); Employment by occupation: 7.1% management, 13.2% professional, 17.0% services, 23.6% sales, 1.9% farming, 8.8% construction, 28.4% production (2000).
Income: Per capita income: $15,055 (2000); Median household income: $31,947 (2000); Poverty rate: 13.8% (2000).
Taxes: Total city taxes per capita: $117 (1997); City property taxes per capita: $74 (1997).
Education: High school graduation rate: 76.4% (2000); College graduation rate: 8.2% (2000).

School District(s)

Hoopeston Area C U School District 11 (PK-12)
2000 Enrollment: 1,509 217-283-6668
Housing: Homeownership rate: 67.8% (2000); Median home value: $48,700 (2000); Median rent: $299 per month (2000); Median age of housing: 50 years (2000).
Hospitals: Hoopeston Community Memorial Hospital (25 beds)
Newspapers: Chronicle (2 x week)
Transportation: Commute to work: 93.6% car, 0.0% public transportation, 3.3% walk, 2.8% work from home (2000); Travel time to work: 54.2% less than 15 minutes, 10.5% 15 to 30 minutes, 17.4% 30 to 45 minutes, 8.8% 45 to 60 minutes, 9.1% 60 minutes or more (2000)

INDIANOLA (village). Covers a land area of 0.386 square miles and a water area of 0 square miles. Located at 39.92° N. Lat.; 87.74° W. Long. Elevation is 674 feet.
Population: 207 (2000); Race: 96.2% White, 0.0% Black, 0.9% Asian, 0.0% American Indian and Alaska Native, 1.3% Hispanic of any race, 3.0% two or more races (2000); Density: 535.8 persons per square mile (2000); Age: 26.5% under 18, 8.1% over 64 (2000); Marriage status: 19.7% never married,

62.8% now married, 9.6% widowed, 8.0% divorced (2000); Foreign born: 1.3% (2000); Ancestry (includes multiple ancestries): 27.4% United States or American, 14.1% German, 9.0% Other groups, 8.5% English, 8.1% Irish (2000).
Economy: In agricultural and bituminous-coal area. Employment by occupation: 0.9% management, 9.5% professional, 20.7% services, 25.0% sales, 0.0% farming, 12.9% construction, 31.0% production (2000).
Income: Per capita income: $16,284 (2000); Median household income: $42,125 (2000); Poverty rate: 6.0% (2000).
Taxes: Total city taxes per capita: $12 (1997); City property taxes per capita: $12 (1997).
Education: High school graduation rate: 80.5% (2000); College graduation rate: 5.7% (2000).
Housing: Homeownership rate: 88.1% (2000); Median home value: $53,100 (2000); Median rent: $333 per month (2000); Median age of housing: 37 years (2000).
Transportation: Commute to work: 100.0% car, 0.0% public transportation, 0.0% walk, 0.0% work from home (2000); Travel time to work: 10.1% less than 15 minutes, 34.9% 15 to 30 minutes, 36.7% 30 to 45 minutes, 12.8% 45 to 60 minutes, 5.5% 60 minutes or more (2000)

MUNCIE (village). Covers a land area of 0.180 square miles and a water area of 0 square miles. Located at 40.11° N. Lat.; 87.84° W. Long. Elevation is 659 feet.
Population: 155 (2000); Race: 98.8% White, 0.0% Black, 1.2% Asian, 0.0% American Indian and Alaska Native, 0.0% Hispanic of any race, 0.0% two or more races (2000); Density: 859.5 persons per square mile (2000); Age: 27.8% under 18, 8.0% over 64 (2000); Marriage status: 26.1% never married, 59.7% now married, 5.0% widowed, 9.2% divorced (2000); Foreign born: 0.0% (2000); Ancestry (includes multiple ancestries): 19.8% United States or American, 19.8% English, 11.1% German, 6.2% Irish, 4.3% Other groups (2000).
Economy: Single-family building permits issued: 0 (2001) / 1 (2000); Multi-family building permits issued: 0 (2001) / 0 (2000); Employment by occupation: 2.5% management, 31.6% professional, 15.2% services, 16.5% sales, 1.3% farming, 17.7% construction, 15.2% production (2000).
Income: Per capita income: $14,822 (2000); Median household income: $36,964 (2000); Poverty rate: 8.0% (2000).
Taxes: Total city taxes per capita: $18 (1997); City property taxes per capita: $6 (1997).
Education: High school graduation rate: 76.9% (2000); College graduation rate: 16.3% (2000).
Housing: Homeownership rate: 79.4% (2000); Median home value: $44,400 (2000); Median rent: $367 per month (2000); Median age of housing: 56 years (2000).
Transportation: Commute to work: 87.3% car, 0.0% public transportation, 6.3% walk, 6.3% work from home (2000); Travel time to work: 23.0% less than 15 minutes, 45.9% 15 to 30 minutes, 31.1% 30 to 45 minutes, 0.0% 45 to 60 minutes, 0.0% 60 minutes or more (2000)

OAKWOOD (village). Covers a land area of 0.899 square miles and a water area of 0 square miles. Located at 40.11° N. Lat.; 87.77° W. Long. Elevation is 645 feet.
Population: 1,502 (2000); Race: 98.4% White, 0.0% Black, 0.2% Asian, 0.4% American Indian and Alaska Native, 0.9% Hispanic of any race, 1.0% two or more races (2000); Density: 1,669.8 persons per square mile (2000); Age: 26.3% under 18, 12.5% over 64 (2000); Marriage status: 21.8% never married, 54.5% now married, 9.4% widowed, 14.3% divorced (2000); Foreign born: 0.4% (2000); Ancestry (includes multiple ancestries): 17.0% German, 16.0% United States or American, 14.2% Irish, 11.4% English, 10.0% Other groups (2000).
Economy: Single-family building permits issued: 0 (2001) / 0 (2000); Multi-family building permits issued: 2 (2001) / 2 (2000); Employment by occupation: 7.5% management, 9.5% professional, 16.6% services, 27.8% sales, 0.3% farming, 12.3% construction, 26.1% production (2000).
Income: Per capita income: $18,655 (2000); Median household income: $41,477 (2000); Poverty rate: 8.1% (2000).
Taxes: Total city taxes per capita: $3 (1997); City property taxes per capita: $3 (1997).
Education: High school graduation rate: 85.9% (2000); College graduation rate: 10.5% (2000).

School District(s)

Vermilion Assoc for Special Education (06-10)
2000 Enrollment: 13 217-443-8273

Housing: Homeownership rate: 83.4% (2000); Median home value: $61,700 (2000); Median rent: $307 per month (2000); Median age of housing: 28 years (2000).
Transportation: Commute to work: 96.1% car, 0.0% public transportation, 1.6% walk, 2.1% work from home (2000); Travel time to work: 22.7% less than 15 minutes, 50.8% 15 to 30 minutes, 19.4% 30 to 45 minutes, 4.0% 45 to 60 minutes, 3.1% 60 minutes or more (2000)

POTOMAC (village). Covers a land area of 0.483 square miles and a water area of 0 square miles. Located at 40.30° N. Lat.; 87.80° W. Long. Elevation is 670 feet.
Population: 681 (2000); Race: 97.6% White, 0.0% Black, 0.0% Asian, 0.0% American Indian and Alaska Native, 2.7% Hispanic of any race, 0.0% two or more races (2000); Density: 1,408.5 persons per square mile (2000); Age: 30.1% under 18, 10.6% over 64 (2000); Marriage status: 22.4% never married, 59.2% now married, 8.4% widowed, 10.0% divorced (2000); Foreign born: 0.0% (2000); Ancestry (includes multiple ancestries): 27.1% German, 18.1% English, 15.0% Irish, 12.2% United States or American, 7.1% Other groups (2000).
Economy: In agricultural and bituminous-coal area. Single-family building permits issued: 0 (2001) / 3 (2000); Multi-family building permits issued: 0 (2001) / 0 (2000); Employment by occupation: 8.5% management, 9.8% professional, 18.6% services, 24.1% sales, 0.6% farming, 7.3% construction, 31.1% production (2000).
Income: Per capita income: $15,197 (2000); Median household income: $40,221 (2000); Poverty rate: 9.1% (2000).
Taxes: Total city taxes per capita: $30 (1997); City property taxes per capita: $30 (1997).
Education: High school graduation rate: 83.5% (2000); College graduation rate: 9.9% (2000).

School District(s)

Potomac C U School District 10 (PK-08)
2000 Enrollment: 229 217-987-6155

Housing: Homeownership rate: 82.2% (2000); Median home value: $43,100 (2000); Median rent: $320 per month (2000); Median age of housing: 54 years (2000).
Transportation: Commute to work: 91.1% car, 0.0% public transportation, 3.1% walk, 3.7% work from home (2000); Travel time to work: 21.1% less than 15 minutes, 25.2% 15 to 30 minutes, 34.8% 30 to 45 minutes, 13.7% 45 to 60 minutes, 5.1% 60 minutes or more (2000)

RANKIN (village). Covers a land area of 0.572 square miles and a water area of 0 square miles. Located at 40.46° N. Lat.; 87.89° W. Long. Elevation is 710 feet.
Population: 617 (2000); Race: 88.8% White, 0.8% Black, 0.0% Asian, 0.3% American Indian and Alaska Native, 13.2% Hispanic of any race, 0.0% two or more races (2000); Density: 1,078.3 persons per square mile (2000); Age: 27.7% under 18, 16.0% over 64 (2000); Marriage status: 22.2% never married, 56.8% now married, 10.9% widowed, 10.0% divorced (2000); Foreign born: 7.7% (2000); Ancestry (includes multiple ancestries): 14.7% German, 13.7% Other groups, 9.8% United States or American, 9.3% Irish, 6.7% English (2000).
Economy: Agriculture: grain; livestock, poultry; dairy products. Single-family building permits issued: 0 (2001) / 0 (2000); Multi-family building permits issued: 0 (2001) / 2 (2000); Employment by occupation: 8.4% management, 8.8% professional, 20.3% services, 17.6% sales, 0.0% farming, 11.0% construction, 33.9% production (2000).
Income: Per capita income: $14,005 (2000); Median household income: $29,063 (2000); Poverty rate: 13.6% (2000).
Taxes: Total city taxes per capita: $64 (1997); City property taxes per capita: $22 (1997).
Education: High school graduation rate: 73.9% (2000); College graduation rate: 7.2% (2000).
Housing: Homeownership rate: 81.9% (2000); Median home value: $38,800 (2000); Median rent: $268 per month (2000); Median age of housing: 60 years (2000).
Transportation: Commute to work: 96.9% car, 0.4% public transportation, 1.3% walk, 1.3% work from home (2000); Travel time to work: 20.9% less than 15 minutes, 28.9% 15 to 30 minutes, 28.4% 30 to 45 minutes, 10.7% 45 to 60 minutes, 11.1% 60 minutes or more (2000)

RIDGE FARM (village). Covers a land area of 3.127 square miles and a water area of 0 square miles. Located at 39.89° N. Lat.; 87.65° W. Long. Elevation is 700 feet.
History: Ridge Farm was platted in 1853 and incorporated as a village in 1874. It developed as a trading center.

Population: 912 (2000); Race: 99.1% White, 0.0% Black, 0.0% Asian, 0.0% American Indian and Alaska Native, 0.4% Hispanic of any race, 0.7% two or more races (2000); Density: 291.6 persons per square mile (2000); Age: 26.4% under 18, 22.7% over 64 (2000); Marriage status: 15.6% never married, 63.7% now married, 10.1% widowed, 10.6% divorced (2000); Foreign born: 0.2% (2000); Ancestry (includes multiple ancestries): 22.3% United States or American, 17.6% German, 11.9% Irish, 7.8% English, 6.7% Other groups (2000).
Economy: Single-family building permits issued: 2 (2001) / 0 (2000); Multi-family building permits issued: 0 (2001) / 0 (2000); Employment by occupation: 6.1% management, 10.8% professional, 19.7% services, 20.6% sales, 0.0% farming, 16.4% construction, 26.4% production (2000).
Income: Per capita income: $16,624 (2000); Median household income: $33,333 (2000); Poverty rate: 10.5% (2000).
Taxes: Total city taxes per capita: $61 (1997); City property taxes per capita: $61 (1997).
Education: High school graduation rate: 80.3% (2000); College graduation rate: 10.4% (2000).
Housing: Homeownership rate: 76.2% (2000); Median home value: $44,400 (2000); Median rent: $245 per month (2000); Median age of housing: 47 years (2000).
Transportation: Commute to work: 94.9% car, 0.0% public transportation, 1.1% walk, 1.7% work from home (2000); Travel time to work: 17.1% less than 15 minutes, 22.9% 15 to 30 minutes, 46.9% 30 to 45 minutes, 7.7% 45 to 60 minutes, 5.4% 60 minutes or more (2000)

ROSSVILLE (village). Covers a land area of 1.345 square miles and a water area of 0 square miles. Located at 40.38° N. Lat.; 87.66° W. Long. Elevation is 706 feet.
History: Rossville was laid out in 1857 and named for early settler Jacob Ross. The site at the intersection of two roads had previously been called Henpeck.
Population: 1,217 (2000); Race: 98.2% White, 0.0% Black, 0.0% Asian, 0.0% American Indian and Alaska Native, 1.5% Hispanic of any race, 0.8% two or more races (2000); Density: 905.1 persons per square mile (2000); Age: 23.5% under 18, 18.6% over 64 (2000); Marriage status: 21.9% never married, 56.9% now married, 10.1% widowed, 11.1% divorced (2000); Foreign born: 1.0% (2000); Ancestry (includes multiple ancestries): 20.5% German, 17.0% English, 11.6% United States or American, 10.9% Irish, 8.3% Other groups (2000).
Economy: Single-family building permits issued: 2 (2001) / 5 (2000); Multi-family building permits issued: 0 (2001) / 0 (2000); Employment by occupation: 8.8% management, 12.6% professional, 14.2% services, 28.1% sales, 1.1% farming, 8.2% construction, 27.0% production (2000).
Income: Per capita income: $16,794 (2000); Median household income: $36,442 (2000); Poverty rate: 9.8% (2000).
Taxes: Total city taxes per capita: $20 (1997); City property taxes per capita: $16 (1997).
Education: High school graduation rate: 81.4% (2000); College graduation rate: 12.8% (2000).

School District(s)

Rossville-Alvin Cu School District 7 (PK-12)
2000 Enrollment: 448 217-748-6600

Housing: Homeownership rate: 77.2% (2000); Median home value: $58,200 (2000); Median rent: $285 per month (2000); Median age of housing: 60+ years (2000).
Transportation: Commute to work: 93.3% car, 0.2% public transportation, 3.9% walk, 1.7% work from home (2000); Travel time to work: 38.0% less than 15 minutes, 23.6% 15 to 30 minutes, 31.6% 30 to 45 minutes, 2.5% 45 to 60 minutes, 4.4% 60 minutes or more (2000)

SIDELL (village). Covers a land area of 0.928 square miles and a water area of 0 square miles. Located at 39.91° N. Lat.; 87.82° W. Long. Elevation is 685 feet.
Population: 626 (2000); Race: 100.0% White, 0.0% Black, 0.0% Asian, 0.0% American Indian and Alaska Native, 0.0% Hispanic of any race, 0.0% two or more races (2000); Density: 674.7 persons per square mile (2000); Age: 27.5% under 18, 14.4% over 64 (2000); Marriage status: 18.4% never married, 63.9% now married, 6.1% widowed, 11.7% divorced (2000); Foreign born: 0.3% (2000); Ancestry (includes multiple ancestries): 33.5% United States or American, 12.5% German, 11.8% Irish, 11.3% English, 8.7% Other groups (2000).
Economy: In agricultural and bituminous coal area. Single-family building permits issued: 0 (2001) / 0 (2000); Multi-family building permits issued: 0 (2001) / 0 (2000); Employment by occupation: 4.2% management, 14.6% professional, 13.5% services, 26.9% sales, 1.5% farming, 5.0% construction, 34.2% production (2000).
Income: Per capita income: $15,061 (2000); Median household income: $31,923 (2000); Poverty rate: 9.6% (2000).
Taxes: Total city taxes per capita: $15 (1997); City property taxes per capita: $13 (1997).
Education: High school graduation rate: 76.5% (2000); College graduation rate: 6.4% (2000).

School District(s)

Jamaica C U School District 12 (PK-12)
2000 Enrollment: 502 217-288-9306

Housing: Homeownership rate: 84.2% (2000); Median home value: $43,600 (2000); Median rent: $296 per month (2000); Median age of housing: 56 years (2000).
Newspapers: Sidell Reporter (1 x week)
Transportation: Commute to work: 91.5% car, 1.2% public transportation, 1.9% walk, 4.7% work from home (2000); Travel time to work: 29.7% less than 15 minutes, 18.7% 15 to 30 minutes, 33.3% 30 to 45 minutes, 17.5% 45 to 60 minutes, 0.8% 60 minutes or more (2000)

TILTON (village). Covers a land area of 3.098 square miles and a water area of 0.028 square miles. Located at 40.09° N. Lat.; 87.64° W. Long. Elevation is 648 feet.
History: Incorporated 1884.
Population: 2,976 (2000); Race: 97.2% White, 0.5% Black, 0.0% Asian, 0.3% American Indian and Alaska Native, 1.0% Hispanic of any race, 2.1% two or more races (2000); Density: 960.5 persons per square mile (2000); Age: 22.8% under 18, 18.5% over 64 (2000); Marriage status: 18.5% never married, 55.1% now married, 8.5% widowed, 17.9% divorced (2000); Foreign born: 0.9% (2000); Ancestry (includes multiple ancestries): 18.6% German, 16.5% United States or American, 13.1% Irish, 10.6% English, 9.5% Other groups (2000).
Economy: Railroad junction. Manufacturing of metal stampings, prefabricated garages, aluminum castings and patterns. Single-family building permits issued: 0 (2001) / 1 (2000); Multi-family building permits issued: 0 (2001) / 0 (2000); Employment by occupation: 9.1% management, 10.0% professional, 23.7% services, 23.9% sales, 0.3% farming, 12.4% construction, 20.6% production (2000).
Income: Per capita income: $16,276 (2000); Median household income: $31,810 (2000); Poverty rate: 8.6% (2000).
Taxes: Total city taxes per capita: $382 (1997); City property taxes per capita: $11 (1997).
Education: High school graduation rate: 77.4% (2000); College graduation rate: 5.2% (2000).
Housing: Homeownership rate: 75.7% (2000); Median home value: $49,700 (2000); Median rent: $290 per month (2000); Median age of housing: 48 years (2000).
Transportation: Commute to work: 96.4% car, 0.4% public transportation, 0.0% walk, 2.4% work from home (2000); Travel time to work: 45.0% less than 15 minutes, 40.9% 15 to 30 minutes, 9.6% 30 to 45 minutes, 2.9% 45 to 60 minutes, 1.7% 60 minutes or more (2000)

WESTVILLE (village). Covers a land area of 1.595 square miles and a water area of 0 square miles. Located at 40.04° N. Lat.; 87.63° W. Long. Elevation is 671 feet.
History: Westville was named for W.P. and E.A. West, who laid out the town in 1873. Coal mining was the first major industry.
Population: 3,175 (2000); Race: 97.3% White, 0.0% Black, 0.7% Asian, 0.0% American Indian and Alaska Native, 1.1% Hispanic of any race, 1.8% two or more races (2000); Density: 1,990.6 persons per square mile (2000); Age: 22.0% under 18, 19.5% over 64 (2000); Marriage status: 21.7% never married, 58.1% now married, 9.3% widowed, 10.9% divorced (2000); Foreign born: 0.7% (2000); Ancestry (includes multiple ancestries): 13.6% German, 12.4% United States or American, 11.5% Irish, 10.3% English, 10.2% Other groups (2000).
Economy: Single-family building permits issued: 0 (2001) / 3 (2000); Multi-family building permits issued: 0 (2001) / 0 (2000); Employment by occupation: 7.7% management, 11.1% professional, 18.1% services, 27.8% sales, 0.0% farming, 9.6% construction, 25.6% production (2000).
Income: Per capita income: $17,538 (2000); Median household income: $34,654 (2000); Poverty rate: 7.4% (2000).
Taxes: Total city taxes per capita: $357 (1997); City property taxes per capita: $103 (1997).
Education: High school graduation rate: 79.2% (2000); College graduation rate: 8.4% (2000).

School District(s)

Westville C U School District 2 (PK-12)
2000 Enrollment: 1,320 217-267-3141

Housing: Homeownership rate: 80.2% (2000); Median home value: $55,500 (2000); Median rent: $312 per month (2000); Median age of housing: 46 years (2000).

Transportation: Commute to work: 97.0% car, 0.5% public transportation, 0.9% walk, 1.6% work from home (2000); Travel time to work: 26.8% less than 15 minutes, 52.1% 15 to 30 minutes, 12.4% 30 to 45 minutes, 4.9% 45 to 60 minutes, 3.9% 60 minutes or more (2000)

Wabash County

Located in southeastern Illinois; bounded on the east and south by the Wabash River, and the Indiana border. Covers a land area of 223.50 square miles, a water area of 4.30 square miles, and is located in the Central Time Zone. The county government was organized in 1824. County seat is Mount Carmel.

Population: 12,937 (2000); Race: 98.0% White, 0.3% Black, 0.3% Asian, 0.2% American Indian and Alaska Native, 0.7% Hispanic of any race, 1.1% two or more races (2000); Density: 57.9 persons per square mile (2000); Age: 24.2% under 18, 17.0% over 64 (2000).

Religion: Five largest groups: 12.7% Catholic Church, 9.9% The United Methodist Church, 9.5% Christian Churches and Churches of Christ, 5.2% Christian Church (Disciples of Christ), 4.2% Southern Baptist Convention (2000).

Economy: Unemployment rate: 7.0% (11/2002); Total civilian labor force: 4,549 (11/2002); Leading industries: 22.2% health care and social assistance; 15.5% manufacturing; 12.0% retail trade (2000); Companies that employ more than 1,000 persons: 0 (2000); Companies that employ more than 100 persons: 7 (2000); Farms: 212 totaling 121,664 acres (1997); Minority business ownership rate: 0.0% (1997); Women business ownership rate: 25.9% (1997); Retail sales per capita: $5,965 (1997). Single-family building permits issued: 12 (2001) / 13 (2000); Multi-family building permits issued: 0 (2001) / 0 (2000).

Income: Per capita income: $16,747 (2000); Median household income: $34,473 (2000); Poverty rate: 14.1% (2000); Bankruptcy rate: 3.26% (2001).

Taxes: Total county taxes per capita: $122 (1997); County property taxes per capita: $81 (1997).

Education: High school graduation rate: 82.2% (2000); College graduation rate: 12.5% (2000).

Housing: Homeownership rate: 75.2% (2000); Median home value: $56,200 (2000); Median rent: $241 per month (2000); Median age of housing: 42 years (2000).

Health: Birth rate: 112.9 per 10,000 population (1998); Age adjusted death rate: 84.7 per 10,000 population (1999); Age adjusted cancer mortality rate: 192.3 deaths per 100,000 population (1999). Air Quality Index: 98% good, 2% moderate, 0% unhealthy (percent of days in 2000). Number of physicians: 7.0 per 10,000 population (1999); Number of hospital beds: 40.2 per 10,000 population (1999).

Elections: 2000 Presidential election results: 36.1% Gore, 61.8% Bush, 1.4% Nader, 0.5% Buchanan

National and State Parks: Beall Woods State Conservation and Natural Area

Additional Information Contacts

Wabash County Government Offices.......................... 618-262-4561
Wabash County Chamber of Commerce 618-262-5116

Wabash County Communities

ALLENDALE (village). Aka Orio. Covers a land area of 0.301 square miles and a water area of 0 square miles. Located at 38.52° N. Lat.; 87.71° W. Long. Elevation is 500 feet.

Population: 528 (2000); Race: 97.6% White, 0.0% Black, 0.7% Asian, 0.0% American Indian and Alaska Native, 0.4% Hispanic of any race, 1.3% two or more races (2000); Density: 1,755.5 persons per square mile (2000); Age: 33.6% under 18, 9.8% over 64 (2000); Marriage status: 25.4% never married, 62.1% now married, 7.7% widowed, 4.9% divorced (2000); Foreign born: 2.0% (2000); Ancestry (includes multiple ancestries): 20.1% German, 16.1% United States or American, 13.3% Other groups, 11.8% Irish, 11.3% English (2000).

Economy: In agricultural area: mixed grain. Oil, coal; sand, gravel. Single-family building permits issued: 1 (2001) / 0 (2000); Multi-family building permits issued: 0 (2001) / 0 (2000); Employment by occupation: 5.8% management, 20.3% professional, 15.4% services, 22.0% sales, 0.0% farming, 12.9% construction, 23.7% production (2000).

Income: Per capita income: $12,117 (2000); Median household income: $31,705 (2000); Poverty rate: 16.6% (2000).

Taxes: Total city taxes per capita: $13 (1997); City property taxes per capita: $9 (1997).

Education: High school graduation rate: 89.4% (2000); College graduation rate: 12.9% (2000).

School District(s)

Allendale C C School District 17 (PK-08)
2000 Enrollment: 140 618-299-3161

Housing: Homeownership rate: 87.2% (2000); Median home value: $54,700 (2000); Median rent: $296 per month (2000); Median age of housing: 27 years (2000).

Transportation: Commute to work: 96.2% car, 0.0% public transportation, 0.9% walk, 2.1% work from home (2000); Travel time to work: 29.6% less than 15 minutes, 44.3% 15 to 30 minutes, 16.1% 30 to 45 minutes, 7.8% 45 to 60 minutes, 2.2% 60 minutes or more (2000)

BELLMONT (village). Covers a land area of 0.365 square miles and a water area of 0 square miles. Located at 38.38° N. Lat.; 87.90° W. Long. Elevation is 430 feet.

Population: 297 (2000); Race: 99.3% White, 0.7% Black, 0.0% Asian, 0.0% American Indian and Alaska Native, 0.7% Hispanic of any race, 0.0% two or more races (2000); Density: 813.9 persons per square mile (2000); Age: 26.1% under 18, 11.6% over 64 (2000); Marriage status: 17.3% never married, 66.7% now married, 6.1% widowed, 10.0% divorced (2000); Foreign born: 1.0% (2000); Ancestry (includes multiple ancestries): 30.0% German, 18.2% English, 9.6% Irish, 9.6% United States or American, 8.3% Other groups (2000).

Economy: In agricultural area: grain. Oil, natural gas, coal. Employment by occupation: 4.4% management, 8.1% professional, 9.6% services, 25.9% sales, 0.0% farming, 12.6% construction, 39.3% production (2000).

Income: Per capita income: $14,263 (2000); Median household income: $30,000 (2000); Poverty rate: 11.9% (2000).

Taxes: Total city taxes per capita: $15 (1997); City property taxes per capita: $11 (1997).

Education: High school graduation rate: 90.5% (2000); College graduation rate: 6.3% (2000).

Housing: Homeownership rate: 75.2% (2000); Median home value: $37,500 (2000); Median rent: $195 per month (2000); Median age of housing: 42 years (2000).

Transportation: Commute to work: 93.3% car, 0.0% public transportation, 4.4% walk, 2.2% work from home (2000); Travel time to work: 35.6% less than 15 minutes, 33.3% 15 to 30 minutes, 15.9% 30 to 45 minutes, 6.8% 45 to 60 minutes, 8.3% 60 minutes or more (2000)

KEENSBURG (village). Covers a land area of 0.258 square miles and a water area of 0 square miles. Located at 38.35° N. Lat.; 87.86° W. Long. Elevation is 425 feet.

Population: 252 (2000); Race: 100.0% White, 0.0% Black, 0.0% Asian, 0.0% American Indian and Alaska Native, 0.0% Hispanic of any race, 0.0% two or more races (2000); Density: 978.6 persons per square mile (2000); Age: 22.4% under 18, 10.5% over 64 (2000); Marriage status: 25.0% never married, 61.2% now married, 6.1% widowed, 7.7% divorced (2000); Foreign born: 0.0% (2000); Ancestry (includes multiple ancestries): 24.9% German, 16.5% United States or American, 14.3% Other groups, 8.9% Scottish, 8.9% Irish (2000).

Economy: In agricultural area. Employment by occupation: 2.9% management, 7.2% professional, 11.6% services, 21.7% sales, 2.2% farming, 10.1% construction, 44.2% production (2000).

Income: Per capita income: $14,889 (2000); Median household income: $30,375 (2000); Poverty rate: 5.6% (2000).

Taxes: Total city taxes per capita: $8 (1997); City property taxes per capita: $8 (1997).

Education: High school graduation rate: 78.0% (2000); College graduation rate: 6.0% (2000).

Housing: Homeownership rate: 84.0% (2000); Median home value: $26,300 (2000); Median rent: $275 per month (2000); Median age of housing: 38 years (2000).

Transportation: Commute to work: 96.3% car, 0.0% public transportation, 0.0% walk, 0.0% work from home (2000); Travel time to work: 30.9% less than 15 minutes, 40.4% 15 to 30 minutes, 13.2% 30 to 45 minutes, 6.6% 45 to 60 minutes, 8.8% 60 minutes or more (2000)

MOUNT CARMEL (city). Aka Sugar Creek. Covers a land area of 4.617 square miles and a water area of 0.153 square miles. Located at 38.41° N. Lat.; 87.76° W. Long. Elevation is 450 feet.
History: Mount Carmel was founded in 1818 by Rev. Thomas S. Hinde of Ohio, who hoped for a "moral, temperate, and industrious village." A mussel and pearl industry began here in 1900.
Population: 7,982 (2000); Race: 97.8% White, 0.4% Black, 0.4% Asian, 0.3% American Indian and Alaska Native, 0.7% Hispanic of any race, 1.0% two or more races (2000); Density: 1,728.7 persons per square mile (2000); Age: 23.9% under 18, 18.9% over 64 (2000); Marriage status: 22.1% never married, 56.5% now married, 9.3% widowed, 12.1% divorced (2000); Foreign born: 0.6% (2000); Ancestry (includes multiple ancestries): 24.5% German, 17.4% United States or American, 10.8% Irish, 9.3% English, 9.2% Other groups (2000).
Economy: Single-family building permits issued: 11 (2001) / 13 (2000); Multi-family building permits issued: 0 (2001) / 0 (2000); Employment by occupation: 6.1% management, 13.8% professional, 21.6% services, 22.7% sales, 0.3% farming, 12.2% construction, 23.3% production (2000).
Income: Per capita income: $16,391 (2000); Median household income: $31,715 (2000); Poverty rate: 15.8% (2000).
Taxes: Total city taxes per capita: $107 (1997); City property taxes per capita: $64 (1997).
Education: High school graduation rate: 79.7% (2000); College graduation rate: 12.9% (2000).

School District(s)

Wabash C U School District 348 (PK-12)
2000 Enrollment: 2,008 618-262-4181

Two-year College(s)

Illinois Eastern Community Colleges-Wabash Valley College (Public)
2001 Enrollment: 2,643 618-393-2982
2001 Tuition: In-state $5,618; Out-of-state $6,961

Housing: Homeownership rate: 68.1% (2000); Median home value: $51,200 (2000); Median rent: $241 per month (2000); Median age of housing: 46 years (2000).
Hospitals: Wabash General Hospital District (56 beds)
Newspapers: Daily Republican Register (5 x week)
Transportation: Commute to work: 91.4% car, 0.0% public transportation, 5.1% walk, 2.7% work from home (2000); Travel time to work: 54.8% less than 15 minutes, 21.7% 15 to 30 minutes, 7.1% 30 to 45 minutes, 8.7% 45 to 60 minutes, 7.7% 60 minutes or more (2000)
Airports: Mount Carmel Municipal
Additional Information Contacts
Wabash County Chamber of Commerce 618-262-5116

Warren County

Located in western Illinois; drained by Henderson Creek. Covers a land area of 542.50 square miles, a water area of 0.60 square miles, and is located in the Central Time Zone. The county government was organized in 1825. County seat is Monmouth.

Weather Station: Monmouth — Elevation: 744 feet

	Jan	Feb	Mar	Apr	May	Jun	Jul	Aug	Sep	Oct	Nov	Dec
High	31	38	50	64	75	83	87	84	78	65	49	36
Low	14	20	30	40	51	60	64	62	54	43	31	21
Precip	1.6	1.7	2.9	3.8	4.3	4.1	4.4	4.2	3.7	3.0	2.7	2.3
Snow	8.6	5.8	3.5	1.6	0.0	0.0	0.0	0.0	0.0	tr	2.3	6.4

High and Low temperatures in degrees Fahrenheit; Precipitation and Snow in inches

Population: 18,735 (2000); Race: 95.8% White, 1.4% Black, 0.4% Asian, 0.1% American Indian and Alaska Native, 2.8% Hispanic of any race, 1.2% two or more races (2000); Density: 34.5 persons per square mile (2000); Age: 23.1% under 18, 16.4% over 64 (2000).
Religion: Five largest groups: 11.0% Catholic Church, 9.6% The United Methodist Church, 7.1% Presbyterian Church (U.S.A.), 5.1% Christian Churches and Churches of Christ, 4.6% Christian Church (Disciples of Christ) (2000).
Economy: Unemployment rate: 5.7% (11/2002); Total civilian labor force: 9,669 (11/2002); Leading industries: 26.0% manufacturing; 18.6% health care and social assistance; 12.2% retail trade (2000); Companies that employ more than 1,000 persons: 0 (2000); Companies that employ more than 100 persons: 6 (2000); Farms: 710 totaling 315,067 acres (1997); Minority business ownership rate: 0.0% (1997); Women business ownership rate: 20.3% (1997); Retail sales per capita: $5,162 (1997). Single-family building permits issued: 24 (2001) / 38 (2000); Multi-family building permits issued: 0 (2001) / 0 (2000).
Income: Per capita income: $16,946 (2000); Median household income: $36,224 (2000); Poverty rate: 9.2% (2000); Bankruptcy rate: 6.49% (2001).
Taxes: Total county taxes per capita: $91 (1997); County property taxes per capita: $91 (1997).
Education: High school graduation rate: 82.3% (2000); College graduation rate: 15.8% (2000).
Housing: Homeownership rate: 74.4% (2000); Median home value: $57,600 (2000); Median rent: $276 per month (2000); Median age of housing: 54 years (2000).
Health: Birth rate: 114.8 per 10,000 population (1998); Age adjusted death rate: 90.6 per 10,000 population (1999); Age adjusted cancer mortality rate: 231.6 deaths per 100,000 population (1999). Number of physicians: 6.4 per 10,000 population (1999); Number of hospital beds: 36.3 per 10,000 population (1999).
Elections: 2000 Presidential election results: 46.2% Gore, 51.1% Bush, 1.7% Nader, 0.7% Buchanan
Additional Information Contacts
Warren County Government Offices 309-734-8592
Monmouth Area Chamber of Commerce 309-734-3181

Warren County Communities

ALEXIS (village). Covers a land area of 0.485 square miles and a water area of 0 square miles. Located at 41.06° N. Lat.; 90.55° W. Long. Elevation is 696 feet.
Population: 863 (2000); Race: 100.0% White, 0.0% Black, 0.0% Asian, 0.0% American Indian and Alaska Native, 2.9% Hispanic of any race, 0.0% two or more races (2000); Density: 1,778.5 persons per square mile (2000); Age: 23.4% under 18, 18.4% over 64 (2000); Marriage status: 17.9% never married, 61.4% now married, 11.7% widowed, 9.0% divorced (2000); Foreign born: 0.0% (2000); Ancestry (includes multiple ancestries): 23.0% Irish, 20.6% German, 15.4% Swedish, 12.1% English, 9.4% United States or American (2000).
Economy: Single-family building permits issued: 2 (2001) / 1 (2000); Multi-family building permits issued: 0 (2001) / 0 (2000); Employment by occupation: 6.1% management, 13.3% professional, 12.6% services, 24.5% sales, 1.9% farming, 11.2% construction, 30.3% production (2000).
Income: Per capita income: $17,059 (2000); Median household income: $36,705 (2000); Poverty rate: 5.9% (2000).
Taxes: Total city taxes per capita: $100 (1997); City property taxes per capita: $25 (1997).
Education: High school graduation rate: 88.6% (2000); College graduation rate: 10.6% (2000).

School District(s)

Alexis C U School District 400 (KG-12)
2000 Enrollment: 308 309-482-3344

Housing: Homeownership rate: 84.2% (2000); Median home value: $53,600 (2000); Median rent: $283 per month (2000); Median age of housing: 60+ years (2000).
Transportation: Commute to work: 95.3% car, 0.0% public transportation, 3.0% walk, 1.7% work from home (2000); Travel time to work: 22.6% less than 15 minutes, 46.1% 15 to 30 minutes, 20.3% 30 to 45 minutes, 5.3% 45 to 60 minutes, 5.8% 60 minutes or more (2000)

BERWICK (unincorporated postal area, zip code 61417). Covers a land area of 28.943 square miles and a water area of 0 square miles. Located at 40.78° N. Lat.; 90.52° W. Long. Elevation is 710 feet.
Population: 324 (2000); Race: 100.0% White, 0.0% Black, 0.0% Asian, 0.0% American Indian and Alaska Native, 0.0% Hispanic of any race, 0.0% two or more races (2000); Density: 11.2 persons per square mile (2000); Age: 14.0% under 18, 12.2% over 64 (2000); Marriage status: 17.6% never married, 69.3% now married, 3.0% widowed, 10.1% divorced (2000); Foreign born: 0.0% (2000); Ancestry (includes multiple ancestries): 31.3% United States or American, 11.9% English, 8.8% Swedish, 6.1% Irish, 4.9% German (2000).
Economy: Employment by occupation: 23.2% management, 6.2% professional, 10.0% services, 19.9% sales, 1.4% farming, 8.5% construction, 30.8% production (2000).
Income: Per capita income: $19,834 (2000); Median household income: $40,268 (2000); Poverty rate: 3.1% (2000).
Education: High school graduation rate: 91.6% (2000); College graduation rate: 10.4% (2000).
Housing: Homeownership rate: 72.1% (2000); Median home value: $48,300 (2000); Median rent: $269 per month (2000); Median age of housing: 60+ years (2000).

Transportation: Commute to work: 86.4% car, 0.0% public transportation, 2.4% walk, 11.2% work from home (2000); Travel time to work: 31.7% less than 15 minutes, 13.1% 15 to 30 minutes, 43.7% 30 to 45 minutes, 6.0% 45 to 60 minutes, 5.5% 60 minutes or more (2000)

CAMERON (unincorporated postal area, zip code 61423). Covers a land area of 53.529 square miles and a water area of 0 square miles. Located at 40.88° N. Lat.; 90.50° W. Long. Elevation is 775 feet.
Population: 779 (2000); Race: 100.0% White, 0.0% Black, 0.0% Asian, 0.0% American Indian and Alaska Native, 2.9% Hispanic of any race, 0.0% two or more races (2000); Density: 14.6 persons per square mile (2000); Age: 26.1% under 18, 11.9% over 64 (2000); Marriage status: 19.0% never married, 74.4% now married, 2.2% widowed, 4.3% divorced (2000); Foreign born: 0.0% (2000); Ancestry (includes multiple ancestries): 23.9% United States or American, 17.7% German, 16.9% Irish, 13.9% English, 12.0% Swedish (2000).
Economy: Employment by occupation: 11.3% management, 16.9% professional, 17.3% services, 14.9% sales, 2.9% farming, 5.6% construction, 31.1% production (2000).
Income: Per capita income: $19,469 (2000); Median household income: $47,596 (2000); Poverty rate: 6.0% (2000).
Education: High school graduation rate: 85.8% (2000); College graduation rate: 10.7% (2000).
Housing: Homeownership rate: 89.0% (2000); Median home value: $75,000 (2000); Median rent: $304 per month (2000); Median age of housing: 48 years (2000).
Transportation: Commute to work: 95.8% car, 0.0% public transportation, 0.7% walk, 2.8% work from home (2000); Travel time to work: 15.3% less than 15 minutes, 59.6% 15 to 30 minutes, 7.2% 30 to 45 minutes, 0.7% 45 to 60 minutes, 17.2% 60 minutes or more (2000)

GERLAW (unincorporated postal area, zip code 61435). Covers a land area of 9.520 square miles and a water area of 0 square miles. Located at 40.97° N. Lat.; 90.54° W. Long. Elevation is 734 feet.
Population: 85 (2000); Race: 100.0% White, 0.0% Black, 0.0% Asian, 0.0% American Indian and Alaska Native, 0.0% Hispanic of any race, 0.0% two or more races (2000); Density: 8.9 persons per square mile (2000); Age: 31.6% under 18, 14.0% over 64 (2000); Marriage status: 27.9% never married, 62.8% now married, 0.0% widowed, 9.3% divorced (2000); Foreign born: 0.0% (2000); Ancestry (includes multiple ancestries): 29.8% United States or American, 26.3% English, 19.3% German, 14.0% Swedish, 5.3% Scandinavian (2000).
Economy: Employment by occupation: 33.3% management, 12.5% professional, 0.0% services, 41.7% sales, 0.0% farming, 0.0% construction, 12.5% production (2000).
Income: Per capita income: $14,618 (2000); Median household income: $29,063 (2000); Poverty rate: 7.0% (2000).
Education: High school graduation rate: 91.7% (2000); College graduation rate: 8.3% (2000).
Housing: Homeownership rate: 63.6% (2000); Median home value: $105,000 (2000); Median age of housing: 60+ years (2000).
Transportation: Commute to work: 66.7% car, 0.0% public transportation, 12.5% walk, 20.8% work from home (2000); Travel time to work: 31.6% less than 15 minutes, 68.4% 15 to 30 minutes, 0.0% 30 to 45 minutes, 0.0% 45 to 60 minutes, 0.0% 60 minutes or more (2000)

KIRKWOOD (village). Covers a land area of 0.909 square miles and a water area of 0 square miles. Located at 40.86° N. Lat.; 90.75° W. Long. Elevation is 737 feet.
Population: 794 (2000); Race: 99.7% White, 0.0% Black, 0.3% Asian, 0.0% American Indian and Alaska Native, 1.2% Hispanic of any race, 0.0% two or more races (2000); Density: 873.7 persons per square mile (2000); Age: 22.4% under 18, 13.4% over 64 (2000); Marriage status: 20.2% never married, 63.7% now married, 7.9% widowed, 8.2% divorced (2000); Foreign born: 0.5% (2000); Ancestry (includes multiple ancestries): 23.5% United States or American, 14.7% German, 11.3% Irish, 9.9% English, 5.9% Swedish (2000).
Economy: In agricultural area. Single-family building permits issued: 0 (2001) / 1 (2000); Multi-family building permits issued: 0 (2001) / 0 (2000); Employment by occupation: 6.1% management, 13.0% professional, 12.5% services, 22.4% sales, 3.8% farming, 11.5% construction, 30.8% production (2000).
Income: Per capita income: $15,040 (2000); Median household income: $34,167 (2000); Poverty rate: 3.4% (2000).
Taxes: Total city taxes per capita: $18 (1997); City property taxes per capita: $18 (1997).
Education: High school graduation rate: 85.5% (2000); College graduation rate: 7.8% (2000).
Housing: Homeownership rate: 85.8% (2000); Median home value: $47,300 (2000); Median rent: $264 per month (2000); Median age of housing: 60+ years (2000).
Transportation: Commute to work: 93.1% car, 0.0% public transportation, 0.5% walk, 1.6% work from home (2000); Travel time to work: 24.4% less than 15 minutes, 31.6% 15 to 30 minutes, 26.5% 30 to 45 minutes, 6.7% 45 to 60 minutes, 10.7% 60 minutes or more (2000)

LITTLE YORK (village). Covers a land area of 0.258 square miles and a water area of 0 square miles. Located at 41.01° N. Lat.; 90.74° W. Long. Elevation is 620 feet.
Population: 269 (2000); Race: 100.0% White, 0.0% Black, 0.0% Asian, 0.0% American Indian and Alaska Native, 0.0% Hispanic of any race, 0.0% two or more races (2000); Density: 1,043.3 persons per square mile (2000); Age: 27.8% under 18, 16.6% over 64 (2000); Marriage status: 21.9% never married, 51.9% now married, 11.4% widowed, 14.8% divorced (2000); Foreign born: 0.0% (2000); Ancestry (includes multiple ancestries): 17.3% German, 15.2% Swedish, 14.1% English, 11.9% United States or American, 10.5% Irish (2000).
Economy: In agricultural area. Employment by occupation: 8.1% management, 12.1% professional, 14.8% services, 20.8% sales, 1.3% farming, 10.1% construction, 32.9% production (2000).
Income: Per capita income: $15,121 (2000); Median household income: $29,688 (2000); Poverty rate: 14.8% (2000).
Taxes: Total city taxes per capita: $12 (1997); City property taxes per capita: $12 (1997).
Education: High school graduation rate: 79.8% (2000); College graduation rate: 5.2% (2000).
Housing: Homeownership rate: 79.3% (2000); Median home value: $38,800 (2000); Median rent: $150 per month (2000); Median age of housing: 60+ years (2000).
Transportation: Commute to work: 91.7% car, 0.0% public transportation, 1.4% walk, 6.9% work from home (2000); Travel time to work: 24.6% less than 15 minutes, 34.3% 15 to 30 minutes, 15.7% 30 to 45 minutes, 9.7% 45 to 60 minutes, 15.7% 60 minutes or more (2000)

MONMOUTH (city). Covers a land area of 4.029 square miles and a water area of 0.021 square miles. Located at 40.91° N. Lat.; 90.64° W. Long. Elevation is 770 feet.
History: Monmouth was named in remembrance of the Revolutionary War battle that took place at Monmouth, New Jersey. Monmouth was established in 1831, and grew as the seat of Warren County.
Population: 9,841 (2000); Race: 92.5% White, 2.6% Black, 0.7% Asian, 0.2% American Indian and Alaska Native, 4.8% Hispanic of any race, 2.0% two or more races (2000); Density: 2,442.3 persons per square mile (2000); Age: 23.2% under 18, 15.6% over 64 (2000); Marriage status: 27.1% never married, 52.3% now married, 9.4% widowed, 11.2% divorced (2000); Foreign born: 2.2% (2000); Ancestry (includes multiple ancestries): 16.5% German, 14.2% English, 13.0% Other groups, 11.2% United States or American, 10.7% Irish (2000).
Economy: Single-family building permits issued: 3 (2001) / 1 (2000); Multi-family building permits issued: 0 (2001) / 0 (2000); Employment by occupation: 9.6% management, 15.2% professional, 20.3% services, 25.6% sales, 0.3% farming, 6.7% construction, 22.3% production (2000).
Income: Per capita income: $15,839 (2000); Median household income: $33,641 (2000); Poverty rate: 11.1% (2000).
Taxes: Total city taxes per capita: $183 (1997); City property taxes per capita: $120 (1997).
Education: High school graduation rate: 78.1% (2000); College graduation rate: 17.6% (2000).

School District(s)

Henderson/Mercer/Warren Roe (07-12)
2000 Enrollment: 51 309-734-6822
Monmouth Unit School District 38 (PK-12)
2000 Enrollment: 1,489 309-734-4712
Warren C U School District 222 (KG-12)
2000 Enrollment: 390 309-734-9411
Yorkwood C U School District 225 (PK-12)
2000 Enrollment: 410 309-734-8514

Four-year College(s)

Monmouth College (Private, Not-for-profit, Presbyterian Church (USA))
2001 Enrollment: 1,072 309-457-2345
2001 Tuition: In-state $17,000; Out-of-state $17,000

Housing: Homeownership rate: 70.2% (2000); Median home value: $52,900 (2000); Median rent: $280 per month (2000); Median age of housing: 54 years (2000).
Hospitals: Community Medical Center (99 beds)
Newspapers: Daily Review Atlas (6 x week)
Transportation: Commute to work: 88.0% car, 0.1% public transportation, 7.4% walk, 3.5% work from home (2000); Travel time to work: 63.4% less than 15 minutes, 22.3% 15 to 30 minutes, 9.6% 30 to 45 minutes, 1.4% 45 to 60 minutes, 3.3% 60 minutes or more (2000)
Additional Information Contacts
Monmouth Area Chamber of Commerce 309-734-3181

ROSEVILLE (village). Covers a land area of 0.812 square miles and a water area of 0 square miles. Located at 40.73° N. Lat.; 90.66° W. Long. Elevation is 750 feet.
History: Roseville grew as a trading center and shipping point for oats and soy beans. The town was first called Hat Grove, referring to the shape of a particular grove of trees.
Population: 1,083 (2000); Race: 99.3% White, 0.0% Black, 0.0% Asian, 0.0% American Indian and Alaska Native, 0.0% Hispanic of any race, 0.7% two or more races (2000); Density: 1,333.3 persons per square mile (2000); Age: 23.6% under 18, 24.6% over 64 (2000); Marriage status: 16.5% never married, 58.2% now married, 15.7% widowed, 9.6% divorced (2000); Foreign born: 0.2% (2000); Ancestry (includes multiple ancestries): 22.6% German, 16.5% United States or American, 14.0% Irish, 13.8% English, 5.6% Swedish (2000).
Economy: Single-family building permits issued: 0 (2001) / 0 (2000); Multi-family building permits issued: 0 (2001) / 0 (2000); Employment by occupation: 11.0% management, 19.2% professional, 17.8% services, 21.6% sales, 1.4% farming, 8.6% construction, 20.4% production (2000).
Income: Per capita income: $16,225 (2000); Median household income: $32,031 (2000); Poverty rate: 10.8% (2000).
Taxes: Total city taxes per capita: $23 (1997); City property taxes per capita: $20 (1997).
Education: High school graduation rate: 78.6% (2000); College graduation rate: 14.5% (2000).

School District(s)

Roseville C U School District 200 (PK-12)
2000 Enrollment: 379 309-426-2157
Housing: Homeownership rate: 82.6% (2000); Median home value: $53,200 (2000); Median rent: $238 per month (2000); Median age of housing: 58 years (2000).
Newspapers: Roseville Independent (1 x week)
Transportation: Commute to work: 94.2% car, 0.0% public transportation, 3.3% walk, 2.5% work from home (2000); Travel time to work: 38.6% less than 15 minutes, 34.3% 15 to 30 minutes, 19.0% 30 to 45 minutes, 5.5% 45 to 60 minutes, 2.6% 60 minutes or more (2000)

SMITHSHIRE (unincorporated postal area, zip code 61478). Covers a land area of 36.926 square miles and a water area of 0 square miles. Located at 40.77° N. Lat.; 90.76° W. Long. Elevation is 737 feet.
Population: 337 (2000); Race: 100.0% White, 0.0% Black, 0.0% Asian, 0.0% American Indian and Alaska Native, 0.7% Hispanic of any race, 0.0% two or more races (2000); Density: 9.1 persons per square mile (2000); Age: 22.2% under 18, 18.5% over 64 (2000); Marriage status: 11.6% never married, 72.6% now married, 11.2% widowed, 4.6% divorced (2000); Foreign born: 0.7% (2000); Ancestry (includes multiple ancestries): 19.9% German, 13.2% United States or American, 12.3% English, 8.3% Irish, 6.0% Other groups (2000).
Economy: Employment by occupation: 6.9% management, 13.8% professional, 19.2% services, 27.7% sales, 3.1% farming, 6.9% construction, 22.3% production (2000).
Income: Per capita income: $19,660 (2000); Median household income: $36,250 (2000); Poverty rate: 8.9% (2000).
Education: High school graduation rate: 74.5% (2000); College graduation rate: 6.9% (2000).
Housing: Homeownership rate: 82.5% (2000); Median home value: $38,600 (2000); Median rent: $186 per month (2000); Median age of housing: 53 years (2000).
Transportation: Commute to work: 83.8% car, 0.0% public transportation, 2.3% walk, 13.8% work from home (2000); Travel time to work: 20.5% less than 15 minutes, 35.7% 15 to 30 minutes, 35.7% 30 to 45 minutes, 8.0% 45 to 60 minutes, 0.0% 60 minutes or more (2000)

Washington County

Located in southwestern Illinois; bounded on the north by the Kaskaskia River; drained by the Little Muddy River. Covers a land area of 562.60 square miles, a water area of 1.50 square miles, and is located in the Central Time Zone. The county government was organized in 1818. County seat is Nashville.

Weather Station: Nashville 4 NE — Elevation: 515 feet

	Jan	Feb	Mar	Apr	May	Jun	Jul	Aug	Sep	Oct	Nov	Dec
High	38	44	55	67	76	85	88	87	80	69	54	43
Low	21	26	35	45	55	64	68	65	58	47	37	27
Precip	2.2	2.3	3.5	3.9	4.1	3.6	3.4	2.7	3.2	3.1	3.7	3.0
Snow	5.8	4.3	1.5	0.6	0.0	0.0	0.0	0.0	0.0	tr	0.9	3.2

High and Low temperatures in degrees Fahrenheit; Precipitation and Snow in inches

Population: 15,148 (2000); Race: 98.6% White, 0.2% Black, 0.1% Asian, 0.4% American Indian and Alaska Native, 0.4% Hispanic of any race, 0.6% two or more races (2000); Density: 26.9 persons per square mile (2000); Age: 25.3% under 18, 16.7% over 64 (2000).
Religion: Five largest groups: 29.9% Catholic Church, 18.2% Lutheran Church—Missouri Synod, 15.4% United Church of Christ, 6.7% Southern Baptist Convention, 4.9% The United Methodist Church (2000).
Economy: Unemployment rate: 4.2% (11/2002); Total civilian labor force: 8,736 (11/2002); Leading industries: 32.0% manufacturing; 13.1% retail trade; 12.3% health care and social assistance (2000); Companies that employ more than 1,000 persons: 0 (2000); Companies that employ more than 100 persons: 7 (2000); Farms: 777 totaling 308,576 acres (1997); Minority business ownership rate: 0.0% (1997); Women business ownership rate: 22.5% (1997); Retail sales per capita: $10,237 (1997). Single-family building permits issued: 58 (2001) / 67 (2000); Multi-family building permits issued: 0 (2001) / 4 (2000).
Income: Per capita income: $19,108 (2000); Median household income: $40,932 (2000); Poverty rate: 6.0% (2000); Bankruptcy rate: 3.71% (2001).
Taxes: Total county taxes per capita: $110 (2000); County property taxes per capita: $104 (2000).
Education: High school graduation rate: 79.1% (2000); College graduation rate: 13.4% (2000).
Housing: Homeownership rate: 81.0% (2000); Median home value: $74,300 (2000); Median rent: $300 per month (2000); Median age of housing: 39 years (2000).
Health: Birth rate: 109.6 per 10,000 population (1998); Age adjusted death rate: 92.1 per 10,000 population (1999); Age adjusted cancer mortality rate: 161.6 deaths per 100,000 population (1999). Number of physicians: 2.0 per 10,000 population (1999); Number of hospital beds: 38.9 per 10,000 population (1999).
Elections: 2000 Presidential election results: 37.0% Gore, 61.0% Bush, 1.3% Nader, 0.5% Buchanan
National and State Parks: Washington County State Conservation Area
Additional Information Contacts
Washington County Government Offices 618-327-8314
Nashville Chamber of Commerce 618-327-3700
Okawville Chamber of Commerce 618-243-5694

Washington County Communities

ADDIEVILLE (village). Covers a land area of 1.053 square miles and a water area of 0 square miles. Located at 38.39° N. Lat.; 89.48° W. Long. Elevation is 475 feet.
Population: 267 (2000); Race: 100.0% White, 0.0% Black, 0.0% Asian, 0.0% American Indian and Alaska Native, 0.0% Hispanic of any race, 0.0% two or more races (2000); Density: 253.6 persons per square mile (2000); Age: 25.1% under 18, 12.4% over 64 (2000); Marriage status: 21.8% never married, 67.8% now married, 2.5% widowed, 7.9% divorced (2000); Foreign born: 0.0% (2000); Ancestry (includes multiple ancestries): 61.4% German, 11.2% United States or American, 6.4% Other groups, 5.2% Irish, 4.9% Polish (2000).
Economy: In agricultural area. Employment by occupation: 5.7% management, 14.9% professional, 13.5% services, 22.0% sales, 2.8% farming, 15.6% construction, 25.5% production (2000).
Income: Per capita income: $16,415 (2000); Median household income: $46,667 (2000); Poverty rate: 2.7% (2000).
Taxes: Total city taxes per capita: $34 (1997); City property taxes per capita: $31 (1997).
Education: High school graduation rate: 83.3% (2000); College graduation rate: 12.1% (2000).

Housing: Homeownership rate: 89.3% (2000); Median home value: $66,000 (2000); Median rent: $175 per month (2000); Median age of housing: 60+ years (2000).
Transportation: Commute to work: 95.8% car, 0.0% public transportation, 1.4% walk, 0.0% work from home (2000); Travel time to work: 19.6% less than 15 minutes, 27.3% 15 to 30 minutes, 14.7% 30 to 45 minutes, 20.3% 45 to 60 minutes, 18.2% 60 minutes or more (2000)

ASHLEY (city). Covers a land area of 1.107 square miles and a water area of 0.022 square miles. Located at 38.32° N. Lat.; 89.18° W. Long. Elevation is 550 feet.
History: Ashley was named for early settler John Ashley.
Population: 613 (2000); Race: 99.4% White, 0.0% Black, 0.0% Asian, 0.0% American Indian and Alaska Native, 0.0% Hispanic of any race, 0.6% two or more races (2000); Density: 553.6 persons per square mile (2000); Age: 29.3% under 18, 17.0% over 64 (2000); Marriage status: 21.7% never married, 47.7% now married, 14.8% widowed, 15.8% divorced (2000); Foreign born: 1.0% (2000); Ancestry (includes multiple ancestries): 31.1% German, 16.7% Polish, 13.9% Irish, 11.2% United States or American, 9.1% English (2000).
Economy: Single-family building permits issued: 0 (2001) / 0 (2000); Multi-family building permits issued: 0 (2001) / 0 (2000); Employment by occupation: 2.8% management, 8.0% professional, 22.3% services, 10.0% sales, 0.0% farming, 20.3% construction, 36.7% production (2000).
Income: Per capita income: $14,694 (2000); Median household income: $31,429 (2000); Poverty rate: 17.0% (2000).
Taxes: Total city taxes per capita: $65 (1997); City property taxes per capita: $61 (1997).
Education: High school graduation rate: 73.5% (2000); College graduation rate: 3.8% (2000).

School District(s)

Ashley C C School Districtrict 15 (PK-08)
2000 Enrollment: 207 618-485-6611

Housing: Homeownership rate: 73.8% (2000); Median home value: $34,500 (2000); Median rent: $271 per month (2000); Median age of housing: 55 years (2000).
Transportation: Commute to work: 93.5% car, 0.0% public transportation, 0.8% walk, 4.9% work from home (2000); Travel time to work: 14.2% less than 15 minutes, 48.5% 15 to 30 minutes, 17.6% 30 to 45 minutes, 4.7% 45 to 60 minutes, 15.0% 60 minutes or more (2000)

DU BOIS (village). Covers a land area of 1.068 square miles and a water area of 0 square miles. Located at 38.22° N. Lat.; 89.21° W. Long. Elevation is 524 feet.
Population: 222 (2000); Race: 100.0% White, 0.0% Black, 0.0% Asian, 0.0% American Indian and Alaska Native, 4.3% Hispanic of any race, 0.0% two or more races (2000); Density: 207.8 persons per square mile (2000); Age: 33.3% under 18, 17.1% over 64 (2000); Marriage status: 19.0% never married, 49.0% now married, 15.6% widowed, 16.3% divorced (2000); Foreign born: 0.0% (2000); Ancestry (includes multiple ancestries): 51.0% Polish, 15.2% German, 5.7% Other groups, 4.3% Italian, 2.9% United States or American (2000).
Economy: In agricultural area: wheat, corn, soybeans, sorghum; hogs; coal, oil. Single-family building permits issued: 0 (2001) / 0 (2000); Multi-family building permits issued: 0 (2001) / 0 (2000); Employment by occupation: 8.3% management, 4.8% professional, 21.4% services, 21.4% sales, 3.6% farming, 10.7% construction, 29.8% production (2000).
Income: Per capita income: $12,367 (2000); Median household income: $30,417 (2000); Poverty rate: 15.7% (2000).
Taxes: Total city taxes per capita: $48 (1997); City property taxes per capita: $29 (1997).
Education: High school graduation rate: 68.8% (2000); College graduation rate: 1.6% (2000).
Housing: Homeownership rate: 83.9% (2000); Median home value: $35,000 (2000); Median rent: $260 per month (2000); Median age of housing: 46 years (2000).
Transportation: Commute to work: 75.6% car, 0.0% public transportation, 12.2% walk, 7.3% work from home (2000); Travel time to work: 22.4% less than 15 minutes, 38.2% 15 to 30 minutes, 25.0% 30 to 45 minutes, 0.0% 45 to 60 minutes, 14.5% 60 minutes or more (2000)

HOYLETON (village). Covers a land area of 0.750 square miles and a water area of 0 square miles. Located at 38.44° N. Lat.; 89.27° W. Long. Elevation is 525 feet.
Population: 520 (2000); Race: 97.7% White, 1.9% Black, 0.0% Asian, 0.0% American Indian and Alaska Native, 0.0% Hispanic of any race, 0.4% two or more races (2000); Density: 692.9 persons per square mile (2000); Age: 31.1% under 18, 14.8% over 64 (2000); Marriage status: 26.1% never married, 54.7% now married, 10.9% widowed, 8.2% divorced (2000); Foreign born: 0.4% (2000); Ancestry (includes multiple ancestries): 53.6% German, 9.8% Other groups, 8.5% Irish, 6.6% United States or American, 4.0% Polish (2000).
Economy: In agricultural area. Single-family building permits issued: 0 (2001) / 0 (2000); Multi-family building permits issued: 0 (2001) / 0 (2000); Employment by occupation: 8.6% management, 13.9% professional, 16.4% services, 16.0% sales, 2.5% farming, 12.3% construction, 30.3% production (2000).
Income: Per capita income: $16,543 (2000); Median household income: $43,250 (2000); Poverty rate: 6.5% (2000).
Taxes: Total city taxes per capita: $30 (1997); City property taxes per capita: $28 (1997).
Education: High school graduation rate: 75.3% (2000); College graduation rate: 15.2% (2000).

School District(s)

Hoyleton Cons School Districtrict 29 (PK-08)
2000 Enrollment: 85 618-493-7787

Housing: Homeownership rate: 75.0% (2000); Median home value: $55,800 (2000); Median rent: $364 per month (2000); Median age of housing: 56 years (2000).
Transportation: Commute to work: 78.8% car, 6.6% public transportation, 8.7% walk, 3.7% work from home (2000); Travel time to work: 34.9% less than 15 minutes, 44.8% 15 to 30 minutes, 15.5% 30 to 45 minutes, 1.3% 45 to 60 minutes, 3.4% 60 minutes or more (2000)

IRVINGTON (village). Covers a land area of 0.838 square miles and a water area of 0 square miles. Located at 38.43° N. Lat.; 89.16° W. Long. Elevation is 530 feet.
History: Irvington was a major strawberry-producing center in the 1890's, when special trains took the produce to Chicago.
Population: 736 (2000); Race: 94.8% White, 0.3% Black, 0.9% Asian, 0.0% American Indian and Alaska Native, 0.7% Hispanic of any race, 4.0% two or more races (2000); Density: 878.6 persons per square mile (2000); Age: 30.3% under 18, 11.6% over 64 (2000); Marriage status: 21.3% never married, 59.1% now married, 6.6% widowed, 13.0% divorced (2000); Foreign born: 0.1% (2000); Ancestry (includes multiple ancestries): 39.6% German, 13.7% Irish, 10.5% Other groups, 7.2% English, 5.9% United States or American (2000).
Economy: Single-family building permits issued: 0 (2001) / 2 (2000); Multi-family building permits issued: 0 (2001) / 0 (2000); Employment by occupation: 10.3% management, 16.8% professional, 14.5% services, 20.4% sales, 0.0% farming, 10.9% construction, 27.1% production (2000).
Income: Per capita income: $16,541 (2000); Median household income: $41,875 (2000); Poverty rate: 9.0% (2000).
Taxes: Total city taxes per capita: $23 (1997); City property taxes per capita: $23 (1997).
Education: High school graduation rate: 82.7% (2000); College graduation rate: 12.1% (2000).

School District(s)

Irvington C C School Districtrict 11 (PK-08)
2000 Enrollment: 94 618-249-6439

Housing: Homeownership rate: 71.6% (2000); Median home value: $63,700 (2000); Median rent: $296 per month (2000); Median age of housing: 30 years (2000).
Transportation: Commute to work: 91.5% car, 0.0% public transportation, 2.8% walk, 4.3% work from home (2000); Travel time to work: 44.5% less than 15 minutes, 36.5% 15 to 30 minutes, 14.2% 30 to 45 minutes, 0.9% 45 to 60 minutes, 3.9% 60 minutes or more (2000)

NASHVILLE (city). Covers a land area of 2.681 square miles and a water area of 0.089 square miles. Located at 38.34° N. Lat.; 89.38° W. Long. Elevation is 530 feet.
History: Incorporated 1853.
Population: 3,147 (2000); Race: 98.6% White, 0.0% Black, 0.0% Asian, 1.0% American Indian and Alaska Native, 0.0% Hispanic of any race, 0.0% two or more races (2000); Density: 1,173.9 persons per square mile (2000); Age: 24.7% under 18, 18.2% over 64 (2000); Marriage status: 21.0% never married, 60.6% now married, 10.3% widowed, 8.1% divorced (2000); Foreign born: 0.3% (2000); Ancestry (includes multiple ancestries): 49.0% German, 15.2% Polish, 12.6% United States or American, 9.1% Irish, 8.7% English (2000).
Economy: Manufacturing: machinery. Agriculture: corn, wheat, fruit, seed; livestock, poultry. Single-family building permits issued: 9 (2001) / 9 (2000);

Multi-family building permits issued: 0 (2001) / 4 (2000); Employment by occupation: 10.4% management, 22.4% professional, 19.0% services, 23.9% sales, 0.7% farming, 7.1% construction, 16.5% production (2000).
Income: Per capita income: $21,935 (2000); Median household income: $42,097 (2000); Poverty rate: 4.4% (2000).
Taxes: Total city taxes per capita: $422 (1997); City property taxes per capita: $53 (1997).
Education: High school graduation rate: 84.8% (2000); College graduation rate: 21.8% (2000).

School District(s)

Nashville C C School Districtrict 49 (PK-08)
2000 Enrollment: 562 618-327-3055
Nashville Community H S District 99 (09-12)
2000 Enrollment: 546 618-327-8286
Housing: Homeownership rate: 72.4% (2000); Median home value: $79,900 (2000); Median rent: $337 per month (2000); Median age of housing: 44 years (2000).
Hospitals: Washington County Hospital (61 beds)
Newspapers: The Nashville News (1 x week)
Transportation: Commute to work: 91.1% car, 1.3% public transportation, 2.6% walk, 3.3% work from home (2000); Travel time to work: 63.5% less than 15 minutes, 13.0% 15 to 30 minutes, 12.3% 30 to 45 minutes, 3.4% 45 to 60 minutes, 7.9% 60 minutes or more (2000)
Additional Information Contacts
Nashville Chamber of Commerce 618-327-3700

NEW MINDEN (village). Covers a land area of 0.275 square miles and a water area of 0 square miles. Located at 38.43° N. Lat.; 89.36° W. Long. Elevation is 465 feet.
Population: 204 (2000); Race: 98.5% White, 0.0% Black, 0.0% Asian, 0.0% American Indian and Alaska Native, 0.0% Hispanic of any race, 1.5% two or more races (2000); Density: 741.8 persons per square mile (2000); Age: 25.0% under 18, 14.7% over 64 (2000); Marriage status: 16.6% never married, 62.6% now married, 13.5% widowed, 7.4% divorced (2000); Foreign born: 0.0% (2000); Ancestry (includes multiple ancestries): 50.0% German, 7.8% Polish, 5.9% Dutch, 5.9% Other groups, 4.9% English (2000).
Economy: In agricultural area: wheat, corn, soybeans; hogs, poultry. Coal; oil. Employment by occupation: 12.9% management, 8.6% professional, 19.0% services, 25.9% sales, 9.5% farming, 10.3% construction, 13.8% production (2000).
Income: Per capita income: $17,942 (2000); Median household income: $41,875 (2000); Poverty rate: 2.5% (2000).
Taxes: Total city taxes per capita: $9 (1997); City property taxes per capita: $9 (1997).
Education: High school graduation rate: 77.1% (2000); College graduation rate: 13.2% (2000).
Housing: Homeownership rate: 86.2% (2000); Median home value: $59,000 (2000); Median rent: $283 per month (2000); Median age of housing: 44 years (2000).
Transportation: Commute to work: 93.8% car, 0.0% public transportation, 3.5% walk, 1.8% work from home (2000); Travel time to work: 33.3% less than 15 minutes, 23.4% 15 to 30 minutes, 23.4% 30 to 45 minutes, 8.1% 45 to 60 minutes, 11.7% 60 minutes or more (2000)

OAKDALE (village). Covers a land area of 1.660 square miles and a water area of 0 square miles. Located at 38.26° N. Lat.; 89.50° W. Long. Elevation is 520 feet.
Population: 213 (2000); Race: 97.5% White, 0.0% Black, 0.0% Asian, 1.5% American Indian and Alaska Native, 0.0% Hispanic of any race, 1.0% two or more races (2000); Density: 128.3 persons per square mile (2000); Age: 24.4% under 18, 14.4% over 64 (2000); Marriage status: 20.0% never married, 68.1% now married, 6.9% widowed, 5.0% divorced (2000); Foreign born: 0.0% (2000); Ancestry (includes multiple ancestries): 46.3% German, 14.9% Irish, 12.4% English, 5.5% United States or American, 5.0% French (except Basque) (2000).
Economy: Employment by occupation: 8.8% management, 17.6% professional, 14.3% services, 13.2% sales, 2.2% farming, 9.9% construction, 34.1% production (2000).
Income: Per capita income: $18,651 (2000); Median household income: $40,938 (2000); Poverty rate: 3.0% (2000).
Taxes: Total city taxes per capita: $14 (1997); City property taxes per capita: $14 (1997).
Education: High school graduation rate: 86.4% (2000); College graduation rate: 10.6% (2000).

School District(s)

Oakdale C C School District 1 (KG-08)
2000 Enrollment: 75 618-329-5292
Housing: Homeownership rate: 88.2% (2000); Median home value: $52,500 (2000); Median rent: $270 per month (2000); Median age of housing: 47 years (2000).
Transportation: Commute to work: 86.8% car, 0.0% public transportation, 5.5% walk, 7.7% work from home (2000); Travel time to work: 29.8% less than 15 minutes, 38.1% 15 to 30 minutes, 7.1% 30 to 45 minutes, 9.5% 45 to 60 minutes, 15.5% 60 minutes or more (2000)

OKAWVILLE (village). Covers a land area of 2.027 square miles and a water area of 0 square miles. Located at 38.43° N. Lat.; 89.54° W. Long. Elevation is 440 feet.
Population: 1,355 (2000); Race: 97.5% White, 0.0% Black, 0.0% Asian, 0.9% American Indian and Alaska Native, 1.2% Hispanic of any race, 0.8% two or more races (2000); Density: 668.6 persons per square mile (2000); Age: 24.7% under 18, 15.7% over 64 (2000); Marriage status: 20.8% never married, 59.8% now married, 9.6% widowed, 9.8% divorced (2000); Foreign born: 1.3% (2000); Ancestry (includes multiple ancestries): 52.5% German, 9.8% Irish, 9.1% United States or American, 7.1% Other groups, 4.7% English (2000).
Economy: Health resort, with mineral springs. Single-family building permits issued: 6 (2001) / 6 (2000); Multi-family building permits issued: 0 (2001) / 0 (2000); Employment by occupation: 11.3% management, 18.4% professional, 19.1% services, 21.4% sales, 0.8% farming, 13.1% construction, 15.9% production (2000).
Income: Per capita income: $19,476 (2000); Median household income: $37,448 (2000); Poverty rate: 6.5% (2000).
Taxes: Total city taxes per capita: $66 (1997); City property taxes per capita: $50 (1997).
Education: High school graduation rate: 80.2% (2000); College graduation rate: 17.5% (2000).

School District(s)

West Washington Co C U District 10 (KG-12)
2000 Enrollment: 697 618-243-6454
Housing: Homeownership rate: 77.9% (2000); Median home value: $78,400 (2000); Median rent: $322 per month (2000); Median age of housing: 43 years (2000).
Newspapers: Okawville Times (1 x week)
Transportation: Commute to work: 94.5% car, 0.4% public transportation, 2.2% walk, 1.7% work from home (2000); Travel time to work: 36.9% less than 15 minutes, 18.4% 15 to 30 minutes, 24.0% 30 to 45 minutes, 12.0% 45 to 60 minutes, 8.7% 60 minutes or more (2000)
Additional Information Contacts
Okawville Chamber of Commerce 618-243-5694

RADOM (village). Covers a land area of 1.037 square miles and a water area of 0 square miles. Located at 38.28° N. Lat.; 89.19° W. Long. Elevation is 533 feet.
Population: 395 (2000); Race: 99.5% White, 0.0% Black, 0.0% Asian, 0.0% American Indian and Alaska Native, 1.0% Hispanic of any race, 0.0% two or more races (2000); Density: 381.0 persons per square mile (2000); Age: 16.5% under 18, 49.2% over 64 (2000); Marriage status: 25.1% never married, 41.7% now married, 32.1% widowed, 1.1% divorced (2000); Foreign born: 0.0% (2000); Ancestry (includes multiple ancestries): 38.8% Polish, 24.7% German, 12.7% Irish, 10.6% United States or American, 3.4% English (2000).
Economy: In agricultural area. Employment by occupation: 3.8% management, 4.8% professional, 13.5% services, 26.0% sales, 2.9% farming, 9.6% construction, 39.4% production (2000).
Income: Per capita income: $13,882 (2000); Median household income: $30,000 (2000); Poverty rate: 8.3% (2000).
Taxes: Total city taxes per capita: $56 (1997); City property taxes per capita: $56 (1997).
Education: High school graduation rate: 43.9% (2000); College graduation rate: 3.3% (2000).
Housing: Homeownership rate: 100.0% (2000); Median home value: $45,000 (2000); Median age of housing: 35 years (2000).
Transportation: Commute to work: 96.1% car, 0.0% public transportation, 1.9% walk, 0.0% work from home (2000); Travel time to work: 18.4% less than 15 minutes, 45.6% 15 to 30 minutes, 27.2% 30 to 45 minutes, 3.9% 45 to 60 minutes, 4.9% 60 minutes or more (2000)

RICHVIEW (village). Covers a land area of 1.112 square miles and a water area of 0 square miles. Located at 38.37° N. Lat.; 89.18° W. Long. Elevation is 540 feet.
Population: 308 (2000); Race: 100.0% White, 0.0% Black, 0.0% Asian, 0.0% American Indian and Alaska Native, 0.0% Hispanic of any race, 0.0% two or more races (2000); Density: 276.9 persons per square mile (2000); Age: 29.0% under 18, 10.3% over 64 (2000); Marriage status: 26.8% never married, 55.8% now married, 4.9% widowed, 12.5% divorced (2000); Foreign born: 0.0% (2000); Ancestry (includes multiple ancestries): 30.0% German, 14.8% United States or American, 12.3% Irish, 11.0% Polish, 9.4% English (2000).
Economy: In agricultural area. Single-family building permits issued: 1 (2001) / 0 (2000); Multi-family building permits issued: 0 (2001) / 0 (2000); Employment by occupation: 2.1% management, 15.4% professional, 22.4% services, 12.6% sales, 0.0% farming, 6.3% construction, 41.3% production (2000).
Income: Per capita income: $15,546 (2000); Median household income: $38,125 (2000); Poverty rate: 8.8% (2000).
Taxes: Total city taxes per capita: $31 (1997); City property taxes per capita: $28 (1997).
Education: High school graduation rate: 78.5% (2000); College graduation rate: 8.1% (2000).
Housing: Homeownership rate: 79.6% (2000); Median home value: $63,200 (2000); Median rent: $258 per month (2000); Median age of housing: 27 years (2000).
Transportation: Commute to work: 92.4% car, 0.0% public transportation, 2.1% walk, 3.5% work from home (2000); Travel time to work: 23.7% less than 15 minutes, 48.2% 15 to 30 minutes, 15.1% 30 to 45 minutes, 4.3% 45 to 60 minutes, 8.6% 60 minutes or more (2000)

VENEDY (village). Covers a land area of 0.286 square miles and a water area of 0 square miles. Located at 38.39° N. Lat.; 89.64° W. Long. Elevation is 460 feet.
Population: 137 (2000); Race: 97.7% White, 0.0% Black, 2.3% Asian, 0.0% American Indian and Alaska Native, 1.5% Hispanic of any race, 0.0% two or more races (2000); Density: 479.1 persons per square mile (2000); Age: 23.5% under 18, 15.2% over 64 (2000); Marriage status: 18.7% never married, 68.2% now married, 6.5% widowed, 6.5% divorced (2000); Foreign born: 0.0% (2000); Ancestry (includes multiple ancestries): 53.0% German, 20.5% Irish, 12.1% English, 6.8% United States or American, 6.8% Italian (2000).
Economy: In agricultural area: wheat, corn, soybeans, sorghum; hogs, poultry; dairying. Employment by occupation: 8.1% management, 17.6% professional, 18.9% services, 18.9% sales, 0.0% farming, 10.8% construction, 25.7% production (2000).
Income: Per capita income: $18,061 (2000); Median household income: $41,389 (2000); Poverty rate: 4.5% (2000).
Taxes: Total city taxes per capita: $31 (1997); City property taxes per capita: $25 (1997).
Education: High school graduation rate: 72.7% (2000); College graduation rate: 8.0% (2000).
Housing: Homeownership rate: 94.4% (2000); Median home value: $58,800 (2000); Median rent: $300 per month (2000); Median age of housing: 46 years (2000).
Transportation: Commute to work: 89.7% car, 7.4% public transportation, 0.0% walk, 2.9% work from home (2000); Travel time to work: 24.2% less than 15 minutes, 34.8% 15 to 30 minutes, 9.1% 30 to 45 minutes, 24.2% 45 to 60 minutes, 7.6% 60 minutes or more (2000)

Wayne County

Located in southeastern Illinois; drained by the Little Wabash River. Covers a land area of 713.90 square miles, a water area of 1.70 square miles, and is located in the Central Time Zone. The county government was organized in 1819. County seat is Fairfield.

Weather Station: Fairfield Radio WFIW — Elevation: 429 feet

	Jan	Feb	Mar	Apr	May	Jun	Jul	Aug	Sep	Oct	Nov	Dec
High	38	44	55	67	76	85	88	87	80	69	54	43
Low	21	25	34	44	53	62	66	63	56	45	36	26
Precip	2.8	2.6	4.6	4.9	4.7	4.0	3.8	3.2	2.9	3.4	4.3	3.5
Snow	5.2	3.7	2.4	0.3	0.0	0.0	0.0	0.0	0.0	tr	0.7	2.9

High and Low temperatures in degrees Fahrenheit; Precipitation and Snow in inches

Population: 17,151 (2000); Race: 98.3% White, 0.1% Black, 0.7% Asian, 0.2% American Indian and Alaska Native, 0.8% Hispanic of any race, 0.5% two or more races (2000); Density: 24.0 persons per square mile (2000); Age: 23.8% under 18, 18.8% over 64 (2000).
Religion: Five largest groups: 23.4% Southern Baptist Convention, 12.5% Christian Churches and Churches of Christ, 8.4% The United Methodist Church, 3.6% Cumberland Presbyterian Church, 1.8% National Association of Free Will Baptists (2000).
Economy: Unemployment rate: 5.7% (11/2002); Total civilian labor force: 7,570 (11/2002); Leading industries: 32.5% manufacturing; 16.6% retail trade; 15.1% health care and social assistance (2000); Companies that employ more than 1,000 persons: 1 (2000); Companies that employ more than 100 persons: 5 (2000); Farms: 972 totaling 320,773 acres (1997); Minority business ownership rate: 0.0% (1997); Women business ownership rate: 12.1% (1997); Retail sales per capita: $6,086 (1997). Single-family building permits issued: 4 (2001) / 8 (2000); Multi-family building permits issued: 0 (2001) / 46 (2000).
Income: Per capita income: $15,793 (2000); Median household income: $30,481 (2000); Poverty rate: 12.4% (2000); Bankruptcy rate: 3.57% (2001).
Taxes: Total county taxes per capita: $58 (1997); County property taxes per capita: $58 (1997).
Education: High school graduation rate: 75.2% (2000); College graduation rate: 10.0% (2000).
Housing: Homeownership rate: 79.6% (2000); Median home value: $48,600 (2000); Median rent: $218 per month (2000); Median age of housing: 38 years (2000).
Health: Birth rate: 116.0 per 10,000 population (1998); Age adjusted death rate: 102.8 per 10,000 population (1999); Age adjusted cancer mortality rate: 276.7 deaths per 100,000 population (1999). Number of physicians: 7.0 per 10,000 population (1999); Number of hospital beds: 95.0 per 10,000 population (1999).
Elections: 2000 Presidential election results: 28.7% Gore, 69.5% Bush, 1.0% Nader, 0.5% Buchanan
National and State Parks: Sam Dale Lake State Conservation Area
Additional Information Contacts
Wayne County Government Offices 618-842-5182
Fairfield Chamber of Commerce 618-842-6116

Wayne County Communities

BARNHILL (unincorporated postal area, zip code 62809). Aka Barn Hill. Covers a land area of 14.526 square miles and a water area of 0.026 square miles. Located at 38.26° N. Lat.; 88.34° W. Long. Elevation is 410 feet.
Population: 239 (2000); Race: 98.6% White, 0.0% Black, 0.0% Asian, 1.4% American Indian and Alaska Native, 2.7% Hispanic of any race, 0.0% two or more races (2000); Density: 16.5 persons per square mile (2000); Age: 22.8% under 18, 13.7% over 64 (2000); Marriage status: 11.1% never married, 72.2% now married, 4.4% widowed, 12.2% divorced (2000); Foreign born: 0.0% (2000); Ancestry (includes multiple ancestries): 27.9% United States or American, 13.2% English, 10.0% Other groups, 9.6% German, 5.5% Irish (2000).
Economy: Employment by occupation: 14.0% management, 11.4% professional, 5.3% services, 25.4% sales, 0.0% farming, 9.6% construction, 34.2% production (2000).
Income: Per capita income: $16,212 (2000); Median household income: $31,250 (2000); Poverty rate: 6.4% (2000).
Education: High school graduation rate: 80.1% (2000); College graduation rate: 8.7% (2000).
Housing: Homeownership rate: 83.7% (2000); Median home value: $33,100 (2000); Median rent: $267 per month (2000); Median age of housing: 32 years (2000).
Transportation: Commute to work: 89.1% car, 1.8% public transportation, 5.5% walk, 1.8% work from home (2000); Travel time to work: 51.9% less than 15 minutes, 26.9% 15 to 30 minutes, 5.6% 30 to 45 minutes, 10.2% 45 to 60 minutes, 5.6% 60 minutes or more (2000)

CISNE (village). Covers a land area of 0.638 square miles and a water area of 0 square miles. Located at 38.51° N. Lat.; 88.43° W. Long. Elevation is 457 feet.
Population: 673 (2000); Race: 98.5% White, 0.3% Black, 0.9% Asian, 0.0% American Indian and Alaska Native, 0.9% Hispanic of any race, 0.0% two or more races (2000); Density: 1,054.8 persons per square mile (2000); Age: 23.7% under 18, 24.0% over 64 (2000); Marriage status: 17.8% never married, 60.8% now married, 10.7% widowed, 10.7% divorced (2000); Foreign born: 0.6% (2000); Ancestry (includes multiple ancestries): 15.4%

English, 13.8% United States or American, 12.9% German, 11.5% Other groups, 6.4% Irish (2000).
Economy: In agricultural area; oil wells. Employment by occupation: 7.7% management, 17.9% professional, 19.0% services, 20.4% sales, 1.8% farming, 9.5% construction, 23.7% production (2000).
Income: Per capita income: $14,044 (2000); Median household income: $26,172 (2000); Poverty rate: 15.5% (2000).
Taxes: Total city taxes per capita: $18 (1997); City property taxes per capita: $14 (1997).
Education: High school graduation rate: 69.5% (2000); College graduation rate: 11.4% (2000).

School District(s)

North Wayne C U School District 200 (PK-12)
2000 Enrollment: 476 618-673-2151

Housing: Homeownership rate: 81.2% (2000); Median home value: $38,900 (2000); Median rent: $211 per month (2000); Median age of housing: 44 years (2000).
Transportation: Commute to work: 95.6% car, 0.4% public transportation, 1.8% walk, 1.8% work from home (2000); Travel time to work: 27.3% less than 15 minutes, 45.3% 15 to 30 minutes, 17.2% 30 to 45 minutes, 4.1% 45 to 60 minutes, 6.0% 60 minutes or more (2000)

FAIRFIELD (city). Aka Thomas Prairie. Covers a land area of 3.616 square miles and a water area of 0.034 square miles. Located at 38.38° N. Lat.; 88.36° W. Long. Elevation is 441 feet.
History: Fairfield was established in 1819, and developed as the seat of Wayne County. Clothing and automobile parts manufacturing were early industries.
Population: 5,421 (2000); Race: 97.0% White, 0.1% Black, 1.8% Asian, 0.3% American Indian and Alaska Native, 1.3% Hispanic of any race, 0.7% two or more races (2000); Density: 1,499.0 persons per square mile (2000); Age: 20.3% under 18, 25.3% over 64 (2000); Marriage status: 15.4% never married, 57.4% now married, 14.2% widowed, 13.0% divorced (2000); Foreign born: 2.3% (2000); Ancestry (includes multiple ancestries): 20.2% United States or American, 14.6% German, 14.3% English, 10.3% Other groups, 8.2% Irish (2000).
Economy: Single-family building permits issued: 4 (2001) / 8 (2000); Multi-family building permits issued: 0 (2001) / 46 (2000); Employment by occupation: 6.3% management, 16.4% professional, 15.4% services, 26.3% sales, 0.6% farming, 8.1% construction, 27.0% production (2000).
Income: Per capita income: $16,791 (2000); Median household income: $25,797 (2000); Poverty rate: 13.1% (2000).
Taxes: Total city taxes per capita: $339 (1997); City property taxes per capita: $140 (1997).
Education: High school graduation rate: 73.8% (2000); College graduation rate: 11.7% (2000).

School District(s)

Fairfield Community H S District 225 (09-12)
2000 Enrollment: 514 618-842-2649
Fairfield Public School District 112 (PK-08)
2000 Enrollment: 617 618-842-6501
Jasper Community Cons School District 17 (KG-08)
2000 Enrollment: 151 618-842-3048
Merriam Community Cons School District 19 (KG-08)
2000 Enrollment: 124 618-842-3101
New Hope C C School District 6 (KG-08)
2000 Enrollment: 186 618-842-3296

Two-year College(s)

Illinois Eastern Community College-Frontier Community College (Public)
2001 Enrollment: 1,913 618-393-2982
2001 Tuition: In-state $5,618; Out-of-state $6,961

Housing: Homeownership rate: 68.6% (2000); Median home value: $46,300 (2000); Median rent: $217 per month (2000); Median age of housing: 47 years (2000).
Hospitals: Fairfield Memorial Hospital (80 beds)
Newspapers: Wayne County Press (2 x week)
Transportation: Commute to work: 93.3% car, 0.6% public transportation, 4.1% walk, 1.3% work from home (2000); Travel time to work: 71.2% less than 15 minutes, 10.2% 15 to 30 minutes, 12.3% 30 to 45 minutes, 3.4% 45 to 60 minutes, 2.8% 60 minutes or more (2000)
Airports: Fairfield Municipal
Additional Information Contacts
Fairfield Chamber of Commerce 618-842-6116

GEFF (unincorporated postal area, zip code 62842). Aka Jeffersonville. Covers a land area of 41.983 square miles and a water area of 0.010 square miles. Located at 38.44° N. Lat.; 88.41° W. Long. Elevation is 457 feet.
Population: 840 (2000); Race: 97.6% White, 0.0% Black, 0.0% Asian, 0.0% American Indian and Alaska Native, 2.3% Hispanic of any race, 1.5% two or more races (2000); Density: 20.0 persons per square mile (2000); Age: 25.7% under 18, 18.4% over 64 (2000); Marriage status: 18.2% never married, 65.1% now married, 9.0% widowed, 7.6% divorced (2000); Foreign born: 0.2% (2000); Ancestry (includes multiple ancestries): 16.4% Other groups, 16.0% United States or American, 12.6% German, 10.3% English, 7.4% Irish (2000).
Economy: Employment by occupation: 15.8% management, 7.0% professional, 16.8% services, 14.2% sales, 4.8% farming, 8.6% construction, 32.9% production (2000).
Income: Per capita income: $14,504 (2000); Median household income: $30,040 (2000); Poverty rate: 10.9% (2000).
Education: High school graduation rate: 74.5% (2000); College graduation rate: 8.2% (2000).

School District(s)

Geff C C School District 14 (KG-08)
2000 Enrollment: 120 618-897-2465

Housing: Homeownership rate: 85.3% (2000); Median home value: $39,800 (2000); Median rent: $252 per month (2000); Median age of housing: 34 years (2000).
Transportation: Commute to work: 93.0% car, 0.0% public transportation, 0.0% walk, 6.5% work from home (2000); Travel time to work: 35.9% less than 15 minutes, 35.7% 15 to 30 minutes, 19.4% 30 to 45 minutes, 4.9% 45 to 60 minutes, 4.1% 60 minutes or more (2000)

GOLDEN GATE (village). Aka Goldengate. Covers a land area of 0.077 square miles and a water area of 0 square miles. Located at 38.35° N. Lat.; 88.20° W. Long. Elevation is 400 feet.
Population: 100 (2000); Race: 97.6% White, 0.0% Black, 0.0% Asian, 0.0% American Indian and Alaska Native, 6.4% Hispanic of any race, 0.0% two or more races (2000); Density: 1,306.6 persons per square mile (2000); Age: 28.0% under 18, 11.2% over 64 (2000); Marriage status: 20.0% never married, 63.2% now married, 4.2% widowed, 12.6% divorced (2000); Foreign born: 0.0% (2000); Ancestry (includes multiple ancestries): 16.8% United States or American, 13.6% Other groups, 12.8% German, 11.2% Irish, 7.2% English (2000).
Economy: In agricultural area. Employment by occupation: 13.2% management, 5.7% professional, 7.5% services, 15.1% sales, 7.5% farming, 5.7% construction, 45.3% production (2000).
Income: Per capita income: $10,214 (2000); Median household income: $21,250 (2000); Poverty rate: 19.2% (2000).
Taxes: Total city taxes per capita: $42 (1997); City property taxes per capita: $42 (1997).
Education: High school graduation rate: 75.6% (2000); College graduation rate: 2.6% (2000).
Housing: Homeownership rate: 91.3% (2000); Median home value: $19,400 (2000); Median rent: $225 per month (2000); Median age of housing: 29 years (2000).
Transportation: Commute to work: 94.3% car, 0.0% public transportation, 5.7% walk, 0.0% work from home (2000); Travel time to work: 3.8% less than 15 minutes, 60.4% 15 to 30 minutes, 15.1% 30 to 45 minutes, 17.0% 45 to 60 minutes, 3.8% 60 minutes or more (2000)

JEFFERSONVILLE (village). Aka Geff. Covers a land area of 1.020 square miles and a water area of 0 square miles. Located at 38.44° N. Lat.; 88.40° W. Long.
History: Also known as Geff.
Population: 366 (2000); Race: 96.4% White, 0.0% Black, 0.0% Asian, 0.0% American Indian and Alaska Native, 4.9% Hispanic of any race, 1.5% two or more races (2000); Density: 358.8 persons per square mile (2000); Age: 30.2% under 18, 14.6% over 64 (2000); Marriage status: 19.4% never married, 56.1% now married, 12.5% widowed, 12.1% divorced (2000); Foreign born: 0.0% (2000); Ancestry (includes multiple ancestries): 19.4% German, 17.6% United States or American, 17.4% Other groups, 9.0% Irish, 8.2% English (2000).
Economy: In agricultural area. Employment by occupation: 6.3% management, 12.0% professional, 22.2% services, 22.8% sales, 0.0% farming, 6.3% construction, 30.4% production (2000).
Income: Per capita income: $11,882 (2000); Median household income: $25,521 (2000); Poverty rate: 19.7% (2000).

Taxes: Total city taxes per capita: $9 (1997); City property taxes per capita: $9 (1997).
Education: High school graduation rate: 77.4% (2000); College graduation rate: 6.3% (2000).
Housing: Homeownership rate: 82.7% (2000); Median home value: $30,200 (2000); Median rent: $238 per month (2000); Median age of housing: 32 years (2000).
Transportation: Commute to work: 95.6% car, 0.0% public transportation, 0.0% walk, 4.4% work from home (2000); Travel time to work: 43.0% less than 15 minutes, 35.1% 15 to 30 minutes, 15.9% 30 to 45 minutes, 0.0% 45 to 60 minutes, 6.0% 60 minutes or more (2000)

JOHNSONVILLE (village). Covers a land area of 0.212 square miles and a water area of 0 square miles. Located at 38.52° N. Lat.; 88.53° W. Long. Elevation is 548 feet.
Population: 69 (2000); Race: 100.0% White, 0.0% Black, 0.0% Asian, 0.0% American Indian and Alaska Native, 0.0% Hispanic of any race, 0.0% two or more races (2000); Density: 325.9 persons per square mile (2000); Age: 22.4% under 18, 10.5% over 64 (2000); Marriage status: 24.6% never married, 59.0% now married, 4.9% widowed, 11.5% divorced (2000); Foreign born: 0.0% (2000); Ancestry (includes multiple ancestries): 26.3% German, 23.7% Other groups, 18.4% Irish, 10.5% English, 6.6% United States or American (2000).
Economy: In agricultural area; oil wells. Employment by occupation: 4.2% management, 14.6% professional, 6.3% services, 18.8% sales, 6.3% farming, 2.1% construction, 47.9% production (2000).
Income: Per capita income: $15,411 (2000); Median household income: $45,000 (2000); Poverty rate: 0.0% (2000).
Taxes: Total city taxes per capita: $30 (1997); City property taxes per capita: $15 (1997).
Education: High school graduation rate: 80.0% (2000); College graduation rate: 12.0% (2000).
Housing: Homeownership rate: 96.4% (2000); Median home value: $31,300 (2000); Median rent: $175 per month (2000); Median age of housing: 52 years (2000).
Transportation: Commute to work: 93.3% car, 0.0% public transportation, 0.0% walk, 0.0% work from home (2000); Travel time to work: 6.7% less than 15 minutes, 48.9% 15 to 30 minutes, 33.3% 30 to 45 minutes, 0.0% 45 to 60 minutes, 11.1% 60 minutes or more (2000)

KEENES (village). Covers a land area of 0.130 square miles and a water area of 0 square miles. Located at 38.33° N. Lat.; 88.64° W. Long. Elevation is 450 feet.
Population: 99 (2000); Race: 100.0% White, 0.0% Black, 0.0% Asian, 0.0% American Indian and Alaska Native, 0.0% Hispanic of any race, 0.0% two or more races (2000); Density: 762.2 persons per square mile (2000); Age: 30.9% under 18, 12.8% over 64 (2000); Marriage status: 13.2% never married, 63.2% now married, 4.4% widowed, 19.1% divorced (2000); Foreign born: 0.0% (2000); Ancestry (includes multiple ancestries): 16.0% United States or American, 14.9% English, 4.3% French (except Basque), 4.3% Other groups, 2.1% Scottish (2000).
Economy: Employment by occupation: 0.0% management, 0.0% professional, 36.6% services, 19.5% sales, 4.9% farming, 4.9% construction, 34.1% production (2000).
Income: Per capita income: $9,034 (2000); Median household income: $16,875 (2000); Poverty rate: 40.4% (2000).
Education: High school graduation rate: 66.7% (2000); College graduation rate: 1.9% (2000).
Housing: Homeownership rate: 95.0% (2000); Median home value: $27,500 (2000); Median age of housing: 34 years (2000).
Transportation: Commute to work: 82.9% car, 4.9% public transportation, 0.0% walk, 0.0% work from home (2000); Travel time to work: 48.8% less than 15 minutes, 17.1% 15 to 30 minutes, 12.2% 30 to 45 minutes, 17.1% 45 to 60 minutes, 4.9% 60 minutes or more (2000)

MOUNT ERIE (village). Covers a land area of 0.389 square miles and a water area of 0 square miles. Located at 38.51° N. Lat.; 88.23° W. Long. Elevation is 515 feet.
Population: 105 (2000); Race: 98.0% White, 0.0% Black, 0.0% Asian, 2.0% American Indian and Alaska Native, 2.0% Hispanic of any race, 0.0% two or more races (2000); Density: 269.7 persons per square mile (2000); Age: 27.3% under 18, 24.2% over 64 (2000); Marriage status: 5.6% never married, 77.8% now married, 12.5% widowed, 4.2% divorced (2000); Foreign born: 2.0% (2000); Ancestry (includes multiple ancestries): 20.2% United States or American, 10.1% English, 7.1% Irish, 6.1% German, 2.0% Norwegian (2000).
Economy: In agricultural area. Employment by occupation: 12.5% management, 9.4% professional, 15.6% services, 21.9% sales, 0.0% farming, 0.0% construction, 40.6% production (2000).
Income: Per capita income: $10,532 (2000); Median household income: $23,750 (2000); Poverty rate: 19.2% (2000).
Taxes: Total city taxes per capita: $15 (1997); City property taxes per capita: $15 (1997).
Education: High school graduation rate: 65.6% (2000); College graduation rate: 6.6% (2000).
Housing: Homeownership rate: 69.6% (2000); Median home value: $28,800 (2000); Median rent: $210 per month (2000); Median age of housing: 37 years (2000).
Transportation: Commute to work: 96.6% car, 0.0% public transportation, 0.0% walk, 3.4% work from home (2000); Travel time to work: 7.1% less than 15 minutes, 28.6% 15 to 30 minutes, 32.1% 30 to 45 minutes, 10.7% 45 to 60 minutes, 21.4% 60 minutes or more (2000)

RINARD (unincorporated postal area, zip code 62878). Covers a land area of 44.117 square miles and a water area of 0.011 square miles. Located at 38.57° N. Lat.; 88.49° W. Long. Elevation is 458 feet.
Population: 463 (2000); Race: 100.0% White, 0.0% Black, 0.0% Asian, 0.0% American Indian and Alaska Native, 0.0% Hispanic of any race, 0.0% two or more races (2000); Density: 10.5 persons per square mile (2000); Age: 21.2% under 18, 20.8% over 64 (2000); Marriage status: 12.5% never married, 63.7% now married, 11.0% widowed, 12.8% divorced (2000); Foreign born: 0.0% (2000); Ancestry (includes multiple ancestries): 18.6% United States or American, 14.1% German, 4.3% English, 4.1% Other groups, 3.8% Irish (2000).
Economy: Employment by occupation: 14.1% management, 22.4% professional, 13.5% services, 5.7% sales, 0.0% farming, 10.4% construction, 33.9% production (2000).
Income: Per capita income: $16,474 (2000); Median household income: $33,000 (2000); Poverty rate: 7.4% (2000).
Education: High school graduation rate: 65.6% (2000); College graduation rate: 11.8% (2000).
Housing: Homeownership rate: 85.1% (2000); Median home value: $36,100 (2000); Median rent: $196 per month (2000); Median age of housing: 42 years (2000).
Transportation: Commute to work: 92.0% car, 2.1% public transportation, 0.0% walk, 5.9% work from home (2000); Travel time to work: 14.2% less than 15 minutes, 45.5% 15 to 30 minutes, 27.3% 30 to 45 minutes, 5.1% 45 to 60 minutes, 8.0% 60 minutes or more (2000)

SIMS (village). Covers a land area of 1.200 square miles and a water area of 0 square miles. Located at 38.36° N. Lat.; 88.53° W. Long. Elevation is 415 feet.
Population: 273 (2000); Race: 100.0% White, 0.0% Black, 0.0% Asian, 0.0% American Indian and Alaska Native, 0.0% Hispanic of any race, 0.0% two or more races (2000); Density: 227.5 persons per square mile (2000); Age: 28.4% under 18, 9.6% over 64 (2000); Marriage status: 24.7% never married, 51.0% now married, 8.6% widowed, 15.7% divorced (2000); Foreign born: 0.8% (2000); Ancestry (includes multiple ancestries): 19.5% United States or American, 10.0% Irish, 8.8% German, 7.7% English, 5.0% Canadian (2000).
Economy: In agricultural area; oil wells. Employment by occupation: 1.0% management, 3.8% professional, 21.2% services, 13.5% sales, 0.0% farming, 20.2% construction, 40.4% production (2000).
Income: Per capita income: $10,870 (2000); Median household income: $22,083 (2000); Poverty rate: 31.0% (2000).
Taxes: Total city taxes per capita: $12 (1997); City property taxes per capita: $12 (1997).
Education: High school graduation rate: 69.6% (2000); College graduation rate: 1.2% (2000).
Housing: Homeownership rate: 78.4% (2000); Median home value: $25,000 (2000); Median rent: $244 per month (2000); Median age of housing: 46 years (2000).
Transportation: Commute to work: 96.1% car, 0.0% public transportation, 0.0% walk, 2.0% work from home (2000); Travel time to work: 18.0% less than 15 minutes, 36.0% 15 to 30 minutes, 30.0% 30 to 45 minutes, 15.0% 45 to 60 minutes, 1.0% 60 minutes or more (2000)

WAYNE CITY (village). Covers a land area of 1.677 square miles and a water area of 0 square miles. Located at 38.34° N. Lat.; 88.59° W. Long. Elevation is 437 feet.
Population: 1,089 (2000); Race: 98.3% White, 0.0% Black, 0.0% Asian, 1.1% American Indian and Alaska Native, 0.8% Hispanic of any race, 0.6%

two or more races (2000); Density: 649.3 persons per square mile (2000); Age: 29.0% under 18, 21.1% over 64 (2000); Marriage status: 18.3% never married, 56.8% now married, 13.0% widowed, 11.8% divorced (2000); Foreign born: 0.3% (2000); Ancestry (includes multiple ancestries): 26.8% United States or American, 11.5% English, 9.7% German, 4.9% Other groups, 4.5% Irish (2000).
Economy: In agricultural area. Employment by occupation: 8.7% management, 18.7% professional, 11.4% services, 16.4% sales, 0.7% farming, 10.7% construction, 33.5% production (2000).
Income: Per capita income: $13,333 (2000); Median household income: $27,009 (2000); Poverty rate: 18.4% (2000).
Taxes: Total city taxes per capita: $26 (1997); City property taxes per capita: $26 (1997).
Education: High school graduation rate: 69.7% (2000); College graduation rate: 9.2% (2000).

School District(s)

Wayne City C U School District 100 (PK-12)
2000 Enrollment: 684 618-895-3103
Housing: Homeownership rate: 74.8% (2000); Median home value: $49,400 (2000); Median rent: $229 per month (2000); Median age of housing: 28 years (2000).
Transportation: Commute to work: 95.4% car, 0.0% public transportation, 2.1% walk, 2.1% work from home (2000); Travel time to work: 30.0% less than 15 minutes, 37.8% 15 to 30 minutes, 24.4% 30 to 45 minutes, 3.3% 45 to 60 minutes, 4.5% 60 minutes or more (2000)

White County

Located in southeastern Illinois; bounded on the east by the Wabash River and the Indiana border; drained by the Little Wabash River. Covers a land area of 494.90 square miles, a water area of 6.80 square miles, and is located in the Central Time Zone. The county government was organized in 1815. County seat is Carmi.

Weather Station: Fulton Lock & Dam 13 — Elevation: 590 feet

	Jan	Feb	Mar	Apr	May	Jun	Jul	Aug	Sep	Oct	Nov	Dec
High	28	33	45	59	71	80	84	82	74	63	47	33
Low	11	16	27	39	51	60	64	62	54	42	30	18
Precip	1.3	1.2	2.4	3.4	3.9	4.2	3.4	4.5	3.3	2.7	2.7	1.8
Snow	6.4	3.8	2.0	0.8	0.0	0.0	0.0	0.0	0.0	tr	0.9	3.8

High and Low temperatures in degrees Fahrenheit; Precipitation and Snow in inches

Weather Station: Morrison — Elevation: 600 feet

	Jan	Feb	Mar	Apr	May	Jun	Jul	Aug	Sep	Oct	Nov	Dec
High	29	34	47	61	73	82	85	83	76	64	48	34
Low	10	15	27	38	49	58	62	60	51	39	29	17
Precip	1.5	1.4	2.8	3.7	4.7	4.2	3.8	4.8	3.1	2.9	2.9	2.1
Snow	10.7	6.8	4.6	1.4	0.0	0.0	0.0	0.0	0.0	tr	2.2	8.3

High and Low temperatures in degrees Fahrenheit; Precipitation and Snow in inches

Population: 15,371 (2000); Race: 98.3% White, 0.3% Black, 0.1% Asian, 0.3% American Indian and Alaska Native, 0.2% Hispanic of any race, 1.1% two or more races (2000); Density: 31.1 persons per square mile (2000); Age: 21.5% under 18, 20.9% over 64 (2000).
Religion: Five largest groups: 17.6% Southern Baptist Convention, 12.9% Christian Churches and Churches of Christ, 10.6% The United Methodist Church, 5.4% Catholic Church, 2.9% Independent, Charismatic Churches (2000).
Economy: Unemployment rate: 5.0% (11/2002); Total civilian labor force: 7,472 (11/2002); Leading industries: 19.6% retail trade; 17.5% health care and social assistance; 11.9% manufacturing (2000); Companies that employ more than 1,000 persons: 0 (2000); Companies that employ more than 100 persons: 7 (2000); Farms: 432 totaling 256,393 acres (1997); Minority business ownership rate: 0.0% (1997); Women business ownership rate: 24.8% (1997); Retail sales per capita: $6,993 (1997). Single-family building permits issued: 1 (2001) / 2 (2000); Multi-family building permits issued: 0 (2001) / 0 (2000).
Income: Per capita income: $16,412 (2000); Median household income: $29,601 (2000); Poverty rate: 12.5% (2000); Bankruptcy rate: 6.02% (2001).
Taxes: Total county taxes per capita: $59 (1997); County property taxes per capita: $54 (1997).
Education: High school graduation rate: 74.6% (2000); College graduation rate: 10.4% (2000).
Housing: Homeownership rate: 78.0% (2000); Median home value: $43,100 (2000); Median rent: $210 per month (2000); Median age of housing: 42 years (2000).
Health: Birth rate: 96.3 per 10,000 population (1998); Age adjusted death rate: 100.7 per 10,000 population (1999); Age adjusted cancer mortality rate: 255.8 deaths per 100,000 population (1999). Number of physicians: 6.5 per 10,000 population (1999); Number of hospital beds: 72.9 per 10,000 population (1999).
Elections: 2000 Presidential election results: 38.7% Gore, 59.2% Bush, 1.5% Nader, 0.5% Buchanan

Additional Information Contacts

White County Government Offices 618-382-7211
Carmi Chamber of Commerce 618-382-7606
Grayville Chamber of Commerce 618-375-7518

White County Communities

BURNT PRAIRIE (village). Aka Liberty. Covers a land area of 0.080 square miles and a water area of 0 square miles. Located at 38.25° N. Lat.; 88.25° W. Long. Elevation is 450 feet.
Population: 58 (2000); Race: 95.7% White, 0.0% Black, 0.0% Asian, 0.0% American Indian and Alaska Native, 0.0% Hispanic of any race, 4.3% two or more races (2000); Density: 728.3 persons per square mile (2000); Age: 4.3% under 18, 26.1% over 64 (2000); Marriage status: 25.0% never married, 52.3% now married, 13.6% widowed, 9.1% divorced (2000); Foreign born: 0.0% (2000); Ancestry (includes multiple ancestries): 21.7% German, 19.6% United States or American, 17.4% English, 4.3% Austrian, 4.3% Scotch-Irish (2000).
Economy: Employment by occupation: 0.0% management, 9.1% professional, 27.3% services, 18.2% sales, 0.0% farming, 18.2% construction, 27.3% production (2000).
Income: Per capita income: $14,572 (2000); Median household income: $18,125 (2000); Poverty rate: 28.3% (2000).
Taxes: Total city taxes per capita: $14 (1997); City property taxes per capita: $14 (1997).
Education: High school graduation rate: 66.7% (2000); College graduation rate: 6.1% (2000).
Housing: Homeownership rate: 59.4% (2000); Median home value: $14,200 (2000); Median rent: $142 per month (2000); Median age of housing: 55 years (2000).
Transportation: Commute to work: 75.0% car, 0.0% public transportation, 10.0% walk, 0.0% work from home (2000); Travel time to work: 30.0% less than 15 minutes, 30.0% 15 to 30 minutes, 25.0% 30 to 45 minutes, 0.0% 45 to 60 minutes, 15.0% 60 minutes or more (2000)

CARMI (city). Covers a land area of 2.478 square miles and a water area of 0.034 square miles. Located at 38.08° N. Lat.; 88.16° W. Long. Elevation is 383 feet.
History: Carmi, platted in 1816, developed as the seat of White County.
Population: 5,422 (2000); Race: 97.8% White, 0.8% Black, 0.0% Asian, 0.3% American Indian and Alaska Native, 0.1% Hispanic of any race, 1.0% two or more races (2000); Density: 2,187.7 persons per square mile (2000); Age: 20.0% under 18, 25.6% over 64 (2000); Marriage status: 16.2% never married, 59.2% now married, 12.2% widowed, 12.4% divorced (2000); Foreign born: 0.2% (2000); Ancestry (includes multiple ancestries): 16.7% German, 12.0% English, 11.6% United States or American, 11.6% Irish, 7.9% Other groups (2000).
Economy: Employment by occupation: 6.5% management, 14.0% professional, 23.9% services, 22.4% sales, 1.4% farming, 12.5% construction, 19.3% production (2000).
Income: Per capita income: $15,886 (2000); Median household income: $25,667 (2000); Poverty rate: 15.1% (2000).
Taxes: Total city taxes per capita: $298 (1997); City property taxes per capita: $22 (1997).
Education: High school graduation rate: 71.5% (2000); College graduation rate: 10.5% (2000).

School District(s)

Carmi-White County C U S District 5 (PK-12)
2000 Enrollment: 1,603 618-382-2341
Housing: Homeownership rate: 69.7% (2000); Median home value: $44,200 (2000); Median rent: $233 per month (2000); Median age of housing: 44 years (2000).
Hospitals: White County Medical Center (49 beds)
Newspapers: Times (5 x week); The Shopper News (1 x week)
Transportation: Commute to work: 93.7% car, 1.0% public transportation, 2.4% walk, 1.9% work from home (2000); Travel time to work: 57.0% less than 15 minutes, 17.4% 15 to 30 minutes, 8.5% 30 to 45 minutes, 6.2% 45 to 60 minutes, 10.9% 60 minutes or more (2000)

Additional Information Contacts
Carmi Chamber of Commerce 618-382-7606

CROSSVILLE (village). Covers a land area of 0.642 square miles and a water area of 0 square miles. Located at 38.16° N. Lat.; 88.06° W. Long. Elevation is 395 feet.
Population: 782 (2000); Race: 97.3% White, 0.0% Black, 0.0% Asian, 0.0% American Indian and Alaska Native, 0.0% Hispanic of any race, 2.7% two or more races (2000); Density: 1,217.1 persons per square mile (2000); Age: 26.1% under 18, 22.5% over 64 (2000); Marriage status: 14.9% never married, 65.7% now married, 12.3% widowed, 7.1% divorced (2000); Foreign born: 0.7% (2000); Ancestry (includes multiple ancestries): 17.4% United States or American, 16.9% German, 11.4% English, 9.7% Irish, 8.7% Other groups (2000).
Economy: Agriculture: corn, wheat; livestock. Single-family building permits issued: 0 (2001) / 0 (2000); Multi-family building permits issued: 0 (2001) / 0 (2000); Employment by occupation: 7.0% management, 15.2% professional, 21.6% services, 13.1% sales, 1.5% farming, 11.6% construction, 30.1% production (2000).
Income: Per capita income: $14,835 (2000); Median household income: $31,202 (2000); Poverty rate: 16.4% (2000).
Taxes: Total city taxes per capita: $107 (1997); City property taxes per capita: $60 (1997).
Education: High school graduation rate: 68.5% (2000); College graduation rate: 6.3% (2000).
Housing: Homeownership rate: 80.6% (2000); Median home value: $39,500 (2000); Median rent: $219 per month (2000); Median age of housing: 43 years (2000).
Transportation: Commute to work: 93.6% car, 0.0% public transportation, 3.0% walk, 2.1% work from home (2000); Travel time to work: 33.5% less than 15 minutes, 32.0% 15 to 30 minutes, 16.5% 30 to 45 minutes, 10.2% 45 to 60 minutes, 7.8% 60 minutes or more (2000)

ENFIELD (village). Covers a land area of 1.160 square miles and a water area of 0 square miles. Located at 38.09° N. Lat.; 88.34° W. Long. Elevation is 470 feet.
History: Enfield was settled in 1813.
Population: 625 (2000); Race: 100.0% White, 0.0% Black, 0.0% Asian, 0.0% American Indian and Alaska Native, 0.0% Hispanic of any race, 0.0% two or more races (2000); Density: 538.8 persons per square mile (2000); Age: 23.5% under 18, 22.2% over 64 (2000); Marriage status: 22.2% never married, 52.2% now married, 14.7% widowed, 10.8% divorced (2000); Foreign born: 0.0% (2000); Ancestry (includes multiple ancestries): 14.2% United States or American, 10.3% German, 4.6% English, 4.2% Irish, 3.2% Other groups (2000).
Economy: Employment by occupation: 5.1% management, 13.9% professional, 17.7% services, 13.9% sales, 0.8% farming, 18.6% construction, 30.0% production (2000).
Income: Per capita income: $13,455 (2000); Median household income: $23,750 (2000); Poverty rate: 24.7% (2000).
Taxes: Total city taxes per capita: $55 (1997); City property taxes per capita: $55 (1997).
Education: High school graduation rate: 62.6% (2000); College graduation rate: 6.8% (2000).
Housing: Homeownership rate: 80.6% (2000); Median home value: $28,700 (2000); Median rent: $155 per month (2000); Median age of housing: 42 years (2000).
Transportation: Commute to work: 95.4% car, 0.8% public transportation, 2.1% walk, 1.7% work from home (2000); Travel time to work: 38.6% less than 15 minutes, 28.8% 15 to 30 minutes, 5.2% 30 to 45 minutes, 13.3% 45 to 60 minutes, 14.2% 60 minutes or more (2000)

GRAYVILLE (city). Covers a land area of 1.489 square miles and a water area of 0.043 square miles. Located at 38.25° N. Lat.; 87.99° W. Long.
Population: 1,725 (2000); Race: 99.4% White, 0.0% Black, 0.0% Asian, 0.0% American Indian and Alaska Native, 0.5% Hispanic of any race, 0.2% two or more races (2000); Density: 1,158.2 persons per square mile (2000); Age: 23.0% under 18, 19.8% over 64 (2000); Marriage status: 21.2% never married, 55.6% now married, 11.2% widowed, 12.0% divorced (2000); Foreign born: 0.4% (2000); Ancestry (includes multiple ancestries): 20.8% United States or American, 13.9% English, 12.6% German, 10.4% Other groups, 8.7% Irish (2000).
Economy: Single-family building permits issued: 1 (2001) / 2 (2000); Multi-family building permits issued: 0 (2001) / 0 (2000); Employment by occupation: 7.1% management, 10.1% professional, 19.6% services, 23.9% sales, 0.4% farming, 12.5% construction, 26.3% production (2000).
Income: Per capita income: $14,318 (2000); Median household income: $30,000 (2000); Poverty rate: 13.3% (2000).
Taxes: Total city taxes per capita: $199 (1997); City property taxes per capita: $113 (1997).
Education: High school graduation rate: 77.4% (2000); College graduation rate: 5.8% (2000).

School District(s)
Grayville C U School District 1 (PK-12)
2000 Enrollment: 351 618-375-6521

Housing: Homeownership rate: 70.6% (2000); Median home value: $37,100 (2000); Median rent: $185 per month (2000); Median age of housing: 48 years (2000).
Transportation: Commute to work: 92.9% car, 0.0% public transportation, 3.4% walk, 2.4% work from home (2000); Travel time to work: 47.1% less than 15 minutes, 21.0% 15 to 30 minutes, 16.1% 30 to 45 minutes, 9.7% 45 to 60 minutes, 6.1% 60 minutes or more (2000)

Additional Information Contacts
Grayville Chamber of Commerce 618-375-7518

MAUNIE (village). Covers a land area of 0.161 square miles and a water area of 0 square miles. Located at 38.03° N. Lat.; 88.04° W. Long. Elevation is 374 feet.
Population: 177 (2000); Race: 90.3% White, 1.6% Black, 1.1% Asian, 0.0% American Indian and Alaska Native, 0.0% Hispanic of any race, 7.0% two or more races (2000); Density: 1,096.2 persons per square mile (2000); Age: 16.2% under 18, 16.2% over 64 (2000); Marriage status: 19.4% never married, 49.0% now married, 9.7% widowed, 21.9% divorced (2000); Foreign born: 1.1% (2000); Ancestry (includes multiple ancestries): 25.9% German, 14.6% Irish, 13.0% Other groups, 10.8% French (except Basque), 10.3% United States or American (2000).
Economy: In agricultural area: corn, wheat, soybeans; oil and natural gas. Employment by occupation: 0.0% management, 16.0% professional, 25.3% services, 10.7% sales, 9.3% farming, 5.3% construction, 33.3% production (2000).
Income: Per capita income: $10,165 (2000); Median household income: $15,500 (2000); Poverty rate: 26.0% (2000).
Taxes: Total city taxes per capita: $19 (1997); City property taxes per capita: $6 (1997).
Education: High school graduation rate: 50.0% (2000); College graduation rate: 0.0% (2000).
Housing: Homeownership rate: 82.1% (2000); Median home value: $15,800 (2000); Median rent: $200 per month (2000); Median age of housing: 40 years (2000).
Transportation: Commute to work: 92.6% car, 0.0% public transportation, 0.0% walk, 0.0% work from home (2000); Travel time to work: 20.6% less than 15 minutes, 32.4% 15 to 30 minutes, 19.1% 30 to 45 minutes, 5.9% 45 to 60 minutes, 22.1% 60 minutes or more (2000)

MILL SHOALS (village). Covers a land area of 0.783 square miles and a water area of 0 square miles. Located at 38.24° N. Lat.; 88.34° W. Long. Elevation is 380 feet.
Population: 235 (2000); Race: 96.4% White, 0.0% Black, 0.0% Asian, 0.0% American Indian and Alaska Native, 1.3% Hispanic of any race, 3.6% two or more races (2000); Density: 299.9 persons per square mile (2000); Age: 22.9% under 18, 19.7% over 64 (2000); Marriage status: 12.0% never married, 71.0% now married, 7.1% widowed, 9.8% divorced (2000); Foreign born: 0.0% (2000); Ancestry (includes multiple ancestries): 17.0% United States or American, 15.2% German, 12.1% English, 11.7% Irish, 7.2% Other groups (2000).
Economy: In agricultural area. Employment by occupation: 14.1% management, 4.0% professional, 18.2% services, 23.2% sales, 0.0% farming, 6.1% construction, 34.3% production (2000).
Income: Per capita income: $14,355 (2000); Median household income: $27,292 (2000); Poverty rate: 9.9% (2000).
Taxes: Total city taxes per capita: $20 (1997); City property taxes per capita: $20 (1997).
Education: High school graduation rate: 67.9% (2000); College graduation rate: 6.4% (2000).
Housing: Homeownership rate: 89.6% (2000); Median home value: $22,500 (2000); Median rent: $175 per month (2000); Median age of housing: 38 years (2000).
Transportation: Commute to work: 94.9% car, 0.0% public transportation, 2.0% walk, 3.0% work from home (2000); Travel time to work: 22.9% less than 15 minutes, 58.3% 15 to 30 minutes, 6.3% 30 to 45 minutes, 2.1% 45 to 60 minutes, 10.4% 60 minutes or more (2000)

NORRIS CITY (village). Covers a land area of 1.159 square miles and a water area of 0 square miles. Located at 37.98° N. Lat.; 88.32° W. Long. Elevation is 443 feet.
History: Norris City was named for pioneer settler William Norris. It developed as an agricultural and coal mining trading area.
Population: 1,057 (2000); Race: 98.9% White, 0.0% Black, 0.0% Asian, 0.5% American Indian and Alaska Native, 0.0% Hispanic of any race, 0.7% two or more races (2000); Density: 911.6 persons per square mile (2000); Age: 21.1% under 18, 22.4% over 64 (2000); Marriage status: 15.8% never married, 61.3% now married, 11.3% widowed, 11.6% divorced (2000); Foreign born: 0.2% (2000); Ancestry (includes multiple ancestries): 17.5% German, 14.5% Irish, 8.7% English, 8.4% United States or American, 8.3% Other groups (2000).
Economy: Employment by occupation: 4.0% management, 14.0% professional, 19.0% services, 20.5% sales, 0.5% farming, 13.3% construction, 28.6% production (2000).
Income: Per capita income: $13,671 (2000); Median household income: $22,121 (2000); Poverty rate: 14.4% (2000).
Taxes: Total city taxes per capita: $64 (1997); City property taxes per capita: $64 (1997).
Education: High school graduation rate: 77.0% (2000); College graduation rate: 7.5% (2000).

School District(s)

Norris City-Omaha-Enfield CUSD 3 (PK-12)
2000 Enrollment: 771 618-378-3222
Housing: Homeownership rate: 79.2% (2000); Median home value: $33,400 (2000); Median rent: $171 per month (2000); Median age of housing: 45 years (2000).
Newspapers: Norris City Banner (1 x week)
Transportation: Commute to work: 94.2% car, 0.0% public transportation, 3.9% walk, 1.5% work from home (2000); Travel time to work: 34.3% less than 15 minutes, 23.5% 15 to 30 minutes, 21.0% 30 to 45 minutes, 9.1% 45 to 60 minutes, 12.1% 60 minutes or more (2000)

PHILLIPSTOWN (village). Covers a land area of 0.271 square miles and a water area of 0 square miles. Located at 38.14° N. Lat.; 88.02° W. Long. Elevation is 492 feet.
Population: 28 (2000); Race: 100.0% White, 0.0% Black, 0.0% Asian, 0.0% American Indian and Alaska Native, 0.0% Hispanic of any race, 0.0% two or more races (2000); Density: 103.3 persons per square mile (2000); Age: 16.0% under 18, 24.0% over 64 (2000); Marriage status: 0.0% never married, 71.4% now married, 9.5% widowed, 19.0% divorced (2000); Foreign born: 0.0% (2000); Ancestry (includes multiple ancestries): 32.0% United States or American, 8.0% Other groups, 8.0% German, 4.0% Irish, 4.0% Norwegian (2000).
Economy: Employment by occupation: 0.0% management, 40.0% professional, 13.3% services, 20.0% sales, 0.0% farming, 20.0% construction, 6.7% production (2000).
Income: Per capita income: $21,188 (2000); Median household income: $42,917 (2000); Poverty rate: 4.0% (2000).
Taxes: Total city taxes per capita: $21 (1997); City property taxes per capita: $21 (1997).
Education: High school graduation rate: 100.0% (2000); College graduation rate: 23.8% (2000).
Housing: Homeownership rate: 73.3% (2000); Median home value: $56,300 (2000); Median age of housing: 17 years (2000).
Transportation: Commute to work: 86.7% car, 0.0% public transportation, 0.0% walk, 13.3% work from home (2000); Travel time to work: 23.1% less than 15 minutes, 7.7% 15 to 30 minutes, 38.5% 30 to 45 minutes, 15.4% 45 to 60 minutes, 15.4% 60 minutes or more (2000)

SPRINGERTON (village). Aka Springer. Covers a land area of 0.125 square miles and a water area of 0 square miles. Located at 38.17° N. Lat.; 88.35° W. Long. Elevation is 440 feet.
Population: 134 (2000); Race: 96.5% White, 0.0% Black, 0.0% Asian, 0.0% American Indian and Alaska Native, 0.0% Hispanic of any race, 3.5% two or more races (2000); Density: 1,068.7 persons per square mile (2000); Age: 26.2% under 18, 19.9% over 64 (2000); Marriage status: 12.5% never married, 74.0% now married, 9.6% widowed, 3.8% divorced (2000); Foreign born: 0.0% (2000); Ancestry (includes multiple ancestries): 18.4% German, 14.9% Other groups, 9.9% United States or American, 9.2% Irish, 7.1% French (except Basque) (2000).
Economy: In agricultural area. Employment by occupation: 10.3% management, 22.4% professional, 13.8% services, 15.5% sales, 8.6% farming, 5.2% construction, 24.1% production (2000).
Income: Per capita income: $12,568 (2000); Median household income: $26,000 (2000); Poverty rate: 10.6% (2000).
Taxes: Total city taxes per capita: $19 (1997); City property taxes per capita: $6 (1997).
Education: High school graduation rate: 62.1% (2000); College graduation rate: 3.2% (2000).
Housing: Homeownership rate: 95.1% (2000); Median home value: $26,700 (2000); Median age of housing: 47 years (2000).
Transportation: Commute to work: 100.0% car, 0.0% public transportation, 0.0% walk, 0.0% work from home (2000); Travel time to work: 28.6% less than 15 minutes, 44.6% 15 to 30 minutes, 3.6% 30 to 45 minutes, 10.7% 45 to 60 minutes, 12.5% 60 minutes or more (2000)

Whiteside County

Located in northwestern Illinois; bounded on the northwest by the Mississippi River and the Iowa border; drained by the Rock River. Covers a land area of 684.80 square miles, a water area of 12.20 square miles, and is located in the Central Time Zone. The county government was organized in 1836. County seat is Morrison.

Weather Station: Fulton Lock & Dam 13 — Elevation: 590 feet

	Jan	Feb	Mar	Apr	May	Jun	Jul	Aug	Sep	Oct	Nov	Dec
High	28	33	45	59	71	80	84	82	74	63	47	33
Low	11	16	27	39	51	60	64	62	54	42	30	18
Precip	1.3	1.2	2.4	3.4	3.9	4.2	3.4	4.5	3.3	2.7	2.7	1.8
Snow	6.4	3.8	2.0	0.8	0.0	0.0	0.0	0.0	0.0	tr	0.9	3.8

High and Low temperatures in degrees Fahrenheit; Precipitation and Snow in inches

Weather Station: Morrison — Elevation: 600 feet

	Jan	Feb	Mar	Apr	May	Jun	Jul	Aug	Sep	Oct	Nov	Dec
High	29	34	47	61	73	82	85	83	76	64	48	34
Low	10	15	27	38	49	58	62	60	51	39	29	17
Precip	1.5	1.4	2.8	3.7	4.7	4.2	3.8	4.8	3.1	2.9	2.9	2.1
Snow	10.7	6.8	4.6	1.4	0.0	0.0	0.0	0.0	0.0	tr	2.2	8.3

High and Low temperatures in degrees Fahrenheit; Precipitation and Snow in inches

Population: 60,653 (2000); Race: 92.2% White, 1.0% Black, 0.4% Asian, 0.5% American Indian and Alaska Native, 8.9% Hispanic of any race, 1.8% two or more races (2000); Density: 88.6 persons per square mile (2000); Age: 25.1% under 18, 16.1% over 64 (2000).
Religion: Five largest groups: 22.7% Catholic Church, 8.3% The United Methodist Church, 6.6% Evangelical Lutheran Church in America, 5.6% Reformed Church in America, 3.1% Lutheran Church—Missouri Synod (2000).
Economy: Unemployment rate: 6.8% (11/2002); Total civilian labor force: 28,893 (11/2002); Leading industries: 31.0% manufacturing; 16.2% health care and social assistance; 15.6% retail trade (2000); Companies that employ more than 1,000 persons: 1 (2000); Companies that employ more than 100 persons: 37 (2000); Farms: 1,039 totaling 384,738 acres (1997); Minority business ownership rate: 4.5% (1997); Women business ownership rate: 28.0% (1997); Retail sales per capita: $8,575 (1997). Single-family building permits issued: 117 (2001) / 126 (2000); Multi-family building permits issued: 22 (2001) / 10 (2000).
Income: Per capita income: $19,296 (2000); Median household income: $40,354 (2000); Poverty rate: 8.5% (2000); Bankruptcy rate: 6.05% (2001).
Taxes: Total county taxes per capita: $110 (2000); County property taxes per capita: $81 (2000).
Education: High school graduation rate: 79.8% (2000); College graduation rate: 11.3% (2000).
Housing: Homeownership rate: 74.5% (2000); Median home value: $75,700 (2000); Median rent: $367 per month (2000); Median age of housing: 44 years (2000).
Health: Birth rate: 136.5 per 10,000 population (1998); Age adjusted death rate: 85.7 per 10,000 population (1999); Age adjusted cancer mortality rate: 182.2 deaths per 100,000 population (1999). Number of physicians: 11.2 per 10,000 population (1999); Number of hospital beds: 27.0 per 10,000 population (1999).
Elections: 2000 Presidential election results: 51.9% Gore, 45.3% Bush, 2.1% Nader, 0.5% Buchanan
National and State Parks: Big Bend State Conservation Area; Morrison-Rockwood State Park; Prophetstown State Park
Additional Information Contacts
Whiteside County Government Offices 815-772-5100
Fulton Chamber of Commerce 815-589-4545
Morrison Chamber of Commerce 815-772-3757

Rock Falls Chamber of Commerce 815-625-4500
Sterling Area Chamber of Commerce 815-625-2400
Whiteside County Association of Realtors 815-626-8148

Whiteside County Communities

ALBANY (village). Covers a land area of 1.000 square miles and a water area of 0 square miles. Located at 41.78° N. Lat.; 90.21° W. Long. Elevation is 600 feet.

Population: 895 (2000); Race: 96.8% White, 0.0% Black, 0.7% Asian, 0.0% American Indian and Alaska Native, 1.5% Hispanic of any race, 1.2% two or more races (2000); Density: 894.8 persons per square mile (2000); Age: 31.4% under 18, 11.7% over 64 (2000); Marriage status: 17.8% never married, 65.0% now married, 8.5% widowed, 8.8% divorced (2000); Foreign born: 0.5% (2000); Ancestry (includes multiple ancestries): 31.0% German, 15.4% United States or American, 15.0% Irish, 12.9% Dutch, 12.0% English (2000).

Economy: In agricultural area: corn, soybeans, oats, cattle, hogs. Single-family building permits issued: 9 (2001) / 3 (2000); Multi-family building permits issued: 0 (2001) / 0 (2000); Employment by occupation: 9.9% management, 17.8% professional, 14.2% services, 22.4% sales, 0.0% farming, 9.9% construction, 25.8% production (2000).

Income: Per capita income: $18,780 (2000); Median household income: $46,719 (2000); Poverty rate: 5.3% (2000).

Taxes: Total city taxes per capita: $124 (1997); City property taxes per capita: $72 (1997).

Education: High school graduation rate: 86.3% (2000); College graduation rate: 12.8% (2000).

Housing: Homeownership rate: 87.5% (2000); Median home value: $82,200 (2000); Median rent: $359 per month (2000); Median age of housing: 38 years (2000).

Transportation: Commute to work: 94.6% car, 0.0% public transportation, 3.2% walk, 1.2% work from home (2000); Travel time to work: 30.8% less than 15 minutes, 41.3% 15 to 30 minutes, 12.8% 30 to 45 minutes, 11.3% 45 to 60 minutes, 4.0% 60 minutes or more (2000)

COLETA (village). Covers a land area of 0.455 square miles and a water area of 0 square miles. Located at 41.90° N. Lat.; 89.80° W. Long. Elevation is 815 feet.

Population: 155 (2000); Race: 91.3% White, 0.0% Black, 0.0% Asian, 1.3% American Indian and Alaska Native, 1.9% Hispanic of any race, 7.5% two or more races (2000); Density: 341.0 persons per square mile (2000); Age: 27.5% under 18, 16.9% over 64 (2000); Marriage status: 25.4% never married, 57.2% now married, 4.3% widowed, 13.0% divorced (2000); Foreign born: 7.5% (2000); Ancestry (includes multiple ancestries): 24.4% German, 11.9% Irish, 9.4% United States or American, 7.5% French (except Basque), 6.9% English (2000).

Economy: In agricultural area: corn; cattle, hogs. Manufacturing: sporting goods. Employment by occupation: 23.9% management, 1.5% professional, 6.0% services, 31.3% sales, 0.0% farming, 10.4% construction, 26.9% production (2000).

Income: Per capita income: $17,439 (2000); Median household income: $40,000 (2000); Poverty rate: 8.8% (2000).

Taxes: Total city taxes per capita: $7 (1997); City property taxes per capita: $7 (1997).

Education: High school graduation rate: 82.7% (2000); College graduation rate: 3.6% (2000).

Housing: Homeownership rate: 94.8% (2000); Median home value: $58,900 (2000); Median age of housing: 60+ years (2000).

Transportation: Commute to work: 92.4% car, 0.0% public transportation, 4.5% walk, 3.0% work from home (2000); Travel time to work: 31.3% less than 15 minutes, 50.0% 15 to 30 minutes, 9.4% 30 to 45 minutes, 7.8% 45 to 60 minutes, 1.6% 60 minutes or more (2000)

DEER GROVE (village). Covers a land area of 0.456 square miles and a water area of 0 square miles. Located at 41.60° N. Lat.; 89.69° W. Long. Elevation is 645 feet.

Population: 48 (2000); Race: 100.0% White, 0.0% Black, 0.0% Asian, 0.0% American Indian and Alaska Native, 3.8% Hispanic of any race, 0.0% two or more races (2000); Density: 105.3 persons per square mile (2000); Age: 24.5% under 18, 7.5% over 64 (2000); Marriage status: 40.5% never married, 45.2% now married, 9.5% widowed, 4.8% divorced (2000); Foreign born: 0.0% (2000); Ancestry (includes multiple ancestries): 37.7% Irish, 37.7% German, 11.3% Swedish, 11.3% Belgian, 9.4% Other groups (2000).

Economy: In agricultural area. Employment by occupation: 3.1% management, 0.0% professional, 28.1% services, 25.0% sales, 0.0% farming, 12.5% construction, 31.3% production (2000).

Income: Per capita income: $16,651 (2000); Median household income: $44,167 (2000); Poverty rate: 5.7% (2000).

Taxes: Total city taxes per capita: $44 (1997); City property taxes per capita: $22 (1997).

Education: High school graduation rate: 79.4% (2000); College graduation rate: 5.9% (2000).

Housing: Homeownership rate: 90.0% (2000); Median home value: $47,100 (2000); Median rent: $225 per month (2000); Median age of housing: 60+ years (2000).

Transportation: Commute to work: 71.9% car, 0.0% public transportation, 0.0% walk, 28.1% work from home (2000); Travel time to work: 17.4% less than 15 minutes, 52.2% 15 to 30 minutes, 21.7% 30 to 45 minutes, 8.7% 45 to 60 minutes, 0.0% 60 minutes or more (2000)

ERIE (village). Covers a land area of 1.403 square miles and a water area of 0.009 square miles. Located at 41.65° N. Lat.; 90.07° W. Long. Elevation is 590 feet.

History: Incorporated 1872.

Population: 1,589 (2000); Race: 98.2% White, 0.4% Black, 0.5% Asian, 0.2% American Indian and Alaska Native, 0.7% Hispanic of any race, 0.6% two or more races (2000); Density: 1,132.7 persons per square mile (2000); Age: 27.0% under 18, 16.7% over 64 (2000); Marriage status: 21.3% never married, 60.6% now married, 8.3% widowed, 9.8% divorced (2000); Foreign born: 1.1% (2000); Ancestry (includes multiple ancestries): 30.1% German, 14.0% Irish, 11.1% English, 9.5% Dutch, 7.1% Swedish (2000).

Economy: In agricultural area. Single-family building permits issued: 6 (2001) / 2 (2000); Multi-family building permits issued: 0 (2001) / 0 (2000); Employment by occupation: 10.4% management, 12.0% professional, 15.0% services, 21.2% sales, 1.3% farming, 11.2% construction, 28.9% production (2000).

Income: Per capita income: $18,775 (2000); Median household income: $41,806 (2000); Poverty rate: 5.1% (2000).

Taxes: Total city taxes per capita: $132 (1997); City property taxes per capita: $86 (1997).

Education: High school graduation rate: 84.9% (2000); College graduation rate: 12.4% (2000).

School District(s)

Erie Community Unit School District 1 (PK-12)
2000 Enrollment: 760 309-659-2239

Housing: Homeownership rate: 77.0% (2000); Median home value: $82,200 (2000); Median rent: $290 per month (2000); Median age of housing: 41 years (2000).

Newspapers: The Review (1 x week)

Transportation: Commute to work: 95.5% car, 0.4% public transportation, 2.7% walk, 1.1% work from home (2000); Travel time to work: 32.9% less than 15 minutes, 31.0% 15 to 30 minutes, 24.6% 30 to 45 minutes, 6.5% 45 to 60 minutes, 5.0% 60 minutes or more (2000)

FENTON (unincorporated postal area, zip code 61251). Covers a land area of 17.109 square miles and a water area of 0 square miles. Located at 41.73° N. Lat.; 90.06° W. Long. Elevation is 640 feet.

Population: 317 (2000); Race: 100.0% White, 0.0% Black, 0.0% Asian, 0.0% American Indian and Alaska Native, 0.0% Hispanic of any race, 0.0% two or more races (2000); Density: 18.5 persons per square mile (2000); Age: 29.2% under 18, 9.4% over 64 (2000); Marriage status: 24.2% never married, 70.3% now married, 3.7% widowed, 1.9% divorced (2000); Foreign born: 0.0% (2000); Ancestry (includes multiple ancestries): 23.1% English, 21.3% Irish, 14.6% German, 13.7% Scotch-Irish, 12.9% Dutch (2000).

Economy: Employment by occupation: 13.4% management, 12.7% professional, 15.9% services, 8.9% sales, 5.1% farming, 10.8% construction, 33.1% production (2000).

Income: Per capita income: $15,537 (2000); Median household income: $47,813 (2000); Poverty rate: 0.0% (2000).

Education: High school graduation rate: 90.7% (2000); College graduation rate: 11.8% (2000).

Housing: Homeownership rate: 85.7% (2000); Median home value: $66,200 (2000); Median rent: $225 per month (2000); Median age of housing: 60+ years (2000).

Transportation: Commute to work: 100.0% car, 0.0% public transportation, 0.0% walk, 0.0% work from home (2000); Travel time to work: 19.7% less than 15 minutes, 40.1% 15 to 30 minutes, 26.1% 30 to 45 minutes, 10.8% 45 to 60 minutes, 3.2% 60 minutes or more (2000)

FULTON (city). Covers a land area of 2.272 square miles and a water area of 0.071 square miles. Located at 41.86° N. Lat.; 90.15° W. Long. Elevation is 610 feet.
History: The name of Fulton honors the inventor of the steamboat, and the city itself owes its early development to river commerce. Later it became the center of an agricultural area, producing tomatoes and cucumbers.
Population: 3,881 (2000); Race: 97.3% White, 0.0% Black, 0.6% Asian, 0.5% American Indian and Alaska Native, 1.2% Hispanic of any race, 1.2% two or more races (2000); Density: 1,708.0 persons per square mile (2000); Age: 23.6% under 18, 20.0% over 64 (2000); Marriage status: 22.0% never married, 62.1% now married, 8.3% widowed, 7.6% divorced (2000); Foreign born: 2.0% (2000); Ancestry (includes multiple ancestries): 37.3% Dutch, 30.4% German, 11.8% Irish, 9.0% English, 5.5% United States or American (2000).
Economy: Single-family building permits issued: 27 (2001) / 5 (2000); Multi-family building permits issued: 0 (2001) / 0 (2000); Employment by occupation: 8.1% management, 19.2% professional, 11.9% services, 19.8% sales, 0.0% farming, 10.2% construction, 30.9% production (2000).
Income: Per capita income: $19,845 (2000); Median household income: $37,068 (2000); Poverty rate: 5.8% (2000).
Taxes: Total city taxes per capita: $55 (1997); City property taxes per capita: $0 (1997).
Education: High school graduation rate: 79.0% (2000); College graduation rate: 12.7% (2000).

School District(s)

River Bend Community Unit District 2 (PK-12)
2000 Enrollment: 1,244 815-589-2711
Housing: Homeownership rate: 76.5% (2000); Median home value: $76,500 (2000); Median rent: $348 per month (2000); Median age of housing: 50 years (2000).
Newspapers: The Whiteside Shopper (1 x week); Fulton Journal (1 x week)
Transportation: Commute to work: 93.5% car, 0.0% public transportation, 3.3% walk, 1.5% work from home (2000); Travel time to work: 53.4% less than 15 minutes, 34.0% 15 to 30 minutes, 5.7% 30 to 45 minutes, 4.2% 45 to 60 minutes, 2.8% 60 minutes or more (2000)
Additional Information Contacts
Fulton Chamber of Commerce. 815-589-4545

LYNDON (village). Covers a land area of 0.821 square miles and a water area of 0 square miles. Located at 41.71° N. Lat.; 89.92° W. Long. Elevation is 615 feet.
Population: 566 (2000); Race: 100.0% White, 0.0% Black, 0.0% Asian, 0.0% American Indian and Alaska Native, 0.7% Hispanic of any race, 0.0% two or more races (2000); Density: 689.6 persons per square mile (2000); Age: 19.9% under 18, 16.3% over 64 (2000); Marriage status: 26.3% never married, 56.6% now married, 5.7% widowed, 11.5% divorced (2000); Foreign born: 0.7% (2000); Ancestry (includes multiple ancestries): 25.4% German, 11.2% Irish, 9.8% United States or American, 9.3% English, 8.8% Dutch (2000).
Economy: In agricultural area. Single-family building permits issued: 0 (2001) / 0 (2000); Multi-family building permits issued: 0 (2001) / 0 (2000); Employment by occupation: 6.9% management, 10.2% professional, 18.8% services, 15.1% sales, 0.0% farming, 13.8% construction, 35.2% production (2000).
Income: Per capita income: $16,870 (2000); Median household income: $37,375 (2000); Poverty rate: 6.8% (2000).
Taxes: Total city taxes per capita: $70 (1997); City property taxes per capita: $62 (1997).
Education: High school graduation rate: 75.7% (2000); College graduation rate: 5.3% (2000).
Housing: Homeownership rate: 86.8% (2000); Median home value: $65,000 (2000); Median rent: $270 per month (2000); Median age of housing: 47 years (2000).
Transportation: Commute to work: 92.3% car, 1.0% public transportation, 3.3% walk, 1.7% work from home (2000); Travel time to work: 35.7% less than 15 minutes, 38.4% 15 to 30 minutes, 16.3% 30 to 45 minutes, 5.4% 45 to 60 minutes, 4.1% 60 minutes or more (2000)

MORRISON (city). Covers a land area of 2.141 square miles and a water area of 0 square miles. Located at 41.80° N. Lat.; 89.96° W. Long. Elevation is 670 feet.
History: Morrison developed when the Chicago & North Western Railway built its station here. It was in Morrison in 1874 that James Sargent installed the first time lock in the First National Bank of Morrison.
Population: 4,447 (2000); Race: 96.9% White, 1.5% Black, 0.0% Asian, 0.3% American Indian and Alaska Native, 2.0% Hispanic of any race, 1.3% two or more races (2000); Density: 2,077.6 persons per square mile (2000); Age: 21.9% under 18, 20.8% over 64 (2000); Marriage status: 20.5% never married, 59.2% now married, 11.3% widowed, 9.0% divorced (2000); Foreign born: 0.5% (2000); Ancestry (includes multiple ancestries): 29.9% German, 23.2% Dutch, 10.9% English, 10.1% Irish, 5.3% United States or American (2000).
Economy: Single-family building permits issued: 3 (2001) / 7 (2000); Multi-family building permits issued: 0 (2001) / 0 (2000); Employment by occupation: 7.9% management, 19.1% professional, 15.5% services, 21.1% sales, 0.9% farming, 10.6% construction, 24.9% production (2000).
Income: Per capita income: $20,179 (2000); Median household income: $40,313 (2000); Poverty rate: 6.1% (2000).
Taxes: Total city taxes per capita: $125 (1997); City property taxes per capita: $53 (1997).
Education: High school graduation rate: 83.7% (2000); College graduation rate: 14.8% (2000).

School District(s)

Morrison Community Unit School District 6 (KG-12)
2000 Enrollment: 1,260 815-772-2064

Two-year College(s)

Morrison Institute of Technology (Private, Not-for-profit)
2001 Enrollment: 149 815-772-7218
2001 Tuition: In-state $9,050; Out-of-state $9,050
Housing: Homeownership rate: 76.0% (2000); Median home value: $76,600 (2000); Median rent: $352 per month (2000); Median age of housing: 51 years (2000).
Hospitals: Morrison Community Hospital (76 beds)
Newspapers: Whiteside News Sentinel (1 x week)
Transportation: Commute to work: 90.4% car, 0.3% public transportation, 7.1% walk, 0.8% work from home (2000); Travel time to work: 47.2% less than 15 minutes, 30.5% 15 to 30 minutes, 15.3% 30 to 45 minutes, 3.5% 45 to 60 minutes, 3.5% 60 minutes or more (2000)
Additional Information Contacts
Morrison Chamber of Commerce. 815-772-3757

PROPHETSTOWN (city). Covers a land area of 1.363 square miles and a water area of 0.021 square miles. Located at 41.67° N. Lat.; 89.93° W. Long. Elevation is 618 feet.
History: The name of Prophetstown refers to the Indian prophet White Cloud, who warned his people about the loss of their lands. The town was founded on the Rock River, where White Cloud had lived.
Population: 2,023 (2000); Race: 98.4% White, 0.3% Black, 0.0% Asian, 0.1% American Indian and Alaska Native, 1.7% Hispanic of any race, 0.6% two or more races (2000); Density: 1,484.5 persons per square mile (2000); Age: 22.7% under 18, 22.5% over 64 (2000); Marriage status: 18.6% never married, 64.1% now married, 9.3% widowed, 8.0% divorced (2000); Foreign born: 1.2% (2000); Ancestry (includes multiple ancestries): 34.8% German, 15.9% Irish, 11.7% English, 8.7% Swedish, 6.9% Other groups (2000).
Economy: Single-family building permits issued: 2 (2001) / 2 (2000); Multi-family building permits issued: 0 (2001) / 0 (2000); Employment by occupation: 13.3% management, 13.1% professional, 15.5% services, 20.0% sales, 1.6% farming, 7.0% construction, 29.5% production (2000).
Income: Per capita income: $19,572 (2000); Median household income: $37,452 (2000); Poverty rate: 9.5% (2000).
Taxes: Total city taxes per capita: $64 (1997); City property taxes per capita: $53 (1997).
Education: High school graduation rate: 86.7% (2000); College graduation rate: 13.8% (2000).

School District(s)

Prophetstown-Lyndon-Tampico CUSD3 (PK-12)
2000 Enrollment: 1,011 815-537-5101
Housing: Homeownership rate: 77.1% (2000); Median home value: $72,900 (2000); Median rent: $307 per month (2000); Median age of housing: 52 years (2000).
Newspapers: Prophetstown Echo (1 x week)
Transportation: Commute to work: 91.1% car, 0.3% public transportation, 4.7% walk, 3.3% work from home (2000); Travel time to work: 54.6% less than 15 minutes, 24.2% 15 to 30 minutes, 11.4% 30 to 45 minutes, 6.3% 45 to 60 minutes, 3.5% 60 minutes or more (2000)

ROCK FALLS (city). Covers a land area of 3.317 square miles and a water area of 0.114 square miles. Located at 41.77° N. Lat.; 89.69° W. Long. Elevation is 641 feet.

History: Rock Falls was platted in 1837. Development came when a dam was built across the river, and later when a feeder canal connected Rock Falls and the Rock River with the Illinois & Mississippi Canal.
Population: 9,580 (2000); Race: 90.0% White, 1.5% Black, 0.1% Asian, 0.7% American Indian and Alaska Native, 11.8% Hispanic of any race, 3.2% two or more races (2000); Density: 2,888.0 persons per square mile (2000); Age: 25.8% under 18, 15.6% over 64 (2000); Marriage status: 22.9% never married, 53.5% now married, 8.4% widowed, 15.2% divorced (2000); Foreign born: 3.3% (2000); Ancestry (includes multiple ancestries): 27.9% German, 15.9% Other groups, 15.3% Irish, 9.0% English, 7.6% United States or American (2000).
Economy: Single-family building permits issued: 3 (2001) / 7 (2000); Multi-family building permits issued: 2 (2001) / 4 (2000); Employment by occupation: 6.0% management, 11.7% professional, 19.0% services, 22.2% sales, 0.4% farming, 7.9% construction, 33.0% production (2000).
Income: Per capita income: $16,524 (2000); Median household income: $34,442 (2000); Poverty rate: 11.5% (2000).
Taxes: Total city taxes per capita: $71 (1997); City property taxes per capita: $60 (1997).
Education: High school graduation rate: 72.5% (2000); College graduation rate: 5.9% (2000).

School District(s)

East Coloma School District 12 (KG-08)
2000 Enrollment: 227 815-625-4400
Montmorency C C School District 145 (KG-08)
2000 Enrollment: 317 815-625-6616
Nelson Elementary School District 8 (KG-08)
2000 Enrollment: 40 815-251-4412
Riverdale School District 14 (KG-08)
2000 Enrollment: 97 815-625-5280
Rock Falls Elementary School District 13 (PK-08)
2000 Enrollment: 1,101 815-626-2604
Rock Falls Township H S District 301 (09-12)
2000 Enrollment: 639 815-625-3886

Housing: Homeownership rate: 63.7% (2000); Median home value: $62,800 (2000); Median rent: $362 per month (2000); Median age of housing: 45 years (2000).
Transportation: Commute to work: 92.9% car, 0.5% public transportation, 3.5% walk, 1.4% work from home (2000); Travel time to work: 60.3% less than 15 minutes, 24.2% 15 to 30 minutes, 6.2% 30 to 45 minutes, 3.7% 45 to 60 minutes, 5.6% 60 minutes or more (2000)

Additional Information Contacts

Rock Falls Chamber of Commerce 815-625-4500

STERLING (city). Covers a land area of 4.672 square miles and a water area of 0.188 square miles. Located at 41.79° N. Lat.; 89.69° W. Long. Elevation is 660 feet.
History: Sterling originated in 1839 from the union of Chatham and Harrisburg in the hopes that the new town would become the seat of Whiteside County. Though Sterling was chosen, it soon lost the honor to Morrison.
Population: 15,451 (2000); Race: 84.1% White, 1.9% Black, 0.9% Asian, 0.7% American Indian and Alaska Native, 18.6% Hispanic of any race, 2.9% two or more races (2000); Density: 3,307.0 persons per square mile (2000); Age: 24.8% under 18, 17.7% over 64 (2000); Marriage status: 24.0% never married, 54.8% now married, 8.5% widowed, 12.6% divorced (2000); Foreign born: 5.4% (2000); Ancestry (includes multiple ancestries): 25.8% German, 24.6% Other groups, 14.7% Irish, 7.7% English, 6.5% United States or American (2000).
Vital Statistics: Birth rate: 179.9 per 10,000 population (1998)
Economy: Single-family building permits issued: 8 (2001) / 25 (2000); Multi-family building permits issued: 20 (2001) / 6 (2000); Employment by occupation: 9.7% management, 15.0% professional, 17.8% services, 22.5% sales, 0.4% farming, 8.1% construction, 26.5% production (2000).
Income: Per capita income: $19,432 (2000); Median household income: $37,664 (2000); Poverty rate: 10.8% (2000).
Taxes: Total city taxes per capita: $148 (2000); City property taxes per capita: $131 (2000).
Education: High school graduation rate: 78.4% (2000); College graduation rate: 12.1% (2000).

School District(s)

Sterling C U District 5 (PK-12)
2000 Enrollment: 3,747 815-626-5050
Whiteside Roe (07-08)
2000 Enrollment: 3 815-625-1495

Housing: Homeownership rate: 62.9% (2000); Median home value: $70,700 (2000); Median rent: $391 per month (2000); Median age of housing: 47 years (2000).
Hospitals: CGH Medical Center (139 beds)
Newspapers: Sauk Valley Sunday; The Daily Gazette (7 x week)
Transportation: Commute to work: 92.1% car, 1.7% public transportation, 2.3% walk, 2.3% work from home (2000); Travel time to work: 61.0% less than 15 minutes, 23.5% 15 to 30 minutes, 8.5% 30 to 45 minutes, 4.0% 45 to 60 minutes, 3.0% 60 minutes or more (2000)
Airports: Whiteside Co Airport-Jos H Bittorf Field

Additional Information Contacts

Sterling Area Chamber of Commerce 815-625-2400
Whiteside County Association of Realtors 815-626-8148

TAMPICO (village). Covers a land area of 0.398 square miles and a water area of 0 square miles. Located at 41.63° N. Lat.; 89.78° W. Long. Elevation is 640 feet.
History: Birthplace of Ronald Reagan.
Population: 772 (2000); Race: 99.5% White, 0.0% Black, 0.0% Asian, 0.0% American Indian and Alaska Native, 1.9% Hispanic of any race, 0.3% two or more races (2000); Density: 1,941.3 persons per square mile (2000); Age: 29.9% under 18, 13.6% over 64 (2000); Marriage status: 18.7% never married, 63.9% now married, 8.7% widowed, 8.7% divorced (2000); Foreign born: 0.8% (2000); Ancestry (includes multiple ancestries): 34.9% German, 14.9% Irish, 12.8% English, 10.4% United States or American, 6.5% Belgian (2000).
Economy: In agricultural area; ships grain. Single-family building permits issued: 0 (2001) / 2 (2000); Multi-family building permits issued: 0 (2001) / 0 (2000); Employment by occupation: 6.6% management, 8.3% professional, 19.3% services, 19.8% sales, 1.4% farming, 12.1% construction, 32.5% production (2000).
Income: Per capita income: $14,467 (2000); Median household income: $40,221 (2000); Poverty rate: 8.5% (2000).
Taxes: Total city taxes per capita: $54 (1997); City property taxes per capita: $47 (1997).
Education: High school graduation rate: 79.8% (2000); College graduation rate: 9.1% (2000).
Housing: Homeownership rate: 79.4% (2000); Median home value: $65,600 (2000); Median rent: $317 per month (2000); Median age of housing: 60+ years (2000).
Transportation: Commute to work: 92.7% car, 0.0% public transportation, 3.7% walk, 2.8% work from home (2000); Travel time to work: 19.8% less than 15 minutes, 39.8% 15 to 30 minutes, 26.5% 30 to 45 minutes, 7.8% 45 to 60 minutes, 6.1% 60 minutes or more (2000)

Will County

Located in northeastern Illinois; bounded on the east by Indiana; drained by the Des Plaines, Du Page, and Kankakee Rivers. Covers a land area of 836.90 square miles, a water area of 12.40 square miles, and is located in the Central Time Zone. The county government was organized in 1836. County seat is Joliet.

Will County is part of the Chicago, IL PMSA. The entire metro area includes: Cook County; DeKalb County; DuPage County; Grundy County; Kane County; Kendall County; Lake County; McHenry County; Will County

Weather Station: Marion 4 NNE Elevation: 475 feet

	Jan	Feb	Mar	Apr	May	Jun	Jul	Aug	Sep	Oct	Nov	Dec
High	38	44	55	66	75	83	87	86	79	68	55	43
Low	20	24	34	43	53	62	66	64	56	44	35	25
Precip	3.0	3.0	4.6	4.7	5.0	4.1	3.8	3.8	3.3	3.1	4.9	3.7
Snow	5.9	5.4	2.5	0.5	0.0	0.0	0.0	0.0	0.0	0.2	0.8	2.9

High and Low temperatures in degrees Fahrenheit; Precipitation and Snow in inches

Population: 502,266 (2000); Race: 81.8% White, 10.3% Black, 2.2% Asian, 0.2% American Indian and Alaska Native, 8.8% Hispanic of any race, 1.7% two or more races (2000); Density: 600.1 persons per square mile (2000); Age: 29.9% under 18, 8.2% over 64 (2000).
Religion: Five largest groups: 38.8% Catholic Church, 2.3% Evangelical Lutheran Church in America, 2.0% The United Methodist Church, 1.9% Lutheran Church—Missouri Synod, 1.2% United Church of Christ (2000).
Economy: Unemployment rate: 6.5% (11/2002); Total civilian labor force: 246,782 (11/2002); Leading industries: 17.9% manufacturing; 14.1% retail trade; 11.3% construction (2000); Companies that employ more than 1,000 persons: 9 (2000); Companies that employ more than 100 persons: 217

(2000); Farms: 910 totaling 293,526 acres (1997); Minority business ownership rate: 9.6% (1997); Women business ownership rate: 26.3% (1997); Retail sales per capita: $7,388 (1997). Single-family building permits issued: 7,047 (2001) / 6,478 (2000); Multi-family building permits issued: 349 (2001) / 681 (2000).
Income: Per capita income: $24,613 (2000); Median household income: $62,238 (2000); Poverty rate: 4.9% (2000); Bankruptcy rate: 6.27% (2001).
Taxes: Total county taxes per capita: $131 (2000); County property taxes per capita: $124 (2000).
Education: High school graduation rate: 86.9% (2000); College graduation rate: 25.5% (2000).
Housing: Homeownership rate: 83.2% (2000); Median home value: $154,300 (2000); Median rent: $554 per month (2000); Median age of housing: 23 years (2000).
Health: Birth rate: 147.4 per 10,000 population (1998); Age adjusted death rate: 84.1 per 10,000 population (1999); Infant mortality rate: 10.1 per 1,000 live births (1998); Age adjusted cancer mortality rate: 212.4 deaths per 100,000 population (1999). Air Quality Index: 77% good, 23% moderate, 0% unhealthy (percent of days in 2000). Number of physicians: 10.6 per 10,000 population (1999); Number of hospital beds: 11.5 per 10,000 population (1999).
Elections: 2000 Presidential election results: 47.4% Gore, 50.0% Bush, 2.0% Nader, 0.4% Buchanan
National and State Parks: Channahon Parkway State Park; Des Plaines State Conservation Area; Kankakee River State Park; Midewin National Tallgrass Prairie
Additional Information Contacts
Will County Government Offices 815-740-4602
Crete Chamber of Commerce 708-672-9216
Frankfort Chamber of Commerce 815-469-3356
Heritage Corridor Convention & Visitors Bureau 815-727-2323
Joliet Region Chamber of Commerce 815-727-5371
Lockport Chamber of Commerce 815-838-3357
Manhattan Chamber of Commerce 815-478-3811
Mokena Chamber of Commerce 708-479-2468
Monee Chamber of Commerce 708-534-5332
New Lenox Chamber of Commerce 815-485-4241
Peotone Chamber of Commerce 708-258-9450
Plainfield Chamber of Commerce 815-436-4431
Romeoville Chamber of Commerce 815-886-2076
Shorewood Chamber of Commerce 815-725-2900
Will Grundy Association of Realtors 815-744-4520

Will County Communities

BEECHER (village). Covers a land area of 2.108 square miles and a water area of 0 square miles. Located at 41.34° N. Lat.; 87.62° W. Long. Elevation is 736 feet.
History: Beecher was platted in 1870 when the Chicago & Eastern Illinois Railway was being built here. The village was named for Henry Ward Beecher.
Population: 2,033 (2000); Race: 98.1% White, 0.0% Black, 0.8% Asian, 0.0% American Indian and Alaska Native, 1.1% Hispanic of any race, 1.0% two or more races (2000); Density: 964.4 persons per square mile (2000); Age: 22.2% under 18, 16.5% over 64 (2000); Marriage status: 21.7% never married, 62.4% now married, 8.7% widowed, 7.2% divorced (2000); Foreign born: 2.5% (2000); Ancestry (includes multiple ancestries): 44.2% German, 12.7% Irish, 10.1% Polish, 8.6% Italian, 7.9% English (2000).
Economy: Single-family building permits issued: 51 (2001) / 19 (2000); Multi-family building permits issued: 0 (2001) / 0 (2000); Employment by occupation: 16.3% management, 11.6% professional, 12.9% services, 30.8% sales, 0.3% farming, 12.3% construction, 15.8% production (2000).
Income: Per capita income: $23,454 (2000); Median household income: $51,250 (2000); Poverty rate: 4.0% (2000).
Taxes: Total city taxes per capita: $195 (1997); City property taxes per capita: $173 (1997).
Education: High school graduation rate: 86.7% (2000); College graduation rate: 16.3% (2000).

School District(s)
Beecher C U School District 200u (KG-12)
2000 Enrollment: 741 708-946-2266
Housing: Homeownership rate: 76.9% (2000); Median home value: $148,900 (2000); Median rent: $489 per month (2000); Median age of housing: 39 years (2000).
Transportation: Commute to work: 92.5% car, 1.3% public transportation, 3.5% walk, 2.4% work from home (2000); Travel time to work: 29.1% less than 15 minutes, 28.8% 15 to 30 minutes, 22.5% 30 to 45 minutes, 9.3% 45 to 60 minutes, 10.3% 60 minutes or more (2000)

BOLINGBROOK (village). Covers a land area of 20.506 square miles and a water area of 0.237 square miles. Located at 41.69° N. Lat.; 88.08° W. Long. Elevation is 703 feet.
Population: 56,321 (2000); Race: 64.1% White, 20.1% Black, 6.7% Asian, 0.2% American Indian and Alaska Native, 13.0% Hispanic of any race, 3.2% two or more races (2000); Density: 2,746.5 persons per square mile (2000); Age: 32.3% under 18, 4.3% over 64 (2000); Marriage status: 25.8% never married, 62.9% now married, 3.7% widowed, 7.6% divorced (2000); Foreign born: 14.4% (2000); Ancestry (includes multiple ancestries): 38.0% Other groups, 19.6% German, 12.8% Irish, 9.8% Polish, 7.7% Italian (2000).
Vital Statistics: Birth rate: 165.8 per 10,000 population (1998)
Economy: Unemployment rate: 6.3% (11/2002); Total civilian labor force: 31,769 (11/2002); Single-family building permits issued: 637 (2001) / 457 (2000); Multi-family building permits issued: 0 (2001) / 400 (2000); Employment by occupation: 15.8% management, 21.0% professional, 11.5% services, 28.8% sales, 0.1% farming, 9.2% construction, 13.7% production (2000).
Income: Per capita income: $23,468 (2000); Median household income: $67,852 (2000); Poverty rate: 4.1% (2000).
Taxes: Total city taxes per capita: $374 (2000); City property taxes per capita: $146 (2000).
Education: High school graduation rate: 87.2% (2000); College graduation rate: 29.2% (2000).
Housing: Homeownership rate: 85.2% (2000); Median home value: $142,000 (2000); Median rent: $712 per month (2000); Median age of housing: 22 years (2000).
Transportation: Commute to work: 91.3% car, 4.1% public transportation, 1.0% walk, 3.0% work from home (2000); Travel time to work: 19.5% less than 15 minutes, 28.4% 15 to 30 minutes, 24.6% 30 to 45 minutes, 12.5% 45 to 60 minutes, 15.0% 60 minutes or more (2000)
Airports: Clow International

BRAIDWOOD (city). Covers a land area of 4.629 square miles and a water area of 0.126 square miles. Located at 41.27° N. Lat.; 88.21° W. Long. Elevation is 575 feet.
History: Braidwood was a crowded coal-mining town in the 1880's, with many mining syndicates operating. The first coal vein was discovered in 1865 by settler William Henneberry. By 1873 Braidwood was incorporated as a city.
Population: 5,203 (2000); Race: 97.5% White, 0.0% Black, 0.0% Asian, 0.0% American Indian and Alaska Native, 5.4% Hispanic of any race, 0.9% two or more races (2000); Density: 1,124.0 persons per square mile (2000); Age: 29.8% under 18, 9.2% over 64 (2000); Marriage status: 23.1% never married, 60.3% now married, 5.3% widowed, 11.3% divorced (2000); Foreign born: 1.5% (2000); Ancestry (includes multiple ancestries): 27.4% German, 14.9% Irish, 14.7% Italian, 9.8% Other groups, 8.9% Polish (2000).
Economy: Single-family building permits issued: 54 (2001) / 33 (2000); Multi-family building permits issued: 0 (2001) / 12 (2000); Employment by occupation: 8.8% management, 12.0% professional, 17.3% services, 19.1% sales, 0.0% farming, 18.2% construction, 24.5% production (2000).
Income: Per capita income: $20,545 (2000); Median household income: $54,375 (2000); Poverty rate: 5.5% (2000).
Taxes: Total city taxes per capita: $250 (1997); City property taxes per capita: $114 (1997).
Education: High school graduation rate: 85.2% (2000); College graduation rate: 9.1% (2000).

School District(s)
Reed Custer C U School District 255u (PK-12)
2000 Enrollment: 1,763 815-458-2307
Housing: Homeownership rate: 85.3% (2000); Median home value: $114,200 (2000); Median rent: $474 per month (2000); Median age of housing: 18 years (2000).
Transportation: Commute to work: 97.1% car, 0.3% public transportation, 0.8% walk, 1.3% work from home (2000); Travel time to work: 29.1% less than 15 minutes, 24.9% 15 to 30 minutes, 24.6% 30 to 45 minutes, 6.9% 45 to 60 minutes, 14.4% 60 minutes or more (2000)

CHANNAHON (village). Covers a land area of 7.207 square miles and a water area of 0.669 square miles. Located at 41.43° N. Lat.; 88.21° W. Long. Elevation is 540 feet.

History: Channahon was settled in 1832 and developed when the Illinois & Michigan Canal was built. Early industries included grain shipping, quarrying, and the manufacture of farm equipment.
Population: 7,344 (2000); Race: 98.3% White, 0.3% Black, 0.0% Asian, 0.0% American Indian and Alaska Native, 2.7% Hispanic of any race, 1.0% two or more races (2000); Density: 1,019.0 persons per square mile (2000); Age: 31.9% under 18, 5.1% over 64 (2000); Marriage status: 19.3% never married, 73.0% now married, 2.5% widowed, 5.2% divorced (2000); Foreign born: 1.3% (2000); Ancestry (includes multiple ancestries): 29.2% German, 21.2% Irish, 14.0% Italian, 8.4% Polish, 7.3% English (2000).
Economy: Single-family building permits issued: 152 (2001) / 147 (2000); Multi-family building permits issued: 86 (2001) / 103 (2000); Employment by occupation: 11.7% management, 18.4% professional, 12.6% services, 25.0% sales, 0.2% farming, 14.1% construction, 17.9% production (2000).
Income: Per capita income: $22,867 (2000); Median household income: $71,991 (2000); Poverty rate: 1.7% (2000).
Taxes: Total city taxes per capita: $104 (1997); City property taxes per capita: $39 (1997).
Education: High school graduation rate: 94.0% (2000); College graduation rate: 18.6% (2000).

School District(s)

Channahon School District 17 (PK-08)
2000 Enrollment: 1,355 815-467-4315
Housing: Homeownership rate: 93.3% (2000); Median home value: $157,700 (2000); Median rent: $663 per month (2000); Median age of housing: 14 years (2000).
Newspapers: Chanooka Weekly (1 x week)
Transportation: Commute to work: 96.6% car, 0.5% public transportation, 0.5% walk, 2.4% work from home (2000); Travel time to work: 21.0% less than 15 minutes, 40.5% 15 to 30 minutes, 16.2% 30 to 45 minutes, 11.3% 45 to 60 minutes, 11.0% 60 minutes or more (2000)

CREST HILL (city). Covers a land area of 7.161 square miles and a water area of 0.106 square miles. Located at 41.56° N. Lat.; 88.10° W. Long. Elevation is 640 feet.
Population: 13,329 (2000); Race: 75.3% White, 18.5% Black, 1.3% Asian, 0.1% American Indian and Alaska Native, 8.7% Hispanic of any race, 2.1% two or more races (2000); Density: 1,861.2 persons per square mile (2000); Age: 17.9% under 18, 9.5% over 64 (2000); Marriage status: 22.8% never married, 55.5% now married, 6.0% widowed, 15.7% divorced (2000); Foreign born: 4.4% (2000); Ancestry (includes multiple ancestries): 21.1% German, 13.9% Other groups, 12.3% Irish, 9.3% Polish, 9.1% Italian (2000).
Vital Statistics: Birth rate: 108.8 per 10,000 population (1998)
Economy: Manufacturing: motor vehicle parts, machinery, fiberglass boats, consumer goods. Stateville Correction Center to North. Single-family building permits issued: 246 (2001) / 110 (2000); Multi-family building permits issued: 69 (2001) / 99 (2000); Employment by occupation: 10.3% management, 17.7% professional, 17.5% services, 29.7% sales, 0.0% farming, 11.4% construction, 13.4% production (2000).
Income: Per capita income: $22,317 (2000); Median household income: $45,313 (2000); Poverty rate: 4.8% (2000).
Taxes: Total city taxes per capita: $88 (1997); City property taxes per capita: $62 (1997).
Education: High school graduation rate: 72.2% (2000); College graduation rate: 11.9% (2000).

School District(s)

Chaney-Monge School Districtrict 88 (KG-08)
2000 Enrollment: 413 815-722-6673
Richland School District 88a (KG-08)
2000 Enrollment: 359 815-744-6166
Housing: Homeownership rate: 65.2% (2000); Median home value: $111,400 (2000); Median rent: $593 per month (2000); Median age of housing: 27 years (2000).
Transportation: Commute to work: 96.8% car, 0.9% public transportation, 1.4% walk, 0.8% work from home (2000); Travel time to work: 29.0% less than 15 minutes, 32.9% 15 to 30 minutes, 17.2% 30 to 45 minutes, 12.0% 45 to 60 minutes, 8.8% 60 minutes or more (2000)

CRETE (village). Covers a land area of 6.378 square miles and a water area of 0.025 square miles. Located at 41.45° N. Lat.; 87.61° W. Long. Elevation is 730 feet.
History: Crete was laid out in 1849 by William Wood, operator of a tavern for travelers on the Chicago-Vincennes Road.
Population: 7,346 (2000); Race: 88.4% White, 10.0% Black, 0.0% Asian, 0.0% American Indian and Alaska Native, 3.2% Hispanic of any race, 1.2% two or more races (2000); Density: 1,151.8 persons per square mile (2000); Age: 25.4% under 18, 13.6% over 64 (2000); Marriage status: 19.6% never married, 67.2% now married, 6.0% widowed, 7.2% divorced (2000); Foreign born: 1.6% (2000); Ancestry (includes multiple ancestries): 36.7% German, 16.6% Irish, 12.8% Other groups, 10.2% Polish, 9.9% English (2000).
Economy: Single-family building permits issued: 39 (2001) / 35 (2000); Multi-family building permits issued: 4 (2001) / 2 (2000); Employment by occupation: 16.9% management, 20.5% professional, 12.3% services, 26.5% sales, 0.1% farming, 11.8% construction, 11.9% production (2000).
Income: Per capita income: $29,671 (2000); Median household income: $67,671 (2000); Poverty rate: 1.6% (2000).
Taxes: Total city taxes per capita: $227 (1997); City property taxes per capita: $193 (1997).
Education: High school graduation rate: 93.2% (2000); College graduation rate: 28.0% (2000).

School District(s)

Crete Monee C U School District 201u (PK-12)
2000 Enrollment: 4,443 708-672-2670
Housing: Homeownership rate: 88.7% (2000); Median home value: $154,900 (2000); Median rent: $573 per month (2000); Median age of housing: 26 years (2000).
Transportation: Commute to work: 92.5% car, 3.4% public transportation, 0.2% walk, 3.9% work from home (2000); Travel time to work: 23.4% less than 15 minutes, 33.3% 15 to 30 minutes, 18.6% 30 to 45 minutes, 8.2% 45 to 60 minutes, 16.5% 60 minutes or more (2000)
Additional Information Contacts
Crete Chamber of Commerce.......................... 708-672-9216

CRYSTAL LAWNS (CDP). Covers a land area of 0.993 square miles and a water area of 0 square miles. Located at 41.57° N. Lat.; 88.15° W. Long.
Population: 2,933 (2000); Race: 95.6% White, 0.1% Black, 0.0% Asian, 0.2% American Indian and Alaska Native, 6.2% Hispanic of any race, 2.4% two or more races (2000); Density: 2,954.5 persons per square mile (2000); Age: 29.6% under 18, 9.5% over 64 (2000); Marriage status: 22.8% never married, 61.7% now married, 5.1% widowed, 10.4% divorced (2000); Foreign born: 2.9% (2000); Ancestry (includes multiple ancestries): 28.1% German, 13.9% Irish, 12.6% English, 8.7% Other groups, 8.1% Polish (2000).
Economy: Employment by occupation: 10.5% management, 21.4% professional, 12.8% services, 27.2% sales, 0.0% farming, 16.8% construction, 11.4% production (2000).
Income: Per capita income: $20,369 (2000); Median household income: $53,750 (2000); Poverty rate: 6.2% (2000).
Education: High school graduation rate: 89.5% (2000); College graduation rate: 15.6% (2000).
Housing: Homeownership rate: 93.0% (2000); Median home value: $121,000 (2000); Median rent: $911 per month (2000); Median age of housing: 36 years (2000).
Transportation: Commute to work: 94.7% car, 3.2% public transportation, 0.0% walk, 1.0% work from home (2000); Travel time to work: 24.3% less than 15 minutes, 34.3% 15 to 30 minutes, 18.1% 30 to 45 minutes, 12.2% 45 to 60 minutes, 11.0% 60 minutes or more (2000)

ELWOOD (village). Covers a land area of 2.711 square miles and a water area of 0 square miles. Located at 41.41° N. Lat.; 88.11° W. Long. Elevation is 648 feet.
Population: 1,620 (2000); Race: 97.1% White, 0.2% Black, 1.5% Asian, 0.0% American Indian and Alaska Native, 2.8% Hispanic of any race, 1.2% two or more races (2000); Density: 597.6 persons per square mile (2000); Age: 25.5% under 18, 13.9% over 64 (2000); Marriage status: 18.1% never married, 63.9% now married, 9.1% widowed, 9.0% divorced (2000); Foreign born: 2.0% (2000); Ancestry (includes multiple ancestries): 31.2% German, 19.7% Irish, 13.6% Italian, 9.7% Other groups, 9.4% Polish (2000).
Economy: In agricultural area. U.S. Army arsenal, now abandoned, nearby. Much of arsenal to become tall-grass prairie. Single-family building permits issued: 21 (2001) / 50 (2000); Multi-family building permits issued: 27 (2001) / 0 (2000); Employment by occupation: 8.3% management, 13.4% professional, 12.6% services, 27.9% sales, 0.3% farming, 18.3% construction, 19.2% production (2000).
Income: Per capita income: $22,442 (2000); Median household income: $53,125 (2000); Poverty rate: 4.6% (2000).
Taxes: Total city taxes per capita: $110 (1997); City property taxes per capita: $18 (1997).
Education: High school graduation rate: 88.6% (2000); College graduation rate: 10.5% (2000).

School District(s)

Elwood C C School District 203 (KG-08)
2000 Enrollment: 310 815-423-5588

Housing: Homeownership rate: 83.1% (2000); Median home value: $132,300 (2000); Median rent: $391 per month (2000); Median age of housing: 9 years (2000).
Transportation: Commute to work: 95.5% car, 0.7% public transportation, 0.7% walk, 2.4% work from home (2000); Travel time to work: 10.9% less than 15 minutes, 47.0% 15 to 30 minutes, 19.3% 30 to 45 minutes, 10.7% 45 to 60 minutes, 12.0% 60 minutes or more (2000)

FAIRMONT (CDP). Covers a land area of 1.648 square miles and a water area of 0 square miles. Located at 41.56° N. Lat.; 88.06° W. Long. Elevation is 630 feet.
Population: 2,563 (2000); Race: 35.7% White, 57.1% Black, 0.6% Asian, 0.0% American Indian and Alaska Native, 8.6% Hispanic of any race, 1.9% two or more races (2000); Density: 1,555.6 persons per square mile (2000); Age: 25.4% under 18, 13.6% over 64 (2000); Marriage status: 35.4% never married, 45.1% now married, 9.0% widowed, 10.5% divorced (2000); Foreign born: 4.7% (2000); Ancestry (includes multiple ancestries): 56.9% Other groups, 10.1% Irish, 9.5% German, 4.2% English, 2.6% Polish (2000).
Economy: Employment by occupation: 8.6% management, 8.6% professional, 19.9% services, 33.0% sales, 0.0% farming, 6.8% construction, 23.1% production (2000).
Income: Per capita income: $17,260 (2000); Median household income: $40,907 (2000); Poverty rate: 14.0% (2000).
Education: High school graduation rate: 73.1% (2000); College graduation rate: 4.8% (2000).
Housing: Homeownership rate: 75.7% (2000); Median home value: $82,200 (2000); Median rent: $460 per month (2000); Median age of housing: 45 years (2000).
Transportation: Commute to work: 93.4% car, 2.6% public transportation, 0.5% walk, 0.4% work from home (2000); Travel time to work: 17.3% less than 15 minutes, 43.3% 15 to 30 minutes, 20.3% 30 to 45 minutes, 12.3% 45 to 60 minutes, 6.8% 60 minutes or more (2000)

FRANKFORT (village). Covers a land area of 10.907 square miles and a water area of 0 square miles. Located at 41.49° N. Lat.; 87.85° W. Long. Elevation is 767 feet.
Population: 10,391 (2000); Race: 93.8% White, 2.4% Black, 2.5% Asian, 0.2% American Indian and Alaska Native, 1.5% Hispanic of any race, 0.7% two or more races (2000); Density: 952.7 persons per square mile (2000); Age: 29.4% under 18, 10.6% over 64 (2000); Marriage status: 18.7% never married, 72.2% now married, 3.9% widowed, 5.1% divorced (2000); Foreign born: 4.3% (2000); Ancestry (includes multiple ancestries): 26.5% German, 21.8% Irish, 14.2% Polish, 12.7% Italian, 7.8% English (2000).
Economy: In suburbanizing area. Single-family building permits issued: 277 (2001) / 276 (2000); Multi-family building permits issued: 0 (2001) / 0 (2000); Employment by occupation: 21.6% management, 27.2% professional, 7.0% services, 27.2% sales, 0.0% farming, 8.2% construction, 8.8% production (2000).
Income: Per capita income: $33,968 (2000); Median household income: $83,055 (2000); Poverty rate: 2.3% (2000).
Taxes: Total city taxes per capita: $486 (1997); City property taxes per capita: $149 (1997).
Education: High school graduation rate: 94.9% (2000); College graduation rate: 40.7% (2000).

School District(s)

Frankfort C C School District 157c (PK-08)
2000 Enrollment: 1,596 815-469-5922
Summit Hill School District 161 (PK-08)
2000 Enrollment: 2,842 815-469-9103

Housing: Homeownership rate: 92.3% (2000); Median home value: $245,900 (2000); Median rent: $638 per month (2000); Median age of housing: 16 years (2000).
Transportation: Commute to work: 86.3% car, 6.9% public transportation, 1.2% walk, 5.2% work from home (2000); Travel time to work: 23.9% less than 15 minutes, 26.8% 15 to 30 minutes, 21.6% 30 to 45 minutes, 10.3% 45 to 60 minutes, 17.3% 60 minutes or more (2000)

Additional Information Contacts

Frankfort Chamber of Commerce 815-469-3356

FRANKFORT SQUARE (CDP). Covers a land area of 2.096 square miles and a water area of 0 square miles. Located at 41.51° N. Lat.; 87.80° W. Long.
Population: 7,766 (2000); Race: 94.1% White, 1.9% Black, 1.7% Asian, 0.0% American Indian and Alaska Native, 4.0% Hispanic of any race, 0.5% two or more races (2000); Density: 3,705.4 persons per square mile (2000); Age: 34.2% under 18, 2.2% over 64 (2000); Marriage status: 23.6% never married, 64.4% now married, 2.3% widowed, 9.7% divorced (2000); Foreign born: 3.3% (2000); Ancestry (includes multiple ancestries): 27.8% Irish, 27.6% German, 20.7% Polish, 11.0% Italian, 9.4% Other groups (2000).
Economy: Employment by occupation: 14.1% management, 17.5% professional, 9.1% services, 31.1% sales, 0.0% farming, 13.0% construction, 15.2% production (2000).
Income: Per capita income: $22,038 (2000); Median household income: $69,459 (2000); Poverty rate: 2.4% (2000).
Education: High school graduation rate: 94.3% (2000); College graduation rate: 22.2% (2000).
Housing: Homeownership rate: 95.5% (2000); Median home value: $153,300 (2000); Median rent: $726 per month (2000); Median age of housing: 20 years (2000).
Transportation: Commute to work: 85.3% car, 10.9% public transportation, 0.5% walk, 2.5% work from home (2000); Travel time to work: 20.7% less than 15 minutes, 27.5% 15 to 30 minutes, 19.1% 30 to 45 minutes, 9.1% 45 to 60 minutes, 23.6% 60 minutes or more (2000)

GODLEY (village). Covers a land area of 1.086 square miles and a water area of 0 square miles. Located at 41.23° N. Lat.; 88.24° W. Long. Elevation is 582 feet.
History: Godley began as a coal town settled by Scotch, Irish, and Welsh miners in the 1880's. The population declined when the mines closed in the early 1900's.
Population: 594 (2000); Race: 92.1% White, 0.7% Black, 0.0% Asian, 0.0% American Indian and Alaska Native, 10.4% Hispanic of any race, 1.0% two or more races (2000); Density: 547.0 persons per square mile (2000); Age: 42.1% under 18, 3.9% over 64 (2000); Marriage status: 18.6% never married, 63.6% now married, 4.1% widowed, 13.7% divorced (2000); Foreign born: 1.9% (2000); Ancestry (includes multiple ancestries): 22.3% Other groups, 16.4% German, 15.9% Irish, 11.3% English, 8.9% Italian (2000).
Economy: Single-family building permits issued: 4 (2001) / 4 (2000); Multi-family building permits issued: 0 (2001) / 4 (2000); Employment by occupation: 6.5% management, 7.8% professional, 21.2% services, 19.0% sales, 0.0% farming, 20.3% construction, 25.1% production (2000).
Income: Per capita income: $14,238 (2000); Median household income: $42,857 (2000); Poverty rate: 14.2% (2000).
Taxes: Total city taxes per capita: $41 (1997); City property taxes per capita: $11 (1997).
Education: High school graduation rate: 78.1% (2000); College graduation rate: 3.8% (2000).
Housing: Homeownership rate: 78.9% (2000); Median home value: $100,500 (2000); Median rent: $475 per month (2000); Median age of housing: 12 years (2000).
Transportation: Commute to work: 91.5% car, 0.4% public transportation, 0.4% walk, 0.4% work from home (2000); Travel time to work: 28.7% less than 15 minutes, 28.3% 15 to 30 minutes, 17.0% 30 to 45 minutes, 11.2% 45 to 60 minutes, 14.8% 60 minutes or more (2000)

GOODINGS GROVE (CDP). Covers a land area of 9.420 square miles and a water area of 0.009 square miles. Located at 41.62° N. Lat.; 87.94° W. Long. Elevation is 757 feet.
Population: 17,084 (2000); Race: 97.0% White, 0.3% Black, 1.3% Asian, 0.1% American Indian and Alaska Native, 3.2% Hispanic of any race, 1.3% two or more races (2000); Density: 1,813.6 persons per square mile (2000); Age: 30.9% under 18, 5.5% over 64 (2000); Marriage status: 23.3% never married, 69.7% now married, 3.2% widowed, 3.8% divorced (2000); Foreign born: 8.0% (2000); Ancestry (includes multiple ancestries): 28.2% Polish, 24.7% Irish, 23.5% German, 15.7% Italian, 5.7% Other groups (2000).
Economy: Employment by occupation: 18.0% management, 18.0% professional, 10.2% services, 31.6% sales, 0.0% farming, 11.4% construction, 10.7% production (2000).
Income: Per capita income: $29,452 (2000); Median household income: $84,484 (2000); Poverty rate: 1.8% (2000).
Education: High school graduation rate: 92.3% (2000); College graduation rate: 30.4% (2000).
Housing: Homeownership rate: 98.2% (2000); Median home value: $219,500 (2000); Median rent: $830 per month (2000); Median age of housing: 16 years (2000).
Transportation: Commute to work: 93.8% car, 2.7% public transportation, 0.3% walk, 2.6% work from home (2000); Travel time to work: 13.9% less

than 15 minutes, 24.1% 15 to 30 minutes, 26.7% 30 to 45 minutes, 18.2% 45 to 60 minutes, 17.1% 60 minutes or more (2000)

INGALLS PARK (CDP). Covers a land area of 1.081 square miles and a water area of 0 square miles. Located at 41.52° N. Lat.; 88.03° W. Long. Elevation is 620 feet.

Population: 3,082 (2000); Race: 91.9% White, 1.8% Black, 0.0% Asian, 0.2% American Indian and Alaska Native, 12.5% Hispanic of any race, 3.5% two or more races (2000); Density: 2,850.3 persons per square mile (2000); Age: 25.4% under 18, 12.0% over 64 (2000); Marriage status: 24.4% never married, 58.3% now married, 5.0% widowed, 12.3% divorced (2000); Foreign born: 4.0% (2000); Ancestry (includes multiple ancestries): 31.5% German, 22.9% Irish, 20.5% Other groups, 11.4% Italian, 10.0% English (2000).

Economy: Employment by occupation: 8.0% management, 8.7% professional, 12.4% services, 29.8% sales, 0.0% farming, 14.9% construction, 26.2% production (2000).

Income: Per capita income: $18,628 (2000); Median household income: $44,076 (2000); Poverty rate: 5.1% (2000).

Education: High school graduation rate: 82.9% (2000); College graduation rate: 5.9% (2000).

Housing: Homeownership rate: 75.7% (2000); Median home value: $83,500 (2000); Median rent: $502 per month (2000); Median age of housing: 52 years (2000).

Transportation: Commute to work: 95.3% car, 1.4% public transportation, 0.6% walk, 1.9% work from home (2000); Travel time to work: 33.1% less than 15 minutes, 36.5% 15 to 30 minutes, 15.3% 30 to 45 minutes, 8.0% 45 to 60 minutes, 7.2% 60 minutes or more (2000)

JOLIET (city). Covers a land area of 38.059 square miles and a water area of 0.286 square miles. Located at 41.53° N. Lat.; 88.10° W. Long. Elevation is 600 feet.

History: The town of Joliet was laid out in 1834 with the name of Juliet (a neighboring village was Romeo) and incorporated in 1837 as the seat of Will County. Industry bloomed in Joliet when the Illinois & Michigan Canal was completed here in 1848. Limestone from the Joliet quarries was shipped across the country. Steel manufacturing in the late 1800's was replaced by the production of wallpaper as a leading industry.

Population: 106,221 (2000); Race: 69.3% White, 18.3% Black, 1.3% Asian, 0.4% American Indian and Alaska Native, 18.2% Hispanic of any race, 2.1% two or more races (2000); Density: 2,790.9 persons per square mile (2000); Age: 29.3% under 18, 11.0% over 64 (2000); Marriage status: 27.9% never married, 56.0% now married, 7.0% widowed, 9.1% divorced (2000); Foreign born: 10.9% (2000); Ancestry (includes multiple ancestries): 34.4% Other groups, 18.0% German, 13.8% Irish, 8.7% Italian, 7.7% Polish (2000).

Vital Statistics: Birth rate: 173.5 per 10,000 population (1998)

Economy: Unemployment rate: 8.3% (11/2002); Total civilian labor force: 44,932 (11/2002); Single-family building permits issued: 1,893 (2001) / 1,522 (2000); Multi-family building permits issued: 144 (2001) / 16 (2000); Employment by occupation: 10.0% management, 17.7% professional, 16.2% services, 27.4% sales, 0.2% farming, 10.4% construction, 18.3% production (2000).

Income: Per capita income: $19,390 (2000); Median household income: $47,761 (2000); Poverty rate: 10.8% (2000).

Taxes: Total city taxes per capita: $321 (2000); City property taxes per capita: $118 (2000).

Education: High school graduation rate: 78.8% (2000); College graduation rate: 18.6% (2000).

School District(s)

Joliet Public School District 86 (PK-08)
2000 Enrollment: 9,271 815-740-3196

Joliet Township HS District 204 (09-12)
2000 Enrollment: 4,401 815-727-6970

Laraway C C School District 70c (PK-08)
2000 Enrollment: 506 815-727-5115

Rockdale School District 84 (KG-08)
2000 Enrollment: 256 815-725-5321

S Will Co Coop for Special Ed (01-12)
2000 Enrollment: 60 815-741-7777

Troy Community Cons School District 30c (PK-08)
2000 Enrollment: 2,832 815-725-8307

Union School District 81 (KG-08)
2000 Enrollment: 170 815-726-5218

Four-year College(s)

University of Saint Francis (Private, Not-for-profit, Roman Catholic)
2001 Enrollment: 3,919 815-740-3360
2001 Tuition: In-state $14,680; Out-of-state $14,680

Two-year College(s)

Joliet Junior College (Public)
2001 Enrollment: 12,089 815-729-9020
2001 Tuition: In-state $5,249; Out-of-state $6,594

Housing: Homeownership rate: 70.3% (2000); Median home value: $119,900 (2000); Median rent: $487 per month (2000); Median age of housing: 36 years (2000).

Hospitals: Silver Cross Hospital; Saint Joseph Medical Center (545 beds); Stateville Correctional Center Hospital (32 beds)

Safety: Violent crime rate: n/a; Property crime rate: 412.3 per 10,000 population (2001).

Newspapers: Herald-News (7 x week); The Times Weekly Newspaper (1 x week)

Transportation: Commute to work: 92.8% car, 2.6% public transportation, 1.6% walk, 1.8% work from home (2000); Travel time to work: 28.9% less than 15 minutes, 29.9% 15 to 30 minutes, 18.1% 30 to 45 minutes, 10.8% 45 to 60 minutes, 12.4% 60 minutes or more (2000); Amtrak: Service available.

Additional Information Contacts

Heritage Corridor Convention & Visitors Bureau 815-727-2323
Joliet Region Chamber of Commerce 815-727-5371
Will Grundy Association of Realtors 815-744-4520

LAKEWOOD SHORES (CDP). Covers a land area of 2.321 square miles and a water area of 0.423 square miles. Located at 41.26° N. Lat.; 88.13° W. Long. Elevation is 565 feet.

Population: 1,487 (2000); Race: 97.1% White, 0.0% Black, 0.0% Asian, 0.6% American Indian and Alaska Native, 3.6% Hispanic of any race, 0.2% two or more races (2000); Density: 640.7 persons per square mile (2000); Age: 32.1% under 18, 4.8% over 64 (2000); Marriage status: 22.1% never married, 62.2% now married, 2.5% widowed, 13.2% divorced (2000); Foreign born: 1.3% (2000); Ancestry (includes multiple ancestries): 22.5% Irish, 16.7% German, 13.7% Polish, 11.0% English, 10.7% United States or American (2000).

Economy: Employment by occupation: 6.2% management, 8.0% professional, 11.7% services, 21.8% sales, 0.0% farming, 25.1% construction, 27.2% production (2000).

Income: Per capita income: $18,414 (2000); Median household income: $52,097 (2000); Poverty rate: 2.6% (2000).

Education: High school graduation rate: 81.6% (2000); College graduation rate: 5.5% (2000).

Housing: Homeownership rate: 89.5% (2000); Median home value: $107,100 (2000); Median rent: $623 per month (2000); Median age of housing: 39 years (2000).

Transportation: Commute to work: 92.1% car, 0.0% public transportation, 0.9% walk, 7.1% work from home (2000); Travel time to work: 18.8% less than 15 minutes, 36.5% 15 to 30 minutes, 25.2% 30 to 45 minutes, 9.0% 45 to 60 minutes, 10.5% 60 minutes or more (2000)

LOCKPORT (city). Covers a land area of 7.084 square miles and a water area of 0.011 square miles. Located at 41.58° N. Lat.; 88.04° W. Long. Elevation is 650 feet.

History: Lockport developed as a shipping and transfer point on the Illinois & Michigan Canal. This was the location of the lock that controlled the volume of water from Lake Michigan. The canal company offices were located here also.

Population: 15,191 (2000); Race: 96.2% White, 0.3% Black, 0.7% Asian, 0.1% American Indian and Alaska Native, 4.9% Hispanic of any race, 1.5% two or more races (2000); Density: 2,144.3 persons per square mile (2000); Age: 27.3% under 18, 10.4% over 64 (2000); Marriage status: 22.9% never married, 63.6% now married, 5.5% widowed, 8.0% divorced (2000); Foreign born: 4.0% (2000); Ancestry (includes multiple ancestries): 31.0% German, 24.5% Irish, 20.5% Polish, 16.2% Italian, 8.1% Other groups (2000).

Economy: Single-family building permits issued: 382 (2001) / 425 (2000); Multi-family building permits issued: 0 (2001) / 18 (2000); Employment by occupation: 12.3% management, 19.6% professional, 11.4% services, 28.8% sales, 0.0% farming, 12.8% construction, 15.0% production (2000).

Income: Per capita income: $24,939 (2000); Median household income: $59,179 (2000); Poverty rate: 3.5% (2000).

Taxes: Total city taxes per capita: $263 (1997); City property taxes per capita: $178 (1997).

Education: High school graduation rate: 89.5% (2000); College graduation rate: 22.6% (2000).

School District(s)

Fairmont School District 89 (PK-08)
2000 Enrollment: 388 815-726-6318
Homer Community Cons School District 33c (KG-08)
2000 Enrollment: 2,848 708-301-3034
Lockport School District 91 (KG-08)
2000 Enrollment: 762 815-838-0737
Lockport Township HS District 205 (09-12)
2000 Enrollment: 2,945 815-588-8100
Taft School District 90 (KG-08)
2000 Enrollment: 314 815-838-0408
Will County School District 92 (KG-08)
2000 Enrollment: 1,805 815-838-8031

Housing: Homeownership rate: 79.1% (2000); Median home value: $149,700 (2000); Median rent: $576 per month (2000); Median age of housing: 28 years (2000).
Transportation: Commute to work: 93.2% car, 3.7% public transportation, 0.7% walk, 1.8% work from home (2000); Travel time to work: 19.3% less than 15 minutes, 28.7% 15 to 30 minutes, 23.1% 30 to 45 minutes, 11.7% 45 to 60 minutes, 17.1% 60 minutes or more (2000)
Additional Information Contacts
Lockport Chamber of Commerce 815-838-3357

MANHATTAN (village). Covers a land area of 3.366 square miles and a water area of 0 square miles. Located at 41.42° N. Lat.; 87.98° W. Long. Elevation is 685 feet.
Population: 3,330 (2000); Race: 97.3% White, 0.4% Black, 0.2% Asian, 0.0% American Indian and Alaska Native, 2.7% Hispanic of any race, 0.7% two or more races (2000); Density: 989.3 persons per square mile (2000); Age: 31.1% under 18, 7.5% over 64 (2000); Marriage status: 23.6% never married, 61.9% now married, 5.3% widowed, 9.2% divorced (2000); Foreign born: 2.5% (2000); Ancestry (includes multiple ancestries): 34.0% German, 31.3% Irish, 11.8% Polish, 10.1% English, 9.9% Italian (2000).
Economy: In agricultural area. Single-family building permits issued: 33 (2001) / 40 (2000); Multi-family building permits issued: 4 (2001) / 2 (2000); Employment by occupation: 13.0% management, 18.7% professional, 12.8% services, 25.9% sales, 0.2% farming, 15.5% construction, 13.9% production (2000).
Income: Per capita income: $21,666 (2000); Median household income: $55,559 (2000); Poverty rate: 3.6% (2000).
Taxes: Total city taxes per capita: $215 (1997); City property taxes per capita: $186 (1997).
Education: High school graduation rate: 92.9% (2000); College graduation rate: 19.2% (2000).

School District(s)

Manhattan School District 114 (PK-08)
2000 Enrollment: 874 815-478-6090

Housing: Homeownership rate: 79.3% (2000); Median home value: $150,500 (2000); Median rent: $574 per month (2000); Median age of housing: 23 years (2000).
Transportation: Commute to work: 92.5% car, 2.5% public transportation, 2.0% walk, 2.7% work from home (2000); Travel time to work: 22.2% less than 15 minutes, 35.8% 15 to 30 minutes, 20.7% 30 to 45 minutes, 9.1% 45 to 60 minutes, 12.2% 60 minutes or more (2000)
Additional Information Contacts
Manhattan Chamber of Commerce 815-478-3811

MOKENA (village). Covers a land area of 5.995 square miles and a water area of 0.004 square miles. Located at 41.53° N. Lat.; 87.87° W. Long. Elevation is 706 feet.
Population: 14,583 (2000); Race: 97.0% White, 0.1% Black, 1.2% Asian, 0.0% American Indian and Alaska Native, 3.2% Hispanic of any race, 0.6% two or more races (2000); Density: 2,432.4 persons per square mile (2000); Age: 32.1% under 18, 6.3% over 64 (2000); Marriage status: 23.7% never married, 68.5% now married, 2.6% widowed, 5.2% divorced (2000); Foreign born: 4.1% (2000); Ancestry (includes multiple ancestries): 29.4% Irish, 29.1% German, 18.5% Polish, 14.5% Italian, 6.3% Other groups (2000).
Economy: In agricultural area: corn, soybeans; dairying. Manufacturing: water pollution control equipment; galvanized ducts and fittings; food processing equipment, plastic injection molds. Single-family building permits issued: 199 (2001) / 184 (2000); Multi-family building permits issued: 0 (2001) / 0 (2000); Employment by occupation: 19.1% management, 22.6% professional, 9.0% services, 30.5% sales, 0.0% farming, 10.9% construction, 7.9% production (2000).
Income: Per capita income: $26,737 (2000); Median household income: $74,703 (2000); Poverty rate: 1.0% (2000).
Taxes: Total city taxes per capita: $102 (1997); City property taxes per capita: $43 (1997).
Education: High school graduation rate: 94.6% (2000); College graduation rate: 34.7% (2000).

School District(s)

Mokena School District 159 (PK-08)
2000 Enrollment: 2,267 708-479-3100

Housing: Homeownership rate: 87.5% (2000); Median home value: $217,000 (2000); Median rent: $613 per month (2000); Median age of housing: 9 years (2000).
Transportation: Commute to work: 86.5% car, 9.9% public transportation, 1.0% walk, 2.4% work from home (2000); Travel time to work: 18.9% less than 15 minutes, 28.7% 15 to 30 minutes, 20.9% 30 to 45 minutes, 11.3% 45 to 60 minutes, 20.1% 60 minutes or more (2000)
Additional Information Contacts
Mokena Chamber of Commerce 708-479-2468

MONEE (village). Covers a land area of 3.100 square miles and a water area of 0 square miles. Located at 41.41° N. Lat.; 87.74° W. Long. Elevation is 800 feet.
Population: 2,924 (2000); Race: 95.7% White, 1.5% Black, 0.0% Asian, 0.0% American Indian and Alaska Native, 2.9% Hispanic of any race, 1.2% two or more races (2000); Density: 943.3 persons per square mile (2000); Age: 22.2% under 18, 16.3% over 64 (2000); Marriage status: 13.3% never married, 71.3% now married, 5.5% widowed, 9.9% divorced (2000); Foreign born: 1.7% (2000); Ancestry (includes multiple ancestries): 30.4% German, 24.5% Irish, 13.6% Polish, 12.5% Italian, 8.5% Other groups (2000).
Economy: In agricultural area. Single-family building permits issued: 125 (2001) / 123 (2000); Multi-family building permits issued: 3 (2001) / 3 (2000); Employment by occupation: 14.1% management, 16.8% professional, 11.5% services, 28.8% sales, 0.3% farming, 13.0% construction, 15.6% production (2000).
Income: Per capita income: $27,687 (2000); Median household income: $58,625 (2000); Poverty rate: 3.4% (2000).
Taxes: Total city taxes per capita: $277 (1997); City property taxes per capita: $194 (1997).
Education: High school graduation rate: 86.5% (2000); College graduation rate: 17.1% (2000).
Housing: Homeownership rate: 87.3% (2000); Median home value: $151,900 (2000); Median rent: $545 per month (2000); Median age of housing: 5 years (2000).
Transportation: Commute to work: 88.5% car, 3.9% public transportation, 1.6% walk, 4.7% work from home (2000); Travel time to work: 19.8% less than 15 minutes, 35.2% 15 to 30 minutes, 20.1% 30 to 45 minutes, 9.0% 45 to 60 minutes, 15.9% 60 minutes or more (2000)
Additional Information Contacts
Monee Chamber of Commerce 708-534-5332

NEW LENOX (village). Covers a land area of 10.094 square miles and a water area of 0.018 square miles. Located at 41.50° N. Lat.; 87.97° W. Long. Elevation is 625 feet.
History: New Lenox was first settled in the 1820's along Hickory Creek.
Population: 17,771 (2000); Race: 97.7% White, 0.1% Black, 0.5% Asian, 0.1% American Indian and Alaska Native, 2.9% Hispanic of any race, 0.8% two or more races (2000); Density: 1,760.5 persons per square mile (2000); Age: 32.8% under 18, 7.7% over 64 (2000); Marriage status: 21.2% never married, 67.8% now married, 4.4% widowed, 6.6% divorced (2000); Foreign born: 1.3% (2000); Ancestry (includes multiple ancestries): 31.5% German, 27.9% Irish, 16.8% Polish, 13.4% Italian, 7.9% English (2000).
Economy: Single-family building permits issued: 324 (2001) / 313 (2000); Multi-family building permits issued: 0 (2001) / 0 (2000); Employment by occupation: 15.0% management, 20.2% professional, 8.8% services, 30.8% sales, 0.1% farming, 13.0% construction, 12.1% production (2000).
Income: Per capita income: $25,161 (2000); Median household income: $67,697 (2000); Poverty rate: 2.4% (2000).
Taxes: Total city taxes per capita: $86 (1997); City property taxes per capita: $67 (1997).
Education: High school graduation rate: 92.5% (2000); College graduation rate: 26.2% (2000).

School District(s)

Lincoln Way Community H S District 210 (09-12)
2000 Enrollment: 4,961 815-485-7600
Lincoln-Way Area Special Education Ja District (09-12)
2000 Enrollment: 21 815-485-6969
New Lenox School District 122 (PK-08)
2000 Enrollment: 4,435 815-485-2169

Housing: Homeownership rate: 90.1% (2000); Median home value: $180,000 (2000); Median rent: $631 per month (2000); Median age of housing: 13 years (2000).
Transportation: Commute to work: 89.4% car, 6.1% public transportation, 0.5% walk, 3.1% work from home (2000); Travel time to work: 21.2% less than 15 minutes, 27.3% 15 to 30 minutes, 21.1% 30 to 45 minutes, 11.6% 45 to 60 minutes, 18.9% 60 minutes or more (2000)
Additional Information Contacts
New Lenox Chamber of Commerce. 815-485-4241

PEOTONE (village). Covers a land area of 1.516 square miles and a water area of 0.003 square miles. Located at 41.32° N. Lat.; 87.79° W. Long. Elevation is 702 feet.
History: Incorporated 1869.
Population: 3,385 (2000); Race: 97.8% White, 0.3% Black, 0.3% Asian, 0.0% American Indian and Alaska Native, 1.0% Hispanic of any race, 1.6% two or more races (2000); Density: 2,232.4 persons per square mile (2000); Age: 30.3% under 18, 10.5% over 64 (2000); Marriage status: 21.9% never married, 60.6% now married, 7.1% widowed, 10.4% divorced (2000); Foreign born: 1.0% (2000); Ancestry (includes multiple ancestries): 39.7% German, 23.9% Irish, 14.7% English, 11.7% Polish, 9.9% Italian (2000).
Economy: In agricultural area. Manufacturing of steel products. Single-family building permits issued: 22 (2001) / 19 (2000); Multi-family building permits issued: 0 (2001) / 0 (2000); Employment by occupation: 10.0% management, 19.0% professional, 10.9% services, 28.5% sales, 2.2% farming, 17.4% construction, 12.0% production (2000).
Income: Per capita income: $23,415 (2000); Median household income: $56,404 (2000); Poverty rate: 0.8% (2000).
Taxes: Total city taxes per capita: $219 (1997); City property taxes per capita: $132 (1997).
Education: High school graduation rate: 90.7% (2000); College graduation rate: 21.3% (2000).

School District(s)

Peotone C U School District 207u (PK-12)
2000 Enrollment: 1,752 708-258-3246
Housing: Homeownership rate: 68.7% (2000); Median home value: $148,600 (2000); Median rent: $514 per month (2000); Median age of housing: 36 years (2000).
Newspapers: Peotone Vedette (1 x week); New Lenox Community Reporter (1 x week); Monee Monitor (1 x week); Manhattan American (1 x week); Grant Park Gazette (1 x week); Crete Record (1 x week); Beecher Herald (1 x week)
Transportation: Commute to work: 92.9% car, 3.0% public transportation, 2.8% walk, 0.8% work from home (2000); Travel time to work: 32.0% less than 15 minutes, 26.5% 15 to 30 minutes, 20.2% 30 to 45 minutes, 6.7% 45 to 60 minutes, 14.6% 60 minutes or more (2000)
Additional Information Contacts
Peotone Chamber of Commerce. 708-258-9450

PLAINFIELD (village). Covers a land area of 11.612 square miles and a water area of 0.835 square miles. Located at 41.61° N. Lat.; 88.20° W. Long. Elevation is 615 feet.
History: Plainfield began as a trading post founded by the Frenchman Du Pazhe about 1790, and later operated by Vetel Vermette for the American Fur Trading Company. The town grew around a cabin built by Captain James Walker in 1829, and was first known as Walker's Grove. The name of Plainfield refers to the flat prairie setting.
Population: 13,038 (2000); Race: 94.6% White, 0.7% Black, 2.0% Asian, 0.0% American Indian and Alaska Native, 4.8% Hispanic of any race, 0.7% two or more races (2000); Density: 1,122.8 persons per square mile (2000); Age: 31.2% under 18, 6.3% over 64 (2000); Marriage status: 19.4% never married, 71.3% now married, 4.0% widowed, 5.3% divorced (2000); Foreign born: 3.9% (2000); Ancestry (includes multiple ancestries): 31.1% German, 20.2% Irish, 16.0% Italian, 15.4% Polish, 9.2% English (2000).
Economy: Single-family building permits issued: 627 (2001) / 602 (2000); Multi-family building permits issued: 12 (2001) / 0 (2000); Employment by occupation: 18.9% management, 23.5% professional, 8.1% services, 29.4% sales, 0.0% farming, 10.3% construction, 9.8% production (2000).
Income: Per capita income: $28,242 (2000); Median household income: $80,799 (2000); Poverty rate: 1.8% (2000).
Taxes: Total city taxes per capita: $272 (1997); City property taxes per capita: $128 (1997).
Education: High school graduation rate: 94.4% (2000); College graduation rate: 33.9% (2000).

School District(s)

Plainfield School District 202 (KG-12)
2000 Enrollment: 11,986 815-439-3240
Housing: Homeownership rate: 88.1% (2000); Median home value: $198,300 (2000); Median rent: $631 per month (2000); Median age of housing: 6 years (2000).
Newspapers: The Enterprise (1 x week)
Transportation: Commute to work: 92.5% car, 2.2% public transportation, 1.0% walk, 3.8% work from home (2000); Travel time to work: 18.3% less than 15 minutes, 27.1% 15 to 30 minutes, 24.6% 30 to 45 minutes, 14.9% 45 to 60 minutes, 15.1% 60 minutes or more (2000)
Additional Information Contacts
Plainfield Chamber of Commerce 815-436-4431

PRESTON HEIGHTS (CDP). Covers a land area of 1.494 square miles and a water area of 0 square miles. Located at 41.49° N. Lat.; 88.07° W. Long. Elevation is 605 feet.
Population: 2,527 (2000); Race: 31.9% White, 62.3% Black, 0.0% Asian, 0.0% American Indian and Alaska Native, 6.6% Hispanic of any race, 3.0% two or more races (2000); Density: 1,691.4 persons per square mile (2000); Age: 30.1% under 18, 10.8% over 64 (2000); Marriage status: 32.2% never married, 51.7% now married, 6.5% widowed, 9.5% divorced (2000); Foreign born: 3.5% (2000); Ancestry (includes multiple ancestries): 62.2% Other groups, 8.6% German, 6.2% Irish, 4.0% Italian, 3.8% United States or American (2000).
Economy: Employment by occupation: 7.1% management, 9.0% professional, 20.8% services, 30.9% sales, 0.0% farming, 7.7% construction, 24.5% production (2000).
Income: Per capita income: $18,681 (2000); Median household income: $42,500 (2000); Poverty rate: 9.7% (2000).
Education: High school graduation rate: 77.9% (2000); College graduation rate: 10.2% (2000).
Housing: Homeownership rate: 67.2% (2000); Median home value: $101,400 (2000); Median rent: $504 per month (2000); Median age of housing: 36 years (2000).
Transportation: Commute to work: 93.1% car, 4.2% public transportation, 0.7% walk, 1.6% work from home (2000); Travel time to work: 28.3% less than 15 minutes, 38.2% 15 to 30 minutes, 13.5% 30 to 45 minutes, 9.9% 45 to 60 minutes, 10.1% 60 minutes or more (2000)

ROCKDALE (village). Covers a land area of 0.794 square miles and a water area of 0 square miles. Located at 41.50° N. Lat.; 88.11° W. Long. Elevation is 550 feet.
History: Incorporated 1903.
Population: 1,888 (2000); Race: 83.4% White, 1.6% Black, 0.6% Asian, 0.8% American Indian and Alaska Native, 21.8% Hispanic of any race, 4.7% two or more races (2000); Density: 2,377.4 persons per square mile (2000); Age: 25.3% under 18, 12.8% over 64 (2000); Marriage status: 26.7% never married, 51.8% now married, 8.7% widowed, 12.8% divorced (2000); Foreign born: 9.1% (2000); Ancestry (includes multiple ancestries): 27.6% Other groups, 18.7% German, 14.8% Irish, 12.7% Italian, 9.2% Polish (2000).
Economy: In agricultural area. Manufacturing of construction materials. Illinois Youth Center is here. Single-family building permits issued: 0 (2001) / 3 (2000); Multi-family building permits issued: 0 (2001) / 0 (2000); Employment by occupation: 7.4% management, 7.7% professional, 15.0% services, 27.3% sales, 0.0% farming, 16.9% construction, 25.7% production (2000).
Income: Per capita income: $18,738 (2000); Median household income: $39,954 (2000); Poverty rate: 9.3% (2000).
Taxes: Total city taxes per capita: $205 (1997); City property taxes per capita: $57 (1997).
Education: High school graduation rate: 77.2% (2000); College graduation rate: 7.4% (2000).
Housing: Homeownership rate: 56.7% (2000); Median home value: $94,300 (2000); Median rent: $499 per month (2000); Median age of housing: 52 years (2000).
Transportation: Commute to work: 92.1% car, 1.1% public transportation, 3.5% walk, 0.7% work from home (2000); Travel time to work: 42.4% less than 15 minutes, 25.9% 15 to 30 minutes, 15.6% 30 to 45 minutes, 6.6% 45 to 60 minutes, 9.5% 60 minutes or more (2000)

ROMEOVILLE (village). Aka Romeo. Covers a land area of 14.514 square miles and a water area of 0.381 square miles. Located at 41.64° N. Lat.; 88.10° W. Long. Elevation is 614 feet.

History: Romeoville developed along the Illinois & Michigan Canal. An early industry was the Globe Oil Refinery.
Population: 21,153 (2000); Race: 84.5% White, 5.5% Black, 2.9% Asian, 0.3% American Indian and Alaska Native, 13.1% Hispanic of any race, 2.1% two or more races (2000); Density: 1,457.4 persons per square mile (2000); Age: 28.6% under 18, 5.3% over 64 (2000); Marriage status: 28.2% never married, 62.1% now married, 3.4% widowed, 6.3% divorced (2000); Foreign born: 9.4% (2000); Ancestry (includes multiple ancestries): 22.8% German, 22.5% Other groups, 19.3% Irish, 15.7% Polish, 9.8% Italian (2000).
Vital Statistics: Birth rate: 132.4 per 10,000 population (1998)
Economy: Single-family building permits issued: 1,148 (2001) / 1,175 (2000); Multi-family building permits issued: 0 (2001) / 0 (2000); Employment by occupation: 12.2% management, 16.3% professional, 10.9% services, 31.5% sales, 0.0% farming, 10.9% construction, 18.1% production (2000).
Income: Per capita income: $21,221 (2000); Median household income: $60,738 (2000); Poverty rate: 1.9% (2000).
Taxes: Total city taxes per capita: $216 (1997); City property taxes per capita: $57 (1997).
Education: High school graduation rate: 84.3% (2000); College graduation rate: 19.3% (2000).

School District(s)

Valley View CUSD #365u (PK-12)
2000 Enrollment: 13,558 815-886-2700

Four-year College(s)

Lewis University (Private, Not-for-profit, Roman Catholic)
2001 Enrollment: 4,407 815-838-0500
2001 Tuition: In-state $14,976; Out-of-state $14,976

Housing: Homeownership rate: 86.1% (2000); Median home value: $118,100 (2000); Median rent: $808 per month (2000); Median age of housing: 21 years (2000).
Newspapers: Catholic Explorer (1 x week)
Transportation: Commute to work: 92.4% car, 2.6% public transportation, 3.0% walk, 1.4% work from home (2000); Travel time to work: 23.0% less than 15 minutes, 23.4% 15 to 30 minutes, 24.2% 30 to 45 minutes, 14.6% 45 to 60 minutes, 14.7% 60 minutes or more (2000)
Airports: Lewis University
Additional Information Contacts
Romeoville Chamber of Commerce 815-886-2076

SHOREWOOD (village). Covers a land area of 3.887 square miles and a water area of 0.065 square miles. Located at 41.51° N. Lat.; 88.20° W. Long. Elevation is 581 feet.
Population: 7,686 (2000); Race: 92.2% White, 1.7% Black, 2.2% Asian, 0.1% American Indian and Alaska Native, 5.5% Hispanic of any race, 1.8% two or more races (2000); Density: 1,977.2 persons per square mile (2000); Age: 31.9% under 18, 5.6% over 64 (2000); Marriage status: 22.5% never married, 65.8% now married, 3.7% widowed, 7.9% divorced (2000); Foreign born: 4.3% (2000); Ancestry (includes multiple ancestries): 29.6% German, 18.3% Irish, 13.5% Italian, 13.4% Polish, 10.8% Other groups (2000).
Economy: Single-family building permits issued: 159 (2001) / 101 (2000); Multi-family building permits issued: 0 (2001) / 22 (2000); Employment by occupation: 16.2% management, 22.5% professional, 8.9% services, 27.8% sales, 0.0% farming, 10.1% construction, 14.5% production (2000).
Income: Per capita income: $28,199 (2000); Median household income: $76,842 (2000); Poverty rate: 2.0% (2000).
Taxes: Total city taxes per capita: $176 (1997); City property taxes per capita: $92 (1997).
Education: High school graduation rate: 93.0% (2000); College graduation rate: 33.6% (2000).
Housing: Homeownership rate: 95.9% (2000); Median home value: $162,900 (2000); Median rent: $894 per month (2000); Median age of housing: 18 years (2000).
Transportation: Commute to work: 95.0% car, 0.6% public transportation, 1.0% walk, 2.9% work from home (2000); Travel time to work: 25.9% less than 15 minutes, 37.2% 15 to 30 minutes, 15.2% 30 to 45 minutes, 11.3% 45 to 60 minutes, 10.4% 60 minutes or more (2000)
Additional Information Contacts
Shorewood Chamber of Commerce 815-725-2900

STEGER (village). Covers a land area of 3.524 square miles and a water area of 0 square miles. Located at 41.47° N. Lat.; 87.63° W. Long.
History: Steger grew up around the piano factory founded by John V. Steger.
Population: 9,682 (2000); Race: 87.3% White, 7.0% Black, 0.4% Asian, 0.1% American Indian and Alaska Native, 7.7% Hispanic of any race, 2.3% two or more races (2000); Density: 2,747.3 persons per square mile (2000); Age: 24.9% under 18, 12.3% over 64 (2000); Marriage status: 27.5% never married, 54.1% now married, 6.6% widowed, 11.8% divorced (2000); Foreign born: 4.6% (2000); Ancestry (includes multiple ancestries): 25.1% German, 17.0% Irish, 16.4% Other groups, 15.5% Italian, 11.0% Polish (2000).
Economy: Single-family building permits issued: 52 (2001) / 36 (2000); Multi-family building permits issued: 0 (2001) / 0 (2000); Employment by occupation: 10.6% management, 12.9% professional, 13.5% services, 28.1% sales, 0.1% farming, 13.8% construction, 21.0% production (2000).
Income: Per capita income: $19,816 (2000); Median household income: $43,275 (2000); Poverty rate: 8.5% (2000).
Taxes: Total city taxes per capita: $160 (1997); City property taxes per capita: $122 (1997).
Education: High school graduation rate: 81.4% (2000); College graduation rate: 10.5% (2000).

School District(s)

Steger School District 194 (PK-08)
2000 Enrollment: 1,588 708-755-0022

Housing: Homeownership rate: 66.0% (2000); Median home value: $98,000 (2000); Median rent: $563 per month (2000); Median age of housing: 36 years (2000).
Transportation: Commute to work: 89.8% car, 4.6% public transportation, 2.3% walk, 2.0% work from home (2000); Travel time to work: 29.9% less than 15 minutes, 33.4% 15 to 30 minutes, 17.6% 30 to 45 minutes, 5.9% 45 to 60 minutes, 13.2% 60 minutes or more (2000)

SYMERTON (village). Covers a land area of 0.051 square miles and a water area of 0 square miles. Located at 41.32° N. Lat.; 88.05° W. Long. Elevation is 635 feet.
Population: 106 (2000); Race: 100.0% White, 0.0% Black, 0.0% Asian, 0.0% American Indian and Alaska Native, 1.0% Hispanic of any race, 0.0% two or more races (2000); Density: 2,064.1 persons per square mile (2000); Age: 33.0% under 18, 6.0% over 64 (2000); Marriage status: 13.0% never married, 66.7% now married, 11.6% widowed, 8.7% divorced (2000); Foreign born: 0.0% (2000); Ancestry (includes multiple ancestries): 37.0% German, 32.0% Irish, 22.0% Italian, 16.0% English, 8.0% Other groups (2000).
Economy: In agricultural area. Employment by occupation: 23.8% management, 0.0% professional, 33.3% services, 11.9% sales, 0.0% farming, 7.1% construction, 23.8% production (2000).
Income: Per capita income: $17,863 (2000); Median household income: $60,357 (2000); Poverty rate: 0.0% (2000).
Taxes: Total city taxes per capita: $28 (1997); City property taxes per capita: $9 (1997).
Education: High school graduation rate: 86.4% (2000); College graduation rate: 5.1% (2000).
Housing: Homeownership rate: 93.9% (2000); Median home value: $93,000 (2000); Median rent: $950 per month (2000); Median age of housing: 60+ years (2000).
Transportation: Commute to work: 100.0% car, 0.0% public transportation, 0.0% walk, 0.0% work from home (2000); Travel time to work: 23.8% less than 15 minutes, 26.2% 15 to 30 minutes, 38.1% 30 to 45 minutes, 11.9% 45 to 60 minutes, 0.0% 60 minutes or more (2000)

UNIVERSITY PARK (village). Aka Park Forest South. Covers a land area of 9.758 square miles and a water area of 0.008 square miles. Located at 41.43° N. Lat.; 87.69° W. Long.
History: Seat of Governors State University.
Population: 6,662 (2000); Race: 10.0% White, 85.6% Black, 0.2% Asian, 0.0% American Indian and Alaska Native, 3.7% Hispanic of any race, 3.5% two or more races (2000); Density: 682.7 persons per square mile (2000); Age: 35.5% under 18, 6.1% over 64 (2000); Marriage status: 36.2% never married, 47.4% now married, 5.3% widowed, 11.2% divorced (2000); Foreign born: 3.7% (2000); Ancestry (includes multiple ancestries): 80.7% Other groups, 3.2% German, 3.0% United States or American, 1.1% Guyanese, 1.0% Jamaican (2000).
Economy: Manufacturing: electronic equipment, plastic products, food products, machinery, paper products. Single-family building permits issued: 39 (2001) / 27 (2000); Multi-family building permits issued: 0 (2001) / 0 (2000); Employment by occupation: 12.2% management, 20.0% professional, 14.2% services, 34.6% sales, 0.0% farming, 6.5% construction, 12.5% production (2000).
Income: Per capita income: $20,017 (2000); Median household income: $50,652 (2000); Poverty rate: 9.1% (2000).
Taxes: Total city taxes per capita: $1,016 (2000); City property taxes per capita: $863 (2000).

Education: High school graduation rate: 92.1% (2000); College graduation rate: 25.4% (2000).

Four-year College(s)

Governors State University (Public)
2001 Enrollment: 5,860 708-534-5000
2001 Tuition: In-state $2,352; Out-of-state $7,056

Housing: Homeownership rate: 58.5% (2000); Median home value: $94,000 (2000); Median rent: $630 per month (2000); Median age of housing: 26 years (2000).

Transportation: Commute to work: 84.4% car, 12.5% public transportation, 1.1% walk, 1.6% work from home (2000); Travel time to work: 15.0% less than 15 minutes, 29.1% 15 to 30 minutes, 13.8% 30 to 45 minutes, 14.4% 45 to 60 minutes, 27.7% 60 minutes or more (2000)

WILLOWBROOK (CDP). Covers a land area of 3.376 square miles and a water area of 0.016 square miles. Located at 41.45° N. Lat.; 87.54° W. Long.

Population: 2,130 (2000); Race: 72.1% White, 24.4% Black, 0.0% Asian, 0.0% American Indian and Alaska Native, 3.8% Hispanic of any race, 0.8% two or more races (2000); Density: 631.0 persons per square mile (2000); Age: 21.2% under 18, 12.2% over 64 (2000); Marriage status: 18.2% never married, 71.1% now married, 6.8% widowed, 4.0% divorced (2000); Foreign born: 3.7% (2000); Ancestry (includes multiple ancestries): 27.4% Other groups, 20.1% German, 16.4% Irish, 15.2% Polish, 10.8% Italian (2000).

Economy: Employment by occupation: 21.8% management, 24.8% professional, 8.3% services, 26.5% sales, 0.0% farming, 9.8% construction, 8.8% production (2000).

Income: Per capita income: $33,177 (2000); Median household income: $88,137 (2000); Poverty rate: 2.9% (2000).

Education: High school graduation rate: 93.9% (2000); College graduation rate: 33.3% (2000).

Housing: Homeownership rate: 97.4% (2000); Median home value: $240,700 (2000); Median rent: $534 per month (2000); Median age of housing: 16 years (2000).

Transportation: Commute to work: 92.1% car, 2.8% public transportation, 0.0% walk, 5.1% work from home (2000); Travel time to work: 11.5% less than 15 minutes, 27.0% 15 to 30 minutes, 25.4% 30 to 45 minutes, 10.4% 45 to 60 minutes, 25.7% 60 minutes or more (2000)

WILMINGTON (city). Covers a land area of 4.214 square miles and a water area of 0.310 square miles. Located at 41.30° N. Lat.; 88.14° W. Long. Elevation is 565 feet.

History: Wilmington was laid out in the 1840's by Thomas Fox, who called it Winchester. In 1854 it was incorporated as a village with the name of Wilmington. The village grew around grist, saw, and carding mills operated by Fox.

Population: 5,134 (2000); Race: 96.6% White, 0.1% Black, 0.0% Asian, 0.4% American Indian and Alaska Native, 2.0% Hispanic of any race, 2.0% two or more races (2000); Density: 1,218.3 persons per square mile (2000); Age: 24.7% under 18, 14.0% over 64 (2000); Marriage status: 23.4% never married, 59.3% now married, 8.6% widowed, 8.7% divorced (2000); Foreign born: 1.4% (2000); Ancestry (includes multiple ancestries): 26.4% German, 22.6% Irish, 13.0% English, 8.5% Italian, 7.5% Polish (2000).

Economy: Single-family building permits issued: 19 (2001) / 14 (2000); Multi-family building permits issued: 0 (2001) / 0 (2000); Employment by occupation: 6.6% management, 14.4% professional, 13.7% services, 27.7% sales, 0.0% farming, 14.8% construction, 22.8% production (2000).

Income: Per capita income: $24,357 (2000); Median household income: $45,659 (2000); Poverty rate: 5.2% (2000).

Taxes: Total city taxes per capita: $254 (1997); City property taxes per capita: $155 (1997).

Education: High school graduation rate: 86.0% (2000); College graduation rate: 10.2% (2000).

School District(s)

Wilmington C U School District 209u (PK-12)
2000 Enrollment: 1,542 815-476-2594

Housing: Homeownership rate: 70.8% (2000); Median home value: $107,000 (2000); Median rent: $423 per month (2000); Median age of housing: 38 years (2000).

Newspapers: The Prairie Shopper (1 x week); Braidwood Journal (1 x week); Free Press Advocate (2 x week); Outdoor Times (8 x year)

Transportation: Commute to work: 96.3% car, 0.3% public transportation, 0.4% walk, 3.0% work from home (2000); Travel time to work: 26.6% less than 15 minutes, 26.2% 15 to 30 minutes, 26.1% 30 to 45 minutes, 8.6% 45 to 60 minutes, 12.6% 60 minutes or more (2000)

Williamson County

Located in southern Illinois; drained by the Big Muddy and South Fork of the Saline River; includes Crab Orchard Lake. Covers a land area of 423.40 square miles, a water area of 21.00 square miles, and is located in the Central Time Zone. The county government was organized in 1839. County seat is Marion.

Weather Station: Marion 4 NNE Elevation: 475 feet

	Jan	Feb	Mar	Apr	May	Jun	Jul	Aug	Sep	Oct	Nov	Dec
High	38	44	55	66	75	83	87	86	79	68	55	43
Low	20	24	34	43	53	62	66	64	56	44	35	25
Precip	3.0	3.0	4.6	4.7	5.0	4.1	3.8	3.8	3.3	3.1	4.9	3.7
Snow	5.9	5.4	2.5	0.5	0.0	0.0	0.0	0.0	0.0	0.2	0.8	2.9

High and Low temperatures in degrees Fahrenheit; Precipitation and Snow in inches

Population: 61,296 (2000); Race: 95.4% White, 2.6% Black, 0.3% Asian, 0.3% American Indian and Alaska Native, 1.5% Hispanic of any race, 0.9% two or more races (2000); Density: 144.8 persons per square mile (2000); Age: 22.9% under 18, 16.5% over 64 (2000).

Religion: Five largest groups: 24.3% Southern Baptist Convention, 7.6% Catholic Church, 5.2% The United Methodist Church, 2.9% Christian Churches and Churches of Christ, 2.5% American Baptist Churches in the USA (2000).

Economy: Unemployment rate: 5.1% (11/2002); Total civilian labor force: 28,938 (11/2002); Leading industries: 18.8% administration, support, waste management, remediation services; 16.5% health care and social assistance; 15.5% retail trade (2000); Companies that employ more than 1,000 persons: 3 (2000); Companies that employ more than 100 persons: 32 (2000); Farms: 585 totaling 92,289 acres (1997); Minority business ownership rate: 4.0% (1997); Women business ownership rate: 21.7% (1997); Retail sales per capita: $9,414 (1997). Single-family building permits issued: 157 (2001) / 135 (2000); Multi-family building permits issued: 2 (2001) / 10 (2000).

Income: Per capita income: $17,779 (2000); Median household income: $31,991 (2000); Poverty rate: 14.6% (2000); Bankruptcy rate: 7.84% (2001).

Taxes: Total county taxes per capita: $81 (2000); County property taxes per capita: $76 (2000).

Education: High school graduation rate: 79.8% (2000); College graduation rate: 17.2% (2000).

Housing: Homeownership rate: 73.6% (2000); Median home value: $63,300 (2000); Median rent: $311 per month (2000); Median age of housing: 32 years (2000).

Health: Birth rate: 114.7 per 10,000 population (1998); Age adjusted death rate: 97.4 per 10,000 population (1999); Age adjusted cancer mortality rate: 253.2 deaths per 100,000 population (1999). Number of physicians: 15.8 per 10,000 population (1999); Number of hospital beds: 46.5 per 10,000 population (1999).

Elections: 2000 Presidential election results: 45.3% Gore, 52.0% Bush, 1.8% Nader, 0.6% Buchanan

National and State Parks: Crab Orchard National Wildlife Refuge

Additional Information Contacts

Williamson County Government Offices. 618-997-1301
Carterville Chamber of Commerce 618-985-6942
Herrin Chamber of Commerce. 618-942-5163
Marion Chamber of Commerce 618-997-6311
Regional Economic Development 618-998-8252

Williamson County Communities

BUSH (village). Covers a land area of 0.461 square miles and a water area of 0.006 square miles. Located at 37.84° N. Lat.; 89.13° W. Long. Elevation is 410 feet.

Population: 257 (2000); Race: 100.0% White, 0.0% Black, 0.0% Asian, 0.0% American Indian and Alaska Native, 0.0% Hispanic of any race, 0.0% two or more races (2000); Density: 558.0 persons per square mile (2000); Age: 23.7% under 18, 12.7% over 64 (2000); Marriage status: 22.2% never married, 53.4% now married, 9.5% widowed, 14.8% divorced (2000); Foreign born: 0.4% (2000); Ancestry (includes multiple ancestries): 30.1% United States or American, 8.9% Irish, 8.5% German, 7.2% English, 4.2% Polish (2000).

Economy: In bituminous-coal-mining and agricultural area. Employment by occupation: 2.3% management, 15.1% professional, 14.0% services, 19.8% sales, 1.2% farming, 18.6% construction, 29.1% production (2000).

Income: Per capita income: $11,503 (2000); Median household income: $14,821 (2000); Poverty rate: 38.1% (2000).

Taxes: Total city taxes per capita: $36 (1997); City property taxes per capita: $11 (1997).
Education: High school graduation rate: 57.1% (2000); College graduation rate: 2.6% (2000).
Housing: Homeownership rate: 87.2% (2000); Median home value: $20,800 (2000); Median rent: $175 per month (2000); Median age of housing: 44 years (2000).
Transportation: Commute to work: 95.1% car, 0.0% public transportation, 0.0% walk, 4.9% work from home (2000); Travel time to work: 6.4% less than 15 minutes, 44.9% 15 to 30 minutes, 28.2% 30 to 45 minutes, 5.1% 45 to 60 minutes, 15.4% 60 minutes or more (2000)

CAMBRIA (village). Covers a land area of 1.365 square miles and a water area of 0.010 square miles. Located at 37.78° N. Lat.; 89.11° W. Long. Elevation is 420 feet.
Population: 1,330 (2000); Race: 93.9% White, 3.3% Black, 0.4% Asian, 0.4% American Indian and Alaska Native, 2.0% Hispanic of any race, 1.0% two or more races (2000); Density: 974.3 persons per square mile (2000); Age: 27.8% under 18, 10.1% over 64 (2000); Marriage status: 24.8% never married, 55.1% now married, 7.7% widowed, 12.4% divorced (2000); Foreign born: 0.9% (2000); Ancestry (includes multiple ancestries): 15.3% German, 14.4% Irish, 12.4% Other groups, 10.6% United States or American, 9.4% English (2000).
Economy: In bituminous-coal mining and agricultural area. Employment by occupation: 7.3% management, 13.3% professional, 18.5% services, 31.0% sales, 0.0% farming, 11.0% construction, 18.8% production (2000).
Income: Per capita income: $12,913 (2000); Median household income: $25,870 (2000); Poverty rate: 23.2% (2000).
Taxes: Total city taxes per capita: $61 (1997); City property taxes per capita: $23 (1997).
Education: High school graduation rate: 73.7% (2000); College graduation rate: 12.9% (2000).
Housing: Homeownership rate: 68.4% (2000); Median home value: $54,800 (2000); Median rent: $309 per month (2000); Median age of housing: 25 years (2000).
Transportation: Commute to work: 96.4% car, 0.3% public transportation, 1.6% walk, 1.0% work from home (2000); Travel time to work: 27.4% less than 15 minutes, 57.5% 15 to 30 minutes, 10.7% 30 to 45 minutes, 1.5% 45 to 60 minutes, 3.0% 60 minutes or more (2000)

CARTERVILLE (city). Covers a land area of 4.347 square miles and a water area of 0.010 square miles. Located at 37.76° N. Lat.; 89.08° W. Long. Elevation is 457 feet.
History: Incorporated 1892.
Population: 4,616 (2000); Race: 96.5% White, 1.3% Black, 0.2% Asian, 0.7% American Indian and Alaska Native, 1.4% Hispanic of any race, 1.0% two or more races (2000); Density: 1,061.8 persons per square mile (2000); Age: 25.3% under 18, 13.2% over 64 (2000); Marriage status: 24.8% never married, 57.1% now married, 5.3% widowed, 12.7% divorced (2000); Foreign born: 1.7% (2000); Ancestry (includes multiple ancestries): 25.5% German, 15.0% Irish, 13.6% English, 12.5% Other groups, 7.9% United States or American (2000).
Economy: Area of urban growth between Marion and Carbondale. In bituminous coal mining and agricultural (sorghum, dairy products, fruit) area. Manufacturing: electrical equipment, consumer goods, light manufacturing. Single-family building permits issued: 41 (2001) / 13 (2000); Multi-family building permits issued: 0 (2001) / 4 (2000); Employment by occupation: 10.8% management, 29.0% professional, 14.2% services, 27.8% sales, 0.3% farming, 6.2% construction, 11.7% production (2000).
Income: Per capita income: $18,884 (2000); Median household income: $36,969 (2000); Poverty rate: 14.6% (2000).
Taxes: Total city taxes per capita: $173 (1997); City property taxes per capita: $76 (1997).
Education: High school graduation rate: 86.1% (2000); College graduation rate: 31.6% (2000).

School District(s)

Carterville C U School District 5 (PK-12)
2000 Enrollment: 1,653 618-985-4826

Two-year College(s)

John A Logan College (Public)
2001 Enrollment: 6,546 618-985-3741
2001 Tuition: In-state $4,257; Out-of-state $6,413

Housing: Homeownership rate: 69.6% (2000); Median home value: $75,200 (2000); Median rent: $389 per month (2000); Median age of housing: 28 years (2000).
Transportation: Commute to work: 95.4% car, 0.0% public transportation, 0.7% walk, 3.5% work from home (2000); Travel time to work: 37.2% less than 15 minutes, 48.0% 15 to 30 minutes, 7.8% 30 to 45 minutes, 1.8% 45 to 60 minutes, 5.2% 60 minutes or more (2000)
Additional Information Contacts
Carterville Chamber of Commerce 618-985-6942

COLP (village). Covers a land area of 0.142 square miles and a water area of 0 square miles. Located at 37.80° N. Lat.; 89.07° W. Long. Elevation is 400 feet.
Population: 224 (2000); Race: 78.8% White, 20.8% Black, 0.4% Asian, 0.0% American Indian and Alaska Native, 0.0% Hispanic of any race, 0.0% two or more races (2000); Density: 1,576.4 persons per square mile (2000); Age: 19.9% under 18, 19.5% over 64 (2000); Marriage status: 26.9% never married, 39.2% now married, 19.4% widowed, 14.5% divorced (2000); Foreign born: 2.2% (2000); Ancestry (includes multiple ancestries): 26.5% Other groups, 10.6% German, 9.7% Irish, 9.3% Polish, 8.8% Dutch (2000).
Economy: In bituminous-coal-mining and agricultural area. Employment by occupation: 13.4% management, 2.4% professional, 24.4% services, 14.6% sales, 0.0% farming, 4.9% construction, 40.2% production (2000).
Income: Per capita income: $13,769 (2000); Median household income: $14,722 (2000); Poverty rate: 37.6% (2000).
Taxes: Total city taxes per capita: $25 (1997); City property taxes per capita: $12 (1997).
Education: High school graduation rate: 80.1% (2000); College graduation rate: 3.8% (2000).
Housing: Homeownership rate: 79.4% (2000); Median home value: $38,600 (2000); Median rent: $263 per month (2000); Median age of housing: 45 years (2000).
Transportation: Commute to work: 97.5% car, 0.0% public transportation, 0.0% walk, 2.5% work from home (2000); Travel time to work: 48.1% less than 15 minutes, 27.3% 15 to 30 minutes, 15.6% 30 to 45 minutes, 3.9% 45 to 60 minutes, 5.2% 60 minutes or more (2000)

CRAINVILLE (village). Covers a land area of 1.397 square miles and a water area of 0 square miles. Located at 37.74° N. Lat.; 89.06° W. Long. Elevation is 473 feet.
Population: 992 (2000); Race: 98.6% White, 0.7% Black, 0.0% Asian, 0.3% American Indian and Alaska Native, 0.0% Hispanic of any race, 0.4% two or more races (2000); Density: 709.9 persons per square mile (2000); Age: 21.3% under 18, 13.2% over 64 (2000); Marriage status: 21.9% never married, 54.8% now married, 7.9% widowed, 15.4% divorced (2000); Foreign born: 0.0% (2000); Ancestry (includes multiple ancestries): 18.5% German, 16.9% English, 16.5% United States or American, 11.3% Irish, 6.3% Other groups (2000).
Economy: In bituminous coal-mining and agricultural area. Single-family building permits issued: 8 (2001) / 8 (2000); Multi-family building permits issued: 0 (2001) / 0 (2000); Employment by occupation: 7.5% management, 21.5% professional, 20.5% services, 28.9% sales, 0.0% farming, 8.1% construction, 13.6% production (2000).
Income: Per capita income: $17,911 (2000); Median household income: $35,750 (2000); Poverty rate: 8.8% (2000).
Taxes: Total city taxes per capita: $73 (2000); City property taxes per capita: $30 (2000).
Education: High school graduation rate: 89.1% (2000); College graduation rate: 26.4% (2000).
Housing: Homeownership rate: 71.2% (2000); Median home value: $64,500 (2000); Median rent: $323 per month (2000); Median age of housing: 27 years (2000).
Transportation: Commute to work: 97.0% car, 0.0% public transportation, 1.6% walk, 1.0% work from home (2000); Travel time to work: 47.6% less than 15 minutes, 37.6% 15 to 30 minutes, 8.7% 30 to 45 minutes, 1.6% 45 to 60 minutes, 4.5% 60 minutes or more (2000)

CREAL SPRINGS (city). Covers a land area of 0.990 square miles and a water area of 0.007 square miles. Located at 37.62° N. Lat.; 88.83° W. Long. Elevation is 500 feet.
Population: 702 (2000); Race: 95.4% White, 0.5% Black, 0.3% Asian, 0.8% American Indian and Alaska Native, 2.1% Hispanic of any race, 2.9% two or more races (2000); Density: 709.1 persons per square mile (2000); Age: 24.0% under 18, 17.9% over 64 (2000); Marriage status: 17.4% never married, 58.4% now married, 14.6% widowed, 9.6% divorced (2000); Foreign born: 0.2% (2000); Ancestry (includes multiple ancestries): 24.0% United States or American, 17.6% Irish, 15.9% Other groups, 9.6% German, 6.6% English (2000).

Economy: Some agriculture. Employment by occupation: 4.8% management, 3.5% professional, 34.1% services, 17.9% sales, 1.7% farming, 15.7% construction, 22.3% production (2000).
Income: Per capita income: $13,483 (2000); Median household income: $25,272 (2000); Poverty rate: 23.7% (2000).
Taxes: Total city taxes per capita: $44 (1997); City property taxes per capita: $38 (1997).
Education: High school graduation rate: 60.0% (2000); College graduation rate: 7.2% (2000).
Housing: Homeownership rate: 79.7% (2000); Median home value: $32,700 (2000); Median rent: $230 per month (2000); Median age of housing: 42 years (2000).
Transportation: Commute to work: 92.9% car, 0.9% public transportation, 1.3% walk, 4.0% work from home (2000); Travel time to work: 24.0% less than 15 minutes, 35.0% 15 to 30 minutes, 26.3% 30 to 45 minutes, 6.0% 45 to 60 minutes, 8.8% 60 minutes or more (2000)

ENERGY (village). Covers a land area of 1.186 square miles and a water area of 0.009 square miles. Located at 37.77° N. Lat.; 89.02° W. Long. Elevation is 455 feet.
Population: 1,175 (2000); Race: 97.6% White, 0.8% Black, 0.6% Asian, 0.0% American Indian and Alaska Native, 1.0% Hispanic of any race, 0.9% two or more races (2000); Density: 990.9 persons per square mile (2000); Age: 16.0% under 18, 22.1% over 64 (2000); Marriage status: 19.3% never married, 58.7% now married, 9.1% widowed, 12.9% divorced (2000); Foreign born: 0.9% (2000); Ancestry (includes multiple ancestries): 15.4% German, 15.0% Irish, 10.8% United States or American, 10.8% English, 8.7% Other groups (2000).
Economy: In coal-mining and agricultural area. Single-family building permits issued: 0 (2001) / 0 (2000); Multi-family building permits issued: 2 (2001) / 0 (2000); Employment by occupation: 10.8% management, 13.3% professional, 16.0% services, 32.9% sales, 0.0% farming, 8.4% construction, 18.6% production (2000).
Income: Per capita income: $14,656 (2000); Median household income: $28,750 (2000); Poverty rate: 12.1% (2000).
Taxes: Total city taxes per capita: $93 (1997); City property taxes per capita: $54 (1997).
Education: High school graduation rate: 76.1% (2000); College graduation rate: 15.2% (2000).
Housing: Homeownership rate: 58.0% (2000); Median home value: $72,300 (2000); Median rent: $331 per month (2000); Median age of housing: 25 years (2000).
Transportation: Commute to work: 95.4% car, 0.0% public transportation, 2.0% walk, 2.6% work from home (2000); Travel time to work: 40.5% less than 15 minutes, 36.7% 15 to 30 minutes, 12.2% 30 to 45 minutes, 5.3% 45 to 60 minutes, 5.1% 60 minutes or more (2000)

HERRIN (city). Covers a land area of 8.202 square miles and a water area of 0.174 square miles. Located at 37.80° N. Lat.; 89.02° W. Long. Elevation is 430 feet.
History: Coal mining began in Herrin in 1895. It was incorporated as a village in 1898 and as a city in 1900.
Population: 11,298 (2000); Race: 96.5% White, 1.8% Black, 0.7% Asian, 0.1% American Indian and Alaska Native, 0.9% Hispanic of any race, 0.6% two or more races (2000); Density: 1,377.5 persons per square mile (2000); Age: 21.9% under 18, 20.6% over 64 (2000); Marriage status: 19.0% never married, 56.6% now married, 11.7% widowed, 12.7% divorced (2000); Foreign born: 1.6% (2000); Ancestry (includes multiple ancestries): 14.6% German, 13.2% Irish, 13.1% United States or American, 11.7% English, 11.5% Other groups (2000).
Vital Statistics: Birth rate: 131.0 per 10,000 population (1998)
Economy: Single-family building permits issued: 44 (2001) / 48 (2000); Multi-family building permits issued: 0 (2001) / 6 (2000); Employment by occupation: 9.5% management, 17.0% professional, 18.5% services, 27.7% sales, 0.2% farming, 8.8% construction, 18.3% production (2000).
Income: Per capita income: $16,782 (2000); Median household income: $28,532 (2000); Poverty rate: 16.0% (2000).
Taxes: Total city taxes per capita: $63 (1997); City property taxes per capita: $55 (1997).
Education: High school graduation rate: 79.0% (2000); College graduation rate: 17.1% (2000).

School District(s)

Herrin C U School District 4 (PK-12)
2000 Enrollment: 2,236 618-988-8024

Housing: Homeownership rate: 71.0% (2000); Median home value: $49,200 (2000); Median rent: $296 per month (2000); Median age of housing: 46 years (2000).
Hospitals: Herrin Hospital (92 beds)
Newspapers: The Spokesman (2 x week)
Transportation: Commute to work: 93.3% car, 0.0% public transportation, 4.1% walk, 1.6% work from home (2000); Travel time to work: 44.4% less than 15 minutes, 31.5% 15 to 30 minutes, 14.4% 30 to 45 minutes, 4.5% 45 to 60 minutes, 5.2% 60 minutes or more (2000)
Additional Information Contacts
Herrin Chamber of Commerce 618-942-5163

HURST (city). Covers a land area of 0.861 square miles and a water area of 0 square miles. Located at 37.83° N. Lat.; 89.14° W. Long. Elevation is 390 feet.
Population: 805 (2000); Race: 96.9% White, 0.0% Black, 0.5% Asian, 0.0% American Indian and Alaska Native, 2.3% Hispanic of any race, 1.0% two or more races (2000); Density: 935.1 persons per square mile (2000); Age: 23.2% under 18, 17.2% over 64 (2000); Marriage status: 26.0% never married, 47.6% now married, 12.9% widowed, 13.5% divorced (2000); Foreign born: 1.7% (2000); Ancestry (includes multiple ancestries): 16.3% Irish, 12.7% Other groups, 12.6% German, 10.2% English, 6.0% United States or American (2000).
Economy: In bituminous coal-mining and agricultural area. Single-family building permits issued: 0 (2001) / 0 (2000); Multi-family building permits issued: 0 (2001) / 0 (2000); Employment by occupation: 7.3% management, 8.5% professional, 20.3% services, 28.8% sales, 0.6% farming, 13.6% construction, 20.9% production (2000).
Income: Per capita income: $12,583 (2000); Median household income: $21,765 (2000); Poverty rate: 24.8% (2000).
Taxes: Total city taxes per capita: $45 (1997); City property taxes per capita: $42 (1997).
Education: High school graduation rate: 66.8% (2000); College graduation rate: 7.3% (2000).
Housing: Homeownership rate: 71.6% (2000); Median home value: $31,300 (2000); Median rent: $199 per month (2000); Median age of housing: 48 years (2000).
Transportation: Commute to work: 95.1% car, 0.7% public transportation, 0.7% walk, 3.6% work from home (2000); Travel time to work: 13.6% less than 15 minutes, 56.8% 15 to 30 minutes, 17.0% 30 to 45 minutes, 8.8% 45 to 60 minutes, 3.7% 60 minutes or more (2000)

JOHNSTON CITY (city). Covers a land area of 1.953 square miles and a water area of 0.058 square miles. Located at 37.82° N. Lat.; 88.92° W. Long. Elevation is 450 feet.
History: Incorporated 1896.
Population: 3,557 (2000); Race: 98.4% White, 0.0% Black, 0.0% Asian, 0.3% American Indian and Alaska Native, 3.8% Hispanic of any race, 1.3% two or more races (2000); Density: 1,820.9 persons per square mile (2000); Age: 22.9% under 18, 18.9% over 64 (2000); Marriage status: 22.1% never married, 56.8% now married, 11.6% widowed, 9.5% divorced (2000); Foreign born: 1.3% (2000); Ancestry (includes multiple ancestries): 17.5% German, 14.9% Irish, 11.7% United States or American, 10.4% Other groups, 8.7% English (2000).
Economy: In bituminous-coal mining and agricultural area: corn, wheat, hay. Single-family building permits issued: 2 (2001) / 2 (2000); Multi-family building permits issued: 0 (2001) / 0 (2000); Employment by occupation: 6.4% management, 11.9% professional, 25.7% services, 23.7% sales, 0.0% farming, 10.6% construction, 21.7% production (2000).
Income: Per capita income: $12,764 (2000); Median household income: $25,143 (2000); Poverty rate: 22.5% (2000).
Taxes: Total city taxes per capita: $42 (1997); City property taxes per capita: $42 (1997).
Education: High school graduation rate: 71.2% (2000); College graduation rate: 7.5% (2000).

School District(s)

Johnston City C U School District 1 (PK-12)
2000 Enrollment: 1,287 618-983-8021

Housing: Homeownership rate: 74.8% (2000); Median home value: $35,600 (2000); Median rent: $264 per month (2000); Median age of housing: 60+ years (2000).
Transportation: Commute to work: 93.0% car, 0.0% public transportation, 5.5% walk, 1.6% work from home (2000); Travel time to work: 36.3% less than 15 minutes, 38.5% 15 to 30 minutes, 13.1% 30 to 45 minutes, 8.7% 45 to 60 minutes, 3.5% 60 minutes or more (2000)

MARION (city). Covers a land area of 12.826 square miles and a water area of 0.697 square miles. Located at 37.73° N. Lat.; 88.93° W. Long. Elevation is 448 feet.
History: Marion was established in the mid-1800's. Early residents were Robert G. Ingersoll and John A. Logan, both of whom became colonels serving in the Civil War.
Population: 16,035 (2000); Race: 93.6% White, 4.3% Black, 0.1% Asian, 0.2% American Indian and Alaska Native, 2.1% Hispanic of any race, 1.4% two or more races (2000); Density: 1,250.2 persons per square mile (2000); Age: 23.0% under 18, 20.2% over 64 (2000); Marriage status: 19.0% never married, 55.9% now married, 10.6% widowed, 14.5% divorced (2000); Foreign born: 0.9% (2000); Ancestry (includes multiple ancestries): 15.5% German, 13.2% English, 12.0% Other groups, 11.2% United States or American, 11.1% Irish (2000).
Vital Statistics: Birth rate: 141.6 per 10,000 population (1998)
Economy: Single-family building permits issued: 62 (2001) / 64 (2000); Multi-family building permits issued: 0 (2001) / 0 (2000); Employment by occupation: 12.8% management, 18.0% professional, 19.3% services, 28.7% sales, 0.0% farming, 6.7% construction, 14.5% production (2000).
Income: Per capita income: $19,073 (2000); Median household income: $30,364 (2000); Poverty rate: 14.9% (2000).
Taxes: Total city taxes per capita: $316 (2000); City property taxes per capita: $141 (2000).
Education: High school graduation rate: 79.5% (2000); College graduation rate: 16.8% (2000).

School District(s)

Crab Orchard C U School District 3 (KG-12)
2000 Enrollment: 391 618-982-2181
Marion Community Unit School District 2 (PK-12)
2000 Enrollment: 3,902 618-993-2321
Williamson Co Special Education District (08-12)
2000 Enrollment: 4 618-993-2138

Housing: Homeownership rate: 64.9% (2000); Median home value: $67,100 (2000); Median rent: $338 per month (2000); Median age of housing: 33 years (2000).
Hospitals: Marion Memorial Hospital (99 beds); US Penitentiary Infirmary; Veterans Affairs Medical Center (39 beds)
Newspapers: The Marion Daily Republican (6 x week); The Williamson County Extra (1 x week)
Transportation: Commute to work: 96.4% car, 0.1% public transportation, 0.9% walk, 2.0% work from home (2000); Travel time to work: 52.2% less than 15 minutes, 28.5% 15 to 30 minutes, 11.8% 30 to 45 minutes, 2.7% 45 to 60 minutes, 4.7% 60 minutes or more (2000)
Airports: Williamson County Regional (primary service)

Additional Information Contacts

Marion Chamber of Commerce 618-997-6311
Regional Economic Development 618-998-8252

PITTSBURG (village). Covers a land area of 2.085 square miles and a water area of 0.027 square miles. Located at 37.77° N. Lat.; 88.85° W. Long. Elevation is 466 feet.
Population: 575 (2000); Race: 99.6% White, 0.0% Black, 0.0% Asian, 0.0% American Indian and Alaska Native, 0.4% Hispanic of any race, 0.4% two or more races (2000); Density: 275.8 persons per square mile (2000); Age: 20.8% under 18, 15.7% over 64 (2000); Marriage status: 23.9% never married, 61.3% now married, 6.9% widowed, 8.0% divorced (2000); Foreign born: 0.4% (2000); Ancestry (includes multiple ancestries): 19.0% German, 13.2% Irish, 12.1% Other groups, 11.7% United States or American, 7.1% English (2000).
Economy: In bituminous-coal-mining and agricultural area. Employment by occupation: 1.6% management, 12.7% professional, 39.6% services, 22.0% sales, 0.0% farming, 12.7% construction, 11.4% production (2000).
Income: Per capita income: $14,186 (2000); Median household income: $29,722 (2000); Poverty rate: 11.3% (2000).
Taxes: Total city taxes per capita: $53 (1997); City property taxes per capita: $16 (1997).
Education: High school graduation rate: 76.5% (2000); College graduation rate: 6.4% (2000).
Housing: Homeownership rate: 86.5% (2000); Median home value: $40,800 (2000); Median rent: $244 per month (2000); Median age of housing: 57 years (2000).
Transportation: Commute to work: 99.2% car, 0.0% public transportation, 0.8% walk, 0.0% work from home (2000); Travel time to work: 19.4% less than 15 minutes, 42.6% 15 to 30 minutes, 16.1% 30 to 45 minutes, 14.0% 45 to 60 minutes, 7.9% 60 minutes or more (2000)

SPILLERTOWN (village). Covers a land area of 0.311 square miles and a water area of 0 square miles. Located at 37.76° N. Lat.; 88.91° W. Long. Elevation is 483 feet.
Population: 220 (2000); Race: 98.6% White, 0.0% Black, 0.0% Asian, 0.0% American Indian and Alaska Native, 1.4% Hispanic of any race, 0.0% two or more races (2000); Density: 707.5 persons per square mile (2000); Age: 20.5% under 18, 19.5% over 64 (2000); Marriage status: 26.8% never married, 51.4% now married, 12.6% widowed, 9.3% divorced (2000); Foreign born: 0.9% (2000); Ancestry (includes multiple ancestries): 16.8% Other groups, 10.5% United States or American, 10.0% Irish, 9.1% English, 8.2% German (2000).
Economy: Employment by occupation: 12.0% management, 8.0% professional, 17.0% services, 30.0% sales, 0.0% farming, 16.0% construction, 17.0% production (2000).
Income: Per capita income: $18,674 (2000); Median household income: $33,125 (2000); Poverty rate: 6.4% (2000).
Taxes: Total city taxes per capita: $16 (1997); City property taxes per capita: $12 (1997).
Education: High school graduation rate: 71.9% (2000); College graduation rate: 3.4% (2000).
Housing: Homeownership rate: 83.0% (2000); Median home value: $58,800 (2000); Median rent: $300 per month (2000); Median age of housing: 44 years (2000).
Transportation: Commute to work: 91.0% car, 0.0% public transportation, 0.0% walk, 2.0% work from home (2000); Travel time to work: 40.8% less than 15 minutes, 39.8% 15 to 30 minutes, 16.3% 30 to 45 minutes, 0.0% 45 to 60 minutes, 3.1% 60 minutes or more (2000)

STONEFORT (village). Covers a land area of 1.461 square miles and a water area of 0.003 square miles. Located at 37.61° N. Lat.; 88.70° W. Long. Elevation is 410 feet.
History: Stonefort was built on the ruins of an old stone fort, a prehistoric structure on a cliff with a stone barricade on the approachable side. In 1872 the town was moved to take advantage of the arrival of the railroad.
Population: 292 (2000); Race: 97.8% White, 0.0% Black, 0.0% Asian, 0.0% American Indian and Alaska Native, 0.0% Hispanic of any race, 2.2% two or more races (2000); Density: 199.9 persons per square mile (2000); Age: 15.6% under 18, 22.6% over 64 (2000); Marriage status: 14.1% never married, 62.7% now married, 8.7% widowed, 14.5% divorced (2000); Foreign born: 0.0% (2000); Ancestry (includes multiple ancestries): 14.4% United States or American, 12.6% German, 11.1% English, 10.7% Irish, 6.3% Other groups (2000).
Economy: Employment by occupation: 9.7% management, 11.1% professional, 34.7% services, 13.9% sales, 0.0% farming, 15.3% construction, 15.3% production (2000).
Income: Per capita income: $16,937 (2000); Median household income: $28,654 (2000); Poverty rate: 16.9% (2000).
Taxes: Total city taxes per capita: $12 (1997); City property taxes per capita: $12 (1997).
Education: High school graduation rate: 68.2% (2000); College graduation rate: 6.8% (2000).
Housing: Homeownership rate: 89.1% (2000); Median home value: $32,700 (2000); Median rent: $181 per month (2000); Median age of housing: 44 years (2000).
Transportation: Commute to work: 98.5% car, 0.0% public transportation, 0.0% walk, 1.5% work from home (2000); Travel time to work: 11.9% less than 15 minutes, 31.3% 15 to 30 minutes, 38.8% 30 to 45 minutes, 4.5% 45 to 60 minutes, 13.4% 60 minutes or more (2000)

WHITEASH (village). Covers a land area of 0.870 square miles and a water area of 0.024 square miles. Located at 37.78° N. Lat.; 88.92° W. Long.
Population: 268 (2000); Race: 98.9% White, 0.0% Black, 0.0% Asian, 0.0% American Indian and Alaska Native, 3.2% Hispanic of any race, 0.0% two or more races (2000); Density: 308.1 persons per square mile (2000); Age: 25.7% under 18, 12.1% over 64 (2000); Marriage status: 14.9% never married, 63.1% now married, 13.1% widowed, 9.0% divorced (2000); Foreign born: 1.1% (2000); Ancestry (includes multiple ancestries): 16.1% German, 16.1% English, 15.0% United States or American, 11.8% Irish, 8.2% Other groups (2000).
Economy: In bituminous-coal-mining and agricultural area: grain; dairying. Employment by occupation: 3.7% management, 13.8% professional, 19.3% services, 33.0% sales, 2.8% farming, 11.0% construction, 16.5% production (2000).
Income: Per capita income: $11,780 (2000); Median household income: $24,167 (2000); Poverty rate: 23.3% (2000).

Taxes: Total city taxes per capita: $11 (1997); City property taxes per capita: $4 (1997).
Education: High school graduation rate: 74.0% (2000); College graduation rate: 2.1% (2000).
Housing: Homeownership rate: 76.7% (2000); Median home value: $58,000 (2000); Median rent: $238 per month (2000); Median age of housing: 32 years (2000).
Transportation: Commute to work: 95.3% car, 0.0% public transportation, 0.9% walk, 1.9% work from home (2000); Travel time to work: 22.9% less than 15 minutes, 51.4% 15 to 30 minutes, 20.0% 30 to 45 minutes, 1.9% 45 to 60 minutes, 3.8% 60 minutes or more (2000)

Winnebago County

Located in northern Illinois; bounded on the north by Wisconsin; drained by the Rock, Pecatonica, and Kishwaukee Rivers. Covers a land area of 513.70 square miles, a water area of 5.50 square miles, and is located in the Central Time Zone. The county government was organized in 1836. County seat is Rockford.

Winnebago County is part of the Rockford, IL MSA. The entire metro area includes: Boone County; Ogle County; Winnebago County

Weather Station: Rockford Greater Rockford Arpt. Elevation: 679 feet

	Jan	Feb	Mar	Apr	May	Jun	Jul	Aug	Sep	Oct	Nov	Dec
High	27	32	45	59	71	81	84	82	74	62	46	33
Low	10	16	26	37	48	58	63	61	52	40	29	17
Precip	1.4	1.3	2.4	3.6	4.0	4.7	4.1	4.1	3.6	2.7	2.6	2.0
Snow	10.1	7.6	5.7	1.6	tr	tr	tr	tr	0.0	tr	2.6	9.8

High and Low temperatures in degrees Fahrenheit; Precipitation and Snow in inches

Population: 278,418 (2000); Race: 82.2% White, 10.6% Black, 1.6% Asian, 0.3% American Indian and Alaska Native, 6.8% Hispanic of any race, 2.2% two or more races (2000); Density: 541.9 persons per square mile (2000); Age: 26.4% under 18, 12.7% over 64 (2000).
Religion: Five largest groups: 22.2% Catholic Church, 7.1% Evangelical Lutheran Church in America, 3.6% The United Methodist Church, 2.3% Assemblies of God, 1.9% Lutheran Church—Missouri Synod (2000).
Economy: Unemployment rate: 7.9% (11/2002); Total civilian labor force: 146,222 (11/2002); Leading industries: 27.0% manufacturing; 13.1% health care and social assistance; 12.7% retail trade (2000); Companies that employ more than 1,000 persons: 7 (2000); Companies that employ more than 100 persons: 239 (2000); Farms: 687 totaling 195,621 acres (1997); Minority business ownership rate: 7.2% (1997); Women business ownership rate: 26.4% (1997); Retail sales per capita: $10,316 (1997). Single-family building permits issued: 912 (2001) / 1,013 (2000); Multi-family building permits issued: 521 (2001) / 250 (2000).
Income: Per capita income: $21,194 (2000); Median household income: $43,886 (2000); Poverty rate: 9.6% (2000); Bankruptcy rate: 8.34% (2001).
Taxes: Total county taxes per capita: $93 (2000); County property taxes per capita: $89 (2000).
Education: High school graduation rate: 81.4% (2000); College graduation rate: 19.4% (2000).
Housing: Homeownership rate: 70.1% (2000); Median home value: $91,900 (2000); Median rent: $436 per month (2000); Median age of housing: 35 years (2000).
Health: Birth rate: 142.4 per 10,000 population (1998); Age adjusted death rate: 90.4 per 10,000 population (1999); Infant mortality rate: 6.0 per 1,000 live births (1998); Age adjusted cancer mortality rate: 210.3 deaths per 100,000 population (1999). Air Quality Index: 84% good, 16% moderate, 0% unhealthy (percent of days in 2000). Number of physicians: 24.6 per 10,000 population (1999); Number of hospital beds: 37.4 per 10,000 population (1999).
Elections: 2000 Presidential election results: 47.6% Gore, 49.2% Bush, 2.4% Nader, 0.3% Buchanan
National and State Parks: Rock Cut State Park
Additional Information Contacts
Winnebago County Government Offices 815-987-2590
Loves Park Chamber of Commerce 815-633-3999
Rockford Area Association of Realtors 815-395-6776
Rockford Area Chamber of Commerce 815-987-8100
Rockton Chamber of Commerce 815-624-7625
Roscoe Chamber of Commerce 815-623-9065

Winnebago County Communities

CHERRY VALLEY (village). Covers a land area of 3.757 square miles and a water area of 0.049 square miles. Located at 42.23° N. Lat.; 88.96° W. Long. Elevation is 730 feet.
Population: 2,191 (2000); Race: 90.3% White, 2.1% Black, 5.4% Asian, 0.2% American Indian and Alaska Native, 2.5% Hispanic of any race, 2.0% two or more races (2000); Density: 583.3 persons per square mile (2000); Age: 29.7% under 18, 6.9% over 64 (2000); Marriage status: 22.7% never married, 64.7% now married, 2.9% widowed, 9.7% divorced (2000); Foreign born: 5.1% (2000); Ancestry (includes multiple ancestries): 28.8% German, 18.1% Irish, 14.0% Other groups, 10.9% English, 10.6% Swedish (2000).
Economy: In agricultural area. Employment by occupation: 12.4% management, 15.1% professional, 8.0% services, 35.9% sales, 0.0% farming, 10.3% construction, 18.3% production (2000).
Income: Per capita income: $23,725 (2000); Median household income: $59,871 (2000); Poverty rate: 6.3% (2000).
Taxes: Total city taxes per capita: $64 (1997); City property taxes per capita: $10 (1997).
Education: High school graduation rate: 90.7% (2000); College graduation rate: 23.9% (2000).
Housing: Homeownership rate: 76.8% (2000); Median home value: $134,200 (2000); Median rent: $473 per month (2000); Median age of housing: 18 years (2000).
Transportation: Commute to work: 98.3% car, 0.0% public transportation, 0.0% walk, 1.3% work from home (2000); Travel time to work: 35.1% less than 15 minutes, 39.6% 15 to 30 minutes, 11.4% 30 to 45 minutes, 4.6% 45 to 60 minutes, 9.3% 60 minutes or more (2000)

DURAND (village). Covers a land area of 0.900 square miles and a water area of 0 square miles. Located at 42.43° N. Lat.; 89.32° W. Long. Elevation is 770 feet.
Population: 1,081 (2000); Race: 98.2% White, 0.7% Black, 0.0% Asian, 0.0% American Indian and Alaska Native, 0.8% Hispanic of any race, 0.6% two or more races (2000); Density: 1,200.9 persons per square mile (2000); Age: 31.7% under 18, 12.1% over 64 (2000); Marriage status: 23.0% never married, 57.6% now married, 6.4% widowed, 12.9% divorced (2000); Foreign born: 0.2% (2000); Ancestry (includes multiple ancestries): 36.2% German, 22.7% Irish, 11.0% English, 11.0% United States or American, 7.5% Norwegian (2000).
Economy: In dairying and grain area. Employment by occupation: 7.5% management, 18.4% professional, 15.2% services, 24.4% sales, 0.8% farming, 10.4% construction, 23.4% production (2000).
Income: Per capita income: $19,211 (2000); Median household income: $43,988 (2000); Poverty rate: 5.6% (2000).
Taxes: Total city taxes per capita: $78 (1997); City property taxes per capita: $28 (1997).
Education: High school graduation rate: 88.4% (2000); College graduation rate: 16.4% (2000).

School District(s)
Durand C U School District 322 (PK-12)
2000 Enrollment: 758 815-248-2171
Housing: Homeownership rate: 66.4% (2000); Median home value: $86,700 (2000); Median rent: $381 per month (2000); Median age of housing: 40 years (2000).
Newspapers: The Volunteer (1 x week)
Transportation: Commute to work: 91.8% car, 0.0% public transportation, 3.7% walk, 3.3% work from home (2000); Travel time to work: 24.0% less than 15 minutes, 20.2% 15 to 30 minutes, 42.6% 30 to 45 minutes, 6.7% 45 to 60 minutes, 6.5% 60 minutes or more (2000)

LAKE SUMMERSET (CDP). Covers a land area of 2.071 square miles and a water area of 0.425 square miles. Located at 42.44° N. Lat.; 89.39° W. Long. Elevation is 900 feet.
Population: 2,061 (2000); Race: 96.4% White, 1.1% Black, 0.4% Asian, 0.0% American Indian and Alaska Native, 0.6% Hispanic of any race, 0.3% two or more races (2000); Density: 995.3 persons per square mile (2000); Age: 20.0% under 18, 22.2% over 64 (2000); Marriage status: 12.5% never married, 74.6% now married, 3.6% widowed, 9.3% divorced (2000); Foreign born: 1.9% (2000); Ancestry (includes multiple ancestries): 34.0% German, 21.4% Irish, 14.3% English, 8.8% Swedish, 7.0% Norwegian (2000).
Economy: Employment by occupation: 16.4% management, 23.9% professional, 7.3% services, 26.7% sales, 0.0% farming, 9.5% construction, 16.2% production (2000).

Income: Per capita income: $27,160 (2000); Median household income: $59,648 (2000); Poverty rate: 0.8% (2000).
Education: High school graduation rate: 94.4% (2000); College graduation rate: 30.6% (2000).
Housing: Homeownership rate: 97.0% (2000); Median home value: $122,800 (2000); Median rent: $648 per month (2000); Median age of housing: 15 years (2000).
Transportation: Commute to work: 95.5% car, 0.0% public transportation, 0.0% walk, 3.2% work from home (2000); Travel time to work: 13.1% less than 15 minutes, 14.3% 15 to 30 minutes, 48.7% 30 to 45 minutes, 13.4% 45 to 60 minutes, 10.6% 60 minutes or more (2000)

LOVES PARK (city). Covers a land area of 14.450 square miles and a water area of 0.368 square miles. Located at 42.32° N. Lat.; 89.02° W. Long. Elevation is 730 feet.
History: Incorporated 1947.
Population: 20,044 (2000); Race: 91.9% White, 1.9% Black, 2.1% Asian, 0.2% American Indian and Alaska Native, 2.9% Hispanic of any race, 2.3% two or more races (2000); Density: 1,387.2 persons per square mile (2000); Age: 25.6% under 18, 11.4% over 64 (2000); Marriage status: 23.7% never married, 57.2% now married, 6.7% widowed, 12.3% divorced (2000); Foreign born: 4.2% (2000); Ancestry (includes multiple ancestries): 29.1% German, 14.7% Irish, 11.1% Other groups, 10.8% Swedish, 10.0% English (2000).
Vital Statistics: Birth rate: 128.7 per 10,000 population (1998)
Economy: Single-family building permits issued: 109 (2001) / 150 (2000); Multi-family building permits issued: 152 (2001) / 85 (2000); Employment by occupation: 11.1% management, 18.3% professional, 10.4% services, 28.6% sales, 0.1% farming, 8.4% construction, 23.1% production (2000).
Income: Per capita income: $20,781 (2000); Median household income: $45,238 (2000); Poverty rate: 5.0% (2000).
Taxes: Total city taxes per capita: $28 (1997); City property taxes per capita: $4 (1997).
Education: High school graduation rate: 86.4% (2000); College graduation rate: 17.2% (2000).

School District(s)

Boone/Winnebago Roe (07-12)
2000 Enrollment: 241 815-636-3060
Harlem Unit District 122 (PK-12)
2000 Enrollment: 7,425 815-654-4500

Housing: Homeownership rate: 70.4% (2000); Median home value: $88,800 (2000); Median rent: $533 per month (2000); Median age of housing: 26 years (2000).
Transportation: Commute to work: 95.7% car, 0.6% public transportation, 0.5% walk, 2.6% work from home (2000); Travel time to work: 34.1% less than 15 minutes, 49.0% 15 to 30 minutes, 8.8% 30 to 45 minutes, 3.1% 45 to 60 minutes, 5.0% 60 minutes or more (2000)

Additional Information Contacts
Loves Park Chamber of Commerce 815-633-3999

MACHESNEY PARK (village). Covers a land area of 12.008 square miles and a water area of 0.381 square miles. Located at 42.35° N. Lat.; 89.04° W. Long. Elevation is 727 feet.
Population: 20,759 (2000); Race: 95.2% White, 1.5% Black, 1.2% Asian, 0.2% American Indian and Alaska Native, 2.5% Hispanic of any race, 1.2% two or more races (2000); Density: 1,728.8 persons per square mile (2000); Age: 26.6% under 18, 9.3% over 64 (2000); Marriage status: 22.5% never married, 60.7% now married, 5.1% widowed, 11.8% divorced (2000); Foreign born: 2.0% (2000); Ancestry (includes multiple ancestries): 29.0% German, 14.8% Irish, 10.8% Other groups, 9.4% English, 8.9% Swedish (2000).
Vital Statistics: Birth rate: 109.8 per 10,000 population (1998)
Economy: Diversified light manufacturing. Single-family building permits issued: 65 (2001) / 80 (2000); Multi-family building permits issued: 8 (2001) / 4 (2000); Employment by occupation: 9.9% management, 14.1% professional, 11.6% services, 27.8% sales, 0.1% farming, 9.9% construction, 26.6% production (2000).
Income: Per capita income: $19,685 (2000); Median household income: $48,315 (2000); Poverty rate: 5.3% (2000).
Taxes: Total city taxes per capita: $25 (1997); City property taxes per capita: $6 (1997).
Education: High school graduation rate: 80.4% (2000); College graduation rate: 11.2% (2000).
Housing: Homeownership rate: 83.5% (2000); Median home value: $90,400 (2000); Median rent: $501 per month (2000); Median age of housing: 30 years (2000).
Newspapers: Senior Courier (1 x month); Rockford Journal (1 x week); The Post Journal (1 x week); Gazette (1 x week)
Transportation: Commute to work: 96.4% car, 0.1% public transportation, 0.4% walk, 1.7% work from home (2000); Travel time to work: 32.1% less than 15 minutes, 51.3% 15 to 30 minutes, 10.9% 30 to 45 minutes, 1.5% 45 to 60 minutes, 4.2% 60 minutes or more (2000)

NEW MILLFORD (village). Covers a land area of 1.089 square miles and a water area of 0.025 square miles. Located at 42.18° N. Lat.; 89.07° W. Long.
Population: 541 (2000); Race: 94.4% White, 0.7% Black, 0.4% Asian, 0.0% American Indian and Alaska Native, 6.8% Hispanic of any race, 3.3% two or more races (2000); Density: 496.6 persons per square mile (2000); Age: 27.4% under 18, 6.1% over 64 (2000); Marriage status: 20.0% never married, 61.2% now married, 5.3% widowed, 13.5% divorced (2000); Foreign born: 1.1% (2000); Ancestry (includes multiple ancestries): 24.4% German, 18.4% Other groups, 16.8% Irish, 14.2% Swedish, 8.4% English (2000).
Economy: Employment by occupation: 8.0% management, 12.1% professional, 15.5% services, 24.5% sales, 0.0% farming, 12.4% construction, 27.6% production (2000).
Income: Per capita income: $22,937 (2000); Median household income: $39,531 (2000); Poverty rate: 9.9% (2000).
Taxes: Total city taxes per capita: $32 (1997); City property taxes per capita: $2 (1997).
Education: High school graduation rate: 76.6% (2000); College graduation rate: 8.1% (2000).
Housing: Homeownership rate: 80.7% (2000); Median home value: $150,000 (2000); Median rent: $375 per month (2000); Median age of housing: 22 years (2000).
Transportation: Commute to work: 95.0% car, 0.0% public transportation, 0.6% walk, 4.4% work from home (2000); Travel time to work: 34.6% less than 15 minutes, 44.1% 15 to 30 minutes, 12.1% 30 to 45 minutes, 2.9% 45 to 60 minutes, 6.2% 60 minutes or more (2000)

PECATONICA (village). Covers a land area of 1.243 square miles and a water area of 0.018 square miles. Located at 42.31° N. Lat.; 89.35° W. Long. Elevation is 759 feet.
History: Incorporated 1869.
Population: 1,997 (2000); Race: 97.8% White, 0.6% Black, 0.0% Asian, 0.0% American Indian and Alaska Native, 1.8% Hispanic of any race, 0.4% two or more races (2000); Density: 1,607.2 persons per square mile (2000); Age: 24.9% under 18, 14.2% over 64 (2000); Marriage status: 20.7% never married, 61.7% now married, 7.3% widowed, 10.3% divorced (2000); Foreign born: 0.7% (2000); Ancestry (includes multiple ancestries): 42.4% German, 13.7% Irish, 11.3% English, 11.2% Swedish, 5.6% United States or American (2000).
Economy: In agricultural area: dairying. Manufacturing of consumer goods. Single-family building permits issued: 5 (2001) / 27 (2000); Multi-family building permits issued: 4 (2001) / 0 (2000); Employment by occupation: 8.4% management, 14.6% professional, 14.8% services, 26.6% sales, 1.3% farming, 11.3% construction, 23.0% production (2000).
Income: Per capita income: $20,420 (2000); Median household income: $47,361 (2000); Poverty rate: 4.7% (2000).
Taxes: Total city taxes per capita: $203 (1997); City property taxes per capita: $40 (1997).
Education: High school graduation rate: 88.4% (2000); College graduation rate: 13.6% (2000).

School District(s)

Pecatonica C U School District 321 (PK-12)
2000 Enrollment: 790 815-239-1639

Housing: Homeownership rate: 78.7% (2000); Median home value: $91,300 (2000); Median rent: $383 per month (2000); Median age of housing: 47 years (2000).
Transportation: Commute to work: 92.2% car, 0.2% public transportation, 4.3% walk, 2.3% work from home (2000); Travel time to work: 29.5% less than 15 minutes, 38.7% 15 to 30 minutes, 26.5% 30 to 45 minutes, 2.9% 45 to 60 minutes, 2.5% 60 minutes or more (2000)

ROCKFORD (city). Covers a land area of 56.005 square miles and a water area of 0.713 square miles. Located at 42.27° N. Lat.; 89.07° W. Long. Elevation is 740 feet.
History: Rockford was named for the ford across the Rock River where the stagecoach crossed before the town was built. Rockford was settled by New Englanders after Germanicus Kent and Thatcher Blake of Galena laid out the town and opened a sawmill. The availability of water power accounted for Rockford's growth, and it was incorporated in 1839 along with a village that

had grown up on the other side of the river. In the 1850's both the Rockford Water Power Company and the Manny Company, producer of reaper-mower machines, were founded. After 1852, when the Chicago & Galena Union Railroad arrived, many people of Swedish descent settled here.
Population: 150,115 (2000); Race: 73.0% White, 17.3% Black, 2.0% Asian, 0.3% American Indian and Alaska Native, 10.2% Hispanic of any race, 2.7% two or more races (2000); Density: 2,680.4 persons per square mile (2000); Age: 26.5% under 18, 14.2% over 64 (2000); Marriage status: 28.2% never married, 51.8% now married, 7.3% widowed, 12.7% divorced (2000); Foreign born: 8.7% (2000); Ancestry (includes multiple ancestries): 28.2% Other groups, 19.7% German, 11.2% Irish, 9.8% Swedish, 7.9% English (2000).
Vital Statistics: Birth rate: 186.0 per 10,000 population (1998)
Economy: Unemployment rate: 9.9% (11/2002); Total civilian labor force: 75,749 (11/2002); Single-family building permits issued: 225 (2001) / 212 (2000); Multi-family building permits issued: 313 (2001) / 89 (2000); Employment by occupation: 10.9% management, 18.3% professional, 14.8% services, 26.0% sales, 0.2% farming, 7.3% construction, 22.6% production (2000).
Income: Per capita income: $19,781 (2000); Median household income: $37,667 (2000); Poverty rate: 14.0% (2000).
Taxes: Total city taxes per capita: $313 (2000); City property taxes per capita: $244 (2000).
Education: High school graduation rate: 77.8% (2000); College graduation rate: 19.8% (2000).

School District(s)

Rockford School District 205 (PK-12)
2000 Enrollment: 27,399 815-966-3101

Four-year College(s)

Rockford College (Private, Not-for-profit)
2001 Enrollment: 1,359 815-226-4000
2001 Tuition: In-state $17,450; Out-of-state $17,450
Saint Anthony College of Nursing (Private, Not-for-profit, Roman Catholic)
2001 Enrollment: 77 815-395-5091
2001 Tuition: In-state $12,000; Out-of-state $12,000
Swedish-American Hospital School of Medical Techn (Private, Not-for-profit)
2001 Enrollment: n/a 815-968-4400

Two-year College(s)

Rock Valley College (Public)
2001 Enrollment: 8,542 815-654-4250
2001 Tuition: In-state $5,563; Out-of-state $8,504
Rockford Business College (Private, For-profit)
2001 Enrollment: 357 815-965-8616
2001 Tuition: In-state $7,760; Out-of-state $7,760
Rockford Memorial Hospital School of X-ray Techn (Private, Not-for-profit)
2001 Enrollment: n/a 815-971-5480
2001 Tuition: In-state $4,530; Out-of-state $5,530
Swedish American Hospital School of Radiography (Private, Not-for-profit)
2001 Enrollment: n/a 815-489-4966
Swedish-American Hospital School of Radiation Therapy (Private, Not-for-profit)
2001 Enrollment: n/a 815-968-4400

Housing: Homeownership rate: 61.3% (2000); Median home value: $79,900 (2000); Median rent: $423 per month (2000); Median age of housing: 42 years (2000).
Hospitals: H. Douglas Singer Mental Health & Development Center (161 beds); Rockford Memorial Hospital; Saint Anthony Medical Center (254 beds); Swedish American Hospital (397 beds)
Safety: Violent crime rate: n/a; Property crime rate: 772.9 per 10,000 population (2001).
Newspapers: Rock River Times (1 x week); Rockford Register Star (7 x week); The Observer (1 x week); Rockford Labor News (1 x week)
Transportation: Commute to work: 93.1% car, 1.8% public transportation, 1.9% walk, 2.3% work from home (2000); Travel time to work: 39.6% less than 15 minutes, 44.0% 15 to 30 minutes, 8.2% 30 to 45 minutes, 2.8% 45 to 60 minutes, 5.5% 60 minutes or more (2000); Amtrak: Service available.
Airports: Greater Rockford (commercial service)

Additional Information Contacts

Rockford Area Association of Realtors 815-395-6776
Rockford Area Chamber of Commerce 815-987-8100

ROCKTON (village). Covers a land area of 3.518 square miles and a water area of 0.182 square miles. Located at 42.45° N. Lat.; 89.06° W. Long. Elevation is 750 feet.
History: Incorporated 1847.
Population: 5,296 (2000); Race: 97.6% White, 1.6% Black, 0.2% Asian, 0.0% American Indian and Alaska Native, 1.5% Hispanic of any race, 0.6% two or more races (2000); Density: 1,505.5 persons per square mile (2000); Age: 30.8% under 18, 10.5% over 64 (2000); Marriage status: 15.3% never married, 73.0% now married, 4.3% widowed, 7.3% divorced (2000); Foreign born: 1.8% (2000); Ancestry (includes multiple ancestries): 36.6% German, 14.2% English, 14.0% Irish, 8.9% Norwegian, 7.4% Swedish (2000).
Economy: Agriculture. Manufacturing of wood products. Employment by occupation: 15.4% management, 24.9% professional, 11.7% services, 24.5% sales, 0.0% farming, 8.7% construction, 14.9% production (2000).
Income: Per capita income: $24,078 (2000); Median household income: $57,292 (2000); Poverty rate: 1.3% (2000).
Taxes: Total city taxes per capita: $176 (1997); City property taxes per capita: $142 (1997).
Education: High school graduation rate: 93.2% (2000); College graduation rate: 29.6% (2000).

School District(s)

Hononegah Community H S District 207 (09-12)
2000 Enrollment: 1,719 815-624-5010
Rockton School District 140 (PK-08)
2000 Enrollment: 1,315 815-624-7143

Housing: Homeownership rate: 80.4% (2000); Median home value: $120,500 (2000); Median rent: $504 per month (2000); Median age of housing: 16 years (2000).
Newspapers: Candlework/Poplar Grove Herald (1 x month)
Transportation: Commute to work: 94.9% car, 0.3% public transportation, 2.2% walk, 2.4% work from home (2000); Travel time to work: 34.4% less than 15 minutes, 35.1% 15 to 30 minutes, 23.9% 30 to 45 minutes, 2.2% 45 to 60 minutes, 4.5% 60 minutes or more (2000)

Additional Information Contacts

Rockton Chamber of Commerce 815-624-7625

ROSCOE (village). Covers a land area of 9.249 square miles and a water area of 0.072 square miles. Located at 42.41° N. Lat.; 89.01° W. Long. Elevation is 741 feet.
Population: 6,244 (2000); Race: 92.7% White, 2.2% Black, 1.7% Asian, 0.2% American Indian and Alaska Native, 2.4% Hispanic of any race, 1.7% two or more races (2000); Density: 675.1 persons per square mile (2000); Age: 32.7% under 18, 6.5% over 64 (2000); Marriage status: 18.6% never married, 71.2% now married, 2.9% widowed, 7.3% divorced (2000); Foreign born: 3.1% (2000); Ancestry (includes multiple ancestries): 25.6% German, 17.7% Irish, 10.7% Other groups, 9.0% English, 7.9% United States or American (2000).
Economy: Manufacturing: level controls, valve actuators, motion control systems. Employment by occupation: 18.4% management, 18.0% professional, 10.9% services, 22.9% sales, 0.2% farming, 9.3% construction, 20.4% production (2000).
Income: Per capita income: $25,324 (2000); Median household income: $59,267 (2000); Poverty rate: 2.9% (2000).
Taxes: Total city taxes per capita: $165 (1997); City property taxes per capita: $154 (1997).
Education: High school graduation rate: 90.5% (2000); College graduation rate: 21.5% (2000).

School District(s)

Kinnikinnick C C School District 131 (PK-08)
2000 Enrollment: 1,631 815-623-2837

Housing: Homeownership rate: 73.5% (2000); Median home value: $119,600 (2000); Median rent: $621 per month (2000); Median age of housing: 7 years (2000).
Transportation: Commute to work: 97.6% car, 0.3% public transportation, 0.3% walk, 1.8% work from home (2000); Travel time to work: 22.0% less than 15 minutes, 50.3% 15 to 30 minutes, 19.2% 30 to 45 minutes, 2.4% 45 to 60 minutes, 6.0% 60 minutes or more (2000)

Additional Information Contacts

Roscoe Chamber of Commerce 815-623-9065

SOUTH BELOIT (city). Covers a land area of 3.960 square miles and a water area of 0.125 square miles. Located at 42.48° N. Lat.; 89.03° W. Long. Elevation is 740 feet.
History: Incorporated 1917.
Population: 5,397 (2000); Race: 90.4% White, 4.4% Black, 0.9% Asian, 0.9% American Indian and Alaska Native, 6.0% Hispanic of any race, 2.0% two or more races (2000); Density: 1,362.9 persons per square mile (2000); Age: 27.0% under 18, 13.6% over 64 (2000); Marriage status: 25.0% never married, 55.2% now married, 7.2% widowed, 12.6% divorced (2000); Foreign born: 2.2% (2000); Ancestry (includes multiple ancestries): 28.1%

German, 17.0% Other groups, 11.0% Irish, 9.9% English, 7.3% Norwegian (2000).
Economy: Agriculture includes corn; cattle, hogs; dairying. Manufacturing: fabricated metal products, high-speed cutting tools, concrete products, foods, building materials, chemicals. Employment by occupation: 8.0% management, 13.4% professional, 12.5% services, 21.2% sales, 0.3% farming, 10.1% construction, 34.6% production (2000).
Income: Per capita income: $18,363 (2000); Median household income: $35,597 (2000); Poverty rate: 10.0% (2000).
Taxes: Total city taxes per capita: $411 (1997); City property taxes per capita: $228 (1997).
Education: High school graduation rate: 73.7% (2000); College graduation rate: 7.4% (2000).

School District(s)

Prairie Hill C C School District 133 (KG-08)
2000 Enrollment: 446 815-389-4694
South Beloit C U School District 320 (PK-12)
2000 Enrollment: 1,036 815-389-3478

Housing: Homeownership rate: 66.9% (2000); Median home value: $86,200 (2000); Median rent: $438 per month (2000); Median age of housing: 35 years (2000).
Transportation: Commute to work: 95.0% car, 0.2% public transportation, 2.0% walk, 1.4% work from home (2000); Travel time to work: 40.5% less than 15 minutes, 37.4% 15 to 30 minutes, 17.0% 30 to 45 minutes, 2.4% 45 to 60 minutes, 2.7% 60 minutes or more (2000); Amtrak: Service available.

WINNEBAGO (village). Covers a land area of 1.392 square miles and a water area of 0 square miles. Located at 42.26° N. Lat.; 89.24° W. Long. Elevation is 869 feet.
Population: 2,958 (2000); Race: 98.9% White, 0.2% Black, 0.0% Asian, 0.1% American Indian and Alaska Native, 2.2% Hispanic of any race, 0.8% two or more races (2000); Density: 2,125.3 persons per square mile (2000); Age: 33.7% under 18, 11.1% over 64 (2000); Marriage status: 20.3% never married, 68.1% now married, 4.9% widowed, 6.7% divorced (2000); Foreign born: 0.6% (2000); Ancestry (includes multiple ancestries): 36.1% German, 13.5% Irish, 10.2% Swedish, 9.9% English, 7.3% Italian (2000).
Economy: In agricultural area. Single-family building permits issued: 7 (2001) / 15 (2000); Multi-family building permits issued: 0 (2001) / 0 (2000); Employment by occupation: 12.2% management, 17.5% professional, 12.6% services, 25.6% sales, 0.5% farming, 11.4% construction, 20.2% production (2000).
Income: Per capita income: $21,019 (2000); Median household income: $59,891 (2000); Poverty rate: 1.1% (2000).
Taxes: Total city taxes per capita: $72 (1997); City property taxes per capita: $53 (1997).
Education: High school graduation rate: 90.4% (2000); College graduation rate: 19.6% (2000).

School District(s)

Winnebago C U School District 323 (PK-12)
2000 Enrollment: 1,688 815-335-2456

Housing: Homeownership rate: 89.0% (2000); Median home value: $110,600 (2000); Median rent: $353 per month (2000); Median age of housing: 24 years (2000).
Transportation: Commute to work: 96.2% car, 0.0% public transportation, 1.5% walk, 2.3% work from home (2000); Travel time to work: 26.4% less than 15 minutes, 55.2% 15 to 30 minutes, 15.4% 30 to 45 minutes, 1.1% 45 to 60 minutes, 1.8% 60 minutes or more (2000)

Woodford County

Located in central Illinois; bounded on the west by the Illinois River; drained by the Mackinaw River. Covers a land area of 528.00 square miles, a water area of 14.80 square miles, and is located in the Central Time Zone. The county government was organized in 1841. County seat is Eureka.

Woodford County is part of the Peoria-Pekin, IL MSA. The entire metro area includes: Peoria County; Tazewell County; Woodford County

Weather Station: Minonk — Elevation: 748 feet

	Jan	Feb	Mar	Apr	May	Jun	Jul	Aug	Sep	Oct	Nov	Dec
High	30	36	48	62	74	83	86	84	78	66	49	36
Low	13	18	28	38	49	59	63	60	52	41	30	19
Precip	1.8	1.9	3.2	3.7	4.4	3.7	3.8	3.4	3.3	2.9	3.3	2.4
Snow	9.0	6.8	3.6	0.9	tr	0.0	0.0	0.0	0.0	tr	1.6	6.2

High and Low temperatures in degrees Fahrenheit; Precipitation and Snow in inches

Population: 35,469 (2000); Race: 98.3% White, 0.4% Black, 0.3% Asian, 0.1% American Indian and Alaska Native, 0.9% Hispanic of any race, 0.6% two or more races (2000); Density: 67.2 persons per square mile (2000); Age: 26.7% under 18, 14.9% over 64 (2000).
Religion: Five largest groups: 15.9% Catholic Church, 7.3% The United Methodist Church, 7.2% Apostolic Christian Church of America, Inc., 4.2% United Church of Christ, 3.9% Lutheran Church—Missouri Synod (2000).
Economy: Unemployment rate: 3.5% (11/2002); Total civilian labor force: 18,574 (11/2002); Leading industries: 25.0% manufacturing; 13.6% health care and social assistance; 13.4% retail trade (2000); Companies that employ more than 1,000 persons: 0 (2000); Companies that employ more than 100 persons: 15 (2000); Farms: 923 totaling 299,763 acres (1997); Minority business ownership rate: 0.0% (1997); Women business ownership rate: 23.3% (1997); Retail sales per capita: $6,585 (1997). Single-family building permits issued: 159 (2001) / 155 (2000); Multi-family building permits issued: 41 (2001) / 26 (2000).
Income: Per capita income: $21,956 (2000); Median household income: $51,394 (2000); Poverty rate: 4.3% (2000); Bankruptcy rate: 3.04% (2001).
Taxes: Total county taxes per capita: $98 (2000); County property taxes per capita: $61 (2000).
Education: High school graduation rate: 87.8% (2000); College graduation rate: 21.1% (2000).
Housing: Homeownership rate: 82.7% (2000); Median home value: $102,900 (2000); Median rent: $396 per month (2000); Median age of housing: 35 years (2000).
Health: Birth rate: 117.6 per 10,000 population (1998); Age adjusted death rate: 83.7 per 10,000 population (1999); Age adjusted cancer mortality rate: 205.7 deaths per 100,000 population (1999). Number of physicians: 5.9 per 10,000 population (1999); Number of hospital beds: n/a (1999).
Elections: 2000 Presidential election results: 32.9% Gore, 64.9% Bush, 1.6% Nader, 0.4% Buchanan
National and State Parks: Woodford County State Conservation Area
Additional Information Contacts
Woodford County Government Offices 309-467-2822

Woodford County Communities

BAY VIEW GARDENS (village). Covers a land area of 0.178 square miles and a water area of 0 square miles. Located at 40.81° N. Lat.; 89.51° W. Long.
Population: 366 (2000); Race: 97.8% White, 0.0% Black, 0.0% Asian, 0.0% American Indian and Alaska Native, 2.2% Hispanic of any race, 2.2% two or more races (2000); Density: 2,057.0 persons per square mile (2000); Age: 29.8% under 18, 10.2% over 64 (2000); Marriage status: 23.6% never married, 63.0% now married, 6.9% widowed, 6.5% divorced (2000); Foreign born: 0.0% (2000); Ancestry (includes multiple ancestries): 26.0% German, 14.4% Other groups, 13.8% English, 9.4% Irish, 7.2% United States or American (2000).
Economy: Single-family building permits issued: 0 (2001) / 0 (2000); Multi-family building permits issued: 0 (2001) / 0 (2000); Employment by occupation: 4.5% management, 11.8% professional, 17.4% services, 29.8% sales, 0.0% farming, 14.0% construction, 22.5% production (2000).
Income: Per capita income: $15,230 (2000); Median household income: $32,750 (2000); Poverty rate: 5.3% (2000).
Taxes: Total city taxes per capita: $29 (1997); City property taxes per capita: $14 (1997).
Education: High school graduation rate: 73.6% (2000); College graduation rate: 6.2% (2000).
Housing: Homeownership rate: 74.1% (2000); Median home value: $70,400 (2000); Median rent: $465 per month (2000); Median age of housing: 39 years (2000).
Transportation: Commute to work: 94.9% car, 0.0% public transportation, 2.8% walk, 1.7% work from home (2000); Travel time to work: 27.2% less than 15 minutes, 43.4% 15 to 30 minutes, 19.7% 30 to 45 minutes, 6.4% 45 to 60 minutes, 3.5% 60 minutes or more (2000)

BENSON (village). Covers a land area of 0.174 square miles and a water area of 0 square miles. Located at 40.85° N. Lat.; 89.12° W. Long. Elevation is 769 feet.
Population: 408 (2000); Race: 100.0% White, 0.0% Black, 0.0% Asian, 0.0% American Indian and Alaska Native, 0.0% Hispanic of any race, 0.0% two or more races (2000); Density: 2,338.6 persons per square mile (2000); Age: 20.5% under 18, 27.3% over 64 (2000); Marriage status: 17.8% never married, 64.2% now married, 10.1% widowed, 8.0% divorced (2000); Foreign born: 1.2% (2000); Ancestry (includes multiple ancestries): 59.0%

German, 10.2% Irish, 7.6% English, 4.4% United States or American, 3.7% Italian (2000).
Economy: In agricultural area. Single-family building permits issued: 0 (2001) / 1 (2000); Multi-family building permits issued: 0 (2001) / 0 (2000); Employment by occupation: 11.0% management, 6.8% professional, 19.4% services, 23.6% sales, 0.0% farming, 18.8% construction, 20.4% production (2000).
Income: Per capita income: $19,358 (2000); Median household income: $40,500 (2000); Poverty rate: 4.1% (2000).
Taxes: Total city taxes per capita: $30 (1997); City property taxes per capita: $25 (1997).
Education: High school graduation rate: 86.8% (2000); College graduation rate: 5.2% (2000).
Housing: Homeownership rate: 86.0% (2000); Median home value: $65,500 (2000); Median rent: $344 per month (2000); Median age of housing: 52 years (2000).
Transportation: Commute to work: 93.2% car, 0.0% public transportation, 4.2% walk, 2.6% work from home (2000); Travel time to work: 39.0% less than 15 minutes, 22.5% 15 to 30 minutes, 22.5% 30 to 45 minutes, 10.7% 45 to 60 minutes, 5.3% 60 minutes or more (2000)

CONGERVILLE (village). Covers a land area of 0.757 square miles and a water area of 0.004 square miles. Located at 40.61° N. Lat.; 89.20° W. Long. Elevation is 745 feet.
Population: 466 (2000); Race: 99.3% White, 0.0% Black, 0.4% Asian, 0.0% American Indian and Alaska Native, 0.0% Hispanic of any race, 0.2% two or more races (2000); Density: 615.3 persons per square mile (2000); Age: 30.8% under 18, 8.0% over 64 (2000); Marriage status: 24.1% never married, 66.0% now married, 6.3% widowed, 3.6% divorced (2000); Foreign born: 0.7% (2000); Ancestry (includes multiple ancestries): 50.0% German, 12.3% United States or American, 11.6% Swiss, 6.5% Irish, 4.5% English (2000).
Economy: Corn, soybeans; cattle; metal fabricating. Single-family building permits issued: 1 (2001) / 6 (2000); Multi-family building permits issued: 0 (2001) / 0 (2000); Employment by occupation: 8.8% management, 9.6% professional, 24.9% services, 22.1% sales, 0.8% farming, 11.6% construction, 22.1% production (2000).
Income: Per capita income: $20,795 (2000); Median household income: $51,786 (2000); Poverty rate: 0.7% (2000).
Taxes: Total city taxes per capita: $40 (1997); City property taxes per capita: $29 (1997).
Education: High school graduation rate: 91.6% (2000); College graduation rate: 14.7% (2000).
Housing: Homeownership rate: 78.5% (2000); Median home value: $98,900 (2000); Median rent: $405 per month (2000); Median age of housing: 29 years (2000).
Transportation: Commute to work: 94.8% car, 0.0% public transportation, 1.6% walk, 3.6% work from home (2000); Travel time to work: 24.7% less than 15 minutes, 45.6% 15 to 30 minutes, 23.0% 30 to 45 minutes, 2.1% 45 to 60 minutes, 4.6% 60 minutes or more (2000)

EL PASO (city). Covers a land area of 1.545 square miles and a water area of 0 square miles. Located at 40.73° N. Lat.; 89.01° W. Long. Elevation is 752 feet.
History: El Paso was the home of Lester Pfister who developed a hybrid corn that gave a high yield.
Population: 2,695 (2000); Race: 98.8% White, 0.4% Black, 0.5% Asian, 0.0% American Indian and Alaska Native, 0.0% Hispanic of any race, 0.3% two or more races (2000); Density: 1,743.9 persons per square mile (2000); Age: 26.4% under 18, 15.1% over 64 (2000); Marriage status: 19.9% never married, 60.2% now married, 9.0% widowed, 10.8% divorced (2000); Foreign born: 1.0% (2000); Ancestry (includes multiple ancestries): 35.4% German, 16.6% Irish, 12.2% English, 9.7% United States or American, 3.9% French (except Basque) (2000).
Economy: Single-family building permits issued: 9 (2001) / 13 (2000); Multi-family building permits issued: 4 (2001) / 0 (2000); Employment by occupation: 11.6% management, 17.9% professional, 17.1% services, 27.6% sales, 0.6% farming, 6.7% construction, 18.5% production (2000).
Income: Per capita income: $21,730 (2000); Median household income: $47,745 (2000); Poverty rate: 3.2% (2000).
Taxes: Total city taxes per capita: $90 (1997); City property taxes per capita: $83 (1997).
Education: High school graduation rate: 83.2% (2000); College graduation rate: 18.8% (2000).

School District(s)

El Paso C U District 375 (PK-12)
2000 Enrollment: 917 309-527-4410

Housing: Homeownership rate: 74.8% (2000); Median home value: $88,800 (2000); Median rent: $415 per month (2000); Median age of housing: 46 years (2000).
Transportation: Commute to work: 92.2% car, 0.0% public transportation, 2.3% walk, 3.6% work from home (2000); Travel time to work: 48.2% less than 15 minutes, 18.5% 15 to 30 minutes, 27.5% 30 to 45 minutes, 4.1% 45 to 60 minutes, 1.7% 60 minutes or more (2000)

EUREKA (city). Covers a land area of 2.690 square miles and a water area of 0.048 square miles. Located at 40.71° N. Lat.; 89.27° W. Long. Elevation is 760 feet.
History: Eureka was settled in the 1830's, and developed around Eureka College, which began in 1848 as a seminary founded by the Disciples of Christ. Eureka was named the seat of Woodford County in 1896.
Population: 4,871 (2000); Race: 97.2% White, 0.4% Black, 0.4% Asian, 0.2% American Indian and Alaska Native, 1.7% Hispanic of any race, 0.7% two or more races (2000); Density: 1,810.5 persons per square mile (2000); Age: 26.3% under 18, 20.5% over 64 (2000); Marriage status: 26.5% never married, 56.0% now married, 12.3% widowed, 5.3% divorced (2000); Foreign born: 1.8% (2000); Ancestry (includes multiple ancestries): 36.1% German, 11.3% Irish, 9.3% English, 6.3% United States or American, 5.3% Other groups (2000).
Economy: Single-family building permits issued: 11 (2001) / 6 (2000); Multi-family building permits issued: 19 (2001) / 0 (2000); Employment by occupation: 10.3% management, 21.9% professional, 16.7% services, 26.3% sales, 0.8% farming, 8.0% construction, 16.0% production (2000).
Income: Per capita income: $20,460 (2000); Median household income: $44,744 (2000); Poverty rate: 2.4% (2000).
Taxes: Total city taxes per capita: $59 (1997); City property taxes per capita: $54 (1997).
Education: High school graduation rate: 82.4% (2000); College graduation rate: 21.6% (2000).

School District(s)

Eureka C U District 140 (PK-12)
2000 Enrollment: 1,645 309-467-3737

Four-year College(s)

Eureka College (Private, Not-for-profit, Christian Church (Disciples of Christ))
2001 Enrollment: 514 309-467-3721
2001 Tuition: In-state $16,600; Out-of-state $16,600

Housing: Homeownership rate: 70.2% (2000); Median home value: $98,800 (2000); Median rent: $394 per month (2000); Median age of housing: 35 years (2000).
Hospitals: Eureka Community Hospital (34 beds)
Newspapers: The Woodford County Journal (1 x week); Woodford Star (1 x week)
Transportation: Commute to work: 89.5% car, 0.0% public transportation, 7.7% walk, 1.7% work from home (2000); Travel time to work: 52.3% less than 15 minutes, 21.1% 15 to 30 minutes, 22.8% 30 to 45 minutes, 2.0% 45 to 60 minutes, 1.9% 60 minutes or more (2000)

GERMANTOWN HILLS (village). Aka Oak Grove Park. Covers a land area of 1.285 square miles and a water area of 0.043 square miles. Located at 40.76° N. Lat.; 89.46° W. Long. Elevation is 800 feet.
Population: 2,111 (2000); Race: 98.4% White, 0.0% Black, 0.3% Asian, 0.2% American Indian and Alaska Native, 0.9% Hispanic of any race, 0.7% two or more races (2000); Density: 1,643.2 persons per square mile (2000); Age: 32.9% under 18, 6.3% over 64 (2000); Marriage status: 19.1% never married, 71.0% now married, 4.4% widowed, 5.5% divorced (2000); Foreign born: 1.0% (2000); Ancestry (includes multiple ancestries): 41.4% German, 13.3% Irish, 11.6% English, 6.9% United States or American, 4.2% Swedish (2000).
Economy: Agricultural area. Single-family building permits issued: 45 (2001) / 34 (2000); Multi-family building permits issued: 10 (2001) / 8 (2000); Employment by occupation: 19.2% management, 31.4% professional, 9.7% services, 24.6% sales, 0.0% farming, 5.7% construction, 9.4% production (2000).
Income: Per capita income: $27,350 (2000); Median household income: $73,594 (2000); Poverty rate: 2.5% (2000).
Taxes: Total city taxes per capita: $65 (1997); City property taxes per capita: $49 (1997).
Education: High school graduation rate: 94.4% (2000); College graduation rate: 42.0% (2000).
Housing: Homeownership rate: 90.6% (2000); Median home value: $156,400 (2000); Median rent: $367 per month (2000); Median age of housing: 11 years (2000).

Transportation: Commute to work: 96.4% car, 0.0% public transportation, 0.6% walk, 2.6% work from home (2000); Travel time to work: 18.3% less than 15 minutes, 64.0% 15 to 30 minutes, 12.2% 30 to 45 minutes, 1.8% 45 to 60 minutes, 3.7% 60 minutes or more (2000)

GOODFIELD (village). Covers a land area of 1.447 square miles and a water area of 0.007 square miles. Located at 40.62° N. Lat.; 89.27° W. Long. Elevation is 748 feet.

Population: 686 (2000); Race: 98.8% White, 0.0% Black, 0.9% Asian, 0.0% American Indian and Alaska Native, 0.3% Hispanic of any race, 0.3% two or more races (2000); Density: 474.2 persons per square mile (2000); Age: 33.7% under 18, 12.1% over 64 (2000); Marriage status: 20.0% never married, 73.5% now married, 3.3% widowed, 3.3% divorced (2000); Foreign born: 0.9% (2000); Ancestry (includes multiple ancestries): 51.4% German, 14.4% Irish, 10.0% United States or American, 7.2% English, 7.2% Swiss (2000).

Economy: Grain, soybeans; cattle; dairying. Manufacturing: feeds, plows and other agricultural equipment. Single-family building permits issued: 7 (2001) / 7 (2000); Multi-family building permits issued: 0 (2001) / 0 (2000); Employment by occupation: 10.1% management, 22.8% professional, 15.4% services, 22.8% sales, 0.6% farming, 11.0% construction, 17.2% production (2000).

Income: Per capita income: $20,099 (2000); Median household income: $60,069 (2000); Poverty rate: 3.2% (2000).

Taxes: Total city taxes per capita: $123 (1997); City property taxes per capita: $29 (1997).

Education: High school graduation rate: 89.4% (2000); College graduation rate: 27.8% (2000).

Housing: Homeownership rate: 88.6% (2000); Median home value: $114,000 (2000); Median rent: $381 per month (2000); Median age of housing: 30 years (2000).

Transportation: Commute to work: 95.8% car, 0.0% public transportation, 0.6% walk, 3.6% work from home (2000); Travel time to work: 32.4% less than 15 minutes, 44.2% 15 to 30 minutes, 16.8% 30 to 45 minutes, 4.0% 45 to 60 minutes, 2.5% 60 minutes or more (2000)

KAPPA (village). Covers a land area of 0.228 square miles and a water area of 0 square miles. Located at 40.67° N. Lat.; 89.00° W. Long. Elevation is 735 feet.

Population: 170 (2000); Race: 97.7% White, 0.0% Black, 0.0% Asian, 2.3% American Indian and Alaska Native, 0.0% Hispanic of any race, 0.0% two or more races (2000); Density: 747.1 persons per square mile (2000); Age: 30.8% under 18, 4.7% over 64 (2000); Marriage status: 18.4% never married, 69.6% now married, 4.8% widowed, 7.2% divorced (2000); Foreign born: 0.0% (2000); Ancestry (includes multiple ancestries): 40.7% German, 25.6% Irish, 18.6% United States or American, 10.5% English, 5.8% Swiss (2000).

Economy: Agriculture area. Single-family building permits issued: 1 (2001) / 1 (2000); Multi-family building permits issued: 0 (2001) / 0 (2000); Employment by occupation: 8.4% management, 15.8% professional, 22.1% services, 28.4% sales, 0.0% farming, 14.7% construction, 10.5% production (2000).

Income: Per capita income: $17,451 (2000); Median household income: $46,786 (2000); Poverty rate: 9.6% (2000).

Taxes: Total city taxes per capita: $41 (1997); City property taxes per capita: $21 (1997).

Education: High school graduation rate: 89.8% (2000); College graduation rate: 13.0% (2000).

Housing: Homeownership rate: 68.2% (2000); Median home value: $83,800 (2000); Median rent: $288 per month (2000); Median age of housing: 28 years (2000).

Transportation: Commute to work: 90.1% car, 0.0% public transportation, 0.0% walk, 9.9% work from home (2000); Travel time to work: 32.9% less than 15 minutes, 41.5% 15 to 30 minutes, 19.5% 30 to 45 minutes, 2.4% 45 to 60 minutes, 3.7% 60 minutes or more (2000)

LOWPOINT (unincorporated postal area, zip code 61545). Aka Low Point. Covers a land area of 31.763 square miles and a water area of 0.031 square miles. Located at 40.87° N. Lat.; 89.37° W. Long.

Population: 651 (2000); Race: 100.0% White, 0.0% Black, 0.0% Asian, 0.0% American Indian and Alaska Native, 0.0% Hispanic of any race, 0.0% two or more races (2000); Density: 20.5 persons per square mile (2000); Age: 29.6% under 18, 12.6% over 64 (2000); Marriage status: 19.7% never married, 66.8% now married, 8.5% widowed, 5.0% divorced (2000); Foreign born: 0.0% (2000); Ancestry (includes multiple ancestries): 48.5% German, 15.5% English, 8.4% Irish, 7.5% Other groups, 5.3% Swiss (2000).

Economy: Employment by occupation: 13.2% management, 16.5% professional, 15.9% services, 14.7% sales, 2.4% farming, 13.2% construction, 24.3% production (2000).

Income: Per capita income: $16,658 (2000); Median household income: $44,167 (2000); Poverty rate: 8.2% (2000).

Education: High school graduation rate: 82.0% (2000); College graduation rate: 9.9% (2000).

Housing: Homeownership rate: 86.2% (2000); Median home value: $69,000 (2000); Median rent: $444 per month (2000); Median age of housing: 59 years (2000).

Transportation: Commute to work: 94.3% car, 0.0% public transportation, 2.1% walk, 1.8% work from home (2000); Travel time to work: 24.4% less than 15 minutes, 36.0% 15 to 30 minutes, 17.4% 30 to 45 minutes, 12.8% 45 to 60 minutes, 9.5% 60 minutes or more (2000)

METAMORA (village). Covers a land area of 1.389 square miles and a water area of 0.002 square miles. Located at 40.79° N. Lat.; 89.36° W. Long. Elevation is 821 feet.

History: Former capital of Woodford county. Old courthouse is now state memorial to Lincoln, who often argued cases here. Incorporated 1845.

Population: 2,700 (2000); Race: 98.3% White, 1.0% Black, 0.0% Asian, 0.4% American Indian and Alaska Native, 1.0% Hispanic of any race, 0.3% two or more races (2000); Density: 1,944.4 persons per square mile (2000); Age: 24.0% under 18, 25.4% over 64 (2000); Marriage status: 15.9% never married, 65.8% now married, 12.0% widowed, 6.2% divorced (2000); Foreign born: 1.2% (2000); Ancestry (includes multiple ancestries): 46.4% German, 14.3% English, 12.5% Irish, 6.5% French (except Basque), 4.6% United States or American (2000).

Economy: In agricultural area; canned foods. Single-family building permits issued: 8 (2001) / 5 (2000); Multi-family building permits issued: 0 (2001) / 12 (2000); Employment by occupation: 11.3% management, 24.9% professional, 14.4% services, 22.3% sales, 0.0% farming, 11.4% construction, 15.7% production (2000).

Income: Per capita income: $20,200 (2000); Median household income: $46,691 (2000); Poverty rate: 2.9% (2000).

Taxes: Total city taxes per capita: $272 (1997); City property taxes per capita: $155 (1997).

Education: High school graduation rate: 87.1% (2000); College graduation rate: 22.7% (2000).

School District(s)

Germantown Hills School District 69 (PK-08)
2000 Enrollment: 758 309-383-2121
Metamora C C School District 1 (PK-08)
2000 Enrollment: 715 309-367-2361
Metamora Township H S District 122 (09-12)
2000 Enrollment: 860 309-367-4151

Housing: Homeownership rate: 75.3% (2000); Median home value: $94,000 (2000); Median rent: $396 per month (2000); Median age of housing: 37 years (2000).

Newspapers: Woodford County Shopper (1 x week); Washburn Leader (1 x week); Metamora Herald (1 x week)

Transportation: Commute to work: 90.5% car, 0.0% public transportation, 5.3% walk, 3.4% work from home (2000); Travel time to work: 39.8% less than 15 minutes, 33.2% 15 to 30 minutes, 17.0% 30 to 45 minutes, 6.2% 45 to 60 minutes, 3.7% 60 minutes or more (2000)

MINONK (city). Covers a land area of 1.366 square miles and a water area of 0 square miles. Located at 40.90° N. Lat.; 89.03° W. Long. Elevation is 750 feet.

History: Incorporated 1867.

Population: 2,168 (2000); Race: 98.2% White, 0.0% Black, 0.0% Asian, 0.0% American Indian and Alaska Native, 1.5% Hispanic of any race, 1.4% two or more races (2000); Density: 1,587.6 persons per square mile (2000); Age: 27.3% under 18, 20.2% over 64 (2000); Marriage status: 18.6% never married, 59.3% now married, 11.3% widowed, 10.8% divorced (2000); Foreign born: 0.7% (2000); Ancestry (includes multiple ancestries): 39.8% German, 15.1% Irish, 7.6% United States or American, 7.4% Polish, 7.1% English (2000).

Economy: Manufacturing: paper products. Agriculture: dairy products; livestock; grain. Single-family building permits issued: 5 (2001) / 2 (2000); Multi-family building permits issued: 0 (2001) / 0 (2000); Employment by occupation: 9.0% management, 15.6% professional, 17.6% services, 26.7% sales, 0.9% farming, 9.0% construction, 21.3% production (2000).

Income: Per capita income: $17,688 (2000); Median household income: $44,028 (2000); Poverty rate: 8.6% (2000).

Taxes: Total city taxes per capita: $164 (1997); City property taxes per capita: $113 (1997).
Education: High school graduation rate: 83.8% (2000); College graduation rate: 13.9% (2000).

School District(s)

Fieldcrest CUSD #6 (PK-12)
2000 Enrollment: 1,301 309-432-2177

Housing: Homeownership rate: 78.2% (2000); Median home value: $74,200 (2000); Median rent: $351 per month (2000); Median age of housing: 47 years (2000).
Newspapers: Minonk News Dispatch (1 x week)
Transportation: Commute to work: 92.4% car, 0.3% public transportation, 3.7% walk, 3.1% work from home (2000); Travel time to work: 39.2% less than 15 minutes, 18.7% 15 to 30 minutes, 26.7% 30 to 45 minutes, 10.8% 45 to 60 minutes, 4.6% 60 minutes or more (2000)

PANOLA (village). Covers a land area of 0.202 square miles and a water area of 0 square miles. Located at 40.78° N. Lat.; 89.02° W. Long. Elevation is 734 feet.
Population: 33 (2000); Race: 100.0% White, 0.0% Black, 0.0% Asian, 0.0% American Indian and Alaska Native, 0.0% Hispanic of any race, 0.0% two or more races (2000); Density: 163.5 persons per square mile (2000); Age: 6.3% under 18, 18.8% over 64 (2000); Marriage status: 28.1% never married, 46.9% now married, 0.0% widowed, 25.0% divorced (2000); Foreign born: 0.0% (2000); Ancestry (includes multiple ancestries): 59.4% German, 12.5% Welsh, 12.5% French (except Basque), 6.3% English, 3.1% United States or American (2000).
Economy: In agricultural area. Employment by occupation: 0.0% management, 25.0% professional, 10.0% services, 20.0% sales, 0.0% farming, 20.0% construction, 25.0% production (2000).
Income: Per capita income: $24,259 (2000); Median household income: $41,875 (2000); Poverty rate: 0.0% (2000).
Taxes: Total city taxes per capita: $22 (1997); City property taxes per capita: $22 (1997).
Education: High school graduation rate: 92.3% (2000); College graduation rate: 7.7% (2000).
Housing: Homeownership rate: 100.0% (2000); Median home value: $68,800 (2000); Median age of housing: 60+ years (2000).
Transportation: Commute to work: 90.0% car, 0.0% public transportation, 0.0% walk, 10.0% work from home (2000); Travel time to work: 22.2% less than 15 minutes, 33.3% 15 to 30 minutes, 44.4% 30 to 45 minutes, 0.0% 45 to 60 minutes, 0.0% 60 minutes or more (2000)

ROANOKE (village). Covers a land area of 0.910 square miles and a water area of 0.037 square miles. Located at 40.79° N. Lat.; 89.20° W. Long. Elevation is 735 feet.
History: Incorporated 1874.
Population: 1,994 (2000); Race: 98.5% White, 0.2% Black, 0.1% Asian, 0.1% American Indian and Alaska Native, 1.1% Hispanic of any race, 0.6% two or more races (2000); Density: 2,192.0 persons per square mile (2000); Age: 24.3% under 18, 21.9% over 64 (2000); Marriage status: 20.0% never married, 66.3% now married, 7.4% widowed, 6.3% divorced (2000); Foreign born: 0.4% (2000); Ancestry (includes multiple ancestries): 56.3% German, 8.8% Irish, 8.0% Swiss, 8.0% Italian, 7.7% English (2000).
Economy: In agricultural area. Single-family building permits issued: 2 (2001) / 5 (2000); Multi-family building permits issued: 0 (2001) / 2 (2000); Employment by occupation: 10.7% management, 16.7% professional, 16.5% services, 27.3% sales, 1.9% farming, 9.7% construction, 17.3% production (2000).
Income: Per capita income: $24,489 (2000); Median household income: $43,125 (2000); Poverty rate: 4.9% (2000).
Taxes: Total city taxes per capita: $57 (1997); City property taxes per capita: $54 (1997).
Education: High school graduation rate: 87.8% (2000); College graduation rate: 15.4% (2000).

School District(s)

Roanoke Benson C U S District 60 (PK-12)
2000 Enrollment: 601 309-923-8921

Housing: Homeownership rate: 81.8% (2000); Median home value: $84,500 (2000); Median rent: $416 per month (2000); Median age of housing: 43 years (2000).
Newspapers: The Roanoke Review (1 x week)
Transportation: Commute to work: 94.4% car, 0.0% public transportation, 3.0% walk, 2.6% work from home (2000); Travel time to work: 46.0% less than 15 minutes, 21.4% 15 to 30 minutes, 25.3% 30 to 45 minutes, 5.3% 45 to 60 minutes, 2.0% 60 minutes or more (2000)

SECOR (village). Covers a land area of 0.355 square miles and a water area of 0 square miles. Located at 40.74° N. Lat.; 89.13° W. Long. Elevation is 735 feet.
Population: 379 (2000); Race: 95.5% White, 0.0% Black, 0.0% Asian, 0.0% American Indian and Alaska Native, 0.0% Hispanic of any race, 4.5% two or more races (2000); Density: 1,068.7 persons per square mile (2000); Age: 24.7% under 18, 16.8% over 64 (2000); Marriage status: 18.4% never married, 63.5% now married, 5.8% widowed, 12.3% divorced (2000); Foreign born: 0.0% (2000); Ancestry (includes multiple ancestries): 40.4% German, 10.8% Other groups, 10.2% Irish, 7.9% English, 5.8% Dutch (2000).
Economy: In agricultural area. Single-family building permits issued: 0 (2001) / 0 (2000); Multi-family building permits issued: 0 (2001) / 0 (2000); Employment by occupation: 5.1% management, 12.5% professional, 23.3% services, 19.3% sales, 1.1% farming, 9.7% construction, 29.0% production (2000).
Income: Per capita income: $22,635 (2000); Median household income: $44,205 (2000); Poverty rate: 8.2% (2000).
Taxes: Total city taxes per capita: $76 (1997); City property taxes per capita: $71 (1997).
Education: High school graduation rate: 74.4% (2000); College graduation rate: 5.0% (2000).
Housing: Homeownership rate: 83.4% (2000); Median home value: $59,700 (2000); Median rent: $311 per month (2000); Median age of housing: 53 years (2000).
Transportation: Commute to work: 93.7% car, 0.0% public transportation, 0.6% walk, 5.2% work from home (2000); Travel time to work: 35.2% less than 15 minutes, 20.0% 15 to 30 minutes, 33.9% 30 to 45 minutes, 7.3% 45 to 60 minutes, 3.6% 60 minutes or more (2000)

SPRING BAY (village). Covers a land area of 0.806 square miles and a water area of 0.331 square miles. Located at 40.82° N. Lat.; 89.52° W. Long. Elevation is 471 feet.
Population: 436 (2000); Race: 98.9% White, 0.4% Black, 0.0% Asian, 0.0% American Indian and Alaska Native, 0.7% Hispanic of any race, 0.7% two or more races (2000); Density: 541.0 persons per square mile (2000); Age: 19.0% under 18, 12.6% over 64 (2000); Marriage status: 22.6% never married, 61.2% now married, 6.6% widowed, 9.7% divorced (2000); Foreign born: 0.0% (2000); Ancestry (includes multiple ancestries): 30.7% German, 11.5% United States or American, 10.2% Other groups, 10.2% Irish, 9.8% English (2000).
Economy: In agricultural area. Single-family building permits issued: 7 (2001) / 7 (2000); Multi-family building permits issued: 8 (2001) / 4 (2000); Employment by occupation: 3.9% management, 11.2% professional, 14.7% services, 24.7% sales, 1.2% farming, 14.7% construction, 29.7% production (2000).
Income: Per capita income: $18,915 (2000); Median household income: $42,500 (2000); Poverty rate: 4.8% (2000).
Taxes: Total city taxes per capita: $27 (1997); City property taxes per capita: $16 (1997).
Education: High school graduation rate: 85.4% (2000); College graduation rate: 8.4% (2000).
Housing: Homeownership rate: 85.2% (2000); Median home value: $75,900 (2000); Median rent: $339 per month (2000); Median age of housing: 32 years (2000).
Transportation: Commute to work: 98.4% car, 0.0% public transportation, 0.8% walk, 0.0% work from home (2000); Travel time to work: 26.5% less than 15 minutes, 46.2% 15 to 30 minutes, 17.8% 30 to 45 minutes, 3.6% 45 to 60 minutes, 5.9% 60 minutes or more (2000)

WASHBURN (village). Covers a land area of 0.727 square miles and a water area of 0 square miles. Located at 40.92° N. Lat.; 89.29° W. Long. Elevation is 690 feet.
Population: 1,147 (2000); Race: 97.3% White, 0.0% Black, 0.0% Asian, 0.0% American Indian and Alaska Native, 2.1% Hispanic of any race, 1.5% two or more races (2000); Density: 1,576.6 persons per square mile (2000); Age: 29.8% under 18, 13.9% over 64 (2000); Marriage status: 26.9% never married, 61.0% now married, 6.1% widowed, 6.0% divorced (2000); Foreign born: 1.0% (2000); Ancestry (includes multiple ancestries): 37.4% German, 10.5% Irish, 9.6% English, 9.2% United States or American, 7.0% Other groups (2000).
Economy: In agricultural area: corn, soybeans; cattle. Single-family building permits issued: 0 (2001) / 0 (2000); Multi-family building permits issued: 0 (2001) / 0 (2000); Employment by occupation: 8.2% management, 13.7%

professional, 15.4% services, 25.3% sales, 2.4% farming, 11.5% construction, 23.4% production (2000).
Income: Per capita income: $17,619 (2000); Median household income: $44,167 (2000); Poverty rate: 8.4% (2000).
Taxes: Total city taxes per capita: $40 (1997); City property taxes per capita: $34 (1997).
Education: High school graduation rate: 84.9% (2000); College graduation rate: 11.8% (2000).

School District(s)

Lowpoint-Washburn C U S District 21 (PK-12)
2000 Enrollment: 460 309-248-7522

Housing: Homeownership rate: 81.1% (2000); Median home value: $71,600 (2000); Median rent: $304 per month (2000); Median age of housing: 57 years (2000).
Transportation: Commute to work: 95.7% car, 0.0% public transportation, 2.2% walk, 1.7% work from home (2000); Travel time to work: 25.2% less than 15 minutes, 23.9% 15 to 30 minutes, 31.1% 30 to 45 minutes, 16.4% 45 to 60 minutes, 3.4% 60 minutes or more (2000)

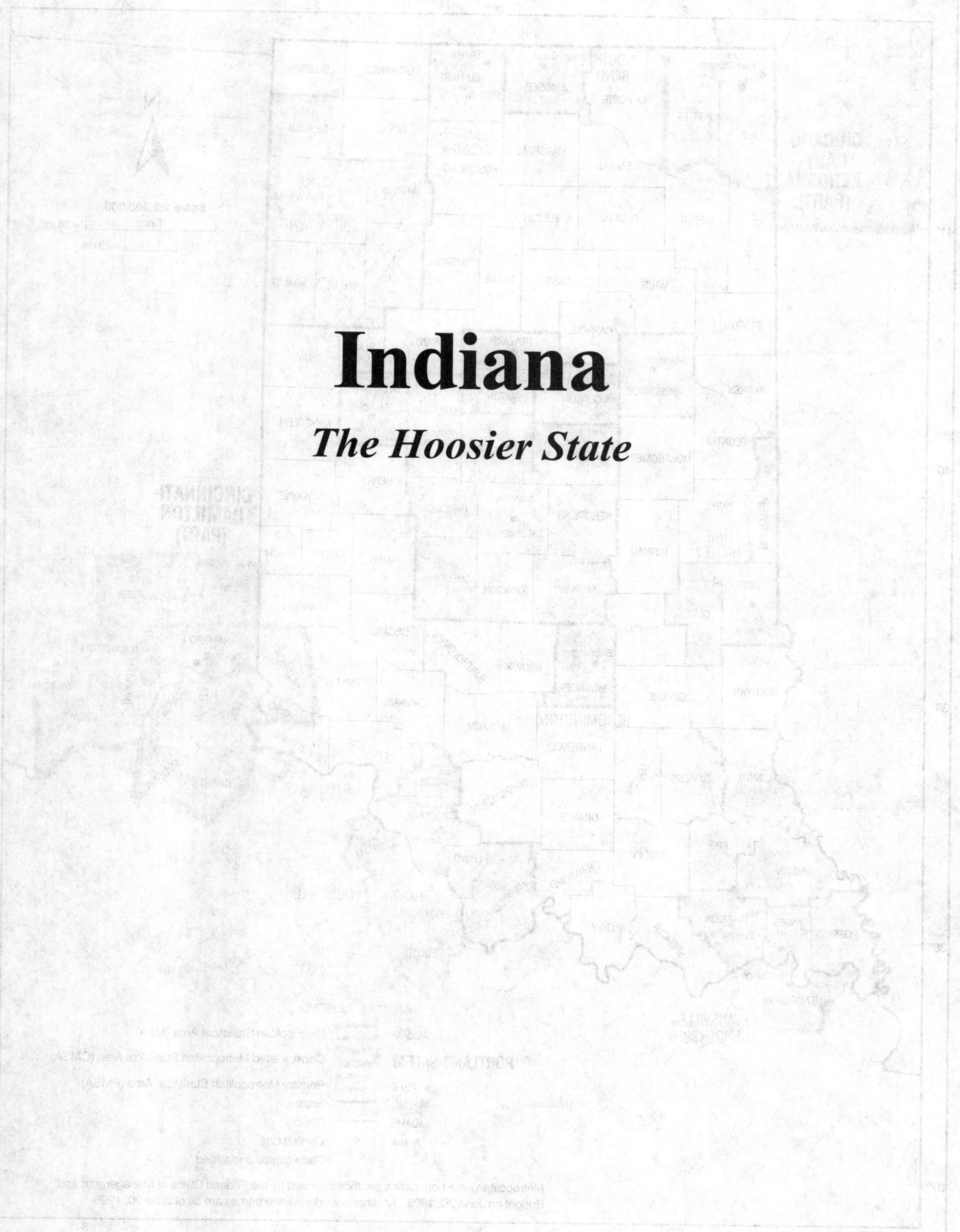

Indiana

The Hoosier State

INDIANA –Metropolitan Areas, Counties, and Central Cities

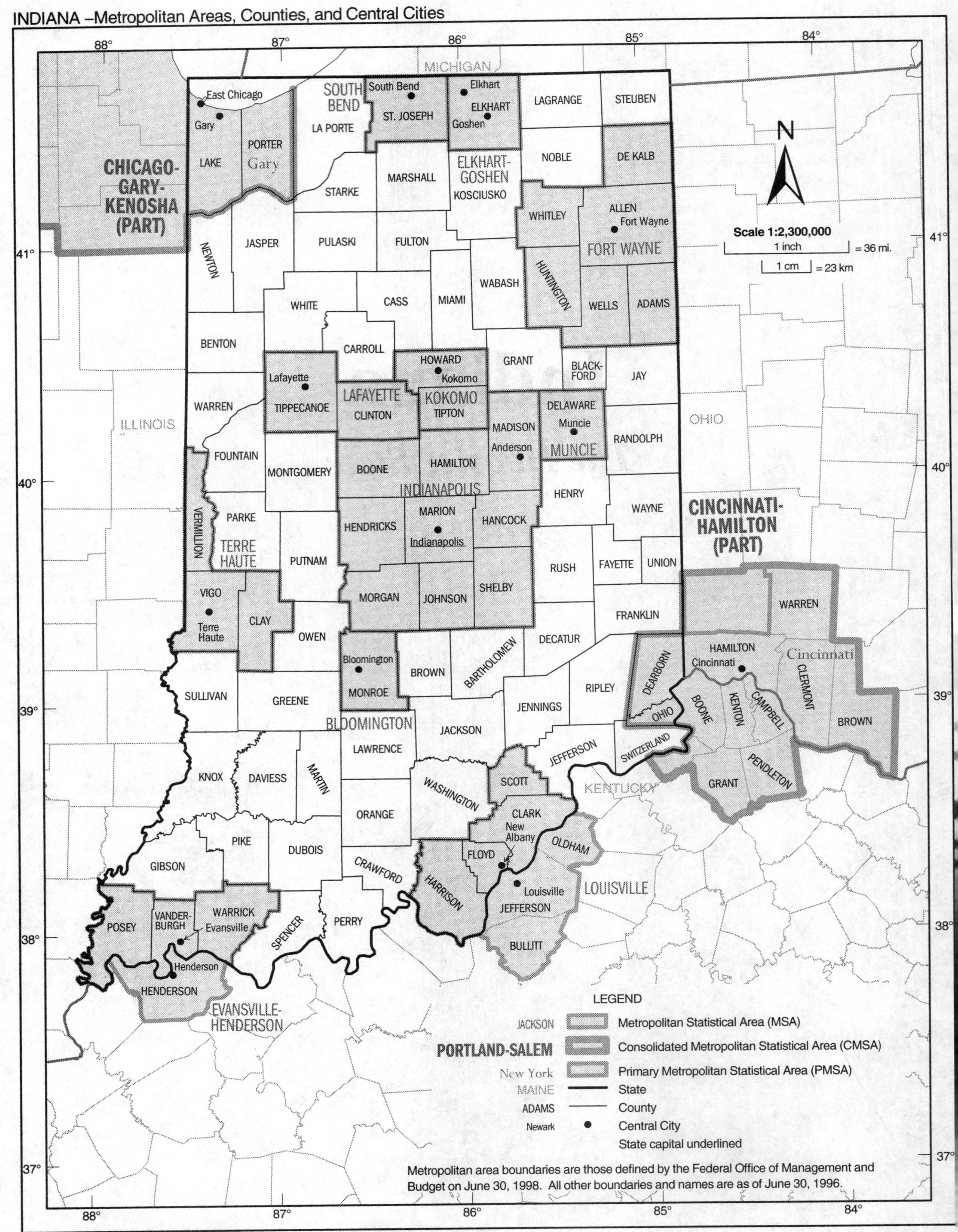

A

B

C

D

E

F

CDP = *Census Designated Place*

CDP = Census Designated Place

N

O

P

Q

R

S

T

U

CDP = Census Designated Place

V

W

Y

Z

Adams County

Located in eastern Indiana; bounded on the east by Ohio. Covers a land area of 339.40 square miles, a water area of 0.60 square miles, and is located in the Eastern Time Zone. The county government was organized in 1835. County seat is Decatur.

Adams County is part of the Fort Wayne, IN MSA. The entire metro area includes: Adams County; Allen County; DeKalb County; Huntington County; Wells County; Whitley County

Weather Station: Berne Elevation: 859 feet

	Jan	Feb	Mar	Apr	May	Jun	Jul	Aug	Sep	Oct	Nov	Dec
High	32	37	48	61	72	81	85	83	76	64	50	38
Low	17	21	30	40	50	60	64	62	55	43	34	24
Precip	2.1	2.1	2.9	3.8	3.8	4.4	4.1	3.6	3.0	2.6	3.2	2.7
Snow	9.4	7.2	4.4	1.1	0.0	0.0	0.0	0.0	0.0	0.4	2.1	6.1

High and Low temperatures in degrees Fahrenheit; Precipitation and Snow in inches

Population: 33,625 (2000); Race: 97.4% White, 0.1% Black, 0.2% Asian, 0.0% American Indian and Alaska Native, 3.2% Hispanic of any race, 0.8% two or more races (2000); Density: 99.1 persons per square mile (2000); Age: 31.2% under 18, 13.5% over 64 (2000).
Religion: Five largest groups: 14.3% Catholic Church, 11.6% Lutheran Church—Missouri Synod, 8.0% The United Methodist Church, 8.0% Old Order Amish Church, 4.5% United Church of Christ (2000).
Economy: Unemployment rate: 3.9% (11/2002); Total civilian labor force: 16,445 (11/2002); Leading industries: 49.7% manufacturing; 13.6% retail trade; 8.7% health care and social assistance (2000); Companies that employ more than 1,000 persons: 1 (2000); Companies that employ more than 100 persons: 28 (2000); Farms: 1,093 totaling 208,653 acres (1997); Minority business ownership rate: 0.0% (1997); Women business ownership rate: 30.3% (1997); Retail sales per capita: $10,528 (1997). Single-family building permits issued: 94 (2001) / 103 (2000); Multi-family building permits issued: 2 (2001) / 18 (2000).
Income: Per capita income: $16,704 (2000); Median household income: $40,625 (2000); Poverty rate: 9.1% (2000); Bankruptcy rate: 4.48% (2001).
Taxes: Total county taxes per capita: $196 (2000); County property taxes per capita: $144 (2000).
Education: High school graduation rate: 80.0% (2000); College graduation rate: 10.7% (2000).
Housing: Homeownership rate: 77.0% (2000); Median home value: $85,400 (2000); Median rent: $320 per month (2000); Median age of housing: 37 years (2000).
Health: Birth rate: 189.7 per 10,000 population (1998); Age adjusted death rate: 69.6 per 10,000 population (1999); Age adjusted cancer mortality rate: 99.2 deaths per 100,000 population (1999). Number of physicians: 4.5 per 10,000 population (1999); Number of hospital beds: 25.9 per 10,000 population (1999).
Elections: 2000 Presidential election results: 30.0% Gore, 68.0% Bush, 0.4% Nader, 1.2% Buchanan
National and State Parks: Limberlost State Memorial
Additional Information Contacts
Adams County Government Offices 219-724-2600
Berne Chamber of Commerce 219-589-8080
Decatur Chamber of Commerce. 219-724-2604

Adams County Communities

BERNE (city). Covers a land area of 1.799 square miles and a water area of 0 square miles. Located at 40.65° N. Lat.; 84.95° W. Long. Elevation is 861 feet.
History: Mennonite immigrants from Berne, Switzerland, settled here in 1852 and named Berne for their former home. The Mennonite Book Concern was established here in 1882.
Population: 4,150 (2000); Race: 97.1% White, 0.0% Black, 0.0% Asian, 0.0% American Indian and Alaska Native, 2.2% Hispanic of any race, 1.1% two or more races (2000); Density: 2,307.3 persons per square mile (2000); Age: 25.2% under 18, 24.4% over 64 (2000); Marriage status: 17.8% never married, 64.9% now married, 11.3% widowed, 6.0% divorced (2000); Foreign born: 1.9% (2000); Ancestry (includes multiple ancestries): 28.7% German, 28.0% Swiss, 10.0% Irish, 7.7% United States or American, 5.5% Other groups (2000).
Economy: Single-family building permits issued: 8 (2001) / 3 (2000); Multi-family building permits issued: 0 (2001) / 16 (2000); Employment by occupation: 11.5% management, 18.6% professional, 15.4% services, 23.2% sales, 1.6% farming, 6.6% construction, 23.0% production (2000).
Income: Per capita income: $17,394 (2000); Median household income: $35,491 (2000); Poverty rate: 3.6% (2000).
Taxes: Total city taxes per capita: $196 (1997); City property taxes per capita: $150 (1997).
Education: High school graduation rate: 82.1% (2000); College graduation rate: 17.8% (2000).

School District(s)

South Adams Schools (KG-12)
2000 Enrollment: 1,497 219-589-3133
Housing: Homeownership rate: 67.7% (2000); Median home value: $79,000 (2000); Median rent: $348 per month (2000); Median age of housing: 37 years (2000).
Safety: Violent crime rate: 0.0 per 10,000 population; Property crime rate: 115.0 per 10,000 population (2001).
Newspapers: Berne Tri-Weekly News (3 x week)
Transportation: Commute to work: 93.5% car, 0.0% public transportation, 3.2% walk, 1.9% work from home (2000); Travel time to work: 66.7% less than 15 minutes, 20.6% 15 to 30 minutes, 4.1% 30 to 45 minutes, 4.0% 45 to 60 minutes, 4.6% 60 minutes or more (2000)
Additional Information Contacts
Berne Chamber of Commerce 219-589-8080

DECATUR (city). Covers a land area of 4.923 square miles and a water area of 0.006 square miles. Located at 40.83° N. Lat.; 84.92° W. Long. Elevation is 794 feet.
History: Decatur was named for Stephen Decatur, American naval hero. Novelist Gene Stratton Porter (1868-1924) lived here for three years.
Population: 9,528 (2000); Race: 93.9% White, 0.3% Black, 0.6% Asian, 0.1% American Indian and Alaska Native, 7.8% Hispanic of any race, 1.3% two or more races (2000); Density: 1,935.4 persons per square mile (2000); Age: 27.0% under 18, 15.1% over 64 (2000); Marriage status: 22.5% never married, 56.5% now married, 8.1% widowed, 12.8% divorced (2000); Foreign born: 1.9% (2000); Ancestry (includes multiple ancestries): 32.4% German, 12.0% Other groups, 9.9% United States or American, 8.6% Irish, 8.0% English (2000).
Economy: Single-family building permits issued: 32 (2001) / 20 (2000); Multi-family building permits issued: 2 (2001) / 0 (2000); Employment by occupation: 8.8% management, 13.2% professional, 16.8% services, 20.3% sales, 0.1% farming, 10.3% construction, 30.5% production (2000).
Income: Per capita income: $18,186 (2000); Median household income: $37,234 (2000); Poverty rate: 7.7% (2000).
Taxes: Total city taxes per capita: $261 (1997); City property taxes per capita: $203 (1997).
Education: High school graduation rate: 85.0% (2000); College graduation rate: 11.2% (2000).

School District(s)

North Adams Community Schools (KG-12)
2000 Enrollment: 2,360 219-724-7146
Housing: Homeownership rate: 68.8% (2000); Median home value: $77,900 (2000); Median rent: $327 per month (2000); Median age of housing: 42 years (2000).
Hospitals: Adams County Memorial Hospital (87 beds)
Safety: Violent crime rate: 12.5 per 10,000 population; Property crime rate: 167.0 per 10,000 population (2001).
Newspapers: Decatur Daily Democrat (6 x week)
Transportation: Commute to work: 93.3% car, 0.2% public transportation, 2.0% walk, 2.4% work from home (2000); Travel time to work: 57.3% less than 15 minutes, 16.1% 15 to 30 minutes, 14.7% 30 to 45 minutes, 7.7% 45 to 60 minutes, 4.3% 60 minutes or more (2000)
Additional Information Contacts
Decatur Chamber of Commerce. 219-724-2604

GENEVA (town). Covers a land area of 1.148 square miles and a water area of 0.126 square miles. Located at 40.59° N. Lat.; 84.96° W. Long. Elevation is 849 feet.
History: Geneva was the home of novelist Gene Stratton Porter from 1893 to 1913. Her books were set in the Limberlost Swamps here.
Population: 1,368 (2000); Race: 95.8% White, 0.5% Black, 0.2% Asian, 0.0% American Indian and Alaska Native, 0.9% Hispanic of any race, 3.0% two or more races (2000); Density: 1,192.1 persons per square mile (2000); Age: 25.6% under 18, 14.2% over 64 (2000); Marriage status: 20.6% never married, 57.4% now married, 7.6% widowed, 14.3% divorced (2000); Foreign born: 0.8% (2000); Ancestry (includes multiple ancestries): 25.9%

German, 10.3% United States or American, 9.4% English, 9.1% Irish, 7.3% Other groups (2000).
Economy: Single-family building permits issued: 3 (2001) / 1 (2000); Multi-family building permits issued: 0 (2001) / 0 (2000); Employment by occupation: 5.9% management, 11.1% professional, 12.8% services, 21.6% sales, 0.9% farming, 11.2% construction, 36.6% production (2000).
Income: Per capita income: $16,435 (2000); Median household income: $33,942 (2000); Poverty rate: 11.9% (2000).
Taxes: Total city taxes per capita: $323 (1997); City property taxes per capita: $276 (1997).
Education: High school graduation rate: 81.2% (2000); College graduation rate: 7.0% (2000).
Housing: Homeownership rate: 65.9% (2000); Median home value: $62,100 (2000); Median rent: $251 per month (2000); Median age of housing: 38 years (2000).
Transportation: Commute to work: 96.3% car, 0.4% public transportation, 1.2% walk, 0.9% work from home (2000); Travel time to work: 36.9% less than 15 minutes, 37.2% 15 to 30 minutes, 14.5% 30 to 45 minutes, 3.0% 45 to 60 minutes, 8.3% 60 minutes or more (2000)

MONROE (town). Covers a land area of 0.480 square miles and a water area of 0 square miles. Located at 40.74° N. Lat.; 84.94° W. Long. Elevation is 825 feet.
Population: 734 (2000); Race: 96.3% White, 0.0% Black, 0.0% Asian, 0.0% American Indian and Alaska Native, 4.7% Hispanic of any race, 2.3% two or more races (2000); Density: 1,529.3 persons per square mile (2000); Age: 28.6% under 18, 14.0% over 64 (2000); Marriage status: 18.2% never married, 66.9% now married, 5.8% widowed, 9.1% divorced (2000); Foreign born: 0.0% (2000); Ancestry (includes multiple ancestries): 35.4% German, 12.6% United States or American, 12.4% Swiss, 11.5% Other groups, 5.7% English (2000).
Economy: Manufacturing: truck trailers. Single-family building permits issued: 4 (2001) / 2 (2000); Multi-family building permits issued: 0 (2001) / 0 (2000); Employment by occupation: 5.9% management, 15.4% professional, 12.9% services, 20.8% sales, 0.5% farming, 12.9% construction, 31.5% production (2000).
Income: Per capita income: $16,682 (2000); Median household income: $42,946 (2000); Poverty rate: 4.0% (2000).
Taxes: Total city taxes per capita: $159 (1997); City property taxes per capita: $111 (1997).
Education: High school graduation rate: 88.6% (2000); College graduation rate: 12.0% (2000).

School District(s)

Adams Central Community Schools (KG-12)
2000 Enrollment: 1,234 219-692-6193

Housing: Homeownership rate: 84.4% (2000); Median home value: $83,000 (2000); Median rent: $310 per month (2000); Median age of housing: 44 years (2000).
Transportation: Commute to work: 93.2% car, 0.5% public transportation, 1.9% walk, 3.3% work from home (2000); Travel time to work: 52.5% less than 15 minutes, 22.6% 15 to 30 minutes, 6.2% 30 to 45 minutes, 15.3% 45 to 60 minutes, 3.4% 60 minutes or more (2000)

Allen County

Located in northeastern Indiana; bounded on the east by Ohio; crossed by the St. Joseph, St. Marys, and Maumee Rivers. Covers a land area of 657.20 square miles, a water area of 2.90 square miles, and is located in the Eastern Time Zone. The county government was organized in 1823. County seat is Fort Wayne.

Allen County is part of the Fort Wayne, IN MSA. The entire metro area includes: Adams County; Allen County; DeKalb County; Huntington County; Wells County; Whitley County

Weather Station: Fort Wayne Baer Field — Elevation: 790 feet

	Jan	Feb	Mar	Apr	May	Jun	Jul	Aug	Sep	Oct	Nov	Dec
High	31	35	47	60	72	81	85	82	76	63	49	37
Low	16	19	29	39	50	59	63	61	53	42	33	23
Precip	2.0	1.9	2.9	3.7	3.7	3.8	3.7	3.5	2.8	2.7	3.0	2.7
Snow	9.9	7.7	4.6	1.2	tr	tr	0.0	tr	0.0	0.5	3.0	7.9

High and Low temperatures in degrees Fahrenheit; Precipitation and Snow in inches

Population: 331,849 (2000); Race: 83.0% White, 11.2% Black, 1.3% Asian, 0.4% American Indian and Alaska Native, 4.2% Hispanic of any race, 1.8% two or more races (2000); Density: 504.9 persons per square mile (2000); Age: 27.6% under 18, 11.4% over 64 (2000).
Religion: Five largest groups: 17.3% Catholic Church, 7.6% Lutheran Church—Missouri Synod, 4.5% The United Methodist Church, 3.7% Evangelical Lutheran Church in America, 1.4% Christian Churches and Churches of Christ (2000).
Economy: Unemployment rate: 4.7% (11/2002); Total civilian labor force: 176,397 (11/2002); Leading industries: 19.4% manufacturing; 12.3% health care and social assistance; 12.3% retail trade (2000); Companies that employ more than 1,000 persons: 12 (2000); Companies that employ more than 100 persons: 279 (2000); Farms: 1,440 totaling 276,385 acres (1997); Minority business ownership rate: 5.5% (1997); Women business ownership rate: 24.2% (1997); Retail sales per capita: $11,335 (1997). Single-family building permits issued: 1,817 (2001) / 1,649 (2000); Multi-family building permits issued: 444 (2001) / 142 (2000).
Income: Per capita income: $21,544 (2000); Median household income: $42,671 (2000); Poverty rate: 9.1% (2000); Bankruptcy rate: 7.41% (2001).
Taxes: Total county taxes per capita: $222 (2000); County property taxes per capita: $158 (2000).
Education: High school graduation rate: 85.7% (2000); College graduation rate: 22.7% (2000).
Housing: Homeownership rate: 71.0% (2000); Median home value: $88,700 (2000); Median rent: $426 per month (2000); Median age of housing: 32 years (2000).
Health: Birth rate: 152.9 per 10,000 population (1998); Age adjusted death rate: 90.9 per 10,000 population (1999); Infant mortality rate: 9.5 per 1,000 live births (1998); Age adjusted cancer mortality rate: 227.9 deaths per 100,000 population (1999). Air Quality Index: 71% good, 29% moderate, 0% unhealthy (percent of days in 2000). Number of physicians: 23.4 per 10,000 population (1999); Number of hospital beds: 50.9 per 10,000 population (1999).
Elections: 2000 Presidential election results: 36.4% Gore, 61.6% Bush, 0.5% Nader, 0.8% Buchanan

Additional Information Contacts

Allen County Government Offices 219-449-3155
Fort Wayne Area Association of Realtors 219-426-4700
Fort Wayne Chamber of Commerce 219-424-1435
New Haven Chamber of Commerce 219-749-4484

Allen County Communities

FORT WAYNE (city). Covers a land area of 78.952 square miles and a water area of 0.169 square miles. Located at 41.07° N. Lat.; 85.12° W. Long. Elevation is 781 feet.
History: The first fort at the site of Fort Wayne was Fort Miami, established in the 1680's by the French. Another stockade was built by Anthony Wayne in 1794. By 1819 a trading post and gristmill were started and more settlers appeared. When Allen County was organized in 1824, Fort Wayne was named as county seat. It was incorporated in 1829. The building of the Wabash & Erie Canal between 1832 and 1840 was a boost for Fort Wayne's economy. Fort Wayne may have claims to the first baseball game played under the lights at its League Park, where in 1883 an arc-lighting system illuminated the field for a game between a professional team from Quincy, Illinois, and a team of students from a Fort Wayne college.
Population: 205,727 (2000); Race: 75.4% White, 17.3% Black, 1.5% Asian, 0.4% American Indian and Alaska Native, 5.7% Hispanic of any race, 2.3% two or more races (2000); Density: 2,605.7 persons per square mile (2000); Age: 27.1% under 18, 12.4% over 64 (2000); Marriage status: 30.3% never married, 49.5% now married, 7.3% widowed, 12.9% divorced (2000); Foreign born: 4.9% (2000); Ancestry (includes multiple ancestries): 27.5% German, 24.9% Other groups, 10.5% Irish, 7.6% English, 7.0% United States or American (2000).
Vital Statistics: Birth rate: 183.0 per 10,000 population (1998)
Economy: Unemployment rate: 5.8% (11/2002); Total civilian labor force: 99,679 (11/2002); Single-family building permits issued: 265 (2001) / 133 (2000); Multi-family building permits issued: 331 (2001) / 94 (2000); Employment by occupation: 10.4% management, 18.3% professional, 14.8% services, 27.9% sales, 0.1% farming, 8.1% construction, 20.4% production (2000).
Income: Per capita income: $18,517 (2000); Median household income: $36,518 (2000); Poverty rate: 12.5% (2000).
Taxes: Total city taxes per capita: $281 (2000); City property taxes per capita: $221 (2000).
Education: High school graduation rate: 83.2% (2000); College graduation rate: 19.4% (2000).

School District(s)

Fort Wayne Community Schools (PK-12)
2000 Enrollment: 31,843 219-425-7272
M S D Southwest Allen County (PK-12)
2000 Enrollment: 5,759 219-431-2010
Northwest Allen County Schools (PK-12)
2000 Enrollment: 4,559 219-637-3155

Four-year College(s)

Concordia Theological Seminary (Private, Not-for-profit, Lutheran Church - Missouri Synod)
2001 Enrollment: 401 219-452-2100
Taylor University-Ft Wayne (Private, Not-for-profit, Interdenominational)
2001 Enrollment: 511 219-744-8600
2001 Tuition: In-state $14,090; Out-of-state $14,090
Indiana University-Purdue University-Fort Wayne (Public)
2001 Enrollment: 11,128 219-481-6100
2001 Tuition: In-state $2,815; Out-of-state $7,023
Indiana Institute of Technology (Private, Not-for-profit)
2001 Enrollment: 3,588 219-422-5561
2001 Tuition: In-state $13,560; Out-of-state $13,560
International Business College (Private, For-profit)
2001 Enrollment: 635 219-459-4500
2001 Tuition: In-state $9,200; Out-of-state $9,200
ITT Technical Institute (Private, For-profit)
2001 Enrollment: 509 219-484-4107
2001 Tuition: In-state $11,304; Out-of-state $11,304
University of Saint Francis (Private, Not-for-profit, Roman Catholic)
2001 Enrollment: 1,683 219-434-3100
2001 Tuition: In-state $13,100; Out-of-state $13,100
Tri-State University-Fort Wayne Campus (Private, Not-for-profit)
2001 Enrollment: 100 219-483-4949
2001 Tuition: In-state $5,880; Out-of-state $5,880

Two-year College(s)

Ivy Tech State College-Northeast (Public)
2001 Enrollment: 4,019 219-482-9171
2001 Tuition: In-state $1,986; Out-of-state $4,029
Masters of Cosmetology College (Private, For-profit)
2001 Enrollment: 15 219-747-3363
Fort Wayne School of Radiography (Private, Not-for-profit, Roman Catholic)
2001 Enrollment: n/a 219-425-3990
Michiana College (Private, For-profit)
2001 Enrollment: 343 219-484-4400
2001 Tuition: In-state $5,616; Out-of-state $5,616
Indiana Business College-Ft Wayne (Private, For-profit)
2001 Enrollment: 170 219-471-7667
2001 Tuition: In-state $8,460; Out-of-state $8,460

Housing: Homeownership rate: 61.6% (2000); Median home value: $74,600 (2000); Median rent: $415 per month (2000); Median age of housing: 38 years (2000).
Hospitals: Fort Wayne State Development Center (458 beds); Lutheran Hospital of Indiana (377 beds); Orthopaedic Hospital at Parkview North; Park View Behavioral Health (97 beds); Parkview Memorial Hospital (656 beds); Parkview North Hospital; Saint Joseph Hospital (191 beds); VA Northern Indiana Health Care System (363 beds)
Safety: Violent crime rate: 51.8 per 10,000 population; Property crime rate: 590.6 per 10,000 population (2001).
Newspapers: The News-Sentinel (6 x week); The Journal Gazette (7 x week); Frost Illustrated (1 x week); Today's Catholic (1 x week)
Transportation: Commute to work: 94.0% car, 1.2% public transportation, 2.1% walk, 2.0% work from home (2000); Travel time to work: 32.7% less than 15 minutes, 48.9% 15 to 30 minutes, 12.3% 30 to 45 minutes, 2.7% 45 to 60 minutes, 3.3% 60 minutes or more (2000)
Airports: Fort Wayne International (primary service); Smith Field (primary service)

Additional Information Contacts

Fort Wayne Area Association of Realtors 219-426-4700
Fort Wayne Chamber of Commerce 219-424-1435

GRABILL (town). Covers a land area of 0.617 square miles and a water area of 0 square miles. Located at 41.21° N. Lat.; 84.96° W. Long. Elevation is 825 feet.
Population: 1,113 (2000); Race: 98.6% White, 0.0% Black, 0.9% Asian, 0.0% American Indian and Alaska Native, 2.2% Hispanic of any race, 0.3% two or more races (2000); Density: 1,805.1 persons per square mile (2000); Age: 33.5% under 18, 8.4% over 64 (2000); Marriage status: 23.5% never married, 62.0% now married, 5.3% widowed, 9.3% divorced (2000); Foreign born: 2.3% (2000); Ancestry (includes multiple ancestries): 38.1% German, 10.6% English, 10.1% Irish, 7.3% Other groups, 5.2% French (except Basque) (2000).
Economy: In agricultural area. Manufacturing: furniture, reinforced fiberglass moldings, feed mixing, steering wheels. Employment by occupation: 8.9% management, 13.8% professional, 12.6% services, 26.9% sales, 0.7% farming, 11.3% construction, 25.8% production (2000).
Income: Per capita income: $17,252 (2000); Median household income: $42,240 (2000); Poverty rate: 8.2% (2000).
Taxes: Total city taxes per capita: $173 (1997); City property taxes per capita: $118 (1997).
Education: High school graduation rate: 85.1% (2000); College graduation rate: 17.2% (2000).
Housing: Homeownership rate: 83.7% (2000); Median home value: $92,400 (2000); Median rent: $349 per month (2000); Median age of housing: 19 years (2000).
Newspapers: East Allen Courier (1 x week)
Transportation: Commute to work: 92.0% car, 0.7% public transportation, 3.1% walk, 3.8% work from home (2000); Travel time to work: 33.6% less than 15 minutes, 39.2% 15 to 30 minutes, 21.9% 30 to 45 minutes, 2.4% 45 to 60 minutes, 2.9% 60 minutes or more (2000)

HARLAN (unincorporated postal area, zip code 46743). Covers a land area of 16.232 square miles and a water area of 0 square miles. Located at 41.21° N. Lat.; 84.85° W. Long. Elevation is 794 feet.
Population: 1,183 (2000); Race: 99.4% White, 0.0% Black, 0.0% Asian, 0.0% American Indian and Alaska Native, 0.0% Hispanic of any race, 0.6% two or more races (2000); Density: 72.9 persons per square mile (2000); Age: 25.2% under 18, 15.1% over 64 (2000); Marriage status: 24.1% never married, 65.4% now married, 4.0% widowed, 6.5% divorced (2000); Foreign born: 0.0% (2000); Ancestry (includes multiple ancestries): 26.1% German, 11.1% United States or American, 10.9% English, 6.3% Other groups, 5.2% French (except Basque) (2000).
Economy: Manufacturing: cabinets. Corn, soybeans. Employment by occupation: 14.6% management, 10.6% professional, 9.0% services, 24.0% sales, 1.3% farming, 13.5% construction, 27.0% production (2000).
Income: Per capita income: $19,923 (2000); Median household income: $47,798 (2000); Poverty rate: 2.8% (2000).
Education: High school graduation rate: 82.7% (2000); College graduation rate: 14.1% (2000).
Housing: Homeownership rate: 86.0% (2000); Median home value: $111,500 (2000); Median rent: $421 per month (2000); Median age of housing: 40 years (2000).
Transportation: Commute to work: 94.4% car, 0.0% public transportation, 1.1% walk, 4.5% work from home (2000); Travel time to work: 23.0% less than 15 minutes, 44.7% 15 to 30 minutes, 20.8% 30 to 45 minutes, 9.1% 45 to 60 minutes, 2.3% 60 minutes or more (2000)

HOAGLAND (unincorporated postal area, zip code 46745). Covers a land area of 17.536 square miles and a water area of 0 square miles. Located at 40.95° N. Lat.; 85.00° W. Long. Elevation is 830 feet.
History: Laid out 1872.
Population: 1,606 (2000); Race: 98.5% White, 0.0% Black, 1.5% Asian, 0.0% American Indian and Alaska Native, 0.8% Hispanic of any race, 0.0% two or more races (2000); Density: 91.6 persons per square mile (2000); Age: 29.6% under 18, 12.2% over 64 (2000); Marriage status: 23.4% never married, 67.3% now married, 4.7% widowed, 4.6% divorced (2000); Foreign born: 1.8% (2000); Ancestry (includes multiple ancestries): 57.1% German, 10.8% Irish, 10.2% United States or American, 6.4% French (except Basque), 4.4% Swiss (2000).
Economy: Corn, oats, soybeans. Manufacturing: wooden cabinets. Employment by occupation: 14.2% management, 17.1% professional, 13.3% services, 24.2% sales, 0.0% farming, 8.3% construction, 23.0% production (2000).
Income: Per capita income: $19,818 (2000); Median household income: $56,034 (2000); Poverty rate: 3.5% (2000).
Education: High school graduation rate: 87.6% (2000); College graduation rate: 15.5% (2000).
Housing: Homeownership rate: 90.6% (2000); Median home value: $102,600 (2000); Median rent: $375 per month (2000); Median age of housing: 30 years (2000).
Transportation: Commute to work: 91.9% car, 0.0% public transportation, 1.3% walk, 5.6% work from home (2000); Travel time to work: 13.6% less than 15 minutes, 50.2% 15 to 30 minutes, 34.3% 30 to 45 minutes, 1.2% 45 to 60 minutes, 0.7% 60 minutes or more (2000)

HUNTERTOWN (town). Covers a land area of 1.626 square miles and a water area of 0 square miles. Located at 41.22° N. Lat.; 85.16° W. Long. Elevation is 838 feet.
History: Settled 1830s.
Population: 1,771 (2000); Race: 97.7% White, 0.6% Black, 0.2% Asian, 0.0% American Indian and Alaska Native, 1.0% Hispanic of any race, 1.3% two or more races (2000); Density: 1,089.4 persons per square mile (2000); Age: 27.8% under 18, 9.1% over 64 (2000); Marriage status: 19.6% never married, 64.3% now married, 4.9% widowed, 11.2% divorced (2000); Foreign born: 1.0% (2000); Ancestry (includes multiple ancestries): 36.0% German, 9.0% United States or American, 9.0% Irish, 8.7% English, 7.1% Other groups (2000).
Economy: Manufacturing: machinery, asphalt. Corn, soybeans. Employment by occupation: 13.9% management, 15.9% professional, 13.5% services, 23.7% sales, 0.0% farming, 11.0% construction, 22.0% production (2000).
Income: Per capita income: $21,232 (2000); Median household income: $52,250 (2000); Poverty rate: 4.2% (2000).
Taxes: Total city taxes per capita: $62 (1997); City property taxes per capita: $25 (1997).
Education: High school graduation rate: 90.1% (2000); College graduation rate: 18.8% (2000).
Housing: Homeownership rate: 80.7% (2000); Median home value: $92,200 (2000); Median rent: $521 per month (2000); Median age of housing: 25 years (2000).
Transportation: Commute to work: 95.5% car, 0.0% public transportation, 0.8% walk, 2.8% work from home (2000); Travel time to work: 21.6% less than 15 minutes, 45.6% 15 to 30 minutes, 24.4% 30 to 45 minutes, 3.5% 45 to 60 minutes, 4.9% 60 minutes or more (2000)

LEO (unincorporated postal area, zip code 46765). Aka Leo-Cedarville. Covers a land area of 10.898 square miles and a water area of 0.028 square miles. Located at 41.22° N. Lat.; 85.02° W. Long.
History: Laid out 1849.
Population: 3,948 (2000); Race: 97.0% White, 0.1% Black, 0.0% Asian, 0.5% American Indian and Alaska Native, 0.9% Hispanic of any race, 0.1% two or more races (2000); Density: 362.3 persons per square mile (2000); Age: 31.8% under 18, 10.7% over 64 (2000); Marriage status: 20.5% never married, 70.7% now married, 4.8% widowed, 4.0% divorced (2000); Foreign born: 0.8% (2000); Ancestry (includes multiple ancestries): 39.8% German, 10.9% English, 9.6% United States or American, 6.7% French (except Basque), 6.4% Irish (2000).
Economy: Corn, soybeans; cattle. Manufacturing: furniture. Employment by occupation: 15.4% management, 20.2% professional, 7.8% services, 28.0% sales, 0.0% farming, 7.3% construction, 21.3% production (2000).
Income: Per capita income: $22,688 (2000); Median household income: $67,011 (2000); Poverty rate: 2.3% (2000).
Education: High school graduation rate: 90.4% (2000); College graduation rate: 26.2% (2000).
Housing: Homeownership rate: 92.5% (2000); Median home value: $131,100 (2000); Median rent: $590 per month (2000); Median age of housing: 24 years (2000).
Transportation: Commute to work: 96.5% car, 0.0% public transportation, 0.2% walk, 3.2% work from home (2000); Travel time to work: 17.1% less than 15 minutes, 60.9% 15 to 30 minutes, 17.6% 30 to 45 minutes, 2.3% 45 to 60 minutes, 2.1% 60 minutes or more (2000)

LEO-CEDARVILLE (town). Aka Leo. Covers a land area of 3.733 square miles and a water area of 0.136 square miles. Located at 41.21° N. Lat.; 85.01° W. Long.
Population: 2,782 (2000); Race: 98.8% White, 0.1% Black, 0.1% Asian, 0.8% American Indian and Alaska Native, 0.7% Hispanic of any race, 0.2% two or more races (2000); Density: 745.1 persons per square mile (2000); Age: 33.4% under 18, 8.6% over 64 (2000); Marriage status: 21.3% never married, 70.0% now married, 3.8% widowed, 4.9% divorced (2000); Foreign born: 1.5% (2000); Ancestry (includes multiple ancestries): 39.8% German, 11.0% English, 8.6% United States or American, 6.4% Irish, 4.6% Dutch (2000).
Economy: Employment by occupation: 16.4% management, 18.9% professional, 9.8% services, 28.1% sales, 0.0% farming, 6.8% construction, 20.0% production (2000).
Income: Per capita income: $22,170 (2000); Median household income: $66,652 (2000); Poverty rate: 1.2% (2000).
Taxes: Total city taxes per capita: $26 (1997); City property taxes per capita: $26 (1997).
Education: High school graduation rate: 93.5% (2000); College graduation rate: 26.0% (2000).
Housing: Homeownership rate: 93.7% (2000); Median home value: $131,800 (2000); Median rent: $491 per month (2000); Median age of housing: 26 years (2000).
Transportation: Commute to work: 97.5% car, 0.0% public transportation, 0.4% walk, 1.8% work from home (2000); Travel time to work: 20.8% less than 15 minutes, 54.9% 15 to 30 minutes, 20.0% 30 to 45 minutes, 1.9% 45 to 60 minutes, 2.5% 60 minutes or more (2000)

MONROEVILLE (town). Covers a land area of 0.751 square miles and a water area of 0 square miles. Located at 40.97° N. Lat.; 84.86° W. Long. Elevation is 810 feet.
History: Settled 1841, incorporated 1865.
Population: 1,236 (2000); Race: 95.4% White, 0.0% Black, 0.2% Asian, 0.1% American Indian and Alaska Native, 2.7% Hispanic of any race, 4.0% two or more races (2000); Density: 1,645.8 persons per square mile (2000); Age: 31.3% under 18, 14.0% over 64 (2000); Marriage status: 23.3% never married, 58.1% now married, 8.5% widowed, 10.0% divorced (2000); Foreign born: 0.8% (2000); Ancestry (includes multiple ancestries): 38.9% German, 12.5% Irish, 9.2% United States or American, 8.5% Other groups, 7.8% French (except Basque) (2000).
Economy: In agricultural area: corn, soybeans. Manufacturing: fertilizer blending. Employment by occupation: 7.2% management, 11.5% professional, 13.6% services, 20.6% sales, 0.0% farming, 15.0% construction, 32.1% production (2000).
Income: Per capita income: $16,242 (2000); Median household income: $35,795 (2000); Poverty rate: 10.0% (2000).
Taxes: Total city taxes per capita: $151 (2000); City property taxes per capita: $122 (2000).
Education: High school graduation rate: 83.5% (2000); College graduation rate: 10.5% (2000).
Housing: Homeownership rate: 82.3% (2000); Median home value: $74,600 (2000); Median rent: $315 per month (2000); Median age of housing: 41 years (2000).
Newspapers: The Monroeville News (1 x week)
Transportation: Commute to work: 91.9% car, 0.4% public transportation, 5.1% walk, 2.3% work from home (2000); Travel time to work: 21.7% less than 15 minutes, 37.3% 15 to 30 minutes, 28.7% 30 to 45 minutes, 4.5% 45 to 60 minutes, 7.9% 60 minutes or more (2000)

NEW HAVEN (city). Covers a land area of 8.151 square miles and a water area of 0.004 square miles. Located at 41.06° N. Lat.; 85.02° W. Long. Elevation is 758 feet.
History: New Haven was settled when the Wabash & Erie Canal was built. Its first residents, who came from New England, named it for the city in Connecticut.
Population: 12,406 (2000); Race: 96.7% White, 0.6% Black, 0.9% Asian, 0.2% American Indian and Alaska Native, 1.7% Hispanic of any race, 0.8% two or more races (2000); Density: 1,522.0 persons per square mile (2000); Age: 24.9% under 18, 13.4% over 64 (2000); Marriage status: 23.2% never married, 58.0% now married, 6.5% widowed, 12.2% divorced (2000); Foreign born: 1.7% (2000); Ancestry (includes multiple ancestries): 37.6% German, 11.7% Irish, 11.2% United States or American, 10.2% English, 9.1% Other groups (2000).
Vital Statistics: Birth rate: 115.3 per 10,000 population (1998)
Economy: Employment by occupation: 10.5% management, 13.1% professional, 14.4% services, 27.1% sales, 0.0% farming, 10.3% construction, 24.6% production (2000).
Income: Per capita income: $19,960 (2000); Median household income: $41,802 (2000); Poverty rate: 6.6% (2000).
Taxes: Total city taxes per capita: $303 (1997); City property taxes per capita: $221 (1997).
Education: High school graduation rate: 83.6% (2000); College graduation rate: 12.4% (2000).

School District(s)

East Allen County Schools (PK-12)
2000 Enrollment: 9,604 219-446-0100
Housing: Homeownership rate: 80.6% (2000); Median home value: $77,600 (2000); Median rent: $418 per month (2000); Median age of housing: 34 years (2000).
Safety: Violent crime rate: 23.2 per 10,000 population; Property crime rate: 347.9 per 10,000 population (2001).
Newspapers: The Allen County Times (1 x week)
Transportation: Commute to work: 95.0% car, 0.1% public transportation, 1.2% walk, 3.0% work from home (2000); Travel time to work: 36.9% less

than 15 minutes, 46.0% 15 to 30 minutes, 12.2% 30 to 45 minutes, 1.9% 45 to 60 minutes, 3.0% 60 minutes or more (2000)
Additional Information Contacts
New Haven Chamber of Commerce 219-749-4484

WOODBURN (city). Aka Shirley City. Covers a land area of 0.918 square miles and a water area of 0 square miles. Located at 41.12° N. Lat.; 84.85° W. Long. Elevation is 756 feet.
History: Laid out 1865. Until 1936, called Shirley City.
Population: 1,579 (2000); Race: 98.5% White, 0.6% Black, 0.1% Asian, 0.3% American Indian and Alaska Native, 0.3% Hispanic of any race, 0.1% two or more races (2000); Density: 1,720.5 persons per square mile (2000); Age: 31.7% under 18, 8.7% over 64 (2000); Marriage status: 21.9% never married, 59.3% now married, 5.6% widowed, 13.2% divorced (2000); Foreign born: 0.6% (2000); Ancestry (includes multiple ancestries): 42.7% German, 10.9% Irish, 6.8% United States or American, 6.6% French (except Basque), 5.8% English (2000).
Economy: In agricultural area: corn, soybeans. Manufacturing: grain processing, metal fabrication, tires. Employment by occupation: 7.8% management, 12.4% professional, 14.8% services, 27.8% sales, 0.6% farming, 14.7% construction, 21.9% production (2000).
Income: Per capita income: $18,061 (2000); Median household income: $40,833 (2000); Poverty rate: 5.8% (2000).
Taxes: Total city taxes per capita: $117 (1997); City property taxes per capita: $73 (1997).
Education: High school graduation rate: 83.9% (2000); College graduation rate: 10.2% (2000).
Housing: Homeownership rate: 75.7% (2000); Median home value: $70,900 (2000); Median rent: $379 per month (2000); Median age of housing: 23 years (2000).
Transportation: Commute to work: 95.1% car, 0.0% public transportation, 3.3% walk, 0.9% work from home (2000); Travel time to work: 21.6% less than 15 minutes, 39.3% 15 to 30 minutes, 28.8% 30 to 45 minutes, 5.8% 45 to 60 minutes, 4.5% 60 minutes or more (2000)

YODER (unincorporated postal area, zip code 46798). Covers a land area of 20.927 square miles and a water area of 0.013 square miles. Located at 40.94° N. Lat.; 85.23° W. Long. Elevation is 810 feet.
Population: 1,872 (2000); Race: 97.9% White, 0.0% Black, 0.4% Asian, 0.0% American Indian and Alaska Native, 2.3% Hispanic of any race, 0.7% two or more races (2000); Density: 89.5 persons per square mile (2000); Age: 27.8% under 18, 8.1% over 64 (2000); Marriage status: 20.9% never married, 64.8% now married, 5.7% widowed, 8.7% divorced (2000); Foreign born: 1.8% (2000); Ancestry (includes multiple ancestries): 42.6% German, 13.1% Irish, 10.8% United States or American, 10.5% English, 10.0% Other groups (2000).
Economy: Employment by occupation: 9.7% management, 13.3% professional, 10.1% services, 27.3% sales, 0.0% farming, 11.2% construction, 28.3% production (2000).
Income: Per capita income: $20,389 (2000); Median household income: $49,500 (2000); Poverty rate: 3.5% (2000).
Education: High school graduation rate: 85.4% (2000); College graduation rate: 10.5% (2000).
Housing: Homeownership rate: 94.0% (2000); Median home value: $94,100 (2000); Median rent: $519 per month (2000); Median age of housing: 26 years (2000).
Transportation: Commute to work: 97.4% car, 0.0% public transportation, 0.2% walk, 2.4% work from home (2000); Travel time to work: 28.8% less than 15 minutes, 49.3% 15 to 30 minutes, 14.1% 30 to 45 minutes, 4.0% 45 to 60 minutes, 3.7% 60 minutes or more (2000)

ZANESVILLE (town). Covers a land area of 0.746 square miles and a water area of 0 square miles. Located at 40.91° N. Lat.; 85.28° W. Long.
Population: 602 (2000); Race: 99.5% White, 0.0% Black, 0.0% Asian, 0.0% American Indian and Alaska Native, 0.5% Hispanic of any race, 0.0% two or more races (2000); Density: 806.6 persons per square mile (2000); Age: 29.1% under 18, 6.6% over 64 (2000); Marriage status: 17.2% never married, 70.5% now married, 1.6% widowed, 10.7% divorced (2000); Foreign born: 0.5% (2000); Ancestry (includes multiple ancestries): 45.7% German, 13.1% Irish, 10.5% Other groups, 9.8% Dutch, 7.6% English (2000).
Economy: Employment by occupation: 9.6% management, 14.4% professional, 12.2% services, 24.9% sales, 0.0% farming, 8.8% construction, 30.0% production (2000).
Income: Per capita income: $20,606 (2000); Median household income: $57,727 (2000); Poverty rate: 4.9% (2000).
Taxes: Total city taxes per capita: $48 (1997); City property taxes per capita: $33 (1997).
Education: High school graduation rate: 95.8% (2000); College graduation rate: 13.8% (2000).
Housing: Homeownership rate: 85.3% (2000); Median home value: $87,800 (2000); Median rent: $395 per month (2000); Median age of housing: 29 years (2000).
Transportation: Commute to work: 92.9% car, 0.0% public transportation, 5.1% walk, 0.9% work from home (2000); Travel time to work: 28.4% less than 15 minutes, 44.8% 15 to 30 minutes, 19.0% 30 to 45 minutes, 4.3% 45 to 60 minutes, 3.4% 60 minutes or more (2000)

Bartholomew County

Located in south central Indiana; drained by the East Fork of the White River. Covers a land area of 406.80 square miles, a water area of 2.50 square miles, and is located in the Eastern Time Zone. The county government was organized in 1821. County seat is Columbus.

Weather Station: Columbus — Elevation: 620 feet

	Jan	Feb	Mar	Apr	May	Jun	Jul	Aug	Sep	Oct	Nov	Dec
High	36	41	52	64	74	82	86	85	79	67	53	42
Low	19	22	31	41	51	61	65	62	54	42	34	25
Precip	2.6	2.5	3.7	4.5	4.5	3.4	4.0	3.8	3.0	2.8	3.7	3.1
Snow	5.1	3.5	1.9	tr	tr	0.0	0.0	0.0	0.0	tr	0.5	2.1

High and Low temperatures in degrees Fahrenheit; Precipitation and Snow in inches

Population: 71,435 (2000); Race: 94.1% White, 1.8% Black, 1.7% Asian, 0.3% American Indian and Alaska Native, 2.4% Hispanic of any race, 0.9% two or more races (2000); Density: 175.6 persons per square mile (2000); Age: 26.4% under 18, 12.2% over 64 (2000).
Religion: Five largest groups: 8.6% Christian Churches and Churches of Christ, 8.4% Lutheran Church—Missouri Synod, 7.6% Catholic Church, 7.6% The United Methodist Church, 5.6% American Baptist Churches in the USA (2000).
Economy: Unemployment rate: 3.6% (11/2002); Total civilian labor force: 37,006 (11/2002); Leading industries: 33.8% manufacturing; 12.1% retail trade; 10.2% health care and social assistance (2000); Companies that employ more than 1,000 persons: 3 (2000); Companies that employ more than 100 persons: 61 (2000); Farms: 577 totaling 166,612 acres (1997); Minority business ownership rate: 3.3% (1997); Women business ownership rate: 28.5% (1997); Retail sales per capita: $9,888 (1997). Single-family building permits issued: 219 (2001) / 210 (2000); Multi-family building permits issued: 4 (2001) / 2 (2000).
Income: Per capita income: $21,536 (2000); Median household income: $44,184 (2000); Poverty rate: 7.3% (2000); Bankruptcy rate: 7.93% (2001).
Taxes: Total county taxes per capita: $297 (2000); County property taxes per capita: $150 (2000).
Education: High school graduation rate: 83.8% (2000); College graduation rate: 22.0% (2000).
Housing: Homeownership rate: 74.2% (2000); Median home value: $105,300 (2000); Median rent: $475 per month (2000); Median age of housing: 31 years (2000).
Health: Birth rate: 149.0 per 10,000 population (1998); Age adjusted death rate: 94.9 per 10,000 population (1999); Age adjusted cancer mortality rate: 241.3 deaths per 100,000 population (1999). Number of physicians: 23.5 per 10,000 population (1999); Number of hospital beds: 42.0 per 10,000 population (1999).
Elections: 2000 Presidential election results: 35.0% Gore, 62.9% Bush, 0.7% Nader, 0.8% Buchanan
Additional Information Contacts
Columbus Area Chamber of Commerce 812-379-4457
Columbus Board of Realtors 812-378-2626

Bartholomew County Communities

CLIFFORD (town). Covers a land area of 0.100 square miles and a water area of 0 square miles. Located at 39.28° N. Lat.; 85.87° W. Long. Elevation is 662 feet.
Population: 291 (2000); Race: 97.8% White, 0.0% Black, 0.0% Asian, 0.7% American Indian and Alaska Native, 0.0% Hispanic of any race, 1.5% two or more races (2000); Density: 2,899.4 persons per square mile (2000); Age: 28.8% under 18, 12.2% over 64 (2000); Marriage status: 22.7% never married, 57.1% now married, 6.9% widowed, 13.3% divorced (2000); Foreign born: 0.0% (2000); Ancestry (includes multiple ancestries): 22.5%

United States or American, 17.0% German, 8.5% Irish, 8.1% English, 7.7% Other groups (2000).
Economy: Agricultural area. Employment by occupation: 5.6% management, 6.5% professional, 8.9% services, 29.8% sales, 0.0% farming, 23.4% construction, 25.8% production (2000).
Income: Per capita income: $13,132 (2000); Median household income: $25,000 (2000); Poverty rate: 15.1% (2000).
Taxes: Total city taxes per capita: $58 (1997); City property taxes per capita: $58 (1997).
Education: High school graduation rate: 68.7% (2000); College graduation rate: 1.4% (2000).
Housing: Homeownership rate: 65.5% (2000); Median home value: $68,300 (2000); Median rent: $413 per month (2000); Median age of housing: 41 years (2000).
Transportation: Commute to work: 96.8% car, 0.0% public transportation, 3.2% walk, 0.0% work from home (2000); Travel time to work: 23.4% less than 15 minutes, 57.3% 15 to 30 minutes, 12.9% 30 to 45 minutes, 3.2% 45 to 60 minutes, 3.2% 60 minutes or more (2000)

COLUMBUS (city). Covers a land area of 25.948 square miles and a water area of 0.425 square miles. Located at 39.21° N. Lat.; 85.91° W. Long. Elevation is 640 feet.
History: Columbus was settled by General John Tipton, John Lindsay, and Luke Bonesteel in 1820, and was called Tiptonia. In 1821 General Tipton offered land for a county seat if the new town were named for him. The county commissioners accepted the land, but named the town Columbus.
Population: 39,059 (2000); Race: 91.5% White, 2.7% Black, 2.7% Asian, 0.2% American Indian and Alaska Native, 2.9% Hispanic of any race, 1.1% two or more races (2000); Density: 1,505.3 persons per square mile (2000); Age: 25.7% under 18, 13.7% over 64 (2000); Marriage status: 20.5% never married, 59.8% now married, 6.7% widowed, 13.0% divorced (2000); Foreign born: 5.5% (2000); Ancestry (includes multiple ancestries): 21.9% German, 15.8% United States or American, 12.9% Other groups, 11.3% English, 10.3% Irish (2000).
Vital Statistics: Birth rate: 175.6 per 10,000 population (1998)
Economy: Unemployment rate: 4.0% (11/2002); Total civilian labor force: 18,196 (11/2002); Employment by occupation: 12.9% management, 22.2% professional, 12.2% services, 23.3% sales, 0.1% farming, 6.4% construction, 22.9% production (2000).
Income: Per capita income: $22,055 (2000); Median household income: $41,723 (2000); Poverty rate: 8.1% (2000).
Taxes: Total city taxes per capita: $356 (2000); City property taxes per capita: $353 (2000).
Education: High school graduation rate: 84.8% (2000); College graduation rate: 27.6% (2000).

School District(s)

Bartholomew Con School Corp (PK-12)
2000 Enrollment: 10,465 812-376-4220

Two-year College(s)

Ivy Tech State College-Columbus (Public)
2001 Enrollment: 1,600 812-372-9925
2001 Tuition: In-state $1,986; Out-of-state $4,029
Indiana Business College (Private, For-profit)
2001 Enrollment: 209 812-379-9000
2001 Tuition: In-state $8,460; Out-of-state $8,460

Housing: Homeownership rate: 64.6% (2000); Median home value: $111,900 (2000); Median rent: $488 per month (2000); Median age of housing: 32 years (2000).
Hospitals: Behavioral Healthcare-Columbus (70 beds); Columbus Regional Hospital (325 beds)
Safety: Violent crime rate: 20.9 per 10,000 population; Property crime rate: 615.3 per 10,000 population (2001).
Newspapers: The Republic (7 x week)
Transportation: Commute to work: 94.5% car, 0.5% public transportation, 1.6% walk, 2.1% work from home (2000); Travel time to work: 59.8% less than 15 minutes, 26.8% 15 to 30 minutes, 6.1% 30 to 45 minutes, 3.4% 45 to 60 minutes, 3.9% 60 minutes or more (2000)
Airports: Columbus Municipal
Additional Information Contacts
Columbus Area Chamber of Commerce 812-379-4457
Columbus Board of Realtors 812-378-2626

ELIZABETHTOWN (town). Covers a land area of 0.252 square miles and a water area of 0 square miles. Located at 39.13° N. Lat.; 85.81° W. Long. Elevation is 644 feet.
Population: 391 (2000); Race: 96.2% White, 0.0% Black, 0.0% Asian, 1.5% American Indian and Alaska Native, 1.5% Hispanic of any race, 0.8% two or more races (2000); Density: 1,552.9 persons per square mile (2000); Age: 26.2% under 18, 16.8% over 64 (2000); Marriage status: 17.7% never married, 61.0% now married, 6.6% widowed, 14.8% divorced (2000); Foreign born: 1.3% (2000); Ancestry (includes multiple ancestries): 18.8% United States or American, 14.5% Other groups, 11.2% German, 6.6% Irish, 5.1% English (2000).
Economy: In agricultural area. Employment by occupation: 6.8% management, 5.1% professional, 14.2% services, 22.7% sales, 0.0% farming, 18.8% construction, 32.4% production (2000).
Income: Per capita income: $16,373 (2000); Median household income: $36,364 (2000); Poverty rate: 12.7% (2000).
Taxes: Total city taxes per capita: $24 (1997); City property taxes per capita: $11 (1997).
Education: High school graduation rate: 57.4% (2000); College graduation rate: 1.6% (2000).
Housing: Homeownership rate: 86.2% (2000); Median home value: $65,700 (2000); Median rent: $455 per month (2000); Median age of housing: 30 years (2000).
Transportation: Commute to work: 100.0% car, 0.0% public transportation, 0.0% walk, 0.0% work from home (2000); Travel time to work: 16.5% less than 15 minutes, 54.5% 15 to 30 minutes, 16.5% 30 to 45 minutes, 1.1% 45 to 60 minutes, 11.4% 60 minutes or more (2000)

HARTSVILLE (town). Covers a land area of 0.332 square miles and a water area of 0 square miles. Located at 39.26° N. Lat.; 85.69° W. Long. Elevation is 761 feet.
History: Hartsville was the first location of Hartsville College, founded in 1850 by the United Brethren denomination but moved to Huntington in 1898.
Population: 376 (2000); Race: 98.3% White, 0.0% Black, 0.0% Asian, 0.8% American Indian and Alaska Native, 0.8% Hispanic of any race, 0.8% two or more races (2000); Density: 1,131.3 persons per square mile (2000); Age: 27.6% under 18, 11.9% over 64 (2000); Marriage status: 23.9% never married, 62.0% now married, 5.6% widowed, 8.5% divorced (2000); Foreign born: 0.0% (2000); Ancestry (includes multiple ancestries): 24.3% United States or American, 19.1% Other groups, 14.1% German, 9.7% English, 8.8% Irish (2000).
Economy: Employment by occupation: 8.9% management, 11.5% professional, 14.7% services, 23.6% sales, 0.0% farming, 10.5% construction, 30.9% production (2000).
Income: Per capita income: $18,372 (2000); Median household income: $50,000 (2000); Poverty rate: 7.7% (2000).
Taxes: Total city taxes per capita: $37 (1997); City property taxes per capita: $22 (1997).
Education: High school graduation rate: 76.5% (2000); College graduation rate: 5.7% (2000).
Housing: Homeownership rate: 84.4% (2000); Median home value: $77,900 (2000); Median rent: $268 per month (2000); Median age of housing: 52 years (2000).
Transportation: Commute to work: 97.3% car, 0.0% public transportation, 0.5% walk, 2.2% work from home (2000); Travel time to work: 6.2% less than 15 minutes, 67.4% 15 to 30 minutes, 17.4% 30 to 45 minutes, 1.1% 45 to 60 minutes, 7.9% 60 minutes or more (2000)

HOPE (town). Covers a land area of 0.954 square miles and a water area of 0 square miles. Located at 39.30° N. Lat.; 85.76° W. Long. Elevation is 723 feet.
Population: 2,140 (2000); Race: 98.5% White, 0.3% Black, 0.0% Asian, 0.0% American Indian and Alaska Native, 1.3% Hispanic of any race, 0.9% two or more races (2000); Density: 2,242.3 persons per square mile (2000); Age: 32.3% under 18, 12.8% over 64 (2000); Marriage status: 19.0% never married, 61.2% now married, 9.4% widowed, 10.5% divorced (2000); Foreign born: 0.7% (2000); Ancestry (includes multiple ancestries): 26.7% United States or American, 16.8% German, 10.5% Other groups, 9.0% Irish, 5.5% English (2000).
Economy: In agricultural area. Manufacturing: meat processing, special machinery, plastics, lumber, steel fabricating. Single-family building permits issued: 9 (2001) / 2 (2000); Multi-family building permits issued: 0 (2001) / 0 (2000); Employment by occupation: 6.9% management, 12.5% professional, 17.3% services, 21.5% sales, 0.2% farming, 11.3% construction, 30.3% production (2000).
Income: Per capita income: $14,099 (2000); Median household income: $33,347 (2000); Poverty rate: 11.0% (2000).
Taxes: Total city taxes per capita: $69 (1997); City property taxes per capita: $66 (1997).

Education: High school graduation rate: 76.1% (2000); College graduation rate: 5.9% (2000).

School District(s)

Flat Rock-Hawcreek School Corp (KG-12)
2000 Enrollment: 1,152 812-546-4922

Housing: Homeownership rate: 76.6% (2000); Median home value: $74,400 (2000); Median rent: $450 per month (2000); Median age of housing: 39 years (2000).

Newspapers: The Star-Journal (1 x week)

Transportation: Commute to work: 94.5% car, 0.8% public transportation, 1.2% walk, 2.2% work from home (2000); Travel time to work: 18.5% less than 15 minutes, 51.4% 15 to 30 minutes, 17.7% 30 to 45 minutes, 5.1% 45 to 60 minutes, 7.3% 60 minutes or more (2000)

JONESVILLE (town). Covers a land area of 0.129 square miles and a water area of 0 square miles. Located at 39.06° N. Lat.; 85.89° W. Long. Elevation is 595 feet.

History: Laid out 1851.

Population: 220 (2000); Race: 90.9% White, 0.0% Black, 0.0% Asian, 9.1% American Indian and Alaska Native, 6.9% Hispanic of any race, 0.0% two or more races (2000); Density: 1,701.8 persons per square mile (2000); Age: 27.6% under 18, 15.1% over 64 (2000); Marriage status: 14.6% never married, 62.2% now married, 8.6% widowed, 14.6% divorced (2000); Foreign born: 0.0% (2000); Ancestry (includes multiple ancestries): 19.4% English, 16.8% Irish, 16.8% Other groups, 16.4% German, 15.5% United States or American (2000).

Economy: In agricultural area. Manufacturing: furniture and wood products. Employment by occupation: 5.6% management, 11.2% professional, 18.7% services, 33.6% sales, 0.0% farming, 0.0% construction, 30.8% production (2000).

Income: Per capita income: $17,995 (2000); Median household income: $30,694 (2000); Poverty rate: 4.7% (2000).

Taxes: Total city taxes per capita: $25 (1997); City property taxes per capita: $21 (1997).

Education: High school graduation rate: 71.2% (2000); College graduation rate: 3.1% (2000).

Housing: Homeownership rate: 72.4% (2000); Median home value: $77,100 (2000); Median rent: $400 per month (2000); Median age of housing: 44 years (2000).

Transportation: Commute to work: 100.0% car, 0.0% public transportation, 0.0% walk, 0.0% work from home (2000); Travel time to work: 19.2% less than 15 minutes, 64.4% 15 to 30 minutes, 16.3% 30 to 45 minutes, 0.0% 45 to 60 minutes, 0.0% 60 minutes or more (2000)

TAYLORSVILLE (CDP). Covers a land area of 1.045 square miles and a water area of 0 square miles. Located at 39.29° N. Lat.; 85.94° W. Long. Elevation is 653 feet.

History: Laid out 1849.

Population: 936 (2000); Race: 99.0% White, 0.0% Black, 0.0% Asian, 0.0% American Indian and Alaska Native, 0.0% Hispanic of any race, 1.0% two or more races (2000); Density: 895.5 persons per square mile (2000); Age: 31.2% under 18, 6.9% over 64 (2000); Marriage status: 16.7% never married, 66.5% now married, 4.5% widowed, 12.3% divorced (2000); Foreign born: 0.0% (2000); Ancestry (includes multiple ancestries): 26.8% German, 15.7% Irish, 11.8% United States or American, 8.2% English, 6.7% Other groups (2000).

Economy: Agricultural area. Service center for Camp Atterbury military reserve to West. Employment by occupation: 4.2% management, 13.7% professional, 12.0% services, 18.8% sales, 0.0% farming, 10.9% construction, 40.4% production (2000).

Income: Per capita income: $15,566 (2000); Median household income: $36,923 (2000); Poverty rate: 9.2% (2000).

Education: High school graduation rate: 72.2% (2000); College graduation rate: 4.9% (2000).

Housing: Homeownership rate: 80.6% (2000); Median home value: $85,500 (2000); Median rent: $194 per month (2000); Median age of housing: 36 years (2000).

Transportation: Commute to work: 90.0% car, 2.2% public transportation, 0.0% walk, 5.1% work from home (2000); Travel time to work: 32.6% less than 15 minutes, 57.6% 15 to 30 minutes, 2.1% 30 to 45 minutes, 2.6% 45 to 60 minutes, 5.2% 60 minutes or more (2000)

Benton County

Located in western Indiana; bounded on the west by Illinois. Covers a land area of 406.30 square miles, a water area of 0.10 square miles, and is located in the Eastern Time Zone. The county government was organized in 1840. County seat is Fowler.

Population: 9,421 (2000); Race: 96.5% White, 0.2% Black, 0.1% Asian, 0.1% American Indian and Alaska Native, 3.0% Hispanic of any race, 1.5% two or more races (2000); Density: 23.2 persons per square mile (2000); Age: 27.5% under 18, 15.8% over 64 (2000).

Religion: Five largest groups: 34.6% Catholic Church, 11.1% The United Methodist Church, 10.6% Christian Churches and Churches of Christ, 2.9% Evangelical Lutheran Church in America, 2.7% Southern Baptist Convention (2000).

Economy: Unemployment rate: 4.8% (11/2002); Total civilian labor force: 5,011 (11/2002); Leading industries: 30.3% manufacturing; 22.3% retail trade; 8.9% health care and social assistance (2000); Companies that employ more than 1,000 persons: 0 (2000); Companies that employ more than 100 persons: 3 (2000); Farms: 433 totaling 256,820 acres (1997); Minority business ownership rate: 0.0% (1997); Women business ownership rate: 19.0% (1997); Retail sales per capita: $7,243 (1997). Single-family building permits issued: 24 (2001) / 26 (2000); Multi-family building permits issued: 0 (2001) / 2 (2000).

Income: Per capita income: $17,220 (2000); Median household income: $39,813 (2000); Poverty rate: 5.5% (2000); Bankruptcy rate: 6.29% (2001).

Taxes: Total county taxes per capita: $288 (1997); County property taxes per capita: $212 (1997).

Education: High school graduation rate: 86.3% (2000); College graduation rate: 13.0% (2000).

Housing: Homeownership rate: 75.8% (2000); Median home value: $75,000 (2000); Median rent: $341 per month (2000); Median age of housing: 53 years (2000).

Health: Birth rate: 130.6 per 10,000 population (1998); Age adjusted death rate: 93.3 per 10,000 population (1999); Age adjusted cancer mortality rate: 246.9 deaths per 100,000 population (1999). Number of physicians: 6.4 per 10,000 population (1999); Number of hospital beds: n/a (1999).

Elections: 2000 Presidential election results: 34.3% Gore, 63.0% Bush, 0.5% Nader, 1.2% Buchanan

Additional Information Contacts

Benton County Government Offices 765-884-0930

Benton County Communities

AMBIA (town). Covers a land area of 0.146 square miles and a water area of 0 square miles. Located at 40.49° N. Lat.; 87.51° W. Long. Elevation is 731 feet.

Population: 197 (2000); Race: 77.3% White, 3.6% Black, 0.0% Asian, 0.0% American Indian and Alaska Native, 39.7% Hispanic of any race, 0.0% two or more races (2000); Density: 1,350.9 persons per square mile (2000); Age: 35.1% under 18, 10.8% over 64 (2000); Marriage status: 14.8% never married, 75.6% now married, 6.7% widowed, 3.0% divorced (2000); Foreign born: 4.1% (2000); Ancestry (includes multiple ancestries): 43.3% Other groups, 14.9% German, 12.4% United States or American, 7.2% English, 5.2% Irish (2000).

Economy: In agricultural area. Employment by occupation: 10.7% management, 9.3% professional, 5.3% services, 21.3% sales, 0.0% farming, 14.7% construction, 38.7% production (2000).

Income: Per capita income: $14,169 (2000); Median household income: $36,667 (2000); Poverty rate: 0.5% (2000).

Taxes: Total city taxes per capita: $47 (1997); City property taxes per capita: $47 (1997).

Education: High school graduation rate: 85.6% (2000); College graduation rate: 4.2% (2000).

Housing: Homeownership rate: 91.3% (2000); Median home value: $28,800 (2000); Median rent: $375 per month (2000); Median age of housing: 60+ years (2000).

Transportation: Commute to work: 88.0% car, 0.0% public transportation, 8.0% walk, 4.0% work from home (2000); Travel time to work: 15.3% less than 15 minutes, 36.1% 15 to 30 minutes, 16.7% 30 to 45 minutes, 12.5% 45 to 60 minutes, 19.4% 60 minutes or more (2000)

BOSWELL (town). Covers a land area of 0.474 square miles and a water area of 0 square miles. Located at 40.51° N. Lat.; 87.38° W. Long. Elevation is 760 feet.

Population: 827 (2000); Race: 93.6% White, 0.0% Black, 0.2% Asian, 0.0% American Indian and Alaska Native, 10.8% Hispanic of any race, 0.0% two or more races (2000); Density: 1,743.3 persons per square mile (2000); Age: 28.7% under 18, 21.3% over 64 (2000); Marriage status: 23.2% never married, 50.7% now married, 12.1% widowed, 14.0% divorced (2000); Foreign born: 1.5% (2000); Ancestry (includes multiple ancestries): 17.8% United States or American, 17.1% Other groups, 16.2% German, 14.9% Irish, 10.4% English (2000).
Economy: In grain area; sawmill. Manufacturing: pallets, planters. Employment by occupation: 6.0% management, 8.7% professional, 22.3% services, 21.5% sales, 0.3% farming, 8.7% construction, 32.6% production (2000).
Income: Per capita income: $14,401 (2000); Median household income: $33,224 (2000); Poverty rate: 8.3% (2000).
Taxes: Total city taxes per capita: $132 (1997); City property taxes per capita: $132 (1997).
Education: High school graduation rate: 75.6% (2000); College graduation rate: 6.1% (2000).
Housing: Homeownership rate: 80.1% (2000); Median home value: $59,300 (2000); Median rent: $353 per month (2000); Median age of housing: 58 years (2000).
Newspapers: Boswell Enterprise (1 x week)
Transportation: Commute to work: 88.2% car, 0.0% public transportation, 3.4% walk, 6.2% work from home (2000); Travel time to work: 37.0% less than 15 minutes, 28.1% 15 to 30 minutes, 17.0% 30 to 45 minutes, 12.8% 45 to 60 minutes, 5.1% 60 minutes or more (2000)

EARL PARK (town). Covers a land area of 0.943 square miles and a water area of 0 square miles. Located at 40.68° N. Lat.; 87.41° W. Long. Elevation is 780 feet.
History: Laid out 1872.
Population: 485 (2000); Race: 99.6% White, 0.2% Black, 0.0% Asian, 0.0% American Indian and Alaska Native, 0.2% Hispanic of any race, 0.0% two or more races (2000); Density: 514.5 persons per square mile (2000); Age: 31.5% under 18, 17.2% over 64 (2000); Marriage status: 24.3% never married, 47.0% now married, 18.0% widowed, 10.7% divorced (2000); Foreign born: 0.0% (2000); Ancestry (includes multiple ancestries): 27.4% German, 13.7% Irish, 9.0% French (except Basque), 8.4% Other groups, 8.2% English (2000).
Economy: In agricultural area. Single-family building permits issued: 0 (2001) / 0 (2000); Multi-family building permits issued: 0 (2001) / 0 (2000); Employment by occupation: 12.4% management, 11.4% professional, 6.4% services, 24.8% sales, 1.5% farming, 14.4% construction, 29.2% production (2000).
Income: Per capita income: $14,369 (2000); Median household income: $32,981 (2000); Poverty rate: 10.4% (2000).
Taxes: Total city taxes per capita: $70 (1997); City property taxes per capita: $68 (1997).
Education: High school graduation rate: 78.4% (2000); College graduation rate: 7.3% (2000).
Housing: Homeownership rate: 72.4% (2000); Median home value: $57,300 (2000); Median rent: $364 per month (2000); Median age of housing: 59 years (2000).
Transportation: Commute to work: 92.0% car, 0.0% public transportation, 2.0% walk, 3.5% work from home (2000); Travel time to work: 44.6% less than 15 minutes, 33.7% 15 to 30 minutes, 8.3% 30 to 45 minutes, 12.4% 45 to 60 minutes, 1.0% 60 minutes or more (2000)

FOWLER (town). Covers a land area of 1.395 square miles and a water area of 0.006 square miles. Located at 40.61° N. Lat.; 87.31° W. Long. Elevation is 826 feet.
History: Laid out 1872.
Population: 2,415 (2000); Race: 96.6% White, 0.0% Black, 0.0% Asian, 0.0% American Indian and Alaska Native, 3.1% Hispanic of any race, 1.7% two or more races (2000); Density: 1,730.6 persons per square mile (2000); Age: 27.8% under 18, 18.0% over 64 (2000); Marriage status: 18.4% never married, 60.1% now married, 10.1% widowed, 11.4% divorced (2000); Foreign born: 0.0% (2000); Ancestry (includes multiple ancestries): 29.0% German, 13.3% United States or American, 12.5% Irish, 12.0% Other groups, 8.4% French (except Basque) (2000).
Economy: Corn, oats, soybeans; hogs, poultry. Manufacturing: paper bags, steel fabrication, concrete patio stone. Single-family building permits issued: 4 (2001) / 4 (2000); Multi-family building permits issued: 0 (2001) / 0 (2000); Employment by occupation: 13.8% management, 12.7% professional, 13.3% services, 27.1% sales, 0.0% farming, 10.1% construction, 23.1% production (2000).
Income: Per capita income: $17,881 (2000); Median household income: $40,396 (2000); Poverty rate: 5.8% (2000).
Taxes: Total city taxes per capita: $181 (1997); City property taxes per capita: $177 (1997).
Education: High school graduation rate: 87.6% (2000); College graduation rate: 15.1% (2000).

School District(s)

Benton Community School Corp (KG-12)
2000 Enrollment: 2,122 765-884-0850
Housing: Homeownership rate: 74.2% (2000); Median home value: $77,100 (2000); Median rent: $330 per month (2000); Median age of housing: 50 years (2000).
Newspapers: Benton Review (1 x week)
Transportation: Commute to work: 95.3% car, 0.4% public transportation, 2.0% walk, 2.4% work from home (2000); Travel time to work: 45.8% less than 15 minutes, 18.7% 15 to 30 minutes, 20.4% 30 to 45 minutes, 10.1% 45 to 60 minutes, 4.9% 60 minutes or more (2000)

OTTERBEIN (town). Covers a land area of 0.572 square miles and a water area of 0 square miles. Located at 40.48° N. Lat.; 87.09° W. Long.
History: Laid out 1872.
Population: 1,312 (2000); Race: 98.5% White, 0.0% Black, 0.0% Asian, 0.2% American Indian and Alaska Native, 1.1% Hispanic of any race, 0.8% two or more races (2000); Density: 2,291.9 persons per square mile (2000); Age: 29.2% under 18, 13.2% over 64 (2000); Marriage status: 21.2% never married, 58.4% now married, 8.4% widowed, 12.1% divorced (2000); Foreign born: 0.3% (2000); Ancestry (includes multiple ancestries): 22.9% German, 12.6% United States or American, 11.7% Irish, 9.1% Other groups, 7.0% English (2000).
Economy: Manufacturing: building components, transportation equipment. Agricultural area: corn, soybeans; livestock. Employment by occupation: 9.8% management, 9.3% professional, 19.2% services, 21.9% sales, 0.6% farming, 10.7% construction, 28.5% production (2000).
Income: Per capita income: $17,128 (2000); Median household income: $40,524 (2000); Poverty rate: 6.9% (2000).
Taxes: Total city taxes per capita: $155 (1997); City property taxes per capita: $141 (1997).
Education: High school graduation rate: 88.2% (2000); College graduation rate: 13.1% (2000).
Housing: Homeownership rate: 75.1% (2000); Median home value: $78,400 (2000); Median rent: $433 per month (2000); Median age of housing: 42 years (2000).
Transportation: Commute to work: 93.2% car, 0.5% public transportation, 0.8% walk, 4.4% work from home (2000); Travel time to work: 27.5% less than 15 minutes, 48.1% 15 to 30 minutes, 18.8% 30 to 45 minutes, 3.7% 45 to 60 minutes, 1.9% 60 minutes or more (2000)

OXFORD (town). Covers a land area of 0.513 square miles and a water area of 0 square miles. Located at 40.52° N. Lat.; 87.25° W. Long. Elevation is 732 feet.
History: In 1896 in Oxford a racehorse named Dan Patch was born, and brought a measure of fame to the town for the records he set. For a time, Oxford was the seat of Benton County.
Population: 1,271 (2000); Race: 96.0% White, 0.3% Black, 0.1% Asian, 0.2% American Indian and Alaska Native, 1.2% Hispanic of any race, 2.6% two or more races (2000); Density: 2,476.0 persons per square mile (2000); Age: 28.5% under 18, 15.7% over 64 (2000); Marriage status: 18.1% never married, 56.0% now married, 14.1% widowed, 11.8% divorced (2000); Foreign born: 0.4% (2000); Ancestry (includes multiple ancestries): 20.9% German, 16.7% United States or American, 10.9% Irish, 6.3% Other groups, 6.1% English (2000).
Economy: Employment by occupation: 6.3% management, 13.5% professional, 16.4% services, 22.9% sales, 1.5% farming, 13.2% construction, 26.2% production (2000).
Income: Per capita income: $16,472 (2000); Median household income: $39,375 (2000); Poverty rate: 5.1% (2000).
Taxes: Total city taxes per capita: $103 (1997); City property taxes per capita: $102 (1997).
Education: High school graduation rate: 83.4% (2000); College graduation rate: 9.7% (2000).
Housing: Homeownership rate: 79.1% (2000); Median home value: $72,200 (2000); Median rent: $319 per month (2000); Median age of housing: 48 years (2000).
Transportation: Commute to work: 94.5% car, 0.5% public transportation, 3.1% walk, 1.5% work from home (2000); Travel time to work: 31.0% less

than 15 minutes, 28.7% 15 to 30 minutes, 26.2% 30 to 45 minutes, 10.2% 45 to 60 minutes, 3.9% 60 minutes or more (2000)

Blackford County

Located in eastern Indiana; drained by the Salamonie River. Covers a land area of 165.10 square miles, a water area of 0.30 square miles, and is located in the Eastern Time Zone. The county government was organized in 1838. County seat is Hartford City.

Weather Station: Hartford City 4 ESE — Elevation: 941 feet

	Jan	Feb	Mar	Apr	May	Jun	Jul	Aug	Sep	Oct	Nov	Dec
High	31	36	47	60	71	80	83	81	75	63	49	37
Low	15	19	29	39	50	59	63	60	53	42	33	22
Precip	1.9	2.0	2.8	3.4	3.7	4.5	4.1	4.1	2.8	2.4	3.3	2.6
Snow	7.6	6.0	3.5	1.0	tr	0.0	0.0	0.0	0.0	0.4	1.6	5.9

High and Low temperatures in degrees Fahrenheit; Precipitation and Snow in inches

Population: 14,048 (2000); Race: 98.1% White, 0.0% Black, 0.2% Asian, 0.3% American Indian and Alaska Native, 1.1% Hispanic of any race, 1.0% two or more races (2000); Density: 85.1 persons per square mile (2000); Age: 24.7% under 18, 15.4% over 64 (2000).
Religion: Five largest groups: 8.5% The United Methodist Church, 5.9% Catholic Church, 3.4% Church of the Nazarene, 3.0% Christian Church (Disciples of Christ), 2.6% Evangelical Lutheran Church in America (2000).
Economy: Unemployment rate: 6.5% (11/2002); Total civilian labor force: 6,036 (11/2002); Leading industries: 51.6% manufacturing; 13.1% retail trade; 9.5% health care and social assistance (2000); Companies that employ more than 1,000 persons: 0 (2000); Companies that employ more than 100 persons: 10 (2000); Farms: 303 totaling 85,958 acres (1997); Minority business ownership rate: 0.0% (1997); Women business ownership rate: 18.7% (1997); Retail sales per capita: $5,924 (1997). Single-family building permits issued: 25 (2001) / 28 (2000); Multi-family building permits issued: 0 (2001) / 68 (2000).
Income: Per capita income: $16,543 (2000); Median household income: $34,760 (2000); Poverty rate: 8.7% (2000); Bankruptcy rate: 8.39% (2001).
Taxes: Total county taxes per capita: $242 (1997); County property taxes per capita: $165 (1997).
Education: High school graduation rate: 81.3% (2000); College graduation rate: 10.3% (2000).
Housing: Homeownership rate: 78.6% (2000); Median home value: $58,900 (2000); Median rent: $301 per month (2000); Median age of housing: 46 years (2000).
Health: Birth rate: 135.3 per 10,000 population (1998); Age adjusted death rate: 92.1 per 10,000 population (1999); Age adjusted cancer mortality rate: 196.6 deaths per 100,000 population (1999). Number of physicians: 6.4 per 10,000 population (1999); Number of hospital beds: 17.8 per 10,000 population (1999).
Elections: 2000 Presidential election results: 43.0% Gore, 55.2% Bush, 0.4% Nader, 0.9% Buchanan

Additional Information Contacts
Blackford County Government Offices 765-348-1620
Blackford County Economic Corp.......................... 765-348-4944
Hartford City Chamber of Commerce 765-348-1905

Blackford County Communities

HARTFORD CITY (city). Covers a land area of 3.721 square miles and a water area of 0.006 square miles. Located at 40.45° N. Lat.; 85.36° W. Long. Elevation is 922 feet.
History: Settled 1832, laid out 1839.
Population: 6,928 (2000); Race: 97.3% White, 0.0% Black, 0.4% Asian, 0.5% American Indian and Alaska Native, 1.7% Hispanic of any race, 1.1% two or more races (2000); Density: 1,861.7 persons per square mile (2000); Age: 25.5% under 18, 17.3% over 64 (2000); Marriage status: 18.9% never married, 59.4% now married, 9.4% widowed, 12.3% divorced (2000); Foreign born: 0.2% (2000); Ancestry (includes multiple ancestries): 15.1% German, 14.0% United States or American, 10.2% Other groups, 8.8% Irish, 7.6% English (2000).
Economy: In rich agricultural area: livestock; dairy products; soybeans, grain. Natural gas and oil fields nearby. Manufacturing: glass, rubber products, transportation equipment, concrete products, canned goods, consumer goods, lumber products. Employment by occupation: 5.8% management, 13.1% professional, 14.6% services, 21.3% sales, 0.2% farming, 9.1% construction, 36.0% production (2000).
Income: Per capita income: $15,596 (2000); Median household income: $31,531 (2000); Poverty rate: 10.4% (2000).
Taxes: Total city taxes per capita: $215 (2000); City property taxes per capita: $209 (2000).
Education: High school graduation rate: 79.8% (2000); College graduation rate: 11.4% (2000).

School District(s)
Blackford County Schools (KG-12)
2000 Enrollment: 2,310 765-348-7550
Housing: Homeownership rate: 74.8% (2000); Median home value: $54,100 (2000); Median rent: $312 per month (2000); Median age of housing: 46 years (2000).
Hospitals: Blackford County Hospital (65 beds)
Safety: Violent crime rate: 2.9 per 10,000 population; Property crime rate: 249.7 per 10,000 population (2001).
Newspapers: News-Times (6 x week); Market Basket (1 x week)
Transportation: Commute to work: 93.7% car, 0.0% public transportation, 1.8% walk, 3.4% work from home (2000); Travel time to work: 51.4% less than 15 minutes, 18.1% 15 to 30 minutes, 20.2% 30 to 45 minutes, 5.3% 45 to 60 minutes, 4.9% 60 minutes or more (2000)

Additional Information Contacts
Blackford County Economic Corp.......................... 765-348-4944
Hartford City Chamber of Commerce 765-348-1905

MONTPELIER (city). Covers a land area of 1.097 square miles and a water area of 0 square miles. Located at 40.55° N. Lat.; 85.28° W. Long. Elevation is 870 feet.
History: Settled 1836, laid out 1837, incorporated 1937.
Population: 1,929 (2000); Race: 97.3% White, 0.1% Black, 0.0% Asian, 0.5% American Indian and Alaska Native, 0.2% Hispanic of any race, 2.1% two or more races (2000); Density: 1,757.9 persons per square mile (2000); Age: 25.9% under 18, 14.2% over 64 (2000); Marriage status: 16.3% never married, 56.8% now married, 9.2% widowed, 17.7% divorced (2000); Foreign born: 0.0% (2000); Ancestry (includes multiple ancestries): 19.7% German, 11.2% Irish, 10.2% United States or American, 6.9% English, 5.9% Other groups (2000).
Economy: In agricultural area: livestock; dairy products; soybeans, corn, grain. Manufacturing: grip nuts, corrugated containers, glass products, gloves; old natural gas and oil wells; stone quarries. Employment by occupation: 6.8% management, 8.3% professional, 12.1% services, 16.4% sales, 1.2% farming, 11.6% construction, 43.7% production (2000).
Income: Per capita income: $15,076 (2000); Median household income: $30,175 (2000); Poverty rate: 9.5% (2000).
Taxes: Total city taxes per capita: $113 (1997); City property taxes per capita: $97 (1997).
Education: High school graduation rate: 75.9% (2000); College graduation rate: 6.4% (2000).
Housing: Homeownership rate: 67.9% (2000); Median home value: $46,600 (2000); Median rent: $279 per month (2000); Median age of housing: 48 years (2000).
Newspapers: The Montpelier Herald (1 x week)
Transportation: Commute to work: 93.6% car, 0.0% public transportation, 3.4% walk, 2.7% work from home (2000); Travel time to work: 31.6% less than 15 minutes, 32.9% 15 to 30 minutes, 19.8% 30 to 45 minutes, 7.4% 45 to 60 minutes, 8.3% 60 minutes or more (2000)

SHAMROCK LAKES (town). Covers a land area of 0.268 square miles and a water area of 0.051 square miles. Located at 40.41° N. Lat.; 85.42° W. Long. Elevation is 917 feet.
Population: 168 (2000); Race: 97.4% White, 0.0% Black, 0.0% Asian, 0.0% American Indian and Alaska Native, 0.0% Hispanic of any race, 2.6% two or more races (2000); Density: 626.3 persons per square mile (2000); Age: 20.5% under 18, 6.4% over 64 (2000); Marriage status: 18.8% never married, 68.4% now married, 3.0% widowed, 9.8% divorced (2000); Foreign born: 0.0% (2000); Ancestry (includes multiple ancestries): 30.8% English, 17.3% German, 16.7% Irish, 12.8% United States or American, 5.1% Swiss (2000).
Economy: Employment by occupation: 8.9% management, 40.0% professional, 2.2% services, 25.6% sales, 2.2% farming, 4.4% construction, 16.7% production (2000).
Income: Per capita income: $21,088 (2000); Median household income: $61,875 (2000); Poverty rate: 2.6% (2000).
Taxes: Total city taxes per capita: $55 (1997); City property taxes per capita: $40 (1997).
Education: High school graduation rate: 97.2% (2000); College graduation rate: 23.1% (2000).

Housing: Homeownership rate: 86.7% (2000); Median home value: $105,400 (2000); Median rent: $450 per month (2000); Median age of housing: 33 years (2000).
Transportation: Commute to work: 100.0% car, 0.0% public transportation, 0.0% walk, 0.0% work from home (2000); Travel time to work: 20.5% less than 15 minutes, 39.8% 15 to 30 minutes, 19.3% 30 to 45 minutes, 3.4% 45 to 60 minutes, 17.0% 60 minutes or more (2000)

Boone County

Located in central Indiana; drained by Sugar and Raccoon Creeks and the Eel River. Covers a land area of 422.90 square miles, a water area of 0.40 square miles, and is located in the Eastern Time Zone. The county government was organized in 1830. County seat is Lebanon.

Boone County is part of the Indianapolis, IN MSA. The entire metro area includes: Boone County; Hamilton County; Hancock County; Hendricks County; Johnson County; Madison County; Marion County; Morgan County; Shelby County

Weather Station: Whitestown Elevation: 935 feet

	Jan	Feb	Mar	Apr	May	Jun	Jul	Aug	Sep	Oct	Nov	Dec
High	33	39	50	63	74	83	86	84	78	66	51	39
Low	16	20	29	40	50	59	63	60	53	42	33	23
Precip	2.4	2.3	3.4	3.9	4.5	4.1	4.6	3.5	3.0	3.0	3.7	3.0
Snow	9.1	6.0	3.0	0.3	0.0	0.0	0.0	0.0	0.0	0.3	1.0	5.7

High and Low temperatures in degrees Fahrenheit; Precipitation and Snow in inches

Population: 46,107 (2000); Race: 98.0% White, 0.2% Black, 0.5% Asian, 0.1% American Indian and Alaska Native, 1.0% Hispanic of any race, 1.0% two or more races (2000); Density: 109.0 persons per square mile (2000); Age: 28.3% under 18, 11.7% over 64 (2000).
Religion: Five largest groups: 10.0% Catholic Church, 6.4% The United Methodist Church, 5.8% Presbyterian Church (U.S.A.), 5.0% Christian Church (Disciples of Christ), 4.7% Christian Churches and Churches of Christ (2000).
Economy: Unemployment rate: 3.5% (11/2002); Total civilian labor force: 25,913 (11/2002); Leading industries: 17.5% manufacturing; 14.3% retail trade; 13.5% health care and social assistance (2000); Companies that employ more than 1,000 persons: 0 (2000); Companies that employ more than 100 persons: 18 (2000); Farms: 611 totaling 228,328 acres (1997); Minority business ownership rate: 0.0% (1997); Women business ownership rate: 22.0% (1997); Retail sales per capita: $6,068 (1997). Single-family building permits issued: 438 (2001) / 410 (2000); Multi-family building permits issued: 53 (2001) / 268 (2000).
Income: Per capita income: $24,182 (2000); Median household income: $49,632 (2000); Poverty rate: 5.2% (2000); Bankruptcy rate: 6.26% (2001).
Taxes: Total county taxes per capita: $259 (2000); County property taxes per capita: $128 (2000).
Education: High school graduation rate: 88.3% (2000); College graduation rate: 27.6% (2000).
Housing: Homeownership rate: 78.7% (2000); Median home value: $131,100 (2000); Median rent: $463 per month (2000); Median age of housing: 29 years (2000).
Health: Birth rate: 125.1 per 10,000 population (1998); Age adjusted death rate: 81.7 per 10,000 population (1999); Age adjusted cancer mortality rate: 212.5 deaths per 100,000 population (1999). Air Quality Index: 52% good, 48% moderate, 0% unhealthy (percent of days in 2000). Number of physicians: 42.1 per 10,000 population (1999); Number of hospital beds: 10.6 per 10,000 population (1999).
Elections: 2000 Presidential election results: 25.9% Gore, 71.5% Bush, 1.1% Nader, 0.6% Buchanan
Additional Information Contacts
Boone County Government Offices 765-482-2940
Lebanon Chamber of Commerce 765-482-1320
Zionsville Chamber of Commerce 317-873-3836

Boone County Communities

ADVANCE (town). Covers a land area of 0.625 square miles and a water area of 0 square miles. Located at 39.99° N. Lat.; 86.61° W. Long. Elevation is 934 feet.
Population: 562 (2000); Race: 99.5% White, 0.0% Black, 0.0% Asian, 0.0% American Indian and Alaska Native, 0.9% Hispanic of any race, 0.0% two or more races (2000); Density: 898.7 persons per square mile (2000); Age: 31.9% under 18, 8.7% over 64 (2000); Marriage status: 15.5% never married, 65.1% now married, 5.7% widowed, 13.8% divorced (2000); Foreign born: 0.0% (2000); Ancestry (includes multiple ancestries): 15.2% German, 13.3% Irish, 13.3% Other groups, 10.1% United States or American, 6.7% English (2000).
Economy: Agricultural area; steel fabricating. Employment by occupation: 8.1% management, 13.9% professional, 11.5% services, 28.8% sales, 1.4% farming, 16.3% construction, 20.0% production (2000).
Income: Per capita income: $17,169 (2000); Median household income: $45,000 (2000); Poverty rate: 6.9% (2000).
Taxes: Total city taxes per capita: $116 (1997); City property taxes per capita: $53 (1997).
Education: High school graduation rate: 82.2% (2000); College graduation rate: 6.3% (2000).
Housing: Homeownership rate: 80.5% (2000); Median home value: $83,300 (2000); Median rent: $442 per month (2000); Median age of housing: 60+ years (2000).
Transportation: Commute to work: 95.3% car, 0.0% public transportation, 0.7% walk, 3.4% work from home (2000); Travel time to work: 14.3% less than 15 minutes, 39.9% 15 to 30 minutes, 24.1% 30 to 45 minutes, 16.4% 45 to 60 minutes, 5.2% 60 minutes or more (2000)

JAMESTOWN (town). Covers a land area of 0.516 square miles and a water area of 0 square miles. Located at 39.92° N. Lat.; 86.62° W. Long. Elevation is 946 feet.
History: Jamestown developed as a stop on the stagecoach route, and later as a station on the New York Central Railroad.
Population: 886 (2000); Race: 98.9% White, 0.4% Black, 0.0% Asian, 0.0% American Indian and Alaska Native, 1.3% Hispanic of any race, 0.4% two or more races (2000); Density: 1,717.6 persons per square mile (2000); Age: 25.1% under 18, 12.4% over 64 (2000); Marriage status: 18.6% never married, 65.6% now married, 5.9% widowed, 9.9% divorced (2000); Foreign born: 0.0% (2000); Ancestry (includes multiple ancestries): 27.3% German, 18.3% English, 14.6% United States or American, 13.2% Irish, 9.9% Other groups (2000).
Economy: Single-family building permits issued: 0 (2001) / 4 (2000); Multi-family building permits issued: 30 (2001) / 0 (2000); Employment by occupation: 10.2% management, 15.0% professional, 17.8% services, 25.0% sales, 0.2% farming, 12.2% construction, 19.8% production (2000).
Income: Per capita income: $19,821 (2000); Median household income: $46,250 (2000); Poverty rate: 7.8% (2000).
Taxes: Total city taxes per capita: $98 (1997); City property taxes per capita: $44 (1997).
Education: High school graduation rate: 82.6% (2000); College graduation rate: 10.9% (2000).
Housing: Homeownership rate: 73.4% (2000); Median home value: $97,700 (2000); Median rent: $422 per month (2000); Median age of housing: 47 years (2000).
Transportation: Commute to work: 93.9% car, 0.0% public transportation, 4.5% walk, 1.6% work from home (2000); Travel time to work: 17.2% less than 15 minutes, 32.5% 15 to 30 minutes, 28.4% 30 to 45 minutes, 16.4% 45 to 60 minutes, 5.6% 60 minutes or more (2000)

LEBANON (city). Covers a land area of 7.283 square miles and a water area of 0 square miles. Located at 40.05° N. Lat.; 86.47° W. Long. Elevation is 948 feet.
History: Lebanon received its biblical name because the forests surrounding it reminded one of its founders of the Cedars of Lebanon. Lebanon was the home of Samuel M. Ralston (1857-1925), governor of Indiana and U.S. senator.
Population: 14,222 (2000); Race: 97.6% White, 0.3% Black, 0.1% Asian, 0.1% American Indian and Alaska Native, 1.7% Hispanic of any race, 1.1% two or more races (2000); Density: 1,952.9 persons per square mile (2000); Age: 26.0% under 18, 13.6% over 64 (2000); Marriage status: 20.6% never married, 57.9% now married, 9.1% widowed, 12.4% divorced (2000); Foreign born: 1.2% (2000); Ancestry (includes multiple ancestries): 22.9% German, 14.6% United States or American, 12.0% Irish, 11.0% English, 10.4% Other groups (2000).
Vital Statistics: Birth rate: 165.9 per 10,000 population (1998)
Economy: Single-family building permits issued: 74 (2001) / 66 (2000); Multi-family building permits issued: 4 (2001) / 0 (2000); Employment by occupation: 8.9% management, 13.3% professional, 19.2% services, 26.8% sales, 0.0% farming, 10.4% construction, 21.4% production (2000).
Income: Per capita income: $18,245 (2000); Median household income: $37,791 (2000); Poverty rate: 7.1% (2000).
Taxes: Total city taxes per capita: $243 (2000); City property taxes per capita: $116 (2000).

Education: High school graduation rate: 83.2% (2000); College graduation rate: 14.5% (2000).

School District(s)

Lebanon Community School Corp (PK-12)
2000 Enrollment: 3,265 765-482-0380

Housing: Homeownership rate: 66.8% (2000); Median home value: $90,900 (2000); Median rent: $429 per month (2000); Median age of housing: 33 years (2000).
Hospitals: Witham Memorial Hospital (80 beds)
Newspapers: The Reporter (6 x week)
Transportation: Commute to work: 95.0% car, 0.1% public transportation, 1.4% walk, 2.7% work from home (2000); Travel time to work: 42.9% less than 15 minutes, 23.1% 15 to 30 minutes, 25.1% 30 to 45 minutes, 5.9% 45 to 60 minutes, 3.0% 60 minutes or more (2000)
Additional Information Contacts
Lebanon Chamber of Commerce 765-482-1320

THORNTOWN (town). Covers a land area of 0.571 square miles and a water area of 0 square miles. Located at 40.12° N. Lat.; 86.60° W. Long. Elevation is 861 feet.
History: Thorntown was called Keewaskee, meaning "place of thorns," when a trading post was established here by Jesuit missionaries. Thorntown was platted in 1829 by Cornelius Westfall.
Population: 1,562 (2000); Race: 99.2% White, 0.0% Black, 0.2% Asian, 0.0% American Indian and Alaska Native, 0.2% Hispanic of any race, 0.7% two or more races (2000); Density: 2,736.1 persons per square mile (2000); Age: 27.8% under 18, 12.7% over 64 (2000); Marriage status: 17.3% never married, 61.2% now married, 7.3% widowed, 14.1% divorced (2000); Foreign born: 0.5% (2000); Ancestry (includes multiple ancestries): 17.8% United States or American, 17.0% German, 9.2% Irish, 8.5% English, 7.7% Other groups (2000).
Economy: Single-family building permits issued: 5 (2001) / 2 (2000); Multi-family building permits issued: 0 (2001) / 0 (2000); Employment by occupation: 6.7% management, 7.6% professional, 19.9% services, 25.1% sales, 1.0% farming, 15.4% construction, 24.3% production (2000).
Income: Per capita income: $19,109 (2000); Median household income: $38,289 (2000); Poverty rate: 6.6% (2000).
Taxes: Total city taxes per capita: $96 (1997); City property taxes per capita: $48 (1997).
Education: High school graduation rate: 82.0% (2000); College graduation rate: 6.4% (2000).

School District(s)

Western Boone Co Com School District (PK-12)
2000 Enrollment: 1,884 765-482-6333

Housing: Homeownership rate: 73.9% (2000); Median home value: $84,500 (2000); Median rent: $405 per month (2000); Median age of housing: 52 years (2000).
Transportation: Commute to work: 90.4% car, 0.4% public transportation, 4.6% walk, 2.7% work from home (2000); Travel time to work: 27.2% less than 15 minutes, 39.9% 15 to 30 minutes, 17.5% 30 to 45 minutes, 11.9% 45 to 60 minutes, 3.5% 60 minutes or more (2000)

ULEN (town). Covers a land area of 0.063 square miles and a water area of 0 square miles. Located at 40.06° N. Lat.; 86.46° W. Long. Elevation is 940 feet.
Population: 123 (2000); Race: 100.0% White, 0.0% Black, 0.0% Asian, 0.0% American Indian and Alaska Native, 0.0% Hispanic of any race, 0.0% two or more races (2000); Density: 1,946.9 persons per square mile (2000); Age: 28.6% under 18, 27.6% over 64 (2000); Marriage status: 16.7% never married, 82.1% now married, 0.0% widowed, 1.2% divorced (2000); Foreign born: 0.0% (2000); Ancestry (includes multiple ancestries): 46.7% German, 33.3% English, 17.1% Dutch, 13.3% Irish, 9.5% Italian (2000).
Economy: Agricultural area. Employment by occupation: 22.0% management, 36.6% professional, 0.0% services, 24.4% sales, 0.0% farming, 9.8% construction, 7.3% production (2000).
Income: Per capita income: $41,557 (2000); Median household income: $57,083 (2000); Poverty rate: 0.0% (2000).
Taxes: Total city taxes per capita: $219 (1997); City property taxes per capita: $103 (1997).
Education: High school graduation rate: 100.0% (2000); College graduation rate: 58.7% (2000).
Housing: Homeownership rate: 100.0% (2000); Median home value: $238,900 (2000); Median age of housing: 60+ years (2000).
Transportation: Commute to work: 100.0% car, 0.0% public transportation, 0.0% walk, 0.0% work from home (2000); Travel time to work: 48.7% less than 15 minutes, 25.6% 15 to 30 minutes, 17.9% 30 to 45 minutes, 7.7% 45 to 60 minutes, 0.0% 60 minutes or more (2000)

WHITESTOWN (town). Covers a land area of 0.255 square miles and a water area of 0 square miles. Located at 39.99° N. Lat.; 86.34° W. Long. Elevation is 940 feet.
History: Laid out 1851.
Population: 471 (2000); Race: 100.0% White, 0.0% Black, 0.0% Asian, 0.0% American Indian and Alaska Native, 0.0% Hispanic of any race, 0.0% two or more races (2000); Density: 1,843.9 persons per square mile (2000); Age: 32.6% under 18, 8.5% over 64 (2000); Marriage status: 21.0% never married, 56.0% now married, 5.8% widowed, 17.2% divorced (2000); Foreign born: 0.9% (2000); Ancestry (includes multiple ancestries): 24.7% United States or American, 17.4% German, 13.6% English, 10.9% Irish, 7.7% Other groups (2000).
Economy: In agricultural area; manufacturing of machinery, vinyl signs. Single-family building permits issued: 0 (2001) / 27 (2000); Multi-family building permits issued: 0 (2001) / 0 (2000); Employment by occupation: 8.7% management, 11.4% professional, 17.7% services, 27.2% sales, 0.0% farming, 15.0% construction, 20.1% production (2000).
Income: Per capita income: $21,674 (2000); Median household income: $46,528 (2000); Poverty rate: 7.3% (2000).
Taxes: Total city taxes per capita: $139 (1997); City property taxes per capita: $73 (1997).
Education: High school graduation rate: 79.8% (2000); College graduation rate: 13.8% (2000).
Housing: Homeownership rate: 79.0% (2000); Median home value: $91,700 (2000); Median rent: $570 per month (2000); Median age of housing: 60+ years (2000).
Safety: Violent crime rate: 63.3 per 10,000 population; Property crime rate: 84.4 per 10,000 population (2001).
Transportation: Commute to work: 91.1% car, 0.0% public transportation, 2.4% walk, 5.7% work from home (2000); Travel time to work: 20.2% less than 15 minutes, 57.5% 15 to 30 minutes, 20.2% 30 to 45 minutes, 1.3% 45 to 60 minutes, 0.9% 60 minutes or more (2000)

ZIONSVILLE (town). Covers a land area of 5.800 square miles and a water area of 0.066 square miles. Located at 39.95° N. Lat.; 86.26° W. Long. Elevation is 849 feet.
History: On his way to his inauguration in Washington in 1861, Abraham Lincoln spoke from the back of a train in Zionsville, saying, "I would like to spend more time here, but there is an event to take place in Washington which cannot start until I get there."
Population: 8,775 (2000); Race: 98.4% White, 0.0% Black, 0.3% Asian, 0.0% American Indian and Alaska Native, 1.2% Hispanic of any race, 1.0% two or more races (2000); Density: 1,512.9 persons per square mile (2000); Age: 31.9% under 18, 10.6% over 64 (2000); Marriage status: 17.0% never married, 70.8% now married, 4.1% widowed, 8.1% divorced (2000); Foreign born: 2.5% (2000); Ancestry (includes multiple ancestries): 24.3% German, 15.4% English, 12.3% United States or American, 10.1% Irish, 5.2% Scottish (2000).
Economy: Single-family building permits issued: 112 (2001) / 98 (2000); Multi-family building permits issued: 0 (2001) / 268 (2000); Employment by occupation: 31.0% management, 25.6% professional, 7.7% services, 25.5% sales, 0.0% farming, 6.9% construction, 3.3% production (2000).
Income: Per capita income: $35,049 (2000); Median household income: $81,770 (2000); Poverty rate: 4.0% (2000).
Taxes: Total city taxes per capita: $287 (1997); City property taxes per capita: $143 (1997).
Education: High school graduation rate: 94.4% (2000); College graduation rate: 60.1% (2000).

School District(s)

Zionsville Community Schools (PK-12)
2000 Enrollment: 3,475 317-873-2858

Housing: Homeownership rate: 81.3% (2000); Median home value: $246,300 (2000); Median rent: $625 per month (2000); Median age of housing: 19 years (2000).
Newspapers: Zionsville Times Sentinel (1 x week)
Transportation: Commute to work: 91.8% car, 0.2% public transportation, 1.9% walk, 5.6% work from home (2000); Travel time to work: 27.1% less than 15 minutes, 37.1% 15 to 30 minutes, 30.2% 30 to 45 minutes, 4.2% 45 to 60 minutes, 1.4% 60 minutes or more (2000)
Additional Information Contacts
Zionsville Chamber of Commerce 317-873-3836

Brown County

Located in south central Indiana; drained by Salt Creek and its north fork. Covers a land area of 312.30 square miles, a water area of 4.40 square miles, and is located in the Eastern Time Zone. The county government was organized in 1836. County seat is Nashville.
Population: 14,957 (2000); Race: 97.4% White, 0.4% Black, 0.3% Asian, 0.3% American Indian and Alaska Native, 0.6% Hispanic of any race, 1.2% two or more races (2000); Density: 47.9 persons per square mile (2000); Age: 23.3% under 18, 12.9% over 64 (2000).
Religion: Five largest groups: 7.0% Catholic Church, 5.9% Christian Churches and Churches of Christ, 5.1% American Baptist Churches in the USA, 3.8% The United Methodist Church, 1.6% Church of the Nazarene (2000).
Economy: Unemployment rate: 4.7% (11/2002); Total civilian labor force: 8,352 (11/2002); Leading industries: 29.2% accommodation & food services; 19.2% retail trade; 10.2% health care and social assistance (2000); Companies that employ more than 1,000 persons: 0 (2000); Companies that employ more than 100 persons: 2 (2000); Farms: 173 totaling 21,707 acres (1997); Minority business ownership rate: 0.0% (1997); Women business ownership rate: 35.4% (1997); Retail sales per capita: $2,709 (1997). Single-family building permits issued: 124 (2001) / 136 (2000); Multi-family building permits issued: 6 (2001) / 4 (2000).
Income: Per capita income: $20,548 (2000); Median household income: $43,708 (2000); Poverty rate: 8.9% (2000); Bankruptcy rate: 5.55% (2001).
Taxes: Total county taxes per capita: $181 (1997); County property taxes per capita: $63 (1997).
Education: High school graduation rate: 83.6% (2000); College graduation rate: 18.5% (2000).
Housing: Homeownership rate: 85.0% (2000); Median home value: $114,500 (2000); Median rent: $455 per month (2000); Median age of housing: 25 years (2000).
Health: Birth rate: 97.6 per 10,000 population (1998); Age adjusted death rate: 84.4 per 10,000 population (1999); Age adjusted cancer mortality rate: 205.0 deaths per 100,000 population (1999). Number of physicians: 4.7 per 10,000 population (1999); Number of hospital beds: n/a (1999).
Elections: 2000 Presidential election results: 38.3% Gore, 56.8% Bush, 3.1% Nader, 1.0% Buchanan
National and State Parks: Brown County State Park; Middle Fork State Wildlife Refuge; TC Steele State Memorial; Yellowwood State Forest
Additional Information Contacts
Brown County Government Offices....................... 812-988-5485
Nashville Chamber of Commerce 812-988-6647

Brown County Communities

NASHVILLE (town). Covers a land area of 0.950 square miles and a water area of 0.006 square miles. Located at 39.20° N. Lat.; 86.23° W. Long. Elevation is 629 feet.
History: Local tradition in Nashville tells of the Liars' Bench on the courthouse lawn which accommodated six tellers of tall and unlikely tales. When a bigger and better story was told by someone standing, one of the seated liars would be pushed off the end of the bench to make room for the bigger liar.
Population: 825 (2000); Race: 94.8% White, 0.9% Black, 0.0% Asian, 0.9% American Indian and Alaska Native, 2.9% Hispanic of any race, 0.7% two or more races (2000); Density: 868.6 persons per square mile (2000); Age: 13.9% under 18, 31.4% over 64 (2000); Marriage status: 18.2% never married, 46.8% now married, 18.6% widowed, 16.4% divorced (2000); Foreign born: 1.9% (2000); Ancestry (includes multiple ancestries): 17.9% German, 15.9% Irish, 12.5% English, 6.8% Other groups, 5.2% French (except Basque) (2000).
Economy: Employment by occupation: 11.7% management, 23.5% professional, 15.5% services, 34.4% sales, 0.0% farming, 5.2% construction, 9.7% production (2000).
Income: Per capita income: $24,723 (2000); Median household income: $27,330 (2000); Poverty rate: 16.5% (2000).
Taxes: Total city taxes per capita: $270 (1997); City property taxes per capita: $128 (1997).
Education: High school graduation rate: 96.7% (2000); College graduation rate: 30.7% (2000).

School District(s)

County School Corp of Brown Co (PK-12)
2000 Enrollment: 2,408 812-988-6601

Housing: Homeownership rate: 48.7% (2000); Median home value: $146,900 (2000); Median rent: $444 per month (2000); Median age of housing: 37 years (2000).
Newspapers: The Brown County Democrat (1 x week)
Transportation: Commute to work: 86.0% car, 0.0% public transportation, 7.6% walk, 5.0% work from home (2000); Travel time to work: 47.1% less than 15 minutes, 11.7% 15 to 30 minutes, 21.2% 30 to 45 minutes, 6.8% 45 to 60 minutes, 13.2% 60 minutes or more (2000)
Additional Information Contacts
Nashville Chamber of Commerce 812-988-6647

Carroll County

Located in northwest central Indiana; crossed by the Wabash River; drained by the Tippecanoe River. Covers a land area of 372.30 square miles, a water area of 2.80 square miles, and is located in the Eastern Time Zone. The county government was organized in 1828. County seat is Delphi.

Weather Station: Delphi 3 S — Elevation: 669 feet

	Jan	Feb	Mar	Apr	May	Jun	Jul	Aug	Sep	Oct	Nov	Dec
High	33	38	50	63	74	83	86	83	78	66	51	39
Low	17	21	31	40	50	60	63	61	54	43	34	24
Precip	1.9	1.9	3.0	3.6	3.9	3.9	4.2	4.1	3.0	2.7	3.1	2.7
Snow	6.2	4.6	2.5	0.8	tr	0.0	0.0	0.0	0.0	0.2	0.9	5.3

High and Low temperatures in degrees Fahrenheit; Precipitation and Snow in inches

Population: 20,165 (2000); Race: 97.8% White, 0.2% Black, 0.1% Asian, 0.2% American Indian and Alaska Native, 3.4% Hispanic of any race, 0.3% two or more races (2000); Density: 54.2 persons per square mile (2000); Age: 26.3% under 18, 14.0% over 64 (2000).
Religion: Five largest groups: 7.4% The United Methodist Church, 4.8% Presbyterian Church (U.S.A.), 4.5% Christian Churches and Churches of Christ, 4.0% Catholic Church, 3.5% Assemblies of God (2000).
Economy: Unemployment rate: 4.5% (11/2002); Total civilian labor force: 11,853 (11/2002); Leading industries: 46.3% manufacturing; 12.2% retail trade; 9.5% health care and social assistance (2000); Companies that employ more than 1,000 persons: 1 (2000); Companies that employ more than 100 persons: 4 (2000); Farms: 563 totaling 218,170 acres (1997); Minority business ownership rate: 0.0% (1997); Women business ownership rate: 28.4% (1997); Retail sales per capita: $4,567 (1997). Single-family building permits issued: 90 (2001) / 92 (2000); Multi-family building permits issued: 10 (2001) / 0 (2000).
Income: Per capita income: $19,436 (2000); Median household income: $42,677 (2000); Poverty rate: 6.8% (2000); Bankruptcy rate: 5.08% (2001).
Taxes: Total county taxes per capita: $243 (2000); County property taxes per capita: $133 (2000).
Education: High school graduation rate: 83.2% (2000); College graduation rate: 12.9% (2000).
Housing: Homeownership rate: 79.7% (2000); Median home value: $87,200 (2000); Median rent: $350 per month (2000); Median age of housing: 44 years (2000).
Health: Birth rate: 130.9 per 10,000 population (1998); Age adjusted death rate: 89.1 per 10,000 population (1999); Age adjusted cancer mortality rate: 177.4 deaths per 100,000 population (1999). Air Quality Index: 61% good, 39% moderate, 0% unhealthy (percent of days in 2000). Number of physicians: 3.5 per 10,000 population (1999); Number of hospital beds: n/a (1999).
Elections: 2000 Presidential election results: 35.9% Gore, 61.7% Bush, 1.1% Nader, 0.8% Buchanan
Additional Information Contacts
Carroll County Government Offices 317-564-3172
Carroll County Board of Realtors 317-564-6451

Carroll County Communities

BRINGHURST (unincorporated postal area, zip code 46913). Covers a land area of 32.909 square miles and a water area of 0 square miles. Located at 40.50° N. Lat.; 86.50° W. Long. Elevation is 721 feet.
Population: 1,379 (2000); Race: 98.8% White, 0.7% Black, 0.0% Asian, 0.0% American Indian and Alaska Native, 1.1% Hispanic of any race, 0.5% two or more races (2000); Density: 41.9 persons per square mile (2000); Age: 29.1% under 18, 10.1% over 64 (2000); Marriage status: 19.1% never married, 74.7% now married, 2.6% widowed, 3.6% divorced (2000); Foreign born: 0.4% (2000); Ancestry (includes multiple ancestries): 18.8% United States or American, 15.6% German, 13.1% English, 12.5% Other groups, 6.8% Irish (2000).

Economy: Employment by occupation: 6.8% management, 18.8% professional, 12.4% services, 17.9% sales, 0.0% farming, 14.0% construction, 30.0% production (2000).
Income: Per capita income: $19,559 (2000); Median household income: $57,574 (2000); Poverty rate: 5.3% (2000).
Education: High school graduation rate: 84.6% (2000); College graduation rate: 16.5% (2000).
Housing: Homeownership rate: 94.0% (2000); Median home value: $99,500 (2000); Median rent: $350 per month (2000); Median age of housing: 39 years (2000).
Transportation: Commute to work: 94.1% car, 0.0% public transportation, 0.7% walk, 3.3% work from home (2000); Travel time to work: 22.3% less than 15 minutes, 33.0% 15 to 30 minutes, 22.8% 30 to 45 minutes, 14.2% 45 to 60 minutes, 7.7% 60 minutes or more (2000)

BURLINGTON (town). Covers a land area of 0.541 square miles and a water area of 0 square miles. Located at 40.48° N. Lat.; 86.39° W. Long. Elevation is 780 feet.
History: Burlington was founded in 1832 as a stagecoach and tavern stop on the Michigan Road. It was named for Wyandotte Chief Burlington.
Population: 444 (2000); Race: 99.1% White, 0.0% Black, 0.0% Asian, 0.0% American Indian and Alaska Native, 0.9% Hispanic of any race, 0.5% two or more races (2000); Density: 820.0 persons per square mile (2000); Age: 17.1% under 18, 20.5% over 64 (2000); Marriage status: 23.4% never married, 50.5% now married, 12.6% widowed, 13.4% divorced (2000); Foreign born: 0.0% (2000); Ancestry (includes multiple ancestries): 18.9% German, 12.8% English, 10.3% Irish, 9.1% United States or American, 7.5% Other groups (2000).
Economy: Employment by occupation: 5.8% management, 11.6% professional, 21.0% services, 13.4% sales, 0.0% farming, 17.4% construction, 30.8% production (2000).
Income: Per capita income: $22,482 (2000); Median household income: $38,472 (2000); Poverty rate: 5.5% (2000).
Taxes: Total city taxes per capita: $132 (1997); City property taxes per capita: $122 (1997).
Education: High school graduation rate: 89.8% (2000); College graduation rate: 15.3% (2000).
Housing: Homeownership rate: 74.9% (2000); Median home value: $86,500 (2000); Median rent: $333 per month (2000); Median age of housing: 43 years (2000).
Transportation: Commute to work: 89.9% car, 0.0% public transportation, 8.8% walk, 0.0% work from home (2000); Travel time to work: 30.4% less than 15 minutes, 24.4% 15 to 30 minutes, 42.9% 30 to 45 minutes, 1.4% 45 to 60 minutes, 0.9% 60 minutes or more (2000)

CAMDEN (town). Covers a land area of 0.260 square miles and a water area of <.001 square miles. Located at 40.60° N. Lat.; 86.53° W. Long. Elevation is 670 feet.
Population: 582 (2000); Race: 97.8% White, 0.8% Black, 0.0% Asian, 0.5% American Indian and Alaska Native, 0.5% Hispanic of any race, 0.3% two or more races (2000); Density: 2,240.7 persons per square mile (2000); Age: 27.6% under 18, 11.1% over 64 (2000); Marriage status: 18.0% never married, 67.1% now married, 6.6% widowed, 8.3% divorced (2000); Foreign born: 0.0% (2000); Ancestry (includes multiple ancestries): 22.4% United States or American, 18.5% German, 11.3% Irish, 9.4% English, 6.9% Other groups (2000).
Economy: In agricultural area. Employment by occupation: 5.0% management, 7.1% professional, 21.1% services, 22.3% sales, 0.9% farming, 13.0% construction, 30.7% production (2000).
Income: Per capita income: $19,476 (2000); Median household income: $44,250 (2000); Poverty rate: 4.2% (2000).
Taxes: Total city taxes per capita: $113 (1997); City property taxes per capita: $103 (1997).
Education: High school graduation rate: 85.1% (2000); College graduation rate: 13.0% (2000).
Housing: Homeownership rate: 77.5% (2000); Median home value: $70,500 (2000); Median rent: $318 per month (2000); Median age of housing: 60+ years (2000).
Transportation: Commute to work: 92.7% car, 0.6% public transportation, 3.5% walk, 2.9% work from home (2000); Travel time to work: 32.6% less than 15 minutes, 29.9% 15 to 30 minutes, 18.8% 30 to 45 minutes, 16.1% 45 to 60 minutes, 2.6% 60 minutes or more (2000)

CUTLER (unincorporated postal area, zip code 46920). Covers a land area of 32.669 square miles and a water area of 0 square miles. Located at 40.47° N. Lat.; 86.47° W. Long. Elevation is 740 feet.
Population: 1,487 (2000); Race: 99.2% White, 0.0% Black, 0.0% Asian, 0.0% American Indian and Alaska Native, 2.2% Hispanic of any race, 0.7% two or more races (2000); Density: 45.5 persons per square mile (2000); Age: 29.1% under 18, 13.4% over 64 (2000); Marriage status: 18.3% never married, 66.5% now married, 6.0% widowed, 9.2% divorced (2000); Foreign born: 0.6% (2000); Ancestry (includes multiple ancestries): 19.8% German, 17.2% United States or American, 11.9% Other groups, 11.0% Irish, 7.9% English (2000).
Economy: Employment by occupation: 8.5% management, 11.9% professional, 13.2% services, 17.3% sales, 0.9% farming, 13.5% construction, 34.7% production (2000).
Income: Per capita income: $23,432 (2000); Median household income: $45,833 (2000); Poverty rate: 3.2% (2000).
Education: High school graduation rate: 93.7% (2000); College graduation rate: 12.9% (2000).
Housing: Homeownership rate: 82.1% (2000); Median home value: $89,000 (2000); Median rent: $353 per month (2000); Median age of housing: 42 years (2000).
Transportation: Commute to work: 93.1% car, 0.0% public transportation, 3.3% walk, 3.2% work from home (2000); Travel time to work: 24.4% less than 15 minutes, 28.2% 15 to 30 minutes, 36.9% 30 to 45 minutes, 9.2% 45 to 60 minutes, 1.4% 60 minutes or more (2000)

DELPHI (city). Covers a land area of 2.557 square miles and a water area of 0 square miles. Located at 40.58° N. Lat.; 86.67° W. Long. Elevation is 580 feet.
History: Delphi was named by Samuel Milroy (1780-1845), a member of the State Constitutional Convention of 1816, who sold the first town lots in 1828. Poet James Whitcomb Riley was a resident here.
Population: 3,015 (2000); Race: 92.3% White, 0.1% Black, 0.0% Asian, 0.0% American Indian and Alaska Native, 13.6% Hispanic of any race, 0.4% two or more races (2000); Density: 1,179.3 persons per square mile (2000); Age: 26.1% under 18, 19.0% over 64 (2000); Marriage status: 18.9% never married, 57.0% now married, 10.7% widowed, 13.4% divorced (2000); Foreign born: 10.8% (2000); Ancestry (includes multiple ancestries): 22.6% United States or American, 19.3% German, 14.4% Other groups, 14.1% Irish, 8.6% English (2000).
Economy: Employment by occupation: 6.8% management, 13.8% professional, 18.3% services, 20.7% sales, 0.7% farming, 8.3% construction, 31.4% production (2000).
Income: Per capita income: $16,703 (2000); Median household income: $34,388 (2000); Poverty rate: 13.4% (2000).
Taxes: Total city taxes per capita: $246 (1997); City property taxes per capita: $243 (1997).
Education: High school graduation rate: 81.2% (2000); College graduation rate: 12.2% (2000).

School District(s)

Delphi Community School Corp (KG-12)
2000 Enrollment: 1,750 765-564-2100

Housing: Homeownership rate: 62.8% (2000); Median home value: $79,500 (2000); Median rent: $346 per month (2000); Median age of housing: 60+ years (2000).
Safety: Violent crime rate: 6.6 per 10,000 population; Property crime rate: 108.8 per 10,000 population (2001).
Transportation: Commute to work: 91.7% car, 0.4% public transportation, 2.7% walk, 3.8% work from home (2000); Travel time to work: 50.5% less than 15 minutes, 19.3% 15 to 30 minutes, 21.7% 30 to 45 minutes, 4.5% 45 to 60 minutes, 4.0% 60 minutes or more (2000)
Additional Information Contacts
Carroll County Board of Realtors 317-564-6451

FLORA (town). Covers a land area of 1.032 square miles and a water area of 0 square miles. Located at 40.54° N. Lat.; 86.52° W. Long. Elevation is 710 feet.
History: Laid out 1872, incorporated 1898.
Population: 2,227 (2000); Race: 96.6% White, 0.5% Black, 0.0% Asian, 0.0% American Indian and Alaska Native, 5.0% Hispanic of any race, 0.0% two or more races (2000); Density: 2,157.4 persons per square mile (2000); Age: 23.9% under 18, 21.6% over 64 (2000); Marriage status: 19.0% never married, 58.9% now married, 12.2% widowed, 9.9% divorced (2000); Foreign born: 1.4% (2000); Ancestry (includes multiple ancestries): 22.2% German, 18.5% United States or American, 12.0% Irish, 11.6% Other groups, 7.9% English (2000).
Economy: In livestock and grain area; plumbing products, cement products; timber. Single-family building permits issued: 4 (2001) / 2 (2000); Multi-family building permits issued: 10 (2001) / 0 (2000); Employment by

occupation: 8.3% management, 14.0% professional, 15.3% services, 20.8% sales, 0.9% farming, 11.2% construction, 29.3% production (2000).
Income: Per capita income: $18,863 (2000); Median household income: $37,400 (2000); Poverty rate: 6.3% (2000).
Taxes: Total city taxes per capita: $191 (1997); City property taxes per capita: $172 (1997).
Education: High school graduation rate: 77.7% (2000); College graduation rate: 11.9% (2000).

School District(s)

Carroll Consolidated Sch Corp (KG-12)
2000 Enrollment: 1,166 219-967-4113
Housing: Homeownership rate: 74.3% (2000); Median home value: $78,100 (2000); Median rent: $328 per month (2000); Median age of housing: 52 years (2000).
Newspapers: Carroll County Comet (1 x week)
Transportation: Commute to work: 92.7% car, 0.3% public transportation, 3.9% walk, 2.3% work from home (2000); Travel time to work: 44.9% less than 15 minutes, 15.1% 15 to 30 minutes, 27.9% 30 to 45 minutes, 9.1% 45 to 60 minutes, 3.0% 60 minutes or more (2000)

YEOMAN (town). Covers a land area of 0.122 square miles and a water area of 0 square miles. Located at 40.66° N. Lat.; 86.72° W. Long. Elevation is 663 feet.
History: Laid out 1880.
Population: 96 (2000); Race: 100.0% White, 0.0% Black, 0.0% Asian, 0.0% American Indian and Alaska Native, 0.0% Hispanic of any race, 0.0% two or more races (2000); Density: 787.3 persons per square mile (2000); Age: 17.0% under 18, 1.1% over 64 (2000); Marriage status: 30.0% never married, 63.7% now married, 0.0% widowed, 6.3% divorced (2000); Foreign born: 3.2% (2000); Ancestry (includes multiple ancestries): 20.2% German, 14.9% United States or American, 12.8% Dutch, 9.6% Irish, 2.1% Other groups (2000).
Economy: In agricultural area. Employment by occupation: 27.4% management, 0.0% professional, 14.5% services, 4.8% sales, 0.0% farming, 11.3% construction, 41.9% production (2000).
Income: Per capita income: $20,315 (2000); Median household income: $53,214 (2000); Poverty rate: 2.1% (2000).
Taxes: Total city taxes per capita: $8 (1997); City property taxes per capita: $8 (1997).
Education: High school graduation rate: 71.2% (2000); College graduation rate: 5.1% (2000).
Housing: Homeownership rate: 87.2% (2000); Median home value: $81,900 (2000); Median rent: $242 per month (2000); Median age of housing: 60+ years (2000).
Transportation: Commute to work: 100.0% car, 0.0% public transportation, 0.0% walk, 0.0% work from home (2000); Travel time to work: 25.8% less than 15 minutes, 45.2% 15 to 30 minutes, 16.1% 30 to 45 minutes, 9.7% 45 to 60 minutes, 3.2% 60 minutes or more (2000)

Cass County

Located in north central Indiana; intersected by the Wabash River; drained by the Eel River and Deer Creek. Covers a land area of 412.90 square miles, a water area of 2.10 square miles, and is located in the Eastern Time Zone. The county government was organized in 1828. County seat is Logansport.
Population: 40,930 (2000); Race: 93.6% White, 1.0% Black, 0.6% Asian, 0.4% American Indian and Alaska Native, 6.9% Hispanic of any race, 1.3% two or more races (2000); Density: 99.1 persons per square mile (2000); Age: 25.8% under 18, 14.4% over 64 (2000).
Religion: Five largest groups: 10.1% Catholic Church, 7.2% The United Methodist Church, 3.4% American Baptist Churches in the USA, 2.4% Christian Churches and Churches of Christ, 2.0% Presbyterian Church (U.S.A.) (2000).
Economy: Unemployment rate: 6.0% (11/2002); Total civilian labor force: 19,530 (11/2002); Leading industries: 42.6% manufacturing; 16.4% health care and social assistance; 12.6% retail trade (2000); Companies that employ more than 1,000 persons: 1 (2000); Companies that employ more than 100 persons: 24 (2000); Farms: 700 totaling 205,380 acres (1997); Minority business ownership rate: 0.0% (1997); Women business ownership rate: 25.1% (1997); Retail sales per capita: $8,755 (1997). Single-family building permits issued: 82 (2001) / 87 (2000); Multi-family building permits issued: 0 (2001) / 0 (2000).
Income: Per capita income: $18,892 (2000); Median household income: $39,193 (2000); Poverty rate: 7.6% (2000); Bankruptcy rate: 5.69% (2001).
Taxes: Total county taxes per capita: $298 (2000); County property taxes per capita: $208 (2000).
Education: High school graduation rate: 81.8% (2000); College graduation rate: 12.0% (2000).
Housing: Homeownership rate: 73.6% (2000); Median home value: $71,500 (2000); Median rent: $350 per month (2000); Median age of housing: 48 years (2000).
Health: Birth rate: 149.3 per 10,000 population (1998); Age adjusted death rate: 93.5 per 10,000 population (1999); Age adjusted cancer mortality rate: 212.8 deaths per 100,000 population (1999). Number of physicians: 10.5 per 10,000 population (1999); Number of hospital beds: 122.2 per 10,000 population (1999).
Elections: 2000 Presidential election results: 35.8% Gore, 61.6% Bush, 0.0% Nader, 1.1% Buchanan
Additional Information Contacts
Cass County Government Offices 219-753-7720
Cass County Board of Realtors 219-722-3648
Logansport Chamber of Commerce 219-753-6388

Cass County Communities

GALVESTON (town). Covers a land area of 0.567 square miles and a water area of 0 square miles. Located at 40.57° N. Lat.; 86.19° W. Long. Elevation is 820 feet.
Population: 1,532 (2000); Race: 96.2% White, 0.0% Black, 0.8% Asian, 0.6% American Indian and Alaska Native, 2.2% Hispanic of any race, 2.2% two or more races (2000); Density: 2,702.9 persons per square mile (2000); Age: 23.5% under 18, 11.6% over 64 (2000); Marriage status: 20.3% never married, 63.4% now married, 5.9% widowed, 10.4% divorced (2000); Foreign born: 0.8% (2000); Ancestry (includes multiple ancestries): 17.9% German, 16.3% United States or American, 12.7% Other groups, 10.3% English, 7.0% Irish (2000).
Economy: In agricultural area. Single-family building permits issued: 0 (2001) / 0 (2000); Multi-family building permits issued: 0 (2001) / 0 (2000); Employment by occupation: 9.5% management, 14.6% professional, 12.8% services, 24.5% sales, 0.4% farming, 14.1% construction, 24.3% production (2000).
Income: Per capita income: $22,880 (2000); Median household income: $45,450 (2000); Poverty rate: 4.4% (2000).
Taxes: Total city taxes per capita: $107 (1997); City property taxes per capita: $102 (1997).
Education: High school graduation rate: 85.5% (2000); College graduation rate: 13.3% (2000).
Housing: Homeownership rate: 76.9% (2000); Median home value: $80,600 (2000); Median rent: $438 per month (2000); Median age of housing: 39 years (2000).
Transportation: Commute to work: 95.0% car, 0.0% public transportation, 4.4% walk, 0.3% work from home (2000); Travel time to work: 23.4% less than 15 minutes, 60.3% 15 to 30 minutes, 9.8% 30 to 45 minutes, 3.1% 45 to 60 minutes, 3.3% 60 minutes or more (2000)

LOGANSPORT (city). Covers a land area of 8.260 square miles and a water area of 0.165 square miles. Located at 40.75° N. Lat.; 86.36° W. Long. Elevation is 602 feet.
History: Logansport began as a trading post situated at the junction of the Wabash and Eel Rivers. The first permanent settler was Alexander Chamberlain, who built the Log Pioneer Inn in 1828.
Population: 19,684 (2000); Race: 89.9% White, 1.9% Black, 0.7% Asian, 0.4% American Indian and Alaska Native, 12.4% Hispanic of any race, 1.5% two or more races (2000); Density: 2,383.0 persons per square mile (2000); Age: 25.4% under 18, 14.9% over 64 (2000); Marriage status: 24.9% never married, 51.3% now married, 8.8% widowed, 14.9% divorced (2000); Foreign born: 7.1% (2000); Ancestry (includes multiple ancestries): 20.8% German, 14.5% Other groups, 12.8% United States or American, 8.4% Irish, 5.2% English (2000).
Vital Statistics: Birth rate: 193.1 per 10,000 population (1998)
Economy: Employment by occupation: 5.1% management, 11.5% professional, 18.1% services, 22.0% sales, 0.5% farming, 9.8% construction, 33.0% production (2000).
Income: Per capita income: $17,085 (2000); Median household income: $33,483 (2000); Poverty rate: 10.1% (2000).
Taxes: Total city taxes per capita: $280 (2000); City property taxes per capita: $275 (2000).
Education: High school graduation rate: 75.3% (2000); College graduation rate: 9.9% (2000).

School District(s)

Logansport Community Sch Corp (PK-12)
2000 Enrollment: 4,263 219-722-2911

Housing: Homeownership rate: 61.4% (2000); Median home value: $59,400 (2000); Median rent: $352 per month (2000); Median age of housing: 59 years (2000).

Hospitals: Logansport State Hospital (396 beds); Memorial Hospital (104 beds)

Safety: Violent crime rate: 14.1 per 10,000 population; Property crime rate: 391.0 per 10,000 population (2001).

Newspapers: Pharos-Tribune (7 x week)

Transportation: Commute to work: 92.9% car, 1.9% public transportation, 2.5% walk, 1.4% work from home (2000); Travel time to work: 61.6% less than 15 minutes, 20.0% 15 to 30 minutes, 7.8% 30 to 45 minutes, 5.4% 45 to 60 minutes, 5.2% 60 minutes or more (2000)

Airports: Logansport Municipal

Additional Information Contacts

Cass County Board of Realtors 219-722-3648
Logansport Chamber of Commerce 219-753-6388

LUCERNE (unincorporated postal area, zip code 46950). Covers a land area of 29.291 square miles and a water area of 0 square miles. Located at 40.88° N. Lat.; 86.38° W. Long. Elevation is 800 feet.

Population: 665 (2000); Race: 100.0% White, 0.0% Black, 0.0% Asian, 0.0% American Indian and Alaska Native, 0.0% Hispanic of any race, 0.0% two or more races (2000); Density: 22.7 persons per square mile (2000); Age: 20.1% under 18, 22.6% over 64 (2000); Marriage status: 14.0% never married, 76.6% now married, 7.8% widowed, 1.6% divorced (2000); Foreign born: 0.0% (2000); Ancestry (includes multiple ancestries): 19.4% German, 14.0% English, 6.4% United States or American, 5.1% Other groups, 4.1% Irish (2000).

Economy: In agricultural area: corn, soybeans, hogs. Manufacturing: food grinding, fertilizer blending. Employment by occupation: 16.8% management, 15.2% professional, 10.9% services, 24.8% sales, 5.6% farming, 18.7% construction, 8.0% production (2000).

Income: Per capita income: $21,232 (2000); Median household income: $39,722 (2000); Poverty rate: 3.6% (2000).

Education: High school graduation rate: 91.5% (2000); College graduation rate: 16.1% (2000).

Housing: Homeownership rate: 79.0% (2000); Median home value: $69,200 (2000); Median rent: $272 per month (2000); Median age of housing: 52 years (2000).

Transportation: Commute to work: 82.9% car, 4.1% public transportation, 1.9% walk, 7.6% work from home (2000); Travel time to work: 12.9% less than 15 minutes, 55.4% 15 to 30 minutes, 16.1% 30 to 45 minutes, 0.0% 45 to 60 minutes, 15.5% 60 minutes or more (2000)

ONWARD (town). Covers a land area of 0.087 square miles and a water area of 0 square miles. Located at 40.69° N. Lat.; 86.19° W. Long. Elevation is 765 feet.

Population: 81 (2000); Race: 100.0% White, 0.0% Black, 0.0% Asian, 0.0% American Indian and Alaska Native, 0.0% Hispanic of any race, 0.0% two or more races (2000); Density: 935.6 persons per square mile (2000); Age: 19.7% under 18, 21.3% over 64 (2000); Marriage status: 8.2% never married, 77.6% now married, 14.3% widowed, 0.0% divorced (2000); Foreign born: 0.0% (2000); Ancestry (includes multiple ancestries): 27.9% Irish, 11.5% Other groups, 9.8% Scottish, 6.6% United States or American, 6.6% French (except Basque) (2000).

Economy: In agricultural area. Employment by occupation: 0.0% management, 0.0% professional, 5.9% services, 29.4% sales, 0.0% farming, 26.5% construction, 38.2% production (2000).

Income: Per capita income: $15,993 (2000); Median household income: $40,625 (2000); Poverty rate: 6.6% (2000).

Taxes: Total city taxes per capita: $136 (1997); City property taxes per capita: $136 (1997).

Education: High school graduation rate: 71.1% (2000); College graduation rate: 0.0% (2000).

Housing: Homeownership rate: 56.0% (2000); Median home value: $55,000 (2000); Median rent: $288 per month (2000); Median age of housing: 31 years (2000).

Transportation: Commute to work: 88.2% car, 0.0% public transportation, 0.0% walk, 11.8% work from home (2000); Travel time to work: 13.3% less than 15 minutes, 73.3% 15 to 30 minutes, 0.0% 30 to 45 minutes, 0.0% 45 to 60 minutes, 13.3% 60 minutes or more (2000)

ROYAL CENTER (town). Covers a land area of 0.501 square miles and a water area of 0 square miles. Located at 40.86° N. Lat.; 86.50° W. Long. Elevation is 740 feet.

History: Laid out 1846.

Population: 832 (2000); Race: 99.2% White, 0.2% Black, 0.0% Asian, 0.0% American Indian and Alaska Native, 0.9% Hispanic of any race, 0.0% two or more races (2000); Density: 1,660.5 persons per square mile (2000); Age: 30.5% under 18, 18.0% over 64 (2000); Marriage status: 20.0% never married, 63.2% now married, 10.8% widowed, 6.0% divorced (2000); Foreign born: 0.6% (2000); Ancestry (includes multiple ancestries): 26.3% German, 14.5% United States or American, 12.7% Irish, 8.5% Other groups, 8.4% English (2000).

Economy: Agricultural area. Lumber. Manufacturing: machinery, wood products. Employment by occupation: 8.2% management, 16.6% professional, 16.1% services, 21.7% sales, 0.0% farming, 6.1% construction, 31.3% production (2000).

Income: Per capita income: $17,440 (2000); Median household income: $40,625 (2000); Poverty rate: 4.7% (2000).

Taxes: Total city taxes per capita: $119 (1997); City property taxes per capita: $106 (1997).

Education: High school graduation rate: 86.0% (2000); College graduation rate: 9.3% (2000).

School District(s)

Pioneer Regional School Corp (KG-12)
2000 Enrollment: 991 219-643-2605

Housing: Homeownership rate: 85.3% (2000); Median home value: $55,900 (2000); Median rent: $328 per month (2000); Median age of housing: 56 years (2000).

Newspapers: Royal Center Record (1 x week)

Transportation: Commute to work: 93.3% car, 0.0% public transportation, 2.9% walk, 2.9% work from home (2000); Travel time to work: 29.2% less than 15 minutes, 51.5% 15 to 30 minutes, 10.4% 30 to 45 minutes, 1.7% 45 to 60 minutes, 7.2% 60 minutes or more (2000)

TWELVE MILE (unincorporated postal area, zip code 46988). Covers a land area of 26.364 square miles and a water area of 0.006 square miles. Located at 40.87° N. Lat.; 86.23° W. Long. Elevation is 794 feet.

Population: 1,104 (2000); Race: 96.3% White, 1.5% Black, 0.0% Asian, 1.5% American Indian and Alaska Native, 0.0% Hispanic of any race, 0.8% two or more races (2000); Density: 41.9 persons per square mile (2000); Age: 22.3% under 18, 12.1% over 64 (2000); Marriage status: 20.9% never married, 55.8% now married, 6.9% widowed, 16.4% divorced (2000); Foreign born: 0.0% (2000); Ancestry (includes multiple ancestries): 17.0% German, 12.2% Other groups, 11.6% Irish, 8.0% United States or American, 4.8% English (2000).

Economy: Employment by occupation: 4.3% management, 17.9% professional, 8.5% services, 22.4% sales, 0.0% farming, 15.5% construction, 31.4% production (2000).

Income: Per capita income: $15,559 (2000); Median household income: $36,360 (2000); Poverty rate: 7.0% (2000).

Education: High school graduation rate: 81.7% (2000); College graduation rate: 9.6% (2000).

Housing: Homeownership rate: 78.4% (2000); Median home value: $69,100 (2000); Median rent: $198 per month (2000); Median age of housing: 34 years (2000).

Transportation: Commute to work: 90.8% car, 0.0% public transportation, 0.0% walk, 9.2% work from home (2000); Travel time to work: 14.8% less than 15 minutes, 47.7% 15 to 30 minutes, 18.0% 30 to 45 minutes, 5.7% 45 to 60 minutes, 13.8% 60 minutes or more (2000)

WALTON (town). Covers a land area of 0.431 square miles and a water area of 0 square miles. Located at 40.66° N. Lat.; 86.24° W. Long. Elevation is 765 feet.

History: Laid out 1852.

Population: 1,069 (2000); Race: 86.1% White, 0.4% Black, 2.3% Asian, 0.5% American Indian and Alaska Native, 15.1% Hispanic of any race, 2.6% two or more races (2000); Density: 2,477.8 persons per square mile (2000); Age: 25.5% under 18, 12.4% over 64 (2000); Marriage status: 20.8% never married, 59.9% now married, 9.0% widowed, 10.3% divorced (2000); Foreign born: 12.8% (2000); Ancestry (includes multiple ancestries): 17.9% German, 17.9% Other groups, 11.6% United States or American, 10.7% English, 9.6% Irish (2000).

Economy: Agricultural area. Manufacturing: houseplant and lawn fertilizers, wire springs; grain mixing. Single-family building permits issued: 3 (2001) / 1 (2000); Multi-family building permits issued: 0 (2001) / 0 (2000);

Employment by occupation: 7.2% management, 16.4% professional, 13.2% services, 22.6% sales, 0.6% farming, 5.8% construction, 34.1% production (2000).
Income: Per capita income: $19,087 (2000); Median household income: $41,429 (2000); Poverty rate: 6.0% (2000).
Taxes: Total city taxes per capita: $95 (1997); City property taxes per capita: $82 (1997).
Education: High school graduation rate: 75.3% (2000); College graduation rate: 10.5% (2000).

School District(s)

Southeastern School Corp (KG-12)
2000 Enrollment: 1,695 219-626-2525
Housing: Homeownership rate: 71.9% (2000); Median home value: $68,000 (2000); Median rent: $303 per month (2000); Median age of housing: 46 years (2000).
Transportation: Commute to work: 96.2% car, 0.4% public transportation, 1.6% walk, 0.4% work from home (2000); Travel time to work: 25.3% less than 15 minutes, 50.9% 15 to 30 minutes, 16.0% 30 to 45 minutes, 2.2% 45 to 60 minutes, 5.7% 60 minutes or more (2000)

Clark County

Located in southeastern Indiana; bounded on the southeast by the Ohio River and the Kentucky border; drained by Silver Creek. Covers a land area of 375.00 square miles, a water area of 1.20 square miles, and is located in the Eastern Time Zone. The county government was organized in 1801. County seat is Jeffersonville.

Clark County is part of the Louisville, KY-IN MSA. The entire metro area includes: Clark County, IN; Floyd County, IN; Harrison County, IN; Scott County, IN; Bullitt County, KY; Jefferson County, KY; Oldham County, KY

Population: 96,472 (2000); Race: 90.4% White, 6.3% Black, 0.4% Asian, 0.3% American Indian and Alaska Native, 1.9% Hispanic of any race, 1.7% two or more races (2000); Density: 257.2 persons per square mile (2000); Age: 24.2% under 18, 12.4% over 64 (2000).
Religion: Five largest groups: 12.7% Catholic Church, 8.3% Southern Baptist Convention, 4.1% The United Methodist Church, 2.7% Christian Churches and Churches of Christ, 2.1% Christian Church (Disciples of Christ) (2000).
Economy: Unemployment rate: 4.5% (11/2002); Total civilian labor force: 55,022 (11/2002); Leading industries: 18.5% retail trade; 17.4% manufacturing; 12.0% transportation & warehousing (2000); Companies that employ more than 1,000 persons: 3 (2000); Companies that employ more than 100 persons: 70 (2000); Farms: 647 totaling 108,773 acres (1997); Minority business ownership rate: 4.9% (1997); Women business ownership rate: 25.9% (1997); Retail sales per capita: $13,530 (1997). Single-family building permits issued: 871 (2001) / 731 (2000); Multi-family building permits issued: 196 (2001) / 62 (2000).
Income: Per capita income: $19,936 (2000); Median household income: $40,111 (2000); Poverty rate: 8.1% (2000); Bankruptcy rate: 9.49% (2001).
Taxes: Total county taxes per capita: $143 (2000); County property taxes per capita: $131 (2000).
Education: High school graduation rate: 79.9% (2000); College graduation rate: 14.3% (2000).
Housing: Homeownership rate: 70.0% (2000); Median home value: $89,900 (2000); Median rent: $423 per month (2000); Median age of housing: 29 years (2000).
Health: Birth rate: 131.9 per 10,000 population (1998); Age adjusted death rate: 99.8 per 10,000 population (1999); Age adjusted cancer mortality rate: 230.2 deaths per 100,000 population (1999). Air Quality Index: 59% good, 41% moderate, 0% unhealthy (percent of days in 2000). Number of physicians: 14.1 per 10,000 population (1999); Number of hospital beds: 33.0 per 10,000 population (1999).
Elections: 2000 Presidential election results: 46.5% Gore, 52.0% Bush, 0.6% Nader, 0.6% Buchanan
National and State Parks: Deam Lake State Recreation Area; Falls of the Ohio State Park
Additional Information Contacts
Southern Indiana Realtors Association 812-941-7472

Clark County Communities

BORDEN (town). Aka New Providence. Covers a land area of 1.111 square miles and a water area of 0 square miles. Located at 38.47° N. Lat.; 85.94° W. Long. Elevation is 560 feet.
Population: 818 (2000); Race: 99.5% White, 0.0% Black, 0.0% Asian, 0.0% American Indian and Alaska Native, 1.3% Hispanic of any race, 0.3% two or more races (2000); Density: 736.4 persons per square mile (2000); Age: 27.2% under 18, 11.0% over 64 (2000); Marriage status: 20.6% never married, 63.8% now married, 4.3% widowed, 11.2% divorced (2000); Foreign born: 0.4% (2000); Ancestry (includes multiple ancestries): 24.9% German, 18.1% United States or American, 13.7% Irish, 11.3% English, 7.6% Other groups (2000).
Economy: Employment by occupation: 7.7% management, 10.5% professional, 14.3% services, 27.0% sales, 0.0% farming, 11.8% construction, 28.7% production (2000).
Income: Per capita income: $17,417 (2000); Median household income: $40,962 (2000); Poverty rate: 11.0% (2000).
Education: High school graduation rate: 80.7% (2000); College graduation rate: 9.9% (2000).
Housing: Homeownership rate: 76.7% (2000); Median home value: $81,200 (2000); Median rent: $363 per month (2000); Median age of housing: 32 years (2000).
Transportation: Commute to work: 95.7% car, 0.5% public transportation, 3.4% walk, 0.0% work from home (2000); Travel time to work: 14.6% less than 15 minutes, 33.8% 15 to 30 minutes, 41.2% 30 to 45 minutes, 4.7% 45 to 60 minutes, 5.6% 60 minutes or more (2000)

CHARLESTOWN (city). Covers a land area of 2.332 square miles and a water area of 0 square miles. Located at 38.45° N. Lat.; 85.66° W. Long. Elevation is 590 feet.
History: Charleston was platted in 1808, and served as the seat of Clark County from 1811 to 1878. In 1940 the E.I. du Pont de Nemours Company built a plant here, followed by the Goodyear Tire and Rubber Company's plant.
Population: 5,993 (2000); Race: 93.5% White, 1.1% Black, 0.2% Asian, 0.8% American Indian and Alaska Native, 4.9% Hispanic of any race, 2.0% two or more races (2000); Density: 2,570.0 persons per square mile (2000); Age: 28.4% under 18, 10.3% over 64 (2000); Marriage status: 23.0% never married, 52.3% now married, 7.9% widowed, 16.8% divorced (2000); Foreign born: 2.7% (2000); Ancestry (includes multiple ancestries): 24.1% United States or American, 13.4% Other groups, 11.4% Irish, 11.3% German, 7.2% English (2000).
Economy: Single-family building permits issued: 14 (2001) / 14 (2000); Multi-family building permits issued: 6 (2001) / 9 (2000); Employment by occupation: 8.8% management, 8.6% professional, 20.6% services, 23.8% sales, 0.0% farming, 11.0% construction, 27.2% production (2000).
Income: Per capita income: $13,892 (2000); Median household income: $28,238 (2000); Poverty rate: 19.2% (2000).
Taxes: Total city taxes per capita: $83 (1997); City property taxes per capita: $80 (1997).
Education: High school graduation rate: 69.6% (2000); College graduation rate: 6.0% (2000).
Housing: Homeownership rate: 57.6% (2000); Median home value: $70,900 (2000); Median rent: $348 per month (2000); Median age of housing: 41 years (2000).
Hospitals: Medical Center of Southern Indiana (96 beds)
Safety: Violent crime rate: 21.6 per 10,000 population; Property crime rate: 453.0 per 10,000 population (2001).
Newspapers: The Leader (1 x week)
Transportation: Commute to work: 94.3% car, 0.5% public transportation, 1.7% walk, 2.6% work from home (2000); Travel time to work: 25.6% less than 15 minutes, 36.6% 15 to 30 minutes, 23.7% 30 to 45 minutes, 9.3% 45 to 60 minutes, 4.8% 60 minutes or more (2000)

CLARKSVILLE (town). Covers a land area of 10.091 square miles and a water area of 0.084 square miles. Located at 38.31° N. Lat.; 85.76° W. Long. Elevation is 455 feet.
History: Clarksville was founded in 1784 by George Rogers Clark on land given to Clark by the State of Virginia in reward for his military service. Clarksville was the site of the duel between Henry Clay and Humphrey Marshall in which each was wounded.
Population: 21,400 (2000); Race: 90.7% White, 5.2% Black, 0.6% Asian, 0.4% American Indian and Alaska Native, 2.8% Hispanic of any race, 1.9% two or more races (2000); Density: 2,120.6 persons per square mile (2000); Age: 23.1% under 18, 15.2% over 64 (2000); Marriage status: 23.5% never married, 53.2% now married, 9.4% widowed, 13.9% divorced (2000);

Foreign born: 2.9% (2000); Ancestry (includes multiple ancestries): 20.0% German, 13.5% Irish, 12.8% Other groups, 12.8% United States or American, 8.8% English (2000).
Vital Statistics: Birth rate: 38.3 per 10,000 population (1998)
Economy: Single-family building permits issued: 170 (2001) / 61 (2000); Multi-family building permits issued: 0 (2001) / 0 (2000); Employment by occupation: 9.8% management, 14.5% professional, 14.0% services, 31.4% sales, 0.2% farming, 9.8% construction, 20.3% production (2000).
Income: Per capita income: $20,315 (2000); Median household income: $35,473 (2000); Poverty rate: 8.1% (2000).
Taxes: Total city taxes per capita: $305 (1997); City property taxes per capita: $299 (1997).
Education: High school graduation rate: 77.6% (2000); College graduation rate: 13.3% (2000).

School District(s)

Clarksville Com School Corp (KG-12)
2000 Enrollment: 1,420 812-282-7753

Two-year College(s)

PJ's College of Cosmetology (Private, For-profit)
2001 Enrollment: 61 317-846-6444

Housing: Homeownership rate: 60.3% (2000); Median home value: $89,300 (2000); Median rent: $462 per month (2000); Median age of housing: 32 years (2000).
Safety: Violent crime rate: 26.5 per 10,000 population; Property crime rate: 950.7 per 10,000 population (2001).
Transportation: Commute to work: 94.0% car, 0.8% public transportation, 2.0% walk, 2.1% work from home (2000); Travel time to work: 36.7% less than 15 minutes, 45.5% 15 to 30 minutes, 13.6% 30 to 45 minutes, 1.8% 45 to 60 minutes, 2.4% 60 minutes or more (2000)
Additional Information Contacts
Southern Indiana Realtors Association 812-941-7472

HENRYVILLE (CDP). Covers a land area of 2.884 square miles and a water area of 0 square miles. Located at 38.54° N. Lat.; 85.76° W. Long. Elevation is 501 feet.
Population: 1,545 (2000); Race: 99.6% White, 0.0% Black, 0.0% Asian, 0.0% American Indian and Alaska Native, 0.0% Hispanic of any race, 0.4% two or more races (2000); Density: 535.6 persons per square mile (2000); Age: 26.1% under 18, 6.4% over 64 (2000); Marriage status: 20.2% never married, 63.5% now married, 3.6% widowed, 12.7% divorced (2000); Foreign born: 0.0% (2000); Ancestry (includes multiple ancestries): 21.8% German, 18.2% United States or American, 17.1% Irish, 15.1% English, 4.6% Other groups (2000).
Economy: Cattle; corn. Employment by occupation: 10.5% management, 12.5% professional, 10.2% services, 26.2% sales, 0.0% farming, 13.5% construction, 27.1% production (2000).
Income: Per capita income: $17,745 (2000); Median household income: $49,405 (2000); Poverty rate: 4.9% (2000).
Education: High school graduation rate: 82.7% (2000); College graduation rate: 13.1% (2000).
Housing: Homeownership rate: 72.5% (2000); Median home value: $85,100 (2000); Median rent: $422 per month (2000); Median age of housing: 26 years (2000).
Transportation: Commute to work: 96.4% car, 0.5% public transportation, 0.0% walk, 1.9% work from home (2000); Travel time to work: 15.6% less than 15 minutes, 34.8% 15 to 30 minutes, 33.0% 30 to 45 minutes, 11.1% 45 to 60 minutes, 5.5% 60 minutes or more (2000)

JEFFERSONVILLE (city). Covers a land area of 13.581 square miles and a water area of <.001 square miles. Located at 38.29° N. Lat.; 85.73° W. Long. Elevation is 450 feet.
History: Jeffersonville was platted in 1802 and named by William Henry Harrison for Thomas Jefferson, who had suggested the plan. The Howard Shipyards were founded in 1834 and influenced the economy of Jeffersonville for a century. The city sustained heavy damage in the 1937 flooding of the Ohio River.
Population: 27,362 (2000); Race: 82.6% White, 13.5% Black, 0.5% Asian, 0.3% American Indian and Alaska Native, 1.8% Hispanic of any race, 2.2% two or more races (2000); Density: 2,014.7 persons per square mile (2000); Age: 23.8% under 18, 12.7% over 64 (2000); Marriage status: 23.8% never married, 54.3% now married, 6.7% widowed, 15.3% divorced (2000); Foreign born: 1.7% (2000); Ancestry (includes multiple ancestries): 19.4% Other groups, 18.9% German, 12.9% United States or American, 12.8% Irish, 8.1% English (2000).
Vital Statistics: Birth rate: 152.0 per 10,000 population (1998)
Economy: Unemployment rate: 5.0% (11/2002); Total civilian labor force: 13,416 (11/2002); Single-family building permits issued: 212 (2001) / 197 (2000); Multi-family building permits issued: 168 (2001) / 32 (2000); Employment by occupation: 11.1% management, 15.8% professional, 14.9% services, 29.8% sales, 0.0% farming, 8.9% construction, 19.6% production (2000).
Income: Per capita income: $19,656 (2000); Median household income: $37,234 (2000); Poverty rate: 10.1% (2000).
Taxes: Total city taxes per capita: $250 (1997); City property taxes per capita: $241 (1997).
Education: High school graduation rate: 80.3% (2000); College graduation rate: 14.9% (2000).

School District(s)

Greater Clark County Schools (PK-12)
2000 Enrollment: 9,725 812-283-0701

Four-year College(s)

Mid-America College of Funeral Service (Private, Not-for-profit)
2001 Enrollment: 51 812-288-8878
2001 Tuition: In-state $6,000; Out-of-state $6,000

Housing: Homeownership rate: 62.1% (2000); Median home value: $85,900 (2000); Median rent: $405 per month (2000); Median age of housing: 30 years (2000).
Hospitals: Clark Memorial Hospital (262 beds)
Safety: Violent crime rate: 37.1 per 10,000 population; Property crime rate: 501.5 per 10,000 population (2001).
Newspapers: Sunnyside Weekly (1 x week); The Evening News (6 x week)
Transportation: Commute to work: 94.4% car, 1.2% public transportation, 2.1% walk, 1.3% work from home (2000); Travel time to work: 35.9% less than 15 minutes, 46.8% 15 to 30 minutes, 12.6% 30 to 45 minutes, 2.5% 45 to 60 minutes, 2.2% 60 minutes or more (2000); Amtrak: Service available.
Airports: Clark County

MARYSVILLE (unincorporated postal area, zip code 47141). Covers a land area of 32.033 square miles and a water area of 0 square miles. Located at 38.54° N. Lat.; 85.60° W. Long. Elevation is 712 feet.
Population: 1,414 (2000); Race: 97.8% White, 0.7% Black, 0.0% Asian, 0.0% American Indian and Alaska Native, 0.3% Hispanic of any race, 1.6% two or more races (2000); Density: 44.1 persons per square mile (2000); Age: 26.0% under 18, 12.2% over 64 (2000); Marriage status: 13.3% never married, 71.1% now married, 6.1% widowed, 9.5% divorced (2000); Foreign born: 0.0% (2000); Ancestry (includes multiple ancestries): 26.0% United States or American, 12.1% German, 8.6% Irish, 8.4% English, 7.5% Other groups (2000).
Economy: Employment by occupation: 10.0% management, 12.5% professional, 11.1% services, 23.5% sales, 1.7% farming, 9.8% construction, 31.3% production (2000).
Income: Per capita income: $19,161 (2000); Median household income: $37,750 (2000); Poverty rate: 6.6% (2000).
Education: High school graduation rate: 73.4% (2000); College graduation rate: 10.0% (2000).
Housing: Homeownership rate: 88.8% (2000); Median home value: $96,900 (2000); Median rent: $275 per month (2000); Median age of housing: 25 years (2000).
Transportation: Commute to work: 96.7% car, 1.1% public transportation, 0.0% walk, 2.2% work from home (2000); Travel time to work: 10.2% less than 15 minutes, 24.8% 15 to 30 minutes, 32.6% 30 to 45 minutes, 24.8% 45 to 60 minutes, 7.5% 60 minutes or more (2000)

MEMPHIS (CDP). Covers a land area of 2.499 square miles and a water area of 0 square miles. Located at 38.48° N. Lat.; 85.76° W. Long. Elevation is 487 feet.
Population: 400 (2000); Race: 95.0% White, 0.0% Black, 0.0% Asian, 1.2% American Indian and Alaska Native, 0.0% Hispanic of any race, 3.8% two or more races (2000); Density: 160.1 persons per square mile (2000); Age: 5.9% under 18, 19.2% over 64 (2000); Marriage status: 13.5% never married, 64.8% now married, 11.6% widowed, 10.1% divorced (2000); Foreign born: 0.0% (2000); Ancestry (includes multiple ancestries): 34.0% German, 25.7% English, 14.5% Irish, 6.5% Swedish, 4.4% United States or American (2000).
Economy: Agricultural area. Manufacturing: beef and pork processing. Employment by occupation: 8.3% management, 10.7% professional, 22.0% services, 20.5% sales, 0.0% farming, 11.2% construction, 27.3% production (2000).
Income: Per capita income: $20,054 (2000); Median household income: $35,658 (2000); Poverty rate: 5.9% (2000).
Education: High school graduation rate: 73.7% (2000); College graduation rate: 2.3% (2000).

Housing: Homeownership rate: 91.8% (2000); Median home value: $83,900 (2000); Median rent: $414 per month (2000); Median age of housing: 36 years (2000).
Transportation: Commute to work: 96.9% car, 0.0% public transportation, 3.1% walk, 0.0% work from home (2000); Travel time to work: 24.5% less than 15 minutes, 43.4% 15 to 30 minutes, 23.5% 30 to 45 minutes, 8.7% 45 to 60 minutes, 0.0% 60 minutes or more (2000)

NABB (unincorporated postal area, zip code 47147). Covers a land area of 32.001 square miles and a water area of 0.006 square miles. Located at 38.59° N. Lat.; 85.53° W. Long.
Population: 1,062 (2000); Race: 96.7% White, 2.2% Black, 0.0% Asian, 0.0% American Indian and Alaska Native, 1.1% Hispanic of any race, 1.1% two or more races (2000); Density: 33.2 persons per square mile (2000); Age: 27.0% under 18, 9.4% over 64 (2000); Marriage status: 18.5% never married, 65.9% now married, 7.4% widowed, 8.2% divorced (2000); Foreign born: 0.0% (2000); Ancestry (includes multiple ancestries): 25.5% German, 16.0% United States or American, 10.3% English, 10.1% Irish, 5.9% Other groups (2000).
Economy: Employment by occupation: 6.3% management, 12.5% professional, 10.8% services, 30.9% sales, 0.0% farming, 12.0% construction, 27.6% production (2000).
Income: Per capita income: $17,847 (2000); Median household income: $43,958 (2000); Poverty rate: 6.9% (2000).
Education: High school graduation rate: 86.3% (2000); College graduation rate: 7.1% (2000).
Housing: Homeownership rate: 88.1% (2000); Median home value: $73,100 (2000); Median rent: $309 per month (2000); Median age of housing: 42 years (2000).
Transportation: Commute to work: 97.6% car, 0.0% public transportation, 0.0% walk, 1.7% work from home (2000); Travel time to work: 12.5% less than 15 minutes, 19.4% 15 to 30 minutes, 37.2% 30 to 45 minutes, 15.6% 45 to 60 minutes, 15.3% 60 minutes or more (2000)

NEW WASHINGTON (CDP). Aka New Otto. Covers a land area of 5.221 square miles and a water area of 0 square miles. Located at 38.56° N. Lat.; 85.54° W. Long. Elevation is 721 feet.
Population: 547 (2000); Race: 100.0% White, 0.0% Black, 0.0% Asian, 0.0% American Indian and Alaska Native, 0.0% Hispanic of any race, 0.0% two or more races (2000); Density: 104.8 persons per square mile (2000); Age: 17.4% under 18, 14.4% over 64 (2000); Marriage status: 18.2% never married, 68.5% now married, 6.0% widowed, 7.3% divorced (2000); Foreign born: 0.0% (2000); Ancestry (includes multiple ancestries): 30.4% German, 17.7% Irish, 15.5% English, 10.6% United States or American, 8.2% Dutch (2000).
Economy: Cattle, poultry. Employment by occupation: 5.5% management, 12.4% professional, 13.4% services, 37.1% sales, 0.0% farming, 12.4% construction, 19.2% production (2000).
Income: Per capita income: $19,343 (2000); Median household income: $37,368 (2000); Poverty rate: 8.2% (2000).
Education: High school graduation rate: 82.9% (2000); College graduation rate: 15.1% (2000).
Housing: Homeownership rate: 83.8% (2000); Median home value: $67,500 (2000); Median rent: $316 per month (2000); Median age of housing: 48 years (2000).
Transportation: Commute to work: 91.6% car, 0.0% public transportation, 2.1% walk, 4.9% work from home (2000); Travel time to work: 25.1% less than 15 minutes, 14.4% 15 to 30 minutes, 41.3% 30 to 45 minutes, 14.0% 45 to 60 minutes, 5.2% 60 minutes or more (2000)

OAK PARK (CDP). Covers a land area of 2.234 square miles and a water area of 0.009 square miles. Located at 38.30° N. Lat.; 85.69° W. Long. Elevation is 460 feet.
Population: 5,379 (2000); Race: 87.7% White, 8.5% Black, 1.0% Asian, 0.0% American Indian and Alaska Native, 1.4% Hispanic of any race, 2.0% two or more races (2000); Density: 2,407.8 persons per square mile (2000); Age: 24.6% under 18, 12.6% over 64 (2000); Marriage status: 21.0% never married, 63.9% now married, 5.9% widowed, 9.1% divorced (2000); Foreign born: 1.3% (2000); Ancestry (includes multiple ancestries): 25.8% German, 14.7% United States or American, 14.1% Irish, 12.8% Other groups, 10.4% English (2000).
Economy: Employment by occupation: 12.1% management, 21.2% professional, 14.4% services, 26.2% sales, 0.0% farming, 8.4% construction, 17.6% production (2000).
Income: Per capita income: $22,445 (2000); Median household income: $51,663 (2000); Poverty rate: 3.4% (2000).
Education: High school graduation rate: 88.6% (2000); College graduation rate: 22.5% (2000).
Housing: Homeownership rate: 81.7% (2000); Median home value: $96,100 (2000); Median rent: $509 per month (2000); Median age of housing: 29 years (2000).
Transportation: Commute to work: 95.3% car, 0.8% public transportation, 0.3% walk, 2.9% work from home (2000); Travel time to work: 25.1% less than 15 minutes, 53.5% 15 to 30 minutes, 16.4% 30 to 45 minutes, 2.7% 45 to 60 minutes, 2.3% 60 minutes or more (2000)

OTISCO (unincorporated postal area, zip code 47163). Covers a land area of 20.286 square miles and a water area of 0.046 square miles. Located at 38.54° N. Lat.; 85.66° W. Long. Elevation is 660 feet.
Population: 1,733 (2000); Race: 98.9% White, 0.8% Black, 0.3% Asian, 0.0% American Indian and Alaska Native, 0.0% Hispanic of any race, 0.0% two or more races (2000); Density: 85.4 persons per square mile (2000); Age: 23.6% under 18, 11.7% over 64 (2000); Marriage status: 17.0% never married, 69.8% now married, 3.9% widowed, 9.3% divorced (2000); Foreign born: 0.4% (2000); Ancestry (includes multiple ancestries): 19.0% German, 17.1% United States or American, 12.7% English, 11.0% Irish, 5.7% Other groups (2000).
Economy: Employment by occupation: 8.1% management, 14.8% professional, 10.2% services, 27.0% sales, 0.7% farming, 15.8% construction, 23.4% production (2000).
Income: Per capita income: $18,444 (2000); Median household income: $44,653 (2000); Poverty rate: 2.7% (2000).
Education: High school graduation rate: 77.9% (2000); College graduation rate: 11.8% (2000).
Housing: Homeownership rate: 95.0% (2000); Median home value: $98,800 (2000); Median rent: $275 per month (2000); Median age of housing: 19 years (2000).
Transportation: Commute to work: 91.2% car, 0.0% public transportation, 1.8% walk, 5.2% work from home (2000); Travel time to work: 13.6% less than 15 minutes, 30.4% 15 to 30 minutes, 45.1% 30 to 45 minutes, 9.9% 45 to 60 minutes, 1.0% 60 minutes or more (2000)

SELLERSBURG (town). Covers a land area of 4.005 square miles and a water area of 0.012 square miles. Located at 38.38° N. Lat.; 85.75° W. Long. Elevation is 500 feet.
History: Laid out 1846.
Population: 6,071 (2000); Race: 99.3% White, 0.1% Black, 0.2% Asian, 0.0% American Indian and Alaska Native, 0.9% Hispanic of any race, 0.2% two or more races (2000); Density: 1,515.8 persons per square mile (2000); Age: 24.1% under 18, 12.6% over 64 (2000); Marriage status: 18.0% never married, 60.2% now married, 6.7% widowed, 15.1% divorced (2000); Foreign born: 1.2% (2000); Ancestry (includes multiple ancestries): 27.3% German, 17.9% Irish, 12.1% English, 11.7% United States or American, 8.6% Other groups (2000).
Economy: Agricultural area. Diversified manufacturing. Single-family building permits issued: 37 (2001) / 31 (2000); Multi-family building permits issued: 0 (2001) / 0 (2000); Employment by occupation: 8.1% management, 13.8% professional, 14.9% services, 29.7% sales, 0.0% farming, 11.1% construction, 22.4% production (2000).
Income: Per capita income: $18,648 (2000); Median household income: $39,832 (2000); Poverty rate: 5.3% (2000).
Taxes: Total city taxes per capita: $174 (1997); City property taxes per capita: $169 (1997).
Education: High school graduation rate: 84.6% (2000); College graduation rate: 12.9% (2000).

School District(s)

West Clark Community Schools (KG-12)
2000 Enrollment: 3,133 812-246-3375

Two-year College(s)

Ivy Tech State College-South Central (Public)
2001 Enrollment: 2,035 812-246-3301
2001 Tuition: In-state $1,986; Out-of-state $4,029

Housing: Homeownership rate: 83.0% (2000); Median home value: $89,600 (2000); Median rent: $392 per month (2000); Median age of housing: 33 years (2000).
Safety: Violent crime rate: 9.8 per 10,000 population; Property crime rate: 201.5 per 10,000 population (2001).
Transportation: Commute to work: 97.2% car, 0.8% public transportation, 0.9% walk, 1.0% work from home (2000); Travel time to work: 29.6% less than 15 minutes, 48.8% 15 to 30 minutes, 14.9% 30 to 45 minutes, 2.2% 45 to 60 minutes, 4.4% 60 minutes or more (2000)

UNDERWOOD (unincorporated postal area, zip code 47177). Covers a land area of 6.332 square miles and a water area of 0.027 square miles. Located at 38.60° N. Lat.; 85.76° W. Long. Elevation is 620 feet.
Population: 620 (2000); Race: 100.0% White, 0.0% Black, 0.0% Asian, 0.0% American Indian and Alaska Native, 1.1% Hispanic of any race, 0.0% two or more races (2000); Density: 97.9 persons per square mile (2000); Age: 28.9% under 18, 14.4% over 64 (2000); Marriage status: 22.9% never married, 63.1% now married, 5.6% widowed, 8.4% divorced (2000); Foreign born: 0.0% (2000); Ancestry (includes multiple ancestries): 32.1% United States or American, 18.6% German, 16.3% English, 6.0% Other groups, 3.3% Welsh (2000).
Economy: Employment by occupation: 9.4% management, 3.4% professional, 22.1% services, 28.5% sales, 1.9% farming, 12.7% construction, 22.1% production (2000).
Income: Per capita income: $18,229 (2000); Median household income: $42,083 (2000); Poverty rate: 6.3% (2000).
Education: High school graduation rate: 68.7% (2000); College graduation rate: 6.9% (2000).
Housing: Homeownership rate: 95.1% (2000); Median home value: $76,600 (2000); Median rent: $175 per month (2000); Median age of housing: 29 years (2000).
Transportation: Commute to work: 100.0% car, 0.0% public transportation, 0.0% walk, 0.0% work from home (2000); Travel time to work: 13.9% less than 15 minutes, 30.9% 15 to 30 minutes, 43.2% 30 to 45 minutes, 6.9% 45 to 60 minutes, 5.0% 60 minutes or more (2000)

UTICA (town). Covers a land area of 0.434 square miles and a water area of 0 square miles. Located at 38.33° N. Lat.; 85.65° W. Long. Elevation is 450 feet.
History: Laid out 1816.
Population: 591 (2000); Race: 99.1% White, 0.0% Black, 0.0% Asian, 0.0% American Indian and Alaska Native, 1.0% Hispanic of any race, 0.9% two or more races (2000); Density: 1,361.7 persons per square mile (2000); Age: 19.1% under 18, 10.7% over 64 (2000); Marriage status: 18.5% never married, 63.2% now married, 5.4% widowed, 12.9% divorced (2000); Foreign born: 0.9% (2000); Ancestry (includes multiple ancestries): 20.5% German, 17.9% United States or American, 14.7% Irish, 5.3% English, 4.8% Other groups (2000).
Economy: Agricultural area. Manufacturing of boats, barges, dry docks. Single-family building permits issued: 10 (2001) / 12 (2000); Multi-family building permits issued: 0 (2001) / 0 (2000); Employment by occupation: 12.3% management, 8.6% professional, 13.3% services, 26.2% sales, 0.3% farming, 14.6% construction, 24.6% production (2000).
Income: Per capita income: $23,518 (2000); Median household income: $36,023 (2000); Poverty rate: 8.1% (2000).
Taxes: Total city taxes per capita: $75 (1997); City property taxes per capita: $68 (1997).
Education: High school graduation rate: 69.8% (2000); College graduation rate: 9.0% (2000).
Housing: Homeownership rate: 78.8% (2000); Median home value: $86,500 (2000); Median rent: $456 per month (2000); Median age of housing: 32 years (2000).
Transportation: Commute to work: 93.3% car, 0.0% public transportation, 1.0% walk, 3.0% work from home (2000); Travel time to work: 11.4% less than 15 minutes, 57.8% 15 to 30 minutes, 20.4% 30 to 45 minutes, 3.5% 45 to 60 minutes, 6.9% 60 minutes or more (2000)

Clay County

Located in western Indiana; drained by the Eel River and Small Birch Creek. Covers a land area of 357.60 square miles, a water area of 2.80 square miles, and is located in the Eastern Time Zone. The county government was organized in 1825. County seat is Brazil.

Clay County is part of the Terre Haute, IN MSA. The entire metro area includes: Clay County; Vermillion County; Vigo County

Population: 26,556 (2000); Race: 98.2% White, 0.3% Black, 0.2% Asian, 0.3% American Indian and Alaska Native, 0.5% Hispanic of any race, 0.5% two or more races (2000); Density: 74.3 persons per square mile (2000); Age: 26.2% under 18, 15.1% over 64 (2000).
Religion: Five largest groups: 8.0% The United Methodist Church, 5.4% Christian Churches and Churches of Christ, 4.0% American Baptist Churches in the USA, 3.5% Catholic Church, 3.0% United Church of Christ (2000).
Economy: Unemployment rate: 5.3% (11/2002); Total civilian labor force: 12,958 (11/2002); Leading industries: 36.9% manufacturing; 18.9% retail trade; 8.6% health care and social assistance (2000); Companies that employ more than 1,000 persons: 1 (2000); Companies that employ more than 100 persons: 5 (2000); Farms: 520 totaling 159,441 acres (1997); Minority business ownership rate: 0.0% (1997); Women business ownership rate: 24.1% (1997); Retail sales per capita: $7,172 (1997). Single-family building permits issued: 48 (2001) / 59 (2000); Multi-family building permits issued: 0 (2001) / 3 (2000).
Income: Per capita income: $16,364 (2000); Median household income: $36,865 (2000); Poverty rate: 8.7% (2000); Bankruptcy rate: 7.21% (2001).
Taxes: Total county taxes per capita: $136 (1997); County property taxes per capita: $62 (1997).
Education: High school graduation rate: 82.3% (2000); College graduation rate: 12.8% (2000).
Housing: Homeownership rate: 79.1% (2000); Median home value: $72,600 (2000); Median rent: $303 per month (2000); Median age of housing: 41 years (2000).
Health: Birth rate: 128.4 per 10,000 population (1998); Age adjusted death rate: 90.7 per 10,000 population (1999); Age adjusted cancer mortality rate: 252.1 deaths per 100,000 population (1999). Number of physicians: 6.4 per 10,000 population (1999); Number of hospital beds: 13.6 per 10,000 population (1999).
Elections: 2000 Presidential election results: 35.5% Gore, 62.9% Bush, 0.2% Nader, 0.8% Buchanan
Additional Information Contacts
Clay County Government Offices 812-448-9005

Clay County Communities

BOWLING GREEN (unincorporated postal area, zip code 47833). Covers a land area of 35.048 square miles and a water area of 0 square miles. Located at 39.36° N. Lat.; 86.99° W. Long. Elevation is 664 feet.
History: Bowling Green was founded in 1825 on the bluffs along the Eel River. For a time it served as the seat of Clay County.
Population: 953 (2000); Race: 94.6% White, 5.4% Black, 0.0% Asian, 0.0% American Indian and Alaska Native, 0.0% Hispanic of any race, 0.0% two or more races (2000); Density: 27.2 persons per square mile (2000); Age: 29.3% under 18, 9.7% over 64 (2000); Marriage status: 22.0% never married, 63.8% now married, 5.3% widowed, 8.9% divorced (2000); Foreign born: 0.0% (2000); Ancestry (includes multiple ancestries): 31.2% United States or American, 18.4% German, 8.3% Irish, 4.3% Scotch-Irish, 3.4% Other groups (2000).
Economy: Employment by occupation: 8.1% management, 6.3% professional, 10.6% services, 26.3% sales, 1.8% farming, 12.6% construction, 34.3% production (2000).
Income: Per capita income: $14,218 (2000); Median household income: $38,676 (2000); Poverty rate: 15.7% (2000).
Education: High school graduation rate: 71.2% (2000); College graduation rate: 7.6% (2000).
Housing: Homeownership rate: 84.2% (2000); Median home value: $71,700 (2000); Median rent: $512 per month (2000); Median age of housing: 27 years (2000).
Transportation: Commute to work: 95.7% car, 0.0% public transportation, 0.0% walk, 4.3% work from home (2000); Travel time to work: 12.5% less than 15 minutes, 28.1% 15 to 30 minutes, 25.6% 30 to 45 minutes, 19.4% 45 to 60 minutes, 14.4% 60 minutes or more (2000)

BRAZIL (city). Covers a land area of 3.341 square miles and a water area of 0.028 square miles. Located at 39.52° N. Lat.; 87.12° W. Long. Elevation is 659 feet.
History: Brazil's development was based on its coal mines and clay plants, which manufactured glazed building bricks and tiles. Brazil was named for the country in South America, the name suggested by resident William Stewart who had just read a magazine article about Brazil.
Population: 8,188 (2000); Race: 97.7% White, 0.3% Black, 0.4% Asian, 0.6% American Indian and Alaska Native, 0.6% Hispanic of any race, 0.3% two or more races (2000); Density: 2,450.6 persons per square mile (2000); Age: 26.4% under 18, 16.3% over 64 (2000); Marriage status: 20.1% never married, 55.0% now married, 10.6% widowed, 14.3% divorced (2000); Foreign born: 1.0% (2000); Ancestry (includes multiple ancestries): 21.2% United States or American, 17.4% German, 11.3% English, 10.4% Irish, 6.3% Other groups (2000).
Economy: Single-family building permits issued: 48 (2001) / 56 (2000); Multi-family building permits issued: 0 (2001) / 0 (2000); Employment by

occupation: 8.6% management, 12.4% professional, 17.7% services, 21.2% sales, 0.3% farming, 9.6% construction, 30.1% production (2000).
Income: Per capita income: $15,123 (2000); Median household income: $30,902 (2000); Poverty rate: 13.2% (2000).
Taxes: Total city taxes per capita: $188 (2000); City property taxes per capita: $163 (2000).
Education: High school graduation rate: 76.5% (2000); College graduation rate: 11.4% (2000).
Housing: Homeownership rate: 64.8% (2000); Median home value: $59,300 (2000); Median rent: $291 per month (2000); Median age of housing: 48 years (2000).
Hospitals: Saint Vincent Clay Hospital (58 beds)
Newspapers: The Brazil Times (6 x week)
Transportation: Commute to work: 94.9% car, 0.0% public transportation, 2.1% walk, 1.9% work from home (2000); Travel time to work: 42.0% less than 15 minutes, 25.0% 15 to 30 minutes, 21.4% 30 to 45 minutes, 4.9% 45 to 60 minutes, 6.8% 60 minutes or more (2000)

CARBON (town). Covers a land area of 0.158 square miles and a water area of 0 square miles. Located at 39.59° N. Lat.; 87.10° W. Long. Elevation is 687 feet.
Population: 334 (2000); Race: 93.8% White, 0.0% Black, 1.8% Asian, 0.0% American Indian and Alaska Native, 0.0% Hispanic of any race, 4.4% two or more races (2000); Density: 2,109.4 persons per square mile (2000); Age: 33.5% under 18, 9.7% over 64 (2000); Marriage status: 17.3% never married, 67.9% now married, 4.5% widowed, 10.3% divorced (2000); Foreign born: 2.6% (2000); Ancestry (includes multiple ancestries): 19.1% United States or American, 11.8% German, 7.9% Irish, 7.4% Other groups, 2.9% French (except Basque) (2000).
Economy: In agricultural and bituminous-coal area. Sawmill. Employment by occupation: 9.9% management, 3.3% professional, 15.1% services, 19.1% sales, 2.6% farming, 12.5% construction, 37.5% production (2000).
Income: Per capita income: $13,089 (2000); Median household income: $35,208 (2000); Poverty rate: 14.8% (2000).
Taxes: Total city taxes per capita: $18 (1997); City property taxes per capita: $16 (1997).
Education: High school graduation rate: 75.0% (2000); College graduation rate: 3.1% (2000).
Housing: Homeownership rate: 86.9% (2000); Median home value: $38,800 (2000); Median rent: $313 per month (2000); Median age of housing: 46 years (2000).
Transportation: Commute to work: 100.0% car, 0.0% public transportation, 0.0% walk, 0.0% work from home (2000); Travel time to work: 17.2% less than 15 minutes, 29.8% 15 to 30 minutes, 23.8% 30 to 45 minutes, 13.2% 45 to 60 minutes, 15.9% 60 minutes or more (2000)

CENTER POINT (town). Aka Centerpoint. Covers a land area of 0.740 square miles and a water area of 0.022 square miles. Located at 39.41° N. Lat.; 87.07° W. Long. Elevation is 671 feet.
Population: 292 (2000); Race: 99.6% White, 0.0% Black, 0.0% Asian, 0.0% American Indian and Alaska Native, 0.0% Hispanic of any race, 0.4% two or more races (2000); Density: 394.7 persons per square mile (2000); Age: 35.3% under 18, 10.2% over 64 (2000); Marriage status: 25.1% never married, 56.3% now married, 5.6% widowed, 13.0% divorced (2000); Foreign born: 0.0% (2000); Ancestry (includes multiple ancestries): 20.8% German, 18.7% United States or American, 7.1% English, 5.3% Irish, 3.5% Scotch-Irish (2000).
Economy: In agricultural and bituminous-coal area. Old-surface coal mines. Employment by occupation: 13.7% management, 21.4% professional, 20.6% services, 11.5% sales, 0.0% farming, 8.4% construction, 24.4% production (2000).
Income: Per capita income: $17,110 (2000); Median household income: $50,833 (2000); Poverty rate: 6.6% (2000).
Taxes: Total city taxes per capita: $14 (1997); City property taxes per capita: $14 (1997).
Education: High school graduation rate: 82.0% (2000); College graduation rate: 16.8% (2000).
Housing: Homeownership rate: 77.6% (2000); Median home value: $60,000 (2000); Median rent: $242 per month (2000); Median age of housing: 55 years (2000).
Transportation: Commute to work: 92.4% car, 0.0% public transportation, 2.3% walk, 5.3% work from home (2000); Travel time to work: 16.9% less than 15 minutes, 43.5% 15 to 30 minutes, 21.8% 30 to 45 minutes, 4.0% 45 to 60 minutes, 13.7% 60 minutes or more (2000)

CLAY CITY (town). Covers a land area of 0.534 square miles and a water area of 0 square miles. Located at 39.27° N. Lat.; 87.11° W. Long. Elevation is 587 feet.
History: Settled 1873, incorporated 1888.
Population: 1,019 (2000); Race: 99.6% White, 0.1% Black, 0.0% Asian, 0.0% American Indian and Alaska Native, 0.7% Hispanic of any race, 0.3% two or more races (2000); Density: 1,906.9 persons per square mile (2000); Age: 24.3% under 18, 20.8% over 64 (2000); Marriage status: 16.2% never married, 61.2% now married, 11.3% widowed, 11.2% divorced (2000); Foreign born: 0.0% (2000); Ancestry (includes multiple ancestries): 22.1% United States or American, 15.6% German, 8.6% Irish, 7.6% Other groups, 6.6% English (2000).
Economy: In agricultural area. Manufacturing: hardwood, preserves, pottery; clay pits, bituminous coal mines. Employment by occupation: 6.4% management, 11.3% professional, 16.2% services, 27.0% sales, 0.4% farming, 16.4% construction, 22.3% production (2000).
Income: Per capita income: $15,281 (2000); Median household income: $31,316 (2000); Poverty rate: 8.9% (2000).
Taxes: Total city taxes per capita: $52 (1997); City property taxes per capita: $51 (1997).
Education: High school graduation rate: 77.8% (2000); College graduation rate: 9.1% (2000).
Housing: Homeownership rate: 76.0% (2000); Median home value: $58,500 (2000); Median rent: $232 per month (2000); Median age of housing: 51 years (2000).
Newspapers: The News (1 x week)
Transportation: Commute to work: 93.5% car, 0.0% public transportation, 3.1% walk, 2.6% work from home (2000); Travel time to work: 25.7% less than 15 minutes, 15.4% 15 to 30 minutes, 33.6% 30 to 45 minutes, 17.4% 45 to 60 minutes, 7.8% 60 minutes or more (2000)

CORY (unincorporated postal area, zip code 47846). Covers a land area of 34.372 square miles and a water area of 0.146 square miles. Located at 39.37° N. Lat.; 87.20° W. Long. Elevation is 621 feet.
Population: 725 (2000); Race: 97.1% White, 0.0% Black, 0.8% Asian, 0.0% American Indian and Alaska Native, 0.0% Hispanic of any race, 2.1% two or more races (2000); Density: 21.1 persons per square mile (2000); Age: 27.0% under 18, 18.2% over 64 (2000); Marriage status: 17.8% never married, 61.9% now married, 10.3% widowed, 10.0% divorced (2000); Foreign born: 0.8% (2000); Ancestry (includes multiple ancestries): 19.0% German, 17.1% United States or American, 13.2% English, 11.9% Irish, 7.6% Other groups (2000).
Economy: Employment by occupation: 4.8% management, 8.7% professional, 17.0% services, 33.8% sales, 1.3% farming, 19.3% construction, 15.1% production (2000).
Income: Per capita income: $15,040 (2000); Median household income: $35,625 (2000); Poverty rate: 0.9% (2000).
Education: High school graduation rate: 96.7% (2000); College graduation rate: 8.0% (2000).
Housing: Homeownership rate: 91.4% (2000); Median home value: $93,300 (2000); Median rent: $325 per month (2000); Median age of housing: 30 years (2000).
Transportation: Commute to work: 91.0% car, 1.9% public transportation, 0.0% walk, 7.1% work from home (2000); Travel time to work: 8.7% less than 15 minutes, 48.8% 15 to 30 minutes, 28.4% 30 to 45 minutes, 2.1% 45 to 60 minutes, 12.1% 60 minutes or more (2000)

HARMONY (town). Covers a land area of 0.754 square miles and a water area of 0 square miles. Located at 39.53° N. Lat.; 87.07° W. Long. Elevation is 673 feet.
History: Harmony was once a prosperous coal-mining town.
Population: 589 (2000); Race: 98.3% White, 0.0% Black, 0.0% Asian, 0.0% American Indian and Alaska Native, 1.7% Hispanic of any race, 0.7% two or more races (2000); Density: 781.0 persons per square mile (2000); Age: 24.4% under 18, 14.0% over 64 (2000); Marriage status: 19.3% never married, 53.4% now married, 11.1% widowed, 16.1% divorced (2000); Foreign born: 0.0% (2000); Ancestry (includes multiple ancestries): 16.6% United States or American, 14.7% German, 9.7% Irish, 9.3% English, 3.7% Other groups (2000).
Economy: Single-family building permits issued: 0 (2001) / 3 (2000); Multi-family building permits issued: 0 (2001) / 3 (2000); Employment by occupation: 7.0% management, 12.2% professional, 16.8% services, 29.0% sales, 1.0% farming, 6.6% construction, 27.3% production (2000).
Income: Per capita income: $16,276 (2000); Median household income: $33,438 (2000); Poverty rate: 8.2% (2000).

Taxes: Total city taxes per capita: $34 (1997); City property taxes per capita: $33 (1997).
Education: High school graduation rate: 82.7% (2000); College graduation rate: 10.1% (2000).
Housing: Homeownership rate: 73.1% (2000); Median home value: $58,600 (2000); Median rent: $317 per month (2000); Median age of housing: 43 years (2000).
Transportation: Commute to work: 95.8% car, 0.0% public transportation, 1.4% walk, 2.8% work from home (2000); Travel time to work: 46.5% less than 15 minutes, 25.1% 15 to 30 minutes, 21.5% 30 to 45 minutes, 3.3% 45 to 60 minutes, 3.6% 60 minutes or more (2000)

KNIGHTSVILLE (town). Covers a land area of 1.020 square miles and a water area of 0 square miles. Located at 39.52° N. Lat.; 87.09° W. Long. Elevation is 680 feet.
Population: 624 (2000); Race: 100.0% White, 0.0% Black, 0.0% Asian, 0.0% American Indian and Alaska Native, 0.0% Hispanic of any race, 0.0% two or more races (2000); Density: 611.5 persons per square mile (2000); Age: 23.6% under 18, 24.1% over 64 (2000); Marriage status: 16.6% never married, 70.8% now married, 6.1% widowed, 6.5% divorced (2000); Foreign born: 0.0% (2000); Ancestry (includes multiple ancestries): 24.4% United States or American, 12.5% English, 12.5% German, 4.7% Irish, 3.8% Other groups (2000).
Economy: In agricultural and bituminous-coal area. Employment by occupation: 9.2% management, 8.4% professional, 11.9% services, 27.6% sales, 1.1% farming, 9.2% construction, 32.6% production (2000).
Income: Per capita income: $14,123 (2000); Median household income: $38,417 (2000); Poverty rate: 5.0% (2000).
Taxes: Total city taxes per capita: $19 (1997); City property taxes per capita: $18 (1997).
Education: High school graduation rate: 66.6% (2000); College graduation rate: 7.0% (2000).

School District(s)

Clay Community Schools (KG-12)
2000 Enrollment: 4,672 812-443-4461
Housing: Homeownership rate: 84.2% (2000); Median home value: $68,000 (2000); Median rent: $254 per month (2000); Median age of housing: 51 years (2000).
Transportation: Commute to work: 94.5% car, 0.0% public transportation, 2.7% walk, 2.0% work from home (2000); Travel time to work: 50.2% less than 15 minutes, 25.9% 15 to 30 minutes, 15.1% 30 to 45 minutes, 1.6% 45 to 60 minutes, 7.2% 60 minutes or more (2000)

POLAND (unincorporated postal area, zip code 47868). Covers a land area of 65.362 square miles and a water area of 0.173 square miles. Located at 39.41° N. Lat.; 86.90° W. Long. Elevation is 700 feet.
Population: 3,212 (2000); Race: 98.6% White, 0.0% Black, 0.0% Asian, 0.4% American Indian and Alaska Native, 0.0% Hispanic of any race, 1.0% two or more races (2000); Density: 49.1 persons per square mile (2000); Age: 26.1% under 18, 14.2% over 64 (2000); Marriage status: 15.2% never married, 67.0% now married, 5.1% widowed, 12.6% divorced (2000); Foreign born: 0.3% (2000); Ancestry (includes multiple ancestries): 19.4% German, 18.6% United States or American, 11.0% Other groups, 10.6% Irish, 7.3% English (2000).
Economy: Employment by occupation: 8.6% management, 10.2% professional, 10.8% services, 23.3% sales, 0.5% farming, 16.7% construction, 29.9% production (2000).
Income: Per capita income: $16,592 (2000); Median household income: $36,321 (2000); Poverty rate: 13.2% (2000).
Education: High school graduation rate: 74.3% (2000); College graduation rate: 7.2% (2000).
Housing: Homeownership rate: 89.2% (2000); Median home value: $79,600 (2000); Median rent: $363 per month (2000); Median age of housing: 24 years (2000).
Transportation: Commute to work: 95.9% car, 0.0% public transportation, 0.0% walk, 2.7% work from home (2000); Travel time to work: 6.5% less than 15 minutes, 24.0% 15 to 30 minutes, 23.3% 30 to 45 minutes, 16.7% 45 to 60 minutes, 29.5% 60 minutes or more (2000)

STAUNTON (town). Covers a land area of 0.341 square miles and a water area of 0 square miles. Located at 39.48° N. Lat.; 87.18° W. Long. Elevation is 646 feet.
History: Founded 1851.
Population: 550 (2000); Race: 98.7% White, 0.0% Black, 0.0% Asian, 0.0% American Indian and Alaska Native, 0.0% Hispanic of any race, 0.0% two or more races (2000); Density: 1,614.0 persons per square mile (2000); Age: 31.4% under 18, 11.3% over 64 (2000); Marriage status: 21.1% never married, 64.9% now married, 4.2% widowed, 9.8% divorced (2000); Foreign born: 0.5% (2000); Ancestry (includes multiple ancestries): 26.8% German, 20.6% United States or American, 9.9% Irish, 9.0% Other groups, 7.5% English (2000).
Economy: Agricultural and bituminous-coal area (surface mines). Employment by occupation: 1.9% management, 10.5% professional, 16.0% services, 28.0% sales, 1.6% farming, 7.8% construction, 34.2% production (2000).
Income: Per capita income: $14,192 (2000); Median household income: $38,750 (2000); Poverty rate: 6.5% (2000).
Taxes: Total city taxes per capita: $133 (1997); City property taxes per capita: $101 (1997).
Education: High school graduation rate: 83.9% (2000); College graduation rate: 4.2% (2000).
Housing: Homeownership rate: 90.5% (2000); Median home value: $53,300 (2000); Median rent: $368 per month (2000); Median age of housing: 37 years (2000).
Transportation: Commute to work: 95.3% car, 0.0% public transportation, 2.0% walk, 1.2% work from home (2000); Travel time to work: 25.2% less than 15 minutes, 37.6% 15 to 30 minutes, 22.0% 30 to 45 minutes, 7.2% 45 to 60 minutes, 8.0% 60 minutes or more (2000)

Clinton County

Located in central Indiana; drained by Sugar Creek. Covers a land area of 405.10 square miles, a water area of 0.20 square miles, and is located in the Eastern Time Zone. The county government was organized in 1830. County seat is Frankfort.

Clinton County is part of the Lafayette, IN MSA. The entire metro area includes: Clinton County; Tippecanoe County

Weather Station: Frankfort Disposal Plant — Elevation: 833 feet

	Jan	Feb	Mar	Apr	May	Jun	Jul	Aug	Sep	Oct	Nov	Dec
High	32	37	49	61	72	81	84	82	77	64	50	38
Low	17	20	30	39	50	59	63	61	54	42	33	23
Precip	2.0	2.0	3.2	3.7	4.1	4.3	4.2	4.0	3.0	2.9	3.4	2.9
Snow	8.0	5.8	3.5	0.6	tr	0.0	0.0	0.0	0.0	0.4	1.1	6.2

High and Low temperatures in degrees Fahrenheit; Precipitation and Snow in inches

Population: 33,866 (2000); Race: 94.2% White, 0.2% Black, 0.1% Asian, 0.1% American Indian and Alaska Native, 7.2% Hispanic of any race, 0.6% two or more races (2000); Density: 83.6 persons per square mile (2000); Age: 27.3% under 18, 14.6% over 64 (2000).
Religion: Five largest groups: 7.3% The United Methodist Church, 6.5% Christian Churches and Churches of Christ, 4.2% Catholic Church, 3.0% Presbyterian Church (U.S.A.), 2.9% Southern Baptist Convention (2000).
Economy: Unemployment rate: 4.6% (11/2002); Total civilian labor force: 16,844 (11/2002); Leading industries: 45.1% manufacturing; 13.7% health care and social assistance; 10.9% retail trade (2000); Companies that employ more than 1,000 persons: 0 (2000); Companies that employ more than 100 persons: 19 (2000); Farms: 585 totaling 236,320 acres (1997); Minority business ownership rate: 0.0% (1997); Women business ownership rate: 25.6% (1997); Retail sales per capita: $5,835 (1997). Single-family building permits issued: 88 (2001) / 73 (2000); Multi-family building permits issued: 12 (2001) / 4 (2000).
Income: Per capita income: $17,862 (2000); Median household income: $40,759 (2000); Poverty rate: 8.6% (2000); Bankruptcy rate: 8.26% (2001).
Taxes: Total county taxes per capita: $256 (2000); County property taxes per capita: $159 (2000).
Education: High school graduation rate: 80.1% (2000); College graduation rate: 10.1% (2000).
Housing: Homeownership rate: 72.9% (2000); Median home value: $85,000 (2000); Median rent: $418 per month (2000); Median age of housing: 49 years (2000).
Health: Birth rate: 147.4 per 10,000 population (1998); Age adjusted death rate: 97.7 per 10,000 population (1999); Age adjusted cancer mortality rate: 223.8 deaths per 100,000 population (1999). Number of physicians: 5.9 per 10,000 population (1999); Number of hospital beds: 15.6 per 10,000 population (1999).
Elections: 2000 Presidential election results: 33.2% Gore, 65.0% Bush, 0.4% Nader, 0.8% Buchanan
Additional Information Contacts
Clinton County Government Offices 765-659-6330
Frankfort Board of Realtors 765-654-4456

Frankfort Chamber of Commerce 765-654-5507

Clinton County Communities

COLFAX (town). Covers a land area of 0.362 square miles and a water area of 0 square miles. Located at 40.19° N. Lat.; 86.66° W. Long. Elevation is 845 feet.
Population: 768 (2000); Race: 100.0% White, 0.0% Black, 0.0% Asian, 0.0% American Indian and Alaska Native, 0.8% Hispanic of any race, 0.0% two or more races (2000); Density: 2,118.9 persons per square mile (2000); Age: 32.1% under 18, 10.2% over 64 (2000); Marriage status: 22.1% never married, 63.0% now married, 7.4% widowed, 7.5% divorced (2000); Foreign born: 0.3% (2000); Ancestry (includes multiple ancestries): 22.7% German, 12.2% Other groups, 11.2% Irish, 9.8% United States or American, 8.8% English (2000).
Economy: In agricultural area; meat processing. Employment by occupation: 3.6% management, 11.4% professional, 17.8% services, 21.4% sales, 0.0% farming, 10.2% construction, 35.5% production (2000).
Income: Per capita income: $14,482 (2000); Median household income: $42,688 (2000); Poverty rate: 7.8% (2000).
Taxes: Total city taxes per capita: $108 (1997); City property taxes per capita: $99 (1997).
Education: High school graduation rate: 74.2% (2000); College graduation rate: 3.9% (2000).
Housing: Homeownership rate: 82.9% (2000); Median home value: $72,500 (2000); Median rent: $229 per month (2000); Median age of housing: 60+ years (2000).
Transportation: Commute to work: 92.3% car, 0.6% public transportation, 2.5% walk, 4.6% work from home (2000); Travel time to work: 15.8% less than 15 minutes, 46.8% 15 to 30 minutes, 25.2% 30 to 45 minutes, 7.4% 45 to 60 minutes, 4.8% 60 minutes or more (2000)

FOREST (unincorporated postal area, zip code 46039). Covers a land area of 27.750 square miles and a water area of 0.014 square miles. Located at 40.36° N. Lat.; 86.30° W. Long. Elevation is 882 feet.
Population: 839 (2000); Race: 100.0% White, 0.0% Black, 0.0% Asian, 0.0% American Indian and Alaska Native, 0.0% Hispanic of any race, 0.0% two or more races (2000); Density: 30.2 persons per square mile (2000); Age: 22.5% under 18, 15.8% over 64 (2000); Marriage status: 16.5% never married, 63.8% now married, 8.2% widowed, 11.4% divorced (2000); Foreign born: 0.0% (2000); Ancestry (includes multiple ancestries): 25.1% United States or American, 18.7% German, 18.1% Irish, 14.4% English, 5.2% Scotch-Irish (2000).
Economy: Employment by occupation: 5.3% management, 22.1% professional, 5.6% services, 15.7% sales, 4.8% farming, 13.7% construction, 32.7% production (2000).
Income: Per capita income: $22,456 (2000); Median household income: $51,625 (2000); Poverty rate: 10.7% (2000).
Education: High school graduation rate: 92.1% (2000); College graduation rate: 13.4% (2000).
Housing: Homeownership rate: 93.5% (2000); Median home value: $86,700 (2000); Median rent: $363 per month (2000); Median age of housing: 60+ years (2000).
Transportation: Commute to work: 96.8% car, 0.0% public transportation, 1.3% walk, 0.0% work from home (2000); Travel time to work: 16.8% less than 15 minutes, 53.9% 15 to 30 minutes, 22.4% 30 to 45 minutes, 1.8% 45 to 60 minutes, 5.0% 60 minutes or more (2000)

FRANKFORT (city). Covers a land area of 5.142 square miles and a water area of 0 square miles. Located at 40.28° N. Lat.; 86.51° W. Long. Elevation is 855 feet.
History: Frankfort was named for Frankfurt am Main, Germany, the home of the grandfather of the Pence brothers who owned the land on which the city was founded. Frankfort developed as the county seat of Clinton County.
Population: 16,662 (2000); Race: 89.4% White, 0.2% Black, 0.1% Asian, 0.1% American Indian and Alaska Native, 13.9% Hispanic of any race, 0.9% two or more races (2000); Density: 3,240.5 persons per square mile (2000); Age: 27.3% under 18, 16.3% over 64 (2000); Marriage status: 22.6% never married, 57.2% now married, 9.3% widowed, 10.9% divorced (2000); Foreign born: 9.0% (2000); Ancestry (includes multiple ancestries): 17.9% Other groups, 16.0% German, 15.0% United States or American, 10.9% Irish, 7.6% English (2000).
Vital Statistics: Birth rate: 156.6 per 10,000 population (1998)
Economy: Single-family building permits issued: 24 (2001) / 30 (2000); Multi-family building permits issued: 8 (2001) / 4 (2000); Employment by occupation: 6.7% management, 6.5% professional, 12.9% services, 20.8% sales, 1.9% farming, 11.3% construction, 39.9% production (2000).
Income: Per capita income: $15,393 (2000); Median household income: $33,275 (2000); Poverty rate: 11.7% (2000).
Taxes: Total city taxes per capita: $207 (2000); City property taxes per capita: $206 (2000).
Education: High school graduation rate: 73.8% (2000); College graduation rate: 7.8% (2000).

School District(s)

Clinton Prairie School Corp (KG-12)
2000 Enrollment: 1,117 765-659-1339
Community Schools of Frankfort (PK-12)
2000 Enrollment: 3,192 765-654-5585

Housing: Homeownership rate: 61.7% (2000); Median home value: $76,600 (2000); Median rent: $422 per month (2000); Median age of housing: 49 years (2000).
Hospitals: Saint Vincent Frankfort Hospital (88 beds)
Safety: Violent crime rate: 24.5 per 10,000 population; Property crime rate: 476.8 per 10,000 population (2001).
Newspapers: The Times (6 x week)
Transportation: Commute to work: 93.2% car, 1.0% public transportation, 1.3% walk, 1.4% work from home (2000); Travel time to work: 60.5% less than 15 minutes, 14.1% 15 to 30 minutes, 17.8% 30 to 45 minutes, 6.2% 45 to 60 minutes, 1.5% 60 minutes or more (2000)

Additional Information Contacts

Frankfort Board of Realtors 765-654-4456
Frankfort Chamber of Commerce 765-654-5507

KIRKLIN (town). Covers a land area of 0.323 square miles and a water area of 0 square miles. Located at 40.19° N. Lat.; 86.36° W. Long. Elevation is 919 feet.
History: Kirklin was established at the junction of the Michigan Road with a state road. Nathan Kirklin bought the land here in 1828 and built a tavern.
Population: 766 (2000); Race: 96.7% White, 0.9% Black, 0.0% Asian, 0.9% American Indian and Alaska Native, 2.3% Hispanic of any race, 0.5% two or more races (2000); Density: 2,371.2 persons per square mile (2000); Age: 35.6% under 18, 10.5% over 64 (2000); Marriage status: 19.6% never married, 55.9% now married, 7.8% widowed, 16.6% divorced (2000); Foreign born: 1.5% (2000); Ancestry (includes multiple ancestries): 20.6% German, 14.8% Irish, 12.8% United States or American, 10.7% Other groups, 3.7% English (2000).
Economy: Employment by occupation: 5.8% management, 12.3% professional, 9.9% services, 23.7% sales, 1.2% farming, 21.3% construction, 25.7% production (2000).
Income: Per capita income: $14,633 (2000); Median household income: $39,167 (2000); Poverty rate: 12.0% (2000).
Taxes: Total city taxes per capita: $108 (1997); City property taxes per capita: $100 (1997).
Education: High school graduation rate: 73.8% (2000); College graduation rate: 5.4% (2000).
Housing: Homeownership rate: 77.6% (2000); Median home value: $74,100 (2000); Median rent: $435 per month (2000); Median age of housing: 49 years (2000).
Transportation: Commute to work: 95.5% car, 0.0% public transportation, 1.8% walk, 2.7% work from home (2000); Travel time to work: 14.7% less than 15 minutes, 28.7% 15 to 30 minutes, 29.7% 30 to 45 minutes, 14.1% 45 to 60 minutes, 12.8% 60 minutes or more (2000)

MICHIGANTOWN (town). Covers a land area of 0.265 square miles and a water area of 0 square miles. Located at 40.32° N. Lat.; 86.39° W. Long. Elevation is 872 feet.
History: Michigantown was founded in 1830 and named for the Michigan Road, for which it served as a stage stop.
Population: 406 (2000); Race: 98.8% White, 0.0% Black, 0.0% Asian, 0.7% American Indian and Alaska Native, 1.7% Hispanic of any race, 0.5% two or more races (2000); Density: 1,533.6 persons per square mile (2000); Age: 24.0% under 18, 19.5% over 64 (2000); Marriage status: 19.7% never married, 60.0% now married, 11.0% widowed, 9.3% divorced (2000); Foreign born: 0.5% (2000); Ancestry (includes multiple ancestries): 22.3% United States or American, 19.5% German, 13.5% Irish, 10.7% French (except Basque), 9.5% Other groups (2000).
Economy: Employment by occupation: 7.2% management, 11.3% professional, 22.7% services, 10.8% sales, 1.5% farming, 10.8% construction, 35.6% production (2000).
Income: Per capita income: $21,102 (2000); Median household income: $37,500 (2000); Poverty rate: 5.0% (2000).

Taxes: Total city taxes per capita: $67 (1997); City property taxes per capita: $63 (1997).
Education: High school graduation rate: 88.4% (2000); College graduation rate: 10.3% (2000).

School District(s)

Clinton Central School Corp (KG-12)
2000 Enrollment: 1,078 765-249-2515

Housing: Homeownership rate: 77.6% (2000); Median home value: $72,500 (2000); Median rent: $392 per month (2000); Median age of housing: 59 years (2000).
Transportation: Commute to work: 87.3% car, 0.0% public transportation, 10.6% walk, 2.1% work from home (2000); Travel time to work: 30.3% less than 15 minutes, 41.1% 15 to 30 minutes, 17.3% 30 to 45 minutes, 7.6% 45 to 60 minutes, 3.8% 60 minutes or more (2000)

MULBERRY (town). Covers a land area of 0.588 square miles and a water area of 0 square miles. Located at 40.34° N. Lat.; 86.66° W. Long. Elevation is 770 feet.
History: Laid out 1858.
Population: 1,387 (2000); Race: 98.6% White, 0.0% Black, 0.0% Asian, 0.0% American Indian and Alaska Native, 1.2% Hispanic of any race, 0.8% two or more races (2000); Density: 2,360.2 persons per square mile (2000); Age: 23.9% under 18, 24.9% over 64 (2000); Marriage status: 17.5% never married, 61.0% now married, 12.7% widowed, 8.8% divorced (2000); Foreign born: 1.2% (2000); Ancestry (includes multiple ancestries): 20.6% German, 13.7% United States or American, 9.5% Irish, 8.9% English, 6.6% Dutch (2000).
Economy: In agricultural area: corn, soybeans, hogs. Single-family building permits issued: 0 (2001) / 0 (2000); Multi-family building permits issued: 0 (2001) / 0 (2000); Employment by occupation: 7.3% management, 16.0% professional, 13.7% services, 22.9% sales, 1.3% farming, 9.5% construction, 29.4% production (2000).
Income: Per capita income: $18,635 (2000); Median household income: $45,000 (2000); Poverty rate: 5.0% (2000).
Taxes: Total city taxes per capita: $66 (1997); City property taxes per capita: $61 (1997).
Education: High school graduation rate: 80.0% (2000); College graduation rate: 10.2% (2000).
Housing: Homeownership rate: 74.3% (2000); Median home value: $87,200 (2000); Median rent: $381 per month (2000); Median age of housing: 60+ years (2000).
Transportation: Commute to work: 95.6% car, 0.0% public transportation, 2.0% walk, 2.1% work from home (2000); Travel time to work: 17.9% less than 15 minutes, 59.0% 15 to 30 minutes, 17.9% 30 to 45 minutes, 3.3% 45 to 60 minutes, 1.8% 60 minutes or more (2000)

ROSSVILLE (town). Covers a land area of 0.516 square miles and a water area of 0 square miles. Located at 40.41° N. Lat.; 86.59° W. Long. Elevation is 722 feet.
History: Laid out 1834.
Population: 1,513 (2000); Race: 99.3% White, 0.1% Black, 0.1% Asian, 0.1% American Indian and Alaska Native, 0.2% Hispanic of any race, 0.3% two or more races (2000); Density: 2,929.8 persons per square mile (2000); Age: 27.4% under 18, 18.4% over 64 (2000); Marriage status: 17.6% never married, 69.5% now married, 4.9% widowed, 8.0% divorced (2000); Foreign born: 0.2% (2000); Ancestry (includes multiple ancestries): 23.2% German, 15.6% United States or American, 13.3% English, 9.9% Irish, 4.0% Other groups (2000).
Economy: In agricultural area; fertilizer blending. Single-family building permits issued: n/a (2001) / 0 (2000); Multi-family building permits issued: n/a (2001) / 0 (2000); Employment by occupation: 13.5% management, 13.4% professional, 13.4% services, 24.7% sales, 0.3% farming, 12.4% construction, 22.4% production (2000).
Income: Per capita income: $19,765 (2000); Median household income: $48,333 (2000); Poverty rate: 3.7% (2000).
Taxes: Total city taxes per capita: $155 (1997); City property taxes per capita: $146 (1997).
Education: High school graduation rate: 83.8% (2000); College graduation rate: 12.3% (2000).

School District(s)

Rossville Con School District (KG-12)
2000 Enrollment: 949 765-379-2990

Housing: Homeownership rate: 82.6% (2000); Median home value: $97,800 (2000); Median rent: $417 per month (2000); Median age of housing: 36 years (2000).
Transportation: Commute to work: 94.4% car, 0.0% public transportation, 1.5% walk, 3.9% work from home (2000); Travel time to work: 17.5% less than 15 minutes, 46.5% 15 to 30 minutes, 29.4% 30 to 45 minutes, 3.6% 45 to 60 minutes, 3.1% 60 minutes or more (2000)

Crawford County

Located in southern Indiana; bounded on the south by the Ohio River and the Kentucky border; drained by the Blue and Little Blue Rivers. Covers a land area of 305.70 square miles, a water area of 3.20 square miles, and is located in the Eastern Time Zone. The county government was organized in 1818. County seat is English.

Weather Station: English 4 S — Elevation: 508 feet

	Jan	Feb	Mar	Apr	May	Jun	Jul	Aug	Sep	Oct	Nov	Dec
High	41	47	58	68	77	84	88	87	81	70	57	46
Low	21	24	32	41	49	58	63	61	53	41	34	25
Precip	3.5	3.2	4.9	5.0	5.1	4.9	4.2	3.8	3.5	3.3	4.3	4.0
Snow	2.4	na	0.5	tr	0.0	0.0	0.0	0.0	0.0	tr	0.3	0.5

High and Low temperatures in degrees Fahrenheit; Precipitation and Snow in inches

Population: 10,743 (2000); Race: 98.9% White, 0.1% Black, 0.2% Asian, 0.4% American Indian and Alaska Native, 0.3% Hispanic of any race, 0.3% two or more races (2000); Density: 35.1 persons per square mile (2000); Age: 25.6% under 18, 12.8% over 64 (2000).
Religion: Five largest groups: 15.4% Christian Churches and Churches of Christ, 7.0% The United Methodist Church, 5.7% The Wesleyan Church, 2.6% General Association of Regular Baptist Churches, 2.4% The Church of Jesus Christ of Latter-day Saints (
Economy: Unemployment rate: 5.3% (11/2002); Total civilian labor force: 6,434 (11/2002); Leading industries: 22.7% retail trade; 14.7% construction; 10.8% accommodation & food services (2000); Companies that employ more than 1,000 persons: 0 (2000); Companies that employ more than 100 persons: 1 (2000); Farms: 410 totaling 61,320 acres (1997); Minority business ownership rate: 0.0% (1997); Women business ownership rate: 18.7% (1997); Retail sales per capita: $3,483 (1997). Single-family building permits issued: 4 (2001) / 6 (2000); Multi-family building permits issued: 0 (2001) / 0 (2000).
Income: Per capita income: $15,926 (2000); Median household income: $32,646 (2000); Poverty rate: 16.8% (2000); Bankruptcy rate: 6.99% (2001).
Taxes: Total county taxes per capita: $143 (1997); County property taxes per capita: $143 (1997).
Education: High school graduation rate: 70.6% (2000); College graduation rate: 8.4% (2000).
Housing: Homeownership rate: 82.9% (2000); Median home value: $64,600 (2000); Median rent: $276 per month (2000); Median age of housing: 25 years (2000).
Health: Birth rate: 118.2 per 10,000 population (1998); Age adjusted death rate: 83.9 per 10,000 population (1999); Age adjusted cancer mortality rate: 196.3 deaths per 100,000 population (1999). Number of physicians: 0.9 per 10,000 population (1999); Number of hospital beds: n/a (1999).
Elections: 2000 Presidential election results: 43.2% Gore, 55.3% Bush, 0.4% Nader, 0.8% Buchanan
National and State Parks: Hilands Overlook State Park
Additional Information Contacts
Crawford County Government Offices 812-338-2601

Crawford County Communities

ALTON (town). Covers a land area of 0.170 square miles and a water area of 0.025 square miles. Located at 38.12° N. Lat.; 86.42° W. Long. Elevation is 425 feet.
Population: 53 (2000); Race: 100.0% White, 0.0% Black, 0.0% Asian, 0.0% American Indian and Alaska Native, 0.0% Hispanic of any race, 0.0% two or more races (2000); Density: 312.3 persons per square mile (2000); Age: 32.6% under 18, 18.6% over 64 (2000); Marriage status: 3.3% never married, 66.7% now married, 26.7% widowed, 3.3% divorced (2000); Foreign born: 0.0% (2000); Ancestry (includes multiple ancestries): 30.2% Irish, 16.3% German, 9.3% Dutch, 7.0% French (except Basque), 4.7% English (2000).
Economy: Agricultural area. Employment by occupation: 0.0% management, 11.1% professional, 11.1% services, 22.2% sales, 16.7% farming, 0.0% construction, 38.9% production (2000).
Income: Per capita income: $11,167 (2000); Median household income: $19,375 (2000); Poverty rate: 9.3% (2000).
Taxes: Total city taxes per capita: $107 (1997); City property taxes per capita: $89 (1997).

Education: High school graduation rate: 40.0% (2000); College graduation rate: 0.0% (2000).
Housing: Homeownership rate: 100.0% (2000); Median home value: $36,300 (2000); Median age of housing: 44 years (2000).
Transportation: Commute to work: 100.0% car, 0.0% public transportation, 0.0% walk, 0.0% work from home (2000); Travel time to work: 22.2% less than 15 minutes, 33.3% 15 to 30 minutes, 22.2% 30 to 45 minutes, 0.0% 45 to 60 minutes, 22.2% 60 minutes or more (2000)

ECKERTY (unincorporated postal area, zip code 47116). Covers a land area of 33.242 square miles and a water area of 0.044 square miles. Located at 38.32° N. Lat.; 86.61° W. Long. Elevation is 731 feet.
Population: 854 (2000); Race: 100.0% White, 0.0% Black, 0.0% Asian, 0.0% American Indian and Alaska Native, 1.4% Hispanic of any race, 0.0% two or more races (2000); Density: 25.7 persons per square mile (2000); Age: 21.6% under 18, 13.6% over 64 (2000); Marriage status: 20.5% never married, 61.7% now married, 2.9% widowed, 14.8% divorced (2000); Foreign born: 0.1% (2000); Ancestry (includes multiple ancestries): 21.9% Irish, 18.6% German, 16.3% Other groups, 7.1% English, 6.3% United States or American (2000).
Economy: Employment by occupation: 9.7% management, 11.9% professional, 17.8% services, 15.8% sales, 5.9% farming, 11.1% construction, 27.7% production (2000).
Income: Per capita income: $15,721 (2000); Median household income: $41,319 (2000); Poverty rate: 18.9% (2000).
Education: High school graduation rate: 70.5% (2000); College graduation rate: 6.4% (2000).
Housing: Homeownership rate: 91.5% (2000); Median home value: $63,900 (2000); Median rent: $325 per month (2000); Median age of housing: 23 years (2000).
Transportation: Commute to work: 93.3% car, 0.0% public transportation, 0.0% walk, 2.7% work from home (2000); Travel time to work: 7.9% less than 15 minutes, 21.6% 15 to 30 minutes, 44.5% 30 to 45 minutes, 10.9% 45 to 60 minutes, 15.0% 60 minutes or more (2000)

ENGLISH (town). Covers a land area of 3.052 square miles and a water area of 0 square miles. Located at 38.33° N. Lat.; 86.46° W. Long. Elevation is 512 feet.
History: The town of English was laid out in 1839, and grew when it became the county seat in 1893. The town was named for William Hayden English, a U.S. congressman from Indiana.
Population: 673 (2000); Race: 99.0% White, 0.0% Black, 0.0% Asian, 1.0% American Indian and Alaska Native, 0.0% Hispanic of any race, 0.0% two or more races (2000); Density: 220.5 persons per square mile (2000); Age: 29.5% under 18, 18.5% over 64 (2000); Marriage status: 19.1% never married, 50.5% now married, 17.6% widowed, 12.8% divorced (2000); Foreign born: 1.1% (2000); Ancestry (includes multiple ancestries): 26.9% United States or American, 12.2% German, 7.6% English, 5.1% Irish, 4.3% Other groups (2000).
Economy: Single-family building permits issued: 4 (2001) / 4 (2000); Multi-family building permits issued: 0 (2001) / 0 (2000); Employment by occupation: 4.8% management, 8.4% professional, 10.0% services, 30.4% sales, 1.2% farming, 9.6% construction, 35.6% production (2000).
Income: Per capita income: $11,065 (2000); Median household income: $20,870 (2000); Poverty rate: 33.9% (2000).
Taxes: Total city taxes per capita: $33 (1997); City property taxes per capita: $4 (1997).
Education: High school graduation rate: 57.1% (2000); College graduation rate: 7.1% (2000).
Housing: Homeownership rate: 67.3% (2000); Median home value: $60,500 (2000); Median rent: <$100 per month (2000); Median age of housing: 26 years (2000).
Transportation: Commute to work: 95.2% car, 0.0% public transportation, 0.0% walk, 4.0% work from home (2000); Travel time to work: 29.6% less than 15 minutes, 12.1% 15 to 30 minutes, 21.7% 30 to 45 minutes, 18.8% 45 to 60 minutes, 17.9% 60 minutes or more (2000)

GRANTSBURG (unincorporated postal area, zip code 47123). Covers a land area of 0.288 square miles and a water area of 0 square miles. Located at 38.28° N. Lat.; 86.46° W. Long. Elevation is 609 feet.
Population: 30 (2000); Race: 100.0% White, 0.0% Black, 0.0% Asian, 0.0% American Indian and Alaska Native, 0.0% Hispanic of any race, 0.0% two or more races (2000); Density: 104.2 persons per square mile (2000); Age: 0.0% under 18, 47.6% over 64 (2000); Marriage status: 0.0% never married, 47.6% now married, 52.4% widowed, 0.0% divorced (2000); Foreign born: 0.0% (2000); Ancestry (includes multiple ancestries): 52.4% United States or American (2000).
Economy: Employment by occupation: 0.0% management, 0.0% professional, 0.0% services, 100.0% sales, 0.0% farming, 0.0% construction, 0.0% production (2000).
Income: Per capita income: $7,138 (2000); Median household income: $4,318 (2000); Poverty rate: 52.4% (2000).
Education: High school graduation rate: 52.4% (2000); College graduation rate: 0.0% (2000).
Housing: Homeownership rate: 100.0% (2000); Median home value: $55,000 (2000); Median age of housing: 15 years (2000).
Transportation: Commute to work: 100.0% car, 0.0% public transportation, 0.0% walk, 0.0% work from home (2000); Travel time to work: 0.0% less than 15 minutes, 0.0% 15 to 30 minutes, 100.0% 30 to 45 minutes, 0.0% 45 to 60 minutes, 0.0% 60 minutes or more (2000)

LEAVENWORTH (town). Covers a land area of 0.834 square miles and a water area of 0.050 square miles. Located at 38.19° N. Lat.; 86.34° W. Long. Elevation is 668 feet.
History: Leavenworth was founded in 1818 and served as Crawford County's seat from 1843 to 1893. A boat-building industry was established in 1830 by David Lyon, and Leavenworth became a shipping point on the Ohio River. The 1937 flooding of the Ohio River destroyed most of the town, which was rebuilt on the hills behind the original site.
Population: 353 (2000); Race: 93.6% White, 4.1% Black, 0.0% Asian, 0.0% American Indian and Alaska Native, 0.6% Hispanic of any race, 1.7% two or more races (2000); Density: 423.3 persons per square mile (2000); Age: 18.6% under 18, 33.9% over 64 (2000); Marriage status: 25.8% never married, 41.1% now married, 16.0% widowed, 17.1% divorced (2000); Foreign born: 1.7% (2000); Ancestry (includes multiple ancestries): 18.3% United States or American, 9.6% European, 5.8% German, 4.9% English, 3.5% Irish (2000).
Economy: Single-family building permits issued: 0 (2001) / 0 (2000); Multi-family building permits issued: 0 (2001) / 0 (2000); Employment by occupation: 0.9% management, 12.2% professional, 30.4% services, 11.3% sales, 0.0% farming, 15.7% construction, 29.6% production (2000).
Income: Per capita income: $15,717 (2000); Median household income: $24,375 (2000); Poverty rate: 18.6% (2000).
Taxes: Total city taxes per capita: $28 (1997); City property taxes per capita: $0 (1997).
Education: High school graduation rate: 51.0% (2000); College graduation rate: 11.8% (2000).
Housing: Homeownership rate: 61.3% (2000); Median home value: $70,600 (2000); Median rent: $183 per month (2000); Median age of housing: 41 years (2000).
Transportation: Commute to work: 93.9% car, 0.0% public transportation, 3.5% walk, 2.6% work from home (2000); Travel time to work: 33.9% less than 15 minutes, 28.6% 15 to 30 minutes, 17.0% 30 to 45 minutes, 8.9% 45 to 60 minutes, 11.6% 60 minutes or more (2000)

MARENGO (town). Covers a land area of 0.765 square miles and a water area of 0 square miles. Located at 38.37° N. Lat.; 86.34° W. Long. Elevation is 590 feet.
History: Marengo grew as a resort village in an area of coldwater springs and caves. Quarrying was an early industry.
Population: 829 (2000); Race: 99.3% White, 0.0% Black, 0.0% Asian, 0.1% American Indian and Alaska Native, 0.0% Hispanic of any race, 0.6% two or more races (2000); Density: 1,083.5 persons per square mile (2000); Age: 30.1% under 18, 14.5% over 64 (2000); Marriage status: 17.7% never married, 52.3% now married, 13.1% widowed, 16.9% divorced (2000); Foreign born: 1.0% (2000); Ancestry (includes multiple ancestries): 14.2% German, 10.9% Irish, 8.5% United States or American, 7.5% Other groups, 4.7% English (2000).
Economy: Single-family building permits issued: 0 (2001) / 0 (2000); Multi-family building permits issued: 0 (2001) / 0 (2000); Employment by occupation: 5.7% management, 12.2% professional, 19.1% services, 22.8% sales, 1.2% farming, 6.5% construction, 32.5% production (2000).
Income: Per capita income: $11,194 (2000); Median household income: $23,542 (2000); Poverty rate: 23.9% (2000).
Taxes: Total city taxes per capita: $33 (1997); City property taxes per capita: $5 (1997).
Education: High school graduation rate: 68.9% (2000); College graduation rate: 4.7% (2000).

School District(s)

Crawford Co Com School Corp (PK-12)
2000 Enrollment: 1,851 812-365-2135

Housing: Homeownership rate: 63.9% (2000); Median home value: $53,600 (2000); Median rent: $263 per month (2000); Median age of housing: 41 years (2000).
Transportation: Commute to work: 97.5% car, 0.0% public transportation, 0.0% walk, 1.7% work from home (2000); Travel time to work: 23.2% less than 15 minutes, 19.7% 15 to 30 minutes, 22.3% 30 to 45 minutes, 23.2% 45 to 60 minutes, 11.6% 60 minutes or more (2000)

SULPHUR (unincorporated postal area, zip code 47174). Covers a land area of 1.713 square miles and a water area of 0 square miles. Located at 38.21° N. Lat.; 86.46° W. Long. Elevation is 715 feet.
History: Sulphur was named for the sulphur springs located nearby. White Sulphur Spring was discovered in the 1860's by men who were drilling for oil. A hotel was built for the visitors who came for the medicinal value of the water, which was also bottled and sold.
Population: 104 (2000); Race: 100.0% White, 0.0% Black, 0.0% Asian, 0.0% American Indian and Alaska Native, 0.0% Hispanic of any race, 0.0% two or more races (2000); Density: 60.7 persons per square mile (2000); Age: 27.8% under 18, 6.9% over 64 (2000); Marriage status: 7.7% never married, 55.8% now married, 9.6% widowed, 26.9% divorced (2000); Foreign born: 0.0% (2000); Ancestry (includes multiple ancestries): 40.3% English, 27.8% German, 26.4% Irish, 20.8% United States or American, 13.9% Dutch (2000).
Economy: Employment by occupation: 0.0% management, 10.6% professional, 19.1% services, 42.6% sales, 0.0% farming, 17.0% construction, 10.6% production (2000).
Income: Per capita income: $23,731 (2000); Median household income: $75,406 (2000); Poverty rate: 0.0% (2000).
Education: High school graduation rate: 100.0% (2000); College graduation rate: 31.3% (2000).
Housing: Homeownership rate: 100.0% (2000); Median age of housing: 6 years (2000).
Transportation: Commute to work: 100.0% car, 0.0% public transportation, 0.0% walk, 0.0% work from home (2000); Travel time to work: 0.0% less than 15 minutes, 72.3% 15 to 30 minutes, 10.6% 30 to 45 minutes, 0.0% 45 to 60 minutes, 17.0% 60 minutes or more (2000)

TASWELL (unincorporated postal area, zip code 47175). Covers a land area of 20.554 square miles and a water area of 0.001 square miles. Located at 38.35° N. Lat.; 86.55° W. Long. Elevation is 779 feet.
Population: 819 (2000); Race: 100.0% White, 0.0% Black, 0.0% Asian, 0.0% American Indian and Alaska Native, 0.0% Hispanic of any race, 0.0% two or more races (2000); Density: 39.8 persons per square mile (2000); Age: 21.6% under 18, 11.2% over 64 (2000); Marriage status: 18.2% never married, 64.1% now married, 7.5% widowed, 10.2% divorced (2000); Foreign born: 0.0% (2000); Ancestry (includes multiple ancestries): 22.7% United States or American, 16.4% English, 13.9% Irish, 9.8% German, 3.8% Other groups (2000).
Economy: Employment by occupation: 8.9% management, 11.2% professional, 3.6% services, 20.0% sales, 0.0% farming, 11.8% construction, 44.4% production (2000).
Income: Per capita income: $33,405 (2000); Median household income: $39,219 (2000); Poverty rate: 8.8% (2000).
Education: High school graduation rate: 74.0% (2000); College graduation rate: 12.4% (2000).
Housing: Homeownership rate: 90.2% (2000); Median home value: $84,000 (2000); Median rent: $125 per month (2000); Median age of housing: 21 years (2000).
Transportation: Commute to work: 92.5% car, 0.0% public transportation, 0.0% walk, 5.7% work from home (2000); Travel time to work: 7.7% less than 15 minutes, 23.7% 15 to 30 minutes, 35.5% 30 to 45 minutes, 16.4% 45 to 60 minutes, 16.7% 60 minutes or more (2000)

Daviess County

Located in southwestern Indiana; bounded on the south by the East Fork of the White River, on the west by the West Fork of the White River. Covers a land area of 430.70 square miles, a water area of 6.20 square miles, and is located in the Eastern Time Zone. The county government was organized in 1816. County seat is Washington.

Weather Station: Washington Elevation: 524 feet

	Jan	Feb	Mar	Apr	May	Jun	Jul	Aug	Sep	Oct	Nov	Dec
High	39	45	56	67	77	85	88	86	80	69	55	44
Low	23	27	36	45	55	64	68	66	58	47	38	28
Precip	2.7	2.6	4.2	4.2	5.4	4.0	4.9	3.7	2.9	3.2	4.3	3.4
Snow	4.2	3.0	1.8	tr	tr	0.0	0.0	0.0	0.0	tr	0.3	2.2

High and Low temperatures in degrees Fahrenheit; Precipitation and Snow in inches

Population: 29,820 (2000); Race: 97.4% White, 0.4% Black, 0.3% Asian, 0.3% American Indian and Alaska Native, 2.0% Hispanic of any race, 0.5% two or more races (2000); Density: 69.2 persons per square mile (2000); Age: 29.0% under 18, 14.6% over 64 (2000).
Religion: Five largest groups: 14.0% Catholic Church, 9.8% Christian Churches and Churches of Christ, 8.5% The United Methodist Church, 5.0% American Baptist Churches in the USA, 3.8% Old Order Amish Church (2000).
Economy: Unemployment rate: 3.7% (11/2002); Total civilian labor force: 13,380 (11/2002); Leading industries: 21.9% manufacturing; 17.7% retail trade; 12.9% health care and social assistance (2000); Companies that employ more than 1,000 persons: 0 (2000); Companies that employ more than 100 persons: 10 (2000); Farms: 1,101 totaling 217,131 acres (1997); Minority business ownership rate: 0.0% (1997); Women business ownership rate: 16.9% (1997); Retail sales per capita: $9,033 (1997). Single-family building permits issued: 17 (2001) / 22 (2000); Multi-family building permits issued: 0 (2001) / 0 (2000).
Income: Per capita income: $16,015 (2000); Median household income: $34,064 (2000); Poverty rate: 13.8% (2000); Bankruptcy rate: 4.47% (2001).
Taxes: Total county taxes per capita: $197 (2000); County property taxes per capita: $114 (2000).
Education: High school graduation rate: 71.8% (2000); College graduation rate: 9.7% (2000).
Housing: Homeownership rate: 78.6% (2000); Median home value: $70,800 (2000); Median rent: $276 per month (2000); Median age of housing: 37 years (2000).
Health: Birth rate: 138.5 per 10,000 population (1998); Age adjusted death rate: 95.3 per 10,000 population (1999); Age adjusted cancer mortality rate: 195.0 deaths per 100,000 population (1999). Air Quality Index: 100% good, 0% moderate, 0% unhealthy (percent of days in 2000). Number of physicians: 4.4 per 10,000 population (1999); Number of hospital beds: 25.2 per 10,000 population (1999).
Elections: 2000 Presidential election results: 27.6% Gore, 70.4% Bush, 0.5% Nader, 0.9% Buchanan
National and State Parks: Glendale State Fish and Wildlife Area
Additional Information Contacts
Daviess County Government Offices.................. 812-254-8662
Washington Chamber of Commerce 812-254-5262

Daviess County Communities

ALFORDSVILLE (town). Covers a land area of 0.068 square miles and a water area of 0 square miles. Located at 38.56° N. Lat.; 86.94° W. Long. Elevation is 520 feet.
History: Laid out 1845.
Population: 112 (2000); Race: 100.0% White, 0.0% Black, 0.0% Asian, 0.0% American Indian and Alaska Native, 0.0% Hispanic of any race, 0.0% two or more races (2000); Density: 1,638.4 persons per square mile (2000); Age: 31.5% under 18, 6.5% over 64 (2000); Marriage status: 28.0% never married, 62.0% now married, 3.0% widowed, 7.0% divorced (2000); Foreign born: 0.0% (2000); Ancestry (includes multiple ancestries): 29.8% United States or American, 19.4% Other groups, 16.9% German, 3.2% English, 1.6% Welsh (2000).
Economy: Employment by occupation: 6.8% management, 0.0% professional, 6.8% services, 35.6% sales, 0.0% farming, 11.9% construction, 39.0% production (2000).
Income: Per capita income: $21,111 (2000); Median household income: $54,375 (2000); Poverty rate: 18.5% (2000).
Taxes: Total city taxes per capita: $61 (1997); City property taxes per capita: $61 (1997).
Education: High school graduation rate: 60.8% (2000); College graduation rate: 0.0% (2000).
Housing: Homeownership rate: 91.1% (2000); Median home value: $55,000 (2000); Median rent: $275 per month (2000); Median age of housing: 32 years (2000).
Transportation: Commute to work: 86.4% car, 0.0% public transportation, 8.5% walk, 5.1% work from home (2000); Travel time to work: 8.9% less

than 15 minutes, 48.2% 15 to 30 minutes, 25.0% 30 to 45 minutes, 10.7% 45 to 60 minutes, 7.1% 60 minutes or more (2000)

CANNELBURG (town). Covers a land area of 0.187 square miles and a water area of 0 square miles. Located at 38.66° N. Lat.; 86.99° W. Long. Elevation is 524 feet.
Population: 140 (2000); Race: 100.0% White, 0.0% Black, 0.0% Asian, 0.0% American Indian and Alaska Native, 0.0% Hispanic of any race, 0.0% two or more races (2000); Density: 747.3 persons per square mile (2000); Age: 28.1% under 18, 5.0% over 64 (2000); Marriage status: 25.3% never married, 70.3% now married, 1.1% widowed, 3.3% divorced (2000); Foreign born: 0.0% (2000); Ancestry (includes multiple ancestries): 38.8% United States or American, 24.8% German, 7.4% Irish, 5.0% English, 3.3% French (except Basque) (2000).
Economy: In agricultural area. Employment by occupation: 14.0% management, 10.5% professional, 15.8% services, 19.3% sales, 0.0% farming, 7.0% construction, 33.3% production (2000).
Income: Per capita income: $12,674 (2000); Median household income: $37,917 (2000); Poverty rate: 14.9% (2000).
Taxes: Total city taxes per capita: $59 (1997); City property taxes per capita: $59 (1997).
Education: High school graduation rate: 68.1% (2000); College graduation rate: 2.9% (2000).
Housing: Homeownership rate: 88.6% (2000); Median home value: $73,000 (2000); Median rent: $325 per month (2000); Median age of housing: 32 years (2000).
Transportation: Commute to work: 94.7% car, 0.0% public transportation, 5.3% walk, 0.0% work from home (2000); Travel time to work: 42.1% less than 15 minutes, 35.1% 15 to 30 minutes, 8.8% 30 to 45 minutes, 0.0% 45 to 60 minutes, 14.0% 60 minutes or more (2000)

ELNORA (town). Covers a land area of 0.947 square miles and a water area of 0 square miles. Located at 38.87° N. Lat.; 87.08° W. Long. Elevation is 476 feet.
Population: 721 (2000); Race: 97.8% White, 0.0% Black, 0.3% Asian, 0.0% American Indian and Alaska Native, 0.0% Hispanic of any race, 1.9% two or more races (2000); Density: 761.7 persons per square mile (2000); Age: 24.1% under 18, 20.7% over 64 (2000); Marriage status: 20.6% never married, 58.7% now married, 10.1% widowed, 10.6% divorced (2000); Foreign born: 0.3% (2000); Ancestry (includes multiple ancestries): 23.3% German, 19.7% United States or American, 13.7% Irish, 6.0% English, 5.1% Other groups (2000).
Economy: In farming and dairying area; cheese, cargo trailers. Employment by occupation: 7.2% management, 11.4% professional, 18.6% services, 24.0% sales, 1.9% farming, 12.5% construction, 24.3% production (2000).
Income: Per capita income: $14,337 (2000); Median household income: $27,321 (2000); Poverty rate: 17.6% (2000).
Taxes: Total city taxes per capita: $34 (1997); City property taxes per capita: $32 (1997).
Education: High school graduation rate: 69.3% (2000); College graduation rate: 6.8% (2000).

School District(s)

North Daviess Com Schools (KG-12)
2000 Enrollment: 1,176 812-636-7654
Housing: Homeownership rate: 83.8% (2000); Median home value: $34,700 (2000); Median rent: $225 per month (2000); Median age of housing: 53 years (2000).
Transportation: Commute to work: 92.7% car, 0.0% public transportation, 2.3% walk, 3.8% work from home (2000); Travel time to work: 40.8% less than 15 minutes, 26.0% 15 to 30 minutes, 18.0% 30 to 45 minutes, 6.0% 45 to 60 minutes, 9.2% 60 minutes or more (2000)

MONTGOMERY (town). Covers a land area of 0.241 square miles and a water area of 0 square miles. Located at 38.66° N. Lat.; 87.04° W. Long. Elevation is 533 feet.
History: Montgomery grew up around St. Peter's Church which was founded in 1818.
Population: 368 (2000); Race: 99.7% White, 0.3% Black, 0.0% Asian, 0.0% American Indian and Alaska Native, 0.5% Hispanic of any race, 0.0% two or more races (2000); Density: 1,527.7 persons per square mile (2000); Age: 23.9% under 18, 12.6% over 64 (2000); Marriage status: 20.5% never married, 61.6% now married, 8.8% widowed, 9.1% divorced (2000); Foreign born: 0.0% (2000); Ancestry (includes multiple ancestries): 24.7% German, 23.7% Irish, 15.6% United States or American, 11.6% English, 9.4% Other groups (2000).
Economy: Employment by occupation: 7.6% management, 14.2% professional, 7.6% services, 23.7% sales, 2.4% farming, 16.6% construction, 28.0% production (2000).
Income: Per capita income: $15,156 (2000); Median household income: $36,944 (2000); Poverty rate: 10.8% (2000).
Taxes: Total city taxes per capita: $73 (1997); City property taxes per capita: $73 (1997).
Education: High school graduation rate: 76.8% (2000); College graduation rate: 7.9% (2000).

School District(s)

Barr-Reeve Com Schools Inc (KG-12)
2000 Enrollment: 741 812-486-3220
Housing: Homeownership rate: 72.3% (2000); Median home value: $54,500 (2000); Median rent: $254 per month (2000); Median age of housing: 60 years (2000).
Transportation: Commute to work: 90.0% car, 0.0% public transportation, 3.8% walk, 6.2% work from home (2000); Travel time to work: 38.8% less than 15 minutes, 24.0% 15 to 30 minutes, 24.5% 30 to 45 minutes, 7.1% 45 to 60 minutes, 5.6% 60 minutes or more (2000)

ODON (town). Covers a land area of 0.943 square miles and a water area of 0.011 square miles. Located at 38.84° N. Lat.; 86.99° W. Long. Elevation is 535 feet.
History: Odon grew as a farm town on a site at a spring where George Rogers Clark and his soldiers stopped for water and to hunt buffalo.
Population: 1,376 (2000); Race: 98.6% White, 0.1% Black, 0.0% Asian, 1.1% American Indian and Alaska Native, 0.3% Hispanic of any race, 0.1% two or more races (2000); Density: 1,458.4 persons per square mile (2000); Age: 22.3% under 18, 23.9% over 64 (2000); Marriage status: 16.6% never married, 60.3% now married, 13.2% widowed, 9.8% divorced (2000); Foreign born: 0.0% (2000); Ancestry (includes multiple ancestries): 21.8% German, 16.4% United States or American, 9.9% English, 8.1% Irish, 6.4% Other groups (2000).
Economy: Employment by occupation: 11.6% management, 16.5% professional, 13.6% services, 22.2% sales, 0.2% farming, 10.4% construction, 25.5% production (2000).
Income: Per capita income: $20,020 (2000); Median household income: $34,667 (2000); Poverty rate: 11.1% (2000).
Taxes: Total city taxes per capita: $57 (1997); City property taxes per capita: $56 (1997).
Education: High school graduation rate: 77.1% (2000); College graduation rate: 11.4% (2000).
Housing: Homeownership rate: 71.8% (2000); Median home value: $56,600 (2000); Median rent: $238 per month (2000); Median age of housing: 42 years (2000).
Newspapers: The Odon Journal (1 x week)
Transportation: Commute to work: 93.9% car, 0.0% public transportation, 3.4% walk, 1.1% work from home (2000); Travel time to work: 32.8% less than 15 minutes, 32.2% 15 to 30 minutes, 14.5% 30 to 45 minutes, 12.9% 45 to 60 minutes, 7.6% 60 minutes or more (2000)

PLAINVILLE (town). Covers a land area of 0.330 square miles and a water area of 0 square miles. Located at 38.80° N. Lat.; 87.15° W. Long. Elevation is 475 feet.
Population: 513 (2000); Race: 96.5% White, 0.0% Black, 0.0% Asian, 1.9% American Indian and Alaska Native, 3.1% Hispanic of any race, 0.6% two or more races (2000); Density: 1,555.3 persons per square mile (2000); Age: 25.9% under 18, 16.1% over 64 (2000); Marriage status: 14.3% never married, 67.3% now married, 10.6% widowed, 7.8% divorced (2000); Foreign born: 1.4% (2000); Ancestry (includes multiple ancestries): 19.7% United States or American, 18.0% German, 12.2% Irish, 8.9% English, 8.7% Other groups (2000).
Economy: Agricultural area. Oil wells. Employment by occupation: 8.7% management, 16.2% professional, 11.8% services, 22.7% sales, 0.4% farming, 13.1% construction, 27.1% production (2000).
Income: Per capita income: $16,335 (2000); Median household income: $37,969 (2000); Poverty rate: 9.8% (2000).
Taxes: Total city taxes per capita: $48 (1997); City property taxes per capita: $46 (1997).
Education: High school graduation rate: 82.5% (2000); College graduation rate: 10.8% (2000).
Housing: Homeownership rate: 78.5% (2000); Median home value: $55,500 (2000); Median rent: $231 per month (2000); Median age of housing: 60 years (2000).
Transportation: Commute to work: 96.4% car, 0.0% public transportation, 2.2% walk, 0.9% work from home (2000); Travel time to work: 22.9% less

than 15 minutes, 37.2% 15 to 30 minutes, 23.3% 30 to 45 minutes, 3.6% 45 to 60 minutes, 13.0% 60 minutes or more (2000)

WASHINGTON (city). Aka Hyatt. Covers a land area of 4.734 square miles and a water area of 0.028 square miles. Located at 38.65° N. Lat.; 87.17° W. Long. Elevation is 504 feet.
History: Washington was founded by Emmanuel Van Trees, who settled here in 1817 on the site where Fort Flora had been built in 1805. The town developed around the Baltimore & Ohio Railroad shops, and became a trading and industrial center.
Population: 11,380 (2000); Race: 94.6% White, 0.8% Black, 0.3% Asian, 0.5% American Indian and Alaska Native, 4.7% Hispanic of any race, 1.0% two or more races (2000); Density: 2,404.0 persons per square mile (2000); Age: 24.6% under 18, 18.3% over 64 (2000); Marriage status: 20.2% never married, 55.3% now married, 9.6% widowed, 14.9% divorced (2000); Foreign born: 4.0% (2000); Ancestry (includes multiple ancestries): 22.3% United States or American, 20.2% German, 12.3% Irish, 10.6% Other groups, 7.1% English (2000).
Vital Statistics: Birth rate: 132.7 per 10,000 population (1998)
Economy: Single-family building permits issued: 17 (2001) / 22 (2000); Multi-family building permits issued: 0 (2001) / 0 (2000); Employment by occupation: 6.3% management, 15.2% professional, 16.2% services, 24.6% sales, 0.5% farming, 8.9% construction, 28.3% production (2000).
Income: Per capita income: $16,721 (2000); Median household income: $29,055 (2000); Poverty rate: 14.3% (2000).
Taxes: Total city taxes per capita: $201 (2000); City property taxes per capita: $194 (2000).
Education: High school graduation rate: 74.7% (2000); College graduation rate: 9.2% (2000).

School District(s)

Twin Rivers Vocational Area
2000 Enrollment: n/a 812-254-1189
Washington Com Schools Inc (KG-12)
2000 Enrollment: 2,567 812-254-5536

Housing: Homeownership rate: 67.5% (2000); Median home value: $63,600 (2000); Median rent: $281 per month (2000); Median age of housing: 44 years (2000).
Hospitals: Davies County Hospital (136 beds)
Newspapers: The Washington Times-Herald (6 x week)
Transportation: Commute to work: 96.2% car, 0.3% public transportation, 2.1% walk, 0.3% work from home (2000); Travel time to work: 60.1% less than 15 minutes, 14.2% 15 to 30 minutes, 12.8% 30 to 45 minutes, 7.4% 45 to 60 minutes, 5.5% 60 minutes or more (2000)
Additional Information Contacts
Washington Chamber of Commerce 812-254-5262

De Kalb County

Located in northeastern Indiana; bounded on the east by Ohio; drained by the St. Joseph River and Cedar and Fish Creeks. Covers a land area of 362.90 square miles, a water area of 1.00 square miles, and is located in the Eastern Time Zone. The county government was organized in 1835. County seat is Auburn.

De Kalb County is part of the Fort Wayne, IN MSA. The entire metro area includes: Adams County; Allen County; DeKalb County; Huntington County; Wells County; Whitley County

Population: 40,285 (2000); Race: 98.1% White, 0.2% Black, 0.4% Asian, 0.2% American Indian and Alaska Native, 1.3% Hispanic of any race, 0.7% two or more races (2000); Density: 111.0 persons per square mile (2000); Age: 28.2% under 18, 11.4% over 64 (2000).
Religion: Five largest groups: 8.2% Catholic Church, 6.4% The United Methodist Church, 5.4% Christian Churches and Churches of Christ, 2.5% Evangelical Lutheran Church in America, 2.5% Lutheran Church—Missouri Synod (2000).
Economy: Unemployment rate: 4.8% (11/2002); Total civilian labor force: 21,974 (11/2002); Leading industries: 57.1% manufacturing; 8.0% retail trade; 7.3% construction (2000); Companies that employ more than 1,000 persons: 0 (2000); Companies that employ more than 100 persons: 42 (2000); Farms: 785 totaling 162,936 acres (1997); Minority business ownership rate: 0.0% (1997); Women business ownership rate: 27.2% (1997); Retail sales per capita: $7,492 (1997). Single-family building permits issued: 198 (2001) / 190 (2000); Multi-family building permits issued: 0 (2001) / 2 (2000).
Income: Per capita income: $19,448 (2000); Median household income: $44,909 (2000); Poverty rate: 5.9% (2000); Bankruptcy rate: 8.45% (2001).
Taxes: Total county taxes per capita: $267 (2000); County property taxes per capita: $155 (2000).
Education: High school graduation rate: 84.7% (2000); College graduation rate: 12.4% (2000).
Housing: Homeownership rate: 81.5% (2000); Median home value: $88,000 (2000); Median rent: $387 per month (2000); Median age of housing: 37 years (2000).
Health: Birth rate: 157.1 per 10,000 population (1998); Age adjusted death rate: 92.8 per 10,000 population (1999); Age adjusted cancer mortality rate: 243.9 deaths per 100,000 population (1999). Air Quality Index: 98% good, 2% moderate, 0% unhealthy (percent of days in 2000). Number of physicians: 8.7 per 10,000 population (1999); Number of hospital beds: 11.2 per 10,000 population (1999).
Elections: 2000 Presidential election results: 34.7% Gore, 63.1% Bush, 0.5% Nader, 1.1% Buchanan
Additional Information Contacts
De Kalb County Government Offices 219-925-2362
Ashley Hudson Chamber of Commerce 219-587-3300
Auburn Chamber of Commerce 219-925-2100
Butler Chamber of Commerce 219-868-5299
Garrett Chamber of Commerce 219-357-4600

De Kalb County Communities

ALTONA (town). Covers a land area of 0.252 square miles and a water area of 0 square miles. Located at 41.35° N. Lat.; 85.15° W. Long. Elevation is 890 feet.
Population: 198 (2000); Race: 100.0% White, 0.0% Black, 0.0% Asian, 0.0% American Indian and Alaska Native, 1.5% Hispanic of any race, 0.0% two or more races (2000); Density: 787.2 persons per square mile (2000); Age: 18.0% under 18, 21.5% over 64 (2000); Marriage status: 20.2% never married, 51.2% now married, 11.9% widowed, 16.7% divorced (2000); Foreign born: 0.0% (2000); Ancestry (includes multiple ancestries): 26.0% German, 17.5% English, 14.5% United States or American, 9.5% Irish, 7.5% Other groups (2000).
Economy: Single-family building permits issued: 0 (2001) / 0 (2000); Multi-family building permits issued: 0 (2001) / 0 (2000); Employment by occupation: 0.0% management, 10.1% professional, 14.7% services, 31.2% sales, 0.0% farming, 3.7% construction, 40.4% production (2000).
Income: Per capita income: $18,530 (2000); Median household income: $28,958 (2000); Poverty rate: 12.1% (2000).
Taxes: Total city taxes per capita: $80 (1997); City property taxes per capita: $74 (1997).
Education: High school graduation rate: 75.2% (2000); College graduation rate: 10.7% (2000).
Housing: Homeownership rate: 82.2% (2000); Median home value: $59,500 (2000); Median rent: $330 per month (2000); Median age of housing: 60+ years (2000).
Transportation: Commute to work: 94.9% car, 0.0% public transportation, 2.0% walk, 3.1% work from home (2000); Travel time to work: 41.1% less than 15 minutes, 36.8% 15 to 30 minutes, 18.9% 30 to 45 minutes, 1.1% 45 to 60 minutes, 2.1% 60 minutes or more (2000)

ASHLEY (town). Aka Ashley-Hudson. Covers a land area of 0.807 square miles and a water area of 0 square miles. Located at 41.52° N. Lat.; 85.06° W. Long.
Population: 1,010 (2000); Race: 97.3% White, 0.9% Black, 0.0% Asian, 0.5% American Indian and Alaska Native, 1.4% Hispanic of any race, 1.1% two or more races (2000); Density: 1,251.5 persons per square mile (2000); Age: 32.6% under 18, 9.7% over 64 (2000); Marriage status: 25.2% never married, 56.2% now married, 3.7% widowed, 14.9% divorced (2000); Foreign born: 1.5% (2000); Ancestry (includes multiple ancestries): 27.2% German, 11.9% United States or American, 11.7% English, 9.9% Other groups, 6.2% Irish (2000).
Economy: Employment by occupation: 6.8% management, 4.5% professional, 11.6% services, 18.0% sales, 0.0% farming, 9.9% construction, 49.2% production (2000).
Income: Per capita income: $14,922 (2000); Median household income: $35,893 (2000); Poverty rate: 12.8% (2000).
Taxes: Total city taxes per capita: $310 (1997); City property taxes per capita: $268 (1997).
Education: High school graduation rate: 80.0% (2000); College graduation rate: 3.1% (2000).

Housing: Homeownership rate: 71.5% (2000); Median home value: $70,200 (2000); Median rent: $308 per month (2000); Median age of housing: 38 years (2000).
Transportation: Commute to work: 89.1% car, 0.6% public transportation, 4.8% walk, 3.8% work from home (2000); Travel time to work: 41.0% less than 15 minutes, 38.6% 15 to 30 minutes, 14.8% 30 to 45 minutes, 3.1% 45 to 60 minutes, 2.4% 60 minutes or more (2000)
Additional Information Contacts
Ashley Hudson Chamber of Commerce.................. 219-587-3300

AUBURN (city). Covers a land area of 6.648 square miles and a water area of 0 square miles. Located at 41.36° N. Lat.; 85.05° W. Long. Elevation is 869 feet.
History: Auburn developed as a trading center for the surrounding farmlands, and as the seat of DeKalb County.
Population: 12,074 (2000); Race: 98.3% White, 0.3% Black, 0.1% Asian, 0.1% American Indian and Alaska Native, 1.6% Hispanic of any race, 1.1% two or more races (2000); Density: 1,816.2 persons per square mile (2000); Age: 26.8% under 18, 13.5% over 64 (2000); Marriage status: 20.8% never married, 57.7% now married, 8.1% widowed, 13.4% divorced (2000); Foreign born: 0.5% (2000); Ancestry (includes multiple ancestries): 35.2% German, 14.6% United States or American, 9.6% Irish, 9.3% English, 7.0% Other groups (2000).
Economy: Single-family building permits issued: 63 (2001) / 53 (2000); Multi-family building permits issued: 0 (2001) / 2 (2000); Employment by occupation: 10.5% management, 14.7% professional, 9.1% services, 22.0% sales, 0.2% farming, 9.8% construction, 33.7% production (2000).
Income: Per capita income: $20,945 (2000); Median household income: $42,762 (2000); Poverty rate: 5.2% (2000).
Taxes: Total city taxes per capita: $329 (2000); City property taxes per capita: $291 (2000).
Education: High school graduation rate: 85.5% (2000); College graduation rate: 17.4% (2000).
Housing: Homeownership rate: 75.8% (2000); Median home value: $93,800 (2000); Median rent: $409 per month (2000); Median age of housing: 28 years (2000).
Hospitals: Dekalb Memorial Hospital (47 beds)
Newspapers: The Evening Star (7 x week); Evening Star Plus (1 x week)
Transportation: Commute to work: 94.7% car, 0.4% public transportation, 2.7% walk, 1.4% work from home (2000); Travel time to work: 55.6% less than 15 minutes, 26.4% 15 to 30 minutes, 11.8% 30 to 45 minutes, 4.3% 45 to 60 minutes, 1.9% 60 minutes or more (2000)
Airports: De Kalb County
Additional Information Contacts
Auburn Chamber of Commerce......................... 219-925-2100

BUTLER (city). Covers a land area of 1.789 square miles and a water area of 0 square miles. Located at 41.43° N. Lat.; 84.87° W. Long. Elevation is 876 feet.
Population: 2,725 (2000); Race: 96.2% White, 0.0% Black, 0.0% Asian, 0.8% American Indian and Alaska Native, 2.5% Hispanic of any race, 0.1% two or more races (2000); Density: 1,523.6 persons per square mile (2000); Age: 30.6% under 18, 9.6% over 64 (2000); Marriage status: 22.0% never married, 59.0% now married, 7.5% widowed, 11.5% divorced (2000); Foreign born: 0.0% (2000); Ancestry (includes multiple ancestries): 21.9% German, 12.2% United States or American, 10.6% Irish, 10.3% Other groups, 7.3% English (2000).
Economy: Employment by occupation: 4.7% management, 7.8% professional, 12.3% services, 17.9% sales, 0.0% farming, 7.6% construction, 49.7% production (2000).
Income: Per capita income: $15,040 (2000); Median household income: $37,250 (2000); Poverty rate: 9.7% (2000).
Taxes: Total city taxes per capita: $171 (1997); City property taxes per capita: $149 (1997).
Education: High school graduation rate: 72.8% (2000); College graduation rate: 6.4% (2000).

School District(s)

Dekalb Co Eastern Com School District (PK-12)
2000 Enrollment: 1,452............................. 219-868-2125
Housing: Homeownership rate: 72.5% (2000); Median home value: $63,900 (2000); Median rent: $369 per month (2000); Median age of housing: 45 years (2000).
Newspapers: The Butler Bulletin (1 x week)
Transportation: Commute to work: 93.4% car, 0.0% public transportation, 2.3% walk, 2.3% work from home (2000); Travel time to work: 40.2% less than 15 minutes, 34.7% 15 to 30 minutes, 17.2% 30 to 45 minutes, 6.3% 45 to 60 minutes, 1.5% 60 minutes or more (2000)
Additional Information Contacts
Butler Chamber of Commerce......................... 219-868-5299

CORUNNA (town). Covers a land area of 0.174 square miles and a water area of 0 square miles. Located at 41.43° N. Lat.; 85.14° W. Long. Elevation is 980 feet.
Population: 254 (2000); Race: 98.3% White, 0.0% Black, 0.0% Asian, 0.9% American Indian and Alaska Native, 2.2% Hispanic of any race, 0.9% two or more races (2000); Density: 1,456.4 persons per square mile (2000); Age: 30.9% under 18, 10.0% over 64 (2000); Marriage status: 26.6% never married, 50.3% now married, 11.6% widowed, 11.6% divorced (2000); Foreign born: 0.0% (2000); Ancestry (includes multiple ancestries): 14.8% German, 12.6% English, 12.2% Irish, 11.3% Other groups, 9.6% United States or American (2000).
Economy: Employment by occupation: 5.6% management, 5.6% professional, 14.8% services, 19.4% sales, 1.9% farming, 11.1% construction, 41.7% production (2000).
Income: Per capita income: $19,301 (2000); Median household income: $40,625 (2000); Poverty rate: 4.8% (2000).
Taxes: Total city taxes per capita: $163 (1997); City property taxes per capita: $163 (1997).
Education: High school graduation rate: 66.9% (2000); College graduation rate: 3.1% (2000).
Housing: Homeownership rate: 91.5% (2000); Median home value: $62,900 (2000); Median rent: $213 per month (2000); Median age of housing: 60+ years (2000).
Transportation: Commute to work: 91.7% car, 0.0% public transportation, 3.7% walk, 0.0% work from home (2000); Travel time to work: 29.6% less than 15 minutes, 57.4% 15 to 30 minutes, 4.6% 30 to 45 minutes, 4.6% 45 to 60 minutes, 3.7% 60 minutes or more (2000)

GARRETT (city). Covers a land area of 3.126 square miles and a water area of 0 square miles. Located at 41.34° N. Lat.; 85.13° W. Long. Elevation is 880 feet.
History: Garrett developed around the Baltimore & Ohio Railroad shops and roundhouse, and served the surrounding farms.
Population: 5,803 (2000); Race: 98.5% White, 0.0% Black, 1.1% Asian, 0.0% American Indian and Alaska Native, 1.2% Hispanic of any race, 0.0% two or more races (2000); Density: 1,856.5 persons per square mile (2000); Age: 30.3% under 18, 11.7% over 64 (2000); Marriage status: 18.5% never married, 62.1% now married, 6.9% widowed, 12.5% divorced (2000); Foreign born: 1.4% (2000); Ancestry (includes multiple ancestries): 31.4% German, 16.9% United States or American, 7.7% Other groups, 7.3% Irish, 7.3% English (2000).
Economy: Employment by occupation: 7.9% management, 10.7% professional, 14.9% services, 20.7% sales, 0.0% farming, 8.2% construction, 37.6% production (2000).
Income: Per capita income: $17,260 (2000); Median household income: $41,747 (2000); Poverty rate: 6.0% (2000).
Taxes: Total city taxes per capita: $171 (1997); City property taxes per capita: $147 (1997).
Education: High school graduation rate: 85.5% (2000); College graduation rate: 8.0% (2000).

School District(s)

Garrett-Keyser-Butler Com (KG-12)
2000 Enrollment: 1,562............................. 219-357-3185
Housing: Homeownership rate: 78.1% (2000); Median home value: $75,300 (2000); Median rent: $387 per month (2000); Median age of housing: 58 years (2000).
Newspapers: The Garrett Clipper (2 x week)
Transportation: Commute to work: 95.7% car, 0.0% public transportation, 1.9% walk, 1.9% work from home (2000); Travel time to work: 49.6% less than 15 minutes, 27.8% 15 to 30 minutes, 15.7% 30 to 45 minutes, 3.7% 45 to 60 minutes, 3.2% 60 minutes or more (2000)
Additional Information Contacts
Garrett Chamber of Commerce........................ 219-357-4600

SAINT JOE (town). Covers a land area of 0.283 square miles and a water area of 0 square miles. Located at 41.31° N. Lat.; 84.90° W. Long. Elevation is 825 feet.
Population: 478 (2000); Race: 96.5% White, 0.4% Black, 0.0% Asian, 0.0% American Indian and Alaska Native, 1.5% Hispanic of any race, 2.1% two or more races (2000); Density: 1,687.7 persons per square mile (2000); Age: 34.6% under 18, 10.0% over 64 (2000); Marriage status: 23.0% never

married, 60.4% now married, 5.7% widowed, 10.9% divorced (2000); Foreign born: 1.0% (2000); Ancestry (includes multiple ancestries): 27.0% United States or American, 22.0% German, 7.5% English, 7.1% Irish, 3.1% Other groups (2000).
Economy: Employment by occupation: 6.4% management, 4.7% professional, 19.6% services, 17.0% sales, 0.0% farming, 6.8% construction, 45.5% production (2000).
Income: Per capita income: $14,570 (2000); Median household income: $36,417 (2000); Poverty rate: 5.5% (2000).
Education: High school graduation rate: 77.6% (2000); College graduation rate: 3.4% (2000).
Housing: Homeownership rate: 78.3% (2000); Median home value: $55,500 (2000); Median rent: $371 per month (2000); Median age of housing: 60+ years (2000).
Transportation: Commute to work: 95.7% car, 0.0% public transportation, 3.4% walk, 0.9% work from home (2000); Travel time to work: 20.7% less than 15 minutes, 50.0% 15 to 30 minutes, 14.7% 30 to 45 minutes, 7.8% 45 to 60 minutes, 6.9% 60 minutes or more (2000)

SPENCERVILLE (unincorporated postal area, zip code 46788). Covers a land area of 34.654 square miles and a water area of 0.113 square miles. Located at 41.26° N. Lat.; 84.93° W. Long. Elevation is 817 feet.
Population: 2,834 (2000); Race: 97.9% White, 0.0% Black, 1.1% Asian, 0.0% American Indian and Alaska Native, 0.0% Hispanic of any race, 1.0% two or more races (2000); Density: 81.8 persons per square mile (2000); Age: 35.5% under 18, 5.7% over 64 (2000); Marriage status: 23.1% never married, 69.0% now married, 2.9% widowed, 5.0% divorced (2000); Foreign born: 1.1% (2000); Ancestry (includes multiple ancestries): 34.1% German, 9.4% Irish, 6.8% English, 5.5% United States or American, 4.3% Other groups (2000).
Economy: Employment by occupation: 9.3% management, 18.5% professional, 9.4% services, 19.0% sales, 0.9% farming, 13.7% construction, 29.2% production (2000).
Income: Per capita income: $17,839 (2000); Median household income: $58,621 (2000); Poverty rate: 7.6% (2000).
Education: High school graduation rate: 83.2% (2000); College graduation rate: 21.1% (2000).
Housing: Homeownership rate: 92.6% (2000); Median home value: $127,900 (2000); Median rent: $415 per month (2000); Median age of housing: 26 years (2000).
Transportation: Commute to work: 91.1% car, 0.7% public transportation, 5.5% walk, 0.7% work from home (2000); Travel time to work: 23.2% less than 15 minutes, 35.2% 15 to 30 minutes, 29.8% 30 to 45 minutes, 7.0% 45 to 60 minutes, 4.8% 60 minutes or more (2000)

WATERLOO (town). Covers a land area of 1.500 square miles and a water area of 0 square miles. Located at 41.43° N. Lat.; 85.02° W. Long. Elevation is 904 feet.
Population: 2,200 (2000); Race: 96.0% White, 0.5% Black, 0.0% Asian, 1.1% American Indian and Alaska Native, 2.4% Hispanic of any race, 0.7% two or more races (2000); Density: 1,466.6 persons per square mile (2000); Age: 33.0% under 18, 8.0% over 64 (2000); Marriage status: 20.8% never married, 57.6% now married, 6.8% widowed, 14.8% divorced (2000); Foreign born: 1.4% (2000); Ancestry (includes multiple ancestries): 22.0% German, 13.8% United States or American, 9.1% Other groups, 7.0% Irish, 6.9% English (2000).
Economy: Employment by occupation: 6.3% management, 8.6% professional, 10.4% services, 20.9% sales, 0.1% farming, 7.3% construction, 46.4% production (2000).
Income: Per capita income: $16,248 (2000); Median household income: $39,831 (2000); Poverty rate: 12.4% (2000).
Taxes: Total city taxes per capita: $190 (1997); City property taxes per capita: $164 (1997).
Education: High school graduation rate: 81.4% (2000); College graduation rate: 6.1% (2000).

School District(s)

Dekalb Co Ctl United School District (PK-12)
2000 Enrollment: 4,009 219-925-3914
Housing: Homeownership rate: 75.6% (2000); Median home value: $68,300 (2000); Median rent: $364 per month (2000); Median age of housing: 52 years (2000).
Transportation: Commute to work: 93.4% car, 0.2% public transportation, 1.3% walk, 2.7% work from home (2000); Travel time to work: 39.4% less than 15 minutes, 44.5% 15 to 30 minutes, 10.6% 30 to 45 minutes, 1.9% 45 to 60 minutes, 3.7% 60 minutes or more (2000); Amtrak: Service available.

Dearborn County

Located in southeastern Indiana; bounded on the east by Ohio, and on the southeast by the Ohio River and the Kentucky border; drained by the Whitewater River. Covers a land area of 305.20 square miles, a water area of 1.80 square miles, and is located in the Eastern Time Zone. The county government was organized in 1803. County seat is Lawrenceburg.

Dearborn County is part of the Cincinnati, OH-KY-IN PMSA. The entire metro area includes: Dearborn County, IN; Ohio County, IN; Boone County, KY; Campbell County, KY; Gallatin County, KY; Grant County, KY; Kenton County, KY; Pendleton County, KY; Brown County, OH; Clermont County, OH; Hamilton County, OH; Warren County, OH

Population: 46,109 (2000); Race: 97.9% White, 0.7% Black, 0.2% Asian, 0.1% American Indian and Alaska Native, 0.4% Hispanic of any race, 0.7% two or more races (2000); Density: 151.1 persons per square mile (2000); Age: 27.6% under 18, 11.1% over 64 (2000).
Religion: Five largest groups: 18.7% Catholic Church, 4.5% The United Methodist Church, 4.2% American Baptist Churches in the USA, 3.4% Christian Churches and Churches of Christ, 3.1% Lutheran Church—Missouri Synod (2000).
Economy: Unemployment rate: 4.1% (11/2002); Total civilian labor force: 24,363 (11/2002); Leading industries: 16.3% manufacturing; 16.2% retail trade; 12.1% health care and social assistance (2000); Companies that employ more than 1,000 persons: 1 (2000); Companies that employ more than 100 persons: 11 (2000); Farms: 679 totaling 81,383 acres (1997); Minority business ownership rate: 0.0% (1997); Women business ownership rate: 36.9% (1997); Retail sales per capita: $7,424 (1997). Single-family building permits issued: 306 (2001) / 340 (2000); Multi-family building permits issued: 33 (2001) / 34 (2000).
Income: Per capita income: $20,431 (2000); Median household income: $48,899 (2000); Poverty rate: 6.6% (2000); Bankruptcy rate: 4.39% (2001).
Taxes: Total county taxes per capita: $243 (2000); County property taxes per capita: $178 (2000).
Education: High school graduation rate: 82.0% (2000); College graduation rate: 15.4% (2000).
Housing: Homeownership rate: 78.6% (2000); Median home value: $120,600 (2000); Median rent: $429 per month (2000); Median age of housing: 26 years (2000).
Health: Birth rate: 139.2 per 10,000 population (1998); Age adjusted death rate: 84.0 per 10,000 population (1999); Age adjusted cancer mortality rate: 215.3 deaths per 100,000 population (1999). Air Quality Index: 99% good, 1% moderate, 0% unhealthy (percent of days in 2000). Number of physicians: 8.2 per 10,000 population (1999); Number of hospital beds: 18.9 per 10,000 population (1999).
Elections: 2000 Presidential election results: 34.1% Gore, 64.9% Bush, 0.0% Nader, 0.5% Buchanan

Additional Information Contacts

Dearborn County Government Offices 812-537-8824
Dearborn County Chamber of Commerce 812-537-0814
Southeastern Indiana Board of Realtors. 812-926-4644

Dearborn County Communities

AURORA (city). Covers a land area of 2.776 square miles and a water area of 0.143 square miles. Located at 39.05° N. Lat.; 84.90° W. Long. Elevation is 501 feet.
History: Aurora was founded in 1819 along the Ohio River. Judge Jesse Holman of the Indiana Supreme Court suggested that the town be named for the goddess of the dawn. Aurora was severely damaged in the 1937 flood of the Ohio River.
Population: 3,965 (2000); Race: 97.6% White, 0.0% Black, 0.3% Asian, 0.2% American Indian and Alaska Native, 0.1% Hispanic of any race, 0.5% two or more races (2000); Density: 1,428.2 persons per square mile (2000); Age: 27.8% under 18, 12.6% over 64 (2000); Marriage status: 22.9% never married, 55.2% now married, 7.9% widowed, 13.9% divorced (2000); Foreign born: 1.1% (2000); Ancestry (includes multiple ancestries): 30.5% German, 17.2% United States or American, 12.2% Irish, 11.1% English, 10.4% Other groups (2000).
Economy: Single-family building permits issued: 4 (2001) / 3 (2000); Multi-family building permits issued: 4 (2001) / 2 (2000); Employment by occupation: 7.3% management, 9.7% professional, 23.1% services, 24.3% sales, 0.6% farming, 16.4% construction, 18.5% production (2000).

Income: Per capita income: $16,587 (2000); Median household income: $32,500 (2000); Poverty rate: 10.4% (2000).
Taxes: Total city taxes per capita: $231 (2000); City property taxes per capita: $176 (2000).
Education: High school graduation rate: 74.8% (2000); College graduation rate: 12.7% (2000).

School District(s)

South Dearborn Com School Corp (PK-12)
2000 Enrollment: 3,111 812-926-2090

Housing: Homeownership rate: 57.5% (2000); Median home value: $87,300 (2000); Median rent: $429 per month (2000); Median age of housing: 53 years (2000).
Safety: Violent crime rate: 5.0 per 10,000 population; Property crime rate: 514.2 per 10,000 population (2001).
Transportation: Commute to work: 94.2% car, 0.0% public transportation, 1.9% walk, 1.7% work from home (2000); Travel time to work: 40.0% less than 15 minutes, 24.5% 15 to 30 minutes, 17.4% 30 to 45 minutes, 12.0% 45 to 60 minutes, 6.1% 60 minutes or more (2000)
Additional Information Contacts
Southeastern Indiana Board of Realtors 812-926-4644

BRIGHT (CDP). Covers a land area of 14.309 square miles and a water area of 0 square miles. Located at 39.21° N. Lat.; 84.86° W. Long. Elevation is 931 feet.
Population: 5,405 (2000); Race: 98.6% White, 0.1% Black, 0.3% Asian, 0.5% American Indian and Alaska Native, 0.5% Hispanic of any race, 0.5% two or more races (2000); Density: 377.7 persons per square mile (2000); Age: 31.5% under 18, 5.7% over 64 (2000); Marriage status: 19.7% never married, 70.3% now married, 2.5% widowed, 7.5% divorced (2000); Foreign born: 1.5% (2000); Ancestry (includes multiple ancestries): 39.4% German, 13.0% United States or American, 10.9% Irish, 10.1% English, 5.5% Other groups (2000).
Economy: Satellite community of Cincinnati. Cattle; wheat. Employment by occupation: 14.0% management, 18.4% professional, 6.0% services, 28.7% sales, 0.0% farming, 14.7% construction, 18.2% production (2000).
Income: Per capita income: $22,401 (2000); Median household income: $63,813 (2000); Poverty rate: 1.7% (2000).
Education: High school graduation rate: 88.4% (2000); College graduation rate: 22.5% (2000).
Housing: Homeownership rate: 86.7% (2000); Median home value: $145,000 (2000); Median rent: $518 per month (2000); Median age of housing: 19 years (2000).
Transportation: Commute to work: 96.4% car, 1.3% public transportation, 0.3% walk, 2.0% work from home (2000); Travel time to work: 17.6% less than 15 minutes, 26.1% 15 to 30 minutes, 32.0% 30 to 45 minutes, 16.3% 45 to 60 minutes, 8.0% 60 minutes or more (2000)

DILLSBORO (town). Covers a land area of 1.010 square miles and a water area of 0 square miles. Located at 39.01° N. Lat.; 85.05° W. Long. Elevation is 868 feet.
Population: 1,436 (2000); Race: 96.9% White, 0.0% Black, 0.4% Asian, 0.0% American Indian and Alaska Native, 1.6% Hispanic of any race, 1.4% two or more races (2000); Density: 1,421.6 persons per square mile (2000); Age: 24.1% under 18, 25.9% over 64 (2000); Marriage status: 20.8% never married, 49.6% now married, 18.8% widowed, 10.8% divorced (2000); Foreign born: 0.6% (2000); Ancestry (includes multiple ancestries): 31.1% German, 13.3% Irish, 11.8% United States or American, 7.5% English, 6.9% Other groups (2000).
Economy: In agricultural area; timber. Employment by occupation: 5.2% management, 8.6% professional, 17.5% services, 18.2% sales, 1.2% farming, 14.4% construction, 34.9% production (2000).
Income: Per capita income: $14,984 (2000); Median household income: $28,462 (2000); Poverty rate: 10.5% (2000).
Taxes: Total city taxes per capita: $112 (1997); City property taxes per capita: $89 (1997).
Education: High school graduation rate: 67.4% (2000); College graduation rate: 4.1% (2000).
Housing: Homeownership rate: 52.6% (2000); Median home value: $90,000 (2000); Median rent: $384 per month (2000); Median age of housing: 30 years (2000).
Transportation: Commute to work: 94.9% car, 0.4% public transportation, 0.4% walk, 3.4% work from home (2000); Travel time to work: 23.5% less than 15 minutes, 27.6% 15 to 30 minutes, 23.5% 30 to 45 minutes, 11.8% 45 to 60 minutes, 13.7% 60 minutes or more (2000)

GREENDALE (city). Covers a land area of 6.046 square miles and a water area of 0.035 square miles. Located at 39.12° N. Lat.; 84.85° W. Long. Elevation is 528 feet.
History: Greendale became associated with the distilling of whiskey in 1809, when the local manufacture of distilled liquors began. The Joseph E. Seagram Company purchased a plant in Greendale in 1933.
Population: 4,296 (2000); Race: 97.8% White, 0.6% Black, 0.1% Asian, 0.0% American Indian and Alaska Native, 0.9% Hispanic of any race, 1.3% two or more races (2000); Density: 710.5 persons per square mile (2000); Age: 21.7% under 18, 16.5% over 64 (2000); Marriage status: 20.7% never married, 59.7% now married, 8.7% widowed, 10.9% divorced (2000); Foreign born: 0.8% (2000); Ancestry (includes multiple ancestries): 35.7% German, 16.0% Irish, 13.9% United States or American, 10.5% English, 6.2% Other groups (2000).
Economy: Employment by occupation: 10.5% management, 18.3% professional, 15.3% services, 29.8% sales, 0.0% farming, 7.3% construction, 18.8% production (2000).
Income: Per capita income: $23,452 (2000); Median household income: $45,926 (2000); Poverty rate: 5.1% (2000).
Taxes: Total city taxes per capita: $375 (1997); City property taxes per capita: $274 (1997).
Education: High school graduation rate: 83.2% (2000); College graduation rate: 21.0% (2000).
Housing: Homeownership rate: 77.9% (2000); Median home value: $113,000 (2000); Median rent: $402 per month (2000); Median age of housing: 41 years (2000).
Transportation: Commute to work: 95.8% car, 0.0% public transportation, 2.4% walk, 1.2% work from home (2000); Travel time to work: 41.6% less than 15 minutes, 27.2% 15 to 30 minutes, 20.3% 30 to 45 minutes, 5.3% 45 to 60 minutes, 5.6% 60 minutes or more (2000)

GUILFORD (unincorporated postal area, zip code 47022). Aka Kennedy. Covers a land area of 39.872 square miles and a water area of 0 square miles. Located at 39.20° N. Lat.; 84.94° W. Long. Elevation is 532 feet.
Population: 3,044 (2000); Race: 98.2% White, 0.0% Black, 0.3% Asian, 0.0% American Indian and Alaska Native, 0.0% Hispanic of any race, 1.2% two or more races (2000); Density: 76.3 persons per square mile (2000); Age: 31.0% under 18, 9.3% over 64 (2000); Marriage status: 19.9% never married, 71.3% now married, 2.7% widowed, 6.1% divorced (2000); Foreign born: 0.6% (2000); Ancestry (includes multiple ancestries): 46.3% German, 13.9% United States or American, 12.1% English, 11.9% Irish, 3.9% Other groups (2000).
Economy: Employment by occupation: 19.3% management, 15.1% professional, 15.4% services, 22.4% sales, 0.3% farming, 10.6% construction, 16.9% production (2000).
Income: Per capita income: $20,585 (2000); Median household income: $52,250 (2000); Poverty rate: 2.7% (2000).
Education: High school graduation rate: 87.0% (2000); College graduation rate: 16.8% (2000).
Housing: Homeownership rate: 91.5% (2000); Median home value: $140,800 (2000); Median rent: $426 per month (2000); Median age of housing: 25 years (2000).
Transportation: Commute to work: 91.5% car, 1.2% public transportation, 2.0% walk, 4.3% work from home (2000); Travel time to work: 12.1% less than 15 minutes, 28.8% 15 to 30 minutes, 29.7% 30 to 45 minutes, 16.6% 45 to 60 minutes, 12.7% 60 minutes or more (2000)

HIDDEN VALLEY (CDP). Covers a land area of 4.216 square miles and a water area of 0.300 square miles. Located at 39.16° N. Lat.; 84.84° W. Long.
Population: 4,417 (2000); Race: 98.4% White, 0.0% Black, 0.0% Asian, 0.0% American Indian and Alaska Native, 0.6% Hispanic of any race, 1.1% two or more races (2000); Density: 1,047.8 persons per square mile (2000); Age: 29.6% under 18, 7.6% over 64 (2000); Marriage status: 16.8% never married, 72.8% now married, 2.1% widowed, 8.2% divorced (2000); Foreign born: 0.7% (2000); Ancestry (includes multiple ancestries): 36.6% German, 17.7% Irish, 10.6% United States or American, 10.3% English, 6.3% Other groups (2000).
Economy: Employment by occupation: 19.0% management, 19.0% professional, 12.4% services, 29.9% sales, 0.0% farming, 9.6% construction, 10.1% production (2000).
Income: Per capita income: $25,464 (2000); Median household income: $70,444 (2000); Poverty rate: 2.8% (2000).
Education: High school graduation rate: 95.9% (2000); College graduation rate: 29.0% (2000).

Housing: Homeownership rate: 96.7% (2000); Median home value: $145,900 (2000); Median rent: $923 per month (2000); Median age of housing: 9 years (2000).
Transportation: Commute to work: 94.4% car, 0.0% public transportation, 1.2% walk, 4.4% work from home (2000); Travel time to work: 13.2% less than 15 minutes, 30.9% 15 to 30 minutes, 35.1% 30 to 45 minutes, 13.8% 45 to 60 minutes, 7.0% 60 minutes or more (2000)

LAWRENCEBURG (city). Covers a land area of 4.900 square miles and a water area of 0.142 square miles. Located at 39.09° N. Lat.; 84.85° W. Long. Elevation is 478 feet.
History: Lawrenceburg was founded in 1801 by Captain Samuel C. Vance. It developed as a port on the Ohio River. In 1937 the river flooded the town, reaching a crest of 82.6 feet. Lawrenceburg was the site of the church where Henry Ward Beecher was pastor in 1837.
Population: 4,685 (2000); Race: 93.0% White, 5.1% Black, 0.0% Asian, 0.0% American Indian and Alaska Native, 0.1% Hispanic of any race, 1.1% two or more races (2000); Density: 956.1 persons per square mile (2000); Age: 25.3% under 18, 15.0% over 64 (2000); Marriage status: 28.8% never married, 48.8% now married, 8.3% widowed, 14.1% divorced (2000); Foreign born: 0.5% (2000); Ancestry (includes multiple ancestries): 24.0% German, 19.1% United States or American, 10.3% Other groups, 9.3% Irish, 7.9% English (2000).
Economy: Employment by occupation: 6.8% management, 10.8% professional, 22.8% services, 26.1% sales, 0.0% farming, 9.9% construction, 23.6% production (2000).
Income: Per capita income: $15,656 (2000); Median household income: $29,306 (2000); Poverty rate: 14.9% (2000).
Taxes: Total city taxes per capita: $555 (2000); City property taxes per capita: $452 (2000).
Education: High school graduation rate: 70.7% (2000); College graduation rate: 6.9% (2000).

School District(s)

Lawrenceburg Com School Corp (KG-12)
2000 Enrollment: 1,557 812-537-7200
Housing: Homeownership rate: 41.4% (2000); Median home value: $88,100 (2000); Median rent: $404 per month (2000); Median age of housing: 31 years (2000).
Hospitals: Dearborn County Hospital (87 beds)
Newspapers: The Journal-Press (1 x week); The Dearborn County Register (1 x week); The Marketplace (1 x week)
Transportation: Commute to work: 90.7% car, 0.0% public transportation, 7.2% walk, 0.0% work from home (2000); Travel time to work: 38.5% less than 15 minutes, 32.6% 15 to 30 minutes, 15.7% 30 to 45 minutes, 9.1% 45 to 60 minutes, 4.0% 60 minutes or more (2000)

Additional Information Contacts

Dearborn County Chamber of Commerce 812-537-0814

MOORES HILL (town). Covers a land area of 0.475 square miles and a water area of 0 square miles. Located at 39.11° N. Lat.; 85.08° W. Long. Elevation is 994 feet.
History: Laid out 1838.
Population: 635 (2000); Race: 96.5% White, 0.0% Black, 0.3% Asian, 1.7% American Indian and Alaska Native, 0.6% Hispanic of any race, 1.3% two or more races (2000); Density: 1,336.7 persons per square mile (2000); Age: 39.3% under 18, 7.4% over 64 (2000); Marriage status: 20.1% never married, 66.4% now married, 4.3% widowed, 9.2% divorced (2000); Foreign born: 0.5% (2000); Ancestry (includes multiple ancestries): 28.8% United States or American, 15.3% German, 9.9% Irish, 8.0% Other groups, 5.7% English (2000).
Economy: In agricultural area. Employment by occupation: 2.4% management, 2.4% professional, 14.2% services, 27.3% sales, 0.0% farming, 18.2% construction, 35.6% production (2000).
Income: Per capita income: $12,832 (2000); Median household income: $38,295 (2000); Poverty rate: 17.0% (2000).
Taxes: Total city taxes per capita: $45 (1997); City property taxes per capita: $36 (1997).
Education: High school graduation rate: 71.1% (2000); College graduation rate: 2.0% (2000).
Housing: Homeownership rate: 72.1% (2000); Median home value: $75,500 (2000); Median rent: $388 per month (2000); Median age of housing: 43 years (2000).
Transportation: Commute to work: 96.3% car, 0.0% public transportation, 0.8% walk, 2.4% work from home (2000); Travel time to work: 14.2% less than 15 minutes, 35.0% 15 to 30 minutes, 16.7% 30 to 45 minutes, 15.8% 45 to 60 minutes, 18.3% 60 minutes or more (2000)

SAINT LEON (town). Covers a land area of 7.161 square miles and a water area of 0 square miles. Located at 39.28° N. Lat.; 84.96° W. Long. Elevation is 1,016 feet.
Population: 387 (2000); Race: 100.0% White, 0.0% Black, 0.0% Asian, 0.0% American Indian and Alaska Native, 0.0% Hispanic of any race, 0.0% two or more races (2000); Density: 54.0 persons per square mile (2000); Age: 26.0% under 18, 19.9% over 64 (2000); Marriage status: 21.6% never married, 65.5% now married, 7.7% widowed, 5.2% divorced (2000); Foreign born: 0.5% (2000); Ancestry (includes multiple ancestries): 69.4% German, 11.7% United States or American, 6.4% Irish, 4.6% English, 1.5% Scottish (2000).
Economy: Employment by occupation: 9.5% management, 15.3% professional, 16.8% services, 34.7% sales, 1.1% farming, 5.8% construction, 16.8% production (2000).
Income: Per capita income: $19,225 (2000); Median household income: $39,821 (2000); Poverty rate: 8.4% (2000).
Education: High school graduation rate: 73.3% (2000); College graduation rate: 8.3% (2000).
Housing: Homeownership rate: 89.0% (2000); Median home value: $135,400 (2000); Median rent: $242 per month (2000); Median age of housing: 31 years (2000).
Transportation: Commute to work: 92.1% car, 0.0% public transportation, 3.2% walk, 3.7% work from home (2000); Travel time to work: 30.6% less than 15 minutes, 36.1% 15 to 30 minutes, 19.7% 30 to 45 minutes, 8.7% 45 to 60 minutes, 4.9% 60 minutes or more (2000)

WEST HARRISON (town). Covers a land area of 0.091 square miles and a water area of 0.009 square miles. Located at 39.26° N. Lat.; 84.82° W. Long. Elevation is 520 feet.
History: West Harrison was founded in 1813. General John Hunt Morgan and his Confederate cavalry raided West Harrison in 1863 before moving on to Ohio.
Population: 284 (2000); Race: 97.8% White, 0.0% Black, 0.0% Asian, 0.0% American Indian and Alaska Native, 0.0% Hispanic of any race, 2.2% two or more races (2000); Density: 3,120.3 persons per square mile (2000); Age: 27.6% under 18, 10.3% over 64 (2000); Marriage status: 34.7% never married, 39.0% now married, 8.0% widowed, 18.3% divorced (2000); Foreign born: 0.0% (2000); Ancestry (includes multiple ancestries): 28.3% German, 18.4% Irish, 7.7% English, 6.3% Other groups, 4.0% United States or American (2000).
Economy: Employment by occupation: 10.7% management, 10.7% professional, 13.2% services, 26.4% sales, 2.5% farming, 17.4% construction, 19.0% production (2000).
Income: Per capita income: $12,667 (2000); Median household income: $21,500 (2000); Poverty rate: 31.6% (2000).
Taxes: Total city taxes per capita: $124 (1997); City property taxes per capita: $83 (1997).
Education: High school graduation rate: 64.2% (2000); College graduation rate: 3.8% (2000).
Housing: Homeownership rate: 42.3% (2000); Median home value: $79,600 (2000); Median rent: $333 per month (2000); Median age of housing: 60+ years (2000).
Transportation: Commute to work: 89.7% car, 1.7% public transportation, 2.6% walk, 3.4% work from home (2000); Travel time to work: 37.5% less than 15 minutes, 19.6% 15 to 30 minutes, 25.9% 30 to 45 minutes, 11.6% 45 to 60 minutes, 5.4% 60 minutes or more (2000)

Decatur County

Located in southeast central Indiana; drained by Flatrock, Small Duck, Clifty, and Sand Creeks. Covers a land area of 372.60 square miles, a water area of 0.80 square miles, and is located in the Eastern Time Zone. The county government was organized in 1821. County seat is Greensburg.

Weather Station: Greensburg Elevation: 935 feet

	Jan	Feb	Mar	Apr	May	Jun	Jul	Aug	Sep	Oct	Nov	Dec
High	35	40	51	63	73	81	85	83	77	65	52	40
Low	19	23	32	42	52	61	65	62	56	44	35	25
Precip	2.5	2.3	3.7	4.4	4.9	4.2	4.1	4.2	3.0	3.1	3.8	3.2
Snow	6.4	4.0	2.8	0.5	tr	0.0	0.0	0.0	0.0	0.2	0.8	3.3

High and Low temperatures in degrees Fahrenheit; Precipitation and Snow in inches

Population: 24,555 (2000); Race: 97.8% White, 0.1% Black, 1.3% Asian, 0.0% American Indian and Alaska Native, 0.5% Hispanic of any race, 0.7%

two or more races (2000); Density: 65.9 persons per square mile (2000); Age: 26.3% under 18, 13.3% over 64 (2000).
Religion: Five largest groups: 22.1% Catholic Church, 16.0% American Baptist Churches in the USA, 6.5% The United Methodist Church, 4.1% Christian Churches and Churches of Christ, 2.6% Christian Church (Disciples of Christ) (2000).
Economy: Unemployment rate: 2.9% (11/2002); Total civilian labor force: 16,399 (11/2002); Leading industries: 46.4% manufacturing; 13.8% retail trade; 8.4% professional, scientific & technical services (2000); Companies that employ more than 1,000 persons: 2 (2000); Companies that employ more than 100 persons: 19 (2000); Farms: 654 totaling 198,614 acres (1997); Minority business ownership rate: 0.0% (1997); Women business ownership rate: 23.9% (1997); Retail sales per capita: $9,099 (1997). Single-family building permits issued: 100 (2001) / 100 (2000); Multi-family building permits issued: 34 (2001) / 0 (2000).
Income: Per capita income: $18,582 (2000); Median household income: $40,401 (2000); Poverty rate: 9.3% (2000); Bankruptcy rate: 7.29% (2001).
Taxes: Total county taxes per capita: $230 (2000); County property taxes per capita: $128 (2000).
Education: High school graduation rate: 79.1% (2000); College graduation rate: 11.5% (2000).
Housing: Homeownership rate: 73.2% (2000); Median home value: $86,400 (2000); Median rent: $380 per month (2000); Median age of housing: 36 years (2000).
Health: Birth rate: 160.1 per 10,000 population (1998); Age adjusted death rate: 91.2 per 10,000 population (1999); Age adjusted cancer mortality rate: 232.2 deaths per 100,000 population (1999). Number of physicians: 8.1 per 10,000 population (1999); Number of hospital beds: 26.9 per 10,000 population (1999).
Elections: 2000 Presidential election results: 31.5% Gore, 66.7% Bush, 0.1% Nader, 1.1% Buchanan
National and State Parks: Greenburg Reservoir State Fishing Area
Additional Information Contacts
Decatur County Government Offices.................... 812-663-2570
Decatur County Board of Realtors...................... 812-663-2114
Greensburg Chamber of Commerce...................... 812-663-2832

Decatur County Communities

GREENSBURG (city). Covers a land area of 4.794 square miles and a water area of 0.039 square miles. Located at 39.34° N. Lat.; 85.48° W. Long. Elevation is 971 feet.
History: Greensburg developed as a residential center.
Population: 10,260 (2000); Race: 95.5% White, 0.2% Black, 3.0% Asian, 0.1% American Indian and Alaska Native, 0.6% Hispanic of any race, 1.1% two or more races (2000); Density: 2,140.4 persons per square mile (2000); Age: 24.3% under 18, 15.4% over 64 (2000); Marriage status: 21.8% never married, 55.6% now married, 8.5% widowed, 14.0% divorced (2000); Foreign born: 3.6% (2000); Ancestry (includes multiple ancestries): 21.0% German, 12.7% United States or American, 9.1% English, 8.7% Other groups, 8.3% Irish (2000).
Economy: Single-family building permits issued: 31 (2001) / 20 (2000); Multi-family building permits issued: 34 (2001) / 0 (2000); Employment by occupation: 8.6% management, 13.8% professional, 13.5% services, 20.5% sales, 0.3% farming, 8.2% construction, 35.1% production (2000).
Income: Per capita income: $18,829 (2000); Median household income: $38,029 (2000); Poverty rate: 11.4% (2000).
Taxes: Total city taxes per capita: $248 (2000); City property taxes per capita: $242 (2000).
Education: High school graduation rate: 77.4% (2000); College graduation rate: 12.7% (2000).

School District(s)

Decatur County Com Schools (PK-12)
2000 Enrollment: 2,236 812-663-4595
Greensburg Community Schools (PK-12)
2000 Enrollment: 1,993 812-663-4774

Housing: Homeownership rate: 62.7% (2000); Median home value: $85,100 (2000); Median rent: $395 per month (2000); Median age of housing: 37 years (2000).
Hospitals: Decatur County Memorial Hospital (115 beds)
Newspapers: Greensburg Daily News (6 x week); The Greensburg Times (1 x week)
Transportation: Commute to work: 94.7% car, 0.0% public transportation, 2.9% walk, 2.0% work from home (2000); Travel time to work: 75.3% less than 15 minutes, 12.1% 15 to 30 minutes, 6.3% 30 to 45 minutes, 1.9% 45 to 60 minutes, 4.3% 60 minutes or more (2000)
Additional Information Contacts
Decatur County Board of Realtors...................... 812-663-2114
Greensburg Chamber of Commerce...................... 812-663-2832

MILFORD (town). Aka Clifty. Covers a land area of 0.090 square miles and a water area of 0 square miles. Located at 39.35° N. Lat.; 85.61° W. Long. Elevation is 843 feet.
History: Laid out 1835.
Population: 121 (2000); Race: 96.0% White, 0.0% Black, 0.0% Asian, 0.0% American Indian and Alaska Native, 0.0% Hispanic of any race, 4.0% two or more races (2000); Density: 1,349.1 persons per square mile (2000); Age: 23.0% under 18, 20.6% over 64 (2000); Marriage status: 21.0% never married, 68.6% now married, 8.6% widowed, 1.9% divorced (2000); Foreign born: 0.0% (2000); Ancestry (includes multiple ancestries): 22.2% United States or American, 21.4% Other groups, 21.4% Irish, 7.9% German, 7.1% English (2000).
Economy: Employment by occupation: 12.0% management, 8.0% professional, 8.0% services, 6.0% sales, 4.0% farming, 20.0% construction, 42.0% production (2000).
Income: Per capita income: $12,506 (2000); Median household income: $30,781 (2000); Poverty rate: 15.9% (2000).
Taxes: Total city taxes per capita: $29 (1997); City property taxes per capita: $29 (1997).
Education: High school graduation rate: 48.1% (2000); College graduation rate: 0.0% (2000).
Housing: Homeownership rate: 71.7% (2000); Median home value: $57,500 (2000); Median rent: $416 per month (2000); Median age of housing: 37 years (2000).
Transportation: Commute to work: 100.0% car, 0.0% public transportation, 0.0% walk, 0.0% work from home (2000); Travel time to work: 4.3% less than 15 minutes, 56.5% 15 to 30 minutes, 17.4% 30 to 45 minutes, 6.5% 45 to 60 minutes, 15.2% 60 minutes or more (2000)

MILLHOUSEN (town). Covers a land area of 1.012 square miles and a water area of 0 square miles. Located at 39.21° N. Lat.; 85.43° W. Long. Elevation is 904 feet.
History: Settled 1838, plotted 1858.
Population: 136 (2000); Race: 100.0% White, 0.0% Black, 0.0% Asian, 0.0% American Indian and Alaska Native, 0.0% Hispanic of any race, 0.0% two or more races (2000); Density: 134.3 persons per square mile (2000); Age: 34.7% under 18, 21.8% over 64 (2000); Marriage status: 9.9% never married, 68.3% now married, 12.9% widowed, 8.9% divorced (2000); Foreign born: 0.0% (2000); Ancestry (includes multiple ancestries): 46.9% German, 5.4% United States or American, 4.1% English, 2.0% Irish, 1.4% Dutch (2000).
Economy: In agricultural area. Employment by occupation: 7.9% management, 17.5% professional, 7.9% services, 20.6% sales, 0.0% farming, 15.9% construction, 30.2% production (2000).
Income: Per capita income: $17,646 (2000); Median household income: $39,250 (2000); Poverty rate: 2.7% (2000).
Taxes: Total city taxes per capita: $33 (1997); City property taxes per capita: $33 (1997).
Education: High school graduation rate: 81.3% (2000); College graduation rate: 7.7% (2000).
Housing: Homeownership rate: 96.1% (2000); Median home value: $93,000 (2000); Median rent: $225 per month (2000); Median age of housing: 60+ years (2000).
Transportation: Commute to work: 93.7% car, 0.0% public transportation, 3.2% walk, 3.2% work from home (2000); Travel time to work: 6.6% less than 15 minutes, 57.4% 15 to 30 minutes, 21.3% 30 to 45 minutes, 9.8% 45 to 60 minutes, 4.9% 60 minutes or more (2000)

NEWPOINT (town). Aka New Point. Covers a land area of 0.273 square miles and a water area of 0 square miles. Located at 39.31° N. Lat.; 85.32° W. Long.
Population: 290 (2000); Race: 99.7% White, 0.0% Black, 0.0% Asian, 0.0% American Indian and Alaska Native, 0.0% Hispanic of any race, 0.3% two or more races (2000); Density: 1,061.8 persons per square mile (2000); Age: 27.1% under 18, 13.0% over 64 (2000); Marriage status: 16.8% never married, 67.3% now married, 7.1% widowed, 8.8% divorced (2000); Foreign born: 0.0% (2000); Ancestry (includes multiple ancestries): 18.5% German, 11.0% United States or American, 5.5% English, 4.8% Irish, 4.1% European (2000).

Economy: Employment by occupation: 5.3% management, 6.0% professional, 14.7% services, 19.3% sales, 0.0% farming, 6.7% construction, 48.0% production (2000).
Income: Per capita income: $21,116 (2000); Median household income: $39,583 (2000); Poverty rate: 7.3% (2000).
Education: High school graduation rate: 67.0% (2000); College graduation rate: 1.6% (2000).
Housing: Homeownership rate: 76.4% (2000); Median home value: $73,100 (2000); Median rent: $373 per month (2000); Median age of housing: 60+ years (2000).
Transportation: Commute to work: 88.4% car, 0.0% public transportation, 6.8% walk, 4.8% work from home (2000); Travel time to work: 31.4% less than 15 minutes, 60.0% 15 to 30 minutes, 4.3% 30 to 45 minutes, 1.4% 45 to 60 minutes, 2.9% 60 minutes or more (2000)

SAINT PAUL (town). Covers a land area of 0.308 square miles and a water area of 0 square miles. Located at 39.42° N. Lat.; 85.62° W. Long. Elevation is 858 feet.
Population: 1,022 (2000); Race: 98.7% White, 0.3% Black, 0.0% Asian, 0.4% American Indian and Alaska Native, 0.0% Hispanic of any race, 0.7% two or more races (2000); Density: 3,314.7 persons per square mile (2000); Age: 30.7% under 18, 6.0% over 64 (2000); Marriage status: 24.1% never married, 62.8% now married, 3.7% widowed, 9.4% divorced (2000); Foreign born: 0.3% (2000); Ancestry (includes multiple ancestries): 20.6% German, 17.4% United States or American, 13.1% Irish, 10.5% English, 9.1% Other groups (2000).
Economy: Employment by occupation: 5.0% management, 4.6% professional, 15.6% services, 22.9% sales, 0.0% farming, 14.1% construction, 37.8% production (2000).
Income: Per capita income: $14,819 (2000); Median household income: $39,079 (2000); Poverty rate: 9.1% (2000).
Education: High school graduation rate: 70.8% (2000); College graduation rate: 2.7% (2000).
Housing: Homeownership rate: 74.8% (2000); Median home value: $77,100 (2000); Median rent: $407 per month (2000); Median age of housing: 45 years (2000).
Transportation: Commute to work: 93.3% car, 0.0% public transportation, 3.9% walk, 2.2% work from home (2000); Travel time to work: 18.6% less than 15 minutes, 56.6% 15 to 30 minutes, 9.4% 30 to 45 minutes, 4.6% 45 to 60 minutes, 10.8% 60 minutes or more (2000)

WESTPORT (town). Covers a land area of 1.326 square miles and a water area of 0.012 square miles. Located at 39.17° N. Lat.; 85.57° W. Long. Elevation is 806 feet.
History: Laid out 1836.
Population: 1,515 (2000); Race: 99.1% White, 0.0% Black, 0.0% Asian, 0.0% American Indian and Alaska Native, 0.0% Hispanic of any race, 0.7% two or more races (2000); Density: 1,142.7 persons per square mile (2000); Age: 25.1% under 18, 13.2% over 64 (2000); Marriage status: 21.7% never married, 56.8% now married, 9.1% widowed, 12.4% divorced (2000); Foreign born: 0.6% (2000); Ancestry (includes multiple ancestries): 16.3% German, 14.6% United States or American, 8.3% Irish, 7.9% English, 4.0% Other groups (2000).
Economy: In agricultural area; manufacturing of plastic and glass products. Employment by occupation: 3.6% management, 14.7% professional, 14.7% services, 19.4% sales, 0.3% farming, 10.2% construction, 37.1% production (2000).
Income: Per capita income: $18,298 (2000); Median household income: $37,500 (2000); Poverty rate: 10.5% (2000).
Taxes: Total city taxes per capita: $65 (1997); City property taxes per capita: $54 (1997).
Education: High school graduation rate: 82.9% (2000); College graduation rate: 9.8% (2000).
Housing: Homeownership rate: 75.0% (2000); Median home value: $77,100 (2000); Median rent: $317 per month (2000); Median age of housing: 36 years (2000).
Transportation: Commute to work: 95.0% car, 0.0% public transportation, 1.5% walk, 2.2% work from home (2000); Travel time to work: 22.0% less than 15 minutes, 45.5% 15 to 30 minutes, 18.5% 30 to 45 minutes, 6.4% 45 to 60 minutes, 7.6% 60 minutes or more (2000)

Delaware County

Located in eastern Indiana; drained by the Mississinewa River and the West Fork of the White River. Covers a land area of 393.30 square miles, a water area of 2.60 square miles, and is located in the Eastern Time Zone. The county government was organized in 1827. County seat is Muncie.

Delaware County is part of the Muncie, IN MSA. The entire metro area includes: Delaware County

Weather Station: Muncie — Elevation: 977 feet

	Jan	Feb	Mar	Apr	May	Jun	Jul	Aug	Sep	Oct	Nov	Dec
High	32	37	48	61	72	81	85	83	77	64	50	38
Low	17	20	30	40	51	60	64	62	54	42	33	23
Precip	2.1	2.2	3.2	3.6	4.1	4.2	3.9	3.4	2.9	2.7	3.3	3.0
Snow	8.4	6.0	3.0	0.5	tr	0.0	0.0	0.0	0.0	0.2	1.2	6.3

High and Low temperatures in degrees Fahrenheit; Precipitation and Snow in inches

Population: 118,769 (2000); Race: 90.9% White, 6.5% Black, 0.6% Asian, 0.2% American Indian and Alaska Native, 1.3% Hispanic of any race, 1.2% two or more races (2000); Density: 302.0 persons per square mile (2000); Age: 22.1% under 18, 13.5% over 64 (2000).
Religion: Five largest groups: 5.9% Catholic Church, 5.8% The United Methodist Church, 2.4% Church of the Nazarene, 1.6% Southern Baptist Convention, 1.2% Christian Church (Disciples of Christ) (2000).
Economy: Unemployment rate: 4.5% (11/2002); Total civilian labor force: 61,618 (11/2002); Leading industries: 19.1% manufacturing; 15.5% health care and social assistance; 15.1% retail trade (2000); Companies that employ more than 1,000 persons: 5 (2000); Companies that employ more than 100 persons: 67 (2000); Farms: 635 totaling 173,443 acres (1997); Minority business ownership rate: 2.6% (1997); Women business ownership rate: 23.2% (1997); Retail sales per capita: $9,504 (1997). Single-family building permits issued: 302 (2001) / 270 (2000); Multi-family building permits issued: 34 (2001) / 132 (2000).
Income: Per capita income: $19,233 (2000); Median household income: $34,659 (2000); Poverty rate: 15.1% (2000); Bankruptcy rate: 7.16% (2001).
Taxes: Total county taxes per capita: $185 (2000); County property taxes per capita: $156 (2000).
Education: High school graduation rate: 81.6% (2000); College graduation rate: 20.4% (2000).
Housing: Homeownership rate: 67.2% (2000); Median home value: $75,400 (2000); Median rent: $390 per month (2000); Median age of housing: 40 years (2000).
Health: Birth rate: 125.0 per 10,000 population (1998); Age adjusted death rate: 93.2 per 10,000 population (1999); Age adjusted cancer mortality rate: 202.0 deaths per 100,000 population (1999). Air Quality Index: 55% good, 45% moderate, 0% unhealthy (percent of days in 2000). Number of physicians: 26.9 per 10,000 population (1999); Number of hospital beds: 34.9 per 10,000 population (1999).
Elections: 2000 Presidential election results: 47.3% Gore, 50.1% Bush, 0.9% Nader, 0.9% Buchanan
Additional Information Contacts
Delaware County Government Offices 765-747-7726
Mid-Eastern Indiana of Realtors 765-747-7197
Muncie-Delaware County Chamber 765-288-6681

Delaware County Communities

ALBANY (town). Covers a land area of 1.651 square miles and a water area of 0 square miles. Located at 40.30° N. Lat.; 85.23° W. Long. Elevation is 954 feet.
Population: 2,368 (2000); Race: 96.2% White, 2.6% Black, 0.5% Asian, 0.0% American Indian and Alaska Native, 0.2% Hispanic of any race, 0.8% two or more races (2000); Density: 1,434.2 persons per square mile (2000); Age: 25.5% under 18, 16.6% over 64 (2000); Marriage status: 20.6% never married, 61.1% now married, 7.3% widowed, 10.9% divorced (2000); Foreign born: 0.6% (2000); Ancestry (includes multiple ancestries): 19.7% United States or American, 15.2% German, 11.7% English, 9.9% Other groups, 9.4% Irish (2000).
Economy: Single-family building permits issued: 17 (2001) / 10 (2000); Multi-family building permits issued: 0 (2001) / 0 (2000); Employment by occupation: 4.8% management, 8.8% professional, 13.1% services, 29.0% sales, 0.0% farming, 12.1% construction, 32.2% production (2000).
Income: Per capita income: $16,620 (2000); Median household income: $33,314 (2000); Poverty rate: 5.9% (2000).
Taxes: Total city taxes per capita: $130 (1997); City property taxes per capita: $110 (1997).
Education: High school graduation rate: 87.9% (2000); College graduation rate: 8.2% (2000).

Housing: Homeownership rate: 71.6% (2000); Median home value: $65,800 (2000); Median rent: $323 per month (2000); Median age of housing: 43 years (2000).
Transportation: Commute to work: 94.2% car, 0.0% public transportation, 4.4% walk, 1.0% work from home (2000); Travel time to work: 33.1% less than 15 minutes, 40.0% 15 to 30 minutes, 17.2% 30 to 45 minutes, 2.9% 45 to 60 minutes, 6.8% 60 minutes or more (2000)

DALEVILLE (town). Covers a land area of 1.992 square miles and a water area of 0.020 square miles. Located at 40.12° N. Lat.; 85.55° W. Long. Elevation is 912 feet.
History: When Daleville was platted in 1838, it was expected that a canal would be built here. Instead, the railroad came in 1852.
Population: 1,658 (2000); Race: 98.7% White, 0.3% Black, 0.0% Asian, 0.6% American Indian and Alaska Native, 0.7% Hispanic of any race, 0.4% two or more races (2000); Density: 832.4 persons per square mile (2000); Age: 28.8% under 18, 13.2% over 64 (2000); Marriage status: 18.7% never married, 63.4% now married, 7.5% widowed, 10.4% divorced (2000); Foreign born: 0.3% (2000); Ancestry (includes multiple ancestries): 19.8% German, 11.4% Irish, 11.2% United States or American, 8.3% English, 7.0% Other groups (2000).
Economy: Single-family building permits issued: 2 (2001) / 3 (2000); Multi-family building permits issued: 0 (2001) / 0 (2000); Employment by occupation: 8.1% management, 14.9% professional, 17.6% services, 26.3% sales, 1.2% farming, 13.2% construction, 18.7% production (2000).
Income: Per capita income: $18,020 (2000); Median household income: $40,592 (2000); Poverty rate: 2.7% (2000).
Taxes: Total city taxes per capita: $118 (1997); City property taxes per capita: $87 (1997).
Education: High school graduation rate: 84.2% (2000); College graduation rate: 15.8% (2000).

School District(s)

Daleville Community Schools (KG-12)
2000 Enrollment: 628 765-378-3329

Housing: Homeownership rate: 72.0% (2000); Median home value: $78,000 (2000); Median rent: $433 per month (2000); Median age of housing: 45 years (2000).
Transportation: Commute to work: 97.2% car, 0.3% public transportation, 1.2% walk, 1.2% work from home (2000); Travel time to work: 24.7% less than 15 minutes, 51.3% 15 to 30 minutes, 13.2% 30 to 45 minutes, 5.0% 45 to 60 minutes, 5.9% 60 minutes or more (2000)

EATON (town). Covers a land area of 1.119 square miles and a water area of <.001 square miles. Located at 40.34° N. Lat.; 85.35° W. Long. Elevation is 914 feet.
Population: 1,603 (2000); Race: 98.8% White, 0.0% Black, 0.0% Asian, 0.0% American Indian and Alaska Native, 0.5% Hispanic of any race, 0.9% two or more races (2000); Density: 1,432.0 persons per square mile (2000); Age: 31.7% under 18, 9.0% over 64 (2000); Marriage status: 21.1% never married, 59.7% now married, 7.2% widowed, 12.0% divorced (2000); Foreign born: 0.8% (2000); Ancestry (includes multiple ancestries): 20.3% United States or American, 15.5% German, 9.5% Irish, 8.9% English, 8.1% Other groups (2000).
Economy: Single-family building permits issued: 2 (2001) / 2 (2000); Multi-family building permits issued: 0 (2001) / 0 (2000); Employment by occupation: 6.1% management, 6.6% professional, 14.3% services, 25.9% sales, 0.1% farming, 15.7% construction, 31.2% production (2000).
Income: Per capita income: $13,833 (2000); Median household income: $31,563 (2000); Poverty rate: 11.1% (2000).
Taxes: Total city taxes per capita: $110 (1997); City property taxes per capita: $92 (1997).
Education: High school graduation rate: 80.1% (2000); College graduation rate: 4.8% (2000).
Housing: Homeownership rate: 81.4% (2000); Median home value: $55,700 (2000); Median rent: $331 per month (2000); Median age of housing: 50 years (2000).
Transportation: Commute to work: 94.6% car, 0.0% public transportation, 2.1% walk, 2.8% work from home (2000); Travel time to work: 21.1% less than 15 minutes, 48.8% 15 to 30 minutes, 20.4% 30 to 45 minutes, 4.5% 45 to 60 minutes, 5.1% 60 minutes or more (2000)

GASTON (town). Covers a land area of 0.351 square miles and a water area of 0 square miles. Located at 40.31° N. Lat.; 85.50° W. Long. Elevation is 890 feet.
Population: 1,010 (2000); Race: 96.7% White, 0.6% Black, 0.0% Asian, 0.3% American Indian and Alaska Native, 0.0% Hispanic of any race, 2.4% two or more races (2000); Density: 2,881.0 persons per square mile (2000); Age: 32.9% under 18, 7.8% over 64 (2000); Marriage status: 26.2% never married, 54.1% now married, 4.6% widowed, 15.1% divorced (2000); Foreign born: 0.0% (2000); Ancestry (includes multiple ancestries): 28.5% United States or American, 18.5% German, 6.8% English, 4.9% Irish, 4.0% Other groups (2000).
Economy: Single-family building permits issued: 4 (2001) / 0 (2000); Multi-family building permits issued: 0 (2001) / 0 (2000); Employment by occupation: 5.6% management, 18.9% professional, 21.7% services, 16.7% sales, 0.0% farming, 18.3% construction, 18.7% production (2000).
Income: Per capita income: $15,357 (2000); Median household income: $31,853 (2000); Poverty rate: 11.8% (2000).
Taxes: Total city taxes per capita: $129 (1997); City property taxes per capita: $111 (1997).
Education: High school graduation rate: 72.4% (2000); College graduation rate: 10.9% (2000).

School District(s)

Harrison-Wash Com School Corp (KG-12)
2000 Enrollment: 963 765-358-4006

Housing: Homeownership rate: 74.1% (2000); Median home value: $57,700 (2000); Median rent: $338 per month (2000); Median age of housing: 51 years (2000).
Transportation: Commute to work: 85.3% car, 0.0% public transportation, 3.3% walk, 4.9% work from home (2000); Travel time to work: 29.3% less than 15 minutes, 36.8% 15 to 30 minutes, 18.8% 30 to 45 minutes, 7.9% 45 to 60 minutes, 7.1% 60 minutes or more (2000)

MUNCIE (city). Covers a land area of 24.184 square miles and a water area of 0.015 square miles. Located at 40.19° N. Lat.; 85.38° W. Long. Elevation is 952 feet.
History: A railroad station and some factories were the impetus for the growth of Muncie, which was platted in 1827 and called Munseytown. Incorporation as a town came in 1847, and by 1865 Muncie was declared a city. About 1887 natural gas wells began to bring many new industries to Muncie. One of these was the Ball Brothers Company, producers of canning jars.
Population: 67,430 (2000); Race: 86.2% White, 10.5% Black, 0.9% Asian, 0.2% American Indian and Alaska Native, 1.7% Hispanic of any race, 1.5% two or more races (2000); Density: 2,788.2 persons per square mile (2000); Age: 19.9% under 18, 13.4% over 64 (2000); Marriage status: 38.0% never married, 42.6% now married, 7.7% widowed, 11.8% divorced (2000); Foreign born: 1.9% (2000); Ancestry (includes multiple ancestries): 17.5% German, 15.3% Other groups, 12.8% United States or American, 9.3% Irish, 9.0% English (2000).
Vital Statistics: Birth rate: 156.9 per 10,000 population (1998)
Economy: Unemployment rate: 5.8% (11/2002); Total civilian labor force: 35,319 (11/2002); Single-family building permits issued: 58 (2001) / 41 (2000); Multi-family building permits issued: 34 (2001) / 132 (2000); Employment by occupation: 7.3% management, 20.3% professional, 20.4% services, 28.0% sales, 0.2% farming, 6.6% construction, 17.1% production (2000).
Income: Per capita income: $15,814 (2000); Median household income: $26,613 (2000); Poverty rate: 23.1% (2000).
Taxes: Total city taxes per capita: $313 (2000); City property taxes per capita: $261 (2000).
Education: High school graduation rate: 75.8% (2000); College graduation rate: 19.0% (2000).

School District(s)

Cowan Community School Corp (KG-12)
2000 Enrollment: 665 765-289-4866
Delaware Community School Corp (KG-12)
2000 Enrollment: 2,904 765-284-5074
Muncie Community Schools (PK-12)
2000 Enrollment: 8,418 765-747-5205
University Schools (KG-12)
2000 Enrollment: 797 765-285-3262

Four-year College(s)

Ball State University (Public)
2001 Enrollment: n/a 765-289-1241
2001 Tuition: In-state $3,924; Out-of-state $10,800

Two-year College(s)

Ball Memorial Hospital School of Radiologic Techn (Private, Not-for-profit)
2001 Enrollment: n/a 765-747-4372
Ivy Tech State College-East Central (Public)
2001 Enrollment: 4,052 765-289-2291
2001 Tuition: In-state $1,986; Out-of-state $4,029

Indiana Business College (Private, For-profit)
2001 Enrollment: 281 765-288-8681
2001 Tuition: In-state $8,640; Out-of-state $8,640

Housing: Homeownership rate: 55.8% (2000); Median home value: $59,300 (2000); Median rent: $380 per month (2000); Median age of housing: 44 years (2000).

Hospitals: Ball Memorial Hospital (436 beds)

Safety: Violent crime rate: 42.6 per 10,000 population; Property crime rate: 388.1 per 10,000 population (2001).

Newspapers: The Star Press (7 x week); Muncie Times (2 x month); The Advertiser - Central Edition (1 x week); Ball State Daily News (5 x week)

Transportation: Commute to work: 86.8% car, 1.7% public transportation, 7.9% walk, 2.5% work from home (2000); Travel time to work: 56.4% less than 15 minutes, 28.7% 15 to 30 minutes, 7.1% 30 to 45 minutes, 2.8% 45 to 60 minutes, 5.0% 60 minutes or more (2000)

Airports: Delaware County - Johnson Field

Additional Information Contacts

Mid-Eastern Indiana of Realtors 765-747-7197
Muncie-Delaware County Chamber. 765-288-6681

SELMA (town). Covers a land area of 0.848 square miles and a water area of 0 square miles. Located at 40.19° N. Lat.; 85.27° W. Long. Elevation is 1,009 feet.

Population: 880 (2000); Race: 97.2% White, 1.6% Black, 0.0% Asian, 0.3% American Indian and Alaska Native, 1.6% Hispanic of any race, 0.9% two or more races (2000); Density: 1,037.2 persons per square mile (2000); Age: 29.1% under 18, 11.9% over 64 (2000); Marriage status: 18.3% never married, 67.4% now married, 5.6% widowed, 8.7% divorced (2000); Foreign born: 0.0% (2000); Ancestry (includes multiple ancestries): 20.1% German, 15.5% United States or American, 9.5% English, 9.3% Irish, 9.1% Other groups (2000).

Economy: Single-family building permits issued: 1 (2001) / 1 (2000); Multi-family building permits issued: 0 (2001) / 0 (2000); Employment by occupation: 6.1% management, 13.9% professional, 15.8% services, 27.7% sales, 0.0% farming, 10.9% construction, 25.5% production (2000).

Income: Per capita income: $18,361 (2000); Median household income: $44,423 (2000); Poverty rate: 4.7% (2000).

Taxes: Total city taxes per capita: $79 (1997); City property taxes per capita: $66 (1997).

Education: High school graduation rate: 85.9% (2000); College graduation rate: 11.5% (2000).

School District(s)

Liberty-Perry Com School Corp (KG-12)
2000 Enrollment: 1,186 765-282-5615

Housing: Homeownership rate: 77.4% (2000); Median home value: $76,200 (2000); Median rent: $378 per month (2000); Median age of housing: 46 years (2000).

Transportation: Commute to work: 97.3% car, 0.0% public transportation, 2.7% walk, 0.0% work from home (2000); Travel time to work: 24.7% less than 15 minutes, 59.3% 15 to 30 minutes, 9.9% 30 to 45 minutes, 1.2% 45 to 60 minutes, 4.8% 60 minutes or more (2000)

YORKTOWN (town). Covers a land area of 3.526 square miles and a water area of 0.061 square miles. Located at 40.17° N. Lat.; 85.48° W. Long. Elevation is 907 feet.

Population: 4,785 (2000); Race: 95.8% White, 1.6% Black, 0.2% Asian, 0.4% American Indian and Alaska Native, 0.4% Hispanic of any race, 2.0% two or more races (2000); Density: 1,357.0 persons per square mile (2000); Age: 27.4% under 18, 14.2% over 64 (2000); Marriage status: 17.4% never married, 63.1% now married, 7.7% widowed, 11.8% divorced (2000); Foreign born: 1.0% (2000); Ancestry (includes multiple ancestries): 23.9% German, 16.5% Irish, 11.3% United States or American, 10.7% English, 7.5% Other groups (2000).

Economy: Single-family building permits issued: 41 (2001) / 41 (2000); Multi-family building permits issued: 0 (2001) / 0 (2000); Employment by occupation: 13.9% management, 21.2% professional, 17.3% services, 20.5% sales, 0.2% farming, 6.8% construction, 20.0% production (2000).

Income: Per capita income: $26,065 (2000); Median household income: $50,974 (2000); Poverty rate: 4.1% (2000).

Taxes: Total city taxes per capita: $141 (1997); City property taxes per capita: $117 (1997).

Education: High school graduation rate: 90.5% (2000); College graduation rate: 25.4% (2000).

School District(s)

Mount Pleasant Township Com Sch Corp (KG-12)
2000 Enrollment: 2,102 765-759-8230

Housing: Homeownership rate: 76.5% (2000); Median home value: $85,800 (2000); Median rent: $404 per month (2000); Median age of housing: 33 years (2000).

Transportation: Commute to work: 99.3% car, 0.0% public transportation, 0.0% walk, 0.7% work from home (2000); Travel time to work: 38.2% less than 15 minutes, 38.5% 15 to 30 minutes, 8.4% 30 to 45 minutes, 3.3% 45 to 60 minutes, 11.7% 60 minutes or more (2000)

Dubois County

Located in southwestern Indiana; bounded on the north by the East Fork of the White River; drained by the Patoka River. Covers a land area of 430.10 square miles, a water area of 5.10 square miles, and is located in the Eastern Time Zone. The county government was organized in 1817. County seat is Jasper.

Weather Station: Dubois S Ind. Forage Farm — Elevation: 688 feet

	Jan	Feb	Mar	Apr	May	Jun	Jul	Aug	Sep	Oct	Nov	Dec
High	37	43	53	65	74	82	86	85	79	67	54	43
Low	20	23	33	43	52	61	65	63	56	44	35	25
Precip	2.9	2.6	4.2	4.7	5.3	4.7	4.4	4.0	3.5	3.3	4.2	3.5
Snow	na	na	na	tr	0.0	0.0	0.0	0.0	0.0	0.2	tr	na

High and Low temperatures in degrees Fahrenheit; Precipitation and Snow in inches

Population: 39,674 (2000); Race: 97.8% White, 0.1% Black, 0.1% Asian, 0.1% American Indian and Alaska Native, 2.5% Hispanic of any race, 0.7% two or more races (2000); Density: 92.2 persons per square mile (2000); Age: 27.4% under 18, 12.9% over 64 (2000).

Religion: Five largest groups: 58.0% Catholic Church, 6.4% Evangelical Lutheran Church in America, 5.1% United Church of Christ, 3.0% Christian Churches and Churches of Christ, 2.8% The United Methodist Church (2000).

Economy: Unemployment rate: 3.4% (11/2002); Total civilian labor force: 22,725 (11/2002); Leading industries: 46.3% manufacturing; 11.5% retail trade; 8.4% health care and social assistance (2000); Companies that employ more than 1,000 persons: 1 (2000); Companies that employ more than 100 persons: 57 (2000); Farms: 812 totaling 191,053 acres (1997); Minority business ownership rate: 0.0% (1997); Women business ownership rate: 21.0% (1997); Retail sales per capita: $14,133 (1997). Single-family building permits issued: 176 (2001) / 208 (2000); Multi-family building permits issued: 0 (2001) / 42 (2000).

Income: Per capita income: $20,225 (2000); Median household income: $44,169 (2000); Poverty rate: 5.3% (2000); Bankruptcy rate: 4.13% (2001).

Taxes: Total county taxes per capita: $112 (2000); County property taxes per capita: $106 (2000).

Education: High school graduation rate: 80.2% (2000); College graduation rate: 14.5% (2000).

Housing: Homeownership rate: 78.0% (2000); Median home value: $92,700 (2000); Median rent: $357 per month (2000); Median age of housing: 29 years (2000).

Health: Birth rate: 134.9 per 10,000 population (1998); Age adjusted death rate: 92.5 per 10,000 population (1999); Age adjusted cancer mortality rate: 195.7 deaths per 100,000 population (1999). Air Quality Index: 100% good, 0% moderate, 0% unhealthy (percent of days in 2000). Number of physicians: 13.9 per 10,000 population (1999); Number of hospital beds: 46.4 per 10,000 population (1999).

Elections: 2000 Presidential election results: 32.8% Gore, 65.4% Bush, 0.3% Nader, 0.8% Buchanan

National and State Parks: Lick Fork State Recreation Area

Additional Information Contacts

Dubois County Government Offices 812-481-7000
Ferdinand Chamber of Commerce 812-367-0550
Huntingburg Chamber of Commerce 812-683-5699
Jasper Chamber of Commerce 812-482-6866

Dubois County Communities

BIRDSEYE (town). Covers a land area of 0.642 square miles and a water area of 0 square miles. Located at 38.31° N. Lat.; 86.69° W. Long. Elevation is 719 feet.

History: Laid out 1880.

Population: 465 (2000); Race: 95.9% White, 0.0% Black, 0.0% Asian, 0.6% American Indian and Alaska Native, 0.4% Hispanic of any race, 3.4% two or more races (2000); Density: 724.8 persons per square mile (2000); Age: 27.7% under 18, 13.1% over 64 (2000); Marriage status: 17.1% never married, 61.0% now married, 12.3% widowed, 9.7% divorced (2000);

Foreign born: 0.0% (2000); Ancestry (includes multiple ancestries): 25.6% United States or American, 20.6% German, 9.9% Other groups, 9.5% English, 7.1% Irish (2000).
Economy: In agricultural area. Employment by occupation: 1.0% management, 6.9% professional, 11.3% services, 16.7% sales, 1.0% farming, 18.1% construction, 45.1% production (2000).
Income: Per capita income: $13,690 (2000); Median household income: $30,156 (2000); Poverty rate: 14.0% (2000).
Taxes: Total city taxes per capita: $68 (1997); City property taxes per capita: $41 (1997).
Education: High school graduation rate: 59.7% (2000); College graduation rate: 2.4% (2000).
Housing: Homeownership rate: 74.4% (2000); Median home value: $64,100 (2000); Median rent: $180 per month (2000); Median age of housing: 29 years (2000).
Transportation: Commute to work: 97.0% car, 0.0% public transportation, 2.0% walk, 1.0% work from home (2000); Travel time to work: 15.5% less than 15 minutes, 42.5% 15 to 30 minutes, 25.0% 30 to 45 minutes, 4.0% 45 to 60 minutes, 13.0% 60 minutes or more (2000)

CELESTINE (unincorporated postal area, zip code 47521). Covers a land area of 17.548 square miles and a water area of 0.010 square miles. Located at 38.38° N. Lat.; 86.74° W. Long. Elevation is 596 feet.
Population: 797 (2000); Race: 100.0% White, 0.0% Black, 0.0% Asian, 0.0% American Indian and Alaska Native, 0.0% Hispanic of any race, 0.0% two or more races (2000); Density: 45.4 persons per square mile (2000); Age: 29.6% under 18, 5.6% over 64 (2000); Marriage status: 20.5% never married, 71.3% now married, 5.3% widowed, 3.0% divorced (2000); Foreign born: 0.0% (2000); Ancestry (includes multiple ancestries): 60.3% German, 6.8% United States or American, 4.9% Other groups, 3.0% Irish, 2.9% Italian (2000).
Economy: Agricultural area. Manufacturing: wooden cabinets. Employment by occupation: 4.2% management, 9.5% professional, 6.8% services, 24.1% sales, 2.5% farming, 16.3% construction, 36.6% production (2000).
Income: Per capita income: $18,503 (2000); Median household income: $56,625 (2000); Poverty rate: 0.0% (2000).
Education: High school graduation rate: 83.7% (2000); College graduation rate: 12.0% (2000).
Housing: Homeownership rate: 100.0% (2000); Median home value: $100,000 (2000); Median age of housing: 20 years (2000).
Transportation: Commute to work: 96.8% car, 0.0% public transportation, 0.0% walk, 3.2% work from home (2000); Travel time to work: 19.0% less than 15 minutes, 60.3% 15 to 30 minutes, 13.3% 30 to 45 minutes, 0.0% 45 to 60 minutes, 7.4% 60 minutes or more (2000)

DUBOIS (unincorporated postal area, zip code 47527). Covers a land area of 57.222 square miles and a water area of 0.014 square miles. Located at 38.47° N. Lat.; 86.77° W. Long. Elevation is 500 feet.
Population: 1,672 (2000); Race: 100.0% White, 0.0% Black, 0.0% Asian, 0.0% American Indian and Alaska Native, 0.0% Hispanic of any race, 0.0% two or more races (2000); Density: 29.2 persons per square mile (2000); Age: 23.9% under 18, 12.8% over 64 (2000); Marriage status: 21.4% never married, 59.7% now married, 6.8% widowed, 12.1% divorced (2000); Foreign born: 0.0% (2000); Ancestry (includes multiple ancestries): 48.5% German, 16.2% United States or American, 11.6% Irish, 4.8% English, 1.8% Scottish (2000).
Economy: Agriculture: poultry feed, furniture, processed eggs. Employment by occupation: 9.5% management, 7.2% professional, 5.8% services, 26.9% sales, 7.3% farming, 10.4% construction, 32.9% production (2000).
Income: Per capita income: $17,774 (2000); Median household income: $39,141 (2000); Poverty rate: 3.7% (2000).
Education: High school graduation rate: 80.1% (2000); College graduation rate: 2.8% (2000).

School District(s)

Northeast Dubois Co Sch Corp (PK-12)
2000 Enrollment: 995 812-678-2781

Housing: Homeownership rate: 84.6% (2000); Median home value: $79,400 (2000); Median rent: $232 per month (2000); Median age of housing: 30 years (2000).
Transportation: Commute to work: 93.8% car, 0.0% public transportation, 3.3% walk, 2.9% work from home (2000); Travel time to work: 27.1% less than 15 minutes, 42.8% 15 to 30 minutes, 20.7% 30 to 45 minutes, 4.5% 45 to 60 minutes, 4.9% 60 minutes or more (2000)

FERDINAND (town). Covers a land area of 2.238 square miles and a water area of 0 square miles. Located at 38.22° N. Lat.; 86.86° W. Long. Elevation is 541 feet.
History: Ferdinand was settled by German Catholics. It was the southern terminus of the Ferdinand Railroad, the shortest steam line in Indiana, with one locomotive making the eight-mile trip north to Huntingburg twice a day.
Population: 2,277 (2000); Race: 99.4% White, 0.0% Black, 0.2% Asian, 0.1% American Indian and Alaska Native, 0.5% Hispanic of any race, 0.3% two or more races (2000); Density: 1,017.3 persons per square mile (2000); Age: 24.1% under 18, 22.1% over 64 (2000); Marriage status: 20.1% never married, 66.7% now married, 7.5% widowed, 5.7% divorced (2000); Foreign born: 0.3% (2000); Ancestry (includes multiple ancestries): 63.7% German, 6.7% United States or American, 6.3% Irish, 4.0% French (except Basque), 3.7% English (2000).
Economy: Single-family building permits issued: 5 (2001) / 12 (2000); Multi-family building permits issued: 0 (2001) / 0 (2000); Employment by occupation: 12.3% management, 17.2% professional, 14.3% services, 17.0% sales, 0.2% farming, 8.5% construction, 30.6% production (2000).
Income: Per capita income: $18,335 (2000); Median household income: $41,326 (2000); Poverty rate: 9.9% (2000).
Taxes: Total city taxes per capita: $202 (1997); City property taxes per capita: $103 (1997).
Education: High school graduation rate: 78.8% (2000); College graduation rate: 24.4% (2000).

School District(s)

Southeast Dubois Co Sch Corp (KG-12)
2000 Enrollment: 1,519 812-367-1653

Housing: Homeownership rate: 78.0% (2000); Median home value: $87,600 (2000); Median rent: $329 per month (2000); Median age of housing: 35 years (2000).
Newspapers: The Spencer County Leader (1 x week); The Ferdinand News (1 x week)
Transportation: Commute to work: 94.3% car, 0.0% public transportation, 2.1% walk, 3.3% work from home (2000); Travel time to work: 39.3% less than 15 minutes, 42.8% 15 to 30 minutes, 7.9% 30 to 45 minutes, 3.3% 45 to 60 minutes, 6.6% 60 minutes or more (2000)

Additional Information Contacts

Ferdinand Chamber of Commerce 812-367-0550

HOLLAND (town). Covers a land area of 0.350 square miles and a water area of <.001 square miles. Located at 38.24° N. Lat.; 87.03° W. Long. Elevation is 544 feet.
Population: 695 (2000); Race: 99.7% White, 0.0% Black, 0.3% Asian, 0.0% American Indian and Alaska Native, 0.0% Hispanic of any race, 0.0% two or more races (2000); Density: 1,988.5 persons per square mile (2000); Age: 28.3% under 18, 15.1% over 64 (2000); Marriage status: 21.2% never married, 59.4% now married, 7.7% widowed, 11.6% divorced (2000); Foreign born: 0.3% (2000); Ancestry (includes multiple ancestries): 59.2% German, 10.3% United States or American, 9.6% Irish, 6.1% English, 3.8% French (except Basque) (2000).
Economy: In agricultural area. Manufacturing: ice cream. Employment by occupation: 5.5% management, 12.9% professional, 15.0% services, 24.3% sales, 0.8% farming, 9.8% construction, 31.7% production (2000).
Income: Per capita income: $16,179 (2000); Median household income: $35,500 (2000); Poverty rate: 9.2% (2000).
Taxes: Total city taxes per capita: $177 (1997); City property taxes per capita: $111 (1997).
Education: High school graduation rate: 85.6% (2000); College graduation rate: 10.2% (2000).
Housing: Homeownership rate: 81.9% (2000); Median home value: $62,000 (2000); Median rent: $221 per month (2000); Median age of housing: 43 years (2000).
Transportation: Commute to work: 90.1% car, 0.0% public transportation, 5.9% walk, 3.5% work from home (2000); Travel time to work: 29.9% less than 15 minutes, 46.0% 15 to 30 minutes, 16.6% 30 to 45 minutes, 4.7% 45 to 60 minutes, 2.8% 60 minutes or more (2000)

HUNTINGBURG (city). Covers a land area of 3.627 square miles and a water area of 0 square miles. Located at 38.29° N. Lat.; 86.95° W. Long. Elevation is 475 feet.
History: Huntingburg, settled by German immigrants, developed around clay mines and poettery works.
Population: 5,598 (2000); Race: 92.7% White, 0.1% Black, 0.1% Asian, 0.1% American Indian and Alaska Native, 9.2% Hispanic of any race, 0.5% two or more races (2000); Density: 1,543.3 persons per square mile (2000);

Age: 26.4% under 18, 16.0% over 64 (2000); Marriage status: 24.8% never married, 53.1% now married, 9.5% widowed, 12.6% divorced (2000); Foreign born: 7.4% (2000); Ancestry (includes multiple ancestries): 39.8% German, 13.5% Other groups, 12.5% United States or American, 8.0% Irish, 6.2% English (2000).
Economy: Single-family building permits issued: 28 (2001) / 40 (2000); Multi-family building permits issued: 0 (2001) / 42 (2000); Employment by occupation: 7.8% management, 10.1% professional, 13.1% services, 22.3% sales, 0.3% farming, 9.2% construction, 37.2% production (2000).
Income: Per capita income: $15,882 (2000); Median household income: $33,415 (2000); Poverty rate: 10.8% (2000).
Taxes: Total city taxes per capita: $219 (2000); City property taxes per capita: $152 (2000).
Education: High school graduation rate: 69.5% (2000); College graduation rate: 10.1% (2000).

School District(s)

Southwest Dubois Co Sch Corp (PK-12)
2000 Enrollment: 1,830 812-683-3971

Housing: Homeownership rate: 66.7% (2000); Median home value: $69,300 (2000); Median rent: $319 per month (2000); Median age of housing: 45 years (2000).
Hospitals: Deaconess Saint Joseph's Hospital (87 beds)
Safety: Violent crime rate: 0.0 per 10,000 population; Property crime rate: 135.0 per 10,000 population (2001).
Newspapers: The Huntingburg Press (1 x week)
Transportation: Commute to work: 93.9% car, 0.1% public transportation, 3.0% walk, 1.7% work from home (2000); Travel time to work: 51.4% less than 15 minutes, 38.1% 15 to 30 minutes, 4.0% 30 to 45 minutes, 2.4% 45 to 60 minutes, 4.1% 60 minutes or more (2000)
Airports: Huntingburg
Additional Information Contacts
Huntingburg Chamber of Commerce 812-683-5699

JASPER (city). Covers a land area of 9.224 square miles and a water area of 0.039 square miles. Located at 38.39° N. Lat.; 86.93° W. Long. Elevation is 472 feet.
History: Jasper was settled by German Catholics in 1838, on a site where a town had been founded about 20 years earlier. An early industry was desk manufacturing.
Population: 12,100 (2000); Race: 97.9% White, 0.0% Black, 0.1% Asian, 0.0% American Indian and Alaska Native, 3.3% Hispanic of any race, 0.9% two or more races (2000); Density: 1,311.8 persons per square mile (2000); Age: 25.3% under 18, 15.8% over 64 (2000); Marriage status: 23.2% never married, 58.3% now married, 7.3% widowed, 11.2% divorced (2000); Foreign born: 2.8% (2000); Ancestry (includes multiple ancestries): 54.3% German, 11.0% United States or American, 8.4% Irish, 6.7% English, 5.9% Other groups (2000).
Vital Statistics: Birth rate: 156.2 per 10,000 population (1998)
Economy: Single-family building permits issued: 80 (2001) / 83 (2000); Multi-family building permits issued: 0 (2001) / 0 (2000); Employment by occupation: 12.3% management, 15.1% professional, 12.2% services, 25.8% sales, 0.1% farming, 7.9% construction, 26.7% production (2000).
Income: Per capita income: $23,547 (2000); Median household income: $42,051 (2000); Poverty rate: 5.6% (2000).
Taxes: Total city taxes per capita: $417 (2000); City property taxes per capita: $287 (2000).
Education: High school graduation rate: 80.7% (2000); College graduation rate: 19.8% (2000).

School District(s)

Greater Jasper Con Schools (PK-12)
2000 Enrollment: 3,056 812-482-1801

Housing: Homeownership rate: 66.5% (2000); Median home value: $96,100 (2000); Median rent: $380 per month (2000); Median age of housing: 29 years (2000).
Hospitals: Memorial Hospital and Health Care Center (131 beds)
Safety: Violent crime rate: 4.9 per 10,000 population; Property crime rate: 194.8 per 10,000 population (2001).
Newspapers: The Herald (6 x week)
Transportation: Commute to work: 96.0% car, 0.1% public transportation, 1.4% walk, 2.1% work from home (2000); Travel time to work: 72.0% less than 15 minutes, 20.0% 15 to 30 minutes, 3.3% 30 to 45 minutes, 1.6% 45 to 60 minutes, 3.0% 60 minutes or more (2000)
Additional Information Contacts
Jasper Chamber of Commerce 812-482-6866

SAINT ANTHONY (unincorporated postal area, zip code 47575). Covers a land area of 21.388 square miles and a water area of 0.019 square miles. Located at 38.31° N. Lat.; 86.81° W. Long. Elevation is 560 feet.
Population: 970 (2000); Race: 100.0% White, 0.0% Black, 0.0% Asian, 0.0% American Indian and Alaska Native, 0.0% Hispanic of any race, 0.0% two or more races (2000); Density: 45.4 persons per square mile (2000); Age: 25.5% under 18, 7.4% over 64 (2000); Marriage status: 21.7% never married, 59.5% now married, 9.6% widowed, 9.2% divorced (2000); Foreign born: 0.0% (2000); Ancestry (includes multiple ancestries): 57.8% German, 12.9% United States or American, 4.1% Irish, 2.9% French (except Basque), 2.3% Other groups (2000).
Economy: Employment by occupation: 11.5% management, 9.3% professional, 6.7% services, 20.6% sales, 3.9% farming, 14.4% construction, 33.6% production (2000).
Income: Per capita income: $17,837 (2000); Median household income: $42,143 (2000); Poverty rate: 1.3% (2000).
Education: High school graduation rate: 78.1% (2000); College graduation rate: 8.8% (2000).
Housing: Homeownership rate: 92.2% (2000); Median home value: $105,900 (2000); Median rent: $275 per month (2000); Median age of housing: 26 years (2000).
Transportation: Commute to work: 91.9% car, 0.0% public transportation, 1.9% walk, 6.2% work from home (2000); Travel time to work: 26.8% less than 15 minutes, 65.7% 15 to 30 minutes, 4.5% 30 to 45 minutes, 0.9% 45 to 60 minutes, 2.1% 60 minutes or more (2000)

SCHNELLVILLE (unincorporated postal area, zip code 47580). Covers a land area of 1.921 square miles and a water area of 0 square miles. Located at 38.34° N. Lat.; 86.75° W. Long. Elevation is 655 feet.
Population: 170 (2000); Race: 100.0% White, 0.0% Black, 0.0% Asian, 0.0% American Indian and Alaska Native, 0.0% Hispanic of any race, 0.0% two or more races (2000); Density: 88.5 persons per square mile (2000); Age: 25.5% under 18, 23.0% over 64 (2000); Marriage status: 24.4% never married, 55.0% now married, 16.8% widowed, 3.8% divorced (2000); Foreign born: 0.0% (2000); Ancestry (includes multiple ancestries): 57.0% German, 8.5% Dutch, 6.1% Scotch-Irish, 5.5% European, 4.2% Irish (2000).
Economy: Employment by occupation: 4.2% management, 12.5% professional, 0.0% services, 16.7% sales, 7.3% farming, 7.3% construction, 52.1% production (2000).
Income: Per capita income: $19,002 (2000); Median household income: $36,250 (2000); Poverty rate: 0.0% (2000).
Education: High school graduation rate: 72.4% (2000); College graduation rate: 7.3% (2000).
Housing: Homeownership rate: 75.7% (2000); Median home value: $75,800 (2000); Median rent: $425 per month (2000); Median age of housing: 60 years (2000).
Transportation: Commute to work: 84.4% car, 0.0% public transportation, 0.0% walk, 7.3% work from home (2000); Travel time to work: 14.6% less than 15 minutes, 50.6% 15 to 30 minutes, 34.8% 30 to 45 minutes, 0.0% 45 to 60 minutes, 0.0% 60 minutes or more (2000)

Elkhart County

Located in northern Indiana; bounded on the north by Michigan; drained by the Elkhart and St. Joseph Rivers. Covers a land area of 463.80 square miles, a water area of 4.00 square miles, and is located in the Eastern Time Zone. The county government was organized in 1830. County seat is Goshen.

Elkhart County is part of the Elkhart-Goshen, IN MSA. The entire metro area includes: Elkhart County

Weather Station: Goshen College — Elevation: 872 feet

	Jan	Feb	Mar	Apr	May	Jun	Jul	Aug	Sep	Oct	Nov	Dec
High	31	35	47	60	72	81	84	82	75	62	48	36
Low	17	20	29	39	49	59	63	61	54	43	33	23
Precip	1.8	1.7	2.7	3.4	3.4	4.0	3.5	4.0	3.7	3.0	2.8	2.6
Snow	10.7	8.0	5.0	1.3	tr	0.0	0.0	0.0	0.0	0.4	3.9	8.9

High and Low temperatures in degrees Fahrenheit; Precipitation and Snow in inches

Population: 182,791 (2000); Race: 86.1% White, 5.1% Black, 0.9% Asian, 0.4% American Indian and Alaska Native, 8.9% Hispanic of any race, 2.0% two or more races (2000); Density: 394.1 persons per square mile (2000); Age: 28.8% under 18, 10.9% over 64 (2000).

Religion: Five largest groups: 6.2% Catholic Church, 4.7% Mennonite Church USA, 4.5% The United Methodist Church, 2.9% The Missionary Church, 2.6% Old Order Amish Church (2000).
Economy: Unemployment rate: 4.3% (11/2002); Total civilian labor force: 97,227 (11/2002); Leading industries: 51.8% manufacturing; 9.3% retail trade; 6.1% health care and social assistance (2000); Companies that employ more than 1,000 persons: 8 (2000); Companies that employ more than 100 persons: 241 (2000); Farms: 1,335 totaling 182,771 acres (1997); Minority business ownership rate: 2.5% (1997); Women business ownership rate: 22.6% (1997); Retail sales per capita: $11,555 (1997). Single-family building permits issued: 884 (2001) / 896 (2000); Multi-family building permits issued: 170 (2001) / 400 (2000).
Income: Per capita income: $20,250 (2000); Median household income: $44,478 (2000); Poverty rate: 7.8% (2000); Bankruptcy rate: 6.37% (2001).
Taxes: Total county taxes per capita: $318 (2000); County property taxes per capita: $199 (2000).
Education: High school graduation rate: 75.7% (2000); College graduation rate: 15.5% (2000).
Housing: Homeownership rate: 72.2% (2000); Median home value: $98,100 (2000); Median rent: $465 per month (2000); Median age of housing: 30 years (2000).
Health: Birth rate: 163.5 per 10,000 population (1998); Age adjusted death rate: 88.2 per 10,000 population (1999); Age adjusted cancer mortality rate: 197.8 deaths per 100,000 population (1999). Air Quality Index: 97% good, 3% moderate, 0% unhealthy (percent of days in 2000). Number of physicians: 12.6 per 10,000 population (1999); Number of hospital beds: 25.5 per 10,000 population (1999).
Elections: 2000 Presidential election results: 30.1% Gore, 67.5% Bush, 1.2% Nader, 0.7% Buchanan
Additional Information Contacts
Elkhart County Government Offices 219-534-3541
Elkhart County Board of Realtors 574-875-3283
Goshen Chamber of Commerce 219-533-2102
Nappanee Chamber of Commerce 219-773-7812
Wakarusa Chamber of Commerce 219-862-4344

Elkhart County Communities

BRISTOL (town). Covers a land area of 2.383 square miles and a water area of 0.113 square miles. Located at 41.72° N. Lat.; 85.81° W. Long. Elevation is 772 feet.
Population: 1,382 (2000); Race: 88.4% White, 0.4% Black, 3.8% Asian, 0.1% American Indian and Alaska Native, 5.6% Hispanic of any race, 4.1% two or more races (2000); Density: 579.8 persons per square mile (2000); Age: 27.9% under 18, 10.9% over 64 (2000); Marriage status: 24.3% never married, 58.8% now married, 4.8% widowed, 12.0% divorced (2000); Foreign born: 4.3% (2000); Ancestry (includes multiple ancestries): 31.6% German, 16.8% Other groups, 10.2% Irish, 9.2% United States or American, 7.0% French (except Basque) (2000).
Economy: Manufacturing: fabricated metal products, construction materials, plastic products, transportation equipment, machinery, textiles, wood products, fiberglass parts, meat processing. Employment by occupation: 9.2% management, 8.9% professional, 9.9% services, 29.7% sales, 0.0% farming, 11.0% construction, 31.3% production (2000).
Income: Per capita income: $20,373 (2000); Median household income: $46,136 (2000); Poverty rate: 5.9% (2000).
Taxes: Total city taxes per capita: $355 (1997); City property taxes per capita: $351 (1997).
Education: High school graduation rate: 80.6% (2000); College graduation rate: 13.3% (2000).
Housing: Homeownership rate: 58.4% (2000); Median home value: $96,800 (2000); Median rent: $483 per month (2000); Median age of housing: 36 years (2000).
Transportation: Commute to work: 90.8% car, 0.3% public transportation, 4.4% walk, 3.4% work from home (2000); Travel time to work: 29.1% less than 15 minutes, 51.4% 15 to 30 minutes, 13.4% 30 to 45 minutes, 4.0% 45 to 60 minutes, 2.1% 60 minutes or more (2000)

DUNLAP (CDP). Covers a land area of 4.234 square miles and a water area of 0.006 square miles. Located at 41.63° N. Lat.; 85.91° W. Long. Elevation is 777 feet.
Population: 5,887 (2000); Race: 93.9% White, 1.2% Black, 1.9% Asian, 0.1% American Indian and Alaska Native, 2.8% Hispanic of any race, 0.9% two or more races (2000); Density: 1,390.4 persons per square mile (2000); Age: 29.5% under 18, 10.2% over 64 (2000); Marriage status: 20.9% never married, 67.8% now married, 4.1% widowed, 7.2% divorced (2000); Foreign born: 4.6% (2000); Ancestry (includes multiple ancestries): 31.7% German, 12.4% Other groups, 10.3% Irish, 9.5% English, 7.7% United States or American (2000).
Economy: Suburb of Elkhart. Employment by occupation: 9.6% management, 16.1% professional, 10.2% services, 27.2% sales, 0.0% farming, 6.4% construction, 30.5% production (2000).
Income: Per capita income: $19,733 (2000); Median household income: $52,083 (2000); Poverty rate: 6.1% (2000).
Education: High school graduation rate: 85.2% (2000); College graduation rate: 14.9% (2000).
Housing: Homeownership rate: 87.9% (2000); Median home value: $98,000 (2000); Median rent: $561 per month (2000); Median age of housing: 30 years (2000).
Transportation: Commute to work: 95.3% car, 0.4% public transportation, 0.7% walk, 3.1% work from home (2000); Travel time to work: 37.2% less than 15 minutes, 49.5% 15 to 30 minutes, 9.5% 30 to 45 minutes, 2.0% 45 to 60 minutes, 1.8% 60 minutes or more (2000)

ELKHART (city). Covers a land area of 21.365 square miles and a water area of 0.894 square miles. Located at 41.68° N. Lat.; 85.96° W. Long. Elevation is 750 feet.
History: Elkhart was named for an island, thought by some to be shaped like an elk's heart, at the place where two rivers meet. The town was platted in 1832 by Dr. Havilah Beardsley. Elkhart grew when the Michigan Southern Railway Company built its shops here in 1870. It was incorporated in 1873. The musical instrument company begun here in 1875 by Charles G. Conn became the largest band instrument manufacturer in the world.
Population: 51,874 (2000); Race: 70.5% White, 15.0% Black, 1.0% Asian, 0.7% American Indian and Alaska Native, 15.7% Hispanic of any race, 2.8% two or more races (2000); Density: 2,428.0 persons per square mile (2000); Age: 28.4% under 18, 11.5% over 64 (2000); Marriage status: 27.8% never married, 50.4% now married, 6.8% widowed, 15.0% divorced (2000); Foreign born: 11.4% (2000); Ancestry (includes multiple ancestries): 30.3% Other groups, 18.7% German, 8.2% Irish, 7.0% United States or American, 6.6% English (2000).
Vital Statistics: Birth rate: 221.7 per 10,000 population (1998)
Economy: Unemployment rate: 5.8% (11/2002); Total civilian labor force: 26,823 (11/2002); Single-family building permits issued: 64 (2001) / 62 (2000); Multi-family building permits issued: 82 (2001) / 42 (2000); Employment by occupation: 9.2% management, 10.8% professional, 11.4% services, 21.4% sales, 0.3% farming, 7.6% construction, 39.3% production (2000).
Income: Per capita income: $17,890 (2000); Median household income: $34,863 (2000); Poverty rate: 13.6% (2000).
Taxes: Total city taxes per capita: $393 (2000); City property taxes per capita: $337 (2000).
Education: High school graduation rate: 71.5% (2000); College graduation rate: 13.4% (2000).

School District(s)
Baugo Community Schools (KG-12)
2000 Enrollment: 1,724 219-293-8583
Concord Community Schools (KG-12)
2000 Enrollment: 4,317 219-875-5161
Elkhart Community Schools (PK-12)
2000 Enrollment: 12,728 219-262-5516

Four-year College(s)
Associated Mennonite Biblical Seminary (Private, Not-for-profit, Mennonite Church)
2001 Enrollment: 162 219-295-3726

Housing: Homeownership rate: 53.7% (2000); Median home value: $78,200 (2000); Median rent: $474 per month (2000); Median age of housing: 40 years (2000).
Hospitals: Elkhart General Hospital (300 beds)
Safety: Violent crime rate: 52.7 per 10,000 population; Property crime rate: 861.9 per 10,000 population (2001).
Newspapers: The Elkhart Truth (7 x week)
Transportation: Commute to work: 93.4% car, 1.3% public transportation, 2.1% walk, 2.1% work from home (2000); Travel time to work: 41.6% less than 15 minutes, 41.0% 15 to 30 minutes, 12.5% 30 to 45 minutes, 2.8% 45 to 60 minutes, 2.2% 60 minutes or more (2000); Amtrak: Service available.
Airports: Elkhart Municipal
Additional Information Contacts
Elkhart County Board of Realtors 574-875-3283

GOSHEN (city). Covers a land area of 13.190 square miles and a water area of 0.209 square miles. Located at 41.58° N. Lat.; 85.83° W. Long. Elevation is 806 feet.
History: Goshen was established by Mennonite settlers, who in 1894 founded Elkhart Academy which became Goshen College.
Population: 29,383 (2000); Race: 82.2% White, 1.2% Black, 1.3% Asian, 0.2% American Indian and Alaska Native, 20.0% Hispanic of any race, 2.3% two or more races (2000); Density: 2,227.7 persons per square mile (2000); Age: 25.7% under 18, 13.6% over 64 (2000); Marriage status: 25.9% never married, 57.6% now married, 6.9% widowed, 9.6% divorced (2000); Foreign born: 15.8% (2000); Ancestry (includes multiple ancestries): 25.4% German, 23.7% Other groups, 11.2% United States or American, 7.2% Irish, 5.4% Swiss (2000).
Vital Statistics: Birth rate: 163.4 per 10,000 population (1998)
Economy: Unemployment rate: 4.0% (11/2002); Total civilian labor force: 14,757 (11/2002); Single-family building permits issued: 87 (2001) / 127 (2000); Multi-family building permits issued: 8 (2001) / 58 (2000); Employment by occupation: 9.7% management, 15.1% professional, 12.1% services, 20.0% sales, 0.3% farming, 7.7% construction, 35.1% production (2000).
Income: Per capita income: $18,899 (2000); Median household income: $39,383 (2000); Poverty rate: 9.3% (2000).
Taxes: Total city taxes per capita: $227 (2000); City property taxes per capita: $194 (2000).
Education: High school graduation rate: 71.9% (2000); College graduation rate: 18.5% (2000).

School District(s)

Fairfield Community Schools (KG-12)
2000 Enrollment: 1,997 219-831-2188
Goshen Community Schools (KG-12)
2000 Enrollment: 5,454 219-533-8631

Four-year College(s)

Goshen College (Private, Not-for-profit, Mennonite Church)
2001 Enrollment: 986 219-535-7000
2001 Tuition: In-state $13,600; Out-of-state $13,600
Housing: Homeownership rate: 64.0% (2000); Median home value: $93,700 (2000); Median rent: $436 per month (2000); Median age of housing: 31 years (2000).
Hospitals: Goshen General Hospital (160 beds); Oaklawn Psychiatric Center (92 beds)
Safety: Violent crime rate: 82.6 per 10,000 population; Property crime rate: 469.4 per 10,000 population (2001).
Newspapers: The Goshen News (7 x week); El Puente (1 x month)
Transportation: Commute to work: 91.9% car, 0.2% public transportation, 3.9% walk, 1.8% work from home (2000); Travel time to work: 46.6% less than 15 minutes, 36.8% 15 to 30 minutes, 12.2% 30 to 45 minutes, 2.2% 45 to 60 minutes, 2.2% 60 minutes or more (2000)
Airports: Goshen Municipal
Additional Information Contacts
Goshen Chamber of Commerce 219-533-2102

MIDDLEBURY (town). Covers a land area of 3.398 square miles and a water area of 0.004 square miles. Located at 41.67° N. Lat.; 85.70° W. Long. Elevation is 837 feet.
History: Laid out 1835.
Population: 2,956 (2000); Race: 96.3% White, 0.0% Black, 2.5% Asian, 0.0% American Indian and Alaska Native, 0.0% Hispanic of any race, 1.1% two or more races (2000); Density: 869.8 persons per square mile (2000); Age: 32.1% under 18, 10.0% over 64 (2000); Marriage status: 18.0% never married, 68.0% now married, 5.6% widowed, 8.4% divorced (2000); Foreign born: 3.3% (2000); Ancestry (includes multiple ancestries): 33.4% German, 14.1% United States or American, 7.5% Irish, 7.2% English, 6.1% Swiss (2000).
Economy: In agricultural area; livestock. Manufacturing: plastics, recreational vehicles, modular and prefabricated homes, furniture, wood products, transportation equipment, window blinds, wire harnesses, store display fixtures, and agricultural machinery; food processing. Employment by occupation: 15.8% management, 12.9% professional, 9.1% services, 27.0% sales, 0.0% farming, 11.5% construction, 23.9% production (2000).
Income: Per capita income: $24,613 (2000); Median household income: $55,000 (2000); Poverty rate: 1.7% (2000).
Taxes: Total city taxes per capita: $347 (1997); City property taxes per capita: $305 (1997).
Education: High school graduation rate: 81.2% (2000); College graduation rate: 17.7% (2000).

School District(s)

Middlebury Community Schools (KG-12)
2000 Enrollment: 3,538 219-825-9425
Housing: Homeownership rate: 75.4% (2000); Median home value: $118,400 (2000); Median rent: $458 per month (2000); Median age of housing: 22 years (2000).
Newspapers: The Middlebury Independent (1 x week)
Transportation: Commute to work: 94.8% car, 0.0% public transportation, 2.5% walk, 2.1% work from home (2000); Travel time to work: 54.8% less than 15 minutes, 29.1% 15 to 30 minutes, 13.1% 30 to 45 minutes, 1.3% 45 to 60 minutes, 1.6% 60 minutes or more (2000)

MILLERSBURG (town). Covers a land area of 0.527 square miles and a water area of 0 square miles. Located at 41.52° N. Lat.; 85.69° W. Long. Elevation is 880 feet.
History: Laid out 1855.
Population: 868 (2000); Race: 98.2% White, 0.0% Black, 0.0% Asian, 0.0% American Indian and Alaska Native, 2.7% Hispanic of any race, 0.4% two or more races (2000); Density: 1,646.6 persons per square mile (2000); Age: 31.3% under 18, 11.6% over 64 (2000); Marriage status: 14.8% never married, 71.1% now married, 4.2% widowed, 9.9% divorced (2000); Foreign born: 0.9% (2000); Ancestry (includes multiple ancestries): 24.4% German, 15.2% United States or American, 10.4% Irish, 6.7% English, 4.8% Other groups (2000).
Economy: Manufacturing: motor vehicles. Employment by occupation: 9.7% management, 10.3% professional, 12.2% services, 19.1% sales, 0.7% farming, 9.2% construction, 38.9% production (2000).
Income: Per capita income: $19,700 (2000); Median household income: $43,750 (2000); Poverty rate: 4.0% (2000).
Taxes: Total city taxes per capita: $273 (2000); City property taxes per capita: $248 (2000).
Education: High school graduation rate: 74.6% (2000); College graduation rate: 10.8% (2000).
Housing: Homeownership rate: 83.1% (2000); Median home value: $78,900 (2000); Median rent: $383 per month (2000); Median age of housing: 34 years (2000).
Transportation: Commute to work: 90.3% car, 0.7% public transportation, 2.6% walk, 3.2% work from home (2000); Travel time to work: 28.1% less than 15 minutes, 54.9% 15 to 30 minutes, 11.8% 30 to 45 minutes, 3.6% 45 to 60 minutes, 1.7% 60 minutes or more (2000)

NAPPANEE (city). Covers a land area of 3.689 square miles and a water area of 0 square miles. Located at 41.44° N. Lat.; 85.99° W. Long. Elevation is 878 feet.
History: Nappanee grew up along the Baltimore & Ohio Railroad. Furniture manufacturing was an early industry in Nappanee, which was platted in 1874.
Population: 6,710 (2000); Race: 96.0% White, 0.3% Black, 0.0% Asian, 0.1% American Indian and Alaska Native, 4.6% Hispanic of any race, 0.8% two or more races (2000); Density: 1,818.9 persons per square mile (2000); Age: 30.4% under 18, 10.9% over 64 (2000); Marriage status: 23.8% never married, 62.9% now married, 5.4% widowed, 7.9% divorced (2000); Foreign born: 2.6% (2000); Ancestry (includes multiple ancestries): 32.4% German, 13.3% United States or American, 7.7% Other groups, 7.1% Irish, 4.7% English (2000).
Economy: Single-family building permits issued: 16 (2001) / 23 (2000); Multi-family building permits issued: 16 (2001) / 0 (2000); Employment by occupation: 8.0% management, 10.3% professional, 12.4% services, 22.6% sales, 0.0% farming, 9.2% construction, 37.7% production (2000).
Income: Per capita income: $19,229 (2000); Median household income: $45,988 (2000); Poverty rate: 4.6% (2000).
Taxes: Total city taxes per capita: $342 (1997); City property taxes per capita: $284 (1997).
Education: High school graduation rate: 76.5% (2000); College graduation rate: 11.4% (2000).

School District(s)

Wa-Nee Community Schools (KG-12)
2000 Enrollment: 2,993 219-773-3131
Housing: Homeownership rate: 68.6% (2000); Median home value: $86,800 (2000); Median rent: $448 per month (2000); Median age of housing: 34 years (2000).
Safety: Violent crime rate: 11.9 per 10,000 population; Property crime rate: 211.9 per 10,000 population (2001).
Newspapers: Nappanee Advance News (1 x week)
Transportation: Commute to work: 93.8% car, 0.0% public transportation, 1.2% walk, 3.0% work from home (2000); Travel time to work: 56.5% less

than 15 minutes, 27.6% 15 to 30 minutes, 12.2% 30 to 45 minutes, 3.1% 45 to 60 minutes, 0.5% 60 minutes or more (2000); Amtrak: Service available.
Additional Information Contacts
Nappanee Chamber of Commerce 219-773-7812

NEW PARIS (CDP). Covers a land area of 0.832 square miles and a water area of 0 square miles. Located at 41.50° N. Lat.; 85.82° W. Long. Elevation is 819 feet.
History: Laid out 1838.
Population: 1,006 (2000); Race: 96.6% White, 0.0% Black, 0.0% Asian, 0.0% American Indian and Alaska Native, 3.4% Hispanic of any race, 0.0% two or more races (2000); Density: 1,209.3 persons per square mile (2000); Age: 36.2% under 18, 14.4% over 64 (2000); Marriage status: 16.4% never married, 68.1% now married, 8.5% widowed, 7.1% divorced (2000); Foreign born: 2.7% (2000); Ancestry (includes multiple ancestries): 31.1% German, 17.2% United States or American, 10.8% Irish, 10.7% English, 3.6% French (except Basque) (2000).
Economy: Railroad Junction. Manufacturing: motor vehicles, dairy products, furniture, boats, wire products, feed. Cattle, poultry; dairying. Employment by occupation: 11.8% management, 7.1% professional, 9.4% services, 21.7% sales, 0.0% farming, 6.1% construction, 43.9% production (2000).
Income: Per capita income: $17,270 (2000); Median household income: $42,446 (2000); Poverty rate: 5.0% (2000).
Education: High school graduation rate: 67.6% (2000); College graduation rate: 11.5% (2000).
Housing: Homeownership rate: 73.0% (2000); Median home value: $83,500 (2000); Median rent: $476 per month (2000); Median age of housing: 45 years (2000).
Transportation: Commute to work: 92.7% car, 0.0% public transportation, 1.0% walk, 2.6% work from home (2000); Travel time to work: 54.4% less than 15 minutes, 31.0% 15 to 30 minutes, 11.7% 30 to 45 minutes, 1.7% 45 to 60 minutes, 1.3% 60 minutes or more (2000)

SIMONTON LAKE (CDP). Covers a land area of 3.261 square miles and a water area of 0.413 square miles. Located at 41.74° N. Lat.; 85.97° W. Long. Elevation is 780 feet.
Population: 4,053 (2000); Race: 95.7% White, 1.0% Black, 0.4% Asian, 2.3% American Indian and Alaska Native, 0.4% Hispanic of any race, 0.2% two or more races (2000); Density: 1,243.0 persons per square mile (2000); Age: 25.4% under 18, 11.3% over 64 (2000); Marriage status: 20.4% never married, 65.3% now married, 4.7% widowed, 9.6% divorced (2000); Foreign born: 1.1% (2000); Ancestry (includes multiple ancestries): 23.3% German, 10.9% Irish, 10.3% United States or American, 8.9% Other groups, 8.5% Italian (2000).
Economy: Employment by occupation: 14.3% management, 9.9% professional, 13.2% services, 31.6% sales, 0.0% farming, 9.3% construction, 21.6% production (2000).
Income: Per capita income: $27,327 (2000); Median household income: $56,539 (2000); Poverty rate: 2.8% (2000).
Education: High school graduation rate: 90.5% (2000); College graduation rate: 20.0% (2000).
Housing: Homeownership rate: 86.9% (2000); Median home value: $112,900 (2000); Median rent: $493 per month (2000); Median age of housing: 27 years (2000).
Transportation: Commute to work: 97.2% car, 0.0% public transportation, 0.0% walk, 2.8% work from home (2000); Travel time to work: 37.0% less than 15 minutes, 44.3% 15 to 30 minutes, 13.8% 30 to 45 minutes, 1.7% 45 to 60 minutes, 3.2% 60 minutes or more (2000)

WAKARUSA (town). Covers a land area of 2.260 square miles and a water area of 0 square miles. Located at 41.53° N. Lat.; 86.01° W. Long. Elevation is 847 feet.
History: Laid out 1852.
Population: 1,618 (2000); Race: 97.2% White, 0.6% Black, 0.9% Asian, 0.0% American Indian and Alaska Native, 2.3% Hispanic of any race, 1.0% two or more races (2000); Density: 716.0 persons per square mile (2000); Age: 25.2% under 18, 20.6% over 64 (2000); Marriage status: 18.2% never married, 59.7% now married, 15.2% widowed, 6.9% divorced (2000); Foreign born: 1.6% (2000); Ancestry (includes multiple ancestries): 34.4% German, 19.0% United States or American, 6.2% Irish, 6.0% Swiss, 5.9% Other groups (2000).
Economy: In agricultural area: dairy products; grain. Manufacturing: transportation equipment, cookers and roasters. Employment by occupation: 7.5% management, 16.5% professional, 9.9% services, 29.4% sales, 1.0% farming, 9.9% construction, 25.8% production (2000).
Income: Per capita income: $19,615 (2000); Median household income: $41,515 (2000); Poverty rate: 4.0% (2000).
Taxes: Total city taxes per capita: $271 (1997); City property taxes per capita: $242 (1997).
Education: High school graduation rate: 83.2% (2000); College graduation rate: 11.8% (2000).
Housing: Homeownership rate: 80.9% (2000); Median home value: $96,100 (2000); Median rent: $392 per month (2000); Median age of housing: 48 years (2000).
Newspapers: Wakarusa Tribune (1 x week)
Transportation: Commute to work: 90.9% car, 0.0% public transportation, 5.1% walk, 2.6% work from home (2000); Travel time to work: 46.2% less than 15 minutes, 38.2% 15 to 30 minutes, 12.0% 30 to 45 minutes, 1.4% 45 to 60 minutes, 2.2% 60 minutes or more (2000)
Additional Information Contacts
Wakarusa Chamber of Commerce 219-862-4344

Fayette County

Located in eastern Indiana; drained by the Whitewater River. Covers a land area of 215.00 square miles, a water area of 0.20 square miles, and is located in the Eastern Time Zone. The county government was organized in 1818. County seat is Connersville.
Population: 25,588 (2000); Race: 97.6% White, 1.2% Black, 0.2% Asian, 0.1% American Indian and Alaska Native, 0.6% Hispanic of any race, 0.6% two or more races (2000); Density: 119.0 persons per square mile (2000); Age: 24.4% under 18, 15.6% over 64 (2000).
Religion: Five largest groups: 11.1% Catholic Church, 6.1% The United Methodist Church, 3.6% Southern Baptist Convention, 3.5% Christian Churches and Churches of Christ, 3.3% Independent, Non-Charismatic Churches (2000).
Economy: Unemployment rate: 8.1% (11/2002); Total civilian labor force: 9,864 (11/2002); Leading industries: 45.0% manufacturing; 14.8% health care and social assistance; 12.3% retail trade (2000); Companies that employ more than 1,000 persons: 1 (2000); Companies that employ more than 100 persons: 8 (2000); Farms: 420 totaling 106,737 acres (1997); Minority business ownership rate: 0.0% (1997); Women business ownership rate: 23.4% (1997); Retail sales per capita: $7,403 (1997). Single-family building permits issued: 62 (2001) / 88 (2000); Multi-family building permits issued: 0 (2001) / 0 (2000).
Income: Per capita income: $18,624 (2000); Median household income: $38,840 (2000); Poverty rate: 7.9% (2000); Bankruptcy rate: 9.55% (2001).
Taxes: Total county taxes per capita: $406 (2000); County property taxes per capita: $190 (2000).
Education: High school graduation rate: 73.7% (2000); College graduation rate: 7.8% (2000).
Housing: Homeownership rate: 71.6% (2000); Median home value: $78,500 (2000); Median rent: $364 per month (2000); Median age of housing: 43 years (2000).
Health: Birth rate: 132.9 per 10,000 population (1998); Age adjusted death rate: 102.5 per 10,000 population (1999); Age adjusted cancer mortality rate: 235.9 deaths per 100,000 population (1999). Number of physicians: 10.2 per 10,000 population (1999); Number of hospital beds: 43.4 per 10,000 population (1999).
Elections: 2000 Presidential election results: 39.5% Gore, 58.5% Bush, 0.4% Nader, 1.1% Buchanan
Additional Information Contacts
Fayette County Government Offices 765-825-8987
Connersville Chamber of Commerce 765-825-2561
East Central Indiana Board of Realtors 765-825-0094

Fayette County Communities

CONNERSVILLE (city). Covers a land area of 8.135 square miles and a water area of 0.012 square miles. Located at 39.65° N. Lat.; 85.13° W. Long. Elevation is 828 feet.
History: Settlement at Connersville began in 1808 when John Conner established a fur-trading post here. He founded the town of Connersville in 1813 and served as its first sheriff, in addition to operating the gristmill, sawmill, tavern, and store.
Population: 15,411 (2000); Race: 96.8% White, 1.9% Black, 0.3% Asian, 0.1% American Indian and Alaska Native, 0.6% Hispanic of any race, 0.7% two or more races (2000); Density: 1,894.5 persons per square mile (2000); Age: 23.4% under 18, 16.9% over 64 (2000); Marriage status: 19.8% never married, 56.7% now married, 9.5% widowed, 14.0% divorced (2000);

Foreign born: 0.6% (2000); Ancestry (includes multiple ancestries): 20.7% United States or American, 12.7% German, 10.1% Irish, 9.4% Other groups, 8.7% English (2000).
Vital Statistics: Birth rate: 162.2 per 10,000 population (1998)
Economy: Employment by occupation: 6.5% management, 10.5% professional, 17.7% services, 18.1% sales, 0.0% farming, 8.8% construction, 38.6% production (2000).
Income: Per capita income: $16,839 (2000); Median household income: $33,911 (2000); Poverty rate: 10.5% (2000).
Taxes: Total city taxes per capita: $321 (1997); City property taxes per capita: $241 (1997).
Education: High school graduation rate: 70.8% (2000); College graduation rate: 6.2% (2000).

School District(s)

Fayette County School Corp (PK-12)
2000 Enrollment: 4,239 765-825-2178
Housing: Homeownership rate: 63.6% (2000); Median home value: $69,300 (2000); Median rent: $365 per month (2000); Median age of housing: 49 years (2000).
Hospitals: Fayette Memorial Hospital (140 beds)
Safety: Violent crime rate: 18.1 per 10,000 population; Property crime rate: 586.5 per 10,000 population (2001).
Newspapers: Connersville News-Examiner (6 x week)
Transportation: Commute to work: 95.5% car, 0.0% public transportation, 2.2% walk, 1.6% work from home (2000); Travel time to work: 55.4% less than 15 minutes, 18.0% 15 to 30 minutes, 11.1% 30 to 45 minutes, 8.3% 45 to 60 minutes, 7.1% 60 minutes or more (2000); Amtrak: Service available.
Additional Information Contacts
Connersville Chamber of Commerce 765-825-2561
East Central Indiana Board of Realtors 765-825-0094

Floyd County

Located in southern Indiana; hilly region, bounded on the south by the Ohio River and the Kentucky border; drained by tributaries of the Ohio River. Covers a land area of 148.00 square miles, a water area of 0.30 square miles, and is located in the Eastern Time Zone. The county government was organized in 1819. County seat is New Albany.

Floyd County is part of the Louisville, KY-IN MSA. The entire metro area includes: Clark County, IN; Floyd County, IN; Harrison County, IN; Scott County, IN; Bullitt County, KY; Jefferson County, KY; Oldham County, KY

Population: 70,823 (2000); Race: 93.3% White, 4.6% Black, 0.5% Asian, 0.1% American Indian and Alaska Native, 1.0% Hispanic of any race, 1.3% two or more races (2000); Density: 478.5 persons per square mile (2000); Age: 25.8% under 18, 12.2% over 64 (2000).
Religion: Five largest groups: 20.8% Catholic Church, 15.5% Southern Baptist Convention, 6.9% The United Methodist Church, 5.1% Christian Churches and Churches of Christ, 2.1% Christian Church (Disciples of Christ) (2000).
Economy: Unemployment rate: 3.8% (11/2002); Total civilian labor force: 40,374 (11/2002); Leading industries: 27.9% manufacturing; 14.0% health care and social assistance; 11.0% retail trade (2000); Companies that employ more than 1,000 persons: 2 (2000); Companies that employ more than 100 persons: 33 (2000); Farms: 310 totaling 28,708 acres (1997); Minority business ownership rate: 0.0% (1997); Women business ownership rate: 28.3% (1997); Retail sales per capita: $4,631 (1997). Single-family building permits issued: 343 (2001) / 353 (2000); Multi-family building permits issued: 31 (2001) / 72 (2000).
Income: Per capita income: $21,852 (2000); Median household income: $44,022 (2000); Poverty rate: 8.7% (2000); Bankruptcy rate: 6.42% (2001).
Taxes: Total county taxes per capita: $172 (2000); County property taxes per capita: $168 (2000).
Education: High school graduation rate: 82.4% (2000); College graduation rate: 20.4% (2000).
Housing: Homeownership rate: 72.5% (2000); Median home value: $104,300 (2000); Median rent: $425 per month (2000); Median age of housing: 30 years (2000).
Health: Birth rate: 115.4 per 10,000 population (1998); Age adjusted death rate: 100.2 per 10,000 population (1999); Age adjusted cancer mortality rate: 225.6 deaths per 100,000 population (1999). Air Quality Index: 77% good, 23% moderate, 0% unhealthy (percent of days in 2000). Number of physicians: 20.8 per 10,000 population (1999); Number of hospital beds: 36.4 per 10,000 population (1999).
Elections: 2000 Presidential election results: 44.0% Gore, 54.9% Bush, 0.2% Nader, 0.5% Buchanan
Additional Information Contacts
Floyd County Government Offices 812-948-5466
Southern Indiana Chamber of Commerce 812-945-0266

Floyd County Communities

FLOYDS KNOBS (unincorporated postal area, zip code 47119). Covers a land area of 41.579 square miles and a water area of 0.027 square miles. Located at 38.34° N. Lat.; 85.89° W. Long. Elevation is 800 feet.
History: James B. Moore of New York built a gristmill here in 1815, and the community called Mooresville grew up around it. Another early industry was the making of beaver top hats. The name was changed in 1843 to honor Colonel Davis Floyd of Jeffersonville. The Knobs part of the name refers to the hills in the area, noted for its strawberry growing.
Population: 9,777 (2000); Race: 99.5% White, 0.1% Black, 0.0% Asian, 0.1% American Indian and Alaska Native, 1.1% Hispanic of any race, 0.3% two or more races (2000); Density: 235.1 persons per square mile (2000); Age: 27.6% under 18, 8.9% over 64 (2000); Marriage status: 21.5% never married, 64.4% now married, 4.8% widowed, 9.4% divorced (2000); Foreign born: 0.8% (2000); Ancestry (includes multiple ancestries): 35.7% German, 14.2% Irish, 11.7% United States or American, 11.5% English, 7.6% French (except Basque) (2000).
Economy: Employment by occupation: 17.2% management, 19.8% professional, 10.5% services, 28.0% sales, 0.2% farming, 7.3% construction, 17.0% production (2000).
Income: Per capita income: $29,877 (2000); Median household income: $63,732 (2000); Poverty rate: 2.8% (2000).
Education: High school graduation rate: 90.0% (2000); College graduation rate: 29.2% (2000).
Housing: Homeownership rate: 91.6% (2000); Median home value: $141,800 (2000); Median rent: $460 per month (2000); Median age of housing: 24 years (2000).
Transportation: Commute to work: 94.1% car, 0.7% public transportation, 0.3% walk, 4.1% work from home (2000); Travel time to work: 21.2% less than 15 minutes, 48.0% 15 to 30 minutes, 23.2% 30 to 45 minutes, 4.6% 45 to 60 minutes, 3.0% 60 minutes or more (2000)

GALENA (CDP). Covers a land area of 2.649 square miles and a water area of 0 square miles. Located at 38.35° N. Lat.; 85.94° W. Long. Elevation is 811 feet.
History: Galena was laid out in 1836, when it was called Germantown for the German immigrants who settled here. The Galena Mill, built in 1857, was a steam-powered flour mill.
Population: 1,831 (2000); Race: 99.1% White, 0.9% Black, 0.0% Asian, 0.0% American Indian and Alaska Native, 0.0% Hispanic of any race, 0.0% two or more races (2000); Density: 691.2 persons per square mile (2000); Age: 30.1% under 18, 11.5% over 64 (2000); Marriage status: 18.7% never married, 64.2% now married, 5.6% widowed, 11.4% divorced (2000); Foreign born: 0.7% (2000); Ancestry (includes multiple ancestries): 39.7% German, 17.5% Irish, 11.6% United States or American, 10.7% Other groups, 9.7% English (2000).
Economy: Employment by occupation: 9.5% management, 19.9% professional, 10.9% services, 27.5% sales, 0.8% farming, 14.3% construction, 17.1% production (2000).
Income: Per capita income: $23,824 (2000); Median household income: $60,313 (2000); Poverty rate: 2.9% (2000).
Education: High school graduation rate: 90.8% (2000); College graduation rate: 27.3% (2000).
Housing: Homeownership rate: 87.7% (2000); Median home value: $132,800 (2000); Median rent: $558 per month (2000); Median age of housing: 18 years (2000).
Transportation: Commute to work: 93.2% car, 0.0% public transportation, 0.0% walk, 5.3% work from home (2000); Travel time to work: 9.9% less than 15 minutes, 44.6% 15 to 30 minutes, 38.8% 30 to 45 minutes, 5.3% 45 to 60 minutes, 1.5% 60 minutes or more (2000)

GEORGETOWN (town). Covers a land area of 1.792 square miles and a water area of 0.016 square miles. Located at 38.30° N. Lat.; 85.97° W. Long. Elevation is 714 feet.
Population: 2,227 (2000); Race: 97.9% White, 0.5% Black, 0.3% Asian, 0.1% American Indian and Alaska Native, 0.8% Hispanic of any race, 0.9% two or more races (2000); Density: 1,242.4 persons per square mile (2000); Age: 30.1% under 18, 6.7% over 64 (2000); Marriage status: 20.6% never

married, 64.1% now married, 4.3% widowed, 11.0% divorced (2000); Foreign born: 0.7% (2000); Ancestry (includes multiple ancestries): 26.2% German, 14.7% Irish, 14.0% United States or American, 11.5% English, 6.7% Other groups (2000).
Economy: Agricultural area; wood trusses. Single-family building permits issued: 17 (2001) / 27 (2000); Multi-family building permits issued: 0 (2001) / 0 (2000); Employment by occupation: 7.7% management, 19.8% professional, 13.9% services, 24.7% sales, 0.2% farming, 14.9% construction, 18.7% production (2000).
Income: Per capita income: $18,645 (2000); Median household income: $48,795 (2000); Poverty rate: 3.1% (2000).
Taxes: Total city taxes per capita: $85 (1997); City property taxes per capita: $61 (1997).
Education: High school graduation rate: 88.7% (2000); College graduation rate: 13.7% (2000).
Housing: Homeownership rate: 90.8% (2000); Median home value: $94,100 (2000); Median rent: $398 per month (2000); Median age of housing: 25 years (2000).
Safety: Violent crime rate: 8.9 per 10,000 population; Property crime rate: 67.0 per 10,000 population (2001).
Transportation: Commute to work: 95.5% car, 0.3% public transportation, 1.4% walk, 2.4% work from home (2000); Travel time to work: 11.4% less than 15 minutes, 51.0% 15 to 30 minutes, 31.1% 30 to 45 minutes, 3.7% 45 to 60 minutes, 2.9% 60 minutes or more (2000)

GREENVILLE (town). Covers a land area of 0.619 square miles and a water area of 0 square miles. Located at 38.37° N. Lat.; 85.98° W. Long. Elevation is 808 feet.
History: Greenville was settled in 1807 and laid out in 1816 as a station on the Old Stage Road. A ready supply of white-oak timber led to the town becoming a center for the production of barrels, wine kegs, and wooden clocks.
Population: 591 (2000); Race: 98.1% White, 0.5% Black, 0.0% Asian, 0.5% American Indian and Alaska Native, 0.5% Hispanic of any race, 1.0% two or more races (2000); Density: 954.9 persons per square mile (2000); Age: 31.1% under 18, 11.3% over 64 (2000); Marriage status: 19.8% never married, 65.6% now married, 6.5% widowed, 8.2% divorced (2000); Foreign born: 0.2% (2000); Ancestry (includes multiple ancestries): 31.9% German, 16.8% Irish, 12.4% United States or American, 10.6% English, 6.9% French (except Basque) (2000).
Economy: Employment by occupation: 20.5% management, 17.5% professional, 9.9% services, 23.2% sales, 0.0% farming, 9.9% construction, 19.0% production (2000).
Income: Per capita income: $24,343 (2000); Median household income: $49,271 (2000); Poverty rate: 4.0% (2000).
Taxes: Total city taxes per capita: $19 (1997); City property taxes per capita: $17 (1997).
Education: High school graduation rate: 83.7% (2000); College graduation rate: 20.1% (2000).
Housing: Homeownership rate: 92.2% (2000); Median home value: $102,000 (2000); Median rent: $425 per month (2000); Median age of housing: 31 years (2000).
Transportation: Commute to work: 93.0% car, 0.0% public transportation, 0.0% walk, 5.5% work from home (2000); Travel time to work: 14.0% less than 15 minutes, 52.5% 15 to 30 minutes, 24.8% 30 to 45 minutes, 8.3% 45 to 60 minutes, 0.4% 60 minutes or more (2000)

NEW ALBANY (city). Covers a land area of 14.625 square miles and a water area of 0.169 square miles. Located at 38.30° N. Lat.; 85.82° W. Long. Elevation is 467 feet.
History: New Albany began as a river town, utilizing its location on the Ohio River for shipping and industry. The town was platted in 1813 by three brothers from New York, who named it for the capital of their former home state. New Albany received its city charter in 1838. Shipyards here built many vessels in the mid-1800's, including the "Robert E. Lee" built in 1866 for Captain John W. Cannon.
Population: 37,603 (2000); Race: 90.2% White, 7.0% Black, 0.6% Asian, 0.2% American Indian and Alaska Native, 0.8% Hispanic of any race, 1.8% two or more races (2000); Density: 2,571.1 persons per square mile (2000); Age: 23.8% under 18, 15.3% over 64 (2000); Marriage status: 24.8% never married, 51.9% now married, 8.5% widowed, 14.8% divorced (2000); Foreign born: 1.3% (2000); Ancestry (includes multiple ancestries): 21.7% German, 15.3% Other groups, 14.9% United States or American, 11.7% Irish, 9.1% English (2000).
Vital Statistics: Birth rate: 147.9 per 10,000 population (1998)
Economy: Unemployment rate: 4.6% (11/2002); Total civilian labor force: 22,128 (11/2002); Single-family building permits issued: 62 (2001) / 55 (2000); Multi-family building permits issued: 31 (2001) / 72 (2000); Employment by occupation: 9.4% management, 16.1% professional, 15.7% services, 28.1% sales, 0.1% farming, 9.9% construction, 20.8% production (2000).
Income: Per capita income: $18,365 (2000); Median household income: $34,923 (2000); Poverty rate: 13.7% (2000).
Taxes: Total city taxes per capita: $229 (1997); City property taxes per capita: $200 (1997).
Education: High school graduation rate: 76.1% (2000); College graduation rate: 15.9% (2000).

School District(s)

New Albany-Floyd Co Con Sch (PK-12)
2000 Enrollment: 11,115 812-949-4200

Four-year College(s)

Indiana University-Southeast (Public)
2001 Enrollment: 6,557 812-941-2000
2001 Tuition: In-state $3,221; Out-of-state $8,520

Housing: Homeownership rate: 59.5% (2000); Median home value: $87,300 (2000); Median rent: $409 per month (2000); Median age of housing: 41 years (2000).
Hospitals: Floyd Memorial Hospital and Health Services (245 beds); Southern Indiana Rehabilitation Hospital (60 beds)
Safety: Violent crime rate: 64.0 per 10,000 population; Property crime rate: 761.1 per 10,000 population (2001).
Newspapers: Tribune (6 x week)
Transportation: Commute to work: 94.2% car, 0.9% public transportation, 2.1% walk, 2.0% work from home (2000); Travel time to work: 36.7% less than 15 minutes, 45.8% 15 to 30 minutes, 12.6% 30 to 45 minutes, 1.7% 45 to 60 minutes, 3.2% 60 minutes or more (2000)
Additional Information Contacts
Southern Indiana Chamber of Commerce 812-945-0266

Fountain County

Located in western Indiana; bounded on the west and north by the Wabash River; drained by Coal Creek. Covers a land area of 395.70 square miles, a water area of 2.20 square miles, and is located in the Eastern Time Zone. The county government was organized in 1825. County seat is Covington.
Population: 17,954 (2000); Race: 98.7% White, 0.0% Black, 0.3% Asian, 0.4% American Indian and Alaska Native, 0.5% Hispanic of any race, 0.5% two or more races (2000); Density: 45.4 persons per square mile (2000); Age: 26.3% under 18, 15.6% over 64 (2000).
Religion: Five largest groups: 9.0% Christian Churches and Churches of Christ, 7.7% The United Methodist Church, 4.9% Catholic Church, 4.1% New Testament Association of Independent Baptist Churches and other Fundamental Baptist Associations, 2.8% C
Economy: Unemployment rate: 5.2% (11/2002); Total civilian labor force: 8,566 (11/2002); Leading industries: 52.8% manufacturing; 14.2% retail trade; 8.4% accommodation & food services (2000); Companies that employ more than 1,000 persons: 0 (2000); Companies that employ more than 100 persons: 6 (2000); Farms: 550 totaling 204,554 acres (1997); Minority business ownership rate: 0.0% (1997); Women business ownership rate: 33.0% (1997); Retail sales per capita: $6,616 (1997). Single-family building permits issued: 9 (2001) / 8 (2000); Multi-family building permits issued: 0 (2001) / 0 (2000).
Income: Per capita income: $17,779 (2000); Median household income: $38,119 (2000); Poverty rate: 8.5% (2000); Bankruptcy rate: 7.94% (2001).
Taxes: Total county taxes per capita: $261 (2000); County property taxes per capita: $165 (2000).
Education: High school graduation rate: 80.7% (2000); College graduation rate: 10.1% (2000).
Housing: Homeownership rate: 77.9% (2000); Median home value: $69,200 (2000); Median rent: $310 per month (2000); Median age of housing: 44 years (2000).
Health: Birth rate: 143.1 per 10,000 population (1998); Age adjusted death rate: 100.8 per 10,000 population (1999); Age adjusted cancer mortality rate: 261.0 deaths per 100,000 population (1999). Air Quality Index: 100% good, 0% moderate, 0% unhealthy (percent of days in 2000). Number of physicians: 2.2 per 10,000 population (1999); Number of hospital beds: n/a (1999).
Elections: 2000 Presidential election results: 37.3% Gore, 60.5% Bush, 0.3% Nader, 1.4% Buchanan
National and State Parks: Shades State Park
Additional Information Contacts

Fountain County Government Offices 765-793-2243

Fountain County Communities

ATTICA (city). Covers a land area of 1.517 square miles and a water area of 0 square miles. Located at 40.29° N. Lat.; 87.24° W. Long. Elevation is 547 feet.

History: Attica developed in the late 1840's when the Wabash & Erie Canal was extended here. A prominent resident of Attica was Dr. John Evans (1814-1897), a physician who later served as Territorial Governor of Colorado and as a U.S. senator.

Population: 3,491 (2000); Race: 98.7% White, 0.0% Black, 0.5% Asian, 0.5% American Indian and Alaska Native, 0.5% Hispanic of any race, 0.4% two or more races (2000); Density: 2,300.6 persons per square mile (2000); Age: 25.6% under 18, 17.3% over 64 (2000); Marriage status: 18.7% never married, 57.6% now married, 12.6% widowed, 11.1% divorced (2000); Foreign born: 1.4% (2000); Ancestry (includes multiple ancestries): 19.1% United States or American, 14.0% German, 12.0% Irish, 7.3% Other groups, 6.1% English (2000).

Economy: Single-family building permits issued: 5 (2001) / 6 (2000); Multi-family building permits issued: 0 (2001) / 0 (2000); Employment by occupation: 5.1% management, 9.1% professional, 19.7% services, 22.3% sales, 0.6% farming, 7.2% construction, 36.0% production (2000).

Income: Per capita income: $16,802 (2000); Median household income: $33,191 (2000); Poverty rate: 11.3% (2000).

Taxes: Total city taxes per capita: $149 (1997); City property taxes per capita: $144 (1997).

Education: High school graduation rate: 72.2% (2000); College graduation rate: 8.1% (2000).

School District(s)

Attica Consolidated Sch Corp (PK-12)
2000 Enrollment: 949 765-762-3236

Housing: Homeownership rate: 64.8% (2000); Median home value: $70,500 (2000); Median rent: $324 per month (2000); Median age of housing: 50 years (2000).

Newspapers: The Messenger (1 x week); Fountain County Neighbor (1 x week)

Transportation: Commute to work: 92.7% car, 0.0% public transportation, 4.4% walk, 1.4% work from home (2000); Travel time to work: 51.2% less than 15 minutes, 12.1% 15 to 30 minutes, 18.2% 30 to 45 minutes, 13.6% 45 to 60 minutes, 4.9% 60 minutes or more (2000)

COVINGTON (city). Covers a land area of 1.168 square miles and a water area of 0 square miles. Located at 40.14° N. Lat.; 87.39° W. Long. Elevation is 560 feet.

History: Covington was laid out in 1826 along the east bank of the Wabash River. A prominent resident was Edward A. Hannegan (1807-1859), U.S. senator and minister to Prussia, where he is said to have dazzled the court. Back home, Hannegan's bid for the presidency was ended when he stabbed his brother-in-law to death.

Population: 2,565 (2000); Race: 98.2% White, 0.2% Black, 0.5% Asian, 0.4% American Indian and Alaska Native, 0.0% Hispanic of any race, 0.7% two or more races (2000); Density: 2,196.1 persons per square mile (2000); Age: 20.7% under 18, 21.2% over 64 (2000); Marriage status: 18.1% never married, 56.0% now married, 15.4% widowed, 10.5% divorced (2000); Foreign born: 1.8% (2000); Ancestry (includes multiple ancestries): 19.4% German, 19.4% United States or American, 9.6% English, 5.6% Irish, 3.0% Other groups (2000).

Economy: Single-family building permits issued: 4 (2001) / 2 (2000); Multi-family building permits issued: 0 (2001) / 0 (2000); Employment by occupation: 10.1% management, 15.7% professional, 11.7% services, 27.2% sales, 1.0% farming, 6.8% construction, 27.4% production (2000).

Income: Per capita income: $20,776 (2000); Median household income: $40,432 (2000); Poverty rate: 7.4% (2000).

Taxes: Total city taxes per capita: $176 (1997); City property taxes per capita: $174 (1997).

Education: High school graduation rate: 84.7% (2000); College graduation rate: 14.9% (2000).

School District(s)

Covington Community Sch Corp (KG-12)
2000 Enrollment: 965 765-793-4877

Housing: Homeownership rate: 75.0% (2000); Median home value: $75,600 (2000); Median rent: $314 per month (2000); Median age of housing: 44 years (2000).

Transportation: Commute to work: 93.3% car, 0.0% public transportation, 3.6% walk, 2.8% work from home (2000); Travel time to work: 41.6% less than 15 minutes, 35.7% 15 to 30 minutes, 11.6% 30 to 45 minutes, 6.7% 45 to 60 minutes, 4.5% 60 minutes or more (2000)

HILLSBORO (town). Aka Hillsborough. Covers a land area of 0.320 square miles and a water area of 0 square miles. Located at 40.10° N. Lat.; 87.15° W. Long. Elevation is 715 feet.

History: Early industry in Hillsboro was based on the clay soil used in the manufacture of tiles and bricks.

Population: 489 (2000); Race: 97.0% White, 0.0% Black, 0.0% Asian, 0.0% American Indian and Alaska Native, 1.9% Hispanic of any race, 2.1% two or more races (2000); Density: 1,527.5 persons per square mile (2000); Age: 26.8% under 18, 18.4% over 64 (2000); Marriage status: 17.1% never married, 66.7% now married, 8.0% widowed, 8.3% divorced (2000); Foreign born: 0.9% (2000); Ancestry (includes multiple ancestries): 24.6% German, 14.6% United States or American, 14.3% Irish, 11.8% English, 11.3% Other groups (2000).

Economy: Employment by occupation: 6.6% management, 15.3% professional, 16.6% services, 20.1% sales, 0.0% farming, 6.6% construction, 34.9% production (2000).

Income: Per capita income: $16,630 (2000); Median household income: $41,806 (2000); Poverty rate: 9.5% (2000).

Taxes: Total city taxes per capita: $62 (1997); City property taxes per capita: $60 (1997).

Education: High school graduation rate: 86.9% (2000); College graduation rate: 11.1% (2000).

Housing: Homeownership rate: 78.3% (2000); Median home value: $63,300 (2000); Median rent: $354 per month (2000); Median age of housing: 59 years (2000).

Transportation: Commute to work: 92.0% car, 0.0% public transportation, 6.2% walk, 1.8% work from home (2000); Travel time to work: 32.9% less than 15 minutes, 32.9% 15 to 30 minutes, 20.3% 30 to 45 minutes, 10.4% 45 to 60 minutes, 3.6% 60 minutes or more (2000)

KINGMAN (town). Covers a land area of 0.816 square miles and a water area of 0 square miles. Located at 39.96° N. Lat.; 87.27° W. Long. Elevation is 705 feet.

Population: 538 (2000); Race: 100.0% White, 0.0% Black, 0.0% Asian, 0.0% American Indian and Alaska Native, 0.0% Hispanic of any race, 0.0% two or more races (2000); Density: 659.2 persons per square mile (2000); Age: 26.9% under 18, 15.1% over 64 (2000); Marriage status: 23.4% never married, 51.5% now married, 12.3% widowed, 12.8% divorced (2000); Foreign born: 0.6% (2000); Ancestry (includes multiple ancestries): 17.2% German, 9.2% United States or American, 4.9% English, 4.3% Irish, 2.6% Polish (2000).

Economy: Agriculture. Manufacturing: fiberglass gloves, steel products and safety clothing. Employment by occupation: 2.7% management, 9.0% professional, 13.1% services, 17.6% sales, 1.4% farming, 9.0% construction, 47.1% production (2000).

Income: Per capita income: $12,815 (2000); Median household income: $28,438 (2000); Poverty rate: 16.2% (2000).

Taxes: Total city taxes per capita: $52 (1997); City property taxes per capita: $51 (1997).

Education: High school graduation rate: 80.6% (2000); College graduation rate: 7.7% (2000).

Housing: Homeownership rate: 65.9% (2000); Median home value: $45,000 (2000); Median rent: $263 per month (2000); Median age of housing: 47 years (2000).

Transportation: Commute to work: 95.9% car, 0.0% public transportation, 2.7% walk, 0.0% work from home (2000); Travel time to work: 23.5% less than 15 minutes, 37.1% 15 to 30 minutes, 24.0% 30 to 45 minutes, 3.6% 45 to 60 minutes, 11.8% 60 minutes or more (2000)

MELLOTT (town). Covers a land area of 0.157 square miles and a water area of 0 square miles. Located at 40.16° N. Lat.; 87.14° W. Long. Elevation is 712 feet.

Population: 207 (2000); Race: 99.1% White, 0.0% Black, 0.0% Asian, 0.9% American Indian and Alaska Native, 2.6% Hispanic of any race, 0.0% two or more races (2000); Density: 1,317.8 persons per square mile (2000); Age: 28.9% under 18, 14.5% over 64 (2000); Marriage status: 8.6% never married, 59.3% now married, 11.1% widowed, 21.0% divorced (2000); Foreign born: 0.0% (2000); Ancestry (includes multiple ancestries): 17.5% United States or American, 14.5% German, 12.3% Other groups, 7.9% English, 6.1% Dutch (2000).

Economy: Agriculture. Employment by occupation: 0.0% management, 9.9% professional, 22.0% services, 3.3% sales, 2.2% farming, 12.1% construction, 50.5% production (2000).

Income: Per capita income: $19,694 (2000); Median household income: $29,375 (2000); Poverty rate: 11.1% (2000).
Taxes: Total city taxes per capita: $21 (1997); City property taxes per capita: $21 (1997).
Education: High school graduation rate: 71.5% (2000); College graduation rate: 6.3% (2000).
Housing: Homeownership rate: 73.5% (2000); Median home value: $49,300 (2000); Median rent: $325 per month (2000); Median age of housing: 30 years (2000).
Transportation: Commute to work: 95.6% car, 0.0% public transportation, 0.0% walk, 2.2% work from home (2000); Travel time to work: 18.0% less than 15 minutes, 33.7% 15 to 30 minutes, 24.7% 30 to 45 minutes, 14.6% 45 to 60 minutes, 9.0% 60 minutes or more (2000)

NEWTOWN (town). Covers a land area of 0.504 square miles and a water area of 0 square miles. Located at 40.20° N. Lat.; 87.14° W. Long. Elevation is 711 feet.
Population: 162 (2000); Race: 100.0% White, 0.0% Black, 0.0% Asian, 0.0% American Indian and Alaska Native, 0.0% Hispanic of any race, 0.0% two or more races (2000); Density: 321.3 persons per square mile (2000); Age: 28.3% under 18, 11.4% over 64 (2000); Marriage status: 15.0% never married, 60.9% now married, 5.3% widowed, 18.8% divorced (2000); Foreign born: 0.0% (2000); Ancestry (includes multiple ancestries): 19.9% Irish, 14.5% United States or American, 13.9% German, 7.8% Other groups, 4.2% English (2000).
Economy: Agricultural area. Employment by occupation: 11.1% management, 13.9% professional, 22.2% services, 4.2% sales, 0.0% farming, 6.9% construction, 41.7% production (2000).
Income: Per capita income: $25,441 (2000); Median household income: $41,250 (2000); Poverty rate: 8.0% (2000).
Taxes: Total city taxes per capita: $32 (1997); City property taxes per capita: $32 (1997).
Education: High school graduation rate: 82.4% (2000); College graduation rate: 10.2% (2000).
Housing: Homeownership rate: 86.4% (2000); Median home value: $57,500 (2000); Median rent: $325 per month (2000); Median age of housing: 48 years (2000).
Transportation: Commute to work: 97.2% car, 0.0% public transportation, 2.8% walk, 0.0% work from home (2000); Travel time to work: 11.1% less than 15 minutes, 29.2% 15 to 30 minutes, 44.4% 30 to 45 minutes, 15.3% 45 to 60 minutes, 0.0% 60 minutes or more (2000)

VEEDERSBURG (town). Covers a land area of 2.716 square miles and a water area of 0 square miles. Located at 40.11° N. Lat.; 87.26° W. Long. Elevation is 612 feet.
History: Veedersburg was a brick manufacturing center. The Veedersburg Paver Company furnished the brick for paving the Indianapolis Motor Speedway.
Population: 2,299 (2000); Race: 98.1% White, 0.0% Black, 0.2% Asian, 0.7% American Indian and Alaska Native, 2.2% Hispanic of any race, 0.6% two or more races (2000); Density: 846.4 persons per square mile (2000); Age: 27.5% under 18, 15.1% over 64 (2000); Marriage status: 17.3% never married, 62.3% now married, 7.4% widowed, 13.0% divorced (2000); Foreign born: 0.9% (2000); Ancestry (includes multiple ancestries): 18.8% German, 15.5% United States or American, 10.2% English, 7.1% Irish, 6.9% Other groups (2000).
Economy: Employment by occupation: 4.2% management, 12.3% professional, 16.2% services, 15.7% sales, 0.6% farming, 8.9% construction, 42.2% production (2000).
Income: Per capita income: $17,435 (2000); Median household income: $35,944 (2000); Poverty rate: 10.9% (2000).
Taxes: Total city taxes per capita: $72 (1997); City property taxes per capita: $70 (1997).
Education: High school graduation rate: 76.9% (2000); College graduation rate: 5.2% (2000).

School District(s)

Southeast Fountain School Corp (KG-12)
2000 Enrollment: 1,373 765-294-2254

Housing: Homeownership rate: 73.2% (2000); Median home value: $59,900 (2000); Median rent: $306 per month (2000); Median age of housing: 43 years (2000).
Transportation: Commute to work: 96.0% car, 0.0% public transportation, 1.6% walk, 1.8% work from home (2000); Travel time to work: 40.2% less than 15 minutes, 21.5% 15 to 30 minutes, 23.6% 30 to 45 minutes, 8.7% 45 to 60 minutes, 6.1% 60 minutes or more (2000)

WALLACE (town). Covers a land area of 0.085 square miles and a water area of 0 square miles. Located at 39.98° N. Lat.; 87.14° W. Long. Elevation is 708 feet.
History: Laid out 1832.
Population: 100 (2000); Race: 100.0% White, 0.0% Black, 0.0% Asian, 0.0% American Indian and Alaska Native, 0.0% Hispanic of any race, 0.0% two or more races (2000); Density: 1,182.8 persons per square mile (2000); Age: 35.8% under 18, 10.1% over 64 (2000); Marriage status: 26.8% never married, 59.2% now married, 7.0% widowed, 7.0% divorced (2000); Foreign born: 17.4% (2000); Ancestry (includes multiple ancestries): 25.7% United States or American, 11.0% Other groups, 11.0% German, 6.4% French (except Basque), 6.4% Irish (2000).
Economy: Agricultural area. Employment by occupation: 4.5% management, 4.5% professional, 20.5% services, 18.2% sales, 0.0% farming, 9.1% construction, 43.2% production (2000).
Income: Per capita income: $10,386 (2000); Median household income: $39,583 (2000); Poverty rate: 23.4% (2000).
Education: High school graduation rate: 69.4% (2000); College graduation rate: 11.3% (2000).
Housing: Homeownership rate: 76.5% (2000); Median home value: $46,700 (2000); Median rent: $275 per month (2000); Median age of housing: 60+ years (2000).
Transportation: Commute to work: 79.5% car, 0.0% public transportation, 18.2% walk, 2.3% work from home (2000); Travel time to work: 32.6% less than 15 minutes, 23.3% 15 to 30 minutes, 39.5% 30 to 45 minutes, 0.0% 45 to 60 minutes, 4.7% 60 minutes or more (2000)

Franklin County

Located in southeastern Indiana; bounded on the east by Ohio; drained by the Whitewater River and its East Fork. Covers a land area of 386.00 square miles, a water area of 5.30 square miles, and is located in the Eastern Time Zone. The county government was organized in 1810. County seat is Brookville.

Weather Station: Brookville — Elevation: 629 feet

	Jan	Feb	Mar	Apr	May	Jun	Jul	Aug	Sep	Oct	Nov	Dec
High	36	41	52	64	75	83	87	85	79	67	54	42
Low	17	20	29	38	48	58	62	60	52	40	32	23
Precip	2.8	2.6	3.7	4.0	4.6	4.0	4.3	3.9	2.6	3.0	3.7	3.3
Snow	na	3.8	2.3	0.3	tr	0.0	0.0	0.0	0.0	tr	1.1	2.8

High and Low temperatures in degrees Fahrenheit; Precipitation and Snow in inches

Population: 22,151 (2000); Race: 98.8% White, 0.0% Black, 0.2% Asian, 0.1% American Indian and Alaska Native, 0.4% Hispanic of any race, 0.7% two or more races (2000); Density: 57.4 persons per square mile (2000); Age: 28.1% under 18, 12.7% over 64 (2000).
Religion: Five largest groups: 24.4% Catholic Church, 9.5% Southern Baptist Convention, 9.1% Christian Churches and Churches of Christ, 4.2% The United Methodist Church, 2.1% Evangelical Lutheran Church in America (2000).
Economy: Unemployment rate: 4.4% (11/2002); Total civilian labor force: 11,959 (11/2002); Leading industries: 21.6% manufacturing; 12.4% accommodation & food services; 12.0% retail trade (2000); Companies that employ more than 1,000 persons: 0 (2000); Companies that employ more than 100 persons: 5 (2000); Farms: 776 totaling 138,635 acres (1997); Minority business ownership rate: 0.0% (1997); Women business ownership rate: 24.4% (1997); Retail sales per capita: $3,097 (1997). Single-family building permits issued: 96 (2001) / 88 (2000); Multi-family building permits issued: 0 (2001) / 0 (2000).
Income: Per capita income: $18,624 (2000); Median household income: $43,530 (2000); Poverty rate: 7.1% (2000); Bankruptcy rate: 4.64% (2001).
Taxes: Total county taxes per capita: $159 (2000); County property taxes per capita: $56 (2000).
Education: High school graduation rate: 76.1% (2000); College graduation rate: 12.5% (2000).
Housing: Homeownership rate: 81.4% (2000); Median home value: $100,100 (2000); Median rent: $316 per month (2000); Median age of housing: 27 years (2000).
Health: Birth rate: 126.0 per 10,000 population (1998); Age adjusted death rate: 73.4 per 10,000 population (1999); Age adjusted cancer mortality rate: 158.2 deaths per 100,000 population (1999). Number of physicians: 2.3 per 10,000 population (1999); Number of hospital beds: n/a (1999).
Elections: 2000 Presidential election results: 31.1% Gore, 67.0% Bush, 0.3% Nader, 1.0% Buchanan

National and State Parks: Mounds State Recreation Area
Additional Information Contacts
Franklin County Government Offices 765-647-4631
Brookville Chamber of Commerce 765-647-3177

Franklin County Communities

BATH (unincorporated postal area, zip code 47010). Aka New Bath. Covers a land area of 12.152 square miles and a water area of 0.051 square miles. Located at 39.51° N. Lat.; 84.82° W. Long. Elevation is 1,014 feet.
Population: 399 (2000); Race: 95.1% White, 0.0% Black, 0.0% Asian, 0.0% American Indian and Alaska Native, 0.0% Hispanic of any race, 4.9% two or more races (2000); Density: 32.8 persons per square mile (2000); Age: 18.1% under 18, 22.6% over 64 (2000); Marriage status: 14.3% never married, 71.7% now married, 4.2% widowed, 9.8% divorced (2000); Foreign born: 1.7% (2000); Ancestry (includes multiple ancestries): 28.9% German, 18.1% Irish, 11.5% United States or American, 6.0% French (except Basque), 4.9% Other groups (2000).
Economy: Employment by occupation: 14.7% management, 7.1% professional, 11.5% services, 23.7% sales, 0.0% farming, 26.3% construction, 16.7% production (2000).
Income: Per capita income: $16,022 (2000); Median household income: $35,139 (2000); Poverty rate: 11.5% (2000).
Education: High school graduation rate: 75.4% (2000); College graduation rate: 17.3% (2000).
Housing: Homeownership rate: 70.3% (2000); Median home value: $78,600 (2000); Median rent: $325 per month (2000); Median age of housing: 39 years (2000).
Transportation: Commute to work: 92.1% car, 0.0% public transportation, 0.0% walk, 4.6% work from home (2000); Travel time to work: 37.5% less than 15 minutes, 31.9% 15 to 30 minutes, 21.5% 30 to 45 minutes, 3.5% 45 to 60 minutes, 5.6% 60 minutes or more (2000)

BROOKVILLE (town). Covers a land area of 1.338 square miles and a water area of 0 square miles. Located at 39.42° N. Lat.; 85.01° W. Long. Elevation is 671 feet.
History: Brookville was laid out in 1808 on a site selected by Amos Butler and Jesse Brooks Thomas. They called their settlement Brooksville in honor of Thomas' mother, whose maiden name was Brooks. The "s" was removed when Franklin County was organized a few years later and Brookville became the county seat. Thomas became a U.S. senator from Illinois and was instrumental in the Missouri Compromise of 1820.
Population: 2,652 (2000); Race: 98.0% White, 0.0% Black, 0.5% Asian, 0.0% American Indian and Alaska Native, 0.7% Hispanic of any race, 0.7% two or more races (2000); Density: 1,982.4 persons per square mile (2000); Age: 22.2% under 18, 23.3% over 64 (2000); Marriage status: 19.6% never married, 53.1% now married, 12.9% widowed, 14.4% divorced (2000); Foreign born: 1.1% (2000); Ancestry (includes multiple ancestries): 36.9% German, 12.8% Other groups, 11.0% United States or American, 11.0% Irish, 8.6% English (2000).
Economy: Employment by occupation: 11.8% management, 14.5% professional, 13.4% services, 20.8% sales, 0.0% farming, 8.6% construction, 30.9% production (2000).
Income: Per capita income: $17,360 (2000); Median household income: $29,390 (2000); Poverty rate: 8.0% (2000).
Taxes: Total city taxes per capita: $78 (1997); City property taxes per capita: $52 (1997).
Education: High school graduation rate: 70.2% (2000); College graduation rate: 9.2% (2000).

School District(s)

Franklin County Com Sch Corp (PK-12)
2000 Enrollment: 3,014 765-647-4128
Housing: Homeownership rate: 59.4% (2000); Median home value: $85,800 (2000); Median rent: $323 per month (2000); Median age of housing: 53 years (2000).
Newspapers: The Brookville Democrat (1 x week); The Brookville American (1 x week)
Transportation: Commute to work: 88.7% car, 0.0% public transportation, 8.4% walk, 2.8% work from home (2000); Travel time to work: 50.9% less than 15 minutes, 15.6% 15 to 30 minutes, 18.8% 30 to 45 minutes, 6.5% 45 to 60 minutes, 8.2% 60 minutes or more (2000)
Additional Information Contacts
Brookville Chamber of Commerce 765-647-3177

CEDAR GROVE (town). Covers a land area of 0.149 square miles and a water area of 0 square miles. Located at 39.35° N. Lat.; 84.93° W. Long. Elevation is 609 feet.
Population: 185 (2000); Race: 100.0% White, 0.0% Black, 0.0% Asian, 0.0% American Indian and Alaska Native, 0.0% Hispanic of any race, 0.0% two or more races (2000); Density: 1,240.3 persons per square mile (2000); Age: 19.8% under 18, 14.8% over 64 (2000); Marriage status: 21.3% never married, 56.7% now married, 10.0% widowed, 12.0% divorced (2000); Foreign born: 0.0% (2000); Ancestry (includes multiple ancestries): 58.8% German, 13.7% United States or American, 11.5% Irish, 6.0% Dutch, 3.8% Italian (2000).
Economy: Agricultural area. Employment by occupation: 10.3% management, 15.0% professional, 12.1% services, 17.8% sales, 1.9% farming, 17.8% construction, 25.2% production (2000).
Income: Per capita income: $23,483 (2000); Median household income: $40,833 (2000); Poverty rate: 6.6% (2000).
Taxes: Total city taxes per capita: $12 (1997); City property taxes per capita: $8 (1997).
Education: High school graduation rate: 90.9% (2000); College graduation rate: 12.9% (2000).
Housing: Homeownership rate: 54.5% (2000); Median home value: $94,300 (2000); Median rent: $365 per month (2000); Median age of housing: 60+ years (2000).
Transportation: Commute to work: 95.3% car, 1.9% public transportation, 1.9% walk, 0.9% work from home (2000); Travel time to work: 25.5% less than 15 minutes, 22.6% 15 to 30 minutes, 23.6% 30 to 45 minutes, 14.2% 45 to 60 minutes, 14.2% 60 minutes or more (2000)

LAUREL (town). Covers a land area of 0.238 square miles and a water area of 0 square miles. Located at 39.50° N. Lat.; 85.18° W. Long. Elevation is 809 feet.
History: Laurel was founded in 1836 by James Conwell, who named it for Laurel, Delaware. It began as a farming community, becoming a mill town and shipping center during the canal period.
Population: 579 (2000); Race: 98.4% White, 0.0% Black, 0.0% Asian, 0.0% American Indian and Alaska Native, 1.2% Hispanic of any race, 1.6% two or more races (2000); Density: 2,434.6 persons per square mile (2000); Age: 28.7% under 18, 13.7% over 64 (2000); Marriage status: 23.9% never married, 54.0% now married, 12.1% widowed, 10.0% divorced (2000); Foreign born: 0.0% (2000); Ancestry (includes multiple ancestries): 29.4% United States or American, 7.1% German, 6.4% Other groups, 5.9% Irish, 2.3% English (2000).
Economy: Employment by occupation: 4.8% management, 6.7% professional, 21.0% services, 11.9% sales, 0.0% farming, 11.4% construction, 44.3% production (2000).
Income: Per capita income: $12,035 (2000); Median household income: $29,375 (2000); Poverty rate: 13.6% (2000).
Taxes: Total city taxes per capita: $115 (1997); City property taxes per capita: $115 (1997).
Education: High school graduation rate: 51.1% (2000); College graduation rate: 5.3% (2000).
Housing: Homeownership rate: 62.7% (2000); Median home value: $49,800 (2000); Median rent: $319 per month (2000); Median age of housing: 52 years (2000).
Transportation: Commute to work: 93.2% car, 0.0% public transportation, 4.9% walk, 2.0% work from home (2000); Travel time to work: 12.9% less than 15 minutes, 12.4% 15 to 30 minutes, 41.3% 30 to 45 minutes, 21.4% 45 to 60 minutes, 11.9% 60 minutes or more (2000)

METAMORA (unincorporated postal area, zip code 47030). Covers a land area of 33.836 square miles and a water area of 0 square miles. Located at 39.42° N. Lat.; 85.13° W. Long. Elevation is 679 feet.
History: The community of Metamora developed around the Whitewater Canal, where a number of mills and factories were located.
Population: 1,553 (2000); Race: 99.6% White, 0.1% Black, 0.0% Asian, 0.0% American Indian and Alaska Native, 0.0% Hispanic of any race, 0.3% two or more races (2000); Density: 45.9 persons per square mile (2000); Age: 30.1% under 18, 11.4% over 64 (2000); Marriage status: 22.0% never married, 63.1% now married, 5.5% widowed, 9.5% divorced (2000); Foreign born: 0.0% (2000); Ancestry (includes multiple ancestries): 20.3% German, 17.4% United States or American, 8.3% Other groups, 7.6% Irish, 5.9% English (2000).
Economy: Employment by occupation: 9.3% management, 12.1% professional, 7.3% services, 18.7% sales, 0.0% farming, 16.3% construction, 36.3% production (2000).

Income: Per capita income: $15,701 (2000); Median household income: $40,298 (2000); Poverty rate: 8.8% (2000).
Education: High school graduation rate: 64.0% (2000); College graduation rate: 8.7% (2000).
Housing: Homeownership rate: 84.6% (2000); Median home value: $90,400 (2000); Median rent: $309 per month (2000); Median age of housing: 25 years (2000).
Transportation: Commute to work: 92.9% car, 0.0% public transportation, 0.7% walk, 3.7% work from home (2000); Travel time to work: 6.6% less than 15 minutes, 21.1% 15 to 30 minutes, 32.0% 30 to 45 minutes, 15.7% 45 to 60 minutes, 24.6% 60 minutes or more (2000)

MOUNT CARMEL (town). Covers a land area of 0.042 square miles and a water area of 0 square miles. Located at 39.40° N. Lat.; 84.87° W. Long. Elevation is 1,023 feet.
Population: 106 (2000); Race: 100.0% White, 0.0% Black, 0.0% Asian, 0.0% American Indian and Alaska Native, 0.0% Hispanic of any race, 0.0% two or more races (2000); Density: 2,526.0 persons per square mile (2000); Age: 33.9% under 18, 11.3% over 64 (2000); Marriage status: 21.2% never married, 60.0% now married, 3.5% widowed, 15.3% divorced (2000); Foreign born: 0.0% (2000); Ancestry (includes multiple ancestries): 41.1% German, 12.9% Other groups, 9.7% Irish, 9.7% United States or American, 6.5% Dutch (2000).
Economy: In agricultural area. Employment by occupation: 10.9% management, 4.3% professional, 10.9% services, 19.6% sales, 0.0% farming, 21.7% construction, 32.6% production (2000).
Income: Per capita income: $9,586 (2000); Median household income: $25,000 (2000); Poverty rate: 27.0% (2000).
Taxes: Total city taxes per capita: $18 (1997); City property taxes per capita: $18 (1997).
Education: High school graduation rate: 52.5% (2000); College graduation rate: 1.7% (2000).
Housing: Homeownership rate: 83.7% (2000); Median home value: $58,000 (2000); Median rent: $425 per month (2000); Median age of housing: 60+ years (2000).
Transportation: Commute to work: 87.0% car, 0.0% public transportation, 2.2% walk, 8.7% work from home (2000); Travel time to work: 23.8% less than 15 minutes, 40.5% 15 to 30 minutes, 11.9% 30 to 45 minutes, 16.7% 45 to 60 minutes, 7.1% 60 minutes or more (2000)

OLDENBURG (town). Covers a land area of 0.416 square miles and a water area of 0 square miles. Located at 39.33° N. Lat.; 85.20° W. Long. Elevation is 881 feet.
History: Oldenburg was founded in 1837 by German immigrants. It was once a brick manufacturing center.
Population: 647 (2000); Race: 100.0% White, 0.0% Black, 0.0% Asian, 0.0% American Indian and Alaska Native, 0.0% Hispanic of any race, 0.0% two or more races (2000); Density: 1,554.2 persons per square mile (2000); Age: 17.0% under 18, 34.2% over 64 (2000); Marriage status: 41.9% never married, 46.0% now married, 10.1% widowed, 2.0% divorced (2000); Foreign born: 0.0% (2000); Ancestry (includes multiple ancestries): 64.1% German, 14.8% Irish, 9.2% English, 3.9% United States or American, 3.9% French (except Basque) (2000).
Economy: Employment by occupation: 8.6% management, 21.1% professional, 15.5% services, 22.4% sales, 0.7% farming, 8.9% construction, 23.0% production (2000).
Income: Per capita income: $19,620 (2000); Median household income: $42,292 (2000); Poverty rate: 17.7% (2000).
Taxes: Total city taxes per capita: $66 (1997); City property taxes per capita: $56 (1997).
Education: High school graduation rate: 87.1% (2000); College graduation rate: 42.0% (2000).
Housing: Homeownership rate: 69.2% (2000); Median home value: $112,900 (2000); Median rent: $321 per month (2000); Median age of housing: 48 years (2000).
Transportation: Commute to work: 75.3% car, 0.0% public transportation, 14.4% walk, 10.3% work from home (2000); Travel time to work: 69.1% less than 15 minutes, 16.4% 15 to 30 minutes, 5.0% 30 to 45 minutes, 3.4% 45 to 60 minutes, 6.1% 60 minutes or more (2000)

Fulton County

Located in northern Indiana; drained by the Tippecanoe River. Covers a land area of 368.50 square miles, a water area of 2.90 square miles, and is located in the Eastern Time Zone. The county government was organized in 1835. County seat is Rochester.

Weather Station: Rochester — Elevation: 767 feet

	Jan	Feb	Mar	Apr	May	Jun	Jul	Aug	Sep	Oct	Nov	Dec
High	30	35	46	59	71	80	84	82	75	63	48	36
Low	14	17	27	37	48	58	62	60	52	40	31	21
Precip	2.0	1.7	2.7	3.9	4.1	4.0	3.9	3.6	3.5	2.9	3.4	2.7
Snow	9.5	8.3	3.8	1.2	0.0	0.0	0.0	0.0	0.0	0.3	2.7	6.7

High and Low temperatures in degrees Fahrenheit; Precipitation and Snow in inches

Population: 20,511 (2000); Race: 95.7% White, 0.8% Black, 0.3% Asian, 0.4% American Indian and Alaska Native, 2.3% Hispanic of any race, 1.4% two or more races (2000); Density: 55.7 persons per square mile (2000); Age: 25.8% under 18, 15.3% over 64 (2000).
Religion: Five largest groups: 9.3% The United Methodist Church, 5.2% Catholic Church, 3.1% American Baptist Churches in the USA, 2.4% New Testament Association of Independent Baptist Churches and other Fundamental Baptist Associations, 2.3% Christ
Economy: Unemployment rate: 7.0% (11/2002); Total civilian labor force: 8,965 (11/2002); Leading industries: 42.8% manufacturing; 14.9% retail trade; 9.0% accommodation & food services (2000); Companies that employ more than 1,000 persons: 0 (2000); Companies that employ more than 100 persons: 12 (2000); Farms: 622 totaling 170,645 acres (1997); Minority business ownership rate: 0.0% (1997); Women business ownership rate: 28.8% (1997); Retail sales per capita: $7,051 (1997). Single-family building permits issued: 35 (2001) / 32 (2000); Multi-family building permits issued: 0 (2001) / 0 (2000).
Income: Per capita income: $17,950 (2000); Median household income: $38,290 (2000); Poverty rate: 7.6% (2000); Bankruptcy rate: 7.66% (2001).
Taxes: Total county taxes per capita: $217 (2000); County property taxes per capita: $136 (2000).
Education: High school graduation rate: 80.2% (2000); College graduation rate: 10.3% (2000).
Housing: Homeownership rate: 78.3% (2000); Median home value: $77,000 (2000); Median rent: $357 per month (2000); Median age of housing: 37 years (2000).
Health: Birth rate: 129.2 per 10,000 population (1998); Age adjusted death rate: 80.3 per 10,000 population (1999); Age adjusted cancer mortality rate: 214.3 deaths per 100,000 population (1999). Number of physicians: 8.3 per 10,000 population (1999); Number of hospital beds: 16.6 per 10,000 population (1999).
Elections: 2000 Presidential election results: 35.6% Gore, 62.7% Bush, 0.4% Nader, 1.0% Buchanan

Additional Information Contacts
Fulton County Government Offices 219-223-2912
Rochester Chamber of Commerce 219-224-2666

Fulton County Communities

AKRON (town). Covers a land area of 0.455 square miles and a water area of 0 square miles. Located at 41.03° N. Lat.; 86.02° W. Long. Elevation is 859 feet.
Population: 1,076 (2000); Race: 90.9% White, 0.0% Black, 0.0% Asian, 0.7% American Indian and Alaska Native, 13.3% Hispanic of any race, 1.3% two or more races (2000); Density: 2,365.8 persons per square mile (2000); Age: 29.5% under 18, 14.7% over 64 (2000); Marriage status: 22.4% never married, 58.8% now married, 10.0% widowed, 8.7% divorced (2000); Foreign born: 9.0% (2000); Ancestry (includes multiple ancestries): 22.2% Other groups, 20.2% German, 14.7% United States or American, 10.2% English, 7.8% Irish (2000).
Economy: In agricultural area. Manufactures hand tools, lumber, concrete products, electric motors. Single-family building permits issued: 1 (2001) / 1 (2000); Multi-family building permits issued: 0 (2001) / 0 (2000); Employment by occupation: 6.5% management, 13.3% professional, 11.2% services, 15.9% sales, 1.6% farming, 4.9% construction, 46.8% production (2000).
Income: Per capita income: $14,878 (2000); Median household income: $31,406 (2000); Poverty rate: 7.6% (2000).
Taxes: Total city taxes per capita: $156 (1997); City property taxes per capita: $154 (1997).
Education: High school graduation rate: 78.6% (2000); College graduation rate: 9.8% (2000).

School District(s)
Tippecanoe Valley School Corp (KG-12)
2000 Enrollment: 2,152 219-353-7741

Housing: Homeownership rate: 72.1% (2000); Median home value: $70,600 (2000); Median rent: $325 per month (2000); Median age of housing: 60+ years (2000).
Transportation: Commute to work: 92.9% car, 0.0% public transportation, 6.0% walk, 0.8% work from home (2000); Travel time to work: 34.0% less than 15 minutes, 36.8% 15 to 30 minutes, 20.8% 30 to 45 minutes, 6.0% 45 to 60 minutes, 2.4% 60 minutes or more (2000)

FULTON (town). Covers a land area of 0.181 square miles and a water area of 0 square miles. Located at 40.94° N. Lat.; 86.26° W. Long. Elevation is 787 feet.
Population: 326 (2000); Race: 100.0% White, 0.0% Black, 0.0% Asian, 0.0% American Indian and Alaska Native, 0.0% Hispanic of any race, 0.0% two or more races (2000); Density: 1,797.9 persons per square mile (2000); Age: 24.0% under 18, 14.7% over 64 (2000); Marriage status: 24.1% never married, 58.3% now married, 7.1% widowed, 10.5% divorced (2000); Foreign born: 2.4% (2000); Ancestry (includes multiple ancestries): 19.8% German, 18.6% United States or American, 9.6% Irish, 7.8% Dutch, 6.3% English (2000).
Economy: Agricultural area; light manufacturing. Employment by occupation: 4.4% management, 17.6% professional, 9.4% services, 19.5% sales, 0.0% farming, 9.4% construction, 39.6% production (2000).
Income: Per capita income: $16,732 (2000); Median household income: $44,375 (2000); Poverty rate: 2.4% (2000).
Taxes: Total city taxes per capita: $60 (1997); City property taxes per capita: $60 (1997).
Education: High school graduation rate: 87.6% (2000); College graduation rate: 8.3% (2000).

School District(s)

Caston School Corporation (KG-12)
2000 Enrollment: 795 219-857-2035
Housing: Homeownership rate: 88.5% (2000); Median home value: $50,300 (2000); Median rent: $388 per month (2000); Median age of housing: 60+ years (2000).
Transportation: Commute to work: 84.2% car, 0.0% public transportation, 8.2% walk, 7.6% work from home (2000); Travel time to work: 28.1% less than 15 minutes, 34.9% 15 to 30 minutes, 24.7% 30 to 45 minutes, 8.2% 45 to 60 minutes, 4.1% 60 minutes or more (2000)

KEWANNA (town). Covers a land area of 0.524 square miles and a water area of 0 square miles. Located at 41.01° N. Lat.; 86.41° W. Long. Elevation is 773 feet.
Population: 614 (2000); Race: 97.2% White, 0.3% Black, 0.0% Asian, 0.0% American Indian and Alaska Native, 1.5% Hispanic of any race, 2.2% two or more races (2000); Density: 1,171.5 persons per square mile (2000); Age: 25.0% under 18, 22.1% over 64 (2000); Marriage status: 11.5% never married, 54.2% now married, 19.4% widowed, 14.9% divorced (2000); Foreign born: 1.0% (2000); Ancestry (includes multiple ancestries): 23.8% German, 14.1% Irish, 12.5% English, 12.1% United States or American, 4.5% French (except Basque) (2000).
Economy: Agricultural area. Manufacturing: metal products. Employment by occupation: 4.5% management, 10.6% professional, 15.2% services, 16.7% sales, 0.8% farming, 9.8% construction, 42.4% production (2000).
Income: Per capita income: $15,718 (2000); Median household income: $22,292 (2000); Poverty rate: 13.0% (2000).
Taxes: Total city taxes per capita: $126 (1997); City property taxes per capita: $125 (1997).
Education: High school graduation rate: 77.1% (2000); College graduation rate: 6.4% (2000).

School District(s)

Union Township Schools
2000 Enrollment: n/a 219-653-2445
Housing: Homeownership rate: 71.4% (2000); Median home value: $46,200 (2000); Median rent: $306 per month (2000); Median age of housing: 57 years (2000).
Newspapers: The Observer (1 x week)
Transportation: Commute to work: 93.5% car, 0.0% public transportation, 5.0% walk, 0.8% work from home (2000); Travel time to work: 32.9% less than 15 minutes, 38.4% 15 to 30 minutes, 10.1% 30 to 45 minutes, 8.9% 45 to 60 minutes, 9.7% 60 minutes or more (2000)

ROCHESTER (city). Aka Pershing. Covers a land area of 4.557 square miles and a water area of 1.111 square miles. Located at 41.06° N. Lat.; 86.20° W. Long. Elevation is 779 feet.
History: Rochester was founded in 1831 as a trading post, and became a resort town on Lake Manitou.
Population: 6,414 (2000); Race: 95.4% White, 0.6% Black, 0.0% Asian, 0.9% American Indian and Alaska Native, 2.3% Hispanic of any race, 1.1% two or more races (2000); Density: 1,407.4 persons per square mile (2000); Age: 22.6% under 18, 17.9% over 64 (2000); Marriage status: 19.9% never married, 53.2% now married, 11.5% widowed, 15.4% divorced (2000); Foreign born: 1.3% (2000); Ancestry (includes multiple ancestries): 20.4% German, 20.4% United States or American, 12.0% Irish, 8.0% English, 7.6% Other groups (2000).
Economy: Single-family building permits issued: 34 (2001) / 31 (2000); Multi-family building permits issued: 0 (2001) / 0 (2000); Employment by occupation: 6.7% management, 10.2% professional, 13.6% services, 25.2% sales, 0.5% farming, 9.8% construction, 33.9% production (2000).
Income: Per capita income: $18,866 (2000); Median household income: $33,424 (2000); Poverty rate: 11.9% (2000).
Taxes: Total city taxes per capita: $192 (1997); City property taxes per capita: $186 (1997).
Education: High school graduation rate: 76.6% (2000); College graduation rate: 9.6% (2000).

School District(s)

Rochester Community Sch Corp (PK-12)
2000 Enrollment: 2,032 219-223-2159
Housing: Homeownership rate: 66.6% (2000); Median home value: $69,800 (2000); Median rent: $384 per month (2000); Median age of housing: 39 years (2000).
Hospitals: Woodlawn Hospital (49 beds)
Newspapers: The Rochester Sentinel (6 x week); The Shopping Guide News (1 x week)
Transportation: Commute to work: 94.5% car, 0.0% public transportation, 0.9% walk, 3.8% work from home (2000); Travel time to work: 62.6% less than 15 minutes, 10.0% 15 to 30 minutes, 14.6% 30 to 45 minutes, 3.7% 45 to 60 minutes, 9.1% 60 minutes or more (2000)
Additional Information Contacts
Rochester Chamber of Commerce 219-224-2666

Gibson County

Located in southwestern Indiana; bounded on the west by the Wabash River and the Illinois border, and on the north by the White River; also drained by the Patoka and Black Rivers. Covers a land area of 488.80 square miles, a water area of 10.30 square miles, and is located in the Central Time Zone. The county government was organized in 1813. County seat is Princeton.

Weather Station: Princeton 1 W — Elevation: 479 feet

	Jan	Feb	Mar	Apr	May	Jun	Jul	Aug	Sep	Oct	Nov	Dec
High	37	44	55	66	76	85	88	86	80	69	54	43
Low	22	26	35	45	55	64	68	66	58	47	37	27
Precip	2.7	2.8	4.3	4.7	5.1	4.0	4.0	3.8	3.1	3.4	4.4	3.6
Snow	na	3.8	1.0	0.3	0.0	0.0	0.0	0.0	0.0	0.1	0.3	2.1

High and Low temperatures in degrees Fahrenheit; Precipitation and Snow in inches

Population: 32,500 (2000); Race: 96.6% White, 2.1% Black, 0.4% Asian, 0.1% American Indian and Alaska Native, 0.8% Hispanic of any race, 0.5% two or more races (2000); Density: 66.5 persons per square mile (2000); Age: 24.8% under 18, 15.6% over 64 (2000).
Religion: Five largest groups: 18.6% Catholic Church, 7.5% The United Methodist Church, 3.1% Church of the Nazarene, 2.5% Assemblies of God, 2.0% United Church of Christ (2000).
Economy: Unemployment rate: 3.4% (11/2002); Total civilian labor force: 20,559 (11/2002); Leading industries: 32.6% manufacturing; 13.3% retail trade; 9.5% health care and social assistance (2000); Companies that employ more than 1,000 persons: 1 (2000); Companies that employ more than 100 persons: 21 (2000); Farms: 579 totaling 232,839 acres (1997); Minority business ownership rate: 0.0% (1997); Women business ownership rate: 19.2% (1997); Retail sales per capita: $7,859 (1997). Single-family building permits issued: 35 (2001) / 18 (2000); Multi-family building permits issued: 0 (2001) / 161 (2000).
Income: Per capita income: $18,169 (2000); Median household income: $37,515 (2000); Poverty rate: 8.2% (2000); Bankruptcy rate: 5.61% (2001).
Taxes: Total county taxes per capita: $215 (2000); County property taxes per capita: $211 (2000).
Education: High school graduation rate: 80.9% (2000); College graduation rate: 12.4% (2000).
Housing: Homeownership rate: 77.9% (2000); Median home value: $74,700 (2000); Median rent: $309 per month (2000); Median age of housing: 37 years (2000).

Health: Birth rate: 130.8 per 10,000 population (1998); Age adjusted death rate: 88.1 per 10,000 population (1999); Age adjusted cancer mortality rate: 186.0 deaths per 100,000 population (1999). Air Quality Index: 87% good, 13% moderate, 0% unhealthy (percent of days in 2000). Number of physicians: 6.5 per 10,000 population (1999); Number of hospital beds: 36.6 per 10,000 population (1999).
Elections: 2000 Presidential election results: 42.1% Gore, 56.2% Bush, 0.6% Nader, 0.7% Buchanan
Additional Information Contacts
Gibson County Government Offices 812-385-4927
Princeton Chamber of Commerce 812-385-2134

Gibson County Communities

BUCKSKIN (unincorporated postal area, zip code 47647). Covers a land area of 1.220 square miles and a water area of 0 square miles. Located at 38.21° N. Lat.; 87.42° W. Long. Elevation is 435 feet.
Population: 86 (2000); Race: 91.6% White, 0.0% Black, 0.0% Asian, 8.4% American Indian and Alaska Native, 0.0% Hispanic of any race, 0.0% two or more races (2000); Density: 70.5 persons per square mile (2000); Age: 10.8% under 18, 38.6% over 64 (2000); Marriage status: 17.6% never married, 9.5% now married, 52.7% widowed, 20.3% divorced (2000); Foreign born: 0.0% (2000); Ancestry (includes multiple ancestries): 72.3% German, 47.0% Irish, 19.3% English, 8.4% Other groups (2000).
Economy: Employment by occupation: 0.0% management, 0.0% professional, 46.4% services, 0.0% sales, 0.0% farming, 25.0% construction, 28.6% production (2000).
Income: Per capita income: $13,642 (2000); Median household income: $30,156 (2000); Poverty rate: 0.0% (2000).
Education: High school graduation rate: 46.8% (2000); College graduation rate: 0.0% (2000).
Housing: Homeownership rate: 84.4% (2000); Median home value: $85,000 (2000); Median rent: $275 per month (2000); Median age of housing: 60+ years (2000).
Transportation: Commute to work: 71.4% car, 0.0% public transportation, 0.0% walk, 28.6% work from home (2000); Travel time to work: 0.0% less than 15 minutes, 0.0% 15 to 30 minutes, 60.0% 30 to 45 minutes, 0.0% 45 to 60 minutes, 40.0% 60 minutes or more (2000)

FORT BRANCH (town). Covers a land area of 0.741 square miles and a water area of 0 square miles. Located at 38.24° N. Lat.; 87.57° W. Long. Elevation is 450 feet.
History: The town of Fort Branch was named for Old Fort Branch, built in 1811.
Population: 2,320 (2000); Race: 98.8% White, 0.0% Black, 0.6% Asian, 0.2% American Indian and Alaska Native, 0.4% Hispanic of any race, 0.5% two or more races (2000); Density: 3,131.0 persons per square mile (2000); Age: 26.5% under 18, 15.9% over 64 (2000); Marriage status: 20.4% never married, 61.7% now married, 9.4% widowed, 8.5% divorced (2000); Foreign born: 0.4% (2000); Ancestry (includes multiple ancestries): 38.6% German, 11.1% English, 10.9% United States or American, 9.2% Irish, 8.6% Other groups (2000).
Economy: Employment by occupation: 8.7% management, 10.4% professional, 16.3% services, 26.7% sales, 0.2% farming, 9.1% construction, 28.6% production (2000).
Income: Per capita income: $17,180 (2000); Median household income: $35,964 (2000); Poverty rate: 4.4% (2000).
Taxes: Total city taxes per capita: $63 (1997); City property taxes per capita: $60 (1997).
Education: High school graduation rate: 83.8% (2000); College graduation rate: 11.8% (2000).

School District(s)

South Gibson School Corp (KG-12)
2000 Enrollment: 1,843 812-753-4230
Housing: Homeownership rate: 75.3% (2000); Median home value: $79,400 (2000); Median rent: $316 per month (2000); Median age of housing: 44 years (2000).
Newspapers: The South Gibson Star-Times (1 x week)
Transportation: Commute to work: 94.8% car, 0.3% public transportation, 2.0% walk, 2.0% work from home (2000); Travel time to work: 34.6% less than 15 minutes, 30.8% 15 to 30 minutes, 24.6% 30 to 45 minutes, 5.1% 45 to 60 minutes, 4.9% 60 minutes or more (2000)

FRANCISCO (town). Covers a land area of 0.545 square miles and a water area of 0 square miles. Located at 38.33° N. Lat.; 87.44° W. Long. Elevation is 470 feet.
History: Francisco developed when the Wabash & Erie Canal was built, and was named for a Spanish laborer on the canal.
Population: 543 (2000); Race: 97.1% White, 0.0% Black, 0.0% Asian, 2.5% American Indian and Alaska Native, 0.0% Hispanic of any race, 0.4% two or more races (2000); Density: 995.5 persons per square mile (2000); Age: 22.9% under 18, 13.1% over 64 (2000); Marriage status: 23.0% never married, 53.4% now married, 11.1% widowed, 12.5% divorced (2000); Foreign born: 0.2% (2000); Ancestry (includes multiple ancestries): 22.7% United States or American, 19.4% German, 5.7% Irish, 5.5% English, 4.0% Other groups (2000).
Economy: Employment by occupation: 5.8% management, 10.0% professional, 12.7% services, 26.3% sales, 2.3% farming, 8.1% construction, 34.7% production (2000).
Income: Per capita income: $15,499 (2000); Median household income: $28,750 (2000); Poverty rate: 9.5% (2000).
Taxes: Total city taxes per capita: $41 (1997); City property taxes per capita: $41 (1997).
Education: High school graduation rate: 75.2% (2000); College graduation rate: 9.2% (2000).
Housing: Homeownership rate: 83.1% (2000); Median home value: $49,400 (2000); Median rent: $322 per month (2000); Median age of housing: 52 years (2000).
Transportation: Commute to work: 99.6% car, 0.0% public transportation, 0.0% walk, 0.0% work from home (2000); Travel time to work: 22.4% less than 15 minutes, 39.6% 15 to 30 minutes, 23.6% 30 to 45 minutes, 8.4% 45 to 60 minutes, 6.0% 60 minutes or more (2000)

HAUBSTADT (town). Covers a land area of 0.685 square miles and a water area of 0 square miles. Located at 38.20° N. Lat.; 87.57° W. Long. Elevation is 473 feet.
Population: 1,529 (2000); Race: 99.3% White, 0.5% Black, 0.1% Asian, 0.0% American Indian and Alaska Native, 0.4% Hispanic of any race, 0.0% two or more races (2000); Density: 2,232.1 persons per square mile (2000); Age: 26.1% under 18, 15.6% over 64 (2000); Marriage status: 18.6% never married, 64.1% now married, 7.1% widowed, 10.2% divorced (2000); Foreign born: 0.1% (2000); Ancestry (includes multiple ancestries): 54.5% German, 11.9% United States or American, 9.2% Irish, 4.2% English, 2.5% Other groups (2000).
Economy: In grain-growing area. Manufacturing:meatpacking; specialty machinery. Employment by occupation: 11.8% management, 13.2% professional, 14.5% services, 21.4% sales, 0.0% farming, 14.8% construction, 24.3% production (2000).
Income: Per capita income: $22,482 (2000); Median household income: $42,837 (2000); Poverty rate: 5.7% (2000).
Taxes: Total city taxes per capita: $97 (1997); City property taxes per capita: $94 (1997).
Education: High school graduation rate: 86.4% (2000); College graduation rate: 16.1% (2000).
Housing: Homeownership rate: 79.1% (2000); Median home value: $101,500 (2000); Median rent: $286 per month (2000); Median age of housing: 30 years (2000).
Transportation: Commute to work: 93.0% car, 0.0% public transportation, 1.3% walk, 5.0% work from home (2000); Travel time to work: 28.0% less than 15 minutes, 32.7% 15 to 30 minutes, 31.9% 30 to 45 minutes, 5.4% 45 to 60 minutes, 2.2% 60 minutes or more (2000)

HAZLETON (town). Aka Buena Vista. Covers a land area of 0.342 square miles and a water area of 0 square miles. Located at 38.48° N. Lat.; 87.54° W. Long. Elevation is 423 feet.
History: Also spelled Hazelton.
Population: 288 (2000); Race: 100.0% White, 0.0% Black, 0.0% Asian, 0.0% American Indian and Alaska Native, 0.0% Hispanic of any race, 0.0% two or more races (2000); Density: 841.0 persons per square mile (2000); Age: 22.4% under 18, 13.8% over 64 (2000); Marriage status: 25.1% never married, 49.8% now married, 13.2% widowed, 11.9% divorced (2000); Foreign born: 0.0% (2000); Ancestry (includes multiple ancestries): 13.4% German, 10.3% United States or American, 10.0% Irish, 6.2% English, 3.8% Other groups (2000).
Economy: Oil wells. Employment by occupation: 3.4% management, 12.9% professional, 17.2% services, 24.1% sales, 0.0% farming, 12.9% construction, 29.3% production (2000).

Income: Per capita income: $13,156 (2000); Median household income: $31,875 (2000); Poverty rate: 25.9% (2000).
Taxes: Total city taxes per capita: $38 (1997); City property taxes per capita: $35 (1997).
Education: High school graduation rate: 73.9% (2000); College graduation rate: 1.0% (2000).
Housing: Homeownership rate: 91.5% (2000); Median home value: $48,300 (2000); Median rent: $195 per month (2000); Median age of housing: 60+ years (2000).
Transportation: Commute to work: 89.5% car, 0.0% public transportation, 4.4% walk, 3.5% work from home (2000); Travel time to work: 16.4% less than 15 minutes, 32.7% 15 to 30 minutes, 31.8% 30 to 45 minutes, 7.3% 45 to 60 minutes, 11.8% 60 minutes or more (2000)

MACKEY (town). Covers a land area of 0.082 square miles and a water area of 0 square miles. Located at 38.25° N. Lat.; 87.39° W. Long. Elevation is 450 feet.
Population: 142 (2000); Race: 100.0% White, 0.0% Black, 0.0% Asian, 0.0% American Indian and Alaska Native, 0.0% Hispanic of any race, 0.0% two or more races (2000); Density: 1,721.8 persons per square mile (2000); Age: 26.8% under 18, 25.9% over 64 (2000); Marriage status: 11.9% never married, 51.2% now married, 15.5% widowed, 21.4% divorced (2000); Foreign born: 0.0% (2000); Ancestry (includes multiple ancestries): 24.1% German, 15.2% United States or American, 7.1% French (except Basque), 7.1% English, 3.6% Dutch (2000).
Economy: Employment by occupation: 4.7% management, 9.3% professional, 11.6% services, 27.9% sales, 4.7% farming, 4.7% construction, 37.2% production (2000).
Income: Per capita income: $14,282 (2000); Median household income: $33,750 (2000); Poverty rate: 8.0% (2000).
Taxes: Total city taxes per capita: $67 (1997); City property taxes per capita: $67 (1997).
Education: High school graduation rate: 76.9% (2000); College graduation rate: 12.8% (2000).
Housing: Homeownership rate: 79.3% (2000); Median home value: $57,500 (2000); Median rent: $400 per month (2000); Median age of housing: 55 years (2000).
Transportation: Commute to work: 88.4% car, 0.0% public transportation, 4.7% walk, 4.7% work from home (2000); Travel time to work: 19.5% less than 15 minutes, 29.3% 15 to 30 minutes, 41.5% 30 to 45 minutes, 4.9% 45 to 60 minutes, 4.9% 60 minutes or more (2000)

OAKLAND CITY (city). Covers a land area of 1.100 square miles and a water area of 0 square miles. Located at 38.33° N. Lat.; 87.34° W. Long. Elevation is 461 feet.
History: Oakland City developed around Oakland City College, established by the Baptist church in 1891.
Population: 2,588 (2000); Race: 96.4% White, 1.0% Black, 0.2% Asian, 0.0% American Indian and Alaska Native, 2.2% Hispanic of any race, 1.4% two or more races (2000); Density: 2,352.6 persons per square mile (2000); Age: 20.5% under 18, 21.6% over 64 (2000); Marriage status: 26.3% never married, 50.0% now married, 9.1% widowed, 14.6% divorced (2000); Foreign born: 1.7% (2000); Ancestry (includes multiple ancestries): 21.3% German, 13.1% Irish, 11.3% English, 11.0% Other groups, 9.3% United States or American (2000).
Economy: Employment by occupation: 8.1% management, 14.7% professional, 18.0% services, 23.5% sales, 1.0% farming, 10.9% construction, 23.8% production (2000).
Income: Per capita income: $13,806 (2000); Median household income: $28,532 (2000); Poverty rate: 11.9% (2000).
Taxes: Total city taxes per capita: $86 (1997); City property taxes per capita: $80 (1997).
Education: High school graduation rate: 74.7% (2000); College graduation rate: 14.7% (2000).

School District(s)

East Gibson School Corporation (PK-12)
2000 Enrollment: 1,094 812-749-4755
Gibson-Pike-Warrick Coop
2000 Enrollment: n/a 812-749-3925

Four-year College(s)

Oakland City University (Private, Not-for-profit, Baptist)
2001 Enrollment: 1,738 812-749-4781
2001 Tuition: In-state $10,950; Out-of-state $10,950

Housing: Homeownership rate: 65.8% (2000); Median home value: $57,100 (2000); Median rent: $286 per month (2000); Median age of housing: 43 years (2000).
Hospitals: Wirth Regional Hospital
Transportation: Commute to work: 86.1% car, 0.7% public transportation, 9.0% walk, 3.0% work from home (2000); Travel time to work: 36.1% less than 15 minutes, 19.2% 15 to 30 minutes, 25.4% 30 to 45 minutes, 15.1% 45 to 60 minutes, 4.1% 60 minutes or more (2000)

OWENSVILLE (town). Covers a land area of 0.496 square miles and a water area of 0 square miles. Located at 38.27° N. Lat.; 87.69° W. Long. Elevation is 510 feet.
History: Laid out 1817; incorporated 1881.
Population: 1,322 (2000); Race: 97.9% White, 0.6% Black, 0.5% Asian, 0.0% American Indian and Alaska Native, 1.4% Hispanic of any race, 0.2% two or more races (2000); Density: 2,665.3 persons per square mile (2000); Age: 25.2% under 18, 24.7% over 64 (2000); Marriage status: 14.5% never married, 58.8% now married, 11.3% widowed, 15.4% divorced (2000); Foreign born: 0.5% (2000); Ancestry (includes multiple ancestries): 19.3% German, 14.0% English, 14.0% United States or American, 11.8% Irish, 6.9% Other groups (2000).
Economy: Agriculture; gas and oil wells; bituminous-coal; timber; feed mill. Employment by occupation: 3.6% management, 12.9% professional, 17.4% services, 23.6% sales, 1.3% farming, 10.1% construction, 31.0% production (2000).
Income: Per capita income: $15,916 (2000); Median household income: $34,306 (2000); Poverty rate: 8.9% (2000).
Taxes: Total city taxes per capita: $205 (1997); City property taxes per capita: $202 (1997).
Education: High school graduation rate: 77.1% (2000); College graduation rate: 11.0% (2000).
Housing: Homeownership rate: 78.5% (2000); Median home value: $65,500 (2000); Median rent: $222 per month (2000); Median age of housing: 40 years (2000).
Transportation: Commute to work: 94.5% car, 0.0% public transportation, 1.5% walk, 1.3% work from home (2000); Travel time to work: 25.0% less than 15 minutes, 38.8% 15 to 30 minutes, 17.6% 30 to 45 minutes, 14.7% 45 to 60 minutes, 3.9% 60 minutes or more (2000)

PATOKA (town). Covers a land area of 0.704 square miles and a water area of 0 square miles. Located at 38.40° N. Lat.; 87.58° W. Long. Elevation is 440 feet.
History: Patoka was settled in 1789 on the Patoka River, and platted in 1813. It was a stagecoach stop on the Vincennes-Evansville line. The name is of Indian origin meaning "logs on the bottom."
Population: 749 (2000); Race: 96.4% White, 2.9% Black, 0.0% Asian, 0.0% American Indian and Alaska Native, 0.0% Hispanic of any race, 0.1% two or more races (2000); Density: 1,064.2 persons per square mile (2000); Age: 29.5% under 18, 11.9% over 64 (2000); Marriage status: 19.1% never married, 57.6% now married, 7.4% widowed, 15.8% divorced (2000); Foreign born: 0.1% (2000); Ancestry (includes multiple ancestries): 18.5% United States or American, 16.5% German, 12.5% English, 9.3% Other groups, 8.5% Irish (2000).
Economy: Employment by occupation: 5.9% management, 8.1% professional, 14.8% services, 22.7% sales, 0.7% farming, 12.1% construction, 35.7% production (2000).
Income: Per capita income: $16,587 (2000); Median household income: $35,208 (2000); Poverty rate: 10.8% (2000).
Taxes: Total city taxes per capita: $18 (1997); City property taxes per capita: $16 (1997).
Education: High school graduation rate: 74.4% (2000); College graduation rate: 8.2% (2000).
Housing: Homeownership rate: 83.4% (2000); Median home value: $54,200 (2000); Median rent: $275 per month (2000); Median age of housing: 29 years (2000).
Transportation: Commute to work: 90.0% car, 0.0% public transportation, 3.6% walk, 4.1% work from home (2000); Travel time to work: 41.0% less than 15 minutes, 27.6% 15 to 30 minutes, 16.6% 30 to 45 minutes, 9.9% 45 to 60 minutes, 4.8% 60 minutes or more (2000)

PRINCETON (city). Covers a land area of 4.850 square miles and a water area of 0 square miles. Located at 38.35° N. Lat.; 87.57° W. Long. Elevation is 500 feet.
History: Princeton was founded in 1814 and named for Captain William Prince. An early industry was Evans Mill, a wool-carding mill which had Abraham Lincoln as a customer in 1827.
Population: 8,175 (2000); Race: 91.6% White, 6.2% Black, 0.3% Asian, 0.0% American Indian and Alaska Native, 2.0% Hispanic of any race, 1.1% two or more races (2000); Density: 1,685.6 persons per square mile (2000);

Age: 24.1% under 18, 19.9% over 64 (2000); Marriage status: 21.2% never married, 53.6% now married, 11.5% widowed, 13.7% divorced (2000); Foreign born: 1.6% (2000); Ancestry (includes multiple ancestries): 17.3% German, 16.8% United States or American, 13.2% Irish, 11.7% English, 11.3% Other groups (2000).
Economy: Single-family building permits issued: 35 (2001) / 18 (2000); Multi-family building permits issued: 0 (2001) / 161 (2000); Employment by occupation: 6.3% management, 11.4% professional, 24.1% services, 21.8% sales, 0.5% farming, 8.7% construction, 27.2% production (2000).
Income: Per capita income: $15,049 (2000); Median household income: $26,689 (2000); Poverty rate: 15.8% (2000).
Taxes: Total city taxes per capita: $229 (2000); City property taxes per capita: $227 (2000).
Education: High school graduation rate: 74.5% (2000); College graduation rate: 9.3% (2000).

School District(s)

North Gibson School Corp (KG-12)
2000 Enrollment: 2,115 812-385-4851
Housing: Homeownership rate: 62.3% (2000); Median home value: $56,400 (2000); Median rent: $313 per month (2000); Median age of housing: 47 years (2000).
Hospitals: Gibson General Hospital (109 beds)
Newspapers: Princeton Daily Clarion (5 x week); Oakland City Journal (1 x week)
Transportation: Commute to work: 92.9% car, 0.0% public transportation, 4.8% walk, 1.2% work from home (2000); Travel time to work: 56.5% less than 15 minutes, 18.2% 15 to 30 minutes, 12.5% 30 to 45 minutes, 9.4% 45 to 60 minutes, 3.4% 60 minutes or more (2000)
Additional Information Contacts
Princeton Chamber of Commerce 812-385-2134

SOMERVILLE (town). Covers a land area of 0.294 square miles and a water area of 0 square miles. Located at 38.27° N. Lat.; 87.37° W. Long. Elevation is 480 feet.
Population: 312 (2000); Race: 99.4% White, 0.0% Black, 0.6% Asian, 0.0% American Indian and Alaska Native, 0.0% Hispanic of any race, 0.0% two or more races (2000); Density: 1,061.5 persons per square mile (2000); Age: 33.2% under 18, 10.9% over 64 (2000); Marriage status: 13.3% never married, 70.8% now married, 7.5% widowed, 8.3% divorced (2000); Foreign born: 0.6% (2000); Ancestry (includes multiple ancestries): 15.8% United States or American, 12.6% German, 8.6% English, 3.4% Irish, 2.0% Other groups (2000).
Economy: Agricultural and bituminous-coal area. Employment by occupation: 6.0% management, 9.7% professional, 20.1% services, 16.4% sales, 0.0% farming, 7.5% construction, 40.3% production (2000).
Income: Per capita income: $12,147 (2000); Median household income: $34,464 (2000); Poverty rate: 5.2% (2000).
Taxes: Total city taxes per capita: $4 (1997); City property taxes per capita: $4 (1997).
Education: High school graduation rate: 72.3% (2000); College graduation rate: 10.3% (2000).
Housing: Homeownership rate: 92.1% (2000); Median home value: $48,900 (2000); Median rent: $300 per month (2000); Median age of housing: 44 years (2000).
Transportation: Commute to work: 94.6% car, 0.0% public transportation, 1.5% walk, 3.8% work from home (2000); Travel time to work: 10.4% less than 15 minutes, 24.8% 15 to 30 minutes, 43.2% 30 to 45 minutes, 16.8% 45 to 60 minutes, 4.8% 60 minutes or more (2000)

Grant County

Located in east central Indiana; drained by the Mississinewa River. Covers a land area of 414.00 square miles, a water area of 0.80 square miles, and is located in the Eastern Time Zone. The county government was organized in 1831. County seat is Marion.

Weather Station: Marion 2 N — Elevation: 787 feet

	Jan	Feb	Mar	Apr	May	Jun	Jul	Aug	Sep	Oct	Nov	Dec
High	32	36	47	60	72	81	85	82	76	64	50	38
Low	16	19	28	38	49	58	63	60	53	41	33	22
Precip	2.1	2.0	3.0	3.7	4.2	3.9	4.7	3.7	2.8	2.6	3.4	2.8
Snow	7.7	6.8	3.2	1.0	0.0	0.0	0.0	0.0	0.0	0.4	1.1	6.0

High and Low temperatures in degrees Fahrenheit; Precipitation and Snow in inches

Population: 73,403 (2000); Race: 89.2% White, 6.9% Black, 0.6% Asian, 0.5% American Indian and Alaska Native, 2.3% Hispanic of any race, 1.7% two or more races (2000); Density: 177.3 persons per square mile (2000); Age: 23.7% under 18, 14.9% over 64 (2000).
Religion: Five largest groups: 8.5% The Wesleyan Church, 6.4% Southern Baptist Convention, 5.7% Catholic Church, 5.3% The United Methodist Church, 3.1% Christian Church (Disciples of Christ) (2000).
Economy: Unemployment rate: 6.1% (11/2002); Total civilian labor force: 31,282 (11/2002); Leading industries: 28.5% manufacturing; 15.7% health care and social assistance; 12.3% retail trade (2000); Companies that employ more than 1,000 persons: 5 (2000); Companies that employ more than 100 persons: 38 (2000); Farms: 575 totaling 192,292 acres (1997); Minority business ownership rate: 5.5% (1997); Women business ownership rate: 27.5% (1997); Retail sales per capita: $8,641 (1997). Single-family building permits issued: 214 (2001) / 215 (2000); Multi-family building permits issued: 20 (2001) / 22 (2000).
Income: Per capita income: $18,003 (2000); Median household income: $36,162 (2000); Poverty rate: 11.8% (2000); Bankruptcy rate: 7.95% (2001).
Taxes: Total county taxes per capita: $243 (2000); County property taxes per capita: $168 (2000).
Education: High school graduation rate: 79.2% (2000); College graduation rate: 14.1% (2000).
Housing: Homeownership rate: 73.2% (2000); Median home value: $68,500 (2000); Median rent: $350 per month (2000); Median age of housing: 40 years (2000).
Health: Birth rate: 128.2 per 10,000 population (1998); Age adjusted death rate: 94.1 per 10,000 population (1999); Age adjusted cancer mortality rate: 237.8 deaths per 100,000 population (1999). Number of physicians: 14.4 per 10,000 population (1999); Number of hospital beds: 26.3 per 10,000 population (1999).
Elections: 2000 Presidential election results: 36.8% Gore, 61.2% Bush, 0.3% Nader, 1.0% Buchanan
Additional Information Contacts
Grant County Government Offices 765-668-8871
Gas City Chamber of Commerce 765-674-7545
Marion Area Board of Realtors 765-664-3232
Marion Chamber of Commerce 765-664-5107

Grant County Communities

FAIRMOUNT (town). Covers a land area of 1.472 square miles and a water area of 0 square miles. Located at 40.41° N. Lat.; 85.64° W. Long. Elevation is 870 feet.
History: Fairmount developed around the Wesleyan Camp Meeting Grounds, site of state and national conferences of the Methodist Church.
Population: 2,992 (2000); Race: 98.4% White, 0.0% Black, 0.0% Asian, 0.5% American Indian and Alaska Native, 1.1% Hispanic of any race, 0.8% two or more races (2000); Density: 2,033.0 persons per square mile (2000); Age: 23.4% under 18, 14.7% over 64 (2000); Marriage status: 19.7% never married, 58.1% now married, 9.2% widowed, 13.1% divorced (2000); Foreign born: 0.0% (2000); Ancestry (includes multiple ancestries): 16.6% German, 14.1% United States or American, 12.6% Irish, 8.6% Other groups, 6.4% English (2000).
Economy: Employment by occupation: 8.5% management, 14.8% professional, 18.0% services, 24.1% sales, 1.0% farming, 9.2% construction, 24.5% production (2000).
Income: Per capita income: $18,029 (2000); Median household income: $33,843 (2000); Poverty rate: 9.1% (2000).
Taxes: Total city taxes per capita: $125 (1997); City property taxes per capita: $92 (1997).
Education: High school graduation rate: 79.9% (2000); College graduation rate: 7.7% (2000).

School District(s)

Madison-Grant United Sch Corp (KG-12)
2000 Enrollment: 1,627 765-948-4143
Housing: Homeownership rate: 76.8% (2000); Median home value: $58,600 (2000); Median rent: $311 per month (2000); Median age of housing: 44 years (2000).
Safety: Violent crime rate: 13.3 per 10,000 population; Property crime rate: 182.8 per 10,000 population (2001).
Newspapers: News-Sun (1 x week)
Transportation: Commute to work: 94.4% car, 0.0% public transportation, 3.9% walk, 0.9% work from home (2000); Travel time to work: 23.6% less than 15 minutes, 48.7% 15 to 30 minutes, 18.0% 30 to 45 minutes, 3.1% 45 to 60 minutes, 6.6% 60 minutes or more (2000)

FOWLERTON (town). Covers a land area of 0.188 square miles and a water area of 0 square miles. Located at 40.41° N. Lat.; 85.57° W. Long. Elevation is 883 feet.
Population: 298 (2000); Race: 99.3% White, 0.0% Black, 0.0% Asian, 0.0% American Indian and Alaska Native, 1.4% Hispanic of any race, 0.7% two or more races (2000); Density: 1,584.0 persons per square mile (2000); Age: 27.1% under 18, 13.7% over 64 (2000); Marriage status: 14.7% never married, 67.9% now married, 5.5% widowed, 11.9% divorced (2000); Foreign born: 0.0% (2000); Ancestry (includes multiple ancestries): 35.4% United States or American, 8.6% Other groups, 7.2% German, 5.5% Irish, 3.8% English (2000).
Economy: In agricultural area. Employment by occupation: 3.4% management, 7.8% professional, 25.9% services, 26.7% sales, 0.0% farming, 10.3% construction, 25.9% production (2000).
Income: Per capita income: $12,615 (2000); Median household income: $28,750 (2000); Poverty rate: 18.6% (2000).
Taxes: Total city taxes per capita: $52 (1997); City property taxes per capita: $38 (1997).
Education: High school graduation rate: 72.3% (2000); College graduation rate: 2.1% (2000).
Housing: Homeownership rate: 76.3% (2000); Median home value: $48,100 (2000); Median rent: $313 per month (2000); Median age of housing: 38 years (2000).
Transportation: Commute to work: 94.7% car, 0.0% public transportation, 0.0% walk, 5.3% work from home (2000); Travel time to work: 14.0% less than 15 minutes, 47.7% 15 to 30 minutes, 21.5% 30 to 45 minutes, 1.9% 45 to 60 minutes, 15.0% 60 minutes or more (2000)

GAS CITY (city). Covers a land area of 3.714 square miles and a water area of 0 square miles. Located at 40.48° N. Lat.; 85.60° W. Long. Elevation is 853 feet.
History: Natural gas was discovered here in 1887, giving brief fortune to Gas City. The Owens-Illinois Glass Company Plant was founded here during the gas boom.
Population: 5,940 (2000); Race: 97.3% White, 0.5% Black, 0.2% Asian, 0.8% American Indian and Alaska Native, 1.4% Hispanic of any race, 0.5% two or more races (2000); Density: 1,599.2 persons per square mile (2000); Age: 25.6% under 18, 13.5% over 64 (2000); Marriage status: 19.9% never married, 56.9% now married, 8.8% widowed, 14.3% divorced (2000); Foreign born: 1.0% (2000); Ancestry (includes multiple ancestries): 17.5% German, 15.3% United States or American, 10.0% Irish, 9.5% Other groups, 7.5% English (2000).
Economy: Single-family building permits issued: 16 (2001) / 19 (2000); Multi-family building permits issued: 8 (2001) / 4 (2000); Employment by occupation: 8.4% management, 13.7% professional, 13.1% services, 25.5% sales, 0.0% farming, 8.1% construction, 31.2% production (2000).
Income: Per capita income: $18,295 (2000); Median household income: $35,940 (2000); Poverty rate: 10.2% (2000).
Taxes: Total city taxes per capita: $139 (1997); City property taxes per capita: $98 (1997).
Education: High school graduation rate: 79.8% (2000); College graduation rate: 9.1% (2000).

School District(s)

Mississinewa Community School Corp (PK-12)
2000 Enrollment: 2,054 765-674-8528

Housing: Homeownership rate: 73.9% (2000); Median home value: $65,800 (2000); Median rent: $379 per month (2000); Median age of housing: 40 years (2000).
Safety: Violent crime rate: 8.4 per 10,000 population; Property crime rate: 339.9 per 10,000 population (2001).
Newspapers: The Courier (1 x week); Twin City Journal-Reporter (1 x week); Oak Hill Times (1 x week)
Transportation: Commute to work: 96.0% car, 0.0% public transportation, 1.9% walk, 1.3% work from home (2000); Travel time to work: 39.7% less than 15 minutes, 39.1% 15 to 30 minutes, 10.1% 30 to 45 minutes, 4.3% 45 to 60 minutes, 6.8% 60 minutes or more (2000)

Additional Information Contacts

Gas City Chamber of Commerce 765-674-7545

JONESBORO (city). Covers a land area of 0.849 square miles and a water area of 0 square miles. Located at 40.47° N. Lat.; 85.63° W. Long. Elevation is 850 feet.
History: Jonesboro was founded in 1837 by Obadiah Jones. Its location on the Mississinewa River made it a trading center.
Population: 1,887 (2000); Race: 96.5% White, 0.3% Black, 0.1% Asian, 0.1% American Indian and Alaska Native, 3.3% Hispanic of any race, 1.6% two or more races (2000); Density: 2,221.8 persons per square mile (2000); Age: 25.6% under 18, 12.3% over 64 (2000); Marriage status: 17.0% never married, 62.2% now married, 5.6% widowed, 15.2% divorced (2000); Foreign born: 0.5% (2000); Ancestry (includes multiple ancestries): 17.1% United States or American, 14.7% Other groups, 12.1% German, 7.7% Irish, 6.4% English (2000).
Economy: Employment by occupation: 7.7% management, 9.6% professional, 15.7% services, 18.1% sales, 0.0% farming, 8.8% construction, 40.1% production (2000).
Income: Per capita income: $16,723 (2000); Median household income: $36,974 (2000); Poverty rate: 6.5% (2000).
Taxes: Total city taxes per capita: $80 (1997); City property taxes per capita: $58 (1997).
Education: High school graduation rate: 78.4% (2000); College graduation rate: 8.0% (2000).
Housing: Homeownership rate: 82.6% (2000); Median home value: $57,500 (2000); Median rent: $301 per month (2000); Median age of housing: 52 years (2000).
Transportation: Commute to work: 96.7% car, 0.3% public transportation, 0.8% walk, 1.9% work from home (2000); Travel time to work: 37.1% less than 15 minutes, 42.4% 15 to 30 minutes, 7.9% 30 to 45 minutes, 8.6% 45 to 60 minutes, 4.0% 60 minutes or more (2000)

MARION (city). Covers a land area of 13.297 square miles and a water area of 0.044 square miles. Located at 40.54° N. Lat.; 85.66° W. Long. Elevation is 815 feet.
History: The first settlers came to Marion in 1826. The town was laid out in 1831 and named for General Francis Marion, cavalry officer in the American Revolution. Marion grew rapidly when natural gas and oil were discovered here in the 1880's, but the boom was short-lived. Diversified industry replaced the oil wells.
Population: 31,320 (2000); Race: 79.2% White, 15.4% Black, 0.7% Asian, 0.6% American Indian and Alaska Native, 3.4% Hispanic of any race, 2.7% two or more races (2000); Density: 2,355.5 persons per square mile (2000); Age: 23.1% under 18, 16.6% over 64 (2000); Marriage status: 25.2% never married, 50.7% now married, 10.1% widowed, 14.0% divorced (2000); Foreign born: 1.8% (2000); Ancestry (includes multiple ancestries): 22.5% Other groups, 13.9% German, 13.6% United States or American, 7.7% English, 7.0% Irish (2000).
Vital Statistics: Birth rate: 171.8 per 10,000 population (1998)
Economy: Unemployment rate: 8.6% (11/2002); Total civilian labor force: 12,925 (11/2002); Employment by occupation: 7.0% management, 15.9% professional, 18.7% services, 21.5% sales, 0.1% farming, 7.2% construction, 29.5% production (2000).
Income: Per capita income: $16,378 (2000); Median household income: $30,440 (2000); Poverty rate: 16.9% (2000).
Taxes: Total city taxes per capita: $347 (1997); City property taxes per capita: $238 (1997).
Education: High school graduation rate: 73.3% (2000); College graduation rate: 13.4% (2000).

School District(s)

Eastbrook Community Sch Corp (KG-12)
2000 Enrollment: 1,734 765-664-0624
Marion Community Schools (PK-12)
2000 Enrollment: 5,943 765-662-2546

Four-year College(s)

Indiana Wesleyan University (Private, Not-for-profit, Wesleyan)
2001 Enrollment: 7,929 317-674-6901
2001 Tuition: In-state $12,740; Out-of-state $12,740

Two-year College(s)

Indiana Business College (Private, For-profit)
2001 Enrollment: 168 765-662-7497
2001 Tuition: In-state $8,460; Out-of-state $8,460

Housing: Homeownership rate: 61.6% (2000); Median home value: $57,000 (2000); Median rent: $343 per month (2000); Median age of housing: 45 years (2000).
Hospitals: Marion General Hospital (191 beds)
Safety: Violent crime rate: 82.9 per 10,000 population; Property crime rate: 634.0 per 10,000 population (2001).
Newspapers: Chronicle-Tribune (7 x week)
Transportation: Commute to work: 88.7% car, 0.9% public transportation, 5.9% walk, 2.7% work from home (2000); Travel time to work: 61.3% less than 15 minutes, 21.4% 15 to 30 minutes, 8.5% 30 to 45 minutes, 3.9% 45 to 60 minutes, 4.9% 60 minutes or more (2000)

Additional Information Contacts
Marion Area Board of Realtors 765-664-3232
Marion Chamber of Commerce 765-664-5107

MATTHEWS (town). Covers a land area of 0.348 square miles and a water area of 0 square miles. Located at 40.38° N. Lat.; 85.49° W. Long. Elevation is 870 feet.
History: Matthews was established in 1833 with a gristmill, sawmill, blacksmith shop, and general store.
Population: 595 (2000); Race: 99.8% White, 0.0% Black, 0.0% Asian, 0.2% American Indian and Alaska Native, 0.0% Hispanic of any race, 0.0% two or more races (2000); Density: 1,707.7 persons per square mile (2000); Age: 25.2% under 18, 15.6% over 64 (2000); Marriage status: 13.3% never married, 71.3% now married, 6.5% widowed, 8.9% divorced (2000); Foreign born: 0.0% (2000); Ancestry (includes multiple ancestries): 22.3% United States or American, 15.3% German, 11.1% Irish, 9.4% English, 8.7% Other groups (2000).
Economy: Employment by occupation: 7.9% management, 18.8% professional, 19.4% services, 13.5% sales, 0.7% farming, 9.2% construction, 30.6% production (2000).
Income: Per capita income: $17,283 (2000); Median household income: $33,125 (2000); Poverty rate: 5.5% (2000).
Taxes: Total city taxes per capita: $105 (1997); City property taxes per capita: $71 (1997).
Education: High school graduation rate: 79.8% (2000); College graduation rate: 9.4% (2000).
Housing: Homeownership rate: 85.5% (2000); Median home value: $61,500 (2000); Median rent: $278 per month (2000); Median age of housing: 42 years (2000).
Transportation: Commute to work: 91.6% car, 0.0% public transportation, 4.1% walk, 3.4% work from home (2000); Travel time to work: 22.4% less than 15 minutes, 31.8% 15 to 30 minutes, 33.2% 30 to 45 minutes, 5.9% 45 to 60 minutes, 6.6% 60 minutes or more (2000)

SWAYZEE (town). Covers a land area of 0.472 square miles and a water area of 0 square miles. Located at 40.50° N. Lat.; 85.82° W. Long. Elevation is 866 feet.
Population: 1,011 (2000); Race: 98.6% White, 0.0% Black, 0.0% Asian, 0.0% American Indian and Alaska Native, 1.2% Hispanic of any race, 0.0% two or more races (2000); Density: 2,141.5 persons per square mile (2000); Age: 25.7% under 18, 13.3% over 64 (2000); Marriage status: 16.4% never married, 67.1% now married, 7.0% widowed, 9.5% divorced (2000); Foreign born: 0.0% (2000); Ancestry (includes multiple ancestries): 21.4% United States or American, 19.5% German, 12.5% English, 9.7% Irish, 7.7% Other groups (2000).
Economy: In agricultural area; canned tomato products. Single-family building permits issued: 1 (2001) / 0 (2000); Multi-family building permits issued: 0 (2001) / 0 (2000); Employment by occupation: 8.3% management, 17.2% professional, 12.1% services, 21.2% sales, 1.1% farming, 10.6% construction, 29.7% production (2000).
Income: Per capita income: $17,476 (2000); Median household income: $41,146 (2000); Poverty rate: 6.0% (2000).
Taxes: Total city taxes per capita: $93 (1997); City property taxes per capita: $70 (1997).
Education: High school graduation rate: 86.3% (2000); College graduation rate: 12.6% (2000).
Housing: Homeownership rate: 86.7% (2000); Median home value: $71,700 (2000); Median rent: $350 per month (2000); Median age of housing: 44 years (2000).
Transportation: Commute to work: 89.9% car, 0.0% public transportation, 7.1% walk, 2.4% work from home (2000); Travel time to work: 24.3% less than 15 minutes, 51.1% 15 to 30 minutes, 12.5% 30 to 45 minutes, 5.3% 45 to 60 minutes, 6.8% 60 minutes or more (2000)

SWEETSER (town). Covers a land area of 0.975 square miles and a water area of 0.009 square miles. Located at 40.57° N. Lat.; 85.76° W. Long. Elevation is 847 feet.
History: Laid out 1871.
Population: 906 (2000); Race: 96.8% White, 0.0% Black, 0.0% Asian, 0.8% American Indian and Alaska Native, 2.9% Hispanic of any race, 0.8% two or more races (2000); Density: 929.2 persons per square mile (2000); Age: 24.1% under 18, 19.5% over 64 (2000); Marriage status: 18.5% never married, 62.8% now married, 8.6% widowed, 10.2% divorced (2000); Foreign born: 0.1% (2000); Ancestry (includes multiple ancestries): 22.2% German, 13.3% English, 12.5% Irish, 10.7% United States or American, 8.4% Other groups (2000).
Economy: Vegetables, soybeans, corn; hogs. Employment by occupation: 5.1% management, 17.3% professional, 9.5% services, 31.5% sales, 0.0% farming, 14.9% construction, 21.7% production (2000).
Income: Per capita income: $19,907 (2000); Median household income: $39,722 (2000); Poverty rate: 5.0% (2000).
Taxes: Total city taxes per capita: $66 (1997); City property taxes per capita: $47 (1997).
Education: High school graduation rate: 84.0% (2000); College graduation rate: 13.2% (2000).
Housing: Homeownership rate: 86.3% (2000); Median home value: $71,800 (2000); Median rent: $386 per month (2000); Median age of housing: 43 years (2000).
Transportation: Commute to work: 92.5% car, 0.5% public transportation, 3.3% walk, 3.3% work from home (2000); Travel time to work: 38.2% less than 15 minutes, 44.2% 15 to 30 minutes, 12.4% 30 to 45 minutes, 1.8% 45 to 60 minutes, 3.4% 60 minutes or more (2000)

UPLAND (town). Covers a land area of 3.932 square miles and a water area of 0.009 square miles. Located at 40.46° N. Lat.; 85.50° W. Long. Elevation is 932 feet.
History: Upland was laid out in 1867 when the railroad arrived and a sawmill was built. Many of the early settlers were Quakers.
Population: 3,803 (2000); Race: 92.8% White, 0.7% Black, 2.2% Asian, 0.3% American Indian and Alaska Native, 1.5% Hispanic of any race, 2.0% two or more races (2000); Density: 967.1 persons per square mile (2000); Age: 14.1% under 18, 8.0% over 64 (2000); Marriage status: 42.9% never married, 48.8% now married, 5.0% widowed, 3.2% divorced (2000); Foreign born: 1.3% (2000); Ancestry (includes multiple ancestries): 25.7% German, 9.7% English, 8.5% United States or American, 8.2% Irish, 6.9% Other groups (2000).
Economy: Employment by occupation: 6.3% management, 28.7% professional, 23.6% services, 25.1% sales, 0.3% farming, 5.6% construction, 10.5% production (2000).
Income: Per capita income: $11,761 (2000); Median household income: $36,827 (2000); Poverty rate: 14.5% (2000).
Taxes: Total city taxes per capita: $64 (1997); City property taxes per capita: $46 (1997).
Education: High school graduation rate: 87.2% (2000); College graduation rate: 34.9% (2000).

Four-year College(s)

Taylor University-Upland (Private, Not-for-profit, Interdenominational)
2001 Enrollment: 1,856 765-998-2751
2001 Tuition: In-state $16,350; Out-of-state $16,350

Housing: Homeownership rate: 70.6% (2000); Median home value: $76,100 (2000); Median rent: $360 per month (2000); Median age of housing: 36 years (2000).
Transportation: Commute to work: 65.7% car, 0.1% public transportation, 24.2% walk, 7.0% work from home (2000); Travel time to work: 61.4% less than 15 minutes, 25.7% 15 to 30 minutes, 6.4% 30 to 45 minutes, 1.7% 45 to 60 minutes, 4.9% 60 minutes or more (2000)

VAN BUREN (town). Covers a land area of 0.584 square miles and a water area of 0 square miles. Located at 40.61° N. Lat.; 85.50° W. Long. Elevation is 850 feet.
Population: 935 (2000); Race: 97.9% White, 0.0% Black, 0.1% Asian, 0.5% American Indian and Alaska Native, 2.2% Hispanic of any race, 0.1% two or more races (2000); Density: 1,599.8 persons per square mile (2000); Age: 33.0% under 18, 12.1% over 64 (2000); Marriage status: 13.4% never married, 68.3% now married, 7.1% widowed, 11.2% divorced (2000); Foreign born: 0.7% (2000); Ancestry (includes multiple ancestries): 18.5% German, 14.2% Other groups, 11.2% Irish, 7.9% English, 7.0% United States or American (2000).
Economy: Agricultural area; popcorn. Employment by occupation: 7.1% management, 11.8% professional, 15.4% services, 26.2% sales, 0.8% farming, 10.1% construction, 28.7% production (2000).
Income: Per capita income: $14,403 (2000); Median household income: $36,719 (2000); Poverty rate: 9.6% (2000).
Taxes: Total city taxes per capita: $143 (1997); City property taxes per capita: $107 (1997).
Education: High school graduation rate: 81.3% (2000); College graduation rate: 8.3% (2000).
Housing: Homeownership rate: 83.0% (2000); Median home value: $57,900 (2000); Median rent: $316 per month (2000); Median age of housing: 53 years (2000).
Transportation: Commute to work: 93.8% car, 0.0% public transportation, 2.8% walk, 3.1% work from home (2000); Travel time to work: 22.1% less

than 15 minutes, 52.8% 15 to 30 minutes, 16.3% 30 to 45 minutes, 2.9% 45 to 60 minutes, 5.9% 60 minutes or more (2000)

Greene County

Located in southwestern Indiana; drained by the West Fork of White River and the Eel River. Covers a land area of 541.70 square miles, a water area of 4.20 square miles, and is located in the Eastern Time Zone. The county government was organized in 1821. County seat is Bloomfield.
Population: 33,157 (2000); Race: 98.5% White, 0.1% Black, 0.1% Asian, 0.4% American Indian and Alaska Native, 0.8% Hispanic of any race, 0.6% two or more races (2000); Density: 61.2 persons per square mile (2000); Age: 24.7% under 18, 15.3% over 64 (2000).
Religion: Five largest groups: 7.8% Christian Churches and Churches of Christ, 6.2% The United Methodist Church, 6.2% American Baptist Churches in the USA, 2.5% Churches of Christ, 2.4% Catholic Church (2000).
Economy: Unemployment rate: 6.4% (11/2002); Total civilian labor force: 13,596 (11/2002); Leading industries: 23.1% retail trade; 17.2% health care and social assistance; 15.3% manufacturing (2000); Companies that employ more than 1,000 persons: 0 (2000); Companies that employ more than 100 persons: 8 (2000); Farms: 878 totaling 205,628 acres (1997); Minority business ownership rate: 0.0% (1997); Women business ownership rate: 20.1% (1997); Retail sales per capita: $5,398 (1997). Single-family building permits issued: 0 (2001) / 0 (2000); Multi-family building permits issued: 0 (2001) / 0 (2000).
Income: Per capita income: $16,834 (2000); Median household income: $33,998 (2000); Poverty rate: 11.0% (2000); Bankruptcy rate: 7.65% (2001).
Taxes: Total county taxes per capita: $183 (2000); County property taxes per capita: $123 (2000).
Education: High school graduation rate: 79.2% (2000); College graduation rate: 10.5% (2000).
Housing: Homeownership rate: 80.0% (2000); Median home value: $66,800 (2000); Median rent: $274 per month (2000); Median age of housing: 31 years (2000).
Health: Birth rate: 112.8 per 10,000 population (1998); Age adjusted death rate: 83.9 per 10,000 population (1999); Age adjusted cancer mortality rate: 205.2 deaths per 100,000 population (1999). Air Quality Index: 48% good, 52% moderate, 0% unhealthy (percent of days in 2000). Number of physicians: 6.3 per 10,000 population (1999); Number of hospital beds: 12.1 per 10,000 population (1999).
Elections: 2000 Presidential election results: 38.8% Gore, 59.1% Bush, 0.5% Nader, 0.8% Buchanan

Additional Information Contacts

Greene County Government Offices 812-384-8532
Bloomfield Chamber of Commerce 812-384-8995
Greene County Board of Realtors 812-847-3300
Linton Chamber of Commerce 812-847-4846

Greene County Communities

BLOOMFIELD (town). Covers a land area of 1.381 square miles and a water area of 0 square miles. Located at 39.02° N. Lat.; 86.94° W. Long. Elevation is 605 feet.
Population: 2,542 (2000); Race: 98.0% White, 0.0% Black, 0.0% Asian, 0.8% American Indian and Alaska Native, 1.9% Hispanic of any race, 0.8% two or more races (2000); Density: 1,841.1 persons per square mile (2000); Age: 20.3% under 18, 20.1% over 64 (2000); Marriage status: 18.7% never married, 51.7% now married, 12.8% widowed, 16.9% divorced (2000); Foreign born: 1.0% (2000); Ancestry (includes multiple ancestries): 20.9% German, 13.0% English, 11.2% Irish, 10.1% United States or American, 5.1% Other groups (2000).
Economy: Agricultural area. Manufacturing: hydraulic jacks, ceramic tile, medical supplies, limestone products, concrete. Single-family building permits issued: 0 (2001) / 0 (2000); Multi-family building permits issued: 0 (2001) / 0 (2000); Employment by occupation: 6.6% management, 20.6% professional, 11.4% services, 31.3% sales, 0.0% farming, 10.3% construction, 19.9% production (2000).
Income: Per capita income: $18,045 (2000); Median household income: $30,224 (2000); Poverty rate: 16.6% (2000).
Taxes: Total city taxes per capita: $122 (1997); City property taxes per capita: $61 (1997).
Education: High school graduation rate: 84.2% (2000); College graduation rate: 15.5% (2000).

School District(s)

Bloomfield School District (KG-12)
2000 Enrollment: 1,081 812-384-4507
Eastern School District of Greene Co (PK-12)
2000 Enrollment: 1,336 812-825-5621

Housing: Homeownership rate: 62.9% (2000); Median home value: $66,900 (2000); Median rent: $298 per month (2000); Median age of housing: 43 years (2000).
Newspapers: The Evening World (5 x week); Bloomfield News (1 x week)
Transportation: Commute to work: 89.5% car, 0.0% public transportation, 6.1% walk, 2.0% work from home (2000); Travel time to work: 32.4% less than 15 minutes, 26.0% 15 to 30 minutes, 21.3% 30 to 45 minutes, 11.7% 45 to 60 minutes, 8.6% 60 minutes or more (2000)

Additional Information Contacts

Bloomfield Chamber of Commerce 812-384-8995

JASONVILLE (city). Covers a land area of 1.302 square miles and a water area of <.001 square miles. Located at 39.16° N. Lat.; 87.20° W. Long. Elevation is 640 feet.
History: Laid out 1859.
Population: 2,490 (2000); Race: 97.1% White, 0.7% Black, 0.0% Asian, 0.7% American Indian and Alaska Native, 0.5% Hispanic of any race, 1.3% two or more races (2000); Density: 1,912.0 persons per square mile (2000); Age: 26.3% under 18, 18.0% over 64 (2000); Marriage status: 19.3% never married, 54.2% now married, 11.6% widowed, 14.8% divorced (2000); Foreign born: 0.6% (2000); Ancestry (includes multiple ancestries): 20.8% United States or American, 16.9% German, 12.3% Irish, 11.0% Other groups, 8.6% English (2000).
Economy: In agricultural area: grain, fruit. Manufacturing: electrical equipment, telephone line coils, wood products; bituminous-coal mines. Employment by occupation: 3.9% management, 11.2% professional, 17.4% services, 14.1% sales, 0.0% farming, 15.5% construction, 37.9% production (2000).
Income: Per capita income: $11,558 (2000); Median household income: $23,208 (2000); Poverty rate: 19.9% (2000).
Taxes: Total city taxes per capita: $139 (1997); City property taxes per capita: $73 (1997).
Education: High school graduation rate: 72.7% (2000); College graduation rate: 5.8% (2000).

School District(s)

M S D Shakamak Schools (PK-12)
2000 Enrollment: 1,019 812-665-3550

Housing: Homeownership rate: 67.1% (2000); Median home value: $45,300 (2000); Median rent: $236 per month (2000); Median age of housing: 47 years (2000).
Newspapers: The Jasonville Leader (1 x week)
Transportation: Commute to work: 92.4% car, 0.0% public transportation, 4.3% walk, 1.2% work from home (2000); Travel time to work: 32.2% less than 15 minutes, 16.5% 15 to 30 minutes, 19.6% 30 to 45 minutes, 18.6% 45 to 60 minutes, 13.1% 60 minutes or more (2000)

LINTON (city). Covers a land area of 2.962 square miles and a water area of 0 square miles. Located at 39.03° N. Lat.; 87.16° W. Long. Elevation is 531 feet.
History: Linton developed as a coal-mining town.
Population: 5,774 (2000); Race: 98.0% White, 0.1% Black, 0.2% Asian, 0.3% American Indian and Alaska Native, 1.6% Hispanic of any race, 1.2% two or more races (2000); Density: 1,949.7 persons per square mile (2000); Age: 21.5% under 18, 24.2% over 64 (2000); Marriage status: 16.1% never married, 58.6% now married, 12.9% widowed, 12.4% divorced (2000); Foreign born: 0.7% (2000); Ancestry (includes multiple ancestries): 21.0% United States or American, 14.0% German, 11.9% Irish, 8.2% English, 7.9% Other groups (2000).
Economy: Employment by occupation: 6.7% management, 14.6% professional, 21.2% services, 21.0% sales, 1.0% farming, 13.7% construction, 21.8% production (2000).
Income: Per capita income: $15,554 (2000); Median household income: $26,477 (2000); Poverty rate: 12.3% (2000).
Taxes: Total city taxes per capita: $169 (2000); City property taxes per capita: $103 (2000).
Education: High school graduation rate: 74.0% (2000); College graduation rate: 7.6% (2000).

School District(s)

Greene-Sullivan Special Education Coop
2000 Enrollment: n/a 812-847-8497

Linton-Stockton School Corp (PK-12)
2000 Enrollment: 1,390 812-847-6020
Housing: Homeownership rate: 70.5% (2000); Median home value: $54,900 (2000); Median rent: $274 per month (2000); Median age of housing: 41 years (2000).
Hospitals: Greene County General Hospital (76 beds)
Newspapers: Greene-Sullivan Weekender; Linton Daily Citizen (6 x week)
Transportation: Commute to work: 92.6% car, 0.0% public transportation, 3.7% walk, 2.3% work from home (2000); Travel time to work: 40.5% less than 15 minutes, 19.7% 15 to 30 minutes, 11.8% 30 to 45 minutes, 11.2% 45 to 60 minutes, 16.8% 60 minutes or more (2000)
Additional Information Contacts
Greene County Board of Realtors 812-847-3300
Linton Chamber of Commerce 812-847-4846

LYONS (town). Covers a land area of 0.865 square miles and a water area of 0 square miles. Located at 38.98° N. Lat.; 87.08° W. Long. Elevation is 521 feet.
Population: 748 (2000); Race: 98.1% White, 0.0% Black, 1.2% Asian, 0.4% American Indian and Alaska Native, 0.0% Hispanic of any race, 0.3% two or more races (2000); Density: 864.5 persons per square mile (2000); Age: 25.4% under 18, 20.0% over 64 (2000); Marriage status: 16.6% never married, 62.8% now married, 10.1% widowed, 10.4% divorced (2000); Foreign born: 0.9% (2000); Ancestry (includes multiple ancestries): 18.1% United States or American, 17.2% German, 11.3% English, 9.9% Other groups, 8.1% Irish (2000).
Economy: In agricultural and bituminous-coal area. Employment by occupation: 4.0% management, 17.3% professional, 20.2% services, 22.1% sales, 1.5% farming, 16.9% construction, 18.0% production (2000).
Income: Per capita income: $12,771 (2000); Median household income: $25,592 (2000); Poverty rate: 20.7% (2000).
Taxes: Total city taxes per capita: $102 (1997); City property taxes per capita: $61 (1997).
Education: High school graduation rate: 72.7% (2000); College graduation rate: 5.3% (2000).
Housing: Homeownership rate: 68.9% (2000); Median home value: $39,900 (2000); Median rent: $216 per month (2000); Median age of housing: 42 years (2000).
Transportation: Commute to work: 94.8% car, 0.0% public transportation, 3.0% walk, 1.5% work from home (2000); Travel time to work: 29.1% less than 15 minutes, 31.7% 15 to 30 minutes, 16.6% 30 to 45 minutes, 12.5% 45 to 60 minutes, 10.2% 60 minutes or more (2000)

NEWBERRY (town). Covers a land area of 0.489 square miles and a water area of 0 square miles. Located at 38.92° N. Lat.; 87.01° W. Long. Elevation is 554 feet.
History: Laid out 1822.
Population: 206 (2000); Race: 100.0% White, 0.0% Black, 0.0% Asian, 0.0% American Indian and Alaska Native, 0.0% Hispanic of any race, 0.0% two or more races (2000); Density: 420.9 persons per square mile (2000); Age: 14.3% under 18, 12.4% over 64 (2000); Marriage status: 19.2% never married, 57.0% now married, 9.3% widowed, 14.5% divorced (2000); Foreign born: 0.0% (2000); Ancestry (includes multiple ancestries): 26.3% United States or American, 13.4% German, 9.7% French (except Basque), 6.9% Irish, 5.5% Other groups (2000).
Economy: In agricultural area: corn, wheat; turkeys. Manufacturing: poultry products. Employment by occupation: 10.5% management, 12.9% professional, 21.0% services, 18.5% sales, 0.8% farming, 11.3% construction, 25.0% production (2000).
Income: Per capita income: $18,313 (2000); Median household income: $36,964 (2000); Poverty rate: 12.9% (2000).
Taxes: Total city taxes per capita: $83 (1997); City property taxes per capita: $48 (1997).
Education: High school graduation rate: 84.5% (2000); College graduation rate: 3.9% (2000).
Housing: Homeownership rate: 81.3% (2000); Median home value: $31,900 (2000); Median rent: $139 per month (2000); Median age of housing: 55 years (2000).
Transportation: Commute to work: 98.4% car, 0.0% public transportation, 0.0% walk, 0.0% work from home (2000); Travel time to work: 8.2% less than 15 minutes, 60.7% 15 to 30 minutes, 5.7% 30 to 45 minutes, 16.4% 45 to 60 minutes, 9.0% 60 minutes or more (2000)

OWENSBURG (unincorporated postal area, zip code 47453). Covers a land area of 11.208 square miles and a water area of 0.023 square miles. Located at 38.92° N. Lat.; 86.74° W. Long. Elevation is 630 feet.
Population: 533 (2000); Race: 100.0% White, 0.0% Black, 0.0% Asian, 0.0% American Indian and Alaska Native, 1.3% Hispanic of any race, 0.0% two or more races (2000); Density: 47.6 persons per square mile (2000); Age: 33.0% under 18, 11.4% over 64 (2000); Marriage status: 9.9% never married, 67.1% now married, 9.6% widowed, 13.4% divorced (2000); Foreign born: 0.0% (2000); Ancestry (includes multiple ancestries): 20.8% United States or American, 13.6% German, 12.9% French (except Basque), 7.7% English, 6.5% Other groups (2000).
Economy: Employment by occupation: 0.0% management, 4.7% professional, 12.4% services, 18.3% sales, 0.0% farming, 37.9% construction, 26.6% production (2000).
Income: Per capita income: $14,454 (2000); Median household income: $27,188 (2000); Poverty rate: 18.3% (2000).
Education: High school graduation rate: 88.8% (2000); College graduation rate: 4.6% (2000).
Housing: Homeownership rate: 86.5% (2000); Median home value: $59,400 (2000); Median rent: $325 per month (2000); Median age of housing: 13 years (2000).
Transportation: Commute to work: 100.0% car, 0.0% public transportation, 0.0% walk, 0.0% work from home (2000); Travel time to work: 10.1% less than 15 minutes, 12.4% 15 to 30 minutes, 58.0% 30 to 45 minutes, 10.7% 45 to 60 minutes, 8.9% 60 minutes or more (2000)

SOLSBERRY (unincorporated postal area, zip code 47459). Covers a land area of 58.893 square miles and a water area of 0 square miles. Located at 39.11° N. Lat.; 86.74° W. Long. Elevation is 789 feet.
History: Laid out 1848.
Population: 3,477 (2000); Race: 98.8% White, 0.0% Black, 0.0% Asian, 0.7% American Indian and Alaska Native, 0.0% Hispanic of any race, 0.5% two or more races (2000); Density: 59.0 persons per square mile (2000); Age: 26.9% under 18, 8.0% over 64 (2000); Marriage status: 17.9% never married, 67.5% now married, 3.5% widowed, 11.1% divorced (2000); Foreign born: 0.2% (2000); Ancestry (includes multiple ancestries): 15.6% United States or American, 13.6% German, 9.3% Irish, 7.5% English, 5.6% Other groups (2000).
Economy: Forested area; cattle. Manufacturing: beef processing. Large railroad trestle nearby to West. Employment by occupation: 10.5% management, 12.6% professional, 13.4% services, 18.6% sales, 0.8% farming, 19.6% construction, 24.5% production (2000).
Income: Per capita income: $17,620 (2000); Median household income: $39,389 (2000); Poverty rate: 8.4% (2000).
Education: High school graduation rate: 78.6% (2000); College graduation rate: 12.0% (2000).
Housing: Homeownership rate: 88.5% (2000); Median home value: $84,300 (2000); Median rent: $331 per month (2000); Median age of housing: 19 years (2000).
Transportation: Commute to work: 94.4% car, 0.0% public transportation, 2.2% walk, 3.1% work from home (2000); Travel time to work: 10.3% less than 15 minutes, 44.8% 15 to 30 minutes, 34.7% 30 to 45 minutes, 4.1% 45 to 60 minutes, 6.1% 60 minutes or more (2000)

SWITZ CITY (town). Covers a land area of 0.224 square miles and a water area of 0 square miles. Located at 39.03° N. Lat.; 87.05° W. Long. Elevation is 523 feet.
History: Switz City grew up around the nearby strip-mining coal fields.
Population: 311 (2000); Race: 100.0% White, 0.0% Black, 0.0% Asian, 0.0% American Indian and Alaska Native, 0.0% Hispanic of any race, 0.0% two or more races (2000); Density: 1,386.8 persons per square mile (2000); Age: 29.3% under 18, 10.7% over 64 (2000); Marriage status: 17.2% never married, 67.6% now married, 5.9% widowed, 9.2% divorced (2000); Foreign born: 0.6% (2000); Ancestry (includes multiple ancestries): 21.8% United States or American, 9.5% German, 8.8% Irish, 6.9% English, 2.2% Other groups (2000).
Economy: Employment by occupation: 10.7% management, 9.4% professional, 17.4% services, 21.5% sales, 0.0% farming, 18.8% construction, 22.1% production (2000).
Income: Per capita income: $13,493 (2000); Median household income: $33,750 (2000); Poverty rate: 10.7% (2000).
Taxes: Total city taxes per capita: $50 (1997); City property taxes per capita: $25 (1997).
Education: High school graduation rate: 78.6% (2000); College graduation rate: 3.0% (2000).

School District(s)

White River Valley School District (KG-12)
2000 Enrollment: 1,002 812-659-1424

Housing: Homeownership rate: 78.7% (2000); Median home value: $39,300 (2000); Median rent: $318 per month (2000); Median age of housing: 47 years (2000).
Transportation: Commute to work: 97.9% car, 0.0% public transportation, 0.0% walk, 2.1% work from home (2000); Travel time to work: 37.1% less than 15 minutes, 25.2% 15 to 30 minutes, 11.9% 30 to 45 minutes, 15.4% 45 to 60 minutes, 10.5% 60 minutes or more (2000)

WORTHINGTON (town). Covers a land area of 0.807 square miles and a water area of 0 square miles. Located at 39.11° N. Lat.; 86.98° W. Long. Elevation is 523 feet.
History: Laid out 1849.
Population: 1,481 (2000); Race: 98.0% White, 0.0% Black, 0.3% Asian, 0.5% American Indian and Alaska Native, 0.5% Hispanic of any race, 1.2% two or more races (2000); Density: 1,834.4 persons per square mile (2000); Age: 22.1% under 18, 20.7% over 64 (2000); Marriage status: 18.4% never married, 54.8% now married, 12.6% widowed, 14.1% divorced (2000); Foreign born: 0.3% (2000); Ancestry (includes multiple ancestries): 19.1% German, 13.4% United States or American, 11.5% Irish, 11.1% English, 6.1% Other groups (2000).
Economy: In agricultural area: grain; livestock. Manufacturing: pork slaughtering and processing. Bituminous-coal mines nearby. Employment by occupation: 5.5% management, 16.4% professional, 14.4% services, 18.8% sales, 0.6% farming, 12.7% construction, 31.6% production (2000).
Income: Per capita income: $18,761 (2000); Median household income: $27,778 (2000); Poverty rate: 13.0% (2000).
Taxes: Total city taxes per capita: $111 (1997); City property taxes per capita: $58 (1997).
Education: High school graduation rate: 76.5% (2000); College graduation rate: 11.7% (2000).
Housing: Homeownership rate: 78.0% (2000); Median home value: $49,300 (2000); Median rent: $252 per month (2000); Median age of housing: 55 years (2000).
Transportation: Commute to work: 94.0% car, 0.3% public transportation, 2.5% walk, 2.3% work from home (2000); Travel time to work: 34.5% less than 15 minutes, 20.8% 15 to 30 minutes, 15.7% 30 to 45 minutes, 12.0% 45 to 60 minutes, 17.0% 60 minutes or more (2000)

Hamilton County

Located in central Indiana; drained by the West Fork of the White River, and by several creeks. Covers a land area of 397.90 square miles, a water area of 4.80 square miles, and is located in the Eastern Time Zone. The county government was organized in 1823. County seat is Noblesville.

Hamilton County is part of the Indianapolis, IN MSA. The entire metro area includes: Boone County; Hamilton County; Hancock County; Hendricks County; Johnson County; Madison County; Marion County; Morgan County; Shelby County

Population: 182,740 (2000); Race: 94.5% White, 1.3% Black, 2.3% Asian, 0.2% American Indian and Alaska Native, 1.8% Hispanic of any race, 1.1% two or more races (2000); Density: 459.2 persons per square mile (2000); Age: 30.7% under 18, 7.5% over 64 (2000).
Religion: Five largest groups: 20.1% Catholic Church, 4.9% The United Methodist Church, 3.8% Christian Churches and Churches of Christ, 2.1% Evangelical Lutheran Church in America, 1.5% Christian Church (Disciples of Christ) (2000).
Economy: Unemployment rate: 2.8% (11/2002); Total civilian labor force: 102,624 (11/2002); Leading industries: 14.2% finance & insurance; 13.1% retail trade; 9.2% health care and social assistance (2000); Companies that employ more than 1,000 persons: 3 (2000); Companies that employ more than 100 persons: 119 (2000); Farms: 591 totaling 140,813 acres (1997); Minority business ownership rate: 3.9% (1997); Women business ownership rate: 29.2% (1997); Retail sales per capita: $11,525 (1997). Single-family building permits issued: 3,714 (2001) / 3,514 (2000); Multi-family building permits issued: 534 (2001) / 768 (2000).
Income: Per capita income: $33,109 (2000); Median household income: $71,026 (2000); Poverty rate: 2.9% (2000); Bankruptcy rate: 5.06% (2001).
Taxes: Total county taxes per capita: $213 (2000); County property taxes per capita: $146 (2000).
Education: High school graduation rate: 94.2% (2000); College graduation rate: 48.9% (2000).
Housing: Homeownership rate: 80.9% (2000); Median home value: $166,300 (2000); Median rent: $618 per month (2000); Median age of housing: 12 years (2000).
Health: Birth rate: 150.8 per 10,000 population (1998); Age adjusted death rate: 77.9 per 10,000 population (1999); Age adjusted cancer mortality rate: 170.7 deaths per 100,000 population (1999). Air Quality Index: 54% good, 46% moderate, 0% unhealthy (percent of days in 2000). Number of physicians: 46.0 per 10,000 population (1999); Number of hospital beds: 7.1 per 10,000 population (1999).
Elections: 2000 Presidential election results: 23.7% Gore, 74.3% Bush, 0.9% Nader, 0.4% Buchanan

Additional Information Contacts

Hamilton County Government Offices 317-776-9601
Carmel Chamber of Commerce 317-846-1049
Cicero Chamber of Commerce 317-984-4079
Fishers Chamber of Commerce 317-578-0700
Noblesville Chamber of Commerce 317-773-0086
Sheridan Chamber of Commerce 317-758-1311
Westfield Chamber of Commerce 317-896-2378

Hamilton County Communities

ARCADIA (town). Covers a land area of 0.550 square miles and a water area of 0 square miles. Located at 40.17° N. Lat.; 86.02° W. Long. Elevation is 863 feet.
Population: 1,747 (2000); Race: 96.1% White, 1.4% Black, 0.3% Asian, 0.3% American Indian and Alaska Native, 0.9% Hispanic of any race, 1.6% two or more races (2000); Density: 3,176.1 persons per square mile (2000); Age: 25.4% under 18, 11.4% over 64 (2000); Marriage status: 23.8% never married, 59.8% now married, 5.7% widowed, 10.7% divorced (2000); Foreign born: 0.6% (2000); Ancestry (includes multiple ancestries): 15.6% German, 12.4% United States or American, 8.8% Irish, 7.5% English, 5.5% Other groups (2000).
Economy: In agricultural area. Single-family building permits issued: 7 (2001) / 6 (2000); Multi-family building permits issued: 0 (2001) / 0 (2000); Employment by occupation: 6.0% management, 15.5% professional, 11.8% services, 26.0% sales, 1.1% farming, 19.2% construction, 20.3% production (2000).
Income: Per capita income: $17,159 (2000); Median household income: $44,063 (2000); Poverty rate: 10.5% (2000).
Taxes: Total city taxes per capita: $140 (1997); City property taxes per capita: $43 (1997).
Education: High school graduation rate: 71.0% (2000); College graduation rate: 10.5% (2000).

School District(s)

Hamilton Heights School Corp (PK-12)
2000 Enrollment: 2,326 317-984-3538

Housing: Homeownership rate: 74.1% (2000); Median home value: $87,800 (2000); Median rent: $377 per month (2000); Median age of housing: 42 years (2000).
Transportation: Commute to work: 94.8% car, 0.0% public transportation, 3.1% walk, 1.8% work from home (2000); Travel time to work: 22.4% less than 15 minutes, 35.5% 15 to 30 minutes, 22.8% 30 to 45 minutes, 12.7% 45 to 60 minutes, 6.5% 60 minutes or more (2000)

ATLANTA (town). Covers a land area of 0.300 square miles and a water area of 0 square miles. Located at 40.21° N. Lat.; 86.02° W. Long. Elevation is 862 feet.
Population: 761 (2000); Race: 96.5% White, 0.0% Black, 0.0% Asian, 1.0% American Indian and Alaska Native, 0.8% Hispanic of any race, 2.0% two or more races (2000); Density: 2,533.9 persons per square mile (2000); Age: 34.4% under 18, 7.7% over 64 (2000); Marriage status: 25.0% never married, 51.9% now married, 10.8% widowed, 12.3% divorced (2000); Foreign born: 0.0% (2000); Ancestry (includes multiple ancestries): 18.7% German, 15.7% Irish, 14.7% English, 12.4% United States or American, 11.9% Other groups (2000).
Economy: Corn, soybeans; hogs. Single-family building permits issued: 6 (2001) / 6 (2000); Multi-family building permits issued: 0 (2001) / 0 (2000); Employment by occupation: 8.7% management, 12.3% professional, 19.8% services, 29.6% sales, 0.0% farming, 14.2% construction, 15.4% production (2000).
Income: Per capita income: $16,342 (2000); Median household income: $43,036 (2000); Poverty rate: 7.0% (2000).
Taxes: Total city taxes per capita: $137 (1997); City property taxes per capita: $74 (1997).

Education: High school graduation rate: 83.0% (2000); College graduation rate: 7.7% (2000).
Housing: Homeownership rate: 74.1% (2000); Median home value: $81,800 (2000); Median rent: $515 per month (2000); Median age of housing: 60+ years (2000).
Transportation: Commute to work: 91.0% car, 0.0% public transportation, 3.1% walk, 5.1% work from home (2000); Travel time to work: 23.1% less than 15 minutes, 22.3% 15 to 30 minutes, 32.6% 30 to 45 minutes, 14.2% 45 to 60 minutes, 7.7% 60 minutes or more (2000)

CARMEL (city). Covers a land area of 17.812 square miles and a water area of 0.107 square miles. Located at 39.97° N. Lat.; 86.10° W. Long. Elevation is 829 feet.
Population: 37,733 (2000); Race: 92.8% White, 1.2% Black, 4.3% Asian, 0.3% American Indian and Alaska Native, 1.5% Hispanic of any race, 1.1% two or more races (2000); Density: 2,118.4 persons per square mile (2000); Age: 30.3% under 18, 9.8% over 64 (2000); Marriage status: 17.9% never married, 70.7% now married, 4.2% widowed, 7.2% divorced (2000); Foreign born: 7.3% (2000); Ancestry (includes multiple ancestries): 28.1% German, 15.1% Irish, 15.0% English, 10.3% Other groups, 7.7% United States or American (2000).
Vital Statistics: Birth rate: 196.6 per 10,000 population (1998)
Economy: Agricultural area. Manufacturing: electronics and machinery, construction materials, printing, consumer goods, publishing, fabricated metal products. Unemployment rate: 2.5% (11/2002); Total civilian labor force: 23,768 (11/2002); Single-family building permits issued: 850 (2001) / 875 (2000); Multi-family building permits issued: 318 (2001) / 428 (2000); Employment by occupation: 26.7% management, 29.4% professional, 8.1% services, 28.2% sales, 0.1% farming, 3.1% construction, 4.3% production (2000).
Income: Per capita income: $38,906 (2000); Median household income: $81,583 (2000); Poverty rate: 2.5% (2000).
Taxes: Total city taxes per capita: $529 (2000); City property taxes per capita: $238 (2000).
Education: High school graduation rate: 97.0% (2000); College graduation rate: 58.4% (2000).

School District(s)

Carmel Clay Schools (PK-12)
2000 Enrollment: 12,073 317-844-9961

Housing: Homeownership rate: 79.0% (2000); Median home value: $205,400 (2000); Median rent: $658 per month (2000); Median age of housing: 18 years (2000).
Hospitals: Saint Vincent Carmel Hospital (100 beds)
Safety: Violent crime rate: 4.2 per 10,000 population; Property crime rate: 184.2 per 10,000 population (2001).
Transportation: Commute to work: 93.4% car, 0.1% public transportation, 0.9% walk, 5.1% work from home (2000); Travel time to work: 27.8% less than 15 minutes, 37.7% 15 to 30 minutes, 24.2% 30 to 45 minutes, 6.5% 45 to 60 minutes, 3.8% 60 minutes or more (2000)
Additional Information Contacts
Carmel Chamber of Commerce 317-846-1049

CICERO (town). Covers a land area of 1.495 square miles and a water area of 0.433 square miles. Located at 40.12° N. Lat.; 86.01° W. Long. Elevation is 838 feet.
History: Cicero, named for a Delaware chief, grew around a Seventh-Day Adventist academy nearby.
Population: 4,303 (2000); Race: 97.3% White, 0.0% Black, 0.0% Asian, 0.0% American Indian and Alaska Native, 3.6% Hispanic of any race, 0.6% two or more races (2000); Density: 2,877.8 persons per square mile (2000); Age: 25.6% under 18, 8.9% over 64 (2000); Marriage status: 15.7% never married, 62.1% now married, 5.0% widowed, 17.2% divorced (2000); Foreign born: 2.4% (2000); Ancestry (includes multiple ancestries): 26.5% United States or American, 18.5% German, 10.2% English, 9.8% Irish, 3.8% Other groups (2000).
Economy: Employment by occupation: 6.9% management, 25.4% professional, 16.9% services, 31.9% sales, 0.8% farming, 6.5% construction, 11.5% production (2000).
Income: Per capita income: $23,169 (2000); Median household income: $54,561 (2000); Poverty rate: 1.7% (2000).
Taxes: Total city taxes per capita: $247 (1997); City property taxes per capita: $118 (1997).
Education: High school graduation rate: 91.6% (2000); College graduation rate: 23.3% (2000).
Housing: Homeownership rate: 79.1% (2000); Median home value: $112,600 (2000); Median rent: $520 per month (2000); Median age of housing: 22 years (2000).
Transportation: Commute to work: 96.2% car, 0.0% public transportation, 1.7% walk, 2.1% work from home (2000); Travel time to work: 25.8% less than 15 minutes, 29.7% 15 to 30 minutes, 24.8% 30 to 45 minutes, 10.5% 45 to 60 minutes, 9.2% 60 minutes or more (2000)
Additional Information Contacts
Cicero Chamber of Commerce 317-984-4079

FISHERS (town). Aka Fishers Station. Covers a land area of 21.690 square miles and a water area of 0.096 square miles. Located at 39.95° N. Lat.; 86.01° W. Long. Elevation is 824 feet.
Population: 37,835 (2000); Race: 92.0% White, 2.7% Black, 3.0% Asian, 0.2% American Indian and Alaska Native, 2.1% Hispanic of any race, 1.5% two or more races (2000); Density: 1,744.3 persons per square mile (2000); Age: 32.1% under 18, 3.3% over 64 (2000); Marriage status: 19.0% never married, 70.9% now married, 1.8% widowed, 8.3% divorced (2000); Foreign born: 4.0% (2000); Ancestry (includes multiple ancestries): 29.2% German, 13.3% English, 13.3% Irish, 11.2% Other groups, 7.2% United States or American (2000).
Economy: Unemployment rate: 1.1% (11/2002); Total civilian labor force: 17,444 (11/2002); Single-family building permits issued: 1,301 (2001) / 1,254 (2000); Multi-family building permits issued: 0 (2001) / 0 (2000); Employment by occupation: 28.2% management, 27.3% professional, 7.2% services, 30.6% sales, 0.1% farming, 2.9% construction, 3.8% production (2000).
Income: Per capita income: $31,891 (2000); Median household income: $75,638 (2000); Poverty rate: 1.8% (2000).
Taxes: Total city taxes per capita: $406 (1997); City property taxes per capita: $184 (1997).
Education: High school graduation rate: 98.2% (2000); College graduation rate: 60.1% (2000).

School District(s)

Hamilton Southeastern Schools (PK-12)
2000 Enrollment: 8,777 317-594-4100

Housing: Homeownership rate: 77.9% (2000); Median home value: $161,500 (2000); Median rent: $718 per month (2000); Median age of housing: 5 years (2000).
Newspapers: Noblesville Ledger (2 x week); North Side Topics (1 x week); Lawrence Topics (1 x week); Fishers Sun-Herald (1 x week); Carmel News-Tribune (1 x week)
Transportation: Commute to work: 94.0% car, 0.1% public transportation, 0.4% walk, 4.9% work from home (2000); Travel time to work: 21.5% less than 15 minutes, 40.9% 15 to 30 minutes, 28.3% 30 to 45 minutes, 5.8% 45 to 60 minutes, 3.5% 60 minutes or more (2000)
Additional Information Contacts
Fishers Chamber of Commerce 317-578-0700

NOBLESVILLE (city). Covers a land area of 17.916 square miles and a water area of 1.150 square miles. Located at 40.05° N. Lat.; 86.02° W. Long. Elevation is 772 feet.
History: Noblesville was founded in 1823 by William Conner who had built a trading post nearby in 1818. Noblesville became the seat of Hamilton County, and Conner became a state senator.
Population: 28,590 (2000); Race: 97.3% White, 1.1% Black, 0.4% Asian, 0.1% American Indian and Alaska Native, 1.7% Hispanic of any race, 0.7% two or more races (2000); Density: 1,595.8 persons per square mile (2000); Age: 29.3% under 18, 8.6% over 64 (2000); Marriage status: 18.7% never married, 67.4% now married, 5.2% widowed, 8.7% divorced (2000); Foreign born: 2.0% (2000); Ancestry (includes multiple ancestries): 27.8% German, 13.8% Irish, 13.4% English, 11.1% United States or American, 7.4% Other groups (2000).
Vital Statistics: Birth rate: 180.1 per 10,000 population (1998)
Economy: Unemployment rate: 3.1% (11/2002); Total civilian labor force: 16,138 (11/2002); Single-family building permits issued: 934 (2001) / 787 (2000); Multi-family building permits issued: 44 (2001) / 278 (2000); Employment by occupation: 18.4% management, 25.5% professional, 10.3% services, 28.1% sales, 0.1% farming, 7.2% construction, 10.3% production (2000).
Income: Per capita income: $28,813 (2000); Median household income: $61,455 (2000); Poverty rate: 5.4% (2000).
Taxes: Total city taxes per capita: $472 (2000); City property taxes per capita: $225 (2000).
Education: High school graduation rate: 90.8% (2000); College graduation rate: 40.9% (2000).

School District(s)

Noblesville Schools (PK-12)
2000 Enrollment: 6,430 317-773-3171

Housing: Homeownership rate: 75.3% (2000); Median home value: $144,900 (2000); Median rent: $548 per month (2000); Median age of housing: 15 years (2000).

Hospitals: Riverview Hospital (163 beds)

Safety: Violent crime rate: 9.7 per 10,000 population; Property crime rate: 253.2 per 10,000 population (2001).

Newspapers: The Noblesville Times (1 x week)

Transportation: Commute to work: 93.8% car, 0.2% public transportation, 1.3% walk, 3.9% work from home (2000); Travel time to work: 23.1% less than 15 minutes, 28.5% 15 to 30 minutes, 29.5% 30 to 45 minutes, 13.2% 45 to 60 minutes, 5.7% 60 minutes or more (2000)

Additional Information Contacts

Noblesville Chamber of Commerce 317-773-0086

SHERIDAN (town). Covers a land area of 1.318 square miles and a water area of 0 square miles. Located at 40.13° N. Lat.; 86.22° W. Long. Elevation is 949 feet.

History: Laid out 1860.

Population: 2,520 (2000); Race: 99.2% White, 0.0% Black, 0.8% Asian, 0.0% American Indian and Alaska Native, 0.3% Hispanic of any race, 0.0% two or more races (2000); Density: 1,912.4 persons per square mile (2000); Age: 24.5% under 18, 17.9% over 64 (2000); Marriage status: 23.0% never married, 57.2% now married, 7.6% widowed, 12.2% divorced (2000); Foreign born: 0.8% (2000); Ancestry (includes multiple ancestries): 37.1% United States or American, 12.2% German, 8.3% English, 6.7% Irish, 6.2% Other groups (2000).

Economy: Agricultural area: grain; livestock; dairying. Manufacturing: animal feeds, screw-machine products, computers. Single-family building permits issued: 13 (2001) / 31 (2000); Multi-family building permits issued: 2 (2001) / 0 (2000); Employment by occupation: 12.5% management, 16.5% professional, 14.3% services, 28.1% sales, 1.1% farming, 15.0% construction, 12.6% production (2000).

Income: Per capita income: $17,802 (2000); Median household income: $38,390 (2000); Poverty rate: 5.9% (2000).

Taxes: Total city taxes per capita: $354 (1997); City property taxes per capita: $180 (1997).

Education: High school graduation rate: 84.1% (2000); College graduation rate: 15.9% (2000).

School District(s)

Marion-Adams Schools (PK-12)
2000 Enrollment: 1,191 317-758-4172

Housing: Homeownership rate: 72.0% (2000); Median home value: $89,000 (2000); Median rent: $356 per month (2000); Median age of housing: 46 years (2000).

Transportation: Commute to work: 89.7% car, 0.0% public transportation, 3.2% walk, 5.6% work from home (2000); Travel time to work: 26.1% less than 15 minutes, 42.4% 15 to 30 minutes, 15.8% 30 to 45 minutes, 9.4% 45 to 60 minutes, 6.3% 60 minutes or more (2000)

Additional Information Contacts

Sheridan Chamber of Commerce 317-758-1311

WESTFIELD (town). Covers a land area of 7.629 square miles and a water area of 0.013 square miles. Located at 40.03° N. Lat.; 86.12° W. Long. Elevation is 899 feet.

History: Westfield was founded in 1834 by a group of Quakers, and was an important station on the Underground Railroad for slaves fleeing to the north.

Population: 9,293 (2000); Race: 93.4% White, 0.9% Black, 1.4% Asian, 0.5% American Indian and Alaska Native, 3.8% Hispanic of any race, 1.3% two or more races (2000); Density: 1,218.2 persons per square mile (2000); Age: 32.3% under 18, 7.2% over 64 (2000); Marriage status: 20.3% never married, 61.8% now married, 5.2% widowed, 12.7% divorced (2000); Foreign born: 3.7% (2000); Ancestry (includes multiple ancestries): 29.1% German, 15.1% Irish, 13.9% English, 10.9% Other groups, 8.7% United States or American (2000).

Economy: Single-family building permits issued: 577 (2001) / 522 (2000); Multi-family building permits issued: 170 (2001) / 62 (2000); Employment by occupation: 18.0% management, 24.2% professional, 10.0% services, 31.4% sales, 0.4% farming, 7.8% construction, 8.1% production (2000).

Income: Per capita income: $22,160 (2000); Median household income: $52,963 (2000); Poverty rate: 4.0% (2000).

Taxes: Total city taxes per capita: $218 (1997); City property taxes per capita: $92 (1997).

Education: High school graduation rate: 90.5% (2000); College graduation rate: 35.6% (2000).

School District(s)

Westfield-Washington Schools (PK-12)
2000 Enrollment: 3,701 317-896-2841

Housing: Homeownership rate: 70.5% (2000); Median home value: $133,100 (2000); Median rent: $545 per month (2000); Median age of housing: 8 years (2000).

Safety: Violent crime rate: 20.3 per 10,000 population; Property crime rate: 210.8 per 10,000 population (2001).

Transportation: Commute to work: 95.9% car, 0.5% public transportation, 0.9% walk, 2.1% work from home (2000); Travel time to work: 31.3% less than 15 minutes, 33.2% 15 to 30 minutes, 23.4% 30 to 45 minutes, 8.4% 45 to 60 minutes, 3.7% 60 minutes or more (2000)

Additional Information Contacts

Westfield Chamber of Commerce 317-896-2378

Hancock County

Located in central Indiana; drained by the Big Blue River and by Sugar and Brandywine Creeks. Covers a land area of 306.10 square miles, a water area of 0.60 square miles, and is located in the Eastern Time Zone. The county government was organized in 1827. County seat is Greenfield.

Hancock County is part of the Indianapolis, IN MSA. The entire metro area includes: Boone County; Hamilton County; Hancock County; Hendricks County; Johnson County; Madison County; Marion County; Morgan County; Shelby County

Weather Station: Greenfield — Elevation: 862 feet

	Jan	Feb	Mar	Apr	May	Jun	Jul	Aug	Sep	Oct	Nov	Dec
High	33	38	50	62	73	82	86	84	78	65	51	39
Low	17	20	30	40	51	60	64	62	55	43	33	23
Precip	2.5	2.4	3.3	4.1	4.7	4.4	5.0	4.0	3.1	3.1	3.9	3.1
Snow	na	na	1.5	0.2	0.0	0.0	0.0	0.0	0.0	tr	0.7	3.0

High and Low temperatures in degrees Fahrenheit; Precipitation and Snow in inches

Population: 55,391 (2000); Race: 98.4% White, 0.0% Black, 0.4% Asian, 0.2% American Indian and Alaska Native, 0.5% Hispanic of any race, 0.9% two or more races (2000); Density: 180.9 persons per square mile (2000); Age: 26.4% under 18, 11.3% over 64 (2000).

Religion: Five largest groups: 9.1% The United Methodist Church, 7.2% Catholic Church, 5.3% Christian Churches and Churches of Christ, 2.2% Church of the Nazarene, 2.1% Southern Baptist Convention (2000).

Economy: Unemployment rate: 3.6% (11/2002); Total civilian labor force: 31,900 (11/2002); Leading industries: 20.1% manufacturing; 13.2% health care and social assistance; 12.3% retail trade (2000); Companies that employ more than 1,000 persons: 1 (2000); Companies that employ more than 100 persons: 13 (2000); Farms: 549 totaling 163,704 acres (1997); Minority business ownership rate: 0.0% (1997); Women business ownership rate: 26.4% (1997); Retail sales per capita: $6,419 (1997). Single-family building permits issued: 944 (2001) / 603 (2000); Multi-family building permits issued: 128 (2001) / 96 (2000).

Income: Per capita income: $24,966 (2000); Median household income: $56,416 (2000); Poverty rate: 3.0% (2000); Bankruptcy rate: 6.57% (2001).

Taxes: Total county taxes per capita: $262 (2000); County property taxes per capita: $117 (2000).

Education: High school graduation rate: 87.8% (2000); College graduation rate: 22.2% (2000).

Housing: Homeownership rate: 81.4% (2000); Median home value: $129,700 (2000); Median rent: $469 per month (2000); Median age of housing: 25 years (2000).

Health: Birth rate: 131.4 per 10,000 population (1998); Age adjusted death rate: 82.3 per 10,000 population (1999); Age adjusted cancer mortality rate: 190.1 deaths per 100,000 population (1999). Air Quality Index: 53% good, 46% moderate, 1% unhealthy (percent of days in 2000). Number of physicians: 13.0 per 10,000 population (1999); Number of hospital beds: 18.2 per 10,000 population (1999).

Elections: 2000 Presidential election results: 28.3% Gore, 69.5% Bush, 0.6% Nader, 0.8% Buchanan

Additional Information Contacts

Hancock County Government Offices 317-462-1106
Greenfield Chamber of Commerce 317-462-4188
New Palestine Chamber of Commerce 317-861-9299

Hancock County Communities

CHARLOTTESVILLE (unincorporated postal area, zip code 46117). Aka Charlottsvillle. Covers a land area of 10.456 square miles and a water area of 0.005 square miles. Located at 39.80° N. Lat.; 85.61° W. Long. Elevation is 942 feet.
Population: 662 (2000); Race: 100.0% White, 0.0% Black, 0.0% Asian, 0.0% American Indian and Alaska Native, 0.0% Hispanic of any race, 0.0% two or more races (2000); Density: 63.3 persons per square mile (2000); Age: 27.8% under 18, 13.1% over 64 (2000); Marriage status: 16.5% never married, 72.2% now married, 7.9% widowed, 3.4% divorced (2000); Foreign born: 0.0% (2000); Ancestry (includes multiple ancestries): 26.1% United States or American, 23.7% English, 20.4% Irish, 14.2% German, 4.2% Scottish (2000).
Economy: Employment by occupation: 2.5% management, 6.5% professional, 8.4% services, 37.1% sales, 0.0% farming, 26.8% construction, 18.7% production (2000).
Income: Per capita income: $20,061 (2000); Median household income: $57,583 (2000); Poverty rate: 1.0% (2000).
Education: High school graduation rate: 80.7% (2000); College graduation rate: 7.6% (2000).

School District(s)

Eastern Hancock Co Com Sch Corp (PK-12)
2000 Enrollment: 1,096 317-467-0064

Housing: Homeownership rate: 90.9% (2000); Median home value: $114,300 (2000); Median rent: $653 per month (2000); Median age of housing: 45 years (2000).
Transportation: Commute to work: 97.2% car, 0.0% public transportation, 0.0% walk, 2.8% work from home (2000); Travel time to work: 15.5% less than 15 minutes, 38.2% 15 to 30 minutes, 16.8% 30 to 45 minutes, 12.0% 45 to 60 minutes, 17.5% 60 minutes or more (2000)

FORTVILLE (town). Covers a land area of 1.216 square miles and a water area of 0 square miles. Located at 39.93° N. Lat.; 85.84° W. Long. Elevation is 859 feet.
History: Fortville was founded in 1849 by Cephas Fort.
Population: 3,444 (2000); Race: 100.0% White, 0.0% Black, 0.0% Asian, 0.0% American Indian and Alaska Native, 0.3% Hispanic of any race, 0.0% two or more races (2000); Density: 2,831.8 persons per square mile (2000); Age: 28.9% under 18, 11.4% over 64 (2000); Marriage status: 25.1% never married, 53.2% now married, 6.5% widowed, 15.1% divorced (2000); Foreign born: 0.0% (2000); Ancestry (includes multiple ancestries): 21.6% German, 21.2% United States or American, 15.4% Irish, 5.7% Other groups, 5.3% Italian (2000).
Economy: Employment by occupation: 11.9% management, 8.2% professional, 11.6% services, 37.0% sales, 0.0% farming, 10.9% construction, 20.4% production (2000).
Income: Per capita income: $17,745 (2000); Median household income: $42,642 (2000); Poverty rate: 6.5% (2000).
Taxes: Total city taxes per capita: $125 (1997); City property taxes per capita: $123 (1997).
Education: High school graduation rate: 79.5% (2000); College graduation rate: 15.6% (2000).

School District(s)

Mount Vernon Community Sch Corp (PK-12)
2000 Enrollment: 2,603 317-485-3100

Housing: Homeownership rate: 68.1% (2000); Median home value: $98,200 (2000); Median rent: $393 per month (2000); Median age of housing: 30 years (2000).
Transportation: Commute to work: 93.3% car, 0.0% public transportation, 3.6% walk, 2.5% work from home (2000); Travel time to work: 15.1% less than 15 minutes, 34.4% 15 to 30 minutes, 31.0% 30 to 45 minutes, 13.6% 45 to 60 minutes, 5.8% 60 minutes or more (2000)

GREENFIELD (city). Covers a land area of 8.031 square miles and a water area of 0.039 square miles. Located at 39.79° N. Lat.; 85.77° W. Long. Elevation is 888 feet.
History: Greenfield was the birthplace in 1849 of poet James Whitcomb Riley. An early industry here was tomato canning.
Population: 14,600 (2000); Race: 98.5% White, 0.0% Black, 0.3% Asian, 0.4% American Indian and Alaska Native, 1.2% Hispanic of any race, 0.4% two or more races (2000); Density: 1,818.0 persons per square mile (2000); Age: 25.1% under 18, 14.4% over 64 (2000); Marriage status: 19.9% never married, 59.0% now married, 8.6% widowed, 12.5% divorced (2000); Foreign born: 0.9% (2000); Ancestry (includes multiple ancestries): 22.6% German, 13.8% United States or American, 12.7% English, 10.7% Irish, 9.5% Other groups (2000).
Vital Statistics: Birth rate: 169.9 per 10,000 population (1998)
Economy: Single-family building permits issued: 354 (2001) / 212 (2000); Multi-family building permits issued: 26 (2001) / 14 (2000); Employment by occupation: 10.9% management, 16.4% professional, 15.8% services, 26.5% sales, 0.2% farming, 11.8% construction, 18.5% production (2000).
Income: Per capita income: $22,509 (2000); Median household income: $42,035 (2000); Poverty rate: 4.3% (2000).
Taxes: Total city taxes per capita: $220 (2000); City property taxes per capita: $214 (2000).
Education: High school graduation rate: 83.8% (2000); College graduation rate: 18.9% (2000).

School District(s)

Greenfield-Central Com Schools (PK-12)
2000 Enrollment: 3,806 317-462-4434

Housing: Homeownership rate: 66.3% (2000); Median home value: $106,300 (2000); Median rent: $526 per month (2000); Median age of housing: 28 years (2000).
Hospitals: Hancock Memorial Hospital and Health Services (120 beds)
Safety: Violent crime rate: 6.8 per 10,000 population; Property crime rate: 158.7 per 10,000 population (2001).
Newspapers: Daily Reporter (6 x week); Warren Township Image (1 x week); Hancock County Image (1 x week)
Transportation: Commute to work: 95.1% car, 0.3% public transportation, 1.0% walk, 2.6% work from home (2000); Travel time to work: 41.0% less than 15 minutes, 20.3% 15 to 30 minutes, 24.7% 30 to 45 minutes, 10.3% 45 to 60 minutes, 3.7% 60 minutes or more (2000)
Additional Information Contacts
Greenfield Chamber of Commerce 317-462-4188

MCCORDSVILLE (town). Covers a land area of 3.203 square miles and a water area of 0 square miles. Located at 39.89° N. Lat.; 85.92° W. Long.
History: Laid out 1865.
Population: 1,134 (2000); Race: 94.4% White, 0.0% Black, 0.0% Asian, 0.0% American Indian and Alaska Native, 2.0% Hispanic of any race, 5.0% two or more races (2000); Density: 354.0 persons per square mile (2000); Age: 29.0% under 18, 9.7% over 64 (2000); Marriage status: 15.9% never married, 68.0% now married, 7.0% widowed, 9.2% divorced (2000); Foreign born: 0.0% (2000); Ancestry (includes multiple ancestries): 23.4% German, 21.1% Irish, 19.5% United States or American, 17.1% English, 11.5% Other groups (2000).
Economy: Manufacturing: machinery, fabricated metal products. Corn, soybeans. Employment by occupation: 25.5% management, 23.5% professional, 9.6% services, 30.2% sales, 0.0% farming, 3.6% construction, 7.6% production (2000).
Income: Per capita income: $30,250 (2000); Median household income: $68,750 (2000); Poverty rate: 0.0% (2000).
Taxes: Total city taxes per capita: $196 (1997); City property taxes per capita: $196 (1997).
Education: High school graduation rate: 87.8% (2000); College graduation rate: 35.5% (2000).
Housing: Homeownership rate: 89.5% (2000); Median home value: $150,800 (2000); Median rent: $416 per month (2000); Median age of housing: 26 years (2000).
Transportation: Commute to work: 92.8% car, 0.0% public transportation, 0.8% walk, 6.4% work from home (2000); Travel time to work: 19.8% less than 15 minutes, 37.1% 15 to 30 minutes, 32.7% 30 to 45 minutes, 6.0% 45 to 60 minutes, 4.4% 60 minutes or more (2000)

NEW PALESTINE (town). Covers a land area of 0.750 square miles and a water area of 0 square miles. Located at 39.72° N. Lat.; 85.89° W. Long. Elevation is 827 feet.
History: Laid out 1838.
Population: 1,264 (2000); Race: 98.3% White, 0.0% Black, 0.3% Asian, 0.0% American Indian and Alaska Native, 0.0% Hispanic of any race, 1.4% two or more races (2000); Density: 1,685.7 persons per square mile (2000); Age: 24.9% under 18, 9.4% over 64 (2000); Marriage status: 16.4% never married, 71.0% now married, 5.9% widowed, 6.7% divorced (2000); Foreign born: 0.5% (2000); Ancestry (includes multiple ancestries): 25.4% German, 22.9% United States or American, 12.2% Irish, 11.6% English, 4.1% Other groups (2000).
Economy: In agricultural area: grain. Single-family building permits issued: 21 (2001) / 29 (2000); Multi-family building permits issued: 0 (2001) / 0 (2000); Employment by occupation: 18.6% management, 14.6% professional,

13.0% services, 25.3% sales, 0.0% farming, 13.0% construction, 15.5% production (2000).
Income: Per capita income: $27,821 (2000); Median household income: $61,875 (2000); Poverty rate: 2.6% (2000).
Taxes: Total city taxes per capita: $141 (1997); City property taxes per capita: $124 (1997).
Education: High school graduation rate: 88.8% (2000); College graduation rate: 23.1% (2000).

School District(s)

Southern Hancock Co Com Sch Corp (PK-12)
2000 Enrollment: 2,728 317-861-4463

Housing: Homeownership rate: 81.0% (2000); Median home value: $129,100 (2000); Median rent: $440 per month (2000); Median age of housing: 34 years (2000).
Newspapers: New Palestine Press (1 x week)
Transportation: Commute to work: 94.8% car, 0.0% public transportation, 2.1% walk, 3.1% work from home (2000); Travel time to work: 18.9% less than 15 minutes, 35.5% 15 to 30 minutes, 28.2% 30 to 45 minutes, 10.9% 45 to 60 minutes, 6.5% 60 minutes or more (2000)
Additional Information Contacts
New Palestine Chamber of Commerce 317-861-9299

SHIRLEY (town). Covers a land area of 0.370 square miles and a water area of 0 square miles. Located at 39.89° N. Lat.; 85.58° W. Long.
Population: 806 (2000); Race: 97.0% White, 0.4% Black, 0.0% Asian, 0.0% American Indian and Alaska Native, 0.6% Hispanic of any race, 2.1% two or more races (2000); Density: 2,178.1 persons per square mile (2000); Age: 27.1% under 18, 16.1% over 64 (2000); Marriage status: 22.2% never married, 62.7% now married, 8.7% widowed, 6.5% divorced (2000); Foreign born: 0.4% (2000); Ancestry (includes multiple ancestries): 19.2% German, 11.4% United States or American, 8.2% English, 7.5% Irish, 5.9% Other groups (2000).
Economy: Employment by occupation: 3.2% management, 8.8% professional, 16.0% services, 21.3% sales, 0.0% farming, 21.0% construction, 29.8% production (2000).
Income: Per capita income: $16,603 (2000); Median household income: $37,000 (2000); Poverty rate: 6.3% (2000).
Taxes: Total city taxes per capita: $127 (1997); City property taxes per capita: $126 (1997).
Education: High school graduation rate: 77.7% (2000); College graduation rate: 7.0% (2000).
Housing: Homeownership rate: 77.5% (2000); Median home value: $80,900 (2000); Median rent: $296 per month (2000); Median age of housing: 60+ years (2000).
Transportation: Commute to work: 92.9% car, 0.0% public transportation, 0.8% walk, 3.2% work from home (2000); Travel time to work: 22.1% less than 15 minutes, 37.7% 15 to 30 minutes, 13.9% 30 to 45 minutes, 17.5% 45 to 60 minutes, 8.7% 60 minutes or more (2000)

SPRING LAKE (town). Covers a land area of 0.154 square miles and a water area of 0.007 square miles. Located at 39.77° N. Lat.; 85.85° W. Long. Elevation is 845 feet.
History: Settled 1884, laid out 1912.
Population: 262 (2000); Race: 98.1% White, 0.0% Black, 0.0% Asian, 0.0% American Indian and Alaska Native, 3.8% Hispanic of any race, 1.1% two or more races (2000); Density: 1,697.2 persons per square mile (2000); Age: 12.9% under 18, 10.6% over 64 (2000); Marriage status: 8.7% never married, 79.5% now married, 3.5% widowed, 8.3% divorced (2000); Foreign born: 0.8% (2000); Ancestry (includes multiple ancestries): 17.5% United States or American, 17.1% German, 9.1% Other groups, 7.6% English, 6.8% Irish (2000).
Economy: Agricultural area. Employment by occupation: 10.5% management, 26.1% professional, 11.8% services, 21.6% sales, 0.0% farming, 13.1% construction, 17.0% production (2000).
Income: Per capita income: $24,468 (2000); Median household income: $52,222 (2000); Poverty rate: 2.7% (2000).
Taxes: Total city taxes per capita: $53 (1997); City property taxes per capita: $53 (1997).
Education: High school graduation rate: 88.8% (2000); College graduation rate: 16.8% (2000).
Housing: Homeownership rate: 94.3% (2000); Median home value: $116,700 (2000); Median rent: $600 per month (2000); Median age of housing: 45 years (2000).
Transportation: Commute to work: 98.0% car, 0.0% public transportation, 0.0% walk, 2.0% work from home (2000); Travel time to work: 22.3% less than 15 minutes, 45.3% 15 to 30 minutes, 16.9% 30 to 45 minutes, 12.8% 45 to 60 minutes, 2.7% 60 minutes or more (2000)

WILKINSON (town). Covers a land area of 0.216 square miles and a water area of 0 square miles. Located at 39.88° N. Lat.; 85.60° W. Long. Elevation is 1,009 feet.
History: Laid out 1883.
Population: 356 (2000); Race: 100.0% White, 0.0% Black, 0.0% Asian, 0.0% American Indian and Alaska Native, 0.0% Hispanic of any race, 0.0% two or more races (2000); Density: 1,651.6 persons per square mile (2000); Age: 14.3% under 18, 22.0% over 64 (2000); Marriage status: 14.0% never married, 66.1% now married, 8.4% widowed, 11.5% divorced (2000); Foreign born: 0.7% (2000); Ancestry (includes multiple ancestries): 20.7% United States or American, 14.8% German, 10.6% Irish, 9.1% English, 3.7% Dutch (2000).
Economy: In agricultural area; manufacturing of agricultural equipment. Single-family building permits issued: 3 (2001) / 0 (2000); Multi-family building permits issued: 0 (2001) / 0 (2000); Employment by occupation: 4.0% management, 12.6% professional, 16.7% services, 33.8% sales, 0.0% farming, 13.6% construction, 19.2% production (2000).
Income: Per capita income: $21,289 (2000); Median household income: $48,750 (2000); Poverty rate: 2.5% (2000).
Taxes: Total city taxes per capita: $125 (1997); City property taxes per capita: $125 (1997).
Education: High school graduation rate: 78.8% (2000); College graduation rate: 5.5% (2000).
Housing: Homeownership rate: 85.2% (2000); Median home value: $92,800 (2000); Median rent: $385 per month (2000); Median age of housing: 55 years (2000).
Transportation: Commute to work: 93.4% car, 0.0% public transportation, 2.5% walk, 0.0% work from home (2000); Travel time to work: 12.6% less than 15 minutes, 33.8% 15 to 30 minutes, 33.8% 30 to 45 minutes, 11.1% 45 to 60 minutes, 8.6% 60 minutes or more (2000)

Harrison County

Located in southern Indiana; bounded on the east, south, and southwest by the Ohio River and the Kentucky border, and on the west by the Blue River. Covers a land area of 485.20 square miles, a water area of 1.70 square miles, and is located in the Eastern Time Zone. The county government was organized in 1808. County seat is Corydon.

Harrison County is part of the Louisville, KY-IN MSA. The entire metro area includes: Clark County, IN; Floyd County, IN; Harrison County, IN; Scott County, IN; Bullitt County, KY; Jefferson County, KY; Oldham County, KY

Population: 34,325 (2000); Race: 98.5% White, 0.3% Black, 0.2% Asian, 0.4% American Indian and Alaska Native, 1.1% Hispanic of any race, 0.3% two or more races (2000); Density: 70.7 persons per square mile (2000); Age: 26.0% under 18, 11.4% over 64 (2000).
Religion: Five largest groups: 18.5% Catholic Church, 12.1% The United Methodist Church, 4.8% Christian Church (Disciples of Christ), 4.0% Southern Baptist Convention, 2.8% Christian Churches and Churches of Christ (2000).
Economy: Unemployment rate: 3.6% (11/2002); Total civilian labor force: 19,540 (11/2002); Leading industries: 32.2% manufacturing; 18.0% retail trade; 11.7% health care and social assistance (2000); Companies that employ more than 1,000 persons: 0 (2000); Companies that employ more than 100 persons: 13 (2000); Farms: 1,108 totaling 161,378 acres (1997); Minority business ownership rate: 5.0% (1997); Women business ownership rate: 25.6% (1997); Retail sales per capita: $6,894 (1997). Single-family building permits issued: 185 (2001) / 204 (2000); Multi-family building permits issued: 2 (2001) / 0 (2000).
Income: Per capita income: $19,643 (2000); Median household income: $43,423 (2000); Poverty rate: 6.4% (2000); Bankruptcy rate: 6.93% (2001).
Taxes: Total county taxes per capita: $226 (2000); County property taxes per capita: $148 (2000).
Education: High school graduation rate: 80.3% (2000); College graduation rate: 13.1% (2000).
Housing: Homeownership rate: 84.1% (2000); Median home value: $95,700 (2000); Median rent: $376 per month (2000); Median age of housing: 24 years (2000).
Health: Birth rate: 130.8 per 10,000 population (1998); Age adjusted death rate: 88.3 per 10,000 population (1999); Age adjusted cancer mortality rate: 218.8 deaths per 100,000 population (1999). Number of physicians: 7.0 per

10,000 population (1999); Number of hospital beds: 13.7 per 10,000 population (1999).
Elections: 2000 Presidential election results: 39.4% Gore, 58.5% Bush, 0.7% Nader, 0.9% Buchanan
Additional Information Contacts
Harrison County Government Offices 812-738-8241
Corydon Chamber of Commerce 812-738-2137

Harrison County Communities

CORYDON (town). Covers a land area of 1.590 square miles and a water area of 0 square miles. Located at 38.21° N. Lat.; 86.12° W. Long. Elevation is 549 feet.
History: Corydon was named by General William Henry Harrison, who owned the land on which the town was platted. Harrison chose the name for the young shepherd in the song "Pastoral Elegy," a favorite of the day. Corydon served as the capital of Indiana for a time, and was the site of the only Civil War battle fought in Indiana. The Battle of Corydon occurred in 1863, when General John Hunt Morgan and his Confederate troops crossed the Ohio River and invaded the town.
Population: 2,715 (2000); Race: 96.9% White, 1.7% Black, 0.0% Asian, 0.8% American Indian and Alaska Native, 1.9% Hispanic of any race, 0.6% two or more races (2000); Density: 1,708.1 persons per square mile (2000); Age: 21.7% under 18, 24.1% over 64 (2000); Marriage status: 20.7% never married, 55.9% now married, 12.2% widowed, 11.2% divorced (2000); Foreign born: 0.2% (2000); Ancestry (includes multiple ancestries): 20.7% German, 13.7% Irish, 13.2% United States or American, 9.0% English, 5.7% Other groups (2000).
Economy: Employment by occupation: 6.2% management, 12.6% professional, 19.6% services, 21.8% sales, 0.8% farming, 11.1% construction, 27.8% production (2000).
Income: Per capita income: $20,740 (2000); Median household income: $33,823 (2000); Poverty rate: 10.3% (2000).
Taxes: Total city taxes per capita: $218 (2000); City property taxes per capita: $197 (2000).
Education: High school graduation rate: 69.3% (2000); College graduation rate: 15.1% (2000).

School District(s)

South Harrison Com Schools (KG-12)
2000 Enrollment: 3,089 812-738-2168
Housing: Homeownership rate: 61.9% (2000); Median home value: $78,800 (2000); Median rent: $382 per month (2000); Median age of housing: 48 years (2000).
Hospitals: Harrison County Hospital (68 beds)
Safety: Violent crime rate: 3.7 per 10,000 population; Property crime rate: 186.8 per 10,000 population (2001).
Newspapers: The Corydon Democrat (1 x week); The Clarion News (1 x week)
Transportation: Commute to work: 97.3% car, 0.0% public transportation, 1.5% walk, 0.4% work from home (2000); Travel time to work: 47.2% less than 15 minutes, 19.6% 15 to 30 minutes, 25.5% 30 to 45 minutes, 1.7% 45 to 60 minutes, 6.0% 60 minutes or more (2000)
Additional Information Contacts
Corydon Chamber of Commerce 812-738-2137

CRANDALL (town). Covers a land area of 0.103 square miles and a water area of 0 square miles. Located at 38.28° N. Lat.; 86.06° W. Long. Elevation is 659 feet.
Population: 131 (2000); Race: 94.9% White, 1.9% Black, 0.0% Asian, 0.0% American Indian and Alaska Native, 0.0% Hispanic of any race, 3.2% two or more races (2000); Density: 1,276.6 persons per square mile (2000); Age: 15.9% under 18, 13.4% over 64 (2000); Marriage status: 21.5% never married, 45.9% now married, 8.9% widowed, 23.7% divorced (2000); Foreign born: 0.0% (2000); Ancestry (includes multiple ancestries): 24.2% United States or American, 14.6% Irish, 14.0% English, 12.7% Other groups, 12.1% German (2000).
Economy: In agricultural area. Employment by occupation: 9.9% management, 9.9% professional, 12.7% services, 9.9% sales, 0.0% farming, 11.3% construction, 46.5% production (2000).
Income: Per capita income: $15,224 (2000); Median household income: $33,333 (2000); Poverty rate: 9.6% (2000).
Education: High school graduation rate: 63.7% (2000); College graduation rate: 8.8% (2000).
Housing: Homeownership rate: 84.1% (2000); Median home value: $73,800 (2000); Median rent: $325 per month (2000); Median age of housing: 60+ years (2000).
Transportation: Commute to work: 100.0% car, 0.0% public transportation, 0.0% walk, 0.0% work from home (2000); Travel time to work: 15.9% less than 15 minutes, 42.0% 15 to 30 minutes, 20.3% 30 to 45 minutes, 13.0% 45 to 60 minutes, 8.7% 60 minutes or more (2000)

DEPAUW (unincorporated postal area, zip code 47115). Covers a land area of 52.186 square miles and a water area of 0 square miles. Located at 38.35° N. Lat.; 86.22° W. Long. Elevation is 652 feet.
Population: 2,351 (2000); Race: 98.8% White, 0.0% Black, 0.0% Asian, 0.3% American Indian and Alaska Native, 0.0% Hispanic of any race, 0.8% two or more races (2000); Density: 45.1 persons per square mile (2000); Age: 25.1% under 18, 17.0% over 64 (2000); Marriage status: 20.3% never married, 61.5% now married, 8.9% widowed, 9.3% divorced (2000); Foreign born: 0.0% (2000); Ancestry (includes multiple ancestries): 19.7% German, 13.5% United States or American, 8.7% French (except Basque), 8.7% Irish, 8.2% English (2000).
Economy: Employment by occupation: 11.9% management, 16.4% professional, 10.1% services, 22.6% sales, 2.2% farming, 13.8% construction, 22.9% production (2000).
Income: Per capita income: $19,944 (2000); Median household income: $38,597 (2000); Poverty rate: 9.2% (2000).
Education: High school graduation rate: 78.2% (2000); College graduation rate: 12.2% (2000).
Housing: Homeownership rate: 86.9% (2000); Median home value: $79,000 (2000); Median rent: $234 per month (2000); Median age of housing: 26 years (2000).
Transportation: Commute to work: 88.7% car, 0.0% public transportation, 1.4% walk, 7.8% work from home (2000); Travel time to work: 26.6% less than 15 minutes, 18.0% 15 to 30 minutes, 25.2% 30 to 45 minutes, 19.1% 45 to 60 minutes, 11.1% 60 minutes or more (2000)

ELIZABETH (town). Covers a land area of 0.137 square miles and a water area of 0 square miles. Located at 38.12° N. Lat.; 85.97° W. Long. Elevation is 750 feet.
Population: 137 (2000); Race: 100.0% White, 0.0% Black, 0.0% Asian, 0.0% American Indian and Alaska Native, 0.0% Hispanic of any race, 0.0% two or more races (2000); Density: 997.1 persons per square mile (2000); Age: 24.8% under 18, 32.8% over 64 (2000); Marriage status: 16.0% never married, 60.4% now married, 13.2% widowed, 10.4% divorced (2000); Foreign born: 0.0% (2000); Ancestry (includes multiple ancestries): 43.1% United States or American, 19.0% German, 10.9% English, 5.8% Irish, 5.8% Other groups (2000).
Economy: In agricultural area. Employment by occupation: 6.7% management, 16.7% professional, 23.3% services, 25.0% sales, 0.0% farming, 1.7% construction, 26.7% production (2000).
Income: Per capita income: $15,208 (2000); Median household income: $31,563 (2000); Poverty rate: 10.2% (2000).
Taxes: Total city taxes per capita: $12 (1997); City property taxes per capita: $12 (1997).
Education: High school graduation rate: 57.0% (2000); College graduation rate: 5.0% (2000).
Housing: Homeownership rate: 70.5% (2000); Median home value: $69,000 (2000); Median rent: $446 per month (2000); Median age of housing: 58 years (2000).
Transportation: Commute to work: 100.0% car, 0.0% public transportation, 0.0% walk, 0.0% work from home (2000); Travel time to work: 35.0% less than 15 minutes, 3.3% 15 to 30 minutes, 31.7% 30 to 45 minutes, 23.3% 45 to 60 minutes, 6.7% 60 minutes or more (2000)

LACONIA (town). Covers a land area of 0.050 square miles and a water area of 0 square miles. Located at 38.03° N. Lat.; 86.08° W. Long. Elevation is 667 feet.
History: Laid out 1816.
Population: 29 (2000); Race: 100.0% White, 0.0% Black, 0.0% Asian, 0.0% American Indian and Alaska Native, 0.0% Hispanic of any race, 0.0% two or more races (2000); Density: 583.2 persons per square mile (2000); Age: 45.8% under 18, 29.2% over 64 (2000); Marriage status: 0.0% never married, 23.1% now married, 53.8% widowed, 23.1% divorced (2000); Foreign born: 0.0% (2000); Ancestry (includes multiple ancestries): 50.0% German, 50.0% English, 20.8% United States or American, 16.7% Irish, 8.3% Other groups (2000).

Economy: In agricultural area. Employment by occupation: 0.0% management, 0.0% professional, 100.0% services, 0.0% sales, 0.0% farming, 0.0% construction, 0.0% production (2000).
Income: Per capita income: $9,779 (2000); Median household income: $16,667 (2000); Poverty rate: 50.0% (2000).
Taxes: Total city taxes per capita: $13 (1997); City property taxes per capita: $0 (1997).
Education: High school graduation rate: 84.6% (2000); College graduation rate: 23.1% (2000).
Housing: Homeownership rate: 72.7% (2000); Median home value: $45,000 (2000); Median rent: $375 per month (2000); Median age of housing: 38 years (2000).
Transportation: Commute to work: 100.0% car, 0.0% public transportation, 0.0% walk, 0.0% work from home (2000); Travel time to work: 0.0% less than 15 minutes, 0.0% 15 to 30 minutes, 0.0% 30 to 45 minutes, 0.0% 45 to 60 minutes, 100.0% 60 minutes or more (2000)

LANESVILLE (town). Covers a land area of 0.402 square miles and a water area of 0 square miles. Located at 38.23° N. Lat.; 85.98° W. Long. Elevation is 730 feet.
History: Lanesville was settled in 1792 as a stage stop and trading center for surrounding farms. It was platted in 1817, and named for General Lane, a surveyor who was an early resident.
Population: 614 (2000); Race: 98.6% White, 0.0% Black, 0.8% Asian, 0.0% American Indian and Alaska Native, 0.8% Hispanic of any race, 0.6% two or more races (2000); Density: 1,527.5 persons per square mile (2000); Age: 32.2% under 18, 8.9% over 64 (2000); Marriage status: 22.6% never married, 64.6% now married, 6.3% widowed, 6.5% divorced (2000); Foreign born: 1.6% (2000); Ancestry (includes multiple ancestries): 42.7% German, 18.2% Irish, 14.7% United States or American, 10.5% English, 6.3% Dutch (2000).
Economy: Employment by occupation: 10.2% management, 23.2% professional, 9.8% services, 29.8% sales, 0.0% farming, 8.9% construction, 18.1% production (2000).
Income: Per capita income: $18,914 (2000); Median household income: $54,219 (2000); Poverty rate: 2.1% (2000).
Taxes: Total city taxes per capita: $18 (1997); City property taxes per capita: $18 (1997).
Education: High school graduation rate: 90.8% (2000); College graduation rate: 20.5% (2000).

School District(s)

Lanesville Community School Corp (KG-12)
2000 Enrollment: 592 812-952-2555

Housing: Homeownership rate: 82.2% (2000); Median home value: $90,500 (2000); Median rent: $473 per month (2000); Median age of housing: 32 years (2000).
Transportation: Commute to work: 93.2% car, 0.0% public transportation, 1.0% walk, 4.8% work from home (2000); Travel time to work: 11.1% less than 15 minutes, 54.4% 15 to 30 minutes, 27.7% 30 to 45 minutes, 4.1% 45 to 60 minutes, 2.7% 60 minutes or more (2000)

MAUCKPORT (town). Covers a land area of 0.136 square miles and a water area of 0.016 square miles. Located at 38.02° N. Lat.; 86.20° W. Long. Elevation is 423 feet.
Population: 83 (2000); Race: 100.0% White, 0.0% Black, 0.0% Asian, 0.0% American Indian and Alaska Native, 0.0% Hispanic of any race, 0.0% two or more races (2000); Density: 610.8 persons per square mile (2000); Age: 18.0% under 18, 5.6% over 64 (2000); Marriage status: 17.3% never married, 37.3% now married, 5.3% widowed, 40.0% divorced (2000); Foreign born: 0.0% (2000); Ancestry (includes multiple ancestries): 9.0% Irish, 9.0% German, 5.6% Other groups, 3.4% United States or American, 2.2% Dutch (2000).
Economy: In agricultural area; hardwood veneer. Employment by occupation: 2.5% management, 5.0% professional, 37.5% services, 15.0% sales, 2.5% farming, 12.5% construction, 25.0% production (2000).
Income: Per capita income: $15,946 (2000); Median household income: $36,964 (2000); Poverty rate: 18.0% (2000).
Taxes: Total city taxes per capita: $19 (1997); City property taxes per capita: $19 (1997).
Education: High school graduation rate: 65.2% (2000); College graduation rate: 5.8% (2000).
Housing: Homeownership rate: 54.0% (2000); Median home value: $33,100 (2000); Median rent: $257 per month (2000); Median age of housing: 60+ years (2000).
Transportation: Commute to work: 88.9% car, 0.0% public transportation, 0.0% walk, 2.8% work from home (2000); Travel time to work: 8.6% less than 15 minutes, 48.6% 15 to 30 minutes, 20.0% 30 to 45 minutes, 14.3% 45 to 60 minutes, 8.6% 60 minutes or more (2000)

MILLTOWN (town). Covers a land area of 1.407 square miles and a water area of 0 square miles. Located at 38.34° N. Lat.; 86.27° W. Long.
Population: 932 (2000); Race: 97.7% White, 0.0% Black, 0.0% Asian, 1.0% American Indian and Alaska Native, 0.4% Hispanic of any race, 1.3% two or more races (2000); Density: 662.2 persons per square mile (2000); Age: 26.1% under 18, 15.9% over 64 (2000); Marriage status: 18.1% never married, 61.0% now married, 5.2% widowed, 15.6% divorced (2000); Foreign born: 0.2% (2000); Ancestry (includes multiple ancestries): 23.5% German, 15.1% Irish, 14.8% United States or American, 7.9% Other groups, 7.2% English (2000).
Economy: Single-family building permits issued: 0 (2001) / 2 (2000); Multi-family building permits issued: 0 (2001) / 0 (2000); Employment by occupation: 9.0% management, 15.2% professional, 13.7% services, 24.2% sales, 0.9% farming, 13.9% construction, 23.1% production (2000).
Income: Per capita income: $17,746 (2000); Median household income: $37,344 (2000); Poverty rate: 13.5% (2000).
Education: High school graduation rate: 73.4% (2000); College graduation rate: 8.5% (2000).
Housing: Homeownership rate: 71.0% (2000); Median home value: $62,200 (2000); Median rent: $246 per month (2000); Median age of housing: 38 years (2000).
Transportation: Commute to work: 97.5% car, 0.0% public transportation, 0.7% walk, 1.8% work from home (2000); Travel time to work: 19.3% less than 15 minutes, 29.2% 15 to 30 minutes, 22.6% 30 to 45 minutes, 21.2% 45 to 60 minutes, 7.8% 60 minutes or more (2000)

NEW MIDDLETOWN (town). Covers a land area of 0.042 square miles and a water area of 0 square miles. Located at 38.16° N. Lat.; 86.05° W. Long. Elevation is 700 feet.
Population: 77 (2000); Race: 87.5% White, 0.0% Black, 0.0% Asian, 0.0% American Indian and Alaska Native, 7.8% Hispanic of any race, 4.7% two or more races (2000); Density: 1,833.9 persons per square mile (2000); Age: 23.4% under 18, 6.3% over 64 (2000); Marriage status: 26.5% never married, 59.2% now married, 8.2% widowed, 6.1% divorced (2000); Foreign born: 7.8% (2000); Ancestry (includes multiple ancestries): 28.1% United States or American, 17.2% Irish, 17.2% Other groups, 10.9% German, 4.7% Canadian (2000).
Economy: In agricultural area. Employment by occupation: 0.0% management, 0.0% professional, 11.8% services, 17.6% sales, 0.0% farming, 29.4% construction, 41.2% production (2000).
Income: Per capita income: $33,423 (2000); Median household income: $45,000 (2000); Poverty rate: 6.3% (2000).
Education: High school graduation rate: 83.7% (2000); College graduation rate: 0.0% (2000).
Housing: Homeownership rate: 84.6% (2000); Median home value: $73,000 (2000); Median rent: $425 per month (2000); Median age of housing: 60+ years (2000).
Transportation: Commute to work: 100.0% car, 0.0% public transportation, 0.0% walk, 0.0% work from home (2000); Travel time to work: 9.4% less than 15 minutes, 40.6% 15 to 30 minutes, 40.6% 30 to 45 minutes, 9.4% 45 to 60 minutes, 0.0% 60 minutes or more (2000)

NEW SALISBURY (unincorporated postal area, zip code 47161). Aka Corydon Junction. Covers a land area of 23.072 square miles and a water area of 0.021 square miles. Located at 38.31° N. Lat.; 86.09° W. Long. Elevation is 746 feet.
History: Laid out 1830.
Population: 3,426 (2000); Race: 99.1% White, 0.0% Black, 0.5% Asian, 0.3% American Indian and Alaska Native, 2.3% Hispanic of any race, 0.1% two or more races (2000); Density: 148.5 persons per square mile (2000); Age: 28.9% under 18, 6.1% over 64 (2000); Marriage status: 20.9% never married, 63.7% now married, 4.8% widowed, 10.6% divorced (2000); Foreign born: 2.3% (2000); Ancestry (includes multiple ancestries): 22.7% United States or American, 20.7% German, 11.5% Irish, 8.3% Other groups, 5.4% English (2000).
Economy: Railroad junction. Manufacturing: furniture, lumber. Employment by occupation: 11.8% management, 10.8% professional, 10.0% services, 26.2% sales, 0.3% farming, 15.8% construction, 25.1% production (2000).
Income: Per capita income: $19,170 (2000); Median household income: $47,804 (2000); Poverty rate: 9.4% (2000).
Education: High school graduation rate: 83.6% (2000); College graduation rate: 9.4% (2000).

Housing: Homeownership rate: 86.9% (2000); Median home value: $95,300 (2000); Median rent: $363 per month (2000); Median age of housing: 22 years (2000).
Transportation: Commute to work: 94.8% car, 0.0% public transportation, 2.0% walk, 3.2% work from home (2000); Travel time to work: 20.3% less than 15 minutes, 28.0% 15 to 30 minutes, 29.0% 30 to 45 minutes, 17.6% 45 to 60 minutes, 5.2% 60 minutes or more (2000)

PALMYRA (town). Covers a land area of 0.928 square miles and a water area of 0.058 square miles. Located at 38.40° N. Lat.; 86.11° W. Long. Elevation is 770 feet.
History: Palmyra was founded in 1810 as a farming village.
Population: 633 (2000); Race: 97.7% White, 0.0% Black, 0.0% Asian, 0.0% American Indian and Alaska Native, 0.0% Hispanic of any race, 2.3% two or more races (2000); Density: 682.5 persons per square mile (2000); Age: 26.1% under 18, 15.0% over 64 (2000); Marriage status: 25.3% never married, 56.1% now married, 9.0% widowed, 9.6% divorced (2000); Foreign born: 0.2% (2000); Ancestry (includes multiple ancestries): 32.2% German, 20.3% United States or American, 13.8% English, 8.8% Irish, 6.6% Other groups (2000).
Economy: Employment by occupation: 7.2% management, 13.1% professional, 15.5% services, 30.6% sales, 0.0% farming, 15.1% construction, 18.6% production (2000).
Income: Per capita income: $15,114 (2000); Median household income: $36,964 (2000); Poverty rate: 7.8% (2000).
Taxes: Total city taxes per capita: $25 (1997); City property taxes per capita: $22 (1997).
Education: High school graduation rate: 74.2% (2000); College graduation rate: 10.1% (2000).
Housing: Homeownership rate: 81.7% (2000); Median home value: $85,000 (2000); Median rent: $425 per month (2000); Median age of housing: 35 years (2000).
Transportation: Commute to work: 92.4% car, 0.0% public transportation, 5.5% walk, 1.4% work from home (2000); Travel time to work: 15.7% less than 15 minutes, 31.4% 15 to 30 minutes, 36.6% 30 to 45 minutes, 12.2% 45 to 60 minutes, 4.2% 60 minutes or more (2000)

RAMSEY (unincorporated postal area, zip code 47166). Covers a land area of 14.357 square miles and a water area of 0 square miles. Located at 38.31° N. Lat.; 86.16° W. Long. Elevation is 715 feet.
Population: 1,245 (2000); Race: 99.6% White, 0.0% Black, 0.0% Asian, 0.4% American Indian and Alaska Native, 0.0% Hispanic of any race, 0.0% two or more races (2000); Density: 86.7 persons per square mile (2000); Age: 24.9% under 18, 6.2% over 64 (2000); Marriage status: 18.2% never married, 61.3% now married, 6.3% widowed, 14.2% divorced (2000); Foreign born: 1.1% (2000); Ancestry (includes multiple ancestries): 21.7% German, 14.6% United States or American, 14.5% Irish, 6.9% Other groups, 4.0% French (except Basque) (2000).
Economy: Employment by occupation: 11.2% management, 10.7% professional, 13.7% services, 21.9% sales, 1.0% farming, 11.6% construction, 29.9% production (2000).
Income: Per capita income: $17,202 (2000); Median household income: $49,896 (2000); Poverty rate: 4.6% (2000).
Education: High school graduation rate: 82.2% (2000); College graduation rate: 16.6% (2000).

School District(s)

North Harrison Com School Corp (KG-12)
2000 Enrollment: 2,364 812-347-2407

Housing: Homeownership rate: 87.0% (2000); Median home value: $87,500 (2000); Median rent: $423 per month (2000); Median age of housing: 21 years (2000).
Transportation: Commute to work: 95.3% car, 0.0% public transportation, 1.8% walk, 2.9% work from home (2000); Travel time to work: 20.6% less than 15 minutes, 27.1% 15 to 30 minutes, 23.9% 30 to 45 minutes, 18.4% 45 to 60 minutes, 10.1% 60 minutes or more (2000)

Hendricks County

Located in central Indiana; drained by the Eel and Whitelick Rivers and Mill Creek. Covers a land area of 408.40 square miles, a water area of 0.50 square miles, and is located in the Eastern Time Zone. The county government was organized in 1823. County seat is Danville.

Hendricks County is part of the Indianapolis, IN MSA. The entire metro area includes: Boone County; Hamilton County; Hancock County; Hendricks County; Johnson County; Madison County; Marion County; Morgan County; Shelby County

Population: 104,093 (2000); Race: 96.3% White, 1.0% Black, 0.6% Asian, 0.2% American Indian and Alaska Native, 1.0% Hispanic of any race, 1.5% two or more races (2000); Density: 254.9 persons per square mile (2000); Age: 28.0% under 18, 9.7% over 64 (2000).
Religion: Five largest groups: 11.8% Catholic Church, 9.4% Christian Churches and Churches of Christ, 4.6% The United Methodist Church, 3.7% General Association of Regular Baptist Churches, 2.2% New Testament Association of Independent Baptist Chur
Economy: Unemployment rate: 3.6% (11/2002); Total civilian labor force: 57,076 (11/2002); Leading industries: 21.3% retail trade; 12.9% accommodation & food services; 12.4% health care and social assistance (2000); Companies that employ more than 1,000 persons: 0 (2000); Companies that employ more than 100 persons: 44 (2000); Farms: 631 totaling 167,228 acres (1997); Minority business ownership rate: 3.5% (1997); Women business ownership rate: 25.0% (1997); Retail sales per capita: $8,208 (1997). Single-family building permits issued: 2,103 (2001) / 1,727 (2000); Multi-family building permits issued: 280 (2001) / 174 (2000).
Income: Per capita income: $23,129 (2000); Median household income: $55,208 (2000); Poverty rate: 3.6% (2000); Bankruptcy rate: 7.40% (2001).
Taxes: Total county taxes per capita: $206 (2000); County property taxes per capita: $79 (2000).
Education: High school graduation rate: 88.5% (2000); College graduation rate: 23.1% (2000).
Housing: Homeownership rate: 82.9% (2000); Median home value: $133,300 (2000); Median rent: $551 per month (2000); Median age of housing: 22 years (2000).
Health: Birth rate: 114.0 per 10,000 population (1998); Age adjusted death rate: 87.5 per 10,000 population (1999); Age adjusted cancer mortality rate: 210.7 deaths per 100,000 population (1999). Air Quality Index: 54% good, 46% moderate, 0% unhealthy (percent of days in 2000). Number of physicians: 12.5 per 10,000 population (1999); Number of hospital beds: 12.6 per 10,000 population (1999).
Elections: 2000 Presidential election results: 26.8% Gore, 71.2% Bush, 0.4% Nader, 0.8% Buchanan

Additional Information Contacts

Hendricks County Government Offices 317-745-9221
Brownsburg Chamber of Commerce 317-852-7885
Danville Chamber of Commerce 317-745-0670
Plainfield Chamber of Commerce 317-839-7222

Hendricks County Communities

AMO (town). Covers a land area of 0.610 square miles and a water area of 0 square miles. Located at 39.68° N. Lat.; 86.61° W. Long. Elevation is 822 feet.
Population: 414 (2000); Race: 100.0% White, 0.0% Black, 0.0% Asian, 0.0% American Indian and Alaska Native, 0.0% Hispanic of any race, 0.0% two or more races (2000); Density: 679.1 persons per square mile (2000); Age: 30.4% under 18, 12.6% over 64 (2000); Marriage status: 20.6% never married, 55.7% now married, 9.8% widowed, 13.9% divorced (2000); Foreign born: 0.0% (2000); Ancestry (includes multiple ancestries): 40.6% United States or American, 14.6% German, 8.2% English, 6.2% Irish, 3.5% Other groups (2000).
Economy: In agricultural area. Employment by occupation: 9.8% management, 13.0% professional, 17.1% services, 31.1% sales, 0.0% farming, 13.0% construction, 16.1% production (2000).
Income: Per capita income: $15,994 (2000); Median household income: $41,167 (2000); Poverty rate: 6.7% (2000).
Education: High school graduation rate: 83.7% (2000); College graduation rate: 11.9% (2000).
Housing: Homeownership rate: 85.1% (2000); Median home value: $83,700 (2000); Median rent: $475 per month (2000); Median age of housing: 55 years (2000).
Transportation: Commute to work: 84.3% car, 0.0% public transportation, 6.8% walk, 8.4% work from home (2000); Travel time to work: 18.3% less than 15 minutes, 28.0% 15 to 30 minutes, 20.0% 30 to 45 minutes, 20.0% 45 to 60 minutes, 13.7% 60 minutes or more (2000)

AVON (town). Covers a land area of 6.381 square miles and a water area of 0.012 square miles. Located at 39.76° N. Lat.; 86.38° W. Long. Elevation is 840 feet.

Population: 6,248 (2000); Race: 94.8% White, 0.5% Black, 1.3% Asian, 0.1% American Indian and Alaska Native, 1.6% Hispanic of any race, 3.2% two or more races (2000); Density: 979.2 persons per square mile (2000); Age: 31.3% under 18, 5.7% over 64 (2000); Marriage status: 15.1% never married, 73.1% now married, 2.7% widowed, 9.0% divorced (2000); Foreign born: 3.6% (2000); Ancestry (includes multiple ancestries): 24.7% German, 13.1% Irish, 13.0% United States or American, 9.8% Other groups, 8.3% English (2000).
Economy: Single-family building permits issued: 141 (2001) / 92 (2000); Multi-family building permits issued: 0 (2001) / 10 (2000); Employment by occupation: 19.7% management, 15.6% professional, 10.5% services, 27.2% sales, 0.0% farming, 9.9% construction, 17.1% production (2000).
Income: Per capita income: $24,740 (2000); Median household income: $66,782 (2000); Poverty rate: 2.9% (2000).
Education: High school graduation rate: 92.4% (2000); College graduation rate: 28.3% (2000).

School District(s)

Avon Community School Corp (KG-12)
2000 Enrollment: 5,153 317-272-2920
Housing: Homeownership rate: 91.3% (2000); Median home value: $145,300 (2000); Median rent: $701 per month (2000); Median age of housing: 5 years (2000).
Transportation: Commute to work: 97.3% car, 0.3% public transportation, 0.0% walk, 2.1% work from home (2000); Travel time to work: 25.4% less than 15 minutes, 39.6% 15 to 30 minutes, 24.6% 30 to 45 minutes, 6.7% 45 to 60 minutes, 3.8% 60 minutes or more (2000)

BROWNSBURG (town). Covers a land area of 7.320 square miles and a water area of 0 square miles. Located at 39.84° N. Lat.; 86.39° W. Long. Elevation is 884 feet.
Population: 14,520 (2000); Race: 98.0% White, 0.1% Black, 0.5% Asian, 0.3% American Indian and Alaska Native, 1.8% Hispanic of any race, 0.8% two or more races (2000); Density: 1,983.5 persons per square mile (2000); Age: 29.9% under 18, 11.4% over 64 (2000); Marriage status: 17.2% never married, 68.3% now married, 6.1% widowed, 8.4% divorced (2000); Foreign born: 1.9% (2000); Ancestry (includes multiple ancestries): 25.8% German, 17.9% United States or American, 13.4% Irish, 12.5% English, 8.1% Other groups (2000).
Economy: Manufacturing: aircraft sheet metal, consumer goods. Single-family building permits issued: 282 (2001) / 299 (2000); Multi-family building permits issued: 36 (2001) / 88 (2000); Employment by occupation: 15.1% management, 26.7% professional, 7.4% services, 31.2% sales, 0.0% farming, 6.4% construction, 13.2% production (2000).
Income: Per capita income: $23,196 (2000); Median household income: $53,629 (2000); Poverty rate: 2.3% (2000).
Taxes: Total city taxes per capita: $263 (1997); City property taxes per capita: $210 (1997).
Education: High school graduation rate: 92.5% (2000); College graduation rate: 32.3% (2000).

School District(s)

Brownsburg Community Sch Corp (PK-12)
2000 Enrollment: 5,041 317-852-5726
Housing: Homeownership rate: 80.0% (2000); Median home value: $124,000 (2000); Median rent: $541 per month (2000); Median age of housing: 13 years (2000).
Safety: Violent crime rate: 41.1 per 10,000 population; Property crime rate: 241.1 per 10,000 population (2001).
Transportation: Commute to work: 95.1% car, 0.3% public transportation, 0.3% walk, 3.0% work from home (2000); Travel time to work: 21.2% less than 15 minutes, 37.4% 15 to 30 minutes, 30.0% 30 to 45 minutes, 7.1% 45 to 60 minutes, 4.3% 60 minutes or more (2000)
Additional Information Contacts
Brownsburg Chamber of Commerce 317-852-7885

CLAYTON (town). Covers a land area of 0.497 square miles and a water area of 0 square miles. Located at 39.68° N. Lat.; 86.52° W. Long. Elevation is 872 feet.
Population: 693 (2000); Race: 97.7% White, 0.4% Black, 0.0% Asian, 0.0% American Indian and Alaska Native, 0.7% Hispanic of any race, 1.2% two or more races (2000); Density: 1,394.7 persons per square mile (2000); Age: 29.7% under 18, 9.8% over 64 (2000); Marriage status: 16.4% never married, 64.2% now married, 6.2% widowed, 13.1% divorced (2000); Foreign born: 0.0% (2000); Ancestry (includes multiple ancestries): 26.7% United States or American, 14.9% Irish, 14.7% German, 8.4% English, 6.0% Other groups (2000).
Economy: Fruit, grain. Employment by occupation: 10.5% management, 13.0% professional, 13.6% services, 34.9% sales, 0.6% farming, 13.3% construction, 14.1% production (2000).
Income: Per capita income: $21,387 (2000); Median household income: $45,066 (2000); Poverty rate: 4.9% (2000).
Taxes: Total city taxes per capita: $136 (1997); City property taxes per capita: $113 (1997).
Education: High school graduation rate: 87.3% (2000); College graduation rate: 6.4% (2000).

School District(s)

Mill Creek Community Sch Corp (PK-12)
2000 Enrollment: 1,571 317-539-9200
Housing: Homeownership rate: 85.6% (2000); Median home value: $87,900 (2000); Median rent: $619 per month (2000); Median age of housing: 60+ years (2000).
Transportation: Commute to work: 96.1% car, 0.0% public transportation, 1.4% walk, 0.8% work from home (2000); Travel time to work: 13.5% less than 15 minutes, 30.7% 15 to 30 minutes, 32.1% 30 to 45 minutes, 14.6% 45 to 60 minutes, 9.0% 60 minutes or more (2000)

COATESVILLE (town). Covers a land area of 0.664 square miles and a water area of 0 square miles. Located at 39.68° N. Lat.; 86.66° W. Long. Elevation is 873 feet.
Population: 516 (2000); Race: 99.6% White, 0.0% Black, 0.0% Asian, 0.0% American Indian and Alaska Native, 0.0% Hispanic of any race, 0.0% two or more races (2000); Density: 776.7 persons per square mile (2000); Age: 33.3% under 18, 11.3% over 64 (2000); Marriage status: 19.2% never married, 61.9% now married, 7.7% widowed, 11.2% divorced (2000); Foreign born: 0.0% (2000); Ancestry (includes multiple ancestries): 18.1% German, 14.7% English, 12.1% United States or American, 10.4% Irish, 6.0% Other groups (2000).
Economy: In dairy, grain, and livestock area; timber. Manufacturing: lawn mowers. Employment by occupation: 5.5% management, 10.6% professional, 12.3% services, 26.4% sales, 0.0% farming, 21.3% construction, 23.8% production (2000).
Income: Per capita income: $15,387 (2000); Median household income: $40,357 (2000); Poverty rate: 4.2% (2000).
Taxes: Total city taxes per capita: $112 (1997); City property taxes per capita: $84 (1997).
Education: High school graduation rate: 77.0% (2000); College graduation rate: 8.4% (2000).
Housing: Homeownership rate: 81.7% (2000); Median home value: $83,600 (2000); Median rent: $414 per month (2000); Median age of housing: 50 years (2000).
Transportation: Commute to work: 95.3% car, 0.0% public transportation, 0.9% walk, 3.9% work from home (2000); Travel time to work: 12.5% less than 15 minutes, 26.3% 15 to 30 minutes, 23.2% 30 to 45 minutes, 17.4% 45 to 60 minutes, 20.5% 60 minutes or more (2000)

DANVILLE (town). Covers a land area of 6.126 square miles and a water area of 0.003 square miles. Located at 39.76° N. Lat.; 86.51° W. Long. Elevation is 954 feet.
History: Danville was settled in 1824 by Daniel Clark, a justice of the peace, for whom the town was named. In 1878 citizens of Danville carried off the desks, bookcases, and books of Central Normal College at Ladoga, and re-established it in Danville.
Population: 6,418 (2000); Race: 97.8% White, 0.0% Black, 1.2% Asian, 0.4% American Indian and Alaska Native, 1.1% Hispanic of any race, 0.7% two or more races (2000); Density: 1,047.7 persons per square mile (2000); Age: 28.6% under 18, 13.1% over 64 (2000); Marriage status: 21.2% never married, 61.8% now married, 8.2% widowed, 8.8% divorced (2000); Foreign born: 1.6% (2000); Ancestry (includes multiple ancestries): 24.9% United States or American, 15.6% German, 15.2% Irish, 10.8% English, 6.5% Other groups (2000).
Economy: Single-family building permits issued: 93 (2001) / 94 (2000); Multi-family building permits issued: 10 (2001) / 34 (2000); Employment by occupation: 8.1% management, 18.7% professional, 13.1% services, 32.2% sales, 1.0% farming, 12.6% construction, 14.4% production (2000).
Income: Per capita income: $22,209 (2000); Median household income: $54,330 (2000); Poverty rate: 2.5% (2000).
Taxes: Total city taxes per capita: $193 (1997); City property taxes per capita: $135 (1997).
Education: High school graduation rate: 88.2% (2000); College graduation rate: 21.5% (2000).

School District(s)

Danville Community School Corp (PK-12)
2000 Enrollment: 2,183 317-745-2212

Housing: Homeownership rate: 73.5% (2000); Median home value: $125,500 (2000); Median rent: $467 per month (2000); Median age of housing: 31 years (2000).
Hospitals: Hendricks Community Hospital (160 beds)
Newspapers: The Republican (1 x week)
Transportation: Commute to work: 93.8% car, 0.0% public transportation, 0.2% walk, 4.8% work from home (2000); Travel time to work: 33.2% less than 15 minutes, 26.9% 15 to 30 minutes, 25.9% 30 to 45 minutes, 10.7% 45 to 60 minutes, 3.3% 60 minutes or more (2000)
Additional Information Contacts
Danville Chamber of Commerce 317-745-0670

LIZTON (town). Covers a land area of 0.285 square miles and a water area of 0 square miles. Located at 39.88° N. Lat.; 86.54° W. Long. Elevation is 958 feet.
History: The area in which Lizton was established in 1851 was swamp land, but a drainage system converted it into fertile farm land. James Whitcomb Riley wrote about Lizton in his poem, "The Lizton Humorist."
Population: 372 (2000); Race: 99.0% White, 0.0% Black, 0.8% Asian, 0.0% American Indian and Alaska Native, 0.0% Hispanic of any race, 0.3% two or more races (2000); Density: 1,303.3 persons per square mile (2000); Age: 35.0% under 18, 7.3% over 64 (2000); Marriage status: 19.6% never married, 55.6% now married, 5.9% widowed, 18.9% divorced (2000); Foreign born: 2.3% (2000); Ancestry (includes multiple ancestries): 18.7% United States or American, 17.9% German, 10.4% English, 6.5% Irish, 6.2% Italian (2000).
Economy: Single-family building permits issued: 3 (2001) / 1 (2000); Multi-family building permits issued: 0 (2001) / 0 (2000); Employment by occupation: 5.3% management, 14.3% professional, 15.9% services, 29.1% sales, 0.0% farming, 14.3% construction, 21.2% production (2000).
Income: Per capita income: $20,269 (2000); Median household income: $40,694 (2000); Poverty rate: 3.1% (2000).
Taxes: Total city taxes per capita: $83 (1997); City property taxes per capita: $79 (1997).
Education: High school graduation rate: 89.0% (2000); College graduation rate: 11.4% (2000).

School District(s)

North West Hendricks Schools (KG-12)
2000 Enrollment: 1,480 317-994-4100

Housing: Homeownership rate: 61.7% (2000); Median home value: $92,600 (2000); Median rent: $428 per month (2000); Median age of housing: 58 years (2000).
Transportation: Commute to work: 99.5% car, 0.0% public transportation, 0.0% walk, 0.5% work from home (2000); Travel time to work: 10.9% less than 15 minutes, 44.3% 15 to 30 minutes, 16.9% 30 to 45 minutes, 19.1% 45 to 60 minutes, 8.7% 60 minutes or more (2000)

NORTH SALEM (town). Covers a land area of 0.262 square miles and a water area of 0 square miles. Located at 39.85° N. Lat.; 86.64° W. Long. Elevation is 879 feet.
History: Laid out 1835.
Population: 591 (2000); Race: 99.7% White, 0.0% Black, 0.2% Asian, 0.0% American Indian and Alaska Native, 0.0% Hispanic of any race, 0.2% two or more races (2000); Density: 2,251.6 persons per square mile (2000); Age: 29.0% under 18, 11.7% over 64 (2000); Marriage status: 20.3% never married, 56.3% now married, 6.8% widowed, 16.7% divorced (2000); Foreign born: 0.2% (2000); Ancestry (includes multiple ancestries): 22.7% German, 14.9% English, 14.3% Irish, 11.7% United States or American, 9.6% Other groups (2000).
Economy: In agricultural area: corn, soybeans; hogs. Employment by occupation: 9.4% management, 14.6% professional, 12.0% services, 31.1% sales, 0.0% farming, 11.6% construction, 21.3% production (2000).
Income: Per capita income: $18,034 (2000); Median household income: $36,923 (2000); Poverty rate: 9.1% (2000).
Taxes: Total city taxes per capita: $197 (1997); City property taxes per capita: $197 (1997).
Education: High school graduation rate: 81.0% (2000); College graduation rate: 9.5% (2000).
Housing: Homeownership rate: 79.5% (2000); Median home value: $77,400 (2000); Median rent: $429 per month (2000); Median age of housing: 60+ years (2000).
Transportation: Commute to work: 92.2% car, 0.0% public transportation, 3.1% walk, 1.9% work from home (2000); Travel time to work: 21.7% less than 15 minutes, 23.3% 15 to 30 minutes, 26.9% 30 to 45 minutes, 15.4% 45 to 60 minutes, 12.6% 60 minutes or more (2000)

PITTSBORO (town). Covers a land area of 1.527 square miles and a water area of 0 square miles. Located at 39.86° N. Lat.; 86.46° W. Long. Elevation is 940 feet.
Population: 1,588 (2000); Race: 99.3% White, 0.1% Black, 0.0% Asian, 0.0% American Indian and Alaska Native, 0.8% Hispanic of any race, 0.5% two or more races (2000); Density: 1,040.0 persons per square mile (2000); Age: 28.6% under 18, 12.4% over 64 (2000); Marriage status: 17.5% never married, 65.9% now married, 7.3% widowed, 9.2% divorced (2000); Foreign born: 0.2% (2000); Ancestry (includes multiple ancestries): 31.6% United States or American, 16.9% German, 9.3% Irish, 6.5% English, 4.1% Other groups (2000).
Economy: Agricultural area: corn, soybeans; cattle, sheep, hogs. Single-family building permits issued: 95 (2001) / 74 (2000); Multi-family building permits issued: 0 (2001) / 0 (2000); Employment by occupation: 13.8% management, 18.4% professional, 11.3% services, 31.4% sales, 0.2% farming, 9.9% construction, 15.0% production (2000).
Income: Per capita income: $20,904 (2000); Median household income: $47,740 (2000); Poverty rate: 3.0% (2000).
Taxes: Total city taxes per capita: $266 (1997); City property taxes per capita: $170 (1997).
Education: High school graduation rate: 89.5% (2000); College graduation rate: 20.3% (2000).
Housing: Homeownership rate: 78.8% (2000); Median home value: $115,500 (2000); Median rent: $514 per month (2000); Median age of housing: 14 years (2000).
Transportation: Commute to work: 94.7% car, 0.2% public transportation, 1.1% walk, 3.2% work from home (2000); Travel time to work: 23.8% less than 15 minutes, 31.5% 15 to 30 minutes, 34.5% 30 to 45 minutes, 6.5% 45 to 60 minutes, 3.7% 60 minutes or more (2000)

PLAINFIELD (town). Covers a land area of 17.981 square miles and a water area of 0.047 square miles. Located at 39.69° N. Lat.; 86.38° W. Long. Elevation is 739 feet.
History: Plainfield, which called itself the Village of Friendly Folk, developed as the headquarters of the Society of Friends. It was in Plainfield in 1842 that Martin Van Buren, campaigning for the 1844 election, was dumped into a mudhole when his carriage was purposely upset by residents who wanted him to pay attention to the need for road improvements.
Population: 18,396 (2000); Race: 94.4% White, 2.5% Black, 0.5% Asian, 0.4% American Indian and Alaska Native, 1.4% Hispanic of any race, 1.4% two or more races (2000); Density: 1,023.1 persons per square mile (2000); Age: 27.3% under 18, 12.4% over 64 (2000); Marriage status: 22.4% never married, 58.5% now married, 6.3% widowed, 12.8% divorced (2000); Foreign born: 1.5% (2000); Ancestry (includes multiple ancestries): 23.7% German, 17.2% United States or American, 12.0% Irish, 11.9% English, 9.9% Other groups (2000).
Vital Statistics: Birth rate: 151.7 per 10,000 population (1998)
Economy: Single-family building permits issued: 453 (2001) / 454 (2000); Multi-family building permits issued: 26 (2001) / 34 (2000); Employment by occupation: 11.4% management, 15.5% professional, 14.3% services, 30.5% sales, 0.0% farming, 12.2% construction, 16.1% production (2000).
Income: Per capita income: $21,083 (2000); Median household income: $46,782 (2000); Poverty rate: 5.2% (2000).
Taxes: Total city taxes per capita: $252 (1997); City property taxes per capita: $155 (1997).
Education: High school graduation rate: 83.7% (2000); College graduation rate: 18.2% (2000).

School District(s)

Plainfield Community Sch Corp (KG-12)
2000 Enrollment: 3,766 317-839-2578

Housing: Homeownership rate: 68.9% (2000); Median home value: $124,900 (2000); Median rent: $545 per month (2000); Median age of housing: 23 years (2000).
Safety: Violent crime rate: 13.5 per 10,000 population; Property crime rate: 458.4 per 10,000 population (2001).
Newspapers: Hendricks County Flyer (1 x week)
Transportation: Commute to work: 93.9% car, 0.0% public transportation, 1.3% walk, 3.2% work from home (2000); Travel time to work: 34.5% less than 15 minutes, 31.9% 15 to 30 minutes, 25.4% 30 to 45 minutes, 5.4% 45 to 60 minutes, 2.9% 60 minutes or more (2000)
Additional Information Contacts
Plainfield Chamber of Commerce 317-839-7222

STILESVILLE (town). Covers a land area of 0.282 square miles and a water area of 0 square miles. Located at 39.64° N. Lat.; 86.63° W. Long. Elevation is 795 feet.
History: Laid out 1828.
Population: 261 (2000); Race: 99.3% White, 0.7% Black, 0.0% Asian, 0.0% American Indian and Alaska Native, 0.7% Hispanic of any race, 0.0% two or more races (2000); Density: 925.7 persons per square mile (2000); Age: 19.3% under 18, 18.2% over 64 (2000); Marriage status: 15.2% never married, 65.0% now married, 10.1% widowed, 9.7% divorced (2000); Foreign born: 0.0% (2000); Ancestry (includes multiple ancestries): 22.5% United States or American, 14.0% English, 13.7% German, 11.2% Irish, 8.4% European (2000).
Economy: In agricultural area: corn, soybeans; hogs, cattle. Employment by occupation: 11.8% management, 9.0% professional, 10.4% services, 20.1% sales, 2.1% farming, 20.8% construction, 25.7% production (2000).
Income: Per capita income: $20,494 (2000); Median household income: $37,857 (2000); Poverty rate: 0.0% (2000).
Taxes: Total city taxes per capita: $53 (1997); City property taxes per capita: $47 (1997).
Education: High school graduation rate: 79.6% (2000); College graduation rate: 8.2% (2000).
Housing: Homeownership rate: 74.6% (2000); Median home value: $83,600 (2000); Median rent: $438 per month (2000); Median age of housing: 48 years (2000).
Transportation: Commute to work: 96.5% car, 0.0% public transportation, 0.0% walk, 0.0% work from home (2000); Travel time to work: 15.3% less than 15 minutes, 20.1% 15 to 30 minutes, 36.8% 30 to 45 minutes, 14.6% 45 to 60 minutes, 13.2% 60 minutes or more (2000)

Henry County

Located in eastern Indiana; drained by the Big Blue River, Flatrock and Fall Creeks. Covers a land area of 392.90 square miles, a water area of 2.00 square miles, and is located in the Eastern Time Zone. The county government was organized in 1821. County seat is New Castle.

Weather Station: New Castle 4 N — Elevation: 1,062 feet

	Jan	Feb	Mar	Apr	May	Jun	Jul	Aug	Sep	Oct	Nov	Dec
High	33	37	48	60	72	80	84	82	76	64	50	39
Low	16	19	29	38	48	58	62	60	53	41	32	23
Precip	2.2	2.2	3.0	4.0	4.6	4.6	4.7	3.5	2.8	3.0	3.6	2.8
Snow	na	na	2.2	0.3	tr	0.0	0.0	0.0	0.0	tr	0.8	na

High and Low temperatures in degrees Fahrenheit; Precipitation and Snow in inches

Population: 48,508 (2000); Race: 98.4% White, 0.7% Black, 0.1% Asian, 0.2% American Indian and Alaska Native, 0.8% Hispanic of any race, 0.4% two or more races (2000); Density: 123.5 persons per square mile (2000); Age: 24.1% under 18, 15.7% over 64 (2000).
Religion: Five largest groups: 4.6% Southern Baptist Convention, 4.6% Church of the Nazarene, 4.3% The United Methodist Church, 4.3% Christian Churches and Churches of Christ, 4.2% Christian Church (Disciples of Christ) (2000).
Economy: Unemployment rate: 5.3% (11/2002); Total civilian labor force: 23,460 (11/2002); Leading industries: 28.9% manufacturing; 18.1% retail trade; 17.0% health care and social assistance (2000); Companies that employ more than 1,000 persons: 1 (2000); Companies that employ more than 100 persons: 13 (2000); Farms: 770 totaling 177,601 acres (1997); Minority business ownership rate: 0.0% (1997); Women business ownership rate: 27.0% (1997); Retail sales per capita: $8,727 (1997). Single-family building permits issued: 136 (2001) / 175 (2000); Multi-family building permits issued: 90 (2001) / 34 (2000).
Income: Per capita income: $19,355 (2000); Median household income: $38,150 (2000); Poverty rate: 7.8% (2000); Bankruptcy rate: 9.73% (2001).
Taxes: Total county taxes per capita: $213 (2000); County property taxes per capita: $127 (2000).
Education: High school graduation rate: 79.6% (2000); College graduation rate: 11.7% (2000).
Housing: Homeownership rate: 77.1% (2000); Median home value: $84,100 (2000); Median rent: $367 per month (2000); Median age of housing: 45 years (2000).
Health: Birth rate: 125.6 per 10,000 population (1998); Age adjusted death rate: 87.7 per 10,000 population (1999); Age adjusted cancer mortality rate: 219.9 deaths per 100,000 population (1999). Number of physicians: 9.3 per 10,000 population (1999); Number of hospital beds: 22.1 per 10,000 population (1999).
Elections: 2000 Presidential election results: 41.8% Gore, 56.4% Bush, 0.1% Nader, 1.2% Buchanan
Additional Information Contacts
Henry County Government Offices 765-529-6401
Knightstown Chamber of Commerce 765-345-5290
New Castle Chamber of Commerce 765-529-5210

Henry County Communities

BLOUNTSVILLE (town). Covers a land area of 0.121 square miles and a water area of 0 square miles. Located at 40.06° N. Lat.; 85.23° W. Long. Elevation is 1,096 feet.
Population: 166 (2000); Race: 100.0% White, 0.0% Black, 0.0% Asian, 0.0% American Indian and Alaska Native, 0.0% Hispanic of any race, 0.0% two or more races (2000); Density: 1,372.9 persons per square mile (2000); Age: 40.0% under 18, 10.0% over 64 (2000); Marriage status: 7.3% never married, 73.6% now married, 1.8% widowed, 17.3% divorced (2000); Foreign born: 0.0% (2000); Ancestry (includes multiple ancestries): 26.1% United States or American, 19.4% German, 10.6% Other groups, 0.6% English, 0.6% Swiss (2000).
Economy: In agricultural area. Employment by occupation: 0.0% management, 6.6% professional, 14.8% services, 9.8% sales, 0.0% farming, 21.3% construction, 47.5% production (2000).
Income: Per capita income: $11,382 (2000); Median household income: $31,023 (2000); Poverty rate: 8.9% (2000).
Taxes: Total city taxes per capita: $37 (1997); City property taxes per capita: $31 (1997).
Education: High school graduation rate: 84.5% (2000); College graduation rate: 0.0% (2000).
Housing: Homeownership rate: 81.8% (2000); Median home value: $45,000 (2000); Median rent: $313 per month (2000); Median age of housing: 58 years (2000).
Transportation: Commute to work: 100.0% car, 0.0% public transportation, 0.0% walk, 0.0% work from home (2000); Travel time to work: 0.0% less than 15 minutes, 24.0% 15 to 30 minutes, 54.0% 30 to 45 minutes, 2.0% 45 to 60 minutes, 20.0% 60 minutes or more (2000)

CADIZ (town). Covers a land area of 0.145 square miles and a water area of 0 square miles. Located at 39.95° N. Lat.; 85.48° W. Long. Elevation is 1,074 feet.
Population: 161 (2000); Race: 96.9% White, 0.0% Black, 0.0% Asian, 0.0% American Indian and Alaska Native, 3.1% Hispanic of any race, 0.0% two or more races (2000); Density: 1,106.9 persons per square mile (2000); Age: 25.6% under 18, 5.6% over 64 (2000); Marriage status: 32.5% never married, 48.8% now married, 7.3% widowed, 11.4% divorced (2000); Foreign born: 2.5% (2000); Ancestry (includes multiple ancestries): 26.9% United States or American, 12.5% German, 10.0% Irish, 6.9% French (except Basque), 6.3% Other groups (2000).
Economy: In agricultural area. Employment by occupation: 4.8% management, 22.9% professional, 31.3% services, 10.8% sales, 0.0% farming, 10.8% construction, 19.3% production (2000).
Income: Per capita income: $12,013 (2000); Median household income: $42,813 (2000); Poverty rate: 13.1% (2000).
Taxes: Total city taxes per capita: $24 (1997); City property taxes per capita: $19 (1997).
Education: High school graduation rate: 78.3% (2000); College graduation rate: 6.0% (2000).
Housing: Homeownership rate: 68.6% (2000); Median home value: $61,500 (2000); Median rent: $306 per month (2000); Median age of housing: 53 years (2000).
Transportation: Commute to work: 100.0% car, 0.0% public transportation, 0.0% walk, 0.0% work from home (2000); Travel time to work: 24.4% less than 15 minutes, 45.1% 15 to 30 minutes, 29.3% 30 to 45 minutes, 1.2% 45 to 60 minutes, 0.0% 60 minutes or more (2000)

DUNREITH (town). Covers a land area of 0.140 square miles and a water area of 0 square miles. Located at 39.80° N. Lat.; 85.43° W. Long. Elevation is 1,036 feet.
History: Dunreith developed around the Pennsylvania Railroad station.
Population: 184 (2000); Race: 100.0% White, 0.0% Black, 0.0% Asian, 0.0% American Indian and Alaska Native, 1.8% Hispanic of any race, 0.0% two or more races (2000); Density: 1,316.7 persons per square mile (2000); Age: 20.6% under 18, 14.1% over 64 (2000); Marriage status: 23.6% never married, 58.8% now married, 5.4% widowed, 12.2% divorced (2000); Foreign born: 0.0% (2000); Ancestry (includes multiple ancestries): 31.8%

United States or American, 20.0% German, 10.6% English, 7.6% Irish, 5.3% French (except Basque) (2000).
Economy: Employment by occupation: 6.5% management, 19.4% professional, 9.7% services, 30.1% sales, 0.0% farming, 6.5% construction, 28.0% production (2000).
Income: Per capita income: $20,697 (2000); Median household income: $39,250 (2000); Poverty rate: 4.7% (2000).
Taxes: Total city taxes per capita: $190 (2000); City property taxes per capita: $125 (2000).
Education: High school graduation rate: 76.2% (2000); College graduation rate: 11.5% (2000).
Housing: Homeownership rate: 73.0% (2000); Median home value: $64,600 (2000); Median rent: $333 per month (2000); Median age of housing: 56 years (2000).
Transportation: Commute to work: 81.6% car, 0.0% public transportation, 13.8% walk, 4.6% work from home (2000); Travel time to work: 26.5% less than 15 minutes, 50.6% 15 to 30 minutes, 0.0% 30 to 45 minutes, 15.7% 45 to 60 minutes, 7.2% 60 minutes or more (2000)

GREENSBORO (town). Covers a land area of 0.122 square miles and a water area of 0 square miles. Located at 39.87° N. Lat.; 85.46° W. Long. Elevation is 1,000 feet.
Population: 174 (2000); Race: 100.0% White, 0.0% Black, 0.0% Asian, 0.0% American Indian and Alaska Native, 0.0% Hispanic of any race, 0.0% two or more races (2000); Density: 1,424.3 persons per square mile (2000); Age: 19.8% under 18, 15.9% over 64 (2000); Marriage status: 14.4% never married, 63.0% now married, 16.4% widowed, 6.2% divorced (2000); Foreign born: 0.0% (2000); Ancestry (includes multiple ancestries): 15.4% United States or American, 8.8% Other groups, 7.7% German, 4.9% English, 4.4% British (2000).
Economy: Agricultural area. Employment by occupation: 2.6% management, 3.9% professional, 27.3% services, 19.5% sales, 0.0% farming, 15.6% construction, 31.2% production (2000).
Income: Per capita income: $14,118 (2000); Median household income: $24,375 (2000); Poverty rate: 5.5% (2000).
Taxes: Total city taxes per capita: $33 (1997); City property taxes per capita: $24 (1997).
Education: High school graduation rate: 65.2% (2000); College graduation rate: 0.0% (2000).
Housing: Homeownership rate: 81.4% (2000); Median home value: $68,400 (2000); Median rent: $214 per month (2000); Median age of housing: 60+ years (2000).
Transportation: Commute to work: 96.1% car, 0.0% public transportation, 0.0% walk, 3.9% work from home (2000); Travel time to work: 29.7% less than 15 minutes, 33.8% 15 to 30 minutes, 10.8% 30 to 45 minutes, 12.2% 45 to 60 minutes, 13.5% 60 minutes or more (2000)

KENNARD (town). Covers a land area of 0.290 square miles and a water area of 0 square miles. Located at 39.90° N. Lat.; 85.51° W. Long. Elevation is 1,041 feet.
Population: 455 (2000); Race: 99.8% White, 0.0% Black, 0.0% Asian, 0.0% American Indian and Alaska Native, 0.0% Hispanic of any race, 0.2% two or more races (2000); Density: 1,568.5 persons per square mile (2000); Age: 35.1% under 18, 15.9% over 64 (2000); Marriage status: 18.4% never married, 60.2% now married, 10.7% widowed, 10.7% divorced (2000); Foreign born: 0.2% (2000); Ancestry (includes multiple ancestries): 16.9% German, 12.9% United States or American, 10.9% Irish, 9.2% Other groups, 8.5% English (2000).
Economy: In agricultural area. Employment by occupation: 10.9% management, 9.6% professional, 10.9% services, 24.4% sales, 0.0% farming, 10.3% construction, 34.0% production (2000).
Income: Per capita income: $14,139 (2000); Median household income: $31,364 (2000); Poverty rate: 10.0% (2000).
Taxes: Total city taxes per capita: $71 (1997); City property taxes per capita: $53 (1997).
Education: High school graduation rate: 78.9% (2000); College graduation rate: 5.0% (2000).
Housing: Homeownership rate: 88.7% (2000); Median home value: $72,200 (2000); Median rent: $338 per month (2000); Median age of housing: 52 years (2000).
Transportation: Commute to work: 94.9% car, 0.0% public transportation, 0.0% walk, 3.8% work from home (2000); Travel time to work: 15.3% less than 15 minutes, 40.0% 15 to 30 minutes, 20.0% 30 to 45 minutes, 10.7% 45 to 60 minutes, 14.0% 60 minutes or more (2000)

KNIGHTSTOWN (town). Covers a land area of 0.710 square miles and a water area of 0 square miles. Located at 39.79° N. Lat.; 85.52° W. Long. Elevation is 938 feet.
History: Knightstown was named for John Knight, an engineer who was involved in the construction of the National Road here.
Population: 2,148 (2000); Race: 100.0% White, 0.0% Black, 0.0% Asian, 0.0% American Indian and Alaska Native, 0.0% Hispanic of any race, 0.0% two or more races (2000); Density: 3,026.2 persons per square mile (2000); Age: 24.1% under 18, 19.5% over 64 (2000); Marriage status: 18.5% never married, 57.1% now married, 8.7% widowed, 15.7% divorced (2000); Foreign born: 0.2% (2000); Ancestry (includes multiple ancestries): 24.1% German, 15.9% English, 12.1% Irish, 10.5% United States or American, 10.4% Other groups (2000).
Economy: Single-family building permits issued: 5 (2001) / 2 (2000); Multi-family building permits issued: 0 (2001) / 0 (2000); Employment by occupation: 8.5% management, 10.9% professional, 15.8% services, 24.2% sales, 0.8% farming, 10.9% construction, 28.9% production (2000).
Income: Per capita income: $22,466 (2000); Median household income: $35,639 (2000); Poverty rate: 7.1% (2000).
Taxes: Total city taxes per capita: $166 (1997); City property taxes per capita: $115 (1997).
Education: High school graduation rate: 83.5% (2000); College graduation rate: 10.9% (2000).

School District(s)

C A Beard Memorial School Corp (KG-12)
2000 Enrollment: 1,411 765-345-5101
Housing: Homeownership rate: 68.3% (2000); Median home value: $86,300 (2000); Median rent: $319 per month (2000); Median age of housing: 60+ years (2000).
Transportation: Commute to work: 96.2% car, 0.0% public transportation, 2.4% walk, 1.3% work from home (2000); Travel time to work: 25.1% less than 15 minutes, 30.6% 15 to 30 minutes, 16.0% 30 to 45 minutes, 18.8% 45 to 60 minutes, 9.5% 60 minutes or more (2000)
Additional Information Contacts
Knightstown Chamber of Commerce. 765-345-5290

LEWISVILLE (town). Covers a land area of 0.327 square miles and a water area of 0 square miles. Located at 39.80° N. Lat.; 85.35° W. Long. Elevation is 1,050 feet.
History: Laid out 1829.
Population: 395 (2000); Race: 99.3% White, 0.0% Black, 0.7% Asian, 0.0% American Indian and Alaska Native, 0.0% Hispanic of any race, 0.0% two or more races (2000); Density: 1,206.4 persons per square mile (2000); Age: 30.4% under 18, 14.5% over 64 (2000); Marriage status: 22.3% never married, 58.6% now married, 6.1% widowed, 13.1% divorced (2000); Foreign born: 1.4% (2000); Ancestry (includes multiple ancestries): 38.6% United States or American, 8.7% Irish, 8.7% German, 6.3% Other groups, 4.1% English (2000).
Economy: In agricultural area. Employment by occupation: 6.3% management, 9.8% professional, 17.8% services, 24.1% sales, 1.7% farming, 9.2% construction, 31.0% production (2000).
Income: Per capita income: $15,476 (2000); Median household income: $37,841 (2000); Poverty rate: 8.3% (2000).
Taxes: Total city taxes per capita: $53 (1997); City property taxes per capita: $40 (1997).
Education: High school graduation rate: 75.6% (2000); College graduation rate: 7.9% (2000).
Housing: Homeownership rate: 75.8% (2000); Median home value: $62,100 (2000); Median rent: $383 per month (2000); Median age of housing: 60+ years (2000).
Transportation: Commute to work: 90.1% car, 0.0% public transportation, 4.3% walk, 4.3% work from home (2000); Travel time to work: 24.7% less than 15 minutes, 48.1% 15 to 30 minutes, 6.5% 30 to 45 minutes, 13.6% 45 to 60 minutes, 7.1% 60 minutes or more (2000)

MIDDLETOWN (town). Covers a land area of 1.101 square miles and a water area of 0 square miles. Located at 40.05° N. Lat.; 85.54° W. Long. Elevation is 965 feet.
History: Laid out 1829.
Population: 2,488 (2000); Race: 98.7% White, 0.0% Black, 0.4% Asian, 0.0% American Indian and Alaska Native, 0.8% Hispanic of any race, 0.7% two or more races (2000); Density: 2,260.4 persons per square mile (2000); Age: 26.2% under 18, 15.2% over 64 (2000); Marriage status: 19.0% never married, 54.3% now married, 10.4% widowed, 16.3% divorced (2000); Foreign born: 0.5% (2000); Ancestry (includes multiple ancestries): 23.3%

United States or American, 17.1% German, 10.7% Other groups, 9.7% Irish, 7.1% English (2000).
Economy: Livestock; grain, tomatoes. Manufacturing: bedding materials. Employment by occupation: 6.7% management, 11.7% professional, 17.4% services, 29.7% sales, 0.0% farming, 17.7% construction, 16.8% production (2000).
Income: Per capita income: $16,017 (2000); Median household income: $32,591 (2000); Poverty rate: 8.2% (2000).
Taxes: Total city taxes per capita: $131 (1997); City property taxes per capita: $86 (1997).
Education: High school graduation rate: 81.4% (2000); College graduation rate: 10.3% (2000).

School District(s)

Shenandoah School Corporation (KG-12)
2000 Enrollment: 1,389 765-354-2266
Housing: Homeownership rate: 67.4% (2000); Median home value: $73,100 (2000); Median rent: $381 per month (2000); Median age of housing: 46 years (2000).
Newspapers: The Middletown News (1 x week)
Transportation: Commute to work: 91.9% car, 0.4% public transportation, 2.4% walk, 3.8% work from home (2000); Travel time to work: 25.7% less than 15 minutes, 39.8% 15 to 30 minutes, 12.7% 30 to 45 minutes, 10.2% 45 to 60 minutes, 11.5% 60 minutes or more (2000)

MOORELAND (town). Covers a land area of 0.140 square miles and a water area of 0 square miles. Located at 39.99° N. Lat.; 85.25° W. Long. Elevation is 1,124 feet.
History: Mooreland was named for early settler Philip Moore.
Population: 393 (2000); Race: 100.0% White, 0.0% Black, 0.0% Asian, 0.0% American Indian and Alaska Native, 0.0% Hispanic of any race, 0.0% two or more races (2000); Density: 2,800.5 persons per square mile (2000); Age: 29.8% under 18, 15.8% over 64 (2000); Marriage status: 16.0% never married, 67.6% now married, 6.0% widowed, 10.3% divorced (2000); Foreign born: 0.0% (2000); Ancestry (includes multiple ancestries): 15.3% United States or American, 12.0% German, 10.4% English, 10.2% Other groups, 8.9% Irish (2000).
Economy: Employment by occupation: 4.9% management, 8.6% professional, 19.6% services, 20.9% sales, 1.8% farming, 13.5% construction, 30.7% production (2000).
Income: Per capita income: $13,176 (2000); Median household income: $35,556 (2000); Poverty rate: 10.2% (2000).
Taxes: Total city taxes per capita: $64 (1997); City property taxes per capita: $50 (1997).
Education: High school graduation rate: 75.8% (2000); College graduation rate: 6.6% (2000).
Housing: Homeownership rate: 83.3% (2000); Median home value: $59,700 (2000); Median rent: $304 per month (2000); Median age of housing: 60 years (2000).
Transportation: Commute to work: 100.0% car, 0.0% public transportation, 0.0% walk, 0.0% work from home (2000); Travel time to work: 10.7% less than 15 minutes, 40.7% 15 to 30 minutes, 30.7% 30 to 45 minutes, 10.7% 45 to 60 minutes, 7.3% 60 minutes or more (2000)

MOUNT SUMMIT (town). Covers a land area of 0.179 square miles and a water area of 0 square miles. Located at 40.00° N. Lat.; 85.38° W. Long. Elevation is 1,097 feet.
History: Mount Summit is at one of the highest elevations in Henry County.
Population: 313 (2000); Race: 100.0% White, 0.0% Black, 0.0% Asian, 0.0% American Indian and Alaska Native, 5.3% Hispanic of any race, 0.0% two or more races (2000); Density: 1,747.0 persons per square mile (2000); Age: 24.6% under 18, 9.6% over 64 (2000); Marriage status: 20.5% never married, 64.0% now married, 5.4% widowed, 10.0% divorced (2000); Foreign born: 0.0% (2000); Ancestry (includes multiple ancestries): 16.9% United States or American, 12.0% German, 11.0% Irish, 10.3% Other groups, 6.3% English (2000).
Economy: Employment by occupation: 13.8% management, 12.6% professional, 13.2% services, 22.2% sales, 0.0% farming, 20.4% construction, 18.0% production (2000).
Income: Per capita income: $20,895 (2000); Median household income: $48,000 (2000); Poverty rate: 5.3% (2000).
Taxes: Total city taxes per capita: $53 (1997); City property taxes per capita: $53 (1997).
Education: High school graduation rate: 90.9% (2000); College graduation rate: 19.1% (2000).

School District(s)

Blue River Valley Schools (PK-12)
2000 Enrollment: 845 765-836-4816
Housing: Homeownership rate: 80.0% (2000); Median home value: $69,300 (2000); Median rent: $340 per month (2000); Median age of housing: 50 years (2000).
Transportation: Commute to work: 89.7% car, 0.0% public transportation, 7.9% walk, 2.4% work from home (2000); Travel time to work: 37.9% less than 15 minutes, 40.4% 15 to 30 minutes, 9.3% 30 to 45 minutes, 9.3% 45 to 60 minutes, 3.1% 60 minutes or more (2000)

NEW CASTLE (city). Covers a land area of 5.951 square miles and a water area of 0 square miles. Located at 39.92° N. Lat.; 85.36° W. Long. Elevation is 1,058 feet.
History: New Castle was the birthplace in 1867 of Wilbur Wright, who with his brother Orville flew the first heavier-than-air craft in 1903 in North Carolina. New Castle developed as an industrial city.
Population: 17,780 (2000); Race: 96.8% White, 1.6% Black, 0.2% Asian, 0.4% American Indian and Alaska Native, 1.0% Hispanic of any race, 0.6% two or more races (2000); Density: 2,987.5 persons per square mile (2000); Age: 23.4% under 18, 17.1% over 64 (2000); Marriage status: 21.4% never married, 54.1% now married, 10.5% widowed, 13.9% divorced (2000); Foreign born: 0.6% (2000); Ancestry (includes multiple ancestries): 21.9% United States or American, 11.7% German, 9.3% English, 9.2% Other groups, 7.6% Irish (2000).
Vital Statistics: Birth rate: 155.2 per 10,000 population (1998)
Economy: Single-family building permits issued: 13 (2001) / 25 (2000); Multi-family building permits issued: 90 (2001) / 34 (2000); Employment by occupation: 6.8% management, 14.3% professional, 20.4% services, 21.2% sales, 0.1% farming, 11.0% construction, 26.3% production (2000).
Income: Per capita income: $17,587 (2000); Median household income: $30,688 (2000); Poverty rate: 12.4% (2000).
Taxes: Total city taxes per capita: $334 (1997); City property taxes per capita: $210 (1997).
Education: High school graduation rate: 72.8% (2000); College graduation rate: 10.2% (2000).

School District(s)

New Castle Community Sch Corp (PK-12)
2000 Enrollment: 3,974 765-521-7201
Housing: Homeownership rate: 65.9% (2000); Median home value: $67,900 (2000); Median rent: $360 per month (2000); Median age of housing: 49 years (2000).
Hospitals: Henry County Memorial Hospital (107 beds)
Safety: Violent crime rate: 7.8 per 10,000 population; Property crime rate: 1,023.5 per 10,000 population (2001).
Newspapers: The Courier-Times (6 x week)
Transportation: Commute to work: 94.7% car, 0.2% public transportation, 2.7% walk, 1.6% work from home (2000); Travel time to work: 56.7% less than 15 minutes, 14.1% 15 to 30 minutes, 13.4% 30 to 45 minutes, 7.4% 45 to 60 minutes, 8.3% 60 minutes or more (2000)
Additional Information Contacts
New Castle Chamber of Commerce. 765-529-5210

SPICELAND (town). Covers a land area of 0.439 square miles and a water area of 0 square miles. Located at 39.83° N. Lat.; 85.43° W. Long. Elevation is 1,050 feet.
History: Spiceland was settled in 1828 by a group of Quakers from North Carolina. From Spiceland Academy, founded in 1834, came historian Charles Austin Beard.
Population: 807 (2000); Race: 98.4% White, 0.0% Black, 0.0% Asian, 0.9% American Indian and Alaska Native, 0.5% Hispanic of any race, 0.7% two or more races (2000); Density: 1,838.6 persons per square mile (2000); Age: 25.5% under 18, 11.4% over 64 (2000); Marriage status: 18.2% never married, 65.3% now married, 9.5% widowed, 7.0% divorced (2000); Foreign born: 0.5% (2000); Ancestry (includes multiple ancestries): 20.5% German, 13.2% United States or American, 11.2% English, 6.7% Irish, 5.5% Other groups (2000).
Economy: Employment by occupation: 8.9% management, 14.8% professional, 14.3% services, 19.4% sales, 0.0% farming, 10.5% construction, 32.1% production (2000).
Income: Per capita income: $20,419 (2000); Median household income: $45,875 (2000); Poverty rate: 2.5% (2000).
Taxes: Total city taxes per capita: $72 (1997); City property taxes per capita: $53 (1997).
Education: High school graduation rate: 88.3% (2000); College graduation rate: 12.5% (2000).

School District(s)

South Henry School Corp (KG-12)
2000 Enrollment: 838 765-987-7882

Housing: Homeownership rate: 80.0% (2000); Median home value: $75,800 (2000); Median rent: $375 per month (2000); Median age of housing: 58 years (2000).

Transportation: Commute to work: 95.2% car, 0.0% public transportation, 2.1% walk, 2.1% work from home (2000); Travel time to work: 37.6% less than 15 minutes, 26.7% 15 to 30 minutes, 9.5% 30 to 45 minutes, 13.9% 45 to 60 minutes, 12.3% 60 minutes or more (2000)

SPRINGPORT (town). Covers a land area of 0.133 square miles and a water area of 0 square miles. Located at 40.04° N. Lat.; 85.39° W. Long. Elevation is 1,050 feet.

Population: 174 (2000); Race: 96.8% White, 0.0% Black, 0.0% Asian, 0.0% American Indian and Alaska Native, 0.0% Hispanic of any race, 3.2% two or more races (2000); Density: 1,309.1 persons per square mile (2000); Age: 31.8% under 18, 14.6% over 64 (2000); Marriage status: 19.4% never married, 66.1% now married, 2.4% widowed, 12.1% divorced (2000); Foreign born: 0.0% (2000); Ancestry (includes multiple ancestries): 20.4% German, 16.6% United States or American, 11.5% English, 9.6% Other groups, 8.9% Irish (2000).

Economy: In agricultural area. Employment by occupation: 14.3% management, 18.6% professional, 24.3% services, 11.4% sales, 0.0% farming, 10.0% construction, 21.4% production (2000).

Income: Per capita income: $17,217 (2000); Median household income: $43,125 (2000); Poverty rate: 9.6% (2000).

Taxes: Total city taxes per capita: $60 (1997); City property taxes per capita: $45 (1997).

Education: High school graduation rate: 79.8% (2000); College graduation rate: 10.1% (2000).

Housing: Homeownership rate: 77.3% (2000); Median home value: $76,000 (2000); Median rent: $317 per month (2000); Median age of housing: 60+ years (2000).

Transportation: Commute to work: 92.9% car, 0.0% public transportation, 4.3% walk, 2.9% work from home (2000); Travel time to work: 10.3% less than 15 minutes, 63.2% 15 to 30 minutes, 5.9% 30 to 45 minutes, 7.4% 45 to 60 minutes, 13.2% 60 minutes or more (2000)

STRAUGHN (town). Covers a land area of 0.140 square miles and a water area of 0 square miles. Located at 39.80° N. Lat.; 85.29° W. Long. Elevation is 1,080 feet.

Population: 263 (2000); Race: 99.6% White, 0.0% Black, 0.0% Asian, 0.0% American Indian and Alaska Native, 0.4% Hispanic of any race, 0.0% two or more races (2000); Density: 1,882.2 persons per square mile (2000); Age: 28.1% under 18, 13.5% over 64 (2000); Marriage status: 29.0% never married, 61.1% now married, 7.7% widowed, 2.3% divorced (2000); Foreign born: 0.4% (2000); Ancestry (includes multiple ancestries): 18.5% English, 14.6% German, 10.7% United States or American, 10.7% Irish, 5.0% Dutch (2000).

Economy: In agricultural area. Employment by occupation: 9.2% management, 16.9% professional, 16.9% services, 26.2% sales, 2.3% farming, 4.6% construction, 23.8% production (2000).

Income: Per capita income: $13,693 (2000); Median household income: $31,944 (2000); Poverty rate: 15.3% (2000).

Taxes: Total city taxes per capita: $42 (1997); City property taxes per capita: $30 (1997).

Education: High school graduation rate: 74.9% (2000); College graduation rate: 9.9% (2000).

Housing: Homeownership rate: 94.1% (2000); Median home value: $64,200 (2000); Median rent: <$100 per month (2000); Median age of housing: 60+ years (2000).

Transportation: Commute to work: 98.5% car, 0.0% public transportation, 1.5% walk, 0.0% work from home (2000); Travel time to work: 24.6% less than 15 minutes, 47.7% 15 to 30 minutes, 16.2% 30 to 45 minutes, 4.6% 45 to 60 minutes, 6.9% 60 minutes or more (2000)

SULPHUR SPRINGS (town). Covers a land area of 0.302 square miles and a water area of 0 square miles. Located at 40.00° N. Lat.; 85.44° W. Long. Elevation is 1,055 feet.

History: Laid out 1853.

Population: 346 (2000); Race: 99.4% White, 0.0% Black, 0.0% Asian, 0.0% American Indian and Alaska Native, 0.0% Hispanic of any race, 0.6% two or more races (2000); Density: 1,145.0 persons per square mile (2000); Age: 22.4% under 18, 18.6% over 64 (2000); Marriage status: 14.5% never married, 69.3% now married, 10.5% widowed, 5.7% divorced (2000); Foreign born: 0.0% (2000); Ancestry (includes multiple ancestries): 28.3% United States or American, 19.7% German, 10.8% English, 7.2% Irish, 3.3% Other groups (2000).

Economy: In agricultural area. Employment by occupation: 6.8% management, 23.7% professional, 15.8% services, 19.2% sales, 0.0% farming, 13.6% construction, 20.9% production (2000).

Income: Per capita income: $19,838 (2000); Median household income: $46,328 (2000); Poverty rate: 3.9% (2000).

Taxes: Total city taxes per capita: $64 (1997); City property taxes per capita: $45 (1997).

Education: High school graduation rate: 82.4% (2000); College graduation rate: 12.1% (2000).

Housing: Homeownership rate: 91.2% (2000); Median home value: $75,300 (2000); Median rent: $335 per month (2000); Median age of housing: 50 years (2000).

Transportation: Commute to work: 94.4% car, 0.0% public transportation, 1.7% walk, 4.0% work from home (2000); Travel time to work: 29.4% less than 15 minutes, 41.8% 15 to 30 minutes, 22.4% 30 to 45 minutes, 3.5% 45 to 60 minutes, 2.9% 60 minutes or more (2000)

Howard County

Located in central Indiana; drained by Wildcat Creek. Covers a land area of 293.10 square miles, a water area of 0.90 square miles, and is located in the Eastern Time Zone. The county government was organized in 1844. County seat is Kokomo.

Howard County is part of the Kokomo, IN MSA. The entire metro area includes: Howard County; Tipton County

Weather Station: Kokomo 3 WSW — Elevation: 816 feet

	Jan	Feb	Mar	Apr	May	Jun	Jul	Aug	Sep	Oct	Nov	Dec
High	30	35	47	60	71	81	84	82	76	64	49	36
Low	14	18	27	37	48	58	62	59	51	40	31	21
Precip	2.5	2.3	3.3	3.9	4.0	3.9	4.5	4.2	3.1	3.1	3.7	3.1
Snow	13.2	10.3	6.1	1.4	tr	0.0	0.0	0.0	0.0	0.4	2.1	9.6

High and Low temperatures in degrees Fahrenheit; Precipitation and Snow in inches

Population: 84,964 (2000); Race: 90.0% White, 6.4% Black, 0.8% Asian, 0.4% American Indian and Alaska Native, 2.1% Hispanic of any race, 1.5% two or more races (2000); Density: 289.9 persons per square mile (2000); Age: 25.6% under 18, 13.4% over 64 (2000).

Religion: Five largest groups: 11.2% Catholic Church, 4.8% The United Methodist Church, 3.7% Christian Churches and Churches of Christ, 2.2% Christian Church (Disciples of Christ), 1.9% Independent, Non-Charismatic Churches (2000).

Economy: Unemployment rate: 5.4% (11/2002); Total civilian labor force: 41,003 (11/2002); Leading industries: 45.0% manufacturing; 13.1% retail trade; 10.5% health care and social assistance (2000); Companies that employ more than 1,000 persons: 4 (2000); Companies that employ more than 100 persons: 44 (2000); Farms: 486 totaling 147,750 acres (1997); Minority business ownership rate: 5.0% (1997); Women business ownership rate: 23.7% (1997); Retail sales per capita: $11,455 (1997). Single-family building permits issued: 335 (2001) / 374 (2000); Multi-family building permits issued: 47 (2001) / 34 (2000).

Income: Per capita income: $22,049 (2000); Median household income: $43,487 (2000); Poverty rate: 9.5% (2000); Bankruptcy rate: 7.93% (2001).

Taxes: Total county taxes per capita: $335 (2000); County property taxes per capita: $284 (2000).

Education: High school graduation rate: 83.3% (2000); College graduation rate: 18.1% (2000).

Housing: Homeownership rate: 71.7% (2000); Median home value: $89,000 (2000); Median rent: $432 per month (2000); Median age of housing: 37 years (2000).

Health: Birth rate: 137.0 per 10,000 population (1998); Age adjusted death rate: 99.2 per 10,000 population (1999); Age adjusted cancer mortality rate: 228.9 deaths per 100,000 population (1999). Number of physicians: 16.4 per 10,000 population (1999); Number of hospital beds: 43.8 per 10,000 population (1999).

Elections: 2000 Presidential election results: 37.8% Gore, 59.6% Bush, 1.0% Nader, 0.9% Buchanan

Additional Information Contacts

Howard County Government Offices. 765-456-2216
Kokomo Chamber of Commerce 765-457-5301
Realtors Association of Central Indiana. 765-457-0089

Howard County Communities

GREENTOWN (town). Covers a land area of 1.004 square miles and a water area of 0 square miles. Located at 40.47° N. Lat.; 85.96° W. Long. Elevation is 844 feet.

History: Greentown was named for Miami Chief Green. It was founded in 1848 by English, German, Scotch, and Dutch immigrants who received the land from the U.S. government.

Population: 2,546 (2000); Race: 98.9% White, 0.0% Black, 0.0% Asian, 0.7% American Indian and Alaska Native, 0.7% Hispanic of any race, 0.4% two or more races (2000); Density: 2,534.8 persons per square mile (2000); Age: 28.0% under 18, 14.4% over 64 (2000); Marriage status: 19.8% never married, 60.1% now married, 8.7% widowed, 11.4% divorced (2000); Foreign born: 0.0% (2000); Ancestry (includes multiple ancestries): 22.0% United States or American, 20.1% German, 12.7% Irish, 8.1% English, 7.2% Other groups (2000).

Economy: Single-family building permits issued: 4 (2001) / 4 (2000); Multi-family building permits issued: 0 (2001) / 0 (2000); Employment by occupation: 7.9% management, 14.4% professional, 16.2% services, 27.6% sales, 0.0% farming, 8.8% construction, 25.1% production (2000).

Income: Per capita income: $20,057 (2000); Median household income: $43,750 (2000); Poverty rate: 9.2% (2000).

Taxes: Total city taxes per capita: $106 (1997); City property taxes per capita: $86 (1997).

Education: High school graduation rate: 89.8% (2000); College graduation rate: 12.7% (2000).

School District(s)

Eastern Howard School Corp (KG-12)
2000 Enrollment: 1,373 765-628-3391

Housing: Homeownership rate: 72.9% (2000); Median home value: $88,800 (2000); Median rent: $375 per month (2000); Median age of housing: 37 years (2000).

Transportation: Commute to work: 94.9% car, 0.0% public transportation, 2.8% walk, 2.3% work from home (2000); Travel time to work: 29.1% less than 15 minutes, 53.7% 15 to 30 minutes, 7.4% 30 to 45 minutes, 1.7% 45 to 60 minutes, 8.1% 60 minutes or more (2000)

INDIAN HEIGHTS (CDP). Covers a land area of 0.861 square miles and a water area of 0 square miles. Located at 40.42° N. Lat.; 86.11° W. Long. Elevation is 870 feet.

Population: 3,274 (2000); Race: 93.7% White, 3.5% Black, 0.0% Asian, 0.4% American Indian and Alaska Native, 2.1% Hispanic of any race, 1.7% two or more races (2000); Density: 3,802.5 persons per square mile (2000); Age: 30.4% under 18, 10.7% over 64 (2000); Marriage status: 19.3% never married, 61.9% now married, 6.9% widowed, 12.0% divorced (2000); Foreign born: 0.6% (2000); Ancestry (includes multiple ancestries): 22.1% United States or American, 14.4% German, 12.9% Other groups, 10.7% Irish, 10.5% English (2000).

Economy: Employment by occupation: 6.0% management, 8.7% professional, 15.9% services, 25.5% sales, 0.0% farming, 10.3% construction, 33.5% production (2000).

Income: Per capita income: $18,062 (2000); Median household income: $45,444 (2000); Poverty rate: 4.6% (2000).

Education: High school graduation rate: 82.6% (2000); College graduation rate: 6.7% (2000).

Housing: Homeownership rate: 81.9% (2000); Median home value: $66,300 (2000); Median rent: $544 per month (2000); Median age of housing: 37 years (2000).

Transportation: Commute to work: 97.9% car, 0.0% public transportation, 0.5% walk, 1.7% work from home (2000); Travel time to work: 44.4% less than 15 minutes, 33.6% 15 to 30 minutes, 11.3% 30 to 45 minutes, 5.6% 45 to 60 minutes, 5.1% 60 minutes or more (2000)

KOKOMO (city). Covers a land area of 16.196 square miles and a water area of 0.059 square miles. Located at 40.48° N. Lat.; 86.13° W. Long. Elevation is 810 feet.

History: Kokomo was platted in 1844. The coming of the railroad in 1853 and the discovery of natural gas in 1886 brought growth to the town. Kokomo was named for a Miami chief.

Population: 46,113 (2000); Race: 85.5% White, 10.2% Black, 0.8% Asian, 0.4% American Indian and Alaska Native, 2.6% Hispanic of any race, 1.9% two or more races (2000); Density: 2,847.2 persons per square mile (2000); Age: 24.9% under 18, 14.3% over 64 (2000); Marriage status: 24.3% never married, 50.8% now married, 8.8% widowed, 16.1% divorced (2000); Foreign born: 2.0% (2000); Ancestry (includes multiple ancestries): 21.2% Other groups, 15.8% German, 15.1% United States or American, 8.8% Irish, 7.7% English (2000).

Vital Statistics: Birth rate: 190.4 per 10,000 population (1998)

Economy: Unemployment rate: 6.6% (11/2002); Total civilian labor force: 22,033 (11/2002); Single-family building permits issued: 206 (2001) / 198 (2000); Multi-family building permits issued: 28 (2001) / 22 (2000); Employment by occupation: 6.9% management, 16.8% professional, 17.3% services, 21.1% sales, 0.1% farming, 9.7% construction, 28.0% production (2000).

Income: Per capita income: $20,083 (2000); Median household income: $36,258 (2000); Poverty rate: 13.0% (2000).

Taxes: Total city taxes per capita: $515 (2000); City property taxes per capita: $382 (2000).

Education: High school graduation rate: 79.4% (2000); College graduation rate: 15.8% (2000).

School District(s)

Kokomo-Center Township Con Sch Corp (PK-12)
2000 Enrollment: 7,256 765-455-8000

Northwestern School Corp (KG-12)
2000 Enrollment: 1,761 765-454-2321

Taylor Community School Corp (KG-12)
2000 Enrollment: 1,511 765-453-3035

Four-year College(s)

Indiana University-Kokomo (Public)
2001 Enrollment: 2,741 765-453-2000
2001 Tuition: In-state $3,221; Out-of-state $8,520

Two-year College(s)

Ivy Tech State College-Kokomo (Public)
2001 Enrollment: 2,003 765-459-0561
2001 Tuition: In-state $1,986; Out-of-state $4,029

Housing: Homeownership rate: 60.9% (2000); Median home value: $74,000 (2000); Median rent: $426 per month (2000); Median age of housing: 43 years (2000).

Hospitals: Howard Community Hospital (115 beds); Saint Joseph Hospital & Health Center (156 beds)

Safety: Violent crime rate: 51.8 per 10,000 population; Property crime rate: 601.2 per 10,000 population (2001).

Newspapers: Kokomo Herald; The Kokomo Tribune (7 x week)

Transportation: Commute to work: 94.4% car, 0.5% public transportation, 2.2% walk, 1.8% work from home (2000); Travel time to work: 58.5% less than 15 minutes, 27.8% 15 to 30 minutes, 5.9% 30 to 45 minutes, 3.2% 45 to 60 minutes, 4.7% 60 minutes or more (2000)

Airports: Kokomo Municipal

Additional Information Contacts

Kokomo Chamber of Commerce 765-457-5301
Realtors Association of Central Indiana. 765-457-0089

RUSSIAVILLE (town). Covers a land area of 0.802 square miles and a water area of 0 square miles. Located at 40.41° N. Lat.; 86.27° W. Long. Elevation is 850 feet.

History: Laid out 1845.

Population: 1,092 (2000); Race: 99.0% White, 0.0% Black, 0.3% Asian, 0.3% American Indian and Alaska Native, 2.4% Hispanic of any race, 0.2% two or more races (2000); Density: 1,361.4 persons per square mile (2000); Age: 28.1% under 18, 12.6% over 64 (2000); Marriage status: 15.3% never married, 67.2% now married, 7.8% widowed, 9.7% divorced (2000); Foreign born: 0.7% (2000); Ancestry (includes multiple ancestries): 19.8% German, 16.4% United States or American, 13.1% English, 10.0% Other groups, 8.0% Irish (2000).

Economy: Corn, soybeans; hogs. Manufacturing: energy management equipment. Sawmill. Single-family building permits issued: 13 (2001) / 14 (2000); Multi-family building permits issued: 0 (2001) / 0 (2000); Employment by occupation: 4.2% management, 15.1% professional, 17.7% services, 21.2% sales, 0.0% farming, 9.7% construction, 32.1% production (2000).

Income: Per capita income: $20,804 (2000); Median household income: $40,875 (2000); Poverty rate: 5.7% (2000).

Taxes: Total city taxes per capita: $1,407 (1997); City property taxes per capita: $1,251 (1997).

Education: High school graduation rate: 87.6% (2000); College graduation rate: 11.0% (2000).

School District(s)

Western School Corp (KG-12)
2000 Enrollment: 2,210 765-883-5576

Housing: Homeownership rate: 83.4% (2000); Median home value: $82,600 (2000); Median rent: $358 per month (2000); Median age of housing: 36 years (2000).
Transportation: Commute to work: 94.6% car, 0.4% public transportation, 2.2% walk, 2.4% work from home (2000); Travel time to work: 25.6% less than 15 minutes, 47.4% 15 to 30 minutes, 16.4% 30 to 45 minutes, 3.1% 45 to 60 minutes, 7.6% 60 minutes or more (2000)

Huntington County

Located in northeast central Indiana; drained by the Wabash, Salamonie, and Little Rivers. Covers a land area of 382.60 square miles, a water area of 5.30 square miles, and is located in the Eastern Time Zone. The county government was organized in 1832. County seat is Huntington.

Huntington County is part of the Fort Wayne, IN MSA. The entire metro area includes: Adams County; Allen County; DeKalb County; Huntington County; Wells County; Whitley County

Population: 38,075 (2000); Race: 97.8% White, 0.3% Black, 0.3% Asian, 0.4% American Indian and Alaska Native, 1.1% Hispanic of any race, 0.9% two or more races (2000); Density: 99.5 persons per square mile (2000); Age: 26.2% under 18, 14.0% over 64 (2000).
Religion: Five largest groups: 13.2% Catholic Church, 7.7% The United Methodist Church, 4.7% The Salvation Army, 4.1% United Church of Christ, 3.8% Christian Churches and Churches of Christ (2000).
Economy: Unemployment rate: 6.4% (11/2002); Total civilian labor force: 20,854 (11/2002); Leading industries: 40.4% manufacturing; 12.3% retail trade; 10.1% health care and social assistance (2000); Companies that employ more than 1,000 persons: 0 (2000); Companies that employ more than 100 persons: 28 (2000); Farms: 651 totaling 184,137 acres (1997); Minority business ownership rate: 0.0% (1997); Women business ownership rate: 22.5% (1997); Retail sales per capita: $8,417 (1997). Single-family building permits issued: 150 (2001) / 153 (2000); Multi-family building permits issued: 0 (2001) / 0 (2000).
Income: Per capita income: $19,480 (2000); Median household income: $41,620 (2000); Poverty rate: 5.5% (2000); Bankruptcy rate: 7.37% (2001).
Taxes: Total county taxes per capita: $227 (2000); County property taxes per capita: $134 (2000).
Education: High school graduation rate: 85.0% (2000); College graduation rate: 14.2% (2000).
Housing: Homeownership rate: 77.0% (2000); Median home value: $81,600 (2000); Median rent: $406 per month (2000); Median age of housing: 47 years (2000).
Health: Birth rate: 134.2 per 10,000 population (1998); Age adjusted death rate: 90.9 per 10,000 population (1999); Age adjusted cancer mortality rate: 193.5 deaths per 100,000 population (1999). Air Quality Index: 61% good, 39% moderate, 0% unhealthy (percent of days in 2000). Number of physicians: 10.5 per 10,000 population (1999); Number of hospital beds: 6.3 per 10,000 population (1999).
Elections: 2000 Presidential election results: 28.2% Gore, 69.2% Bush, 1.1% Nader, 0.9% Buchanan
National and State Parks: Kil-So-Quah State Recreation Area; Little Turtle State Recreation Area; Markle State Recreation Area; Mount Etna State Recreation Area
Additional Information Contacts
Huntington County Government Offices 219-358-4822
Huntington Area Association of Realtors 219-358-1200
Huntington Chamber of Commerce 219-356-5300
Warren Area Chamber of Commerce 219-375-3175

Huntington County Communities

ANDREWS (town). Covers a land area of 0.496 square miles and a water area of 0 square miles. Located at 40.86° N. Lat.; 85.60° W. Long. Elevation is 737 feet.
History: Andrews was the birthplace of educator Ellwood Patterson Cubberley who graduated from Indiana University in 1891 and went on to be president of Vincennes University and instrumental in the early days of Stanford University.
Population: 1,290 (2000); Race: 96.6% White, 0.2% Black, 1.0% Asian, 1.3% American Indian and Alaska Native, 1.0% Hispanic of any race, 0.7% two or more races (2000); Density: 2,602.2 persons per square mile (2000); Age: 30.4% under 18, 11.1% over 64 (2000); Marriage status: 21.3% never married, 57.8% now married, 6.5% widowed, 14.3% divorced (2000); Foreign born: 1.0% (2000); Ancestry (includes multiple ancestries): 20.9% German, 13.8% United States or American, 8.2% Other groups, 7.3% Irish, 6.1% English (2000).
Economy: Employment by occupation: 4.8% management, 6.1% professional, 14.6% services, 11.7% sales, 0.0% farming, 14.1% construction, 48.8% production (2000).
Income: Per capita income: $15,198 (2000); Median household income: $35,125 (2000); Poverty rate: 8.2% (2000).
Taxes: Total city taxes per capita: $123 (1997); City property taxes per capita: $123 (1997).
Education: High school graduation rate: 71.1% (2000); College graduation rate: 3.3% (2000).
Housing: Homeownership rate: 70.8% (2000); Median home value: $59,500 (2000); Median rent: $358 per month (2000); Median age of housing: 48 years (2000).
Transportation: Commute to work: 93.5% car, 0.0% public transportation, 2.5% walk, 1.8% work from home (2000); Travel time to work: 27.2% less than 15 minutes, 40.3% 15 to 30 minutes, 16.2% 30 to 45 minutes, 12.4% 45 to 60 minutes, 3.9% 60 minutes or more (2000)

HUNTINGTON (city). Covers a land area of 8.345 square miles and a water area of 0.086 square miles. Located at 40.88° N. Lat.; 85.49° W. Long. Elevation is 743 feet.
History: Huntington was named in 1831 for Samuel Huntington, a member of the first Continental Congress. Previous to that the community was known as Wepecheange, meaning "place of flints." Huntington was the home of John R. Kissinger, on whom Dr. Walter Reed experimented with yellow fever tests in 1900 in Cuba.
Population: 17,450 (2000); Race: 97.5% White, 0.4% Black, 0.2% Asian, 0.3% American Indian and Alaska Native, 1.3% Hispanic of any race, 0.9% two or more races (2000); Density: 2,091.0 persons per square mile (2000); Age: 26.2% under 18, 13.8% over 64 (2000); Marriage status: 26.9% never married, 54.5% now married, 6.0% widowed, 12.6% divorced (2000); Foreign born: 1.0% (2000); Ancestry (includes multiple ancestries): 28.5% German, 13.6% United States or American, 9.8% Irish, 7.4% Other groups, 6.6% English (2000).
Vital Statistics: Birth rate: 166.8 per 10,000 population (1998)
Economy: Employment by occupation: 8.1% management, 12.2% professional, 16.6% services, 21.5% sales, 0.1% farming, 7.7% construction, 33.9% production (2000).
Income: Per capita income: $18,242 (2000); Median household income: $35,600 (2000); Poverty rate: 8.1% (2000).
Taxes: Total city taxes per capita: $346 (2000); City property taxes per capita: $346 (2000).
Education: High school graduation rate: 81.0% (2000); College graduation rate: 13.7% (2000).

School District(s)

Huntington Co Com Sch Corp (KG-12)
2000 Enrollment: 6,523 219-356-7812

Four-year College(s)

Huntington College (Private, Not-for-profit, United Brethren Church)
2001 Enrollment: 989 219-356-6000
2001 Tuition: In-state $14,270; Out-of-state $14,270

Housing: Homeownership rate: 68.4% (2000); Median home value: $71,100 (2000); Median rent: $401 per month (2000); Median age of housing: 56 years (2000).
Hospitals: Parkview Huntington Hospital (24 beds)
Safety: Violent crime rate: 13.7 per 10,000 population; Property crime rate: 233.1 per 10,000 population (2001).
Newspapers: The Huntington County Tab (2 x week); Huntington Herald-Press (6 x week)
Transportation: Commute to work: 89.5% car, 0.1% public transportation, 5.3% walk, 3.4% work from home (2000); Travel time to work: 56.3% less than 15 minutes, 19.9% 15 to 30 minutes, 15.3% 30 to 45 minutes, 5.7% 45 to 60 minutes, 2.7% 60 minutes or more (2000)
Airports: Huntington Municipal
Additional Information Contacts
Huntington Area Association of Realtors 219-358-1200
Huntington Chamber of Commerce 219-356-5300

MARKLE (town). Covers a land area of 0.987 square miles and a water area of 0.030 square miles. Located at 40.82° N. Lat.; 85.33° W. Long.
Population: 1,102 (2000); Race: 98.6% White, 0.5% Black, 0.0% Asian, 0.2% American Indian and Alaska Native, 1.0% Hispanic of any race, 0.0% two or more races (2000); Density: 1,116.3 persons per square mile (2000); Age: 23.5% under 18, 17.6% over 64 (2000); Marriage status: 18.4% never

married, 55.2% now married, 12.2% widowed, 14.2% divorced (2000); Foreign born: 0.4% (2000); Ancestry (includes multiple ancestries): 26.9% German, 12.7% English, 11.2% Irish, 9.7% United States or American, 8.6% Other groups (2000).
Economy: Employment by occupation: 11.5% management, 10.0% professional, 11.3% services, 25.3% sales, 0.6% farming, 12.8% construction, 28.5% production (2000).
Income: Per capita income: $18,504 (2000); Median household income: $37,039 (2000); Poverty rate: 6.7% (2000).
Taxes: Total city taxes per capita: $129 (1997); City property taxes per capita: $128 (1997).
Education: High school graduation rate: 85.4% (2000); College graduation rate: 12.3% (2000).
Housing: Homeownership rate: 74.9% (2000); Median home value: $75,200 (2000); Median rent: $322 per month (2000); Median age of housing: 49 years (2000).
Transportation: Commute to work: 92.7% car, 0.0% public transportation, 3.7% walk, 2.5% work from home (2000); Travel time to work: 25.6% less than 15 minutes, 44.4% 15 to 30 minutes, 25.0% 30 to 45 minutes, 3.2% 45 to 60 minutes, 1.8% 60 minutes or more (2000)

MOUNT ETNA (town). Covers a land area of 0.082 square miles and a water area of 0 square miles. Located at 40.74° N. Lat.; 85.56° W. Long. Elevation is 813 feet.
History: Mount Etna was founded in 1839, and named for Mt. Etna in Sicily.
Population: 110 (2000); Race: 97.2% White, 0.0% Black, 0.0% Asian, 0.0% American Indian and Alaska Native, 0.0% Hispanic of any race, 2.8% two or more races (2000); Density: 1,343.1 persons per square mile (2000); Age: 29.2% under 18, 14.2% over 64 (2000); Marriage status: 21.6% never married, 54.5% now married, 9.1% widowed, 14.8% divorced (2000); Foreign born: 1.9% (2000); Ancestry (includes multiple ancestries): 33.0% German, 22.6% United States or American, 18.9% English, 12.3% Irish, 3.8% Scottish (2000).
Economy: Employment by occupation: 5.7% management, 7.5% professional, 15.1% services, 34.0% sales, 0.0% farming, 5.7% construction, 32.1% production (2000).
Income: Per capita income: $13,421 (2000); Median household income: $37,500 (2000); Poverty rate: 10.7% (2000).
Taxes: Total city taxes per capita: $28 (1997); City property taxes per capita: $18 (1997).
Education: High school graduation rate: 66.7% (2000); College graduation rate: 19.4% (2000).
Housing: Homeownership rate: 100.0% (2000); Median home value: $78,800 (2000); Median age of housing: 60+ years (2000).
Transportation: Commute to work: 100.0% car, 0.0% public transportation, 0.0% walk, 0.0% work from home (2000); Travel time to work: 7.5% less than 15 minutes, 66.0% 15 to 30 minutes, 5.7% 30 to 45 minutes, 9.4% 45 to 60 minutes, 11.3% 60 minutes or more (2000)

ROANOKE (town). Covers a land area of 0.623 square miles and a water area of 0 square miles. Located at 40.96° N. Lat.; 85.37° W. Long. Elevation is 780 feet.
History: Roanoke was known for the Roanoke Classical Seminary founded in 1861 by Frederick S. Reefy. The emphasis in culture provided by the seminary gave Roanoke the reputation as the Athens of Indiana.
Population: 1,495 (2000); Race: 99.5% White, 0.0% Black, 0.3% Asian, 0.0% American Indian and Alaska Native, 0.7% Hispanic of any race, 0.2% two or more races (2000); Density: 2,400.5 persons per square mile (2000); Age: 27.1% under 18, 11.6% over 64 (2000); Marriage status: 21.1% never married, 64.2% now married, 6.2% widowed, 8.5% divorced (2000); Foreign born: 0.3% (2000); Ancestry (includes multiple ancestries): 40.7% German, 12.6% Irish, 10.9% United States or American, 7.4% English, 5.9% Other groups (2000).
Economy: Employment by occupation: 11.9% management, 15.6% professional, 13.7% services, 20.7% sales, 0.2% farming, 9.7% construction, 28.2% production (2000).
Income: Per capita income: $20,373 (2000); Median household income: $47,250 (2000); Poverty rate: 5.4% (2000).
Taxes: Total city taxes per capita: $138 (1997); City property taxes per capita: $136 (1997).
Education: High school graduation rate: 88.0% (2000); College graduation rate: 17.6% (2000).
Housing: Homeownership rate: 78.7% (2000); Median home value: $89,400 (2000); Median rent: $400 per month (2000); Median age of housing: 32 years (2000).
Transportation: Commute to work: 96.8% car, 0.5% public transportation, 2.1% walk, 0.6% work from home (2000); Travel time to work: 31.6% less than 15 minutes, 38.7% 15 to 30 minutes, 23.4% 30 to 45 minutes, 2.7% 45 to 60 minutes, 3.5% 60 minutes or more (2000)

WARREN (town). Covers a land area of 0.912 square miles and a water area of 0 square miles. Located at 40.68° N. Lat.; 85.42° W. Long. Elevation is 830 feet.
History: Laid out 1836.
Population: 1,272 (2000); Race: 98.7% White, 0.4% Black, 0.1% Asian, 0.0% American Indian and Alaska Native, 1.0% Hispanic of any race, 0.2% two or more races (2000); Density: 1,395.1 persons per square mile (2000); Age: 30.1% under 18, 13.8% over 64 (2000); Marriage status: 19.7% never married, 60.1% now married, 6.7% widowed, 13.6% divorced (2000); Foreign born: 0.3% (2000); Ancestry (includes multiple ancestries): 28.0% German, 19.0% United States or American, 12.3% English, 9.4% Irish, 5.1% Other groups (2000).
Economy: In agricultural area: poultry, livestock; soybeans, grain. Manufacturing includes corrugated containers, poultry processing, feed grinding. Employment by occupation: 7.7% management, 11.3% professional, 22.1% services, 16.6% sales, 1.3% farming, 11.1% construction, 29.8% production (2000).
Income: Per capita income: $17,145 (2000); Median household income: $38,550 (2000); Poverty rate: 3.1% (2000).
Taxes: Total city taxes per capita: $140 (1997); City property taxes per capita: $137 (1997).
Education: High school graduation rate: 86.5% (2000); College graduation rate: 10.5% (2000).
Housing: Homeownership rate: 80.2% (2000); Median home value: $65,800 (2000); Median rent: $343 per month (2000); Median age of housing: 60+ years (2000).
Transportation: Commute to work: 93.1% car, 0.3% public transportation, 4.7% walk, 1.6% work from home (2000); Travel time to work: 36.4% less than 15 minutes, 30.1% 15 to 30 minutes, 22.7% 30 to 45 minutes, 7.0% 45 to 60 minutes, 3.9% 60 minutes or more (2000)
Additional Information Contacts
Warren Area Chamber of Commerce. 219-375-3175

Jackson County

Located in southern Indiana; bounded on the south by the Muscatatuck River; drained by the East Fork of the White River. Covers a land area of 509.30 square miles, a water area of 4.40 square miles, and is located in the Eastern Time Zone. The county government was organized in 1815. County seat is Brownstown.

Weather Station: Seymour 2 N Elevation: 567 feet

	Jan	Feb	Mar	Apr	May	Jun	Jul	Aug	Sep	Oct	Nov	Dec
High	37	42	53	65	74	82	85	84	79	67	54	42
Low	19	22	31	40	51	60	64	61	53	40	33	24
Precip	3.1	2.7	3.8	4.7	4.9	4.0	4.4	4.3	3.0	3.3	4.0	3.4
Snow	na	na	2.3	tr	0.0	0.0	0.0	0.0	0.0	0.2	0.6	1.9

High and Low temperatures in degrees Fahrenheit; Precipitation and Snow in inches

Population: 41,335 (2000); Race: 95.8% White, 0.8% Black, 0.8% Asian, 0.2% American Indian and Alaska Native, 1.9% Hispanic of any race, 1.1% two or more races (2000); Density: 81.2 persons per square mile (2000); Age: 25.6% under 18, 13.3% over 64 (2000).
Religion: Five largest groups: 17.5% Lutheran Church—Missouri Synod, 9.7% Christian Churches and Churches of Christ, 5.4% American Baptist Churches in the USA, 5.2% Church of the Nazarene, 4.4% The United Methodist Church (2000).
Economy: Unemployment rate: 4.4% (11/2002); Total civilian labor force: 22,651 (11/2002); Leading industries: 36.0% manufacturing; 13.2% retail trade; 10.7% health care and social assistance (2000); Companies that employ more than 1,000 persons: 3 (2000); Companies that employ more than 100 persons: 31 (2000); Farms: 809 totaling 201,006 acres (1997); Minority business ownership rate: 0.0% (1997); Women business ownership rate: 26.5% (1997); Retail sales per capita: $9,513 (1997). Single-family building permits issued: 154 (2001) / 156 (2000); Multi-family building permits issued: 26 (2001) / 47 (2000).
Income: Per capita income: $18,400 (2000); Median household income: $39,401 (2000); Poverty rate: 8.5% (2000); Bankruptcy rate: 8.86% (2001).
Taxes: Total county taxes per capita: $197 (2000); County property taxes per capita: $102 (2000).

Education: High school graduation rate: 79.8% (2000); College graduation rate: 11.5% (2000).
Housing: Homeownership rate: 74.2% (2000); Median home value: $87,500 (2000); Median rent: $401 per month (2000); Median age of housing: 31 years (2000).
Health: Birth rate: 143.5 per 10,000 population (1998); Age adjusted death rate: 91.1 per 10,000 population (1999); Age adjusted cancer mortality rate: 212.8 deaths per 100,000 population (1999). Air Quality Index: 55% good, 45% moderate, 0% unhealthy (percent of days in 2000). Number of physicians: 9.4 per 10,000 population (1999); Number of hospital beds: 27.1 per 10,000 population (1999).
Elections: 2000 Presidential election results: 36.5% Gore, 62.0% Bush, 0.2% Nader, 0.9% Buchanan
National and State Parks: Starve Hollow State Beach
Additional Information Contacts
Jackson County Government Offices.................... 812-358-6116
Brownstown Chamber of Commerce.................... 812-358-2930
Jackson County Board of Realtors.................... 812-522-3223
Seymour Chamber of Commerce.................... 812-522-3681

Jackson County Communities

BROWNSTOWN (town). Covers a land area of 1.431 square miles and a water area of 0 square miles. Located at 38.88° N. Lat.; 86.04° W. Long. Elevation is 627 feet.
History: Brownstown was founded in 1816 as a farm town and seat of Jackson County.
Population: 2,978 (2000); Race: 99.0% White, 0.2% Black, 0.0% Asian, 0.0% American Indian and Alaska Native, 1.6% Hispanic of any race, 0.3% two or more races (2000); Density: 2,080.6 persons per square mile (2000); Age: 27.7% under 18, 15.9% over 64 (2000); Marriage status: 19.5% never married, 58.3% now married, 8.7% widowed, 13.4% divorced (2000); Foreign born: 1.6% (2000); Ancestry (includes multiple ancestries): 21.4% German, 21.3% United States or American, 9.5% English, 8.8% Irish, 5.3% Other groups (2000).
Economy: Employment by occupation: 8.3% management, 13.8% professional, 15.5% services, 22.0% sales, 0.4% farming, 10.0% construction, 30.0% production (2000).
Income: Per capita income: $15,525 (2000); Median household income: $35,000 (2000); Poverty rate: 11.7% (2000).
Taxes: Total city taxes per capita: $99 (1997); City property taxes per capita: $88 (1997).
Education: High school graduation rate: 82.6% (2000); College graduation rate: 11.6% (2000).

School District(s)

Brownstown Cnt Com Sch Corp (PK-12)
2000 Enrollment: 1,740 812-358-4271
Housing: Homeownership rate: 69.5% (2000); Median home value: $80,100 (2000); Median rent: $340 per month (2000); Median age of housing: 30 years (2000).
Newspapers: Jackson County Banner (2 x week)
Transportation: Commute to work: 93.9% car, 0.4% public transportation, 2.2% walk, 2.9% work from home (2000); Travel time to work: 41.2% less than 15 minutes, 35.3% 15 to 30 minutes, 11.0% 30 to 45 minutes, 7.1% 45 to 60 minutes, 5.4% 60 minutes or more (2000)
Additional Information Contacts
Brownstown Chamber of Commerce.................... 812-358-2930

CROTHERSVILLE (town). Covers a land area of 1.144 square miles and a water area of 0 square miles. Located at 38.79° N. Lat.; 85.84° W. Long. Elevation is 565 feet.
Population: 1,570 (2000); Race: 99.0% White, 0.3% Black, 0.0% Asian, 0.3% American Indian and Alaska Native, 0.4% Hispanic of any race, 0.4% two or more races (2000); Density: 1,372.2 persons per square mile (2000); Age: 23.9% under 18, 14.1% over 64 (2000); Marriage status: 18.8% never married, 60.8% now married, 7.3% widowed, 13.0% divorced (2000); Foreign born: 0.4% (2000); Ancestry (includes multiple ancestries): 26.9% United States or American, 14.8% German, 7.8% Irish, 6.2% English, 5.6% Other groups (2000).
Economy: Manufacturing: shoes. Employment by occupation: 4.3% management, 7.8% professional, 13.0% services, 25.0% sales, 0.5% farming, 7.2% construction, 42.2% production (2000).
Income: Per capita income: $18,182 (2000); Median household income: $32,768 (2000); Poverty rate: 8.8% (2000).
Taxes: Total city taxes per capita: $83 (1997); City property taxes per capita: $56 (1997).
Education: High school graduation rate: 75.4% (2000); College graduation rate: 5.2% (2000).

School District(s)

Crothersville Community Schools (KG-12)
2000 Enrollment: 537 812-793-2601
Housing: Homeownership rate: 75.6% (2000); Median home value: $70,700 (2000); Median rent: $327 per month (2000); Median age of housing: 38 years (2000).
Newspapers: Crothersville Times (1 x week)
Transportation: Commute to work: 96.3% car, 0.0% public transportation, 1.2% walk, 1.9% work from home (2000); Travel time to work: 23.3% less than 15 minutes, 46.2% 15 to 30 minutes, 21.6% 30 to 45 minutes, 4.8% 45 to 60 minutes, 4.1% 60 minutes or more (2000)

FREETOWN (unincorporated postal area, zip code 47235). Covers a land area of 48.294 square miles and a water area of 0.071 square miles. Located at 38.98° N. Lat.; 86.13° W. Long. Elevation is 632 feet.
Population: 1,938 (2000); Race: 98.1% White, 0.4% Black, 0.0% Asian, 0.3% American Indian and Alaska Native, 0.9% Hispanic of any race, 0.6% two or more races (2000); Density: 40.1 persons per square mile (2000); Age: 24.1% under 18, 10.0% over 64 (2000); Marriage status: 21.6% never married, 67.9% now married, 3.3% widowed, 7.2% divorced (2000); Foreign born: 0.0% (2000); Ancestry (includes multiple ancestries): 30.8% United States or American, 16.2% German, 9.7% English, 9.1% Other groups, 5.5% Irish (2000).
Economy: On East edge of Hoosier National Forest. Vegetables, livestock. Timber. Near the Knobstone Escarpment. Employment by occupation: 14.4% management, 16.4% professional, 6.1% services, 18.6% sales, 1.1% farming, 16.0% construction, 27.4% production (2000).
Income: Per capita income: $19,434 (2000); Median household income: $45,781 (2000); Poverty rate: 6.8% (2000).
Education: High school graduation rate: 79.9% (2000); College graduation rate: 18.2% (2000).
Housing: Homeownership rate: 89.6% (2000); Median home value: $96,600 (2000); Median rent: $245 per month (2000); Median age of housing: 27 years (2000).
Transportation: Commute to work: 94.3% car, 2.3% public transportation, 0.0% walk, 2.8% work from home (2000); Travel time to work: 5.7% less than 15 minutes, 36.2% 15 to 30 minutes, 37.3% 30 to 45 minutes, 13.3% 45 to 60 minutes, 7.5% 60 minutes or more (2000)

MEDORA (town). Covers a land area of 0.319 square miles and a water area of 0 square miles. Located at 38.82° N. Lat.; 86.17° W. Long. Elevation is 526 feet.
Population: 565 (2000); Race: 99.1% White, 0.0% Black, 0.0% Asian, 0.0% American Indian and Alaska Native, 0.7% Hispanic of any race, 0.9% two or more races (2000); Density: 1,773.5 persons per square mile (2000); Age: 24.4% under 18, 15.6% over 64 (2000); Marriage status: 27.0% never married, 50.6% now married, 12.9% widowed, 9.5% divorced (2000); Foreign born: 0.5% (2000); Ancestry (includes multiple ancestries): 20.3% German, 14.2% United States or American, 11.6% Irish, 8.0% Other groups, 7.5% English (2000).
Economy: In agricultural area. Single-family building permits issued: 0 (2001) / 0 (2000); Multi-family building permits issued: 0 (2001) / 0 (2000); Employment by occupation: 3.0% management, 6.0% professional, 14.3% services, 18.5% sales, 6.4% farming, 12.1% construction, 39.6% production (2000).
Income: Per capita income: $13,262 (2000); Median household income: $27,813 (2000); Poverty rate: 10.9% (2000).
Taxes: Total city taxes per capita: $49 (1997); City property taxes per capita: $44 (1997).
Education: High school graduation rate: 69.1% (2000); College graduation rate: 3.9% (2000).

School District(s)

Medora Community School Corp (KG-12)
2000 Enrollment: 307 812-966-2210
Housing: Homeownership rate: 86.3% (2000); Median home value: $53,900 (2000); Median rent: $342 per month (2000); Median age of housing: 37 years (2000).
Transportation: Commute to work: 91.4% car, 0.8% public transportation, 6.7% walk, 0.0% work from home (2000); Travel time to work: 20.4% less than 15 minutes, 22.7% 15 to 30 minutes, 35.7% 30 to 45 minutes, 10.6% 45 to 60 minutes, 10.6% 60 minutes or more (2000)

NORMAN (unincorporated postal area, zip code 47264). Covers a land area of 99.737 square miles and a water area of 0.149 square miles. Located at 38.96° N. Lat.; 86.27° W. Long. Elevation is 870 feet.
Population: 1,428 (2000); Race: 99.7% White, 0.0% Black, 0.0% Asian, 0.1% American Indian and Alaska Native, 0.0% Hispanic of any race, 0.1% two or more races (2000); Density: 14.3 persons per square mile (2000); Age: 16.6% under 18, 16.0% over 64 (2000); Marriage status: 13.3% never married, 74.9% now married, 4.3% widowed, 7.4% divorced (2000); Foreign born: 0.0% (2000); Ancestry (includes multiple ancestries): 17.5% United States or American, 14.6% German, 11.4% Irish, 8.7% English, 6.1% Other groups (2000).
Economy: Employment by occupation: 7.4% management, 3.0% professional, 14.1% services, 12.8% sales, 6.0% farming, 20.8% construction, 35.8% production (2000).
Income: Per capita income: $17,232 (2000); Median household income: $35,625 (2000); Poverty rate: 8.1% (2000).
Education: High school graduation rate: 68.7% (2000); College graduation rate: 4.5% (2000).
Housing: Homeownership rate: 89.7% (2000); Median home value: $73,500 (2000); Median rent: $248 per month (2000); Median age of housing: 34 years (2000).
Transportation: Commute to work: 95.2% car, 0.0% public transportation, 0.3% walk, 3.2% work from home (2000); Travel time to work: 3.0% less than 15 minutes, 36.7% 15 to 30 minutes, 32.2% 30 to 45 minutes, 19.4% 45 to 60 minutes, 8.6% 60 minutes or more (2000)

SEYMOUR (city). Covers a land area of 10.837 square miles and a water area of 0 square miles. Located at 38.95° N. Lat.; 85.89° W. Long. Elevation is 605 feet.
History: Seymour developed as a factory town at the junction of three railroads.
Population: 18,101 (2000); Race: 92.5% White, 1.4% Black, 1.3% Asian, 0.1% American Indian and Alaska Native, 3.7% Hispanic of any race, 1.6% two or more races (2000); Density: 1,670.3 persons per square mile (2000); Age: 25.2% under 18, 13.7% over 64 (2000); Marriage status: 20.9% never married, 57.8% now married, 7.8% widowed, 13.5% divorced (2000); Foreign born: 4.4% (2000); Ancestry (includes multiple ancestries): 23.9% German, 20.1% United States or American, 10.3% Other groups, 8.9% Irish, 6.3% English (2000).
Vital Statistics: Birth rate: 167.4 per 10,000 population (1998)
Economy: Single-family building permits issued: 96 (2001) / 98 (2000); Multi-family building permits issued: 26 (2001) / 47 (2000); Employment by occupation: 7.6% management, 12.8% professional, 10.4% services, 22.7% sales, 1.0% farming, 10.1% construction, 35.3% production (2000).
Income: Per capita income: $18,222 (2000); Median household income: $36,883 (2000); Poverty rate: 10.0% (2000).
Taxes: Total city taxes per capita: $231 (1997); City property taxes per capita: $200 (1997).
Education: High school graduation rate: 77.9% (2000); College graduation rate: 12.0% (2000).

School District(s)
Seymour Community Schools (PK-12)
2000 Enrollment: 3,792 812-522-3340
Housing: Homeownership rate: 64.0% (2000); Median home value: $82,500 (2000); Median rent: $421 per month (2000); Median age of housing: 32 years (2000).
Hospitals: Memorial Hospital (166 beds)
Safety: Violent crime rate: 47.2 per 10,000 population; Property crime rate: 662.5 per 10,000 population (2001).
Newspapers: The Tribune (6 x week)
Transportation: Commute to work: 95.1% car, 0.0% public transportation, 1.8% walk, 1.7% work from home (2000); Travel time to work: 57.4% less than 15 minutes, 25.3% 15 to 30 minutes, 10.3% 30 to 45 minutes, 2.7% 45 to 60 minutes, 4.3% 60 minutes or more (2000)
Airports: Freeman Municipal
Additional Information Contacts
Jackson County Board of Realtors 812-522-3223
Seymour Chamber of Commerce 812-522-3681

VALLONIA (unincorporated postal area, zip code 47281). Covers a land area of 52.840 square miles and a water area of 0.269 square miles. Located at 38.80° N. Lat.; 86.09° W. Long. Elevation is 560 feet.
History: Vallonia is on the site of old Fort Vallonia, built in 1805. Vallonia was platted in 1810, and was the first seat of Jackson County.
Population: 1,392 (2000); Race: 99.6% White, 0.0% Black, 0.0% Asian, 0.0% American Indian and Alaska Native, 0.0% Hispanic of any race, 0.4% two or more races (2000); Density: 26.3 persons per square mile (2000); Age: 22.9% under 18, 16.3% over 64 (2000); Marriage status: 13.7% never married, 68.0% now married, 7.2% widowed, 11.0% divorced (2000); Foreign born: 0.0% (2000); Ancestry (includes multiple ancestries): 21.6% German, 19.0% United States or American, 10.7% Other groups, 5.5% Irish, 3.9% English (2000).
Economy: Employment by occupation: 12.8% management, 11.3% professional, 6.8% services, 15.4% sales, 4.1% farming, 15.5% construction, 34.1% production (2000).
Income: Per capita income: $16,292 (2000); Median household income: $32,188 (2000); Poverty rate: 6.2% (2000).
Education: High school graduation rate: 69.8% (2000); College graduation rate: 7.2% (2000).
Housing: Homeownership rate: 84.4% (2000); Median home value: $91,600 (2000); Median rent: $191 per month (2000); Median age of housing: 35 years (2000).
Transportation: Commute to work: 91.1% car, 0.0% public transportation, 0.0% walk, 7.8% work from home (2000); Travel time to work: 16.8% less than 15 minutes, 39.7% 15 to 30 minutes, 23.2% 30 to 45 minutes, 11.2% 45 to 60 minutes, 9.1% 60 minutes or more (2000)

Jasper County

Located in northwestern Indiana; bounded on the north by the Kankakee River; drained by the Iroquois River. Covers a land area of 559.90 square miles, a water area of 1.40 square miles, and is located in the Central Time Zone. The county government was organized in 1835. County seat is Rensselaer.

Weather Station: Rensselaer — Elevation: 649 feet

	Jan	Feb	Mar	Apr	May	Jun	Jul	Aug	Sep	Oct	Nov	Dec
High	31	36	47	60	72	81	85	82	76	64	49	36
Low	15	19	29	39	50	60	64	61	53	41	32	21
Precip	2.0	1.7	3.2	3.5	4.3	4.4	3.8	3.5	3.5	3.1	3.2	2.7
Snow	na	na	na	0.3	0.0	0.0	0.0	0.0	0.0	tr	0.5	na

High and Low temperatures in degrees Fahrenheit; Precipitation and Snow in inches

Population: 30,043 (2000); Race: 97.5% White, 0.2% Black, 0.1% Asian, 0.2% American Indian and Alaska Native, 2.8% Hispanic of any race, 1.1% two or more races (2000); Density: 53.7 persons per square mile (2000); Age: 27.5% under 18, 12.4% over 64 (2000).
Religion: Five largest groups: 13.6% Catholic Church, 5.3% The United Methodist Church, 5.2% Reformed Church in America, 4.8% Christian Reformed Church in North America, 2.8% Lutheran Church—Missouri Synod (2000).
Economy: Unemployment rate: 5.0% (11/2002); Total civilian labor force: 14,857 (11/2002); Leading industries: 18.2% retail trade; 16.1% manufacturing; 9.9% administration, support, waste management, remediation services (2000); Companies that employ more than 1,000 persons: 0 (2000); Companies that employ more than 100 persons: 13 (2000); Farms: 618 totaling 282,915 acres (1997); Minority business ownership rate: 0.0% (1997); Women business ownership rate: 17.1% (1997); Retail sales per capita: $9,737 (1997). Single-family building permits issued: 241 (2001) / 236 (2000); Multi-family building permits issued: 34 (2001) / 34 (2000).
Income: Per capita income: $19,012 (2000); Median household income: $43,369 (2000); Poverty rate: 6.7% (2000); Bankruptcy rate: 6.39% (2001).
Taxes: Total county taxes per capita: $276 (2000); County property taxes per capita: $178 (2000).
Education: High school graduation rate: 82.4% (2000); College graduation rate: 13.0% (2000).
Housing: Homeownership rate: 77.5% (2000); Median home value: $105,700 (2000); Median rent: $386 per month (2000); Median age of housing: 27 years (2000).
Health: Birth rate: 128.8 per 10,000 population (1998); Age adjusted death rate: 94.0 per 10,000 population (1999); Age adjusted cancer mortality rate: 200.1 deaths per 100,000 population (1999). Air Quality Index: 100% good, 0% moderate, 0% unhealthy (percent of days in 2000). Number of physicians: 6.0 per 10,000 population (1999); Number of hospital beds: 22.0 per 10,000 population (1999).
Elections: 2000 Presidential election results: 33.5% Gore, 64.6% Bush, 0.6% Nader, 0.6% Buchanan
Additional Information Contacts
Jasper County Government Offices 219-866-4930
Demotte Chamber of Commerce 219-987-5800

Rensselaer & Remington Chamber 219-866-8223

Jasper County Communities

COLLEGEVILLE (CDP). Covers a land area of 1.290 square miles and a water area of 0 square miles. Located at 40.91° N. Lat.; 87.15° W. Long. Elevation is 660 feet.
History: Seat of St. Joseph's College.
Population: 865 (2000); Race: 97.7% White, 1.6% Black, 0.0% Asian, 0.0% American Indian and Alaska Native, 3.7% Hispanic of any race, 0.7% two or more races (2000); Density: 670.5 persons per square mile (2000); Age: 5.5% under 18, 3.6% over 64 (2000); Marriage status: 46.7% never married, 48.3% now married, 4.4% widowed, 0.6% divorced (2000); Foreign born: 0.7% (2000); Ancestry (includes multiple ancestries): 23.7% German, 15.2% Irish, 11.0% Italian, 9.8% Other groups, 6.2% Polish (2000).
Economy: Employment by occupation: 10.4% management, 25.4% professional, 14.1% services, 35.2% sales, 1.4% farming, 3.7% construction, 9.9% production (2000).
Income: Per capita income: $8,587 (2000); Median household income: $44,821 (2000); Poverty rate: 19.5% (2000).
Education: High school graduation rate: 100.0% (2000); College graduation rate: 20.1% (2000).
Housing: Homeownership rate: 95.4% (2000); Median home value: $109,800 (2000); Median rent: $575 per month (2000); Median age of housing: 27 years (2000).
Transportation: Commute to work: 59.7% car, 0.0% public transportation, 33.4% walk, 3.2% work from home (2000); Travel time to work: 75.6% less than 15 minutes, 12.5% 15 to 30 minutes, 3.3% 30 to 45 minutes, 8.6% 45 to 60 minutes, 0.0% 60 minutes or more (2000)

DE MOTTE (town). Aka Demotte. Covers a land area of 3.590 square miles and a water area of 0 square miles. Located at 41.19° N. Lat.; 87.19° W. Long. Elevation is 668 feet.
Population: 3,234 (2000); Race: 96.6% White, 0.0% Black, 0.2% Asian, 0.0% American Indian and Alaska Native, 2.2% Hispanic of any race, 1.7% two or more races (2000); Density: 900.7 persons per square mile (2000); Age: 25.1% under 18, 21.1% over 64 (2000); Marriage status: 20.1% never married, 59.4% now married, 11.3% widowed, 9.2% divorced (2000); Foreign born: 2.4% (2000); Ancestry (includes multiple ancestries): 25.0% German, 19.5% Dutch, 12.5% Irish, 10.4% English, 7.9% Polish (2000).
Economy: Single-family building permits issued: 69 (2001) / 69 (2000); Multi-family building permits issued: 6 (2001) / 6 (2000); Employment by occupation: 8.8% management, 16.9% professional, 17.7% services, 16.6% sales, 1.1% farming, 14.3% construction, 24.6% production (2000).
Income: Per capita income: $19,059 (2000); Median household income: $37,557 (2000); Poverty rate: 7.7% (2000).
Education: High school graduation rate: 79.2% (2000); College graduation rate: 13.2% (2000).
Housing: Homeownership rate: 65.8% (2000); Median home value: $111,100 (2000); Median rent: $457 per month (2000); Median age of housing: 21 years (2000).
Newspapers: Kankakee Valley Post-News (1 x week); Action Plus Shopper (1 x week)
Transportation: Commute to work: 93.4% car, 0.6% public transportation, 2.6% walk, 2.0% work from home (2000); Travel time to work: 32.4% less than 15 minutes, 18.0% 15 to 30 minutes, 22.8% 30 to 45 minutes, 16.2% 45 to 60 minutes, 10.6% 60 minutes or more (2000)
Additional Information Contacts
Demotte Chamber of Commerce 219-987-5800

FAIR OAKS (unincorporated postal area, zip code 47943). Covers a land area of 60.150 square miles and a water area of 0.024 square miles. Located at 41.07° N. Lat.; 87.26° W. Long. Elevation is 696 feet.
Population: 763 (2000); Race: 97.5% White, 0.0% Black, 0.6% Asian, 1.2% American Indian and Alaska Native, 3.8% Hispanic of any race, 0.0% two or more races (2000); Density: 12.7 persons per square mile (2000); Age: 29.3% under 18, 7.3% over 64 (2000); Marriage status: 20.8% never married, 69.0% now married, 3.8% widowed, 6.4% divorced (2000); Foreign born: 1.2% (2000); Ancestry (includes multiple ancestries): 21.9% German, 14.6% Dutch, 13.5% United States or American, 13.4% Irish, 6.6% Polish (2000).
Economy: Employment by occupation: 12.9% management, 9.5% professional, 3.7% services, 16.7% sales, 1.2% farming, 13.7% construction, 42.3% production (2000).
Income: Per capita income: $19,114 (2000); Median household income: $47,143 (2000); Poverty rate: 6.1% (2000).
Education: High school graduation rate: 85.1% (2000); College graduation rate: 10.6% (2000).
Housing: Homeownership rate: 72.9% (2000); Median home value: $113,100 (2000); Median rent: $409 per month (2000); Median age of housing: 27 years (2000).
Transportation: Commute to work: 85.9% car, 2.1% public transportation, 8.1% walk, 3.9% work from home (2000); Travel time to work: 18.8% less than 15 minutes, 39.7% 15 to 30 minutes, 15.9% 30 to 45 minutes, 17.8% 45 to 60 minutes, 7.8% 60 minutes or more (2000)

REMINGTON (town). Covers a land area of 1.034 square miles and a water area of 0 square miles. Located at 40.76° N. Lat.; 87.15° W. Long. Elevation is 724 feet.
History: Laid out 1860.
Population: 1,323 (2000); Race: 99.2% White, 0.3% Black, 0.0% Asian, 0.0% American Indian and Alaska Native, 0.8% Hispanic of any race, 0.3% two or more races (2000); Density: 1,279.7 persons per square mile (2000); Age: 28.0% under 18, 14.5% over 64 (2000); Marriage status: 19.1% never married, 56.7% now married, 9.9% widowed, 14.3% divorced (2000); Foreign born: 0.9% (2000); Ancestry (includes multiple ancestries): 31.1% German, 13.8% Irish, 11.2% English, 9.1% United States or American, 6.4% Other groups (2000).
Economy: In grain and livestock area. Manufacturing: soy protein, carbon alloy forming. Single-family building permits issued: 0 (2001) / 0 (2000); Multi-family building permits issued: 0 (2001) / 0 (2000); Employment by occupation: 13.7% management, 10.3% professional, 11.5% services, 21.1% sales, 2.5% farming, 12.1% construction, 28.8% production (2000).
Income: Per capita income: $17,184 (2000); Median household income: $37,037 (2000); Poverty rate: 7.5% (2000).
Taxes: Total city taxes per capita: $127 (1997); City property taxes per capita: $121 (1997).
Education: High school graduation rate: 86.0% (2000); College graduation rate: 9.2% (2000).
Housing: Homeownership rate: 68.6% (2000); Median home value: $80,700 (2000); Median rent: $386 per month (2000); Median age of housing: 50 years (2000).
Transportation: Commute to work: 92.9% car, 0.0% public transportation, 4.3% walk, 2.1% work from home (2000); Travel time to work: 55.4% less than 15 minutes, 21.8% 15 to 30 minutes, 11.0% 30 to 45 minutes, 4.5% 45 to 60 minutes, 7.2% 60 minutes or more (2000)

RENSSELAER (city). Covers a land area of 2.901 square miles and a water area of 0.060 square miles. Located at 40.93° N. Lat.; 87.15° W. Long. Elevation is 657 feet.
History: Rensselaer was founded in 1837 by James Van Rensselaer, a merchant from New York who operated a gristmill here. Rensselaer soon became a trading center for the surrounding farming community.
Population: 5,294 (2000); Race: 94.9% White, 0.3% Black, 0.2% Asian, 0.8% American Indian and Alaska Native, 2.5% Hispanic of any race, 2.7% two or more races (2000); Density: 1,824.8 persons per square mile (2000); Age: 24.7% under 18, 19.5% over 64 (2000); Marriage status: 21.9% never married, 55.3% now married, 11.5% widowed, 11.2% divorced (2000); Foreign born: 1.9% (2000); Ancestry (includes multiple ancestries): 25.0% German, 11.9% Irish, 11.7% English, 10.8% United States or American, 7.6% Other groups (2000).
Economy: Single-family building permits issued: 21 (2001) / 14 (2000); Multi-family building permits issued: 26 (2001) / 22 (2000); Employment by occupation: 9.0% management, 16.3% professional, 15.6% services, 18.6% sales, 0.2% farming, 12.9% construction, 27.4% production (2000).
Income: Per capita income: $20,872 (2000); Median household income: $34,821 (2000); Poverty rate: 10.0% (2000).
Taxes: Total city taxes per capita: $152 (2000); City property taxes per capita: $150 (2000).
Education: High school graduation rate: 79.6% (2000); College graduation rate: 17.5% (2000).

School District(s)

Rensselaer Central School Corp (PK-12)
2000 Enrollment: 1,717 219-866-7822

Four-year College(s)

Saint Josephs College (Private, Not-for-profit, Roman Catholic)
2001 Enrollment: 914 219-866-6000
2001 Tuition: In-state $15,880; Out-of-state $15,880

Housing: Homeownership rate: 63.7% (2000); Median home value: $82,800 (2000); Median rent: $348 per month (2000); Median age of housing: 49 years (2000).
Hospitals: Jasper County Hospital (86 beds)

Safety: Violent crime rate: 16.9 per 10,000 population; Property crime rate: 520.3 per 10,000 population (2001).
Newspapers: Rensselaer Republican (6 x week); Shoppers News (1 x week); Remington Press (1 x week)
Transportation: Commute to work: 90.9% car, 0.0% public transportation, 5.5% walk, 1.6% work from home (2000); Travel time to work: 69.7% less than 15 minutes, 13.1% 15 to 30 minutes, 4.7% 30 to 45 minutes, 7.7% 45 to 60 minutes, 4.8% 60 minutes or more (2000); Amtrak: Service available.
Additional Information Contacts
Rensselaer & Remington Chamber 219-866-8223

ROSELAWN (CDP). Covers a land area of 8.119 square miles and a water area of 0 square miles. Located at 41.15° N. Lat.; 87.28° W. Long.
Population: 3,933 (2000); Race: 95.6% White, 0.4% Black, 0.2% Asian, 0.3% American Indian and Alaska Native, 3.8% Hispanic of any race, 2.5% two or more races (2000); Density: 484.4 persons per square mile (2000); Age: 26.4% under 18, 7.9% over 64 (2000); Marriage status: 18.7% never married, 68.5% now married, 6.4% widowed, 6.3% divorced (2000); Foreign born: 2.8% (2000); Ancestry (includes multiple ancestries): 25.2% German, 13.5% Irish, 12.5% United States or American, 8.1% Other groups, 7.6% English (2000).
Economy: Employment by occupation: 8.3% management, 8.9% professional, 17.3% services, 19.9% sales, 0.9% farming, 20.5% construction, 24.2% production (2000).
Income: Per capita income: $19,136 (2000); Median household income: $48,625 (2000); Poverty rate: 3.9% (2000).
Education: High school graduation rate: 81.9% (2000); College graduation rate: 5.3% (2000).
Housing: Homeownership rate: 94.9% (2000); Median home value: $108,500 (2000); Median rent: $388 per month (2000); Median age of housing: 19 years (2000).
Transportation: Commute to work: 94.5% car, 0.0% public transportation, 1.0% walk, 3.4% work from home (2000); Travel time to work: 20.3% less than 15 minutes, 18.4% 15 to 30 minutes, 17.2% 30 to 45 minutes, 22.8% 45 to 60 minutes, 21.3% 60 minutes or more (2000)

WHEATFIELD (town). Covers a land area of 0.552 square miles and a water area of 0 square miles. Located at 41.19° N. Lat.; 87.05° W. Long. Elevation is 663 feet.
Population: 772 (2000); Race: 99.4% White, 0.6% Black, 0.0% Asian, 0.0% American Indian and Alaska Native, 0.0% Hispanic of any race, 0.0% two or more races (2000); Density: 1,398.4 persons per square mile (2000); Age: 31.3% under 18, 12.9% over 64 (2000); Marriage status: 28.7% never married, 52.9% now married, 6.6% widowed, 11.9% divorced (2000); Foreign born: 0.0% (2000); Ancestry (includes multiple ancestries): 21.1% German, 12.1% United States or American, 11.3% Dutch, 9.6% Irish, 7.8% Polish (2000).
Economy: Agricultural area; marble products. Jasper-Pulaski State Fish and Wildlife Area and Nursery nearby to Southeast. Single-family building permits issued: 5 (2001) / 6 (2000); Multi-family building permits issued: 0 (2001) / 0 (2000); Employment by occupation: 11.2% management, 8.8% professional, 18.9% services, 17.7% sales, 1.5% farming, 21.2% construction, 20.6% production (2000).
Income: Per capita income: $15,003 (2000); Median household income: $38,021 (2000); Poverty rate: 7.5% (2000).
Taxes: Total city taxes per capita: $127 (1997); City property taxes per capita: $127 (1997).
Education: High school graduation rate: 77.2% (2000); College graduation rate: 6.5% (2000).

School District(s)
Kankakee Valley School Corp (KG-12)
2000 Enrollment: 3,229 219-987-4711

Housing: Homeownership rate: 76.4% (2000); Median home value: $82,800 (2000); Median rent: $418 per month (2000); Median age of housing: 39 years (2000).
Transportation: Commute to work: 93.1% car, 0.0% public transportation, 4.2% walk, 1.5% work from home (2000); Travel time to work: 36.6% less than 15 minutes, 18.3% 15 to 30 minutes, 22.3% 30 to 45 minutes, 10.7% 45 to 60 minutes, 12.2% 60 minutes or more (2000)

Jay County

Located in eastern Indiana; bounded on the east by Ohio; drained by the Salamonie River. Covers a land area of 383.60 square miles, a water area of 0.20 square miles, and is located in the Eastern Time Zone. The county government was organized in 1835. County seat is Portland.

Weather Station: Portland 1 SW — Elevation: 908 feet

	Jan	Feb	Mar	Apr	May	Jun	Jul	Aug	Sep	Oct	Nov	Dec
High	32	36	47	60	71	80	84	82	76	63	50	37
Low	16	18	27	38	49	58	62	60	52	40	32	22
Precip	1.9	1.9	2.6	3.6	3.9	4.1	4.5	3.9	2.7	2.6	3.1	2.5
Snow	6.3	5.8	2.9	0.4	0.0	0.0	0.0	0.0	0.0	0.2	0.7	4.7

High and Low temperatures in degrees Fahrenheit; Precipitation and Snow in inches

Population: 21,806 (2000); Race: 97.0% White, 0.2% Black, 0.4% Asian, 0.0% American Indian and Alaska Native, 1.9% Hispanic of any race, 0.9% two or more races (2000); Density: 56.8 persons per square mile (2000); Age: 26.9% under 18, 14.7% over 64 (2000).
Religion: Five largest groups: 9.4% Catholic Church, 8.0% The United Methodist Church, 5.3% Church of the Nazarene, 3.5% Christian Churches and Churches of Christ, 3.4% New Testament Association of Independent Baptist Churches and other Fundamental
Economy: Unemployment rate: 6.5% (11/2002); Total civilian labor force: 10,530 (11/2002); Leading industries: 43.6% manufacturing; 13.8% health care and social assistance; 11.0% retail trade (2000); Companies that employ more than 1,000 persons: 0 (2000); Companies that employ more than 100 persons: 13 (2000); Farms: 839 totaling 179,794 acres (1997); Minority business ownership rate: 0.0% (1997); Women business ownership rate: 17.3% (1997); Retail sales per capita: $5,308 (1997). Single-family building permits issued: 68 (2001) / 65 (2000); Multi-family building permits issued: 2 (2001) / 0 (2000).
Income: Per capita income: $16,686 (2000); Median household income: $35,700 (2000); Poverty rate: 9.1% (2000); Bankruptcy rate: 6.34% (2001).
Taxes: Total county taxes per capita: $235 (2000); County property taxes per capita: $161 (2000).
Education: High school graduation rate: 78.5% (2000); College graduation rate: 9.9% (2000).
Housing: Homeownership rate: 77.8% (2000); Median home value: $62,500 (2000); Median rent: $275 per month (2000); Median age of housing: 52 years (2000).
Health: Birth rate: 151.3 per 10,000 population (1998); Age adjusted death rate: 95.1 per 10,000 population (1999); Age adjusted cancer mortality rate: 200.9 deaths per 100,000 population (1999). Number of physicians: 6.0 per 10,000 population (1999); Number of hospital beds: 25.2 per 10,000 population (1999).
Elections: 2000 Presidential election results: 39.4% Gore, 58.4% Bush, 0.2% Nader, 1.2% Buchanan
National and State Parks: Limberlost State Game Reserve
Additional Information Contacts
Jay County Government Offices 219-726-7575
Portland Area Chamber of Commerce 219-726-4481

Jay County Communities

BRYANT (town). Aka Briant. Covers a land area of 0.303 square miles and a water area of 0 square miles. Located at 40.53° N. Lat.; 84.96° W. Long. Elevation is 875 feet.
Population: 272 (2000); Race: 98.3% White, 0.0% Black, 0.0% Asian, 0.0% American Indian and Alaska Native, 0.0% Hispanic of any race, 1.7% two or more races (2000); Density: 897.9 persons per square mile (2000); Age: 31.3% under 18, 8.8% over 64 (2000); Marriage status: 11.0% never married, 72.6% now married, 3.7% widowed, 12.8% divorced (2000); Foreign born: 0.0% (2000); Ancestry (includes multiple ancestries): 34.3% United States or American, 20.9% German, 10.4% Other groups, 9.8% Irish, 6.7% Swiss (2000).
Economy: In agriculture area. Single-family building permits issued: 1 (2001) / 0 (2000); Multi-family building permits issued: 0 (2001) / 0 (2000); Employment by occupation: 0.0% management, 1.9% professional, 11.5% services, 18.6% sales, 0.0% farming, 16.7% construction, 51.3% production (2000).
Income: Per capita income: $13,416 (2000); Median household income: $34,821 (2000); Poverty rate: 4.4% (2000).
Taxes: Total city taxes per capita: $24 (1997); City property taxes per capita: $24 (1997).
Education: High school graduation rate: 81.1% (2000); College graduation rate: 2.1% (2000).
Housing: Homeownership rate: 93.3% (2000); Median home value: $43,300 (2000); Median rent: $308 per month (2000); Median age of housing: 60+ years (2000).

Transportation: Commute to work: 93.3% car, 0.0% public transportation, 2.0% walk, 1.3% work from home (2000); Travel time to work: 49.0% less than 15 minutes, 31.3% 15 to 30 minutes, 15.0% 30 to 45 minutes, 2.0% 45 to 60 minutes, 2.7% 60 minutes or more (2000)

DUNKIRK (city). Covers a land area of 1.125 square miles and a water area of 0 square miles. Located at 40.37° N. Lat.; 85.21° W. Long. Elevation is 954 feet.
Population: 2,646 (2000); Race: 99.1% White, 0.3% Black, 0.0% Asian, 0.0% American Indian and Alaska Native, 1.0% Hispanic of any race, 0.6% two or more races (2000); Density: 2,351.4 persons per square mile (2000); Age: 24.6% under 18, 16.2% over 64 (2000); Marriage status: 20.7% never married, 59.6% now married, 8.8% widowed, 10.9% divorced (2000); Foreign born: 0.4% (2000); Ancestry (includes multiple ancestries): 16.9% United States or American, 15.5% German, 9.4% Irish, 7.1% English, 2.7% Other groups (2000).
Economy: Employment by occupation: 4.6% management, 4.7% professional, 16.0% services, 17.7% sales, 0.8% farming, 13.2% construction, 42.9% production (2000).
Income: Per capita income: $15,128 (2000); Median household income: $33,750 (2000); Poverty rate: 10.5% (2000).
Taxes: Total city taxes per capita: $211 (1997); City property taxes per capita: $160 (1997).
Education: High school graduation rate: 71.3% (2000); College graduation rate: 4.4% (2000).
Housing: Homeownership rate: 74.8% (2000); Median home value: $46,400 (2000); Median rent: $256 per month (2000); Median age of housing: 55 years (2000).
Newspapers: Dunkirk News and Sun (1 x week)
Transportation: Commute to work: 96.3% car, 0.0% public transportation, 2.0% walk, 1.3% work from home (2000); Travel time to work: 40.2% less than 15 minutes, 32.3% 15 to 30 minutes, 18.2% 30 to 45 minutes, 3.4% 45 to 60 minutes, 5.8% 60 minutes or more (2000)

PENNVILLE (town). Covers a land area of 0.392 square miles and a water area of 0 square miles. Located at 40.49° N. Lat.; 85.14° W. Long. Elevation is 885 feet.
Population: 706 (2000); Race: 97.3% White, 0.7% Black, 0.4% Asian, 0.0% American Indian and Alaska Native, 1.1% Hispanic of any race, 1.5% two or more races (2000); Density: 1,800.0 persons per square mile (2000); Age: 28.5% under 18, 13.6% over 64 (2000); Marriage status: 19.7% never married, 53.7% now married, 5.1% widowed, 21.6% divorced (2000); Foreign born: 0.4% (2000); Ancestry (includes multiple ancestries): 21.5% German, 18.3% United States or American, 5.8% English, 4.6% Other groups, 4.6% Irish (2000).
Economy: In agricultural area. Manufacturing of food products. Employment by occupation: 3.5% management, 7.0% professional, 12.5% services, 22.0% sales, 0.6% farming, 15.3% construction, 39.0% production (2000).
Income: Per capita income: $14,182 (2000); Median household income: $29,688 (2000); Poverty rate: 9.4% (2000).
Taxes: Total city taxes per capita: $67 (1997); City property taxes per capita: $66 (1997).
Education: High school graduation rate: 78.1% (2000); College graduation rate: 5.9% (2000).
Housing: Homeownership rate: 66.2% (2000); Median home value: $39,400 (2000); Median rent: $244 per month (2000); Median age of housing: 49 years (2000).
Transportation: Commute to work: 92.4% car, 0.0% public transportation, 2.0% walk, 5.6% work from home (2000); Travel time to work: 10.1% less than 15 minutes, 52.1% 15 to 30 minutes, 25.5% 30 to 45 minutes, 8.0% 45 to 60 minutes, 4.2% 60 minutes or more (2000)

PORTLAND (city). Covers a land area of 4.108 square miles and a water area of 0.007 square miles. Located at 40.43° N. Lat.; 84.98° W. Long. Elevation is 908 feet.
History: Portland was the birthplace of Elwood Haynes (1857-1925) who invented the first successful clutch-driven automobile.
Population: 6,437 (2000); Race: 94.0% White, 0.2% Black, 1.4% Asian, 0.0% American Indian and Alaska Native, 3.6% Hispanic of any race, 1.3% two or more races (2000); Density: 1,566.8 persons per square mile (2000); Age: 22.9% under 18, 17.9% over 64 (2000); Marriage status: 21.0% never married, 55.8% now married, 10.7% widowed, 12.4% divorced (2000); Foreign born: 3.3% (2000); Ancestry (includes multiple ancestries): 20.0% United States or American, 18.1% German, 9.2% Other groups, 7.9% Irish, 7.5% English (2000).
Economy: Single-family building permits issued: n/a (2001) / 0 (2000); Multi-family building permits issued: n/a (2001) / 0 (2000); Employment by occupation: 7.4% management, 11.2% professional, 13.8% services, 19.5% sales, 0.5% farming, 10.7% construction, 36.9% production (2000).
Income: Per capita income: $18,375 (2000); Median household income: $31,045 (2000); Poverty rate: 9.6% (2000).
Taxes: Total city taxes per capita: $230 (1997); City property taxes per capita: $213 (1997).
Education: High school graduation rate: 77.2% (2000); College graduation rate: 11.0% (2000).

School District(s)

Jay School Corp (PK-12)
2000 Enrollment: 3,927 219-726-9341
Housing: Homeownership rate: 68.5% (2000); Median home value: $63,200 (2000); Median rent: $306 per month (2000); Median age of housing: 55 years (2000).
Hospitals: Jay County Hospital (65 beds)
Safety: Violent crime rate: 15.4 per 10,000 population; Property crime rate: 427.9 per 10,000 population (2001).
Newspapers: The Commercial Review (6 x week)
Transportation: Commute to work: 93.5% car, 0.3% public transportation, 2.5% walk, 1.7% work from home (2000); Travel time to work: 63.7% less than 15 minutes, 17.6% 15 to 30 minutes, 11.2% 30 to 45 minutes, 5.3% 45 to 60 minutes, 2.2% 60 minutes or more (2000)
Airports: Portland Municipal
Additional Information Contacts
Portland Area Chamber of Commerce 219-726-4481

REDKEY (town). Aka Red Key. Covers a land area of 0.935 square miles and a water area of 0.005 square miles. Located at 40.35° N. Lat.; 85.15° W. Long. Elevation is 964 feet.
Population: 1,427 (2000); Race: 99.2% White, 0.2% Black, 0.0% Asian, 0.1% American Indian and Alaska Native, 0.6% Hispanic of any race, 0.5% two or more races (2000); Density: 1,526.8 persons per square mile (2000); Age: 24.3% under 18, 15.0% over 64 (2000); Marriage status: 21.4% never married, 55.2% now married, 9.4% widowed, 14.0% divorced (2000); Foreign born: 0.0% (2000); Ancestry (includes multiple ancestries): 22.1% United States or American, 13.0% German, 10.9% Irish, 6.7% Other groups, 5.2% English (2000).
Economy: Employment by occupation: 5.4% management, 7.6% professional, 15.1% services, 21.5% sales, 0.5% farming, 13.4% construction, 36.6% production (2000).
Income: Per capita income: $13,906 (2000); Median household income: $30,732 (2000); Poverty rate: 14.0% (2000).
Taxes: Total city taxes per capita: $94 (1997); City property taxes per capita: $94 (1997).
Education: High school graduation rate: 76.2% (2000); College graduation rate: 6.3% (2000).
Housing: Homeownership rate: 73.4% (2000); Median home value: $45,800 (2000); Median rent: $242 per month (2000); Median age of housing: 56 years (2000).
Transportation: Commute to work: 96.2% car, 0.0% public transportation, 1.5% walk, 1.1% work from home (2000); Travel time to work: 22.6% less than 15 minutes, 37.5% 15 to 30 minutes, 21.2% 30 to 45 minutes, 9.9% 45 to 60 minutes, 8.8% 60 minutes or more (2000)

SALAMONIA (town). Covers a land area of 0.367 square miles and a water area of 0 square miles. Located at 40.38° N. Lat.; 84.86° W. Long. Elevation is 970 feet.
Population: 158 (2000); Race: 97.0% White, 0.0% Black, 0.0% Asian, 0.0% American Indian and Alaska Native, 0.0% Hispanic of any race, 3.0% two or more races (2000); Density: 429.9 persons per square mile (2000); Age: 44.5% under 18, 1.8% over 64 (2000); Marriage status: 21.1% never married, 55.8% now married, 12.6% widowed, 10.5% divorced (2000); Foreign born: 0.6% (2000); Ancestry (includes multiple ancestries): 36.6% United States or American, 10.4% German, 6.1% Irish, 4.3% English, 3.7% Other groups (2000).
Economy: In agricultural area. Employment by occupation: 1.3% management, 20.0% professional, 13.3% services, 16.0% sales, 2.7% farming, 9.3% construction, 37.3% production (2000).
Income: Per capita income: $11,734 (2000); Median household income: $36,458 (2000); Poverty rate: 16.1% (2000).
Taxes: Total city taxes per capita: $35 (1997); City property taxes per capita: $35 (1997).
Education: High school graduation rate: 91.0% (2000); College graduation rate: 2.6% (2000).

Housing: Homeownership rate: 81.8% (2000); Median home value: $40,600 (2000); Median rent: $225 per month (2000); Median age of housing: 60+ years (2000).
Transportation: Commute to work: 94.3% car, 0.0% public transportation, 0.0% walk, 2.9% work from home (2000); Travel time to work: 45.6% less than 15 minutes, 27.9% 15 to 30 minutes, 16.2% 30 to 45 minutes, 2.9% 45 to 60 minutes, 7.4% 60 minutes or more (2000)

Jefferson County

Located in southeastern Indiana; bounded on the south partly by the Ohio River and the Kentucky border; drained by Big Creek. Covers a land area of 361.40 square miles, a water area of 1.60 square miles, and is located in the Eastern Time Zone. The county government was organized in 1810. County seat is Madison.

Weather Station: Madison Sewage Plant — Elevation: 459 feet

	Jan	Feb	Mar	Apr	May	Jun	Jul	Aug	Sep	Oct	Nov	Dec
High	40	46	56	67	76	84	87	86	80	69	56	45
Low	23	26	35	43	53	62	67	65	58	46	37	28
Precip	3.0	2.8	4.3	4.3	4.9	4.3	4.3	4.0	2.9	3.3	3.8	3.6
Snow	5.7	4.2	2.4	tr	tr	0.0	0.0	0.0	0.0	0.1	tr	2.9

High and Low temperatures in degrees Fahrenheit; Precipitation and Snow in inches

Population: 31,705 (2000); Race: 96.5% White, 1.5% Black, 0.3% Asian, 0.3% American Indian and Alaska Native, 1.4% Hispanic of any race, 1.1% two or more races (2000); Density: 87.7 persons per square mile (2000); Age: 24.4% under 18, 13.1% over 64 (2000).
Religion: Five largest groups: 12.1% American Baptist Churches in the USA, 9.1% Catholic Church, 8.2% Southern Baptist Convention, 5.5% The United Methodist Church, 4.8% Christian Churches and Churches of Christ (2000).
Economy: Unemployment rate: 4.4% (11/2002); Total civilian labor force: 14,044 (11/2002); Leading industries: 30.0% manufacturing; 17.2% health care and social assistance; 16.6% retail trade (2000); Companies that employ more than 1,000 persons: 0 (2000); Companies that employ more than 100 persons: 17 (2000); Farms: 796 totaling 126,379 acres (1997); Minority business ownership rate: 0.0% (1997); Women business ownership rate: 14.8% (1997); Retail sales per capita: $8,963 (1997). Single-family building permits issued: 156 (2001) / 153 (2000); Multi-family building permits issued: 27 (2001) / 16 (2000).
Income: Per capita income: $17,412 (2000); Median household income: $38,189 (2000); Poverty rate: 9.6% (2000); Bankruptcy rate: 6.30% (2001).
Taxes: Total county taxes per capita: $171 (2000); County property taxes per capita: $165 (2000).
Education: High school graduation rate: 81.0% (2000); College graduation rate: 16.4% (2000).
Housing: Homeownership rate: 74.6% (2000); Median home value: $85,800 (2000); Median rent: $340 per month (2000); Median age of housing: 29 years (2000).
Health: Birth rate: 122.7 per 10,000 population (1998); Age adjusted death rate: 103.3 per 10,000 population (1999); Age adjusted cancer mortality rate: 258.6 deaths per 100,000 population (1999). Air Quality Index: 100% good, 0% moderate, 0% unhealthy (percent of days in 2000). Number of physicians: 16.4 per 10,000 population (1999); Number of hospital beds: 135.9 per 10,000 population (1999).
Elections: 2000 Presidential election results: 42.9% Gore, 55.2% Bush, 0.7% Nader, 0.8% Buchanan
National and State Parks: Clifty Falls State Park
Additional Information Contacts
Jefferson County Government Offices.................. 812-265-8921
Jefferson County Board of Realtors.................. 812-574-1101
Madison Chamber of Commerce.................. 812-265-3135
Small Business Development Center.................. 812-265-3127

Jefferson County Communities

BROOKSBURG (town). Covers a land area of 0.110 square miles and a water area of 0.002 square miles. Located at 38.73° N. Lat.; 85.24° W. Long. Elevation is 470 feet.
Population: 74 (2000); Race: 94.9% White, 0.0% Black, 0.0% Asian, 0.0% American Indian and Alaska Native, 0.0% Hispanic of any race, 5.1% two or more races (2000); Density: 673.5 persons per square mile (2000); Age: 22.8% under 18, 8.9% over 64 (2000); Marriage status: 7.9% never married, 54.0% now married, 12.7% widowed, 25.4% divorced (2000); Foreign born: 0.0% (2000); Ancestry (includes multiple ancestries): 25.3% Irish, 21.5% Other groups, 13.9% United States or American, 10.1% English, 2.5% Scottish (2000).
Economy: In agricultural area. Employment by occupation: 4.8% management, 19.0% professional, 19.0% services, 14.3% sales, 0.0% farming, 21.4% construction, 21.4% production (2000).
Income: Per capita income: $19,016 (2000); Median household income: $37,500 (2000); Poverty rate: 2.5% (2000).
Taxes: Total city taxes per capita: $26 (1997); City property taxes per capita: $26 (1997).
Education: High school graduation rate: 81.4% (2000); College graduation rate: 6.8% (2000).
Housing: Homeownership rate: 84.8% (2000); Median home value: $51,000 (2000); Median rent: $225 per month (2000); Median age of housing: 60+ years (2000).
Transportation: Commute to work: 95.2% car, 0.0% public transportation, 4.8% walk, 0.0% work from home (2000); Travel time to work: 19.0% less than 15 minutes, 59.5% 15 to 30 minutes, 11.9% 30 to 45 minutes, 4.8% 45 to 60 minutes, 4.8% 60 minutes or more (2000)

CANAAN (unincorporated postal area, zip code 47224). Covers a land area of 28.808 square miles and a water area of 0.040 square miles. Located at 38.89° N. Lat.; 85.21° W. Long. Elevation is 950 feet.
Population: 653 (2000); Race: 99.1% White, 0.9% Black, 0.0% Asian, 0.0% American Indian and Alaska Native, 0.0% Hispanic of any race, 0.0% two or more races (2000); Density: 22.7 persons per square mile (2000); Age: 15.6% under 18, 4.5% over 64 (2000); Marriage status: 19.9% never married, 71.0% now married, 0.8% widowed, 8.3% divorced (2000); Foreign born: 0.0% (2000); Ancestry (includes multiple ancestries): 33.6% United States or American, 19.1% German, 10.5% Other groups, 5.1% Irish, 4.9% English (2000).
Economy: Employment by occupation: 3.1% management, 6.4% professional, 23.1% services, 23.7% sales, 2.5% farming, 20.6% construction, 20.6% production (2000).
Income: Per capita income: $17,668 (2000); Median household income: $43,170 (2000); Poverty rate: 8.0% (2000).
Education: High school graduation rate: 72.7% (2000); College graduation rate: 2.9% (2000).
Housing: Homeownership rate: 76.1% (2000); Median home value: $74,700 (2000); Median rent: $287 per month (2000); Median age of housing: 25 years (2000).
Transportation: Commute to work: 95.0% car, 0.0% public transportation, 1.7% walk, 3.3% work from home (2000); Travel time to work: 17.9% less than 15 minutes, 35.2% 15 to 30 minutes, 19.9% 30 to 45 minutes, 12.1% 45 to 60 minutes, 15.0% 60 minutes or more (2000)

DEPUTY (unincorporated postal area, zip code 47230). Covers a land area of 42.876 square miles and a water area of 0.169 square miles. Located at 38.80° N. Lat.; 85.62° W. Long. Elevation is 620 feet.
Population: 1,776 (2000); Race: 99.3% White, 0.0% Black, 0.0% Asian, 0.0% American Indian and Alaska Native, 0.3% Hispanic of any race, 0.5% two or more races (2000); Density: 41.4 persons per square mile (2000); Age: 28.6% under 18, 9.4% over 64 (2000); Marriage status: 15.2% never married, 67.2% now married, 6.4% widowed, 11.2% divorced (2000); Foreign born: 0.3% (2000); Ancestry (includes multiple ancestries): 24.4% United States or American, 9.5% German, 8.2% Irish, 7.3% Other groups, 4.2% English (2000).
Economy: Employment by occupation: 3.7% management, 9.5% professional, 11.7% services, 16.6% sales, 0.8% farming, 20.7% construction, 37.0% production (2000).
Income: Per capita income: $13,405 (2000); Median household income: $32,948 (2000); Poverty rate: 8.2% (2000).
Education: High school graduation rate: 71.2% (2000); College graduation rate: 4.3% (2000).
Housing: Homeownership rate: 89.6% (2000); Median home value: $72,200 (2000); Median rent: $338 per month (2000); Median age of housing: 28 years (2000).
Transportation: Commute to work: 98.0% car, 0.0% public transportation, 0.0% walk, 2.0% work from home (2000); Travel time to work: 10.4% less than 15 minutes, 37.2% 15 to 30 minutes, 29.4% 30 to 45 minutes, 13.8% 45 to 60 minutes, 9.2% 60 minutes or more (2000)

DUPONT (town). Aka Du Pont. Covers a land area of 1.026 square miles and a water area of 0 square miles. Located at 38.89° N. Lat.; 85.51° W. Long. Elevation is 783 feet.
History: Laid out 1849.

Population: 392 (2000); Race: 94.0% White, 0.0% Black, 0.8% Asian, 0.0% American Indian and Alaska Native, 4.2% Hispanic of any race, 1.8% two or more races (2000); Density: 382.1 persons per square mile (2000); Age: 38.1% under 18, 4.2% over 64 (2000); Marriage status: 22.0% never married, 49.4% now married, 4.6% widowed, 23.9% divorced (2000); Foreign born: 3.4% (2000); Ancestry (includes multiple ancestries): 21.1% German, 17.2% Other groups, 12.5% United States or American, 11.2% English, 9.9% Irish (2000).
Economy: Agricultural area. Employment by occupation: 9.1% management, 17.6% professional, 13.9% services, 16.4% sales, 1.2% farming, 12.1% construction, 29.7% production (2000).
Income: Per capita income: $13,966 (2000); Median household income: $37,188 (2000); Poverty rate: 19.3% (2000).
Education: High school graduation rate: 75.9% (2000); College graduation rate: 7.5% (2000).
Housing: Homeownership rate: 75.5% (2000); Median home value: $65,900 (2000); Median rent: $338 per month (2000); Median age of housing: 46 years (2000).
Transportation: Commute to work: 98.8% car, 0.0% public transportation, 1.2% walk, 0.0% work from home (2000); Travel time to work: 10.9% less than 15 minutes, 52.1% 15 to 30 minutes, 19.4% 30 to 45 minutes, 9.1% 45 to 60 minutes, 8.5% 60 minutes or more (2000)

HANOVER (town). Covers a land area of 2.100 square miles and a water area of 0 square miles. Located at 38.71° N. Lat.; 85.47° W. Long. Elevation is 780 feet.
History: Hanover developed around Hanover College, founded in 1827 by the Presbyterian denomination as a manual labor academy.
Population: 2,834 (2000); Race: 96.1% White, 2.4% Black, 0.0% Asian, 0.0% American Indian and Alaska Native, 2.9% Hispanic of any race, 0.7% two or more races (2000); Density: 1,349.2 persons per square mile (2000); Age: 26.2% under 18, 13.5% over 64 (2000); Marriage status: 20.4% never married, 58.2% now married, 7.1% widowed, 14.3% divorced (2000); Foreign born: 0.9% (2000); Ancestry (includes multiple ancestries): 20.4% United States or American, 19.7% German, 12.4% Other groups, 10.0% Irish, 9.1% English (2000).
Economy: Single-family building permits issued: 12 (2001) / 12 (2000); Multi-family building permits issued: 0 (2001) / 0 (2000); Employment by occupation: 6.9% management, 20.8% professional, 17.0% services, 21.2% sales, 0.0% farming, 13.1% construction, 21.0% production (2000).
Income: Per capita income: $16,520 (2000); Median household income: $37,944 (2000); Poverty rate: 8.5% (2000).
Taxes: Total city taxes per capita: $32 (1997); City property taxes per capita: $27 (1997).
Education: High school graduation rate: 77.0% (2000); College graduation rate: 15.9% (2000).

School District(s)

Southwestern-Jefferson Co Con (PK-12)
2000 Enrollment: 1,574 812-866-6250

Four-year College(s)

Hanover College (Private, Not-for-profit, Presbyterian Church (USA))
2001 Enrollment: 1,111 812-866-7000
2001 Tuition: In-state $12,000; Out-of-state $12,000

Housing: Homeownership rate: 64.9% (2000); Median home value: $70,900 (2000); Median rent: $409 per month (2000); Median age of housing: 27 years (2000).
Transportation: Commute to work: 87.7% car, 0.0% public transportation, 7.9% walk, 3.2% work from home (2000); Travel time to work: 42.3% less than 15 minutes, 35.5% 15 to 30 minutes, 8.5% 30 to 45 minutes, 4.5% 45 to 60 minutes, 9.3% 60 minutes or more (2000)

MADISON (city). Covers a land area of 8.556 square miles and a water area of 0.327 square miles. Located at 38.75° N. Lat.; 85.39° W. Long. Elevation is 497 feet.
History: Madison was settled in 1805, and the town was platted in 1809 by Colonel John Paul, a Revolutionary War soldier, who named it for President James Madison. Shipyards flourished here in the 1830's, and by 1850 Madison was the largest city in Indiana. Tobacco was an important part of the economy in the early 1900's.
Population: 12,004 (2000); Race: 95.1% White, 2.5% Black, 0.2% Asian, 0.4% American Indian and Alaska Native, 1.9% Hispanic of any race, 1.4% two or more races (2000); Density: 1,402.9 persons per square mile (2000); Age: 21.9% under 18, 17.0% over 64 (2000); Marriage status: 21.4% never married, 55.4% now married, 9.4% widowed, 13.8% divorced (2000); Foreign born: 1.4% (2000); Ancestry (includes multiple ancestries): 21.5% German, 14.4% United States or American, 11.3% English, 10.6% Irish, 8.8% Other groups (2000).
Vital Statistics: Birth rate: 135.8 per 10,000 population (1998)
Economy: Single-family building permits issued: 70 (2001) / 61 (2000); Multi-family building permits issued: 27 (2001) / 16 (2000); Employment by occupation: 12.0% management, 18.3% professional, 14.7% services, 24.9% sales, 0.2% farming, 7.8% construction, 22.1% production (2000).
Income: Per capita income: $18,923 (2000); Median household income: $35,092 (2000); Poverty rate: 12.3% (2000).
Taxes: Total city taxes per capita: $251 (2000); City property taxes per capita: $248 (2000).
Education: High school graduation rate: 82.0% (2000); College graduation rate: 21.6% (2000).

School District(s)

Madison Consolidated Schools (PK-12)
2000 Enrollment: 3,408 812-273-8511

Two-year College(s)

Ivy Tech State College-Southeast (Public)
2001 Enrollment: 1,495 812-265-2580
2001 Tuition: In-state $1,986; Out-of-state $4,029
Kings Daughters Hospital-School of Rad Techn (Private, Not-for-profit)
2001 Enrollment: n/a 312-902-1100

Housing: Homeownership rate: 63.2% (2000); Median home value: $92,000 (2000); Median rent: $327 per month (2000); Median age of housing: 39 years (2000).
Hospitals: King's Daughters' Hospital (142 beds); Madison State Hospital (400 beds)
Safety: Violent crime rate: 19.1 per 10,000 population; Property crime rate: 377.7 per 10,000 population (2001).
Newspapers: The Madison Courier (6 x week); Weekly Herald (1 x week)
Transportation: Commute to work: 92.5% car, 1.1% public transportation, 3.3% walk, 2.1% work from home (2000); Travel time to work: 63.5% less than 15 minutes, 18.6% 15 to 30 minutes, 7.3% 30 to 45 minutes, 4.9% 45 to 60 minutes, 5.6% 60 minutes or more (2000)
Airports: Madison Municipal
Additional Information Contacts
Jefferson County Board of Realtors 812-574-1101
Madison Chamber of Commerce 812-265-3135
Small Business Development Center 812-265-3127

Jennings County

Located in southeastern Indiana; drained by Vernon, Graham, and Sand Creeks. Covers a land area of 377.20 square miles, a water area of 1.10 square miles, and is located in the Eastern Time Zone. The county government was organized in 1816. County seat is Vernon.

Weather Station: North Vernon 1 NW Elevation: 744 feet

	Jan	Feb	Mar	Apr	May	Jun	Jul	Aug	Sep	Oct	Nov	Dec
High	39	45	55	67	75	84	87	85	na	68	54	44
Low	21	25	34	43	52	61	65	63	na	45	36	27
Precip	2.3	2.6	3.7	4.5	4.5	3.7	4.4	4.4	2.9	3.2	4.0	3.3
Snow	4.0	2.8	1.7	0.1	tr	0.0	0.0	0.0	0.0	0.0	0.2	na

High and Low temperatures in degrees Fahrenheit; Precipitation and Snow in inches

Population: 27,554 (2000); Race: 97.0% White, 0.7% Black, 0.3% Asian, 0.4% American Indian and Alaska Native, 0.9% Hispanic of any race, 1.2% two or more races (2000); Density: 73.0 persons per square mile (2000); Age: 27.7% under 18, 10.7% over 64 (2000).
Religion: Five largest groups: 13.0% American Baptist Churches in the USA, 9.4% Catholic Church, 4.1% The United Methodist Church, 3.5% Christian Churches and Churches of Christ, 1.4% The Church of Jesus Christ of Latter-day Saints (2000).
Economy: Unemployment rate: 5.7% (11/2002); Total civilian labor force: 14,039 (11/2002); Leading industries: 38.5% manufacturing; 11.8% retail trade; 9.1% construction (2000); Companies that employ more than 1,000 persons: 0 (2000); Companies that employ more than 100 persons: 13 (2000); Farms: 605 totaling 130,373 acres (1997); Minority business ownership rate: 0.0% (1997); Women business ownership rate: 30.6% (1997); Retail sales per capita: $5,012 (1997). Single-family building permits issued: 192 (2001) / 208 (2000); Multi-family building permits issued: 19 (2001) / 0 (2000).
Income: Per capita income: $17,059 (2000); Median household income: $39,402 (2000); Poverty rate: 9.2% (2000); Bankruptcy rate: 10.93% (2001).
Taxes: Total county taxes per capita: $142 (1997); County property taxes per capita: $74 (1997).

Education: High school graduation rate: 76.2% (2000); College graduation rate: 8.4% (2000).
Housing: Homeownership rate: 79.1% (2000); Median home value: $81,900 (2000); Median rent: $371 per month (2000); Median age of housing: 25 years (2000).
Health: Birth rate: 153.2 per 10,000 population (1998); Age adjusted death rate: 92.3 per 10,000 population (1999); Age adjusted cancer mortality rate: 207.5 deaths per 100,000 population (1999). Number of physicians: 3.6 per 10,000 population (1999); Number of hospital beds: 9.1 per 10,000 population (1999).
Elections: 2000 Presidential election results: 37.4% Gore, 60.4% Bush, 0.5% Nader, 1.1% Buchanan
National and State Parks: Brush Creek State Fish and Wildlife Area; Crosley State Fish and Wildlife Area; Muscatatuck National Wildlife Refuge; Muscatatuck State Park; Selmier State Forest
Additional Information Contacts
Jennings County Government Offices 812-346-2131
Muscatatuck Board of Realtors 812-346-4982
North Vernon Chamber of Commerce 812-346-2339

Jennings County Communities

BUTLERVILLE (unincorporated postal area, zip code 47223). Covers a land area of 62.492 square miles and a water area of 0.285 square miles. Located at 39.04° N. Lat.; 85.49° W. Long. Elevation is 814 feet.
Population: 1,943 (2000); Race: 95.2% White, 1.1% Black, 0.0% Asian, 1.9% American Indian and Alaska Native, 0.0% Hispanic of any race, 1.7% two or more races (2000); Density: 31.1 persons per square mile (2000); Age: 23.3% under 18, 10.6% over 64 (2000); Marriage status: 12.0% never married, 73.8% now married, 6.8% widowed, 7.5% divorced (2000); Foreign born: 0.0% (2000); Ancestry (includes multiple ancestries): 14.5% German, 13.1% United States or American, 10.2% English, 9.7% Irish, 2.6% Other groups (2000).
Economy: Agricultural area. Manufacturing: boxes, pallets. Employment by occupation: 14.0% management, 5.5% professional, 19.1% services, 20.9% sales, 1.0% farming, 6.6% construction, 32.9% production (2000).
Income: Per capita income: $18,252 (2000); Median household income: $40,379 (2000); Poverty rate: 15.2% (2000).
Education: High school graduation rate: 68.1% (2000); College graduation rate: 5.5% (2000).
Housing: Homeownership rate: 82.6% (2000); Median home value: $76,300 (2000); Median rent: $334 per month (2000); Median age of housing: 36 years (2000).
Transportation: Commute to work: 87.2% car, 1.1% public transportation, 2.4% walk, 9.3% work from home (2000); Travel time to work: 24.4% less than 15 minutes, 27.6% 15 to 30 minutes, 28.8% 30 to 45 minutes, 7.7% 45 to 60 minutes, 11.3% 60 minutes or more (2000)

COMMISKEY (unincorporated postal area, zip code 47227). Covers a land area of 44.476 square miles and a water area of 0.118 square miles. Located at 38.87° N. Lat.; 85.64° W. Long. Elevation is 695 feet.
Population: 1,370 (2000); Race: 97.9% White, 0.0% Black, 0.5% Asian, 0.0% American Indian and Alaska Native, 2.1% Hispanic of any race, 0.0% two or more races (2000); Density: 30.8 persons per square mile (2000); Age: 30.2% under 18, 13.4% over 64 (2000); Marriage status: 16.2% never married, 70.9% now married, 3.5% widowed, 9.3% divorced (2000); Foreign born: 0.4% (2000); Ancestry (includes multiple ancestries): 18.3% United States or American, 15.2% German, 10.7% Irish, 7.2% Other groups, 4.5% English (2000).
Economy: Employment by occupation: 13.0% management, 13.6% professional, 11.6% services, 13.6% sales, 3.0% farming, 19.7% construction, 25.6% production (2000).
Income: Per capita income: $17,236 (2000); Median household income: $40,610 (2000); Poverty rate: 6.9% (2000).
Education: High school graduation rate: 72.3% (2000); College graduation rate: 10.9% (2000).
Housing: Homeownership rate: 81.5% (2000); Median home value: $89,700 (2000); Median rent: $300 per month (2000); Median age of housing: 23 years (2000).
Transportation: Commute to work: 96.6% car, 0.0% public transportation, 0.0% walk, 2.5% work from home (2000); Travel time to work: 3.8% less than 15 minutes, 48.0% 15 to 30 minutes, 31.1% 30 to 45 minutes, 8.1% 45 to 60 minutes, 9.0% 60 minutes or more (2000)

NORTH VERNON (city). Covers a land area of 4.389 square miles and a water area of 0.010 square miles. Located at 39.00° N. Lat.; 85.62° W. Long. Elevation is 725 feet.
History: North Vernon was platted in 1854 as a railroad town and trading center.
Population: 6,515 (2000); Race: 96.7% White, 1.2% Black, 0.7% Asian, 0.6% American Indian and Alaska Native, 0.4% Hispanic of any race, 0.7% two or more races (2000); Density: 1,484.4 persons per square mile (2000); Age: 27.2% under 18, 14.3% over 64 (2000); Marriage status: 20.3% never married, 56.5% now married, 9.1% widowed, 14.1% divorced (2000); Foreign born: 0.8% (2000); Ancestry (includes multiple ancestries): 19.0% German, 15.3% United States or American, 10.4% English, 8.6% Other groups, 6.9% Irish (2000).
Economy: Employment by occupation: 8.5% management, 16.5% professional, 15.2% services, 19.9% sales, 1.0% farming, 10.8% construction, 28.1% production (2000).
Income: Per capita income: $16,836 (2000); Median household income: $34,244 (2000); Poverty rate: 11.8% (2000).
Taxes: Total city taxes per capita: $110 (1997); City property taxes per capita: $110 (1997).
Education: High school graduation rate: 75.2% (2000); College graduation rate: 12.6% (2000).

School District(s)

Jennings County Schools (PK-12)
2000 Enrollment: 5,121 812-346-4483
Housing: Homeownership rate: 62.5% (2000); Median home value: $72,600 (2000); Median rent: $359 per month (2000); Median age of housing: 31 years (2000).
Hospitals: Saint Vincent Jennings Hospital (25 beds)
Safety: Violent crime rate: 41.2 per 10,000 population; Property crime rate: 409.0 per 10,000 population (2001).
Newspapers: The North Vernon Sun (1 x week); North Vernon Plain Dealer (1 x week)
Transportation: Commute to work: 95.9% car, 0.6% public transportation, 1.7% walk, 1.8% work from home (2000); Travel time to work: 58.6% less than 15 minutes, 17.5% 15 to 30 minutes, 17.3% 30 to 45 minutes, 2.7% 45 to 60 minutes, 3.9% 60 minutes or more (2000)
Additional Information Contacts
Muscatatuck Board of Realtors 812-346-4982
North Vernon Chamber of Commerce 812-346-2339

PARIS CROSSING (unincorporated postal area, zip code 47270). Covers a land area of 19.361 square miles and a water area of 0.058 square miles. Located at 38.83° N. Lat.; 85.71° W. Long. Elevation is 625 feet.
Population: 819 (2000); Race: 98.4% White, 0.0% Black, 0.0% Asian, 0.0% American Indian and Alaska Native, 0.0% Hispanic of any race, 1.6% two or more races (2000); Density: 42.3 persons per square mile (2000); Age: 29.0% under 18, 6.3% over 64 (2000); Marriage status: 11.7% never married, 75.0% now married, 3.3% widowed, 10.0% divorced (2000); Foreign born: 0.0% (2000); Ancestry (includes multiple ancestries): 20.0% German, 17.8% United States or American, 9.8% English, 7.2% Irish, 4.0% Dutch (2000).
Economy: Employment by occupation: 10.8% management, 6.3% professional, 8.0% services, 21.4% sales, 0.0% farming, 20.5% construction, 33.0% production (2000).
Income: Per capita income: $16,066 (2000); Median household income: $35,417 (2000); Poverty rate: 9.1% (2000).
Education: High school graduation rate: 80.3% (2000); College graduation rate: 3.3% (2000).
Housing: Homeownership rate: 86.5% (2000); Median home value: $78,400 (2000); Median rent: $275 per month (2000); Median age of housing: 23 years (2000).
Transportation: Commute to work: 100.0% car, 0.0% public transportation, 0.0% walk, 0.0% work from home (2000); Travel time to work: 5.6% less than 15 minutes, 42.8% 15 to 30 minutes, 33.4% 30 to 45 minutes, 12.0% 45 to 60 minutes, 6.2% 60 minutes or more (2000)

SCIPIO (unincorporated postal area, zip code 47273). Covers a land area of 29.239 square miles and a water area of 0.046 square miles. Located at 39.08° N. Lat.; 85.73° W. Long. Elevation is 686 feet.
Population: 1,863 (2000); Race: 97.0% White, 0.2% Black, 0.0% Asian, 0.0% American Indian and Alaska Native, 1.7% Hispanic of any race, 2.1% two or more races (2000); Density: 63.7 persons per square mile (2000); Age: 29.3% under 18, 8.8% over 64 (2000); Marriage status: 15.0% never married, 70.1% now married, 2.8% widowed, 12.1% divorced (2000); Foreign born: 1.4% (2000); Ancestry (includes multiple ancestries): 21.7% United States or

American, 21.4% German, 13.2% Other groups, 9.8% Irish, 8.1% English (2000).
Economy: Employment by occupation: 9.0% management, 8.4% professional, 12.9% services, 23.8% sales, 0.0% farming, 10.7% construction, 35.2% production (2000).
Income: Per capita income: $19,022 (2000); Median household income: $49,400 (2000); Poverty rate: 4.6% (2000).
Education: High school graduation rate: 86.5% (2000); College graduation rate: 5.8% (2000).
Housing: Homeownership rate: 90.2% (2000); Median home value: $85,800 (2000); Median rent: $400 per month (2000); Median age of housing: 29 years (2000).
Transportation: Commute to work: 94.4% car, 0.0% public transportation, 2.6% walk, 2.3% work from home (2000); Travel time to work: 15.2% less than 15 minutes, 51.7% 15 to 30 minutes, 28.3% 30 to 45 minutes, 2.6% 45 to 60 minutes, 2.3% 60 minutes or more (2000)

VERNON (town). Covers a land area of 0.239 square miles and a water area of 0 square miles. Located at 38.98° N. Lat.; 85.61° W. Long. Elevation is 665 feet.
History: The land grant that established Vernon in 1815 stipulated that it should be the county seat forever.
Population: 330 (2000); Race: 97.2% White, 1.9% Black, 0.0% Asian, 0.9% American Indian and Alaska Native, 0.0% Hispanic of any race, 0.0% two or more races (2000); Density: 1,383.2 persons per square mile (2000); Age: 28.3% under 18, 14.6% over 64 (2000); Marriage status: 35.3% never married, 39.1% now married, 13.6% widowed, 12.0% divorced (2000); Foreign born: 0.0% (2000); Ancestry (includes multiple ancestries): 15.8% German, 11.5% United States or American, 10.2% Irish, 4.0% French (except Basque), 3.4% Other groups (2000).
Economy: Employment by occupation: 6.6% management, 8.0% professional, 13.9% services, 21.2% sales, 0.0% farming, 11.7% construction, 38.7% production (2000).
Income: Per capita income: $17,367 (2000); Median household income: $29,750 (2000); Poverty rate: 9.5% (2000).
Taxes: Total city taxes per capita: $77 (1997); City property taxes per capita: $27 (1997).
Education: High school graduation rate: 80.8% (2000); College graduation rate: 8.8% (2000).
Housing: Homeownership rate: 61.1% (2000); Median home value: $81,300 (2000); Median rent: $388 per month (2000); Median age of housing: 60+ years (2000).
Transportation: Commute to work: 93.1% car, 0.0% public transportation, 2.3% walk, 4.6% work from home (2000); Travel time to work: 28.0% less than 15 minutes, 28.8% 15 to 30 minutes, 22.4% 30 to 45 minutes, 15.2% 45 to 60 minutes, 5.6% 60 minutes or more (2000)

Johnson County

Located in central Indiana; drained by the West Fork of the White River. Covers a land area of 320.20 square miles, a water area of 1.40 square miles, and is located in the Eastern Time Zone. The county government was organized in 1822. County seat is Franklin.

Johnson County is part of the Indianapolis, IN MSA. The entire metro area includes: Boone County; Hamilton County; Hancock County; Hendricks County; Johnson County; Madison County; Marion County; Morgan County; Shelby County

Weather Station: New Whiteland Elevation: 784 feet

	Jan	Feb	Mar	Apr	May	Jun	Jul	Aug	Sep	Oct	Nov	Dec
High	33	38	51	62	73	82	85	83	77	65	51	39
Low	16	19	30	40	51	60	63	61	53	41	32	22
Precip	2.2	2.1	3.6	4.2	4.5	4.0	4.3	3.6	2.9	2.9	4.0	3.1
Snow	na	na	na	0.4	0.0	0.0	0.0	0.0	0.0	0.3	0.4	na

High and Low temperatures in degrees Fahrenheit; Precipitation and Snow in inches

Population: 115,209 (2000); Race: 97.0% White, 0.9% Black, 0.8% Asian, 0.1% American Indian and Alaska Native, 1.0% Hispanic of any race, 0.7% two or more races (2000); Density: 359.8 persons per square mile (2000); Age: 27.2% under 18, 11.0% over 64 (2000).
Religion: Five largest groups: 8.5% Catholic Church, 7.1% Christian Churches and Churches of Christ, 5.1% Independent, Non-Charismatic Churches, 2.9% The United Methodist Church, 2.3% General Association of Regular Baptist Churches (2000).
Economy: Unemployment rate: 3.6% (11/2002); Total civilian labor force: 65,847 (11/2002); Leading industries: 22.6% retail trade; 18.3% manufacturing; 12.2% health care and social assistance (2000); Companies that employ more than 1,000 persons: 2 (2000); Companies that employ more than 100 persons: 60 (2000); Farms: 526 totaling 135,563 acres (1997); Minority business ownership rate: 3.5% (1997); Women business ownership rate: 27.7% (1997); Retail sales per capita: $10,957 (1997). Single-family building permits issued: 1,388 (2001) / 1,450 (2000); Multi-family building permits issued: 118 (2001) / 30 (2000).
Income: Per capita income: $22,976 (2000); Median household income: $52,693 (2000); Poverty rate: 5.6% (2000); Bankruptcy rate: 9.14% (2001).
Taxes: Total county taxes per capita: $207 (2000); County property taxes per capita: $86 (2000).
Education: High school graduation rate: 85.7% (2000); College graduation rate: 23.1% (2000).
Housing: Homeownership rate: 76.5% (2000); Median home value: $122,500 (2000); Median rent: $512 per month (2000); Median age of housing: 22 years (2000).
Health: Birth rate: 138.9 per 10,000 population (1998); Age adjusted death rate: 89.0 per 10,000 population (1999); Age adjusted cancer mortality rate: 226.8 deaths per 100,000 population (1999). Air Quality Index: 53% good, 47% moderate, 0% unhealthy (percent of days in 2000). Number of physicians: 18.3 per 10,000 population (1999); Number of hospital beds: 25.3 per 10,000 population (1999).
Elections: 2000 Presidential election results: 28.3% Gore, 69.5% Bush, 0.4% Nader, 0.9% Buchanan
National and State Parks: Atterbury State Fish and Wildlife Area
Additional Information Contacts
Johnson County Government Offices 317-736-5000
Franklin Chamber of Commerce 317-736-6334
Greenwood Chamber of Commerce. 317-888-4856

Johnson County Communities

BARGERSVILLE (town). Covers a land area of 1.092 square miles and a water area of 0 square miles. Located at 39.52° N. Lat.; 86.16° W. Long. Elevation is 819 feet.
Population: 2,120 (2000); Race: 98.6% White, 0.0% Black, 0.0% Asian, 0.6% American Indian and Alaska Native, 0.2% Hispanic of any race, 0.8% two or more races (2000); Density: 1,941.4 persons per square mile (2000); Age: 31.1% under 18, 7.2% over 64 (2000); Marriage status: 18.1% never married, 63.2% now married, 4.6% widowed, 14.0% divorced (2000); Foreign born: 0.6% (2000); Ancestry (includes multiple ancestries): 26.4% United States or American, 20.3% German, 10.3% Irish, 8.3% English, 7.3% Other groups (2000).
Economy: Agricultural area. Manufacturing: wood furniture, robotics, machinery. Single-family building permits issued: 33 (2001) / 23 (2000); Multi-family building permits issued: 0 (2001) / 0 (2000); Employment by occupation: 9.0% management, 12.1% professional, 14.9% services, 27.2% sales, 0.3% farming, 16.2% construction, 20.4% production (2000).
Income: Per capita income: $19,499 (2000); Median household income: $48,264 (2000); Poverty rate: 4.3% (2000).
Taxes: Total city taxes per capita: $82 (1997); City property taxes per capita: $80 (1997).
Education: High school graduation rate: 87.0% (2000); College graduation rate: 11.9% (2000).
Housing: Homeownership rate: 75.7% (2000); Median home value: $90,900 (2000); Median rent: $503 per month (2000); Median age of housing: 28 years (2000).
Transportation: Commute to work: 96.2% car, 0.0% public transportation, 1.2% walk, 2.6% work from home (2000); Travel time to work: 21.6% less than 15 minutes, 34.1% 15 to 30 minutes, 26.9% 30 to 45 minutes, 12.0% 45 to 60 minutes, 5.4% 60 minutes or more (2000)

EDINBURGH (town). Covers a land area of 2.843 square miles and a water area of 0 square miles. Located at 39.35° N. Lat.; 85.96° W. Long. Elevation is 670 feet.
Population: 4,505 (2000); Race: 99.4% White, 0.0% Black, 0.0% Asian, 0.2% American Indian and Alaska Native, 0.9% Hispanic of any race, 0.2% two or more races (2000); Density: 1,584.8 persons per square mile (2000); Age: 27.5% under 18, 10.5% over 64 (2000); Marriage status: 20.0% never married, 58.3% now married, 6.0% widowed, 15.7% divorced (2000); Foreign born: 0.7% (2000); Ancestry (includes multiple ancestries): 15.0% United States or American, 13.3% English, 11.3% German, 5.8% Other groups, 5.7% Irish (2000).

Economy: Single-family building permits issued: 3 (2001) / 4 (2000); Multi-family building permits issued: 10 (2001) / 6 (2000); Employment by occupation: 6.7% management, 5.6% professional, 13.7% services, 20.2% sales, 0.4% farming, 11.1% construction, 42.4% production (2000).
Income: Per capita income: $14,486 (2000); Median household income: $32,170 (2000); Poverty rate: 12.4% (2000).
Taxes: Total city taxes per capita: $248 (1997); City property taxes per capita: $244 (1997).
Education: High school graduation rate: 59.4% (2000); College graduation rate: 2.8% (2000).

School District(s)
Edinburgh Community Sch Corp (KG-12)
2000 Enrollment: 983 812-526-2681
Housing: Homeownership rate: 63.6% (2000); Median home value: $87,400 (2000); Median rent: $395 per month (2000); Median age of housing: 37 years (2000).
Transportation: Commute to work: 89.4% car, 0.0% public transportation, 6.2% walk, 0.6% work from home (2000); Travel time to work: 49.8% less than 15 minutes, 30.8% 15 to 30 minutes, 8.6% 30 to 45 minutes, 7.5% 45 to 60 minutes, 3.4% 60 minutes or more (2000)

FRANKLIN (city). Covers a land area of 11.263 square miles and a water area of 0 square miles. Located at 39.49° N. Lat.; 86.05° W. Long. Elevation is 728 feet.
History: Franklin developed as a shipping center for grain and tomatoes. In 1834 Franklin College was established as the Indiana Baptist Manual Labor Institute.
Population: 19,463 (2000); Race: 96.1% White, 1.6% Black, 0.6% Asian, 0.2% American Indian and Alaska Native, 1.1% Hispanic of any race, 0.6% two or more races (2000); Density: 1,728.1 persons per square mile (2000); Age: 25.7% under 18, 15.7% over 64 (2000); Marriage status: 23.6% never married, 57.7% now married, 7.8% widowed, 10.9% divorced (2000); Foreign born: 1.5% (2000); Ancestry (includes multiple ancestries): 19.1% German, 13.8% United States or American, 12.3% Irish, 10.8% Other groups, 9.8% English (2000).
Vital Statistics: Birth rate: 170.6 per 10,000 population (1998)
Economy: Single-family building permits issued: 200 (2001) / 292 (2000); Multi-family building permits issued: 0 (2001) / 6 (2000); Employment by occupation: 11.0% management, 16.7% professional, 14.7% services, 25.0% sales, 0.6% farming, 11.0% construction, 21.0% production (2000).
Income: Per capita income: $18,937 (2000); Median household income: $45,414 (2000); Poverty rate: 7.6% (2000).
Taxes: Total city taxes per capita: $213 (1997); City property taxes per capita: $200 (1997).
Education: High school graduation rate: 79.4% (2000); College graduation rate: 17.9% (2000).

School District(s)
Franklin Community School Corp (KG-12)
2000 Enrollment: 4,196 317-738-5800

Four-year College(s)
Franklin College of Indiana (Private, Not-for-profit, American Baptist)
2001 Enrollment: 1,028 317-738-8000
2001 Tuition: In-state $14,750; Out-of-state $14,750
Housing: Homeownership rate: 67.9% (2000); Median home value: $103,000 (2000); Median rent: $492 per month (2000); Median age of housing: 20 years (2000).
Hospitals: Johnson Memorial Hospital (160 beds)
Safety: Violent crime rate: 6.6 per 10,000 population; Property crime rate: 556.4 per 10,000 population (2001).
Newspapers: Daily Journal (6 x week); Franklin Challenger (1 x week)
Transportation: Commute to work: 94.0% car, 0.2% public transportation, 2.8% walk, 1.4% work from home (2000); Travel time to work: 45.4% less than 15 minutes, 25.0% 15 to 30 minutes, 18.6% 30 to 45 minutes, 7.0% 45 to 60 minutes, 4.0% 60 minutes or more (2000)
Additional Information Contacts
Franklin Chamber of Commerce 317-736-6334

GREENWOOD (city). Covers a land area of 14.273 square miles and a water area of <.001 square miles. Located at 39.61° N. Lat.; 86.11° W. Long. Elevation is 812 feet.
History: Greenwood developed as an industrial town with automobile-parts factories and a canning company.
Population: 36,037 (2000); Race: 96.7% White, 0.6% Black, 1.0% Asian, 0.1% American Indian and Alaska Native, 1.8% Hispanic of any race, 1.0% two or more races (2000); Density: 2,524.8 persons per square mile (2000); Age: 25.1% under 18, 12.1% over 64 (2000); Marriage status: 23.1% never married, 58.4% now married, 6.9% widowed, 11.6% divorced (2000); Foreign born: 2.4% (2000); Ancestry (includes multiple ancestries): 24.8% German, 14.6% United States or American, 13.0% Irish, 10.7% English, 7.8% Other groups (2000).
Vital Statistics: Birth rate: 178.4 per 10,000 population (1998)
Economy: Unemployment rate: 2.6% (11/2002); Total civilian labor force: 20,780 (11/2002); Single-family building permits issued: 592 (2001) / 584 (2000); Multi-family building permits issued: 108 (2001) / 14 (2000); Employment by occupation: 14.9% management, 20.7% professional, 12.0% services, 30.0% sales, 0.1% farming, 10.0% construction, 12.3% production (2000).
Income: Per capita income: $23,003 (2000); Median household income: $46,176 (2000); Poverty rate: 7.0% (2000).
Taxes: Total city taxes per capita: $111 (2000); City property taxes per capita: $111 (2000).
Education: High school graduation rate: 87.6% (2000); College graduation rate: 23.7% (2000).

School District(s)
Center Grove Com Sch Corp (KG-12)
2000 Enrollment: 6,676 317-881-9326
Central Nine Career Center
2000 Enrollment: n/a 317-888-4401
Greenwood Community Sch Corp (PK-12)
2000 Enrollment: 3,839 317-889-4060

Four-year College(s)
Heritage Baptist University (Private, Not-for-profit, Baptist)
2001 Enrollment: n/a 317-882-2327
Housing: Homeownership rate: 62.5% (2000); Median home value: $116,400 (2000); Median rent: $528 per month (2000); Median age of housing: 20 years (2000).
Hospitals: Valle Vista Health System (88 beds)
Safety: Violent crime rate: 38.9 per 10,000 population; Property crime rate: 504.7 per 10,000 population (2001).
Newspapers: Greenwood and Southside Challenger (1 x week)
Transportation: Commute to work: 95.9% car, 0.1% public transportation, 1.7% walk, 1.9% work from home (2000); Travel time to work: 25.7% less than 15 minutes, 37.4% 15 to 30 minutes, 26.9% 30 to 45 minutes, 7.2% 45 to 60 minutes, 2.9% 60 minutes or more (2000)
Additional Information Contacts
Greenwood Chamber of Commerce 317-888-4856

NEEDHAM (unincorporated postal area, zip code 46162). Covers a land area of 11.140 square miles and a water area of 0 square miles. Located at 39.54° N. Lat.; 85.95° W. Long. Elevation is 729 feet.
Population: 411 (2000); Race: 100.0% White, 0.0% Black, 0.0% Asian, 0.0% American Indian and Alaska Native, 0.0% Hispanic of any race, 0.0% two or more races (2000); Density: 36.9 persons per square mile (2000); Age: 22.6% under 18, 11.3% over 64 (2000); Marriage status: 37.6% never married, 50.3% now married, 8.2% widowed, 3.9% divorced (2000); Foreign born: 1.9% (2000); Ancestry (includes multiple ancestries): 27.0% English, 14.3% Dutch, 12.7% Other groups, 10.5% German, 6.2% Irish (2000).
Economy: Employment by occupation: 27.5% management, 12.0% professional, 16.5% services, 11.5% sales, 3.0% farming, 16.0% construction, 13.5% production (2000).
Income: Per capita income: $16,440 (2000); Median household income: $55,278 (2000); Poverty rate: 9.9% (2000).
Education: High school graduation rate: 75.0% (2000); College graduation rate: 3.4% (2000).
Housing: Homeownership rate: 79.0% (2000); Median home value: $92,200 (2000); Median rent: $193 per month (2000); Median age of housing: 57 years (2000).
Transportation: Commute to work: 79.0% car, 4.0% public transportation, 0.0% walk, 17.0% work from home (2000); Travel time to work: 32.5% less than 15 minutes, 25.9% 15 to 30 minutes, 7.8% 30 to 45 minutes, 12.0% 45 to 60 minutes, 21.7% 60 minutes or more (2000)

NEW WHITELAND (town). Covers a land area of 1.229 square miles and a water area of 0 square miles. Located at 39.56° N. Lat.; 86.09° W. Long. Elevation is 806 feet.
Population: 4,579 (2000); Race: 99.3% White, 0.0% Black, 0.0% Asian, 0.0% American Indian and Alaska Native, 0.7% Hispanic of any race, 0.3% two or more races (2000); Density: 3,725.5 persons per square mile (2000); Age: 30.2% under 18, 9.6% over 64 (2000); Marriage status: 17.9% never married, 69.4% now married, 4.0% widowed, 8.7% divorced (2000); Foreign born: 0.9% (2000); Ancestry (includes multiple ancestries): 24.3% German,

15.6% United States or American, 13.9% Irish, 11.0% English, 8.6% Other groups (2000).
Economy: Single-family building permits issued: 0 (2001) / 3 (2000); Multi-family building permits issued: 0 (2001) / 0 (2000); Employment by occupation: 9.8% management, 11.1% professional, 11.4% services, 28.8% sales, 0.0% farming, 16.3% construction, 22.6% production (2000).
Income: Per capita income: $18,221 (2000); Median household income: $52,907 (2000); Poverty rate: 3.0% (2000).
Taxes: Total city taxes per capita: $95 (1997); City property taxes per capita: $92 (1997).
Education: High school graduation rate: 85.5% (2000); College graduation rate: 9.8% (2000).
Housing: Homeownership rate: 90.6% (2000); Median home value: $89,500 (2000); Median rent: $710 per month (2000); Median age of housing: 36 years (2000).
Safety: Violent crime rate: 8.7 per 10,000 population; Property crime rate: 119.4 per 10,000 population (2001).
Transportation: Commute to work: 95.3% car, 0.0% public transportation, 0.4% walk, 2.5% work from home (2000); Travel time to work: 22.0% less than 15 minutes, 31.6% 15 to 30 minutes, 31.4% 30 to 45 minutes, 11.0% 45 to 60 minutes, 4.1% 60 minutes or more (2000)

NINEVEH (unincorporated postal area, zip code 46164). Covers a land area of 22.920 square miles and a water area of 0.845 square miles. Located at 39.32° N. Lat.; 86.11° W. Long. Elevation is 772 feet.
Population: 4,133 (2000); Race: 97.5% White, 0.4% Black, 0.4% Asian, 0.2% American Indian and Alaska Native, 0.6% Hispanic of any race, 0.7% two or more races (2000); Density: 180.3 persons per square mile (2000); Age: 23.1% under 18, 11.5% over 64 (2000); Marriage status: 18.1% never married, 66.7% now married, 5.0% widowed, 10.2% divorced (2000); Foreign born: 0.8% (2000); Ancestry (includes multiple ancestries): 26.9% German, 14.7% Irish, 12.1% English, 7.6% Other groups, 7.0% United States or American (2000).
Economy: Employment by occupation: 11.5% management, 14.3% professional, 11.5% services, 25.5% sales, 0.1% farming, 19.0% construction, 18.2% production (2000).
Income: Per capita income: $20,532 (2000); Median household income: $46,810 (2000); Poverty rate: 7.6% (2000).
Education: High school graduation rate: 87.2% (2000); College graduation rate: 14.0% (2000).
Housing: Homeownership rate: 94.2% (2000); Median home value: $116,300 (2000); Median rent: $540 per month (2000); Median age of housing: 24 years (2000).
Transportation: Commute to work: 98.0% car, 0.0% public transportation, 0.0% walk, 2.0% work from home (2000); Travel time to work: 8.1% less than 15 minutes, 31.1% 15 to 30 minutes, 25.4% 30 to 45 minutes, 14.8% 45 to 60 minutes, 20.6% 60 minutes or more (2000)

PRINCES LAKES (town). Covers a land area of 1.281 square miles and a water area of 0.193 square miles. Located at 39.35° N. Lat.; 86.10° W. Long. Elevation is 880 feet.
Population: 1,506 (2000); Race: 98.2% White, 0.4% Black, 0.6% Asian, 0.0% American Indian and Alaska Native, 1.6% Hispanic of any race, 0.8% two or more races (2000); Density: 1,175.3 persons per square mile (2000); Age: 29.1% under 18, 9.4% over 64 (2000); Marriage status: 18.0% never married, 64.5% now married, 4.6% widowed, 12.9% divorced (2000); Foreign born: 0.9% (2000); Ancestry (includes multiple ancestries): 21.9% German, 12.7% Irish, 10.1% English, 9.3% United States or American, 8.5% Other groups (2000).
Economy: Single-family building permits issued: 8 (2001) / 5 (2000); Multi-family building permits issued: 0 (2001) / 0 (2000); Employment by occupation: 8.7% management, 14.5% professional, 12.0% services, 23.5% sales, 0.3% farming, 15.8% construction, 25.2% production (2000).
Income: Per capita income: $19,378 (2000); Median household income: $46,339 (2000); Poverty rate: 6.2% (2000).
Taxes: Total city taxes per capita: $116 (1997); City property taxes per capita: $107 (1997).
Education: High school graduation rate: 85.2% (2000); College graduation rate: 13.4% (2000).
Housing: Homeownership rate: 90.9% (2000); Median home value: $103,300 (2000); Median rent: $535 per month (2000); Median age of housing: 37 years (2000).
Transportation: Commute to work: 96.1% car, 0.0% public transportation, 0.0% walk, 3.9% work from home (2000); Travel time to work: 10.0% less than 15 minutes, 39.0% 15 to 30 minutes, 22.7% 30 to 45 minutes, 16.5% 45 to 60 minutes, 11.8% 60 minutes or more (2000)

TRAFALGAR (town). Covers a land area of 1.289 square miles and a water area of 0 square miles. Located at 39.41° N. Lat.; 86.15° W. Long. Elevation is 828 feet.
History: Laid out 1850.
Population: 798 (2000); Race: 99.8% White, 0.2% Black, 0.0% Asian, 0.0% American Indian and Alaska Native, 1.0% Hispanic of any race, 0.0% two or more races (2000); Density: 619.2 persons per square mile (2000); Age: 36.2% under 18, 7.5% over 64 (2000); Marriage status: 19.3% never married, 62.9% now married, 2.5% widowed, 15.3% divorced (2000); Foreign born: 0.2% (2000); Ancestry (includes multiple ancestries): 22.3% German, 12.6% Irish, 11.5% United States or American, 10.5% English, 8.6% Other groups (2000).
Economy: In agricultural area. Manufacturing of wood products. Single-family building permits issued: 12 (2001) / 22 (2000); Multi-family building permits issued: 0 (2001) / 0 (2000); Employment by occupation: 8.9% management, 13.1% professional, 10.8% services, 23.9% sales, 0.0% farming, 14.5% construction, 28.8% production (2000).
Income: Per capita income: $17,079 (2000); Median household income: $50,357 (2000); Poverty rate: 8.4% (2000).
Taxes: Total city taxes per capita: $84 (1997); City property taxes per capita: $76 (1997).
Education: High school graduation rate: 78.2% (2000); College graduation rate: 13.8% (2000).

School District(s)

Nineveh-Hensley-Jackson United (KG-12)
2000 Enrollment: 1,796 317-878-2100

Housing: Homeownership rate: 75.0% (2000); Median home value: $101,500 (2000); Median rent: $485 per month (2000); Median age of housing: 17 years (2000).
Transportation: Commute to work: 94.6% car, 1.0% public transportation, 3.1% walk, 1.3% work from home (2000); Travel time to work: 22.3% less than 15 minutes, 36.8% 15 to 30 minutes, 20.7% 30 to 45 minutes, 15.5% 45 to 60 minutes, 4.7% 60 minutes or more (2000)

WHITELAND (town). Covers a land area of 2.272 square miles and a water area of 0 square miles. Located at 39.54° N. Lat.; 86.08° W. Long. Elevation is 800 feet.
Population: 3,958 (2000); Race: 98.0% White, 0.3% Black, 0.4% Asian, 0.0% American Indian and Alaska Native, 0.0% Hispanic of any race, 1.3% two or more races (2000); Density: 1,742.4 persons per square mile (2000); Age: 34.6% under 18, 5.0% over 64 (2000); Marriage status: 16.5% never married, 68.5% now married, 2.5% widowed, 12.5% divorced (2000); Foreign born: 0.6% (2000); Ancestry (includes multiple ancestries): 23.3% German, 15.8% United States or American, 14.7% Irish, 13.7% English, 9.3% Other groups (2000).
Economy: Single-family building permits issued: 41 (2001) / 33 (2000); Multi-family building permits issued: 0 (2001) / 4 (2000); Employment by occupation: 13.3% management, 15.5% professional, 12.0% services, 27.2% sales, 0.0% farming, 10.2% construction, 21.9% production (2000).
Income: Per capita income: $21,169 (2000); Median household income: $56,944 (2000); Poverty rate: 1.9% (2000).
Taxes: Total city taxes per capita: $67 (1997); City property taxes per capita: $55 (1997).
Education: High school graduation rate: 92.5% (2000); College graduation rate: 20.7% (2000).

School District(s)

Clark-Pleasant Com School Corp (KG-12)
2000 Enrollment: 3,348 317-535-7579

Housing: Homeownership rate: 88.7% (2000); Median home value: $107,300 (2000); Median rent: $722 per month (2000); Median age of housing: 14 years (2000).
Transportation: Commute to work: 97.6% car, 0.0% public transportation, 0.0% walk, 1.8% work from home (2000); Travel time to work: 17.0% less than 15 minutes, 41.1% 15 to 30 minutes, 28.8% 30 to 45 minutes, 6.6% 45 to 60 minutes, 6.5% 60 minutes or more (2000)

Knox County

Located in southwestern Indiana; bounded on the west by the Wabash River and the Illinois border, on the east by the West Fork of the White River, and on the south by the White River. Covers a land area of 515.80 square miles, a water area of 8.20 square miles, and is located in the Eastern Time Zone. The county government was organized in 1790. County seat is Vincennes.

Population: 39,256 (2000); Race: 96.2% White, 1.8% Black, 0.6% Asian, 0.3% American Indian and Alaska Native, 1.0% Hispanic of any race, 0.7% two or more races (2000); Density: 76.1 persons per square mile (2000); Age: 23.0% under 18, 15.3% over 64 (2000).
Religion: Five largest groups: 14.4% Catholic Church, 6.0% The United Methodist Church, 5.0% American Baptist Churches in the USA, 3.8% United Church of Christ, 3.5% Christian Churches and Churches of Christ (2000).
Economy: Unemployment rate: 3.3% (11/2002); Total civilian labor force: 19,154 (11/2002); Leading industries: 23.6% health care and social assistance; 18.2% retail trade; 10.7% accommodation & food services (2000); Companies that employ more than 1,000 persons: 1 (2000); Companies that employ more than 100 persons: 17 (2000); Farms: 584 totaling 280,628 acres (1997); Minority business ownership rate: 0.0% (1997); Women business ownership rate: 22.0% (1997); Retail sales per capita: $10,099 (1997). Single-family building permits issued: 63 (2001) / 48 (2000); Multi-family building permits issued: 20 (2001) / 16 (2000).
Income: Per capita income: $16,085 (2000); Median household income: $31,362 (2000); Poverty rate: 16.0% (2000); Bankruptcy rate: 5.60% (2001).
Taxes: Total county taxes per capita: $160 (2000); County property taxes per capita: $118 (2000).
Education: High school graduation rate: 81.7% (2000); College graduation rate: 14.4% (2000).
Housing: Homeownership rate: 68.9% (2000); Median home value: $63,600 (2000); Median rent: $316 per month (2000); Median age of housing: 46 years (2000).
Health: Birth rate: 120.2 per 10,000 population (1998); Age adjusted death rate: 101.3 per 10,000 population (1999); Age adjusted cancer mortality rate: 220.1 deaths per 100,000 population (1999). Number of physicians: 17.3 per 10,000 population (1999); Number of hospital beds: 61.6 per 10,000 population (1999).
Elections: 2000 Presidential election results: 41.9% Gore, 56.4% Bush, 0.5% Nader, 0.7% Buchanan
National and State Parks: George Rogers Clark National Historical Park; George Rogers Clark State Memorial; White Oak State Fishing Area
Additional Information Contacts
Knox County Government Offices. 812-885-2502
Knox County Board of Realtors 812-895-5669
Vincennes Chamber of Commerce. 812-882-6440

Knox County Communities

BICKNELL (city). Covers a land area of 1.524 square miles and a water area of 0 square miles. Located at 38.77° N. Lat.; 87.30° W. Long. Elevation is 530 feet.
History: Coal mining began in Bicknell in 1875, and was responsible for the growth of the community. The town was founded by a Bicknell, an ancestor of Ernest P. Bicknell (1862-1930) who directed American Red Cross activities abroad.
Population: 3,378 (2000); Race: 98.8% White, 0.1% Black, 0.2% Asian, 0.1% American Indian and Alaska Native, 0.8% Hispanic of any race, 0.8% two or more races (2000); Density: 2,216.8 persons per square mile (2000); Age: 25.8% under 18, 17.1% over 64 (2000); Marriage status: 19.1% never married, 57.8% now married, 9.0% widowed, 14.0% divorced (2000); Foreign born: 1.7% (2000); Ancestry (includes multiple ancestries): 18.4% United States or American, 15.9% German, 8.7% Irish, 7.2% Other groups, 7.1% English (2000).
Economy: Single-family building permits issued: 0 (2001) / 0 (2000); Multi-family building permits issued: 0 (2001) / 0 (2000); Employment by occupation: 6.3% management, 11.2% professional, 21.2% services, 24.1% sales, 1.0% farming, 12.8% construction, 23.4% production (2000).
Income: Per capita income: $13,027 (2000); Median household income: $23,046 (2000); Poverty rate: 26.3% (2000).
Taxes: Total city taxes per capita: $114 (1997); City property taxes per capita: $114 (1997).
Education: High school graduation rate: 73.7% (2000); College graduation rate: 4.2% (2000).

School District(s)

North Knox School Corp (KG-12)
2000 Enrollment: 1,638 812-735-4434
Housing: Homeownership rate: 68.6% (2000); Median home value: $42,200 (2000); Median rent: $272 per month (2000); Median age of housing: 56 years (2000).
Transportation: Commute to work: 92.5% car, 0.0% public transportation, 3.8% walk, 1.1% work from home (2000); Travel time to work: 34.7% less than 15 minutes, 30.2% 15 to 30 minutes, 23.6% 30 to 45 minutes, 2.4% 45 to 60 minutes, 9.2% 60 minutes or more (2000)

BRUCEVILLE (town). Covers a land area of 0.294 square miles and a water area of 0 square miles. Located at 38.75° N. Lat.; 87.41° W. Long. Elevation is 513 feet.
History: Bruceville was first settled by Major William Bruce in 1805, who built a fort on his land. The town was founded in 1811. Major Bruce operated a tavern and inn here, and raised his family of 25 children. Abraham Lincoln was a guest of Bruce in 1844.
Population: 469 (2000); Race: 96.5% White, 0.0% Black, 1.1% Asian, 0.4% American Indian and Alaska Native, 2.9% Hispanic of any race, 0.9% two or more races (2000); Density: 1,597.2 persons per square mile (2000); Age: 28.6% under 18, 16.2% over 64 (2000); Marriage status: 21.5% never married, 55.3% now married, 8.5% widowed, 14.7% divorced (2000); Foreign born: 1.1% (2000); Ancestry (includes multiple ancestries): 21.1% United States or American, 15.7% European, 11.3% German, 10.0% Other groups, 5.5% Irish (2000).
Economy: Employment by occupation: 5.8% management, 18.8% professional, 20.2% services, 28.8% sales, 0.0% farming, 6.7% construction, 19.7% production (2000).
Income: Per capita income: $13,829 (2000); Median household income: $24,028 (2000); Poverty rate: 14.0% (2000).
Taxes: Total city taxes per capita: $74 (1997); City property taxes per capita: $70 (1997).
Education: High school graduation rate: 81.5% (2000); College graduation rate: 6.0% (2000).
Housing: Homeownership rate: 78.2% (2000); Median home value: $50,700 (2000); Median rent: $288 per month (2000); Median age of housing: 60+ years (2000).
Transportation: Commute to work: 94.2% car, 0.0% public transportation, 1.9% walk, 1.9% work from home (2000); Travel time to work: 25.7% less than 15 minutes, 58.9% 15 to 30 minutes, 6.9% 30 to 45 minutes, 5.4% 45 to 60 minutes, 3.0% 60 minutes or more (2000)

DECKER (town). Covers a land area of 0.262 square miles and a water area of 0.007 square miles. Located at 38.51° N. Lat.; 87.52° W. Long. Elevation is 450 feet.
Population: 283 (2000); Race: 100.0% White, 0.0% Black, 0.0% Asian, 0.0% American Indian and Alaska Native, 0.0% Hispanic of any race, 0.0% two or more races (2000); Density: 1,081.0 persons per square mile (2000); Age: 36.5% under 18, 12.3% over 64 (2000); Marriage status: 27.1% never married, 45.7% now married, 8.5% widowed, 18.6% divorced (2000); Foreign born: 0.0% (2000); Ancestry (includes multiple ancestries): 30.7% United States or American, 10.5% German, 10.1% Irish, 6.9% Other groups, 2.2% French (except Basque) (2000).
Economy: In agricultural area. Employment by occupation: 5.4% management, 3.2% professional, 22.6% services, 25.8% sales, 3.2% farming, 15.1% construction, 24.7% production (2000).
Income: Per capita income: $15,482 (2000); Median household income: $24,821 (2000); Poverty rate: 21.3% (2000).
Taxes: Total city taxes per capita: $14 (1997); City property taxes per capita: $14 (1997).
Education: High school graduation rate: 66.0% (2000); College graduation rate: 5.2% (2000).
Housing: Homeownership rate: 88.6% (2000); Median home value: $35,600 (2000); Median rent: $175 per month (2000); Median age of housing: 60+ years (2000).
Transportation: Commute to work: 100.0% car, 0.0% public transportation, 0.0% walk, 0.0% work from home (2000); Travel time to work: 21.7% less than 15 minutes, 56.5% 15 to 30 minutes, 17.4% 30 to 45 minutes, 4.3% 45 to 60 minutes, 0.0% 60 minutes or more (2000)

EDWARDSPORT (town). Covers a land area of 0.278 square miles and a water area of 0 square miles. Located at 38.81° N. Lat.; 87.25° W. Long. Elevation is 512 feet.
History: Edwardsport developed as a docking place for the flatboats on the White River. Later, the Indiana Public Service Company used water power and coal from the nearby strip mines to generate electricity for many parts of southwestern Indiana.
Population: 363 (2000); Race: 96.4% White, 0.0% Black, 0.0% Asian, 0.6% American Indian and Alaska Native, 0.6% Hispanic of any race, 3.1% two or more races (2000); Density: 1,305.3 persons per square mile (2000); Age: 22.8% under 18, 12.5% over 64 (2000); Marriage status: 19.7% never married, 62.4% now married, 10.3% widowed, 7.6% divorced (2000); Foreign born: 0.6% (2000); Ancestry (includes multiple ancestries): 20.6%

German, 15.8% Irish, 11.4% English, 10.0% United States or American, 8.6% Other groups (2000).
Economy: Employment by occupation: 11.5% management, 7.7% professional, 15.4% services, 19.2% sales, 3.3% farming, 10.4% construction, 32.4% production (2000).
Income: Per capita income: $13,541 (2000); Median household income: $26,750 (2000); Poverty rate: 20.5% (2000).
Taxes: Total city taxes per capita: $37 (1997); City property taxes per capita: $34 (1997).
Education: High school graduation rate: 75.5% (2000); College graduation rate: 1.3% (2000).
Housing: Homeownership rate: 81.8% (2000); Median home value: $30,200 (2000); Median rent: $261 per month (2000); Median age of housing: 60+ years (2000).
Transportation: Commute to work: 96.2% car, 0.0% public transportation, 2.2% walk, 0.0% work from home (2000); Travel time to work: 36.2% less than 15 minutes, 24.3% 15 to 30 minutes, 29.7% 30 to 45 minutes, 4.3% 45 to 60 minutes, 5.4% 60 minutes or more (2000)

MONROE CITY (town). Covers a land area of 0.269 square miles and a water area of 0 square miles. Located at 38.61° N. Lat.; 87.35° W. Long. Elevation is 520 feet.
Population: 548 (2000); Race: 98.1% White, 0.0% Black, 0.0% Asian, 0.0% American Indian and Alaska Native, 0.9% Hispanic of any race, 1.3% two or more races (2000); Density: 2,039.4 persons per square mile (2000); Age: 25.7% under 18, 18.4% over 64 (2000); Marriage status: 20.2% never married, 60.5% now married, 8.5% widowed, 10.8% divorced (2000); Foreign born: 0.0% (2000); Ancestry (includes multiple ancestries): 17.3% United States or American, 15.4% German, 10.6% English, 7.6% Irish, 5.4% Other groups (2000).
Economy: In agricultural and bituminous-coal area. Employment by occupation: 7.2% management, 14.0% professional, 11.4% services, 27.1% sales, 2.1% farming, 12.3% construction, 25.8% production (2000).
Income: Per capita income: $15,579 (2000); Median household income: $32,788 (2000); Poverty rate: 7.1% (2000).
Taxes: Total city taxes per capita: $25 (1997); City property taxes per capita: $24 (1997).
Education: High school graduation rate: 82.2% (2000); College graduation rate: 9.6% (2000).
Housing: Homeownership rate: 71.9% (2000); Median home value: $48,600 (2000); Median rent: $288 per month (2000); Median age of housing: 46 years (2000).
Transportation: Commute to work: 93.6% car, 0.0% public transportation, 3.0% walk, 3.4% work from home (2000); Travel time to work: 24.3% less than 15 minutes, 43.4% 15 to 30 minutes, 11.9% 30 to 45 minutes, 7.5% 45 to 60 minutes, 12.8% 60 minutes or more (2000)

OAKTOWN (town). Covers a land area of 0.281 square miles and a water area of 0 square miles. Located at 38.87° N. Lat.; 87.44° W. Long. Elevation is 475 feet.
History: Laid out 1867.
Population: 633 (2000); Race: 96.9% White, 0.0% Black, 0.0% Asian, 0.3% American Indian and Alaska Native, 3.6% Hispanic of any race, 2.8% two or more races (2000); Density: 2,250.4 persons per square mile (2000); Age: 22.0% under 18, 20.0% over 64 (2000); Marriage status: 23.4% never married, 55.3% now married, 8.9% widowed, 12.4% divorced (2000); Foreign born: 3.1% (2000); Ancestry (includes multiple ancestries): 15.9% United States or American, 15.8% German, 11.1% Other groups, 8.3% English, 4.7% Irish (2000).
Economy: Fruit (especially watermelons), wheat, corn. Oil wells. Employment by occupation: 6.7% management, 13.1% professional, 22.9% services, 20.5% sales, 6.4% farming, 9.8% construction, 20.5% production (2000).
Income: Per capita income: $14,417 (2000); Median household income: $30,481 (2000); Poverty rate: 17.6% (2000).
Taxes: Total city taxes per capita: $43 (1997); City property taxes per capita: $41 (1997).
Education: High school graduation rate: 77.4% (2000); College graduation rate: 6.2% (2000).
Housing: Homeownership rate: 71.4% (2000); Median home value: $50,300 (2000); Median rent: $225 per month (2000); Median age of housing: 59 years (2000).
Transportation: Commute to work: 89.0% car, 0.0% public transportation, 2.4% walk, 3.1% work from home (2000); Travel time to work: 27.8% less than 15 minutes, 35.2% 15 to 30 minutes, 24.6% 30 to 45 minutes, 6.8% 45 to 60 minutes, 5.7% 60 minutes or more (2000)

SANDBORN (town). Covers a land area of 0.400 square miles and a water area of 0 square miles. Located at 38.89° N. Lat.; 87.18° W. Long. Elevation is 480 feet.
Population: 451 (2000); Race: 97.2% White, 0.0% Black, 0.0% Asian, 2.0% American Indian and Alaska Native, 0.4% Hispanic of any race, 0.4% two or more races (2000); Density: 1,127.5 persons per square mile (2000); Age: 23.2% under 18, 21.3% over 64 (2000); Marriage status: 13.8% never married, 69.7% now married, 8.9% widowed, 7.6% divorced (2000); Foreign born: 0.4% (2000); Ancestry (includes multiple ancestries): 22.8% German, 18.2% United States or American, 9.1% Other groups, 9.1% English, 7.6% Irish (2000).
Economy: In agricultural and bituminous-coal area: surface mines. Employment by occupation: 9.0% management, 18.1% professional, 17.0% services, 17.6% sales, 3.7% farming, 18.1% construction, 16.5% production (2000).
Income: Per capita income: $17,878 (2000); Median household income: $31,000 (2000); Poverty rate: 11.5% (2000).
Taxes: Total city taxes per capita: $62 (1997); City property taxes per capita: $60 (1997).
Education: High school graduation rate: 78.0% (2000); College graduation rate: 7.5% (2000).
Housing: Homeownership rate: 91.7% (2000); Median home value: $41,500 (2000); Median rent: $292 per month (2000); Median age of housing: 60+ years (2000).
Transportation: Commute to work: 92.5% car, 0.0% public transportation, 3.8% walk, 3.8% work from home (2000); Travel time to work: 20.1% less than 15 minutes, 26.8% 15 to 30 minutes, 35.8% 30 to 45 minutes, 6.1% 45 to 60 minutes, 11.2% 60 minutes or more (2000)

VINCENNES (city). Covers a land area of 7.137 square miles and a water area of 0.068 square miles. Located at 38.67° N. Lat.; 87.51° W. Long. Elevation is 429 feet.
History: Vincennes had its beginnings about 1732, when Francois Morgane de Vincennes built a fort here. The French flag flew over Vincennes until 1763, when it was ceded to Great Britain by the Treaty of Paris. The American flag replaced the Union Jack in 1779 when George Rogers Clark captured Fort Sackville. Vincennes was the first seat of government for the Indiana Territory created in 1800, with William Henry Harrison as governor.
Population: 18,701 (2000); Race: 94.0% White, 3.1% Black, 0.9% Asian, 0.5% American Indian and Alaska Native, 1.2% Hispanic of any race, 0.9% two or more races (2000); Density: 2,620.3 persons per square mile (2000); Age: 20.2% under 18, 14.9% over 64 (2000); Marriage status: 34.4% never married, 44.7% now married, 9.0% widowed, 11.9% divorced (2000); Foreign born: 1.4% (2000); Ancestry (includes multiple ancestries): 19.9% German, 17.5% United States or American, 8.7% Irish, 8.4% Other groups, 8.3% English (2000).
Vital Statistics: Birth rate: 138.5 per 10,000 population (1998)
Economy: Single-family building permits issued: 5 (2001) / 12 (2000); Multi-family building permits issued: 12 (2001) / 8 (2000); Employment by occupation: 7.4% management, 17.7% professional, 22.9% services, 27.7% sales, 0.8% farming, 7.4% construction, 16.2% production (2000).
Income: Per capita income: $14,993 (2000); Median household income: $26,289 (2000); Poverty rate: 20.7% (2000).
Taxes: Total city taxes per capita: $166 (1997); City property taxes per capita: $160 (1997).
Education: High school graduation rate: 80.0% (2000); College graduation rate: 15.2% (2000).

School District(s)

South Knox School Corp (KG-12)
2000 Enrollment: 1,103 812-726-4440
Vincennes Community Sch Corp (KG-12)
2000 Enrollment: 3,208 812-882-4844

Two-year College(s)

Good Samaritan Hospital School of Radiologic Tech (Public)
2001 Enrollment: 20 812-885-8011
2001 Tuition: In-state $1,200; Out-of-state $1,200
Vincennes University (Public)
2001 Enrollment: 18,285 812-888-8888
2001 Tuition: In-state $2,500; Out-of-state $6,240

Housing: Homeownership rate: 57.9% (2000); Median home value: $62,000 (2000); Median rent: $334 per month (2000); Median age of housing: 47 years (2000).
Hospitals: Good Samaritan Hospital (289 beds)
Safety: Violent crime rate: 18.6 per 10,000 population; Property crime rate: 646.1 per 10,000 population (2001).

Newspapers: Vincennes Sun-Commercial (6 x week)
Transportation: Commute to work: 91.2% car, 0.1% public transportation, 6.4% walk, 1.7% work from home (2000); Travel time to work: 69.7% less than 15 minutes, 17.8% 15 to 30 minutes, 6.8% 30 to 45 minutes, 1.9% 45 to 60 minutes, 3.8% 60 minutes or more (2000)
Additional Information Contacts
Knox County Board of Realtors........................812-895-5669
Vincennes Chamber of Commerce........................812-882-6440

WHEATLAND (town). Covers a land area of 0.414 square miles and a water area of 0 square miles. Located at 38.66° N. Lat.; 87.30° W. Long. Elevation is 490 feet.
History: Laid out 1858.
Population: 504 (2000); Race: 99.6% White, 0.4% Black, 0.0% Asian, 0.0% American Indian and Alaska Native, 0.0% Hispanic of any race, 0.0% two or more races (2000); Density: 1,218.2 persons per square mile (2000); Age: 27.5% under 18, 15.2% over 64 (2000); Marriage status: 16.4% never married, 60.2% now married, 6.5% widowed, 16.9% divorced (2000); Foreign born: 1.2% (2000); Ancestry (includes multiple ancestries): 19.5% United States or American, 16.8% German, 12.5% English, 7.0% Scottish, 5.3% Irish (2000).
Economy: Agricultural area: wheat, melons, fruit, corn, soybeans. Employment by occupation: 6.9% management, 15.7% professional, 14.7% services, 31.8% sales, 1.4% farming, 9.2% construction, 20.3% production (2000).
Income: Per capita income: $14,646 (2000); Median household income: $27,174 (2000); Poverty rate: 16.3% (2000).
Taxes: Total city taxes per capita: $33 (1997); City property taxes per capita: $31 (1997).
Education: High school graduation rate: 75.7% (2000); College graduation rate: 5.9% (2000).
Housing: Homeownership rate: 69.6% (2000); Median home value: $40,800 (2000); Median rent: $275 per month (2000); Median age of housing: 50 years (2000).
Transportation: Commute to work: 90.6% car, 0.0% public transportation, 5.7% walk, 3.8% work from home (2000); Travel time to work: 17.6% less than 15 minutes, 54.9% 15 to 30 minutes, 18.1% 30 to 45 minutes, 3.9% 45 to 60 minutes, 5.4% 60 minutes or more (2000)

Kosciusko County

Located in northern Indiana; drained by the Tippecanoe and Eel Rivers; includes Wawasee and Winona Lakes. Covers a land area of 537.50 square miles, a water area of 16.80 square miles, and is located in the Eastern Time Zone. The county government was organized in 1835. County seat is Warsaw.

Weather Station: Warsaw — Elevation: 807 feet

	Jan	Feb	Mar	Apr	May	Jun	Jul	Aug	Sep	Oct	Nov	Dec
High	31	36	47	59	71	80	83	81	75	63	49	37
Low	15	18	28	38	49	58	62	60	53	42	32	22
Precip	1.8	1.4	2.1	3.5	3.8	4.4	4.0	4.0	3.2	3.3	2.9	2.5
Snow	na	na	na	0.2	0.0	0.0	0.0	0.0	0.0	tr	na	na

High and Low temperatures in degrees Fahrenheit; Precipitation and Snow in inches

Population: 74,057 (2000); Race: 94.4% White, 0.5% Black, 0.5% Asian, 0.2% American Indian and Alaska Native, 4.9% Hispanic of any race, 1.3% two or more races (2000); Density: 137.8 persons per square mile (2000); Age: 27.7% under 18, 12.0% over 64 (2000).
Religion: Five largest groups: 7.1% The United Methodist Church, 6.4% Catholic Church, 4.4% Christian Churches and Churches of Christ, 3.2% Independent, Non-Charismatic Churches, 2.5% The Wesleyan Church (2000).
Economy: Unemployment rate: 4.6% (11/2002); Total civilian labor force: 37,895 (11/2002); Leading industries: 50.1% manufacturing; 10.9% retail trade; 7.6% health care and social assistance (2000); Companies that employ more than 1,000 persons: 3 (2000); Companies that employ more than 100 persons: 51 (2000); Farms: 1,130 totaling 246,907 acres (1997); Minority business ownership rate: 5.2% (1997); Women business ownership rate: 28.3% (1997); Retail sales per capita: $7,832 (1997). Single-family building permits issued: 411 (2001) / 403 (2000); Multi-family building permits issued: 64 (2001) / 30 (2000).
Income: Per capita income: $19,806 (2000); Median household income: $43,939 (2000); Poverty rate: 6.4% (2000); Bankruptcy rate: 7.45% (2001).
Taxes: Total county taxes per capita: $177 (2000); County property taxes per capita: $125 (2000).
Education: High school graduation rate: 81.6% (2000); College graduation rate: 14.9% (2000).
Housing: Homeownership rate: 78.9% (2000); Median home value: $95,500 (2000); Median rent: $403 per month (2000); Median age of housing: 29 years (2000).
Health: Birth rate: 146.8 per 10,000 population (1998); Age adjusted death rate: 91.5 per 10,000 population (1999); Age adjusted cancer mortality rate: 240.4 deaths per 100,000 population (1999). Number of physicians: 6.2 per 10,000 population (1999); Number of hospital beds: 9.7 per 10,000 population (1999).
Elections: 2000 Presidential election results: 22.9% Gore, 75.3% Bush, 0.4% Nader, 0.7% Buchanan
National and State Parks: Tri-County State Fish And Game Area
Additional Information Contacts
Kosciusko County Government Offices..................574-267-4444
Kosciusko Board of Realtors..........................219-269-6706
North Webster Chamber of Commerce....................219-834-7076
Syracuse-Wawasee Chamber of Commerce.................219-457-5637
Warsaw Chamber of Commerce...........................219-267-6311

Kosciusko County Communities

BURKET (town). Covers a land area of 0.073 square miles and a water area of 0 square miles. Located at 41.15° N. Lat.; 85.96° W. Long. Elevation is 860 feet.
Population: 195 (2000); Race: 98.0% White, 2.0% Black, 0.0% Asian, 0.0% American Indian and Alaska Native, 4.5% Hispanic of any race, 0.0% two or more races (2000); Density: 2,685.1 persons per square mile (2000); Age: 28.6% under 18, 7.5% over 64 (2000); Marriage status: 26.8% never married, 48.3% now married, 10.7% widowed, 14.1% divorced (2000); Foreign born: 0.0% (2000); Ancestry (includes multiple ancestries): 22.1% United States or American, 20.6% Other groups, 13.6% German, 11.6% Irish, 9.0% Dutch (2000).
Economy: In agricultural area: eggs; poultry. Employment by occupation: 2.0% management, 9.1% professional, 17.2% services, 13.1% sales, 0.0% farming, 6.1% construction, 52.5% production (2000).
Income: Per capita income: $13,098 (2000); Median household income: $27,500 (2000); Poverty rate: 11.6% (2000).
Taxes: Total city taxes per capita: $65 (1997); City property taxes per capita: $42 (1997).
Education: High school graduation rate: 63.6% (2000); College graduation rate: 1.8% (2000).
Housing: Homeownership rate: 87.8% (2000); Median home value: $53,300 (2000); Median rent: $275 per month (2000); Median age of housing: 60+ years (2000).
Transportation: Commute to work: 82.8% car, 0.0% public transportation, 7.1% walk, 9.1% work from home (2000); Travel time to work: 16.7% less than 15 minutes, 56.7% 15 to 30 minutes, 15.6% 30 to 45 minutes, 8.9% 45 to 60 minutes, 2.2% 60 minutes or more (2000)

CLAYPOOL (town). Covers a land area of 0.361 square miles and a water area of 0 square miles. Located at 41.12° N. Lat.; 85.88° W. Long. Elevation is 900 feet.
Population: 311 (2000); Race: 95.3% White, 1.9% Black, 0.6% Asian, 0.0% American Indian and Alaska Native, 2.2% Hispanic of any race, 1.3% two or more races (2000); Density: 861.7 persons per square mile (2000); Age: 29.7% under 18, 8.5% over 64 (2000); Marriage status: 22.0% never married, 65.1% now married, 5.4% widowed, 7.5% divorced (2000); Foreign born: 0.9% (2000); Ancestry (includes multiple ancestries): 30.0% German, 17.0% United States or American, 16.1% Irish, 9.1% English, 7.9% Other groups (2000).
Economy: In agricultural area. Employment by occupation: 6.0% management, 4.5% professional, 14.2% services, 12.7% sales, 0.0% farming, 6.0% construction, 56.7% production (2000).
Income: Per capita income: $12,021 (2000); Median household income: $33,833 (2000); Poverty rate: 9.5% (2000).
Taxes: Total city taxes per capita: $91 (1997); City property taxes per capita: $68 (1997).
Education: High school graduation rate: 62.4% (2000); College graduation rate: 1.6% (2000).
Housing: Homeownership rate: 77.6% (2000); Median home value: $62,500 (2000); Median rent: $367 per month (2000); Median age of housing: 60+ years (2000).
Transportation: Commute to work: 96.1% car, 0.0% public transportation, 3.1% walk, 0.8% work from home (2000); Travel time to work: 31.5% less

than 15 minutes, 48.0% 15 to 30 minutes, 18.9% 30 to 45 minutes, 0.0% 45 to 60 minutes, 1.6% 60 minutes or more (2000)

ETNA GREEN (town). Covers a land area of 0.470 square miles and a water area of <.001 square miles. Located at 41.27° N. Lat.; 86.04° W. Long. Elevation is 818 feet.
Population: 663 (2000); Race: 99.5% White, 0.5% Black, 0.0% Asian, 0.0% American Indian and Alaska Native, 0.6% Hispanic of any race, 0.0% two or more races (2000); Density: 1,411.3 persons per square mile (2000); Age: 36.5% under 18, 9.9% over 64 (2000); Marriage status: 30.0% never married, 52.7% now married, 5.6% widowed, 11.8% divorced (2000); Foreign born: 0.0% (2000); Ancestry (includes multiple ancestries): 21.4% German, 15.4% United States or American, 14.2% Irish, 7.3% English, 2.6% Dutch (2000).
Economy: In agricultural area. Manufacturing: modular wooden houses and mobile homes. Single-family building permits issued: 0 (2001) / 2 (2000); Multi-family building permits issued: 0 (2001) / 0 (2000); Employment by occupation: 2.0% management, 12.7% professional, 11.7% services, 23.1% sales, 0.0% farming, 9.4% construction, 41.1% production (2000).
Income: Per capita income: $14,110 (2000); Median household income: $35,625 (2000); Poverty rate: 4.9% (2000).
Taxes: Total city taxes per capita: $100 (1997); City property taxes per capita: $72 (1997).
Education: High school graduation rate: 81.2% (2000); College graduation rate: 7.0% (2000).
Housing: Homeownership rate: 81.5% (2000); Median home value: $72,100 (2000); Median rent: $375 per month (2000); Median age of housing: 39 years (2000).
Transportation: Commute to work: 85.4% car, 0.0% public transportation, 3.1% walk, 5.8% work from home (2000); Travel time to work: 29.1% less than 15 minutes, 55.8% 15 to 30 minutes, 11.9% 30 to 45 minutes, 1.4% 45 to 60 minutes, 1.8% 60 minutes or more (2000)

LEESBURG (town). Covers a land area of 0.232 square miles and a water area of 0 square miles. Located at 41.33° N. Lat.; 85.85° W. Long. Elevation is 853 feet.
History: Laid out 1835.
Population: 625 (2000); Race: 90.9% White, 0.5% Black, 1.0% Asian, 1.3% American Indian and Alaska Native, 6.8% Hispanic of any race, 3.3% two or more races (2000); Density: 2,689.8 persons per square mile (2000); Age: 26.8% under 18, 7.9% over 64 (2000); Marriage status: 15.2% never married, 70.7% now married, 4.2% widowed, 9.9% divorced (2000); Foreign born: 3.8% (2000); Ancestry (includes multiple ancestries): 27.1% German, 18.0% United States or American, 15.9% Other groups, 8.1% Irish, 5.1% Dutch (2000).
Economy: In agricultural area. Employment by occupation: 12.9% management, 8.2% professional, 11.0% services, 19.9% sales, 0.0% farming, 10.1% construction, 37.9% production (2000).
Income: Per capita income: $20,031 (2000); Median household income: $46,750 (2000); Poverty rate: 5.2% (2000).
Taxes: Total city taxes per capita: $116 (1997); City property taxes per capita: $89 (1997).
Education: High school graduation rate: 84.5% (2000); College graduation rate: 13.8% (2000).
Housing: Homeownership rate: 82.0% (2000); Median home value: $81,600 (2000); Median rent: $410 per month (2000); Median age of housing: 52 years (2000).
Transportation: Commute to work: 93.4% car, 0.0% public transportation, 0.6% walk, 4.7% work from home (2000); Travel time to work: 40.7% less than 15 minutes, 47.7% 15 to 30 minutes, 7.0% 30 to 45 minutes, 3.3% 45 to 60 minutes, 1.3% 60 minutes or more (2000)

MENTONE (town). Covers a land area of 0.630 square miles and a water area of 0 square miles. Located at 41.17° N. Lat.; 86.03° W. Long. Elevation is 839 feet.
Population: 898 (2000); Race: 89.0% White, 0.0% Black, 0.0% Asian, 0.5% American Indian and Alaska Native, 11.1% Hispanic of any race, 2.1% two or more races (2000); Density: 1,424.6 persons per square mile (2000); Age: 31.5% under 18, 13.2% over 64 (2000); Marriage status: 23.9% never married, 59.6% now married, 7.8% widowed, 8.7% divorced (2000); Foreign born: 4.5% (2000); Ancestry (includes multiple ancestries): 23.2% German, 15.6% United States or American, 14.3% Other groups, 8.1% Irish, 6.2% English (2000).
Economy: In agricultural area; eggs, chickens; lumber. Manufacturing: livestock feed mixing, poultry processing; mechanical springs, powder coating. Single-family building permits issued: 3 (2001) / 3 (2000); Multi-family building permits issued: 0 (2001) / 0 (2000); Employment by occupation: 6.1% management, 9.0% professional, 16.3% services, 21.9% sales, 2.4% farming, 9.0% construction, 35.3% production (2000).
Income: Per capita income: $15,372 (2000); Median household income: $38,750 (2000); Poverty rate: 6.3% (2000).
Taxes: Total city taxes per capita: $174 (1997); City property taxes per capita: $122 (1997).
Education: High school graduation rate: 78.0% (2000); College graduation rate: 8.6% (2000).
Housing: Homeownership rate: 77.6% (2000); Median home value: $64,300 (2000); Median rent: $367 per month (2000); Median age of housing: 60+ years (2000).
Transportation: Commute to work: 86.4% car, 0.0% public transportation, 7.2% walk, 3.0% work from home (2000); Travel time to work: 36.6% less than 15 minutes, 44.0% 15 to 30 minutes, 14.1% 30 to 45 minutes, 3.1% 45 to 60 minutes, 2.3% 60 minutes or more (2000)

MILFORD (town). Covers a land area of 1.079 square miles and a water area of 0.002 square miles. Located at 41.40° N. Lat.; 85.84° W. Long. Elevation is 835 feet.
History: Laid out 1836.
Population: 1,550 (2000); Race: 91.2% White, 0.0% Black, 0.0% Asian, 0.0% American Indian and Alaska Native, 12.8% Hispanic of any race, 2.1% two or more races (2000); Density: 1,436.8 persons per square mile (2000); Age: 25.8% under 18, 16.5% over 64 (2000); Marriage status: 17.5% never married, 61.5% now married, 7.3% widowed, 13.8% divorced (2000); Foreign born: 5.4% (2000); Ancestry (includes multiple ancestries): 22.4% German, 18.5% Other groups, 13.6% United States or American, 9.4% Irish, 7.4% English (2000).
Economy: Poultry area. Manufacturing: motor vehicles, grain bins, livestock feeding and watering equipment, poultry processing, feed mixing, mobile restrooms. Employment by occupation: 8.3% management, 8.3% professional, 9.9% services, 18.3% sales, 0.3% farming, 13.3% construction, 41.6% production (2000).
Income: Per capita income: $17,247 (2000); Median household income: $36,458 (2000); Poverty rate: 4.0% (2000).
Taxes: Total city taxes per capita: $198 (1997); City property taxes per capita: $135 (1997).
Education: High school graduation rate: 70.0% (2000); College graduation rate: 8.0% (2000).
Housing: Homeownership rate: 67.2% (2000); Median home value: $78,600 (2000); Median rent: $377 per month (2000); Median age of housing: 37 years (2000).
Newspapers: Senior Life - Northwest Indiana Edition (1 x month); The Kosciusko County Paper (1 x week); The Elkhart County Paper (1 x week); The Elkhart City Paper (1 x week); The Mail-Journal (1 x week); Senior Life-Allen Edition (1 x month); Senior Life-Elkhart/Kosciusko Edition (1 x month); Senior Life-Saint Joseph Edition (1 x month)
Transportation: Commute to work: 90.8% car, 0.0% public transportation, 5.4% walk, 2.7% work from home (2000); Travel time to work: 45.3% less than 15 minutes, 40.2% 15 to 30 minutes, 8.7% 30 to 45 minutes, 3.4% 45 to 60 minutes, 2.3% 60 minutes or more (2000)

NORTH WEBSTER (town). Covers a land area of 0.717 square miles and a water area of 0 square miles. Located at 41.32° N. Lat.; 85.69° W. Long. Elevation is 880 feet.
Population: 1,067 (2000); Race: 96.8% White, 0.7% Black, 0.7% Asian, 0.2% American Indian and Alaska Native, 1.7% Hispanic of any race, 1.0% two or more races (2000); Density: 1,488.0 persons per square mile (2000); Age: 22.5% under 18, 18.0% over 64 (2000); Marriage status: 19.3% never married, 64.1% now married, 7.6% widowed, 9.0% divorced (2000); Foreign born: 1.1% (2000); Ancestry (includes multiple ancestries): 23.4% United States or American, 21.9% German, 9.9% English, 9.2% Other groups, 7.4% Irish (2000).
Economy: In agricultural area. Manufacturing: heaters. Recreation area. Employment by occupation: 9.0% management, 10.9% professional, 9.2% services, 29.2% sales, 0.0% farming, 11.1% construction, 30.6% production (2000).
Income: Per capita income: $18,824 (2000); Median household income: $39,038 (2000); Poverty rate: 6.5% (2000).
Taxes: Total city taxes per capita: $260 (1997); City property taxes per capita: $175 (1997).
Education: High school graduation rate: 80.7% (2000); College graduation rate: 14.0% (2000).
Housing: Homeownership rate: 71.2% (2000); Median home value: $95,300 (2000); Median rent: $413 per month (2000); Median age of housing: 33 years (2000).

Transportation: Commute to work: 92.3% car, 0.0% public transportation, 4.3% walk, 2.1% work from home (2000); Travel time to work: 32.7% less than 15 minutes, 41.2% 15 to 30 minutes, 17.5% 30 to 45 minutes, 3.5% 45 to 60 minutes, 5.2% 60 minutes or more (2000)
Additional Information Contacts
North Webster Chamber of Commerce 219-834-7076

PIERCETON (town). Covers a land area of 0.915 square miles and a water area of 0 square miles. Located at 41.20° N. Lat.; 85.70° W. Long. Elevation is 928 feet.
Population: 695 (2000); Race: 96.4% White, 2.0% Black, 0.0% Asian, 0.0% American Indian and Alaska Native, 3.5% Hispanic of any race, 0.0% two or more races (2000); Density: 759.3 persons per square mile (2000); Age: 31.8% under 18, 7.4% over 64 (2000); Marriage status: 20.2% never married, 59.9% now married, 6.6% widowed, 13.2% divorced (2000); Foreign born: 0.0% (2000); Ancestry (includes multiple ancestries): 26.7% German, 23.6% United States or American, 11.4% Other groups, 7.9% Irish, 7.3% English (2000).
Economy: Manufacturing: fabricated metal products. Corn, soybeans; poultry, cattle; lumber. Resort lakes nearby to North. Employment by occupation: 6.7% management, 7.3% professional, 15.1% services, 20.9% sales, 0.0% farming, 9.3% construction, 40.7% production (2000).
Income: Per capita income: $14,436 (2000); Median household income: $37,188 (2000); Poverty rate: 11.9% (2000).
Taxes: Total city taxes per capita: $131 (1997); City property taxes per capita: $92 (1997).
Education: High school graduation rate: 76.0% (2000); College graduation rate: 5.7% (2000).

School District(s)
Whitko Community School Corp (KG-12)
2000 Enrollment: 2,000 219-594-2658
Housing: Homeownership rate: 73.4% (2000); Median home value: $64,000 (2000); Median rent: $405 per month (2000); Median age of housing: 43 years (2000).
Transportation: Commute to work: 96.1% car, 0.0% public transportation, 0.6% walk, 3.3% work from home (2000); Travel time to work: 23.7% less than 15 minutes, 55.5% 15 to 30 minutes, 12.8% 30 to 45 minutes, 3.1% 45 to 60 minutes, 5.0% 60 minutes or more (2000)

SIDNEY (town). Covers a land area of 0.130 square miles and a water area of 0.005 square miles. Located at 41.10° N. Lat.; 85.74° W. Long. Elevation is 976 feet.
Population: 168 (2000); Race: 100.0% White, 0.0% Black, 0.0% Asian, 0.0% American Indian and Alaska Native, 0.0% Hispanic of any race, 0.0% two or more races (2000); Density: 1,291.2 persons per square mile (2000); Age: 29.2% under 18, 15.7% over 64 (2000); Marriage status: 19.6% never married, 66.4% now married, 5.6% widowed, 8.4% divorced (2000); Foreign born: 1.1% (2000); Ancestry (includes multiple ancestries): 36.8% United States or American, 14.1% Irish, 9.2% German, 8.1% Other groups, 4.3% Swiss (2000).
Economy: In agricultural area. Single-family building permits issued: 0 (2001) / 0 (2000); Multi-family building permits issued: 0 (2001) / 0 (2000); Employment by occupation: 1.2% management, 5.9% professional, 15.3% services, 30.6% sales, 0.0% farming, 9.4% construction, 37.6% production (2000).
Income: Per capita income: $14,959 (2000); Median household income: $30,000 (2000); Poverty rate: 8.6% (2000).
Taxes: Total city taxes per capita: $38 (1997); City property taxes per capita: $19 (1997).
Education: High school graduation rate: 69.8% (2000); College graduation rate: 5.2% (2000).
Housing: Homeownership rate: 89.1% (2000); Median home value: $53,600 (2000); Median rent: $508 per month (2000); Median age of housing: 60+ years (2000).
Transportation: Commute to work: 97.5% car, 0.0% public transportation, 0.0% walk, 2.5% work from home (2000); Travel time to work: 7.7% less than 15 minutes, 76.9% 15 to 30 minutes, 7.7% 30 to 45 minutes, 0.0% 45 to 60 minutes, 7.7% 60 minutes or more (2000)

SILVER LAKE (town). Covers a land area of 0.291 square miles and a water area of 0 square miles. Located at 41.07° N. Lat.; 85.89° W. Long. Elevation is 912 feet.
History: Laid out 1859.
Population: 546 (2000); Race: 90.9% White, 0.0% Black, 0.0% Asian, 0.0% American Indian and Alaska Native, 8.6% Hispanic of any race, 2.2% two or more races (2000); Density: 1,874.9 persons per square mile (2000); Age: 28.7% under 18, 16.1% over 64 (2000); Marriage status: 20.7% never married, 62.3% now married, 8.2% widowed, 8.9% divorced (2000); Foreign born: 3.5% (2000); Ancestry (includes multiple ancestries): 21.4% English, 18.6% United States or American, 13.0% German, 10.6% Other groups, 7.7% Irish (2000).
Economy: Agricultural area. Manufacturing of fabricated steel products. Resort lakes (fishing) nearby. Employment by occupation: 11.2% management, 9.1% professional, 21.1% services, 17.8% sales, 2.5% farming, 4.1% construction, 34.3% production (2000).
Income: Per capita income: $13,561 (2000); Median household income: $33,088 (2000); Poverty rate: 12.1% (2000).
Taxes: Total city taxes per capita: $129 (1997); City property taxes per capita: $90 (1997).
Education: High school graduation rate: 66.9% (2000); College graduation rate: 4.0% (2000).
Housing: Homeownership rate: 79.2% (2000); Median home value: $64,100 (2000); Median rent: $319 per month (2000); Median age of housing: 51 years (2000).
Transportation: Commute to work: 91.9% car, 0.0% public transportation, 5.1% walk, 0.0% work from home (2000); Travel time to work: 25.8% less than 15 minutes, 48.7% 15 to 30 minutes, 15.3% 30 to 45 minutes, 3.8% 45 to 60 minutes, 6.4% 60 minutes or more (2000)

SYRACUSE (town). Covers a land area of 1.609 square miles and a water area of 0.309 square miles. Located at 41.42° N. Lat.; 85.75° W. Long. Elevation is 870 feet.
History: Syracuse was settled as a summer resort town on Lakes Syracuse, Wawasee, and Papakeechee.
Population: 3,038 (2000); Race: 90.5% White, 1.4% Black, 0.0% Asian, 0.0% American Indian and Alaska Native, 6.7% Hispanic of any race, 2.6% two or more races (2000); Density: 1,888.5 persons per square mile (2000); Age: 26.9% under 18, 12.8% over 64 (2000); Marriage status: 23.8% never married, 54.6% now married, 6.3% widowed, 15.3% divorced (2000); Foreign born: 1.4% (2000); Ancestry (includes multiple ancestries): 24.2% German, 12.7% Irish, 12.3% Other groups, 10.8% United States or American, 7.7% English (2000).
Economy: Employment by occupation: 8.6% management, 4.7% professional, 14.4% services, 24.3% sales, 0.4% farming, 14.2% construction, 33.5% production (2000).
Income: Per capita income: $18,822 (2000); Median household income: $40,000 (2000); Poverty rate: 5.7% (2000).
Taxes: Total city taxes per capita: $421 (1997); City property taxes per capita: $290 (1997).
Education: High school graduation rate: 83.8% (2000); College graduation rate: 9.5% (2000).

School District(s)
Wawasee Community School Corp (KG-12)
2000 Enrollment: 3,552 219-457-3188
Housing: Homeownership rate: 66.9% (2000); Median home value: $85,300 (2000); Median rent: $412 per month (2000); Median age of housing: 32 years (2000).
Transportation: Commute to work: 91.7% car, 0.0% public transportation, 4.8% walk, 1.9% work from home (2000); Travel time to work: 47.7% less than 15 minutes, 36.0% 15 to 30 minutes, 9.8% 30 to 45 minutes, 3.0% 45 to 60 minutes, 3.5% 60 minutes or more (2000)
Additional Information Contacts
Syracuse-Wawasee Chamber of Commerce 219-457-5637

WARSAW (city). Covers a land area of 10.481 square miles and a water area of 1.067 square miles. Located at 41.24° N. Lat.; 85.84° W. Long. Elevation is 826 feet.
History: In its name, Warsaw remembers the Polish nationality of Thaddeus Kosciusko (1746-1817), for whom Kosciusko County was named. Kosciusko was an aide to General Washington during the Revolutionary War, in addition to being a Polish national hero.
Population: 12,415 (2000); Race: 90.0% White, 1.3% Black, 1.6% Asian, 0.4% American Indian and Alaska Native, 10.9% Hispanic of any race, 1.9% two or more races (2000); Density: 1,184.6 persons per square mile (2000); Age: 25.9% under 18, 13.3% over 64 (2000); Marriage status: 23.9% never married, 56.5% now married, 7.1% widowed, 12.4% divorced (2000); Foreign born: 7.0% (2000); Ancestry (includes multiple ancestries): 23.0% German, 16.3% Other groups, 12.4% United States or American, 10.3% English, 10.2% Irish (2000).
Vital Statistics: Birth rate: 240.8 per 10,000 population (1998)
Economy: Single-family building permits issued: 13 (2001) / 11 (2000); Multi-family building permits issued: 60 (2001) / 24 (2000); Employment by

occupation: 10.4% management, 13.8% professional, 11.1% services, 25.3% sales, 0.8% farming, 8.5% construction, 30.1% production (2000).
Income: Per capita income: $19,262 (2000); Median household income: $36,564 (2000); Poverty rate: 9.2% (2000).
Taxes: Total city taxes per capita: $550 (1997); City property taxes per capita: $382 (1997).
Education: High school graduation rate: 79.6% (2000); College graduation rate: 17.5% (2000).

School District(s)

Warsaw Community Schools (KG-12)
2000 Enrollment: 6,369 219-267-3238

Housing: Homeownership rate: 63.0% (2000); Median home value: $84,100 (2000); Median rent: $412 per month (2000); Median age of housing: 34 years (2000).
Hospitals: Kosciusko Community Hospital (72 beds)
Safety: Violent crime rate: 17.6 per 10,000 population; Property crime rate: 242.7 per 10,000 population (2001).
Newspapers: Times-Union (6 x week)
Transportation: Commute to work: 91.6% car, 1.7% public transportation, 2.6% walk, 2.9% work from home (2000); Travel time to work: 62.3% less than 15 minutes, 20.9% 15 to 30 minutes, 9.6% 30 to 45 minutes, 3.8% 45 to 60 minutes, 3.3% 60 minutes or more (2000)
Airports: Warsaw Municipal
Additional Information Contacts
Kosciusko Board of Realtors 219-269-6706
Warsaw Chamber of Commerce 219-267-6311

WINONA LAKE (town). Covers a land area of 2.898 square miles and a water area of 0.350 square miles. Located at 41.22° N. Lat.; 85.81° W. Long. Elevation is 830 feet.
History: Winona Lake is a vacation retreat area. Evangelist Billy Sunday built a tabernacle here that influenced the character of the town.
Population: 3,987 (2000); Race: 92.4% White, 0.2% Black, 0.2% Asian, 0.0% American Indian and Alaska Native, 6.5% Hispanic of any race, 2.2% two or more races (2000); Density: 1,375.7 persons per square mile (2000); Age: 28.1% under 18, 13.0% over 64 (2000); Marriage status: 25.9% never married, 57.3% now married, 7.6% widowed, 9.3% divorced (2000); Foreign born: 4.0% (2000); Ancestry (includes multiple ancestries): 27.9% German, 14.5% United States or American, 12.2% English, 8.6% Other groups, 8.4% Irish (2000).
Economy: Single-family building permits issued: 41 (2001) / 25 (2000); Multi-family building permits issued: 0 (2001) / 0 (2000); Employment by occupation: 10.1% management, 19.4% professional, 13.7% services, 22.8% sales, 0.0% farming, 7.5% construction, 26.5% production (2000).
Income: Per capita income: $19,025 (2000); Median household income: $42,454 (2000); Poverty rate: 6.7% (2000).
Taxes: Total city taxes per capita: $182 (1997); City property taxes per capita: $126 (1997).
Education: High school graduation rate: 87.9% (2000); College graduation rate: 28.8% (2000).

Four-year College(s)

Grace College and Theological Seminary (Private, Not-for-profit, Brethren Church)
2001 Enrollment: 1,357 219-372-5100
2001 Tuition: In-state $11,440; Out-of-state $11,440

Housing: Homeownership rate: 69.5% (2000); Median home value: $96,300 (2000); Median rent: $378 per month (2000); Median age of housing: 31 years (2000).
Transportation: Commute to work: 94.5% car, 0.9% public transportation, 1.7% walk, 2.9% work from home (2000); Travel time to work: 54.5% less than 15 minutes, 29.2% 15 to 30 minutes, 11.9% 30 to 45 minutes, 1.5% 45 to 60 minutes, 3.0% 60 minutes or more (2000)

La Grange County

Located in northeastern Indiana; bounded on the north by Michigan; drained by the Pigeon and Short Little Elkhart Rivers. Covers a land area of 379.60 square miles, a water area of 7.20 square miles, and is located in the Eastern Time Zone. The county government was organized in 1832. County seat is Lagrange.

Weather Station: Lagrange Sewage Plant — Elevation: 892 feet

	Jan	Feb	Mar	Apr	May	Jun	Jul	Aug	Sep	Oct	Nov	Dec
High	29	34	45	58	70	79	83	81	74	61	47	35
Low	14	17	26	36	47	57	61	59	52	40	31	21
Precip	1.8	1.7	2.7	3.4	3.6	4.1	3.7	3.9	3.5	2.8	2.9	2.6
Snow	10.7	8.1	5.0	1.5	tr	0.0	0.0	0.0	0.0	0.5	3.4	9.5

High and Low temperatures in degrees Fahrenheit; Precipitation and Snow in inches

Population: 34,909 (2000); Race: 96.6% White, 0.3% Black, 0.4% Asian, 0.2% American Indian and Alaska Native, 3.0% Hispanic of any race, 0.6% two or more races (2000); Density: 92.0 persons per square mile (2000); Age: 33.7% under 18, 10.0% over 64 (2000).
Religion: Five largest groups: 17.1% Old Order Amish Church, 6.1% The United Methodist Church, 4.6% Mennonite Church USA, 2.3% Christian Churches and Churches of Christ, 2.0% Catholic Church (2000).
Economy: Unemployment rate: 4.4% (11/2002); Total civilian labor force: 15,662 (11/2002); Leading industries: 54.4% manufacturing; 11.9% retail trade; 6.7% accommodation & food services (2000); Companies that employ more than 1,000 persons: 0 (2000); Companies that employ more than 100 persons: 21 (2000); Farms: 1,392 totaling 189,932 acres (1997); Minority business ownership rate: 6.6% (1997); Women business ownership rate: 18.7% (1997); Retail sales per capita: $6,200 (1997). Single-family building permits issued: 209 (2001) / 215 (2000); Multi-family building permits issued: 2 (2001) / 2 (2000).
Income: Per capita income: $16,481 (2000); Median household income: $42,848 (2000); Poverty rate: 7.7% (2000); Bankruptcy rate: 4.99% (2001).
Taxes: Total county taxes per capita: $239 (2000); County property taxes per capita: $123 (2000).
Education: High school graduation rate: 60.2% (2000); College graduation rate: 8.9% (2000).
Housing: Homeownership rate: 81.4% (2000); Median home value: $99,800 (2000); Median rent: $388 per month (2000); Median age of housing: 30 years (2000).
Health: Birth rate: 201.4 per 10,000 population (1998); Age adjusted death rate: 78.7 per 10,000 population (1999); Age adjusted cancer mortality rate: 179.2 deaths per 100,000 population (1999). Number of physicians: 4.3 per 10,000 population (1999); Number of hospital beds: 15.2 per 10,000 population (1999).
Elections: 2000 Presidential election results: 32.8% Gore, 65.3% Bush, 0.6% Nader, 0.9% Buchanan
National and State Parks: Pigeon River State Fish and Wildlife Area
Additional Information Contacts
LaGrange County Government Offices 219-463-3442
Lagrange Chamber of Commerce 219-463-2443
Lagrange County Convention & Visitors Bureau 219-768-4008
Topeka Area Chamber of Commerce. 219-593-2138

La Grange County Communities

HOWE (unincorporated postal area, zip code 46746). Covers a land area of 75.122 square miles and a water area of 1.106 square miles. Located at 41.72° N. Lat.; 85.39° W. Long. Elevation is 877 feet.
History: Howe was laid out in 1834 on the site of a large apple orchard, said to have been planted by Johnny Appleseed. First called Lima, Howe was renamed in 1884 to honor John B. Howe, the founder of Howe School.
Population: 4,106 (2000); Race: 94.1% White, 0.3% Black, 1.1% Asian, 0.7% American Indian and Alaska Native, 7.2% Hispanic of any race, 0.3% two or more races (2000); Density: 54.7 persons per square mile (2000); Age: 27.0% under 18, 11.6% over 64 (2000); Marriage status: 21.0% never married, 64.8% now married, 5.4% widowed, 8.8% divorced (2000); Foreign born: 5.4% (2000); Ancestry (includes multiple ancestries): 23.0% German, 16.3% Other groups, 14.0% United States or American, 10.1% English, 8.6% Irish (2000).
Economy: Employment by occupation: 10.7% management, 13.5% professional, 13.0% services, 16.0% sales, 2.0% farming, 8.3% construction, 36.5% production (2000).
Income: Per capita income: $16,841 (2000); Median household income: $38,594 (2000); Poverty rate: 7.4% (2000).
Education: High school graduation rate: 77.0% (2000); College graduation rate: 14.8% (2000).
Housing: Homeownership rate: 80.5% (2000); Median home value: $92,200 (2000); Median rent: $387 per month (2000); Median age of housing: 36 years (2000).
Transportation: Commute to work: 90.5% car, 1.1% public transportation, 3.6% walk, 2.4% work from home (2000); Travel time to work: 40.0% less

than 15 minutes, 30.0% 15 to 30 minutes, 19.8% 30 to 45 minutes, 5.7% 45 to 60 minutes, 4.5% 60 minutes or more (2000)

LAGRANGE (town). Covers a land area of 1.699 square miles and a water area of 0 square miles. Located at 41.64° N. Lat.; 85.41° W. Long. Elevation is 920 feet.

History: LaGrange became the seat of LaGrange County in 1844. The town was named in 1836 for the Marquis de LaFayette's country residence near Paris, by the French immigrants who settled here. LaGrange was incorporated in 1855.

Population: 2,919 (2000); Race: 90.7% White, 0.9% Black, 0.3% Asian, 0.2% American Indian and Alaska Native, 7.5% Hispanic of any race, 1.4% two or more races (2000); Density: 1,717.8 persons per square mile (2000); Age: 27.8% under 18, 15.4% over 64 (2000); Marriage status: 24.3% never married, 53.1% now married, 9.3% widowed, 13.3% divorced (2000); Foreign born: 5.3% (2000); Ancestry (includes multiple ancestries): 19.1% German, 15.3% United States or American, 11.6% Other groups, 8.8% English, 6.5% Irish (2000).

Economy: Employment by occupation: 5.9% management, 10.0% professional, 15.6% services, 18.1% sales, 2.1% farming, 9.2% construction, 39.2% production (2000).

Income: Per capita income: $17,865 (2000); Median household income: $32,054 (2000); Poverty rate: 7.1% (2000).

Taxes: Total city taxes per capita: $125 (1997); City property taxes per capita: $91 (1997).

Education: High school graduation rate: 74.9% (2000); College graduation rate: 13.0% (2000).

School District(s)

Lakeland School Corporation (KG-12)
2000 Enrollment: 2,305 219-463-7101

Prairie Heights Com Sch Corp (KG-12)
2000 Enrollment: 1,842 219-351-3214

Housing: Homeownership rate: 60.9% (2000); Median home value: $80,800 (2000); Median rent: $364 per month (2000); Median age of housing: 46 years (2000).

Hospitals: LaGrange Community Hospital (62 beds)

Newspapers: Lagrange Standard (1 x week); Lagrange News (1 x week); Lagrange-Countian (1 x week); The Crystal Valley Trading Post (1 x week)

Transportation: Commute to work: 91.5% car, 0.0% public transportation, 5.1% walk, 2.5% work from home (2000); Travel time to work: 56.9% less than 15 minutes, 26.7% 15 to 30 minutes, 11.0% 30 to 45 minutes, 1.2% 45 to 60 minutes, 4.2% 60 minutes or more (2000)

Additional Information Contacts

Lagrange Chamber of Commerce 219-463-2443

SHIPSHEWANA (town). Covers a land area of 0.920 square miles and a water area of 0 square miles. Located at 41.67° N. Lat.; 85.58° W. Long. Elevation is 904 feet.

History: Shipshewana began as a trading center for Amish farmers in the area.

Population: 536 (2000); Race: 97.2% White, 0.4% Black, 0.0% Asian, 0.0% American Indian and Alaska Native, 2.6% Hispanic of any race, 1.9% two or more races (2000); Density: 582.7 persons per square mile (2000); Age: 19.3% under 18, 18.7% over 64 (2000); Marriage status: 24.1% never married, 59.7% now married, 9.2% widowed, 7.0% divorced (2000); Foreign born: 0.6% (2000); Ancestry (includes multiple ancestries): 25.4% German, 23.9% United States or American, 9.3% Swiss, 6.7% Irish, 5.8% English (2000).

Economy: Employment by occupation: 12.3% management, 7.7% professional, 12.9% services, 28.7% sales, 1.0% farming, 8.1% construction, 29.4% production (2000).

Income: Per capita income: $26,270 (2000); Median household income: $30,156 (2000); Poverty rate: 8.0% (2000).

Taxes: Total city taxes per capita: $892 (1997); City property taxes per capita: $646 (1997).

Education: High school graduation rate: 56.4% (2000); College graduation rate: 3.8% (2000).

Housing: Homeownership rate: 48.7% (2000); Median home value: $114,300 (2000); Median rent: $399 per month (2000); Median age of housing: 26 years (2000).

Transportation: Commute to work: 80.0% car, 0.3% public transportation, 6.1% walk, 4.8% work from home (2000); Travel time to work: 55.3% less than 15 minutes, 34.2% 15 to 30 minutes, 9.8% 30 to 45 minutes, 0.0% 45 to 60 minutes, 0.7% 60 minutes or more (2000)

Additional Information Contacts

Lagrange County Convention & Visitors Bureau 219-768-4008

TOPEKA (town). Covers a land area of 1.378 square miles and a water area of 0 square miles. Located at 41.53° N. Lat.; 85.54° W. Long. Elevation is 938 feet.

History: Laid out 1843.

Population: 1,159 (2000); Race: 96.1% White, 0.0% Black, 1.6% Asian, 0.0% American Indian and Alaska Native, 2.2% Hispanic of any race, 1.6% two or more races (2000); Density: 841.2 persons per square mile (2000); Age: 30.9% under 18, 10.3% over 64 (2000); Marriage status: 22.6% never married, 58.6% now married, 4.8% widowed, 14.0% divorced (2000); Foreign born: 3.7% (2000); Ancestry (includes multiple ancestries): 28.0% German, 13.7% United States or American, 10.7% Other groups, 8.8% Irish, 6.7% English (2000).

Economy: Agricultural area: hay; poultry; dairying. Manufacturing: boats, carbide-tipped tools, modular homes, trailers. Employment by occupation: 5.6% management, 8.4% professional, 12.2% services, 15.2% sales, 0.0% farming, 9.8% construction, 48.8% production (2000).

Income: Per capita income: $17,269 (2000); Median household income: $37,105 (2000); Poverty rate: 9.1% (2000).

Taxes: Total city taxes per capita: $507 (1997); City property taxes per capita: $435 (1997).

Education: High school graduation rate: 64.7% (2000); College graduation rate: 8.0% (2000).

School District(s)

Westview School Corporation (KG-12)
2000 Enrollment: 2,231 219-768-4404

Housing: Homeownership rate: 64.9% (2000); Median home value: $79,600 (2000); Median rent: $331 per month (2000); Median age of housing: 35 years (2000).

Transportation: Commute to work: 88.5% car, 0.0% public transportation, 3.2% walk, 3.2% work from home (2000); Travel time to work: 43.4% less than 15 minutes, 38.0% 15 to 30 minutes, 14.0% 30 to 45 minutes, 1.6% 45 to 60 minutes, 3.0% 60 minutes or more (2000)

Additional Information Contacts

Topeka Area Chamber of Commerce 219-593-2138

La Porte County

Located in northwestern Indiana; bounded on the northwest by Lake Michigan, on the north by Michigan, and partly on the south by the Kankakee River. Covers a land area of 598.20 square miles, a water area of 14.80 square miles, and is located in the Central Time Zone. The county government was organized in 1832. County seat is La Porte.

Weather Station: La Porte — Elevation: 807 feet

	Jan	Feb	Mar	Apr	May	Jun	Jul	Aug	Sep	Oct	Nov	Dec
High	30	35	46	58	70	79	83	81	74	62	47	35
Low	16	20	29	39	50	59	64	62	55	44	33	23
Precip	2.3	1.9	3.1	3.6	3.5	4.4	3.8	4.1	3.9	3.3	3.8	3.1
Snow	21.6	12.6	7.1	1.4	tr	0.0	0.0	0.0	0.0	0.3	4.8	13.7

High and Low temperatures in degrees Fahrenheit; Precipitation and Snow in inches

Population: 110,106 (2000); Race: 86.2% White, 10.0% Black, 0.3% Asian, 0.2% American Indian and Alaska Native, 2.9% Hispanic of any race, 2.0% two or more races (2000); Density: 184.1 persons per square mile (2000); Age: 24.5% under 18, 13.6% over 64 (2000).

Religion: Five largest groups: 22.9% Catholic Church, 3.4% Lutheran Church—Missouri Synod, 2.7% Evangelical Lutheran Church in America, 2.7% The United Methodist Church, 2.3% Christian Churches and Churches of Christ (2000).

Economy: Unemployment rate: 6.5% (11/2002); Total civilian labor force: 55,792 (11/2002); Leading industries: 24.3% manufacturing; 16.4% retail trade; 12.2% health care and social assistance (2000); Companies that employ more than 1,000 persons: 3 (2000); Companies that employ more than 100 persons: 63 (2000); Farms: 749 totaling 247,756 acres (1997); Minority business ownership rate: 7.9% (1997); Women business ownership rate: 23.8% (1997); Retail sales per capita: $9,501 (1997). Single-family building permits issued: 406 (2001) / 418 (2000); Multi-family building permits issued: 36 (2001) / 22 (2000).

Income: Per capita income: $18,913 (2000); Median household income: $41,430 (2000); Poverty rate: 8.7% (2000); Bankruptcy rate: 9.42% (2001).

Taxes: Total county taxes per capita: $321 (2000); County property taxes per capita: $229 (2000).

Education: High school graduation rate: 80.6% (2000); College graduation rate: 14.0% (2000).

Housing: Homeownership rate: 75.2% (2000); Median home value: $93,500 (2000); Median rent: $410 per month (2000); Median age of housing: 40 years (2000).
Health: Birth rate: 127.6 per 10,000 population (1998); Age adjusted death rate: 94.7 per 10,000 population (1999); Age adjusted cancer mortality rate: 234.2 deaths per 100,000 population (1999). Air Quality Index: 73% good, 27% moderate, <1% unhealthy (percent of days in 2000). Number of physicians: 15.7 per 10,000 population (1999); Number of hospital beds: 41.0 per 10,000 population (1999).
Elections: 2000 Presidential election results: 49.7% Gore, 47.8% Bush, 1.0% Nader, 0.9% Buchanan
National and State Parks: Kingsbury State Fish And Game Area; Kingsbury State Fish and Wildlife Area
Additional Information Contacts
LaPorte County Government Offices 219-326-6808
La Porte Chamber of Commerce 219-362-3178
La Porte County Convention & Visitors Bureau 219-872-5055
Laporte County Association of Realtors 219-324-8120
Michigan City Chamber of Commerce 219-874-6221

La Porte County Communities

HANNA (unincorporated postal area, zip code 46340). Covers a land area of 35.426 square miles and a water area of 0.165 square miles. Located at 41.39° N. Lat.; 86.76° W. Long. Elevation is 706 feet.
History: Laid out 1858.
Population: 1,068 (2000); Race: 93.0% White, 1.5% Black, 0.2% Asian, 0.0% American Indian and Alaska Native, 0.0% Hispanic of any race, 5.3% two or more races (2000); Density: 30.1 persons per square mile (2000); Age: 24.5% under 18, 14.8% over 64 (2000); Marriage status: 18.1% never married, 70.0% now married, 6.5% widowed, 5.4% divorced (2000); Foreign born: 0.2% (2000); Ancestry (includes multiple ancestries): 35.6% German, 19.5% Irish, 9.2% United States or American, 7.7% Polish, 5.1% English (2000).
Economy: Railroad junction. Dairying; fruit. Employment by occupation: 9.6% management, 16.9% professional, 10.0% services, 20.6% sales, 1.4% farming, 19.4% construction, 22.0% production (2000).
Income: Per capita income: $19,064 (2000); Median household income: $48,056 (2000); Poverty rate: 6.3% (2000).
Education: High school graduation rate: 86.4% (2000); College graduation rate: 11.7% (2000).
Housing: Homeownership rate: 90.2% (2000); Median home value: $95,200 (2000); Median rent: $377 per month (2000); Median age of housing: 35 years (2000).
Transportation: Commute to work: 86.7% car, 0.0% public transportation, 4.5% walk, 8.8% work from home (2000); Travel time to work: 22.1% less than 15 minutes, 31.8% 15 to 30 minutes, 26.6% 30 to 45 minutes, 16.1% 45 to 60 minutes, 3.4% 60 minutes or more (2000)

KINGSBURY (town). Covers a land area of 0.584 square miles and a water area of 0 square miles. Located at 41.52° N. Lat.; 86.70° W. Long. Elevation is 750 feet.
History: Kingsbury developed around the Wabash and the Grand Trunk Railroads in the mid-1800's.
Population: 229 (2000); Race: 97.1% White, 0.0% Black, 0.0% Asian, 0.0% American Indian and Alaska Native, 0.0% Hispanic of any race, 2.9% two or more races (2000); Density: 391.8 persons per square mile (2000); Age: 23.3% under 18, 8.6% over 64 (2000); Marriage status: 23.2% never married, 68.5% now married, 2.4% widowed, 6.0% divorced (2000); Foreign born: 3.8% (2000); Ancestry (includes multiple ancestries): 32.9% German, 13.8% Irish, 9.0% United States or American, 9.0% Polish, 9.0% French (except Basque) (2000).
Economy: Single-family building permits issued: 0 (2001) / 1 (2000); Multi-family building permits issued: 0 (2001) / 0 (2000); Employment by occupation: 0.8% management, 8.2% professional, 8.2% services, 29.5% sales, 0.0% farming, 11.5% construction, 41.8% production (2000).
Income: Per capita income: $18,096 (2000); Median household income: $50,000 (2000); Poverty rate: 9.7% (2000).
Taxes: Total city taxes per capita: $57 (1997); City property taxes per capita: $53 (1997).
Education: High school graduation rate: 84.6% (2000); College graduation rate: 12.5% (2000).
Housing: Homeownership rate: 79.5% (2000); Median home value: $87,700 (2000); Median rent: $363 per month (2000); Median age of housing: 49 years (2000).
Transportation: Commute to work: 95.9% car, 0.0% public transportation, 3.3% walk, 0.0% work from home (2000); Travel time to work: 32.0% less than 15 minutes, 38.5% 15 to 30 minutes, 19.7% 30 to 45 minutes, 4.9% 45 to 60 minutes, 4.9% 60 minutes or more (2000)

KINGSFORD HEIGHTS (town). Covers a land area of 0.941 square miles and a water area of 0 square miles. Located at 41.48° N. Lat.; 86.69° W. Long. Elevation is 717 feet.
Population: 1,453 (2000); Race: 85.2% White, 12.3% Black, 0.2% Asian, 0.0% American Indian and Alaska Native, 0.7% Hispanic of any race, 1.4% two or more races (2000); Density: 1,543.7 persons per square mile (2000); Age: 34.1% under 18, 8.3% over 64 (2000); Marriage status: 21.7% never married, 54.9% now married, 7.1% widowed, 16.3% divorced (2000); Foreign born: 1.0% (2000); Ancestry (includes multiple ancestries): 20.7% United States or American, 19.8% Other groups, 15.6% German, 11.0% Irish, 6.6% Polish (2000).
Economy: Single-family building permits issued: 1 (2001) / 4 (2000); Multi-family building permits issued: 0 (2001) / 0 (2000); Employment by occupation: 5.8% management, 4.9% professional, 9.4% services, 21.7% sales, 0.0% farming, 8.9% construction, 49.3% production (2000).
Income: Per capita income: $13,961 (2000); Median household income: $32,169 (2000); Poverty rate: 13.4% (2000).
Taxes: Total city taxes per capita: $61 (1997); City property taxes per capita: $57 (1997).
Education: High school graduation rate: 73.2% (2000); College graduation rate: 5.0% (2000).
Housing: Homeownership rate: 75.9% (2000); Median home value: $54,700 (2000); Median rent: $409 per month (2000); Median age of housing: 44 years (2000).
Transportation: Commute to work: 98.0% car, 0.4% public transportation, 1.1% walk, 0.5% work from home (2000); Travel time to work: 16.7% less than 15 minutes, 60.1% 15 to 30 minutes, 8.7% 30 to 45 minutes, 8.2% 45 to 60 minutes, 6.3% 60 minutes or more (2000)

LA CROSSE (town). Covers a land area of 0.539 square miles and a water area of 0 square miles. Located at 41.31° N. Lat.; 86.89° W. Long. Elevation is 678 feet.
Population: 561 (2000); Race: 98.1% White, 0.0% Black, 0.0% Asian, 0.7% American Indian and Alaska Native, 0.0% Hispanic of any race, 1.1% two or more races (2000); Density: 1,040.0 persons per square mile (2000); Age: 24.3% under 18, 15.8% over 64 (2000); Marriage status: 22.2% never married, 62.8% now married, 5.3% widowed, 9.7% divorced (2000); Foreign born: 0.4% (2000); Ancestry (includes multiple ancestries): 39.1% German, 12.8% Irish, 11.3% English, 10.2% Polish, 6.5% Dutch (2000).
Economy: Agricultural area. Single-family building permits issued: 2 (2001) / 2 (2000); Multi-family building permits issued: 0 (2001) / 0 (2000); Employment by occupation: 5.4% management, 9.3% professional, 12.8% services, 30.4% sales, 0.8% farming, 14.8% construction, 26.5% production (2000).
Income: Per capita income: $17,962 (2000); Median household income: $36,667 (2000); Poverty rate: 1.5% (2000).
Taxes: Total city taxes per capita: $107 (1997); City property taxes per capita: $107 (1997).
Education: High school graduation rate: 88.5% (2000); College graduation rate: 9.0% (2000).
Housing: Homeownership rate: 85.8% (2000); Median home value: $76,400 (2000); Median rent: $342 per month (2000); Median age of housing: 60+ years (2000).
Transportation: Commute to work: 99.2% car, 0.0% public transportation, 0.0% walk, 0.8% work from home (2000); Travel time to work: 21.8% less than 15 minutes, 34.1% 15 to 30 minutes, 27.4% 30 to 45 minutes, 9.5% 45 to 60 minutes, 7.1% 60 minutes or more (2000)

LA PORTE (city). Covers a land area of 11.459 square miles and a water area of 0.711 square miles. Located at 41.60° N. Lat.; 86.71° W. Long. Elevation is 817 feet.
History: La Porte was founded in 1830 when the Michigan Road was under construction. Its name is French for "the door," and through La Porte passed much commerce.
Population: 21,621 (2000); Race: 93.4% White, 1.8% Black, 0.2% Asian, 0.1% American Indian and Alaska Native, 6.5% Hispanic of any race, 1.2% two or more races (2000); Density: 1,886.8 persons per square mile (2000); Age: 24.1% under 18, 17.0% over 64 (2000); Marriage status: 22.0% never married, 53.6% now married, 9.5% widowed, 15.0% divorced (2000); Foreign born: 4.2% (2000); Ancestry (includes multiple ancestries): 29.7%

German, 12.8% Other groups, 11.8% Irish, 10.9% Polish, 9.3% United States or American (2000).
Vital Statistics: Birth rate: 169.3 per 10,000 population (1998)
Economy: Single-family building permits issued: 23 (2001) / 28 (2000); Multi-family building permits issued: 0 (2001) / 0 (2000); Employment by occupation: 8.9% management, 13.0% professional, 16.7% services, 21.7% sales, 0.4% farming, 11.0% construction, 28.3% production (2000).
Income: Per capita income: $17,900 (2000); Median household income: $35,376 (2000); Poverty rate: 11.0% (2000).
Education: High school graduation rate: 79.2% (2000); College graduation rate: 13.0% (2000).

School District(s)

Cass Township Schools (KG-08)
2000 Enrollment: 249 219-326-6808
Dewey Township Schools (KG-12)
2000 Enrollment: 188 219-326-6808
Laporte Community School Corp (PK-12)
2000 Enrollment: 6,326 219-362-7056

Housing: Homeownership rate: 63.4% (2000); Median home value: $82,400 (2000); Median rent: $405 per month (2000); Median age of housing: 50 years (2000).
Hospitals: LaPorte Regional Health System (227 beds)
Safety: Violent crime rate: 23.0 per 10,000 population; Property crime rate: 517.4 per 10,000 population (2001).
Newspapers: The La Porte Herald-Argus (6 x week); The Regional News (1 x week)
Transportation: Commute to work: 93.4% car, 0.5% public transportation, 3.0% walk, 1.2% work from home (2000); Travel time to work: 52.3% less than 15 minutes, 25.0% 15 to 30 minutes, 11.3% 30 to 45 minutes, 6.2% 45 to 60 minutes, 5.2% 60 minutes or more (2000)
Additional Information Contacts
La Porte Chamber of Commerce 219-362-3178
Laporte County Association of Realtors 219-324-8120

LONG BEACH (town). Covers a land area of 1.042 square miles and a water area of 2.111 square miles. Located at 41.74° N. Lat.; 86.85° W. Long. Elevation is 610 feet.
Population: 1,559 (2000); Race: 97.5% White, 0.0% Black, 0.6% Asian, 0.5% American Indian and Alaska Native, 2.2% Hispanic of any race, 1.4% two or more races (2000); Density: 1,495.7 persons per square mile (2000); Age: 22.5% under 18, 20.5% over 64 (2000); Marriage status: 18.3% never married, 68.6% now married, 6.1% widowed, 7.0% divorced (2000); Foreign born: 2.9% (2000); Ancestry (includes multiple ancestries): 41.2% Irish, 27.2% German, 13.4% English, 9.3% Polish, 8.4% Other groups (2000).
Economy: Single-family building permits issued: 9 (2001) / 5 (2000); Multi-family building permits issued: 0 (2001) / 0 (2000); Employment by occupation: 30.9% management, 32.8% professional, 7.0% services, 22.0% sales, 0.0% farming, 4.1% construction, 3.2% production (2000).
Income: Per capita income: $43,159 (2000); Median household income: $71,364 (2000); Poverty rate: 0.9% (2000).
Taxes: Total city taxes per capita: $256 (1997); City property taxes per capita: $245 (1997).
Education: High school graduation rate: 98.1% (2000); College graduation rate: 56.9% (2000).
Housing: Homeownership rate: 94.9% (2000); Median home value: $217,500 (2000); Median rent: $600 per month (2000); Median age of housing: 47 years (2000).
Safety: Violent crime rate: 15.8 per 10,000 population; Property crime rate: 163.2 per 10,000 population (2001).
Transportation: Commute to work: 86.9% car, 4.5% public transportation, 0.9% walk, 5.6% work from home (2000); Travel time to work: 32.7% less than 15 minutes, 29.8% 15 to 30 minutes, 9.5% 30 to 45 minutes, 6.3% 45 to 60 minutes, 21.7% 60 minutes or more (2000)

MICHIANA SHORES (town). Covers a land area of 0.346 square miles and a water area of 0 square miles. Located at 41.75° N. Lat.; 86.81° W. Long. Elevation is 610 feet.
Population: 330 (2000); Race: 96.8% White, 0.0% Black, 0.0% Asian, 0.0% American Indian and Alaska Native, 4.6% Hispanic of any race, 2.5% two or more races (2000); Density: 954.0 persons per square mile (2000); Age: 11.7% under 18, 29.2% over 64 (2000); Marriage status: 16.3% never married, 54.4% now married, 9.5% widowed, 19.8% divorced (2000); Foreign born: 10.3% (2000); Ancestry (includes multiple ancestries): 21.7% German, 19.6% Irish, 10.3% Polish, 9.3% Swedish, 8.2% United States or American (2000).
Economy: Tourist area. Single-family building permits issued: 4 (2001) / 4 (2000); Multi-family building permits issued: 0 (2001) / 0 (2000); Employment by occupation: 17.1% management, 21.4% professional, 7.1% services, 30.7% sales, 0.0% farming, 7.9% construction, 15.7% production (2000).
Income: Per capita income: $30,633 (2000); Median household income: $46,250 (2000); Poverty rate: 2.5% (2000).
Taxes: Total city taxes per capita: $177 (1997); City property taxes per capita: $161(1997).
Education: High school graduation rate: 94.3% (2000); College graduation rate: 35.7% (2000).
Housing: Homeownership rate: 89.5% (2000); Median home value: $154,200 (2000); Median rent: $538 per month (2000); Median age of housing: 38 years (2000).
Transportation: Commute to work: 91.3% car, 2.9% public transportation, 2.2% walk, 3.6% work from home (2000); Travel time to work: 44.4% less than 15 minutes, 23.3% 15 to 30 minutes, 9.8% 30 to 45 minutes, 2.3% 45 to 60 minutes, 20.3% 60 minutes or more (2000)

MICHIGAN CITY (city). Covers a land area of 19.600 square miles and a water area of 3.517 square miles. Located at 41.70° N. Lat.; 86.88° W. Long. Elevation is 625 feet.
History: It was in Michigan City that Daniel Webster made a Fourth of July speech in 1837. The city was founded in 1832 at the northern end of the Michigan Road, on Lake Michigan. From the early 1840's it served as a port for shipping interests and later for a fishing fleet.
Population: 32,900 (2000); Race: 69.2% White, 26.3% Black, 0.2% Asian, 0.4% American Indian and Alaska Native, 2.9% Hispanic of any race, 3.3% two or more races (2000); Density: 1,678.6 persons per square mile (2000); Age: 24.9% under 18, 14.4% over 64 (2000); Marriage status: 28.1% never married, 47.2% now married, 8.6% widowed, 16.1% divorced (2000); Foreign born: 2.1% (2000); Ancestry (includes multiple ancestries): 28.3% Other groups, 20.2% German, 11.1% Polish, 9.8% Irish, 7.2% United States or American (2000).
Economy: Unemployment rate: 8.9% (11/2002); Total civilian labor force: 17,289 (11/2002); Single-family building permits issued: 52 (2001) / 50 (2000); Multi-family building permits issued: 8 (2001) / 22 (2000); Employment by occupation: 8.5% management, 12.8% professional, 21.3% services, 25.7% sales, 0.2% farming, 9.3% construction, 22.2% production (2000).
Income: Per capita income: $16,995 (2000); Median household income: $33,732 (2000); Poverty rate: 13.3% (2000).
Taxes: Total city taxes per capita: $505 (2000); City property taxes per capita: $390 (2000).
Education: High school graduation rate: 76.3% (2000); College graduation rate: 12.1% (2000).

School District(s)

Michigan City Area Schools (PK-12)
2000 Enrollment: 6,990 219-873-2000

Two-year College(s)

Commonwealth Business College-Michigan City (Private, For-profit)
2001 Enrollment: 385 219-877-3100
2001 Tuition: In-state $5,328; Out-of-state $5,328
Lakeshore Medical Laboratory Training Program (Private, Not-for-profit)
2001 Enrollment: n/a 219-872-7032

Housing: Homeownership rate: 60.8% (2000); Median home value: $76,600 (2000); Median rent: $411 per month (2000); Median age of housing: 44 years (2000).
Hospitals: Saint Anthony Memorial Health Centers (190 beds)
Safety: Violent crime rate: 36.6 per 10,000 population; Property crime rate: 771.6 per 10,000 population (2001).
Newspapers: The News-Dispatch (7 x week)
Transportation: Commute to work: 93.2% car, 1.8% public transportation, 2.6% walk, 1.4% work from home (2000); Travel time to work: 54.1% less than 15 minutes, 26.8% 15 to 30 minutes, 8.7% 30 to 45 minutes, 5.5% 45 to 60 minutes, 4.9% 60 minutes or more (2000); Amtrak: Service available.
Airports: Michigan City Municipal
Additional Information Contacts
La Porte County Convention & Visitors Bureau 219-872-5055
Michigan City Chamber of Commerce 219-874-6221

MILL CREEK (unincorporated postal area, zip code 46365). Covers a land area of 23.309 square miles and a water area of 0.101 square miles. Located at 41.59° N. Lat.; 86.53° W. Long.
Population: 1,003 (2000); Race: 100.0% White, 0.0% Black, 0.0% Asian, 0.0% American Indian and Alaska Native, 0.0% Hispanic of any race, 0.0%

two or more races (2000); Density: 43.0 persons per square mile (2000); Age: 32.6% under 18, 2.8% over 64 (2000); Marriage status: 20.6% never married, 68.0% now married, 4.0% widowed, 7.3% divorced (2000); Foreign born: 0.7% (2000); Ancestry (includes multiple ancestries): 32.5% German, 14.8% Irish, 12.4% Polish, 8.3% United States or American, 8.2% English (2000).
Economy: Employment by occupation: 8.9% management, 18.2% professional, 7.6% services, 21.9% sales, 2.4% farming, 17.7% construction, 23.3% production (2000).
Income: Per capita income: $20,208 (2000); Median household income: $53,125 (2000); Poverty rate: 1.6% (2000).
Education: High school graduation rate: 90.7% (2000); College graduation rate: 15.1% (2000).
Housing: Homeownership rate: 88.3% (2000); Median home value: $110,700 (2000); Median rent: $460 per month (2000); Median age of housing: 25 years (2000).
Transportation: Commute to work: 93.5% car, 0.0% public transportation, 2.7% walk, 2.0% work from home (2000); Travel time to work: 22.5% less than 15 minutes, 40.1% 15 to 30 minutes, 26.3% 30 to 45 minutes, 10.1% 45 to 60 minutes, 1.0% 60 minutes or more (2000)

POTTAWATTAMIE PARK (town). Aka Pottawattomie Park. Covers a land area of 0.251 square miles and a water area of 0 square miles. Located at 41.72° N. Lat.; 86.86° W. Long.
Population: 300 (2000); Race: 86.0% White, 10.6% Black, 1.3% Asian, 0.0% American Indian and Alaska Native, 1.0% Hispanic of any race, 1.0% two or more races (2000); Density: 1,196.9 persons per square mile (2000); Age: 23.3% under 18, 29.6% over 64 (2000); Marriage status: 20.4% never married, 66.0% now married, 8.0% widowed, 5.6% divorced (2000); Foreign born: 8.0% (2000); Ancestry (includes multiple ancestries): 28.2% German, 15.3% Other groups, 14.0% English, 7.3% Polish, 6.3% Lebanese (2000).
Economy: Employment by occupation: 19.8% management, 36.6% professional, 8.9% services, 26.7% sales, 0.0% farming, 6.9% construction, 1.0% production (2000).
Income: Per capita income: $24,383 (2000); Median household income: $37,500 (2000); Poverty rate: 8.6% (2000).
Taxes: Total city taxes per capita: $124 (1997); City property taxes per capita: $116 (1997).
Education: High school graduation rate: 88.4% (2000); College graduation rate: 42.4% (2000).
Housing: Homeownership rate: 93.4% (2000); Median home value: $137,100 (2000); Median rent: $475 per month (2000); Median age of housing: 41 years (2000).
Transportation: Commute to work: 97.0% car, 2.0% public transportation, 0.0% walk, 1.0% work from home (2000); Travel time to work: 58.2% less than 15 minutes, 15.3% 15 to 30 minutes, 0.0% 30 to 45 minutes, 12.2% 45 to 60 minutes, 14.3% 60 minutes or more (2000)

ROLLING PRAIRIE (unincorporated postal area, zip code 46371). Covers a land area of 37.421 square miles and a water area of 0.667 square miles. Located at 41.67° N. Lat.; 86.60° W. Long. Elevation is 822 feet.
History: The site for Rolling Prairie was chosen in 1831 by Ezekial Provolt, who built a cabin here in 1834. The town was laid out in 1853.
Population: 3,132 (2000); Race: 98.4% White, 0.6% Black, 0.5% Asian, 0.0% American Indian and Alaska Native, 1.1% Hispanic of any race, 0.3% two or more races (2000); Density: 83.7 persons per square mile (2000); Age: 24.5% under 18, 11.7% over 64 (2000); Marriage status: 16.9% never married, 63.7% now married, 8.1% widowed, 11.2% divorced (2000); Foreign born: 0.3% (2000); Ancestry (includes multiple ancestries): 31.3% German, 13.7% Irish, 13.2% Polish, 9.0% English, 6.7% United States or American (2000).
Economy: Employment by occupation: 9.0% management, 12.7% professional, 20.3% services, 17.7% sales, 0.9% farming, 13.9% construction, 25.4% production (2000).
Income: Per capita income: $19,422 (2000); Median household income: $50,548 (2000); Poverty rate: 4.1% (2000).
Education: High school graduation rate: 85.1% (2000); College graduation rate: 10.3% (2000).
Housing: Homeownership rate: 91.6% (2000); Median home value: $98,700 (2000); Median rent: $446 per month (2000); Median age of housing: 38 years (2000).
Transportation: Commute to work: 90.2% car, 1.2% public transportation, 3.5% walk, 4.7% work from home (2000); Travel time to work: 27.1% less than 15 minutes, 45.9% 15 to 30 minutes, 13.9% 30 to 45 minutes, 7.2% 45 to 60 minutes, 5.9% 60 minutes or more (2000)

TRAIL CREEK (town). Covers a land area of 1.218 square miles and a water area of 0 square miles. Located at 41.69° N. Lat.; 86.85° W. Long. Elevation is 632 feet.
Population: 2,296 (2000); Race: 95.4% White, 2.2% Black, 0.0% Asian, 0.0% American Indian and Alaska Native, 0.9% Hispanic of any race, 2.0% two or more races (2000); Density: 1,884.6 persons per square mile (2000); Age: 22.3% under 18, 23.8% over 64 (2000); Marriage status: 13.0% never married, 69.1% now married, 10.6% widowed, 7.3% divorced (2000); Foreign born: 1.6% (2000); Ancestry (includes multiple ancestries): 42.7% German, 25.0% Polish, 13.3% Irish, 11.2% English, 5.5% Other groups (2000).
Economy: Single-family building permits issued: 1 (2001) / 2 (2000); Multi-family building permits issued: 0 (2001) / 0 (2000); Employment by occupation: 14.0% management, 20.1% professional, 12.3% services, 26.6% sales, 0.3% farming, 10.8% construction, 15.9% production (2000).
Income: Per capita income: $20,289 (2000); Median household income: $43,750 (2000); Poverty rate: 5.3% (2000).
Taxes: Total city taxes per capita: $96 (1997); City property taxes per capita: $89 (1997).
Education: High school graduation rate: 84.7% (2000); College graduation rate: 18.0% (2000).
Housing: Homeownership rate: 93.3% (2000); Median home value: $98,900 (2000); Median rent: $458 per month (2000); Median age of housing: 39 years (2000).
Transportation: Commute to work: 94.9% car, 0.9% public transportation, 0.8% walk, 3.3% work from home (2000); Travel time to work: 60.2% less than 15 minutes, 22.3% 15 to 30 minutes, 8.2% 30 to 45 minutes, 5.0% 45 to 60 minutes, 4.4% 60 minutes or more (2000)

UNION MILLS (unincorporated postal area, zip code 46382). Covers a land area of 49.412 square miles and a water area of 0.036 square miles. Located at 41.48° N. Lat.; 86.77° W. Long. Elevation is 735 feet.
Population: 1,990 (2000); Race: 99.3% White, 0.4% Black, 0.0% Asian, 0.0% American Indian and Alaska Native, 0.0% Hispanic of any race, 0.4% two or more races (2000); Density: 40.3 persons per square mile (2000); Age: 27.3% under 18, 13.5% over 64 (2000); Marriage status: 15.1% never married, 71.5% now married, 4.7% widowed, 8.7% divorced (2000); Foreign born: 0.0% (2000); Ancestry (includes multiple ancestries): 38.8% German, 11.7% Irish, 10.8% English, 8.4% United States or American, 6.2% Polish (2000).
Economy: Employment by occupation: 7.7% management, 9.1% professional, 16.5% services, 22.5% sales, 1.8% farming, 18.5% construction, 23.9% production (2000).
Income: Per capita income: $17,184 (2000); Median household income: $41,302 (2000); Poverty rate: 2.4% (2000).
Education: High school graduation rate: 88.1% (2000); College graduation rate: 8.9% (2000).

School District(s)

South Central Com School Corp (KG-12)
2000 Enrollment: 855 219-767-2263

Housing: Homeownership rate: 91.6% (2000); Median home value: $93,300 (2000); Median rent: $526 per month (2000); Median age of housing: 32 years (2000).
Transportation: Commute to work: 92.5% car, 0.8% public transportation, 0.8% walk, 5.9% work from home (2000); Travel time to work: 17.7% less than 15 minutes, 47.8% 15 to 30 minutes, 14.4% 30 to 45 minutes, 12.4% 45 to 60 minutes, 7.7% 60 minutes or more (2000)

WANATAH (town). Covers a land area of 1.370 square miles and a water area of 0 square miles. Located at 41.43° N. Lat.; 86.89° W. Long. Elevation is 725 feet.
History: Wanatah is named for an Indian chief whose name means "keep knee deep in mud."
Population: 1,013 (2000); Race: 96.2% White, 0.1% Black, 0.2% Asian, 0.0% American Indian and Alaska Native, 3.8% Hispanic of any race, 3.2% two or more races (2000); Density: 739.2 persons per square mile (2000); Age: 26.8% under 18, 10.2% over 64 (2000); Marriage status: 20.5% never married, 63.1% now married, 6.5% widowed, 9.9% divorced (2000); Foreign born: 0.2% (2000); Ancestry (includes multiple ancestries): 36.8% German, 13.7% Irish, 9.8% English, 8.6% Other groups, 7.8% United States or American (2000).
Economy: Single-family building permits issued: 1 (2001) / 3 (2000); Multi-family building permits issued: 0 (2001) / 0 (2000); Employment by occupation: 9.9% management, 11.3% professional, 12.4% services, 26.3% sales, 1.1% farming, 18.2% construction, 20.8% production (2000).

Income: Per capita income: $19,945 (2000); Median household income: $50,625 (2000); Poverty rate: 5.3% (2000).
Taxes: Total city taxes per capita: $128 (1997); City property taxes per capita: $124 (1997).
Education: High school graduation rate: 85.7% (2000); College graduation rate: 14.3% (2000).
Housing: Homeownership rate: 85.8% (2000); Median home value: $98,800 (2000); Median rent: $445 per month (2000); Median age of housing: 39 years (2000).
Transportation: Commute to work: 91.0% car, 0.2% public transportation, 3.4% walk, 4.6% work from home (2000); Travel time to work: 34.4% less than 15 minutes, 32.4% 15 to 30 minutes, 22.4% 30 to 45 minutes, 5.8% 45 to 60 minutes, 5.0% 60 minutes or more (2000)

WESTVILLE (town). Covers a land area of 3.126 square miles and a water area of 0 square miles. Located at 41.54° N. Lat.; 86.90° W. Long. Elevation is 805 feet.
History: Settled 1836, laid out 1851.
Population: 2,116 (2000); Race: 95.5% White, 2.1% Black, 0.5% Asian, 0.0% American Indian and Alaska Native, 0.8% Hispanic of any race, 1.4% two or more races (2000); Density: 677.0 persons per square mile (2000); Age: 23.9% under 18, 12.3% over 64 (2000); Marriage status: 22.3% never married, 53.4% now married, 7.0% widowed, 17.2% divorced (2000); Foreign born: 1.2% (2000); Ancestry (includes multiple ancestries): 27.1% German, 16.2% Irish, 9.0% Other groups, 8.7% English, 7.2% United States or American (2000).
Economy: In agricultural area; manufacturing of feed and fertilizer blending. Single-family building permits issued: 2 (2001) / 2 (2000); Multi-family building permits issued: 0 (2001) / 0 (2000); Employment by occupation: 7.4% management, 10.0% professional, 15.3% services, 27.6% sales, 0.7% farming, 11.1% construction, 27.8% production (2000).
Income: Per capita income: $18,306 (2000); Median household income: $36,761 (2000); Poverty rate: 6.3% (2000).
Taxes: Total city taxes per capita: $35 (1997); City property taxes per capita: $35 (1997).
Education: High school graduation rate: 80.1% (2000); College graduation rate: 8.6% (2000).

School District(s)

M S D of New Durham Township (KG-12)
2000 Enrollment: 703 219-785-2239

Four-year College(s)

Purdue University-North Central Campus (Public)
2001 Enrollment: 3,493 219-785-5200
2001 Tuition: In-state $3,053; Out-of-state $7,748

Housing: Homeownership rate: 78.2% (2000); Median home value: $74,500 (2000); Median rent: $387 per month (2000); Median age of housing: 22 years (2000).
Safety: Violent crime rate: 4.7 per 10,000 population; Property crime rate: 446.4 per 10,000 population (2001).
Newspapers: Westville Indicator (1 x week)
Transportation: Commute to work: 96.7% car, 0.9% public transportation, 1.5% walk, 0.4% work from home (2000); Travel time to work: 27.1% less than 15 minutes, 46.2% 15 to 30 minutes, 15.4% 30 to 45 minutes, 6.5% 45 to 60 minutes, 4.9% 60 minutes or more (2000)

Lake County

Located in northwestern Indiana; bounded on the north by Lake Michigan, on the west by Illinois, and on the south by the Kankakee River; crossed by the Grand Calumet and Little Calumet Rivers. Covers a land area of 497.00 square miles, a water area of 129.40 square miles, and is located in the Central Time Zone. The county government was organized in 1836. County seat is Crown Point.

Lake County is part of the Gary, IN PMSA. The entire metro area includes: Lake County; Porter County

Weather Station: Hobart 2 WNW — Elevation: 639 feet

	Jan	Feb	Mar	Apr	May	Jun	Jul	Aug	Sep	Oct	Nov	Dec
High	32	37	48	60	72	81	85	83	77	65	50	37
Low	15	20	29	38	47	58	63	61	54	43	33	22
Precip	1.9	1.6	2.7	3.6	3.9	4.4	3.5	3.7	3.7	3.0	3.5	2.4
Snow	9.1	7.4	3.2	0.8	tr	0.0	0.0	0.0	0.0	tr	1.1	5.8

High and Low temperatures in degrees Fahrenheit; Precipitation and Snow in inches

Weather Station: Lowell — Elevation: 662 feet

	Jan	Feb	Mar	Apr	May	Jun	Jul	Aug	Sep	Oct	Nov	Dec
High	30	35	47	60	72	81	84	82	76	64	48	36
Low	13	17	28	37	48	58	62	60	52	40	31	20
Precip	1.8	1.7	3.0	4.2	4.4	4.6	4.0	3.9	3.5	3.1	3.6	2.7
Snow	10.7	9.2	4.0	0.5	tr	0.0	0.0	0.0	0.0	0.2	1.9	6.6

High and Low temperatures in degrees Fahrenheit; Precipitation and Snow in inches

Population: 484,564 (2000); Race: 66.7% White, 25.2% Black, 0.8% Asian, 0.3% American Indian and Alaska Native, 12.1% Hispanic of any race, 2.0% two or more races (2000); Density: 975.0 persons per square mile (2000); Age: 26.8% under 18, 13.0% over 64 (2000).
Religion: Five largest groups: 26.4% Catholic Church, 2.2% Southern Baptist Convention, 1.9% Lutheran Church—Missouri Synod, 1.6% The United Methodist Church, 1.2% Christian Churches and Churches of Christ (2000).
Economy: Unemployment rate: 5.7% (11/2002); Total civilian labor force: 218,024 (11/2002); Leading industries: 18.9% manufacturing; 15.1% health care and social assistance; 14.8% retail trade (2000); Companies that employ more than 1,000 persons: 12 (2000); Companies that employ more than 100 persons: 254 (2000); Farms: 442 totaling 148,872 acres (1997); Minority business ownership rate: 16.9% (1997); Women business ownership rate: 26.6% (1997); Retail sales per capita: $9,100 (1997). Single-family building permits issued: 1,470 (2001) / 1,549 (2000); Multi-family building permits issued: 577 (2001) / 379 (2000).
Income: Per capita income: $19,639 (2000); Median household income: $41,829 (2000); Poverty rate: 12.2% (2000); Bankruptcy rate: 9.09% (2001).
Taxes: Total county taxes per capita: $363 (2000); County property taxes per capita: $349 (2000).
Education: High school graduation rate: 80.7% (2000); College graduation rate: 16.2% (2000).
Housing: Homeownership rate: 69.0% (2000); Median home value: $97,500 (2000); Median rent: $445 per month (2000); Median age of housing: 40 years (2000).
Health: Birth rate: 147.6 per 10,000 population (1998); Age adjusted death rate: 103.8 per 10,000 population (1999); Infant mortality rate: 10.2 per 1,000 live births (1998); Age adjusted cancer mortality rate: 250.0 deaths per 100,000 population (1999). Air Quality Index: 69% good, 31% moderate, 0% unhealthy (percent of days in 2000). Number of physicians: 16.9 per 10,000 population (1999); Number of hospital beds: 44.7 per 10,000 population (1999).
Elections: 2000 Presidential election results: 62.0% Gore, 36.0% Bush, 0.9% Nader, 0.6% Buchanan
National and State Parks: Hoosier Prairie State Nature Preserve
Additional Information Contacts
Lake County Government Offices 219-755-3200
Cedar Lake Chamber of Commerce. 219-374-6157
Crown Point Chamber of Commerce 219-663-1800
Dyer Chamber of Commerce 219-865-1045
East Chicago Chamber of Commerce 219-398-1600
Gary Chamber of Commerce 219-885-7407
Greater Northwest Indiana Association of Realtors. 219-795-3600
Griffith Chamber of Commerce 219-924-2155
Hammond Chamber of Commerce. 219-931-1000
Highland Chamber of Commerce. 219-923-3666
Hobart Chamber of Commerce 219-942-5774
Lowell Chamber of Commerce 219-696-0231
Merrillville Chamber of Commerce. 219-769-8180
Schererville Chamber of Commerce 219-322-5412
St. John Chamber of Commerce. 219-365-4686
Whiting Chamber of Commerce 219-659-0292

Lake County Communities

CEDAR LAKE (town). Covers a land area of 6.791 square miles and a water area of 1.325 square miles. Located at 41.36° N. Lat.; 87.43° W. Long. Elevation is 725 feet.
Population: 9,279 (2000); Race: 97.1% White, 0.1% Black, 0.2% Asian, 0.1% American Indian and Alaska Native, 3.2% Hispanic of any race, 2.3% two or more races (2000); Density: 1,366.3 persons per square mile (2000); Age: 28.1% under 18, 9.0% over 64 (2000); Marriage status: 24.1% never married, 60.7% now married, 5.6% widowed, 9.6% divorced (2000); Foreign born: 1.2% (2000); Ancestry (includes multiple ancestries): 28.2% German, 15.4% Irish, 10.1% Polish, 7.6% Other groups, 7.5% English (2000).
Economy: Single-family building permits issued: 54 (2001) / 51 (2000); Multi-family building permits issued: 10 (2001) / 0 (2000); Employment by

occupation: 6.2% management, 11.6% professional, 13.1% services, 25.9% sales, 0.5% farming, 22.2% construction, 20.6% production (2000).
Income: Per capita income: $17,825 (2000); Median household income: $43,987 (2000); Poverty rate: 6.6% (2000).
Taxes: Total city taxes per capita: $136 (1997); City property taxes per capita: $117 (1997).
Education: High school graduation rate: 82.4% (2000); College graduation rate: 7.4% (2000).

School District(s)

Hanover Community School Corp (KG-12)
2000 Enrollment: 1,557 219-374-3500
Housing: Homeownership rate: 74.4% (2000); Median home value: $97,200 (2000); Median rent: $473 per month (2000); Median age of housing: 41 years (2000).
Safety: Violent crime rate: 73.9 per 10,000 population; Property crime rate: 334.4 per 10,000 population (2001).
Transportation: Commute to work: 95.1% car, 0.6% public transportation, 1.2% walk, 2.0% work from home (2000); Travel time to work: 20.2% less than 15 minutes, 35.5% 15 to 30 minutes, 22.9% 30 to 45 minutes, 12.6% 45 to 60 minutes, 8.7% 60 minutes or more (2000)
Additional Information Contacts
Cedar Lake Chamber of Commerce 219-374-6157

CROWN POINT (city). Covers a land area of 16.620 square miles and a water area of 0.006 square miles. Located at 41.42° N. Lat.; 87.35° W. Long. Elevation is 735 feet.
History: Crown Point was founded by Solon Robinson, who came here from Connecticut in 1834 and built a cabin. Robinson, who served as Lake County's first justice of the peace, built the first courthouse for Lake County when Crown Point was chosen as the county seat. The town was first called Robinson's Prairie; the later name refers to Robinson's nickname of King of the Squatters.
Population: 19,806 (2000); Race: 95.0% White, 1.8% Black, 0.7% Asian, 0.0% American Indian and Alaska Native, 4.2% Hispanic of any race, 1.5% two or more races (2000); Density: 1,191.7 persons per square mile (2000); Age: 22.1% under 18, 17.6% over 64 (2000); Marriage status: 22.8% never married, 59.4% now married, 8.4% widowed, 9.4% divorced (2000); Foreign born: 6.4% (2000); Ancestry (includes multiple ancestries): 26.6% German, 15.4% Irish, 11.7% Polish, 9.1% English, 8.6% Other groups (2000).
Vital Statistics: Birth rate: 232.3 per 10,000 population (1998)
Economy: Single-family building permits issued: 205 (2001) / 239 (2000); Multi-family building permits issued: 8 (2001) / 16 (2000); Employment by occupation: 11.7% management, 19.7% professional, 14.2% services, 30.4% sales, 0.2% farming, 10.0% construction, 13.9% production (2000).
Income: Per capita income: $24,568 (2000); Median household income: $52,889 (2000); Poverty rate: 3.7% (2000).
Taxes: Total city taxes per capita: $280 (2000); City property taxes per capita: $249 (2000).
Education: High school graduation rate: 88.5% (2000); College graduation rate: 25.0% (2000).

School District(s)

Crown Point Community Sch Corp (PK-12)
2000 Enrollment: 5,460 219-663-3371
Northwest Indiana Special Education Coop
2000 Enrollment: n/a 219-663-6500

Four-year College(s)

Hyles-Anderson College (Private, Not-for-profit)
2001 Enrollment: n/a 219-769-4901
Housing: Homeownership rate: 74.1% (2000); Median home value: $125,900 (2000); Median rent: $579 per month (2000); Median age of housing: 28 years (2000).
Hospitals: Saint Anthony Medical Center (411 beds)
Safety: Violent crime rate: 5.5 per 10,000 population; Property crime rate: 156.6 per 10,000 population (2001).
Newspapers: Winfield News (1 x week); Pennysaver (1 x week); Cedar Lake/Lowell Star (1 x week); Crown Point Shopper (1 x week); Crown Point Star (1 x week); Merrillville Herald (1 x week); Lowell Shopping News (1 x week); Lofs Shopping News (1 x week)
Transportation: Commute to work: 94.1% car, 1.2% public transportation, 1.9% walk, 2.2% work from home (2000); Travel time to work: 36.9% less than 15 minutes, 22.7% 15 to 30 minutes, 22.5% 30 to 45 minutes, 8.4% 45 to 60 minutes, 9.4% 60 minutes or more (2000)
Additional Information Contacts
Crown Point Chamber of Commerce 219-663-1800

DYER (town). Covers a land area of 5.960 square miles and a water area of 0 square miles. Located at 41.50° N. Lat.; 87.51° W. Long. Elevation is 630 feet.
Population: 13,895 (2000); Race: 95.7% White, 1.0% Black, 1.2% Asian, 0.1% American Indian and Alaska Native, 5.6% Hispanic of any race, 0.6% two or more races (2000); Density: 2,331.3 persons per square mile (2000); Age: 26.3% under 18, 12.2% over 64 (2000); Marriage status: 20.1% never married, 67.5% now married, 5.8% widowed, 6.6% divorced (2000); Foreign born: 4.9% (2000); Ancestry (includes multiple ancestries): 22.2% German, 21.0% Polish, 17.6% Irish, 10.0% Italian, 9.7% Other groups (2000).
Vital Statistics: Birth rate: 110.1 per 10,000 population (1998)
Economy: Machinery parts. Single-family building permits issued: 131 (2001) / 128 (2000); Multi-family building permits issued: 0 (2001) / 0 (2000); Employment by occupation: 13.5% management, 22.4% professional, 11.0% services, 29.2% sales, 0.1% farming, 11.6% construction, 12.2% production (2000).
Income: Per capita income: $27,390 (2000); Median household income: $63,045 (2000); Poverty rate: 3.4% (2000).
Taxes: Total city taxes per capita: $229 (1997); City property taxes per capita: $201 (1997).
Education: High school graduation rate: 90.3% (2000); College graduation rate: 25.4% (2000).

Four-year College(s)

Mid-America Reformed Seminary (Private, Not-for-profit, Other Protestant)
2001 Enrollment: n/a 219-864-2400
Housing: Homeownership rate: 91.5% (2000); Median home value: $141,000 (2000); Median rent: $622 per month (2000); Median age of housing: 22 years (2000).
Hospitals: Saint Margaret Mercy Healthcare Centers (794 beds)
Safety: Violent crime rate: 10.0 per 10,000 population; Property crime rate: 227.6 per 10,000 population (2001).
Transportation: Commute to work: 90.4% car, 4.8% public transportation, 0.7% walk, 3.5% work from home (2000); Travel time to work: 19.0% less than 15 minutes, 34.3% 15 to 30 minutes, 23.6% 30 to 45 minutes, 7.0% 45 to 60 minutes, 16.0% 60 minutes or more (2000); Amtrak: Service available.
Additional Information Contacts
Dyer Chamber of Commerce 219-865-1045

EAST CHICAGO (city). Covers a land area of 11.977 square miles and a water area of 3.654 square miles. Located at 41.63° N. Lat.; 87.46° W. Long. Elevation is 592 feet.
History: East Chicago was incorporated as a town in 1889. Growth was slow until 1901, when a steel mill was built and work was begun on the Indiana Harbor and Ship Canal. Other industries followed, and East Chicago became an important petroleum refining area.
Population: 32,414 (2000); Race: 36.5% White, 36.0% Black, 0.1% Asian, 0.5% American Indian and Alaska Native, 51.6% Hispanic of any race, 2.7% two or more races (2000); Density: 2,706.3 persons per square mile (2000); Age: 30.6% under 18, 13.8% over 64 (2000); Marriage status: 38.4% never married, 42.8% now married, 8.3% widowed, 10.5% divorced (2000); Foreign born: 14.7% (2000); Ancestry (includes multiple ancestries): 77.6% Other groups, 4.8% Polish, 1.5% German, 1.2% Irish, 0.8% Italian (2000).
Vital Statistics: Birth rate: 196.2 per 10,000 population (1998)
Economy: Unemployment rate: 9.7% (11/2002); Total civilian labor force: 12,826 (11/2002); Single-family building permits issued: 11 (2001) / 16 (2000); Multi-family building permits issued: 0 (2001) / 0 (2000); Employment by occupation: 5.5% management, 11.7% professional, 21.7% services, 23.8% sales, 0.1% farming, 9.1% construction, 28.0% production (2000).
Income: Per capita income: $13,517 (2000); Median household income: $26,538 (2000); Poverty rate: 24.4% (2000).
Taxes: Total city taxes per capita: $894 (2000); City property taxes per capita: $886 (2000).
Education: High school graduation rate: 60.6% (2000); College graduation rate: 7.1% (2000).

School District(s)

School City of East Chicago (PK-12)
2000 Enrollment: 6,212 219-391-4100
Housing: Homeownership rate: 44.6% (2000); Median home value: $69,900 (2000); Median rent: $337 per month (2000); Median age of housing: 53 years (2000).
Hospitals: Saint Catherine Hospital of East Chicago (290 beds)
Safety: Violent crime rate: 304.9 per 10,000 population; Property crime rate: 573.4 per 10,000 population (2001).

Transportation: Commute to work: 88.1% car, 3.1% public transportation, 5.6% walk, 1.5% work from home (2000); Travel time to work: 37.3% less than 15 minutes, 35.1% 15 to 30 minutes, 16.5% 30 to 45 minutes, 4.2% 45 to 60 minutes, 6.8% 60 minutes or more (2000)
Additional Information Contacts
East Chicago Chamber of Commerce 219-398-1600

GARY (city). Covers a land area of 50.229 square miles and a water area of 7.015 square miles. Located at 41.58° N. Lat.; 87.34° W. Long. Elevation is 600 feet.
History: The site of Gary was selected by the United States Steel Corporation in 1905 as the location of a new plant, as reported by Judge Elbert H. Gary in the Corporation's annual report. What was at first a work camp was expanded by the Gary Land Company into the city of Gary. Since the area was all sand where no grass would grow, soil had to be imported and trees and shrubs planted. Other industries soon joined the steel company, and Gary's industrial character was fixed.
Population: 102,746 (2000); Race: 11.8% White, 84.0% Black, 0.2% Asian, 0.3% American Indian and Alaska Native, 4.7% Hispanic of any race, 1.6% two or more races (2000); Density: 2,045.5 persons per square mile (2000); Age: 29.9% under 18, 12.7% over 64 (2000); Marriage status: 38.8% never married, 38.4% now married, 9.4% widowed, 13.5% divorced (2000); Foreign born: 1.6% (2000); Ancestry (includes multiple ancestries): 74.3% Other groups, 2.0% United States or American, 1.9% German, 1.7% Irish, 1.3% African (2000).
Vital Statistics: Birth rate: 195.5 per 10,000 population (1998)
Economy: Unemployment rate: 11.5% (11/2002); Total civilian labor force: 45,102 (11/2002); Single-family building permits issued: 4 (2001) / 6 (2000); Multi-family building permits issued: 0 (2001) / 0 (2000); Employment by occupation: 6.5% management, 14.1% professional, 24.0% services, 26.8% sales, 0.0% farming, 7.3% construction, 21.3% production (2000).
Income: Per capita income: $14,383 (2000); Median household income: $27,195 (2000); Poverty rate: 25.8% (2000).
Taxes: Total city taxes per capita: $590 (2000); City property taxes per capita: $574 (2000).
Education: High school graduation rate: 72.7% (2000); College graduation rate: 10.1% (2000).

School District(s)

Gary Community School Corp (PK-12)
2000 Enrollment: 19,206 219-881-5401
Lake Ridge Schools (KG-12)
2000 Enrollment: 2,426 219-838-1819

Four-year College(s)

Indiana University-Northwest (Public)
2001 Enrollment: 4,639 219-980-6500
2001 Tuition: In-state $3,221; Out-of-state $8,520

Two-year College(s)

Ivy Tech State College-Northwest (Public)
2001 Enrollment: 5,146 219-981-1111
2001 Tuition: In-state $1,986; Out-of-state $4,029

Housing: Homeownership rate: 55.9% (2000); Median home value: $53,400 (2000); Median rent: $361 per month (2000); Median age of housing: 45 years (2000).
Hospitals: Methodist Hospitals-North Lake Campus (469 beds)
Safety: Violent crime rate: 87.2 per 10,000 population; Property crime rate: 506.3 per 10,000 population (2001).
Newspapers: Gary Info (1 x week); The Gary Crusader (1 x week)
Transportation: Commute to work: 90.1% car, 4.7% public transportation, 2.5% walk, 1.7% work from home (2000); Travel time to work: 22.0% less than 15 minutes, 44.6% 15 to 30 minutes, 20.0% 30 to 45 minutes, 5.2% 45 to 60 minutes, 8.2% 60 minutes or more (2000)
Airports: Gary/Chicago (primary service)
Additional Information Contacts
Gary Chamber of Commerce 219-885-7407

GRIFFITH (town). Covers a land area of 7.170 square miles and a water area of 0 square miles. Located at 41.53° N. Lat.; 87.42° W. Long. Elevation is 625 feet.
History: Settled c.1854. Incorporated 1904.
Population: 17,334 (2000); Race: 84.4% White, 9.9% Black, 1.0% Asian, 0.2% American Indian and Alaska Native, 8.3% Hispanic of any race, 1.4% two or more races (2000); Density: 2,417.7 persons per square mile (2000); Age: 25.6% under 18, 11.0% over 64 (2000); Marriage status: 26.3% never married, 56.9% now married, 7.0% widowed, 9.8% divorced (2000); Foreign born: 3.1% (2000); Ancestry (includes multiple ancestries): 23.5% German, 20.2% Other groups, 13.7% Polish, 13.3% Irish, 6.3% English (2000).
Vital Statistics: Birth rate: 135.6 per 10,000 population (1998)
Economy: Primarily residential town in the Chicago metropolitan area. Manufactuirng includes fabricated metal products, chemicals, electronic equipment, construction materials. Single-family building permits issued: 8 (2001) / 18 (2000); Multi-family building permits issued: 0 (2001) / 0 (2000); Employment by occupation: 9.8% management, 16.1% professional, 13.7% services, 30.4% sales, 0.2% farming, 12.0% construction, 17.8% production (2000).
Income: Per capita income: $21,866 (2000); Median household income: $50,030 (2000); Poverty rate: 3.9% (2000).
Taxes: Total city taxes per capita: $165 (1997); City property taxes per capita: $156 (1997).
Education: High school graduation rate: 89.1% (2000); College graduation rate: 15.1% (2000).

School District(s)

Griffith Public Schools (KG-12)
2000 Enrollment: 2,708 219-924-4250

Housing: Homeownership rate: 66.9% (2000); Median home value: $108,600 (2000); Median rent: $612 per month (2000); Median age of housing: 35 years (2000).
Safety: Violent crime rate: 21.8 per 10,000 population; Property crime rate: 335.0 per 10,000 population (2001).
Transportation: Commute to work: 93.2% car, 3.3% public transportation, 1.4% walk, 1.5% work from home (2000); Travel time to work: 27.3% less than 15 minutes, 38.7% 15 to 30 minutes, 15.4% 30 to 45 minutes, 5.4% 45 to 60 minutes, 13.2% 60 minutes or more (2000)
Airports: Griffith-Merrillville
Additional Information Contacts
Griffith Chamber of Commerce 219-924-2155

HAMMOND (city). Covers a land area of 22.878 square miles and a water area of 1.951 square miles. Located at 41.61° N. Lat.; 87.49° W. Long. Elevation is 585 feet.
History: George H. Hammond, a Detroit butcher, opened a slaughterhouse in what was to become Hammond in 1869, when the refrigerator box was invented by the Davis brothers in Detroit and shipping of dressed beef became possible. Before Hammond was incorporated as a city in 1884, it had been known as Hohman for an early settler, and as State Line for its location on the Indiana-Illinois border. Hammond's slaughterhouse was the beginning of much industry in Hammond.
Population: 83,048 (2000); Race: 72.2% White, 14.1% Black, 0.5% Asian, 0.4% American Indian and Alaska Native, 21.0% Hispanic of any race, 3.2% two or more races (2000); Density: 3,630.0 persons per square mile (2000); Age: 27.3% under 18, 12.8% over 64 (2000); Marriage status: 30.4% never married, 49.7% now married, 8.5% widowed, 11.4% divorced (2000); Foreign born: 7.3% (2000); Ancestry (includes multiple ancestries): 34.7% Other groups, 14.0% German, 12.3% Polish, 11.5% Irish, 4.7% English (2000).
Vital Statistics: Birth rate: 151.4 per 10,000 population (1998)
Economy: Unemployment rate: 6.0% (11/2002); Total civilian labor force: 38,329 (11/2002); Single-family building permits issued: 9 (2001) / 12 (2000); Multi-family building permits issued: 0 (2001) / 0 (2000); Employment by occupation: 7.9% management, 12.6% professional, 17.6% services, 28.7% sales, 0.0% farming, 10.9% construction, 22.4% production (2000).
Income: Per capita income: $16,254 (2000); Median household income: $35,528 (2000); Poverty rate: 14.3% (2000).
Taxes: Total city taxes per capita: $408 (2000); City property taxes per capita: $399 (2000).
Education: High school graduation rate: 75.6% (2000); College graduation rate: 11.3% (2000).

School District(s)

School City of Hammond (PK-12)
2000 Enrollment: 12,725 219-933-2400

Four-year College(s)

Purdue University-Calumet Campus (Public)
2001 Enrollment: 9,103 219-989-2400
2001 Tuition: In-state $3,272; Out-of-state $8,228
Saint Margaret Hospital Medical Technology Program (Private, Not-for-profit, Roman Catholic)
2001 Enrollment: n/a 219-932-2300

Two-year College(s)

Indiana College of Commerce (Private, For-profit)
2001 Enrollment: n/a 219-845-2400

Sawyer College-Hammond (Private, For-profit)
2001 Enrollment: 102 219-931-0436
2001 Tuition: In-state $6,000; Out-of-state $6,000
Housing: Homeownership rate: 63.2% (2000); Median home value: $78,400 (2000); Median rent: $439 per month (2000); Median age of housing: 49 years (2000).
Hospitals: Community Hospital (350 beds); Saint Margaret Mercy Health Care Centers (475 beds)
Safety: Violent crime rate: 91.2 per 10,000 population; Property crime rate: 613.5 per 10,000 population (2001).
Transportation: Commute to work: 90.4% car, 4.6% public transportation, 2.6% walk, 1.5% work from home (2000); Travel time to work: 27.1% less than 15 minutes, 38.4% 15 to 30 minutes, 18.3% 30 to 45 minutes, 7.3% 45 to 60 minutes, 9.0% 60 minutes or more (2000); Amtrak: Service available.
Additional Information Contacts
Hammond Chamber of Commerce. 219-931-1000

HIGHLAND (town). Aka Highlands. Covers a land area of 6.868 square miles and a water area of 0.023 square miles. Located at 41.55° N. Lat.; 87.45° W. Long. Elevation is 620 feet.
History: Highland was settled by people of Dutch descent, who established truck-gardening farms in the area.
Population: 23,546 (2000); Race: 94.7% White, 1.2% Black, 1.0% Asian, 0.1% American Indian and Alaska Native, 6.5% Hispanic of any race, 1.4% two or more races (2000); Density: 3,428.3 persons per square mile (2000); Age: 21.4% under 18, 16.8% over 64 (2000); Marriage status: 23.4% never married, 59.7% now married, 8.2% widowed, 8.7% divorced (2000); Foreign born: 4.5% (2000); Ancestry (includes multiple ancestries): 22.5% German, 17.6% Polish, 14.9% Irish, 11.2% Other groups, 9.2% English (2000).
Vital Statistics: Birth rate: 107.5 per 10,000 population (1998)
Economy: Single-family building permits issued: 57 (2001) / 50 (2000); Multi-family building permits issued: 20 (2001) / 42 (2000); Employment by occupation: 13.0% management, 19.8% professional, 13.0% services, 30.3% sales, 0.0% farming, 9.6% construction, 14.2% production (2000).
Income: Per capita income: $24,530 (2000); Median household income: $51,297 (2000); Poverty rate: 3.0% (2000).
Taxes: Total city taxes per capita: $246 (1997); City property taxes per capita: $226 (1997).
Education: High school graduation rate: 87.8% (2000); College graduation rate: 22.1% (2000).

School District(s)

School Town of Highland (KG-12)
2000 Enrollment: 3,264 219-922-5615
Housing: Homeownership rate: 78.6% (2000); Median home value: $123,000 (2000); Median rent: $626 per month (2000); Median age of housing: 34 years (2000).
Safety: Violent crime rate: 16.9 per 10,000 population; Property crime rate: 460.7 per 10,000 population (2001).
Newspapers: Calumet Press (2 x month)
Transportation: Commute to work: 92.4% car, 4.0% public transportation, 1.4% walk, 2.0% work from home (2000); Travel time to work: 33.3% less than 15 minutes, 38.6% 15 to 30 minutes, 13.0% 30 to 45 minutes, 6.3% 45 to 60 minutes, 8.9% 60 minutes or more (2000)
Additional Information Contacts
Highland Chamber of Commerce. 219-923-3666

HOBART (city). Covers a land area of 26.215 square miles and a water area of 0.492 square miles. Located at 41.52° N. Lat.; 87.26° W. Long. Elevation is 632 feet.
History: Hobart was founded by George Earle, an Englishman who built a home here and named the town for his brother. The town was platted in 1849.
Population: 25,363 (2000); Race: 93.6% White, 1.5% Black, 0.5% Asian, 0.3% American Indian and Alaska Native, 8.1% Hispanic of any race, 1.6% two or more races (2000); Density: 967.5 persons per square mile (2000); Age: 23.6% under 18, 15.3% over 64 (2000); Marriage status: 24.0% never married, 57.7% now married, 8.1% widowed, 10.2% divorced (2000); Foreign born: 2.9% (2000); Ancestry (includes multiple ancestries): 23.7% German, 15.5% Irish, 14.0% Other groups, 11.3% Polish, 10.0% English (2000).
Vital Statistics: Birth rate: 168.0 per 10,000 population (1998)
Economy: Unemployment rate: 3.2% (11/2002); Total civilian labor force: 10,866 (11/2002); Single-family building permits issued: 203 (2001) / 161 (2000); Multi-family building permits issued: 60 (2001) / 156 (2000); Employment by occupation: 9.4% management, 15.9% professional, 14.2% services, 26.9% sales, 0.1% farming, 15.1% construction, 18.5% production (2000).
Income: Per capita income: $21,508 (2000); Median household income: $47,759 (2000); Poverty rate: 4.8% (2000).
Taxes: Total city taxes per capita: $275 (1997); City property taxes per capita: $255 (1997).
Education: High school graduation rate: 84.3% (2000); College graduation rate: 14.2% (2000).

School District(s)

River Forest Community Sch Corp (PK-12)
2000 Enrollment: 1,420 219-962-2909
School City of Hobart (KG-12)
2000 Enrollment: 3,518 219-942-8885

Two-year College(s)

College of Court Reporting Inc (Private, For-profit)
2001 Enrollment: n/a 219-942-1459
2001 Tuition: In-state $4,844; Out-of-state $4,844
Housing: Homeownership rate: 80.3% (2000); Median home value: $97,700 (2000); Median rent: $539 per month (2000); Median age of housing: 40 years (2000).
Hospitals: Saint Mary Medical Center (194 beds)
Newspapers: Hobart Gazette (1 x week)
Transportation: Commute to work: 94.5% car, 1.6% public transportation, 0.9% walk, 2.1% work from home (2000); Travel time to work: 26.4% less than 15 minutes, 40.8% 15 to 30 minutes, 20.6% 30 to 45 minutes, 4.5% 45 to 60 minutes, 7.7% 60 minutes or more (2000)
Additional Information Contacts
Hobart Chamber of Commerce 219-942-5774

LAKE DALECARLIA (CDP). Covers a land area of 1.420 square miles and a water area of 0.280 square miles. Located at 41.33° N. Lat.; 87.40° W. Long. Elevation is 720 feet.
Population: 1,285 (2000); Race: 97.4% White, 0.0% Black, 0.0% Asian, 0.0% American Indian and Alaska Native, 0.0% Hispanic of any race, 2.6% two or more races (2000); Density: 904.7 persons per square mile (2000); Age: 26.8% under 18, 13.1% over 64 (2000); Marriage status: 21.9% never married, 59.5% now married, 9.4% widowed, 9.3% divorced (2000); Foreign born: 4.3% (2000); Ancestry (includes multiple ancestries): 20.2% Irish, 19.4% German, 18.5% Polish, 10.4% Italian, 9.5% English (2000).
Economy: Employment by occupation: 7.9% management, 20.2% professional, 11.7% services, 22.5% sales, 0.0% farming, 19.7% construction, 18.0% production (2000).
Income: Per capita income: $25,068 (2000); Median household income: $52,454 (2000); Poverty rate: 4.1% (2000).
Education: High school graduation rate: 90.6% (2000); College graduation rate: 20.2% (2000).
Housing: Homeownership rate: 90.5% (2000); Median home value: $117,100 (2000); Median rent: $390 per month (2000); Median age of housing: 44 years (2000).
Transportation: Commute to work: 96.8% car, 0.0% public transportation, 0.0% walk, 0.0% work from home (2000); Travel time to work: 20.8% less than 15 minutes, 23.3% 15 to 30 minutes, 34.2% 30 to 45 minutes, 9.6% 45 to 60 minutes, 12.1% 60 minutes or more (2000)

LAKE STATION (city). Covers a land area of 8.297 square miles and a water area of 0.170 square miles. Located at 41.57° N. Lat.; 87.26° W. Long. Elevation is 614 feet.
Population: 13,948 (2000); Race: 86.2% White, 0.3% Black, 0.4% Asian, 0.2% American Indian and Alaska Native, 19.8% Hispanic of any race, 3.0% two or more races (2000); Density: 1,681.0 persons per square mile (2000); Age: 27.2% under 18, 10.1% over 64 (2000); Marriage status: 29.0% never married, 52.6% now married, 7.1% widowed, 11.3% divorced (2000); Foreign born: 4.3% (2000); Ancestry (includes multiple ancestries): 25.5% Other groups, 15.9% German, 14.6% Irish, 5.8% United States or American, 5.5% English (2000).
Vital Statistics: Birth rate: 131.2 per 10,000 population (1998)
Economy: In the Calumet industrial region. Manufacturing: surgical instruments, cement blocks. Single-family building permits issued: 20 (2001) / 12 (2000); Multi-family building permits issued: 0 (2001) / 0 (2000); Employment by occupation: 5.7% management, 6.9% professional, 19.1% services, 24.5% sales, 0.3% farming, 18.3% construction, 25.2% production (2000).
Income: Per capita income: $15,319 (2000); Median household income: $36,984 (2000); Poverty rate: 14.6% (2000).
Taxes: Total city taxes per capita: $130 (1997); City property taxes per capita: $122 (1997).
Education: High school graduation rate: 74.0% (2000); College graduation rate: 4.8% (2000).

School District(s)

Lake Station Community Schools (PK-12)
2000 Enrollment: 1,430 219-962-1159

Housing: Homeownership rate: 79.0% (2000); Median home value: $73,600 (2000); Median rent: $437 per month (2000); Median age of housing: 44 years (2000).

Transportation: Commute to work: 95.7% car, 1.1% public transportation, 1.1% walk, 0.8% work from home (2000); Travel time to work: 25.4% less than 15 minutes, 45.4% 15 to 30 minutes, 19.1% 30 to 45 minutes, 4.0% 45 to 60 minutes, 6.1% 60 minutes or more (2000)

LAKES OF THE FOUR SEASONS (CDP). Covers a land area of 2.680 square miles and a water area of 0.414 square miles. Located at 41.40° N. Lat.; 87.21° W. Long.

Population: 7,291 (2000); Race: 96.2% White, 0.0% Black, 2.2% Asian, 0.0% American Indian and Alaska Native, 4.4% Hispanic of any race, 0.9% two or more races (2000); Density: 2,720.3 persons per square mile (2000); Age: 27.0% under 18, 10.1% over 64 (2000); Marriage status: 22.1% never married, 68.9% now married, 3.4% widowed, 5.7% divorced (2000); Foreign born: 5.2% (2000); Ancestry (includes multiple ancestries): 28.0% German, 16.0% Irish, 13.8% Polish, 10.8% English, 8.2% Other groups (2000).

Economy: Employment by occupation: 14.4% management, 22.9% professional, 11.1% services, 27.6% sales, 0.0% farming, 10.6% construction, 13.4% production (2000).

Income: Per capita income: $25,537 (2000); Median household income: $67,528 (2000); Poverty rate: 2.6% (2000).

Education: High school graduation rate: 95.2% (2000); College graduation rate: 30.4% (2000).

Housing: Homeownership rate: 97.4% (2000); Median home value: $142,100 (2000); Median rent: $858 per month (2000); Median age of housing: 19 years (2000).

Transportation: Commute to work: 96.2% car, 0.0% public transportation, 0.0% walk, 3.8% work from home (2000); Travel time to work: 11.4% less than 15 minutes, 33.3% 15 to 30 minutes, 26.2% 30 to 45 minutes, 14.3% 45 to 60 minutes, 14.8% 60 minutes or more (2000)

LOWELL (town). Covers a land area of 4.081 square miles and a water area of 0.081 square miles. Located at 41.29° N. Lat.; 87.41° W. Long. Elevation is 684 feet.

History: Settled 1849, laid out 1853.

Population: 7,505 (2000); Race: 97.0% White, 0.0% Black, 0.6% Asian, 0.8% American Indian and Alaska Native, 3.7% Hispanic of any race, 0.7% two or more races (2000); Density: 1,839.2 persons per square mile (2000); Age: 29.4% under 18, 10.6% over 64 (2000); Marriage status: 22.2% never married, 63.0% now married, 5.8% widowed, 9.1% divorced (2000); Foreign born: 1.4% (2000); Ancestry (includes multiple ancestries): 32.2% German, 17.1% Irish, 12.0% Polish, 11.3% English, 7.6% Other groups (2000).

Economy: Consumer goods, automotive parts, furniture. Single-family building permits issued: 57 (2001) / 60 (2000); Multi-family building permits issued: 0 (2001) / 0 (2000); Employment by occupation: 10.5% management, 15.7% professional, 13.8% services, 25.7% sales, 0.5% farming, 14.9% construction, 19.0% production (2000).

Income: Per capita income: $19,752 (2000); Median household income: $49,173 (2000); Poverty rate: 6.5% (2000).

Taxes: Total city taxes per capita: $185 (1997); City property taxes per capita: $171 (1997).

Education: High school graduation rate: 87.2% (2000); College graduation rate: 14.8% (2000).

School District(s)

Tri-Creek School Corp (KG-12)
2000 Enrollment: 3,186 219-696-6661

Housing: Homeownership rate: 77.6% (2000); Median home value: $112,800 (2000); Median rent: $487 per month (2000); Median age of housing: 28 years (2000).

Safety: Violent crime rate: 35.8 per 10,000 population; Property crime rate: 239.8 per 10,000 population (2001).

Newspapers: South Lake Advertiser (1 x week); Northern Star (1 x week); Lowell Tribune (1 x week); Cedar Lake Journal (1 x week)

Transportation: Commute to work: 95.8% car, 0.5% public transportation, 1.7% walk, 1.6% work from home (2000); Travel time to work: 31.2% less than 15 minutes, 22.2% 15 to 30 minutes, 23.8% 30 to 45 minutes, 11.5% 45 to 60 minutes, 11.2% 60 minutes or more (2000)

Additional Information Contacts

Lowell Chamber of Commerce 219-696-0231

MERRILLVILLE (town). Covers a land area of 33.283 square miles and a water area of 0.034 square miles. Located at 41.48° N. Lat.; 87.33° W. Long. Elevation is 650 feet.

History: Merrillville was settled at the place where many smaller trails met with the Sauk Trail.

Population: 30,560 (2000); Race: 70.3% White, 22.8% Black, 1.4% Asian, 0.4% American Indian and Alaska Native, 9.4% Hispanic of any race, 1.9% two or more races (2000); Density: 918.2 persons per square mile (2000); Age: 24.4% under 18, 14.8% over 64 (2000); Marriage status: 25.4% never married, 56.8% now married, 8.0% widowed, 9.7% divorced (2000); Foreign born: 7.0% (2000); Ancestry (includes multiple ancestries): 32.7% Other groups, 16.0% German, 10.6% Irish, 9.8% Polish, 5.5% English (2000).

Vital Statistics: Birth rate: 130.9 per 10,000 population (1998)

Economy: Unemployment rate: 2.7% (11/2002); Total civilian labor force: 13,839 (11/2002); Single-family building permits issued: 55 (2001) / 52 (2000); Multi-family building permits issued: 164 (2001) / 68 (2000); Employment by occupation: 9.7% management, 18.6% professional, 14.3% services, 28.0% sales, 0.1% farming, 9.6% construction, 19.7% production (2000).

Income: Per capita income: $22,293 (2000); Median household income: $49,545 (2000); Poverty rate: 4.3% (2000).

Taxes: Total city taxes per capita: $185 (2000); City property taxes per capita: $162 (2000).

Education: High school graduation rate: 86.5% (2000); College graduation rate: 20.2% (2000).

School District(s)

Merrillville Community School (KG-12)
2000 Enrollment: 6,064 219-650-5300

Four-year College(s)

Davenport University-Western Region-Merrillville (Private, Not-for-profit)
2001 Enrollment: 650 219-769-5556
2001 Tuition: In-state $7,515; Out-of-state $7,515

Keller Graduate School of Management Inc (Private, For-profit)
2001 Enrollment: 99 219-736-7440

Two-year College(s)

Commonwealth Business College-Main Campus (Private, For-profit)
2001 Enrollment: 317 219-769-3321
2001 Tuition: In-state $5,328; Out-of-state $5,328

Sawyer College-Merrillville (Private, For-profit)
2001 Enrollment: 105 219-947-4555
2001 Tuition: In-state $6,000; Out-of-state $6,000

Housing: Homeownership rate: 70.8% (2000); Median home value: $101,300 (2000); Median rent: $631 per month (2000); Median age of housing: 30 years (2000).

Safety: Violent crime rate: 11.1 per 10,000 population; Property crime rate: 324.4 per 10,000 population (2001).

Newspapers: Post-Tribune (7 x week); Northwest Indiana Catholic (1 x week)

Transportation: Commute to work: 94.5% car, 2.1% public transportation, 1.2% walk, 1.5% work from home (2000); Travel time to work: 24.8% less than 15 minutes, 36.5% 15 to 30 minutes, 20.3% 30 to 45 minutes, 6.5% 45 to 60 minutes, 11.9% 60 minutes or more (2000)

Additional Information Contacts

Greater Northwest Indiana Association of Realtors 219-795-3600
Merrillville Chamber of Commerce 219-769-8180

MUNSTER (town). Covers a land area of 7.540 square miles and a water area of 0.054 square miles. Located at 41.55° N. Lat.; 87.50° W. Long. Elevation is 600 feet.

History: Settled 1855.

Population: 21,511 (2000); Race: 92.1% White, 0.9% Black, 4.4% Asian, 0.2% American Indian and Alaska Native, 5.0% Hispanic of any race, 1.6% two or more races (2000); Density: 2,852.8 persons per square mile (2000); Age: 24.1% under 18, 18.5% over 64 (2000); Marriage status: 20.7% never married, 63.6% now married, 9.4% widowed, 6.4% divorced (2000); Foreign born: 7.9% (2000); Ancestry (includes multiple ancestries): 19.5% German, 19.4% Polish, 14.1% Irish, 12.1% Other groups, 8.0% Italian (2000).

Vital Statistics: Birth rate: 80.0 per 10,000 population (1998)

Economy: Light manufacturing: soft drinks, printing, aluminum alloys. It is a primarily residential suburb in the industrialized Hammond-East Chicago area. Single-family building permits issued: 67 (2001) / 87 (2000); Multi-family building permits issued: 115 (2001) / 0 (2000); Employment by occupation: 15.2% management, 31.1% professional, 9.1% services, 24.4% sales, 0.3% farming, 7.3% construction, 12.6% production (2000).

Income: Per capita income: $30,952 (2000); Median household income: $63,243 (2000); Poverty rate: 4.3% (2000).
Taxes: Total city taxes per capita: $248 (1997); City property taxes per capita: $215 (1997).
Education: High school graduation rate: 93.0% (2000); College graduation rate: 39.2% (2000).

School District(s)

School Town of Munster (KG-12)
2000 Enrollment: 3,887 219-836-9111

Housing: Homeownership rate: 89.1% (2000); Median home value: $163,800 (2000); Median rent: $641 per month (2000); Median age of housing: 32 years (2000).
Safety: Violent crime rate: 12.5 per 10,000 population; Property crime rate: 242.7 per 10,000 population (2001).
Newspapers: The Times-Illinois Edition (7 x week); The Times (7 x week)
Transportation: Commute to work: 89.7% car, 4.4% public transportation, 1.5% walk, 3.8% work from home (2000); Travel time to work: 32.0% less than 15 minutes, 34.9% 15 to 30 minutes, 13.9% 30 to 45 minutes, 7.3% 45 to 60 minutes, 12.0% 60 minutes or more (2000)

NEW CHICAGO (town). Covers a land area of 0.672 square miles and a water area of 0 square miles. Located at 41.55° N. Lat.; 87.27° W. Long. Elevation is 630 feet.
History: New Chicago was the home of the United States Electric Carriage Company, which built the first electric buggy in 1898.
Population: 2,063 (2000); Race: 85.6% White, 0.4% Black, 0.2% Asian, 0.2% American Indian and Alaska Native, 22.1% Hispanic of any race, 2.6% two or more races (2000); Density: 3,071.3 persons per square mile (2000); Age: 24.4% under 18, 15.0% over 64 (2000); Marriage status: 25.9% never married, 48.9% now married, 7.6% widowed, 17.6% divorced (2000); Foreign born: 4.7% (2000); Ancestry (includes multiple ancestries): 27.3% Other groups, 17.4% German, 13.0% Irish, 11.7% Polish, 8.7% United States or American (2000).
Economy: Single-family building permits issued: 4 (2001) / 9 (2000); Multi-family building permits issued: 0 (2001) / 0 (2000); Employment by occupation: 5.5% management, 10.8% professional, 20.5% services, 22.6% sales, 0.0% farming, 19.5% construction, 21.1% production (2000).
Income: Per capita income: $16,342 (2000); Median household income: $32,759 (2000); Poverty rate: 14.2% (2000).
Taxes: Total city taxes per capita: $99 (1997); City property taxes per capita: $91 (1997).
Education: High school graduation rate: 65.8% (2000); College graduation rate: 3.3% (2000).
Housing: Homeownership rate: 79.1% (2000); Median home value: $69,600 (2000); Median rent: $456 per month (2000); Median age of housing: 38 years (2000).
Safety: Violent crime rate: 43.4 per 10,000 population; Property crime rate: 308.4 per 10,000 population (2001).
Transportation: Commute to work: 96.5% car, 0.6% public transportation, 0.8% walk, 1.3% work from home (2000); Travel time to work: 23.0% less than 15 minutes, 44.7% 15 to 30 minutes, 20.9% 30 to 45 minutes, 5.7% 45 to 60 minutes, 5.6% 60 minutes or more (2000)

SAINT JOHN (town). Covers a land area of 6.724 square miles and a water area of 0.048 square miles. Located at 41.44° N. Lat.; 87.47° W. Long. Elevation is 750 feet.
Population: 8,382 (2000); Race: 97.1% White, 0.1% Black, 0.3% Asian, 0.2% American Indian and Alaska Native, 2.5% Hispanic of any race, 2.2% two or more races (2000); Density: 1,246.6 persons per square mile (2000); Age: 30.3% under 18, 9.3% over 64 (2000); Marriage status: 18.9% never married, 72.0% now married, 5.7% widowed, 3.4% divorced (2000); Foreign born: 3.3% (2000); Ancestry (includes multiple ancestries): 24.0% German, 23.1% Polish, 17.2% Irish, 12.4% Italian, 8.4% Dutch (2000).
Economy: Single-family building permits issued: 111 (2001) / 129 (2000); Multi-family building permits issued: 10 (2001) / 22 (2000); Employment by occupation: 16.7% management, 20.2% professional, 7.8% services, 28.2% sales, 0.0% farming, 14.9% construction, 12.2% production (2000).
Income: Per capita income: $25,106 (2000); Median household income: $71,378 (2000); Poverty rate: 1.7% (2000).
Education: High school graduation rate: 93.2% (2000); College graduation rate: 25.1% (2000).

School District(s)

Lake Central School Corp (PK-12)
2000 Enrollment: 8,354 219-365-8507

Housing: Homeownership rate: 96.6% (2000); Median home value: $172,100 (2000); Median rent: $380 per month (2000); Median age of housing: 11 years (2000).
Transportation: Commute to work: 95.3% car, 2.5% public transportation, 0.8% walk, 1.1% work from home (2000); Travel time to work: 14.7% less than 15 minutes, 31.3% 15 to 30 minutes, 27.1% 30 to 45 minutes, 12.9% 45 to 60 minutes, 13.9% 60 minutes or more (2000)
Additional Information Contacts
St. John Chamber of Commerce. 219-365-4686

SCHERERVILLE (town). Covers a land area of 13.610 square miles and a water area of 0.031 square miles. Located at 41.48° N. Lat.; 87.44° W. Long. Elevation is 626 feet.
History: Laid out 1866.
Population: 24,851 (2000); Race: 92.2% White, 2.2% Black, 2.1% Asian, 0.1% American Indian and Alaska Native, 6.3% Hispanic of any race, 2.0% two or more races (2000); Density: 1,825.9 persons per square mile (2000); Age: 24.6% under 18, 10.4% over 64 (2000); Marriage status: 23.0% never married, 62.6% now married, 5.9% widowed, 8.5% divorced (2000); Foreign born: 8.3% (2000); Ancestry (includes multiple ancestries): 22.9% German, 17.3% Polish, 15.1% Irish, 13.0% Other groups, 6.8% English (2000).
Vital Statistics: Birth rate: 83.3 per 10,000 population (1998)
Economy: Manufacturing: scrap metal processing, foil and decals, water treatment chemicals, pipe coatings, steel fabricating. Single-family building permits issued: 143 (2001) / 176 (2000); Multi-family building permits issued: 100 (2001) / 6 (2000); Employment by occupation: 14.4% management, 21.2% professional, 12.4% services, 25.9% sales, 0.0% farming, 11.2% construction, 14.9% production (2000).
Income: Per capita income: $28,528 (2000); Median household income: $59,243 (2000); Poverty rate: 3.1% (2000).
Taxes: Total city taxes per capita: $244 (2000); City property taxes per capita: $182 (2000).
Education: High school graduation rate: 92.0% (2000); College graduation rate: 29.5% (2000).
Housing: Homeownership rate: 73.7% (2000); Median home value: $157,900 (2000); Median rent: $579 per month (2000); Median age of housing: 18 years (2000).
Safety: Violent crime rate: 8.0 per 10,000 population; Property crime rate: 265.7 per 10,000 population (2001).
Transportation: Commute to work: 93.4% car, 2.2% public transportation, 1.4% walk, 2.1% work from home (2000); Travel time to work: 18.2% less than 15 minutes, 37.1% 15 to 30 minutes, 25.1% 30 to 45 minutes, 7.3% 45 to 60 minutes, 12.3% 60 minutes or more (2000)
Additional Information Contacts
Schererville Chamber of Commerce 219-322-5412

SCHNEIDER (town). Covers a land area of 0.878 square miles and a water area of 0 square miles. Located at 41.18° N. Lat.; 87.44° W. Long. Elevation is 636 feet.
Population: 317 (2000); Race: 96.0% White, 0.9% Black, 0.6% Asian, 0.0% American Indian and Alaska Native, 0.0% Hispanic of any race, 2.6% two or more races (2000); Density: 361.0 persons per square mile (2000); Age: 31.8% under 18, 10.0% over 64 (2000); Marriage status: 25.1% never married, 61.8% now married, 5.8% widowed, 7.3% divorced (2000); Foreign born: 1.1% (2000); Ancestry (includes multiple ancestries): 23.8% German, 22.6% Irish, 14.6% Other groups, 13.5% English, 8.9% Italian (2000).
Economy: Agricultural area. LaSalle State Fish and Wildlife Area nearby to Southwest. Single-family building permits issued: 0 (2001) / 0 (2000); Multi-family building permits issued: 0 (2001) / 0 (2000); Employment by occupation: 7.2% management, 2.2% professional, 15.9% services, 16.7% sales, 0.0% farming, 27.5% construction, 30.4% production (2000).
Income: Per capita income: $16,463 (2000); Median household income: $46,339 (2000); Poverty rate: 5.9% (2000).
Taxes: Total city taxes per capita: $224 (1997); City property taxes per capita: $218 (1997).
Education: High school graduation rate: 77.1% (2000); College graduation rate: 0.0% (2000).
Housing: Homeownership rate: 77.7% (2000); Median home value: $74,100 (2000); Median rent: $330 per month (2000); Median age of housing: 50 years (2000).
Transportation: Commute to work: 96.3% car, 0.0% public transportation, 2.2% walk, 1.5% work from home (2000); Travel time to work: 24.6% less than 15 minutes, 33.6% 15 to 30 minutes, 14.9% 30 to 45 minutes, 14.2% 45 to 60 minutes, 12.7% 60 minutes or more (2000)

WHITING (city). Covers a land area of 1.763 square miles and a water area of 1.519 square miles. Located at 41.67° N. Lat.; 87.49° W. Long. Elevation is 585 feet.
History: Whiting was settled by German immigrants. For many years a Standard Oil Company plant, established in 1889, was the major industry.
Population: 5,137 (2000); Race: 85.6% White, 0.2% Black, 2.0% Asian, 0.2% American Indian and Alaska Native, 24.7% Hispanic of any race, 2.3% two or more races (2000); Density: 2,914.1 persons per square mile (2000); Age: 26.2% under 18, 14.6% over 64 (2000); Marriage status: 31.5% never married, 48.0% now married, 9.3% widowed, 11.3% divorced (2000); Foreign born: 10.8% (2000); Ancestry (includes multiple ancestries): 29.5% Other groups, 18.0% Slovak, 17.1% Polish, 16.1% Irish, 11.5% German (2000).
Economy: Single-family building permits issued: 1 (2001) / 0 (2000); Multi-family building permits issued: 0 (2001) / 0 (2000); Employment by occupation: 8.0% management, 16.0% professional, 14.4% services, 27.2% sales, 0.0% farming, 11.8% construction, 22.5% production (2000).
Income: Per capita income: $17,518 (2000); Median household income: $34,972 (2000); Poverty rate: 12.3% (2000).
Taxes: Total city taxes per capita: $1,213 (1997); City property taxes per capita: $1,199 (1997).
Education: High school graduation rate: 79.2% (2000); College graduation rate: 15.8% (2000).

School District(s)

Whiting School City (PK-12)
2000 Enrollment: 877 219-659-0656

Four-year College(s)

Calumet College of Saint Joseph (Private, Not-for-profit, Roman Catholic)
2001 Enrollment: 1,000 219-473-7770
2001 Tuition: In-state $7,500; Out-of-state $7,500
Housing: Homeownership rate: 53.8% (2000); Median home value: $91,200 (2000); Median rent: $389 per month (2000); Median age of housing: 60+ years (2000).
Transportation: Commute to work: 86.3% car, 1.8% public transportation, 9.9% walk, 1.7% work from home (2000); Travel time to work: 43.3% less than 15 minutes, 27.5% 15 to 30 minutes, 17.4% 30 to 45 minutes, 6.8% 45 to 60 minutes, 5.0% 60 minutes or more (2000); Amtrak: Service available.
Additional Information Contacts
Whiting Chamber of Commerce 219-659-0292

WINFIELD (town). Covers a land area of 12.298 square miles and a water area of 0 square miles. Located at 41.41° N. Lat.; 87.26° W. Long. Elevation is 707 feet.
Population: 2,298 (2000); Race: 95.2% White, 0.4% Black, 1.5% Asian, 0.2% American Indian and Alaska Native, 4.3% Hispanic of any race, 1.9% two or more races (2000); Density: 186.9 persons per square mile (2000); Age: 26.0% under 18, 15.6% over 64 (2000); Marriage status: 19.3% never married, 63.7% now married, 10.7% widowed, 6.3% divorced (2000); Foreign born: 9.0% (2000); Ancestry (includes multiple ancestries): 27.9% German, 12.7% Irish, 12.2% Polish, 9.2% Other groups, 8.0% English (2000).
Economy: Single-family building permits issued: 114 (2001) / 108 (2000); Multi-family building permits issued: 0 (2001) / 0 (2000); Employment by occupation: 15.7% management, 20.6% professional, 10.3% services, 27.0% sales, 0.2% farming, 14.2% construction, 12.0% production (2000).
Income: Per capita income: $24,765 (2000); Median household income: $65,641 (2000); Poverty rate: 2.8% (2000).
Taxes: Total city taxes per capita: $83 (1997); City property taxes per capita: $63 (1997).
Education: High school graduation rate: 85.3% (2000); College graduation rate: 28.1% (2000).
Housing: Homeownership rate: 90.4% (2000); Median home value: $180,100 (2000); Median rent: $546 per month (2000); Median age of housing: 5 years (2000).
Transportation: Commute to work: 94.3% car, 0.9% public transportation, 0.2% walk, 4.5% work from home (2000); Travel time to work: 15.4% less than 15 minutes, 37.1% 15 to 30 minutes, 23.8% 30 to 45 minutes, 14.4% 45 to 60 minutes, 9.3% 60 minutes or more (2000)

Lawrence County

Located in southern Indiana; drained by Salt Creek and the East Fork of the White River. Covers a land area of 448.80 square miles, a water area of 3.20 square miles, and is located in the Eastern Time Zone. The county government was organized in 1819. County seat is Bedford.

Weather Station: Oolitic Purdue Exp. Farm — Elevation: 649 feet

	Jan	Feb	Mar	Apr	May	Jun	Jul	Aug	Sep	Oct	Nov	Dec
High	37	42	53	64	74	82	86	84	78	67	54	42
Low	18	21	30	40	50	59	64	62	53	41	33	24
Precip	2.7	2.6	3.8	4.6	5.0	3.9	4.4	4.1	2.9	3.3	3.9	3.3
Snow	5.8	3.8	2.7	tr	tr	0.0	0.0	0.0	0.0	tr	0.4	2.6

High and Low temperatures in degrees Fahrenheit; Precipitation and Snow in inches

Population: 45,922 (2000); Race: 97.5% White, 0.5% Black, 0.4% Asian, 0.3% American Indian and Alaska Native, 0.7% Hispanic of any race, 1.0% two or more races (2000); Density: 102.3 persons per square mile (2000); Age: 24.5% under 18, 14.8% over 64 (2000).
Religion: Five largest groups: 8.7% Christian Churches and Churches of Christ, 8.0% American Baptist Churches in the USA, 5.5% Catholic Church, 3.0% Churches of Christ, 2.9% The United Methodist Church (2000).
Economy: Unemployment rate: 7.4% (11/2002); Total civilian labor force: 22,337 (11/2002); Leading industries: 34.8% manufacturing; 16.2% retail trade; 13.8% health care and social assistance (2000); Companies that employ more than 1,000 persons: 2 (2000); Companies that employ more than 100 persons: 19 (2000); Farms: 875 totaling 170,811 acres (1997); Minority business ownership rate: 0.0% (1997); Women business ownership rate: 18.6% (1997); Retail sales per capita: $8,183 (1997). Single-family building permits issued: 34 (2001) / 41 (2000); Multi-family building permits issued: 2 (2001) / 0 (2000).
Income: Per capita income: $17,653 (2000); Median household income: $36,280 (2000); Poverty rate: 9.8% (2000); Bankruptcy rate: 7.95% (2001).
Taxes: Total county taxes per capita: $230 (2000); County property taxes per capita: $103 (2000).
Education: High school graduation rate: 77.4% (2000); College graduation rate: 10.7% (2000).
Housing: Homeownership rate: 78.9% (2000); Median home value: $75,400 (2000); Median rent: $341 per month (2000); Median age of housing: 32 years (2000).
Health: Birth rate: 127.4 per 10,000 population (1998); Age adjusted death rate: 86.1 per 10,000 population (1999); Age adjusted cancer mortality rate: 209.2 deaths per 100,000 population (1999). Number of physicians: 12.4 per 10,000 population (1999); Number of hospital beds: 37.5 per 10,000 population (1999).
Elections: 2000 Presidential election results: 31.4% Gore, 66.1% Bush, 0.6% Nader, 1.1% Buchanan
National and State Parks: Spring Mill State Park
Additional Information Contacts
Lawrence County Government Offices 812-275-7543
Bedford Area Chamber of Commerce 812-275-4493
Bedford Board of Realtors 812-277-1861
Mitchell Chamber of Commerce 812-849-4441

Lawrence County Communities

BEDFORD (city). Aka Eureka. Covers a land area of 11.898 square miles and a water area of 0 square miles. Located at 38.86° N. Lat.; 86.49° W. Long. Elevation is 710 feet.
History: Beford developed as the center of a limestone industry, providing stone for such buildings as the Empire State Building and the Chicago Museum of Fine Arts.
Population: 13,768 (2000); Race: 96.8% White, 1.1% Black, 0.2% Asian, 0.6% American Indian and Alaska Native, 0.8% Hispanic of any race, 1.0% two or more races (2000); Density: 1,157.1 persons per square mile (2000); Age: 21.1% under 18, 22.2% over 64 (2000); Marriage status: 19.1% never married, 54.4% now married, 11.9% widowed, 14.6% divorced (2000); Foreign born: 1.1% (2000); Ancestry (includes multiple ancestries): 18.3% United States or American, 12.6% German, 9.8% Irish, 9.1% English, 8.8% Other groups (2000).
Vital Statistics: Birth rate: 127.1 per 10,000 population (1998)
Economy: Single-family building permits issued: 13 (2001) / 18 (2000); Multi-family building permits issued: 2 (2001) / 0 (2000); Employment by occupation: 8.8% management, 17.3% professional, 18.9% services, 23.3% sales, 0.1% farming, 8.3% construction, 23.3% production (2000).
Income: Per capita income: $17,649 (2000); Median household income: $31,022 (2000); Poverty rate: 11.5% (2000).
Taxes: Total city taxes per capita: $214 (1997); City property taxes per capita: $209 (1997).
Education: High school graduation rate: 74.0% (2000); College graduation rate: 12.5% (2000).

School District(s)

North Lawrence Com Schools (PK-12)
2000 Enrollment: 5,298 812-279-3521

Housing: Homeownership rate: 65.6% (2000); Median home value: $69,900 (2000); Median rent: $358 per month (2000); Median age of housing: 48 years (2000).
Hospitals: Bedford Regional Medical Center (49 beds); Dunn Memorial Hospital (137 beds)
Safety: Violent crime rate: 12.3 per 10,000 population; Property crime rate: 420.3 per 10,000 population (2001).
Newspapers: The Times-Mail (7 x week)
Transportation: Commute to work: 93.5% car, 1.1% public transportation, 2.5% walk, 1.6% work from home (2000); Travel time to work: 50.8% less than 15 minutes, 16.7% 15 to 30 minutes, 22.9% 30 to 45 minutes, 5.6% 45 to 60 minutes, 3.9% 60 minutes or more (2000)
Additional Information Contacts
Bedford Area Chamber of Commerce 812-275-4493
Bedford Board of Realtors 812-277-1861

HELTONVILLE (unincorporated postal area, zip code 47436). Covers a land area of 43.054 square miles and a water area of 0.010 square miles. Located at 38.97° N. Lat.; 86.41° W. Long. Elevation is 700 feet.
Population: 1,232 (2000); Race: 95.3% White, 3.2% Black, 0.7% Asian, 0.0% American Indian and Alaska Native, 0.0% Hispanic of any race, 0.8% two or more races (2000); Density: 28.6 persons per square mile (2000); Age: 22.3% under 18, 10.6% over 64 (2000); Marriage status: 17.6% never married, 57.0% now married, 7.2% widowed, 18.1% divorced (2000); Foreign born: 0.6% (2000); Ancestry (includes multiple ancestries): 17.5% United States or American, 9.5% English, 9.1% Irish, 8.5% German, 8.2% Other groups (2000).
Economy: Employment by occupation: 6.5% management, 20.1% professional, 10.3% services, 21.8% sales, 1.0% farming, 10.9% construction, 29.4% production (2000).
Income: Per capita income: $19,392 (2000); Median household income: $40,481 (2000); Poverty rate: 9.0% (2000).
Education: High school graduation rate: 82.2% (2000); College graduation rate: 8.7% (2000).
Housing: Homeownership rate: 87.4% (2000); Median home value: $78,900 (2000); Median rent: $363 per month (2000); Median age of housing: 30 years (2000).
Transportation: Commute to work: 98.0% car, 0.0% public transportation, 0.0% walk, 2.0% work from home (2000); Travel time to work: 11.4% less than 15 minutes, 20.9% 15 to 30 minutes, 50.4% 30 to 45 minutes, 7.0% 45 to 60 minutes, 10.4% 60 minutes or more (2000)

MITCHELL (city). Covers a land area of 3.394 square miles and a water area of 0.005 square miles. Located at 38.73° N. Lat.; 86.47° W. Long. Elevation is 687 feet.
History: The first settlers came to Mitchell in 1813. The town was platted about 1852 when the Louisville, New Albany, & Salem Railroad came through Lawrence County. The town was named for O.M. Mitchell, a construction engineer for the Ohio & Mississippi Railroad which crossed the original line in 1856.
Population: 4,567 (2000); Race: 98.6% White, 0.5% Black, 0.0% Asian, 0.1% American Indian and Alaska Native, 0.2% Hispanic of any race, 0.8% two or more races (2000); Density: 1,345.6 persons per square mile (2000); Age: 25.8% under 18, 16.4% over 64 (2000); Marriage status: 20.3% never married, 54.7% now married, 11.2% widowed, 13.8% divorced (2000); Foreign born: 0.7% (2000); Ancestry (includes multiple ancestries): 20.1% United States or American, 17.8% English, 13.2% German, 7.2% Irish, 5.2% Other groups (2000).
Economy: Single-family building permits issued: 20 (2001) / 23 (2000); Multi-family building permits issued: 0 (2001) / 0 (2000); Employment by occupation: 4.3% management, 9.9% professional, 17.9% services, 20.5% sales, 0.3% farming, 11.2% construction, 35.8% production (2000).
Income: Per capita income: $13,894 (2000); Median household income: $28,559 (2000); Poverty rate: 16.9% (2000).
Taxes: Total city taxes per capita: $111 (1997); City property taxes per capita: $111 (1997).
Education: High school graduation rate: 69.4% (2000); College graduation rate: 5.3% (2000).

School District(s)

Mitchell Community Schools (PK-12)
2000 Enrollment: 2,097 812-849-4481

Housing: Homeownership rate: 71.8% (2000); Median home value: $59,300 (2000); Median rent: $308 per month (2000); Median age of housing: 35 years (2000).
Newspapers: The Mitchell Tribune (1 x week)
Transportation: Commute to work: 94.9% car, 0.3% public transportation, 1.2% walk, 2.0% work from home (2000); Travel time to work: 40.4% less than 15 minutes, 29.3% 15 to 30 minutes, 14.3% 30 to 45 minutes, 8.9% 45 to 60 minutes, 7.2% 60 minutes or more (2000)
Additional Information Contacts
Mitchell Chamber of Commerce 812-849-4441

OOLITIC (town). Covers a land area of 0.805 square miles and a water area of 0 square miles. Located at 38.89° N. Lat.; 86.52° W. Long. Elevation is 589 feet.
History: Oolitic was named for the oolitic texture of the limestone in the quarries that surround it, which provided the town with its early industry.
Population: 1,152 (2000); Race: 97.9% White, 0.0% Black, 0.3% Asian, 0.0% American Indian and Alaska Native, 0.0% Hispanic of any race, 1.6% two or more races (2000); Density: 1,431.1 persons per square mile (2000); Age: 22.5% under 18, 13.3% over 64 (2000); Marriage status: 19.5% never married, 58.0% now married, 7.2% widowed, 15.4% divorced (2000); Foreign born: 0.8% (2000); Ancestry (includes multiple ancestries): 16.4% United States or American, 9.4% Irish, 8.9% English, 8.5% German, 6.4% Other groups (2000).
Economy: Single-family building permits issued: 1 (2001) / 0 (2000); Multi-family building permits issued: 0 (2001) / 0 (2000); Employment by occupation: 5.5% management, 14.4% professional, 15.7% services, 22.1% sales, 1.1% farming, 11.4% construction, 29.9% production (2000).
Income: Per capita income: $16,889 (2000); Median household income: $31,250 (2000); Poverty rate: 13.2% (2000).
Taxes: Total city taxes per capita: $64 (1997); City property taxes per capita: $61 (1997).
Education: High school graduation rate: 80.9% (2000); College graduation rate: 9.8% (2000).
Housing: Homeownership rate: 69.2% (2000); Median home value: $70,200 (2000); Median rent: $302 per month (2000); Median age of housing: 37 years (2000).
Transportation: Commute to work: 95.2% car, 0.0% public transportation, 1.2% walk, 1.4% work from home (2000); Travel time to work: 42.7% less than 15 minutes, 22.3% 15 to 30 minutes, 23.2% 30 to 45 minutes, 5.2% 45 to 60 minutes, 6.5% 60 minutes or more (2000)

SPRINGVILLE (unincorporated postal area, zip code 47462). Covers a land area of 75.918 square miles and a water area of 0.049 square miles. Located at 38.96° N. Lat.; 86.63° W. Long. Elevation is 640 feet.
History: Laid out 1832.
Population: 4,834 (2000); Race: 97.1% White, 0.0% Black, 0.8% Asian, 0.3% American Indian and Alaska Native, 0.2% Hispanic of any race, 1.7% two or more races (2000); Density: 63.7 persons per square mile (2000); Age: 24.7% under 18, 10.2% over 64 (2000); Marriage status: 16.7% never married, 68.1% now married, 4.8% widowed, 10.4% divorced (2000); Foreign born: 0.2% (2000); Ancestry (includes multiple ancestries): 16.1% United States or American, 10.6% Irish, 10.4% German, 9.0% Other groups, 5.1% English (2000).
Economy: Limestone quarries. Manufacturing: plastic products, crushed stone, agricultural lime, asphalt products. Employment by occupation: 7.4% management, 14.6% professional, 15.2% services, 18.0% sales, 0.4% farming, 13.8% construction, 30.6% production (2000).
Income: Per capita income: $18,517 (2000); Median household income: $41,930 (2000); Poverty rate: 8.4% (2000).
Education: High school graduation rate: 76.5% (2000); College graduation rate: 7.2% (2000).
Housing: Homeownership rate: 90.1% (2000); Median home value: $81,000 (2000); Median rent: $337 per month (2000); Median age of housing: 23 years (2000).
Transportation: Commute to work: 95.5% car, 0.0% public transportation, 0.6% walk, 3.4% work from home (2000); Travel time to work: 13.6% less than 15 minutes, 47.3% 15 to 30 minutes, 27.1% 30 to 45 minutes, 6.3% 45 to 60 minutes, 5.7% 60 minutes or more (2000)

WILLIAMS (unincorporated postal area, zip code 47470). Covers a land area of 75.964 square miles and a water area of 0.137 square miles. Located at 38.84° N. Lat.; 86.68° W. Long. Elevation is 680 feet.
Population: 1,691 (2000); Race: 99.3% White, 0.0% Black, 0.0% Asian, 0.0% American Indian and Alaska Native, 0.0% Hispanic of any race, 0.7% two or more races (2000); Density: 22.3 persons per square mile (2000); Age:

29.8% under 18, 10.9% over 64 (2000); Marriage status: 20.0% never married, 64.0% now married, 8.5% widowed, 7.6% divorced (2000); Foreign born: 0.7% (2000); Ancestry (includes multiple ancestries): 23.3% United States or American, 19.5% Other groups, 19.4% German, 15.0% Irish, 11.2% English (2000).
Economy: Employment by occupation: 6.7% management, 16.5% professional, 11.8% services, 18.4% sales, 2.4% farming, 11.6% construction, 32.6% production (2000).
Income: Per capita income: $19,183 (2000); Median household income: $36,389 (2000); Poverty rate: 13.3% (2000).
Education: High school graduation rate: 81.7% (2000); College graduation rate: 11.9% (2000).
Housing: Homeownership rate: 85.7% (2000); Median home value: $69,700 (2000); Median rent: $250 per month (2000); Median age of housing: 27 years (2000).
Transportation: Commute to work: 93.5% car, 0.0% public transportation, 2.2% walk, 2.3% work from home (2000); Travel time to work: 13.2% less than 15 minutes, 50.9% 15 to 30 minutes, 13.2% 30 to 45 minutes, 14.3% 45 to 60 minutes, 8.5% 60 minutes or more (2000)

Madison County

Located in east central Indiana; drained by the West Fork of the White River and by many creeks. Covers a land area of 452.10 square miles, a water area of 0.80 square miles, and is located in the Eastern Time Zone. The county government was organized in 1823. County seat is Anderson.

Madison County is part of the Indianapolis, IN MSA. The entire metro area includes: Boone County; Hamilton County; Hancock County; Hendricks County; Johnson County; Madison County; Marion County; Morgan County; Shelby County

Weather Station: Anderson Sewage Plant — Elevation: 843 feet

	Jan	Feb	Mar	Apr	May	Jun	Jul	Aug	Sep	Oct	Nov	Dec
High	33	38	49	61	71	80	84	82	75	64	50	38
Low	19	23	31	40	51	60	64	62	54	43	35	24
Precip	2.1	2.3	3.2	3.8	4.1	4.2	4.3	3.3	3.0	2.8	3.7	2.8
Snow	6.6	4.6	2.1	0.2	0.0	0.0	0.0	0.0	0.0	tr	0.7	3.6

High and Low temperatures in degrees Fahrenheit; Precipitation and Snow in inches

Weather Station: Elwood Wastewater Plant — Elevation: 839 feet

	Jan	Feb	Mar	Apr	May	Jun	Jul	Aug	Sep	Oct	Nov	Dec
High	32	37	48	61	72	81	85	83	77	65	51	38
Low	15	19	28	38	48	58	62	59	52	40	32	22
Precip	2.3	1.9	3.0	3.8	4.1	4.3	4.5	3.9	3.2	2.7	3.6	3.0
Snow	na	na	na	tr	0.0	0.0	0.0	0.0	0.0	tr	tr	na

High and Low temperatures in degrees Fahrenheit; Precipitation and Snow in inches

Population: 133,358 (2000); Race: 89.9% White, 7.8% Black, 0.4% Asian, 0.3% American Indian and Alaska Native, 1.4% Hispanic of any race, 1.0% two or more races (2000); Density: 295.0 persons per square mile (2000); Age: 23.8% under 18, 14.9% over 64 (2000).
Religion: Five largest groups: 6.0% Catholic Church, 4.4% The United Methodist Church, 4.1% Church of God (Anderson, Indiana), 3.0% American Baptist Churches in the USA, 2.6% Christian Church (Disciples of Christ) (2000).
Economy: Unemployment rate: 4.7% (11/2002); Total civilian labor force: 67,632 (11/2002); Leading industries: 22.3% manufacturing; 16.2% retail trade; 14.8% health care and social assistance (2000); Companies that employ more than 1,000 persons: 5 (2000); Companies that employ more than 100 persons: 54 (2000); Farms: 738 totaling 223,751 acres (1997); Minority business ownership rate: 4.1% (1997); Women business ownership rate: 26.1% (1997); Retail sales per capita: $8,510 (1997). Single-family building permits issued: 359 (2001) / 334 (2000); Multi-family building permits issued: 14 (2001) / 22 (2000).
Income: Per capita income: $20,090 (2000); Median household income: $38,925 (2000); Poverty rate: 9.3% (2000); Bankruptcy rate: 9.14% (2001).
Taxes: Total county taxes per capita: $193 (2000); County property taxes per capita: $153 (2000).
Education: High school graduation rate: 80.1% (2000); College graduation rate: 14.4% (2000).
Housing: Homeownership rate: 74.2% (2000); Median home value: $81,600 (2000); Median rent: $398 per month (2000); Median age of housing: 42 years (2000).
Health: Birth rate: 130.6 per 10,000 population (1998); Age adjusted death rate: 98.5 per 10,000 population (1999); Age adjusted cancer mortality rate: 219.9 deaths per 100,000 population (1999). Air Quality Index: 59% good, 41% moderate, 1% unhealthy (percent of days in 2000). Number of physicians: 12.6 per 10,000 population (1999); Number of hospital beds: 19.0 per 10,000 population (1999).
Elections: 2000 Presidential election results: 44.8% Gore, 53.5% Bush, 0.0% Nader, 1.0% Buchanan
National and State Parks: Mounds State Park
Additional Information Contacts
Madison County Government Offices 765-641-9470
Alexandria Chamber of Commerce 765-724-3144
Anderson Chamber of Commerce 765-642-0264
Anderson Madison County Association of Realtors 765-649-8106
Elwood Chamber of Commerce 765-552-0180
Pendleton Chamber of Commerce 765-778-1741

Madison County Communities

ALEXANDRIA (city). Covers a land area of 2.712 square miles and a water area of 0 square miles. Located at 40.26° N. Lat.; 85.67° W. Long. Elevation is 866 feet.
History: In Alexandria the Johns-Manville Company operated the first rock-wool insulation factory in the world, utilizing the argillaceous limestone found here.
Population: 6,260 (2000); Race: 97.7% White, 0.1% Black, 0.2% Asian, 0.0% American Indian and Alaska Native, 1.7% Hispanic of any race, 2.0% two or more races (2000); Density: 2,308.6 persons per square mile (2000); Age: 30.0% under 18, 13.5% over 64 (2000); Marriage status: 16.7% never married, 63.7% now married, 6.7% widowed, 12.9% divorced (2000); Foreign born: 1.0% (2000); Ancestry (includes multiple ancestries): 19.5% German, 15.1% English, 13.5% Other groups, 10.9% Irish, 5.5% United States or American (2000).
Economy: Single-family building permits issued: 5 (2001) / 13 (2000); Multi-family building permits issued: 0 (2001) / 0 (2000); Employment by occupation: 10.5% management, 12.2% professional, 15.0% services, 24.1% sales, 0.0% farming, 12.0% construction, 26.2% production (2000).
Income: Per capita income: $15,578 (2000); Median household income: $35,359 (2000); Poverty rate: 7.0% (2000).
Taxes: Total city taxes per capita: $234 (1997); City property taxes per capita: $188 (1997).
Education: High school graduation rate: 75.6% (2000); College graduation rate: 9.7% (2000).

School District(s)

Alexandria Com School Corp (PK-12)
2000 Enrollment: 1,878 765-724-4496
Housing: Homeownership rate: 68.6% (2000); Median home value: $72,800 (2000); Median rent: $400 per month (2000); Median age of housing: 52 years (2000).
Safety: Violent crime rate: 15.9 per 10,000 population; Property crime rate: 300.2 per 10,000 population (2001).
Newspapers: Alexandria Times-Tribune (1 x week)
Transportation: Commute to work: 93.6% car, 0.0% public transportation, 1.9% walk, 0.0% work from home (2000); Travel time to work: 33.1% less than 15 minutes, 37.3% 15 to 30 minutes, 12.5% 30 to 45 minutes, 4.8% 45 to 60 minutes, 12.3% 60 minutes or more (2000)
Additional Information Contacts
Alexandria Chamber of Commerce 765-724-3144

ANDERSON (city). Covers a land area of 40.047 square miles and a water area of 0.109 square miles. Located at 40.10° N. Lat.; 85.68° W. Long. Elevation is 887 feet.
History: Anderson was platted in 1823 and named for Delaware Chief Kikthawenund, who was called Captain Anderson by the settlers. It was incorporated as Andersontown in 1838, and reincorporated as a city in 1865. The discovery of natural gas in 1886 brought industrial development, followed by the automotive industry.
Population: 59,734 (2000); Race: 82.2% White, 14.8% Black, 0.5% Asian, 0.4% American Indian and Alaska Native, 1.9% Hispanic of any race, 1.2% two or more races (2000); Density: 1,491.6 persons per square mile (2000); Age: 23.2% under 18, 16.4% over 64 (2000); Marriage status: 25.3% never married, 50.8% now married, 8.9% widowed, 14.9% divorced (2000); Foreign born: 1.8% (2000); Ancestry (includes multiple ancestries): 18.9% Other groups, 15.9% United States or American, 14.8% German, 9.0% English, 7.8% Irish (2000).
Vital Statistics: Birth rate: 157.7 per 10,000 population (1998)

Economy: Unemployment rate: 6.0% (11/2002); Total civilian labor force: 30,648 (11/2002); Single-family building permits issued: 110 (2001) / 120 (2000); Multi-family building permits issued: 8 (2001) / 16 (2000); Employment by occupation: 8.6% management, 14.2% professional, 19.0% services, 26.9% sales, 0.1% farming, 9.5% construction, 21.6% production (2000).
Income: Per capita income: $19,142 (2000); Median household income: $32,577 (2000); Poverty rate: 13.4% (2000).
Taxes: Total city taxes per capita: $405 (2000); City property taxes per capita: $295 (2000).
Education: High school graduation rate: 77.4% (2000); College graduation rate: 13.1% (2000).

School District(s)

Anderson Community School Corp (PK-12)
2000 Enrollment: 10,412 765-641-2028
Frankton-Lapel Community Schools (PK-12)
2000 Enrollment: 2,253 765-734-1261

Four-year College(s)

Anderson University (Private, Not-for-profit, Church of God)
2001 Enrollment: 2,427 765-649-9071
2001 Tuition: In-state $15,380; Out-of-state $15,380

Two-year College(s)

Indiana Business College (Private, For-profit)
2001 Enrollment: 241 765-644-7514
2001 Tuition: In-state $8,460; Out-of-state $8,460

Housing: Homeownership rate: 63.8% (2000); Median home value: $67,900 (2000); Median rent: $400 per month (2000); Median age of housing: 44 years (2000).
Hospitals: Community Hospital of Anderson & Madison Company (207 beds); Saint John's Health System (332 beds)
Newspapers: The Herald-Bulletin (7 x week)
Transportation: Commute to work: 92.5% car, 1.0% public transportation, 3.6% walk, 2.4% work from home (2000); Travel time to work: 43.4% less than 15 minutes, 26.8% 15 to 30 minutes, 13.7% 30 to 45 minutes, 9.8% 45 to 60 minutes, 6.4% 60 minutes or more (2000)
Airports: Anderson Municipal-Darlington Field
Additional Information Contacts
Anderson Chamber of Commerce 765-642-0264
Anderson Madison County Association of Realtors 765-649-8106

CHESTERFIELD (town). Covers a land area of 1.148 square miles and a water area of 0 square miles. Located at 40.11° N. Lat.; 85.59° W. Long. Elevation is 908 feet.
History: The Chesterfield Spiritualist Camp was built here in 1890 by Dr. J. Westerfield and his followers.
Population: 2,969 (2000); Race: 98.3% White, 0.7% Black, 0.0% Asian, 0.2% American Indian and Alaska Native, 0.9% Hispanic of any race, 0.5% two or more races (2000); Density: 2,586.5 persons per square mile (2000); Age: 23.8% under 18, 14.6% over 64 (2000); Marriage status: 21.1% never married, 57.1% now married, 9.2% widowed, 12.6% divorced (2000); Foreign born: 1.4% (2000); Ancestry (includes multiple ancestries): 19.2% United States or American, 13.0% German, 9.8% English, 6.4% Irish, 4.3% Other groups (2000).
Economy: Single-family building permits issued: 0 (2001) / 0 (2000); Multi-family building permits issued: 0 (2001) / 0 (2000); Employment by occupation: 6.7% management, 14.2% professional, 16.2% services, 25.6% sales, 0.6% farming, 11.6% construction, 25.1% production (2000).
Income: Per capita income: $18,738 (2000); Median household income: $37,143 (2000); Poverty rate: 5.9% (2000).
Taxes: Total city taxes per capita: $197 (1997); City property taxes per capita: $171 (1997).
Education: High school graduation rate: 83.3% (2000); College graduation rate: 15.0% (2000).
Housing: Homeownership rate: 78.4% (2000); Median home value: $68,600 (2000); Median rent: $373 per month (2000); Median age of housing: 42 years (2000).
Safety: Violent crime rate: 16.7 per 10,000 population; Property crime rate: 408.6 per 10,000 population (2001).
Transportation: Commute to work: 95.6% car, 0.0% public transportation, 1.9% walk, 2.1% work from home (2000); Travel time to work: 28.5% less than 15 minutes, 43.5% 15 to 30 minutes, 10.4% 30 to 45 minutes, 10.3% 45 to 60 minutes, 7.3% 60 minutes or more (2000)

COUNTRY CLUB HEIGHTS (town). Covers a land area of 0.306 square miles and a water area of 0 square miles. Located at 40.12° N. Lat.; 85.68° W. Long. Elevation is 860 feet.
Population: 91 (2000); Race: 93.5% White, 6.5% Black, 0.0% Asian, 0.0% American Indian and Alaska Native, 0.0% Hispanic of any race, 0.0% two or more races (2000); Density: 297.8 persons per square mile (2000); Age: 12.9% under 18, 24.7% over 64 (2000); Marriage status: 10.5% never married, 77.9% now married, 3.5% widowed, 8.1% divorced (2000); Foreign born: 0.0% (2000); Ancestry (includes multiple ancestries): 19.4% English, 18.3% German, 9.7% Scotch-Irish, 7.5% French (except Basque), 6.5% Irish (2000).
Economy: Single-family building permits issued: 0 (2001) / 0 (2000); Multi-family building permits issued: 0 (2001) / 0 (2000); Employment by occupation: 25.0% management, 40.9% professional, 0.0% services, 29.5% sales, 0.0% farming, 0.0% construction, 4.5% production (2000).
Income: Per capita income: $52,273 (2000); Median household income: $97,723 (2000); Poverty rate: 4.3% (2000).
Taxes: Total city taxes per capita: $224 (1997); City property taxes per capita: $187 (1997).
Education: High school graduation rate: 92.4% (2000); College graduation rate: 51.9% (2000).
Housing: Homeownership rate: 100.0% (2000); Median home value: $192,000 (2000); Median age of housing: 39 years (2000).
Transportation: Commute to work: 100.0% car, 0.0% public transportation, 0.0% walk, 0.0% work from home (2000); Travel time to work: 81.8% less than 15 minutes, 9.1% 15 to 30 minutes, 4.5% 30 to 45 minutes, 0.0% 45 to 60 minutes, 4.5% 60 minutes or more (2000)

EDGEWOOD (town). Covers a land area of 0.805 square miles and a water area of 0 square miles. Located at 40.10° N. Lat.; 85.73° W. Long. Elevation is 876 feet.
History: Edgewood grew as a residential suburb for employees of the manufacturing plants in nearby Anderson.
Population: 1,988 (2000); Race: 96.6% White, 2.4% Black, 0.2% Asian, 0.2% American Indian and Alaska Native, 0.2% Hispanic of any race, 0.5% two or more races (2000); Density: 2,468.9 persons per square mile (2000); Age: 19.3% under 18, 23.0% over 64 (2000); Marriage status: 13.3% never married, 70.1% now married, 8.1% widowed, 8.5% divorced (2000); Foreign born: 1.5% (2000); Ancestry (includes multiple ancestries): 23.7% German, 17.1% English, 15.5% Irish, 15.0% United States or American, 5.5% Other groups (2000).
Economy: Single-family building permits issued: 0 (2001) / 0 (2000); Multi-family building permits issued: 4 (2001) / 6 (2000); Employment by occupation: 16.2% management, 31.6% professional, 6.7% services, 30.2% sales, 0.0% farming, 5.7% construction, 9.5% production (2000).
Income: Per capita income: $30,383 (2000); Median household income: $57,857 (2000); Poverty rate: 1.9% (2000).
Taxes: Total city taxes per capita: $105 (1997); City property taxes per capita: $75 (1997).
Education: High school graduation rate: 95.8% (2000); College graduation rate: 38.8% (2000).
Housing: Homeownership rate: 93.3% (2000); Median home value: $102,600 (2000); Median rent: $468 per month (2000); Median age of housing: 44 years (2000).
Transportation: Commute to work: 97.0% car, 0.0% public transportation, 0.0% walk, 2.6% work from home (2000); Travel time to work: 50.0% less than 15 minutes, 29.7% 15 to 30 minutes, 9.7% 30 to 45 minutes, 5.9% 45 to 60 minutes, 4.7% 60 minutes or more (2000)

ELWOOD (city). Covers a land area of 3.550 square miles and a water area of 0 square miles. Located at 40.27° N. Lat.; 85.83° W. Long. Elevation is 865 feet.
History: Elwood was the birthplace of Wendell L. Wilkie, presidential nominee in 1940, who lived here until 1919. His speech accepting the nomination was made in Elwood.
Population: 9,737 (2000); Race: 97.7% White, 0.0% Black, 1.1% Asian, 0.5% American Indian and Alaska Native, 0.8% Hispanic of any race, 0.2% two or more races (2000); Density: 2,743.1 persons per square mile (2000); Age: 25.2% under 18, 15.5% over 64 (2000); Marriage status: 17.7% never married, 60.6% now married, 7.0% widowed, 14.6% divorced (2000); Foreign born: 1.3% (2000); Ancestry (includes multiple ancestries): 29.3% United States or American, 17.5% German, 11.1% Irish, 8.8% English, 8.7% Other groups (2000).
Economy: Single-family building permits issued: 8 (2001) / 6 (2000); Multi-family building permits issued: 0 (2001) / 0 (2000); Employment by occupation: 6.6% management, 10.8% professional, 16.8% services, 20.6% sales, 0.0% farming, 10.9% construction, 34.2% production (2000).
Income: Per capita income: $15,402 (2000); Median household income: $30,986 (2000); Poverty rate: 15.2% (2000).

Taxes: Total city taxes per capita: $234 (1997); City property taxes per capita: $186 (1997).
Education: High school graduation rate: 67.4% (2000); College graduation rate: 5.9% (2000).

School District(s)

Elwood Community School Corp (PK-12)
2000 Enrollment: 2,091 765-552-9861

Housing: Homeownership rate: 72.2% (2000); Median home value: $64,000 (2000); Median rent: $390 per month (2000); Median age of housing: 60+ years (2000).
Hospitals: Saint Vincent Mercy Hospital (49 beds)
Safety: Violent crime rate: 0.0 per 10,000 population; Property crime rate: 422.8 per 10,000 population (2001).
Newspapers: The Call-Leader (6 x week)
Transportation: Commute to work: 96.3% car, 0.0% public transportation, 2.9% walk, 0.3% work from home (2000); Travel time to work: 49.7% less than 15 minutes, 15.3% 15 to 30 minutes, 20.3% 30 to 45 minutes, 8.9% 45 to 60 minutes, 5.9% 60 minutes or more (2000)

Additional Information Contacts

Elwood Chamber of Commerce. 765-552-0180

FRANKTON (town). Covers a land area of 1.009 square miles and a water area of 0 square miles. Located at 40.22° N. Lat.; 85.77° W. Long. Elevation is 862 feet.
Population: 1,905 (2000); Race: 97.9% White, 0.0% Black, 0.5% Asian, 0.0% American Indian and Alaska Native, 1.6% Hispanic of any race, 0.5% two or more races (2000); Density: 1,888.0 persons per square mile (2000); Age: 28.8% under 18, 14.4% over 64 (2000); Marriage status: 20.6% never married, 61.1% now married, 8.1% widowed, 10.2% divorced (2000); Foreign born: 0.7% (2000); Ancestry (includes multiple ancestries): 23.2% English, 20.3% German, 12.5% Irish, 8.2% United States or American, 8.0% Other groups (2000).
Economy: In agricultural area. Single-family building permits issued: 14 (2001) / 0 (2000); Multi-family building permits issued: 0 (2001) / 0 (2000); Employment by occupation: 8.2% management, 11.9% professional, 17.9% services, 24.1% sales, 0.3% farming, 10.5% construction, 27.0% production (2000).
Income: Per capita income: $17,232 (2000); Median household income: $39,130 (2000); Poverty rate: 8.1% (2000).
Taxes: Total city taxes per capita: $106 (1997); City property taxes per capita: $93 (1997).
Education: High school graduation rate: 81.8% (2000); College graduation rate: 8.8% (2000).
Housing: Homeownership rate: 86.0% (2000); Median home value: $79,000 (2000); Median rent: $377 per month (2000); Median age of housing: 40 years (2000).
Transportation: Commute to work: 97.5% car, 0.0% public transportation, 0.8% walk, 1.1% work from home (2000); Travel time to work: 22.5% less than 15 minutes, 37.9% 15 to 30 minutes, 22.0% 30 to 45 minutes, 9.4% 45 to 60 minutes, 8.2% 60 minutes or more (2000)

INGALLS (town). Covers a land area of 0.686 square miles and a water area of 0 square miles. Located at 39.95° N. Lat.; 85.80° W. Long. Elevation is 869 feet.
Population: 1,168 (2000); Race: 98.9% White, 0.0% Black, 0.0% Asian, 0.0% American Indian and Alaska Native, 0.4% Hispanic of any race, 1.1% two or more races (2000); Density: 1,703.7 persons per square mile (2000); Age: 29.4% under 18, 10.0% over 64 (2000); Marriage status: 19.8% never married, 64.2% now married, 5.3% widowed, 10.7% divorced (2000); Foreign born: 0.4% (2000); Ancestry (includes multiple ancestries): 32.2% United States or American, 12.5% German, 8.5% English, 7.2% Other groups, 6.7% Irish (2000).
Economy: In agricultural area. Single-family building permits issued: 8 (2001) / 10 (2000); Multi-family building permits issued: 0 (2001) / 0 (2000); Employment by occupation: 10.8% management, 5.0% professional, 15.5% services, 25.4% sales, 0.0% farming, 14.4% construction, 28.9% production (2000).
Income: Per capita income: $16,988 (2000); Median household income: $43,456 (2000); Poverty rate: 5.4% (2000).
Taxes: Total city taxes per capita: $88 (1997); City property taxes per capita: $71 (1997).
Education: High school graduation rate: 71.5% (2000); College graduation rate: 3.0% (2000).
Housing: Homeownership rate: 83.7% (2000); Median home value: $78,900 (2000); Median rent: $467 per month (2000); Median age of housing: 34 years (2000).
Transportation: Commute to work: 94.7% car, 0.0% public transportation, 0.4% walk, 2.5% work from home (2000); Travel time to work: 15.2% less than 15 minutes, 26.2% 15 to 30 minutes, 37.4% 30 to 45 minutes, 15.7% 45 to 60 minutes, 5.6% 60 minutes or more (2000)

LAPEL (town). Covers a land area of 0.766 square miles and a water area of 0 square miles. Located at 40.06° N. Lat.; 85.84° W. Long. Elevation is 858 feet.
History: Laid out 1876.
Population: 1,855 (2000); Race: 98.9% White, 0.1% Black, 0.0% Asian, 0.2% American Indian and Alaska Native, 0.3% Hispanic of any race, 0.7% two or more races (2000); Density: 2,421.5 persons per square mile (2000); Age: 30.5% under 18, 13.5% over 64 (2000); Marriage status: 20.5% never married, 58.7% now married, 8.2% widowed, 12.6% divorced (2000); Foreign born: 0.5% (2000); Ancestry (includes multiple ancestries): 27.0% United States or American, 18.9% German, 9.5% Irish, 8.3% English, 6.9% Other groups (2000).
Economy: In livestock and grain area; glass products. Single-family building permits issued: 11 (2001) / 13 (2000); Multi-family building permits issued: 2 (2001) / 0 (2000); Employment by occupation: 9.9% management, 15.4% professional, 13.0% services, 28.3% sales, 0.2% farming, 13.3% construction, 19.9% production (2000).
Income: Per capita income: $18,887 (2000); Median household income: $41,389 (2000); Poverty rate: 5.7% (2000).
Taxes: Total city taxes per capita: $104 (1997); City property taxes per capita: $84 (1997).
Education: High school graduation rate: 84.4% (2000); College graduation rate: 11.3% (2000).
Housing: Homeownership rate: 72.0% (2000); Median home value: $82,900 (2000); Median rent: $391 per month (2000); Median age of housing: 45 years (2000).
Newspapers: Lapel Post (1 x week)
Transportation: Commute to work: 96.1% car, 0.0% public transportation, 2.3% walk, 1.3% work from home (2000); Travel time to work: 20.5% less than 15 minutes, 47.1% 15 to 30 minutes, 19.9% 30 to 45 minutes, 7.7% 45 to 60 minutes, 4.7% 60 minutes or more (2000)

MARKLEVILLE (town). Covers a land area of 0.406 square miles and a water area of 0 square miles. Located at 39.98° N. Lat.; 85.61° W. Long. Elevation is 954 feet.
History: Laid out 1852.
Population: 383 (2000); Race: 97.0% White, 0.0% Black, 0.4% Asian, 0.0% American Indian and Alaska Native, 2.6% Hispanic of any race, 0.0% two or more races (2000); Density: 943.7 persons per square mile (2000); Age: 24.2% under 18, 5.6% over 64 (2000); Marriage status: 26.0% never married, 59.2% now married, 2.9% widowed, 11.8% divorced (2000); Foreign born: 0.0% (2000); Ancestry (includes multiple ancestries): 31.7% United States or American, 11.5% Irish, 9.9% German, 7.7% Other groups, 7.3% English (2000).
Economy: Agricultural area. Manufacturing: building materials, wood products. Employment by occupation: 8.9% management, 10.6% professional, 19.1% services, 23.8% sales, 0.0% farming, 13.5% construction, 24.1% production (2000).
Income: Per capita income: $17,395 (2000); Median household income: $48,438 (2000); Poverty rate: 0.8% (2000).
Taxes: Total city taxes per capita: $91 (1997); City property taxes per capita: $62 (1997).
Education: High school graduation rate: 91.3% (2000); College graduation rate: 6.4% (2000).
Housing: Homeownership rate: 90.6% (2000); Median home value: $78,000 (2000); Median rent: $467 per month (2000); Median age of housing: 51 years (2000).
Transportation: Commute to work: 95.9% car, 0.0% public transportation, 3.0% walk, 1.0% work from home (2000); Travel time to work: 14.7% less than 15 minutes, 53.2% 15 to 30 minutes, 18.4% 30 to 45 minutes, 9.6% 45 to 60 minutes, 4.1% 60 minutes or more (2000)

ORESTES (town). Covers a land area of 0.394 square miles and a water area of 0 square miles. Located at 40.27° N. Lat.; 85.72° W. Long. Elevation is 874 feet.
Population: 334 (2000); Race: 97.3% White, 0.0% Black, 0.0% Asian, 0.0% American Indian and Alaska Native, 2.2% Hispanic of any race, 1.9% two or more races (2000); Density: 848.5 persons per square mile (2000); Age: 23.5% under 18, 13.8% over 64 (2000); Marriage status: 24.2% never married, 56.0% now married, 4.8% widowed, 15.0% divorced (2000); Foreign born: 0.8% (2000); Ancestry (includes multiple ancestries): 23.5%

English, 20.8% United States or American, 14.9% German, 14.3% Irish, 11.1% Other groups (2000).
Economy: Agricultural area. Manufacturing: food. Employment by occupation: 2.3% management, 3.5% professional, 14.6% services, 32.2% sales, 0.0% farming, 15.8% construction, 31.6% production (2000).
Income: Per capita income: $18,037 (2000); Median household income: $39,219 (2000); Poverty rate: 3.8% (2000).
Taxes: Total city taxes per capita: $91 (1997); City property taxes per capita: $76 (1997).
Education: High school graduation rate: 69.9% (2000); College graduation rate: 1.6% (2000).
Housing: Homeownership rate: 80.7% (2000); Median home value: $57,600 (2000); Median rent: $319 per month (2000); Median age of housing: 60 years (2000).
Transportation: Commute to work: 98.8% car, 0.0% public transportation, 0.0% walk, 1.2% work from home (2000); Travel time to work: 26.7% less than 15 minutes, 29.1% 15 to 30 minutes, 33.9% 30 to 45 minutes, 7.3% 45 to 60 minutes, 3.0% 60 minutes or more (2000)

PENDLETON (town). Covers a land area of 6.705 square miles and a water area of 0.055 square miles. Located at 40.00° N. Lat.; 85.74° W. Long. Elevation is 860 feet.
History: Pendleton was the county seat in the 1820's.
Population: 3,873 (2000); Race: 98.9% White, 0.9% Black, 0.0% Asian, 0.0% American Indian and Alaska Native, 0.2% Hispanic of any race, 0.0% two or more races (2000); Density: 577.6 persons per square mile (2000); Age: 28.8% under 18, 15.7% over 64 (2000); Marriage status: 16.5% never married, 60.7% now married, 8.5% widowed, 14.3% divorced (2000); Foreign born: 0.0% (2000); Ancestry (includes multiple ancestries): 17.7% United States or American, 16.8% German, 10.5% English, 4.6% Irish, 4.4% Other groups (2000).
Economy: Single-family building permits issued: 11 (2001) / 14 (2000); Multi-family building permits issued: 0 (2001) / 0 (2000); Employment by occupation: 13.8% management, 14.9% professional, 10.3% services, 29.1% sales, 0.0% farming, 10.9% construction, 21.0% production (2000).
Income: Per capita income: $20,074 (2000); Median household income: $46,204 (2000); Poverty rate: 4.1% (2000).
Taxes: Total city taxes per capita: $310 (1997); City property taxes per capita: $249 (1997).
Education: High school graduation rate: 88.0% (2000); College graduation rate: 26.3% (2000).

School District(s)

South Madison Com Sch Corp (KG-12)
2000 Enrollment: 3,466 765-778-2152

Housing: Homeownership rate: 64.7% (2000); Median home value: $110,700 (2000); Median rent: $508 per month (2000); Median age of housing: 43 years (2000).
Newspapers: The Pendleton Times (1 x week)
Transportation: Commute to work: 95.0% car, 0.0% public transportation, 0.0% walk, 5.0% work from home (2000); Travel time to work: 34.6% less than 15 minutes, 30.1% 15 to 30 minutes, 22.9% 30 to 45 minutes, 9.9% 45 to 60 minutes, 2.5% 60 minutes or more (2000)
Additional Information Contacts
Pendleton Chamber of Commerce 765-778-1741

RIVER FOREST (town). Covers a land area of 0.016 square miles and a water area of 0 square miles. Located at 40.11° N. Lat.; 85.72° W. Long. Elevation is 850 feet.
Population: 28 (2000); Race: 100.0% White, 0.0% Black, 0.0% Asian, 0.0% American Indian and Alaska Native, 0.0% Hispanic of any race, 0.0% two or more races (2000); Density: 1,745.0 persons per square mile (2000); Age: 41.4% under 18, 17.2% over 64 (2000); Marriage status: 15.0% never married, 85.0% now married, 0.0% widowed, 0.0% divorced (2000); Foreign born: 0.0% (2000); Ancestry (includes multiple ancestries): 69.0% United States or American, 13.8% English, 6.9% French (except Basque), 6.9% Scottish, 6.9% Other groups (2000).
Economy: Employment by occupation: 25.0% management, 0.0% professional, 12.5% services, 62.5% sales, 0.0% farming, 0.0% construction, 0.0% production (2000).
Income: Per capita income: $37,421 (2000); Median household income: $110,555 (2000); Poverty rate: 0.0% (2000).
Taxes: Total city taxes per capita: $188 (1997); City property taxes per capita: $188 (1997).
Education: High school graduation rate: 100.0% (2000); College graduation rate: 29.4% (2000).
Housing: Homeownership rate: 100.0% (2000); Median home value: $156,300 (2000); Median age of housing: 45 years (2000).
Transportation: Commute to work: 100.0% car, 0.0% public transportation, 0.0% walk, 0.0% work from home (2000); Travel time to work: 12.5% less than 15 minutes, 50.0% 15 to 30 minutes, 37.5% 30 to 45 minutes, 0.0% 45 to 60 minutes, 0.0% 60 minutes or more (2000)

SUMMITVILLE (town). Covers a land area of 0.539 square miles and a water area of 0 square miles. Located at 40.33° N. Lat.; 85.64° W. Long. Elevation is 883 feet.
History: Laid out 1867.
Population: 1,090 (2000); Race: 97.9% White, 0.0% Black, 0.3% Asian, 0.0% American Indian and Alaska Native, 0.7% Hispanic of any race, 1.1% two or more races (2000); Density: 2,023.6 persons per square mile (2000); Age: 25.5% under 18, 12.5% over 64 (2000); Marriage status: 17.3% never married, 67.3% now married, 6.3% widowed, 9.1% divorced (2000); Foreign born: 0.0% (2000); Ancestry (includes multiple ancestries): 16.2% United States or American, 14.3% German, 10.2% Irish, 9.4% English, 6.6% Other groups (2000).
Economy: In agricultural area. Manufacturing of wooden pallets, tools. Single-family building permits issued: 4 (2001) / 6 (2000); Multi-family building permits issued: 0 (2001) / 0 (2000); Employment by occupation: 11.5% management, 12.5% professional, 15.8% services, 19.9% sales, 0.4% farming, 10.2% construction, 29.7% production (2000).
Income: Per capita income: $18,311 (2000); Median household income: $37,303 (2000); Poverty rate: 7.9% (2000).
Taxes: Total city taxes per capita: $120 (1997); City property taxes per capita: $99 (1997).
Education: High school graduation rate: 77.8% (2000); College graduation rate: 8.2% (2000).
Housing: Homeownership rate: 84.0% (2000); Median home value: $63,300 (2000); Median rent: $311 per month (2000); Median age of housing: 52 years (2000).
Transportation: Commute to work: 91.5% car, 0.0% public transportation, 4.9% walk, 2.5% work from home (2000); Travel time to work: 20.2% less than 15 minutes, 38.2% 15 to 30 minutes, 27.5% 30 to 45 minutes, 9.5% 45 to 60 minutes, 4.6% 60 minutes or more (2000)

WOODLAWN HEIGHTS (town). Covers a land area of 0.120 square miles and a water area of 0 square miles. Located at 40.11° N. Lat.; 85.69° W. Long. Elevation is 880 feet.
Population: 73 (2000); Race: 96.2% White, 0.0% Black, 0.0% Asian, 0.0% American Indian and Alaska Native, 3.8% Hispanic of any race, 0.0% two or more races (2000); Density: 607.0 persons per square mile (2000); Age: 7.5% under 18, 9.4% over 64 (2000); Marriage status: 8.2% never married, 91.8% now married, 0.0% widowed, 0.0% divorced (2000); Foreign born: 0.0% (2000); Ancestry (includes multiple ancestries): 49.1% English, 28.3% German, 13.2% Irish, 13.2% Dutch, 11.3% French (except Basque) (2000).
Economy: Employment by occupation: 45.5% management, 33.3% professional, 0.0% services, 12.1% sales, 0.0% farming, 9.1% construction, 0.0% production (2000).
Income: Per capita income: $66,385 (2000); Median household income: $111,324 (2000); Poverty rate: 5.7% (2000).
Taxes: Total city taxes per capita: $48 (1997); City property taxes per capita: $38 (1997).
Education: High school graduation rate: 100.0% (2000); College graduation rate: 69.4% (2000).
Housing: Homeownership rate: 92.6% (2000); Median home value: $232,500 (2000); Median rent: $275 per month (2000); Median age of housing: 28 years (2000).
Transportation: Commute to work: 100.0% car, 0.0% public transportation, 0.0% walk, 0.0% work from home (2000); Travel time to work: 51.5% less than 15 minutes, 24.2% 15 to 30 minutes, 15.2% 30 to 45 minutes, 0.0% 45 to 60 minutes, 9.1% 60 minutes or more (2000)

Marion County

Located in central Indiana; drained by the West Fork of the White River. Covers a land area of 396.20 square miles, a water area of 6.80 square miles, and is located in the Eastern Time Zone. The county government was organized in 1821. County seat is Indianapolis.

Marion County is part of the Indianapolis, IN MSA. The entire metro area includes: Boone County; Hamilton County; Hancock County; Hendricks

County; Johnson County; Madison County; Marion County; Morgan County; Shelby County

Weather Station: Indianapolis Int'l Airport — Elevation: 790 feet

	Jan	Feb	Mar	Apr	May	Jun	Jul	Aug	Sep	Oct	Nov	Dec
High	34	40	51	63	74	82	86	84	78	66	52	40
Low	18	22	32	42	52	62	66	64	56	44	34	25
Precip	2.5	2.4	3.5	3.7	4.3	4.0	4.5	3.7	2.8	2.8	3.6	3.0
Snow	9.2	6.3	3.0	0.4	tr	tr	0.0	tr	0.0	0.4	1.3	5.8

High and Low temperatures in degrees Fahrenheit; Precipitation and Snow in inches

Weather Station: Indianapolis SE Side — Elevation: 843 feet

	Jan	Feb	Mar	Apr	May	Jun	Jul	Aug	Sep	Oct	Nov	Dec
High	34	39	50	62	73	81	85	83	77	65	51	40
Low	18	21	31	41	52	61	65	63	55	43	34	24
Precip	2.0	2.0	3.1	3.8	4.6	4.1	4.9	3.6	2.5	2.8	3.7	2.8
Snow	na	na	0.9	0.1	tr	0.0	0.0	0.0	0.0	0.2	0.2	1.4

High and Low temperatures in degrees Fahrenheit; Precipitation and Snow in inches

Weather Station: Oaklandon Geist Reservoir — Elevation: 793 feet

	Jan	Feb	Mar	Apr	May	Jun	Jul	Aug	Sep	Oct	Nov	Dec
High	33	38	49	62	72	81	84	83	77	65	51	39
Low	17	19	29	39	50	60	64	61	54	42	33	23
Precip	2.3	2.3	3.4	4.0	4.8	4.1	4.7	4.0	3.4	3.1	3.9	3.2
Snow	7.6	5.7	2.8	0.4	0.0	0.0	0.0	0.0	0.0	0.3	0.9	5.4

High and Low temperatures in degrees Fahrenheit; Precipitation and Snow in inches

Population: 860,454 (2000); Race: 70.4% White, 24.1% Black, 1.3% Asian, 0.3% American Indian and Alaska Native, 3.7% Hispanic of any race, 1.8% two or more races (2000); Density: 2,171.5 persons per square mile (2000); Age: 25.7% under 18, 11.1% over 64 (2000).
Religion: Five largest groups: 12.6% Catholic Church, 3.6% The United Methodist Church, 2.8% Christian Churches and Churches of Christ, 2.6% Independent, Non-Charismatic Churches, 2.0% Christian Church (Disciples of Christ) (2000).
Economy: Unemployment rate: 5.2% (11/2002); Total civilian labor force: 468,593 (11/2002); Leading industries: 12.8% health care and social assistance; 11.9% manufacturing; 11.0% retail trade (2000); Companies that employ more than 1,000 persons: 44 (2000); Companies that employ more than 100 persons: 937 (2000); Farms: 225 totaling 29,034 acres (1997); Minority business ownership rate: 11.1% (1997); Women business ownership rate: 26.3% (1997); Retail sales per capita: $13,203 (1997). Single-family building permits issued: 5,217 (2001) / 3,952 (2000); Multi-family building permits issued: 1,310 (2001) / 1,264 (2000).
Income: Per capita income: $21,789 (2000); Median household income: $40,421 (2000); Poverty rate: 11.4% (2000); Bankruptcy rate: 10.99% (2001).
Education: High school graduation rate: 81.6% (2000); College graduation rate: 25.4% (2000).
Housing: Homeownership rate: 59.3% (2000); Median home value: $99,000 (2000); Median rent: $488 per month (2000); Median age of housing: 34 years (2000).
Health: Birth rate: 161.9 per 10,000 population (1998); Age adjusted death rate: 106.4 per 10,000 population (1999); Infant mortality rate: 7.9 per 1,000 live births (1998); Age adjusted cancer mortality rate: 252.4 deaths per 100,000 population (1999). Air Quality Index: 72% good, 28% moderate, 0% unhealthy (percent of days in 2000). Number of physicians: 41.2 per 10,000 population (1999); Number of hospital beds: 54.3 per 10,000 population (1999).
Elections: 2000 Presidential election results: 47.9% Gore, 49.2% Bush, 1.1% Nader, 0.5% Buchanan
Additional Information Contacts
Marion County Government Offices 317-236-3200
Indiana Association of Realtors 317-842-0890
Indiana Commercial Board of Realtors 317-632-2509
Indianapolis Black Chamber 317-924-9840
Indianapolis Chamber of Commerce 317-541-9876
Metropolitan Indianapolis Board of Realtors 317-956-1912

Marion County Communities

BEECH GROVE (city). Covers a land area of 4.297 square miles and a water area of 0 square miles. Located at 39.71° N. Lat.; 86.09° W. Long. Elevation is 800 feet.
History: Incorporated 1906.
Population: 14,880 (2000); Race: 96.5% White, 1.4% Black, 0.5% Asian, 0.1% American Indian and Alaska Native, 1.4% Hispanic of any race, 0.5% two or more races (2000); Density: 3,462.5 persons per square mile (2000); Age: 26.1% under 18, 16.3% over 64 (2000); Marriage status: 25.2% never married, 52.1% now married, 8.4% widowed, 14.4% divorced (2000); Foreign born: 1.7% (2000); Ancestry (includes multiple ancestries): 27.9% German, 20.2% United States or American, 18.8% Irish, 11.8% English, 8.3% Other groups (2000).
Vital Statistics: Birth rate: 120.3 per 10,000 population (1998)
Economy: Primarily residential, it has some manufacturing: flour and wheat milling, Railroad repair, chemicals. Single-family building permits issued: 18 (2001) / 16 (2000); Multi-family building permits issued: 0 (2001) / 11 (2000); Employment by occupation: 8.2% management, 16.8% professional, 15.9% services, 29.1% sales, 0.0% farming, 10.7% construction, 19.3% production (2000).
Income: Per capita income: $19,647 (2000); Median household income: $41,548 (2000); Poverty rate: 6.1% (2000).
Taxes: Total city taxes per capita: $323 (1997); City property taxes per capita: $261 (1997).
Education: High school graduation rate: 80.6% (2000); College graduation rate: 16.7% (2000).

School District(s)
Beech Grove City Schools (PK-12)
2000 Enrollment: 2,396 317-788-4481

Four-year College(s)
Saint Francis Hospital and Health Centers (Private, Not-for-profit, Roman Catholic)
2001 Enrollment: n/a

Housing: Homeownership rate: 60.9% (2000); Median home value: $94,000 (2000); Median rent: $502 per month (2000); Median age of housing: 37 years (2000).
Hospitals: Saint Francis Beech Grove (500 beds)
Safety: Violent crime rate: 8.0 per 10,000 population; Property crime rate: 299.4 per 10,000 population (2001).
Newspapers: Southside Times (1 x week)
Transportation: Commute to work: 93.8% car, 1.4% public transportation, 2.0% walk, 2.3% work from home (2000); Travel time to work: 28.2% less than 15 minutes, 41.0% 15 to 30 minutes, 17.0% 30 to 45 minutes, 3.3% 45 to 60 minutes, 10.5% 60 minutes or more (2000)

CAMBY (unincorporated postal area, zip code 46113). Part of the City of Indianapolis. Covers a land area of 17.365 square miles and a water area of 0.074 square miles. Located at 39.63° N. Lat.; 86.31° W. Long. Elevation is 779 feet.
Population: 6,666 (2000); Race: 98.1% White, 0.0% Black, 0.7% Asian, 0.3% American Indian and Alaska Native, 0.0% Hispanic of any race, 0.8% two or more races (2000); Density: 383.9 persons per square mile (2000); Age: 26.9% under 18, 10.1% over 64 (2000); Marriage status: 17.3% never married, 67.2% now married, 4.5% widowed, 11.0% divorced (2000); Foreign born: 1.0% (2000); Ancestry (includes multiple ancestries): 21.8% German, 14.9% Irish, 13.4% United States or American, 11.1% Other groups, 8.7% English (2000).
Economy: Employment by occupation: 12.7% management, 11.1% professional, 12.6% services, 30.4% sales, 0.5% farming, 17.1% construction, 15.5% production (2000).
Income: Per capita income: $20,324 (2000); Median household income: $52,352 (2000); Poverty rate: 7.0% (2000).
Education: High school graduation rate: 80.8% (2000); College graduation rate: 12.5% (2000).
Housing: Homeownership rate: 89.3% (2000); Median home value: $118,300 (2000); Median rent: $460 per month (2000); Median age of housing: 21 years (2000).
Transportation: Commute to work: 96.8% car, 0.0% public transportation, 0.5% walk, 1.6% work from home (2000); Travel time to work: 18.1% less than 15 minutes, 40.9% 15 to 30 minutes, 29.9% 30 to 45 minutes, 6.7% 45 to 60 minutes, 4.3% 60 minutes or more (2000)

CLERMONT (town). Covers a land area of 0.681 square miles and a water area of 0 square miles. Located at 39.81° N. Lat.; 86.32° W. Long. Elevation is 833 feet.
History: When Clermont was platted in 1849 it was called Mechanicsburg, but the name was changed in 1855.
Population: 1,477 (2000); Race: 93.1% White, 3.0% Black, 1.8% Asian, 0.0% American Indian and Alaska Native, 0.5% Hispanic of any race, 2.1% two or more races (2000); Density: 2,167.7 persons per square mile (2000); Age: 22.5% under 18, 13.8% over 64 (2000); Marriage status: 24.0% never married, 60.2% now married, 6.6% widowed, 9.2% divorced (2000); Foreign born: 2.4% (2000); Ancestry (includes multiple ancestries): 25.3% German,

15.7% Irish, 12.1% Other groups, 11.5% English, 9.5% United States or American (2000).
Economy: Employment by occupation: 16.7% management, 15.9% professional, 8.6% services, 35.2% sales, 0.0% farming, 11.3% construction, 12.3% production (2000).
Income: Per capita income: $25,149 (2000); Median household income: $51,875 (2000); Poverty rate: 6.8% (2000).
Taxes: Total city taxes per capita: $158 (1997); City property taxes per capita: $154 (1997).
Education: High school graduation rate: 89.9% (2000); College graduation rate: 26.0% (2000).
Housing: Homeownership rate: 86.1% (2000); Median home value: $98,600 (2000); Median rent: $607 per month (2000); Median age of housing: 36 years (2000).
Transportation: Commute to work: 97.0% car, 0.0% public transportation, 0.0% walk, 3.0% work from home (2000); Travel time to work: 10.1% less than 15 minutes, 57.5% 15 to 30 minutes, 26.4% 30 to 45 minutes, 2.4% 45 to 60 minutes, 3.7% 60 minutes or more (2000)

CROWS NEST (town). Covers a land area of 0.446 square miles and a water area of 0 square miles. Located at 39.85° N. Lat.; 86.17° W. Long. Elevation is 750 feet.
History: Joined Indianapolis in 1970.
Population: 96 (2000); Race: 100.0% White, 0.0% Black, 0.0% Asian, 0.0% American Indian and Alaska Native, 0.0% Hispanic of any race, 0.0% two or more races (2000); Density: 215.2 persons per square mile (2000); Age: 11.9% under 18, 15.5% over 64 (2000); Marriage status: 18.2% never married, 66.2% now married, 0.0% widowed, 15.6% divorced (2000); Foreign born: 0.0% (2000); Ancestry (includes multiple ancestries): 36.9% English, 13.1% German, 10.7% Swedish, 8.3% Scotch-Irish, 7.1% French (except Basque) (2000).
Economy: Employment by occupation: 42.2% management, 42.2% professional, 0.0% services, 6.7% sales, 0.0% farming, 0.0% construction, 8.9% production (2000).
Income: Per capita income: $100,565 (2000); Median household income: $154,780 (2000); Poverty rate: 0.0% (2000).
Education: High school graduation rate: 100.0% (2000); College graduation rate: 74.2% (2000).
Housing: Homeownership rate: 79.5% (2000); Median home value: $625,000 (2000); Median rent: $1,125 per month (2000); Median age of housing: 60+ years (2000).
Transportation: Commute to work: 100.0% car, 0.0% public transportation, 0.0% walk, 0.0% work from home (2000); Travel time to work: 13.3% less than 15 minutes, 86.7% 15 to 30 minutes, 0.0% 30 to 45 minutes, 0.0% 45 to 60 minutes, 0.0% 60 minutes or more (2000)

CUMBERLAND (town). Covers a land area of 1.892 square miles and a water area of 0.035 square miles. Located at 39.78° N. Lat.; 85.95° W. Long. Elevation is 856 feet.
Population: 5,500 (2000); Race: 85.5% White, 9.1% Black, 2.6% Asian, 0.5% American Indian and Alaska Native, 0.9% Hispanic of any race, 1.7% two or more races (2000); Density: 2,907.0 persons per square mile (2000); Age: 29.5% under 18, 8.6% over 64 (2000); Marriage status: 24.1% never married, 61.7% now married, 4.8% widowed, 9.4% divorced (2000); Foreign born: 2.9% (2000); Ancestry (includes multiple ancestries): 26.4% German, 16.5% Other groups, 11.3% United States or American, 11.3% Irish, 9.7% English (2000).
Economy: Now part of City of Indianapolis. Single-family building permits issued: 10 (2001) / 9 (2000); Multi-family building permits issued: 0 (2001) / 0 (2000); Employment by occupation: 15.6% management, 19.0% professional, 10.3% services, 32.8% sales, 0.0% farming, 8.5% construction, 13.8% production (2000).
Income: Per capita income: $24,746 (2000); Median household income: $57,875 (2000); Poverty rate: 6.6% (2000).
Education: High school graduation rate: 88.6% (2000); College graduation rate: 28.2% (2000).
Housing: Homeownership rate: 72.7% (2000); Median home value: $142,900 (2000); Median rent: $435 per month (2000); Median age of housing: 17 years (2000).
Transportation: Commute to work: 92.6% car, 1.5% public transportation, 1.3% walk, 3.7% work from home (2000); Travel time to work: 24.4% less than 15 minutes, 40.4% 15 to 30 minutes, 29.2% 30 to 45 minutes, 3.2% 45 to 60 minutes, 2.8% 60 minutes or more (2000)

HOMECROFT (town). Covers a land area of 0.232 square miles and a water area of 0 square miles. Located at 39.66° N. Lat.; 86.13° W. Long. Elevation is 764 feet.
Population: 751 (2000); Race: 98.8% White, 0.3% Black, 0.0% Asian, 0.0% American Indian and Alaska Native, 0.0% Hispanic of any race, 0.9% two or more races (2000); Density: 3,243.5 persons per square mile (2000); Age: 21.6% under 18, 17.1% over 64 (2000); Marriage status: 20.1% never married, 62.0% now married, 7.5% widowed, 10.3% divorced (2000); Foreign born: 2.0% (2000); Ancestry (includes multiple ancestries): 32.1% German, 13.9% United States or American, 13.0% Irish, 10.4% English, 3.9% Other groups (2000).
Economy: Employment by occupation: 17.7% management, 26.0% professional, 12.2% services, 27.6% sales, 0.0% farming, 6.0% construction, 10.4% production (2000).
Income: Per capita income: $28,888 (2000); Median household income: $60,156 (2000); Poverty rate: 2.1% (2000).
Taxes: Total city taxes per capita: $86 (1997); City property taxes per capita: $69 (1997).
Education: High school graduation rate: 95.0% (2000); College graduation rate: 35.8% (2000).
Housing: Homeownership rate: 93.2% (2000); Median home value: $113,700 (2000); Median rent: $670 per month (2000); Median age of housing: 52 years (2000).
Transportation: Commute to work: 93.7% car, 0.5% public transportation, 1.3% walk, 3.9% work from home (2000); Travel time to work: 26.4% less than 15 minutes, 48.2% 15 to 30 minutes, 18.8% 30 to 45 minutes, 3.0% 45 to 60 minutes, 3.5% 60 minutes or more (2000)

INDIANAPOLIS (special city). Covers a land area of 361.480 square miles and a water area of 6.678 square miles. Located at 39.79° N. Lat.; 86.14° W. Long. Elevation is 717 feet.
History: Settlement began in Indianapolis in 1820, when several families built cabins here and called it Fall Creek. That same year, Fall Creek was selected as the site for Indiana's capital because of its location near the center of the state. The new city was named Indianapolis in 1821; the first legislature met here in 1825. Indianapolis was incorporated as a city in 1847. Henry Ward Beecher, well-known writer, preacher, and brother of Harriet Beecher Stowe, lived in Indianapolis at that time.
Population: 781,870 (2000); Race: 69.1% White, 25.4% Black, 1.3% Asian, 0.3% American Indian and Alaska Native, 3.8% Hispanic of any race, 1.8% two or more races (2000); Density: 2,163.0 persons per square mile (2000); Age: 25.6% under 18, 11.0% over 64 (2000); Marriage status: 31.8% never married, 48.7% now married, 6.4% widowed, 13.1% divorced (2000); Foreign born: 4.6% (2000); Ancestry (includes multiple ancestries): 30.0% Other groups, 16.6% German, 10.2% Irish, 9.3% United States or American, 7.7% English (2000).
Vital Statistics: Birth rate: 172.2 per 10,000 population (1998)
Economy: Unemployment rate: 5.3% (11/2002); Total civilian labor force: 435,694 (11/2002); Single-family building permits issued: 4,765 (2001) / 3,534 (2000); Multi-family building permits issued: 1,108 (2001) / 1,253 (2000); Employment by occupation: 13.1% management, 19.6% professional, 14.9% services, 28.3% sales, 0.1% farming, 8.6% construction, 15.2% production (2000).
Income: Per capita income: $21,640 (2000); Median household income: $40,051 (2000); Poverty rate: 11.9% (2000).
Education: High school graduation rate: 81.3% (2000); College graduation rate: 25.4% (2000).

School District(s)

Franklin Township Com Sch Corp (PK-12)
2000 Enrollment: 5,694 317-862-2411
In Department of Correction (05-12)
2000 Enrollment: 726 317-232-5770
In Department of Mental Health (PK-12)
2000 Enrollment: n/a 317-232-7844
In State Department of Health (PK-12)
2000 Enrollment: 574 317-233-7852
Indianapolis Public Schools (PK-12)
2000 Enrollment: 41,008 317-226-4411
M S D Decatur Township (KG-12)
2000 Enrollment: 5,394 317-856-5265
M S D Lawrence Township (PK-12)
2000 Enrollment: 15,692 317-546-4921
M S D Perry Township (PK-12)
2000 Enrollment: 11,969 317-780-4200

M S D Pike Township (PK-12)
2000 Enrollment: 9,754 317-293-0393
M S D Warren Township (PK-12)
2000 Enrollment: 10,611 317-532-6100
M S D Washington Township (PK-12)
2000 Enrollment: 10,162 317-845-9400
M S D Wayne Township (PK-12)
2000 Enrollment: 13,263 317-243-8251

Four-year College(s)

Butler University (Private, Not-for-profit)
2001 Enrollment: 4,264 317-940-8000
2001 Tuition: In-state $18,940; Out-of-state $18,940
Christian Theological Seminary (Private, Not-for-profit, Christian Church (Disciples of Christ))
2001 Enrollment: 280 317-924-1331
Indiana University-Purdue University-Indianapolis (Public)
2001 Enrollment: 28,339 317-274-5555
2001 Tuition: In-state $3,839; Out-of-state $11,940
Indiana Bible College (Private, Not-for-profit, Pentecostal Holiness Church)
2001 Enrollment: n/a 317-784-8069
University of Indianapolis (Private, Not-for-profit, United Methodist)
2001 Enrollment: 3,708 317-788-3368
2001 Tuition: In-state $15,350; Out-of-state $15,350
ITT Technical Institute (Private, For-profit)
2001 Enrollment: 798 317-875-8640
2001 Tuition: In-state $11,304; Out-of-state $11,304
Marian College (Private, Not-for-profit, Roman Catholic)
2001 Enrollment: 1,260 317-955-6000
2001 Tuition: In-state $15,226; Out-of-state $15,226
Martin University (Private, Not-for-profit)
2001 Enrollment: 536 317-543-3235
2001 Tuition: In-state $8,850; Out-of-state $8,850

Two-year College(s)

Ivy Tech State College-Central Indiana (Public)
2001 Enrollment: 7,357 317-921-4488
2001 Tuition: In-state $1,986; Out-of-state $4,029
Indiana Business College (Private, For-profit)
2001 Enrollment: 812 317-264-5656
2001 Tuition: In-state $8,460; Out-of-state $8,460
International Business College-Indianapolis (Private, For-profit)
2001 Enrollment: 255 317-841-6400
2001 Tuition: In-state $9,200; Out-of-state $9,200
Lincoln Technical Institute (Private, For-profit)
2001 Enrollment: 703 317-632-5553
Professional Careers Institute (Private, For-profit)
2001 Enrollment: 536 317-299-6001
2001 Tuition: In-state $7,150; Out-of-state $7,150
Wilson College (Private, For-profit)
2001 Enrollment: n/a 317-787-6863
Indiana Business College (Private, For-profit)
2001 Enrollment: 353 317-783-5100
2001 Tuition: In-state $8,460; Out-of-state $8,460
American Trans Air Aviation Training Academy (Private, For-profit)
2001 Enrollment: 219 317-243-4514

Housing: Homeownership rate: 58.7% (2000); Median home value: $98,200 (2000); Median rent: $486 per month (2000); Median age of housing: 34 years (2000).
Hospitals: Community Health Network (1,025 beds); Community Hospital-North (290 beds); Community Hospital-South (150 beds); Fairbanks Hospital (96 beds); Larue D. Carter Memorial Hospital (146 beds); Methodist Hospital of Indiana (1,120 beds); Riley Hospital & Indiana University Hospital; Roudebush Veterans Affairs Medical Center (191 beds); Saint Vincent Indianapolis Hospital (650 beds); Saint Francis Indianapolis; Westview Hospital (120 beds); Winona Memorial Hospital (317 beds); Wishard Health Services (518 beds); Women's Hospital of Indianapolis (182 beds)
Safety: Violent crime rate: 93.1 per 10,000 population; Property crime rate: 421.3 per 10,000 population (2001).
Newspapers: Franklin Township Informer (1 x week); West Side Community News (1 x week); The Court and Commercial Record (3 x week); The Indianapolis Star (7 x week); Northeast Reporter (1 x week); East Side Herald (1 x week); National Jewish Post and Opinion (1 x week); Indiana Herald (1 x week); The Criterion (1 x week); The Spotlight (1 x week); Indianapolis Recorder (1 x week); NUVO Newsweekly (1 x week)
Transportation: Commute to work: 92.3% car, 2.4% public transportation, 2.0% walk, 2.5% work from home (2000); Travel time to work: 25.8% less than 15 minutes, 47.6% 15 to 30 minutes, 18.8% 30 to 45 minutes, 3.8% 45 to 60 minutes, 4.0% 60 minutes or more (2000); Amtrak: Service available.
Airports: Indianapolis International (primary service/medium hub); Indianapolis Metropolitan (primary service/medium hub); Eagle Creek Airpark (primary service/medium hub); Mount Comfort (primary service/medium hub); Indianapolis Terry (primary service/medium hub); Greenwood Municipal (primary service/medium hub)
Additional Information Contacts
Indiana Association of Realtors 317-842-0890
Indiana Commercial Board of Realtors 317-632-2509
Indianapolis Black Chamber 317-924-9840
Indianapolis Chamber of Commerce 317-541-9876
Metropolitan Indianapolis Board of Realtors 317-956-1912

LAWRENCE (city). Covers a land area of 20.082 square miles and a water area of 0.102 square miles. Located at 39.86° N. Lat.; 85.99° W. Long. Elevation is 860 feet.
History: Fort Benjamin Harrison is here.
Population: 38,915 (2000); Race: 77.7% White, 15.6% Black, 1.5% Asian, 0.3% American Indian and Alaska Native, 4.8% Hispanic of any race, 2.9% two or more races (2000); Density: 1,937.8 persons per square mile (2000); Age: 29.5% under 18, 8.0% over 64 (2000); Marriage status: 25.1% never married, 57.6% now married, 4.3% widowed, 13.0% divorced (2000); Foreign born: 5.5% (2000); Ancestry (includes multiple ancestries): 25.5% Other groups, 20.0% German, 12.7% Irish, 10.1% United States or American, 8.5% English (2000).
Vital Statistics: Birth rate: 8.2 per 10,000 population (1998)
Economy: Light manufacturing. Unemployment rate: 4.7% (11/2002); Total civilian labor force: 15,924 (11/2002); Single-family building permits issued: 434 (2001) / 402 (2000); Multi-family building permits issued: 10 (2001) / 0 (2000); Employment by occupation: 16.0% management, 20.0% professional, 11.4% services, 31.0% sales, 0.1% farming, 8.7% construction, 12.8% production (2000).
Income: Per capita income: $22,543 (2000); Median household income: $47,838 (2000); Poverty rate: 6.7% (2000).
Taxes: Total city taxes per capita: $153 (1997); City property taxes per capita: $118 (1997).
Education: High school graduation rate: 85.6% (2000); College graduation rate: 26.8% (2000).
Housing: Homeownership rate: 75.5% (2000); Median home value: $116,200 (2000); Median rent: $515 per month (2000); Median age of housing: 18 years (2000).
Safety: Violent crime rate: 45.5 per 10,000 population; Property crime rate: 249.1 per 10,000 population (2001).
Newspapers: Lawrence Community Journal (1 x week)
Transportation: Commute to work: 95.8% car, 0.5% public transportation, 0.7% walk, 2.5% work from home (2000); Travel time to work: 20.6% less than 15 minutes, 43.3% 15 to 30 minutes, 26.3% 30 to 45 minutes, 5.6% 45 to 60 minutes, 4.3% 60 minutes or more (2000)

MERIDIAN HILLS (town). Covers a land area of 1.484 square miles and a water area of 0.002 square miles. Located at 39.88° N. Lat.; 86.15° W. Long. Elevation is 800 feet.
History: Former municipality, merged with Indianapolis 1970.
Population: 1,713 (2000); Race: 98.2% White, 1.0% Black, 0.3% Asian, 0.4% American Indian and Alaska Native, 0.0% Hispanic of any race, 0.0% two or more races (2000); Density: 1,154.3 persons per square mile (2000); Age: 25.7% under 18, 18.1% over 64 (2000); Marriage status: 14.9% never married, 72.9% now married, 6.3% widowed, 5.9% divorced (2000); Foreign born: 2.1% (2000); Ancestry (includes multiple ancestries): 33.8% German, 18.5% English, 15.1% Irish, 6.1% Italian, 6.1% French (except Basque) (2000).
Economy: Employment by occupation: 29.2% management, 35.6% professional, 3.9% services, 28.7% sales, 0.0% farming, 1.2% construction, 1.3% production (2000).
Income: Per capita income: $59,829 (2000); Median household income: $107,009 (2000); Poverty rate: 0.2% (2000).
Taxes: Total city taxes per capita: $124 (1997); City property taxes per capita: $119 (1997).
Education: High school graduation rate: 99.0% (2000); College graduation rate: 78.3% (2000).
Housing: Homeownership rate: 95.6% (2000); Median home value: $281,900 (2000); Median rent: $1,250 per month (2000); Median age of housing: 45 years (2000).
Transportation: Commute to work: 96.7% car, 0.0% public transportation, 0.0% walk, 3.0% work from home (2000); Travel time to work: 25.3% less

than 15 minutes, 60.2% 15 to 30 minutes, 10.6% 30 to 45 minutes, 1.1% 45 to 60 minutes, 2.8% 60 minutes or more (2000)

NORTH CROWS NEST (town). Covers a land area of 0.064 square miles and a water area of 0 square miles. Located at 39.86° N. Lat.; 86.16° W. Long. Elevation is 775 feet.
Population: 42 (2000); Race: 100.0% White, 0.0% Black, 0.0% Asian, 0.0% American Indian and Alaska Native, 0.0% Hispanic of any race, 0.0% two or more races (2000); Density: 654.0 persons per square mile (2000); Age: 11.9% under 18, 26.2% over 64 (2000); Marriage status: 21.4% never married, 71.4% now married, 0.0% widowed, 7.1% divorced (2000); Foreign born: 0.0% (2000); Ancestry (includes multiple ancestries): 38.1% English, 23.8% Italian, 19.0% German, 19.0% Scottish, 11.9% Serbian (2000).
Economy: Employment by occupation: 25.0% management, 37.5% professional, 0.0% services, 37.5% sales, 0.0% farming, 0.0% construction, 0.0% production (2000).
Income: Per capita income: $48,029 (2000); Median household income: $132,364 (2000); Poverty rate: 0.0% (2000).
Taxes: Total city taxes per capita: $214 (2000); City property taxes per capita: $190 (2000).
Education: High school graduation rate: 100.0% (2000); College graduation rate: 84.8% (2000).
Housing: Homeownership rate: 100.0% (2000); Median home value: $598,200 (2000); Median age of housing: 60+ years (2000).
Transportation: Commute to work: 87.5% car, 0.0% public transportation, 12.5% walk, 0.0% work from home (2000); Travel time to work: 50.0% less than 15 minutes, 50.0% 15 to 30 minutes, 0.0% 30 to 45 minutes, 0.0% 45 to 60 minutes, 0.0% 60 minutes or more (2000)

ROCKY RIPPLE (town). Covers a land area of 0.304 square miles and a water area of 0 square miles. Located at 39.84° N. Lat.; 86.17° W. Long. Elevation is 705 feet.
Population: 712 (2000); Race: 92.6% White, 5.4% Black, 0.0% Asian, 0.0% American Indian and Alaska Native, 2.7% Hispanic of any race, 1.7% two or more races (2000); Density: 2,338.5 persons per square mile (2000); Age: 21.9% under 18, 17.2% over 64 (2000); Marriage status: 29.0% never married, 52.6% now married, 7.0% widowed, 11.4% divorced (2000); Foreign born: 2.4% (2000); Ancestry (includes multiple ancestries): 29.1% German, 17.2% Irish, 15.2% Other groups, 13.4% English, 8.7% United States or American (2000).
Economy: Employment by occupation: 15.4% management, 23.8% professional, 15.7% services, 24.1% sales, 0.0% farming, 9.2% construction, 11.8% production (2000).
Income: Per capita income: $22,691 (2000); Median household income: $44,464 (2000); Poverty rate: 2.4% (2000).
Taxes: Total city taxes per capita: $14 (1997); City property taxes per capita: $14 (1997).
Education: High school graduation rate: 82.6% (2000); College graduation rate: 32.1% (2000).
Housing: Homeownership rate: 78.7% (2000); Median home value: $80,100 (2000); Median rent: $558 per month (2000); Median age of housing: 48 years (2000).
Transportation: Commute to work: 92.0% car, 1.1% public transportation, 1.3% walk, 3.2% work from home (2000); Travel time to work: 22.9% less than 15 minutes, 55.1% 15 to 30 minutes, 14.6% 30 to 45 minutes, 1.7% 45 to 60 minutes, 5.8% 60 minutes or more (2000)

SOUTHPORT (city). Covers a land area of 0.642 square miles and a water area of 0 square miles. Located at 39.66° N. Lat.; 86.11° W. Long. Elevation is 775 feet.
History: Laid out 1852.
Population: 1,852 (2000); Race: 95.9% White, 0.3% Black, 0.3% Asian, 0.0% American Indian and Alaska Native, 3.6% Hispanic of any race, 0.7% two or more races (2000); Density: 2,886.2 persons per square mile (2000); Age: 24.4% under 18, 11.6% over 64 (2000); Marriage status: 24.4% never married, 58.8% now married, 7.1% widowed, 9.7% divorced (2000); Foreign born: 3.4% (2000); Ancestry (includes multiple ancestries): 26.8% German, 13.3% United States or American, 12.0% English, 10.8% Other groups, 8.8% Irish (2000).
Economy: Single-family building permits issued: 0 (2001) / 0 (2000); Multi-family building permits issued: 0 (2001) / 0 (2000); Employment by occupation: 12.4% management, 17.4% professional, 14.0% services, 25.8% sales, 0.3% farming, 11.9% construction, 18.2% production (2000).
Income: Per capita income: $24,374 (2000); Median household income: $56,719 (2000); Poverty rate: 6.2% (2000).
Taxes: Total city taxes per capita: $79 (1997); City property taxes per capita: $60 (1997).
Education: High school graduation rate: 88.9% (2000); College graduation rate: 22.5% (2000).
Housing: Homeownership rate: 76.5% (2000); Median home value: $103,600 (2000); Median rent: $582 per month (2000); Median age of housing: 38 years (2000).
Transportation: Commute to work: 92.7% car, 0.7% public transportation, 0.4% walk, 4.3% work from home (2000); Travel time to work: 20.1% less than 15 minutes, 38.8% 15 to 30 minutes, 33.4% 30 to 45 minutes, 5.1% 45 to 60 minutes, 2.6% 60 minutes or more (2000)

SPEEDWAY (town). Covers a land area of 4.755 square miles and a water area of 0.008 square miles. Located at 39.79° N. Lat.; 86.25° W. Long. Elevation is 744 feet.
History: Speedway, laid out in 1912 by Carl Fisher, James T. Allison, and Frank H. Wheeler, gained fame as the home of the Indianapolis Motor Speedway.
Population: 12,881 (2000); Race: 84.0% White, 11.5% Black, 2.4% Asian, 0.1% American Indian and Alaska Native, 2.3% Hispanic of any race, 1.3% two or more races (2000); Density: 2,708.9 persons per square mile (2000); Age: 20.3% under 18, 17.8% over 64 (2000); Marriage status: 28.6% never married, 47.3% now married, 8.3% widowed, 15.8% divorced (2000); Foreign born: 4.5% (2000); Ancestry (includes multiple ancestries): 22.7% German, 17.5% Other groups, 12.8% Irish, 11.4% English, 10.1% United States or American (2000).
Vital Statistics: Birth rate: 57.5 per 10,000 population (1998)
Economy: Single-family building permits issued: 0 (2001) / 0 (2000); Multi-family building permits issued: 192 (2001) / 0 (2000); Employment by occupation: 11.8% management, 19.8% professional, 14.8% services, 29.9% sales, 0.2% farming, 6.5% construction, 17.0% production (2000).
Income: Per capita income: $21,467 (2000); Median household income: $37,713 (2000); Poverty rate: 8.8% (2000).
Taxes: Total city taxes per capita: $301 (1997); City property taxes per capita: $235 (1997).
Education: High school graduation rate: 88.0% (2000); College graduation rate: 22.4% (2000).

School District(s)

School Town of Speedway (KG-12)
2000 Enrollment: 1,626 317-244-0236
Housing: Homeownership rate: 46.6% (2000); Median home value: $98,700 (2000); Median rent: $499 per month (2000); Median age of housing: 38 years (2000).
Safety: Violent crime rate: 31.7 per 10,000 population; Property crime rate: 231.6 per 10,000 population (2001).
Newspapers: The Press (1 x week)
Transportation: Commute to work: 92.3% car, 2.2% public transportation, 3.0% walk, 1.4% work from home (2000); Travel time to work: 29.0% less than 15 minutes, 48.4% 15 to 30 minutes, 16.1% 30 to 45 minutes, 2.6% 45 to 60 minutes, 3.9% 60 minutes or more (2000)

SPRING HILL (town). Covers a land area of 0.110 square miles and a water area of 0 square miles. Located at 39.83° N. Lat.; 86.19° W. Long.
Population: 97 (2000); Race: 98.4% White, 1.6% Black, 0.0% Asian, 0.0% American Indian and Alaska Native, 0.0% Hispanic of any race, 0.0% two or more races (2000); Density: 881.1 persons per square mile (2000); Age: 13.6% under 18, 16.0% over 64 (2000); Marriage status: 31.5% never married, 54.6% now married, 4.6% widowed, 9.3% divorced (2000); Foreign born: 4.0% (2000); Ancestry (includes multiple ancestries): 13.6% United States or American, 12.8% Greek, 12.0% Irish, 11.2% Italian, 11.2% English (2000).
Economy: Employment by occupation: 8.6% management, 32.1% professional, 13.6% services, 45.7% sales, 0.0% farming, 0.0% construction, 0.0% production (2000).
Income: Per capita income: $77,390 (2000); Median household income: $103,337 (2000); Poverty rate: 10.4% (2000).
Education: High school graduation rate: 94.2% (2000); College graduation rate: 81.4% (2000).
Housing: Homeownership rate: 73.6% (2000); Median home value: $270,800 (2000); Median rent: $1,400 per month (2000); Median age of housing: 18 years (2000).
Transportation: Commute to work: 94.3% car, 0.0% public transportation, 0.0% walk, 5.7% work from home (2000); Travel time to work: 9.1% less than 15 minutes, 80.3% 15 to 30 minutes, 10.6% 30 to 45 minutes, 0.0% 45 to 60 minutes, 0.0% 60 minutes or more (2000)

WARREN PARK (town). Covers a land area of 0.450 square miles and a water area of 0 square miles. Located at 39.78° N. Lat.; 86.05° W. Long. Elevation is 814 feet.
Population: 1,656 (2000); Race: 92.0% White, 4.2% Black, 1.5% Asian, 0.0% American Indian and Alaska Native, 1.7% Hispanic of any race, 0.6% two or more races (2000); Density: 3,683.3 persons per square mile (2000); Age: 17.4% under 18, 36.5% over 64 (2000); Marriage status: 15.2% never married, 42.6% now married, 27.6% widowed, 14.6% divorced (2000); Foreign born: 3.1% (2000); Ancestry (includes multiple ancestries): 20.5% German, 19.7% Irish, 13.3% English, 12.7% Other groups, 10.7% United States or American (2000).
Economy: Employment by occupation: 13.7% management, 17.5% professional, 11.3% services, 35.4% sales, 0.0% farming, 9.7% construction, 12.4% production (2000).
Income: Per capita income: $24,836 (2000); Median household income: $25,185 (2000); Poverty rate: 6.2% (2000).
Taxes: Total city taxes per capita: $59 (1997); City property taxes per capita: $56 (1997).
Education: High school graduation rate: 78.5% (2000); College graduation rate: 15.9% (2000).
Housing: Homeownership rate: 31.8% (2000); Median home value: $104,300 (2000); Median rent: $532 per month (2000); Median age of housing: 38 years (2000).
Transportation: Commute to work: 92.1% car, 1.0% public transportation, 3.8% walk, 2.5% work from home (2000); Travel time to work: 32.0% less than 15 minutes, 44.1% 15 to 30 minutes, 22.1% 30 to 45 minutes, 1.8% 45 to 60 minutes, 0.0% 60 minutes or more (2000)

WILLIAMS CREEK (town). Covers a land area of 0.338 square miles and a water area of 0 square miles. Located at 39.90° N. Lat.; 86.14° W. Long. Elevation is 775 feet.
Population: 413 (2000); Race: 98.8% White, 1.2% Black, 0.0% Asian, 0.0% American Indian and Alaska Native, 0.0% Hispanic of any race, 0.0% two or more races (2000); Density: 1,221.1 persons per square mile (2000); Age: 28.5% under 18, 12.9% over 64 (2000); Marriage status: 16.0% never married, 69.0% now married, 5.8% widowed, 9.2% divorced (2000); Foreign born: 1.5% (2000); Ancestry (includes multiple ancestries): 30.5% German, 20.5% English, 18.5% Irish, 6.8% Scotch-Irish, 5.9% Italian (2000).
Economy: Employment by occupation: 36.1% management, 32.7% professional, 5.4% services, 19.8% sales, 0.0% farming, 1.5% construction, 4.5% production (2000).
Income: Per capita income: $82,132 (2000); Median household income: $172,996 (2000); Poverty rate: 1.2% (2000).
Taxes: Total city taxes per capita: $200 (1997); City property taxes per capita: $193 (1997).
Education: High school graduation rate: 99.3% (2000); College graduation rate: 77.6% (2000).
Housing: Homeownership rate: 100.0% (2000); Median home value: $553,600 (2000); Median age of housing: 50 years (2000).
Transportation: Commute to work: 92.5% car, 0.0% public transportation, 4.0% walk, 3.5% work from home (2000); Travel time to work: 35.4% less than 15 minutes, 40.6% 15 to 30 minutes, 22.9% 30 to 45 minutes, 1.0% 45 to 60 minutes, 0.0% 60 minutes or more (2000)

WYNNEDALE (town). Covers a land area of 0.167 square miles and a water area of 0 square miles. Located at 39.83° N. Lat.; 86.19° W. Long. Elevation is 750 feet.
Population: 275 (2000); Race: 68.0% White, 32.0% Black, 0.0% Asian, 0.0% American Indian and Alaska Native, 0.0% Hispanic of any race, 0.0% two or more races (2000); Density: 1,643.6 persons per square mile (2000); Age: 24.0% under 18, 19.5% over 64 (2000); Marriage status: 21.5% never married, 64.4% now married, 7.8% widowed, 6.3% divorced (2000); Foreign born: 0.0% (2000); Ancestry (includes multiple ancestries): 28.1% Other groups, 24.9% German, 20.4% English, 9.8% Italian, 8.0% Scottish (2000).
Economy: Employment by occupation: 25.2% management, 43.6% professional, 10.4% services, 17.8% sales, 0.0% farming, 0.0% construction, 3.1% production (2000).
Income: Per capita income: $50,323 (2000); Median household income: $93,778 (2000); Poverty rate: 0.9% (2000).
Taxes: Total city taxes per capita: $91 (1997); City property taxes per capita: $87 (1997).
Education: High school graduation rate: 90.8% (2000); College graduation rate: 67.9% (2000).
Housing: Homeownership rate: 100.0% (2000); Median home value: $183,000 (2000); Median age of housing: 41 years (2000).
Transportation: Commute to work: 92.6% car, 1.2% public transportation, 0.0% walk, 6.1% work from home (2000); Travel time to work: 32.7% less than 15 minutes, 63.4% 15 to 30 minutes, 3.9% 30 to 45 minutes, 0.0% 45 to 60 minutes, 0.0% 60 minutes or more (2000)

Marshall County

Located in northern Indiana; drained by the Yellow and Tippecanoe River; includes several lakes. Covers a land area of 444.30 square miles, a water area of 5.70 square miles, and is located in the Eastern Time Zone. The county government was organized in 1835. County seat is Plymouth.
Population: 45,128 (2000); Race: 95.3% White, 0.2% Black, 0.3% Asian, 0.2% American Indian and Alaska Native, 5.9% Hispanic of any race, 1.1% two or more races (2000); Density: 101.6 persons per square mile (2000); Age: 28.0% under 18, 13.2% over 64 (2000).
Religion: Five largest groups: 10.2% Catholic Church, 7.1% The United Methodist Church, 3.1% United Church of Christ, 3.0% The Wesleyan Church, 2.7% Lutheran Church—Missouri Synod (2000).
Economy: Unemployment rate: 5.5% (11/2002); Total civilian labor force: 22,517 (11/2002); Leading industries: 44.3% manufacturing; 11.1% retail trade; 9.2% health care and social assistance (2000); Companies that employ more than 1,000 persons: 0 (2000); Companies that employ more than 100 persons: 38 (2000); Farms: 865 totaling 201,637 acres (1997); Minority business ownership rate: 0.0% (1997); Women business ownership rate: 22.8% (1997); Retail sales per capita: $8,115 (1997). Single-family building permits issued: 189 (2001) / 224 (2000); Multi-family building permits issued: 28 (2001) / 62 (2000).
Income: Per capita income: $18,427 (2000); Median household income: $42,581 (2000); Poverty rate: 6.8% (2000); Bankruptcy rate: 6.40% (2001).
Taxes: Total county taxes per capita: $202 (1997); County property taxes per capita: $117 (1997).
Education: High school graduation rate: 79.8% (2000); College graduation rate: 14.9% (2000).
Housing: Homeownership rate: 76.8% (2000); Median home value: $88,100 (2000); Median rent: $398 per month (2000); Median age of housing: 34 years (2000).
Health: Birth rate: 151.1 per 10,000 population (1998); Age adjusted death rate: 82.3 per 10,000 population (1999); Age adjusted cancer mortality rate: 189.6 deaths per 100,000 population (1999). Number of physicians: 8.6 per 10,000 population (1999); Number of hospital beds: 29.9 per 10,000 population (1999).
Elections: 2000 Presidential election results: 34.3% Gore, 63.6% Bush, 0.7% Nader, 1.0% Buchanan
National and State Parks: Menominee State Wetlands
Additional Information Contacts
Marshall County Government Offices 219-935-8555
Bremen Chamber of Commerce. 219-546-2044
Culver Chamber of Commerce. 219-842-5253
North Central Indiana Association of Realtors 219-935-3940
Plymouth Chamber of Commerce 219-936-2323

Marshall County Communities

ARGOS (town). Covers a land area of 0.678 square miles and a water area of 0 square miles. Located at 41.23° N. Lat.; 86.24° W. Long. Elevation is 828 feet.
History: Argos began as a stagecoach stop on the Michigan Road. The name was chosen by Schuyler Colfax, vice-president under the Grant administration.
Population: 1,613 (2000); Race: 97.3% White, 0.9% Black, 0.4% Asian, 0.0% American Indian and Alaska Native, 1.4% Hispanic of any race, 0.8% two or more races (2000); Density: 2,378.2 persons per square mile (2000); Age: 30.7% under 18, 10.3% over 64 (2000); Marriage status: 19.8% never married, 59.9% now married, 7.6% widowed, 12.7% divorced (2000); Foreign born: 0.3% (2000); Ancestry (includes multiple ancestries): 35.0% German, 12.5% Irish, 10.8% English, 9.2% United States or American, 7.7% Other groups (2000).
Economy: Single-family building permits issued: 5 (2001) / 23 (2000); Multi-family building permits issued: 0 (2001) / 0 (2000); Employment by occupation: 5.9% management, 10.2% professional, 12.6% services, 23.1% sales, 0.8% farming, 8.4% construction, 39.1% production (2000).
Income: Per capita income: $15,643 (2000); Median household income: $35,000 (2000); Poverty rate: 11.5% (2000).
Taxes: Total city taxes per capita: $445 (2000); City property taxes per capita: $405 (2000).

Education: High school graduation rate: 82.5% (2000); College graduation rate: 12.7% (2000).

School District(s)

Argos Community Schools (KG-12)
2000 Enrollment: 801 219-892-5139

Housing: Homeownership rate: 69.5% (2000); Median home value: $73,100 (2000); Median rent: $375 per month (2000); Median age of housing: 52 years (2000).

Transportation: Commute to work: 93.3% car, 0.0% public transportation, 3.6% walk, 2.3% work from home (2000); Travel time to work: 41.8% less than 15 minutes, 32.2% 15 to 30 minutes, 12.5% 30 to 45 minutes, 5.3% 45 to 60 minutes, 8.2% 60 minutes or more (2000)

BOURBON (town). Covers a land area of 1.037 square miles and a water area of 0.004 square miles. Located at 41.29° N. Lat.; 86.11° W. Long. Elevation is 850 feet.

Population: 1,691 (2000); Race: 97.6% White, 0.0% Black, 0.6% Asian, 0.4% American Indian and Alaska Native, 4.2% Hispanic of any race, 0.0% two or more races (2000); Density: 1,630.3 persons per square mile (2000); Age: 31.5% under 18, 11.9% over 64 (2000); Marriage status: 23.4% never married, 59.0% now married, 6.0% widowed, 11.6% divorced (2000); Foreign born: 2.9% (2000); Ancestry (includes multiple ancestries): 30.8% German, 14.5% United States or American, 10.7% Other groups, 10.6% Irish, 7.4% English (2000).

Economy: In agricultural area: livestock, poultry; grain; feed milling, meat processing. Manufacturing: plastic products, hardwood lumber, windows, transportation products, wire; foundry. Single-family building permits issued: 4 (2001) / 7 (2000); Multi-family building permits issued: 0 (2001) / 0 (2000); Employment by occupation: 4.9% management, 14.2% professional, 12.1% services, 23.3% sales, 0.2% farming, 11.4% construction, 33.9% production (2000).

Income: Per capita income: $17,054 (2000); Median household income: $40,292 (2000); Poverty rate: 5.9% (2000).

Taxes: Total city taxes per capita: $115 (1997); City property taxes per capita: $114 (1997).

Education: High school graduation rate: 81.2% (2000); College graduation rate: 12.2% (2000).

School District(s)

Triton School Corporation (KG-12)
2000 Enrollment: 1,103 219-342-2255

Housing: Homeownership rate: 72.9% (2000); Median home value: $73,300 (2000); Median rent: $373 per month (2000); Median age of housing: 49 years (2000).

Newspapers: Bourbon News-Mirror (1 x week)

Transportation: Commute to work: 92.7% car, 0.5% public transportation, 4.7% walk, 2.1% work from home (2000); Travel time to work: 36.4% less than 15 minutes, 44.1% 15 to 30 minutes, 9.9% 30 to 45 minutes, 5.3% 45 to 60 minutes, 4.4% 60 minutes or more (2000)

BREMEN (town). Covers a land area of 2.280 square miles and a water area of 0 square miles. Located at 41.44° N. Lat.; 86.14° W. Long. Elevation is 854 feet.

History: Bremen reports that its fire department was the 1882 and 1887 winner of the hose and engine maneuvers at the state championships.

Population: 4,486 (2000); Race: 90.5% White, 0.0% Black, 0.0% Asian, 0.0% American Indian and Alaska Native, 12.0% Hispanic of any race, 2.1% two or more races (2000); Density: 1,967.8 persons per square mile (2000); Age: 28.8% under 18, 15.6% over 64 (2000); Marriage status: 21.3% never married, 63.3% now married, 7.0% widowed, 8.4% divorced (2000); Foreign born: 8.2% (2000); Ancestry (includes multiple ancestries): 33.6% German, 17.3% Other groups, 9.6% United States or American, 9.4% Irish, 8.2% English (2000).

Economy: Single-family building permits issued: 10 (2001) / 14 (2000); Multi-family building permits issued: 0 (2001) / 36 (2000); Employment by occupation: 11.6% management, 14.0% professional, 10.6% services, 16.9% sales, 0.7% farming, 8.6% construction, 37.6% production (2000).

Income: Per capita income: $17,073 (2000); Median household income: $40,185 (2000); Poverty rate: 6.5% (2000).

Taxes: Total city taxes per capita: $328 (2000); City property taxes per capita: $327 (2000).

Education: High school graduation rate: 75.3% (2000); College graduation rate: 12.2% (2000).

School District(s)

Bremen Public Schools (KG-12)
2000 Enrollment: 1,474 219-546-3929

Housing: Homeownership rate: 71.9% (2000); Median home value: $85,500 (2000); Median rent: $385 per month (2000); Median age of housing: 36 years (2000).

Hospitals: Community Hospital of Bremen (24 beds)

Safety: Violent crime rate: 6.7 per 10,000 population; Property crime rate: 277.1 per 10,000 population (2001).

Newspapers: Bremen Enquirer (1 x week)

Transportation: Commute to work: 93.6% car, 0.0% public transportation, 3.5% walk, 1.8% work from home (2000); Travel time to work: 56.1% less than 15 minutes, 22.6% 15 to 30 minutes, 15.4% 30 to 45 minutes, 3.5% 45 to 60 minutes, 2.4% 60 minutes or more (2000)

Additional Information Contacts

Bremen Chamber of Commerce 219-546-2044

CULVER (town). Covers a land area of 0.785 square miles and a water area of 0 square miles. Located at 41.21° N. Lat.; 86.42° W. Long. Elevation is 754 feet.

History: Culver developed as a resort town near Lake Maxinkuckee. It was named for Henry Harrison Culver of St. Louis who founded Culver Military Academy in 1894.

Population: 1,539 (2000); Race: 95.4% White, 0.2% Black, 1.1% Asian, 0.5% American Indian and Alaska Native, 3.4% Hispanic of any race, 1.9% two or more races (2000); Density: 1,961.7 persons per square mile (2000); Age: 23.1% under 18, 23.3% over 64 (2000); Marriage status: 23.8% never married, 53.3% now married, 11.8% widowed, 11.1% divorced (2000); Foreign born: 1.7% (2000); Ancestry (includes multiple ancestries): 31.4% German, 15.5% English, 11.9% Irish, 9.0% United States or American, 7.3% Other groups (2000).

Economy: Single-family building permits issued: 4 (2001) / 4 (2000); Multi-family building permits issued: 0 (2001) / 0 (2000); Employment by occupation: 12.4% management, 24.5% professional, 16.4% services, 20.1% sales, 0.7% farming, 9.1% construction, 16.7% production (2000).

Income: Per capita income: $18,938 (2000); Median household income: $33,047 (2000); Poverty rate: 10.4% (2000).

Taxes: Total city taxes per capita: $267 (1997); City property taxes per capita: $262 (1997).

Education: High school graduation rate: 84.5% (2000); College graduation rate: 25.5% (2000).

School District(s)

Culver Community Schools Corp (KG-12)
2000 Enrollment: 1,182 219-842-3364

Housing: Homeownership rate: 70.6% (2000); Median home value: $81,500 (2000); Median rent: $323 per month (2000); Median age of housing: 53 years (2000).

Safety: Violent crime rate: 0.0 per 10,000 population; Property crime rate: 200.3 per 10,000 population (2001).

Newspapers: The Culver Citizen (1 x week)

Transportation: Commute to work: 85.0% car, 0.9% public transportation, 8.4% walk, 4.1% work from home (2000); Travel time to work: 44.3% less than 15 minutes, 27.4% 15 to 30 minutes, 12.6% 30 to 45 minutes, 6.4% 45 to 60 minutes, 9.3% 60 minutes or more (2000)

Additional Information Contacts

Culver Chamber of Commerce 219-842-5253

LA PAZ (town). Aka Lapaz. Covers a land area of 0.515 square miles and a water area of 0 square miles. Located at 41.45° N. Lat.; 86.30° W. Long. Elevation is 879 feet.

Population: 489 (2000); Race: 87.1% White, 0.0% Black, 0.6% Asian, 2.0% American Indian and Alaska Native, 4.0% Hispanic of any race, 6.7% two or more races (2000); Density: 948.6 persons per square mile (2000); Age: 23.4% under 18, 9.5% over 64 (2000); Marriage status: 24.3% never married, 52.5% now married, 5.4% widowed, 17.9% divorced (2000); Foreign born: 1.2% (2000); Ancestry (includes multiple ancestries): 32.5% German, 16.9% Other groups, 14.5% United States or American, 7.3% Irish, 4.8% Dutch (2000).

Economy: Employment by occupation: 2.8% management, 5.2% professional, 15.3% services, 26.8% sales, 0.0% farming, 10.1% construction, 39.7% production (2000).

Income: Per capita income: $16,658 (2000); Median household income: $37,961 (2000); Poverty rate: 5.2% (2000).

Taxes: Total city taxes per capita: $65 (1997); City property taxes per capita: $65 (1997).

Education: High school graduation rate: 77.4% (2000); College graduation rate: 0.9% (2000).

Housing: Homeownership rate: 60.0% (2000); Median home value: $66,100 (2000); Median rent: $406 per month (2000); Median age of housing: 48 years (2000).
Transportation: Commute to work: 90.5% car, 0.7% public transportation, 3.2% walk, 1.8% work from home (2000); Travel time to work: 33.9% less than 15 minutes, 36.4% 15 to 30 minutes, 22.1% 30 to 45 minutes, 0.0% 45 to 60 minutes, 7.5% 60 minutes or more (2000)

PLYMOUTH (city). Covers a land area of 6.959 square miles and a water area of 0.015 square miles. Located at 41.34° N. Lat.; 86.31° W. Long. Elevation is 799 feet.
History: Plymouth was founded in 1834 as a shipping center and county seat.
Population: 9,840 (2000); Race: 90.0% White, 0.2% Black, 0.6% Asian, 0.4% American Indian and Alaska Native, 16.3% Hispanic of any race, 1.3% two or more races (2000); Density: 1,414.0 persons per square mile (2000); Age: 26.3% under 18, 14.1% over 64 (2000); Marriage status: 23.7% never married, 52.7% now married, 9.6% widowed, 14.0% divorced (2000); Foreign born: 11.7% (2000); Ancestry (includes multiple ancestries): 25.3% German, 20.0% Other groups, 9.4% Irish, 9.3% United States or American, 7.7% English (2000).
Economy: Single-family building permits issued: 112 (2001) / 115 (2000); Multi-family building permits issued: 28 (2001) / 26 (2000); Employment by occupation: 6.9% management, 11.3% professional, 13.6% services, 20.4% sales, 0.4% farming, 8.6% construction, 38.7% production (2000).
Income: Per capita income: $15,417 (2000); Median household income: $34,505 (2000); Poverty rate: 13.1% (2000).
Taxes: Total city taxes per capita: $332 (2000); City property taxes per capita: $328 (2000).
Education: High school graduation rate: 74.2% (2000); College graduation rate: 12.4% (2000).

School District(s)

Plymouth Community School Corp (PK-12)
2000 Enrollment: 3,301 219-936-3115

Housing: Homeownership rate: 56.9% (2000); Median home value: $74,900 (2000); Median rent: $415 per month (2000); Median age of housing: 36 years (2000).
Hospitals: BHC of Northern Indiana (80 beds); Saint Joseph's Regional Medical Center - Plymouth Campus (58 beds)
Safety: Violent crime rate: 10.1 per 10,000 population; Property crime rate: 454.8 per 10,000 population (2001).
Newspapers: Pilot News (6 x week)
Transportation: Commute to work: 91.0% car, 0.9% public transportation, 4.2% walk, 2.5% work from home (2000); Travel time to work: 59.1% less than 15 minutes, 20.6% 15 to 30 minutes, 9.5% 30 to 45 minutes, 5.9% 45 to 60 minutes, 4.9% 60 minutes or more (2000)

Additional Information Contacts

North Central Indiana Association of Realtors 219-935-3940
Plymouth Chamber of Commerce 219-936-2323

TIPPECANOE (unincorporated postal area, zip code 46570). Covers a land area of 21.095 square miles and a water area of 0.036 square miles. Located at 41.20° N. Lat.; 86.12° W. Long. Elevation is 780 feet.
History: Laid out 1882.
Population: 1,053 (2000); Race: 95.4% White, 0.0% Black, 0.0% Asian, 0.0% American Indian and Alaska Native, 3.5% Hispanic of any race, 1.8% two or more races (2000); Density: 49.9 persons per square mile (2000); Age: 27.8% under 18, 12.5% over 64 (2000); Marriage status: 19.7% never married, 61.7% now married, 8.7% widowed, 9.9% divorced (2000); Foreign born: 2.7% (2000); Ancestry (includes multiple ancestries): 26.0% German, 15.8% Irish, 11.3% English, 10.4% United States or American, 9.9% Other groups (2000).
Economy: Agriculture includes soybeans, corn; cattle; dairying. Manufacturing includes steel roofing, fabricated structural metal. Employment by occupation: 5.2% management, 4.3% professional, 17.5% services, 17.3% sales, 0.5% farming, 13.7% construction, 41.4% production (2000).
Income: Per capita income: $17,102 (2000); Median household income: $40,385 (2000); Poverty rate: 5.4% (2000).
Education: High school graduation rate: 67.6% (2000); College graduation rate: 5.3% (2000).
Housing: Homeownership rate: 87.8% (2000); Median home value: $72,500 (2000); Median rent: $267 per month (2000); Median age of housing: 32 years (2000).
Transportation: Commute to work: 91.0% car, 0.9% public transportation, 3.8% walk, 2.4% work from home (2000); Travel time to work: 25.8% less than 15 minutes, 31.1% 15 to 30 minutes, 22.8% 30 to 45 minutes, 6.0% 45 to 60 minutes, 14.2% 60 minutes or more (2000)

Martin County

Located in southwestern Indiana; drained by the Lost River and East Fork of the White River. Covers a land area of 336.10 square miles, a water area of 4.40 square miles, and is located in the Eastern Time Zone. The county government was organized in 1820. County seat is Shoals.

Weather Station: Crane Naval Depot — Elevation: 728 feet

	Jan	Feb	Mar	Apr	May	Jun	Jul	Aug	Sep	Oct	Nov	Dec
High	39	45	56	67	77	84	88	86	81	69	56	45
Low	21	26	34	44	54	62	67	65	58	46	37	27
Precip	3.0	2.7	4.1	5.0	5.5	3.9	4.9	4.0	3.3	3.4	4.2	3.4
Snow	na	na	1.8	tr	0.0	0.0	0.0	0.0	0.0	tr	tr	na

High and Low temperatures in degrees Fahrenheit; Precipitation and Snow in inches

Weather Station: Shoals Hiway 50 Bridge — Elevation: 547 feet

	Jan	Feb	Mar	Apr	May	Jun	Jul	Aug	Sep	Oct	Nov	Dec
High	37	43	54	66	75	83	87	85	79	68	55	43
Low	19	22	31	40	50	59	64	62	54	42	34	25
Precip	3.0	2.8	4.3	4.6	5.6	4.2	4.7	3.6	3.3	3.3	4.4	3.5
Snow	5.7	4.0	2.8	tr	0.0	0.0	0.0	0.0	0.0	0.1	0.3	2.7

High and Low temperatures in degrees Fahrenheit; Precipitation and Snow in inches

Population: 10,369 (2000); Race: 98.9% White, 0.1% Black, 0.0% Asian, 0.3% American Indian and Alaska Native, 0.1% Hispanic of any race, 0.6% two or more races (2000); Density: 30.8 persons per square mile (2000); Age: 25.2% under 18, 14.3% over 64 (2000).
Religion: Five largest groups: 25.3% Catholic Church, 10.9% The United Methodist Church, 9.8% Christian Churches and Churches of Christ, 3.5% Evangelical Lutheran Church in America, 2.8% Old Order Amish Church (2000).
Economy: Unemployment rate: 4.8% (11/2002); Total civilian labor force: 4,999 (11/2002); Leading industries: 31.6% manufacturing; 14.5% retail trade; 11.1% accommodation & food services (2000); Companies that employ more than 1,000 persons: 0 (2000); Companies that employ more than 100 persons: 4 (2000); Farms: 335 totaling 70,105 acres (1997); Minority business ownership rate: 0.0% (1997); Women business ownership rate: 17.9% (1997); Retail sales per capita: $5,562 (1997). Single-family building permits issued: 6 (2001) / 7 (2000); Multi-family building permits issued: 0 (2001) / 0 (2000).
Income: Per capita income: $17,054 (2000); Median household income: $36,411 (2000); Poverty rate: 11.2% (2000); Bankruptcy rate: 3.90% (2001).
Taxes: Total county taxes per capita: $197 (1997); County property taxes per capita: $136 (1997).
Education: High school graduation rate: 74.2% (2000); College graduation rate: 8.8% (2000).
Housing: Homeownership rate: 81.3% (2000); Median home value: $64,200 (2000); Median rent: $243 per month (2000); Median age of housing: 32 years (2000).
Health: Birth rate: 139.8 per 10,000 population (1998); Age adjusted death rate: 104.7 per 10,000 population (1999); Age adjusted cancer mortality rate: 314.3 deaths per 100,000 population (1999). Number of physicians: 3.9 per 10,000 population (1999); Number of hospital beds: n/a (1999).
Elections: 2000 Presidential election results: 32.9% Gore, 65.3% Bush, 0.3% Nader, 1.0% Buchanan
National and State Parks: Martin County State Forest; Martin State Forest

Additional Information Contacts

Martin County Government Offices...................... 812-247-3731
Martin County Chamber of Commerce 812-295-4093

Martin County Communities

CRANE (town). Covers a land area of 0.119 square miles and a water area of 0 square miles. Located at 38.89° N. Lat.; 86.90° W. Long. Elevation is 545 feet.
Population: 203 (2000); Race: 100.0% White, 0.0% Black, 0.0% Asian, 0.0% American Indian and Alaska Native, 0.0% Hispanic of any race, 0.0% two or more races (2000); Density: 1,705.5 persons per square mile (2000); Age: 28.0% under 18, 17.1% over 64 (2000); Marriage status: 10.5% never married, 65.0% now married, 7.0% widowed, 17.5% divorced (2000); Foreign born: 0.0% (2000); Ancestry (includes multiple ancestries): 16.1% German, 15.0% Irish, 13.0% United States or American, 9.8% English, 9.3% French (except Basque) (2000).

Economy: Heavily forested. Situated on the Northwest corner of the Crane Naval Weapons Support Center, which manufactures ordnance and microwave systems. Employment by occupation: 0.0% management, 18.6% professional, 20.9% services, 17.4% sales, 0.0% farming, 19.8% construction, 23.3% production (2000).
Income: Per capita income: $16,853 (2000); Median household income: $36,250 (2000); Poverty rate: 13.6% (2000).
Taxes: Total city taxes per capita: $124 (1997); City property taxes per capita: $60 (1997).
Education: High school graduation rate: 78.1% (2000); College graduation rate: 7.3% (2000).
Housing: Homeownership rate: 66.7% (2000); Median home value: $31,300 (2000); Median rent: $320 per month (2000); Median age of housing: 49 years (2000).
Transportation: Commute to work: 88.8% car, 0.0% public transportation, 4.5% walk, 3.4% work from home (2000); Travel time to work: 38.4% less than 15 minutes, 4.7% 15 to 30 minutes, 12.8% 30 to 45 minutes, 33.7% 45 to 60 minutes, 10.5% 60 minutes or more (2000)

LOOGOOTEE (city). Covers a land area of 1.566 square miles and a water area of 0 square miles. Located at 38.67° N. Lat.; 86.91° W. Long. Elevation is 537 feet.
History: Loogootee grew when natural gas was found here in 1899, and several glass factories were established. The town was named for Lowe, an engineer on the first railroad, and Gootee, who owned the land on which the town was built.
Population: 2,741 (2000); Race: 97.7% White, 0.0% Black, 0.0% Asian, 0.3% American Indian and Alaska Native, 0.3% Hispanic of any race, 1.7% two or more races (2000); Density: 1,750.5 persons per square mile (2000); Age: 23.1% under 18, 18.4% over 64 (2000); Marriage status: 20.8% never married, 54.0% now married, 10.8% widowed, 14.4% divorced (2000); Foreign born: 0.6% (2000); Ancestry (includes multiple ancestries): 21.4% United States or American, 20.1% German, 16.3% Irish, 7.8% English, 5.6% Other groups (2000).
Economy: Single-family building permits issued: 6 (2001) / 7 (2000); Multi-family building permits issued: 0 (2001) / 0 (2000); Employment by occupation: 9.2% management, 17.4% professional, 17.3% services, 21.2% sales, 0.0% farming, 13.8% construction, 20.9% production (2000).
Income: Per capita income: $17,321 (2000); Median household income: $30,492 (2000); Poverty rate: 16.4% (2000).
Education: High school graduation rate: 73.6% (2000); College graduation rate: 10.8% (2000).

School District(s)

Loogootee Community Sch Corp (KG-12)
2000 Enrollment: 1,070 812-295-2595
Housing: Homeownership rate: 71.8% (2000); Median home value: $66,600 (2000); Median rent: $263 per month (2000); Median age of housing: 36 years (2000).
Safety: Violent crime rate: 14.5 per 10,000 population; Property crime rate: 188.7 per 10,000 population (2001).
Newspapers: Loogootee Tribune (1 x week)
Transportation: Commute to work: 92.6% car, 0.0% public transportation, 2.7% walk, 4.4% work from home (2000); Travel time to work: 43.6% less than 15 minutes, 20.2% 15 to 30 minutes, 27.5% 30 to 45 minutes, 4.9% 45 to 60 minutes, 3.7% 60 minutes or more (2000)
Additional Information Contacts
Martin County Chamber of Commerce 812-295-4093

SHOALS (town). Covers a land area of 1.801 square miles and a water area of 0.095 square miles. Located at 38.66° N. Lat.; 86.79° W. Long. Elevation is 450 feet.
History: Shoals was founded in 1816 and named for the shallow place in the White River that afforded a crossing. The area was known as a haven for moonshiners and bootleggers during prohibition.
Population: 807 (2000); Race: 98.0% White, 0.9% Black, 0.3% Asian, 0.0% American Indian and Alaska Native, 0.0% Hispanic of any race, 0.9% two or more races (2000); Density: 448.0 persons per square mile (2000); Age: 13.7% under 18, 24.7% over 64 (2000); Marriage status: 13.8% never married, 55.3% now married, 13.2% widowed, 17.7% divorced (2000); Foreign born: 0.6% (2000); Ancestry (includes multiple ancestries): 24.1% United States or American, 16.4% Other groups, 10.5% German, 7.4% English, 6.0% Irish (2000).
Economy: Employment by occupation: 9.0% management, 11.2% professional, 23.9% services, 20.1% sales, 0.7% farming, 8.6% construction, 26.5% production (2000).
Income: Per capita income: $14,234 (2000); Median household income: $23,750 (2000); Poverty rate: 20.4% (2000).
Taxes: Total city taxes per capita: $148 (1997); City property taxes per capita: $93 (1997).
Education: High school graduation rate: 66.7% (2000); College graduation rate: 4.4% (2000).

School District(s)

Shoals Community School Corp (PK-12)
2000 Enrollment: 788 812-247-2060
Housing: Homeownership rate: 69.2% (2000); Median home value: $59,500 (2000); Median rent: $204 per month (2000); Median age of housing: 36 years (2000).
Newspapers: The Shoals News (1 x week)
Transportation: Commute to work: 91.8% car, 0.0% public transportation, 4.5% walk, 2.6% work from home (2000); Travel time to work: 41.0% less than 15 minutes, 21.5% 15 to 30 minutes, 21.8% 30 to 45 minutes, 7.3% 45 to 60 minutes, 8.4% 60 minutes or more (2000)

Miami County

Located in north central Indiana; crossed by the Wabash, Mississinewa, and Eel Rivers. Covers a land area of 375.60 square miles, a water area of 1.70 square miles, and is located in the Eastern Time Zone. The county government was organized in 1832. County seat is Peru.
Population: 36,082 (2000); Race: 93.5% White, 2.6% Black, 0.4% Asian, 0.8% American Indian and Alaska Native, 1.8% Hispanic of any race, 1.8% two or more races (2000); Density: 96.1 persons per square mile (2000); Age: 26.0% under 18, 12.9% over 64 (2000).
Religion: Five largest groups: 7.3% American Baptist Churches in the USA, 6.7% Catholic Church, 5.8% The United Methodist Church, 5.0% Christian Churches and Churches of Christ, 3.3% Lutheran Church—Missouri Synod (2000).
Economy: Unemployment rate: 8.2% (11/2002); Total civilian labor force: 16,741 (11/2002); Leading industries: 30.7% manufacturing; 13.9% retail trade; 11.6% health care and social assistance (2000); Companies that employ more than 1,000 persons: 0 (2000); Companies that employ more than 100 persons: 11 (2000); Farms: 678 totaling 197,198 acres (1997); Minority business ownership rate: 0.0% (1997); Women business ownership rate: 21.8% (1997); Retail sales per capita: $6,171 (1997). Single-family building permits issued: 102 (2001) / 115 (2000); Multi-family building permits issued: 0 (2001) / 0 (2000).
Income: Per capita income: $17,726 (2000); Median household income: $39,184 (2000); Poverty rate: 8.0% (2000); Bankruptcy rate: 7.61% (2001).
Taxes: Total county taxes per capita: $138 (2000); County property taxes per capita: $117 (2000).
Education: High school graduation rate: 81.9% (2000); College graduation rate: 10.4% (2000).
Housing: Homeownership rate: 76.0% (2000); Median home value: $71,100 (2000); Median rent: $365 per month (2000); Median age of housing: 46 years (2000).
Health: Birth rate: 125.3 per 10,000 population (1998); Age adjusted death rate: 92.1 per 10,000 population (1999); Age adjusted cancer mortality rate: 230.4 deaths per 100,000 population (1999). Number of physicians: 8.0 per 10,000 population (1999); Number of hospital beds: 20.8 per 10,000 population (1999).
Elections: 2000 Presidential election results: 32.1% Gore, 65.0% Bush, 0.3% Nader, 1.5% Buchanan
National and State Parks: Frances Slocum State Forest
Additional Information Contacts
Miami County Government Offices. 765-472-3901
Miami County Board of Realtors 765-472-2461
Peru-Miami Chamber of Commerce 765-472-1923

Miami County Communities

AMBOY (town). Covers a land area of 0.354 square miles and a water area of 0 square miles. Located at 40.60° N. Lat.; 85.92° W. Long. Elevation is 815 feet.
Population: 360 (2000); Race: 91.2% White, 0.0% Black, 1.1% Asian, 0.6% American Indian and Alaska Native, 2.5% Hispanic of any race, 2.3% two or more races (2000); Density: 1,017.8 persons per square mile (2000); Age: 22.9% under 18, 16.9% over 64 (2000); Marriage status: 14.6% never married, 75.3% now married, 4.5% widowed, 5.6% divorced (2000); Foreign born: 1.7% (2000); Ancestry (includes multiple ancestries): 19.2% German,

13.3% United States or American, 10.5% Other groups, 6.8% Swiss, 6.5% Dutch (2000).
Economy: In agricultural area. Manufactures doors. Employment by occupation: 8.6% management, 16.6% professional, 12.3% services, 28.8% sales, 0.0% farming, 14.1% construction, 19.6% production (2000).
Income: Per capita income: $19,503 (2000); Median household income: $41,397 (2000); Poverty rate: 7.1% (2000).
Taxes: Total city taxes per capita: $74 (1997); City property taxes per capita: $49 (1997).
Education: High school graduation rate: 75.1% (2000); College graduation rate: 6.6% (2000).
Housing: Homeownership rate: 86.8% (2000); Median home value: $57,800 (2000); Median rent: $329 per month (2000); Median age of housing: 60+ years (2000).
Transportation: Commute to work: 96.3% car, 0.0% public transportation, 0.0% walk, 2.5% work from home (2000); Travel time to work: 14.5% less than 15 minutes, 34.6% 15 to 30 minutes, 36.5% 30 to 45 minutes, 3.1% 45 to 60 minutes, 11.3% 60 minutes or more (2000)

BUNKER HILL (town). Covers a land area of 0.436 square miles and a water area of 0 square miles. Located at 40.65° N. Lat.; 86.10° W. Long. Elevation is 810 feet.
Population: 987 (2000); Race: 96.4% White, 0.8% Black, 0.2% Asian, 0.8% American Indian and Alaska Native, 1.2% Hispanic of any race, 1.4% two or more races (2000); Density: 2,262.6 persons per square mile (2000); Age: 29.1% under 18, 12.0% over 64 (2000); Marriage status: 19.3% never married, 61.2% now married, 5.7% widowed, 13.8% divorced (2000); Foreign born: 2.6% (2000); Ancestry (includes multiple ancestries): 22.7% German, 13.8% English, 12.4% United States or American, 9.0% Irish, 8.4% Other groups (2000).
Economy: In livestock and grain area; dairy products. Limestone. Single-family building permits issued: 8 (2001) / 8 (2000); Multi-family building permits issued: 0 (2001) / 0 (2000); Employment by occupation: 5.9% management, 7.2% professional, 14.5% services, 26.0% sales, 0.7% farming, 17.4% construction, 28.4% production (2000).
Income: Per capita income: $17,000 (2000); Median household income: $36,154 (2000); Poverty rate: 7.1% (2000).
Taxes: Total city taxes per capita: $155 (1997); City property taxes per capita: $130 (1997).
Education: High school graduation rate: 85.6% (2000); College graduation rate: 10.7% (2000).

School District(s)

Maconaquah School Corp (PK-12)
2000 Enrollment: 2,277 765-689-9131
Housing: Homeownership rate: 70.3% (2000); Median home value: $64,900 (2000); Median rent: $290 per month (2000); Median age of housing: 43 years (2000).
Transportation: Commute to work: 94.1% car, 0.0% public transportation, 2.6% walk, 1.7% work from home (2000); Travel time to work: 27.8% less than 15 minutes, 46.6% 15 to 30 minutes, 18.8% 30 to 45 minutes, 0.4% 45 to 60 minutes, 6.4% 60 minutes or more (2000)

CONVERSE (town). Covers a land area of 0.891 square miles and a water area of 0 square miles. Located at 40.58° N. Lat.; 85.86° W. Long. Elevation is 832 feet.
Population: 1,137 (2000); Race: 98.9% White, 0.0% Black, 0.2% Asian, 0.5% American Indian and Alaska Native, 2.3% Hispanic of any race, 0.0% two or more races (2000); Density: 1,276.4 persons per square mile (2000); Age: 29.3% under 18, 16.5% over 64 (2000); Marriage status: 18.0% never married, 60.7% now married, 9.5% widowed, 11.8% divorced (2000); Foreign born: 0.4% (2000); Ancestry (includes multiple ancestries): 21.8% German, 13.8% United States or American, 9.3% English, 8.7% Irish, 5.9% Other groups (2000).
Economy: In livestock and grain area; canned goods. Single-family building permits issued: 2 (2001) / 5 (2000); Multi-family building permits issued: 0 (2001) / 0 (2000); Employment by occupation: 11.2% management, 17.2% professional, 14.1% services, 23.7% sales, 0.0% farming, 8.1% construction, 25.7% production (2000).
Income: Per capita income: $16,317 (2000); Median household income: $33,333 (2000); Poverty rate: 15.7% (2000).
Taxes: Total city taxes per capita: $182 (1997); City property taxes per capita: $135 (1997).
Education: High school graduation rate: 81.2% (2000); College graduation rate: 12.8% (2000).

School District(s)

Oak Hill United School Corp (PK-12)
2000 Enrollment: 1,551 765-395-3341
Housing: Homeownership rate: 78.6% (2000); Median home value: $62,700 (2000); Median rent: $303 per month (2000); Median age of housing: 48 years (2000).
Transportation: Commute to work: 92.3% car, 0.6% public transportation, 5.8% walk, 0.4% work from home (2000); Travel time to work: 22.8% less than 15 minutes, 43.9% 15 to 30 minutes, 27.1% 30 to 45 minutes, 3.0% 45 to 60 minutes, 3.2% 60 minutes or more (2000)

DENVER (town). Covers a land area of 0.233 square miles and a water area of 0 square miles. Located at 40.86° N. Lat.; 86.07° W. Long. Elevation is 709 feet.
Population: 541 (2000); Race: 94.2% White, 0.0% Black, 0.0% Asian, 0.5% American Indian and Alaska Native, 0.8% Hispanic of any race, 5.3% two or more races (2000); Density: 2,318.0 persons per square mile (2000); Age: 30.2% under 18, 10.3% over 64 (2000); Marriage status: 21.6% never married, 58.3% now married, 5.7% widowed, 14.4% divorced (2000); Foreign born: 0.0% (2000); Ancestry (includes multiple ancestries): 29.8% German, 13.4% Irish, 12.7% United States or American, 9.7% Other groups, 6.9% English (2000).
Economy: Poultry, fruit, dairy products, grain. Employment by occupation: 11.3% management, 4.4% professional, 16.0% services, 24.4% sales, 3.3% farming, 5.8% construction, 34.9% production (2000).
Income: Per capita income: $15,224 (2000); Median household income: $36,250 (2000); Poverty rate: 9.5% (2000).
Taxes: Total city taxes per capita: $47 (1997); City property taxes per capita: $38 (1997).
Education: High school graduation rate: 85.0% (2000); College graduation rate: 3.3% (2000).

School District(s)

North Miami Community Schools (PK-12)
2000 Enrollment: 1,201 765-985-3891
Housing: Homeownership rate: 88.0% (2000); Median home value: $58,200 (2000); Median rent: $392 per month (2000); Median age of housing: 60+ years (2000).
Transportation: Commute to work: 94.1% car, 0.0% public transportation, 0.0% walk, 5.9% work from home (2000); Travel time to work: 21.3% less than 15 minutes, 56.7% 15 to 30 minutes, 18.1% 30 to 45 minutes, 1.2% 45 to 60 minutes, 2.8% 60 minutes or more (2000)

GRISSOM AFB (CDP). Covers a land area of 4.197 square miles and a water area of 0 square miles. Located at 40.67° N. Lat.; 86.15° W. Long.
Population: 1,652 (2000); Race: 85.2% White, 6.4% Black, 0.6% Asian, 0.0% American Indian and Alaska Native, 4.0% Hispanic of any race, 7.9% two or more races (2000); Density: 393.6 persons per square mile (2000); Age: 34.8% under 18, 1.2% over 64 (2000); Marriage status: 24.6% never married, 61.1% now married, 0.6% widowed, 13.8% divorced (2000); Foreign born: 1.2% (2000); Ancestry (includes multiple ancestries): 25.9% German, 18.4% Other groups, 11.3% United States or American, 9.0% Irish, 7.3% English (2000).
Economy: Employment by occupation: 10.5% management, 7.8% professional, 20.6% services, 31.0% sales, 0.0% farming, 6.2% construction, 23.8% production (2000).
Income: Per capita income: $15,869 (2000); Median household income: $45,000 (2000); Poverty rate: 8.9% (2000).
Education: High school graduation rate: 90.6% (2000); College graduation rate: 16.8% (2000).
Housing: Homeownership rate: 25.7% (2000); Median home value: $87,500 (2000); Median rent: $547 per month (2000); Median age of housing: 37 years (2000).
Transportation: Commute to work: 98.0% car, 0.0% public transportation, 0.7% walk, 0.7% work from home (2000); Travel time to work: 24.6% less than 15 minutes, 52.2% 15 to 30 minutes, 15.7% 30 to 45 minutes, 3.3% 45 to 60 minutes, 4.1% 60 minutes or more (2000)

MACY (town). Covers a land area of 0.141 square miles and a water area of 0 square miles. Located at 40.96° N. Lat.; 86.12° W. Long. Elevation is 882 feet.
History: Laid out 1860.
Population: 248 (2000); Race: 96.1% White, 0.0% Black, 0.0% Asian, 0.0% American Indian and Alaska Native, 0.0% Hispanic of any race, 3.9% two or more races (2000); Density: 1,755.5 persons per square mile (2000); Age: 32.2% under 18, 6.4% over 64 (2000); Marriage status: 20.2% never married, 73.8% now married, 5.4% widowed, 0.6% divorced (2000); Foreign born:

0.0% (2000); Ancestry (includes multiple ancestries): 21.5% German, 14.6% United States or American, 10.3% Irish, 8.6% English, 5.6% Other groups (2000).
Economy: In agricultural area. Employment by occupation: 0.0% management, 16.1% professional, 15.3% services, 22.0% sales, 0.0% farming, 12.7% construction, 33.9% production (2000).
Income: Per capita income: $14,692 (2000); Median household income: $37,188 (2000); Poverty rate: 2.6% (2000).
Taxes: Total city taxes per capita: $79 (1997); City property taxes per capita: $63 (1997).
Education: High school graduation rate: 83.0% (2000); College graduation rate: 7.1% (2000).
Housing: Homeownership rate: 85.2% (2000); Median home value: $51,300 (2000); Median rent: $194 per month (2000); Median age of housing: 60+ years (2000).
Transportation: Commute to work: 98.2% car, 0.0% public transportation, 1.8% walk, 0.0% work from home (2000); Travel time to work: 10.7% less than 15 minutes, 63.4% 15 to 30 minutes, 14.3% 30 to 45 minutes, 8.0% 45 to 60 minutes, 3.6% 60 minutes or more (2000)

MEXICO (CDP). Covers a land area of 5.479 square miles and a water area of 0 square miles. Located at 40.82° N. Lat.; 86.11° W. Long. Elevation is 700 feet.
History: Mexico was settled largely by German Baptists as a stagecoach stop between Indianapolis and Michigan City.
Population: 984 (2000); Race: 97.4% White, 0.0% Black, 0.0% Asian, 0.0% American Indian and Alaska Native, 0.0% Hispanic of any race, 2.6% two or more races (2000); Density: 179.6 persons per square mile (2000); Age: 26.3% under 18, 10.5% over 64 (2000); Marriage status: 21.3% never married, 58.9% now married, 8.9% widowed, 10.9% divorced (2000); Foreign born: 0.0% (2000); Ancestry (includes multiple ancestries): 29.9% German, 18.6% United States or American, 11.7% Dutch, 7.7% Irish, 6.6% Other groups (2000).
Economy: Employment by occupation: 9.8% management, 11.9% professional, 10.7% services, 27.7% sales, 0.0% farming, 12.6% construction, 27.3% production (2000).
Income: Per capita income: $19,150 (2000); Median household income: $49,234 (2000); Poverty rate: 5.1% (2000).
Education: High school graduation rate: 89.5% (2000); College graduation rate: 9.6% (2000).
Housing: Homeownership rate: 84.9% (2000); Median home value: $84,600 (2000); Median rent: $286 per month (2000); Median age of housing: 35 years (2000).
Transportation: Commute to work: 94.5% car, 0.0% public transportation, 2.9% walk, 1.6% work from home (2000); Travel time to work: 43.8% less than 15 minutes, 26.6% 15 to 30 minutes, 21.4% 30 to 45 minutes, 4.7% 45 to 60 minutes, 3.5% 60 minutes or more (2000)

PERU (city). Aka Bunker Hill Air Force Base. Covers a land area of 4.615 square miles and a water area of 0.043 square miles. Located at 40.75° N. Lat.; 86.06° W. Long. Elevation is 656 feet.
History: Peru's reputation as the Circus City of the World, serving as winter quarters for many circuses, began in the late 1800's when Ben Wallace started the Hagenbeck-Wallace Circus.
Population: 12,994 (2000); Race: 92.9% White, 2.7% Black, 0.4% Asian, 1.1% American Indian and Alaska Native, 2.1% Hispanic of any race, 1.7% two or more races (2000); Density: 2,815.5 persons per square mile (2000); Age: 26.4% under 18, 16.3% over 64 (2000); Marriage status: 21.4% never married, 53.8% now married, 10.3% widowed, 14.4% divorced (2000); Foreign born: 1.2% (2000); Ancestry (includes multiple ancestries): 20.9% German, 13.2% United States or American, 11.7% Irish, 10.2% Other groups, 7.8% English (2000).
Vital Statistics: Birth rate: 159.3 per 10,000 population (1998)
Economy: Single-family building permits issued: 30 (2001) / 21 (2000); Multi-family building permits issued: 0 (2001) / 0 (2000); Employment by occupation: 6.7% management, 11.7% professional, 16.4% services, 21.9% sales, 0.4% farming, 9.6% construction, 33.2% production (2000).
Income: Per capita income: $17,497 (2000); Median household income: $30,668 (2000); Poverty rate: 11.8% (2000).
Taxes: Total city taxes per capita: $280 (2000); City property taxes per capita: $211 (2000).
Education: High school graduation rate: 77.7% (2000); College graduation rate: 8.6% (2000).

School District(s)

Peru Community Schools (KG-12)
2000 Enrollment: 2,544 765-473-3081

Housing: Homeownership rate: 69.0% (2000); Median home value: $55,400 (2000); Median rent: $345 per month (2000); Median age of housing: 59 years (2000).
Hospitals: Dukes Memorial Hospital (158 beds)
Newspapers: The Peru Daily Tribune (6 x week)
Transportation: Commute to work: 92.0% car, 0.1% public transportation, 3.9% walk, 3.2% work from home (2000); Travel time to work: 55.2% less than 15 minutes, 24.4% 15 to 30 minutes, 10.5% 30 to 45 minutes, 4.2% 45 to 60 minutes, 5.8% 60 minutes or more (2000)
Additional Information Contacts
Miami County Board of Realtors 765-472-2461
Peru-Miami Chamber of Commerce 765-472-1923

Monroe County

Located in south central Indiana; drained by the West Fork of the White River, and several creeks. Covers a land area of 394.30 square miles, a water area of 17.00 square miles, and is located in the Eastern Time Zone. The county government was organized in 1818. County seat is Bloomington.

Monroe County is part of the Bloomington, IN MSA. The entire metro area includes: Monroe County

Weather Station: Bloomington Indiana Univ. Elevation: 830 feet

	Jan	Feb	Mar	Apr	May	Jun	Jul	Aug	Sep	Oct	Nov	Dec
High	36	42	52	64	74	82	86	85	78	67	54	42
Low	19	23	32	42	52	62	66	64	56	44	36	25
Precip	2.6	2.6	3.7	4.5	5.1	4.1	4.3	3.9	3.5	3.1	4.0	3.3
Snow	na	na	na	tr	0.0	0.0	0.0	0.0	0.0	0.2	tr	1.6

High and Low temperatures in degrees Fahrenheit; Precipitation and Snow in inches

Population: 120,563 (2000); Race: 91.0% White, 3.0% Black, 3.2% Asian, 0.2% American Indian and Alaska Native, 1.7% Hispanic of any race, 1.8% two or more races (2000); Density: 305.7 persons per square mile (2000); Age: 17.9% under 18, 9.1% over 64 (2000).
Religion: Five largest groups: 10.4% Catholic Church, 4.0% Christian Churches and Churches of Christ, 3.7% The United Methodist Church, 1.9% American Baptist Churches in the USA, 1.7% Churches of Christ (2000).
Economy: Unemployment rate: 2.9% (11/2002); Total civilian labor force: 64,038 (11/2002); Leading industries: 17.1% manufacturing; 15.6% retail trade; 15.1% health care and social assistance (2000); Companies that employ more than 1,000 persons: 4 (2000); Companies that employ more than 100 persons: 54 (2000); Farms: 473 totaling 62,149 acres (1997); Minority business ownership rate: 3.1% (1997); Women business ownership rate: 27.0% (1997); Retail sales per capita: $9,262 (1997). Single-family building permits issued: 495 (2001) / 480 (2000); Multi-family building permits issued: 384 (2001) / 140 (2000).
Income: Per capita income: $18,534 (2000); Median household income: $33,311 (2000); Poverty rate: 18.9% (2000); Bankruptcy rate: 4.57% (2001).
Taxes: Total county taxes per capita: $243 (2000); County property taxes per capita: $173 (2000).
Education: High school graduation rate: 88.5% (2000); College graduation rate: 39.6% (2000).
Housing: Homeownership rate: 53.9% (2000); Median home value: $113,100 (2000); Median rent: $488 per month (2000); Median age of housing: 24 years (2000).
Health: Birth rate: 104.8 per 10,000 population (1998); Age adjusted death rate: 80.5 per 10,000 population (1999); Age adjusted cancer mortality rate: 222.4 deaths per 100,000 population (1999). Number of physicians: 24.0 per 10,000 population (1999); Number of hospital beds: 82.9 per 10,000 population (1999).
Elections: 2000 Presidential election results: 43.6% Gore, 47.6% Bush, 7.4% Nader, 0.4% Buchanan
National and State Parks: Allens Creek State Recreation Area; Fairfax State Recreation Area; North Fork State Wildlife Refuge; Paynetown State Recreation Area
Additional Information Contacts
Monroe County Government Offices.................... 812-349-2550
Bloomington Board of Realtors 812-339-1301
Bloomington Chamber of Commerce 812-336-6381
Ellettsville Chamber of Commerce 812-876-6611
Small Business Development Center.................. 812-339-8937

Monroe County Communities

BLOOMINGTON (city). Covers a land area of 19.735 square miles and a water area of 0.199 square miles. Located at 39.16° N. Lat.; 86.52° W. Long. Elevation is 745 feet.
History: Bloomington was settled in 1815 and developed around the stone quarries and mills. In 1820 Indiana University was founded here. Bloomington was named by a group of early settlers who enjoyed the many flowers on the hillsides.
Population: 69,291 (2000); Race: 87.5% White, 4.2% Black, 5.0% Asian, 0.3% American Indian and Alaska Native, 2.2% Hispanic of any race, 2.1% two or more races (2000); Density: 3,511.1 persons per square mile (2000); Age: 12.4% under 18, 8.0% over 64 (2000); Marriage status: 60.0% never married, 29.0% now married, 3.5% widowed, 7.5% divorced (2000); Foreign born: 8.1% (2000); Ancestry (includes multiple ancestries): 24.9% German, 15.7% Other groups, 13.3% Irish, 10.9% English, 6.7% United States or American (2000).
Vital Statistics: Birth rate: 112.4 per 10,000 population (1998)
Economy: Unemployment rate: 3.5% (11/2002); Total civilian labor force: 33,402 (11/2002); Employment by occupation: 10.8% management, 33.1% professional, 20.0% services, 25.4% sales, 0.1% farming, 4.1% construction, 6.4% production (2000).
Income: Per capita income: $16,481 (2000); Median household income: $25,377 (2000); Poverty rate: 29.6% (2000).
Taxes: Total city taxes per capita: $291 (2000); City property taxes per capita: $209 (2000).
Education: High school graduation rate: 91.2% (2000); College graduation rate: 54.8% (2000).

School District(s)

Monroe County Com Sch Corp (PK-12)
2000 Enrollment: 10,540 812-330-7700

Four-year College(s)

Indiana University-Bloomington (Public)
2001 Enrollment: 37,963 812-855-4848
2001 Tuition: In-state $4,196; Out-of-state $13,930
Housing: Homeownership rate: 35.5% (2000); Median home value: $126,000 (2000); Median rent: $491 per month (2000); Median age of housing: 26 years (2000).
Hospitals: Bloomington Hospital (297 beds)
Safety: Violent crime rate: 16.2 per 10,000 population; Property crime rate: 350.5 per 10,000 population (2001).
Newspapers: Sunday Herald-Times; Herald-Times (7 x week); Indiana Daily Student (5 x week)
Transportation: Commute to work: 76.0% car, 3.0% public transportation, 14.5% walk, 3.3% work from home (2000); Travel time to work: 60.9% less than 15 minutes, 28.6% 15 to 30 minutes, 4.9% 30 to 45 minutes, 1.8% 45 to 60 minutes, 3.8% 60 minutes or more (2000)
Airports: Monroe County
Additional Information Contacts
Bloomington Board of Realtors 812-339-1301
Bloomington Chamber of Commerce 812-336-6381
Small Business Development Center 812-339-8937

ELLETTSVILLE (town). Covers a land area of 2.155 square miles and a water area of 0 square miles. Located at 39.23° N. Lat.; 86.62° W. Long. Elevation is 722 feet.
History: Ellettsville developed around the stone quarries, some of which specialized in fine carving and ornamentation. Ellettsville was platted in 1837 and named for Edward Elletts who had operated a tavern here in the early 1800's.
Population: 5,078 (2000); Race: 96.5% White, 1.8% Black, 0.4% Asian, 0.5% American Indian and Alaska Native, 1.4% Hispanic of any race, 0.9% two or more races (2000); Density: 2,356.8 persons per square mile (2000); Age: 31.4% under 18, 10.0% over 64 (2000); Marriage status: 21.9% never married, 52.4% now married, 6.1% widowed, 19.6% divorced (2000); Foreign born: 1.4% (2000); Ancestry (includes multiple ancestries): 20.0% German, 16.0% United States or American, 13.5% English, 12.2% Other groups, 10.3% Irish (2000).
Economy: Single-family building permits issued: 18 (2001) / 13 (2000); Multi-family building permits issued: 0 (2001) / 16 (2000); Employment by occupation: 11.0% management, 17.5% professional, 14.7% services, 25.7% sales, 0.0% farming, 9.2% construction, 21.8% production (2000).
Income: Per capita income: $16,120 (2000); Median household income: $37,276 (2000); Poverty rate: 9.2% (2000).
Taxes: Total city taxes per capita: $162 (1997); City property taxes per capita: $107 (1997).
Education: High school graduation rate: 85.4% (2000); College graduation rate: 16.9% (2000).

School District(s)

Richland-Bean Blossom C S C (PK-12)
2000 Enrollment: 2,735 812-876-7100
Housing: Homeownership rate: 69.4% (2000); Median home value: $85,100 (2000); Median rent: $421 per month (2000); Median age of housing: 23 years (2000).
Newspapers: The Journal (1 x week)
Transportation: Commute to work: 93.4% car, 0.8% public transportation, 2.9% walk, 1.1% work from home (2000); Travel time to work: 27.9% less than 15 minutes, 51.9% 15 to 30 minutes, 13.4% 30 to 45 minutes, 3.1% 45 to 60 minutes, 3.7% 60 minutes or more (2000)
Additional Information Contacts
Ellettsville Chamber of Commerce 812-876-6611

STINESVILLE (town). Covers a land area of 0.109 square miles and a water area of 0 square miles. Located at 39.29° N. Lat.; 86.65° W. Long. Elevation is 610 feet.
History: Old limestone quarries. Laid out 1855.
Population: 194 (2000); Race: 100.0% White, 0.0% Black, 0.0% Asian, 0.0% American Indian and Alaska Native, 3.4% Hispanic of any race, 0.0% two or more races (2000); Density: 1,783.8 persons per square mile (2000); Age: 37.9% under 18, 13.1% over 64 (2000); Marriage status: 15.1% never married, 59.7% now married, 11.5% widowed, 13.7% divorced (2000); Foreign born: 0.0% (2000); Ancestry (includes multiple ancestries): 35.9% Other groups, 18.0% United States or American, 16.0% German, 9.7% Irish, 6.3% English (2000).
Economy: In agricultural area. Employment by occupation: 7.0% management, 14.1% professional, 29.6% services, 18.3% sales, 0.0% farming, 8.5% construction, 22.5% production (2000).
Income: Per capita income: $11,411 (2000); Median household income: $31,875 (2000); Poverty rate: 1.0% (2000).
Taxes: Total city taxes per capita: $43 (1997); City property taxes per capita: $29 (1997).
Education: High school graduation rate: 57.7% (2000); College graduation rate: 8.1% (2000).
Housing: Homeownership rate: 80.0% (2000); Median home value: $50,000 (2000); Median rent: $450 per month (2000); Median age of housing: 60+ years (2000).
Transportation: Commute to work: 90.6% car, 0.0% public transportation, 6.3% walk, 3.1% work from home (2000); Travel time to work: 11.3% less than 15 minutes, 37.1% 15 to 30 minutes, 24.2% 30 to 45 minutes, 8.1% 45 to 60 minutes, 19.4% 60 minutes or more (2000)

UNIONVILLE (unincorporated postal area, zip code 47468). Covers a land area of 21.994 square miles and a water area of 1.637 square miles. Located at 39.25° N. Lat.; 86.39° W. Long. Elevation is 878 feet.
Population: 1,215 (2000); Race: 99.4% White, 0.0% Black, 0.0% Asian, 0.0% American Indian and Alaska Native, 0.0% Hispanic of any race, 0.3% two or more races (2000); Density: 55.2 persons per square mile (2000); Age: 31.6% under 18, 9.5% over 64 (2000); Marriage status: 19.8% never married, 65.2% now married, 7.3% widowed, 7.7% divorced (2000); Foreign born: 6.2% (2000); Ancestry (includes multiple ancestries): 22.3% German, 14.2% United States or American, 13.2% English, 11.9% Irish, 9.6% Other groups (2000).
Economy: Employment by occupation: 18.0% management, 22.9% professional, 5.8% services, 23.4% sales, 0.0% farming, 10.8% construction, 19.1% production (2000).
Income: Per capita income: $18,520 (2000); Median household income: $45,441 (2000); Poverty rate: 12.8% (2000).
Education: High school graduation rate: 81.9% (2000); College graduation rate: 31.2% (2000).
Housing: Homeownership rate: 85.5% (2000); Median home value: $116,300 (2000); Median rent: $460 per month (2000); Median age of housing: 27 years (2000).
Transportation: Commute to work: 88.6% car, 0.6% public transportation, 5.0% walk, 5.0% work from home (2000); Travel time to work: 8.8% less than 15 minutes, 37.9% 15 to 30 minutes, 25.5% 30 to 45 minutes, 9.7% 45 to 60 minutes, 18.1% 60 minutes or more (2000)

Montgomery County

Located in west central Indiana; drained by Sugar and Raccoon Creeks. Covers a land area of 504.50 square miles, a water area of 0.80 square miles, and is located in the Eastern Time Zone. The county government was organized in 1823. County seat is Crawfordsville.

Population: 37,629 (2000); Race: 96.8% White, 0.8% Black, 0.1% Asian, 0.1% American Indian and Alaska Native, 1.6% Hispanic of any race, 0.8% two or more races (2000); Density: 74.6 persons per square mile (2000); Age: 25.9% under 18, 13.9% over 64 (2000).

Religion: Five largest groups: 11.6% Christian Churches and Churches of Christ, 6.8% The United Methodist Church, 5.2% Catholic Church, 4.3% American Baptist Churches in the USA, 3.6% Christian Church (Disciples of Christ) (2000).

Economy: Unemployment rate: 4.0% (11/2002); Total civilian labor force: 17,261 (11/2002); Leading industries: 41.7% manufacturing; 12.3% retail trade; 9.4% health care and social assistance (2000); Companies that employ more than 1,000 persons: 1 (2000); Companies that employ more than 100 persons: 26 (2000); Farms: 681 totaling 273,258 acres (1997); Minority business ownership rate: 0.0% (1997); Women business ownership rate: 26.1% (1997); Retail sales per capita: $8,096 (1997). Single-family building permits issued: 134 (2001) / 116 (2000); Multi-family building permits issued: 100 (2001) / 0 (2000).

Income: Per capita income: $18,938 (2000); Median household income: $41,297 (2000); Poverty rate: 8.3% (2000); Bankruptcy rate: 7.80% (2001).

Taxes: Total county taxes per capita: $212 (2000); County property taxes per capita: $139 (2000).

Education: High school graduation rate: 85.7% (2000); College graduation rate: 14.7% (2000).

Housing: Homeownership rate: 73.3% (2000); Median home value: $88,800 (2000); Median rent: $388 per month (2000); Median age of housing: 41 years (2000).

Health: Birth rate: 124.9 per 10,000 population (1998); Age adjusted death rate: 97.6 per 10,000 population (1999); Age adjusted cancer mortality rate: 219.0 deaths per 100,000 population (1999). Number of physicians: 10.1 per 10,000 population (1999); Number of hospital beds: 23.7 per 10,000 population (1999).

Elections: 2000 Presidential election results: 29.8% Gore, 67.9% Bush, 1.0% Nader, 0.8% Buchanan

Additional Information Contacts

Montgomery County Government Offices. 765-364-6430
Crawfordsville Chamber of Commerce 765-362-6800
Montgomery County Economic Development. 765-362-6851

Montgomery County Communities

ALAMO (town). Covers a land area of 0.057 square miles and a water area of 0 square miles. Located at 39.98° N. Lat.; 87.05° W. Long. Elevation is 811 feet.

Population: 137 (2000); Race: 80.6% White, 0.0% Black, 0.0% Asian, 0.9% American Indian and Alaska Native, 0.0% Hispanic of any race, 13.9% two or more races (2000); Density: 2,388.5 persons per square mile (2000); Age: 43.5% under 18, 13.9% over 64 (2000); Marriage status: 17.6% never married, 72.1% now married, 0.0% widowed, 10.3% divorced (2000); Foreign born: 6.5% (2000); Ancestry (includes multiple ancestries): 26.9% Other groups, 15.7% United States or American, 12.0% German, 8.3% English, 7.4% Dutch (2000).

Economy: In agricultural area. Employment by occupation: 0.0% management, 0.0% professional, 9.4% services, 21.9% sales, 0.0% farming, 18.8% construction, 50.0% production (2000).

Income: Per capita income: $8,800 (2000); Median household income: $17,500 (2000); Poverty rate: 29.6% (2000).

Taxes: Total city taxes per capita: $33 (1997); City property taxes per capita: $25 (1997).

Education: High school graduation rate: 75.0% (2000); College graduation rate: 3.3% (2000).

Housing: Homeownership rate: 71.8% (2000); Median home value: $24,300 (2000); Median rent: $417 per month (2000); Median age of housing: 36 years (2000).

Transportation: Commute to work: 86.2% car, 0.0% public transportation, 6.9% walk, 6.9% work from home (2000); Travel time to work: 14.8% less than 15 minutes, 66.7% 15 to 30 minutes, 18.5% 30 to 45 minutes, 0.0% 45 to 60 minutes, 0.0% 60 minutes or more (2000)

CRAWFORDSVILLE (city). Covers a land area of 8.378 square miles and a water area of 0 square miles. Located at 40.03° N. Lat.; 86.89° W. Long. Elevation is 769 feet.

History: Crawfordsville was laid out in 1823 by Major Ambrose Whitlock, and named for Colonel William Crawford of Virginia. A prominent resident of Crawfordsville was Civil War General Lew Wallace, better known as the author of the novel "Ben Hur."

Population: 15,243 (2000); Race: 93.5% White, 1.9% Black, 0.3% Asian, 0.2% American Indian and Alaska Native, 3.1% Hispanic of any race, 1.2% two or more races (2000); Density: 1,819.4 persons per square mile (2000); Age: 23.4% under 18, 16.5% over 64 (2000); Marriage status: 25.5% never married, 51.6% now married, 9.8% widowed, 13.1% divorced (2000); Foreign born: 2.9% (2000); Ancestry (includes multiple ancestries): 17.4% German, 12.5% Irish, 10.7% United States or American, 10.5% Other groups, 9.1% English (2000).

Vital Statistics: Birth rate: 148.9 per 10,000 population (1998)

Economy: Single-family building permits issued: 24 (2001) / 11 (2000); Multi-family building permits issued: 100 (2001) / 0 (2000); Employment by occupation: 8.4% management, 14.1% professional, 15.7% services, 23.3% sales, 0.6% farming, 7.7% construction, 30.1% production (2000).

Income: Per capita income: $16,945 (2000); Median household income: $34,571 (2000); Poverty rate: 12.9% (2000).

Taxes: Total city taxes per capita: $361 (2000); City property taxes per capita: $208 (2000).

Education: High school graduation rate: 80.5% (2000); College graduation rate: 14.3% (2000).

School District(s)

Crawfordsville Com Schools (PK-12)
2000 Enrollment: 2,488 765-362-2342

Four-year College(s)

Wabash College (Private, Not-for-profit)
2001 Enrollment: 849 765-361-6100
2001 Tuition: In-state $18,893; Out-of-state $18,893

Housing: Homeownership rate: 58.8% (2000); Median home value: $80,000 (2000); Median rent: $399 per month (2000); Median age of housing: 44 years (2000).

Safety: Violent crime rate: 13.7 per 10,000 population; Property crime rate: 549.3 per 10,000 population (2001).

Newspapers: Journal-Review (6 x week)

Transportation: Commute to work: 90.5% car, 0.3% public transportation, 6.2% walk, 2.0% work from home (2000); Travel time to work: 68.3% less than 15 minutes, 15.6% 15 to 30 minutes, 6.2% 30 to 45 minutes, 5.6% 45 to 60 minutes, 4.3% 60 minutes or more (2000); Amtrak: Service available.

Airports: Crawfordsville Municipal

Additional Information Contacts

Crawfordsville Chamber of Commerce 765-362-6800
Montgomery County Economic Development. 765-362-6851

DARLINGTON (town). Covers a land area of 0.315 square miles and a water area of 0 square miles. Located at 40.10° N. Lat.; 86.77° W. Long. Elevation is 765 feet.

Population: 854 (2000); Race: 99.5% White, 0.0% Black, 0.1% Asian, 0.0% American Indian and Alaska Native, 0.0% Hispanic of any race, 0.0% two or more races (2000); Density: 2,706.9 persons per square mile (2000); Age: 31.1% under 18, 17.4% over 64 (2000); Marriage status: 15.3% never married, 57.0% now married, 12.3% widowed, 15.4% divorced (2000); Foreign born: 0.2% (2000); Ancestry (includes multiple ancestries): 22.5% German, 17.7% Irish, 12.2% English, 7.6% United States or American, 4.9% Other groups (2000).

Economy: Employment by occupation: 5.6% management, 12.2% professional, 11.5% services, 25.3% sales, 0.0% farming, 12.2% construction, 33.2% production (2000).

Income: Per capita income: $15,154 (2000); Median household income: $36,250 (2000); Poverty rate: 7.1% (2000).

Taxes: Total city taxes per capita: $90 (1997); City property taxes per capita: $60 (1997).

Education: High school graduation rate: 85.4% (2000); College graduation rate: 10.3% (2000).

Housing: Homeownership rate: 83.4% (2000); Median home value: $76,600 (2000); Median rent: $303 per month (2000); Median age of housing: 55 years (2000).

Transportation: Commute to work: 93.7% car, 0.8% public transportation, 2.6% walk, 2.9% work from home (2000); Travel time to work: 27.5% less than 15 minutes, 44.7% 15 to 30 minutes, 16.2% 30 to 45 minutes, 5.9% 45 to 60 minutes, 5.7% 60 minutes or more (2000)

LADOGA (town). Covers a land area of 0.502 square miles and a water area of 0 square miles. Located at 39.91° N. Lat.; 86.79° W. Long. Elevation is 826 feet.

Population: 1,047 (2000); Race: 99.3% White, 0.0% Black, 0.0% Asian, 0.0% American Indian and Alaska Native, 0.7% Hispanic of any race, 0.0%

two or more races (2000); Density: 2,085.4 persons per square mile (2000); Age: 30.5% under 18, 17.3% over 64 (2000); Marriage status: 16.6% never married, 67.6% now married, 6.3% widowed, 9.5% divorced (2000); Foreign born: 0.0% (2000); Ancestry (includes multiple ancestries): 16.4% German, 16.2% United States or American, 8.3% Irish, 7.5% English, 5.6% Other groups (2000).

Economy: Agricultural area: corn, soybeans; livestock. Employment by occupation: 9.3% management, 10.4% professional, 17.6% services, 22.3% sales, 0.0% farming, 8.1% construction, 32.3% production (2000).

Income: Per capita income: $16,163 (2000); Median household income: $40,781 (2000); Poverty rate: 7.7% (2000).

Taxes: Total city taxes per capita: $118 (1997); City property taxes per capita: $75 (1997).

Education: High school graduation rate: 85.4% (2000); College graduation rate: 11.5% (2000).

Housing: Homeownership rate: 73.7% (2000); Median home value: $78,000 (2000); Median rent: $403 per month (2000); Median age of housing: 60+ years (2000).

Transportation: Commute to work: 94.6% car, 0.0% public transportation, 3.3% walk, 1.6% work from home (2000); Travel time to work: 27.4% less than 15 minutes, 41.2% 15 to 30 minutes, 11.4% 30 to 45 minutes, 10.7% 45 to 60 minutes, 9.3% 60 minutes or more (2000)

LINDEN (town). Covers a land area of 0.259 square miles and a water area of 0 square miles. Located at 40.18° N. Lat.; 86.90° W. Long. Elevation is 787 feet.

Population: 700 (2000); Race: 99.9% White, 0.1% Black, 0.0% Asian, 0.0% American Indian and Alaska Native, 1.4% Hispanic of any race, 0.0% two or more races (2000); Density: 2,703.8 persons per square mile (2000); Age: 24.8% under 18, 15.1% over 64 (2000); Marriage status: 15.0% never married, 63.6% now married, 8.2% widowed, 13.2% divorced (2000); Foreign born: 0.7% (2000); Ancestry (includes multiple ancestries): 15.0% German, 14.9% United States or American, 7.4% English, 6.9% Irish, 4.5% Other groups (2000).

Economy: In agricultural area. Employment by occupation: 6.5% management, 9.7% professional, 18.9% services, 23.9% sales, 0.0% farming, 7.4% construction, 33.6% production (2000).

Income: Per capita income: $16,733 (2000); Median household income: $36,750 (2000); Poverty rate: 5.0% (2000).

Taxes: Total city taxes per capita: $82 (1997); City property taxes per capita: $54 (1997).

Education: High school graduation rate: 87.5% (2000); College graduation rate: 10.0% (2000).

School District(s)

North Montgomery Com Sch Corp (KG-12)
2000 Enrollment: 2,069 765-339-7262

Housing: Homeownership rate: 76.4% (2000); Median home value: $77,800 (2000); Median rent: $330 per month (2000); Median age of housing: 44 years (2000).

Transportation: Commute to work: 94.2% car, 0.0% public transportation, 3.0% walk, 2.1% work from home (2000); Travel time to work: 28.8% less than 15 minutes, 35.3% 15 to 30 minutes, 20.7% 30 to 45 minutes, 4.6% 45 to 60 minutes, 10.5% 60 minutes or more (2000)

NEW MARKET (town). Covers a land area of 0.320 square miles and a water area of 0 square miles. Located at 39.95° N. Lat.; 86.92° W. Long. Elevation is 810 feet.

Population: 659 (2000); Race: 99.7% White, 0.0% Black, 0.0% Asian, 0.0% American Indian and Alaska Native, 0.0% Hispanic of any race, 0.3% two or more races (2000); Density: 2,059.2 persons per square mile (2000); Age: 31.1% under 18, 11.6% over 64 (2000); Marriage status: 13.4% never married, 70.1% now married, 6.9% widowed, 9.6% divorced (2000); Foreign born: 1.1% (2000); Ancestry (includes multiple ancestries): 19.0% United States or American, 15.6% German, 8.3% Irish, 6.2% English, 2.6% French (except Basque) (2000).

Economy: In agricultural area. Manufacturing: grain mixing. Employment by occupation: 5.4% management, 16.7% professional, 9.6% services, 19.2% sales, 0.6% farming, 12.8% construction, 35.6% production (2000).

Income: Per capita income: $17,937 (2000); Median household income: $45,385 (2000); Poverty rate: 0.5% (2000).

Taxes: Total city taxes per capita: $93 (1997); City property taxes per capita: $71 (1997).

Education: High school graduation rate: 93.0% (2000); College graduation rate: 8.2% (2000).

School District(s)

South Montgomery Com Sch Corp (KG-12)
2000 Enrollment: 2,141 765-866-0203

Housing: Homeownership rate: 77.5% (2000); Median home value: $75,700 (2000); Median rent: $367 per month (2000); Median age of housing: 46 years (2000).

Transportation: Commute to work: 91.2% car, 0.0% public transportation, 3.6% walk, 5.2% work from home (2000); Travel time to work: 32.8% less than 15 minutes, 46.9% 15 to 30 minutes, 7.9% 30 to 45 minutes, 4.5% 45 to 60 minutes, 7.9% 60 minutes or more (2000)

NEW RICHMOND (town). Covers a land area of 0.179 square miles and a water area of 0 square miles. Located at 40.19° N. Lat.; 86.97° W. Long. Elevation is 782 feet.

Population: 349 (2000); Race: 96.8% White, 1.2% Black, 0.0% Asian, 0.0% American Indian and Alaska Native, 0.3% Hispanic of any race, 2.1% two or more races (2000); Density: 1,950.0 persons per square mile (2000); Age: 26.3% under 18, 15.9% over 64 (2000); Marriage status: 16.8% never married, 68.3% now married, 8.4% widowed, 6.5% divorced (2000); Foreign born: 0.0% (2000); Ancestry (includes multiple ancestries): 20.9% German, 9.7% United States or American, 7.7% Irish, 7.4% Other groups, 5.6% English (2000).

Economy: In agricultural area. Alfalfa. Employment by occupation: 8.6% management, 14.2% professional, 7.4% services, 23.5% sales, 0.0% farming, 11.7% construction, 34.6% production (2000).

Income: Per capita income: $17,001 (2000); Median household income: $43,438 (2000); Poverty rate: 3.8% (2000).

Taxes: Total city taxes per capita: $123 (1997); City property taxes per capita: $82 (1997).

Education: High school graduation rate: 80.6% (2000); College graduation rate: 7.9% (2000).

Housing: Homeownership rate: 85.2% (2000); Median home value: $69,800 (2000); Median rent: $308 per month (2000); Median age of housing: 57 years (2000).

Transportation: Commute to work: 94.8% car, 1.3% public transportation, 0.0% walk, 3.9% work from home (2000); Travel time to work: 18.2% less than 15 minutes, 34.5% 15 to 30 minutes, 29.7% 30 to 45 minutes, 8.8% 45 to 60 minutes, 8.8% 60 minutes or more (2000)

NEW ROSS (town). Covers a land area of 0.290 square miles and a water area of 0 square miles. Located at 39.96° N. Lat.; 86.71° W. Long. Elevation is 890 feet.

History: New Ross grew as a trading center for surrounding farms.

Population: 334 (2000); Race: 96.0% White, 0.0% Black, 0.0% Asian, 0.0% American Indian and Alaska Native, 4.0% Hispanic of any race, 0.0% two or more races (2000); Density: 1,153.2 persons per square mile (2000); Age: 32.0% under 18, 11.0% over 64 (2000); Marriage status: 11.0% never married, 67.8% now married, 12.3% widowed, 8.9% divorced (2000); Foreign born: 0.6% (2000); Ancestry (includes multiple ancestries): 21.6% German, 14.6% Other groups, 6.7% Scottish, 6.1% United States or American, 5.5% Irish (2000).

Economy: Employment by occupation: 10.6% management, 11.2% professional, 13.7% services, 13.7% sales, 0.0% farming, 21.1% construction, 29.8% production (2000).

Income: Per capita income: $15,834 (2000); Median household income: $38,250 (2000); Poverty rate: 4.9% (2000).

Taxes: Total city taxes per capita: $55 (1997); City property taxes per capita: $35 (1997).

Education: High school graduation rate: 89.8% (2000); College graduation rate: 9.7% (2000).

Housing: Homeownership rate: 91.9% (2000); Median home value: $74,400 (2000); Median rent: $336 per month (2000); Median age of housing: 60+ years (2000).

Transportation: Commute to work: 95.6% car, 0.0% public transportation, 3.2% walk, 0.0% work from home (2000); Travel time to work: 16.5% less than 15 minutes, 48.7% 15 to 30 minutes, 23.4% 30 to 45 minutes, 8.9% 45 to 60 minutes, 2.5% 60 minutes or more (2000)

WAVELAND (town). Covers a land area of 0.361 square miles and a water area of 0 square miles. Located at 39.87° N. Lat.; 87.04° W. Long. Elevation is 731 feet.

History: Laid out 1835.

Population: 416 (2000); Race: 98.3% White, 0.0% Black, 0.0% Asian, 0.0% American Indian and Alaska Native, 1.7% Hispanic of any race, 0.0% two or more races (2000); Density: 1,151.6 persons per square mile (2000); Age: 20.7% under 18, 19.5% over 64 (2000); Marriage status: 17.8% never

married, 64.4% now married, 7.6% widowed, 10.2% divorced (2000); Foreign born: 0.0% (2000); Ancestry (includes multiple ancestries): 20.2% United States or American, 19.3% German, 14.0% Irish, 11.2% English, 5.2% Dutch (2000).
Economy: Agricultural area: grain; livestock. Employment by occupation: 1.4% management, 17.4% professional, 15.0% services, 18.8% sales, 1.4% farming, 16.0% construction, 30.0% production (2000).
Income: Per capita income: $17,970 (2000); Median household income: $43,036 (2000); Poverty rate: 2.9% (2000).
Taxes: Total city taxes per capita: $34 (1997); City property taxes per capita: $16 (1997).
Education: High school graduation rate: 82.2% (2000); College graduation rate: 12.2% (2000).
Housing: Homeownership rate: 84.8% (2000); Median home value: $70,600 (2000); Median rent: $392 per month (2000); Median age of housing: 60+ years (2000).
Transportation: Commute to work: 92.9% car, 0.0% public transportation, 5.2% walk, 1.9% work from home (2000); Travel time to work: 18.9% less than 15 minutes, 50.0% 15 to 30 minutes, 13.6% 30 to 45 minutes, 1.5% 45 to 60 minutes, 16.0% 60 minutes or more (2000)

WAYNETOWN (town). Covers a land area of 0.436 square miles and a water area of 0 square miles. Located at 40.08° N. Lat.; 87.06° W. Long. Elevation is 750 feet.
History: Waynetown developed around the tile factories and brick kilns that made use of the clay in the area.
Population: 909 (2000); Race: 98.4% White, 0.4% Black, 0.0% Asian, 0.0% American Indian and Alaska Native, 1.0% Hispanic of any race, 1.2% two or more races (2000); Density: 2,085.8 persons per square mile (2000); Age: 22.9% under 18, 15.0% over 64 (2000); Marriage status: 17.1% never married, 64.5% now married, 7.6% widowed, 10.8% divorced (2000); Foreign born: 1.1% (2000); Ancestry (includes multiple ancestries): 15.6% United States or American, 15.3% German, 8.2% Irish, 7.6% English, 5.9% Other groups (2000).
Economy: Employment by occupation: 6.9% management, 12.2% professional, 10.4% services, 28.0% sales, 1.1% farming, 8.0% construction, 33.3% production (2000).
Income: Per capita income: $16,328 (2000); Median household income: $37,188 (2000); Poverty rate: 8.6% (2000).
Taxes: Total city taxes per capita: $86 (1997); City property taxes per capita: $56 (1997).
Education: High school graduation rate: 88.2% (2000); College graduation rate: 9.5% (2000).
Housing: Homeownership rate: 78.2% (2000); Median home value: $74,700 (2000); Median rent: $306 per month (2000); Median age of housing: 56 years (2000).
Transportation: Commute to work: 91.4% car, 0.5% public transportation, 4.5% walk, 2.9% work from home (2000); Travel time to work: 13.6% less than 15 minutes, 61.7% 15 to 30 minutes, 9.8% 30 to 45 minutes, 7.9% 45 to 60 minutes, 7.0% 60 minutes or more (2000)

WINGATE (town). Covers a land area of 0.275 square miles and a water area of 0 square miles. Located at 40.17° N. Lat.; 87.07° W. Long. Elevation is 769 feet.
Population: 299 (2000); Race: 100.0% White, 0.0% Black, 0.0% Asian, 0.0% American Indian and Alaska Native, 0.0% Hispanic of any race, 0.0% two or more races (2000); Density: 1,086.0 persons per square mile (2000); Age: 36.5% under 18, 18.6% over 64 (2000); Marriage status: 18.6% never married, 55.0% now married, 11.4% widowed, 15.0% divorced (2000); Foreign born: 0.0% (2000); Ancestry (includes multiple ancestries): 23.0% United States or American, 6.0% German, 5.7% English, 5.3% Scotch-Irish, 4.7% Other groups (2000).
Economy: In agricultural area. Employment by occupation: 0.8% management, 19.2% professional, 13.6% services, 16.0% sales, 0.0% farming, 4.0% construction, 46.4% production (2000).
Income: Per capita income: $14,123 (2000); Median household income: $28,750 (2000); Poverty rate: 22.2% (2000).
Taxes: Total city taxes per capita: $197 (1997); City property taxes per capita: $129 (1997).
Education: High school graduation rate: 82.4% (2000); College graduation rate: 3.7% (2000).
Housing: Homeownership rate: 62.0% (2000); Median home value: $62,200 (2000); Median rent: $333 per month (2000); Median age of housing: 46 years (2000).
Transportation: Commute to work: 97.4% car, 0.0% public transportation, 1.7% walk, 0.0% work from home (2000); Travel time to work: 6.8% less than 15 minutes, 45.3% 15 to 30 minutes, 26.5% 30 to 45 minutes, 17.1% 45 to 60 minutes, 4.3% 60 minutes or more (2000)

Morgan County

Located in central Indiana; drained by the West Fork of the White River, Whitelick River, and Camp Creek. Covers a land area of 406.50 square miles, a water area of 2.90 square miles, and is located in the Eastern Time Zone. The county government was organized in 1821. County seat is Martinsville.

Morgan County is part of the Indianapolis, IN MSA. The entire metro area includes: Boone County; Hamilton County; Hancock County; Hendricks County; Johnson County; Madison County; Marion County; Morgan County; Shelby County

Weather Station: Martinsville 2 SW Elevation: 606 feet

	Jan	Feb	Mar	Apr	May	Jun	Jul	Aug	Sep	Oct	Nov	Dec
High	36	41	51	63	73	81	85	84	78	66	53	41
Low	18	21	30	40	49	59	63	61	52	40	33	24
Precip	2.5	2.4	3.5	4.3	4.8	3.9	4.2	4.0	3.1	3.0	3.9	3.0
Snow	6.7	4.8	2.6	tr	0.0	0.0	0.0	0.0	0.0	0.2	0.7	2.7

High and Low temperatures in degrees Fahrenheit; Precipitation and Snow in inches

Population: 66,689 (2000); Race: 98.3% White, 0.1% Black, 0.4% Asian, 0.3% American Indian and Alaska Native, 0.4% Hispanic of any race, 0.8% two or more races (2000); Density: 164.1 persons per square mile (2000); Age: 27.2% under 18, 10.7% over 64 (2000).
Religion: Five largest groups: 5.5% Christian Churches and Churches of Christ, 4.8% Southern Baptist Convention, 4.7% Catholic Church, 4.0% American Baptist Churches in the USA, 3.6% Christian Church (Disciples of Christ) (2000).
Economy: Unemployment rate: 3.9% (11/2002); Total civilian labor force: 37,192 (11/2002); Leading industries: 20.3% manufacturing; 20.1% retail trade; 12.9% health care and social assistance (2000); Companies that employ more than 1,000 persons: 1 (2000); Companies that employ more than 100 persons: 16 (2000); Farms: 601 totaling 133,958 acres (1997); Minority business ownership rate: 0.0% (1997); Women business ownership rate: 20.1% (1997); Retail sales per capita: $6,688 (1997). Single-family building permits issued: 502 (2001) / 551 (2000); Multi-family building permits issued: 22 (2001) / 32 (2000).
Income: Per capita income: $20,657 (2000); Median household income: $47,739 (2000); Poverty rate: 6.6% (2000); Bankruptcy rate: 7.33% (2001).
Taxes: Total county taxes per capita: $280 (2000); County property taxes per capita: $169 (2000).
Education: High school graduation rate: 80.7% (2000); College graduation rate: 12.6% (2000).
Housing: Homeownership rate: 79.7% (2000); Median home value: $116,200 (2000); Median rent: $436 per month (2000); Median age of housing: 27 years (2000).
Health: Birth rate: 138.9 per 10,000 population (1998); Age adjusted death rate: 87.9 per 10,000 population (1999); Age adjusted cancer mortality rate: 212.5 deaths per 100,000 population (1999). Air Quality Index: 51% good, 49% moderate, 0% unhealthy (percent of days in 2000). Number of physicians: 8.7 per 10,000 population (1999); Number of hospital beds: 21.0 per 10,000 population (1999).
Elections: 2000 Presidential election results: 28.3% Gore, 69.4% Bush, 0.7% Nader, 0.9% Buchanan
National and State Parks: Bradford Woods State Reservation; Morgan Monroe State Forest
Additional Information Contacts
Morgan County Government Offices 765-342-1001
Martinsville Chamber of Commerce 765-342-8110
Mooresville Chamber of Commerce 317-831-6509

Morgan County Communities

BETHANY (town). Covers a land area of 0.083 square miles and a water area of 0.011 square miles. Located at 39.53° N. Lat.; 86.37° W. Long. Elevation is 648 feet.
Population: 94 (2000); Race: 100.0% White, 0.0% Black, 0.0% Asian, 0.0% American Indian and Alaska Native, 0.0% Hispanic of any race, 0.0% two or more races (2000); Density: 1,133.6 persons per square mile (2000); Age: 38.5% under 18, 1.9% over 64 (2000); Marriage status: 38.6% never married, 43.2% now married, 0.0% widowed, 18.2% divorced (2000); Foreign born: 0.0% (2000); Ancestry (includes multiple ancestries): 30.8% United States or

American, 23.1% Other groups, 3.8% Irish, 3.8% Czech, 3.8% German (2000).
Economy: Employment by occupation: 0.0% management, 0.0% professional, 8.0% services, 32.0% sales, 0.0% farming, 40.0% construction, 20.0% production (2000).
Income: Per capita income: $16,967 (2000); Median household income: $22,344 (2000); Poverty rate: 1.9% (2000).
Taxes: Total city taxes per capita: $40 (1997); City property taxes per capita: $40 (1997).
Education: High school graduation rate: 95.7% (2000); College graduation rate: 8.7% (2000).
Housing: Homeownership rate: 81.0% (2000); Median home value: $65,000 (2000); Median rent: $400 per month (2000); Median age of housing: 60+ years (2000).
Transportation: Commute to work: 92.0% car, 0.0% public transportation, 0.0% walk, 8.0% work from home (2000); Travel time to work: 0.0% less than 15 minutes, 17.4% 15 to 30 minutes, 39.1% 30 to 45 minutes, 13.0% 45 to 60 minutes, 30.4% 60 minutes or more (2000)

BROOKLYN (town). Covers a land area of 0.777 square miles and a water area of 0.019 square miles. Located at 39.54° N. Lat.; 86.37° W. Long. Elevation is 646 feet.
History: A supply of clay near Brooklyn provided the material for the manufacture of drain tile and brick. A brief gold rush took place in the early 1900's at Gold Creek, near Brooklyn.
Population: 1,545 (2000); Race: 95.5% White, 0.0% Black, 0.0% Asian, 0.6% American Indian and Alaska Native, 1.4% Hispanic of any race, 3.7% two or more races (2000); Density: 1,988.5 persons per square mile (2000); Age: 27.2% under 18, 8.3% over 64 (2000); Marriage status: 20.4% never married, 62.7% now married, 6.3% widowed, 10.6% divorced (2000); Foreign born: 0.6% (2000); Ancestry (includes multiple ancestries): 19.3% German, 14.0% United States or American, 12.2% Other groups, 10.6% Irish, 9.5% English (2000).
Economy: Employment by occupation: 7.0% management, 10.2% professional, 12.7% services, 28.3% sales, 0.4% farming, 19.3% construction, 22.1% production (2000).
Income: Per capita income: $18,242 (2000); Median household income: $42,880 (2000); Poverty rate: 9.5% (2000).
Taxes: Total city taxes per capita: $40 (1997); City property taxes per capita: $40 (1997).
Education: High school graduation rate: 76.6% (2000); College graduation rate: 8.3% (2000).
Housing: Homeownership rate: 77.5% (2000); Median home value: $99,100 (2000); Median rent: $459 per month (2000); Median age of housing: 25 years (2000).
Transportation: Commute to work: 96.0% car, 0.5% public transportation, 0.2% walk, 2.6% work from home (2000); Travel time to work: 17.5% less than 15 minutes, 30.2% 15 to 30 minutes, 37.5% 30 to 45 minutes, 11.8% 45 to 60 minutes, 3.0% 60 minutes or more (2000)

MARTINSVILLE (city). Covers a land area of 4.464 square miles and a water area of 0.010 square miles. Located at 39.42° N. Lat.; 86.42° W. Long. Elevation is 607 feet.
History: Prospectors drilling for gas in Martinsville discovered artesian wells of therapeutic waters, giving the town the nickname of Artesian City.
Population: 11,698 (2000); Race: 98.5% White, 0.1% Black, 0.1% Asian, 0.0% American Indian and Alaska Native, 0.5% Hispanic of any race, 0.8% two or more races (2000); Density: 2,620.6 persons per square mile (2000); Age: 25.0% under 18, 15.5% over 64 (2000); Marriage status: 20.7% never married, 55.1% now married, 9.5% widowed, 14.6% divorced (2000); Foreign born: 0.7% (2000); Ancestry (includes multiple ancestries): 28.0% United States or American, 15.5% German, 11.0% Irish, 8.8% Other groups, 6.8% English (2000).
Vital Statistics: Birth rate: 204.3 per 10,000 population (1998)
Economy: Single-family building permits issued: 49 (2001) / 32 (2000); Multi-family building permits issued: 12 (2001) / 10 (2000); Employment by occupation: 8.1% management, 11.6% professional, 17.8% services, 23.6% sales, 0.1% farming, 18.8% construction, 19.9% production (2000).
Income: Per capita income: $17,664 (2000); Median household income: $32,746 (2000); Poverty rate: 11.6% (2000).
Taxes: Total city taxes per capita: $182 (1997); City property taxes per capita: $168 (1997).
Education: High school graduation rate: 71.6% (2000); College graduation rate: 10.7% (2000).

School District(s)

M S D Martinsville Schools (PK-12)
2000 Enrollment: 5,421 765-342-6641
Housing: Homeownership rate: 60.6% (2000); Median home value: $90,100 (2000); Median rent: $413 per month (2000); Median age of housing: 38 years (2000).
Hospitals: Morgan Hospital Medical Centre (106 beds)
Safety: Violent crime rate: 18.7 per 10,000 population; Property crime rate: 630.7 per 10,000 population (2001).
Newspapers: Reporter-Times (7 x week)
Transportation: Commute to work: 92.5% car, 0.1% public transportation, 3.8% walk, 2.0% work from home (2000); Travel time to work: 47.2% less than 15 minutes, 11.6% 15 to 30 minutes, 17.3% 30 to 45 minutes, 14.2% 45 to 60 minutes, 9.7% 60 minutes or more (2000)
Additional Information Contacts
Martinsville Chamber of Commerce 765-342-8110

MONROVIA (town). Covers a land area of 0.886 square miles and a water area of 0 square miles. Located at 39.57° N. Lat.; 86.48° W. Long. Elevation is 808 feet.
History: Laid out 1834.
Population: 628 (2000); Race: 99.7% White, 0.0% Black, 0.0% Asian, 0.0% American Indian and Alaska Native, 0.0% Hispanic of any race, 0.3% two or more races (2000); Density: 709.1 persons per square mile (2000); Age: 20.6% under 18, 16.2% over 64 (2000); Marriage status: 22.5% never married, 59.6% now married, 6.1% widowed, 11.8% divorced (2000); Foreign born: 0.0% (2000); Ancestry (includes multiple ancestries): 26.9% United States or American, 21.1% German, 8.4% Irish, 5.5% Other groups, 4.9% English (2000).
Economy: Hogs; soybeans, corn, apples. Employment by occupation: 6.8% management, 14.8% professional, 12.8% services, 29.1% sales, 0.6% farming, 16.3% construction, 19.6% production (2000).
Income: Per capita income: $20,366 (2000); Median household income: $49,583 (2000); Poverty rate: 8.6% (2000).
Education: High school graduation rate: 84.1% (2000); College graduation rate: 11.1% (2000).

School District(s)

Monroe-Gregg School District (PK-12)
2000 Enrollment: 1,335 317-996-3720
Housing: Homeownership rate: 75.7% (2000); Median home value: $88,800 (2000); Median rent: $441 per month (2000); Median age of housing: 48 years (2000).
Transportation: Commute to work: 92.2% car, 0.0% public transportation, 4.5% walk, 2.7% work from home (2000); Travel time to work: 17.9% less than 15 minutes, 26.9% 15 to 30 minutes, 43.2% 30 to 45 minutes, 11.4% 45 to 60 minutes, 0.6% 60 minutes or more (2000)

MOORESVILLE (town). Covers a land area of 5.536 square miles and a water area of 0.016 square miles. Located at 39.60° N. Lat.; 86.36° W. Long. Elevation is 690 feet.
History: Laid out 1824.
Population: 9,273 (2000); Race: 99.0% White, 0.0% Black, 0.0% Asian, 0.4% American Indian and Alaska Native, 0.3% Hispanic of any race, 0.6% two or more races (2000); Density: 1,675.0 persons per square mile (2000); Age: 26.7% under 18, 11.5% over 64 (2000); Marriage status: 20.1% never married, 59.6% now married, 6.9% widowed, 13.4% divorced (2000); Foreign born: 0.3% (2000); Ancestry (includes multiple ancestries): 26.3% United States or American, 22.0% German, 12.9% Irish, 8.1% English, 5.3% Other groups (2000).
Economy: Agricultural area: grain, fruit; dairy products. Varied manufacturing. Single-family building permits issued: 230 (2001) / 219 (2000); Multi-family building permits issued: 10 (2001) / 22 (2000); Employment by occupation: 10.4% management, 14.1% professional, 15.2% services, 27.6% sales, 0.0% farming, 13.8% construction, 19.0% production (2000).
Income: Per capita income: $21,504 (2000); Median household income: $47,292 (2000); Poverty rate: 4.3% (2000).
Taxes: Total city taxes per capita: $257 (1997); City property taxes per capita: $205 (1997).
Education: High school graduation rate: 84.3% (2000); College graduation rate: 15.5% (2000).

School District(s)

Mooresville Con School Corp (PK-12)
2000 Enrollment: 4,023 317-831-0950

Housing: Homeownership rate: 71.0% (2000); Median home value: $112,700 (2000); Median rent: $444 per month (2000); Median age of housing: 28 years (2000).
Hospitals: Saint Francis Mooresville
Safety: Violent crime rate: 9.7 per 10,000 population; Property crime rate: 320.6 per 10,000 population (2001).
Newspapers: The Times (2 x week)
Transportation: Commute to work: 95.0% car, 0.0% public transportation, 1.9% walk, 1.9% work from home (2000); Travel time to work: 29.8% less than 15 minutes, 37.2% 15 to 30 minutes, 24.9% 30 to 45 minutes, 4.5% 45 to 60 minutes, 3.5% 60 minutes or more (2000)
Additional Information Contacts
Mooresville Chamber of Commerce 317-831-6509

MORGANTOWN (town). Covers a land area of 0.382 square miles and a water area of 0 square miles. Located at 39.37° N. Lat.; 86.26° W. Long. Elevation is 680 feet.
History: Laid out 1831.
Population: 964 (2000); Race: 99.2% White, 0.0% Black, 0.2% Asian, 0.2% American Indian and Alaska Native, 0.5% Hispanic of any race, 0.0% two or more races (2000); Density: 2,521.6 persons per square mile (2000); Age: 24.1% under 18, 18.7% over 64 (2000); Marriage status: 21.0% never married, 51.8% now married, 17.1% widowed, 10.1% divorced (2000); Foreign born: 0.2% (2000); Ancestry (includes multiple ancestries): 32.6% United States or American, 16.6% Irish, 14.3% German, 12.3% English, 9.3% Other groups (2000).
Economy: In agricultural area. Single-family building permits issued: 2 (2001) / 4 (2000); Multi-family building permits issued: 0 (2001) / 0 (2000); Employment by occupation: 6.7% management, 6.1% professional, 21.5% services, 25.7% sales, 0.6% farming, 20.0% construction, 19.4% production (2000).
Income: Per capita income: $17,504 (2000); Median household income: $33,158 (2000); Poverty rate: 8.3% (2000).
Taxes: Total city taxes per capita: $107 (1997); City property taxes per capita: $103 (1997).
Education: High school graduation rate: 72.5% (2000); College graduation rate: 6.1% (2000).
Housing: Homeownership rate: 63.9% (2000); Median home value: $79,200 (2000); Median rent: $433 per month (2000); Median age of housing: 46 years (2000).
Transportation: Commute to work: 86.4% car, 0.0% public transportation, 11.0% walk, 2.5% work from home (2000); Travel time to work: 24.2% less than 15 minutes, 25.5% 15 to 30 minutes, 23.5% 30 to 45 minutes, 14.6% 45 to 60 minutes, 12.2% 60 minutes or more (2000)

PARAGON (town). Covers a land area of 0.251 square miles and a water area of 0 square miles. Located at 39.39° N. Lat.; 86.56° W. Long. Elevation is 580 feet.
Population: 663 (2000); Race: 99.2% White, 0.0% Black, 0.0% Asian, 0.0% American Indian and Alaska Native, 0.9% Hispanic of any race, 0.8% two or more races (2000); Density: 2,640.8 persons per square mile (2000); Age: 28.4% under 18, 12.3% over 64 (2000); Marriage status: 15.0% never married, 67.3% now married, 5.8% widowed, 11.9% divorced (2000); Foreign born: 0.3% (2000); Ancestry (includes multiple ancestries): 22.3% United States or American, 15.2% German, 12.3% Other groups, 11.7% English, 8.6% Irish (2000).
Economy: Agricultural area. Single-family building permits issued: 0 (2001) / 0 (2000); Multi-family building permits issued: 0 (2001) / 0 (2000); Employment by occupation: 5.1% management, 2.4% professional, 11.8% services, 15.8% sales, 0.0% farming, 21.9% construction, 43.1% production (2000).
Income: Per capita income: $14,193 (2000); Median household income: $37,333 (2000); Poverty rate: 13.3% (2000).
Taxes: Total city taxes per capita: $70 (1997); City property taxes per capita: $60 (1997).
Education: High school graduation rate: 65.4% (2000); College graduation rate: 1.0% (2000).
Housing: Homeownership rate: 67.9% (2000); Median home value: $76,400 (2000); Median rent: $429 per month (2000); Median age of housing: 44 years (2000).
Transportation: Commute to work: 85.4% car, 2.7% public transportation, 9.2% walk, 1.4% work from home (2000); Travel time to work: 22.1% less than 15 minutes, 38.3% 15 to 30 minutes, 12.8% 30 to 45 minutes, 14.8% 45 to 60 minutes, 12.1% 60 minutes or more (2000)

Newton County

Located in northwestern Indiana; bounded on the west by Illinois, and on the north by the Kankakee River; also drained by the Iroquois River. Covers a land area of 401.80 square miles, a water area of 1.70 square miles, and is located in the Central Time Zone. The county government was organized in 1857. County seat is Kentland.

Weather Station: Kentland — Elevation: 692 feet

	Jan	Feb	Mar	Apr	May	Jun	Jul	Aug	Sep	Oct	Nov	Dec
High	31	37	49	62	74	83	86	84	78	66	50	37
Low	15	19	30	39	50	60	63	61	54	42	33	21
Precip	1.6	1.5	2.8	3.5	4.3	4.3	4.2	3.9	3.6	2.9	3.4	2.6
Snow	7.5	6.8	3.2	0.8	0.0	0.0	0.0	0.0	0.0	0.1	2.0	6.3

High and Low temperatures in degrees Fahrenheit; Precipitation and Snow in inches

Population: 14,566 (2000); Race: 97.1% White, 0.2% Black, 0.4% Asian, 0.5% American Indian and Alaska Native, 2.9% Hispanic of any race, 0.6% two or more races (2000); Density: 36.2 persons per square mile (2000); Age: 26.5% under 18, 13.0% over 64 (2000).
Religion: Five largest groups: 9.0% Catholic Church, 7.5% The United Methodist Church, 3.8% Christian Church (Disciples of Christ), 3.7% American Baptist Churches in the USA, 3.1% Southern Baptist Convention (2000).
Economy: Unemployment rate: 5.8% (11/2002); Total civilian labor force: 6,139 (11/2002); Leading industries: 45.9% manufacturing; 14.2% retail trade; 8.3% construction (2000); Companies that employ more than 1,000 persons: 0 (2000); Companies that employ more than 100 persons: 6 (2000); Farms: 381 totaling 207,315 acres (1997); Minority business ownership rate: 0.0% (1997); Women business ownership rate: 20.6% (1997); Retail sales per capita: $4,804 (1997). Single-family building permits issued: 82 (2001) / 87 (2000); Multi-family building permits issued: 0 (2001) / 11 (2000).
Income: Per capita income: $17,755 (2000); Median household income: $40,944 (2000); Poverty rate: 6.9% (2000); Bankruptcy rate: 6.39% (2001).
Taxes: Total county taxes per capita: $289 (1997); County property taxes per capita: $212 (1997).
Education: High school graduation rate: 78.7% (2000); College graduation rate: 9.6% (2000).
Housing: Homeownership rate: 80.0% (2000); Median home value: $87,500 (2000); Median rent: $352 per month (2000); Median age of housing: 38 years (2000).
Health: Birth rate: 106.4 per 10,000 population (1998); Age adjusted death rate: 91.6 per 10,000 population (1999); Age adjusted cancer mortality rate: 216.5 deaths per 100,000 population (1999). Number of physicians: 1.4 per 10,000 population (1999); Number of hospital beds: n/a (1999).
Elections: 2000 Presidential election results: 38.1% Gore, 59.0% Bush, 0.5% Nader, 1.6% Buchanan
National and State Parks: La Salle State Fish and Wildlife Area; Willow Slough State Game Preserve
Additional Information Contacts
Newton County Government Offices 219-474-6081
Brook Chamber of Commerce 219-275-7731
Kentland Area Chamber of Commerce 219-474-6665

Newton County Communities

BROOK (town). Covers a land area of 0.661 square miles and a water area of 0.009 square miles. Located at 40.86° N. Lat.; 87.36° W. Long. Elevation is 646 feet.
History: An early industry in Brook was the Hess Manufacturing Company, whose cosmetics line started when a local druggist concocted witch hazel lotion in a copper clothes boiler.
Population: 1,062 (2000); Race: 94.2% White, 0.4% Black, 0.4% Asian, 0.8% American Indian and Alaska Native, 10.4% Hispanic of any race, 0.3% two or more races (2000); Density: 1,607.2 persons per square mile (2000); Age: 28.6% under 18, 13.0% over 64 (2000); Marriage status: 25.1% never married, 61.2% now married, 6.1% widowed, 7.6% divorced (2000); Foreign born: 5.7% (2000); Ancestry (includes multiple ancestries): 15.6% German, 14.1% English, 13.9% United States or American, 12.2% Other groups, 8.4% Irish (2000).
Economy: Single-family building permits issued: 2 (2001) / 2 (2000); Multi-family building permits issued: 0 (2001) / 0 (2000); Employment by occupation: 8.2% management, 7.2% professional, 15.4% services, 20.6% sales, 1.0% farming, 11.0% construction, 36.6% production (2000).
Income: Per capita income: $14,826 (2000); Median household income: $34,881 (2000); Poverty rate: 7.9% (2000).

Taxes: Total city taxes per capita: $122 (1997); City property taxes per capita: $121 (1997).
Education: High school graduation rate: 80.7% (2000); College graduation rate: 9.4% (2000).
Housing: Homeownership rate: 73.6% (2000); Median home value: $65,500 (2000); Median rent: $317 per month (2000); Median age of housing: 60+ years (2000).
Transportation: Commute to work: 94.6% car, 0.0% public transportation, 2.7% walk, 0.8% work from home (2000); Travel time to work: 33.3% less than 15 minutes, 41.1% 15 to 30 minutes, 12.2% 30 to 45 minutes, 4.5% 45 to 60 minutes, 8.9% 60 minutes or more (2000)
Additional Information Contacts
Brook Chamber of Commerce 219-275-7731

GOODLAND (town). Covers a land area of 0.784 square miles and a water area of 0 square miles. Located at 40.76° N. Lat.; 87.29° W. Long. Elevation is 727 feet.
Population: 1,096 (2000); Race: 99.3% White, 0.0% Black, 0.0% Asian, 0.2% American Indian and Alaska Native, 0.1% Hispanic of any race, 0.5% two or more races (2000); Density: 1,397.1 persons per square mile (2000); Age: 26.3% under 18, 17.3% over 64 (2000); Marriage status: 21.8% never married, 56.1% now married, 10.2% widowed, 11.8% divorced (2000); Foreign born: 0.0% (2000); Ancestry (includes multiple ancestries): 29.6% German, 14.3% Irish, 12.2% English, 11.0% United States or American, 7.4% Other groups (2000).
Economy: In agricultural area: corn, soybeans; cattle; dairy products. Manufacturing: plastic molding, transformers; stone quarrying. Single-family building permits issued: 3 (2001) / 3 (2000); Multi-family building permits issued: 0 (2001) / 0 (2000); Employment by occupation: 7.8% management, 9.7% professional, 16.3% services, 15.1% sales, 1.2% farming, 13.2% construction, 36.8% production (2000).
Income: Per capita income: $15,715 (2000); Median household income: $35,952 (2000); Poverty rate: 6.2% (2000).
Taxes: Total city taxes per capita: $110 (1997); City property taxes per capita: $110 (1997).
Education: High school graduation rate: 77.4% (2000); College graduation rate: 8.6% (2000).
Housing: Homeownership rate: 77.3% (2000); Median home value: $62,100 (2000); Median rent: $353 per month (2000); Median age of housing: 57 years (2000).
Transportation: Commute to work: 91.0% car, 0.0% public transportation, 5.1% walk, 3.1% work from home (2000); Travel time to work: 50.4% less than 15 minutes, 26.6% 15 to 30 minutes, 12.3% 30 to 45 minutes, 6.9% 45 to 60 minutes, 3.8% 60 minutes or more (2000)

KENTLAND (town). Covers a land area of 1.457 square miles and a water area of 0 square miles. Located at 40.77° N. Lat.; 87.44° W. Long. Elevation is 680 feet.
History: Kentland was the birthplace in 1866 of George Ade, Hoosier author, humorist, and playwright. An early industry here was the Whole Milk Cheese Factory.
Population: 1,822 (2000); Race: 99.6% White, 0.0% Black, 0.1% Asian, 0.1% American Indian and Alaska Native, 3.4% Hispanic of any race, 0.2% two or more races (2000); Density: 1,250.5 persons per square mile (2000); Age: 25.8% under 18, 15.4% over 64 (2000); Marriage status: 24.5% never married, 53.8% now married, 9.5% widowed, 12.2% divorced (2000); Foreign born: 2.6% (2000); Ancestry (includes multiple ancestries): 21.5% German, 15.0% Irish, 11.2% English, 10.7% United States or American, 8.6% Other groups (2000).
Economy: Single-family building permits issued: 3 (2001) / 3 (2000); Multi-family building permits issued: 0 (2001) / 0 (2000); Employment by occupation: 8.7% management, 12.1% professional, 16.2% services, 22.0% sales, 0.8% farming, 10.1% construction, 30.1% production (2000).
Income: Per capita income: $17,797 (2000); Median household income: $34,732 (2000); Poverty rate: 7.5% (2000).
Taxes: Total city taxes per capita: $118 (1997); City property taxes per capita: $111 (1997).
Education: High school graduation rate: 83.1% (2000); College graduation rate: 13.4% (2000).

School District(s)

South Newton School Corp (PK-12)
2000 Enrollment: 1,063 219-474-5184
Housing: Homeownership rate: 67.9% (2000); Median home value: $71,600 (2000); Median rent: $355 per month (2000); Median age of housing: 51 years (2000).
Newspapers: Newton County Enterprise (1 x week)
Transportation: Commute to work: 92.2% car, 0.2% public transportation, 3.9% walk, 2.5% work from home (2000); Travel time to work: 62.3% less than 15 minutes, 20.3% 15 to 30 minutes, 5.9% 30 to 45 minutes, 4.6% 45 to 60 minutes, 7.0% 60 minutes or more (2000)
Additional Information Contacts
Kentland Area Chamber of Commerce 219-474-6665

LAKE VILLAGE (CDP). Covers a land area of 3.978 square miles and a water area of 0 square miles. Located at 41.13° N. Lat.; 87.44° W. Long. Elevation is 656 feet.
History: Lake Village was located on land that had been reclaimed from a swamp. It grew as the center of a farming and goat-raising area.
Population: 855 (2000); Race: 97.5% White, 0.0% Black, 0.0% Asian, 0.0% American Indian and Alaska Native, 2.5% Hispanic of any race, 1.4% two or more races (2000); Density: 215.0 persons per square mile (2000); Age: 29.8% under 18, 11.8% over 64 (2000); Marriage status: 16.3% never married, 55.5% now married, 6.7% widowed, 21.6% divorced (2000); Foreign born: 1.1% (2000); Ancestry (includes multiple ancestries): 24.8% German, 16.1% Irish, 11.8% Polish, 10.7% Other groups, 10.2% United States or American (2000).
Economy: Employment by occupation: 10.5% management, 10.5% professional, 16.2% services, 11.1% sales, 0.0% farming, 22.8% construction, 28.8% production (2000).
Income: Per capita income: $17,280 (2000); Median household income: $39,474 (2000); Poverty rate: 5.2% (2000).
Education: High school graduation rate: 76.4% (2000); College graduation rate: 4.8% (2000).
Housing: Homeownership rate: 84.1% (2000); Median home value: $89,600 (2000); Median rent: $381 per month (2000); Median age of housing: 31 years (2000).
Transportation: Commute to work: 94.6% car, 0.0% public transportation, 0.0% walk, 5.4% work from home (2000); Travel time to work: 12.3% less than 15 minutes, 17.8% 15 to 30 minutes, 25.0% 30 to 45 minutes, 27.1% 45 to 60 minutes, 17.8% 60 minutes or more (2000)

MOROCCO (town). Covers a land area of 0.579 square miles and a water area of 0 square miles. Located at 40.94° N. Lat.; 87.45° W. Long. Elevation is 698 feet.
History: The area in which Morocco was sited was once known as Beaver Prairie for the abundance of beaver in the streams.
Population: 1,127 (2000); Race: 99.2% White, 0.0% Black, 0.0% Asian, 0.0% American Indian and Alaska Native, 1.1% Hispanic of any race, 0.5% two or more races (2000); Density: 1,947.0 persons per square mile (2000); Age: 20.7% under 18, 20.2% over 64 (2000); Marriage status: 21.9% never married, 53.8% now married, 13.7% widowed, 10.6% divorced (2000); Foreign born: 0.9% (2000); Ancestry (includes multiple ancestries): 28.0% German, 15.3% Irish, 14.1% English, 10.4% United States or American, 9.5% Other groups (2000).
Economy: Single-family building permits issued: 2 (2001) / 2 (2000); Multi-family building permits issued: 0 (2001) / 0 (2000); Employment by occupation: 8.6% management, 14.2% professional, 13.8% services, 18.8% sales, 1.6% farming, 12.8% construction, 30.2% production (2000).
Income: Per capita income: $17,776 (2000); Median household income: $32,176 (2000); Poverty rate: 9.3% (2000).
Taxes: Total city taxes per capita: $136 (1997); City property taxes per capita: $134 (1997).
Education: High school graduation rate: 76.9% (2000); College graduation rate: 11.4% (2000).

School District(s)

North Newton School Corp (KG-12)
2000 Enrollment: 1,759 219-285-2228
Housing: Homeownership rate: 72.4% (2000); Median home value: $65,500 (2000); Median rent: $340 per month (2000); Median age of housing: 56 years (2000).
Newspapers: Morocco Courier (1 x week)
Transportation: Commute to work: 94.4% car, 0.4% public transportation, 1.7% walk, 2.8% work from home (2000); Travel time to work: 37.2% less than 15 minutes, 29.7% 15 to 30 minutes, 12.1% 30 to 45 minutes, 8.9% 45 to 60 minutes, 12.1% 60 minutes or more (2000)

MOUNT AYR (town). Covers a land area of 0.149 square miles and a water area of 0 square miles. Located at 40.95° N. Lat.; 87.29° W. Long. Elevation is 699 feet.
Population: 147 (2000); Race: 100.0% White, 0.0% Black, 0.0% Asian, 0.0% American Indian and Alaska Native, 0.0% Hispanic of any race, 0.0% two or more races (2000); Density: 983.8 persons per square mile (2000);

Age: 36.2% under 18, 8.0% over 64 (2000); Marriage status: 22.5% never married, 52.5% now married, 13.3% widowed, 11.7% divorced (2000); Foreign born: 0.0% (2000); Ancestry (includes multiple ancestries): 31.6% United States or American, 16.1% German, 11.5% Irish, 10.3% Dutch, 6.9% Italian (2000).
Economy: In agricultural area. Single-family building permits issued: 0 (2001) / 0 (2000); Multi-family building permits issued: 0 (2001) / 0 (2000); Employment by occupation: 0.0% management, 10.5% professional, 8.4% services, 25.3% sales, 0.0% farming, 8.4% construction, 47.4% production (2000).
Income: Per capita income: $18,195 (2000); Median household income: $52,000 (2000); Poverty rate: 0.0% (2000).
Taxes: Total city taxes per capita: $33 (1997); City property taxes per capita: $33 (1997).
Education: High school graduation rate: 72.3% (2000); College graduation rate: 5.0% (2000).
Housing: Homeownership rate: 96.0% (2000); Median home value: $56,300 (2000); Median rent: $425 per month (2000); Median age of housing: 60+ years (2000).
Transportation: Commute to work: 96.8% car, 0.0% public transportation, 0.0% walk, 3.2% work from home (2000); Travel time to work: 19.6% less than 15 minutes, 39.1% 15 to 30 minutes, 16.3% 30 to 45 minutes, 16.3% 45 to 60 minutes, 8.7% 60 minutes or more (2000)

Noble County

Located in northeastern Indiana; drained by the Elkhart River; includes many small lakes. Covers a land area of 411.10 square miles, a water area of 6.50 square miles, and is located in the Eastern Time Zone. The county government was organized in 1835. County seat is Albion.
Population: 46,275 (2000); Race: 94.2% White, 0.3% Black, 0.6% Asian, 0.1% American Indian and Alaska Native, 7.0% Hispanic of any race, 0.9% two or more races (2000); Density: 112.6 persons per square mile (2000); Age: 28.9% under 18, 11.0% over 64 (2000).
Religion: Five largest groups: 7.7% Catholic Church, 7.6% The United Methodist Church, 5.5% Lutheran Church—Missouri Synod, 1.4% Assemblies of God, 1.1% Evangelical Lutheran Church in America (2000).
Economy: Unemployment rate: 5.0% (11/2002); Total civilian labor force: 23,991 (11/2002); Leading industries: 61.5% manufacturing; 9.1% retail trade; 6.1% health care and social assistance (2000); Companies that employ more than 1,000 persons: 0 (2000); Companies that employ more than 100 persons: 44 (2000); Farms: 942 totaling 181,963 acres (1997); Minority business ownership rate: 0.0% (1997); Women business ownership rate: 22.4% (1997); Retail sales per capita: $6,159 (1997). Single-family building permits issued: 239 (2001) / 221 (2000); Multi-family building permits issued: 19 (2001) / 23 (2000).
Income: Per capita income: $17,896 (2000); Median household income: $42,700 (2000); Poverty rate: 7.9% (2000); Bankruptcy rate: 7.86% (2001).
Taxes: Total county taxes per capita: $190 (2000); County property taxes per capita: $98 (2000).
Education: High school graduation rate: 77.3% (2000); College graduation rate: 11.1% (2000).
Housing: Homeownership rate: 78.0% (2000); Median home value: $88,600 (2000); Median rent: $382 per month (2000); Median age of housing: 33 years (2000).
Health: Birth rate: 156.2 per 10,000 population (1998); Age adjusted death rate: 99.8 per 10,000 population (1999); Age adjusted cancer mortality rate: 257.7 deaths per 100,000 population (1999). Number of physicians: 5.8 per 10,000 population (1999); Number of hospital beds: 9.3 per 10,000 population (1999).
Elections: 2000 Presidential election results: 33.9% Gore, 64.0% Bush, 0.5% Nader, 1.0% Buchanan
National and State Parks: Chain O'Lakes State Park; Gene Stratton Porter State Memorial
Additional Information Contacts
Noble County Government Offices 219-636-2658
Kendallville Chamber of Commerce 260-347-1554
Northeastern Indiana Association of Realtors 260-347-1593
Rome City Chamber of Commerce 219-854-2412

Noble County Communities

ALBION (town). Covers a land area of 1.396 square miles and a water area of 0 square miles. Located at 41.39° N. Lat.; 85.42° W. Long. Elevation is 963 feet.
History: Albion was first called The Center. The name was changed to Albion about 1845, when the town was successful in its bid to become the new seat of Noble County. Albion was a station on the Underground Railroad, helping slaves to escape to freedom.
Population: 2,284 (2000); Race: 97.2% White, 0.4% Black, 0.2% Asian, 0.0% American Indian and Alaska Native, 2.0% Hispanic of any race, 1.3% two or more races (2000); Density: 1,636.5 persons per square mile (2000); Age: 30.1% under 18, 8.3% over 64 (2000); Marriage status: 26.3% never married, 50.6% now married, 6.0% widowed, 17.1% divorced (2000); Foreign born: 0.6% (2000); Ancestry (includes multiple ancestries): 28.1% German, 13.1% United States or American, 11.0% Other groups, 8.5% Irish, 7.2% English (2000).
Economy: Single-family building permits issued: 6 (2001) / 8 (2000); Multi-family building permits issued: 0 (2001) / 6 (2000); Employment by occupation: 6.0% management, 9.3% professional, 13.2% services, 18.0% sales, 0.4% farming, 9.2% construction, 43.8% production (2000).
Income: Per capita income: $16,405 (2000); Median household income: $36,282 (2000); Poverty rate: 4.7% (2000).
Taxes: Total city taxes per capita: $155 (1997); City property taxes per capita: $147 (1997).
Education: High school graduation rate: 81.3% (2000); College graduation rate: 9.6% (2000).

School District(s)
Central Noble Com School Corp (KG-12)
2000 Enrollment: 1,501 219-636-2175
Housing: Homeownership rate: 70.9% (2000); Median home value: $76,300 (2000); Median rent: $393 per month (2000); Median age of housing: 33 years (2000).
Newspapers: Albion New Era (1 x week)
Transportation: Commute to work: 94.7% car, 0.4% public transportation, 3.1% walk, 0.6% work from home (2000); Travel time to work: 50.4% less than 15 minutes, 31.1% 15 to 30 minutes, 9.1% 30 to 45 minutes, 3.8% 45 to 60 minutes, 5.6% 60 minutes or more (2000)

AVILLA (town). Covers a land area of 1.367 square miles and a water area of 0 square miles. Located at 41.36° N. Lat.; 85.23° W. Long. Elevation is 972 feet.
Population: 2,049 (2000); Race: 96.8% White, 0.4% Black, 0.2% Asian, 0.3% American Indian and Alaska Native, 0.8% Hispanic of any race, 2.3% two or more races (2000); Density: 1,499.1 persons per square mile (2000); Age: 25.7% under 18, 18.3% over 64 (2000); Marriage status: 19.8% never married, 57.6% now married, 12.2% widowed, 10.3% divorced (2000); Foreign born: 1.3% (2000); Ancestry (includes multiple ancestries): 36.1% German, 11.5% Irish, 8.2% United States or American, 6.6% English, 6.2% Other groups (2000).
Economy: In agricultural area. Single-family building permits issued: 28 (2001) / 19 (2000); Multi-family building permits issued: 7 (2001) / 0 (2000); Employment by occupation: 7.4% management, 12.6% professional, 14.2% services, 19.4% sales, 1.0% farming, 5.8% construction, 39.6% production (2000).
Income: Per capita income: $17,591 (2000); Median household income: $42,014 (2000); Poverty rate: 5.7% (2000).
Taxes: Total city taxes per capita: $112 (1997); City property taxes per capita: $104 (1997).
Education: High school graduation rate: 82.9% (2000); College graduation rate: 7.6% (2000).
Housing: Homeownership rate: 66.5% (2000); Median home value: $91,300 (2000); Median rent: $433 per month (2000); Median age of housing: 22 years (2000).
Transportation: Commute to work: 96.1% car, 0.0% public transportation, 2.2% walk, 1.1% work from home (2000); Travel time to work: 39.0% less than 15 minutes, 38.5% 15 to 30 minutes, 15.4% 30 to 45 minutes, 4.2% 45 to 60 minutes, 2.9% 60 minutes or more (2000)

CROMWELL (town). Covers a land area of 0.297 square miles and a water area of 0 square miles. Located at 41.40° N. Lat.; 85.61° W. Long. Elevation is 953 feet.
Population: 452 (2000); Race: 96.4% White, 0.0% Black, 0.0% Asian, 0.0% American Indian and Alaska Native, 5.0% Hispanic of any race, 1.0% two or more races (2000); Density: 1,523.3 persons per square mile (2000); Age: 26.5% under 18, 10.0% over 64 (2000); Marriage status: 20.9% never married, 61.0% now married, 7.1% widowed, 11.0% divorced (2000); Foreign born: 1.9% (2000); Ancestry (includes multiple ancestries): 21.5% German, 15.3% Irish, 14.1% Other groups, 13.4% United States or American, 5.5% English (2000).

Economy: In agricultural area. Manufacturing: wire products. Single-family building permits issued: 9 (2001) / 6 (2000); Multi-family building permits issued: 0 (2001) / 0 (2000); Employment by occupation: 4.9% management, 4.4% professional, 17.3% services, 20.0% sales, 0.9% farming, 13.8% construction, 38.7% production (2000).
Income: Per capita income: $15,664 (2000); Median household income: $38,438 (2000); Poverty rate: 14.7% (2000).
Taxes: Total city taxes per capita: $186 (2000); City property taxes per capita: $175 (2000).
Education: High school graduation rate: 73.9% (2000); College graduation rate: 3.4% (2000).
Housing: Homeownership rate: 67.0% (2000); Median home value: $63,900 (2000); Median rent: $280 per month (2000); Median age of housing: 53 years (2000).
Transportation: Commute to work: 88.7% car, 0.0% public transportation, 5.4% walk, 5.9% work from home (2000); Travel time to work: 39.9% less than 15 minutes, 38.9% 15 to 30 minutes, 13.9% 30 to 45 minutes, 3.4% 45 to 60 minutes, 3.8% 60 minutes or more (2000)

KENDALLVILLE (city). Covers a land area of 5.088 square miles and a water area of 0.224 square miles. Located at 41.44° N. Lat.; 85.26° W. Long. Elevation is 982 feet.
History: Kendallville was settled in 1833 when David Bundle opened a tavern to serve the many travelers that passed this way. When the New York Central Railroad came through in 1857, the village grew. The Flint & Walling Manufacturing Plant was founded here in 1865 as a machine shop, and became a producer of windmills and pumps.
Population: 9,616 (2000); Race: 96.5% White, 0.1% Black, 1.1% Asian, 0.1% American Indian and Alaska Native, 2.7% Hispanic of any race, 0.8% two or more races (2000); Density: 1,890.0 persons per square mile (2000); Age: 26.8% under 18, 15.2% over 64 (2000); Marriage status: 21.9% never married, 54.1% now married, 9.0% widowed, 15.0% divorced (2000); Foreign born: 2.4% (2000); Ancestry (includes multiple ancestries): 25.9% German, 19.0% United States or American, 10.3% Irish, 10.0% Other groups, 9.5% English (2000).
Economy: Single-family building permits issued: 35 (2001) / 31 (2000); Multi-family building permits issued: 12 (2001) / 17 (2000); Employment by occupation: 8.0% management, 10.1% professional, 12.9% services, 21.0% sales, 0.4% farming, 10.0% construction, 37.6% production (2000).
Income: Per capita income: $16,335 (2000); Median household income: $33,899 (2000); Poverty rate: 9.9% (2000).
Taxes: Total city taxes per capita: $355 (2000); City property taxes per capita: $349 (2000).
Education: High school graduation rate: 75.1% (2000); College graduation rate: 11.9% (2000).

School District(s)

East Noble School Corp (PK-12)
2000 Enrollment: 3,941 219-347-2502
Housing: Homeownership rate: 66.4% (2000); Median home value: $81,100 (2000); Median rent: $361 per month (2000); Median age of housing: 38 years (2000).
Hospitals: Parkview Noble Hospital (66 beds)
Safety: Violent crime rate: 19.6 per 10,000 population; Property crime rate: 527.4 per 10,000 population (2001).
Newspapers: The News-Sun (7 x week)
Transportation: Commute to work: 93.9% car, 0.1% public transportation, 3.2% walk, 2.1% work from home (2000); Travel time to work: 59.7% less than 15 minutes, 21.7% 15 to 30 minutes, 10.7% 30 to 45 minutes, 4.0% 45 to 60 minutes, 3.9% 60 minutes or more (2000)
Additional Information Contacts
Kendallville Chamber of Commerce 260-347-1554
Northeastern Indiana Association of Realtors 260-347-1593

KIMMELL (unincorporated postal area, zip code 46760). Covers a land area of 24.386 square miles and a water area of 0.422 square miles. Located at 41.36° N. Lat.; 85.56° W. Long. Elevation is 920 feet.
History: Kimmell achieved a degree of fame as a producer of onions. In 1936 Andrew W. Milnar of Kimmell grew 1,471 bushels of onions on one acre of land.
Population: 1,368 (2000); Race: 99.1% White, 0.0% Black, 0.0% Asian, 0.0% American Indian and Alaska Native, 0.5% Hispanic of any race, 0.9% two or more races (2000); Density: 56.1 persons per square mile (2000); Age: 28.7% under 18, 9.0% over 64 (2000); Marriage status: 20.2% never married, 58.6% now married, 5.9% widowed, 15.3% divorced (2000); Foreign born: 0.5% (2000); Ancestry (includes multiple ancestries): 32.5% German, 14.3% United States or American, 12.3% English, 8.2% Irish, 3.5% Dutch (2000).
Economy: Employment by occupation: 9.3% management, 12.3% professional, 7.1% services, 24.8% sales, 3.2% farming, 8.0% construction, 35.2% production (2000).
Income: Per capita income: $18,128 (2000); Median household income: $39,821 (2000); Poverty rate: 2.4% (2000).
Education: High school graduation rate: 85.0% (2000); College graduation rate: 11.2% (2000).
Housing: Homeownership rate: 82.7% (2000); Median home value: $74,000 (2000); Median rent: $325 per month (2000); Median age of housing: 50 years (2000).
Transportation: Commute to work: 87.7% car, 0.0% public transportation, 3.8% walk, 8.4% work from home (2000); Travel time to work: 22.5% less than 15 minutes, 39.3% 15 to 30 minutes, 24.5% 30 to 45 minutes, 7.4% 45 to 60 minutes, 6.4% 60 minutes or more (2000)

LAOTTO (unincorporated postal area, zip code 46763). Aka La Otto. Covers a land area of 24.578 square miles and a water area of 0 square miles. Located at 41.28° N. Lat.; 85.22° W. Long. Elevation is 872 feet.
History: Laid out 1871.
Population: 1,684 (2000); Race: 100.0% White, 0.0% Black, 0.0% Asian, 0.0% American Indian and Alaska Native, 0.7% Hispanic of any race, 0.0% two or more races (2000); Density: 68.5 persons per square mile (2000); Age: 27.7% under 18, 9.8% over 64 (2000); Marriage status: 19.2% never married, 71.3% now married, 3.4% widowed, 6.1% divorced (2000); Foreign born: 0.4% (2000); Ancestry (includes multiple ancestries): 31.4% German, 15.2% English, 12.8% United States or American, 8.1% Irish, 5.5% French (except Basque) (2000).
Economy: Manufacturing: metal products. Corn, wheat; cattle. Employment by occupation: 14.0% management, 13.8% professional, 12.3% services, 20.8% sales, 0.6% farming, 12.5% construction, 26.1% production (2000).
Income: Per capita income: $20,062 (2000); Median household income: $48,654 (2000); Poverty rate: 6.1% (2000).
Education: High school graduation rate: 88.6% (2000); College graduation rate: 14.7% (2000).
Housing: Homeownership rate: 91.0% (2000); Median home value: $104,800 (2000); Median rent: $398 per month (2000); Median age of housing: 31 years (2000).
Transportation: Commute to work: 87.0% car, 0.0% public transportation, 7.7% walk, 5.3% work from home (2000); Travel time to work: 31.0% less than 15 minutes, 34.4% 15 to 30 minutes, 24.0% 30 to 45 minutes, 4.4% 45 to 60 minutes, 6.2% 60 minutes or more (2000)

LIGONIER (city). Covers a land area of 2.250 square miles and a water area of 0 square miles. Located at 41.46° N. Lat.; 85.59° W. Long. Elevation is 880 feet.
History: Ligonier was settled along the Elkhart River. Many of the early residents were Jewish.
Population: 4,357 (2000); Race: 73.9% White, 0.1% Black, 0.1% Asian, 0.1% American Indian and Alaska Native, 34.5% Hispanic of any race, 1.5% two or more races (2000); Density: 1,936.7 persons per square mile (2000); Age: 31.3% under 18, 10.0% over 64 (2000); Marriage status: 25.8% never married, 55.6% now married, 7.5% widowed, 11.1% divorced (2000); Foreign born: 23.5% (2000); Ancestry (includes multiple ancestries): 35.8% Other groups, 18.3% German, 11.4% United States or American, 7.0% Irish, 6.0% English (2000).
Economy: Single-family building permits issued: 19 (2001) / 15 (2000); Multi-family building permits issued: 0 (2001) / 0 (2000); Employment by occupation: 4.2% management, 7.6% professional, 10.5% services, 15.9% sales, 0.9% farming, 6.5% construction, 54.5% production (2000).
Income: Per capita income: $14,448 (2000); Median household income: $36,546 (2000); Poverty rate: 14.3% (2000).
Taxes: Total city taxes per capita: $167 (1997); City property taxes per capita: $164 (1997).
Education: High school graduation rate: 64.3% (2000); College graduation rate: 7.7% (2000).

School District(s)

West Noble School Corporation (KG-12)
2000 Enrollment: 2,513 219-894-3191
Housing: Homeownership rate: 66.1% (2000); Median home value: $72,500 (2000); Median rent: $375 per month (2000); Median age of housing: 40 years (2000).
Safety: Violent crime rate: 13.7 per 10,000 population; Property crime rate: 299.0 per 10,000 population (2001).
Newspapers: Northeast Indiana Advertiser (1 x week); Advance-Leader (1 x week)

Transportation: Commute to work: 95.0% car, 0.0% public transportation, 0.9% walk, 2.3% work from home (2000); Travel time to work: 48.5% less than 15 minutes, 31.5% 15 to 30 minutes, 14.8% 30 to 45 minutes, 2.6% 45 to 60 minutes, 2.6% 60 minutes or more (2000)

ROME CITY (town). Covers a land area of 1.193 square miles and a water area of 0.979 square miles. Located at 41.49° N. Lat.; 85.36° W. Long. Elevation is 930 feet.
History: Rome City developed when a dam was built across a tributary of the Elkhart River, forming Sylvan Lake. The settlement, which became a resort community, was platted in 1839 and named by the Irish construction workers.
Population: 1,615 (2000); Race: 98.2% White, 0.1% Black, 0.3% Asian, 0.1% American Indian and Alaska Native, 0.4% Hispanic of any race, 1.3% two or more races (2000); Density: 1,354.0 persons per square mile (2000); Age: 24.6% under 18, 11.9% over 64 (2000); Marriage status: 18.1% never married, 64.9% now married, 6.4% widowed, 10.6% divorced (2000); Foreign born: 0.3% (2000); Ancestry (includes multiple ancestries): 23.2% German, 18.6% United States or American, 11.0% Irish, 9.9% Other groups, 7.7% English (2000).
Economy: Single-family building permits issued: 9 (2001) / 15 (2000); Multi-family building permits issued: 0 (2001) / 0 (2000); Employment by occupation: 8.7% management, 10.1% professional, 12.4% services, 18.3% sales, 0.3% farming, 8.9% construction, 41.3% production (2000).
Income: Per capita income: $19,612 (2000); Median household income: $41,118 (2000); Poverty rate: 9.3% (2000).
Taxes: Total city taxes per capita: $152 (1997); City property taxes per capita: $141 (1997).
Education: High school graduation rate: 70.0% (2000); College graduation rate: 11.0% (2000).
Housing: Homeownership rate: 77.5% (2000); Median home value: $123,600 (2000); Median rent: $419 per month (2000); Median age of housing: 48 years (2000).
Transportation: Commute to work: 95.6% car, 0.6% public transportation, 0.7% walk, 1.3% work from home (2000); Travel time to work: 24.6% less than 15 minutes, 43.4% 15 to 30 minutes, 14.2% 30 to 45 minutes, 11.8% 45 to 60 minutes, 5.9% 60 minutes or more (2000)
Additional Information Contacts
Rome City Chamber of Commerce 219-854-2412

WAWAKA (unincorporated postal area, zip code 46794). Covers a land area of 28.473 square miles and a water area of 0.203 square miles. Located at 41.46° N. Lat.; 85.45° W. Long. Elevation is 902 feet.
History: The name Wawaka is of Indian origin meaning "big heron." The town was founded in 1857 when the New York Central Railroad was built through the area.
Population: 1,640 (2000); Race: 98.1% White, 0.0% Black, 1.0% Asian, 0.0% American Indian and Alaska Native, 0.5% Hispanic of any race, 0.3% two or more races (2000); Density: 57.6 persons per square mile (2000); Age: 33.8% under 18, 9.1% over 64 (2000); Marriage status: 23.0% never married, 66.1% now married, 2.9% widowed, 8.0% divorced (2000); Foreign born: 1.4% (2000); Ancestry (includes multiple ancestries): 25.7% German, 15.2% United States or American, 6.4% Irish, 5.6% Other groups, 5.3% English (2000).
Economy: Employment by occupation: 14.9% management, 7.4% professional, 10.4% services, 11.2% sales, 1.1% farming, 12.9% construction, 42.0% production (2000).
Income: Per capita income: $16,489 (2000); Median household income: $49,100 (2000); Poverty rate: 8.7% (2000).
Education: High school graduation rate: 74.1% (2000); College graduation rate: 8.3% (2000).
Housing: Homeownership rate: 91.6% (2000); Median home value: $92,900 (2000); Median rent: $378 per month (2000); Median age of housing: 36 years (2000).
Transportation: Commute to work: 92.5% car, 0.0% public transportation, 2.2% walk, 5.3% work from home (2000); Travel time to work: 34.4% less than 15 minutes, 39.2% 15 to 30 minutes, 14.2% 30 to 45 minutes, 5.5% 45 to 60 minutes, 6.7% 60 minutes or more (2000)

WOLCOTTVILLE (town). Covers a land area of 1.025 square miles and a water area of 0 square miles. Located at 41.52° N. Lat.; 85.36° W. Long. Elevation is 934 feet.
History: Wolcottville grew around a gristmill, sawmill, and distillery established by George Wolcott from Connecticut. The number of nearby lakes made Wolcottville a vacation center as well.
Population: 933 (2000); Race: 95.6% White, 0.0% Black, 0.2% Asian, 0.2% American Indian and Alaska Native, 0.2% Hispanic of any race, 4.0% two or more races (2000); Density: 910.1 persons per square mile (2000); Age: 32.8% under 18, 8.6% over 64 (2000); Marriage status: 17.5% never married, 60.4% now married, 4.7% widowed, 17.5% divorced (2000); Foreign born: 0.4% (2000); Ancestry (includes multiple ancestries): 20.4% United States or American, 14.3% German, 11.4% Other groups, 7.6% English, 4.2% Irish (2000).
Economy: Employment by occupation: 2.6% management, 6.1% professional, 10.0% services, 14.2% sales, 0.4% farming, 11.4% construction, 55.2% production (2000).
Income: Per capita income: $16,974 (2000); Median household income: $35,833 (2000); Poverty rate: 10.9% (2000).
Taxes: Total city taxes per capita: $166 (1997); City property taxes per capita: $135 (1997).
Education: High school graduation rate: 66.2% (2000); College graduation rate: 2.8% (2000).
Housing: Homeownership rate: 62.3% (2000); Median home value: $68,400 (2000); Median rent: $410 per month (2000); Median age of housing: 43 years (2000).
Transportation: Commute to work: 94.4% car, 0.0% public transportation, 3.3% walk, 0.7% work from home (2000); Travel time to work: 18.0% less than 15 minutes, 54.2% 15 to 30 minutes, 17.5% 30 to 45 minutes, 4.9% 45 to 60 minutes, 5.4% 60 minutes or more (2000)

Ohio County

Located in southeastern Indiana; bounded on the east by the Ohio River and the Kentucky border. Covers a land area of 86.70 square miles, a water area of 0.70 square miles, and is located in the Eastern Time Zone. The county government was organized in 1844. County seat is Rising Sun.

Ohio County is part of the Cincinnati, OH-KY-IN PMSA. The entire metro area includes: Dearborn County, IN; Ohio County, IN; Boone County, KY; Campbell County, KY; Gallatin County, KY; Grant County, KY; Kenton County, KY; Pendleton County, KY; Brown County, OH; Clermont County, OH; Hamilton County, OH; Warren County, OH

Population: 5,623 (2000); Race: 98.8% White, 0.4% Black, 0.0% Asian, 0.0% American Indian and Alaska Native, 0.6% Hispanic of any race, 0.6% two or more races (2000); Density: 64.8 persons per square mile (2000); Age: 24.8% under 18, 13.8% over 64 (2000).
Religion: Five largest groups: 10.9% Christian Churches and Churches of Christ, 7.5% American Baptist Churches in the USA, 5.6% The United Methodist Church, 4.1% Evangelical Lutheran Church in America, 3.3% United Church of Christ (2000).
Economy: Unemployment rate: 3.6% (11/2002); Total civilian labor force: 2,722 (11/2002); Leading industries: Companies that employ more than 1,000 persons: 1 (2000); Companies that employ more than 100 persons: 1 (2000); Farms: 252 totaling 29,880 acres (1997); Minority business ownership rate: 0.0% (1997); Women business ownership rate: 0.0% (1997); Retail sales per capita: $2,520 (1997). Single-family building permits issued: 31 (2001) / 23 (2000); Multi-family building permits issued: 0 (2001) / 0 (2000).
Income: Per capita income: $19,627 (2000); Median household income: $41,348 (2000); Poverty rate: 7.1% (2000); Bankruptcy rate: 11.76% (2001).
Taxes: Total county taxes per capita: $181 (1997); County property taxes per capita: $109 (1997).
Education: High school graduation rate: 78.4% (2000); College graduation rate: 11.6% (2000).
Housing: Homeownership rate: 77.6% (2000); Median home value: $97,100 (2000); Median rent: $389 per month (2000); Median age of housing: 29 years (2000).
Health: Birth rate: 112.0 per 10,000 population (1998); Age adjusted death rate: 54.3 per 10,000 population (1999); Age adjusted cancer mortality rate: 142.7 (Unreliable figure as per CDC) deaths per 100,000 population (1999). Number of physicians: 1.8 per 10,000 population (1999); Number of hospital beds: n/a (1999).
Elections: 2000 Presidential election results: 38.2% Gore, 60.8% Bush, 0.2% Nader, 0.4% Buchanan
Additional Information Contacts
Ohio County Government Offices 812-438-2062
Rising Sun-Ohio County Chamber. 812-438-3130

Ohio County Communities

RISING SUN (city). Covers a land area of 1.484 square miles and a water area of 0.102 square miles. Located at 38.95° N. Lat.; 84.85° W. Long. Elevation is 520 feet.
History: Rising Sun was platted in 1814 along the Ohio River, and grew as a shipping center.
Population: 2,470 (2000); Race: 98.8% White, 0.8% Black, 0.0% Asian, 0.0% American Indian and Alaska Native, 0.7% Hispanic of any race, 0.4% two or more races (2000); Density: 1,664.4 persons per square mile (2000); Age: 24.1% under 18, 17.7% over 64 (2000); Marriage status: 22.4% never married, 57.7% now married, 11.9% widowed, 8.0% divorced (2000); Foreign born: 0.0% (2000); Ancestry (includes multiple ancestries): 22.8% German, 20.1% United States or American, 15.1% Irish, 12.4% English, 4.2% Other groups (2000).
Economy: Single-family building permits issued: 0 (2001) / 2 (2000); Multi-family building permits issued: 0 (2001) / 0 (2000); Employment by occupation: 11.5% management, 14.4% professional, 21.9% services, 19.3% sales, 0.9% farming, 9.5% construction, 22.4% production (2000).
Income: Per capita income: $17,221 (2000); Median household income: $33,750 (2000); Poverty rate: 10.3% (2000).
Taxes: Total city taxes per capita: $526 (1997); City property taxes per capita: $71 (1997).
Education: High school graduation rate: 76.9% (2000); College graduation rate: 12.6% (2000).

School District(s)

Rising Sun-Ohio Co Com (KG-12)
2000 Enrollment: 1,027 812-438-2655
Housing: Homeownership rate: 65.2% (2000); Median home value: $89,100 (2000); Median rent: $373 per month (2000); Median age of housing: 44 years (2000).
Newspapers: The Rising Sun Recorder (1 x week); Ohio County News (1 x week)
Transportation: Commute to work: 90.3% car, 0.0% public transportation, 4.3% walk, 3.6% work from home (2000); Travel time to work: 41.7% less than 15 minutes, 26.1% 15 to 30 minutes, 13.1% 30 to 45 minutes, 12.3% 45 to 60 minutes, 6.8% 60 minutes or more (2000)
Additional Information Contacts
Rising Sun-Ohio County Chamber. 812-438-3130

Orange County

Located in southern Indiana; drained by the Lick, Lost, and Potoka Rivers. Covers a land area of 399.50 square miles, a water area of 8.70 square miles, and is located in the Eastern Time Zone. The county government was organized in 1815. County seat is Paoli.

Weather Station: Paoli Elevation: 557 feet

	Jan	Feb	Mar	Apr	May	Jun	Jul	Aug	Sep	Oct	Nov	Dec
High	39	45	55	66	76	84	88	86	80	69	55	44
Low	19	22	31	41	51	60	64	62	54	42	33	24
Precip	3.1	2.9	4.5	5.1	5.1	4.2	4.4	4.0	3.3	3.1	4.2	3.5
Snow	na	na	1.3	0.1	0.0	0.0	0.0	0.0	0.0	0.0	0.2	2.4

High and Low temperatures in degrees Fahrenheit; Precipitation and Snow in inches

Population: 19,306 (2000); Race: 97.7% White, 0.3% Black, 0.0% Asian, 0.5% American Indian and Alaska Native, 0.8% Hispanic of any race, 1.2% two or more races (2000); Density: 48.3 persons per square mile (2000); Age: 25.7% under 18, 14.8% over 64 (2000).
Religion: Five largest groups: 12.6% Christian Churches and Churches of Christ, 8.4% American Baptist Churches in the USA, 7.2% The United Methodist Church, 3.0% Catholic Church, 3.0% The Wesleyan Church (2000).
Economy: Unemployment rate: 8.8% (11/2002); Total civilian labor force: 8,149 (11/2002); Leading industries: 35.6% manufacturing; 14.8% construction; 14.1% health care and social assistance (2000); Companies that employ more than 1,000 persons: 0 (2000); Companies that employ more than 100 persons: 15 (2000); Farms: 531 totaling 123,343 acres (1997); Minority business ownership rate: 0.0% (1997); Women business ownership rate: 21.6% (1997); Retail sales per capita: $5,325 (1997). Single-family building permits issued: 0 (2001) / 5 (2000); Multi-family building permits issued: 0 (2001) / 0 (2000).
Income: Per capita income: $16,717 (2000); Median household income: $31,564 (2000); Poverty rate: 12.4% (2000); Bankruptcy rate: 8.99% (2001).
Taxes: Total county taxes per capita: $162 (1997); County property taxes per capita: $98 (1997).
Education: High school graduation rate: 73.8% (2000); College graduation rate: 10.2% (2000).
Housing: Homeownership rate: 79.2% (2000); Median home value: $63,500 (2000); Median rent: $275 per month (2000); Median age of housing: 29 years (2000).
Health: Birth rate: 121.2 per 10,000 population (1998); Age adjusted death rate: 100.9 per 10,000 population (1999); Age adjusted cancer mortality rate: 241.7 deaths per 100,000 population (1999). Number of physicians: 7.8 per 10,000 population (1999); Number of hospital beds: 24.9 per 10,000 population (1999).
Elections: 2000 Presidential election results: 34.9% Gore, 62.9% Bush, 0.6% Nader, 1.0% Buchanan
National and State Parks: Hoosier National Forest; Jackson State Recreation Area; Newton-Stewart State Recreation Area; Pioneer Mothers State Wayside; Springs Valley State Fish and Wildlife Area; Tillery Hill State Recreation Area
Additional Information Contacts
Orange County Government Offices 812-723-2649
French Lick Chamber of Commerce 812-936-2405
Paoli Chamber of Commerce 812-723-4769

Orange County Communities

FRENCH LICK (town). Covers a land area of 1.623 square miles and a water area of 0 square miles. Located at 38.54° N. Lat.; 86.61° W. Long. Elevation is 511 feet.
History: French Lick was founded in 1811 on the site of mineral springs where a trading post had been operated by the French in the early 1700's. The French Lick Springs Hotel was opened in 1840 by Dr. William A. Bowles, who not only entertained visitors to the medicinal springs, but marketed the spring water by boiling and bottling it as Pluto Water.
Population: 1,941 (2000); Race: 97.2% White, 2.3% Black, 0.0% Asian, 0.5% American Indian and Alaska Native, 0.5% Hispanic of any race, 0.0% two or more races (2000); Density: 1,196.3 persons per square mile (2000); Age: 22.3% under 18, 21.1% over 64 (2000); Marriage status: 17.4% never married, 55.6% now married, 11.3% widowed, 15.7% divorced (2000); Foreign born: 1.4% (2000); Ancestry (includes multiple ancestries): 18.7% German, 17.9% United States or American, 13.6% Irish, 10.8% Other groups, 6.6% English (2000).
Economy: Single-family building permits issued: 0 (2001) / 4 (2000); Multi-family building permits issued: 0 (2001) / 0 (2000); Employment by occupation: 6.1% management, 15.1% professional, 15.4% services, 24.7% sales, 1.0% farming, 4.9% construction, 32.8% production (2000).
Income: Per capita income: $15,113 (2000); Median household income: $27,197 (2000); Poverty rate: 18.7% (2000).
Taxes: Total city taxes per capita: $137 (1997); City property taxes per capita: $113 (1997).
Education: High school graduation rate: 71.4% (2000); College graduation rate: 12.2% (2000).

School District(s)

Springs Valley Com School Corp (KG-12)
2000 Enrollment: 939 812-936-4474
Housing: Homeownership rate: 63.0% (2000); Median home value: $52,800 (2000); Median rent: $272 per month (2000); Median age of housing: 38 years (2000).
Newspapers: Springs Valley Herald (1 x week)
Transportation: Commute to work: 89.8% car, 0.0% public transportation, 7.2% walk, 3.0% work from home (2000); Travel time to work: 45.0% less than 15 minutes, 20.1% 15 to 30 minutes, 21.4% 30 to 45 minutes, 6.8% 45 to 60 minutes, 6.6% 60 minutes or more (2000)
Additional Information Contacts
French Lick Chamber of Commerce 812-936-2405

ORLEANS (town). Covers a land area of 1.568 square miles and a water area of 0 square miles. Located at 38.66° N. Lat.; 86.45° W. Long. Elevation is 635 feet.
History: Orleans was founded in 1815 shortly after General Jackson's victory at New Orleans, and the town was named for that event. Orleans developed as an orchard and dairy center.
Population: 2,273 (2000); Race: 98.5% White, 0.0% Black, 0.0% Asian, 0.0% American Indian and Alaska Native, 1.5% Hispanic of any race, 1.4% two or more races (2000); Density: 1,449.3 persons per square mile (2000); Age: 26.8% under 18, 17.8% over 64 (2000); Marriage status: 15.7% never married, 60.2% now married, 11.2% widowed, 12.9% divorced (2000); Foreign born: 0.2% (2000); Ancestry (includes multiple ancestries): 26.0% United States or American, 12.4% German, 11.0% Other groups, 8.2% English, 6.4% Irish (2000).

Economy: Employment by occupation: 8.1% management, 5.9% professional, 21.6% services, 21.2% sales, 1.0% farming, 9.3% construction, 32.8% production (2000).
Income: Per capita income: $14,476 (2000); Median household income: $27,138 (2000); Poverty rate: 17.2% (2000).
Taxes: Total city taxes per capita: $132 (1997); City property taxes per capita: $113 (1997).
Education: High school graduation rate: 78.0% (2000); College graduation rate: 5.9% (2000).

School District(s)

Orleans Community Schools (KG-12)
2000 Enrollment: 816 812-865-2688
Housing: Homeownership rate: 70.5% (2000); Median home value: $61,500 (2000); Median rent: $280 per month (2000); Median age of housing: 36 years (2000).
Newspapers: The Progress Examiner (1 x week)
Transportation: Commute to work: 95.0% car, 0.0% public transportation, 0.7% walk, 2.8% work from home (2000); Travel time to work: 47.0% less than 15 minutes, 32.5% 15 to 30 minutes, 7.3% 30 to 45 minutes, 8.7% 45 to 60 minutes, 4.4% 60 minutes or more (2000)

PAOLI (town). Covers a land area of 3.783 square miles and a water area of 0 square miles. Located at 38.55° N. Lat.; 86.46° W. Long. Elevation is 615 feet.
History: The Orange County Courthouse was constructed in 1850 in Paoli, the county seat.
Population: 3,844 (2000); Race: 96.3% White, 0.3% Black, 0.0% Asian, 0.8% American Indian and Alaska Native, 1.7% Hispanic of any race, 2.1% two or more races (2000); Density: 1,016.0 persons per square mile (2000); Age: 25.7% under 18, 17.6% over 64 (2000); Marriage status: 17.4% never married, 59.9% now married, 9.6% widowed, 13.1% divorced (2000); Foreign born: 2.3% (2000); Ancestry (includes multiple ancestries): 22.7% United States or American, 13.8% German, 12.2% Irish, 10.9% English, 10.5% Other groups (2000).
Economy: Employment by occupation: 7.4% management, 15.8% professional, 15.5% services, 20.1% sales, 0.8% farming, 10.1% construction, 30.5% production (2000).
Income: Per capita income: $14,313 (2000); Median household income: $26,962 (2000); Poverty rate: 15.1% (2000).
Taxes: Total city taxes per capita: $124 (1997); City property taxes per capita: $113 (1997).
Education: High school graduation rate: 68.0% (2000); College graduation rate: 13.7% (2000).

School District(s)

Paoli Community School Corp (KG-12)
2000 Enrollment: 1,694 812-723-4717
Housing: Homeownership rate: 68.2% (2000); Median home value: $56,300 (2000); Median rent: $262 per month (2000); Median age of housing: 34 years (2000).
Hospitals: Bloomington Hospital of Orange County (25 beds)
Newspapers: Paoli Republican (1 x week); Paoli News (1 x week); The Orange Countian (1 x week)
Transportation: Commute to work: 95.1% car, 0.0% public transportation, 2.7% walk, 2.2% work from home (2000); Travel time to work: 56.9% less than 15 minutes, 24.2% 15 to 30 minutes, 10.2% 30 to 45 minutes, 3.1% 45 to 60 minutes, 5.6% 60 minutes or more (2000)
Additional Information Contacts
Paoli Chamber of Commerce 812-723-4769

WEST BADEN SPRINGS (town). Aka West Baden. Covers a land area of 1.069 square miles and a water area of 0 square miles. Located at 38.56° N. Lat.; 86.61° W. Long. Elevation is 500 feet.
Population: 618 (2000); Race: 97.7% White, 0.0% Black, 0.2% Asian, 0.6% American Indian and Alaska Native, 1.1% Hispanic of any race, 1.1% two or more races (2000); Density: 577.8 persons per square mile (2000); Age: 23.1% under 18, 15.0% over 64 (2000); Marriage status: 22.6% never married, 59.6% now married, 6.2% widowed, 11.5% divorced (2000); Foreign born: 0.2% (2000); Ancestry (includes multiple ancestries): 30.7% United States or American, 10.1% English, 8.4% German, 6.7% Other groups, 3.4% Irish (2000).
Economy: Single-family building permits issued: 0 (2001) / 1 (2000); Multi-family building permits issued: 0 (2001) / 0 (2000); Employment by occupation: 5.0% management, 14.6% professional, 10.7% services, 15.4% sales, 0.0% farming, 13.6% construction, 40.7% production (2000).
Income: Per capita income: $14,532 (2000); Median household income: $32,750 (2000); Poverty rate: 9.7% (2000).
Taxes: Total city taxes per capita: $163 (1997); City property taxes per capita: $129 (1997).
Education: High school graduation rate: 68.2% (2000); College graduation rate: 10.3% (2000).
Housing: Homeownership rate: 78.8% (2000); Median home value: $56,400 (2000); Median rent: $259 per month (2000); Median age of housing: 32 years (2000).
Transportation: Commute to work: 98.6% car, 0.0% public transportation, 0.0% walk, 0.7% work from home (2000); Travel time to work: 43.7% less than 15 minutes, 9.4% 15 to 30 minutes, 27.1% 30 to 45 minutes, 13.4% 45 to 60 minutes, 6.5% 60 minutes or more (2000)

Owen County

Located in southwest central Indiana; drained by the West Fork of the White River and Mill Creek. Covers a land area of 385.20 square miles, a water area of 2.70 square miles, and is located in the Eastern Time Zone. The county government was organized in 1818. County seat is Spencer.

Weather Station: Spencer — Elevation: 547 feet

	Jan	Feb	Mar	Apr	May	Jun	Jul	Aug	Sep	Oct	Nov	Dec
High	35	41	51	63	73	81	85	84	78	66	52	41
Low	16	19	29	38	48	58	62	60	52	39	31	22
Precip	2.5	2.5	3.8	4.5	5.0	4.6	4.7	4.5	3.2	3.1	4.0	3.3
Snow	5.8	5.0	2.3	0.3	0.0	0.0	0.0	0.0	0.0	tr	0.5	3.0

High and Low temperatures in degrees Fahrenheit; Precipitation and Snow in inches

Population: 21,786 (2000); Race: 97.9% White, 0.3% Black, 0.1% Asian, 0.4% American Indian and Alaska Native, 0.8% Hispanic of any race, 1.0% two or more races (2000); Density: 56.6 persons per square mile (2000); Age: 26.7% under 18, 12.8% over 64 (2000).
Religion: Five largest groups: 5.5% American Baptist Churches in the USA, 4.7% Christian Churches and Churches of Christ, 3.9% The United Methodist Church, 2.2% Independent, Non-Charismatic Churches, 2.1% Church of the Nazarene (2000).
Economy: Unemployment rate: 5.1% (11/2002); Total civilian labor force: 11,446 (11/2002); Leading industries: 40.5% manufacturing; 13.7% retail trade; 9.8% accommodation & food services (2000); Companies that employ more than 1,000 persons: 0 (2000); Companies that employ more than 100 persons: 4 (2000); Farms: 569 totaling 107,265 acres (1997); Minority business ownership rate: 0.0% (1997); Women business ownership rate: 22.2% (1997); Retail sales per capita: $3,519 (1997). Single-family building permits issued: 2 (2001) / 1 (2000); Multi-family building permits issued: 0 (2001) / 4 (2000).
Income: Per capita income: $16,884 (2000); Median household income: $36,529 (2000); Poverty rate: 9.4% (2000); Bankruptcy rate: 6.17% (2001).
Taxes: Total county taxes per capita: $176 (1997); County property taxes per capita: $104 (1997).
Education: High school graduation rate: 74.9% (2000); College graduation rate: 9.2% (2000).
Housing: Homeownership rate: 81.6% (2000); Median home value: $84,600 (2000); Median rent: $340 per month (2000); Median age of housing: 26 years (2000).
Health: Birth rate: 101.0 per 10,000 population (1998); Age adjusted death rate: 83.0 per 10,000 population (1999); Age adjusted cancer mortality rate: 162.5 deaths per 100,000 population (1999). Number of physicians: 2.3 per 10,000 population (1999); Number of hospital beds: n/a (1999).
Elections: 2000 Presidential election results: 34.7% Gore, 61.8% Bush, 1.3% Nader, 1.1% Buchanan
National and State Parks: McCormicks Creek State Park
Additional Information Contacts
Owen County Government Offices 812-829-5000
Spencer-Owen Chamber of Commerce 812-829-3245

Owen County Communities

COAL CITY (unincorporated postal area, zip code 47427). Covers a land area of 54.586 square miles and a water area of 0.307 square miles. Located at 39.23° N. Lat.; 87.03° W. Long. Elevation is 655 feet.
History: Old surface coal mines nearby. Laid out 1875.
Population: 1,091 (2000); Race: 99.0% White, 0.0% Black, 0.0% Asian, 0.0% American Indian and Alaska Native, 0.0% Hispanic of any race, 0.0% two or more races (2000); Density: 20.0 persons per square mile (2000); Age: 26.8% under 18, 11.6% over 64 (2000); Marriage status: 14.3% never married, 72.0% now married, 6.7% widowed, 7.0% divorced (2000); Foreign born: 0.0% (2000); Ancestry (includes multiple ancestries): 21.0% German,

17.0% United States or American, 7.8% Irish, 7.0% Other groups, 5.0% English (2000).
Economy: Bituminous-coal area. Employment by occupation: 7.3% management, 10.4% professional, 14.4% services, 14.2% sales, 2.2% farming, 15.9% construction, 35.6% production (2000).
Income: Per capita income: $14,313 (2000); Median household income: $33,276 (2000); Poverty rate: 17.5% (2000).
Education: High school graduation rate: 77.5% (2000); College graduation rate: 7.2% (2000).
Housing: Homeownership rate: 92.9% (2000); Median home value: $59,500 (2000); Median rent: $305 per month (2000); Median age of housing: 33 years (2000).
Transportation: Commute to work: 87.3% car, 0.0% public transportation, 1.8% walk, 7.6% work from home (2000); Travel time to work: 11.6% less than 15 minutes, 24.6% 15 to 30 minutes, 27.4% 30 to 45 minutes, 22.8% 45 to 60 minutes, 13.6% 60 minutes or more (2000)

FREEDOM (unincorporated postal area, zip code 47431). Covers a land area of 36.485 square miles and a water area of 0.040 square miles. Located at 39.23° N. Lat.; 86.88° W. Long. Elevation is 537 feet.
Population: 1,279 (2000); Race: 97.9% White, 1.0% Black, 0.2% Asian, 0.0% American Indian and Alaska Native, 0.0% Hispanic of any race, 0.8% two or more races (2000); Density: 35.1 persons per square mile (2000); Age: 26.2% under 18, 14.1% over 64 (2000); Marriage status: 18.9% never married, 62.2% now married, 5.6% widowed, 13.4% divorced (2000); Foreign born: 0.2% (2000); Ancestry (includes multiple ancestries): 31.8% United States or American, 15.2% German, 7.4% English, 7.1% Other groups, 7.0% French (except Basque) (2000).
Economy: Employment by occupation: 5.6% management, 10.6% professional, 17.4% services, 12.9% sales, 0.0% farming, 19.6% construction, 34.0% production (2000).
Income: Per capita income: $13,807 (2000); Median household income: $29,743 (2000); Poverty rate: 9.5% (2000).
Education: High school graduation rate: 71.0% (2000); College graduation rate: 8.4% (2000).
Housing: Homeownership rate: 87.5% (2000); Median home value: $82,100 (2000); Median rent: $247 per month (2000); Median age of housing: 24 years (2000).
Transportation: Commute to work: 93.2% car, 0.0% public transportation, 2.6% walk, 3.0% work from home (2000); Travel time to work: 15.0% less than 15 minutes, 31.4% 15 to 30 minutes, 11.7% 30 to 45 minutes, 10.7% 45 to 60 minutes, 31.2% 60 minutes or more (2000)

GOSPORT (town). Covers a land area of 0.383 square miles and a water area of 0 square miles. Located at 39.35° N. Lat.; 86.66° W. Long. Elevation is 650 feet.
History: Gosport was laid out in 1829 as a shipping point for trade on the White River.
Population: 715 (2000); Race: 98.6% White, 0.0% Black, 0.0% Asian, 0.3% American Indian and Alaska Native, 2.3% Hispanic of any race, 0.7% two or more races (2000); Density: 1,868.6 persons per square mile (2000); Age: 27.1% under 18, 16.2% over 64 (2000); Marriage status: 19.0% never married, 55.2% now married, 10.6% widowed, 15.1% divorced (2000); Foreign born: 0.3% (2000); Ancestry (includes multiple ancestries): 12.1% United States or American, 11.7% German, 7.8% Irish, 7.4% Other groups, 4.3% English (2000).
Economy: Employment by occupation: 4.8% management, 11.1% professional, 15.9% services, 19.2% sales, 0.0% farming, 9.6% construction, 39.5% production (2000).
Income: Per capita income: $14,101 (2000); Median household income: $31,833 (2000); Poverty rate: 17.2% (2000).
Taxes: Total city taxes per capita: $53 (1997); City property taxes per capita: $40 (1997).
Education: High school graduation rate: 69.5% (2000); College graduation rate: 8.2% (2000).
Housing: Homeownership rate: 66.5% (2000); Median home value: $76,300 (2000); Median rent: $346 per month (2000); Median age of housing: 53 years (2000).
Transportation: Commute to work: 91.5% car, 0.0% public transportation, 6.2% walk, 0.4% work from home (2000); Travel time to work: 17.1% less than 15 minutes, 34.1% 15 to 30 minutes, 25.2% 30 to 45 minutes, 8.5% 45 to 60 minutes, 15.1% 60 minutes or more (2000)

QUINCY (unincorporated postal area, zip code 47456). Covers a land area of 21.676 square miles and a water area of 0.124 square miles. Located at 39.44° N. Lat.; 86.73° W. Long. Elevation is 759 feet.
Population: 799 (2000); Race: 99.1% White, 0.0% Black, 0.0% Asian, 0.0% American Indian and Alaska Native, 0.0% Hispanic of any race, 0.9% two or more races (2000); Density: 36.9 persons per square mile (2000); Age: 36.3% under 18, 7.2% over 64 (2000); Marriage status: 8.9% never married, 74.5% now married, 5.5% widowed, 11.1% divorced (2000); Foreign born: 0.0% (2000); Ancestry (includes multiple ancestries): 15.3% Irish, 15.1% United States or American, 13.8% German, 7.7% Swedish, 5.2% English (2000).
Economy: Employment by occupation: 5.2% management, 14.0% professional, 16.5% services, 14.9% sales, 0.0% farming, 23.1% construction, 26.2% production (2000).
Income: Per capita income: $16,421 (2000); Median household income: $36,071 (2000); Poverty rate: 12.4% (2000).
Education: High school graduation rate: 62.6% (2000); College graduation rate: 5.0% (2000).
Housing: Homeownership rate: 91.7% (2000); Median home value: $76,200 (2000); Median rent: $266 per month (2000); Median age of housing: 25 years (2000).
Transportation: Commute to work: 92.4% car, 0.0% public transportation, 0.0% walk, 5.1% work from home (2000); Travel time to work: 1.5% less than 15 minutes, 34.0% 15 to 30 minutes, 12.1% 30 to 45 minutes, 29.9% 45 to 60 minutes, 22.5% 60 minutes or more (2000)

SPENCER (town). Covers a land area of 1.264 square miles and a water area of 0 square miles. Located at 39.28° N. Lat.; 86.76° W. Long. Elevation is 566 feet.
History: Spencer was a farming, coal mining, and quarrying center named for Captain Spencer of Kentucky, who was killed at the Battle of Tippecanoe. Spencer was the hometown of poets William Herschell (1873-1939) and William Vaughn Moody (1869-1910).
Population: 2,508 (2000); Race: 98.8% White, 0.0% Black, 0.2% Asian, 0.2% American Indian and Alaska Native, 0.5% Hispanic of any race, 0.6% two or more races (2000); Density: 1,984.6 persons per square mile (2000); Age: 27.2% under 18, 17.6% over 64 (2000); Marriage status: 21.9% never married, 50.5% now married, 10.7% widowed, 17.0% divorced (2000); Foreign born: 0.1% (2000); Ancestry (includes multiple ancestries): 17.3% German, 16.6% United States or American, 14.6% Irish, 9.2% English, 8.1% Other groups (2000).
Economy: Single-family building permits issued: 2 (2001) / 1 (2000); Multi-family building permits issued: 0 (2001) / 4 (2000); Employment by occupation: 8.1% management, 12.9% professional, 11.0% services, 25.9% sales, 0.5% farming, 11.9% construction, 29.6% production (2000).
Income: Per capita income: $15,843 (2000); Median household income: $28,664 (2000); Poverty rate: 9.5% (2000).
Taxes: Total city taxes per capita: $140 (1997); City property taxes per capita: $131 (1997).
Education: High school graduation rate: 72.0% (2000); College graduation rate: 9.0% (2000).

School District(s)

Spencer-Owen Community Schools (PK-12)
2000 Enrollment: 3,174 812-829-2233
Housing: Homeownership rate: 57.0% (2000); Median home value: $78,400 (2000); Median rent: $346 per month (2000); Median age of housing: 41 years (2000).
Newspapers: Spencer Evening World (5 x week); The Owen Leader (1 x week)
Transportation: Commute to work: 92.4% car, 0.0% public transportation, 5.2% walk, 1.9% work from home (2000); Travel time to work: 42.1% less than 15 minutes, 14.6% 15 to 30 minutes, 21.0% 30 to 45 minutes, 6.5% 45 to 60 minutes, 15.8% 60 minutes or more (2000)
Additional Information Contacts
Spencer-Owen Chamber of Commerce 812-829-3245

Parke County

Located in western Indiana; bounded on the west by the Wabash River; drained by Sugar and Raccoon Creeks. Covers a land area of 444.80 square miles, a water area of 5.30 square miles, and is located in the Eastern Time Zone. The county government was organized in 1821. County seat is Rockville.

Weather Station: Rockville Elevation: 688 feet

	Jan	Feb	Mar	Apr	May	Jun	Jul	Aug	Sep	Oct	Nov	Dec
High	36	42	53	66	76	84	87	85	79	68	53	41
Low	18	22	32	42	52	61	65	62	56	44	35	25
Precip	2.5	2.2	3.7	4.3	4.8	4.1	4.8	4.2	3.2	3.1	4.3	3.5
Snow	5.0	3.3	2.2	0.2	tr	0.0	0.0	0.0	0.0	0.0	0.4	5.2

High and Low temperatures in degrees Fahrenheit; Precipitation and Snow in inches

Population: 17,241 (2000); Race: 96.8% White, 1.8% Black, 0.2% Asian, 0.4% American Indian and Alaska Native, 0.6% Hispanic of any race, 0.7% two or more races (2000); Density: 38.8 persons per square mile (2000); Age: 24.0% under 18, 14.7% over 64 (2000).
Religion: Five largest groups: 11.6% Christian Churches and Churches of Christ, 4.9% The United Methodist Church, 2.8% Friends (Quakers), 2.6% Southern Baptist Convention, 2.3% Christian Church (Disciples of Christ) (2000).
Economy: Unemployment rate: 4.9% (11/2002); Total civilian labor force: 7,569 (11/2002); Leading industries: 28.8% manufacturing; 17.7% retail trade; 14.7% health care and social assistance (2000); Companies that employ more than 1,000 persons: 0 (2000); Companies that employ more than 100 persons: 2 (2000); Farms: 471 totaling 188,816 acres (1997); Minority business ownership rate: 0.0% (1997); Women business ownership rate: 23.2% (1997); Retail sales per capita: $2,944 (1997). Single-family building permits issued: 48 (2001) / 43 (2000); Multi-family building permits issued: 0 (2001) / 0 (2000).
Income: Per capita income: $16,986 (2000); Median household income: $35,724 (2000); Poverty rate: 11.5% (2000); Bankruptcy rate: 5.21% (2001).
Taxes: Total county taxes per capita: $223 (2000); County property taxes per capita: $137 (2000).
Education: High school graduation rate: 80.5% (2000); College graduation rate: 11.6% (2000).
Housing: Homeownership rate: 80.3% (2000); Median home value: $64,900 (2000); Median rent: $280 per month (2000); Median age of housing: 34 years (2000).
Health: Birth rate: 106.1 per 10,000 population (1998); Age adjusted death rate: 82.6 per 10,000 population (1999); Age adjusted cancer mortality rate: 182.1 deaths per 100,000 population (1999). Number of physicians: 5.8 per 10,000 population (1999); Number of hospital beds: n/a (1999).
Elections: 2000 Presidential election results: 38.5% Gore, 59.6% Bush, 0.3% Nader, 1.0% Buchanan
National and State Parks: Raccoon Lake State Recreation Area; Turkey Run State Park
Additional Information Contacts
Parke County Government Offices 765-569-3422
Parke County Chamber of Commerce 765-569-5565

Parke County Communities

BLOOMINGDALE (town). Covers a land area of 0.571 square miles and a water area of 0 square miles. Located at 39.83° N. Lat.; 87.25° W. Long. Elevation is 650 feet.
Population: 319 (2000); Race: 99.0% White, 0.3% Black, 0.0% Asian, 0.0% American Indian and Alaska Native, 0.0% Hispanic of any race, 0.7% two or more races (2000); Density: 558.7 persons per square mile (2000); Age: 22.9% under 18, 14.0% over 64 (2000); Marriage status: 18.9% never married, 63.8% now married, 7.4% widowed, 9.9% divorced (2000); Foreign born: 0.7% (2000); Ancestry (includes multiple ancestries): 25.3% German, 22.5% English, 14.7% Irish, 11.6% United States or American, 6.1% French (except Basque) (2000).
Economy: In agricultural area. Manufacturing: plastic products and hardwood lumber. Employment by occupation: 5.7% management, 17.6% professional, 23.3% services, 24.5% sales, 0.0% farming, 8.8% construction, 20.1% production (2000).
Income: Per capita income: $17,928 (2000); Median household income: $36,500 (2000); Poverty rate: 2.0% (2000).
Taxes: Total city taxes per capita: $132 (2000); City property taxes per capita: $119 (2000).
Education: High school graduation rate: 92.0% (2000); College graduation rate: 13.7% (2000).
Housing: Homeownership rate: 93.0% (2000); Median home value: $53,300 (2000); Median rent: $250 per month (2000); Median age of housing: 60+ years (2000).
Transportation: Commute to work: 84.6% car, 0.0% public transportation, 12.2% walk, 3.2% work from home (2000); Travel time to work: 46.4% less than 15 minutes, 22.5% 15 to 30 minutes, 9.9% 30 to 45 minutes, 13.2% 45 to 60 minutes, 7.9% 60 minutes or more (2000)

BRIDGETON (unincorporated postal area, zip code 47836). Covers a land area of 2.929 square miles and a water area of 0.006 square miles. Located at 39.64° N. Lat.; 87.17° W. Long. Elevation is 560 feet.
History: Covered bridge here and many others in the surrounding area. Laid out 1857.
Population: 126 (2000); Race: 100.0% White, 0.0% Black, 0.0% Asian, 0.0% American Indian and Alaska Native, 0.0% Hispanic of any race, 0.0% two or more races (2000); Density: 43.0 persons per square mile (2000); Age: 31.6% under 18, 4.4% over 64 (2000); Marriage status: 18.8% never married, 63.5% now married, 5.9% widowed, 11.8% divorced (2000); Foreign born: 4.4% (2000); Ancestry (includes multiple ancestries): 45.6% Irish, 17.5% French (except Basque), 17.5% Other groups, 11.4% German, 5.3% English (2000).
Economy: Agricultural area: corn; hogs. Seasonal tourist site, especially in autumn. Employment by occupation: 18.0% management, 8.2% professional, 41.0% services, 6.6% sales, 8.2% farming, 9.8% construction, 8.2% production (2000).
Income: Per capita income: $11,926 (2000); Median household income: $16,000 (2000); Poverty rate: 45.6% (2000).
Education: High school graduation rate: 93.2% (2000); College graduation rate: 0.0% (2000).
Housing: Homeownership rate: 100.0% (2000); Median home value: $45,700 (2000); Median age of housing: 35 years (2000).
Transportation: Commute to work: 100.0% car, 0.0% public transportation, 0.0% walk, 0.0% work from home (2000); Travel time to work: 18.0% less than 15 minutes, 70.5% 15 to 30 minutes, 0.0% 30 to 45 minutes, 11.5% 45 to 60 minutes, 0.0% 60 minutes or more (2000)

MARSHALL (town). Covers a land area of 0.246 square miles and a water area of 0 square miles. Located at 39.84° N. Lat.; 87.18° W. Long. Elevation is 700 feet.
History: Covered bridges in area. Laid out 1878.
Population: 360 (2000); Race: 97.4% White, 0.5% Black, 0.0% Asian, 0.0% American Indian and Alaska Native, 1.0% Hispanic of any race, 2.1% two or more races (2000); Density: 1,464.4 persons per square mile (2000); Age: 32.9% under 18, 10.4% over 64 (2000); Marriage status: 24.9% never married, 55.9% now married, 4.6% widowed, 14.6% divorced (2000); Foreign born: 0.0% (2000); Ancestry (includes multiple ancestries): 25.6% United States or American, 12.0% English, 7.6% German, 5.7% Irish, 4.4% Other groups (2000).
Economy: Agricultural area. Manufacturing: plastic products. Tourist area around Turkey Run State Park to North; canoeing on Sugar Creek. Employment by occupation: 4.4% management, 6.6% professional, 18.1% services, 18.1% sales, 1.1% farming, 9.3% construction, 42.3% production (2000).
Income: Per capita income: $12,889 (2000); Median household income: $33,906 (2000); Poverty rate: 16.7% (2000).
Taxes: Total city taxes per capita: $27 (1997); City property taxes per capita: $27 (1997).
Education: High school graduation rate: 82.3% (2000); College graduation rate: 7.7% (2000).

School District(s)

Turkey Run Community Sch Corp (PK-12)
2000 Enrollment: 694 765-597-2750
Housing: Homeownership rate: 81.2% (2000); Median home value: $57,300 (2000); Median rent: $288 per month (2000); Median age of housing: 51 years (2000).
Transportation: Commute to work: 98.3% car, 0.0% public transportation, 1.7% walk, 0.0% work from home (2000); Travel time to work: 36.7% less than 15 minutes, 23.3% 15 to 30 minutes, 28.3% 30 to 45 minutes, 4.4% 45 to 60 minutes, 7.2% 60 minutes or more (2000)

MECCA (town). Covers a land area of 0.402 square miles and a water area of 0 square miles. Located at 39.72° N. Lat.; 87.33° W. Long. Elevation is 495 feet.
History: Covered bridges in area. Laid out 1890.
Population: 355 (2000); Race: 94.2% White, 0.0% Black, 4.0% Asian, 0.0% American Indian and Alaska Native, 0.6% Hispanic of any race, 1.2% two or more races (2000); Density: 884.1 persons per square mile (2000); Age: 29.2% under 18, 7.3% over 64 (2000); Marriage status: 25.4% never married, 50.4% now married, 7.0% widowed, 17.2% divorced (2000); Foreign born: 1.5% (2000); Ancestry (includes multiple ancestries): 13.7% German, 13.7% Irish, 9.1% Other groups, 5.8% United States or American, 4.9% English (2000).

Economy: Hogs, cattle; wheat, corn. Single-family building permits issued: 0 (2001) / 0 (2000); Multi-family building permits issued: 0 (2001) / 0 (2000); Employment by occupation: 4.2% management, 7.2% professional, 22.9% services, 18.1% sales, 1.2% farming, 6.0% construction, 40.4% production (2000).
Income: Per capita income: $12,094 (2000); Median household income: $31,375 (2000); Poverty rate: 8.6% (2000).
Taxes: Total city taxes per capita: $12 (1997); City property taxes per capita: $12 (1997).
Education: High school graduation rate: 69.5% (2000); College graduation rate: 1.0% (2000).
Housing: Homeownership rate: 78.5% (2000); Median home value: $37,500 (2000); Median rent: $311 per month (2000); Median age of housing: 40 years (2000).
Transportation: Commute to work: 95.1% car, 0.0% public transportation, 3.1% walk, 1.9% work from home (2000); Travel time to work: 32.1% less than 15 minutes, 35.8% 15 to 30 minutes, 21.4% 30 to 45 minutes, 5.7% 45 to 60 minutes, 5.0% 60 minutes or more (2000)

MONTEZUMA (town). Covers a land area of 0.618 square miles and a water area of 0 square miles. Located at 39.79° N. Lat.; 87.37° W. Long. Elevation is 501 feet.
History: When the Wabash & Erie Canal was completed in 1848, Montezuma became a commercial center on the Wabash River. Montezuma was settled by Samuel Hill in 1821, and named for the Aztec emperor of Mexico.
Population: 1,179 (2000); Race: 97.3% White, 1.3% Black, 0.3% Asian, 0.3% American Indian and Alaska Native, 0.6% Hispanic of any race, 0.9% two or more races (2000); Density: 1,908.1 persons per square mile (2000); Age: 27.4% under 18, 13.7% over 64 (2000); Marriage status: 21.4% never married, 54.2% now married, 8.8% widowed, 15.7% divorced (2000); Foreign born: 0.5% (2000); Ancestry (includes multiple ancestries): 22.7% United States or American, 17.9% German, 9.6% Irish, 5.5% Other groups, 5.2% English (2000).
Economy: Single-family building permits issued: 0 (2001) / 0 (2000); Multi-family building permits issued: 0 (2001) / 0 (2000); Employment by occupation: 6.6% management, 6.6% professional, 18.8% services, 25.1% sales, 2.4% farming, 16.2% construction, 24.2% production (2000).
Income: Per capita income: $13,754 (2000); Median household income: $31,111 (2000); Poverty rate: 20.1% (2000).
Taxes: Total city taxes per capita: $53 (1997); City property taxes per capita: $49 (1997).
Education: High school graduation rate: 80.9% (2000); College graduation rate: 3.5% (2000).

School District(s)

Southwest Parke Com Sch Corp (KG-12)
2000 Enrollment: 1,037 765-569-2073

Housing: Homeownership rate: 73.3% (2000); Median home value: $46,200 (2000); Median rent: $296 per month (2000); Median age of housing: 48 years (2000).
Transportation: Commute to work: 94.3% car, 0.0% public transportation, 1.2% walk, 1.0% work from home (2000); Travel time to work: 35.5% less than 15 minutes, 33.0% 15 to 30 minutes, 18.0% 30 to 45 minutes, 4.4% 45 to 60 minutes, 9.1% 60 minutes or more (2000)

ROCKVILLE (town). Covers a land area of 1.437 square miles and a water area of 0 square miles. Located at 39.76° N. Lat.; 87.22° W. Long. Elevation is 711 feet.
History: Joseph A. Wright, a governor of Indiana, began his law practice in Rockville.
Population: 2,765 (2000); Race: 97.2% White, 0.0% Black, 0.0% Asian, 1.7% American Indian and Alaska Native, 0.3% Hispanic of any race, 1.1% two or more races (2000); Density: 1,924.4 persons per square mile (2000); Age: 20.9% under 18, 22.8% over 64 (2000); Marriage status: 20.3% never married, 52.7% now married, 14.5% widowed, 12.4% divorced (2000); Foreign born: 0.8% (2000); Ancestry (includes multiple ancestries): 20.1% German, 16.0% United States or American, 11.6% English, 9.3% Irish, 7.2% Other groups (2000).
Economy: Single-family building permits issued: 3 (2001) / 5 (2000); Multi-family building permits issued: 0 (2001) / 0 (2000); Employment by occupation: 7.3% management, 15.4% professional, 23.8% services, 25.7% sales, 0.6% farming, 8.3% construction, 19.0% production (2000).
Income: Per capita income: $18,431 (2000); Median household income: $27,813 (2000); Poverty rate: 15.4% (2000).
Taxes: Total city taxes per capita: $172 (1997); City property taxes per capita: $169 (1997).
Education: High school graduation rate: 82.9% (2000); College graduation rate: 13.1% (2000).

School District(s)

Rockville Community Schools (KG-12)
2000 Enrollment: 944 765-569-5582

Housing: Homeownership rate: 62.0% (2000); Median home value: $66,900 (2000); Median rent: $263 per month (2000); Median age of housing: 45 years (2000).
Newspapers: Parke County Sentinel (1 x week)
Transportation: Commute to work: 89.5% car, 0.0% public transportation, 4.0% walk, 5.3% work from home (2000); Travel time to work: 54.8% less than 15 minutes, 15.8% 15 to 30 minutes, 18.1% 30 to 45 minutes, 5.8% 45 to 60 minutes, 5.6% 60 minutes or more (2000)
Additional Information Contacts
Parke County Chamber of Commerce 765-569-5565

ROSEDALE (town). Covers a land area of 0.397 square miles and a water area of 0 square miles. Located at 39.62° N. Lat.; 87.28° W. Long. Elevation is 542 feet.
History: Settled c.1819.
Population: 750 (2000); Race: 99.3% White, 0.0% Black, 0.0% Asian, 0.3% American Indian and Alaska Native, 1.1% Hispanic of any race, 0.4% two or more races (2000); Density: 1,890.6 persons per square mile (2000); Age: 28.4% under 18, 16.6% over 64 (2000); Marriage status: 21.7% never married, 59.0% now married, 9.2% widowed, 10.1% divorced (2000); Foreign born: 0.3% (2000); Ancestry (includes multiple ancestries): 21.6% United States or American, 15.3% English, 14.1% German, 8.8% Irish, 5.2% Other groups (2000).
Economy: In agricultural area; machine shop. Employment by occupation: 6.0% management, 13.9% professional, 12.9% services, 29.0% sales, 0.6% farming, 10.1% construction, 27.4% production (2000).
Income: Per capita income: $15,301 (2000); Median household income: $34,519 (2000); Poverty rate: 14.0% (2000).
Taxes: Total city taxes per capita: $41 (1997); City property taxes per capita: $40 (1997).
Education: High school graduation rate: 85.9% (2000); College graduation rate: 10.8% (2000).
Housing: Homeownership rate: 83.9% (2000); Median home value: $50,100 (2000); Median rent: $217 per month (2000); Median age of housing: 60+ years (2000).
Transportation: Commute to work: 96.8% car, 0.0% public transportation, 2.3% walk, 0.0% work from home (2000); Travel time to work: 18.8% less than 15 minutes, 40.3% 15 to 30 minutes, 27.3% 30 to 45 minutes, 10.1% 45 to 60 minutes, 3.6% 60 minutes or more (2000)

Perry County

Located in southern Indiana; bounded on the south and partly on the east by the Ohio River and the Kentucky border; drained by the Anderson River. Covers a land area of 381.40 square miles, a water area of 4.90 square miles, and is located in the Eastern Time Zone. The county government was organized in 1814. County seat is Cannelton.

Weather Station: Tell City — Elevation: 396 feet

	Jan	Feb	Mar	Apr	May	Jun	Jul	Aug	Sep	Oct	Nov	Dec
High	40	45	55	67	76	84	88	87	81	69	56	45
Low	23	26	35	44	54	63	68	66	59	46	37	29
Precip	3.2	3.2	4.6	4.9	5.1	4.3	4.6	3.7	3.3	3.2	4.1	4.0
Snow	4.4	2.6	0.7	0.1	0.0	0.0	0.0	0.0	0.0	0.0	0.4	1.0

High and Low temperatures in degrees Fahrenheit; Precipitation and Snow in inches

Population: 18,899 (2000); Race: 97.8% White, 1.4% Black, 0.0% Asian, 0.0% American Indian and Alaska Native, 0.6% Hispanic of any race, 0.6% two or more races (2000); Density: 49.6 persons per square mile (2000); Age: 23.0% under 18, 14.9% over 64 (2000).
Religion: Five largest groups: 33.0% Catholic Church, 4.8% United Church of Christ, 3.8% American Baptist Churches in the USA, 3.2% The United Methodist Church, 2.0% Churches of Christ (2000).
Economy: Unemployment rate: 4.5% (11/2002); Total civilian labor force: 8,920 (11/2002); Leading industries: 35.2% manufacturing; 18.6% retail trade; 14.0% health care and social assistance (2000); Companies that employ more than 1,000 persons: 0 (2000); Companies that employ more than 100 persons: 7 (2000); Farms: 484 totaling 84,251 acres (1997); Minority business ownership rate: 0.0% (1997); Women business ownership rate: 23.1% (1997); Retail sales per capita: $6,797 (1997). Single-family building

permits issued: 41 (2001) / 50 (2000); Multi-family building permits issued: 0 (2001) / 6 (2000).
Income: Per capita income: $16,673 (2000); Median household income: $36,246 (2000); Poverty rate: 9.4% (2000); Bankruptcy rate: 6.26% (2001).
Taxes: Total county taxes per capita: $300 (2000); County property taxes per capita: $116 (2000).
Education: High school graduation rate: 74.8% (2000); College graduation rate: 9.6% (2000).
Housing: Homeownership rate: 79.2% (2000); Median home value: $71,200 (2000); Median rent: $302 per month (2000); Median age of housing: 33 years (2000).
Health: Birth rate: 111.7 per 10,000 population (1998); Age adjusted death rate: 92.7 per 10,000 population (1999); Age adjusted cancer mortality rate: 234.0 deaths per 100,000 population (1999). Air Quality Index: 60% good, 40% moderate, 0% unhealthy (percent of days in 2000). Number of physicians: 4.2 per 10,000 population (1999); Number of hospital beds: 20.1 per 10,000 population (1999).
Elections: 2000 Presidential election results: 51.8% Gore, 46.9% Bush, 0.4% Nader, 0.5% Buchanan
National and State Parks: Ferdinand State Forest; Harrison-Crawford State Forest
Additional Information Contacts
Perry County Government Offices 812-547-6427
Tell City Chamber of Commerce 812-547-2385

Perry County Communities

BRANCHVILLE (unincorporated postal area, zip code 47514). Covers a land area of 6.299 square miles and a water area of 0 square miles. Located at 38.13° N. Lat.; 86.58° W. Long. Elevation is 434 feet.
Population: 253 (2000); Race: 100.0% White, 0.0% Black, 0.0% Asian, 0.0% American Indian and Alaska Native, 0.0% Hispanic of any race, 0.0% two or more races (2000); Density: 40.2 persons per square mile (2000); Age: 40.1% under 18, 7.4% over 64 (2000); Marriage status: 17.8% never married, 69.9% now married, 7.3% widowed, 5.0% divorced (2000); Foreign born: 0.0% (2000); Ancestry (includes multiple ancestries): 33.2% German, 21.4% United States or American, 19.6% English, 13.4% French (except Basque), 13.4% Irish (2000).
Economy: Employment by occupation: 16.4% management, 8.2% professional, 6.7% services, 13.4% sales, 0.0% farming, 13.4% construction, 41.8% production (2000).
Income: Per capita income: $15,241 (2000); Median household income: $52,250 (2000); Poverty rate: 6.2% (2000).
Education: High school graduation rate: 69.7% (2000); College graduation rate: 16.8% (2000).
Housing: Homeownership rate: 100.0% (2000); Median home value: $67,400 (2000); Median age of housing: 25 years (2000).
Transportation: Commute to work: 82.8% car, 0.0% public transportation, 0.0% walk, 17.2% work from home (2000); Travel time to work: 18.0% less than 15 minutes, 22.5% 15 to 30 minutes, 27.0% 30 to 45 minutes, 20.7% 45 to 60 minutes, 11.7% 60 minutes or more (2000)

BRISTOW (unincorporated postal area, zip code 47515). Covers a land area of 61.816 square miles and a water area of 0.028 square miles. Located at 38.18° N. Lat.; 86.71° W. Long. Elevation is 416 feet.
Population: 1,111 (2000); Race: 99.6% White, 0.0% Black, 0.0% Asian, 0.0% American Indian and Alaska Native, 0.0% Hispanic of any race, 0.4% two or more races (2000); Density: 18.0 persons per square mile (2000); Age: 29.2% under 18, 12.7% over 64 (2000); Marriage status: 17.8% never married, 67.5% now married, 3.7% widowed, 11.0% divorced (2000); Foreign born: 0.0% (2000); Ancestry (includes multiple ancestries): 39.0% German, 15.5% United States or American, 6.6% English, 5.9% Irish, 2.1% French (except Basque) (2000).
Economy: Employment by occupation: 8.5% management, 7.1% professional, 11.1% services, 16.0% sales, 0.5% farming, 15.2% construction, 41.6% production (2000).
Income: Per capita income: $16,762 (2000); Median household income: $40,982 (2000); Poverty rate: 6.2% (2000).
Education: High school graduation rate: 70.6% (2000); College graduation rate: 4.1% (2000).
Housing: Homeownership rate: 87.9% (2000); Median home value: $71,000 (2000); Median rent: $200 per month (2000); Median age of housing: 29 years (2000).
Transportation: Commute to work: 92.5% car, 0.0% public transportation, 0.0% walk, 7.5% work from home (2000); Travel time to work: 8.5% less than 15 minutes, 41.9% 15 to 30 minutes, 23.4% 30 to 45 minutes, 14.1% 45 to 60 minutes, 12.2% 60 minutes or more (2000)

CANNELTON (city). Covers a land area of 1.482 square miles and a water area of 0.071 square miles. Located at 37.91° N. Lat.; 86.74° W. Long. Elevation is 426 feet.
History: Cannelton was founded in 1837 as a coal-mining town and shipping port on the Ohio River.
Population: 1,209 (2000); Race: 99.4% White, 0.0% Black, 0.2% Asian, 0.0% American Indian and Alaska Native, 0.9% Hispanic of any race, 0.2% two or more races (2000); Density: 816.0 persons per square mile (2000); Age: 25.4% under 18, 15.4% over 64 (2000); Marriage status: 24.8% never married, 49.0% now married, 9.5% widowed, 16.7% divorced (2000); Foreign born: 0.2% (2000); Ancestry (includes multiple ancestries): 24.4% German, 14.6% United States or American, 14.1% English, 10.7% Irish, 8.3% Other groups (2000).
Economy: Single-family building permits issued: 0 (2001) / 0 (2000); Multi-family building permits issued: 0 (2001) / 0 (2000); Employment by occupation: 7.1% management, 6.4% professional, 18.3% services, 20.5% sales, 0.4% farming, 11.2% construction, 36.1% production (2000).
Income: Per capita income: $13,578 (2000); Median household income: $27,361 (2000); Poverty rate: 16.0% (2000).
Taxes: Total city taxes per capita: $314 (2000); City property taxes per capita: $188 (2000).
Education: High school graduation rate: 74.8% (2000); College graduation rate: 6.4% (2000).

School District(s)

Cannelton City Schools (KG-12)
2000 Enrollment: 232 812-547-2637
Housing: Homeownership rate: 64.9% (2000); Median home value: $56,600 (2000); Median rent: $284 per month (2000); Median age of housing: 45 years (2000).
Transportation: Commute to work: 92.6% car, 0.0% public transportation, 3.8% walk, 0.8% work from home (2000); Travel time to work: 48.5% less than 15 minutes, 25.2% 15 to 30 minutes, 13.6% 30 to 45 minutes, 8.1% 45 to 60 minutes, 4.7% 60 minutes or more (2000)

DERBY (unincorporated postal area, zip code 47525). Covers a land area of 34.266 square miles and a water area of 0.074 square miles. Located at 38.03° N. Lat.; 86.55° W. Long. Elevation is 409 feet.
Population: 418 (2000); Race: 97.8% White, 0.0% Black, 0.0% Asian, 0.0% American Indian and Alaska Native, 0.0% Hispanic of any race, 2.2% two or more races (2000); Density: 12.2 persons per square mile (2000); Age: 26.2% under 18, 6.5% over 64 (2000); Marriage status: 23.3% never married, 65.5% now married, 4.0% widowed, 7.2% divorced (2000); Foreign born: 0.0% (2000); Ancestry (includes multiple ancestries): 23.6% United States or American, 21.0% German, 14.3% Irish, 11.3% English, 8.0% Other groups (2000).
Economy: Employment by occupation: 2.2% management, 14.9% professional, 15.8% services, 18.4% sales, 5.7% farming, 9.6% construction, 33.3% production (2000).
Income: Per capita income: $14,597 (2000); Median household income: $38,333 (2000); Poverty rate: 3.4% (2000).
Education: High school graduation rate: 86.6% (2000); College graduation rate: 13.8% (2000).
Housing: Homeownership rate: 91.0% (2000); Median home value: $65,600 (2000); Median rent: $255 per month (2000); Median age of housing: 20 years (2000).
Transportation: Commute to work: 94.5% car, 0.0% public transportation, 1.8% walk, 3.7% work from home (2000); Travel time to work: 6.2% less than 15 minutes, 37.8% 15 to 30 minutes, 25.4% 30 to 45 minutes, 14.4% 45 to 60 minutes, 16.3% 60 minutes or more (2000)

LEOPOLD (unincorporated postal area, zip code 47551). Covers a land area of 44.776 square miles and a water area of 0.011 square miles. Located at 38.12° N. Lat.; 86.55° W. Long. Elevation is 725 feet.
Population: 568 (2000); Race: 97.3% White, 0.0% Black, 0.0% Asian, 0.0% American Indian and Alaska Native, 0.0% Hispanic of any race, 2.7% two or more races (2000); Density: 12.7 persons per square mile (2000); Age: 19.6% under 18, 9.2% over 64 (2000); Marriage status: 25.3% never married, 61.4% now married, 2.7% widowed, 10.6% divorced (2000); Foreign born: 0.0% (2000); Ancestry (includes multiple ancestries): 28.5% German, 17.2% French (except Basque), 15.3% United States or American, 11.5% Irish, 6.8% English (2000).

Economy: Employment by occupation: 8.9% management, 19.0% professional, 15.2% services, 14.6% sales, 0.0% farming, 8.2% construction, 34.2% production (2000).
Income: Per capita income: $17,196 (2000); Median household income: $37,500 (2000); Poverty rate: 8.3% (2000).
Education: High school graduation rate: 84.1% (2000); College graduation rate: 11.1% (2000).

School District(s)

Perry Central Com Schools Corp (PK-12)
2000 Enrollment: 1,181 812-843-5576

Housing: Homeownership rate: 92.5% (2000); Median home value: $76,400 (2000); Median rent: $375 per month (2000); Median age of housing: 24 years (2000).
Transportation: Commute to work: 93.7% car, 1.3% public transportation, 1.3% walk, 3.8% work from home (2000); Travel time to work: 15.5% less than 15 minutes, 27.3% 15 to 30 minutes, 19.4% 30 to 45 minutes, 16.8% 45 to 60 minutes, 21.1% 60 minutes or more (2000)

ROME (unincorporated postal area, zip code 47574). Covers a land area of 12.940 square miles and a water area of 0 square miles. Located at 37.93° N. Lat.; 86.56° W. Long. Elevation is 406 feet.
Population: 167 (2000); Race: 100.0% White, 0.0% Black, 0.0% Asian, 0.0% American Indian and Alaska Native, 0.0% Hispanic of any race, 0.0% two or more races (2000); Density: 12.9 persons per square mile (2000); Age: 16.7% under 18, 17.6% over 64 (2000); Marriage status: 14.1% never married, 76.8% now married, 4.0% widowed, 5.1% divorced (2000); Foreign born: 2.8% (2000); Ancestry (includes multiple ancestries): 38.0% German, 10.2% Other groups, 8.3% Italian, 6.5% French (except Basque), 6.5% Scottish (2000).
Economy: Employment by occupation: 11.8% management, 0.0% professional, 11.8% services, 29.4% sales, 0.0% farming, 0.0% construction, 47.1% production (2000).
Income: Per capita income: $13,219 (2000); Median household income: $27,188 (2000); Poverty rate: 14.8% (2000).
Education: High school graduation rate: 70.0% (2000); College graduation rate: 0.0% (2000).
Housing: Homeownership rate: 90.4% (2000); Median home value: $20,700 (2000); Median age of housing: 24 years (2000).
Transportation: Commute to work: 82.4% car, 0.0% public transportation, 0.0% walk, 17.6% work from home (2000); Travel time to work: 25.0% less than 15 minutes, 41.1% 15 to 30 minutes, 17.9% 30 to 45 minutes, 16.1% 45 to 60 minutes, 0.0% 60 minutes or more (2000)

SAINT CROIX (unincorporated postal area, zip code 47576). Covers a land area of 29.809 square miles and a water area of 0.671 square miles. Located at 38.19° N. Lat.; 86.60° W. Long. Elevation is 761 feet.
Population: 462 (2000); Race: 100.0% White, 0.0% Black, 0.0% Asian, 0.0% American Indian and Alaska Native, 0.0% Hispanic of any race, 0.0% two or more races (2000); Density: 15.5 persons per square mile (2000); Age: 18.1% under 18, 17.5% over 64 (2000); Marriage status: 19.2% never married, 70.6% now married, 6.2% widowed, 4.0% divorced (2000); Foreign born: 0.0% (2000); Ancestry (includes multiple ancestries): 35.8% German, 14.0% Irish, 13.5% United States or American, 8.1% French (except Basque), 7.8% English (2000).
Economy: Employment by occupation: 7.0% management, 17.1% professional, 17.1% services, 26.7% sales, 2.1% farming, 8.0% construction, 21.9% production (2000).
Income: Per capita income: $16,913 (2000); Median household income: $38,250 (2000); Poverty rate: 7.8% (2000).
Education: High school graduation rate: 78.9% (2000); College graduation rate: 15.0% (2000).
Housing: Homeownership rate: 87.0% (2000); Median home value: $77,500 (2000); Median rent: $304 per month (2000); Median age of housing: 27 years (2000).
Transportation: Commute to work: 94.7% car, 0.0% public transportation, 0.0% walk, 3.2% work from home (2000); Travel time to work: 9.4% less than 15 minutes, 26.5% 15 to 30 minutes, 39.8% 30 to 45 minutes, 18.2% 45 to 60 minutes, 6.1% 60 minutes or more (2000)

TELL CITY (city). Covers a land area of 4.557 square miles and a water area of 0.051 square miles. Located at 37.95° N. Lat.; 86.76° W. Long. Elevation is 436 feet.
History: Tell City was settled in 1857 by a group of Swiss immigrants, and named for the legendary Swiss hero William Tell. An early industry was furniture making.
Population: 7,845 (2000); Race: 99.4% White, 0.1% Black, 0.0% Asian, 0.0% American Indian and Alaska Native, 0.7% Hispanic of any race, 0.5% two or more races (2000); Density: 1,721.4 persons per square mile (2000); Age: 22.5% under 18, 20.7% over 64 (2000); Marriage status: 19.9% never married, 56.5% now married, 9.8% widowed, 13.7% divorced (2000); Foreign born: 0.2% (2000); Ancestry (includes multiple ancestries): 27.0% German, 11.9% United States or American, 11.8% Irish, 8.5% English, 5.7% French (except Basque) (2000).
Economy: Single-family building permits issued: 11 (2001) / 20 (2000); Multi-family building permits issued: 0 (2001) / 4 (2000); Employment by occupation: 6.1% management, 13.2% professional, 16.5% services, 23.6% sales, 0.0% farming, 10.7% construction, 30.0% production (2000).
Income: Per capita income: $17,443 (2000); Median household income: $31,045 (2000); Poverty rate: 11.2% (2000).
Taxes: Total city taxes per capita: $195 (2000); City property taxes per capita: $153 (2000).
Education: High school graduation rate: 72.2% (2000); College graduation rate: 11.1% (2000).

School District(s)

Tell City-Troy Township School Corp (PK-12)
2000 Enrollment: 1,722 812-547-3300

Housing: Homeownership rate: 70.8% (2000); Median home value: $69,800 (2000); Median rent: $301 per month (2000); Median age of housing: 39 years (2000).
Hospitals: Perry County Memorial Hospital
Safety: Violent crime rate: 10.1 per 10,000 population; Property crime rate: 320.7 per 10,000 population (2001).
Newspapers: The Perry County News (2 x week)
Transportation: Commute to work: 94.7% car, 0.4% public transportation, 1.6% walk, 1.4% work from home (2000); Travel time to work: 56.3% less than 15 minutes, 18.2% 15 to 30 minutes, 12.3% 30 to 45 minutes, 7.6% 45 to 60 minutes, 5.6% 60 minutes or more (2000)
Additional Information Contacts
Tell City Chamber of Commerce 812-547-2385

TROY (town). Covers a land area of 0.314 square miles and a water area of 0 square miles. Located at 37.99° N. Lat.; 86.79° W. Long. Elevation is 430 feet.
History: Troy was founded by families from Virginia. It served as the seat of Perry County until 1818.
Population: 392 (2000); Race: 97.5% White, 1.8% Black, 0.0% Asian, 0.8% American Indian and Alaska Native, 0.0% Hispanic of any race, 0.0% two or more races (2000); Density: 1,248.4 persons per square mile (2000); Age: 23.4% under 18, 13.1% over 64 (2000); Marriage status: 26.7% never married, 49.1% now married, 8.8% widowed, 15.4% divorced (2000); Foreign born: 0.0% (2000); Ancestry (includes multiple ancestries): 30.2% German, 21.9% Irish, 12.8% United States or American, 12.1% French (except Basque), 11.6% Other groups (2000).
Economy: Single-family building permits issued: 0 (2001) / 1 (2000); Multi-family building permits issued: 0 (2001) / 2 (2000); Employment by occupation: 5.2% management, 5.2% professional, 14.5% services, 16.8% sales, 0.0% farming, 16.8% construction, 41.6% production (2000).
Income: Per capita income: $13,891 (2000); Median household income: $30,536 (2000); Poverty rate: 19.6% (2000).
Taxes: Total city taxes per capita: $38 (1997); City property taxes per capita: $28 (1997).
Education: High school graduation rate: 71.8% (2000); College graduation rate: 3.8% (2000).
Housing: Homeownership rate: 74.4% (2000); Median home value: $65,700 (2000); Median rent: $260 per month (2000); Median age of housing: 39 years (2000).
Transportation: Commute to work: 97.0% car, 0.0% public transportation, 2.4% walk, 0.0% work from home (2000); Travel time to work: 43.2% less than 15 minutes, 14.8% 15 to 30 minutes, 18.3% 30 to 45 minutes, 16.0% 45 to 60 minutes, 7.7% 60 minutes or more (2000)

Pike County

Located in southwestern Indiana; bounded on the north by the White River; drained by the Patoka River. Covers a land area of 336.20 square miles, a water area of 4.90 square miles, and is located in the Eastern Time Zone. The county government was organized in 1816. County seat is Petersburg.
Population: 12,837 (2000); Race: 98.5% White, 0.1% Black, 0.5% Asian, 0.1% American Indian and Alaska Native, 0.8% Hispanic of any race, 0.5%

two or more races (2000); Density: 38.2 persons per square mile (2000); Age: 24.0% under 18, 15.3% over 64 (2000).
Religion: Five largest groups: 8.7% The United Methodist Church, 2.5% Catholic Church, 2.5% American Baptist Churches in the USA, 2.2% Christian Churches and Churches of Christ, 2.0% Church of the Nazarene (2000).
Economy: Unemployment rate: 5.1% (11/2002); Total civilian labor force: 6,245 (11/2002); Leading industries: 14.2% health care and social assistance; 13.4% retail trade; 10.9% transportation & warehousing (2000); Companies that employ more than 1,000 persons: 0 (2000); Companies that employ more than 100 persons: 3 (2000); Farms: 288 totaling 84,237 acres (1997); Minority business ownership rate: 0.0% (1997); Women business ownership rate: 0.0% (1997); Retail sales per capita: $3,209 (1997). Single-family building permits issued: 55 (2001) / 61 (2000); Multi-family building permits issued: 4 (2001) / 12 (2000).
Income: Per capita income: $16,217 (2000); Median household income: $34,759 (2000); Poverty rate: 8.0% (2000); Bankruptcy rate: 6.28% (2001).
Taxes: Total county taxes per capita: $222 (1997); County property taxes per capita: $219 (1997).
Education: High school graduation rate: 75.6% (2000); College graduation rate: 8.4% (2000).
Housing: Homeownership rate: 82.7% (2000); Median home value: $59,300 (2000); Median rent: $235 per month (2000); Median age of housing: 31 years (2000).
Health: Birth rate: 127.8 per 10,000 population (1998); Age adjusted death rate: 92.4 per 10,000 population (1999); Age adjusted cancer mortality rate: 201.9 deaths per 100,000 population (1999). Air Quality Index: 98% good, 2% moderate, 0% unhealthy (percent of days in 2000). Number of physicians: 2.3 per 10,000 population (1999); Number of hospital beds: n/a (1999).
Elections: 2000 Presidential election results: 41.3% Gore, 56.6% Bush, 0.1% Nader, 1.4% Buchanan
National and State Parks: Patoka State Fish and Wildlife Area; Pike State Forest
Additional Information Contacts
Pike County Government Offices 812-354-8448
Petersburg Chamber of Commerce 812-354-8155

Pike County Communities

OTWELL (unincorporated postal area, zip code 47564). Covers a land area of 38.002 square miles and a water area of 0.228 square miles. Located at 38.47° N. Lat.; 87.09° W. Long. Elevation is 490 feet.
History: Old surface mines.
Population: 1,418 (2000); Race: 98.7% White, 0.0% Black, 0.4% Asian, 0.2% American Indian and Alaska Native, 0.0% Hispanic of any race, 0.7% two or more races (2000); Density: 37.3 persons per square mile (2000); Age: 29.9% under 18, 15.1% over 64 (2000); Marriage status: 16.9% never married, 68.7% now married, 8.3% widowed, 6.1% divorced (2000); Foreign born: 0.9% (2000); Ancestry (includes multiple ancestries): 23.8% German, 22.3% United States or American, 11.2% English, 10.1% Irish, 6.4% French (except Basque) (2000).
Economy: Agriculture: wheat, corn; cattle, hogs. Bituminous coal. Employment by occupation: 9.3% management, 15.2% professional, 8.5% services, 17.6% sales, 0.8% farming, 13.0% construction, 35.6% production (2000).
Income: Per capita income: $17,579 (2000); Median household income: $36,974 (2000); Poverty rate: 5.7% (2000).
Education: High school graduation rate: 77.2% (2000); College graduation rate: 11.8% (2000).
Housing: Homeownership rate: 84.8% (2000); Median home value: $65,300 (2000); Median rent: $200 per month (2000); Median age of housing: 24 years (2000).
Transportation: Commute to work: 94.2% car, 0.0% public transportation, 0.6% walk, 4.2% work from home (2000); Travel time to work: 26.9% less than 15 minutes, 53.2% 15 to 30 minutes, 14.6% 30 to 45 minutes, 1.4% 45 to 60 minutes, 3.9% 60 minutes or more (2000)

PETERSBURG (city). Aka Hosmer. Covers a land area of 1.464 square miles and a water area of 0 square miles. Located at 38.49° N. Lat.; 87.28° W. Long. Elevation is 439 feet.
History: Laid out 1817, incorporated 1924.
Population: 2,570 (2000); Race: 99.6% White, 0.2% Black, 0.0% Asian, 0.0% American Indian and Alaska Native, 0.0% Hispanic of any race, 0.2% two or more races (2000); Density: 1,755.3 persons per square mile (2000); Age: 20.7% under 18, 22.2% over 64 (2000); Marriage status: 20.4% never married, 55.3% now married, 12.0% widowed, 12.3% divorced (2000); Foreign born: 0.6% (2000); Ancestry (includes multiple ancestries): 16.3% United States or American, 14.4% German, 9.8% Irish, 9.8% English, 3.8% Other groups (2000).
Economy: Surface coal (bituminous) mines; oil wells; timber. Agricultural area. Manufacturing (steel fabrication). Electricity generation. Employment by occupation: 6.8% management, 15.2% professional, 18.2% services, 16.8% sales, 1.9% farming, 8.0% construction, 33.1% production (2000).
Income: Per capita income: $15,158 (2000); Median household income: $27,054 (2000); Poverty rate: 11.6% (2000).
Taxes: Total city taxes per capita: $157 (2000); City property taxes per capita: $137 (2000).
Education: High school graduation rate: 66.5% (2000); College graduation rate: 7.4% (2000).

School District(s)
Pike County School Corp (PK-12)
2000 Enrollment: 2,202 812-354-8731
Housing: Homeownership rate: 67.7% (2000); Median home value: $50,100 (2000); Median rent: $246 per month (2000); Median age of housing: 38 years (2000).
Newspapers: The Press-Dispatch (1 x week)
Transportation: Commute to work: 94.1% car, 0.0% public transportation, 2.9% walk, 2.1% work from home (2000); Travel time to work: 46.2% less than 15 minutes, 21.6% 15 to 30 minutes, 17.8% 30 to 45 minutes, 8.9% 45 to 60 minutes, 5.5% 60 minutes or more (2000)
Additional Information Contacts
Petersburg Chamber of Commerce 812-354-8155

SPURGEON (town). Covers a land area of 0.175 square miles and a water area of 0 square miles. Located at 38.25° N. Lat.; 87.25° W. Long. Elevation is 509 feet.
History: Laid out 1860.
Population: 227 (2000); Race: 95.9% White, 1.8% Black, 0.0% Asian, 0.0% American Indian and Alaska Native, 3.6% Hispanic of any race, 0.0% two or more races (2000); Density: 1,299.1 persons per square mile (2000); Age: 22.5% under 18, 17.1% over 64 (2000); Marriage status: 17.1% never married, 68.6% now married, 10.9% widowed, 3.4% divorced (2000); Foreign born: 3.2% (2000); Ancestry (includes multiple ancestries): 22.5% German, 12.6% United States or American, 11.7% Irish, 8.1% Other groups, 6.3% English (2000).
Economy: In agricultural and bituminous-coal-mining area (surface mining). Employment by occupation: 2.1% management, 15.6% professional, 15.6% services, 30.2% sales, 2.1% farming, 2.1% construction, 32.3% production (2000).
Income: Per capita income: $16,850 (2000); Median household income: $36,429 (2000); Poverty rate: 4.1% (2000).
Taxes: Total city taxes per capita: $74 (1997); City property taxes per capita: $61 (1997).
Education: High school graduation rate: 70.5% (2000); College graduation rate: 6.2% (2000).
Housing: Homeownership rate: 85.9% (2000); Median home value: $53,300 (2000); Median rent: $225 per month (2000); Median age of housing: 60+ years (2000).
Transportation: Commute to work: 92.6% car, 0.0% public transportation, 0.0% walk, 7.4% work from home (2000); Travel time to work: 3.4% less than 15 minutes, 20.7% 15 to 30 minutes, 52.9% 30 to 45 minutes, 23.0% 45 to 60 minutes, 0.0% 60 minutes or more (2000)

STENDAL (unincorporated postal area, zip code 47585). Covers a land area of 37.225 square miles and a water area of 0.415 square miles. Located at 38.26° N. Lat.; 87.14° W. Long. Elevation is 626 feet.
Population: 473 (2000); Race: 90.1% White, 0.0% Black, 9.9% Asian, 0.0% American Indian and Alaska Native, 0.0% Hispanic of any race, 0.0% two or more races (2000); Density: 12.7 persons per square mile (2000); Age: 17.5% under 18, 17.0% over 64 (2000); Marriage status: 28.4% never married, 63.2% now married, 6.4% widowed, 1.9% divorced (2000); Foreign born: 2.8% (2000); Ancestry (includes multiple ancestries): 30.3% German, 17.5% United States or American, 12.6% Other groups, 9.0% English, 6.9% Norwegian (2000).
Economy: Employment by occupation: 13.0% management, 6.0% professional, 13.9% services, 17.1% sales, 3.2% farming, 15.7% construction, 31.0% production (2000).
Income: Per capita income: $17,624 (2000); Median household income: $48,594 (2000); Poverty rate: 3.7% (2000).
Education: High school graduation rate: 64.4% (2000); College graduation rate: 10.3% (2000).

Housing: Homeownership rate: 100.0% (2000); Median home value: $71,300 (2000); Median age of housing: 23 years (2000).
Transportation: Commute to work: 94.4% car, 0.0% public transportation, 0.0% walk, 5.6% work from home (2000); Travel time to work: 10.8% less than 15 minutes, 43.1% 15 to 30 minutes, 27.9% 30 to 45 minutes, 8.8% 45 to 60 minutes, 9.3% 60 minutes or more (2000)

VELPEN (unincorporated postal area, zip code 47590). Covers a land area of 40.595 square miles and a water area of 0.183 square miles. Located at 38.35° N. Lat.; 87.10° W. Long. Elevation is 489 feet.
Population: 747 (2000); Race: 100.0% White, 0.0% Black, 0.0% Asian, 0.0% American Indian and Alaska Native, 0.0% Hispanic of any race, 0.0% two or more races (2000); Density: 18.4 persons per square mile (2000); Age: 29.1% under 18, 8.0% over 64 (2000); Marriage status: 24.0% never married, 63.0% now married, 3.5% widowed, 9.5% divorced (2000); Foreign born: 0.8% (2000); Ancestry (includes multiple ancestries): 26.8% German, 26.4% United States or American, 13.1% Other groups, 4.9% English, 4.4% French (except Basque) (2000).
Economy: Employment by occupation: 4.2% management, 8.3% professional, 6.1% services, 27.2% sales, 3.3% farming, 17.5% construction, 33.3% production (2000).
Income: Per capita income: $17,467 (2000); Median household income: $35,813 (2000); Poverty rate: 3.5% (2000).
Education: High school graduation rate: 78.1% (2000); College graduation rate: 3.6% (2000).
Housing: Homeownership rate: 80.4% (2000); Median home value: $65,000 (2000); Median rent: $211 per month (2000); Median age of housing: 22 years (2000).
Transportation: Commute to work: 96.4% car, 1.7% public transportation, 1.9% walk, 0.0% work from home (2000); Travel time to work: 12.2% less than 15 minutes, 53.3% 15 to 30 minutes, 15.3% 30 to 45 minutes, 3.9% 45 to 60 minutes, 15.3% 60 minutes or more (2000)

WINSLOW (town). Covers a land area of 0.644 square miles and a water area of 0 square miles. Located at 38.38° N. Lat.; 87.21° W. Long. Elevation is 440 feet.
History: Winslow developed as a coal-mining town
Population: 881 (2000); Race: 95.0% White, 0.0% Black, 1.1% Asian, 1.3% American Indian and Alaska Native, 0.9% Hispanic of any race, 2.6% two or more races (2000); Density: 1,367.1 persons per square mile (2000); Age: 28.9% under 18, 12.7% over 64 (2000); Marriage status: 20.8% never married, 53.1% now married, 9.6% widowed, 16.5% divorced (2000); Foreign born: 0.1% (2000); Ancestry (includes multiple ancestries): 18.0% United States or American, 14.9% German, 14.2% Irish, 13.4% Other groups, 12.3% English (2000).
Economy: Employment by occupation: 6.7% management, 10.6% professional, 22.7% services, 15.5% sales, 0.8% farming, 10.3% construction, 33.3% production (2000).
Income: Per capita income: $13,986 (2000); Median household income: $28,672 (2000); Poverty rate: 13.5% (2000).
Taxes: Total city taxes per capita: $116 (1997); City property taxes per capita: $98 (1997).
Education: High school graduation rate: 74.5% (2000); College graduation rate: 7.7% (2000).
Housing: Homeownership rate: 75.2% (2000); Median home value: $48,500 (2000); Median rent: $213 per month (2000); Median age of housing: 58 years (2000).
Transportation: Commute to work: 93.1% car, 0.5% public transportation, 4.0% walk, 1.3% work from home (2000); Travel time to work: 20.6% less than 15 minutes, 29.7% 15 to 30 minutes, 27.3% 30 to 45 minutes, 15.5% 45 to 60 minutes, 7.0% 60 minutes or more (2000)

Porter County

Located in northwestern Indiana; bounded on the north by Lake Michigan, and on the south by the Kankakee River; drained by the Little Calumet and Grand Calumet Rivers. Covers a land area of 418.10 square miles, a water area of 103.50 square miles, and is located in the Central Time Zone. The county government was organized in 1835. County seat is Valparaiso.

Porter County is part of the Gary, IN PMSA. The entire metro area includes: Lake County; Porter County

Weather Station: Valparaiso Waterworks — Elevation: 797 feet

	Jan	Feb	Mar	Apr	May	Jun	Jul	Aug	Sep	Oct	Nov	Dec
High	30	36	47	60	71	80	83	81	75	63	49	36
Low	15	19	29	38	49	58	63	61	54	43	33	22
Precip	2.1	1.8	3.0	3.7	3.9	4.5	3.9	3.9	3.8	3.2	3.6	2.8
Snow	11.8	9.2	5.7	1.1	tr	0.0	0.0	0.0	0.0	0.2	3.2	8.6

High and Low temperatures in degrees Fahrenheit; Precipitation and Snow in inches

Weather Station: Wanatah 2 WNW — Elevation: 734 feet

	Jan	Feb	Mar	Apr	May	Jun	Jul	Aug	Sep	Oct	Nov	Dec
High	30	35	46	58	70	80	83	81	75	63	48	36
Low	13	18	27	37	48	58	61	59	51	40	31	20
Precip	1.6	1.6	2.8	3.6	3.7	4.3	4.2	3.7	3.8	2.9	3.4	2.5
Snow	13.5	10.9	6.4	1.2	tr	0.0	0.0	0.0	0.0	0.3	3.3	8.9

High and Low temperatures in degrees Fahrenheit; Precipitation and Snow in inches

Population: 146,798 (2000); Race: 95.0% White, 1.1% Black, 0.7% Asian, 0.2% American Indian and Alaska Native, 4.8% Hispanic of any race, 1.6% two or more races (2000); Density: 351.1 persons per square mile (2000); Age: 25.6% under 18, 10.9% over 64 (2000).
Religion: Five largest groups: 20.7% Catholic Church, 3.3% Lutheran Church—Missouri Synod, 2.5% The United Methodist Church, 2.2% Evangelical Lutheran Church in America, 1.7% Church of the Nazarene (2000).
Economy: Unemployment rate: 3.9% (11/2002); Total civilian labor force: 73,509 (11/2002); Leading industries: 23.6% manufacturing; 13.2% retail trade; 10.5% health care and social assistance (2000); Companies that employ more than 1,000 persons: 4 (2000); Companies that employ more than 100 persons: 68 (2000); Farms: 476 totaling 134,505 acres (1997); Minority business ownership rate: 3.8% (1997); Women business ownership rate: 28.0% (1997); Retail sales per capita: $7,215 (1997). Single-family building permits issued: 860 (2001) / 846 (2000); Multi-family building permits issued: 468 (2001) / 261 (2000).
Income: Per capita income: $23,957 (2000); Median household income: $53,100 (2000); Poverty rate: 5.9% (2000); Bankruptcy rate: 7.54% (2001).
Taxes: Total county taxes per capita: $158 (2000); County property taxes per capita: $152 (2000).
Education: High school graduation rate: 88.3% (2000); College graduation rate: 22.6% (2000).
Housing: Homeownership rate: 76.6% (2000); Median home value: $127,000 (2000); Median rent: $535 per month (2000); Median age of housing: 26 years (2000).
Health: Birth rate: 118.5 per 10,000 population (1998); Age adjusted death rate: 92.1 per 10,000 population (1999); Age adjusted cancer mortality rate: 240.0 deaths per 100,000 population (1999). Air Quality Index: 72% good, 28% moderate, 0% unhealthy (percent of days in 2000). Number of physicians: 16.7 per 10,000 population (1999); Number of hospital beds: 19.0 per 10,000 population (1999).
Elections: 2000 Presidential election results: 45.1% Gore, 52.5% Bush, 1.0% Nader, 0.9% Buchanan
National and State Parks: Indiana Dunes National Lakeshore; Indiana Dunes State Park
Additional Information Contacts
Porter County Government Offices 219-465-3332
Duneland Chamber of Commerce 219-926-5513
Hebron Chamber of Commerce 219-996-5678
Kouts Chamber of Commerce 219-766-2867
Portage Chamber of Commerce 219-762-3300
Valparaiso Chamber of Commerce 219-462-1105

Porter County Communities

BEVERLY SHORES (town). Covers a land area of 3.577 square miles and a water area of 2.269 square miles. Located at 41.68° N. Lat.; 86.98° W. Long. Elevation is 650 feet.
Population: 708 (2000); Race: 98.1% White, 1.2% Black, 0.0% Asian, 0.3% American Indian and Alaska Native, 0.0% Hispanic of any race, 0.4% two or more races (2000); Density: 197.9 persons per square mile (2000); Age: 8.9% under 18, 21.7% over 64 (2000); Marriage status: 26.0% never married, 58.6% now married, 6.6% widowed, 8.7% divorced (2000); Foreign born: 9.5% (2000); Ancestry (includes multiple ancestries): 28.0% German, 18.5% Irish, 14.7% Lithuanian, 7.7% English, 7.4% Polish (2000).
Economy: Developed as a resort village and residential community. Single-family building permits issued: 5 (2001) / 3 (2000); Multi-family building permits issued: 0 (2001) / 0 (2000); Employment by occupation:

23.2% management, 29.0% professional, 11.0% services, 22.7% sales, 0.0% farming, 5.5% construction, 8.6% production (2000).
Income: Per capita income: $40,825 (2000); Median household income: $59,107 (2000); Poverty rate: 4.9% (2000).
Taxes: Total city taxes per capita: $449 (1997); City property taxes per capita: $426 (1997).
Education: High school graduation rate: 93.9% (2000); College graduation rate: 56.6% (2000).
Housing: Homeownership rate: 84.4% (2000); Median home value: $238,000 (2000); Median rent: $538 per month (2000); Median age of housing: 38 years (2000).
Transportation: Commute to work: 77.4% car, 11.7% public transportation, 0.8% walk, 9.3% work from home (2000); Travel time to work: 12.3% less than 15 minutes, 29.9% 15 to 30 minutes, 15.2% 30 to 45 minutes, 7.9% 45 to 60 minutes, 34.6% 60 minutes or more (2000)

BURNS HARBOR (town). Aka Westport. Covers a land area of 6.834 square miles and a water area of 0.079 square miles. Located at 41.61° N. Lat.; 87.12° W. Long. Elevation is 620 feet.
Population: 766 (2000); Race: 92.5% White, 0.3% Black, 0.6% Asian, 2.0% American Indian and Alaska Native, 1.5% Hispanic of any race, 4.1% two or more races (2000); Density: 112.1 persons per square mile (2000); Age: 23.7% under 18, 9.2% over 64 (2000); Marriage status: 19.3% never married, 63.7% now married, 3.1% widowed, 13.8% divorced (2000); Foreign born: 2.2% (2000); Ancestry (includes multiple ancestries): 21.1% Irish, 20.7% German, 11.8% Other groups, 11.0% English, 6.8% United States or American (2000).
Economy: Steel and steel products. Single-family building permits issued: 0 (2001) / 0 (2000); Multi-family building permits issued: 0 (2001) / 0 (2000); Employment by occupation: 5.7% management, 8.4% professional, 21.2% services, 19.8% sales, 0.0% farming, 16.9% construction, 27.9% production (2000).
Income: Per capita income: $23,344 (2000); Median household income: $53,929 (2000); Poverty rate: 6.3% (2000).
Taxes: Total city taxes per capita: $963 (1997); City property taxes per capita: $946 (1997).
Education: High school graduation rate: 85.8% (2000); College graduation rate: 9.2% (2000).
Housing: Homeownership rate: 88.1% (2000); Median home value: $94,600 (2000); Median rent: $571 per month (2000); Median age of housing: 40 years (2000).
Safety: Violent crime rate: 13.0 per 10,000 population; Property crime rate: 545.5 per 10,000 population (2001).
Transportation: Commute to work: 91.9% car, 0.5% public transportation, 3.7% walk, 2.0% work from home (2000); Travel time to work: 37.7% less than 15 minutes, 27.9% 15 to 30 minutes, 17.1% 30 to 45 minutes, 5.0% 45 to 60 minutes, 12.3% 60 minutes or more (2000)

CHESTERTON (town). Covers a land area of 8.513 square miles and a water area of 0.113 square miles. Located at 41.60° N. Lat.; 87.05° W. Long. Elevation is 640 feet.
Population: 10,488 (2000); Race: 96.3% White, 0.9% Black, 1.3% Asian, 0.0% American Indian and Alaska Native, 3.7% Hispanic of any race, 0.7% two or more races (2000); Density: 1,232.0 persons per square mile (2000); Age: 26.8% under 18, 10.0% over 64 (2000); Marriage status: 23.9% never married, 58.5% now married, 6.6% widowed, 10.9% divorced (2000); Foreign born: 2.2% (2000); Ancestry (includes multiple ancestries): 25.6% German, 19.4% Irish, 12.0% English, 10.2% Polish, 9.7% Other groups (2000).
Economy: Agricultural area: fruit; poultry; dairy products; diversified manufacturing. Single-family building permits issued: 81 (2001) / 84 (2000); Multi-family building permits issued: 66 (2001) / 22 (2000); Employment by occupation: 15.4% management, 24.8% professional, 10.9% services, 24.2% sales, 0.2% farming, 10.9% construction, 13.7% production (2000).
Income: Per capita income: $26,539 (2000); Median household income: $55,530 (2000); Poverty rate: 4.3% (2000).
Taxes: Total city taxes per capita: $226 (1997); City property taxes per capita: $214 (1997).
Education: High school graduation rate: 92.7% (2000); College graduation rate: 29.5% (2000).

School District(s)

Duneland School Corporation (KG-12)
2000 Enrollment: 5,326 219-983-3605
Housing: Homeownership rate: 69.4% (2000); Median home value: $133,500 (2000); Median rent: $563 per month (2000); Median age of housing: 29 years (2000).
Safety: Violent crime rate: 10.4 per 10,000 population; Property crime rate: 289.2 per 10,000 population (2001).
Newspapers: Duneland News (1 x week); Chesterton Tribune (5 x week); Valparaiso News (1 x week)
Transportation: Commute to work: 92.7% car, 2.7% public transportation, 1.7% walk, 2.3% work from home (2000); Travel time to work: 36.3% less than 15 minutes, 31.3% 15 to 30 minutes, 17.6% 30 to 45 minutes, 6.3% 45 to 60 minutes, 8.6% 60 minutes or more (2000)
Additional Information Contacts
Duneland Chamber of Commerce 219-926-5513

DUNE ACRES (town). Covers a land area of 2.137 square miles and a water area of 1.380 square miles. Located at 41.64° N. Lat.; 87.08° W. Long. Elevation is 621 feet.
Population: 213 (2000); Race: 96.4% White, 0.0% Black, 0.0% Asian, 0.0% American Indian and Alaska Native, 1.6% Hispanic of any race, 3.6% two or more races (2000); Density: 99.7 persons per square mile (2000); Age: 8.8% under 18, 34.7% over 64 (2000); Marriage status: 12.4% never married, 77.5% now married, 3.4% widowed, 6.7% divorced (2000); Foreign born: 8.3% (2000); Ancestry (includes multiple ancestries): 24.9% German, 19.2% English, 17.1% Irish, 8.8% Polish, 8.8% Scottish (2000).
Economy: Single-family building permits issued: 1 (2001) / 4 (2000); Multi-family building permits issued: 0 (2001) / 0 (2000); Employment by occupation: 17.1% management, 47.6% professional, 3.8% services, 23.8% sales, 0.0% farming, 3.8% construction, 3.8% production (2000).
Income: Per capita income: $68,051 (2000); Median household income: $94,843 (2000); Poverty rate: 0.0% (2000).
Taxes: Total city taxes per capita: $569 (1997); City property taxes per capita: $553 (1997).
Education: High school graduation rate: 99.4% (2000); College graduation rate: 78.8% (2000).
Housing: Homeownership rate: 91.3% (2000); Median home value: $390,600 (2000); Median rent: $1,500 per month (2000); Median age of housing: 39 years (2000).
Transportation: Commute to work: 81.9% car, 2.9% public transportation, 0.0% walk, 15.2% work from home (2000); Travel time to work: 20.2% less than 15 minutes, 30.3% 15 to 30 minutes, 14.6% 30 to 45 minutes, 18.0% 45 to 60 minutes, 16.9% 60 minutes or more (2000)

HEBRON (town). Covers a land area of 1.549 square miles and a water area of 0 square miles. Located at 41.32° N. Lat.; 87.20° W. Long. Elevation is 703 feet.
Population: 3,596 (2000); Race: 94.7% White, 0.0% Black, 0.4% Asian, 0.4% American Indian and Alaska Native, 4.3% Hispanic of any race, 2.9% two or more races (2000); Density: 2,321.5 persons per square mile (2000); Age: 29.5% under 18, 12.1% over 64 (2000); Marriage status: 24.7% never married, 56.1% now married, 8.7% widowed, 10.5% divorced (2000); Foreign born: 1.8% (2000); Ancestry (includes multiple ancestries): 27.5% German, 17.7% Irish, 14.2% Polish, 12.2% Other groups, 7.6% English (2000).
Economy: Agricultural area. Single-family building permits issued: 6 (2001) / 2 (2000); Multi-family building permits issued: 0 (2001) / 0 (2000); Employment by occupation: 6.8% management, 16.5% professional, 12.2% services, 30.5% sales, 0.0% farming, 17.0% construction, 17.0% production (2000).
Income: Per capita income: $18,119 (2000); Median household income: $42,103 (2000); Poverty rate: 4.2% (2000).
Taxes: Total city taxes per capita: $95 (1997); City property taxes per capita: $85 (1997).
Education: High school graduation rate: 88.9% (2000); College graduation rate: 11.7% (2000).

School District(s)

M S D Boone Township (KG-12)
2000 Enrollment: 1,171 219-996-6016
Housing: Homeownership rate: 70.5% (2000); Median home value: $100,800 (2000); Median rent: $485 per month (2000); Median age of housing: 23 years (2000).
Safety: Violent crime rate: 19.4 per 10,000 population; Property crime rate: 118.9 per 10,000 population (2001).
Transportation: Commute to work: 96.1% car, 0.4% public transportation, 1.7% walk, 0.9% work from home (2000); Travel time to work: 19.7% less than 15 minutes, 35.0% 15 to 30 minutes, 19.7% 30 to 45 minutes, 13.0% 45 to 60 minutes, 12.6% 60 minutes or more (2000)
Additional Information Contacts
Hebron Chamber of Commerce 219-996-5678

KOUTS (town). Covers a land area of 1.116 square miles and a water area of 0 square miles. Located at 41.31° N. Lat.; 87.02° W. Long. Elevation is 684 feet.
History: Laid out 1864.
Population: 1,698 (2000); Race: 98.7% White, 0.0% Black, 0.0% Asian, 0.0% American Indian and Alaska Native, 1.8% Hispanic of any race, 0.3% two or more races (2000); Density: 1,522.0 persons per square mile (2000); Age: 25.0% under 18, 15.7% over 64 (2000); Marriage status: 20.0% never married, 62.3% now married, 7.0% widowed, 10.7% divorced (2000); Foreign born: 0.7% (2000); Ancestry (includes multiple ancestries): 41.5% German, 14.4% Irish, 9.7% English, 7.7% United States or American, 6.8% Polish (2000).
Economy: Manufacturing: animal feed, spring wire. Single-family building permits issued: 15 (2001) / 15 (2000); Multi-family building permits issued: 0 (2001) / 0 (2000); Employment by occupation: 10.2% management, 20.5% professional, 11.7% services, 21.8% sales, 0.0% farming, 13.0% construction, 22.9% production (2000).
Income: Per capita income: $19,239 (2000); Median household income: $44,850 (2000); Poverty rate: 3.2% (2000).
Taxes: Total city taxes per capita: $151 (1997); City property taxes per capita: $146 (1997).
Education: High school graduation rate: 88.7% (2000); College graduation rate: 16.1% (2000).

School District(s)

East Porter County School Corp (KG-12)
2000 Enrollment: 1,928 219-462-5841
Housing: Homeownership rate: 82.2% (2000); Median home value: $101,900 (2000); Median rent: $465 per month (2000); Median age of housing: 34 years (2000).
Safety: Violent crime rate: 11.7 per 10,000 population; Property crime rate: 515.2 per 10,000 population (2001).
Transportation: Commute to work: 96.0% car, 0.6% public transportation, 2.4% walk, 0.6% work from home (2000); Travel time to work: 23.7% less than 15 minutes, 40.5% 15 to 30 minutes, 16.4% 30 to 45 minutes, 11.2% 45 to 60 minutes, 8.3% 60 minutes or more (2000)
Additional Information Contacts
Kouts Chamber of Commerce 219-766-2867

OGDEN DUNES (town). Aka Wickliffe. Covers a land area of 0.730 square miles and a water area of 0.712 square miles. Located at 41.62° N. Lat.; 87.19° W. Long. Elevation is 700 feet.
History: In 1916, on the site that became Ogden Dunes, a woman was found living alone and avoiding contact with other people. The newspapers called her Diana of the Dunes, and many stories were told about her.
Population: 1,313 (2000); Race: 97.9% White, 0.7% Black, 0.7% Asian, 0.0% American Indian and Alaska Native, 3.0% Hispanic of any race, 0.5% two or more races (2000); Density: 1,798.3 persons per square mile (2000); Age: 18.0% under 18, 20.9% over 64 (2000); Marriage status: 16.7% never married, 66.8% now married, 7.6% widowed, 8.9% divorced (2000); Foreign born: 3.4% (2000); Ancestry (includes multiple ancestries): 20.6% German, 16.7% Irish, 14.8% English, 10.2% Polish, 6.7% Italian (2000).
Economy: Single-family building permits issued: 0 (2001) / 0 (2000); Multi-family building permits issued: 0 (2001) / 0 (2000); Employment by occupation: 24.9% management, 35.6% professional, 7.9% services, 20.9% sales, 0.0% farming, 4.1% construction, 6.5% production (2000).
Income: Per capita income: $49,852 (2000); Median household income: $76,924 (2000); Poverty rate: 4.1% (2000).
Taxes: Total city taxes per capita: $1,040 (1997); City property taxes per capita: $1,024 (1997).
Education: High school graduation rate: 97.2% (2000); College graduation rate: 55.0% (2000).
Housing: Homeownership rate: 89.9% (2000); Median home value: $222,000 (2000); Median rent: $835 per month (2000); Median age of housing: 40 years (2000).
Transportation: Commute to work: 88.2% car, 6.2% public transportation, 0.0% walk, 5.0% work from home (2000); Travel time to work: 14.0% less than 15 minutes, 32.8% 15 to 30 minutes, 25.3% 30 to 45 minutes, 8.5% 45 to 60 minutes, 19.4% 60 minutes or more (2000)

PORTAGE (city). Covers a land area of 25.456 square miles and a water area of 1.970 square miles. Located at 41.58° N. Lat.; 87.18° W. Long. Elevation is 644 feet.
History: A new port, accommodating ocean vessels, began operating here in the early 1970s (Burns International Harbor). Incorporated 1959.
Population: 33,496 (2000); Race: 92.3% White, 1.7% Black, 0.3% Asian, 0.1% American Indian and Alaska Native, 10.4% Hispanic of any race, 2.5% two or more races (2000); Density: 1,315.8 persons per square mile (2000); Age: 25.9% under 18, 11.7% over 64 (2000); Marriage status: 23.5% never married, 55.7% now married, 8.2% widowed, 12.6% divorced (2000); Foreign born: 3.0% (2000); Ancestry (includes multiple ancestries): 22.0% German, 18.3% Other groups, 15.3% Irish, 8.8% English, 8.6% Polish (2000).
Vital Statistics: Birth rate: 139.7 per 10,000 population (1998)
Economy: Manufacturing includes steel, steel products. Unemployment rate: 5.0% (11/2002); Total civilian labor force: 15,831 (11/2002); Single-family building permits issued: 172 (2001) / 180 (2000); Multi-family building permits issued: 200 (2001) / 8 (2000); Employment by occupation: 7.9% management, 12.8% professional, 16.8% services, 23.5% sales, 0.0% farming, 15.7% construction, 23.2% production (2000).
Income: Per capita income: $20,146 (2000); Median household income: $47,500 (2000); Poverty rate: 7.5% (2000).
Taxes: Total city taxes per capita: $227 (2000); City property taxes per capita: $214 (2000).
Education: High school graduation rate: 82.1% (2000); College graduation rate: 10.1% (2000).

School District(s)

Portage Township Schools (PK-12)
2000 Enrollment: 8,033 219-762-6511
Housing: Homeownership rate: 72.2% (2000); Median home value: $109,000 (2000); Median rent: $516 per month (2000); Median age of housing: 25 years (2000).
Safety: Violent crime rate: 14.2 per 10,000 population; Property crime rate: 332.2 per 10,000 population (2001).
Newspapers: Portage News (1 x week)
Transportation: Commute to work: 96.2% car, 1.3% public transportation, 0.4% walk, 1.2% work from home (2000); Travel time to work: 27.8% less than 15 minutes, 38.3% 15 to 30 minutes, 21.8% 30 to 45 minutes, 5.0% 45 to 60 minutes, 7.1% 60 minutes or more (2000)
Additional Information Contacts
Portage Chamber of Commerce 219-762-3300

PORTER (town). Covers a land area of 6.304 square miles and a water area of 0.305 square miles. Located at 41.62° N. Lat.; 87.07° W. Long. Elevation is 640 feet.
History: Laid out 1855.
Population: 4,972 (2000); Race: 95.3% White, 0.7% Black, 0.3% Asian, 0.3% American Indian and Alaska Native, 4.4% Hispanic of any race, 2.4% two or more races (2000); Density: 788.8 persons per square mile (2000); Age: 28.5% under 18, 8.6% over 64 (2000); Marriage status: 24.5% never married, 55.7% now married, 5.4% widowed, 14.5% divorced (2000); Foreign born: 2.4% (2000); Ancestry (includes multiple ancestries): 25.3% German, 16.9% Irish, 11.8% English, 11.7% Polish, 8.5% Other groups (2000).
Economy: Manufacturing: steel processing. Single-family building permits issued: 31 (2001) / 33 (2000); Multi-family building permits issued: 6 (2001) / 12 (2000); Employment by occupation: 11.5% management, 17.9% professional, 13.8% services, 26.9% sales, 0.0% farming, 15.1% construction, 14.8% production (2000).
Income: Per capita income: $24,615 (2000); Median household income: $50,625 (2000); Poverty rate: 6.5% (2000).
Taxes: Total city taxes per capita: $189 (1997); City property taxes per capita: $162 (1997).
Education: High school graduation rate: 91.0% (2000); College graduation rate: 24.7% (2000).
Housing: Homeownership rate: 71.4% (2000); Median home value: $123,700 (2000); Median rent: $563 per month (2000); Median age of housing: 31 years (2000).
Transportation: Commute to work: 88.1% car, 7.5% public transportation, 2.1% walk, 1.5% work from home (2000); Travel time to work: 34.2% less than 15 minutes, 28.5% 15 to 30 minutes, 15.1% 30 to 45 minutes, 5.1% 45 to 60 minutes, 17.1% 60 minutes or more (2000)

SOUTH HAVEN (CDP). Covers a land area of 1.244 square miles and a water area of 0 square miles. Located at 41.54° N. Lat.; 87.13° W. Long. Elevation is 650 feet.
Population: 5,619 (2000); Race: 96.8% White, 0.7% Black, 0.3% Asian, 0.4% American Indian and Alaska Native, 4.9% Hispanic of any race, 0.9% two or more races (2000); Density: 4,515.3 persons per square mile (2000); Age: 30.5% under 18, 7.5% over 64 (2000); Marriage status: 23.9% never married, 60.3% now married, 5.0% widowed, 10.8% divorced (2000);

Foreign born: 0.9% (2000); Ancestry (includes multiple ancestries): 22.0% German, 18.6% Irish, 11.5% English, 11.3% Other groups, 9.5% United States or American (2000).
Economy: Employment by occupation: 5.3% management, 10.6% professional, 23.4% services, 23.2% sales, 0.0% farming, 13.0% construction, 24.5% production (2000).
Income: Per capita income: $18,112 (2000); Median household income: $52,583 (2000); Poverty rate: 5.8% (2000).
Education: High school graduation rate: 84.6% (2000); College graduation rate: 6.6% (2000).
Housing: Homeownership rate: 79.4% (2000); Median home value: $84,100 (2000); Median rent: $557 per month (2000); Median age of housing: 33 years (2000).
Transportation: Commute to work: 96.9% car, 0.9% public transportation, 1.3% walk, 0.7% work from home (2000); Travel time to work: 26.1% less than 15 minutes, 43.4% 15 to 30 minutes, 17.2% 30 to 45 minutes, 5.9% 45 to 60 minutes, 7.4% 60 minutes or more (2000)

TOWN OF PINES (town). Covers a land area of 2.276 square miles and a water area of 0 square miles. Located at 41.68° N. Lat.; 86.94° W. Long. Elevation is 620 feet.
Population: 798 (2000); Race: 97.0% White, 0.0% Black, 0.2% Asian, 1.7% American Indian and Alaska Native, 0.2% Hispanic of any race, 1.0% two or more races (2000); Density: 350.5 persons per square mile (2000); Age: 22.1% under 18, 9.2% over 64 (2000); Marriage status: 23.4% never married, 56.3% now married, 5.6% widowed, 14.7% divorced (2000); Foreign born: 2.1% (2000); Ancestry (includes multiple ancestries): 28.4% German, 14.9% United States or American, 12.3% Other groups, 10.2% Irish, 9.7% Polish (2000).
Economy: Indiana Dunes National Lakeshore to North. Single-family building permits issued: 2 (2001) / 3 (2000); Multi-family building permits issued: 0 (2001) / 0 (2000); Employment by occupation: 6.0% management, 9.3% professional, 14.6% services, 25.8% sales, 0.0% farming, 19.5% construction, 24.8% production (2000).
Income: Per capita income: $19,856 (2000); Median household income: $41,875 (2000); Poverty rate: 8.7% (2000).
Education: High school graduation rate: 75.7% (2000); College graduation rate: 7.6% (2000).
Housing: Homeownership rate: 79.4% (2000); Median home value: $80,900 (2000); Median rent: $434 per month (2000); Median age of housing: 41 years (2000).
Transportation: Commute to work: 90.6% car, 2.2% public transportation, 0.0% walk, 4.6% work from home (2000); Travel time to work: 43.7% less than 15 minutes, 32.0% 15 to 30 minutes, 11.7% 30 to 45 minutes, 7.1% 45 to 60 minutes, 5.6% 60 minutes or more (2000)

VALPARAISO (city). Covers a land area of 10.904 square miles and a water area of 0.085 square miles. Located at 41.47° N. Lat.; 87.05° W. Long. Elevation is 738 feet.
History: Valparaiso was sited on the Old Sauk Trail. In 1859 the Valparaiso Male and Female College was founded here by the Methodist Church. The College, purchased by the Lutheran Church in 1925, became Valparaiso University.
Population: 27,428 (2000); Race: 94.0% White, 1.5% Black, 1.6% Asian, 0.2% American Indian and Alaska Native, 3.2% Hispanic of any race, 1.6% two or more races (2000); Density: 2,515.4 persons per square mile (2000); Age: 21.3% under 18, 13.2% over 64 (2000); Marriage status: 31.5% never married, 50.4% now married, 7.5% widowed, 10.6% divorced (2000); Foreign born: 4.1% (2000); Ancestry (includes multiple ancestries): 32.9% German, 16.2% Irish, 11.9% English, 9.2% Polish, 8.9% Other groups (2000).
Vital Statistics: Birth rate: 177.9 per 10,000 population (1998)
Economy: Unemployment rate: 3.0% (11/2002); Total civilian labor force: 14,105 (11/2002); Single-family building permits issued: 103 (2001) / 70 (2000); Multi-family building permits issued: 186 (2001) / 186 (2000); Employment by occupation: 11.4% management, 26.9% professional, 14.4% services, 26.5% sales, 0.0% farming, 9.2% construction, 11.7% production (2000).
Income: Per capita income: $22,509 (2000); Median household income: $45,799 (2000); Poverty rate: 9.1% (2000).
Taxes: Total city taxes per capita: $283 (1997); City property taxes per capita: $270 (1997).
Education: High school graduation rate: 90.6% (2000); College graduation rate: 34.5% (2000).

School District(s)

Porter County Education Interlocal
2000 Enrollment: n/a 219-464-9607
Porter Township School Corp (KG-12)
2000 Enrollment: 1,624 219-477-4933
Valparaiso Community Schools (KG-12)
2000 Enrollment: 6,035 219-531-3000

Four-year College(s)

Valparaiso University (Private, Not-for-profit, Lutheran Church - Missouri Synod)
2001 Enrollment: 3,533 219-464-5000
2001 Tuition: In-state $18,100; Out-of-state $18,100

Two-year College(s)

Porter Memorial Hospital School of Radiography (Public)
2001 Enrollment: n/a 219-465-4883

Housing: Homeownership rate: 54.8% (2000); Median home value: $121,700 (2000); Median rent: $548 per month (2000); Median age of housing: 29 years (2000).
Hospitals: Porter Memorial Hospital (402 beds)
Safety: Violent crime rate: 19.2 per 10,000 population; Property crime rate: 306.0 per 10,000 population (2001).
Newspapers: The Vidette Times (7 x week)
Transportation: Commute to work: 87.3% car, 0.7% public transportation, 7.8% walk, 2.9% work from home (2000); Travel time to work: 48.8% less than 15 minutes, 24.5% 15 to 30 minutes, 14.7% 30 to 45 minutes, 6.4% 45 to 60 minutes, 5.6% 60 minutes or more (2000)
Airports: Porter County Municipal
Additional Information Contacts
Valparaiso Chamber of Commerce 219-462-1105

Posey County

Located in southwestern Indiana; bounded on the west by the Wabash River and the Illinois border, and on the south by the Ohio River and the Kentucky border; drained by Big Creek. Covers a land area of 408.50 square miles, a water area of 10.90 square miles, and is located in the Central Time Zone. The county government was organized in 1814. County seat is Mount Vernon.

Posey County is part of the Evansville-Henderson, IN-KY MSA. The entire metro area includes: Posey County, IN; Vanderburgh County, IN; Warrick County, IN; Henderson County, KY

Weather Station: Mount Vernon — Elevation: 419 feet

	Jan	Feb	Mar	Apr	May	Jun	Jul	Aug	Sep	Oct	Nov	Dec
High	39	44	55	66	76	85	88	87	81	69	56	44
Low	22	26	35	45	55	64	68	65	58	46	37	28
Precip	3.2	3.0	4.7	4.5	5.4	3.9	4.2	3.0	2.8	3.0	4.3	3.7
Snow	4.5	3.8	2.3	0.4	0.0	0.0	0.0	0.0	0.0	0.1	0.4	2.2

High and Low temperatures in degrees Fahrenheit; Precipitation and Snow in inches

Population: 27,061 (2000); Race: 97.9% White, 1.0% Black, 0.1% Asian, 0.2% American Indian and Alaska Native, 0.5% Hispanic of any race, 0.7% two or more races (2000); Density: 66.2 persons per square mile (2000); Age: 27.3% under 18, 12.4% over 64 (2000).
Religion: Five largest groups: 20.8% Catholic Church, 7.9% The United Methodist Church, 6.8% United Church of Christ, 3.3% Southern Baptist Convention, 2.8% Assemblies of God (2000).
Economy: Unemployment rate: 3.9% (11/2002); Total civilian labor force: 13,917 (11/2002); Leading industries: 36.4% manufacturing; 13.0% retail trade; 9.9% construction (2000); Companies that employ more than 1,000 persons: 1 (2000); Companies that employ more than 100 persons: 9 (2000); Farms: 437 totaling 195,305 acres (1997); Minority business ownership rate: 0.0% (1997); Women business ownership rate: 30.7% (1997); Retail sales per capita: $5,726 (1997). Single-family building permits issued: 93 (2001) / 97 (2000); Multi-family building permits issued: 2 (2001) / 0 (2000).
Income: Per capita income: $19,516 (2000); Median household income: $44,209 (2000); Poverty rate: 7.4% (2000); Bankruptcy rate: 4.28% (2001).
Taxes: Total county taxes per capita: $241 (2000); County property taxes per capita: $239 (2000).
Education: High school graduation rate: 84.4% (2000); College graduation rate: 14.8% (2000).
Housing: Homeownership rate: 81.9% (2000); Median home value: $89,800 (2000); Median rent: $318 per month (2000); Median age of housing: 31 years (2000).

Health: Birth rate: 104.6 per 10,000 population (1998); Age adjusted death rate: 86.3 per 10,000 population (1999); Age adjusted cancer mortality rate: 202.2 deaths per 100,000 population (1999). Air Quality Index: 56% good, 44% moderate, 0% unhealthy (percent of days in 2000). Number of physicians: 3.7 per 10,000 population (1999); Number of hospital beds: n/a (1999).
Elections: 2000 Presidential election results: 39.9% Gore, 58.5% Bush, 0.5% Nader, 0.8% Buchanan
National and State Parks: Angel Mounds State Memorial; Harmonie State Park; New Harmony State Memorial; The Labyrinth State Memorial
Additional Information Contacts
Posey County Government Offices 812-838-1300
Mt Vernon Chamber of Commerce 812-838-3639

Posey County Communities

CYNTHIANA (town). Covers a land area of 0.402 square miles and a water area of 0 square miles. Located at 38.18° N. Lat.; 87.70° W. Long. Elevation is 440 feet.
Population: 693 (2000); Race: 98.8% White, 1.0% Black, 0.0% Asian, 0.0% American Indian and Alaska Native, 0.4% Hispanic of any race, 0.1% two or more races (2000); Density: 1,725.1 persons per square mile (2000); Age: 22.4% under 18, 11.7% over 64 (2000); Marriage status: 19.9% never married, 63.3% now married, 6.6% widowed, 10.3% divorced (2000); Foreign born: 0.7% (2000); Ancestry (includes multiple ancestries): 28.7% German, 18.5% United States or American, 14.3% Other groups, 10.9% Irish, 5.6% English (2000).
Economy: In agricultural area. Employment by occupation: 5.7% management, 7.8% professional, 15.1% services, 17.6% sales, 0.5% farming, 14.6% construction, 38.6% production (2000).
Income: Per capita income: $15,313 (2000); Median household income: $37,589 (2000); Poverty rate: 9.7% (2000).
Taxes: Total city taxes per capita: $81 (2000); City property taxes per capita: $74 (2000).
Education: High school graduation rate: 78.3% (2000); College graduation rate: 5.9% (2000).
Housing: Homeownership rate: 74.9% (2000); Median home value: $57,300 (2000); Median rent: $275 per month (2000); Median age of housing: 50 years (2000).
Transportation: Commute to work: 93.9% car, 0.0% public transportation, 1.1% walk, 5.0% work from home (2000); Travel time to work: 21.7% less than 15 minutes, 33.0% 15 to 30 minutes, 32.2% 30 to 45 minutes, 11.0% 45 to 60 minutes, 2.0% 60 minutes or more (2000)

GRIFFIN (town). Covers a land area of 0.068 square miles and a water area of 0 square miles. Located at 38.20° N. Lat.; 87.91° W. Long. Elevation is 385 feet.
History: Laid out 1881.
Population: 160 (2000); Race: 100.0% White, 0.0% Black, 0.0% Asian, 0.0% American Indian and Alaska Native, 0.0% Hispanic of any race, 0.0% two or more races (2000); Density: 2,363.3 persons per square mile (2000); Age: 20.7% under 18, 18.6% over 64 (2000); Marriage status: 13.6% never married, 55.2% now married, 17.6% widowed, 13.6% divorced (2000); Foreign born: 0.0% (2000); Ancestry (includes multiple ancestries): 13.8% German, 13.8% United States or American, 9.0% Irish, 5.5% British, 2.8% European (2000).
Economy: In agricultural and petroleum area. Employment by occupation: 1.5% management, 7.4% professional, 10.3% services, 33.8% sales, 0.0% farming, 11.8% construction, 35.3% production (2000).
Income: Per capita income: $18,074 (2000); Median household income: $26,786 (2000); Poverty rate: 17.9% (2000).
Taxes: Total city taxes per capita: $58 (1997); City property taxes per capita: $58 (1997).
Education: High school graduation rate: 74.8% (2000); College graduation rate: 3.9% (2000).
Housing: Homeownership rate: 72.7% (2000); Median home value: $47,300 (2000); Median rent: $300 per month (2000); Median age of housing: 55 years (2000).
Transportation: Commute to work: 97.1% car, 2.9% public transportation, 0.0% walk, 0.0% work from home (2000); Travel time to work: 11.8% less than 15 minutes, 17.6% 15 to 30 minutes, 39.7% 30 to 45 minutes, 19.1% 45 to 60 minutes, 11.8% 60 minutes or more (2000)

MOUNT VERNON (city). Covers a land area of 2.463 square miles and a water area of 0.066 square miles. Located at 37.93° N. Lat.; 87.89° W. Long. Elevation is 398 feet.
History: Mount Vernon, founded in 1805 by Irish trader Andrew McFadden, was first called McFadden's Landing. The name was changed in 1816.
Population: 7,478 (2000); Race: 96.0% White, 2.9% Black, 0.1% Asian, 0.1% American Indian and Alaska Native, 0.7% Hispanic of any race, 0.7% two or more races (2000); Density: 3,036.0 persons per square mile (2000); Age: 26.6% under 18, 14.6% over 64 (2000); Marriage status: 17.9% never married, 59.8% now married, 9.6% widowed, 12.7% divorced (2000); Foreign born: 1.0% (2000); Ancestry (includes multiple ancestries): 28.1% German, 12.9% United States or American, 11.9% English, 11.1% Irish, 8.2% Other groups (2000).
Economy: Employment by occupation: 10.6% management, 20.4% professional, 15.0% services, 24.0% sales, 0.7% farming, 8.4% construction, 20.9% production (2000).
Income: Per capita income: $19,264 (2000); Median household income: $36,543 (2000); Poverty rate: 12.5% (2000).
Taxes: Total city taxes per capita: $234 (2000); City property taxes per capita: $231 (2000).
Education: High school graduation rate: 81.0% (2000); College graduation rate: 13.7% (2000).

School District(s)

M S D Mount Vernon (PK-12)
2000 Enrollment: 2,815 812-838-4471
Housing: Homeownership rate: 70.9% (2000); Median home value: $81,700 (2000); Median rent: $325 per month (2000); Median age of housing: 36 years (2000).
Safety: Violent crime rate: 5.3 per 10,000 population; Property crime rate: 122.3 per 10,000 population (2001).
Newspapers: The Posey Advantage (1 x week); Mount Vernon Democrat (1 x week)
Transportation: Commute to work: 94.0% car, 0.0% public transportation, 2.6% walk, 3.0% work from home (2000); Travel time to work: 54.9% less than 15 minutes, 17.1% 15 to 30 minutes, 18.1% 30 to 45 minutes, 5.8% 45 to 60 minutes, 4.1% 60 minutes or more (2000)
Additional Information Contacts
Mt Vernon Chamber of Commerce 812-838-3639

NEW HARMONY (town). Covers a land area of 0.635 square miles and a water area of 0.009 square miles. Located at 38.12° N. Lat.; 87.93° W. Long. Elevation is 384 feet.
History: New Harmony was the site of two social experiments. In 1815 the Rappites, a religious group of Germans from Pennsylvania, founded the village of Harmonie, trying to create a society based on cooperative living. After ten years their hard work had created a prosperous town out of the wildnerness, but also created discontent. They sold the village to Robert Owen, a Welsh philanthropist and social reformer whose dream was to found a communal society. Owen called his community New Harmony. The experiment as Owen envisioned it was a failure within two years, but New Harmony continued to be an intellectual center.
Population: 916 (2000); Race: 98.0% White, 0.2% Black, 0.8% Asian, 0.7% American Indian and Alaska Native, 0.0% Hispanic of any race, 0.3% two or more races (2000); Density: 1,441.5 persons per square mile (2000); Age: 20.8% under 18, 30.3% over 64 (2000); Marriage status: 17.7% never married, 55.5% now married, 16.8% widowed, 10.0% divorced (2000); Foreign born: 0.8% (2000); Ancestry (includes multiple ancestries): 20.5% German, 15.6% English, 7.5% Irish, 7.4% United States or American, 5.4% Other groups (2000).
Economy: Single-family building permits issued: 3 (2001) / 3 (2000); Multi-family building permits issued: 0 (2001) / 0 (2000); Employment by occupation: 11.7% management, 19.4% professional, 22.0% services, 17.9% sales, 0.0% farming, 7.3% construction, 21.8% production (2000).
Income: Per capita income: $17,349 (2000); Median household income: $28,182 (2000); Poverty rate: 12.4% (2000).
Taxes: Total city taxes per capita: $87 (1997); City property taxes per capita: $82 (1997).
Education: High school graduation rate: 75.9% (2000); College graduation rate: 19.4% (2000).

School District(s)

New Harmony Town & Township Con Sch (PK-12)
2000 Enrollment: 231 812-682-4401
Housing: Homeownership rate: 71.6% (2000); Median home value: $71,500 (2000); Median rent: $310 per month (2000); Median age of housing: 58 years (2000).

Transportation: Commute to work: 83.9% car, 0.0% public transportation, 9.0% walk, 6.3% work from home (2000); Travel time to work: 45.6% less than 15 minutes, 21.2% 15 to 30 minutes, 20.1% 30 to 45 minutes, 10.2% 45 to 60 minutes, 2.9% 60 minutes or more (2000)

POSEYVILLE (town). Covers a land area of 0.664 square miles and a water area of 0 square miles. Located at 38.16° N. Lat.; 87.78° W. Long. Elevation is 434 feet.
Population: 1,187 (2000); Race: 99.8% White, 0.0% Black, 0.0% Asian, 0.0% American Indian and Alaska Native, 0.0% Hispanic of any race, 0.2% two or more races (2000); Density: 1,788.2 persons per square mile (2000); Age: 27.9% under 18, 21.4% over 64 (2000); Marriage status: 18.9% never married, 60.2% now married, 10.8% widowed, 10.1% divorced (2000); Foreign born: 0.2% (2000); Ancestry (includes multiple ancestries): 35.6% German, 14.1% United States or American, 10.5% Irish, 9.0% English, 5.6% Other groups (2000).
Economy: Agricultural area; feed milling. Employment by occupation: 13.1% management, 14.7% professional, 12.3% services, 23.2% sales, 0.0% farming, 15.3% construction, 21.5% production (2000).
Income: Per capita income: $18,815 (2000); Median household income: $37,604 (2000); Poverty rate: 5.2% (2000).
Taxes: Total city taxes per capita: $110 (1997); City property taxes per capita: $107 (1997).
Education: High school graduation rate: 85.2% (2000); College graduation rate: 10.4% (2000).

School District(s)

M S D North Posey Co Schools (PK-12)
2000 Enrollment: 1,662 812-874-2243
Housing: Homeownership rate: 79.7% (2000); Median home value: $67,600 (2000); Median rent: $285 per month (2000); Median age of housing: 44 years (2000).
Newspapers: The Posey County News (1 x week)
Transportation: Commute to work: 95.0% car, 0.3% public transportation, 2.2% walk, 1.2% work from home (2000); Travel time to work: 41.3% less than 15 minutes, 17.7% 15 to 30 minutes, 27.8% 30 to 45 minutes, 7.9% 45 to 60 minutes, 5.3% 60 minutes or more (2000)

WADESVILLE (unincorporated postal area, zip code 47638). Covers a land area of 50.665 square miles and a water area of 0.015 square miles. Located at 38.08° N. Lat.; 87.78° W. Long. Elevation is 476 feet.
Population: 3,444 (2000); Race: 99.4% White, 0.0% Black, 0.0% Asian, 0.3% American Indian and Alaska Native, 0.3% Hispanic of any race, 0.3% two or more races (2000); Density: 68.0 persons per square mile (2000); Age: 29.4% under 18, 8.6% over 64 (2000); Marriage status: 19.0% never married, 69.5% now married, 3.8% widowed, 7.8% divorced (2000); Foreign born: 0.2% (2000); Ancestry (includes multiple ancestries): 40.1% German, 12.7% United States or American, 11.9% English, 9.5% Irish, 6.8% Other groups (2000).
Economy: Employment by occupation: 13.2% management, 19.3% professional, 8.2% services, 23.6% sales, 0.4% farming, 14.8% construction, 20.4% production (2000).
Income: Per capita income: $20,263 (2000); Median household income: $51,103 (2000); Poverty rate: 5.3% (2000).
Education: High school graduation rate: 88.0% (2000); College graduation rate: 16.1% (2000).
Housing: Homeownership rate: 83.1% (2000); Median home value: $102,700 (2000); Median rent: $303 per month (2000); Median age of housing: 28 years (2000).
Transportation: Commute to work: 92.4% car, 0.0% public transportation, 2.0% walk, 4.6% work from home (2000); Travel time to work: 15.2% less than 15 minutes, 45.1% 15 to 30 minutes, 32.2% 30 to 45 minutes, 3.8% 45 to 60 minutes, 3.7% 60 minutes or more (2000)

Pulaski County

Located in northwestern Indiana; drained by the Tippecanoe River. Covers a land area of 433.70 square miles, a water area of 0.90 square miles, and is located in the Eastern Time Zone. The county government was organized in 1835. County seat is Winamac.

Weather Station: Winamac 2 SSE — Elevation: 688 feet

	Jan	Feb	Mar	Apr	May	Jun	Jul	Aug	Sep	Oct	Nov	Dec
High	31	36	48	61	72	80	84	81	75	63	49	37
Low	14	18	28	39	50	59	63	61	53	42	32	21
Precip	1.9	1.6	2.8	3.7	3.8	4.1	3.9	3.8	3.4	3.0	3.1	2.5
Snow	8.5	5.3	3.2	1.2	tr	0.0	0.0	0.0	0.0	0.1	2.1	5.4

High and Low temperatures in degrees Fahrenheit; Precipitation and Snow in inches

Population: 13,755 (2000); Race: 96.9% White, 1.3% Black, 0.2% Asian, 0.2% American Indian and Alaska Native, 1.2% Hispanic of any race, 1.1% two or more races (2000); Density: 31.7 persons per square mile (2000); Age: 26.9% under 18, 15.3% over 64 (2000).
Religion: Five largest groups: 17.8% Catholic Church, 5.5% The United Methodist Church, 5.4% Christian Churches and Churches of Christ, 4.2% Christian Church (Disciples of Christ), 3.4% Lutheran Church—Missouri Synod (2000).
Economy: Unemployment rate: 6.9% (11/2002); Total civilian labor force: 5,641 (11/2002); Leading industries: 31.4% manufacturing; 15.7% health care and social assistance; 15.2% retail trade (2000); Companies that employ more than 1,000 persons: 0 (2000); Companies that employ more than 100 persons: 3 (2000); Farms: 531 totaling 236,332 acres (1997); Minority business ownership rate: 0.0% (1997); Women business ownership rate: 24.3% (1997); Retail sales per capita: $5,539 (1997). Single-family building permits issued: 56 (2001) / 69 (2000); Multi-family building permits issued: 24 (2001) / 4 (2000).
Income: Per capita income: $16,835 (2000); Median household income: $35,422 (2000); Poverty rate: 8.3% (2000); Bankruptcy rate: 5.69% (2001).
Taxes: Total county taxes per capita: $305 (2000); County property taxes per capita: $222 (2000).
Education: High school graduation rate: 79.8% (2000); College graduation rate: 10.3% (2000).
Housing: Homeownership rate: 80.7% (2000); Median home value: $72,500 (2000); Median rent: $307 per month (2000); Median age of housing: 40 years (2000).
Health: Birth rate: 134.5 per 10,000 population (1998); Age adjusted death rate: 89.1 per 10,000 population (1999); Age adjusted cancer mortality rate: 180.4 deaths per 100,000 population (1999). Number of physicians: 5.1 per 10,000 population (1999); Number of hospital beds: 18.2 per 10,000 population (1999).
Elections: 2000 Presidential election results: 34.8% Gore, 63.4% Bush, 0.3% Nader, 0.9% Buchanan
National and State Parks: Winamac State Fish and Wildlife Area
Additional Information Contacts
Pulaski County Government Offices 219-946-3653
Winamac Chamber of Commerce 219-946-3869

Pulaski County Communities

FRANCESVILLE (town). Covers a land area of 0.306 square miles and a water area of 0 square miles. Located at 40.98° N. Lat.; 86.88° W. Long. Elevation is 681 feet.
Population: 905 (2000); Race: 97.4% White, 0.0% Black, 0.0% Asian, 0.0% American Indian and Alaska Native, 2.4% Hispanic of any race, 1.9% two or more races (2000); Density: 2,954.7 persons per square mile (2000); Age: 26.4% under 18, 16.2% over 64 (2000); Marriage status: 21.3% never married, 59.0% now married, 8.9% widowed, 10.7% divorced (2000); Foreign born: 0.1% (2000); Ancestry (includes multiple ancestries): 36.5% German, 16.0% Irish, 11.8% Other groups, 7.9% United States or American, 7.2% French (except Basque) (2000).
Economy: Manufacturing: truck wheels and rims, plastic tubing, feed, crushed stone products. Single-family building permits issued: 1 (2001) / 3 (2000); Multi-family building permits issued: 0 (2001) / 0 (2000); Employment by occupation: 8.1% management, 13.8% professional, 13.1% services, 21.8% sales, 3.5% farming, 8.7% construction, 31.0% production (2000).
Income: Per capita income: $16,469 (2000); Median household income: $39,464 (2000); Poverty rate: 4.2% (2000).
Taxes: Total city taxes per capita: $92 (1997); City property taxes per capita: $82 (1997).
Education: High school graduation rate: 81.6% (2000); College graduation rate: 8.5% (2000).

School District(s)

West Central School Corp (KG-12)
2000 Enrollment: 999 219-567-9161
Housing: Homeownership rate: 80.8% (2000); Median home value: $67,100 (2000); Median rent: $319 per month (2000); Median age of housing: 56 years (2000).
Newspapers: Francesville Tribune (1 x week)
Transportation: Commute to work: 91.5% car, 0.4% public transportation, 4.0% walk, 2.7% work from home (2000); Travel time to work: 44.2% less than 15 minutes, 22.0% 15 to 30 minutes, 20.1% 30 to 45 minutes, 5.5% 45 to 60 minutes, 8.2% 60 minutes or more (2000)

MEDARYVILLE (town). Covers a land area of 0.456 square miles and a water area of 0 square miles. Located at 41.08° N. Lat.; 86.88° W. Long. Elevation is 685 feet.
Population: 565 (2000); Race: 98.1% White, 0.0% Black, 0.0% Asian, 0.0% American Indian and Alaska Native, 4.2% Hispanic of any race, 0.5% two or more races (2000); Density: 1,240.4 persons per square mile (2000); Age: 23.2% under 18, 18.9% over 64 (2000); Marriage status: 18.7% never married, 60.4% now married, 8.1% widowed, 12.8% divorced (2000); Foreign born: 0.5% (2000); Ancestry (includes multiple ancestries): 31.2% German, 12.1% Irish, 9.5% United States or American, 8.5% Other groups, 6.9% English (2000).
Economy: Agriculture; apparel. Medaryville Correctional Unit nearby. Employment by occupation: 4.6% management, 3.1% professional, 11.6% services, 15.4% sales, 3.1% farming, 10.0% construction, 52.1% production (2000).
Income: Per capita income: $14,937 (2000); Median household income: $31,750 (2000); Poverty rate: 4.9% (2000).
Taxes: Total city taxes per capita: $102 (1997); City property taxes per capita: $101 (1997).
Education: High school graduation rate: 71.8% (2000); College graduation rate: 1.7% (2000).
Housing: Homeownership rate: 87.2% (2000); Median home value: $57,400 (2000); Median rent: $360 per month (2000); Median age of housing: 53 years (2000).
Transportation: Commute to work: 86.3% car, 0.0% public transportation, 8.2% walk, 2.3% work from home (2000); Travel time to work: 28.4% less than 15 minutes, 30.8% 15 to 30 minutes, 17.6% 30 to 45 minutes, 5.6% 45 to 60 minutes, 17.6% 60 minutes or more (2000)

MONTEREY (town). Covers a land area of 0.171 square miles and a water area of 0 square miles. Located at 41.15° N. Lat.; 86.48° W. Long. Elevation is 725 feet.
History: Laid out 1849.
Population: 231 (2000); Race: 98.8% White, 0.0% Black, 0.0% Asian, 0.0% American Indian and Alaska Native, 0.0% Hispanic of any race, 1.2% two or more races (2000); Density: 1,353.5 persons per square mile (2000); Age: 30.9% under 18, 14.4% over 64 (2000); Marriage status: 19.3% never married, 61.3% now married, 6.6% widowed, 12.7% divorced (2000); Foreign born: 0.0% (2000); Ancestry (includes multiple ancestries): 34.6% German, 12.3% Irish, 10.3% United States or American, 7.0% Polish, 6.6% Other groups (2000).
Economy: In agricultural area. Employment by occupation: 18.3% management, 8.3% professional, 23.9% services, 18.3% sales, 4.6% farming, 11.0% construction, 15.6% production (2000).
Income: Per capita income: $14,479 (2000); Median household income: $24,779 (2000); Poverty rate: 14.5% (2000).
Taxes: Total city taxes per capita: $140 (1997); City property taxes per capita: $127 (1997).
Education: High school graduation rate: 78.1% (2000); College graduation rate: 5.2% (2000).
Housing: Homeownership rate: 83.5% (2000); Median home value: $55,000 (2000); Median rent: $310 per month (2000); Median age of housing: 60+ years (2000).
Transportation: Commute to work: 88.1% car, 0.0% public transportation, 9.2% walk, 2.8% work from home (2000); Travel time to work: 33.0% less than 15 minutes, 33.0% 15 to 30 minutes, 18.9% 30 to 45 minutes, 7.5% 45 to 60 minutes, 7.5% 60 minutes or more (2000)

STAR CITY (CDP). Covers a land area of 1.056 square miles and a water area of 0 square miles. Located at 40.97° N. Lat.; 86.55° W. Long. Elevation is 719 feet.
History: Laid out 1859.
Population: 377 (2000); Race: 100.0% White, 0.0% Black, 0.0% Asian, 0.0% American Indian and Alaska Native, 0.0% Hispanic of any race, 0.0% two or more races (2000); Density: 357.1 persons per square mile (2000); Age: 20.3% under 18, 15.7% over 64 (2000); Marriage status: 20.4% never married, 73.4% now married, 0.0% widowed, 6.2% divorced (2000); Foreign born: 0.0% (2000); Ancestry (includes multiple ancestries): 33.1% German, 18.3% Irish, 15.1% English, 8.1% United States or American, 3.8% French (except Basque) (2000).
Economy: In agricultural area: corn, soybeans; livestock. Manufacturing: feed milling, grain grinding and mixing. Employment by occupation: 0.0% management, 8.3% professional, 17.6% services, 9.8% sales, 6.4% farming, 13.7% construction, 44.1% production (2000).
Income: Per capita income: $14,168 (2000); Median household income: $39,432 (2000); Poverty rate: 0.0% (2000).
Education: High school graduation rate: 87.8% (2000); College graduation rate: 0.4% (2000).
Housing: Homeownership rate: 80.0% (2000); Median home value: $44,400 (2000); Median rent: $272 per month (2000); Median age of housing: 60+ years (2000).
Transportation: Commute to work: 95.1% car, 0.0% public transportation, 0.0% walk, 4.9% work from home (2000); Travel time to work: 52.6% less than 15 minutes, 21.6% 15 to 30 minutes, 22.7% 30 to 45 minutes, 0.0% 45 to 60 minutes, 3.1% 60 minutes or more (2000)

WINAMAC (town). Covers a land area of 1.291 square miles and a water area of 0 square miles. Located at 41.05° N. Lat.; 86.60° W. Long. Elevation is 710 feet.
History: Winamac was founded in 1835 along the Tippecanoe River, and was named for Potawatomi Chief Winamac.
Population: 2,418 (2000); Race: 95.4% White, 0.4% Black, 0.2% Asian, 0.5% American Indian and Alaska Native, 2.2% Hispanic of any race, 2.4% two or more races (2000); Density: 1,872.5 persons per square mile (2000); Age: 23.8% under 18, 20.6% over 64 (2000); Marriage status: 21.6% never married, 48.0% now married, 15.0% widowed, 15.4% divorced (2000); Foreign born: 1.5% (2000); Ancestry (includes multiple ancestries): 33.5% German, 12.1% Irish, 9.4% United States or American, 9.2% English, 7.8% Other groups (2000).
Economy: Single-family building permits issued: 4 (2001) / 10 (2000); Multi-family building permits issued: 24 (2001) / 4 (2000); Employment by occupation: 10.3% management, 15.7% professional, 13.3% services, 21.0% sales, 0.6% farming, 8.0% construction, 31.1% production (2000).
Income: Per capita income: $16,447 (2000); Median household income: $31,413 (2000); Poverty rate: 8.2% (2000).
Taxes: Total city taxes per capita: $137 (1997); City property taxes per capita: $119 (1997).
Education: High school graduation rate: 77.4% (2000); College graduation rate: 14.1% (2000).

School District(s)

Eastern Pulaski Com Sch Corp (KG-12)
2000 Enrollment: 1,539 219-946-4010

Housing: Homeownership rate: 66.4% (2000); Median home value: $68,000 (2000); Median rent: $319 per month (2000); Median age of housing: 47 years (2000).
Hospitals: Pulaski Memorial Hospital (29 beds)
Newspapers: Pulaski County Journal (1 x week); The Independent (1 x week)
Transportation: Commute to work: 95.9% car, 0.0% public transportation, 2.9% walk, 1.3% work from home (2000); Travel time to work: 63.1% less than 15 minutes, 17.9% 15 to 30 minutes, 12.3% 30 to 45 minutes, 2.4% 45 to 60 minutes, 4.3% 60 minutes or more (2000)
Additional Information Contacts
Winamac Chamber of Commerce 219-946-3869

Putnam County

Located in central Indiana; drained by the Eel River. Covers a land area of 480.30 square miles, a water area of 2.30 square miles, and is located in the Eastern Time Zone. The county government was organized in 1821. County seat is Greencastle.

Weather Station: Greencastle 1 SE — Elevation: 859 feet

	Jan	Feb	Mar	Apr	May	Jun	Jul	Aug	Sep	Oct	Nov	Dec
High	34	40	51	63	74	82	86	84	78	66	52	39
Low	17	22	31	42	52	61	65	63	56	44	34	24
Precip	2.4	2.5	3.7	3.8	4.7	4.2	5.2	4.2	3.2	3.1	3.9	3.1
Snow	9.3	6.5	3.6	0.5	tr	0.0	0.0	0.0	0.0	0.2	1.5	5.7

High and Low temperatures in degrees Fahrenheit; Precipitation and Snow in inches

Population: 36,019 (2000); Race: 94.8% White, 2.9% Black, 0.7% Asian, 0.3% American Indian and Alaska Native, 1.4% Hispanic of any race, 0.9% two or more races (2000); Density: 75.0 persons per square mile (2000); Age: 23.7% under 18, 12.4% over 64 (2000).
Religion: Five largest groups: 5.6% Christian Church (Disciples of Christ), 5.3% Christian Churches and Churches of Christ, 4.2% The United Methodist Church, 4.1% American Baptist Churches in the USA, 2.8% Catholic Church (2000).
Economy: Unemployment rate: 3.3% (11/2002); Total civilian labor force: 17,859 (11/2002); Leading industries: 25.8% manufacturing; 11.1% retail

trade; 10.5% health care and social assistance (2000); Companies that employ more than 1,000 persons: 1 (2000); Companies that employ more than 100 persons: 15 (2000); Farms: 794 totaling 195,377 acres (1997); Minority business ownership rate: 0.0% (1997); Women business ownership rate: 18.5% (1997); Retail sales per capita: $5,485 (1997). Single-family building permits issued: 151 (2001) / 38 (2000); Multi-family building permits issued: 0 (2001) / 2 (2000).
Income: Per capita income: $17,163 (2000); Median household income: $38,882 (2000); Poverty rate: 8.0% (2000); Bankruptcy rate: 7.93% (2001).
Taxes: Total county taxes per capita: $243 (2000); County property taxes per capita: $154 (2000).
Education: High school graduation rate: 81.2% (2000); College graduation rate: 13.1% (2000).
Housing: Homeownership rate: 78.6% (2000); Median home value: $94,300 (2000); Median rent: $373 per month (2000); Median age of housing: 30 years (2000).
Health: Birth rate: 124.7 per 10,000 population (1998); Age adjusted death rate: 82.5 per 10,000 population (1999); Age adjusted cancer mortality rate: 216.1 deaths per 100,000 population (1999). Air Quality Index: 98% good, 2% moderate, 0% unhealthy (percent of days in 2000). Number of physicians: 5.8 per 10,000 population (1999); Number of hospital beds: 23.6 per 10,000 population (1999).
Elections: 2000 Presidential election results: 34.7% Gore, 61.9% Bush, 1.2% Nader, 1.3% Buchanan
National and State Parks: Owen-Putnam State Forest; Richard Lieber State Park
Additional Information Contacts
Putnam County Government Offices 765-653-4603
Cloverdale Chamber of Commerce 765-795-3993
Greencastle Chamber of Commerce...................... 765-653-4517
Putnam County Board of Realtors 765-526-2321

Putnam County Communities

BAINBRIDGE (town). Covers a land area of 0.378 square miles and a water area of 0 square miles. Located at 39.76° N. Lat.; 86.81° W. Long. Elevation is 929 feet.
Population: 743 (2000); Race: 96.1% White, 0.1% Black, 0.4% Asian, 0.1% American Indian and Alaska Native, 1.9% Hispanic of any race, 1.4% two or more races (2000); Density: 1,964.9 persons per square mile (2000); Age: 32.8% under 18, 9.4% over 64 (2000); Marriage status: 21.0% never married, 62.5% now married, 4.2% widowed, 12.3% divorced (2000); Foreign born: 1.5% (2000); Ancestry (includes multiple ancestries): 21.5% German, 20.1% United States or American, 12.5% English, 12.0% Irish, 9.4% Other groups (2000).
Economy: In agricultural area. Single-family building permits issued: 1 (2001) / 3 (2000); Multi-family building permits issued: 0 (2001) / 2 (2000); Employment by occupation: 10.3% management, 8.1% professional, 14.1% services, 21.4% sales, 0.5% farming, 16.3% construction, 29.3% production (2000).
Income: Per capita income: $14,231 (2000); Median household income: $36,852 (2000); Poverty rate: 5.5% (2000).
Taxes: Total city taxes per capita: $92 (1997); City property taxes per capita: $78 (1997).
Education: High school graduation rate: 83.3% (2000); College graduation rate: 7.9% (2000).
School District(s)
North Putnam Community Schools (PK-12)
2000 Enrollment: 1,831 765-522-6218
Housing: Homeownership rate: 73.4% (2000); Median home value: $83,400 (2000); Median rent: $414 per month (2000); Median age of housing: 46 years (2000).
Transportation: Commute to work: 96.3% car, 0.8% public transportation, 1.1% walk, 1.1% work from home (2000); Travel time to work: 14.6% less than 15 minutes, 27.8% 15 to 30 minutes, 21.8% 30 to 45 minutes, 20.6% 45 to 60 minutes, 15.2% 60 minutes or more (2000)

CLOVERDALE (town). Covers a land area of 3.481 square miles and a water area of 0.065 square miles. Located at 39.51° N. Lat.; 86.80° W. Long. Elevation is 779 feet.
Population: 2,243 (2000); Race: 98.2% White, 0.0% Black, 0.3% Asian, 0.0% American Indian and Alaska Native, 0.3% Hispanic of any race, 1.2% two or more races (2000); Density: 644.3 persons per square mile (2000); Age: 25.9% under 18, 14.4% over 64 (2000); Marriage status: 22.8% never married, 57.0% now married, 7.6% widowed, 12.6% divorced (2000); Foreign born: 1.0% (2000); Ancestry (includes multiple ancestries): 21.2% German, 16.3% United States or American, 11.6% Irish, 7.8% English, 6.7% Other groups (2000).
Economy: Hogs, cattle grain. Manufacturing: plastics. Limestone quarries, crushed stone. Single-family building permits issued: 6 (2001) / 9 (2000); Multi-family building permits issued: 0 (2001) / 0 (2000); Employment by occupation: 7.2% management, 8.0% professional, 22.0% services, 25.5% sales, 0.0% farming, 13.6% construction, 23.6% production (2000).
Income: Per capita income: $16,982 (2000); Median household income: $36,402 (2000); Poverty rate: 7.4% (2000).
Taxes: Total city taxes per capita: $86 (2000); City property taxes per capita: $73 (2000).
Education: High school graduation rate: 77.8% (2000); College graduation rate: 7.8% (2000).
School District(s)
Cloverdale Community Schools (PK-12)
2000 Enrollment: 1,554 765-795-4664
Housing: Homeownership rate: 73.7% (2000); Median home value: $83,100 (2000); Median rent: $376 per month (2000); Median age of housing: 21 years (2000).
Newspapers: Hoosier Topics (1 x week)
Transportation: Commute to work: 92.3% car, 0.5% public transportation, 2.0% walk, 4.9% work from home (2000); Travel time to work: 28.0% less than 15 minutes, 31.6% 15 to 30 minutes, 16.5% 30 to 45 minutes, 13.3% 45 to 60 minutes, 10.7% 60 minutes or more (2000)
Additional Information Contacts
Cloverdale Chamber of Commerce 765-795-3993

FILLMORE (town). Covers a land area of 1.903 square miles and a water area of 0 square miles. Located at 39.67° N. Lat.; 86.75° W. Long. Elevation is 847 feet.
History: Laid out 1837.
Population: 545 (2000); Race: 97.9% White, 0.0% Black, 0.0% Asian, 0.0% American Indian and Alaska Native, 2.9% Hispanic of any race, 0.0% two or more races (2000); Density: 286.4 persons per square mile (2000); Age: 34.1% under 18, 11.2% over 64 (2000); Marriage status: 16.3% never married, 72.2% now married, 4.6% widowed, 6.8% divorced (2000); Foreign born: 0.0% (2000); Ancestry (includes multiple ancestries): 19.0% United States or American, 12.0% Irish, 11.6% German, 9.3% Other groups, 3.4% French (except Basque) (2000).
Economy: Hogs, cattle. Manufacturing. Employment by occupation: 5.3% management, 8.2% professional, 27.5% services, 16.8% sales, 0.8% farming, 15.6% construction, 25.8% production (2000).
Income: Per capita income: $13,514 (2000); Median household income: $38,269 (2000); Poverty rate: 8.0% (2000).
Taxes: Total city taxes per capita: $49 (1997); City property taxes per capita: $47 (1997).
Education: High school graduation rate: 78.2% (2000); College graduation rate: 4.8% (2000).
Housing: Homeownership rate: 81.0% (2000); Median home value: $75,200 (2000); Median rent: $375 per month (2000); Median age of housing: 49 years (2000).
Transportation: Commute to work: 97.1% car, 0.0% public transportation, 0.0% walk, 2.1% work from home (2000); Travel time to work: 21.5% less than 15 minutes, 35.2% 15 to 30 minutes, 21.5% 30 to 45 minutes, 14.6% 45 to 60 minutes, 7.3% 60 minutes or more (2000)

GREENCASTLE (city). Covers a land area of 5.299 square miles and a water area of 0.047 square miles. Located at 39.64° N. Lat.; 86.85° W. Long. Elevation is 849 feet.
History: Indiana Asbury University, which later became DePauw University, was founded in 1837 in Greencastle by the Methodist Episcopal Church.
Population: 9,880 (2000); Race: 95.4% White, 1.9% Black, 1.6% Asian, 0.1% American Indian and Alaska Native, 1.4% Hispanic of any race, 0.5% two or more races (2000); Density: 1,864.6 persons per square mile (2000); Age: 19.3% under 18, 15.2% over 64 (2000); Marriage status: 30.3% never married, 51.3% now married, 9.2% widowed, 9.3% divorced (2000); Foreign born: 2.2% (2000); Ancestry (includes multiple ancestries): 20.5% German, 13.3% United States or American, 12.2% Irish, 12.1% Other groups, 10.2% English (2000).
Economy: Single-family building permits issued: 15 (2001) / 22 (2000); Multi-family building permits issued: 0 (2001) / 0 (2000); Employment by occupation: 5.9% management, 20.6% professional, 17.1% services, 25.0% sales, 0.0% farming, 6.7% construction, 24.8% production (2000).
Income: Per capita income: $15,351 (2000); Median household income: $29,798 (2000); Poverty rate: 9.8% (2000).

Taxes: Total city taxes per capita: $148 (1997); City property taxes per capita: $131 (1997).
Education: High school graduation rate: 80.5% (2000); College graduation rate: 17.5% (2000).

School District(s)

Greencastle Community Sch Corp (KG-12)
2000 Enrollment: 2,009 765-653-9771
South Putnam Community Schools (KG-12)
2000 Enrollment: 1,429 765-653-3119

Four-year College(s)

DePauw University (Private, Not-for-profit, United Methodist)
2001 Enrollment: 2,219 765-658-4800
2001 Tuition: In-state $21,100; Out-of-state $21,100

Housing: Homeownership rate: 57.5% (2000); Median home value: $85,500 (2000); Median rent: $377 per month (2000); Median age of housing: 41 years (2000).
Hospitals: Putnam County Hospital (85 beds)
Newspapers: Banner-Graphic (6 x week)
Transportation: Commute to work: 80.9% car, 0.0% public transportation, 16.6% walk, 0.9% work from home (2000); Travel time to work: 71.8% less than 15 minutes, 12.0% 15 to 30 minutes, 6.0% 30 to 45 minutes, 3.4% 45 to 60 minutes, 6.7% 60 minutes or more (2000)

Additional Information Contacts

Greencastle Chamber of Commerce. 765-653-4517
Putnam County Board of Realtors 765-526-2321

REELSVILLE (unincorporated postal area, zip code 46171). Covers a land area of 38.867 square miles and a water area of 0.073 square miles. Located at 39.52° N. Lat.; 86.96° W. Long. Elevation is 614 feet.
Population: 1,679 (2000); Race: 98.3% White, 1.1% Black, 0.0% Asian, 0.5% American Indian and Alaska Native, 0.0% Hispanic of any race, 0.0% two or more races (2000); Density: 43.2 persons per square mile (2000); Age: 27.5% under 18, 15.6% over 64 (2000); Marriage status: 15.7% never married, 68.9% now married, 7.1% widowed, 8.2% divorced (2000); Foreign born: 0.0% (2000); Ancestry (includes multiple ancestries): 22.5% German, 17.3% Other groups, 11.0% Irish, 9.3% English, 5.7% United States or American (2000).
Economy: Employment by occupation: 15.6% management, 11.4% professional, 11.9% services, 18.7% sales, 0.9% farming, 15.6% construction, 26.1% production (2000).
Income: Per capita income: $16,740 (2000); Median household income: $40,847 (2000); Poverty rate: 8.1% (2000).
Education: High school graduation rate: 75.6% (2000); College graduation rate: 9.8% (2000).
Housing: Homeownership rate: 93.8% (2000); Median home value: $84,700 (2000); Median rent: $275 per month (2000); Median age of housing: 32 years (2000).
Transportation: Commute to work: 92.4% car, 0.0% public transportation, 0.6% walk, 4.0% work from home (2000); Travel time to work: 15.2% less than 15 minutes, 33.4% 15 to 30 minutes, 16.6% 30 to 45 minutes, 12.6% 45 to 60 minutes, 22.1% 60 minutes or more (2000)

ROACHDALE (town). Covers a land area of 0.510 square miles and a water area of 0 square miles. Located at 39.85° N. Lat.; 86.80° W. Long. Elevation is 846 feet.
History: Laid out 1879.
Population: 975 (2000); Race: 99.1% White, 0.4% Black, 0.0% Asian, 0.0% American Indian and Alaska Native, 0.0% Hispanic of any race, 0.5% two or more races (2000); Density: 1,910.2 persons per square mile (2000); Age: 24.6% under 18, 17.2% over 64 (2000); Marriage status: 19.0% never married, 60.0% now married, 9.1% widowed, 11.9% divorced (2000); Foreign born: 0.0% (2000); Ancestry (includes multiple ancestries): 16.7% United States or American, 12.6% Irish, 11.0% German, 9.9% English, 7.0% Other groups (2000).
Economy: In agricultural area; dairy products; grain, soybeans; livestock. Single-family building permits issued: 1 (2001) / 4 (2000); Multi-family building permits issued: 0 (2001) / 0 (2000); Employment by occupation: 7.1% management, 9.1% professional, 16.4% services, 21.3% sales, 0.0% farming, 13.3% construction, 32.7% production (2000).
Income: Per capita income: $17,112 (2000); Median household income: $31,932 (2000); Poverty rate: 12.6% (2000).
Taxes: Total city taxes per capita: $116 (1997); City property taxes per capita: $100 (1997).
Education: High school graduation rate: 75.6% (2000); College graduation rate: 9.8% (2000).
Housing: Homeownership rate: 72.9% (2000); Median home value: $75,800 (2000); Median rent: $316 per month (2000); Median age of housing: 53 years (2000).
Transportation: Commute to work: 92.6% car, 0.5% public transportation, 1.8% walk, 5.2% work from home (2000); Travel time to work: 27.1% less than 15 minutes, 24.9% 15 to 30 minutes, 26.1% 30 to 45 minutes, 10.7% 45 to 60 minutes, 11.2% 60 minutes or more (2000)

RUSSELLVILLE (town). Covers a land area of 0.199 square miles and a water area of 0 square miles. Located at 39.85° N. Lat.; 86.98° W. Long. Elevation is 831 feet.
History: Laid out 1828.
Population: 340 (2000); Race: 97.2% White, 0.0% Black, 0.0% Asian, 0.0% American Indian and Alaska Native, 0.6% Hispanic of any race, 2.8% two or more races (2000); Density: 1,712.7 persons per square mile (2000); Age: 28.5% under 18, 19.1% over 64 (2000); Marriage status: 10.7% never married, 62.9% now married, 15.4% widowed, 11.0% divorced (2000); Foreign born: 0.0% (2000); Ancestry (includes multiple ancestries): 30.9% United States or American, 10.2% Irish, 8.8% German, 7.5% Other groups, 4.4% English (2000).
Economy: Agriculture includes grain; livestock. Manufacturing: wood products, limestone products, metal heat sinks. Limestone quarries. Employment by occupation: 5.8% management, 7.8% professional, 13.6% services, 18.2% sales, 1.3% farming, 16.2% construction, 37.0% production (2000).
Income: Per capita income: $15,236 (2000); Median household income: $34,375 (2000); Poverty rate: 6.1% (2000).
Taxes: Total city taxes per capita: $63 (1997); City property taxes per capita: $41 (1997).
Education: High school graduation rate: 80.4% (2000); College graduation rate: 2.4% (2000).
Housing: Homeownership rate: 85.1% (2000); Median home value: $58,900 (2000); Median rent: $238 per month (2000); Median age of housing: 60+ years (2000).
Transportation: Commute to work: 97.4% car, 0.0% public transportation, 1.3% walk, 1.3% work from home (2000); Travel time to work: 19.3% less than 15 minutes, 43.3% 15 to 30 minutes, 17.3% 30 to 45 minutes, 12.0% 45 to 60 minutes, 8.0% 60 minutes or more (2000)

Randolph County

Located in eastern Indiana; bounded on the east by Ohio; drained by the Mississinewa and Whitewater Rivers and the West Fork of the White River; includes the highest point in Indiana (1,240 ft). Covers a land area of 452.80 square miles, a water area of 0.40 square miles, and is located in the Eastern Time Zone. The county government was organized in 1818. County seat is Winchester.

Weather Station: Farmland 5 NNW — Elevation: 964 feet

	Jan	Feb	Mar	Apr	May	Jun	Jul	Aug	Sep	Oct	Nov	Dec
High	32	37	47	60	71	80	84	82	76	64	50	38
Low	15	18	27	38	49	59	62	59	52	40	32	22
Precip	1.9	1.8	2.7	3.5	4.0	4.4	4.4	3.6	2.9	2.7	3.2	2.6
Snow	8.1	6.2	4.0	0.7	tr	0.0	0.0	0.0	0.0	0.2	1.3	5.2

High and Low temperatures in degrees Fahrenheit; Precipitation and Snow in inches

Weather Station: Winchester Airport 3E — Elevation: 1,108 feet

	Jan	Feb	Mar	Apr	May	Jun	Jul	Aug	Sep	Oct	Nov	Dec
High	32	36	47	60	71	80	83	81	76	63	49	38
Low	16	19	29	39	50	60	63	61	54	43	33	23
Precip	1.8	1.6	2.9	3.7	4.1	4.3	4.3	3.5	2.7	2.7	3.2	2.8
Snow	5.1	4.9	2.7	0.3	tr	0.0	tr	0.0	0.0	tr	0.6	2.7

High and Low temperatures in degrees Fahrenheit; Precipitation and Snow in inches

Population: 27,401 (2000); Race: 98.1% White, 0.2% Black, 0.1% Asian, 0.1% American Indian and Alaska Native, 1.0% Hispanic of any race, 0.8% two or more races (2000); Density: 60.5 persons per square mile (2000); Age: 25.3% under 18, 15.8% over 64 (2000).
Religion: Five largest groups: 6.0% The United Methodist Church, 4.7% Christian Church (Disciples of Christ), 3.7% Catholic Church, 3.6% Friends (Quakers), 3.4% Church of the Nazarene (2000).
Economy: Unemployment rate: 6.3% (11/2002); Total civilian labor force: 11,645 (11/2002); Leading industries: 47.2% manufacturing; 14.1% retail trade; 9.3% health care and social assistance (2000); Companies that employ more than 1,000 persons: 0 (2000); Companies that employ more than 100 persons: 11 (2000); Farms: 851 totaling 223,817 acres (1997); Minority

business ownership rate: 0.0% (1997); Women business ownership rate: 18.3% (1997); Retail sales per capita: $5,532 (1997). Single-family building permits issued: 57 (2001) / 60 (2000); Multi-family building permits issued: 8 (2001) / 0 (2000).
Income: Per capita income: $16,954 (2000); Median household income: $34,544 (2000); Poverty rate: 11.1% (2000); Bankruptcy rate: 8.13% (2001).
Taxes: Total county taxes per capita: $234 (2000); County property taxes per capita: $156 (2000).
Education: High school graduation rate: 79.6% (2000); College graduation rate: 9.9% (2000).
Housing: Homeownership rate: 75.9% (2000); Median home value: $64,600 (2000); Median rent: $285 per month (2000); Median age of housing: 52 years (2000).
Health: Birth rate: 131.8 per 10,000 population (1998); Age adjusted death rate: 88.5 per 10,000 population (1999); Age adjusted cancer mortality rate: 198.8 deaths per 100,000 population (1999). Number of physicians: 4.0 per 10,000 population (1999); Number of hospital beds: 9.1 per 10,000 population (1999).
Elections: 2000 Presidential election results: 38.6% Gore, 59.4% Bush, 0.2% Nader, 1.2% Buchanan

Additional Information Contacts

Randolph County Government Offices 765-584-7070
Randolph County Board of Realtors 765-584-1011
Union City Chamber of Commerce 765-964-5409
Winchester Chamber of Commerce 765-584-3731

Randolph County Communities

FARMLAND (town). Covers a land area of 0.502 square miles and a water area of 0 square miles. Located at 40.18° N. Lat.; 85.12° W. Long. Elevation is 1,039 feet.
History: Farmland was settled as a trading town for the surrounding farming area.
Population: 1,456 (2000); Race: 99.0% White, 0.0% Black, 0.0% Asian, 0.1% American Indian and Alaska Native, 0.3% Hispanic of any race, 0.8% two or more races (2000); Density: 2,898.1 persons per square mile (2000); Age: 27.7% under 18, 15.7% over 64 (2000); Marriage status: 19.1% never married, 62.9% now married, 7.8% widowed, 10.2% divorced (2000); Foreign born: 0.3% (2000); Ancestry (includes multiple ancestries): 16.4% German, 16.2% United States or American, 11.3% Irish, 10.9% English, 7.5% Other groups (2000).
Economy: Employment by occupation: 7.2% management, 13.4% professional, 15.8% services, 23.3% sales, 0.3% farming, 11.7% construction, 28.2% production (2000).
Income: Per capita income: $18,405 (2000); Median household income: $36,250 (2000); Poverty rate: 6.5% (2000).
Taxes: Total city taxes per capita: $117 (1997); City property taxes per capita: $91 (1997).
Education: High school graduation rate: 84.0% (2000); College graduation rate: 8.7% (2000).
Housing: Homeownership rate: 77.5% (2000); Median home value: $60,800 (2000); Median rent: $280 per month (2000); Median age of housing: 48 years (2000).
Transportation: Commute to work: 92.3% car, 0.0% public transportation, 4.2% walk, 3.5% work from home (2000); Travel time to work: 22.0% less than 15 minutes, 36.9% 15 to 30 minutes, 29.1% 30 to 45 minutes, 3.7% 45 to 60 minutes, 8.3% 60 minutes or more (2000)

LOSANTVILLE (town). Aka Bronson. Covers a land area of 0.177 square miles and a water area of 0 square miles. Located at 40.02° N. Lat.; 85.18° W. Long. Elevation is 1,138 feet.
History: Also called Bronson.
Population: 280 (2000); Race: 100.0% White, 0.0% Black, 0.0% Asian, 0.0% American Indian and Alaska Native, 0.0% Hispanic of any race, 0.0% two or more races (2000); Density: 1,584.8 persons per square mile (2000); Age: 36.2% under 18, 13.4% over 64 (2000); Marriage status: 12.9% never married, 68.2% now married, 7.5% widowed, 11.4% divorced (2000); Foreign born: 0.0% (2000); Ancestry (includes multiple ancestries): 14.4% United States or American, 12.8% Irish, 7.0% English, 5.0% Other groups, 3.4% German (2000).
Economy: Agricultural area. Employment by occupation: 5.3% management, 13.2% professional, 17.5% services, 23.7% sales, 2.6% farming, 19.3% construction, 18.4% production (2000).
Income: Per capita income: $12,885 (2000); Median household income: $30,000 (2000); Poverty rate: 15.8% (2000).
Taxes: Total city taxes per capita: $105 (1997); City property taxes per capita: $98 (1997).
Education: High school graduation rate: 80.6% (2000); College graduation rate: 3.9% (2000).
Housing: Homeownership rate: 78.1% (2000); Median home value: $66,100 (2000); Median rent: $353 per month (2000); Median age of housing: 60+ years (2000).
Transportation: Commute to work: 92.2% car, 0.0% public transportation, 2.6% walk, 0.9% work from home (2000); Travel time to work: 23.5% less than 15 minutes, 27.0% 15 to 30 minutes, 39.1% 30 to 45 minutes, 5.2% 45 to 60 minutes, 5.2% 60 minutes or more (2000)

LYNN (town). Covers a land area of 0.564 square miles and a water area of 0 square miles. Located at 40.04° N. Lat.; 84.94° W. Long. Elevation is 1,180 feet.
History: Lynn was established in 1847. The arrival of the railroad in 1852 brought a period of prosperity.
Population: 1,143 (2000); Race: 96.1% White, 0.6% Black, 0.0% Asian, 0.3% American Indian and Alaska Native, 0.0% Hispanic of any race, 3.0% two or more races (2000); Density: 2,027.3 persons per square mile (2000); Age: 28.4% under 18, 14.1% over 64 (2000); Marriage status: 21.3% never married, 57.9% now married, 8.9% widowed, 11.9% divorced (2000); Foreign born: 0.0% (2000); Ancestry (includes multiple ancestries): 15.7% United States or American, 15.4% German, 12.0% English, 9.7% Irish, 9.1% Other groups (2000).
Economy: Employment by occupation: 5.4% management, 12.0% professional, 16.6% services, 18.3% sales, 0.6% farming, 8.3% construction, 38.8% production (2000).
Income: Per capita income: $15,148 (2000); Median household income: $32,368 (2000); Poverty rate: 10.2% (2000).
Taxes: Total city taxes per capita: $104 (1997); City property taxes per capita: $103 (1997).
Education: High school graduation rate: 77.7% (2000); College graduation rate: 5.2% (2000).

School District(s)

Randolph Southern School Corp (KG-12)
2000 Enrollment: 646 765-874-1181

Housing: Homeownership rate: 72.1% (2000); Median home value: $63,700 (2000); Median rent: $290 per month (2000); Median age of housing: 57 years (2000).
Transportation: Commute to work: 90.5% car, 0.0% public transportation, 6.9% walk, 2.2% work from home (2000); Travel time to work: 36.0% less than 15 minutes, 35.0% 15 to 30 minutes, 22.5% 30 to 45 minutes, 1.3% 45 to 60 minutes, 5.1% 60 minutes or more (2000)

MODOC (town). Covers a land area of 0.118 square miles and a water area of 0 square miles. Located at 40.04° N. Lat.; 85.12° W. Long. Elevation is 1,177 feet.
Population: 225 (2000); Race: 100.0% White, 0.0% Black, 0.0% Asian, 0.0% American Indian and Alaska Native, 0.0% Hispanic of any race, 0.0% two or more races (2000); Density: 1,908.1 persons per square mile (2000); Age: 24.6% under 18, 16.1% over 64 (2000); Marriage status: 17.9% never married, 59.3% now married, 9.3% widowed, 13.6% divorced (2000); Foreign born: 0.0% (2000); Ancestry (includes multiple ancestries): 18.6% United States or American, 9.5% Irish, 6.0% German, 6.0% Scotch-Irish, 2.5% British (2000).
Economy: Employment by occupation: 6.0% management, 6.0% professional, 14.5% services, 18.1% sales, 0.0% farming, 9.6% construction, 45.8% production (2000).
Income: Per capita income: $13,230 (2000); Median household income: $28,333 (2000); Poverty rate: 14.6% (2000).
Taxes: Total city taxes per capita: $173 (1997); City property taxes per capita: $73 (1997).
Education: High school graduation rate: 71.1% (2000); College graduation rate: 1.5% (2000).

School District(s)

Union School Corporation (KG-12)
2000 Enrollment: 498 765-853-5464

Housing: Homeownership rate: 85.4% (2000); Median home value: $40,800 (2000); Median rent: $242 per month (2000); Median age of housing: 60+ years (2000).
Transportation: Commute to work: 90.4% car, 0.0% public transportation, 6.0% walk, 3.6% work from home (2000); Travel time to work: 13.8% less than 15 minutes, 37.5% 15 to 30 minutes, 23.8% 30 to 45 minutes, 13.8% 45 to 60 minutes, 11.3% 60 minutes or more (2000)

PARKER CITY (town). Covers a land area of 0.579 square miles and a water area of 0 square miles. Located at 40.19° N. Lat.; 85.20° W. Long. Elevation is 1,025 feet.
History: Parker City was settled as a center for trading for the nearby farming communities.
Population: 1,416 (2000); Race: 99.4% White, 0.0% Black, 0.0% Asian, 0.2% American Indian and Alaska Native, 0.4% Hispanic of any race, 0.0% two or more races (2000); Density: 2,444.0 persons per square mile (2000); Age: 24.2% under 18, 16.7% over 64 (2000); Marriage status: 17.9% never married, 60.9% now married, 7.8% widowed, 13.4% divorced (2000); Foreign born: 0.5% (2000); Ancestry (includes multiple ancestries): 19.7% United States or American, 17.4% German, 10.2% English, 8.4% Irish, 5.3% Other groups (2000).
Economy: Employment by occupation: 8.7% management, 15.5% professional, 19.4% services, 25.2% sales, 0.0% farming, 9.3% construction, 21.9% production (2000).
Income: Per capita income: $16,552 (2000); Median household income: $34,500 (2000); Poverty rate: 12.8% (2000).
Taxes: Total city taxes per capita: $108 (1997); City property taxes per capita: $75 (1997).
Education: High school graduation rate: 80.2% (2000); College graduation rate: 11.3% (2000).

School District(s)

Monroe Central School Corp (KG-12)
2000 Enrollment: 1,070 765-468-6868

Housing: Homeownership rate: 78.1% (2000); Median home value: $58,100 (2000); Median rent: $311 per month (2000); Median age of housing: 43 years (2000).
Transportation: Commute to work: 92.4% car, 0.0% public transportation, 4.9% walk, 1.6% work from home (2000); Travel time to work: 19.7% less than 15 minutes, 52.5% 15 to 30 minutes, 17.4% 30 to 45 minutes, 4.3% 45 to 60 minutes, 6.0% 60 minutes or more (2000)

RIDGEVILLE (town). Covers a land area of 0.590 square miles and a water area of 0 square miles. Located at 40.29° N. Lat.; 85.02° W. Long. Elevation is 1,000 feet.
History: Settled 1817, laid out 1837, incorporated 1868.
Population: 843 (2000); Race: 98.2% White, 0.0% Black, 0.0% Asian, 0.2% American Indian and Alaska Native, 1.5% Hispanic of any race, 0.6% two or more races (2000); Density: 1,429.4 persons per square mile (2000); Age: 27.3% under 18, 10.5% over 64 (2000); Marriage status: 18.0% never married, 62.6% now married, 6.6% widowed, 12.8% divorced (2000); Foreign born: 1.2% (2000); Ancestry (includes multiple ancestries): 14.8% German, 13.1% United States or American, 10.1% English, 7.9% Irish, 7.8% Other groups (2000).
Economy: Livestock and grain area. Manufacturing of mobile homes; stone quarrying. Employment by occupation: 7.0% management, 7.7% professional, 8.5% services, 23.4% sales, 0.5% farming, 17.9% construction, 35.0% production (2000).
Income: Per capita income: $14,547 (2000); Median household income: $33,819 (2000); Poverty rate: 8.3% (2000).
Taxes: Total city taxes per capita: $113 (1997); City property taxes per capita: $89 (1997).
Education: High school graduation rate: 70.2% (2000); College graduation rate: 5.1% (2000).
Housing: Homeownership rate: 80.3% (2000); Median home value: $42,300 (2000); Median rent: $262 per month (2000); Median age of housing: 60+ years (2000).
Transportation: Commute to work: 91.4% car, 0.5% public transportation, 4.7% walk, 2.5% work from home (2000); Travel time to work: 25.3% less than 15 minutes, 39.6% 15 to 30 minutes, 16.7% 30 to 45 minutes, 10.1% 45 to 60 minutes, 8.3% 60 minutes or more (2000)

SARATOGA (town). Covers a land area of 0.264 square miles and a water area of 0 square miles. Located at 40.23° N. Lat.; 84.91° W. Long. Elevation is 1,050 feet.
History: Laid out 1875.
Population: 288 (2000); Race: 99.0% White, 0.0% Black, 0.0% Asian, 0.0% American Indian and Alaska Native, 1.4% Hispanic of any race, 1.0% two or more races (2000); Density: 1,090.9 persons per square mile (2000); Age: 22.2% under 18, 19.8% over 64 (2000); Marriage status: 16.5% never married, 63.6% now married, 7.4% widowed, 12.6% divorced (2000); Foreign born: 1.0% (2000); Ancestry (includes multiple ancestries): 35.8% United States or American, 9.4% German, 8.0% Irish, 6.3% Other groups, 5.6% English (2000).
Economy: In agricultural area. Manufacturing: farm gates, steel tubing. Employment by occupation: 1.4% management, 6.3% professional, 19.6% services, 17.5% sales, 0.0% farming, 7.7% construction, 47.6% production (2000).
Income: Per capita income: $14,669 (2000); Median household income: $30,000 (2000); Poverty rate: 6.9% (2000).
Taxes: Total city taxes per capita: $423 (1997); City property taxes per capita: $127 (1997).
Education: High school graduation rate: 70.4% (2000); College graduation rate: 0.0% (2000).
Housing: Homeownership rate: 63.8% (2000); Median home value: $44,400 (2000); Median rent: $310 per month (2000); Median age of housing: 60+ years (2000).
Transportation: Commute to work: 81.6% car, 0.0% public transportation, 12.8% walk, 2.8% work from home (2000); Travel time to work: 54.0% less than 15 minutes, 30.7% 15 to 30 minutes, 8.8% 30 to 45 minutes, 2.2% 45 to 60 minutes, 4.4% 60 minutes or more (2000)

UNION CITY (city). Covers a land area of 1.815 square miles and a water area of 0.007 square miles. Located at 40.20° N. Lat.; 84.81° W. Long. Elevation is 1,114 feet.
History: Union City was formed straddling the state line with Ohio. Isaac Pusey Gray, governor of Indiana from 1885-1889, lived here.
Population: 3,622 (2000); Race: 93.7% White, 0.3% Black, 0.0% Asian, 0.0% American Indian and Alaska Native, 5.0% Hispanic of any race, 1.7% two or more races (2000); Density: 1,995.1 persons per square mile (2000); Age: 24.7% under 18, 17.9% over 64 (2000); Marriage status: 18.9% never married, 56.6% now married, 9.3% widowed, 15.2% divorced (2000); Foreign born: 2.8% (2000); Ancestry (includes multiple ancestries): 25.2% United States or American, 23.3% German, 12.4% Other groups, 11.5% Irish, 6.6% English (2000).
Economy: Employment by occupation: 7.7% management, 5.3% professional, 15.6% services, 20.2% sales, 1.5% farming, 7.4% construction, 42.2% production (2000).
Income: Per capita income: $13,981 (2000); Median household income: $26,526 (2000); Poverty rate: 19.7% (2000).
Taxes: Total city taxes per capita: $309 (1997); City property taxes per capita: $232 (1997).
Education: High school graduation rate: 72.1% (2000); College graduation rate: 7.8% (2000).

School District(s)

Randolph Eastern School Corp (KG-12)
2000 Enrollment: 919 765-964-4994

Housing: Homeownership rate: 65.7% (2000); Median home value: $55,600 (2000); Median rent: $310 per month (2000); Median age of housing: 51 years (2000).
Safety: Violent crime rate: 19.2 per 10,000 population; Property crime rate: 230.6 per 10,000 population (2001).
Transportation: Commute to work: 92.9% car, 0.0% public transportation, 4.2% walk, 2.3% work from home (2000); Travel time to work: 44.6% less than 15 minutes, 29.7% 15 to 30 minutes, 15.4% 30 to 45 minutes, 4.4% 45 to 60 minutes, 5.8% 60 minutes or more (2000)
Additional Information Contacts
Union City Chamber of Commerce 765-964-5409

WINCHESTER (city). Covers a land area of 3.102 square miles and a water area of <.001 square miles. Located at 40.17° N. Lat.; 84.97° W. Long. Elevation is 1,097 feet.
History: Winchester developed as a grain and livestock shipping center, and as the seat of Randolph County.
Population: 5,037 (2000); Race: 98.9% White, 0.4% Black, 0.0% Asian, 0.4% American Indian and Alaska Native, 0.8% Hispanic of any race, 0.3% two or more races (2000); Density: 1,623.8 persons per square mile (2000); Age: 23.0% under 18, 18.9% over 64 (2000); Marriage status: 18.3% never married, 57.2% now married, 10.1% widowed, 14.4% divorced (2000); Foreign born: 0.4% (2000); Ancestry (includes multiple ancestries): 20.3% United States or American, 18.3% German, 9.6% English, 7.3% Irish, 3.9% Other groups (2000).
Economy: Employment by occupation: 7.7% management, 15.1% professional, 19.9% services, 17.3% sales, 0.6% farming, 10.4% construction, 29.0% production (2000).
Income: Per capita income: $17,753 (2000); Median household income: $28,500 (2000); Poverty rate: 15.0% (2000).
Taxes: Total city taxes per capita: $255 (1997); City property taxes per capita: $170 (1997).

Education: High school graduation rate: 75.4% (2000); College graduation rate: 10.1% (2000).

School District(s)

Randolph Central School Corp (KG-12)
2000 Enrollment: 1,661 765-584-1401

Housing: Homeownership rate: 63.6% (2000); Median home value: $58,600 (2000); Median rent: $258 per month (2000); Median age of housing: 57 years (2000).

Hospitals: Saint Vincent Randolph Hospital (25 beds)

Safety: Violent crime rate: 9.9 per 10,000 population; Property crime rate: 310.0 per 10,000 population (2001).

Newspapers: The News-Gazette (6 x week)

Transportation: Commute to work: 92.8% car, 0.0% public transportation, 4.8% walk, 1.1% work from home (2000); Travel time to work: 57.7% less than 15 minutes, 15.6% 15 to 30 minutes, 15.3% 30 to 45 minutes, 5.4% 45 to 60 minutes, 5.9% 60 minutes or more (2000)

Airports: Randolph County

Additional Information Contacts
Randolph County Board of Realtors 765-584-1011
Winchester Chamber of Commerce 765-584-3731

Ripley County

Located in southeastern Indiana; drained by Laughery and Graham Creeks. Covers a land area of 446.40 square miles, a water area of 1.60 square miles, and is located in the Eastern Time Zone. The county government was organized in 1816. County seat is Versailles.

Population: 26,523 (2000); Race: 98.5% White, 0.0% Black, 0.2% Asian, 0.3% American Indian and Alaska Native, 0.6% Hispanic of any race, 0.5% two or more races (2000); Density: 59.4 persons per square mile (2000); Age: 28.1% under 18, 13.4% over 64 (2000).

Religion: Five largest groups: 34.6% Catholic Church, 11.8% American Baptist Churches in the USA, 8.3% Evangelical Lutheran Church in America, 6.3% The United Methodist Church, 4.8% Christian Churches and Churches of Christ (2000).

Economy: Unemployment rate: 3.8% (11/2002); Total civilian labor force: 14,735 (11/2002); Leading industries: 33.1% manufacturing; 10.2% retail trade; 9.9% health care and social assistance (2000); Companies that employ more than 1,000 persons: 1 (2000); Companies that employ more than 100 persons: 17 (2000); Farms: 821 totaling 159,460 acres (1997); Minority business ownership rate: 0.0% (1997); Women business ownership rate: 32.0% (1997); Retail sales per capita: $7,269 (1997). Single-family building permits issued: 146 (2001) / 157 (2000); Multi-family building permits issued: 118 (2001) / 53 (2000).

Income: Per capita income: $17,559 (2000); Median household income: $41,426 (2000); Poverty rate: 7.5% (2000); Bankruptcy rate: 5.36% (2001).

Taxes: Total county taxes per capita: $222 (2000); County property taxes per capita: $121 (2000).

Education: High school graduation rate: 78.9% (2000); College graduation rate: 11.5% (2000).

Housing: Homeownership rate: 76.9% (2000); Median home value: $94,900 (2000); Median rent: $356 per month (2000); Median age of housing: 31 years (2000).

Health: Birth rate: 152.3 per 10,000 population (1998); Age adjusted death rate: 88.3 per 10,000 population (1999); Age adjusted cancer mortality rate: 223.9 deaths per 100,000 population (1999). Number of physicians: 13.6 per 10,000 population (1999); Number of hospital beds: 29.8 per 10,000 population (1999).

Elections: 2000 Presidential election results: 32.8% Gore, 65.5% Bush, 0.2% Nader, 1.0% Buchanan

National and State Parks: Versailles State Park

Additional Information Contacts
Ripley County Government Offices 812-689-6115
Batesville Chamber of Commerce 812-934-3101
Ripley County Chamber of Commerce 812-689-6654

Ripley County Communities

BATESVILLE (city). Covers a land area of 5.822 square miles and a water area of 0.066 square miles. Located at 39.29° N. Lat.; 85.22° W. Long. Elevation is 983 feet.

History: Batesville was settled by German immigrants, and developed as a furniture manufacturing center.

Population: 6,033 (2000); Race: 99.2% White, 0.0% Black, 0.1% Asian, 0.4% American Indian and Alaska Native, 0.2% Hispanic of any race, 0.2% two or more races (2000); Density: 1,036.2 persons per square mile (2000); Age: 28.0% under 18, 14.4% over 64 (2000); Marriage status: 20.7% never married, 62.4% now married, 7.6% widowed, 9.3% divorced (2000); Foreign born: 0.6% (2000); Ancestry (includes multiple ancestries): 50.1% German, 11.3% Irish, 9.1% English, 8.6% United States or American, 4.3% Other groups (2000).

Economy: Single-family building permits issued: 19 (2001) / 26 (2000); Multi-family building permits issued: 76 (2001) / 4 (2000); Employment by occupation: 11.5% management, 22.0% professional, 11.5% services, 25.4% sales, 0.2% farming, 6.0% construction, 23.5% production (2000).

Income: Per capita income: $21,892 (2000); Median household income: $50,115 (2000); Poverty rate: 3.5% (2000).

Taxes: Total city taxes per capita: $260 (1997); City property taxes per capita: $230 (1997).

Education: High school graduation rate: 86.9% (2000); College graduation rate: 25.1% (2000).

School District(s)

Batesville Community Sch Corp (PK-12)
2000 Enrollment: 1,810 812-934-2194

Housing: Homeownership rate: 70.6% (2000); Median home value: $118,500 (2000); Median rent: $434 per month (2000); Median age of housing: 30 years (2000).

Hospitals: Margaret Mary Community Hospital (79 beds)

Safety: Violent crime rate: 0.0 per 10,000 population; Property crime rate: 69.2 per 10,000 population (2001).

Newspapers: The Herald Tribune (2 x week)

Transportation: Commute to work: 92.0% car, 0.0% public transportation, 3.1% walk, 4.8% work from home (2000); Travel time to work: 67.9% less than 15 minutes, 13.4% 15 to 30 minutes, 5.2% 30 to 45 minutes, 5.6% 45 to 60 minutes, 7.9% 60 minutes or more (2000)

Additional Information Contacts
Batesville Chamber of Commerce 812-934-3101

CROSS PLAINS (unincorporated postal area, zip code 47017). Covers a land area of 15.567 square miles and a water area of 0.078 square miles. Located at 38.93° N. Lat.; 85.19° W. Long. Elevation is 963 feet.

Population: 484 (2000); Race: 100.0% White, 0.0% Black, 0.0% Asian, 0.0% American Indian and Alaska Native, 0.0% Hispanic of any race, 0.0% two or more races (2000); Density: 31.1 persons per square mile (2000); Age: 23.3% under 18, 22.8% over 64 (2000); Marriage status: 16.6% never married, 53.4% now married, 21.2% widowed, 8.9% divorced (2000); Foreign born: 0.0% (2000); Ancestry (includes multiple ancestries): 25.5% German, 15.5% United States or American, 4.8% English, 3.8% Dutch, 3.8% Irish (2000).

Economy: Employment by occupation: 5.2% management, 21.1% professional, 13.4% services, 26.3% sales, 0.0% farming, 12.9% construction, 21.1% production (2000).

Income: Per capita income: $16,376 (2000); Median household income: $36,023 (2000); Poverty rate: 4.0% (2000).

Education: High school graduation rate: 79.5% (2000); College graduation rate: 9.4% (2000).

Housing: Homeownership rate: 93.8% (2000); Median home value: $90,300 (2000); Median rent: $196 per month (2000); Median age of housing: 42 years (2000).

Transportation: Commute to work: 100.0% car, 0.0% public transportation, 0.0% walk, 0.0% work from home (2000); Travel time to work: 21.6% less than 15 minutes, 37.6% 15 to 30 minutes, 21.1% 30 to 45 minutes, 12.4% 45 to 60 minutes, 7.2% 60 minutes or more (2000)

FRIENDSHIP (unincorporated postal area, zip code 47021). Covers a land area of 0.473 square miles and a water area of 0 square miles. Located at 38.96° N. Lat.; 85.14° W. Long. Elevation is 650 feet.

Population: 49 (2000); Race: 100.0% White, 0.0% Black, 0.0% Asian, 0.0% American Indian and Alaska Native, 0.0% Hispanic of any race, 0.0% two or more races (2000); Density: 103.5 persons per square mile (2000); Age: 39.7% under 18, 7.9% over 64 (2000); Marriage status: 9.5% never married, 45.2% now married, 23.8% widowed, 21.4% divorced (2000); Foreign born: 0.0% (2000); Ancestry (includes multiple ancestries): 54.0% German, 23.8% English, 22.2% Other groups, 22.2% Scotch-Irish, 7.9% Italian (2000).

Economy: Employment by occupation: 15.2% management, 12.1% professional, 0.0% services, 42.4% sales, 0.0% farming, 0.0% construction, 30.3% production (2000).

Income: Per capita income: $14,056 (2000); Median household income: $43,092 (2000); Poverty rate: 17.5% (2000).

Education: High school graduation rate: 63.2% (2000); College graduation rate: 0.0% (2000).

Housing: Homeownership rate: 66.7% (2000); Median home value: $59,200 (2000); Median rent: $375 per month (2000); Median age of housing: 60+ years (2000).
Transportation: Commute to work: 100.0% car, 0.0% public transportation, 0.0% walk, 0.0% work from home (2000); Travel time to work: 15.2% less than 15 minutes, 12.1% 15 to 30 minutes, 0.0% 30 to 45 minutes, 0.0% 45 to 60 minutes, 72.7% 60 minutes or more (2000)

HOLTON (town). Covers a land area of 1.794 square miles and a water area of 0 square miles. Located at 39.07° N. Lat.; 85.38° W. Long. Elevation is 911 feet.
Population: 407 (2000); Race: 100.0% White, 0.0% Black, 0.0% Asian, 0.0% American Indian and Alaska Native, 0.0% Hispanic of any race, 0.0% two or more races (2000); Density: 226.9 persons per square mile (2000); Age: 26.9% under 18, 9.1% over 64 (2000); Marriage status: 19.9% never married, 59.5% now married, 5.3% widowed, 15.3% divorced (2000); Foreign born: 0.0% (2000); Ancestry (includes multiple ancestries): 21.4% United States or American, 13.0% German, 6.3% English, 5.3% Irish, 4.3% Other groups (2000).
Economy: Cattle, poultry, corn. Employment by occupation: 6.1% management, 12.1% professional, 23.7% services, 15.7% sales, 1.5% farming, 14.6% construction, 26.3% production (2000).
Income: Per capita income: $12,357 (2000); Median household income: $28,750 (2000); Poverty rate: 22.6% (2000).
Taxes: Total city taxes per capita: $59 (1997); City property taxes per capita: $55 (1997).
Education: High school graduation rate: 62.6% (2000); College graduation rate: 3.9% (2000).
Housing: Homeownership rate: 76.9% (2000); Median home value: $60,000 (2000); Median rent: $361 per month (2000); Median age of housing: 54 years (2000).
Transportation: Commute to work: 98.0% car, 0.0% public transportation, 0.0% walk, 1.5% work from home (2000); Travel time to work: 29.0% less than 15 minutes, 29.5% 15 to 30 minutes, 22.3% 30 to 45 minutes, 7.8% 45 to 60 minutes, 11.4% 60 minutes or more (2000)

MILAN (town). Covers a land area of 1.901 square miles and a water area of 0.034 square miles. Located at 39.12° N. Lat.; 85.13° W. Long. Elevation is 990 feet.
History: Laid out 1854.
Population: 1,816 (2000); Race: 99.0% White, 0.3% Black, 0.0% Asian, 0.3% American Indian and Alaska Native, 0.9% Hispanic of any race, 0.3% two or more races (2000); Density: 955.2 persons per square mile (2000); Age: 27.3% under 18, 17.0% over 64 (2000); Marriage status: 21.9% never married, 51.1% now married, 13.0% widowed, 14.0% divorced (2000); Foreign born: 0.1% (2000); Ancestry (includes multiple ancestries): 31.0% German, 16.7% United States or American, 12.2% Irish, 10.7% Other groups, 9.2% English (2000).
Economy: In agricultural area. Employment by occupation: 4.1% management, 11.4% professional, 19.2% services, 17.9% sales, 0.2% farming, 10.1% construction, 37.1% production (2000).
Income: Per capita income: $16,191 (2000); Median household income: $36,066 (2000); Poverty rate: 9.0% (2000).
Taxes: Total city taxes per capita: $89 (1997); City property taxes per capita: $81 (1997).
Education: High school graduation rate: 71.7% (2000); College graduation rate: 8.3% (2000).

School District(s)

Milan Community Schools (KG-12)
2000 Enrollment: 1,190 812-654-2365
Housing: Homeownership rate: 64.6% (2000); Median home value: $78,200 (2000); Median rent: $390 per month (2000); Median age of housing: 40 years (2000).
Transportation: Commute to work: 95.2% car, 0.0% public transportation, 1.9% walk, 2.4% work from home (2000); Travel time to work: 21.5% less than 15 minutes, 33.2% 15 to 30 minutes, 20.1% 30 to 45 minutes, 12.5% 45 to 60 minutes, 12.8% 60 minutes or more (2000)

NAPOLEON (town). Covers a land area of 0.188 square miles and a water area of 0 square miles. Located at 39.20° N. Lat.; 85.32° W. Long. Elevation is 970 feet.
History: Laid out 1820.
Population: 238 (2000); Race: 100.0% White, 0.0% Black, 0.0% Asian, 0.0% American Indian and Alaska Native, 0.0% Hispanic of any race, 0.0% two or more races (2000); Density: 1,266.1 persons per square mile (2000); Age: 26.4% under 18, 20.3% over 64 (2000); Marriage status: 18.7% never married, 66.3% now married, 9.3% widowed, 5.7% divorced (2000); Foreign born: 1.7% (2000); Ancestry (includes multiple ancestries): 59.3% German, 19.5% United States or American, 12.6% Irish, 10.0% Other groups, 4.3% English (2000).
Economy: In agricultural area. Manufacturing of wood products. Employment by occupation: 13.6% management, 6.8% professional, 11.0% services, 20.3% sales, 0.0% farming, 5.1% construction, 43.2% production (2000).
Income: Per capita income: $16,187 (2000); Median household income: $39,844 (2000); Poverty rate: 11.3% (2000).
Taxes: Total city taxes per capita: $20 (1997); City property taxes per capita: $16 (1997).
Education: High school graduation rate: 74.7% (2000); College graduation rate: 7.4% (2000).
Housing: Homeownership rate: 75.0% (2000); Median home value: $76,700 (2000); Median rent: $338 per month (2000); Median age of housing: 40 years (2000).
Transportation: Commute to work: 71.2% car, 1.7% public transportation, 20.3% walk, 6.8% work from home (2000); Travel time to work: 33.6% less than 15 minutes, 57.3% 15 to 30 minutes, 6.4% 30 to 45 minutes, 2.7% 45 to 60 minutes, 0.0% 60 minutes or more (2000)

OSGOOD (town). Covers a land area of 1.299 square miles and a water area of 0.031 square miles. Located at 39.12° N. Lat.; 85.29° W. Long. Elevation is 990 feet.
History: Laid out 1857.
Population: 1,669 (2000); Race: 98.9% White, 0.0% Black, 0.1% Asian, 0.8% American Indian and Alaska Native, 0.8% Hispanic of any race, 0.2% two or more races (2000); Density: 1,285.0 persons per square mile (2000); Age: 27.8% under 18, 17.2% over 64 (2000); Marriage status: 18.7% never married, 58.8% now married, 10.9% widowed, 11.6% divorced (2000); Foreign born: 0.4% (2000); Ancestry (includes multiple ancestries): 25.2% German, 14.6% United States or American, 13.7% Irish, 9.5% Other groups, 6.8% English (2000).
Economy: Farm trading center, with some manufacturing: cement products, shoes; grain milling, timber; limestone quarries. Employment by occupation: 7.4% management, 5.8% professional, 16.4% services, 18.2% sales, 0.4% farming, 10.3% construction, 41.5% production (2000).
Income: Per capita income: $13,842 (2000); Median household income: $29,659 (2000); Poverty rate: 11.0% (2000).
Taxes: Total city taxes per capita: $105 (1997); City property taxes per capita: $89 (1997).
Education: High school graduation rate: 67.1% (2000); College graduation rate: 4.5% (2000).

School District(s)

Jac-Cen-Del Community Sch Corp (KG-12)
2000 Enrollment: 970 812-689-4114
Housing: Homeownership rate: 61.9% (2000); Median home value: $72,100 (2000); Median rent: $296 per month (2000); Median age of housing: 44 years (2000).
Transportation: Commute to work: 92.1% car, 0.4% public transportation, 6.2% walk, 1.3% work from home (2000); Travel time to work: 34.2% less than 15 minutes, 24.7% 15 to 30 minutes, 28.7% 30 to 45 minutes, 4.5% 45 to 60 minutes, 7.9% 60 minutes or more (2000)

SUNMAN (town). Covers a land area of 1.014 square miles and a water area of 0 square miles. Located at 39.23° N. Lat.; 85.09° W. Long. Elevation is 1,021 feet.
History: Laid out 1856.
Population: 805 (2000); Race: 96.1% White, 0.3% Black, 0.3% Asian, 0.1% American Indian and Alaska Native, 3.7% Hispanic of any race, 0.0% two or more races (2000); Density: 793.8 persons per square mile (2000); Age: 30.2% under 18, 14.1% over 64 (2000); Marriage status: 27.4% never married, 50.1% now married, 9.9% widowed, 12.6% divorced (2000); Foreign born: 3.3% (2000); Ancestry (includes multiple ancestries): 40.0% German, 13.2% United States or American, 12.0% Other groups, 11.9% Irish, 5.7% English (2000).
Economy: In agricultural area. Manufacturing: offset printing. Employment by occupation: 5.6% management, 8.9% professional, 12.6% services, 22.8% sales, 0.5% farming, 19.6% construction, 29.8% production (2000).
Income: Per capita income: $14,828 (2000); Median household income: $33,819 (2000); Poverty rate: 9.6% (2000).
Taxes: Total city taxes per capita: $93 (1997); City property taxes per capita: $93 (1997).
Education: High school graduation rate: 70.4% (2000); College graduation rate: 7.6% (2000).

School District(s)

Sunman-Dearborn Com Sch Corp (KG-12)
2000 Enrollment: 4,128 812-623-2291

Housing: Homeownership rate: 60.4% (2000); Median home value: $92,800 (2000); Median rent: $332 per month (2000); Median age of housing: 30 years (2000).

Transportation: Commute to work: 90.6% car, 0.0% public transportation, 7.2% walk, 1.7% work from home (2000); Travel time to work: 32.5% less than 15 minutes, 30.2% 15 to 30 minutes, 21.5% 30 to 45 minutes, 11.9% 45 to 60 minutes, 4.0% 60 minutes or more (2000)

VERSAILLES (town). Covers a land area of 1.526 square miles and a water area of 0 square miles. Located at 39.06° N. Lat.; 85.25° W. Long. Elevation is 968 feet.

History: Versailles was founded in 1818 as a farming center. General John Morgan and his men came to Versailles in 1863 and looted the office of the county treasurer.

Population: 1,784 (2000); Race: 98.5% White, 0.0% Black, 0.0% Asian, 0.7% American Indian and Alaska Native, 0.4% Hispanic of any race, 0.4% two or more races (2000); Density: 1,168.9 persons per square mile (2000); Age: 25.8% under 18, 14.9% over 64 (2000); Marriage status: 20.3% never married, 56.8% now married, 9.2% widowed, 13.7% divorced (2000); Foreign born: 0.6% (2000); Ancestry (includes multiple ancestries): 23.1% German, 12.6% United States or American, 11.2% English, 9.0% Irish, 6.2% Other groups (2000).

Economy: Employment by occupation: 7.9% management, 15.6% professional, 17.2% services, 22.2% sales, 0.0% farming, 8.1% construction, 28.9% production (2000).

Income: Per capita income: $17,352 (2000); Median household income: $35,144 (2000); Poverty rate: 8.7% (2000).

Taxes: Total city taxes per capita: $100 (1997); City property taxes per capita: $99 (1997).

Education: High school graduation rate: 80.6% (2000); College graduation rate: 14.9% (2000).

School District(s)

South Ripley Com Sch Corp (KG-12)
2000 Enrollment: 1,441 812-689-6282

Southeastern Career Center
2000 Enrollment: n/a 812-689-5253

Housing: Homeownership rate: 68.8% (2000); Median home value: $81,800 (2000); Median rent: $338 per month (2000); Median age of housing: 36 years (2000).

Newspapers: Versailles Republican (1 x week); Osgood Journal (1 x week); Spotlight-Advertiser (1 x week)

Transportation: Commute to work: 91.4% car, 0.4% public transportation, 2.8% walk, 5.1% work from home (2000); Travel time to work: 38.1% less than 15 minutes, 22.4% 15 to 30 minutes, 27.2% 30 to 45 minutes, 5.1% 45 to 60 minutes, 7.3% 60 minutes or more (2000)

Additional Information Contacts

Ripley County Chamber of Commerce 812-689-6654

Rush County

Located in east central Indiana; drained by the Big Blue River and Flatrock Creek. Covers a land area of 408.30 square miles, a water area of 0.30 square miles, and is located in the Eastern Time Zone. The county government was organized in 1821. County seat is Rushville.

Weather Station: Rushville Sewage Plant — Elevation: 958 feet

	Jan	Feb	Mar	Apr	May	Jun	Jul	Aug	Sep	Oct	Nov	Dec
High	33	39	49	62	73	81	84	83	77	65	51	39
Low	16	19	29	39	50	59	63	60	53	41	32	23
Precip	2.6	2.5	3.2	4.2	4.9	4.2	4.5	3.5	2.9	2.9	3.6	3.1
Snow	5.7	4.4	2.0	0.3	tr	0.0	0.0	0.0	0.0	0.3	0.6	2.8

High and Low temperatures in degrees Fahrenheit; Precipitation and Snow in inches

Population: 18,261 (2000); Race: 97.2% White, 1.0% Black, 0.1% Asian, 0.4% American Indian and Alaska Native, 0.7% Hispanic of any race, 1.2% two or more races (2000); Density: 44.7 persons per square mile (2000); Age: 26.7% under 18, 14.8% over 64 (2000).

Religion: Five largest groups: 9.7% Catholic Church, 9.6% Christian Churches and Churches of Christ, 8.0% Christian Church (Disciples of Christ), 6.5% The United Methodist Church, 5.1% Southern Baptist Convention (2000).

Economy: Unemployment rate: 4.3% (11/2002); Total civilian labor force: 9,547 (11/2002); Leading industries: 27.8% manufacturing; 15.6% retail trade; 15.0% health care and social assistance (2000); Companies that employ more than 1,000 persons: 0 (2000); Companies that employ more than 100 persons: 8 (2000); Farms: 663 totaling 227,874 acres (1997); Minority business ownership rate: 0.0% (1997); Women business ownership rate: 24.6% (1997); Retail sales per capita: $6,257 (1997). Single-family building permits issued: 52 (2001) / 75 (2000); Multi-family building permits issued: 0 (2001) / 2 (2000).

Income: Per capita income: $17,997 (2000); Median household income: $38,152 (2000); Poverty rate: 7.3% (2000); Bankruptcy rate: 9.67% (2001).

Taxes: Total county taxes per capita: $278 (1997); County property taxes per capita: $193 (1997).

Education: High school graduation rate: 79.6% (2000); College graduation rate: 10.3% (2000).

Housing: Homeownership rate: 74.1% (2000); Median home value: $82,300 (2000); Median rent: $337 per month (2000); Median age of housing: 55 years (2000).

Health: Birth rate: 134.2 per 10,000 population (1998); Age adjusted death rate: 103.7 per 10,000 population (1999); Age adjusted cancer mortality rate: 225.8 deaths per 100,000 population (1999). Number of physicians: 4.4 per 10,000 population (1999); Number of hospital beds: 13.7 per 10,000 population (1999).

Elections: 2000 Presidential election results: 32.5% Gore, 65.2% Bush, 0.3% Nader, 1.1% Buchanan

Additional Information Contacts

Rush County Government Offices 765-932-2077
Rushville Chamber of Commerce 765-932-2880

Rush County Communities

ARLINGTON (unincorporated postal area, zip code 46104). Covers a land area of 29.822 square miles and a water area of 0.032 square miles. Located at 39.64° N. Lat.; 85.60° W. Long. Elevation is 922 feet.

History: Arlington was established around a stone quarry.

Population: 1,124 (2000); Race: 98.5% White, 0.0% Black, 0.0% Asian, 0.0% American Indian and Alaska Native, 0.0% Hispanic of any race, 1.5% two or more races (2000); Density: 37.7 persons per square mile (2000); Age: 30.5% under 18, 12.6% over 64 (2000); Marriage status: 15.9% never married, 68.9% now married, 8.2% widowed, 6.9% divorced (2000); Foreign born: 0.0% (2000); Ancestry (includes multiple ancestries): 20.1% German, 17.0% United States or American, 15.5% Irish, 7.9% English, 4.2% Other groups (2000).

Economy: Employment by occupation: 16.7% management, 15.6% professional, 18.7% services, 11.6% sales, 1.3% farming, 6.2% construction, 29.8% production (2000).

Income: Per capita income: $16,479 (2000); Median household income: $36,550 (2000); Poverty rate: 2.5% (2000).

Education: High school graduation rate: 84.9% (2000); College graduation rate: 15.0% (2000).

Housing: Homeownership rate: 86.8% (2000); Median home value: $69,200 (2000); Median rent: $429 per month (2000); Median age of housing: 60+ years (2000).

Transportation: Commute to work: 95.2% car, 0.8% public transportation, 1.3% walk, 2.7% work from home (2000); Travel time to work: 23.9% less than 15 minutes, 33.6% 15 to 30 minutes, 23.2% 30 to 45 minutes, 10.6% 45 to 60 minutes, 8.9% 60 minutes or more (2000)

CARTHAGE (town). Covers a land area of 0.574 square miles and a water area of 0 square miles. Located at 39.73° N. Lat.; 85.57° W. Long. Elevation is 886 feet.

Population: 928 (2000); Race: 98.2% White, 0.0% Black, 0.0% Asian, 0.5% American Indian and Alaska Native, 0.7% Hispanic of any race, 1.1% two or more races (2000); Density: 1,616.3 persons per square mile (2000); Age: 27.7% under 18, 12.1% over 64 (2000); Marriage status: 17.3% never married, 65.6% now married, 7.1% widowed, 10.0% divorced (2000); Foreign born: 0.1% (2000); Ancestry (includes multiple ancestries): 19.9% United States or American, 16.7% German, 13.6% Irish, 12.2% English, 5.0% Other groups (2000).

Economy: Agricultural area: corn; hogs, poultry; lumber, paperboard. Employment by occupation: 8.3% management, 6.0% professional, 15.4% services, 23.5% sales, 0.5% farming, 16.4% construction, 30.0% production (2000).

Income: Per capita income: $15,598 (2000); Median household income: $35,417 (2000); Poverty rate: 7.2% (2000).

Taxes: Total city taxes per capita: $85 (1997); City property taxes per capita: $84 (1997).

Education: High school graduation rate: 74.4% (2000); College graduation rate: 6.3% (2000).
Housing: Homeownership rate: 70.5% (2000); Median home value: $70,500 (2000); Median rent: $365 per month (2000); Median age of housing: 60+ years (2000).
Transportation: Commute to work: 93.3% car, 0.0% public transportation, 4.1% walk, 2.6% work from home (2000); Travel time to work: 17.3% less than 15 minutes, 29.9% 15 to 30 minutes, 16.8% 30 to 45 minutes, 20.2% 45 to 60 minutes, 15.8% 60 minutes or more (2000)

FALMOUTH (unincorporated postal area, zip code 46127). Covers a land area of 22.286 square miles and a water area of 0 square miles. Located at 39.71° N. Lat.; 85.32° W. Long. Elevation is 1,046 feet.
Population: 374 (2000); Race: 100.0% White, 0.0% Black, 0.0% Asian, 0.0% American Indian and Alaska Native, 0.0% Hispanic of any race, 0.0% two or more races (2000); Density: 16.8 persons per square mile (2000); Age: 22.9% under 18, 23.5% over 64 (2000); Marriage status: 13.0% never married, 59.7% now married, 6.0% widowed, 21.3% divorced (2000); Foreign born: 0.0% (2000); Ancestry (includes multiple ancestries): 67.0% United States or American, 6.9% English, 6.6% Irish, 1.7% German (2000).
Economy: Employment by occupation: 15.8% management, 7.2% professional, 11.8% services, 9.2% sales, 7.9% farming, 15.1% construction, 32.9% production (2000).
Income: Per capita income: $14,315 (2000); Median household income: $27,150 (2000); Poverty rate: 6.6% (2000).
Education: High school graduation rate: 75.9% (2000); College graduation rate: 5.0% (2000).
Housing: Homeownership rate: 80.6% (2000); Median home value: $87,500 (2000); Median rent: $382 per month (2000); Median age of housing: 60+ years (2000).
Transportation: Commute to work: 100.0% car, 0.0% public transportation, 0.0% walk, 0.0% work from home (2000); Travel time to work: 16.4% less than 15 minutes, 33.6% 15 to 30 minutes, 46.7% 30 to 45 minutes, 3.3% 45 to 60 minutes, 0.0% 60 minutes or more (2000)

GLENWOOD (town). Covers a land area of 0.173 square miles and a water area of 0 square miles. Located at 39.62° N. Lat.; 85.30° W. Long. Elevation is 1,082 feet.
Population: 318 (2000); Race: 99.4% White, 0.0% Black, 0.0% Asian, 0.0% American Indian and Alaska Native, 0.0% Hispanic of any race, 0.6% two or more races (2000); Density: 1,839.9 persons per square mile (2000); Age: 32.1% under 18, 18.2% over 64 (2000); Marriage status: 18.7% never married, 64.8% now married, 4.8% widowed, 11.7% divorced (2000); Foreign born: 0.0% (2000); Ancestry (includes multiple ancestries): 42.9% United States or American, 14.0% German, 9.7% Irish, 4.2% Other groups, 3.9% English (2000).
Economy: Employment by occupation: 10.7% management, 4.5% professional, 15.2% services, 20.5% sales, 0.0% farming, 6.3% construction, 42.9% production (2000).
Income: Per capita income: $13,171 (2000); Median household income: $33,750 (2000); Poverty rate: 14.5% (2000).
Taxes: Total city taxes per capita: $122 (1997); City property taxes per capita: $115 (1997).
Education: High school graduation rate: 76.4% (2000); College graduation rate: 2.7% (2000).
Housing: Homeownership rate: 86.1% (2000); Median home value: $63,800 (2000); Median rent: $338 per month (2000); Median age of housing: 60+ years (2000).
Transportation: Commute to work: 94.6% car, 0.0% public transportation, 5.4% walk, 0.0% work from home (2000); Travel time to work: 32.1% less than 15 minutes, 27.7% 15 to 30 minutes, 21.4% 30 to 45 minutes, 12.5% 45 to 60 minutes, 6.3% 60 minutes or more (2000)

MANILLA (unincorporated postal area, zip code 46150). Covers a land area of 26.940 square miles and a water area of 0.009 square miles. Located at 39.56° N. Lat.; 85.61° W. Long. Elevation is 893 feet.
Population: 928 (2000); Race: 98.3% White, 0.0% Black, 0.0% Asian, 0.0% American Indian and Alaska Native, 1.7% Hispanic of any race, 0.0% two or more races (2000); Density: 34.4 persons per square mile (2000); Age: 25.6% under 18, 19.0% over 64 (2000); Marriage status: 16.7% never married, 63.1% now married, 11.0% widowed, 9.2% divorced (2000); Foreign born: 1.2% (2000); Ancestry (includes multiple ancestries): 23.3% German, 10.0% United States or American, 9.4% Irish, 9.4% Other groups, 6.7% English (2000).
Economy: Employment by occupation: 9.0% management, 8.8% professional, 9.9% services, 22.5% sales, 2.9% farming, 22.3% construction, 24.5% production (2000).
Income: Per capita income: $18,098 (2000); Median household income: $42,159 (2000); Poverty rate: 6.1% (2000).
Education: High school graduation rate: 82.9% (2000); College graduation rate: 13.4% (2000).
Housing: Homeownership rate: 86.4% (2000); Median home value: $65,500 (2000); Median rent: $425 per month (2000); Median age of housing: 58 years (2000).
Transportation: Commute to work: 92.8% car, 3.7% public transportation, 0.0% walk, 3.5% work from home (2000); Travel time to work: 19.3% less than 15 minutes, 42.7% 15 to 30 minutes, 13.0% 30 to 45 minutes, 7.7% 45 to 60 minutes, 17.3% 60 minutes or more (2000)

MILROY (unincorporated postal area, zip code 46156). Covers a land area of 40.307 square miles and a water area of 0.038 square miles. Located at 39.48° N. Lat.; 85.47° W. Long. Elevation is 967 feet.
History: Laid out 1830.
Population: 1,575 (2000); Race: 100.0% White, 0.0% Black, 0.0% Asian, 0.0% American Indian and Alaska Native, 0.4% Hispanic of any race, 0.0% two or more races (2000); Density: 39.1 persons per square mile (2000); Age: 30.1% under 18, 8.5% over 64 (2000); Marriage status: 22.0% never married, 60.1% now married, 8.2% widowed, 9.6% divorced (2000); Foreign born: 0.5% (2000); Ancestry (includes multiple ancestries): 29.6% United States or American, 23.9% German, 12.1% Irish, 4.8% Other groups, 4.6% English (2000).
Economy: Manufacturing: paper products, canned tomatoes. Hogs; corn, wheat. Employment by occupation: 9.1% management, 3.8% professional, 11.1% services, 16.7% sales, 1.4% farming, 16.9% construction, 41.0% production (2000).
Income: Per capita income: $14,936 (2000); Median household income: $37,448 (2000); Poverty rate: 10.6% (2000).
Education: High school graduation rate: 72.5% (2000); College graduation rate: 1.0% (2000).
Housing: Homeownership rate: 72.9% (2000); Median home value: $75,600 (2000); Median rent: $353 per month (2000); Median age of housing: 52 years (2000).
Transportation: Commute to work: 87.7% car, 0.3% public transportation, 4.6% walk, 7.4% work from home (2000); Travel time to work: 24.3% less than 15 minutes, 40.2% 15 to 30 minutes, 10.2% 30 to 45 minutes, 7.4% 45 to 60 minutes, 17.9% 60 minutes or more (2000)

RUSHVILLE (city). Covers a land area of 2.246 square miles and a water area of 0 square miles. Located at 39.61° N. Lat.; 85.44° W. Long. Elevation is 966 feet.
History: Rushville was founded in 1822 and named for Benjamin F. Rush, a Revolutionary War soldier and a signer of the Declaration of Independence.
Population: 5,995 (2000); Race: 95.2% White, 2.9% Black, 0.4% Asian, 1.0% American Indian and Alaska Native, 0.8% Hispanic of any race, 0.5% two or more races (2000); Density: 2,668.8 persons per square mile (2000); Age: 25.5% under 18, 17.4% over 64 (2000); Marriage status: 19.5% never married, 54.9% now married, 9.7% widowed, 15.9% divorced (2000); Foreign born: 0.6% (2000); Ancestry (includes multiple ancestries): 30.1% United States or American, 17.5% German, 10.8% Other groups, 10.5% English, 10.2% Irish (2000).
Economy: Employment by occupation: 6.1% management, 8.1% professional, 14.5% services, 20.1% sales, 0.4% farming, 9.3% construction, 41.5% production (2000).
Income: Per capita income: $17,072 (2000); Median household income: $30,233 (2000); Poverty rate: 11.0% (2000).
Taxes: Total city taxes per capita: $354 (1997); City property taxes per capita: $351 (1997).
Education: High school graduation rate: 73.3% (2000); College graduation rate: 7.1% (2000).

School District(s)

Rush County Schools (PK-12)
2000 Enrollment: 2,668 765-932-4186
Housing: Homeownership rate: 61.1% (2000); Median home value: $79,100 (2000); Median rent: $333 per month (2000); Median age of housing: 60+ years (2000).
Hospitals: Rush Memorial Hospital (15 beds)
Safety: Violent crime rate: 13.3 per 10,000 population; Property crime rate: 277.0 per 10,000 population (2001).
Newspapers: Rushville Republican (6 x week); Rushville Telegram (1 x week)

Transportation: Commute to work: 92.4% car, 1.0% public transportation, 3.0% walk, 2.7% work from home (2000); Travel time to work: 50.0% less than 15 minutes, 16.0% 15 to 30 minutes, 18.3% 30 to 45 minutes, 7.1% 45 to 60 minutes, 8.6% 60 minutes or more (2000)

Additional Information Contacts

Rushville Chamber of Commerce 765-932-2880

Saint Joseph County

Located in northern Indiana; bounded on the north by Michigan; drained by the St. Joseph, Yellow, and Kankakee Rivers. Covers a land area of 457.30 square miles, a water area of 3.60 square miles, and is located in the Eastern Time Zone. The county government was organized in 1830. County seat is South Bend.

Saint Joseph County is part of the South Bend, IN MSA. The entire metro area includes: St. Joseph County

Weather Station: South Bend Michiana Regional — Elevation: 770 feet

	Jan	Feb	Mar	Apr	May	Jun	Jul	Aug	Sep	Oct	Nov	Dec
High	31	35	46	59	71	80	83	81	74	62	48	36
Low	17	20	29	39	49	59	63	62	54	43	34	23
Precip	2.2	2.0	2.9	3.7	3.5	4.1	3.8	4.0	3.9	3.3	3.4	3.1
Snow	22.9	15.5	9.2	2.0	tr	tr	tr	tr	tr	0.5	7.7	18.8

High and Low temperatures in degrees Fahrenheit; Precipitation and Snow in inches

Population: 265,559 (2000); Race: 82.7% White, 11.2% Black, 1.3% Asian, 0.3% American Indian and Alaska Native, 4.6% Hispanic of any race, 2.1% two or more races (2000); Density: 580.7 persons per square mile (2000); Age: 25.7% under 18, 13.6% over 64 (2000).

Religion: Five largest groups: 23.8% Catholic Church, 3.8% The United Methodist Church, 1.6% Evangelical Lutheran Church in America, 1.1% Presbyterian Church (U.S.A.), 1.1% Assemblies of God (2000).

Economy: Unemployment rate: 4.4% (11/2002); Total civilian labor force: 135,545 (11/2002); Leading industries: 17.0% manufacturing; 14.1% retail trade; 12.0% health care and social assistance (2000); Companies that employ more than 1,000 persons: 4 (2000); Companies that employ more than 100 persons: 218 (2000); Farms: 666 totaling 154,142 acres (1997); Minority business ownership rate: 6.9% (1997); Women business ownership rate: 25.3% (1997); Retail sales per capita: $10,780 (1997). Single-family building permits issued: 780 (2001) / 889 (2000); Multi-family building permits issued: 154 (2001) / 776 (2000).

Income: Per capita income: $19,756 (2000); Median household income: $40,420 (2000); Poverty rate: 10.4% (2000); Bankruptcy rate: 7.23% (2001).

Taxes: Total county taxes per capita: $241 (2000); County property taxes per capita: $229 (2000).

Education: High school graduation rate: 82.4% (2000); College graduation rate: 23.6% (2000).

Housing: Homeownership rate: 71.7% (2000); Median home value: $85,700 (2000); Median rent: $456 per month (2000); Median age of housing: 41 years (2000).

Health: Birth rate: 150.2 per 10,000 population (1998); Age adjusted death rate: 92.0 per 10,000 population (1999); Age adjusted cancer mortality rate: 224.9 deaths per 100,000 population (1999). Air Quality Index: 61% good, 38% moderate, 1% unhealthy (percent of days in 2000). Number of physicians: 22.1 per 10,000 population (1999); Number of hospital beds: 31.8 per 10,000 population (1999).

Elections: 2000 Presidential election results: 48.9% Gore, 48.8% Bush, 0.9% Nader, 0.6% Buchanan

National and State Parks: Potato Creek State Park

Additional Information Contacts

St. Joseph County Government Offices 219-235-9534
Greater South Bend- Mishawaka Association of Realtors 219-289-6378
North Liberty Chamber of Commerce 219-656-3393
St. Joseph Chamber of Commerce 219-234-0051
Walkerton Chamber of Commerce 219-586-3100

Saint Joseph County Communities

GEORGETOWN (CDP). Covers a land area of 1.940 square miles and a water area of 0.009 square miles. Located at 41.72° N. Lat.; 86.22° W. Long.

Population: 4,497 (2000); Race: 85.8% White, 6.9% Black, 2.0% Asian, 2.3% American Indian and Alaska Native, 3.1% Hispanic of any race, 1.4% two or more races (2000); Density: 2,318.1 persons per square mile (2000); Age: 21.0% under 18, 14.3% over 64 (2000); Marriage status: 28.0% never married, 57.3% now married, 7.1% widowed, 7.6% divorced (2000); Foreign born: 4.7% (2000); Ancestry (includes multiple ancestries): 31.6% German, 17.2% Irish, 14.2% Other groups, 12.3% Polish, 7.5% English (2000).

Economy: Employment by occupation: 14.3% management, 35.7% professional, 12.3% services, 24.7% sales, 0.0% farming, 4.6% construction, 8.2% production (2000).

Income: Per capita income: $24,302 (2000); Median household income: $51,019 (2000); Poverty rate: 10.2% (2000).

Education: High school graduation rate: 93.4% (2000); College graduation rate: 40.9% (2000).

Housing: Homeownership rate: 57.6% (2000); Median home value: $118,800 (2000); Median rent: $628 per month (2000); Median age of housing: 25 years (2000).

Transportation: Commute to work: 98.5% car, 0.2% public transportation, 0.4% walk, 0.6% work from home (2000); Travel time to work: 39.3% less than 15 minutes, 44.9% 15 to 30 minutes, 8.3% 30 to 45 minutes, 3.2% 45 to 60 minutes, 4.2% 60 minutes or more (2000)

GRANGER (CDP). Covers a land area of 26.219 square miles and a water area of 0.001 square miles. Located at 41.73° N. Lat.; 86.14° W. Long. Elevation is 805 feet.

Population: 28,284 (2000); Race: 94.2% White, 1.8% Black, 2.9% Asian, 0.0% American Indian and Alaska Native, 0.8% Hispanic of any race, 0.8% two or more races (2000); Density: 1,078.8 persons per square mile (2000); Age: 31.9% under 18, 7.5% over 64 (2000); Marriage status: 17.8% never married, 75.1% now married, 3.0% widowed, 4.1% divorced (2000); Foreign born: 4.5% (2000); Ancestry (includes multiple ancestries): 28.1% German, 16.9% Irish, 11.4% English, 10.9% Polish, 7.6% Other groups (2000).

Economy: Manufacturing: transportation equipment, machinery, lumber, fabricated steel. Employment by occupation: 22.5% management, 28.2% professional, 8.4% services, 28.2% sales, 0.0% farming, 4.6% construction, 8.0% production (2000).

Income: Per capita income: $31,367 (2000); Median household income: $80,744 (2000); Poverty rate: 1.4% (2000).

Education: High school graduation rate: 95.5% (2000); College graduation rate: 49.5% (2000).

Four-year College(s)

Davenport University-Western Region-South Bend (Private, Not-for-profit)
2001 Enrollment: 551 219-277-8447
2001 Tuition: In-state $6,764; Out-of-state $6,764

Housing: Homeownership rate: 97.5% (2000); Median home value: $154,600 (2000); Median rent: $985 per month (2000); Median age of housing: 16 years (2000).

Transportation: Commute to work: 95.5% car, 0.2% public transportation, 0.8% walk, 3.3% work from home (2000); Travel time to work: 26.7% less than 15 minutes, 53.2% 15 to 30 minutes, 13.8% 30 to 45 minutes, 3.4% 45 to 60 minutes, 3.0% 60 minutes or more (2000)

GULIVOIRE PARK (CDP). Covers a land area of 1.373 square miles and a water area of 0 square miles. Located at 41.61° N. Lat.; 86.24° W. Long.

Population: 2,974 (2000); Race: 97.2% White, 2.3% Black, 0.0% Asian, 0.0% American Indian and Alaska Native, 0.5% Hispanic of any race, 0.3% two or more races (2000); Density: 2,165.4 persons per square mile (2000); Age: 22.5% under 18, 20.9% over 64 (2000); Marriage status: 18.2% never married, 65.9% now married, 8.3% widowed, 7.6% divorced (2000); Foreign born: 1.4% (2000); Ancestry (includes multiple ancestries): 29.6% German, 17.9% Polish, 11.8% Irish, 11.3% Hungarian, 8.9% English (2000).

Economy: Employment by occupation: 13.9% management, 14.7% professional, 9.6% services, 29.2% sales, 0.0% farming, 13.3% construction, 19.3% production (2000).

Income: Per capita income: $20,432 (2000); Median household income: $46,156 (2000); Poverty rate: 3.9% (2000).

Education: High school graduation rate: 87.4% (2000); College graduation rate: 19.5% (2000).

Housing: Homeownership rate: 95.1% (2000); Median home value: $95,900 (2000); Median rent: $475 per month (2000); Median age of housing: 40 years (2000).

Transportation: Commute to work: 97.6% car, 0.0% public transportation, 0.5% walk, 1.9% work from home (2000); Travel time to work: 29.0% less than 15 minutes, 58.2% 15 to 30 minutes, 7.7% 30 to 45 minutes, 3.0% 45 to 60 minutes, 2.1% 60 minutes or more (2000)

INDIAN VILLAGE (town). Covers a land area of 0.097 square miles and a water area of 0 square miles. Located at 41.71° N. Lat.; 86.23° W. Long. Elevation is 730 feet.

Population: 144 (2000); Race: 97.9% White, 1.4% Black, 0.0% Asian, 0.0% American Indian and Alaska Native, 2.9% Hispanic of any race, 0.7% two or more races (2000); Density: 1,490.2 persons per square mile (2000); Age: 23.6% under 18, 12.9% over 64 (2000); Marriage status: 26.1% never married, 54.6% now married, 5.9% widowed, 13.4% divorced (2000); Foreign born: 2.9% (2000); Ancestry (includes multiple ancestries): 42.9% German, 21.4% Irish, 13.6% Polish, 10.7% Austrian, 7.9% Swiss (2000).
Economy: Employment by occupation: 10.3% management, 36.8% professional, 11.8% services, 25.0% sales, 0.0% farming, 5.9% construction, 10.3% production (2000).
Income: Per capita income: $18,791 (2000); Median household income: $43,750 (2000); Poverty rate: 4.3% (2000).
Taxes: Total city taxes per capita: $14 (1997); City property taxes per capita: $14 (1997).
Education: High school graduation rate: 85.9% (2000); College graduation rate: 36.4% (2000).
Housing: Homeownership rate: 93.0% (2000); Median home value: $108,600 (2000); Median rent: $825 per month (2000); Median age of housing: 40 years (2000).
Transportation: Commute to work: 92.6% car, 0.0% public transportation, 0.0% walk, 2.9% work from home (2000); Travel time to work: 50.0% less than 15 minutes, 37.9% 15 to 30 minutes, 9.1% 30 to 45 minutes, 0.0% 45 to 60 minutes, 3.0% 60 minutes or more (2000)

LAKEVILLE (town). Covers a land area of 0.524 square miles and a water area of 0 square miles. Located at 41.52° N. Lat.; 86.27° W. Long. Elevation is 833 feet.
Population: 567 (2000); Race: 96.6% White, 0.0% Black, 0.0% Asian, 0.0% American Indian and Alaska Native, 2.5% Hispanic of any race, 3.0% two or more races (2000); Density: 1,082.5 persons per square mile (2000); Age: 23.7% under 18, 16.5% over 64 (2000); Marriage status: 27.6% never married, 40.0% now married, 12.1% widowed, 20.3% divorced (2000); Foreign born: 0.0% (2000); Ancestry (includes multiple ancestries): 28.0% German, 19.0% Irish, 7.0% United States or American, 6.3% Other groups, 5.4% Belgian (2000).
Economy: Manufacturing: transportation equipment. Agriculture. Employment by occupation: 10.7% management, 5.0% professional, 17.7% services, 20.1% sales, 0.0% farming, 13.7% construction, 32.8% production (2000).
Income: Per capita income: $15,885 (2000); Median household income: $28,438 (2000); Poverty rate: 13.6% (2000).
Taxes: Total city taxes per capita: $114 (1997); City property taxes per capita: $106 (1997).
Education: High school graduation rate: 77.2% (2000); College graduation rate: 8.1% (2000).

School District(s)

Union-North United School Corp (KG-12)
2000 Enrollment: 1,299 219-784-8141
Housing: Homeownership rate: 62.2% (2000); Median home value: $61,400 (2000); Median rent: $338 per month (2000); Median age of housing: 54 years (2000).
Transportation: Commute to work: 94.6% car, 1.4% public transportation, 2.7% walk, 0.7% work from home (2000); Travel time to work: 20.1% less than 15 minutes, 51.5% 15 to 30 minutes, 16.7% 30 to 45 minutes, 6.1% 45 to 60 minutes, 5.5% 60 minutes or more (2000)

MISHAWAKA (city). Covers a land area of 15.711 square miles and a water area of 0.336 square miles. Located at 41.66° N. Lat.; 86.17° W. Long. Elevation is 722 feet.
History: Mishawaka, situated along the St. Joseph River, developed around the Mishawaka Woolen and Rubber Manufacturing Company plant where felt, rubberboots, and raincoats were produced. Mishawaka was named for the daughter of Shawnee Chief Elkhart.
Population: 46,557 (2000); Race: 91.3% White, 3.4% Black, 1.5% Asian, 0.5% American Indian and Alaska Native, 2.7% Hispanic of any race, 2.2% two or more races (2000); Density: 2,963.3 persons per square mile (2000); Age: 24.0% under 18, 14.1% over 64 (2000); Marriage status: 29.8% never married, 48.0% now married, 8.2% widowed, 14.0% divorced (2000); Foreign born: 4.4% (2000); Ancestry (includes multiple ancestries): 27.2% German, 14.0% Irish, 12.1% Other groups, 9.4% Polish, 8.1% English (2000).
Vital Statistics: Birth rate: 162.4 per 10,000 population (1998)
Economy: Unemployment rate: 4.2% (11/2002); Total civilian labor force: 24,736 (11/2002); Single-family building permits issued: 108 (2001) / 99 (2000); Multi-family building permits issued: 78 (2001) / 743 (2000); Employment by occupation: 11.1% management, 16.1% professional, 15.5% services, 29.0% sales, 0.1% farming, 8.2% construction, 20.1% production (2000).
Income: Per capita income: $18,434 (2000); Median household income: $33,986 (2000); Poverty rate: 9.9% (2000).
Taxes: Total city taxes per capita: $390 (2000); City property taxes per capita: $370 (2000).
Education: High school graduation rate: 80.8% (2000); College graduation rate: 18.1% (2000).

School District(s)

Penn-Harris-Madison Sch Corp (KG-12)
2000 Enrollment: 9,838 219-259-7941
School City of Mishawaka (PK-12)
2000 Enrollment: 5,237 219-254-4500

Four-year College(s)

Bethel College (Private, Not-for-profit, Missionary Church Inc)
2001 Enrollment: 1,660 219-259-8511
2001 Tuition: In-state $13,300; Out-of-state $13,300
Housing: Homeownership rate: 56.8% (2000); Median home value: $77,400 (2000); Median rent: $461 per month (2000); Median age of housing: 34 years (2000).
Hospitals: Ancilla Health Care (125 beds)
Safety: Violent crime rate: 48.3 per 10,000 population; Property crime rate: 907.3 per 10,000 population (2001).
Newspapers: Mishawaka Enterprise (1 x week)
Transportation: Commute to work: 93.9% car, 1.0% public transportation, 3.2% walk, 1.3% work from home (2000); Travel time to work: 36.6% less than 15 minutes, 44.8% 15 to 30 minutes, 12.1% 30 to 45 minutes, 2.3% 45 to 60 minutes, 4.2% 60 minutes or more (2000)

NEW CARLISLE (town). Covers a land area of 1.835 square miles and a water area of 0 square miles. Located at 41.70° N. Lat.; 86.50° W. Long. Elevation is 780 feet.
History: New Carlisle was founded in 1835 and named for its founder, Richard R. Carlisle, who was an adventurer. The town became a trading center for the surrounding farm lands.
Population: 1,505 (2000); Race: 98.1% White, 0.0% Black, 0.8% Asian, 0.0% American Indian and Alaska Native, 2.2% Hispanic of any race, 1.2% two or more races (2000); Density: 820.3 persons per square mile (2000); Age: 27.0% under 18, 15.0% over 64 (2000); Marriage status: 22.8% never married, 56.2% now married, 8.5% widowed, 12.5% divorced (2000); Foreign born: 0.8% (2000); Ancestry (includes multiple ancestries): 31.3% German, 14.0% Polish, 13.1% Irish, 12.0% English, 5.6% United States or American (2000).
Economy: Single-family building permits issued: 6 (2001) / 6 (2000); Multi-family building permits issued: 48 (2001) / 0 (2000); Employment by occupation: 10.5% management, 14.7% professional, 17.4% services, 25.3% sales, 0.3% farming, 11.1% construction, 20.7% production (2000).
Income: Per capita income: $18,597 (2000); Median household income: $36,542 (2000); Poverty rate: 6.6% (2000).
Taxes: Total city taxes per capita: $149 (1997); City property taxes per capita: $139 (1997).
Education: High school graduation rate: 87.0% (2000); College graduation rate: 13.1% (2000).

School District(s)

New Prairie United School Corp (KG-12)
2000 Enrollment: 2,554 219-654-7273
Housing: Homeownership rate: 75.7% (2000); Median home value: $80,600 (2000); Median rent: $364 per month (2000); Median age of housing: 47 years (2000).
Transportation: Commute to work: 95.9% car, 0.0% public transportation, 3.1% walk, 0.6% work from home (2000); Travel time to work: 32.2% less than 15 minutes, 39.3% 15 to 30 minutes, 17.7% 30 to 45 minutes, 6.0% 45 to 60 minutes, 4.8% 60 minutes or more (2000)

NORTH LIBERTY (town). Covers a land area of 0.749 square miles and a water area of 0 square miles. Located at 41.53° N. Lat.; 86.43° W. Long. Elevation is 733 feet.
History: Laid out 1836.
Population: 1,402 (2000); Race: 97.6% White, 0.4% Black, 0.2% Asian, 0.1% American Indian and Alaska Native, 1.0% Hispanic of any race, 1.6% two or more races (2000); Density: 1,872.6 persons per square mile (2000); Age: 32.1% under 18, 11.7% over 64 (2000); Marriage status: 20.3% never married, 58.4% now married, 8.9% widowed, 12.4% divorced (2000); Foreign born: 0.8% (2000); Ancestry (includes multiple ancestries): 27.3% German, 16.9% Irish, 13.1% Polish, 9.3% United States or American, 8.6% English (2000).

Economy: Dairy products, grain. Manufacturing: aluminum extrusions. Employment by occupation: 8.2% management, 18.9% professional, 12.3% services, 23.3% sales, 0.0% farming, 11.6% construction, 25.7% production (2000).
Income: Per capita income: $16,469 (2000); Median household income: $34,850 (2000); Poverty rate: 10.1% (2000).
Taxes: Total city taxes per capita: $139 (1997); City property taxes per capita: $131 (1997).
Education: High school graduation rate: 82.8% (2000); College graduation rate: 11.7% (2000).
Housing: Homeownership rate: 66.5% (2000); Median home value: $79,200 (2000); Median rent: $392 per month (2000); Median age of housing: 53 years (2000).
Transportation: Commute to work: 93.1% car, 0.0% public transportation, 2.8% walk, 2.9% work from home (2000); Travel time to work: 27.3% less than 15 minutes, 30.1% 15 to 30 minutes, 30.0% 30 to 45 minutes, 8.8% 45 to 60 minutes, 3.9% 60 minutes or more (2000)
Additional Information Contacts
North Liberty Chamber of Commerce 219-656-3393

NOTRE DAME (unincorporated postal area, zip code 46556). Covers a land area of 0.570 square miles and a water area of 0.031 square miles. Located at 41.59° N. Lat.; 86.29° W. Long.
Population: 6,747 (2000); Race: 89.1% White, 2.7% Black, 1.9% Asian, 0.4% American Indian and Alaska Native, 6.6% Hispanic of any race, 3.3% two or more races (2000); Density: 11,836.8 persons per square mile (2000); Age: 0.4% under 18, 1.4% over 64 (2000); Marriage status: 82.1% never married, 17.8% now married, 0.1% widowed, 0.0% divorced (2000); Foreign born: 2.2% (2000); Ancestry (includes multiple ancestries): 38.6% Irish, 29.6% German, 15.7% Italian, 13.7% Other groups, 10.5% Polish (2000).
Economy: Employment by occupation: 5.0% management, 37.2% professional, 20.4% services, 33.4% sales, 0.0% farming, 0.5% construction, 3.5% production (2000).
Income: Per capita income: $4,448 (2000); Median household income: $26,250 (2000); Poverty rate: 26.4% (2000).
Education: High school graduation rate: 98.4% (2000); College graduation rate: 87.4% (2000).

Four-year College(s)

University of Notre Dame (Private, Not-for-profit, Roman Catholic)
2001 Enrollment: 11,054 219-631-5000
2001 Tuition: In-state $24,320; Out-of-state $24,320
Saint Mary's College (Private, Not-for-profit, Roman Catholic)
2001 Enrollment: 1,523 219-284-4000
2001 Tuition: In-state $19,240; Out-of-state $19,240

Two-year College(s)

Holy Cross College (Private, Not-for-profit, Roman Catholic)
2001 Enrollment: 558 219-239-8400
2001 Tuition: In-state $8,500; Out-of-state $8,500
Housing: Homeownership rate: 0.0% (2000); Median rent: <$100 per month (2000); Median age of housing: 50 years (2000).
Newspapers: The Observer (5 x week)
Transportation: Commute to work: 7.2% car, 0.0% public transportation, 82.9% walk, 5.6% work from home (2000); Travel time to work: 88.3% less than 15 minutes, 9.8% 15 to 30 minutes, 0.9% 30 to 45 minutes, 0.6% 45 to 60 minutes, 0.3% 60 minutes or more (2000)

OSCEOLA (town). Covers a land area of 1.366 square miles and a water area of 0.009 square miles. Located at 41.66° N. Lat.; 86.07° W. Long. Elevation is 735 feet.
Population: 1,859 (2000); Race: 98.2% White, 0.5% Black, 0.3% Asian, 0.0% American Indian and Alaska Native, 0.1% Hispanic of any race, 0.9% two or more races (2000); Density: 1,361.2 persons per square mile (2000); Age: 26.2% under 18, 13.5% over 64 (2000); Marriage status: 24.7% never married, 58.1% now married, 5.2% widowed, 12.0% divorced (2000); Foreign born: 1.9% (2000); Ancestry (includes multiple ancestries): 25.9% German, 14.6% Irish, 12.7% United States or American, 9.0% English, 6.5% Polish (2000).
Economy: Light manufacturing. Employment by occupation: 9.5% management, 10.0% professional, 12.9% services, 24.9% sales, 0.0% farming, 15.2% construction, 27.6% production (2000).
Income: Per capita income: $18,051 (2000); Median household income: $43,657 (2000); Poverty rate: 3.7% (2000).
Taxes: Total city taxes per capita: $70 (1997); City property taxes per capita: $66 (1997).
Education: High school graduation rate: 78.8% (2000); College graduation rate: 8.7% (2000).
Housing: Homeownership rate: 84.2% (2000); Median home value: $77,200 (2000); Median rent: $554 per month (2000); Median age of housing: 47 years (2000).
Transportation: Commute to work: 95.6% car, 0.0% public transportation, 1.3% walk, 2.5% work from home (2000); Travel time to work: 29.0% less than 15 minutes, 52.5% 15 to 30 minutes, 13.9% 30 to 45 minutes, 2.6% 45 to 60 minutes, 1.9% 60 minutes or more (2000)

ROSELAND (town). Covers a land area of 0.389 square miles and a water area of 0 square miles. Located at 41.71° N. Lat.; 86.25° W. Long. Elevation is 725 feet.
History: Wild roses that grew in the countryside were the inspiration for the name of Roseland. In 1855 St. Mary's College was founded here by the Roman Catholic Church as a sister institution to Notre Dame University.
Population: 1,809 (2000); Race: 91.9% White, 2.9% Black, 1.7% Asian, 0.5% American Indian and Alaska Native, 3.4% Hispanic of any race, 1.5% two or more races (2000); Density: 4,655.5 persons per square mile (2000); Age: 6.6% under 18, 6.6% over 64 (2000); Marriage status: 66.9% never married, 25.8% now married, 2.7% widowed, 4.6% divorced (2000); Foreign born: 3.1% (2000); Ancestry (includes multiple ancestries): 23.8% German, 20.7% Irish, 14.5% Polish, 10.6% Other groups, 6.0% Italian (2000).
Economy: Employment by occupation: 5.5% management, 16.9% professional, 12.6% services, 46.1% sales, 0.0% farming, 5.9% construction, 13.1% production (2000).
Income: Per capita income: $9,450 (2000); Median household income: $33,214 (2000); Poverty rate: 5.7% (2000).
Taxes: Total city taxes per capita: $243 (1997); City property taxes per capita: $226 (1997).
Education: High school graduation rate: 79.3% (2000); College graduation rate: 15.9% (2000).
Housing: Homeownership rate: 68.4% (2000); Median home value: $69,800 (2000); Median rent: $396 per month (2000); Median age of housing: 51 years (2000).
Transportation: Commute to work: 44.5% car, 1.1% public transportation, 51.1% walk, 2.0% work from home (2000); Travel time to work: 74.7% less than 15 minutes, 19.0% 15 to 30 minutes, 2.7% 30 to 45 minutes, 1.2% 45 to 60 minutes, 2.3% 60 minutes or more (2000)

SOUTH BEND (city). Covers a land area of 38.684 square miles and a water area of 0.427 square miles. Located at 41.67° N. Lat.; 86.25° W. Long. Elevation is 725 feet.
History: South Bend was founded in 1823 by Alexis Coquillard, who called it Big St. Joseph Station. The location at a bend of the St. Joseph River caused settlers to refer to their community as The Bend, and in 1830 the Post Office officially named it South Bend. Early industries in South Bend were the Studebaker blacksmith and wagon shop which later became an automobile manufacturer, and the Oliver Chilled Plow Works, which used a process for chilling and hardening steel to increase its uses.
Population: 107,789 (2000); Race: 66.6% White, 24.3% Black, 1.1% Asian, 0.4% American Indian and Alaska Native, 8.5% Hispanic of any race, 2.9% two or more races (2000); Density: 2,786.4 persons per square mile (2000); Age: 27.3% under 18, 14.8% over 64 (2000); Marriage status: 32.0% never married, 47.7% now married, 8.4% widowed, 11.8% divorced (2000); Foreign born: 6.4% (2000); Ancestry (includes multiple ancestries): 32.7% Other groups, 17.6% German, 10.7% Polish, 10.5% Irish, 5.9% English (2000).
Vital Statistics: Birth rate: 198.0 per 10,000 population (1998)
Economy: Unemployment rate: 6.1% (11/2002); Total civilian labor force: 55,951 (11/2002); Employment by occupation: 9.8% management, 18.3% professional, 16.9% services, 25.6% sales, 0.1% farming, 7.2% construction, 22.0% production (2000).
Income: Per capita income: $17,121 (2000); Median household income: $32,439 (2000); Poverty rate: 16.7% (2000).
Taxes: Total city taxes per capita: $393 (2000); City property taxes per capita: $381 (2000).
Education: High school graduation rate: 77.7% (2000); College graduation rate: 20.3% (2000).

School District(s)

South Bend Community Sch Corp (PK-12)
2000 Enrollment: 21,536 219-283-8000

Four-year College(s)

Indiana University-South Bend (Public)
2001 Enrollment: 7,417 219-237-4111
2001 Tuition: In-state $3,278; Out-of-state $9,147
Indiana Christian University (Private, Not-for-profit, Other Protestant)
2001 Enrollment: n/a 219-291-3292

Tri-State University-South Bend Campus (Private, Not-for-profit)
2001 Enrollment: 91 219-234-4810
2001 Tuition: In-state $5,880; Out-of-state $5,880

Two-year College(s)

Ivy Tech State College (Public)
2001 Enrollment: 3,784 219-289-7001
2001 Tuition: In-state $1,986; Out-of-state $4,029
Michiana College (Private, For-profit)
2001 Enrollment: 398 219-237-0774
2001 Tuition: In-state $5,616; Out-of-state $5,616

Housing: Homeownership rate: 63.1% (2000); Median home value: $66,600 (2000); Median rent: $447 per month (2000); Median age of housing: 48 years (2000).
Hospitals: Memorial Hospital of South Bend (526 beds); Saint Joseph's Regional Medical Center (339 beds)
Safety: Violent crime rate: 81.9 per 10,000 population; Property crime rate: 759.6 per 10,000 population (2001).
Newspapers: South Bend Tribune (7 x week); Tri-County News (1 x week)
Transportation: Commute to work: 91.8% car, 2.7% public transportation, 2.1% walk, 2.4% work from home (2000); Travel time to work: 40.3% less than 15 minutes, 41.0% 15 to 30 minutes, 12.6% 30 to 45 minutes, 2.6% 45 to 60 minutes, 3.4% 60 minutes or more (2000); Amtrak: Service available.
Airports: South Bend Regional (primary service/small hub)
Additional Information Contacts
Greater South Bend- Mishawaka Association of Realtors..... 219-289-6378
St. Joseph Chamber of Commerce 219-234-0051

WALKERTON (town). Covers a land area of 1.735 square miles and a water area of 0 square miles. Located at 41.46° N. Lat.; 86.48° W. Long. Elevation is 707 feet.
History: Walkerton was known as one of the largest peppermint-growing centers in the country.
Population: 2,274 (2000); Race: 94.7% White, 0.0% Black, 0.4% Asian, 0.0% American Indian and Alaska Native, 7.3% Hispanic of any race, 0.6% two or more races (2000); Density: 1,310.6 persons per square mile (2000); Age: 29.7% under 18, 15.7% over 64 (2000); Marriage status: 24.2% never married, 53.8% now married, 8.3% widowed, 13.7% divorced (2000); Foreign born: 2.3% (2000); Ancestry (includes multiple ancestries): 26.5% German, 17.8% Irish, 10.6% Other groups, 7.8% English, 7.6% United States or American (2000).
Economy: Single-family building permits issued: 2 (2001) / 2 (2000); Multi-family building permits issued: 0 (2001) / 0 (2000); Employment by occupation: 6.7% management, 18.1% professional, 15.3% services, 24.6% sales, 0.5% farming, 12.7% construction, 22.1% production (2000).
Income: Per capita income: $15,122 (2000); Median household income: $36,481 (2000); Poverty rate: 14.5% (2000).
Taxes: Total city taxes per capita: $181 (1997); City property taxes per capita: $169 (1997).
Education: High school graduation rate: 75.0% (2000); College graduation rate: 14.9% (2000).

School District(s)

John Glenn School Corporation (PK-12)
2000 Enrollment: 1,739 219-586-3129

Housing: Homeownership rate: 68.8% (2000); Median home value: $76,400 (2000); Median rent: $348 per month (2000); Median age of housing: 46 years (2000).
Newspapers: Independent News (1 x week)
Transportation: Commute to work: 88.5% car, 0.0% public transportation, 6.5% walk, 3.9% work from home (2000); Travel time to work: 38.5% less than 15 minutes, 20.4% 15 to 30 minutes, 22.8% 30 to 45 minutes, 13.2% 45 to 60 minutes, 5.1% 60 minutes or more (2000)
Additional Information Contacts
Walkerton Chamber of Commerce........................ 219-586-3100

Scott County

Located in southeastern Indiana; bounded on the north by the Muscatatuck River, and drained by its tributaries. Covers a land area of 190.40 square miles, a water area of 2.30 square miles, and is located in the Eastern Time Zone. The county government was organized in 1820. County seat is Scottsburg.

Scott County is part of the Louisville, KY-IN MSA. The entire metro area includes: Clark County, IN; Floyd County, IN; Harrison County, IN; Scott County, IN; Bullitt County, KY; Jefferson County, KY; Oldham County, KY

Weather Station: Scottsburg — Elevation: 547 feet

	Jan	Feb	Mar	Apr	May	Jun	Jul	Aug	Sep	Oct	Nov	Dec
High	38	44	54	66	75	84	87	86	80	68	55	44
Low	20	23	32	42	52	61	65	63	55	42	34	25
Precip	3.0	2.7	4.2	4.4	4.7	4.2	4.3	4.3	3.0	3.0	3.6	3.3
Snow	5.1	4.8	3.7	0.1	0.0	0.0	0.0	0.0	0.0	0.1	0.5	2.4

High and Low temperatures in degrees Fahrenheit; Precipitation and Snow in inches

Population: 22,960 (2000); Race: 98.2% White, 0.3% Black, 0.1% Asian, 0.5% American Indian and Alaska Native, 0.8% Hispanic of any race, 0.7% two or more races (2000); Density: 120.6 persons per square mile (2000); Age: 26.2% under 18, 11.1% over 64 (2000).
Religion: Five largest groups: 18.0% Christian Churches and Churches of Christ, 13.2% American Baptist Churches in the USA, 3.1% Church of God (Cleveland, Tennessee), 2.9% The United Methodist Church, 2.8% Catholic Church (2000).
Economy: Unemployment rate: 5.3% (11/2002); Total civilian labor force: 11,640 (11/2002); Leading industries: 40.9% manufacturing; 17.7% retail trade; 10.6% health care and social assistance (2000); Companies that employ more than 1,000 persons: 0 (2000); Companies that employ more than 100 persons: 13 (2000); Farms: 348 totaling 57,372 acres (1997); Minority business ownership rate: 0.0% (1997); Women business ownership rate: 28.0% (1997); Retail sales per capita: $7,366 (1997). Single-family building permits issued: 116 (2001) / 117 (2000); Multi-family building permits issued: 99 (2001) / 88 (2000).
Income: Per capita income: $16,065 (2000); Median household income: $34,656 (2000); Poverty rate: 13.1% (2000); Bankruptcy rate: 10.02% (2001).
Taxes: Total county taxes per capita: $365 (2000); County property taxes per capita: $177 (2000).
Education: High school graduation rate: 71.4% (2000); College graduation rate: 8.8% (2000).
Housing: Homeownership rate: 75.8% (2000); Median home value: $76,900 (2000); Median rent: $395 per month (2000); Median age of housing: 27 years (2000).
Health: Birth rate: 125.9 per 10,000 population (1998); Age adjusted death rate: 121.4 per 10,000 population (1999); Age adjusted cancer mortality rate: 355.3 deaths per 100,000 population (1999). Number of physicians: 7.4 per 10,000 population (1999); Number of hospital beds: 19.6 per 10,000 population (1999).
Elections: 2000 Presidential election results: 49.9% Gore, 47.9% Bush, 0.5% Nader, 1.1% Buchanan
Additional Information Contacts
Scott County Government Offices 812-752-8408
Scottsburg Chamber of Commerce 812-752-4080

Scott County Communities

AUSTIN (town). Covers a land area of 2.427 square miles and a water area of 0 square miles. Located at 38.74° N. Lat.; 85.80° W. Long. Elevation is 575 feet.
History: The Morgan Packing Company plant established the community of Austin as a canning center.
Population: 4,724 (2000); Race: 98.3% White, 0.3% Black, 0.0% Asian, 0.3% American Indian and Alaska Native, 1.7% Hispanic of any race, 0.1% two or more races (2000); Density: 1,946.4 persons per square mile (2000); Age: 29.6% under 18, 9.6% over 64 (2000); Marriage status: 21.0% never married, 56.9% now married, 7.5% widowed, 14.7% divorced (2000); Foreign born: 0.8% (2000); Ancestry (includes multiple ancestries): 21.3% United States or American, 8.5% Other groups, 7.3% German, 6.6% Irish, 3.4% English (2000).
Economy: Single-family building permits issued: 22 (2001) / 28 (2000); Multi-family building permits issued: 0 (2001) / 0 (2000); Employment by occupation: 4.6% management, 6.5% professional, 16.4% services, 16.3% sales, 0.5% farming, 10.5% construction, 45.1% production (2000).
Income: Per capita income: $12,431 (2000); Median household income: $28,495 (2000); Poverty rate: 19.1% (2000).
Taxes: Total city taxes per capita: $82 (1997); City property taxes per capita: $54 (1997).
Education: High school graduation rate: 60.3% (2000); College graduation rate: 3.7% (2000).

School District(s)

Scott County School District 1 (KG-12)
2000 Enrollment: 1,410 812-794-8750

Housing: Homeownership rate: 65.2% (2000); Median home value: $59,700 (2000); Median rent: $344 per month (2000); Median age of housing: 35 years (2000).
Transportation: Commute to work: 96.1% car, 0.9% public transportation, 2.2% walk, 0.4% work from home (2000); Travel time to work: 42.4% less than 15 minutes, 22.0% 15 to 30 minutes, 21.3% 30 to 45 minutes, 9.5% 45 to 60 minutes, 4.8% 60 minutes or more (2000)

LEXINGTON (unincorporated postal area, zip code 47138). Covers a land area of 75.189 square miles and a water area of 0.487 square miles. Located at 38.67° N. Lat.; 85.61° W. Long. Elevation is 622 feet.
History: Founded c.1811.
Population: 4,270 (2000); Race: 98.2% White, 1.1% Black, 0.4% Asian, 0.0% American Indian and Alaska Native, 0.4% Hispanic of any race, 0.3% two or more races (2000); Density: 56.8 persons per square mile (2000); Age: 26.3% under 18, 9.5% over 64 (2000); Marriage status: 18.6% never married, 64.8% now married, 5.1% widowed, 11.4% divorced (2000); Foreign born: 0.7% (2000); Ancestry (includes multiple ancestries): 22.6% United States or American, 17.7% German, 9.8% Irish, 9.2% Other groups, 8.7% English (2000).
Economy: In agricultural area. Lumber, crushed stone, agricultural lime. Employment by occupation: 4.0% management, 12.3% professional, 15.2% services, 20.3% sales, 0.7% farming, 12.4% construction, 35.2% production (2000).
Income: Per capita income: $15,748 (2000); Median household income: $39,891 (2000); Poverty rate: 11.3% (2000).
Education: High school graduation rate: 74.5% (2000); College graduation rate: 7.4% (2000).
Housing: Homeownership rate: 86.7% (2000); Median home value: $91,300 (2000); Median rent: $340 per month (2000); Median age of housing: 25 years (2000).
Transportation: Commute to work: 95.8% car, 0.5% public transportation, 0.3% walk, 2.6% work from home (2000); Travel time to work: 15.0% less than 15 minutes, 43.1% 15 to 30 minutes, 21.6% 30 to 45 minutes, 12.6% 45 to 60 minutes, 7.8% 60 minutes or more (2000)

SCOTTSBURG (city). Covers a land area of 4.804 square miles and a water area of 0.011 square miles. Located at 38.68° N. Lat.; 85.77° W. Long. Elevation is 570 feet.
History: Laid out 1871.
Population: 6,040 (2000); Race: 98.4% White, 0.1% Black, 0.0% Asian, 0.6% American Indian and Alaska Native, 0.5% Hispanic of any race, 0.8% two or more races (2000); Density: 1,257.2 persons per square mile (2000); Age: 23.9% under 18, 14.9% over 64 (2000); Marriage status: 20.8% never married, 53.3% now married, 9.3% widowed, 16.6% divorced (2000); Foreign born: 0.1% (2000); Ancestry (includes multiple ancestries): 24.4% United States or American, 14.7% German, 11.5% Irish, 8.9% Other groups, 8.8% English (2000).
Economy: In agricultural area: grain; livestock, poultry. Manufacturing: plastics, rubber products, lumber. Employment by occupation: 11.2% management, 13.0% professional, 15.7% services, 22.0% sales, 0.5% farming, 7.9% construction, 29.6% production (2000).
Income: Per capita income: $16,552 (2000); Median household income: $30,687 (2000); Poverty rate: 15.5% (2000).
Taxes: Total city taxes per capita: $321 (2000); City property taxes per capita: $221 (2000).
Education: High school graduation rate: 72.4% (2000); College graduation rate: 11.2% (2000).

School District(s)

Scott County School District 2 (KG-12)
2000 Enrollment: 2,692 812-752-8946

Housing: Homeownership rate: 62.6% (2000); Median home value: $77,100 (2000); Median rent: $432 per month (2000); Median age of housing: 31 years (2000).
Hospitals: Scott Memorial Hospital (107 beds)
Safety: Violent crime rate: 29.6 per 10,000 population; Property crime rate: 385.2 per 10,000 population (2001).
Newspapers: Scott County Journal (1 x week); The Austin Chronicle (1 x week); The Giveaway (1 x week)
Transportation: Commute to work: 94.9% car, 0.3% public transportation, 2.4% walk, 1.4% work from home (2000); Travel time to work: 55.7% less than 15 minutes, 11.2% 15 to 30 minutes, 19.1% 30 to 45 minutes, 8.3% 45 to 60 minutes, 5.8% 60 minutes or more (2000)
Additional Information Contacts
Scottsburg Chamber of Commerce 812-752-4080

Shelby County

Located in central Indiana; drained by the Big Blue River. Covers a land area of 412.60 square miles, a water area of 0.50 square miles, and is located in the Eastern Time Zone. The county government was organized in 1821. County seat is Shelbyville.

Shelby County is part of the Indianapolis, IN MSA. The entire metro area includes: Boone County; Hamilton County; Hancock County; Hendricks County; Johnson County; Madison County; Marion County; Morgan County; Shelby County

Population: 43,445 (2000); Race: 97.4% White, 0.6% Black, 0.4% Asian, 0.2% American Indian and Alaska Native, 1.1% Hispanic of any race, 1.2% two or more races (2000); Density: 105.3 persons per square mile (2000); Age: 26.6% under 18, 12.1% over 64 (2000).
Religion: Five largest groups: 9.0% Catholic Church, 7.7% American Baptist Churches in the USA, 6.3% The United Methodist Church, 3.3% Christian Churches and Churches of Christ, 1.5% Christian Church (Disciples of Christ) (2000).
Economy: Unemployment rate: 4.8% (11/2002); Total civilian labor force: 24,550 (11/2002); Leading industries: 41.7% manufacturing; 10.5% retail trade; 9.8% health care and social assistance (2000); Companies that employ more than 1,000 persons: 0 (2000); Companies that employ more than 100 persons: 24 (2000); Farms: 641 totaling 200,661 acres (1997); Minority business ownership rate: 0.0% (1997); Women business ownership rate: 26.1% (1997); Retail sales per capita: $7,199 (1997). Single-family building permits issued: 144 (2001) / 145 (2000); Multi-family building permits issued: 9 (2001) / 16 (2000).
Income: Per capita income: $20,324 (2000); Median household income: $43,649 (2000); Poverty rate: 7.6% (2000); Bankruptcy rate: 6.07% (2001).
Taxes: Total county taxes per capita: $274 (2000); County property taxes per capita: $163 (2000).
Education: High school graduation rate: 79.8% (2000); College graduation rate: 12.7% (2000).
Housing: Homeownership rate: 73.4% (2000); Median home value: $98,600 (2000); Median rent: $445 per month (2000); Median age of housing: 39 years (2000).
Health: Birth rate: 124.8 per 10,000 population (1998); Age adjusted death rate: 79.1 per 10,000 population (1999); Age adjusted cancer mortality rate: 172.2 deaths per 100,000 population (1999). Air Quality Index: 45% good, 55% moderate, 0% unhealthy (percent of days in 2000). Number of physicians: 6.7 per 10,000 population (1999); Number of hospital beds: 13.4 per 10,000 population (1999).
Elections: 2000 Presidential election results: 35.1% Gore, 62.6% Bush, 0.5% Nader, 0.9% Buchanan
Additional Information Contacts
Shelby County Government Offices 317-392-6330
Shelbyville Chamber of Commerce 765-398-6647

Shelby County Communities

BOGGSTOWN (unincorporated postal area, zip code 46110). Covers a land area of 12.724 square miles and a water area of 0 square miles. Located at 39.56° N. Lat.; 85.92° W. Long. Elevation is 756 feet.
Population: 501 (2000); Race: 100.0% White, 0.0% Black, 0.0% Asian, 0.0% American Indian and Alaska Native, 0.0% Hispanic of any race, 0.0% two or more races (2000); Density: 39.4 persons per square mile (2000); Age: 33.6% under 18, 11.1% over 64 (2000); Marriage status: 18.5% never married, 75.5% now married, 3.2% widowed, 2.9% divorced (2000); Foreign born: 0.0% (2000); Ancestry (includes multiple ancestries): 27.4% German, 17.7% United States or American, 15.0% French (except Basque), 13.9% Irish, 10.5% Other groups (2000).
Economy: In agricultural area. Manufacturing: meat processing, fertilizer blending. Employment by occupation: 12.7% management, 25.4% professional, 0.0% services, 20.5% sales, 4.6% farming, 24.0% construction, 12.7% production (2000).
Income: Per capita income: $18,661 (2000); Median household income: $44,861 (2000); Poverty rate: 16.5% (2000).
Education: High school graduation rate: 87.5% (2000); College graduation rate: 16.8% (2000).
Housing: Homeownership rate: 72.8% (2000); Median home value: $155,900 (2000); Median rent: $409 per month (2000); Median age of housing: 60+ years (2000).

Transportation: Commute to work: 100.0% car, 0.0% public transportation, 0.0% walk, 0.0% work from home (2000); Travel time to work: 13.5% less than 15 minutes, 52.8% 15 to 30 minutes, 13.1% 30 to 45 minutes, 16.3% 45 to 60 minutes, 4.4% 60 minutes or more (2000)

FAIRLAND (CDP). Covers a land area of 3.470 square miles and a water area of 0.016 square miles. Located at 39.58° N. Lat.; 85.86° W. Long. Elevation is 778 feet.

Population: 1,276 (2000); Race: 98.7% White, 0.0% Black, 0.0% Asian, 0.0% American Indian and Alaska Native, 0.0% Hispanic of any race, 1.3% two or more races (2000); Density: 367.7 persons per square mile (2000); Age: 32.9% under 18, 9.1% over 64 (2000); Marriage status: 32.7% never married, 44.2% now married, 9.9% widowed, 13.2% divorced (2000); Foreign born: 0.4% (2000); Ancestry (includes multiple ancestries): 31.7% United States or American, 22.1% German, 12.7% Other groups, 10.4% Irish, 7.0% English (2000).

Economy: Agricultural area. Manufacturing: wooden cabinets, fiberglass insulation, diesel piston parts. Employment by occupation: 13.9% management, 10.2% professional, 11.9% services, 18.7% sales, 1.3% farming, 15.0% construction, 29.0% production (2000).

Income: Per capita income: $17,406 (2000); Median household income: $45,972 (2000); Poverty rate: 10.3% (2000).

Education: High school graduation rate: 79.1% (2000); College graduation rate: 10.8% (2000).

School District(s)

Northwestern Con School Corp (KG-12)
2000 Enrollment: 1,546 317-835-7461

Housing: Homeownership rate: 88.9% (2000); Median home value: $85,600 (2000); Median rent: $450 per month (2000); Median age of housing: 37 years (2000).

Transportation: Commute to work: 91.7% car, 0.0% public transportation, 1.0% walk, 3.3% work from home (2000); Travel time to work: 13.8% less than 15 minutes, 44.7% 15 to 30 minutes, 23.3% 30 to 45 minutes, 12.7% 45 to 60 minutes, 5.5% 60 minutes or more (2000)

FLAT ROCK (unincorporated postal area, zip code 47234). Covers a land area of 36.032 square miles and a water area of 0 square miles. Located at 39.37° N. Lat.; 85.78° W. Long. Elevation is 692 feet.

Population: 1,441 (2000); Race: 98.7% White, 0.0% Black, 0.0% Asian, 0.0% American Indian and Alaska Native, 0.0% Hispanic of any race, 1.3% two or more races (2000); Density: 40.0 persons per square mile (2000); Age: 24.3% under 18, 12.2% over 64 (2000); Marriage status: 21.9% never married, 67.9% now married, 4.3% widowed, 5.9% divorced (2000); Foreign born: 2.7% (2000); Ancestry (includes multiple ancestries): 24.6% United States or American, 18.7% German, 8.1% Irish, 7.9% English, 2.6% Other groups (2000).

Economy: Employment by occupation: 18.0% management, 9.1% professional, 6.1% services, 20.6% sales, 3.0% farming, 13.2% construction, 30.0% production (2000).

Income: Per capita income: $17,966 (2000); Median household income: $41,230 (2000); Poverty rate: 5.4% (2000).

Education: High school graduation rate: 80.3% (2000); College graduation rate: 9.4% (2000).

Housing: Homeownership rate: 80.5% (2000); Median home value: $84,600 (2000); Median rent: $331 per month (2000); Median age of housing: 58 years (2000).

Transportation: Commute to work: 96.3% car, 0.0% public transportation, 0.6% walk, 2.3% work from home (2000); Travel time to work: 15.3% less than 15 minutes, 58.6% 15 to 30 minutes, 10.4% 30 to 45 minutes, 6.7% 45 to 60 minutes, 9.1% 60 minutes or more (2000)

FOUNTAINTOWN (unincorporated postal area, zip code 46130). Covers a land area of 26.502 square miles and a water area of 0 square miles. Located at 39.68° N. Lat.; 85.83° W. Long. Elevation is 854 feet.

Population: 2,219 (2000); Race: 100.0% White, 0.0% Black, 0.0% Asian, 0.0% American Indian and Alaska Native, 0.4% Hispanic of any race, 0.0% two or more races (2000); Density: 83.7 persons per square mile (2000); Age: 30.7% under 18, 6.7% over 64 (2000); Marriage status: 23.7% never married, 64.3% now married, 4.8% widowed, 7.2% divorced (2000); Foreign born: 0.4% (2000); Ancestry (includes multiple ancestries): 32.5% German, 23.1% Irish, 15.0% English, 10.7% United States or American, 5.3% Polish (2000).

Economy: Employment by occupation: 17.6% management, 10.5% professional, 9.7% services, 29.7% sales, 0.0% farming, 16.2% construction, 16.3% production (2000).

Income: Per capita income: $24,238 (2000); Median household income: $63,500 (2000); Poverty rate: 2.6% (2000).

Education: High school graduation rate: 91.0% (2000); College graduation rate: 19.1% (2000).

Housing: Homeownership rate: 84.4% (2000); Median home value: $118,200 (2000); Median rent: $405 per month (2000); Median age of housing: 30 years (2000).

Transportation: Commute to work: 93.6% car, 0.0% public transportation, 2.1% walk, 4.4% work from home (2000); Travel time to work: 11.9% less than 15 minutes, 38.8% 15 to 30 minutes, 31.5% 30 to 45 minutes, 11.7% 45 to 60 minutes, 6.1% 60 minutes or more (2000)

MORRISTOWN (town). Covers a land area of 0.958 square miles and a water area of 0 square miles. Located at 39.67° N. Lat.; 85.69° W. Long. Elevation is 830 feet.

History: Laid out 1828.

Population: 1,133 (2000); Race: 99.2% White, 0.0% Black, 0.0% Asian, 0.0% American Indian and Alaska Native, 0.7% Hispanic of any race, 0.8% two or more races (2000); Density: 1,182.2 persons per square mile (2000); Age: 29.8% under 18, 16.8% over 64 (2000); Marriage status: 21.9% never married, 55.0% now married, 11.1% widowed, 12.0% divorced (2000); Foreign born: 0.4% (2000); Ancestry (includes multiple ancestries): 22.4% German, 19.9% United States or American, 13.0% Irish, 11.7% Other groups, 11.1% English (2000).

Economy: In agricultural area. Manufacturing: motor vehicle leaf springs, seals, steering components, hamburger buns, plastic moldings, windows and doors. Single-family building permits issued: 0 (2001) / 0 (2000); Multi-family building permits issued: 3 (2001) / 6 (2000); Employment by occupation: 6.7% management, 10.1% professional, 21.6% services, 19.4% sales, 0.4% farming, 12.5% construction, 29.3% production (2000).

Income: Per capita income: $16,129 (2000); Median household income: $36,417 (2000); Poverty rate: 5.5% (2000).

Taxes: Total city taxes per capita: $130 (1997); City property taxes per capita: $115 (1997).

Education: High school graduation rate: 80.9% (2000); College graduation rate: 7.1% (2000).

Housing: Homeownership rate: 74.1% (2000); Median home value: $81,400 (2000); Median rent: $375 per month (2000); Median age of housing: 44 years (2000).

Transportation: Commute to work: 92.6% car, 0.2% public transportation, 3.7% walk, 1.0% work from home (2000); Travel time to work: 35.8% less than 15 minutes, 26.0% 15 to 30 minutes, 15.2% 30 to 45 minutes, 16.7% 45 to 60 minutes, 6.3% 60 minutes or more (2000)

SHELBYVILLE (city). Covers a land area of 8.873 square miles and a water area of 0.106 square miles. Located at 39.52° N. Lat.; 85.77° W. Long. Elevation is 764 feet.

History: Shelbyville was laid out in 1822 and named for the first governor of Kentucky. Shelbyville was the home of Vice President Thomas A. Hendricks (1819-1885).

Population: 17,951 (2000); Race: 95.5% White, 1.3% Black, 0.9% Asian, 0.2% American Indian and Alaska Native, 2.1% Hispanic of any race, 1.8% two or more races (2000); Density: 2,023.0 persons per square mile (2000); Age: 26.0% under 18, 13.2% over 64 (2000); Marriage status: 23.8% never married, 53.0% now married, 7.4% widowed, 15.7% divorced (2000); Foreign born: 2.8% (2000); Ancestry (includes multiple ancestries): 25.5% German, 23.1% United States or American, 10.7% Irish, 9.8% Other groups, 6.3% English (2000).

Vital Statistics: Birth rate: 146.0 per 10,000 population (1998)

Economy: Single-family building permits issued: 33 (2001) / 34 (2000); Multi-family building permits issued: 4 (2001) / 8 (2000); Employment by occupation: 9.2% management, 13.3% professional, 15.6% services, 21.8% sales, 0.1% farming, 9.2% construction, 30.7% production (2000).

Income: Per capita income: $18,670 (2000); Median household income: $36,824 (2000); Poverty rate: 9.1% (2000).

Taxes: Total city taxes per capita: $250 (2000); City property taxes per capita: $245 (2000).

Education: High school graduation rate: 74.8% (2000); College graduation rate: 10.6% (2000).

School District(s)

Blue River Career Programs
2000 Enrollment: n/a 317-392-4191

Blue River Special Education Coop (PK-PK)
2000 Enrollment: n/a 317-398-4468

Shelby Eastern Schools (KG-12)
2000 Enrollment: 1,715 765-544-2246

Shelbyville Central Schools (KG-12)
2000 Enrollment: 3,828 317-392-2505

Southwestern Con Sch Shelby Co (KG-12)
2000 Enrollment: 770 317-729-5746
Housing: Homeownership rate: 58.0% (2000); Median home value: $86,900 (2000); Median rent: $461 per month (2000); Median age of housing: 43 years (2000).
Hospitals: Major Hospital (89 beds)
Newspapers: The Shelbyville News (6 x week)
Transportation: Commute to work: 92.7% car, 0.2% public transportation, 3.0% walk, 1.7% work from home (2000); Travel time to work: 61.8% less than 15 minutes, 15.0% 15 to 30 minutes, 11.5% 30 to 45 minutes, 7.4% 45 to 60 minutes, 4.3% 60 minutes or more (2000)
Airports: Shelbyville Municipal
Additional Information Contacts
Shelbyville Chamber of Commerce 765-398-6647

WALDRON (unincorporated postal area, zip code 46182). Covers a land area of 35.820 square miles and a water area of 0.021 square miles. Located at 39.45° N. Lat.; 85.67° W. Long. Elevation is 824 feet.
History: Laid out 1854.
Population: 1,971 (2000); Race: 97.6% White, 0.0% Black, 0.0% Asian, 2.4% American Indian and Alaska Native, 0.4% Hispanic of any race, 0.0% two or more races (2000); Density: 55.0 persons per square mile (2000); Age: 28.5% under 18, 17.0% over 64 (2000); Marriage status: 11.4% never married, 67.8% now married, 6.6% widowed, 14.3% divorced (2000); Foreign born: 0.0% (2000); Ancestry (includes multiple ancestries): 32.1% German, 17.2% United States or American, 12.0% Irish, 10.2% English, 3.8% Other groups (2000).
Economy: Corn, wheat; hogs. Employment by occupation: 11.7% management, 10.1% professional, 11.9% services, 24.4% sales, 0.0% farming, 13.4% construction, 28.5% production (2000).
Income: Per capita income: $18,073 (2000); Median household income: $41,524 (2000); Poverty rate: 7.2% (2000).
Education: High school graduation rate: 82.2% (2000); College graduation rate: 11.0% (2000).
Housing: Homeownership rate: 83.0% (2000); Median home value: $88,400 (2000); Median rent: $388 per month (2000); Median age of housing: 53 years (2000).
Transportation: Commute to work: 95.0% car, 0.0% public transportation, 4.1% walk, 0.0% work from home (2000); Travel time to work: 30.8% less than 15 minutes, 48.7% 15 to 30 minutes, 10.0% 30 to 45 minutes, 9.6% 45 to 60 minutes, 0.8% 60 minutes or more (2000)

Spencer County

Located in southwestern Indiana; bounded on the south by the Ohio River and the Kentucky border; drained by the Anderson River and Little Pigeon Creek. Covers a land area of 398.70 square miles, a water area of 2.50 square miles, and is located in the Central Time Zone. The county government was organized in 1818. County seat is Rockport.

Weather Station: Saint Meinrad — Elevation: 508 feet

	Jan	Feb	Mar	Apr	May	Jun	Jul	Aug	Sep	Oct	Nov	Dec
High	40	47	57	68	77	84	87	86	81	70	57	46
Low	23	27	36	45	53	62	66	65	58	46	37	28
Precip	3.1	3.0	4.4	4.7	4.7	4.1	4.7	3.8	3.3	3.0	4.0	3.7
Snow	3.8	2.8	1.4	tr	0.0	0.0	0.0	0.0	0.0	tr	0.1	1.6

High and Low temperatures in degrees Fahrenheit; Precipitation and Snow in inches

Population: 20,391 (2000); Race: 97.8% White, 0.5% Black, 0.2% Asian, 0.4% American Indian and Alaska Native, 1.1% Hispanic of any race, 0.3% two or more races (2000); Density: 51.1 persons per square mile (2000); Age: 26.5% under 18, 12.9% over 64 (2000).
Religion: Five largest groups: 22.3% Catholic Church, 10.3% The United Methodist Church, 4.7% American Baptist Churches in the USA, 3.8% Southern Baptist Convention, 3.4% Christian Churches and Churches of Christ (2000).
Economy: Unemployment rate: 4.1% (11/2002); Total civilian labor force: 10,421 (11/2002); Leading industries: 27.6% manufacturing; 20.5% transportation & warehousing; 11.1% retail trade (2000); Companies that employ more than 1,000 persons: 1 (2000); Companies that employ more than 100 persons: 12 (2000); Farms: 638 totaling 172,687 acres (1997); Minority business ownership rate: 0.0% (1997); Women business ownership rate: 28.0% (1997); Retail sales per capita: $4,556 (1997). Single-family building permits issued: 125 (2001) / 145 (2000); Multi-family building permits issued: 6 (2001) / 2 (2000).
Income: Per capita income: $18,000 (2000); Median household income: $42,451 (2000); Poverty rate: 6.9% (2000); Bankruptcy rate: 6.27% (2001).
Taxes: Total county taxes per capita: $210 (2000); County property taxes per capita: $192 (2000).
Education: High school graduation rate: 81.2% (2000); College graduation rate: 13.0% (2000).
Housing: Homeownership rate: 83.4% (2000); Median home value: $85,100 (2000); Median rent: $309 per month (2000); Median age of housing: 27 years (2000).
Health: Birth rate: 125.1 per 10,000 population (1998); Age adjusted death rate: 82.8 per 10,000 population (1999); Age adjusted cancer mortality rate: 205.6 deaths per 100,000 population (1999). Air Quality Index: 99% good, 1% moderate, 0% unhealthy (percent of days in 2000). Number of physicians: 3.4 per 10,000 population (1999); Number of hospital beds: n/a (1999).
Elections: 2000 Presidential election results: 41.8% Gore, 56.7% Bush, 0.5% Nader, 0.7% Buchanan
National and State Parks: Lincoln Boyhood National Memorial; Lincoln State Park; Nancy Hanks Lincoln State Memorial; Spencer County State Forest
Additional Information Contacts
Spencer County Government Offices. 812-649-4376
Dale Chamber of Commerce 812-937-7196
Santa Claus Chamber of Commerce 812-937-2848
Spencer County Regional Chamber 812-649-2186
St. Meinrad Chamber of Commerce. 812-357-7342

Spencer County Communities

CHRISNEY (town). Covers a land area of 0.366 square miles and a water area of 0 square miles. Located at 38.01° N. Lat.; 87.03° W. Long. Elevation is 441 feet.
Population: 544 (2000); Race: 94.8% White, 0.0% Black, 0.0% Asian, 0.9% American Indian and Alaska Native, 2.9% Hispanic of any race, 1.4% two or more races (2000); Density: 1,484.9 persons per square mile (2000); Age: 28.9% under 18, 18.4% over 64 (2000); Marriage status: 14.3% never married, 60.4% now married, 12.3% widowed, 13.0% divorced (2000); Foreign born: 0.4% (2000); Ancestry (includes multiple ancestries): 20.9% United States or American, 17.5% German, 17.0% Other groups, 11.7% English, 9.6% Irish (2000).
Economy: In agricultural and bituminous-coal area. Employment by occupation: 5.0% management, 11.6% professional, 11.6% services, 24.5% sales, 0.0% farming, 10.0% construction, 37.3% production (2000).
Income: Per capita income: $14,127 (2000); Median household income: $34,464 (2000); Poverty rate: 15.1% (2000).
Taxes: Total city taxes per capita: $81 (1997); City property taxes per capita: $45 (1997).
Education: High school graduation rate: 74.4% (2000); College graduation rate: 6.7% (2000).
Housing: Homeownership rate: 74.7% (2000); Median home value: $61,600 (2000); Median rent: $306 per month (2000); Median age of housing: 52 years (2000).
Transportation: Commute to work: 97.5% car, 0.0% public transportation, 0.8% walk, 1.7% work from home (2000); Travel time to work: 17.6% less than 15 minutes, 42.1% 15 to 30 minutes, 17.6% 30 to 45 minutes, 15.9% 45 to 60 minutes, 6.9% 60 minutes or more (2000)

DALE (town). Covers a land area of 1.529 square miles and a water area of 0 square miles. Located at 38.16° N. Lat.; 86.98° W. Long. Elevation is 470 feet.
History: Dale was named for Robert Dale Owen, who founded the colony at New Harmony.
Population: 1,568 (2000); Race: 89.5% White, 0.6% Black, 0.1% Asian, 0.1% American Indian and Alaska Native, 10.5% Hispanic of any race, 0.5% two or more races (2000); Density: 1,025.4 persons per square mile (2000); Age: 24.4% under 18, 16.0% over 64 (2000); Marriage status: 18.4% never married, 58.2% now married, 9.1% widowed, 14.4% divorced (2000); Foreign born: 7.9% (2000); Ancestry (includes multiple ancestries): 30.9% German, 14.5% Other groups, 9.5% English, 9.3% Irish, 7.8% United States or American (2000).
Economy: Single-family building permits issued: 10 (2001) / 8 (2000); Multi-family building permits issued: 0 (2001) / 2 (2000); Employment by occupation: 4.0% management, 10.2% professional, 11.6% services, 20.7% sales, 1.1% farming, 10.0% construction, 42.5% production (2000).
Income: Per capita income: $16,163 (2000); Median household income: $36,295 (2000); Poverty rate: 4.5% (2000).

Taxes: Total city taxes per capita: $93 (1997); City property taxes per capita: $66 (1997).
Education: High school graduation rate: 73.4% (2000); College graduation rate: 10.7% (2000).
Housing: Homeownership rate: 69.6% (2000); Median home value: $71,400 (2000); Median rent: $291 per month (2000); Median age of housing: 29 years (2000).
Transportation: Commute to work: 96.4% car, 0.0% public transportation, 2.3% walk, 1.3% work from home (2000); Travel time to work: 37.7% less than 15 minutes, 33.1% 15 to 30 minutes, 19.7% 30 to 45 minutes, 5.6% 45 to 60 minutes, 3.9% 60 minutes or more (2000)
Additional Information Contacts
Dale Chamber of Commerce 812-937-7196

EVANSTON (unincorporated postal area, zip code 47531). Covers a land area of 24.974 square miles and a water area of 0.020 square miles. Located at 38.05° N. Lat.; 86.82° W. Long. Elevation is 413 feet.
Population: 715 (2000); Race: 100.0% White, 0.0% Black, 0.0% Asian, 0.0% American Indian and Alaska Native, 0.0% Hispanic of any race, 0.0% two or more races (2000); Density: 28.6 persons per square mile (2000); Age: 22.4% under 18, 10.1% over 64 (2000); Marriage status: 14.9% never married, 75.6% now married, 4.3% widowed, 5.2% divorced (2000); Foreign born: 1.0% (2000); Ancestry (includes multiple ancestries): 31.9% German, 12.1% English, 10.5% Irish, 9.8% United States or American, 3.7% French (except Basque) (2000).
Economy: Employment by occupation: 7.5% management, 10.4% professional, 5.2% services, 31.0% sales, 0.0% farming, 18.0% construction, 27.8% production (2000).
Income: Per capita income: $17,945 (2000); Median household income: $45,682 (2000); Poverty rate: 2.7% (2000).
Education: High school graduation rate: 84.7% (2000); College graduation rate: 10.3% (2000).
Housing: Homeownership rate: 100.0% (2000); Median home value: $75,600 (2000); Median age of housing: 32 years (2000).
Transportation: Commute to work: 90.7% car, 0.0% public transportation, 2.6% walk, 4.1% work from home (2000); Travel time to work: 10.0% less than 15 minutes, 47.1% 15 to 30 minutes, 18.4% 30 to 45 minutes, 13.3% 45 to 60 minutes, 11.2% 60 minutes or more (2000)

GENTRYVILLE (town). Covers a land area of 0.389 square miles and a water area of 0 square miles. Located at 38.10° N. Lat.; 87.03° W. Long. Elevation is 405 feet.
History: Abraham Lincoln was a clerk in the store of James Gentry, one of the first merchants in Gentryville and the man for whom the town was named.
Population: 262 (2000); Race: 100.0% White, 0.0% Black, 0.0% Asian, 0.0% American Indian and Alaska Native, 0.0% Hispanic of any race, 0.0% two or more races (2000); Density: 674.1 persons per square mile (2000); Age: 25.6% under 18, 12.8% over 64 (2000); Marriage status: 29.2% never married, 64.1% now married, 0.0% widowed, 6.7% divorced (2000); Foreign born: 0.8% (2000); Ancestry (includes multiple ancestries): 32.4% United States or American, 21.2% Other groups, 19.6% German, 10.4% English, 6.0% Irish (2000).
Economy: Single-family building permits issued: 0 (2001) / 0 (2000); Multi-family building permits issued: 0 (2001) / 0 (2000); Employment by occupation: 4.4% management, 6.2% professional, 24.8% services, 16.8% sales, 0.0% farming, 18.6% construction, 29.2% production (2000).
Income: Per capita income: $15,752 (2000); Median household income: $38,750 (2000); Poverty rate: 9.6% (2000).
Taxes: Total city taxes per capita: $38 (1997); City property taxes per capita: $27 (1997).
Education: High school graduation rate: 76.8% (2000); College graduation rate: 3.7% (2000).
Housing: Homeownership rate: 89.1% (2000); Median home value: $72,500 (2000); Median rent: $238 per month (2000); Median age of housing: 27 years (2000).
Transportation: Commute to work: 96.5% car, 0.0% public transportation, 0.0% walk, 1.8% work from home (2000); Travel time to work: 28.8% less than 15 minutes, 27.9% 15 to 30 minutes, 18.0% 30 to 45 minutes, 21.6% 45 to 60 minutes, 3.6% 60 minutes or more (2000)

GRANDVIEW (town). Aka Grand View. Covers a land area of 0.957 square miles and a water area of 0 square miles. Located at 37.93° N. Lat.; 86.98° W. Long. Elevation is 390 feet.
History: Grandview was named for its location on a bluff which afforded a view for five miles up and down the river.
Population: 696 (2000); Race: 97.7% White, 1.8% Black, 0.0% Asian, 0.0% American Indian and Alaska Native, 0.3% Hispanic of any race, 0.4% two or more races (2000); Density: 727.5 persons per square mile (2000); Age: 29.4% under 18, 8.1% over 64 (2000); Marriage status: 19.0% never married, 61.7% now married, 5.6% widowed, 13.7% divorced (2000); Foreign born: 0.0% (2000); Ancestry (includes multiple ancestries): 31.8% United States or American, 17.9% German, 6.2% English, 5.6% Irish, 4.9% Other groups (2000).
Economy: Single-family building permits issued: 6 (2001) / 6 (2000); Multi-family building permits issued: 0 (2001) / 0 (2000); Employment by occupation: 3.6% management, 6.9% professional, 27.5% services, 19.6% sales, 0.6% farming, 9.7% construction, 32.0% production (2000).
Income: Per capita income: $13,928 (2000); Median household income: $35,417 (2000); Poverty rate: 12.0% (2000).
Taxes: Total city taxes per capita: $61 (1997); City property taxes per capita: $51 (1997).
Education: High school graduation rate: 72.0% (2000); College graduation rate: 5.0% (2000).
Housing: Homeownership rate: 72.7% (2000); Median home value: $63,300 (2000); Median rent: $278 per month (2000); Median age of housing: 31 years (2000).
Transportation: Commute to work: 96.9% car, 0.0% public transportation, 0.6% walk, 2.5% work from home (2000); Travel time to work: 32.3% less than 15 minutes, 22.5% 15 to 30 minutes, 29.1% 30 to 45 minutes, 11.1% 45 to 60 minutes, 5.1% 60 minutes or more (2000)

LAMAR (unincorporated postal area, zip code 47550). Covers a land area of 37.740 square miles and a water area of 0.106 square miles. Located at 38.07° N. Lat.; 86.92° W. Long. Elevation is 412 feet.
Population: 772 (2000); Race: 100.0% White, 0.0% Black, 0.0% Asian, 0.0% American Indian and Alaska Native, 0.0% Hispanic of any race, 0.0% two or more races (2000); Density: 20.5 persons per square mile (2000); Age: 28.1% under 18, 7.9% over 64 (2000); Marriage status: 28.5% never married, 60.5% now married, 3.0% widowed, 8.1% divorced (2000); Foreign born: 0.0% (2000); Ancestry (includes multiple ancestries): 28.4% German, 18.9% United States or American, 7.3% Irish, 6.9% English, 6.8% Other groups (2000).
Economy: Bituminous-coal mining and processing. Employment by occupation: 5.1% management, 18.9% professional, 15.6% services, 18.7% sales, 1.0% farming, 18.3% construction, 22.5% production (2000).
Income: Per capita income: $15,386 (2000); Median household income: $44,013 (2000); Poverty rate: 17.3% (2000).
Education: High school graduation rate: 77.4% (2000); College graduation rate: 12.8% (2000).
Housing: Homeownership rate: 92.5% (2000); Median home value: $90,400 (2000); Median rent: $307 per month (2000); Median age of housing: 31 years (2000).
Transportation: Commute to work: 96.1% car, 0.0% public transportation, 0.6% walk, 3.3% work from home (2000); Travel time to work: 21.0% less than 15 minutes, 25.8% 15 to 30 minutes, 32.4% 30 to 45 minutes, 13.3% 45 to 60 minutes, 7.4% 60 minutes or more (2000)

LINCOLN CITY (unincorporated postal area, zip code 47552). Covers a land area of 3.977 square miles and a water area of 0.090 square miles. Located at 38.11° N. Lat.; 86.99° W. Long. Elevation is 437 feet.
History: Lincoln City was platted in 1872 on land that had been part of the farm of Thomas Lincoln, father of Abraham Lincoln, who settled here in 1816 when Abe was seven years old.
Population: 177 (2000); Race: 100.0% White, 0.0% Black, 0.0% Asian, 0.0% American Indian and Alaska Native, 0.0% Hispanic of any race, 0.0% two or more races (2000); Density: 44.5 persons per square mile (2000); Age: 31.0% under 18, 8.6% over 64 (2000); Marriage status: 19.6% never married, 75.0% now married, 5.4% widowed, 0.0% divorced (2000); Foreign born: 0.0% (2000); Ancestry (includes multiple ancestries): 31.0% German, 14.2% United States or American, 10.7% English (2000).
Economy: Employment by occupation: 9.6% management, 35.1% professional, 16.0% services, 0.0% sales, 0.0% farming, 17.0% construction, 22.3% production (2000).
Income: Per capita income: $15,027 (2000); Median household income: $40,833 (2000); Poverty rate: 0.0% (2000).
Education: High school graduation rate: 70.0% (2000); College graduation rate: 14.6% (2000).

School District(s)
North Spencer County Sch Corp (PK-12)
2000 Enrollment: 2,379 812-937-2400

Housing: Homeownership rate: 100.0% (2000); Median home value: $68,100 (2000); Median age of housing: 37 years (2000).
Transportation: Commute to work: 81.9% car, 0.0% public transportation, 0.0% walk, 18.1% work from home (2000); Travel time to work: 46.8% less than 15 minutes, 24.7% 15 to 30 minutes, 20.8% 30 to 45 minutes, 7.8% 45 to 60 minutes, 0.0% 60 minutes or more (2000)

RICHLAND (unincorporated postal area, zip code 47634). Covers a land area of 51.242 square miles and a water area of 0.056 square miles. Located at 37.93° N. Lat.; 87.19° W. Long.
Population: 2,530 (2000); Race: 98.1% White, 0.0% Black, 1.1% Asian, 0.2% American Indian and Alaska Native, 0.0% Hispanic of any race, 0.6% two or more races (2000); Density: 49.4 persons per square mile (2000); Age: 26.0% under 18, 13.4% over 64 (2000); Marriage status: 19.2% never married, 59.4% now married, 7.5% widowed, 13.8% divorced (2000); Foreign born: 1.0% (2000); Ancestry (includes multiple ancestries): 22.4% German, 18.0% United States or American, 12.6% Irish, 8.7% Other groups, 8.0% English (2000).
Economy: Employment by occupation: 4.6% management, 10.0% professional, 17.5% services, 28.6% sales, 2.4% farming, 14.2% construction, 22.6% production (2000).
Income: Per capita income: $16,523 (2000); Median household income: $37,987 (2000); Poverty rate: 3.5% (2000).
Education: High school graduation rate: 82.3% (2000); College graduation rate: 7.3% (2000).
Housing: Homeownership rate: 87.8% (2000); Median home value: $75,300 (2000); Median rent: $286 per month (2000); Median age of housing: 33 years (2000).
Transportation: Commute to work: 94.4% car, 0.6% public transportation, 0.0% walk, 4.6% work from home (2000); Travel time to work: 15.2% less than 15 minutes, 31.3% 15 to 30 minutes, 28.3% 30 to 45 minutes, 16.9% 45 to 60 minutes, 8.3% 60 minutes or more (2000)

ROCKPORT (city). Covers a land area of 1.172 square miles and a water area of 0.019 square miles. Located at 37.88° N. Lat.; 87.05° W. Long. Elevation is 445 feet.
History: Rockport was first settled by Daniel Grass in 1807. The Lincoln family, and especially Abraham Lincoln, were visitors in Rockport when they lived 16 miles north. John Pitcher, a Rockport attorney, was a friend of Abe's who allowed him to use his extensive library of law, history, and fiction.
Population: 2,160 (2000); Race: 95.5% White, 3.3% Black, 0.0% Asian, 0.2% American Indian and Alaska Native, 0.3% Hispanic of any race, 1.0% two or more races (2000); Density: 1,843.6 persons per square mile (2000); Age: 26.1% under 18, 15.7% over 64 (2000); Marriage status: 20.7% never married, 57.6% now married, 12.8% widowed, 8.8% divorced (2000); Foreign born: 0.0% (2000); Ancestry (includes multiple ancestries): 23.9% German, 14.9% Irish, 13.0% United States or American, 8.8% Other groups, 6.6% English (2000).
Economy: Single-family building permits issued: 4 (2001) / 29 (2000); Multi-family building permits issued: 0 (2001) / 0 (2000); Employment by occupation: 3.1% management, 13.6% professional, 20.0% services, 24.3% sales, 0.3% farming, 12.9% construction, 25.9% production (2000).
Income: Per capita income: $14,298 (2000); Median household income: $27,275 (2000); Poverty rate: 14.9% (2000).
Taxes: Total city taxes per capita: $350 (1997); City property taxes per capita: $285 (1997).
Education: High school graduation rate: 76.8% (2000); College graduation rate: 11.2% (2000).

School District(s)

South Spencer County Sch Corp (PK-12)
2000 Enrollment: 1,477 812-649-2591
Housing: Homeownership rate: 62.9% (2000); Median home value: $63,800 (2000); Median rent: $279 per month (2000); Median age of housing: 39 years (2000).
Newspapers: The Spencer County Journal-Democrat (1 x week)
Transportation: Commute to work: 93.1% car, 0.0% public transportation, 3.8% walk, 1.5% work from home (2000); Travel time to work: 38.1% less than 15 minutes, 25.6% 15 to 30 minutes, 18.5% 30 to 45 minutes, 10.3% 45 to 60 minutes, 7.5% 60 minutes or more (2000)
Additional Information Contacts
Spencer County Regional Chamber 812-649-2186

SAINT MEINRAD (unincorporated postal area, zip code 47577). Covers a land area of 22.356 square miles and a water area of 0.052 square miles. Located at 38.16° N. Lat.; 86.81° W. Long. Elevation is 426 feet.
History: The community of St. Meinrad grew up near the St. Meinrad Abbey, founded in 1854 by Benedictine Fathers and named for a ninth-century Swiss hermit. The massive sandstone Abbey Church dominated the village.
Population: 1,131 (2000); Race: 100.0% White, 0.0% Black, 0.0% Asian, 0.0% American Indian and Alaska Native, 0.0% Hispanic of any race, 0.0% two or more races (2000); Density: 50.6 persons per square mile (2000); Age: 23.8% under 18, 16.1% over 64 (2000); Marriage status: 24.5% never married, 59.7% now married, 9.5% widowed, 6.3% divorced (2000); Foreign born: 0.0% (2000); Ancestry (includes multiple ancestries): 55.2% German, 14.0% United States or American, 6.1% Irish, 2.2% French (except Basque), 2.0% Other groups (2000).
Economy: Employment by occupation: 7.2% management, 10.4% professional, 6.8% services, 24.8% sales, 2.5% farming, 4.3% construction, 43.9% production (2000).
Income: Per capita income: $15,074 (2000); Median household income: $39,653 (2000); Poverty rate: 19.4% (2000).
Education: High school graduation rate: 75.9% (2000); College graduation rate: 12.1% (2000).

Four-year College(s)

Saint Meinrad School of Theology (Private, Not-for-profit, Roman Catholic)
2001 Enrollment: 117 812-357-6611
Housing: Homeownership rate: 85.0% (2000); Median home value: $71,600 (2000); Median rent: $132 per month (2000); Median age of housing: 37 years (2000).
Transportation: Commute to work: 88.6% car, 0.0% public transportation, 5.4% walk, 4.8% work from home (2000); Travel time to work: 35.4% less than 15 minutes, 28.7% 15 to 30 minutes, 26.5% 30 to 45 minutes, 4.6% 45 to 60 minutes, 4.8% 60 minutes or more (2000)
Additional Information Contacts
St. Meinrad Chamber of Commerce. 812-357-7342

SANTA CLAUS (town). Covers a land area of 5.183 square miles and a water area of 0.384 square miles. Located at 38.11° N. Lat.; 86.92° W. Long. Elevation is 510 feet.
History: Santa Claus was laid out in 1846. The suggested name of Santa Fe was rejected by the post office, and Santa Claus was suggested as a joke, since it was near Christmas. The name served to bring hundreds of letters through the Santa Claus post office each December, where Jim Martin, postmaster from 1897 to 1935, played Santa Claus.
Population: 2,041 (2000); Race: 99.1% White, 0.1% Black, 0.2% Asian, 0.0% American Indian and Alaska Native, 0.4% Hispanic of any race, 0.2% two or more races (2000); Density: 393.8 persons per square mile (2000); Age: 30.6% under 18, 8.6% over 64 (2000); Marriage status: 16.0% never married, 75.0% now married, 3.0% widowed, 6.1% divorced (2000); Foreign born: 0.8% (2000); Ancestry (includes multiple ancestries): 46.3% German, 13.6% English, 9.9% Irish, 8.5% United States or American, 6.4% Other groups (2000).
Economy: Single-family building permits issued: 25 (2001) / 41 (2000); Multi-family building permits issued: 0 (2001) / 0 (2000); Employment by occupation: 22.6% management, 23.0% professional, 7.2% services, 23.3% sales, 0.2% farming, 4.2% construction, 19.5% production (2000).
Income: Per capita income: $23,957 (2000); Median household income: $60,388 (2000); Poverty rate: 1.2% (2000).
Taxes: Total city taxes per capita: $300 (1997); City property taxes per capita: $224 (1997).
Education: High school graduation rate: 95.5% (2000); College graduation rate: 35.6% (2000).
Housing: Homeownership rate: 87.9% (2000); Median home value: $133,400 (2000); Median rent: $615 per month (2000); Median age of housing: 9 years (2000).
Transportation: Commute to work: 96.9% car, 0.4% public transportation, 0.6% walk, 2.0% work from home (2000); Travel time to work: 30.4% less than 15 minutes, 27.5% 15 to 30 minutes, 27.6% 30 to 45 minutes, 7.7% 45 to 60 minutes, 6.9% 60 minutes or more (2000)
Additional Information Contacts
Santa Claus Chamber of Commerce 812-937-2848

Starke County

Located in northwestern Indiana; bounded on the northwest by the Kankakee River; drained by the Yellow River. Covers a land area of 309.30 square miles, a water area of 3.00 square miles, and is located in the Central Time Zone. The county government was organized in 1835. County seat is Knox.

Population: 23,556 (2000); Race: 97.1% White, 0.2% Black, 0.7% Asian, 0.2% American Indian and Alaska Native, 1.9% Hispanic of any race, 0.6% two or more races (2000); Density: 76.2 persons per square mile (2000); Age: 26.7% under 18, 13.8% over 64 (2000).
Religion: Five largest groups: 6.6% Catholic Church, 5.7% Lutheran Church—Missouri Synod, 2.5% The United Methodist Church, 1.1% Assemblies of God, 1.0% New Testament Association of Independent Baptist Churches and other Fundamental Baptist Associ
Economy: Unemployment rate: 7.2% (11/2002); Total civilian labor force: 9,758 (11/2002); Leading industries: 34.6% manufacturing; 20.4% health care and social assistance; 19.5% retail trade (2000); Companies that employ more than 1,000 persons: 0 (2000); Companies that employ more than 100 persons: 7 (2000); Farms: 410 totaling 135,643 acres (1997); Minority business ownership rate: 0.0% (1997); Women business ownership rate: 17.8% (1997); Retail sales per capita: $4,657 (1997). Single-family building permits issued: 104 (2001) / 111 (2000); Multi-family building permits issued: 0 (2001) / 0 (2000).
Income: Per capita income: $16,466 (2000); Median household income: $37,243 (2000); Poverty rate: 11.1% (2000); Bankruptcy rate: 10.02% (2001).
Taxes: Total county taxes per capita: $155 (1997); County property taxes per capita: $130 (1997).
Education: High school graduation rate: 72.0% (2000); College graduation rate: 8.4% (2000).
Housing: Homeownership rate: 80.8% (2000); Median home value: $80,000 (2000); Median rent: $335 per month (2000); Median age of housing: 35 years (2000).
Health: Birth rate: 130.3 per 10,000 population (1998); Age adjusted death rate: 95.5 per 10,000 population (1999); Age adjusted cancer mortality rate: 251.1 deaths per 100,000 population (1999). Number of physicians: 4.2 per 10,000 population (1999); Number of hospital beds: 14.9 per 10,000 population (1999).
Elections: 2000 Presidential election results: 47.5% Gore, 50.0% Bush, 0.3% Nader, 1.3% Buchanan
National and State Parks: Bass Lake State Beach; Kaukakee State Fish and Wildlife Area

Additional Information Contacts

Starke County Government Offices 219-772-9101
Knox Chamber of Commerce. 574-772-5548
Starke County Board of Realtors 574-772-5300

Starke County Communities

BASS LAKE (CDP). Covers a land area of 9.150 square miles and a water area of 2.139 square miles. Located at 41.23° N. Lat.; 86.58° W. Long. Elevation is 715 feet.
Population: 1,249 (2000); Race: 93.3% White, 0.0% Black, 0.0% Asian, 0.0% American Indian and Alaska Native, 6.3% Hispanic of any race, 0.0% two or more races (2000); Density: 136.5 persons per square mile (2000); Age: 22.8% under 18, 17.1% over 64 (2000); Marriage status: 16.0% never married, 66.2% now married, 7.1% widowed, 10.7% divorced (2000); Foreign born: 5.2% (2000); Ancestry (includes multiple ancestries): 36.5% German, 18.9% Irish, 18.6% Polish, 9.0% Other groups, 8.1% English (2000).
Economy: Employment by occupation: 14.0% management, 11.7% professional, 12.2% services, 22.8% sales, 0.0% farming, 13.8% construction, 25.5% production (2000).
Income: Per capita income: $19,407 (2000); Median household income: $42,440 (2000); Poverty rate: 14.7% (2000).
Education: High school graduation rate: 76.6% (2000); College graduation rate: 7.0% (2000).
Housing: Homeownership rate: 85.8% (2000); Median home value: $88,300 (2000); Median rent: $396 per month (2000); Median age of housing: 35 years (2000).
Transportation: Commute to work: 98.2% car, 0.0% public transportation, 0.0% walk, 1.8% work from home (2000); Travel time to work: 28.5% less than 15 minutes, 22.0% 15 to 30 minutes, 16.4% 30 to 45 minutes, 7.1% 45 to 60 minutes, 26.0% 60 minutes or more (2000)

GROVERTOWN (unincorporated postal area, zip code 46531). Covers a land area of 23.807 square miles and a water area of 0.009 square miles. Located at 41.35° N. Lat.; 86.51° W. Long. Elevation is 725 feet.
Population: 1,335 (2000); Race: 95.4% White, 0.0% Black, 0.0% Asian, 0.0% American Indian and Alaska Native, 4.8% Hispanic of any race, 0.0% two or more races (2000); Density: 56.1 persons per square mile (2000); Age: 24.0% under 18, 12.6% over 64 (2000); Marriage status: 24.5% never married, 62.1% now married, 4.7% widowed, 8.8% divorced (2000); Foreign born: 4.0% (2000); Ancestry (includes multiple ancestries): 20.6% Irish, 14.7% United States or American, 12.2% German, 11.1% Polish, 9.7% Other groups (2000).
Economy: Employment by occupation: 5.7% management, 9.5% professional, 11.3% services, 18.8% sales, 0.0% farming, 17.5% construction, 37.3% production (2000).
Income: Per capita income: $18,485 (2000); Median household income: $41,765 (2000); Poverty rate: 7.9% (2000).
Education: High school graduation rate: 69.0% (2000); College graduation rate: 5.4% (2000).
Housing: Homeownership rate: 86.1% (2000); Median home value: $92,800 (2000); Median rent: $321 per month (2000); Median age of housing: 26 years (2000).
Transportation: Commute to work: 92.0% car, 0.0% public transportation, 1.3% walk, 6.7% work from home (2000); Travel time to work: 30.7% less than 15 minutes, 29.9% 15 to 30 minutes, 20.3% 30 to 45 minutes, 8.8% 45 to 60 minutes, 10.4% 60 minutes or more (2000)

HAMLET (town). Covers a land area of 0.965 square miles and a water area of 0.009 square miles. Located at 41.38° N. Lat.; 86.58° W. Long. Elevation is 697 feet.
History: Hamlet was sited at the crossing of the Pennsylvania and New York Central Railroads. It was platted in 1863 by John Hamlet, for whom it was named, and soon became a shipping center.
Population: 820 (2000); Race: 98.1% White, 0.0% Black, 0.0% Asian, 0.7% American Indian and Alaska Native, 1.0% Hispanic of any race, 0.7% two or more races (2000); Density: 849.5 persons per square mile (2000); Age: 35.4% under 18, 7.1% over 64 (2000); Marriage status: 17.3% never married, 64.0% now married, 5.6% widowed, 13.1% divorced (2000); Foreign born: 1.0% (2000); Ancestry (includes multiple ancestries): 27.8% German, 14.9% Irish, 13.3% United States or American, 7.5% Other groups, 6.4% English (2000).
Economy: Single-family building permits issued: 0 (2001) / 0 (2000); Multi-family building permits issued: 0 (2001) / 0 (2000); Employment by occupation: 8.5% management, 6.3% professional, 15.4% services, 19.7% sales, 2.6% farming, 12.8% construction, 34.8% production (2000).
Income: Per capita income: $12,811 (2000); Median household income: $30,750 (2000); Poverty rate: 17.3% (2000).
Taxes: Total city taxes per capita: $147 (1997); City property taxes per capita: $111 (1997).
Education: High school graduation rate: 74.5% (2000); College graduation rate: 3.2% (2000).

School District(s)

Oregon-Davis School Corp (KG-12)
2000 Enrollment: 742 219-867-2111
Housing: Homeownership rate: 81.2% (2000); Median home value: $64,000 (2000); Median rent: $386 per month (2000); Median age of housing: 47 years (2000).
Transportation: Commute to work: 95.9% car, 0.6% public transportation, 0.3% walk, 2.4% work from home (2000); Travel time to work: 32.0% less than 15 minutes, 43.8% 15 to 30 minutes, 10.6% 30 to 45 minutes, 5.1% 45 to 60 minutes, 8.5% 60 minutes or more (2000)

KNOX (city). Covers a land area of 3.928 square miles and a water area of 0 square miles. Located at 41.29° N. Lat.; 86.62° W. Long. Elevation is 702 feet.
History: Knox developed as a trading center for the surrounding farmlands.
Population: 3,721 (2000); Race: 96.8% White, 0.2% Black, 0.0% Asian, 0.6% American Indian and Alaska Native, 1.7% Hispanic of any race, 0.9% two or more races (2000); Density: 947.3 persons per square mile (2000); Age: 25.9% under 18, 16.8% over 64 (2000); Marriage status: 21.1% never married, 52.7% now married, 11.0% widowed, 15.2% divorced (2000); Foreign born: 4.6% (2000); Ancestry (includes multiple ancestries): 20.7% German, 13.8% Irish, 13.1% United States or American, 10.4% Other groups, 8.6% English (2000).
Economy: Single-family building permits issued: 12 (2001) / 19 (2000); Multi-family building permits issued: 0 (2001) / 0 (2000); Employment by occupation: 6.7% management, 12.5% professional, 14.0% services, 17.4% sales, 0.5% farming, 9.0% construction, 39.8% production (2000).
Income: Per capita income: $16,184 (2000); Median household income: $29,891 (2000); Poverty rate: 15.5% (2000).
Taxes: Total city taxes per capita: $191 (1997); City property taxes per capita: $143 (1997).

Education: High school graduation rate: 68.3% (2000); College graduation rate: 9.4% (2000).

School District(s)

Knox Community School Corp (KG-12)
2000 Enrollment: 2,081 219-772-1600

Housing: Homeownership rate: 66.6% (2000); Median home value: $65,800 (2000); Median rent: $325 per month (2000); Median age of housing: 42 years (2000).
Hospitals: Starke Memorial Hospital (49 beds)
Safety: Violent crime rate: 18.7 per 10,000 population; Property crime rate: 486.4 per 10,000 population (2001).
Newspapers: The Leader (1 x week); The Review (1 x week)
Transportation: Commute to work: 94.2% car, 0.0% public transportation, 4.6% walk, 0.4% work from home (2000); Travel time to work: 57.7% less than 15 minutes, 8.9% 15 to 30 minutes, 19.5% 30 to 45 minutes, 4.3% 45 to 60 minutes, 9.5% 60 minutes or more (2000)

Additional Information Contacts

Knox Chamber of Commerce. 574-772-5548
Starke County Board of Realtors 574-772-5300

KOONTZ LAKE (CDP). Covers a land area of 3.385 square miles and a water area of 0.503 square miles. Located at 41.41° N. Lat.; 86.48° W. Long. Elevation is 735 feet.
Population: 1,554 (2000); Race: 95.8% White, 1.8% Black, 0.0% Asian, 0.0% American Indian and Alaska Native, 4.3% Hispanic of any race, 0.6% two or more races (2000); Density: 459.1 persons per square mile (2000); Age: 22.0% under 18, 17.2% over 64 (2000); Marriage status: 23.5% never married, 61.6% now married, 7.5% widowed, 7.4% divorced (2000); Foreign born: 2.5% (2000); Ancestry (includes multiple ancestries): 29.2% German, 17.7% Irish, 12.8% United States or American, 8.8% Polish, 7.8% Other groups (2000).
Economy: Recreation. Employment by occupation: 9.0% management, 9.5% professional, 11.5% services, 22.3% sales, 0.0% farming, 15.0% construction, 32.7% production (2000).
Income: Per capita income: $21,429 (2000); Median household income: $37,137 (2000); Poverty rate: 7.7% (2000).
Education: High school graduation rate: 73.3% (2000); College graduation rate: 6.2% (2000).
Housing: Homeownership rate: 82.7% (2000); Median home value: $77,100 (2000); Median rent: $406 per month (2000); Median age of housing: 41 years (2000).
Transportation: Commute to work: 95.9% car, 0.0% public transportation, 0.0% walk, 3.4% work from home (2000); Travel time to work: 38.6% less than 15 minutes, 24.8% 15 to 30 minutes, 12.6% 30 to 45 minutes, 10.4% 45 to 60 minutes, 13.6% 60 minutes or more (2000)

NORTH JUDSON (town). Covers a land area of 0.920 square miles and a water area of 0 square miles. Located at 41.21° N. Lat.; 86.77° W. Long. Elevation is 700 feet.
History: Laid out 1861.
Population: 1,675 (2000); Race: 93.6% White, 0.2% Black, 0.0% Asian, 0.1% American Indian and Alaska Native, 6.7% Hispanic of any race, 1.3% two or more races (2000); Density: 1,820.1 persons per square mile (2000); Age: 35.0% under 18, 12.8% over 64 (2000); Marriage status: 19.1% never married, 56.8% now married, 11.3% widowed, 12.7% divorced (2000); Foreign born: 2.3% (2000); Ancestry (includes multiple ancestries): 21.4% German, 14.8% Other groups, 13.0% Irish, 10.7% United States or American, 6.1% Polish (2000).
Economy: Agriculture: grain; livestock. Manufacturing: dried foliage, meatpacking, furnaces and air conditioners. Single-family building permits issued: 3 (2001) / 3 (2000); Multi-family building permits issued: 0 (2001) / 0 (2000); Employment by occupation: 7.6% management, 12.6% professional, 17.4% services, 20.3% sales, 0.3% farming, 15.2% construction, 26.6% production (2000).
Income: Per capita income: $13,052 (2000); Median household income: $29,779 (2000); Poverty rate: 12.7% (2000).
Taxes: Total city taxes per capita: $209 (1997); City property taxes per capita: $200 (1997).
Education: High school graduation rate: 74.9% (2000); College graduation rate: 9.1% (2000).

School District(s)

North Judson-San Pierre Sch Corp (KG-12)
2000 Enrollment: 1,583 219-896-2155

Housing: Homeownership rate: 63.8% (2000); Median home value: $72,700 (2000); Median rent: $327 per month (2000); Median age of housing: 54 years (2000).
Transportation: Commute to work: 96.0% car, 0.0% public transportation, 2.0% walk, 2.0% work from home (2000); Travel time to work: 30.0% less than 15 minutes, 25.7% 15 to 30 minutes, 14.7% 30 to 45 minutes, 14.6% 45 to 60 minutes, 15.1% 60 minutes or more (2000)

SAN PIERRE (CDP). Covers a land area of 0.142 square miles and a water area of 0 square miles. Located at 41.19° N. Lat.; 86.89° W. Long. Elevation is 704 feet.
Population: 156 (2000); Race: 100.0% White, 0.0% Black, 0.0% Asian, 0.0% American Indian and Alaska Native, 0.0% Hispanic of any race, 0.0% two or more races (2000); Density: 1,100.2 persons per square mile (2000); Age: 28.1% under 18, 11.9% over 64 (2000); Marriage status: 49.0% never married, 18.1% now married, 14.8% widowed, 18.1% divorced (2000); Foreign born: 0.0% (2000); Ancestry (includes multiple ancestries): 26.3% United States or American, 13.1% German, 8.1% French (except Basque), 5.0% Dutch (2000).
Economy: Employment by occupation: 0.0% management, 19.0% professional, 15.2% services, 13.9% sales, 0.0% farming, 12.7% construction, 39.2% production (2000).
Income: Per capita income: $13,552 (2000); Median household income: $30,500 (2000); Poverty rate: 0.0% (2000).
Education: High school graduation rate: 93.8% (2000); College graduation rate: 16.7% (2000).
Housing: Homeownership rate: 81.2% (2000); Median home value: $68,600 (2000); Median rent: $425 per month (2000); Median age of housing: 47 years (2000).
Transportation: Commute to work: 91.1% car, 0.0% public transportation, 8.9% walk, 0.0% work from home (2000); Travel time to work: 54.4% less than 15 minutes, 0.0% 15 to 30 minutes, 38.0% 30 to 45 minutes, 7.6% 45 to 60 minutes, 0.0% 60 minutes or more (2000)

Steuben County

Located in northeastern Indiana; bounded on the north by Michigan, and on the east by Ohio; drained by Pigeon Creek; includes several lakes. Covers a land area of 308.70 square miles, a water area of 13.80 square miles, and is located in the Eastern Time Zone. The county government was organized in 1835. County seat is Angola.

Weather Station: Angola — Elevation: 1,007 feet

	Jan	Feb	Mar	Apr	May	Jun	Jul	Aug	Sep	Oct	Nov	Dec
High	29	33	43	57	69	78	82	80	73	61	47	35
Low	14	15	24	35	47	56	61	59	51	39	30	20
Precip	2.0	1.8	2.7	3.5	4.0	3.7	3.9	3.9	3.4	2.7	3.2	2.7
Snow	10.4	7.8	4.2	0.7	tr	0.0	0.0	0.0	0.0	0.3	2.2	8.0

High and Low temperatures in degrees Fahrenheit; Precipitation and Snow in inches

Population: 33,214 (2000); Race: 96.9% White, 0.5% Black, 0.4% Asian, 0.4% American Indian and Alaska Native, 1.8% Hispanic of any race, 1.0% two or more races (2000); Density: 107.6 persons per square mile (2000); Age: 25.6% under 18, 11.9% over 64 (2000).
Religion: Five largest groups: 5.0% The United Methodist Church, 5.0% Catholic Church, 2.7% The Missionary Church, 2.7% Christian Churches and Churches of Christ, 2.1% Lutheran Church—Missouri Synod (2000).
Economy: Unemployment rate: 6.7% (11/2002); Total civilian labor force: 15,839 (11/2002); Leading industries: 36.5% manufacturing; 21.9% administration, support, waste management, remediation services; 12.7% retail trade (2000); Companies that employ more than 1,000 persons: 2 (2000); Companies that employ more than 100 persons: 42 (2000); Farms: 581 totaling 123,953 acres (1997); Minority business ownership rate: 0.0% (1997); Women business ownership rate: 16.0% (1997); Retail sales per capita: $12,813 (1997). Single-family building permits issued: 247 (2001) / 240 (2000); Multi-family building permits issued: 49 (2001) / 35 (2000).
Income: Per capita income: $20,647 (2000); Median household income: $44,089 (2000); Poverty rate: 6.7% (2000); Bankruptcy rate: 6.14% (2001).
Taxes: Total county taxes per capita: $271 (2000); County property taxes per capita: $160 (2000).
Education: High school graduation rate: 84.3% (2000); College graduation rate: 15.5% (2000).
Housing: Homeownership rate: 78.3% (2000); Median home value: $106,200 (2000); Median rent: $418 per month (2000); Median age of housing: 27 years (2000).
Health: Birth rate: 131.6 per 10,000 population (1998); Age adjusted death rate: 98.6 per 10,000 population (1999); Age adjusted cancer mortality rate: 215.2 deaths per 100,000 population (1999). Number of physicians: 7.8 per

10,000 population (1999); Number of hospital beds: 9.0 per 10,000 population (1999).
Elections: 2000 Presidential election results: 36.4% Gore, 61.7% Bush, 0.4% Nader, 0.8% Buchanan
National and State Parks: Cedar Lake Marsh State Fish and Wildlife Area; Marsh Lake Wetlands State Fish and Wildlife Area; Pokagon State Park
Additional Information Contacts
Steuben County Government Offices.................... 219-668-1000
Angola Chamber of Commerce.................... 219-665-3512
Fremont Area Chamber of Commerce.................... 219-495-9010
Hamilton Area Chamber.................... 219-488-4881

Steuben County Communities

ANGOLA (city). Covers a land area of 4.229 square miles and a water area of 0.015 square miles. Located at 41.63° N. Lat.; 85.00° W. Long. Elevation is 950 feet.
Population: 7,344 (2000); Race: 93.3% White, 1.3% Black, 1.3% Asian, 0.4% American Indian and Alaska Native, 3.3% Hispanic of any race, 1.9% two or more races (2000); Density: 1,736.4 persons per square mile (2000); Age: 22.8% under 18, 12.7% over 64 (2000); Marriage status: 29.9% never married, 49.8% now married, 8.1% widowed, 12.2% divorced (2000); Foreign born: 2.3% (2000); Ancestry (includes multiple ancestries): 27.0% German, 11.5% English, 9.6% United States or American, 9.1% Irish, 8.7% Other groups (2000).
Economy: Agriculture and some manufacturing: feed, brick, tile, automobile and boat parts, dock equipment, wire baskets, sheet-metal fabrication, electrical equipment, paint, needles. Resort area. Single-family building permits issued: 33 (2001) / 33 (2000); Multi-family building permits issued: 49 (2001) / 35 (2000); Employment by occupation: 7.6% management, 21.1% professional, 14.3% services, 22.6% sales, 0.0% farming, 5.9% construction, 28.5% production (2000).
Income: Per capita income: $16,750 (2000); Median household income: $34,925 (2000); Poverty rate: 10.5% (2000).
Taxes: Total city taxes per capita: $175 (1997); City property taxes per capita: $172 (1997).
Education: High school graduation rate: 81.2% (2000); College graduation rate: 19.7% (2000).

School District(s)
M S D Steuben County (KG-12)
2000 Enrollment: 3,009.................... 219-665-2854

Four-year College(s)
Tri-State University (Private, Not-for-profit)
2001 Enrollment: 1,268.................... 219-665-4100
2001 Tuition: In-state $15,950; Out-of-state $15,950

Housing: Homeownership rate: 50.8% (2000); Median home value: $91,500 (2000); Median rent: $414 per month (2000); Median age of housing: 28 years (2000).
Hospitals: Cameron Memorial Community Hospital (32 beds)
Safety: Violent crime rate: 21.7 per 10,000 population; Property crime rate: 697.4 per 10,000 population (2001).
Newspapers: Herald-Republican (2 x week)
Transportation: Commute to work: 91.8% car, 0.7% public transportation, 5.1% walk, 1.1% work from home (2000); Travel time to work: 66.0% less than 15 minutes, 21.2% 15 to 30 minutes, 5.8% 30 to 45 minutes, 2.3% 45 to 60 minutes, 4.8% 60 minutes or more (2000)
Airports: Tri-State Steuben County
Additional Information Contacts
Angola Chamber of Commerce.................... 219-665-3512

CLEAR LAKE (town). Covers a land area of 1.045 square miles and a water area of 1.313 square miles. Located at 41.73° N. Lat.; 84.84° W. Long. Elevation is 1,050 feet.
Population: 244 (2000); Race: 100.0% White, 0.0% Black, 0.0% Asian, 0.0% American Indian and Alaska Native, 0.0% Hispanic of any race, 0.0% two or more races (2000); Density: 233.4 persons per square mile (2000); Age: 14.2% under 18, 21.2% over 64 (2000); Marriage status: 13.7% never married, 72.6% now married, 6.9% widowed, 6.9% divorced (2000); Foreign born: 0.0% (2000); Ancestry (includes multiple ancestries): 50.4% German, 16.4% English, 9.1% Irish, 9.1% United States or American, 8.4% French (except Basque) (2000).
Economy: Resort area. Single-family building permits issued: 4 (2001) / 4 (2000); Multi-family building permits issued: 0 (2001) / 0 (2000); Employment by occupation: 22.1% management, 14.8% professional, 18.8% services, 24.8% sales, 0.0% farming, 6.7% construction, 12.8% production (2000).
Income: Per capita income: $23,092 (2000); Median household income: $49,250 (2000); Poverty rate: 4.4% (2000).
Taxes: Total city taxes per capita: $341 (1997); City property taxes per capita: $308 (1997).
Education: High school graduation rate: 96.9% (2000); College graduation rate: 24.3% (2000).
Housing: Homeownership rate: 94.4% (2000); Median home value: $275,000 (2000); Median rent: $381 per month (2000); Median age of housing: 45 years (2000).
Transportation: Commute to work: 95.2% car, 0.0% public transportation, 2.8% walk, 2.1% work from home (2000); Travel time to work: 33.1% less than 15 minutes, 34.5% 15 to 30 minutes, 4.2% 30 to 45 minutes, 11.3% 45 to 60 minutes, 16.9% 60 minutes or more (2000)

FREMONT (town). Covers a land area of 2.226 square miles and a water area of 0.006 square miles. Located at 41.73° N. Lat.; 84.93° W. Long. Elevation is 1,030 feet.
Population: 1,696 (2000); Race: 97.6% White, 0.1% Black, 0.6% Asian, 0.4% American Indian and Alaska Native, 2.4% Hispanic of any race, 0.8% two or more races (2000); Density: 761.9 persons per square mile (2000); Age: 35.4% under 18, 8.1% over 64 (2000); Marriage status: 22.4% never married, 54.6% now married, 6.2% widowed, 16.7% divorced (2000); Foreign born: 1.8% (2000); Ancestry (includes multiple ancestries): 28.8% German, 10.7% Other groups, 10.7% English, 9.5% United States or American, 6.9% Irish (2000).
Economy: Agriculture: lumber milling. Manufacturing: aluminum auto wheels, camper axles, pressure tanks, steel wire, plastic containers, baked goods, machine forgings, gaskets. Employment by occupation: 8.0% management, 9.8% professional, 13.1% services, 24.5% sales, 0.0% farming, 8.0% construction, 36.6% production (2000).
Income: Per capita income: $16,067 (2000); Median household income: $38,462 (2000); Poverty rate: 7.3% (2000).
Taxes: Total city taxes per capita: $194 (1997); City property taxes per capita: $190 (1997).
Education: High school graduation rate: 83.3% (2000); College graduation rate: 12.6% (2000).

School District(s)
Fremont Community Schools (KG-12)
2000 Enrollment: 1,263.................... 219-495-5005

Housing: Homeownership rate: 75.2% (2000); Median home value: $85,000 (2000); Median rent: $406 per month (2000); Median age of housing: 23 years (2000).
Transportation: Commute to work: 93.1% car, 1.0% public transportation, 4.4% walk, 1.5% work from home (2000); Travel time to work: 57.2% less than 15 minutes, 27.5% 15 to 30 minutes, 7.2% 30 to 45 minutes, 4.2% 45 to 60 minutes, 3.9% 60 minutes or more (2000)
Additional Information Contacts
Fremont Area Chamber of Commerce.................... 219-495-9010

HAMILTON (town). Covers a land area of 1.656 square miles and a water area of 0.359 square miles. Located at 41.53° N. Lat.; 84.91° W. Long. Elevation is 900 feet.
History: Hamilton was called Enterprise when it was founded in 1836 at a site that provided water power. The town was incorporated in 1914.
Population: 1,233 (2000); Race: 98.6% White, 0.0% Black, 0.0% Asian, 0.2% American Indian and Alaska Native, 1.5% Hispanic of any race, 0.7% two or more races (2000); Density: 744.5 persons per square mile (2000); Age: 24.7% under 18, 14.0% over 64 (2000); Marriage status: 18.8% never married, 59.3% now married, 8.7% widowed, 13.2% divorced (2000); Foreign born: 0.2% (2000); Ancestry (includes multiple ancestries): 30.8% German, 11.4% English, 11.3% Irish, 10.0% United States or American, 5.8% Other groups (2000).
Economy: Employment by occupation: 8.2% management, 10.7% professional, 11.4% services, 24.6% sales, 0.0% farming, 12.9% construction, 32.2% production (2000).
Income: Per capita income: $19,834 (2000); Median household income: $40,391 (2000); Poverty rate: 9.2% (2000).
Taxes: Total city taxes per capita: $262 (1997); City property taxes per capita: $250 (1997).
Education: High school graduation rate: 82.3% (2000); College graduation rate: 10.0% (2000).

School District(s)
Hamilton Community Schools (KG-12)
2000 Enrollment: 730.................... 219-488-2513

Housing: Homeownership rate: 72.7% (2000); Median home value: $95,500 (2000); Median rent: $342 per month (2000); Median age of housing: 29 years (2000).
Newspapers: The Hamilton News (1 x week)
Transportation: Commute to work: 94.4% car, 0.3% public transportation, 1.6% walk, 3.2% work from home (2000); Travel time to work: 34.1% less than 15 minutes, 42.9% 15 to 30 minutes, 11.8% 30 to 45 minutes, 7.8% 45 to 60 minutes, 3.5% 60 minutes or more (2000)
Additional Information Contacts
Hamilton Area Chamber 219-488-4881

HUDSON (town). Covers a land area of 0.819 square miles and a water area of 0 square miles. Located at 41.53° N. Lat.; 85.08° W. Long. Elevation is 990 feet.
Population: 596 (2000); Race: 95.1% White, 0.0% Black, 0.2% Asian, 1.1% American Indian and Alaska Native, 3.1% Hispanic of any race, 0.5% two or more races (2000); Density: 728.1 persons per square mile (2000); Age: 28.5% under 18, 5.9% over 64 (2000); Marriage status: 22.6% never married, 58.8% now married, 3.3% widowed, 15.4% divorced (2000); Foreign born: 3.6% (2000); Ancestry (includes multiple ancestries): 28.0% German, 14.4% United States or American, 14.3% Other groups, 8.9% English, 3.9% Irish (2000).
Economy: Potatoes, onions. Manufacturing: metal furniture, extruded plastics, metal stampings. Employment by occupation: 5.6% management, 6.5% professional, 7.2% services, 17.4% sales, 0.0% farming, 12.8% construction, 50.5% production (2000).
Income: Per capita income: $17,282 (2000); Median household income: $42,321 (2000); Poverty rate: 4.3% (2000).
Taxes: Total city taxes per capita: $122 (1997); City property taxes per capita: $108 (1997).
Education: High school graduation rate: 76.6% (2000); College graduation rate: 5.0% (2000).
Housing: Homeownership rate: 88.4% (2000); Median home value: $67,400 (2000); Median rent: $436 per month (2000); Median age of housing: 60+ years (2000).
Transportation: Commute to work: 93.4% car, 0.9% public transportation, 0.6% walk, 4.4% work from home (2000); Travel time to work: 41.8% less than 15 minutes, 37.8% 15 to 30 minutes, 10.9% 30 to 45 minutes, 6.3% 45 to 60 minutes, 3.3% 60 minutes or more (2000)

ORLAND (town). Covers a land area of 0.665 square miles and a water area of 0 square miles. Located at 41.73° N. Lat.; 85.17° W. Long. Elevation is 962 feet.
History: Laid out 1838.
Population: 341 (2000); Race: 97.0% White, 0.0% Black, 0.0% Asian, 0.0% American Indian and Alaska Native, 3.0% Hispanic of any race, 3.0% two or more races (2000); Density: 512.8 persons per square mile (2000); Age: 33.7% under 18, 14.2% over 64 (2000); Marriage status: 24.1% never married, 48.9% now married, 8.5% widowed, 18.5% divorced (2000); Foreign born: 1.1% (2000); Ancestry (includes multiple ancestries): 32.6% German, 12.6% Irish, 11.5% United States or American, 9.0% English, 4.4% Dutch (2000).
Economy: Manufacturing: plastic products, wire products, food, transportation equipment, fabricated metal products. Fawn River State Fish Hatchery nearby to Northwest. Employment by occupation: 5.0% management, 10.6% professional, 11.3% services, 25.6% sales, 0.0% farming, 13.1% construction, 34.4% production (2000).
Income: Per capita income: $15,188 (2000); Median household income: $38,542 (2000); Poverty rate: 7.9% (2000).
Taxes: Total city taxes per capita: $154 (1997); City property taxes per capita: $149 (1997).
Education: High school graduation rate: 82.6% (2000); College graduation rate: 8.5% (2000).
Housing: Homeownership rate: 79.7% (2000); Median home value: $75,900 (2000); Median rent: $308 per month (2000); Median age of housing: 60+ years (2000).
Transportation: Commute to work: 94.4% car, 0.0% public transportation, 3.8% walk, 1.9% work from home (2000); Travel time to work: 25.5% less than 15 minutes, 49.0% 15 to 30 minutes, 11.5% 30 to 45 minutes, 6.4% 45 to 60 minutes, 7.6% 60 minutes or more (2000)

PLEASANT LAKE (unincorporated postal area, zip code 46779). Covers a land area of 34.863 square miles and a water area of 0.656 square miles. Located at 41.57° N. Lat.; 85.03° W. Long. Elevation is 963 feet.
History: The community of Pleasant Lake was named for the nearby lake, which was called Nipcondish, meaning "pleasant waters," by the Indians.
Population: 2,191 (2000); Race: 98.5% White, 0.0% Black, 0.4% Asian, 0.0% American Indian and Alaska Native, 0.7% Hispanic of any race, 0.8% two or more races (2000); Density: 62.8 persons per square mile (2000); Age: 27.1% under 18, 12.7% over 64 (2000); Marriage status: 25.1% never married, 60.1% now married, 4.5% widowed, 10.3% divorced (2000); Foreign born: 0.9% (2000); Ancestry (includes multiple ancestries): 20.3% German, 12.0% United States or American, 10.4% English, 9.7% Other groups, 7.4% Irish (2000).
Economy: Employment by occupation: 10.9% management, 6.9% professional, 14.5% services, 26.8% sales, 0.6% farming, 15.8% construction, 24.6% production (2000).
Income: Per capita income: $19,893 (2000); Median household income: $41,992 (2000); Poverty rate: 6.1% (2000).
Education: High school graduation rate: 84.6% (2000); College graduation rate: 10.0% (2000).
Housing: Homeownership rate: 84.5% (2000); Median home value: $88,800 (2000); Median rent: $418 per month (2000); Median age of housing: 29 years (2000).
Transportation: Commute to work: 95.6% car, 0.7% public transportation, 1.4% walk, 2.3% work from home (2000); Travel time to work: 40.4% less than 15 minutes, 41.5% 15 to 30 minutes, 9.7% 30 to 45 minutes, 4.2% 45 to 60 minutes, 4.2% 60 minutes or more (2000)

Sullivan County

Located in southwestern Indiana; bounded on the west by the Wabash River and the Illinois border; drained by Busseron and Maria Creeks. Covers a land area of 447.20 square miles, a water area of 6.80 square miles, and is located in the Eastern Time Zone. The county government was organized in 1816. County seat is Sullivan.
Population: 21,751 (2000); Race: 93.8% White, 4.2% Black, 0.1% Asian, 0.4% American Indian and Alaska Native, 0.9% Hispanic of any race, 1.1% two or more races (2000); Density: 48.6 persons per square mile (2000); Age: 22.6% under 18, 14.1% over 64 (2000).
Religion: Five largest groups: 8.0% Christian Churches and Churches of Christ, 6.9% American Baptist Churches in the USA, 6.6% The United Methodist Church, 3.7% Churches of Christ, 2.2% Southern Baptist Convention (2000).
Economy: Unemployment rate: 5.5% (11/2002); Total civilian labor force: 9,151 (11/2002); Leading industries: 16.9% retail trade; 15.1% manufacturing; 13.3% health care and social assistance (2000); Companies that employ more than 1,000 persons: 0 (2000); Companies that employ more than 100 persons: 10 (2000); Farms: 473 totaling 176,895 acres (1997); Minority business ownership rate: 0.0% (1997); Women business ownership rate: 19.7% (1997); Retail sales per capita: $4,445 (1997). Single-family building permits issued: 21 (2001) / 19 (2000); Multi-family building permits issued: 0 (2001) / 2 (2000).
Income: Per capita income: $16,234 (2000); Median household income: $32,976 (2000); Poverty rate: 10.9% (2000); Bankruptcy rate: 7.60% (2001).
Taxes: Total county taxes per capita: $173 (2000); County property taxes per capita: $171 (2000).
Education: High school graduation rate: 80.8% (2000); College graduation rate: 9.4% (2000).
Housing: Homeownership rate: 79.8% (2000); Median home value: $58,900 (2000); Median rent: $275 per month (2000); Median age of housing: 39 years (2000).
Health: Birth rate: 105.3 per 10,000 population (1998); Age adjusted death rate: 101.4 per 10,000 population (1999); Age adjusted cancer mortality rate: 194.3 deaths per 100,000 population (1999). Air Quality Index: 99% good, 1% moderate, 0% unhealthy (percent of days in 2000). Number of physicians: 3.7 per 10,000 population (1999); Number of hospital beds: 17.0 per 10,000 population (1999).
Elections: 2000 Presidential election results: 46.4% Gore, 52.3% Bush, 0.1% Nader, 0.6% Buchanan
National and State Parks: Greene-Sullivan State Forest
Additional Information Contacts
Sullivan County Government Offices 812-268-4491

Sullivan County Communities

CARLISLE (town). Covers a land area of 0.537 square miles and a water area of 0 square miles. Located at 38.96° N. Lat.; 87.40° W. Long. Elevation is 504 feet.
History: Carlisle was settled in 1803 on land granted to Samuel Ledgerwood for services to the U.S. government. Its early industry was coal mining.

Population: 2,660 (2000); Race: 64.5% White, 31.2% Black, 0.0% Asian, 1.5% American Indian and Alaska Native, 2.4% Hispanic of any race, 2.1% two or more races (2000); Density: 4,953.5 persons per square mile (2000); Age: 6.5% under 18, 5.2% over 64 (2000); Marriage status: 46.3% never married, 30.5% now married, 5.0% widowed, 18.2% divorced (2000); Foreign born: 0.0% (2000); Ancestry (includes multiple ancestries): 19.7% Other groups, 10.8% German, 9.0% United States or American, 7.0% Irish, 4.6% English (2000).
Economy: Employment by occupation: 4.3% management, 18.4% professional, 22.7% services, 17.1% sales, 1.0% farming, 13.7% construction, 22.7% production (2000).
Income: Per capita income: $12,822 (2000); Median household income: $29,875 (2000); Poverty rate: 13.4% (2000).
Taxes: Total city taxes per capita: $66 (1997); City property taxes per capita: $66 (1997).
Education: High school graduation rate: 76.0% (2000); College graduation rate: 3.7% (2000).
Housing: Homeownership rate: 71.3% (2000); Median home value: $45,700 (2000); Median rent: $294 per month (2000); Median age of housing: 60+ years (2000).
Transportation: Commute to work: 95.3% car, 0.0% public transportation, 2.2% walk, 2.5% work from home (2000); Travel time to work: 41.7% less than 15 minutes, 20.7% 15 to 30 minutes, 20.7% 30 to 45 minutes, 9.2% 45 to 60 minutes, 7.7% 60 minutes or more (2000)

DUGGER (town). Covers a land area of 0.582 square miles and a water area of 0 square miles. Located at 39.07° N. Lat.; 87.26° W. Long. Elevation is 684 feet.
Population: 955 (2000); Race: 98.8% White, 0.0% Black, 0.0% Asian, 0.4% American Indian and Alaska Native, 0.7% Hispanic of any race, 0.4% two or more races (2000); Density: 1,641.1 persons per square mile (2000); Age: 22.1% under 18, 16.4% over 64 (2000); Marriage status: 21.5% never married, 57.2% now married, 9.0% widowed, 12.4% divorced (2000); Foreign born: 0.0% (2000); Ancestry (includes multiple ancestries): 11.2% United States or American, 10.7% Other groups, 9.7% German, 8.5% English, 6.6% Irish (2000).
Economy: In agricultural area; crushed stone, bituminous coal. Employment by occupation: 3.7% management, 21.0% professional, 20.3% services, 22.0% sales, 0.5% farming, 11.2% construction, 21.3% production (2000).
Income: Per capita income: $15,255 (2000); Median household income: $31,071 (2000); Poverty rate: 7.8% (2000).
Taxes: Total city taxes per capita: $51 (1997); City property taxes per capita: $50 (1997).
Education: High school graduation rate: 84.0% (2000); College graduation rate: 5.3% (2000).
Housing: Homeownership rate: 85.2% (2000); Median home value: $41,000 (2000); Median rent: $225 per month (2000); Median age of housing: 58 years (2000).
Transportation: Commute to work: 96.6% car, 0.0% public transportation, 1.2% walk, 2.2% work from home (2000); Travel time to work: 26.5% less than 15 minutes, 32.8% 15 to 30 minutes, 16.4% 30 to 45 minutes, 11.3% 45 to 60 minutes, 13.0% 60 minutes or more (2000)

FAIRBANKS (unincorporated postal area, zip code 47849). Covers a land area of 24.176 square miles and a water area of 0.072 square miles. Located at 39.19° N. Lat.; 87.54° W. Long. Elevation is 548 feet.
History: The community of Fairbanks was named for Lt. Fairbanks who was killed near here in 1812, while escorting a wagonload of supplies to Fort Harrison.
Population: 415 (2000); Race: 100.0% White, 0.0% Black, 0.0% Asian, 0.0% American Indian and Alaska Native, 0.0% Hispanic of any race, 0.0% two or more races (2000); Density: 17.2 persons per square mile (2000); Age: 26.4% under 18, 18.7% over 64 (2000); Marriage status: 5.1% never married, 87.3% now married, 5.7% widowed, 2.0% divorced (2000); Foreign born: 0.0% (2000); Ancestry (includes multiple ancestries): 17.1% English, 11.4% Other groups, 8.4% United States or American, 7.5% German, 7.0% Irish (2000).
Economy: Employment by occupation: 3.6% management, 9.9% professional, 18.2% services, 29.7% sales, 0.0% farming, 25.0% construction, 13.5% production (2000).
Income: Per capita income: $17,100 (2000); Median household income: $39,583 (2000); Poverty rate: 14.9% (2000).
Education: High school graduation rate: 83.5% (2000); College graduation rate: 14.0% (2000).
Housing: Homeownership rate: 87.2% (2000); Median home value: $56,700 (2000); Median rent: $288 per month (2000); Median age of housing: 37 years (2000).
Transportation: Commute to work: 100.0% car, 0.0% public transportation, 0.0% walk, 0.0% work from home (2000); Travel time to work: 0.0% less than 15 minutes, 36.5% 15 to 30 minutes, 28.1% 30 to 45 minutes, 16.9% 45 to 60 minutes, 18.5% 60 minutes or more (2000)

FARMERSBURG (town). Covers a land area of 0.726 square miles and a water area of 0 square miles. Located at 39.25° N. Lat.; 87.38° W. Long. Elevation is 559 feet.
History: Farmersburg developed as a supply center for the surrounding farming community.
Population: 1,180 (2000); Race: 94.4% White, 0.2% Black, 1.1% Asian, 1.1% American Indian and Alaska Native, 1.2% Hispanic of any race, 2.3% two or more races (2000); Density: 1,626.4 persons per square mile (2000); Age: 26.0% under 18, 16.7% over 64 (2000); Marriage status: 22.4% never married, 54.3% now married, 9.0% widowed, 14.4% divorced (2000); Foreign born: 1.1% (2000); Ancestry (includes multiple ancestries): 17.5% United States or American, 14.8% German, 13.8% English, 10.0% Irish, 7.0% Other groups (2000).
Economy: Employment by occupation: 10.8% management, 14.8% professional, 19.4% services, 25.3% sales, 1.1% farming, 9.5% construction, 19.0% production (2000).
Income: Per capita income: $14,873 (2000); Median household income: $30,478 (2000); Poverty rate: 11.0% (2000).
Taxes: Total city taxes per capita: $43 (1997); City property taxes per capita: $42 (1997).
Education: High school graduation rate: 82.1% (2000); College graduation rate: 10.3% (2000).
Housing: Homeownership rate: 79.6% (2000); Median home value: $57,500 (2000); Median rent: $335 per month (2000); Median age of housing: 41 years (2000).
Transportation: Commute to work: 97.0% car, 0.0% public transportation, 1.3% walk, 1.7% work from home (2000); Travel time to work: 21.8% less than 15 minutes, 36.2% 15 to 30 minutes, 31.3% 30 to 45 minutes, 6.8% 45 to 60 minutes, 4.0% 60 minutes or more (2000)

HYMERA (town). Covers a land area of 0.703 square miles and a water area of 0 square miles. Located at 39.18° N. Lat.; 87.30° W. Long. Elevation is 524 feet.
History: Hymera was platted in 1870 and named Pittsburg, after coal was discovered nearby. Postmaster John Badders changed the name to High Mary, referring to his daughter, and the name was later shortened to Hymera.
Population: 833 (2000); Race: 98.8% White, 0.0% Black, 0.0% Asian, 0.0% American Indian and Alaska Native, 0.0% Hispanic of any race, 1.2% two or more races (2000); Density: 1,184.5 persons per square mile (2000); Age: 23.7% under 18, 16.2% over 64 (2000); Marriage status: 23.0% never married, 55.4% now married, 14.0% widowed, 7.5% divorced (2000); Foreign born: 0.0% (2000); Ancestry (includes multiple ancestries): 19.4% United States or American, 11.9% English, 11.4% German, 7.5% Irish, 4.1% Other groups (2000).
Economy: Employment by occupation: 4.3% management, 7.7% professional, 20.7% services, 21.9% sales, 0.0% farming, 15.1% construction, 30.2% production (2000).
Income: Per capita income: $13,113 (2000); Median household income: $28,938 (2000); Poverty rate: 17.2% (2000).
Taxes: Total city taxes per capita: $70 (1997); City property taxes per capita: $68 (1997).
Education: High school graduation rate: 71.8% (2000); College graduation rate: 6.2% (2000).

School District(s)

Northeast School Corp (PK-12)
2000 Enrollment: 1,564 812-383-5761
Housing: Homeownership rate: 79.5% (2000); Median home value: $37,600 (2000); Median rent: $189 per month (2000); Median age of housing: 57 years (2000).
Transportation: Commute to work: 94.9% car, 0.3% public transportation, 3.8% walk, 1.0% work from home (2000); Travel time to work: 18.3% less than 15 minutes, 27.2% 15 to 30 minutes, 25.0% 30 to 45 minutes, 14.7% 45 to 60 minutes, 14.7% 60 minutes or more (2000)

MEROM (town). Covers a land area of 0.361 square miles and a water area of 0 square miles. Located at 39.05° N. Lat.; 87.56° W. Long. Elevation is 437 feet.

History: From 1817 to 1842 Merom was the seat of Sullivan County and a shipping center. The name, which means "high ground along the waters," reflects Merom's location on a bluff of the Wabash River.
Population: 294 (2000); Race: 97.7% White, 1.0% Black, 0.0% Asian, 0.0% American Indian and Alaska Native, 0.0% Hispanic of any race, 1.3% two or more races (2000); Density: 813.7 persons per square mile (2000); Age: 29.0% under 18, 9.2% over 64 (2000); Marriage status: 21.9% never married, 65.3% now married, 5.0% widowed, 7.9% divorced (2000); Foreign born: 0.3% (2000); Ancestry (includes multiple ancestries): 17.2% United States or American, 13.5% German, 11.9% Irish, 9.6% Other groups, 9.2% English (2000).
Economy: Employment by occupation: 8.8% management, 10.4% professional, 8.8% services, 16.0% sales, 1.6% farming, 12.0% construction, 42.4% production (2000).
Income: Per capita income: $13,087 (2000); Median household income: $31,528 (2000); Poverty rate: 14.5% (2000).
Taxes: Total city taxes per capita: $46 (1997); City property taxes per capita: $46 (1997).
Education: High school graduation rate: 81.9% (2000); College graduation rate: 8.3% (2000).
Housing: Homeownership rate: 82.6% (2000); Median home value: $42,900 (2000); Median rent: $333 per month (2000); Median age of housing: 60+ years (2000).
Transportation: Commute to work: 90.9% car, 0.0% public transportation, 7.4% walk, 0.0% work from home (2000); Travel time to work: 25.6% less than 15 minutes, 46.3% 15 to 30 minutes, 3.3% 30 to 45 minutes, 17.4% 45 to 60 minutes, 7.4% 60 minutes or more (2000)

SHELBURN (town). Covers a land area of 0.658 square miles and a water area of 0 square miles. Located at 39.18° N. Lat.; 87.39° W. Long. Elevation is 540 feet.
History: Shelburn was founded in 1818. Growth was seen when the first coal mine was established in 1868.
Population: 1,268 (2000); Race: 97.6% White, 0.3% Black, 0.0% Asian, 0.0% American Indian and Alaska Native, 0.9% Hispanic of any race, 1.8% two or more races (2000); Density: 1,926.0 persons per square mile (2000); Age: 26.3% under 18, 13.0% over 64 (2000); Marriage status: 18.5% never married, 54.4% now married, 8.9% widowed, 18.2% divorced (2000); Foreign born: 0.2% (2000); Ancestry (includes multiple ancestries): 18.0% United States or American, 13.0% English, 11.3% German, 10.2% Irish, 6.4% Other groups (2000).
Economy: Employment by occupation: 7.0% management, 9.8% professional, 20.5% services, 17.9% sales, 1.1% farming, 15.8% construction, 27.9% production (2000).
Income: Per capita income: $12,752 (2000); Median household income: $25,714 (2000); Poverty rate: 18.0% (2000).
Taxes: Total city taxes per capita: $40 (1997); City property taxes per capita: $39 (1997).
Education: High school graduation rate: 74.7% (2000); College graduation rate: 3.7% (2000).
Housing: Homeownership rate: 74.8% (2000); Median home value: $42,200 (2000); Median rent: $230 per month (2000); Median age of housing: 39 years (2000).
Transportation: Commute to work: 92.8% car, 0.0% public transportation, 2.1% walk, 2.7% work from home (2000); Travel time to work: 31.1% less than 15 minutes, 28.3% 15 to 30 minutes, 21.7% 30 to 45 minutes, 12.7% 45 to 60 minutes, 6.2% 60 minutes or more (2000)

SULLIVAN (city). Covers a land area of 1.916 square miles and a water area of 0 square miles. Located at 39.09° N. Lat.; 87.40° W. Long. Elevation is 532 feet.
History: Sullivan was laid out in 1842 as the seat of Sullivan County, which was moved from Merom to the more central location. The early economy of Sullivan was based on coal mining.
Population: 4,617 (2000); Race: 97.9% White, 0.2% Black, 0.0% Asian, 0.5% American Indian and Alaska Native, 1.0% Hispanic of any race, 1.2% two or more races (2000); Density: 2,410.1 persons per square mile (2000); Age: 24.1% under 18, 21.5% over 64 (2000); Marriage status: 17.8% never married, 50.1% now married, 16.8% widowed, 15.3% divorced (2000); Foreign born: 0.0% (2000); Ancestry (includes multiple ancestries): 14.5% United States or American, 13.1% English, 12.7% German, 10.7% Other groups, 9.6% Irish (2000).
Economy: Single-family building permits issued: 21 (2001) / 19 (2000); Multi-family building permits issued: 0 (2001) / 2 (2000); Employment by occupation: 6.3% management, 14.4% professional, 21.0% services, 26.1% sales, 0.0% farming, 12.1% construction, 20.1% production (2000).
Income: Per capita income: $17,717 (2000); Median household income: $26,115 (2000); Poverty rate: 16.6% (2000).
Taxes: Total city taxes per capita: $153 (2000); City property taxes per capita: $147 (2000).
Education: High school graduation rate: 78.1% (2000); College graduation rate: 8.6% (2000).

School District(s)

Southwest School Corp (PK-12)
2000 Enrollment: 1,995 812-268-6311
Housing: Homeownership rate: 67.1% (2000); Median home value: $55,100 (2000); Median rent: $253 per month (2000); Median age of housing: 52 years (2000).
Hospitals: Sullivan County Community Hospital
Newspapers: Sullivan Daily Times (5 x week)
Transportation: Commute to work: 94.6% car, 0.0% public transportation, 2.5% walk, 1.7% work from home (2000); Travel time to work: 45.0% less than 15 minutes, 24.5% 15 to 30 minutes, 15.5% 30 to 45 minutes, 8.4% 45 to 60 minutes, 6.6% 60 minutes or more (2000)

Switzerland County

Located in southeastern Indiana; bounded on the east and south by the Ohio River and the Kentucky border. Covers a land area of 221.20 square miles, a water area of 2.30 square miles, and is located in the Eastern Time Zone. The county government was organized in 1814. County seat is Vevay.

Weather Station: Vevay Elevation: 469 feet

	Jan	Feb	Mar	Apr	May	Jun	Jul	Aug	Sep	Oct	Nov	Dec
High	40	46	57	68	77	85	88	87	80	69	56	45
Low	23	25	34	42	52	61	66	64	57	45	36	28
Precip	3.1	2.9	4.1	4.3	4.7	4.6	3.8	3.9	3.1	3.1	3.6	3.7
Snow	6.5	5.1	3.3	0.1	tr	0.0	0.0	0.0	0.0	0.3	0.6	2.7

High and Low temperatures in degrees Fahrenheit; Precipitation and Snow in inches

Population: 9,065 (2000); Race: 99.0% White, 0.0% Black, 0.4% Asian, 0.1% American Indian and Alaska Native, 0.7% Hispanic of any race, 0.3% two or more races (2000); Density: 41.0 persons per square mile (2000); Age: 26.2% under 18, 12.7% over 64 (2000).
Religion: Five largest groups: 13.4% American Baptist Churches in the USA, 5.1% Christian Churches and Churches of Christ, 3.3% The United Methodist Church, 1.6% Old Order Amish Church, 1.6% Catholic Church (2000).
Economy: Unemployment rate: 5.3% (11/2002); Total civilian labor force: 3,734 (11/2002); Leading industries: 17.4% manufacturing; 15.5% health care and social assistance; 14.8% accommodation & food services (2000); Companies that employ more than 1,000 persons: 0 (2000); Companies that employ more than 100 persons: 0 (2000); Farms: 541 totaling 67,881 acres (1997); Minority business ownership rate: 0.0% (1997); Women business ownership rate: 0.0% (1997); Retail sales per capita: $1,971 (1997). Single-family building permits issued: 124 (2001) / 122 (2000); Multi-family building permits issued: 0 (2001) / 0 (2000).
Income: Per capita income: $17,466 (2000); Median household income: $37,092 (2000); Poverty rate: 13.9% (2000); Bankruptcy rate: 7.68% (2001).
Taxes: Total county taxes per capita: $152 (1997); County property taxes per capita: $110 (1997).
Education: High school graduation rate: 71.4% (2000); College graduation rate: 7.6% (2000).
Housing: Homeownership rate: 77.8% (2000); Median home value: $78,400 (2000); Median rent: $318 per month (2000); Median age of housing: 28 years (2000).
Health: Birth rate: 123.6 per 10,000 population (1998); Age adjusted death rate: 79.8 per 10,000 population (1999); Age adjusted cancer mortality rate: 149.9 (Unreliable figure as per CDC) deaths per 100,000 population (1999). Number of physicians: 2.2 per 10,000 population (1999); Number of hospital beds: n/a (1999).
Elections: 2000 Presidential election results: 41.3% Gore, 56.5% Bush, 0.5% Nader, 1.1% Buchanan

Additional Information Contacts

Switzerland County Government Offices 812-427-3302

Switzerland County Communities

BENNINGTON (unincorporated postal area, zip code 47011). Covers a land area of 26.942 square miles and a water area of 0.067 square miles. Located at 38.84° N. Lat.; 85.07° W. Long. Elevation is 891 feet.
Population: 674 (2000); Race: 100.0% White, 0.0% Black, 0.0% Asian, 0.0% American Indian and Alaska Native, 0.0% Hispanic of any race, 0.0%

two or more races (2000); Density: 25.0 persons per square mile (2000); Age: 36.8% under 18, 9.2% over 64 (2000); Marriage status: 23.7% never married, 66.1% now married, 3.9% widowed, 6.2% divorced (2000); Foreign born: 0.0% (2000); Ancestry (includes multiple ancestries): 36.0% German, 13.4% Irish, 11.9% United States or American, 3.0% Swiss, 2.2% Other groups (2000).
Economy: Employment by occupation: 9.6% management, 16.9% professional, 11.1% services, 9.9% sales, 0.0% farming, 16.6% construction, 36.0% production (2000).
Income: Per capita income: $12,270 (2000); Median household income: $28,676 (2000); Poverty rate: 32.6% (2000).
Education: High school graduation rate: 73.0% (2000); College graduation rate: 14.4% (2000).
Housing: Homeownership rate: 83.7% (2000); Median home value: $74,600 (2000); Median rent: $192 per month (2000); Median age of housing: 24 years (2000).
Transportation: Commute to work: 92.0% car, 0.0% public transportation, 2.2% walk, 4.1% work from home (2000); Travel time to work: 11.3% less than 15 minutes, 34.2% 15 to 30 minutes, 20.3% 30 to 45 minutes, 18.6% 45 to 60 minutes, 15.6% 60 minutes or more (2000)

FLORENCE (unincorporated postal area, zip code 47020). Covers a land area of 22.617 square miles and a water area of 0 square miles. Located at 38.81° N. Lat.; 84.94° W. Long. Elevation is 480 feet.
Population: 1,037 (2000); Race: 100.0% White, 0.0% Black, 0.0% Asian, 0.0% American Indian and Alaska Native, 1.4% Hispanic of any race, 0.0% two or more races (2000); Density: 45.9 persons per square mile (2000); Age: 27.1% under 18, 10.0% over 64 (2000); Marriage status: 19.5% never married, 61.4% now married, 8.3% widowed, 10.8% divorced (2000); Foreign born: 0.0% (2000); Ancestry (includes multiple ancestries): 27.7% United States or American, 15.9% German, 8.1% Other groups, 6.1% Irish, 5.0% English (2000).
Economy: Employment by occupation: 8.4% management, 6.1% professional, 17.0% services, 17.6% sales, 0.0% farming, 22.2% construction, 28.7% production (2000).
Income: Per capita income: $25,455 (2000); Median household income: $40,859 (2000); Poverty rate: 10.1% (2000).
Education: High school graduation rate: 58.7% (2000); College graduation rate: 3.8% (2000).
Housing: Homeownership rate: 80.4% (2000); Median home value: $87,300 (2000); Median rent: $429 per month (2000); Median age of housing: 18 years (2000).
Transportation: Commute to work: 95.7% car, 0.0% public transportation, 2.2% walk, 2.2% work from home (2000); Travel time to work: 12.4% less than 15 minutes, 31.6% 15 to 30 minutes, 23.4% 30 to 45 minutes, 16.6% 45 to 60 minutes, 16.0% 60 minutes or more (2000)

PATRIOT (town). Covers a land area of 0.223 square miles and a water area of 0.038 square miles. Located at 38.83° N. Lat.; 84.82° W. Long. Elevation is 466 feet.
History: Suffered during flood of 1937. Laid out 1820.
Population: 202 (2000); Race: 100.0% White, 0.0% Black, 0.0% Asian, 0.0% American Indian and Alaska Native, 0.0% Hispanic of any race, 0.0% two or more races (2000); Density: 906.7 persons per square mile (2000); Age: 26.4% under 18, 13.7% over 64 (2000); Marriage status: 34.4% never married, 48.6% now married, 8.7% widowed, 8.2% divorced (2000); Foreign born: 0.0% (2000); Ancestry (includes multiple ancestries): 41.5% United States or American, 17.0% German, 11.3% English, 9.4% Irish, 6.1% Other groups (2000).
Economy: In agricultural area. Manufacturing: fiberglass, motor vehicle parts. Sand and gravel. Employment by occupation: 4.3% management, 10.8% professional, 14.0% services, 17.2% sales, 0.0% farming, 9.7% construction, 44.1% production (2000).
Income: Per capita income: $16,866 (2000); Median household income: $37,500 (2000); Poverty rate: 10.4% (2000).
Taxes: Total city taxes per capita: $24 (1997); City property taxes per capita: $19 (1997).
Education: High school graduation rate: 60.9% (2000); College graduation rate: 4.5% (2000).
Housing: Homeownership rate: 76.6% (2000); Median home value: $76,700 (2000); Median rent: $346 per month (2000); Median age of housing: 46 years (2000).
Transportation: Commute to work: 85.7% car, 0.0% public transportation, 9.9% walk, 0.0% work from home (2000); Travel time to work: 25.3% less than 15 minutes, 19.8% 15 to 30 minutes, 18.7% 30 to 45 minutes, 7.7% 45 to 60 minutes, 28.6% 60 minutes or more (2000)

VEVAY (town). Covers a land area of 1.481 square miles and a water area of 0.054 square miles. Located at 38.74° N. Lat.; 85.07° W. Long. Elevation is 489 feet.
History: Vevay was founded in 1801 by Swiss immigrants, who planted vineyards and became known for their fine wines. Vevay was the birthplace of Edward Eggleston, author of "The Hoosier Schoolmaster."
Population: 1,735 (2000); Race: 97.2% White, 0.0% Black, 1.3% Asian, 0.0% American Indian and Alaska Native, 1.4% Hispanic of any race, 0.2% two or more races (2000); Density: 1,171.3 persons per square mile (2000); Age: 23.4% under 18, 20.2% over 64 (2000); Marriage status: 24.0% never married, 48.6% now married, 9.7% widowed, 17.7% divorced (2000); Foreign born: 1.5% (2000); Ancestry (includes multiple ancestries): 19.2% United States or American, 12.5% Other groups, 12.4% German, 9.6% Irish, 7.1% English (2000).
Economy: Employment by occupation: 9.5% management, 13.2% professional, 22.4% services, 18.9% sales, 0.0% farming, 11.8% construction, 24.1% production (2000).
Income: Per capita income: $15,477 (2000); Median household income: $27,448 (2000); Poverty rate: 15.1% (2000).
Taxes: Total city taxes per capita: $169 (1997); City property taxes per capita: $141 (1997).
Education: High school graduation rate: 73.0% (2000); College graduation rate: 8.9% (2000).

School District(s)

Switzerland County School Corp (PK-12)
2000 Enrollment: 1,639 812-427-2611

Housing: Homeownership rate: 58.7% (2000); Median home value: $75,600 (2000); Median rent: $298 per month (2000); Median age of housing: 43 years (2000).
Newspapers: Vevay Reveille Enterprise (1 x week); Switzerland Democrat (1 x week)
Transportation: Commute to work: 88.6% car, 0.3% public transportation, 7.8% walk, 2.0% work from home (2000); Travel time to work: 48.7% less than 15 minutes, 14.0% 15 to 30 minutes, 19.9% 30 to 45 minutes, 7.0% 45 to 60 minutes, 10.5% 60 minutes or more (2000)

Tippecanoe County

Located in west central Indiana; crossed by the Wabash River; drained by the Tippecanoe River. Covers a land area of 499.80 square miles, a water area of 3.30 square miles, and is located in the Eastern Time Zone. The county government was organized in 1826. County seat is Lafayette.

Tippecanoe County is part of the Lafayette, IN MSA. The entire metro area includes: Clinton County; Tippecanoe County

Weather Station: Lafayette 8 S — Elevation: 731 feet

	Jan	Feb	Mar	Apr	May	Jun	Jul	Aug	Sep	Oct	Nov	Dec
High	31	37	48	61	72	81	85	83	77	65	50	37
Low	15	19	29	39	50	59	63	61	53	42	32	22
Precip	1.8	1.7	3.0	3.5	4.1	4.2	4.0	3.7	2.8	2.5	3.0	2.5
Snow	7.5	4.6	2.6	0.7	tr	0.0	0.0	0.0	0.0	0.5	0.8	5.1

High and Low temperatures in degrees Fahrenheit; Precipitation and Snow in inches

Weather Station: West Lafayette 6 NW — Elevation: 702 feet

	Jan	Feb	Mar	Apr	May	Jun	Jul	Aug	Sep	Oct	Nov	Dec
High	31	36	48	60	72	81	84	82	77	64	50	37
Low	15	19	29	39	50	60	63	61	53	42	32	22
Precip	1.8	1.5	2.9	3.8	4.2	4.1	4.0	3.7	3.1	2.8	3.1	2.4
Snow	7.4	4.8	2.4	0.7	0.0	0.0	0.0	0.0	0.0	0.2	1.0	5.0

High and Low temperatures in degrees Fahrenheit; Precipitation and Snow in inches

Weather Station: West Lafayette Purdue Univ. Arpt. — Elevation: 597 feet

	Jan	Feb	Mar	Apr	May	Jun	Jul	Aug	Sep	Oct	Nov	Dec
High	32	37	49	62	73	83	86	84	77	65	50	38
Low	16	20	31	40	50	60	64	63	55	43	34	24
Precip	1.7	1.5	3.0	3.7	3.8	4.1	3.9	3.9	2.9	2.4	3.0	2.5
Snow	7.2	4.8	2.1	0.6	tr	0.0	0.0	0.0	0.0	0.3	0.9	5.7

High and Low temperatures in degrees Fahrenheit; Precipitation and Snow in inches

Population: 148,955 (2000); Race: 88.9% White, 2.3% Black, 4.5% Asian, 0.4% American Indian and Alaska Native, 5.2% Hispanic of any race, 1.6% two or more races (2000); Density: 298.0 persons per square mile (2000); Age: 20.9% under 18, 9.0% over 64 (2000).

Religion: Five largest groups: 13.1% Catholic Church, 4.0% The United Methodist Church, 2.8% Presbyterian Church (U.S.A.), 1.8% Lutheran Church—Missouri Synod, 1.3% Independent, Charismatic Churches (2000).
Economy: Unemployment rate: 3.8% (11/2002); Total civilian labor force: 78,820 (11/2002); Leading industries: 27.2% manufacturing; 15.4% retail trade; 11.2% health care and social assistance (2000); Companies that employ more than 1,000 persons: 10 (2000); Companies that employ more than 100 persons: 93 (2000); Farms: 665 totaling 241,539 acres (1997); Minority business ownership rate: 5.2% (1997); Women business ownership rate: 29.7% (1997); Retail sales per capita: $10,682 (1997). Single-family building permits issued: 835 (2001) / 769 (2000); Multi-family building permits issued: 641 (2001) / 941 (2000).
Income: Per capita income: $19,375 (2000); Median household income: $38,652 (2000); Poverty rate: 15.4% (2000); Bankruptcy rate: 5.33% (2001).
Taxes: Total county taxes per capita: $110 (2000); County property taxes per capita: $61 (2000).
Education: High school graduation rate: 87.8% (2000); College graduation rate: 33.2% (2000).
Housing: Homeownership rate: 55.9% (2000); Median home value: $112,200 (2000); Median rent: $500 per month (2000); Median age of housing: 29 years (2000).
Health: Birth rate: 119.1 per 10,000 population (1998); Age adjusted death rate: 97.8 per 10,000 population (1999); Age adjusted cancer mortality rate: 236.6 deaths per 100,000 population (1999). Number of physicians: 21.9 per 10,000 population (1999); Number of hospital beds: 32.8 per 10,000 population (1999).
Elections: 2000 Presidential election results: 39.4% Gore, 56.4% Bush, 2.3% Nader, 0.9% Buchanan
Additional Information Contacts
Tippecanoe County Government Offices.................. 765-423-9326
Lafayette Chamber of Commerce 765-742-4041
Lafayette Convention & Visitors Bureau.................. 765-447-9999
Lafayette Regional Association of Realtors................ 765-429-5411
Small Business Development Center 765-742-2394

Tippecanoe County Communities

BATTLE GROUND (town). Covers a land area of 1.148 square miles and a water area of 0 square miles. Located at 40.50° N. Lat.; 86.84° W. Long. Elevation is 575 feet.
History: A memorial park marks scene of the Battle of Tippecanoe (1811) between Native Americans and U.S. soldiers under Gen. W. H. Harrison.
Population: 1,323 (2000); Race: 97.8% White, 0.3% Black, 0.7% Asian, 0.2% American Indian and Alaska Native, 1.0% Hispanic of any race, 0.6% two or more races (2000); Density: 1,152.5 persons per square mile (2000); Age: 38.3% under 18, 4.2% over 64 (2000); Marriage status: 22.4% never married, 62.5% now married, 3.6% widowed, 11.5% divorced (2000); Foreign born: 1.0% (2000); Ancestry (includes multiple ancestries): 34.7% German, 16.6% Irish, 11.5% English, 8.1% Other groups, 7.3% United States or American (2000).
Economy: Employment by occupation: 14.3% management, 21.2% professional, 17.7% services, 20.5% sales, 0.9% farming, 7.1% construction, 18.3% production (2000).
Income: Per capita income: $18,012 (2000); Median household income: $52,857 (2000); Poverty rate: 5.0% (2000).
Taxes: Total city taxes per capita: $135 (1997); City property taxes per capita: $106 (1997).
Education: High school graduation rate: 95.1% (2000); College graduation rate: 30.2% (2000).
Housing: Homeownership rate: 85.7% (2000); Median home value: $101,800 (2000); Median rent: $430 per month (2000); Median age of housing: 27 years (2000).
Transportation: Commute to work: 94.4% car, 0.0% public transportation, 2.0% walk, 3.3% work from home (2000); Travel time to work: 23.8% less than 15 minutes, 60.2% 15 to 30 minutes, 11.0% 30 to 45 minutes, 1.9% 45 to 60 minutes, 3.1% 60 minutes or more (2000)

CLARKS HILL (town). Covers a land area of 0.275 square miles and a water area of 0 square miles. Located at 40.24° N. Lat.; 86.72° W. Long. Elevation is 826 feet.
Population: 680 (2000); Race: 99.7% White, 0.0% Black, 0.3% Asian, 0.0% American Indian and Alaska Native, 0.0% Hispanic of any race, 0.0% two or more races (2000); Density: 2,474.5 persons per square mile (2000); Age: 37.6% under 18, 9.4% over 64 (2000); Marriage status: 15.3% never married, 69.4% now married, 4.3% widowed, 11.1% divorced (2000); Foreign born: 0.6% (2000); Ancestry (includes multiple ancestries): 29.0% United States or American, 13.1% Irish, 8.4% German, 7.1% Other groups, 4.8% English (2000).
Economy: Agricultural area. Employment by occupation: 3.8% management, 7.2% professional, 19.2% services, 18.5% sales, 1.4% farming, 17.5% construction, 32.5% production (2000).
Income: Per capita income: $12,773 (2000); Median household income: $35,893 (2000); Poverty rate: 10.1% (2000).
Taxes: Total city taxes per capita: $63 (1997); City property taxes per capita: $45 (1997).
Education: High school graduation rate: 71.0% (2000); College graduation rate: 3.1% (2000).
Housing: Homeownership rate: 77.0% (2000); Median home value: $76,500 (2000); Median rent: $380 per month (2000); Median age of housing: 43 years (2000).
Transportation: Commute to work: 98.6% car, 0.0% public transportation, 0.7% walk, 0.7% work from home (2000); Travel time to work: 9.9% less than 15 minutes, 56.0% 15 to 30 minutes, 22.3% 30 to 45 minutes, 4.3% 45 to 60 minutes, 7.4% 60 minutes or more (2000)

DAYTON (town). Covers a land area of 1.038 square miles and a water area of 0 square miles. Located at 40.37° N. Lat.; 86.76° W. Long. Elevation is 673 feet.
Population: 1,120 (2000); Race: 96.7% White, 0.3% Black, 0.0% Asian, 0.5% American Indian and Alaska Native, 3.3% Hispanic of any race, 0.8% two or more races (2000); Density: 1,079.2 persons per square mile (2000); Age: 33.9% under 18, 7.4% over 64 (2000); Marriage status: 22.5% never married, 59.7% now married, 4.1% widowed, 13.8% divorced (2000); Foreign born: 0.8% (2000); Ancestry (includes multiple ancestries): 25.1% German, 14.4% United States or American, 9.2% Irish, 8.6% Other groups, 5.9% English (2000).
Economy: Corn, wheat, cattle. Employment by occupation: 8.9% management, 13.1% professional, 12.9% services, 26.4% sales, 0.4% farming, 8.9% construction, 29.5% production (2000).
Income: Per capita income: $17,401 (2000); Median household income: $44,792 (2000); Poverty rate: 7.9% (2000).
Taxes: Total city taxes per capita: $100 (1997); City property taxes per capita: $71 (1997).
Education: High school graduation rate: 88.5% (2000); College graduation rate: 15.8% (2000).
Housing: Homeownership rate: 74.6% (2000); Median home value: $93,800 (2000); Median rent: $446 per month (2000); Median age of housing: 25 years (2000).
Transportation: Commute to work: 95.2% car, 0.0% public transportation, 1.9% walk, 2.0% work from home (2000); Travel time to work: 35.2% less than 15 minutes, 50.0% 15 to 30 minutes, 10.6% 30 to 45 minutes, 2.3% 45 to 60 minutes, 1.9% 60 minutes or more (2000)

LAFAYETTE (city). Covers a land area of 20.095 square miles and a water area of 0 square miles. Located at 40.41° N. Lat.; 86.87° W. Long. Elevation is 567 feet.
History: Lafayette was founded in 1824 by William Digby, and named for the Marquis de Lafayette. Lafayette was an early shipping center along the Wabash River. It was from Lafayette that the balloon carrying the first airmail in the U.S. was launched. The flight failed to reach its destination and the mail continued on by train.
Population: 56,397 (2000); Race: 89.1% White, 2.5% Black, 1.5% Asian, 0.5% American Indian and Alaska Native, 9.4% Hispanic of any race, 2.0% two or more races (2000); Density: 2,806.5 persons per square mile (2000); Age: 23.1% under 18, 12.1% over 64 (2000); Marriage status: 30.6% never married, 50.9% now married, 6.5% widowed, 12.1% divorced (2000); Foreign born: 7.9% (2000); Ancestry (includes multiple ancestries): 21.7% German, 17.5% Other groups, 11.7% United States or American, 11.5% Irish, 9.3% English (2000).
Vital Statistics: Birth rate: 174.0 per 10,000 population (1998)
Economy: Unemployment rate: 3.7% (11/2002); Total civilian labor force: 27,978 (11/2002); Single-family building permits issued: 266 (2001) / 262 (2000); Multi-family building permits issued: 90 (2001) / 321 (2000); Employment by occupation: 9.0% management, 20.8% professional, 16.7% services, 24.1% sales, 0.3% farming, 8.0% construction, 21.2% production (2000).
Income: Per capita income: $19,217 (2000); Median household income: $35,859 (2000); Poverty rate: 12.1% (2000).
Taxes: Total city taxes per capita: $328 (2000); City property taxes per capita: $264 (2000).

Education: High school graduation rate: 83.1% (2000); College graduation rate: 23.7% (2000).

School District(s)

Lafayette School Corporation (KG-12)
2000 Enrollment: 7,405 765-771-6000
Tippecanoe School Corp (KG-12)
2000 Enrollment: 9,711 765-474-2481

Two-year College(s)

Ivy Tech State College-Lafayette (Public)
2001 Enrollment: 4,143 765-772-9100
2001 Tuition: In-state $1,986; Out-of-state $4,029
Indiana Business College (Private, For-profit)
2001 Enrollment: 155 765-447-9550
2001 Tuition: In-state $8,460; Out-of-state $8,460
Saint Elizabeth School of Nursing (Private, Not-for-profit)
2001 Enrollment: 108 765-423-6400
2001 Tuition: In-state $9,940; Out-of-state $9,940

Housing: Homeownership rate: 52.6% (2000); Median home value: $89,700 (2000); Median rent: $491 per month (2000); Median age of housing: 37 years (2000).

Hospitals: Lafayette Home Hospital (365 beds); Saint Elizabeth Medical Center (375 beds); Wabash Valley Hospital

Safety: Violent crime rate: 23.1 per 10,000 population; Property crime rate: 479.4 per 10,000 population (2001).

Newspapers: Journal and Courier (7 x week); The Catholic Moment (1 x week); Lafayette Leader (1 x week)

Transportation: Commute to work: 92.3% car, 1.8% public transportation, 2.4% walk, 2.2% work from home (2000); Travel time to work: 51.7% less than 15 minutes, 36.4% 15 to 30 minutes, 6.1% 30 to 45 minutes, 1.7% 45 to 60 minutes, 4.2% 60 minutes or more (2000); Amtrak: Service available.

Airports: Purdue University (primary service)

Additional Information Contacts

Lafayette Chamber of Commerce 765-742-4041
Lafayette Convention & Visitors Bureau. 765-447-9999
Lafayette Regional Association of Realtors. 765-429-5411
Small Business Development Center. 765-742-2394

ROMNEY (unincorporated postal area, zip code 47981). Covers a land area of 38.107 square miles and a water area of 0 square miles. Located at 40.24° N. Lat.; 86.91° W. Long. Elevation is 733 feet.

History: Founded c.1831.

Population: 786 (2000); Race: 100.0% White, 0.0% Black, 0.0% Asian, 0.0% American Indian and Alaska Native, 0.0% Hispanic of any race, 0.0% two or more races (2000); Density: 20.6 persons per square mile (2000); Age: 34.4% under 18, 12.3% over 64 (2000); Marriage status: 11.9% never married, 66.2% now married, 9.8% widowed, 12.1% divorced (2000); Foreign born: 0.0% (2000); Ancestry (includes multiple ancestries): 22.2% United States or American, 20.7% English, 12.4% German, 11.2% Scottish, 7.0% Dutch (2000).

Economy: In agricultural area: corn, soybeans; livestock. Manufacturing: popcorn; wheat-, soybean-seed improvement. Employment by occupation: 16.3% management, 12.5% professional, 16.9% services, 18.7% sales, 0.0% farming, 10.8% construction, 24.8% production (2000).

Income: Per capita income: $19,936 (2000); Median household income: $46,932 (2000); Poverty rate: 1.7% (2000).

Education: High school graduation rate: 90.5% (2000); College graduation rate: 17.9% (2000).

Housing: Homeownership rate: 75.0% (2000); Median home value: $113,700 (2000); Median rent: $368 per month (2000); Median age of housing: 43 years (2000).

Transportation: Commute to work: 84.5% car, 0.0% public transportation, 5.5% walk, 7.6% work from home (2000); Travel time to work: 22.1% less than 15 minutes, 41.6% 15 to 30 minutes, 34.4% 30 to 45 minutes, 1.9% 45 to 60 minutes, 0.0% 60 minutes or more (2000)

SHADELAND (town). Covers a land area of 27.132 square miles and a water area of 0.232 square miles. Located at 40.36° N. Lat.; 86.94° W. Long. Elevation is 622 feet.

History: Laid out 1824.

Population: 1,682 (2000); Race: 98.8% White, 0.3% Black, 0.3% Asian, 0.0% American Indian and Alaska Native, 2.2% Hispanic of any race, 0.2% two or more races (2000); Density: 62.0 persons per square mile (2000); Age: 25.9% under 18, 8.7% over 64 (2000); Marriage status: 26.2% never married, 64.3% now married, 3.9% widowed, 5.5% divorced (2000); Foreign born: 0.9% (2000); Ancestry (includes multiple ancestries): 25.7% German, 13.9% United States or American, 12.3% English, 10.4% Irish, 6.0% Dutch (2000).

Economy: Agricultural area. Employment by occupation: 10.4% management, 15.2% professional, 14.9% services, 26.8% sales, 1.3% farming, 13.5% construction, 17.8% production (2000).

Income: Per capita income: $20,631 (2000); Median household income: $48,750 (2000); Poverty rate: 3.1% (2000).

Taxes: Total city taxes per capita: $114 (1997); City property taxes per capita: $114 (1997).

Education: High school graduation rate: 83.5% (2000); College graduation rate: 17.1% (2000).

Housing: Homeownership rate: 84.9% (2000); Median home value: $120,700 (2000); Median rent: $438 per month (2000); Median age of housing: 32 years (2000).

Transportation: Commute to work: 92.3% car, 1.0% public transportation, 0.7% walk, 4.3% work from home (2000); Travel time to work: 22.1% less than 15 minutes, 60.1% 15 to 30 minutes, 13.3% 30 to 45 minutes, 2.5% 45 to 60 minutes, 1.9% 60 minutes or more (2000)

WEST LAFAYETTE (city). Covers a land area of 5.513 square miles and a water area of 0.010 square miles. Located at 40.44° N. Lat.; 86.91° W. Long. Elevation is 617 feet.

History: Purdue University was founded in 1874 in West Lafayette.

Population: 28,778 (2000); Race: 83.7% White, 2.6% Black, 10.9% Asian, 0.2% American Indian and Alaska Native, 2.7% Hispanic of any race, 1.6% two or more races (2000); Density: 5,219.6 persons per square mile (2000); Age: 10.3% under 18, 7.8% over 64 (2000); Marriage status: 62.5% never married, 31.6% now married, 3.1% widowed, 2.8% divorced (2000); Foreign born: 13.3% (2000); Ancestry (includes multiple ancestries): 26.7% German, 17.0% Other groups, 12.2% Irish, 11.5% English, 5.9% Polish (2000).

Vital Statistics: Birth rate: 110.2 per 10,000 population (1998)

Economy: Unemployment rate: 4.9% (11/2002); Total civilian labor force: 14,817 (11/2002); Single-family building permits issued: 24 (2001) / 40 (2000); Multi-family building permits issued: 485 (2001) / 18 (2000); Employment by occupation: 9.7% management, 43.0% professional, 16.9% services, 20.6% sales, 1.1% farming, 2.6% construction, 6.0% production (2000).

Income: Per capita income: $18,337 (2000); Median household income: $24,869 (2000); Poverty rate: 38.3% (2000).

Taxes: Total city taxes per capita: $246 (1997); City property taxes per capita: $171 (1997).

Education: High school graduation rate: 96.2% (2000); College graduation rate: 69.7% (2000).

School District(s)

West Lafayette Com School Corp (KG-12)
2000 Enrollment: 1,876 765-746-1641

Four-year College(s)

Purdue University-Main Campus (Public)
2001 Enrollment: 39,882 765-494-4600
2001 Tuition: In-state $3,830; Out-of-state $13,538

Housing: Homeownership rate: 32.9% (2000); Median home value: $145,400 (2000); Median rent: $542 per month (2000); Median age of housing: 25 years (2000).

Safety: Violent crime rate: 13.1 per 10,000 population; Property crime rate: 193.2 per 10,000 population (2001).

Newspapers: The Purdue Exponent (5 x week)

Transportation: Commute to work: 74.0% car, 1.9% public transportation, 19.3% walk, 2.7% work from home (2000); Travel time to work: 62.1% less than 15 minutes, 29.9% 15 to 30 minutes, 4.1% 30 to 45 minutes, 1.3% 45 to 60 minutes, 2.6% 60 minutes or more (2000)

WESTPOINT (unincorporated postal area, zip code 47992). Aka West Point. Covers a land area of 36.562 square miles and a water area of 0.162 square miles. Located at 40.31° N. Lat.; 87.04° W. Long. Elevation is 670 feet.

History: The community of Westpoint was laid out in 1833 as a stagecoach stop between Lafayette and Attica.

Population: 1,328 (2000); Race: 96.9% White, 2.6% Black, 0.0% Asian, 0.0% American Indian and Alaska Native, 0.4% Hispanic of any race, 0.5% two or more races (2000); Density: 36.3 persons per square mile (2000); Age: 28.4% under 18, 14.2% over 64 (2000); Marriage status: 17.5% never married, 67.5% now married, 4.8% widowed, 10.2% divorced (2000); Foreign born: 0.0% (2000); Ancestry (includes multiple ancestries): 21.5% German, 12.3% Other groups, 11.8% Irish, 9.8% English, 9.4% United States or American (2000).

Economy: Employment by occupation: 6.1% management, 14.7% professional, 15.6% services, 29.2% sales, 2.2% farming, 9.3% construction, 22.9% production (2000).

Income: Per capita income: $22,300 (2000); Median household income: $58,611 (2000); Poverty rate: 1.6% (2000).
Education: High school graduation rate: 87.1% (2000); College graduation rate: 16.9% (2000).
Housing: Homeownership rate: 91.9% (2000); Median home value: $96,000 (2000); Median rent: $454 per month (2000); Median age of housing: 39 years (2000).
Transportation: Commute to work: 94.0% car, 0.0% public transportation, 0.0% walk, 6.0% work from home (2000); Travel time to work: 6.8% less than 15 minutes, 52.8% 15 to 30 minutes, 31.0% 30 to 45 minutes, 2.8% 45 to 60 minutes, 6.6% 60 minutes or more (2000)

Tipton County

Located in central Indiana; drained by Cicero and Turkey Creeks. Covers a land area of 260.40 square miles, a water area of 0 square miles, and is located in the Eastern Time Zone. The county government was organized in 1844. County seat is Tipton.

Tipton County is part of the Kokomo, IN MSA. The entire metro area includes: Howard County; Tipton County

Population: 16,577 (2000); Race: 98.2% White, 0.0% Black, 0.6% Asian, 0.2% American Indian and Alaska Native, 0.8% Hispanic of any race, 0.7% two or more races (2000); Density: 63.7 persons per square mile (2000); Age: 25.0% under 18, 14.6% over 64 (2000).
Religion: Five largest groups: 9.2% Catholic Church, 8.8% Christian Churches and Churches of Christ, 6.8% Christian Church (Disciples of Christ), 4.8% The United Methodist Church, 3.5% The Wesleyan Church (2000).
Economy: Unemployment rate: 4.3% (11/2002); Total civilian labor force: 8,487 (11/2002); Leading industries: 29.1% manufacturing; 15.9% health care and social assistance; 13.6% retail trade (2000); Companies that employ more than 1,000 persons: 0 (2000); Companies that employ more than 100 persons: 5 (2000); Farms: 415 totaling 158,440 acres (1997); Minority business ownership rate: 0.0% (1997); Women business ownership rate: 15.7% (1997); Retail sales per capita: $7,189 (1997). Single-family building permits issued: 46 (2001) / 53 (2000); Multi-family building permits issued: 0 (2001) / 0 (2000).
Income: Per capita income: $21,926 (2000); Median household income: $48,546 (2000); Poverty rate: 5.1% (2000); Bankruptcy rate: 7.03% (2001).
Taxes: Total county taxes per capita: $263 (2000); County property taxes per capita: $143 (2000).
Education: High school graduation rate: 83.7% (2000); College graduation rate: 12.4% (2000).
Housing: Homeownership rate: 79.9% (2000); Median home value: $88,300 (2000); Median rent: $396 per month (2000); Median age of housing: 41 years (2000).
Health: Birth rate: 122.5 per 10,000 population (1998); Age adjusted death rate: 84.7 per 10,000 population (1999); Age adjusted cancer mortality rate: 194.7 deaths per 100,000 population (1999). Number of physicians: 7.8 per 10,000 population (1999); Number of hospital beds: 61.5 per 10,000 population (1999).
Elections: 2000 Presidential election results: 32.7% Gore, 65.4% Bush, 0.1% Nader, 1.1% Buchanan

Additional Information Contacts

Tipton County Government Offices. 765-675-2794
Tipton County Chamber of Commerce 765-675-7533
Tipton County Economic Development. 765-675-7417

Tipton County Communities

KEMPTON (town). Covers a land area of 0.163 square miles and a water area of 0 square miles. Located at 40.28° N. Lat.; 86.23° W. Long. Elevation is 928 feet.
Population: 380 (2000); Race: 98.7% White, 0.0% Black, 0.0% Asian, 0.0% American Indian and Alaska Native, 1.8% Hispanic of any race, 0.5% two or more races (2000); Density: 2,335.8 persons per square mile (2000); Age: 29.5% under 18, 15.6% over 64 (2000); Marriage status: 19.4% never married, 65.1% now married, 5.3% widowed, 10.2% divorced (2000); Foreign born: 0.8% (2000); Ancestry (includes multiple ancestries): 19.6% German, 15.1% United States or American, 7.8% English, 6.3% Other groups, 5.5% Irish (2000).
Economy: In agricultural area. Single-family building permits issued: 1 (2001) / 1 (2000); Multi-family building permits issued: 0 (2001) / 0 (2000); Employment by occupation: 3.1% management, 13.0% professional, 12.4% services, 13.7% sales, 2.5% farming, 12.4% construction, 42.9% production (2000).
Income: Per capita income: $15,620 (2000); Median household income: $40,625 (2000); Poverty rate: 4.5% (2000).
Taxes: Total city taxes per capita: $79 (1997); City property taxes per capita: $79 (1997).
Education: High school graduation rate: 78.8% (2000); College graduation rate: 5.5% (2000).
Housing: Homeownership rate: 85.7% (2000); Median home value: $66,800 (2000); Median rent: $320 per month (2000); Median age of housing: 60+ years (2000).
Transportation: Commute to work: 96.9% car, 0.0% public transportation, 1.3% walk, 0.6% work from home (2000); Travel time to work: 9.5% less than 15 minutes, 41.1% 15 to 30 minutes, 22.8% 30 to 45 minutes, 12.0% 45 to 60 minutes, 14.6% 60 minutes or more (2000)

SHARPSVILLE (town). Covers a land area of 0.221 square miles and a water area of 0 square miles. Located at 40.37° N. Lat.; 86.08° W. Long. Elevation is 881 feet.
History: Laid out 1850.
Population: 618 (2000); Race: 98.1% White, 0.2% Black, 0.0% Asian, 0.7% American Indian and Alaska Native, 2.7% Hispanic of any race, 0.0% two or more races (2000); Density: 2,795.4 persons per square mile (2000); Age: 25.3% under 18, 12.5% over 64 (2000); Marriage status: 20.3% never married, 63.4% now married, 7.3% widowed, 9.1% divorced (2000); Foreign born: 1.2% (2000); Ancestry (includes multiple ancestries): 18.6% United States or American, 17.4% German, 11.3% English, 7.9% Other groups, 5.8% Irish (2000).
Economy: Agricultural area. Manufacturing: commercial seeds; meat processing. Employment by occupation: 6.3% management, 9.3% professional, 13.8% services, 22.7% sales, 0.0% farming, 10.8% construction, 37.2% production (2000).
Income: Per capita income: $22,480 (2000); Median household income: $52,292 (2000); Poverty rate: 2.8% (2000).
Taxes: Total city taxes per capita: $86 (1997); City property taxes per capita: $81 (1997).
Education: High school graduation rate: 79.6% (2000); College graduation rate: 7.3% (2000).

School District(s)

Northern Com Sch Tipton Co (KG-12)
2000 Enrollment: 1,044 765-963-2585

Housing: Homeownership rate: 88.4% (2000); Median home value: $74,200 (2000); Median rent: $438 per month (2000); Median age of housing: 49 years (2000).
Transportation: Commute to work: 98.1% car, 0.0% public transportation, 0.0% walk, 1.9% work from home (2000); Travel time to work: 28.2% less than 15 minutes, 50.2% 15 to 30 minutes, 11.2% 30 to 45 minutes, 8.1% 45 to 60 minutes, 2.3% 60 minutes or more (2000)

TIPTON (city). Covers a land area of 1.852 square miles and a water area of 0 square miles. Located at 40.28° N. Lat.; 86.04° W. Long. Elevation is 864 feet.
History: Laid out 1839.
Population: 5,251 (2000); Race: 97.8% White, 0.0% Black, 1.0% Asian, 0.4% American Indian and Alaska Native, 0.0% Hispanic of any race, 0.8% two or more races (2000); Density: 2,834.9 persons per square mile (2000); Age: 22.9% under 18, 18.6% over 64 (2000); Marriage status: 18.4% never married, 55.5% now married, 12.2% widowed, 13.9% divorced (2000); Foreign born: 1.2% (2000); Ancestry (includes multiple ancestries): 26.9% United States or American, 16.3% German, 10.0% English, 8.8% Irish, 6.0% Other groups (2000).
Economy: In agricultural area: grain; livestock. Manufacturing: sheet metal fabricating, hybrid corn and soybean seeds, fiberglass boats, packaged meats, motor vehicle stampings. Single-family building permits issued: 15 (2001) / 21 (2000); Multi-family building permits issued: 0 (2001) / 0 (2000); Employment by occupation: 8.6% management, 10.1% professional, 22.7% services, 22.2% sales, 1.5% farming, 12.1% construction, 22.8% production (2000).
Income: Per capita income: $19,489 (2000); Median household income: $34,075 (2000); Poverty rate: 7.2% (2000).
Taxes: Total city taxes per capita: $279 (2000); City property taxes per capita: $276 (2000).
Education: High school graduation rate: 77.8% (2000); College graduation rate: 10.8% (2000).

School District(s)
Tipton Community School Corp (KG-12)
2000 Enrollment: 1,856 765-675-2147
Housing: Homeownership rate: 69.9% (2000); Median home value: $73,200 (2000); Median rent: $401 per month (2000); Median age of housing: 51 years (2000).
Hospitals: Tipton County Memorial Hospital (136 beds)
Safety: Violent crime rate: 7.6 per 10,000 population; Property crime rate: 337.1 per 10,000 population (2001).
Newspapers: Tipton County Tribune (6 x week)
Transportation: Commute to work: 95.4% car, 0.0% public transportation, 3.3% walk, 0.8% work from home (2000); Travel time to work: 46.5% less than 15 minutes, 23.4% 15 to 30 minutes, 20.8% 30 to 45 minutes, 7.8% 45 to 60 minutes, 1.6% 60 minutes or more (2000)
Additional Information Contacts
Tipton County Chamber of Commerce 765-675-7533
Tipton County Economic Development. 765-675-7417

WINDFALL CITY (town). Aka Windfall. Covers a land area of 0.291 square miles and a water area of 0 square miles. Located at 40.36° N. Lat.; 85.95° W. Long.
Population: 712 (2000); Race: 98.0% White, 0.0% Black, 0.4% Asian, 0.0% American Indian and Alaska Native, 0.7% Hispanic of any race, 1.6% two or more races (2000); Density: 2,444.3 persons per square mile (2000); Age: 23.0% under 18, 14.7% over 64 (2000); Marriage status: 15.8% never married, 68.3% now married, 9.2% widowed, 6.7% divorced (2000); Foreign born: 0.0% (2000); Ancestry (includes multiple ancestries): 16.6% United States or American, 14.0% German, 10.2% Other groups, 8.0% Irish, 6.0% English (2000).
Economy: Single-family building permits issued: 2 (2001) / 2 (2000); Multi-family building permits issued: 0 (2001) / 0 (2000); Employment by occupation: 7.0% management, 9.3% professional, 16.8% services, 17.4% sales, 0.0% farming, 11.3% construction, 38.3% production (2000).
Income: Per capita income: $18,948 (2000); Median household income: $40,000 (2000); Poverty rate: 9.7% (2000).
Taxes: Total city taxes per capita: $98 (1997); City property taxes per capita: $98 (1997).
Education: High school graduation rate: 71.1% (2000); College graduation rate: 3.8% (2000).
Housing: Homeownership rate: 76.9% (2000); Median home value: $60,500 (2000); Median rent: $336 per month (2000); Median age of housing: 45 years (2000).
Transportation: Commute to work: 97.1% car, 0.0% public transportation, 2.4% walk, 0.0% work from home (2000); Travel time to work: 20.9% less than 15 minutes, 47.9% 15 to 30 minutes, 19.1% 30 to 45 minutes, 7.1% 45 to 60 minutes, 5.0% 60 minutes or more (2000)

Union County

Located in eastern Indiana; bounded on the east by Ohio; drained by the East Fork of the Whitewater River. Covers a land area of 161.50 square miles, a water area of 3.70 square miles, and is located in the Eastern Time Zone. The county government was organized in 1821. County seat is Liberty.
Population: 7,349 (2000); Race: 98.6% White, 0.4% Black, 0.4% Asian, 0.2% American Indian and Alaska Native, 0.1% Hispanic of any race, 0.4% two or more races (2000); Density: 45.5 persons per square mile (2000); Age: 27.2% under 18, 12.9% over 64 (2000).
Religion: Five largest groups: 11.6% The United Methodist Church, 8.3% Catholic Church, 6.3% Christian Churches and Churches of Christ, 3.4% New Testament Association of Independent Baptist Churches and other Fundamental Baptist Associations, 3.1%
Economy: Unemployment rate: 3.8% (11/2002); Total civilian labor force: 3,632 (11/2002); Leading industries: 22.8% retail trade; 10.9% finance & insurance; 10.6% wholesale trade (2000); Companies that employ more than 1,000 persons: 0 (2000); Companies that employ more than 100 persons: 0 (2000); Farms: 268 totaling 82,500 acres (1997); Minority business ownership rate: 0.0% (1997); Women business ownership rate: 22.6% (1997); Retail sales per capita: $3,965 (1997). Single-family building permits issued: 41 (2001) / 39 (2000); Multi-family building permits issued: 2 (2001) / 0 (2000).
Income: Per capita income: $19,549 (2000); Median household income: $36,672 (2000); Poverty rate: 9.7% (2000); Bankruptcy rate: 5.82% (2001).
Taxes: Total county taxes per capita: $272 (1997); County property taxes per capita: $194 (1997).
Education: High school graduation rate: 79.9% (2000); College graduation rate: 11.1% (2000).
Housing: Homeownership rate: 75.0% (2000); Median home value: $82,600 (2000); Median rent: $332 per month (2000); Median age of housing: 38 years (2000).
Health: Birth rate: 130.6 per 10,000 population (1998); Age adjusted death rate: 72.5 per 10,000 population (1999); Age adjusted cancer mortality rate: 135.1 (Unreliable figure as per CDC) deaths per 100,000 population (1999). Number of physicians: 1.4 per 10,000 population (1999); Number of hospital beds: n/a (1999).
Elections: 2000 Presidential election results: 32.8% Gore, 65.0% Bush, 0.4% Nader, 1.1% Buchanan
National and State Parks: Whitewater State Park
Additional Information Contacts
Union County Government Offices 765-458-5464

Union County Communities

BROWNSVILLE (unincorporated postal area, zip code 47325). Covers a land area of 25.762 square miles and a water area of 0 square miles. Located at 39.68° N. Lat.; 85.02° W. Long. Elevation is 790 feet.
Population: 775 (2000); Race: 95.3% White, 0.0% Black, 3.3% Asian, 0.0% American Indian and Alaska Native, 0.0% Hispanic of any race, 1.4% two or more races (2000); Density: 30.1 persons per square mile (2000); Age: 26.1% under 18, 8.0% over 64 (2000); Marriage status: 8.9% never married, 83.8% now married, 0.9% widowed, 6.4% divorced (2000); Foreign born: 1.0% (2000); Ancestry (includes multiple ancestries): 19.4% United States or American, 15.1% German, 9.1% Irish, 8.0% English, 5.0% Other groups (2000).
Economy: Employment by occupation: 18.2% management, 9.5% professional, 12.6% services, 12.3% sales, 0.0% farming, 13.5% construction, 33.8% production (2000).
Income: Per capita income: $43,652 (2000); Median household income: $45,735 (2000); Poverty rate: 14.9% (2000).
Education: High school graduation rate: 75.5% (2000); College graduation rate: 8.9% (2000).
Housing: Homeownership rate: 85.6% (2000); Median home value: $77,400 (2000); Median rent: $313 per month (2000); Median age of housing: 28 years (2000).
Transportation: Commute to work: 93.1% car, 0.0% public transportation, 1.6% walk, 5.3% work from home (2000); Travel time to work: 8.6% less than 15 minutes, 50.0% 15 to 30 minutes, 22.8% 30 to 45 minutes, 9.6% 45 to 60 minutes, 8.9% 60 minutes or more (2000)

LIBERTY (town). Covers a land area of 0.871 square miles and a water area of 0 square miles. Located at 39.63° N. Lat.; 84.92° W. Long. Elevation is 992 feet.
History: Liberty was the home from 1824 to 1843 of Ambrose Burnside who achieved military distinction during the Civil War, and later served as governor of Rhode Island and as a U.S. senator.
Population: 2,061 (2000); Race: 97.8% White, 0.6% Black, 0.0% Asian, 0.6% American Indian and Alaska Native, 0.0% Hispanic of any race, 0.9% two or more races (2000); Density: 2,366.6 persons per square mile (2000); Age: 22.7% under 18, 22.3% over 64 (2000); Marriage status: 20.1% never married, 54.2% now married, 11.4% widowed, 14.3% divorced (2000); Foreign born: 0.8% (2000); Ancestry (includes multiple ancestries): 26.0% United States or American, 13.7% German, 8.0% Irish, 6.9% English, 6.1% Other groups (2000).
Economy: Employment by occupation: 9.6% management, 12.8% professional, 19.5% services, 27.1% sales, 0.0% farming, 11.4% construction, 19.7% production (2000).
Income: Per capita income: $15,440 (2000); Median household income: $30,296 (2000); Poverty rate: 11.0% (2000).
Taxes: Total city taxes per capita: $202 (1997); City property taxes per capita: $182 (1997).
Education: High school graduation rate: 75.2% (2000); College graduation rate: 9.2% (2000).

School District(s)
Union Co/Clg Corner Joint School District (PK-12)
2000 Enrollment: 1,609 765-458-7471
Housing: Homeownership rate: 63.0% (2000); Median home value: $68,200 (2000); Median rent: $325 per month (2000); Median age of housing: 50 years (2000).
Newspapers: Union County Review (1 x week); The Liberty Herald (1 x week)

Transportation: Commute to work: 89.6% car, 0.0% public transportation, 6.3% walk, 2.8% work from home (2000); Travel time to work: 36.9% less than 15 minutes, 39.8% 15 to 30 minutes, 14.9% 30 to 45 minutes, 3.7% 45 to 60 minutes, 4.7% 60 minutes or more (2000)

WEST COLLEGE CORNER (town). Covers a land area of 0.263 square miles and a water area of 0 square miles. Located at 39.56° N. Lat.; 84.81° W. Long. Elevation is 989 feet.
Population: 634 (2000); Race: 96.6% White, 1.2% Black, 0.6% Asian, 0.0% American Indian and Alaska Native, 0.0% Hispanic of any race, 0.0% two or more races (2000); Density: 2,410.4 persons per square mile (2000); Age: 37.6% under 18, 7.4% over 64 (2000); Marriage status: 17.4% never married, 64.5% now married, 6.3% widowed, 11.8% divorced (2000); Foreign born: 0.8% (2000); Ancestry (includes multiple ancestries): 22.6% German, 21.8% United States or American, 15.6% Irish, 10.5% English, 5.1% Other groups (2000).
Economy: Employment by occupation: 6.5% management, 7.8% professional, 24.2% services, 22.9% sales, 0.0% farming, 18.8% construction, 19.8% production (2000).
Income: Per capita income: $13,528 (2000); Median household income: $34,625 (2000); Poverty rate: 16.1% (2000).
Taxes: Total city taxes per capita: $116 (1997); City property taxes per capita: $93 (1997).
Education: High school graduation rate: 75.9% (2000); College graduation rate: 5.4% (2000).
Housing: Homeownership rate: 57.4% (2000); Median home value: $75,000 (2000); Median rent: $321 per month (2000); Median age of housing: 41 years (2000).
Transportation: Commute to work: 91.5% car, 0.0% public transportation, 4.9% walk, 3.5% work from home (2000); Travel time to work: 46.9% less than 15 minutes, 29.7% 15 to 30 minutes, 7.7% 30 to 45 minutes, 4.8% 45 to 60 minutes, 11.0% 60 minutes or more (2000)

Vanderburgh County

Located in southwestern Indiana; bounded on the south by the Ohio River and the Kentucky border; drained by Pigeon Creek. Covers a land area of 234.60 square miles, a water area of 1.20 square miles, and is located in the Central Time Zone. The county government was organized in 1818. County seat is Evansville.

Vanderburgh County is part of the Evansville-Henderson, IN-KY MSA. The entire metro area includes: Posey County, IN; Vanderburgh County, IN; Warrick County, IN; Henderson County, KY

Weather Station: Evansville Museum — Elevation: 377 feet

	Jan	Feb	Mar	Apr	May	Jun	Jul	Aug	Sep	Oct	Nov	Dec
High	40	47	58	69	78	87	90	88	82	70	57	46
Low	24	28	38	47	56	65	69	67	60	48	39	30
Precip	2.8	3.3	4.7	4.7	4.9	3.9	4.2	3.3	3.2	3.1	4.5	3.7
Snow	4.9	3.5	2.6	0.5	tr	0.0	0.0	0.0	0.0	tr	0.3	2.0

High and Low temperatures in degrees Fahrenheit; Precipitation and Snow in inches

Weather Station: Evansville Regional Airport — Elevation: 380 feet

	Jan	Feb	Mar	Apr	May	Jun	Jul	Aug	Sep	Oct	Nov	Dec
High	39	45	56	67	77	86	89	87	81	69	56	45
Low	23	27	36	45	55	64	68	66	58	45	37	28
Precip	2.8	2.9	4.4	4.7	5.0	4.1	3.7	3.1	2.9	3.0	4.1	3.5
Snow	4.7	4.1	2.5	0.4	tr	tr	0.0	0.0	tr	0.2	0.4	2.5

High and Low temperatures in degrees Fahrenheit; Precipitation and Snow in inches

Population: 171,922 (2000); Race: 89.2% White, 7.9% Black, 0.9% Asian, 0.2% American Indian and Alaska Native, 1.0% Hispanic of any race, 1.2% two or more races (2000); Density: 732.9 persons per square mile (2000); Age: 23.1% under 18, 15.3% over 64 (2000).
Religion: Five largest groups: 18.3% Catholic Church, 11.1% Southern Baptist Convention, 4.2% United Church of Christ, 4.1% The United Methodist Church, 1.9% Lutheran Church—Missouri Synod (2000).
Economy: Unemployment rate: 4.2% (11/2002); Total civilian labor force: 91,339 (11/2002); Leading industries: 15.7% manufacturing; 14.8% health care and social assistance; 13.4% retail trade (2000); Companies that employ more than 1,000 persons: 8 (2000); Companies that employ more than 100 persons: 175 (2000); Farms: 271 totaling 72,112 acres (1997); Minority business ownership rate: 6.6% (1997); Women business ownership rate: 23.4% (1997); Retail sales per capita: $13,565 (1997). Single-family building permits issued: 520 (2001) / 566 (2000); Multi-family building permits issued: 17 (2001) / 474 (2000).
Income: Per capita income: $20,655 (2000); Median household income: $36,823 (2000); Poverty rate: 11.2% (2000); Bankruptcy rate: 6.85% (2001).
Taxes: Total county taxes per capita: $502 (2000); County property taxes per capita: $195 (2000).
Education: High school graduation rate: 83.1% (2000); College graduation rate: 19.3% (2000).
Housing: Homeownership rate: 66.8% (2000); Median home value: $82,400 (2000); Median rent: $376 per month (2000); Median age of housing: 41 years (2000).
Health: Birth rate: 132.9 per 10,000 population (1998); Age adjusted death rate: 95.4 per 10,000 population (1999); Age adjusted cancer mortality rate: 216.8 deaths per 100,000 population (1999). Air Quality Index: 75% good, 25% moderate, 0% unhealthy (percent of days in 2000). Number of physicians: 31.6 per 10,000 population (1999); Number of hospital beds: 82.0 per 10,000 population (1999).
Elections: 2000 Presidential election results: 44.1% Gore, 54.1% Bush, 0.6% Nader, 0.7% Buchanan
Additional Information Contacts
Vanderburgh County Government Offices 812-435-5241
Evansville Area Association of Realtors 812-473-3333
Evansville Chamber of Commerce. 812-425-8147

Vanderburgh County Communities

DARMSTADT (town). Covers a land area of 4.721 square miles and a water area of 0.018 square miles. Located at 38.09° N. Lat.; 87.57° W. Long. Elevation is 483 feet.
History: Established 1860.
Population: 1,313 (2000); Race: 99.8% White, 0.2% Black, 0.0% Asian, 0.0% American Indian and Alaska Native, 0.0% Hispanic of any race, 0.0% two or more races (2000); Density: 278.1 persons per square mile (2000); Age: 26.1% under 18, 15.5% over 64 (2000); Marriage status: 18.6% never married, 71.7% now married, 5.0% widowed, 4.7% divorced (2000); Foreign born: 0.0% (2000); Ancestry (includes multiple ancestries): 43.7% German, 13.4% English, 11.6% United States or American, 10.6% Irish, 3.6% French (except Basque) (2000).
Economy: Wheat, corn. Employment by occupation: 16.0% management, 20.1% professional, 13.5% services, 22.7% sales, 0.9% farming, 12.3% construction, 14.5% production (2000).
Income: Per capita income: $31,898 (2000); Median household income: $68,359 (2000); Poverty rate: 1.1% (2000).
Taxes: Total city taxes per capita: $63 (1997); City property taxes per capita: $46 (1997).
Education: High school graduation rate: 93.8% (2000); College graduation rate: 28.2% (2000).
Housing: Homeownership rate: 91.2% (2000); Median home value: $142,100 (2000); Median rent: $431 per month (2000); Median age of housing: 37 years (2000).
Transportation: Commute to work: 94.3% car, 0.3% public transportation, 0.8% walk, 4.3% work from home (2000); Travel time to work: 24.6% less than 15 minutes, 56.8% 15 to 30 minutes, 14.6% 30 to 45 minutes, 3.1% 45 to 60 minutes, 1.0% 60 minutes or more (2000)

EVANSVILLE (city). Covers a land area of 40.704 square miles and a water area of 0.059 square miles. Located at 37.97° N. Lat.; 87.55° W. Long. Elevation is 388 feet.
History: Colonel Hugh McGary established a ferry at this spot on the Ohio River in 1812, and a village called McGary's Ferry grew up around it. McGary sold part of his holdings to General Robert Evans in 1818. When the community was designated as the seat of the new Vanderburgh County, it was named Evansville. The town had a good inland harbor, and soon became a transportation hub. It was chartered as a city in 1848.
Population: 121,582 (2000); Race: 86.2% White, 10.5% Black, 0.9% Asian, 0.2% American Indian and Alaska Native, 1.2% Hispanic of any race, 1.6% two or more races (2000); Density: 2,987.0 persons per square mile (2000); Age: 22.8% under 18, 16.3% over 64 (2000); Marriage status: 26.5% never married, 49.8% now married, 8.4% widowed, 15.3% divorced (2000); Foreign born: 1.6% (2000); Ancestry (includes multiple ancestries): 24.6% German, 15.8% Other groups, 10.7% United States or American, 10.4% Irish, 9.1% English (2000).
Vital Statistics: Birth rate: 163.7 per 10,000 population (1998)
Economy: Unemployment rate: 4.8% (11/2002); Total civilian labor force: 68,457 (11/2002); Single-family building permits issued: 89 (2001) / 135

(2000); Multi-family building permits issued: 8 (2001) / 24 (2000); Employment by occupation: 9.2% management, 15.8% professional, 17.3% services, 28.6% sales, 0.1% farming, 9.0% construction, 19.9% production (2000).
Income: Per capita income: $18,388 (2000); Median household income: $31,963 (2000); Poverty rate: 13.7% (2000).
Taxes: Total city taxes per capita: $337 (2000); City property taxes per capita: $244 (2000).
Education: High school graduation rate: 80.7% (2000); College graduation rate: 16.7% (2000).

School District(s)

Evansville-Vanderburgh Sch Corp (PK-12)
2000 Enrollment: 22,875 812-435-8477

Four-year College(s)

University of Evansville (Private, Not-for-profit, United Methodist)
2001 Enrollment: 2,555 812-479-2468
2001 Tuition: In-state $17,050; Out-of-state $17,050
University of Southern Indiana (Public)
2001 Enrollment: 9,362 812-464-8600
2001 Tuition: In-state $2,774; Out-of-state $6,790

Two-year College(s)

Ivy Tech State College-Southwest (Public)
2001 Enrollment: 4,290 812-426-2865
2001 Tuition: In-state $1,986; Out-of-state $4,029
Indiana Business College (Private, For-profit)
2001 Enrollment: 245 812-476-6000
2001 Tuition: In-state $8,460; Out-of-state $8,460

Housing: Homeownership rate: 59.9% (2000); Median home value: $69,700 (2000); Median rent: $370 per month (2000); Median age of housing: 46 years (2000).
Hospitals: Deaconess Cross Pointe; Deaconess Hospital; Evansville Psychiatric Children Center (28 beds); Evansville State Hospital; HealthSouth Tri-State Rehabilitation Hospital (80 beds); Saint Mary's Medical Center of Evansville (502 beds)
Safety: Violent crime rate: 57.8 per 10,000 population; Property crime rate: 487.5 per 10,000 population (2001).
Newspapers: The Evansville Courier & Press (7 x week); Message (1 x week)
Transportation: Commute to work: 92.5% car, 1.7% public transportation, 3.2% walk, 1.8% work from home (2000); Travel time to work: 43.3% less than 15 minutes, 42.7% 15 to 30 minutes, 8.0% 30 to 45 minutes, 2.3% 45 to 60 minutes, 3.7% 60 minutes or more (2000)
Airports: Evansville Regional (primary service)

Additional Information Contacts

Evansville Area Association of Realtors 812-473-3333
Evansville Chamber of Commerce. 812-425-8147

HIGHLAND (CDP). Covers a land area of 2.300 square miles and a water area of 0.004 square miles. Located at 38.04° N. Lat.; 87.56° W. Long. Elevation is 492 feet.
Population: 4,107 (2000); Race: 97.2% White, 0.4% Black, 1.6% Asian, 0.0% American Indian and Alaska Native, 0.2% Hispanic of any race, 0.8% two or more races (2000); Density: 1,785.3 persons per square mile (2000); Age: 25.0% under 18, 13.2% over 64 (2000); Marriage status: 18.8% never married, 69.8% now married, 5.8% widowed, 5.6% divorced (2000); Foreign born: 2.5% (2000); Ancestry (includes multiple ancestries): 41.7% German, 16.7% Irish, 16.3% English, 12.2% United States or American, 5.4% Other groups (2000).
Economy: Employment by occupation: 15.0% management, 22.3% professional, 8.1% services, 33.9% sales, 0.0% farming, 5.3% construction, 15.4% production (2000).
Income: Per capita income: $36,716 (2000); Median household income: $69,975 (2000); Poverty rate: 0.7% (2000).
Education: High school graduation rate: 93.1% (2000); College graduation rate: 30.5% (2000).
Housing: Homeownership rate: 95.5% (2000); Median home value: $134,800 (2000); Median rent: $595 per month (2000); Median age of housing: 18 years (2000).
Transportation: Commute to work: 98.7% car, 0.0% public transportation, 0.3% walk, 1.1% work from home (2000); Travel time to work: 28.1% less than 15 minutes, 55.2% 15 to 30 minutes, 11.0% 30 to 45 minutes, 3.1% 45 to 60 minutes, 2.6% 60 minutes or more (2000)

MELODY HILL (CDP). Covers a land area of 1.361 square miles and a water area of 0.007 square miles. Located at 38.02° N. Lat.; 87.51° W. Long. Elevation is 430 feet.
Population: 3,066 (2000); Race: 95.8% White, 0.9% Black, 2.7% Asian, 0.0% American Indian and Alaska Native, 0.2% Hispanic of any race, 0.4% two or more races (2000); Density: 2,252.0 persons per square mile (2000); Age: 25.9% under 18, 15.4% over 64 (2000); Marriage status: 16.3% never married, 71.9% now married, 5.4% widowed, 6.5% divorced (2000); Foreign born: 2.8% (2000); Ancestry (includes multiple ancestries): 40.9% German, 14.3% Irish, 12.0% English, 11.1% United States or American, 9.3% Other groups (2000).
Economy: Employment by occupation: 13.5% management, 20.3% professional, 10.5% services, 36.0% sales, 0.6% farming, 2.6% construction, 16.7% production (2000).
Income: Per capita income: $23,880 (2000); Median household income: $60,764 (2000); Poverty rate: 1.1% (2000).
Education: High school graduation rate: 94.8% (2000); College graduation rate: 28.2% (2000).
Housing: Homeownership rate: 95.7% (2000); Median home value: $112,000 (2000); Median rent: $491 per month (2000); Median age of housing: 30 years (2000).
Transportation: Commute to work: 97.6% car, 0.0% public transportation, 0.0% walk, 2.4% work from home (2000); Travel time to work: 43.8% less than 15 minutes, 45.2% 15 to 30 minutes, 6.6% 30 to 45 minutes, 0.6% 45 to 60 minutes, 3.8% 60 minutes or more (2000)

Vermillion County

Located in western Indiana; bounded on the west by Illinois, and on the east by the Wabash River; drained by the Vermilion River. Covers a land area of 256.90 square miles, a water area of 3.00 square miles, and is located in the Eastern Time Zone. The county government was organized in 1824. County seat is Newport.

Vermillion County is part of the Terre Haute, IN MSA. The entire metro area includes: Clay County; Vermillion County; Vigo County

Population: 16,788 (2000); Race: 97.8% White, 0.3% Black, 0.1% Asian, 0.3% American Indian and Alaska Native, 0.9% Hispanic of any race, 1.0% two or more races (2000); Density: 65.4 persons per square mile (2000); Age: 23.8% under 18, 15.9% over 64 (2000).
Religion: Five largest groups: 6.8% Catholic Church, 6.7% The United Methodist Church, 4.9% American Baptist Churches in the USA, 4.0% Christian Churches and Churches of Christ, 2.0% The Church of Jesus Christ of Latter-day Saints (2000).
Economy: Unemployment rate: 5.7% (11/2002); Total civilian labor force: 8,000 (11/2002); Leading industries: 32.1% manufacturing; 13.9% retail trade; 11.0% health care and social assistance (2000); Companies that employ more than 1,000 persons: 1 (2000); Companies that employ more than 100 persons: 10 (2000); Farms: 249 totaling 118,065 acres (1997); Minority business ownership rate: 0.0% (1997); Women business ownership rate: 26.8% (1997); Retail sales per capita: $7,293 (1997). Single-family building permits issued: 37 (2001) / 41 (2000); Multi-family building permits issued: 0 (2001) / 0 (2000).
Income: Per capita income: $18,579 (2000); Median household income: $34,837 (2000); Poverty rate: 9.5% (2000); Bankruptcy rate: 6.40% (2001).
Taxes: Total county taxes per capita: $228 (2000); County property taxes per capita: $211 (2000).
Education: High school graduation rate: 81.2% (2000); College graduation rate: 11.2% (2000).
Housing: Homeownership rate: 79.2% (2000); Median home value: $59,500 (2000); Median rent: $276 per month (2000); Median age of housing: 53 years (2000).
Health: Birth rate: 122.7 per 10,000 population (1998); Age adjusted death rate: 95.5 per 10,000 population (1999); Age adjusted cancer mortality rate: 237.5 deaths per 100,000 population (1999). Number of physicians: 4.2 per 10,000 population (1999); Number of hospital beds: 16.1 per 10,000 population (1999).
Elections: 2000 Presidential election results: 50.8% Gore, 47.2% Bush, 0.2% Nader, 1.2% Buchanan

Additional Information Contacts

Vermillion County Government Offices 765-492-3570
Clinton Chamber of Commerce 765-832-3844

Vermillion County Communities

CAYUGA (town). Covers a land area of 1.002 square miles and a water area of 0 square miles. Located at 39.94° N. Lat.; 87.46° W. Long. Elevation is 511 feet.
Population: 1,109 (2000); Race: 97.7% White, 0.0% Black, 0.2% Asian, 0.6% American Indian and Alaska Native, 0.9% Hispanic of any race, 1.6% two or more races (2000); Density: 1,106.8 persons per square mile (2000); Age: 23.7% under 18, 15.6% over 64 (2000); Marriage status: 19.9% never married, 60.7% now married, 10.3% widowed, 9.1% divorced (2000); Foreign born: 0.2% (2000); Ancestry (includes multiple ancestries): 25.3% United States or American, 13.0% German, 10.7% English, 9.2% Irish, 5.1% Other groups (2000).
Economy: Agricultural and bituminous-coal area. Manufacturing: canned goods, brick, corrugated shipping containers, feeds, ice cream. Electric power plant nearby. Single-family building permits issued: 5 (2001) / 5 (2000); Multi-family building permits issued: 0 (2001) / 0 (2000); Employment by occupation: 4.0% management, 10.6% professional, 19.7% services, 16.5% sales, 0.6% farming, 15.9% construction, 32.7% production (2000).
Income: Per capita income: $16,042 (2000); Median household income: $31,053 (2000); Poverty rate: 9.9% (2000).
Taxes: Total city taxes per capita: $141 (1997); City property taxes per capita: $137 (1997).
Education: High school graduation rate: 79.3% (2000); College graduation rate: 7.1% (2000).

School District(s)

North Vermillion Com Sch Corp (KG-12)
2000 Enrollment: 847 765-492-4033
Housing: Homeownership rate: 90.1% (2000); Median home value: $53,200 (2000); Median rent: $275 per month (2000); Median age of housing: 44 years (2000).
Newspapers: Herald News (1 x week)
Transportation: Commute to work: 94.5% car, 0.0% public transportation, 3.7% walk, 1.4% work from home (2000); Travel time to work: 35.3% less than 15 minutes, 24.0% 15 to 30 minutes, 27.7% 30 to 45 minutes, 8.3% 45 to 60 minutes, 4.8% 60 minutes or more (2000)

CLINTON (city). Covers a land area of 2.244 square miles and a water area of 0.018 square miles. Located at 39.66° N. Lat.; 87.40° W. Long. Elevation is 498 feet.
History: Clinton was laid out along the Wabash River in 1829, and named for DeWitt Clinton (1769-1828), governor of New York. Clinton developed as a coal-mining town.
Population: 5,126 (2000); Race: 97.0% White, 0.3% Black, 0.0% Asian, 0.3% American Indian and Alaska Native, 1.7% Hispanic of any race, 1.5% two or more races (2000); Density: 2,284.5 persons per square mile (2000); Age: 23.0% under 18, 21.2% over 64 (2000); Marriage status: 20.3% never married, 51.7% now married, 15.3% widowed, 12.7% divorced (2000); Foreign born: 1.3% (2000); Ancestry (includes multiple ancestries): 16.5% German, 12.4% Irish, 12.1% English, 11.3% Italian, 10.0% Other groups (2000).
Economy: Single-family building permits issued: 1 (2001) / 1 (2000); Multi-family building permits issued: 0 (2001) / 0 (2000); Employment by occupation: 5.6% management, 13.9% professional, 21.4% services, 22.1% sales, 0.0% farming, 11.4% construction, 25.6% production (2000).
Income: Per capita income: $14,601 (2000); Median household income: $29,330 (2000); Poverty rate: 12.5% (2000).
Taxes: Total city taxes per capita: $101 (1997); City property taxes per capita: $98 (1997).
Education: High school graduation rate: 76.5% (2000); College graduation rate: 10.2% (2000).

School District(s)

South Vermillion Com Sch Corp (KG-12)
2000 Enrollment: 1,948 765-832-2426
Housing: Homeownership rate: 68.8% (2000); Median home value: $51,800 (2000); Median rent: $248 per month (2000); Median age of housing: 60+ years (2000).
Hospitals: West Central Community Hospital (56 beds)
Newspapers: The Daily Clintonian (5 x week)
Transportation: Commute to work: 93.1% car, 0.5% public transportation, 3.0% walk, 2.4% work from home (2000); Travel time to work: 39.4% less than 15 minutes, 36.0% 15 to 30 minutes, 19.0% 30 to 45 minutes, 4.0% 45 to 60 minutes, 1.7% 60 minutes or more (2000)
Additional Information Contacts
Clinton Chamber of Commerce 765-832-3844

DANA (town). Covers a land area of 0.294 square miles and a water area of 0 square miles. Located at 39.80° N. Lat.; 87.49° W. Long. Elevation is 637 feet.
History: Ernie Pyle State Memorial.
Population: 662 (2000); Race: 92.4% White, 3.2% Black, 0.0% Asian, 0.3% American Indian and Alaska Native, 4.0% Hispanic of any race, 1.5% two or more races (2000); Density: 2,255.4 persons per square mile (2000); Age: 33.6% under 18, 12.8% over 64 (2000); Marriage status: 11.3% never married, 69.1% now married, 6.8% widowed, 12.9% divorced (2000); Foreign born: 2.6% (2000); Ancestry (includes multiple ancestries): 26.4% United States or American, 19.8% German, 11.2% Other groups, 8.2% Irish, 7.0% English (2000).
Economy: Single-family building permits issued: 9 (2001) / 9 (2000); Multi-family building permits issued: 0 (2001) / 0 (2000); Employment by occupation: 10.0% management, 10.7% professional, 16.3% services, 19.6% sales, 3.0% farming, 15.2% construction, 25.2% production (2000).
Income: Per capita income: $15,603 (2000); Median household income: $34,750 (2000); Poverty rate: 9.9% (2000).
Taxes: Total city taxes per capita: $253 (1997); City property taxes per capita: $251 (1997).
Education: High school graduation rate: 83.5% (2000); College graduation rate: 5.2% (2000).
Housing: Homeownership rate: 75.1% (2000); Median home value: $50,200 (2000); Median rent: $353 per month (2000); Median age of housing: 60+ years (2000).
Transportation: Commute to work: 91.7% car, 0.0% public transportation, 5.7% walk, 0.8% work from home (2000); Travel time to work: 25.9% less than 15 minutes, 40.7% 15 to 30 minutes, 19.8% 30 to 45 minutes, 10.6% 45 to 60 minutes, 3.0% 60 minutes or more (2000)

FAIRVIEW PARK (town). Covers a land area of 0.905 square miles and a water area of 0 square miles. Located at 39.68° N. Lat.; 87.41° W. Long. Elevation is 572 feet.
History: Laid out 1902.
Population: 1,496 (2000); Race: 98.2% White, 0.1% Black, 0.1% Asian, 0.1% American Indian and Alaska Native, 1.1% Hispanic of any race, 1.3% two or more races (2000); Density: 1,652.4 persons per square mile (2000); Age: 23.7% under 18, 14.7% over 64 (2000); Marriage status: 18.5% never married, 64.5% now married, 5.9% widowed, 11.1% divorced (2000); Foreign born: 0.6% (2000); Ancestry (includes multiple ancestries): 18.6% United States or American, 16.5% German, 11.3% English, 10.6% Italian, 9.3% Irish (2000).
Economy: In agricultural and bituminous-coal area. Employment by occupation: 8.1% management, 14.7% professional, 17.3% services, 28.2% sales, 0.3% farming, 13.2% construction, 18.2% production (2000).
Income: Per capita income: $21,459 (2000); Median household income: $36,078 (2000); Poverty rate: 10.1% (2000).
Taxes: Total city taxes per capita: $45 (1997); City property taxes per capita: $43 (1997).
Education: High school graduation rate: 86.9% (2000); College graduation rate: 11.2% (2000).
Housing: Homeownership rate: 78.3% (2000); Median home value: $78,900 (2000); Median rent: $356 per month (2000); Median age of housing: 29 years (2000).
Transportation: Commute to work: 96.4% car, 0.3% public transportation, 0.9% walk, 2.1% work from home (2000); Travel time to work: 40.6% less than 15 minutes, 31.4% 15 to 30 minutes, 19.5% 30 to 45 minutes, 2.8% 45 to 60 minutes, 5.7% 60 minutes or more (2000)

HILLSDALE (unincorporated postal area, zip code 47854). Covers a land area of 33.968 square miles and a water area of 0.010 square miles. Located at 39.82° N. Lat.; 87.41° W. Long. Elevation is 600 feet.
Population: 961 (2000); Race: 94.2% White, 0.6% Black, 1.2% Asian, 1.8% American Indian and Alaska Native, 0.0% Hispanic of any race, 1.5% two or more races (2000); Density: 28.3 persons per square mile (2000); Age: 25.4% under 18, 10.3% over 64 (2000); Marriage status: 14.2% never married, 67.3% now married, 5.9% widowed, 12.6% divorced (2000); Foreign born: 0.9% (2000); Ancestry (includes multiple ancestries): 18.4% German, 15.0% Other groups, 12.7% United States or American, 11.6% English, 9.1% Irish (2000).
Economy: Corn, wheat; cattle. Employment by occupation: 12.9% management, 9.9% professional, 13.8% services, 16.3% sales, 0.0% farming, 21.1% construction, 26.0% production (2000).
Income: Per capita income: $25,532 (2000); Median household income: $43,542 (2000); Poverty rate: 3.5% (2000).

Education: High school graduation rate: 88.7% (2000); College graduation rate: 12.3% (2000).
Housing: Homeownership rate: 90.2% (2000); Median home value: $72,900 (2000); Median rent: $282 per month (2000); Median age of housing: 35 years (2000).
Transportation: Commute to work: 97.6% car, 0.0% public transportation, 1.7% walk, 0.0% work from home (2000); Travel time to work: 30.6% less than 15 minutes, 29.0% 15 to 30 minutes, 26.4% 30 to 45 minutes, 8.8% 45 to 60 minutes, 5.2% 60 minutes or more (2000)

NEWPORT (town). Covers a land area of 0.809 square miles and a water area of 0 square miles. Located at 39.88° N. Lat.; 87.40° W. Long. Elevation is 498 feet.
Population: 578 (2000); Race: 98.9% White, 0.0% Black, 1.1% Asian, 0.0% American Indian and Alaska Native, 0.0% Hispanic of any race, 0.0% two or more races (2000); Density: 714.8 persons per square mile (2000); Age: 30.0% under 18, 17.2% over 64 (2000); Marriage status: 17.5% never married, 50.1% now married, 14.1% widowed, 18.2% divorced (2000); Foreign born: 0.9% (2000); Ancestry (includes multiple ancestries): 33.6% United States or American, 9.9% German, 4.5% Irish, 4.3% English, 2.5% Other groups (2000).
Economy: Manufacturing: ordnance, chemicals. Corn, wheat; cattle. Single-family building permits issued: 0 (2001) / 0 (2000); Multi-family building permits issued: 0 (2001) / 0 (2000); Employment by occupation: 10.6% management, 5.1% professional, 20.0% services, 22.1% sales, 1.3% farming, 13.2% construction, 27.7% production (2000).
Income: Per capita income: $16,771 (2000); Median household income: $33,571 (2000); Poverty rate: 9.1% (2000).
Taxes: Total city taxes per capita: $52 (1997); City property taxes per capita: $52 (1997).
Education: High school graduation rate: 78.8% (2000); College graduation rate: 4.7% (2000).
Housing: Homeownership rate: 82.7% (2000); Median home value: $44,300 (2000); Median rent: $257 per month (2000); Median age of housing: 57 years (2000).
Transportation: Commute to work: 88.5% car, 0.9% public transportation, 7.5% walk, 1.3% work from home (2000); Travel time to work: 37.7% less than 15 minutes, 29.1% 15 to 30 minutes, 13.5% 30 to 45 minutes, 12.6% 45 to 60 minutes, 7.2% 60 minutes or more (2000)

PERRYSVILLE (town). Covers a land area of 0.252 square miles and a water area of 0 square miles. Located at 40.05° N. Lat.; 87.43° W. Long. Elevation is 542 feet.
Population: 502 (2000); Race: 100.0% White, 0.0% Black, 0.0% Asian, 0.0% American Indian and Alaska Native, 0.0% Hispanic of any race, 0.0% two or more races (2000); Density: 1,995.4 persons per square mile (2000); Age: 22.6% under 18, 17.1% over 64 (2000); Marriage status: 15.6% never married, 61.8% now married, 5.8% widowed, 16.8% divorced (2000); Foreign born: 0.2% (2000); Ancestry (includes multiple ancestries): 22.2% United States or American, 12.8% English, 8.2% German, 6.2% Other groups, 5.4% Dutch (2000).
Economy: Agricultural and bituminous-coal area. Employment by occupation: 8.6% management, 7.8% professional, 16.3% services, 18.8% sales, 0.0% farming, 9.0% construction, 39.6% production (2000).
Income: Per capita income: $15,455 (2000); Median household income: $33,929 (2000); Poverty rate: 9.2% (2000).
Taxes: Total city taxes per capita: $34 (1997); City property taxes per capita: $34 (1997).
Education: High school graduation rate: 78.6% (2000); College graduation rate: 5.3% (2000).
Housing: Homeownership rate: 82.0% (2000); Median home value: $55,700 (2000); Median rent: $277 per month (2000); Median age of housing: 52 years (2000).
Transportation: Commute to work: 95.9% car, 1.2% public transportation, 1.7% walk, 0.4% work from home (2000); Travel time to work: 22.4% less than 15 minutes, 49.0% 15 to 30 minutes, 19.1% 30 to 45 minutes, 5.8% 45 to 60 minutes, 3.7% 60 minutes or more (2000)

UNIVERSAL (town). Covers a land area of 0.284 square miles and a water area of 0 square miles. Located at 39.62° N. Lat.; 87.45° W. Long. Elevation is 482 feet.
History: Laid out 1911.
Population: 419 (2000); Race: 99.3% White, 0.0% Black, 0.0% Asian, 0.7% American Indian and Alaska Native, 0.9% Hispanic of any race, 0.0% two or more races (2000); Density: 1,477.5 persons per square mile (2000); Age: 19.0% under 18, 7.4% over 64 (2000); Marriage status: 23.7% never married, 58.3% now married, 4.2% widowed, 13.8% divorced (2000); Foreign born: 0.0% (2000); Ancestry (includes multiple ancestries): 18.5% German, 12.3% Italian, 10.6% Other groups, 10.2% Irish, 10.2% English (2000).
Economy: In agricultural and bituminous-coal area: surface mines. Employment by occupation: 6.9% management, 15.5% professional, 10.6% services, 22.4% sales, 0.4% farming, 20.4% construction, 23.7% production (2000).
Income: Per capita income: $17,930 (2000); Median household income: $36,042 (2000); Poverty rate: 9.3% (2000).
Taxes: Total city taxes per capita: $15 (1997); City property taxes per capita: $12 (1997).
Education: High school graduation rate: 79.7% (2000); College graduation rate: 4.5% (2000).
Housing: Homeownership rate: 69.3% (2000); Median home value: $45,500 (2000); Median rent: $306 per month (2000); Median age of housing: 60+ years (2000).
Transportation: Commute to work: 100.0% car, 0.0% public transportation, 0.0% walk, 0.0% work from home (2000); Travel time to work: 30.7% less than 15 minutes, 43.7% 15 to 30 minutes, 17.2% 30 to 45 minutes, 5.0% 45 to 60 minutes, 3.4% 60 minutes or more (2000)

Vigo County

Located in western Indiana; bounded on the west by Illinois; crossed by the Wabash River; drained by Honey Creek. Covers a land area of 403.30 square miles, a water area of 7.20 square miles, and is located in the Eastern Time Zone. The county government was organized in 1818. County seat is Terre Haute.

Vigo County is part of the Terre Haute, IN MSA. The entire metro area includes: Clay County; Vermillion County; Vigo County

Weather Station: Terre Haute Indiana State — Elevation: 505 feet

	Jan	Feb	Mar	Apr	May	Jun	Jul	Aug	Sep	Oct	Nov	Dec
High	35	40	52	64	75	83	87	85	79	68	53	41
Low	17	21	32	42	52	61	65	63	55	43	33	23
Precip	2.2	2.5	3.7	4.2	4.4	4.0	4.4	3.8	3.0	2.8	3.7	3.1
Snow	na	na	1.6	tr	0.0	0.0	0.0	0.0	0.0	0.0	0.5	2.2

High and Low temperatures in degrees Fahrenheit; Precipitation and Snow in inches

Population: 105,848 (2000); Race: 90.6% White, 6.1% Black, 1.0% Asian, 0.3% American Indian and Alaska Native, 1.2% Hispanic of any race, 1.6% two or more races (2000); Density: 262.5 persons per square mile (2000); Age: 22.8% under 18, 14.3% over 64 (2000).
Religion: Five largest groups: 8.7% Catholic Church, 4.9% The United Methodist Church, 2.7% Christian Churches and Churches of Christ, 2.3% American Baptist Churches in the USA, 1.7% Assemblies of God (2000).
Economy: Unemployment rate: 5.0% (11/2002); Total civilian labor force: 51,308 (11/2002); Leading industries: 20.3% retail trade; 16.7% manufacturing; 16.0% health care and social assistance (2000); Companies that employ more than 1,000 persons: 2 (2000); Companies that employ more than 100 persons: 78 (2000); Farms: 455 totaling 114,889 acres (1997); Minority business ownership rate: 3.8% (1997); Women business ownership rate: 24.7% (1997); Retail sales per capita: $21,958 (1997). Single-family building permits issued: 328 (2001) / 281 (2000); Multi-family building permits issued: 96 (2001) / 31 (2000).
Income: Per capita income: $17,620 (2000); Median household income: $33,184 (2000); Poverty rate: 14.1% (2000); Bankruptcy rate: 7.21% (2001).
Taxes: Total county taxes per capita: $167 (2000); County property taxes per capita: $156 (2000).
Education: High school graduation rate: 81.0% (2000); College graduation rate: 21.4% (2000).
Housing: Homeownership rate: 67.4% (2000); Median home value: $72,500 (2000); Median rent: $360 per month (2000); Median age of housing: 43 years (2000).
Health: Birth rate: 133.0 per 10,000 population (1998); Age adjusted death rate: 107.7 per 10,000 population (1999); Age adjusted cancer mortality rate: 248.9 deaths per 100,000 population (1999). Air Quality Index: 70% good, 30% moderate, 0% unhealthy (percent of days in 2000). Number of physicians: 25.2 per 10,000 population (1999); Number of hospital beds: 57.9 per 10,000 population (1999).
Elections: 2000 Presidential election results: 48.5% Gore, 49.7% Bush, 0.4% Nader, 0.6% Buchanan

Additional Information Contacts

Vigo County Government Offices 812-462-3367
Terre Haute Area Association of Realtors 812-234-8732

Terre Haute Convention & Visitors Bureau 812-234-5555

Vigo County Communities

LEWIS (unincorporated postal area, zip code 47858). Covers a land area of 37.772 square miles and a water area of 0.039 square miles. Located at 39.25° N. Lat.; 87.23° W. Long. Elevation is 617 feet.
Population: 694 (2000); Race: 96.1% White, 0.0% Black, 0.8% Asian, 0.0% American Indian and Alaska Native, 0.0% Hispanic of any race, 3.2% two or more races (2000); Density: 18.4 persons per square mile (2000); Age: 25.6% under 18, 15.8% over 64 (2000); Marriage status: 14.3% never married, 71.5% now married, 4.7% widowed, 9.4% divorced (2000); Foreign born: 0.8% (2000); Ancestry (includes multiple ancestries): 29.2% German, 14.0% English, 11.3% Irish, 9.2% Other groups, 5.9% Italian (2000).
Economy: Employment by occupation: 15.3% management, 2.2% professional, 19.3% services, 26.5% sales, 0.0% farming, 11.5% construction, 25.2% production (2000).
Income: Per capita income: $18,312 (2000); Median household income: $34,489 (2000); Poverty rate: 1.5% (2000).
Education: High school graduation rate: 86.3% (2000); College graduation rate: 14.6% (2000).
Housing: Homeownership rate: 94.1% (2000); Median home value: $86,500 (2000); Median rent: $125 per month (2000); Median age of housing: 27 years (2000).
Transportation: Commute to work: 83.2% car, 0.0% public transportation, 0.0% walk, 16.8% work from home (2000); Travel time to work: 15.4% less than 15 minutes, 23.2% 15 to 30 minutes, 37.5% 30 to 45 minutes, 10.1% 45 to 60 minutes, 13.9% 60 minutes or more (2000)

NORTH TERRE HAUTE (CDP). Covers a land area of 3.578 square miles and a water area of 0 square miles. Located at 39.53° N. Lat.; 87.36° W. Long. Elevation is 487 feet.
History: The Markle Mill was built in 1816 on the banks of Otter Creek, near the site of North Terre Haute, and the town developed around it.
Population: 4,606 (2000); Race: 96.4% White, 2.0% Black, 0.0% Asian, 0.0% American Indian and Alaska Native, 1.1% Hispanic of any race, 1.7% two or more races (2000); Density: 1,287.3 persons per square mile (2000); Age: 27.6% under 18, 13.6% over 64 (2000); Marriage status: 21.3% never married, 57.1% now married, 7.4% widowed, 14.2% divorced (2000); Foreign born: 0.9% (2000); Ancestry (includes multiple ancestries): 19.7% German, 14.9% United States or American, 11.7% Irish, 10.5% English, 6.2% Other groups (2000).
Economy: Employment by occupation: 6.0% management, 15.0% professional, 17.8% services, 30.4% sales, 0.0% farming, 9.4% construction, 21.4% production (2000).
Income: Per capita income: $15,729 (2000); Median household income: $34,617 (2000); Poverty rate: 9.6% (2000).
Education: High school graduation rate: 82.6% (2000); College graduation rate: 13.0% (2000).
Housing: Homeownership rate: 72.2% (2000); Median home value: $74,300 (2000); Median rent: $344 per month (2000); Median age of housing: 35 years (2000).
Transportation: Commute to work: 97.5% car, 0.0% public transportation, 0.0% walk, 1.7% work from home (2000); Travel time to work: 34.7% less than 15 minutes, 47.6% 15 to 30 minutes, 10.4% 30 to 45 minutes, 1.1% 45 to 60 minutes, 6.2% 60 minutes or more (2000)

PIMENTO (unincorporated postal area, zip code 47866). Covers a land area of 17.602 square miles and a water area of 0.090 square miles. Located at 39.29° N. Lat.; 87.31° W. Long. Elevation is 600 feet.
Population: 412 (2000); Race: 100.0% White, 0.0% Black, 0.0% Asian, 0.0% American Indian and Alaska Native, 0.0% Hispanic of any race, 0.0% two or more races (2000); Density: 23.4 persons per square mile (2000); Age: 21.6% under 18, 23.9% over 64 (2000); Marriage status: 27.9% never married, 65.7% now married, 5.4% widowed, 1.1% divorced (2000); Foreign born: 1.1% (2000); Ancestry (includes multiple ancestries): 22.6% German, 19.4% English, 11.6% Irish, 6.8% Other groups, 4.8% Welsh (2000).
Economy: Employment by occupation: 9.0% management, 19.5% professional, 19.5% services, 16.2% sales, 0.0% farming, 15.2% construction, 20.5% production (2000).
Income: Per capita income: $24,021 (2000); Median household income: $47,625 (2000); Poverty rate: 1.6% (2000).
Education: High school graduation rate: 91.5% (2000); College graduation rate: 9.7% (2000).
Housing: Homeownership rate: 90.5% (2000); Median home value: $75,000 (2000); Median rent: $466 per month (2000); Median age of housing: 36 years (2000).
Transportation: Commute to work: 84.3% car, 0.0% public transportation, 4.8% walk, 9.5% work from home (2000); Travel time to work: 10.0% less than 15 minutes, 71.6% 15 to 30 minutes, 14.2% 30 to 45 minutes, 4.2% 45 to 60 minutes, 0.0% 60 minutes or more (2000)

RILEY (town). Covers a land area of 0.092 square miles and a water area of 0 square miles. Located at 39.39° N. Lat.; 87.30° W. Long. Elevation is 568 feet.
History: Riley, first known as Lockport, developed around a coal mine.
Population: 160 (2000); Race: 100.0% White, 0.0% Black, 0.0% Asian, 0.0% American Indian and Alaska Native, 0.0% Hispanic of any race, 0.0% two or more races (2000); Density: 1,747.7 persons per square mile (2000); Age: 26.9% under 18, 18.6% over 64 (2000); Marriage status: 12.3% never married, 68.9% now married, 9.4% widowed, 9.4% divorced (2000); Foreign born: 0.0% (2000); Ancestry (includes multiple ancestries): 46.2% United States or American, 26.2% German, 9.0% Irish, 6.9% Dutch, 3.4% English (2000).
Economy: Employment by occupation: 17.2% management, 5.2% professional, 24.1% services, 27.6% sales, 0.0% farming, 10.3% construction, 15.5% production (2000).
Income: Per capita income: $13,616 (2000); Median household income: $28,333 (2000); Poverty rate: 12.0% (2000).
Taxes: Total city taxes per capita: $59 (1997); City property taxes per capita: $46 (1997).
Education: High school graduation rate: 84.3% (2000); College graduation rate: 18.1% (2000).
Housing: Homeownership rate: 75.7% (2000); Median home value: $74,600 (2000); Median rent: $358 per month (2000); Median age of housing: 40 years (2000).
Transportation: Commute to work: 100.0% car, 0.0% public transportation, 0.0% walk, 0.0% work from home (2000); Travel time to work: 25.5% less than 15 minutes, 69.1% 15 to 30 minutes, 5.5% 30 to 45 minutes, 0.0% 45 to 60 minutes, 0.0% 60 minutes or more (2000)

SAINT MARY OF THE WOODS (unincorporated postal area, zip code 47876). Covers a land area of 0.042 square miles and a water area of 0 square miles. Located at 39.43° N. Lat.; 87.41° W. Long.
Population: 427 (2000); Race: 98.1% White, 1.9% Black, 0.0% Asian, 0.0% American Indian and Alaska Native, 0.0% Hispanic of any race, 0.0% two or more races (2000); Density: 10,166.7 persons per square mile (2000); Age: 0.0% under 18, 55.5% over 64 (2000); Marriage status: 78.0% never married, 20.9% now married, 1.2% widowed, 0.0% divorced (2000); Foreign born: 1.4% (2000); Ancestry (includes multiple ancestries): 34.8% German, 19.5% Irish, 6.7% Polish, 3.2% Dutch, 3.2% Other groups (2000).
Economy: Employment by occupation: 4.6% management, 10.1% professional, 44.0% services, 36.7% sales, 4.6% farming, 0.0% construction, 0.0% production (2000).
Income: Per capita income: $5,353 (2000); Median household income: $0 (2000); Poverty rate: 0.0% (2000).
Education: High school graduation rate: 95.3% (2000); College graduation rate: 93.4% (2000).

Four-year College(s)

Saint Mary-of-the-Woods College (Private, Not-for-profit, Roman Catholic)
2001 Enrollment: 1,502 812-535-5151
2001 Tuition: In-state $15,090; Out-of-state $15,090

Housing: Homeownership rate: 0.0% (2000); Median age of housing: n/a years (2000).
Transportation: Commute to work: 12.6% car, 0.0% public transportation, 82.5% walk, 0.0% work from home (2000); Travel time to work: 87.4% less than 15 minutes, 12.6% 15 to 30 minutes, 0.0% 30 to 45 minutes, 0.0% 45 to 60 minutes, 0.0% 60 minutes or more (2000)

SEELYVILLE (town). Covers a land area of 0.862 square miles and a water area of 0.010 square miles. Located at 39.49° N. Lat.; 87.26° W. Long. Elevation is 588 feet.
History: Seelyville was established as a mining center.
Population: 1,182 (2000); Race: 98.2% White, 0.3% Black, 0.0% Asian, 0.4% American Indian and Alaska Native, 1.3% Hispanic of any race, 0.0% two or more races (2000); Density: 1,371.4 persons per square mile (2000); Age: 23.0% under 18, 10.9% over 64 (2000); Marriage status: 22.2% never married, 58.0% now married, 5.7% widowed, 14.2% divorced (2000); Foreign born: 0.3% (2000); Ancestry (includes multiple ancestries): 20.3%

United States or American, 19.4% German, 13.7% Irish, 10.3% English, 4.4% Other groups (2000).
Economy: Employment by occupation: 6.6% management, 14.7% professional, 17.5% services, 28.1% sales, 0.0% farming, 12.4% construction, 20.8% production (2000).
Income: Per capita income: $17,588 (2000); Median household income: $35,114 (2000); Poverty rate: 7.4% (2000).
Taxes: Total city taxes per capita: $23 (1997); City property taxes per capita: $22 (1997).
Education: High school graduation rate: 84.7% (2000); College graduation rate: 13.3% (2000).
Housing: Homeownership rate: 78.3% (2000); Median home value: $73,700 (2000); Median rent: $382 per month (2000); Median age of housing: 41 years (2000).
Transportation: Commute to work: 96.5% car, 0.0% public transportation, 0.0% walk, 2.8% work from home (2000); Travel time to work: 20.3% less than 15 minutes, 62.8% 15 to 30 minutes, 8.8% 30 to 45 minutes, 4.6% 45 to 60 minutes, 3.4% 60 minutes or more (2000)

TERRE HAUTE (city). Covers a land area of 31.238 square miles and a water area of 0.864 square miles. Located at 39.47° N. Lat.; 87.39° W. Long. Elevation is 501 feet.
History: Terre Haute's name, meaning "high land," was given to it by French traders in the early 1700's. The city itself was established in 1816 by the Terre Haute Town Company, a group of Indiana and Kentucky businessmen. It was soon selected as the seat of Vigo County, and was incorporated as a town in 1832. Coal mining was the major industry in Terre Haute after 1875. It's reputation as a "union town" was influenced in part by Eugene V. Debs who lived and worked here.
Population: 59,614 (2000); Race: 86.1% White, 9.9% Black, 0.9% Asian, 0.4% American Indian and Alaska Native, 1.5% Hispanic of any race, 2.2% two or more races (2000); Density: 1,908.4 persons per square mile (2000); Age: 21.4% under 18, 14.9% over 64 (2000); Marriage status: 32.8% never married, 45.7% now married, 8.9% widowed, 12.5% divorced (2000); Foreign born: 2.1% (2000); Ancestry (includes multiple ancestries): 18.7% German, 15.2% Other groups, 13.1% United States or American, 10.6% Irish, 9.6% English (2000).
Vital Statistics: Birth rate: 160.0 per 10,000 population (1998)
Economy: Unemployment rate: 6.1% (11/2002); Total civilian labor force: 26,098 (11/2002); Single-family building permits issued: 135 (2001) / 103 (2000); Multi-family building permits issued: 32 (2001) / 31 (2000); Employment by occupation: 8.5% management, 20.0% professional, 20.5% services, 28.6% sales, 0.2% farming, 6.9% construction, 15.2% production (2000).
Income: Per capita income: $15,728 (2000); Median household income: $28,018 (2000); Poverty rate: 19.2% (2000).
Taxes: Total city taxes per capita: $322 (1997); City property taxes per capita: $316 (1997).
Education: High school graduation rate: 77.7% (2000); College graduation rate: 19.7% (2000).

School District(s)

Covered Bridge Special Education District
2000 Enrollment: n/a 812-462-4364
Vigo County School Corp (PK-12)
2000 Enrollment: 16,545 812-462-4216

Four-year College(s)

Indiana State University (Public)
2001 Enrollment: 11,321 812-237-6311
2001 Tuition: In-state $3,672; Out-of-state $9,166
Rose-Hulman Institute of Technology (Private, Not-for-profit)
2001 Enrollment: 1,749 812-877-1511
2001 Tuition: In-state $21,263; Out-of-state $21,263

Two-year College(s)

Ivy Tech State College-Wabash Valley (Public)
2001 Enrollment: 3,810 812-299-1121
2001 Tuition: In-state $1,986; Out-of-state $4,029
Indiana Business College (Private, For-profit)
2001 Enrollment: 282 812-232-4458
2001 Tuition: In-state $8,460; Out-of-state $8,460

Housing: Homeownership rate: 59.3% (2000); Median home value: $60,400 (2000); Median rent: $353 per month (2000); Median age of housing: 54 years (2000).
Hospitals: Hamilton Center (16 beds); Terre Haute Regional Hospital (278 beds); Union Hospital (343 beds)
Safety: Violent crime rate: 25.0 per 10,000 population; Property crime rate: 913.4 per 10,000 population (2001).
Newspapers: The Tribune-Star (7 x week)
Transportation: Commute to work: 89.7% car, 0.5% public transportation, 6.7% walk, 1.8% work from home (2000); Travel time to work: 53.5% less than 15 minutes, 34.3% 15 to 30 minutes, 6.7% 30 to 45 minutes, 2.1% 45 to 60 minutes, 3.4% 60 minutes or more (2000)
Airports: Terre Haute International-Hulman Field

Additional Information Contacts

Terre Haute Area Association of Realtors 812-234-8732
Terre Haute Convention & Visitors Bureau. 812-234-5555

WEST TERRE HAUTE (town). Covers a land area of 0.756 square miles and a water area of 0 square miles. Located at 39.46° N. Lat.; 87.44° W. Long. Elevation is 476 feet.
History: West Terre Haute began as a coal-mining town.
Population: 2,330 (2000); Race: 96.8% White, 0.0% Black, 0.2% Asian, 0.8% American Indian and Alaska Native, 0.8% Hispanic of any race, 2.1% two or more races (2000); Density: 3,082.4 persons per square mile (2000); Age: 29.4% under 18, 12.0% over 64 (2000); Marriage status: 23.8% never married, 52.6% now married, 9.9% widowed, 13.8% divorced (2000); Foreign born: 0.4% (2000); Ancestry (includes multiple ancestries): 19.6% United States or American, 11.1% Other groups, 10.4% German, 9.7% Irish, 4.7% English (2000).
Economy: Employment by occupation: 2.1% management, 9.0% professional, 22.0% services, 26.0% sales, 0.0% farming, 19.6% construction, 21.2% production (2000).
Income: Per capita income: $11,887 (2000); Median household income: $25,954 (2000); Poverty rate: 20.7% (2000).
Taxes: Total city taxes per capita: $80 (1997); City property taxes per capita: $78 (1997).
Education: High school graduation rate: 63.7% (2000); College graduation rate: 5.1% (2000).
Housing: Homeownership rate: 71.5% (2000); Median home value: $42,900 (2000); Median rent: $288 per month (2000); Median age of housing: 56 years (2000).
Safety: Violent crime rate: n/a; Property crime rate: 405.5 per 10,000 population (2001).
Transportation: Commute to work: 92.2% car, 0.0% public transportation, 3.5% walk, 2.8% work from home (2000); Travel time to work: 34.2% less than 15 minutes, 49.9% 15 to 30 minutes, 9.6% 30 to 45 minutes, 3.3% 45 to 60 minutes, 3.0% 60 minutes or more (2000)

Wabash County

Located in northeast central Indiana; drained by the Wabash, Eel, Salamonie, and Mississinewa Rivers. Covers a land area of 413.20 square miles, a water area of 7.90 square miles, and is located in the Eastern Time Zone. The county government was organized in 1832. County seat is Wabash.
Population: 34,960 (2000); Race: 97.0% White, 0.3% Black, 0.7% Asian, 0.9% American Indian and Alaska Native, 0.9% Hispanic of any race, 0.9% two or more races (2000); Density: 84.6 persons per square mile (2000); Age: 24.5% under 18, 15.6% over 64 (2000).
Religion: Five largest groups: 9.3% The United Methodist Church, 8.4% Christian Churches and Churches of Christ, 7.2% Catholic Church, 4.4% Church of the Brethren, 2.5% Evangelical Lutheran Church in America (2000).
Economy: Unemployment rate: 4.8% (11/2002); Total civilian labor force: 16,776 (11/2002); Leading industries: 40.2% manufacturing; 14.2% retail trade; 13.3% health care and social assistance (2000); Companies that employ more than 1,000 persons: 0 (2000); Companies that employ more than 100 persons: 25 (2000); Farms: 762 totaling 188,230 acres (1997); Minority business ownership rate: 0.0% (1997); Women business ownership rate: 30.5% (1997); Retail sales per capita: $8,336 (1997). Single-family building permits issued: 101 (2001) / 88 (2000); Multi-family building permits issued: 0 (2001) / 0 (2000).
Income: Per capita income: $18,192 (2000); Median household income: $40,413 (2000); Poverty rate: 6.9% (2000); Bankruptcy rate: 7.81% (2001).
Taxes: Total county taxes per capita: $213 (2000); County property taxes per capita: $118 (2000).
Education: High school graduation rate: 81.7% (2000); College graduation rate: 13.7% (2000).
Housing: Homeownership rate: 75.9% (2000); Median home value: $78,400 (2000); Median rent: $337 per month (2000); Median age of housing: 45 years (2000).
Health: Birth rate: 111.3 per 10,000 population (1998); Age adjusted death rate: 90.2 per 10,000 population (1999); Age adjusted cancer mortality rate:

207.1 deaths per 100,000 population (1999). Number of physicians: 9.2 per 10,000 population (1999); Number of hospital beds: 20.3 per 10,000 population (1999).
Elections: 2000 Presidential election results: 33.2% Gore, 64.6% Bush, 1.0% Nader, 0.9% Buchanan
National and State Parks: Doranew Holland State Recreation Area; Frances Slocum State Recreation Area; Hogback Ridge State Recreation Area; Lost Bridge State Recreation Area; Miami State Recreation Area; Mount Hope State Recreation Area; Pearson Mill State Recreation Area; Red Bridge State Recreation Area; Salamonie River State Forest
Additional Information Contacts
Wabash County Government Offices.......................219-563-0661
North Manchester Chamber of Commerce 219-982-7644
Wabash Area Chamber of Commerce 260-563-1168
Wabash County Board of Realtors...........................260-563-8009

Wabash County Communities

LA FONTAINE (town). Covers a land area of 0.612 square miles and a water area of 0 square miles. Located at 40.67° N. Lat.; 85.72° W. Long. Elevation is 808 feet.
Population: 900 (2000); Race: 98.0% White, 0.0% Black, 0.0% Asian, 1.1% American Indian and Alaska Native, 1.3% Hispanic of any race, 0.0% two or more races (2000); Density: 1,470.2 persons per square mile (2000); Age: 23.7% under 18, 20.2% over 64 (2000); Marriage status: 18.4% never married, 60.2% now married, 11.7% widowed, 9.6% divorced (2000); Foreign born: 0.0% (2000); Ancestry (includes multiple ancestries): 25.3% German, 19.4% United States or American, 10.4% Other groups, 9.4% Irish, 8.3% English (2000).
Economy: In agricultural area. Employment by occupation: 7.4% management, 15.6% professional, 12.9% services, 21.6% sales, 0.5% farming, 5.8% construction, 36.2% production (2000).
Income: Per capita income: $17,203 (2000); Median household income: $43,393 (2000); Poverty rate: 3.8% (2000).
Taxes: Total city taxes per capita: $102 (1997); City property taxes per capita: $85 (1997).
Education: High school graduation rate: 83.2% (2000); College graduation rate: 8.3% (2000).
Housing: Homeownership rate: 73.8% (2000); Median home value: $58,800 (2000); Median rent: $273 per month (2000); Median age of housing: 60+ years (2000).
Transportation: Commute to work: 94.3% car, 2.0% public transportation, 2.2% walk, 0.5% work from home (2000); Travel time to work: 21.0% less than 15 minutes, 58.8% 15 to 30 minutes, 14.8% 30 to 45 minutes, 1.0% 45 to 60 minutes, 4.4% 60 minutes or more (2000)

LAGRO (town). Covers a land area of 0.598 square miles and a water area of 0.007 square miles. Located at 40.83° N. Lat.; 85.72° W. Long. Elevation is 681 feet.
History: The Wabash & Erie Canal was the impetus for the settlement of Lagro, named for an Indian chief, Les Gros.
Population: 454 (2000); Race: 97.0% White, 0.4% Black, 0.0% Asian, 1.1% American Indian and Alaska Native, 0.0% Hispanic of any race, 1.5% two or more races (2000); Density: 758.7 persons per square mile (2000); Age: 35.9% under 18, 10.1% over 64 (2000); Marriage status: 17.2% never married, 67.7% now married, 5.5% widowed, 9.5% divorced (2000); Foreign born: 0.0% (2000); Ancestry (includes multiple ancestries): 32.7% United States or American, 12.7% German, 9.7% Other groups, 7.2% Irish, 5.7% English (2000).
Economy: Employment by occupation: 3.6% management, 5.2% professional, 23.8% services, 9.3% sales, 0.0% farming, 15.5% construction, 42.5% production (2000).
Income: Per capita income: $13,186 (2000); Median household income: $34,327 (2000); Poverty rate: 6.5% (2000).
Taxes: Total city taxes per capita: $113 (1997); City property taxes per capita: $101 (1997).
Education: High school graduation rate: 60.7% (2000); College graduation rate: 4.4% (2000).
Housing: Homeownership rate: 89.9% (2000); Median home value: $43,900 (2000); Median rent: $319 per month (2000); Median age of housing: 55 years (2000).
Transportation: Commute to work: 100.0% car, 0.0% public transportation, 0.0% walk, 0.0% work from home (2000); Travel time to work: 23.4% less than 15 minutes, 58.0% 15 to 30 minutes, 8.0% 30 to 45 minutes, 4.8% 45 to 60 minutes, 5.9% 60 minutes or more (2000)

NORTH MANCHESTER (town). Covers a land area of 3.607 square miles and a water area of 0 square miles. Located at 41.00° N. Lat.; 85.77° W. Long. Elevation is 773 feet.
History: Among the early residents in North Manchester was a group of Dunkers, members of a religious sect founded in Germany in 1708. Thomas R. Marshall, Vice President of the United States under Woodrow Wilson, was born in North Manchester.
Population: 6,260 (2000); Race: 96.4% White, 0.7% Black, 1.5% Asian, 0.2% American Indian and Alaska Native, 1.0% Hispanic of any race, 0.9% two or more races (2000); Density: 1,735.5 persons per square mile (2000); Age: 17.5% under 18, 22.3% over 64 (2000); Marriage status: 25.9% never married, 53.4% now married, 12.0% widowed, 8.7% divorced (2000); Foreign born: 0.9% (2000); Ancestry (includes multiple ancestries): 30.4% German, 12.2% United States or American, 9.3% Irish, 8.3% English, 4.6% Other groups (2000).
Economy: Single-family building permits issued: 11 (2001) / 2 (2000); Multi-family building permits issued: 0 (2001) / 0 (2000); Employment by occupation: 9.7% management, 19.5% professional, 18.1% services, 24.2% sales, 1.4% farming, 4.7% construction, 22.4% production (2000).
Income: Per capita income: $17,140 (2000); Median household income: $35,448 (2000); Poverty rate: 8.7% (2000).
Taxes: Total city taxes per capita: $174 (1997); City property taxes per capita: $123 (1997).
Education: High school graduation rate: 84.9% (2000); College graduation rate: 25.3% (2000).

School District(s)

Manchester Community Schools (KG-12)
2000 Enrollment: 1,661 219-982-7518

Four-year College(s)

Manchester College (Private, Not-for-profit, Church of Brethren)
2001 Enrollment: 1,137 219-982-5000
2001 Tuition: In-state $15,230; Out-of-state $15,230
Housing: Homeownership rate: 66.6% (2000); Median home value: $84,000 (2000); Median rent: $326 per month (2000); Median age of housing: 46 years (2000).
Safety: Violent crime rate: 3.2 per 10,000 population; Property crime rate: 316.1 per 10,000 population (2001).
Newspapers: The News-Journal (1 x week)
Transportation: Commute to work: 84.3% car, 0.0% public transportation, 11.7% walk, 3.0% work from home (2000); Travel time to work: 62.5% less than 15 minutes, 15.7% 15 to 30 minutes, 14.2% 30 to 45 minutes, 5.8% 45 to 60 minutes, 1.8% 60 minutes or more (2000)
Additional Information Contacts
North Manchester Chamber of Commerce 219-982-7644

ROANN (town). Covers a land area of 0.180 square miles and a water area of 0 square miles. Located at 40.91° N. Lat.; 85.92° W. Long. Elevation is 750 feet.
History: Laid out 1853.
Population: 400 (2000); Race: 100.0% White, 0.0% Black, 0.0% Asian, 0.0% American Indian and Alaska Native, 0.0% Hispanic of any race, 0.0% two or more races (2000); Density: 2,226.4 persons per square mile (2000); Age: 20.1% under 18, 14.0% over 64 (2000); Marriage status: 20.1% never married, 62.8% now married, 8.1% widowed, 9.0% divorced (2000); Foreign born: 0.0% (2000); Ancestry (includes multiple ancestries): 26.9% German, 16.5% English, 11.7% Irish, 5.1% United States or American, 4.1% Other groups (2000).
Economy: In agricultural area. Employment by occupation: 9.0% management, 5.8% professional, 6.3% services, 24.2% sales, 2.2% farming, 6.7% construction, 45.7% production (2000).
Income: Per capita income: $20,880 (2000); Median household income: $41,000 (2000); Poverty rate: 9.5% (2000).
Taxes: Total city taxes per capita: $102 (1997); City property taxes per capita: $102 (1997).
Education: High school graduation rate: 72.6% (2000); College graduation rate: 8.9% (2000).
Housing: Homeownership rate: 83.7% (2000); Median home value: $53,000 (2000); Median rent: $341 per month (2000); Median age of housing: 60+ years (2000).
Transportation: Commute to work: 98.1% car, 0.0% public transportation, 1.9% walk, 0.0% work from home (2000); Travel time to work: 7.0% less than 15 minutes, 67.9% 15 to 30 minutes, 20.5% 30 to 45 minutes, 4.7% 45 to 60 minutes, 0.0% 60 minutes or more (2000)

URBANA (unincorporated postal area, zip code 46990). Covers a land area of 30.034 square miles and a water area of 0.031 square miles. Located at 40.89° N. Lat.; 85.74° W. Long. Elevation is 795 feet.
History: Laid out 1854.
Population: 851 (2000); Race: 100.0% White, 0.0% Black, 0.0% Asian, 0.0% American Indian and Alaska Native, 0.0% Hispanic of any race, 0.0% two or more races (2000); Density: 28.3 persons per square mile (2000); Age: 33.5% under 18, 8.2% over 64 (2000); Marriage status: 13.2% never married, 78.2% now married, 4.1% widowed, 4.5% divorced (2000); Foreign born: 0.0% (2000); Ancestry (includes multiple ancestries): 23.1% German, 9.0% United States or American, 7.7% English, 4.1% Irish, 3.8% Scotch-Irish (2000).
Economy: Manufacturing: tanks and hoppers, sheet metal fabricating. Soybeans, corn; livestock. Employment by occupation: 21.7% management, 10.0% professional, 9.0% services, 26.4% sales, 2.4% farming, 5.7% construction, 24.8% production (2000).
Income: Per capita income: $16,664 (2000); Median household income: $46,063 (2000); Poverty rate: 5.6% (2000).
Education: High school graduation rate: 94.1% (2000); College graduation rate: 22.9% (2000).
Housing: Homeownership rate: 87.7% (2000); Median home value: $82,000 (2000); Median rent: $406 per month (2000); Median age of housing: 60+ years (2000).
Transportation: Commute to work: 84.4% car, 0.0% public transportation, 4.0% walk, 8.2% work from home (2000); Travel time to work: 35.1% less than 15 minutes, 40.3% 15 to 30 minutes, 4.6% 30 to 45 minutes, 9.5% 45 to 60 minutes, 10.5% 60 minutes or more (2000)

WABASH (city). Covers a land area of 8.903 square miles and a water area of 0.249 square miles. Located at 40.80° N. Lat.; 85.82° W. Long. Elevation is 984 feet.
History: Its location along the Wabash River gave the town of Wabash its name, which comes from the Indian "oubache," meaning "water over white stones." The Wabash & Erie Canal was completed through this area in 1835, bringing Irish immigrants as canal workers.
Population: 11,743 (2000); Race: 96.2% White, 0.3% Black, 1.0% Asian, 1.1% American Indian and Alaska Native, 0.7% Hispanic of any race, 1.2% two or more races (2000); Density: 1,319.0 persons per square mile (2000); Age: 24.3% under 18, 16.1% over 64 (2000); Marriage status: 23.0% never married, 54.3% now married, 9.5% widowed, 13.2% divorced (2000); Foreign born: 1.2% (2000); Ancestry (includes multiple ancestries): 22.8% German, 12.4% United States or American, 12.1% English, 10.5% Irish, 8.1% Other groups (2000).
Vital Statistics: Birth rate: 132.0 per 10,000 population (1998)
Economy: Single-family building permits issued: 22 (2001) / 18 (2000); Multi-family building permits issued: 0 (2001) / 0 (2000); Employment by occupation: 8.4% management, 11.7% professional, 15.0% services, 24.7% sales, 0.6% farming, 7.2% construction, 32.5% production (2000).
Income: Per capita income: $18,210 (2000); Median household income: $34,401 (2000); Poverty rate: 9.3% (2000).
Taxes: Total city taxes per capita: $212 (1997); City property taxes per capita: $205 (1997).
Education: High school graduation rate: 78.2% (2000); College graduation rate: 11.1% (2000).

School District(s)

Heartland Career Center
  2000 Enrollment: n/a 219-563-7481
M S D Wabash County Schools (KG-12)
  2000 Enrollment: 2,644 219-563-7438
Wabash City Schools (PK-12)
  2000 Enrollment: 1,706 219-563-2151

Housing: Homeownership rate: 67.9% (2000); Median home value: $70,000 (2000); Median rent: $333 per month (2000); Median age of housing: 49 years (2000).
Hospitals: Wabash County Hospital (99 beds)
Safety: Violent crime rate: 6.8 per 10,000 population; Property crime rate: 187.1 per 10,000 population (2001).
Newspapers: Wabash Plain Dealer (6 x week); The Paper of Wabash County (1 x week)
Transportation: Commute to work: 95.3% car, 0.2% public transportation, 1.9% walk, 1.9% work from home (2000); Travel time to work: 65.1% less than 15 minutes, 17.3% 15 to 30 minutes, 10.0% 30 to 45 minutes, 3.4% 45 to 60 minutes, 4.2% 60 minutes or more (2000)

Additional Information Contacts

Wabash Area Chamber of Commerce 260-563-1168
Wabash County Board of Realtors 260-563-8009

Warren County

Located in western Indiana; bounded on the west by Illinois, and on the southeast by the Wabash River. Covers a land area of 364.90 square miles, a water area of 1.70 square miles, and is located in the Eastern Time Zone. The county government was organized in 1827. County seat is Williamsport.
Population: 8,419 (2000); Race: 99.0% White, 0.0% Black, 0.1% Asian, 0.2% American Indian and Alaska Native, 0.7% Hispanic of any race, 0.6% two or more races (2000); Density: 23.1 persons per square mile (2000); Age: 26.3% under 18, 14.0% over 64 (2000).
Religion: Five largest groups: 19.5% Christian Churches and Churches of Christ, 9.6% The United Methodist Church, 5.3% Independent, Non-Charismatic Churches, 2.7% Catholic Church, 2.2% Church of the Nazarene (2000).
Economy: Unemployment rate: 5.1% (11/2002); Total civilian labor force: 3,927 (11/2002); Leading industries: 33.7% manufacturing; 11.9% wholesale trade; 2.1% professional, scientific & technical services (2000); Companies that employ more than 1,000 persons: 0 (2000); Companies that employ more than 100 persons: 2 (2000); Farms: 378 totaling 184,653 acres (1997); Minority business ownership rate: 0.0% (1997); Women business ownership rate: 0.0% (1997); Retail sales per capita: $2,398 (1997). Single-family building permits issued: 54 (2001) / 63 (2000); Multi-family building permits issued: 0 (2001) / 4 (2000).
Income: Per capita income: $18,070 (2000); Median household income: $41,825 (2000); Poverty rate: 6.5% (2000); Bankruptcy rate: 6.64% (2001).
Taxes: Total county taxes per capita: $315 (1997); County property taxes per capita: $194 (1997).
Education: High school graduation rate: 85.0% (2000); College graduation rate: 14.0% (2000).
Housing: Homeownership rate: 80.9% (2000); Median home value: $74,100 (2000); Median rent: $310 per month (2000); Median age of housing: 41 years (2000).
Health: Birth rate: 120.0 per 10,000 population (1998); Age adjusted death rate: 96.5 per 10,000 population (1999); Age adjusted cancer mortality rate: 206.1 (Unreliable figure as per CDC) deaths per 100,000 population (1999). Number of physicians: 3.6 per 10,000 population (1999); Number of hospital beds: 26.1 per 10,000 population (1999).
Elections: 2000 Presidential election results: 39.0% Gore, 58.9% Bush, 0.6% Nader, 1.0% Buchanan

Additional Information Contacts

Warren County Government Offices 765-762-3275

Warren County Communities

PINE VILLAGE (town). Covers a land area of 0.126 square miles and a water area of 0 square miles. Located at 40.45° N. Lat.; 87.25° W. Long. Elevation is 667 feet.
Population: 255 (2000); Race: 99.6% White, 0.0% Black, 0.4% Asian, 0.0% American Indian and Alaska Native, 1.6% Hispanic of any race, 0.0% two or more races (2000); Density: 2,031.5 persons per square mile (2000); Age: 17.3% under 18, 17.3% over 64 (2000); Marriage status: 24.8% never married, 51.8% now married, 7.1% widowed, 16.4% divorced (2000); Foreign born: 1.6% (2000); Ancestry (includes multiple ancestries): 18.1% United States or American, 17.3% Irish, 16.1% German, 10.2% English, 6.3% Other groups (2000).
Economy: Agricultural area. Employment by occupation: 15.9% management, 6.9% professional, 9.0% services, 19.3% sales, 2.1% farming, 11.7% construction, 35.2% production (2000).
Income: Per capita income: $18,952 (2000); Median household income: $38,875 (2000); Poverty rate: 7.1% (2000).
Taxes: Total city taxes per capita: $100 (1997); City property taxes per capita: $91 (1997).
Education: High school graduation rate: 80.4% (2000); College graduation rate: 14.9% (2000).
Housing: Homeownership rate: 71.6% (2000); Median home value: $60,000 (2000); Median rent: $380 per month (2000); Median age of housing: 60+ years (2000).
Transportation: Commute to work: 84.9% car, 0.0% public transportation, 5.5% walk, 4.8% work from home (2000); Travel time to work: 22.3% less than 15 minutes, 25.9% 15 to 30 minutes, 33.8% 30 to 45 minutes, 10.1% 45 to 60 minutes, 7.9% 60 minutes or more (2000)

STATE LINE CITY (town). Aka State Line. Covers a land area of 0.135 square miles and a water area of 0 square miles. Located at 40.19° N. Lat.; 87.52° W. Long.
Population: 141 (2000); Race: 100.0% White, 0.0% Black, 0.0% Asian, 0.0% American Indian and Alaska Native, 0.0% Hispanic of any race, 0.0% two or more races (2000); Density: 1,046.9 persons per square mile (2000); Age: 28.4% under 18, 12.7% over 64 (2000); Marriage status: 26.5% never married, 65.5% now married, 5.3% widowed, 2.7% divorced (2000); Foreign born: 0.0% (2000); Ancestry (includes multiple ancestries): 26.1% Irish, 23.9% German, 9.0% English, 6.7% United States or American, 4.5% Other groups (2000).
Economy: Employment by occupation: 1.6% management, 10.9% professional, 14.1% services, 29.7% sales, 0.0% farming, 9.4% construction, 34.4% production (2000).
Income: Per capita income: $15,685 (2000); Median household income: $34,250 (2000); Poverty rate: 3.7% (2000).
Taxes: Total city taxes per capita: $54 (1997); City property taxes per capita: $49 (1997).
Education: High school graduation rate: 84.1% (2000); College graduation rate: 4.5% (2000).
Housing: Homeownership rate: 88.2% (2000); Median home value: $34,700 (2000); Median rent: $275 per month (2000); Median age of housing: 45 years (2000).
Transportation: Commute to work: 86.4% car, 3.4% public transportation, 0.0% walk, 10.2% work from home (2000); Travel time to work: 37.7% less than 15 minutes, 47.2% 15 to 30 minutes, 1.9% 30 to 45 minutes, 0.0% 45 to 60 minutes, 13.2% 60 minutes or more (2000)

WEST LEBANON (town). Covers a land area of 0.616 square miles and a water area of 0 square miles. Located at 40.27° N. Lat.; 87.38° W. Long. Elevation is 714 feet.
History: Laid out 1830.
Population: 793 (2000); Race: 99.7% White, 0.3% Black, 0.0% Asian, 0.0% American Indian and Alaska Native, 0.5% Hispanic of any race, 0.0% two or more races (2000); Density: 1,287.1 persons per square mile (2000); Age: 29.9% under 18, 11.2% over 64 (2000); Marriage status: 18.9% never married, 58.8% now married, 6.9% widowed, 15.4% divorced (2000); Foreign born: 0.4% (2000); Ancestry (includes multiple ancestries): 16.1% German, 11.4% United States or American, 11.2% Other groups, 8.6% Irish, 8.2% English (2000).
Economy: Grain. Manufacturing: fabricated metal products, prefabricated buildings; seed. Employment by occupation: 6.9% management, 11.1% professional, 12.0% services, 16.9% sales, 0.6% farming, 16.0% construction, 36.6% production (2000).
Income: Per capita income: $15,424 (2000); Median household income: $34,844 (2000); Poverty rate: 8.1% (2000).
Taxes: Total city taxes per capita: $6 (1997); City property taxes per capita: $6 (1997).
Education: High school graduation rate: 74.5% (2000); College graduation rate: 9.5% (2000).
Housing: Homeownership rate: 79.7% (2000); Median home value: $55,400 (2000); Median rent: $237 per month (2000); Median age of housing: 40 years (2000).
Transportation: Commute to work: 96.3% car, 0.0% public transportation, 0.6% walk, 2.0% work from home (2000); Travel time to work: 38.8% less than 15 minutes, 31.5% 15 to 30 minutes, 13.2% 30 to 45 minutes, 9.4% 45 to 60 minutes, 7.1% 60 minutes or more (2000)

WILLIAMSPORT (town). Covers a land area of 1.053 square miles and a water area of 0 square miles. Located at 40.28° N. Lat.; 87.29° W. Long. Elevation is 630 feet.
History: The land on which Williamsport was founded was owned by General William Henry Harrison. A spur of the Wabash & Erie Canal was built to Williamsport, giving an early boost to commerce and bringing the nickname of Side Cut City.
Population: 1,935 (2000); Race: 99.1% White, 0.0% Black, 0.4% Asian, 0.0% American Indian and Alaska Native, 0.4% Hispanic of any race, 0.6% two or more races (2000); Density: 1,838.4 persons per square mile (2000); Age: 25.8% under 18, 19.6% over 64 (2000); Marriage status: 18.6% never married, 58.0% now married, 13.1% widowed, 10.3% divorced (2000); Foreign born: 0.3% (2000); Ancestry (includes multiple ancestries): 18.4% United States or American, 16.4% German, 8.5% English, 6.5% Irish, 6.1% Other groups (2000).
Economy: Employment by occupation: 7.1% management, 12.7% professional, 16.6% services, 21.0% sales, 1.1% farming, 8.1% construction, 33.5% production (2000).
Income: Per capita income: $17,026 (2000); Median household income: $39,605 (2000); Poverty rate: 5.4% (2000).
Taxes: Total city taxes per capita: $30 (1997); City property taxes per capita: $11 (1997).
Education: High school graduation rate: 79.7% (2000); College graduation rate: 8.4% (2000).

School District(s)

M S D Warren County (KG-12)
2000 Enrollment: 1,369 765-762-3364

Housing: Homeownership rate: 70.5% (2000); Median home value: $69,200 (2000); Median rent: $330 per month (2000); Median age of housing: 41 years (2000).
Hospitals: St Vincent Williamsport (16 beds)
Newspapers: The Review-Republican (1 x week)
Transportation: Commute to work: 95.3% car, 0.0% public transportation, 2.0% walk, 1.9% work from home (2000); Travel time to work: 52.4% less than 15 minutes, 14.3% 15 to 30 minutes, 12.3% 30 to 45 minutes, 14.6% 45 to 60 minutes, 6.4% 60 minutes or more (2000)

Warrick County

Located in southwestern Indiana; bounded on the south by the Ohio River and the Kentucky border. Covers a land area of 384.10 square miles, a water area of 6.80 square miles, and is located in the Central Time Zone. The county government was organized in 1813. County seat is Boonville.

Warrick County is part of the Evansville-Henderson, IN-KY MSA. The entire metro area includes: Posey County, IN; Vanderburgh County, IN; Warrick County, IN; Henderson County, KY

Population: 52,383 (2000); Race: 98.1% White, 0.6% Black, 0.5% Asian, 0.2% American Indian and Alaska Native, 0.6% Hispanic of any race, 0.4% two or more races (2000); Density: 136.4 persons per square mile (2000); Age: 26.8% under 18, 10.8% over 64 (2000).
Religion: Five largest groups: 13.1% Catholic Church, 6.2% The United Methodist Church, 4.8% Southern Baptist Convention, 3.1% United Church of Christ, 1.8% Christian Churches and Churches of Christ (2000).
Economy: Unemployment rate: 3.6% (11/2002); Total civilian labor force: 29,258 (11/2002); Leading industries: 30.3% manufacturing; 14.4% health care and social assistance; 12.3% retail trade (2000); Companies that employ more than 1,000 persons: 1 (2000); Companies that employ more than 100 persons: 15 (2000); Farms: 356 totaling 98,549 acres (1997); Minority business ownership rate: 0.0% (1997); Women business ownership rate: 25.6% (1997); Retail sales per capita: $4,303 (1997). Single-family building permits issued: 357 (2001) / 366 (2000); Multi-family building permits issued: 18 (2001) / 73 (2000).
Income: Per capita income: $21,893 (2000); Median household income: $48,814 (2000); Poverty rate: 5.3% (2000); Bankruptcy rate: 5.27% (2001).
Taxes: Total county taxes per capita: $280 (2000); County property taxes per capita: $223 (2000).
Education: High school graduation rate: 86.3% (2000); College graduation rate: 21.8% (2000).
Housing: Homeownership rate: 83.3% (2000); Median home value: $104,400 (2000); Median rent: $380 per month (2000); Median age of housing: 24 years (2000).
Health: Birth rate: 118.4 per 10,000 population (1998); Age adjusted death rate: 97.7 per 10,000 population (1999); Age adjusted cancer mortality rate: 187.1 deaths per 100,000 population (1999). Air Quality Index: 61% good, 39% moderate, 0% unhealthy (percent of days in 2000). Number of physicians: 25.2 per 10,000 population (1999); Number of hospital beds: 5.5 per 10,000 population (1999).
Elections: 2000 Presidential election results: 39.2% Gore, 59.2% Bush, 0.5% Nader, 0.7% Buchanan

Additional Information Contacts

Warrick County Government Offices 812-897-6120
Newburgh Chamber of Commerce. 812-853-5078
Warrick County Chamber of Commerce 812-897-2340

Warrick County Communities

BOONVILLE (city). Covers a land area of 2.947 square miles and a water area of 0.018 square miles. Located at 38.04° N. Lat.; 87.27° W. Long. Elevation is 430 feet.
History: Boonville was laid out in 1818 as a coal-mining and farming center at a place where several wagon trails crossed. It was named for Jesse Boon, the father of Ratliff Boon who was the first treasurer of Warrick County, the first state representative from Warrick County in 1816, and a representative in Congress from 1825-1839.
Population: 6,834 (2000); Race: 99.3% White, 0.7% Black, 0.0% Asian, 0.0% American Indian and Alaska Native, 0.1% Hispanic of any race, 0.0% two or more races (2000); Density: 2,318.9 persons per square mile (2000); Age: 27.2% under 18, 15.0% over 64 (2000); Marriage status: 20.9% never married, 56.2% now married, 13.5% widowed, 9.4% divorced (2000); Foreign born: 0.4% (2000); Ancestry (includes multiple ancestries): 21.3% German, 20.3% United States or American, 9.5% Irish, 6.7% English, 5.0% Other groups (2000).
Economy: Employment by occupation: 8.1% management, 15.2% professional, 16.5% services, 24.7% sales, 0.4% farming, 15.1% construction, 20.0% production (2000).
Income: Per capita income: $15,869 (2000); Median household income: $34,913 (2000); Poverty rate: 9.2% (2000).
Taxes: Total city taxes per capita: $265 (1997); City property taxes per capita: $188 (1997).
Education: High school graduation rate: 75.7% (2000); College graduation rate: 10.9% (2000).

School District(s)
Warrick County School Corp (KG-12)
2000 Enrollment: 8,981 812-897-0400
Housing: Homeownership rate: 73.7% (2000); Median home value: $68,500 (2000); Median rent: $358 per month (2000); Median age of housing: 42 years (2000).
Hospitals: Saint Mary's Warrick (48 beds)
Safety: Violent crime rate: 107.7 per 10,000 population; Property crime rate: 394.3 per 10,000 population (2001).
Newspapers: The Boonville Standard (1 x week); The Warrick East (1 x week); The Warrick West Shopper (1 x week)
Transportation: Commute to work: 95.9% car, 0.3% public transportation, 1.8% walk, 1.4% work from home (2000); Travel time to work: 40.4% less than 15 minutes, 21.7% 15 to 30 minutes, 26.3% 30 to 45 minutes, 8.0% 45 to 60 minutes, 3.6% 60 minutes or more (2000)
Additional Information Contacts
Warrick County Chamber of Commerce 812-897-2340

CHANDLER (town). Covers a land area of 1.689 square miles and a water area of 0 square miles. Located at 38.04° N. Lat.; 87.36° W. Long. Elevation is 421 feet.
Population: 3,094 (2000); Race: 100.0% White, 0.0% Black, 0.0% Asian, 0.0% American Indian and Alaska Native, 0.0% Hispanic of any race, 0.0% two or more races (2000); Density: 1,831.9 persons per square mile (2000); Age: 26.2% under 18, 9.3% over 64 (2000); Marriage status: 20.3% never married, 62.0% now married, 6.6% widowed, 11.0% divorced (2000); Foreign born: 0.2% (2000); Ancestry (includes multiple ancestries): 16.7% German, 13.1% United States or American, 10.6% Irish, 9.3% English, 6.3% Other groups (2000).
Economy: In agricultural and bituminous-coal area. Manufacturing: electronics, hardwoods, kiln dried lumber. Single-family building permits issued: 9 (2001) / 2 (2000); Multi-family building permits issued: 0 (2001) / 0 (2000); Employment by occupation: 3.4% management, 4.5% professional, 19.5% services, 28.2% sales, 0.7% farming, 14.7% construction, 28.9% production (2000).
Income: Per capita income: $16,172 (2000); Median household income: $36,047 (2000); Poverty rate: 14.1% (2000).
Taxes: Total city taxes per capita: $107 (1997); City property taxes per capita: $87 (1997).
Education: High school graduation rate: 74.6% (2000); College graduation rate: 4.5% (2000).
Housing: Homeownership rate: 81.9% (2000); Median home value: $66,600 (2000); Median rent: $328 per month (2000); Median age of housing: 34 years (2000).
Transportation: Commute to work: 96.1% car, 0.0% public transportation, 1.8% walk, 0.5% work from home (2000); Travel time to work: 20.2% less than 15 minutes, 49.0% 15 to 30 minutes, 21.4% 30 to 45 minutes, 4.4% 45 to 60 minutes, 5.0% 60 minutes or more (2000)

ELBERFELD (town). Covers a land area of 0.310 square miles and a water area of 0 square miles. Located at 38.16° N. Lat.; 87.44° W. Long. Elevation is 445 feet.
Population: 636 (2000); Race: 100.0% White, 0.0% Black, 0.0% Asian, 0.0% American Indian and Alaska Native, 0.3% Hispanic of any race, 0.0% two or more races (2000); Density: 2,050.7 persons per square mile (2000); Age: 21.0% under 18, 13.6% over 64 (2000); Marriage status: 19.8% never married, 61.8% now married, 7.1% widowed, 11.2% divorced (2000); Foreign born: 0.3% (2000); Ancestry (includes multiple ancestries): 37.5% German, 18.4% United States or American, 9.3% Irish, 8.8% English, 7.4% Other groups (2000).
Economy: In agricultural and bituminous-coal area. Surface mines. Employment by occupation: 6.3% management, 11.7% professional, 19.5% services, 27.6% sales, 0.6% farming, 14.1% construction, 20.1% production (2000).
Income: Per capita income: $19,236 (2000); Median household income: $40,833 (2000); Poverty rate: 4.2% (2000).
Taxes: Total city taxes per capita: $78 (1997); City property taxes per capita: $60 (1997).
Education: High school graduation rate: 82.2% (2000); College graduation rate: 8.9% (2000).
Housing: Homeownership rate: 84.2% (2000); Median home value: $81,900 (2000); Median rent: $266 per month (2000); Median age of housing: 46 years (2000).
Transportation: Commute to work: 93.7% car, 0.3% public transportation, 1.8% walk, 3.6% work from home (2000); Travel time to work: 14.0% less than 15 minutes, 42.4% 15 to 30 minutes, 35.2% 30 to 45 minutes, 4.4% 45 to 60 minutes, 4.0% 60 minutes or more (2000)

LYNNVILLE (town). Covers a land area of 1.707 square miles and a water area of 0.229 square miles. Located at 38.20° N. Lat.; 87.31° W. Long. Elevation is 497 feet.
Population: 781 (2000); Race: 98.3% White, 0.0% Black, 0.0% Asian, 0.0% American Indian and Alaska Native, 0.0% Hispanic of any race, 1.7% two or more races (2000); Density: 457.5 persons per square mile (2000); Age: 25.2% under 18, 15.8% over 64 (2000); Marriage status: 18.0% never married, 61.4% now married, 8.6% widowed, 12.0% divorced (2000); Foreign born: 0.0% (2000); Ancestry (includes multiple ancestries): 25.2% United States or American, 15.7% German, 13.4% Irish, 10.3% English, 7.6% Other groups (2000).
Economy: In agricultural and bituminous-coal area. Employment by occupation: 5.7% management, 12.5% professional, 18.8% services, 21.4% sales, 0.6% farming, 14.0% construction, 27.1% production (2000).
Income: Per capita income: $16,288 (2000); Median household income: $35,556 (2000); Poverty rate: 8.0% (2000).
Taxes: Total city taxes per capita: $69 (1997); City property taxes per capita: $54 (1997).
Education: High school graduation rate: 78.2% (2000); College graduation rate: 9.5% (2000).
Housing: Homeownership rate: 82.3% (2000); Median home value: $70,700 (2000); Median rent: $287 per month (2000); Median age of housing: 33 years (2000).
Transportation: Commute to work: 98.2% car, 0.0% public transportation, 1.2% walk, 0.6% work from home (2000); Travel time to work: 16.6% less than 15 minutes, 25.6% 15 to 30 minutes, 37.3% 30 to 45 minutes, 14.5% 45 to 60 minutes, 6.0% 60 minutes or more (2000)

NEWBURGH (town). Aka House Estates. Covers a land area of 1.358 square miles and a water area of 0.002 square miles. Located at 37.94° N. Lat.; 87.40° W. Long. Elevation is 393 feet.
History: Settled 1803, laid out 1818.
Population: 3,088 (2000); Race: 99.3% White, 0.0% Black, 0.0% Asian, 0.4% American Indian and Alaska Native, 0.7% Hispanic of any race, 0.3% two or more races (2000); Density: 2,274.6 persons per square mile (2000); Age: 23.1% under 18, 12.7% over 64 (2000); Marriage status: 18.8% never married, 61.1% now married, 7.4% widowed, 12.6% divorced (2000); Foreign born: 1.3% (2000); Ancestry (includes multiple ancestries): 29.6% German, 14.9% Irish, 14.4% English, 11.7% United States or American, 6.1% Other groups (2000).
Economy: Manufacturing: aluminum ingots. Single-family building permits issued: 21 (2001) / 50 (2000); Multi-family building permits issued: 0 (2001) / 0 (2000); Employment by occupation: 16.6% management, 19.7% professional, 17.1% services, 26.4% sales, 0.0% farming, 4.9% construction, 15.2% production (2000).

Income: Per capita income: $24,537 (2000); Median household income: $41,581 (2000); Poverty rate: 2.5% (2000).
Taxes: Total city taxes per capita: $192 (1997); City property taxes per capita: $144 (1997).
Education: High school graduation rate: 89.8% (2000); College graduation rate: 32.8% (2000).

Four-year College(s)

ITT Technical Institute (Private, For-profit)
2001 Enrollment: 364 812-858-1600
2001 Tuition: In-state $10,548; Out-of-state $10,548
Trinity Theological Seminary-Trinity College (Private, Not-for-profit)
2001 Enrollment: 7,144 812-853-0611
2001 Tuition: In-state $2,200; Out-of-state $2,200

Housing: Homeownership rate: 73.3% (2000); Median home value: $99,600 (2000); Median rent: $346 per month (2000); Median age of housing: 34 years (2000).
Newspapers: Newburgh/Chandler Register (1 x week)
Transportation: Commute to work: 97.3% car, 0.0% public transportation, 1.1% walk, 1.6% work from home (2000); Travel time to work: 24.9% less than 15 minutes, 56.8% 15 to 30 minutes, 11.7% 30 to 45 minutes, 3.7% 45 to 60 minutes, 2.9% 60 minutes or more (2000)
Additional Information Contacts
Newburgh Chamber of Commerce. 812-853-5078

TENNYSON (town). Covers a land area of 0.251 square miles and a water area of 0 square miles. Located at 38.08° N. Lat.; 87.11° W. Long. Elevation is 435 feet.
Population: 290 (2000); Race: 97.2% White, 0.7% Black, 0.0% Asian, 0.0% American Indian and Alaska Native, 1.1% Hispanic of any race, 2.1% two or more races (2000); Density: 1,155.1 persons per square mile (2000); Age: 36.5% under 18, 8.1% over 64 (2000); Marriage status: 28.4% never married, 48.3% now married, 9.0% widowed, 14.4% divorced (2000); Foreign born: 0.0% (2000); Ancestry (includes multiple ancestries): 17.9% German, 15.4% United States or American, 10.9% English, 7.0% Irish, 6.3% Other groups (2000).
Economy: Agricultural area. Employment by occupation: 8.4% management, 4.2% professional, 22.7% services, 8.4% sales, 0.0% farming, 18.5% construction, 37.8% production (2000).
Income: Per capita income: $13,660 (2000); Median household income: $36,250 (2000); Poverty rate: 16.8% (2000).
Taxes: Total city taxes per capita: $48 (1997); City property taxes per capita: $38 (1997).
Education: High school graduation rate: 59.4% (2000); College graduation rate: 4.4% (2000).
Housing: Homeownership rate: 79.4% (2000); Median home value: $52,900 (2000); Median rent: $181 per month (2000); Median age of housing: 31 years (2000).
Transportation: Commute to work: 86.6% car, 0.0% public transportation, 4.2% walk, 5.9% work from home (2000); Travel time to work: 8.0% less than 15 minutes, 30.4% 15 to 30 minutes, 36.6% 30 to 45 minutes, 15.2% 45 to 60 minutes, 9.8% 60 minutes or more (2000)

Washington County

Located in southern Indiana; bounded on the north by the Muscatatuck River and the East Fork of the White River; drained by the Blue and Lost Rivers. Covers a land area of 514.40 square miles, a water area of 2.10 square miles, and is located in the Eastern Time Zone. The county government was organized in 1813. County seat is Salem.

Weather Station: Salem — Elevation: 797 feet

	Jan	Feb	Mar	Apr	May	Jun	Jul	Aug	Sep	Oct	Nov	Dec
High	39	45	55	67	76	84	87	86	80	69	55	44
Low	22	25	33	42	52	61	65	63	56	44	36	27
Precip	3.2	2.9	4.3	4.7	5.1	3.9	4.4	3.5	2.9	2.9	4.0	3.9
Snow	5.7	5.6	3.4	0.2	0.0	0.0	0.0	0.0	0.0	0.2	0.5	2.4

High and Low temperatures in degrees Fahrenheit; Precipitation and Snow in inches

Population: 27,223 (2000); Race: 98.7% White, 0.2% Black, 0.2% Asian, 0.0% American Indian and Alaska Native, 0.6% Hispanic of any race, 0.6% two or more races (2000); Density: 52.9 persons per square mile (2000); Age: 26.5% under 18, 12.1% over 64 (2000).
Religion: Five largest groups: 13.8% Christian Churches and Churches of Christ, 7.4% American Baptist Churches in the USA, 5.9% Churches of Christ, 4.1% The United Methodist Church, 3.8% Christian Church (Disciples of Christ) (2000).
Economy: Unemployment rate: 5.9% (11/2002); Total civilian labor force: 11,597 (11/2002); Leading industries: 49.2% manufacturing; 12.0% retail trade; 10.9% health care and social assistance (2000); Companies that employ more than 1,000 persons: 0 (2000); Companies that employ more than 100 persons: 8 (2000); Farms: 914 totaling 181,298 acres (1997); Minority business ownership rate: 0.0% (1997); Women business ownership rate: 17.4% (1997); Retail sales per capita: $6,495 (1997). Single-family building permits issued: 30 (2001) / 35 (2000); Multi-family building permits issued: 50 (2001) / 0 (2000).
Income: Per capita income: $16,748 (2000); Median household income: $36,630 (2000); Poverty rate: 10.6% (2000); Bankruptcy rate: 7.33% (2001).
Taxes: Total county taxes per capita: $216 (2000); County property taxes per capita: $145 (2000).
Education: High school graduation rate: 75.2% (2000); College graduation rate: 10.2% (2000).
Housing: Homeownership rate: 81.1% (2000); Median home value: $77,500 (2000); Median rent: $319 per month (2000); Median age of housing: 27 years (2000).
Health: Birth rate: 127.5 per 10,000 population (1998); Age adjusted death rate: 90.9 per 10,000 population (1999); Age adjusted cancer mortality rate: 235.2 deaths per 100,000 population (1999). Number of physicians: 6.6 per 10,000 population (1999); Number of hospital beds: 21.3 per 10,000 population (1999).
Elections: 2000 Presidential election results: 37.5% Gore, 59.9% Bush, 0.5% Nader, 1.3% Buchanan
National and State Parks: Clark State Forest; Jackson-Washington State Forest
Additional Information Contacts
Washington County Government Offices 812-883-4805
Washington County Board of Realtors 812-883-5695

Washington County Communities

CAMPBELLSBURG (town). Covers a land area of 0.978 square miles and a water area of 0 square miles. Located at 38.65° N. Lat.; 86.26° W. Long. Elevation is 830 feet.
Population: 578 (2000); Race: 100.0% White, 0.0% Black, 0.0% Asian, 0.0% American Indian and Alaska Native, 1.6% Hispanic of any race, 0.0% two or more races (2000); Density: 591.2 persons per square mile (2000); Age: 27.7% under 18, 14.8% over 64 (2000); Marriage status: 29.4% never married, 49.8% now married, 11.9% widowed, 8.9% divorced (2000); Foreign born: 0.0% (2000); Ancestry (includes multiple ancestries): 15.1% United States or American, 11.1% English, 8.4% Other groups, 7.8% Irish, 7.3% German (2000).
Economy: In agricultural area. Employment by occupation: 3.3% management, 11.4% professional, 13.8% services, 8.1% sales, 1.6% farming, 14.6% construction, 47.2% production (2000).
Income: Per capita income: $13,672 (2000); Median household income: $23,438 (2000); Poverty rate: 15.3% (2000).
Taxes: Total city taxes per capita: $51 (1997); City property taxes per capita: $48 (1997).
Education: High school graduation rate: 65.7% (2000); College graduation rate: 6.4% (2000).

School District(s)

South Central Area Special Ed
2000 Enrollment: n/a 812-755-4868
West Washington School Corp (PK-12)
2000 Enrollment: 1,098 812-755-4872

Housing: Homeownership rate: 68.0% (2000); Median home value: $52,600 (2000); Median rent: $258 per month (2000); Median age of housing: 40 years (2000).
Transportation: Commute to work: 95.0% car, 0.0% public transportation, 4.2% walk, 0.8% work from home (2000); Travel time to work: 32.6% less than 15 minutes, 44.1% 15 to 30 minutes, 8.9% 30 to 45 minutes, 6.4% 45 to 60 minutes, 8.1% 60 minutes or more (2000)

FREDERICKSBURG (town). Covers a land area of 1.003 square miles and a water area of 0 square miles. Located at 38.43° N. Lat.; 86.19° W. Long. Elevation is 615 feet.
History: Fredericksburg was settled in 1805 and became a toll station on the plank road between New Albany and Vincennes. Many of the settlers here were Quakers who built the Lick Creek Friends Church in 1815.
Population: 92 (2000); Race: 100.0% White, 0.0% Black, 0.0% Asian, 0.0% American Indian and Alaska Native, 0.0% Hispanic of any race, 0.0% two or more races (2000); Density: 91.7 persons per square mile (2000); Age: 21.4%

under 18, 13.3% over 64 (2000); Marriage status: 23.9% never married, 47.7% now married, 5.7% widowed, 22.7% divorced (2000); Foreign born: 0.0% (2000); Ancestry (includes multiple ancestries): 17.3% United States or American, 13.3% French (except Basque), 12.2% German, 11.2% Irish, 11.2% Other groups (2000).
Economy: Employment by occupation: 7.7% management, 0.0% professional, 15.4% services, 20.5% sales, 0.0% farming, 25.6% construction, 30.8% production (2000).
Income: Per capita income: $10,626 (2000); Median household income: $21,250 (2000); Poverty rate: 23.5% (2000).
Taxes: Total city taxes per capita: $56 (1997); City property taxes per capita: $56 (1997).
Education: High school graduation rate: 75.0% (2000); College graduation rate: 0.0% (2000).
Housing: Homeownership rate: 57.8% (2000); Median home value: $61,700 (2000); Median rent: $361 per month (2000); Median age of housing: 43 years (2000).
Transportation: Commute to work: 97.3% car, 0.0% public transportation, 0.0% walk, 2.7% work from home (2000); Travel time to work: 0.0% less than 15 minutes, 19.4% 15 to 30 minutes, 55.6% 30 to 45 minutes, 25.0% 45 to 60 minutes, 0.0% 60 minutes or more (2000)

HARDINSBURG (town). Covers a land area of 2.039 square miles and a water area of 0 square miles. Located at 38.46° N. Lat.; 86.27° W. Long. Elevation is 700 feet.
History: Laid out 1838.
Population: 244 (2000); Race: 98.8% White, 0.0% Black, 0.0% Asian, 0.0% American Indian and Alaska Native, 7.9% Hispanic of any race, 0.0% two or more races (2000); Density: 119.7 persons per square mile (2000); Age: 32.9% under 18, 11.9% over 64 (2000); Marriage status: 18.6% never married, 59.0% now married, 7.7% widowed, 14.8% divorced (2000); Foreign born: 0.0% (2000); Ancestry (includes multiple ancestries): 17.1% Irish, 14.7% German, 13.5% Polish, 12.7% English, 11.9% United States or American (2000).
Economy: Agricultural area. Wood furniture. Employment by occupation: 8.3% management, 12.5% professional, 5.2% services, 21.9% sales, 0.0% farming, 14.6% construction, 37.5% production (2000).
Income: Per capita income: $14,112 (2000); Median household income: $23,125 (2000); Poverty rate: 13.9% (2000).
Taxes: Total city taxes per capita: $9 (1997); City property taxes per capita: $9 (1997).
Education: High school graduation rate: 75.3% (2000); College graduation rate: 8.0% (2000).

School District(s)

South Central Area Vocational
2000 Enrollment: n/a 812-472-3885
Housing: Homeownership rate: 68.7% (2000); Median home value: $63,300 (2000); Median rent: $355 per month (2000); Median age of housing: 54 years (2000).
Transportation: Commute to work: 92.7% car, 3.1% public transportation, 0.0% walk, 2.1% work from home (2000); Travel time to work: 9.6% less than 15 minutes, 19.1% 15 to 30 minutes, 44.7% 30 to 45 minutes, 12.8% 45 to 60 minutes, 13.8% 60 minutes or more (2000)

LITTLE YORK (town). Covers a land area of 0.977 square miles and a water area of 0 square miles. Located at 38.70° N. Lat.; 85.90° W. Long. Elevation is 563 feet.
History: Laid out 1831.
Population: 185 (2000); Race: 100.0% White, 0.0% Black, 0.0% Asian, 0.0% American Indian and Alaska Native, 0.0% Hispanic of any race, 0.0% two or more races (2000); Density: 189.3 persons per square mile (2000); Age: 20.2% under 18, 13.9% over 64 (2000); Marriage status: 20.0% never married, 71.7% now married, 2.8% widowed, 5.5% divorced (2000); Foreign born: 0.0% (2000); Ancestry (includes multiple ancestries): 15.6% United States or American, 14.5% German, 6.9% English, 5.2% Irish, 5.2% Other groups (2000).
Economy: Agricultural area. Employment by occupation: 11.3% management, 12.3% professional, 11.3% services, 19.8% sales, 1.9% farming, 1.9% construction, 41.5% production (2000).
Income: Per capita income: $16,994 (2000); Median household income: $42,500 (2000); Poverty rate: 4.6% (2000).
Taxes: Total city taxes per capita: $6 (1997); City property taxes per capita: $6 (1997).
Education: High school graduation rate: 81.1% (2000); College graduation rate: 14.8% (2000).
Housing: Homeownership rate: 82.2% (2000); Median home value: $87,500 (2000); Median rent: $505 per month (2000); Median age of housing: 41 years (2000).
Transportation: Commute to work: 94.1% car, 0.0% public transportation, 2.0% walk, 2.0% work from home (2000); Travel time to work: 42.0% less than 15 minutes, 35.0% 15 to 30 minutes, 14.0% 30 to 45 minutes, 5.0% 45 to 60 minutes, 4.0% 60 minutes or more (2000)

LIVONIA (town). Covers a land area of 1.045 square miles and a water area of 0 square miles. Located at 38.55° N. Lat.; 86.27° W. Long. Elevation is 780 feet.
History: Laid out 1819.
Population: 112 (2000); Race: 100.0% White, 0.0% Black, 0.0% Asian, 0.0% American Indian and Alaska Native, 0.0% Hispanic of any race, 0.0% two or more races (2000); Density: 107.2 persons per square mile (2000); Age: 24.3% under 18, 5.8% over 64 (2000); Marriage status: 35.4% never married, 54.9% now married, 4.9% widowed, 4.9% divorced (2000); Foreign born: 0.0% (2000); Ancestry (includes multiple ancestries): 14.6% United States or American, 9.7% German, 7.8% Irish, 6.8% English, 4.9% Other groups (2000).
Economy: Agricultural area. Employment by occupation: 5.1% management, 13.6% professional, 22.0% services, 16.9% sales, 3.4% farming, 8.5% construction, 30.5% production (2000).
Income: Per capita income: $14,233 (2000); Median household income: $32,321 (2000); Poverty rate: 11.2% (2000).
Taxes: Total city taxes per capita: $7 (1997); City property taxes per capita: $7 (1997).
Education: High school graduation rate: 60.3% (2000); College graduation rate: 9.5% (2000).
Housing: Homeownership rate: 77.3% (2000); Median home value: $61,900 (2000); Median rent: $275 per month (2000); Median age of housing: 39 years (2000).
Transportation: Commute to work: 89.8% car, 3.4% public transportation, 6.8% walk, 0.0% work from home (2000); Travel time to work: 27.1% less than 15 minutes, 28.8% 15 to 30 minutes, 11.9% 30 to 45 minutes, 15.3% 45 to 60 minutes, 16.9% 60 minutes or more (2000)

NEW PEKIN (town). Aka Pekin. Covers a land area of 2.335 square miles and a water area of 0.035 square miles. Located at 38.50° N. Lat.; 86.01° W. Long. Elevation is 703 feet.
Population: 1,334 (2000); Race: 96.3% White, 0.4% Black, 0.0% Asian, 0.0% American Indian and Alaska Native, 2.7% Hispanic of any race, 1.5% two or more races (2000); Density: 571.4 persons per square mile (2000); Age: 26.9% under 18, 10.6% over 64 (2000); Marriage status: 21.7% never married, 57.8% now married, 5.3% widowed, 15.2% divorced (2000); Foreign born: 0.8% (2000); Ancestry (includes multiple ancestries): 14.2% United States or American, 12.2% Other groups, 10.7% German, 10.3% Irish, 6.5% English (2000).
Economy: Employment by occupation: 3.4% management, 7.1% professional, 18.1% services, 16.1% sales, 1.5% farming, 13.6% construction, 40.2% production (2000).
Income: Per capita income: $14,710 (2000); Median household income: $32,546 (2000); Poverty rate: 17.1% (2000).
Taxes: Total city taxes per capita: $51 (1997); City property taxes per capita: $51 (1997).
Education: High school graduation rate: 64.2% (2000); College graduation rate: 3.9% (2000).
Housing: Homeownership rate: 66.0% (2000); Median home value: $66,300 (2000); Median rent: $312 per month (2000); Median age of housing: 25 years (2000).
Transportation: Commute to work: 93.1% car, 0.0% public transportation, 3.0% walk, 2.0% work from home (2000); Travel time to work: 24.9% less than 15 minutes, 26.8% 15 to 30 minutes, 23.7% 30 to 45 minutes, 15.9% 45 to 60 minutes, 8.8% 60 minutes or more (2000)

PEKIN (unincorporated postal area, zip code 47165). Aka New Pekin. Covers a land area of 77.457 square miles and a water area of 0.160 square miles. Located at 38.51° N. Lat.; 86.01° W. Long. Elevation is 685 feet.
Population: 5,825 (2000); Race: 98.1% White, 0.1% Black, 0.1% Asian, 0.1% American Indian and Alaska Native, 1.5% Hispanic of any race, 0.9% two or more races (2000); Density: 75.2 persons per square mile (2000); Age: 27.9% under 18, 9.1% over 64 (2000); Marriage status: 18.7% never married, 65.1% now married, 4.7% widowed, 11.4% divorced (2000); Foreign born: 0.5% (2000); Ancestry (includes multiple ancestries): 20.5% German, 13.3% Irish, 12.8% United States or American, 9.5% Other groups, 8.4% English (2000).

Economy: In agricultural area. Employment by occupation: 8.8% management, 15.5% professional, 13.1% services, 20.8% sales, 1.8% farming, 11.9% construction, 28.1% production (2000).
Income: Per capita income: $16,551 (2000); Median household income: $40,149 (2000); Poverty rate: 9.1% (2000).
Education: High school graduation rate: 78.1% (2000); College graduation rate: 10.7% (2000).

School District(s)

East Washington School Corp (KG-12)
2000 Enrollment: 1,696 812-967-3926
Housing: Homeownership rate: 82.7% (2000); Median home value: $81,500 (2000); Median rent: $296 per month (2000); Median age of housing: 22 years (2000).
Newspapers: The Banner-Gazette (1 x week)
Transportation: Commute to work: 94.5% car, 0.7% public transportation, 0.6% walk, 3.1% work from home (2000); Travel time to work: 14.4% less than 15 minutes, 20.9% 15 to 30 minutes, 32.7% 30 to 45 minutes, 21.7% 45 to 60 minutes, 10.3% 60 minutes or more (2000)

SALEM (city). Covers a land area of 3.890 square miles and a water area of 0.017 square miles. Located at 38.60° N. Lat.; 86.09° W. Long. Elevation is 747 feet.
History: Salem was founded in 1814 and named for Salem, North Carolina, the former home of the wife of the county surveyor. John Hay, statesman, diplomat, poet, and historian, was born in 1838 in Salem. In 1863 Salem was burned and looted by General Morgan and his raiders.
Population: 6,172 (2000); Race: 99.2% White, 0.0% Black, 0.3% Asian, 0.1% American Indian and Alaska Native, 0.1% Hispanic of any race, 0.3% two or more races (2000); Density: 1,586.8 persons per square mile (2000); Age: 21.3% under 18, 20.7% over 64 (2000); Marriage status: 20.8% never married, 54.8% now married, 10.7% widowed, 13.7% divorced (2000); Foreign born: 0.9% (2000); Ancestry (includes multiple ancestries): 17.0% United States or American, 13.9% German, 11.0% English, 8.6% Irish, 7.1% Other groups (2000).
Economy: Single-family building permits issued: 30 (2001) / 35 (2000); Multi-family building permits issued: 50 (2001) / 0 (2000); Employment by occupation: 7.5% management, 12.7% professional, 17.7% services, 19.3% sales, 0.7% farming, 8.4% construction, 33.7% production (2000).
Income: Per capita income: $16,299 (2000); Median household income: $29,256 (2000); Poverty rate: 11.6% (2000).
Taxes: Total city taxes per capita: $187 (1997); City property taxes per capita: $153 (1997).
Education: High school graduation rate: 70.1% (2000); College graduation rate: 9.2% (2000).

School District(s)

Salem Community Schools (KG-12)
2000 Enrollment: 1,978 812-883-4437
Housing: Homeownership rate: 70.7% (2000); Median home value: $67,200 (2000); Median rent: $326 per month (2000); Median age of housing: 40 years (2000).
Hospitals: Washington County Memorial Hospital (70 beds)
Safety: Violent crime rate: 8.1 per 10,000 population; Property crime rate: 67.7 per 10,000 population (2001).
Newspapers: The Salem Leader (1 x week); The Salem Democrat (1 x week); Your Ad-vantage (1 x week)
Transportation: Commute to work: 94.0% car, 0.2% public transportation, 3.5% walk, 1.3% work from home (2000); Travel time to work: 56.4% less than 15 minutes, 17.4% 15 to 30 minutes, 8.9% 30 to 45 minutes, 10.5% 45 to 60 minutes, 6.8% 60 minutes or more (2000)
Additional Information Contacts
Washington County Board of Realtors 812-883-5695

SALTILLO (town). Covers a land area of 1.163 square miles and a water area of 0 square miles. Located at 38.66° N. Lat.; 86.29° W. Long. Elevation is 800 feet.
Population: 107 (2000); Race: 100.0% White, 0.0% Black, 0.0% Asian, 0.0% American Indian and Alaska Native, 0.0% Hispanic of any race, 0.0% two or more races (2000); Density: 92.0 persons per square mile (2000); Age: 25.9% under 18, 20.7% over 64 (2000); Marriage status: 17.6% never married, 65.9% now married, 7.7% widowed, 8.8% divorced (2000); Foreign born: 0.0% (2000); Ancestry (includes multiple ancestries): 25.0% United States or American, 12.9% German, 11.2% Other groups, 5.2% English, 0.9% Irish (2000).
Economy: In agricultural area. Employment by occupation: 4.3% management, 15.2% professional, 19.6% services, 15.2% sales, 0.0% farming, 8.7% construction, 37.0% production (2000).
Income: Per capita income: $16,253 (2000); Median household income: $22,500 (2000); Poverty rate: 12.1% (2000).
Taxes: Total city taxes per capita: $8 (1997); City property taxes per capita: $8 (1997).
Education: High school graduation rate: 63.4% (2000); College graduation rate: 11.0% (2000).
Housing: Homeownership rate: 82.4% (2000); Median home value: $29,600 (2000); Median rent: $275 per month (2000); Median age of housing: 24 years (2000).
Transportation: Commute to work: 100.0% car, 0.0% public transportation, 0.0% walk, 0.0% work from home (2000); Travel time to work: 23.9% less than 15 minutes, 37.0% 15 to 30 minutes, 13.0% 30 to 45 minutes, 13.0% 45 to 60 minutes, 13.0% 60 minutes or more (2000)

Wayne County

Located in eastern Indiana; bounded on the east by Ohio; drained by the Whitewater River and its East Fork. Covers a land area of 403.60 square miles, a water area of 0.80 square miles, and is located in the Eastern Time Zone. The county government was organized in 1810. County seat is Richmond.

Weather Station: Cambridge City 3 N — Elevation: 997 feet

	Jan	Feb	Mar	Apr	May	Jun	Jul	Aug	Sep	Oct	Nov	Dec
High	33	38	49	61	71	80	83	82	76	64	51	39
Low	15	18	28	37	48	57	61	59	51	39	31	22
Precip	2.4	2.3	3.4	4.2	4.8	4.4	4.2	3.5	2.8	2.8	3.5	3.0
Snow	7.2	5.4	3.5	0.5	tr	0.0	0.0	0.0	0.0	0.1	1.1	4.0

High and Low temperatures in degrees Fahrenheit; Precipitation and Snow in inches

Weather Station: Richmond Water Works — Elevation: 1,013 feet

	Jan	Feb	Mar	Apr	May	Jun	Jul	Aug	Sep	Oct	Nov	Dec
High	34	39	50	62	73	81	85	83	77	64	51	40
Low	17	20	30	39	49	58	62	60	53	41	33	24
Precip	2.5	2.3	3.2	3.9	4.3	4.2	3.8	3.6	2.5	3.1	3.3	2.9
Snow	6.7	4.7	2.4	0.7	tr	0.0	0.0	0.0	0.0	0.2	0.9	3.1

High and Low temperatures in degrees Fahrenheit; Precipitation and Snow in inches

Population: 71,097 (2000); Race: 92.0% White, 4.6% Black, 0.7% Asian, 0.3% American Indian and Alaska Native, 1.3% Hispanic of any race, 1.7% two or more races (2000); Density: 176.2 persons per square mile (2000); Age: 24.2% under 18, 15.9% over 64 (2000).
Religion: Five largest groups: 7.7% Catholic Church, 5.1% The United Methodist Church, 4.3% Christian Churches and Churches of Christ, 3.6% Southern Baptist Convention, 3.2% Evangelical Lutheran Church in America (2000).
Economy: Unemployment rate: 5.1% (11/2002); Total civilian labor force: 35,532 (11/2002); Leading industries: 27.3% manufacturing; 14.3% retail trade; 14.2% health care and social assistance (2000); Companies that employ more than 1,000 persons: 4 (2000); Companies that employ more than 100 persons: 55 (2000); Farms: 814 totaling 172,860 acres (1997); Minority business ownership rate: 4.2% (1997); Women business ownership rate: 28.8% (1997); Retail sales per capita: $9,612 (1997). Single-family building permits issued: 126 (2001) / 142 (2000); Multi-family building permits issued: 0 (2001) / 4 (2000).
Income: Per capita income: $17,727 (2000); Median household income: $34,885 (2000); Poverty rate: 11.4% (2000); Bankruptcy rate: 7.61% (2001).
Taxes: Total county taxes per capita: $393 (2000); County property taxes per capita: $299 (2000).
Education: High school graduation rate: 78.1% (2000); College graduation rate: 13.7% (2000).
Housing: Homeownership rate: 68.7% (2000); Median home value: $80,300 (2000); Median rent: $362 per month (2000); Median age of housing: 46 years (2000).
Health: Birth rate: 132.1 per 10,000 population (1998); Age adjusted death rate: 93.6 per 10,000 population (1999); Age adjusted cancer mortality rate: 245.7 deaths per 100,000 population (1999). Air Quality Index: 100% good, 0% moderate, 0% unhealthy (percent of days in 2000). Number of physicians: 17.3 per 10,000 population (1999); Number of hospital beds: 76.9 per 10,000 population (1999).
Elections: 2000 Presidential election results: 40.9% Gore, 56.8% Bush, 0.8% Nader, 1.0% Buchanan
Additional Information Contacts
Wayne County Government Offices 765-973-9200
Hagerstown Chamber of Commerce 765-489-5071
Richmond Association of Realtors. 765-962-7687

Richmond Chamber of Commerce........................765-962-1511
Wayne County Convention Bureau.....................765-935-8687

Wayne County Communities

BOSTON (town). Covers a land area of 0.211 square miles and a water area of 0 square miles. Located at 39.74° N. Lat.; 84.85° W. Long. Elevation is 1,136 feet.

Population: 177 (2000); Race: 100.0% White, 0.0% Black, 0.0% Asian, 0.0% American Indian and Alaska Native, 0.0% Hispanic of any race, 0.0% two or more races (2000); Density: 838.5 persons per square mile (2000); Age: 25.8% under 18, 4.5% over 64 (2000); Marriage status: 18.2% never married, 70.8% now married, 0.6% widowed, 10.4% divorced (2000); Foreign born: 0.0% (2000); Ancestry (includes multiple ancestries): 26.8% German, 25.8% United States or American, 21.7% Irish, 9.1% English, 4.0% Other groups (2000).

Economy: Employment by occupation: 13.0% management, 8.7% professional, 9.6% services, 21.7% sales, 0.0% farming, 14.8% construction, 32.2% production (2000).

Income: Per capita income: $19,852 (2000); Median household income: $50,625 (2000); Poverty rate: 2.5% (2000).

Taxes: Total city taxes per capita: $13 (1997); City property taxes per capita: $0 (1997).

Education: High school graduation rate: 73.2% (2000); College graduation rate: 5.7% (2000).

Housing: Homeownership rate: 89.9% (2000); Median home value: $61,900 (2000); Median rent: $242 per month (2000); Median age of housing: 60+ years (2000).

Transportation: Commute to work: 92.9% car, 2.7% public transportation, 2.7% walk, 0.0% work from home (2000); Travel time to work: 34.5% less than 15 minutes, 48.7% 15 to 30 minutes, 5.3% 30 to 45 minutes, 2.7% 45 to 60 minutes, 8.8% 60 minutes or more (2000)

CAMBRIDGE CITY (town). Covers a land area of 1.045 square miles and a water area of 0 square miles. Located at 39.81° N. Lat.; 85.17° W. Long. Elevation is 937 feet.

History: Founded in 1836 as a depot on the Whitewater Canal, Cambridge City was a shipping center for Indianapolis merchants for a time.

Population: 2,121 (2000); Race: 99.8% White, 0.0% Black, 0.2% Asian, 0.0% American Indian and Alaska Native, 0.8% Hispanic of any race, 0.0% two or more races (2000); Density: 2,030.6 persons per square mile (2000); Age: 25.6% under 18, 16.0% over 64 (2000); Marriage status: 20.1% never married, 55.1% now married, 10.9% widowed, 13.8% divorced (2000); Foreign born: 0.2% (2000); Ancestry (includes multiple ancestries): 18.0% United States or American, 17.5% German, 9.1% Irish, 7.6% English, 6.1% Other groups (2000).

Economy: Single-family building permits issued: 3 (2001) / 5 (2000); Multi-family building permits issued: 0 (2001) / 0 (2000); Employment by occupation: 9.6% management, 12.7% professional, 14.7% services, 25.4% sales, 0.8% farming, 11.4% construction, 25.5% production (2000).

Income: Per capita income: $17,691 (2000); Median household income: $33,750 (2000); Poverty rate: 8.6% (2000).

Taxes: Total city taxes per capita: $144 (1997); City property taxes per capita: $125 (1997).

Education: High school graduation rate: 77.9% (2000); College graduation rate: 12.3% (2000).

Housing: Homeownership rate: 62.8% (2000); Median home value: $77,700 (2000); Median rent: $323 per month (2000); Median age of housing: 60+ years (2000).

Newspapers: Western Wayne News (1 x week)

Transportation: Commute to work: 92.9% car, 0.0% public transportation, 3.8% walk, 1.9% work from home (2000); Travel time to work: 40.7% less than 15 minutes, 32.7% 15 to 30 minutes, 15.8% 30 to 45 minutes, 4.4% 45 to 60 minutes, 6.4% 60 minutes or more (2000)

CENTERVILLE (town). Covers a land area of 1.002 square miles and a water area of 0 square miles. Located at 39.81° N. Lat.; 84.99° W. Long. Elevation is 1,002 feet.

History: Centerville was once the seat of Wayne County. It reluctantly gave up the county records to Richmond on August 14, 1873, when shots were fired into the jail where the Centerville citizens had barricaded themselves and the records.

Population: 2,427 (2000); Race: 98.1% White, 0.6% Black, 0.1% Asian, 0.0% American Indian and Alaska Native, 2.6% Hispanic of any race, 0.6% two or more races (2000); Density: 2,421.5 persons per square mile (2000); Age: 28.1% under 18, 17.6% over 64 (2000); Marriage status: 17.4% never married, 59.2% now married, 10.4% widowed, 13.0% divorced (2000); Foreign born: 0.4% (2000); Ancestry (includes multiple ancestries): 22.9% United States or American, 19.7% German, 10.0% Irish, 9.3% English, 6.4% Other groups (2000).

Economy: Single-family building permits issued: 13 (2001) / 11 (2000); Multi-family building permits issued: 0 (2001) / 0 (2000); Employment by occupation: 10.7% management, 14.5% professional, 19.8% services, 23.5% sales, 0.0% farming, 9.2% construction, 22.3% production (2000).

Income: Per capita income: $15,526 (2000); Median household income: $32,219 (2000); Poverty rate: 6.7% (2000).

Taxes: Total city taxes per capita: $143 (1997); City property taxes per capita: $123 (1997).

Education: High school graduation rate: 82.7% (2000); College graduation rate: 11.3% (2000).

School District(s)

Centerville-Abington Com Schools (PK-12)
2000 Enrollment: 1,680..........................765-855-3475

Housing: Homeownership rate: 70.4% (2000); Median home value: $77,200 (2000); Median rent: $411 per month (2000); Median age of housing: 46 years (2000).

Transportation: Commute to work: 90.5% car, 0.5% public transportation, 4.8% walk, 3.7% work from home (2000); Travel time to work: 31.3% less than 15 minutes, 51.8% 15 to 30 minutes, 8.9% 30 to 45 minutes, 1.9% 45 to 60 minutes, 6.1% 60 minutes or more (2000)

DUBLIN (town). Covers a land area of 0.538 square miles and a water area of 0 square miles. Located at 39.81° N. Lat.; 85.20° W. Long. Elevation is 1,050 feet.

History: Located on the Old National Road, Dublin was the site of The Maples, a tavern built in 1825.

Population: 697 (2000); Race: 100.0% White, 0.0% Black, 0.0% Asian, 0.0% American Indian and Alaska Native, 0.8% Hispanic of any race, 0.0% two or more races (2000); Density: 1,295.0 persons per square mile (2000); Age: 28.5% under 18, 16.6% over 64 (2000); Marriage status: 19.9% never married, 66.7% now married, 7.0% widowed, 6.3% divorced (2000); Foreign born: 0.0% (2000); Ancestry (includes multiple ancestries): 19.6% United States or American, 14.5% German, 7.6% Irish, 5.7% Other groups, 5.0% English (2000).

Economy: Employment by occupation: 7.7% management, 13.6% professional, 13.9% services, 25.1% sales, 0.0% farming, 8.0% construction, 31.7% production (2000).

Income: Per capita income: $13,656 (2000); Median household income: $31,111 (2000); Poverty rate: 13.9% (2000).

Taxes: Total city taxes per capita: $45 (1997); City property taxes per capita: $28 (1997).

Education: High school graduation rate: 74.6% (2000); College graduation rate: 8.1% (2000).

Housing: Homeownership rate: 85.4% (2000); Median home value: $61,900 (2000); Median rent: $378 per month (2000); Median age of housing: 60+ years (2000).

Transportation: Commute to work: 95.7% car, 0.0% public transportation, 2.1% walk, 1.2% work from home (2000); Travel time to work: 30.1% less than 15 minutes, 32.9% 15 to 30 minutes, 24.8% 30 to 45 minutes, 8.4% 45 to 60 minutes, 3.7% 60 minutes or more (2000)

EAST GERMANTOWN (town). Aka Pershing. Covers a land area of 0.127 square miles and a water area of 0 square miles. Located at 39.81° N. Lat.; 85.13° W. Long. Elevation is 1,050 feet.

Population: 243 (2000); Race: 93.4% White, 0.0% Black, 0.0% Asian, 0.0% American Indian and Alaska Native, 6.6% Hispanic of any race, 0.0% two or more races (2000); Density: 1,913.2 persons per square mile (2000); Age: 34.9% under 18, 14.0% over 64 (2000); Marriage status: 11.3% never married, 63.7% now married, 11.3% widowed, 13.8% divorced (2000); Foreign born: 4.4% (2000); Ancestry (includes multiple ancestries): 44.1% United States or American, 10.5% German, 10.0% Other groups, 7.9% Irish, 3.9% English (2000).

Economy: In agricultural area. Single-family building permits issued: 0 (2001) / 0 (2000); Multi-family building permits issued: 0 (2001) / 0 (2000); Employment by occupation: 5.3% management, 16.8% professional, 11.6% services, 15.8% sales, 0.0% farming, 7.4% construction, 43.2% production (2000).

Income: Per capita income: $12,827 (2000); Median household income: $30,714 (2000); Poverty rate: 15.3% (2000).

Taxes: Total city taxes per capita: $11 (1997); City property taxes per capita: $3 (1997).

Education: High school graduation rate: 69.0% (2000); College graduation rate: 8.3% (2000).
Housing: Homeownership rate: 79.8% (2000); Median home value: $66,700 (2000); Median rent: $400 per month (2000); Median age of housing: 56 years (2000).
Transportation: Commute to work: 89.5% car, 0.0% public transportation, 5.3% walk, 2.1% work from home (2000); Travel time to work: 40.9% less than 15 minutes, 40.9% 15 to 30 minutes, 12.9% 30 to 45 minutes, 3.2% 45 to 60 minutes, 2.2% 60 minutes or more (2000)

ECONOMY (town). Covers a land area of 0.097 square miles and a water area of 0 square miles. Located at 39.97° N. Lat.; 85.08° W. Long. Elevation is 1,146 feet.
History: Economy was the site in 1936 of Dr. James R. King's experiment in cooperative medical care, the Economy Mutual Health Association.
Population: 200 (2000); Race: 98.5% White, 0.0% Black, 0.0% Asian, 0.0% American Indian and Alaska Native, 3.1% Hispanic of any race, 1.5% two or more races (2000); Density: 2,062.6 persons per square mile (2000); Age: 30.9% under 18, 9.3% over 64 (2000); Marriage status: 16.4% never married, 66.4% now married, 5.5% widowed, 11.6% divorced (2000); Foreign born: 2.1% (2000); Ancestry (includes multiple ancestries): 24.7% German, 20.6% United States or American, 19.1% Irish, 7.7% English, 5.7% French (except Basque) (2000).
Economy: Employment by occupation: 0.0% management, 6.4% professional, 14.1% services, 41.0% sales, 2.6% farming, 9.0% construction, 26.9% production (2000).
Income: Per capita income: $17,609 (2000); Median household income: $37,083 (2000); Poverty rate: 16.0% (2000).
Taxes: Total city taxes per capita: $86 (1997); City property taxes per capita: $86 (1997).
Education: High school graduation rate: 78.2% (2000); College graduation rate: 7.6% (2000).
Housing: Homeownership rate: 89.0% (2000); Median home value: $51,900 (2000); Median rent: $260 per month (2000); Median age of housing: 60+ years (2000).
Transportation: Commute to work: 93.4% car, 0.0% public transportation, 5.3% walk, 0.0% work from home (2000); Travel time to work: 7.9% less than 15 minutes, 64.5% 15 to 30 minutes, 22.4% 30 to 45 minutes, 2.6% 45 to 60 minutes, 2.6% 60 minutes or more (2000)

FOUNTAIN CITY (town). Covers a land area of 0.263 square miles and a water area of 0 square miles. Located at 39.95° N. Lat.; 84.92° W. Long. Elevation is 1,114 feet.
History: Fountain was incorporated as Newport in 1834, but the name was changed to Fountain City when water from an underground lake was found to rise to the surface when pipes were sunk to it. Fountain City was a major station on the Underground Railroad of freedom for fugitive slaves.
Population: 735 (2000); Race: 96.3% White, 0.7% Black, 0.0% Asian, 0.3% American Indian and Alaska Native, 0.0% Hispanic of any race, 2.4% two or more races (2000); Density: 2,795.5 persons per square mile (2000); Age: 26.0% under 18, 15.2% over 64 (2000); Marriage status: 21.9% never married, 58.8% now married, 8.7% widowed, 10.6% divorced (2000); Foreign born: 0.3% (2000); Ancestry (includes multiple ancestries): 18.9% German, 16.9% United States or American, 16.7% Other groups, 11.9% Irish, 7.9% English (2000).
Economy: Single-family building permits issued: 1 (2001) / 0 (2000); Multi-family building permits issued: 0 (2001) / 0 (2000); Employment by occupation: 5.9% management, 16.7% professional, 14.7% services, 24.3% sales, 0.0% farming, 11.0% construction, 27.4% production (2000).
Income: Per capita income: $15,669 (2000); Median household income: $34,722 (2000); Poverty rate: 8.8% (2000).
Taxes: Total city taxes per capita: $132 (1997); City property taxes per capita: $114 (1997).
Education: High school graduation rate: 74.7% (2000); College graduation rate: 9.9% (2000).

School District(s)

Northeastern Wayne Schools (PK-12)
2000 Enrollment: 1,155 765-847-2821
Housing: Homeownership rate: 76.7% (2000); Median home value: $72,900 (2000); Median rent: $355 per month (2000); Median age of housing: 48 years (2000).
Transportation: Commute to work: 91.1% car, 0.0% public transportation, 1.4% walk, 3.7% work from home (2000); Travel time to work: 25.6% less than 15 minutes, 63.1% 15 to 30 minutes, 4.8% 30 to 45 minutes, 1.2% 45 to 60 minutes, 5.4% 60 minutes or more (2000)

GREENS FORK (town). Covers a land area of 0.151 square miles and a water area of 0 square miles. Located at 39.89° N. Lat.; 85.04° W. Long. Elevation is 1,010 feet.
History: Laid out 1818.
Population: 371 (2000); Race: 100.0% White, 0.0% Black, 0.0% Asian, 0.0% American Indian and Alaska Native, 0.5% Hispanic of any race, 0.0% two or more races (2000); Density: 2,462.8 persons per square mile (2000); Age: 33.1% under 18, 10.2% over 64 (2000); Marriage status: 29.8% never married, 52.9% now married, 5.2% widowed, 12.1% divorced (2000); Foreign born: 0.0% (2000); Ancestry (includes multiple ancestries): 17.2% English, 16.4% German, 14.8% United States or American, 10.4% Irish, 6.8% Other groups (2000).
Economy: In agricultural area. Single-family building permits issued: 1 (2001) / 0 (2000); Multi-family building permits issued: 0 (2001) / 0 (2000); Employment by occupation: 4.9% management, 7.6% professional, 25.0% services, 23.4% sales, 0.0% farming, 8.2% construction, 31.0% production (2000).
Income: Per capita income: $13,605 (2000); Median household income: $36,406 (2000); Poverty rate: 8.2% (2000).
Taxes: Total city taxes per capita: $109 (1997); City property taxes per capita: $89 (1997).
Education: High school graduation rate: 82.6% (2000); College graduation rate: 6.4% (2000).
Housing: Homeownership rate: 88.4% (2000); Median home value: $53,800 (2000); Median rent: $363 per month (2000); Median age of housing: 60+ years (2000).
Transportation: Commute to work: 98.4% car, 0.0% public transportation, 0.0% walk, 1.6% work from home (2000); Travel time to work: 18.2% less than 15 minutes, 49.7% 15 to 30 minutes, 19.3% 30 to 45 minutes, 5.0% 45 to 60 minutes, 7.7% 60 minutes or more (2000)

HAGERSTOWN (town). Covers a land area of 1.386 square miles and a water area of 0 square miles. Located at 39.91° N. Lat.; 85.16° W. Long. Elevation is 1,015 feet.
Population: 1,768 (2000); Race: 98.5% White, 0.0% Black, 0.0% Asian, 0.0% American Indian and Alaska Native, 0.0% Hispanic of any race, 1.5% two or more races (2000); Density: 1,276.0 persons per square mile (2000); Age: 22.0% under 18, 18.5% over 64 (2000); Marriage status: 18.6% never married, 60.4% now married, 11.1% widowed, 10.0% divorced (2000); Foreign born: 0.0% (2000); Ancestry (includes multiple ancestries): 22.7% German, 16.6% United States or American, 12.2% English, 10.3% Irish, 8.7% Other groups (2000).
Economy: Trading center in livestock and grain area. Manufacturing: candy, consumer goods, wood products. Single-family building permits issued: 1 (2001) / 3 (2000); Multi-family building permits issued: 0 (2001) / 0 (2000); Employment by occupation: 8.1% management, 16.5% professional, 14.9% services, 29.8% sales, 0.3% farming, 12.1% construction, 18.2% production (2000).
Income: Per capita income: $20,901 (2000); Median household income: $36,691 (2000); Poverty rate: 1.8% (2000).
Taxes: Total city taxes per capita: $221 (1997); City property taxes per capita: $200 (1997).
Education: High school graduation rate: 86.8% (2000); College graduation rate: 16.7% (2000).

School District(s)

Nettle Creek School Corp (PK-12)
2000 Enrollment: 1,317 765-489-4543
Housing: Homeownership rate: 73.3% (2000); Median home value: $84,600 (2000); Median rent: $307 per month (2000); Median age of housing: 55 years (2000).
Safety: Violent crime rate: 11.2 per 10,000 population; Property crime rate: 281.2 per 10,000 population (2001).
Newspapers: The Hagerstown Exponent (1 x week)
Transportation: Commute to work: 92.5% car, 0.0% public transportation, 4.6% walk, 1.1% work from home (2000); Travel time to work: 33.8% less than 15 minutes, 35.7% 15 to 30 minutes, 16.9% 30 to 45 minutes, 4.8% 45 to 60 minutes, 8.8% 60 minutes or more (2000)

Additional Information Contacts

Hagerstown Chamber of Commerce 765-489-5071

MILTON (town). Covers a land area of 0.271 square miles and a water area of 0 square miles. Located at 39.78° N. Lat.; 85.15° W. Long. Elevation is 929 feet.
Population: 611 (2000); Race: 99.5% White, 0.0% Black, 0.0% Asian, 0.0% American Indian and Alaska Native, 0.0% Hispanic of any race, 0.5% two or

more races (2000); Density: 2,251.3 persons per square mile (2000); Age: 27.7% under 18, 12.2% over 64 (2000); Marriage status: 19.3% never married, 58.7% now married, 6.0% widowed, 16.0% divorced (2000); Foreign born: 0.3% (2000); Ancestry (includes multiple ancestries): 22.3% United States or American, 11.4% German, 9.1% Irish, 5.1% English, 4.6% Other groups (2000).
Economy: Employment by occupation: 4.3% management, 9.3% professional, 18.0% services, 18.7% sales, 0.0% farming, 12.7% construction, 37.0% production (2000).
Income: Per capita income: $15,131 (2000); Median household income: $35,167 (2000); Poverty rate: 11.3% (2000).
Education: High school graduation rate: 68.4% (2000); College graduation rate: 4.9% (2000).
Housing: Homeownership rate: 75.2% (2000); Median home value: $58,000 (2000); Median rent: $320 per month (2000); Median age of housing: 60+ years (2000).
Transportation: Commute to work: 89.4% car, 0.0% public transportation, 4.4% walk, 2.7% work from home (2000); Travel time to work: 36.8% less than 15 minutes, 30.5% 15 to 30 minutes, 20.7% 30 to 45 minutes, 5.6% 45 to 60 minutes, 6.3% 60 minutes or more (2000)

MOUNT AUBURN (town). Covers a land area of 0.222 square miles and a water area of 0.009 square miles. Located at 39.81° N. Lat.; 85.19° W. Long. Elevation is 995 feet.
Population: 75 (2000); Race: 100.0% White, 0.0% Black, 0.0% Asian, 0.0% American Indian and Alaska Native, 0.0% Hispanic of any race, 0.0% two or more races (2000); Density: 337.7 persons per square mile (2000); Age: 8.1% under 18, 45.2% over 64 (2000); Marriage status: 3.4% never married, 91.5% now married, 3.4% widowed, 1.7% divorced (2000); Foreign born: 0.0% (2000); Ancestry (includes multiple ancestries): 27.4% United States or American, 11.3% Irish, 3.2% Swiss, 3.2% Scotch-Irish, 1.6% English (2000).
Economy: Employment by occupation: 20.8% management, 8.3% professional, 0.0% services, 25.0% sales, 0.0% farming, 20.8% construction, 25.0% production (2000).
Income: Per capita income: $17,624 (2000); Median household income: $30,313 (2000); Poverty rate: 3.2% (2000).
Taxes: Total city taxes per capita: $92 (1997); City property taxes per capita: $57 (1997).
Education: High school graduation rate: 63.2% (2000); College graduation rate: 7.0% (2000).
Housing: Homeownership rate: 92.9% (2000); Median home value: $77,500 (2000); Median rent: $425 per month (2000); Median age of housing: 60+ years (2000).
Transportation: Commute to work: 100.0% car, 0.0% public transportation, 0.0% walk, 0.0% work from home (2000); Travel time to work: 40.9% less than 15 minutes, 36.4% 15 to 30 minutes, 0.0% 30 to 45 minutes, 0.0% 45 to 60 minutes, 22.7% 60 minutes or more (2000)

RICHMOND (city). Covers a land area of 23.215 square miles and a water area of 0.060 square miles. Located at 39.83° N. Lat.; 84.89° W. Long. Elevation is 966 feet.
History: Richmond was founded in 1805 by soldiers who had been with George Rogers Clark at the capture of Fort Sackville. They were joined by other settlers, many of them Quakers who founded Earlham College in 1847. Richmond was known for its greenhouses and rose cultivation, including the Richmond Rose hybrid developed in 1905.
Population: 39,124 (2000); Race: 86.7% White, 8.0% Black, 1.2% Asian, 0.5% American Indian and Alaska Native, 1.9% Hispanic of any race, 2.5% two or more races (2000); Density: 1,685.3 persons per square mile (2000); Age: 23.4% under 18, 16.5% over 64 (2000); Marriage status: 24.5% never married, 53.1% now married, 8.9% widowed, 13.6% divorced (2000); Foreign born: 2.4% (2000); Ancestry (includes multiple ancestries): 17.9% German, 14.4% Other groups, 13.6% United States or American, 10.1% Irish, 8.7% English (2000).
Vital Statistics: Birth rate: 160.3 per 10,000 population (1998)
Economy: Unemployment rate: 6.0% (11/2002); Total civilian labor force: 18,464 (11/2002); Single-family building permits issued: 26 (2001) / 30 (2000); Multi-family building permits issued: 0 (2001) / 0 (2000); Employment by occupation: 8.5% management, 15.4% professional, 17.0% services, 25.2% sales, 0.3% farming, 8.0% construction, 25.7% production (2000).
Income: Per capita income: $17,096 (2000); Median household income: $30,210 (2000); Poverty rate: 15.7% (2000).
Taxes: Total city taxes per capita: $292 (2000); City property taxes per capita: $266 (2000).
Education: High school graduation rate: 74.6% (2000); College graduation rate: 13.8% (2000).

School District(s)

Richmond Community School Corp (PK-12)
 2000 Enrollment: 6,178 765-973-3300

Four-year College(s)

Bethany Theological Seminary (Private, Not-for-profit, Church of Brethren)
 2001 Enrollment: 64 765-983-1800
Earlham College (Private, Not-for-profit, Friends)
 2001 Enrollment: 1,145 765-983-1200
 2001 Tuition: In-state $21,700; Out-of-state $21,700
Indiana University-East (Public)
 2001 Enrollment: 2,469 765-973-8200
 2001 Tuition: In-state $3,221; Out-of-state $8,520

Two-year College(s)

Ivy Tech State College-Whitewater (Public)
 2001 Enrollment: 1,469 765-966-2656
 2001 Tuition: In-state $1,986; Out-of-state $4,029
Reid Hospital & Health Care Service School of Rad Techn (Public)
 2001 Enrollment: n/a 765-983-3000

Housing: Homeownership rate: 58.5% (2000); Median home value: $73,000 (2000); Median rent: $364 per month (2000); Median age of housing: 49 years (2000).
Hospitals: Reid Hospital and Health Care Services (238 beds); Richmond State Hospital (324 beds)
Newspapers: Palladium-Item (7 x week)
Transportation: Commute to work: 91.8% car, 1.0% public transportation, 4.0% walk, 1.7% work from home (2000); Travel time to work: 62.1% less than 15 minutes, 26.8% 15 to 30 minutes, 6.1% 30 to 45 minutes, 1.7% 45 to 60 minutes, 3.3% 60 minutes or more (2000)
Airports: Richmond Municipal
Additional Information Contacts
Richmond Association of Realtors 765-962-7687
Richmond Chamber of Commerce 765-962-1511
Wayne County Convention Bureau 765-935-8687

SPRING GROVE (town). Covers a land area of 0.317 square miles and a water area of 0 square miles. Located at 39.84° N. Lat.; 84.89° W. Long. Elevation is 1,010 feet.
Population: 386 (2000); Race: 96.4% White, 0.5% Black, 1.7% Asian, 0.0% American Indian and Alaska Native, 0.0% Hispanic of any race, 1.0% two or more races (2000); Density: 1,216.7 persons per square mile (2000); Age: 12.4% under 18, 42.2% over 64 (2000); Marriage status: 14.1% never married, 57.6% now married, 17.8% widowed, 10.6% divorced (2000); Foreign born: 1.5% (2000); Ancestry (includes multiple ancestries): 17.2% English, 15.5% German, 12.1% United States or American, 11.9% Irish, 6.6% Other groups (2000).
Economy: Single-family building permits issued: 0 (2001) / 0 (2000); Multi-family building permits issued: 0 (2001) / 4 (2000); Employment by occupation: 11.7% management, 29.2% professional, 9.1% services, 23.4% sales, 0.0% farming, 8.4% construction, 18.2% production (2000).
Income: Per capita income: $24,705 (2000); Median household income: $45,781 (2000); Poverty rate: 10.1% (2000).
Taxes: Total city taxes per capita: $133 (1997); City property taxes per capita: $100 (1997).
Education: High school graduation rate: 71.9% (2000); College graduation rate: 22.9% (2000).
Housing: Homeownership rate: 76.3% (2000); Median home value: $94,300 (2000); Median rent: $493 per month (2000); Median age of housing: 47 years (2000).
Transportation: Commute to work: 92.9% car, 0.0% public transportation, 1.3% walk, 5.8% work from home (2000); Travel time to work: 73.1% less than 15 minutes, 18.6% 15 to 30 minutes, 2.1% 30 to 45 minutes, 4.8% 45 to 60 minutes, 1.4% 60 minutes or more (2000)

WEBSTER (unincorporated postal area, zip code 47392). Covers a land area of 0.064 square miles and a water area of 0 square miles. Located at 39.90° N. Lat.; 84.94° W. Long. Elevation is 1,051 feet.
Population: 68 (2000); Race: 100.0% White, 0.0% Black, 0.0% Asian, 0.0% American Indian and Alaska Native, 0.0% Hispanic of any race, 0.0% two or more races (2000); Density: 1,055.1 persons per square mile (2000); Age: 10.2% under 18, 51.0% over 64 (2000); Marriage status: 18.4% never married, 73.5% now married, 0.0% widowed, 8.2% divorced (2000); Foreign born: 0.0% (2000); Ancestry (includes multiple ancestries): 20.4% English, 20.4% Irish, 10.2% German, 10.2% Dutch (2000).

Economy: Employment by occupation: 0.0% management, 0.0% professional, 0.0% services, 0.0% sales, 0.0% farming, 40.0% construction, 60.0% production (2000).
Income: Per capita income: $8,847 (2000); Median household income: $28,750 (2000); Poverty rate: 0.0% (2000).
Education: High school graduation rate: 77.3% (2000); College graduation rate: 0.0% (2000).
Housing: Homeownership rate: 100.0% (2000); Median home value: $71,000 (2000); Median age of housing: 60+ years (2000).
Transportation: Commute to work: 100.0% car, 0.0% public transportation, 0.0% walk, 0.0% work from home (2000); Travel time to work: 0.0% less than 15 minutes, 100.0% 15 to 30 minutes, 0.0% 30 to 45 minutes, 0.0% 45 to 60 minutes, 0.0% 60 minutes or more (2000)

WHITEWATER (town). Covers a land area of 0.080 square miles and a water area of 0 square miles. Located at 39.94° N. Lat.; 84.83° W. Long. Elevation is 1,127 feet.
Population: 78 (2000); Race: 100.0% White, 0.0% Black, 0.0% Asian, 0.0% American Indian and Alaska Native, 0.0% Hispanic of any race, 0.0% two or more races (2000); Density: 976.0 persons per square mile (2000); Age: 20.0% under 18, 11.7% over 64 (2000); Marriage status: 18.4% never married, 55.1% now married, 4.1% widowed, 22.4% divorced (2000); Foreign born: 0.0% (2000); Ancestry (includes multiple ancestries): 28.3% Irish, 25.0% German, 10.0% English, 3.3% United States or American, 3.3% Dutch (2000).
Economy: Employment by occupation: 0.0% management, 0.0% professional, 12.5% services, 15.6% sales, 0.0% farming, 21.9% construction, 50.0% production (2000).
Income: Per capita income: $13,987 (2000); Median household income: $31,875 (2000); Poverty rate: 6.7% (2000).
Taxes: Total city taxes per capita: $18 (1997); City property taxes per capita: $0 (1997).
Education: High school graduation rate: 81.6% (2000); College graduation rate: 2.6% (2000).
Housing: Homeownership rate: 70.8% (2000); Median home value: $61,300 (2000); Median rent: $183 per month (2000); Median age of housing: 50 years (2000).
Transportation: Commute to work: 100.0% car, 0.0% public transportation, 0.0% walk, 0.0% work from home (2000); Travel time to work: 18.8% less than 15 minutes, 68.8% 15 to 30 minutes, 6.3% 30 to 45 minutes, 0.0% 45 to 60 minutes, 6.3% 60 minutes or more (2000)

WILLIAMSBURG (unincorporated postal area, zip code 47393). Covers a land area of 35.675 square miles and a water area of 0 square miles. Located at 39.95° N. Lat.; 84.99° W. Long. Elevation is 1,065 feet.
Population: 1,562 (2000); Race: 99.0% White, 0.4% Black, 0.3% Asian, 0.0% American Indian and Alaska Native, 1.7% Hispanic of any race, 0.0% two or more races (2000); Density: 43.8 persons per square mile (2000); Age: 25.7% under 18, 18.4% over 64 (2000); Marriage status: 19.2% never married, 74.4% now married, 1.9% widowed, 4.5% divorced (2000); Foreign born: 0.6% (2000); Ancestry (includes multiple ancestries): 25.7% United States or American, 12.0% English, 10.4% Irish, 7.8% German, 6.1% Other groups (2000).
Economy: Employment by occupation: 9.8% management, 12.3% professional, 17.9% services, 25.9% sales, 1.6% farming, 11.0% construction, 21.5% production (2000).
Income: Per capita income: $16,632 (2000); Median household income: $40,750 (2000); Poverty rate: 7.0% (2000).
Education: High school graduation rate: 81.0% (2000); College graduation rate: 9.2% (2000).
Housing: Homeownership rate: 87.2% (2000); Median home value: $83,900 (2000); Median rent: $216 per month (2000); Median age of housing: 39 years (2000).
Transportation: Commute to work: 95.2% car, 0.0% public transportation, 0.0% walk, 4.3% work from home (2000); Travel time to work: 24.9% less than 15 minutes, 62.1% 15 to 30 minutes, 5.4% 30 to 45 minutes, 5.1% 45 to 60 minutes, 2.6% 60 minutes or more (2000)

Wells County

Located in eastern Indiana; drained by the Wabash and Salamonie Rivers. Covers a land area of 370.00 square miles, a water area of 0.40 square miles, and is located in the Eastern Time Zone. The county government was organized in 1835. County seat is Bluffton.

Wells County is part of the Fort Wayne, IN MSA. The entire metro area includes: Adams County; Allen County; DeKalb County; Huntington County; Wells County; Whitley County

Weather Station: Bluffton 1 N — Elevation: 823 feet

	Jan	Feb	Mar	Apr	May	Jun	Jul	Aug	Sep	Oct	Nov	Dec
High	30	35	46	59	71	80	84	81	75	63	48	37
Low	15	17	28	38	49	59	62	60	52	41	32	22
Precip	2.1	1.8	2.6	3.3	4.1	3.8	4.0	3.6	3.0	2.5	3.1	2.7
Snow	8.4	7.1	3.7	1.1	0.0	0.0	tr	0.0	0.0	0.2	1.8	5.6

High and Low temperatures in degrees Fahrenheit; Precipitation and Snow in inches

Population: 27,600 (2000); Race: 98.3% White, 0.2% Black, 0.2% Asian, 0.2% American Indian and Alaska Native, 1.5% Hispanic of any race, 0.8% two or more races (2000); Density: 74.6 persons per square mile (2000); Age: 27.4% under 18, 14.1% over 64 (2000).
Religion: Five largest groups: 17.7% Catholic Church, 8.7% The United Methodist Church, 7.8% Apostolic Christian Church of America, Inc., 3.5% The Wesleyan Church, 3.3% Evangelical Lutheran Church in America (2000).
Economy: Unemployment rate: 3.5% (11/2002); Total civilian labor force: 14,538 (11/2002); Leading industries: 32.7% manufacturing; 15.2% wholesale trade; 12.7% health care and social assistance (2000); Companies that employ more than 1,000 persons: 1 (2000); Companies that employ more than 100 persons: 22 (2000); Farms: 660 totaling 195,901 acres (1997); Minority business ownership rate: 7.7% (1997); Women business ownership rate: 24.7% (1997); Retail sales per capita: $6,132 (1997). Single-family building permits issued: 116 (2001) / 111 (2000); Multi-family building permits issued: 28 (2001) / 12 (2000).
Income: Per capita income: $19,158 (2000); Median household income: $43,934 (2000); Poverty rate: 5.9% (2000); Bankruptcy rate: 5.25% (2001).
Taxes: Total county taxes per capita: $345 (2000); County property taxes per capita: $254 (2000).
Education: High school graduation rate: 87.3% (2000); College graduation rate: 14.3% (2000).
Housing: Homeownership rate: 80.8% (2000); Median home value: $87,900 (2000); Median rent: $358 per month (2000); Median age of housing: 38 years (2000).
Health: Birth rate: 125.0 per 10,000 population (1998); Age adjusted death rate: 87.9 per 10,000 population (1999); Age adjusted cancer mortality rate: 219.0 deaths per 100,000 population (1999). Number of physicians: 14.1 per 10,000 population (1999); Number of hospital beds: 33.3 per 10,000 population (1999).
Elections: 2000 Presidential election results: 29.4% Gore, 68.7% Bush, 0.3% Nader, 1.1% Buchanan
National and State Parks: Ouabache State Park
Additional Information Contacts
Wells County Government Offices 219-824-6470
Adams Jay Wells County Board of Realtors 219-827-0791
Wells County Chamber Commerce 219-824-0510

Wells County Communities

BLUFFTON (city). Covers a land area of 6.610 square miles and a water area of 0.007 square miles. Located at 40.73° N. Lat.; 85.17° W. Long. Elevation is 828 feet.
History: Established in the mid-1800's, Bluffton was built on the bluffs overlooking the Wabash River.
Population: 9,536 (2000); Race: 97.8% White, 0.4% Black, 0.1% Asian, 0.4% American Indian and Alaska Native, 3.0% Hispanic of any race, 0.9% two or more races (2000); Density: 1,442.7 persons per square mile (2000); Age: 25.1% under 18, 17.2% over 64 (2000); Marriage status: 21.1% never married, 55.9% now married, 9.9% widowed, 13.1% divorced (2000); Foreign born: 1.1% (2000); Ancestry (includes multiple ancestries): 27.4% German, 10.8% United States or American, 10.3% Other groups, 8.7% Irish, 8.1% English (2000).
Economy: Employment by occupation: 8.7% management, 14.7% professional, 15.7% services, 23.7% sales, 0.7% farming, 9.0% construction, 27.5% production (2000).
Income: Per capita income: $19,118 (2000); Median household income: $37,416 (2000); Poverty rate: 9.0% (2000).
Taxes: Total city taxes per capita: $99 (2000); City property taxes per capita: $97 (2000).
Education: High school graduation rate: 81.6% (2000); College graduation rate: 14.2% (2000).

School District(s)

M S D Bluffton-Harrison (KG-12)
2000 Enrollment: 1,584 219-824-2620

Housing: Homeownership rate: 71.2% (2000); Median home value: $78,300 (2000); Median rent: $342 per month (2000); Median age of housing: 40 years (2000).

Hospitals: Caylor-Nickel Medical Center (99 beds); Wells Community Hospital (38 beds)

Safety: Violent crime rate: 9.4 per 10,000 population; Property crime rate: 201.3 per 10,000 population (2001).

Newspapers: News-Banner (6 x week); The Echo (1 x week)

Transportation: Commute to work: 92.6% car, 0.0% public transportation, 4.2% walk, 2.6% work from home (2000); Travel time to work: 62.0% less than 15 minutes, 18.9% 15 to 30 minutes, 11.7% 30 to 45 minutes, 4.7% 45 to 60 minutes, 2.8% 60 minutes or more (2000)

Additional Information Contacts

Adams Jay Wells County Board of Realtors 219-827-0791
Wells County Chamber Commerce 219-824-0510

CRAIGVILLE (unincorporated postal area, zip code 46731). Covers a land area of 15.391 square miles and a water area of 0 square miles. Located at 40.79° N. Lat.; 85.09° W. Long. Elevation is 850 feet.

Population: 651 (2000); Race: 100.0% White, 0.0% Black, 0.0% Asian, 0.0% American Indian and Alaska Native, 3.9% Hispanic of any race, 0.0% two or more races (2000); Density: 42.3 persons per square mile (2000); Age: 34.8% under 18, 13.0% over 64 (2000); Marriage status: 16.6% never married, 79.3% now married, 3.1% widowed, 1.0% divorced (2000); Foreign born: 1.1% (2000); Ancestry (includes multiple ancestries): 44.0% German, 10.0% English, 9.9% Swiss, 4.7% Other groups, 4.0% United States or American (2000).

Economy: Employment by occupation: 15.3% management, 17.7% professional, 4.9% services, 32.4% sales, 0.0% farming, 5.2% construction, 24.5% production (2000).

Income: Per capita income: $21,627 (2000); Median household income: $61,579 (2000); Poverty rate: 3.9% (2000).

Education: High school graduation rate: 84.9% (2000); College graduation rate: 19.1% (2000).

Housing: Homeownership rate: 91.8% (2000); Median home value: $118,200 (2000); Median rent: $500 per month (2000); Median age of housing: 59 years (2000).

Transportation: Commute to work: 92.7% car, 0.0% public transportation, 0.0% walk, 7.3% work from home (2000); Travel time to work: 35.0% less than 15 minutes, 32.3% 15 to 30 minutes, 28.1% 30 to 45 minutes, 3.0% 45 to 60 minutes, 1.7% 60 minutes or more (2000)

KEYSTONE (unincorporated postal area, zip code 46759). Covers a land area of 29.208 square miles and a water area of 0 square miles. Located at 40.59° N. Lat.; 85.17° W. Long. Elevation is 851 feet.

Population: 765 (2000); Race: 89.6% White, 0.0% Black, 0.0% Asian, 0.8% American Indian and Alaska Native, 1.7% Hispanic of any race, 8.0% two or more races (2000); Density: 26.2 persons per square mile (2000); Age: 32.8% under 18, 13.5% over 64 (2000); Marriage status: 16.0% never married, 69.5% now married, 8.9% widowed, 5.6% divorced (2000); Foreign born: 2.0% (2000); Ancestry (includes multiple ancestries): 21.1% German, 18.4% United States or American, 12.2% Other groups, 5.6% Irish, 2.9% Scottish (2000).

Economy: Employment by occupation: 5.6% management, 13.6% professional, 11.5% services, 27.2% sales, 1.9% farming, 5.4% construction, 34.9% production (2000).

Income: Per capita income: $14,501 (2000); Median household income: $39,750 (2000); Poverty rate: 3.9% (2000).

Education: High school graduation rate: 88.2% (2000); College graduation rate: 10.3% (2000).

Housing: Homeownership rate: 83.1% (2000); Median home value: $91,500 (2000); Median rent: $278 per month (2000); Median age of housing: 48 years (2000).

Transportation: Commute to work: 91.3% car, 0.0% public transportation, 0.0% walk, 7.0% work from home (2000); Travel time to work: 27.7% less than 15 minutes, 48.6% 15 to 30 minutes, 12.3% 30 to 45 minutes, 7.8% 45 to 60 minutes, 3.5% 60 minutes or more (2000)

LIBERTY CENTER (unincorporated postal area, zip code 46766). Covers a land area of 16.638 square miles and a water area of 0.026 square miles. Located at 40.70° N. Lat.; 85.29° W. Long. Elevation is 855 feet.

Population: 631 (2000); Race: 95.2% White, 0.0% Black, 3.6% Asian, 0.0% American Indian and Alaska Native, 0.0% Hispanic of any race, 1.2% two or more races (2000); Density: 37.9 persons per square mile (2000); Age: 25.7% under 18, 10.2% over 64 (2000); Marriage status: 16.0% never married, 68.5% now married, 6.5% widowed, 9.0% divorced (2000); Foreign born: 2.6% (2000); Ancestry (includes multiple ancestries): 30.0% German, 14.7% United States or American, 8.7% Other groups, 8.6% English, 4.0% Czech (2000).

Economy: Employment by occupation: 9.0% management, 10.1% professional, 10.1% services, 27.0% sales, 2.2% farming, 10.4% construction, 31.2% production (2000).

Income: Per capita income: $18,316 (2000); Median household income: $50,625 (2000); Poverty rate: 10.0% (2000).

Education: High school graduation rate: 91.5% (2000); College graduation rate: 14.2% (2000).

Housing: Homeownership rate: 83.0% (2000); Median home value: $70,000 (2000); Median rent: $375 per month (2000); Median age of housing: 60+ years (2000).

Transportation: Commute to work: 92.6% car, 1.1% public transportation, 2.6% walk, 1.7% work from home (2000); Travel time to work: 27.3% less than 15 minutes, 55.2% 15 to 30 minutes, 8.7% 30 to 45 minutes, 6.7% 45 to 60 minutes, 2.0% 60 minutes or more (2000)

OSSIAN (town). Covers a land area of 1.492 square miles and a water area of 0 square miles. Located at 40.88° N. Lat.; 85.16° W. Long. Elevation is 830 feet.

History: Laid out 1850.

Population: 2,943 (2000); Race: 98.9% White, 0.0% Black, 0.1% Asian, 0.0% American Indian and Alaska Native, 1.4% Hispanic of any race, 0.4% two or more races (2000); Density: 1,972.0 persons per square mile (2000); Age: 29.2% under 18, 14.5% over 64 (2000); Marriage status: 20.1% never married, 61.1% now married, 8.6% widowed, 10.1% divorced (2000); Foreign born: 0.9% (2000); Ancestry (includes multiple ancestries): 31.8% German, 12.6% English, 10.6% United States or American, 9.0% Irish, 5.3% Other groups (2000).

Economy: Agricultural area: soybeans, corn. Manufacturing: food products, transportation equipment; meat processing. Employment by occupation: 7.8% management, 17.9% professional, 12.7% services, 26.6% sales, 0.3% farming, 10.2% construction, 24.5% production (2000).

Income: Per capita income: $18,925 (2000); Median household income: $45,449 (2000); Poverty rate: 4.4% (2000).

Taxes: Total city taxes per capita: $85 (1997); City property taxes per capita: $83 (1997).

Education: High school graduation rate: 88.9% (2000); College graduation rate: 17.7% (2000).

School District(s)

Northern Wells Com Schools (PK-12)
2000 Enrollment: 2,714 219-622-4125

Housing: Homeownership rate: 78.0% (2000); Median home value: $86,800 (2000); Median rent: $413 per month (2000); Median age of housing: 26 years (2000).

Newspapers: Sunriser News (1 x week); The Ossian Journal (1 x week)

Transportation: Commute to work: 95.8% car, 0.6% public transportation, 0.0% walk, 3.1% work from home (2000); Travel time to work: 27.3% less than 15 minutes, 46.8% 15 to 30 minutes, 20.8% 30 to 45 minutes, 2.7% 45 to 60 minutes, 2.4% 60 minutes or more (2000)

PONETO (town). Covers a land area of 0.115 square miles and a water area of 0 square miles. Located at 40.65° N. Lat.; 85.22° W. Long. Elevation is 852 feet.

Population: 240 (2000); Race: 100.0% White, 0.0% Black, 0.0% Asian, 0.0% American Indian and Alaska Native, 0.0% Hispanic of any race, 0.0% two or more races (2000); Density: 2,078.5 persons per square mile (2000); Age: 29.7% under 18, 7.1% over 64 (2000); Marriage status: 13.5% never married, 74.8% now married, 8.4% widowed, 3.2% divorced (2000); Foreign born: 0.0% (2000); Ancestry (includes multiple ancestries): 25.9% German, 14.6% United States or American, 8.0% English, 8.0% Other groups, 3.8% Polish (2000).

Economy: Agricultural area. Employment by occupation: 7.6% management, 4.2% professional, 16.0% services, 19.3% sales, 1.7% farming, 15.1% construction, 36.1% production (2000).

Income: Per capita income: $15,820 (2000); Median household income: $43,125 (2000); Poverty rate: 5.2% (2000).

Taxes: Total city taxes per capita: $64 (1997); City property taxes per capita: $64 (1997).

Education: High school graduation rate: 85.4% (2000); College graduation rate: 3.1% (2000).

School District(s)

Southern Wells Com Schools (KG-12)

2000 Enrollment: 869 765-728-5537

Housing: Homeownership rate: 86.5% (2000); Median home value: $55,800 (2000); Median rent: $375 per month (2000); Median age of housing: 56 years (2000).

Transportation: Commute to work: 94.1% car, 0.0% public transportation, 3.4% walk, 2.5% work from home (2000); Travel time to work: 29.3% less than 15 minutes, 51.7% 15 to 30 minutes, 11.2% 30 to 45 minutes, 5.2% 45 to 60 minutes, 2.6% 60 minutes or more (2000)

UNIONDALE (town). Covers a land area of 0.216 square miles and a water area of 0.001 square miles. Located at 40.82° N. Lat.; 85.24° W. Long. Elevation is 817 feet.

History: Laid out 1883.

Population: 277 (2000); Race: 100.0% White, 0.0% Black, 0.0% Asian, 0.0% American Indian and Alaska Native, 0.0% Hispanic of any race, 0.0% two or more races (2000); Density: 1,280.9 persons per square mile (2000); Age: 27.3% under 18, 19.6% over 64 (2000); Marriage status: 22.7% never married, 57.6% now married, 8.6% widowed, 11.1% divorced (2000); Foreign born: 0.0% (2000); Ancestry (includes multiple ancestries): 41.2% German, 15.8% English, 15.0% Irish, 6.2% United States or American, 6.2% French (except Basque) (2000).

Economy: In agricultural area. Manufacturing: feed mixing. Employment by occupation: 16.4% management, 14.7% professional, 9.5% services, 25.0% sales, 0.0% farming, 19.0% construction, 15.5% production (2000).

Income: Per capita income: $18,743 (2000); Median household income: $40,469 (2000); Poverty rate: 2.3% (2000).

Taxes: Total city taxes per capita: $52 (1997); City property taxes per capita: $52 (1997).

Education: High school graduation rate: 86.2% (2000); College graduation rate: 6.6% (2000).

Housing: Homeownership rate: 89.2% (2000); Median home value: $58,600 (2000); Median rent: $413 per month (2000); Median age of housing: 60+ years (2000).

Transportation: Commute to work: 95.7% car, 0.0% public transportation, 2.6% walk, 1.7% work from home (2000); Travel time to work: 17.7% less than 15 minutes, 46.0% 15 to 30 minutes, 27.4% 30 to 45 minutes, 8.8% 45 to 60 minutes, 0.0% 60 minutes or more (2000)

VERA CRUZ (town). Covers a land area of 0.087 square miles and a water area of 0 square miles. Located at 40.70° N. Lat.; 85.07° W. Long. Elevation is 825 feet.

History: Laid out 1848.

Population: 55 (2000); Race: 100.0% White, 0.0% Black, 0.0% Asian, 0.0% American Indian and Alaska Native, 0.0% Hispanic of any race, 0.0% two or more races (2000); Density: 635.1 persons per square mile (2000); Age: 39.6% under 18, 18.8% over 64 (2000); Marriage status: 21.2% never married, 54.5% now married, 18.2% widowed, 6.1% divorced (2000); Foreign born: 0.0% (2000); Ancestry (includes multiple ancestries): 29.2% German, 20.8% Irish, 16.7% United States or American, 4.2% French (except Basque), 4.2% English (2000).

Economy: In agricultural area. Employment by occupation: 0.0% management, 23.1% professional, 0.0% services, 15.4% sales, 23.1% farming, 15.4% construction, 23.1% production (2000).

Income: Per capita income: $11,963 (2000); Median household income: $20,625 (2000); Poverty rate: 0.0% (2000).

Taxes: Total city taxes per capita: $24 (1997); City property taxes per capita: $12 (1997).

Education: High school graduation rate: 73.1% (2000); College graduation rate: 0.0% (2000).

Housing: Homeownership rate: 75.0% (2000); Median home value: $65,000 (2000); Median rent: $400 per month (2000); Median age of housing: 60+ years (2000).

Transportation: Commute to work: 100.0% car, 0.0% public transportation, 0.0% walk, 0.0% work from home (2000); Travel time to work: 61.5% less than 15 minutes, 38.5% 15 to 30 minutes, 0.0% 30 to 45 minutes, 0.0% 45 to 60 minutes, 0.0% 60 minutes or more (2000)

White County

Located in northwestern Indiana; bounded on the east by the Tippecanoe River; drained by the Tippecanoe River. Covers a land area of 505.20 square miles, a water area of 3.60 square miles, and is located in the Eastern Time Zone. The county government was organized in 1834. County seat is Monticello.

Population: 25,267 (2000); Race: 94.9% White, 0.1% Black, 0.4% Asian, 0.4% American Indian and Alaska Native, 5.3% Hispanic of any race, 1.3% two or more races (2000); Density: 50.0 persons per square mile (2000); Age: 25.7% under 18, 14.9% over 64 (2000).

Religion: Five largest groups: 6.9% The United Methodist Church, 6.3% Catholic Church, 5.0% American Baptist Churches in the USA, 4.1% Christian Church (Disciples of Christ), 2.4% Lutheran Church—Missouri Synod (2000).

Economy: Unemployment rate: 7.4% (11/2002); Total civilian labor force: 12,670 (11/2002); Leading industries: 42.4% manufacturing; 17.2% retail trade; 7.1% accommodation & food services (2000); Companies that employ more than 1,000 persons: 1 (2000); Companies that employ more than 100 persons: 17 (2000); Farms: 620 totaling 272,072 acres (1997); Minority business ownership rate: 0.0% (1997); Women business ownership rate: 29.3% (1997); Retail sales per capita: $8,370 (1997). Single-family building permits issued: 80 (2001) / 126 (2000); Multi-family building permits issued: 10 (2001) / 8 (2000).

Income: Per capita income: $18,323 (2000); Median household income: $40,707 (2000); Poverty rate: 7.0% (2000); Bankruptcy rate: 8.01% (2001).

Taxes: Total county taxes per capita: $209 (2000); County property taxes per capita: $118 (2000).

Education: High school graduation rate: 82.1% (2000); College graduation rate: 10.5% (2000).

Housing: Homeownership rate: 76.6% (2000); Median home value: $86,200 (2000); Median rent: $396 per month (2000); Median age of housing: 35 years (2000).

Health: Birth rate: 141.3 per 10,000 population (1998); Age adjusted death rate: 83.3 per 10,000 population (1999); Age adjusted cancer mortality rate: 192.9 deaths per 100,000 population (1999). Number of physicians: 7.1 per 10,000 population (1999); Number of hospital beds: 23.4 per 10,000 population (1999).

Elections: 2000 Presidential election results: 36.9% Gore, 61.0% Bush, 0.4% Nader, 1.1% Buchanan

Additional Information Contacts

White County Government Offices 219-583-5761

Greater Monticello Chamber 219-583-7220

White County Association of Realtors 219-583-4507

White County Communities

BROOKSTON (town). Covers a land area of 0.593 square miles and a water area of 0 square miles. Located at 40.60° N. Lat.; 86.86° W. Long. Elevation is 674 feet.

Population: 1,717 (2000); Race: 98.3% White, 0.0% Black, 0.0% Asian, 0.0% American Indian and Alaska Native, 1.2% Hispanic of any race, 1.0% two or more races (2000); Density: 2,895.8 persons per square mile (2000); Age: 27.8% under 18, 10.1% over 64 (2000); Marriage status: 20.1% never married, 61.6% now married, 5.9% widowed, 12.4% divorced (2000); Foreign born: 0.5% (2000); Ancestry (includes multiple ancestries): 26.0% German, 14.6% United States or American, 12.7% English, 12.0% Irish, 8.4% Other groups (2000).

Economy: In agricultural area. Manufacturing: machinery, paper products. Employment by occupation: 9.5% management, 14.9% professional, 14.2% services, 25.8% sales, 0.0% farming, 11.2% construction, 24.3% production (2000).

Income: Per capita income: $18,291 (2000); Median household income: $41,422 (2000); Poverty rate: 5.2% (2000).

Taxes: Total city taxes per capita: $45 (1997); City property taxes per capita: $39 (1997).

Education: High school graduation rate: 88.2% (2000); College graduation rate: 12.6% (2000).

Housing: Homeownership rate: 78.1% (2000); Median home value: $82,900 (2000); Median rent: $415 per month (2000); Median age of housing: 36 years (2000).

Transportation: Commute to work: 95.2% car, 0.2% public transportation, 1.1% walk, 3.0% work from home (2000); Travel time to work: 12.8% less than 15 minutes, 56.5% 15 to 30 minutes, 23.2% 30 to 45 minutes, 1.7% 45 to 60 minutes, 5.7% 60 minutes or more (2000)

BUFFALO (CDP). Covers a land area of 2.385 square miles and a water area of 0.164 square miles. Located at 40.88° N. Lat.; 86.74° W. Long. Elevation is 672 feet.

Population: 672 (2000); Race: 98.9% White, 0.0% Black, 0.0% Asian, 0.0% American Indian and Alaska Native, 2.5% Hispanic of any race, 1.1% two or more races (2000); Density: 281.7 persons per square mile (2000); Age: 26.9% under 18, 20.7% over 64 (2000); Marriage status: 19.8% never married, 61.5% now married, 7.1% widowed, 11.5% divorced (2000); Foreign born: 0.0% (2000); Ancestry (includes multiple ancestries): 36.0% United States or American, 15.4% Irish, 13.2% German, 8.1% Other groups, 7.3% English (2000).
Economy: Employment by occupation: 10.4% management, 12.7% professional, 24.3% services, 19.1% sales, 3.6% farming, 14.3% construction, 15.5% production (2000).
Income: Per capita income: $15,062 (2000); Median household income: $29,583 (2000); Poverty rate: 10.5% (2000).
Education: High school graduation rate: 77.4% (2000); College graduation rate: 3.4% (2000).
Housing: Homeownership rate: 84.4% (2000); Median home value: $88,000 (2000); Median rent: $466 per month (2000); Median age of housing: 25 years (2000).
Transportation: Commute to work: 91.2% car, 0.0% public transportation, 3.6% walk, 5.2% work from home (2000); Travel time to work: 8.8% less than 15 minutes, 44.1% 15 to 30 minutes, 29.8% 30 to 45 minutes, 5.5% 45 to 60 minutes, 11.8% 60 minutes or more (2000)

BURNETTSVILLE (town). Covers a land area of 0.739 square miles and a water area of 0 square miles. Located at 40.76° N. Lat.; 86.59° W. Long. Elevation is 710 feet.
Population: 373 (2000); Race: 99.5% White, 0.0% Black, 0.0% Asian, 0.0% American Indian and Alaska Native, 0.5% Hispanic of any race, 0.5% two or more races (2000); Density: 504.6 persons per square mile (2000); Age: 27.0% under 18, 13.8% over 64 (2000); Marriage status: 14.6% never married, 65.4% now married, 8.8% widowed, 11.2% divorced (2000); Foreign born: 0.0% (2000); Ancestry (includes multiple ancestries): 15.9% German, 15.1% United States or American, 8.2% English, 7.7% Irish, 6.3% Italian (2000).
Economy: Employment by occupation: 9.3% management, 15.2% professional, 13.7% services, 26.0% sales, 0.0% farming, 6.9% construction, 28.9% production (2000).
Income: Per capita income: $22,005 (2000); Median household income: $36,563 (2000); Poverty rate: 9.0% (2000).
Taxes: Total city taxes per capita: $16 (1997); City property taxes per capita: $14 (1997).
Education: High school graduation rate: 84.8% (2000); College graduation rate: 9.8% (2000).
Housing: Homeownership rate: 82.3% (2000); Median home value: $63,800 (2000); Median rent: $315 per month (2000); Median age of housing: 60+ years (2000).
Transportation: Commute to work: 84.7% car, 1.5% public transportation, 9.4% walk, 0.5% work from home (2000); Travel time to work: 22.8% less than 15 minutes, 56.9% 15 to 30 minutes, 10.4% 30 to 45 minutes, 6.4% 45 to 60 minutes, 3.5% 60 minutes or more (2000)

CHALMERS (town). Covers a land area of 0.250 square miles and a water area of 0 square miles. Located at 40.66° N. Lat.; 86.86° W. Long. Elevation is 705 feet.
Population: 513 (2000); Race: 99.6% White, 0.0% Black, 0.0% Asian, 0.0% American Indian and Alaska Native, 1.6% Hispanic of any race, 0.4% two or more races (2000); Density: 2,055.7 persons per square mile (2000); Age: 25.0% under 18, 10.4% over 64 (2000); Marriage status: 24.3% never married, 58.5% now married, 7.8% widowed, 9.4% divorced (2000); Foreign born: 1.2% (2000); Ancestry (includes multiple ancestries): 29.5% German, 19.0% United States or American, 12.6% English, 10.6% Irish, 8.8% Dutch (2000).
Economy: In agricultural area. Employment by occupation: 7.9% management, 9.0% professional, 15.8% services, 30.8% sales, 0.0% farming, 4.5% construction, 32.0% production (2000).
Income: Per capita income: $19,258 (2000); Median household income: $51,591 (2000); Poverty rate: 3.6% (2000).
Taxes: Total city taxes per capita: $88 (1997); City property taxes per capita: $86 (1997).
Education: High school graduation rate: 89.6% (2000); College graduation rate: 12.3% (2000).

School District(s)

Frontier School Corporation (KG-12)
2000 Enrollment: 878 219-984-5009

Housing: Homeownership rate: 78.6% (2000); Median home value: $78,700 (2000); Median rent: $375 per month (2000); Median age of housing: 60+ years (2000).
Transportation: Commute to work: 91.1% car, 0.8% public transportation, 3.1% walk, 3.5% work from home (2000); Travel time to work: 15.2% less than 15 minutes, 32.8% 15 to 30 minutes, 44.8% 30 to 45 minutes, 4.0% 45 to 60 minutes, 3.2% 60 minutes or more (2000)

IDAVILLE (unincorporated postal area, zip code 47950). Covers a land area of 36.650 square miles and a water area of 0 square miles. Located at 40.79° N. Lat.; 86.65° W. Long. Elevation is 705 feet.
Population: 854 (2000); Race: 94.6% White, 0.0% Black, 2.1% Asian, 0.0% American Indian and Alaska Native, 3.3% Hispanic of any race, 0.0% two or more races (2000); Density: 23.3 persons per square mile (2000); Age: 32.3% under 18, 7.4% over 64 (2000); Marriage status: 22.5% never married, 45.9% now married, 10.9% widowed, 20.7% divorced (2000); Foreign born: 2.1% (2000); Ancestry (includes multiple ancestries): 20.7% German, 14.3% United States or American, 8.5% Other groups, 7.4% Irish, 4.8% Italian (2000).
Economy: Dairying; soybeans, corn; hogs. Employment by occupation: 12.8% management, 5.3% professional, 7.7% services, 19.4% sales, 1.4% farming, 13.0% construction, 40.3% production (2000).
Income: Per capita income: $21,381 (2000); Median household income: $42,256 (2000); Poverty rate: 3.3% (2000).
Education: High school graduation rate: 88.0% (2000); College graduation rate: 5.3% (2000).
Housing: Homeownership rate: 84.4% (2000); Median home value: $73,500 (2000); Median rent: $365 per month (2000); Median age of housing: 60+ years (2000).
Transportation: Commute to work: 98.8% car, 0.0% public transportation, 0.0% walk, 1.2% work from home (2000); Travel time to work: 23.9% less than 15 minutes, 45.6% 15 to 30 minutes, 18.7% 30 to 45 minutes, 7.5% 45 to 60 minutes, 4.4% 60 minutes or more (2000)

MONON (town). Covers a land area of 0.562 square miles and a water area of 0 square miles. Located at 40.86° N. Lat.; 86.88° W. Long. Elevation is 668 feet.
History: Laid out 1853, incorporated 1879.
Population: 1,733 (2000); Race: 83.3% White, 0.0% Black, 0.5% Asian, 1.0% American Indian and Alaska Native, 20.6% Hispanic of any race, 1.9% two or more races (2000); Density: 3,083.8 persons per square mile (2000); Age: 27.7% under 18, 13.3% over 64 (2000); Marriage status: 25.3% never married, 55.9% now married, 8.4% widowed, 10.5% divorced (2000); Foreign born: 13.2% (2000); Ancestry (includes multiple ancestries): 21.1% Other groups, 16.5% German, 13.4% United States or American, 8.9% Irish, 4.7% English (2000).
Economy: Railroad junction. Agricultural area: corn, oats, soybeans. Diversified manufacturing; stone quarrying. Employment by occupation: 3.4% management, 7.7% professional, 11.5% services, 18.2% sales, 4.4% farming, 8.3% construction, 46.4% production (2000).
Income: Per capita income: $13,567 (2000); Median household income: $32,235 (2000); Poverty rate: 16.4% (2000).
Taxes: Total city taxes per capita: $96 (1997); City property taxes per capita: $87 (1997).
Education: High school graduation rate: 71.5% (2000); College graduation rate: 4.4% (2000).

School District(s)

North White School Corp (KG-12)
2000 Enrollment: 1,139 219-253-6618

Housing: Homeownership rate: 66.5% (2000); Median home value: $57,700 (2000); Median rent: $330 per month (2000); Median age of housing: 46 years (2000).
Newspapers: The News & Review (1 x week)
Transportation: Commute to work: 88.7% car, 0.7% public transportation, 6.4% walk, 2.4% work from home (2000); Travel time to work: 38.7% less than 15 minutes, 32.4% 15 to 30 minutes, 12.0% 30 to 45 minutes, 10.7% 45 to 60 minutes, 6.1% 60 minutes or more (2000)

MONTICELLO (city). Covers a land area of 2.795 square miles and a water area of 0.215 square miles. Located at 40.74° N. Lat.; 86.76° W. Long. Elevation is 682 feet.
History: Monticello was established as a resort town on the Tippecanoe River. When the Indiana Hydroelectric Power Company built dams across the river in 1923 and 1925, several lakes were formed which provided recreation sites.

Population: 5,723 (2000); Race: 91.5% White, 0.0% Black, 0.8% Asian, 0.8% American Indian and Alaska Native, 10.3% Hispanic of any race, 1.2% two or more races (2000); Density: 2,047.9 persons per square mile (2000); Age: 24.3% under 18, 19.0% over 64 (2000); Marriage status: 20.2% never married, 52.5% now married, 15.4% widowed, 11.9% divorced (2000); Foreign born: 6.6% (2000); Ancestry (includes multiple ancestries): 20.3% German, 18.2% Other groups, 11.8% United States or American, 10.4% English, 7.1% Irish (2000).
Economy: Employment by occupation: 6.3% management, 14.6% professional, 12.5% services, 19.8% sales, 0.0% farming, 7.8% construction, 38.9% production (2000).
Income: Per capita income: $17,066 (2000); Median household income: $35,537 (2000); Poverty rate: 8.1% (2000).
Taxes: Total city taxes per capita: $245 (2000); City property taxes per capita: $196 (2000).
Education: High school graduation rate: 76.7% (2000); College graduation rate: 10.3% (2000).

School District(s)

Twin Lakes School Corp (PK-12)
2000 Enrollment: 2,734 219-583-7211

Housing: Homeownership rate: 62.4% (2000); Median home value: $79,000 (2000); Median rent: $438 per month (2000); Median age of housing: 35 years (2000).
Hospitals: White County Memorial Hospital (59 beds)
Newspapers: Herald Journal (6 x week)
Transportation: Commute to work: 91.3% car, 0.0% public transportation, 5.8% walk, 2.8% work from home (2000); Travel time to work: 61.2% less than 15 minutes, 13.6% 15 to 30 minutes, 12.4% 30 to 45 minutes, 9.8% 45 to 60 minutes, 2.9% 60 minutes or more (2000)
Airports: White County
Additional Information Contacts
Greater Monticello Chamber 219-583-7220
White County Association of Realtors 219-583-4507

NORWAY (CDP). Covers a land area of 0.889 square miles and a water area of 0.064 square miles. Located at 40.78° N. Lat.; 86.76° W. Long. Elevation is 655 feet.
Population: 437 (2000); Race: 100.0% White, 0.0% Black, 0.0% Asian, 0.0% American Indian and Alaska Native, 0.0% Hispanic of any race, 0.0% two or more races (2000); Density: 491.4 persons per square mile (2000); Age: 17.9% under 18, 12.8% over 64 (2000); Marriage status: 20.8% never married, 41.6% now married, 12.4% widowed, 25.2% divorced (2000); Foreign born: 0.0% (2000); Ancestry (includes multiple ancestries): 30.9% German, 23.0% United States or American, 9.8% Irish, 8.5% English, 6.7% Other groups (2000).
Economy: Employment by occupation: 22.6% management, 3.1% professional, 25.2% services, 10.2% sales, 3.1% farming, 8.4% construction, 27.4% production (2000).
Income: Per capita income: $16,681 (2000); Median household income: $28,214 (2000); Poverty rate: 19.5% (2000).
Education: High school graduation rate: 68.2% (2000); College graduation rate: 7.8% (2000).
Housing: Homeownership rate: 61.5% (2000); Median home value: $83,600 (2000); Median rent: $413 per month (2000); Median age of housing: 44 years (2000).
Transportation: Commute to work: 92.5% car, 3.5% public transportation, 0.0% walk, 0.0% work from home (2000); Travel time to work: 58.0% less than 15 minutes, 14.6% 15 to 30 minutes, 11.1% 30 to 45 minutes, 13.7% 45 to 60 minutes, 2.7% 60 minutes or more (2000)

REYNOLDS (town). Covers a land area of 0.528 square miles and a water area of 0 square miles. Located at 40.75° N. Lat.; 86.87° W. Long. Elevation is 700 feet.
Population: 547 (2000); Race: 87.2% White, 0.0% Black, 0.0% Asian, 1.1% American Indian and Alaska Native, 12.0% Hispanic of any race, 0.0% two or more races (2000); Density: 1,036.2 persons per square mile (2000); Age: 32.2% under 18, 14.6% over 64 (2000); Marriage status: 23.5% never married, 62.8% now married, 5.6% widowed, 8.1% divorced (2000); Foreign born: 6.9% (2000); Ancestry (includes multiple ancestries): 23.0% German, 20.6% Other groups, 10.6% United States or American, 8.3% English, 6.5% Irish (2000).
Economy: Railroad junction in agricultural area. Employment by occupation: 4.9% management, 10.5% professional, 14.2% services, 32.4% sales, 0.0% farming, 10.5% construction, 27.5% production (2000).
Income: Per capita income: $16,188 (2000); Median household income: $40,833 (2000); Poverty rate: 4.6% (2000).
Taxes: Total city taxes per capita: $51 (1997); City property taxes per capita: $49 (1997).
Education: High school graduation rate: 75.6% (2000); College graduation rate: 7.6% (2000).
Housing: Homeownership rate: 66.7% (2000); Median home value: $67,500 (2000); Median rent: $366 per month (2000); Median age of housing: 45 years (2000).
Transportation: Commute to work: 96.3% car, 0.0% public transportation, 0.8% walk, 1.2% work from home (2000); Travel time to work: 40.3% less than 15 minutes, 26.1% 15 to 30 minutes, 24.4% 30 to 45 minutes, 6.3% 45 to 60 minutes, 2.9% 60 minutes or more (2000)

WOLCOTT (town). Covers a land area of 0.536 square miles and a water area of 0 square miles. Located at 40.75° N. Lat.; 87.04° W. Long. Elevation is 718 feet.
History: Laid out 1861.
Population: 989 (2000); Race: 97.1% White, 0.8% Black, 0.0% Asian, 0.0% American Indian and Alaska Native, 1.5% Hispanic of any race, 1.7% two or more races (2000); Density: 1,846.8 persons per square mile (2000); Age: 29.1% under 18, 16.2% over 64 (2000); Marriage status: 16.8% never married, 62.3% now married, 11.3% widowed, 9.6% divorced (2000); Foreign born: 1.2% (2000); Ancestry (includes multiple ancestries): 32.8% German, 19.2% Other groups, 16.1% Irish, 13.0% English, 11.9% United States or American (2000).
Economy: In agricultural area. Manufacturing: consumer goods, fertilizer. Employment by occupation: 11.1% management, 10.6% professional, 16.9% services, 19.2% sales, 2.1% farming, 10.6% construction, 29.4% production (2000).
Income: Per capita income: $14,875 (2000); Median household income: $37,563 (2000); Poverty rate: 8.4% (2000).
Taxes: Total city taxes per capita: $88 (1997); City property taxes per capita: $76 (1997).
Education: High school graduation rate: 81.8% (2000); College graduation rate: 9.9% (2000).

School District(s)

Tri-County School Corp (KG-12)
2000 Enrollment: 844 219-279-2418

Housing: Homeownership rate: 77.4% (2000); Median home value: $69,900 (2000); Median rent: $345 per month (2000); Median age of housing: 49 years (2000).
Newspapers: Wolcott Enterprise (1 x week)
Transportation: Commute to work: 92.9% car, 0.0% public transportation, 3.0% walk, 1.3% work from home (2000); Travel time to work: 59.0% less than 15 minutes, 13.3% 15 to 30 minutes, 16.6% 30 to 45 minutes, 6.8% 45 to 60 minutes, 4.4% 60 minutes or more (2000)

Whitley County

Located in northeastern Indiana; drained by the Eel River. Covers a land area of 335.50 square miles, a water area of 2.40 square miles, and is located in the Eastern Time Zone. The county government was organized in 1835. County seat is Columbia City.

Whitley County is part of the Fort Wayne, IN MSA. The entire metro area includes: Adams County; Allen County; DeKalb County; Huntington County; Wells County; Whitley County

Weather Station: Columbia City — Elevation: 849 feet

	Jan	Feb	Mar	Apr	May	Jun	Jul	Aug	Sep	Oct	Nov	Dec
High	31	35	46	59	71	80	83	81	75	62	48	36
Low	14	17	27	37	48	57	61	59	51	40	31	21
Precip	2.1	1.8	2.9	3.8	3.6	4.3	3.9	3.5	3.6	2.9	3.3	2.8
Snow	9.4	7.4	4.1	1.0	tr	0.0	0.0	0.0	0.0	0.3	2.1	7.2

High and Low temperatures in degrees Fahrenheit; Precipitation and Snow in inches

Population: 30,707 (2000); Race: 98.4% White, 0.3% Black, 0.4% Asian, 0.2% American Indian and Alaska Native, 0.6% Hispanic of any race, 0.4% two or more races (2000); Density: 91.5 persons per square mile (2000); Age: 26.8% under 18, 13.1% over 64 (2000).
Religion: Five largest groups: 8.6% Catholic Church, 7.8% The United Methodist Church, 4.4% Churches of God, General Conference, 3.9% Lutheran Church—Missouri Synod, 3.1% Evangelical Lutheran Church in America (2000).
Economy: Unemployment rate: 4.5% (11/2002); Total civilian labor force: 16,781 (11/2002); Leading industries: 41.2% manufacturing; 14.9% retail trade; 9.2% health care and social assistance (2000); Companies that employ

more than 1,000 persons: 0 (2000); Companies that employ more than 100 persons: 23 (2000); Farms: 787 totaling 165,067 acres (1997); Minority business ownership rate: 0.0% (1997); Women business ownership rate: 20.1% (1997); Retail sales per capita: $7,371 (1997). Single-family building permits issued: 196 (2001) / 210 (2000); Multi-family building permits issued: 4 (2001) / 2 (2000).
Income: Per capita income: $20,519 (2000); Median household income: $45,503 (2000); Poverty rate: 4.9% (2000); Bankruptcy rate: 6.56% (2001).
Taxes: Total county taxes per capita: $227 (1997); County property taxes per capita: $136 (1997).
Education: High school graduation rate: 86.2% (2000); College graduation rate: 13.3% (2000).
Housing: Homeownership rate: 83.3% (2000); Median home value: $96,000 (2000); Median rent: $372 per month (2000); Median age of housing: 36 years (2000).
Health: Birth rate: 138.4 per 10,000 population (1998); Age adjusted death rate: 81.0 per 10,000 population (1999); Age adjusted cancer mortality rate: 159.9 deaths per 100,000 population (1999). Number of physicians: 6.5 per 10,000 population (1999); Number of hospital beds: 39.4 per 10,000 population (1999).
Elections: 2000 Presidential election results: 33.0% Gore, 65.0% Bush, 0.2% Nader, 1.0% Buchanan
Additional Information Contacts
Whitley County Government Offices. 219-248-3100
Columbia City Chamber of Commerce 219-248-8131

Whitley County Communities

CHURUBUSCO (town). Covers a land area of 0.888 square miles and a water area of 0 square miles. Located at 41.23° N. Lat.; 85.32° W. Long. Elevation is 909 feet.
History: Churubusco got its name from a Mexican town where American forces won a battle during the war with Mexico.
Population: 1,666 (2000); Race: 99.0% White, 0.2% Black, 0.0% Asian, 0.4% American Indian and Alaska Native, 0.5% Hispanic of any race, 0.4% two or more races (2000); Density: 1,876.8 persons per square mile (2000); Age: 30.2% under 18, 12.2% over 64 (2000); Marriage status: 29.0% never married, 50.9% now married, 10.6% widowed, 9.5% divorced (2000); Foreign born: 0.9% (2000); Ancestry (includes multiple ancestries): 33.6% German, 14.2% Irish, 11.5% United States or American, 5.8% English, 4.3% Other groups (2000).
Economy: Single-family building permits issued: 13 (2001) / 18 (2000); Multi-family building permits issued: 0 (2001) / 0 (2000); Employment by occupation: 7.0% management, 12.5% professional, 15.3% services, 25.9% sales, 0.6% farming, 8.4% construction, 30.3% production (2000).
Income: Per capita income: $17,814 (2000); Median household income: $39,583 (2000); Poverty rate: 4.9% (2000).
Taxes: Total city taxes per capita: $131 (1997); City property taxes per capita: $102 (1997).
Education: High school graduation rate: 83.2% (2000); College graduation rate: 9.3% (2000).

School District(s)

Smith-Green Community Schools (PK-12)
2000 Enrollment: 1,447 219-693-2007
Housing: Homeownership rate: 78.7% (2000); Median home value: $75,400 (2000); Median rent: $377 per month (2000); Median age of housing: 44 years (2000).
Newspapers: Churubusco News (1 x week)
Transportation: Commute to work: 90.5% car, 0.2% public transportation, 5.8% walk, 3.1% work from home (2000); Travel time to work: 28.4% less than 15 minutes, 45.1% 15 to 30 minutes, 18.2% 30 to 45 minutes, 4.6% 45 to 60 minutes, 3.7% 60 minutes or more (2000)

COLUMBIA CITY (city). Covers a land area of 5.205 square miles and a water area of 0 square miles. Located at 41.15° N. Lat.; 85.48° W. Long. Elevation is 861 feet.
History: Columbia City was the home of Thomas Riley Marshall (1854-1925), Vice-President under Woodrow Wilson, governor of Indiana from 1909-1913, and author of the statement, "What this country really needs is a good five-cent cigar." Also from Columbia City was historical novelist Lloyd C. Douglas, who was born here in 1877.
Population: 7,077 (2000); Race: 97.8% White, 0.3% Black, 0.8% Asian, 0.6% American Indian and Alaska Native, 0.4% Hispanic of any race, 0.4% two or more races (2000); Density: 1,359.5 persons per square mile (2000); Age: 23.4% under 18, 18.0% over 64 (2000); Marriage status: 20.0% never married, 54.9% now married, 9.4% widowed, 15.7% divorced (2000); Foreign born: 1.1% (2000); Ancestry (includes multiple ancestries): 33.5% German, 11.0% United States or American, 8.5% English, 7.9% Irish, 6.3% Other groups (2000).
Economy: Single-family building permits issued: 50 (2001) / 43 (2000); Multi-family building permits issued: 4 (2001) / 0 (2000); Employment by occupation: 9.8% management, 12.6% professional, 14.6% services, 24.7% sales, 0.3% farming, 9.4% construction, 28.5% production (2000).
Income: Per capita income: $19,296 (2000); Median household income: $36,112 (2000); Poverty rate: 6.4% (2000).
Taxes: Total city taxes per capita: $190 (2000); City property taxes per capita: $185 (2000).
Education: High school graduation rate: 81.6% (2000); College graduation rate: 11.8% (2000).

School District(s)

Whitley Co Cons Schools (PK-12)
2000 Enrollment: 3,609 219-244-5772
Housing: Homeownership rate: 71.7% (2000); Median home value: $82,100 (2000); Median rent: $361 per month (2000); Median age of housing: 37 years (2000).
Hospitals: Parkview Whitley Hospital (45 beds)
Newspapers: Post & Mail (6 x week)
Transportation: Commute to work: 94.9% car, 0.3% public transportation, 1.0% walk, 2.1% work from home (2000); Travel time to work: 50.2% less than 15 minutes, 21.4% 15 to 30 minutes, 19.7% 30 to 45 minutes, 6.9% 45 to 60 minutes, 1.8% 60 minutes or more (2000)
Additional Information Contacts
Columbia City Chamber of Commerce 219-248-8131

LARWILL (town). Covers a land area of 0.223 square miles and a water area of 0 square miles. Located at 41.17° N. Lat.; 85.62° W. Long. Elevation is 940 feet.
History: Laid out 1854.
Population: 282 (2000); Race: 95.6% White, 0.0% Black, 0.0% Asian, 0.0% American Indian and Alaska Native, 4.4% Hispanic of any race, 0.0% two or more races (2000); Density: 1,266.9 persons per square mile (2000); Age: 32.8% under 18, 9.8% over 64 (2000); Marriage status: 21.8% never married, 56.4% now married, 9.5% widowed, 12.3% divorced (2000); Foreign born: 0.0% (2000); Ancestry (includes multiple ancestries): 18.9% United States or American, 18.3% German, 8.2% Irish, 6.0% Other groups, 1.3% English (2000).
Economy: In agricultural area. Employment by occupation: 8.5% management, 14.0% professional, 8.5% services, 6.2% sales, 0.0% farming, 10.9% construction, 51.9% production (2000).
Income: Per capita income: $13,154 (2000); Median household income: $36,563 (2000); Poverty rate: 10.7% (2000).
Taxes: Total city taxes per capita: $39 (1997); City property taxes per capita: $39 (1997).
Education: High school graduation rate: 76.0% (2000); College graduation rate: 5.2% (2000).
Housing: Homeownership rate: 81.1% (2000); Median home value: $58,200 (2000); Median rent: $342 per month (2000); Median age of housing: 60+ years (2000).
Transportation: Commute to work: 92.1% car, 0.0% public transportation, 0.0% walk, 1.6% work from home (2000); Travel time to work: 29.0% less than 15 minutes, 36.3% 15 to 30 minutes, 8.9% 30 to 45 minutes, 10.5% 45 to 60 minutes, 15.3% 60 minutes or more (2000)

SOUTH WHITLEY (town). Covers a land area of 0.735 square miles and a water area of 0 square miles. Located at 41.08° N. Lat.; 85.62° W. Long. Elevation is 808 feet.
History: Laid out 1837.
Population: 1,782 (2000); Race: 98.6% White, 0.0% Black, 0.0% Asian, 0.1% American Indian and Alaska Native, 0.6% Hispanic of any race, 1.0% two or more races (2000); Density: 2,423.2 persons per square mile (2000); Age: 27.3% under 18, 15.7% over 64 (2000); Marriage status: 20.6% never married, 56.7% now married, 8.4% widowed, 14.3% divorced (2000); Foreign born: 0.2% (2000); Ancestry (includes multiple ancestries): 31.9% German, 13.0% United States or American, 7.1% English, 6.8% Other groups, 6.2% Irish (2000).
Economy: In grain and livestock area; ships grain. Manufacturing: machinery, musical instruments, fabricated metal products, electrical equipment, paper goods, mobile office buildings. Single-family building permits issued: 7 (2001) / 4 (2000); Multi-family building permits issued: 0 (2001) / 2 (2000); Employment by occupation: 6.8% management, 11.7%

professional, 13.5% services, 19.5% sales, 0.3% farming, 10.1% construction, 38.0% production (2000).
Income: Per capita income: $19,766 (2000); Median household income: $35,114 (2000); Poverty rate: 8.2% (2000).
Taxes: Total city taxes per capita: $160 (1997); City property taxes per capita: $129 (1997).
Education: High school graduation rate: 82.6% (2000); College graduation rate: 11.9% (2000).
Housing: Homeownership rate: 73.7% (2000); Median home value: $71,900 (2000); Median rent: $318 per month (2000); Median age of housing: 49 years (2000).
Newspapers: Tribune-News (1 x week)
Transportation: Commute to work: 93.4% car, 0.0% public transportation, 4.7% walk, 1.4% work from home (2000); Travel time to work: 38.4% less than 15 minutes, 26.9% 15 to 30 minutes, 17.8% 30 to 45 minutes, 10.9% 45 to 60 minutes, 6.0% 60 minutes or more (2000)

TRI-LAKES (CDP). Covers a land area of 35.160 square miles and a water area of 0.898 square miles. Located at 41.22° N. Lat.; 85.47° W. Long. Elevation is 911 feet.
Population: 3,925 (2000); Race: 98.8% White, 0.0% Black, 0.4% Asian, 0.4% American Indian and Alaska Native, 0.7% Hispanic of any race, 0.3% two or more races (2000); Density: 111.6 persons per square mile (2000); Age: 26.7% under 18, 11.9% over 64 (2000); Marriage status: 16.2% never married, 68.2% now married, 4.1% widowed, 11.5% divorced (2000); Foreign born: 0.5% (2000); Ancestry (includes multiple ancestries): 28.6% German, 13.6% United States or American, 9.7% Irish, 9.3% English, 6.4% Other groups (2000).
Economy: Employment by occupation: 14.6% management, 17.7% professional, 10.4% services, 24.5% sales, 1.1% farming, 13.2% construction, 18.5% production (2000).
Income: Per capita income: $22,590 (2000); Median household income: $52,429 (2000); Poverty rate: 1.8% (2000).
Education: High school graduation rate: 90.4% (2000); College graduation rate: 18.8% (2000).
Housing: Homeownership rate: 92.2% (2000); Median home value: $126,200 (2000); Median rent: $421 per month (2000); Median age of housing: 36 years (2000).
Transportation: Commute to work: 97.7% car, 0.0% public transportation, 0.6% walk, 1.6% work from home (2000); Travel time to work: 26.9% less than 15 minutes, 24.2% 15 to 30 minutes, 31.6% 30 to 45 minutes, 13.0% 45 to 60 minutes, 4.3% 60 minutes or more (2000)

Iowa

The Hawkeye State

IOWA –Metropolitan Areas, Counties, and Central Cities

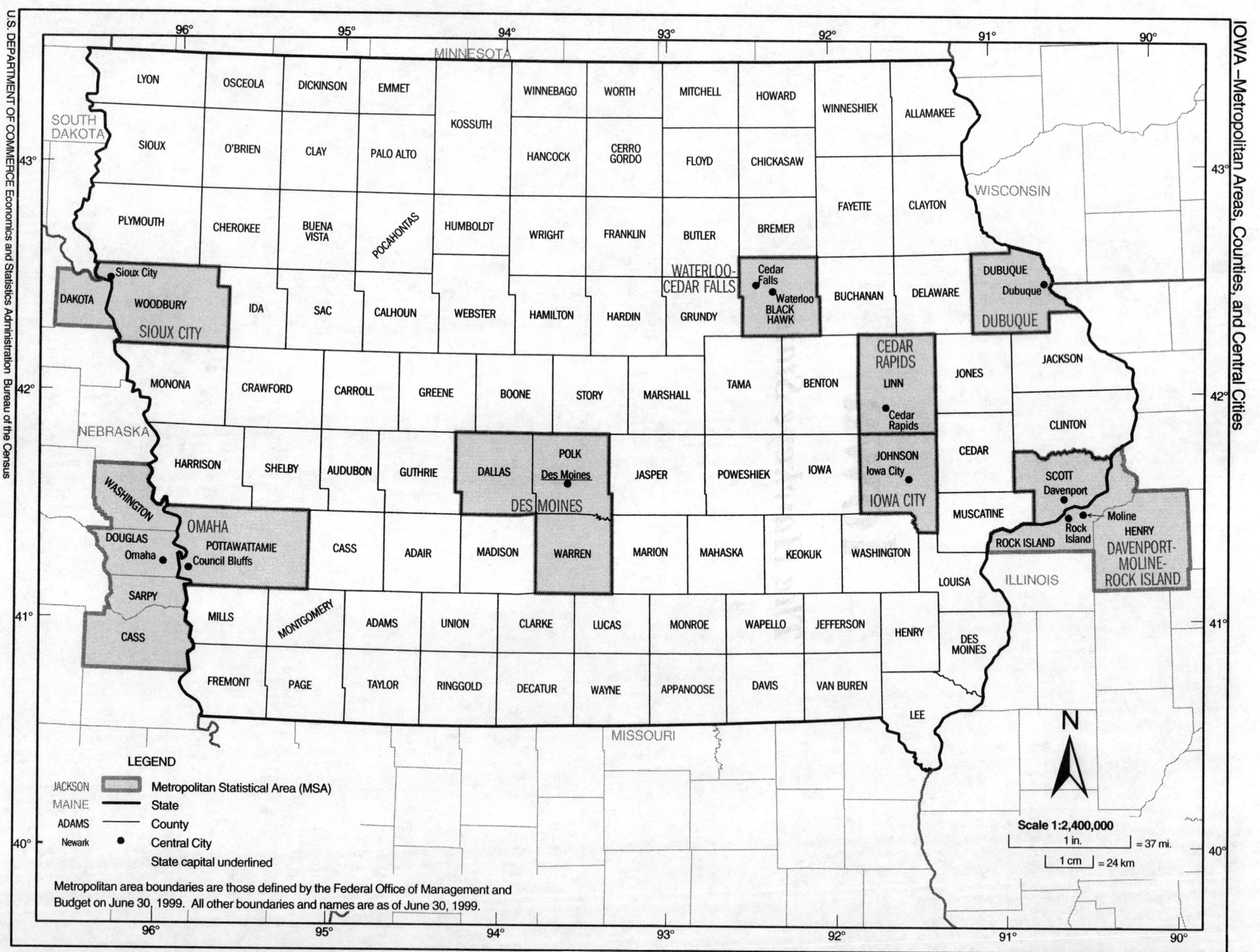

U.S. DEPARTMENT OF COMMERCE Economics and Statistics Administration Bureau of the Census

A

B

C

D

CDP = Census Designated Place

CDP = Census Designated Place

CDP = Census Designated Place

Adair County

Located in southwestern Iowa; drained by the Middle, North, and Thompson Rivers, and by the Middle and East Branches of the Nodaway. Covers a land area of 569.30 square miles, a water area of 1.00 square miles, and is located in the Central Time Zone. The county government was organized in 1851. County seat is Greenfield.

Weather Station: Greenfield Elevation: 1,338 feet

	Jan	Feb	Mar	Apr	May	Jun	Jul	Aug	Sep	Oct	Nov	Dec
High	30	37	49	63	74	83	87	84	77	65	48	35
Low	12	18	28	40	51	60	65	62	54	42	29	18
Precip	1.0	1.0	2.3	3.7	4.4	4.2	4.6	3.8	4.0	2.6	2.2	1.3
Snow	7.7	6.4	3.4	1.2	tr	0.0	tr	0.0	0.0	0.3	2.7	5.4

High and Low temperatures in degrees Fahrenheit; Precipitation and Snow in inches

Population: 8,243 (2000); Race: 99.2% White, 0.1% Black, 0.2% Asian, 0.1% American Indian and Alaska Native, 0.7% Hispanic of any race, 0.3% two or more races (2000); Density: 14.5 persons per square mile (2000); Age: 24.0% under 18, 22.1% over 64 (2000).
Religion: Five largest groups: 23.6% The United Methodist Church, 15.4% Lutheran Church—Missouri Synod, 12.2% Catholic Church, 11.9% Evangelical Lutheran Church in America, 2.4% Presbyterian Church (U.S.A.) (2000).
Economy: Unemployment rate: 3.1% (11/2002); Total civilian labor force: 4,570 (11/2002); Leading industries: 24.9% manufacturing; 19.3% health care and social assistance; 13.0% retail trade (2000); Companies that employ more than 1,000 persons: 0 (2000); Companies that employ more than 100 persons: 2 (2000); Farms: 792 totaling 335,756 acres (1997); Minority business ownership rate: 0.0% (1997); Women business ownership rate: 28.3% (1997); Retail sales per capita: $5,671 (1997). Single-family building permits issued: 19 (2001) / 25 (2000); Multi-family building permits issued: 0 (2001) / 36 (2000).
Income: Per capita income: $17,262 (2000); Median household income: $35,179 (2000); Poverty rate: 7.6% (2000); Bankruptcy rate: 1.97% (2001).
Taxes: Total county taxes per capita: $217 (2000); County property taxes per capita: $209 (2000).
Education: High school graduation rate: 87.8% (2000); College graduation rate: 11.2% (2000).
Housing: Homeownership rate: 75.3% (2000); Median home value: $59,300 (2000); Median rent: $264 per month (2000); Median age of housing: 53 years (2000).
Health: Birth rate: 92.2 per 10,000 population (1998); Age adjusted death rate: 86.5 per 10,000 population (1999); Age adjusted cancer mortality rate: 186.7 deaths per 100,000 population (1999). Number of physicians: 1.2 per 10,000 population (1999); Number of hospital beds: 26.7 per 10,000 population (1999).
Elections: 2000 Presidential election results: 42.5% Gore, 55.2% Bush, 1.6% Nader, 0.3% Buchanan
National and State Parks: Meadow Lake State Public Hunting Area
Additional Information Contacts
Adair County Government Offices 641-743-2445
Community Development Corp 641-743-8205
Greenfield Chamber of Commerce 641-743-8444

Adair County Communities

ADAIR (city). Covers a land area of 2.201 square miles and a water area of 0.017 square miles. Located at 41.50° N. Lat.; 94.64° W. Long.
History: Adair was named for General John Adair, who fought in the War of 1812. In 1873 Jesse James and his gang here derailed a train of five coaches. Estimates of the loot obtained from the passengers ranged from a small amount to $3,000. Afterwards, the James boys said that the engineer's death made this the "only job we regret."
Population: 839 (2000); Race: 99.0% White, 0.0% Black, 0.0% Asian, 0.0% American Indian and Alaska Native, 1.5% Hispanic of any race, 1.0% two or more races (2000); Density: 381.1 persons per square mile (2000); Age: 22.8% under 18, 25.9% over 64 (2000); Marriage status: 15.2% never married, 63.2% now married, 14.1% widowed, 7.5% divorced (2000); Foreign born: 1.3% (2000); Ancestry (includes multiple ancestries): 37.2% German, 12.8% United States or American, 9.6% English, 9.4% Danish, 5.9% Irish (2000).
Economy: Single-family building permits issued: 3 (2001) / 3 (2000); Multi-family building permits issued: 0 (2001) / 0 (2000); Employment by occupation: 11.7% management, 10.7% professional, 17.8% services, 26.5% sales, 1.0% farming, 14.2% construction, 18.1% production (2000).
Income: Per capita income: $15,557 (2000); Median household income: $31,319 (2000); Poverty rate: 6.5% (2000).
Taxes: Total city taxes per capita: $224 (1997); City property taxes per capita: $215 (1997).
Education: High school graduation rate: 85.1% (2000); College graduation rate: 13.4% (2000).

School District(s)

Adair-Casey Community School District (KG-12)
2000 Enrollment: 391 641-746-2241
Housing: Homeownership rate: 79.7% (2000); Median home value: $53,600 (2000); Median rent: $250 per month (2000); Median age of housing: 41 years (2000).
Newspapers: The Adair News (1 x week)
Transportation: Commute to work: 89.3% car, 0.5% public transportation, 3.1% walk, 6.0% work from home (2000); Travel time to work: 62.9% less than 15 minutes, 12.2% 15 to 30 minutes, 9.7% 30 to 45 minutes, 7.8% 45 to 60 minutes, 7.5% 60 minutes or more (2000)

BRIDGEWATER (city). Covers a land area of 0.287 square miles and a water area of 0 square miles. Located at 41.24° N. Lat.; 94.66° W. Long. Elevation is 1,188 feet.
History: Bridgewater was established in 1885. The name refers to the 640-foot railroad bridge over the Nodaway River, built by the Chicago, Burlington & Quincy Railroad.
Population: 178 (2000); Race: 100.0% White, 0.0% Black, 0.0% Asian, 0.0% American Indian and Alaska Native, 1.3% Hispanic of any race, 0.0% two or more races (2000); Density: 620.7 persons per square mile (2000); Age: 17.1% under 18, 38.6% over 64 (2000); Marriage status: 24.5% never married, 51.7% now married, 15.4% widowed, 8.4% divorced (2000); Foreign born: 0.0% (2000); Ancestry (includes multiple ancestries): 34.8% German, 23.4% Irish, 10.8% English, 9.5% Other groups, 5.1% French (except Basque) (2000).
Economy: Employment by occupation: 7.8% management, 14.3% professional, 24.7% services, 16.9% sales, 0.0% farming, 9.1% construction, 27.3% production (2000).
Income: Per capita income: $18,780 (2000); Median household income: $30,536 (2000); Poverty rate: 7.0% (2000).
Taxes: Total city taxes per capita: $63 (1997); City property taxes per capita: $63 (1997).
Education: High school graduation rate: 85.4% (2000); College graduation rate: 13.8% (2000).
Housing: Homeownership rate: 80.5% (2000); Median home value: $14,800 (2000); Median rent: $290 per month (2000); Median age of housing: 60+ years (2000).
Transportation: Commute to work: 84.4% car, 0.0% public transportation, 7.8% walk, 3.9% work from home (2000); Travel time to work: 27.0% less than 15 minutes, 28.4% 15 to 30 minutes, 35.1% 30 to 45 minutes, 1.4% 45 to 60 minutes, 8.1% 60 minutes or more (2000)

FONTANELLE (city). Covers a land area of 0.892 square miles and a water area of 0 square miles. Located at 41.29° N. Lat.; 94.56° W. Long. Elevation is 1,244 feet.
History: Fontanelle, formerly called Summerset, was the first county seat. A line of the Underground Railway, which helped slaves to escape from the South, passed through the town between 1850 and 1861.
Population: 692 (2000); Race: 98.1% White, 0.0% Black, 0.0% Asian, 0.3% American Indian and Alaska Native, 1.3% Hispanic of any race, 0.3% two or more races (2000); Density: 775.6 persons per square mile (2000); Age: 17.8% under 18, 34.9% over 64 (2000); Marriage status: 18.1% never married, 62.1% now married, 12.1% widowed, 7.7% divorced (2000); Foreign born: 0.7% (2000); Ancestry (includes multiple ancestries): 32.9% German, 11.0% United States or American, 10.7% Irish, 8.2% English, 6.7% Danish (2000).
Economy: Single-family building permits issued: 1 (2001) / 2 (2000); Multi-family building permits issued: 0 (2001) / 12 (2000); Employment by occupation: 10.7% management, 8.8% professional, 9.8% services, 23.3% sales, 0.0% farming, 16.1% construction, 31.2% production (2000).
Income: Per capita income: $16,352 (2000); Median household income: $31,328 (2000); Poverty rate: 5.8% (2000).
Taxes: Total city taxes per capita: $131 (1997); City property taxes per capita: $130 (1997).
Education: High school graduation rate: 80.0% (2000); College graduation rate: 6.5% (2000).

School District(s)

Bridgewater-Fontanelle Community School District (N -N)
2000 Enrollment: n/a 515-745-2671

Housing: Homeownership rate: 82.2% (2000); Median home value: $47,300 (2000); Median rent: $177 per month (2000); Median age of housing: 56 years (2000).
Newspapers: Fontanelle Observer (1 x week)
Transportation: Commute to work: 94.0% car, 1.3% public transportation, 1.6% walk, 3.2% work from home (2000); Travel time to work: 60.0% less than 15 minutes, 19.0% 15 to 30 minutes, 7.9% 30 to 45 minutes, 4.9% 45 to 60 minutes, 8.2% 60 minutes or more (2000)

GREENFIELD (city). Covers a land area of 1.816 square miles and a water area of 0 square miles. Located at 41.30° N. Lat.; 94.45° W. Long. Elevation is 1,368 feet.
History: Greenfield's name was chosen as descriptive of its setting, in green fields.
Population: 2,129 (2000); Race: 99.2% White, 0.0% Black, 0.3% Asian, 0.3% American Indian and Alaska Native, 0.5% Hispanic of any race, 0.0% two or more races (2000); Density: 1,172.6 persons per square mile (2000); Age: 22.2% under 18, 26.3% over 64 (2000); Marriage status: 16.8% never married, 64.2% now married, 10.5% widowed, 8.4% divorced (2000); Foreign born: 1.1% (2000); Ancestry (includes multiple ancestries): 32.0% German, 13.4% Irish, 11.3% English, 10.9% United States or American, 5.8% Danish (2000).
Economy: Single-family building permits issued: 2 (2001) / 6 (2000); Multi-family building permits issued: 0 (2001) / 0 (2000); Employment by occupation: 8.8% management, 14.7% professional, 13.6% services, 22.7% sales, 1.3% farming, 11.5% construction, 27.5% production (2000).
Income: Per capita income: $19,444 (2000); Median household income: $33,869 (2000); Poverty rate: 10.6% (2000).
Taxes: Total city taxes per capita: $263 (1997); City property taxes per capita: $261 (1997).
Education: High school graduation rate: 88.2% (2000); College graduation rate: 8.5% (2000).

School District(s)

Nodaway Valley Community School District (KG-12)
2000 Enrollment: 851 641-743-6127
Housing: Homeownership rate: 73.2% (2000); Median home value: $60,700 (2000); Median rent: $270 per month (2000); Median age of housing: 48 years (2000).
Hospitals: Adair County Memorial Hospital (31 beds)
Newspapers: Adair County Free Press (1 x week)
Transportation: Commute to work: 90.1% car, 0.4% public transportation, 6.1% walk, 2.2% work from home (2000); Travel time to work: 72.5% less than 15 minutes, 6.1% 15 to 30 minutes, 12.1% 30 to 45 minutes, 3.0% 45 to 60 minutes, 6.3% 60 minutes or more (2000)
Additional Information Contacts
Community Development Corp 641-743-8205
Greenfield Chamber of Commerce 641-743-8444

ORIENT (city). Covers a land area of 0.466 square miles and a water area of 0 square miles. Located at 41.20° N. Lat.; 94.41° W. Long. Elevation is 1,344 feet.
History: It is believed that Orient was named by the Chicago, Burlington & Quincy Railroad Company upon establishing a station there in 1879.
Population: 402 (2000); Race: 100.0% White, 0.0% Black, 0.0% Asian, 0.0% American Indian and Alaska Native, 0.2% Hispanic of any race, 0.0% two or more races (2000); Density: 863.4 persons per square mile (2000); Age: 29.5% under 18, 17.4% over 64 (2000); Marriage status: 18.5% never married, 66.0% now married, 8.6% widowed, 6.8% divorced (2000); Foreign born: 0.5% (2000); Ancestry (includes multiple ancestries): 35.5% German, 10.9% Irish, 10.4% United States or American, 6.7% Other groups, 5.6% English (2000).
Economy: Single-family building permits issued: 2 (2001) / 2 (2000); Multi-family building permits issued: 0 (2001) / 0 (2000); Employment by occupation: 5.4% management, 16.5% professional, 16.1% services, 28.1% sales, 2.2% farming, 18.8% construction, 12.9% production (2000).
Income: Per capita income: $13,937 (2000); Median household income: $35,750 (2000); Poverty rate: 6.5% (2000).
Taxes: Total city taxes per capita: $117 (1997); City property taxes per capita: $112 (1997).
Education: High school graduation rate: 90.4% (2000); College graduation rate: 9.3% (2000).

School District(s)

Orient-Macksburg Community School District (PK-12)
2000 Enrollment: 343 641-337-5061
Housing: Homeownership rate: 83.8% (2000); Median home value: $45,400 (2000); Median rent: $253 per month (2000); Median age of housing: 56 years (2000).
Transportation: Commute to work: 86.9% car, 0.0% public transportation, 8.6% walk, 1.4% work from home (2000); Travel time to work: 37.4% less than 15 minutes, 45.2% 15 to 30 minutes, 7.3% 30 to 45 minutes, 0.5% 45 to 60 minutes, 9.6% 60 minutes or more (2000)

Adams County

Located in southwestern Iowa; in rolling prairie land, drained by the Middle and East Branches of the Nodaway and by the Little Platte River. Covers a land area of 423.50 square miles, a water area of 1.90 square miles, and is located in the Central Time Zone. The county government was organized in 1851. County seat is Corning.

Weather Station: Corning Elevation: 1,213 feet

	Jan	Feb	Mar	Apr	May	Jun	Jul	Aug	Sep	Oct	Nov	Dec
High	30	36	48	61	72	82	86	84	76	64	48	35
Low	9	15	26	37	48	58	63	60	51	39	27	15
Precip	0.9	1.0	2.4	3.5	4.6	4.4	4.4	4.4	4.5	2.7	2.2	1.2
Snow	6.0	5.8	3.6	1.4	tr	0.0	0.0	0.0	0.0	0.2	2.3	5.3

High and Low temperatures in degrees Fahrenheit; Precipitation and Snow in inches

Population: 4,482 (2000); Race: 99.1% White, 0.3% Black, 0.2% Asian, 0.3% American Indian and Alaska Native, 0.2% Hispanic of any race, 0.1% two or more races (2000); Density: 10.6 persons per square mile (2000); Age: 23.8% under 18, 21.3% over 64 (2000).
Religion: Five largest groups: 15.4% The United Methodist Church, 9.9% Catholic Church, 6.3% Presbyterian Church (U.S.A.), 4.3% Lutheran Church—Missouri Synod, 2.9% Evangelical Lutheran Church in America (2000).
Economy: Unemployment rate: 5.4% (11/2002); Total civilian labor force: 1,960 (11/2002); Leading industries: 33.1% health care and social assistance; 20.0% manufacturing; 4.9% wholesale trade (2000); Companies that employ more than 1,000 persons: 0 (2000); Companies that employ more than 100 persons: 3 (2000); Farms: 573 totaling 235,441 acres (1997); Minority business ownership rate: 0.0% (1997); Women business ownership rate: 0.0% (1997); Retail sales per capita: $3,621 (1997). Single-family building permits issued: 5 (2001) / 2 (2000); Multi-family building permits issued: 0 (2001) / 0 (2000).
Income: Per capita income: $15,550 (2000); Median household income: $30,453 (2000); Poverty rate: 9.3% (2000); Bankruptcy rate: 3.37% (2001).
Taxes: Total county taxes per capita: $282 (1997); County property taxes per capita: $281 (1997).
Education: High school graduation rate: 84.5% (2000); College graduation rate: 12.0% (2000).
Housing: Homeownership rate: 74.8% (2000); Median home value: $46,500 (2000); Median rent: $237 per month (2000); Median age of housing: 2000 years (2000).
Health: Birth rate: 107.1 per 10,000 population (1998); Age adjusted death rate: 88.8 per 10,000 population (1999); Age adjusted cancer mortality rate: 124.5 (Unreliable figure as per CDC) deaths per 100,000 population (1999). Number of physicians: 8.9 per 10,000 population (1999); Number of hospital beds: 44.6 per 10,000 population (1999).
Elections: 2000 Presidential election results: 41.8% Gore, 54.6% Bush, 2.4% Nader, 0.8% Buchanan
Additional Information Contacts
Adams County Government Offices 515-322-3340
Corning Chamber of Commerce 641-322-3243

Adams County Communities

CARBON (city). Covers a land area of 0.709 square miles and a water area of 0 square miles. Located at 41.05° N. Lat.; 94.82° W. Long. Elevation is 1,115 feet.
History: Extensive coal deposits nearby brought the name of Carbon to this community.
Population: 28 (2000); Race: 100.0% White, 0.0% Black, 0.0% Asian, 0.0% American Indian and Alaska Native, 0.0% Hispanic of any race, 0.0% two or more races (2000); Density: 39.5 persons per square mile (2000); Age: 0.0% under 18, 13.6% over 64 (2000); Marriage status: 63.6% never married, 9.1% now married, 13.6% widowed, 13.6% divorced (2000); Foreign born: 0.0% (2000); Ancestry (includes multiple ancestries): 31.8% Irish, 22.7% French (except Basque), 22.7% Italian, 22.7% German, 13.6% Other groups (2000).

Economy: Employment by occupation: 35.7% management, 0.0% professional, 7.1% services, 0.0% sales, 0.0% farming, 14.3% construction, 42.9% production (2000).
Income: Per capita income: $9,891 (2000); Median household income: $10,500 (2000); Poverty rate: 45.5% (2000).
Taxes: Total city taxes per capita: $56 (1997); City property taxes per capita: $56 (1997).
Education: High school graduation rate: 60.0% (2000); College graduation rate: 5.0% (2000).
Housing: Homeownership rate: 86.7% (2000); Median home value: <$10,000 (2000); Median age of housing: 60+ years (2000).
Transportation: Commute to work: 100.0% car, 0.0% public transportation, 0.0% walk, 0.0% work from home (2000); Travel time to work: 14.3% less than 15 minutes, 28.6% 15 to 30 minutes, 57.1% 30 to 45 minutes, 0.0% 45 to 60 minutes, 0.0% 60 minutes or more (2000)

CORNING (city). Covers a land area of 1.575 square miles and a water area of 0.004 square miles. Located at 40.99° N. Lat.; 94.73° W. Long. Elevation is 1,117 feet.
History: Corning was platted in 1855 by D. M. Smith of Chariton, who named it for a friend, Erastus Corning of Corning, New York. Corning was the home of Dan W. Turner, Governor of Iowa (1930-1932).
Population: 1,783 (2000); Race: 99.3% White, 0.7% Black, 0.0% Asian, 0.0% American Indian and Alaska Native, 0.3% Hispanic of any race, 0.0% two or more races (2000); Density: 1,132.3 persons per square mile (2000); Age: 22.7% under 18, 26.0% over 64 (2000); Marriage status: 16.9% never married, 60.5% now married, 14.6% widowed, 8.0% divorced (2000); Foreign born: 0.0% (2000); Ancestry (includes multiple ancestries): 18.6% German, 12.1% English, 10.1% Irish, 8.7% United States or American, 4.5% Dutch (2000).
Economy: Single-family building permits issued: 1 (2001) / 0 (2000); Multi-family building permits issued: 0 (2001) / 0 (2000); Employment by occupation: 11.1% management, 13.2% professional, 22.9% services, 21.2% sales, 0.5% farming, 11.0% construction, 20.3% production (2000).
Income: Per capita income: $15,836 (2000); Median household income: $28,977 (2000); Poverty rate: 7.5% (2000).
Taxes: Total city taxes per capita: $219 (2000); City property taxes per capita: $216 (2000).
Education: High school graduation rate: 83.1% (2000); College graduation rate: 10.0% (2000).

School District(s)

Corning Community School District (KG-12)
2000 Enrollment: 654 641-322-4242
Housing: Homeownership rate: 70.0% (2000); Median home value: $50,700 (2000); Median rent: $264 per month (2000); Median age of housing: 50 years (2000).
Newspapers: Adams County Free Press (1 x week)
Transportation: Commute to work: 90.6% car, 0.5% public transportation, 6.7% walk, 1.6% work from home (2000); Travel time to work: 70.4% less than 15 minutes, 8.3% 15 to 30 minutes, 10.8% 30 to 45 minutes, 3.4% 45 to 60 minutes, 7.1% 60 minutes or more (2000)
Additional Information Contacts
Corning Chamber of Commerce 641-322-3243

NODAWAY (city). Covers a land area of 0.520 square miles and a water area of 0 square miles. Located at 40.93° N. Lat.; 94.89° W. Long. Elevation is 1,084 feet.
History: Nodaway was named for the local East Nodaway River.
Population: 132 (2000); Race: 98.4% White, 0.0% Black, 0.0% Asian, 0.0% American Indian and Alaska Native, 0.0% Hispanic of any race, 1.6% two or more races (2000); Density: 254.0 persons per square mile (2000); Age: 17.8% under 18, 18.6% over 64 (2000); Marriage status: 9.4% never married, 73.6% now married, 12.3% widowed, 4.7% divorced (2000); Foreign born: 0.0% (2000); Ancestry (includes multiple ancestries): 20.2% German, 17.8% Irish, 9.3% United States or American, 8.5% Other groups, 7.8% Dutch (2000).
Economy: Employment by occupation: 15.0% management, 10.0% professional, 13.3% services, 23.3% sales, 0.0% farming, 13.3% construction, 25.0% production (2000).
Income: Per capita income: $16,722 (2000); Median household income: $34,375 (2000); Poverty rate: 11.6% (2000).
Taxes: Total city taxes per capita: $126 (1997); City property taxes per capita: $126 (1997).
Education: High school graduation rate: 80.2% (2000); College graduation rate: 9.9% (2000).
Housing: Homeownership rate: 86.2% (2000); Median home value: $23,200 (2000); Median rent: $175 per month (2000); Median age of housing: 60+ years (2000).
Transportation: Commute to work: 81.7% car, 0.0% public transportation, 3.3% walk, 10.0% work from home (2000); Travel time to work: 38.9% less than 15 minutes, 33.3% 15 to 30 minutes, 9.3% 30 to 45 minutes, 0.0% 45 to 60 minutes, 18.5% 60 minutes or more (2000)

PRESCOTT (city). Covers a land area of 0.400 square miles and a water area of 0 square miles. Located at 41.02° N. Lat.; 94.61° W. Long. Elevation is 1,153 feet.
History: Prescott had also been called Motley and Glendale. The name was changed to Prescott in 1869 to honor a railroad man when the Burlington & Missouri River Railroad was completed there.
Population: 266 (2000); Race: 99.3% White, 0.0% Black, 0.0% Asian, 0.0% American Indian and Alaska Native, 0.0% Hispanic of any race, 0.7% two or more races (2000); Density: 664.7 persons per square mile (2000); Age: 29.6% under 18, 15.2% over 64 (2000); Marriage status: 20.9% never married, 62.1% now married, 11.2% widowed, 5.8% divorced (2000); Foreign born: 0.0% (2000); Ancestry (includes multiple ancestries): 23.7% German, 16.3% Irish, 10.7% English, 9.3% United States or American, 4.4% Other groups (2000).
Economy: Employment by occupation: 5.8% management, 25.0% professional, 13.3% services, 10.8% sales, 2.5% farming, 19.2% construction, 23.3% production (2000).
Income: Per capita income: $11,714 (2000); Median household income: $28,500 (2000); Poverty rate: 7.8% (2000).
Taxes: Total city taxes per capita: $105 (1997); City property taxes per capita: $102 (1997).
Education: High school graduation rate: 83.6% (2000); College graduation rate: 7.6% (2000).

School District(s)

Prescott Community School District (KG-12)
2000 Enrollment: 56 641-335-2212
Housing: Homeownership rate: 84.5% (2000); Median home value: $17,800 (2000); Median rent: $182 per month (2000); Median age of housing: 60+ years (2000).
Transportation: Commute to work: 94.2% car, 0.0% public transportation, 4.2% walk, 1.7% work from home (2000); Travel time to work: 11.0% less than 15 minutes, 65.3% 15 to 30 minutes, 14.4% 30 to 45 minutes, 0.0% 45 to 60 minutes, 9.3% 60 minutes or more (2000)

Allamakee County

Located in northeastern Iowa; bounded on the north by Minnesota, and on the east by the Mississippi River and the Wisconsin border; rolling prairie area drained by the Upper Iowa River. Covers a land area of 639.60 square miles, a water area of 19.10 square miles, and is located in the Central Time Zone. The county government was organized in 1847. County seat is Waukon.

Weather Station: Waukon 1 NNE Elevation: 1,243 feet

	Jan	Feb	Mar	Apr	May	Jun	Jul	Aug	Sep	Oct	Nov	Dec
High	23	29	42	57	69	78	82	79	71	60	42	28
Low	6	12	24	36	48	57	62	60	51	39	26	13
Precip	0.6	0.4	1.6	3.4	3.6	4.6	4.5	4.4	3.4	2.2	2.0	0.8
Snow	9.8	6.7	6.1	2.0	tr	0.0	0.0	0.0	0.0	tr	3.8	7.0

High and Low temperatures in degrees Fahrenheit; Precipitation and Snow in inches

Population: 14,675 (2000); Race: 95.7% White, 0.1% Black, 0.3% Asian, 0.3% American Indian and Alaska Native, 3.7% Hispanic of any race, 0.7% two or more races (2000); Density: 22.9 persons per square mile (2000); Age: 25.5% under 18, 18.4% over 64 (2000).
Religion: Five largest groups: 45.7% Catholic Church, 24.0% Evangelical Lutheran Church in America, 8.1% Presbyterian Church (U.S.A.), 6.9% United Church of Christ, 4.0% The United Methodist Church (2000).
Economy: Unemployment rate: 4.1% (11/2002); Total civilian labor force: 7,724 (11/2002); Leading industries: 32.9% manufacturing; 17.6% health care and social assistance; 14.6% retail trade (2000); Companies that employ more than 1,000 persons: 0 (2000); Companies that employ more than 100 persons: 9 (2000); Farms: 958 totaling 295,778 acres (1997); Minority business ownership rate: 0.0% (1997); Women business ownership rate: 9.7% (1997); Retail sales per capita: $7,224 (1997). Single-family building permits issued: 65 (2001) / 63 (2000); Multi-family building permits issued: 24 (2001) / 12 (2000).
Income: Per capita income: $16,599 (2000); Median household income: $33,967 (2000); Poverty rate: 9.6% (2000); Bankruptcy rate: 1.27% (2001).

Taxes: Total county taxes per capita: $237 (1997); County property taxes per capita: $235 (1997).
Education: High school graduation rate: 81.4% (2000); College graduation rate: 14.4% (2000).
Housing: Homeownership rate: 76.5% (2000); Median home value: $68,100 (2000); Median rent: $275 per month (2000); Median age of housing: 42 years (2000).
Health: Birth rate: 117.2 per 10,000 population (1998); Age adjusted death rate: 72.8 per 10,000 population (1999); Age adjusted cancer mortality rate: 210.1 deaths per 100,000 population (1999). Number of physicians: 7.5 per 10,000 population (1999); Number of hospital beds: 17.0 per 10,000 population (1999).
Elections: 2000 Presidential election results: 44.6% Gore, 50.7% Bush, 3.1% Nader, 1.1% Buchanan
National and State Parks: Yellow River State Forest; Yellow River State Forest Trail
Additional Information Contacts
Allamakee County Government Offices 563-568-3522
Postville Chamber of Commerce 563-864-7247
Waukon Chamber of Commerce 563-568-4110

Allamakee County Communities

DORCHESTER (unincorporated postal area, zip code 52140). Covers a land area of 74.517 square miles and a water area of 0.051 square miles. Located at 43.44° N. Lat.; 91.53° W. Long. Elevation is 795 feet.
History: Dorchester was named for Dorchester, England.
Population: 594 (2000); Race: 99.5% White, 0.0% Black, 0.5% Asian, 0.0% American Indian and Alaska Native, 0.0% Hispanic of any race, 0.0% two or more races (2000); Density: 8.0 persons per square mile (2000); Age: 19.8% under 18, 12.2% over 64 (2000); Marriage status: 19.5% never married, 73.5% now married, 2.3% widowed, 4.6% divorced (2000); Foreign born: 0.5% (2000); Ancestry (includes multiple ancestries): 39.6% German, 31.1% Norwegian, 22.5% Irish, 7.7% English, 6.1% United States or American (2000).
Economy: Employment by occupation: 24.0% management, 6.5% professional, 11.5% services, 12.8% sales, 11.2% farming, 17.8% construction, 16.2% production (2000).
Income: Per capita income: $15,481 (2000); Median household income: $37,639 (2000); Poverty rate: 3.8% (2000).
Education: High school graduation rate: 82.1% (2000); College graduation rate: 8.7% (2000).
Housing: Homeownership rate: 87.7% (2000); Median home value: $47,200 (2000); Median age of housing: 60+ years (2000).
Transportation: Commute to work: 66.9% car, 1.6% public transportation, 10.4% walk, 19.6% work from home (2000); Travel time to work: 37.6% less than 15 minutes, 38.8% 15 to 30 minutes, 7.5% 30 to 45 minutes, 10.2% 45 to 60 minutes, 5.9% 60 minutes or more (2000)

HARPERS FERRY (city). Covers a land area of 0.611 square miles and a water area of 0.017 square miles. Located at 43.20° N. Lat.; 91.15° W. Long. Elevation is 645 feet.
History: Harpers Ferry, named in 1860 for David Harper, was an important river landing in the early days of river traffic. At that time, the town was a community of pearl fishermen.
Population: 330 (2000); Race: 97.6% White, 0.0% Black, 0.0% Asian, 2.4% American Indian and Alaska Native, 0.3% Hispanic of any race, 0.0% two or more races (2000); Density: 539.7 persons per square mile (2000); Age: 13.5% under 18, 32.6% over 64 (2000); Marriage status: 12.6% never married, 69.7% now married, 9.2% widowed, 8.5% divorced (2000); Foreign born: 1.8% (2000); Ancestry (includes multiple ancestries): 47.6% German, 28.7% Irish, 9.3% English, 9.0% Norwegian, 6.0% French (except Basque) (2000).
Economy: Single-family building permits issued: 1 (2001) / 0 (2000); Multi-family building permits issued: 0 (2001) / 0 (2000); Employment by occupation: 17.4% management, 5.2% professional, 24.3% services, 16.5% sales, 0.0% farming, 10.4% construction, 26.1% production (2000).
Income: Per capita income: $17,566 (2000); Median household income: $29,091 (2000); Poverty rate: 7.5% (2000).
Taxes: Total city taxes per capita: $268 (1997); City property taxes per capita: $191 (1997).
Education: High school graduation rate: 79.4% (2000); College graduation rate: 8.4% (2000).
Housing: Homeownership rate: 93.5% (2000); Median home value: $73,000 (2000); Median rent: $225 per month (2000); Median age of housing: 35 years (2000).
Transportation: Commute to work: 82.1% car, 0.0% public transportation, 7.1% walk, 10.7% work from home (2000); Travel time to work: 19.0% less than 15 minutes, 45.0% 15 to 30 minutes, 20.0% 30 to 45 minutes, 4.0% 45 to 60 minutes, 12.0% 60 minutes or more (2000)

LANSING (city). Covers a land area of 1.077 square miles and a water area of 0.089 square miles. Located at 43.36° N. Lat.; 91.22° W. Long. Elevation is 630 feet.
History: The first claim on the town site of Lansing was staked in 1848 by H. H. Houghton.
Population: 1,012 (2000); Race: 98.7% White, 0.8% Black, 0.2% Asian, 0.0% American Indian and Alaska Native, 0.2% Hispanic of any race, 0.1% two or more races (2000); Density: 939.4 persons per square mile (2000); Age: 19.1% under 18, 28.9% over 64 (2000); Marriage status: 20.7% never married, 52.5% now married, 16.0% widowed, 10.8% divorced (2000); Foreign born: 0.6% (2000); Ancestry (includes multiple ancestries): 48.0% German, 30.5% Irish, 14.9% Norwegian, 7.4% English, 4.6% United States or American (2000).
Economy: Employment by occupation: 9.2% management, 10.1% professional, 14.4% services, 23.0% sales, 1.1% farming, 15.5% construction, 26.6% production (2000).
Income: Per capita income: $17,372 (2000); Median household income: $29,482 (2000); Poverty rate: 6.8% (2000).
Taxes: Total city taxes per capita: $328 (1997); City property taxes per capita: $271 (1997).
Education: High school graduation rate: 82.9% (2000); College graduation rate: 8.7% (2000).

School District(s)

Eastern Allamakee Community School District (KG-12)
2000 Enrollment: 510 319-538-4202
Housing: Homeownership rate: 75.8% (2000); Median home value: $70,400 (2000); Median rent: $265 per month (2000); Median age of housing: 60+ years (2000).
Newspapers: Allamakee Journal (1 x week); Lansing Livewire (1 x week)
Transportation: Commute to work: 82.4% car, 0.0% public transportation, 10.0% walk, 7.2% work from home (2000); Travel time to work: 59.0% less than 15 minutes, 15.1% 15 to 30 minutes, 8.3% 30 to 45 minutes, 11.2% 45 to 60 minutes, 6.3% 60 minutes or more (2000)

NEW ALBIN (city). Covers a land area of 0.220 square miles and a water area of 0 square miles. Located at 43.49° N. Lat.; 91.28° W. Long.
History: New Albin was involved in a boundary dispute between Iowa and Minnesota in the winter of 1851-52.
Population: 527 (2000); Race: 99.8% White, 0.0% Black, 0.0% Asian, 0.2% American Indian and Alaska Native, 3.4% Hispanic of any race, 0.0% two or more races (2000); Density: 2,390.8 persons per square mile (2000); Age: 32.5% under 18, 16.3% over 64 (2000); Marriage status: 22.5% never married, 56.4% now married, 10.8% widowed, 10.3% divorced (2000); Foreign born: 0.8% (2000); Ancestry (includes multiple ancestries): 56.8% German, 23.1% Irish, 14.1% Norwegian, 8.6% English, 5.8% Other groups (2000).
Economy: Single-family building permits issued: 0 (2001) / 0 (2000); Multi-family building permits issued: 0 (2001) / 0 (2000); Employment by occupation: 8.5% management, 8.5% professional, 15.1% services, 25.9% sales, 2.8% farming, 15.1% construction, 24.1% production (2000).
Income: Per capita income: $14,049 (2000); Median household income: $32,981 (2000); Poverty rate: 6.6% (2000).
Taxes: Total city taxes per capita: $235 (1997); City property taxes per capita: $176 (1997).
Education: High school graduation rate: 80.3% (2000); College graduation rate: 6.8% (2000).
Housing: Homeownership rate: 88.7% (2000); Median home value: $43,500 (2000); Median rent: $235 per month (2000); Median age of housing: 56 years (2000).
Transportation: Commute to work: 85.6% car, 0.0% public transportation, 9.6% walk, 2.9% work from home (2000); Travel time to work: 43.1% less than 15 minutes, 19.8% 15 to 30 minutes, 23.8% 30 to 45 minutes, 11.9% 45 to 60 minutes, 1.5% 60 minutes or more (2000)

POSTVILLE (city). Covers a land area of 2.078 square miles and a water area of 0 square miles. Located at 43.08° N. Lat.; 91.57° W. Long. Elevation is 1,192 feet.
History: Postville was named for Joel Post, who built a house here in 1841.

Population: 2,273 (2000); Race: 78.4% White, 0.5% Black, 0.8% Asian, 0.2% American Indian and Alaska Native, 20.1% Hispanic of any race, 2.1% two or more races (2000); Density: 1,093.6 persons per square mile (2000); Age: 24.1% under 18, 15.8% over 64 (2000); Marriage status: 18.4% never married, 66.3% now married, 8.4% widowed, 6.8% divorced (2000); Foreign born: 33.0% (2000); Ancestry (includes multiple ancestries): 32.1% German, 27.1% Other groups, 11.1% Norwegian, 6.6% English, 6.1% Ukrainian (2000).
Economy: Single-family building permits issued: 4 (2001) / 2 (2000); Multi-family building permits issued: 24 (2001) / 12 (2000); Employment by occupation: 7.8% management, 9.0% professional, 9.9% services, 17.4% sales, 2.2% farming, 8.5% construction, 45.2% production (2000).
Income: Per capita income: $14,264 (2000); Median household income: $32,667 (2000); Poverty rate: 12.7% (2000).
Taxes: Total city taxes per capita: $307 (1997); City property taxes per capita: $220 (1997).
Education: High school graduation rate: 72.4% (2000); College graduation rate: 16.8% (2000).

School District(s)

Postville Community School District (KG-12)
2000 Enrollment: 590 319-864-7651
Housing: Homeownership rate: 67.4% (2000); Median home value: $64,300 (2000); Median rent: $333 per month (2000); Median age of housing: 49 years (2000).
Newspapers: Postville Herald-Leader (1 x week)
Transportation: Commute to work: 73.2% car, 0.0% public transportation, 22.6% walk, 1.2% work from home (2000); Travel time to work: 69.8% less than 15 minutes, 22.0% 15 to 30 minutes, 5.7% 30 to 45 minutes, 0.8% 45 to 60 minutes, 1.8% 60 minutes or more (2000)
Additional Information Contacts
Postville Chamber of Commerce 563-864-7247

WATERVILLE (city). Covers a land area of 0.434 square miles and a water area of 0 square miles. Located at 43.20° N. Lat.; 91.29° W. Long.
History: Waterville was once known as Waterville Mill and was once the site of a grist mill and saw mill.
Population: 145 (2000); Race: 100.0% White, 0.0% Black, 0.0% Asian, 0.0% American Indian and Alaska Native, 0.0% Hispanic of any race, 0.0% two or more races (2000); Density: 333.9 persons per square mile (2000); Age: 33.1% under 18, 12.5% over 64 (2000); Marriage status: 17.6% never married, 74.5% now married, 5.9% widowed, 2.0% divorced (2000); Foreign born: 0.0% (2000); Ancestry (includes multiple ancestries): 44.9% Norwegian, 36.0% German, 9.6% Irish, 8.8% United States or American, 8.1% French (except Basque) (2000).
Economy: Employment by occupation: 15.0% management, 5.0% professional, 20.0% services, 26.7% sales, 1.7% farming, 10.0% construction, 21.7% production (2000).
Income: Per capita income: $12,277 (2000); Median household income: $35,625 (2000); Poverty rate: 10.3% (2000).
Taxes: Total city taxes per capita: $126 (1997); City property taxes per capita: $63 (1997).
Education: High school graduation rate: 89.9% (2000); College graduation rate: 12.4% (2000).
Housing: Homeownership rate: 92.5% (2000); Median home value: $32,500 (2000); Median rent: $300 per month (2000); Median age of housing: 60+ years (2000).
Transportation: Commute to work: 78.3% car, 0.0% public transportation, 16.7% walk, 5.0% work from home (2000); Travel time to work: 21.1% less than 15 minutes, 45.6% 15 to 30 minutes, 19.3% 30 to 45 minutes, 0.0% 45 to 60 minutes, 14.0% 60 minutes or more (2000)

WAUKON (city). Covers a land area of 2.942 square miles and a water area of 0 square miles. Located at 43.26° N. Lat.; 91.47° W. Long. Elevation is 1,216 feet.
History: Waukon is believed to have been named for a prominent chief of the Winnebagos.
Population: 4,131 (2000); Race: 98.1% White, 0.0% Black, 0.4% Asian, 0.3% American Indian and Alaska Native, 0.6% Hispanic of any race, 1.2% two or more races (2000); Density: 1,404.3 persons per square mile (2000); Age: 23.3% under 18, 24.6% over 64 (2000); Marriage status: 22.2% never married, 55.2% now married, 14.7% widowed, 8.0% divorced (2000); Foreign born: 1.0% (2000); Ancestry (includes multiple ancestries): 43.9% German, 23.3% Norwegian, 22.8% Irish, 7.2% United States or American, 6.0% English (2000).
Economy: Single-family building permits issued: 14 (2001) / 14 (2000); Multi-family building permits issued: 0 (2001) / 0 (2000); Employment by occupation: 5.7% management, 19.1% professional, 16.3% services, 26.1% sales, 2.8% farming, 9.1% construction, 21.0% production (2000).
Income: Per capita income: $17,047 (2000); Median household income: $30,325 (2000); Poverty rate: 12.3% (2000).
Taxes: Total city taxes per capita: $352 (1997); City property taxes per capita: $266 (1997).
Education: High school graduation rate: 80.4% (2000); College graduation rate: 16.6% (2000).

School District(s)

Allamakee Community School District (PK-12)
2000 Enrollment: 1,497 319-568-3409
Housing: Homeownership rate: 70.2% (2000); Median home value: $67,900 (2000); Median rent: $270 per month (2000); Median age of housing: 45 years (2000).
Hospitals: Veterans Memorial Hospital (40 beds)
Newspapers: Waukon Standard (1 x week); Northeast Iowa Extra (1 x week)
Transportation: Commute to work: 91.7% car, 0.2% public transportation, 5.5% walk, 2.3% work from home (2000); Travel time to work: 66.2% less than 15 minutes, 17.7% 15 to 30 minutes, 9.6% 30 to 45 minutes, 2.3% 45 to 60 minutes, 4.1% 60 minutes or more (2000)
Additional Information Contacts
Waukon Chamber of Commerce 563-568-4110

Appanoose County

Located in south central Iowa; bounded on the south by Missouri. Covers a land area of 496.30 square miles, a water area of 20.10 square miles, and is located in the Central Time Zone. The county government was organized in 1843. County seat is Centerville.

Weather Station: Centerville — Elevation: 977 feet

	Jan	Feb	Mar	Apr	May	Jun	Jul	Aug	Sep	Oct	Nov	Dec
High	31	38	50	63	73	82	87	84	76	65	49	36
Low	14	19	30	41	52	61	66	63	55	43	31	20
Precip	0.9	0.9	2.3	3.5	4.7	4.3	5.3	4.4	4.1	3.0	2.4	1.3
Snow	6.1	5.7	3.1	2.0	0.0	0.0	0.0	0.0	0.0	0.3	1.7	4.5

High and Low temperatures in degrees Fahrenheit; Precipitation and Snow in inches

Weather Station: Rathbun Dam — Elevation: 964 feet

	Jan	Feb	Mar	Apr	May	Jun	Jul	Aug	Sep	Oct	Nov	Dec
High	30	36	48	61	71	81	86	84	76	64	48	35
Low	11	16	27	40	50	60	65	62	53	41	29	17
Precip	0.9	1.1	2.2	3.4	4.7	4.4	5.1	4.3	4.2	3.0	2.4	1.4
Snow	5.5	5.2	2.5	0.8	0.0	0.0	0.0	0.0	0.0	tr	0.7	4.0

High and Low temperatures in degrees Fahrenheit; Precipitation and Snow in inches

Population: 13,721 (2000); Race: 97.8% White, 0.5% Black, 0.5% Asian, 0.1% American Indian and Alaska Native, 1.1% Hispanic of any race, 0.8% two or more races (2000); Density: 27.6 persons per square mile (2000); Age: 23.8% under 18, 20.0% over 64 (2000).
Religion: Five largest groups: 10.9% Catholic Church, 8.4% The United Methodist Church, 7.2% Christian Church (Disciples of Christ), 2.6% American Baptist Churches in the USA, 2.3% Church of the Nazarene (2000).
Economy: Unemployment rate: 4.2% (11/2002); Total civilian labor force: 6,891 (11/2002); Leading industries: 30.3% manufacturing; 19.6% retail trade; 17.4% health care and social assistance (2000); Companies that employ more than 1,000 persons: 0 (2000); Companies that employ more than 100 persons: 6 (2000); Farms: 797 totaling 241,094 acres (1997); Minority business ownership rate: 0.0% (1997); Women business ownership rate: 28.3% (1997); Retail sales per capita: $6,843 (1997). Single-family building permits issued: 4 (2001) / 16 (2000); Multi-family building permits issued: 0 (2001) / 0 (2000).
Income: Per capita income: $14,644 (2000); Median household income: $28,612 (2000); Poverty rate: 14.5% (2000); Bankruptcy rate: 4.00% (2001).
Taxes: Total county taxes per capita: $231 (1997); County property taxes per capita: $231 (1997).
Education: High school graduation rate: 81.4% (2000); College graduation rate: 12.2% (2000).
Housing: Homeownership rate: 74.1% (2000); Median home value: $45,400 (2000); Median rent: $259 per month (2000); Median age of housing: 45 years (2000).
Health: Birth rate: 111.5 per 10,000 population (1998); Age adjusted death rate: 88.7 per 10,000 population (1999); Age adjusted cancer mortality rate: 236.5 deaths per 100,000 population (1999). Number of physicians: 8.7 per

10,000 population (1999); Number of hospital beds: 41.5 per 10,000 population (1999).
Elections: 2000 Presidential election results: 44.9% Gore, 52.5% Bush, 1.8% Nader, 0.3% Buchanan
National and State Parks: Sharon Bluffs State Park
Additional Information Contacts
Appanoose County Government Offices 515-856-6101
Centerville Chamber of Commerce 641-437-4102

Appanoose County Communities

CENTERVILLE (city). Covers a land area of 4.520 square miles and a water area of 0.039 square miles. Located at 40.73° N. Lat.; 92.87° W. Long. Elevation is 1,014 feet.
History: In 1846 the village was platted as Chaldea by J. F. Stratton. The residents, however, called the town Sentersville in honor of Governor Senter of Tennessee. When the name was submitted to the General Assembly in 1847, the legislators changed it to Centerville, believing there was an error in spelling.
Population: 5,924 (2000); Race: 96.5% White, 1.2% Black, 0.9% Asian, 0.1% American Indian and Alaska Native, 2.0% Hispanic of any race, 0.8% two or more races (2000); Density: 1,310.5 persons per square mile (2000); Age: 23.7% under 18, 22.6% over 64 (2000); Marriage status: 22.6% never married, 54.6% now married, 11.2% widowed, 11.6% divorced (2000); Foreign born: 1.6% (2000); Ancestry (includes multiple ancestries): 21.1% German, 13.4% United States or American, 9.6% English, 8.4% Other groups, 8.0% Irish (2000).
Economy: Single-family building permits issued: 3 (2001) / 3 (2000); Multi-family building permits issued: 0 (2001) / 0 (2000); Employment by occupation: 8.3% management, 14.7% professional, 14.8% services, 25.5% sales, 1.0% farming, 9.6% construction, 26.0% production (2000).
Income: Per capita income: $13,574 (2000); Median household income: $25,498 (2000); Poverty rate: 18.2% (2000).
Taxes: Total city taxes per capita: $210 (1997); City property taxes per capita: $202 (1997).
Education: High school graduation rate: 79.0% (2000); College graduation rate: 14.2% (2000).

School District(s)
Centerville Community School District (KG-12)
2000 Enrollment: 1,656 641-856-0601
Housing: Homeownership rate: 63.1% (2000); Median home value: $45,700 (2000); Median rent: $267 per month (2000); Median age of housing: 52 years (2000).
Hospitals: Mercy Medical Center - Centerville (58 beds)
Safety: Violent crime rate: 38.9 per 10,000 population; Property crime rate: 483.3 per 10,000 population (2001).
Newspapers: Daily Iowegian (5 x week)
Transportation: Commute to work: 94.0% car, 0.1% public transportation, 2.6% walk, 1.8% work from home (2000); Travel time to work: 78.4% less than 15 minutes, 6.8% 15 to 30 minutes, 4.3% 30 to 45 minutes, 3.1% 45 to 60 minutes, 7.5% 60 minutes or more (2000)
Airports: Centerville Municipal
Additional Information Contacts
Centerville Chamber of Commerce 641-437-4102

CINCINNATI (city). Covers a land area of 1.741 square miles and a water area of 0 square miles. Located at 40.63° N. Lat.; 92.92° W. Long. Elevation is 1,034 feet.
History: The name of Cincinnati refers to the Roman patriot Cincinnatus. This Cincinnati was established after the Cincinnati in Ohio.
Population: 428 (2000); Race: 96.7% White, 0.0% Black, 0.0% Asian, 0.0% American Indian and Alaska Native, 0.7% Hispanic of any race, 3.3% two or more races (2000); Density: 245.9 persons per square mile (2000); Age: 26.4% under 18, 14.3% over 64 (2000); Marriage status: 25.5% never married, 50.3% now married, 9.8% widowed, 14.4% divorced (2000); Foreign born: 0.0% (2000); Ancestry (includes multiple ancestries): 20.9% German, 12.4% Irish, 11.9% English, 8.1% United States or American, 5.9% French (except Basque) (2000).
Economy: Employment by occupation: 4.5% management, 3.9% professional, 22.3% services, 20.1% sales, 0.0% farming, 5.6% construction, 43.6% production (2000).
Income: Per capita income: $12,489 (2000); Median household income: $26,641 (2000); Poverty rate: 11.4% (2000).
Taxes: Total city taxes per capita: $56 (1997); City property taxes per capita: $56 (1997).
Education: High school graduation rate: 75.9% (2000); College graduation rate: 8.3% (2000).
Housing: Homeownership rate: 95.0% (2000); Median home value: $18,400 (2000); Median rent: $175 per month (2000); Median age of housing: 55 years (2000).
Transportation: Commute to work: 98.3% car, 0.6% public transportation, 1.1% walk, 0.0% work from home (2000); Travel time to work: 43.6% less than 15 minutes, 43.6% 15 to 30 minutes, 3.9% 30 to 45 minutes, 1.1% 45 to 60 minutes, 7.8% 60 minutes or more (2000)

EXLINE (city). Covers a land area of 0.993 square miles and a water area of 0 square miles. Located at 40.65° N. Lat.; 92.84° W. Long.
History: When Exline was first platted in 1874, it was called Caldwell City. The name was changed to honor merchant David Exline, on whose land the town was situated.
Population: 191 (2000); Race: 100.0% White, 0.0% Black, 0.0% Asian, 0.0% American Indian and Alaska Native, 0.0% Hispanic of any race, 0.0% two or more races (2000); Density: 192.3 persons per square mile (2000); Age: 25.9% under 18, 10.2% over 64 (2000); Marriage status: 33.8% never married, 50.0% now married, 9.7% widowed, 6.5% divorced (2000); Foreign born: 0.0% (2000); Ancestry (includes multiple ancestries): 10.7% German, 10.7% Irish, 9.1% English, 5.6% Other groups, 3.6% United States or American (2000).
Economy: Employment by occupation: 2.4% management, 15.3% professional, 23.5% services, 14.1% sales, 0.0% farming, 15.3% construction, 29.4% production (2000).
Income: Per capita income: $11,896 (2000); Median household income: $22,019 (2000); Poverty rate: 27.4% (2000).
Taxes: Total city taxes per capita: $31 (1997); City property taxes per capita: $31 (1997).
Education: High school graduation rate: 64.6% (2000); College graduation rate: 0.0% (2000).
Housing: Homeownership rate: 87.0% (2000); Median home value: $33,100 (2000); Median rent: $213 per month (2000); Median age of housing: 55 years (2000).
Transportation: Commute to work: 97.6% car, 0.0% public transportation, 0.0% walk, 2.4% work from home (2000); Travel time to work: 44.6% less than 15 minutes, 45.8% 15 to 30 minutes, 6.0% 30 to 45 minutes, 0.0% 45 to 60 minutes, 3.6% 60 minutes or more (2000)

MORAVIA (city). Covers a land area of 1.158 square miles and a water area of 0.001 square miles. Located at 40.89° N. Lat.; 92.81° W. Long. Elevation is 1,001 feet.
History: Moravia was founded by a religious community from North Carolina known as the Moravian Society.
Population: 713 (2000); Race: 97.2% White, 0.0% Black, 0.0% Asian, 0.0% American Indian and Alaska Native, 1.8% Hispanic of any race, 1.0% two or more races (2000); Density: 615.8 persons per square mile (2000); Age: 23.6% under 18, 26.1% over 64 (2000); Marriage status: 19.9% never married, 53.4% now married, 16.4% widowed, 10.3% divorced (2000); Foreign born: 1.2% (2000); Ancestry (includes multiple ancestries): 19.0% United States or American, 16.9% German, 13.0% English, 6.2% Irish, 4.7% Other groups (2000).
Economy: Employment by occupation: 10.6% management, 12.3% professional, 16.4% services, 20.8% sales, 2.0% farming, 7.5% construction, 30.4% production (2000).
Income: Per capita income: $15,821 (2000); Median household income: $26,042 (2000); Poverty rate: 13.8% (2000).
Taxes: Total city taxes per capita: $84 (1997); City property taxes per capita: $83 (1997).
Education: High school graduation rate: 86.3% (2000); College graduation rate: 9.3% (2000).

School District(s)
Moravia Community School District (PK-12)
2000 Enrollment: 395 641-724-3240
Housing: Homeownership rate: 76.6% (2000); Median home value: $42,400 (2000); Median rent: $187 per month (2000); Median age of housing: 45 years (2000).
Newspapers: Moravia Union (1 x week)
Transportation: Commute to work: 92.2% car, 0.0% public transportation, 4.8% walk, 1.7% work from home (2000); Travel time to work: 34.0% less than 15 minutes, 37.8% 15 to 30 minutes, 16.3% 30 to 45 minutes, 6.9% 45 to 60 minutes, 4.9% 60 minutes or more (2000)

MOULTON (city). Covers a land area of 1.016 square miles and a water area of 0 square miles. Located at 40.68° N. Lat.; 92.67° W. Long. Elevation is 987 feet.
History: Moulton was settled in 1867 and platted in 1868 as Elizabethtown. It was renamed for J. J. Moulton, a railroad surveyor.
Population: 658 (2000); Race: 95.7% White, 0.0% Black, 0.8% Asian, 1.1% American Indian and Alaska Native, 0.0% Hispanic of any race, 2.4% two or more races (2000); Density: 647.8 persons per square mile (2000); Age: 23.5% under 18, 20.4% over 64 (2000); Marriage status: 22.1% never married, 52.4% now married, 12.3% widowed, 13.1% divorced (2000); Foreign born: 0.8% (2000); Ancestry (includes multiple ancestries): 16.0% German, 13.0% United States or American, 10.8% Irish, 8.4% English, 4.3% Other groups (2000).
Economy: Employment by occupation: 8.6% management, 16.0% professional, 9.3% services, 23.4% sales, 1.5% farming, 11.9% construction, 29.4% production (2000).
Income: Per capita income: $14,744 (2000); Median household income: $22,692 (2000); Poverty rate: 14.8% (2000).
Taxes: Total city taxes per capita: $79 (1997); City property taxes per capita: $76 (1997).
Education: High school graduation rate: 76.7% (2000); College graduation rate: 7.0% (2000).

School District(s)

Moulton-Udell Community School District (PK-12)
2000 Enrollment: 310 641-642-3665
Housing: Homeownership rate: 71.2% (2000); Median home value: $29,300 (2000); Median rent: $227 per month (2000); Median age of housing: 39 years (2000).
Transportation: Commute to work: 88.0% car, 0.0% public transportation, 8.6% walk, 2.6% work from home (2000); Travel time to work: 39.6% less than 15 minutes, 35.0% 15 to 30 minutes, 18.8% 30 to 45 minutes, 2.3% 45 to 60 minutes, 4.2% 60 minutes or more (2000)

MYSTIC (city). Covers a land area of 2.929 square miles and a water area of 0 square miles. Located at 40.77° N. Lat.; 92.94° W. Long. Elevation is 896 feet.
History: Mystic was established in the 1880's as a mining center following the discovery of a rich vein of coal. Dennis Vandyke named the town for his birthplace, Mystic, Connecticut.
Population: 588 (2000); Race: 99.6% White, 0.2% Black, 0.0% Asian, 0.0% American Indian and Alaska Native, 1.9% Hispanic of any race, 0.2% two or more races (2000); Density: 200.7 persons per square mile (2000); Age: 29.8% under 18, 9.0% over 64 (2000); Marriage status: 20.4% never married, 61.1% now married, 5.0% widowed, 13.5% divorced (2000); Foreign born: 0.4% (2000); Ancestry (includes multiple ancestries): 20.1% German, 16.8% English, 13.8% Irish, 9.2% Other groups, 4.6% United States or American (2000).
Economy: Employment by occupation: 6.1% management, 7.9% professional, 17.0% services, 17.0% sales, 0.0% farming, 12.7% construction, 39.3% production (2000).
Income: Per capita income: $11,846 (2000); Median household income: $25,568 (2000); Poverty rate: 22.9% (2000).
Taxes: Total city taxes per capita: $83 (1997); City property taxes per capita: $83 (1997).
Education: High school graduation rate: 73.3% (2000); College graduation rate: 4.6% (2000).
Housing: Homeownership rate: 81.1% (2000); Median home value: $32,200 (2000); Median rent: $183 per month (2000); Median age of housing: 52 years (2000).
Transportation: Commute to work: 90.2% car, 1.8% public transportation, 3.6% walk, 1.8% work from home (2000); Travel time to work: 36.7% less than 15 minutes, 45.2% 15 to 30 minutes, 4.5% 30 to 45 minutes, 7.7% 45 to 60 minutes, 5.9% 60 minutes or more (2000)

NUMA (city). Covers a land area of 0.444 square miles and a water area of 0 square miles. Located at 40.68° N. Lat.; 92.97° W. Long. Elevation is 1,037 feet.
Population: 109 (2000); Race: 94.6% White, 0.0% Black, 2.7% Asian, 0.0% American Indian and Alaska Native, 0.0% Hispanic of any race, 2.7% two or more races (2000); Density: 245.7 persons per square mile (2000); Age: 12.5% under 18, 11.6% over 64 (2000); Marriage status: 25.7% never married, 65.3% now married, 2.0% widowed, 6.9% divorced (2000); Foreign born: 2.7% (2000); Ancestry (includes multiple ancestries): 32.1% Irish, 24.1% German, 16.1% English, 11.6% United States or American, 10.7% Dutch (2000).
Economy: Employment by occupation: 0.0% management, 22.6% professional, 11.3% services, 11.3% sales, 0.0% farming, 14.5% construction, 40.3% production (2000).
Income: Per capita income: $15,694 (2000); Median household income: $26,625 (2000); Poverty rate: 10.7% (2000).
Taxes: Total city taxes per capita: $59 (1997); City property taxes per capita: $59 (1997).
Education: High school graduation rate: 84.5% (2000); College graduation rate: 14.3% (2000).
Housing: Homeownership rate: 84.0% (2000); Median home value: $30,400 (2000); Median rent: $358 per month (2000); Median age of housing: 60+ years (2000).
Transportation: Commute to work: 100.0% car, 0.0% public transportation, 0.0% walk, 0.0% work from home (2000); Travel time to work: 8.1% less than 15 minutes, 51.6% 15 to 30 minutes, 19.4% 30 to 45 minutes, 6.5% 45 to 60 minutes, 14.5% 60 minutes or more (2000)

PLANO (city). Covers a land area of 0.565 square miles and a water area of 0 square miles. Located at 40.75° N. Lat.; 93.04° W. Long.
History: Plano was named for Plano, Illinois, by a group of Seventh Day Adventists from that town.
Population: 58 (2000); Race: 100.0% White, 0.0% Black, 0.0% Asian, 0.0% American Indian and Alaska Native, 0.0% Hispanic of any race, 0.0% two or more races (2000); Density: 102.7 persons per square mile (2000); Age: 3.1% under 18, 23.1% over 64 (2000); Marriage status: 15.4% never married, 63.1% now married, 9.2% widowed, 12.3% divorced (2000); Foreign born: 0.0% (2000); Ancestry (includes multiple ancestries): 21.5% English, 12.3% Scottish, 6.2% Other groups, 6.2% Irish, 4.6% United States or American (2000).
Economy: Employment by occupation: 9.7% management, 16.1% professional, 9.7% services, 19.4% sales, 0.0% farming, 32.3% construction, 12.9% production (2000).
Income: Per capita income: $22,474 (2000); Median household income: $30,625 (2000); Poverty rate: 23.1% (2000).
Taxes: Total city taxes per capita: $27 (1997); City property taxes per capita: $27 (1997).
Education: High school graduation rate: 72.9% (2000); College graduation rate: 6.8% (2000).
Housing: Homeownership rate: 86.5% (2000); Median home value: $33,400 (2000); Median rent: $263 per month (2000); Median age of housing: 29 years (2000).
Transportation: Commute to work: 96.8% car, 0.0% public transportation, 3.2% walk, 0.0% work from home (2000); Travel time to work: 3.2% less than 15 minutes, 83.9% 15 to 30 minutes, 6.5% 30 to 45 minutes, 6.5% 45 to 60 minutes, 0.0% 60 minutes or more (2000)

RATHBUN (city). Covers a land area of 0.215 square miles and a water area of 0 square miles. Located at 40.80° N. Lat.; 92.88° W. Long.
History: Rathbun was named for the general manager of mining operations at this location for the Star Coal Company of Streator, Illinois.
Population: 88 (2000); Race: 100.0% White, 0.0% Black, 0.0% Asian, 0.0% American Indian and Alaska Native, 0.0% Hispanic of any race, 0.0% two or more races (2000); Density: 408.7 persons per square mile (2000); Age: 28.4% under 18, 11.4% over 64 (2000); Marriage status: 22.5% never married, 69.0% now married, 1.4% widowed, 7.0% divorced (2000); Foreign born: 0.0% (2000); Ancestry (includes multiple ancestries): 23.9% United States or American, 21.6% German, 17.0% English, 10.2% Croatian, 10.2% Irish (2000).
Economy: Employment by occupation: 12.8% management, 6.4% professional, 17.0% services, 19.1% sales, 0.0% farming, 14.9% construction, 29.8% production (2000).
Income: Per capita income: $14,749 (2000); Median household income: $40,000 (2000); Poverty rate: 17.0% (2000).
Taxes: Total city taxes per capita: $22 (1997); City property taxes per capita: $22 (1997).
Education: High school graduation rate: 82.1% (2000); College graduation rate: 7.1% (2000).
Housing: Homeownership rate: 83.3% (2000); Median home value: $29,400 (2000); Median rent: $288 per month (2000); Median age of housing: 60+ years (2000).
Transportation: Commute to work: 100.0% car, 0.0% public transportation, 0.0% walk, 0.0% work from home (2000); Travel time to work: 19.1% less than 15 minutes, 68.1% 15 to 30 minutes, 0.0% 30 to 45 minutes, 4.3% 45 to 60 minutes, 8.5% 60 minutes or more (2000)

UDELL (city). Covers a land area of 0.317 square miles and a water area of 0 square miles. Located at 40.78° N. Lat.; 92.74° W. Long. Elevation is 996 feet.
History: It is believed that Udell was named after state senator Dr. Nathan Udell.
Population: 58 (2000); Race: 100.0% White, 0.0% Black, 0.0% Asian, 0.0% American Indian and Alaska Native, 0.0% Hispanic of any race, 0.0% two or more races (2000); Density: 183.0 persons per square mile (2000); Age: 46.2% under 18, 1.5% over 64 (2000); Marriage status: 22.9% never married, 51.4% now married, 2.9% widowed, 22.9% divorced (2000); Foreign born: 0.0% (2000); Ancestry (includes multiple ancestries): 21.5% United States or American, 6.2% English, 4.6% German, 3.1% Dutch (2000).
Economy: Employment by occupation: 0.0% management, 0.0% professional, 11.8% services, 29.4% sales, 0.0% farming, 11.8% construction, 47.1% production (2000).
Income: Per capita income: $7,294 (2000); Median household income: $24,688 (2000); Poverty rate: 15.3% (2000).
Taxes: Total city taxes per capita: $26 (1997); City property taxes per capita: $26 (1997).
Education: High school graduation rate: 74.3% (2000); College graduation rate: 11.4% (2000).
Housing: Homeownership rate: 47.4% (2000); Median home value: $26,900 (2000); Median rent: $358 per month (2000); Median age of housing: 47 years (2000).
Transportation: Commute to work: 100.0% car, 0.0% public transportation, 0.0% walk, 0.0% work from home (2000); Travel time to work: 0.0% less than 15 minutes, 58.8% 15 to 30 minutes, 41.2% 30 to 45 minutes, 0.0% 45 to 60 minutes, 0.0% 60 minutes or more (2000)

UNIONVILLE (city). Covers a land area of 0.745 square miles and a water area of 0 square miles. Located at 40.81° N. Lat.; 92.69° W. Long. Elevation is 936 feet.
Population: 127 (2000); Race: 100.0% White, 0.0% Black, 0.0% Asian, 0.0% American Indian and Alaska Native, 0.8% Hispanic of any race, 0.0% two or more races (2000); Density: 170.5 persons per square mile (2000); Age: 29.0% under 18, 12.1% over 64 (2000); Marriage status: 23.2% never married, 65.3% now married, 7.4% widowed, 4.2% divorced (2000); Foreign born: 0.8% (2000); Ancestry (includes multiple ancestries): 36.3% United States or American, 16.1% German, 10.5% Italian, 10.5% English, 10.5% Swedish (2000).
Economy: In agricultural area. Employment by occupation: 3.6% management, 37.5% professional, 1.8% services, 12.5% sales, 7.1% farming, 17.9% construction, 19.6% production (2000).
Income: Per capita income: $13,856 (2000); Median household income: $33,333 (2000); Poverty rate: 11.3% (2000).
Taxes: Total city taxes per capita: $44 (1997); City property taxes per capita: $44 (1997).
Education: High school graduation rate: 82.3% (2000); College graduation rate: 21.5% (2000).
Housing: Homeownership rate: 93.3% (2000); Median home value: $28,800 (2000); Median rent: $275 per month (2000); Median age of housing: 39 years (2000).
Transportation: Commute to work: 96.4% car, 0.0% public transportation, 0.0% walk, 3.6% work from home (2000); Travel time to work: 11.1% less than 15 minutes, 42.6% 15 to 30 minutes, 31.5% 30 to 45 minutes, 1.9% 45 to 60 minutes, 13.0% 60 minutes or more (2000)

Audubon County

Located in west central Iowa; drained by the East Nishnabotna River. Covers a land area of 443.10 square miles, a water area of 0.40 square miles, and is located in the Central Time Zone. The county government was organized in 1851. County seat is Audubon.

Weather Station: Audubon 1 SSE — Elevation: 1,289 feet

	Jan	Feb	Mar	Apr	May	Jun	Jul	Aug	Sep	Oct	Nov	Dec
High	29	35	48	63	73	83	86	84	76	64	46	33
Low	10	16	26	38	49	59	63	61	52	40	27	16
Precip	0.9	0.9	2.3	3.4	4.3	4.3	4.4	3.8	3.6	2.8	1.9	1.1
Snow	6.9	5.8	5.0	1.9	0.0	0.0	0.0	0.0	tr	0.6	3.0	6.4

High and Low temperatures in degrees Fahrenheit; Precipitation and Snow in inches

Population: 6,830 (2000); Race: 98.9% White, 0.2% Black, 0.4% Asian, 0.1% American Indian and Alaska Native, 0.2% Hispanic of any race, 0.4% two or more races (2000); Density: 15.4 persons per square mile (2000); Age: 25.8% under 18, 23.6% over 64 (2000).
Religion: Five largest groups: 35.7% Evangelical Lutheran Church in America, 12.5% The United Methodist Church, 11.9% Catholic Church, 6.5% Lutheran Church—Missouri Synod, 4.7% Christian Church (Disciples of Christ) (2000).
Economy: Unemployment rate: 2.6% (11/2002); Total civilian labor force: 3,474 (11/2002); Leading industries: 23.3% health care and social assistance; 16.1% retail trade; 14.2% manufacturing (2000); Companies that employ more than 1,000 persons: 0 (2000); Companies that employ more than 100 persons: 1 (2000); Farms: 649 totaling 272,258 acres (1997); Minority business ownership rate: 0.0% (1997); Women business ownership rate: 21.5% (1997); Retail sales per capita: $7,607 (1997). Single-family building permits issued: 11 (2001) / 2 (2000); Multi-family building permits issued: 0 (2001) / 0 (2000).
Income: Per capita income: $17,489 (2000); Median household income: $32,215 (2000); Poverty rate: 7.7% (2000); Bankruptcy rate: 1.47% (2001).
Taxes: Total county taxes per capita: $385 (1997); County property taxes per capita: $384 (1997).
Education: High school graduation rate: 82.5% (2000); College graduation rate: 12.3% (2000).
Housing: Homeownership rate: 79.0% (2000); Median home value: $48,700 (2000); Median rent: $225 per month (2000); Median age of housing: 58 years (2000).
Health: Birth rate: 105.4 per 10,000 population (1998); Age adjusted death rate: 57.4 per 10,000 population (1999); Age adjusted cancer mortality rate: 112.6 (Unreliable figure as per CDC) deaths per 100,000 population (1999). Number of physicians: 1.5 per 10,000 population (1999); Number of hospital beds: 42.5 per 10,000 population (1999).
Elections: 2000 Presidential election results: 47.0% Gore, 50.5% Bush, 1.5% Nader, 0.6% Buchanan
Additional Information Contacts
Audubon County Government Offices. 712-563-2584

Audubon County Communities

AUDUBON (city). Covers a land area of 1.759 square miles and a water area of 0 square miles. Located at 41.72° N. Lat.; 94.92° W. Long. Elevation is 1,373 feet.
History: Audubon was platted in 1878 and named for the naturalist, John James Audubon.
Population: 2,382 (2000); Race: 99.5% White, 0.2% Black, 0.0% Asian, 0.0% American Indian and Alaska Native, 0.3% Hispanic of any race, 0.3% two or more races (2000); Density: 1,354.2 persons per square mile (2000); Age: 22.4% under 18, 31.6% over 64 (2000); Marriage status: 16.3% never married, 61.1% now married, 13.2% widowed, 9.4% divorced (2000); Foreign born: 0.2% (2000); Ancestry (includes multiple ancestries): 30.9% Danish, 30.7% German, 10.3% Irish, 9.3% English, 5.5% United States or American (2000).
Economy: Single-family building permits issued: 4 (2001) / 0 (2000); Multi-family building permits issued: 0 (2001) / 0 (2000); Employment by occupation: 11.8% management, 19.7% professional, 20.9% services, 20.7% sales, 2.4% farming, 9.2% construction, 15.3% production (2000).
Income: Per capita income: $20,128 (2000); Median household income: $33,068 (2000); Poverty rate: 6.7% (2000).
Taxes: Total city taxes per capita: $248 (1997); City property taxes per capita: $246 (1997).
Education: High school graduation rate: 79.5% (2000); College graduation rate: 13.7% (2000).

School District(s)
Audubon Community School District (PK-12)
2000 Enrollment: 838 712-563-2607
Housing: Homeownership rate: 81.3% (2000); Median home value: $52,500 (2000); Median rent: $240 per month (2000); Median age of housing: 48 years (2000).
Hospitals: Audubon County Memorial Hospital (25 beds)
Safety: Violent crime rate: 8.4 per 10,000 population; Property crime rate: 222.8 per 10,000 population (2001).
Newspapers: Audubon County Advocate Journal (1 x week); Nishna Valley Tribune (1 x week)
Transportation: Commute to work: 90.0% car, 0.0% public transportation, 5.8% walk, 4.2% work from home (2000); Travel time to work: 76.8% less than 15 minutes, 9.9% 15 to 30 minutes, 8.7% 30 to 45 minutes, 0.7% 45 to 60 minutes, 3.9% 60 minutes or more (2000)

BRAYTON (city). Covers a land area of 0.616 square miles and a water area of 0 square miles. Located at 41.54° N. Lat.; 94.92° W. Long. Elevation is 1,209 feet.
History: Brayton was named for one of the civil engineers working on the Chicago, Rock Island & Pacific Railroad here in 1878-79.
Population: 145 (2000); Race: 98.1% White, 0.0% Black, 1.9% Asian, 0.0% American Indian and Alaska Native, 0.0% Hispanic of any race, 0.0% two or more races (2000); Density: 235.4 persons per square mile (2000); Age: 18.7% under 18, 35.5% over 64 (2000); Marriage status: 30.2% never married, 58.1% now married, 3.9% widowed, 7.8% divorced (2000); Foreign born: 1.9% (2000); Ancestry (includes multiple ancestries): 33.5% Danish, 29.0% German, 5.8% Scotch-Irish, 5.8% United States or American, 5.2% Irish (2000).
Economy: Single-family building permits issued: 0 (2001) / 0 (2000); Multi-family building permits issued: 0 (2001) / 0 (2000); Employment by occupation: 0.0% management, 6.9% professional, 19.0% services, 10.3% sales, 3.4% farming, 17.2% construction, 43.1% production (2000).
Income: Per capita income: $12,166 (2000); Median household income: $25,875 (2000); Poverty rate: 3.9% (2000).
Taxes: Total city taxes per capita: $78 (1997); City property taxes per capita: $78 (1997).
Education: High school graduation rate: 65.1% (2000); College graduation rate: 9.4% (2000).
Housing: Homeownership rate: 66.7% (2000); Median home value: $23,800 (2000); Median rent: $200 per month (2000); Median age of housing: 60+ years (2000).
Transportation: Commute to work: 92.7% car, 0.0% public transportation, 0.0% walk, 7.3% work from home (2000); Travel time to work: 27.5% less than 15 minutes, 43.1% 15 to 30 minutes, 17.6% 30 to 45 minutes, 0.0% 45 to 60 minutes, 11.8% 60 minutes or more (2000)

EXIRA (city). Covers a land area of 1.024 square miles and a water area of 0 square miles. Located at 41.59° N. Lat.; 94.87° W. Long. Elevation is 1,227 feet.
History: Exira was founded by Judge D. M. Harris in 1857. The town was named for Exira Eckman of Ohio, who, with her father, Judge John Eckman, was visiting relatives when the town was platted. One of the promoters of the town had intended to call it Viola, for his own daughter, but when Judge Eckman offered to buy a town lot if the town was named for his daughter, the change was made.
Population: 810 (2000); Race: 97.9% White, 0.0% Black, 0.5% Asian, 0.6% American Indian and Alaska Native, 0.0% Hispanic of any race, 1.0% two or more races (2000); Density: 791.0 persons per square mile (2000); Age: 20.7% under 18, 34.0% over 64 (2000); Marriage status: 21.9% never married, 51.7% now married, 18.2% widowed, 8.2% divorced (2000); Foreign born: 0.5% (2000); Ancestry (includes multiple ancestries): 36.9% Danish, 29.8% German, 14.6% Irish, 10.6% English, 4.7% Other groups (2000).
Economy: Single-family building permits issued: 1 (2001) / 0 (2000); Multi-family building permits issued: 0 (2001) / 0 (2000); Employment by occupation: 11.3% management, 12.0% professional, 23.8% services, 19.6% sales, 2.1% farming, 9.2% construction, 22.0% production (2000).
Income: Per capita income: $15,124 (2000); Median household income: $26,319 (2000); Poverty rate: 11.7% (2000).
Taxes: Total city taxes per capita: $155 (1997); City property taxes per capita: $150 (1997).
Education: High school graduation rate: 76.8% (2000); College graduation rate: 9.1% (2000).

School District(s)

Exira Community School District (PK-12)
2000 Enrollment: 310 712-268-5555

Housing: Homeownership rate: 84.5% (2000); Median home value: $38,500 (2000); Median rent: $186 per month (2000); Median age of housing: 53 years (2000).
Transportation: Commute to work: 89.2% car, 0.0% public transportation, 4.8% walk, 4.2% work from home (2000); Travel time to work: 59.9% less than 15 minutes, 24.6% 15 to 30 minutes, 3.6% 30 to 45 minutes, 4.1% 45 to 60 minutes, 7.7% 60 minutes or more (2000)

GRAY (city). Covers a land area of 1.001 square miles and a water area of 0 square miles. Located at 41.84° N. Lat.; 94.98° W. Long. Elevation is 1,374 feet.
History: Gray was founded in 1881 on land belonging to George B. Gray, and named for him.
Population: 82 (2000); Race: 97.6% White, 0.0% Black, 2.4% Asian, 0.0% American Indian and Alaska Native, 0.0% Hispanic of any race, 0.0% two or more races (2000); Density: 81.9 persons per square mile (2000); Age: 14.3% under 18, 26.2% over 64 (2000); Marriage status: 19.2% never married, 68.5% now married, 12.3% widowed, 0.0% divorced (2000); Foreign born: 2.4% (2000); Ancestry (includes multiple ancestries): 52.4% German, 17.9% Danish, 11.9% Irish, 9.5% English, 4.8% Other groups (2000).
Economy: Employment by occupation: 4.7% management, 23.3% professional, 18.6% services, 4.7% sales, 4.7% farming, 4.7% construction, 39.5% production (2000).
Income: Per capita income: $18,190 (2000); Median household income: $35,750 (2000); Poverty rate: 2.4% (2000).
Taxes: Total city taxes per capita: $105 (1997); City property taxes per capita: $105 (1997).
Education: High school graduation rate: 66.1% (2000); College graduation rate: 16.1% (2000).
Housing: Homeownership rate: 93.9% (2000); Median home value: $14,600 (2000); Median rent: $275 per month (2000); Median age of housing: 60+ years (2000).
Transportation: Commute to work: 90.7% car, 0.0% public transportation, 9.3% walk, 0.0% work from home (2000); Travel time to work: 16.3% less than 15 minutes, 51.2% 15 to 30 minutes, 14.0% 30 to 45 minutes, 7.0% 45 to 60 minutes, 11.6% 60 minutes or more (2000)

HAMLIN (unincorporated postal area, zip code 50117). Covers a land area of 29.890 square miles and a water area of 0.028 square miles. Located at 41.67° N. Lat.; 94.84° W. Long. Elevation is 1,266 feet.
History: Hamlin was named for Nathaniel H. Hamlin, first settler in the county, and was at one time considered as a site for the county seat.
Population: 251 (2000); Race: 100.0% White, 0.0% Black, 0.0% Asian, 0.0% American Indian and Alaska Native, 0.0% Hispanic of any race, 0.0% two or more races (2000); Density: 8.4 persons per square mile (2000); Age: 18.3% under 18, 10.7% over 64 (2000); Marriage status: 15.3% never married, 81.5% now married, 3.2% widowed, 0.0% divorced (2000); Foreign born: 0.0% (2000); Ancestry (includes multiple ancestries): 31.3% Danish, 22.2% German, 21.8% United States or American, 12.7% English, 9.1% Swedish (2000).
Economy: Employment by occupation: 12.6% management, 17.9% professional, 4.6% services, 15.9% sales, 0.0% farming, 24.5% construction, 24.5% production (2000).
Income: Per capita income: $16,685 (2000); Median household income: $27,262 (2000); Poverty rate: 9.5% (2000).
Education: High school graduation rate: 100.0% (2000); College graduation rate: 8.9% (2000).
Housing: Homeownership rate: 86.3% (2000); Median home value: $76,700 (2000); Median rent: $405 per month (2000); Median age of housing: 60+ years (2000).
Transportation: Commute to work: 98.0% car, 0.0% public transportation, 0.0% walk, 2.0% work from home (2000); Travel time to work: 54.7% less than 15 minutes, 26.4% 15 to 30 minutes, 8.1% 30 to 45 minutes, 4.7% 45 to 60 minutes, 6.1% 60 minutes or more (2000)

KIMBALLTON (city). Covers a land area of 0.760 square miles and a water area of 0 square miles. Located at 41.62° N. Lat.; 95.07° W. Long. Elevation is 1,290 feet.
History: Kimballton was founded by people of Danish descent.
Population: 342 (2000); Race: 100.0% White, 0.0% Black, 0.0% Asian, 0.0% American Indian and Alaska Native, 0.0% Hispanic of any race, 0.0% two or more races (2000); Density: 450.0 persons per square mile (2000); Age: 29.0% under 18, 19.7% over 64 (2000); Marriage status: 21.9% never married, 60.7% now married, 9.9% widowed, 7.4% divorced (2000); Foreign born: 4.2% (2000); Ancestry (includes multiple ancestries): 58.1% Danish, 22.3% German, 11.9% Irish, 4.5% Norwegian, 3.2% Swedish (2000).
Economy: Single-family building permits issued: 0 (2001) / 0 (2000); Multi-family building permits issued: 0 (2001) / 0 (2000); Employment by occupation: 6.8% management, 9.5% professional, 27.7% services, 25.0% sales, 0.0% farming, 8.8% construction, 22.3% production (2000).
Income: Per capita income: $13,514 (2000); Median household income: $32,188 (2000); Poverty rate: 11.9% (2000).
Taxes: Total city taxes per capita: $75 (1997); City property taxes per capita: $71 (1997).
Education: High school graduation rate: 80.5% (2000); College graduation rate: 10.7% (2000).
Housing: Homeownership rate: 80.4% (2000); Median home value: $38,200 (2000); Median rent: $188 per month (2000); Median age of housing: 60+ years (2000).

Transportation: Commute to work: 91.0% car, 1.4% public transportation, 2.8% walk, 4.8% work from home (2000); Travel time to work: 39.9% less than 15 minutes, 44.2% 15 to 30 minutes, 0.0% 30 to 45 minutes, 2.2% 45 to 60 minutes, 13.8% 60 minutes or more (2000)

Benton County

Located in east central Iowa; drained by the Cedar River. Covers a land area of 716.40 square miles, a water area of 2.10 square miles, and is located in the Central Time Zone. The county government was organized in 1837. County seat is Vinton.

Weather Station: Belle Plaine — Elevation: 807 feet

	Jan	Feb	Mar	Apr	May	Jun	Jul	Aug	Sep	Oct	Nov	Dec
High	28	34	46	60	72	81	85	83	75	63	46	33
Low	9	15	27	38	49	59	63	61	52	40	28	16
Precip	1.0	1.1	2.4	3.6	4.3	4.6	4.2	4.8	3.7	2.8	2.3	1.4
Snow	8.1	6.5	4.4	2.3	tr	0.0	0.0	0.0	0.0	0.4	3.0	6.3

High and Low temperatures in degrees Fahrenheit; Precipitation and Snow in inches

Weather Station: Vinton — Elevation: 849 feet

	Jan	Feb	Mar	Apr	May	Jun	Jul	Aug	Sep	Oct	Nov	Dec
High	27	33	46	62	73	82	86	83	76	63	45	32
Low	9	15	27	38	49	58	62	60	51	40	27	16
Precip	1.0	1.0	2.2	3.3	4.2	4.3	3.9	4.3	3.8	2.6	2.3	1.3
Snow	8.1	6.3	4.8	1.9	tr	0.0	0.0	0.0	0.0	0.3	3.5	6.4

High and Low temperatures in degrees Fahrenheit; Precipitation and Snow in inches

Population: 25,308 (2000); Race: 99.0% White, 0.2% Black, 0.2% Asian, 0.1% American Indian and Alaska Native, 0.4% Hispanic of any race, 0.5% two or more races (2000); Density: 35.3 persons per square mile (2000); Age: 27.3% under 18, 15.4% over 64 (2000).
Religion: Five largest groups: 18.9% Catholic Church, 18.1% Lutheran Church—Missouri Synod, 7.8% The United Methodist Church, 4.9% Presbyterian Church (U.S.A.), 2.9% Evangelical Lutheran Church in America (2000).
Economy: Unemployment rate: 4.9% (11/2002); Total civilian labor force: 12,203 (11/2002); Leading industries: 18.5% retail trade; 14.7% health care and social assistance; 12.5% manufacturing (2000); Companies that employ more than 1,000 persons: 0 (2000); Companies that employ more than 100 persons: 4 (2000); Farms: 1,210 totaling 418,483 acres (1997); Minority business ownership rate: 0.0% (1997); Women business ownership rate: 14.2% (1997); Retail sales per capita: $5,768 (1997). Single-family building permits issued: 74 (2001) / 85 (2000); Multi-family building permits issued: 23 (2001) / 10 (2000).
Income: Per capita income: $18,891 (2000); Median household income: $42,427 (2000); Poverty rate: 6.1% (2000); Bankruptcy rate: 2.47% (2001).
Taxes: Total county taxes per capita: $212 (2000); County property taxes per capita: $212 (2000).
Education: High school graduation rate: 87.8% (2000); College graduation rate: 13.9% (2000).
Housing: Homeownership rate: 79.4% (2000); Median home value: $82,700 (2000); Median rent: $300 per month (2000); Median age of housing: 46 years (2000).
Health: Birth rate: 128.8 per 10,000 population (1998); Age adjusted death rate: 69.8 per 10,000 population (1999); Age adjusted cancer mortality rate: 157.9 deaths per 100,000 population (1999). Number of physicians: 2.4 per 10,000 population (1999); Number of hospital beds: 34.4 per 10,000 population (1999).
Elections: 2000 Presidential election results: 50.3% Gore, 46.5% Bush, 2.0% Nader, 0.8% Buchanan
National and State Parks: Dudgeon Lake State Wildlife Mgt Area
Additional Information Contacts
Benton County Government Offices 319-472-2365
Benton County Board of Realtors 319-228-8148

Benton County Communities

ATKINS (city). Covers a land area of 0.816 square miles and a water area of 0 square miles. Located at 41.99° N. Lat.; 91.86° W. Long.
History: Atkins was settled by Germans and originally known as Hague. The name was changed in 1882 by railroad officials.
Population: 977 (2000); Race: 100.0% White, 0.0% Black, 0.0% Asian, 0.0% American Indian and Alaska Native, 0.0% Hispanic of any race, 0.0% two or more races (2000); Density: 1,197.6 persons per square mile (2000); Age: 29.3% under 18, 12.2% over 64 (2000); Marriage status: 18.6% never married, 68.9% now married, 5.2% widowed, 7.3% divorced (2000); Foreign born: 0.0% (2000); Ancestry (includes multiple ancestries): 51.2% German, 18.3% Irish, 8.3% Czech, 8.1% English, 5.3% Norwegian (2000).
Economy: Single-family building permits issued: 14 (2001) / 17 (2000); Multi-family building permits issued: 0 (2001) / 0 (2000); Employment by occupation: 15.4% management, 15.0% professional, 11.6% services, 28.5% sales, 1.0% farming, 12.0% construction, 16.4% production (2000).
Income: Per capita income: $20,507 (2000); Median household income: $50,833 (2000); Poverty rate: 3.9% (2000).
Taxes: Total city taxes per capita: $205 (1997); City property taxes per capita: $201 (1997).
Education: High school graduation rate: 90.0% (2000); College graduation rate: 17.0% (2000).
Housing: Homeownership rate: 84.8% (2000); Median home value: $100,700 (2000); Median rent: $318 per month (2000); Median age of housing: 31 years (2000).
Transportation: Commute to work: 94.8% car, 0.0% public transportation, 0.2% walk, 5.0% work from home (2000); Travel time to work: 18.0% less than 15 minutes, 67.1% 15 to 30 minutes, 12.5% 30 to 45 minutes, 1.3% 45 to 60 minutes, 1.1% 60 minutes or more (2000)

BELLE PLAINE (city). Covers a land area of 3.232 square miles and a water area of 0.012 square miles. Located at 41.89° N. Lat.; 92.27° W. Long. Elevation is 824 feet.
History: Belle Plaine was known as Gwinsville until 1862, when the post office was established. In July 1894, a fire destroyed two blocks of buildings in the heart of town.
Population: 2,878 (2000); Race: 99.0% White, 0.5% Black, 0.0% Asian, 0.0% American Indian and Alaska Native, 1.5% Hispanic of any race, 0.4% two or more races (2000); Density: 890.6 persons per square mile (2000); Age: 26.2% under 18, 21.6% over 64 (2000); Marriage status: 20.7% never married, 58.4% now married, 10.1% widowed, 10.8% divorced (2000); Foreign born: 0.9% (2000); Ancestry (includes multiple ancestries): 32.8% German, 12.9% Irish, 11.6% English, 11.2% Czech, 7.1% United States or American (2000).
Economy: Single-family building permits issued: 5 (2001) / 5 (2000); Multi-family building permits issued: 0 (2001) / 0 (2000); Employment by occupation: 8.4% management, 10.9% professional, 15.8% services, 26.0% sales, 0.0% farming, 10.3% construction, 28.6% production (2000).
Income: Per capita income: $16,321 (2000); Median household income: $36,316 (2000); Poverty rate: 7.0% (2000).
Taxes: Total city taxes per capita: $244 (1997); City property taxes per capita: $241 (1997).
Education: High school graduation rate: 81.4% (2000); College graduation rate: 13.6% (2000).

School District(s)
Belle Plaine Community School District (PK-12)
2000 Enrollment: 767 319-444-3611
Housing: Homeownership rate: 74.5% (2000); Median home value: $57,400 (2000); Median rent: $234 per month (2000); Median age of housing: 60+ years (2000).
Newspapers: South Benton Star-Press (1 x week); Belle Plaine Union (1 x week)
Transportation: Commute to work: 95.5% car, 0.0% public transportation, 1.4% walk, 3.1% work from home (2000); Travel time to work: 42.6% less than 15 minutes, 11.8% 15 to 30 minutes, 24.4% 30 to 45 minutes, 14.6% 45 to 60 minutes, 6.5% 60 minutes or more (2000)

BLAIRSTOWN (city). Covers a land area of 0.475 square miles and a water area of 0 square miles. Located at 41.90° N. Lat.; 92.08° W. Long. Elevation is 839 feet.
History: Blairstown is where the Hickory Grove Debating Society was organized in 1858.
Population: 682 (2000); Race: 99.9% White, 0.0% Black, 0.0% Asian, 0.0% American Indian and Alaska Native, 0.3% Hispanic of any race, 0.0% two or more races (2000); Density: 1,434.7 persons per square mile (2000); Age: 25.9% under 18, 21.3% over 64 (2000); Marriage status: 20.2% never married, 64.2% now married, 7.5% widowed, 8.1% divorced (2000); Foreign born: 0.3% (2000); Ancestry (includes multiple ancestries): 49.9% German, 10.9% United States or American, 10.4% Irish, 5.1% English, 4.9% Czech (2000).
Economy: Single-family building permits issued: 4 (2001) / 1 (2000); Multi-family building permits issued: 0 (2001) / 0 (2000); Employment by occupation: 6.1% management, 9.9% professional, 13.5% services, 28.9% sales, 1.7% farming, 11.8% construction, 28.1% production (2000).

Income: Per capita income: $16,828 (2000); Median household income: $40,662 (2000); Poverty rate: 11.0% (2000).
Taxes: Total city taxes per capita: $151 (1997); City property taxes per capita: $149 (1997).
Education: High school graduation rate: 85.7% (2000); College graduation rate: 8.8% (2000).
Housing: Homeownership rate: 73.8% (2000); Median home value: $84,400 (2000); Median rent: $355 per month (2000); Median age of housing: 49 years (2000).
Transportation: Commute to work: 87.1% car, 0.0% public transportation, 8.1% walk, 3.9% work from home (2000); Travel time to work: 33.8% less than 15 minutes, 30.0% 15 to 30 minutes, 29.7% 30 to 45 minutes, 4.1% 45 to 60 minutes, 2.3% 60 minutes or more (2000)

GARRISON (city). Covers a land area of 0.247 square miles and a water area of 0 square miles. Located at 42.14° N. Lat.; 92.14° W. Long. Elevation is 859 feet.
History: Originally known as Benton, after the county, Garrison was later named for landowner Nelson Garrison, on whose property the post office was established in 1873.
Population: 413 (2000); Race: 98.7% White, 0.0% Black, 0.5% Asian, 0.0% American Indian and Alaska Native, 0.0% Hispanic of any race, 0.8% two or more races (2000); Density: 1,673.3 persons per square mile (2000); Age: 27.1% under 18, 13.5% over 64 (2000); Marriage status: 17.1% never married, 63.2% now married, 9.0% widowed, 10.7% divorced (2000); Foreign born: 1.3% (2000); Ancestry (includes multiple ancestries): 27.3% German, 16.3% United States or American, 7.3% Irish, 6.5% Norwegian, 4.8% English (2000).
Economy: Employment by occupation: 8.4% management, 6.8% professional, 20.9% services, 21.5% sales, 2.6% farming, 13.1% construction, 26.7% production (2000).
Income: Per capita income: $14,719 (2000); Median household income: $26,389 (2000); Poverty rate: 13.0% (2000).
Taxes: Total city taxes per capita: $133 (1997); City property taxes per capita: $130 (1997).
Education: High school graduation rate: 73.4% (2000); College graduation rate: 4.8% (2000).
Housing: Homeownership rate: 78.2% (2000); Median home value: $41,800 (2000); Median rent: $267 per month (2000); Median age of housing: 60+ years (2000).
Transportation: Commute to work: 94.7% car, 0.0% public transportation, 4.3% walk, 0.0% work from home (2000); Travel time to work: 26.2% less than 15 minutes, 35.3% 15 to 30 minutes, 3.2% 30 to 45 minutes, 21.9% 45 to 60 minutes, 13.4% 60 minutes or more (2000)

KEYSTONE (city). Covers a land area of 0.370 square miles and a water area of 0 square miles. Located at 42.00° N. Lat.; 92.19° W. Long. Elevation is 875 feet.
History: Keystone was settled by the Pennsylvania Dutch.
Population: 687 (2000); Race: 99.3% White, 0.0% Black, 0.0% Asian, 0.0% American Indian and Alaska Native, 0.0% Hispanic of any race, 0.7% two or more races (2000); Density: 1,855.3 persons per square mile (2000); Age: 28.8% under 18, 24.8% over 64 (2000); Marriage status: 14.2% never married, 65.5% now married, 13.3% widowed, 6.9% divorced (2000); Foreign born: 1.3% (2000); Ancestry (includes multiple ancestries): 52.4% German, 7.4% Irish, 6.4% United States or American, 3.9% Danish, 2.9% Norwegian (2000).
Economy: Single-family building permits issued: 1 (2001) / 0 (2000); Multi-family building permits issued: 0 (2001) / 0 (2000); Employment by occupation: 7.9% management, 24.1% professional, 14.6% services, 27.6% sales, 1.0% farming, 9.8% construction, 14.9% production (2000).
Income: Per capita income: $18,215 (2000); Median household income: $36,458 (2000); Poverty rate: 2.7% (2000).
Taxes: Total city taxes per capita: $196 (1997); City property taxes per capita: $194 (1997).
Education: High school graduation rate: 80.8% (2000); College graduation rate: 14.4% (2000).
Housing: Homeownership rate: 79.8% (2000); Median home value: $69,100 (2000); Median rent: $344 per month (2000); Median age of housing: 53 years (2000).
Transportation: Commute to work: 88.5% car, 0.7% public transportation, 6.6% walk, 4.3% work from home (2000); Travel time to work: 28.4% less than 15 minutes, 16.1% 15 to 30 minutes, 32.9% 30 to 45 minutes, 17.8% 45 to 60 minutes, 4.8% 60 minutes or more (2000)

LUZERNE (city). Covers a land area of 0.126 square miles and a water area of 0 square miles. Located at 41.90° N. Lat.; 92.18° W. Long.
History: Luzerne was named after the town of Luzerne, Switzerland. The name was given by Isaac B. Howe, owner of the land where the town was built.
Population: 105 (2000); Race: 100.0% White, 0.0% Black, 0.0% Asian, 0.0% American Indian and Alaska Native, 0.0% Hispanic of any race, 0.0% two or more races (2000); Density: 834.5 persons per square mile (2000); Age: 26.7% under 18, 24.4% over 64 (2000); Marriage status: 25.3% never married, 57.3% now married, 6.7% widowed, 10.7% divorced (2000); Foreign born: 0.0% (2000); Ancestry (includes multiple ancestries): 45.3% German, 38.4% United States or American, 10.5% Irish, 7.0% English, 5.8% Czech (2000).
Economy: Employment by occupation: 0.0% management, 8.6% professional, 8.6% services, 28.6% sales, 0.0% farming, 22.9% construction, 31.4% production (2000).
Income: Per capita income: $14,747 (2000); Median household income: $28,750 (2000); Poverty rate: 0.0% (2000).
Taxes: Total city taxes per capita: $97 (1997); City property taxes per capita: $97 (1997).
Education: High school graduation rate: 89.5% (2000); College graduation rate: 5.3% (2000).
Housing: Homeownership rate: 94.4% (2000); Median home value: $43,000 (2000); Median rent: $125 per month (2000); Median age of housing: 60+ years (2000).
Transportation: Commute to work: 77.1% car, 0.0% public transportation, 17.1% walk, 5.7% work from home (2000); Travel time to work: 54.5% less than 15 minutes, 21.2% 15 to 30 minutes, 18.2% 30 to 45 minutes, 6.1% 45 to 60 minutes, 0.0% 60 minutes or more (2000)

MOUNT AUBURN (city). Covers a land area of 0.267 square miles and a water area of 0 square miles. Located at 42.25° N. Lat.; 92.09° W. Long. Elevation is 863 feet.
History: Mount Auburn is believed to be named after Mount Auburn, Illinois.
Population: 160 (2000); Race: 99.4% White, 0.0% Black, 0.0% Asian, 0.0% American Indian and Alaska Native, 0.0% Hispanic of any race, 0.6% two or more races (2000); Density: 598.5 persons per square mile (2000); Age: 23.3% under 18, 17.8% over 64 (2000); Marriage status: 17.6% never married, 67.9% now married, 6.1% widowed, 8.4% divorced (2000); Foreign born: 0.0% (2000); Ancestry (includes multiple ancestries): 37.4% German, 18.4% English, 8.6% Irish, 7.4% United States or American, 3.7% French (except Basque) (2000).
Economy: Employment by occupation: 12.2% management, 5.4% professional, 14.9% services, 29.7% sales, 4.1% farming, 18.9% construction, 14.9% production (2000).
Income: Per capita income: $15,909 (2000); Median household income: $39,250 (2000); Poverty rate: 0.0% (2000).
Taxes: Total city taxes per capita: $129 (1997); City property taxes per capita: $115 (1997).
Education: High school graduation rate: 89.1% (2000); College graduation rate: 13.6% (2000).
Housing: Homeownership rate: 100.0% (2000); Median home value: $43,300 (2000); Median age of housing: 60+ years (2000).
Transportation: Commute to work: 91.9% car, 0.0% public transportation, 2.7% walk, 2.7% work from home (2000); Travel time to work: 16.7% less than 15 minutes, 25.0% 15 to 30 minutes, 36.1% 30 to 45 minutes, 12.5% 45 to 60 minutes, 9.7% 60 minutes or more (2000)

NEWHALL (city). Covers a land area of 0.299 square miles and a water area of 0 square miles. Located at 41.99° N. Lat.; 91.96° W. Long. Elevation is 899 feet.
History: Newhall was named for famed Iowa author John B. Newhall.
Population: 886 (2000); Race: 100.0% White, 0.0% Black, 0.0% Asian, 0.0% American Indian and Alaska Native, 0.0% Hispanic of any race, 0.0% two or more races (2000); Density: 2,966.2 persons per square mile (2000); Age: 27.6% under 18, 21.7% over 64 (2000); Marriage status: 22.4% never married, 62.1% now married, 9.3% widowed, 6.3% divorced (2000); Foreign born: 0.0% (2000); Ancestry (includes multiple ancestries): 54.8% German, 11.2% Irish, 6.8% United States or American, 5.3% Norwegian, 4.9% Czech (2000).
Economy: Single-family building permits issued: 8 (2001) / 5 (2000); Multi-family building permits issued: 0 (2001) / 0 (2000); Employment by occupation: 13.2% management, 21.0% professional, 11.9% services, 24.0% sales, 0.0% farming, 6.6% construction, 23.3% production (2000).

Income: Per capita income: $20,124 (2000); Median household income: $43,269 (2000); Poverty rate: 2.3% (2000).
Taxes: Total city taxes per capita: $201 (1997); City property taxes per capita: $198 (1997).
Education: High school graduation rate: 88.0% (2000); College graduation rate: 13.7% (2000).
Housing: Homeownership rate: 83.8% (2000); Median home value: $92,200 (2000); Median rent: $288 per month (2000); Median age of housing: 38 years (2000).
Transportation: Commute to work: 95.2% car, 0.0% public transportation, 4.4% walk, 0.5% work from home (2000); Travel time to work: 25.1% less than 15 minutes, 34.3% 15 to 30 minutes, 34.8% 30 to 45 minutes, 1.6% 45 to 60 minutes, 4.2% 60 minutes or more (2000)

NORWAY (city). Covers a land area of 0.455 square miles and a water area of 0 square miles. Located at 41.90° N. Lat.; 91.92° W. Long. Elevation is 796 feet.
History: Norway was platted in 1863. The town was named by a Norwegian who donated land to the railroad.
Population: 601 (2000); Race: 99.5% White, 0.0% Black, 0.0% Asian, 0.0% American Indian and Alaska Native, 0.2% Hispanic of any race, 0.0% two or more races (2000); Density: 1,320.9 persons per square mile (2000); Age: 27.7% under 18, 13.1% over 64 (2000); Marriage status: 22.4% never married, 63.2% now married, 4.9% widowed, 9.4% divorced (2000); Foreign born: 0.7% (2000); Ancestry (includes multiple ancestries): 50.9% German, 12.5% Irish, 9.8% English, 6.8% United States or American, 5.4% Czech (2000).
Economy: Single-family building permits issued: 1 (2001) / 3 (2000); Multi-family building permits issued: 0 (2001) / 0 (2000); Employment by occupation: 13.7% management, 12.7% professional, 15.0% services, 22.7% sales, 0.7% farming, 12.7% construction, 22.7% production (2000).
Income: Per capita income: $20,300 (2000); Median household income: $44,018 (2000); Poverty rate: 5.1% (2000).
Taxes: Total city taxes per capita: $140 (1997); City property taxes per capita: $137 (1997).
Education: High school graduation rate: 91.4% (2000); College graduation rate: 13.1% (2000).
Housing: Homeownership rate: 79.7% (2000); Median home value: $82,000 (2000); Median rent: $263 per month (2000); Median age of housing: 51 years (2000).
Transportation: Commute to work: 94.0% car, 0.0% public transportation, 3.3% walk, 2.7% work from home (2000); Travel time to work: 27.7% less than 15 minutes, 47.6% 15 to 30 minutes, 20.2% 30 to 45 minutes, 2.1% 45 to 60 minutes, 2.4% 60 minutes or more (2000)

SHELLSBURG (city). Covers a land area of 0.720 square miles and a water area of 0 square miles. Located at 42.09° N. Lat.; 91.87° W. Long. Elevation is 774 feet.
History: Shellsburg is named after Shellsburg, Pennsylvania.
Population: 938 (2000); Race: 99.4% White, 0.0% Black, 0.0% Asian, 0.0% American Indian and Alaska Native, 1.4% Hispanic of any race, 0.6% two or more races (2000); Density: 1,302.8 persons per square mile (2000); Age: 28.2% under 18, 15.0% over 64 (2000); Marriage status: 22.0% never married, 63.2% now married, 5.0% widowed, 9.8% divorced (2000); Foreign born: 0.8% (2000); Ancestry (includes multiple ancestries): 36.7% German, 14.6% Irish, 12.1% English, 7.2% Other groups, 6.2% United States or American (2000).
Economy: Single-family building permits issued: 2 (2001) / 4 (2000); Multi-family building permits issued: 0 (2001) / 0 (2000); Employment by occupation: 9.5% management, 14.0% professional, 11.8% services, 31.4% sales, 0.4% farming, 7.5% construction, 25.4% production (2000).
Income: Per capita income: $17,352 (2000); Median household income: $41,912 (2000); Poverty rate: 8.3% (2000).
Taxes: Total city taxes per capita: $196 (1997); City property taxes per capita: $191 (1997).
Education: High school graduation rate: 85.1% (2000); College graduation rate: 15.4% (2000).
Housing: Homeownership rate: 79.6% (2000); Median home value: $91,600 (2000); Median rent: $365 per month (2000); Median age of housing: 37 years (2000).
Transportation: Commute to work: 92.9% car, 0.0% public transportation, 3.9% walk, 2.6% work from home (2000); Travel time to work: 16.3% less than 15 minutes, 46.4% 15 to 30 minutes, 28.7% 30 to 45 minutes, 5.1% 45 to 60 minutes, 3.5% 60 minutes or more (2000)

URBANA (city). Covers a land area of 0.674 square miles and a water area of 0 square miles. Located at 42.22° N. Lat.; 91.87° W. Long. Elevation is 940 feet.
History: Urbana was named by postal officials in 1857.
Population: 1,019 (2000); Race: 99.5% White, 0.0% Black, 0.0% Asian, 0.4% American Indian and Alaska Native, 0.0% Hispanic of any race, 0.1% two or more races (2000); Density: 1,512.5 persons per square mile (2000); Age: 32.4% under 18, 7.8% over 64 (2000); Marriage status: 16.1% never married, 70.5% now married, 4.4% widowed, 9.0% divorced (2000); Foreign born: 0.0% (2000); Ancestry (includes multiple ancestries): 45.7% German, 19.1% Irish, 8.0% English, 5.9% Norwegian, 5.0% United States or American (2000).
Economy: Single-family building permits issued: 26 (2001) / 25 (2000); Multi-family building permits issued: 2 (2001) / 2 (2000); Employment by occupation: 8.6% management, 14.0% professional, 10.4% services, 27.5% sales, 0.2% farming, 13.7% construction, 25.7% production (2000).
Income: Per capita income: $18,005 (2000); Median household income: $49,063 (2000); Poverty rate: 1.1% (2000).
Taxes: Total city taxes per capita: $158 (1997); City property taxes per capita: $149 (1997).
Education: High school graduation rate: 90.5% (2000); College graduation rate: 15.7% (2000).
Housing: Homeownership rate: 89.1% (2000); Median home value: $91,000 (2000); Median rent: $306 per month (2000); Median age of housing: 26 years (2000).
Transportation: Commute to work: 98.1% car, 0.0% public transportation, 1.3% walk, 0.6% work from home (2000); Travel time to work: 17.7% less than 15 minutes, 37.6% 15 to 30 minutes, 35.9% 30 to 45 minutes, 5.8% 45 to 60 minutes, 3.0% 60 minutes or more (2000)

VAN HORNE (city). Covers a land area of 0.710 square miles and a water area of 0 square miles. Located at 42.00° N. Lat.; 92.08° W. Long.
History: Van Horne was named for railroad superintendent Cornelius Van Horne.
Population: 716 (2000); Race: 97.7% White, 1.2% Black, 0.7% Asian, 0.0% American Indian and Alaska Native, 0.0% Hispanic of any race, 0.4% two or more races (2000); Density: 1,008.2 persons per square mile (2000); Age: 25.8% under 18, 16.4% over 64 (2000); Marriage status: 17.4% never married, 61.8% now married, 9.0% widowed, 11.8% divorced (2000); Foreign born: 0.8% (2000); Ancestry (includes multiple ancestries): 48.0% German, 14.7% Irish, 7.0% French (except Basque), 6.8% United States or American, 5.0% Czech (2000).
Economy: Single-family building permits issued: 1 (2001) / 1 (2000); Multi-family building permits issued: 0 (2001) / 4 (2000); Employment by occupation: 11.7% management, 20.6% professional, 10.2% services, 26.4% sales, 0.7% farming, 12.7% construction, 17.7% production (2000).
Income: Per capita income: $19,439 (2000); Median household income: $45,000 (2000); Poverty rate: 2.9% (2000).
Taxes: Total city taxes per capita: $152 (1997); City property taxes per capita: $149 (1997).
Education: High school graduation rate: 89.7% (2000); College graduation rate: 15.8% (2000).

School District(s)

Benton Community School District (PK-12)
2000 Enrollment: 1,673 319-228-8701

Housing: Homeownership rate: 79.9% (2000); Median home value: $83,600 (2000); Median rent: $245 per month (2000); Median age of housing: 42 years (2000).
Transportation: Commute to work: 95.4% car, 0.0% public transportation, 2.3% walk, 2.3% work from home (2000); Travel time to work: 44.6% less than 15 minutes, 22.5% 15 to 30 minutes, 22.7% 30 to 45 minutes, 7.3% 45 to 60 minutes, 2.9% 60 minutes or more (2000)

Additional Information Contacts

Benton County Board of Realtors 319-228-8148

VINTON (city). Covers a land area of 4.296 square miles and a water area of 0 square miles. Located at 42.16° N. Lat.; 92.02° W. Long. Elevation is 810 feet.
History: Vinton was settled in 1839 by Reuben Daskirk and was first known as Northport, later as Fremont. In 1846 the post office in Benton County was established here, and the name changed to Vinton for Plym Vinton, a Congressman from Ohio, who paid $50 for the honor.
Population: 5,102 (2000); Race: 99.1% White, 0.0% Black, 0.3% Asian, 0.0% American Indian and Alaska Native, 0.2% Hispanic of any race, 0.6% two or more races (2000); Density: 1,187.7 persons per square mile (2000);

Age: 24.7% under 18, 19.3% over 64 (2000); Marriage status: 20.3% never married, 61.4% now married, 8.9% widowed, 9.5% divorced (2000); Foreign born: 1.1% (2000); Ancestry (includes multiple ancestries): 37.1% German, 14.4% Irish, 12.0% English, 10.7% United States or American, 4.0% Czech (2000).
Economy: Single-family building permits issued: 6 (2001) / 7 (2000); Multi-family building permits issued: 21 (2001) / 4 (2000); Employment by occupation: 8.9% management, 19.0% professional, 19.7% services, 23.8% sales, 0.0% farming, 11.5% construction, 17.1% production (2000).
Income: Per capita income: $19,808 (2000); Median household income: $35,114 (2000); Poverty rate: 9.8% (2000).
Taxes: Total city taxes per capita: $205 (1997); City property taxes per capita: $201 (1997).
Education: High school graduation rate: 86.3% (2000); College graduation rate: 16.1% (2000).

School District(s)

Iowa Braille & Sight Saving School (N -N)
2000 Enrollment: n/a 319-472-5221
Vinton-Shellsburg Community School District (PK-12)
2000 Enrollment: 1,854 319-436-4728

Housing: Homeownership rate: 71.3% (2000); Median home value: $73,900 (2000); Median rent: $297 per month (2000); Median age of housing: 48 years (2000).
Hospitals: Virginia Gay Hospital (99 beds)
Newspapers: Cedar Valley Times (5 x week)
Transportation: Commute to work: 94.8% car, 1.0% public transportation, 1.6% walk, 1.7% work from home (2000); Travel time to work: 50.2% less than 15 minutes, 8.4% 15 to 30 minutes, 25.2% 30 to 45 minutes, 14.0% 45 to 60 minutes, 2.3% 60 minutes or more (2000)

WALFORD (city). Covers a land area of 0.959 square miles and a water area of 0 square miles. Located at 41.87° N. Lat.; 91.83° W. Long. Elevation is 806 feet.
Population: 1,224 (2000); Race: 98.5% White, 0.0% Black, 0.6% Asian, 0.7% American Indian and Alaska Native, 0.9% Hispanic of any race, 0.2% two or more races (2000); Density: 1,276.8 persons per square mile (2000); Age: 37.2% under 18, 4.0% over 64 (2000); Marriage status: 19.0% never married, 75.1% now married, 1.8% widowed, 4.1% divorced (2000); Foreign born: 1.0% (2000); Ancestry (includes multiple ancestries): 49.7% German, 17.0% Irish, 10.7% Czech, 9.0% English, 6.7% Norwegian (2000).
Economy: Single-family building permits issued: 6 (2001) / 17 (2000); Multi-family building permits issued: 0 (2001) / 0 (2000); Employment by occupation: 15.5% management, 22.1% professional, 8.1% services, 29.6% sales, 0.6% farming, 7.8% construction, 16.4% production (2000).
Income: Per capita income: $21,370 (2000); Median household income: $67,833 (2000); Poverty rate: 0.4% (2000).
Taxes: Total city taxes per capita: $125 (1997); City property taxes per capita: $111 (1997).
Education: High school graduation rate: 97.1% (2000); College graduation rate: 29.6% (2000).
Housing: Homeownership rate: 89.0% (2000); Median home value: $156,500 (2000); Median rent: $392 per month (2000); Median age of housing: 5 years (2000).
Transportation: Commute to work: 96.2% car, 0.0% public transportation, 1.1% walk, 2.4% work from home (2000); Travel time to work: 17.4% less than 15 minutes, 66.8% 15 to 30 minutes, 14.3% 30 to 45 minutes, 0.3% 45 to 60 minutes, 1.2% 60 minutes or more (2000)

WATKINS (unincorporated postal area, zip code 52354). Covers a land area of 25.082 square miles and a water area of 0 square miles. Located at 41.90° N. Lat.; 91.98° W. Long.
History: Watkins was named for Chicago & North Western Railroad officer J. B. Watkins.
Population: 404 (2000); Race: 98.8% White, 0.0% Black, 1.2% Asian, 0.0% American Indian and Alaska Native, 0.0% Hispanic of any race, 0.0% two or more races (2000); Density: 16.1 persons per square mile (2000); Age: 26.9% under 18, 11.3% over 64 (2000); Marriage status: 23.7% never married, 56.4% now married, 7.1% widowed, 12.8% divorced (2000); Foreign born: 1.2% (2000); Ancestry (includes multiple ancestries): 65.6% German, 15.6% Irish, 14.2% Czech, 6.4% Other groups, 6.4% European (2000).
Economy: Employment by occupation: 8.8% management, 5.2% professional, 24.4% services, 17.1% sales, 6.2% farming, 14.0% construction, 24.4% production (2000).
Income: Per capita income: $18,606 (2000); Median household income: $42,500 (2000); Poverty rate: 0.0% (2000).
Education: High school graduation rate: 83.3% (2000); College graduation rate: 5.3% (2000).
Housing: Homeownership rate: 75.4% (2000); Median home value: $58,200 (2000); Median rent: $519 per month (2000); Median age of housing: 48 years (2000).
Transportation: Commute to work: 94.8% car, 0.0% public transportation, 0.0% walk, 5.2% work from home (2000); Travel time to work: 10.4% less than 15 minutes, 30.6% 15 to 30 minutes, 39.3% 30 to 45 minutes, 13.7% 45 to 60 minutes, 6.0% 60 minutes or more (2000)

Black Hawk County

Located in east central Iowa; prairie area, drained by the Cedar River. Covers a land area of 567.10 square miles, a water area of 4.80 square miles, and is located in the Central Time Zone. The county government was organized in 1843. County seat is Waterloo.

Black Hawk County is part of the Waterloo-Cedar Falls, IA MSA. The entire metro area includes: Black Hawk County

Weather Station: Waterloo Municipal Airport — Elevation: 862 feet

	Jan	Feb	Mar	Apr	May	Jun	Jul	Aug	Sep	Oct	Nov	Dec
High	24	30	44	59	71	81	84	82	74	61	44	30
Low	6	13	25	36	49	58	62	60	50	38	26	14
Precip	0.8	1.0	2.2	3.2	4.1	4.7	4.2	4.1	3.1	2.6	2.1	1.2
Snow	8.0	7.2	4.9	2.1	tr	tr	0.0	0.0	0.0	0.1	4.6	7.5

High and Low temperatures in degrees Fahrenheit; Precipitation and Snow in inches

Population: 128,012 (2000); Race: 88.4% White, 7.7% Black, 1.0% Asian, 0.2% American Indian and Alaska Native, 1.9% Hispanic of any race, 1.6% two or more races (2000); Density: 225.7 persons per square mile (2000); Age: 23.1% under 18, 14.0% over 64 (2000).
Religion: Five largest groups: 19.9% Catholic Church, 11.2% Evangelical Lutheran Church in America, 5.2% The United Methodist Church, 3.5% Lutheran Church—Missouri Synod, 2.7% The Wesleyan Church (2000).
Economy: Unemployment rate: 4.1% (11/2002); Total civilian labor force: 69,419 (11/2002); Leading industries: 21.6% manufacturing; 15.4% health care and social assistance; 15.1% retail trade (2000); Companies that employ more than 1,000 persons: 5 (2000); Companies that employ more than 100 persons: 88 (2000); Farms: 1,002 totaling 285,972 acres (1997); Minority business ownership rate: 4.2% (1997); Women business ownership rate: 30.5% (1997); Retail sales per capita: $11,082 (1997). Single-family building permits issued: 233 (2001) / 251 (2000); Multi-family building permits issued: 255 (2001) / 128 (2000).
Income: Per capita income: $18,885 (2000); Median household income: $37,266 (2000); Poverty rate: 13.1% (2000); Bankruptcy rate: 3.33% (2001).
Taxes: Total county taxes per capita: $182 (2000); County property taxes per capita: $174 (2000).
Education: High school graduation rate: 86.5% (2000); College graduation rate: 23.0% (2000).
Housing: Homeownership rate: 68.9% (2000); Median home value: $77,000 (2000); Median rent: $393 per month (2000); Median age of housing: 41 years (2000).
Health: Birth rate: 128.0 per 10,000 population (1998); Age adjusted death rate: 87.9 per 10,000 population (1999); Age adjusted cancer mortality rate: 213.5 deaths per 100,000 population (1999). Air Quality Index: 96% good, 4% moderate, 0% unhealthy (percent of days in 2000). Number of physicians: 19.0 per 10,000 population (1999); Number of hospital beds: 43.9 per 10,000 population (1999).
Elections: 2000 Presidential election results: 54.7% Gore, 42.6% Bush, 2.1% Nader, 0.3% Buchanan
National and State Parks: McFarlane State Park
Additional Information Contacts
Black Hawk County Government Offices 319-833-3003
Cedar Falls Chamber of Commerce 319-266-3593
Dunkerton Chamber of Commerce 319-822-3300
Waterloo Cedar Falls Board of Realtors 319-234-1731
Waterloo Chamber of Commerce. 319-233-8431
Waterloo Convention & Visitors Bureau 319-233-8350

Black Hawk County Communities

CEDAR FALLS (city). Covers a land area of 28.300 square miles and a water area of 0.585 square miles. Located at 42.52° N. Lat.; 92.44° W. Long. Elevation is 854 feet.

History: The first settlers in Cedar Falls were William Sturgis and his family, who built a cabin on the west side of the Cedar River in 1845. Work on a major railroad (later known as the Illinois Central) stopped in Cedar Falls in 1861 due to a lack of funds and the outbreak of the Civil War. Railroad construction resumed in 1869.
Population: 36,145 (2000); Race: 95.3% White, 1.1% Black, 1.6% Asian, 0.5% American Indian and Alaska Native, 0.9% Hispanic of any race, 1.1% two or more races (2000); Density: 1,277.2 persons per square mile (2000); Age: 17.6% under 18, 11.8% over 64 (2000); Marriage status: 43.3% never married, 44.6% now married, 5.3% widowed, 6.7% divorced (2000); Foreign born: 2.7% (2000); Ancestry (includes multiple ancestries): 43.4% German, 12.9% Irish, 10.5% English, 8.7% Norwegian, 6.0% Other groups (2000).
Vital Statistics: Birth rate: 88.0 per 10,000 population (1998)
Economy: Unemployment rate: 3.4% (11/2002); Total civilian labor force: 20,803 (11/2002); Single-family building permits issued: 112 (2001) / 107 (2000); Multi-family building permits issued: 213 (2001) / 60 (2000); Employment by occupation: 11.9% management, 25.4% professional, 17.9% services, 28.8% sales, 0.4% farming, 5.5% construction, 10.2% production (2000).
Income: Per capita income: $19,140 (2000); Median household income: $40,226 (2000); Poverty rate: 16.7% (2000).
Taxes: Total city taxes per capita: $408 (2000); City property taxes per capita: $290 (2000).
Education: High school graduation rate: 92.6% (2000); College graduation rate: 39.2% (2000).

School District(s)
Cedar Falls Community School District (PK-12)
2000 Enrollment: 4,465 319-277-8800
Price Laboratory School (N -N)
2000 Enrollment: n/a 319-273-6136

Four-year College(s)
University of Northern Iowa (Public)
2001 Enrollment: 14,410 319-273-2311
2001 Tuition: In-state $3,116; Out-of-state $8,438

Two-year College(s)
La James College of Hairstyling (Private, For-profit)
2001 Enrollment: 66 319-277-2150
Hamilton College (Private, For-profit)
2001 Enrollment: 437 319-277-0220
2001 Tuition: In-state $9,360; Out-of-state $9,360

Housing: Homeownership rate: 64.4% (2000); Median home value: $102,500 (2000); Median rent: $432 per month (2000); Median age of housing: 36 years (2000).
Hospitals: Sartori Memorial Hospital (101 beds)
Safety: Violent crime rate: 30.5 per 10,000 population; Property crime rate: 286.1 per 10,000 population (2001).
Transportation: Commute to work: 85.9% car, 0.5% public transportation, 9.6% walk, 2.7% work from home (2000); Travel time to work: 59.6% less than 15 minutes, 33.8% 15 to 30 minutes, 3.6% 30 to 45 minutes, 1.0% 45 to 60 minutes, 2.0% 60 minutes or more (2000)
Additional Information Contacts
Cedar Falls Chamber of Commerce 319-266-3593

DUNKERTON (city). Covers a land area of 0.945 square miles and a water area of 0 square miles. Located at 42.56° N. Lat.; 92.16° W. Long. Elevation is 947 feet.
History: Dunkerton, a station on the Diagonal railroad across the state, was named for James and Thomas Dunkerton who owned the land. It was platted in 1886.
Population: 749 (2000); Race: 99.4% White, 0.0% Black, 0.6% Asian, 0.0% American Indian and Alaska Native, 0.0% Hispanic of any race, 0.0% two or more races (2000); Density: 792.9 persons per square mile (2000); Age: 29.8% under 18, 9.1% over 64 (2000); Marriage status: 25.1% never married, 67.0% now married, 3.8% widowed, 4.2% divorced (2000); Foreign born: 0.6% (2000); Ancestry (includes multiple ancestries): 53.3% German, 17.7% Irish, 7.2% English, 6.9% Norwegian, 5.7% Swedish (2000).
Economy: Single-family building permits issued: 8 (2001) / 5 (2000); Multi-family building permits issued: 0 (2001) / 0 (2000); Employment by occupation: 12.8% management, 13.4% professional, 11.9% services, 29.0% sales, 0.9% farming, 15.5% construction, 16.5% production (2000).
Income: Per capita income: $15,863 (2000); Median household income: $41,771 (2000); Poverty rate: 5.9% (2000).
Taxes: Total city taxes per capita: $229 (1997); City property taxes per capita: $133 (1997).
Education: High school graduation rate: 88.2% (2000); College graduation rate: 11.3% (2000).

School District(s)
Dunkerton Community School District (PK-12)
2000 Enrollment: 522 319-822-4295

Housing: Homeownership rate: 79.5% (2000); Median home value: $82,800 (2000); Median rent: $300 per month (2000); Median age of housing: 28 years (2000).
Transportation: Commute to work: 94.2% car, 0.0% public transportation, 3.0% walk, 1.5% work from home (2000); Travel time to work: 25.4% less than 15 minutes, 49.8% 15 to 30 minutes, 20.7% 30 to 45 minutes, 3.4% 45 to 60 minutes, 0.6% 60 minutes or more (2000)
Additional Information Contacts
Dunkerton Chamber of Commerce 319-822-3300

ELK RUN HEIGHTS (city). Covers a land area of 0.992 square miles and a water area of 0 square miles. Located at 42.46° N. Lat.; 92.25° W. Long.
Population: 1,052 (2000); Race: 96.2% White, 0.0% Black, 0.0% Asian, 0.3% American Indian and Alaska Native, 1.3% Hispanic of any race, 3.5% two or more races (2000); Density: 1,060.1 persons per square mile (2000); Age: 26.3% under 18, 14.2% over 64 (2000); Marriage status: 22.2% never married, 63.1% now married, 4.9% widowed, 9.8% divorced (2000); Foreign born: 2.1% (2000); Ancestry (includes multiple ancestries): 48.2% German, 16.1% Irish, 7.6% United States or American, 6.3% English, 6.2% French (except Basque) (2000).
Economy: Single-family building permits issued: 2 (2001) / 2 (2000); Multi-family building permits issued: 0 (2001) / 0 (2000); Employment by occupation: 11.2% management, 16.0% professional, 10.8% services, 27.8% sales, 0.0% farming, 11.9% construction, 22.2% production (2000).
Income: Per capita income: $18,129 (2000); Median household income: $45,179 (2000); Poverty rate: 1.6% (2000).
Taxes: Total city taxes per capita: $180 (1997); City property taxes per capita: $87 (1997).
Education: High school graduation rate: 81.2% (2000); College graduation rate: 8.9% (2000).
Housing: Homeownership rate: 90.6% (2000); Median home value: $71,500 (2000); Median rent: $424 per month (2000); Median age of housing: 42 years (2000).
Transportation: Commute to work: 95.7% car, 0.0% public transportation, 0.4% walk, 3.1% work from home (2000); Travel time to work: 43.2% less than 15 minutes, 46.8% 15 to 30 minutes, 2.7% 30 to 45 minutes, 3.3% 45 to 60 minutes, 4.0% 60 minutes or more (2000)

EVANSDALE (city). Covers a land area of 4.210 square miles and a water area of 0.018 square miles. Located at 42.46° N. Lat.; 92.28° W. Long. Elevation is 841 feet.
History: Two men responsible for the incorporation of Evansdale, District Judge William T. Evans and attorney Dale Van Eman, contributed parts of their names to form the name of the town.
Population: 4,526 (2000); Race: 96.6% White, 1.7% Black, 0.0% Asian, 0.0% American Indian and Alaska Native, 0.9% Hispanic of any race, 1.5% two or more races (2000); Density: 1,075.0 persons per square mile (2000); Age: 25.3% under 18, 13.7% over 64 (2000); Marriage status: 24.2% never married, 55.1% now married, 7.4% widowed, 13.4% divorced (2000); Foreign born: 0.3% (2000); Ancestry (includes multiple ancestries): 42.3% German, 17.2% Irish, 9.6% English, 7.0% United States or American, 6.9% Other groups (2000).
Economy: Single-family building permits issued: 15 (2001) / 3 (2000); Multi-family building permits issued: 0 (2001) / 0 (2000); Employment by occupation: 6.2% management, 9.2% professional, 14.5% services, 32.7% sales, 0.1% farming, 12.8% construction, 24.4% production (2000).
Income: Per capita income: $15,363 (2000); Median household income: $31,160 (2000); Poverty rate: 12.0% (2000).
Taxes: Total city taxes per capita: $180 (1997); City property taxes per capita: $87 (1997).
Education: High school graduation rate: 77.9% (2000); College graduation rate: 5.8% (2000).
Housing: Homeownership rate: 70.1% (2000); Median home value: $61,500 (2000); Median rent: $335 per month (2000); Median age of housing: 41 years (2000).
Transportation: Commute to work: 95.1% car, 0.0% public transportation, 0.0% walk, 4.7% work from home (2000); Travel time to work: 44.1% less than 15 minutes, 47.0% 15 to 30 minutes, 5.2% 30 to 45 minutes, 0.5% 45 to 60 minutes, 3.2% 60 minutes or more (2000)

GILBERTVILLE (city). Covers a land area of 0.392 square miles and a water area of 0.004 square miles. Located at 42.41° N. Lat.; 92.21° W. Long.

History: Gilbertville, originally called French Town, began as a frontier "paper town," represented to potential immigrants from the east coast as a booming place when very little existed there.
Population: 767 (2000); Race: 97.7% White, 0.0% Black, 0.7% Asian, 0.9% American Indian and Alaska Native, 0.0% Hispanic of any race, 0.7% two or more races (2000); Density: 1,957.8 persons per square mile (2000); Age: 26.1% under 18, 15.6% over 64 (2000); Marriage status: 26.2% never married, 59.9% now married, 8.1% widowed, 5.8% divorced (2000); Foreign born: 0.4% (2000); Ancestry (includes multiple ancestries): 62.9% German, 10.5% Irish, 4.5% United States or American, 4.2% French (except Basque), 3.7% Other groups (2000).
Economy: Single-family building permits issued: 2 (2001) / 2 (2000); Multi-family building permits issued: 0 (2001) / 0 (2000); Employment by occupation: 8.6% management, 9.4% professional, 20.6% services, 29.5% sales, 0.0% farming, 6.3% construction, 25.6% production (2000).
Income: Per capita income: $18,367 (2000); Median household income: $41,490 (2000); Poverty rate: 4.0% (2000).
Taxes: Total city taxes per capita: $181 (1997); City property taxes per capita: $87 (1997).
Education: High school graduation rate: 80.4% (2000); College graduation rate: 10.1% (2000).
Housing: Homeownership rate: 84.4% (2000); Median home value: $82,300 (2000); Median rent: $296 per month (2000); Median age of housing: 35 years (2000).
Transportation: Commute to work: 90.1% car, 1.0% public transportation, 2.6% walk, 5.8% work from home (2000); Travel time to work: 33.1% less than 15 minutes, 55.0% 15 to 30 minutes, 5.8% 30 to 45 minutes, 3.3% 45 to 60 minutes, 2.8% 60 minutes or more (2000)

HUDSON (city). Covers a land area of 7.700 square miles and a water area of 0.006 square miles. Located at 42.40° N. Lat.; 92.45° W. Long. Elevation is 888 feet.
History: Hudson was once an important station on the old wagon thoroughfare between Waterloo and Eldora.
Population: 2,117 (2000); Race: 98.1% White, 0.0% Black, 1.7% Asian, 0.0% American Indian and Alaska Native, 0.0% Hispanic of any race, 0.2% two or more races (2000); Density: 274.9 persons per square mile (2000); Age: 26.6% under 18, 10.0% over 64 (2000); Marriage status: 19.2% never married, 69.1% now married, 5.9% widowed, 5.8% divorced (2000); Foreign born: 2.3% (2000); Ancestry (includes multiple ancestries): 49.6% German, 15.0% Irish, 10.3% English, 8.1% Norwegian, 4.5% United States or American (2000).
Economy: Single-family building permits issued: 11 (2001) / 8 (2000); Multi-family building permits issued: 4 (2001) / 4 (2000); Employment by occupation: 15.0% management, 21.9% professional, 14.2% services, 24.1% sales, 1.0% farming, 7.9% construction, 15.9% production (2000).
Income: Per capita income: $24,101 (2000); Median household income: $56,065 (2000); Poverty rate: 3.3% (2000).
Taxes: Total city taxes per capita: $268 (1997); City property taxes per capita: $171 (1997).
Education: High school graduation rate: 95.0% (2000); College graduation rate: 25.7% (2000).

School District(s)

Hudson Community School District (KG-12)
2000 Enrollment: 926 319-988-3233
Housing: Homeownership rate: 86.0% (2000); Median home value: $102,500 (2000); Median rent: $356 per month (2000); Median age of housing: 34 years (2000).
Newspapers: The Hudson Herald (1 x week)
Transportation: Commute to work: 93.7% car, 0.4% public transportation, 1.3% walk, 3.0% work from home (2000); Travel time to work: 35.7% less than 15 minutes, 54.2% 15 to 30 minutes, 5.9% 30 to 45 minutes, 1.1% 45 to 60 minutes, 3.0% 60 minutes or more (2000)

LA PORTE CITY (city). Covers a land area of 2.626 square miles and a water area of 0 square miles. Located at 42.31° N. Lat.; 92.18° W. Long. Elevation is 812 feet.
History: La Porte City was first called La Porte for the city of that name in Indiana. Because the names were confused in the mails, the word "city" was added.
Population: 2,275 (2000); Race: 99.1% White, 0.0% Black, 0.0% Asian, 0.0% American Indian and Alaska Native, 0.9% Hispanic of any race, 0.4% two or more races (2000); Density: 866.3 persons per square mile (2000); Age: 26.0% under 18, 17.7% over 64 (2000); Marriage status: 22.5% never married, 60.6% now married, 9.6% widowed, 7.3% divorced (2000); Foreign born: 1.0% (2000); Ancestry (includes multiple ancestries): 46.7% German, 13.4% Irish, 11.7% English, 7.3% United States or American, 4.9% Norwegian (2000).
Economy: Single-family building permits issued: 3 (2001) / 3 (2000); Multi-family building permits issued: 0 (2001) / 0 (2000); Employment by occupation: 8.5% management, 12.6% professional, 12.8% services, 32.1% sales, 0.7% farming, 8.9% construction, 24.5% production (2000).
Income: Per capita income: $19,266 (2000); Median household income: $37,540 (2000); Poverty rate: 6.2% (2000).
Taxes: Total city taxes per capita: $301 (1997); City property taxes per capita: $203 (1997).
Education: High school graduation rate: 88.1% (2000); College graduation rate: 10.2% (2000).

School District(s)

Union Community School District (PK-12)
2000 Enrollment: 1,233 319-342-2674
Housing: Homeownership rate: 75.8% (2000); Median home value: $73,300 (2000); Median rent: $297 per month (2000); Median age of housing: 46 years (2000).
Newspapers: The Progress-Review (1 x week)
Transportation: Commute to work: 93.1% car, 0.0% public transportation, 2.3% walk, 4.3% work from home (2000); Travel time to work: 23.2% less than 15 minutes, 45.9% 15 to 30 minutes, 23.6% 30 to 45 minutes, 4.4% 45 to 60 minutes, 2.9% 60 minutes or more (2000)

RAYMOND (city). Covers a land area of 1.541 square miles and a water area of 0 square miles. Located at 42.46° N. Lat.; 92.22° W. Long.
History: Because a number of early settlers were from the New York and New Jersey area, it is believed that Raymond was named in honor of the co-founder of the New York Times, Jarvis Henry Raymond.
Population: 537 (2000); Race: 99.2% White, 0.0% Black, 0.0% Asian, 0.0% American Indian and Alaska Native, 0.8% Hispanic of any race, 0.8% two or more races (2000); Density: 348.5 persons per square mile (2000); Age: 26.1% under 18, 16.3% over 64 (2000); Marriage status: 14.5% never married, 69.6% now married, 5.6% widowed, 10.2% divorced (2000); Foreign born: 1.1% (2000); Ancestry (includes multiple ancestries): 60.0% German, 11.9% Irish, 6.8% English, 6.8% United States or American, 3.6% Norwegian (2000).
Economy: Single-family building permits issued: 3 (2001) / 4 (2000); Multi-family building permits issued: 0 (2001) / 0 (2000); Employment by occupation: 5.7% management, 11.3% professional, 11.3% services, 34.8% sales, 0.0% farming, 13.0% construction, 23.9% production (2000).
Income: Per capita income: $22,201 (2000); Median household income: $47,813 (2000); Poverty rate: 3.6% (2000).
Taxes: Total city taxes per capita: $190 (1997); City property taxes per capita: $98 (1997).
Education: High school graduation rate: 82.4% (2000); College graduation rate: 7.9% (2000).
Housing: Homeownership rate: 90.2% (2000); Median home value: $84,200 (2000); Median rent: $417 per month (2000); Median age of housing: 38 years (2000).
Transportation: Commute to work: 86.9% car, 0.9% public transportation, 7.0% walk, 5.2% work from home (2000); Travel time to work: 37.8% less than 15 minutes, 49.3% 15 to 30 minutes, 6.9% 30 to 45 minutes, 4.6% 45 to 60 minutes, 1.4% 60 minutes or more (2000)

WATERLOO (city). Covers a land area of 60.735 square miles and a water area of 1.281 square miles. Located at 42.49° N. Lat.; 92.34° W. Long. Elevation is 841 feet.
History: Waterloo was named for the Battle of Waterloo in Belgium.
Population: 68,747 (2000); Race: 81.4% White, 13.7% Black, 1.0% Asian, 0.1% American Indian and Alaska Native, 2.7% Hispanic of any race, 2.1% two or more races (2000); Density: 1,131.9 persons per square mile (2000); Age: 24.7% under 18, 15.4% over 64 (2000); Marriage status: 27.4% never married, 54.2% now married, 8.0% widowed, 10.4% divorced (2000); Foreign born: 5.2% (2000); Ancestry (includes multiple ancestries): 32.0% German, 18.6% Other groups, 12.3% Irish, 7.7% English, 5.8% United States or American (2000).
Vital Statistics: Birth rate: 158.7 per 10,000 population (1998)
Economy: Unemployment rate: 4.9% (11/2002); Total civilian labor force: 35,307 (11/2002); Single-family building permits issued: 51 (2001) / 89 (2000); Multi-family building permits issued: 38 (2001) / 64 (2000); Employment by occupation: 9.6% management, 18.0% professional, 15.6% services, 26.6% sales, 0.2% farming, 8.5% construction, 21.5% production (2000).
Income: Per capita income: $18,558 (2000); Median household income: $34,092 (2000); Poverty rate: 13.7% (2000).

Taxes: Total city taxes per capita: $499 (2000); City property taxes per capita: $368 (2000).
Education: High school graduation rate: 83.8% (2000); College graduation rate: 19.4% (2000).

School District(s)

Waterloo Community School District (PK-12)
2000 Enrollment: 10,498 319-291-4800

Four-year College(s)

Allen College (Private, Not-for-profit)
2001 Enrollment: 259 319-226-2027
2001 Tuition: In-state $7,015; Out-of-state $7,015

Two-year College(s)

Hawkeye Community College (Public)
2001 Enrollment: 4,456 319-296-2320
2001 Tuition: In-state $2,580; Out-of-state $4,860
College of Hair Design (Private, For-profit)
2001 Enrollment: 35 319-232-9995

Housing: Homeownership rate: 67.1% (2000); Median home value: $65,400 (2000); Median rent: $386 per month (2000); Median age of housing: 43 years (2000).
Hospitals: Allen Memorial Hospital (234 beds); Covenant Medical Center (346 beds)
Safety: Violent crime rate: 47.8 per 10,000 population; Property crime rate: 562.7 per 10,000 population (2001).
Newspapers: Waterloo-Cedar Falls Courier (6 x week); Waterloo Courier (1 x week)
Transportation: Commute to work: 94.3% car, 1.2% public transportation, 1.8% walk, 2.0% work from home (2000); Travel time to work: 53.4% less than 15 minutes, 38.2% 15 to 30 minutes, 4.2% 30 to 45 minutes, 1.2% 45 to 60 minutes, 3.0% 60 minutes or more (2000)
Airports: Waterloo Municipal (primary service)

Additional Information Contacts

Waterloo Cedar Falls Board of Realtors 319-234-1731
Waterloo Chamber of Commerce. 319-233-8431
Waterloo Convention & Visitors Bureau 319-233-8350

Boone County

Located in central Iowa; drained by the Des Moines River. Covers a land area of 571.50 square miles, a water area of 2.10 square miles, and is located in the Central Time Zone. The county government was organized in 1846. County seat is Boone.

Weather Station: Ames 8 WSW — Elevation: 1,099 feet

	Jan	Feb	Mar	Apr	May	Jun	Jul	Aug	Sep	Oct	Nov	Dec
High	27	34	46	62	73	82	85	82	76	64	45	32
Low	9	16	27	38	50	59	63	61	52	40	27	15
Precip	0.7	0.8	2.1	3.5	4.4	5.0	4.5	4.5	3.2	2.7	2.0	1.0
Snow	7.6	7.0	5.5	2.1	0.0	0.0	0.0	0.0	0.0	0.3	2.9	6.5

High and Low temperatures in degrees Fahrenheit; Precipitation and Snow in inches

Weather Station: Boone — Elevation: 1,049 feet

	Jan	Feb	Mar	Apr	May	Jun	Jul	Aug	Sep	Oct	Nov	Dec
High	28	34	46	60	72	81	85	83	76	64	46	32
Low	6	12	25	36	47	57	61	59	49	37	25	13
Precip	1.1	1.1	2.5	3.5	4.5	5.3	4.4	4.5	3.3	2.7	2.3	1.4
Snow	8.1	6.7	5.0	1.5	tr	0.0	0.0	0.0	0.0	0.3	3.0	6.4

High and Low temperatures in degrees Fahrenheit; Precipitation and Snow in inches

Population: 26,224 (2000); Race: 98.3% White, 0.6% Black, 0.1% Asian, 0.1% American Indian and Alaska Native, 0.7% Hispanic of any race, 0.8% two or more races (2000); Density: 45.9 persons per square mile (2000); Age: 24.8% under 18, 16.4% over 64 (2000).
Religion: Five largest groups: 12.0% Catholic Church, 9.8% Evangelical Lutheran Church in America, 9.5% The United Methodist Church, 6.5% Lutheran Church—Missouri Synod, 4.0% Christian Church (Disciples of Christ) (2000).
Economy: Unemployment rate: 3.1% (11/2002); Total civilian labor force: 14,961 (11/2002); Leading industries: 25.7% health care and social assistance; 16.7% retail trade; 11.9% manufacturing (2000); Companies that employ more than 1,000 persons: 0 (2000); Companies that employ more than 100 persons: 11 (2000); Farms: 863 totaling 328,906 acres (1997); Minority business ownership rate: 0.0% (1997); Women business ownership rate: 14.1% (1997); Retail sales per capita: $6,618 (1997). Single-family building permits issued: 65 (2001) / 96 (2000); Multi-family building permits issued: 138 (2001) / 6 (2000).
Income: Per capita income: $19,943 (2000); Median household income: $40,763 (2000); Poverty rate: 7.6% (2000); Bankruptcy rate: 4.02% (2001).
Taxes: Total county taxes per capita: $165 (2000); County property taxes per capita: $139 (2000).
Education: High school graduation rate: 89.0% (2000); College graduation rate: 18.8% (2000).
Housing: Homeownership rate: 75.6% (2000); Median home value: $74,900 (2000); Median rent: $359 per month (2000); Median age of housing: 51 years (2000).
Health: Birth rate: 112.5 per 10,000 population (1998); Age adjusted death rate: 84.2 per 10,000 population (1999); Age adjusted cancer mortality rate: 180.3 deaths per 100,000 population (1999). Number of physicians: 5.7 per 10,000 population (1999); Number of hospital beds: 123.6 per 10,000 population (1999).
Elections: 2000 Presidential election results: 51.2% Gore, 45.9% Bush, 2.1% Nader, 0.4% Buchanan
National and State Parks: Barkley Memorial State Park; Holst State Forest; Ledges State Park; Pilot Mound State Forest; Worth State Game Farm

Additional Information Contacts

Boone County Government Offices. 515-433-0502
Boone Chamber of Commerce. 515-432-3342

Boone County Communities

BEAVER (city). Covers a land area of 0.256 square miles and a water area of 0 square miles. Located at 42.03° N. Lat.; 94.14° W. Long.
History: Beaver was named after a nearby stream where beaver were found.
Population: 53 (2000); Race: 94.5% White, 0.0% Black, 5.5% Asian, 0.0% American Indian and Alaska Native, 0.0% Hispanic of any race, 0.0% two or more races (2000); Density: 207.0 persons per square mile (2000); Age: 30.9% under 18, 1.8% over 64 (2000); Marriage status: 24.4% never married, 46.3% now married, 9.8% widowed, 19.5% divorced (2000); Foreign born: 5.5% (2000); Ancestry (includes multiple ancestries): 49.1% German, 32.7% French (except Basque), 23.6% English, 18.2% Belgian, 9.1% Dutch (2000).
Economy: Employment by occupation: 7.1% management, 0.0% professional, 14.3% services, 21.4% sales, 10.7% farming, 17.9% construction, 28.6% production (2000).
Income: Per capita income: $13,020 (2000); Median household income: $30,625 (2000); Poverty rate: 1.8% (2000).
Taxes: Total city taxes per capita: $222 (1997); City property taxes per capita: $178 (1997).
Education: High school graduation rate: 87.9% (2000); College graduation rate: 0.0% (2000).
Housing: Homeownership rate: 90.0% (2000); Median home value: $27,800 (2000); Median rent: $125 per month (2000); Median age of housing: 60+ years (2000).
Transportation: Commute to work: 92.9% car, 0.0% public transportation, 0.0% walk, 7.1% work from home (2000); Travel time to work: 23.1% less than 15 minutes, 26.9% 15 to 30 minutes, 50.0% 30 to 45 minutes, 0.0% 45 to 60 minutes, 0.0% 60 minutes or more (2000)

BERKLEY (city). Covers a land area of 0.209 square miles and a water area of 0 square miles. Located at 41.94° N. Lat.; 94.11° W. Long. Elevation is 973 feet.
Population: 24 (2000); Race: 100.0% White, 0.0% Black, 0.0% Asian, 0.0% American Indian and Alaska Native, 0.0% Hispanic of any race, 0.0% two or more races (2000); Density: 114.6 persons per square mile (2000); Age: 0.0% under 18, 51.9% over 64 (2000); Marriage status: 18.5% never married, 48.1% now married, 22.2% widowed, 11.1% divorced (2000); Foreign born: 0.0% (2000); Ancestry (includes multiple ancestries): 48.1% German, 22.2% Swedish, 11.1% European, 11.1% Scotch-Irish, 7.4% Irish (2000).
Economy: In livestock and grain area. Employment by occupation: 18.2% management, 18.2% professional, 9.1% services, 27.3% sales, 0.0% farming, 27.3% construction, 0.0% production (2000).
Income: Per capita income: $15,822 (2000); Median household income: $30,000 (2000); Poverty rate: 11.1% (2000).
Taxes: Total city taxes per capita: $75 (1997); City property taxes per capita: $25 (1997).
Education: High school graduation rate: 75.0% (2000); College graduation rate: 29.2% (2000).
Housing: Homeownership rate: 83.3% (2000); Median home value: $55,000 (2000); Median rent: $225 per month (2000); Median age of housing: 50 years (2000).
Transportation: Commute to work: 54.5% car, 0.0% public transportation, 0.0% walk, 36.4% work from home (2000); Travel time to work: 14.3% less

than 15 minutes, 85.7% 15 to 30 minutes, 0.0% 30 to 45 minutes, 0.0% 45 to 60 minutes, 0.0% 60 minutes or more (2000)

BOONE (city). Covers a land area of 8.929 square miles and a water area of 0.004 square miles. Located at 42.06° N. Lat.; 93.88° W. Long. Elevation is 1,122 feet.
History: The town was laid out in 1851. It was first known as Boone Station, later as Montana, and then Boone.
Population: 12,803 (2000); Race: 98.1% White, 0.8% Black, 0.1% Asian, 0.2% American Indian and Alaska Native, 1.0% Hispanic of any race, 0.8% two or more races (2000); Density: 1,433.9 persons per square mile (2000); Age: 24.2% under 18, 17.7% over 64 (2000); Marriage status: 24.1% never married, 55.7% now married, 9.7% widowed, 10.5% divorced (2000); Foreign born: 0.6% (2000); Ancestry (includes multiple ancestries): 32.7% German, 12.5% Irish, 10.8% English, 9.4% Swedish, 6.9% Norwegian (2000).
Vital Statistics: Birth rate: 140.6 per 10,000 population (1998)
Economy: Single-family building permits issued: 25 (2001) / 39 (2000); Multi-family building permits issued: 138 (2001) / 0 (2000); Employment by occupation: 8.0% management, 15.5% professional, 20.2% services, 27.7% sales, 0.4% farming, 12.0% construction, 16.1% production (2000).
Income: Per capita income: $18,995 (2000); Median household income: $38,179 (2000); Poverty rate: 8.4% (2000).
Taxes: Total city taxes per capita: $359 (2000); City property taxes per capita: $274 (2000).
Education: High school graduation rate: 89.2% (2000); College graduation rate: 17.8% (2000).

School District(s)

Boone Community School District (PK-12)
2000 Enrollment: 2,302 515-433-0750
United Community School District (KG-12)
2000 Enrollment: 385 515-432-5319

Housing: Homeownership rate: 70.1% (2000); Median home value: $67,400 (2000); Median rent: $355 per month (2000); Median age of housing: 56 years (2000).
Hospitals: Boone County Hospital (49 beds)
Safety: Violent crime rate: 3.1 per 10,000 population; Property crime rate: 246.3 per 10,000 population (2001).
Newspapers: Boone News-Republican (5 x week); Shopping News (1 x week); Boone Today (2 x week); Boone County News-Republican (1 x week)
Transportation: Commute to work: 92.2% car, 0.4% public transportation, 2.9% walk, 3.2% work from home (2000); Travel time to work: 57.2% less than 15 minutes, 22.1% 15 to 30 minutes, 10.5% 30 to 45 minutes, 4.9% 45 to 60 minutes, 5.2% 60 minutes or more (2000)
Additional Information Contacts
Boone Chamber of Commerce 515-432-3342

BOXHOLM (city). Covers a land area of 1.022 square miles and a water area of 0 square miles. Located at 42.17° N. Lat.; 94.10° W. Long. Elevation is 1,146 feet.
History: Boxholm was platted in 1900, and named for the town of Boxholm, Sweden. Many of the first residents were natives of Sweden.
Population: 215 (2000); Race: 100.0% White, 0.0% Black, 0.0% Asian, 0.0% American Indian and Alaska Native, 1.4% Hispanic of any race, 0.0% two or more races (2000); Density: 210.4 persons per square mile (2000); Age: 19.6% under 18, 25.2% over 64 (2000); Marriage status: 12.7% never married, 66.3% now married, 8.3% widowed, 12.7% divorced (2000); Foreign born: 0.0% (2000); Ancestry (includes multiple ancestries): 43.0% German, 26.2% Swedish, 19.6% Irish, 17.3% English, 6.5% Norwegian (2000).
Economy: Single-family building permits issued: 1 (2001) / 0 (2000); Multi-family building permits issued: 0 (2001) / 0 (2000); Employment by occupation: 11.3% management, 8.5% professional, 16.0% services, 19.8% sales, 0.0% farming, 15.1% construction, 29.2% production (2000).
Income: Per capita income: $18,503 (2000); Median household income: $37,083 (2000); Poverty rate: 7.5% (2000).
Taxes: Total city taxes per capita: $186 (1997); City property taxes per capita: $129 (1997).
Education: High school graduation rate: 90.4% (2000); College graduation rate: 7.2% (2000).

School District(s)

Grand Community School District (KG-12)
2000 Enrollment: 129 515-846-6214

Housing: Homeownership rate: 86.1% (2000); Median home value: $37,500 (2000); Median rent: $229 per month (2000); Median age of housing: 60+ years (2000).
Transportation: Commute to work: 88.7% car, 0.0% public transportation, 11.3% walk, 0.0% work from home (2000); Travel time to work: 20.8% less than 15 minutes, 26.4% 15 to 30 minutes, 30.2% 30 to 45 minutes, 12.3% 45 to 60 minutes, 10.4% 60 minutes or more (2000)

FRASER (city). Covers a land area of 0.831 square miles and a water area of 0.050 square miles. Located at 42.12° N. Lat.; 93.96° W. Long.
History: Fraser was platted and named by the Fraser Coal Company.
Population: 137 (2000); Race: 97.1% White, 2.9% Black, 0.0% Asian, 0.0% American Indian and Alaska Native, 0.0% Hispanic of any race, 0.0% two or more races (2000); Density: 164.8 persons per square mile (2000); Age: 23.4% under 18, 12.4% over 64 (2000); Marriage status: 30.4% never married, 60.7% now married, 1.8% widowed, 7.1% divorced (2000); Foreign born: 0.0% (2000); Ancestry (includes multiple ancestries): 21.2% German, 19.7% United States or American, 18.2% English, 16.8% Irish, 9.5% Dutch (2000).
Economy: Employment by occupation: 8.9% management, 0.0% professional, 22.8% services, 16.5% sales, 6.3% farming, 20.3% construction, 25.3% production (2000).
Income: Per capita income: $14,454 (2000); Median household income: $40,313 (2000); Poverty rate: 5.1% (2000).
Taxes: Total city taxes per capita: $89 (1997); City property taxes per capita: $40 (1997).
Education: High school graduation rate: 74.7% (2000); College graduation rate: 0.0% (2000).
Housing: Homeownership rate: 84.6% (2000); Median home value: $28,800 (2000); Median rent: $275 per month (2000); Median age of housing: 35 years (2000).
Transportation: Commute to work: 94.8% car, 0.0% public transportation, 0.0% walk, 2.6% work from home (2000); Travel time to work: 13.3% less than 15 minutes, 41.3% 15 to 30 minutes, 32.0% 30 to 45 minutes, 13.3% 45 to 60 minutes, 0.0% 60 minutes or more (2000)

LUTHER (city). Covers a land area of 0.774 square miles and a water area of 0 square miles. Located at 41.96° N. Lat.; 93.81° W. Long. Elevation is 1,095 feet.
History: The origins of the name of Luther are not clear. Some say it was named for Martin Luther, the religious reformer. Others say it was named after a local store owner.
Population: 158 (2000); Race: 100.0% White, 0.0% Black, 0.0% Asian, 0.0% American Indian and Alaska Native, 0.0% Hispanic of any race, 0.0% two or more races (2000); Density: 204.1 persons per square mile (2000); Age: 34.3% under 18, 12.7% over 64 (2000); Marriage status: 12.2% never married, 77.4% now married, 5.2% widowed, 5.2% divorced (2000); Foreign born: 0.0% (2000); Ancestry (includes multiple ancestries): 44.6% German, 12.0% Norwegian, 11.4% Irish, 10.8% Scottish, 7.2% French (except Basque) (2000).
Economy: Single-family building permits issued: 0 (2001) / 0 (2000); Multi-family building permits issued: 0 (2001) / 0 (2000); Employment by occupation: 7.4% management, 7.4% professional, 27.9% services, 19.1% sales, 0.0% farming, 20.6% construction, 17.6% production (2000).
Income: Per capita income: $14,393 (2000); Median household income: $41,964 (2000); Poverty rate: 13.3% (2000).
Taxes: Total city taxes per capita: $142 (1997); City property taxes per capita: $90 (1997).
Education: High school graduation rate: 88.7% (2000); College graduation rate: 12.4% (2000).
Housing: Homeownership rate: 89.5% (2000); Median home value: $80,600 (2000); Median rent: $317 per month (2000); Median age of housing: 60+ years (2000).
Transportation: Commute to work: 94.0% car, 0.0% public transportation, 0.0% walk, 6.0% work from home (2000); Travel time to work: 17.5% less than 15 minutes, 52.4% 15 to 30 minutes, 22.2% 30 to 45 minutes, 1.6% 45 to 60 minutes, 6.3% 60 minutes or more (2000)

MADRID (city). Covers a land area of 1.150 square miles and a water area of 0 square miles. Located at 41.87° N. Lat.; 93.82° W. Long. Elevation is 1,001 feet.
History: Madrid was platted in 1852 as Swede Point, in honor of many settlers of that nationality. The place was renamed for the capital of Spain in 1855.
Population: 2,264 (2000); Race: 99.8% White, 0.0% Black, 0.0% Asian, 0.2% American Indian and Alaska Native, 0.5% Hispanic of any race, 0.0% two or more races (2000); Density: 1,968.4 persons per square mile (2000); Age: 25.2% under 18, 16.2% over 64 (2000); Marriage status: 19.7% never married, 63.8% now married, 7.1% widowed, 9.5% divorced (2000); Foreign

born: 1.3% (2000); Ancestry (includes multiple ancestries): 32.1% German, 15.3% Irish, 10.9% Swedish, 8.3% English, 7.9% Other groups (2000).
Economy: Single-family building permits issued: 5 (2001) / 4 (2000); Multi-family building permits issued: 0 (2001) / 0 (2000); Employment by occupation: 12.4% management, 12.6% professional, 16.3% services, 35.0% sales, 0.5% farming, 8.5% construction, 14.8% production (2000).
Income: Per capita income: $24,576 (2000); Median household income: $39,706 (2000); Poverty rate: 7.8% (2000).
Taxes: Total city taxes per capita: $190 (1997); City property taxes per capita: $131 (1997).
Education: High school graduation rate: 87.8% (2000); College graduation rate: 16.0% (2000).

School District(s)

Madrid Community School District (KG-12)
2000 Enrollment: 596 515-795-3241
Housing: Homeownership rate: 78.7% (2000); Median home value: $71,800 (2000); Median rent: $353 per month (2000); Median age of housing: 50 years (2000).
Newspapers: Madrid Register-News (1 x week)
Transportation: Commute to work: 92.8% car, 0.0% public transportation, 2.5% walk, 4.1% work from home (2000); Travel time to work: 29.0% less than 15 minutes, 29.2% 15 to 30 minutes, 31.7% 30 to 45 minutes, 4.8% 45 to 60 minutes, 5.2% 60 minutes or more (2000)

OGDEN (city). Covers a land area of 1.374 square miles and a water area of 0 square miles. Located at 42.04° N. Lat.; 94.03° W. Long. Elevation is 1,092 feet.
History: Ogden was named for the capitalist, W. B. Ogden.
Population: 2,023 (2000); Race: 99.8% White, 0.0% Black, 0.2% Asian, 0.0% American Indian and Alaska Native, 0.0% Hispanic of any race, 0.0% two or more races (2000); Density: 1,472.3 persons per square mile (2000); Age: 23.0% under 18, 20.9% over 64 (2000); Marriage status: 17.4% never married, 64.5% now married, 8.6% widowed, 9.5% divorced (2000); Foreign born: 0.3% (2000); Ancestry (includes multiple ancestries): 39.8% German, 13.1% Irish, 9.8% English, 9.5% Swedish, 6.6% Dutch (2000).
Economy: Single-family building permits issued: 6 (2001) / 6 (2000); Multi-family building permits issued: 0 (2001) / 6 (2000); Employment by occupation: 7.9% management, 13.5% professional, 16.4% services, 25.4% sales, 2.1% farming, 13.8% construction, 20.9% production (2000).
Income: Per capita income: $19,542 (2000); Median household income: $41,114 (2000); Poverty rate: 2.9% (2000).
Taxes: Total city taxes per capita: $192 (1997); City property taxes per capita: $142 (1997).
Education: High school graduation rate: 87.0% (2000); College graduation rate: 11.6% (2000).

School District(s)

Ogden Community School District (KG-12)
2000 Enrollment: 800 515-275-2894
Housing: Homeownership rate: 82.0% (2000); Median home value: $77,000 (2000); Median rent: $364 per month (2000); Median age of housing: 47 years (2000).
Newspapers: Ogden Reporter (1 x week)
Transportation: Commute to work: 92.2% car, 0.0% public transportation, 3.2% walk, 3.8% work from home (2000); Travel time to work: 39.5% less than 15 minutes, 39.4% 15 to 30 minutes, 11.2% 30 to 45 minutes, 4.3% 45 to 60 minutes, 5.7% 60 minutes or more (2000)

PILOT MOUND (city). Covers a land area of 0.949 square miles and a water area of 0 square miles. Located at 42.16° N. Lat.; 94.01° W. Long.
History: Pilot Mound got its name from the geography of the area. There was a big hill in the area which was a landmark and meeting place of the time.
Population: 214 (2000); Race: 99.5% White, 0.0% Black, 0.0% Asian, 0.5% American Indian and Alaska Native, 0.0% Hispanic of any race, 0.0% two or more races (2000); Density: 225.6 persons per square mile (2000); Age: 15.8% under 18, 27.1% over 64 (2000); Marriage status: 8.0% never married, 70.1% now married, 13.2% widowed, 8.6% divorced (2000); Foreign born: 0.0% (2000); Ancestry (includes multiple ancestries): 28.1% German, 20.2% English, 15.8% Swedish, 11.3% United States or American, 9.4% Irish (2000).
Economy: Single-family building permits issued: 0 (2001) / 0 (2000); Multi-family building permits issued: 0 (2001) / 0 (2000); Employment by occupation: 8.3% management, 9.4% professional, 29.2% services, 10.4% sales, 4.2% farming, 10.4% construction, 28.1% production (2000).
Income: Per capita income: $14,414 (2000); Median household income: $29,750 (2000); Poverty rate: 8.5% (2000).
Taxes: Total city taxes per capita: $139 (1997); City property taxes per capita: $85 (1997).
Education: High school graduation rate: 78.1% (2000); College graduation rate: 1.3% (2000).
Housing: Homeownership rate: 82.1% (2000); Median home value: $33,900 (2000); Median rent: $221 per month (2000); Median age of housing: 60+ years (2000).
Transportation: Commute to work: 92.8% car, 0.0% public transportation, 5.2% walk, 2.1% work from home (2000); Travel time to work: 28.4% less than 15 minutes, 38.9% 15 to 30 minutes, 9.5% 30 to 45 minutes, 10.5% 45 to 60 minutes, 12.6% 60 minutes or more (2000)

Bremer County

Located in northeastern Iowa, in prairie area; drained by the Cedar, Wapsipinicon, and Shell Rock Rivers. Covers a land area of 437.90 square miles, a water area of 1.70 square miles, and is located in the Central Time Zone. The county government was organized in 1851. County seat is Waverly.

Weather Station: Tripoli — Elevation: 958 feet

	Jan	Feb	Mar	Apr	May	Jun	Jul	Aug	Sep	Oct	Nov	Dec
High	23	30	43	58	71	80	83	81	73	61	43	29
Low	5	12	24	36	48	57	61	59	50	38	26	13
Precip	1.0	1.0	2.1	3.6	4.4	4.8	4.6	5.3	3.4	2.7	2.3	1.1
Snow	9.2	6.6	5.2	2.4	tr	0.0	0.0	0.0	0.0	0.1	4.6	7.9

High and Low temperatures in degrees Fahrenheit; Precipitation and Snow in inches

Population: 23,325 (2000); Race: 98.1% White, 0.4% Black, 0.7% Asian, 0.1% American Indian and Alaska Native, 0.8% Hispanic of any race, 0.7% two or more races (2000); Density: 53.3 persons per square mile (2000); Age: 24.1% under 18, 15.9% over 64 (2000).
Religion: Five largest groups: 34.8% Evangelical Lutheran Church in America, 15.0% Catholic Church, 11.7% The United Methodist Church, 9.5% Lutheran Church—Missouri Synod, 6.4% United Church of Christ (2000).
Economy: Unemployment rate: 2.6% (11/2002); Total civilian labor force: 12,293 (11/2002); Leading industries: 22.5% manufacturing; 14.4% health care and social assistance; 13.1% finance & insurance (2000); Companies that employ more than 1,000 persons: 0 (2000); Companies that employ more than 100 persons: 17 (2000); Farms: 982 totaling 238,528 acres (1997); Minority business ownership rate: 0.0% (1997); Women business ownership rate: 31.4% (1997); Retail sales per capita: $6,211 (1997). Single-family building permits issued: 102 (2001) / 110 (2000); Multi-family building permits issued: 24 (2001) / 28 (2000).
Income: Per capita income: $19,199 (2000); Median household income: $40,826 (2000); Poverty rate: 5.1% (2000); Bankruptcy rate: 2.54% (2001).
Taxes: Total county taxes per capita: $159 (2000); County property taxes per capita: $152 (2000).
Education: High school graduation rate: 87.7% (2000); College graduation rate: 21.5% (2000).
Housing: Homeownership rate: 78.1% (2000); Median home value: $88,000 (2000); Median rent: $316 per month (2000); Median age of housing: 45 years (2000).
Health: Birth rate: 90.0 per 10,000 population (1998); Age adjusted death rate: 74.3 per 10,000 population (1999); Age adjusted cancer mortality rate: 185.2 deaths per 100,000 population (1999). Air Quality Index: 82% good, 18% moderate, 0% unhealthy (percent of days in 2000). Number of physicians: 8.6 per 10,000 population (1999); Number of hospital beds: 21.9 per 10,000 population (1999).
Elections: 2000 Presidential election results: 46.3% Gore, 50.8% Bush, 2.3% Nader, 0.3% Buchanan
National and State Parks: Sweet Marsh State Wildlife Management Area
Additional Information Contacts
Bremer County Government Offices 319-352-0340
Bremer Butler Chickasaw Board of Realtors 319-352-1713
Waverly Chamber of Commerce 319-352-4526

Bremer County Communities

DENVER (city). Covers a land area of 1.381 square miles and a water area of 0 square miles. Located at 42.67° N. Lat.; 92.33° W. Long. Elevation is 943 feet.
History: Denver was previously named both Jefferson City and Breckenridge. In 1863, when a regular post office was established, the name was changed to Denver.

Population: 1,627 (2000); Race: 98.5% White, 0.1% Black, 0.1% Asian, 0.0% American Indian and Alaska Native, 0.2% Hispanic of any race, 1.1% two or more races (2000); Density: 1,177.9 persons per square mile (2000); Age: 27.9% under 18, 16.0% over 64 (2000); Marriage status: 19.5% never married, 64.0% now married, 8.9% widowed, 7.6% divorced (2000); Foreign born: 0.4% (2000); Ancestry (includes multiple ancestries): 58.3% German, 8.2% Irish, 7.6% United States or American, 7.6% Norwegian, 6.8% English (2000).
Economy: Employment by occupation: 15.2% management, 19.7% professional, 11.1% services, 30.6% sales, 0.1% farming, 8.4% construction, 14.9% production (2000).
Income: Per capita income: $20,791 (2000); Median household income: $44,375 (2000); Poverty rate: 2.4% (2000).
Taxes: Total city taxes per capita: $181 (1997); City property taxes per capita: $175 (1997).
Education: High school graduation rate: 92.6% (2000); College graduation rate: 23.9% (2000).

School District(s)

Denver Community School District (KG-12)
2000 Enrollment: 759 319-984-6323
Housing: Homeownership rate: 76.9% (2000); Median home value: $92,900 (2000); Median rent: $355 per month (2000); Median age of housing: 32 years (2000).
Newspapers: Forum (1 x week)
Transportation: Commute to work: 92.7% car, 0.5% public transportation, 4.5% walk, 2.2% work from home (2000); Travel time to work: 26.2% less than 15 minutes, 55.5% 15 to 30 minutes, 12.5% 30 to 45 minutes, 0.7% 45 to 60 minutes, 5.1% 60 minutes or more (2000)

FREDERIKA (city). Covers a land area of 0.200 square miles and a water area of 0 square miles. Located at 42.88° N. Lat.; 92.30° W. Long. Elevation is 1,050 feet.
History: Frederika was named for Frederika Bremer (1801-1865), a popular Swedish novelist who visited the United States around 1849 and 1850.
Population: 199 (2000); Race: 99.5% White, 0.0% Black, 0.0% Asian, 0.0% American Indian and Alaska Native, 0.5% Hispanic of any race, 0.0% two or more races (2000); Density: 993.5 persons per square mile (2000); Age: 15.0% under 18, 32.0% over 64 (2000); Marriage status: 13.3% never married, 70.6% now married, 12.8% widowed, 3.3% divorced (2000); Foreign born: 0.5% (2000); Ancestry (includes multiple ancestries): 46.6% German, 9.2% English, 8.7% Irish, 4.4% Italian, 1.9% United States or American (2000).
Economy: Employment by occupation: 5.9% management, 8.8% professional, 10.3% services, 23.5% sales, 0.0% farming, 26.5% construction, 25.0% production (2000).
Income: Per capita income: $20,224 (2000); Median household income: $36,250 (2000); Poverty rate: 12.6% (2000).
Taxes: Total city taxes per capita: $181 (2000); City property taxes per capita: $90 (2000).
Education: High school graduation rate: 73.1% (2000); College graduation rate: 4.5% (2000).
Housing: Homeownership rate: 76.5% (2000); Median home value: $60,900 (2000); Median rent: $195 per month (2000); Median age of housing: 55 years (2000).
Transportation: Commute to work: 95.6% car, 0.0% public transportation, 4.4% walk, 0.0% work from home (2000); Travel time to work: 10.3% less than 15 minutes, 25.0% 15 to 30 minutes, 50.0% 30 to 45 minutes, 4.4% 45 to 60 minutes, 10.3% 60 minutes or more (2000)

JANESVILLE (city). Covers a land area of 1.448 square miles and a water area of 0.045 square miles. Located at 42.64° N. Lat.; 92.46° W. Long. Elevation is 891 feet.
History: Janesville was named in 1849 by John T. Barrick, first settler, in honor of his wife. Janesville was the first town in the county.
Population: 829 (2000); Race: 99.1% White, 0.0% Black, 0.7% Asian, 0.0% American Indian and Alaska Native, 0.1% Hispanic of any race, 0.1% two or more races (2000); Density: 572.5 persons per square mile (2000); Age: 26.8% under 18, 14.6% over 64 (2000); Marriage status: 18.3% never married, 63.6% now married, 9.1% widowed, 9.1% divorced (2000); Foreign born: 1.0% (2000); Ancestry (includes multiple ancestries): 47.2% German, 13.1% Irish, 12.0% United States or American, 9.2% English, 5.1% Danish (2000).
Economy: Employment by occupation: 6.5% management, 15.0% professional, 11.4% services, 26.2% sales, 0.0% farming, 15.4% construction, 25.5% production (2000).
Income: Per capita income: $18,878 (2000); Median household income: $40,060 (2000); Poverty rate: 3.5% (2000).
Taxes: Total city taxes per capita: $296 (1997); City property taxes per capita: $269 (1997).
Education: High school graduation rate: 82.8% (2000); College graduation rate: 10.1% (2000).

School District(s)

Janesville Consolidated School District (PK-12)
2000 Enrollment: 317 319-987-2581
Housing: Homeownership rate: 79.5% (2000); Median home value: $77,600 (2000); Median rent: $257 per month (2000); Median age of housing: 40 years (2000).
Transportation: Commute to work: 96.9% car, 0.2% public transportation, 0.2% walk, 2.6% work from home (2000); Travel time to work: 28.3% less than 15 minutes, 55.4% 15 to 30 minutes, 8.8% 30 to 45 minutes, 2.2% 45 to 60 minutes, 5.4% 60 minutes or more (2000)

PLAINFIELD (city). Covers a land area of 0.325 square miles and a water area of 0 square miles. Located at 42.84° N. Lat.; 92.53° W. Long. Elevation is 942 feet.
History: Plainfield was named for Plainfield, Illinois, former home of many of the settlers.
Population: 438 (2000); Race: 99.4% White, 0.0% Black, 0.0% Asian, 0.4% American Indian and Alaska Native, 0.0% Hispanic of any race, 0.2% two or more races (2000); Density: 1,347.4 persons per square mile (2000); Age: 23.3% under 18, 15.1% over 64 (2000); Marriage status: 18.6% never married, 66.6% now married, 7.8% widowed, 7.0% divorced (2000); Foreign born: 0.9% (2000); Ancestry (includes multiple ancestries): 52.9% German, 16.0% Irish, 8.6% Norwegian, 7.6% United States or American, 5.4% English (2000).
Economy: Single-family building permits issued: 0 (2001) / 1 (2000); Multi-family building permits issued: 0 (2001) / 0 (2000); Employment by occupation: 10.1% management, 8.6% professional, 19.4% services, 19.0% sales, 0.0% farming, 11.2% construction, 31.7% production (2000).
Income: Per capita income: $18,156 (2000); Median household income: $39,688 (2000); Poverty rate: 8.0% (2000).
Taxes: Total city taxes per capita: $178 (1997); City property taxes per capita: $176 (1997).
Education: High school graduation rate: 89.4% (2000); College graduation rate: 6.0% (2000).
Housing: Homeownership rate: 77.8% (2000); Median home value: $66,100 (2000); Median rent: $309 per month (2000); Median age of housing: 54 years (2000).
Transportation: Commute to work: 88.7% car, 0.0% public transportation, 5.4% walk, 5.8% work from home (2000); Travel time to work: 26.0% less than 15 minutes, 43.4% 15 to 30 minutes, 16.5% 30 to 45 minutes, 9.1% 45 to 60 minutes, 5.0% 60 minutes or more (2000)

READLYN (city). Covers a land area of 0.322 square miles and a water area of 0 square miles. Located at 42.70° N. Lat.; 92.22° W. Long. Elevation is 1,032 feet.
History: Readlyn was named after an official with the Chicago Great Western Railroad.
Population: 786 (2000); Race: 99.4% White, 0.0% Black, 0.0% Asian, 0.6% American Indian and Alaska Native, 0.0% Hispanic of any race, 0.0% two or more races (2000); Density: 2,444.4 persons per square mile (2000); Age: 30.3% under 18, 19.2% over 64 (2000); Marriage status: 15.7% never married, 67.7% now married, 11.1% widowed, 5.5% divorced (2000); Foreign born: 0.0% (2000); Ancestry (includes multiple ancestries): 72.8% German, 7.2% Irish, 4.2% United States or American, 4.2% English, 3.9% Norwegian (2000).
Economy: Employment by occupation: 14.6% management, 15.7% professional, 11.7% services, 27.9% sales, 1.1% farming, 11.7% construction, 17.3% production (2000).
Income: Per capita income: $17,721 (2000); Median household income: $41,625 (2000); Poverty rate: 2.7% (2000).
Taxes: Total city taxes per capita: $195 (1997); City property taxes per capita: $194 (1997).
Education: High school graduation rate: 81.8% (2000); College graduation rate: 12.8% (2000).
Housing: Homeownership rate: 86.3% (2000); Median home value: $78,200 (2000); Median rent: $261 per month (2000); Median age of housing: 51 years (2000).
Transportation: Commute to work: 90.5% car, 0.0% public transportation, 4.1% walk, 4.9% work from home (2000); Travel time to work: 27.4% less

than 15 minutes, 39.9% 15 to 30 minutes, 27.1% 30 to 45 minutes, 2.0% 45 to 60 minutes, 3.7% 60 minutes or more (2000)

SUMNER (city). Covers a land area of 2.526 square miles and a water area of 0 square miles. Located at 42.85° N. Lat.; 92.10° W. Long. Elevation is 1,063 feet.
History: Sumner was named for Massachusetts senator Charles Sumner.
Population: 2,106 (2000); Race: 99.1% White, 0.2% Black, 0.0% Asian, 0.0% American Indian and Alaska Native, 1.0% Hispanic of any race, 0.4% two or more races (2000); Density: 833.8 persons per square mile (2000); Age: 22.4% under 18, 25.2% over 64 (2000); Marriage status: 16.7% never married, 59.5% now married, 16.1% widowed, 7.8% divorced (2000); Foreign born: 0.6% (2000); Ancestry (includes multiple ancestries): 52.7% German, 10.8% United States or American, 9.2% English, 8.5% Irish, 7.2% Norwegian (2000).
Economy: Single-family building permits issued: 6 (2001) / 3 (2000); Multi-family building permits issued: 0 (2001) / 0 (2000); Employment by occupation: 6.6% management, 12.1% professional, 14.0% services, 21.5% sales, 1.5% farming, 11.6% construction, 32.6% production (2000).
Income: Per capita income: $18,029 (2000); Median household income: $33,417 (2000); Poverty rate: 4.2% (2000).
Taxes: Total city taxes per capita: $216 (1997); City property taxes per capita: $212 (1997).
Education: High school graduation rate: 85.2% (2000); College graduation rate: 14.6% (2000).

School District(s)

Sumner Community School District (KG-12)
2000 Enrollment: 688 319-578-3425
Housing: Homeownership rate: 82.8% (2000); Median home value: $68,100 (2000); Median rent: $286 per month (2000); Median age of housing: 59 years (2000).
Hospitals: Community Memorial Hospital (25 beds)
Newspapers: Sumner Gazette (1 x week); AD-Paper (1 x week)
Transportation: Commute to work: 88.7% car, 0.0% public transportation, 6.5% walk, 4.0% work from home (2000); Travel time to work: 61.6% less than 15 minutes, 12.8% 15 to 30 minutes, 14.6% 30 to 45 minutes, 6.9% 45 to 60 minutes, 4.2% 60 minutes or more (2000)

TRIPOLI (city). Covers a land area of 1.402 square miles and a water area of 0 square miles. Located at 42.80° N. Lat.; 92.25° W. Long. Elevation is 1,050 feet.
History: Tripoli was incorporated in 1885 and is believed to be named for the Battle of Tripoli.
Population: 1,310 (2000); Race: 98.9% White, 0.0% Black, 0.1% Asian, 0.0% American Indian and Alaska Native, 0.2% Hispanic of any race, 1.1% two or more races (2000); Density: 934.7 persons per square mile (2000); Age: 28.7% under 18, 19.6% over 64 (2000); Marriage status: 21.6% never married, 59.5% now married, 11.1% widowed, 7.8% divorced (2000); Foreign born: 0.8% (2000); Ancestry (includes multiple ancestries): 60.6% German, 8.5% United States or American, 5.9% Irish, 4.8% English, 4.5% Norwegian (2000).
Economy: Employment by occupation: 8.7% management, 13.4% professional, 12.3% services, 30.4% sales, 1.2% farming, 13.2% construction, 20.8% production (2000).
Income: Per capita income: $16,882 (2000); Median household income: $34,444 (2000); Poverty rate: 9.6% (2000).
Taxes: Total city taxes per capita: $241 (1997); City property taxes per capita: $237 (1997).
Education: High school graduation rate: 77.5% (2000); College graduation rate: 12.0% (2000).

School District(s)

Tripoli Community School District (KG-12)
2000 Enrollment: 530 319-882-4201
Housing: Homeownership rate: 81.0% (2000); Median home value: $64,800 (2000); Median rent: $278 per month (2000); Median age of housing: 55 years (2000).
Newspapers: Tripoli Leader (1 x week)
Transportation: Commute to work: 88.7% car, 0.9% public transportation, 6.9% walk, 3.2% work from home (2000); Travel time to work: 33.3% less than 15 minutes, 30.5% 15 to 30 minutes, 21.8% 30 to 45 minutes, 9.5% 45 to 60 minutes, 4.9% 60 minutes or more (2000)

WAVERLY (city). Covers a land area of 11.163 square miles and a water area of 0.309 square miles. Located at 42.72° N. Lat.; 92.47° W. Long. Elevation is 936 feet.
History: Waverly was to have been named Harmon for its founder, W. P. Harmon. But the chief speaker at the meeting formally naming the town had spent the morning reading one of the Waverly novels, and in the midst of his address pronounced Waverly instead of Harmon. Harmon raised no objections, and the name was retained.
Population: 8,968 (2000); Race: 96.7% White, 0.9% Black, 1.5% Asian, 0.1% American Indian and Alaska Native, 0.7% Hispanic of any race, 0.8% two or more races (2000); Density: 803.4 persons per square mile (2000); Age: 21.7% under 18, 16.5% over 64 (2000); Marriage status: 30.1% never married, 56.2% now married, 8.8% widowed, 4.9% divorced (2000); Foreign born: 2.0% (2000); Ancestry (includes multiple ancestries): 50.6% German, 12.1% Irish, 10.4% English, 8.2% Norwegian, 4.4% United States or American (2000).
Economy: Single-family building permits issued: 37 (2001) / 55 (2000); Multi-family building permits issued: 24 (2001) / 28 (2000); Employment by occupation: 12.0% management, 24.9% professional, 16.4% services, 26.8% sales, 1.1% farming, 6.4% construction, 12.4% production (2000).
Income: Per capita income: $18,285 (2000); Median household income: $39,587 (2000); Poverty rate: 6.3% (2000).
Taxes: Total city taxes per capita: $375 (2000); City property taxes per capita: $358 (2000).
Education: High school graduation rate: 88.4% (2000); College graduation rate: 31.5% (2000).

School District(s)

Waverly-Shell Rock Community School District (PK-12)
2000 Enrollment: 2,061 319-352-3630

Four-year College(s)

Wartburg College (Private, Not-for-profit, Evangelical Lutheran Church)
2001 Enrollment: 1,649 319-352-8200
2001 Tuition: In-state $16,210; Out-of-state $16,210
Housing: Homeownership rate: 70.7% (2000); Median home value: $95,800 (2000); Median rent: $345 per month (2000); Median age of housing: 36 years (2000).
Hospitals: Waverly Municipal Hospital (45 beds)
Safety: Violent crime rate: 11.2 per 10,000 population; Property crime rate: 187.5 per 10,000 population (2001).
Newspapers: The Waverly Democrat (1 x week); The Bremer County Independent (1 x week)
Transportation: Commute to work: 84.6% car, 0.2% public transportation, 11.4% walk, 2.6% work from home (2000); Travel time to work: 67.5% less than 15 minutes, 18.6% 15 to 30 minutes, 11.1% 30 to 45 minutes, 1.6% 45 to 60 minutes, 1.1% 60 minutes or more (2000)

Additional Information Contacts

Bremer Butler Chickasaw Board of Realtors 319-352-1713
Waverly Chamber of Commerce 319-352-4526

Buchanan County

Located in eastern Iowa; prairie area, drained by the Wapsipinicon River and Buffalo Creek. Covers a land area of 571.30 square miles, a water area of 2.10 square miles, and is located in the Central Time Zone. The county government was organized in 1837. County seat is Independence.
Population: 21,093 (2000); Race: 98.2% White, 0.3% Black, 0.5% Asian, 0.2% American Indian and Alaska Native, 1.0% Hispanic of any race, 0.6% two or more races (2000); Density: 36.9 persons per square mile (2000); Age: 28.5% under 18, 14.5% over 64 (2000).
Religion: Five largest groups: 34.0% Catholic Church, 11.2% The United Methodist Church, 9.1% Evangelical Lutheran Church in America, 3.8% Presbyterian Church (U.S.A.), 3.0% Lutheran Church—Missouri Synod (2000).
Economy: Unemployment rate: 4.2% (11/2002); Total civilian labor force: 10,967 (11/2002); Leading industries: 26.2% manufacturing; 18.5% health care and social assistance; 17.8% retail trade (2000); Companies that employ more than 1,000 persons: 0 (2000); Companies that employ more than 100 persons: 9 (2000); Farms: 1,136 totaling 336,863 acres (1997); Minority business ownership rate: 0.0% (1997); Women business ownership rate: 29.5% (1997); Retail sales per capita: $7,322 (1997). Single-family building permits issued: 29 (2001) / 38 (2000); Multi-family building permits issued: 4 (2001) / 4 (2000).
Income: Per capita income: $18,405 (2000); Median household income: $38,036 (2000); Poverty rate: 9.4% (2000); Bankruptcy rate: 3.10% (2001).
Taxes: Total county taxes per capita: $209 (2000); County property taxes per capita: $202 (2000).
Education: High school graduation rate: 84.6% (2000); College graduation rate: 12.7% (2000).

Housing: Homeownership rate: 78.1% (2000); Median home value: $73,900 (2000); Median rent: $282 per month (2000); Median age of housing: 40 years (2000).
Health: Birth rate: 146.5 per 10,000 population (1998); Age adjusted death rate: 89.6 per 10,000 population (1999); Age adjusted cancer mortality rate: 176.7 deaths per 100,000 population (1999). Number of physicians: 6.6 per 10,000 population (1999); Number of hospital beds: 123.3 per 10,000 population (1999).
Elections: 2000 Presidential election results: 53.6% Gore, 43.5% Bush, 1.8% Nader, 0.6% Buchanan
National and State Parks: Cedar Rock State Park; Troy Mills State Fish And Game Area
Additional Information Contacts
Buchanan County Government Offices 319-334-2196
Independence Chamber of Commerce 319-334-7178
Jesup Chamber of Commerce. 319-827-3100

Buchanan County Communities

AURORA (city). Covers a land area of 0.573 square miles and a water area of 0 square miles. Located at 42.61° N. Lat.; 91.72° W. Long. Elevation is 1,135 feet.
History: Aurora was named for East Aurora, New York, the birthplace of Bishop Warren, the founder of the town.
Population: 194 (2000); Race: 94.5% White, 0.0% Black, 0.0% Asian, 0.0% American Indian and Alaska Native, 0.0% Hispanic of any race, 5.5% two or more races (2000); Density: 338.5 persons per square mile (2000); Age: 26.0% under 18, 15.0% over 64 (2000); Marriage status: 19.9% never married, 68.2% now married, 6.6% widowed, 5.3% divorced (2000); Foreign born: 1.0% (2000); Ancestry (includes multiple ancestries): 28.5% German, 20.5% United States or American, 11.0% English, 9.5% Irish, 3.0% Norwegian (2000).
Economy: Employment by occupation: 15.7% management, 2.2% professional, 3.4% services, 27.0% sales, 3.4% farming, 14.6% construction, 33.7% production (2000).
Income: Per capita income: $16,254 (2000); Median household income: $38,750 (2000); Poverty rate: 19.5% (2000).
Taxes: Total city taxes per capita: $170 (1997); City property taxes per capita: $105 (1997).
Education: High school graduation rate: 76.2% (2000); College graduation rate: 8.5% (2000).
Housing: Homeownership rate: 82.9% (2000); Median home value: $46,700 (2000); Median rent: $239 per month (2000); Median age of housing: 60+ years (2000).
Transportation: Commute to work: 74.4% car, 3.7% public transportation, 17.1% walk, 2.4% work from home (2000); Travel time to work: 40.0% less than 15 minutes, 32.5% 15 to 30 minutes, 1.3% 30 to 45 minutes, 15.0% 45 to 60 minutes, 11.3% 60 minutes or more (2000)

BRANDON (city). Covers a land area of 0.312 square miles and a water area of 0 square miles. Located at 42.31° N. Lat.; 92.00° W. Long.
History: In 1851, Thomas Brandon established a trading post on the Wapsipinicon River. The town of Brandon grew up around this spot.
Population: 311 (2000); Race: 95.8% White, 0.0% Black, 0.0% Asian, 4.2% American Indian and Alaska Native, 0.0% Hispanic of any race, 0.0% two or more races (2000); Density: 997.9 persons per square mile (2000); Age: 18.2% under 18, 17.3% over 64 (2000); Marriage status: 27.7% never married, 56.3% now married, 10.2% widowed, 5.9% divorced (2000); Foreign born: 0.0% (2000); Ancestry (includes multiple ancestries): 37.8% German, 14.7% Irish, 14.3% United States or American, 8.8% Other groups, 6.8% English (2000).
Economy: Employment by occupation: 11.9% management, 15.0% professional, 7.5% services, 21.3% sales, 1.9% farming, 23.1% construction, 19.4% production (2000).
Income: Per capita income: $17,428 (2000); Median household income: $34,219 (2000); Poverty rate: 9.4% (2000).
Taxes: Total city taxes per capita: $87 (1997); City property taxes per capita: $84 (1997).
Education: High school graduation rate: 78.3% (2000); College graduation rate: 6.3% (2000).
Housing: Homeownership rate: 78.5% (2000); Median home value: $54,700 (2000); Median rent: $290 per month (2000); Median age of housing: 60+ years (2000).
Transportation: Commute to work: 87.5% car, 2.5% public transportation, 4.4% walk, 2.5% work from home (2000); Travel time to work: 15.4% less than 15 minutes, 22.4% 15 to 30 minutes, 55.1% 30 to 45 minutes, 7.1% 45 to 60 minutes, 0.0% 60 minutes or more (2000)

FAIRBANK (city). Covers a land area of 0.592 square miles and a water area of 0.013 square miles. Located at 42.64° N. Lat.; 92.04° W. Long. Elevation is 996 feet.
History: Fairbank was originally an Amish-Mennonite settlement.
Population: 1,041 (2000); Race: 99.7% White, 0.0% Black, 0.0% Asian, 0.0% American Indian and Alaska Native, 0.9% Hispanic of any race, 0.2% two or more races (2000); Density: 1,758.9 persons per square mile (2000); Age: 29.1% under 18, 14.0% over 64 (2000); Marriage status: 17.5% never married, 65.3% now married, 8.6% widowed, 8.6% divorced (2000); Foreign born: 0.2% (2000); Ancestry (includes multiple ancestries): 47.4% German, 14.9% Irish, 6.9% United States or American, 5.9% Norwegian, 5.8% English (2000).
Economy: Single-family building permits issued: 0 (2001) / 0 (2000); Multi-family building permits issued: 0 (2001) / 0 (2000); Employment by occupation: 9.6% management, 12.6% professional, 14.7% services, 27.7% sales, 0.8% farming, 9.8% construction, 24.8% production (2000).
Income: Per capita income: $17,262 (2000); Median household income: $36,900 (2000); Poverty rate: 8.9% (2000).
Taxes: Total city taxes per capita: $148 (1997); City property taxes per capita: $145 (1997).
Education: High school graduation rate: 88.0% (2000); College graduation rate: 12.7% (2000).

School District(s)

Wapsie Valley Community School District (KG-12)
2000 Enrollment: 709 319-638-6711
Housing: Homeownership rate: 80.9% (2000); Median home value: $77,100 (2000); Median rent: $210 per month (2000); Median age of housing: 32 years (2000).
Transportation: Commute to work: 92.1% car, 0.0% public transportation, 3.4% walk, 3.9% work from home (2000); Travel time to work: 28.5% less than 15 minutes, 30.4% 15 to 30 minutes, 33.5% 30 to 45 minutes, 4.5% 45 to 60 minutes, 3.1% 60 minutes or more (2000)

HAZLETON (city). Covers a land area of 0.744 square miles and a water area of 0.038 square miles. Located at 42.61° N. Lat.; 91.90° W. Long. Elevation is 995 feet.
History: Hazleton was first known as Superior, but was renamed in 1863.
Population: 950 (2000); Race: 98.3% White, 0.2% Black, 0.1% Asian, 0.0% American Indian and Alaska Native, 1.5% Hispanic of any race, 1.2% two or more races (2000); Density: 1,276.4 persons per square mile (2000); Age: 29.0% under 18, 12.2% over 64 (2000); Marriage status: 20.2% never married, 61.7% now married, 6.6% widowed, 11.5% divorced (2000); Foreign born: 0.3% (2000); Ancestry (includes multiple ancestries): 37.6% German, 13.0% Irish, 11.1% United States or American, 6.4% English, 5.7% Other groups (2000).
Economy: Employment by occupation: 8.7% management, 8.3% professional, 15.7% services, 20.7% sales, 0.0% farming, 14.2% construction, 32.5% production (2000).
Income: Per capita income: $14,955 (2000); Median household income: $32,625 (2000); Poverty rate: 11.6% (2000).
Taxes: Total city taxes per capita: $80 (1997); City property taxes per capita: $71 (1997).
Education: High school graduation rate: 84.3% (2000); College graduation rate: 4.7% (2000).
Housing: Homeownership rate: 77.6% (2000); Median home value: $44,000 (2000); Median rent: $301 per month (2000); Median age of housing: 28 years (2000).
Transportation: Commute to work: 92.0% car, 0.2% public transportation, 4.2% walk, 2.9% work from home (2000); Travel time to work: 40.0% less than 15 minutes, 32.7% 15 to 30 minutes, 10.8% 30 to 45 minutes, 8.5% 45 to 60 minutes, 8.0% 60 minutes or more (2000)

INDEPENDENCE (city). Covers a land area of 3.708 square miles and a water area of 0.135 square miles. Located at 42.47° N. Lat.; 91.89° W. Long. Elevation is 921 feet.
History: Independence was given its name because the town was organized on July 4, 1847. The town owes its founding to Rufus B. Clark, a trapper, who saw the possibilities of utilizing water power from the Wapsipinicon River.
Population: 6,014 (2000); Race: 97.1% White, 0.4% Black, 1.3% Asian, 0.0% American Indian and Alaska Native, 1.5% Hispanic of any race, 0.6% two or more races (2000); Density: 1,621.8 persons per square mile (2000); Age: 24.5% under 18, 19.8% over 64 (2000); Marriage status: 22.1% never

married, 59.4% now married, 11.7% widowed, 6.8% divorced (2000); Foreign born: 2.1% (2000); Ancestry (includes multiple ancestries): 38.9% German, 16.9% Irish, 9.2% English, 8.0% United States or American, 4.3% French (except Basque) (2000).
Economy: Single-family building permits issued: 25 (2001) / 28 (2000); Multi-family building permits issued: 4 (2001) / 4 (2000); Employment by occupation: 11.1% management, 17.6% professional, 17.3% services, 22.9% sales, 0.9% farming, 9.3% construction, 20.9% production (2000).
Income: Per capita income: $20,683 (2000); Median household income: $36,554 (2000); Poverty rate: 7.0% (2000).
Taxes: Total city taxes per capita: $318 (1997); City property taxes per capita: $307 (1997).
Education: High school graduation rate: 85.5% (2000); College graduation rate: 17.2% (2000).

School District(s)

Independence Community School District (PK-12)
2000 Enrollment: 1,630 319-334-7400
Mental Health Institute (N -N)
2000 Enrollment: n/a 319-334-2583

Housing: Homeownership rate: 72.9% (2000); Median home value: $75,600 (2000); Median rent: $296 per month (2000); Median age of housing: 50 years (2000).
Hospitals: Mental Health Institute (382 beds); People's Memorial Hospital (50 beds)
Safety: Violent crime rate: 11.7 per 10,000 population; Property crime rate: 331.2 per 10,000 population (2001).
Newspapers: The Weekend Express (2 x week); Bulletin Journal (2 x week)
Transportation: Commute to work: 88.7% car, 0.0% public transportation, 6.6% walk, 4.0% work from home (2000); Travel time to work: 61.8% less than 15 minutes, 11.8% 15 to 30 minutes, 13.2% 30 to 45 minutes, 7.9% 45 to 60 minutes, 5.2% 60 minutes or more (2000)

Additional Information Contacts

Independence Chamber of Commerce 319-334-7178

JESUP (city). Covers a land area of 1.678 square miles and a water area of 0 square miles. Located at 42.47° N. Lat.; 92.06° W. Long. Elevation is 980 feet.
History: Jesup, settled in 1858, was named for a railroad official. One morning in 1866, a giant prairie fire was viewed in the distance heading towards the village. The settlers, instead of fleeing, started backfires so that as the great fire advanced it would meet only long strips of burned grass and would die out from lack of fuel.
Population: 2,212 (2000); Race: 99.4% White, 0.3% Black, 0.0% Asian, 0.0% American Indian and Alaska Native, 1.1% Hispanic of any race, 0.2% two or more races (2000); Density: 1,318.6 persons per square mile (2000); Age: 28.4% under 18, 17.7% over 64 (2000); Marriage status: 20.4% never married, 65.0% now married, 8.8% widowed, 5.7% divorced (2000); Foreign born: 0.3% (2000); Ancestry (includes multiple ancestries): 48.5% German, 12.3% Irish, 12.1% English, 7.5% United States or American, 3.9% Norwegian (2000).
Economy: Single-family building permits issued: 3 (2001) / 7 (2000); Multi-family building permits issued: 0 (2001) / 0 (2000); Employment by occupation: 12.4% management, 17.6% professional, 11.3% services, 22.0% sales, 0.0% farming, 12.5% construction, 24.1% production (2000).
Income: Per capita income: $17,160 (2000); Median household income: $42,109 (2000); Poverty rate: 3.5% (2000).
Taxes: Total city taxes per capita: $263 (1997); City property taxes per capita: $256 (1997).
Education: High school graduation rate: 84.3% (2000); College graduation rate: 7.8% (2000).

School District(s)

Jesup Community School District (KG-12)
2000 Enrollment: 857 319-827-1700

Housing: Homeownership rate: 82.6% (2000); Median home value: $82,400 (2000); Median rent: $298 per month (2000); Median age of housing: 30 years (2000).
Newspapers: Citizen Herald (1 x week)
Transportation: Commute to work: 93.1% car, 0.0% public transportation, 4.4% walk, 1.6% work from home (2000); Travel time to work: 31.8% less than 15 minutes, 43.3% 15 to 30 minutes, 16.7% 30 to 45 minutes, 5.6% 45 to 60 minutes, 2.6% 60 minutes or more (2000)

Additional Information Contacts

Jesup Chamber of Commerce 319-827-3100

LAMONT (city). Covers a land area of 0.601 square miles and a water area of 0 square miles. Located at 42.60° N. Lat.; 91.64° W. Long.
History: There is no recorded reason for selecting the name of Lamont. The town has also been known as Erie and Ward's Corners.
Population: 503 (2000); Race: 99.0% White, 0.0% Black, 0.4% Asian, 0.0% American Indian and Alaska Native, 0.0% Hispanic of any race, 0.6% two or more races (2000); Density: 837.2 persons per square mile (2000); Age: 30.4% under 18, 13.4% over 64 (2000); Marriage status: 17.4% never married, 67.8% now married, 7.6% widowed, 7.3% divorced (2000); Foreign born: 0.0% (2000); Ancestry (includes multiple ancestries): 35.6% German, 8.6% English, 7.8% United States or American, 7.5% Irish, 5.7% Other groups (2000).
Economy: Single-family building permits issued: 1 (2001) / 3 (2000); Multi-family building permits issued: 0 (2001) / 0 (2000); Employment by occupation: 8.0% management, 9.0% professional, 15.1% services, 19.1% sales, 2.0% farming, 17.1% construction, 29.6% production (2000).
Income: Per capita income: $15,201 (2000); Median household income: $30,000 (2000); Poverty rate: 11.1% (2000).
Taxes: Total city taxes per capita: $205 (1997); City property taxes per capita: $132 (1997).
Education: High school graduation rate: 83.3% (2000); College graduation rate: 6.9% (2000).
Housing: Homeownership rate: 72.9% (2000); Median home value: $37,500 (2000); Median rent: $215 per month (2000); Median age of housing: 60+ years (2000).
Newspapers: Lamont Leader (1 x week)
Transportation: Commute to work: 93.9% car, 0.0% public transportation, 3.5% walk, 1.5% work from home (2000); Travel time to work: 28.7% less than 15 minutes, 32.3% 15 to 30 minutes, 14.9% 30 to 45 minutes, 6.2% 45 to 60 minutes, 17.9% 60 minutes or more (2000)

QUASQUETON (city). Covers a land area of 1.146 square miles and a water area of 0.033 square miles. Located at 42.39° N. Lat.; 91.75° W. Long.
History: Quasqueton, settled in 1842, derives its name from the Indian word meaning "swift running water."
Population: 574 (2000); Race: 97.1% White, 2.0% Black, 0.0% Asian, 0.0% American Indian and Alaska Native, 1.3% Hispanic of any race, 0.0% two or more races (2000); Density: 501.0 persons per square mile (2000); Age: 28.5% under 18, 14.2% over 64 (2000); Marriage status: 17.4% never married, 65.2% now married, 10.3% widowed, 7.2% divorced (2000); Foreign born: 0.9% (2000); Ancestry (includes multiple ancestries): 37.5% German, 18.1% Irish, 10.8% English, 10.1% United States or American, 6.5% Other groups (2000).
Economy: Employment by occupation: 3.9% management, 10.7% professional, 14.2% services, 19.7% sales, 2.1% farming, 18.5% construction, 30.9% production (2000).
Income: Per capita income: $15,913 (2000); Median household income: $36,518 (2000); Poverty rate: 9.9% (2000).
Taxes: Total city taxes per capita: $126 (1997); City property taxes per capita: $125 (1997).
Education: High school graduation rate: 77.3% (2000); College graduation rate: 6.1% (2000).
Housing: Homeownership rate: 82.3% (2000); Median home value: $64,800 (2000); Median rent: $323 per month (2000); Median age of housing: 36 years (2000).
Transportation: Commute to work: 90.7% car, 0.9% public transportation, 5.3% walk, 2.2% work from home (2000); Travel time to work: 28.6% less than 15 minutes, 21.8% 15 to 30 minutes, 20.0% 30 to 45 minutes, 24.1% 45 to 60 minutes, 5.5% 60 minutes or more (2000)

ROWLEY (city). Covers a land area of 0.360 square miles and a water area of 0 square miles. Located at 42.36° N. Lat.; 91.84° W. Long. Elevation is 990 feet.
History: Rowley was named for an official of the Burlington, Cedar Rapids & Northern Railroad, D. W. C. Rowley.
Population: 290 (2000); Race: 100.0% White, 0.0% Black, 0.0% Asian, 0.0% American Indian and Alaska Native, 0.0% Hispanic of any race, 0.0% two or more races (2000); Density: 806.3 persons per square mile (2000); Age: 28.2% under 18, 17.0% over 64 (2000); Marriage status: 13.7% never married, 68.3% now married, 8.4% widowed, 9.7% divorced (2000); Foreign born: 0.0% (2000); Ancestry (includes multiple ancestries): 47.3% German, 15.6% English, 10.2% United States or American, 9.5% Irish, 4.4% Polish (2000).
Economy: Employment by occupation: 13.1% management, 6.6% professional, 19.0% services, 16.1% sales, 0.0% farming, 12.4% construction, 32.8% production (2000).
Income: Per capita income: $17,315 (2000); Median household income: $36,563 (2000); Poverty rate: 7.1% (2000).

Taxes: Total city taxes per capita: $145 (2000); City property taxes per capita: $141 (2000).
Education: High school graduation rate: 80.7% (2000); College graduation rate: 6.1% (2000).
Housing: Homeownership rate: 91.2% (2000); Median home value: $62,300 (2000); Median rent: $350 per month (2000); Median age of housing: 46 years (2000).
Transportation: Commute to work: 92.7% car, 0.0% public transportation, 7.3% walk, 0.0% work from home (2000); Travel time to work: 23.4% less than 15 minutes, 31.4% 15 to 30 minutes, 30.7% 30 to 45 minutes, 10.9% 45 to 60 minutes, 3.6% 60 minutes or more (2000)

STANLEY (city). Covers a land area of 0.240 square miles and a water area of 0 square miles. Located at 42.64° N. Lat.; 91.81° W. Long.
History: Stanley was named for a relative of the landowners of the town site.
Population: 128 (2000); Race: 89.0% White, 1.6% Black, 0.0% Asian, 0.0% American Indian and Alaska Native, 3.1% Hispanic of any race, 9.4% two or more races (2000); Density: 532.5 persons per square mile (2000); Age: 44.1% under 18, 6.3% over 64 (2000); Marriage status: 15.9% never married, 74.4% now married, 4.9% widowed, 4.9% divorced (2000); Foreign born: 0.0% (2000); Ancestry (includes multiple ancestries): 35.4% German, 24.4% United States or American, 15.7% Irish, 15.7% Other groups, 3.9% English (2000).
Economy: Employment by occupation: 0.0% management, 13.7% professional, 17.6% services, 25.5% sales, 0.0% farming, 11.8% construction, 31.4% production (2000).
Income: Per capita income: $9,631 (2000); Median household income: $30,313 (2000); Poverty rate: 22.4% (2000).
Taxes: Total city taxes per capita: $102 (1997); City property taxes per capita: $34 (1997).
Education: High school graduation rate: 87.0% (2000); College graduation rate: 8.7% (2000).
Housing: Homeownership rate: 95.0% (2000); Median home value: $20,000 (2000); Median age of housing: 60+ years (2000).
Transportation: Commute to work: 89.8% car, 0.0% public transportation, 6.1% walk, 0.0% work from home (2000); Travel time to work: 30.6% less than 15 minutes, 49.0% 15 to 30 minutes, 6.1% 30 to 45 minutes, 4.1% 45 to 60 minutes, 10.2% 60 minutes or more (2000)

WINTHROP (city). Covers a land area of 0.580 square miles and a water area of 0 square miles. Located at 42.47° N. Lat.; 91.73° W. Long.
History: Winthrop was named for Winthrop, Maine.
Population: 772 (2000); Race: 98.7% White, 0.0% Black, 0.0% Asian, 0.3% American Indian and Alaska Native, 1.0% Hispanic of any race, 1.0% two or more races (2000); Density: 1,330.9 persons per square mile (2000); Age: 24.9% under 18, 14.9% over 64 (2000); Marriage status: 20.8% never married, 59.1% now married, 12.7% widowed, 7.5% divorced (2000); Foreign born: 0.3% (2000); Ancestry (includes multiple ancestries): 28.4% German, 17.3% Irish, 15.7% United States or American, 9.2% English, 7.1% Other groups (2000).
Economy: Employment by occupation: 9.8% management, 20.1% professional, 12.7% services, 24.0% sales, 0.5% farming, 7.4% construction, 25.5% production (2000).
Income: Per capita income: $19,183 (2000); Median household income: $36,136 (2000); Poverty rate: 5.7% (2000).
Taxes: Total city taxes per capita: $139 (1997); City property taxes per capita: $137 (1997).
Education: High school graduation rate: 91.0% (2000); College graduation rate: 18.9% (2000).

School District(s)

East Buchanan Community School District (PK-12)
2000 Enrollment: 652 319-935-3767

Housing: Homeownership rate: 80.2% (2000); Median home value: $64,000 (2000); Median rent: $267 per month (2000); Median age of housing: 45 years (2000).
Newspapers: The Winthrop News (1 x week)
Transportation: Commute to work: 86.6% car, 0.0% public transportation, 8.9% walk, 4.5% work from home (2000); Travel time to work: 52.8% less than 15 minutes, 21.5% 15 to 30 minutes, 12.4% 30 to 45 minutes, 8.0% 45 to 60 minutes, 5.2% 60 minutes or more (2000)

Buena Vista County

Located in northwestern Iowa; prairie area, drained by the Little Sioux River. Covers a land area of 574.80 square miles, a water area of 5.30 square miles, and is located in the Central Time Zone. The county government was organized in 1851. County seat is Storm Lake.

Weather Station: Sioux Rapids 4 E — Elevation: 1,417 feet

	Jan	Feb	Mar	Apr	May	Jun	Jul	Aug	Sep	Oct	Nov	Dec
High	24	31	43	59	72	81	84	81	74	61	42	28
Low	6	12	23	35	48	57	61	59	50	37	24	11
Precip	0.6	0.6	2.1	3.2	3.7	4.6	3.8	4.6	3.2	2.5	1.7	0.8
Snow	7.5	4.9	5.9	1.9	tr	0.0	0.0	0.0	tr	0.3	na	6.1

High and Low temperatures in degrees Fahrenheit; Precipitation and Snow in inches

Weather Station: Storm Lake 2 E — Elevation: 1,423 feet

	Jan	Feb	Mar	Apr	May	Jun	Jul	Aug	Sep	Oct	Nov	Dec
High	24	30	42	58	70	80	83	81	73	61	42	29
Low	5	12	23	35	47	57	61	59	50	38	24	12
Precip	0.6	0.6	2.0	3.7	4.2	5.1	4.6	4.6	3.6	2.6	1.6	0.9
Snow	7.7	6.7	7.2	2.4	tr	0.0	0.0	0.0	tr	0.3	4.5	7.0

High and Low temperatures in degrees Fahrenheit; Precipitation and Snow in inches

Population: 20,411 (2000); Race: 87.6% White, 0.5% Black, 4.3% Asian, 0.2% American Indian and Alaska Native, 12.5% Hispanic of any race, 1.6% two or more races (2000); Density: 35.5 persons per square mile (2000); Age: 25.3% under 18, 16.8% over 64 (2000).
Religion: Five largest groups: 15.4% Evangelical Lutheran Church in America, 13.0% Lutheran Church—Missouri Synod, 12.3% Catholic Church, 10.5% The United Methodist Church, 6.0% Presbyterian Church (U.S.A.) (2000).
Economy: Unemployment rate: 2.7% (11/2002); Total civilian labor force: 11,150 (11/2002); Leading industries: 34.2% manufacturing; 16.1% retail trade; 13.0% health care and social assistance (2000); Companies that employ more than 1,000 persons: 1 (2000); Companies that employ more than 100 persons: 9 (2000); Farms: 867 totaling 356,751 acres (1997); Minority business ownership rate: 0.0% (1997); Women business ownership rate: 13.2% (1997); Retail sales per capita: $9,784 (1997). Single-family building permits issued: 17 (2001) / 20 (2000); Multi-family building permits issued: 0 (2001) / 2 (2000).
Income: Per capita income: $16,042 (2000); Median household income: $35,300 (2000); Poverty rate: 10.5% (2000); Bankruptcy rate: 2.75% (2001).
Taxes: Total county taxes per capita: $220 (2000); County property taxes per capita: $219 (2000).
Education: High school graduation rate: 81.3% (2000); College graduation rate: 18.7% (2000).
Housing: Homeownership rate: 70.5% (2000); Median home value: $64,900 (2000); Median rent: $320 per month (2000); Median age of housing: 49 years (2000).
Health: Birth rate: 115.1 per 10,000 population (1998); Age adjusted death rate: 84.1 per 10,000 population (1999); Age adjusted cancer mortality rate: 248.2 deaths per 100,000 population (1999). Number of physicians: 7.3 per 10,000 population (1999); Number of hospital beds: 14.7 per 10,000 population (1999).
Elections: 2000 Presidential election results: 41.3% Gore, 54.6% Bush, 2.9% Nader, 0.7% Buchanan
National and State Parks: Storm Lake State Wildlife Management Area
Additional Information Contacts
Buena Vista County Government Offices 712-749-2542
Storm Lake Chamber of Commerce. 712-732-3780
United Counties Board of Realtors 712-732-2143

Buena Vista County Communities

ALBERT CITY (city). Covers a land area of 0.544 square miles and a water area of 0 square miles. Located at 42.78° N. Lat.; 94.95° W. Long. Elevation is 1,325 feet.
History: Albert City was originally called Manthorp. The name was changed in 1900 after a variation of Albertina, the first name of Mrs. George Anderson.
Population: 709 (2000); Race: 98.2% White, 0.0% Black, 1.1% Asian, 0.0% American Indian and Alaska Native, 0.7% Hispanic of any race, 0.7% two or more races (2000); Density: 1,302.9 persons per square mile (2000); Age: 28.5% under 18, 19.1% over 64 (2000); Marriage status: 18.2% never married, 70.5% now married, 7.1% widowed, 4.2% divorced (2000); Foreign born: 4.6% (2000); Ancestry (includes multiple ancestries): 48.1% German, 24.9% Swedish, 10.8% Norwegian, 5.8% Irish, 5.5% United States or American (2000).
Economy: Single-family building permits issued: 0 (2001) / 0 (2000); Multi-family building permits issued: 0 (2001) / 0 (2000); Employment by

occupation: 9.4% management, 17.9% professional, 17.4% services, 19.3% sales, 5.2% farming, 9.4% construction, 21.5% production (2000).
Income: Per capita income: $15,219 (2000); Median household income: $33,188 (2000); Poverty rate: 9.5% (2000).
Taxes: Total city taxes per capita: $331 (2000); City property taxes per capita: $244 (2000).
Education: High school graduation rate: 86.9% (2000); College graduation rate: 14.1% (2000).

School District(s)

Albert City-Truesdale Community School District (PK-12)
2000 Enrollment: 260 712-843-5496
Housing: Homeownership rate: 80.9% (2000); Median home value: $38,100 (2000); Median rent: $245 per month (2000); Median age of housing: 51 years (2000).
Transportation: Commute to work: 86.3% car, 0.0% public transportation, 10.9% walk, 2.5% work from home (2000); Travel time to work: 54.6% less than 15 minutes, 22.1% 15 to 30 minutes, 16.7% 30 to 45 minutes, 2.0% 45 to 60 minutes, 4.6% 60 minutes or more (2000)

ALTA (city). Covers a land area of 1.047 square miles and a water area of 0 square miles. Located at 42.67° N. Lat.; 95.30° W. Long. Elevation is 1,509 feet.
History: Alta was named for Altai Blair, daughter of John Blair, an early settler. George Alfred Carlson (1876-1926), elected Governor of Colorado in 1914, was born in Alta. Aurelia, Iowa, was named for another daughter of John Blair.
Population: 1,865 (2000); Race: 93.0% White, 0.7% Black, 1.2% Asian, 0.1% American Indian and Alaska Native, 10.0% Hispanic of any race, 2.1% two or more races (2000); Density: 1,780.4 persons per square mile (2000); Age: 28.1% under 18, 15.0% over 64 (2000); Marriage status: 22.0% never married, 58.9% now married, 7.8% widowed, 11.3% divorced (2000); Foreign born: 5.0% (2000); Ancestry (includes multiple ancestries): 39.1% German, 15.8% Other groups, 11.0% Irish, 7.0% Norwegian, 6.9% Swedish (2000).
Economy: Single-family building permits issued: 6 (2001) / 1 (2000); Multi-family building permits issued: 0 (2001) / 0 (2000); Employment by occupation: 10.6% management, 14.1% professional, 16.2% services, 25.7% sales, 2.3% farming, 9.2% construction, 21.9% production (2000).
Income: Per capita income: $15,908 (2000); Median household income: $31,941 (2000); Poverty rate: 11.3% (2000).
Taxes: Total city taxes per capita: $183 (1997); City property taxes per capita: $122 (1997).
Education: High school graduation rate: 87.2% (2000); College graduation rate: 16.8% (2000).

School District(s)

Alta Community School District (KG-12)
2000 Enrollment: 626 712-284-1010
Housing: Homeownership rate: 73.0% (2000); Median home value: $69,500 (2000); Median rent: $335 per month (2000); Median age of housing: 47 years (2000).
Transportation: Commute to work: 92.7% car, 0.7% public transportation, 3.3% walk, 3.1% work from home (2000); Travel time to work: 59.9% less than 15 minutes, 29.5% 15 to 30 minutes, 5.0% 30 to 45 minutes, 1.9% 45 to 60 minutes, 3.8% 60 minutes or more (2000)

LAKESIDE (city). Covers a land area of 0.182 square miles and a water area of 0 square miles. Located at 42.62° N. Lat.; 95.17° W. Long.
History: Lakeside is believed to have been part of a local farm, Lakeside Stock Farm
Population: 484 (2000); Race: 66.0% White, 0.0% Black, 10.5% Asian, 2.7% American Indian and Alaska Native, 25.4% Hispanic of any race, 1.2% two or more races (2000); Density: 2,662.6 persons per square mile (2000); Age: 29.5% under 18, 9.1% over 64 (2000); Marriage status: 24.0% never married, 63.4% now married, 6.6% widowed, 6.1% divorced (2000); Foreign born: 21.9% (2000); Ancestry (includes multiple ancestries): 33.0% Other groups, 26.4% German, 9.9% Irish, 7.4% Swedish, 5.4% English (2000).
Economy: Single-family building permits issued: 6 (2001) / 2 (2000); Multi-family building permits issued: 0 (2001) / 0 (2000); Employment by occupation: 8.6% management, 13.4% professional, 11.2% services, 33.2% sales, 0.0% farming, 4.3% construction, 29.3% production (2000).
Income: Per capita income: $15,724 (2000); Median household income: $39,135 (2000); Poverty rate: 7.3% (2000).
Taxes: Total city taxes per capita: $139 (1997); City property taxes per capita: $82 (1997).
Education: High school graduation rate: 78.5% (2000); College graduation rate: 15.5% (2000).
Housing: Homeownership rate: 82.1% (2000); Median home value: $75,300 (2000); Median rent: $369 per month (2000); Median age of housing: 30 years (2000).
Transportation: Commute to work: 97.8% car, 0.0% public transportation, 0.0% walk, 2.2% work from home (2000); Travel time to work: 78.4% less than 15 minutes, 13.7% 15 to 30 minutes, 3.5% 30 to 45 minutes, 0.9% 45 to 60 minutes, 3.5% 60 minutes or more (2000)

LINN GROVE (city). Covers a land area of 0.594 square miles and a water area of 0.014 square miles. Located at 42.89° N. Lat.; 95.24° W. Long. Elevation is 1,257 feet.
History: Linn Grove got its name from the linden trees in the area. The town was also once known as Sweet's Mill.
Population: 211 (2000); Race: 95.7% White, 0.0% Black, 0.0% Asian, 0.0% American Indian and Alaska Native, 4.3% Hispanic of any race, 0.0% two or more races (2000); Density: 355.1 persons per square mile (2000); Age: 22.0% under 18, 23.0% over 64 (2000); Marriage status: 21.1% never married, 54.4% now married, 11.1% widowed, 13.5% divorced (2000); Foreign born: 3.3% (2000); Ancestry (includes multiple ancestries): 43.5% German, 10.5% Irish, 8.6% English, 8.1% Norwegian, 8.1% Danish (2000).
Economy: Employment by occupation: 15.8% management, 16.7% professional, 8.8% services, 19.3% sales, 10.5% farming, 7.0% construction, 21.9% production (2000).
Income: Per capita income: $22,945 (2000); Median household income: $33,125 (2000); Poverty rate: 5.3% (2000).
Taxes: Total city taxes per capita: $146 (1997); City property taxes per capita: $86 (1997).
Education: High school graduation rate: 82.8% (2000); College graduation rate: 21.9% (2000).
Housing: Homeownership rate: 88.0% (2000); Median home value: $21,400 (2000); Median rent: $119 per month (2000); Median age of housing: 60+ years (2000).
Transportation: Commute to work: 96.5% car, 0.0% public transportation, 1.8% walk, 1.8% work from home (2000); Travel time to work: 45.5% less than 15 minutes, 17.0% 15 to 30 minutes, 33.9% 30 to 45 minutes, 1.8% 45 to 60 minutes, 1.8% 60 minutes or more (2000)

MARATHON (city). Covers a land area of 0.732 square miles and a water area of 0 square miles. Located at 42.86° N. Lat.; 94.98° W. Long. Elevation is 1,395 feet.
History: Marathon is believed to be named in honor of the historic Greek battlefield.
Population: 302 (2000); Race: 97.5% White, 0.0% Black, 1.8% Asian, 0.0% American Indian and Alaska Native, 1.4% Hispanic of any race, 0.7% two or more races (2000); Density: 412.7 persons per square mile (2000); Age: 22.5% under 18, 22.5% over 64 (2000); Marriage status: 16.6% never married, 62.3% now married, 9.4% widowed, 11.7% divorced (2000); Foreign born: 1.8% (2000); Ancestry (includes multiple ancestries): 26.1% German, 11.3% English, 9.2% Other groups, 8.1% Irish, 8.1% Swedish (2000).
Economy: Employment by occupation: 3.3% management, 3.3% professional, 26.4% services, 25.6% sales, 4.1% farming, 9.1% construction, 28.1% production (2000).
Income: Per capita income: $12,751 (2000); Median household income: $20,982 (2000); Poverty rate: 22.5% (2000).
Taxes: Total city taxes per capita: $241 (1997); City property taxes per capita: $172 (1997).
Education: High school graduation rate: 82.2% (2000); College graduation rate: 10.3% (2000).
Housing: Homeownership rate: 79.3% (2000); Median home value: $16,200 (2000); Median rent: $157 per month (2000); Median age of housing: 60+ years (2000).
Transportation: Commute to work: 90.5% car, 0.0% public transportation, 5.2% walk, 4.3% work from home (2000); Travel time to work: 29.7% less than 15 minutes, 27.0% 15 to 30 minutes, 22.5% 30 to 45 minutes, 9.9% 45 to 60 minutes, 10.8% 60 minutes or more (2000)

NEWELL (city). Covers a land area of 1.255 square miles and a water area of 0 square miles. Located at 42.60° N. Lat.; 95.00° W. Long. Elevation is 1,264 feet.
History: Newell was founded in 1869 as a station on the Dubuque & Sioux City Railroad line.
Population: 887 (2000); Race: 96.3% White, 0.2% Black, 0.2% Asian, 0.0% American Indian and Alaska Native, 3.5% Hispanic of any race, 0.0% two or more races (2000); Density: 706.9 persons per square mile (2000); Age: 26.5% under 18, 24.7% over 64 (2000); Marriage status: 17.9% never

married, 59.7% now married, 14.0% widowed, 8.4% divorced (2000); Foreign born: 2.2% (2000); Ancestry (includes multiple ancestries): 33.4% German, 11.1% English, 10.0% Danish, 8.3% United States or American, 6.6% Norwegian (2000).
Economy: Single-family building permits issued: 0 (2001) / 1 (2000); Multi-family building permits issued: 0 (2001) / 2 (2000); Employment by occupation: 11.1% management, 17.1% professional, 14.9% services, 25.7% sales, 1.6% farming, 9.8% construction, 19.8% production (2000).
Income: Per capita income: $13,554 (2000); Median household income: $31,204 (2000); Poverty rate: 8.7% (2000).
Taxes: Total city taxes per capita: $223 (1997); City property taxes per capita: $158 (1997).
Education: High school graduation rate: 83.4% (2000); College graduation rate: 14.7% (2000).

School District(s)

Newell-Fonda Community School District (KG-12)
2000 Enrollment: 470 712-272-3324
Housing: Homeownership rate: 84.0% (2000); Median home value: $46,700 (2000); Median rent: $253 per month (2000); Median age of housing: 57 years (2000).
Newspapers: Buena Vista County Journal (1 x week)
Transportation: Commute to work: 84.7% car, 0.0% public transportation, 10.4% walk, 3.0% work from home (2000); Travel time to work: 48.3% less than 15 minutes, 43.8% 15 to 30 minutes, 1.7% 30 to 45 minutes, 1.4% 45 to 60 minutes, 4.8% 60 minutes or more (2000)

REMBRANDT (city). Covers a land area of 0.204 square miles and a water area of 0 square miles. Located at 42.82° N. Lat.; 95.16° W. Long. Elevation is 1,333 feet.
History: Rembrandt grew out of a work camp housing employees during the construction of the Minnesota and St. Louis Railroad. First named in honor of Barney Orsland, on whose farm the town was laid out in 1899, it was later renamed for the Dutch painter.
Population: 228 (2000); Race: 100.0% White, 0.0% Black, 0.0% Asian, 0.0% American Indian and Alaska Native, 0.0% Hispanic of any race, 0.0% two or more races (2000); Density: 1,116.9 persons per square mile (2000); Age: 27.7% under 18, 12.1% over 64 (2000); Marriage status: 16.8% never married, 61.8% now married, 9.2% widowed, 12.1% divorced (2000); Foreign born: 0.0% (2000); Ancestry (includes multiple ancestries): 38.4% German, 16.5% Irish, 14.3% Norwegian, 13.8% English, 10.7% United States or American (2000).
Economy: Single-family building permits issued: 0 (2001) / 0 (2000); Multi-family building permits issued: 0 (2001) / 0 (2000); Employment by occupation: 12.6% management, 7.2% professional, 10.8% services, 33.3% sales, 1.8% farming, 7.2% construction, 27.0% production (2000).
Income: Per capita income: $17,248 (2000); Median household income: $34,375 (2000); Poverty rate: 4.0% (2000).
Taxes: Total city taxes per capita: $111 (1997); City property taxes per capita: $56 (1997).
Education: High school graduation rate: 83.3% (2000); College graduation rate: 11.8% (2000).
Housing: Homeownership rate: 78.9% (2000); Median home value: $30,800 (2000); Median rent: $189 per month (2000); Median age of housing: 57 years (2000).
Transportation: Commute to work: 89.2% car, 0.0% public transportation, 8.1% walk, 2.7% work from home (2000); Travel time to work: 20.4% less than 15 minutes, 39.8% 15 to 30 minutes, 30.6% 30 to 45 minutes, 1.9% 45 to 60 minutes, 7.4% 60 minutes or more (2000)

SIOUX RAPIDS (city). Covers a land area of 0.821 square miles and a water area of 0 square miles. Located at 42.89° N. Lat.; 95.14° W. Long. Elevation is 1,272 feet.
History: Sioux Rapids was platted in 1858 by Luther H. Barnes, who dreamed of seeing a great city grow here on the banks of the Little Sioux River. The community failed to thrive, and when Barnes left, heart-broken and impoverished, the other residents used his former town stakes for kindling wood.
Population: 720 (2000); Race: 98.0% White, 0.0% Black, 0.0% Asian, 0.0% American Indian and Alaska Native, 5.5% Hispanic of any race, 1.2% two or more races (2000); Density: 877.0 persons per square mile (2000); Age: 25.9% under 18, 23.5% over 64 (2000); Marriage status: 17.5% never married, 60.5% now married, 11.0% widowed, 11.0% divorced (2000); Foreign born: 2.6% (2000); Ancestry (includes multiple ancestries): 38.8% German, 12.8% Norwegian, 10.6% Irish, 8.8% English, 8.6% Other groups (2000).
Economy: Single-family building permits issued: 0 (2001) / 0 (2000); Multi-family building permits issued: 0 (2001) / 0 (2000); Employment by occupation: 14.0% management, 15.2% professional, 12.3% services, 20.2% sales, 4.4% farming, 9.6% construction, 24.3% production (2000).
Income: Per capita income: $16,759 (2000); Median household income: $33,250 (2000); Poverty rate: 6.4% (2000).
Taxes: Total city taxes per capita: $215 (1997); City property taxes per capita: $154 (1997).
Education: High school graduation rate: 84.2% (2000); College graduation rate: 13.0% (2000).

School District(s)

Sioux Central Community School District (PK-12)
2000 Enrollment: 574 712-283-2571
Housing: Homeownership rate: 78.2% (2000); Median home value: $39,500 (2000); Median rent: $239 per month (2000); Median age of housing: 60+ years (2000).
Newspapers: Sioux Rapids Bulletin (1 x week)
Transportation: Commute to work: 91.2% car, 0.0% public transportation, 4.8% walk, 3.3% work from home (2000); Travel time to work: 39.4% less than 15 minutes, 30.0% 15 to 30 minutes, 20.3% 30 to 45 minutes, 3.8% 45 to 60 minutes, 6.6% 60 minutes or more (2000)

STORM LAKE (city). Covers a land area of 3.997 square miles and a water area of 0 square miles. Located at 42.64° N. Lat.; 95.20° W. Long. Elevation is 1,434 feet.
History: Buena Vista College (formerly Fort Dodge Presbytery College) was moved to Storm Lake in 1891 after the town donated eight acres of land and $25,000.
Population: 10,076 (2000); Race: 79.5% White, 0.6% Black, 7.6% Asian, 0.3% American Indian and Alaska Native, 20.7% Hispanic of any race, 2.4% two or more races (2000); Density: 2,521.2 persons per square mile (2000); Age: 24.4% under 18, 16.8% over 64 (2000); Marriage status: 33.9% never married, 52.1% now married, 8.4% widowed, 5.6% divorced (2000); Foreign born: 21.5% (2000); Ancestry (includes multiple ancestries): 31.8% German, 27.7% Other groups, 8.6% Irish, 5.7% English, 5.0% Swedish (2000).
Economy: Single-family building permits issued: 5 (2001) / 5 (2000); Multi-family building permits issued: 0 (2001) / 0 (2000); Employment by occupation: 8.8% management, 14.6% professional, 14.0% services, 25.2% sales, 1.1% farming, 6.9% construction, 29.3% production (2000).
Income: Per capita income: $15,150 (2000); Median household income: $35,270 (2000); Poverty rate: 11.6% (2000).
Taxes: Total city taxes per capita: $287 (2000); City property taxes per capita: $212 (2000).
Education: High school graduation rate: 73.3% (2000); College graduation rate: 19.5% (2000).

School District(s)

Storm Lake Community School District (PK-12)
2000 Enrollment: 1,918 712-732-8060

Four-year College(s)

Buena Vista University (Private, Not-for-profit, Presbyterian Church (USA))
2001 Enrollment: 2,910 712-749-2400
2001 Tuition: In-state $17,846; Out-of-state $17,846

Two-year College(s)

Faust Institute of Cosmetology (Private, For-profit)
2001 Enrollment: 33 712-732-6570
Housing: Homeownership rate: 63.6% (2000); Median home value: $71,300 (2000); Median rent: $356 per month (2000); Median age of housing: 45 years (2000).
Hospitals: Buena Vista Regional Medical Centre (54 beds)
Safety: Violent crime rate: 19.9 per 10,000 population; Property crime rate: 257.3 per 10,000 population (2001).
Newspapers: The Storm Lake Times (2 x week); Pilot-Tribune (3 x week); Buena Vista Shopper (1 x week)
Transportation: Commute to work: 84.2% car, 0.3% public transportation, 11.3% walk, 2.5% work from home (2000); Travel time to work: 83.9% less than 15 minutes, 7.8% 15 to 30 minutes, 3.5% 30 to 45 minutes, 2.3% 45 to 60 minutes, 2.4% 60 minutes or more (2000)

Additional Information Contacts

Storm Lake Chamber of Commerce. 712-732-3780
United Counties Board of Realtors 712-732-2143

TRUESDALE (city). Covers a land area of 0.140 square miles and a water area of 0 square miles. Located at 42.72° N. Lat.; 95.18° W. Long. Elevation is 1,360 feet.
History: Truesdale was named for W. H. Truesdale, a Minnesota and St. Louis Railroad official. The first general store was opened in 1901.

Population: 91 (2000); Race: 100.0% White, 0.0% Black, 0.0% Asian, 0.0% American Indian and Alaska Native, 0.0% Hispanic of any race, 0.0% two or more races (2000); Density: 649.3 persons per square mile (2000); Age: 13.9% under 18, 12.9% over 64 (2000); Marriage status: 18.0% never married, 53.9% now married, 6.7% widowed, 21.3% divorced (2000); Foreign born: 0.0% (2000); Ancestry (includes multiple ancestries): 39.6% German, 13.9% Irish, 9.9% Swedish, 7.9% French (except Basque), 5.0% Italian (2000).
Economy: Single-family building permits issued: 0 (2001) / 0 (2000); Multi-family building permits issued: 0 (2001) / 0 (2000); Employment by occupation: 10.3% management, 3.4% professional, 17.2% services, 29.3% sales, 3.4% farming, 22.4% construction, 13.8% production (2000).
Income: Per capita income: $15,410 (2000); Median household income: $29,063 (2000); Poverty rate: 4.0% (2000).
Taxes: Total city taxes per capita: $200 (1997); City property taxes per capita: $136 (1997).
Education: High school graduation rate: 84.8% (2000); College graduation rate: 5.1% (2000).
Housing: Homeownership rate: 91.5% (2000); Median home value: $23,500 (2000); Median rent: $225 per month (2000); Median age of housing: 60 years (2000).
Transportation: Commute to work: 87.9% car, 0.0% public transportation, 6.9% walk, 5.2% work from home (2000); Travel time to work: 47.3% less than 15 minutes, 49.1% 15 to 30 minutes, 3.6% 30 to 45 minutes, 0.0% 45 to 60 minutes, 0.0% 60 minutes or more (2000)

Butler County

Located in north central Iowa; prairie area, drained by the Shell Rock River. Covers a land area of 580.40 square miles, a water area of 1.20 square miles, and is located in the Central Time Zone. The county government was organized in 1851. County seat is Allison.

Weather Station: Allison Elevation: 1,049 feet

	Jan	Feb	Mar	Apr	May	Jun	Jul	Aug	Sep	Oct	Nov	Dec
High	25	31	44	60	72	82	85	82	75	62	44	30
Low	8	14	25	37	49	59	62	60	52	40	27	14
Precip	0.8	0.9	1.8	3.2	4.4	4.8	4.4	4.3	3.5	2.6	2.1	1.0
Snow	8.7	6.9	5.3	1.8	0.0	0.0	0.0	0.0	0.0	tr	4.8	6.4

High and Low temperatures in degrees Fahrenheit; Precipitation and Snow in inches

Population: 15,305 (2000); Race: 99.1% White, 0.1% Black, 0.2% Asian, 0.0% American Indian and Alaska Native, 0.5% Hispanic of any race, 0.5% two or more races (2000); Density: 26.4 persons per square mile (2000); Age: 24.6% under 18, 20.2% over 64 (2000).
Religion: Five largest groups: 25.2% Evangelical Lutheran Church in America, 11.1% Reformed Church in America, 10.6% The United Methodist Church, 7.5% United Church of Christ, 6.7% Catholic Church (2000).
Economy: Unemployment rate: 4.8% (11/2002); Total civilian labor force: 6,841 (11/2002); Leading industries: 22.4% manufacturing; 16.4% retail trade; 16.1% health care and social assistance (2000); Companies that employ more than 1,000 persons: 0 (2000); Companies that employ more than 100 persons: 2 (2000); Farms: 1,085 totaling 324,282 acres (1997); Minority business ownership rate: 0.0% (1997); Women business ownership rate: 21.1% (1997); Retail sales per capita: $4,300 (1997). Single-family building permits issued: 19 (2001) / 21 (2000); Multi-family building permits issued: 0 (2001) / 0 (2000).
Income: Per capita income: $17,036 (2000); Median household income: $35,883 (2000); Poverty rate: 8.0% (2000); Bankruptcy rate: 3.40% (2001).
Taxes: Total county taxes per capita: $260 (2000); County property taxes per capita: $260 (2000).
Education: High school graduation rate: 82.2% (2000); College graduation rate: 12.4% (2000).
Housing: Homeownership rate: 80.4% (2000); Median home value: $62,200 (2000); Median rent: $239 per month (2000); Median age of housing: 55 years (2000).
Health: Birth rate: 105.9 per 10,000 population (1998); Age adjusted death rate: 71.5 per 10,000 population (1999); Age adjusted cancer mortality rate: 184.7 deaths per 100,000 population (1999). Number of physicians: 1.3 per 10,000 population (1999); Number of hospital beds: n/a (1999).
Elections: 2000 Presidential election results: 40.7% Gore, 57.1% Bush, 1.7% Nader, 0.2% Buchanan
National and State Parks: Heery Woods State Park
Additional Information Contacts
Butler County Government Offices 319-267-2670

Butler County Communities

ALLISON (city). Covers a land area of 2.949 square miles and a water area of 0 square miles. Located at 42.75° N. Lat.; 92.79° W. Long. Elevation is 1,044 feet.
History: Allison was named for William Boyd Allison, a U.S. Senator from Iowa.
Population: 1,006 (2000); Race: 100.0% White, 0.0% Black, 0.0% Asian, 0.0% American Indian and Alaska Native, 0.0% Hispanic of any race, 0.0% two or more races (2000); Density: 341.2 persons per square mile (2000); Age: 21.2% under 18, 31.2% over 64 (2000); Marriage status: 13.4% never married, 62.7% now married, 15.4% widowed, 8.4% divorced (2000); Foreign born: 0.8% (2000); Ancestry (includes multiple ancestries): 60.2% German, 7.3% Irish, 6.5% Norwegian, 6.4% English, 5.4% Dutch (2000).
Economy: Single-family building permits issued: 0 (2001) / 0 (2000); Multi-family building permits issued: 0 (2001) / 0 (2000); Employment by occupation: 12.6% management, 13.3% professional, 20.7% services, 23.1% sales, 0.0% farming, 12.9% construction, 17.4% production (2000).
Income: Per capita income: $16,472 (2000); Median household income: $34,338 (2000); Poverty rate: 8.9% (2000).
Taxes: Total city taxes per capita: $226 (1997); City property taxes per capita: $211 (1997).
Education: High school graduation rate: 81.1% (2000); College graduation rate: 11.2% (2000).

School District(s)

Allison-Bristow Community School District (KG-12)
2000 Enrollment: 350 319-267-2205
Housing: Homeownership rate: 81.3% (2000); Median home value: $53,900 (2000); Median rent: $246 per month (2000); Median age of housing: 47 years (2000).
Newspapers: Butler County Tribune Journal (1 x week)
Transportation: Commute to work: 86.8% car, 0.0% public transportation, 6.1% walk, 6.6% work from home (2000); Travel time to work: 46.5% less than 15 minutes, 25.6% 15 to 30 minutes, 14.8% 30 to 45 minutes, 6.6% 45 to 60 minutes, 6.6% 60 minutes or more (2000)

APLINGTON (city). Covers a land area of 0.580 square miles and a water area of 0 square miles. Located at 42.58° N. Lat.; 92.88° W. Long.
History: Aplington was named for Zenas Aplington, the town's first storekeeper.
Population: 1,054 (2000); Race: 100.0% White, 0.0% Black, 0.0% Asian, 0.0% American Indian and Alaska Native, 0.0% Hispanic of any race, 0.0% two or more races (2000); Density: 1,818.0 persons per square mile (2000); Age: 22.2% under 18, 31.5% over 64 (2000); Marriage status: 12.6% never married, 63.5% now married, 16.6% widowed, 7.3% divorced (2000); Foreign born: 1.2% (2000); Ancestry (includes multiple ancestries): 58.9% German, 8.5% United States or American, 7.0% Dutch, 4.7% English, 4.6% Irish (2000).
Economy: Single-family building permits issued: 0 (2001) / 0 (2000); Multi-family building permits issued: 0 (2001) / 0 (2000); Employment by occupation: 10.6% management, 16.2% professional, 20.8% services, 25.6% sales, 1.2% farming, 5.1% construction, 20.5% production (2000).
Income: Per capita income: $17,527 (2000); Median household income: $32,440 (2000); Poverty rate: 8.9% (2000).
Taxes: Total city taxes per capita: $240 (1997); City property taxes per capita: $230 (1997).
Education: High school graduation rate: 72.7% (2000); College graduation rate: 15.9% (2000).

School District(s)

Aplington Community School District (KG-12)
2000 Enrollment: 372 319-347-2394
Housing: Homeownership rate: 83.3% (2000); Median home value: $65,200 (2000); Median rent: $225 per month (2000); Median age of housing: 45 years (2000).
Transportation: Commute to work: 90.5% car, 0.0% public transportation, 5.6% walk, 3.9% work from home (2000); Travel time to work: 46.8% less than 15 minutes, 17.6% 15 to 30 minutes, 23.9% 30 to 45 minutes, 8.7% 45 to 60 minutes, 3.1% 60 minutes or more (2000)

AREDALE (city). Covers a land area of 1.000 square miles and a water area of 0 square miles. Located at 42.83° N. Lat.; 93.00° W. Long. Elevation is 1,023 feet.
Population: 89 (2000); Race: 100.0% White, 0.0% Black, 0.0% Asian, 0.0% American Indian and Alaska Native, 0.0% Hispanic of any race, 0.0% two or more races (2000); Density: 89.0 persons per square mile (2000); Age: 26.7%

under 18, 36.0% over 64 (2000); Marriage status: 3.5% never married, 61.4% now married, 21.1% widowed, 14.0% divorced (2000); Foreign born: 0.0% (2000); Ancestry (includes multiple ancestries): 50.7% German, 17.3% United States or American, 10.7% Other groups, 9.3% English, 5.3% Irish (2000).
Economy: Grain storage. Single-family building permits issued: 0 (2001) / 0 (2000); Multi-family building permits issued: 0 (2001) / 0 (2000); Employment by occupation: 10.0% management, 0.0% professional, 26.7% services, 26.7% sales, 0.0% farming, 26.7% construction, 10.0% production (2000).
Income: Per capita income: $15,579 (2000); Median household income: $32,500 (2000); Poverty rate: 5.3% (2000).
Taxes: Total city taxes per capita: $179 (1997); City property taxes per capita: $167 (1997).
Education: High school graduation rate: 74.5% (2000); College graduation rate: 0.0% (2000).
Housing: Homeownership rate: 94.6% (2000); Median home value: $13,800 (2000); Median age of housing: 60+ years (2000).
Transportation: Commute to work: 66.7% car, 0.0% public transportation, 23.3% walk, 10.0% work from home (2000); Travel time to work: 51.9% less than 15 minutes, 7.4% 15 to 30 minutes, 33.3% 30 to 45 minutes, 0.0% 45 to 60 minutes, 7.4% 60 minutes or more (2000)

BRISTOW (city). Covers a land area of 0.933 square miles and a water area of 0 square miles. Located at 42.77° N. Lat.; 92.90° W. Long.
History: Bristow was first known as West Point.
Population: 202 (2000); Race: 99.0% White, 0.0% Black, 1.0% Asian, 0.0% American Indian and Alaska Native, 0.0% Hispanic of any race, 0.0% two or more races (2000); Density: 216.6 persons per square mile (2000); Age: 27.8% under 18, 12.6% over 64 (2000); Marriage status: 19.3% never married, 70.0% now married, 4.7% widowed, 6.0% divorced (2000); Foreign born: 1.0% (2000); Ancestry (includes multiple ancestries): 61.6% German, 9.1% Irish, 6.6% English, 5.1% Other groups, 4.5% United States or American (2000).
Economy: Single-family building permits issued: 4 (2001) / 0 (2000); Multi-family building permits issued: 0 (2001) / 0 (2000); Employment by occupation: 7.9% management, 2.2% professional, 20.2% services, 21.3% sales, 6.7% farming, 11.2% construction, 30.3% production (2000).
Income: Per capita income: $11,305 (2000); Median household income: $30,625 (2000); Poverty rate: 17.7% (2000).
Taxes: Total city taxes per capita: $77 (1997); City property taxes per capita: $62 (1997).
Education: High school graduation rate: 81.1% (2000); College graduation rate: 0.0% (2000).
Housing: Homeownership rate: 89.3% (2000); Median home value: $27,300 (2000); Median rent: $206 per month (2000); Median age of housing: 60+ years (2000).
Transportation: Commute to work: 96.6% car, 0.0% public transportation, 3.4% walk, 0.0% work from home (2000); Travel time to work: 39.3% less than 15 minutes, 41.6% 15 to 30 minutes, 11.2% 30 to 45 minutes, 7.9% 45 to 60 minutes, 0.0% 60 minutes or more (2000)

CLARKSVILLE (city). Covers a land area of 1.365 square miles and a water area of 0.013 square miles. Located at 42.78° N. Lat.; 92.67° W. Long. Elevation is 924 feet.
History: Clarksville was laid out by Thomas and Jeremiah Clark and D.C. Hilton. The Clarks gave their name to the town.
Population: 1,441 (2000); Race: 98.1% White, 0.2% Black, 0.7% Asian, 0.1% American Indian and Alaska Native, 0.1% Hispanic of any race, 0.8% two or more races (2000); Density: 1,056.0 persons per square mile (2000); Age: 25.0% under 18, 21.5% over 64 (2000); Marriage status: 17.9% never married, 57.9% now married, 14.8% widowed, 9.5% divorced (2000); Foreign born: 0.7% (2000); Ancestry (includes multiple ancestries): 51.9% German, 8.3% Irish, 7.0% English, 6.3% United States or American, 3.6% Dutch (2000).
Economy: Single-family building permits issued: 0 (2001) / 0 (2000); Multi-family building permits issued: 0 (2001) / 0 (2000); Employment by occupation: 7.2% management, 13.6% professional, 19.7% services, 20.0% sales, 1.7% farming, 10.2% construction, 27.6% production (2000).
Income: Per capita income: $14,811 (2000); Median household income: $32,857 (2000); Poverty rate: 9.7% (2000).
Taxes: Total city taxes per capita: $161 (1997); City property taxes per capita: $156 (1997).
Education: High school graduation rate: 76.2% (2000); College graduation rate: 8.7% (2000).

School District(s)
Clarksville Community School District (PK-12)
2000 Enrollment: 408 319-278-4008
Housing: Homeownership rate: 77.0% (2000); Median home value: $52,200 (2000); Median rent: $261 per month (2000); Median age of housing: 59 years (2000).
Newspapers: The Clarksville Star (1 x week)
Transportation: Commute to work: 89.6% car, 0.3% public transportation, 5.3% walk, 4.5% work from home (2000); Travel time to work: 29.9% less than 15 minutes, 44.5% 15 to 30 minutes, 17.1% 30 to 45 minutes, 4.9% 45 to 60 minutes, 3.6% 60 minutes or more (2000)

DUMONT (city). Covers a land area of 1.754 square miles and a water area of 0 square miles. Located at 42.74° N. Lat.; 92.97° W. Long.
History: Dumont was founded by S.B. Dumont, a businessman in the area, and was probably named for him.
Population: 676 (2000); Race: 97.0% White, 0.0% Black, 0.0% Asian, 0.0% American Indian and Alaska Native, 4.5% Hispanic of any race, 0.0% two or more races (2000); Density: 385.4 persons per square mile (2000); Age: 21.0% under 18, 29.0% over 64 (2000); Marriage status: 19.7% never married, 54.2% now married, 17.1% widowed, 9.0% divorced (2000); Foreign born: 3.6% (2000); Ancestry (includes multiple ancestries): 47.2% German, 7.3% United States or American, 7.0% Irish, 6.1% Norwegian, 6.1% English (2000).
Economy: Single-family building permits issued: 1 (2001) / 1 (2000); Multi-family building permits issued: 0 (2001) / 0 (2000); Employment by occupation: 5.6% management, 12.5% professional, 17.5% services, 24.8% sales, 3.0% farming, 10.9% construction, 25.7% production (2000).
Income: Per capita income: $15,260 (2000); Median household income: $27,708 (2000); Poverty rate: 8.7% (2000).
Taxes: Total city taxes per capita: $153 (1997); City property taxes per capita: $140 (1997).
Education: High school graduation rate: 78.4% (2000); College graduation rate: 7.0% (2000).
Housing: Homeownership rate: 80.8% (2000); Median home value: $33,300 (2000); Median rent: $198 per month (2000); Median age of housing: 60+ years (2000).
Transportation: Commute to work: 83.8% car, 0.0% public transportation, 9.6% walk, 2.0% work from home (2000); Travel time to work: 47.1% less than 15 minutes, 30.3% 15 to 30 minutes, 9.1% 30 to 45 minutes, 4.7% 45 to 60 minutes, 8.8% 60 minutes or more (2000)

GREENE (city). Covers a land area of 1.095 square miles and a water area of 0.059 square miles. Located at 42.89° N. Lat.; 92.80° W. Long. Elevation is 955 feet.
History: Greene was named in 1868 for the Burlington, Cedar Rapids & Minnesota Railroad president, Judge George Greene of Cedar Rapids.
Population: 1,099 (2000); Race: 99.9% White, 0.0% Black, 0.0% Asian, 0.0% American Indian and Alaska Native, 0.2% Hispanic of any race, 0.1% two or more races (2000); Density: 1,003.7 persons per square mile (2000); Age: 20.9% under 18, 29.1% over 64 (2000); Marriage status: 16.2% never married, 61.4% now married, 17.0% widowed, 5.3% divorced (2000); Foreign born: 1.4% (2000); Ancestry (includes multiple ancestries): 54.8% German, 13.3% English, 9.9% Irish, 6.0% United States or American, 4.6% Norwegian (2000).
Economy: Single-family building permits issued: 0 (2001) / 2 (2000); Multi-family building permits issued: 0 (2001) / 0 (2000); Employment by occupation: 7.6% management, 17.7% professional, 18.3% services, 27.0% sales, 1.3% farming, 13.3% construction, 14.8% production (2000).
Income: Per capita income: $17,891 (2000); Median household income: $34,063 (2000); Poverty rate: 5.8% (2000).
Taxes: Total city taxes per capita: $224 (1997); City property taxes per capita: $207 (1997).
Education: High school graduation rate: 85.6% (2000); College graduation rate: 17.0% (2000).

School District(s)
Greene Community School District (PK-12)
2000 Enrollment: 459 641-823-5523
Housing: Homeownership rate: 85.2% (2000); Median home value: $52,800 (2000); Median rent: $230 per month (2000); Median age of housing: 60+ years (2000).
Transportation: Commute to work: 88.2% car, 0.0% public transportation, 5.6% walk, 5.8% work from home (2000); Travel time to work: 54.1% less than 15 minutes, 24.0% 15 to 30 minutes, 9.4% 30 to 45 minutes, 6.4% 45 to 60 minutes, 6.1% 60 minutes or more (2000)

KESLEY (unincorporated postal area, zip code 50649). Covers a land area of 0.018 square miles and a water area of 0 square miles. Located at 42.66° N. Lat.; 92.91° W. Long. Elevation is 1,009 feet.
History: Kesley was named for an early farmer in the area, Kesley Green.
Population: 25 (2000); Race: 100.0% White, 0.0% Black, 0.0% Asian, 0.0% American Indian and Alaska Native, 0.0% Hispanic of any race, 0.0% two or more races (2000); Density: 1,397.2 persons per square mile (2000); Age: 8.0% under 18, 40.0% over 64 (2000); Marriage status: 8.7% never married, 56.5% now married, 26.1% widowed, 8.7% divorced (2000); Foreign born: 0.0% (2000); Ancestry (includes multiple ancestries): 88.0% German, 12.0% United States or American, 8.0% Irish, 8.0% Scotch-Irish (2000).
Economy: Employment by occupation: 15.4% management, 15.4% professional, 0.0% services, 30.8% sales, 0.0% farming, 23.1% construction, 15.4% production (2000).
Income: Per capita income: $13,736 (2000); Median household income: $21,250 (2000); Poverty rate: 0.0% (2000).
Education: High school graduation rate: 61.9% (2000); College graduation rate: 0.0% (2000).
Housing: Homeownership rate: 84.6% (2000); Median home value: $55,000 (2000); Median age of housing: 60+ years (2000).
Transportation: Commute to work: 69.2% car, 0.0% public transportation, 30.8% walk, 0.0% work from home (2000); Travel time to work: 76.9% less than 15 minutes, 0.0% 15 to 30 minutes, 7.7% 30 to 45 minutes, 15.4% 45 to 60 minutes, 0.0% 60 minutes or more (2000)

NEW HARTFORD (city). Covers a land area of 0.505 square miles and a water area of 0 square miles. Located at 42.56° N. Lat.; 92.62° W. Long.
History: New Hartford was settled in 1854 and named for Hartford, Connecticut, home of many of the town's first residents.
Population: 659 (2000); Race: 97.6% White, 0.0% Black, 0.0% Asian, 0.0% American Indian and Alaska Native, 0.6% Hispanic of any race, 2.1% two or more races (2000); Density: 1,303.9 persons per square mile (2000); Age: 25.5% under 18, 12.6% over 64 (2000); Marriage status: 25.9% never married, 58.7% now married, 7.3% widowed, 8.2% divorced (2000); Foreign born: 0.0% (2000); Ancestry (includes multiple ancestries): 46.2% German, 12.4% Irish, 9.5% English, 7.3% United States or American, 7.0% Other groups (2000).
Economy: Single-family building permits issued: 0 (2001) / 2 (2000); Multi-family building permits issued: 0 (2001) / 0 (2000); Employment by occupation: 8.0% management, 6.9% professional, 13.2% services, 25.2% sales, 2.0% farming, 13.2% construction, 31.5% production (2000).
Income: Per capita income: $16,771 (2000); Median household income: $34,750 (2000); Poverty rate: 9.0% (2000).
Taxes: Total city taxes per capita: $201 (1997); City property taxes per capita: $188 (1997).
Education: High school graduation rate: 82.4% (2000); College graduation rate: 12.3% (2000).
Housing: Homeownership rate: 73.2% (2000); Median home value: $50,000 (2000); Median rent: $280 per month (2000); Median age of housing: 52 years (2000).
Transportation: Commute to work: 91.3% car, 0.3% public transportation, 2.9% walk, 4.1% work from home (2000); Travel time to work: 18.4% less than 15 minutes, 49.2% 15 to 30 minutes, 23.9% 30 to 45 minutes, 4.2% 45 to 60 minutes, 4.2% 60 minutes or more (2000)

PARKERSBURG (city). Covers a land area of 1.141 square miles and a water area of 0 square miles. Located at 42.57° N. Lat.; 92.78° W. Long. Elevation is 951 feet.
History: Parkersburg was built on a site formerly so covered with heavy brush that pioneers called the place the "brush bed of the beaver." J. T. Parker, hotel keeper and first postmaster, named the town for Nathan H. Parker of Davenport, a well-known writer during the 1850's and 1860's.
Population: 1,889 (2000); Race: 98.7% White, 0.1% Black, 0.0% Asian, 0.1% American Indian and Alaska Native, 0.5% Hispanic of any race, 0.9% two or more races (2000); Density: 1,655.7 persons per square mile (2000); Age: 24.9% under 18, 21.9% over 64 (2000); Marriage status: 19.3% never married, 63.4% now married, 10.7% widowed, 6.7% divorced (2000); Foreign born: 0.6% (2000); Ancestry (includes multiple ancestries): 57.5% German, 7.1% Dutch, 7.0% Irish, 5.3% English, 5.3% United States or American (2000).
Economy: Single-family building permits issued: 3 (2001) / 1 (2000); Multi-family building permits issued: 0 (2001) / 0 (2000); Employment by occupation: 6.8% management, 18.0% professional, 19.5% services, 24.0% sales, 1.6% farming, 12.5% construction, 17.6% production (2000).
Income: Per capita income: $16,978 (2000); Median household income: $32,083 (2000); Poverty rate: 7.3% (2000).
Taxes: Total city taxes per capita: $246 (1997); City property taxes per capita: $232 (1997).
Education: High school graduation rate: 78.0% (2000); College graduation rate: 12.7% (2000).

School District(s)

Parkersburg Community School District (PK-12)
2000 Enrollment: 544 319-346-1012
Housing: Homeownership rate: 79.6% (2000); Median home value: $71,500 (2000); Median rent: $262 per month (2000); Median age of housing: 40 years (2000).
Newspapers: Parkersburg Eclipse-News-Review (1 x week)
Transportation: Commute to work: 92.5% car, 0.0% public transportation, 2.6% walk, 4.6% work from home (2000); Travel time to work: 33.4% less than 15 minutes, 18.0% 15 to 30 minutes, 40.0% 30 to 45 minutes, 7.1% 45 to 60 minutes, 1.6% 60 minutes or more (2000)

SHELL ROCK (city). Covers a land area of 1.564 square miles and a water area of 0.057 square miles. Located at 42.71° N. Lat.; 92.58° W. Long. Elevation is 921 feet.
History: Shell Rock is named after its location on the Shell Rock River.
Population: 1,298 (2000); Race: 98.4% White, 0.0% Black, 0.0% Asian, 0.0% American Indian and Alaska Native, 1.2% Hispanic of any race, 1.2% two or more races (2000); Density: 829.9 persons per square mile (2000); Age: 23.6% under 18, 16.0% over 64 (2000); Marriage status: 22.1% never married, 57.5% now married, 11.0% widowed, 9.4% divorced (2000); Foreign born: 0.9% (2000); Ancestry (includes multiple ancestries): 55.4% German, 10.1% Irish, 9.6% English, 6.8% Dutch, 6.0% United States or American (2000).
Economy: Single-family building permits issued: 1 (2001) / 0 (2000); Multi-family building permits issued: 0 (2001) / 0 (2000); Employment by occupation: 8.0% management, 11.9% professional, 20.1% services, 24.8% sales, 0.4% farming, 9.7% construction, 25.1% production (2000).
Income: Per capita income: $17,064 (2000); Median household income: $36,823 (2000); Poverty rate: 7.2% (2000).
Taxes: Total city taxes per capita: $202 (1997); City property taxes per capita: $199 (1997).
Education: High school graduation rate: 85.5% (2000); College graduation rate: 13.9% (2000).
Housing: Homeownership rate: 78.4% (2000); Median home value: $73,300 (2000); Median rent: $300 per month (2000); Median age of housing: 55 years (2000).
Transportation: Commute to work: 92.1% car, 0.6% public transportation, 3.7% walk, 2.4% work from home (2000); Travel time to work: 44.2% less than 15 minutes, 33.8% 15 to 30 minutes, 16.1% 30 to 45 minutes, 3.2% 45 to 60 minutes, 2.8% 60 minutes or more (2000)

Calhoun County

Located in central Iowa; drained by the Raccoon River. Covers a land area of 570.10 square miles, a water area of 2.10 square miles, and is located in the Central Time Zone. The county government was organized in 1851. County seat is Rockwell City.

Weather Station: Rockwell City — Elevation: 1,194 feet

	Jan	Feb	Mar	Apr	May	Jun	Jul	Aug	Sep	Oct	Nov	Dec
High	26	33	45	61	73	82	85	83	76	63	44	31
Low	8	14	26	37	49	59	63	60	52	40	26	14
Precip	0.8	0.6	2.0	3.2	4.4	4.4	4.1	3.8	3.3	2.5	1.6	0.9
Snow	7.8	6.0	6.3	2.5	tr	0.0	0.0	0.0	tr	0.7	4.2	6.9

High and Low temperatures in degrees Fahrenheit; Precipitation and Snow in inches

Population: 11,115 (2000); Race: 98.1% White, 0.7% Black, 0.1% Asian, 0.1% American Indian and Alaska Native, 0.9% Hispanic of any race, 0.4% two or more races (2000); Density: 19.5 persons per square mile (2000); Age: 22.9% under 18, 22.1% over 64 (2000).
Religion: Five largest groups: 20.7% Evangelical Lutheran Church in America, 16.4% Catholic Church, 15.0% The United Methodist Church, 12.9% Lutheran Church—Missouri Synod, 6.1% Christian Church (Disciples of Christ) (2000).
Economy: Unemployment rate: 3.2% (11/2002); Total civilian labor force: 4,650 (11/2002); Leading industries: 39.8% health care and social assistance; 17.5% retail trade; 6.7% manufacturing (2000); Companies that employ more than 1,000 persons: 0 (2000); Companies that employ more than 100 persons: 2 (2000); Farms: 793 totaling 336,516 acres (1997); Minority business

ownership rate: 0.0% (1997); Women business ownership rate: 22.8% (1997); Retail sales per capita: $7,103 (1997). Single-family building permits issued: 10 (2001) / 11 (2000); Multi-family building permits issued: 0 (2001) / 0 (2000).
Income: Per capita income: $17,498 (2000); Median household income: $33,286 (2000); Poverty rate: 10.1% (2000); Bankruptcy rate: 3.70% (2001).
Taxes: Total county taxes per capita: $311 (2000); County property taxes per capita: $310 (2000).
Education: High school graduation rate: 85.4% (2000); College graduation rate: 15.4% (2000).
Housing: Homeownership rate: 77.4% (2000); Median home value: $54,700 (2000); Median rent: $240 per month (2000); Median age of housing: 54 years (2000).
Health: Birth rate: 102.6 per 10,000 population (1998); Age adjusted death rate: 80.1 per 10,000 population (1999); Age adjusted cancer mortality rate: 217.2 deaths per 100,000 population (1999). Number of physicians: 8.1 per 10,000 population (1999); Number of hospital beds: 47.7 per 10,000 population (1999).
Elections: 2000 Presidential election results: 42.3% Gore, 55.1% Bush, 1.8% Nader, 0.4% Buchanan
National and State Parks: Towhead Lake State Game Management Area; Townhead Lake State Game Mgt Area; Twin Lakes State Park; Twin Lakes State Park West
Additional Information Contacts
Calhoun County Government Offices 712-297-7741
Lake City Chamber of Commerce 712-464-7611
Rockwell City Chamber of Commerce 712-297-8874

Calhoun County Communities

FARNHAMVILLE (city). Covers a land area of 0.652 square miles and a water area of 0.007 square miles. Located at 42.27° N. Lat.; 94.40° W. Long.
History: Farnhamville was established in 1881 as Farnham, probably named for Willford M. Farnham, whose land was purchased by the railroad company to be the site of the town.
Population: 430 (2000); Race: 98.3% White, 0.5% Black, 0.0% Asian, 1.2% American Indian and Alaska Native, 0.0% Hispanic of any race, 0.0% two or more races (2000); Density: 659.6 persons per square mile (2000); Age: 21.9% under 18, 27.1% over 64 (2000); Marriage status: 18.6% never married, 60.1% now married, 11.6% widowed, 9.7% divorced (2000); Foreign born: 0.5% (2000); Ancestry (includes multiple ancestries): 31.8% German, 13.2% Irish, 11.6% English, 9.9% Swedish, 9.4% United States or American (2000).
Economy: Single-family building permits issued: 0 (2001) / 0 (2000); Multi-family building permits issued: 0 (2001) / 0 (2000); Employment by occupation: 12.2% management, 9.6% professional, 14.4% services, 29.8% sales, 1.1% farming, 18.6% construction, 14.4% production (2000).
Income: Per capita income: $21,619 (2000); Median household income: $29,107 (2000); Poverty rate: 10.0% (2000).
Taxes: Total city taxes per capita: $180 (1997); City property taxes per capita: $180 (1997).
Education: High school graduation rate: 89.6% (2000); College graduation rate: 8.7% (2000).
Housing: Homeownership rate: 80.8% (2000); Median home value: $42,300 (2000); Median rent: $254 per month (2000); Median age of housing: 48 years (2000).
Transportation: Commute to work: 94.4% car, 0.0% public transportation, 4.4% walk, 1.1% work from home (2000); Travel time to work: 42.7% less than 15 minutes, 22.5% 15 to 30 minutes, 25.8% 30 to 45 minutes, 4.5% 45 to 60 minutes, 4.5% 60 minutes or more (2000)

JOLLEY (city). Covers a land area of 0.115 square miles and a water area of 0 square miles. Located at 42.47° N. Lat.; 94.71° W. Long. Elevation is 1,232 feet.
History: Jolley was established in 1883 as a station on the Chicago, Milwaukee & St. Paul Railroad. It was named for railroad attorney O.J. Jolley.
Population: 54 (2000); Race: 100.0% White, 0.0% Black, 0.0% Asian, 0.0% American Indian and Alaska Native, 0.0% Hispanic of any race, 0.0% two or more races (2000); Density: 469.1 persons per square mile (2000); Age: 8.8% under 18, 10.5% over 64 (2000); Marriage status: 30.2% never married, 49.1% now married, 15.1% widowed, 5.7% divorced (2000); Foreign born: 0.0% (2000); Ancestry (includes multiple ancestries): 56.1% German, 14.0% Swedish, 14.0% Irish, 12.3% Norwegian, 7.0% English (2000).
Economy: Single-family building permits issued: 0 (2001) / 0 (2000); Multi-family building permits issued: 0 (2001) / 0 (2000); Employment by occupation: 14.8% management, 0.0% professional, 18.5% services, 18.5% sales, 0.0% farming, 40.7% construction, 7.4% production (2000).
Income: Per capita income: $23,268 (2000); Median household income: $24,286 (2000); Poverty rate: 12.3% (2000).
Taxes: Total city taxes per capita: $111 (1997); City property taxes per capita: $111 (1997).
Education: High school graduation rate: 94.9% (2000); College graduation rate: 0.0% (2000).
Housing: Homeownership rate: 82.1% (2000); Median home value: <$10,000 (2000); Median age of housing: 60+ years (2000).
Transportation: Commute to work: 92.6% car, 0.0% public transportation, 0.0% walk, 7.4% work from home (2000); Travel time to work: 16.0% less than 15 minutes, 36.0% 15 to 30 minutes, 28.0% 30 to 45 minutes, 0.0% 45 to 60 minutes, 20.0% 60 minutes or more (2000)

KNIERIM (city). Covers a land area of 1.007 square miles and a water area of 0 square miles. Located at 42.45° N. Lat.; 94.45° W. Long. Elevation is 1,175 feet.
History: Knierim was founded in 1899 when the Central Railroad came through. William and Wilhelmina Knierim sold lots of their farm land to develop the town.
Population: 70 (2000); Race: 100.0% White, 0.0% Black, 0.0% Asian, 0.0% American Indian and Alaska Native, 0.0% Hispanic of any race, 0.0% two or more races (2000); Density: 69.5 persons per square mile (2000); Age: 5.3% under 18, 30.7% over 64 (2000); Marriage status: 23.9% never married, 57.7% now married, 7.0% widowed, 11.3% divorced (2000); Foreign born: 0.0% (2000); Ancestry (includes multiple ancestries): 60.0% German, 12.0% Irish, 10.7% English, 10.7% Norwegian, 6.7% Danish (2000).
Economy: Single-family building permits issued: 0 (2001) / 0 (2000); Multi-family building permits issued: 0 (2001) / 0 (2000); Employment by occupation: 11.9% management, 11.9% professional, 0.0% services, 28.6% sales, 7.1% farming, 7.1% construction, 33.3% production (2000).
Income: Per capita income: $20,280 (2000); Median household income: $26,667 (2000); Poverty rate: 11.0% (2000).
Taxes: Total city taxes per capita: $288 (1997); City property taxes per capita: $288 (1997).
Education: High school graduation rate: 87.0% (2000); College graduation rate: 7.2% (2000).
Housing: Homeownership rate: 94.3% (2000); Median home value: $16,500 (2000); Median rent: $225 per month (2000); Median age of housing: 60+ years (2000).
Transportation: Commute to work: 92.9% car, 0.0% public transportation, 0.0% walk, 0.0% work from home (2000); Travel time to work: 33.3% less than 15 minutes, 35.7% 15 to 30 minutes, 19.0% 30 to 45 minutes, 4.8% 45 to 60 minutes, 7.1% 60 minutes or more (2000)

LAKE CITY (city). Covers a land area of 4.821 square miles and a water area of 0 square miles. Located at 42.26° N. Lat.; 94.73° W. Long. Elevation is 1,232 feet.
History: Lake City was laid out in 1885 by the Western Town Lot Company and incorporated in 1881 when the railroad arrived. The town was named after Lake Creek which nearly surrounds the town.
Population: 1,787 (2000); Race: 98.6% White, 0.0% Black, 0.0% Asian, 0.0% American Indian and Alaska Native, 2.1% Hispanic of any race, 0.4% two or more races (2000); Density: 370.7 persons per square mile (2000); Age: 25.4% under 18, 26.0% over 64 (2000); Marriage status: 18.9% never married, 57.4% now married, 14.8% widowed, 8.9% divorced (2000); Foreign born: 0.4% (2000); Ancestry (includes multiple ancestries): 42.7% German, 14.1% Irish, 8.8% English, 5.6% United States or American, 4.1% Other groups (2000).
Economy: Single-family building permits issued: 1 (2001) / 3 (2000); Multi-family building permits issued: 0 (2001) / 0 (2000); Employment by occupation: 6.8% management, 23.4% professional, 21.2% services, 22.4% sales, 2.0% farming, 12.3% construction, 12.0% production (2000).
Income: Per capita income: $14,969 (2000); Median household income: $31,000 (2000); Poverty rate: 14.1% (2000).
Taxes: Total city taxes per capita: $262 (1997); City property taxes per capita: $259 (1997).
Education: High school graduation rate: 82.7% (2000); College graduation rate: 13.4% (2000).

School District(s)
Southern Cal Community School District (KG-12)
2000 Enrollment: 676 712-464-7210

Housing: Homeownership rate: 76.4% (2000); Median home value: $50,500 (2000); Median rent: $233 per month (2000); Median age of housing: 60+ years (2000).
Hospitals: Stewart Memorial Community Hospital (56 beds)
Newspapers: The Lake City Graphic (1 x week)
Transportation: Commute to work: 92.6% car, 0.0% public transportation, 4.5% walk, 2.2% work from home (2000); Travel time to work: 56.6% less than 15 minutes, 30.5% 15 to 30 minutes, 8.6% 30 to 45 minutes, 2.6% 45 to 60 minutes, 1.7% 60 minutes or more (2000)
Additional Information Contacts
Lake City Chamber of Commerce 712-464-7611

LOHRVILLE (city). Covers a land area of 3.924 square miles and a water area of 0 square miles. Located at 42.26° N. Lat.; 94.54° W. Long. Elevation is 1,149 feet.
History: Lohrville was mapped by the Western Town Lot Company in 1867. The site of the town was originally owned by Jacob A. and Mary Lohr.
Population: 431 (2000); Race: 99.3% White, 0.0% Black, 0.0% Asian, 0.5% American Indian and Alaska Native, 0.7% Hispanic of any race, 0.0% two or more races (2000); Density: 109.8 persons per square mile (2000); Age: 24.7% under 18, 16.6% over 64 (2000); Marriage status: 19.9% never married, 58.1% now married, 7.4% widowed, 14.5% divorced (2000); Foreign born: 0.0% (2000); Ancestry (includes multiple ancestries): 36.3% German, 18.2% Irish, 12.5% English, 7.9% Swedish, 5.8% United States or American (2000).
Economy: Single-family building permits issued: 0 (2001) / 0 (2000); Multi-family building permits issued: 0 (2001) / 0 (2000); Employment by occupation: 8.1% management, 19.0% professional, 25.8% services, 19.5% sales, 5.9% farming, 7.2% construction, 14.5% production (2000).
Income: Per capita income: $15,655 (2000); Median household income: $29,545 (2000); Poverty rate: 12.1% (2000).
Taxes: Total city taxes per capita: $188 (1997); City property taxes per capita: $186 (1997).
Education: High school graduation rate: 84.9% (2000); College graduation rate: 17.7% (2000).
Housing: Homeownership rate: 82.6% (2000); Median home value: $32,100 (2000); Median rent: $227 per month (2000); Median age of housing: 60+ years (2000).
Transportation: Commute to work: 88.5% car, 0.0% public transportation, 9.7% walk, 1.8% work from home (2000); Travel time to work: 44.6% less than 15 minutes, 33.8% 15 to 30 minutes, 13.1% 30 to 45 minutes, 2.8% 45 to 60 minutes, 5.6% 60 minutes or more (2000)

MANSON (city). Covers a land area of 3.193 square miles and a water area of 0 square miles. Located at 42.53° N. Lat.; 94.53° W. Long. Elevation is 1,221 feet.
History: Manson was established in 1872 by the Sioux City and Iowa Town Lot and Land Company. Soon afterward, the town was made a relay station on the Fort Dodge and Sioux City stage line.
Population: 1,893 (2000); Race: 98.2% White, 0.3% Black, 0.5% Asian, 0.0% American Indian and Alaska Native, 0.6% Hispanic of any race, 0.1% two or more races (2000); Density: 592.8 persons per square mile (2000); Age: 24.6% under 18, 24.9% over 64 (2000); Marriage status: 19.4% never married, 58.6% now married, 13.6% widowed, 8.4% divorced (2000); Foreign born: 1.3% (2000); Ancestry (includes multiple ancestries): 47.6% German, 14.1% Irish, 9.0% Swedish, 6.8% United States or American, 5.7% English (2000).
Economy: Single-family building permits issued: 0 (2001) / 0 (2000); Multi-family building permits issued: 0 (2001) / 0 (2000); Employment by occupation: 8.9% management, 22.7% professional, 20.1% services, 23.9% sales, 0.8% farming, 7.2% construction, 16.5% production (2000).
Income: Per capita income: $16,687 (2000); Median household income: $31,331 (2000); Poverty rate: 8.9% (2000).
Taxes: Total city taxes per capita: $288 (1997); City property taxes per capita: $283 (1997).
Education: High school graduation rate: 85.4% (2000); College graduation rate: 22.4% (2000).

School District(s)

Manson Northwest Webster Community School District (KG-12)
2000 Enrollment: 879 712-469-2202
Housing: Homeownership rate: 74.4% (2000); Median home value: $61,200 (2000); Median rent: $285 per month (2000); Median age of housing: 38 years (2000).
Newspapers: Calhoun County Journal Herald (1 x week)
Transportation: Commute to work: 91.0% car, 0.2% public transportation, 3.9% walk, 4.6% work from home (2000); Travel time to work: 47.1% less than 15 minutes, 27.0% 15 to 30 minutes, 22.2% 30 to 45 minutes, 2.0% 45 to 60 minutes, 1.6% 60 minutes or more (2000)

POMEROY (city). Covers a land area of 2.043 square miles and a water area of 0 square miles. Located at 42.54° N. Lat.; 94.68° W. Long.
History: Pomeroy was struck by a terrific cyclone on July 6, 1893. The storm destroyed every building on five nearby farms, then struck the town with full force, destroying all of its buildings.
Population: 710 (2000); Race: 99.7% White, 0.0% Black, 0.0% Asian, 0.0% American Indian and Alaska Native, 0.0% Hispanic of any race, 0.3% two or more races (2000); Density: 347.4 persons per square mile (2000); Age: 22.5% under 18, 26.7% over 64 (2000); Marriage status: 18.6% never married, 56.5% now married, 15.4% widowed, 9.4% divorced (2000); Foreign born: 0.3% (2000); Ancestry (includes multiple ancestries): 46.7% German, 12.4% Irish, 11.1% Swedish, 8.5% English, 4.4% United States or American (2000).
Economy: Single-family building permits issued: 2 (2001) / 0 (2000); Multi-family building permits issued: 0 (2001) / 0 (2000); Employment by occupation: 8.3% management, 19.9% professional, 22.0% services, 19.1% sales, 2.5% farming, 8.7% construction, 19.5% production (2000).
Income: Per capita income: $15,702 (2000); Median household income: $24,531 (2000); Poverty rate: 11.5% (2000).
Taxes: Total city taxes per capita: $142 (1997); City property taxes per capita: $140 (1997).
Education: High school graduation rate: 85.0% (2000); College graduation rate: 13.9% (2000).

School District(s)

Pomeroy-Palmer Community School District (KG-12)
2000 Enrollment: 298 712-468-2268
Housing: Homeownership rate: 73.4% (2000); Median home value: $40,600 (2000); Median rent: $175 per month (2000); Median age of housing: 52 years (2000).
Transportation: Commute to work: 89.5% car, 0.0% public transportation, 5.5% walk, 4.4% work from home (2000); Travel time to work: 43.3% less than 15 minutes, 24.3% 15 to 30 minutes, 18.6% 30 to 45 minutes, 9.9% 45 to 60 minutes, 3.8% 60 minutes or more (2000)

RINARD (city). Covers a land area of 0.999 square miles and a water area of 0 square miles. Located at 42.33° N. Lat.; 94.48° W. Long. Elevation is 1,170 feet.
History: Rinard was founded in 1904 by the Iowa Townsite Company. It was named for an employee of the Chicago Great Western Railway.
Population: 72 (2000); Race: 100.0% White, 0.0% Black, 0.0% Asian, 0.0% American Indian and Alaska Native, 0.0% Hispanic of any race, 0.0% two or more races (2000); Density: 72.1 persons per square mile (2000); Age: 22.6% under 18, 22.6% over 64 (2000); Marriage status: 20.0% never married, 66.0% now married, 0.0% widowed, 14.0% divorced (2000); Foreign born: 0.0% (2000); Ancestry (includes multiple ancestries): 32.3% German, 14.5% Other groups, 11.3% Irish, 11.3% Swedish, 11.3% Scotch-Irish (2000).
Economy: Single-family building permits issued: 0 (2001) / 0 (2000); Multi-family building permits issued: 0 (2001) / 0 (2000); Employment by occupation: 0.0% management, 0.0% professional, 16.0% services, 24.0% sales, 0.0% farming, 24.0% construction, 36.0% production (2000).
Income: Per capita income: $10,706 (2000); Median household income: $16,875 (2000); Poverty rate: 27.4% (2000).
Taxes: Total city taxes per capita: $134 (1997); City property taxes per capita: $134 (1997).
Education: High school graduation rate: 79.5% (2000); College graduation rate: 0.0% (2000).
Housing: Homeownership rate: 96.3% (2000); Median home value: $20,600 (2000); Median age of housing: 60+ years (2000).
Transportation: Commute to work: 100.0% car, 0.0% public transportation, 0.0% walk, 0.0% work from home (2000); Travel time to work: 8.0% less than 15 minutes, 12.0% 15 to 30 minutes, 72.0% 30 to 45 minutes, 8.0% 45 to 60 minutes, 0.0% 60 minutes or more (2000)

ROCKWELL CITY (city). Covers a land area of 4.212 square miles and a water area of 0 square miles. Located at 42.39° N. Lat.; 94.63° W. Long. Elevation is 1,223 feet.
History: Rockwell City was named for J. M. Rockwell, an early settler. The town has been called "the golden buckle on the Corn Belt."
Population: 2,264 (2000); Race: 94.4% White, 3.2% Black, 0.0% Asian, 0.2% American Indian and Alaska Native, 1.8% Hispanic of any race, 1.7% two or more races (2000); Density: 537.5 persons per square mile (2000); Age: 18.0% under 18, 21.7% over 64 (2000); Marriage status: 25.3% never married, 50.8% now married, 11.8% widowed, 12.1% divorced (2000);

Foreign born: 0.3% (2000); Ancestry (includes multiple ancestries): 35.9% German, 10.1% United States or American, 9.7% Irish, 8.3% English, 6.5% Other groups (2000).
Economy: Single-family building permits issued: 0 (2001) / 0 (2000); Multi-family building permits issued: 0 (2001) / 0 (2000); Employment by occupation: 6.4% management, 25.1% professional, 19.3% services, 25.9% sales, 0.0% farming, 10.4% construction, 12.9% production (2000).
Income: Per capita income: $17,671 (2000); Median household income: $31,071 (2000); Poverty rate: 9.5% (2000).
Taxes: Total city taxes per capita: $212 (1997); City property taxes per capita: $210 (1997).
Education: High school graduation rate: 81.4% (2000); College graduation rate: 12.0% (2000).

School District(s)

North Central Correctional Facility (N -N)
2000 Enrollment: n/a 712-297-7521
Rockwell City-Lytton Community School District (PK-12)
2000 Enrollment: 590 712-297-7341

Housing: Homeownership rate: 75.8% (2000); Median home value: $55,100 (2000); Median rent: $270 per month (2000); Median age of housing: 53 years (2000).
Newspapers: Advocate (1 x week)
Transportation: Commute to work: 88.6% car, 0.6% public transportation, 5.3% walk, 4.0% work from home (2000); Travel time to work: 58.3% less than 15 minutes, 18.4% 15 to 30 minutes, 18.7% 30 to 45 minutes, 2.7% 45 to 60 minutes, 1.9% 60 minutes or more (2000)
Additional Information Contacts
Rockwell City Chamber of Commerce 712-297-8874

SOMERS (city). Covers a land area of 0.349 square miles and a water area of 0 square miles. Located at 42.37° N. Lat.; 94.43° W. Long. Elevation is 1,157 feet.
History: Somers was founded in 1900 on the Chicago, Rock Island & Pacific Railroad. The town is thought to be named for a local physician.
Population: 165 (2000); Race: 100.0% White, 0.0% Black, 0.0% Asian, 0.0% American Indian and Alaska Native, 2.4% Hispanic of any race, 0.0% two or more races (2000); Density: 473.1 persons per square mile (2000); Age: 19.8% under 18, 15.0% over 64 (2000); Marriage status: 23.2% never married, 62.7% now married, 4.9% widowed, 9.2% divorced (2000); Foreign born: 0.0% (2000); Ancestry (includes multiple ancestries): 26.9% German, 18.6% English, 13.2% Irish, 9.0% Other groups, 6.6% Norwegian (2000).
Economy: Single-family building permits issued: 0 (2001) / 0 (2000); Multi-family building permits issued: 0 (2001) / 0 (2000); Employment by occupation: 11.9% management, 14.3% professional, 19.0% services, 26.2% sales, 2.4% farming, 15.5% construction, 10.7% production (2000).
Income: Per capita income: $15,777 (2000); Median household income: $31,250 (2000); Poverty rate: 15.9% (2000).
Taxes: Total city taxes per capita: $153 (1997); City property taxes per capita: $153 (1997).
Education: High school graduation rate: 82.3% (2000); College graduation rate: 10.6% (2000).
Housing: Homeownership rate: 82.8% (2000); Median home value: $36,800 (2000); Median rent: $231 per month (2000); Median age of housing: 55 years (2000).
Transportation: Commute to work: 92.7% car, 0.0% public transportation, 2.4% walk, 4.9% work from home (2000); Travel time to work: 33.3% less than 15 minutes, 39.7% 15 to 30 minutes, 21.8% 30 to 45 minutes, 0.0% 45 to 60 minutes, 5.1% 60 minutes or more (2000)

YETTER (city). Covers a land area of 0.123 square miles and a water area of 0 square miles. Located at 42.31° N. Lat.; 94.84° W. Long. Elevation is 1,216 feet.
History: Yetter was named for Mr. and Mrs. L. M. Yetter, owners of the town site. The town was laid out in 1899.
Population: 36 (2000); Race: 100.0% White, 0.0% Black, 0.0% Asian, 0.0% American Indian and Alaska Native, 0.0% Hispanic of any race, 0.0% two or more races (2000); Density: 292.7 persons per square mile (2000); Age: 15.6% under 18, 12.5% over 64 (2000); Marriage status: 48.1% never married, 29.6% now married, 0.0% widowed, 22.2% divorced (2000); Foreign born: 0.0% (2000); Ancestry (includes multiple ancestries): 81.3% German, 12.5% Norwegian, 9.4% Danish, 6.3% Irish (2000).
Economy: Single-family building permits issued: 0 (2001) / 0 (2000); Multi-family building permits issued: 0 (2001) / 0 (2000); Employment by occupation: 9.5% management, 0.0% professional, 19.0% services, 14.3% sales, 0.0% farming, 9.5% construction, 47.6% production (2000).
Income: Per capita income: $21,675 (2000); Median household income: $45,938 (2000); Poverty rate: 0.0% (2000).
Taxes: Total city taxes per capita: $478 (1997); City property taxes per capita: $478 (1997).
Education: High school graduation rate: 81.5% (2000); College graduation rate: 0.0% (2000).
Housing: Homeownership rate: 81.3% (2000); Median home value: <$10,000 (2000); Median age of housing: 60+ years (2000).
Transportation: Commute to work: 100.0% car, 0.0% public transportation, 0.0% walk, 0.0% work from home (2000); Travel time to work: 9.5% less than 15 minutes, 47.6% 15 to 30 minutes, 9.5% 30 to 45 minutes, 9.5% 45 to 60 minutes, 23.8% 60 minutes or more (2000)

Carroll County

Located in west central Iowa; drained by the Raccoon, Middle Raccoon, East and West Nishnabotna Rivers. Covers a land area of 569.30 square miles, a water area of 0.90 square miles, and is located in the Central Time Zone. The county government was organized in 1851. County seat is Carroll.

Weather Station: Carroll — Elevation: 1,240 feet

	Jan	Feb	Mar	Apr	May	Jun	Jul	Aug	Sep	Oct	Nov	Dec
High	27	33	46	61	72	82	86	83	76	63	45	32
Low	9	15	25	36	48	58	62	60	51	39	26	14
Precip	0.9	0.8	2.3	3.4	4.4	4.5	4.8	3.8	3.4	2.5	1.7	0.9
Snow	7.2	5.9	5.9	2.0	tr	0.0	0.0	0.0	tr	0.5	3.2	6.5

High and Low temperatures in degrees Fahrenheit; Precipitation and Snow in inches

Population: 21,421 (2000); Race: 99.1% White, 0.1% Black, 0.3% Asian, 0.1% American Indian and Alaska Native, 0.6% Hispanic of any race, 0.3% two or more races (2000); Density: 37.6 persons per square mile (2000); Age: 27.0% under 18, 18.7% over 64 (2000).
Religion: Five largest groups: 54.7% Catholic Church, 12.1% Lutheran Church—Missouri Synod, 8.6% The United Methodist Church, 3.1% Presbyterian Church (U.S.A.), 2.3% Evangelical Lutheran Church in America (2000).
Economy: Unemployment rate: 2.3% (11/2002); Total civilian labor force: 12,272 (11/2002); Leading industries: 17.5% retail trade; 17.0% health care and social assistance; 13.0% manufacturing (2000); Companies that employ more than 1,000 persons: 0 (2000); Companies that employ more than 100 persons: 16 (2000); Farms: 1,102 totaling 352,698 acres (1997); Minority business ownership rate: 0.0% (1997); Women business ownership rate: 15.7% (1997); Retail sales per capita: $10,454 (1997). Single-family building permits issued: 53 (2001) / 41 (2000); Multi-family building permits issued: 0 (2001) / 0 (2000).
Income: Per capita income: $18,595 (2000); Median household income: $37,275 (2000); Poverty rate: 6.5% (2000); Bankruptcy rate: 2.21% (2001).
Taxes: Total county taxes per capita: $200 (2000); County property taxes per capita: $200 (2000).
Education: High school graduation rate: 83.7% (2000); College graduation rate: 16.0% (2000).
Housing: Homeownership rate: 74.3% (2000); Median home value: $75,900 (2000); Median rent: $321 per month (2000); Median age of housing: 45 years (2000).
Health: Birth rate: 114.8 per 10,000 population (1998); Age adjusted death rate: 85.5 per 10,000 population (1999); Age adjusted cancer mortality rate: 217.3 deaths per 100,000 population (1999). Number of physicians: 9.3 per 10,000 population (1999); Number of hospital beds: 106.9 per 10,000 population (1999).
Elections: 2000 Presidential election results: 46.7% Gore, 51.0% Bush, 1.5% Nader, 0.5% Buchanan
National and State Parks: Swan Lake State Park
Additional Information Contacts
Carroll County Government Offices 712-792-4923
Carroll Board of Realtors 712-792-5840
Carroll Chamber of Commerce 712-792-4383
Manning Information & Development Office 712-653-3131

Carroll County Communities

ARCADIA (city). Covers a land area of 0.977 square miles and a water area of 0 square miles. Located at 42.08° N. Lat.; 95.04° W. Long. Elevation is 1,425 feet.
History: Arcadia was named after a province in ancient Greece. The town was nicknamed "Tip Top" by railroad employees because it was the highest point on the main line through Iowa.

Population: 443 (2000); Race: 99.5% White, 0.0% Black, 0.0% Asian, 0.0% American Indian and Alaska Native, 0.5% Hispanic of any race, 0.0% two or more races (2000); Density: 453.2 persons per square mile (2000); Age: 29.2% under 18, 18.3% over 64 (2000); Marriage status: 20.1% never married, 70.0% now married, 6.9% widowed, 3.0% divorced (2000); Foreign born: 0.0% (2000); Ancestry (includes multiple ancestries): 65.8% German, 5.0% United States or American, 3.8% Irish, 2.5% Other groups, 2.3% French (except Basque) (2000).
Economy: Single-family building permits issued: 1 (2001) / 3 (2000); Multi-family building permits issued: 0 (2001) / 0 (2000); Employment by occupation: 11.3% management, 11.7% professional, 16.1% services, 25.7% sales, 0.0% farming, 7.0% construction, 28.3% production (2000).
Income: Per capita income: $16,584 (2000); Median household income: $34,063 (2000); Poverty rate: 6.1% (2000).
Taxes: Total city taxes per capita: $131 (1997); City property taxes per capita: $128 (1997).
Education: High school graduation rate: 83.2% (2000); College graduation rate: 9.3% (2000).
Housing: Homeownership rate: 89.6% (2000); Median home value: $57,900 (2000); Median rent: $179 per month (2000); Median age of housing: 49 years (2000).
Transportation: Commute to work: 82.6% car, 0.0% public transportation, 10.4% walk, 5.7% work from home (2000); Travel time to work: 47.5% less than 15 minutes, 38.2% 15 to 30 minutes, 6.9% 30 to 45 minutes, 1.8% 45 to 60 minutes, 5.5% 60 minutes or more (2000)

BREDA (city). Covers a land area of 0.478 square miles and a water area of 0 square miles. Located at 42.18° N. Lat.; 94.97° W. Long. Elevation is 1,370 feet.
History: An early resident and owner of the hotel in Breda was John Le Duc, who had come from Breda, Holland.
Population: 477 (2000); Race: 100.0% White, 0.0% Black, 0.0% Asian, 0.0% American Indian and Alaska Native, 0.0% Hispanic of any race, 0.0% two or more races (2000); Density: 998.4 persons per square mile (2000); Age: 21.5% under 18, 29.7% over 64 (2000); Marriage status: 22.4% never married, 59.9% now married, 12.4% widowed, 5.3% divorced (2000); Foreign born: 0.0% (2000); Ancestry (includes multiple ancestries): 65.7% German, 12.1% Irish, 10.6% United States or American, 4.1% English, 3.0% Dutch (2000).
Economy: Single-family building permits issued: 0 (2001) / 0 (2000); Multi-family building permits issued: 0 (2001) / 0 (2000); Employment by occupation: 14.2% management, 10.9% professional, 14.2% services, 23.7% sales, 1.9% farming, 13.7% construction, 21.3% production (2000).
Income: Per capita income: $17,461 (2000); Median household income: $29,783 (2000); Poverty rate: 6.9% (2000).
Taxes: Total city taxes per capita: $86 (1997); City property taxes per capita: $84 (1997).
Education: High school graduation rate: 80.8% (2000); College graduation rate: 9.5% (2000).
Housing: Homeownership rate: 77.4% (2000); Median home value: $61,700 (2000); Median rent: $268 per month (2000); Median age of housing: 49 years (2000).
Newspapers: Breda News (1 x week)
Transportation: Commute to work: 83.9% car, 0.0% public transportation, 9.5% walk, 5.2% work from home (2000); Travel time to work: 49.5% less than 15 minutes, 39.0% 15 to 30 minutes, 6.5% 30 to 45 minutes, 0.0% 45 to 60 minutes, 5.0% 60 minutes or more (2000)

CARROLL (city). Covers a land area of 5.543 square miles and a water area of 0 square miles. Located at 42.07° N. Lat.; 94.86° W. Long. Elevation is 1,266 feet.
History: Carroll was named for Charles Carroll, one of the signers of the Declaration of Independence.
Population: 10,106 (2000); Race: 98.7% White, 0.1% Black, 0.6% Asian, 0.2% American Indian and Alaska Native, 0.6% Hispanic of any race, 0.4% two or more races (2000); Density: 1,823.2 persons per square mile (2000); Age: 25.8% under 18, 19.6% over 64 (2000); Marriage status: 23.8% never married, 58.1% now married, 10.2% widowed, 7.8% divorced (2000); Foreign born: 1.0% (2000); Ancestry (includes multiple ancestries): 61.3% German, 12.8% Irish, 6.9% English, 4.7% United States or American, 2.9% Other groups (2000).
Economy: Single-family building permits issued: 27 (2001) / 27 (2000); Multi-family building permits issued: 0 (2001) / 0 (2000); Employment by occupation: 10.0% management, 16.6% professional, 14.2% services, 32.2% sales, 1.0% farming, 11.0% construction, 15.1% production (2000).
Income: Per capita income: $20,442 (2000); Median household income: $39,853 (2000); Poverty rate: 5.2% (2000).
Taxes: Total city taxes per capita: $391 (2000); City property taxes per capita: $378 (2000).
Education: High school graduation rate: 85.1% (2000); College graduation rate: 20.4% (2000).

School District(s)
Carroll Community School District (PK-12)
2000 Enrollment: 1,816 712-792-8001
Housing: Homeownership rate: 69.7% (2000); Median home value: $86,400 (2000); Median rent: $352 per month (2000); Median age of housing: 34 years (2000).
Hospitals: Saint Anthony Regional Hospital (178 beds)
Safety: Violent crime rate: 6.9 per 10,000 population; Property crime rate: 237.7 per 10,000 population (2001).
Newspapers: Carroll Daily Times-Herald (5 x week); Smart Shopper (1 x week); Carroll Today (1 x week)
Transportation: Commute to work: 92.1% car, 1.2% public transportation, 2.4% walk, 3.6% work from home (2000); Travel time to work: 81.2% less than 15 minutes, 11.3% 15 to 30 minutes, 3.7% 30 to 45 minutes, 0.8% 45 to 60 minutes, 3.0% 60 minutes or more (2000)
Airports: Arthur N Neu
Additional Information Contacts
Carroll Board of Realtors 712-792-5840
Carroll Chamber of Commerce 712-792-4383

COON RAPIDS (city). Covers a land area of 1.738 square miles and a water area of 0 square miles. Located at 41.87° N. Lat.; 94.67° W. Long.
History: The town of Coon Rapids takes its name from its location at a rapids on the Middle Raccoon River. The quantity of raccoons in the area led to the naming of the river.
Population: 1,305 (2000); Race: 98.2% White, 1.5% Black, 0.0% Asian, 0.0% American Indian and Alaska Native, 2.6% Hispanic of any race, 0.0% two or more races (2000); Density: 750.7 persons per square mile (2000); Age: 21.9% under 18, 24.9% over 64 (2000); Marriage status: 19.2% never married, 59.9% now married, 12.6% widowed, 8.3% divorced (2000); Foreign born: 0.4% (2000); Ancestry (includes multiple ancestries): 40.6% German, 14.7% English, 13.6% Irish, 6.6% Other groups, 5.9% United States or American (2000).
Economy: Single-family building permits issued: 10 (2001) / 2 (2000); Multi-family building permits issued: 0 (2001) / 0 (2000); Employment by occupation: 9.7% management, 17.1% professional, 17.8% services, 27.2% sales, 2.9% farming, 11.0% construction, 14.4% production (2000).
Income: Per capita income: $16,765 (2000); Median household income: $32,951 (2000); Poverty rate: 9.4% (2000).
Taxes: Total city taxes per capita: $527 (2000); City property taxes per capita: $325 (2000).
Education: High school graduation rate: 81.1% (2000); College graduation rate: 14.6% (2000).

School District(s)
Coon Rapids-Bayard Community School District (PK-12)
2000 Enrollment: 561 712-999-2207
Housing: Homeownership rate: 73.0% (2000); Median home value: $56,600 (2000); Median rent: $228 per month (2000); Median age of housing: 57 years (2000).
Newspapers: Coon Rapids Enterprise (1 x week)
Transportation: Commute to work: 89.4% car, 0.0% public transportation, 5.9% walk, 4.8% work from home (2000); Travel time to work: 66.1% less than 15 minutes, 10.2% 15 to 30 minutes, 17.5% 30 to 45 minutes, 2.5% 45 to 60 minutes, 3.7% 60 minutes or more (2000)

DEDHAM (city). Covers a land area of 0.579 square miles and a water area of 0 square miles. Located at 41.90° N. Lat.; 94.82° W. Long. Elevation is 1,245 feet.
History: Dedham was named by a surveyor for the Chicago, Milwaukee & St. Paul Railroad, who came from Dedham, Massachusetts.
Population: 280 (2000); Race: 100.0% White, 0.0% Black, 0.0% Asian, 0.0% American Indian and Alaska Native, 2.5% Hispanic of any race, 0.0% two or more races (2000); Density: 483.5 persons per square mile (2000); Age: 27.6% under 18, 19.3% over 64 (2000); Marriage status: 32.4% never married, 51.7% now married, 10.1% widowed, 5.8% divorced (2000); Foreign born: 1.8% (2000); Ancestry (includes multiple ancestries): 56.0% German, 15.6% United States or American, 5.5% Irish, 2.2% Other groups, 1.8% English (2000).
Economy: Single-family building permits issued: 1 (2001) / 1 (2000); Multi-family building permits issued: 0 (2001) / 0 (2000); Employment by

occupation: 6.7% management, 11.2% professional, 14.2% services, 23.9% sales, 1.5% farming, 14.2% construction, 28.4% production (2000).
Income: Per capita income: $13,505 (2000); Median household income: $33,125 (2000); Poverty rate: 9.9% (2000).
Taxes: Total city taxes per capita: $102 (1997); City property taxes per capita: $94 (1997).
Education: High school graduation rate: 73.7% (2000); College graduation rate: 5.4% (2000).
Housing: Homeownership rate: 85.5% (2000); Median home value: $39,600 (2000); Median rent: $150 per month (2000); Median age of housing: 56 years (2000).
Transportation: Commute to work: 89.6% car, 0.0% public transportation, 5.2% walk, 3.7% work from home (2000); Travel time to work: 27.1% less than 15 minutes, 63.6% 15 to 30 minutes, 4.7% 30 to 45 minutes, 1.6% 45 to 60 minutes, 3.1% 60 minutes or more (2000)

GLIDDEN (city). Covers a land area of 1.017 square miles and a water area of 0 square miles. Located at 42.05° N. Lat.; 94.72° W. Long. Elevation is 1,226 feet.
History: Glidden was named for Captain W.T. Glidden, an investor in the Mississippi & Iowa Central Railroad.
Population: 1,253 (2000); Race: 98.9% White, 0.0% Black, 0.0% Asian, 0.2% American Indian and Alaska Native, 0.6% Hispanic of any race, 0.6% two or more races (2000); Density: 1,231.6 persons per square mile (2000); Age: 23.0% under 18, 17.3% over 64 (2000); Marriage status: 30.3% never married, 53.0% now married, 11.1% widowed, 5.6% divorced (2000); Foreign born: 0.5% (2000); Ancestry (includes multiple ancestries): 46.3% German, 9.0% Irish, 6.6% United States or American, 6.0% English, 5.7% Danish (2000).
Economy: Single-family building permits issued: 3 (2001) / 0 (2000); Multi-family building permits issued: 0 (2001) / 0 (2000); Employment by occupation: 8.7% management, 11.6% professional, 13.7% services, 29.0% sales, 2.2% farming, 13.8% construction, 21.0% production (2000).
Income: Per capita income: $17,437 (2000); Median household income: $35,333 (2000); Poverty rate: 5.7% (2000).
Taxes: Total city taxes per capita: $187 (1997); City property taxes per capita: $182 (1997).
Education: High school graduation rate: 79.6% (2000); College graduation rate: 13.2% (2000).

School District(s)

Glidden-Ralston Community School District (KG-12)
2000 Enrollment: 418 712-659-3411
Housing: Homeownership rate: 76.9% (2000); Median home value: $66,200 (2000); Median rent: $268 per month (2000); Median age of housing: 50 years (2000).
Newspapers: Glidden Graphic (1 x week)
Transportation: Commute to work: 89.6% car, 0.0% public transportation, 6.0% walk, 3.6% work from home (2000); Travel time to work: 61.3% less than 15 minutes, 31.0% 15 to 30 minutes, 3.2% 30 to 45 minutes, 0.9% 45 to 60 minutes, 3.5% 60 minutes or more (2000)

HALBUR (city). Covers a land area of 0.205 square miles and a water area of 0 square miles. Located at 42.00° N. Lat.; 94.97° W. Long. Elevation is 1,384 feet.
History: Halbur, laid out in 1881, was named for Anton Halbur, who owned the land adjoining the railroad station. The name was chosen by Orlando H. Manning, who served as lieutenant governor of Iowa (1882-1885).
Population: 202 (2000); Race: 100.0% White, 0.0% Black, 0.0% Asian, 0.0% American Indian and Alaska Native, 0.0% Hispanic of any race, 0.0% two or more races (2000); Density: 987.2 persons per square mile (2000); Age: 37.2% under 18, 9.6% over 64 (2000); Marriage status: 21.2% never married, 63.6% now married, 10.6% widowed, 4.6% divorced (2000); Foreign born: 0.0% (2000); Ancestry (includes multiple ancestries): 80.3% German, 4.6% United States or American, 4.1% Danish, 3.2% Norwegian, 2.8% French (except Basque) (2000).
Economy: Single-family building permits issued: 0 (2001) / 0 (2000); Multi-family building permits issued: 0 (2001) / 0 (2000); Employment by occupation: 9.4% management, 7.5% professional, 15.1% services, 28.3% sales, 2.8% farming, 23.6% construction, 13.2% production (2000).
Income: Per capita income: $16,896 (2000); Median household income: $41,250 (2000); Poverty rate: 4.1% (2000).
Taxes: Total city taxes per capita: $102 (1997); City property taxes per capita: $98 (1997).
Education: High school graduation rate: 81.3% (2000); College graduation rate: 6.5% (2000).
Housing: Homeownership rate: 94.4% (2000); Median home value: $60,900 (2000); Median rent: $125 per month (2000); Median age of housing: 47 years (2000).
Transportation: Commute to work: 90.6% car, 0.0% public transportation, 9.4% walk, 0.0% work from home (2000); Travel time to work: 57.5% less than 15 minutes, 32.1% 15 to 30 minutes, 4.7% 30 to 45 minutes, 0.0% 45 to 60 minutes, 5.7% 60 minutes or more (2000)

LANESBORO (city). Covers a land area of 0.743 square miles and a water area of 0.010 square miles. Located at 42.18° N. Lat.; 94.69° W. Long. Elevation is 1,149 feet.
History: Lanesboro was considered by the Chicago Great Western Railroad to be a model town as developed by them. The town was laid out on land sold to the railroad by farmer George Lane.
Population: 152 (2000); Race: 100.0% White, 0.0% Black, 0.0% Asian, 0.0% American Indian and Alaska Native, 0.0% Hispanic of any race, 0.0% two or more races (2000); Density: 204.5 persons per square mile (2000); Age: 11.7% under 18, 30.6% over 64 (2000); Marriage status: 19.6% never married, 63.7% now married, 12.7% widowed, 3.9% divorced (2000); Foreign born: 0.0% (2000); Ancestry (includes multiple ancestries): 45.9% German, 18.0% English, 14.4% Irish, 11.7% United States or American, 5.4% Norwegian (2000).
Economy: Single-family building permits issued: 1 (2001) / 0 (2000); Multi-family building permits issued: 0 (2001) / 0 (2000); Employment by occupation: 4.1% management, 6.1% professional, 16.3% services, 24.5% sales, 4.1% farming, 32.7% construction, 12.2% production (2000).
Income: Per capita income: $15,397 (2000); Median household income: $25,750 (2000); Poverty rate: 10.8% (2000).
Taxes: Total city taxes per capita: $95 (1997); City property taxes per capita: $89 (1997).
Education: High school graduation rate: 69.1% (2000); College graduation rate: 7.4% (2000).
Housing: Homeownership rate: 98.5% (2000); Median home value: $19,500 (2000); Median rent: $175 per month (2000); Median age of housing: 60+ years (2000).
Transportation: Commute to work: 85.1% car, 0.0% public transportation, 8.5% walk, 6.4% work from home (2000); Travel time to work: 43.2% less than 15 minutes, 36.4% 15 to 30 minutes, 6.8% 30 to 45 minutes, 4.5% 45 to 60 minutes, 9.1% 60 minutes or more (2000)

LIDDERDALE (city). Covers a land area of 2.417 square miles and a water area of 0 square miles. Located at 42.12° N. Lat.; 94.78° W. Long. Elevation is 1,244 feet.
History: Lidderdale was named after an executive of Liverpool 8 Company, an English company which provided large amounts of money to the Chicago Great Western Railroad as it was being built in this area.
Population: 186 (2000); Race: 98.1% White, 0.0% Black, 0.0% Asian, 0.0% American Indian and Alaska Native, 0.0% Hispanic of any race, 1.9% two or more races (2000); Density: 76.9 persons per square mile (2000); Age: 32.7% under 18, 14.4% over 64 (2000); Marriage status: 20.7% never married, 67.9% now married, 5.7% widowed, 5.7% divorced (2000); Foreign born: 0.0% (2000); Ancestry (includes multiple ancestries): 54.3% German, 18.3% Irish, 2.4% English, 2.4% Polish, 1.9% United States or American (2000).
Economy: Employment by occupation: 22.8% management, 8.7% professional, 10.9% services, 20.7% sales, 4.3% farming, 14.1% construction, 18.5% production (2000).
Income: Per capita income: $13,513 (2000); Median household income: $29,306 (2000); Poverty rate: 2.9% (2000).
Taxes: Total city taxes per capita: $304 (1997); City property taxes per capita: $299 (1997).
Education: High school graduation rate: 88.1% (2000); College graduation rate: 5.1% (2000).
Housing: Homeownership rate: 80.0% (2000); Median home value: $47,800 (2000); Median rent: $217 per month (2000); Median age of housing: 60+ years (2000).
Transportation: Commute to work: 85.9% car, 0.0% public transportation, 12.0% walk, 2.2% work from home (2000); Travel time to work: 56.7% less than 15 minutes, 22.2% 15 to 30 minutes, 3.3% 30 to 45 minutes, 15.6% 45 to 60 minutes, 2.2% 60 minutes or more (2000)

MANNING (city). Covers a land area of 2.388 square miles and a water area of 0.007 square miles. Located at 41.90° N. Lat.; 95.06° W. Long. Elevation is 1,355 feet.
History: Manning was platted in 1880 and named in honor of O. H. Manning.

Population: 1,490 (2000); Race: 99.3% White, 0.0% Black, 0.2% Asian, 0.0% American Indian and Alaska Native, 0.6% Hispanic of any race, 0.1% two or more races (2000); Density: 624.0 persons per square mile (2000); Age: 23.9% under 18, 27.1% over 64 (2000); Marriage status: 19.1% never married, 60.0% now married, 15.8% widowed, 5.1% divorced (2000); Foreign born: 0.3% (2000); Ancestry (includes multiple ancestries): 65.4% German, 7.7% United States or American, 6.4% Irish, 4.8% English, 3.7% Danish (2000).
Economy: Single-family building permits issued: 3 (2001) / 2 (2000); Multi-family building permits issued: 0 (2001) / 0 (2000); Employment by occupation: 12.6% management, 15.5% professional, 21.3% services, 20.7% sales, 2.0% farming, 11.6% construction, 16.4% production (2000).
Income: Per capita income: $16,806 (2000); Median household income: $32,083 (2000); Poverty rate: 7.9% (2000).
Taxes: Total city taxes per capita: $200 (1997); City property taxes per capita: $196 (1997).
Education: High school graduation rate: 78.3% (2000); College graduation rate: 14.6% (2000).

School District(s)

Manning Community School District (PK-12)
2000 Enrollment: 584 712-653-3771
Housing: Homeownership rate: 76.7% (2000); Median home value: $53,000 (2000); Median rent: $265 per month (2000); Median age of housing: 53 years (2000).
Hospitals: Manning Regional Healthcare Center (41 beds)
Newspapers: The Manning Monitor (1 x week)
Transportation: Commute to work: 87.9% car, 0.0% public transportation, 9.6% walk, 2.1% work from home (2000); Travel time to work: 72.3% less than 15 minutes, 11.2% 15 to 30 minutes, 12.6% 30 to 45 minutes, 1.2% 45 to 60 minutes, 2.8% 60 minutes or more (2000)
Additional Information Contacts
Manning Information & Development Office 712-653-3131

RALSTON (city). Covers a land area of 1.976 square miles and a water area of 0 square miles. Located at 42.04° N. Lat.; 94.63° W. Long.
History: Ralston was known for many years as Slater Siding. In 1891 when a station was built, the name was changed to honor an officer of the American Express Company.
Population: 98 (2000); Race: 100.0% White, 0.0% Black, 0.0% Asian, 0.0% American Indian and Alaska Native, 0.0% Hispanic of any race, 0.0% two or more races (2000); Density: 49.6 persons per square mile (2000); Age: 28.3% under 18, 5.7% over 64 (2000); Marriage status: 15.4% never married, 79.5% now married, 1.3% widowed, 3.8% divorced (2000); Foreign born: 0.0% (2000); Ancestry (includes multiple ancestries): 41.5% German, 8.5% Italian, 6.6% Other groups, 4.7% United States or American, 3.8% Irish (2000).
Economy: Employment by occupation: 1.8% management, 10.5% professional, 7.0% services, 14.0% sales, 0.0% farming, 14.0% construction, 52.6% production (2000).
Income: Per capita income: $15,746 (2000); Median household income: $34,375 (2000); Poverty rate: 0.9% (2000).
Taxes: Total city taxes per capita: $619 (1997); City property taxes per capita: $619 (1997).
Education: High school graduation rate: 79.2% (2000); College graduation rate: 8.3% (2000).
Housing: Homeownership rate: 82.2% (2000); Median home value: $32,500 (2000); Median rent: $225 per month (2000); Median age of housing: 60+ years (2000).
Transportation: Commute to work: 82.5% car, 0.0% public transportation, 17.5% walk, 0.0% work from home (2000); Travel time to work: 43.9% less than 15 minutes, 29.8% 15 to 30 minutes, 3.5% 30 to 45 minutes, 12.3% 45 to 60 minutes, 10.5% 60 minutes or more (2000)

TEMPLETON (city). Covers a land area of 0.409 square miles and a water area of 0 square miles. Located at 41.91° N. Lat.; 94.94° W. Long.
History: Templeton was platted in 1882 on land owned by William Overmire, and was settled largely by people of German descent. During prohibition the town was known for its bootleg rye whiskey.
Population: 334 (2000); Race: 99.1% White, 0.6% Black, 0.0% Asian, 0.0% American Indian and Alaska Native, 0.0% Hispanic of any race, 0.3% two or more races (2000); Density: 816.7 persons per square mile (2000); Age: 25.6% under 18, 23.3% over 64 (2000); Marriage status: 21.0% never married, 67.5% now married, 5.9% widowed, 5.5% divorced (2000); Foreign born: 0.0% (2000); Ancestry (includes multiple ancestries): 57.0% German, 9.9% United States or American, 9.3% Irish, 4.1% Dutch, 2.6% Danish (2000).
Economy: Single-family building permits issued: 0 (2001) / 0 (2000); Multi-family building permits issued: 0 (2001) / 0 (2000); Employment by occupation: 14.2% management, 11.5% professional, 15.3% services, 29.0% sales, 1.6% farming, 10.9% construction, 17.5% production (2000).
Income: Per capita income: $18,703 (2000); Median household income: $37,500 (2000); Poverty rate: 3.2% (2000).
Taxes: Total city taxes per capita: $227 (1997); City property taxes per capita: $224 (1997).
Education: High school graduation rate: 78.4% (2000); College graduation rate: 12.5% (2000).
Housing: Homeownership rate: 86.7% (2000); Median home value: $62,600 (2000); Median rent: $231 per month (2000); Median age of housing: 52 years (2000).
Transportation: Commute to work: 86.3% car, 0.0% public transportation, 5.5% walk, 7.1% work from home (2000); Travel time to work: 41.4% less than 15 minutes, 37.9% 15 to 30 minutes, 14.2% 30 to 45 minutes, 4.7% 45 to 60 minutes, 1.8% 60 minutes or more (2000)

WILLEY (city). Covers a land area of 0.248 square miles and a water area of 0 square miles. Located at 41.97° N. Lat.; 94.82° W. Long. Elevation is 1,345 feet.
Population: 103 (2000); Race: 100.0% White, 0.0% Black, 0.0% Asian, 0.0% American Indian and Alaska Native, 0.0% Hispanic of any race, 0.0% two or more races (2000); Density: 415.2 persons per square mile (2000); Age: 40.0% under 18, 6.4% over 64 (2000); Marriage status: 40.0% never married, 48.8% now married, 6.3% widowed, 5.0% divorced (2000); Foreign born: 0.0% (2000); Ancestry (includes multiple ancestries): 85.5% German, 4.5% Irish, 2.7% Danish, 2.7% Welsh, 1.8% English (2000).
Economy: Single-family building permits issued: 0 (2001) / 0 (2000); Multi-family building permits issued: 0 (2001) / 0 (2000); Employment by occupation: 12.5% management, 10.7% professional, 10.7% services, 32.1% sales, 0.0% farming, 3.6% construction, 30.4% production (2000).
Income: Per capita income: $12,900 (2000); Median household income: $42,083 (2000); Poverty rate: 8.2% (2000).
Taxes: Total city taxes per capita: $79 (1997); City property taxes per capita: $79 (1997).
Education: High school graduation rate: 81.4% (2000); College graduation rate: 5.1% (2000).
Housing: Homeownership rate: 91.7% (2000); Median home value: $35,800 (2000); Median age of housing: 60+ years (2000).
Transportation: Commute to work: 98.2% car, 0.0% public transportation, 0.0% walk, 1.8% work from home (2000); Travel time to work: 23.6% less than 15 minutes, 67.3% 15 to 30 minutes, 3.6% 30 to 45 minutes, 3.6% 45 to 60 minutes, 1.8% 60 minutes or more (2000)

Cass County

Located in southwestern Iowa; drained by the East Nishnabotna and West Nodaway Rivers. Covers a land area of 564.30 square miles, a water area of 0.70 square miles, and is located in the Central Time Zone. The county government was organized in 1851. County seat is Atlantic.

Weather Station: Atlantic 1 NE — Elevation: 1,158 feet

	Jan	Feb	Mar	Apr	May	Jun	Jul	Aug	Sep	Oct	Nov	Dec
High	29	35	48	62	73	83	86	83	76	64	46	33
Low	9	15	26	37	49	59	63	61	51	39	27	15
Precip	0.9	0.9	2.4	3.5	4.4	4.8	4.6	3.8	3.9	2.8	1.8	1.1
Snow	6.6	5.7	3.6	1.2	0.0	0.0	0.0	0.0	0.0	0.5	2.5	5.1

High and Low temperatures in degrees Fahrenheit; Precipitation and Snow in inches

Population: 14,684 (2000); Race: 98.7% White, 0.2% Black, 0.3% Asian, 0.1% American Indian and Alaska Native, 0.8% Hispanic of any race, 0.3% two or more races (2000); Density: 26.0 persons per square mile (2000); Age: 23.7% under 18, 20.8% over 64 (2000).
Religion: Five largest groups: 17.0% The United Methodist Church, 12.6% Catholic Church, 10.3% Lutheran Church—Missouri Synod, 7.2% Evangelical Lutheran Church in America, 6.7% United Church of Christ (2000).
Economy: Unemployment rate: 3.9% (11/2002); Total civilian labor force: 7,247 (11/2002); Leading industries: 23.6% manufacturing; 17.6% retail trade; 17.6% health care and social assistance (2000); Companies that employ more than 1,000 persons: 0 (2000); Companies that employ more than 100 persons: 7 (2000); Farms: 804 totaling 331,362 acres (1997); Minority business ownership rate: 0.0% (1997); Women business ownership rate: 23.3% (1997); Retail sales per capita: $8,292 (1997). Single-family building

permits issued: 15 (2001) / 31 (2000); Multi-family building permits issued: 2 (2001) / 0 (2000).
Income: Per capita income: $17,067 (2000); Median household income: $32,922 (2000); Poverty rate: 11.1% (2000); Bankruptcy rate: 4.24% (2001).
Taxes: Total county taxes per capita: $219 (2000); County property taxes per capita: $218 (2000).
Education: High school graduation rate: 85.9% (2000); College graduation rate: 16.6% (2000).
Housing: Homeownership rate: 74.6% (2000); Median home value: $59,500 (2000); Median rent: $268 per month (2000); Median age of housing: 57 years (2000).
Health: Birth rate: 98.8 per 10,000 population (1998); Age adjusted death rate: 88.1 per 10,000 population (1999); Age adjusted cancer mortality rate: 211.0 deaths per 100,000 population (1999). Number of physicians: 7.5 per 10,000 population (1999); Number of hospital beds: 49.0 per 10,000 population (1999).
Elections: 2000 Presidential election results: 36.1% Gore, 61.1% Bush, 2.1% Nader, 0.3% Buchanan
National and State Parks: Cold Springs State Park; Lake Anita State Park
Additional Information Contacts
Cass County Government Offices 712-243-4570
Atlantic Chamber of Commerce.......................... 712-243-3017
Massena Chamber of Commerce 712-779-2295

Cass County Communities

ANITA (city). Covers a land area of 1.714 square miles and a water area of 0 square miles. Located at 41.44° N. Lat.; 94.76° W. Long. Elevation is 1,256 feet.
History: Anita was named for Anita Cowles, niece of the surveyor of the town site, Lewis Beason, who platted it in 1869.
Population: 1,049 (2000); Race: 99.5% White, 0.0% Black, 0.0% Asian, 0.0% American Indian and Alaska Native, 0.7% Hispanic of any race, 0.2% two or more races (2000); Density: 612.1 persons per square mile (2000); Age: 21.9% under 18, 25.1% over 64 (2000); Marriage status: 20.4% never married, 57.4% now married, 13.9% widowed, 8.3% divorced (2000); Foreign born: 0.8% (2000); Ancestry (includes multiple ancestries): 36.3% German, 13.4% Danish, 11.2% English, 9.2% Irish, 5.8% United States or American (2000).
Economy: Single-family building permits issued: 1 (2001) / 4 (2000); Multi-family building permits issued: 0 (2001) / 0 (2000); Employment by occupation: 6.6% management, 10.9% professional, 20.3% services, 23.8% sales, 0.0% farming, 9.4% construction, 29.0% production (2000).
Income: Per capita income: $15,672 (2000); Median household income: $28,984 (2000); Poverty rate: 8.1% (2000).
Taxes: Total city taxes per capita: $137 (1997); City property taxes per capita: $125 (1997).
Education: High school graduation rate: 84.0% (2000); College graduation rate: 9.3% (2000).

School District(s)

Anita Community School District (KG-12)
2000 Enrollment: 322 712-762-3231
Housing: Homeownership rate: 77.9% (2000); Median home value: $44,800 (2000); Median rent: $201 per month (2000); Median age of housing: 60+ years (2000).
Newspapers: Anita Tribune (1 x week)
Transportation: Commute to work: 93.3% car, 0.0% public transportation, 3.6% walk, 1.7% work from home (2000); Travel time to work: 45.7% less than 15 minutes, 36.6% 15 to 30 minutes, 6.2% 30 to 45 minutes, 4.5% 45 to 60 minutes, 7.0% 60 minutes or more (2000)

ATLANTIC (city). Covers a land area of 8.150 square miles and a water area of 0.033 square miles. Located at 41.40° N. Lat.; 95.01° W. Long. Elevation is 1,215 feet.
History: Atlantic was thought to be halfway between the two oceans, and its name was to be either Atlantic or Pacific. A coin was flipped and Pacific won. But when it was learned that a number of other midwestern towns already had that name, the decision was reversed.
Population: 7,257 (2000); Race: 98.5% White, 0.2% Black, 0.5% Asian, 0.1% American Indian and Alaska Native, 1.1% Hispanic of any race, 0.4% two or more races (2000); Density: 890.4 persons per square mile (2000); Age: 22.8% under 18, 22.9% over 64 (2000); Marriage status: 19.0% never married, 58.5% now married, 12.2% widowed, 10.3% divorced (2000); Foreign born: 1.1% (2000); Ancestry (includes multiple ancestries): 34.2% German, 15.0% Danish, 11.7% Irish, 9.7% English, 4.9% United States or American (2000).
Economy: Single-family building permits issued: 4 (2001) / 22 (2000); Multi-family building permits issued: 2 (2001) / 0 (2000); Employment by occupation: 12.5% management, 16.8% professional, 15.3% services, 27.2% sales, 0.0% farming, 7.4% construction, 20.9% production (2000).
Income: Per capita income: $17,832 (2000); Median household income: $33,370 (2000); Poverty rate: 12.1% (2000).
Taxes: Total city taxes per capita: $396 (2000); City property taxes per capita: $295 (2000).
Education: High school graduation rate: 84.4% (2000); College graduation rate: 20.7% (2000).

School District(s)

Atlantic Community School District (PK-12)
2000 Enrollment: 1,672 712-243-4252
Housing: Homeownership rate: 70.1% (2000); Median home value: $68,200 (2000); Median rent: $281 per month (2000); Median age of housing: 48 years (2000).
Hospitals: Cass County Memorial Hospital (100 beds)
Newspapers: Atlantic News-Telegraph (6 x week); The Southwest Iowa Shopper (1 x week)
Transportation: Commute to work: 93.0% car, 0.6% public transportation, 3.6% walk, 2.4% work from home (2000); Travel time to work: 74.8% less than 15 minutes, 9.4% 15 to 30 minutes, 5.9% 30 to 45 minutes, 2.0% 45 to 60 minutes, 7.9% 60 minutes or more (2000)
Airports: Atlantic Municipal
Additional Information Contacts
Atlantic Chamber of Commerce.......................... 712-243-3017

CUMBERLAND (city). Covers a land area of 0.602 square miles and a water area of 0 square miles. Located at 41.27° N. Lat.; 94.87° W. Long. Elevation is 1,223 feet.
History: Cumberland was established in 1884. Its name commemorates the sinking of the U.S.S. Cumberland by the Merrimac in the 1862 sea battle.
Population: 281 (2000); Race: 100.0% White, 0.0% Black, 0.0% Asian, 0.0% American Indian and Alaska Native, 0.0% Hispanic of any race, 0.0% two or more races (2000); Density: 466.9 persons per square mile (2000); Age: 18.0% under 18, 30.1% over 64 (2000); Marriage status: 13.7% never married, 69.6% now married, 11.9% widowed, 4.8% divorced (2000); Foreign born: 0.0% (2000); Ancestry (includes multiple ancestries): 30.5% German, 19.2% Irish, 10.2% English, 6.4% United States or American, 3.8% Danish (2000).
Economy: Employment by occupation: 9.9% management, 7.4% professional, 19.0% services, 14.0% sales, 1.7% farming, 11.6% construction, 36.4% production (2000).
Income: Per capita income: $15,662 (2000); Median household income: $28,750 (2000); Poverty rate: 8.3% (2000).
Taxes: Total city taxes per capita: $110 (1997); City property taxes per capita: $107 (1997).
Education: High school graduation rate: 82.9% (2000); College graduation rate: 5.4% (2000).
Housing: Homeownership rate: 78.4% (2000); Median home value: $23,300 (2000); Median rent: $225 per month (2000); Median age of housing: 60+ years (2000).
Transportation: Commute to work: 88.4% car, 0.0% public transportation, 6.6% walk, 5.0% work from home (2000); Travel time to work: 24.3% less than 15 minutes, 44.3% 15 to 30 minutes, 14.8% 30 to 45 minutes, 3.5% 45 to 60 minutes, 13.0% 60 minutes or more (2000)

GRISWOLD (city). Covers a land area of 0.614 square miles and a water area of 0 square miles. Located at 41.23° N. Lat.; 95.14° W. Long. Elevation is 1,098 feet.
History: Griswold was named for J.N.R. Griswold, a New York merchant and banker, who was a director of the Chicago, Burlington & Quincy Railroad.
Population: 1,039 (2000); Race: 99.3% White, 0.0% Black, 0.0% Asian, 0.0% American Indian and Alaska Native, 2.2% Hispanic of any race, 0.2% two or more races (2000); Density: 1,691.0 persons per square mile (2000); Age: 20.2% under 18, 26.0% over 64 (2000); Marriage status: 16.8% never married, 63.9% now married, 10.8% widowed, 8.5% divorced (2000); Foreign born: 0.6% (2000); Ancestry (includes multiple ancestries): 34.2% German, 11.8% English, 11.5% United States or American, 9.7% Irish, 5.3% Other groups (2000).
Economy: Single-family building permits issued: 4 (2001) / 0 (2000); Multi-family building permits issued: 0 (2001) / 0 (2000); Employment by

occupation: 10.9% management, 17.1% professional, 14.5% services, 22.8% sales, 0.6% farming, 12.5% construction, 21.6% production (2000).
Income: Per capita income: $16,430 (2000); Median household income: $31,538 (2000); Poverty rate: 6.6% (2000).
Taxes: Total city taxes per capita: $128 (1997); City property taxes per capita: $117 (1997).
Education: High school graduation rate: 86.4% (2000); College graduation rate: 14.0% (2000).

School District(s)

Griswold Community School District (KG-12)
2000 Enrollment: 691 712-778-2152
Housing: Homeownership rate: 84.9% (2000); Median home value: $50,200 (2000); Median rent: $262 per month (2000); Median age of housing: 60+ years (2000).
Newspapers: Griswold American (1 x week)
Transportation: Commute to work: 86.6% car, 0.0% public transportation, 10.6% walk, 2.0% work from home (2000); Travel time to work: 43.1% less than 15 minutes, 27.6% 15 to 30 minutes, 14.3% 30 to 45 minutes, 7.0% 45 to 60 minutes, 8.0% 60 minutes or more (2000)

LEWIS (city). Covers a land area of 0.500 square miles and a water area of 0 square miles. Located at 41.30° N. Lat.; 95.08° W. Long. Elevation is 1,157 feet.
History: Lewis was named for Lewis Cass, U.S. Senator from Michigan. The town was an active station for the Underground Railway during John Brown's abolition campaign.
Population: 438 (2000); Race: 98.7% White, 0.4% Black, 0.0% Asian, 0.0% American Indian and Alaska Native, 0.4% Hispanic of any race, 0.0% two or more races (2000); Density: 876.0 persons per square mile (2000); Age: 27.2% under 18, 17.8% over 64 (2000); Marriage status: 17.5% never married, 58.0% now married, 11.3% widowed, 13.2% divorced (2000); Foreign born: 0.0% (2000); Ancestry (includes multiple ancestries): 23.4% German, 13.5% United States or American, 8.3% English, 8.3% Danish, 7.9% Irish (2000).
Economy: Single-family building permits issued: 1 (2001) / 0 (2000); Multi-family building permits issued: 0 (2001) / 0 (2000); Employment by occupation: 6.2% management, 7.8% professional, 21.2% services, 15.5% sales, 2.1% farming, 7.8% construction, 39.4% production (2000).
Income: Per capita income: $14,316 (2000); Median household income: $30,114 (2000); Poverty rate: 8.2% (2000).
Taxes: Total city taxes per capita: $88 (1997); City property taxes per capita: $81 (1997).
Education: High school graduation rate: 85.1% (2000); College graduation rate: 7.1% (2000).
Housing: Homeownership rate: 78.8% (2000); Median home value: $45,000 (2000); Median rent: $258 per month (2000); Median age of housing: 60+ years (2000).
Transportation: Commute to work: 92.1% car, 1.0% public transportation, 3.1% walk, 3.7% work from home (2000); Travel time to work: 28.3% less than 15 minutes, 47.8% 15 to 30 minutes, 4.9% 30 to 45 minutes, 12.0% 45 to 60 minutes, 7.1% 60 minutes or more (2000)

MARNE (city). Covers a land area of 0.574 square miles and a water area of 0 square miles. Located at 41.44° N. Lat.; 95.11° W. Long. Elevation is 1,193 feet.
History: Marne was named after Marne, Germany. The town was financed by an investment firm consisting of five German individuals.
Population: 149 (2000); Race: 99.2% White, 0.0% Black, 0.0% Asian, 0.0% American Indian and Alaska Native, 0.0% Hispanic of any race, 0.8% two or more races (2000); Density: 259.5 persons per square mile (2000); Age: 20.8% under 18, 9.6% over 64 (2000); Marriage status: 26.7% never married, 49.5% now married, 3.8% widowed, 20.0% divorced (2000); Foreign born: 0.0% (2000); Ancestry (includes multiple ancestries): 33.6% German, 24.0% Danish, 13.6% Irish, 10.4% United States or American, 10.4% English (2000).
Economy: Employment by occupation: 4.8% management, 0.0% professional, 17.7% services, 24.2% sales, 14.5% farming, 14.5% construction, 24.2% production (2000).
Income: Per capita income: $13,998 (2000); Median household income: $31,875 (2000); Poverty rate: 9.8% (2000).
Taxes: Total city taxes per capita: $111 (1997); City property taxes per capita: $105 (1997).
Education: High school graduation rate: 79.7% (2000); College graduation rate: 7.6% (2000).
Housing: Homeownership rate: 85.0% (2000); Median home value: $38,000 (2000); Median rent: $245 per month (2000); Median age of housing: 60+ years (2000).
Transportation: Commute to work: 82.8% car, 0.0% public transportation, 17.2% walk, 0.0% work from home (2000); Travel time to work: 65.5% less than 15 minutes, 13.8% 15 to 30 minutes, 12.1% 30 to 45 minutes, 0.0% 45 to 60 minutes, 8.6% 60 minutes or more (2000)

MASSENA (city). Covers a land area of 0.695 square miles and a water area of 0 square miles. Located at 41.25° N. Lat.; 94.76° W. Long. Elevation is 1,211 feet.
History: Massena was named for a town in New York from which many of the early settlers came. When the gold fever hit this vicinity in 1859, a number of settlers left for Pike's Peak, Colorado, only to return when the gold was not found.
Population: 414 (2000); Race: 99.5% White, 0.0% Black, 0.0% Asian, 0.5% American Indian and Alaska Native, 0.0% Hispanic of any race, 0.0% two or more races (2000); Density: 595.3 persons per square mile (2000); Age: 25.0% under 18, 18.9% over 64 (2000); Marriage status: 17.8% never married, 59.6% now married, 12.3% widowed, 10.2% divorced (2000); Foreign born: 0.0% (2000); Ancestry (includes multiple ancestries): 35.6% German, 19.8% Irish, 10.6% English, 9.7% United States or American, 5.2% Danish (2000).
Economy: Employment by occupation: 14.3% management, 11.9% professional, 13.8% services, 21.9% sales, 0.0% farming, 16.7% construction, 21.4% production (2000).
Income: Per capita income: $15,012 (2000); Median household income: $30,625 (2000); Poverty rate: 10.6% (2000).
Taxes: Total city taxes per capita: $142 (1997); City property taxes per capita: $129 (1997).
Education: High school graduation rate: 89.1% (2000); College graduation rate: 12.3% (2000).

School District(s)

C and M Community School District (KG-12)
2000 Enrollment: 244 712-779-2211
Housing: Homeownership rate: 89.3% (2000); Median home value: $37,100 (2000); Median rent: $219 per month (2000); Median age of housing: 56 years (2000).
Transportation: Commute to work: 90.0% car, 0.0% public transportation, 6.7% walk, 3.3% work from home (2000); Travel time to work: 50.7% less than 15 minutes, 19.2% 15 to 30 minutes, 15.8% 30 to 45 minutes, 4.4% 45 to 60 minutes, 9.9% 60 minutes or more (2000)
Additional Information Contacts
Massena Chamber of Commerce 712-779-2295

WIOTA (city). Covers a land area of 0.317 square miles and a water area of 0 square miles. Located at 41.40° N. Lat.; 94.88° W. Long. Elevation is 1,202 feet.
History: The name Wiota may have been taken from a Winnebago and Iowa word, niota, meaning "much water."
Population: 149 (2000); Race: 100.0% White, 0.0% Black, 0.0% Asian, 0.0% American Indian and Alaska Native, 0.0% Hispanic of any race, 0.0% two or more races (2000); Density: 469.6 persons per square mile (2000); Age: 18.9% under 18, 15.4% over 64 (2000); Marriage status: 15.6% never married, 57.4% now married, 8.2% widowed, 18.9% divorced (2000); Foreign born: 0.0% (2000); Ancestry (includes multiple ancestries): 41.3% German, 15.4% Danish, 12.6% Irish, 4.9% Italian, 4.2% United States or American (2000).
Economy: Employment by occupation: 11.6% management, 1.2% professional, 12.8% services, 20.9% sales, 8.1% farming, 17.4% construction, 27.9% production (2000).
Income: Per capita income: $15,994 (2000); Median household income: $29,167 (2000); Poverty rate: 20.3% (2000).
Taxes: Total city taxes per capita: $93 (1997); City property taxes per capita: $80 (1997).
Education: High school graduation rate: 82.7% (2000); College graduation rate: 4.8% (2000).
Housing: Homeownership rate: 80.9% (2000); Median home value: $41,700 (2000); Median rent: $284 per month (2000); Median age of housing: 60+ years (2000).
Transportation: Commute to work: 82.6% car, 0.0% public transportation, 2.3% walk, 11.6% work from home (2000); Travel time to work: 44.7% less than 15 minutes, 38.2% 15 to 30 minutes, 6.6% 30 to 45 minutes, 0.0% 45 to 60 minutes, 10.5% 60 minutes or more (2000)

Cedar County

Located in eastern Iowa; drained by the Cedar River. Covers a land area of 579.50 square miles, a water area of 2.40 square miles, and is located in the Central Time Zone. The county government was organized in 1837. County seat is Tipton.

Weather Station: Tipton 4 NE Elevation: 767 feet

	Jan	Feb	Mar	Apr	May	Jun	Jul	Aug	Sep	Oct	Nov	Dec
High	26	33	46	60	72	81	84	82	75	63	46	33
Low	8	14	26	37	49	58	62	59	50	39	27	15
Precip	1.2	1.4	2.4	3.6	4.6	4.4	4.1	4.6	3.7	2.7	2.6	1.9
Snow	6.5	5.8	2.9	1.3	tr	0.0	0.0	0.0	0.0	0.1	2.0	5.6

High and Low temperatures in degrees Fahrenheit; Precipitation and Snow in inches

Population: 18,187 (2000); Race: 98.7% White, 0.1% Black, 0.3% Asian, 0.1% American Indian and Alaska Native, 0.9% Hispanic of any race, 0.5% two or more races (2000); Density: 31.4 persons per square mile (2000); Age: 25.3% under 18, 16.2% over 64 (2000).
Religion: Five largest groups: 11.3% The United Methodist Church, 11.1% United Church of Christ, 11.1% Catholic Church, 8.4% Evangelical Lutheran Church in America, 4.4% Lutheran Church—Missouri Synod (2000).
Economy: Unemployment rate: 3.5% (11/2002); Total civilian labor force: 9,365 (11/2002); Leading industries: 22.5% manufacturing; 16.1% retail trade; 11.6% health care and social assistance (2000); Companies that employ more than 1,000 persons: 0 (2000); Companies that employ more than 100 persons: 4 (2000); Farms: 965 totaling 325,744 acres (1997); Minority business ownership rate: 0.0% (1997); Women business ownership rate: 24.5% (1997); Retail sales per capita: $5,604 (1997). Single-family building permits issued: 67 (2001) / 66 (2000); Multi-family building permits issued: 14 (2001) / 10 (2000).
Income: Per capita income: $19,200 (2000); Median household income: $42,198 (2000); Poverty rate: 5.5% (2000); Bankruptcy rate: 2.53% (2001).
Taxes: Total county taxes per capita: $265 (2000); County property taxes per capita: $260 (2000).
Education: High school graduation rate: 87.7% (2000); College graduation rate: 16.3% (2000).
Housing: Homeownership rate: 76.9% (2000); Median home value: $84,600 (2000); Median rent: $334 per month (2000); Median age of housing: 49 years (2000).
Health: Birth rate: 101.7 per 10,000 population (1998); Age adjusted death rate: 67.7 per 10,000 population (1999); Age adjusted cancer mortality rate: 144.4 deaths per 100,000 population (1999). Number of physicians: 3.3 per 10,000 population (1999); Number of hospital beds: n/a (1999).
Elections: 2000 Presidential election results: 48.3% Gore, 48.3% Bush, 2.5% Nader, 0.4% Buchanan
National and State Parks: Herbert Hoover National Historic Site
Additional Information Contacts
Cedar County Government Offices 563-886-3168
Durant Chamber of Commerce 563-785-6099
Tipton Chamber of Commerce.................... 563-886-6350

Cedar County Communities

BENNETT (city). Covers a land area of 0.206 square miles and a water area of 0 square miles. Located at 41.74° N. Lat.; 90.97° W. Long. Elevation is 742 feet.
History: Bennett was named for Chester Settle Bennett, an agent for the Burlington, Cedar Rapids & Minnesota Railroad.
Population: 395 (2000); Race: 99.5% White, 0.0% Black, 0.0% Asian, 0.0% American Indian and Alaska Native, 0.8% Hispanic of any race, 0.5% two or more races (2000); Density: 1,916.4 persons per square mile (2000); Age: 26.5% under 18, 14.4% over 64 (2000); Marriage status: 24.8% never married, 59.6% now married, 8.3% widowed, 7.3% divorced (2000); Foreign born: 0.5% (2000); Ancestry (includes multiple ancestries): 57.8% German, 10.5% Irish, 9.5% English, 4.4% Dutch, 3.3% Swedish (2000).
Economy: Single-family building permits issued: 1 (2001) / 1 (2000); Multi-family building permits issued: 0 (2001) / 0 (2000); Employment by occupation: 9.3% management, 10.8% professional, 14.7% services, 27.9% sales, 2.5% farming, 14.2% construction, 20.6% production (2000).
Income: Per capita income: $17,320 (2000); Median household income: $41,429 (2000); Poverty rate: 1.8% (2000).
Taxes: Total city taxes per capita: $127 (1997); City property taxes per capita: $127 (1997).
Education: High school graduation rate: 88.4% (2000); College graduation rate: 8.4% (2000).

School District(s)
Bennett Community School District (KG-12)
2000 Enrollment: 245 319-890-2226
Housing: Homeownership rate: 85.5% (2000); Median home value: $62,000 (2000); Median rent: $344 per month (2000); Median age of housing: 60+ years (2000).
Transportation: Commute to work: 85.3% car, 0.0% public transportation, 12.3% walk, 0.0% work from home (2000); Travel time to work: 25.5% less than 15 minutes, 32.4% 15 to 30 minutes, 23.0% 30 to 45 minutes, 14.2% 45 to 60 minutes, 4.9% 60 minutes or more (2000)

CLARENCE (city). Covers a land area of 0.632 square miles and a water area of 0 square miles. Located at 41.88° N. Lat.; 91.05° W. Long. Elevation is 825 feet.
History: Clarence was named for Clarence, New York. It was originally called Onion Grove because of the formerly abundant growth of wild onions in the timber along the banks of nearby Mill Creek.
Population: 1,008 (2000); Race: 99.6% White, 0.2% Black, 0.2% Asian, 0.0% American Indian and Alaska Native, 0.0% Hispanic of any race, 0.0% two or more races (2000); Density: 1,594.3 persons per square mile (2000); Age: 21.0% under 18, 27.2% over 64 (2000); Marriage status: 11.3% never married, 69.4% now married, 13.1% widowed, 6.1% divorced (2000); Foreign born: 0.7% (2000); Ancestry (includes multiple ancestries): 57.6% German, 11.6% Irish, 8.1% English, 5.1% Dutch, 5.0% Norwegian (2000).
Economy: Single-family building permits issued: 0 (2001) / 6 (2000); Multi-family building permits issued: 2 (2001) / 2 (2000); Employment by occupation: 9.5% management, 13.7% professional, 10.8% services, 33.4% sales, 1.7% farming, 10.4% construction, 20.5% production (2000).
Income: Per capita income: $17,157 (2000); Median household income: $36,042 (2000); Poverty rate: 4.9% (2000).
Taxes: Total city taxes per capita: $196 (1997); City property taxes per capita: $194 (1997).
Education: High school graduation rate: 85.9% (2000); College graduation rate: 12.1% (2000).
Housing: Homeownership rate: 74.0% (2000); Median home value: $65,900 (2000); Median rent: $342 per month (2000); Median age of housing: 50 years (2000).
Transportation: Commute to work: 88.1% car, 0.0% public transportation, 6.3% walk, 3.9% work from home (2000); Travel time to work: 45.1% less than 15 minutes, 16.9% 15 to 30 minutes, 15.8% 30 to 45 minutes, 17.4% 45 to 60 minutes, 4.7% 60 minutes or more (2000)

DURANT (city). Covers a land area of 0.995 square miles and a water area of 0 square miles. Located at 41.60° N. Lat.; 90.90° W. Long.
History: Durant was named for Thomas C. Durant, president of the Union Pacific Railroad.
Population: 1,677 (2000); Race: 98.3% White, 0.0% Black, 0.4% Asian, 0.0% American Indian and Alaska Native, 1.1% Hispanic of any race, 0.8% two or more races (2000); Density: 1,685.4 persons per square mile (2000); Age: 25.9% under 18, 17.9% over 64 (2000); Marriage status: 17.7% never married, 61.2% now married, 10.8% widowed, 10.3% divorced (2000); Foreign born: 1.3% (2000); Ancestry (includes multiple ancestries): 54.5% German, 11.6% Irish, 7.0% United States or American, 6.7% English, 5.5% Other groups (2000).
Economy: Single-family building permits issued: 14 (2001) / 5 (2000); Multi-family building permits issued: 0 (2001) / 0 (2000); Employment by occupation: 11.5% management, 10.2% professional, 15.3% services, 28.8% sales, 0.2% farming, 11.2% construction, 22.8% production (2000).
Income: Per capita income: $19,399 (2000); Median household income: $41,681 (2000); Poverty rate: 5.8% (2000).
Taxes: Total city taxes per capita: $238 (1997); City property taxes per capita: $214 (1997).
Education: High school graduation rate: 84.1% (2000); College graduation rate: 12.4% (2000).

School District(s)
Durant Community School District (KG-12)
2000 Enrollment: 700 319-785-4432
Housing: Homeownership rate: 76.6% (2000); Median home value: $89,900 (2000); Median rent: $359 per month (2000); Median age of housing: 46 years (2000).
Transportation: Commute to work: 91.1% car, 0.0% public transportation, 5.2% walk, 2.8% work from home (2000); Travel time to work: 40.3% less than 15 minutes, 27.1% 15 to 30 minutes, 25.4% 30 to 45 minutes, 3.3% 45 to 60 minutes, 3.9% 60 minutes or more (2000)
Additional Information Contacts
Durant Chamber of Commerce 563-785-6099

LOWDEN (city). Covers a land area of 1.011 square miles and a water area of 0 square miles. Located at 41.85° N. Lat.; 90.92° W. Long. Elevation is 717 feet.
History: Lowden is a version of Loudenville, Ohio. The town was named by Thomas Shearer, the owner of the site, who was from Loudenville, Ohio.
Population: 794 (2000); Race: 97.2% White, 0.5% Black, 0.8% Asian, 0.0% American Indian and Alaska Native, 1.9% Hispanic of any race, 1.3% two or more races (2000); Density: 785.3 persons per square mile (2000); Age: 23.1% under 18, 20.9% over 64 (2000); Marriage status: 15.8% never married, 64.7% now married, 11.2% widowed, 8.3% divorced (2000); Foreign born: 2.0% (2000); Ancestry (includes multiple ancestries): 56.3% German, 6.9% United States or American, 6.8% Irish, 5.0% Other groups, 4.0% Czech (2000).
Economy: Single-family building permits issued: 1 (2001) / 0 (2000); Multi-family building permits issued: 0 (2001) / 0 (2000); Employment by occupation: 10.6% management, 9.1% professional, 22.2% services, 22.2% sales, 0.0% farming, 14.4% construction, 21.7% production (2000).
Income: Per capita income: $18,303 (2000); Median household income: $35,714 (2000); Poverty rate: 6.0% (2000).
Taxes: Total city taxes per capita: $139 (1997); City property taxes per capita: $136 (1997).
Education: High school graduation rate: 82.3% (2000); College graduation rate: 12.3% (2000).
Housing: Homeownership rate: 80.4% (2000); Median home value: $66,700 (2000); Median rent: $313 per month (2000); Median age of housing: 56 years (2000).
Newspapers: Sun-News (1 x week)
Transportation: Commute to work: 91.6% car, 0.0% public transportation, 4.3% walk, 4.1% work from home (2000); Travel time to work: 43.9% less than 15 minutes, 23.7% 15 to 30 minutes, 10.9% 30 to 45 minutes, 11.2% 45 to 60 minutes, 10.4% 60 minutes or more (2000)

MECHANICSVILLE (city). Covers a land area of 0.741 square miles and a water area of 0.002 square miles. Located at 41.90° N. Lat.; 91.25° W. Long. Elevation is 895 feet.
History: Mechanicsville was so named because the first four settlers of the town were mechanics.
Population: 1,173 (2000); Race: 98.5% White, 0.0% Black, 0.0% Asian, 0.3% American Indian and Alaska Native, 2.6% Hispanic of any race, 1.0% two or more races (2000); Density: 1,582.5 persons per square mile (2000); Age: 26.3% under 18, 19.7% over 64 (2000); Marriage status: 19.7% never married, 59.2% now married, 11.6% widowed, 9.6% divorced (2000); Foreign born: 0.6% (2000); Ancestry (includes multiple ancestries): 38.0% German, 15.0% Irish, 12.9% English, 7.7% United States or American, 5.7% Other groups (2000).
Economy: Single-family building permits issued: 0 (2001) / 0 (2000); Multi-family building permits issued: 0 (2001) / 0 (2000); Employment by occupation: 9.9% management, 10.8% professional, 16.1% services, 28.0% sales, 0.4% farming, 11.6% construction, 23.3% production (2000).
Income: Per capita income: $16,429 (2000); Median household income: $36,053 (2000); Poverty rate: 7.9% (2000).
Taxes: Total city taxes per capita: $138 (1997); City property taxes per capita: $137 (1997).
Education: High school graduation rate: 80.0% (2000); College graduation rate: 10.7% (2000).
Housing: Homeownership rate: 79.8% (2000); Median home value: $74,100 (2000); Median rent: $317 per month (2000); Median age of housing: 56 years (2000).
Transportation: Commute to work: 90.7% car, 0.4% public transportation, 4.4% walk, 3.6% work from home (2000); Travel time to work: 23.3% less than 15 minutes, 27.1% 15 to 30 minutes, 30.7% 30 to 45 minutes, 10.8% 45 to 60 minutes, 8.1% 60 minutes or more (2000)

STANWOOD (city). Covers a land area of 0.642 square miles and a water area of 0 square miles. Located at 41.89° N. Lat.; 91.15° W. Long.
History: Stanwood was named for an official of the Chicago & North Western Railroad.
Population: 680 (2000); Race: 98.7% White, 0.0% Black, 0.7% Asian, 0.0% American Indian and Alaska Native, 0.0% Hispanic of any race, 0.6% two or more races (2000); Density: 1,059.9 persons per square mile (2000); Age: 27.2% under 18, 15.0% over 64 (2000); Marriage status: 19.6% never married, 61.6% now married, 6.9% widowed, 11.9% divorced (2000); Foreign born: 1.7% (2000); Ancestry (includes multiple ancestries): 41.9% German, 11.5% Irish, 7.9% English, 7.5% Other groups, 4.6% French (except Basque) (2000).
Economy: Single-family building permits issued: 2 (2001) / 2 (2000); Multi-family building permits issued: 0 (2001) / 0 (2000); Employment by occupation: 8.0% management, 19.9% professional, 13.7% services, 21.1% sales, 0.3% farming, 12.0% construction, 25.1% production (2000).
Income: Per capita income: $16,561 (2000); Median household income: $37,102 (2000); Poverty rate: 7.4% (2000).
Taxes: Total city taxes per capita: $140 (1997); City property taxes per capita: $137 (1997).
Education: High school graduation rate: 86.1% (2000); College graduation rate: 16.0% (2000).

School District(s)

North Cedar Community School District (KG-12)
2000 Enrollment: 957 319-942-3358
Housing: Homeownership rate: 79.0% (2000); Median home value: $66,800 (2000); Median rent: $281 per month (2000); Median age of housing: 60 years (2000).
Transportation: Commute to work: 92.0% car, 0.9% public transportation, 4.3% walk, 2.9% work from home (2000); Travel time to work: 29.7% less than 15 minutes, 25.9% 15 to 30 minutes, 25.0% 30 to 45 minutes, 15.9% 45 to 60 minutes, 3.5% 60 minutes or more (2000)

TIPTON (city). Covers a land area of 1.821 square miles and a water area of 0 square miles. Located at 41.77° N. Lat.; 91.12° W. Long. Elevation is 807 feet.
History: Tipton was named by a friend of Indiana senator General John Tipton.
Population: 3,155 (2000); Race: 99.1% White, 0.0% Black, 0.0% Asian, 0.3% American Indian and Alaska Native, 0.4% Hispanic of any race, 0.2% two or more races (2000); Density: 1,732.2 persons per square mile (2000); Age: 23.2% under 18, 20.9% over 64 (2000); Marriage status: 22.1% never married, 58.4% now married, 11.4% widowed, 8.2% divorced (2000); Foreign born: 0.0% (2000); Ancestry (includes multiple ancestries): 36.1% German, 13.2% Irish, 12.8% United States or American, 9.3% English, 3.8% Other groups (2000).
Economy: Single-family building permits issued: 13 (2001) / 4 (2000); Multi-family building permits issued: 0 (2001) / 4 (2000); Employment by occupation: 7.8% management, 16.2% professional, 15.9% services, 25.3% sales, 2.3% farming, 10.2% construction, 22.2% production (2000).
Income: Per capita income: $17,494 (2000); Median household income: $36,778 (2000); Poverty rate: 7.0% (2000).
Taxes: Total city taxes per capita: $202 (1997); City property taxes per capita: $200 (1997).
Education: High school graduation rate: 87.4% (2000); College graduation rate: 16.2% (2000).

School District(s)

Tipton Community School District (PK-12)
2000 Enrollment: 885 319-886-6121
Housing: Homeownership rate: 72.6% (2000); Median home value: $86,500 (2000); Median rent: $320 per month (2000); Median age of housing: 46 years (2000).
Safety: Violent crime rate: 0.0 per 10,000 population; Property crime rate: 161.8 per 10,000 population (2001).
Newspapers: The Tipton Conservative and Advertiser (1 x week); Cedar County Advertiser (1 x week)
Transportation: Commute to work: 90.5% car, 1.0% public transportation, 5.8% walk, 2.7% work from home (2000); Travel time to work: 47.7% less than 15 minutes, 15.9% 15 to 30 minutes, 22.3% 30 to 45 minutes, 10.4% 45 to 60 minutes, 3.7% 60 minutes or more (2000)
Additional Information Contacts
Tipton Chamber of Commerce 563-886-6350

WEST BRANCH (city). Covers a land area of 1.977 square miles and a water area of 0 square miles. Located at 41.67° N. Lat.; 91.34° W. Long. Elevation is 718 feet.
History: West Branch is the birthplace of Herbert Hoover, President of the United States (1929-1933).
Population: 2,188 (2000); Race: 96.6% White, 0.3% Black, 1.4% Asian, 0.0% American Indian and Alaska Native, 1.7% Hispanic of any race, 1.0% two or more races (2000); Density: 1,106.8 persons per square mile (2000); Age: 25.7% under 18, 14.9% over 64 (2000); Marriage status: 20.7% never married, 58.5% now married, 7.5% widowed, 13.3% divorced (2000); Foreign born: 2.0% (2000); Ancestry (includes multiple ancestries): 35.3% German, 19.0% Irish, 12.0% English, 8.4% United States or American, 5.6% Other groups (2000).
Economy: Single-family building permits issued: 9 (2001) / 18 (2000); Multi-family building permits issued: 12 (2001) / 0 (2000); Employment by

occupation: 9.5% management, 24.1% professional, 13.0% services, 27.5% sales, 0.0% farming, 10.0% construction, 15.8% production (2000).
Income: Per capita income: $19,577 (2000); Median household income: $42,500 (2000); Poverty rate: 4.7% (2000).
Taxes: Total city taxes per capita: $309 (2000); City property taxes per capita: $293 (2000).
Education: High school graduation rate: 91.2% (2000); College graduation rate: 23.8% (2000).

School District(s)

West Branch Community School District (PK-12)
2000 Enrollment: 902 319-643-7213
Housing: Homeownership rate: 78.6% (2000); Median home value: $97,200 (2000); Median rent: $367 per month (2000); Median age of housing: 29 years (2000).
Newspapers: West Branch Times (1 x week)
Transportation: Commute to work: 93.2% car, 0.0% public transportation, 2.9% walk, 2.7% work from home (2000); Travel time to work: 27.0% less than 15 minutes, 54.4% 15 to 30 minutes, 13.5% 30 to 45 minutes, 2.9% 45 to 60 minutes, 2.2% 60 minutes or more (2000)

Cerro Gordo County

Located in northern Iowa; drained by the Shell Rock River and Lime Creek. Covers a land area of 568.30 square miles, a water area of 6.80 square miles, and is located in the Central Time Zone. The county government was organized in 1851. County seat is Mason City.

Weather Station: Mason City — Elevation: 1,089 feet

	Jan	Feb	Mar	Apr	May	Jun	Jul	Aug	Sep	Oct	Nov	Dec
High	23	30	42	58	71	81	84	81	74	61	42	28
Low	4	12	23	35	47	57	61	58	49	38	24	11
Precip	0.9	0.8	2.0	3.3	4.4	5.0	4.6	4.7	3.5	2.7	2.1	1.0
Snow	8.3	5.3	5.6	0.9	0.0	0.0	0.0	0.0	0.0	0.2	3.0	na

High and Low temperatures in degrees Fahrenheit; Precipitation and Snow in inches

Weather Station: Mason City Municipal Airport — Elevation: 1,190 feet

	Jan	Feb	Mar	Apr	May	Jun	Jul	Aug	Sep	Oct	Nov	Dec
High	22	29	41	57	71	80	83	81	73	60	42	27
Low	5	12	24	36	47	57	61	59	49	37	24	11
Precip	1.0	0.9	2.3	3.4	4.4	4.8	4.4	4.5	3.3	2.6	2.0	1.1
Snow	10.9	6.6	6.7	2.4	tr	tr	tr	tr	tr	0.5	5.0	8.4

High and Low temperatures in degrees Fahrenheit; Precipitation and Snow in inches

Population: 46,447 (2000); Race: 96.4% White, 0.9% Black, 0.7% Asian, 0.2% American Indian and Alaska Native, 2.6% Hispanic of any race, 1.0% two or more races (2000); Density: 81.7 persons per square mile (2000); Age: 24.0% under 18, 17.7% over 64 (2000).
Religion: Five largest groups: 20.1% Evangelical Lutheran Church in America, 19.1% Catholic Church, 11.4% The United Methodist Church, 2.6% Lutheran Church—Missouri Synod, 1.1% Christian Church (Disciples of Christ) (2000).
Economy: Unemployment rate: 3.6% (11/2002); Total civilian labor force: 26,544 (11/2002); Leading industries: 24.2% health care and social assistance; 17.5% manufacturing; 17.0% retail trade (2000); Companies that employ more than 1,000 persons: 1 (2000); Companies that employ more than 100 persons: 32 (2000); Farms: 822 totaling 300,851 acres (1997); Minority business ownership rate: 0.0% (1997); Women business ownership rate: 22.5% (1997); Retail sales per capita: $13,168 (1997). Single-family building permits issued: 60 (2001) / 66 (2000); Multi-family building permits issued: 19 (2001) / 14 (2000).
Income: Per capita income: $19,184 (2000); Median household income: $35,867 (2000); Poverty rate: 8.5% (2000); Bankruptcy rate: 3.40% (2001).
Taxes: Total county taxes per capita: $217 (2000); County property taxes per capita: $184 (2000).
Education: High school graduation rate: 87.3% (2000); College graduation rate: 20.3% (2000).
Housing: Homeownership rate: 71.5% (2000); Median home value: $75,400 (2000); Median rent: $338 per month (2000); Median age of housing: 47 years (2000).
Health: Birth rate: 113.0 per 10,000 population (1998); Age adjusted death rate: 80.5 per 10,000 population (1999); Age adjusted cancer mortality rate: 196.1 deaths per 100,000 population (1999). Air Quality Index: 98% good, 2% moderate, 0% unhealthy (percent of days in 2000). Number of physicians: 29.3 per 10,000 population (1999); Number of hospital beds: 53.2 per 10,000 population (1999).
Elections: 2000 Presidential election results: 55.0% Gore, 42.4% Bush, 1.8% Nader, 0.4% Buchanan
National and State Parks: Clear Lake State Game Management Area; Clear Lake State Park; Historic Northern Iowa State Historical Marker; McIntosh Woods State Park
Additional Information Contacts
Cerro Gordo County Government Offices 641-421-3021
Cedar Valley Board of Realtors 641-749-5341
Clear Lake Board of Realtors 641-357-6123
Clear Lake Chamber of Commerce 641-357-2159
Greater Mason City Board of Realtors 641-423-1972
Mason City Chamber of Commerce 641-423-5724

Cerro Gordo County Communities

CLEAR LAKE (city). Covers a land area of 10.431 square miles and a water area of 2.596 square miles. Located at 43.13° N. Lat.; 93.38° W. Long. Elevation is 1,233 feet.
History: Clear Lake was named for the six-mile lake on whose shore the town was built.
Population: 8,161 (2000); Race: 97.6% White, 0.1% Black, 0.8% Asian, 0.3% American Indian and Alaska Native, 1.5% Hispanic of any race, 0.7% two or more races (2000); Density: 782.4 persons per square mile (2000); Age: 23.0% under 18, 18.1% over 64 (2000); Marriage status: 23.6% never married, 57.5% now married, 7.7% widowed, 11.2% divorced (2000); Foreign born: 1.7% (2000); Ancestry (includes multiple ancestries): 40.5% German, 16.5% Norwegian, 13.2% Irish, 10.5% English, 4.8% Other groups (2000).
Economy: Single-family building permits issued: 15 (2001) / 10 (2000); Multi-family building permits issued: 6 (2001) / 0 (2000); Employment by occupation: 10.7% management, 16.7% professional, 18.1% services, 26.5% sales, 0.1% farming, 9.8% construction, 18.2% production (2000).
Income: Per capita income: $20,213 (2000); Median household income: $35,097 (2000); Poverty rate: 7.6% (2000).
Taxes: Total city taxes per capita: $403 (1997); City property taxes per capita: $246 (1997).
Education: High school graduation rate: 87.2% (2000); College graduation rate: 24.0% (2000).

School District(s)

Clear Lake Community School District (PK-12)
2000 Enrollment: 1,513 641-357-2181
Housing: Homeownership rate: 74.9% (2000); Median home value: $90,900 (2000); Median rent: $333 per month (2000); Median age of housing: 38 years (2000).
Newspapers: Clear Lake Mirror-Reporter (1 x week); The Advertiser (1 x week)
Transportation: Commute to work: 88.3% car, 1.6% public transportation, 5.7% walk, 3.6% work from home (2000); Travel time to work: 58.3% less than 15 minutes, 33.0% 15 to 30 minutes, 5.6% 30 to 45 minutes, 1.1% 45 to 60 minutes, 1.9% 60 minutes or more (2000)
Additional Information Contacts
Clear Lake Board of Realtors 641-357-6123
Clear Lake Chamber of Commerce 641-357-2159

DOUGHERTY (city). Covers a land area of 0.554 square miles and a water area of 0 square miles. Located at 42.92° N. Lat.; 93.04° W. Long. Elevation is 1,100 feet.
History: The first settler in this area, Daniel Dougherty, gave his name to the town of Dougherty.
Population: 80 (2000); Race: 91.7% White, 0.0% Black, 0.0% Asian, 0.0% American Indian and Alaska Native, 8.3% Hispanic of any race, 0.0% two or more races (2000); Density: 144.5 persons per square mile (2000); Age: 18.1% under 18, 15.3% over 64 (2000); Marriage status: 23.9% never married, 53.7% now married, 11.9% widowed, 10.4% divorced (2000); Foreign born: 8.3% (2000); Ancestry (includes multiple ancestries): 29.2% Irish, 29.2% German, 12.5% Other groups, 9.7% Norwegian, 8.3% United States or American (2000).
Economy: Employment by occupation: 3.9% management, 7.8% professional, 7.8% services, 21.6% sales, 0.0% farming, 13.7% construction, 45.1% production (2000).
Income: Per capita income: $19,569 (2000); Median household income: $36,458 (2000); Poverty rate: 4.2% (2000).
Taxes: Total city taxes per capita: $225 (1997); City property taxes per capita: $118 (1997).

Education: High school graduation rate: 82.5% (2000); College graduation rate: 7.0% (2000).
Housing: Homeownership rate: 100.0% (2000); Median home value: $18,300 (2000); Median age of housing: 60+ years (2000).
Transportation: Commute to work: 94.1% car, 0.0% public transportation, 5.9% walk, 0.0% work from home (2000); Travel time to work: 19.6% less than 15 minutes, 25.5% 15 to 30 minutes, 35.3% 30 to 45 minutes, 19.6% 45 to 60 minutes, 0.0% 60 minutes or more (2000)

MASON CITY (city). Covers a land area of 25.786 square miles and a water area of 0.377 square miles. Located at 43.14° N. Lat.; 93.20° W. Long. Elevation is 1,120 feet.
History: Mason City was orginally known as Masonic Grove, but the name was changed when the town was platted in 1854. Most of the early pioneers were of the Masonic order.
Population: 29,172 (2000); Race: 95.2% White, 1.3% Black, 0.8% Asian, 0.2% American Indian and Alaska Native, 3.3% Hispanic of any race, 1.2% two or more races (2000); Density: 1,131.3 persons per square mile (2000); Age: 23.8% under 18, 17.9% over 64 (2000); Marriage status: 24.4% never married, 54.6% now married, 9.7% widowed, 11.3% divorced (2000); Foreign born: 1.5% (2000); Ancestry (includes multiple ancestries): 40.2% German, 16.3% Norwegian, 13.2% Irish, 9.6% English, 7.7% Other groups (2000).
Vital Statistics: Birth rate: 119.0 per 10,000 population (1998)
Economy: Unemployment rate: 3.2% (11/2002); Total civilian labor force: 16,254 (11/2002); Single-family building permits issued: 31 (2001) / 36 (2000); Multi-family building permits issued: 9 (2001) / 14 (2000); Employment by occupation: 10.5% management, 17.4% professional, 16.6% services, 27.9% sales, 0.2% farming, 7.7% construction, 19.7% production (2000).
Income: Per capita income: $18,899 (2000); Median household income: $33,852 (2000); Poverty rate: 10.0% (2000).
Taxes: Total city taxes per capita: $430 (2000); City property taxes per capita: $292 (2000).
Education: High school graduation rate: 86.5% (2000); College graduation rate: 20.0% (2000).

School District(s)

Mason City Community School District (PK-12)
2000 Enrollment: 4,470 641-421-4400

Four-year College(s)

Hamilton College-Mason City Branch (Private, For-profit)
2001 Enrollment: 286 515-423-2530
2001 Tuition: In-state $9,360; Out-of-state $9,360

Two-year College(s)

La James College of Hairstyling and Cosmetology (Private, For-profit)
2001 Enrollment: 90 641-424-2161

North Iowa Area Community College (Public)
2001 Enrollment: 2,722 641-423-1264
2001 Tuition: In-state $2,073; Out-of-state $3,084

Mercy Medical Center-North Iowa School of Rad Tech (Private, Not-for-profit, Roman Catholic)
2001 Enrollment: n/a 641-422-7200

Housing: Homeownership rate: 67.4% (2000); Median home value: $72,700 (2000); Median rent: $341 per month (2000); Median age of housing: 48 years (2000).
Hospitals: Mercy Medical Center-North Iowa (350 beds)
Safety: Violent crime rate: 17.8 per 10,000 population; Property crime rate: 621.5 per 10,000 population (2001).
Newspapers: Globe-Gazette (7 x week); Mason City Shopper (1 x week); Business Journal (1 x month)
Transportation: Commute to work: 92.4% car, 1.3% public transportation, 3.0% walk, 2.5% work from home (2000); Travel time to work: 70.5% less than 15 minutes, 20.6% 15 to 30 minutes, 4.6% 30 to 45 minutes, 1.7% 45 to 60 minutes, 2.6% 60 minutes or more (2000)
Airports: Mason City Municipal (primary service)

Additional Information Contacts

Cedar Valley Board of Realtors 641-749-5341
Greater Mason City Board of Realtors. 641-423-1972
Mason City Chamber of Commerce. 641-423-5724

MESERVEY (city). Covers a land area of 1.510 square miles and a water area of 0 square miles. Located at 42.91° N. Lat.; 93.47° W. Long. Elevation is 1,246 feet.
History: Meservey was first named Kausville. The name was changed to honor a railroad promoter S. T. Meservey.
Population: 252 (2000); Race: 96.9% White, 0.0% Black, 0.0% Asian, 0.0% American Indian and Alaska Native, 6.6% Hispanic of any race, 1.9% two or more races (2000); Density: 166.9 persons per square mile (2000); Age: 17.5% under 18, 28.0% over 64 (2000); Marriage status: 6.9% never married, 73.1% now married, 9.3% widowed, 10.6% divorced (2000); Foreign born: 2.3% (2000); Ancestry (includes multiple ancestries): 47.1% German, 12.5% Norwegian, 9.3% Irish, 7.4% Other groups, 7.4% United States or American (2000).
Economy: Single-family building permits issued: 0 (2001) / 0 (2000); Multi-family building permits issued: 0 (2001) / 0 (2000); Employment by occupation: 9.1% management, 9.9% professional, 13.2% services, 33.9% sales, 4.1% farming, 8.3% construction, 21.5% production (2000).
Income: Per capita income: $16,043 (2000); Median household income: $32,500 (2000); Poverty rate: 8.9% (2000).
Taxes: Total city taxes per capita: $186 (1997); City property taxes per capita: $75 (1997).
Education: High school graduation rate: 79.8% (2000); College graduation rate: 8.3% (2000).
Housing: Homeownership rate: 83.6% (2000); Median home value: $28,800 (2000); Median rent: $233 per month (2000); Median age of housing: 53 years (2000).
Transportation: Commute to work: 92.4% car, 0.0% public transportation, 5.1% walk, 0.0% work from home (2000); Travel time to work: 25.4% less than 15 minutes, 39.0% 15 to 30 minutes, 22.0% 30 to 45 minutes, 5.1% 45 to 60 minutes, 8.5% 60 minutes or more (2000)

PLYMOUTH (city). Covers a land area of 0.439 square miles and a water area of 0 square miles. Located at 43.24° N. Lat.; 93.12° W. Long. Elevation is 1,128 feet.
History: Plymouth was laid out when the railroad came through the area. It is named after Plymouth, England.
Population: 429 (2000); Race: 97.8% White, 0.0% Black, 0.0% Asian, 0.0% American Indian and Alaska Native, 2.7% Hispanic of any race, 1.3% two or more races (2000); Density: 976.6 persons per square mile (2000); Age: 33.0% under 18, 17.8% over 64 (2000); Marriage status: 17.9% never married, 67.3% now married, 9.4% widowed, 5.5% divorced (2000); Foreign born: 0.7% (2000); Ancestry (includes multiple ancestries): 49.2% German, 17.6% Irish, 11.8% English, 9.1% Norwegian, 7.6% United States or American (2000).
Economy: Single-family building permits issued: 0 (2001) / 0 (2000); Multi-family building permits issued: 0 (2001) / 0 (2000); Employment by occupation: 4.9% management, 10.8% professional, 16.8% services, 30.8% sales, 0.5% farming, 12.4% construction, 23.8% production (2000).
Income: Per capita income: $12,888 (2000); Median household income: $32,344 (2000); Poverty rate: 6.3% (2000).
Taxes: Total city taxes per capita: $119 (1997); City property taxes per capita: $16 (1997).
Education: High school graduation rate: 86.6% (2000); College graduation rate: 6.5% (2000).
Housing: Homeownership rate: 81.1% (2000); Median home value: $54,200 (2000); Median rent: $258 per month (2000); Median age of housing: 60+ years (2000).
Transportation: Commute to work: 94.0% car, 0.0% public transportation, 4.4% walk, 1.6% work from home (2000); Travel time to work: 15.0% less than 15 minutes, 63.9% 15 to 30 minutes, 7.2% 30 to 45 minutes, 5.0% 45 to 60 minutes, 8.9% 60 minutes or more (2000)

ROCK FALLS (city). Covers a land area of 0.211 square miles and a water area of 0 square miles. Located at 43.20° N. Lat.; 93.08° W. Long. Elevation is 1,104 feet.
History: Rock Falls was named for its location on the Shell Rock River.
Population: 170 (2000); Race: 100.0% White, 0.0% Black, 0.0% Asian, 0.0% American Indian and Alaska Native, 0.0% Hispanic of any race, 0.0% two or more races (2000); Density: 806.7 persons per square mile (2000); Age: 17.6% under 18, 25.6% over 64 (2000); Marriage status: 15.5% never married, 72.9% now married, 7.1% widowed, 4.5% divorced (2000); Foreign born: 1.1% (2000); Ancestry (includes multiple ancestries): 40.3% German, 11.9% Norwegian, 9.7% English, 8.5% Czech, 8.0% United States or American (2000).
Economy: Single-family building permits issued: 0 (2001) / 0 (2000); Multi-family building permits issued: 0 (2001) / 0 (2000); Employment by occupation: 14.3% management, 4.4% professional, 14.3% services, 25.3% sales, 0.0% farming, 11.0% construction, 30.8% production (2000).
Income: Per capita income: $17,523 (2000); Median household income: $40,714 (2000); Poverty rate: 1.1% (2000).

Taxes: Total city taxes per capita: $174 (1997); City property taxes per capita: $77 (1997).
Education: High school graduation rate: 91.9% (2000); College graduation rate: 8.9% (2000).
Housing: Homeownership rate: 88.7% (2000); Median home value: $67,100 (2000); Median rent: $275 per month (2000); Median age of housing: 48 years (2000).
Transportation: Commute to work: 94.5% car, 0.0% public transportation, 0.0% walk, 5.5% work from home (2000); Travel time to work: 18.6% less than 15 minutes, 68.6% 15 to 30 minutes, 9.3% 30 to 45 minutes, 0.0% 45 to 60 minutes, 3.5% 60 minutes or more (2000)

ROCKWELL (city). Covers a land area of 2.969 square miles and a water area of 0 square miles. Located at 42.98° N. Lat.; 93.19° W. Long. Elevation is 1,130 feet.
History: Rockwell was named for B. G. Rockwell, at one time owner of the land on which the village stands.
Population: 989 (2000); Race: 97.4% White, 0.0% Black, 0.2% Asian, 0.0% American Indian and Alaska Native, 2.9% Hispanic of any race, 2.0% two or more races (2000); Density: 333.2 persons per square mile (2000); Age: 26.8% under 18, 21.7% over 64 (2000); Marriage status: 17.9% never married, 63.4% now married, 11.4% widowed, 7.3% divorced (2000); Foreign born: 0.5% (2000); Ancestry (includes multiple ancestries): 48.7% German, 15.3% Irish, 15.0% Norwegian, 7.5% English, 5.4% Other groups (2000).
Economy: Single-family building permits issued: 4 (2001) / 3 (2000); Multi-family building permits issued: 0 (2001) / 0 (2000); Employment by occupation: 12.4% management, 11.7% professional, 18.4% services, 26.5% sales, 1.1% farming, 8.4% construction, 21.5% production (2000).
Income: Per capita income: $16,491 (2000); Median household income: $39,219 (2000); Poverty rate: 6.8% (2000).
Taxes: Total city taxes per capita: $253 (1997); City property taxes per capita: $144 (1997).
Education: High school graduation rate: 88.8% (2000); College graduation rate: 9.3% (2000).

School District(s)

Rockwell-Swaledale Community School District (PK-12)
2000 Enrollment: 457 641-822-3236

Housing: Homeownership rate: 85.7% (2000); Median home value: $62,500 (2000); Median rent: $268 per month (2000); Median age of housing: 46 years (2000).
Transportation: Commute to work: 94.4% car, 0.4% public transportation, 1.8% walk, 2.7% work from home (2000); Travel time to work: 30.0% less than 15 minutes, 53.7% 15 to 30 minutes, 10.8% 30 to 45 minutes, 3.2% 45 to 60 minutes, 2.3% 60 minutes or more (2000)

SWALEDALE (city). Covers a land area of 0.255 square miles and a water area of 0 square miles. Located at 42.97° N. Lat.; 93.31° W. Long. Elevation is 1,150 feet.
History: Swaledale is believed to have been named for a railroad associate with the Mason City & Fort Dodge Railroad.
Population: 174 (2000); Race: 100.0% White, 0.0% Black, 0.0% Asian, 0.0% American Indian and Alaska Native, 0.0% Hispanic of any race, 0.0% two or more races (2000); Density: 682.9 persons per square mile (2000); Age: 33.2% under 18, 18.1% over 64 (2000); Marriage status: 14.9% never married, 68.7% now married, 8.2% widowed, 8.2% divorced (2000); Foreign born: 0.0% (2000); Ancestry (includes multiple ancestries): 51.8% German, 23.8% Irish, 15.0% Norwegian, 8.8% Danish, 7.8% United States or American (2000).
Economy: Single-family building permits issued: 0 (2001) / 0 (2000); Multi-family building permits issued: 0 (2001) / 0 (2000); Employment by occupation: 11.0% management, 1.2% professional, 17.1% services, 28.0% sales, 0.0% farming, 15.9% construction, 26.8% production (2000).
Income: Per capita income: $11,710 (2000); Median household income: $28,906 (2000); Poverty rate: 5.2% (2000).
Taxes: Total city taxes per capita: $231 (1997); City property taxes per capita: $124 (1997).
Education: High school graduation rate: 89.9% (2000); College graduation rate: 4.6% (2000).
Housing: Homeownership rate: 80.6% (2000); Median home value: $23,500 (2000); Median rent: $280 per month (2000); Median age of housing: 52 years (2000).
Transportation: Commute to work: 80.5% car, 0.0% public transportation, 8.5% walk, 11.0% work from home (2000); Travel time to work: 16.4% less than 15 minutes, 37.0% 15 to 30 minutes, 35.6% 30 to 45 minutes, 4.1% 45 to 60 minutes, 6.8% 60 minutes or more (2000)

THORNTON (city). Covers a land area of 1.246 square miles and a water area of 0 square miles. Located at 42.94° N. Lat.; 93.38° W. Long. Elevation is 1,192 feet.
History: Thornton was named for the mother of a prominent landowner in the area.
Population: 422 (2000); Race: 100.0% White, 0.0% Black, 0.0% Asian, 0.0% American Indian and Alaska Native, 0.0% Hispanic of any race, 0.0% two or more races (2000); Density: 338.6 persons per square mile (2000); Age: 20.4% under 18, 25.7% over 64 (2000); Marriage status: 21.6% never married, 62.3% now married, 9.1% widowed, 7.0% divorced (2000); Foreign born: 0.0% (2000); Ancestry (includes multiple ancestries): 43.6% German, 11.3% Norwegian, 10.6% English, 9.8% Danish, 9.8% Irish (2000).
Economy: Single-family building permits issued: 1 (2001) / 1 (2000); Multi-family building permits issued: 0 (2001) / 0 (2000); Employment by occupation: 10.8% management, 19.5% professional, 13.0% services, 23.8% sales, 1.1% farming, 9.2% construction, 22.7% production (2000).
Income: Per capita income: $16,622 (2000); Median household income: $35,125 (2000); Poverty rate: 11.0% (2000).
Taxes: Total city taxes per capita: $251 (1997); City property taxes per capita: $140 (1997).
Education: High school graduation rate: 89.2% (2000); College graduation rate: 17.6% (2000).

School District(s)

Meservey-Thornton Community School District (KG-12)
2000 Enrollment: 196 641-998-2315

Housing: Homeownership rate: 81.0% (2000); Median home value: $46,100 (2000); Median rent: $210 per month (2000); Median age of housing: 49 years (2000).
Newspapers: Southern County News (1 x week)
Transportation: Commute to work: 90.7% car, 0.0% public transportation, 6.6% walk, 0.5% work from home (2000); Travel time to work: 29.7% less than 15 minutes, 44.0% 15 to 30 minutes, 24.7% 30 to 45 minutes, 0.0% 45 to 60 minutes, 1.6% 60 minutes or more (2000)

VENTURA (city). Covers a land area of 1.729 square miles and a water area of 0.640 square miles. Located at 43.12° N. Lat.; 93.47° W. Long.
History: Ventura was once known as Thayer's Siding. It was located on the Chicago, Milwaukee & St. Paul Railroad.
Population: 670 (2000); Race: 98.7% White, 0.0% Black, 0.0% Asian, 0.0% American Indian and Alaska Native, 1.3% Hispanic of any race, 0.6% two or more races (2000); Density: 387.4 persons per square mile (2000); Age: 23.0% under 18, 19.0% over 64 (2000); Marriage status: 17.3% never married, 66.7% now married, 6.9% widowed, 9.1% divorced (2000); Foreign born: 0.6% (2000); Ancestry (includes multiple ancestries): 38.8% German, 17.0% Norwegian, 10.7% Irish, 9.8% English, 9.8% United States or American (2000).
Economy: Single-family building permits issued: 0 (2001) / 5 (2000); Multi-family building permits issued: 0 (2001) / 0 (2000); Employment by occupation: 17.9% management, 19.6% professional, 10.4% services, 21.7% sales, 0.6% farming, 12.2% construction, 17.6% production (2000).
Income: Per capita income: $22,994 (2000); Median household income: $41,875 (2000); Poverty rate: 4.0% (2000).
Taxes: Total city taxes per capita: $302 (1997); City property taxes per capita: $183 (1997).
Education: High school graduation rate: 88.7% (2000); College graduation rate: 24.2% (2000).

School District(s)

Ventura Community School District (KG-12)
2000 Enrollment: 339 641-829-4484

Housing: Homeownership rate: 83.0% (2000); Median home value: $88,600 (2000); Median rent: $370 per month (2000); Median age of housing: 40 years (2000).
Transportation: Commute to work: 90.7% car, 0.6% public transportation, 4.8% walk, 3.3% work from home (2000); Travel time to work: 38.0% less than 15 minutes, 44.9% 15 to 30 minutes, 10.6% 30 to 45 minutes, 2.8% 45 to 60 minutes, 3.7% 60 minutes or more (2000)

Cherokee County

Located in northwestern Iowa; drained by the Little Sioux and Maple Rivers. Covers a land area of 577.20 square miles, a water area of 0.20 square miles, and is located in the Central Time Zone. The county government was organized in 1851. County seat is Cherokee.

Weather Station: Cherokee Elevation: 1,177 feet

	Jan	Feb	Mar	Apr	May	Jun	Jul	Aug	Sep	Oct	Nov	Dec
High	25	32	44	59	72	81	85	83	75	62	44	30
Low	5	11	23	35	47	57	62	59	48	36	23	11
Precip	0.6	0.6	2.0	2.8	3.7	4.5	3.9	3.5	3.2	2.1	1.6	0.8
Snow	6.4	5.7	5.7	1.5	0.0	0.0	0.0	0.0	0.0	0.3	4.8	6.7

High and Low temperatures in degrees Fahrenheit; Precipitation and Snow in inches

Population: 13,035 (2000); Race: 98.4% White, 0.6% Black, 0.4% Asian, 0.0% American Indian and Alaska Native, 0.6% Hispanic of any race, 0.3% two or more races (2000); Density: 22.6 persons per square mile (2000); Age: 24.5% under 18, 20.3% over 64 (2000).
Religion: Five largest groups: 21.1% Catholic Church, 16.8% The United Methodist Church, 14.7% Lutheran Church—Missouri Synod, 8.6% Evangelical Lutheran Church in America, 4.9% Presbyterian Church (U.S.A.) (2000).
Economy: Unemployment rate: 3.4% (11/2002); Total civilian labor force: 6,923 (11/2002); Leading industries: 21.3% health care and social assistance; 20.2% manufacturing; 17.3% retail trade (2000); Companies that employ more than 1,000 persons: 0 (2000); Companies that employ more than 100 persons: 6 (2000); Farms: 890 totaling 330,355 acres (1997); Minority business ownership rate: 0.0% (1997); Women business ownership rate: 12.4% (1997); Retail sales per capita: $8,058 (1997). Single-family building permits issued: 15 (2001) / 17 (2000); Multi-family building permits issued: 0 (2001) / 0 (2000).
Income: Per capita income: $17,934 (2000); Median household income: $35,142 (2000); Poverty rate: 7.3% (2000); Bankruptcy rate: 2.99% (2001).
Taxes: Total county taxes per capita: $254 (1997); County property taxes per capita: $247 (1997).
Education: High school graduation rate: 87.5% (2000); College graduation rate: 15.2% (2000).
Housing: Homeownership rate: 73.5% (2000); Median home value: $57,300 (2000); Median rent: $260 per month (2000); Median age of housing: 54 years (2000).
Health: Birth rate: 100.5 per 10,000 population (1998); Age adjusted death rate: 83.5 per 10,000 population (1999); Age adjusted cancer mortality rate: 234.8 deaths per 100,000 population (1999). Number of physicians: 9.2 per 10,000 population (1999); Number of hospital beds: 115.1 per 10,000 population (1999).
Elections: 2000 Presidential election results: 43.2% Gore, 52.5% Bush, 2.4% Nader, 1.3% Buchanan
National and State Parks: Nester Stiles State Preserve; Steele Prairie State Preserve
Additional Information Contacts
Cherokee County Government Offices 712-225-6704
Cherokee Chamber of Commerce 712-225-6414

Cherokee County Communities

AURELIA (city). Covers a land area of 1.046 square miles and a water area of 0 square miles. Located at 42.71° N. Lat.; 95.43° W. Long. Elevation is 1,387 feet.
History: Aurelia was named for Aurelia Blair, daughter of John Blair, an early settler. Alta, Iowa, was named for another daughter of John Blair.
Population: 1,062 (2000); Race: 98.3% White, 0.0% Black, 0.6% Asian, 0.0% American Indian and Alaska Native, 1.1% Hispanic of any race, 0.0% two or more races (2000); Density: 1,015.2 persons per square mile (2000); Age: 24.3% under 18, 28.9% over 64 (2000); Marriage status: 16.3% never married, 64.4% now married, 12.2% widowed, 7.1% divorced (2000); Foreign born: 1.4% (2000); Ancestry (includes multiple ancestries): 53.8% German, 12.8% Swedish, 10.5% English, 10.1% Irish, 4.8% United States or American (2000).
Economy: Single-family building permits issued: 0 (2001) / 0 (2000); Multi-family building permits issued: 0 (2001) / 0 (2000); Employment by occupation: 12.9% management, 19.2% professional, 15.1% services, 22.3% sales, 2.7% farming, 10.4% construction, 17.4% production (2000).
Income: Per capita income: $17,417 (2000); Median household income: $37,250 (2000); Poverty rate: 5.7% (2000).
Taxes: Total city taxes per capita: $259 (1997); City property taxes per capita: $223 (1997).
Education: High school graduation rate: 88.2% (2000); College graduation rate: 18.8% (2000).

School District(s)
Aurelia Community School District (PK-12)
2000 Enrollment: 365 712-434-2284

Housing: Homeownership rate: 82.2% (2000); Median home value: $59,900 (2000); Median rent: $282 per month (2000); Median age of housing: 45 years (2000).
Transportation: Commute to work: 93.4% car, 0.0% public transportation, 5.2% walk, 1.4% work from home (2000); Travel time to work: 44.4% less than 15 minutes, 44.2% 15 to 30 minutes, 6.0% 30 to 45 minutes, 0.4% 45 to 60 minutes, 5.0% 60 minutes or more (2000)

CHEROKEE (city). Covers a land area of 6.408 square miles and a water area of 0.024 square miles. Located at 42.75° N. Lat.; 95.55° W. Long. Elevation is 1,201 feet.
History: The first town of Cherokee was founded in 1856 by a colony from Milford, Massachusetts. The town was moved to the south in 1870 when the railroad was built through the county.
Population: 5,369 (2000); Race: 97.4% White, 1.3% Black, 0.4% Asian, 0.0% American Indian and Alaska Native, 1.1% Hispanic of any race, 0.4% two or more races (2000); Density: 837.8 persons per square mile (2000); Age: 22.5% under 18, 22.1% over 64 (2000); Marriage status: 21.8% never married, 56.2% now married, 12.0% widowed, 10.0% divorced (2000); Foreign born: 1.1% (2000); Ancestry (includes multiple ancestries): 39.9% German, 12.5% Irish, 8.2% United States or American, 6.6% Swedish, 6.3% English (2000).
Economy: Single-family building permits issued: 3 (2001) / 3 (2000); Multi-family building permits issued: 0 (2001) / 0 (2000); Employment by occupation: 10.2% management, 14.2% professional, 17.7% services, 21.2% sales, 1.2% farming, 9.3% construction, 26.2% production (2000).
Income: Per capita income: $17,846 (2000); Median household income: $31,240 (2000); Poverty rate: 7.0% (2000).
Taxes: Total city taxes per capita: $298 (2000); City property taxes per capita: $294 (2000).
Education: High school graduation rate: 84.2% (2000); College graduation rate: 13.3% (2000).

School District(s)
Cherokee Community School District (PK-12)
2000 Enrollment: 1,204 712-225-6767
Mental Health Institute (N -N)
2000 Enrollment: n/a 712-225-2594

Housing: Homeownership rate: 68.8% (2000); Median home value: $54,500 (2000); Median rent: $268 per month (2000); Median age of housing: 50 years (2000).
Hospitals: Mental Health Institute (110 beds); Sioux Valley Memorial Hospital (67 beds)
Newspapers: Chronicle Times (5 x week); Area Advertiser (1 x week); Shopper (1 x week)
Transportation: Commute to work: 91.1% car, 0.4% public transportation, 4.9% walk, 1.6% work from home (2000); Travel time to work: 73.8% less than 15 minutes, 15.3% 15 to 30 minutes, 5.2% 30 to 45 minutes, 2.3% 45 to 60 minutes, 3.4% 60 minutes or more (2000)
Additional Information Contacts
Cherokee Chamber of Commerce 712-225-6414

CLEGHORN (city). Covers a land area of 0.342 square miles and a water area of 0 square miles. Located at 42.81° N. Lat.; 95.71° W. Long.
History: Cleghorn, incorporated in 1901, owes its name to Dr. Cleghorn, who gave or sold all his property to the town on the condition that it was to revert to his estate if "alcoholic liquors are sold or used on the land, other than for medical purposes."
Population: 250 (2000); Race: 100.0% White, 0.0% Black, 0.0% Asian, 0.0% American Indian and Alaska Native, 0.0% Hispanic of any race, 0.0% two or more races (2000); Density: 730.3 persons per square mile (2000); Age: 22.7% under 18, 19.8% over 64 (2000); Marriage status: 12.1% never married, 72.6% now married, 10.8% widowed, 4.5% divorced (2000); Foreign born: 2.2% (2000); Ancestry (includes multiple ancestries): 56.1% German, 18.0% English, 8.6% Swedish, 6.8% Irish, 4.7% Norwegian (2000).
Economy: Single-family building permits issued: 1 (2001) / 1 (2000); Multi-family building permits issued: 0 (2001) / 0 (2000); Employment by occupation: 10.6% management, 16.2% professional, 10.6% services, 23.2% sales, 1.4% farming, 14.8% construction, 23.2% production (2000).
Income: Per capita income: $16,886 (2000); Median household income: $39,167 (2000); Poverty rate: 4.7% (2000).
Taxes: Total city taxes per capita: $176 (1997); City property taxes per capita: $137 (1997).
Education: High school graduation rate: 91.5% (2000); College graduation rate: 13.8% (2000).

Housing: Homeownership rate: 92.5% (2000); Median home value: $55,800 (2000); Median rent: $325 per month (2000); Median age of housing: 60+ years (2000).
Transportation: Commute to work: 86.4% car, 0.0% public transportation, 11.4% walk, 0.0% work from home (2000); Travel time to work: 40.7% less than 15 minutes, 42.1% 15 to 30 minutes, 12.1% 30 to 45 minutes, 3.6% 45 to 60 minutes, 1.4% 60 minutes or more (2000)

LARRABEE (city). Covers a land area of 0.127 square miles and a water area of 0 square miles. Located at 42.86° N. Lat.; 95.54° W. Long. Elevation is 1,366 feet.
History: Larrabee was platted and settled in 1887. The town was named for William Larrabee, Governor of Iowa (1886-1890).
Population: 149 (2000); Race: 100.0% White, 0.0% Black, 0.0% Asian, 0.0% American Indian and Alaska Native, 0.0% Hispanic of any race, 0.0% two or more races (2000); Density: 1,169.3 persons per square mile (2000); Age: 21.8% under 18, 21.0% over 64 (2000); Marriage status: 29.1% never married, 46.6% now married, 11.7% widowed, 12.6% divorced (2000); Foreign born: 0.0% (2000); Ancestry (includes multiple ancestries): 30.6% German, 8.1% Swedish, 7.3% Irish, 4.8% Norwegian, 3.2% English (2000).
Economy: Employment by occupation: 12.9% management, 8.1% professional, 29.0% services, 19.4% sales, 0.0% farming, 4.8% construction, 25.8% production (2000).
Income: Per capita income: $13,306 (2000); Median household income: $22,500 (2000); Poverty rate: 3.2% (2000).
Taxes: Total city taxes per capita: $135 (1997); City property taxes per capita: $106 (1997).
Education: High school graduation rate: 87.5% (2000); College graduation rate: 10.0% (2000).
Housing: Homeownership rate: 86.7% (2000); Median home value: $28,800 (2000); Median rent: $250 per month (2000); Median age of housing: 60+ years (2000).
Transportation: Commute to work: 91.5% car, 0.0% public transportation, 5.1% walk, 3.4% work from home (2000); Travel time to work: 31.6% less than 15 minutes, 61.4% 15 to 30 minutes, 7.0% 30 to 45 minutes, 0.0% 45 to 60 minutes, 0.0% 60 minutes or more (2000)

MARCUS (city). Covers a land area of 1.730 square miles and a water area of 0 square miles. Located at 42.82° N. Lat.; 95.80° W. Long. Elevation is 1,451 feet.
History: Marcus was named for the son of railroad builder John I. Blair.
Population: 1,139 (2000); Race: 97.5% White, 0.0% Black, 1.4% Asian, 0.0% American Indian and Alaska Native, 0.0% Hispanic of any race, 1.1% two or more races (2000); Density: 658.4 persons per square mile (2000); Age: 22.4% under 18, 28.3% over 64 (2000); Marriage status: 18.7% never married, 60.0% now married, 15.1% widowed, 6.2% divorced (2000); Foreign born: 1.2% (2000); Ancestry (includes multiple ancestries): 42.7% German, 11.5% Irish, 10.5% English, 10.4% Swedish, 6.1% United States or American (2000).
Economy: Single-family building permits issued: 0 (2001) / 1 (2000); Multi-family building permits issued: 0 (2001) / 0 (2000); Employment by occupation: 9.7% management, 15.8% professional, 17.0% services, 21.8% sales, 0.8% farming, 9.8% construction, 25.1% production (2000).
Income: Per capita income: $19,381 (2000); Median household income: $37,604 (2000); Poverty rate: 7.8% (2000).
Taxes: Total city taxes per capita: $352 (1997); City property taxes per capita: $311 (1997).
Education: High school graduation rate: 84.7% (2000); College graduation rate: 17.2% (2000).

School District(s)

Marcus-Meriden-Cleghorn Community School District (PK-12)
2000 Enrollment: 596 712-376-4171

Housing: Homeownership rate: 86.0% (2000); Median home value: $62,200 (2000); Median rent: $249 per month (2000); Median age of housing: 59 years (2000).
Newspapers: The Marcus News (1 x week)
Transportation: Commute to work: 90.7% car, 0.0% public transportation, 5.4% walk, 2.9% work from home (2000); Travel time to work: 49.2% less than 15 minutes, 25.9% 15 to 30 minutes, 17.9% 30 to 45 minutes, 2.8% 45 to 60 minutes, 4.2% 60 minutes or more (2000)

MERIDEN (city). Covers a land area of 0.111 square miles and a water area of 0 square miles. Located at 42.79° N. Lat.; 95.63° W. Long. Elevation is 1,402 feet.
History: Meriden was first named Hazzard in honor of a relative of John Blair, an early settler. The townspeople, however, were not fond of Mr. Blair and requested the Post Office Department to change the name.
Population: 184 (2000); Race: 100.0% White, 0.0% Black, 0.0% Asian, 0.0% American Indian and Alaska Native, 0.0% Hispanic of any race, 0.0% two or more races (2000); Density: 1,660.9 persons per square mile (2000); Age: 11.4% under 18, 24.4% over 64 (2000); Marriage status: 15.9% never married, 68.2% now married, 7.4% widowed, 8.5% divorced (2000); Foreign born: 0.0% (2000); Ancestry (includes multiple ancestries): 37.3% German, 13.5% English, 12.4% Irish, 8.8% Scotch-Irish, 8.8% Danish (2000).
Economy: Employment by occupation: 12.4% management, 8.0% professional, 18.6% services, 12.4% sales, 0.9% farming, 15.9% construction, 31.9% production (2000).
Income: Per capita income: $14,755 (2000); Median household income: $24,750 (2000); Poverty rate: 11.4% (2000).
Taxes: Total city taxes per capita: $126 (1997); City property taxes per capita: $95 (1997).
Education: High school graduation rate: 81.5% (2000); College graduation rate: 10.6% (2000).
Housing: Homeownership rate: 77.2% (2000); Median home value: $40,000 (2000); Median rent: $229 per month (2000); Median age of housing: 29 years (2000).
Transportation: Commute to work: 87.6% car, 0.0% public transportation, 7.1% walk, 5.3% work from home (2000); Travel time to work: 47.7% less than 15 minutes, 41.1% 15 to 30 minutes, 7.5% 30 to 45 minutes, 1.9% 45 to 60 minutes, 1.9% 60 minutes or more (2000)

QUIMBY (city). Covers a land area of 0.412 square miles and a water area of 0 square miles. Located at 42.63° N. Lat.; 95.64° W. Long. Elevation is 1,190 feet.
History: Quimby was named for Illinois Central Railroad official F. W. Quimby.
Population: 368 (2000); Race: 100.0% White, 0.0% Black, 0.0% Asian, 0.0% American Indian and Alaska Native, 0.3% Hispanic of any race, 0.0% two or more races (2000); Density: 893.0 persons per square mile (2000); Age: 26.6% under 18, 20.6% over 64 (2000); Marriage status: 20.4% never married, 62.6% now married, 8.3% widowed, 8.7% divorced (2000); Foreign born: 0.3% (2000); Ancestry (includes multiple ancestries): 46.7% German, 14.0% United States or American, 10.9% Irish, 10.6% English, 5.7% Swedish (2000).
Economy: Single-family building permits issued: 1 (2001) / 3 (2000); Multi-family building permits issued: 0 (2001) / 0 (2000); Employment by occupation: 8.3% management, 9.6% professional, 16.6% services, 25.5% sales, 0.0% farming, 12.1% construction, 28.0% production (2000).
Income: Per capita income: $13,017 (2000); Median household income: $25,625 (2000); Poverty rate: 9.2% (2000).
Taxes: Total city taxes per capita: $141 (1997); City property taxes per capita: $141 (1997).
Education: High school graduation rate: 83.8% (2000); College graduation rate: 12.3% (2000).
Housing: Homeownership rate: 72.8% (2000); Median home value: $36,100 (2000); Median rent: $194 per month (2000); Median age of housing: 59 years (2000).
Transportation: Commute to work: 94.7% car, 0.0% public transportation, 5.3% walk, 0.0% work from home (2000); Travel time to work: 21.2% less than 15 minutes, 57.6% 15 to 30 minutes, 8.6% 30 to 45 minutes, 7.3% 45 to 60 minutes, 5.3% 60 minutes or more (2000)

WASHTA (city). Covers a land area of 1.050 square miles and a water area of 0 square miles. Located at 42.57° N. Lat.; 95.71° W. Long. Elevation is 1,157 feet.
History: The name Washta was taken from a Sioux word "waste," meaning "good."
Population: 282 (2000); Race: 100.0% White, 0.0% Black, 0.0% Asian, 0.0% American Indian and Alaska Native, 0.6% Hispanic of any race, 0.0% two or more races (2000); Density: 268.5 persons per square mile (2000); Age: 25.9% under 18, 19.7% over 64 (2000); Marriage status: 23.2% never married, 52.8% now married, 12.2% widowed, 11.8% divorced (2000); Foreign born: 0.0% (2000); Ancestry (includes multiple ancestries): 39.7% German, 11.9% United States or American, 10.3% Norwegian, 9.4% French (except Basque), 7.2% English (2000).
Economy: Single-family building permits issued: 0 (2001) / 0 (2000); Multi-family building permits issued: 0 (2001) / 0 (2000); Employment by occupation: 2.8% management, 19.9% professional, 12.1% services, 20.6% sales, 5.0% farming, 11.3% construction, 28.4% production (2000).

Income: Per capita income: $13,025 (2000); Median household income: $30,673 (2000); Poverty rate: 13.6% (2000).
Taxes: Total city taxes per capita: $52 (1997); City property taxes per capita: $52 (1997).
Education: High school graduation rate: 79.3% (2000); College graduation rate: 9.9% (2000).
Housing: Homeownership rate: 74.8% (2000); Median home value: $26,800 (2000); Median rent: $202 per month (2000); Median age of housing: 60+ years (2000).
Transportation: Commute to work: 92.1% car, 0.0% public transportation, 5.7% walk, 0.7% work from home (2000); Travel time to work: 26.6% less than 15 minutes, 45.3% 15 to 30 minutes, 13.7% 30 to 45 minutes, 12.9% 45 to 60 minutes, 1.4% 60 minutes or more (2000)

Chickasaw County

Located in northeastern Iowa; prairie area, drained by the Cedar, Wapsipinicon, and Little Cedar Rivers. Covers a land area of 504.60 square miles, a water area of 0.80 square miles, and is located in the Central Time Zone. The county government was organized in 1851. County seat is New Hampton.

Weather Station: New Hampton Elevation: 1,158 feet

	Jan	Feb	Mar	Apr	May	Jun	Jul	Aug	Sep	Oct	Nov	Dec
High	23	30	42	58	71	80	83	81	73	61	42	29
Low	6	13	25	37	49	58	62	60	51	40	26	13
Precip	1.1	1.0	2.3	3.8	4.3	4.7	4.6	4.8	3.4	2.7	2.4	1.3
Snow	10.1	6.4	6.9	2.4	tr	0.0	0.0	0.0	tr	0.2	4.9	8.8

High and Low temperatures in degrees Fahrenheit; Precipitation and Snow in inches

Population: 13,095 (2000); Race: 98.6% White, 0.1% Black, 0.5% Asian, 0.0% American Indian and Alaska Native, 0.4% Hispanic of any race, 0.6% two or more races (2000); Density: 25.9 persons per square mile (2000); Age: 26.0% under 18, 17.9% over 64 (2000).
Religion: Five largest groups: 49.3% Catholic Church, 20.2% Evangelical Lutheran Church in America, 8.5% The United Methodist Church, 5.1% United Church of Christ, 3.2% American Baptist Churches in the USA (2000).
Economy: Unemployment rate: 4.4% (11/2002); Total civilian labor force: 6,649 (11/2002); Leading industries: 40.6% manufacturing; 11.4% retail trade; 10.9% health care and social assistance (2000); Companies that employ more than 1,000 persons: 0 (2000); Companies that employ more than 100 persons: 5 (2000); Farms: 926 totaling 272,371 acres (1997); Minority business ownership rate: 0.0% (1997); Women business ownership rate: 18.6% (1997); Retail sales per capita: $5,470 (1997). Single-family building permits issued: 15 (2001) / 5 (2000); Multi-family building permits issued: 0 (2001) / 4 (2000).
Income: Per capita income: $18,237 (2000); Median household income: $37,649 (2000); Poverty rate: 8.3% (2000); Bankruptcy rate: 2.36% (2001).
Taxes: Total county taxes per capita: $228 (1997); County property taxes per capita: $227 (1997).
Education: High school graduation rate: 83.4% (2000); College graduation rate: 12.2% (2000).
Housing: Homeownership rate: 80.4% (2000); Median home value: $71,200 (2000); Median rent: $253 per month (2000); Median age of housing: 50 years (2000).
Health: Birth rate: 97.0 per 10,000 population (1998); Age adjusted death rate: 77.9 per 10,000 population (1999); Age adjusted cancer mortality rate: 198.7 deaths per 100,000 population (1999). Number of physicians: 3.8 per 10,000 population (1999); Number of hospital beds: 45.8 per 10,000 population (1999).
Elections: 2000 Presidential election results: 52.2% Gore, 44.6% Bush, 2.2% Nader, 0.6% Buchanan
Additional Information Contacts
Chickasaw County Government Offices 641-394-2100
New Hampton Chamber of Commerce 641-394-2021

Chickasaw County Communities

ALTA VISTA (city). Covers a land area of 0.756 square miles and a water area of 0 square miles. Located at 43.19° N. Lat.; 92.41° W. Long. Elevation is 1,159 feet.
History: Alta Vista, Spanish for "high view," was originally known as Elk Creek.
Population: 286 (2000); Race: 100.0% White, 0.0% Black, 0.0% Asian, 0.0% American Indian and Alaska Native, 0.0% Hispanic of any race, 0.0% two or more races (2000); Density: 378.5 persons per square mile (2000); Age: 22.8% under 18, 24.7% over 64 (2000); Marriage status: 23.1% never married, 60.2% now married, 11.1% widowed, 5.6% divorced (2000); Foreign born: 0.0% (2000); Ancestry (includes multiple ancestries): 55.6% German, 12.7% Irish, 5.8% Norwegian, 3.9% French (except Basque), 3.5% Scotch-Irish (2000).
Economy: Single-family building permits issued: 0 (2001) / 0 (2000); Multi-family building permits issued: 0 (2001) / 0 (2000); Employment by occupation: 15.1% management, 5.6% professional, 12.7% services, 15.9% sales, 0.0% farming, 22.2% construction, 28.6% production (2000).
Income: Per capita income: $15,378 (2000); Median household income: $26,786 (2000); Poverty rate: 13.9% (2000).
Taxes: Total city taxes per capita: $163 (1997); City property taxes per capita: $159 (1997).
Education: High school graduation rate: 80.2% (2000); College graduation rate: 6.2% (2000).
Housing: Homeownership rate: 86.7% (2000); Median home value: $41,700 (2000); Median rent: $194 per month (2000); Median age of housing: 60+ years (2000).
Transportation: Commute to work: 87.3% car, 1.6% public transportation, 7.1% walk, 2.4% work from home (2000); Travel time to work: 24.4% less than 15 minutes, 33.3% 15 to 30 minutes, 23.6% 30 to 45 minutes, 8.1% 45 to 60 minutes, 10.6% 60 minutes or more (2000)

BASSETT (city). Covers a land area of 0.369 square miles and a water area of 0 square miles. Located at 43.06° N. Lat.; 92.51° W. Long.
History: Bassett was a flag station on the Chicago, Milwaukee & St. Paul Railroad. It was named for a merchant who bought wheat extensively along the route.
Population: 74 (2000); Race: 100.0% White, 0.0% Black, 0.0% Asian, 0.0% American Indian and Alaska Native, 0.0% Hispanic of any race, 0.0% two or more races (2000); Density: 200.8 persons per square mile (2000); Age: 16.4% under 18, 14.9% over 64 (2000); Marriage status: 27.0% never married, 55.6% now married, 1.6% widowed, 15.9% divorced (2000); Foreign born: 0.0% (2000); Ancestry (includes multiple ancestries): 44.8% German, 11.9% Dutch, 7.5% English, 7.5% United States or American, 4.5% Other groups (2000).
Economy: Employment by occupation: 9.1% management, 0.0% professional, 30.3% services, 0.0% sales, 0.0% farming, 9.1% construction, 51.5% production (2000).
Income: Per capita income: $13,131 (2000); Median household income: $30,000 (2000); Poverty rate: 14.9% (2000).
Taxes: Total city taxes per capita: $39 (1997); City property taxes per capita: $39 (1997).
Education: High school graduation rate: 78.8% (2000); College graduation rate: 0.0% (2000).
Housing: Homeownership rate: 89.3% (2000); Median home value: $40,600 (2000); Median rent: $225 per month (2000); Median age of housing: 60+ years (2000).
Transportation: Commute to work: 100.0% car, 0.0% public transportation, 0.0% walk, 0.0% work from home (2000); Travel time to work: 45.5% less than 15 minutes, 30.3% 15 to 30 minutes, 6.1% 30 to 45 minutes, 9.1% 45 to 60 minutes, 9.1% 60 minutes or more (2000)

FREDERICKSBURG (city). Covers a land area of 0.860 square miles and a water area of 0 square miles. Located at 42.96° N. Lat.; 92.19° W. Long. Elevation is 1,076 feet.
History: Fredericksburg was platted in 1856 and named for Frederick Padden, the founder. It was the home of Dr. W. S. Pitts, a physician who wrote the song "Little Brown Church in the Vale."
Population: 984 (2000); Race: 98.7% White, 0.4% Black, 0.4% Asian, 0.0% American Indian and Alaska Native, 0.2% Hispanic of any race, 0.2% two or more races (2000); Density: 1,143.9 persons per square mile (2000); Age: 24.5% under 18, 21.8% over 64 (2000); Marriage status: 20.2% never married, 59.6% now married, 9.4% widowed, 10.8% divorced (2000); Foreign born: 0.3% (2000); Ancestry (includes multiple ancestries): 55.3% German, 9.8% Norwegian, 9.4% English, 8.4% Irish, 3.6% United States or American (2000).
Economy: Single-family building permits issued: 2 (2001) / 0 (2000); Multi-family building permits issued: 0 (2001) / 0 (2000); Employment by occupation: 9.4% management, 11.7% professional, 16.9% services, 17.8% sales, 0.0% farming, 8.5% construction, 35.7% production (2000).
Income: Per capita income: $15,956 (2000); Median household income: $31,938 (2000); Poverty rate: 7.6% (2000).
Taxes: Total city taxes per capita: $144 (1997); City property taxes per capita: $138 (1997).

Education: High school graduation rate: 81.3% (2000); College graduation rate: 10.3% (2000).

School District(s)

Fredericksburg Community School District (KG-12)
2000 Enrollment: 409 319-237-5364

Housing: Homeownership rate: 81.3% (2000); Median home value: $62,400 (2000); Median rent: $227 per month (2000); Median age of housing: 55 years (2000).

Newspapers: Fredericksburg Review (1 x week)

Transportation: Commute to work: 80.4% car, 0.5% public transportation, 14.8% walk, 2.2% work from home (2000); Travel time to work: 61.6% less than 15 minutes, 23.2% 15 to 30 minutes, 9.5% 30 to 45 minutes, 2.2% 45 to 60 minutes, 3.4% 60 minutes or more (2000)

IONIA (city). Covers a land area of 0.558 square miles and a water area of 0 square miles. Located at 43.03° N. Lat.; 92.45° W. Long. Elevation is 1,150 feet.

History: Ionia may have been named for Ionia, Michigan. It was originally known as Dover, but the name was changed by the postal authorities.

Population: 277 (2000); Race: 100.0% White, 0.0% Black, 0.0% Asian, 0.0% American Indian and Alaska Native, 0.0% Hispanic of any race, 0.0% two or more races (2000); Density: 496.3 persons per square mile (2000); Age: 23.6% under 18, 13.9% over 64 (2000); Marriage status: 24.4% never married, 57.9% now married, 8.6% widowed, 9.0% divorced (2000); Foreign born: 0.0% (2000); Ancestry (includes multiple ancestries): 64.4% German, 11.2% Irish, 3.7% French (except Basque), 3.4% Norwegian, 2.6% Hungarian (2000).

Economy: Employment by occupation: 4.5% management, 11.2% professional, 16.4% services, 17.9% sales, 0.0% farming, 16.4% construction, 33.6% production (2000).

Income: Per capita income: $17,355 (2000); Median household income: $35,357 (2000); Poverty rate: 0.0% (2000).

Taxes: Total city taxes per capita: $80 (1997); City property taxes per capita: $74 (1997).

Education: High school graduation rate: 81.8% (2000); College graduation rate: 3.2% (2000).

Housing: Homeownership rate: 82.9% (2000); Median home value: $50,300 (2000); Median rent: $254 per month (2000); Median age of housing: 40 years (2000).

Transportation: Commute to work: 94.7% car, 1.5% public transportation, 0.0% walk, 1.5% work from home (2000); Travel time to work: 43.1% less than 15 minutes, 30.8% 15 to 30 minutes, 6.2% 30 to 45 minutes, 10.8% 45 to 60 minutes, 9.2% 60 minutes or more (2000)

LAWLER (city). Covers a land area of 0.892 square miles and a water area of 0.012 square miles. Located at 43.07° N. Lat.; 92.15° W. Long. Elevation is 1,088 feet.

History: Lawler was named for Chicago, Milwaukee & St. Paul railroad official John Lawler.

Population: 461 (2000); Race: 99.1% White, 0.0% Black, 0.0% Asian, 0.0% American Indian and Alaska Native, 0.0% Hispanic of any race, 0.9% two or more races (2000); Density: 517.1 persons per square mile (2000); Age: 17.9% under 18, 22.7% over 64 (2000); Marriage status: 22.6% never married, 59.0% now married, 12.7% widowed, 5.7% divorced (2000); Foreign born: 1.1% (2000); Ancestry (includes multiple ancestries): 53.3% German, 22.0% Irish, 12.9% Norwegian, 11.1% Czech, 7.7% English (2000).

Economy: Single-family building permits issued: 1 (2001) / 0 (2000); Multi-family building permits issued: 0 (2001) / 0 (2000); Employment by occupation: 14.8% management, 15.3% professional, 16.3% services, 21.2% sales, 1.0% farming, 7.4% construction, 24.1% production (2000).

Income: Per capita income: $21,268 (2000); Median household income: $30,500 (2000); Poverty rate: 16.3% (2000).

Taxes: Total city taxes per capita: $104 (1997); City property taxes per capita: $104 (1997).

Education: High school graduation rate: 81.4% (2000); College graduation rate: 14.0% (2000).

Housing: Homeownership rate: 75.9% (2000); Median home value: $53,800 (2000); Median rent: $255 per month (2000); Median age of housing: 40 years (2000).

Transportation: Commute to work: 89.2% car, 1.0% public transportation, 6.9% walk, 2.5% work from home (2000); Travel time to work: 45.5% less than 15 minutes, 31.3% 15 to 30 minutes, 18.2% 30 to 45 minutes, 0.5% 45 to 60 minutes, 4.5% 60 minutes or more (2000)

NASHUA (city). Covers a land area of 2.458 square miles and a water area of 0.172 square miles. Located at 42.95° N. Lat.; 92.53° W. Long. Elevation is 968 feet.

History: Nashua was named by E. P. Greeley for his old home town in New Hampshire. The settlement was first called Bridgeport and later Woodbridge.

Population: 1,618 (2000); Race: 99.1% White, 0.2% Black, 0.1% Asian, 0.1% American Indian and Alaska Native, 0.1% Hispanic of any race, 0.4% two or more races (2000); Density: 658.2 persons per square mile (2000); Age: 24.2% under 18, 20.6% over 64 (2000); Marriage status: 19.9% never married, 62.6% now married, 9.5% widowed, 8.0% divorced (2000); Foreign born: 0.5% (2000); Ancestry (includes multiple ancestries): 52.1% German, 12.3% Irish, 9.9% English, 4.9% United States or American, 4.8% Norwegian (2000).

Economy: Single-family building permits issued: 4 (2001) / 2 (2000); Multi-family building permits issued: 0 (2001) / 0 (2000); Employment by occupation: 9.3% management, 14.5% professional, 13.0% services, 21.5% sales, 2.7% farming, 8.6% construction, 30.4% production (2000).

Income: Per capita income: $16,031 (2000); Median household income: $31,713 (2000); Poverty rate: 9.0% (2000).

Taxes: Total city taxes per capita: $201 (1997); City property taxes per capita: $197 (1997).

Education: High school graduation rate: 85.9% (2000); College graduation rate: 13.0% (2000).

School District(s)

Nashua-Plainfield Community School District (PK-12)
2000 Enrollment: 868 641-435-4835

Housing: Homeownership rate: 79.9% (2000); Median home value: $56,200 (2000); Median rent: $249 per month (2000); Median age of housing: 54 years (2000).

Newspapers: The Nashua Reporter & Weekly Reporter (1 x week)

Transportation: Commute to work: 93.3% car, 0.0% public transportation, 3.1% walk, 2.3% work from home (2000); Travel time to work: 38.8% less than 15 minutes, 34.7% 15 to 30 minutes, 16.0% 30 to 45 minutes, 5.8% 45 to 60 minutes, 4.7% 60 minutes or more (2000)

NEW HAMPTON (city). Covers a land area of 2.898 square miles and a water area of 0 square miles. Located at 43.06° N. Lat.; 92.31° W. Long. Elevation is 1,159 feet.

History: New Hampton, first known as Chickasaw Center, was later renamed by Osgood Gowen for his old home town in New Hampshire.

Population: 3,692 (2000); Race: 98.0% White, 0.0% Black, 0.9% Asian, 0.0% American Indian and Alaska Native, 0.0% Hispanic of any race, 1.0% two or more races (2000); Density: 1,274.0 persons per square mile (2000); Age: 23.3% under 18, 23.3% over 64 (2000); Marriage status: 23.6% never married, 55.7% now married, 14.3% widowed, 6.4% divorced (2000); Foreign born: 1.2% (2000); Ancestry (includes multiple ancestries): 52.3% German, 20.8% Irish, 14.7% Norwegian, 6.8% English, 4.9% Czech (2000).

Economy: Single-family building permits issued: 8 (2001) / 3 (2000); Multi-family building permits issued: 0 (2001) / 4 (2000); Employment by occupation: 13.0% management, 14.3% professional, 16.4% services, 24.9% sales, 0.8% farming, 9.1% construction, 21.6% production (2000).

Income: Per capita income: $20,255 (2000); Median household income: $40,082 (2000); Poverty rate: 6.1% (2000).

Taxes: Total city taxes per capita: $323 (1997); City property taxes per capita: $317 (1997).

Education: High school graduation rate: 79.0% (2000); College graduation rate: 17.3% (2000).

School District(s)

New Hampton Community School District (PK-12)
2000 Enrollment: 1,273 641-394-2134

Housing: Homeownership rate: 73.9% (2000); Median home value: $77,900 (2000); Median rent: $289 per month (2000); Median age of housing: 44 years (2000).

Hospitals: Mercy Medical Center - New Hampton (49 beds)

Newspapers: New Hampton Tribune (2 x week)

Transportation: Commute to work: 86.7% car, 0.0% public transportation, 6.9% walk, 5.8% work from home (2000); Travel time to work: 70.6% less than 15 minutes, 9.4% 15 to 30 minutes, 9.3% 30 to 45 minutes, 5.1% 45 to 60 minutes, 5.6% 60 minutes or more (2000)

Additional Information Contacts

New Hampton Chamber of Commerce 641-394-2021

NORTH WASHINGTON (city). Covers a land area of 0.196 square miles and a water area of 0 square miles. Located at 43.11° N. Lat.; 92.41° W. Long. Elevation is 1,119 feet.

History: North Washington was named in honor of President George Washington. The "North" was added to set it apart from the many other Washingtons.
Population: 118 (2000); Race: 100.0% White, 0.0% Black, 0.0% Asian, 0.0% American Indian and Alaska Native, 0.0% Hispanic of any race, 0.0% two or more races (2000); Density: 601.2 persons per square mile (2000); Age: 28.1% under 18, 14.9% over 64 (2000); Marriage status: 8.0% never married, 80.5% now married, 8.0% widowed, 3.4% divorced (2000); Foreign born: 0.0% (2000); Ancestry (includes multiple ancestries): 57.0% German, 20.7% United States or American, 16.5% Irish, 7.4% Dutch, 7.4% Norwegian (2000).
Economy: Employment by occupation: 3.2% management, 4.8% professional, 15.9% services, 15.9% sales, 0.0% farming, 15.9% construction, 44.4% production (2000).
Income: Per capita income: $15,611 (2000); Median household income: $38,542 (2000); Poverty rate: 5.8% (2000).
Taxes: Total city taxes per capita: $93 (1997); City property taxes per capita: $93 (1997).
Education: High school graduation rate: 84.4% (2000); College graduation rate: 0.0% (2000).
Housing: Homeownership rate: 77.6% (2000); Median home value: $45,000 (2000); Median rent: $261 per month (2000); Median age of housing: 60+ years (2000).
Transportation: Commute to work: 84.1% car, 0.0% public transportation, 9.5% walk, 3.2% work from home (2000); Travel time to work: 39.3% less than 15 minutes, 39.3% 15 to 30 minutes, 8.2% 30 to 45 minutes, 3.3% 45 to 60 minutes, 9.8% 60 minutes or more (2000)

Clarke County

Located in southern Iowa; prairie area, drained by the Chariton and South Rivers. Covers a land area of 431.10 square miles, a water area of 0.60 square miles, and is located in the Central Time Zone. The county government was organized in 1846. County seat is Osceola.

Weather Station: Osceola — Elevation: 1,108 feet

	Jan	Feb	Mar	Apr	May	Jun	Jul	Aug	Sep	Oct	Nov	Dec
High	30	36	49	63	73	82	87	84	77	64	47	35
Low	11	16	27	39	50	59	64	61	52	40	28	17
Precip	0.9	1.0	2.3	3.5	4.7	4.4	4.6	4.3	4.2	2.9	2.3	1.2
Snow	6.7	6.0	3.9	1.9	0.0	0.0	0.0	0.0	0.0	0.6	2.1	4.2

High and Low temperatures in degrees Fahrenheit; Precipitation and Snow in inches

Population: 9,133 (2000); Race: 96.1% White, 0.0% Black, 0.2% Asian, 0.4% American Indian and Alaska Native, 3.4% Hispanic of any race, 1.1% two or more races (2000); Density: 21.2 persons per square mile (2000); Age: 26.2% under 18, 17.0% over 64 (2000).
Religion: Five largest groups: 11.1% The United Methodist Church, 9.7% Christian Church (Disciples of Christ), 4.9% Catholic Church, 4.7% Christian Churches and Churches of Christ, 3.4% Assemblies of God (2000).
Economy: Unemployment rate: 5.8% (11/2002); Total civilian labor force: 5,061 (11/2002); Leading industries: 32.8% manufacturing; 11.6% retail trade; 9.5% health care and social assistance (2000); Companies that employ more than 1,000 persons: 0 (2000); Companies that employ more than 100 persons: 6 (2000); Farms: 678 totaling 221,848 acres (1997); Minority business ownership rate: 0.0% (1997); Women business ownership rate: 19.2% (1997); Retail sales per capita: $6,239 (1997). Single-family building permits issued: 11 (2001) / 20 (2000); Multi-family building permits issued: 0 (2001) / 0 (2000).
Income: Per capita income: $16,409 (2000); Median household income: $34,474 (2000); Poverty rate: 8.5% (2000); Bankruptcy rate: 3.21% (2001).
Taxes: Total county taxes per capita: $256 (2000); County property taxes per capita: $244 (2000).
Education: High school graduation rate: 84.4% (2000); College graduation rate: 12.1% (2000).
Housing: Homeownership rate: 72.3% (2000); Median home value: $64,700 (2000); Median rent: $349 per month (2000); Median age of housing: 39 years (2000).
Health: Birth rate: 109.5 per 10,000 population (1998); Age adjusted death rate: 84.6 per 10,000 population (1999); Age adjusted cancer mortality rate: 198.9 deaths per 100,000 population (1999). Number of physicians: 4.4 per 10,000 population (1999); Number of hospital beds: 52.6 per 10,000 population (1999).
Elections: 2000 Presidential election results: 49.8% Gore, 47.5% Bush, 1.8% Nader, 0.5% Buchanan
Additional Information Contacts

Clarke County Government Offices. 641-342-3311
Osceola Chamber of Commerce. 641-342-4200
South Central Iowa Board of Realtors 641-342-2141

Clarke County Communities

MURRAY (city). Covers a land area of 0.784 square miles and a water area of 0 square miles. Located at 41.04° N. Lat.; 93.95° W. Long. Elevation is 1,216 feet.
History: Murray was a station on the Burlington & Missouri River Railroad in 1868. It is believed to have been named after a railroad official.
Population: 766 (2000); Race: 99.7% White, 0.0% Black, 0.0% Asian, 0.0% American Indian and Alaska Native, 0.4% Hispanic of any race, 0.0% two or more races (2000); Density: 977.4 persons per square mile (2000); Age: 28.2% under 18, 13.8% over 64 (2000); Marriage status: 19.2% never married, 60.2% now married, 7.7% widowed, 12.9% divorced (2000); Foreign born: 0.1% (2000); Ancestry (includes multiple ancestries): 15.6% German, 14.3% United States or American, 13.6% Irish, 13.5% English, 5.7% Other groups (2000).
Economy: Single-family building permits issued: 2 (2001) / 1 (2000); Multi-family building permits issued: 0 (2001) / 0 (2000); Employment by occupation: 5.9% management, 10.5% professional, 14.5% services, 20.1% sales, 3.7% farming, 12.0% construction, 33.3% production (2000).
Income: Per capita income: $14,879 (2000); Median household income: $29,879 (2000); Poverty rate: 8.2% (2000).
Taxes: Total city taxes per capita: $132 (1997); City property taxes per capita: $130 (1997).
Education: High school graduation rate: 86.3% (2000); College graduation rate: 5.4% (2000).

School District(s)

Murray Community School District (PK-12)
2000 Enrollment: 398 641-447-2517
Housing: Homeownership rate: 72.8% (2000); Median home value: $46,700 (2000); Median rent: $281 per month (2000); Median age of housing: 60+ years (2000).
Transportation: Commute to work: 92.6% car, 0.0% public transportation, 3.2% walk, 3.2% work from home (2000); Travel time to work: 32.0% less than 15 minutes, 38.9% 15 to 30 minutes, 8.4% 30 to 45 minutes, 5.4% 45 to 60 minutes, 15.3% 60 minutes or more (2000)

OSCEOLA (city). Covers a land area of 5.837 square miles and a water area of 0.204 square miles. Located at 41.03° N. Lat.; 93.76° W. Long. Elevation is 1,137 feet.
History: Osceola, first called Osceola City, was settled in 1850 by pioneers from Ohio and Indiana. The town was named for the Seminole chief, Osceola.
Population: 4,659 (2000); Race: 94.8% White, 0.0% Black, 0.2% Asian, 0.0% American Indian and Alaska Native, 6.2% Hispanic of any race, 0.7% two or more races (2000); Density: 798.2 persons per square mile (2000); Age: 25.1% under 18, 19.0% over 64 (2000); Marriage status: 19.1% never married, 57.2% now married, 11.4% widowed, 12.2% divorced (2000); Foreign born: 4.7% (2000); Ancestry (includes multiple ancestries): 18.9% German, 14.3% United States or American, 12.6% English, 11.3% Irish, 9.6% Other groups (2000).
Economy: Single-family building permits issued: 9 (2001) / 19 (2000); Multi-family building permits issued: 0 (2001) / 0 (2000); Employment by occupation: 13.8% management, 14.6% professional, 14.4% services, 22.4% sales, 0.6% farming, 9.8% construction, 24.5% production (2000).
Income: Per capita income: $17,244 (2000); Median household income: $32,701 (2000); Poverty rate: 7.6% (2000).
Taxes: Total city taxes per capita: $474 (1997); City property taxes per capita: $471 (1997).
Education: High school graduation rate: 83.8% (2000); College graduation rate: 14.5% (2000).

School District(s)

Clarke Community School District (PK-12)
2000 Enrollment: 1,486 641-342-4969
Housing: Homeownership rate: 64.7% (2000); Median home value: $67,600 (2000); Median rent: $369 per month (2000); Median age of housing: 38 years (2000).
Hospitals: Clarke County Public Hospital (68 beds)
Safety: Violent crime rate: 10.7 per 10,000 population; Property crime rate: 567.3 per 10,000 population (2001).
Newspapers: Osceola Sentinel-Tribune (1 x week)
Transportation: Commute to work: 90.8% car, 1.2% public transportation, 3.1% walk, 4.8% work from home (2000); Travel time to work: 73.2% less

than 15 minutes, 6.7% 15 to 30 minutes, 5.9% 30 to 45 minutes, 5.9% 45 to 60 minutes, 8.3% 60 minutes or more (2000); Amtrak: Service available.

Additional Information Contacts

Osceola Chamber of Commerce. 641-342-4200
South Central Iowa Board of Realtors 641-342-2141

WOODBURN (city). Covers a land area of 0.629 square miles and a water area of 0 square miles. Located at 41.01° N. Lat.; 93.59° W. Long. Elevation is 961 feet.

Population: 244 (2000); Race: 96.8% White, 0.0% Black, 0.0% Asian, 0.0% American Indian and Alaska Native, 0.0% Hispanic of any race, 3.2% two or more races (2000); Density: 387.9 persons per square mile (2000); Age: 32.5% under 18, 8.3% over 64 (2000); Marriage status: 24.5% never married, 56.0% now married, 6.0% widowed, 13.6% divorced (2000); Foreign born: 0.0% (2000); Ancestry (includes multiple ancestries): 21.4% United States or American, 17.5% German, 15.5% English, 9.1% Irish, 5.2% Welsh (2000).
Economy: In agricultural area. Employment by occupation: 5.0% management, 2.5% professional, 31.9% services, 21.0% sales, 1.7% farming, 10.1% construction, 27.7% production (2000).
Income: Per capita income: $11,139 (2000); Median household income: $22,500 (2000); Poverty rate: 26.8% (2000).
Taxes: Total city taxes per capita: $63 (1997); City property taxes per capita: $63 (1997).
Education: High school graduation rate: 85.4% (2000); College graduation rate: 4.2% (2000).
Housing: Homeownership rate: 77.8% (2000); Median home value: $34,600 (2000); Median rent: $263 per month (2000); Median age of housing: 40 years (2000).
Transportation: Commute to work: 93.2% car, 3.4% public transportation, 0.0% walk, 3.4% work from home (2000); Travel time to work: 17.7% less than 15 minutes, 53.1% 15 to 30 minutes, 13.3% 30 to 45 minutes, 1.8% 45 to 60 minutes, 14.2% 60 minutes or more (2000)

Clay County

Located in northwestern Iowa; prairie area, drained by the Little Sioux and Ocheyedan Rivers. Covers a land area of 568.90 square miles, a water area of 3.60 square miles, and is located in the Central Time Zone. The county government was organized in 1851. County seat is Spencer.

Weather Station: Elkader 5 SSW — Elevation: 767 feet

	Jan	Feb	Mar	Apr	May	Jun	Jul	Aug	Sep	Oct	Nov	Dec
High	27	33	45	60	72	81	85	82	75	63	45	31
Low	6	12	23	35	46	55	60	58	49	38	26	13
Precip	1.0	1.1	2.1	3.5	4.1	4.4	4.1	4.7	3.2	2.5	2.4	1.2
Snow	9.6	7.0	5.2	2.0	0.0	0.0	0.0	0.0	0.0	0.2	4.0	8.2

High and Low temperatures in degrees Fahrenheit; Precipitation and Snow in inches

Weather Station: Guttenberg Lock & Dam 10 — Elevation: 623 feet

	Jan	Feb	Mar	Apr	May	Jun	Jul	Aug	Sep	Oct	Nov	Dec
High	27	33	45	59	72	81	84	82	74	62	45	32
Low	9	15	27	39	51	60	64	62	54	42	29	16
Precip	1.1	1.1	2.0	3.2	3.9	4.3	4.2	4.4	3.2	2.2	2.2	1.3
Snow	10.7	5.6	4.0	1.2	0.0	0.0	0.0	0.0	0.0	0.1	2.3	7.0

High and Low temperatures in degrees Fahrenheit; Precipitation and Snow in inches

Population: 17,372 (2000); Race: 97.4% White, 0.2% Black, 0.8% Asian, 0.0% American Indian and Alaska Native, 1.2% Hispanic of any race, 0.4% two or more races (2000); Density: 30.5 persons per square mile (2000); Age: 24.7% under 18, 18.0% over 64 (2000).
Religion: Five largest groups: 13.9% Evangelical Lutheran Church in America, 13.6% Catholic Church, 13.6% The United Methodist Church, 8.8% Lutheran Church—Missouri Synod, 4.6% Reformed Church in America (2000).
Economy: Unemployment rate: 3.3% (11/2002); Total civilian labor force: 10,658 (11/2002); Leading industries: 23.0% retail trade; 15.3% health care and social assistance; 14.6% manufacturing (2000); Companies that employ more than 1,000 persons: 0 (2000); Companies that employ more than 100 persons: 10 (2000); Farms: 668 totaling 285,829 acres (1997); Minority business ownership rate: 0.0% (1997); Women business ownership rate: 26.0% (1997); Retail sales per capita: $12,221 (1997). Single-family building permits issued: 42 (2001) / 45 (2000); Multi-family building permits issued: 29 (2001) / 0 (2000).
Income: Per capita income: $19,451 (2000); Median household income: $35,799 (2000); Poverty rate: 8.2% (2000); Bankruptcy rate: 2.42% (2001).
Taxes: Total county taxes per capita: $242 (2000); County property taxes per capita: $204 (2000).
Education: High school graduation rate: 88.0% (2000); College graduation rate: 16.3% (2000).
Housing: Homeownership rate: 69.2% (2000); Median home value: $74,400 (2000); Median rent: $304 per month (2000); Median age of housing: 45 years (2000).
Health: Birth rate: 103.0 per 10,000 population (1998); Age adjusted death rate: 77.0 per 10,000 population (1999); Age adjusted cancer mortality rate: 146.8 deaths per 100,000 population (1999). Number of physicians: 17.3 per 10,000 population (1999); Number of hospital beds: 48.9 per 10,000 population (1999).
Elections: 2000 Presidential election results: 43.5% Gore, 52.7% Bush, 2.2% Nader, 0.7% Buchanan
National and State Parks: Barringer Slough State Game Mgt Area; Dan Green Slough State Game Management Area; Deweys Pasture State Game Management Area; Elk Lake State Game Mgt Area; Mud Lake State Wildlife Management Area; Ocheyedan River State Game Refuge; Pickerel Lake State Wildlife Management Area; Round Lake State Game Management Area; Smiths Slough State Game Management Area; Trumbull Lake State Game Management Area; Wanata State Park; Wapiti Marsh State Game Management Area

Additional Information Contacts

Clay County Government Offices 712-262-1569
Spencer Chamber of Commerce. 712-262-5680

Clay County Communities

DICKENS (city). Covers a land area of 0.838 square miles and a water area of 0 square miles. Located at 43.13° N. Lat.; 95.02° W. Long.
History: The name of Dickens reflects the surname of someone important in the community, either a family of early residents or a railroad construction company employee.
Population: 202 (2000); Race: 98.8% White, 0.0% Black, 0.0% Asian, 0.0% American Indian and Alaska Native, 0.0% Hispanic of any race, 1.2% two or more races (2000); Density: 240.9 persons per square mile (2000); Age: 37.2% under 18, 7.0% over 64 (2000); Marriage status: 18.5% never married, 72.3% now married, 2.3% widowed, 6.9% divorced (2000); Foreign born: 0.0% (2000); Ancestry (includes multiple ancestries): 25.6% German, 9.1% Norwegian, 7.9% United States or American, 6.6% Danish, 5.0% Irish (2000).
Economy: Single-family building permits issued: 0 (2001) / 0 (2000); Multi-family building permits issued: 0 (2001) / 0 (2000); Employment by occupation: 0.0% management, 9.7% professional, 23.4% services, 16.9% sales, 0.0% farming, 7.3% construction, 42.7% production (2000).
Income: Per capita income: $13,344 (2000); Median household income: $44,167 (2000); Poverty rate: 4.5% (2000).
Taxes: Total city taxes per capita: $113 (1997); City property taxes per capita: $113 (1997).
Education: High school graduation rate: 70.4% (2000); College graduation rate: 0.0% (2000).
Housing: Homeownership rate: 91.6% (2000); Median home value: $31,700 (2000); Median rent: $281 per month (2000); Median age of housing: 60+ years (2000).
Transportation: Commute to work: 93.4% car, 0.0% public transportation, 3.3% walk, 0.0% work from home (2000); Travel time to work: 50.8% less than 15 minutes, 30.3% 15 to 30 minutes, 13.1% 30 to 45 minutes, 3.3% 45 to 60 minutes, 2.5% 60 minutes or more (2000)

EVERLY (city). Covers a land area of 1.101 square miles and a water area of 0 square miles. Located at 43.16° N. Lat.; 95.32° W. Long. Elevation is 1,365 feet.
History: First called Clark, the town of Everly was renamed in 1884 when it was platted, probably after a railroad conductor or surveyor.
Population: 647 (2000); Race: 98.9% White, 0.0% Black, 0.0% Asian, 0.0% American Indian and Alaska Native, 0.3% Hispanic of any race, 1.1% two or more races (2000); Density: 587.8 persons per square mile (2000); Age: 28.3% under 18, 15.4% over 64 (2000); Marriage status: 17.4% never married, 61.8% now married, 10.8% widowed, 10.0% divorced (2000); Foreign born: 0.3% (2000); Ancestry (includes multiple ancestries): 47.4% German, 11.1% Norwegian, 11.0% Irish, 8.9% Dutch, 4.7% English (2000).
Economy: Single-family building permits issued: 1 (2001) / 6 (2000); Multi-family building permits issued: 5 (2001) / 0 (2000); Employment by occupation: 5.2% management, 13.0% professional, 14.8% services, 23.6% sales, 4.8% farming, 7.9% construction, 30.6% production (2000).

Income: Per capita income: $15,996 (2000); Median household income: $35,278 (2000); Poverty rate: 3.0% (2000).
Taxes: Total city taxes per capita: $212 (1997); City property taxes per capita: $209 (1997).
Education: High school graduation rate: 90.3% (2000); College graduation rate: 15.7% (2000).
Housing: Homeownership rate: 78.5% (2000); Median home value: $56,500 (2000); Median rent: $267 per month (2000); Median age of housing: 47 years (2000).
Newspapers: Everly-Royal News (1 x week)
Transportation: Commute to work: 91.1% car, 0.0% public transportation, 5.8% walk, 2.5% work from home (2000); Travel time to work: 24.0% less than 15 minutes, 60.9% 15 to 30 minutes, 5.0% 30 to 45 minutes, 1.3% 45 to 60 minutes, 8.8% 60 minutes or more (2000)

FOSTORIA (city). Covers a land area of 0.475 square miles and a water area of 0 square miles. Located at 43.24° N. Lat.; 95.15° W. Long. Elevation is 1,449 feet.
History: Fostoria is the outgrowth of a pioneer settlement begun in 1869 by Thomas Berry, Peter Nelson, G. W. Clark, Joseph O'Brien, and their families.
Population: 230 (2000); Race: 96.5% White, 0.9% Black, 1.7% Asian, 0.0% American Indian and Alaska Native, 0.0% Hispanic of any race, 0.9% two or more races (2000); Density: 483.7 persons per square mile (2000); Age: 30.1% under 18, 10.9% over 64 (2000); Marriage status: 14.0% never married, 68.3% now married, 6.7% widowed, 11.0% divorced (2000); Foreign born: 1.7% (2000); Ancestry (includes multiple ancestries): 55.0% German, 10.9% Norwegian, 9.2% Irish, 7.9% Other groups, 5.2% United States or American (2000).
Economy: Single-family building permits issued: 1 (2001) / 1 (2000); Multi-family building permits issued: 0 (2001) / 0 (2000); Employment by occupation: 17.8% management, 8.5% professional, 16.9% services, 19.5% sales, 0.0% farming, 14.4% construction, 22.9% production (2000).
Income: Per capita income: $15,952 (2000); Median household income: $38,750 (2000); Poverty rate: 2.2% (2000).
Taxes: Total city taxes per capita: $153 (1997); City property taxes per capita: $153 (1997).
Education: High school graduation rate: 87.3% (2000); College graduation rate: 7.6% (2000).
Housing: Homeownership rate: 85.7% (2000); Median home value: $62,200 (2000); Median rent: $356 per month (2000); Median age of housing: 51 years (2000).
Transportation: Commute to work: 96.6% car, 0.0% public transportation, 0.0% walk, 3.4% work from home (2000); Travel time to work: 54.0% less than 15 minutes, 31.0% 15 to 30 minutes, 8.8% 30 to 45 minutes, 3.5% 45 to 60 minutes, 2.7% 60 minutes or more (2000)

GILLETT GROVE (city). Covers a land area of 0.189 square miles and a water area of 0 square miles. Located at 43.01° N. Lat.; 95.03° W. Long. Elevation is 1,300 feet.
History: The first residents of Gillett Grove were brothers Isaiah and George Gillett and their families.
Population: 55 (2000); Race: 91.3% White, 8.7% Black, 0.0% Asian, 0.0% American Indian and Alaska Native, 0.0% Hispanic of any race, 0.0% two or more races (2000); Density: 291.6 persons per square mile (2000); Age: 23.9% under 18, 2.2% over 64 (2000); Marriage status: 27.0% never married, 43.2% now married, 2.7% widowed, 27.0% divorced (2000); Foreign born: 0.0% (2000); Ancestry (includes multiple ancestries): 41.3% German, 32.6% Irish, 8.7% Other groups, 8.7% United States or American, 8.7% Norwegian (2000).
Economy: Employment by occupation: 6.3% management, 0.0% professional, 18.8% services, 18.8% sales, 0.0% farming, 25.0% construction, 31.3% production (2000).
Income: Per capita income: $12,337 (2000); Median household income: $21,429 (2000); Poverty rate: 28.3% (2000).
Taxes: Total city taxes per capita: $75 (1997); City property taxes per capita: $75 (1997).
Education: High school graduation rate: 62.5% (2000); College graduation rate: 8.3% (2000).

School District(s)

South Clay Community School District (PK-12)
2000 Enrollment: 127 712-835-2275

Housing: Homeownership rate: 76.0% (2000); Median home value: $17,500 (2000); Median rent: $163 per month (2000); Median age of housing: 50 years (2000).
Transportation: Commute to work: 100.0% car, 0.0% public transportation, 0.0% walk, 0.0% work from home (2000); Travel time to work: 0.0% less than 15 minutes, 75.0% 15 to 30 minutes, 6.3% 30 to 45 minutes, 0.0% 45 to 60 minutes, 18.8% 60 minutes or more (2000)

GREENVILLE (city). Covers a land area of 0.183 square miles and a water area of 0 square miles. Located at 43.01° N. Lat.; 95.14° W. Long.
History: The first settlers here, Albert and Lizzie Greene, gave their name to the town.
Population: 93 (2000); Race: 100.0% White, 0.0% Black, 0.0% Asian, 0.0% American Indian and Alaska Native, 0.0% Hispanic of any race, 0.0% two or more races (2000); Density: 507.9 persons per square mile (2000); Age: 35.0% under 18, 8.3% over 64 (2000); Marriage status: 16.7% never married, 77.4% now married, 6.0% widowed, 0.0% divorced (2000); Foreign born: 0.0% (2000); Ancestry (includes multiple ancestries): 33.3% German, 18.3% Irish, 7.5% Dutch, 6.7% Norwegian, 5.8% Swedish (2000).
Economy: Single-family building permits issued: 0 (2001) / 0 (2000); Multi-family building permits issued: 0 (2001) / 0 (2000); Employment by occupation: 7.5% management, 0.0% professional, 17.5% services, 30.0% sales, 0.0% farming, 22.5% construction, 22.5% production (2000).
Income: Per capita income: $22,217 (2000); Median household income: $29,531 (2000); Poverty rate: 19.2% (2000).
Taxes: Total city taxes per capita: $62 (1997); City property taxes per capita: $62 (1997).
Education: High school graduation rate: 74.3% (2000); College graduation rate: 0.0% (2000).
Housing: Homeownership rate: 100.0% (2000); Median home value: $25,000 (2000); Median age of housing: 60+ years (2000).
Transportation: Commute to work: 95.2% car, 0.0% public transportation, 0.0% walk, 0.0% work from home (2000); Travel time to work: 26.2% less than 15 minutes, 45.2% 15 to 30 minutes, 23.8% 30 to 45 minutes, 4.8% 45 to 60 minutes, 0.0% 60 minutes or more (2000)

PETERSON (city). Covers a land area of 0.308 square miles and a water area of 0 square miles. Located at 42.91° N. Lat.; 95.34° W. Long. Elevation is 1,238 feet.
History: It is believed that Peterson was named for the original owner of the town site, Adlie Peterson.
Population: 372 (2000); Race: 98.4% White, 0.0% Black, 0.0% Asian, 0.0% American Indian and Alaska Native, 1.6% Hispanic of any race, 0.0% two or more races (2000); Density: 1,208.5 persons per square mile (2000); Age: 18.0% under 18, 30.8% over 64 (2000); Marriage status: 24.1% never married, 50.0% now married, 15.2% widowed, 10.7% divorced (2000); Foreign born: 2.9% (2000); Ancestry (includes multiple ancestries): 40.3% German, 12.7% English, 10.6% Irish, 4.8% Danish, 4.0% Scotch-Irish (2000).
Economy: Single-family building permits issued: 1 (2001) / 1 (2000); Multi-family building permits issued: 0 (2001) / 0 (2000); Employment by occupation: 10.4% management, 11.0% professional, 15.2% services, 25.0% sales, 1.8% farming, 14.6% construction, 22.0% production (2000).
Income: Per capita income: $16,932 (2000); Median household income: $30,000 (2000); Poverty rate: 10.3% (2000).
Taxes: Total city taxes per capita: $195 (1997); City property taxes per capita: $193 (1997).
Education: High school graduation rate: 86.4% (2000); College graduation rate: 7.0% (2000).
Housing: Homeownership rate: 84.3% (2000); Median home value: $35,000 (2000); Median rent: $218 per month (2000); Median age of housing: 60+ years (2000).
Newspapers: Peterson Patriot (1 x week)
Transportation: Commute to work: 86.6% car, 0.0% public transportation, 11.0% walk, 2.4% work from home (2000); Travel time to work: 31.3% less than 15 minutes, 28.1% 15 to 30 minutes, 26.9% 30 to 45 minutes, 1.9% 45 to 60 minutes, 11.9% 60 minutes or more (2000)

ROSSIE (city). Covers a land area of 0.150 square miles and a water area of 0 square miles. Located at 43.01° N. Lat.; 95.18° W. Long. Elevation is 1,409 feet.
History: Rossie is believed to have been named in honor of an engineer on the Chicago, Rock Island & Pacific Railroad.
Population: 58 (2000); Race: 100.0% White, 0.0% Black, 0.0% Asian, 0.0% American Indian and Alaska Native, 0.0% Hispanic of any race, 0.0% two or more races (2000); Density: 385.5 persons per square mile (2000); Age: 27.0% under 18, 4.1% over 64 (2000); Marriage status: 24.6% never married, 59.0% now married, 8.2% widowed, 8.2% divorced (2000); Foreign born: 0.0% (2000); Ancestry (includes multiple ancestries): 41.9% German, 12.2% United States or American, 5.4% Dutch, 5.4% English, 5.4% Australian (2000).

Economy: Single-family building permits issued: 0 (2001) / 0 (2000); Multi-family building permits issued: 0 (2001) / 0 (2000); Employment by occupation: 0.0% management, 25.0% professional, 0.0% services, 19.4% sales, 0.0% farming, 5.6% construction, 50.0% production (2000).
Income: Per capita income: $13,266 (2000); Median household income: $30,833 (2000); Poverty rate: 9.5% (2000).
Taxes: Total city taxes per capita: $56 (1997); City property taxes per capita: $56 (1997).
Education: High school graduation rate: 90.7% (2000); College graduation rate: 3.7% (2000).
Housing: Homeownership rate: 56.7% (2000); Median home value: $31,300 (2000); Median rent: $333 per month (2000); Median age of housing: 53 years (2000).
Transportation: Commute to work: 100.0% car, 0.0% public transportation, 0.0% walk, 0.0% work from home (2000); Travel time to work: 13.9% less than 15 minutes, 58.3% 15 to 30 minutes, 22.2% 30 to 45 minutes, 5.6% 45 to 60 minutes, 0.0% 60 minutes or more (2000)

ROYAL (city). Covers a land area of 0.293 square miles and a water area of 0 square miles. Located at 43.06° N. Lat.; 95.28° W. Long. Elevation is 1,414 feet.
History: The name Royal was bestowed upon the town by its first postmistress Eliza Nelson.
Population: 479 (2000); Race: 98.7% White, 0.0% Black, 0.0% Asian, 0.0% American Indian and Alaska Native, 1.3% Hispanic of any race, 1.3% two or more races (2000); Density: 1,634.2 persons per square mile (2000); Age: 24.5% under 18, 19.8% over 64 (2000); Marriage status: 27.4% never married, 53.5% now married, 8.9% widowed, 10.2% divorced (2000); Foreign born: 0.8% (2000); Ancestry (includes multiple ancestries): 49.2% German, 18.1% Danish, 9.3% Irish, 6.8% Norwegian, 6.1% Dutch (2000).
Economy: Single-family building permits issued: 1 (2001) / 0 (2000); Multi-family building permits issued: 0 (2001) / 0 (2000); Employment by occupation: 7.7% management, 12.3% professional, 15.7% services, 26.4% sales, 0.8% farming, 13.8% construction, 23.4% production (2000).
Income: Per capita income: $18,118 (2000); Median household income: $37,500 (2000); Poverty rate: 4.7% (2000).
Taxes: Total city taxes per capita: $129 (1997); City property taxes per capita: $129 (1997).
Education: High school graduation rate: 84.6% (2000); College graduation rate: 14.4% (2000).

School District(s)

Clay Central-Everly Community School District (PK-12)
2000 Enrollment: 521 712-933-2242

Housing: Homeownership rate: 78.4% (2000); Median home value: $47,500 (2000); Median rent: $220 per month (2000); Median age of housing: 57 years (2000).
Transportation: Commute to work: 87.3% car, 0.0% public transportation, 8.7% walk, 4.0% work from home (2000); Travel time to work: 26.0% less than 15 minutes, 64.9% 15 to 30 minutes, 1.7% 30 to 45 minutes, 5.4% 45 to 60 minutes, 2.1% 60 minutes or more (2000)

SPENCER (city). Covers a land area of 10.122 square miles and a water area of 0.046 square miles. Located at 43.14° N. Lat.; 95.14° W. Long. Elevation is 1,321 feet.
History: Spencer was founded in 1859 and named for U.S. Senator George E. Spencer (1836-1893). Most of the business section was destroyed by a fire due to the careless handling of fireworks on July 4, 1931.
Population: 11,317 (2000); Race: 96.5% White, 0.2% Black, 1.3% Asian, 0.0% American Indian and Alaska Native, 1.4% Hispanic of any race, 0.4% two or more races (2000); Density: 1,118.1 persons per square mile (2000); Age: 24.1% under 18, 19.4% over 64 (2000); Marriage status: 22.2% never married, 58.4% now married, 8.7% widowed, 10.8% divorced (2000); Foreign born: 2.3% (2000); Ancestry (includes multiple ancestries): 41.3% German, 10.2% Norwegian, 9.8% Irish, 8.6% Dutch, 8.0% English (2000).
Vital Statistics: Birth rate: 121.9 per 10,000 population (1998)
Economy: Single-family building permits issued: 31 (2001) / 32 (2000); Multi-family building permits issued: 24 (2001) / 0 (2000); Employment by occupation: 11.2% management, 12.8% professional, 13.8% services, 28.3% sales, 0.5% farming, 9.0% construction, 24.4% production (2000).
Income: Per capita income: $19,153 (2000); Median household income: $32,970 (2000); Poverty rate: 9.5% (2000).
Taxes: Total city taxes per capita: $387 (2000); City property taxes per capita: $288 (2000).
Education: High school graduation rate: 87.3% (2000); College graduation rate: 17.1% (2000).

School District(s)

Spencer Community School District (PK-12)
2000 Enrollment: 2,205 712-262-8950

Housing: Homeownership rate: 65.0% (2000); Median home value: $80,900 (2000); Median rent: $315 per month (2000); Median age of housing: 41 years (2000).
Hospitals: Spencer Municipal Hospital (99 beds)
Safety: Violent crime rate: 2.7 per 10,000 population; Property crime rate: 270.7 per 10,000 population (2001).
Newspapers: Spencer Daily Reporter (5 x week); Northwest Iowa Shopper Weekend (1 x week)
Transportation: Commute to work: 92.3% car, 0.9% public transportation, 3.3% walk, 1.9% work from home (2000); Travel time to work: 78.5% less than 15 minutes, 13.3% 15 to 30 minutes, 5.6% 30 to 45 minutes, 1.3% 45 to 60 minutes, 1.2% 60 minutes or more (2000)
Airports: Spencer Municipal
Additional Information Contacts
Spencer Chamber of Commerce. 712-262-5680

WEBB (city). Covers a land area of 0.503 square miles and a water area of 0 square miles. Located at 42.94° N. Lat.; 95.01° W. Long. Elevation is 1,370 feet.
History: Webb was named for the mother of a local settler.
Population: 165 (2000); Race: 97.8% White, 0.0% Black, 0.0% Asian, 0.5% American Indian and Alaska Native, 0.0% Hispanic of any race, 1.6% two or more races (2000); Density: 328.0 persons per square mile (2000); Age: 36.3% under 18, 17.0% over 64 (2000); Marriage status: 18.2% never married, 57.9% now married, 9.9% widowed, 14.0% divorced (2000); Foreign born: 1.1% (2000); Ancestry (includes multiple ancestries): 29.1% German, 22.0% Irish, 11.0% Swedish, 7.7% English, 6.6% Danish (2000).
Economy: Single-family building permits issued: 0 (2001) / 0 (2000); Multi-family building permits issued: 0 (2001) / 0 (2000); Employment by occupation: 8.5% management, 16.9% professional, 0.0% services, 10.2% sales, 0.0% farming, 22.0% construction, 42.4% production (2000).
Income: Per capita income: $13,087 (2000); Median household income: $27,500 (2000); Poverty rate: 9.8% (2000).
Taxes: Total city taxes per capita: $87 (1997); City property taxes per capita: $87 (1997).
Education: High school graduation rate: 87.9% (2000); College graduation rate: 4.7% (2000).
Housing: Homeownership rate: 94.4% (2000); Median home value: $37,500 (2000); Median rent: $250 per month (2000); Median age of housing: 60 years (2000).
Transportation: Commute to work: 91.2% car, 0.0% public transportation, 3.5% walk, 0.0% work from home (2000); Travel time to work: 35.1% less than 15 minutes, 22.8% 15 to 30 minutes, 26.3% 30 to 45 minutes, 1.8% 45 to 60 minutes, 14.0% 60 minutes or more (2000)

Clayton County

Located in northeastern Iowa; bounded on the east by the Mississippi River and the Wisconsin border; drained by the Turkey and Volga Rivers. Covers a land area of 778.80 square miles, a water area of 14.00 square miles, and is located in the Central Time Zone. The county government was organized in 1837. County seat is Elkader.

Weather Station: Elkader 5 SSW — Elevation: 767 feet

	Jan	Feb	Mar	Apr	May	Jun	Jul	Aug	Sep	Oct	Nov	Dec
High	27	33	45	60	72	81	85	82	75	63	45	31
Low	6	12	23	35	46	55	60	58	49	38	26	13
Precip	1.0	1.1	2.1	3.5	4.1	4.4	4.1	4.7	3.2	2.5	2.4	1.2
Snow	9.6	7.0	5.2	2.0	0.0	0.0	0.0	0.0	0.0	0.2	4.0	8.2

High and Low temperatures in degrees Fahrenheit; Precipitation and Snow in inches

Weather Station: Guttenberg Lock & Dam 10 — Elevation: 623 feet

	Jan	Feb	Mar	Apr	May	Jun	Jul	Aug	Sep	Oct	Nov	Dec
High	27	33	45	59	72	81	84	82	74	62	45	32
Low	9	15	27	39	51	60	64	62	54	42	29	16
Precip	1.1	1.1	2.0	3.2	3.9	4.3	4.2	4.4	3.2	2.2	2.2	1.3
Snow	10.7	5.6	4.0	1.2	0.0	0.0	0.0	0.0	0.0	0.1	2.3	7.0

High and Low temperatures in degrees Fahrenheit; Precipitation and Snow in inches

Population: 18,678 (2000); Race: 98.7% White, 0.4% Black, 0.2% Asian, 0.1% American Indian and Alaska Native, 0.6% Hispanic of any race, 0.4% two or more races (2000); Density: 24.0 persons per square mile (2000); Age: 25.3% under 18, 18.6% over 64 (2000).

Religion: Five largest groups: 32.7% Evangelical Lutheran Church in America, 32.2% Catholic Church, 8.4% The United Methodist Church, 4.2% United Church of Christ, 1.8% Lutheran Church—Missouri Synod (2000).
Economy: Unemployment rate: 5.1% (11/2002); Total civilian labor force: 10,672 (11/2002); Leading industries: 26.0% manufacturing; 16.5% health care and social assistance; 11.6% retail trade (2000); Companies that employ more than 1,000 persons: 0 (2000); Companies that employ more than 100 persons: 10 (2000); Farms: 1,638 totaling 452,050 acres (1997); Minority business ownership rate: 0.0% (1997); Women business ownership rate: 28.9% (1997); Retail sales per capita: $7,099 (1997). Single-family building permits issued: 51 (2001) / 48 (2000); Multi-family building permits issued: 36 (2001) / 48 (2000).
Income: Per capita income: $16,930 (2000); Median household income: $34,068 (2000); Poverty rate: 8.6% (2000); Bankruptcy rate: 2.62% (2001).
Taxes: Total county taxes per capita: $281 (2000); County property taxes per capita: $233 (2000).
Education: High school graduation rate: 82.6% (2000); College graduation rate: 12.8% (2000).
Housing: Homeownership rate: 76.6% (2000); Median home value: $66,400 (2000); Median rent: $272 per month (2000); Median age of housing: 59 years (2000).
Health: Birth rate: 111.4 per 10,000 population (1998); Age adjusted death rate: 94.1 per 10,000 population (1999); Age adjusted cancer mortality rate: 201.6 deaths per 100,000 population (1999). Number of physicians: 4.8 per 10,000 population (1999); Number of hospital beds: 22.0 per 10,000 population (1999).
Elections: 2000 Presidential election results: 49.5% Gore, 47.1% Bush, 2.4% Nader, 0.7% Buchanan
National and State Parks: Bixby State Park; Effigy Mounds National Monument; Giard Tract State Historical Marker; Merritt Forest State Preserve; Mississippi Valley Overlook State Historical Marker; Mossy Glen State Preserve; Pikes Peak State Park; Rentz Memorial Woods State Preserve; Roberts Creek State Preserve; Turkey River Mounds State Monument; Turkey River Mounds State Preserve
Additional Information Contacts
Clayton County Government Offices.................... 563-245-1106
Elkader Chamber of Commerce.......................... 563-245-2857
Mc Gregor Chamber of Commerce 563-873-2186
Monona Chamber of Commerce 563-539-4455
Strawberry Pt Development Fund 563-933-4417

Clayton County Communities

CLAYTON (city). Covers a land area of 0.551 square miles and a water area of 0 square miles. Located at 42.90° N. Lat.; 91.14° W. Long. Elevation is 624 feet.
History: The town of Clayton takes its name from the county. Both names honor Senator J.M. Clayton of Delaware (1796-1856).
Population: 55 (2000); Race: 100.0% White, 0.0% Black, 0.0% Asian, 0.0% American Indian and Alaska Native, 0.0% Hispanic of any race, 0.0% two or more races (2000); Density: 99.8 persons per square mile (2000); Age: 5.3% under 18, 24.6% over 64 (2000); Marriage status: 17.9% never married, 53.6% now married, 16.1% widowed, 12.5% divorced (2000); Foreign born: 0.0% (2000); Ancestry (includes multiple ancestries): 54.4% German, 21.1% English, 10.5% United States or American, 8.8% Czech, 7.0% Norwegian (2000).
Economy: Single-family building permits issued: 1 (2001) / 1 (2000); Multi-family building permits issued: 0 (2001) / 0 (2000); Employment by occupation: 15.2% management, 18.2% professional, 21.2% services, 6.1% sales, 0.0% farming, 15.2% construction, 24.2% production (2000).
Income: Per capita income: $21,214 (2000); Median household income: $31,250 (2000); Poverty rate: 0.0% (2000).
Taxes: Total city taxes per capita: $390 (1997); City property taxes per capita: $341 (1997).
Education: High school graduation rate: 78.4% (2000); College graduation rate: 17.6% (2000).
Housing: Homeownership rate: 100.0% (2000); Median home value: $81,000 (2000); Median age of housing: 45 years (2000).
Transportation: Commute to work: 90.9% car, 0.0% public transportation, 9.1% walk, 0.0% work from home (2000); Travel time to work: 33.3% less than 15 minutes, 33.3% 15 to 30 minutes, 21.2% 30 to 45 minutes, 3.0% 45 to 60 minutes, 9.1% 60 minutes or more (2000)

ELKADER (city). Covers a land area of 1.397 square miles and a water area of 0 square miles. Located at 42.85° N. Lat.; 91.40° W. Long. Elevation is 759 feet.
History: Elkader was named in 1845 for an Algerian chieftain, Abd-el-Kader, who was then making a valiant defense against the inroads of French imperialism in his country.
Population: 1,465 (2000); Race: 99.5% White, 0.3% Black, 0.0% Asian, 0.0% American Indian and Alaska Native, 0.0% Hispanic of any race, 0.1% two or more races (2000); Density: 1,049.0 persons per square mile (2000); Age: 20.6% under 18, 26.9% over 64 (2000); Marriage status: 16.7% never married, 59.0% now married, 14.9% widowed, 9.4% divorced (2000); Foreign born: 0.8% (2000); Ancestry (includes multiple ancestries): 51.6% German, 16.0% Norwegian, 10.5% Irish, 7.4% English, 3.2% Dutch (2000).
Economy: Single-family building permits issued: 1 (2001) / 0 (2000); Multi-family building permits issued: 0 (2001) / 14 (2000); Employment by occupation: 9.4% management, 21.4% professional, 13.9% services, 26.0% sales, 1.6% farming, 11.4% construction, 16.3% production (2000).
Income: Per capita income: $16,785 (2000); Median household income: $32,857 (2000); Poverty rate: 5.2% (2000).
Taxes: Total city taxes per capita: $322 (1997); City property taxes per capita: $268 (1997).
Education: High school graduation rate: 80.8% (2000); College graduation rate: 19.9% (2000).

School District(s)

Central Community School District (KG-12)
2000 Enrollment: 660 319-245-1751
Housing: Homeownership rate: 75.6% (2000); Median home value: $66,000 (2000); Median rent: $224 per month (2000); Median age of housing: 60+ years (2000).
Hospitals: Central Community Hospital (29 beds)
Newspapers: The Clayton County Register (1 x week)
Transportation: Commute to work: 74.8% car, 0.5% public transportation, 17.1% walk, 5.3% work from home (2000); Travel time to work: 71.1% less than 15 minutes, 14.7% 15 to 30 minutes, 11.0% 30 to 45 minutes, 1.1% 45 to 60 minutes, 2.1% 60 minutes or more (2000)
Additional Information Contacts
Elkader Chamber of Commerce.......................... 563-245-2857

ELKPORT (city). Covers a land area of 0.187 square miles and a water area of 0 square miles. Located at 42.74° N. Lat.; 91.27° W. Long. Elevation is 655 feet.
History: Elkport took its name from its location near the mouth of Elk Creek, near the Turkey River.
Population: 88 (2000); Race: 100.0% White, 0.0% Black, 0.0% Asian, 0.0% American Indian and Alaska Native, 0.0% Hispanic of any race, 0.0% two or more races (2000); Density: 470.2 persons per square mile (2000); Age: 36.1% under 18, 18.1% over 64 (2000); Marriage status: 12.8% never married, 53.2% now married, 14.9% widowed, 19.1% divorced (2000); Foreign born: 0.0% (2000); Ancestry (includes multiple ancestries): 45.8% German, 18.1% French (except Basque), 16.7% United States or American, 15.3% Irish, 6.9% Portuguese (2000).
Economy: Single-family building permits issued: 0 (2001) / 0 (2000); Multi-family building permits issued: 0 (2001) / 0 (2000); Employment by occupation: 0.0% management, 17.2% professional, 10.3% services, 24.1% sales, 6.9% farming, 20.7% construction, 20.7% production (2000).
Income: Per capita income: $11,518 (2000); Median household income: $24,375 (2000); Poverty rate: 6.9% (2000).
Taxes: Total city taxes per capita: $100 (1997); City property taxes per capita: $50 (1997).
Education: High school graduation rate: 66.7% (2000); College graduation rate: 6.7% (2000).
Housing: Homeownership rate: 94.3% (2000); Median home value: $40,400 (2000); Median rent: $175 per month (2000); Median age of housing: 60+ years (2000).
Transportation: Commute to work: 100.0% car, 0.0% public transportation, 0.0% walk, 0.0% work from home (2000); Travel time to work: 13.8% less than 15 minutes, 41.4% 15 to 30 minutes, 17.2% 30 to 45 minutes, 3.4% 45 to 60 minutes, 24.1% 60 minutes or more (2000)

FARMERSBURG (city). Aka Famersburg. Covers a land area of 0.402 square miles and a water area of 0 square miles. Located at 42.95° N. Lat.; 91.36° W. Long.
History: Farmersburg, established in 1858, was given its name by Thomas Street, the son of a military man stationed here. The community was earlier known as National.

Population: 300 (2000); Race: 100.0% White, 0.0% Black, 0.0% Asian, 0.0% American Indian and Alaska Native, 0.0% Hispanic of any race, 0.0% two or more races (2000); Density: 745.9 persons per square mile (2000); Age: 28.6% under 18, 20.1% over 64 (2000); Marriage status: 17.4% never married, 60.6% now married, 12.0% widowed, 10.0% divorced (2000); Foreign born: 0.0% (2000); Ancestry (includes multiple ancestries): 63.2% German, 22.0% Norwegian, 14.5% Irish, 4.4% Swiss, 4.1% Other groups (2000).
Economy: Single-family building permits issued: 0 (2001) / 0 (2000); Multi-family building permits issued: 0 (2001) / 0 (2000); Employment by occupation: 4.9% management, 6.7% professional, 11.0% services, 28.8% sales, 4.3% farming, 11.0% construction, 33.1% production (2000).
Income: Per capita income: $14,796 (2000); Median household income: $34,000 (2000); Poverty rate: 6.3% (2000).
Taxes: Total city taxes per capita: $156 (1997); City property taxes per capita: $105 (1997).
Education: High school graduation rate: 86.2% (2000); College graduation rate: 3.8% (2000).
Housing: Homeownership rate: 80.6% (2000); Median home value: $54,800 (2000); Median rent: $247 per month (2000); Median age of housing: 60+ years (2000).
Transportation: Commute to work: 92.5% car, 0.0% public transportation, 0.0% walk, 6.2% work from home (2000); Travel time to work: 29.1% less than 15 minutes, 55.0% 15 to 30 minutes, 15.9% 30 to 45 minutes, 0.0% 45 to 60 minutes, 0.0% 60 minutes or more (2000)

GARBER (city). Covers a land area of 0.237 square miles and a water area of 0 square miles. Located at 42.74° N. Lat.; 91.26° W. Long.
History: First called Elkport and then East Elkport, Garber was later named for landowner John Garber.
Population: 103 (2000); Race: 95.3% White, 0.0% Black, 4.7% Asian, 0.0% American Indian and Alaska Native, 0.0% Hispanic of any race, 0.0% two or more races (2000); Density: 434.9 persons per square mile (2000); Age: 31.1% under 18, 14.2% over 64 (2000); Marriage status: 21.5% never married, 54.4% now married, 10.1% widowed, 13.9% divorced (2000); Foreign born: 3.8% (2000); Ancestry (includes multiple ancestries): 54.7% German, 4.7% Other groups, 1.9% Dutch, 1.9% Irish, 1.9% United States or American (2000).
Economy: Employment by occupation: 4.3% management, 8.5% professional, 10.6% services, 14.9% sales, 8.5% farming, 14.9% construction, 38.3% production (2000).
Income: Per capita income: $11,618 (2000); Median household income: $22,708 (2000); Poverty rate: 16.0% (2000).
Taxes: Total city taxes per capita: $94 (1997); City property taxes per capita: $51 (1997).
Education: High school graduation rate: 74.2% (2000); College graduation rate: 1.6% (2000).
Housing: Homeownership rate: 86.5% (2000); Median home value: $48,300 (2000); Median rent: $188 per month (2000); Median age of housing: 60+ years (2000).
Transportation: Commute to work: 95.7% car, 0.0% public transportation, 0.0% walk, 4.3% work from home (2000); Travel time to work: 11.1% less than 15 minutes, 37.8% 15 to 30 minutes, 24.4% 30 to 45 minutes, 8.9% 45 to 60 minutes, 17.8% 60 minutes or more (2000)

GARNAVILLO (city). Covers a land area of 0.878 square miles and a water area of 0 square miles. Located at 42.86° N. Lat.; 91.23° W. Long. Elevation is 1,065 feet.
History: Garnavillo, named Jacksonville in 1844, was given its present name in 1846 by Judge Samuel Murdock, for a town in Ireland.
Population: 754 (2000); Race: 97.8% White, 2.2% Black, 0.0% Asian, 0.0% American Indian and Alaska Native, 0.0% Hispanic of any race, 0.0% two or more races (2000); Density: 858.3 persons per square mile (2000); Age: 21.4% under 18, 24.9% over 64 (2000); Marriage status: 23.5% never married, 53.4% now married, 13.7% widowed, 9.5% divorced (2000); Foreign born: 0.5% (2000); Ancestry (includes multiple ancestries): 60.3% German, 9.5% Irish, 7.0% English, 5.4% United States or American, 5.2% Norwegian (2000).
Economy: Single-family building permits issued: 0 (2001) / 0 (2000); Multi-family building permits issued: 0 (2001) / 0 (2000); Employment by occupation: 16.8% management, 11.1% professional, 25.5% services, 12.4% sales, 1.6% farming, 9.7% construction, 22.9% production (2000).
Income: Per capita income: $20,964 (2000); Median household income: $35,694 (2000); Poverty rate: 9.3% (2000).
Taxes: Total city taxes per capita: $318 (1997); City property taxes per capita: $266 (1997).
Education: High school graduation rate: 74.5% (2000); College graduation rate: 13.5% (2000).

School District(s)

Garnavillo Community School District (PK-12)
2000 Enrollment: 243 319-964-2441
Housing: Homeownership rate: 81.6% (2000); Median home value: $64,500 (2000); Median rent: $245 per month (2000); Median age of housing: 46 years (2000).
Transportation: Commute to work: 81.0% car, 0.0% public transportation, 10.8% walk, 4.8% work from home (2000); Travel time to work: 47.8% less than 15 minutes, 34.2% 15 to 30 minutes, 11.4% 30 to 45 minutes, 1.4% 45 to 60 minutes, 5.3% 60 minutes or more (2000)

GUTTENBERG (city). Covers a land area of 2.065 square miles and a water area of 0.026 square miles. Located at 42.78° N. Lat.; 91.10° W. Long. Elevation is 625 feet.
History: Guttenberg was first known as Prairie La Porte. The name was later changed to Guttenberg for the German inventor of the printing press, Johann Gutenberg. The change in spelling was due to an error in the first plat of the site filed in the county records. In 1845, the Western Settlement Society of Cincinnati colonized the town with German immigrants, many of whom were intellectuals who had fled from military service in Europe.
Population: 1,987 (2000); Race: 96.8% White, 1.5% Black, 0.7% Asian, 0.2% American Indian and Alaska Native, 0.3% Hispanic of any race, 0.8% two or more races (2000); Density: 962.3 persons per square mile (2000); Age: 20.1% under 18, 28.0% over 64 (2000); Marriage status: 21.9% never married, 54.6% now married, 15.3% widowed, 8.2% divorced (2000); Foreign born: 1.8% (2000); Ancestry (includes multiple ancestries): 60.7% German, 9.5% Irish, 8.1% English, 5.0% Norwegian, 4.3% Other groups (2000).
Economy: Single-family building permits issued: 6 (2001) / 6 (2000); Multi-family building permits issued: 0 (2001) / 4 (2000); Employment by occupation: 10.0% management, 17.2% professional, 19.0% services, 20.2% sales, 2.6% farming, 8.4% construction, 22.6% production (2000).
Income: Per capita income: $17,098 (2000); Median household income: $29,151 (2000); Poverty rate: 8.4% (2000).
Taxes: Total city taxes per capita: $316 (1997); City property taxes per capita: $232 (1997).
Education: High school graduation rate: 73.2% (2000); College graduation rate: 13.5% (2000).

School District(s)

Guttenberg Community School District (KG-12)
2000 Enrollment: 513 319-252-2341
Housing: Homeownership rate: 73.4% (2000); Median home value: $82,200 (2000); Median rent: $274 per month (2000); Median age of housing: 57 years (2000).
Hospitals: Guttenberg Municipal Hospital (25 beds)
Newspapers: Guttenberg Press (1 x week)
Transportation: Commute to work: 86.7% car, 0.0% public transportation, 9.7% walk, 3.6% work from home (2000); Travel time to work: 67.6% less than 15 minutes, 11.3% 15 to 30 minutes, 9.3% 30 to 45 minutes, 6.6% 45 to 60 minutes, 5.3% 60 minutes or more (2000)

LITTLEPORT (city). Covers a land area of 0.333 square miles and a water area of 0 square miles. Located at 42.75° N. Lat.; 91.36° W. Long. Elevation is 708 feet.
History: Littleport, which was settled in 1848, was subject to disastrous floods of the Volga River (named for the river in Russia).
Population: 26 (2000); Race: 100.0% White, 0.0% Black, 0.0% Asian, 0.0% American Indian and Alaska Native, 0.0% Hispanic of any race, 0.0% two or more races (2000); Density: 78.0 persons per square mile (2000); Age: 10.5% under 18, 26.3% over 64 (2000); Marriage status: 21.1% never married, 73.7% now married, 5.3% widowed, 0.0% divorced (2000); Foreign born: 0.0% (2000); Ancestry (includes multiple ancestries): 68.4% German, 10.5% Danish, 10.5% English, 5.3% Swiss (2000).
Economy: Single-family building permits issued: 0 (2001) / 0 (2000); Multi-family building permits issued: 0 (2001) / 0 (2000); Employment by occupation: 14.3% management, 14.3% professional, 28.6% services, 14.3% sales, 0.0% farming, 28.6% construction, 0.0% production (2000).
Income: Per capita income: $16,237 (2000); Median household income: $23,125 (2000); Poverty rate: 15.8% (2000).
Taxes: Total city taxes per capita: $95 (1997); City property taxes per capita: $48 (1997).
Education: High school graduation rate: 82.4% (2000); College graduation rate: 11.8% (2000).

Housing: Homeownership rate: 100.0% (2000); Median home value: $32,500 (2000); Median age of housing: 60+ years (2000).
Transportation: Commute to work: 80.0% car, 20.0% public transportation, 0.0% walk, 0.0% work from home (2000); Travel time to work: 20.0% less than 15 minutes, 60.0% 15 to 30 minutes, 20.0% 30 to 45 minutes, 0.0% 45 to 60 minutes, 0.0% 60 minutes or more (2000)

LUANA (city). Covers a land area of 1.050 square miles and a water area of 0 square miles. Located at 43.06° N. Lat.; 91.45° W. Long.
History: Luana, named for Luana Scott, wife of William S. Scott, an early settler, was organized with the advent of the Chicago, Milwaukee, & St. Paul Railroad in the early 1850's.
Population: 249 (2000); Race: 98.8% White, 0.0% Black, 0.0% Asian, 0.0% American Indian and Alaska Native, 4.5% Hispanic of any race, 1.2% two or more races (2000); Density: 237.1 persons per square mile (2000); Age: 20.1% under 18, 21.7% over 64 (2000); Marriage status: 36.7% never married, 49.5% now married, 10.0% widowed, 3.8% divorced (2000); Foreign born: 3.7% (2000); Ancestry (includes multiple ancestries): 58.6% German, 9.4% Norwegian, 7.8% Other groups, 6.1% English, 3.7% Irish (2000).
Economy: Single-family building permits issued: 0 (2001) / 2 (2000); Multi-family building permits issued: 0 (2001) / 0 (2000); Employment by occupation: 4.9% management, 10.7% professional, 5.7% services, 27.0% sales, 4.9% farming, 11.5% construction, 35.2% production (2000).
Income: Per capita income: $16,165 (2000); Median household income: $29,583 (2000); Poverty rate: 9.9% (2000).
Taxes: Total city taxes per capita: $178 (1997); City property taxes per capita: $131 (1997).
Education: High school graduation rate: 70.5% (2000); College graduation rate: 11.6% (2000).
Housing: Homeownership rate: 77.1% (2000); Median home value: $55,500 (2000); Median rent: $280 per month (2000); Median age of housing: 43 years (2000).
Transportation: Commute to work: 80.8% car, 0.0% public transportation, 10.0% walk, 9.2% work from home (2000); Travel time to work: 51.4% less than 15 minutes, 35.8% 15 to 30 minutes, 8.3% 30 to 45 minutes, 4.6% 45 to 60 minutes, 0.0% 60 minutes or more (2000)

MARQUETTE (city). Covers a land area of 1.220 square miles and a water area of 0.063 square miles. Located at 43.04° N. Lat.; 91.18° W. Long. Elevation is 629 feet.
History: Marquette was first known as North McGregor and later renamed for Father Marquette, who, along with Louis Joliet, viewed the Iowa territory from the mouth of the Wisconsin River in 1673.
Population: 421 (2000); Race: 100.0% White, 0.0% Black, 0.0% Asian, 0.0% American Indian and Alaska Native, 0.6% Hispanic of any race, 0.0% two or more races (2000); Density: 345.2 persons per square mile (2000); Age: 16.7% under 18, 19.4% over 64 (2000); Marriage status: 22.0% never married, 47.2% now married, 14.2% widowed, 16.7% divorced (2000); Foreign born: 1.1% (2000); Ancestry (includes multiple ancestries): 44.7% German, 15.0% Irish, 11.7% Norwegian, 9.2% English, 7.8% French (except Basque) (2000).
Economy: Single-family building permits issued: 4 (2001) / 3 (2000); Multi-family building permits issued: 36 (2001) / 26 (2000); Employment by occupation: 6.0% management, 10.5% professional, 19.5% services, 22.5% sales, 1.5% farming, 11.0% construction, 29.0% production (2000).
Income: Per capita income: $18,037 (2000); Median household income: $30,179 (2000); Poverty rate: 5.6% (2000).
Taxes: Total city taxes per capita: $438 (1997); City property taxes per capita: $384 (1997).
Education: High school graduation rate: 91.6% (2000); College graduation rate: 11.8% (2000).
Housing: Homeownership rate: 76.5% (2000); Median home value: $67,100 (2000); Median rent: $285 per month (2000); Median age of housing: 60+ years (2000).
Transportation: Commute to work: 89.1% car, 0.0% public transportation, 7.3% walk, 3.6% work from home (2000); Travel time to work: 61.6% less than 15 minutes, 28.6% 15 to 30 minutes, 4.3% 30 to 45 minutes, 2.7% 45 to 60 minutes, 2.7% 60 minutes or more (2000)

MCGREGOR (city). Covers a land area of 1.308 square miles and a water area of 0.002 square miles. Located at 43.02° N. Lat.; 91.18° W. Long. Elevation is 627 feet.
History: McGregor was named Coulee des Sioux by early French traders. In 1836 when Alexander McGregor established a ferry from Prairie du Chen, Wisconsin, to the village, it became known as McGregor's Landing.
Population: 871 (2000); Race: 99.8% White, 0.0% Black, 0.0% Asian, 0.2% American Indian and Alaska Native, 0.2% Hispanic of any race, 0.0% two or more races (2000); Density: 665.8 persons per square mile (2000); Age: 22.6% under 18, 22.3% over 64 (2000); Marriage status: 21.6% never married, 49.4% now married, 14.0% widowed, 15.0% divorced (2000); Foreign born: 1.4% (2000); Ancestry (includes multiple ancestries): 46.4% German, 15.8% Irish, 9.3% English, 7.7% Norwegian, 6.9% United States or American (2000).
Economy: Single-family building permits issued: 1 (2001) / 7 (2000); Multi-family building permits issued: 0 (2001) / 0 (2000); Employment by occupation: 8.2% management, 10.5% professional, 20.2% services, 24.2% sales, 0.7% farming, 11.2% construction, 24.9% production (2000).
Income: Per capita income: $15,636 (2000); Median household income: $30,163 (2000); Poverty rate: 9.9% (2000).
Taxes: Total city taxes per capita: $265 (1997); City property taxes per capita: $199 (1997).
Education: High school graduation rate: 80.8% (2000); College graduation rate: 13.2% (2000).
Housing: Homeownership rate: 61.9% (2000); Median home value: $55,600 (2000); Median rent: $287 per month (2000); Median age of housing: 60+ years (2000).
Newspapers: North Iowa Times (1 x week)
Transportation: Commute to work: 83.6% car, 0.0% public transportation, 9.8% walk, 4.5% work from home (2000); Travel time to work: 63.6% less than 15 minutes, 23.0% 15 to 30 minutes, 6.3% 30 to 45 minutes, 0.0% 45 to 60 minutes, 7.1% 60 minutes or more (2000)
Additional Information Contacts
Mc Gregor Chamber of Commerce 563-873-2186

MILLVILLE (city). Covers a land area of 0.067 square miles and a water area of 0 square miles. Located at 42.70° N. Lat.; 91.07° W. Long. Elevation is 639 feet.
History: Millville was originally chosen as a suitable site on the Turkey River for a sawmill and grist mill. The town was settled in 1833.
Population: 23 (2000); Race: 100.0% White, 0.0% Black, 0.0% Asian, 0.0% American Indian and Alaska Native, 0.0% Hispanic of any race, 0.0% two or more races (2000); Density: 342.6 persons per square mile (2000); Age: 28.1% under 18, 0.0% over 64 (2000); Marriage status: 8.0% never married, 76.0% now married, 0.0% widowed, 16.0% divorced (2000); Foreign born: 0.0% (2000); Ancestry (includes multiple ancestries): 65.6% German, 37.5% Irish, 21.9% English, 12.5% United States or American (2000).
Economy: Employment by occupation: 22.2% management, 16.7% professional, 16.7% services, 16.7% sales, 0.0% farming, 16.7% construction, 11.1% production (2000).
Income: Per capita income: $14,378 (2000); Median household income: $29,583 (2000); Poverty rate: 0.0% (2000).
Taxes: Total city taxes per capita: $65 (1997); City property taxes per capita: $32 (1997).
Education: High school graduation rate: 91.3% (2000); College graduation rate: 8.7% (2000).
Housing: Homeownership rate: 100.0% (2000); Median home value: $53,800 (2000); Median age of housing: 59 years (2000).
Transportation: Commute to work: 62.5% car, 0.0% public transportation, 0.0% walk, 37.5% work from home (2000); Travel time to work: 50.0% less than 15 minutes, 0.0% 15 to 30 minutes, 30.0% 30 to 45 minutes, 0.0% 45 to 60 minutes, 20.0% 60 minutes or more (2000)

MONONA (city). Covers a land area of 1.153 square miles and a water area of 0 square miles. Located at 43.05° N. Lat.; 91.39° W. Long.
History: Monona was named for an Indian girl who, believing her white lover had been slain by her people, jumped from a high rock into the Mississippi River. Although the group of men who named the town discovered the girl's name was Winona, the original name was not changed.
Population: 1,550 (2000); Race: 98.5% White, 0.0% Black, 0.2% Asian, 0.8% American Indian and Alaska Native, 0.1% Hispanic of any race, 0.4% two or more races (2000); Density: 1,344.6 persons per square mile (2000); Age: 23.3% under 18, 24.0% over 64 (2000); Marriage status: 21.0% never married, 59.0% now married, 10.3% widowed, 9.7% divorced (2000); Foreign born: 0.7% (2000); Ancestry (includes multiple ancestries): 57.0% German, 13.8% Norwegian, 10.2% Irish, 6.3% English, 3.1% Other groups (2000).
Economy: Single-family building permits issued: 0 (2001) / 1 (2000); Multi-family building permits issued: 0 (2001) / 4 (2000); Employment by occupation: 9.4% management, 15.0% professional, 15.0% services, 23.8% sales, 1.9% farming, 9.0% construction, 25.9% production (2000).

Income: Per capita income: $18,746 (2000); Median household income: $35,000 (2000); Poverty rate: 7.3% (2000).
Taxes: Total city taxes per capita: $209 (1997); City property taxes per capita: $158 (1997).
Education: High school graduation rate: 82.8% (2000); College graduation rate: 13.4% (2000).

School District(s)

Mfl Marmac Community School District (KG-12)
2000 Enrollment: 1,082 319-539-4795
Housing: Homeownership rate: 75.1% (2000); Median home value: $62,500 (2000); Median rent: $278 per month (2000); Median age of housing: 60 years (2000).
Transportation: Commute to work: 90.9% car, 0.0% public transportation, 5.3% walk, 3.8% work from home (2000); Travel time to work: 52.0% less than 15 minutes, 29.9% 15 to 30 minutes, 9.3% 30 to 45 minutes, 2.6% 45 to 60 minutes, 6.1% 60 minutes or more (2000)
Additional Information Contacts
Monona Chamber of Commerce 563-539-4455

NORTH BUENA VISTA (city). Covers a land area of 0.695 square miles and a water area of 0.041 square miles. Located at 42.67° N. Lat.; 90.95° W. Long. Elevation is 626 feet.
History: North Buena Vista was named such for its "beautiful view" and the northerly location on the Mississippi.
Population: 124 (2000); Race: 100.0% White, 0.0% Black, 0.0% Asian, 0.0% American Indian and Alaska Native, 0.0% Hispanic of any race, 0.0% two or more races (2000); Density: 178.4 persons per square mile (2000); Age: 17.9% under 18, 16.3% over 64 (2000); Marriage status: 35.2% never married, 52.4% now married, 7.6% widowed, 4.8% divorced (2000); Foreign born: 0.0% (2000); Ancestry (includes multiple ancestries): 68.3% German, 13.8% Irish, 7.3% Luxemburger, 5.7% United States or American, 4.9% French (except Basque) (2000).
Economy: Employment by occupation: 0.0% management, 1.6% professional, 21.9% services, 6.3% sales, 0.0% farming, 40.6% construction, 29.7% production (2000).
Income: Per capita income: $12,729 (2000); Median household income: $20,625 (2000); Poverty rate: 13.8% (2000).
Taxes: Total city taxes per capita: $83 (1997); City property taxes per capita: $38 (1997).
Education: High school graduation rate: 67.8% (2000); College graduation rate: 0.0% (2000).
Housing: Homeownership rate: 86.0% (2000); Median home value: $56,400 (2000); Median rent: $356 per month (2000); Median age of housing: 19 years (2000).
Transportation: Commute to work: 85.9% car, 0.0% public transportation, 14.1% walk, 0.0% work from home (2000); Travel time to work: 28.1% less than 15 minutes, 20.3% 15 to 30 minutes, 29.7% 30 to 45 minutes, 4.7% 45 to 60 minutes, 17.2% 60 minutes or more (2000)

OSTERDOCK (city). Covers a land area of 0.455 square miles and a water area of 0 square miles. Located at 42.73° N. Lat.; 91.16° W. Long.
History: Osterdock was located near two ice caves in the bluffs bordering the Turkey River.
Population: 50 (2000); Race: 100.0% White, 0.0% Black, 0.0% Asian, 0.0% American Indian and Alaska Native, 0.0% Hispanic of any race, 0.0% two or more races (2000); Density: 109.9 persons per square mile (2000); Age: 10.0% under 18, 22.0% over 64 (2000); Marriage status: 6.5% never married, 84.8% now married, 8.7% widowed, 0.0% divorced (2000); Foreign born: 0.0% (2000); Ancestry (includes multiple ancestries): 32.0% German, 10.0% Norwegian, 6.0% Scottish, 6.0% United States or American, 6.0% Swiss (2000).
Economy: Single-family building permits issued: 1 (2001) / 0 (2000); Multi-family building permits issued: 0 (2001) / 0 (2000); Employment by occupation: 14.3% management, 0.0% professional, 28.6% services, 38.1% sales, 0.0% farming, 0.0% construction, 19.0% production (2000).
Income: Per capita income: $18,566 (2000); Median household income: $31,250 (2000); Poverty rate: 26.0% (2000).
Taxes: Total city taxes per capita: $20 (1997); City property taxes per capita: $20 (1997).
Education: High school graduation rate: 76.7% (2000); College graduation rate: 0.0% (2000).
Housing: Homeownership rate: 100.0% (2000); Median home value: $55,000 (2000); Median age of housing: 60+ years (2000).
Transportation: Commute to work: 85.7% car, 0.0% public transportation, 9.5% walk, 4.8% work from home (2000); Travel time to work: 25.0% less than 15 minutes, 30.0% 15 to 30 minutes, 10.0% 30 to 45 minutes, 35.0% 45 to 60 minutes, 0.0% 60 minutes or more (2000)

SAINT OLAF (city). Covers a land area of 0.247 square miles and a water area of 0 square miles. Located at 42.92° N. Lat.; 91.38° W. Long. Elevation is 845 feet.
Population: 136 (2000); Race: 98.4% White, 0.0% Black, 1.6% Asian, 0.0% American Indian and Alaska Native, 0.0% Hispanic of any race, 0.0% two or more races (2000); Density: 550.8 persons per square mile (2000); Age: 32.3% under 18, 8.7% over 64 (2000); Marriage status: 15.1% never married, 69.9% now married, 6.5% widowed, 8.6% divorced (2000); Foreign born: 1.6% (2000); Ancestry (includes multiple ancestries): 43.3% German, 27.6% Norwegian, 4.7% Irish, 3.9% Swedish, 3.9% English (2000).
Economy: Single-family building permits issued: 0 (2001) / 0 (2000); Multi-family building permits issued: 0 (2001) / 0 (2000); Employment by occupation: 13.6% management, 16.7% professional, 6.1% services, 22.7% sales, 3.0% farming, 7.6% construction, 30.3% production (2000).
Income: Per capita income: $15,284 (2000); Median household income: $34,583 (2000); Poverty rate: 8.1% (2000).
Education: High school graduation rate: 90.5% (2000); College graduation rate: 8.1% (2000).
Housing: Homeownership rate: 83.7% (2000); Median home value: $42,500 (2000); Median rent: $325 per month (2000); Median age of housing: 60+ years (2000).
Transportation: Commute to work: 83.3% car, 0.0% public transportation, 10.6% walk, 6.1% work from home (2000); Travel time to work: 37.1% less than 15 minutes, 30.6% 15 to 30 minutes, 17.7% 30 to 45 minutes, 11.3% 45 to 60 minutes, 3.2% 60 minutes or more (2000)

STRAWBERRY POINT (city). Covers a land area of 2.045 square miles and a water area of 0 square miles. Located at 42.67° N. Lat.; 91.53° W. Long. Elevation is 1,200 feet.
History: Strawberry Point was so named because wild strawberries once grew in abundance.
Population: 1,386 (2000); Race: 98.5% White, 0.0% Black, 0.7% Asian, 0.2% American Indian and Alaska Native, 0.2% Hispanic of any race, 0.6% two or more races (2000); Density: 677.7 persons per square mile (2000); Age: 25.4% under 18, 23.0% over 64 (2000); Marriage status: 18.8% never married, 56.6% now married, 15.8% widowed, 8.8% divorced (2000); Foreign born: 0.9% (2000); Ancestry (includes multiple ancestries): 59.7% German, 17.4% Irish, 12.6% English, 5.5% Other groups, 4.4% Norwegian (2000).
Economy: Single-family building permits issued: 0 (2001) / 2 (2000); Multi-family building permits issued: 0 (2001) / 0 (2000); Employment by occupation: 8.1% management, 12.8% professional, 15.5% services, 18.5% sales, 2.3% farming, 12.2% construction, 30.7% production (2000).
Income: Per capita income: $18,400 (2000); Median household income: $34,766 (2000); Poverty rate: 5.9% (2000).
Taxes: Total city taxes per capita: $207 (1997); City property taxes per capita: $159 (1997).
Education: High school graduation rate: 88.0% (2000); College graduation rate: 15.4% (2000).
Housing: Homeownership rate: 79.3% (2000); Median home value: $63,500 (2000); Median rent: $238 per month (2000); Median age of housing: 55 years (2000).
Newspapers: Strawberry Point Press Journal (1 x week)
Transportation: Commute to work: 86.5% car, 0.3% public transportation, 7.4% walk, 5.1% work from home (2000); Travel time to work: 52.4% less than 15 minutes, 26.5% 15 to 30 minutes, 11.0% 30 to 45 minutes, 3.4% 45 to 60 minutes, 6.8% 60 minutes or more (2000)
Additional Information Contacts
Strawberry Pt Development Fund 563-933-4417

VOLGA (city). Aka Volga City. Covers a land area of 0.787 square miles and a water area of 0 square miles. Located at 42.80° N. Lat.; 91.54° W. Long. Elevation is 794 feet.
History: Volga was named for the Volga River in Russia.
Population: 247 (2000); Race: 100.0% White, 0.0% Black, 0.0% Asian, 0.0% American Indian and Alaska Native, 0.0% Hispanic of any race, 0.0% two or more races (2000); Density: 314.0 persons per square mile (2000); Age: 28.0% under 18, 17.3% over 64 (2000); Marriage status: 23.8% never married, 59.3% now married, 8.9% widowed, 7.9% divorced (2000); Foreign born: 0.0% (2000); Ancestry (includes multiple ancestries): 42.1% German, 19.9% Irish, 13.3% English, 10.7% Norwegian, 7.7% Scottish (2000).
Economy: Single-family building permits issued: 1 (2001) / 3 (2000); Multi-family building permits issued: 0 (2001) / 0 (2000); Employment by

occupation: 8.4% management, 9.2% professional, 10.7% services, 12.2% sales, 7.6% farming, 20.6% construction, 31.3% production (2000).
Income: Per capita income: $13,440 (2000); Median household income: $24,375 (2000); Poverty rate: 18.1% (2000).
Taxes: Total city taxes per capita: $146 (1997); City property taxes per capita: $95 (1997).
Education: High school graduation rate: 84.3% (2000); College graduation rate: 17.4% (2000).
Housing: Homeownership rate: 80.2% (2000); Median home value: $41,700 (2000); Median rent: $225 per month (2000); Median age of housing: 60+ years (2000).
Transportation: Commute to work: 93.7% car, 0.0% public transportation, 3.1% walk, 3.1% work from home (2000); Travel time to work: 33.3% less than 15 minutes, 20.3% 15 to 30 minutes, 25.2% 30 to 45 minutes, 6.5% 45 to 60 minutes, 14.6% 60 minutes or more (2000)

Clinton County

Located in eastern Iowa; bounded on the east by the Mississippi River and the Illinois border, and on the south and southwest by the Wapsipinicon River. Covers a land area of 695.00 square miles, a water area of 15.20 square miles, and is located in the Central Time Zone. The county government was organized in 1837. County seat is Clinton.

Weather Station: Clinton 1 — Elevation: 583 feet

	Jan	Feb	Mar	Apr	May	Jun	Jul	Aug	Sep	Oct	Nov	Dec
High	29	35	48	62	74	82	86	83	76	64	48	34
Low	12	18	28	40	51	60	64	62	54	42	30	19
Precip	1.5	1.4	2.5	3.3	4.1	4.5	3.5	4.5	3.3	2.7	2.4	2.0
Snow	9.8	6.0	3.5	1.2	tr	0.0	0.0	0.0	0.0	0.2	2.2	7.0

High and Low temperatures in degrees Fahrenheit; Precipitation and Snow in inches

Weather Station: Maquoketa 3 S — Elevation: 679 feet

	Jan	Feb	Mar	Apr	May	Jun	Jul	Aug	Sep	Oct	Nov	Dec
High	27	33	45	60	72	81	84	82	74	62	46	33
Low	9	15	26	37	48	58	62	59	51	39	28	16
Precip	1.2	1.3	2.3	3.2	4.1	4.3	3.5	4.6	3.8	2.5	2.5	1.7
Snow	8.8	5.3	3.6	1.8	tr	0.0	0.0	0.0	0.0	0.1	2.3	5.6

High and Low temperatures in degrees Fahrenheit; Precipitation and Snow in inches

Population: 50,149 (2000); Race: 96.6% White, 1.6% Black, 0.6% Asian, 0.3% American Indian and Alaska Native, 1.7% Hispanic of any race, 0.6% two or more races (2000); Density: 72.2 persons per square mile (2000); Age: 25.6% under 18, 15.8% over 64 (2000).
Religion: Five largest groups: 21.0% Catholic Church, 8.0% Evangelical Lutheran Church in America, 6.6% Lutheran Church—Missouri Synod, 5.1% The United Methodist Church, 3.4% United Church of Christ (2000).
Economy: Unemployment rate: 4.9% (11/2002); Total civilian labor force: 26,673 (11/2002); Leading industries: 25.6% manufacturing; 15.7% retail trade; 15.0% health care and social assistance (2000); Companies that employ more than 1,000 persons: 1 (2000); Companies that employ more than 100 persons: 40 (2000); Farms: 1,268 totaling 367,764 acres (1997); Minority business ownership rate: 0.0% (1997); Women business ownership rate: 26.9% (1997); Retail sales per capita: $8,350 (1997). Single-family building permits issued: 92 (2001) / 104 (2000); Multi-family building permits issued: 11 (2001) / 32 (2000).
Income: Per capita income: $17,724 (2000); Median household income: $37,423 (2000); Poverty rate: 10.2% (2000); Bankruptcy rate: 4.55% (2001).
Taxes: Total county taxes per capita: $198 (2000); County property taxes per capita: $163 (2000).
Education: High school graduation rate: 85.6% (2000); College graduation rate: 14.4% (2000).
Housing: Homeownership rate: 72.9% (2000); Median home value: $70,900 (2000); Median rent: $319 per month (2000); Median age of housing: 50 years (2000).
Health: Birth rate: 135.0 per 10,000 population (1998); Age adjusted death rate: 92.6 per 10,000 population (1999); Age adjusted cancer mortality rate: 204.7 deaths per 100,000 population (1999). Air Quality Index: 83% good, 17% moderate, 0% unhealthy (percent of days in 2000). Number of physicians: 12.4 per 10,000 population (1999); Number of hospital beds: 91.1 per 10,000 population (1999).
Elections: 2000 Presidential election results: 55.4% Gore, 41.6% Bush, 2.1% Nader, 0.5% Buchanan
National and State Parks: Barber Creek State Wildlife Management Area; Goose Lake State Wildlife Area; Syracuse State Wildlife Management Area
Additional Information Contacts

Clinton County Government Offices 563-244-0560
Clinton Board of Realtors. 563-242-2906
Clinton Chamber of Commerce 563-242-5702
De Witt Area Association of Realtors 563-659-3445
De Witt Chamber & Economic Development 563-659-8500
Dewitt Developement Co. 563-659-8508

Clinton County Communities

ANDOVER (city). Covers a land area of 0.198 square miles and a water area of 0 square miles. Located at 41.97° N. Lat.; 90.25° W. Long.
History: Andover was named after Andover, Vermont, by C. C. Wheeler of the Chicago & North Western Railroad.
Population: 87 (2000); Race: 100.0% White, 0.0% Black, 0.0% Asian, 0.0% American Indian and Alaska Native, 0.0% Hispanic of any race, 0.0% two or more races (2000); Density: 439.9 persons per square mile (2000); Age: 18.9% under 18, 28.9% over 64 (2000); Marriage status: 13.5% never married, 66.2% now married, 13.5% widowed, 6.8% divorced (2000); Foreign born: 0.0% (2000); Ancestry (includes multiple ancestries): 53.3% German, 8.9% Irish, 6.7% French (except Basque), 5.6% English, 5.6% Polish (2000).
Economy: Employment by occupation: 7.5% management, 15.0% professional, 10.0% services, 15.0% sales, 0.0% farming, 0.0% construction, 52.5% production (2000).
Income: Per capita income: $19,843 (2000); Median household income: $33,750 (2000); Poverty rate: 3.3% (2000).
Taxes: Total city taxes per capita: $69 (1997); City property taxes per capita: $69 (1997).
Education: High school graduation rate: 80.9% (2000); College graduation rate: 2.9% (2000).
Housing: Homeownership rate: 87.5% (2000); Median home value: $48,500 (2000); Median rent: $275 per month (2000); Median age of housing: 60+ years (2000).
Transportation: Commute to work: 90.0% car, 0.0% public transportation, 0.0% walk, 5.0% work from home (2000); Travel time to work: 15.8% less than 15 minutes, 52.6% 15 to 30 minutes, 18.4% 30 to 45 minutes, 13.2% 45 to 60 minutes, 0.0% 60 minutes or more (2000)

BRYANT (unincorporated postal area, zip code 52727). Covers a land area of 27.416 square miles and a water area of 0 square miles. Located at 41.96° N. Lat.; 90.33° W. Long.
History: Bryant was named for American poet and editor William Cullen Bryant. The name was selected by Isaac Howe, an employee of the Midland Railroad.
Population: 457 (2000); Race: 98.1% White, 1.5% Black, 0.0% Asian, 0.0% American Indian and Alaska Native, 0.0% Hispanic of any race, 0.4% two or more races (2000); Density: 16.7 persons per square mile (2000); Age: 34.2% under 18, 11.4% over 64 (2000); Marriage status: 19.2% never married, 68.3% now married, 3.8% widowed, 8.7% divorced (2000); Foreign born: 0.0% (2000); Ancestry (includes multiple ancestries): 51.6% German, 14.0% Irish, 8.7% English, 3.8% French (except Basque), 3.8% Danish (2000).
Economy: Employment by occupation: 18.3% management, 17.9% professional, 8.7% services, 11.5% sales, 2.4% farming, 8.3% construction, 32.9% production (2000).
Income: Per capita income: $16,885 (2000); Median household income: $46,771 (2000); Poverty rate: 12.1% (2000).
Education: High school graduation rate: 95.8% (2000); College graduation rate: 8.7% (2000).
Housing: Homeownership rate: 78.3% (2000); Median home value: $104,900 (2000); Median rent: $354 per month (2000); Median age of housing: 52 years (2000).
Transportation: Commute to work: 86.9% car, 1.6% public transportation, 1.6% walk, 9.9% work from home (2000); Travel time to work: 19.8% less than 15 minutes, 62.6% 15 to 30 minutes, 12.3% 30 to 45 minutes, 5.3% 45 to 60 minutes, 0.0% 60 minutes or more (2000)

CALAMUS (city). Covers a land area of 0.487 square miles and a water area of 0 square miles. Located at 41.82° N. Lat.; 90.76° W. Long.
History: Calamus received its name from a wild marsh plant that formerly grew in abundance around the town pump. The plant has a three-petaled flower resembling a miniature iris, and long thin blades of olive green.
Population: 394 (2000); Race: 98.1% White, 0.0% Black, 1.0% Asian, 0.0% American Indian and Alaska Native, 1.0% Hispanic of any race, 1.0% two or more races (2000); Density: 808.5 persons per square mile (2000); Age: 28.6% under 18, 16.5% over 64 (2000); Marriage status: 19.1% never

married, 63.4% now married, 8.9% widowed, 8.6% divorced (2000); Foreign born: 1.5% (2000); Ancestry (includes multiple ancestries): 55.3% German, 18.2% Irish, 8.3% Belgian, 7.5% Norwegian, 5.8% English (2000).
Economy: Single-family building permits issued: 2 (2001) / 1 (2000); Multi-family building permits issued: 0 (2001) / 0 (2000); Employment by occupation: 9.2% management, 6.7% professional, 11.3% services, 32.3% sales, 0.0% farming, 15.4% construction, 25.1% production (2000).
Income: Per capita income: $15,306 (2000); Median household income: $38,214 (2000); Poverty rate: 9.2% (2000).
Taxes: Total city taxes per capita: $216 (2000); City property taxes per capita: $140 (2000).
Education: High school graduation rate: 87.8% (2000); College graduation rate: 8.1% (2000).
Housing: Homeownership rate: 85.7% (2000); Median home value: $67,500 (2000); Median rent: $319 per month (2000); Median age of housing: 60+ years (2000).
Transportation: Commute to work: 88.2% car, 0.5% public transportation, 5.6% walk, 4.6% work from home (2000); Travel time to work: 28.0% less than 15 minutes, 29.0% 15 to 30 minutes, 20.4% 30 to 45 minutes, 16.7% 45 to 60 minutes, 5.9% 60 minutes or more (2000)

CAMANCHE (city). Covers a land area of 8.724 square miles and a water area of 0.708 square miles. Located at 41.78° N. Lat.; 90.26° W. Long. Elevation is 600 feet.
History: Camanche was designated the first seat of Clinton County. On Sunday, June 3, 1860, a cyclone almost destroyed the town, killing many people.
Population: 4,215 (2000); Race: 99.0% White, 0.0% Black, 0.4% Asian, 0.0% American Indian and Alaska Native, 0.2% Hispanic of any race, 0.6% two or more races (2000); Density: 483.1 persons per square mile (2000); Age: 22.8% under 18, 14.2% over 64 (2000); Marriage status: 22.7% never married, 61.9% now married, 6.4% widowed, 9.0% divorced (2000); Foreign born: 1.2% (2000); Ancestry (includes multiple ancestries): 41.4% German, 14.2% Irish, 9.5% United States or American, 7.1% English, 6.4% Other groups (2000).
Economy: Single-family building permits issued: 12 (2001) / 13 (2000); Multi-family building permits issued: 0 (2001) / 0 (2000); Employment by occupation: 6.9% management, 16.3% professional, 15.8% services, 22.9% sales, 0.0% farming, 11.0% construction, 27.0% production (2000).
Income: Per capita income: $19,456 (2000); Median household income: $42,078 (2000); Poverty rate: 5.2% (2000).
Taxes: Total city taxes per capita: $302 (1997); City property taxes per capita: $213 (1997).
Education: High school graduation rate: 86.3% (2000); College graduation rate: 10.6% (2000).

School District(s)
Camanche Community School District (PK-12)
2000 Enrollment: 981 319-259-3000

Housing: Homeownership rate: 78.7% (2000); Median home value: $80,600 (2000); Median rent: $355 per month (2000); Median age of housing: 32 years (2000).
Safety: Violent crime rate: 9.5 per 10,000 population; Property crime rate: 118.8 per 10,000 population (2001).
Transportation: Commute to work: 95.3% car, 0.0% public transportation, 2.3% walk, 2.2% work from home (2000); Travel time to work: 51.1% less than 15 minutes, 28.1% 15 to 30 minutes, 11.4% 30 to 45 minutes, 4.9% 45 to 60 minutes, 4.4% 60 minutes or more (2000)

CHARLOTTE (city). Covers a land area of 0.571 square miles and a water area of 0 square miles. Located at 41.96° N. Lat.; 90.47° W. Long. Elevation is 681 feet.
History: The post office at Charlotte was established in 1853. Charlotte Gilmore, for whom the town was named, was the wife of the first postmaster, Albert Gilmore.
Population: 421 (2000); Race: 100.0% White, 0.0% Black, 0.0% Asian, 0.0% American Indian and Alaska Native, 0.0% Hispanic of any race, 0.0% two or more races (2000); Density: 737.0 persons per square mile (2000); Age: 30.6% under 18, 15.0% over 64 (2000); Marriage status: 28.5% never married, 59.5% now married, 7.9% widowed, 4.1% divorced (2000); Foreign born: 0.0% (2000); Ancestry (includes multiple ancestries): 57.0% German, 14.3% Irish, 10.2% United States or American, 5.5% English, 2.9% Dutch (2000).
Economy: Single-family building permits issued: 0 (2001) / 3 (2000); Multi-family building permits issued: 0 (2001) / 0 (2000); Employment by occupation: 6.1% management, 13.0% professional, 21.6% services, 16.5% sales, 0.9% farming, 12.6% construction, 29.4% production (2000).
Income: Per capita income: $15,312 (2000); Median household income: $37,500 (2000); Poverty rate: 8.8% (2000).
Taxes: Total city taxes per capita: $160 (1997); City property taxes per capita: $80 (1997).
Education: High school graduation rate: 81.6% (2000); College graduation rate: 10.0% (2000).
Housing: Homeownership rate: 73.3% (2000); Median home value: $62,700 (2000); Median rent: $333 per month (2000); Median age of housing: 46 years (2000).
Transportation: Commute to work: 90.7% car, 0.9% public transportation, 4.4% walk, 3.1% work from home (2000); Travel time to work: 33.6% less than 15 minutes, 36.4% 15 to 30 minutes, 22.7% 30 to 45 minutes, 3.6% 45 to 60 minutes, 3.6% 60 minutes or more (2000)

CLINTON (city). Covers a land area of 35.565 square miles and a water area of 2.751 square miles. Located at 41.84° N. Lat.; 90.20° W. Long. Elevation is 5,489 feet.
History: Elijah Buell was the first settler to arrive in Clinton in 1835. He established a ferry across the Mississippi River to accommodate the many people on their way west. Joseph M. Bartlett laid out the town in 1838, naming it New York. It was later renamed for DeWitt Clinton, one-time Governor of the state of New York.
Population: 27,772 (2000); Race: 94.9% White, 2.8% Black, 0.8% Asian, 0.3% American Indian and Alaska Native, 2.6% Hispanic of any race, 0.7% two or more races (2000); Density: 780.9 persons per square mile (2000); Age: 24.7% under 18, 16.9% over 64 (2000); Marriage status: 23.9% never married, 54.6% now married, 9.2% widowed, 12.3% divorced (2000); Foreign born: 1.5% (2000); Ancestry (includes multiple ancestries): 36.7% German, 15.3% Irish, 9.3% Other groups, 8.5% English, 6.9% United States or American (2000).
Vital Statistics: Birth rate: 145.1 per 10,000 population (1998)
Economy: Unemployment rate: 5.9% (11/2002); Total civilian labor force: 14,932 (11/2002); Single-family building permits issued: 26 (2001) / 34 (2000); Multi-family building permits issued: 9 (2001) / 32 (2000); Employment by occupation: 7.8% management, 14.4% professional, 16.9% services, 25.0% sales, 0.2% farming, 8.9% construction, 26.9% production (2000).
Income: Per capita income: $17,320 (2000); Median household income: $34,159 (2000); Poverty rate: 12.5% (2000).
Taxes: Total city taxes per capita: $454 (2000); City property taxes per capita: $359 (2000).
Education: High school graduation rate: 84.2% (2000); College graduation rate: 14.9% (2000).

School District(s)
Clinton Community School District (PK-12)
2000 Enrollment: 4,574 319-243-9600

Four-year College(s)
Mount Saint Clare College (Private, Not-for-profit, Roman Catholic)
2001 Enrollment: 479 563-242-4023
2001 Tuition: In-state $13,800; Out-of-state $13,800

Housing: Homeownership rate: 69.3% (2000); Median home value: $61,300 (2000); Median rent: $311 per month (2000); Median age of housing: 54 years (2000).
Hospitals: Samaritan Health System (171 beds)
Newspapers: Clinton Herald (6 x week); River Cities News & Advertiser (1 x week)
Transportation: Commute to work: 93.0% car, 1.2% public transportation, 2.7% walk, 2.3% work from home (2000); Travel time to work: 60.5% less than 15 minutes, 26.6% 15 to 30 minutes, 5.6% 30 to 45 minutes, 3.1% 45 to 60 minutes, 4.2% 60 minutes or more (2000)
Airports: Clinton Municipal
Additional Information Contacts
Clinton Board of Realtors. 563-242-2906
Clinton Chamber of Commerce 563-242-5702

DE WITT (city). Covers a land area of 4.870 square miles and a water area of 0 square miles. Located at 41.82° N. Lat.; 90.54° W. Long. Elevation is 683 feet.
History: De Witt, originally called Vanderburg, was named for De Witt Clinton, Governor of New York (1817-1822). It was known as an excellent duck-hunting region.
Population: 5,049 (2000); Race: 99.5% White, 0.0% Black, 0.2% Asian, 0.0% American Indian and Alaska Native, 1.1% Hispanic of any race, 0.4% two or more races (2000); Density: 1,036.8 persons per square mile (2000); Age: 25.8% under 18, 16.6% over 64 (2000); Marriage status: 21.0% never married, 60.9% now married, 10.0% widowed, 8.2% divorced (2000);

Foreign born: 2.5% (2000); Ancestry (includes multiple ancestries): 46.4% German, 14.5% Irish, 8.1% English, 6.7% United States or American, 3.8% Norwegian (2000).
Economy: Single-family building permits issued: 17 (2001) / 14 (2000); Multi-family building permits issued: 2 (2001) / 0 (2000); Employment by occupation: 14.7% management, 15.4% professional, 13.7% services, 28.9% sales, 0.8% farming, 9.1% construction, 17.4% production (2000).
Income: Per capita income: $19,717 (2000); Median household income: $44,720 (2000); Poverty rate: 6.2% (2000).
Taxes: Total city taxes per capita: $466 (2000); City property taxes per capita: $376 (2000).
Education: High school graduation rate: 89.5% (2000); College graduation rate: 19.3% (2000).

School District(s)

Central Clinton Community School District (PK-12)
2000 Enrollment: 1,674 319-659-0700
Housing: Homeownership rate: 69.8% (2000); Median home value: $90,700 (2000); Median rent: $341 per month (2000); Median age of housing: 37 years (2000).
Hospitals: Dewitt Community Hospital (24 beds)
Newspapers: The Observer (2 x week)
Transportation: Commute to work: 90.8% car, 0.0% public transportation, 3.7% walk, 4.2% work from home (2000); Travel time to work: 45.5% less than 15 minutes, 22.1% 15 to 30 minutes, 27.5% 30 to 45 minutes, 2.6% 45 to 60 minutes, 2.3% 60 minutes or more (2000)

Additional Information Contacts

De Witt Area Asociation of Realtors 563-659-3445
De Witt Chamber & Economic Development 563-659-8500
Dewitt Developement Co 563-659-8508

DELMAR (city). Covers a land area of 0.765 square miles and a water area of 0 square miles. Located at 42.00° N. Lat.; 90.60° W. Long. Elevation is 807 feet.
History: When the Midland Railroad was extended from Clinton, Iowa, to Delmar, the first excursion train carried six women whose initials were used to form the name of the town. Fortunately, one of the names began with a D, for the Midland Railroad liked to name their stations alphabetically, and they already had an A, B, and C on this line.
Population: 514 (2000); Race: 98.5% White, 0.0% Black, 0.0% Asian, 0.4% American Indian and Alaska Native, 2.1% Hispanic of any race, 0.0% two or more races (2000); Density: 671.9 persons per square mile (2000); Age: 29.4% under 18, 18.3% over 64 (2000); Marriage status: 18.9% never married, 65.0% now married, 10.9% widowed, 5.2% divorced (2000); Foreign born: 0.0% (2000); Ancestry (includes multiple ancestries): 50.2% German, 26.7% Irish, 8.2% English, 5.9% Other groups, 5.7% Dutch (2000).
Economy: Single-family building permits issued: 2 (2001) / 2 (2000); Multi-family building permits issued: 0 (2001) / 0 (2000); Employment by occupation: 4.9% management, 10.2% professional, 14.6% services, 27.9% sales, 2.2% farming, 12.4% construction, 27.9% production (2000).
Income: Per capita income: $14,469 (2000); Median household income: $29,375 (2000); Poverty rate: 6.7% (2000).
Taxes: Total city taxes per capita: $174 (1997); City property taxes per capita: $73 (1997).
Education: High school graduation rate: 76.8% (2000); College graduation rate: 6.0% (2000).

School District(s)

Delwood Community School District (KG-12)
2000 Enrollment: 148 319-674-4164
Housing: Homeownership rate: 91.8% (2000); Median home value: $58,900 (2000); Median rent: $313 per month (2000); Median age of housing: 60+ years (2000).
Transportation: Commute to work: 92.0% car, 0.0% public transportation, 2.2% walk, 4.5% work from home (2000); Travel time to work: 28.5% less than 15 minutes, 39.3% 15 to 30 minutes, 10.3% 30 to 45 minutes, 17.3% 45 to 60 minutes, 4.7% 60 minutes or more (2000)

ELWOOD (unincorporated postal area, zip code 52226). Covers a land area of 0.543 square miles and a water area of 0 square miles. Located at 41.99° N. Lat.; 90.73° W. Long.
History: Elwood takes its name from settler Kinsey Elwood, on whose land the town was located.
Population: 92 (2000); Race: 95.7% White, 0.0% Black, 0.0% Asian, 0.0% American Indian and Alaska Native, 0.0% Hispanic of any race, 4.3% two or more races (2000); Density: 169.5 persons per square mile (2000); Age: 33.6% under 18, 6.9% over 64 (2000); Marriage status: 18.3% never married, 64.6% now married, 2.4% widowed, 14.6% divorced (2000); Foreign born: 0.0% (2000); Ancestry (includes multiple ancestries): 52.6% German, 25.9% Irish, 8.6% United States or American, 8.6% Austrian, 6.0% Dutch (2000).
Economy: Employment by occupation: 13.5% management, 13.5% professional, 17.3% services, 13.5% sales, 0.0% farming, 23.1% construction, 19.2% production (2000).
Income: Per capita income: $15,403 (2000); Median household income: $36,250 (2000); Poverty rate: 5.4% (2000).
Education: High school graduation rate: 85.7% (2000); College graduation rate: 15.7% (2000).
Housing: Homeownership rate: 75.0% (2000); Median home value: $52,500 (2000); Median rent: $331 per month (2000); Median age of housing: 50 years (2000).
Transportation: Commute to work: 94.2% car, 0.0% public transportation, 0.0% walk, 5.8% work from home (2000); Travel time to work: 14.3% less than 15 minutes, 53.1% 15 to 30 minutes, 6.1% 30 to 45 minutes, 22.4% 45 to 60 minutes, 4.1% 60 minutes or more (2000)

GOOSE LAKE (city). Covers a land area of 0.326 square miles and a water area of 0 square miles. Located at 41.96° N. Lat.; 90.38° W. Long.
History: The name of Goose Lake is descriptive of the location, with a lake nearby where wild geese were plentiful. This name was chosen in 1876, replacing an earlier name of O'Brien.
Population: 232 (2000); Race: 100.0% White, 0.0% Black, 0.0% Asian, 0.0% American Indian and Alaska Native, 0.0% Hispanic of any race, 0.0% two or more races (2000); Density: 710.9 persons per square mile (2000); Age: 32.6% under 18, 9.3% over 64 (2000); Marriage status: 24.1% never married, 57.5% now married, 6.9% widowed, 11.5% divorced (2000); Foreign born: 0.0% (2000); Ancestry (includes multiple ancestries): 50.8% German, 15.3% Irish, 5.1% English, 4.7% Norwegian, 4.2% United States or American (2000).
Economy: Single-family building permits issued: 3 (2001) / 0 (2000); Multi-family building permits issued: 0 (2001) / 0 (2000); Employment by occupation: 1.6% management, 27.8% professional, 25.4% services, 19.0% sales, 0.0% farming, 10.3% construction, 15.9% production (2000).
Income: Per capita income: $15,453 (2000); Median household income: $43,125 (2000); Poverty rate: 2.6% (2000).
Taxes: Total city taxes per capita: $175 (1997); City property taxes per capita: $97 (1997).
Education: High school graduation rate: 92.3% (2000); College graduation rate: 17.6% (2000).

School District(s)

Northeast Community School District (PK-12)
2000 Enrollment: 715 319-577-2249
Housing: Homeownership rate: 93.0% (2000); Median home value: $67,800 (2000); Median rent: $317 per month (2000); Median age of housing: 41 years (2000).
Transportation: Commute to work: 92.1% car, 0.0% public transportation, 6.3% walk, 1.6% work from home (2000); Travel time to work: 36.3% less than 15 minutes, 38.7% 15 to 30 minutes, 14.5% 30 to 45 minutes, 8.9% 45 to 60 minutes, 1.6% 60 minutes or more (2000)

GRAND MOUND (city). Covers a land area of 1.837 square miles and a water area of 0 square miles. Located at 41.82° N. Lat.; 90.64° W. Long.
History: Grand Mound was so named because of a nearby glacial terminal moraine known as Sand Mound.
Population: 676 (2000); Race: 96.9% White, 0.0% Black, 0.0% Asian, 0.0% American Indian and Alaska Native, 1.0% Hispanic of any race, 2.1% two or more races (2000); Density: 367.9 persons per square mile (2000); Age: 30.2% under 18, 11.6% over 64 (2000); Marriage status: 16.2% never married, 70.1% now married, 6.6% widowed, 7.2% divorced (2000); Foreign born: 1.0% (2000); Ancestry (includes multiple ancestries): 44.6% German, 15.4% Irish, 10.0% English, 8.9% Other groups, 7.0% United States or American (2000).
Economy: Single-family building permits issued: 2 (2001) / 3 (2000); Multi-family building permits issued: 0 (2001) / 0 (2000); Employment by occupation: 12.4% management, 9.2% professional, 17.7% services, 24.8% sales, 0.0% farming, 13.2% construction, 22.7% production (2000).
Income: Per capita income: $17,228 (2000); Median household income: $42,411 (2000); Poverty rate: 7.1% (2000).
Taxes: Total city taxes per capita: $222 (1997); City property taxes per capita: $143 (1997).
Education: High school graduation rate: 90.2% (2000); College graduation rate: 15.6% (2000).
Housing: Homeownership rate: 84.2% (2000); Median home value: $72,000 (2000); Median rent: $308 per month (2000); Median age of housing: 60+ years (2000).

Transportation: Commute to work: 88.1% car, 0.3% public transportation, 2.4% walk, 8.4% work from home (2000); Travel time to work: 31.1% less than 15 minutes, 26.5% 15 to 30 minutes, 31.1% 30 to 45 minutes, 9.2% 45 to 60 minutes, 2.0% 60 minutes or more (2000)

LOST NATION (city). Covers a land area of 0.642 square miles and a water area of 0 square miles. Located at 41.96° N. Lat.; 90.81° W. Long. Elevation is 744 feet.
History: The origins of the name Lost Nation are not clear. It may have been named for its wild and inaccessible location.
Population: 497 (2000); Race: 97.8% White, 0.0% Black, 0.0% Asian, 0.0% American Indian and Alaska Native, 0.0% Hispanic of any race, 2.2% two or more races (2000); Density: 773.7 persons per square mile (2000); Age: 25.2% under 18, 17.8% over 64 (2000); Marriage status: 19.9% never married, 58.9% now married, 13.5% widowed, 7.7% divorced (2000); Foreign born: 0.8% (2000); Ancestry (includes multiple ancestries): 44.8% German, 19.4% Irish, 10.2% United States or American, 5.4% English, 4.8% Other groups (2000).
Economy: Single-family building permits issued: 0 (2001) / 0 (2000); Multi-family building permits issued: 0 (2001) / 0 (2000); Employment by occupation: 10.2% management, 15.8% professional, 14.0% services, 20.0% sales, 0.0% farming, 14.4% construction, 25.6% production (2000).
Income: Per capita income: $13,933 (2000); Median household income: $31,354 (2000); Poverty rate: 15.3% (2000).
Taxes: Total city taxes per capita: $191 (1997); City property taxes per capita: $108 (1997).
Education: High school graduation rate: 85.3% (2000); College graduation rate: 8.8% (2000).
Housing: Homeownership rate: 75.8% (2000); Median home value: $50,000 (2000); Median rent: $280 per month (2000); Median age of housing: 60+ years (2000).
Transportation: Commute to work: 82.8% car, 0.0% public transportation, 13.5% walk, 3.7% work from home (2000); Travel time to work: 33.3% less than 15 minutes, 34.8% 15 to 30 minutes, 13.0% 30 to 45 minutes, 12.6% 45 to 60 minutes, 6.3% 60 minutes or more (2000)

LOW MOOR (city). Covers a land area of 0.466 square miles and a water area of 0 square miles. Located at 41.80° N. Lat.; 90.35° W. Long.
History: The trade name "Low Moor" stamped on rails imported from England for use in railroad construction provided inspiration for the town's name. The town was an Underground Railroad station established to aid slaves on their way north.
Population: 240 (2000); Race: 100.0% White, 0.0% Black, 0.0% Asian, 0.0% American Indian and Alaska Native, 0.0% Hispanic of any race, 0.0% two or more races (2000); Density: 514.6 persons per square mile (2000); Age: 20.0% under 18, 17.0% over 64 (2000); Marriage status: 21.9% never married, 68.8% now married, 4.2% widowed, 5.2% divorced (2000); Foreign born: 0.0% (2000); Ancestry (includes multiple ancestries): 38.7% German, 17.4% English, 7.7% Irish, 4.7% European, 4.7% Other groups (2000).
Economy: Single-family building permits issued: 0 (2001) / 0 (2000); Multi-family building permits issued: 0 (2001) / 0 (2000); Employment by occupation: 2.5% management, 15.0% professional, 13.3% services, 15.0% sales, 0.0% farming, 5.0% construction, 49.2% production (2000).
Income: Per capita income: $18,585 (2000); Median household income: $40,417 (2000); Poverty rate: 5.5% (2000).
Taxes: Total city taxes per capita: $176 (1997); City property taxes per capita: $99 (1997).
Education: High school graduation rate: 89.0% (2000); College graduation rate: 7.6% (2000).
Housing: Homeownership rate: 79.3% (2000); Median home value: $69,500 (2000); Median rent: $295 per month (2000); Median age of housing: 60 years (2000).
Transportation: Commute to work: 95.8% car, 0.0% public transportation, 2.5% walk, 1.7% work from home (2000); Travel time to work: 37.1% less than 15 minutes, 44.0% 15 to 30 minutes, 12.1% 30 to 45 minutes, 0.0% 45 to 60 minutes, 6.9% 60 minutes or more (2000)

TORONTO (city). Covers a land area of 0.184 square miles and a water area of 0 square miles. Located at 41.90° N. Lat.; 90.86° W. Long. Elevation is 720 feet.
History: Toronto was named after Toronto, Canada.
Population: 134 (2000); Race: 97.6% White, 0.0% Black, 0.0% Asian, 0.0% American Indian and Alaska Native, 1.6% Hispanic of any race, 2.4% two or more races (2000); Density: 728.6 persons per square mile (2000); Age: 20.5% under 18, 21.3% over 64 (2000); Marriage status: 17.1% never married, 75.2% now married, 4.8% widowed, 2.9% divorced (2000); Foreign born: 0.0% (2000); Ancestry (includes multiple ancestries): 40.9% German, 18.1% Irish, 15.7% Other groups, 7.1% United States or American, 3.1% English (2000).
Economy: Employment by occupation: 0.0% management, 0.0% professional, 29.7% services, 39.1% sales, 0.0% farming, 15.6% construction, 15.6% production (2000).
Income: Per capita income: $13,702 (2000); Median household income: $27,500 (2000); Poverty rate: 6.3% (2000).
Taxes: Total city taxes per capita: $126 (1997); City property taxes per capita: $52 (1997).
Education: High school graduation rate: 80.7% (2000); College graduation rate: 1.1% (2000).
Housing: Homeownership rate: 92.3% (2000); Median home value: $33,100 (2000); Median rent: $250 per month (2000); Median age of housing: 60+ years (2000).
Transportation: Commute to work: 90.6% car, 0.0% public transportation, 1.6% walk, 7.8% work from home (2000); Travel time to work: 18.6% less than 15 minutes, 16.9% 15 to 30 minutes, 27.1% 30 to 45 minutes, 25.4% 45 to 60 minutes, 11.9% 60 minutes or more (2000)

WELTON (city). Covers a land area of 0.114 square miles and a water area of 0 square miles. Located at 41.91° N. Lat.; 90.60° W. Long. Elevation is 701 feet.
History: Welton, dating back to 1850, was so named because of a fancied resemblance in the surroundings to Welton Dale in Hull, England.
Population: 159 (2000); Race: 100.0% White, 0.0% Black, 0.0% Asian, 0.0% American Indian and Alaska Native, 0.0% Hispanic of any race, 0.0% two or more races (2000); Density: 1,388.9 persons per square mile (2000); Age: 29.8% under 18, 4.3% over 64 (2000); Marriage status: 27.8% never married, 56.4% now married, 3.0% widowed, 12.8% divorced (2000); Foreign born: 0.0% (2000); Ancestry (includes multiple ancestries): 47.2% German, 18.0% Irish, 6.2% Other groups, 6.2% Danish, 5.6% United States or American (2000).
Economy: Single-family building permits issued: 1 (2001) / 1 (2000); Multi-family building permits issued: 0 (2001) / 0 (2000); Employment by occupation: 3.9% management, 2.9% professional, 23.3% services, 24.3% sales, 0.0% farming, 6.8% construction, 38.8% production (2000).
Income: Per capita income: $17,680 (2000); Median household income: $48,750 (2000); Poverty rate: 0.0% (2000).
Taxes: Total city taxes per capita: $123 (1997); City property taxes per capita: $80 (1997).
Education: High school graduation rate: 95.7% (2000); College graduation rate: 10.6% (2000).
Housing: Homeownership rate: 83.1% (2000); Median home value: $61,900 (2000); Median rent: $325 per month (2000); Median age of housing: 60+ years (2000).
Transportation: Commute to work: 89.3% car, 0.0% public transportation, 8.7% walk, 1.9% work from home (2000); Travel time to work: 29.7% less than 15 minutes, 41.6% 15 to 30 minutes, 12.9% 30 to 45 minutes, 4.0% 45 to 60 minutes, 11.9% 60 minutes or more (2000)

WHEATLAND (city). Covers a land area of 0.555 square miles and a water area of 0 square miles. Located at 41.83° N. Lat.; 90.83° W. Long. Elevation is 671 feet.
History: Wheatland was named by John L. Bennett, who platted the town in 1858, for the home of President James Buchanan near Lancaster, Pennsylvania.
Population: 772 (2000); Race: 98.7% White, 0.1% Black, 0.4% Asian, 0.0% American Indian and Alaska Native, 0.8% Hispanic of any race, 0.8% two or more races (2000); Density: 1,389.8 persons per square mile (2000); Age: 32.0% under 18, 22.3% over 64 (2000); Marriage status: 17.0% never married, 64.0% now married, 9.0% widowed, 9.9% divorced (2000); Foreign born: 0.6% (2000); Ancestry (includes multiple ancestries): 46.7% German, 10.3% Irish, 7.9% United States or American, 4.5% English, 4.1% Norwegian (2000).
Economy: Employment by occupation: 9.0% management, 13.2% professional, 16.1% services, 26.1% sales, 0.3% farming, 10.3% construction, 24.8% production (2000).
Income: Per capita income: $13,824 (2000); Median household income: $30,875 (2000); Poverty rate: 13.8% (2000).
Taxes: Total city taxes per capita: $136 (1997); City property taxes per capita: $133 (1997).
Education: High school graduation rate: 82.5% (2000); College graduation rate: 10.0% (2000).

School District(s)

Calamus-Wheatland Community School District (PK-12)
2000 Enrollment: 564 319-374-1292

Housing: Homeownership rate: 77.1% (2000); Median home value: $67,800 (2000); Median rent: $328 per month (2000); Median age of housing: 54 years (2000).

Transportation: Commute to work: 83.3% car, 0.0% public transportation, 8.2% walk, 5.2% work from home (2000); Travel time to work: 27.2% less than 15 minutes, 29.7% 15 to 30 minutes, 26.9% 30 to 45 minutes, 12.1% 45 to 60 minutes, 4.1% 60 minutes or more (2000)

Crawford County

Located in western Iowa; drained by the Boyer River. Covers a land area of 714.40 square miles, a water area of 0.60 square miles, and is located in the Central Time Zone. The county government was organized in 1851. County seat is Denison.

Weather Station: Denison Elevation: 1,400 feet

	Jan	Feb	Mar	Apr	May	Jun	Jul	Aug	Sep	Oct	Nov	Dec
High	27	34	46	60	71	81	84	82	75	62	45	32
Low	9	16	26	38	50	60	64	62	53	41	27	15
Precip	0.8	0.7	2.2	3.1	4.2	4.2	3.8	3.3	3.4	2.3	1.6	1.0
Snow	8.1	6.5	6.8	2.3	tr	0.0	0.0	0.0	tr	0.8	4.0	7.6

High and Low temperatures in degrees Fahrenheit; Precipitation and Snow in inches

Population: 16,942 (2000); Race: 92.4% White, 0.8% Black, 0.1% Asian, 1.4% American Indian and Alaska Native, 9.0% Hispanic of any race, 0.7% two or more races (2000); Density: 23.7 persons per square mile (2000); Age: 26.6% under 18, 17.3% over 64 (2000).

Religion: Five largest groups: 34.1% Lutheran Church—Missouri Synod, 17.8% Catholic Church, 6.1% The United Methodist Church, 4.6% Presbyterian Church (U.S.A.), 3.3% United Church of Christ (2000).

Economy: Unemployment rate: 3.0% (11/2002); Total civilian labor force: 8,983 (11/2002); Leading industries: 34.1% manufacturing; 16.7% retail trade; 14.2% health care and social assistance (2000); Companies that employ more than 1,000 persons: 1 (2000); Companies that employ more than 100 persons: 8 (2000); Farms: 1,107 totaling 431,726 acres (1997); Minority business ownership rate: 0.0% (1997); Women business ownership rate: 30.6% (1997); Retail sales per capita: $6,785 (1997). Single-family building permits issued: 30 (2001) / 25 (2000); Multi-family building permits issued: 4 (2001) / 10 (2000).

Income: Per capita income: $15,851 (2000); Median household income: $33,922 (2000); Poverty rate: 11.1% (2000); Bankruptcy rate: 1.51% (2001).

Taxes: Total county taxes per capita: $269 (2000); County property taxes per capita: $264 (2000).

Education: High school graduation rate: 78.5% (2000); College graduation rate: 12.4% (2000).

Housing: Homeownership rate: 73.1% (2000); Median home value: $58,200 (2000); Median rent: $281 per month (2000); Median age of housing: 49 years (2000).

Health: Birth rate: 112.2 per 10,000 population (1998); Age adjusted death rate: 80.4 per 10,000 population (1999); Age adjusted cancer mortality rate: 195.9 deaths per 100,000 population (1999). Number of physicians: 4.7 per 10,000 population (1999); Number of hospital beds: 16.5 per 10,000 population (1999).

Elections: 2000 Presidential election results: 43.3% Gore, 53.1% Bush, 2.2% Nader, 0.8% Buchanan

Additional Information Contacts

Crawford County Government Offices 712-263-3045
Denison Chamber of Commerce 712-263-5621

Crawford County Communities

ARION (city). Covers a land area of 0.475 square miles and a water area of 0 square miles. Located at 41.94° N. Lat.; 95.46° W. Long. Elevation is 1,140 feet.

History: Arion was named by N. Richards, a hotel proprietor. The business section was destroyed by fire in 1909.

Population: 136 (2000); Race: 98.1% White, 0.0% Black, 0.0% Asian, 0.0% American Indian and Alaska Native, 1.9% Hispanic of any race, 1.9% two or more races (2000); Density: 286.4 persons per square mile (2000); Age: 28.4% under 18, 9.0% over 64 (2000); Marriage status: 23.9% never married, 51.3% now married, 6.0% widowed, 18.8% divorced (2000); Foreign born: 0.0% (2000); Ancestry (includes multiple ancestries): 59.4% German, 23.9% Irish, 11.0% English, 7.1% Norwegian, 7.1% Dutch (2000).

Economy: Employment by occupation: 4.2% management, 2.8% professional, 21.1% services, 8.5% sales, 2.8% farming, 4.2% construction, 56.3% production (2000).

Income: Per capita income: $12,654 (2000); Median household income: $33,750 (2000); Poverty rate: 27.7% (2000).

Taxes: Total city taxes per capita: $33 (1997); City property taxes per capita: $33 (1997).

Education: High school graduation rate: 72.0% (2000); College graduation rate: 0.0% (2000).

Housing: Homeownership rate: 85.7% (2000); Median home value: $23,100 (2000); Median rent: $125 per month (2000); Median age of housing: 46 years (2000).

Transportation: Commute to work: 100.0% car, 0.0% public transportation, 0.0% walk, 0.0% work from home (2000); Travel time to work: 62.0% less than 15 minutes, 35.2% 15 to 30 minutes, 0.0% 30 to 45 minutes, 0.0% 45 to 60 minutes, 2.8% 60 minutes or more (2000)

ASPINWALL (city). Covers a land area of 0.099 square miles and a water area of 0 square miles. Located at 41.91° N. Lat.; 95.13° W. Long. Elevation is 1,381 feet.

History: Aspinwall was platted in 1882 by the Milwaukee Land Company.

Population: 58 (2000); Race: 100.0% White, 0.0% Black, 0.0% Asian, 0.0% American Indian and Alaska Native, 0.0% Hispanic of any race, 0.0% two or more races (2000); Density: 584.9 persons per square mile (2000); Age: 1.6% under 18, 30.2% over 64 (2000); Marriage status: 40.3% never married, 51.6% now married, 8.1% widowed, 0.0% divorced (2000); Foreign born: 0.0% (2000); Ancestry (includes multiple ancestries): 47.6% German, 28.6% United States or American, 17.5% Other groups, 7.9% English, 6.3% Danish (2000).

Economy: Employment by occupation: 2.6% management, 15.4% professional, 23.1% services, 20.5% sales, 0.0% farming, 25.6% construction, 12.8% production (2000).

Income: Per capita income: $19,835 (2000); Median household income: $26,786 (2000); Poverty rate: 0.0% (2000).

Taxes: Total city taxes per capita: $200 (1997); City property taxes per capita: $200 (1997).

Education: High school graduation rate: 71.2% (2000); College graduation rate: 7.7% (2000).

Housing: Homeownership rate: 88.5% (2000); Median home value: $38,800 (2000); Median age of housing: 60+ years (2000).

Transportation: Commute to work: 82.1% car, 0.0% public transportation, 0.0% walk, 17.9% work from home (2000); Travel time to work: 15.6% less than 15 minutes, 53.1% 15 to 30 minutes, 31.3% 30 to 45 minutes, 0.0% 45 to 60 minutes, 0.0% 60 minutes or more (2000)

BUCK GROVE (city). Covers a land area of 0.367 square miles and a water area of 0 square miles. Located at 41.91° N. Lat.; 95.39° W. Long. Elevation is 1,302 feet.

History: Buck Grove's name is descriptive of the area where the first settlers located, a wooded area (grove) with many deer.

Population: 49 (2000); Race: 100.0% White, 0.0% Black, 0.0% Asian, 0.0% American Indian and Alaska Native, 0.0% Hispanic of any race, 0.0% two or more races (2000); Density: 133.6 persons per square mile (2000); Age: 12.0% under 18, 20.0% over 64 (2000); Marriage status: 32.7% never married, 57.1% now married, 6.1% widowed, 4.1% divorced (2000); Foreign born: 0.0% (2000); Ancestry (includes multiple ancestries): 72.0% German, 6.0% English, 6.0% French (except Basque), 4.0% Czech, 4.0% Dutch (2000).

Economy: Employment by occupation: 9.7% management, 6.5% professional, 48.4% services, 6.5% sales, 0.0% farming, 12.9% construction, 16.1% production (2000).

Income: Per capita income: $14,492 (2000); Median household income: $25,417 (2000); Poverty rate: 10.0% (2000).

Taxes: Total city taxes per capita: $36 (1997); City property taxes per capita: $36 (1997).

Education: High school graduation rate: 74.3% (2000); College graduation rate: 0.0% (2000).

Housing: Homeownership rate: 77.3% (2000); Median home value: $36,300 (2000); Median rent: $125 per month (2000); Median age of housing: 60 years (2000).

Transportation: Commute to work: 74.2% car, 9.7% public transportation, 16.1% walk, 0.0% work from home (2000); Travel time to work: 58.1% less than 15 minutes, 22.6% 15 to 30 minutes, 0.0% 30 to 45 minutes, 0.0% 45 to 60 minutes, 19.4% 60 minutes or more (2000)

CHARTER OAK (city). Covers a land area of 0.489 square miles and a water area of 0 square miles. Located at 42.06° N. Lat.; 95.58° W. Long. Elevation is 1,232 feet.
History: Charter Oak was named for the Charter Oak of Connecticut.
Population: 530 (2000); Race: 99.6% White, 0.0% Black, 0.0% Asian, 0.0% American Indian and Alaska Native, 1.6% Hispanic of any race, 0.0% two or more races (2000); Density: 1,084.4 persons per square mile (2000); Age: 23.6% under 18, 22.9% over 64 (2000); Marriage status: 16.5% never married, 68.2% now married, 9.8% widowed, 5.5% divorced (2000); Foreign born: 0.0% (2000); Ancestry (includes multiple ancestries): 63.7% German, 8.1% Irish, 5.3% United States or American, 3.8% Norwegian, 3.5% English (2000).
Economy: Single-family building permits issued: 0 (2001) / 0 (2000); Multi-family building permits issued: 0 (2001) / 0 (2000); Employment by occupation: 4.3% management, 17.7% professional, 16.9% services, 21.7% sales, 3.5% farming, 11.8% construction, 24.0% production (2000).
Income: Per capita income: $16,583 (2000); Median household income: $33,482 (2000); Poverty rate: 5.5% (2000).
Taxes: Total city taxes per capita: $243 (1997); City property taxes per capita: $238 (1997).
Education: High school graduation rate: 79.2% (2000); College graduation rate: 14.6% (2000).

School District(s)

Charter Oak-Ute Community School District (KG-12)
2000 Enrollment: 319 712-678-3325

Housing: Homeownership rate: 81.4% (2000); Median home value: $36,100 (2000); Median rent: $233 per month (2000); Median age of housing: 60+ years (2000).
Newspapers: Charter Oak-Ute Newspaper (1 x week)
Transportation: Commute to work: 95.6% car, 0.0% public transportation, 4.0% walk, 0.4% work from home (2000); Travel time to work: 32.7% less than 15 minutes, 51.0% 15 to 30 minutes, 8.8% 30 to 45 minutes, 4.0% 45 to 60 minutes, 3.6% 60 minutes or more (2000)

DELOIT (city). Covers a land area of 0.421 square miles and a water area of 0 square miles. Located at 42.09° N. Lat.; 95.31° W. Long. Elevation is 1,202 feet.
History: Deloit has had two locations and at least five names since the first settlement here in 1857. The first name of Mason's Grove was changed to Bayers Valley, then Bloomington, then Beloit, which became Deloit to distinguish it from another place with the same name. About 1900 the main part of the town was moved to accommodate the railroad depot.
Population: 288 (2000); Race: 89.7% White, 0.0% Black, 3.3% Asian, 0.7% American Indian and Alaska Native, 6.0% Hispanic of any race, 3.3% two or more races (2000); Density: 684.4 persons per square mile (2000); Age: 26.7% under 18, 11.7% over 64 (2000); Marriage status: 18.0% never married, 64.9% now married, 6.6% widowed, 10.5% divorced (2000); Foreign born: 2.3% (2000); Ancestry (includes multiple ancestries): 50.0% German, 11.0% Irish, 9.7% United States or American, 9.0% Other groups, 5.3% English (2000).
Economy: Single-family building permits issued: 2 (2001) / 0 (2000); Multi-family building permits issued: 0 (2001) / 0 (2000); Employment by occupation: 2.4% management, 9.5% professional, 33.7% services, 15.4% sales, 1.8% farming, 5.9% construction, 31.4% production (2000).
Income: Per capita income: $14,446 (2000); Median household income: $36,250 (2000); Poverty rate: 6.0% (2000).
Taxes: Total city taxes per capita: $46 (1997); City property taxes per capita: $46 (1997).
Education: High school graduation rate: 74.5% (2000); College graduation rate: 6.1% (2000).
Housing: Homeownership rate: 75.0% (2000); Median home value: $36,000 (2000); Median rent: $295 per month (2000); Median age of housing: 45 years (2000).
Transportation: Commute to work: 92.9% car, 1.8% public transportation, 5.4% walk, 0.0% work from home (2000); Travel time to work: 55.4% less than 15 minutes, 38.1% 15 to 30 minutes, 3.0% 30 to 45 minutes, 1.8% 45 to 60 minutes, 1.8% 60 minutes or more (2000)

DENISON (city). Covers a land area of 6.191 square miles and a water area of 0.033 square miles. Located at 42.01° N. Lat.; 95.35° W. Long. Elevation is 1,176 feet.
History: Denison was named for its founder, J. W. Denison, a Baptist minister who came here in 1855 as an agent of the Providence Western Land Company.
Population: 7,339 (2000); Race: 85.4% White, 1.5% Black, 0.0% Asian, 3.0% American Indian and Alaska Native, 18.6% Hispanic of any race, 1.0% two or more races (2000); Density: 1,185.5 persons per square mile (2000); Age: 26.3% under 18, 17.5% over 64 (2000); Marriage status: 26.1% never married, 55.1% now married, 10.6% widowed, 8.2% divorced (2000); Foreign born: 12.6% (2000); Ancestry (includes multiple ancestries): 41.0% German, 18.9% Other groups, 10.9% Irish, 8.8% United States or American, 5.6% Danish (2000).
Economy: Single-family building permits issued: 10 (2001) / 17 (2000); Multi-family building permits issued: 4 (2001) / 10 (2000); Employment by occupation: 7.5% management, 12.1% professional, 15.8% services, 20.5% sales, 0.7% farming, 7.8% construction, 35.6% production (2000).
Income: Per capita income: $15,391 (2000); Median household income: $33,187 (2000); Poverty rate: 12.1% (2000).
Taxes: Total city taxes per capita: $362 (2000); City property taxes per capita: $355 (2000).
Education: High school graduation rate: 73.5% (2000); College graduation rate: 13.6% (2000).

School District(s)

Denison Community School District (KG-12)
2000 Enrollment: 1,708 712-263-2176

Housing: Homeownership rate: 65.1% (2000); Median home value: $72,500 (2000); Median rent: $310 per month (2000); Median age of housing: 39 years (2000).
Hospitals: Crawford County Memorial Hospital (72 beds)
Safety: Violent crime rate: 2.7 per 10,000 population; Property crime rate: 240.1 per 10,000 population (2001).
Newspapers: Denison Review (1 x week); Denison Bulletin (1 x week); Meat Empire Saving Guide (2 x week)
Transportation: Commute to work: 93.9% car, 0.1% public transportation, 2.4% walk, 3.3% work from home (2000); Travel time to work: 81.0% less than 15 minutes, 11.2% 15 to 30 minutes, 3.5% 30 to 45 minutes, 0.7% 45 to 60 minutes, 3.5% 60 minutes or more (2000)

Additional Information Contacts

Denison Chamber of Commerce 712-263-5621

DOW CITY (city). Covers a land area of 0.319 square miles and a water area of 0 square miles. Located at 41.92° N. Lat.; 95.49° W. Long. Elevation is 1,131 feet.
History: Dow City was named for S. E. Dow, an early settler.
Population: 503 (2000); Race: 99.6% White, 0.0% Black, 0.0% Asian, 0.0% American Indian and Alaska Native, 0.9% Hispanic of any race, 0.4% two or more races (2000); Density: 1,578.3 persons per square mile (2000); Age: 10.2% under 18, 30.4% over 64 (2000); Marriage status: 14.7% never married, 60.5% now married, 12.6% widowed, 12.1% divorced (2000); Foreign born: 0.9% (2000); Ancestry (includes multiple ancestries): 33.5% German, 10.4% Irish, 9.6% United States or American, 8.3% English, 3.7% Other groups (2000).
Economy: Employment by occupation: 5.4% management, 17.6% professional, 16.1% services, 15.1% sales, 2.4% farming, 5.4% construction, 38.0% production (2000).
Income: Per capita income: $18,108 (2000); Median household income: $30,547 (2000); Poverty rate: 8.0% (2000).
Taxes: Total city taxes per capita: $89 (1997); City property taxes per capita: $86 (1997).
Education: High school graduation rate: 69.1% (2000); College graduation rate: 7.2% (2000).
Housing: Homeownership rate: 70.8% (2000); Median home value: $40,200 (2000); Median rent: $218 per month (2000); Median age of housing: 48 years (2000).
Transportation: Commute to work: 88.8% car, 0.0% public transportation, 8.3% walk, 2.9% work from home (2000); Travel time to work: 41.2% less than 15 minutes, 44.2% 15 to 30 minutes, 8.5% 30 to 45 minutes, 3.0% 45 to 60 minutes, 3.0% 60 minutes or more (2000)

KIRON (city). Covers a land area of 0.204 square miles and a water area of 0 square miles. Located at 42.19° N. Lat.; 95.32° W. Long. Elevation is 1,341 feet.
History: Kiron may have been named by A. Norelius, a financial backer, for a town in Manchuria. It may also have been intended that the town be named Kidron, for a stream near Jerusalem, but the 'd' was accidently omitted in the town records.
Population: 273 (2000); Race: 94.5% White, 0.0% Black, 0.0% Asian, 4.4% American Indian and Alaska Native, 0.0% Hispanic of any race, 1.1% two or more races (2000); Density: 1,337.6 persons per square mile (2000); Age: 25.6% under 18, 23.1% over 64 (2000); Marriage status: 24.8% never

married, 54.2% now married, 10.3% widowed, 10.7% divorced (2000); Foreign born: 1.8% (2000); Ancestry (includes multiple ancestries): 43.6% German, 19.4% Swedish, 11.0% English, 7.7% Irish, 7.3% Dutch (2000).
Economy: Single-family building permits issued: 0 (2001) / 0 (2000); Multi-family building permits issued: 0 (2001) / 0 (2000); Employment by occupation: 4.6% management, 13.7% professional, 16.0% services, 37.4% sales, 0.0% farming, 9.2% construction, 19.1% production (2000).
Income: Per capita income: $16,061 (2000); Median household income: $31,429 (2000); Poverty rate: 14.7% (2000).
Taxes: Total city taxes per capita: $109 (1997); City property taxes per capita: $105 (1997).
Education: High school graduation rate: 91.4% (2000); College graduation rate: 12.4% (2000).
Housing: Homeownership rate: 74.8% (2000); Median home value: $44,600 (2000); Median rent: $320 per month (2000); Median age of housing: 51 years (2000).
Transportation: Commute to work: 88.5% car, 0.0% public transportation, 4.6% walk, 6.9% work from home (2000); Travel time to work: 29.8% less than 15 minutes, 56.2% 15 to 30 minutes, 10.7% 30 to 45 minutes, 1.7% 45 to 60 minutes, 1.7% 60 minutes or more (2000)

MANILLA (city). Covers a land area of 0.792 square miles and a water area of 0 square miles. Located at 41.88° N. Lat.; 95.23° W. Long. Elevation is 1,317 feet.
History: Manilla was named after a Fourth of July celebration. A tug-of-war decided the name.
Population: 839 (2000); Race: 98.1% White, 0.4% Black, 0.6% Asian, 0.1% American Indian and Alaska Native, 0.5% Hispanic of any race, 0.4% two or more races (2000); Density: 1,059.2 persons per square mile (2000); Age: 24.1% under 18, 26.7% over 64 (2000); Marriage status: 18.2% never married, 61.8% now married, 12.9% widowed, 7.1% divorced (2000); Foreign born: 1.4% (2000); Ancestry (includes multiple ancestries): 64.9% German, 12.4% Irish, 7.8% Danish, 5.1% Norwegian, 3.9% Other groups (2000).
Economy: Single-family building permits issued: 3 (2001) / 0 (2000); Multi-family building permits issued: 0 (2001) / 0 (2000); Employment by occupation: 6.2% management, 11.3% professional, 20.8% services, 21.3% sales, 1.3% farming, 14.1% construction, 25.1% production (2000).
Income: Per capita income: $14,011 (2000); Median household income: $31,146 (2000); Poverty rate: 12.1% (2000).
Taxes: Total city taxes per capita: $112 (1997); City property taxes per capita: $109 (1997).
Education: High school graduation rate: 78.8% (2000); College graduation rate: 6.2% (2000).

School District(s)

Ikm Community School District (PK-12)
2000 Enrollment: 453 712-654-2852
Housing: Homeownership rate: 81.9% (2000); Median home value: $37,300 (2000); Median rent: $189 per month (2000); Median age of housing: 60+ years (2000).
Newspapers: The Manilla Times (1 x week)
Transportation: Commute to work: 89.4% car, 0.0% public transportation, 8.0% walk, 2.1% work from home (2000); Travel time to work: 45.2% less than 15 minutes, 30.4% 15 to 30 minutes, 16.1% 30 to 45 minutes, 1.1% 45 to 60 minutes, 7.1% 60 minutes or more (2000)

RICKETTS (city). Covers a land area of 0.255 square miles and a water area of 0 square miles. Located at 42.13° N. Lat.; 95.57° W. Long. Elevation is 1,366 feet.
History: Ricketts was platted in 1899 by the Western Town Lot Company.
Population: 144 (2000); Race: 98.6% White, 0.0% Black, 1.4% Asian, 0.0% American Indian and Alaska Native, 7.0% Hispanic of any race, 0.0% two or more races (2000); Density: 564.6 persons per square mile (2000); Age: 25.2% under 18, 23.1% over 64 (2000); Marriage status: 23.2% never married, 63.4% now married, 9.8% widowed, 3.6% divorced (2000); Foreign born: 7.0% (2000); Ancestry (includes multiple ancestries): 55.2% German, 9.1% Swedish, 8.4% Irish, 6.3% Scottish, 6.3% English (2000).
Economy: Employment by occupation: 3.9% management, 0.0% professional, 43.1% services, 29.4% sales, 0.0% farming, 7.8% construction, 15.7% production (2000).
Income: Per capita income: $12,017 (2000); Median household income: $31,250 (2000); Poverty rate: 12.6% (2000).
Taxes: Total city taxes per capita: $100 (1997); City property taxes per capita: $100 (1997).
Education: High school graduation rate: 65.6% (2000); College graduation rate: 5.4% (2000).
Housing: Homeownership rate: 81.8% (2000); Median home value: $22,800 (2000); Median rent: $325 per month (2000); Median age of housing: 60+ years (2000).
Transportation: Commute to work: 86.3% car, 0.0% public transportation, 9.8% walk, 3.9% work from home (2000); Travel time to work: 24.5% less than 15 minutes, 51.0% 15 to 30 minutes, 8.2% 30 to 45 minutes, 6.1% 45 to 60 minutes, 10.2% 60 minutes or more (2000)

SCHLESWIG (city). Covers a land area of 1.315 square miles and a water area of 0 square miles. Located at 42.16° N. Lat.; 95.43° W. Long. Elevation is 1,497 feet.
History: Schleswig was named for a town in Prussia. It had previously been called Morgan, then Hohenzollern.
Population: 833 (2000); Race: 99.6% White, 0.0% Black, 0.0% Asian, 0.0% American Indian and Alaska Native, 2.2% Hispanic of any race, 0.4% two or more races (2000); Density: 633.5 persons per square mile (2000); Age: 23.8% under 18, 27.5% over 64 (2000); Marriage status: 14.6% never married, 68.5% now married, 10.9% widowed, 5.9% divorced (2000); Foreign born: 0.7% (2000); Ancestry (includes multiple ancestries): 57.6% German, 8.1% United States or American, 7.3% Irish, 5.4% Swedish, 4.4% English (2000).
Economy: Single-family building permits issued: 0 (2001) / 1 (2000); Multi-family building permits issued: 0 (2001) / 0 (2000); Employment by occupation: 9.9% management, 9.4% professional, 18.5% services, 21.6% sales, 2.6% farming, 9.6% construction, 28.4% production (2000).
Income: Per capita income: $15,805 (2000); Median household income: $31,328 (2000); Poverty rate: 4.2% (2000).
Taxes: Total city taxes per capita: $155 (1997); City property taxes per capita: $151 (1997).
Education: High school graduation rate: 72.2% (2000); College graduation rate: 7.8% (2000).

School District(s)

Schleswig Community School District (PK-12)
2000 Enrollment: 182 712-676-3313
Housing: Homeownership rate: 82.1% (2000); Median home value: $46,900 (2000); Median rent: $239 per month (2000); Median age of housing: 56 years (2000).
Transportation: Commute to work: 92.9% car, 0.0% public transportation, 2.4% walk, 2.9% work from home (2000); Travel time to work: 39.5% less than 15 minutes, 49.9% 15 to 30 minutes, 6.5% 30 to 45 minutes, 1.6% 45 to 60 minutes, 2.5% 60 minutes or more (2000)

VAIL (city). Covers a land area of 0.559 square miles and a water area of 0 square miles. Located at 42.06° N. Lat.; 95.20° W. Long. Elevation is 1,260 feet.
History: Vail was named by a railroad official, Thomas Ryan from Tipperary, Ireland. Vail originally had a large Irish population.
Population: 452 (2000); Race: 93.2% White, 2.2% Black, 0.0% Asian, 0.0% American Indian and Alaska Native, 4.2% Hispanic of any race, 1.3% two or more races (2000); Density: 808.0 persons per square mile (2000); Age: 30.0% under 18, 17.7% over 64 (2000); Marriage status: 23.3% never married, 61.1% now married, 8.3% widowed, 7.4% divorced (2000); Foreign born: 3.1% (2000); Ancestry (includes multiple ancestries): 51.9% German, 16.6% Irish, 10.4% Other groups, 7.7% United States or American, 5.5% English (2000).
Economy: Single-family building permits issued: 1 (2001) / 1 (2000); Multi-family building permits issued: 0 (2001) / 0 (2000); Employment by occupation: 5.6% management, 5.2% professional, 20.3% services, 22.0% sales, 1.3% farming, 13.4% construction, 32.3% production (2000).
Income: Per capita income: $15,071 (2000); Median household income: $33,750 (2000); Poverty rate: 7.0% (2000).
Taxes: Total city taxes per capita: $114 (1997); City property taxes per capita: $108 (1997).
Education: High school graduation rate: 88.3% (2000); College graduation rate: 4.8% (2000).
Housing: Homeownership rate: 76.1% (2000); Median home value: $37,000 (2000); Median rent: $253 per month (2000); Median age of housing: 56 years (2000).
Newspapers: The Observer (1 x week)
Transportation: Commute to work: 88.7% car, 0.0% public transportation, 7.0% walk, 3.0% work from home (2000); Travel time to work: 44.8% less than 15 minutes, 37.2% 15 to 30 minutes, 8.1% 30 to 45 minutes, 1.3% 45 to 60 minutes, 8.5% 60 minutes or more (2000)

WESTSIDE (city). Aka West Side. Covers a land area of 1.481 square miles and a water area of 0 square miles. Located at 42.07° N. Lat.; 95.10° W. Long.
History: Westside was so named by railroad officials because the town lies west of a long, steep incline in the roadbed. At first the settlement was principally a community of railroad workers, most of whom were veterans of the Civil War.
Population: 327 (2000); Race: 100.0% White, 0.0% Black, 0.0% Asian, 0.0% American Indian and Alaska Native, 0.0% Hispanic of any race, 0.0% two or more races (2000); Density: 220.8 persons per square mile (2000); Age: 19.6% under 18, 26.8% over 64 (2000); Marriage status: 13.7% never married, 77.9% now married, 5.5% widowed, 3.0% divorced (2000); Foreign born: 0.6% (2000); Ancestry (includes multiple ancestries): 60.1% German, 15.0% United States or American, 6.5% Irish, 5.9% English, 5.0% Dutch (2000).
Economy: Single-family building permits issued: 2 (2001) / 1 (2000); Multi-family building permits issued: 0 (2001) / 0 (2000); Employment by occupation: 5.7% management, 12.5% professional, 13.1% services, 26.1% sales, 1.7% farming, 12.5% construction, 28.4% production (2000).
Income: Per capita income: $31,545 (2000); Median household income: $37,250 (2000); Poverty rate: 3.1% (2000).
Taxes: Total city taxes per capita: $135 (1997); City property taxes per capita: $133 (1997).
Education: High school graduation rate: 92.1% (2000); College graduation rate: 12.0% (2000).

School District(s)

Ar-We-Va Community School District (PK-12)
2000 Enrollment: 484 712-663-4311

Housing: Homeownership rate: 88.1% (2000); Median home value: $58,800 (2000); Median rent: $232 per month (2000); Median age of housing: 54 years (2000).
Transportation: Commute to work: 82.8% car, 0.0% public transportation, 9.8% walk, 7.5% work from home (2000); Travel time to work: 46.0% less than 15 minutes, 48.4% 15 to 30 minutes, 4.3% 30 to 45 minutes, 1.2% 45 to 60 minutes, 0.0% 60 minutes or more (2000)

Dallas County

Located in central Iowa; prairie area, drained by the Raccoon River system and by Beaver Creek. Covers a land area of 586.50 square miles, a water area of 5.30 square miles, and is located in the Central Time Zone. The county government was organized in 1846. County seat is Adel.

Dallas County is part of the Des Moines, IA MSA. The entire metro area includes: Dallas County; Polk County; Warren County

Weather Station: Perry — Elevation: 964 feet

	Jan	Feb	Mar	Apr	May	Jun	Jul	Aug	Sep	Oct	Nov	Dec
High	27	33	46	60	72	81	85	82	75	63	46	32
Low	8	14	26	37	49	59	63	60	51	38	26	14
Precip	0.8	0.7	2.1	3.1	4.3	4.7	4.0	4.2	3.1	2.5	1.8	1.0
Snow	5.9	4.8	4.6	0.6	0.0	0.0	0.0	0.0	0.0	0.1	2.4	4.6

High and Low temperatures in degrees Fahrenheit; Precipitation and Snow in inches

Population: 40,750 (2000); Race: 94.7% White, 1.0% Black, 0.3% Asian, 0.1% American Indian and Alaska Native, 5.3% Hispanic of any race, 0.8% two or more races (2000); Density: 69.5 persons per square mile (2000); Age: 28.2% under 18, 11.1% over 64 (2000).
Religion: Five largest groups: 12.6% Catholic Church, 10.2% The United Methodist Church, 5.8% Christian Church (Disciples of Christ), 4.4% Evangelical Lutheran Church in America, 3.1% Lutheran Church—Missouri Synod (2000).
Economy: Unemployment rate: 3.0% (11/2002); Total civilian labor force: 21,961 (11/2002); Leading industries: 23.6% manufacturing; 15.0% health care and social assistance; 15.0% retail trade (2000); Companies that employ more than 1,000 persons: 0 (2000); Companies that employ more than 100 persons: 18 (2000); Farms: 918 totaling 323,612 acres (1997); Minority business ownership rate: 0.0% (1997); Women business ownership rate: 29.1% (1997); Retail sales per capita: $6,167 (1997). Single-family building permits issued: 269 (2001) / 245 (2000); Multi-family building permits issued: 222 (2001) / 38 (2000).
Income: Per capita income: $22,970 (2000); Median household income: $48,528 (2000); Poverty rate: 5.6% (2000); Bankruptcy rate: 3.78% (2001).
Taxes: Total county taxes per capita: $227 (2000); County property taxes per capita: $222 (2000).
Education: High school graduation rate: 89.5% (2000); College graduation rate: 26.8% (2000).
Housing: Homeownership rate: 76.4% (2000); Median home value: $108,000 (2000); Median rent: $448 per month (2000); Median age of housing: 26 years (2000).
Health: Birth rate: 129.1 per 10,000 population (1998); Age adjusted death rate: 86.4 per 10,000 population (1999); Age adjusted cancer mortality rate: 204.1 deaths per 100,000 population (1999). Number of physicians: 4.7 per 10,000 population (1999); Number of hospital beds: 8.1 per 10,000 population (1999).
Elections: 2000 Presidential election results: 44.3% Gore, 53.3% Bush, 1.7% Nader, 0.3% Buchanan
National and State Parks: Dallas Lake State Wildlife Area; Pleasant Valley State Wildlife Area
Additional Information Contacts
Dallas County Government Offices 515-993-5816
Perry Chamber of Commerce 515-465-4601
Raccoon Valley Board of Realtors 515-453-5632

Dallas County Communities

ADEL (city). Covers a land area of 3.271 square miles and a water area of 0.006 square miles. Located at 41.61° N. Lat.; 94.02° W. Long. Elevation is 930 feet.
History: Adel was in 1850 a station on the Dubuque-Council Bluffs stagecoach route. When the town was settled in 1846 it was called Penoach, but the name was changed in 1849 when the place was made the county seat.
Population: 3,435 (2000); Race: 99.5% White, 0.1% Black, 0.0% Asian, 0.0% American Indian and Alaska Native, 0.9% Hispanic of any race, 0.4% two or more races (2000); Density: 1,050.1 persons per square mile (2000); Age: 28.4% under 18, 14.2% over 64 (2000); Marriage status: 25.6% never married, 54.7% now married, 8.6% widowed, 11.1% divorced (2000); Foreign born: 1.5% (2000); Ancestry (includes multiple ancestries): 34.4% German, 13.0% Irish, 12.1% English, 9.0% United States or American, 5.6% Norwegian (2000).
Economy: Single-family building permits issued: 20 (2001) / 15 (2000); Multi-family building permits issued: 0 (2001) / 0 (2000); Employment by occupation: 18.9% management, 12.7% professional, 13.6% services, 32.9% sales, 0.5% farming, 11.2% construction, 10.3% production (2000).
Income: Per capita income: $19,743 (2000); Median household income: $39,423 (2000); Poverty rate: 4.0% (2000).
Taxes: Total city taxes per capita: $222 (1997); City property taxes per capita: $217 (1997).
Education: High school graduation rate: 88.2% (2000); College graduation rate: 20.4% (2000).

School District(s)

Adel-Desoto-Minburn Community School District (PK-12)
2000 Enrollment: 1,518 515-993-4283

Housing: Homeownership rate: 68.8% (2000); Median home value: $94,600 (2000); Median rent: $420 per month (2000); Median age of housing: 33 years (2000).
Newspapers: Grimes Today (1 x week); Northeast Dallas County Record (1 x week); The Round-Up (1 x week); Dallas County Roundup (1 x week); Dallas County News (1 x week)
Transportation: Commute to work: 89.7% car, 0.4% public transportation, 5.9% walk, 3.5% work from home (2000); Travel time to work: 34.4% less than 15 minutes, 28.7% 15 to 30 minutes, 25.8% 30 to 45 minutes, 9.2% 45 to 60 minutes, 2.0% 60 minutes or more (2000)

BOONEVILLE (unincorporated postal area, zip code 50038). Covers a land area of 4.364 square miles and a water area of 0.051 square miles. Located at 41.52° N. Lat.; 93.90° W. Long.
History: Booneville was established on land owned by William and Susannah Boone, who gave their name to the new town.
Population: 322 (2000); Race: 100.0% White, 0.0% Black, 0.0% Asian, 0.0% American Indian and Alaska Native, 0.0% Hispanic of any race, 0.0% two or more races (2000); Density: 73.8 persons per square mile (2000); Age: 20.2% under 18, 10.9% over 64 (2000); Marriage status: 29.5% never married, 48.8% now married, 4.3% widowed, 17.4% divorced (2000); Foreign born: 0.6% (2000); Ancestry (includes multiple ancestries): 25.2% German, 15.0% Irish, 13.5% English, 11.7% United States or American, 5.3% Norwegian (2000).
Economy: Employment by occupation: 10.1% management, 7.6% professional, 16.7% services, 31.3% sales, 1.0% farming, 12.1% construction, 21.2% production (2000).

Income: Per capita income: $27,049 (2000); Median household income: $39,583 (2000); Poverty rate: 11.8% (2000).
Education: High school graduation rate: 88.2% (2000); College graduation rate: 18.9% (2000).
Housing: Homeownership rate: 89.7% (2000); Median home value: $78,300 (2000); Median rent: $342 per month (2000); Median age of housing: 23 years (2000).
Transportation: Commute to work: 95.4% car, 0.0% public transportation, 1.5% walk, 3.1% work from home (2000); Travel time to work: 18.6% less than 15 minutes, 56.9% 15 to 30 minutes, 23.4% 30 to 45 minutes, 1.1% 45 to 60 minutes, 0.0% 60 minutes or more (2000)

BOUTON (city). Covers a land area of 0.140 square miles and a water area of 0 square miles. Located at 41.85° N. Lat.; 94.00° W. Long. Elevation is 938 feet.
History: Bouton was established on land owned by a Mr. Bouton, and the town took Bouton's name as its own.
Population: 136 (2000); Race: 97.5% White, 0.0% Black, 0.0% Asian, 0.0% American Indian and Alaska Native, 0.0% Hispanic of any race, 2.5% two or more races (2000); Density: 971.3 persons per square mile (2000); Age: 23.3% under 18, 16.7% over 64 (2000); Marriage status: 20.2% never married, 42.6% now married, 13.8% widowed, 23.4% divorced (2000); Foreign born: 0.0% (2000); Ancestry (includes multiple ancestries): 37.5% United States or American, 7.5% Other groups, 5.0% German, 4.2% Irish, 4.2% European (2000).
Economy: Single-family building permits issued: 0 (2001) / 0 (2000); Multi-family building permits issued: 0 (2001) / 0 (2000); Employment by occupation: 7.6% management, 0.0% professional, 16.7% services, 30.3% sales, 0.0% farming, 19.7% construction, 25.8% production (2000).
Income: Per capita income: $17,778 (2000); Median household income: $34,688 (2000); Poverty rate: 6.7% (2000).
Taxes: Total city taxes per capita: $120 (1997); City property taxes per capita: $120 (1997).
Education: High school graduation rate: 80.7% (2000); College graduation rate: 0.0% (2000).
Housing: Homeownership rate: 72.7% (2000); Median home value: $27,500 (2000); Median rent: $388 per month (2000); Median age of housing: 60+ years (2000).
Transportation: Commute to work: 95.3% car, 0.0% public transportation, 0.0% walk, 4.7% work from home (2000); Travel time to work: 34.4% less than 15 minutes, 13.1% 15 to 30 minutes, 41.0% 30 to 45 minutes, 6.6% 45 to 60 minutes, 4.9% 60 minutes or more (2000)

DALLAS CENTER (city). Covers a land area of 4.418 square miles and a water area of 0 square miles. Located at 41.68° N. Lat.; 93.96° W. Long. Elevation is 1,072 feet.
History: Dallas Center was so named because early residents hoped that the county seat would be established here.
Population: 1,595 (2000); Race: 99.2% White, 0.0% Black, 0.0% Asian, 0.0% American Indian and Alaska Native, 0.4% Hispanic of any race, 0.4% two or more races (2000); Density: 361.0 persons per square mile (2000); Age: 26.3% under 18, 16.3% over 64 (2000); Marriage status: 18.2% never married, 66.5% now married, 7.3% widowed, 8.0% divorced (2000); Foreign born: 0.6% (2000); Ancestry (includes multiple ancestries): 34.1% German, 10.9% English, 10.4% Irish, 5.9% Dutch, 5.2% United States or American (2000).
Economy: Single-family building permits issued: 3 (2001) / 4 (2000); Multi-family building permits issued: 0 (2001) / 0 (2000); Employment by occupation: 14.8% management, 17.2% professional, 11.8% services, 29.2% sales, 2.3% farming, 13.2% construction, 11.5% production (2000).
Income: Per capita income: $20,038 (2000); Median household income: $52,883 (2000); Poverty rate: 4.2% (2000).
Taxes: Total city taxes per capita: $352 (1997); City property taxes per capita: $345 (1997).
Education: High school graduation rate: 88.1% (2000); College graduation rate: 18.5% (2000).

School District(s)

Dallas Center-Grimes Community School District (PK-12)
2000 Enrollment: 1,521 515-992-3866

Housing: Homeownership rate: 82.8% (2000); Median home value: $96,600 (2000); Median rent: $354 per month (2000); Median age of housing: 47 years (2000).
Transportation: Commute to work: 96.1% car, 0.0% public transportation, 1.2% walk, 2.4% work from home (2000); Travel time to work: 27.2% less than 15 minutes, 36.5% 15 to 30 minutes, 27.0% 30 to 45 minutes, 7.4% 45 to 60 minutes, 1.9% 60 minutes or more (2000)

DAWSON (city). Covers a land area of 0.478 square miles and a water area of 0 square miles. Located at 41.84° N. Lat.; 94.22° W. Long. Elevation is 948 feet.
History: Dawson was established as a station on the Chicago, Milwaukee & St. Paul Railroad. It was first called Undine.
Population: 155 (2000); Race: 91.5% White, 0.0% Black, 0.0% Asian, 0.0% American Indian and Alaska Native, 3.7% Hispanic of any race, 4.9% two or more races (2000); Density: 324.2 persons per square mile (2000); Age: 30.5% under 18, 13.4% over 64 (2000); Marriage status: 9.4% never married, 82.1% now married, 1.7% widowed, 6.8% divorced (2000); Foreign born: 2.4% (2000); Ancestry (includes multiple ancestries): 29.3% German, 13.4% Danish, 10.4% United States or American, 8.5% Other groups, 7.3% Irish (2000).
Economy: Single-family building permits issued: 0 (2001) / 0 (2000); Multi-family building permits issued: 4 (2001) / 3 (2000); Employment by occupation: 4.7% management, 18.8% professional, 12.5% services, 21.9% sales, 0.0% farming, 21.9% construction, 20.3% production (2000).
Income: Per capita income: $13,524 (2000); Median household income: $38,750 (2000); Poverty rate: 2.4% (2000).
Taxes: Total city taxes per capita: $47 (1997); City property taxes per capita: $47 (1997).
Education: High school graduation rate: 81.8% (2000); College graduation rate: 5.5% (2000).
Housing: Homeownership rate: 95.3% (2000); Median home value: $33,000 (2000); Median rent: $525 per month (2000); Median age of housing: 60+ years (2000).
Transportation: Commute to work: 96.9% car, 0.0% public transportation, 0.0% walk, 3.1% work from home (2000); Travel time to work: 30.6% less than 15 minutes, 32.3% 15 to 30 minutes, 16.1% 30 to 45 minutes, 19.4% 45 to 60 minutes, 1.6% 60 minutes or more (2000)

DE SOTO (city). Covers a land area of 1.481 square miles and a water area of 0 square miles. Located at 41.53° N. Lat.; 94.00° W. Long. Elevation is 975 feet.
History: De Soto was named for an official of the Chicago, Rock Island & Pacific Railroad when the survey was made in 1868.
Population: 1,009 (2000); Race: 99.2% White, 0.0% Black, 0.4% Asian, 0.0% American Indian and Alaska Native, 0.0% Hispanic of any race, 0.4% two or more races (2000); Density: 681.4 persons per square mile (2000); Age: 33.1% under 18, 6.1% over 64 (2000); Marriage status: 21.0% never married, 66.8% now married, 2.3% widowed, 9.9% divorced (2000); Foreign born: 1.1% (2000); Ancestry (includes multiple ancestries): 25.3% German, 14.5% English, 12.9% Irish, 6.8% United States or American, 6.7% Swedish (2000).
Economy: Single-family building permits issued: 10 (2001) / 2 (2000); Multi-family building permits issued: 0 (2001) / 0 (2000); Employment by occupation: 8.3% management, 10.3% professional, 13.7% services, 37.7% sales, 0.4% farming, 12.3% construction, 17.5% production (2000).
Income: Per capita income: $17,464 (2000); Median household income: $48,816 (2000); Poverty rate: 3.3% (2000).
Education: High school graduation rate: 92.8% (2000); College graduation rate: 13.6% (2000).
Housing: Homeownership rate: 88.0% (2000); Median home value: $88,100 (2000); Median rent: $386 per month (2000); Median age of housing: 26 years (2000).
Transportation: Commute to work: 91.9% car, 0.4% public transportation, 2.0% walk, 5.8% work from home (2000); Travel time to work: 13.8% less than 15 minutes, 54.1% 15 to 30 minutes, 26.6% 30 to 45 minutes, 3.3% 45 to 60 minutes, 2.3% 60 minutes or more (2000)

DEXTER (city). Covers a land area of 1.192 square miles and a water area of 0 square miles. Located at 41.51° N. Lat.; 94.22° W. Long. Elevation is 1,150 feet.
History: Dexter was founded in 1868 by the Chicago, Rock Island & Pacific Railroad and named for a race horse. Dr. Nelson Percy, inventor of a blood transfusion device, lived here.
Population: 689 (2000); Race: 99.4% White, 0.0% Black, 0.0% Asian, 0.6% American Indian and Alaska Native, 2.1% Hispanic of any race, 0.0% two or more races (2000); Density: 578.2 persons per square mile (2000); Age: 28.8% under 18, 17.0% over 64 (2000); Marriage status: 17.5% never married, 63.1% now married, 9.2% widowed, 10.2% divorced (2000); Foreign born: 0.4% (2000); Ancestry (includes multiple ancestries): 29.5% German, 12.6% Irish, 12.4% English, 6.2% Other groups, 5.8% United States or American (2000).

Economy: Single-family building permits issued: 3 (2001) / 3 (2000); Multi-family building permits issued: 0 (2001) / 0 (2000); Employment by occupation: 8.6% management, 10.0% professional, 18.3% services, 32.9% sales, 2.0% farming, 13.0% construction, 15.3% production (2000).
Income: Per capita income: $16,990 (2000); Median household income: $39,375 (2000); Poverty rate: 4.6% (2000).
Taxes: Total city taxes per capita: $292 (1997); City property taxes per capita: $291 (1997).
Education: High school graduation rate: 84.8% (2000); College graduation rate: 14.6% (2000).
Housing: Homeownership rate: 82.0% (2000); Median home value: $77,100 (2000); Median rent: $275 per month (2000); Median age of housing: 60+ years (2000).
Transportation: Commute to work: 95.7% car, 0.0% public transportation, 1.7% walk, 2.0% work from home (2000); Travel time to work: 25.4% less than 15 minutes, 15.9% 15 to 30 minutes, 34.6% 30 to 45 minutes, 20.3% 45 to 60 minutes, 3.7% 60 minutes or more (2000)

GRANGER (city). Covers a land area of 0.513 square miles and a water area of 0 square miles. Located at 41.76° N. Lat.; 93.82° W. Long. Elevation is 887 feet.
History: Granger was laid out in 1879. It was named for Ben Granger, an official of the Des Moines Northern Railway, a narrow-gauge railroad running between Des Moines and Boone.
Population: 583 (2000); Race: 98.8% White, 0.0% Black, 0.9% Asian, 0.0% American Indian and Alaska Native, 0.5% Hispanic of any race, 0.0% two or more races (2000); Density: 1,136.6 persons per square mile (2000); Age: 19.5% under 18, 21.6% over 64 (2000); Marriage status: 22.8% never married, 51.1% now married, 15.2% widowed, 10.9% divorced (2000); Foreign born: 0.4% (2000); Ancestry (includes multiple ancestries): 30.7% German, 16.3% Irish, 9.8% English, 9.3% United States or American, 6.7% French (except Basque) (2000).
Economy: Single-family building permits issued: 0 (2001) / 0 (2000); Multi-family building permits issued: 0 (2001) / 0 (2000); Employment by occupation: 9.9% management, 18.1% professional, 21.3% services, 27.3% sales, 0.7% farming, 12.8% construction, 9.9% production (2000).
Income: Per capita income: $19,110 (2000); Median household income: $31,442 (2000); Poverty rate: 5.2% (2000).
Taxes: Total city taxes per capita: $230 (1997); City property taxes per capita: $227 (1997).
Education: High school graduation rate: 85.3% (2000); College graduation rate: 16.2% (2000).
Housing: Homeownership rate: 70.0% (2000); Median home value: $88,300 (2000); Median rent: $383 per month (2000); Median age of housing: 36 years (2000).
Transportation: Commute to work: 89.1% car, 0.0% public transportation, 6.2% walk, 3.3% work from home (2000); Travel time to work: 30.7% less than 15 minutes, 49.8% 15 to 30 minutes, 15.4% 30 to 45 minutes, 2.2% 45 to 60 minutes, 1.9% 60 minutes or more (2000)

LINDEN (city). Covers a land area of 0.790 square miles and a water area of 0 square miles. Located at 41.64° N. Lat.; 94.27° W. Long. Elevation is 1,120 feet.
History: Linden was named for the linden trees in the area.
Population: 226 (2000); Race: 99.6% White, 0.0% Black, 0.0% Asian, 0.4% American Indian and Alaska Native, 0.0% Hispanic of any race, 0.0% two or more races (2000); Density: 286.1 persons per square mile (2000); Age: 27.0% under 18, 12.6% over 64 (2000); Marriage status: 21.4% never married, 67.4% now married, 1.6% widowed, 9.6% divorced (2000); Foreign born: 0.0% (2000); Ancestry (includes multiple ancestries): 22.2% English, 17.0% German, 12.2% Irish, 5.2% United States or American, 5.2% Swedish (2000).
Economy: Employment by occupation: 7.0% management, 13.0% professional, 14.8% services, 29.6% sales, 0.0% farming, 16.5% construction, 19.1% production (2000).
Income: Per capita income: $14,392 (2000); Median household income: $32,500 (2000); Poverty rate: 4.8% (2000).
Taxes: Total city taxes per capita: $89 (1997); City property taxes per capita: $89 (1997).
Education: High school graduation rate: 79.4% (2000); College graduation rate: 3.2% (2000).
Housing: Homeownership rate: 89.9% (2000); Median home value: $39,800 (2000); Median rent: $306 per month (2000); Median age of housing: 60+ years (2000).
Transportation: Commute to work: 93.9% car, 2.6% public transportation, 1.7% walk, 1.7% work from home (2000); Travel time to work: 11.5% less than 15 minutes, 37.2% 15 to 30 minutes, 19.5% 30 to 45 minutes, 16.8% 45 to 60 minutes, 15.0% 60 minutes or more (2000)

MINBURN (city). Covers a land area of 0.271 square miles and a water area of 0 square miles. Located at 41.75° N. Lat.; 94.02° W. Long. Elevation is 1,042 feet.
History: Minburn was platted in 1869 by J. B. Hill and D. F. Rogers. A steam-operated saw- and gristmill was the town's first industrial plant.
Population: 391 (2000); Race: 98.4% White, 0.0% Black, 0.0% Asian, 0.0% American Indian and Alaska Native, 0.7% Hispanic of any race, 0.9% two or more races (2000); Density: 1,440.5 persons per square mile (2000); Age: 27.5% under 18, 8.7% over 64 (2000); Marriage status: 13.5% never married, 67.0% now married, 8.2% widowed, 11.3% divorced (2000); Foreign born: 1.4% (2000); Ancestry (includes multiple ancestries): 39.1% German, 16.7% Irish, 13.9% English, 9.6% United States or American, 7.3% Italian (2000).
Economy: Single-family building permits issued: 0 (2001) / 0 (2000); Multi-family building permits issued: 0 (2001) / 0 (2000); Employment by occupation: 13.3% management, 4.7% professional, 16.7% services, 33.5% sales, 3.9% farming, 8.6% construction, 19.3% production (2000).
Income: Per capita income: $19,421 (2000); Median household income: $44,917 (2000); Poverty rate: 4.5% (2000).
Taxes: Total city taxes per capita: $281 (1997); City property taxes per capita: $281 (1997).
Education: High school graduation rate: 87.7% (2000); College graduation rate: 5.3% (2000).
Housing: Homeownership rate: 80.7% (2000); Median home value: $78,900 (2000); Median rent: $361 per month (2000); Median age of housing: 50 years (2000).
Transportation: Commute to work: 91.3% car, 0.0% public transportation, 1.3% walk, 7.0% work from home (2000); Travel time to work: 24.8% less than 15 minutes, 32.2% 15 to 30 minutes, 27.1% 30 to 45 minutes, 12.1% 45 to 60 minutes, 3.7% 60 minutes or more (2000)

PERRY (city). Covers a land area of 3.705 square miles and a water area of 0.006 square miles. Located at 41.84° N. Lat.; 94.10° W. Long. Elevation is 998 feet.
History: Perry was named for Colonel Perry, one of the owners of the Des Moines Valley Railroad. The town was platted by John Willis in 1887.
Population: 7,633 (2000); Race: 81.8% White, 1.8% Black, 0.1% Asian, 0.2% American Indian and Alaska Native, 24.2% Hispanic of any race, 1.2% two or more races (2000); Density: 2,060.4 persons per square mile (2000); Age: 27.3% under 18, 15.9% over 64 (2000); Marriage status: 26.4% never married, 56.4% now married, 8.3% widowed, 8.8% divorced (2000); Foreign born: 16.4% (2000); Ancestry (includes multiple ancestries): 26.6% Other groups, 23.8% German, 10.4% Irish, 9.0% English, 7.4% United States or American (2000).
Economy: Single-family building permits issued: 15 (2001) / 7 (2000); Multi-family building permits issued: 52 (2001) / 10 (2000); Employment by occupation: 8.0% management, 12.1% professional, 19.9% services, 21.8% sales, 3.3% farming, 6.7% construction, 28.1% production (2000).
Income: Per capita income: $15,935 (2000); Median household income: $35,429 (2000); Poverty rate: 12.2% (2000).
Taxes: Total city taxes per capita: $250 (1997); City property taxes per capita: $241 (1997).
Education: High school graduation rate: 75.5% (2000); College graduation rate: 10.4% (2000).

School District(s)

Perry Community School District (PK-12)
2000 Enrollment: 1,830 515-465-4656
Housing: Homeownership rate: 65.1% (2000); Median home value: $69,000 (2000); Median rent: $390 per month (2000); Median age of housing: 50 years (2000).
Hospitals: Dallas County Hospital (25 beds)
Safety: Violent crime rate: 19.7 per 10,000 population; Property crime rate: 270.2 per 10,000 population (2001).
Newspapers: El Viento del Tropico; Perry Chief (1 x week)
Transportation: Commute to work: 94.3% car, 0.2% public transportation, 2.9% walk, 1.1% work from home (2000); Travel time to work: 55.5% less than 15 minutes, 19.3% 15 to 30 minutes, 15.4% 30 to 45 minutes, 8.2% 45 to 60 minutes, 1.6% 60 minutes or more (2000)
Additional Information Contacts
Perry Chamber of Commerce. 515-465-4601

REDFIELD (city). Covers a land area of 1.382 square miles and a water area of 0 square miles. Located at 41.59° N. Lat.; 94.19° W. Long. Elevation is 958 feet.

History: Redfield was first named New Ireland when the Cavanaugh brothers platted the town in 1850. The post office was known as McKay. The town was renamed in honor of Colonel James Redfield, who was killed during the Civil War.
Population: 833 (2000); Race: 96.6% White, 0.0% Black, 0.0% Asian, 1.2% American Indian and Alaska Native, 0.6% Hispanic of any race, 1.2% two or more races (2000); Density: 602.6 persons per square mile (2000); Age: 26.6% under 18, 14.9% over 64 (2000); Marriage status: 17.8% never married, 62.0% now married, 8.1% widowed, 12.1% divorced (2000); Foreign born: 0.0% (2000); Ancestry (includes multiple ancestries): 23.0% German, 15.2% English, 12.5% Irish, 11.7% United States or American, 6.5% Other groups (2000).
Economy: Single-family building permits issued: 6 (2001) / 3 (2000); Multi-family building permits issued: 0 (2001) / 0 (2000); Employment by occupation: 9.4% management, 7.1% professional, 16.4% services, 26.7% sales, 1.4% farming, 15.7% construction, 23.3% production (2000).
Income: Per capita income: $17,155 (2000); Median household income: $38,333 (2000); Poverty rate: 6.1% (2000).
Taxes: Total city taxes per capita: $113 (1997); City property taxes per capita: $113 (1997).
Education: High school graduation rate: 83.7% (2000); College graduation rate: 9.5% (2000).

School District(s)

Dexfield Community School District (PK-12)
2000 Enrollment: 274 515-833-2331
Housing: Homeownership rate: 80.4% (2000); Median home value: $55,100 (2000); Median rent: $342 per month (2000); Median age of housing: 60+ years (2000).
Transportation: Commute to work: 92.9% car, 0.0% public transportation, 4.3% walk, 2.8% work from home (2000); Travel time to work: 28.5% less than 15 minutes, 20.4% 15 to 30 minutes, 25.5% 30 to 45 minutes, 13.9% 45 to 60 minutes, 11.7% 60 minutes or more (2000)

VAN METER (city). Covers a land area of 0.597 square miles and a water area of 0.018 square miles. Located at 41.53° N. Lat.; 93.95° W. Long. Elevation is 874 feet.
History: Van Meter was named for Jacob Rhodes Van Meter, an early settler who built a flour mill here in 1866.
Population: 866 (2000); Race: 97.1% White, 1.4% Black, 0.5% Asian, 0.0% American Indian and Alaska Native, 0.6% Hispanic of any race, 0.8% two or more races (2000); Density: 1,450.3 persons per square mile (2000); Age: 30.3% under 18, 9.0% over 64 (2000); Marriage status: 21.7% never married, 61.9% now married, 4.6% widowed, 11.8% divorced (2000); Foreign born: 0.8% (2000); Ancestry (includes multiple ancestries): 32.8% German, 12.7% Irish, 11.6% English, 8.3% United States or American, 5.3% Other groups (2000).
Economy: Single-family building permits issued: 6 (2001) / 1 (2000); Multi-family building permits issued: 0 (2001) / 0 (2000); Employment by occupation: 15.1% management, 17.4% professional, 14.7% services, 37.0% sales, 0.0% farming, 9.7% construction, 6.2% production (2000).
Income: Per capita income: $20,272 (2000); Median household income: $50,625 (2000); Poverty rate: 2.7% (2000).
Taxes: Total city taxes per capita: $196 (1997); City property taxes per capita: $179 (1997).
Education: High school graduation rate: 91.7% (2000); College graduation rate: 22.7% (2000).

School District(s)

Van Meter Community School District (KG-12)
2000 Enrollment: 508 515-996-9960
Housing: Homeownership rate: 76.7% (2000); Median home value: $93,100 (2000); Median rent: $373 per month (2000); Median age of housing: 29 years (2000).
Transportation: Commute to work: 92.8% car, 0.0% public transportation, 4.8% walk, 2.1% work from home (2000); Travel time to work: 16.2% less than 15 minutes, 58.2% 15 to 30 minutes, 20.5% 30 to 45 minutes, 1.3% 45 to 60 minutes, 3.8% 60 minutes or more (2000)

WAUKEE (city). Covers a land area of 8.390 square miles and a water area of 0.011 square miles. Located at 41.60° N. Lat.; 93.86° W. Long. Elevation is 1,032 feet.
History: The Wragg Central Nurseries were founded here in 1863.
Population: 5,126 (2000); Race: 98.3% White, 1.4% Black, 0.0% Asian, 0.1% American Indian and Alaska Native, 1.0% Hispanic of any race, 0.2% two or more races (2000); Density: 610.9 persons per square mile (2000); Age: 31.7% under 18, 7.7% over 64 (2000); Marriage status: 15.9% never married, 69.7% now married, 4.6% widowed, 9.9% divorced (2000); Foreign born: 0.4% (2000); Ancestry (includes multiple ancestries): 35.2% German, 15.2% Irish, 9.7% English, 6.8% Swedish, 5.7% United States or American (2000).
Economy: Single-family building permits issued: 122 (2001) / 114 (2000); Multi-family building permits issued: 166 (2001) / 25 (2000); Employment by occupation: 20.3% management, 20.3% professional, 13.3% services, 29.0% sales, 0.0% farming, 9.2% construction, 7.9% production (2000).
Income: Per capita income: $24,351 (2000); Median household income: $58,024 (2000); Poverty rate: 3.0% (2000).
Taxes: Total city taxes per capita: $472 (2000); City property taxes per capita: $398 (2000).
Education: High school graduation rate: 95.1% (2000); College graduation rate: 34.0% (2000).

School District(s)

Waukee Community School District (PK-12)
2000 Enrollment: 2,422 515-987-5161
Housing: Homeownership rate: 84.1% (2000); Median home value: $132,000 (2000); Median rent: $473 per month (2000); Median age of housing: 9 years (2000).
Transportation: Commute to work: 94.8% car, 0.3% public transportation, 0.8% walk, 3.9% work from home (2000); Travel time to work: 23.2% less than 15 minutes, 58.5% 15 to 30 minutes, 15.6% 30 to 45 minutes, 0.8% 45 to 60 minutes, 1.9% 60 minutes or more (2000)
Additional Information Contacts
Raccoon Valley Board of Realtors 515-453-5632

WOODWARD (city). Covers a land area of 0.910 square miles and a water area of 0 square miles. Located at 41.85° N. Lat.; 93.92° W. Long. Elevation is 1,065 feet.
History: Woodward was originally a trading post known as Xenia. When the railroad company surveyed this section in 1880, it gave the site its present name.
Population: 1,200 (2000); Race: 96.5% White, 0.0% Black, 2.4% Asian, 0.4% American Indian and Alaska Native, 0.6% Hispanic of any race, 0.7% two or more races (2000); Density: 1,319.1 persons per square mile (2000); Age: 27.7% under 18, 13.4% over 64 (2000); Marriage status: 21.5% never married, 56.0% now married, 9.5% widowed, 12.9% divorced (2000); Foreign born: 1.8% (2000); Ancestry (includes multiple ancestries): 30.4% German, 17.3% Irish, 9.6% English, 8.3% Other groups, 7.0% United States or American (2000).
Economy: Single-family building permits issued: 1 (2001) / 2 (2000); Multi-family building permits issued: 0 (2001) / 0 (2000); Employment by occupation: 9.7% management, 19.1% professional, 20.6% services, 26.6% sales, 0.8% farming, 10.9% construction, 12.3% production (2000).
Income: Per capita income: $19,501 (2000); Median household income: $35,647 (2000); Poverty rate: 6.9% (2000).
Taxes: Total city taxes per capita: $111 (1997); City property taxes per capita: $110 (1997).
Education: High school graduation rate: 89.5% (2000); College graduation rate: 15.7% (2000).

School District(s)

Woodward-Granger Community School District (KG-12)
2000 Enrollment: 646 515-438-4333
Housing: Homeownership rate: 74.6% (2000); Median home value: $74,200 (2000); Median rent: $352 per month (2000); Median age of housing: 47 years (2000).
Hospitals: Woodward Resource Center (639 beds)
Transportation: Commute to work: 95.6% car, 0.0% public transportation, 2.4% walk, 1.7% work from home (2000); Travel time to work: 31.5% less than 15 minutes, 28.1% 15 to 30 minutes, 29.7% 30 to 45 minutes, 7.1% 45 to 60 minutes, 3.5% 60 minutes or more (2000)

Davis County

Located in southeastern Iowa; bounded on the south by Missouri; drained by the Des Moines, Fox, North Fabius, and Wyaconda Rivers; includes Lake Wapello. Covers a land area of 503.20 square miles, a water area of 1.60 square miles, and is located in the Central Time Zone. The county government was organized in 1843. County seat is Bloomfield.

Weather Station: Bloomfield 1 WNW — Elevation: 810 feet

	Jan	Feb	Mar	Apr	May	Jun	Jul	Aug	Sep	Oct	Nov	Dec
High	32	39	51	64	74	83	87	85	77	66	50	37
Low	14	19	30	41	52	61	65	63	54	43	31	20
Precip	1.1	1.2	2.5	3.6	5.0	4.3	4.8	4.9	4.3	2.9	2.6	1.5
Snow	8.1	6.6	4.3	2.6	tr	0.0	0.0	0.0	0.0	0.2	2.4	5.7

High and Low temperatures in degrees Fahrenheit; Precipitation and Snow in inches

Population: 8,541 (2000); Race: 98.8% White, 0.1% Black, 0.0% Asian, 0.2% American Indian and Alaska Native, 0.8% Hispanic of any race, 0.7% two or more races (2000); Density: 17.0 persons per square mile (2000); Age: 27.2% under 18, 17.4% over 64 (2000).
Religion: Five largest groups: 12.1% The United Methodist Church, 11.6% Christian Church (Disciples of Christ), 5.6% Old Order Amish Church, 2.7% General Association of Regular Baptist Churches, 2.0% Christian Churches and Churches of Christ (2000)
Economy: Unemployment rate: 3.5% (11/2002); Total civilian labor force: 4,399 (11/2002); Leading industries: 26.4% health care and social assistance; 20.8% manufacturing; 17.3% retail trade (2000); Companies that employ more than 1,000 persons: 0 (2000); Companies that employ more than 100 persons: 2 (2000); Farms: 884 totaling 266,508 acres (1997); Minority business ownership rate: 0.0% (1997); Women business ownership rate: 0.0% (1997); Retail sales per capita: $5,129 (1997). Single-family building permits issued: 7 (2001) / 8 (2000); Multi-family building permits issued: 0 (2001) / 0 (2000).
Income: Per capita income: $15,127 (2000); Median household income: $32,864 (2000); Poverty rate: 11.9% (2000); Bankruptcy rate: 4.23% (2001).
Taxes: Total county taxes per capita: $692 (2000); County property taxes per capita: $686 (2000).
Education: High school graduation rate: 78.9% (2000); College graduation rate: 11.4% (2000).
Housing: Homeownership rate: 79.8% (2000); Median home value: $55,000 (2000); Median rent: $271 per month (2000); Median age of housing: 45 years (2000).
Health: Birth rate: 119.4 per 10,000 population (1998); Age adjusted death rate: 69.1 per 10,000 population (1999); Age adjusted cancer mortality rate: 170.1 (Unreliable figure as per CDC) deaths per 100,000 population (1999). Number of physicians: 4.7 per 10,000 population (1999); Number of hospital beds: 78.4 per 10,000 population (1999).
Elections: 2000 Presidential election results: 45.0% Gore, 52.1% Bush, 1.8% Nader, 0.5% Buchanan
National and State Parks: Eldon State Game Area; Lake Wapello State Park
Additional Information Contacts
Davis County Government Offices 515-664-2344
Bloomfield Chamber of Commerce 641-664-1726

Davis County Communities

BLOOMFIELD (city). Covers a land area of 2.272 square miles and a water area of 0.027 square miles. Located at 40.75° N. Lat.; 92.41° W. Long. Elevation is 832 feet.
History: The name Bloomfield was selected by the county commissioners by drawing a slip of paper from a hat. The other two slips bore the names "Jefferson" and "Davis."
Population: 2,601 (2000); Race: 98.9% White, 0.2% Black, 0.0% Asian, 0.4% American Indian and Alaska Native, 0.5% Hispanic of any race, 0.5% two or more races (2000); Density: 1,145.0 persons per square mile (2000); Age: 19.1% under 18, 26.3% over 64 (2000); Marriage status: 17.6% never married, 58.0% now married, 14.4% widowed, 10.1% divorced (2000); Foreign born: 0.7% (2000); Ancestry (includes multiple ancestries): 25.7% German, 13.4% Irish, 12.6% English, 12.0% United States or American, 5.7% Dutch (2000).
Economy: Single-family building permits issued: 4 (2001) / 5 (2000); Multi-family building permits issued: 0 (2001) / 0 (2000); Employment by occupation: 8.1% management, 20.9% professional, 12.7% services, 22.0% sales, 1.5% farming, 13.3% construction, 21.5% production (2000).
Income: Per capita income: $17,962 (2000); Median household income: $31,471 (2000); Poverty rate: 8.6% (2000).
Taxes: Total city taxes per capita: $286 (2000); City property taxes per capita: $279 (2000).
Education: High school graduation rate: 81.5% (2000); College graduation rate: 14.2% (2000).

School District(s)
Davis County Community School District (PK-12)
2000 Enrollment: 1,308 641-664-2200
Housing: Homeownership rate: 73.9% (2000); Median home value: $53,300 (2000); Median rent: $279 per month (2000); Median age of housing: 51 years (2000).
Hospitals: Davis County Hospital (80 beds)
Safety: Violent crime rate: 11.5 per 10,000 population; Property crime rate: 154.0 per 10,000 population (2001).
Newspapers: The Bloomfield Democrat (1 x week)
Transportation: Commute to work: 92.4% car, 1.0% public transportation, 3.8% walk, 2.4% work from home (2000); Travel time to work: 55.8% less than 15 minutes, 15.7% 15 to 30 minutes, 20.1% 30 to 45 minutes, 2.8% 45 to 60 minutes, 5.6% 60 minutes or more (2000)
Additional Information Contacts
Bloomfield Chamber of Commerce 641-664-1726

DRAKESVILLE (city). Covers a land area of 0.248 square miles and a water area of 0 square miles. Located at 40.79° N. Lat.; 92.48° W. Long.
History: Drakesville was named for John Adams Drake, original owner of the townsite and a relative of the Englishman, Sir Francis Drake. Drakesville was laid out around a rectangular square, similar to the greens in England. Francis Marion Drake (1830-1903), one of Iowa's first governors (1896-1898), was born and raised here.
Population: 185 (2000); Race: 89.9% White, 0.7% Black, 0.0% Asian, 0.0% American Indian and Alaska Native, 8.0% Hispanic of any race, 9.4% two or more races (2000); Density: 746.4 persons per square mile (2000); Age: 27.5% under 18, 18.8% over 64 (2000); Marriage status: 12.9% never married, 57.4% now married, 7.9% widowed, 21.8% divorced (2000); Foreign born: 1.4% (2000); Ancestry (includes multiple ancestries): 18.1% English, 12.3% German, 8.7% United States or American, 5.8% Irish, 5.1% Other groups (2000).
Economy: Single-family building permits issued: 0 (2001) / 0 (2000); Multi-family building permits issued: 0 (2001) / 0 (2000); Employment by occupation: 6.0% management, 13.4% professional, 20.9% services, 26.9% sales, 0.0% farming, 10.4% construction, 22.4% production (2000).
Income: Per capita income: $13,063 (2000); Median household income: $26,875 (2000); Poverty rate: 11.6% (2000).
Taxes: Total city taxes per capita: $103 (1997); City property taxes per capita: $97 (1997).
Education: High school graduation rate: 79.1% (2000); College graduation rate: 9.9% (2000).
Housing: Homeownership rate: 81.4% (2000); Median home value: $32,100 (2000); Median rent: $238 per month (2000); Median age of housing: 60 years (2000).
Transportation: Commute to work: 89.6% car, 0.0% public transportation, 0.0% walk, 9.0% work from home (2000); Travel time to work: 27.9% less than 15 minutes, 47.5% 15 to 30 minutes, 11.5% 30 to 45 minutes, 6.6% 45 to 60 minutes, 6.6% 60 minutes or more (2000)

FLORIS (city). Covers a land area of 0.484 square miles and a water area of 0 square miles. Located at 40.86° N. Lat.; 92.33° W. Long. Elevation is 706 feet.
History: The name of Floris was chosen by Dr. O.C. Udell, probably because of the many flowers growing in the area.
Population: 153 (2000); Race: 96.1% White, 0.0% Black, 0.0% Asian, 0.0% American Indian and Alaska Native, 3.9% Hispanic of any race, 0.0% two or more races (2000); Density: 316.3 persons per square mile (2000); Age: 27.0% under 18, 18.4% over 64 (2000); Marriage status: 9.3% never married, 65.3% now married, 17.8% widowed, 7.6% divorced (2000); Foreign born: 1.3% (2000); Ancestry (includes multiple ancestries): 17.8% English, 16.4% United States or American, 13.8% German, 7.2% Swedish, 5.3% Other groups (2000).
Economy: Employment by occupation: 6.5% management, 6.5% professional, 6.5% services, 9.7% sales, 0.0% farming, 3.2% construction, 67.7% production (2000).
Income: Per capita income: $9,438 (2000); Median household income: $19,375 (2000); Poverty rate: 22.4% (2000).
Taxes: Total city taxes per capita: $56 (1997); City property taxes per capita: $51 (1997).
Education: High school graduation rate: 68.8% (2000); College graduation rate: 3.7% (2000).
Housing: Homeownership rate: 67.2% (2000); Median home value: $18,400 (2000); Median rent: $304 per month (2000); Median age of housing: 50 years (2000).
Transportation: Commute to work: 87.1% car, 0.0% public transportation, 12.9% walk, 0.0% work from home (2000); Travel time to work: 22.6% less than 15 minutes, 54.8% 15 to 30 minutes, 22.6% 30 to 45 minutes, 0.0% 45 to 60 minutes, 0.0% 60 minutes or more (2000)

PULASKI (city). Covers a land area of 0.372 square miles and a water area of 0 square miles. Located at 40.69° N. Lat.; 92.27° W. Long.
History: Pulaski was named in 1850 by Columbus Hains, the first postmaster, for Count Pulaski, Polish officer who aided the colonists in the American Revolution.

Population: 249 (2000); Race: 93.4% White, 0.0% Black, 0.0% Asian, 0.0% American Indian and Alaska Native, 0.0% Hispanic of any race, 6.6% two or more races (2000); Density: 669.3 persons per square mile (2000); Age: 27.4% under 18, 16.6% over 64 (2000); Marriage status: 13.1% never married, 70.2% now married, 8.6% widowed, 8.1% divorced (2000); Foreign born: 0.0% (2000); Ancestry (includes multiple ancestries): 38.2% German, 11.6% Irish, 11.6% Dutch, 8.9% United States or American, 7.3% Scotch-Irish (2000).
Economy: Single-family building permits issued: 3 (2001) / 3 (2000); Multi-family building permits issued: 0 (2001) / 0 (2000); Employment by occupation: 4.3% management, 14.7% professional, 10.3% services, 24.1% sales, 2.6% farming, 12.9% construction, 31.0% production (2000).
Income: Per capita income: $14,334 (2000); Median household income: $30,694 (2000); Poverty rate: 10.8% (2000).
Taxes: Total city taxes per capita: $31 (1997); City property taxes per capita: $31 (1997).
Education: High school graduation rate: 84.4% (2000); College graduation rate: 9.2% (2000).
Housing: Homeownership rate: 85.1% (2000); Median home value: $34,800 (2000); Median rent: $213 per month (2000); Median age of housing: 60+ years (2000).
Transportation: Commute to work: 95.6% car, 0.0% public transportation, 0.0% walk, 4.4% work from home (2000); Travel time to work: 15.6% less than 15 minutes, 33.0% 15 to 30 minutes, 28.4% 30 to 45 minutes, 12.8% 45 to 60 minutes, 10.1% 60 minutes or more (2000)

Decatur County

Located in southern Iowa; prairie area, bounded on the south by Missouri; drained by the Thompson and Weldon Rivers. Covers a land area of 531.80 square miles, a water area of 1.50 square miles, and is located in the Central Time Zone. The county government was organized in 1846. County seat is Leon.

Weather Station: Leon 6 ESE Elevation: 997 feet

	Jan	Feb	Mar	Apr	May	Jun	Jul	Aug	Sep	Oct	Nov	Dec
High	31	38	50	63	73	82	87	85	77	65	48	36
Low	12	17	28	38	49	59	64	61	52	40	29	17
Precip	1.0	1.2	2.3	3.7	5.0	4.3	4.6	4.3	4.2	3.2	2.4	1.4
Snow	6.8	5.5	3.6	1.7	0.0	0.0	0.0	0.0	0.0	0.1	2.5	6.1

High and Low temperatures in degrees Fahrenheit; Precipitation and Snow in inches

Population: 8,689 (2000); Race: 97.4% White, 0.8% Black, 0.5% Asian, 0.2% American Indian and Alaska Native, 1.3% Hispanic of any race, 1.0% two or more races (2000); Density: 16.3 persons per square mile (2000); Age: 23.1% under 18, 17.6% over 64 (2000).
Religion: Five largest groups: 11.2% Community of Christ, 7.4% The United Methodist Church, 4.6% Southern Baptist Convention, 3.0% Catholic Church, 2.9% The Church of Jesus Christ of Latter-day Saints (2000).
Economy: Unemployment rate: 4.9% (11/2002); Total civilian labor force: 3,983 (11/2002); Leading industries: 15.4% health care and social assistance; 11.0% retail trade; 8.3% manufacturing (2000); Companies that employ more than 1,000 persons: 0 (2000); Companies that employ more than 100 persons: 2 (2000); Farms: 730 totaling 261,927 acres (1997); Minority business ownership rate: 0.0% (1997); Women business ownership rate: 21.7% (1997); Retail sales per capita: $3,047 (1997). Single-family building permits issued: 5 (2001) / 7 (2000); Multi-family building permits issued: 0 (2001) / 3 (2000).
Income: Per capita income: $14,209 (2000); Median household income: $27,343 (2000); Poverty rate: 15.5% (2000); Bankruptcy rate: 2.86% (2001).
Taxes: Total county taxes per capita: $217 (1997); County property taxes per capita: $212 (1997).
Education: High school graduation rate: 81.7% (2000); College graduation rate: 15.1% (2000).
Housing: Homeownership rate: 71.1% (2000); Median home value: $45,400 (2000); Median rent: $258 per month (2000); Median age of housing: 43 years (2000).
Health: Birth rate: 105.9 per 10,000 population (1998); Age adjusted death rate: 81.8 per 10,000 population (1999); Age adjusted cancer mortality rate: 179.5 deaths per 100,000 population (1999). Number of physicians: 4.6 per 10,000 population (1999); Number of hospital beds: 56.4 per 10,000 population (1999).
Elections: 2000 Presidential election results: 45.1% Gore, 51.3% Bush, 2.5% Nader, 0.4% Buchanan
National and State Parks: Decatur State Wildlife Area; Nine Eagles State Park; Sand Creek State Wildlife Area

Additional Information Contacts
Decatur County Government Offices.................... 641-446-4382

Decatur County Communities

DAVIS CITY (city). Covers a land area of 0.586 square miles and a water area of 0 square miles. Located at 40.64° N. Lat.; 93.81° W. Long. Elevation is 914 feet.
History: Davis City was established at the site of William Davis' water-powered sawmill.
Population: 275 (2000); Race: 98.3% White, 0.0% Black, 0.0% Asian, 1.0% American Indian and Alaska Native, 0.7% Hispanic of any race, 0.0% two or more races (2000); Density: 469.5 persons per square mile (2000); Age: 27.2% under 18, 13.4% over 64 (2000); Marriage status: 22.6% never married, 55.8% now married, 4.0% widowed, 17.7% divorced (2000); Foreign born: 0.0% (2000); Ancestry (includes multiple ancestries): 29.3% German, 13.4% Irish, 13.1% United States or American, 12.1% English, 6.9% Dutch (2000).
Economy: Employment by occupation: 9.2% management, 1.8% professional, 30.3% services, 19.3% sales, 1.8% farming, 12.8% construction, 24.8% production (2000).
Income: Per capita income: $10,091 (2000); Median household income: $23,750 (2000); Poverty rate: 28.6% (2000).
Taxes: Total city taxes per capita: $57 (1997); City property taxes per capita: $49 (1997).
Education: High school graduation rate: 69.3% (2000); College graduation rate: 3.9% (2000).
Housing: Homeownership rate: 63.9% (2000); Median home value: $14,100 (2000); Median rent: $196 per month (2000); Median age of housing: 59 years (2000).
Transportation: Commute to work: 93.4% car, 0.0% public transportation, 1.9% walk, 1.9% work from home (2000); Travel time to work: 39.4% less than 15 minutes, 25.0% 15 to 30 minutes, 9.6% 30 to 45 minutes, 11.5% 45 to 60 minutes, 14.4% 60 minutes or more (2000)

DECATUR CITY (city). Aka Decatur. Covers a land area of 0.391 square miles and a water area of 0.003 square miles. Located at 40.74° N. Lat.; 93.83° W. Long. Elevation is 1,137 feet.
History: Decatur City took its name from the county, named in honor of naval officer Stephen Decatur, a commander in the War of 1812.
Population: 199 (2000); Race: 93.5% White, 2.7% Black, 0.0% Asian, 1.1% American Indian and Alaska Native, 2.7% Hispanic of any race, 0.0% two or more races (2000); Density: 508.5 persons per square mile (2000); Age: 21.0% under 18, 16.7% over 64 (2000); Marriage status: 18.4% never married, 56.3% now married, 16.5% widowed, 8.9% divorced (2000); Foreign born: 1.1% (2000); Ancestry (includes multiple ancestries): 17.7% German, 15.6% Irish, 10.2% Other groups, 9.7% United States or American, 6.5% English (2000).
Economy: Employment by occupation: 6.5% management, 4.3% professional, 13.0% services, 17.4% sales, 2.2% farming, 27.2% construction, 29.3% production (2000).
Income: Per capita income: $14,394 (2000); Median household income: $21,250 (2000); Poverty rate: 26.3% (2000).
Taxes: Total city taxes per capita: $70 (1997); City property taxes per capita: $64 (1997).
Education: High school graduation rate: 73.4% (2000); College graduation rate: 1.4% (2000).
Housing: Homeownership rate: 86.5% (2000); Median home value: $32,900 (2000); Median rent: $263 per month (2000); Median age of housing: 26 years (2000).
Transportation: Commute to work: 95.7% car, 0.0% public transportation, 2.2% walk, 2.2% work from home (2000); Travel time to work: 41.1% less than 15 minutes, 18.9% 15 to 30 minutes, 21.1% 30 to 45 minutes, 2.2% 45 to 60 minutes, 16.7% 60 minutes or more (2000)

GARDEN GROVE (city). Covers a land area of 0.696 square miles and a water area of 0 square miles. Located at 40.82° N. Lat.; 93.60° W. Long. Elevation is 1,110 feet.
History: Garden Grove was established and named by the Mormons as a rest camp and supply depot on the Mormon Trail, providing cabins and services for those heading west. The name remained after the Mormons left.
Population: 250 (2000); Race: 98.7% White, 0.0% Black, 0.0% Asian, 0.0% American Indian and Alaska Native, 0.0% Hispanic of any race, 1.3% two or more races (2000); Density: 359.0 persons per square mile (2000); Age: 29.0% under 18, 16.9% over 64 (2000); Marriage status: 26.9% never

married, 51.6% now married, 9.7% widowed, 11.8% divorced (2000); Foreign born: 0.0% (2000); Ancestry (includes multiple ancestries): 14.7% United States or American, 12.1% German, 10.0% Irish, 7.4% English, 6.1% Other groups (2000).
Economy: Employment by occupation: 5.7% management, 9.2% professional, 34.5% services, 12.6% sales, 2.3% farming, 12.6% construction, 23.0% production (2000).
Income: Per capita income: $10,301 (2000); Median household income: $19,844 (2000); Poverty rate: 35.5% (2000).
Taxes: Total city taxes per capita: $122 (1997); City property taxes per capita: $117 (1997).
Education: High school graduation rate: 69.5% (2000); College graduation rate: 3.5% (2000).
Housing: Homeownership rate: 77.2% (2000); Median home value: $20,000 (2000); Median rent: $257 per month (2000); Median age of housing: 60+ years (2000).
Transportation: Commute to work: 95.2% car, 1.2% public transportation, 2.4% walk, 0.0% work from home (2000); Travel time to work: 17.9% less than 15 minutes, 40.5% 15 to 30 minutes, 13.1% 30 to 45 minutes, 14.3% 45 to 60 minutes, 14.3% 60 minutes or more (2000)

GRAND RIVER (city). Covers a land area of 0.208 square miles and a water area of 0 square miles. Located at 40.81° N. Lat.; 93.96° W. Long. Elevation is 1,010 feet.
History: Grand River takes its name from the river on which it is located.
Population: 225 (2000); Race: 99.5% White, 0.0% Black, 0.5% Asian, 0.0% American Indian and Alaska Native, 0.0% Hispanic of any race, 0.0% two or more races (2000); Density: 1,079.8 persons per square mile (2000); Age: 21.6% under 18, 35.6% over 64 (2000); Marriage status: 14.5% never married, 57.8% now married, 13.3% widowed, 14.5% divorced (2000); Foreign born: 0.5% (2000); Ancestry (includes multiple ancestries): 13.9% German, 13.5% United States or American, 12.0% English, 11.5% Irish, 3.8% Italian (2000).
Economy: Employment by occupation: 9.7% management, 8.3% professional, 9.7% services, 29.2% sales, 2.8% farming, 11.1% construction, 29.2% production (2000).
Income: Per capita income: $14,272 (2000); Median household income: $22,344 (2000); Poverty rate: 14.9% (2000).
Taxes: Total city taxes per capita: $106 (1997); City property taxes per capita: $100 (1997).
Education: High school graduation rate: 76.5% (2000); College graduation rate: 6.7% (2000).
Housing: Homeownership rate: 76.8% (2000); Median home value: $23,300 (2000); Median rent: $225 per month (2000); Median age of housing: 60+ years (2000).
Transportation: Commute to work: 95.8% car, 0.0% public transportation, 4.2% walk, 0.0% work from home (2000); Travel time to work: 15.3% less than 15 minutes, 41.7% 15 to 30 minutes, 23.6% 30 to 45 minutes, 8.3% 45 to 60 minutes, 11.1% 60 minutes or more (2000)

LAMONI (city). Covers a land area of 3.211 square miles and a water area of 0.060 square miles. Located at 40.62° N. Lat.; 93.93° W. Long. Elevation is 1,126 feet.
History: Lamoni was platted in 1879 as a colony for members of the Mormon Church, who had came to Iowa from Missouri and Nauvoo, Illinois. The place was named for a "righteous king" recorded in the Book of Morman.
Population: 2,444 (2000); Race: 93.8% White, 1.9% Black, 1.3% Asian, 0.3% American Indian and Alaska Native, 2.6% Hispanic of any race, 2.4% two or more races (2000); Density: 761.1 persons per square mile (2000); Age: 15.3% under 18, 15.6% over 64 (2000); Marriage status: 47.0% never married, 40.8% now married, 7.0% widowed, 5.1% divorced (2000); Foreign born: 5.7% (2000); Ancestry (includes multiple ancestries): 15.9% German, 14.5% English, 13.2% Irish, 11.4% Other groups, 7.0% United States or American (2000).
Economy: Single-family building permits issued: 3 (2001) / 6 (2000); Multi-family building permits issued: 0 (2001) / 3 (2000); Employment by occupation: 8.0% management, 28.1% professional, 18.9% services, 32.5% sales, 0.6% farming, 5.1% construction, 6.7% production (2000).
Income: Per capita income: $13,105 (2000); Median household income: $24,735 (2000); Poverty rate: 19.6% (2000).
Taxes: Total city taxes per capita: $179 (1997); City property taxes per capita: $171 (1997).
Education: High school graduation rate: 86.4% (2000); College graduation rate: 32.3% (2000).

School District(s)

Lamoni Community School District (PK-12)
2000 Enrollment: 406 641-784-3342

Four-year College(s)

Graceland University-Lamoni (Private, Not-for-profit, Reorganized Latter Day Saints Church)
2001 Enrollment: 2,523 641-784-5000
2001 Tuition: In-state $13,025; Out-of-state $13,025

Housing: Homeownership rate: 53.5% (2000); Median home value: $68,900 (2000); Median rent: $277 per month (2000); Median age of housing: 38 years (2000).
Newspapers: Pony Express (1 x week); Lamoni Chronicle (1 x week)
Transportation: Commute to work: 69.9% car, 0.2% public transportation, 24.9% walk, 3.4% work from home (2000); Travel time to work: 81.2% less than 15 minutes, 6.5% 15 to 30 minutes, 4.3% 30 to 45 minutes, 1.3% 45 to 60 minutes, 6.7% 60 minutes or more (2000)

LE ROY (city). Covers a land area of 0.330 square miles and a water area of 0 square miles. Located at 40.87° N. Lat.; 93.59° W. Long.
History: Le Roy was named for a relative of early settler A. G. Buffum. Land for the town was donated by J. L. Young and E. S. Buffum.
Population: 13 (2000); Race: 100.0% White, 0.0% Black, 0.0% Asian, 0.0% American Indian and Alaska Native, 0.0% Hispanic of any race, 0.0% two or more races (2000); Density: 39.4 persons per square mile (2000); Age: 26.7% under 18, 26.7% over 64 (2000); Marriage status: 15.4% never married, 61.5% now married, 0.0% widowed, 23.1% divorced (2000); Foreign born: 0.0% (2000); Ancestry (includes multiple ancestries): 20.0% Irish, 13.3% United States or American (2000).
Economy: Employment by occupation: 0.0% management, 0.0% professional, 50.0% services, 0.0% sales, 0.0% farming, 0.0% construction, 50.0% production (2000).
Income: Per capita income: $14,560 (2000); Median household income: $33,125 (2000); Poverty rate: 0.0% (2000).
Taxes: Total city taxes per capita: $30 (1997); City property taxes per capita: $30 (1997).
Education: High school graduation rate: 100.0% (2000); College graduation rate: 18.2% (2000).
Housing: Homeownership rate: 100.0% (2000); Median home value: <$10,000 (2000); Median age of housing: 56 years (2000).
Transportation: Commute to work: 50.0% car, 0.0% public transportation, 50.0% walk, 0.0% work from home (2000); Travel time to work: 50.0% less than 15 minutes, 0.0% 15 to 30 minutes, 50.0% 30 to 45 minutes, 0.0% 45 to 60 minutes, 0.0% 60 minutes or more (2000)

LEON (city). Covers a land area of 3.143 square miles and a water area of 0.010 square miles. Located at 40.74° N. Lat.; 93.74° W. Long. Elevation is 1,019 feet.
History: Leon was to be called Independence, but as a settlement of that name had already been established in Iowa, the town was called South Independence until the winter of 1854-55; then the State Legislature changed the name to Leon in response to a petition submitted by citizens of that community.
Population: 1,983 (2000); Race: 99.6% White, 0.3% Black, 0.0% Asian, 0.0% American Indian and Alaska Native, 0.0% Hispanic of any race, 0.2% two or more races (2000); Density: 630.9 persons per square mile (2000); Age: 25.1% under 18, 23.0% over 64 (2000); Marriage status: 15.5% never married, 60.4% now married, 12.6% widowed, 11.5% divorced (2000); Foreign born: 0.0% (2000); Ancestry (includes multiple ancestries): 21.8% German, 12.6% Irish, 12.1% English, 9.4% United States or American, 4.8% Other groups (2000).
Economy: Single-family building permits issued: 2 (2001) / 1 (2000); Multi-family building permits issued: 0 (2001) / 0 (2000); Employment by occupation: 5.9% management, 21.5% professional, 19.1% services, 19.2% sales, 2.3% farming, 11.4% construction, 20.5% production (2000).
Income: Per capita income: $13,015 (2000); Median household income: $24,390 (2000); Poverty rate: 16.6% (2000).
Taxes: Total city taxes per capita: $231 (1997); City property taxes per capita: $224 (1997).
Education: High school graduation rate: 76.1% (2000); College graduation rate: 12.9% (2000).

School District(s)

Central Decatur Community School District (PK-12)
2000 Enrollment: 753 641-446-4818

Housing: Homeownership rate: 66.9% (2000); Median home value: $39,600 (2000); Median rent: $253 per month (2000); Median age of housing: 48 years (2000).

Hospitals: Decatur County Hospital (49 beds)
Newspapers: The Journal-Reporter (1 x week)
Transportation: Commute to work: 86.7% car, 1.4% public transportation, 5.1% walk, 5.4% work from home (2000); Travel time to work: 56.5% less than 15 minutes, 14.6% 15 to 30 minutes, 14.2% 30 to 45 minutes, 3.5% 45 to 60 minutes, 11.2% 60 minutes or more (2000)

PLEASANTON (city). Covers a land area of 0.344 square miles and a water area of 0 square miles. Located at 40.58° N. Lat.; 93.74° W. Long.
History: Pleasanton was once known as Pleasant Plains.
Population: 37 (2000); Race: 100.0% White, 0.0% Black, 0.0% Asian, 0.0% American Indian and Alaska Native, 0.0% Hispanic of any race, 0.0% two or more races (2000); Density: 107.6 persons per square mile (2000); Age: 0.0% under 18, 75.0% over 64 (2000); Marriage status: 0.0% never married, 68.8% now married, 12.5% widowed, 18.8% divorced (2000); Foreign born: 0.0% (2000); Ancestry (includes multiple ancestries): 62.5% German, 31.3% English, 18.8% French (except Basque), 12.5% Swedish, 12.5% Irish (2000).
Economy: Employment by occupation: 100.0% management, 0.0% professional, 0.0% services, 0.0% sales, 0.0% farming, 0.0% construction, 0.0% production (2000).
Income: Per capita income: $29,231 (2000); Median household income: $51,250 (2000); Poverty rate: 12.5% (2000).
Taxes: Total city taxes per capita: $117 (1997); City property taxes per capita: $17 (1997).
Education: High school graduation rate: 87.5% (2000); College graduation rate: 0.0% (2000).
Housing: Homeownership rate: 83.3% (2000); Median home value: $37,500 (2000); Median age of housing: 60+ years (2000).
Transportation: Commute to work: 100.0% car, 0.0% public transportation, 0.0% walk, 0.0% work from home (2000); Travel time to work: 0.0% less than 15 minutes, 0.0% 15 to 30 minutes, 100.0% 30 to 45 minutes, 0.0% 45 to 60 minutes, 0.0% 60 minutes or more (2000)

VAN WERT (city). Covers a land area of 0.331 square miles and a water area of 0.005 square miles. Located at 40.87° N. Lat.; 93.79° W. Long. Elevation is 1,155 feet.
History: Van Wert was named after Van Wert, Ohio.
Population: 231 (2000); Race: 99.1% White, 0.0% Black, 0.9% Asian, 0.0% American Indian and Alaska Native, 1.7% Hispanic of any race, 0.0% two or more races (2000); Density: 697.6 persons per square mile (2000); Age: 13.9% under 18, 12.6% over 64 (2000); Marriage status: 21.8% never married, 61.4% now married, 5.0% widowed, 11.9% divorced (2000); Foreign born: 0.9% (2000); Ancestry (includes multiple ancestries): 23.4% German, 13.0% Other groups, 12.6% Irish, 8.7% Dutch, 8.2% United States or American (2000).
Economy: Employment by occupation: 7.6% management, 6.1% professional, 10.6% services, 25.0% sales, 0.0% farming, 15.9% construction, 34.8% production (2000).
Income: Per capita income: $16,564 (2000); Median household income: $34,375 (2000); Poverty rate: 5.6% (2000).
Taxes: Total city taxes per capita: $51 (1997); City property taxes per capita: $47 (1997).
Education: High school graduation rate: 69.6% (2000); College graduation rate: 7.6% (2000).
Housing: Homeownership rate: 82.5% (2000); Median home value: $33,300 (2000); Median rent: $306 per month (2000); Median age of housing: 45 years (2000).
Transportation: Commute to work: 96.0% car, 0.0% public transportation, 0.0% walk, 1.6% work from home (2000); Travel time to work: 18.5% less than 15 minutes, 59.7% 15 to 30 minutes, 4.8% 30 to 45 minutes, 9.7% 45 to 60 minutes, 7.3% 60 minutes or more (2000)

WELDON (city). Covers a land area of 0.179 square miles and a water area of 0 square miles. Located at 40.89° N. Lat.; 93.73° W. Long. Elevation is 1,146 feet.
History: Weldon was named for the Weldon River.
Population: 145 (2000); Race: 100.0% White, 0.0% Black, 0.0% Asian, 0.0% American Indian and Alaska Native, 0.0% Hispanic of any race, 0.0% two or more races (2000); Density: 808.6 persons per square mile (2000); Age: 33.7% under 18, 7.8% over 64 (2000); Marriage status: 21.0% never married, 58.8% now married, 2.5% widowed, 17.6% divorced (2000); Foreign born: 0.0% (2000); Ancestry (includes multiple ancestries): 25.3% German, 16.3% United States or American, 10.2% Irish, 7.2% Dutch, 7.2% English (2000).
Economy: Employment by occupation: 1.3% management, 7.9% professional, 19.7% services, 11.8% sales, 0.0% farming, 10.5% construction, 48.7% production (2000).
Income: Per capita income: $11,315 (2000); Median household income: $28,750 (2000); Poverty rate: 14.4% (2000).
Taxes: Total city taxes per capita: $53 (1997); City property taxes per capita: $53 (1997).
Education: High school graduation rate: 86.7% (2000); College graduation rate: 1.0% (2000).
Housing: Homeownership rate: 96.8% (2000); Median home value: $26,000 (2000); Median age of housing: 60+ years (2000).
Transportation: Commute to work: 100.0% car, 0.0% public transportation, 0.0% walk, 0.0% work from home (2000); Travel time to work: 10.0% less than 15 minutes, 43.8% 15 to 30 minutes, 6.3% 30 to 45 minutes, 16.3% 45 to 60 minutes, 23.8% 60 minutes or more (2000)

Delaware County

Located in eastern Iowa; prairie area drained by the Maquoketa River. Covers a land area of 577.90 square miles, a water area of 1.20 square miles, and is located in the Central Time Zone. The county government was organized in 1837. County seat is Manchester.

Weather Station: Manchester 2 — Elevation: 987 feet

	Jan	Feb	Mar	Apr	May	Jun	Jul	Aug	Sep	Oct	Nov	Dec
High	25	31	44	58	71	80	83	81	74	61	44	31
Low	6	13	24	35	47	57	61	58	49	37	25	13
Precip	0.9	0.9	1.9	3.3	3.9	4.4	4.5	5.3	3.3	2.7	2.3	1.1
Snow	9.3	6.0	3.8	1.5	tr	0.0	0.0	0.0	0.0	0.2	3.0	7.1

High and Low temperatures in degrees Fahrenheit; Precipitation and Snow in inches

Population: 18,404 (2000); Race: 99.1% White, 0.0% Black, 0.2% Asian, 0.2% American Indian and Alaska Native, 0.6% Hispanic of any race, 0.4% two or more races (2000); Density: 31.8 persons per square mile (2000); Age: 29.0% under 18, 15.0% over 64 (2000).
Religion: Five largest groups: 57.1% Catholic Church, 11.5% The United Methodist Church, 8.8% Evangelical Lutheran Church in America, 3.2% Lutheran Church—Missouri Synod, 3.0% Presbyterian Church (U.S.A.) (2000).
Economy: Unemployment rate: 5.9% (11/2002); Total civilian labor force: 9,819 (11/2002); Leading industries: 33.7% manufacturing; 15.6% retail trade; 12.4% health care and social assistance (2000); Companies that employ more than 1,000 persons: 0 (2000); Companies that employ more than 100 persons: 7 (2000); Farms: 1,278 totaling 326,187 acres (1997); Minority business ownership rate: 0.0% (1997); Women business ownership rate: 15.5% (1997); Retail sales per capita: $6,005 (1997). Single-family building permits issued: 19 (2001) / 17 (2000); Multi-family building permits issued: 2 (2001) / 0 (2000).
Income: Per capita income: $17,327 (2000); Median household income: $37,168 (2000); Poverty rate: 7.9% (2000); Bankruptcy rate: 2.58% (2001).
Taxes: Total county taxes per capita: $228 (2000); County property taxes per capita: $188 (2000).
Education: High school graduation rate: 85.1% (2000); College graduation rate: 13.0% (2000).
Housing: Homeownership rate: 78.0% (2000); Median home value: $79,700 (2000); Median rent: $284 per month (2000); Median age of housing: 40 years (2000).
Health: Birth rate: 134.2 per 10,000 population (1998); Age adjusted death rate: 71.7 per 10,000 population (1999); Age adjusted cancer mortality rate: 151.2 deaths per 100,000 population (1999). Air Quality Index: 100% good, 0% moderate, 0% unhealthy (percent of days in 2000). Number of physicians: 4.3 per 10,000 population (1999); Number of hospital beds: 19.0 per 10,000 population (1999).
Elections: 2000 Presidential election results: 45.6% Gore, 51.2% Bush, 1.9% Nader, 0.5% Buchanan
National and State Parks: Backbone State Forest; Backbone State Park
Additional Information Contacts
Delaware County Government Offices 563-927-2515
Backbone Board of Realtors. 563-556-5721
Manchester Chamber of Commerce. 563-927-4141

Delaware County Communities

COLESBURG (city). Covers a land area of 0.294 square miles and a water area of 0 square miles. Located at 42.64° N. Lat.; 91.20° W. Long. Elevation is 1,157 feet.

History: Both Hiram Cole, a proprietor, and James Cole, a surveyor, were part of the early history of Colesburg, originally spelled Cole's Burgh.
Population: 412 (2000); Race: 100.0% White, 0.0% Black, 0.0% Asian, 0.0% American Indian and Alaska Native, 0.0% Hispanic of any race, 0.0% two or more races (2000); Density: 1,399.9 persons per square mile (2000); Age: 20.7% under 18, 25.7% over 64 (2000); Marriage status: 19.8% never married, 63.5% now married, 10.8% widowed, 5.9% divorced (2000); Foreign born: 1.9% (2000); Ancestry (includes multiple ancestries): 48.8% German, 11.2% United States or American, 6.9% English, 6.2% Irish, 2.1% Other groups (2000).
Economy: Single-family building permits issued: 1 (2001) / 1 (2000); Multi-family building permits issued: 0 (2001) / 0 (2000); Employment by occupation: 8.8% management, 8.8% professional, 12.3% services, 21.1% sales, 0.0% farming, 16.2% construction, 32.8% production (2000).
Income: Per capita income: $16,638 (2000); Median household income: $33,068 (2000); Poverty rate: 5.2% (2000).
Taxes: Total city taxes per capita: $295 (1997); City property taxes per capita: $234 (1997).
Education: High school graduation rate: 80.1% (2000); College graduation rate: 11.1% (2000).
Housing: Homeownership rate: 85.0% (2000); Median home value: $58,000 (2000); Median rent: $154 per month (2000); Median age of housing: 47 years (2000).
Transportation: Commute to work: 92.0% car, 0.0% public transportation, 3.0% walk, 5.0% work from home (2000); Travel time to work: 25.4% less than 15 minutes, 33.9% 15 to 30 minutes, 27.0% 30 to 45 minutes, 8.5% 45 to 60 minutes, 5.3% 60 minutes or more (2000)

DELAWARE (city). Covers a land area of 0.799 square miles and a water area of 0.011 square miles. Located at 42.47° N. Lat.; 91.34° W. Long.
History: Delaware takes its name from the county, which was named by settlers from the state of Delaware.
Population: 188 (2000); Race: 100.0% White, 0.0% Black, 0.0% Asian, 0.0% American Indian and Alaska Native, 3.8% Hispanic of any race, 0.0% two or more races (2000); Density: 235.4 persons per square mile (2000); Age: 23.0% under 18, 13.1% over 64 (2000); Marriage status: 20.0% never married, 68.0% now married, 5.3% widowed, 6.7% divorced (2000); Foreign born: 0.0% (2000); Ancestry (includes multiple ancestries): 57.4% German, 10.9% Irish, 4.4% English, 2.7% Scottish, 2.2% Scotch-Irish (2000).
Economy: Single-family building permits issued: 1 (2001) / 1 (2000); Multi-family building permits issued: 0 (2001) / 0 (2000); Employment by occupation: 1.0% management, 7.9% professional, 21.8% services, 17.8% sales, 0.0% farming, 18.8% construction, 32.7% production (2000).
Income: Per capita income: $18,361 (2000); Median household income: $36,875 (2000); Poverty rate: 4.4% (2000).
Taxes: Total city taxes per capita: $107 (1997); City property taxes per capita: $56 (1997).
Education: High school graduation rate: 76.1% (2000); College graduation rate: 1.4% (2000).
Housing: Homeownership rate: 90.7% (2000); Median home value: $53,800 (2000); Median rent: $242 per month (2000); Median age of housing: 29 years (2000).
Transportation: Commute to work: 87.1% car, 0.0% public transportation, 5.0% walk, 7.9% work from home (2000); Travel time to work: 51.6% less than 15 minutes, 25.8% 15 to 30 minutes, 4.3% 30 to 45 minutes, 5.4% 45 to 60 minutes, 12.9% 60 minutes or more (2000)

DELHI (city). Covers a land area of 0.973 square miles and a water area of 0.054 square miles. Located at 42.42° N. Lat.; 91.33° W. Long. Elevation is 998 feet.
History: Delhi was the home of J. L. McCreery, who wrote the poem "There is No Death."
Population: 458 (2000); Race: 100.0% White, 0.0% Black, 0.0% Asian, 0.0% American Indian and Alaska Native, 0.0% Hispanic of any race, 0.0% two or more races (2000); Density: 470.8 persons per square mile (2000); Age: 22.7% under 18, 21.8% over 64 (2000); Marriage status: 22.9% never married, 57.7% now married, 6.5% widowed, 12.8% divorced (2000); Foreign born: 0.0% (2000); Ancestry (includes multiple ancestries): 44.3% German, 15.8% Irish, 12.8% United States or American, 6.6% English, 4.7% French (except Basque) (2000).
Economy: Single-family building permits issued: 1 (2001) / 0 (2000); Multi-family building permits issued: 0 (2001) / 0 (2000); Employment by occupation: 8.1% management, 20.2% professional, 7.3% services, 25.1% sales, 0.0% farming, 10.5% construction, 28.7% production (2000).
Income: Per capita income: $19,751 (2000); Median household income: $38,636 (2000); Poverty rate: 5.7% (2000).
Taxes: Total city taxes per capita: $286 (1997); City property taxes per capita: $230 (1997).
Education: High school graduation rate: 86.5% (2000); College graduation rate: 16.5% (2000).

School District(s)

Maquoketa Valley Community School District (PK-12)
2000 Enrollment: 991 319-922-9422
Housing: Homeownership rate: 85.5% (2000); Median home value: $83,800 (2000); Median rent: $310 per month (2000); Median age of housing: 35 years (2000).
Transportation: Commute to work: 82.6% car, 0.0% public transportation, 13.4% walk, 4.0% work from home (2000); Travel time to work: 42.6% less than 15 minutes, 25.7% 15 to 30 minutes, 9.3% 30 to 45 minutes, 9.7% 45 to 60 minutes, 12.7% 60 minutes or more (2000)

DUNDEE (city). Covers a land area of 0.405 square miles and a water area of 0 square miles. Located at 42.57° N. Lat.; 91.54° W. Long. Elevation is 998 feet.
History: The name of Dundee probably refers to the Scottish Dundee, and was suggested by the man who donated the land for the railroad right-of-way.
Population: 179 (2000); Race: 100.0% White, 0.0% Black, 0.0% Asian, 0.0% American Indian and Alaska Native, 0.0% Hispanic of any race, 0.0% two or more races (2000); Density: 441.7 persons per square mile (2000); Age: 25.0% under 18, 28.0% over 64 (2000); Marriage status: 17.2% never married, 71.9% now married, 6.3% widowed, 4.7% divorced (2000); Foreign born: 0.0% (2000); Ancestry (includes multiple ancestries): 52.4% German, 12.8% Irish, 9.8% English, 3.7% Other groups, 2.4% Dutch (2000).
Economy: Employment by occupation: 5.1% management, 16.7% professional, 15.4% services, 20.5% sales, 0.0% farming, 14.1% construction, 28.2% production (2000).
Income: Per capita income: $13,531 (2000); Median household income: $26,719 (2000); Poverty rate: 9.8% (2000).
Taxes: Total city taxes per capita: $103 (1997); City property taxes per capita: $52 (1997).
Education: High school graduation rate: 84.3% (2000); College graduation rate: 8.7% (2000).
Housing: Homeownership rate: 85.1% (2000); Median home value: $52,500 (2000); Median rent: $283 per month (2000); Median age of housing: 60+ years (2000).
Transportation: Commute to work: 82.9% car, 0.0% public transportation, 3.9% walk, 13.2% work from home (2000); Travel time to work: 19.7% less than 15 minutes, 47.0% 15 to 30 minutes, 15.2% 30 to 45 minutes, 0.0% 45 to 60 minutes, 18.2% 60 minutes or more (2000)

EARLVILLE (city). Covers a land area of 0.546 square miles and a water area of 0 square miles. Located at 42.48° N. Lat.; 91.27° W. Long.
History: Earlville, originally called Nottingham, was renamed for George M. Earl, an early resident in the vicinity.
Population: 900 (2000); Race: 99.3% White, 0.0% Black, 0.0% Asian, 0.3% American Indian and Alaska Native, 2.0% Hispanic of any race, 0.0% two or more races (2000); Density: 1,648.0 persons per square mile (2000); Age: 30.3% under 18, 17.8% over 64 (2000); Marriage status: 27.1% never married, 56.3% now married, 8.6% widowed, 8.0% divorced (2000); Foreign born: 0.8% (2000); Ancestry (includes multiple ancestries): 50.8% German, 9.5% Irish, 8.4% United States or American, 7.8% English, 3.6% Norwegian (2000).
Economy: Single-family building permits issued: 0 (2001) / 0 (2000); Multi-family building permits issued: 0 (2001) / 0 (2000); Employment by occupation: 7.8% management, 16.9% professional, 16.7% services, 19.8% sales, 1.4% farming, 10.4% construction, 27.1% production (2000).
Income: Per capita income: $14,855 (2000); Median household income: $38,194 (2000); Poverty rate: 6.6% (2000).
Taxes: Total city taxes per capita: $210 (1997); City property taxes per capita: $157 (1997).
Education: High school graduation rate: 81.2% (2000); College graduation rate: 11.2% (2000).
Housing: Homeownership rate: 78.1% (2000); Median home value: $67,300 (2000); Median rent: $307 per month (2000); Median age of housing: 48 years (2000).
Transportation: Commute to work: 90.2% car, 0.0% public transportation, 3.8% walk, 4.5% work from home (2000); Travel time to work: 39.7% less than 15 minutes, 40.9% 15 to 30 minutes, 5.0% 30 to 45 minutes, 4.7% 45 to 60 minutes, 9.7% 60 minutes or more (2000)
Additional Information Contacts
Backbone Board of Realtors. 563-556-5721

EDGEWOOD (city). Covers a land area of 0.845 square miles and a water area of 0 square miles. Located at 42.64° N. Lat.; 91.40° W. Long.
History: Edgewood was first known as Yankee Settlement and renamed in 1875.
Population: 923 (2000); Race: 100.0% White, 0.0% Black, 0.0% Asian, 0.0% American Indian and Alaska Native, 0.0% Hispanic of any race, 0.0% two or more races (2000); Density: 1,092.6 persons per square mile (2000); Age: 25.1% under 18, 20.9% over 64 (2000); Marriage status: 20.4% never married, 55.8% now married, 15.9% widowed, 7.8% divorced (2000); Foreign born: 0.0% (2000); Ancestry (includes multiple ancestries): 48.1% German, 10.6% Irish, 8.1% English, 8.0% United States or American, 3.5% French (except Basque) (2000).
Economy: Single-family building permits issued: 2 (2001) / 1 (2000); Multi-family building permits issued: 2 (2001) / 0 (2000); Employment by occupation: 10.0% management, 17.9% professional, 17.0% services, 16.6% sales, 1.1% farming, 9.1% construction, 28.3% production (2000).
Income: Per capita income: $16,187 (2000); Median household income: $35,455 (2000); Poverty rate: 4.7% (2000).
Taxes: Total city taxes per capita: $301 (1997); City property taxes per capita: $246 (1997).
Education: High school graduation rate: 78.3% (2000); College graduation rate: 11.0% (2000).

School District(s)

Edgewood-Colesburg Community School District (KG-12)
2000 Enrollment: 639 319-928-6411
Housing: Homeownership rate: 78.2% (2000); Median home value: $69,800 (2000); Median rent: $295 per month (2000); Median age of housing: 45 years (2000).
Newspapers: The Edgewood Reminder (1 x week)
Transportation: Commute to work: 85.5% car, 1.5% public transportation, 7.6% walk, 3.9% work from home (2000); Travel time to work: 43.3% less than 15 minutes, 22.8% 15 to 30 minutes, 14.0% 30 to 45 minutes, 7.2% 45 to 60 minutes, 12.6% 60 minutes or more (2000)

GREELEY (city). Covers a land area of 0.378 square miles and a water area of 0 square miles. Located at 42.58° N. Lat.; 91.34° W. Long. Elevation is 1,143 feet.
History: Greeley, first called Plum Spring, was renamed in 1863 in honor of Horace Greeley, the journalist. The Holbert Horse Farm, known by horse breeders thoroughout the world, was established here in 1877.
Population: 276 (2000); Race: 100.0% White, 0.0% Black, 0.0% Asian, 0.0% American Indian and Alaska Native, 0.0% Hispanic of any race, 0.0% two or more races (2000); Density: 729.7 persons per square mile (2000); Age: 22.8% under 18, 14.7% over 64 (2000); Marriage status: 21.1% never married, 63.8% now married, 6.0% widowed, 9.1% divorced (2000); Foreign born: 0.0% (2000); Ancestry (includes multiple ancestries): 37.2% German, 17.9% United States or American, 13.3% Irish, 7.4% English, 3.2% Dutch (2000).
Economy: Employment by occupation: 7.4% management, 3.0% professional, 12.6% services, 20.7% sales, 0.7% farming, 21.5% construction, 34.1% production (2000).
Income: Per capita income: $15,508 (2000); Median household income: $35,000 (2000); Poverty rate: 10.2% (2000).
Taxes: Total city taxes per capita: $124 (1997); City property taxes per capita: $76 (1997).
Education: High school graduation rate: 77.6% (2000); College graduation rate: 5.2% (2000).
Housing: Homeownership rate: 91.2% (2000); Median home value: $48,000 (2000); Median rent: $150 per month (2000); Median age of housing: 59 years (2000).
Transportation: Commute to work: 87.2% car, 0.0% public transportation, 9.8% walk, 1.5% work from home (2000); Travel time to work: 25.2% less than 15 minutes, 42.0% 15 to 30 minutes, 14.5% 30 to 45 minutes, 11.5% 45 to 60 minutes, 6.9% 60 minutes or more (2000)

HOPKINTON (city). Covers a land area of 0.617 square miles and a water area of 0 square miles. Located at 42.34° N. Lat.; 91.24° W. Long. Elevation is 806 feet.
History: One of the founders of Hopkinton came from Hopkinton, Massachusetts, and the town was named for her. The town has also been called Hoptown.
Population: 681 (2000); Race: 98.9% White, 0.0% Black, 0.5% Asian, 0.0% American Indian and Alaska Native, 0.3% Hispanic of any race, 0.6% two or more races (2000); Density: 1,103.5 persons per square mile (2000); Age: 30.0% under 18, 14.6% over 64 (2000); Marriage status: 25.2% never married, 58.2% now married, 9.8% widowed, 6.8% divorced (2000); Foreign born: 0.9% (2000); Ancestry (includes multiple ancestries): 46.2% German, 12.4% Irish, 10.3% English, 8.3% United States or American, 5.0% French (except Basque) (2000).
Economy: Single-family building permits issued: 2 (2001) / 3 (2000); Multi-family building permits issued: 0 (2001) / 0 (2000); Employment by occupation: 5.4% management, 9.5% professional, 14.9% services, 22.0% sales, 0.6% farming, 10.7% construction, 36.9% production (2000).
Income: Per capita income: $13,707 (2000); Median household income: $33,958 (2000); Poverty rate: 4.9% (2000).
Taxes: Total city taxes per capita: $240 (1997); City property taxes per capita: $187 (1997).
Education: High school graduation rate: 85.1% (2000); College graduation rate: 5.7% (2000).
Housing: Homeownership rate: 81.0% (2000); Median home value: $66,100 (2000); Median rent: $220 per month (2000); Median age of housing: 52 years (2000).
Newspapers: Delaware County Leader (1 x week); The Delhi Shopper (1 x week); The Earlville Reminder
Transportation: Commute to work: 91.6% car, 0.0% public transportation, 3.9% walk, 4.2% work from home (2000); Travel time to work: 41.2% less than 15 minutes, 33.6% 15 to 30 minutes, 7.9% 30 to 45 minutes, 11.3% 45 to 60 minutes, 6.0% 60 minutes or more (2000)

MANCHESTER (city). Covers a land area of 4.126 square miles and a water area of 0.015 square miles. Located at 42.48° N. Lat.; 91.45° W. Long. Elevation is 942 feet.
History: Manchester was originally known as Burrington, but the name was changed because of the similarity to Burlington. According to one story, the town name was created by twisting Chesterman, the name of an early settler. But it is more probable that the town was named for Manchester, England, home of many of the early residents.
Population: 5,257 (2000); Race: 98.7% White, 0.0% Black, 0.4% Asian, 0.0% American Indian and Alaska Native, 0.7% Hispanic of any race, 0.8% two or more races (2000); Density: 1,274.0 persons per square mile (2000); Age: 26.4% under 18, 20.0% over 64 (2000); Marriage status: 22.8% never married, 57.0% now married, 11.1% widowed, 9.1% divorced (2000); Foreign born: 1.0% (2000); Ancestry (includes multiple ancestries): 49.8% German, 15.1% Irish, 12.4% English, 7.7% United States or American, 5.6% Other groups (2000).
Economy: Single-family building permits issued: 12 (2001) / 11 (2000); Multi-family building permits issued: 0 (2001) / 0 (2000); Employment by occupation: 8.6% management, 16.7% professional, 16.8% services, 22.2% sales, 0.7% farming, 9.4% construction, 25.5% production (2000).
Income: Per capita income: $18,811 (2000); Median household income: $31,099 (2000); Poverty rate: 9.8% (2000).
Taxes: Total city taxes per capita: $431 (2000); City property taxes per capita: $360 (2000).
Education: High school graduation rate: 84.7% (2000); College graduation rate: 19.1% (2000).

School District(s)

West Delaware County Community School District (KG-12)
2000 Enrollment: 1,931 319-927-3515
Housing: Homeownership rate: 70.8% (2000); Median home value: $75,400 (2000); Median rent: $298 per month (2000); Median age of housing: 42 years (2000).
Hospitals: Regional Medical Center of Northeast Iowa (37 beds)
Newspapers: The Manchester Press (1 x week)
Transportation: Commute to work: 90.0% car, 0.6% public transportation, 5.0% walk, 4.0% work from home (2000); Travel time to work: 65.4% less than 15 minutes, 13.8% 15 to 30 minutes, 5.3% 30 to 45 minutes, 11.2% 45 to 60 minutes, 4.3% 60 minutes or more (2000)
Airports: Manchester Municipal
Additional Information Contacts
Manchester Chamber of Commerce. 563-927-4141

MASONVILLE (city). Covers a land area of 0.330 square miles and a water area of 0 square miles. Located at 42.48° N. Lat.; 91.59° W. Long. Elevation is 1,004 feet.
History: Masonville is named for landowner A. R. Mason. The town was mapped in 1858.
Population: 104 (2000); Race: 99.0% White, 0.0% Black, 0.0% Asian, 0.0% American Indian and Alaska Native, 0.0% Hispanic of any race, 1.0% two or more races (2000); Density: 315.3 persons per square mile (2000); Age: 10.1% under 18, 13.1% over 64 (2000); Marriage status: 32.3% never married, 53.1% now married, 5.2% widowed, 9.4% divorced (2000); Foreign

born: 0.0% (2000); Ancestry (includes multiple ancestries): 39.4% German, 16.2% Irish, 12.1% English, 11.1% United States or American, 8.1% French (except Basque) (2000).
Economy: Employment by occupation: 2.6% management, 7.9% professional, 28.9% services, 17.1% sales, 0.0% farming, 14.5% construction, 28.9% production (2000).
Income: Per capita income: $20,166 (2000); Median household income: $32,000 (2000); Poverty rate: 5.1% (2000).
Taxes: Total city taxes per capita: $315 (1997); City property taxes per capita: $260 (1997).
Education: High school graduation rate: 91.3% (2000); College graduation rate: 5.8% (2000).
Housing: Homeownership rate: 86.0% (2000); Median home value: $38,800 (2000); Median rent: $192 per month (2000); Median age of housing: 60+ years (2000).
Transportation: Commute to work: 84.2% car, 0.0% public transportation, 13.2% walk, 2.6% work from home (2000); Travel time to work: 45.9% less than 15 minutes, 36.5% 15 to 30 minutes, 9.5% 30 to 45 minutes, 2.7% 45 to 60 minutes, 5.4% 60 minutes or more (2000)

RYAN (city). Covers a land area of 0.430 square miles and a water area of 0 square miles. Located at 42.35° N. Lat.; 91.48° W. Long. Elevation is 1,000 feet.
History: Ryan was named for Father Patrick Ryan, first rector of the Catholic Church here.
Population: 410 (2000); Race: 99.8% White, 0.0% Black, 0.0% Asian, 0.0% American Indian and Alaska Native, 0.0% Hispanic of any race, 0.2% two or more races (2000); Density: 953.1 persons per square mile (2000); Age: 33.0% under 18, 8.0% over 64 (2000); Marriage status: 28.6% never married, 61.5% now married, 6.0% widowed, 4.0% divorced (2000); Foreign born: 0.5% (2000); Ancestry (includes multiple ancestries): 39.3% Irish, 33.3% German, 6.1% English, 3.9% French (except Basque), 3.9% Other groups (2000).
Economy: Employment by occupation: 11.0% management, 11.9% professional, 13.7% services, 23.3% sales, 0.0% farming, 15.1% construction, 25.1% production (2000).
Income: Per capita income: $14,576 (2000); Median household income: $34,250 (2000); Poverty rate: 8.7% (2000).
Taxes: Total city taxes per capita: $216 (1997); City property taxes per capita: $161 (1997).
Education: High school graduation rate: 84.1% (2000); College graduation rate: 6.0% (2000).
Housing: Homeownership rate: 81.4% (2000); Median home value: $77,900 (2000); Median rent: $315 per month (2000); Median age of housing: 41 years (2000).
Transportation: Commute to work: 87.6% car, 0.0% public transportation, 6.5% walk, 5.1% work from home (2000); Travel time to work: 26.7% less than 15 minutes, 27.7% 15 to 30 minutes, 26.2% 30 to 45 minutes, 12.6% 45 to 60 minutes, 6.8% 60 minutes or more (2000)

Des Moines County

Located in southeastern Iowa; prairie area bounded on the east by the Mississippi River and the Illinois border, and on the south by the Skunk River. Covers a land area of 416.10 square miles, a water area of 13.60 square miles, and is located in the Central Time Zone. The county government was organized in 1834. County seat is Burlington.

Weather Station: Burlington Radio KBUR — Elevation: 702 feet

	Jan	Feb	Mar	Apr	May	Jun	Jul	Aug	Sep	Oct	Nov	Dec
High	30	36	49	62	73	82	86	83	76	64	49	36
Low	14	20	30	42	52	62	66	64	56	44	32	20
Precip	1.3	1.5	3.0	3.7	4.4	4.3	4.4	4.1	3.8	2.9	2.7	2.1
Snow	7.8	5.6	3.4	1.4	0.0	0.0	0.0	0.0	0.0	tr	2.1	5.6

High and Low temperatures in degrees Fahrenheit; Precipitation and Snow in inches

Population: 42,351 (2000); Race: 94.3% White, 3.3% Black, 0.6% Asian, 0.3% American Indian and Alaska Native, 1.7% Hispanic of any race, 1.1% two or more races (2000); Density: 101.8 persons per square mile (2000); Age: 24.3% under 18, 16.7% over 64 (2000).
Religion: Five largest groups: 12.5% Catholic Church, 7.4% The United Methodist Church, 5.4% Evangelical Lutheran Church in America, 2.8% United Church of Christ, 1.9% Presbyterian Church (U.S.A.) (2000).
Economy: Unemployment rate: 5.6% (11/2002); Total civilian labor force: 22,280 (11/2002); Leading industries: 31.6% manufacturing; 16.1% retail trade; 15.0% health care and social assistance (2000); Companies that employ more than 1,000 persons: 1 (2000); Companies that employ more than 100 persons: 29 (2000); Farms: 650 totaling 192,165 acres (1997); Minority business ownership rate: 0.0% (1997); Women business ownership rate: 19.2% (1997); Retail sales per capita: $11,875 (1997). Single-family building permits issued: 24 (2001) / 35 (2000); Multi-family building permits issued: 8 (2001) / 14 (2000).
Income: Per capita income: $19,701 (2000); Median household income: $36,790 (2000); Poverty rate: 10.7% (2000); Bankruptcy rate: 7.46% (2001).
Taxes: Total county taxes per capita: $182 (2000); County property taxes per capita: $143 (2000).
Education: High school graduation rate: 85.8% (2000); College graduation rate: 16.0% (2000).
Housing: Homeownership rate: 74.2% (2000); Median home value: $70,100 (2000); Median rent: $349 per month (2000); Median age of housing: 51 years (2000).
Health: Birth rate: 121.6 per 10,000 population (1998); Age adjusted death rate: 85.7 per 10,000 population (1999); Age adjusted cancer mortality rate: 186.2 deaths per 100,000 population (1999). Number of physicians: 16.1 per 10,000 population (1999); Number of hospital beds: 73.9 per 10,000 population (1999).
Elections: 2000 Presidential election results: 58.6% Gore, 38.1% Bush, 2.1% Nader, 0.6% Buchanan

Additional Information Contacts

Des Moines County Government Offices 319-753-8203
Burlington Board of Realtors 319-752-5544
Burlington Chamber of Commerce 319-752-6365

Des Moines County Communities

BURLINGTON (city). Covers a land area of 14.051 square miles and a water area of 0.783 square miles. Located at 40.80° N. Lat.; 91.11° W. Long. Elevation is 533 feet.
History: John Gray, a native of Vermont, arrived here in 1834 and was allowed, upon purchasing a lot, to name the settlement Burlington after his home town. Burlington was originally in the Territory of Wisconsin and served as its capital. When the Iowa Territory was created in 1838, Burlington served as its temporary capital.
Population: 26,839 (2000); Race: 92.3% White, 4.7% Black, 0.7% Asian, 0.3% American Indian and Alaska Native, 1.9% Hispanic of any race, 1.2% two or more races (2000); Density: 1,910.1 persons per square mile (2000); Age: 24.1% under 18, 17.3% over 64 (2000); Marriage status: 24.7% never married, 54.9% now married, 8.2% widowed, 12.1% divorced (2000); Foreign born: 1.6% (2000); Ancestry (includes multiple ancestries): 32.4% German, 13.7% Irish, 11.2% Other groups, 9.4% English, 9.0% United States or American (2000).
Vital Statistics: Birth rate: 136.7 per 10,000 population (1998)
Economy: Unemployment rate: 6.4% (11/2002); Total civilian labor force: 13,791 (11/2002); Single-family building permits issued: 20 (2001) / 25 (2000); Multi-family building permits issued: 8 (2001) / 9 (2000); Employment by occupation: 8.1% management, 16.1% professional, 15.0% services, 25.7% sales, 0.2% farming, 10.1% construction, 24.7% production (2000).
Income: Per capita income: $19,450 (2000); Median household income: $33,770 (2000); Poverty rate: 12.6% (2000).
Taxes: Total city taxes per capita: $468 (2000); City property taxes per capita: $307 (2000).
Education: High school graduation rate: 84.0% (2000); College graduation rate: 16.1% (2000).

School District(s)

Burlington Community School District (PK-12)
2000 Enrollment: 4,739 319-753-6791

Two-year College(s)

Daytons School of Hair Design (Private, For-profit)
2001 Enrollment: 26 319-752-3193

Housing: Homeownership rate: 70.1% (2000); Median home value: $63,300 (2000); Median rent: $346 per month (2000); Median age of housing: 60+ years (2000).
Hospitals: Burlington Medical Center (396 beds)
Safety: Violent crime rate: 54.8 per 10,000 population; Property crime rate: 484.9 per 10,000 population (2001).
Newspapers: The Hawk Eye (7 x week)
Transportation: Commute to work: 93.1% car, 0.6% public transportation, 2.5% walk, 2.5% work from home (2000); Travel time to work: 65.6% less than 15 minutes, 24.0% 15 to 30 minutes, 5.4% 30 to 45 minutes, 2.0% 45 to 60 minutes, 2.9% 60 minutes or more (2000); Amtrak: Service available.
Airports: Southeast Iowa Regional (primary service)

Additional Information Contacts
Burlington Board of Realtors 319-752-5544
Burlington Chamber of Commerce 319-752-6365

DANVILLE (city). Covers a land area of 0.756 square miles and a water area of 0 square miles. Located at 40.86° N. Lat.; 91.31° W. Long. Elevation is 726 feet.
History: Danville was settled in 1854 by Alanson and Harriet Messenger.
Population: 914 (2000); Race: 99.2% White, 0.0% Black, 0.2% Asian, 0.0% American Indian and Alaska Native, 0.2% Hispanic of any race, 0.3% two or more races (2000); Density: 1,209.2 persons per square mile (2000); Age: 22.2% under 18, 20.3% over 64 (2000); Marriage status: 15.4% never married, 68.9% now married, 7.1% widowed, 8.6% divorced (2000); Foreign born: 0.4% (2000); Ancestry (includes multiple ancestries): 39.2% German, 12.7% Irish, 8.2% English, 6.7% Swedish, 6.6% United States or American (2000).
Economy: Single-family building permits issued: 0 (2001) / 3 (2000); Multi-family building permits issued: 0 (2001) / 0 (2000); Employment by occupation: 7.5% management, 13.5% professional, 18.0% services, 23.0% sales, 0.8% farming, 14.1% construction, 23.2% production (2000).
Income: Per capita income: $19,659 (2000); Median household income: $45,357 (2000); Poverty rate: 3.1% (2000).
Taxes: Total city taxes per capita: $264 (1997); City property taxes per capita: $162 (1997).
Education: High school graduation rate: 91.0% (2000); College graduation rate: 12.5% (2000).

School District(s)
Danville Community School District (KG-12)
2000 Enrollment: 549 319-392-4223

Housing: Homeownership rate: 81.0% (2000); Median home value: $78,300 (2000); Median rent: $335 per month (2000); Median age of housing: 35 years (2000).
Transportation: Commute to work: 93.4% car, 0.6% public transportation, 4.3% walk, 1.5% work from home (2000); Travel time to work: 36.1% less than 15 minutes, 54.0% 15 to 30 minutes, 7.1% 30 to 45 minutes, 0.0% 45 to 60 minutes, 2.8% 60 minutes or more (2000)

MEDIAPOLIS (city). Covers a land area of 1.205 square miles and a water area of 0 square miles. Located at 41.00° N. Lat.; 91.16° W. Long. Elevation is 764 feet.
History: Mediapolis got its name because of its location halfway between two county seats, Burlington and Wapello.
Population: 1,644 (2000); Race: 98.3% White, 0.0% Black, 0.6% Asian, 0.0% American Indian and Alaska Native, 0.6% Hispanic of any race, 1.1% two or more races (2000); Density: 1,364.3 persons per square mile (2000); Age: 25.2% under 18, 23.1% over 64 (2000); Marriage status: 17.8% never married, 63.6% now married, 8.4% widowed, 10.1% divorced (2000); Foreign born: 0.9% (2000); Ancestry (includes multiple ancestries): 35.4% German, 12.8% Irish, 10.2% United States or American, 9.1% English, 8.2% Swedish (2000).
Economy: Single-family building permits issued: 3 (2001) / 4 (2000); Multi-family building permits issued: 0 (2001) / 5 (2000); Employment by occupation: 6.8% management, 16.6% professional, 16.3% services, 24.5% sales, 0.1% farming, 11.1% construction, 24.6% production (2000).
Income: Per capita income: $17,974 (2000); Median household income: $37,857 (2000); Poverty rate: 8.3% (2000).
Taxes: Total city taxes per capita: $260 (1997); City property taxes per capita: $158 (1997).
Education: High school graduation rate: 86.9% (2000); College graduation rate: 15.5% (2000).

School District(s)
Mediapolis Community School District (KG-12)
2000 Enrollment: 940 319-394-3237

Housing: Homeownership rate: 83.4% (2000); Median home value: $77,700 (2000); Median rent: $270 per month (2000); Median age of housing: 35 years (2000).
Newspapers: The Mediapolis News (1 x week)
Transportation: Commute to work: 91.9% car, 0.0% public transportation, 4.3% walk, 3.0% work from home (2000); Travel time to work: 49.6% less than 15 minutes, 30.5% 15 to 30 minutes, 14.5% 30 to 45 minutes, 2.4% 45 to 60 minutes, 3.1% 60 minutes or more (2000)

MIDDLETOWN (city). Covers a land area of 0.611 square miles and a water area of 0 square miles. Located at 40.82° N. Lat.; 91.26° W. Long.
History: Middletown was laid out in 1839 by Josiah T. Smith of Ohio. The town was first named Lewis Point for an early settler, and was renamed by John Sharp of Pennsylvania in 1847.
Population: 535 (2000); Race: 93.7% White, 2.9% Black, 0.5% Asian, 0.0% American Indian and Alaska Native, 2.0% Hispanic of any race, 1.6% two or more races (2000); Density: 875.2 persons per square mile (2000); Age: 28.8% under 18, 14.6% over 64 (2000); Marriage status: 21.4% never married, 54.5% now married, 11.3% widowed, 12.9% divorced (2000); Foreign born: 1.3% (2000); Ancestry (includes multiple ancestries): 27.1% German, 12.1% English, 11.9% Other groups, 8.3% Irish, 5.8% United States or American (2000).
Economy: Single-family building permits issued: 0 (2001) / 1 (2000); Multi-family building permits issued: 0 (2001) / 0 (2000); Employment by occupation: 5.6% management, 7.9% professional, 22.9% services, 21.4% sales, 0.0% farming, 14.3% construction, 27.8% production (2000).
Income: Per capita income: $16,835 (2000); Median household income: $37,083 (2000); Poverty rate: 19.5% (2000).
Taxes: Total city taxes per capita: $168 (1997); City property taxes per capita: $76 (1997).
Education: High school graduation rate: 90.2% (2000); College graduation rate: 14.5% (2000).
Housing: Homeownership rate: 76.7% (2000); Median home value: $65,000 (2000); Median rent: $294 per month (2000); Median age of housing: 42 years (2000).
Transportation: Commute to work: 90.5% car, 0.8% public transportation, 6.1% walk, 2.7% work from home (2000); Travel time to work: 42.4% less than 15 minutes, 37.0% 15 to 30 minutes, 3.1% 30 to 45 minutes, 13.6% 45 to 60 minutes, 3.9% 60 minutes or more (2000)

SPERRY (unincorporated postal area, zip code 52650). Covers a land area of 39.152 square miles and a water area of 0.086 square miles. Located at 40.95° N. Lat.; 91.16° W. Long.
History: Sperry was named for resident John M. Sperry.
Population: 855 (2000); Race: 98.9% White, 0.0% Black, 0.0% Asian, 0.0% American Indian and Alaska Native, 0.0% Hispanic of any race, 1.1% two or more races (2000); Density: 21.8 persons per square mile (2000); Age: 27.5% under 18, 6.2% over 64 (2000); Marriage status: 27.2% never married, 61.9% now married, 4.3% widowed, 6.6% divorced (2000); Foreign born: 0.0% (2000); Ancestry (includes multiple ancestries): 40.2% German, 13.2% United States or American, 10.8% English, 9.2% Swedish, 6.9% Irish (2000).
Economy: Employment by occupation: 13.7% management, 19.0% professional, 8.7% services, 22.8% sales, 2.8% farming, 10.3% construction, 22.8% production (2000).
Income: Per capita income: $20,918 (2000); Median household income: $52,250 (2000); Poverty rate: 8.6% (2000).
Education: High school graduation rate: 85.2% (2000); College graduation rate: 17.4% (2000).
Housing: Homeownership rate: 87.7% (2000); Median home value: $98,100 (2000); Median rent: $360 per month (2000); Median age of housing: 29 years (2000).
Transportation: Commute to work: 95.2% car, 1.0% public transportation, 0.0% walk, 3.8% work from home (2000); Travel time to work: 20.8% less than 15 minutes, 47.1% 15 to 30 minutes, 24.3% 30 to 45 minutes, 1.4% 45 to 60 minutes, 6.4% 60 minutes or more (2000)

WEST BURLINGTON (city). Covers a land area of 5.028 square miles and a water area of 0 square miles. Located at 40.82° N. Lat.; 91.16° W. Long.
History: West Burlington was formally known as Leffleer's Station. In 1882, Joel West organized the community by bringing the workers at the locomotive shops in the north part of town into a realty company, enabling them to buy lots on the installment plan. Any religious denomination that wanted to build a church here was given two lots.
Population: 3,161 (2000); Race: 94.7% White, 2.3% Black, 0.2% Asian, 0.4% American Indian and Alaska Native, 3.6% Hispanic of any race, 2.1% two or more races (2000); Density: 628.7 persons per square mile (2000); Age: 20.0% under 18, 19.1% over 64 (2000); Marriage status: 21.7% never married, 54.2% now married, 10.0% widowed, 14.1% divorced (2000); Foreign born: 4.2% (2000); Ancestry (includes multiple ancestries): 31.1% German, 15.3% Irish, 11.4% United States or American, 9.8% Other groups, 8.8% English (2000).
Economy: Single-family building permits issued: 1 (2001) / 2 (2000); Multi-family building permits issued: 0 (2001) / 0 (2000); Employment by occupation: 9.2% management, 15.1% professional, 17.3% services, 25.1% sales, 1.7% farming, 7.6% construction, 23.9% production (2000).

Income: Per capita income: $19,659 (2000); Median household income: $38,958 (2000); Poverty rate: 8.2% (2000).
Taxes: Total city taxes per capita: $529 (1997); City property taxes per capita: $395 (1997).
Education: High school graduation rate: 89.1% (2000); College graduation rate: 14.5% (2000).

School District(s)

West Burlington Ind School District (KG-12)
2000 Enrollment: 750 319-752-8747

Two-year College(s)

Southeastern Community College (Public)
2001 Enrollment: 2,835 319-752-2731
2001 Tuition: In-state $2,294; Out-of-state $2,782

Housing: Homeownership rate: 67.2% (2000); Median home value: $64,300 (2000); Median rent: $396 per month (2000); Median age of housing: 40 years (2000).
Safety: Violent crime rate: 12.7 per 10,000 population; Property crime rate: 820.1 per 10,000 population (2001).
Newspapers: Des Moines County News (1 x week)
Transportation: Commute to work: 90.6% car, 1.0% public transportation, 3.7% walk, 2.6% work from home (2000); Travel time to work: 68.9% less than 15 minutes, 19.6% 15 to 30 minutes, 7.2% 30 to 45 minutes, 2.2% 45 to 60 minutes, 2.0% 60 minutes or more (2000)

YARMOUTH (unincorporated postal area, zip code 52660). Covers a land area of 21.753 square miles and a water area of 0.023 square miles. Located at 40.98° N. Lat.; 91.29° W. Long. Elevation is 704 feet.
History: Yarmouth was named for Yarmouth, England.
Population: 238 (2000); Race: 98.3% White, 0.0% Black, 0.0% Asian, 0.0% American Indian and Alaska Native, 0.0% Hispanic of any race, 1.7% two or more races (2000); Density: 10.9 persons per square mile (2000); Age: 17.7% under 18, 23.4% over 64 (2000); Marriage status: 18.0% never married, 59.5% now married, 6.8% widowed, 15.6% divorced (2000); Foreign born: 0.0% (2000); Ancestry (includes multiple ancestries): 37.2% German, 20.8% English, 10.8% Swedish, 7.8% Irish, 6.9% United States or American (2000).
Economy: Employment by occupation: 5.3% management, 19.3% professional, 14.0% services, 17.5% sales, 2.6% farming, 13.2% construction, 28.1% production (2000).
Income: Per capita income: $17,837 (2000); Median household income: $40,938 (2000); Poverty rate: 6.1% (2000).
Education: High school graduation rate: 86.0% (2000); College graduation rate: 20.1% (2000).
Housing: Homeownership rate: 76.2% (2000); Median home value: $45,500 (2000); Median rent: $419 per month (2000); Median age of housing: 60+ years (2000).
Transportation: Commute to work: 89.5% car, 0.0% public transportation, 5.3% walk, 5.3% work from home (2000); Travel time to work: 26.9% less than 15 minutes, 34.3% 15 to 30 minutes, 16.7% 30 to 45 minutes, 4.6% 45 to 60 minutes, 17.6% 60 minutes or more (2000)

Dickinson County

Located in northwestern Iowa; prairie area bounded on the north by Minnesota; drained by the Little Sioux River. Covers a land area of 381.10 square miles, a water area of 22.60 square miles, and is located in the Central Time Zone. The county government was organized in 1851. County seat is Spirit Lake.

Weather Station: Lake Park — Elevation: 1,463 feet

	Jan	Feb	Mar	Apr	May	Jun	Jul	Aug	Sep	Oct	Nov	Dec
High	22	28	39	56	69	79	83	80	72	59	40	27
Low	3	10	21	35	47	57	61	59	49	37	23	10
Precip	0.7	0.6	2.0	2.8	3.5	4.5	3.7	3.8	2.8	2.0	1.6	0.7
Snow	7.9	5.5	8.2	2.7	tr	0.0	0.0	0.0	tr	0.6	6.2	7.3

High and Low temperatures in degrees Fahrenheit; Precipitation and Snow in inches

Weather Station: Milford 4 NW — Elevation: 1,400 feet

	Jan	Feb	Mar	Apr	May	Jun	Jul	Aug	Sep	Oct	Nov	Dec
High	22	29	41	58	71	80	83	81	73	60	41	27
Low	4	11	23	35	47	57	61	59	50	38	24	11
Precip	0.6	0.6	2.0	3.1	3.8	4.6	3.6	3.8	3.0	2.2	1.8	0.8
Snow	na	5.4	6.1	0.8	tr	0.0	0.0	0.0	tr	0.6	3.1	6.5

High and Low temperatures in degrees Fahrenheit; Precipitation and Snow in inches

Population: 16,424 (2000); Race: 98.9% White, 0.3% Black, 0.2% Asian, 0.1% American Indian and Alaska Native, 0.6% Hispanic of any race, 0.5% two or more races (2000); Density: 43.1 persons per square mile (2000); Age: 21.9% under 18, 20.6% over 64 (2000).
Religion: Five largest groups: 25.3% Catholic Church, 15.0% The United Methodist Church, 13.1% Evangelical Lutheran Church in America, 7.4% Lutheran Church—Missouri Synod, 4.0% Presbyterian Church (U.S.A.) (2000).
Economy: Unemployment rate: 3.0% (11/2002); Total civilian labor force: 9,936 (11/2002); Leading industries: 31.4% manufacturing; 15.7% retail trade; 11.3% accommodation & food services (2000); Companies that employ more than 1,000 persons: 0 (2000); Companies that employ more than 100 persons: 8 (2000); Farms: 512 totaling 201,126 acres (1997); Minority business ownership rate: 0.0% (1997); Women business ownership rate: 26.3% (1997); Retail sales per capita: $10,728 (1997). Single-family building permits issued: 152 (2001) / 110 (2000); Multi-family building permits issued: 22 (2001) / 28 (2000).
Income: Per capita income: $21,929 (2000); Median household income: $39,020 (2000); Poverty rate: 6.0% (2000); Bankruptcy rate: 2.12% (2001).
Taxes: Total county taxes per capita: $219 (2000); County property taxes per capita: $214 (2000).
Education: High school graduation rate: 89.2% (2000); College graduation rate: 21.3% (2000).
Housing: Homeownership rate: 78.0% (2000); Median home value: $96,800 (2000); Median rent: $332 per month (2000); Median age of housing: 30 years (2000).
Health: Birth rate: 107.2 per 10,000 population (1998); Age adjusted death rate: 67.6 per 10,000 population (1999); Age adjusted cancer mortality rate: 172.1 deaths per 100,000 population (1999). Number of physicians: 9.1 per 10,000 population (1999); Number of hospital beds: 29.8 per 10,000 population (1999).
Elections: 2000 Presidential election results: 45.1% Gore, 52.0% Bush, 2.1% Nader, 0.4% Buchanan
National and State Parks: Cayler Prairie State Preserve; Cory Marsh State Game Management Area; Emerson Bay State Recreation Area; Freda Haffner Kettlehole State Preserve; Gull Point State Park; Marble Beach State Recreation Area; Marble Lake State Game Management Area; Mini Wakan State Park; Minnewashta Lake State Game Mgt Area; Orleans State Park; Pikes Point State Park; Pillsbury Point State Park; Pleasant Lake State Game Management Area; Silver Lake Fen State Preserve; Spirit Lake State Game Management Area; Spring Run State Game Management Area; Spring Run State Game Management Areas; Trappers Bay State Park; Upper Gar Lake State Game Management Area; Yager Slough State Game Management Area
Additional Information Contacts
Dickinson County Government Offices 712-336-3356
Arnolds Park Chamber of Commerce 712-332-2107
Iowa Great Lakes Board of Realtors 712-332-6444

Dickinson County Communities

ARNOLDS PARK (city). Covers a land area of 1.297 square miles and a water area of <.001 square miles. Located at 43.36° N. Lat.; 95.13° W. Long.
History: Arnolds Park was named in honor of W. B. Arnold.
Population: 1,162 (2000); Race: 97.2% White, 0.2% Black, 0.0% Asian, 0.7% American Indian and Alaska Native, 0.5% Hispanic of any race, 1.9% two or more races (2000); Density: 896.1 persons per square mile (2000); Age: 16.0% under 18, 24.2% over 64 (2000); Marriage status: 17.1% never married, 61.7% now married, 8.6% widowed, 12.6% divorced (2000); Foreign born: 1.0% (2000); Ancestry (includes multiple ancestries): 39.9% German, 12.7% Irish, 11.4% Norwegian, 10.7% English, 7.2% Dutch (2000).
Economy: Single-family building permits issued: 14 (2001) / 9 (2000); Multi-family building permits issued: 0 (2001) / 4 (2000); Employment by occupation: 12.4% management, 9.5% professional, 20.4% services, 26.7% sales, 0.0% farming, 11.6% construction, 19.4% production (2000).
Income: Per capita income: $24,072 (2000); Median household income: $35,441 (2000); Poverty rate: 5.4% (2000).
Taxes: Total city taxes per capita: $702 (1997); City property taxes per capita: $627 (1997).
Education: High school graduation rate: 88.3% (2000); College graduation rate: 16.6% (2000).
Housing: Homeownership rate: 80.1% (2000); Median home value: $90,000 (2000); Median rent: $370 per month (2000); Median age of housing: 28 years (2000).
Transportation: Commute to work: 93.9% car, 0.0% public transportation, 2.2% walk, 3.2% work from home (2000); Travel time to work: 56.5% less

than 15 minutes, 29.8% 15 to 30 minutes, 7.5% 30 to 45 minutes, 2.7% 45 to 60 minutes, 3.4% 60 minutes or more (2000)

Additional Information Contacts

Arnolds Park Chamber of Commerce 712-332-2107

LAKE PARK (city). Covers a land area of 1.488 square miles and a water area of 0.035 square miles. Located at 43.45° N. Lat.; 95.32° W. Long. Elevation is 1,490 feet.

History: Lake Park was named for its location on Silver Lake.

Population: 1,023 (2000); Race: 98.9% White, 0.0% Black, 0.0% Asian, 0.0% American Indian and Alaska Native, 0.7% Hispanic of any race, 1.1% two or more races (2000); Density: 687.7 persons per square mile (2000); Age: 20.9% under 18, 26.9% over 64 (2000); Marriage status: 16.9% never married, 65.0% now married, 9.4% widowed, 8.7% divorced (2000); Foreign born: 1.9% (2000); Ancestry (includes multiple ancestries): 45.4% German, 12.0% Irish, 8.9% English, 8.9% Dutch, 5.2% Norwegian (2000).

Economy: Single-family building permits issued: 5 (2001) / 2 (2000); Multi-family building permits issued: 0 (2001) / 4 (2000); Employment by occupation: 10.0% management, 13.1% professional, 17.3% services, 22.2% sales, 1.0% farming, 10.0% construction, 26.3% production (2000).

Income: Per capita income: $18,094 (2000); Median household income: $35,104 (2000); Poverty rate: 5.8% (2000).

Taxes: Total city taxes per capita: $208 (1997); City property taxes per capita: $206 (1997).

Education: High school graduation rate: 84.3% (2000); College graduation rate: 16.4% (2000).

School District(s)

Harris-Lake Park Community School District (KG-12)
2000 Enrollment: 346 712-832-3640
Sioux Valley (N -N)
2000 Enrollment: n/a 507-839-3673

Housing: Homeownership rate: 80.9% (2000); Median home value: $64,000 (2000); Median rent: $242 per month (2000); Median age of housing: 44 years (2000).

Transportation: Commute to work: 93.8% car, 0.0% public transportation, 2.7% walk, 2.7% work from home (2000); Travel time to work: 37.0% less than 15 minutes, 45.2% 15 to 30 minutes, 16.5% 30 to 45 minutes, 0.0% 45 to 60 minutes, 1.3% 60 minutes or more (2000)

MILFORD (city). Covers a land area of 2.258 square miles and a water area of <.001 square miles. Located at 43.32° N. Lat.; 95.15° W. Long. Elevation is 1,441 feet.

History: Milford came into existence with the building of the Milford flour mills in the summer of 1869. The mill owners platted the town in 1870, but the destruction of crops by grasshoppers for four successive years led to the discontinuance of the mills and retarded the growth of Milford.

Population: 2,474 (2000); Race: 98.4% White, 0.7% Black, 0.3% Asian, 0.0% American Indian and Alaska Native, 0.0% Hispanic of any race, 0.5% two or more races (2000); Density: 1,095.5 persons per square mile (2000); Age: 24.3% under 18, 18.9% over 64 (2000); Marriage status: 22.4% never married, 55.8% now married, 9.2% widowed, 12.5% divorced (2000); Foreign born: 0.6% (2000); Ancestry (includes multiple ancestries): 40.6% German, 12.8% Irish, 10.4% Norwegian, 10.3% English, 6.3% Swedish (2000).

Economy: Single-family building permits issued: 13 (2001) / 14 (2000); Multi-family building permits issued: 0 (2001) / 2 (2000); Employment by occupation: 9.1% management, 14.9% professional, 14.2% services, 24.5% sales, 0.8% farming, 8.4% construction, 28.0% production (2000).

Income: Per capita income: $16,680 (2000); Median household income: $36,063 (2000); Poverty rate: 6.9% (2000).

Taxes: Total city taxes per capita: $294 (1997); City property taxes per capita: $287 (1997).

Education: High school graduation rate: 87.9% (2000); College graduation rate: 15.0% (2000).

School District(s)

Okoboji Community School District (PK-12)
2000 Enrollment: 943 712-338-4757

Housing: Homeownership rate: 73.6% (2000); Median home value: $78,500 (2000); Median rent: $322 per month (2000); Median age of housing: 32 years (2000).

Transportation: Commute to work: 90.1% car, 0.0% public transportation, 6.4% walk, 1.5% work from home (2000); Travel time to work: 56.7% less than 15 minutes, 35.0% 15 to 30 minutes, 4.5% 30 to 45 minutes, 1.1% 45 to 60 minutes, 2.7% 60 minutes or more (2000)

OKOBOJI (city). Covers a land area of 1.783 square miles and a water area of 0.003 square miles. Located at 43.38° N. Lat.; 95.13° W. Long. Elevation is 1,456 feet.

History: Okoboji was established as a post office in the spring of 1855.

Population: 820 (2000); Race: 99.8% White, 0.0% Black, 0.2% Asian, 0.0% American Indian and Alaska Native, 0.0% Hispanic of any race, 0.0% two or more races (2000); Density: 460.0 persons per square mile (2000); Age: 14.7% under 18, 29.6% over 64 (2000); Marriage status: 18.3% never married, 59.1% now married, 10.9% widowed, 11.8% divorced (2000); Foreign born: 1.6% (2000); Ancestry (includes multiple ancestries): 35.9% German, 14.7% Irish, 10.4% Norwegian, 10.2% English, 6.4% Dutch (2000).

Economy: Single-family building permits issued: 8 (2001) / 5 (2000); Multi-family building permits issued: 4 (2001) / 8 (2000); Employment by occupation: 15.8% management, 15.3% professional, 13.1% services, 35.8% sales, 0.0% farming, 7.2% construction, 12.8% production (2000).

Income: Per capita income: $29,297 (2000); Median household income: $37,500 (2000); Poverty rate: 5.3% (2000).

Taxes: Total city taxes per capita: $805 (1997); City property taxes per capita: $623 (1997).

Education: High school graduation rate: 91.2% (2000); College graduation rate: 33.4% (2000).

Housing: Homeownership rate: 79.4% (2000); Median home value: $181,900 (2000); Median rent: $379 per month (2000); Median age of housing: 26 years (2000).

Transportation: Commute to work: 87.5% car, 0.0% public transportation, 4.8% walk, 5.9% work from home (2000); Travel time to work: 81.0% less than 15 minutes, 9.2% 15 to 30 minutes, 5.1% 30 to 45 minutes, 0.5% 45 to 60 minutes, 4.1% 60 minutes or more (2000)

ORLEANS (city). Covers a land area of 1.001 square miles and a water area of 0.004 square miles. Located at 43.44° N. Lat.; 95.10° W. Long.

History: Orleans is named after Orleans, France.

Population: 583 (2000); Race: 99.0% White, 0.0% Black, 0.3% Asian, 0.3% American Indian and Alaska Native, 0.7% Hispanic of any race, 0.0% two or more races (2000); Density: 582.2 persons per square mile (2000); Age: 18.5% under 18, 29.1% over 64 (2000); Marriage status: 17.8% never married, 62.8% now married, 11.7% widowed, 7.7% divorced (2000); Foreign born: 0.3% (2000); Ancestry (includes multiple ancestries): 47.8% German, 15.1% Irish, 14.4% Norwegian, 8.3% English, 8.3% Danish (2000).

Economy: Single-family building permits issued: 5 (2001) / 4 (2000); Multi-family building permits issued: 0 (2001) / 4 (2000); Employment by occupation: 14.0% management, 16.9% professional, 13.0% services, 33.9% sales, 0.0% farming, 9.3% construction, 13.0% production (2000).

Income: Per capita income: $28,451 (2000); Median household income: $41,818 (2000); Poverty rate: 9.2% (2000).

Taxes: Total city taxes per capita: $183 (1997); City property taxes per capita: $176 (1997).

Education: High school graduation rate: 90.2% (2000); College graduation rate: 28.3% (2000).

Housing: Homeownership rate: 83.9% (2000); Median home value: $152,600 (2000); Median rent: $339 per month (2000); Median age of housing: 41 years (2000).

Transportation: Commute to work: 89.4% car, 0.0% public transportation, 1.4% walk, 7.2% work from home (2000); Travel time to work: 56.5% less than 15 minutes, 32.8% 15 to 30 minutes, 6.6% 30 to 45 minutes, 2.6% 45 to 60 minutes, 1.5% 60 minutes or more (2000)

SPIRIT LAKE (city). Covers a land area of 3.328 square miles and a water area of 0.016 square miles. Located at 43.42° N. Lat.; 95.10° W. Long. Elevation is 1,470 feet.

History: Spirit Lake was named after the glacier-created lake of the same name.

Population: 4,261 (2000); Race: 98.9% White, 0.6% Black, 0.0% Asian, 0.0% American Indian and Alaska Native, 1.2% Hispanic of any race, 0.5% two or more races (2000); Density: 1,280.2 persons per square mile (2000); Age: 25.2% under 18, 18.4% over 64 (2000); Marriage status: 24.0% never married, 54.9% now married, 11.6% widowed, 9.5% divorced (2000); Foreign born: 0.6% (2000); Ancestry (includes multiple ancestries): 39.9% German, 12.0% English, 9.9% Irish, 9.3% Norwegian, 4.9% United States or American (2000).

Economy: Single-family building permits issued: 34 (2001) / 29 (2000); Multi-family building permits issued: 12 (2001) / 0 (2000); Employment by occupation: 11.5% management, 15.0% professional, 16.3% services, 27.0% sales, 0.0% farming, 10.8% construction, 19.3% production (2000).

Income: Per capita income: $18,661 (2000); Median household income: $36,224 (2000); Poverty rate: 6.6% (2000).
Taxes: Total city taxes per capita: $586 (2000); City property taxes per capita: $416 (2000).
Education: High school graduation rate: 86.1% (2000); College graduation rate: 20.9% (2000).

School District(s)

Spirit Lake Community School District (KG-12)
2000 Enrollment: 1,316 712-336-2820

Two-year College(s)

Faust Institute of Cosmetology (Private, For-profit)
2001 Enrollment: 19 712-336-3518

Housing: Homeownership rate: 70.7% (2000); Median home value: $91,100 (2000); Median rent: $339 per month (2000); Median age of housing: 34 years (2000).
Hospitals: Dickinson County Memorial Hospital (49 beds)
Newspapers: Dickinson County News (2 x week); Okobojian (2 x week)
Transportation: Commute to work: 91.5% car, 0.0% public transportation, 3.3% walk, 3.7% work from home (2000); Travel time to work: 72.0% less than 15 minutes, 17.6% 15 to 30 minutes, 5.5% 30 to 45 minutes, 2.3% 45 to 60 minutes, 2.6% 60 minutes or more (2000)
Airports: Spirit Lake Municipal
Additional Information Contacts
Iowa Great Lakes Board of Realtors 712-332-6444

SUPERIOR (city). Covers a land area of 0.423 square miles and a water area of 0 square miles. Located at 43.43° N. Lat.; 94.94° W. Long. Elevation is 1,480 feet.
Population: 142 (2000); Race: 98.7% White, 0.0% Black, 0.0% Asian, 0.0% American Indian and Alaska Native, 3.3% Hispanic of any race, 0.0% two or more races (2000); Density: 336.0 persons per square mile (2000); Age: 14.4% under 18, 19.6% over 64 (2000); Marriage status: 15.1% never married, 66.2% now married, 4.3% widowed, 14.4% divorced (2000); Foreign born: 3.3% (2000); Ancestry (includes multiple ancestries): 47.1% German, 28.8% Norwegian, 11.8% English, 9.2% United States or American, 5.2% Other groups (2000).
Economy: Livestock; grain. Single-family building permits issued: 0 (2001) / 0 (2000); Multi-family building permits issued: 0 (2001) / 0 (2000); Employment by occupation: 2.4% management, 8.4% professional, 6.0% services, 18.1% sales, 2.4% farming, 14.5% construction, 48.2% production (2000).
Income: Per capita income: $25,486 (2000); Median household income: $35,000 (2000); Poverty rate: 3.3% (2000).
Taxes: Total city taxes per capita: $463 (1997); City property taxes per capita: $463 (1997).
Education: High school graduation rate: 88.8% (2000); College graduation rate: 2.6% (2000).
Housing: Homeownership rate: 95.7% (2000); Median home value: $39,800 (2000); Median rent: $213 per month (2000); Median age of housing: 56 years (2000).
Transportation: Commute to work: 90.1% car, 0.0% public transportation, 2.5% walk, 7.4% work from home (2000); Travel time to work: 20.0% less than 15 minutes, 61.3% 15 to 30 minutes, 14.7% 30 to 45 minutes, 0.0% 45 to 60 minutes, 4.0% 60 minutes or more (2000)

TERRIL (city). Covers a land area of 0.546 square miles and a water area of 0 square miles. Located at 43.30° N. Lat.; 94.97° W. Long. Elevation is 1,417 feet.
History: Terril was named for the landowner who sold the land for the town site.
Population: 404 (2000); Race: 100.0% White, 0.0% Black, 0.0% Asian, 0.0% American Indian and Alaska Native, 0.5% Hispanic of any race, 0.0% two or more races (2000); Density: 740.0 persons per square mile (2000); Age: 20.9% under 18, 15.5% over 64 (2000); Marriage status: 25.9% never married, 58.4% now married, 6.3% widowed, 9.5% divorced (2000); Foreign born: 0.0% (2000); Ancestry (includes multiple ancestries): 37.6% German, 18.0% Norwegian, 12.1% United States or American, 10.6% Irish, 7.0% Dutch (2000).
Economy: Single-family building permits issued: 0 (2001) / 1 (2000); Multi-family building permits issued: 0 (2001) / 0 (2000); Employment by occupation: 10.0% management, 8.3% professional, 13.5% services, 27.1% sales, 2.6% farming, 14.8% construction, 23.6% production (2000).
Income: Per capita income: $16,283 (2000); Median household income: $34,583 (2000); Poverty rate: 13.8% (2000).
Taxes: Total city taxes per capita: $272 (1997); City property taxes per capita: $269 (1997).
Education: High school graduation rate: 91.6% (2000); College graduation rate: 14.0% (2000).

School District(s)

Terril Community School District (PK-12)
2000 Enrollment: 219 712-853-6111

Housing: Homeownership rate: 74.9% (2000); Median home value: $40,900 (2000); Median rent: $265 per month (2000); Median age of housing: 49 years (2000).
Transportation: Commute to work: 85.8% car, 0.0% public transportation, 8.0% walk, 6.2% work from home (2000); Travel time to work: 24.2% less than 15 minutes, 66.4% 15 to 30 minutes, 8.5% 30 to 45 minutes, 0.5% 45 to 60 minutes, 0.5% 60 minutes or more (2000)

WAHPETON (city). Covers a land area of 1.279 square miles and a water area of 0.028 square miles. Located at 43.37° N. Lat.; 95.17° W. Long.
History: Wahpeton is of Sioux origin and means "dwellers among the leaves."
Population: 462 (2000); Race: 99.5% White, 0.0% Black, 0.0% Asian, 0.0% American Indian and Alaska Native, 2.1% Hispanic of any race, 0.5% two or more races (2000); Density: 361.1 persons per square mile (2000); Age: 15.9% under 18, 34.1% over 64 (2000); Marriage status: 9.3% never married, 73.4% now married, 10.1% widowed, 7.1% divorced (2000); Foreign born: 1.9% (2000); Ancestry (includes multiple ancestries): 47.2% German, 13.8% English, 11.0% Norwegian, 10.0% Irish, 8.2% Danish (2000).
Economy: Single-family building permits issued: 8 (2001) / 5 (2000); Multi-family building permits issued: 0 (2001) / 0 (2000); Employment by occupation: 11.8% management, 21.1% professional, 17.6% services, 17.6% sales, 2.0% farming, 6.9% construction, 23.0% production (2000).
Income: Per capita income: $36,258 (2000); Median household income: $53,125 (2000); Poverty rate: 7.3% (2000).
Taxes: Total city taxes per capita: $555 (1997); City property taxes per capita: $482 (1997).
Education: High school graduation rate: 94.7% (2000); College graduation rate: 27.5% (2000).
Housing: Homeownership rate: 89.5% (2000); Median home value: $152,100 (2000); Median rent: $325 per month (2000); Median age of housing: 29 years (2000).
Transportation: Commute to work: 83.7% car, 0.0% public transportation, 9.9% walk, 6.4% work from home (2000); Travel time to work: 55.8% less than 15 minutes, 27.4% 15 to 30 minutes, 9.5% 30 to 45 minutes, 4.7% 45 to 60 minutes, 2.6% 60 minutes or more (2000)

WEST OKOBOJI (city). Covers a land area of 1.241 square miles and a water area of 0.122 square miles. Located at 43.35° N. Lat.; 95.15° W. Long.
History: West Okoboji was named for Lake Okoboji. The name has a Sioux origin.
Population: 432 (2000); Race: 97.7% White, 1.4% Black, 0.0% Asian, 0.0% American Indian and Alaska Native, 0.0% Hispanic of any race, 0.9% two or more races (2000); Density: 348.2 persons per square mile (2000); Age: 20.8% under 18, 25.7% over 64 (2000); Marriage status: 16.9% never married, 59.3% now married, 11.5% widowed, 12.3% divorced (2000); Foreign born: 0.0% (2000); Ancestry (includes multiple ancestries): 37.3% German, 12.7% Norwegian, 10.9% Irish, 9.5% English, 7.2% Danish (2000).
Economy: Single-family building permits issued: 2 (2001) / 2 (2000); Multi-family building permits issued: 0 (2001) / 0 (2000); Employment by occupation: 15.1% management, 9.3% professional, 16.6% services, 30.7% sales, 1.0% farming, 7.8% construction, 19.5% production (2000).
Income: Per capita income: $24,853 (2000); Median household income: $32,083 (2000); Poverty rate: 16.3% (2000).
Taxes: Total city taxes per capita: $275 (1997); City property taxes per capita: $264 (1997).
Education: High school graduation rate: 90.9% (2000); College graduation rate: 17.2% (2000).
Housing: Homeownership rate: 58.0% (2000); Median home value: $174,300 (2000); Median rent: $371 per month (2000); Median age of housing: 29 years (2000).
Transportation: Commute to work: 91.5% car, 1.0% public transportation, 1.0% walk, 6.5% work from home (2000); Travel time to work: 56.1% less than 15 minutes, 35.3% 15 to 30 minutes, 5.3% 30 to 45 minutes, 0.0% 45 to 60 minutes, 3.2% 60 minutes or more (2000)

Dubuque County

Located in eastern Iowa; bounded on the east by the Mississippi River and the Wisconsin and Illinois borders; prairie area, drained by the North Fork of the Maquoketa River. Covers a land area of 608.20 square miles, a water area of 8.40 square miles, and is located in the Central Time Zone. The county government was organized in 1834. County seat is Dubuque.

Dubuque County is part of the Dubuque, IA MSA. The entire metro area includes: Dubuque County

Weather Station: Cascade — Elevation: 849 feet

	Jan	Feb	Mar	Apr	May	Jun	Jul	Aug	Sep	Oct	Nov	Dec
High	26	32	44	59	71	81	85	82	74	62	45	32
Low	7	13	25	36	48	57	61	59	50	38	27	14
Precip	1.2	1.2	2.3	3.0	3.7	4.5	3.4	4.7	3.5	2.4	2.4	1.5
Snow	9.6	7.0	4.5	1.9	0.0	0.0	0.0	0.0	0.0	tr	2.9	7.0

High and Low temperatures in degrees Fahrenheit; Precipitation and Snow in inches

Weather Station: Dubuque Lock & Dam 11 — Elevation: 620 feet

	Jan	Feb	Mar	Apr	May	Jun	Jul	Aug	Sep	Oct	Nov	Dec
High	27	33	45	59	72	81	85	82	74	62	45	32
Low	10	16	28	40	52	61	66	64	55	44	31	18
Precip	1.1	1.1	2.2	3.3	3.9	4.2	4.3	4.2	3.8	2.4	2.3	1.4
Snow	10.5	6.7	4.4	1.5	tr	0.0	0.0	0.0	0.0	tr	2.6	7.8

High and Low temperatures in degrees Fahrenheit; Precipitation and Snow in inches

Weather Station: Dubuque Regional Airport — Elevation: 1,053 feet

	Jan	Feb	Mar	Apr	May	Jun	Jul	Aug	Sep	Oct	Nov	Dec
High	25	31	43	58	69	79	82	80	72	60	44	30
Low	9	15	26	38	48	58	62	60	52	40	28	16
Precip	1.2	1.4	2.6	3.5	4.0	4.1	3.7	4.7	3.7	2.5	2.5	1.7
Snow	10.2	8.6	7.6	3.2	tr	tr	0.0	0.0	0.0	0.2	4.5	9.5

High and Low temperatures in degrees Fahrenheit; Precipitation and Snow in inches

Population: 89,143 (2000); Race: 97.3% White, 0.8% Black, 0.4% Asian, 0.2% American Indian and Alaska Native, 1.2% Hispanic of any race, 0.9% two or more races (2000); Density: 146.6 persons per square mile (2000); Age: 25.5% under 18, 14.8% over 64 (2000).
Religion: Five largest groups: 64.8% Catholic Church, 3.9% Evangelical Lutheran Church in America, 2.3% The United Methodist Church, 1.7% Lutheran Church—Missouri Synod, 1.4% Presbyterian Church (U.S.A.) (2000).
Economy: Unemployment rate: 3.1% (11/2002); Total civilian labor force: 49,105 (11/2002); Leading industries: 22.4% manufacturing; 14.6% retail trade; 13.3% health care and social assistance (2000); Companies that employ more than 1,000 persons: 3 (2000); Companies that employ more than 100 persons: 86 (2000); Farms: 1,579 totaling 336,497 acres (1997); Minority business ownership rate: 0.0% (1997); Women business ownership rate: 24.9% (1997); Retail sales per capita: $10,608 (1997). Single-family building permits issued: 326 (2001) / 262 (2000); Multi-family building permits issued: 115 (2001) / 79 (2000).
Income: Per capita income: $19,600 (2000); Median household income: $39,582 (2000); Poverty rate: 7.8% (2000); Bankruptcy rate: 2.49% (2001).
Taxes: Total county taxes per capita: $205 (2000); County property taxes per capita: $172 (2000).
Education: High school graduation rate: 85.2% (2000); College graduation rate: 21.3% (2000).
Housing: Homeownership rate: 73.5% (2000); Median home value: $93,300 (2000); Median rent: $364 per month (2000); Median age of housing: 40 years (2000).
Health: Birth rate: 129.2 per 10,000 population (1998); Age adjusted death rate: 84.9 per 10,000 population (1999); Age adjusted cancer mortality rate: 196.0 deaths per 100,000 population (1999). Number of physicians: 22.4 per 10,000 population (1999); Number of hospital beds: 58.8 per 10,000 population (1999).
Elections: 2000 Presidential election results: 55.4% Gore, 40.8% Bush, 2.5% Nader, 0.7% Buchanan
National and State Parks: Mines of Spain State Park; White Pine Hollow State Park
Additional Information Contacts
Dubuque County Government Offices.......... 563-589-4441
Dubuque Board of Realtors.......... 563-556-5721
Dubuque Chamber of Commerce.......... 563-557-9200
Dyersville Chamber of Commerce.......... 563-875-2311

Dubuque County Communities

ASBURY (city). Covers a land area of 2.521 square miles and a water area of 0 square miles. Located at 42.51° N. Lat.; 90.76° W. Long.
Population: 2,450 (2000); Race: 98.5% White, 0.2% Black, 0.4% Asian, 0.0% American Indian and Alaska Native, 0.0% Hispanic of any race, 0.9% two or more races (2000); Density: 971.8 persons per square mile (2000); Age: 31.9% under 18, 6.1% over 64 (2000); Marriage status: 20.7% never married, 73.7% now married, 1.2% widowed, 4.4% divorced (2000); Foreign born: 0.8% (2000); Ancestry (includes multiple ancestries): 56.8% German, 18.8% Irish, 10.2% United States or American, 7.2% English, 4.3% French (except Basque) (2000).
Economy: Three miles West Northwest of Dubuque. Single-family building permits issued: 41 (2001) / 37 (2000); Multi-family building permits issued: 12 (2001) / 0 (2000); Employment by occupation: 15.7% management, 24.3% professional, 9.3% services, 28.8% sales, 0.3% farming, 5.7% construction, 15.8% production (2000).
Income: Per capita income: $21,447 (2000); Median household income: $60,100 (2000); Poverty rate: 4.0% (2000).
Taxes: Total city taxes per capita: $224 (1997); City property taxes per capita: $131 (1997).
Education: High school graduation rate: 94.1% (2000); College graduation rate: 30.8% (2000).
Housing: Homeownership rate: 88.7% (2000); Median home value: $127,800 (2000); Median rent: $420 per month (2000); Median age of housing: 24 years (2000).
Transportation: Commute to work: 97.7% car, 0.3% public transportation, 0.3% walk, 1.7% work from home (2000); Travel time to work: 45.0% less than 15 minutes, 48.9% 15 to 30 minutes, 3.8% 30 to 45 minutes, 0.5% 45 to 60 minutes, 2.0% 60 minutes or more (2000)

BALLTOWN (city). Covers a land area of 0.059 square miles and a water area of 0 square miles. Located at 42.63° N. Lat.; 90.86° W. Long.
Population: 73 (2000); Race: 100.0% White, 0.0% Black, 0.0% Asian, 0.0% American Indian and Alaska Native, 0.0% Hispanic of any race, 0.0% two or more races (2000); Density: 1,233.4 persons per square mile (2000); Age: 18.6% under 18, 18.6% over 64 (2000); Marriage status: 29.2% never married, 66.7% now married, 4.2% widowed, 0.0% divorced (2000); Foreign born: 0.0% (2000); Ancestry (includes multiple ancestries): 54.2% German, 8.5% Irish, 6.8% Norwegian, 1.7% Dutch (2000).
Economy: Employment by occupation: 3.3% management, 3.3% professional, 33.3% services, 16.7% sales, 0.0% farming, 0.0% construction, 43.3% production (2000).
Income: Per capita income: $24,241 (2000); Median household income: $40,625 (2000); Poverty rate: 0.0% (2000).
Taxes: Total city taxes per capita: $79 (1997); City property taxes per capita: $0 (1997).
Education: High school graduation rate: 80.6% (2000); College graduation rate: 2.8% (2000).
Housing: Homeownership rate: 83.3% (2000); Median home value: $91,700 (2000); Median age of housing: 34 years (2000).
Transportation: Commute to work: 83.3% car, 0.0% public transportation, 0.0% walk, 16.7% work from home (2000); Travel time to work: 0.0% less than 15 minutes, 20.0% 15 to 30 minutes, 64.0% 30 to 45 minutes, 16.0% 45 to 60 minutes, 0.0% 60 minutes or more (2000)

BANKSTON (city). Covers a land area of 0.275 square miles and a water area of 0 square miles. Located at 42.50° N. Lat.; 90.96° W. Long.
History: Bankston was founded by Colonel Bankston.
Population: 27 (2000); Race: 100.0% White, 0.0% Black, 0.0% Asian, 0.0% American Indian and Alaska Native, 0.0% Hispanic of any race, 0.0% two or more races (2000); Density: 98.2 persons per square mile (2000); Age: 37.9% under 18, 6.9% over 64 (2000); Marriage status: 62.5% never married, 29.2% now married, 8.3% widowed, 0.0% divorced (2000); Foreign born: 0.0% (2000); Ancestry (includes multiple ancestries): 75.9% German, 6.9% United States or American, 3.4% Irish (2000).
Economy: Employment by occupation: 25.0% management, 0.0% professional, 58.3% services, 8.3% sales, 0.0% farming, 8.3% construction, 0.0% production (2000).
Income: Per capita income: $9,886 (2000); Median household income: $18,750 (2000); Poverty rate: 41.4% (2000).
Taxes: Total city taxes per capita: $83 (1997); City property taxes per capita: $0 (1997).
Education: High school graduation rate: 90.9% (2000); College graduation rate: 0.0% (2000).

Housing: Homeownership rate: 66.7% (2000); Median home value: $75,000 (2000); Median rent: $175 per month (2000); Median age of housing: 57 years (2000).
Transportation: Commute to work: 75.0% car, 0.0% public transportation, 25.0% walk, 0.0% work from home (2000); Travel time to work: 25.0% less than 15 minutes, 33.3% 15 to 30 minutes, 33.3% 30 to 45 minutes, 8.3% 45 to 60 minutes, 0.0% 60 minutes or more (2000)

BERNARD (city). Covers a land area of 0.092 square miles and a water area of 0 square miles. Located at 42.31° N. Lat.; 90.83° W. Long.
History: Bernard, originally known as Melleray, was named after Father Bernard, abbott of the New Melleray monastery.
Population: 97 (2000); Race: 100.0% White, 0.0% Black, 0.0% Asian, 0.0% American Indian and Alaska Native, 0.0% Hispanic of any race, 0.0% two or more races (2000); Density: 1,053.5 persons per square mile (2000); Age: 16.3% under 18, 21.4% over 64 (2000); Marriage status: 34.5% never married, 46.0% now married, 17.2% widowed, 2.3% divorced (2000); Foreign born: 0.0% (2000); Ancestry (includes multiple ancestries): 41.8% German, 36.7% Irish, 8.2% Other groups, 4.1% English, 3.1% Scotch-Irish (2000).
Economy: Employment by occupation: 12.5% management, 1.8% professional, 14.3% services, 19.6% sales, 5.4% farming, 12.5% construction, 33.9% production (2000).
Income: Per capita income: $32,671 (2000); Median household income: $30,000 (2000); Poverty rate: 6.1% (2000).
Taxes: Total city taxes per capita: $112 (1997); City property taxes per capita: $30 (1997).
Education: High school graduation rate: 79.7% (2000); College graduation rate: 4.1% (2000).
Housing: Homeownership rate: 88.0% (2000); Median home value: $65,000 (2000); Median rent: $325 per month (2000); Median age of housing: 56 years (2000).
Transportation: Commute to work: 92.9% car, 0.0% public transportation, 7.1% walk, 0.0% work from home (2000); Travel time to work: 33.9% less than 15 minutes, 41.1% 15 to 30 minutes, 21.4% 30 to 45 minutes, 3.6% 45 to 60 minutes, 0.0% 60 minutes or more (2000)

CASCADE (city). Covers a land area of 1.131 square miles and a water area of 0 square miles. Located at 42.29° N. Lat.; 91.01° W. Long. Elevation is 832 feet.
History: Cascade was named for the cascades in the Maquoketa River. Early settlers, predominantly of Irish ancestry, migrated from the East and attempted to utilize the natural waterfall here as a source of power. Because the dam they built was small and railroad facilities were inadequate, the town did not become the industrial center its founders planned.
Population: 1,958 (2000); Race: 97.3% White, 0.0% Black, 0.0% Asian, 0.0% American Indian and Alaska Native, 0.0% Hispanic of any race, 1.8% two or more races (2000); Density: 1,731.2 persons per square mile (2000); Age: 24.7% under 18, 19.5% over 64 (2000); Marriage status: 20.6% never married, 65.7% now married, 8.8% widowed, 5.0% divorced (2000); Foreign born: 0.4% (2000); Ancestry (includes multiple ancestries): 51.2% German, 28.1% Irish, 9.1% United States or American, 3.8% Other groups, 2.7% Luxemburger (2000).
Economy: Single-family building permits issued: 10 (2001) / 10 (2000); Multi-family building permits issued: 0 (2001) / 3 (2000); Employment by occupation: 11.9% management, 16.0% professional, 15.8% services, 18.4% sales, 1.8% farming, 8.7% construction, 27.5% production (2000).
Income: Per capita income: $18,280 (2000); Median household income: $40,273 (2000); Poverty rate: 11.1% (2000).
Taxes: Total city taxes per capita: $229 (1997); City property taxes per capita: $137 (1997).
Education: High school graduation rate: 82.8% (2000); College graduation rate: 15.8% (2000).
Housing: Homeownership rate: 73.8% (2000); Median home value: $82,900 (2000); Median rent: $323 per month (2000); Median age of housing: 37 years (2000).
Newspapers: Cascade Pioneer (1 x week)
Transportation: Commute to work: 88.2% car, 0.0% public transportation, 7.7% walk, 3.1% work from home (2000); Travel time to work: 56.0% less than 15 minutes, 20.5% 15 to 30 minutes, 17.4% 30 to 45 minutes, 2.0% 45 to 60 minutes, 4.1% 60 minutes or more (2000)

CENTRALIA (city). Covers a land area of 0.549 square miles and a water area of 0 square miles. Located at 42.47° N. Lat.; 90.83° W. Long.
History: Centralia, a hamlet settled in 1837, was platted in 1850 under the name of Dakotah.
Population: 101 (2000); Race: 100.0% White, 0.0% Black, 0.0% Asian, 0.0% American Indian and Alaska Native, 0.0% Hispanic of any race, 0.0% two or more races (2000); Density: 183.9 persons per square mile (2000); Age: 39.5% under 18, 7.3% over 64 (2000); Marriage status: 22.0% never married, 67.0% now married, 2.2% widowed, 8.8% divorced (2000); Foreign born: 0.0% (2000); Ancestry (includes multiple ancestries): 41.1% German, 22.6% Irish, 7.3% United States or American, 5.6% French (except Basque), 4.0% Luxemburger (2000).
Economy: Employment by occupation: 17.5% management, 14.0% professional, 31.6% services, 3.5% sales, 0.0% farming, 7.0% construction, 26.3% production (2000).
Income: Per capita income: $15,269 (2000); Median household income: $43,333 (2000); Poverty rate: 13.8% (2000).
Taxes: Total city taxes per capita: $76 (1997); City property taxes per capita: $0 (1997).
Education: High school graduation rate: 87.7% (2000); College graduation rate: 4.1% (2000).
Housing: Homeownership rate: 84.8% (2000); Median home value: $93,300 (2000); Median rent: $325 per month (2000); Median age of housing: 27 years (2000).
Transportation: Commute to work: 88.3% car, 0.0% public transportation, 0.0% walk, 11.7% work from home (2000); Travel time to work: 26.4% less than 15 minutes, 64.2% 15 to 30 minutes, 7.5% 30 to 45 minutes, 0.0% 45 to 60 minutes, 1.9% 60 minutes or more (2000)

DUBUQUE (city). Covers a land area of 26.483 square miles and a water area of 1.234 square miles. Located at 42.50° N. Lat.; 90.68° W. Long. Elevation is 850 feet.
History: Dubuque was named for Julien Dubuque, a French Canadian who mined lead ore in the area in the 1780's. Originally part of the Wisconsin territory, it became part of Iowa in 1834. The first church in Iowa was built here in 1834, and the first bank in 1836.
Population: 57,686 (2000); Race: 96.5% White, 1.2% Black, 0.4% Asian, 0.2% American Indian and Alaska Native, 1.7% Hispanic of any race, 1.0% two or more races (2000); Density: 2,178.2 persons per square mile (2000); Age: 23.5% under 18, 16.7% over 64 (2000); Marriage status: 28.8% never married, 53.9% now married, 7.9% widowed, 9.4% divorced (2000); Foreign born: 2.5% (2000); Ancestry (includes multiple ancestries): 46.8% German, 22.2% Irish, 7.4% United States or American, 6.8% English, 5.1% Other groups (2000).
Vital Statistics: Birth rate: 138.5 per 10,000 population (1998)
Economy: Unemployment rate: 3.4% (11/2002); Total civilian labor force: 32,413 (11/2002); Single-family building permits issued: 67 (2001) / 40 (2000); Multi-family building permits issued: 43 (2001) / 68 (2000); Employment by occupation: 10.4% management, 19.2% professional, 17.0% services, 27.1% sales, 0.4% farming, 6.4% construction, 19.5% production (2000).
Income: Per capita income: $19,616 (2000); Median household income: $36,785 (2000); Poverty rate: 9.5% (2000).
Taxes: Total city taxes per capita: $449 (2000); City property taxes per capita: $290 (2000).
Education: High school graduation rate: 84.9% (2000); College graduation rate: 23.3% (2000).

School District(s)

Dubuque Community School District (PK-12)
2000 Enrollment: 9,919 319-588-5100

Four-year College(s)

Clarke College (Private, Not-for-profit, Roman Catholic)
2001 Enrollment: 1,201 319-588-6300
2001 Tuition: In-state $14,685; Out-of-state $14,685
University of Dubuque (Private, Not-for-profit, Presbyterian Church (USA))
2001 Enrollment: 1,039 563-589-3000
2001 Tuition: In-state $14,770; Out-of-state $14,770
Emmaus Bible College (Private, Not-for-profit, Brethren Church)
2001 Enrollment: 284 319-588-8000
2001 Tuition: In-state $5,816; Out-of-state $5,816
Loras College (Private, Not-for-profit, Roman Catholic)
2001 Enrollment: 1,758 563-588-7100
2001 Tuition: In-state $15,980; Out-of-state $15,980
Wartburg Theological Seminary (Private, Not-for-profit, Evangelical Lutheran Church)
2001 Enrollment: 172 563-589-0200

Two-year College(s)

Capri College (Private, For-profit)
2001 Enrollment: 86 319-588-2379

Housing: Homeownership rate: 67.7% (2000); Median home value: $88,400 (2000); Median rent: $370 per month (2000); Median age of housing: 46 years (2000).
Hospitals: Finley Hospital (158 beds); Mercy Medical Center (521 beds)
Safety: Violent crime rate: 4.2 per 10,000 population; Property crime rate: 254.1 per 10,000 population (2001).
Newspapers: The Dubuque Leader (1 x week); The Witness (1 x week); Telegraph Herald (7 x week)
Transportation: Commute to work: 90.2% car, 0.8% public transportation, 6.1% walk, 2.3% work from home (2000); Travel time to work: 64.7% less than 15 minutes, 28.8% 15 to 30 minutes, 3.1% 30 to 45 minutes, 1.1% 45 to 60 minutes, 2.3% 60 minutes or more (2000)
Airports: Dubuque Regional (primary service)
Additional Information Contacts
Dubuque Board of Realtors 563-556-5721
Dubuque Chamber of Commerce........................ 563-557-9200

DURANGO (city). Covers a land area of 0.034 square miles and a water area of 0 square miles. Located at 42.56° N. Lat.; 90.77° W. Long.
History: Durango was known in pioneer days as Timber Diggings. Here the notorious outlaw, "Kaintuck" Anderson, was killed in 1837.
Population: 24 (2000); Race: 84.6% White, 0.0% Black, 0.0% Asian, 0.0% American Indian and Alaska Native, 0.0% Hispanic of any race, 0.0% two or more races (2000); Density: 709.8 persons per square mile (2000); Age: 15.4% under 18, 15.4% over 64 (2000); Marriage status: 41.7% never married, 58.3% now married, 0.0% widowed, 0.0% divorced (2000); Foreign born: 0.0% (2000); Ancestry (includes multiple ancestries): 53.8% German, 30.8% Other groups, 7.7% Italian, 7.7% Irish, 7.7% English (2000).
Economy: Single-family building permits issued: 0 (2001) / 0 (2000); Multi-family building permits issued: 0 (2001) / 0 (2000); Employment by occupation: 0.0% management, 0.0% professional, 0.0% services, 30.8% sales, 0.0% farming, 46.2% construction, 23.1% production (2000).
Income: Per capita income: $19,827 (2000); Median household income: $32,188 (2000); Poverty rate: 15.4% (2000).
Education: High school graduation rate: 50.0% (2000); College graduation rate: 0.0% (2000).
Housing: Homeownership rate: 81.8% (2000); Median home value: $72,500 (2000); Median rent: $375 per month (2000); Median age of housing: 39 years (2000).
Transportation: Commute to work: 100.0% car, 0.0% public transportation, 0.0% walk, 0.0% work from home (2000); Travel time to work: 30.8% less than 15 minutes, 69.2% 15 to 30 minutes, 0.0% 30 to 45 minutes, 0.0% 45 to 60 minutes, 0.0% 60 minutes or more (2000)

DYERSVILLE (city). Covers a land area of 4.595 square miles and a water area of 0.007 square miles. Located at 42.48° N. Lat.; 91.12° W. Long.
History: Dyersville was settled in 1837-38 by English families, and in 1848 was named for James Dyer, Jr. St. Francis Xavier church, with two spires thrusting upward 200 feet, was built here in 1888 at a cost of $100,000.
Population: 4,035 (2000); Race: 99.4% White, 0.1% Black, 0.1% Asian, 0.0% American Indian and Alaska Native, 0.1% Hispanic of any race, 0.3% two or more races (2000); Density: 878.1 persons per square mile (2000); Age: 28.3% under 18, 16.4% over 64 (2000); Marriage status: 21.7% never married, 65.5% now married, 9.0% widowed, 3.8% divorced (2000); Foreign born: 0.1% (2000); Ancestry (includes multiple ancestries): 62.6% German, 11.8% Irish, 6.7% United States or American, 6.1% English, 2.0% Dutch (2000).
Economy: Single-family building permits issued: 20 (2001) / 9 (2000); Multi-family building permits issued: 60 (2001) / 0 (2000); Employment by occupation: 11.4% management, 13.9% professional, 16.6% services, 26.8% sales, 1.2% farming, 10.6% construction, 19.6% production (2000).
Income: Per capita income: $17,195 (2000); Median household income: $38,469 (2000); Poverty rate: 4.8% (2000).
Taxes: Total city taxes per capita: $294 (1997); City property taxes per capita: $277 (1997).
Education: High school graduation rate: 81.1% (2000); College graduation rate: 13.9% (2000).
Housing: Homeownership rate: 83.2% (2000); Median home value: $95,000 (2000); Median rent: $292 per month (2000); Median age of housing: 34 years (2000).
Hospitals: Mercy Medical Center - Dyersville (95 beds)
Safety: Violent crime rate: 7.4 per 10,000 population; Property crime rate: 161.3 per 10,000 population (2001).
Newspapers: Eastern Iowa Shopping News (1 x week); Dyersville Commercial (1 x week)
Transportation: Commute to work: 92.6% car, 0.0% public transportation, 3.8% walk, 3.6% work from home (2000); Travel time to work: 61.5% less than 15 minutes, 20.8% 15 to 30 minutes, 13.9% 30 to 45 minutes, 2.6% 45 to 60 minutes, 1.3% 60 minutes or more (2000)
Additional Information Contacts
Dyersville Chamber of Commerce........................ 563-875-2311

EPWORTH (city). Covers a land area of 1.310 square miles and a water area of 0 square miles. Located at 42.44° N. Lat.; 90.93° W. Long.
History: Epworth was named for Epworth, England, birthplace of John Wesley. The Epworth Seminary was opened here in 1857.
Population: 1,428 (2000); Race: 93.4% White, 0.0% Black, 3.9% Asian, 0.0% American Indian and Alaska Native, 1.0% Hispanic of any race, 1.0% two or more races (2000); Density: 1,089.8 persons per square mile (2000); Age: 28.2% under 18, 9.0% over 64 (2000); Marriage status: 34.3% never married, 56.2% now married, 4.7% widowed, 4.9% divorced (2000); Foreign born: 6.7% (2000); Ancestry (includes multiple ancestries): 57.1% German, 27.3% Irish, 6.6% Other groups, 5.9% English, 4.7% United States or American (2000).
Economy: Single-family building permits issued: 15 (2001) / 8 (2000); Multi-family building permits issued: 0 (2001) / 4 (2000); Employment by occupation: 6.8% management, 16.2% professional, 18.4% services, 22.5% sales, 1.5% farming, 7.7% construction, 26.9% production (2000).
Income: Per capita income: $15,869 (2000); Median household income: $39,938 (2000); Poverty rate: 6.2% (2000).
Taxes: Total city taxes per capita: $200 (1997); City property taxes per capita: $106 (1997).
Education: High school graduation rate: 87.0% (2000); College graduation rate: 15.7% (2000).

Four-year College(s)
Divine Word College (Private, Not-for-profit, Roman Catholic)
2001 Enrollment: 76 319-876-3353
2001 Tuition: In-state $8,600; Out-of-state $8,600
Housing: Homeownership rate: 83.2% (2000); Median home value: $85,200 (2000); Median rent: $318 per month (2000); Median age of housing: 27 years (2000).
Transportation: Commute to work: 88.3% car, 0.0% public transportation, 5.8% walk, 5.0% work from home (2000); Travel time to work: 33.8% less than 15 minutes, 39.6% 15 to 30 minutes, 21.6% 30 to 45 minutes, 2.3% 45 to 60 minutes, 2.7% 60 minutes or more (2000)

FARLEY (city). Covers a land area of 1.406 square miles and a water area of 0 square miles. Located at 42.44° N. Lat.; 91.00° W. Long. Elevation is 1,064 feet.
History: Farley was named in honor of Jesse P. Farley of Dubuque, who was connected with the building of the Illinois Central Railroad in 1856-57. The Farmers' Creamery here was awarded a silver medal at the Dairyman's Fair in London, England, in 1878.
Population: 1,334 (2000); Race: 99.1% White, 0.1% Black, 0.1% Asian, 0.0% American Indian and Alaska Native, 1.2% Hispanic of any race, 0.3% two or more races (2000); Density: 948.8 persons per square mile (2000); Age: 30.4% under 18, 12.9% over 64 (2000); Marriage status: 24.0% never married, 63.5% now married, 7.7% widowed, 4.9% divorced (2000); Foreign born: 0.4% (2000); Ancestry (includes multiple ancestries): 56.0% German, 21.3% Irish, 9.7% United States or American, 3.6% English, 2.5% French (except Basque) (2000).
Economy: Single-family building permits issued: 11 (2001) / 8 (2000); Multi-family building permits issued: 0 (2001) / 0 (2000); Employment by occupation: 8.0% management, 10.8% professional, 16.3% services, 27.1% sales, 1.9% farming, 10.3% construction, 25.5% production (2000).
Income: Per capita income: $17,186 (2000); Median household income: $41,333 (2000); Poverty rate: 5.3% (2000).
Taxes: Total city taxes per capita: $215 (1997); City property taxes per capita: $122 (1997).
Education: High school graduation rate: 83.5% (2000); College graduation rate: 9.2% (2000).

School District(s)
Western Dubuque Community School District (KG-12)
2000 Enrollment: 2,719 319-744-3885
Housing: Homeownership rate: 83.1% (2000); Median home value: $87,200 (2000); Median rent: $340 per month (2000); Median age of housing: 40 years (2000).
Transportation: Commute to work: 91.3% car, 0.3% public transportation, 4.3% walk, 4.1% work from home (2000); Travel time to work: 44.3% less than 15 minutes, 28.3% 15 to 30 minutes, 21.3% 30 to 45 minutes, 2.6% 45 to 60 minutes, 3.5% 60 minutes or more (2000)

GRAF (city). Covers a land area of 0.140 square miles and a water area of 0 square miles. Located at 42.49° N. Lat.; 90.87° W. Long.
Population: 73 (2000); Race: 100.0% White, 0.0% Black, 0.0% Asian, 0.0% American Indian and Alaska Native, 0.0% Hispanic of any race, 0.0% two or more races (2000); Density: 521.4 persons per square mile (2000); Age: 41.0% under 18, 2.0% over 64 (2000); Marriage status: 15.9% never married, 76.2% now married, 0.0% widowed, 7.9% divorced (2000); Foreign born: 4.0% (2000); Ancestry (includes multiple ancestries): 92.0% German, 22.0% Irish, 13.0% Swiss, 11.0% Arab/Arabic, 4.0% Moroccan (2000).
Economy: Single-family building permits issued: 0 (2001) / 0 (2000); Multi-family building permits issued: 0 (2001) / 0 (2000); Employment by occupation: 8.2% management, 22.4% professional, 8.2% services, 16.3% sales, 0.0% farming, 28.6% construction, 16.3% production (2000).
Income: Per capita income: $14,438 (2000); Median household income: $56,250 (2000); Poverty rate: 0.0% (2000).
Taxes: Total city taxes per capita: $127 (1997); City property taxes per capita: $48 (1997).
Education: High school graduation rate: 78.4% (2000); College graduation rate: 29.4% (2000).
Housing: Homeownership rate: 96.3% (2000); Median home value: $101,900 (2000); Median age of housing: 26 years (2000).
Transportation: Commute to work: 100.0% car, 0.0% public transportation, 0.0% walk, 0.0% work from home (2000); Travel time to work: 16.3% less than 15 minutes, 42.9% 15 to 30 minutes, 30.6% 30 to 45 minutes, 4.1% 45 to 60 minutes, 6.1% 60 minutes or more (2000)

HOLY CROSS (city). Covers a land area of 0.284 square miles and a water area of 0 square miles. Located at 42.60° N. Lat.; 90.99° W. Long.
History: Holy Cross, founded by German and Irish settlers, was originally established as the Pin Oak post office, with John H. Floyd as postmaster. The name was changed in 1899 to commemorate the large wooden cross with which Bishop Loras had marked the site for a future church.
Population: 339 (2000); Race: 100.0% White, 0.0% Black, 0.0% Asian, 0.0% American Indian and Alaska Native, 0.0% Hispanic of any race, 0.0% two or more races (2000); Density: 1,191.8 persons per square mile (2000); Age: 29.0% under 18, 14.0% over 64 (2000); Marriage status: 22.2% never married, 68.5% now married, 6.5% widowed, 2.8% divorced (2000); Foreign born: 0.0% (2000); Ancestry (includes multiple ancestries): 64.5% German, 17.4% United States or American, 9.7% Irish, 3.7% French (except Basque), 1.2% English (2000).
Economy: Single-family building permits issued: 2 (2001) / 0 (2000); Multi-family building permits issued: 0 (2001) / 0 (2000); Employment by occupation: 8.4% management, 9.0% professional, 10.2% services, 28.3% sales, 1.2% farming, 21.1% construction, 21.7% production (2000).
Income: Per capita income: $16,629 (2000); Median household income: $38,125 (2000); Poverty rate: 8.7% (2000).
Taxes: Total city taxes per capita: $229 (1997); City property taxes per capita: $132 (1997).
Education: High school graduation rate: 82.6% (2000); College graduation rate: 7.0% (2000).
Housing: Homeownership rate: 76.9% (2000); Median home value: $89,500 (2000); Median rent: $238 per month (2000); Median age of housing: 38 years (2000).
Transportation: Commute to work: 81.3% car, 0.0% public transportation, 13.3% walk, 5.4% work from home (2000); Travel time to work: 38.2% less than 15 minutes, 29.9% 15 to 30 minutes, 28.0% 30 to 45 minutes, 2.5% 45 to 60 minutes, 1.3% 60 minutes or more (2000)

LUXEMBURG (city). Covers a land area of 0.455 square miles and a water area of 0 square miles. Located at 42.60° N. Lat.; 91.07° W. Long. Elevation is 1,180 feet.
History: Luxemburg, a German settlement, was once known as Flea Hill. The Holy Trinity Catholic Church here was built in 1876.
Population: 246 (2000); Race: 98.9% White, 0.0% Black, 1.1% Asian, 0.0% American Indian and Alaska Native, 0.0% Hispanic of any race, 0.0% two or more races (2000); Density: 540.2 persons per square mile (2000); Age: 27.0% under 18, 21.1% over 64 (2000); Marriage status: 25.2% never married, 68.3% now married, 6.4% widowed, 0.0% divorced (2000); Foreign born: 1.1% (2000); Ancestry (includes multiple ancestries): 71.5% German, 5.2% Irish, 4.8% Luxemburger, 2.6% Other groups, 1.5% English (2000).
Economy: Single-family building permits issued: 1 (2001) / 1 (2000); Multi-family building permits issued: 0 (2001) / 0 (2000); Employment by occupation: 12.0% management, 9.9% professional, 14.1% services, 25.4% sales, 0.0% farming, 22.5% construction, 16.2% production (2000).
Income: Per capita income: $15,314 (2000); Median household income: $35,833 (2000); Poverty rate: 0.0% (2000).
Taxes: Total city taxes per capita: $233 (1997); City property taxes per capita: $135 (1997).
Education: High school graduation rate: 76.9% (2000); College graduation rate: 7.7% (2000).
Housing: Homeownership rate: 95.9% (2000); Median home value: $80,700 (2000); Median rent: $275 per month (2000); Median age of housing: 44 years (2000).
Transportation: Commute to work: 89.0% car, 0.0% public transportation, 5.9% walk, 3.7% work from home (2000); Travel time to work: 23.7% less than 15 minutes, 31.3% 15 to 30 minutes, 28.2% 30 to 45 minutes, 13.7% 45 to 60 minutes, 3.1% 60 minutes or more (2000)

NEW VIENNA (city). Covers a land area of 0.450 square miles and a water area of 0 square miles. Located at 42.54° N. Lat.; 91.11° W. Long. Elevation is 1,018 feet.
History: New Vienna was founded by German families about 1844.
Population: 400 (2000); Race: 100.0% White, 0.0% Black, 0.0% Asian, 0.0% American Indian and Alaska Native, 0.0% Hispanic of any race, 0.0% two or more races (2000); Density: 889.1 persons per square mile (2000); Age: 18.0% under 18, 25.1% over 64 (2000); Marriage status: 22.9% never married, 63.7% now married, 8.2% widowed, 5.1% divorced (2000); Foreign born: 0.0% (2000); Ancestry (includes multiple ancestries): 70.1% German, 5.8% United States or American, 4.1% Irish, 2.2% French (except Basque), 1.5% Norwegian (2000).
Economy: Single-family building permits issued: 1 (2001) / 2 (2000); Multi-family building permits issued: 0 (2001) / 0 (2000); Employment by occupation: 11.3% management, 6.6% professional, 11.8% services, 24.5% sales, 0.0% farming, 16.0% construction, 29.7% production (2000).
Income: Per capita income: $25,285 (2000); Median household income: $36,500 (2000); Poverty rate: 6.8% (2000).
Taxes: Total city taxes per capita: $267 (1997); City property taxes per capita: $170 (1997).
Education: High school graduation rate: 73.3% (2000); College graduation rate: 2.6% (2000).
Housing: Homeownership rate: 85.6% (2000); Median home value: $81,300 (2000); Median rent: $250 per month (2000); Median age of housing: 39 years (2000).
Transportation: Commute to work: 91.5% car, 0.0% public transportation, 4.7% walk, 2.8% work from home (2000); Travel time to work: 55.8% less than 15 minutes, 9.7% 15 to 30 minutes, 21.4% 30 to 45 minutes, 8.7% 45 to 60 minutes, 4.4% 60 minutes or more (2000)

PEOSTA (city). Covers a land area of 1.348 square miles and a water area of 0 square miles. Located at 42.44° N. Lat.; 90.84° W. Long.
History: It is believed that Peosta was named in honor of the wife of a Fox chief who discovered local lead deposits.
Population: 651 (2000); Race: 98.3% White, 0.2% Black, 0.0% Asian, 0.0% American Indian and Alaska Native, 1.6% Hispanic of any race, 1.6% two or more races (2000); Density: 482.9 persons per square mile (2000); Age: 36.7% under 18, 5.2% over 64 (2000); Marriage status: 17.4% never married, 77.9% now married, 1.4% widowed, 3.3% divorced (2000); Foreign born: 0.0% (2000); Ancestry (includes multiple ancestries): 55.5% German, 22.1% Irish, 7.4% United States or American, 5.6% Other groups, 3.4% Dutch (2000).
Economy: Single-family building permits issued: 20 (2001) / 22 (2000); Multi-family building permits issued: 0 (2001) / 0 (2000); Employment by occupation: 16.0% management, 20.7% professional, 8.6% services, 26.5% sales, 1.2% farming, 4.9% construction, 21.9% production (2000).
Income: Per capita income: $17,499 (2000); Median household income: $56,250 (2000); Poverty rate: 1.7% (2000).
Taxes: Total city taxes per capita: $803 (1997); City property taxes per capita: $765 (1997).
Education: High school graduation rate: 93.7% (2000); College graduation rate: 34.4% (2000).
Housing: Homeownership rate: 86.2% (2000); Median home value: $128,800 (2000); Median rent: $306 per month (2000); Median age of housing: 4 years (2000).
Transportation: Commute to work: 95.4% car, 0.0% public transportation, 0.9% walk, 3.7% work from home (2000); Travel time to work: 28.9% less than 15 minutes, 55.6% 15 to 30 minutes, 11.3% 30 to 45 minutes, 0.6% 45 to 60 minutes, 3.5% 60 minutes or more (2000)

RICKARDSVILLE (city). Covers a land area of 0.860 square miles and a water area of 0 square miles. Located at 42.58° N. Lat.; 90.88° W. Long.
Population: 191 (2000); Race: 100.0% White, 0.0% Black, 0.0% Asian, 0.0% American Indian and Alaska Native, 0.0% Hispanic of any race, 0.0% two or more races (2000); Density: 222.1 persons per square mile (2000); Age: 27.6% under 18, 10.6% over 64 (2000); Marriage status: 25.7% never married, 69.1% now married, 1.7% widowed, 3.4% divorced (2000); Foreign born: 0.0% (2000); Ancestry (includes multiple ancestries): 58.5% German, 9.2% Irish, 6.5% United States or American, 5.1% Scandinavian, 3.2% English (2000).
Economy: Corn; hogs, cattle. Single-family building permits issued: 0 (2001) / 0 (2000); Multi-family building permits issued: 0 (2001) / 0 (2000); Employment by occupation: 9.6% management, 12.0% professional, 4.0% services, 29.6% sales, 3.2% farming, 11.2% construction, 30.4% production (2000).
Income: Per capita income: $22,768 (2000); Median household income: $43,750 (2000); Poverty rate: 3.2% (2000).
Taxes: Total city taxes per capita: $107 (1997); City property taxes per capita: $16 (1997).
Education: High school graduation rate: 81.6% (2000); College graduation rate: 12.8% (2000).
Housing: Homeownership rate: 89.9% (2000); Median home value: $85,500 (2000); Median rent: $375 per month (2000); Median age of housing: 41 years (2000).
Transportation: Commute to work: 94.5% car, 0.0% public transportation, 5.5% walk, 0.0% work from home (2000); Travel time to work: 23.6% less than 15 minutes, 53.5% 15 to 30 minutes, 18.1% 30 to 45 minutes, 0.0% 45 to 60 minutes, 4.7% 60 minutes or more (2000)

SAGEVILLE (city). Covers a land area of 0.626 square miles and a water area of 0 square miles. Located at 42.55° N. Lat.; 90.71° W. Long. Elevation is 616 feet.
Population: 203 (2000); Race: 100.0% White, 0.0% Black, 0.0% Asian, 0.0% American Indian and Alaska Native, 0.0% Hispanic of any race, 0.0% two or more races (2000); Density: 324.5 persons per square mile (2000); Age: 32.1% under 18, 4.6% over 64 (2000); Marriage status: 31.4% never married, 57.7% now married, 3.4% widowed, 7.4% divorced (2000); Foreign born: 0.0% (2000); Ancestry (includes multiple ancestries): 46.8% German, 19.0% United States or American, 18.6% English, 11.8% Irish, 4.6% Norwegian (2000).
Economy: Single-family building permits issued: 0 (2001) / 0 (2000); Multi-family building permits issued: 0 (2001) / 0 (2000); Employment by occupation: 5.3% management, 8.8% professional, 13.3% services, 22.1% sales, 0.0% farming, 9.7% construction, 40.7% production (2000).
Income: Per capita income: $13,700 (2000); Median household income: $29,167 (2000); Poverty rate: 14.8% (2000).
Taxes: Total city taxes per capita: $81 (1997); City property taxes per capita: $0 (1997).
Education: High school graduation rate: 93.7% (2000); College graduation rate: 12.7% (2000).
Housing: Homeownership rate: 93.2% (2000); Median home value: $107,500 (2000); Median rent: $138 per month (2000); Median age of housing: 27 years (2000).
Transportation: Commute to work: 94.7% car, 1.8% public transportation, 1.8% walk, 1.8% work from home (2000); Travel time to work: 42.3% less than 15 minutes, 45.0% 15 to 30 minutes, 9.0% 30 to 45 minutes, 0.0% 45 to 60 minutes, 3.6% 60 minutes or more (2000)

SHERRILL (city). Covers a land area of 0.106 square miles and a water area of 0 square miles. Located at 42.60° N. Lat.; 90.78° W. Long.
History: Sherrill was named after local landowners Adam and Isaac Sherrill.
Population: 186 (2000); Race: 100.0% White, 0.0% Black, 0.0% Asian, 0.0% American Indian and Alaska Native, 0.0% Hispanic of any race, 0.0% two or more races (2000); Density: 1,753.9 persons per square mile (2000); Age: 24.9% under 18, 15.5% over 64 (2000); Marriage status: 23.9% never married, 68.3% now married, 7.7% widowed, 0.0% divorced (2000); Foreign born: 0.0% (2000); Ancestry (includes multiple ancestries): 60.2% German, 16.6% Irish, 9.4% English, 3.9% French (except Basque), 2.2% United States or American (2000).
Economy: Single-family building permits issued: 0 (2001) / 0 (2000); Multi-family building permits issued: 0 (2001) / 0 (2000); Employment by occupation: 5.6% management, 23.6% professional, 13.5% services, 21.3% sales, 0.0% farming, 11.2% construction, 24.7% production (2000).
Income: Per capita income: $21,118 (2000); Median household income: $38,125 (2000); Poverty rate: 3.3% (2000).
Taxes: Total city taxes per capita: $90 (1997); City property taxes per capita: $6 (1997).
Education: High school graduation rate: 80.5% (2000); College graduation rate: 4.9% (2000).
Housing: Homeownership rate: 83.6% (2000); Median home value: $97,100 (2000); Median rent: $404 per month (2000); Median age of housing: 40 years (2000).
Transportation: Commute to work: 92.1% car, 0.0% public transportation, 2.2% walk, 5.6% work from home (2000); Travel time to work: 21.4% less than 15 minutes, 57.1% 15 to 30 minutes, 15.5% 30 to 45 minutes, 2.4% 45 to 60 minutes, 3.6% 60 minutes or more (2000)

WORTHINGTON (city). Covers a land area of 0.310 square miles and a water area of 0 square miles. Located at 42.39° N. Lat.; 91.12° W. Long. Elevation is 920 feet.
History: Worthington was named for local store owner, Amos Worthington.
Population: 381 (2000); Race: 100.0% White, 0.0% Black, 0.0% Asian, 0.0% American Indian and Alaska Native, 0.0% Hispanic of any race, 0.0% two or more races (2000); Density: 1,228.9 persons per square mile (2000); Age: 28.1% under 18, 17.8% over 64 (2000); Marriage status: 21.1% never married, 62.5% now married, 10.4% widowed, 6.0% divorced (2000); Foreign born: 0.0% (2000); Ancestry (includes multiple ancestries): 73.7% German, 25.3% Irish, 2.6% Swedish, 2.6% United States or American, 2.6% English (2000).
Economy: Single-family building permits issued: 0 (2001) / 0 (2000); Multi-family building permits issued: 0 (2001) / 0 (2000); Employment by occupation: 7.3% management, 3.1% professional, 11.0% services, 26.2% sales, 0.0% farming, 13.6% construction, 38.7% production (2000).
Income: Per capita income: $14,119 (2000); Median household income: $36,250 (2000); Poverty rate: 3.9% (2000).
Taxes: Total city taxes per capita: $270 (2000); City property taxes per capita: $144 (2000).
Education: High school graduation rate: 79.4% (2000); College graduation rate: 6.0% (2000).
Housing: Homeownership rate: 89.0% (2000); Median home value: $74,500 (2000); Median rent: $263 per month (2000); Median age of housing: 45 years (2000).
Transportation: Commute to work: 89.2% car, 0.0% public transportation, 9.7% walk, 1.1% work from home (2000); Travel time to work: 47.3% less than 15 minutes, 29.3% 15 to 30 minutes, 15.8% 30 to 45 minutes, 7.6% 45 to 60 minutes, 0.0% 60 minutes or more (2000)

ZWINGLE (city). Covers a land area of 0.156 square miles and a water area of 0 square miles. Located at 42.29° N. Lat.; 90.68° W. Long. Elevation is 902 feet.
History: Zwingle was named for Ulrich Zwingli, the Swiss Protestant reformer.
Population: 100 (2000); Race: 100.0% White, 0.0% Black, 0.0% Asian, 0.0% American Indian and Alaska Native, 0.0% Hispanic of any race, 0.0% two or more races (2000); Density: 640.9 persons per square mile (2000); Age: 25.7% under 18, 18.9% over 64 (2000); Marriage status: 20.0% never married, 53.8% now married, 10.8% widowed, 15.4% divorced (2000); Foreign born: 0.0% (2000); Ancestry (includes multiple ancestries): 51.4% German, 39.2% Irish, 14.9% Other groups, 4.1% Norwegian, 4.1% English (2000).
Economy: Employment by occupation: 11.1% management, 6.7% professional, 17.8% services, 24.4% sales, 0.0% farming, 13.3% construction, 26.7% production (2000).
Income: Per capita income: $18,916 (2000); Median household income: $26,667 (2000); Poverty rate: 1.4% (2000).
Taxes: Total city taxes per capita: $140 (2000); City property taxes per capita: $60 (2000).
Education: High school graduation rate: 62.3% (2000); College graduation rate: 3.8% (2000).
Housing: Homeownership rate: 88.2% (2000); Median home value: $33,100 (2000); Median rent: $375 per month (2000); Median age of housing: 60 years (2000).
Transportation: Commute to work: 100.0% car, 0.0% public transportation, 0.0% walk, 0.0% work from home (2000); Travel time to work: 13.3% less than 15 minutes, 31.1% 15 to 30 minutes, 48.9% 30 to 45 minutes, 6.7% 45 to 60 minutes, 0.0% 60 minutes or more (2000)

Emmet County

Located in northwestern Iowa; bounded on the north by Minnesota; prairie area, dotted with small lakes, drained by the East and West Des Moines Rivers. Covers a land area of 395.70 square miles, a water area of 6.60 square miles, and is located in the Central Time Zone. The county government was organized in 1851. County seat is Estherville.

Weather Station: Estherville 2 N Elevation: 1,299 feet

	Jan	Feb	Mar	Apr	May	Jun	Jul	Aug	Sep	Oct	Nov	Dec
High	22	28	40	56	70	79	83	80	72	60	41	27
Low	4	10	22	34	47	56	60	58	48	36	23	10
Precip	0.6	0.5	1.7	3.2	3.4	4.7	3.4	3.7	2.8	2.2	1.5	0.6
Snow	7.4	5.6	6.8	2.5	0.0	0.0	0.0	0.0	tr	0.7	5.1	7.0

High and Low temperatures in degrees Fahrenheit; Precipitation and Snow in inches

Population: 11,027 (2000); Race: 97.4% White, 0.2% Black, 0.1% Asian, 0.1% American Indian and Alaska Native, 4.4% Hispanic of any race, 0.4% two or more races (2000); Density: 27.9 persons per square mile (2000); Age: 23.8% under 18, 19.2% over 64 (2000).
Religion: Five largest groups: 32.9% Evangelical Lutheran Church in America, 14.2% Catholic Church, 11.6% The United Methodist Church, 7.2% Presbyterian Church (U.S.A.), 4.3% Christian Church (Disciples of Christ) (2000).
Economy: Unemployment rate: 4.1% (11/2002); Total civilian labor force: 5,401 (11/2002); Leading industries: 23.9% manufacturing; 21.4% health care and social assistance; 16.6% retail trade (2000); Companies that employ more than 1,000 persons: 0 (2000); Companies that employ more than 100 persons: 6 (2000); Farms: 519 totaling 220,174 acres (1997); Minority business ownership rate: 0.0% (1997); Women business ownership rate: 17.5% (1997); Retail sales per capita: $7,225 (1997). Single-family building permits issued: 15 (2001) / 18 (2000); Multi-family building permits issued: 0 (2001) / 15 (2000).
Income: Per capita income: $16,619 (2000); Median household income: $33,305 (2000); Poverty rate: 8.2% (2000); Bankruptcy rate: 3.58% (2001).
Taxes: Total county taxes per capita: $263 (2000); County property taxes per capita: $255 (2000).
Education: High school graduation rate: 82.2% (2000); College graduation rate: 13.0% (2000).
Housing: Homeownership rate: 75.2% (2000); Median home value: $53,000 (2000); Median rent: $254 per month (2000); Median age of housing: 54 years (2000).
Health: Birth rate: 117.0 per 10,000 population (1998); Age adjusted death rate: 72.2 per 10,000 population (1999); Age adjusted cancer mortality rate: 192.2 deaths per 100,000 population (1999). Air Quality Index: 100% good, 0% moderate, 0% unhealthy (percent of days in 2000). Number of physicians: 7.3 per 10,000 population (1999); Number of hospital beds: 32.6 per 10,000 population (1999).
Elections: 2000 Presidential election results: 46.8% Gore, 50.4% Bush, 2.1% Nader, 0.4% Buchanan
National and State Parks: Anderson Prairie State Preserve; Birge Lake State Game Management Area; Cheever Lake State Game Mgt Area; Cunningham Slough State Game Management Area; East Swan Lake State Games Management Area; Fort Defiance State Park; Grass Lake State Game Management Area; High Lake State Game Management Area; Ingham Lake State Game Management Area; Iowa Lake State Game Management Area; Okamanpeedam State Park; Ryan Lake State Game Management Area; Tuttle Lake State Game Management Area; Twelvemile Lake State Game Management Area; West Swan Lake State Game Management Area
Additional Information Contacts
Emmet County Government Offices 712-362-4261
Estherville Area Chamber of Commerce 712-362-3541

Emmet County Communities

ARMSTRONG (city). Covers a land area of 0.821 square miles and a water area of 0 square miles. Located at 43.39° N. Lat.; 94.48° W. Long.
History: Armstrong, named for an explorer and early settler, sprang into existence during the construction of the Albert Lea-Estherville branch of the Chicago, Rock Island & Pacific Railroad.
Population: 979 (2000); Race: 98.3% White, 0.4% Black, 0.0% Asian, 0.0% American Indian and Alaska Native, 0.6% Hispanic of any race, 1.1% two or more races (2000); Density: 1,192.7 persons per square mile (2000); Age: 21.4% under 18, 23.8% over 64 (2000); Marriage status: 20.6% never married, 59.4% now married, 13.7% widowed, 6.4% divorced (2000); Foreign born: 0.2% (2000); Ancestry (includes multiple ancestries): 41.1% German, 17.1% Norwegian, 11.3% Irish, 10.3% Danish, 7.8% United States or American (2000).
Economy: Single-family building permits issued: 0 (2001) / 0 (2000); Multi-family building permits issued: 0 (2001) / 0 (2000); Employment by occupation: 9.9% management, 11.4% professional, 15.9% services, 25.7% sales, 1.4% farming, 7.2% construction, 28.4% production (2000).
Income: Per capita income: $16,221 (2000); Median household income: $35,446 (2000); Poverty rate: 8.0% (2000).
Taxes: Total city taxes per capita: $144 (1997); City property taxes per capita: $142 (1997).
Education: High school graduation rate: 80.7% (2000); College graduation rate: 10.8% (2000).

School District(s)

Armstrong-Ringsted Community School District (PK-12)
2000 Enrollment: 453 712-868-3550
Housing: Homeownership rate: 86.4% (2000); Median home value: $44,900 (2000); Median rent: $195 per month (2000); Median age of housing: 48 years (2000).
Newspapers: Ringsted Dispatch (1 x week); Armstrong Journal (1 x week)
Transportation: Commute to work: 91.4% car, 0.0% public transportation, 5.6% walk, 3.0% work from home (2000); Travel time to work: 59.3% less than 15 minutes, 21.8% 15 to 30 minutes, 13.3% 30 to 45 minutes, 1.3% 45 to 60 minutes, 4.2% 60 minutes or more (2000)

DOLLIVER (city). Covers a land area of 0.365 square miles and a water area of 0 square miles. Located at 43.46° N. Lat.; 94.61° W. Long. Elevation is 1,275 feet.
History: Dolliver was named for Jonathan P. Dolliver, U.S. Senator from Iowa (1900-1910).
Population: 77 (2000); Race: 100.0% White, 0.0% Black, 0.0% Asian, 0.0% American Indian and Alaska Native, 6.0% Hispanic of any race, 0.0% two or more races (2000); Density: 210.9 persons per square mile (2000); Age: 17.0% under 18, 18.0% over 64 (2000); Marriage status: 18.8% never married, 61.2% now married, 15.3% widowed, 4.7% divorced (2000); Foreign born: 0.0% (2000); Ancestry (includes multiple ancestries): 47.0% German, 16.0% Norwegian, 12.0% Irish, 8.0% French (except Basque), 3.0% Swedish (2000).
Economy: Single-family building permits issued: 0 (2001) / 0 (2000); Multi-family building permits issued: 0 (2001) / 0 (2000); Employment by occupation: 18.6% management, 8.5% professional, 10.2% services, 20.3% sales, 3.4% farming, 3.4% construction, 35.6% production (2000).
Income: Per capita income: $18,387 (2000); Median household income: $28,036 (2000); Poverty rate: 0.0% (2000).
Taxes: Total city taxes per capita: $122 (1997); City property taxes per capita: $122 (1997).
Education: High school graduation rate: 72.4% (2000); College graduation rate: 2.6% (2000).
Housing: Homeownership rate: 87.0% (2000); Median home value: $27,500 (2000); Median rent: $225 per month (2000); Median age of housing: 60+ years (2000).
Transportation: Commute to work: 100.0% car, 0.0% public transportation, 0.0% walk, 0.0% work from home (2000); Travel time to work: 25.0% less than 15 minutes, 42.9% 15 to 30 minutes, 25.0% 30 to 45 minutes, 0.0% 45 to 60 minutes, 7.1% 60 minutes or more (2000)

ESTHERVILLE (city). Covers a land area of 5.198 square miles and a water area of 0 square miles. Located at 43.40° N. Lat.; 94.83° W. Long. Elevation is 1,298 feet.
History: Estherville was named for Mrs. Esther Ridley, the wife of one of the men who assisted in platting the town in 1857.
Population: 6,656 (2000); Race: 96.4% White, 0.3% Black, 0.2% Asian, 0.0% American Indian and Alaska Native, 6.4% Hispanic of any race, 0.3% two or more races (2000); Density: 1,280.4 persons per square mile (2000); Age: 22.9% under 18, 19.3% over 64 (2000); Marriage status: 27.5% never married, 54.0% now married, 9.7% widowed, 8.8% divorced (2000); Foreign born: 3.6% (2000); Ancestry (includes multiple ancestries): 38.0% German, 18.4% Norwegian, 9.8% Irish, 7.6% Other groups, 6.1% English (2000).
Economy: Single-family building permits issued: 7 (2001) / 5 (2000); Multi-family building permits issued: 0 (2001) / 15 (2000); Employment by occupation: 10.0% management, 11.0% professional, 15.0% services, 26.0% sales, 1.2% farming, 8.4% construction, 28.4% production (2000).
Income: Per capita income: $16,488 (2000); Median household income: $31,279 (2000); Poverty rate: 8.1% (2000).
Taxes: Total city taxes per capita: $177 (1997); City property taxes per capita: $170 (1997).

Education: High school graduation rate: 82.0% (2000); College graduation rate: 13.3% (2000).

School District(s)

Estherville Lincoln Central Com School District (PK-12)
2000 Enrollment: 1,499 712-362-2692

Two-year College(s)

Iowa Lakes Community College (Public)
2001 Enrollment: 2,862 712-362-0433
2001 Tuition: In-state $2,336; Out-of-state $2,400

Housing: Homeownership rate: 72.2% (2000); Median home value: $54,500 (2000); Median rent: $265 per month (2000); Median age of housing: 54 years (2000).

Hospitals: Avera Holy Family Health (58 beds)

Safety: Violent crime rate: 39.1 per 10,000 population; Property crime rate: 270.7 per 10,000 population (2001).

Newspapers: Estherville Daily News (6 x week); The Estherville Spirit (1 x week)

Transportation: Commute to work: 93.1% car, 1.3% public transportation, 2.3% walk, 2.6% work from home (2000); Travel time to work: 61.0% less than 15 minutes, 20.9% 15 to 30 minutes, 12.5% 30 to 45 minutes, 3.6% 45 to 60 minutes, 2.0% 60 minutes or more (2000)

Airports: Estherville Municipal

Additional Information Contacts

Estherville Area Chamber of Commerce 712-362-3541

GRUVER (city). Covers a land area of 0.128 square miles and a water area of 0 square miles. Located at 43.39° N. Lat.; 94.70° W. Long. Elevation is 1,300 feet.

History: Gruver, formerly called Luzon, was platted and settled by John and Anna R. Dows in 1899.

Population: 106 (2000); Race: 100.0% White, 0.0% Black, 0.0% Asian, 0.0% American Indian and Alaska Native, 5.4% Hispanic of any race, 0.0% two or more races (2000); Density: 830.1 persons per square mile (2000); Age: 25.0% under 18, 10.7% over 64 (2000); Marriage status: 24.2% never married, 69.2% now married, 2.2% widowed, 4.4% divorced (2000); Foreign born: 1.8% (2000); Ancestry (includes multiple ancestries): 33.9% German, 29.5% Norwegian, 9.8% Irish, 9.8% Other groups, 6.3% English (2000).

Economy: Single-family building permits issued: 0 (2001) / 0 (2000); Multi-family building permits issued: 0 (2001) / 0 (2000); Employment by occupation: 8.2% management, 14.8% professional, 27.9% services, 27.9% sales, 0.0% farming, 6.6% construction, 14.8% production (2000).

Income: Per capita income: $17,766 (2000); Median household income: $38,125 (2000); Poverty rate: 2.7% (2000).

Taxes: Total city taxes per capita: $94 (1997); City property taxes per capita: $94 (1997).

Education: High school graduation rate: 79.1% (2000); College graduation rate: 9.0% (2000).

Housing: Homeownership rate: 88.9% (2000); Median home value: $37,500 (2000); Median rent: $325 per month (2000); Median age of housing: 55 years (2000).

Transportation: Commute to work: 83.6% car, 0.0% public transportation, 12.7% walk, 3.6% work from home (2000); Travel time to work: 66.0% less than 15 minutes, 22.6% 15 to 30 minutes, 3.8% 30 to 45 minutes, 7.5% 45 to 60 minutes, 0.0% 60 minutes or more (2000)

RINGSTED (city). Covers a land area of 1.078 square miles and a water area of 0 square miles. Located at 43.29° N. Lat.; 94.50° W. Long. Elevation is 1,270 feet.

History: Ringsted was platted by the Western Town Lot Company in 1899. The town was named for Ringsted, Denmark.

Population: 436 (2000); Race: 99.5% White, 0.0% Black, 0.0% Asian, 0.0% American Indian and Alaska Native, 0.0% Hispanic of any race, 0.5% two or more races (2000); Density: 404.4 persons per square mile (2000); Age: 17.6% under 18, 28.2% over 64 (2000); Marriage status: 23.2% never married, 54.8% now married, 14.2% widowed, 7.8% divorced (2000); Foreign born: 0.0% (2000); Ancestry (includes multiple ancestries): 38.8% German, 23.7% Danish, 20.2% Norwegian, 8.6% Irish, 7.1% Swedish (2000).

Economy: Single-family building permits issued: 1 (2001) / 0 (2000); Multi-family building permits issued: 0 (2001) / 0 (2000); Employment by occupation: 12.1% management, 9.2% professional, 12.6% services, 18.4% sales, 5.2% farming, 12.6% construction, 29.9% production (2000).

Income: Per capita income: $16,375 (2000); Median household income: $24,286 (2000); Poverty rate: 7.1% (2000).

Taxes: Total city taxes per capita: $200 (1997); City property taxes per capita: $197 (1997).

Education: High school graduation rate: 83.7% (2000); College graduation rate: 11.2% (2000).

Housing: Homeownership rate: 76.3% (2000); Median home value: $25,000 (2000); Median rent: $215 per month (2000); Median age of housing: 58 years (2000).

Transportation: Commute to work: 92.2% car, 0.0% public transportation, 4.8% walk, 1.2% work from home (2000); Travel time to work: 36.0% less than 15 minutes, 30.5% 15 to 30 minutes, 21.3% 30 to 45 minutes, 6.1% 45 to 60 minutes, 6.1% 60 minutes or more (2000)

WALLINGFORD (city). Covers a land area of 0.975 square miles and a water area of 0 square miles. Located at 43.31° N. Lat.; 94.79° W. Long. Elevation is 1,276 feet.

History: Wallingford is believed to be named after Wallingford, England.

Population: 210 (2000); Race: 100.0% White, 0.0% Black, 0.0% Asian, 0.0% American Indian and Alaska Native, 0.0% Hispanic of any race, 0.0% two or more races (2000); Density: 215.4 persons per square mile (2000); Age: 34.4% under 18, 9.4% over 64 (2000); Marriage status: 18.2% never married, 71.8% now married, 5.9% widowed, 4.1% divorced (2000); Foreign born: 0.0% (2000); Ancestry (includes multiple ancestries): 30.3% German, 28.3% Norwegian, 10.2% United States or American, 8.2% Irish, 4.1% English (2000).

Economy: Single-family building permits issued: 0 (2001) / 1 (2000); Multi-family building permits issued: 0 (2001) / 0 (2000); Employment by occupation: 5.8% management, 5.8% professional, 23.3% services, 15.5% sales, 0.0% farming, 9.7% construction, 39.8% production (2000).

Income: Per capita income: $13,137 (2000); Median household income: $39,500 (2000); Poverty rate: 9.4% (2000).

Taxes: Total city taxes per capita: $111 (1997); City property taxes per capita: $111 (1997).

Education: High school graduation rate: 83.9% (2000); College graduation rate: 11.2% (2000).

Housing: Homeownership rate: 89.0% (2000); Median home value: $40,700 (2000); Median rent: $313 per month (2000); Median age of housing: 60+ years (2000).

Transportation: Commute to work: 92.2% car, 0.0% public transportation, 1.9% walk, 2.9% work from home (2000); Travel time to work: 63.0% less than 15 minutes, 22.0% 15 to 30 minutes, 13.0% 30 to 45 minutes, 2.0% 45 to 60 minutes, 0.0% 60 minutes or more (2000)

Fayette County

Located in northeastern Iowa; drained by the Volga, Maquoketa, and Turkey Rivers. Covers a land area of 730.90 square miles, a water area of 0.50 square miles, and is located in the Central Time Zone. The county government was organized in 1837. County seat is West Union.

Weather Station: Fayette — Elevation: 1,049 feet

	Jan	Feb	Mar	Apr	May	Jun	Jul	Aug	Sep	Oct	Nov	Dec
High	24	30	43	58	71	80	83	81	73	61	43	29
Low	5	11	23	35	46	56	60	58	49	38	25	12
Precip	1.1	1.1	2.2	3.6	4.4	4.6	4.4	4.9	3.5	2.6	2.3	1.3
Snow	10.5	7.7	6.3	2.3	tr	0.0	0.0	0.0	0.0	0.2	4.4	9.0

High and Low temperatures in degrees Fahrenheit; Precipitation and Snow in inches

Weather Station: Oelwein 2 S — Elevation: 1,007 feet

	Jan	Feb	Mar	Apr	May	Jun	Jul	Aug	Sep	Oct	Nov	Dec
High	24	30	43	58	71	80	83	80	73	61	43	30
Low	6	13	25	37	48	58	62	60	51	39	26	13
Precip	1.1	1.1	2.0	3.3	4.0	4.5	4.2	4.9	3.7	2.6	2.1	1.4
Snow	9.4	5.9	5.1	1.4	0.0	0.0	0.0	0.0	0.0	tr	4.0	7.4

High and Low temperatures in degrees Fahrenheit; Precipitation and Snow in inches

Population: 22,008 (2000); Race: 97.7% White, 0.5% Black, 0.5% Asian, 0.1% American Indian and Alaska Native, 1.5% Hispanic of any race, 0.6% two or more races (2000); Density: 30.1 persons per square mile (2000); Age: 25.0% under 18, 19.0% over 64 (2000).

Religion: Five largest groups: 25.8% Catholic Church, 24.5% Evangelical Lutheran Church in America, 10.6% The United Methodist Church, 4.1% Presbyterian Church (U.S.A.), 3.8% Lutheran Church—Missouri Synod (2000).

Economy: Unemployment rate: 3.9% (11/2002); Total civilian labor force: 11,780 (11/2002); Leading industries: 23.4% manufacturing; 15.8% retail trade; 15.3% health care and social assistance (2000); Companies that employ more than 1,000 persons: 0 (2000); Companies that employ more than 100 persons: 10 (2000); Farms: 1,295 totaling 404,407 acres (1997); Minority

business ownership rate: 0.0% (1997); Women business ownership rate: 38.4% (1997); Retail sales per capita: $7,955 (1997). Single-family building permits issued: 18 (2001) / 25 (2000); Multi-family building permits issued: 12 (2001) / 7 (2000).
Income: Per capita income: $17,271 (2000); Median household income: $32,453 (2000); Poverty rate: 10.8% (2000); Bankruptcy rate: 2.83% (2001).
Taxes: Total county taxes per capita: $193 (1997); County property taxes per capita: $185 (1997).
Education: High school graduation rate: 84.8% (2000); College graduation rate: 13.8% (2000).
Housing: Homeownership rate: 75.6% (2000); Median home value: $58,300 (2000); Median rent: $270 per month (2000); Median age of housing: 55 years (2000).
Health: Birth rate: 107.2 per 10,000 population (1998); Age adjusted death rate: 80.6 per 10,000 population (1999); Age adjusted cancer mortality rate: 184.8 deaths per 100,000 population (1999). Number of physicians: 4.1 per 10,000 population (1999); Number of hospital beds: 40.4 per 10,000 population (1999).
Elections: 2000 Presidential election results: 48.2% Gore, 49.3% Bush, 1.8% Nader, 0.3% Buchanan
National and State Parks: Brush Creek Canyon State Park; Echo Valley State Park; Montauk State Historical Site; Volga River State Recreation Area
Additional Information Contacts
Fayette County Government Offices 563-422-3497
Oelwein Chamber of Commerce 319-283-1105

Fayette County Communities

ARLINGTON (city). Covers a land area of 1.048 square miles and a water area of 0 square miles. Located at 42.74° N. Lat.; 91.67° W. Long. Elevation is 1,112 feet.
History: Arlington was originally known as Moetown, and then later as Brush Creek. The name comes from Arlington, England.
Population: 490 (2000); Race: 99.4% White, 0.0% Black, 0.0% Asian, 0.0% American Indian and Alaska Native, 0.0% Hispanic of any race, 0.6% two or more races (2000); Density: 467.4 persons per square mile (2000); Age: 27.7% under 18, 22.1% over 64 (2000); Marriage status: 17.6% never married, 62.3% now married, 13.4% widowed, 6.7% divorced (2000); Foreign born: 0.4% (2000); Ancestry (includes multiple ancestries): 44.7% German, 10.0% Irish, 7.0% English, 5.7% Norwegian, 4.9% United States or American (2000).
Economy: Employment by occupation: 5.0% management, 16.6% professional, 8.5% services, 20.1% sales, 2.0% farming, 9.5% construction, 38.2% production (2000).
Income: Per capita income: $14,643 (2000); Median household income: $30,357 (2000); Poverty rate: 14.9% (2000).
Taxes: Total city taxes per capita: $198 (1997); City property taxes per capita: $147 (1997).
Education: High school graduation rate: 78.9% (2000); College graduation rate: 10.5% (2000).

School District(s)

Starmont Community School District (PK-12)
2000 Enrollment: 913 319-933-4598
Housing: Homeownership rate: 73.0% (2000); Median home value: $34,000 (2000); Median rent: $138 per month (2000); Median age of housing: 60+ years (2000).
Transportation: Commute to work: 88.3% car, 1.0% public transportation, 6.1% walk, 1.0% work from home (2000); Travel time to work: 32.3% less than 15 minutes, 34.9% 15 to 30 minutes, 20.5% 30 to 45 minutes, 1.5% 45 to 60 minutes, 10.8% 60 minutes or more (2000)

CLERMONT (city). Covers a land area of 1.095 square miles and a water area of 0 square miles. Located at 42.99° N. Lat.; 91.65° W. Long. Elevation is 855 feet.
History: Clermont was originally known as Norway. The first settler, a man named Delaplaine, arrived in 1848.
Population: 716 (2000); Race: 100.0% White, 0.0% Black, 0.0% Asian, 0.0% American Indian and Alaska Native, 0.0% Hispanic of any race, 0.0% two or more races (2000); Density: 653.9 persons per square mile (2000); Age: 28.6% under 18, 16.9% over 64 (2000); Marriage status: 22.1% never married, 58.5% now married, 10.2% widowed, 9.2% divorced (2000); Foreign born: 0.0% (2000); Ancestry (includes multiple ancestries): 44.9% German, 29.7% Norwegian, 9.3% Irish, 6.4% United States or American, 5.8% Swiss (2000).
Economy: Single-family building permits issued: 2 (2001) / 4 (2000); Multi-family building permits issued: 0 (2001) / 0 (2000); Employment by occupation: 8.2% management, 10.9% professional, 11.7% services, 26.9% sales, 0.8% farming, 11.4% construction, 30.2% production (2000).
Income: Per capita income: $14,276 (2000); Median household income: $34,712 (2000); Poverty rate: 8.1% (2000).
Taxes: Total city taxes per capita: $227 (1997); City property taxes per capita: $174 (1997).
Education: High school graduation rate: 81.6% (2000); College graduation rate: 13.9% (2000).
Housing: Homeownership rate: 86.2% (2000); Median home value: $70,000 (2000); Median rent: $256 per month (2000); Median age of housing: 52 years (2000).
Transportation: Commute to work: 88.0% car, 0.0% public transportation, 5.7% walk, 2.4% work from home (2000); Travel time to work: 54.0% less than 15 minutes, 24.2% 15 to 30 minutes, 10.0% 30 to 45 minutes, 6.1% 45 to 60 minutes, 5.6% 60 minutes or more (2000)

ELGIN (city). Covers a land area of 0.668 square miles and a water area of 0 square miles. Located at 42.95° N. Lat.; 91.63° W. Long. Elevation is 834 feet.
History: Elgin was surveyed by N.V. Burdick from Elgin, Illinois, and named for his home town.
Population: 676 (2000); Race: 99.4% White, 0.0% Black, 0.6% Asian, 0.0% American Indian and Alaska Native, 0.0% Hispanic of any race, 0.0% two or more races (2000); Density: 1,011.3 persons per square mile (2000); Age: 23.6% under 18, 24.4% over 64 (2000); Marriage status: 20.0% never married, 54.1% now married, 16.3% widowed, 9.5% divorced (2000); Foreign born: 0.6% (2000); Ancestry (includes multiple ancestries): 37.7% German, 25.7% Norwegian, 19.0% Swiss, 7.6% United States or American, 6.0% Irish (2000).
Economy: Single-family building permits issued: 3 (2001) / 2 (2000); Multi-family building permits issued: 0 (2001) / 0 (2000); Employment by occupation: 13.0% management, 16.9% professional, 13.3% services, 30.5% sales, 0.6% farming, 10.7% construction, 14.9% production (2000).
Income: Per capita income: $16,225 (2000); Median household income: $28,833 (2000); Poverty rate: 7.8% (2000).
Taxes: Total city taxes per capita: $173 (1997); City property taxes per capita: $122 (1997).
Education: High school graduation rate: 86.9% (2000); College graduation rate: 12.6% (2000).

School District(s)

Valley Community School District (KG-12)
2000 Enrollment: 598 319-426-5501
Housing: Homeownership rate: 73.1% (2000); Median home value: $58,800 (2000); Median rent: $207 per month (2000); Median age of housing: 48 years (2000).
Newspapers: The Elgin Echo (1x week)
Transportation: Commute to work: 89.8% car, 0.0% public transportation, 7.9% walk, 1.6% work from home (2000); Travel time to work: 48.0% less than 15 minutes, 36.7% 15 to 30 minutes, 8.0% 30 to 45 minutes, 3.3% 45 to 60 minutes, 4.0% 60 minutes or more (2000)

FAYETTE (city). Covers a land area of 1.493 square miles and a water area of 0 square miles. Located at 42.84° N. Lat.; 91.80° W. Long. Elevation is 1,015 feet.
History: Fayette Seminary (later known as Upper Iowa University) was built in Fayette in 1857 after Col. Robert Alexander and Samuel H. Robinson had donated the land and a sum of $50,000.
Population: 1,300 (2000); Race: 85.5% White, 5.4% Black, 3.6% Asian, 0.5% American Indian and Alaska Native, 3.9% Hispanic of any race, 2.9% two or more races (2000); Density: 870.9 persons per square mile (2000); Age: 19.2% under 18, 10.7% over 64 (2000); Marriage status: 49.3% never married, 39.6% now married, 6.3% widowed, 4.8% divorced (2000); Foreign born: 6.0% (2000); Ancestry (includes multiple ancestries): 33.7% German, 17.1% Other groups, 16.0% Irish, 8.4% Norwegian, 7.9% English (2000).
Economy: Single-family building permits issued: 2 (2001) / 0 (2000); Multi-family building permits issued: 12 (2001) / 0 (2000); Employment by occupation: 6.8% management, 24.0% professional, 19.7% services, 24.7% sales, 1.2% farming, 6.3% construction, 17.2% production (2000).
Income: Per capita income: $11,131 (2000); Median household income: $28,750 (2000); Poverty rate: 16.4% (2000).
Taxes: Total city taxes per capita: $238 (1997); City property taxes per capita: $190 (1997).
Education: High school graduation rate: 90.3% (2000); College graduation rate: 27.4% (2000).

Four-year College(s)

Upper Iowa University (Private, Not-for-profit)
2001 Enrollment: 4,557 319-425-5200
2001 Tuition: In-state $12,856; Out-of-state $12,856

Housing: Homeownership rate: 60.8% (2000); Median home value: $55,000 (2000); Median rent: $283 per month (2000); Median age of housing: 57 years (2000).

Newspapers: Fayette Leader (1 x week)

Transportation: Commute to work: 64.3% car, 0.0% public transportation, 29.6% walk, 4.5% work from home (2000); Travel time to work: 68.4% less than 15 minutes, 21.1% 15 to 30 minutes, 6.2% 30 to 45 minutes, 0.5% 45 to 60 minutes, 3.8% 60 minutes or more (2000)

HAWKEYE (city). Covers a land area of 0.666 square miles and a water area of 0 square miles. Located at 42.93° N. Lat.; 91.95° W. Long. Elevation is 1,177 feet.

History: The name of Hawkeye refers either to the Sauk chief Black Hawk, or to a character in "The Last of the Mohicans" by James Fenimore Cooper.

Population: 489 (2000); Race: 98.8% White, 0.0% Black, 0.0% Asian, 0.0% American Indian and Alaska Native, 0.0% Hispanic of any race, 0.0% two or more races (2000); Density: 734.2 persons per square mile (2000); Age: 23.0% under 18, 19.4% over 64 (2000); Marriage status: 21.5% never married, 60.4% now married, 11.1% widowed, 7.0% divorced (2000); Foreign born: 1.2% (2000); Ancestry (includes multiple ancestries): 50.7% German, 11.6% Irish, 11.6% Norwegian, 5.5% English, 4.1% French (except Basque) (2000).

Economy: Single-family building permits issued: 1 (2001) / 1 (2000); Multi-family building permits issued: 0 (2001) / 0 (2000); Employment by occupation: 13.7% management, 9.0% professional, 15.6% services, 17.6% sales, 2.0% farming, 16.4% construction, 25.8% production (2000).

Income: Per capita income: $14,319 (2000); Median household income: $30,333 (2000); Poverty rate: 8.6% (2000).

Taxes: Total city taxes per capita: $174 (1997); City property taxes per capita: $119 (1997).

Education: High school graduation rate: 83.7% (2000); College graduation rate: 11.3% (2000).

Housing: Homeownership rate: 79.4% (2000); Median home value: $48,200 (2000); Median rent: $189 per month (2000); Median age of housing: 60+ years (2000).

Transportation: Commute to work: 89.1% car, 0.0% public transportation, 3.5% walk, 4.7% work from home (2000); Travel time to work: 32.0% less than 15 minutes, 51.6% 15 to 30 minutes, 13.1% 30 to 45 minutes, 3.3% 45 to 60 minutes, 0.0% 60 minutes or more (2000)

MAYNARD (city). Covers a land area of 0.992 square miles and a water area of 0.026 square miles. Located at 42.77° N. Lat.; 91.87° W. Long. Elevation is 1,101 feet.

History: Maynard was named in honor of Henry Maynard.

Population: 500 (2000); Race: 99.6% White, 0.0% Black, 0.0% Asian, 0.0% American Indian and Alaska Native, 0.0% Hispanic of any race, 0.4% two or more races (2000); Density: 504.2 persons per square mile (2000); Age: 25.8% under 18, 22.1% over 64 (2000); Marriage status: 25.4% never married, 53.3% now married, 11.7% widowed, 9.5% divorced (2000); Foreign born: 0.4% (2000); Ancestry (includes multiple ancestries): 56.0% German, 11.4% Irish, 8.3% English, 4.7% United States or American, 3.9% Dutch (2000).

Economy: Single-family building permits issued: 0 (2001) / 4 (2000); Multi-family building permits issued: 0 (2001) / 0 (2000); Employment by occupation: 14.9% management, 24.0% professional, 9.0% services, 14.5% sales, 0.5% farming, 16.7% construction, 20.4% production (2000).

Income: Per capita income: $15,779 (2000); Median household income: $32,639 (2000); Poverty rate: 8.1% (2000).

Taxes: Total city taxes per capita: $162 (1997); City property taxes per capita: $112 (1997).

Education: High school graduation rate: 89.3% (2000); College graduation rate: 21.7% (2000).

School District(s)

West Central Community School District (KG-12)
2000 Enrollment: 340 319-637-2283

Housing: Homeownership rate: 81.6% (2000); Median home value: $51,400 (2000); Median rent: $300 per month (2000); Median age of housing: 40 years (2000).

Transportation: Commute to work: 92.8% car, 0.0% public transportation, 5.4% walk, 1.8% work from home (2000); Travel time to work: 47.5% less than 15 minutes, 37.3% 15 to 30 minutes, 6.0% 30 to 45 minutes, 4.1% 45 to 60 minutes, 5.1% 60 minutes or more (2000)

OELWEIN (city). Covers a land area of 4.794 square miles and a water area of 0.048 square miles. Located at 42.67° N. Lat.; 91.91° W. Long. Elevation is 1,039 feet.

History: Oelwein was named for a German who gave part of his property for the railroad station and right-of-way.

Population: 6,692 (2000); Race: 97.6% White, 0.2% Black, 0.5% Asian, 0.2% American Indian and Alaska Native, 2.8% Hispanic of any race, 0.4% two or more races (2000); Density: 1,395.8 persons per square mile (2000); Age: 24.3% under 18, 23.0% over 64 (2000); Marriage status: 21.2% never married, 54.6% now married, 13.4% widowed, 10.8% divorced (2000); Foreign born: 0.8% (2000); Ancestry (includes multiple ancestries): 46.1% German, 17.0% Irish, 10.1% English, 7.3% Other groups, 6.1% United States or American (2000).

Economy: Single-family building permits issued: 4 (2001) / 11 (2000); Multi-family building permits issued: 0 (2001) / 0 (2000); Employment by occupation: 7.6% management, 15.8% professional, 16.7% services, 26.2% sales, 1.3% farming, 8.9% construction, 23.4% production (2000).

Income: Per capita income: $17,502 (2000); Median household income: $27,347 (2000); Poverty rate: 13.7% (2000).

Taxes: Total city taxes per capita: $303 (2000); City property taxes per capita: $224 (2000).

Education: High school graduation rate: 82.2% (2000); College graduation rate: 12.6% (2000).

School District(s)

Oelwein Community School District (PK-12)
2000 Enrollment: 1,564 319-283-3536

Housing: Homeownership rate: 72.7% (2000); Median home value: $53,300 (2000); Median rent: $297 per month (2000); Median age of housing: 51 years (2000).

Hospitals: Mercy Hospital of Franciscan Sisters (64 beds)

Safety: Violent crime rate: 0.0 per 10,000 population; Property crime rate: 173.5 per 10,000 population (2001).

Newspapers: The Daily Register (6 x week)

Transportation: Commute to work: 92.7% car, 0.0% public transportation, 3.7% walk, 2.7% work from home (2000); Travel time to work: 68.5% less than 15 minutes, 11.7% 15 to 30 minutes, 9.4% 30 to 45 minutes, 7.6% 45 to 60 minutes, 2.8% 60 minutes or more (2000)

Airports: Oelwein Municipal

Additional Information Contacts

Oelwein Chamber of Commerce 319-283-1105

RANDALIA (city). Covers a land area of 0.217 square miles and a water area of 0 square miles. Located at 42.86° N. Lat.; 91.88° W. Long. Elevation is 1,103 feet.

History: Randalia was named for a family of local brothers, the Randall brothers.

Population: 84 (2000); Race: 96.6% White, 0.0% Black, 0.0% Asian, 0.0% American Indian and Alaska Native, 0.0% Hispanic of any race, 3.4% two or more races (2000); Density: 387.3 persons per square mile (2000); Age: 29.2% under 18, 13.5% over 64 (2000); Marriage status: 33.8% never married, 56.3% now married, 0.0% widowed, 9.9% divorced (2000); Foreign born: 2.2% (2000); Ancestry (includes multiple ancestries): 20.2% Other groups, 18.0% German, 15.7% Irish, 15.7% Norwegian, 14.6% English (2000).

Economy: Employment by occupation: 5.0% management, 2.5% professional, 30.0% services, 10.0% sales, 2.5% farming, 10.0% construction, 40.0% production (2000).

Income: Per capita income: $12,018 (2000); Median household income: $36,875 (2000); Poverty rate: 23.6% (2000).

Taxes: Total city taxes per capita: $56 (1997); City property taxes per capita: $56 (1997).

Education: High school graduation rate: 92.5% (2000); College graduation rate: 5.7% (2000).

Housing: Homeownership rate: 67.7% (2000); Median home value: $25,000 (2000); Median rent: $258 per month (2000); Median age of housing: 60+ years (2000).

Transportation: Commute to work: 92.5% car, 0.0% public transportation, 5.0% walk, 2.5% work from home (2000); Travel time to work: 10.3% less than 15 minutes, 74.4% 15 to 30 minutes, 5.1% 30 to 45 minutes, 0.0% 45 to 60 minutes, 10.3% 60 minutes or more (2000)

SAINT LUCAS (city). Covers a land area of 0.268 square miles and a water area of 0 square miles. Located at 43.06° N. Lat.; 91.93° W. Long.

History: St. Lucas was named for the Catholic church in town, St. Luke's.

Population: 178 (2000); Race: 100.0% White, 0.0% Black, 0.0% Asian, 0.0% American Indian and Alaska Native, 0.0% Hispanic of any race, 0.0% two or more races (2000); Density: 664.1 persons per square mile (2000); Age: 14.9% under 18, 33.3% over 64 (2000); Marriage status: 19.3% never married, 63.3% now married, 16.7% widowed, 0.7% divorced (2000); Foreign born: 0.0% (2000); Ancestry (includes multiple ancestries): 59.5% German, 19.0% Irish, 8.9% Norwegian, 5.4% English, 5.4% Czech (2000).
Economy: Employment by occupation: 12.5% management, 22.5% professional, 11.3% services, 31.3% sales, 5.0% farming, 7.5% construction, 10.0% production (2000).
Income: Per capita income: $25,612 (2000); Median household income: $35,625 (2000); Poverty rate: 9.5% (2000).
Education: High school graduation rate: 67.4% (2000); College graduation rate: 14.7% (2000).
Housing: Homeownership rate: 87.0% (2000); Median home value: $52,500 (2000); Median rent: $200 per month (2000); Median age of housing: 44 years (2000).
Transportation: Commute to work: 88.8% car, 0.0% public transportation, 6.3% walk, 5.0% work from home (2000); Travel time to work: 36.8% less than 15 minutes, 42.1% 15 to 30 minutes, 18.4% 30 to 45 minutes, 0.0% 45 to 60 minutes, 2.6% 60 minutes or more (2000)

WADENA (city). Covers a land area of 0.737 square miles and a water area of 0 square miles. Located at 42.84° N. Lat.; 91.65° W. Long.
History: Wadena was named for an Ojibwa chief.
Population: 243 (2000); Race: 100.0% White, 0.0% Black, 0.0% Asian, 0.0% American Indian and Alaska Native, 2.0% Hispanic of any race, 0.0% two or more races (2000); Density: 329.8 persons per square mile (2000); Age: 32.8% under 18, 14.2% over 64 (2000); Marriage status: 19.0% never married, 62.4% now married, 5.3% widowed, 13.2% divorced (2000); Foreign born: 3.2% (2000); Ancestry (includes multiple ancestries): 37.2% German, 18.6% Irish, 13.4% English, 4.7% Swiss, 4.3% French (except Basque) (2000).
Economy: Single-family building permits issued: 0 (2001) / 0 (2000); Multi-family building permits issued: 0 (2001) / 0 (2000); Employment by occupation: 5.7% management, 9.5% professional, 24.8% services, 13.3% sales, 2.9% farming, 24.8% construction, 19.0% production (2000).
Income: Per capita income: $13,861 (2000); Median household income: $25,500 (2000); Poverty rate: 14.3% (2000).
Taxes: Total city taxes per capita: $117 (1997); City property taxes per capita: $69 (1997).
Education: High school graduation rate: 76.6% (2000); College graduation rate: 4.5% (2000).
Housing: Homeownership rate: 67.2% (2000); Median home value: $36,300 (2000); Median rent: $231 per month (2000); Median age of housing: 49 years (2000).
Transportation: Commute to work: 71.8% car, 1.9% public transportation, 17.5% walk, 7.8% work from home (2000); Travel time to work: 37.9% less than 15 minutes, 32.6% 15 to 30 minutes, 7.4% 30 to 45 minutes, 2.1% 45 to 60 minutes, 20.0% 60 minutes or more (2000)

WAUCOMA (city). Covers a land area of 0.431 square miles and a water area of 0 square miles. Located at 43.05° N. Lat.; 92.03° W. Long.
History: It is believed that Waucoma was named for a stream in Wisconsin of the same name.
Population: 299 (2000); Race: 100.0% White, 0.0% Black, 0.0% Asian, 0.0% American Indian and Alaska Native, 0.0% Hispanic of any race, 0.0% two or more races (2000); Density: 693.8 persons per square mile (2000); Age: 16.6% under 18, 28.4% over 64 (2000); Marriage status: 19.7% never married, 58.3% now married, 12.6% widowed, 9.4% divorced (2000); Foreign born: 1.0% (2000); Ancestry (includes multiple ancestries): 40.9% German, 17.6% United States or American, 17.2% Irish, 16.9% Czech, 4.1% English (2000).
Economy: Single-family building permits issued: 0 (2001) / 0 (2000); Multi-family building permits issued: 0 (2001) / 0 (2000); Employment by occupation: 14.4% management, 1.5% professional, 17.4% services, 15.2% sales, 2.3% farming, 5.3% construction, 43.9% production (2000).
Income: Per capita income: $14,323 (2000); Median household income: $22,500 (2000); Poverty rate: 15.5% (2000).
Taxes: Total city taxes per capita: $145 (1997); City property taxes per capita: $87 (1997).
Education: High school graduation rate: 66.2% (2000); College graduation rate: 6.0% (2000).
Housing: Homeownership rate: 78.2% (2000); Median home value: $35,500 (2000); Median rent: $263 per month (2000); Median age of housing: 60+ years (2000).
Transportation: Commute to work: 81.8% car, 0.0% public transportation, 12.1% walk, 4.5% work from home (2000); Travel time to work: 46.0% less than 15 minutes, 27.0% 15 to 30 minutes, 15.1% 30 to 45 minutes, 2.4% 45 to 60 minutes, 9.5% 60 minutes or more (2000)

WEST UNION (city). Covers a land area of 2.690 square miles and a water area of 0 square miles. Located at 42.96° N. Lat.; 91.81° W. Long. Elevation is 1,105 feet.
History: West Union, first called Knob Prairie, became known by its present name in 1849. It has been noted for its many springs.
Population: 2,549 (2000); Race: 97.5% White, 0.0% Black, 0.5% Asian, 0.2% American Indian and Alaska Native, 1.6% Hispanic of any race, 1.0% two or more races (2000); Density: 947.8 persons per square mile (2000); Age: 23.5% under 18, 21.9% over 64 (2000); Marriage status: 22.2% never married, 54.2% now married, 12.9% widowed, 10.7% divorced (2000); Foreign born: 1.4% (2000); Ancestry (includes multiple ancestries): 49.5% German, 17.8% Norwegian, 13.3% Irish, 6.8% English, 4.8% United States or American (2000).
Economy: Single-family building permits issued: 6 (2001) / 3 (2000); Multi-family building permits issued: 0 (2001) / 7 (2000); Employment by occupation: 15.8% management, 14.3% professional, 14.6% services, 21.5% sales, 1.4% farming, 8.4% construction, 24.1% production (2000).
Income: Per capita income: $17,937 (2000); Median household income: $34,515 (2000); Poverty rate: 9.1% (2000).
Taxes: Total city taxes per capita: $287 (1997); City property taxes per capita: $231 (1997).
Education: High school graduation rate: 86.9% (2000); College graduation rate: 16.9% (2000).

School District(s)

North Fayette Community School District (PK-12)
2000 Enrollment: 1,160 319-422-3851
Housing: Homeownership rate: 71.5% (2000); Median home value: $67,500 (2000); Median rent: $275 per month (2000); Median age of housing: 45 years (2000).
Hospitals: Palmer Lutheran Health Center (25 beds)
Newspapers: Fayette County Union (1 x week)
Transportation: Commute to work: 90.6% car, 0.0% public transportation, 3.8% walk, 3.9% work from home (2000); Travel time to work: 74.9% less than 15 minutes, 10.0% 15 to 30 minutes, 5.8% 30 to 45 minutes, 4.4% 45 to 60 minutes, 5.0% 60 minutes or more (2000)

WESTGATE (city). Covers a land area of 0.357 square miles and a water area of 0 square miles. Located at 42.76° N. Lat.; 91.99° W. Long. Elevation is 1,092 feet.
History: Westgate was named for landowner Sylvester S. Westgate and his family.
Population: 234 (2000); Race: 100.0% White, 0.0% Black, 0.0% Asian, 0.0% American Indian and Alaska Native, 0.0% Hispanic of any race, 0.0% two or more races (2000); Density: 655.0 persons per square mile (2000); Age: 27.7% under 18, 19.8% over 64 (2000); Marriage status: 20.0% never married, 63.6% now married, 8.2% widowed, 8.2% divorced (2000); Foreign born: 0.0% (2000); Ancestry (includes multiple ancestries): 42.7% German, 8.7% United States or American, 8.3% English, 5.9% Irish, 5.1% Other groups (2000).
Economy: Single-family building permits issued: 0 (2001) / 0 (2000); Multi-family building permits issued: 0 (2001) / 0 (2000); Employment by occupation: 9.5% management, 12.9% professional, 17.2% services, 22.4% sales, 0.9% farming, 4.3% construction, 32.8% production (2000).
Income: Per capita income: $14,709 (2000); Median household income: $30,750 (2000); Poverty rate: 7.6% (2000).
Taxes: Total city taxes per capita: $144 (1997); City property taxes per capita: $80 (1997).
Education: High school graduation rate: 86.3% (2000); College graduation rate: 4.2% (2000).
Housing: Homeownership rate: 81.6% (2000); Median home value: $39,400 (2000); Median rent: $250 per month (2000); Median age of housing: 60+ years (2000).
Transportation: Commute to work: 90.3% car, 2.7% public transportation, 2.7% walk, 4.4% work from home (2000); Travel time to work: 30.6% less than 15 minutes, 44.4% 15 to 30 minutes, 13.9% 30 to 45 minutes, 4.6% 45 to 60 minutes, 6.5% 60 minutes or more (2000)

Floyd County

Located in northern Iowa; prairie area, drained by the Shell Rock, Cedar, and Little Cedar Rivers. Covers a land area of 500.60 square miles, a water area of 0.70 square miles, and is located in the Central Time Zone. The county government was organized in 1851. County seat is Charles City.

Weather Station: Charles City — Elevation: 1,017 feet

	Jan	Feb	Mar	Apr	May	Jun	Jul	Aug	Sep	Oct	Nov	Dec
High	24	30	43	59	72	81	84	82	74	62	43	29
Low	6	13	24	36	48	58	61	59	50	39	26	13
Precip	0.9	0.8	2.0	3.4	4.2	5.0	4.6	4.5	3.5	2.6	2.1	1.1
Snow	9.8	6.4	6.2	2.9	tr	0.0	0.0	0.0	0.0	0.1	4.4	7.9

High and Low temperatures in degrees Fahrenheit; Precipitation and Snow in inches

Population: 16,900 (2000); Race: 98.5% White, 0.1% Black, 0.3% Asian, 0.1% American Indian and Alaska Native, 1.1% Hispanic of any race, 0.4% two or more races (2000); Density: 33.8 persons per square mile (2000); Age: 25.2% under 18, 19.1% over 64 (2000).
Religion: Five largest groups: 23.9% Catholic Church, 14.7% Evangelical Lutheran Church in America, 14.1% The United Methodist Church, 2.5% United Church of Christ, 2.2% The Wesleyan Church (2000).
Economy: Unemployment rate: 4.4% (11/2002); Total civilian labor force: 7,834 (11/2002); Leading industries: 22.3% manufacturing; 21.4% health care and social assistance; 16.3% retail trade (2000); Companies that employ more than 1,000 persons: 0 (2000); Companies that employ more than 100 persons: 5 (2000); Farms: 850 totaling 300,255 acres (1997); Minority business ownership rate: 0.0% (1997); Women business ownership rate: 27.3% (1997); Retail sales per capita: $7,233 (1997). Single-family building permits issued: 24 (2001) / 9 (2000); Multi-family building permits issued: 0 (2001) / 0 (2000).
Income: Per capita income: $17,091 (2000); Median household income: $35,237 (2000); Poverty rate: 9.3% (2000); Bankruptcy rate: 3.50% (2001).
Taxes: Total county taxes per capita: $212 (2000); County property taxes per capita: $206 (2000).
Education: High school graduation rate: 85.9% (2000); College graduation rate: 14.8% (2000).
Housing: Homeownership rate: 74.1% (2000); Median home value: $64,700 (2000); Median rent: $277 per month (2000); Median age of housing: 47 years (2000).
Health: Birth rate: 116.0 per 10,000 population (1998); Age adjusted death rate: 88.5 per 10,000 population (1999); Age adjusted cancer mortality rate: 214.8 deaths per 100,000 population (1999). Number of physicians: 4.1 per 10,000 population (1999); Number of hospital beds: 18.3 per 10,000 population (1999).
Elections: 2000 Presidential election results: 52.9% Gore, 44.1% Bush, 2.1% Nader, 0.5% Buchanan
National and State Parks: Idlewild State Park
Additional Information Contacts
Floyd County Government Offices 641-257-6131
Charles City Chamber of Commerce 641-228-4234

Floyd County Communities

CHARLES CITY (city). Covers a land area of 6.152 square miles and a water area of 0.087 square miles. Located at 43.06° N. Lat.; 92.67° W. Long. Elevation is 1,013 feet.
History: Charles City was first known as The Ford. The first settlement was made by Joseph Kelly in 1850. The name was changed to Charles City in 1869 in honor of Joseph Kelly's son, Charles. When Charles W. Hart and his college classmate, Charles H. Parr, began building stationary gasoline engines here in 1896, they also started a series of experiments with machines to be used in farming. Because they built traction motors, their advertising manager, W. H. Williams, coined the new name "tractor."
Population: 7,812 (2000); Race: 97.8% White, 0.2% Black, 0.5% Asian, 0.1% American Indian and Alaska Native, 1.5% Hispanic of any race, 0.6% two or more races (2000); Density: 1,269.9 persons per square mile (2000); Age: 23.4% under 18, 24.5% over 64 (2000); Marriage status: 22.2% never married, 54.6% now married, 14.2% widowed, 9.0% divorced (2000); Foreign born: 1.6% (2000); Ancestry (includes multiple ancestries): 44.7% German, 18.0% Irish, 7.3% English, 7.1% United States or American, 5.8% Norwegian (2000).
Economy: Single-family building permits issued: 10 (2001) / 3 (2000); Multi-family building permits issued: 0 (2001) / 0 (2000); Employment by occupation: 9.7% management, 20.9% professional, 23.9% services, 20.9% sales, 0.6% farming, 8.1% construction, 15.8% production (2000).
Income: Per capita income: $16,659 (2000); Median household income: $30,568 (2000); Poverty rate: 11.2% (2000).
Taxes: Total city taxes per capita: $342 (1997); City property taxes per capita: $336 (1997).
Education: High school graduation rate: 84.0% (2000); College graduation rate: 15.6% (2000).

School District(s)

Charles City Community School District (PK-12)
2000 Enrollment: 1,780 641-257-6500
Housing: Homeownership rate: 66.8% (2000); Median home value: $63,600 (2000); Median rent: $290 per month (2000); Median age of housing: 46 years (2000).
Hospitals: Floyd County Memorial Hospital (55 beds)
Safety: Violent crime rate: 15.4 per 10,000 population; Property crime rate: 228.1 per 10,000 population (2001).
Newspapers: Charles City Press (5 x week); 6 County Look & Shop (1 x week)
Transportation: Commute to work: 91.7% car, 0.6% public transportation, 2.6% walk, 3.7% work from home (2000); Travel time to work: 71.4% less than 15 minutes, 10.3% 15 to 30 minutes, 8.2% 30 to 45 minutes, 5.8% 45 to 60 minutes, 4.4% 60 minutes or more (2000)
Additional Information Contacts
Charles City Chamber of Commerce 641-228-4234

COLWELL (city). Covers a land area of 0.184 square miles and a water area of 0 square miles. Located at 43.15° N. Lat.; 92.59° W. Long. Elevation is 1,150 feet.
History: James Colwell, builder of the first three homes in the town of Colwell, gave his name to the place.
Population: 76 (2000); Race: 100.0% White, 0.0% Black, 0.0% Asian, 0.0% American Indian and Alaska Native, 0.0% Hispanic of any race, 0.0% two or more races (2000); Density: 413.8 persons per square mile (2000); Age: 28.0% under 18, 6.7% over 64 (2000); Marriage status: 1.9% never married, 83.3% now married, 9.3% widowed, 5.6% divorced (2000); Foreign born: 0.0% (2000); Ancestry (includes multiple ancestries): 48.0% German, 12.0% Norwegian, 6.7% French (except Basque), 5.3% English, 5.3% Czech (2000).
Economy: Employment by occupation: 10.5% management, 7.9% professional, 10.5% services, 26.3% sales, 0.0% farming, 5.3% construction, 39.5% production (2000).
Income: Per capita income: $12,504 (2000); Median household income: $27,813 (2000); Poverty rate: 10.7% (2000).
Taxes: Total city taxes per capita: $114 (1997); City property taxes per capita: $102 (1997).
Education: High school graduation rate: 86.0% (2000); College graduation rate: 4.7% (2000).
Housing: Homeownership rate: 87.5% (2000); Median home value: $26,900 (2000); Median rent: $300 per month (2000); Median age of housing: 52 years (2000).
Transportation: Commute to work: 89.5% car, 0.0% public transportation, 10.5% walk, 0.0% work from home (2000); Travel time to work: 15.8% less than 15 minutes, 65.8% 15 to 30 minutes, 2.6% 30 to 45 minutes, 5.3% 45 to 60 minutes, 10.5% 60 minutes or more (2000)

FLOYD (city). Covers a land area of 0.589 square miles and a water area of 0 square miles. Located at 43.12° N. Lat.; 92.74° W. Long. Elevation is 1,099 feet.
History: Floyd was named in honor of William Floyd of Long Island, New York, one of the signers of the Declaration of Independence.
Population: 361 (2000); Race: 100.0% White, 0.0% Black, 0.0% Asian, 0.0% American Indian and Alaska Native, 0.0% Hispanic of any race, 0.0% two or more races (2000); Density: 612.7 persons per square mile (2000); Age: 24.1% under 18, 11.0% over 64 (2000); Marriage status: 32.5% never married, 53.8% now married, 4.3% widowed, 9.5% divorced (2000); Foreign born: 0.0% (2000); Ancestry (includes multiple ancestries): 48.5% German, 15.6% Irish, 7.4% English, 6.0% Norwegian, 5.2% Swedish (2000).
Economy: Single-family building permits issued: 0 (2001) / 1 (2000); Multi-family building permits issued: 0 (2001) / 0 (2000); Employment by occupation: 8.2% management, 6.0% professional, 23.0% services, 18.6% sales, 1.1% farming, 12.6% construction, 30.6% production (2000).
Income: Per capita income: $14,723 (2000); Median household income: $35,096 (2000); Poverty rate: 6.4% (2000).
Taxes: Total city taxes per capita: $122 (1997); City property taxes per capita: $102 (1997).
Education: High school graduation rate: 80.4% (2000); College graduation rate: 8.4% (2000).

Housing: Homeownership rate: 88.6% (2000); Median home value: $45,000 (2000); Median rent: $250 per month (2000); Median age of housing: 59 years (2000).
Transportation: Commute to work: 90.9% car, 0.0% public transportation, 8.0% walk, 0.0% work from home (2000); Travel time to work: 31.8% less than 15 minutes, 44.3% 15 to 30 minutes, 18.8% 30 to 45 minutes, 1.1% 45 to 60 minutes, 4.0% 60 minutes or more (2000)

MARBLE ROCK (city). Covers a land area of 0.836 square miles and a water area of 0.037 square miles. Located at 42.96° N. Lat.; 92.86° W. Long. Elevation is 1,002 feet.
History: Marble Rock was so named because of the rock beds on which the town was built.
Population: 326 (2000); Race: 100.0% White, 0.0% Black, 0.0% Asian, 0.0% American Indian and Alaska Native, 0.0% Hispanic of any race, 0.0% two or more races (2000); Density: 390.1 persons per square mile (2000); Age: 21.8% under 18, 22.2% over 64 (2000); Marriage status: 24.6% never married, 55.7% now married, 9.5% widowed, 10.2% divorced (2000); Foreign born: 0.0% (2000); Ancestry (includes multiple ancestries): 45.8% German, 10.8% English, 6.2% United States or American, 5.8% Irish, 4.9% Norwegian (2000).
Economy: Single-family building permits issued: 1 (2001) / 0 (2000); Multi-family building permits issued: 0 (2001) / 0 (2000); Employment by occupation: 16.9% management, 16.2% professional, 5.6% services, 23.9% sales, 4.9% farming, 4.9% construction, 27.5% production (2000).
Income: Per capita income: $17,937 (2000); Median household income: $35,500 (2000); Poverty rate: 7.2% (2000).
Taxes: Total city taxes per capita: $236 (2000); City property taxes per capita: $141 (2000).
Education: High school graduation rate: 80.4% (2000); College graduation rate: 6.1% (2000).
Housing: Homeownership rate: 72.1% (2000); Median home value: $32,500 (2000); Median rent: $211 per month (2000); Median age of housing: 59 years (2000).
Transportation: Commute to work: 92.3% car, 0.0% public transportation, 2.1% walk, 4.2% work from home (2000); Travel time to work: 15.4% less than 15 minutes, 39.0% 15 to 30 minutes, 19.1% 30 to 45 minutes, 11.0% 45 to 60 minutes, 15.4% 60 minutes or more (2000)

NORA SPRINGS (city). Covers a land area of 2.187 square miles and a water area of 0.027 square miles. Located at 43.14° N. Lat.; 93.00° W. Long. Elevation is 1,063 feet.
History: Nora Springs was formerly known as Woodstock, but acquired its present name because of its many springs.
Population: 1,532 (2000); Race: 99.5% White, 0.0% Black, 0.0% Asian, 0.0% American Indian and Alaska Native, 1.4% Hispanic of any race, 0.2% two or more races (2000); Density: 700.5 persons per square mile (2000); Age: 22.2% under 18, 18.2% over 64 (2000); Marriage status: 19.2% never married, 63.5% now married, 8.1% widowed, 9.3% divorced (2000); Foreign born: 0.6% (2000); Ancestry (includes multiple ancestries): 38.7% German, 13.9% Norwegian, 11.9% Irish, 7.8% United States or American, 7.3% English (2000).
Economy: Single-family building permits issued: 3 (2001) / 1 (2000); Multi-family building permits issued: 0 (2001) / 0 (2000); Employment by occupation: 9.1% management, 10.8% professional, 13.3% services, 30.3% sales, 0.0% farming, 13.8% construction, 22.8% production (2000).
Income: Per capita income: $16,246 (2000); Median household income: $34,926 (2000); Poverty rate: 5.3% (2000).
Taxes: Total city taxes per capita: $220 (1997); City property taxes per capita: $201 (1997).
Education: High school graduation rate: 88.1% (2000); College graduation rate: 12.0% (2000).

School District(s)

Nora Springs-Rock Falls Community School District (KG-12)
2000 Enrollment: 498 641-749-5301
Housing: Homeownership rate: 82.1% (2000); Median home value: $64,700 (2000); Median rent: $281 per month (2000); Median age of housing: 49 years (2000).
Newspapers: Shell Rock Valley Times (1 x week)
Transportation: Commute to work: 93.0% car, 0.3% public transportation, 3.1% walk, 2.1% work from home (2000); Travel time to work: 26.0% less than 15 minutes, 51.7% 15 to 30 minutes, 14.4% 30 to 45 minutes, 1.6% 45 to 60 minutes, 6.3% 60 minutes or more (2000)

ROCKFORD (city). Covers a land area of 0.630 square miles and a water area of 0 square miles. Located at 43.05° N. Lat.; 92.94° W. Long. Elevation is 1,021 feet.
History: Rockford was named after Rockford, Illinois.
Population: 907 (2000); Race: 98.7% White, 0.4% Black, 0.0% Asian, 0.0% American Indian and Alaska Native, 0.0% Hispanic of any race, 0.9% two or more races (2000); Density: 1,439.5 persons per square mile (2000); Age: 28.2% under 18, 17.3% over 64 (2000); Marriage status: 19.4% never married, 60.6% now married, 10.2% widowed, 9.8% divorced (2000); Foreign born: 0.3% (2000); Ancestry (includes multiple ancestries): 52.7% German, 12.1% Irish, 8.8% Norwegian, 3.8% Dutch, 3.8% English (2000).
Economy: Single-family building permits issued: 2 (2001) / 0 (2000); Multi-family building permits issued: 0 (2001) / 0 (2000); Employment by occupation: 11.5% management, 15.1% professional, 12.5% services, 24.7% sales, 2.6% farming, 9.9% construction, 23.8% production (2000).
Income: Per capita income: $15,455 (2000); Median household income: $32,143 (2000); Poverty rate: 11.9% (2000).
Taxes: Total city taxes per capita: $146 (1997); City property taxes per capita: $131 (1997).
Education: High school graduation rate: 85.9% (2000); College graduation rate: 11.7% (2000).

School District(s)

Rudd-Rockford-Marble Rk Community School District (KG-12)
2000 Enrollment: 650 641-756-3610
Housing: Homeownership rate: 73.2% (2000); Median home value: $57,700 (2000); Median rent: $205 per month (2000); Median age of housing: 49 years (2000).
Transportation: Commute to work: 91.2% car, 0.0% public transportation, 3.8% walk, 4.3% work from home (2000); Travel time to work: 27.4% less than 15 minutes, 37.8% 15 to 30 minutes, 31.3% 30 to 45 minutes, 0.7% 45 to 60 minutes, 2.7% 60 minutes or more (2000)

RUDD (city). Covers a land area of 0.997 square miles and a water area of 0 square miles. Located at 43.12° N. Lat.; 92.90° W. Long.
History: Rudd was platted as Danville by James Swartwood in 1869, but was renamed for a man who promised to contribute $1,000 for a church if the town were named for him. He allegedly forgot his promise after the renaming.
Population: 431 (2000); Race: 95.9% White, 0.0% Black, 0.5% Asian, 1.2% American Indian and Alaska Native, 0.0% Hispanic of any race, 1.9% two or more races (2000); Density: 432.4 persons per square mile (2000); Age: 31.6% under 18, 16.0% over 64 (2000); Marriage status: 14.1% never married, 67.4% now married, 8.4% widowed, 10.1% divorced (2000); Foreign born: 0.7% (2000); Ancestry (includes multiple ancestries): 45.9% German, 7.7% Irish, 6.5% Norwegian, 5.7% Dutch, 4.8% English (2000).
Economy: Single-family building permits issued: 0 (2001) / 0 (2000); Multi-family building permits issued: 0 (2001) / 0 (2000); Employment by occupation: 14.1% management, 15.6% professional, 15.1% services, 18.2% sales, 3.1% farming, 9.4% construction, 24.5% production (2000).
Income: Per capita income: $17,167 (2000); Median household income: $32,679 (2000); Poverty rate: 7.7% (2000).
Taxes: Total city taxes per capita: $165 (1997); City property taxes per capita: $145 (1997).
Education: High school graduation rate: 82.4% (2000); College graduation rate: 13.7% (2000).
Housing: Homeownership rate: 75.1% (2000); Median home value: $49,100 (2000); Median rent: $286 per month (2000); Median age of housing: 56 years (2000).
Transportation: Commute to work: 89.4% car, 1.6% public transportation, 4.2% walk, 4.8% work from home (2000); Travel time to work: 32.8% less than 15 minutes, 42.8% 15 to 30 minutes, 12.8% 30 to 45 minutes, 6.7% 45 to 60 minutes, 5.0% 60 minutes or more (2000)

Franklin County

Located in north central Iowa; rolling prairie area. Covers a land area of 582.40 square miles, a water area of 0.60 square miles, and is located in the Central Time Zone. The county government was organized in 1851. County seat is Hampton.

Weather Station: Hampton Elevation: 1,227 feet

	Jan	Feb	Mar	Apr	May	Jun	Jul	Aug	Sep	Oct	Nov	Dec
High	24	30	42	58	71	80	83	81	74	61	43	29
Low	7	13	25	36	48	58	62	59	50	39	25	13
Precip	0.9	0.8	2.2	3.2	4.5	4.9	4.7	4.3	3.2	2.6	2.0	1.2
Snow	8.3	6.4	6.0	2.6	tr	0.0	tr	0.0	0.0	0.4	4.2	7.1

High and Low temperatures in degrees Fahrenheit; Precipitation and Snow in inches

Population: 10,704 (2000); Race: 94.3% White, 0.0% Black, 0.3% Asian, 0.2% American Indian and Alaska Native, 6.1% Hispanic of any race, 0.4% two or more races (2000); Density: 18.4 persons per square mile (2000); Age: 24.2% under 18, 20.5% over 64 (2000).
Religion: Five largest groups: 18.7% The United Methodist Church, 14.8% Evangelical Lutheran Church in America, 10.9% Catholic Church, 8.9% United Church of Christ, 7.9% Lutheran Church—Missouri Synod (2000).
Economy: Unemployment rate: 3.6% (11/2002); Total civilian labor force: 5,778 (11/2002); Leading industries: 27.5% manufacturing; 18.9% health care and social assistance; 15.2% retail trade (2000); Companies that employ more than 1,000 persons: 0 (2000); Companies that employ more than 100 persons: 4 (2000); Farms: 856 totaling 344,296 acres (1997); Minority business ownership rate: 0.0% (1997); Women business ownership rate: 24.4% (1997); Retail sales per capita: $5,600 (1997). Single-family building permits issued: 5 (2001) / 8 (2000); Multi-family building permits issued: 0 (2001) / 0 (2000).
Income: Per capita income: $18,767 (2000); Median household income: $36,042 (2000); Poverty rate: 8.0% (2000); Bankruptcy rate: 4.16% (2001).
Taxes: Total county taxes per capita: $355 (2000); County property taxes per capita: $338 (2000).
Education: High school graduation rate: 84.0% (2000); College graduation rate: 14.5% (2000).
Housing: Homeownership rate: 74.8% (2000); Median home value: $55,200 (2000); Median rent: $268 per month (2000); Median age of housing: 56 years (2000).
Health: Birth rate: 104.6 per 10,000 population (1998); Age adjusted death rate: 81.5 per 10,000 population (1999); Age adjusted cancer mortality rate: 134.5 deaths per 100,000 population (1999). Number of physicians: 2.8 per 10,000 population (1999); Number of hospital beds: 71.9 per 10,000 population (1999).
Elections: 2000 Presidential election results: 43.0% Gore, 53.8% Bush, 2.2% Nader, 0.3% Buchanan
National and State Parks: Beeds Lake State Park
Additional Information Contacts
Franklin County Government Offices 641-456-5622
Hampton Chamber of Commerce. 641-456-5668

Franklin County Communities

ALEXANDER (city). Covers a land area of 4.278 square miles and a water area of 0 square miles. Located at 42.80° N. Lat.; 93.47° W. Long. Elevation is 1,253 feet.
History: Alexander, platted in 1855, was named for an employee of the Iowa Central Railroad.
Population: 165 (2000); Race: 93.0% White, 0.0% Black, 0.0% Asian, 0.0% American Indian and Alaska Native, 8.1% Hispanic of any race, 0.0% two or more races (2000); Density: 38.6 persons per square mile (2000); Age: 16.9% under 18, 30.8% over 64 (2000); Marriage status: 19.0% never married, 60.5% now married, 11.6% widowed, 8.8% divorced (2000); Foreign born: 8.7% (2000); Ancestry (includes multiple ancestries): 42.4% German, 15.1% United States or American, 9.9% Other groups, 7.0% Dutch, 6.4% English (2000).
Economy: Single-family building permits issued: 0 (2001) / 0 (2000); Multi-family building permits issued: 0 (2001) / 0 (2000); Employment by occupation: 5.0% management, 6.3% professional, 12.5% services, 23.8% sales, 3.8% farming, 13.8% construction, 35.0% production (2000).
Income: Per capita income: $14,995 (2000); Median household income: $31,250 (2000); Poverty rate: 9.3% (2000).
Taxes: Total city taxes per capita: $88 (1997); City property taxes per capita: $88 (1997).
Education: High school graduation rate: 81.4% (2000); College graduation rate: 7.8% (2000).
Housing: Homeownership rate: 69.5% (2000); Median home value: $36,700 (2000); Median rent: $236 per month (2000); Median age of housing: 56 years (2000).
Transportation: Commute to work: 81.3% car, 0.0% public transportation, 8.8% walk, 7.5% work from home (2000); Travel time to work: 40.5% less than 15 minutes, 39.2% 15 to 30 minutes, 6.8% 30 to 45 minutes, 10.8% 45 to 60 minutes, 2.7% 60 minutes or more (2000)

BRADFORD (unincorporated postal area, zip code 50041). Covers a land area of 0.414 square miles and a water area of 0 square miles. Located at 42.63° N. Lat.; 93.24° W. Long. Elevation is 1,250 feet.
History: Bradford is the home of The Little Brown Church in the Vale, made popular by the hymn written by Dr. W. S. Pitts.
Population: 123 (2000); Race: 100.0% White, 0.0% Black, 0.0% Asian, 0.0% American Indian and Alaska Native, 0.0% Hispanic of any race, 0.0% two or more races (2000); Density: 296.8 persons per square mile (2000); Age: 37.2% under 18, 0.0% over 64 (2000); Marriage status: 16.2% never married, 79.8% now married, 4.0% widowed, 0.0% divorced (2000); Foreign born: 0.0% (2000); Ancestry (includes multiple ancestries): 39.9% German, 35.8% Norwegian, 8.1% Czech, 6.8% English, 4.7% Irish (2000).
Economy: Employment by occupation: 6.8% management, 19.3% professional, 13.6% services, 4.5% sales, 6.8% farming, 8.0% construction, 40.9% production (2000).
Income: Per capita income: $12,224 (2000); Median household income: $36,071 (2000); Poverty rate: 18.9% (2000).
Education: High school graduation rate: 100.0% (2000); College graduation rate: 12.9% (2000).
Housing: Homeownership rate: 75.0% (2000); Median home value: $25,000 (2000); Median rent: $275 per month (2000); Median age of housing: 53 years (2000).
Transportation: Commute to work: 80.5% car, 0.0% public transportation, 14.6% walk, 4.9% work from home (2000); Travel time to work: 24.4% less than 15 minutes, 61.5% 15 to 30 minutes, 14.1% 30 to 45 minutes, 0.0% 45 to 60 minutes, 0.0% 60 minutes or more (2000)

COULTER (city). Covers a land area of 2.454 square miles and a water area of 0 square miles. Located at 42.73° N. Lat.; 93.36° W. Long.
History: Coulter began in the 1880's as a station on the Chicago Great Western Railroad, and was named for a railroad official whose surname was Colter. The spelling change was made by the post office.
Population: 262 (2000); Race: 95.9% White, 0.0% Black, 0.0% Asian, 0.0% American Indian and Alaska Native, 4.9% Hispanic of any race, 1.9% two or more races (2000); Density: 106.8 persons per square mile (2000); Age: 30.1% under 18, 18.0% over 64 (2000); Marriage status: 23.0% never married, 56.9% now married, 5.4% widowed, 14.7% divorced (2000); Foreign born: 3.0% (2000); Ancestry (includes multiple ancestries): 28.6% German, 16.9% Norwegian, 14.7% Other groups, 11.3% Danish, 9.0% English (2000).
Economy: Single-family building permits issued: 0 (2001) / 0 (2000); Multi-family building permits issued: 0 (2001) / 0 (2000); Employment by occupation: 1.6% management, 6.5% professional, 17.1% services, 28.5% sales, 3.3% farming, 22.8% construction, 20.3% production (2000).
Income: Per capita income: $14,056 (2000); Median household income: $35,208 (2000); Poverty rate: 18.4% (2000).
Taxes: Total city taxes per capita: $127 (1997); City property taxes per capita: $127 (1997).
Education: High school graduation rate: 82.9% (2000); College graduation rate: 14.1% (2000).
Housing: Homeownership rate: 68.9% (2000); Median home value: $31,500 (2000); Median rent: $223 per month (2000); Median age of housing: 57 years (2000).
Transportation: Commute to work: 94.3% car, 1.6% public transportation, 0.0% walk, 4.1% work from home (2000); Travel time to work: 46.2% less than 15 minutes, 26.5% 15 to 30 minutes, 6.0% 30 to 45 minutes, 6.8% 45 to 60 minutes, 14.5% 60 minutes or more (2000)

GENEVA (city). Covers a land area of 0.427 square miles and a water area of 0 square miles. Located at 42.67° N. Lat.; 93.13° W. Long. Elevation is 1,092 feet.
History: Geneva was named after Geneva Clock, a pioneer woman who settled in this area with her husband, W.C. Clock.
Population: 171 (2000); Race: 100.0% White, 0.0% Black, 0.0% Asian, 0.0% American Indian and Alaska Native, 0.0% Hispanic of any race, 0.0% two or more races (2000); Density: 400.4 persons per square mile (2000); Age: 20.3% under 18, 30.7% over 64 (2000); Marriage status: 17.5% never married, 67.5% now married, 11.1% widowed, 4.0% divorced (2000); Foreign born: 0.0% (2000); Ancestry (includes multiple ancestries): 65.4% German, 9.8% Irish, 8.5% Dutch, 6.5% Swedish, 3.9% Danish (2000).
Economy: Employment by occupation: 5.9% management, 5.9% professional, 16.2% services, 11.8% sales, 0.0% farming, 14.7% construction, 45.6% production (2000).

Income: Per capita income: $15,112 (2000); Median household income: $33,542 (2000); Poverty rate: 5.9% (2000).
Taxes: Total city taxes per capita: $104 (1997); City property taxes per capita: $73 (1997).
Education: High school graduation rate: 83.6% (2000); College graduation rate: 4.3% (2000).
Housing: Homeownership rate: 89.2% (2000); Median home value: $35,800 (2000); Median rent: $225 per month (2000); Median age of housing: 60+ years (2000).
Transportation: Commute to work: 89.7% car, 0.0% public transportation, 2.9% walk, 0.0% work from home (2000); Travel time to work: 32.4% less than 15 minutes, 41.2% 15 to 30 minutes, 14.7% 30 to 45 minutes, 8.8% 45 to 60 minutes, 2.9% 60 minutes or more (2000)

HAMPTON (city). Covers a land area of 4.276 square miles and a water area of 0 square miles. Located at 42.74° N. Lat.; 93.20° W. Long. Elevation is 1,143 feet.
History: Hampton was founded by Job Garner and George Ryan in 1856. The village was first named Benjamin.
Population: 4,218 (2000); Race: 90.1% White, 0.0% Black, 0.8% Asian, 0.1% American Indian and Alaska Native, 11.2% Hispanic of any race, 0.4% two or more races (2000); Density: 986.4 persons per square mile (2000); Age: 23.6% under 18, 21.9% over 64 (2000); Marriage status: 19.1% never married, 61.0% now married, 12.7% widowed, 7.3% divorced (2000); Foreign born: 8.2% (2000); Ancestry (includes multiple ancestries): 44.8% German, 13.7% Other groups, 9.3% English, 8.9% Irish, 7.0% Norwegian (2000).
Economy: Single-family building permits issued: 3 (2001) / 5 (2000); Multi-family building permits issued: 0 (2001) / 0 (2000); Employment by occupation: 12.6% management, 14.1% professional, 20.9% services, 18.1% sales, 3.9% farming, 6.1% construction, 24.2% production (2000).
Income: Per capita income: $19,907 (2000); Median household income: $33,005 (2000); Poverty rate: 9.4% (2000).
Taxes: Total city taxes per capita: $343 (1997); City property taxes per capita: $326 (1997).
Education: High school graduation rate: 80.7% (2000); College graduation rate: 12.5% (2000).

School District(s)

Hampton-Dumont Community School District (PK-12)
2000 Enrollment: 1,249 641-456-2175
Housing: Homeownership rate: 70.6% (2000); Median home value: $56,900 (2000); Median rent: $288 per month (2000); Median age of housing: 48 years (2000).
Hospitals: Franklin General Hospital (77 beds)
Safety: Violent crime rate: 0.0 per 10,000 population; Property crime rate: 125.8 per 10,000 population (2001).
Newspapers: Hampton Chronicle (1 x week)
Transportation: Commute to work: 84.8% car, 0.7% public transportation, 6.9% walk, 5.8% work from home (2000); Travel time to work: 71.3% less than 15 minutes, 13.1% 15 to 30 minutes, 7.6% 30 to 45 minutes, 4.4% 45 to 60 minutes, 3.6% 60 minutes or more (2000)
Additional Information Contacts
Hampton Chamber of Commerce. 641-456-5668

HANSELL (city). Covers a land area of 0.217 square miles and a water area of 0 square miles. Located at 42.75° N. Lat.; 93.10° W. Long.
History: In 1881 George W. Hansell laid out the town of Hansell as a station on the Dubuque & Dakota Railroad.
Population: 96 (2000); Race: 100.0% White, 0.0% Black, 0.0% Asian, 0.0% American Indian and Alaska Native, 0.0% Hispanic of any race, 0.0% two or more races (2000); Density: 441.8 persons per square mile (2000); Age: 16.7% under 18, 21.9% over 64 (2000); Marriage status: 18.6% never married, 64.7% now married, 10.8% widowed, 5.9% divorced (2000); Foreign born: 1.8% (2000); Ancestry (includes multiple ancestries): 48.2% German, 11.4% Norwegian, 9.6% Irish, 9.6% English, 7.0% Danish (2000).
Economy: Employment by occupation: 7.4% management, 11.1% professional, 13.0% services, 5.6% sales, 0.0% farming, 24.1% construction, 38.9% production (2000).
Income: Per capita income: $17,389 (2000); Median household income: $32,250 (2000); Poverty rate: 12.3% (2000).
Taxes: Total city taxes per capita: $134 (1997); City property taxes per capita: $98 (1997).
Education: High school graduation rate: 88.5% (2000); College graduation rate: 4.6% (2000).
Housing: Homeownership rate: 87.2% (2000); Median home value: $39,200 (2000); Median rent: $163 per month (2000); Median age of housing: 50 years (2000).
Transportation: Commute to work: 88.9% car, 0.0% public transportation, 0.0% walk, 7.4% work from home (2000); Travel time to work: 32.0% less than 15 minutes, 28.0% 15 to 30 minutes, 18.0% 30 to 45 minutes, 4.0% 45 to 60 minutes, 18.0% 60 minutes or more (2000)

LATIMER (city). Covers a land area of 2.337 square miles and a water area of 0 square miles. Located at 42.76° N. Lat.; 93.36° W. Long. Elevation is 1,239 feet.
History: Latimer became a railroad station on the Iowa Central Railroad in 1881. The town was platted in 1882 and named for banker J. F. Lattimer.
Population: 535 (2000); Race: 77.7% White, 0.0% Black, 0.0% Asian, 0.0% American Indian and Alaska Native, 22.3% Hispanic of any race, 1.0% two or more races (2000); Density: 228.9 persons per square mile (2000); Age: 26.9% under 18, 29.4% over 64 (2000); Marriage status: 17.0% never married, 65.3% now married, 11.8% widowed, 6.0% divorced (2000); Foreign born: 13.4% (2000); Ancestry (includes multiple ancestries): 41.7% German, 20.6% Other groups, 8.9% English, 6.9% United States or American, 6.7% Norwegian (2000).
Economy: Single-family building permits issued: 0 (2001) / 0 (2000); Multi-family building permits issued: 0 (2001) / 0 (2000); Employment by occupation: 18.6% management, 8.3% professional, 18.1% services, 19.1% sales, 2.9% farming, 9.8% construction, 23.0% production (2000).
Income: Per capita income: $14,332 (2000); Median household income: $29,028 (2000); Poverty rate: 6.6% (2000).
Taxes: Total city taxes per capita: $252 (1997); City property taxes per capita: $220 (1997).
Education: High school graduation rate: 75.4% (2000); College graduation rate: 12.2% (2000).

School District(s)

Cal Community School District (PK-12)
2000 Enrollment: 282 641-579-6087
Housing: Homeownership rate: 78.4% (2000); Median home value: $40,000 (2000); Median rent: $208 per month (2000); Median age of housing: 56 years (2000).
Transportation: Commute to work: 84.7% car, 0.0% public transportation, 11.4% walk, 4.0% work from home (2000); Travel time to work: 49.0% less than 15 minutes, 22.7% 15 to 30 minutes, 21.6% 30 to 45 minutes, 1.0% 45 to 60 minutes, 5.7% 60 minutes or more (2000)

POPEJOY (city). Covers a land area of 0.731 square miles and a water area of 0 square miles. Located at 42.59° N. Lat.; 93.42° W. Long. Elevation is 1,159 feet.
History: Popejoy was named for local landowner John I. Popejoy.
Population: 78 (2000); Race: 93.8% White, 0.0% Black, 0.0% Asian, 0.0% American Indian and Alaska Native, 0.0% Hispanic of any race, 6.3% two or more races (2000); Density: 106.7 persons per square mile (2000); Age: 16.3% under 18, 25.0% over 64 (2000); Marriage status: 24.6% never married, 66.7% now married, 8.7% widowed, 0.0% divorced (2000); Foreign born: 0.0% (2000); Ancestry (includes multiple ancestries): 28.7% United States or American, 20.0% German, 15.0% Other groups, 13.8% Norwegian, 10.0% English (2000).
Economy: Employment by occupation: 27.9% management, 0.0% professional, 14.0% services, 30.2% sales, 7.0% farming, 11.6% construction, 9.3% production (2000).
Income: Per capita income: $13,666 (2000); Median household income: $29,464 (2000); Poverty rate: 6.3% (2000).
Taxes: Total city taxes per capita: $44 (1997); City property taxes per capita: $44 (1997).
Education: High school graduation rate: 87.5% (2000); College graduation rate: 5.4% (2000).
Housing: Homeownership rate: 94.7% (2000); Median home value: $25,000 (2000); Median rent: $225 per month (2000); Median age of housing: 60+ years (2000).
Transportation: Commute to work: 93.0% car, 0.0% public transportation, 0.0% walk, 0.0% work from home (2000); Travel time to work: 27.9% less than 15 minutes, 67.4% 15 to 30 minutes, 4.7% 30 to 45 minutes, 0.0% 45 to 60 minutes, 0.0% 60 minutes or more (2000)

SHEFFIELD (city). Covers a land area of 5.554 square miles and a water area of 0.029 square miles. Located at 42.89° N. Lat.; 93.21° W. Long. Elevation is 1,076 feet.

History: Sheffield was named for the original owner of the town site. The Bailey Creek Dam, on the creek of that name, was constructed by volunteer labor under the sponsorship of the Sportsmen's Conservation Club.
Population: 930 (2000); Race: 99.1% White, 0.3% Black, 0.0% Asian, 0.5% American Indian and Alaska Native, 0.8% Hispanic of any race, 0.0% two or more races (2000); Density: 167.4 persons per square mile (2000); Age: 23.6% under 18, 26.4% over 64 (2000); Marriage status: 15.4% never married, 61.6% now married, 16.7% widowed, 6.3% divorced (2000); Foreign born: 0.2% (2000); Ancestry (includes multiple ancestries): 57.1% German, 16.3% English, 10.9% Irish, 8.6% Norwegian, 5.0% French (except Basque) (2000).
Economy: Single-family building permits issued: 2 (2001) / 2 (2000); Multi-family building permits issued: 0 (2001) / 0 (2000); Employment by occupation: 10.6% management, 15.4% professional, 13.2% services, 25.0% sales, 0.5% farming, 12.0% construction, 23.3% production (2000).
Income: Per capita income: $16,980 (2000); Median household income: $38,594 (2000); Poverty rate: 5.3% (2000).
Taxes: Total city taxes per capita: $205 (1997); City property taxes per capita: $176 (1997).
Education: High school graduation rate: 84.6% (2000); College graduation rate: 10.9% (2000).

School District(s)

Sheffield-Chapin Community School District (PK-12)
2000 Enrollment: 338 641-892-4160

Housing: Homeownership rate: 86.8% (2000); Median home value: $58,600 (2000); Median rent: $164 per month (2000); Median age of housing: 58 years (2000).
Newspapers: The Sheffield Press (1 x week)
Transportation: Commute to work: 91.9% car, 0.0% public transportation, 2.9% walk, 4.2% work from home (2000); Travel time to work: 41.7% less than 15 minutes, 33.5% 15 to 30 minutes, 21.5% 30 to 45 minutes, 2.3% 45 to 60 minutes, 1.0% 60 minutes or more (2000)

Fremont County

Located in southwestern Iowa; bounded on the south by Missouri and on the west by the Missouri River and the Nebraska border; prairie area, drained by the Nishnabotna River. Covers a land area of 511.10 square miles, a water area of 5.70 square miles, and is located in the Central Time Zone. The county government was organized in 1847. County seat is Sidney.

Weather Station: Sidney Elevation: 1,128 feet

	Jan	Feb	Mar	Apr	May	Jun	Jul	Aug	Sep	Oct	Nov	Dec
High	33	40	52	65	75	84	88	86	79	67	49	37
Low	13	19	30	41	52	62	66	64	55	43	30	19
Precip	0.8	0.9	2.5	3.4	4.5	4.2	5.0	3.9	3.7	2.7	2.1	1.1
Snow	7.0	6.5	5.7	2.3	tr	0.0	0.0	0.0	0.0	0.7	3.3	6.1

High and Low temperatures in degrees Fahrenheit; Precipitation and Snow in inches

Population: 8,010 (2000); Race: 97.9% White, 0.0% Black, 0.4% Asian, 0.1% American Indian and Alaska Native, 1.8% Hispanic of any race, 0.6% two or more races (2000); Density: 15.7 persons per square mile (2000); Age: 24.9% under 18, 19.8% over 64 (2000).
Religion: Five largest groups: 17.6% The United Methodist Church, 9.0% Catholic Church, 5.5% Christian Churches and Churches of Christ, 3.8% United Church of Christ, 3.3% Presbyterian Church (U.S.A.) (2000).
Economy: Unemployment rate: 2.3% (11/2002); Total civilian labor force: 4,629 (11/2002); Leading industries: 20.7% retail trade; 20.2% health care and social assistance; 15.7% manufacturing (2000); Companies that employ more than 1,000 persons: 0 (2000); Companies that employ more than 100 persons: 3 (2000); Farms: 568 totaling 318,355 acres (1997); Minority business ownership rate: 0.0% (1997); Women business ownership rate: 0.0% (1997); Retail sales per capita: $3,434 (1997). Single-family building permits issued: 23 (2001) / 23 (2000); Multi-family building permits issued: 0 (2001) / 0 (2000).
Income: Per capita income: $18,081 (2000); Median household income: $38,345 (2000); Poverty rate: 9.5% (2000); Bankruptcy rate: 4.12% (2001).
Taxes: Total county taxes per capita: $337 (1997); County property taxes per capita: $305 (1997).
Education: High school graduation rate: 85.0% (2000); College graduation rate: 14.0% (2000).
Housing: Homeownership rate: 74.5% (2000); Median home value: $64,400 (2000); Median rent: $268 per month (2000); Median age of housing: 52 years (2000).
Health: Birth rate: 111.1 per 10,000 population (1998); Age adjusted death rate: 88.3 per 10,000 population (1999); Age adjusted cancer mortality rate: 178.1 deaths per 100,000 population (1999). Number of physicians: 2.5 per 10,000 population (1999); Number of hospital beds: 31.2 per 10,000 population (1999).
Elections: 2000 Presidential election results: 40.4% Gore, 57.2% Bush, 1.7% Nader, 0.3% Buchanan
National and State Parks: Bartlett State Wildlife Management Area; Forneys Lake State Wildlife Management Area; McPaul State Wildlife Management Area; Percival State Wildlife Management Area; Scott State Wildlife Management Area; Waubonsie State Park; Waubonsie State Park Trail
Additional Information Contacts
Fremont County Government Offices 712-374-2415

Fremont County Communities

FARRAGUT (city). Covers a land area of 0.366 square miles and a water area of 0 square miles. Located at 40.72° N. Lat.; 95.48° W. Long. Elevation is 959 feet.
History: Farragut was named in honor of Civil War naval officer David Glasgow Farragut.
Population: 509 (2000); Race: 97.2% White, 0.0% Black, 0.4% Asian, 0.0% American Indian and Alaska Native, 1.1% Hispanic of any race, 2.4% two or more races (2000); Density: 1,390.2 persons per square mile (2000); Age: 26.2% under 18, 25.7% over 64 (2000); Marriage status: 14.7% never married, 64.4% now married, 14.5% widowed, 6.4% divorced (2000); Foreign born: 0.7% (2000); Ancestry (includes multiple ancestries): 27.7% German, 15.7% United States or American, 14.0% English, 13.3% Irish, 6.6% Other groups (2000).
Economy: Single-family building permits issued: 0 (2001) / 1 (2000); Multi-family building permits issued: 0 (2001) / 0 (2000); Employment by occupation: 6.7% management, 19.2% professional, 17.2% services, 18.8% sales, 0.8% farming, 10.9% construction, 26.4% production (2000).
Income: Per capita income: $16,667 (2000); Median household income: $34,250 (2000); Poverty rate: 7.5% (2000).
Taxes: Total city taxes per capita: $162 (1997); City property taxes per capita: $131 (1997).
Education: High school graduation rate: 81.6% (2000); College graduation rate: 14.1% (2000).

School District(s)

Farragut Community School District (PK-12)
2000 Enrollment: 355 712-385-8131

Housing: Homeownership rate: 82.4% (2000); Median home value: $57,400 (2000); Median rent: $189 per month (2000); Median age of housing: 43 years (2000).
Transportation: Commute to work: 92.8% car, 0.0% public transportation, 3.8% walk, 2.5% work from home (2000); Travel time to work: 50.0% less than 15 minutes, 33.9% 15 to 30 minutes, 8.3% 30 to 45 minutes, 4.8% 45 to 60 minutes, 3.0% 60 minutes or more (2000)

HAMBURG (city). Covers a land area of 1.120 square miles and a water area of <.001 square miles. Located at 40.60° N. Lat.; 95.65° W. Long. Elevation is 914 feet.
History: Hamburg was named by a settler for his native city, Hamburg, Germany. A trader named Hitchcock once built a cabin directly on the Iowa-Missouri border, two miles to the south, and lived there for several years with a collection of wives. Whenever officers from Iowa visited him to ask for an explanation, he retreated to the Missouri end of his house and when the Missouri officers sought to question him, he took refuge in the Iowa end. It was several years before the officers of the two states joined forces and finally brought him to justice.
Population: 1,240 (2000); Race: 97.1% White, 0.0% Black, 0.2% Asian, 0.2% American Indian and Alaska Native, 5.2% Hispanic of any race, 0.4% two or more races (2000); Density: 1,107.1 persons per square mile (2000); Age: 21.9% under 18, 20.4% over 64 (2000); Marriage status: 21.0% never married, 53.0% now married, 11.7% widowed, 14.3% divorced (2000); Foreign born: 4.5% (2000); Ancestry (includes multiple ancestries): 25.1% German, 12.7% Irish, 8.9% Other groups, 8.8% United States or American, 7.9% English (2000).
Economy: Single-family building permits issued: 3 (2001) / 1 (2000); Multi-family building permits issued: 0 (2001) / 0 (2000); Employment by occupation: 8.9% management, 9.9% professional, 15.8% services, 24.3% sales, 0.7% farming, 9.7% construction, 30.9% production (2000).
Income: Per capita income: $16,050 (2000); Median household income: $29,479 (2000); Poverty rate: 13.9% (2000).

Taxes: Total city taxes per capita: $341 (1997); City property taxes per capita: $307 (1997).
Education: High school graduation rate: 79.2% (2000); College graduation rate: 9.3% (2000).

School District(s)

Hamburg Community School District (PK-12)
2000 Enrollment: 323 712-382-1063

Housing: Homeownership rate: 69.8% (2000); Median home value: $58,900 (2000); Median rent: $273 per month (2000); Median age of housing: 55 years (2000).
Hospitals: Grape Community Hospital (49 beds)
Newspapers: Hamburg Reporter (1 x week)
Transportation: Commute to work: 94.5% car, 0.0% public transportation, 2.5% walk, 1.3% work from home (2000); Travel time to work: 63.0% less than 15 minutes, 20.4% 15 to 30 minutes, 7.9% 30 to 45 minutes, 3.9% 45 to 60 minutes, 4.9% 60 minutes or more (2000)

IMOGENE (city). Covers a land area of 0.200 square miles and a water area of 0 square miles. Located at 40.87° N. Lat.; 95.42° W. Long. Elevation is 1,100 feet.
History: Imogene was settled by a group of Irishmen in the early 1880's. A Roman Catholic church of an elaborate scale was erected in 1915. In 1886, August Werener, a local cabinetmaker, planned to demonstate his "flying machine" at the Fourth of July celebration. When the blades were spun, however, the wooden cogs were sheared off. Werner never recovered from his disappointment, and died in the State Hospital for the Insane at Clarinda.
Population: 66 (2000); Race: 100.0% White, 0.0% Black, 0.0% Asian, 0.0% American Indian and Alaska Native, 0.0% Hispanic of any race, 0.0% two or more races (2000); Density: 330.5 persons per square mile (2000); Age: 8.3% under 18, 25.0% over 64 (2000); Marriage status: 31.8% never married, 47.7% now married, 13.6% widowed, 6.8% divorced (2000); Foreign born: 0.0% (2000); Ancestry (includes multiple ancestries): 45.8% German, 41.7% Irish, 27.1% United States or American, 12.5% English, 10.4% Polish (2000).
Economy: Employment by occupation: 14.8% management, 18.5% professional, 7.4% services, 11.1% sales, 7.4% farming, 11.1% construction, 29.6% production (2000).
Income: Per capita income: $25,329 (2000); Median household income: $41,250 (2000); Poverty rate: 4.2% (2000).
Taxes: Total city taxes per capita: $143 (1997); City property taxes per capita: $107 (1997).
Education: High school graduation rate: 94.6% (2000); College graduation rate: 5.4% (2000).
Housing: Homeownership rate: 59.3% (2000); Median home value: $36,700 (2000); Median rent: $308 per month (2000); Median age of housing: 60+ years (2000).
Transportation: Commute to work: 92.6% car, 0.0% public transportation, 0.0% walk, 7.4% work from home (2000); Travel time to work: 40.0% less than 15 minutes, 16.0% 15 to 30 minutes, 32.0% 30 to 45 minutes, 4.0% 45 to 60 minutes, 8.0% 60 minutes or more (2000)

PERCIVAL (unincorporated postal area, zip code 51648). Covers a land area of 57.157 square miles and a water area of 0.156 square miles. Located at 40.74° N. Lat.; 95.79° W. Long. Elevation is 934 feet.
History: Percival was once known as Gaston. The name was changed after the Civil War to honor a local lawyer, Robert Percival.
Population: 276 (2000); Race: 89.8% White, 0.0% Black, 0.0% Asian, 1.5% American Indian and Alaska Native, 10.2% Hispanic of any race, 0.0% two or more races (2000); Density: 4.8 persons per square mile (2000); Age: 18.2% under 18, 19.3% over 64 (2000); Marriage status: 17.7% never married, 69.7% now married, 5.6% widowed, 6.9% divorced (2000); Foreign born: 6.1% (2000); Ancestry (includes multiple ancestries): 28.8% German, 13.3% Other groups, 9.8% English, 9.8% Irish, 9.5% United States or American (2000).
Economy: Employment by occupation: 23.5% management, 13.1% professional, 10.5% services, 20.9% sales, 1.3% farming, 5.9% construction, 24.8% production (2000).
Income: Per capita income: $22,560 (2000); Median household income: $48,636 (2000); Poverty rate: 0.4% (2000).
Education: High school graduation rate: 88.5% (2000); College graduation rate: 13.0% (2000).
Housing: Homeownership rate: 75.4% (2000); Median home value: $97,500 (2000); Median rent: $163 per month (2000); Median age of housing: 46 years (2000).
Transportation: Commute to work: 94.1% car, 0.0% public transportation, 0.7% walk, 5.2% work from home (2000); Travel time to work: 31.7% less than 15 minutes, 17.2% 15 to 30 minutes, 38.6% 30 to 45 minutes, 12.4% 45 to 60 minutes, 0.0% 60 minutes or more (2000)

RANDOLPH (city). Covers a land area of 0.317 square miles and a water area of 0 square miles. Located at 40.87° N. Lat.; 95.56° W. Long. Elevation is 977 feet.
Population: 209 (2000); Race: 100.0% White, 0.0% Black, 0.0% Asian, 0.0% American Indian and Alaska Native, 0.0% Hispanic of any race, 0.0% two or more races (2000); Density: 658.7 persons per square mile (2000); Age: 35.3% under 18, 7.1% over 64 (2000); Marriage status: 24.4% never married, 57.1% now married, 1.3% widowed, 17.3% divorced (2000); Foreign born: 0.0% (2000); Ancestry (includes multiple ancestries): 31.3% United States or American, 21.9% German, 12.9% English, 6.7% Swedish, 5.8% Irish (2000).
Economy: Livestock; grain. Single-family building permits issued: 0 (2001) / 0 (2000); Multi-family building permits issued: 0 (2001) / 0 (2000); Employment by occupation: 3.5% management, 12.2% professional, 28.7% services, 20.0% sales, 4.3% farming, 6.1% construction, 25.2% production (2000).
Income: Per capita income: $13,925 (2000); Median household income: $34,861 (2000); Poverty rate: 14.3% (2000).
Taxes: Total city taxes per capita: $316 (2000); City property taxes per capita: $91 (2000).
Education: High school graduation rate: 82.7% (2000); College graduation rate: 6.3% (2000).
Housing: Homeownership rate: 79.5% (2000); Median home value: $41,100 (2000); Median rent: $275 per month (2000); Median age of housing: 60+ years (2000).
Transportation: Commute to work: 93.0% car, 0.0% public transportation, 3.5% walk, 0.0% work from home (2000); Travel time to work: 28.7% less than 15 minutes, 29.6% 15 to 30 minutes, 23.5% 30 to 45 minutes, 7.8% 45 to 60 minutes, 10.4% 60 minutes or more (2000)

RIVERTON (city). Covers a land area of 0.598 square miles and a water area of 0 square miles. Located at 40.68° N. Lat.; 95.56° W. Long. Elevation is 926 feet.
Population: 304 (2000); Race: 98.8% White, 0.0% Black, 0.0% Asian, 0.0% American Indian and Alaska Native, 0.0% Hispanic of any race, 1.2% two or more races (2000); Density: 508.1 persons per square mile (2000); Age: 29.7% under 18, 12.9% over 64 (2000); Marriage status: 17.7% never married, 59.1% now married, 7.9% widowed, 15.4% divorced (2000); Foreign born: 0.0% (2000); Ancestry (includes multiple ancestries): 25.3% German, 14.1% United States or American, 10.6% Irish, 7.6% English, 5.3% Dutch (2000).
Economy: Livestock; grain. Single-family building permits issued: 0 (2001) / 0 (2000); Multi-family building permits issued: 0 (2001) / 0 (2000); Employment by occupation: 8.9% management, 10.1% professional, 8.9% services, 29.6% sales, 3.6% farming, 11.8% construction, 27.2% production (2000).
Income: Per capita income: $12,854 (2000); Median household income: $27,500 (2000); Poverty rate: 16.5% (2000).
Taxes: Total city taxes per capita: $111 (1997); City property taxes per capita: $79 (1997).
Education: High school graduation rate: 71.7% (2000); College graduation rate: 4.9% (2000).
Housing: Homeownership rate: 81.8% (2000); Median home value: $30,200 (2000); Median rent: $235 per month (2000); Median age of housing: 60+ years (2000).
Transportation: Commute to work: 100.0% car, 0.0% public transportation, 0.0% walk, 0.0% work from home (2000); Travel time to work: 25.4% less than 15 minutes, 58.6% 15 to 30 minutes, 5.3% 30 to 45 minutes, 0.0% 45 to 60 minutes, 10.7% 60 minutes or more (2000)

SIDNEY (city). Covers a land area of 1.264 square miles and a water area of 0 square miles. Located at 40.74° N. Lat.; 95.64° W. Long. Elevation is 1,049 feet.
History: Sidney was named for Sidney, Ohio, where Milton Richard, who platted the town, once lived.
Population: 1,300 (2000); Race: 98.9% White, 0.0% Black, 0.0% Asian, 0.0% American Indian and Alaska Native, 2.5% Hispanic of any race, 0.2% two or more races (2000); Density: 1,028.6 persons per square mile (2000); Age: 27.1% under 18, 21.4% over 64 (2000); Marriage status: 16.9% never married, 63.4% now married, 9.4% widowed, 10.3% divorced (2000); Foreign born: 1.2% (2000); Ancestry (includes multiple ancestries): 22.3% German, 13.8% Irish, 9.1% English, 9.1% United States or American, 6.2% Other groups (2000).

Economy: Single-family building permits issued: 0 (2001) / 5 (2000); Multi-family building permits issued: 0 (2001) / 0 (2000); Employment by occupation: 11.1% management, 15.0% professional, 20.8% services, 18.9% sales, 0.4% farming, 11.3% construction, 22.4% production (2000).
Income: Per capita income: $15,027 (2000); Median household income: $36,375 (2000); Poverty rate: 9.7% (2000).
Taxes: Total city taxes per capita: $216 (1997); City property taxes per capita: $182 (1997).
Education: High school graduation rate: 85.8% (2000); College graduation rate: 14.3% (2000).

School District(s)

Sidney Community School District (PK-12)
2000 Enrollment: 441 712-374-2141
Housing: Homeownership rate: 71.8% (2000); Median home value: $64,000 (2000); Median rent: $269 per month (2000); Median age of housing: 41 years (2000).
Newspapers: Sidney Argus-Herald (1 x week)
Transportation: Commute to work: 91.8% car, 0.0% public transportation, 4.6% walk, 3.2% work from home (2000); Travel time to work: 46.3% less than 15 minutes, 30.1% 15 to 30 minutes, 7.9% 30 to 45 minutes, 7.0% 45 to 60 minutes, 8.6% 60 minutes or more (2000)

TABOR (city). Covers a land area of 1.277 square miles and a water area of 0 square miles. Located at 40.89° N. Lat.; 95.67° W. Long.
History: Tabor was the scene of some of John Brown's anti-slavery activities of 1858-59.
Population: 993 (2000); Race: 99.5% White, 0.0% Black, 0.3% Asian, 0.0% American Indian and Alaska Native, 0.0% Hispanic of any race, 0.2% two or more races (2000); Density: 777.4 persons per square mile (2000); Age: 23.5% under 18, 27.9% over 64 (2000); Marriage status: 13.8% never married, 65.7% now married, 12.3% widowed, 8.3% divorced (2000); Foreign born: 0.2% (2000); Ancestry (includes multiple ancestries): 25.5% German, 14.9% Irish, 14.6% English, 6.9% United States or American, 5.0% Other groups (2000).
Economy: Single-family building permits issued: 5 (2001) / 6 (2000); Multi-family building permits issued: 0 (2001) / 0 (2000); Employment by occupation: 11.4% management, 16.4% professional, 21.4% services, 25.0% sales, 1.6% farming, 10.7% construction, 13.6% production (2000).
Income: Per capita income: $16,979 (2000); Median household income: $36,750 (2000); Poverty rate: 7.9% (2000).
Taxes: Total city taxes per capita: $128 (1997); City property taxes per capita: $94 (1997).
Education: High school graduation rate: 82.1% (2000); College graduation rate: 12.0% (2000).

School District(s)

Fremont-Mills Community School District (PK-12)
2000 Enrollment: 499 712-629-2325
Housing: Homeownership rate: 71.7% (2000); Median home value: $80,900 (2000); Median rent: $300 per month (2000); Median age of housing: 54 years (2000).
Newspapers: Beacon-Enterprise (1 x week)
Transportation: Commute to work: 94.2% car, 0.5% public transportation, 3.0% walk, 1.9% work from home (2000); Travel time to work: 35.6% less than 15 minutes, 21.0% 15 to 30 minutes, 22.4% 30 to 45 minutes, 14.2% 45 to 60 minutes, 6.8% 60 minutes or more (2000)

THURMAN (city). Covers a land area of 0.557 square miles and a water area of 0 square miles. Located at 40.82° N. Lat.; 95.75° W. Long. Elevation is 972 feet.
History: Thurman had also been known as Fremont City and Plum Hollow. The name Thurman was to honor Vice President Allen G. Thurman of the Cleveland administration.
Population: 236 (2000); Race: 98.2% White, 0.9% Black, 0.0% Asian, 0.9% American Indian and Alaska Native, 0.0% Hispanic of any race, 0.0% two or more races (2000); Density: 424.1 persons per square mile (2000); Age: 33.2% under 18, 8.6% over 64 (2000); Marriage status: 22.8% never married, 66.5% now married, 5.4% widowed, 5.4% divorced (2000); Foreign born: 1.4% (2000); Ancestry (includes multiple ancestries): 28.2% German, 17.3% Irish, 15.0% Other groups, 14.5% English, 11.4% Norwegian (2000).
Economy: Single-family building permits issued: 0 (2001) / 0 (2000); Multi-family building permits issued: 0 (2001) / 0 (2000); Employment by occupation: 7.4% management, 13.7% professional, 24.2% services, 26.3% sales, 0.0% farming, 15.8% construction, 12.6% production (2000).
Income: Per capita income: $13,851 (2000); Median household income: $34,583 (2000); Poverty rate: 16.4% (2000).
Taxes: Total city taxes per capita: $74 (1997); City property taxes per capita: $48 (1997).
Education: High school graduation rate: 78.1% (2000); College graduation rate: 9.5% (2000).
Housing: Homeownership rate: 97.3% (2000); Median home value: $43,800 (2000); Median age of housing: 60+ years (2000).
Transportation: Commute to work: 95.7% car, 0.0% public transportation, 0.0% walk, 4.3% work from home (2000); Travel time to work: 5.6% less than 15 minutes, 25.8% 15 to 30 minutes, 31.5% 30 to 45 minutes, 30.3% 45 to 60 minutes, 6.7% 60 minutes or more (2000)

Greene County

Located in central Iowa; prairie area, drained by the Raccoon River. Covers a land area of 568.40 square miles, a water area of 2.70 square miles, and is located in the Central Time Zone. The county government was organized in 1851. County seat is Jefferson.

Weather Station: Jefferson — Elevation: 1,043 feet

	Jan	Feb	Mar	Apr	May	Jun	Jul	Aug	Sep	Oct	Nov	Dec
High	29	36	48	63	74	84	87	84	78	65	47	33
Low	10	16	27	38	50	60	64	62	53	41	28	16
Precip	1.0	0.9	2.2	3.2	4.3	4.6	4.0	4.0	3.0	2.5	1.9	1.1
Snow	7.4	6.2	5.3	1.7	tr	0.0	0.0	0.0	0.0	0.2	2.9	6.3

High and Low temperatures in degrees Fahrenheit; Precipitation and Snow in inches

Population: 10,366 (2000); Race: 98.2% White, 0.1% Black, 0.1% Asian, 0.3% American Indian and Alaska Native, 1.3% Hispanic of any race, 0.7% two or more races (2000); Density: 18.2 persons per square mile (2000); Age: 25.6% under 18, 21.7% over 64 (2000).
Religion: Five largest groups: 22.4% The United Methodist Church, 16.7% Catholic Church, 7.7% Lutheran Church—Missouri Synod, 7.1% Christian Church (Disciples of Christ), 5.3% American Baptist Churches in the USA (2000).
Economy: Unemployment rate: 3.3% (11/2002); Total civilian labor force: 4,526 (11/2002); Leading industries: 26.5% health care and social assistance; 22.7% manufacturing; 13.1% retail trade (2000); Companies that employ more than 1,000 persons: 0 (2000); Companies that employ more than 100 persons: 4 (2000); Farms: 763 totaling 343,346 acres (1997); Minority business ownership rate: 0.0% (1997); Women business ownership rate: 16.1% (1997); Retail sales per capita: $5,266 (1997). Single-family building permits issued: 24 (2001) / 15 (2000); Multi-family building permits issued: 0 (2001) / 0 (2000).
Income: Per capita income: $16,866 (2000); Median household income: $33,883 (2000); Poverty rate: 8.1% (2000); Bankruptcy rate: 4.20% (2001).
Taxes: Total county taxes per capita: $365 (2000); County property taxes per capita: $359 (2000).
Education: High school graduation rate: 85.6% (2000); College graduation rate: 14.6% (2000).
Housing: Homeownership rate: 75.6% (2000); Median home value: $51,800 (2000); Median rent: $258 per month (2000); Median age of housing: 56 years (2000).
Health: Birth rate: 106.1 per 10,000 population (1998); Age adjusted death rate: 83.2 per 10,000 population (1999); Age adjusted cancer mortality rate: 144.5 deaths per 100,000 population (1999). Number of physicians: 4.8 per 10,000 population (1999); Number of hospital beds: 122.5 per 10,000 population (1999).
Elections: 2000 Presidential election results: 48.8% Gore, 48.4% Bush, 2.3% Nader, 0.3% Buchanan
National and State Parks: Dunbar Slough State Wildlife Management Area; Goose Lake State Wildlife Management Area; McMahon State Wildlife Management Area; Rippey State Access Area; Snake Creek State Game Management Area
Additional Information Contacts
Greene County Government Offices 515-386-2316
Jefferson Chamber of Commerce......................... 515-386-2155

Greene County Communities

CHURDAN (city). Covers a land area of 2.116 square miles and a water area of 0.006 square miles. Located at 42.15° N. Lat.; 94.47° W. Long. Elevation is 1,110 feet.
History: Joseph Churdan, who gave his name to the town of Churdan, was the first postmaster here.
Population: 418 (2000); Race: 98.9% White, 0.4% Black, 0.0% Asian, 0.6% American Indian and Alaska Native, 0.0% Hispanic of any race, 0.0% two or

more races (2000); Density: 197.5 persons per square mile (2000); Age: 21.7% under 18, 29.5% over 64 (2000); Marriage status: 16.2% never married, 59.9% now married, 14.9% widowed, 9.0% divorced (2000); Foreign born: 0.4% (2000); Ancestry (includes multiple ancestries): 28.4% German, 21.9% Irish, 10.8% United States or American, 9.7% English, 7.1% Swedish (2000).
Economy: Single-family building permits issued: 0 (2001) / 0 (2000); Multi-family building permits issued: 0 (2001) / 0 (2000); Employment by occupation: 12.4% management, 11.9% professional, 21.4% services, 20.4% sales, 1.5% farming, 11.4% construction, 20.9% production (2000).
Income: Per capita income: $17,090 (2000); Median household income: $26,932 (2000); Poverty rate: 13.8% (2000).
Taxes: Total city taxes per capita: $171 (1997); City property taxes per capita: $169 (1997).
Education: High school graduation rate: 87.1% (2000); College graduation rate: 11.1% (2000).

School District(s)

Paton-Churdan Community School District (KG-12)
2000 Enrollment: 200 515-389-3111
Housing: Homeownership rate: 82.4% (2000); Median home value: $27,400 (2000); Median rent: $185 per month (2000); Median age of housing: 60+ years (2000).
Transportation: Commute to work: 78.6% car, 0.0% public transportation, 13.3% walk, 8.2% work from home (2000); Travel time to work: 36.7% less than 15 minutes, 32.2% 15 to 30 minutes, 19.4% 30 to 45 minutes, 5.0% 45 to 60 minutes, 6.7% 60 minutes or more (2000)

COOPER (unincorporated postal area, zip code 50059). Covers a land area of 0.500 square miles and a water area of 0 square miles. Located at 41.91° N. Lat.; 94.34° W. Long. Elevation is 1,079 feet.
History: Cooper was laid out in 1881 by the Polk and Hubbell Development Company, and named for Hubbell's father-in-law, Isaac Cooper.
Population: 14 (2000); Race: 100.0% White, 0.0% Black, 0.0% Asian, 0.0% American Indian and Alaska Native, 0.0% Hispanic of any race, 0.0% two or more races (2000); Density: 28.0 persons per square mile (2000); Age: 65.2% under 18, 0.0% over 64 (2000); Marriage status: 0.0% never married, 0.0% now married, 0.0% widowed, 100.0% divorced (2000); Foreign born: 0.0% (2000); Ancestry (includes multiple ancestries): 100.0% German (2000).
Economy: Employment by occupation: 0.0% management, 0.0% professional, 0.0% services, 0.0% sales, 0.0% farming, 0.0% construction, 100.0% production (2000).
Income: Per capita income: $10,135 (2000); Median household income: $28,750 (2000); Poverty rate: 0.0% (2000).
Education: High school graduation rate: 100.0% (2000); College graduation rate: 0.0% (2000).
Housing: Homeownership rate: 100.0% (2000); Median home value: $45,000 (2000); Median age of housing: 60+ years (2000).
Transportation: Commute to work: 0.0% car, 0.0% public transportation, 100.0% walk, 0.0% work from home (2000); Travel time to work: 100.0% less than 15 minutes, 0.0% 15 to 30 minutes, 0.0% 30 to 45 minutes, 0.0% 45 to 60 minutes, 0.0% 60 minutes or more (2000)

DANA (city). Covers a land area of 0.282 square miles and a water area of 0 square miles. Located at 42.10° N. Lat.; 94.24° W. Long. Elevation is 1,118 feet.
History: Samuel Dana founded the town of Dana around 1879, and named it for himself.
Population: 84 (2000); Race: 100.0% White, 0.0% Black, 0.0% Asian, 0.0% American Indian and Alaska Native, 0.0% Hispanic of any race, 0.0% two or more races (2000); Density: 297.5 persons per square mile (2000); Age: 27.9% under 18, 7.4% over 64 (2000); Marriage status: 24.5% never married, 53.1% now married, 4.1% widowed, 18.4% divorced (2000); Foreign born: 0.0% (2000); Ancestry (includes multiple ancestries): 27.9% German, 16.2% Irish, 14.7% United States or American, 7.4% English, 5.9% Other groups (2000).
Economy: Employment by occupation: 0.0% management, 6.9% professional, 37.9% services, 27.6% sales, 6.9% farming, 13.8% construction, 6.9% production (2000).
Income: Per capita income: $11,199 (2000); Median household income: $33,750 (2000); Poverty rate: 8.8% (2000).
Taxes: Total city taxes per capita: $203 (1997); City property taxes per capita: $188 (1997).
Education: High school graduation rate: 72.1% (2000); College graduation rate: 4.7% (2000).
Housing: Homeownership rate: 75.0% (2000); Median home value: $15,000 (2000); Median rent: $325 per month (2000); Median age of housing: 60+ years (2000).
Transportation: Commute to work: 82.8% car, 6.9% public transportation, 10.3% walk, 0.0% work from home (2000); Travel time to work: 31.0% less than 15 minutes, 20.7% 15 to 30 minutes, 20.7% 30 to 45 minutes, 6.9% 45 to 60 minutes, 20.7% 60 minutes or more (2000)

GRAND JUNCTION (city). Covers a land area of 0.965 square miles and a water area of 0 square miles. Located at 42.03° N. Lat.; 94.23° W. Long. Elevation is 1,041 feet.
History: Grand Junction was so named because of the junction here of the Chicago & North Western and the Minnesota & St. Louis Railroads. In 1870 a local newspaper, the "Headlight," was responsible for bringing many immigrants here to settle.
Population: 964 (2000); Race: 96.6% White, 0.0% Black, 0.2% Asian, 0.0% American Indian and Alaska Native, 2.9% Hispanic of any race, 1.4% two or more races (2000); Density: 999.1 persons per square mile (2000); Age: 30.5% under 18, 18.7% over 64 (2000); Marriage status: 22.2% never married, 58.8% now married, 8.9% widowed, 10.1% divorced (2000); Foreign born: 1.4% (2000); Ancestry (includes multiple ancestries): 31.9% German, 15.2% English, 12.0% Irish, 10.0% United States or American, 4.9% Other groups (2000).
Economy: Single-family building permits issued: 2 (2001) / 2 (2000); Multi-family building permits issued: 0 (2001) / 0 (2000); Employment by occupation: 6.0% management, 10.3% professional, 19.9% services, 25.4% sales, 2.0% farming, 10.6% construction, 25.7% production (2000).
Income: Per capita income: $12,733 (2000); Median household income: $27,875 (2000); Poverty rate: 14.6% (2000).
Taxes: Total city taxes per capita: $95 (1997); City property taxes per capita: $93 (1997).
Education: High school graduation rate: 81.5% (2000); College graduation rate: 8.8% (2000).

School District(s)

East Greene Community School District (PK-12)
2000 Enrollment: 455 515-738-5741
Housing: Homeownership rate: 73.2% (2000); Median home value: $37,500 (2000); Median rent: $205 per month (2000); Median age of housing: 60+ years (2000).
Transportation: Commute to work: 95.6% car, 0.0% public transportation, 2.6% walk, 1.3% work from home (2000); Travel time to work: 37.0% less than 15 minutes, 30.7% 15 to 30 minutes, 13.2% 30 to 45 minutes, 7.4% 45 to 60 minutes, 11.6% 60 minutes or more (2000)

JEFFERSON (city). Covers a land area of 5.822 square miles and a water area of 0.055 square miles. Located at 42.01° N. Lat.; 94.37° W. Long. Elevation is 1,078 feet.
History: Jefferson was established after a group of settlers came to Des Moines in 1854 and borrowed $200 to purchase the town site. Named in honor of President Thomas Jefferson, it was first called New Jefferson.
Population: 4,626 (2000); Race: 98.5% White, 0.0% Black, 0.0% Asian, 0.3% American Indian and Alaska Native, 1.0% Hispanic of any race, 1.0% two or more races (2000); Density: 794.6 persons per square mile (2000); Age: 24.7% under 18, 26.8% over 64 (2000); Marriage status: 19.1% never married, 58.2% now married, 14.5% widowed, 8.2% divorced (2000); Foreign born: 0.8% (2000); Ancestry (includes multiple ancestries): 36.4% German, 13.4% English, 13.0% Irish, 10.5% United States or American, 5.1% Norwegian (2000).
Economy: Single-family building permits issued: 2 (2001) / 4 (2000); Multi-family building permits issued: 0 (2001) / 0 (2000); Employment by occupation: 8.8% management, 21.2% professional, 16.6% services, 22.0% sales, 0.9% farming, 11.0% construction, 19.5% production (2000).
Income: Per capita income: $17,441 (2000); Median household income: $32,818 (2000); Poverty rate: 7.3% (2000).
Taxes: Total city taxes per capita: $333 (2000); City property taxes per capita: $324 (2000).
Education: High school graduation rate: 84.5% (2000); College graduation rate: 15.6% (2000).

School District(s)

Jefferson-Scranton Community School District (PK-12)
2000 Enrollment: 1,450 515-386-4168
Housing: Homeownership rate: 74.8% (2000); Median home value: $58,900 (2000); Median rent: $278 per month (2000); Median age of housing: 48 years (2000).
Hospitals: Greene County Medical Center (127 beds)
Newspapers: The Jefferson Herald (1 x week); The Bee (1 x week)

Transportation: Commute to work: 90.7% car, 0.6% public transportation, 3.1% walk, 4.1% work from home (2000); Travel time to work: 69.6% less than 15 minutes, 9.8% 15 to 30 minutes, 10.3% 30 to 45 minutes, 5.8% 45 to 60 minutes, 4.4% 60 minutes or more (2000)
Airports: Jefferson Municipal
Additional Information Contacts
Jefferson Chamber of Commerce 515-386-2155

PATON (city). Covers a land area of 0.566 square miles and a water area of <.001 square miles. Located at 42.16° N. Lat.; 94.25° W. Long. Elevation is 1,101 feet.
History: Paton was named for Scottish immigrant William Paton.
Population: 265 (2000); Race: 95.2% White, 0.0% Black, 0.0% Asian, 0.0% American Indian and Alaska Native, 1.5% Hispanic of any race, 3.7% two or more races (2000); Density: 468.3 persons per square mile (2000); Age: 34.8% under 18, 20.5% over 64 (2000); Marriage status: 16.1% never married, 56.3% now married, 18.2% widowed, 9.4% divorced (2000); Foreign born: 2.6% (2000); Ancestry (includes multiple ancestries): 28.9% German, 14.7% Irish, 7.3% United States or American, 7.0% Swedish, 6.6% English (2000).
Economy: Employment by occupation: 19.0% management, 12.0% professional, 8.0% services, 24.0% sales, 1.0% farming, 13.0% construction, 23.0% production (2000).
Income: Per capita income: $15,256 (2000); Median household income: $32,500 (2000); Poverty rate: 7.8% (2000).
Taxes: Total city taxes per capita: $164 (1997); City property taxes per capita: $160 (1997).
Education: High school graduation rate: 84.8% (2000); College graduation rate: 7.3% (2000).
Housing: Homeownership rate: 88.2% (2000); Median home value: $32,900 (2000); Median rent: $217 per month (2000); Median age of housing: 56 years (2000).
Transportation: Commute to work: 91.2% car, 0.0% public transportation, 6.9% walk, 2.0% work from home (2000); Travel time to work: 26.0% less than 15 minutes, 48.0% 15 to 30 minutes, 14.0% 30 to 45 minutes, 6.0% 45 to 60 minutes, 6.0% 60 minutes or more (2000)

RIPPEY (city). Covers a land area of 0.842 square miles and a water area of 0 square miles. Located at 41.93° N. Lat.; 94.20° W. Long. Elevation is 1,077 feet.
History: Rippey may have been named in honor of an early settler in the area, Judge Robert M. Rippey.
Population: 319 (2000); Race: 96.8% White, 0.0% Black, 0.6% Asian, 0.0% American Indian and Alaska Native, 2.5% Hispanic of any race, 0.0% two or more races (2000); Density: 378.7 persons per square mile (2000); Age: 33.5% under 18, 15.8% over 64 (2000); Marriage status: 14.0% never married, 68.1% now married, 5.7% widowed, 12.2% divorced (2000); Foreign born: 3.2% (2000); Ancestry (includes multiple ancestries): 35.4% German, 13.3% English, 11.1% Irish, 9.2% United States or American, 6.0% Other groups (2000).
Economy: Single-family building permits issued: 0 (2001) / 0 (2000); Multi-family building permits issued: 0 (2001) / 0 (2000); Employment by occupation: 8.3% management, 22.2% professional, 14.6% services, 23.6% sales, 0.0% farming, 8.3% construction, 22.9% production (2000).
Income: Per capita income: $14,344 (2000); Median household income: $33,611 (2000); Poverty rate: 6.6% (2000).
Taxes: Total city taxes per capita: $116 (1997); City property taxes per capita: $116 (1997).
Education: High school graduation rate: 82.1% (2000); College graduation rate: 9.5% (2000).
Housing: Homeownership rate: 85.7% (2000); Median home value: $38,300 (2000); Median rent: <$100 per month (2000); Median age of housing: 59 years (2000).
Transportation: Commute to work: 95.8% car, 0.0% public transportation, 4.2% walk, 0.0% work from home (2000); Travel time to work: 31.9% less than 15 minutes, 47.2% 15 to 30 minutes, 5.6% 30 to 45 minutes, 6.3% 45 to 60 minutes, 9.0% 60 minutes or more (2000)

SCRANTON (city). Covers a land area of 1.878 square miles and a water area of 0 square miles. Located at 42.02° N. Lat.; 94.54° W. Long. Elevation is 1,185 feet.
History: Scranton was named for Scranton, Pennsylvania.
Population: 604 (2000); Race: 96.6% White, 0.0% Black, 0.2% Asian, 0.0% American Indian and Alaska Native, 6.0% Hispanic of any race, 0.0% two or more races (2000); Density: 321.6 persons per square mile (2000); Age: 26.1% under 18, 20.8% over 64 (2000); Marriage status: 19.4% never married, 60.3% now married, 10.5% widowed, 9.8% divorced (2000); Foreign born: 4.6% (2000); Ancestry (includes multiple ancestries): 33.8% German, 13.9% Irish, 12.5% English, 9.6% Other groups, 5.0% Danish (2000).
Economy: Single-family building permits issued: 0 (2001) / 1 (2000); Multi-family building permits issued: 0 (2001) / 0 (2000); Employment by occupation: 9.2% management, 11.7% professional, 10.0% services, 15.5% sales, 5.4% farming, 12.1% construction, 36.0% production (2000).
Income: Per capita income: $13,836 (2000); Median household income: $29,375 (2000); Poverty rate: 13.1% (2000).
Taxes: Total city taxes per capita: $176 (1997); City property taxes per capita: $174 (1997).
Education: High school graduation rate: 80.1% (2000); College graduation rate: 11.7% (2000).
Housing: Homeownership rate: 76.0% (2000); Median home value: $33,300 (2000); Median rent: $234 per month (2000); Median age of housing: 60+ years (2000).
Newspapers: Scranton Journal (1 x week)
Transportation: Commute to work: 90.2% car, 0.0% public transportation, 5.6% walk, 2.1% work from home (2000); Travel time to work: 51.1% less than 15 minutes, 31.0% 15 to 30 minutes, 4.8% 30 to 45 minutes, 2.6% 45 to 60 minutes, 10.5% 60 minutes or more (2000)

Grundy County

Located in central Iowa; rolling prairie area, drained by Wolf Creek. Covers a land area of 502.50 square miles, a water area of 0 square miles, and is located in the Central Time Zone. The county government was organized in 1851. County seat is Grundy Center.

Weather Station: Grundy Center — Elevation: 1,017 feet

	Jan	Feb	Mar	Apr	May	Jun	Jul	Aug	Sep	Oct	Nov	Dec
High	24	31	43	58	70	80	83	81	74	62	44	30
Low	6	12	24	36	48	58	62	59	50	38	25	13
Precip	0.9	1.0	2.3	3.3	4.4	5.0	4.1	3.9	3.1	2.7	2.2	1.2
Snow	9.6	7.6	6.4	2.5	tr	0.0	tr	0.0	0.0	0.3	4.0	7.9

High and Low temperatures in degrees Fahrenheit; Precipitation and Snow in inches

Population: 12,369 (2000); Race: 99.1% White, 0.0% Black, 0.3% Asian, 0.1% American Indian and Alaska Native, 0.6% Hispanic of any race, 0.4% two or more races (2000); Density: 24.6 persons per square mile (2000); Age: 25.2% under 18, 19.3% over 64 (2000).
Religion: Five largest groups: 15.9% The United Methodist Church, 10.9% Evangelical Lutheran Church in America, 9.5% Presbyterian Church (U.S.A.), 6.5% Catholic Church, 6.2% United Church of Christ (2000).
Economy: Unemployment rate: 2.8% (11/2002); Total civilian labor force: 6,267 (11/2002); Leading industries: 21.7% manufacturing; 14.9% retail trade; 11.8% health care and social assistance (2000); Companies that employ more than 1,000 persons: 0 (2000); Companies that employ more than 100 persons: 5 (2000); Farms: 754 totaling 321,389 acres (1997); Minority business ownership rate: 0.0% (1997); Women business ownership rate: 26.6% (1997); Retail sales per capita: $4,991 (1997). Single-family building permits issued: 43 (2001) / 36 (2000); Multi-family building permits issued: 6 (2001) / 24 (2000).
Income: Per capita income: $19,142 (2000); Median household income: $39,396 (2000); Poverty rate: 4.6% (2000); Bankruptcy rate: 1.13% (2001).
Taxes: Total county taxes per capita: $266 (2000); County property taxes per capita: $255 (2000).
Education: High school graduation rate: 86.5% (2000); College graduation rate: 17.2% (2000).
Housing: Homeownership rate: 79.7% (2000); Median home value: $72,500 (2000); Median rent: $275 per month (2000); Median age of housing: 49 years (2000).
Health: Birth rate: 110.0 per 10,000 population (1998); Age adjusted death rate: 72.1 per 10,000 population (1999); Age adjusted cancer mortality rate: 189.5 deaths per 100,000 population (1999). Number of physicians: 5.7 per 10,000 population (1999); Number of hospital beds: 64.7 per 10,000 population (1999).
Elections: 2000 Presidential election results: 35.0% Gore, 63.0% Bush, 1.2% Nader, 0.3% Buchanan
Additional Information Contacts
Grundy County Government Offices 319-824-3122
Grundy Center Chamber of Commerce 319-824-3838

Grundy County Communities

BEAMAN (city). Covers a land area of 0.185 square miles and a water area of 0.008 square miles. Located at 42.22° N. Lat.; 92.82° W. Long.
History: Beaman was named for H. H. Beaman, the original owner of the town site.
Population: 210 (2000); Race: 99.5% White, 0.0% Black, 0.0% Asian, 0.0% American Indian and Alaska Native, 0.5% Hispanic of any race, 0.0% two or more races (2000); Density: 1,138.0 persons per square mile (2000); Age: 27.1% under 18, 20.4% over 64 (2000); Marriage status: 21.4% never married, 61.3% now married, 2.9% widowed, 14.5% divorced (2000); Foreign born: 0.9% (2000); Ancestry (includes multiple ancestries): 46.2% German, 19.9% Irish, 6.8% Czech, 6.8% Norwegian, 6.3% English (2000).
Economy: Single-family building permits issued: 0 (2001) / 1 (2000); Multi-family building permits issued: 0 (2001) / 0 (2000); Employment by occupation: 11.2% management, 15.0% professional, 16.8% services, 27.1% sales, 1.9% farming, 3.7% construction, 24.3% production (2000).
Income: Per capita income: $18,960 (2000); Median household income: $45,750 (2000); Poverty rate: 0.5% (2000).
Taxes: Total city taxes per capita: $283 (1997); City property taxes per capita: $283 (1997).
Education: High school graduation rate: 85.5% (2000); College graduation rate: 12.4% (2000).
Housing: Homeownership rate: 65.9% (2000); Median home value: $43,200 (2000); Median rent: $297 per month (2000); Median age of housing: 57 years (2000).
Transportation: Commute to work: 92.6% car, 0.0% public transportation, 7.4% walk, 0.0% work from home (2000); Travel time to work: 31.5% less than 15 minutes, 53.7% 15 to 30 minutes, 5.6% 30 to 45 minutes, 1.9% 45 to 60 minutes, 7.4% 60 minutes or more (2000)

CONRAD (city). Covers a land area of 1.210 square miles and a water area of 0 square miles. Located at 42.22° N. Lat.; 92.87° W. Long. Elevation is 1,010 feet.
History: An early pioneer, John W. Conrad, named a grove of trees Conrad's Grove. The town of Conrad took its name from the grove.
Population: 1,055 (2000); Race: 97.9% White, 0.0% Black, 0.8% Asian, 0.0% American Indian and Alaska Native, 0.2% Hispanic of any race, 1.3% two or more races (2000); Density: 871.7 persons per square mile (2000); Age: 25.4% under 18, 21.9% over 64 (2000); Marriage status: 15.4% never married, 62.7% now married, 12.1% widowed, 9.9% divorced (2000); Foreign born: 2.2% (2000); Ancestry (includes multiple ancestries): 46.3% German, 14.5% English, 14.3% Irish, 6.0% United States or American, 5.7% Norwegian (2000).
Economy: Single-family building permits issued: 1 (2001) / 5 (2000); Multi-family building permits issued: 2 (2001) / 0 (2000); Employment by occupation: 15.3% management, 19.3% professional, 16.4% services, 27.2% sales, 0.6% farming, 5.4% construction, 15.8% production (2000).
Income: Per capita income: $21,220 (2000); Median household income: $42,396 (2000); Poverty rate: 3.8% (2000).
Taxes: Total city taxes per capita: $411 (1997); City property taxes per capita: $407 (1997).
Education: High school graduation rate: 89.9% (2000); College graduation rate: 25.8% (2000).

School District(s)

BCLUW Community School District (KG-12)
2000 Enrollment: 692 641-366-2819
Housing: Homeownership rate: 78.9% (2000); Median home value: $81,200 (2000); Median rent: $225 per month (2000); Median age of housing: 35 years (2000).
Newspapers: The Record (1 x week)
Transportation: Commute to work: 90.8% car, 0.0% public transportation, 7.0% walk, 1.4% work from home (2000); Travel time to work: 46.1% less than 15 minutes, 37.8% 15 to 30 minutes, 12.3% 30 to 45 minutes, 1.6% 45 to 60 minutes, 2.2% 60 minutes or more (2000)

DIKE (city). Covers a land area of 1.305 square miles and a water area of 0 square miles. Located at 42.46° N. Lat.; 92.62° W. Long. Elevation is 945 feet.
History: Railroadman C.T. Dike, who owned large amounts of land in this area, incorporated the town of Dike in 1900, and named it for himself.
Population: 944 (2000); Race: 98.6% White, 0.0% Black, 1.0% Asian, 0.0% American Indian and Alaska Native, 0.0% Hispanic of any race, 0.4% two or more races (2000); Density: 723.5 persons per square mile (2000); Age: 25.9% under 18, 16.0% over 64 (2000); Marriage status: 17.2% never married, 68.5% now married, 7.6% widowed, 6.6% divorced (2000); Foreign born: 1.2% (2000); Ancestry (includes multiple ancestries): 53.8% German, 12.4% Irish, 11.7% English, 10.7% Danish, 5.0% Swedish (2000).
Economy: Single-family building permits issued: 15 (2001) / 11 (2000); Multi-family building permits issued: 4 (2001) / 0 (2000); Employment by occupation: 10.0% management, 21.5% professional, 14.7% services, 27.2% sales, 1.8% farming, 9.2% construction, 15.5% production (2000).
Income: Per capita income: $20,532 (2000); Median household income: $43,750 (2000); Poverty rate: 4.7% (2000).
Taxes: Total city taxes per capita: $216 (1997); City property taxes per capita: $213 (1997).
Education: High school graduation rate: 85.3% (2000); College graduation rate: 21.8% (2000).

School District(s)

Dike-New Hartford Community School District (PK-12)
2000 Enrollment: 769 319-989-2552
Housing: Homeownership rate: 80.1% (2000); Median home value: $95,200 (2000); Median rent: $320 per month (2000); Median age of housing: 41 years (2000).
Transportation: Commute to work: 88.6% car, 0.0% public transportation, 6.0% walk, 4.3% work from home (2000); Travel time to work: 30.9% less than 15 minutes, 53.8% 15 to 30 minutes, 9.5% 30 to 45 minutes, 3.7% 45 to 60 minutes, 2.2% 60 minutes or more (2000)

GRUNDY CENTER (city). Covers a land area of 2.452 square miles and a water area of 0 square miles. Located at 42.36° N. Lat.; 92.77° W. Long. Elevation is 1,026 feet.
History: Grundy Center is where the writer Herbert Quick (1861-1925) first attended school. Quick was the author of "Vandemark's Folly" and numerous other novels of the days after the log cabin era of Iowa's development.
Population: 2,596 (2000); Race: 98.8% White, 0.2% Black, 0.4% Asian, 0.4% American Indian and Alaska Native, 1.7% Hispanic of any race, 0.3% two or more races (2000); Density: 1,058.9 persons per square mile (2000); Age: 22.0% under 18, 24.0% over 64 (2000); Marriage status: 18.0% never married, 65.6% now married, 10.3% widowed, 6.2% divorced (2000); Foreign born: 0.7% (2000); Ancestry (includes multiple ancestries): 52.6% German, 9.5% English, 9.4% Irish, 8.1% United States or American, 5.1% Norwegian (2000).
Economy: Single-family building permits issued: 5 (2001) / 6 (2000); Multi-family building permits issued: 0 (2001) / 24 (2000); Employment by occupation: 13.1% management, 18.1% professional, 15.7% services, 25.1% sales, 0.3% farming, 6.6% construction, 21.1% production (2000).
Income: Per capita income: $18,859 (2000); Median household income: $37,222 (2000); Poverty rate: 4.5% (2000).
Taxes: Total city taxes per capita: $319 (1997); City property taxes per capita: $316 (1997).
Education: High school graduation rate: 82.5% (2000); College graduation rate: 17.8% (2000).

School District(s)

Grundy Center Community School District (KG-12)
2000 Enrollment: 768 319-824-5418
Housing: Homeownership rate: 79.9% (2000); Median home value: $73,600 (2000); Median rent: $276 per month (2000); Median age of housing: 44 years (2000).
Hospitals: Grundy County Memorial Hospital (25 beds)
Safety: Violent crime rate: 11.6 per 10,000 population; Property crime rate: 158.1 per 10,000 population (2001).
Newspapers: Grundy Register (1 x week)
Transportation: Commute to work: 84.5% car, 0.0% public transportation, 9.1% walk, 4.1% work from home (2000); Travel time to work: 63.3% less than 15 minutes, 9.6% 15 to 30 minutes, 17.6% 30 to 45 minutes, 3.8% 45 to 60 minutes, 5.7% 60 minutes or more (2000)
Additional Information Contacts
Grundy Center Chamber of Commerce 319-824-3838

HOLLAND (city). Covers a land area of 0.250 square miles and a water area of 0 square miles. Located at 42.40° N. Lat.; 92.79° W. Long. Elevation is 995 feet.
History: Holland's name reflects the heritage of its early Dutch settlers.
Population: 250 (2000); Race: 98.2% White, 0.0% Black, 1.1% Asian, 0.0% American Indian and Alaska Native, 0.7% Hispanic of any race, 0.7% two or more races (2000); Density: 1,001.5 persons per square mile (2000); Age: 26.5% under 18, 19.1% over 64 (2000); Marriage status: 18.4% never married, 71.8% now married, 6.3% widowed, 3.4% divorced (2000); Foreign born: 1.1% (2000); Ancestry (includes multiple ancestries): 61.8% German,

15.1% Irish, 8.8% Dutch, 8.1% United States or American, 3.7% English (2000).
Economy: Single-family building permits issued: 0 (2001) / 0 (2000); Multi-family building permits issued: 0 (2001) / 0 (2000); Employment by occupation: 10.8% management, 7.9% professional, 12.2% services, 21.6% sales, 0.7% farming, 10.8% construction, 36.0% production (2000).
Income: Per capita income: $15,370 (2000); Median household income: $34,886 (2000); Poverty rate: 6.3% (2000).
Taxes: Total city taxes per capita: $124 (1997); City property taxes per capita: $119 (1997).
Education: High school graduation rate: 84.0% (2000); College graduation rate: 5.3% (2000).
Housing: Homeownership rate: 88.7% (2000); Median home value: $46,300 (2000); Median rent: $305 per month (2000); Median age of housing: 49 years (2000).
Transportation: Commute to work: 88.1% car, 0.0% public transportation, 6.7% walk, 3.7% work from home (2000); Travel time to work: 46.9% less than 15 minutes, 18.5% 15 to 30 minutes, 28.5% 30 to 45 minutes, 4.6% 45 to 60 minutes, 1.5% 60 minutes or more (2000)

MORRISON (city). Covers a land area of 0.102 square miles and a water area of 0 square miles. Located at 42.34° N. Lat.; 92.67° W. Long.
History: The town of Morrison was named for its founder.
Population: 97 (2000); Race: 98.9% White, 0.0% Black, 0.0% Asian, 1.1% American Indian and Alaska Native, 0.0% Hispanic of any race, 0.0% two or more races (2000); Density: 947.1 persons per square mile (2000); Age: 20.0% under 18, 26.3% over 64 (2000); Marriage status: 19.8% never married, 61.7% now married, 8.6% widowed, 9.9% divorced (2000); Foreign born: 2.1% (2000); Ancestry (includes multiple ancestries): 48.4% German, 9.5% Czech, 8.4% Scottish, 8.4% Danish, 7.4% United States or American (2000).
Economy: Employment by occupation: 11.6% management, 2.3% professional, 39.5% services, 9.3% sales, 0.0% farming, 2.3% construction, 34.9% production (2000).
Income: Per capita income: $12,538 (2000); Median household income: $26,250 (2000); Poverty rate: 11.6% (2000).
Taxes: Total city taxes per capita: $92 (1997); City property taxes per capita: $84 (1997).
Education: High school graduation rate: 74.6% (2000); College graduation rate: 5.6% (2000).
Housing: Homeownership rate: 93.0% (2000); Median home value: $36,000 (2000); Median rent: $275 per month (2000); Median age of housing: 39 years (2000).
Transportation: Commute to work: 81.4% car, 0.0% public transportation, 11.6% walk, 7.0% work from home (2000); Travel time to work: 52.5% less than 15 minutes, 25.0% 15 to 30 minutes, 20.0% 30 to 45 minutes, 2.5% 45 to 60 minutes, 0.0% 60 minutes or more (2000)

REINBECK (city). Covers a land area of 1.819 square miles and a water area of 0 square miles. Located at 42.32° N. Lat.; 92.59° W. Long. Elevation is 926 feet.
History: Reinbeck was named after Reinbeck, Germany.
Population: 1,751 (2000); Race: 99.8% White, 0.0% Black, 0.0% Asian, 0.0% American Indian and Alaska Native, 0.2% Hispanic of any race, 0.0% two or more races (2000); Density: 962.5 persons per square mile (2000); Age: 22.6% under 18, 23.6% over 64 (2000); Marriage status: 18.6% never married, 62.7% now married, 11.0% widowed, 7.8% divorced (2000); Foreign born: 0.6% (2000); Ancestry (includes multiple ancestries): 53.5% German, 9.1% Irish, 9.0% English, 6.9% United States or American, 3.7% Danish (2000).
Economy: Single-family building permits issued: 5 (2001) / 1 (2000); Multi-family building permits issued: 0 (2001) / 0 (2000); Employment by occupation: 11.9% management, 17.7% professional, 13.3% services, 25.4% sales, 1.2% farming, 10.7% construction, 19.8% production (2000).
Income: Per capita income: $19,814 (2000); Median household income: $36,667 (2000); Poverty rate: 4.0% (2000).
Taxes: Total city taxes per capita: $265 (1997); City property taxes per capita: $259 (1997).
Education: High school graduation rate: 86.7% (2000); College graduation rate: 17.3% (2000).

School District(s)

Gladbrook-Reinbeck Community School District (KG-12)
2000 Enrollment: 816 319-345-2712

Housing: Homeownership rate: 78.3% (2000); Median home value: $68,600 (2000); Median rent: $301 per month (2000); Median age of housing: 51 years (2000).
Newspapers: Reinbeck Courier (1 x week)
Transportation: Commute to work: 91.5% car, 0.2% public transportation, 5.2% walk, 2.1% work from home (2000); Travel time to work: 49.3% less than 15 minutes, 21.5% 15 to 30 minutes, 26.2% 30 to 45 minutes, 1.7% 45 to 60 minutes, 1.2% 60 minutes or more (2000)

STOUT (city). Covers a land area of 0.311 square miles and a water area of 0 square miles. Located at 42.52° N. Lat.; 92.71° W. Long. Elevation is 1,020 feet.
History: Stout was named for the owner of the town site, A. V. Stout.
Population: 217 (2000); Race: 97.7% White, 0.0% Black, 0.9% Asian, 0.5% American Indian and Alaska Native, 0.9% Hispanic of any race, 0.0% two or more races (2000); Density: 697.3 persons per square mile (2000); Age: 38.0% under 18, 13.0% over 64 (2000); Marriage status: 29.4% never married, 63.4% now married, 3.3% widowed, 3.9% divorced (2000); Foreign born: 0.5% (2000); Ancestry (includes multiple ancestries): 46.3% German, 15.3% Irish, 12.0% United States or American, 8.3% Scottish, 6.0% Dutch (2000).
Economy: Employment by occupation: 7.9% management, 9.0% professional, 20.2% services, 32.6% sales, 0.0% farming, 19.1% construction, 11.2% production (2000).
Income: Per capita income: $12,504 (2000); Median household income: $40,781 (2000); Poverty rate: 12.5% (2000).
Taxes: Total city taxes per capita: $88 (1997); City property taxes per capita: $88 (1997).
Education: High school graduation rate: 81.5% (2000); College graduation rate: 7.6% (2000).
Housing: Homeownership rate: 76.7% (2000); Median home value: $54,100 (2000); Median rent: $400 per month (2000); Median age of housing: 60+ years (2000).
Transportation: Commute to work: 95.5% car, 0.0% public transportation, 2.2% walk, 2.2% work from home (2000); Travel time to work: 10.3% less than 15 minutes, 33.3% 15 to 30 minutes, 50.6% 30 to 45 minutes, 5.7% 45 to 60 minutes, 0.0% 60 minutes or more (2000)

WELLSBURG (city). Covers a land area of 0.987 square miles and a water area of 0 square miles. Located at 42.43° N. Lat.; 92.92° W. Long. Elevation is 1,058 feet.
History: Wellsburg was named for prominent settlers George and Sarah Wells. The Wells gave one square mile of their land for the development of the town.
Population: 716 (2000); Race: 98.9% White, 0.0% Black, 0.4% Asian, 0.4% American Indian and Alaska Native, 1.0% Hispanic of any race, 0.0% two or more races (2000); Density: 725.6 persons per square mile (2000); Age: 22.0% under 18, 29.1% over 64 (2000); Marriage status: 16.4% never married, 63.1% now married, 16.6% widowed, 4.0% divorced (2000); Foreign born: 0.1% (2000); Ancestry (includes multiple ancestries): 63.7% German, 5.4% Irish, 5.3% Norwegian, 4.7% United States or American, 4.0% Dutch (2000).
Economy: Single-family building permits issued: 0 (2001) / 0 (2000); Multi-family building permits issued: 0 (2001) / 0 (2000); Employment by occupation: 9.1% management, 17.0% professional, 20.5% services, 20.2% sales, 0.0% farming, 8.5% construction, 24.6% production (2000).
Income: Per capita income: $17,636 (2000); Median household income: $30,417 (2000); Poverty rate: 6.0% (2000).
Taxes: Total city taxes per capita: $222 (1997); City property taxes per capita: $220 (1997).
Education: High school graduation rate: 81.6% (2000); College graduation rate: 10.5% (2000).

School District(s)

Wellsburg-Steamboat Rock Community School District (KG-12)
2000 Enrollment: 287 641-869-3732

Housing: Homeownership rate: 84.4% (2000); Median home value: $37,600 (2000); Median rent: $177 per month (2000); Median age of housing: 56 years (2000).
Transportation: Commute to work: 84.2% car, 0.0% public transportation, 10.3% walk, 5.1% work from home (2000); Travel time to work: 40.7% less than 15 minutes, 28.1% 15 to 30 minutes, 16.9% 30 to 45 minutes, 10.8% 45 to 60 minutes, 3.4% 60 minutes or more (2000)

Guthrie County

Located in west central Iowa; prairie area, drained by the Middle Raccoon, South Raccoon, and Middle Rivers. Covers a land area of 590.60 square miles, a water area of 2.50 square miles, and is located in the Central Time

Zone. The county government was organized in 1851. County seat is Guthrie Center.

Weather Station: Guthrie Center Elevation: 1,072 feet

	Jan	Feb	Mar	Apr	May	Jun	Jul	Aug	Sep	Oct	Nov	Dec
High	28	34	46	60	72	82	86	83	76	63	46	33
Low	8	14	25	37	48	58	62	60	50	37	26	14
Precip	0.9	1.0	2.4	3.4	4.6	4.7	4.2	4.5	3.5	2.6	2.0	1.2
Snow	8.0	7.1	4.8	1.7	tr	0.0	0.0	0.0	0.0	0.5	2.6	5.9

High and Low temperatures in degrees Fahrenheit; Precipitation and Snow in inches

Population: 11,353 (2000); Race: 98.5% White, 0.2% Black, 0.0% Asian, 0.1% American Indian and Alaska Native, 1.6% Hispanic of any race, 0.6% two or more races (2000); Density: 19.2 persons per square mile (2000); Age: 23.5% under 18, 20.6% over 64 (2000).
Religion: Five largest groups: 17.3% The United Methodist Church, 11.0% Catholic Church, 7.7% Lutheran Church—Missouri Synod, 5.7% Christian Church (Disciples of Christ), 3.3% Church of the Brethren (2000).
Economy: Unemployment rate: 3.3% (11/2002); Total civilian labor force: 5,963 (11/2002); Leading industries: 20.4% health care and social assistance; 18.9% retail trade; 14.5% accommodation & food services (2000); Companies that employ more than 1,000 persons: 0 (2000); Companies that employ more than 100 persons: 0 (2000); Farms: 847 totaling 304,177 acres (1997); Minority business ownership rate: 0.0% (1997); Women business ownership rate: 21.7% (1997); Retail sales per capita: $5,046 (1997). Single-family building permits issued: 52 (2001) / 59 (2000); Multi-family building permits issued: 0 (2001) / 0 (2000).
Income: Per capita income: $19,726 (2000); Median household income: $36,495 (2000); Poverty rate: 8.0% (2000); Bankruptcy rate: 3.11% (2001).
Taxes: Total county taxes per capita: $320 (1997); County property taxes per capita: $309 (1997).
Education: High school graduation rate: 85.4% (2000); College graduation rate: 14.9% (2000).
Housing: Homeownership rate: 79.6% (2000); Median home value: $61,800 (2000); Median rent: $276 per month (2000); Median age of housing: 46 years (2000).
Health: Birth rate: 107.5 per 10,000 population (1998); Age adjusted death rate: 70.9 per 10,000 population (1999); Age adjusted cancer mortality rate: 173.0 deaths per 100,000 population (1999). Number of physicians: 3.5 per 10,000 population (1999); Number of hospital beds: 22.0 per 10,000 population (1999).
Elections: 2000 Presidential election results: 45.6% Gore, 51.9% Bush, 1.6% Nader, 0.4% Buchanan
National and State Parks: Bays Branch State Wildlife Area; Lakin Slough State Game Management Area; Lennon Mills State Wildlife Area; Lenon Mill State Wildlife Area; McCord Pond State Wildlife Management Area; Milo Ray State Wildlife Area; Sheeder Prairie State Preserve; Springbrook State Park

Additional Information Contacts

Guthrie County Government Offices 641-747-3512
Panora Chamber of Commerce 641-755-3300
Stuart Chamber of Commerce 515-523-2868

Guthrie County Communities

BAGLEY (city). Covers a land area of 0.306 square miles and a water area of 0 square miles. Located at 41.84° N. Lat.; 94.42° W. Long. Elevation is 1,106 feet.
History: Bagley was named for a saloon keeper.
Population: 354 (2000); Race: 91.6% White, 0.0% Black, 0.0% Asian, 0.0% American Indian and Alaska Native, 11.8% Hispanic of any race, 0.0% two or more races (2000); Density: 1,158.2 persons per square mile (2000); Age: 24.6% under 18, 17.6% over 64 (2000); Marriage status: 22.7% never married, 56.8% now married, 10.4% widowed, 10.1% divorced (2000); Foreign born: 1.7% (2000); Ancestry (includes multiple ancestries): 21.4% German, 17.3% Irish, 15.9% Other groups, 8.4% United States or American, 5.5% English (2000).
Economy: Single-family building permits issued: 0 (2001) / 0 (2000); Multi-family building permits issued: 0 (2001) / 0 (2000); Employment by occupation: 9.2% management, 10.4% professional, 17.3% services, 22.5% sales, 4.0% farming, 15.0% construction, 21.4% production (2000).
Income: Per capita income: $13,754 (2000); Median household income: $29,219 (2000); Poverty rate: 16.1% (2000).
Taxes: Total city taxes per capita: $139 (1997); City property taxes per capita: $139 (1997).
Education: High school graduation rate: 79.6% (2000); College graduation rate: 12.9% (2000).
Housing: Homeownership rate: 76.9% (2000); Median home value: $42,000 (2000); Median rent: $156 per month (2000); Median age of housing: 60+ years (2000).
Transportation: Commute to work: 88.8% car, 0.0% public transportation, 5.9% walk, 5.3% work from home (2000); Travel time to work: 21.1% less than 15 minutes, 29.8% 15 to 30 minutes, 21.7% 30 to 45 minutes, 11.2% 45 to 60 minutes, 16.1% 60 minutes or more (2000)

BAYARD (city). Covers a land area of 0.476 square miles and a water area of 0 square miles. Located at 41.85° N. Lat.; 94.55° W. Long. Elevation is 1,135 feet.
History: Bayard was named after Thomas Francis Bayard of Delaware, who once served as Secretary of State.
Population: 536 (2000); Race: 96.4% White, 0.0% Black, 0.0% Asian, 0.4% American Indian and Alaska Native, 4.3% Hispanic of any race, 3.2% two or more races (2000); Density: 1,124.9 persons per square mile (2000); Age: 26.7% under 18, 25.8% over 64 (2000); Marriage status: 20.6% never married, 57.5% now married, 14.5% widowed, 7.5% divorced (2000); Foreign born: 0.0% (2000); Ancestry (includes multiple ancestries): 33.1% German, 17.4% Irish, 14.0% English, 12.5% United States or American, 6.2% Other groups (2000).
Economy: Employment by occupation: 11.3% management, 6.1% professional, 19.8% services, 20.3% sales, 2.4% farming, 10.8% construction, 29.2% production (2000).
Income: Per capita income: $13,073 (2000); Median household income: $24,444 (2000); Poverty rate: 23.2% (2000).
Taxes: Total city taxes per capita: $170 (1997); City property taxes per capita: $165 (1997).
Education: High school graduation rate: 75.5% (2000); College graduation rate: 3.7% (2000).
Housing: Homeownership rate: 71.2% (2000); Median home value: $32,300 (2000); Median rent: $153 per month (2000); Median age of housing: 60+ years (2000).
Newspapers: The News Gazette (1 x week)
Transportation: Commute to work: 91.5% car, 0.0% public transportation, 5.7% walk, 1.9% work from home (2000); Travel time to work: 44.4% less than 15 minutes, 16.9% 15 to 30 minutes, 19.8% 30 to 45 minutes, 6.3% 45 to 60 minutes, 12.6% 60 minutes or more (2000)

CASEY (city). Covers a land area of 0.737 square miles and a water area of 0 square miles. Located at 41.50° N. Lat.; 94.52° W. Long.
History: The name of Casey came from the name of a contractor in the area.
Population: 478 (2000); Race: 98.5% White, 0.4% Black, 0.0% Asian, 0.0% American Indian and Alaska Native, 0.0% Hispanic of any race, 1.0% two or more races (2000); Density: 649.0 persons per square mile (2000); Age: 28.9% under 18, 22.0% over 64 (2000); Marriage status: 17.1% never married, 59.4% now married, 10.6% widowed, 12.9% divorced (2000); Foreign born: 0.6% (2000); Ancestry (includes multiple ancestries): 27.4% German, 14.4% English, 8.8% United States or American, 7.5% Irish, 5.4% Other groups (2000).
Economy: Single-family building permits issued: 1 (2001) / 0 (2000); Multi-family building permits issued: 0 (2001) / 0 (2000); Employment by occupation: 15.5% management, 4.1% professional, 19.2% services, 19.7% sales, 2.6% farming, 19.2% construction, 19.7% production (2000).
Income: Per capita income: $15,189 (2000); Median household income: $35,000 (2000); Poverty rate: 9.2% (2000).
Taxes: Total city taxes per capita: $115 (1997); City property taxes per capita: $115 (1997).
Education: High school graduation rate: 81.9% (2000); College graduation rate: 9.1% (2000).
Housing: Homeownership rate: 81.2% (2000); Median home value: $38,900 (2000); Median rent: $254 per month (2000); Median age of housing: 60+ years (2000).
Transportation: Commute to work: 89.7% car, 0.0% public transportation, 5.4% walk, 3.3% work from home (2000); Travel time to work: 37.1% less than 15 minutes, 31.5% 15 to 30 minutes, 7.3% 30 to 45 minutes, 12.4% 45 to 60 minutes, 11.8% 60 minutes or more (2000)

GUTHRIE CENTER (city). Covers a land area of 2.467 square miles and a water area of 0 square miles. Located at 41.68° N. Lat.; 94.50° W. Long. Elevation is 1,150 feet.
History: The first settlers in Guthrie Center were Pennsylvania Dutch, who came about the middle of the 19th century.

Population: 1,668 (2000); Race: 98.5% White, 0.0% Black, 0.1% Asian, 0.1% American Indian and Alaska Native, 1.0% Hispanic of any race, 0.4% two or more races (2000); Density: 676.0 persons per square mile (2000); Age: 26.0% under 18, 25.7% over 64 (2000); Marriage status: 15.8% never married, 57.1% now married, 16.6% widowed, 10.5% divorced (2000); Foreign born: 1.2% (2000); Ancestry (includes multiple ancestries): 29.6% German, 13.9% Irish, 13.5% English, 9.6% Danish, 7.3% United States or American (2000).
Economy: Single-family building permits issued: 2 (2001) / 3 (2000); Multi-family building permits issued: 0 (2001) / 0 (2000); Employment by occupation: 13.9% management, 17.7% professional, 17.6% services, 21.1% sales, 3.3% farming, 12.6% construction, 13.9% production (2000).
Income: Per capita income: $16,662 (2000); Median household income: $30,714 (2000); Poverty rate: 7.7% (2000).
Taxes: Total city taxes per capita: $212 (1997); City property taxes per capita: $207 (1997).
Education: High school graduation rate: 79.2% (2000); College graduation rate: 13.6% (2000).

School District(s)

Guthrie Center Community School District (PK-12)
2000 Enrollment: 558 641-747-3521

Housing: Homeownership rate: 75.9% (2000); Median home value: $50,500 (2000); Median rent: $323 per month (2000); Median age of housing: 57 years (2000).
Hospitals: Guthrie County Hospital (25 beds)
Newspapers: Guthrie Center Times (1 x week)
Transportation: Commute to work: 90.0% car, 0.0% public transportation, 5.7% walk, 3.4% work from home (2000); Travel time to work: 65.9% less than 15 minutes, 9.0% 15 to 30 minutes, 7.7% 30 to 45 minutes, 7.3% 45 to 60 minutes, 10.2% 60 minutes or more (2000)

JAMAICA (city). Covers a land area of 0.457 square miles and a water area of 0 square miles. Located at 41.84° N. Lat.; 94.30° W. Long. Elevation is 1,048 feet.
History: Local legend tells that the name of Jamaica was selected by a blindfolded mayor pointing at a world map, and randomly hitting on the Caribbean island. Before that, the place was called Van Nest.
Population: 237 (2000); Race: 96.0% White, 0.0% Black, 0.0% Asian, 0.8% American Indian and Alaska Native, 3.2% Hispanic of any race, 0.0% two or more races (2000); Density: 518.1 persons per square mile (2000); Age: 19.3% under 18, 15.3% over 64 (2000); Marriage status: 24.9% never married, 54.2% now married, 9.5% widowed, 11.4% divorced (2000); Foreign born: 1.2% (2000); Ancestry (includes multiple ancestries): 24.1% German, 14.5% Irish, 12.4% English, 10.8% Other groups, 7.2% United States or American (2000).
Economy: Employment by occupation: 8.5% management, 17.0% professional, 17.0% services, 27.0% sales, 0.0% farming, 8.5% construction, 22.0% production (2000).
Income: Per capita income: $18,850 (2000); Median household income: $35,417 (2000); Poverty rate: 14.5% (2000).
Taxes: Total city taxes per capita: $62 (1997); City property taxes per capita: $62 (1997).
Education: High school graduation rate: 84.1% (2000); College graduation rate: 10.0% (2000).
Housing: Homeownership rate: 55.7% (2000); Median home value: $44,200 (2000); Median rent: $225 per month (2000); Median age of housing: 60+ years (2000).
Transportation: Commute to work: 92.9% car, 0.0% public transportation, 1.4% walk, 4.3% work from home (2000); Travel time to work: 14.8% less than 15 minutes, 42.2% 15 to 30 minutes, 23.0% 30 to 45 minutes, 12.6% 45 to 60 minutes, 7.4% 60 minutes or more (2000)

MENLO (city). Covers a land area of 0.468 square miles and a water area of 0 square miles. Located at 41.52° N. Lat.; 94.40° W. Long. Elevation is 1,265 feet.
History: Menlo was located on the Chicago, Rock Island & Pacific Railroad line. It was first known as The Switch and then as Guthrie Switch. The name was changed to Menlo after Guthrie Center was established.
Population: 365 (2000); Race: 100.0% White, 0.0% Black, 0.0% Asian, 0.0% American Indian and Alaska Native, 1.5% Hispanic of any race, 0.0% two or more races (2000); Density: 779.7 persons per square mile (2000); Age: 24.8% under 18, 19.5% over 64 (2000); Marriage status: 16.5% never married, 58.6% now married, 8.4% widowed, 16.5% divorced (2000); Foreign born: 0.0% (2000); Ancestry (includes multiple ancestries): 24.8% German, 18.9% United States or American, 15.3% Irish, 13.6% English, 6.8% Norwegian (2000).
Economy: Single-family building permits issued: 1 (2001) / 3 (2000); Multi-family building permits issued: 0 (2001) / 0 (2000); Employment by occupation: 4.6% management, 8.6% professional, 21.2% services, 23.8% sales, 0.7% farming, 11.9% construction, 29.1% production (2000).
Income: Per capita income: $17,990 (2000); Median household income: $29,375 (2000); Poverty rate: 7.4% (2000).
Taxes: Total city taxes per capita: $188 (1997); City property taxes per capita: $185 (1997).
Education: High school graduation rate: 82.6% (2000); College graduation rate: 10.2% (2000).
Housing: Homeownership rate: 85.6% (2000); Median home value: $46,400 (2000); Median rent: <$100 per month (2000); Median age of housing: 60+ years (2000).
Transportation: Commute to work: 88.0% car, 0.0% public transportation, 3.3% walk, 8.0% work from home (2000); Travel time to work: 30.4% less than 15 minutes, 18.1% 15 to 30 minutes, 13.8% 30 to 45 minutes, 33.3% 45 to 60 minutes, 4.3% 60 minutes or more (2000)

PANORA (city). Covers a land area of 1.802 square miles and a water area of 0 square miles. Located at 41.69° N. Lat.; 94.36° W. Long. Elevation is 1,071 feet.
History: Panora's name is a contraction of "panorama." The story is that pioneers, viewing the site from a hill, exclaimed, "What a beautiful panorama."
Population: 1,175 (2000); Race: 97.2% White, 0.9% Black, 0.0% Asian, 0.3% American Indian and Alaska Native, 1.2% Hispanic of any race, 1.6% two or more races (2000); Density: 652.1 persons per square mile (2000); Age: 28.1% under 18, 20.7% over 64 (2000); Marriage status: 18.3% never married, 52.1% now married, 16.2% widowed, 13.4% divorced (2000); Foreign born: 0.5% (2000); Ancestry (includes multiple ancestries): 37.7% German, 18.0% English, 14.5% Irish, 6.0% Swedish, 5.2% Other groups (2000).
Economy: Single-family building permits issued: 2 (2001) / 3 (2000); Multi-family building permits issued: 0 (2001) / 0 (2000); Employment by occupation: 8.6% management, 13.4% professional, 19.8% services, 24.9% sales, 1.6% farming, 12.3% construction, 19.3% production (2000).
Income: Per capita income: $15,510 (2000); Median household income: $35,000 (2000); Poverty rate: 10.0% (2000).
Taxes: Total city taxes per capita: $288 (1997); City property taxes per capita: $286 (1997).
Education: High school graduation rate: 83.3% (2000); College graduation rate: 7.5% (2000).

School District(s)

Panorama Community School District (PK-12)
2000 Enrollment: 764 641-755-2317

Housing: Homeownership rate: 74.7% (2000); Median home value: $69,500 (2000); Median rent: $356 per month (2000); Median age of housing: 47 years (2000).
Newspapers: Guthrie County Vedette (1 x week)
Transportation: Commute to work: 87.0% car, 0.8% public transportation, 8.4% walk, 3.9% work from home (2000); Travel time to work: 46.4% less than 15 minutes, 6.6% 15 to 30 minutes, 10.8% 30 to 45 minutes, 22.7% 45 to 60 minutes, 13.6% 60 minutes or more (2000)
Additional Information Contacts
Panora Chamber of Commerce 641-755-3300

STUART (city). Covers a land area of 2.024 square miles and a water area of 0 square miles. Located at 41.50° N. Lat.; 94.32° W. Long. Elevation is 1,210 feet.
History: Stuart was founded in 1869 by Captain Charles Stuart of Vermont, for whom the town was named. The town was the home of John Herriott, Lieutenant Governor of Iowa (1902-1907).
Population: 1,712 (2000); Race: 98.6% White, 0.0% Black, 0.5% Asian, 0.0% American Indian and Alaska Native, 1.0% Hispanic of any race, 0.1% two or more races (2000); Density: 846.0 persons per square mile (2000); Age: 22.6% under 18, 21.1% over 64 (2000); Marriage status: 24.3% never married, 55.5% now married, 9.3% widowed, 10.9% divorced (2000); Foreign born: 1.2% (2000); Ancestry (includes multiple ancestries): 30.8% German, 15.4% Irish, 12.6% English, 6.5% United States or American, 6.2% Other groups (2000).
Economy: Single-family building permits issued: 11 (2001) / 12 (2000); Multi-family building permits issued: 0 (2001) / 24 (2000); Employment by occupation: 11.7% management, 11.7% professional, 17.8% services, 28.6% sales, 1.5% farming, 11.3% construction, 17.5% production (2000).
Income: Per capita income: $17,113 (2000); Median household income: $33,491 (2000); Poverty rate: 8.4% (2000).

Taxes: Total city taxes per capita: $266 (2000); City property taxes per capita: $262 (2000).
Education: High school graduation rate: 81.8% (2000); College graduation rate: 13.9% (2000).

School District(s)

Stuart-Menlo Community School District (KG-12)
2000 Enrollment: 655 515-523-2187
Housing: Homeownership rate: 69.6% (2000); Median home value: $76,500 (2000); Median rent: $313 per month (2000); Median age of housing: 45 years (2000).
Newspapers: The Stuart Herald (1 x week)
Transportation: Commute to work: 91.4% car, 0.0% public transportation, 4.9% walk, 2.5% work from home (2000); Travel time to work: 41.5% less than 15 minutes, 13.8% 15 to 30 minutes, 25.3% 30 to 45 minutes, 16.1% 45 to 60 minutes, 3.4% 60 minutes or more (2000)
Additional Information Contacts
Stuart Chamber of Commerce 515-523-2868

YALE (city). Covers a land area of 0.296 square miles and a water area of 0 square miles. Located at 41.77° N. Lat.; 94.35° W. Long. Elevation is 1,128 feet.
History: Yale was named for landowner Milo Yale. The town was laid out in 1882.
Population: 287 (2000); Race: 100.0% White, 0.0% Black, 0.0% Asian, 0.0% American Indian and Alaska Native, 0.0% Hispanic of any race, 0.0% two or more races (2000); Density: 969.8 persons per square mile (2000); Age: 36.1% under 18, 15.2% over 64 (2000); Marriage status: 15.5% never married, 64.3% now married, 10.1% widowed, 10.1% divorced (2000); Foreign born: 0.0% (2000); Ancestry (includes multiple ancestries): 20.6% German, 15.9% United States or American, 14.2% Irish, 9.1% Dutch, 6.8% Other groups (2000).
Economy: Single-family building permits issued: 0 (2001) / 0 (2000); Multi-family building permits issued: 0 (2001) / 0 (2000); Employment by occupation: 9.0% management, 9.9% professional, 19.8% services, 25.2% sales, 3.6% farming, 12.6% construction, 19.8% production (2000).
Income: Per capita income: $12,789 (2000); Median household income: $32,875 (2000); Poverty rate: 11.1% (2000).
Taxes: Total city taxes per capita: $173 (1997); City property taxes per capita: $168 (1997).
Education: High school graduation rate: 86.2% (2000); College graduation rate: 9.9% (2000).
Housing: Homeownership rate: 76.0% (2000); Median home value: $43,700 (2000); Median rent: $186 per month (2000); Median age of housing: 52 years (2000).
Transportation: Commute to work: 94.5% car, 0.0% public transportation, 4.5% walk, 0.0% work from home (2000); Travel time to work: 26.4% less than 15 minutes, 33.6% 15 to 30 minutes, 14.5% 30 to 45 minutes, 8.2% 45 to 60 minutes, 17.3% 60 minutes or more (2000)

Hamilton County

Located in central Iowa; prairie area, drained by the Boone and Skunk Rivers. Covers a land area of 576.70 square miles, a water area of 0.80 square miles, and is located in the Central Time Zone. The county government was organized in 1856. County seat is Webster City.

Weather Station: Webster City — Elevation: 1,167 feet

	Jan	Feb	Mar	Apr	May	Jun	Jul	Aug	Sep	Oct	Nov	Dec
High	26	32	45	60	73	81	85	82	75	63	45	31
Low	7	14	25	37	48	58	62	60	51	39	26	13
Precip	0.8	0.8	1.9	3.1	4.2	5.2	4.3	4.6	3.1	2.6	1.8	1.2
Snow	8.5	6.4	5.4	1.9	0.0	0.0	0.0	0.0	0.0	0.1	3.8	7.3

High and Low temperatures in degrees Fahrenheit; Precipitation and Snow in inches

Population: 16,438 (2000); Race: 97.1% White, 0.1% Black, 1.7% Asian, 0.0% American Indian and Alaska Native, 1.0% Hispanic of any race, 0.7% two or more races (2000); Density: 28.5 persons per square mile (2000); Age: 25.5% under 18, 18.0% over 64 (2000).
Religion: Five largest groups: 20.0% Evangelical Lutheran Church in America, 13.9% The United Methodist Church, 12.6% Catholic Church, 5.6% United Church of Christ, 3.6% Christian Churches and Churches of Christ (2000).
Economy: Unemployment rate: 3.1% (11/2002); Total civilian labor force: 8,413 (11/2002); Leading industries: 45.9% manufacturing; 11.7% wholesale trade; 10.5% retail trade (2000); Companies that employ more than 1,000 persons: 1 (2000); Companies that employ more than 100 persons: 7 (2000); Farms: 790 totaling 348,675 acres (1997); Minority business ownership rate: 0.0% (1997); Women business ownership rate: 38.4% (1997); Retail sales per capita: $5,659 (1997). Single-family building permits issued: 18 (2001) / 33 (2000); Multi-family building permits issued: 4 (2001) / 2 (2000).
Income: Per capita income: $18,801 (2000); Median household income: $38,658 (2000); Poverty rate: 6.3% (2000); Bankruptcy rate: 2.74% (2001).
Taxes: Total county taxes per capita: $240 (2000); County property taxes per capita: $233 (2000).
Education: High school graduation rate: 87.3% (2000); College graduation rate: 17.5% (2000).
Housing: Homeownership rate: 72.8% (2000); Median home value: $70,500 (2000); Median rent: $317 per month (2000); Median age of housing: 49 years (2000).
Health: Birth rate: 132.6 per 10,000 population (1998); Age adjusted death rate: 78.7 per 10,000 population (1999); Age adjusted cancer mortality rate: 205.9 deaths per 100,000 population (1999). Number of physicians: 7.9 per 10,000 population (1999); Number of hospital beds: 24.3 per 10,000 population (1999).
Elections: 2000 Presidential election results: 45.0% Gore, 52.4% Bush, 1.9% Nader, 0.4% Buchanan
Additional Information Contacts
Hamilton County Government Offices 515-832-9530
Wright Hamilton Board of Realtors 515-832-1228

Hamilton County Communities

BLAIRSBURG (city). Covers a land area of 0.645 square miles and a water area of 0 square miles. Located at 42.48° N. Lat.; 93.64° W. Long. Elevation is 1,224 feet.
History: Blairsburg, a station on the Illinois Central Railroad, was platted in 1869 by railroad man John I. Blair, and named for him.
Population: 235 (2000); Race: 100.0% White, 0.0% Black, 0.0% Asian, 0.0% American Indian and Alaska Native, 0.0% Hispanic of any race, 0.0% two or more races (2000); Density: 364.1 persons per square mile (2000); Age: 27.6% under 18, 13.8% over 64 (2000); Marriage status: 19.0% never married, 69.8% now married, 3.7% widowed, 7.4% divorced (2000); Foreign born: 0.0% (2000); Ancestry (includes multiple ancestries): 36.6% German, 11.6% Irish, 10.8% United States or American, 9.5% English, 9.5% Norwegian (2000).
Economy: Single-family building permits issued: 0 (2001) / 0 (2000); Multi-family building permits issued: 0 (2001) / 0 (2000); Employment by occupation: 9.6% management, 11.2% professional, 5.6% services, 24.0% sales, 0.0% farming, 20.8% construction, 28.8% production (2000).
Income: Per capita income: $17,817 (2000); Median household income: $46,667 (2000); Poverty rate: 0.9% (2000).
Taxes: Total city taxes per capita: $122 (1997); City property taxes per capita: $122 (1997).
Education: High school graduation rate: 82.2% (2000); College graduation rate: 14.6% (2000).

School District(s)

Northeast Hamilton Community School District (PK-12)
2000 Enrollment: 304 515-325-6202
Housing: Homeownership rate: 75.3% (2000); Median home value: $53,100 (2000); Median rent: $269 per month (2000); Median age of housing: 48 years (2000).
Transportation: Commute to work: 84.0% car, 0.0% public transportation, 12.8% walk, 3.2% work from home (2000); Travel time to work: 38.8% less than 15 minutes, 45.5% 15 to 30 minutes, 14.0% 30 to 45 minutes, 1.7% 45 to 60 minutes, 0.0% 60 minutes or more (2000)

ELLSWORTH (city). Covers a land area of 0.900 square miles and a water area of 0 square miles. Located at 42.31° N. Lat.; 93.58° W. Long.
History: Platted in 1880 for the Chicago & North Western Railroad, Ellsworth was named to honor Colonel Elmer E. Ellsworth, a Civil War soldier in the volunteer regiment known as the Chicago Zouaves. Ellsworth died in battle in Virginia.
Population: 531 (2000); Race: 92.6% White, 0.4% Black, 0.0% Asian, 0.0% American Indian and Alaska Native, 13.1% Hispanic of any race, 0.0% two or more races (2000); Density: 589.9 persons per square mile (2000); Age: 26.6% under 18, 15.6% over 64 (2000); Marriage status: 22.8% never married, 57.2% now married, 8.2% widowed, 11.9% divorced (2000); Foreign born: 4.0% (2000); Ancestry (includes multiple ancestries): 26.6% Norwegian, 25.7% German, 14.6% Other groups, 7.0% European, 6.1% English (2000).

Economy: Employment by occupation: 9.5% management, 19.3% professional, 11.9% services, 15.6% sales, 4.9% farming, 13.6% construction, 25.1% production (2000).
Income: Per capita income: $15,299 (2000); Median household income: $30,893 (2000); Poverty rate: 11.2% (2000).
Taxes: Total city taxes per capita: $197 (1997); City property taxes per capita: $197 (1997).
Education: High school graduation rate: 82.6% (2000); College graduation rate: 18.7% (2000).
Housing: Homeownership rate: 68.8% (2000); Median home value: $65,700 (2000); Median rent: $283 per month (2000); Median age of housing: 54 years (2000).
Transportation: Commute to work: 86.6% car, 0.0% public transportation, 5.0% walk, 0.4% work from home (2000); Travel time to work: 42.6% less than 15 minutes, 36.3% 15 to 30 minutes, 16.5% 30 to 45 minutes, 0.8% 45 to 60 minutes, 3.8% 60 minutes or more (2000)

JEWELL (unincorporated postal area, zip code 50130). Aka Jewell Junction. Covers a land area of 66.721 square miles and a water area of 0.519 square miles. Located at 42.33° N. Lat.; 93.72° W. Long.
Population: 1,703 (2000); Race: 97.6% White, 0.0% Black, 0.9% Asian, 0.0% American Indian and Alaska Native, 0.9% Hispanic of any race, 0.9% two or more races (2000); Density: 25.5 persons per square mile (2000); Age: 27.3% under 18, 17.2% over 64 (2000); Marriage status: 18.1% never married, 68.1% now married, 7.1% widowed, 6.7% divorced (2000); Foreign born: 1.0% (2000); Ancestry (includes multiple ancestries): 36.1% German, 32.0% Norwegian, 6.9% English, 6.6% Irish, 4.8% Danish (2000).
Economy: Employment by occupation: 16.7% management, 21.5% professional, 13.7% services, 22.0% sales, 2.4% farming, 9.2% construction, 14.5% production (2000).
Income: Per capita income: $19,388 (2000); Median household income: $40,673 (2000); Poverty rate: 5.2% (2000).
Education: High school graduation rate: 92.4% (2000); College graduation rate: 18.6% (2000).

School District(s)

South Hamilton Community School District (KG-12)
2000 Enrollment: 758 515-827-5479
Housing: Homeownership rate: 77.8% (2000); Median home value: $85,900 (2000); Median rent: $382 per month (2000); Median age of housing: 51 years (2000).
Newspapers: South Hamilton Record-News (1 x week)
Transportation: Commute to work: 90.8% car, 0.0% public transportation, 2.8% walk, 6.3% work from home (2000); Travel time to work: 40.6% less than 15 minutes, 33.8% 15 to 30 minutes, 16.5% 30 to 45 minutes, 4.0% 45 to 60 minutes, 5.1% 60 minutes or more (2000)

JEWELL JUNCTION (city). Aka Jewell. Covers a land area of 3.876 square miles and a water area of 0.127 square miles. Located at 42.30° N. Lat.; 93.64° W. Long.
History: First known as Calahan after James Calahan of Des Moines, who owned much land in the state, the name was changed to Jewell Junction by David T. Jewell who had originally owned the town site. The town was established in 1880 when the Toledo & North Western Railroad came through.
Population: 1,239 (2000); Race: 96.7% White, 0.0% Black, 1.2% Asian, 0.0% American Indian and Alaska Native, 1.3% Hispanic of any race, 1.2% two or more races (2000); Density: 319.7 persons per square mile (2000); Age: 29.7% under 18, 16.2% over 64 (2000); Marriage status: 17.7% never married, 66.1% now married, 8.4% widowed, 7.7% divorced (2000); Foreign born: 1.4% (2000); Ancestry (includes multiple ancestries): 36.3% German, 28.5% Norwegian, 8.3% Irish, 6.9% English, 4.2% Danish (2000).
Economy: Single-family building permits issued: 5 (2001) / 4 (2000); Multi-family building permits issued: 0 (2001) / 0 (2000); Employment by occupation: 13.2% management, 22.8% professional, 14.5% services, 22.5% sales, 2.2% farming, 10.2% construction, 14.5% production (2000).
Income: Per capita income: $18,780 (2000); Median household income: $42,614 (2000); Poverty rate: 4.4% (2000).
Taxes: Total city taxes per capita: $225 (1997); City property taxes per capita: $223 (1997).
Education: High school graduation rate: 91.1% (2000); College graduation rate: 19.3% (2000).
Housing: Homeownership rate: 79.9% (2000); Median home value: $82,800 (2000); Median rent: $381 per month (2000); Median age of housing: 50 years (2000).
Transportation: Commute to work: 93.0% car, 0.0% public transportation, 3.8% walk, 3.1% work from home (2000); Travel time to work: 42.4% less than 15 minutes, 32.9% 15 to 30 minutes, 16.6% 30 to 45 minutes, 3.2% 45 to 60 minutes, 4.9% 60 minutes or more (2000)

KAMRAR (city). Covers a land area of 0.830 square miles and a water area of 0 square miles. Located at 42.39° N. Lat.; 93.72° W. Long. Elevation is 1,110 feet.
History: Kamrar was named for a lawyer, Judge J. M. Kamrar, who represented the Chicago & North Western Railroad.
Population: 229 (2000); Race: 96.9% White, 1.8% Black, 0.0% Asian, 0.0% American Indian and Alaska Native, 2.2% Hispanic of any race, 0.0% two or more races (2000); Density: 275.9 persons per square mile (2000); Age: 27.0% under 18, 14.2% over 64 (2000); Marriage status: 18.2% never married, 65.9% now married, 7.4% widowed, 8.5% divorced (2000); Foreign born: 0.0% (2000); Ancestry (includes multiple ancestries): 42.0% German, 15.0% Irish, 11.1% Norwegian, 9.7% United States or American, 6.2% Danish (2000).
Economy: Single-family building permits issued: 0 (2001) / 0 (2000); Multi-family building permits issued: 0 (2001) / 0 (2000); Employment by occupation: 9.3% management, 5.6% professional, 23.4% services, 4.7% sales, 0.0% farming, 12.1% construction, 44.9% production (2000).
Income: Per capita income: $15,892 (2000); Median household income: $37,188 (2000); Poverty rate: 3.1% (2000).
Taxes: Total city taxes per capita: $158 (1997); City property taxes per capita: $158 (1997).
Education: High school graduation rate: 83.6% (2000); College graduation rate: 6.2% (2000).
Housing: Homeownership rate: 78.7% (2000); Median home value: $32,500 (2000); Median rent: $275 per month (2000); Median age of housing: 60+ years (2000).
Transportation: Commute to work: 96.2% car, 0.0% public transportation, 3.8% walk, 0.0% work from home (2000); Travel time to work: 21.0% less than 15 minutes, 53.3% 15 to 30 minutes, 21.0% 30 to 45 minutes, 1.0% 45 to 60 minutes, 3.8% 60 minutes or more (2000)

RANDALL (city). Covers a land area of 0.460 square miles and a water area of 0 square miles. Located at 42.23° N. Lat.; 93.60° W. Long. Elevation is 1,022 feet.
History: Randall was established by the Chicago & North Western Railroad.
Population: 148 (2000); Race: 96.4% White, 0.0% Black, 0.0% Asian, 3.6% American Indian and Alaska Native, 0.0% Hispanic of any race, 0.0% two or more races (2000); Density: 321.8 persons per square mile (2000); Age: 16.4% under 18, 12.9% over 64 (2000); Marriage status: 15.4% never married, 65.8% now married, 12.0% widowed, 6.8% divorced (2000); Foreign born: 0.0% (2000); Ancestry (includes multiple ancestries): 35.7% Norwegian, 31.4% German, 12.9% United States or American, 5.0% English, 4.3% Danish (2000).
Economy: Single-family building permits issued: 1 (2001) / 2 (2000); Multi-family building permits issued: 0 (2001) / 0 (2000); Employment by occupation: 4.2% management, 15.6% professional, 31.3% services, 25.0% sales, 2.1% farming, 9.4% construction, 12.5% production (2000).
Income: Per capita income: $20,991 (2000); Median household income: $30,750 (2000); Poverty rate: 6.4% (2000).
Taxes: Total city taxes per capita: $209 (1997); City property taxes per capita: $209 (1997).
Education: High school graduation rate: 90.5% (2000); College graduation rate: 15.2% (2000).
Housing: Homeownership rate: 89.1% (2000); Median home value: $47,300 (2000); Median rent: $375 per month (2000); Median age of housing: 60+ years (2000).
Transportation: Commute to work: 87.5% car, 0.0% public transportation, 3.1% walk, 9.4% work from home (2000); Travel time to work: 36.8% less than 15 minutes, 48.3% 15 to 30 minutes, 10.3% 30 to 45 minutes, 0.0% 45 to 60 minutes, 4.6% 60 minutes or more (2000)

STANHOPE (city). Covers a land area of 0.983 square miles and a water area of 0 square miles. Located at 42.29° N. Lat.; 93.79° W. Long. Elevation is 1,122 feet.
History: Stanhope was mapped by the Western Town Lot Company in 1883. A railroad official named the town in honor of lecturer and author, Lady Hester L. Stanhope.
Population: 488 (2000); Race: 98.6% White, 0.0% Black, 0.0% Asian, 0.0% American Indian and Alaska Native, 1.4% Hispanic of any race, 1.4% two or more races (2000); Density: 496.4 persons per square mile (2000); Age: 24.8% under 18, 19.4% over 64 (2000); Marriage status: 23.7% never married, 60.6% now married, 7.9% widowed, 7.9% divorced (2000); Foreign born: 1.4% (2000); Ancestry (includes multiple ancestries): 25.5% German,

10.9% United States or American, 9.9% Irish, 9.7% Norwegian, 6.7% Swedish (2000).
Economy: Single-family building permits issued: 0 (2001) / 0 (2000); Multi-family building permits issued: 0 (2001) / 0 (2000); Employment by occupation: 9.0% management, 12.2% professional, 18.8% services, 19.6% sales, 1.6% farming, 6.5% construction, 32.2% production (2000).
Income: Per capita income: $18,592 (2000); Median household income: $39,500 (2000); Poverty rate: 6.1% (2000).
Taxes: Total city taxes per capita: $131 (1997); City property taxes per capita: $129 (1997).
Education: High school graduation rate: 84.8% (2000); College graduation rate: 14.9% (2000).
Housing: Homeownership rate: 77.6% (2000); Median home value: $55,200 (2000); Median rent: $312 per month (2000); Median age of housing: 49 years (2000).
Transportation: Commute to work: 95.4% car, 0.0% public transportation, 1.7% walk, 0.0% work from home (2000); Travel time to work: 21.7% less than 15 minutes, 50.4% 15 to 30 minutes, 21.7% 30 to 45 minutes, 0.8% 45 to 60 minutes, 5.4% 60 minutes or more (2000)

STRATFORD (city). Covers a land area of 1.924 square miles and a water area of 0 square miles. Located at 42.27° N. Lat.; 93.92° W. Long. Elevation is 1,116 feet.
History: Stratford was named after Stratford-upon-Avon, England.
Population: 746 (2000); Race: 98.4% White, 0.0% Black, 0.0% Asian, 0.3% American Indian and Alaska Native, 0.0% Hispanic of any race, 1.3% two or more races (2000); Density: 387.7 persons per square mile (2000); Age: 20.4% under 18, 29.7% over 64 (2000); Marriage status: 19.4% never married, 58.0% now married, 15.8% widowed, 6.8% divorced (2000); Foreign born: 0.3% (2000); Ancestry (includes multiple ancestries): 27.6% Swedish, 25.0% German, 14.1% Irish, 9.8% English, 8.1% Norwegian (2000).
Economy: Employment by occupation: 4.2% management, 10.0% professional, 20.2% services, 26.3% sales, 2.4% farming, 14.8% construction, 22.1% production (2000).
Income: Per capita income: $15,553 (2000); Median household income: $29,375 (2000); Poverty rate: 5.7% (2000).
Taxes: Total city taxes per capita: $152 (1997); City property taxes per capita: $149 (1997).
Education: High school graduation rate: 83.4% (2000); College graduation rate: 9.3% (2000).

School District(s)

Stratford Community School District (PK-12)
2000 Enrollment: 115 515-838-2208
Housing: Homeownership rate: 75.9% (2000); Median home value: $57,800 (2000); Median rent: $271 per month (2000); Median age of housing: 58 years (2000).
Newspapers: Stratford Courier (1 x week)
Transportation: Commute to work: 90.7% car, 0.0% public transportation, 5.0% walk, 2.2% work from home (2000); Travel time to work: 32.9% less than 15 minutes, 20.6% 15 to 30 minutes, 32.0% 30 to 45 minutes, 9.5% 45 to 60 minutes, 5.1% 60 minutes or more (2000)

WEBSTER CITY (city). Covers a land area of 8.557 square miles and a water area of 0.015 square miles. Located at 42.46° N. Lat.; 93.82° W. Long. Elevation is 1,044 feet.
History: Webster City was settled in 1850 by Wilson C. Brewer, and named in 1856 for an owner of a stage line that extended between Belmond and Fort Dodge.
Population: 8,176 (2000); Race: 95.6% White, 0.1% Black, 3.2% Asian, 0.0% American Indian and Alaska Native, 0.5% Hispanic of any race, 0.9% two or more races (2000); Density: 955.5 persons per square mile (2000); Age: 24.1% under 18, 19.6% over 64 (2000); Marriage status: 20.0% never married, 58.5% now married, 9.2% widowed, 12.3% divorced (2000); Foreign born: 3.5% (2000); Ancestry (includes multiple ancestries): 33.8% German, 14.3% Irish, 13.0% Norwegian, 7.4% English, 6.2% United States or American (2000).
Economy: Single-family building permits issued: 12 (2001) / 27 (2000); Multi-family building permits issued: 4 (2001) / 2 (2000); Employment by occupation: 9.7% management, 17.9% professional, 13.9% services, 21.0% sales, 0.9% farming, 9.4% construction, 27.2% production (2000).
Income: Per capita income: $19,057 (2000); Median household income: $36,582 (2000); Poverty rate: 7.3% (2000).
Taxes: Total city taxes per capita: $399 (2000); City property taxes per capita: $386 (2000).
Education: High school graduation rate: 84.8% (2000); College graduation rate: 17.2% (2000).

School District(s)

Webster City Community School District (PK-12)
2000 Enrollment: 1,751 515-832-9200
Housing: Homeownership rate: 70.3% (2000); Median home value: $68,500 (2000); Median rent: $317 per month (2000); Median age of housing: 45 years (2000).
Hospitals: Hamilton County Public Hospital (65 beds)
Safety: Violent crime rate: 28.2 per 10,000 population; Property crime rate: 297.5 per 10,000 population (2001).
Newspapers: The Daily Freeman-Journal (5 x week)
Transportation: Commute to work: 91.9% car, 0.5% public transportation, 3.8% walk, 2.8% work from home (2000); Travel time to work: 78.3% less than 15 minutes, 11.7% 15 to 30 minutes, 5.3% 30 to 45 minutes, 2.8% 45 to 60 minutes, 2.0% 60 minutes or more (2000)
Additional Information Contacts
Wright Hamilton Board of Realtors 515-832-1228

WILLIAMS (city). Covers a land area of 0.877 square miles and a water area of 0 square miles. Located at 42.48° N. Lat.; 93.54° W. Long.
History: Williams was an Irish community settled by Peter Laforge in 1868. It was named for Major William Williams of Fort Dodge. In the 1880's the town was destroyed by a cyclone.
Population: 427 (2000); Race: 100.0% White, 0.0% Black, 0.0% Asian, 0.0% American Indian and Alaska Native, 1.1% Hispanic of any race, 0.0% two or more races (2000); Density: 487.0 persons per square mile (2000); Age: 22.6% under 18, 20.2% over 64 (2000); Marriage status: 19.6% never married, 65.3% now married, 9.1% widowed, 6.1% divorced (2000); Foreign born: 1.8% (2000); Ancestry (includes multiple ancestries): 34.8% German, 13.2% Norwegian, 12.6% Irish, 9.2% English, 7.0% European (2000).
Economy: Employment by occupation: 9.1% management, 17.8% professional, 9.5% services, 26.4% sales, 0.0% farming, 13.6% construction, 23.6% production (2000).
Income: Per capita income: $16,000 (2000); Median household income: $36,250 (2000); Poverty rate: 2.2% (2000).
Taxes: Total city taxes per capita: $110 (1997); City property taxes per capita: $107 (1997).
Education: High school graduation rate: 88.8% (2000); College graduation rate: 10.5% (2000).
Housing: Homeownership rate: 73.1% (2000); Median home value: $54,500 (2000); Median rent: $264 per month (2000); Median age of housing: 60+ years (2000).
Transportation: Commute to work: 92.4% car, 0.0% public transportation, 5.5% walk, 2.1% work from home (2000); Travel time to work: 31.0% less than 15 minutes, 51.7% 15 to 30 minutes, 13.8% 30 to 45 minutes, 0.9% 45 to 60 minutes, 2.6% 60 minutes or more (2000)

Hancock County

Located in northern Iowa; prairie area, drained by branches of the Iowa River. Covers a land area of 571.10 square miles, a water area of 2.00 square miles, and is located in the Central Time Zone. The county government was organized in 1851. County seat is Garner.
Population: 12,100 (2000); Race: 97.8% White, 0.0% Black, 0.3% Asian, 0.1% American Indian and Alaska Native, 3.1% Hispanic of any race, 0.5% two or more races (2000); Density: 21.2 persons per square mile (2000); Age: 26.7% under 18, 17.8% over 64 (2000).
Religion: Five largest groups: 18.3% The United Methodist Church, 17.8% Catholic Church, 13.7% Evangelical Lutheran Church in America, 8.9% Lutheran Church—Missouri Synod, 6.3% United Church of Christ (2000).
Economy: Unemployment rate: 2.1% (11/2002); Total civilian labor force: 6,828 (11/2002); Leading industries: 38.2% manufacturing; 15.1% retail trade; 13.7% health care and social assistance (2000); Companies that employ more than 1,000 persons: 0 (2000); Companies that employ more than 100 persons: 5 (2000); Farms: 849 totaling 334,050 acres (1997); Minority business ownership rate: 0.0% (1997); Women business ownership rate: 15.5% (1997); Retail sales per capita: $4,616 (1997). Single-family building permits issued: 21 (2001) / 28 (2000); Multi-family building permits issued: 0 (2001) / 14 (2000).
Income: Per capita income: $17,957 (2000); Median household income: $37,703 (2000); Poverty rate: 6.0% (2000); Bankruptcy rate: 1.82% (2001).
Taxes: Total county taxes per capita: $346 (1997); County property taxes per capita: $340 (1997).

Education: High school graduation rate: 85.8% (2000); College graduation rate: 15.4% (2000).
Housing: Homeownership rate: 78.2% (2000); Median home value: $59,600 (2000); Median rent: $255 per month (2000); Median age of housing: 48 years (2000).
Health: Birth rate: 111.6 per 10,000 population (1998); Age adjusted death rate: 74.7 per 10,000 population (1999); Age adjusted cancer mortality rate: 152.3 deaths per 100,000 population (1999). Number of physicians: 0.8 per 10,000 population (1999); Number of hospital beds: 20.7 per 10,000 population (1999).
Elections: 2000 Presidential election results: 42.0% Gore, 55.0% Bush, 2.3% Nader, 0.4% Buchanan
National and State Parks: Crystal Lake State Game Mgt Area; Eagle Lake State Game Management Area; Eagle Lake State Park; Pilot Knob State Park; West Twin Lake State Game Management Area
Additional Information Contacts
Hancock County Government Offices 641-923-3163
Britt Chamber of Commerce 641-843-3867
Garner Chamber of Commerce 641-923-3993
North Central Iowa Board of Realtors 641-923-2813

Hancock County Communities

BRITT (city). Covers a land area of 1.221 square miles and a water area of 0 square miles. Located at 43.09° N. Lat.; 93.80° W. Long. Elevation is 1,234 feet.
History: Britt was the home of John Hammill, Governor of Iowa (1925-1931). In 1900, an editor known as "Bailey of Britt" announced that a national Hobo Convention would be held in the town. On the appointed day reporters flocked to Britt from many parts of the county, only to discover that they had been hoaxed. However, they entered into the spirit of the occasion, outdoing each other in inventing stories about hoboes who never existed.
Population: 2,052 (2000); Race: 92.4% White, 0.0% Black, 0.2% Asian, 0.0% American Indian and Alaska Native, 7.6% Hispanic of any race, 1.3% two or more races (2000); Density: 1,680.5 persons per square mile (2000); Age: 24.5% under 18, 23.4% over 64 (2000); Marriage status: 20.1% never married, 60.4% now married, 12.8% widowed, 6.7% divorced (2000); Foreign born: 3.8% (2000); Ancestry (includes multiple ancestries): 40.5% German, 11.4% Norwegian, 8.6% Other groups, 7.0% Irish, 7.0% Czech (2000).
Economy: Single-family building permits issued: 5 (2001) / 5 (2000); Multi-family building permits issued: 0 (2001) / 0 (2000); Employment by occupation: 9.3% management, 12.8% professional, 15.5% services, 20.5% sales, 1.7% farming, 7.5% construction, 32.7% production (2000).
Income: Per capita income: $16,130 (2000); Median household income: $33,150 (2000); Poverty rate: 8.2% (2000).
Taxes: Total city taxes per capita: $159 (1997); City property taxes per capita: $138 (1997).
Education: High school graduation rate: 77.8% (2000); College graduation rate: 10.7% (2000).

School District(s)

West Hancock Community School District (PK-12)
2000 Enrollment: 745 641-843-3863
Housing: Homeownership rate: 78.8% (2000); Median home value: $60,700 (2000); Median rent: $249 per month (2000); Median age of housing: 48 years (2000).
Hospitals: Hancock County Memorial Hospital (26 beds)
Newspapers: Britt News Tribune (1 x week)
Transportation: Commute to work: 91.8% car, 0.3% public transportation, 4.9% walk, 2.7% work from home (2000); Travel time to work: 50.7% less than 15 minutes, 28.7% 15 to 30 minutes, 12.6% 30 to 45 minutes, 4.4% 45 to 60 minutes, 3.6% 60 minutes or more (2000)
Additional Information Contacts
Britt Chamber of Commerce 641-843-3867

CORWITH (city). Covers a land area of 1.561 square miles and a water area of 0 square miles. Located at 42.99° N. Lat.; 93.95° W. Long. Elevation is 1,177 feet.
History: John Erastus Corwith, for whom the town of Corwith was named, owned a lot of land in the area but lived in Galena, Illinois, where he was a stockholder and director of several banks. Corwith was founded in 1880.
Population: 350 (2000); Race: 98.5% White, 0.0% Black, 0.0% Asian, 1.2% American Indian and Alaska Native, 8.2% Hispanic of any race, 0.0% two or more races (2000); Density: 224.2 persons per square mile (2000); Age: 31.9% under 18, 17.8% over 64 (2000); Marriage status: 17.5% never married, 62.2% now married, 11.8% widowed, 8.5% divorced (2000); Foreign born: 1.8% (2000); Ancestry (includes multiple ancestries): 41.2% German, 20.2% United States or American, 14.6% Norwegian, 8.2% Other groups, 6.7% Irish (2000).
Economy: Single-family building permits issued: 0 (2001) / 0 (2000); Multi-family building permits issued: 0 (2001) / 0 (2000); Employment by occupation: 8.8% management, 20.8% professional, 11.2% services, 18.4% sales, 3.2% farming, 8.0% construction, 29.6% production (2000).
Income: Per capita income: $13,054 (2000); Median household income: $27,222 (2000); Poverty rate: 11.4% (2000).
Taxes: Total city taxes per capita: $182 (1997); City property taxes per capita: $124 (1997).
Education: High school graduation rate: 86.2% (2000); College graduation rate: 12.9% (2000).
Housing: Homeownership rate: 80.7% (2000); Median home value: $37,000 (2000); Median rent: $202 per month (2000); Median age of housing: 49 years (2000).
Transportation: Commute to work: 96.7% car, 0.0% public transportation, 0.0% walk, 1.6% work from home (2000); Travel time to work: 43.0% less than 15 minutes, 24.0% 15 to 30 minutes, 12.4% 30 to 45 minutes, 9.9% 45 to 60 minutes, 10.7% 60 minutes or more (2000)

CRYSTAL LAKE (city). Covers a land area of 0.255 square miles and a water area of 0 square miles. Located at 43.22° N. Lat.; 93.79° W. Long. Elevation is 1,295 feet.
History: The town of Crystal Lake takes its name from the lake, which is known for its crystal clear waters.
Population: 285 (2000); Race: 100.0% White, 0.0% Black, 0.0% Asian, 0.0% American Indian and Alaska Native, 1.5% Hispanic of any race, 0.0% two or more races (2000); Density: 1,118.6 persons per square mile (2000); Age: 22.9% under 18, 21.1% over 64 (2000); Marriage status: 32.7% never married, 49.1% now married, 10.6% widowed, 7.5% divorced (2000); Foreign born: 0.0% (2000); Ancestry (includes multiple ancestries): 43.3% German, 20.4% Norwegian, 10.9% Irish, 10.5% Danish, 7.3% English (2000).
Economy: Single-family building permits issued: 0 (2001) / 1 (2000); Multi-family building permits issued: 0 (2001) / 0 (2000); Employment by occupation: 5.8% management, 3.6% professional, 7.9% services, 22.3% sales, 0.0% farming, 7.9% construction, 52.5% production (2000).
Income: Per capita income: $14,927 (2000); Median household income: $29,615 (2000); Poverty rate: 19.1% (2000).
Taxes: Total city taxes per capita: $143 (1997); City property taxes per capita: $89 (1997).
Education: High school graduation rate: 81.5% (2000); College graduation rate: 8.2% (2000).
Housing: Homeownership rate: 80.6% (2000); Median home value: $38,900 (2000); Median rent: $228 per month (2000); Median age of housing: 47 years (2000).
Transportation: Commute to work: 94.1% car, 0.0% public transportation, 2.2% walk, 3.7% work from home (2000); Travel time to work: 28.5% less than 15 minutes, 57.7% 15 to 30 minutes, 5.4% 30 to 45 minutes, 4.6% 45 to 60 minutes, 3.8% 60 minutes or more (2000)

GARNER (city). Covers a land area of 2.089 square miles and a water area of 0 square miles. Located at 43.09° N. Lat.; 93.60° W. Long. Elevation is 1,209 feet.
History: Garner was named for a railroad official. The county seat was transferred from Concord when the railroad was built through Garner, missing Concord.
Population: 2,922 (2000); Race: 99.0% White, 0.0% Black, 0.5% Asian, 0.0% American Indian and Alaska Native, 0.6% Hispanic of any race, 0.2% two or more races (2000); Density: 1,398.7 persons per square mile (2000); Age: 25.1% under 18, 18.8% over 64 (2000); Marriage status: 19.8% never married, 63.0% now married, 10.3% widowed, 7.0% divorced (2000); Foreign born: 0.9% (2000); Ancestry (includes multiple ancestries): 49.3% German, 16.7% Norwegian, 11.3% English, 10.3% Irish, 7.1% Czech (2000).
Economy: Single-family building permits issued: 10 (2001) / 13 (2000); Multi-family building permits issued: 0 (2001) / 14 (2000); Employment by occupation: 12.7% management, 17.5% professional, 13.9% services, 24.3% sales, 0.5% farming, 5.7% construction, 25.4% production (2000).
Income: Per capita income: $18,976 (2000); Median household income: $39,750 (2000); Poverty rate: 5.4% (2000).
Taxes: Total city taxes per capita: $308 (1997); City property taxes per capita: $248 (1997).
Education: High school graduation rate: 89.9% (2000); College graduation rate: 19.1% (2000).

School District(s)

Garner-Hayfield Community School District (PK-12)
2000 Enrollment: 914 641-923-2718

Housing: Homeownership rate: 78.7% (2000); Median home value: $74,000 (2000); Median rent: $310 per month (2000); Median age of housing: 34 years (2000).

Safety: Violent crime rate: 6.9 per 10,000 population; Property crime rate: 205.5 per 10,000 population (2001).

Newspapers: Garner Leader & Signal (1 x week)

Transportation: Commute to work: 91.5% car, 0.3% public transportation, 2.5% walk, 4.4% work from home (2000); Travel time to work: 54.7% less than 15 minutes, 27.5% 15 to 30 minutes, 11.1% 30 to 45 minutes, 3.3% 45 to 60 minutes, 3.4% 60 minutes or more (2000)

Additional Information Contacts

Garner Chamber of Commerce 641-923-3993
North Central Iowa Board of Realtors 641-923-2813

GOODELL (city). Covers a land area of 0.428 square miles and a water area of 0 square miles. Located at 42.92° N. Lat.; 93.61° W. Long. Elevation is 1,236 feet.

History: Goodell was named for financier John Goodell of Cincinnati, who was instrumental in building the railroad through Hancock County.

Population: 174 (2000); Race: 85.6% White, 0.0% Black, 0.0% Asian, 0.0% American Indian and Alaska Native, 12.6% Hispanic of any race, 1.8% two or more races (2000); Density: 406.1 persons per square mile (2000); Age: 22.8% under 18, 7.2% over 64 (2000); Marriage status: 31.0% never married, 45.5% now married, 8.3% widowed, 15.2% divorced (2000); Foreign born: 10.8% (2000); Ancestry (includes multiple ancestries): 35.9% German, 21.6% Norwegian, 12.6% Other groups, 12.0% Irish, 7.8% United States or American (2000).

Economy: Employment by occupation: 9.1% management, 2.0% professional, 11.1% services, 17.2% sales, 8.1% farming, 11.1% construction, 41.4% production (2000).

Income: Per capita income: $14,795 (2000); Median household income: $32,292 (2000); Poverty rate: 3.0% (2000).

Taxes: Total city taxes per capita: $99 (1997); City property taxes per capita: $52 (1997).

Education: High school graduation rate: 71.4% (2000); College graduation rate: 0.0% (2000).

Housing: Homeownership rate: 85.3% (2000); Median home value: $27,500 (2000); Median rent: $175 per month (2000); Median age of housing: 60+ years (2000).

Transportation: Commute to work: 95.9% car, 0.0% public transportation, 4.1% walk, 0.0% work from home (2000); Travel time to work: 56.1% less than 15 minutes, 28.6% 15 to 30 minutes, 11.2% 30 to 45 minutes, 4.1% 45 to 60 minutes, 0.0% 60 minutes or more (2000)

KANAWHA (city). Covers a land area of 2.007 square miles and a water area of 0 square miles. Located at 42.93° N. Lat.; 93.79° W. Long. Elevation is 1,183 feet.

History: A railroad engineer named the town of Kanawha after his hometown in Virginia.

Population: 739 (2000); Race: 97.6% White, 0.0% Black, 0.5% Asian, 0.5% American Indian and Alaska Native, 4.9% Hispanic of any race, 0.8% two or more races (2000); Density: 368.3 persons per square mile (2000); Age: 24.2% under 18, 30.0% over 64 (2000); Marriage status: 15.4% never married, 64.8% now married, 16.8% widowed, 2.9% divorced (2000); Foreign born: 2.7% (2000); Ancestry (includes multiple ancestries): 34.5% German, 24.2% Norwegian, 11.8% Dutch, 8.4% Other groups, 6.5% United States or American (2000).

Economy: Single-family building permits issued: 0 (2001) / 0 (2000); Multi-family building permits issued: 0 (2001) / 0 (2000); Employment by occupation: 12.0% management, 17.5% professional, 14.2% services, 20.9% sales, 2.5% farming, 11.4% construction, 21.5% production (2000).

Income: Per capita income: $18,429 (2000); Median household income: $36,250 (2000); Poverty rate: 5.1% (2000).

Taxes: Total city taxes per capita: $286 (1997); City property taxes per capita: $225 (1997).

Education: High school graduation rate: 77.4% (2000); College graduation rate: 14.8% (2000).

Housing: Homeownership rate: 83.3% (2000); Median home value: $35,400 (2000); Median rent: $196 per month (2000); Median age of housing: 51 years (2000).

Newspapers: The Kanawha Reporter (1 x week)

Transportation: Commute to work: 91.8% car, 0.0% public transportation, 4.4% walk, 2.5% work from home (2000); Travel time to work: 53.4% less than 15 minutes, 24.4% 15 to 30 minutes, 12.5% 30 to 45 minutes, 5.8% 45 to 60 minutes, 3.9% 60 minutes or more (2000)

KLEMME (city). Covers a land area of 0.511 square miles and a water area of 0 square miles. Located at 43.00° N. Lat.; 93.60° W. Long. Elevation is 1,220 feet.

History: Klemme was established along the Burlington, Cedar Rapids & Northern Railroad. The land for the town site was set aside by landowner Harmon J. Klemme.

Population: 593 (2000); Race: 99.2% White, 0.0% Black, 0.0% Asian, 0.0% American Indian and Alaska Native, 2.4% Hispanic of any race, 0.0% two or more races (2000); Density: 1,161.0 persons per square mile (2000); Age: 25.0% under 18, 25.2% over 64 (2000); Marriage status: 19.6% never married, 63.1% now married, 10.2% widowed, 7.1% divorced (2000); Foreign born: 2.4% (2000); Ancestry (includes multiple ancestries): 49.4% German, 15.8% Norwegian, 6.9% United States or American, 6.6% Other groups, 5.5% Irish (2000).

Economy: Single-family building permits issued: 0 (2001) / 0 (2000); Multi-family building permits issued: 0 (2001) / 0 (2000); Employment by occupation: 8.2% management, 7.9% professional, 11.6% services, 16.1% sales, 0.0% farming, 13.5% construction, 42.7% production (2000).

Income: Per capita income: $15,581 (2000); Median household income: $32,614 (2000); Poverty rate: 5.0% (2000).

Taxes: Total city taxes per capita: $232 (1997); City property taxes per capita: $168 (1997).

Education: High school graduation rate: 77.2% (2000); College graduation rate: 7.9% (2000).

Housing: Homeownership rate: 72.6% (2000); Median home value: $37,300 (2000); Median rent: $267 per month (2000); Median age of housing: 56 years (2000).

Transportation: Commute to work: 89.7% car, 0.0% public transportation, 8.0% walk, 1.9% work from home (2000); Travel time to work: 41.1% less than 15 minutes, 34.9% 15 to 30 minutes, 10.9% 30 to 45 minutes, 8.5% 45 to 60 minutes, 4.7% 60 minutes or more (2000)

WODEN (city). Covers a land area of 0.429 square miles and a water area of 0 square miles. Located at 43.23° N. Lat.; 93.90° W. Long.

History: Woden was named for the Norse god Odin.

Population: 243 (2000); Race: 100.0% White, 0.0% Black, 0.0% Asian, 0.0% American Indian and Alaska Native, 0.0% Hispanic of any race, 0.0% two or more races (2000); Density: 565.8 persons per square mile (2000); Age: 17.7% under 18, 24.1% over 64 (2000); Marriage status: 15.2% never married, 62.7% now married, 18.6% widowed, 3.4% divorced (2000); Foreign born: 0.8% (2000); Ancestry (includes multiple ancestries): 60.8% German, 11.8% Norwegian, 8.4% Danish, 5.9% Irish, 5.9% United States or American (2000).

Economy: Single-family building permits issued: 0 (2001) / 0 (2000); Multi-family building permits issued: 0 (2001) / 0 (2000); Employment by occupation: 14.8% management, 10.7% professional, 22.1% services, 17.2% sales, 0.0% farming, 10.7% construction, 24.6% production (2000).

Income: Per capita income: $17,544 (2000); Median household income: $27,083 (2000); Poverty rate: 19.8% (2000).

Taxes: Total city taxes per capita: $157 (1997); City property taxes per capita: $99 (1997).

Education: High school graduation rate: 85.9% (2000); College graduation rate: 9.9% (2000).

School District(s)

Woden-Crystal Lake Community School District (PK-12)
2000 Enrollment: 219 641-926-5311

Housing: Homeownership rate: 82.8% (2000); Median home value: $32,500 (2000); Median rent: $188 per month (2000); Median age of housing: 54 years (2000).

Transportation: Commute to work: 78.7% car, 1.6% public transportation, 11.5% walk, 4.1% work from home (2000); Travel time to work: 56.4% less than 15 minutes, 39.3% 15 to 30 minutes, 0.0% 30 to 45 minutes, 0.0% 45 to 60 minutes, 4.3% 60 minutes or more (2000)

Hardin County

Located in central Iowa; prairie area, drained by the Iowa River. Covers a land area of 569.30 square miles, a water area of 0.70 square miles, and is located in the Central Time Zone. The county government was organized in 1851. County seat is Eldora.

Weather Station: Eldora Elevation: 1,141 feet

	Jan	Feb	Mar	Apr	May	Jun	Jul	Aug	Sep	Oct	Nov	Dec
High	25	31	44	58	71	81	85	82	75	62	44	30
Low	7	13	25	36	48	58	62	60	51	39	26	13
Precip	0.9	0.9	2.1	3.2	4.4	5.3	3.9	4.3	3.2	2.7	2.1	1.1
Snow	8.6	6.8	5.3	1.8	0.0	0.0	0.0	0.0	0.0	tr	3.4	6.6

High and Low temperatures in degrees Fahrenheit; Precipitation and Snow in inches

Weather Station: Iowa Falls Elevation: 1,128 feet

	Jan	Feb	Mar	Apr	May	Jun	Jul	Aug	Sep	Oct	Nov	Dec
High	25	32	44	60	73	82	85	82	75	62	44	30
Low	7	13	26	37	49	58	62	60	51	39	26	14
Precip	1.1	1.0	2.2	3.4	4.3	5.4	4.0	4.4	3.3	2.8	2.2	1.2
Snow	8.9	7.0	5.6	2.1	0.0	0.0	0.0	0.0	0.0	tr	4.1	7.5

High and Low temperatures in degrees Fahrenheit; Precipitation and Snow in inches

Population: 18,812 (2000); Race: 97.4% White, 0.6% Black, 0.4% Asian, 0.0% American Indian and Alaska Native, 2.1% Hispanic of any race, 0.8% two or more races (2000); Density: 33.0 persons per square mile (2000); Age: 24.5% under 18, 20.7% over 64 (2000).
Religion: Five largest groups: 15.7% The United Methodist Church, 11.6% Lutheran Church—Missouri Synod, 11.5% United Church of Christ, 6.6% Evangelical Lutheran Church in America, 6.4% Catholic Church (2000).
Economy: Unemployment rate: 4.4% (11/2002); Total civilian labor force: 9,728 (11/2002); Leading industries: 21.5% manufacturing; 17.1% health care and social assistance; 16.1% wholesale trade (2000); Companies that employ more than 1,000 persons: 0 (2000); Companies that employ more than 100 persons: 11 (2000); Farms: 857 totaling 339,951 acres (1997); Minority business ownership rate: 0.0% (1997); Women business ownership rate: 22.8% (1997); Retail sales per capita: $8,167 (1997). Single-family building permits issued: 21 (2001) / 13 (2000); Multi-family building permits issued: 43 (2001) / 10 (2000).
Income: Per capita income: $17,537 (2000); Median household income: $35,429 (2000); Poverty rate: 8.0% (2000); Bankruptcy rate: 3.57% (2001).
Taxes: Total county taxes per capita: $236 (2000); County property taxes per capita: $199 (2000).
Education: High school graduation rate: 85.7% (2000); College graduation rate: 17.1% (2000).
Housing: Homeownership rate: 74.6% (2000); Median home value: $57,200 (2000); Median rent: $286 per month (2000); Median age of housing: 53 years (2000).
Health: Birth rate: 109.5 per 10,000 population (1998); Age adjusted death rate: 80.1 per 10,000 population (1999); Age adjusted cancer mortality rate: 201.1 deaths per 100,000 population (1999). Number of physicians: 8.0 per 10,000 population (1999); Number of hospital beds: 21.3 per 10,000 population (1999).
Elections: 2000 Presidential election results: 44.3% Gore, 53.2% Bush, 1.7% Nader, 0.4% Buchanan
National and State Parks: Pine Lake State Park; Steamboat Rock Wayside State Park
Additional Information Contacts
Hardin County Government Offices 641-858-3461
Eldora Area Chamber & Development 641-939-3241
Eldora Chamber of Commerce.................... 641-858-3241
Heart of Iowa Board of Realtors 641-648-6656
Iowa Falls Area Development 641-648-5604
Iowa Falls Chamber of Commerce.................... 641-648-5549

Hardin County Communities

ACKLEY (city). Covers a land area of 2.452 square miles and a water area of 0.033 square miles. Located at 42.55° N. Lat.; 93.05° W. Long. Elevation is 1,092 feet.
History: Ackley, originally known as Fontaine, was platted in 1857 by the Dubuque & Pacific Railroad. The town was named for William J. Ackley, president of the Railroad.
Population: 1,809 (2000); Race: 93.1% White, 0.2% Black, 0.4% Asian, 0.0% American Indian and Alaska Native, 9.2% Hispanic of any race, 2.6% two or more races (2000); Density: 737.8 persons per square mile (2000); Age: 22.7% under 18, 27.0% over 64 (2000); Marriage status: 19.4% never married, 61.8% now married, 13.3% widowed, 5.5% divorced (2000); Foreign born: 7.4% (2000); Ancestry (includes multiple ancestries): 54.2% German, 8.8% Other groups, 6.6% Irish, 6.1% United States or American, 6.1% English (2000).
Economy: Single-family building permits issued: 3 (2001) / 4 (2000); Multi-family building permits issued: 0 (2001) / 10 (2000); Employment by occupation: 10.7% management, 17.9% professional, 15.0% services, 22.8% sales, 3.3% farming, 9.1% construction, 21.2% production (2000).
Income: Per capita income: $17,406 (2000); Median household income: $36,250 (2000); Poverty rate: 8.3% (2000).
Taxes: Total city taxes per capita: $320 (1997); City property taxes per capita: $306 (1997).
Education: High school graduation rate: 73.9% (2000); College graduation rate: 14.4% (2000).

School District(s)
Ackley-Geneva Community School District (KG-12)
2000 Enrollment: 509 641-847-2611
Housing: Homeownership rate: 80.0% (2000); Median home value: $48,700 (2000); Median rent: $277 per month (2000); Median age of housing: 52 years (2000).
Newspapers: Ackley World Journal (1 x week)
Transportation: Commute to work: 86.1% car, 0.0% public transportation, 9.9% walk, 3.1% work from home (2000); Travel time to work: 47.4% less than 15 minutes, 31.8% 15 to 30 minutes, 7.9% 30 to 45 minutes, 4.5% 45 to 60 minutes, 8.3% 60 minutes or more (2000)

ALDEN (city). Covers a land area of 1.718 square miles and a water area of 0.015 square miles. Located at 42.51° N. Lat.; 93.37° W. Long. Elevation is 1,168 feet.
History: Alden is believed to be named either for John Alden, a Governor of Plymouth Colony, Massachusetts, or for Henry Alden, an early settler in the area.
Population: 904 (2000); Race: 97.5% White, 0.0% Black, 0.0% Asian, 0.0% American Indian and Alaska Native, 4.6% Hispanic of any race, 0.6% two or more races (2000); Density: 526.2 persons per square mile (2000); Age: 28.9% under 18, 16.2% over 64 (2000); Marriage status: 22.7% never married, 59.8% now married, 10.9% widowed, 6.6% divorced (2000); Foreign born: 1.5% (2000); Ancestry (includes multiple ancestries): 48.0% German, 10.0% Irish, 9.0% Norwegian, 5.7% United States or American, 4.8% Other groups (2000).
Economy: Single-family building permits issued: 0 (2001) / 1 (2000); Multi-family building permits issued: 0 (2001) / 0 (2000); Employment by occupation: 8.2% management, 7.7% professional, 17.6% services, 21.0% sales, 2.9% farming, 13.5% construction, 29.0% production (2000).
Income: Per capita income: $16,011 (2000); Median household income: $35,966 (2000); Poverty rate: 10.6% (2000).
Taxes: Total city taxes per capita: $345 (1997); City property taxes per capita: $286 (1997).
Education: High school graduation rate: 86.5% (2000); College graduation rate: 9.5% (2000).

School District(s)
Alden Comm. School District (KG-12)
2000 Enrollment: 360 515-859-3395
Housing: Homeownership rate: 82.4% (2000); Median home value: $47,300 (2000); Median rent: $266 per month (2000); Median age of housing: 55 years (2000).
Transportation: Commute to work: 89.3% car, 0.0% public transportation, 2.9% walk, 6.1% work from home (2000); Travel time to work: 49.9% less than 15 minutes, 24.3% 15 to 30 minutes, 10.3% 30 to 45 minutes, 10.3% 45 to 60 minutes, 5.2% 60 minutes or more (2000)

BUCKEYE (city). Covers a land area of 1.004 square miles and a water area of 0 square miles. Located at 42.41° N. Lat.; 93.37° W. Long. Elevation is 1,154 feet.
Population: 110 (2000); Race: 100.0% White, 0.0% Black, 0.0% Asian, 0.0% American Indian and Alaska Native, 0.0% Hispanic of any race, 0.0% two or more races (2000); Density: 109.6 persons per square mile (2000); Age: 15.8% under 18, 22.1% over 64 (2000); Marriage status: 23.2% never married, 67.1% now married, 7.3% widowed, 2.4% divorced (2000); Foreign born: 0.0% (2000); Ancestry (includes multiple ancestries): 64.2% German, 15.8% Norwegian, 4.2% French (except Basque), 4.2% Irish, 4.2% United States or American (2000).
Economy: In agricultural area: fertilizer. Employment by occupation: 0.0% management, 3.6% professional, 12.7% services, 32.7% sales, 10.9% farming, 3.6% construction, 36.4% production (2000).
Income: Per capita income: $16,880 (2000); Median household income: $24,750 (2000); Poverty rate: 5.3% (2000).
Taxes: Total city taxes per capita: $433 (1997); City property taxes per capita: $375 (1997).
Education: High school graduation rate: 77.6% (2000); College graduation rate: 6.0% (2000).

Housing: Homeownership rate: 87.5% (2000); Median home value: $22,500 (2000); Median rent: $238 per month (2000); Median age of housing: 60+ years (2000).
Transportation: Commute to work: 94.5% car, 0.0% public transportation, 0.0% walk, 5.5% work from home (2000); Travel time to work: 5.8% less than 15 minutes, 46.2% 15 to 30 minutes, 30.8% 30 to 45 minutes, 9.6% 45 to 60 minutes, 7.7% 60 minutes or more (2000)

ELDORA (city). Covers a land area of 4.346 square miles and a water area of 0 square miles. Located at 42.36° N. Lat.; 93.10° W. Long. Elevation is 1,088 feet.
History: Eldora was first named Eldorado because of a rush for gold here in 1851, but the name was later shortened. John Ellsworth had discovered the glittering particles of gold in the black soil, but no vein was discovered.
Population: 3,035 (2000); Race: 96.5% White, 0.0% Black, 1.6% Asian, 0.0% American Indian and Alaska Native, 1.9% Hispanic of any race, 2.0% two or more races (2000); Density: 698.4 persons per square mile (2000); Age: 28.9% under 18, 20.8% over 64 (2000); Marriage status: 25.8% never married, 52.7% now married, 13.9% widowed, 7.6% divorced (2000); Foreign born: 2.3% (2000); Ancestry (includes multiple ancestries): 34.4% German, 12.5% English, 12.2% United States or American, 11.1% Irish, 6.8% Norwegian (2000).
Economy: Single-family building permits issued: 0 (2001) / 1 (2000); Multi-family building permits issued: 2 (2001) / 0 (2000); Employment by occupation: 14.3% management, 16.4% professional, 21.0% services, 21.6% sales, 1.3% farming, 7.8% construction, 17.7% production (2000).
Income: Per capita income: $15,459 (2000); Median household income: $33,170 (2000); Poverty rate: 6.9% (2000).
Taxes: Total city taxes per capita: $312 (1997); City property taxes per capita: $253 (1997).
Education: High school graduation rate: 84.1% (2000); College graduation rate: 14.4% (2000).

School District(s)

Eldora-New Providence Community School District (PK-12)
2000 Enrollment: 757 641-939-5631
State Training School (N -N)
2000 Enrollment: n/a 515-858-5402

Housing: Homeownership rate: 71.9% (2000); Median home value: $48,800 (2000); Median rent: $261 per month (2000); Median age of housing: 53 years (2000).
Safety: Violent crime rate: 19.8 per 10,000 population; Property crime rate: 277.0 per 10,000 population (2001).
Newspapers: Hardin County Index (1 x week); Eldora Herald-Ledger (1 x week)
Transportation: Commute to work: 87.0% car, 0.0% public transportation, 6.2% walk, 4.9% work from home (2000); Travel time to work: 73.2% less than 15 minutes, 9.8% 15 to 30 minutes, 6.7% 30 to 45 minutes, 4.1% 45 to 60 minutes, 6.2% 60 minutes or more (2000)
Additional Information Contacts
Eldora Area Chamber & Development 641-939-3241
Eldora Chamber of Commerce. 641-858-3241

GARDEN CITY (unincorporated postal area, zip code 50102). Covers a land area of 0.505 square miles and a water area of 0 square miles. Located at 42.24° N. Lat.; 93.39° W. Long. Elevation is 1,200 feet.
Population: 101 (2000); Race: 100.0% White, 0.0% Black, 0.0% Asian, 0.0% American Indian and Alaska Native, 0.0% Hispanic of any race, 0.0% two or more races (2000); Density: 200.1 persons per square mile (2000); Age: 11.3% under 18, 19.6% over 64 (2000); Marriage status: 14.6% never married, 75.3% now married, 0.0% widowed, 10.1% divorced (2000); Foreign born: 0.0% (2000); Ancestry (includes multiple ancestries): 62.9% German, 40.2% Norwegian, 13.4% Swedish, 8.2% English, 5.2% Irish (2000).
Economy: Employment by occupation: 0.0% management, 5.3% professional, 19.3% services, 24.6% sales, 0.0% farming, 21.1% construction, 29.8% production (2000).
Income: Per capita income: $18,322 (2000); Median household income: $35,750 (2000); Poverty rate: 5.2% (2000).
Education: High school graduation rate: 79.0% (2000); College graduation rate: 12.3% (2000).
Housing: Homeownership rate: 80.4% (2000); Median home value: $32,100 (2000); Median rent: $275 per month (2000); Median age of housing: 60+ years (2000).
Transportation: Commute to work: 100.0% car, 0.0% public transportation, 0.0% walk, 0.0% work from home (2000); Travel time to work: 0.0% less than 15 minutes, 49.1% 15 to 30 minutes, 42.1% 30 to 45 minutes, 0.0% 45 to 60 minutes, 8.8% 60 minutes or more (2000)

HUBBARD (city). Covers a land area of 1.837 square miles and a water area of 0 square miles. Located at 42.30° N. Lat.; 93.30° W. Long. Elevation is 1,099 feet.
History: Hubbard was a boyhood home of Herbert Hoover, President of the United States (1929-1933).
Population: 885 (2000); Race: 99.8% White, 0.0% Black, 0.0% Asian, 0.0% American Indian and Alaska Native, 0.0% Hispanic of any race, 0.2% two or more races (2000); Density: 481.7 persons per square mile (2000); Age: 21.8% under 18, 30.8% over 64 (2000); Marriage status: 11.6% never married, 67.9% now married, 13.4% widowed, 7.0% divorced (2000); Foreign born: 0.4% (2000); Ancestry (includes multiple ancestries): 46.4% German, 14.0% Norwegian, 9.5% English, 7.1% United States or American, 7.0% Irish (2000).
Economy: Single-family building permits issued: 1 (2001) / 1 (2000); Multi-family building permits issued: 0 (2001) / 0 (2000); Employment by occupation: 10.1% management, 21.2% professional, 13.8% services, 25.7% sales, 2.9% farming, 5.8% construction, 20.6% production (2000).
Income: Per capita income: $21,805 (2000); Median household income: $35,089 (2000); Poverty rate: 4.8% (2000).
Taxes: Total city taxes per capita: $176 (1997); City property taxes per capita: $118 (1997).
Education: High school graduation rate: 81.9% (2000); College graduation rate: 14.9% (2000).

School District(s)

Hubbard-Radcliffe Community School District (KG-12)
2000 Enrollment: 508 641-864-2211

Housing: Homeownership rate: 85.6% (2000); Median home value: $59,500 (2000); Median rent: $247 per month (2000); Median age of housing: 55 years (2000).
Newspapers: Signal-Review (1 x week)
Transportation: Commute to work: 88.6% car, 0.5% public transportation, 6.9% walk, 2.4% work from home (2000); Travel time to work: 52.0% less than 15 minutes, 16.9% 15 to 30 minutes, 19.3% 30 to 45 minutes, 3.8% 45 to 60 minutes, 7.9% 60 minutes or more (2000)

IOWA FALLS (city). Covers a land area of 4.979 square miles and a water area of 0.068 square miles. Located at 42.52° N. Lat.; 93.26° W. Long. Elevation is 1,107 feet.
History: Iowa Falls was known successively as Rocksylvania and White's Mills before it was incorporated in 1856.
Population: 5,193 (2000); Race: 97.7% White, 1.6% Black, 0.1% Asian, 0.0% American Indian and Alaska Native, 0.5% Hispanic of any race, 0.5% two or more races (2000); Density: 1,043.1 persons per square mile (2000); Age: 20.1% under 18, 22.7% over 64 (2000); Marriage status: 26.3% never married, 52.8% now married, 11.6% widowed, 9.3% divorced (2000); Foreign born: 0.6% (2000); Ancestry (includes multiple ancestries): 45.1% German, 11.9% Irish, 11.5% English, 11.4% Norwegian, 5.2% Dutch (2000).
Economy: Single-family building permits issued: 5 (2001) / 1 (2000); Multi-family building permits issued: 41 (2001) / 0 (2000); Employment by occupation: 11.6% management, 16.9% professional, 14.0% services, 24.2% sales, 0.7% farming, 11.5% construction, 21.1% production (2000).
Income: Per capita income: $18,330 (2000); Median household income: $32,141 (2000); Poverty rate: 10.0% (2000).
Taxes: Total city taxes per capita: $479 (2000); City property taxes per capita: $379 (2000).
Education: High school graduation rate: 86.3% (2000); College graduation rate: 20.2% (2000).

School District(s)

Iowa Falls Community School District (PK-12)
2000 Enrollment: 1,139 641-648-6400

Housing: Homeownership rate: 67.7% (2000); Median home value: $64,000 (2000); Median rent: $317 per month (2000); Median age of housing: 48 years (2000).
Hospitals: Ellsworth Municipal Hospital (42 beds)
Safety: Violent crime rate: 9.6 per 10,000 population; Property crime rate: 323.9 per 10,000 population (2001).
Newspapers: Times Citizen (2 x week); The Advertiser (1 x week)
Transportation: Commute to work: 92.3% car, 0.3% public transportation, 3.0% walk, 3.6% work from home (2000); Travel time to work: 72.4% less than 15 minutes, 14.6% 15 to 30 minutes, 6.2% 30 to 45 minutes, 1.0% 45 to 60 minutes, 5.8% 60 minutes or more (2000)
Additional Information Contacts
Heart of Iowa Board of Realtors 641-648-6656

Iowa Falls Area Development 641-648-5604
Iowa Falls Chamber of Commerce. 641-648-5549

NEW PROVIDENCE (city). Covers a land area of 1.003 square miles and a water area of 0 square miles. Located at 42.28° N. Lat.; 93.17° W. Long. Elevation is 1,130 feet.
History: New Providence is named after Providence township. It is believed to indicate the faith of the pioneers in Providence for guidance.
Population: 227 (2000); Race: 99.6% White, 0.0% Black, 0.0% Asian, 0.0% American Indian and Alaska Native, 0.4% Hispanic of any race, 0.0% two or more races (2000); Density: 226.3 persons per square mile (2000); Age: 27.4% under 18, 14.5% over 64 (2000); Marriage status: 26.6% never married, 57.3% now married, 5.2% widowed, 10.9% divorced (2000); Foreign born: 0.0% (2000); Ancestry (includes multiple ancestries): 34.6% German, 17.1% Irish, 14.5% English, 6.8% European, 6.4% Dutch (2000).
Economy: Employment by occupation: 7.7% management, 19.7% professional, 13.7% services, 26.5% sales, 0.0% farming, 14.5% construction, 17.9% production (2000).
Income: Per capita income: $18,514 (2000); Median household income: $39,583 (2000); Poverty rate: 6.8% (2000).
Taxes: Total city taxes per capita: $87 (1997); City property taxes per capita: $79 (1997).
Education: High school graduation rate: 95.7% (2000); College graduation rate: 27.3% (2000).
Housing: Homeownership rate: 79.4% (2000); Median home value: $50,400 (2000); Median rent: $217 per month (2000); Median age of housing: 55 years (2000).
Transportation: Commute to work: 82.1% car, 0.0% public transportation, 12.8% walk, 3.4% work from home (2000); Travel time to work: 61.1% less than 15 minutes, 24.8% 15 to 30 minutes, 12.4% 30 to 45 minutes, 1.8% 45 to 60 minutes, 0.0% 60 minutes or more (2000)

OWASA (city). Covers a land area of 0.565 square miles and a water area of 0 square miles. Located at 42.43° N. Lat.; 93.20° W. Long. Elevation is 1,085 feet.
Population: 38 (2000); Race: 100.0% White, 0.0% Black, 0.0% Asian, 0.0% American Indian and Alaska Native, 0.0% Hispanic of any race, 0.0% two or more races (2000); Density: 67.3 persons per square mile (2000); Age: 27.8% under 18, 13.9% over 64 (2000); Marriage status: 7.7% never married, 50.0% now married, 19.2% widowed, 23.1% divorced (2000); Foreign born: 0.0% (2000); Ancestry (includes multiple ancestries): 27.8% Irish, 22.2% German, 16.7% English, 8.3% Other groups, 8.3% Danish (2000).
Economy: In agricultural area. Employment by occupation: 21.7% management, 17.4% professional, 4.3% services, 13.0% sales, 17.4% farming, 0.0% construction, 26.1% production (2000).
Income: Per capita income: $17,047 (2000); Median household income: $35,417 (2000); Poverty rate: 6.5% (2000).
Taxes: Total city taxes per capita: $167 (1997); City property taxes per capita: $167 (1997).
Education: High school graduation rate: 100.0% (2000); College graduation rate: 4.2% (2000).
Housing: Homeownership rate: 89.5% (2000); Median home value: $28,800 (2000); Median rent: $275 per month (2000); Median age of housing: 52 years (2000).
Transportation: Commute to work: 91.3% car, 0.0% public transportation, 8.7% walk, 0.0% work from home (2000); Travel time to work: 8.7% less than 15 minutes, 69.6% 15 to 30 minutes, 0.0% 30 to 45 minutes, 21.7% 45 to 60 minutes, 0.0% 60 minutes or more (2000)

RADCLIFFE (city). Covers a land area of 1.004 square miles and a water area of 0 square miles. Located at 42.31° N. Lat.; 93.43° W. Long.
History: Radcliffe was founded in 1884 for the Toledo & North Western Railroad.
Population: 607 (2000); Race: 91.7% White, 0.0% Black, 0.0% Asian, 0.0% American Indian and Alaska Native, 9.0% Hispanic of any race, 1.0% two or more races (2000); Density: 604.3 persons per square mile (2000); Age: 24.9% under 18, 26.3% over 64 (2000); Marriage status: 21.8% never married, 64.2% now married, 8.5% widowed, 5.5% divorced (2000); Foreign born: 3.5% (2000); Ancestry (includes multiple ancestries): 41.9% German, 31.3% Norwegian, 14.3% Other groups, 7.4% English, 6.1% Swedish (2000).
Economy: Single-family building permits issued: 0 (2001) / 0 (2000); Multi-family building permits issued: 0 (2001) / 0 (2000); Employment by occupation: 14.8% management, 12.7% professional, 21.3% services, 24.4% sales, 0.7% farming, 6.5% construction, 19.6% production (2000).
Income: Per capita income: $18,729 (2000); Median household income: $39,417 (2000); Poverty rate: 1.1% (2000).
Taxes: Total city taxes per capita: $164 (1997); City property taxes per capita: $112 (1997).
Education: High school graduation rate: 90.4% (2000); College graduation rate: 16.2% (2000).
Housing: Homeownership rate: 78.4% (2000); Median home value: $63,200 (2000); Median rent: $328 per month (2000); Median age of housing: 48 years (2000).
Transportation: Commute to work: 92.9% car, 0.0% public transportation, 2.1% walk, 4.9% work from home (2000); Travel time to work: 38.3% less than 15 minutes, 27.1% 15 to 30 minutes, 23.8% 30 to 45 minutes, 5.2% 45 to 60 minutes, 5.6% 60 minutes or more (2000)

STEAMBOAT ROCK (city). Covers a land area of 0.544 square miles and a water area of 0 square miles. Located at 42.40° N. Lat.; 93.06° W. Long. Elevation is 978 feet.
History: Steamboat Rock was named for a geographical feature on the river at the site of the town.
Population: 336 (2000); Race: 92.1% White, 2.4% Black, 0.0% Asian, 0.0% American Indian and Alaska Native, 8.2% Hispanic of any race, 1.2% two or more races (2000); Density: 617.6 persons per square mile (2000); Age: 25.8% under 18, 18.8% over 64 (2000); Marriage status: 20.9% never married, 57.3% now married, 11.9% widowed, 9.9% divorced (2000); Foreign born: 6.7% (2000); Ancestry (includes multiple ancestries): 48.6% German, 10.6% English, 10.0% Other groups, 5.5% Irish, 5.5% Norwegian (2000).
Economy: Employment by occupation: 10.5% management, 31.6% professional, 9.0% services, 18.0% sales, 0.0% farming, 11.3% construction, 19.5% production (2000).
Income: Per capita income: $13,777 (2000); Median household income: $28,125 (2000); Poverty rate: 14.6% (2000).
Taxes: Total city taxes per capita: $179 (1997); City property taxes per capita: $134 (1997).
Education: High school graduation rate: 80.0% (2000); College graduation rate: 15.3% (2000).
Housing: Homeownership rate: 67.4% (2000); Median home value: $34,000 (2000); Median rent: $232 per month (2000); Median age of housing: 55 years (2000).
Transportation: Commute to work: 95.5% car, 0.0% public transportation, 2.3% walk, 0.8% work from home (2000); Travel time to work: 48.5% less than 15 minutes, 36.4% 15 to 30 minutes, 6.1% 30 to 45 minutes, 3.0% 45 to 60 minutes, 6.1% 60 minutes or more (2000)

UNION (city). Covers a land area of 0.553 square miles and a water area of 0 square miles. Located at 42.24° N. Lat.; 93.06° W. Long. Elevation is 933 feet.
History: Union is believed to have been named at the time of the Civil War, reflecting the patriotic feeling of the day.
Population: 427 (2000); Race: 100.0% White, 0.0% Black, 0.0% Asian, 0.0% American Indian and Alaska Native, 0.0% Hispanic of any race, 0.0% two or more races (2000); Density: 772.8 persons per square mile (2000); Age: 24.9% under 18, 22.4% over 64 (2000); Marriage status: 17.8% never married, 62.6% now married, 12.6% widowed, 7.0% divorced (2000); Foreign born: 0.5% (2000); Ancestry (includes multiple ancestries): 29.3% German, 10.9% English, 9.5% Irish, 9.2% United States or American, 7.4% Norwegian (2000).
Economy: Single-family building permits issued: 1 (2001) / 1 (2000); Multi-family building permits issued: 0 (2001) / 0 (2000); Employment by occupation: 10.5% management, 8.1% professional, 12.0% services, 17.2% sales, 1.9% farming, 5.3% construction, 45.0% production (2000).
Income: Per capita income: $16,370 (2000); Median household income: $34,792 (2000); Poverty rate: 12.0% (2000).
Taxes: Total city taxes per capita: $207 (1997); City property taxes per capita: $193 (1997).
Education: High school graduation rate: 86.4% (2000); College graduation rate: 14.6% (2000).
Housing: Homeownership rate: 72.7% (2000); Median home value: $46,100 (2000); Median rent: $257 per month (2000); Median age of housing: 44 years (2000).
Transportation: Commute to work: 87.9% car, 1.5% public transportation, 8.7% walk, 1.9% work from home (2000); Travel time to work: 27.2% less than 15 minutes, 40.6% 15 to 30 minutes, 19.3% 30 to 45 minutes, 7.4% 45 to 60 minutes, 5.4% 60 minutes or more (2000)

WHITTEN (city). Covers a land area of 0.545 square miles and a water area of 0.003 square miles. Located at 42.26° N. Lat.; 93.00° W. Long. Elevation is 1,041 feet.

History: The town of Whitten was named for C. C. Whitten. He was instrumental in getting the Chicago & North Western Railroad through the area.
Population: 160 (2000); Race: 98.7% White, 0.0% Black, 1.3% Asian, 0.0% American Indian and Alaska Native, 0.0% Hispanic of any race, 0.0% two or more races (2000); Density: 293.6 persons per square mile (2000); Age: 40.5% under 18, 9.5% over 64 (2000); Marriage status: 18.9% never married, 60.4% now married, 3.8% widowed, 17.0% divorced (2000); Foreign born: 1.3% (2000); Ancestry (includes multiple ancestries): 35.4% German, 16.5% Irish, 8.9% United States or American, 8.2% English, 8.2% Norwegian (2000).
Economy: Employment by occupation: 3.8% management, 9.0% professional, 23.1% services, 16.7% sales, 0.0% farming, 9.0% construction, 38.5% production (2000).
Income: Per capita income: $13,996 (2000); Median household income: $42,656 (2000); Poverty rate: 1.3% (2000).
Taxes: Total city taxes per capita: $104 (1997); City property taxes per capita: $96 (1997).
Education: High school graduation rate: 85.2% (2000); College graduation rate: 8.0% (2000).
Housing: Homeownership rate: 88.9% (2000); Median home value: $34,400 (2000); Median rent: $413 per month (2000); Median age of housing: 60+ years (2000).
Transportation: Commute to work: 89.7% car, 0.0% public transportation, 6.4% walk, 3.8% work from home (2000); Travel time to work: 29.3% less than 15 minutes, 53.3% 15 to 30 minutes, 12.0% 30 to 45 minutes, 0.0% 45 to 60 minutes, 5.3% 60 minutes or more (2000)

Harrison County

Located in western Iowa; bounded on the west by the Missouri River and the Nebraska border; prairie area, drained by the Boyer and Soldier Rivers. Covers a land area of 696.70 square miles, a water area of 4.20 square miles, and is located in the Central Time Zone. The county government was organized in 1851. County seat is Logan.

Weather Station: Logan — Elevation: 987 feet

	Jan	Feb	Mar	Apr	May	Jun	Jul	Aug	Sep	Oct	Nov	Dec
High	30	37	49	63	74	84	87	85	77	65	48	34
Low	10	16	27	39	50	60	64	62	52	39	27	15
Precip	0.8	0.8	2.3	3.2	4.6	4.4	4.1	3.5	3.6	2.6	1.7	1.0
Snow	7.7	6.8	6.1	1.9	0.0	0.0	0.0	0.0	tr	0.9	3.6	6.7

High and Low temperatures in degrees Fahrenheit; Precipitation and Snow in inches

Population: 15,666 (2000); Race: 98.7% White, 0.2% Black, 0.3% Asian, 0.4% American Indian and Alaska Native, 0.5% Hispanic of any race, 0.3% two or more races (2000); Density: 22.5 persons per square mile (2000); Age: 26.2% under 18, 17.7% over 64 (2000).
Religion: Five largest groups: 14.5% Catholic Church, 9.6% The United Methodist Church, 6.0% Christian Churches and Churches of Christ, 5.6% Lutheran Church—Missouri Synod, 4.8% Evangelical Lutheran Church in America (2000).
Economy: Unemployment rate: 3.4% (11/2002); Total civilian labor force: 7,595 (11/2002); Leading industries: 21.0% retail trade; 20.4% health care and social assistance; 12.9% accommodation & food services (2000); Companies that employ more than 1,000 persons: 0 (2000); Companies that employ more than 100 persons: 6 (2000); Farms: 876 totaling 392,708 acres (1997); Minority business ownership rate: 0.0% (1997); Women business ownership rate: 26.7% (1997); Retail sales per capita: $10,919 (1997). Single-family building permits issued: 50 (2001) / 69 (2000); Multi-family building permits issued: 6 (2001) / 4 (2000).
Income: Per capita income: $17,662 (2000); Median household income: $38,141 (2000); Poverty rate: 7.1% (2000); Bankruptcy rate: 3.52% (2001).
Taxes: Total county taxes per capita: $306 (2000); County property taxes per capita: $271 (2000).
Education: High school graduation rate: 85.0% (2000); College graduation rate: 12.7% (2000).
Housing: Homeownership rate: 76.6% (2000); Median home value: $74,900 (2000); Median rent: $305 per month (2000); Median age of housing: 59 years (2000).
Health: Birth rate: 106.0 per 10,000 population (1998); Age adjusted death rate: 100.2 per 10,000 population (1999); Age adjusted cancer mortality rate: 244.8 deaths per 100,000 population (1999). Air Quality Index: 81% good, 19% moderate, 0% unhealthy (percent of days in 2000). Number of physicians: 5.1 per 10,000 population (1999); Number of hospital beds: 16.0 per 10,000 population (1999).
Elections: 2000 Presidential election results: 39.0% Gore, 58.1% Bush, 1.9% Nader, 0.5% Buchanan
National and State Parks: California Bend State Wildlife Refuge; Deer Island State Game Management Area; Nobles Lake State Wildlife Management Area; Round Lake State Wildlife Management Area; Tyson Island State Wildlife Management Area
Additional Information Contacts
Harrison County Government Offices 712-644-2401
Missouri Valley Chamber of Commerce 712-642-2553

Harrison County Communities

DUNLAP (city). Covers a land area of 1.091 square miles and a water area of 0.014 square miles. Located at 41.85° N. Lat.; 95.60° W. Long. Elevation is 1,158 feet.
History: Dunlap was named for George L. Dunlap, a railroad official. The site first attracted settlers because the view was unobstructed for 10 miles up and down the valley of the Boyer River.
Population: 1,139 (2000); Race: 99.3% White, 0.3% Black, 0.0% Asian, 0.0% American Indian and Alaska Native, 0.7% Hispanic of any race, 0.2% two or more races (2000); Density: 1,043.9 persons per square mile (2000); Age: 21.7% under 18, 27.4% over 64 (2000); Marriage status: 19.4% never married, 55.8% now married, 12.4% widowed, 12.5% divorced (2000); Foreign born: 0.3% (2000); Ancestry (includes multiple ancestries): 39.5% German, 18.2% Irish, 16.7% English, 6.5% United States or American, 4.9% Danish (2000).
Economy: Single-family building permits issued: 2 (2001) / 4 (2000); Multi-family building permits issued: 0 (2001) / 4 (2000); Employment by occupation: 9.0% management, 16.8% professional, 14.3% services, 23.8% sales, 2.3% farming, 10.9% construction, 22.8% production (2000).
Income: Per capita income: $17,936 (2000); Median household income: $31,100 (2000); Poverty rate: 10.5% (2000).
Taxes: Total city taxes per capita: $169 (1997); City property taxes per capita: $166 (1997).
Education: High school graduation rate: 81.9% (2000); College graduation rate: 12.4% (2000).

School District(s)

Boyer Valley Community School District (PK-12)
2000 Enrollment: 600 712-643-2251
Housing: Homeownership rate: 76.8% (2000); Median home value: $48,000 (2000); Median rent: $273 per month (2000); Median age of housing: 60+ years (2000).
Newspapers: Dunlap Reporter (1 x week)
Transportation: Commute to work: 91.0% car, 0.0% public transportation, 3.6% walk, 5.1% work from home (2000); Travel time to work: 47.4% less than 15 minutes, 24.0% 15 to 30 minutes, 8.9% 30 to 45 minutes, 5.4% 45 to 60 minutes, 14.3% 60 minutes or more (2000)

LITTLE SIOUX (city). Covers a land area of 0.350 square miles and a water area of 0 square miles. Located at 41.80° N. Lat.; 96.02° W. Long. Elevation is 1,033 feet.
History: Little Sioux was named after the river of the same name.
Population: 217 (2000); Race: 99.6% White, 0.0% Black, 0.0% Asian, 0.0% American Indian and Alaska Native, 0.4% Hispanic of any race, 0.0% two or more races (2000); Density: 620.2 persons per square mile (2000); Age: 22.2% under 18, 23.1% over 64 (2000); Marriage status: 18.6% never married, 62.2% now married, 8.0% widowed, 11.2% divorced (2000); Foreign born: 0.9% (2000); Ancestry (includes multiple ancestries): 26.7% German, 12.4% Irish, 10.7% English, 6.2% Norwegian, 5.8% Swedish (2000).
Economy: Single-family building permits issued: 0 (2001) / 0 (2000); Multi-family building permits issued: 0 (2001) / 0 (2000); Employment by occupation: 11.0% management, 4.0% professional, 20.0% services, 16.0% sales, 3.0% farming, 17.0% construction, 29.0% production (2000).
Income: Per capita income: $20,410 (2000); Median household income: $28,583 (2000); Poverty rate: 17.8% (2000).
Taxes: Total city taxes per capita: $129 (1997); City property taxes per capita: $124 (1997).
Education: High school graduation rate: 76.7% (2000); College graduation rate: 4.4% (2000).
Housing: Homeownership rate: 83.0% (2000); Median home value: $37,100 (2000); Median rent: $188 per month (2000); Median age of housing: 60+ years (2000).
Transportation: Commute to work: 100.0% car, 0.0% public transportation, 0.0% walk, 0.0% work from home (2000); Travel time to work: 15.2% less

than 15 minutes, 14.1% 15 to 30 minutes, 17.2% 30 to 45 minutes, 28.3% 45 to 60 minutes, 25.3% 60 minutes or more (2000)

LOGAN (city). Covers a land area of 1.015 square miles and a water area of 0 square miles. Located at 41.64° N. Lat.; 95.79° W. Long. Elevation is 1,104 feet.

History: Logan was formerly known as Boyer Falls because of its proximity to the falls on the river. The name was changed in 1864 to honor General John A. Logan, an officer in the Civil War.

Population: 1,545 (2000); Race: 98.8% White, 0.5% Black, 0.0% Asian, 0.2% American Indian and Alaska Native, 0.5% Hispanic of any race, 0.3% two or more races (2000); Density: 1,522.8 persons per square mile (2000); Age: 28.1% under 18, 21.5% over 64 (2000); Marriage status: 20.6% never married, 57.9% now married, 13.3% widowed, 8.2% divorced (2000); Foreign born: 0.3% (2000); Ancestry (includes multiple ancestries): 41.1% German, 15.8% English, 15.0% Irish, 7.2% United States or American, 4.7% Other groups (2000).

Economy: Single-family building permits issued: 1 (2001) / 4 (2000); Multi-family building permits issued: 0 (2001) / 0 (2000); Employment by occupation: 9.9% management, 14.8% professional, 17.6% services, 26.1% sales, 1.0% farming, 11.0% construction, 19.5% production (2000).

Income: Per capita income: $18,709 (2000); Median household income: $35,455 (2000); Poverty rate: 9.5% (2000).

Taxes: Total city taxes per capita: $305 (1997); City property taxes per capita: $301 (1997).

Education: High school graduation rate: 83.9% (2000); College graduation rate: 13.6% (2000).

School District(s)

Logan-Magnolia Community School District (PK-12)
2000 Enrollment: 719 712-644-2250

Housing: Homeownership rate: 75.9% (2000); Median home value: $78,300 (2000); Median rent: $317 per month (2000); Median age of housing: 60+ years (2000).

Newspapers: The Logan Herald-Observer (1 x week)

Transportation: Commute to work: 89.4% car, 0.0% public transportation, 6.2% walk, 3.0% work from home (2000); Travel time to work: 45.8% less than 15 minutes, 14.5% 15 to 30 minutes, 18.4% 30 to 45 minutes, 17.0% 45 to 60 minutes, 4.3% 60 minutes or more (2000)

MAGNOLIA (city). Covers a land area of 0.583 square miles and a water area of 0 square miles. Located at 41.69° N. Lat.; 95.87° W. Long. Elevation is 1,300 feet.

History: Magnolia gets its name from the magnolia tree.

Population: 200 (2000); Race: 100.0% White, 0.0% Black, 0.0% Asian, 0.0% American Indian and Alaska Native, 0.0% Hispanic of any race, 0.0% two or more races (2000); Density: 343.2 persons per square mile (2000); Age: 23.7% under 18, 19.1% over 64 (2000); Marriage status: 15.4% never married, 73.5% now married, 5.9% widowed, 5.1% divorced (2000); Foreign born: 0.0% (2000); Ancestry (includes multiple ancestries): 31.2% German, 17.3% Irish, 13.9% English, 6.9% Norwegian, 4.6% Swedish (2000).

Economy: Employment by occupation: 2.3% management, 11.6% professional, 8.1% services, 25.6% sales, 3.5% farming, 24.4% construction, 24.4% production (2000).

Income: Per capita income: $16,533 (2000); Median household income: $30,625 (2000); Poverty rate: 11.0% (2000).

Taxes: Total city taxes per capita: $133 (1997); City property taxes per capita: $128 (1997).

Education: High school graduation rate: 76.7% (2000); College graduation rate: 7.5% (2000).

Housing: Homeownership rate: 90.9% (2000); Median home value: $50,000 (2000); Median rent: $413 per month (2000); Median age of housing: 60+ years (2000).

Transportation: Commute to work: 97.7% car, 0.0% public transportation, 2.3% walk, 0.0% work from home (2000); Travel time to work: 22.1% less than 15 minutes, 15.1% 15 to 30 minutes, 4.7% 30 to 45 minutes, 34.9% 45 to 60 minutes, 23.3% 60 minutes or more (2000)

MISSOURI VALLEY (city). Covers a land area of 3.044 square miles and a water area of 0 square miles. Located at 41.55° N. Lat.; 95.89° W. Long. Elevation is 1,019 feet.

History: The first settler in Missouri Valley was H. B. Henricks, who arrived in 1854. In 1856 the McIntosh brothers came, and the place was first named McIntosh Point, and later St. Johns. When the Chicago & North Western Railroad was built through the area, the name was changed to Missouri Valley.

Population: 2,992 (2000); Race: 99.1% White, 0.2% Black, 0.7% Asian, 0.0% American Indian and Alaska Native, 0.0% Hispanic of any race, 0.0% two or more races (2000); Density: 982.9 persons per square mile (2000); Age: 24.3% under 18, 18.6% over 64 (2000); Marriage status: 19.2% never married, 59.2% now married, 11.0% widowed, 10.5% divorced (2000); Foreign born: 1.3% (2000); Ancestry (includes multiple ancestries): 42.2% German, 23.5% Irish, 14.4% English, 6.2% United States or American, 5.0% Danish (2000).

Economy: Single-family building permits issued: 1 (2001) / 2 (2000); Multi-family building permits issued: 0 (2001) / 0 (2000); Employment by occupation: 10.4% management, 15.2% professional, 17.6% services, 31.4% sales, 0.2% farming, 8.8% construction, 16.3% production (2000).

Income: Per capita income: $18,031 (2000); Median household income: $36,594 (2000); Poverty rate: 5.6% (2000).

Taxes: Total city taxes per capita: $210 (1997); City property taxes per capita: $202 (1997).

Education: High school graduation rate: 83.7% (2000); College graduation rate: 11.6% (2000).

School District(s)

Missouri Valley Community School District (PK-12)
2000 Enrollment: 963 712-642-2706

Housing: Homeownership rate: 66.1% (2000); Median home value: $74,500 (2000); Median rent: $353 per month (2000); Median age of housing: 59 years (2000).

Hospitals: Alegent Health Community Memorial Hospital (25 beds)

Newspapers: Harrison County Merchandiser (1 x week); Missouri Valley Times-News (2 x week)

Transportation: Commute to work: 92.8% car, 0.3% public transportation, 4.5% walk, 2.0% work from home (2000); Travel time to work: 39.4% less than 15 minutes, 21.0% 15 to 30 minutes, 30.9% 30 to 45 minutes, 5.9% 45 to 60 minutes, 2.7% 60 minutes or more (2000)

Additional Information Contacts

Missouri Valley Chamber of Commerce 712-642-2553

MODALE (city). Covers a land area of 1.082 square miles and a water area of 0 square miles. Located at 41.62° N. Lat.; 96.01° W. Long. Elevation is 1,013 feet.

History: The town of Modale was mapped in 1870 and was originally called Martinsville. Four years later the name was changed to Modale.

Population: 303 (2000); Race: 99.0% White, 0.0% Black, 0.0% Asian, 0.0% American Indian and Alaska Native, 0.0% Hispanic of any race, 0.0% two or more races (2000); Density: 280.0 persons per square mile (2000); Age: 21.4% under 18, 21.4% over 64 (2000); Marriage status: 13.6% never married, 62.8% now married, 10.8% widowed, 12.8% divorced (2000); Foreign born: 0.7% (2000); Ancestry (includes multiple ancestries): 25.4% German, 21.1% Irish, 13.0% United States or American, 12.0% English, 7.7% Swedish (2000).

Economy: Single-family building permits issued: 1 (2001) / 1 (2000); Multi-family building permits issued: 0 (2001) / 0 (2000); Employment by occupation: 17.0% management, 11.9% professional, 17.6% services, 23.3% sales, 0.0% farming, 10.1% construction, 20.1% production (2000).

Income: Per capita income: $19,111 (2000); Median household income: $34,688 (2000); Poverty rate: 10.0% (2000).

Taxes: Total city taxes per capita: $200 (1997); City property taxes per capita: $197 (1997).

Education: High school graduation rate: 75.5% (2000); College graduation rate: 7.9% (2000).

Housing: Homeownership rate: 83.3% (2000); Median home value: $63,400 (2000); Median rent: $163 per month (2000); Median age of housing: 44 years (2000).

Transportation: Commute to work: 92.9% car, 0.0% public transportation, 7.1% walk, 0.0% work from home (2000); Travel time to work: 27.6% less than 15 minutes, 25.0% 15 to 30 minutes, 23.1% 30 to 45 minutes, 24.4% 45 to 60 minutes, 0.0% 60 minutes or more (2000)

MONDAMIN (city). Covers a land area of 0.462 square miles and a water area of 0 square miles. Located at 41.71° N. Lat.; 96.02° W. Long. Elevation is 1,025 feet.

History: Mondamin, which comes from an Indian word for "corn," was platted as a railroad town in 1867-68.

Population: 423 (2000); Race: 98.7% White, 0.0% Black, 0.0% Asian, 0.0% American Indian and Alaska Native, 0.0% Hispanic of any race, 1.3% two or more races (2000); Density: 915.0 persons per square mile (2000); Age: 28.2% under 18, 14.8% over 64 (2000); Marriage status: 18.1% never married, 67.5% now married, 7.4% widowed, 7.1% divorced (2000); Foreign born: 0.4% (2000); Ancestry (includes multiple ancestries): 35.1% German,

16.3% English, 12.1% United States or American, 10.3% Irish, 6.3% Dutch (2000).
Economy: Single-family building permits issued: 1 (2001) / 1 (2000); Multi-family building permits issued: 0 (2001) / 0 (2000); Employment by occupation: 10.0% management, 14.0% professional, 16.5% services, 15.0% sales, 3.0% farming, 19.0% construction, 22.5% production (2000).
Income: Per capita income: $18,123 (2000); Median household income: $40,278 (2000); Poverty rate: 3.1% (2000).
Taxes: Total city taxes per capita: $113 (1997); City property taxes per capita: $111 (1997).
Education: High school graduation rate: 79.8% (2000); College graduation rate: 13.5% (2000).

School District(s)

West Harrison Community School District (KG-12)
2000 Enrollment: 497 712-646-2231
Housing: Homeownership rate: 78.2% (2000); Median home value: $66,300 (2000); Median rent: $281 per month (2000); Median age of housing: 49 years (2000).
Transportation: Commute to work: 90.1% car, 0.0% public transportation, 6.9% walk, 1.5% work from home (2000); Travel time to work: 24.6% less than 15 minutes, 18.1% 15 to 30 minutes, 19.1% 30 to 45 minutes, 20.6% 45 to 60 minutes, 17.6% 60 minutes or more (2000)

PERSIA (city). Covers a land area of 0.457 square miles and a water area of 0 square miles. Located at 41.57° N. Lat.; 95.57° W. Long. Elevation is 1,273 feet.
History: The name of Persia may refer to Persian immigrant construction workers on the railroad in that area.
Population: 363 (2000); Race: 99.7% White, 0.0% Black, 0.0% Asian, 0.0% American Indian and Alaska Native, 0.3% Hispanic of any race, 0.3% two or more races (2000); Density: 794.9 persons per square mile (2000); Age: 28.9% under 18, 16.2% over 64 (2000); Marriage status: 20.4% never married, 62.9% now married, 10.7% widowed, 6.1% divorced (2000); Foreign born: 1.3% (2000); Ancestry (includes multiple ancestries): 31.0% German, 10.1% Irish, 10.1% Polish, 9.8% English, 6.4% Danish (2000).
Economy: Single-family building permits issued: 0 (2001) / 1 (2000); Multi-family building permits issued: 0 (2001) / 0 (2000); Employment by occupation: 12.4% management, 10.7% professional, 16.0% services, 16.6% sales, 2.4% farming, 19.5% construction, 22.5% production (2000).
Income: Per capita income: $14,859 (2000); Median household income: $36,563 (2000); Poverty rate: 10.0% (2000).
Taxes: Total city taxes per capita: $126 (1997); City property taxes per capita: $126 (1997).
Education: High school graduation rate: 84.2% (2000); College graduation rate: 10.1% (2000).
Housing: Homeownership rate: 78.5% (2000); Median home value: $59,600 (2000); Median rent: $381 per month (2000); Median age of housing: 60+ years (2000).
Transportation: Commute to work: 94.9% car, 0.0% public transportation, 0.0% walk, 3.8% work from home (2000); Travel time to work: 6.7% less than 15 minutes, 14.7% 15 to 30 minutes, 32.7% 30 to 45 minutes, 36.7% 45 to 60 minutes, 9.3% 60 minutes or more (2000)

PISGAH (city). Covers a land area of 1.005 square miles and a water area of 0 square miles. Located at 41.83° N. Lat.; 95.92° W. Long. Elevation is 1,060 feet.
History: Pisgah was plotted in 1899 by the Western Town Lot Company with the arrival of the Chicago & North Western Railroad.
Population: 316 (2000); Race: 98.7% White, 0.0% Black, 0.0% Asian, 0.3% American Indian and Alaska Native, 0.9% Hispanic of any race, 0.6% two or more races (2000); Density: 314.4 persons per square mile (2000); Age: 25.3% under 18, 31.6% over 64 (2000); Marriage status: 9.4% never married, 60.4% now married, 16.5% widowed, 13.7% divorced (2000); Foreign born: 0.0% (2000); Ancestry (includes multiple ancestries): 26.3% German, 13.3% Other groups, 12.0% English, 12.0% Irish, 8.2% United States or American (2000).
Economy: Employment by occupation: 6.2% management, 5.4% professional, 25.6% services, 21.7% sales, 0.0% farming, 15.5% construction, 25.6% production (2000).
Income: Per capita income: $13,837 (2000); Median household income: $26,125 (2000); Poverty rate: 15.5% (2000).
Taxes: Total city taxes per capita: $158 (1997); City property taxes per capita: $155 (1997).
Education: High school graduation rate: 84.3% (2000); College graduation rate: 7.4% (2000).
Housing: Homeownership rate: 77.2% (2000); Median home value: $39,400 (2000); Median rent: $263 per month (2000); Median age of housing: 60+ years (2000).
Transportation: Commute to work: 90.7% car, 0.0% public transportation, 6.2% walk, 1.6% work from home (2000); Travel time to work: 20.5% less than 15 minutes, 22.0% 15 to 30 minutes, 10.2% 30 to 45 minutes, 24.4% 45 to 60 minutes, 22.8% 60 minutes or more (2000)

WOODBINE (city). Covers a land area of 1.132 square miles and a water area of 0 square miles. Located at 41.73° N. Lat.; 95.70° W. Long. Elevation is 1,078 feet.
History: Woodbine was named by Mrs. Ann Butler, an Englishwoman, around whose home woodbine grew in profusion. The Woodbine Normal School was established in 1887.
Population: 1,564 (2000); Race: 96.8% White, 0.0% Black, 0.3% Asian, 2.0% American Indian and Alaska Native, 0.5% Hispanic of any race, 0.8% two or more races (2000); Density: 1,381.1 persons per square mile (2000); Age: 24.1% under 18, 27.4% over 64 (2000); Marriage status: 18.2% never married, 59.6% now married, 15.1% widowed, 7.0% divorced (2000); Foreign born: 0.6% (2000); Ancestry (includes multiple ancestries): 36.5% German, 17.3% English, 13.9% Irish, 9.0% Other groups, 7.0% Danish (2000).
Economy: Single-family building permits issued: 3 (2001) / 2 (2000); Multi-family building permits issued: 4 (2001) / 0 (2000); Employment by occupation: 11.0% management, 14.8% professional, 15.7% services, 25.3% sales, 0.3% farming, 15.3% construction, 17.6% production (2000).
Income: Per capita income: $15,117 (2000); Median household income: $30,083 (2000); Poverty rate: 10.4% (2000).
Taxes: Total city taxes per capita: $195 (1997); City property taxes per capita: $195 (1997).
Education: High school graduation rate: 85.0% (2000); College graduation rate: 12.7% (2000).

School District(s)

Woodbine Community School District (PK-12)
2000 Enrollment: 560 712-647-2411
Housing: Homeownership rate: 70.4% (2000); Median home value: $72,500 (2000); Median rent: $300 per month (2000); Median age of housing: 60+ years (2000).
Newspapers: The Woodbine Twiner (1 x week)
Transportation: Commute to work: 89.7% car, 0.0% public transportation, 5.6% walk, 4.0% work from home (2000); Travel time to work: 54.8% less than 15 minutes, 16.1% 15 to 30 minutes, 9.0% 30 to 45 minutes, 10.9% 45 to 60 minutes, 9.2% 60 minutes or more (2000)

Henry County

Located in southeastern Iowa; prairie area, drained by the Skunk River. Covers a land area of 434.40 square miles, a water area of 2.20 square miles, and is located in the Central Time Zone. The county government was organized in 1836. County seat is Mount Pleasant.

Weather Station: Mount Pleasant 1 SSW — Elevation: 728 feet

	Jan	Feb	Mar	Apr	May	Jun	Jul	Aug	Sep	Oct	Nov	Dec
High	30	37	49	63	73	82	86	84	77	65	49	36
Low	13	19	29	41	51	61	65	63	54	43	31	20
Precip	1.3	1.3	2.6	3.3	4.4	4.0	4.7	4.6	4.5	2.7	2.7	1.8
Snow	8.1	5.7	3.0	1.4	0.0	0.0	0.0	0.0	0.0	tr	1.8	5.8

High and Low temperatures in degrees Fahrenheit; Precipitation and Snow in inches

Population: 20,336 (2000); Race: 94.3% White, 1.5% Black, 1.9% Asian, 0.3% American Indian and Alaska Native, 1.6% Hispanic of any race, 1.3% two or more races (2000); Density: 46.8 persons per square mile (2000); Age: 24.6% under 18, 14.8% over 64 (2000).
Religion: Five largest groups: 12.1% The United Methodist Church, 6.7% Catholic Church, 4.9% Independent, Charismatic Churches, 4.2% Presbyterian Church (U.S.A.), 4.0% Mennonite Church USA (2000).
Economy: Unemployment rate: 6.5% (11/2002); Total civilian labor force: 10,354 (11/2002); Leading industries: 22.7% manufacturing; 20.8% administration, support, waste management, remediation services; 8.9% health care and social assistance (2000); Companies that employ more than 1,000 persons: 2 (2000); Companies that employ more than 100 persons: 17 (2000); Farms: 835 totaling 244,704 acres (1997); Minority business ownership rate: 0.0% (1997); Women business ownership rate: 24.7% (1997); Retail sales per capita: $8,161 (1997). Single-family building permits issued: 31 (2001) / 51 (2000); Multi-family building permits issued: 8 (2001) / 4 (2000).

Income: Per capita income: $18,192 (2000); Median household income: $39,087 (2000); Poverty rate: 8.8% (2000); Bankruptcy rate: 4.52% (2001).
Taxes: Total county taxes per capita: $227 (2000); County property taxes per capita: $211 (2000).
Education: High school graduation rate: 86.1% (2000); College graduation rate: 16.2% (2000).
Housing: Homeownership rate: 73.1% (2000); Median home value: $76,700 (2000); Median rent: $334 per month (2000); Median age of housing: 37 years (2000).
Health: Birth rate: 122.9 per 10,000 population (1998); Age adjusted death rate: 83.1 per 10,000 population (1999); Age adjusted cancer mortality rate: 219.5 deaths per 100,000 population (1999). Number of physicians: 8.4 per 10,000 population (1999); Number of hospital beds: 92.4 per 10,000 population (1999).
Elections: 2000 Presidential election results: 45.1% Gore, 51.6% Bush, 2.1% Nader, 0.5% Buchanan
National and State Parks: Geode State Park
Additional Information Contacts
Henry County Government Offices 319-385-0759
Mt Pleasant Chamber of Commerce 319-385-3101

Henry County Communities

COPPOCK (city). Covers a land area of 0.234 square miles and a water area of 0.010 square miles. Located at 41.16° N. Lat.; 91.71° W. Long.
Population: 57 (2000); Race: 100.0% White, 0.0% Black, 0.0% Asian, 0.0% American Indian and Alaska Native, 0.0% Hispanic of any race, 0.0% two or more races (2000); Density: 243.7 persons per square mile (2000); Age: 29.0% under 18, 7.2% over 64 (2000); Marriage status: 26.4% never married, 64.2% now married, 9.4% widowed, 0.0% divorced (2000); Foreign born: 0.0% (2000); Ancestry (includes multiple ancestries): 23.2% United States or American, 14.5% Irish, 8.7% Hungarian, 4.3% Dutch, 2.9% German (2000).
Economy: Employment by occupation: 0.0% management, 13.5% professional, 13.5% services, 27.0% sales, 0.0% farming, 24.3% construction, 21.6% production (2000).
Income: Per capita income: $11,051 (2000); Median household income: $26,750 (2000); Poverty rate: 30.4% (2000).
Taxes: Total city taxes per capita: $38 (1997); City property taxes per capita: $19 (1997).
Education: High school graduation rate: 65.1% (2000); College graduation rate: 0.0% (2000).
Housing: Homeownership rate: 78.3% (2000); Median home value: <$10,000 (2000); Median rent: $275 per month (2000); Median age of housing: 26 years (2000).
Transportation: Commute to work: 100.0% car, 0.0% public transportation, 0.0% walk, 0.0% work from home (2000); Travel time to work: 35.1% less than 15 minutes, 35.1% 15 to 30 minutes, 18.9% 30 to 45 minutes, 5.4% 45 to 60 minutes, 5.4% 60 minutes or more (2000)

HILLSBORO (city). Covers a land area of 0.509 square miles and a water area of 0 square miles. Located at 40.83° N. Lat.; 91.71° W. Long.
History: Hillsboro was first called Washington, then Hillsborough, which was simplified to Hillsboro.
Population: 205 (2000); Race: 98.7% White, 0.0% Black, 0.0% Asian, 0.0% American Indian and Alaska Native, 0.0% Hispanic of any race, 1.3% two or more races (2000); Density: 402.7 persons per square mile (2000); Age: 30.3% under 18, 12.0% over 64 (2000); Marriage status: 25.7% never married, 62.0% now married, 4.5% widowed, 7.8% divorced (2000); Foreign born: 0.0% (2000); Ancestry (includes multiple ancestries): 10.3% United States or American, 8.5% Other groups, 8.5% German, 6.4% English, 3.0% Dutch (2000).
Economy: Employment by occupation: 3.7% management, 11.0% professional, 18.3% services, 11.9% sales, 2.8% farming, 16.5% construction, 35.8% production (2000).
Income: Per capita income: $11,985 (2000); Median household income: $35,500 (2000); Poverty rate: 21.8% (2000).
Taxes: Total city taxes per capita: $115 (1997); City property taxes per capita: $69 (1997).
Education: High school graduation rate: 78.8% (2000); College graduation rate: 3.4% (2000).
Housing: Homeownership rate: 80.5% (2000); Median home value: $41,800 (2000); Median rent: $275 per month (2000); Median age of housing: 60+ years (2000).
Transportation: Commute to work: 90.6% car, 0.0% public transportation, 5.7% walk, 3.8% work from home (2000); Travel time to work: 11.8% less than 15 minutes, 56.9% 15 to 30 minutes, 17.6% 30 to 45 minutes, 6.9% 45 to 60 minutes, 6.9% 60 minutes or more (2000)

MOUNT PLEASANT (city). Covers a land area of 7.695 square miles and a water area of 0.015 square miles. Located at 40.96° N. Lat.; 91.55° W. Long. Elevation is 719 feet.
History: Mount Pleasant was the home of the first courthouse in Iowa, built in 1839.
Population: 8,751 (2000); Race: 90.3% White, 3.3% Black, 3.5% Asian, 0.3% American Indian and Alaska Native, 3.1% Hispanic of any race, 1.5% two or more races (2000); Density: 1,137.3 persons per square mile (2000); Age: 22.9% under 18, 14.1% over 64 (2000); Marriage status: 27.7% never married, 50.9% now married, 8.4% widowed, 13.1% divorced (2000); Foreign born: 3.0% (2000); Ancestry (includes multiple ancestries): 30.8% German, 14.2% Irish, 12.1% Other groups, 10.7% United States or American, 10.6% English (2000).
Economy: Single-family building permits issued: 10 (2001) / 15 (2000); Multi-family building permits issued: 8 (2001) / 0 (2000); Employment by occupation: 9.2% management, 18.9% professional, 15.2% services, 22.8% sales, 0.4% farming, 5.5% construction, 28.0% production (2000).
Income: Per capita income: $16,824 (2000); Median household income: $35,558 (2000); Poverty rate: 10.2% (2000).
Taxes: Total city taxes per capita: $375 (2000); City property taxes per capita: $294 (2000).
Education: High school graduation rate: 84.2% (2000); College graduation rate: 18.1% (2000).

School District(s)
Mount Pleasant Community School District (PK-12)
2000 Enrollment: 2,178 319-385-7750
Mount Pleasant Correctional Facility (N -N)
2000 Enrollment: n/a 319-385-9511

Four-year College(s)
Iowa Wesleyan College (Private, Not-for-profit, United Methodist)
2001 Enrollment: 812 319-385-8021
2001 Tuition: In-state $13,530; Out-of-state $13,530

Housing: Homeownership rate: 65.0% (2000); Median home value: $81,700 (2000); Median rent: $335 per month (2000); Median age of housing: 35 years (2000).
Hospitals: Henry County Health Center (99 beds); Mental Health Institute (40 beds)
Safety: Violent crime rate: 20.6 per 10,000 population; Property crime rate: 86.9 per 10,000 population (2001).
Newspapers: The Mount Pleasant News (5 x week)
Transportation: Commute to work: 90.2% car, 0.7% public transportation, 5.9% walk, 1.9% work from home (2000); Travel time to work: 79.9% less than 15 minutes, 7.6% 15 to 30 minutes, 8.1% 30 to 45 minutes, 1.7% 45 to 60 minutes, 2.7% 60 minutes or more (2000); Amtrak: Service available.
Airports: Mount Pleasant Municipal
Additional Information Contacts
Mt Pleasant Chamber of Commerce 319-385-3101

MOUNT UNION (city). Covers a land area of 0.111 square miles and a water area of 0 square miles. Located at 41.05° N. Lat.; 91.39° W. Long. Elevation is 720 feet.
History: The name Mount Union is believed to be an indication of its slight elevation in a flat area and a symbol of the unity of the community.
Population: 132 (2000); Race: 100.0% White, 0.0% Black, 0.0% Asian, 0.0% American Indian and Alaska Native, 0.0% Hispanic of any race, 0.0% two or more races (2000); Density: 1,188.4 persons per square mile (2000); Age: 34.3% under 18, 5.8% over 64 (2000); Marriage status: 24.2% never married, 61.5% now married, 0.0% widowed, 14.3% divorced (2000); Foreign born: 0.0% (2000); Ancestry (includes multiple ancestries): 49.6% German, 13.1% English, 12.4% Irish, 10.9% Swedish, 6.6% Pennsylvania German (2000).
Economy: Employment by occupation: 9.8% management, 11.5% professional, 11.5% services, 13.1% sales, 0.0% farming, 11.5% construction, 42.6% production (2000).
Income: Per capita income: $12,735 (2000); Median household income: $27,500 (2000); Poverty rate: 21.6% (2000).
Taxes: Total city taxes per capita: $160 (1997); City property taxes per capita: $111 (1997).
Education: High school graduation rate: 88.8% (2000); College graduation rate: 11.3% (2000).
Housing: Homeownership rate: 77.4% (2000); Median home value: $39,600 (2000); Median rent: $475 per month (2000); Median age of housing: 60+ years (2000).

Transportation: Commute to work: 78.0% car, 0.0% public transportation, 6.8% walk, 10.2% work from home (2000); Travel time to work: 15.1% less than 15 minutes, 58.5% 15 to 30 minutes, 18.9% 30 to 45 minutes, 7.5% 45 to 60 minutes, 0.0% 60 minutes or more (2000)

NEW LONDON (city). Covers a land area of 1.006 square miles and a water area of 0 square miles. Located at 40.92° N. Lat.; 91.40° W. Long. Elevation is 768 feet.
History: New London, first named Dover in honor of Abraham C. Dover, owner of the site, was the home of Frank Lundeen, world champion horseshoe pitcher in 1922-23.
Population: 1,937 (2000); Race: 98.0% White, 0.2% Black, 0.2% Asian, 0.0% American Indian and Alaska Native, 0.6% Hispanic of any race, 1.3% two or more races (2000); Density: 1,924.9 persons per square mile (2000); Age: 24.7% under 18, 16.3% over 64 (2000); Marriage status: 19.7% never married, 61.9% now married, 7.6% widowed, 10.9% divorced (2000); Foreign born: 0.4% (2000); Ancestry (includes multiple ancestries): 34.1% German, 12.3% Irish, 9.7% English, 4.9% United States or American, 4.8% Other groups (2000).
Economy: Single-family building permits issued: 0 (2001) / 1 (2000); Multi-family building permits issued: 0 (2001) / 0 (2000); Employment by occupation: 9.4% management, 13.1% professional, 15.0% services, 19.6% sales, 0.6% farming, 11.5% construction, 30.7% production (2000).
Income: Per capita income: $18,301 (2000); Median household income: $39,432 (2000); Poverty rate: 6.4% (2000).
Taxes: Total city taxes per capita: $191 (1997); City property taxes per capita: $142 (1997).
Education: High school graduation rate: 88.8% (2000); College graduation rate: 15.0% (2000).

School District(s)

New London Community School District (KG-12)
2000 Enrollment: 574 319-367-0512
Housing: Homeownership rate: 75.4% (2000); Median home value: $61,900 (2000); Median rent: $353 per month (2000); Median age of housing: 44 years (2000).
Newspapers: New London Journal (1 x week)
Transportation: Commute to work: 96.1% car, 0.0% public transportation, 2.5% walk, 0.8% work from home (2000); Travel time to work: 41.5% less than 15 minutes, 43.7% 15 to 30 minutes, 10.2% 30 to 45 minutes, 1.2% 45 to 60 minutes, 3.3% 60 minutes or more (2000)

OLDS (city). Covers a land area of 0.297 square miles and a water area of 0 square miles. Located at 41.13° N. Lat.; 91.54° W. Long.
History: Olds was named for a landowner who donated property for the town with the stipulation the town be named for him.
Population: 249 (2000); Race: 94.1% White, 0.8% Black, 0.0% Asian, 2.5% American Indian and Alaska Native, 2.1% Hispanic of any race, 0.8% two or more races (2000); Density: 839.5 persons per square mile (2000); Age: 31.0% under 18, 7.9% over 64 (2000); Marriage status: 26.5% never married, 58.2% now married, 5.9% widowed, 9.4% divorced (2000); Foreign born: 2.1% (2000); Ancestry (includes multiple ancestries): 31.4% German, 19.7% Irish, 15.1% Other groups, 10.5% United States or American, 6.7% Swedish (2000).
Economy: Single-family building permits issued: 1 (2001) / 0 (2000); Multi-family building permits issued: 0 (2001) / 0 (2000); Employment by occupation: 11.7% management, 12.6% professional, 12.6% services, 24.3% sales, 2.7% farming, 18.9% construction, 17.1% production (2000).
Income: Per capita income: $13,760 (2000); Median household income: $31,875 (2000); Poverty rate: 9.0% (2000).
Taxes: Total city taxes per capita: $176 (1997); City property taxes per capita: $127 (1997).
Education: High school graduation rate: 90.7% (2000); College graduation rate: 11.6% (2000).
Housing: Homeownership rate: 51.5% (2000); Median home value: $48,300 (2000); Median rent: $347 per month (2000); Median age of housing: 55 years (2000).
Transportation: Commute to work: 89.0% car, 0.0% public transportation, 2.8% walk, 8.3% work from home (2000); Travel time to work: 22.0% less than 15 minutes, 45.0% 15 to 30 minutes, 14.0% 30 to 45 minutes, 10.0% 45 to 60 minutes, 9.0% 60 minutes or more (2000)

ROME (city). Covers a land area of 0.130 square miles and a water area of <.001 square miles. Located at 40.98° N. Lat.; 91.68° W. Long.
History: Rome was settled in 1836.
Population: 113 (2000); Race: 96.7% White, 0.0% Black, 0.0% Asian, 0.0% American Indian and Alaska Native, 0.0% Hispanic of any race, 3.3% two or more races (2000); Density: 870.5 persons per square mile (2000); Age: 16.3% under 18, 4.3% over 64 (2000); Marriage status: 33.3% never married, 38.5% now married, 5.1% widowed, 23.1% divorced (2000); Foreign born: 0.0% (2000); Ancestry (includes multiple ancestries): 40.2% United States or American, 31.5% German, 7.6% Other groups, 4.3% Italian, 3.3% Irish (2000).
Economy: Employment by occupation: 9.6% management, 1.9% professional, 13.5% services, 19.2% sales, 0.0% farming, 7.7% construction, 48.1% production (2000).
Income: Per capita income: $12,976 (2000); Median household income: $22,083 (2000); Poverty rate: 27.0% (2000).
Taxes: Total city taxes per capita: $90 (1997); City property taxes per capita: $45 (1997).
Education: High school graduation rate: 85.5% (2000); College graduation rate: 4.8% (2000).
Housing: Homeownership rate: 77.6% (2000); Median home value: $55,000 (2000); Median rent: $313 per month (2000); Median age of housing: 31 years (2000).
Transportation: Commute to work: 90.4% car, 0.0% public transportation, 3.8% walk, 5.8% work from home (2000); Travel time to work: 32.7% less than 15 minutes, 61.2% 15 to 30 minutes, 2.0% 30 to 45 minutes, 4.1% 45 to 60 minutes, 0.0% 60 minutes or more (2000)

SALEM (city). Covers a land area of 0.608 square miles and a water area of 0.004 square miles. Located at 40.85° N. Lat.; 91.62° W. Long. Elevation is 717 feet.
History: Salem was settled about 1835 by Quakers from North and South Carolina, and later from Ohio, Illinois, and Indiana. It was the earliest Quaker settlement west of the Mississippi. Residents were active in assisting slaves to escape by means of the Underground Railroad.
Population: 464 (2000); Race: 99.3% White, 0.0% Black, 0.7% Asian, 0.0% American Indian and Alaska Native, 0.7% Hispanic of any race, 0.0% two or more races (2000); Density: 763.7 persons per square mile (2000); Age: 24.3% under 18, 21.6% over 64 (2000); Marriage status: 21.8% never married, 50.3% now married, 15.0% widowed, 13.0% divorced (2000); Foreign born: 1.4% (2000); Ancestry (includes multiple ancestries): 28.4% German, 10.6% Irish, 9.9% English, 8.6% United States or American, 7.7% Other groups (2000).
Economy: Employment by occupation: 1.0% management, 9.9% professional, 16.3% services, 23.2% sales, 0.0% farming, 12.8% construction, 36.9% production (2000).
Income: Per capita income: $18,585 (2000); Median household income: $31,500 (2000); Poverty rate: 3.2% (2000).
Taxes: Total city taxes per capita: $101 (1997); City property taxes per capita: $57 (1997).
Education: High school graduation rate: 81.4% (2000); College graduation rate: 7.1% (2000).
Housing: Homeownership rate: 71.5% (2000); Median home value: $38,400 (2000); Median rent: $257 per month (2000); Median age of housing: 52 years (2000).
Transportation: Commute to work: 92.8% car, 0.0% public transportation, 5.2% walk, 0.0% work from home (2000); Travel time to work: 22.7% less than 15 minutes, 61.9% 15 to 30 minutes, 4.6% 30 to 45 minutes, 4.1% 45 to 60 minutes, 6.7% 60 minutes or more (2000)

WAYLAND (city). Covers a land area of 0.861 square miles and a water area of 0 square miles. Located at 41.14° N. Lat.; 91.66° W. Long. Elevation is 738 feet.
History: Wayland was originally a colony of Amish-Mennonites.
Population: 945 (2000); Race: 96.0% White, 0.0% Black, 0.7% Asian, 2.0% American Indian and Alaska Native, 0.2% Hispanic of any race, 1.1% two or more races (2000); Density: 1,097.0 persons per square mile (2000); Age: 25.3% under 18, 26.0% over 64 (2000); Marriage status: 19.7% never married, 62.5% now married, 10.8% widowed, 6.9% divorced (2000); Foreign born: 0.8% (2000); Ancestry (includes multiple ancestries): 41.0% German, 9.3% Irish, 7.4% English, 5.9% United States or American, 3.7% Other groups (2000).
Economy: Single-family building permits issued: 3 (2001) / 2 (2000); Multi-family building permits issued: 0 (2001) / 0 (2000); Employment by occupation: 9.5% management, 13.7% professional, 10.2% services, 32.9% sales, 1.7% farming, 9.2% construction, 22.7% production (2000).
Income: Per capita income: $15,717 (2000); Median household income: $35,667 (2000); Poverty rate: 5.7% (2000).
Taxes: Total city taxes per capita: $166 (1997); City property taxes per capita: $120 (1997).

Education: High school graduation rate: 80.5% (2000); College graduation rate: 13.2% (2000).

School District(s)

Waco Community School District (PK-12)
2000 Enrollment: 575 319-256-6200

Housing: Homeownership rate: 75.2% (2000); Median home value: $65,000 (2000); Median rent: $300 per month (2000); Median age of housing: 60+ years (2000).

Transportation: Commute to work: 91.6% car, 0.0% public transportation, 4.3% walk, 3.1% work from home (2000); Travel time to work: 42.3% less than 15 minutes, 35.6% 15 to 30 minutes, 11.7% 30 to 45 minutes, 3.7% 45 to 60 minutes, 6.7% 60 minutes or more (2000)

WESTWOOD (city). Covers a land area of 0.152 square miles and a water area of 0.003 square miles. Located at 40.96° N. Lat.; 91.62° W. Long. Elevation is 700 feet.

Population: 127 (2000); Race: 89.7% White, 3.2% Black, 0.0% Asian, 0.0% American Indian and Alaska Native, 0.0% Hispanic of any race, 7.1% two or more races (2000); Density: 835.1 persons per square mile (2000); Age: 21.4% under 18, 14.3% over 64 (2000); Marriage status: 13.6% never married, 81.8% now married, 1.8% widowed, 2.7% divorced (2000); Foreign born: 0.0% (2000); Ancestry (includes multiple ancestries): 36.5% German, 23.0% English, 13.5% Other groups, 12.7% United States or American, 11.1% Irish (2000).

Economy: Corn, soybeans; cattle, hogs. Single-family building permits issued: 0 (2001) / 0 (2000); Multi-family building permits issued: 0 (2001) / 0 (2000); Employment by occupation: 25.6% management, 38.4% professional, 4.7% services, 25.6% sales, 0.0% farming, 0.0% construction, 5.8% production (2000).

Income: Per capita income: $33,677 (2000); Median household income: $89,522 (2000); Poverty rate: 0.0% (2000).

Taxes: Total city taxes per capita: $255 (1997); City property taxes per capita: $208 (1997).

Education: High school graduation rate: 97.9% (2000); College graduation rate: 61.1% (2000).

Housing: Homeownership rate: 100.0% (2000); Median home value: $140,600 (2000); Median age of housing: 27 years (2000).

Transportation: Commute to work: 100.0% car, 0.0% public transportation, 0.0% walk, 0.0% work from home (2000); Travel time to work: 76.7% less than 15 minutes, 12.8% 15 to 30 minutes, 7.0% 30 to 45 minutes, 1.2% 45 to 60 minutes, 2.3% 60 minutes or more (2000)

WINFIELD (city). Covers a land area of 1.038 square miles and a water area of 0 square miles. Located at 41.12° N. Lat.; 91.43° W. Long. Elevation is 698 feet.

History: The name of Winfield was in honor of General Winfield Scott.

Population: 1,131 (2000); Race: 97.0% White, 0.2% Black, 0.6% Asian, 0.0% American Indian and Alaska Native, 2.2% Hispanic of any race, 1.1% two or more races (2000); Density: 1,089.7 persons per square mile (2000); Age: 30.1% under 18, 20.1% over 64 (2000); Marriage status: 19.0% never married, 57.9% now married, 12.8% widowed, 10.3% divorced (2000); Foreign born: 1.3% (2000); Ancestry (includes multiple ancestries): 32.2% German, 16.2% Irish, 9.2% Other groups, 9.1% English, 8.5% United States or American (2000).

Economy: Single-family building permits issued: 0 (2001) / 1 (2000); Multi-family building permits issued: 0 (2001) / 0 (2000); Employment by occupation: 4.2% management, 10.1% professional, 20.4% services, 23.6% sales, 0.4% farming, 8.9% construction, 32.5% production (2000).

Income: Per capita income: $17,949 (2000); Median household income: $32,500 (2000); Poverty rate: 12.7% (2000).

Taxes: Total city taxes per capita: $151 (1997); City property taxes per capita: $100 (1997).

Education: High school graduation rate: 87.8% (2000); College graduation rate: 12.4% (2000).

School District(s)

Winfield-Mount Union Community School District (KG-12)
2000 Enrollment: 499 319-257-7700

Housing: Homeownership rate: 72.8% (2000); Median home value: $60,800 (2000); Median rent: $265 per month (2000); Median age of housing: 51 years (2000).

Newspapers: Winfield Beacon/Wayland News (1 x week)

Transportation: Commute to work: 90.4% car, 0.0% public transportation, 7.4% walk, 1.2% work from home (2000); Travel time to work: 31.9% less than 15 minutes, 37.2% 15 to 30 minutes, 13.8% 30 to 45 minutes, 10.4% 45 to 60 minutes, 6.7% 60 minutes or more (2000)

Howard County

Located in northeastern Iowa; bounded on the north by Minnesota; prairie area, drained by the Upper Iowa, Wapsipinicon, and Turkey Rivers. Covers a land area of 473.40 square miles, a water area of 0.40 square miles, and is located in the Central Time Zone. The county government was organized in 1851. County seat is Cresco.

Weather Station: Cresco 1 NE — Elevation: 1,253 feet

	Jan	Feb	Mar	Apr	May	Jun	Jul	Aug	Sep	Oct	Nov	Dec
High	21	27	39	55	69	78	82	79	71	59	41	27
Low	3	9	21	34	46	56	60	57	48	36	23	10
Precip	1.0	0.9	2.2	3.6	3.9	4.4	4.6	5.1	3.9	2.5	2.4	1.2
Snow	10.9	7.1	6.9	2.5	tr	0.0	0.0	0.0	0.0	0.4	5.1	8.8

High and Low temperatures in degrees Fahrenheit; Precipitation and Snow in inches

Population: 9,932 (2000); Race: 99.4% White, 0.1% Black, 0.1% Asian, 0.0% American Indian and Alaska Native, 0.2% Hispanic of any race, 0.4% two or more races (2000); Density: 21.0 persons per square mile (2000); Age: 26.2% under 18, 20.0% over 64 (2000).

Religion: Five largest groups: 51.4% Catholic Church, 21.1% Evangelical Lutheran Church in America, 11.4% The United Methodist Church, 2.7% Old Order Amish Church, 1.5% Lutheran Church—Missouri Synod (2000).

Economy: Unemployment rate: 3.3% (11/2002); Total civilian labor force: 5,624 (11/2002); Leading industries: 46.5% manufacturing; 14.4% health care and social assistance; 10.2% retail trade (2000); Companies that employ more than 1,000 persons: 1 (2000); Companies that employ more than 100 persons: 3 (2000); Farms: 862 totaling 269,750 acres (1997); Minority business ownership rate: 0.0% (1997); Women business ownership rate: 17.1% (1997); Retail sales per capita: $5,609 (1997). Single-family building permits issued: 11 (2001) / 16 (2000); Multi-family building permits issued: 0 (2001) / 0 (2000).

Income: Per capita income: $17,842 (2000); Median household income: $34,641 (2000); Poverty rate: 9.3% (2000); Bankruptcy rate: 2.38% (2001).

Taxes: Total county taxes per capita: $259 (1997); County property taxes per capita: $201 (1997).

Education: High school graduation rate: 79.3% (2000); College graduation rate: 12.6% (2000).

Housing: Homeownership rate: 79.2% (2000); Median home value: $59,500 (2000); Median rent: $241 per month (2000); Median age of housing: 56 years (2000).

Health: Birth rate: 113.8 per 10,000 population (1998); Age adjusted death rate: 83.6 per 10,000 population (1999); Age adjusted cancer mortality rate: 193.3 deaths per 100,000 population (1999). Number of physicians: 10.1 per 10,000 population (1999); Number of hospital beds: 32.2 per 10,000 population (1999).

Elections: 2000 Presidential election results: 54.0% Gore, 42.8% Bush, 2.2% Nader, 0.7% Buchanan

National and State Parks: Hayden Prairie State Wildlife Area; Turkey River Access State Wildlife Area

Additional Information Contacts

Howard County Government Offices. 319-547-2880

Howard County Communities

CHESTER (city). Covers a land area of 1.334 square miles and a water area of 0 square miles. Located at 43.49° N. Lat.; 92.36° W. Long.

History: Chester, formerly known as Eatonville, was once a military outlook post on Military Ridge Trail.

Population: 151 (2000); Race: 100.0% White, 0.0% Black, 0.0% Asian, 0.0% American Indian and Alaska Native, 0.0% Hispanic of any race, 0.0% two or more races (2000); Density: 113.2 persons per square mile (2000); Age: 17.1% under 18, 34.8% over 64 (2000); Marriage status: 21.7% never married, 58.7% now married, 15.2% widowed, 4.3% divorced (2000); Foreign born: 0.0% (2000); Ancestry (includes multiple ancestries): 46.2% German, 27.8% Norwegian, 14.6% English, 13.9% Dutch, 5.7% Swedish (2000).

Economy: Single-family building permits issued: 0 (2001) / 0 (2000); Multi-family building permits issued: 0 (2001) / 0 (2000); Employment by occupation: 6.1% management, 12.1% professional, 4.5% services, 25.8% sales, 10.6% farming, 4.5% construction, 36.4% production (2000).

Income: Per capita income: $18,240 (2000); Median household income: $21,875 (2000); Poverty rate: 8.2% (2000).

Taxes: Total city taxes per capita: $282 (1997); City property taxes per capita: $235 (1997).

Education: High school graduation rate: 84.2% (2000); College graduation rate: 11.4% (2000).
Housing: Homeownership rate: 80.6% (2000); Median home value: $49,000 (2000); Median rent: $188 per month (2000); Median age of housing: 60+ years (2000).
Transportation: Commute to work: 72.7% car, 0.0% public transportation, 21.2% walk, 6.1% work from home (2000); Travel time to work: 40.3% less than 15 minutes, 35.5% 15 to 30 minutes, 12.9% 30 to 45 minutes, 8.1% 45 to 60 minutes, 3.2% 60 minutes or more (2000)

CRESCO (city). Covers a land area of 3.298 square miles and a water area of 0 square miles. Located at 43.37° N. Lat.; 92.11° W. Long. Elevation is 1,298 feet.
History: Cresco was named by its founder, Augustus Beadle. W. B. Berry, a farmer, successfully experimented here with growing ears of corn of various colors.
Population: 3,905 (2000); Race: 99.6% White, 0.0% Black, 0.0% Asian, 0.0% American Indian and Alaska Native, 0.1% Hispanic of any race, 0.4% two or more races (2000); Density: 1,184.2 persons per square mile (2000); Age: 25.7% under 18, 22.5% over 64 (2000); Marriage status: 24.0% never married, 56.0% now married, 13.2% widowed, 6.8% divorced (2000); Foreign born: 0.2% (2000); Ancestry (includes multiple ancestries): 42.9% German, 25.2% Norwegian, 16.7% Irish, 12.1% Czech, 8.1% English (2000).
Economy: Single-family building permits issued: 9 (2001) / 16 (2000); Multi-family building permits issued: 0 (2001) / 0 (2000); Employment by occupation: 8.8% management, 15.1% professional, 16.1% services, 24.0% sales, 2.7% farming, 8.7% construction, 24.7% production (2000).
Income: Per capita income: $18,190 (2000); Median household income: $32,236 (2000); Poverty rate: 6.8% (2000).
Taxes: Total city taxes per capita: $358 (1997); City property taxes per capita: $309 (1997).
Education: High school graduation rate: 80.2% (2000); College graduation rate: 17.2% (2000).

School District(s)

Howard-Winneshiek Community School District (PK-12)
2000 Enrollment: 1,576 319-547-2762

Housing: Homeownership rate: 75.4% (2000); Median home value: $63,200 (2000); Median rent: $263 per month (2000); Median age of housing: 55 years (2000).
Hospitals: Regional Health Services of Howard County (32 beds)
Safety: Violent crime rate: 46.1 per 10,000 population; Property crime rate: 312.7 per 10,000 population (2001).
Newspapers: Times-Plain Dealer (1 x week)
Transportation: Commute to work: 92.7% car, 0.0% public transportation, 5.4% walk, 0.8% work from home (2000); Travel time to work: 68.1% less than 15 minutes, 19.9% 15 to 30 minutes, 6.3% 30 to 45 minutes, 1.8% 45 to 60 minutes, 3.8% 60 minutes or more (2000)

ELMA (city). Covers a land area of 1.287 square miles and a water area of 0 square miles. Located at 43.24° N. Lat.; 92.43° W. Long. Elevation is 1,188 feet.
History: Elma was formed from the joining of several communities, including Busti and Howard. It was named for the youngest daughter of Lemuel Potter, on whose land part of the town was built.
Population: 598 (2000); Race: 96.5% White, 1.0% Black, 0.7% Asian, 0.0% American Indian and Alaska Native, 0.3% Hispanic of any race, 1.8% two or more races (2000); Density: 464.5 persons per square mile (2000); Age: 21.4% under 18, 28.1% over 64 (2000); Marriage status: 22.6% never married, 53.8% now married, 18.0% widowed, 5.6% divorced (2000); Foreign born: 1.0% (2000); Ancestry (includes multiple ancestries): 45.6% German, 17.3% Irish, 11.5% Czech, 7.7% Norwegian, 6.3% Other groups (2000).
Economy: Single-family building permits issued: 0 (2001) / 0 (2000); Multi-family building permits issued: 0 (2001) / 0 (2000); Employment by occupation: 8.9% management, 6.6% professional, 27.8% services, 18.5% sales, 3.5% farming, 5.4% construction, 29.3% production (2000).
Income: Per capita income: $15,263 (2000); Median household income: $27,417 (2000); Poverty rate: 17.4% (2000).
Taxes: Total city taxes per capita: $169 (1997); City property taxes per capita: $124 (1997).
Education: High school graduation rate: 75.4% (2000); College graduation rate: 9.2% (2000).
Housing: Homeownership rate: 75.7% (2000); Median home value: $34,400 (2000); Median rent: $231 per month (2000); Median age of housing: 60+ years (2000).
Transportation: Commute to work: 80.3% car, 0.0% public transportation, 15.4% walk, 4.2% work from home (2000); Travel time to work: 45.6% less than 15 minutes, 13.3% 15 to 30 minutes, 24.6% 30 to 45 minutes, 3.2% 45 to 60 minutes, 13.3% 60 minutes or more (2000)

LIME SPRINGS (city). Covers a land area of 1.017 square miles and a water area of 0 square miles. Located at 43.45° N. Lat.; 92.28° W. Long. Elevation is 1,250 feet.
History: Lime Springs was once the home of Governor Larrabee (the 13th Governor of Iowa, 1886-1890).
Population: 496 (2000); Race: 99.0% White, 0.0% Black, 0.2% Asian, 0.0% American Indian and Alaska Native, 1.2% Hispanic of any race, 0.8% two or more races (2000); Density: 487.8 persons per square mile (2000); Age: 28.4% under 18, 22.9% over 64 (2000); Marriage status: 21.6% never married, 59.1% now married, 10.2% widowed, 9.1% divorced (2000); Foreign born: 1.0% (2000); Ancestry (includes multiple ancestries): 40.7% German, 15.3% Norwegian, 7.4% Dutch, 7.2% Irish, 6.3% Other groups (2000).
Economy: Single-family building permits issued: 2 (2001) / 0 (2000); Multi-family building permits issued: 0 (2001) / 0 (2000); Employment by occupation: 16.8% management, 9.1% professional, 13.2% services, 23.6% sales, 0.5% farming, 13.2% construction, 23.6% production (2000).
Income: Per capita income: $15,706 (2000); Median household income: $33,750 (2000); Poverty rate: 5.9% (2000).
Taxes: Total city taxes per capita: $212 (1997); City property taxes per capita: $168 (1997).
Education: High school graduation rate: 85.1% (2000); College graduation rate: 11.9% (2000).
Housing: Homeownership rate: 86.4% (2000); Median home value: $48,300 (2000); Median rent: $192 per month (2000); Median age of housing: 60 years (2000).
Newspapers: Lime Springs Herald (1 x week)
Transportation: Commute to work: 89.4% car, 0.0% public transportation, 8.3% walk, 2.3% work from home (2000); Travel time to work: 42.0% less than 15 minutes, 30.2% 15 to 30 minutes, 5.2% 30 to 45 minutes, 14.6% 45 to 60 minutes, 8.0% 60 minutes or more (2000)

PROTIVIN (city). Covers a land area of 0.478 square miles and a water area of 0 square miles. Located at 43.21° N. Lat.; 92.09° W. Long. Elevation is 1,150 feet.
History: Protivin was named by early settler Frank Chyle. The name was taken from his wife's home of Protivin, Czechoslovakia.
Population: 317 (2000); Race: 100.0% White, 0.0% Black, 0.0% Asian, 0.0% American Indian and Alaska Native, 1.0% Hispanic of any race, 0.0% two or more races (2000); Density: 663.5 persons per square mile (2000); Age: 19.9% under 18, 28.4% over 64 (2000); Marriage status: 25.1% never married, 50.2% now married, 18.9% widowed, 5.8% divorced (2000); Foreign born: 0.0% (2000); Ancestry (includes multiple ancestries): 45.1% Czech, 40.5% German, 8.8% Norwegian, 7.8% Irish, 4.6% Czechoslovakian (2000).
Economy: Employment by occupation: 7.3% management, 6.0% professional, 16.6% services, 15.9% sales, 6.0% farming, 13.9% construction, 34.4% production (2000).
Income: Per capita income: $18,818 (2000); Median household income: $29,779 (2000); Poverty rate: 13.2% (2000).
Taxes: Total city taxes per capita: $197 (1997); City property taxes per capita: $151 (1997).
Education: High school graduation rate: 75.2% (2000); College graduation rate: 6.6% (2000).
Housing: Homeownership rate: 72.7% (2000); Median home value: $45,000 (2000); Median rent: $175 per month (2000); Median age of housing: 39 years (2000).
Transportation: Commute to work: 86.6% car, 0.0% public transportation, 9.4% walk, 4.0% work from home (2000); Travel time to work: 37.1% less than 15 minutes, 35.0% 15 to 30 minutes, 12.6% 30 to 45 minutes, 6.3% 45 to 60 minutes, 9.1% 60 minutes or more (2000)

Humboldt County

Located in north central Iowa; prairie area, drained by the Des Moines and East Des Moines Rivers. Covers a land area of 434.40 square miles, a water area of 1.30 square miles, and is located in the Central Time Zone. The county government was organized in 1851. County seat is Dakota City.

Weather Station: Humboldt 3 W Elevation: 1,108 feet

	Jan	Feb	Mar	Apr	May	Jun	Jul	Aug	Sep	Oct	Nov	Dec
High	25	31	44	60	72	82	84	81	74	62	43	29
Low	6	13	25	37	49	59	62	59	50	38	25	12
Precip	0.9	0.7	2.2	3.1	3.9	4.5	4.1	4.2	3.3	2.4	1.8	1.1
Snow	6.9	5.2	5.1	1.5	0.0	0.0	0.0	0.0	0.0	0.2	3.3	6.9

High and Low temperatures in degrees Fahrenheit; Precipitation and Snow in inches

Population: 10,381 (2000); Race: 97.6% White, 0.3% Black, 0.4% Asian, 0.0% American Indian and Alaska Native, 1.4% Hispanic of any race, 1.1% two or more races (2000); Density: 23.9 persons per square mile (2000); Age: 24.8% under 18, 21.0% over 64 (2000).
Religion: Five largest groups: 29.3% Evangelical Lutheran Church in America, 22.3% The United Methodist Church, 15.9% Catholic Church, 9.8% Lutheran Church—Missouri Synod, 3.4% Baptist General Conference (2000).
Economy: Unemployment rate: 2.6% (11/2002); Total civilian labor force: 5,302 (11/2002); Leading industries: 37.0% manufacturing; 13.2% retail trade; 12.4% health care and social assistance (2000); Companies that employ more than 1,000 persons: 0 (2000); Companies that employ more than 100 persons: 7 (2000); Farms: 600 totaling 257,411 acres (1997); Minority business ownership rate: 0.0% (1997); Women business ownership rate: 14.2% (1997); Retail sales per capita: $6,883 (1997). Single-family building permits issued: 17 (2001) / 17 (2000); Multi-family building permits issued: 0 (2001) / 44 (2000).
Income: Per capita income: $18,300 (2000); Median household income: $38,201 (2000); Poverty rate: 8.3% (2000); Bankruptcy rate: 4.68% (2001).
Taxes: Total county taxes per capita: $295 (2000); County property taxes per capita: $294 (2000).
Education: High school graduation rate: 86.3% (2000); College graduation rate: 15.4% (2000).
Housing: Homeownership rate: 75.9% (2000); Median home value: $71,700 (2000); Median rent: $280 per month (2000); Median age of housing: 48 years (2000).
Health: Birth rate: 93.4 per 10,000 population (1998); Age adjusted death rate: 78.5 per 10,000 population (1999); Age adjusted cancer mortality rate: 151.3 deaths per 100,000 population (1999). Number of physicians: 5.8 per 10,000 population (1999); Number of hospital beds: 47.2 per 10,000 population (1999).
Elections: 2000 Presidential election results: 39.5% Gore, 57.6% Bush, 2.0% Nader, 0.5% Buchanan
National and State Parks: Bradgate State Fishing Access; Frank Gotch State Park; Ottosen Marsh State Game Management Area

Additional Information Contacts

Humboldt County Government Offices 515-332-1571
Humboldt Chamber of Commerce 515-332-1481
Humboldt County Board of Realtors 515-332-1071

Humboldt County Communities

BODE (city). Covers a land area of 0.410 square miles and a water area of 0 square miles. Located at 42.86° N. Lat.; 94.28° W. Long. Elevation is 1,150 feet.
History: Bode, a station on the Burlington, Cedar Rapids & Northern Railroad, may have been named for a railroad engineer or surveyor.
Population: 327 (2000); Race: 94.8% White, 0.0% Black, 3.6% Asian, 0.0% American Indian and Alaska Native, 0.0% Hispanic of any race, 1.6% two or more races (2000); Density: 797.6 persons per square mile (2000); Age: 18.8% under 18, 27.2% over 64 (2000); Marriage status: 21.1% never married, 59.6% now married, 11.7% widowed, 7.5% divorced (2000); Foreign born: 1.3% (2000); Ancestry (includes multiple ancestries): 34.0% German, 29.4% Norwegian, 10.0% English, 7.1% Other groups, 6.8% Irish (2000).
Economy: Employment by occupation: 5.3% management, 16.4% professional, 13.8% services, 27.6% sales, 0.0% farming, 14.5% construction, 22.4% production (2000).
Income: Per capita income: $16,014 (2000); Median household income: $32,917 (2000); Poverty rate: 5.8% (2000).
Taxes: Total city taxes per capita: $136 (1997); City property taxes per capita: $136 (1997).
Education: High school graduation rate: 80.1% (2000); College graduation rate: 15.4% (2000).

School District(s)

Twin Rivers Community School District (PK-12)
2000 Enrollment: 248 515-379-1526

Housing: Homeownership rate: 79.0% (2000); Median home value: $33,000 (2000); Median rent: $242 per month (2000); Median age of housing: 55 years (2000).
Transportation: Commute to work: 87.8% car, 0.0% public transportation, 8.8% walk, 3.4% work from home (2000); Travel time to work: 34.5% less than 15 minutes, 43.7% 15 to 30 minutes, 10.6% 30 to 45 minutes, 8.5% 45 to 60 minutes, 2.8% 60 minutes or more (2000)

BRADGATE (city). Covers a land area of 0.347 square miles and a water area of 0.002 square miles. Located at 42.80° N. Lat.; 94.42° W. Long. Elevation is 1,123 feet.
History: Bradgate was laid out in 1882 by the Western Town Lot Company, and was first called Willow Glen. The name was soon changed to Bradgate by the inhabitants.
Population: 101 (2000); Race: 100.0% White, 0.0% Black, 0.0% Asian, 0.0% American Indian and Alaska Native, 0.0% Hispanic of any race, 0.0% two or more races (2000); Density: 291.1 persons per square mile (2000); Age: 17.8% under 18, 15.8% over 64 (2000); Marriage status: 25.3% never married, 53.8% now married, 4.4% widowed, 16.5% divorced (2000); Foreign born: 3.0% (2000); Ancestry (includes multiple ancestries): 33.7% German, 15.8% United States or American, 9.9% Irish, 9.9% Danish, 5.9% Norwegian (2000).
Economy: Single-family building permits issued: 0 (2001) / 0 (2000); Multi-family building permits issued: 0 (2001) / 0 (2000); Employment by occupation: 3.1% management, 9.4% professional, 12.5% services, 32.8% sales, 3.1% farming, 12.5% construction, 26.6% production (2000).
Income: Per capita income: $16,407 (2000); Median household income: $30,000 (2000); Poverty rate: 16.8% (2000).
Taxes: Total city taxes per capita: $97 (1997); City property taxes per capita: $97 (1997).
Education: High school graduation rate: 84.1% (2000); College graduation rate: 5.8% (2000).
Housing: Homeownership rate: 78.0% (2000); Median home value: $17,800 (2000); Median rent: $183 per month (2000); Median age of housing: 60+ years (2000).
Transportation: Commute to work: 86.4% car, 0.0% public transportation, 13.6% walk, 0.0% work from home (2000); Travel time to work: 33.9% less than 15 minutes, 42.4% 15 to 30 minutes, 23.7% 30 to 45 minutes, 0.0% 45 to 60 minutes, 0.0% 60 minutes or more (2000)

DAKOTA CITY (city). Covers a land area of 0.736 square miles and a water area of 0.036 square miles. Located at 42.72° N. Lat.; 94.20° W. Long. Elevation is 1,125 feet.
History: Dakota City was named for the Dakota (Sioux) Indians. Ed McKnight, founder of the village, built a dam across the East Fork of the Des Moines River.
Population: 911 (2000); Race: 97.0% White, 0.0% Black, 0.3% Asian, 0.0% American Indian and Alaska Native, 2.1% Hispanic of any race, 1.6% two or more races (2000); Density: 1,238.0 persons per square mile (2000); Age: 28.4% under 18, 11.9% over 64 (2000); Marriage status: 20.5% never married, 62.5% now married, 7.2% widowed, 9.8% divorced (2000); Foreign born: 0.3% (2000); Ancestry (includes multiple ancestries): 43.6% German, 18.7% Norwegian, 13.3% Irish, 6.7% Danish, 6.0% United States or American (2000).
Economy: Single-family building permits issued: 1 (2001) / 2 (2000); Multi-family building permits issued: 0 (2001) / 0 (2000); Employment by occupation: 8.7% management, 12.8% professional, 12.3% services, 30.2% sales, 0.6% farming, 9.1% construction, 26.3% production (2000).
Income: Per capita income: $15,441 (2000); Median household income: $33,977 (2000); Poverty rate: 6.6% (2000).
Taxes: Total city taxes per capita: $177 (2000); City property taxes per capita: $176 (2000).
Education: High school graduation rate: 86.3% (2000); College graduation rate: 10.3% (2000).
Housing: Homeownership rate: 82.2% (2000); Median home value: $66,500 (2000); Median rent: $312 per month (2000); Median age of housing: 36 years (2000).
Transportation: Commute to work: 94.5% car, 0.0% public transportation, 2.7% walk, 2.9% work from home (2000); Travel time to work: 62.8% less than 15 minutes, 18.4% 15 to 30 minutes, 12.1% 30 to 45 minutes, 1.1% 45 to 60 minutes, 5.7% 60 minutes or more (2000)

GILMORE CITY (city). Covers a land area of 1.240 square miles and a water area of 0 square miles. Located at 42.73° N. Lat.; 94.44° W. Long. Elevation is 1,207 feet.

History: Gilmore City was named for railroad superintendent C.N. Gilmore of Des Moines.
Population: 556 (2000); Race: 100.0% White, 0.0% Black, 0.0% Asian, 0.0% American Indian and Alaska Native, 1.4% Hispanic of any race, 0.0% two or more races (2000); Density: 448.5 persons per square mile (2000); Age: 26.8% under 18, 18.8% over 64 (2000); Marriage status: 26.4% never married, 53.8% now married, 9.8% widowed, 10.0% divorced (2000); Foreign born: 1.4% (2000); Ancestry (includes multiple ancestries): 41.5% German, 13.7% Irish, 13.5% Norwegian, 11.1% English, 8.5% Danish (2000).
Economy: Single-family building permits issued: 2 (2001) / 0 (2000); Multi-family building permits issued: 0 (2001) / 0 (2000); Employment by occupation: 10.7% management, 9.6% professional, 21.0% services, 18.0% sales, 0.0% farming, 14.0% construction, 26.8% production (2000).
Income: Per capita income: $15,511 (2000); Median household income: $31,827 (2000); Poverty rate: 7.9% (2000).
Taxes: Total city taxes per capita: $97 (1997); City property taxes per capita: $95 (1997).
Education: High school graduation rate: 87.0% (2000); College graduation rate: 5.2% (2000).

School District(s)

Gilmore City-Bradgate Community School District (PK-12)
2000 Enrollment: 170 515-373-6619
Housing: Homeownership rate: 76.6% (2000); Median home value: $39,200 (2000); Median rent: $189 per month (2000); Median age of housing: 60+ years (2000).
Transportation: Commute to work: 93.0% car, 0.0% public transportation, 2.2% walk, 4.8% work from home (2000); Travel time to work: 26.9% less than 15 minutes, 48.1% 15 to 30 minutes, 9.6% 30 to 45 minutes, 9.6% 45 to 60 minutes, 5.8% 60 minutes or more (2000)

HARDY (city). Covers a land area of 0.442 square miles and a water area of 0 square miles. Located at 42.81° N. Lat.; 94.05° W. Long. Elevation is 1,129 feet.
History: Local legend tells that Hardy was named for a railroad engineer who lost his life in a train derailment caused by cattle on the tracks here.
Population: 57 (2000); Race: 96.2% White, 0.0% Black, 0.0% Asian, 0.0% American Indian and Alaska Native, 0.0% Hispanic of any race, 3.8% two or more races (2000); Density: 128.9 persons per square mile (2000); Age: 17.3% under 18, 17.3% over 64 (2000); Marriage status: 28.3% never married, 47.8% now married, 2.2% widowed, 21.7% divorced (2000); Foreign born: 3.8% (2000); Ancestry (includes multiple ancestries): 36.5% Norwegian, 34.6% German, 13.5% English, 5.8% United States or American, 5.8% Scottish (2000).
Economy: Employment by occupation: 22.7% management, 9.1% professional, 9.1% services, 18.2% sales, 0.0% farming, 0.0% construction, 40.9% production (2000).
Income: Per capita income: $12,910 (2000); Median household income: $28,929 (2000); Poverty rate: 15.4% (2000).
Taxes: Total city taxes per capita: $340 (1997); City property taxes per capita: $340 (1997).
Education: High school graduation rate: 63.9% (2000); College graduation rate: 2.8% (2000).
Housing: Homeownership rate: 100.0% (2000); Median home value: $13,200 (2000); Median age of housing: 60+ years (2000).
Transportation: Commute to work: 77.3% car, 0.0% public transportation, 13.6% walk, 9.1% work from home (2000); Travel time to work: 15.0% less than 15 minutes, 50.0% 15 to 30 minutes, 0.0% 30 to 45 minutes, 35.0% 45 to 60 minutes, 0.0% 60 minutes or more (2000)

HUMBOLDT (city). Covers a land area of 4.649 square miles and a water area of 0.152 square miles. Located at 42.72° N. Lat.; 94.22° W. Long. Elevation is 1,088 feet.
History: Humboldt, originally called Springvale, was settled by the Rev. S. H. Taft with a group of abolitionists. It was renamed to honor Baron Alexander von Humboldt, a German scientist (1786-1859).
Population: 4,452 (2000); Race: 95.7% White, 0.8% Black, 0.6% Asian, 0.1% American Indian and Alaska Native, 2.2% Hispanic of any race, 2.0% two or more races (2000); Density: 957.7 persons per square mile (2000); Age: 22.1% under 18, 26.4% over 64 (2000); Marriage status: 18.7% never married, 59.5% now married, 13.5% widowed, 8.3% divorced (2000); Foreign born: 2.4% (2000); Ancestry (includes multiple ancestries): 41.6% German, 16.5% Norwegian, 12.7% Irish, 10.7% English, 5.5% Other groups (2000).
Economy: Single-family building permits issued: 8 (2001) / 10 (2000); Multi-family building permits issued: 0 (2001) / 44 (2000); Employment by occupation: 13.7% management, 17.4% professional, 11.4% services, 26.0% sales, 2.5% farming, 9.3% construction, 19.8% production (2000).
Income: Per capita income: $19,656 (2000); Median household income: $39,338 (2000); Poverty rate: 7.3% (2000).
Taxes: Total city taxes per capita: $264 (1997); City property taxes per capita: $257 (1997).
Education: High school graduation rate: 85.6% (2000); College graduation rate: 19.3% (2000).

School District(s)

Humboldt Community School District (KG-12)
2000 Enrollment: 1,482 515-332-1330
Housing: Homeownership rate: 72.8% (2000); Median home value: $83,700 (2000); Median rent: $291 per month (2000); Median age of housing: 41 years (2000).
Hospitals: Humboldt County Memorial Hospital (49 beds)
Safety: Violent crime rate: 6.7 per 10,000 population; Property crime rate: 112.4 per 10,000 population (2001).
Newspapers: Independent (1 x week)
Transportation: Commute to work: 94.6% car, 0.0% public transportation, 3.4% walk, 0.8% work from home (2000); Travel time to work: 67.7% less than 15 minutes, 16.6% 15 to 30 minutes, 8.2% 30 to 45 minutes, 1.1% 45 to 60 minutes, 6.4% 60 minutes or more (2000)
Additional Information Contacts
Humboldt Chamber of Commerce 515-332-1481
Humboldt County Board of Realtors 515-332-1071

LIVERMORE (city). Covers a land area of 0.699 square miles and a water area of 0 square miles. Located at 42.86° N. Lat.; 94.18° W. Long. Elevation is 1,136 feet.
History: The town of Livermore was mapped and named by railroad officials in 1880.
Population: 431 (2000); Race: 100.0% White, 0.0% Black, 0.0% Asian, 0.0% American Indian and Alaska Native, 0.7% Hispanic of any race, 0.0% two or more races (2000); Density: 616.4 persons per square mile (2000); Age: 23.4% under 18, 17.1% over 64 (2000); Marriage status: 27.3% never married, 46.4% now married, 12.9% widowed, 13.4% divorced (2000); Foreign born: 0.2% (2000); Ancestry (includes multiple ancestries): 31.3% German, 11.3% Irish, 10.6% English, 10.1% Norwegian, 7.2% United States or American (2000).
Economy: Single-family building permits issued: 0 (2001) / 0 (2000); Multi-family building permits issued: 0 (2001) / 0 (2000); Employment by occupation: 10.5% management, 7.9% professional, 13.7% services, 17.9% sales, 0.0% farming, 24.7% construction, 25.3% production (2000).
Income: Per capita income: $13,714 (2000); Median household income: $26,328 (2000); Poverty rate: 12.6% (2000).
Taxes: Total city taxes per capita: $128 (1997); City property taxes per capita: $126 (1997).
Education: High school graduation rate: 77.5% (2000); College graduation rate: 5.5% (2000).
Housing: Homeownership rate: 88.7% (2000); Median home value: $40,300 (2000); Median rent: $184 per month (2000); Median age of housing: 60+ years (2000).
Transportation: Commute to work: 94.1% car, 1.6% public transportation, 2.7% walk, 1.6% work from home (2000); Travel time to work: 19.2% less than 15 minutes, 52.2% 15 to 30 minutes, 10.4% 30 to 45 minutes, 8.8% 45 to 60 minutes, 9.3% 60 minutes or more (2000)

OTTOSEN (city). Covers a land area of 0.570 square miles and a water area of 0 square miles. Located at 42.89° N. Lat.; 94.37° W. Long.
History: Ottosen was named for the prominent citizen and owner of the general store, Chris Ottosen.
Population: 61 (2000); Race: 100.0% White, 0.0% Black, 0.0% Asian, 0.0% American Indian and Alaska Native, 0.0% Hispanic of any race, 0.0% two or more races (2000); Density: 107.1 persons per square mile (2000); Age: 30.2% under 18, 11.3% over 64 (2000); Marriage status: 26.8% never married, 39.0% now married, 14.6% widowed, 19.5% divorced (2000); Foreign born: 0.0% (2000); Ancestry (includes multiple ancestries): 34.0% German, 18.9% Norwegian, 13.2% English, 5.7% Other groups, 3.8% Scottish (2000).
Economy: Employment by occupation: 13.8% management, 6.9% professional, 17.2% services, 17.2% sales, 6.9% farming, 27.6% construction, 10.3% production (2000).
Income: Per capita income: $15,525 (2000); Median household income: $34,000 (2000); Poverty rate: 3.8% (2000).
Taxes: Total city taxes per capita: $239 (1997); City property taxes per capita: $239 (1997).

Education: High school graduation rate: 88.2% (2000); College graduation rate: 0.0% (2000).
Housing: Homeownership rate: 81.8% (2000); Median home value: $12,500 (2000); Median rent: $225 per month (2000); Median age of housing: 60+ years (2000).
Transportation: Commute to work: 75.9% car, 0.0% public transportation, 24.1% walk, 0.0% work from home (2000); Travel time to work: 51.7% less than 15 minutes, 34.5% 15 to 30 minutes, 10.3% 30 to 45 minutes, 0.0% 45 to 60 minutes, 3.4% 60 minutes or more (2000)

PIONEER (city). Covers a land area of 0.063 square miles and a water area of 0 square miles. Located at 42.65° N. Lat.; 94.39° W. Long. Elevation is 1,170 feet.
History: Pioneer was named by an official of the Chicago, Rock Island & Pacific Railroad.
Population: 21 (2000); Race: 100.0% White, 0.0% Black, 0.0% Asian, 0.0% American Indian and Alaska Native, 0.0% Hispanic of any race, 0.0% two or more races (2000); Density: 333.1 persons per square mile (2000); Age: 33.3% under 18, 8.3% over 64 (2000); Marriage status: 0.0% never married, 75.0% now married, 12.5% widowed, 12.5% divorced (2000); Foreign born: 0.0% (2000); Ancestry (includes multiple ancestries): 41.7% Irish, 29.2% Dutch, 20.8% German, 12.5% Czech, 8.3% Other groups (2000).
Economy: Employment by occupation: 0.0% management, 0.0% professional, 50.0% services, 10.0% sales, 0.0% farming, 20.0% construction, 20.0% production (2000).
Income: Per capita income: $10,079 (2000); Median household income: $19,375 (2000); Poverty rate: 50.0% (2000).
Taxes: Total city taxes per capita: $149 (1997); City property taxes per capita: $149 (1997).
Education: High school graduation rate: 75.0% (2000); College graduation rate: 0.0% (2000).
Housing: Homeownership rate: 100.0% (2000); Median home value: $16,900 (2000); Median age of housing: 60+ years (2000).
Transportation: Commute to work: 60.0% car, 0.0% public transportation, 40.0% walk, 0.0% work from home (2000); Travel time to work: 40.0% less than 15 minutes, 40.0% 15 to 30 minutes, 20.0% 30 to 45 minutes, 0.0% 45 to 60 minutes, 0.0% 60 minutes or more (2000)

RENWICK (city). Covers a land area of 0.992 square miles and a water area of 0 square miles. Located at 42.82° N. Lat.; 93.97° W. Long. Elevation is 1,155 feet.
History: Renwick was platted by the Western Town Lot Company in 1882.
Population: 306 (2000); Race: 98.7% White, 0.0% Black, 1.3% Asian, 0.0% American Indian and Alaska Native, 0.0% Hispanic of any race, 0.0% two or more races (2000); Density: 308.4 persons per square mile (2000); Age: 23.9% under 18, 16.5% over 64 (2000); Marriage status: 31.5% never married, 54.0% now married, 9.3% widowed, 5.2% divorced (2000); Foreign born: 2.0% (2000); Ancestry (includes multiple ancestries): 35.7% German, 14.5% Norwegian, 12.5% Irish, 6.7% Other groups, 4.7% English (2000).
Economy: Single-family building permits issued: 0 (2001) / 0 (2000); Multi-family building permits issued: 0 (2001) / 0 (2000); Employment by occupation: 2.8% management, 9.7% professional, 13.8% services, 15.9% sales, 9.7% farming, 6.2% construction, 42.1% production (2000).
Income: Per capita income: $18,609 (2000); Median household income: $33,333 (2000); Poverty rate: 7.5% (2000).
Taxes: Total city taxes per capita: $205 (1997); City property taxes per capita: $205 (1997).
Education: High school graduation rate: 91.1% (2000); College graduation rate: 16.7% (2000).
Housing: Homeownership rate: 87.0% (2000); Median home value: $35,200 (2000); Median rent: $258 per month (2000); Median age of housing: 58 years (2000).
Transportation: Commute to work: 84.7% car, 1.4% public transportation, 0.7% walk, 7.6% work from home (2000); Travel time to work: 33.8% less than 15 minutes, 45.9% 15 to 30 minutes, 12.8% 30 to 45 minutes, 3.0% 45 to 60 minutes, 4.5% 60 minutes or more (2000)

RUTLAND (city). Covers a land area of 0.899 square miles and a water area of 0 square miles. Located at 42.75° N. Lat.; 94.29° W. Long. Elevation is 1,128 feet.
History: Rutland was named after Rutland, Vermont. The town was platted in 1882 by the Western Town Lot Company.
Population: 145 (2000); Race: 97.3% White, 0.0% Black, 0.0% Asian, 0.0% American Indian and Alaska Native, 1.3% Hispanic of any race, 2.7% two or more races (2000); Density: 161.3 persons per square mile (2000); Age: 26.8% under 18, 14.8% over 64 (2000); Marriage status: 21.0% never married, 61.3% now married, 5.0% widowed, 12.6% divorced (2000); Foreign born: 0.0% (2000); Ancestry (includes multiple ancestries): 32.9% German, 22.8% Irish, 14.8% English, 13.4% Other groups, 12.8% Norwegian (2000).
Economy: Single-family building permits issued: 0 (2001) / 0 (2000); Multi-family building permits issued: 0 (2001) / 0 (2000); Employment by occupation: 4.9% management, 6.2% professional, 17.3% services, 14.8% sales, 4.9% farming, 24.7% construction, 27.2% production (2000).
Income: Per capita income: $13,432 (2000); Median household income: $30,556 (2000); Poverty rate: 2.7% (2000).
Taxes: Total city taxes per capita: $169 (1997); City property taxes per capita: $169 (1997).
Education: High school graduation rate: 83.2% (2000); College graduation rate: 5.9% (2000).
Housing: Homeownership rate: 75.4% (2000); Median home value: $36,300 (2000); Median rent: $355 per month (2000); Median age of housing: 60+ years (2000).
Transportation: Commute to work: 97.5% car, 0.0% public transportation, 0.0% walk, 2.5% work from home (2000); Travel time to work: 51.9% less than 15 minutes, 25.3% 15 to 30 minutes, 10.1% 30 to 45 minutes, 6.3% 45 to 60 minutes, 6.3% 60 minutes or more (2000)

THOR (city). Covers a land area of 0.996 square miles and a water area of 0 square miles. Located at 42.68° N. Lat.; 94.04° W. Long. Elevation is 1,152 feet.
History: Thor was mapped in 1882 by the Western Town Lot Company and was named for the Norse god Thor.
Population: 174 (2000); Race: 100.0% White, 0.0% Black, 0.0% Asian, 0.0% American Indian and Alaska Native, 0.0% Hispanic of any race, 0.0% two or more races (2000); Density: 174.6 persons per square mile (2000); Age: 15.2% under 18, 17.6% over 64 (2000); Marriage status: 27.2% never married, 57.1% now married, 5.4% widowed, 10.2% divorced (2000); Foreign born: 0.0% (2000); Ancestry (includes multiple ancestries): 43.6% German, 30.9% Norwegian, 9.7% Swedish, 5.5% Scotch-Irish, 4.8% French (except Basque) (2000).
Economy: Employment by occupation: 15.6% management, 7.3% professional, 13.5% services, 17.7% sales, 2.1% farming, 8.3% construction, 35.4% production (2000).
Income: Per capita income: $18,410 (2000); Median household income: $36,000 (2000); Poverty rate: 10.3% (2000).
Taxes: Total city taxes per capita: $74 (1997); City property taxes per capita: $74 (1997).
Education: High school graduation rate: 82.9% (2000); College graduation rate: 12.4% (2000).
Housing: Homeownership rate: 89.9% (2000); Median home value: $37,900 (2000); Median rent: $325 per month (2000); Median age of housing: 60+ years (2000).
Transportation: Commute to work: 88.0% car, 0.0% public transportation, 9.8% walk, 2.2% work from home (2000); Travel time to work: 22.2% less than 15 minutes, 60.0% 15 to 30 minutes, 15.6% 30 to 45 minutes, 0.0% 45 to 60 minutes, 2.2% 60 minutes or more (2000)

Ida County

Located in western Iowa; prairie area, drained by the Maple and Soldier Rivers. Covers a land area of 431.70 square miles, a water area of 0.50 square miles, and is located in the Central Time Zone. The county government was organized in 1851. County seat is Ida Grove.

Weather Station: Ida Grove 5 NW — Elevation: 1,318 feet

	Jan	Feb	Mar	Apr	May	Jun	Jul	Aug	Sep	Oct	Nov	Dec
High	27	33	46	61	72	82	85	83	75	63	45	31
Low	7	13	24	36	48	58	63	60	51	39	25	13
Precip	0.8	0.6	2.0	3.2	4.0	4.7	3.8	3.8	2.9	2.3	1.4	0.8
Snow	7.2	6.6	6.2	1.7	tr	0.0	0.0	0.0	0.0	0.4	4.1	6.7

High and Low temperatures in degrees Fahrenheit; Precipitation and Snow in inches

Population: 7,837 (2000); Race: 99.0% White, 0.4% Black, 0.1% Asian, 0.2% American Indian and Alaska Native, 0.4% Hispanic of any race, 0.3% two or more races (2000); Density: 18.2 persons per square mile (2000); Age: 25.5% under 18, 21.6% over 64 (2000).
Religion: Five largest groups: 23.2% Lutheran Church—Missouri Synod, 17.3% The United Methodist Church, 13.9% Catholic Church, 12.1% Evangelical Lutheran Church in America, 7.3% Presbyterian Church (U.S.A.) (2000).

Economy: Unemployment rate: 3.0% (11/2002); Total civilian labor force: 3,923 (11/2002); Leading industries: 35.8% manufacturing; 12.6% retail trade; 12.5% health care and social assistance (2000); Companies that employ more than 1,000 persons: 0 (2000); Companies that employ more than 100 persons: 7 (2000); Farms: 637 totaling 253,306 acres (1997); Minority business ownership rate: 0.0% (1997); Women business ownership rate: 0.0% (1997); Retail sales per capita: $6,591 (1997). Single-family building permits issued: 11 (2001) / 8 (2000); Multi-family building permits issued: 0 (2001) / 0 (2000).
Income: Per capita income: $18,675 (2000); Median household income: $34,805 (2000); Poverty rate: 8.8% (2000); Bankruptcy rate: 3.36% (2001).
Taxes: Total county taxes per capita: $239 (1997); County property taxes per capita: $233 (1997).
Education: High school graduation rate: 85.0% (2000); College graduation rate: 13.6% (2000).
Housing: Homeownership rate: 73.2% (2000); Median home value: $55,500 (2000); Median rent: $234 per month (2000); Median age of housing: 59 years (2000).
Health: Birth rate: 114.8 per 10,000 population (1998); Age adjusted death rate: 90.0 per 10,000 population (1999); Age adjusted cancer mortality rate: 179.9 deaths per 100,000 population (1999). Number of physicians: 2.6 per 10,000 population (1999); Number of hospital beds: 45.9 per 10,000 population (1999).
Elections: 2000 Presidential election results: 40.4% Gore, 56.4% Bush, 1.7% Nader, 1.0% Buchanan

Additional Information Contacts
Ida County Government Offices 712-364-2626
Ida Grove Chamber of Commerce 712-364-3404

Ida County Communities

ARTHUR (city). Covers a land area of 0.153 square miles and a water area of 0 square miles. Located at 42.33° N. Lat.; 95.34° W. Long.
History: Arthur was platted in 1885 by the Western Town Lot Company. It was named after U.S. President Chester Arthur.
Population: 245 (2000); Race: 98.3% White, 0.0% Black, 0.0% Asian, 0.8% American Indian and Alaska Native, 0.0% Hispanic of any race, 0.8% two or more races (2000); Density: 1,600.1 persons per square mile (2000); Age: 25.3% under 18, 24.9% over 64 (2000); Marriage status: 23.5% never married, 59.4% now married, 13.4% widowed, 3.7% divorced (2000); Foreign born: 0.0% (2000); Ancestry (includes multiple ancestries): 60.8% German, 24.1% Irish, 16.9% Swedish, 10.5% English, 7.2% United States or American (2000).
Economy: Single-family building permits issued: 0 (2001) / 0 (2000); Multi-family building permits issued: 0 (2001) / 0 (2000); Employment by occupation: 5.3% management, 13.3% professional, 21.2% services, 22.1% sales, 2.7% farming, 16.8% construction, 18.6% production (2000).
Income: Per capita income: $14,007 (2000); Median household income: $25,833 (2000); Poverty rate: 8.0% (2000).
Taxes: Total city taxes per capita: $124 (1997); City property taxes per capita: $124 (1997).
Education: High school graduation rate: 89.3% (2000); College graduation rate: 12.8% (2000).
Housing: Homeownership rate: 73.6% (2000); Median home value: $42,800 (2000); Median rent: $238 per month (2000); Median age of housing: 59 years (2000).
Transportation: Commute to work: 92.9% car, 0.0% public transportation, 5.3% walk, 1.8% work from home (2000); Travel time to work: 71.2% less than 15 minutes, 17.1% 15 to 30 minutes, 5.4% 30 to 45 minutes, 2.7% 45 to 60 minutes, 3.6% 60 minutes or more (2000)

BATTLE CREEK (city). Covers a land area of 0.498 square miles and a water area of 0 square miles. Located at 42.31° N. Lat.; 95.60° W. Long. Elevation is 1,194 feet.
History: Battle Creek was established in 1884 and named after a nearby stream.
Population: 743 (2000); Race: 99.2% White, 0.0% Black, 0.0% Asian, 0.0% American Indian and Alaska Native, 1.9% Hispanic of any race, 0.5% two or more races (2000); Density: 1,490.5 persons per square mile (2000); Age: 17.6% under 18, 28.2% over 64 (2000); Marriage status: 15.4% never married, 59.4% now married, 14.5% widowed, 10.6% divorced (2000); Foreign born: 0.0% (2000); Ancestry (includes multiple ancestries): 52.0% German, 13.7% Irish, 8.5% English, 7.9% Danish, 5.2% Dutch (2000).
Economy: Single-family building permits issued: 0 (2001) / 0 (2000); Multi-family building permits issued: 0 (2001) / 0 (2000); Employment by occupation: 13.0% management, 12.2% professional, 20.9% services, 18.8% sales, 1.2% farming, 8.1% construction, 25.8% production (2000).
Income: Per capita income: $16,106 (2000); Median household income: $31,029 (2000); Poverty rate: 7.3% (2000).
Taxes: Total city taxes per capita: $123 (1997); City property taxes per capita: $119 (1997).
Education: High school graduation rate: 76.8% (2000); College graduation rate: 10.6% (2000).
Housing: Homeownership rate: 79.1% (2000); Median home value: $38,500 (2000); Median rent: $226 per month (2000); Median age of housing: 60+ years (2000).
Transportation: Commute to work: 92.2% car, 0.0% public transportation, 5.8% walk, 1.2% work from home (2000); Travel time to work: 55.7% less than 15 minutes, 32.6% 15 to 30 minutes, 2.9% 30 to 45 minutes, 3.2% 45 to 60 minutes, 5.6% 60 minutes or more (2000)

GALVA (city). Covers a land area of 0.642 square miles and a water area of 0 square miles. Located at 42.50° N. Lat.; 95.41° W. Long. Elevation is 1,286 feet.
History: Galva, platted in 1882, was named after Galva, Illinois, the former home of many early Swedish settlers here, who brought the name ("Gelfe" in Swedish) with them.
Population: 368 (2000); Race: 98.9% White, 0.0% Black, 0.5% Asian, 0.5% American Indian and Alaska Native, 0.0% Hispanic of any race, 0.0% two or more races (2000); Density: 573.2 persons per square mile (2000); Age: 19.5% under 18, 30.8% over 64 (2000); Marriage status: 15.1% never married, 71.1% now married, 7.2% widowed, 6.6% divorced (2000); Foreign born: 0.5% (2000); Ancestry (includes multiple ancestries): 44.8% German, 14.6% Irish, 9.1% English, 7.4% United States or American, 5.5% Swedish (2000).
Economy: Single-family building permits issued: 0 (2001) / 0 (2000); Multi-family building permits issued: 0 (2001) / 0 (2000); Employment by occupation: 13.3% management, 7.8% professional, 20.6% services, 22.2% sales, 2.8% farming, 13.9% construction, 19.4% production (2000).
Income: Per capita income: $24,062 (2000); Median household income: $30,577 (2000); Poverty rate: 6.6% (2000).
Taxes: Total city taxes per capita: $132 (1997); City property taxes per capita: $130 (1997).
Education: High school graduation rate: 79.2% (2000); College graduation rate: 4.9% (2000).
Housing: Homeownership rate: 89.2% (2000); Median home value: $35,500 (2000); Median rent: $144 per month (2000); Median age of housing: 60+ years (2000).
Transportation: Commute to work: 84.6% car, 0.0% public transportation, 9.9% walk, 3.3% work from home (2000); Travel time to work: 54.0% less than 15 minutes, 25.0% 15 to 30 minutes, 14.8% 30 to 45 minutes, 0.0% 45 to 60 minutes, 6.3% 60 minutes or more (2000)

HOLSTEIN (city). Covers a land area of 1.447 square miles and a water area of 0.009 square miles. Located at 42.48° N. Lat.; 95.54° W. Long. Elevation is 1,437 feet.
History: Holstein was founded in 1882 when a branch of the Chicago & North Western Railroad was constructed through the area. The town was named for the area in Prussia where many of the town's first residents lived before migrating to America.
Population: 1,470 (2000); Race: 100.0% White, 0.0% Black, 0.0% Asian, 0.0% American Indian and Alaska Native, 0.0% Hispanic of any race, 0.0% two or more races (2000); Density: 1,016.0 persons per square mile (2000); Age: 23.0% under 18, 27.9% over 64 (2000); Marriage status: 18.3% never married, 61.6% now married, 14.0% widowed, 6.0% divorced (2000); Foreign born: 0.3% (2000); Ancestry (includes multiple ancestries): 60.6% German, 11.4% Irish, 8.2% English, 5.9% United States or American, 5.4% Norwegian (2000).
Economy: Single-family building permits issued: 6 (2001) / 6 (2000); Multi-family building permits issued: 0 (2001) / 0 (2000); Employment by occupation: 9.1% management, 14.2% professional, 16.6% services, 28.1% sales, 1.2% farming, 7.8% construction, 23.0% production (2000).
Income: Per capita income: $17,941 (2000); Median household income: $35,250 (2000); Poverty rate: 9.1% (2000).
Taxes: Total city taxes per capita: $200 (1997); City property taxes per capita: $195 (1997).
Education: High school graduation rate: 85.4% (2000); College graduation rate: 15.8% (2000).

School District(s)
Galva-Holstein Community School District (PK-12)
2000 Enrollment: 560 712-368-4353

Housing: Homeownership rate: 77.7% (2000); Median home value: $59,100 (2000); Median rent: $235 per month (2000); Median age of housing: 57 years (2000).
Newspapers: Advance (1 x week)
Transportation: Commute to work: 85.0% car, 0.6% public transportation, 6.5% walk, 5.9% work from home (2000); Travel time to work: 66.6% less than 15 minutes, 19.5% 15 to 30 minutes, 5.8% 30 to 45 minutes, 3.0% 45 to 60 minutes, 5.1% 60 minutes or more (2000)

IDA GROVE (city). Covers a land area of 2.080 square miles and a water area of 0.011 square miles. Located at 42.34° N. Lat.; 95.47° W. Long. Elevation is 1,236 feet.
History: Ida Grove was founded by settlers from Scotland.
Population: 2,350 (2000); Race: 98.8% White, 0.4% Black, 0.0% Asian, 0.3% American Indian and Alaska Native, 0.9% Hispanic of any race, 0.6% two or more races (2000); Density: 1,129.7 persons per square mile (2000); Age: 23.3% under 18, 22.0% over 64 (2000); Marriage status: 20.0% never married, 58.9% now married, 13.3% widowed, 7.8% divorced (2000); Foreign born: 0.2% (2000); Ancestry (includes multiple ancestries): 53.9% German, 10.4% Irish, 9.5% English, 7.2% United States or American, 5.4% Swedish (2000).
Economy: Single-family building permits issued: 5 (2001) / 2 (2000); Multi-family building permits issued: 0 (2001) / 0 (2000); Employment by occupation: 11.8% management, 19.0% professional, 16.0% services, 21.7% sales, 0.5% farming, 7.1% construction, 23.7% production (2000).
Income: Per capita income: $20,698 (2000); Median household income: $35,341 (2000); Poverty rate: 7.7% (2000).
Taxes: Total city taxes per capita: $262 (1997); City property taxes per capita: $259 (1997).
Education: High school graduation rate: 84.5% (2000); College graduation rate: 15.3% (2000).

School District(s)
Battle Creek-Ida Grove Community School District (PK-12)
2000 Enrollment: 842 712-364-3687
Housing: Homeownership rate: 69.4% (2000); Median home value: $62,600 (2000); Median rent: $229 per month (2000); Median age of housing: 51 years (2000).
Hospitals: Horn Memorial Hospital (42 beds)
Newspapers: The Reminder (1 x week); The Ida County Courier (1 x week)
Transportation: Commute to work: 91.5% car, 0.6% public transportation, 4.9% walk, 2.7% work from home (2000); Travel time to work: 75.5% less than 15 minutes, 12.2% 15 to 30 minutes, 5.0% 30 to 45 minutes, 1.4% 45 to 60 minutes, 6.0% 60 minutes or more (2000)
Additional Information Contacts
Ida Grove Chamber of Commerce 712-364-3404

Iowa County

Located in east central Iowa; prairie area, drained by the Iowa River and forks of the English River. Covers a land area of 586.40 square miles, a water area of 0.90 square miles, and is located in the Central Time Zone. The county government was organized in 1843. County seat is Marengo.

Weather Station: Williamsburg — Elevation: 849 feet

	Jan	Feb	Mar	Apr	May	Jun	Jul	Aug	Sep	Oct	Nov	Dec
High	28	35	47	61	73	82	86	83	76	64	47	34
Low	10	16	27	38	50	60	64	61	53	41	29	17
Precip	1.1	1.0	2.2	3.4	4.8	4.6	4.4	4.9	3.9	2.7	2.6	1.5
Snow	8.9	6.3	4.0	2.1	tr	0.0	0.0	0.0	0.0	0.4	2.6	6.2

High and Low temperatures in degrees Fahrenheit; Precipitation and Snow in inches

Population: 15,671 (2000); Race: 99.0% White, 0.2% Black, 0.2% Asian, 0.0% American Indian and Alaska Native, 0.7% Hispanic of any race, 0.4% two or more races (2000); Density: 26.7 persons per square mile (2000); Age: 26.3% under 18, 17.1% over 64 (2000).
Religion: Five largest groups: 19.1% Lutheran Church—Missouri Synod, 14.4% Catholic Church, 9.1% The United Methodist Church, 4.4% Presbyterian Church (U.S.A.), 2.4% Mennonite Church USA (2000).
Economy: Unemployment rate: 2.6% (11/2002); Total civilian labor force: 9,830 (11/2002); Leading industries: 56.6% manufacturing; 13.5% retail trade; 10.1% accommodation & food services (2000); Companies that employ more than 1,000 persons: 1 (2000); Companies that employ more than 100 persons: 9 (2000); Farms: 976 totaling 331,922 acres (1997); Minority business ownership rate: 0.0% (1997); Women business ownership rate: 27.4% (1997); Retail sales per capita: $9,940 (1997). Single-family building permits issued: 18 (2001) / 25 (2000); Multi-family building permits issued: 2 (2001) / 12 (2000).
Income: Per capita income: $18,884 (2000); Median household income: $41,222 (2000); Poverty rate: 5.0% (2000); Bankruptcy rate: 2.03% (2001).
Taxes: Total county taxes per capita: $291 (2000); County property taxes per capita: $208 (2000).
Education: High school graduation rate: 87.0% (2000); College graduation rate: 15.8% (2000).
Housing: Homeownership rate: 77.9% (2000); Median home value: $85,600 (2000); Median rent: $317 per month (2000); Median age of housing: 50 years (2000).
Health: Birth rate: 111.7 per 10,000 population (1998); Age adjusted death rate: 82.0 per 10,000 population (1999); Age adjusted cancer mortality rate: 175.5 deaths per 100,000 population (1999). Number of physicians: 5.1 per 10,000 population (1999); Number of hospital beds: 24.9 per 10,000 population (1999).
Elections: 2000 Presidential election results: 43.6% Gore, 52.5% Bush, 2.5% Nader, 0.8% Buchanan
Additional Information Contacts
Iowa County Government Offices 319-642-3923
Amana Colonies Convention Bureau 319-622-7622
Williamsburg Chamber of Commerce 319-668-1500

Iowa County Communities

CONROY (unincorporated postal area, zip code 52220). Covers a land area of 0.049 square miles and a water area of 0 square miles. Located at 41.72° N. Lat.; 91.99° W. Long. Elevation is 883 feet.
History: Conroy was named for pioneer settler James Conroy.
Population: 72 (2000); Race: 100.0% White, 0.0% Black, 0.0% Asian, 0.0% American Indian and Alaska Native, 0.0% Hispanic of any race, 0.0% two or more races (2000); Density: 1,474.1 persons per square mile (2000); Age: 27.3% under 18, 7.3% over 64 (2000); Marriage status: 44.3% never married, 42.3% now married, 8.2% widowed, 5.2% divorced (2000); Foreign born: 13.6% (2000); Ancestry (includes multiple ancestries): 38.2% German, 33.6% Norwegian, 26.4% Irish, 19.1% Other groups, 16.4% Welsh (2000).
Economy: Employment by occupation: 14.3% management, 0.0% professional, 7.9% services, 17.5% sales, 0.0% farming, 17.5% construction, 42.9% production (2000).
Income: Per capita income: $16,200 (2000); Median household income: $75,171 (2000); Poverty rate: 0.0% (2000).
Education: High school graduation rate: 81.5% (2000); College graduation rate: 9.3% (2000).
Housing: Homeownership rate: 100.0% (2000); Median home value: $69,300 (2000); Median age of housing: 35 years (2000).
Transportation: Commute to work: 100.0% car, 0.0% public transportation, 0.0% walk, 0.0% work from home (2000); Travel time to work: 31.7% less than 15 minutes, 36.5% 15 to 30 minutes, 15.9% 30 to 45 minutes, 7.9% 45 to 60 minutes, 7.9% 60 minutes or more (2000)

HOMESTEAD (unincorporated postal area, zip code 52236). Covers a land area of 29.916 square miles and a water area of 0.062 square miles. Located at 41.73° N. Lat.; 91.87° W. Long.
History: Homestead was one of the seven villages of the Amana Society.
Population: 449 (2000); Race: 100.0% White, 0.0% Black, 0.0% Asian, 0.0% American Indian and Alaska Native, 1.2% Hispanic of any race, 0.0% two or more races (2000); Density: 15.0 persons per square mile (2000); Age: 19.6% under 18, 24.7% over 64 (2000); Marriage status: 12.5% never married, 73.3% now married, 9.5% widowed, 4.7% divorced (2000); Foreign born: 0.0% (2000); Ancestry (includes multiple ancestries): 64.8% German, 18.3% English, 12.5% Irish, 3.4% Scotch-Irish, 3.2% Czech (2000).
Economy: Employment by occupation: 24.6% management, 14.0% professional, 8.8% services, 21.9% sales, 2.2% farming, 7.5% construction, 21.1% production (2000).
Income: Per capita income: $22,080 (2000); Median household income: $50,781 (2000); Poverty rate: 2.4% (2000).
Education: High school graduation rate: 89.0% (2000); College graduation rate: 9.6% (2000).
Housing: Homeownership rate: 76.4% (2000); Median home value: $107,000 (2000); Median rent: $263 per month (2000); Median age of housing: 56 years (2000).
Transportation: Commute to work: 91.5% car, 0.0% public transportation, 0.0% walk, 8.5% work from home (2000); Travel time to work: 25.4% less than 15 minutes, 54.1% 15 to 30 minutes, 12.7% 30 to 45 minutes, 7.8% 45 to 60 minutes, 0.0% 60 minutes or more (2000)

LADORA (city). Covers a land area of 0.306 square miles and a water area of 0 square miles. Located at 41.75° N. Lat.; 92.18° W. Long. Elevation is 783 feet.
History: Ladora was named by a local music teacher, Mrs. Scofield. The name is a combination of musical syllables la, do, and re.
Population: 287 (2000); Race: 100.0% White, 0.0% Black, 0.0% Asian, 0.0% American Indian and Alaska Native, 0.7% Hispanic of any race, 0.0% two or more races (2000); Density: 937.8 persons per square mile (2000); Age: 28.5% under 18, 12.3% over 64 (2000); Marriage status: 21.4% never married, 55.3% now married, 7.9% widowed, 15.3% divorced (2000); Foreign born: 0.7% (2000); Ancestry (includes multiple ancestries): 41.5% German, 10.9% English, 8.8% United States or American, 8.5% Irish, 4.9% Scottish (2000).
Economy: Employment by occupation: 3.5% management, 7.7% professional, 7.7% services, 31.5% sales, 1.4% farming, 11.2% construction, 37.1% production (2000).
Income: Per capita income: $15,888 (2000); Median household income: $36,875 (2000); Poverty rate: 8.5% (2000).
Taxes: Total city taxes per capita: $156 (1997); City property taxes per capita: $72 (1997).
Education: High school graduation rate: 79.7% (2000); College graduation rate: 4.8% (2000).
Housing: Homeownership rate: 86.1% (2000); Median home value: $35,900 (2000); Median rent: $319 per month (2000); Median age of housing: 60+ years (2000).
Transportation: Commute to work: 95.1% car, 0.0% public transportation, 0.0% walk, 2.1% work from home (2000); Travel time to work: 31.4% less than 15 minutes, 42.9% 15 to 30 minutes, 12.9% 30 to 45 minutes, 7.9% 45 to 60 minutes, 5.0% 60 minutes or more (2000)

MARENGO (city). Covers a land area of 2.094 square miles and a water area of 0.061 square miles. Located at 41.79° N. Lat.; 92.07° W. Long. Elevation is 738 feet.
History: Marengo was named for the plain of Marengo, near Alessandria, Italy, where the Austrians were defeated by Napoleon in 1800.
Population: 2,535 (2000); Race: 99.3% White, 0.2% Black, 0.6% Asian, 0.0% American Indian and Alaska Native, 0.0% Hispanic of any race, 0.0% two or more races (2000); Density: 1,210.5 persons per square mile (2000); Age: 24.8% under 18, 19.3% over 64 (2000); Marriage status: 20.6% never married, 55.4% now married, 12.4% widowed, 11.7% divorced (2000); Foreign born: 1.3% (2000); Ancestry (includes multiple ancestries): 34.8% German, 12.7% Irish, 9.0% English, 7.8% United States or American, 3.6% French (except Basque) (2000).
Economy: Single-family building permits issued: 6 (2001) / 5 (2000); Multi-family building permits issued: 0 (2001) / 0 (2000); Employment by occupation: 10.5% management, 10.9% professional, 17.7% services, 21.0% sales, 1.4% farming, 9.2% construction, 29.2% production (2000).
Income: Per capita income: $17,425 (2000); Median household income: $36,509 (2000); Poverty rate: 7.3% (2000).
Taxes: Total city taxes per capita: $325 (1997); City property taxes per capita: $238 (1997).
Education: High school graduation rate: 86.5% (2000); College graduation rate: 9.2% (2000).

School District(s)

Iowa Valley Community School District (PK-12)
2000 Enrollment: 675 319-642-7714

Housing: Homeownership rate: 71.8% (2000); Median home value: $72,800 (2000); Median rent: $284 per month (2000); Median age of housing: 56 years (2000).
Hospitals: Marengo Memorial Hospital (25 beds)
Newspapers: Marengo Pioneer-Republican (1 x week); Iowa County Advertiser (1 x week)
Transportation: Commute to work: 92.0% car, 0.0% public transportation, 5.3% walk, 2.2% work from home (2000); Travel time to work: 41.4% less than 15 minutes, 30.6% 15 to 30 minutes, 15.4% 30 to 45 minutes, 9.1% 45 to 60 minutes, 3.6% 60 minutes or more (2000)

MIDDLE AMANA (unincorporated postal area, zip code 52307). Aka Middle. Covers a land area of 5.503 square miles and a water area of 0 square miles. Located at 41.79° N. Lat.; 91.91° W. Long.
History: Middle Amana was one of the seven villages of the Amana Society.
Population: 164 (2000); Race: 100.0% White, 0.0% Black, 0.0% Asian, 0.0% American Indian and Alaska Native, 0.0% Hispanic of any race, 0.0% two or more races (2000); Density: 29.8 persons per square mile (2000); Age: 26.7% under 18, 27.3% over 64 (2000); Marriage status: 33.3% never married, 59.5% now married, 7.2% widowed, 0.0% divorced (2000); Foreign born: 0.0% (2000); Ancestry (includes multiple ancestries): 72.2% German, 14.4% Czech, 5.9% English, 4.3% United States or American, 4.3% Northern European (2000).
Economy: Employment by occupation: 6.5% management, 15.1% professional, 24.7% services, 20.4% sales, 0.0% farming, 0.0% construction, 33.3% production (2000).
Income: Per capita income: $18,450 (2000); Median household income: $40,125 (2000); Poverty rate: 4.3% (2000).
Education: High school graduation rate: 83.1% (2000); College graduation rate: 21.2% (2000).
Housing: Homeownership rate: 57.8% (2000); Median home value: $122,900 (2000); Median rent: $344 per month (2000); Median age of housing: 60+ years (2000).
Transportation: Commute to work: 77.4% car, 0.0% public transportation, 22.6% walk, 0.0% work from home (2000); Travel time to work: 83.9% less than 15 minutes, 10.8% 15 to 30 minutes, 5.4% 30 to 45 minutes, 0.0% 45 to 60 minutes, 0.0% 60 minutes or more (2000)

MILLERSBURG (city). Covers a land area of 0.126 square miles and a water area of 0 square miles. Located at 41.57° N. Lat.; 92.15° W. Long. Elevation is 870 feet.
History: Millersburg was platted in 1852 by Rueben Miller.
Population: 184 (2000); Race: 100.0% White, 0.0% Black, 0.0% Asian, 0.0% American Indian and Alaska Native, 0.0% Hispanic of any race, 0.0% two or more races (2000); Density: 1,463.4 persons per square mile (2000); Age: 33.5% under 18, 15.3% over 64 (2000); Marriage status: 29.1% never married, 51.0% now married, 5.3% widowed, 14.6% divorced (2000); Foreign born: 0.0% (2000); Ancestry (includes multiple ancestries): 35.4% German, 12.0% United States or American, 9.1% English, 9.1% Norwegian, 6.7% Irish (2000).
Economy: Single-family building permits issued: 0 (2001) / 1 (2000); Multi-family building permits issued: 0 (2001) / 0 (2000); Employment by occupation: 7.9% management, 2.0% professional, 22.8% services, 12.9% sales, 5.9% farming, 14.9% construction, 33.7% production (2000).
Income: Per capita income: $18,233 (2000); Median household income: $37,500 (2000); Poverty rate: 14.4% (2000).
Taxes: Total city taxes per capita: $134 (1997); City property taxes per capita: $48 (1997).
Education: High school graduation rate: 81.6% (2000); College graduation rate: 4.0% (2000).

School District(s)

Deep River-Millersburg Community School District (PK-12)
2000 Enrollment: 130 319-655-7641

Housing: Homeownership rate: 74.4% (2000); Median home value: $45,300 (2000); Median rent: $269 per month (2000); Median age of housing: 60 years (2000).
Transportation: Commute to work: 84.2% car, 0.0% public transportation, 5.9% walk, 9.9% work from home (2000); Travel time to work: 28.6% less than 15 minutes, 36.3% 15 to 30 minutes, 20.9% 30 to 45 minutes, 0.0% 45 to 60 minutes, 14.3% 60 minutes or more (2000)

NORTH ENGLISH (city). Covers a land area of 0.555 square miles and a water area of 0 square miles. Located at 41.51° N. Lat.; 92.07° W. Long. Elevation is 815 feet.
History: North English is believed to be named after English Township and the North English River.
Population: 991 (2000); Race: 99.3% White, 0.5% Black, 0.2% Asian, 0.0% American Indian and Alaska Native, 0.6% Hispanic of any race, 0.0% two or more races (2000); Density: 1,784.2 persons per square mile (2000); Age: 24.2% under 18, 27.7% over 64 (2000); Marriage status: 19.5% never married, 55.8% now married, 15.1% widowed, 9.6% divorced (2000); Foreign born: 0.2% (2000); Ancestry (includes multiple ancestries): 35.7% German, 8.6% English, 6.6% Irish, 5.0% Dutch, 4.9% Other groups (2000).
Economy: Employment by occupation: 7.5% management, 18.0% professional, 22.4% services, 22.6% sales, 1.1% farming, 7.8% construction, 20.5% production (2000).
Income: Per capita income: $16,158 (2000); Median household income: $32,639 (2000); Poverty rate: 8.2% (2000).
Taxes: Total city taxes per capita: $221 (1997); City property taxes per capita: $135 (1997).
Education: High school graduation rate: 85.3% (2000); College graduation rate: 14.9% (2000).

School District(s)

English Valleys Community School District (PK-12)
2000 Enrollment: 562 319-664-3634

Housing: Homeownership rate: 83.0% (2000); Median home value: $58,200 (2000); Median rent: $286 per month (2000); Median age of housing: 54 years (2000).
Newspapers: North English Record (1 x week)
Transportation: Commute to work: 89.4% car, 0.5% public transportation, 4.8% walk, 4.8% work from home (2000); Travel time to work: 33.3% less than 15 minutes, 24.2% 15 to 30 minutes, 17.9% 30 to 45 minutes, 16.9% 45 to 60 minutes, 7.7% 60 minutes or more (2000)

PARNELL (city). Covers a land area of 0.174 square miles and a water area of 0 square miles. Located at 41.58° N. Lat.; 92.00° W. Long. Elevation is 859 feet.
History: Parnell is named for Irish statesman James Stewart Parnell.
Population: 220 (2000); Race: 100.0% White, 0.0% Black, 0.0% Asian, 0.0% American Indian and Alaska Native, 0.4% Hispanic of any race, 0.0% two or more races (2000); Density: 1,267.8 persons per square mile (2000); Age: 22.7% under 18, 15.6% over 64 (2000); Marriage status: 34.5% never married, 47.5% now married, 9.0% widowed, 9.0% divorced (2000); Foreign born: 0.0% (2000); Ancestry (includes multiple ancestries): 47.6% German, 31.6% Irish, 12.0% English, 7.1% Scottish, 6.2% Czech (2000).
Economy: Single-family building permits issued: 0 (2001) / 1 (2000); Multi-family building permits issued: 0 (2001) / 0 (2000); Employment by occupation: 9.2% management, 7.8% professional, 17.7% services, 25.5% sales, 1.4% farming, 10.6% construction, 27.7% production (2000).
Income: Per capita income: $19,293 (2000); Median household income: $36,667 (2000); Poverty rate: 6.2% (2000).
Taxes: Total city taxes per capita: $190 (1997); City property taxes per capita: $105 (1997).
Education: High school graduation rate: 88.3% (2000); College graduation rate: 11.7% (2000).
Housing: Homeownership rate: 80.9% (2000); Median home value: $68,300 (2000); Median rent: $338 per month (2000); Median age of housing: 36 years (2000).
Transportation: Commute to work: 98.6% car, 0.0% public transportation, 0.0% walk, 1.4% work from home (2000); Travel time to work: 29.2% less than 15 minutes, 35.8% 15 to 30 minutes, 28.5% 30 to 45 minutes, 6.6% 45 to 60 minutes, 0.0% 60 minutes or more (2000)

SOUTH AMANA (unincorporated postal area, zip code 52334). Covers a land area of 16.842 square miles and a water area of 0 square miles. Located at 41.73° N. Lat.; 91.94° W. Long.
History: South Amana was one of the seven villages of the Amana Society.
Population: 285 (2000); Race: 100.0% White, 0.0% Black, 0.0% Asian, 0.0% American Indian and Alaska Native, 0.0% Hispanic of any race, 0.0% two or more races (2000); Density: 16.9 persons per square mile (2000); Age: 22.9% under 18, 13.5% over 64 (2000); Marriage status: 23.6% never married, 67.0% now married, 1.9% widowed, 7.5% divorced (2000); Foreign born: 0.0% (2000); Ancestry (includes multiple ancestries): 70.5% German, 12.7% English, 10.2% Other groups, 6.9% Irish, 5.5% Norwegian (2000).
Economy: Employment by occupation: 19.1% management, 7.3% professional, 7.9% services, 19.7% sales, 3.4% farming, 0.0% construction, 42.7% production (2000).
Income: Per capita income: $20,995 (2000); Median household income: $44,545 (2000); Poverty rate: 0.0% (2000).
Education: High school graduation rate: 88.3% (2000); College graduation rate: 15.7% (2000).
Housing: Homeownership rate: 74.1% (2000); Median home value: $118,800 (2000); Median rent: $354 per month (2000); Median age of housing: 32 years (2000).
Transportation: Commute to work: 89.3% car, 0.0% public transportation, 0.0% walk, 10.7% work from home (2000); Travel time to work: 24.5% less than 15 minutes, 57.9% 15 to 30 minutes, 14.5% 30 to 45 minutes, 3.1% 45 to 60 minutes, 0.0% 60 minutes or more (2000)

VICTOR (city). Covers a land area of 0.473 square miles and a water area of 0 square miles. Located at 41.73° N. Lat.; 92.29° W. Long.
History: Victor was called Greenville when it was settled by groups of immigrants from Ireland, Belgium, and Germany.
Population: 952 (2000); Race: 98.5% White, 0.0% Black, 0.2% Asian, 0.1% American Indian and Alaska Native, 0.5% Hispanic of any race, 0.5% two or more races (2000); Density: 2,010.6 persons per square mile (2000); Age: 25.9% under 18, 19.7% over 64 (2000); Marriage status: 18.8% never married, 63.8% now married, 8.6% widowed, 8.7% divorced (2000); Foreign born: 0.7% (2000); Ancestry (includes multiple ancestries): 42.8% German, 12.3% Irish, 9.8% Belgian, 7.5% English, 7.2% Czech (2000).
Economy: Single-family building permits issued: 3 (2001) / 4 (2000); Multi-family building permits issued: 0 (2001) / 0 (2000); Employment by occupation: 10.4% management, 13.0% professional, 14.2% services, 23.8% sales, 0.6% farming, 11.0% construction, 27.0% production (2000).
Income: Per capita income: $18,837 (2000); Median household income: $38,542 (2000); Poverty rate: 7.9% (2000).
Taxes: Total city taxes per capita: $254 (1997); City property taxes per capita: $171 (1997).
Education: High school graduation rate: 90.4% (2000); College graduation rate: 13.4% (2000).

School District(s)

H-L-V Community School District (PK-12)
2000 Enrollment: 479 319-647-2161

Housing: Homeownership rate: 79.7% (2000); Median home value: $69,300 (2000); Median rent: $260 per month (2000); Median age of housing: 48 years (2000).
Transportation: Commute to work: 86.6% car, 0.0% public transportation, 9.7% walk, 3.2% work from home (2000); Travel time to work: 53.1% less than 15 minutes, 23.8% 15 to 30 minutes, 15.7% 30 to 45 minutes, 5.6% 45 to 60 minutes, 1.7% 60 minutes or more (2000)

WILLIAMSBURG (city). Covers a land area of 3.146 square miles and a water area of 0.008 square miles. Located at 41.66° N. Lat.; 92.01° W. Long. Elevation is 765 feet.
History: Williamsburg was named for its founder Richard Williams.
Population: 2,622 (2000); Race: 97.1% White, 0.2% Black, 0.0% Asian, 0.0% American Indian and Alaska Native, 2.3% Hispanic of any race, 1.3% two or more races (2000); Density: 833.4 persons per square mile (2000); Age: 29.0% under 18, 16.9% over 64 (2000); Marriage status: 21.8% never married, 63.2% now married, 9.3% widowed, 5.7% divorced (2000); Foreign born: 0.6% (2000); Ancestry (includes multiple ancestries): 49.8% German, 15.3% Irish, 7.5% English, 6.3% United States or American, 4.5% Dutch (2000).
Economy: Single-family building permits issued: 9 (2001) / 14 (2000); Multi-family building permits issued: 2 (2001) / 12 (2000); Employment by occupation: 10.2% management, 18.5% professional, 12.8% services, 28.6% sales, 1.1% farming, 9.2% construction, 19.7% production (2000).
Income: Per capita income: $19,712 (2000); Median household income: $36,528 (2000); Poverty rate: 4.3% (2000).
Taxes: Total city taxes per capita: $536 (1997); City property taxes per capita: $414 (1997).
Education: High school graduation rate: 85.3% (2000); College graduation rate: 23.7% (2000).

School District(s)

Williamsburg Community School District (PK-12)
2000 Enrollment: 1,076 319-668-1059

Housing: Homeownership rate: 73.1% (2000); Median home value: $100,200 (2000); Median rent: $367 per month (2000); Median age of housing: 34 years (2000).
Newspapers: The Journal Tribune (1 x week)
Transportation: Commute to work: 93.8% car, 0.0% public transportation, 3.3% walk, 2.9% work from home (2000); Travel time to work: 51.8% less than 15 minutes, 21.0% 15 to 30 minutes, 21.4% 30 to 45 minutes, 4.0% 45 to 60 minutes, 1.8% 60 minutes or more (2000)
Additional Information Contacts
Williamsburg Chamber of Commerce 319-668-1500

Jackson County

Located in eastern Iowa; bounded on the east by the Mississippi River and the Illinois border; prairie area, drained by the Maquoketa and North Fork Maquoketa Rivers. Covers a land area of 636.10 square miles, a water area of 13.70 square miles, and is located in the Central Time Zone. The county government was organized in 1837. County seat is Maquoketa.

Weather Station: Bellevue Lock & Dam 12 — Elevation: 600 feet

	Jan	Feb	Mar	Apr	May	Jun	Jul	Aug	Sep	Oct	Nov	Dec
High	27	33	45	59	71	81	84	82	74	62	46	33
Low	10	15	26	37	48	58	62	60	52	40	28	17
Precip	1.1	1.2	2.3	3.3	3.8	4.4	3.3	4.4	3.8	2.6	2.6	1.6
Snow	10.4	5.9	4.1	1.4	0.1	0.0	0.0	0.0	0.0	tr	1.8	7.1

High and Low temperatures in degrees Fahrenheit; Precipitation and Snow in inches

Population: 20,296 (2000); Race: 99.3% White, 0.1% Black, 0.1% Asian, 0.2% American Indian and Alaska Native, 0.5% Hispanic of any race, 0.2%

two or more races (2000); Density: 31.9 persons per square mile (2000); Age: 26.0% under 18, 17.3% over 64 (2000).
Religion: Five largest groups: 42.9% Catholic Church, 19.5% Evangelical Lutheran Church in America, 4.5% The United Methodist Church, 2.0% United Church of Christ, 1.8% Presbyterian Church (U.S.A.) (2000).
Economy: Unemployment rate: 6.4% (11/2002); Total civilian labor force: 9,508 (11/2002); Leading industries: 26.4% manufacturing; 17.1% retail trade; 15.9% health care and social assistance (2000); Companies that employ more than 1,000 persons: 0 (2000); Companies that employ more than 100 persons: 8 (2000); Farms: 1,280 totaling 334,824 acres (1997); Minority business ownership rate: 0.0% (1997); Women business ownership rate: 17.1% (1997); Retail sales per capita: $8,244 (1997). Single-family building permits issued: 64 (2001) / 49 (2000); Multi-family building permits issued: 12 (2001) / 18 (2000).
Income: Per capita income: $17,329 (2000); Median household income: $34,529 (2000); Poverty rate: 10.3% (2000); Bankruptcy rate: 2.37% (2001).
Taxes: Total county taxes per capita: $216 (2000); County property taxes per capita: $182 (2000).
Education: High school graduation rate: 81.5% (2000); College graduation rate: 12.1% (2000).
Housing: Homeownership rate: 75.8% (2000); Median home value: $76,500 (2000); Median rent: $292 per month (2000); Median age of housing: 42 years (2000).
Health: Birth rate: 116.3 per 10,000 population (1998); Age adjusted death rate: 83.2 per 10,000 population (1999); Age adjusted cancer mortality rate: 215.3 deaths per 100,000 population (1999). Number of physicians: 5.4 per 10,000 population (1999); Number of hospital beds: 30.1 per 10,000 population (1999).
Elections: 2000 Presidential election results: 54.8% Gore, 41.7% Bush, 2.5% Nader, 0.6% Buchanan
National and State Parks: Bellevue State Park; Bellevue State Park; Dalton Pond State Fishing Access Area; Maquoketa Caves State Park
Additional Information Contacts
Jackson County Government Offices 563-652-3144
Bellevue Chamber of Commerce 563-872-5830
Jackson County Board of Realtors 563-652-2772
Maquoketa Chamber of Commerce 563-652-4602

Jackson County Communities

ANDREW (city). Covers a land area of 0.263 square miles and a water area of 0 square miles. Located at 42.15° N. Lat.; 90.59° W. Long.
History: Andrew was the home of Ansel Briggs, first Governor of Iowa (1846-1850). Briggs, who carried the mail along the old Military Road to Dubuque (1836-1846), lived in the Butterworth Tavern, half a mile north of town.
Population: 460 (2000); Race: 100.0% White, 0.0% Black, 0.0% Asian, 0.0% American Indian and Alaska Native, 3.2% Hispanic of any race, 0.0% two or more races (2000); Density: 1,747.9 persons per square mile (2000); Age: 39.4% under 18, 8.8% over 64 (2000); Marriage status: 28.8% never married, 52.5% now married, 7.7% widowed, 11.0% divorced (2000); Foreign born: 3.6% (2000); Ancestry (includes multiple ancestries): 51.6% German, 9.9% Irish, 6.2% United States or American, 6.2% English, 5.4% Other groups (2000).
Economy: Single-family building permits issued: 2 (2001) / 0 (2000); Multi-family building permits issued: 0 (2001) / 0 (2000); Employment by occupation: 6.8% management, 13.2% professional, 18.4% services, 21.1% sales, 0.0% farming, 13.2% construction, 27.4% production (2000).
Income: Per capita income: $12,860 (2000); Median household income: $36,563 (2000); Poverty rate: 9.3% (2000).
Taxes: Total city taxes per capita: $126 (1997); City property taxes per capita: $78 (1997).
Education: High school graduation rate: 82.1% (2000); College graduation rate: 12.3% (2000).

School District(s)
Andrew Community School District (PK-12)
2000 Enrollment: 357 319-672-3221
Housing: Homeownership rate: 72.6% (2000); Median home value: $64,500 (2000); Median rent: $298 per month (2000); Median age of housing: 36 years (2000).
Transportation: Commute to work: 88.2% car, 1.1% public transportation, 2.7% walk, 3.7% work from home (2000); Travel time to work: 28.3% less than 15 minutes, 33.3% 15 to 30 minutes, 21.1% 30 to 45 minutes, 12.8% 45 to 60 minutes, 4.4% 60 minutes or more (2000)

BALDWIN (city). Covers a land area of 0.358 square miles and a water area of 0 square miles. Located at 42.07° N. Lat.; 90.84° W. Long.
History: Baldwin was originally named Fremont after General John C. Fremont. The name was changed to honor Edward Baldwin, the original owner of the site.
Population: 127 (2000); Race: 98.5% White, 1.5% Black, 0.0% Asian, 0.0% American Indian and Alaska Native, 0.0% Hispanic of any race, 0.0% two or more races (2000); Density: 355.0 persons per square mile (2000); Age: 21.5% under 18, 21.5% over 64 (2000); Marriage status: 33.3% never married, 48.7% now married, 6.0% widowed, 12.0% divorced (2000); Foreign born: 0.0% (2000); Ancestry (includes multiple ancestries): 46.9% German, 20.0% United States or American, 5.4% Irish, 3.1% English, 3.1% Danish (2000).
Economy: Single-family building permits issued: 0 (2001) / 0 (2000); Multi-family building permits issued: 0 (2001) / 0 (2000); Employment by occupation: 5.8% management, 0.0% professional, 13.0% services, 11.6% sales, 0.0% farming, 29.0% construction, 40.6% production (2000).
Income: Per capita income: $15,997 (2000); Median household income: $35,313 (2000); Poverty rate: 2.3% (2000).
Taxes: Total city taxes per capita: $112 (1997); City property taxes per capita: $52 (1997).
Education: High school graduation rate: 73.3% (2000); College graduation rate: 5.8% (2000).
Housing: Homeownership rate: 91.1% (2000); Median home value: $31,700 (2000); Median rent: $275 per month (2000); Median age of housing: 60+ years (2000).
Transportation: Commute to work: 92.8% car, 0.0% public transportation, 4.3% walk, 0.0% work from home (2000); Travel time to work: 29.0% less than 15 minutes, 49.3% 15 to 30 minutes, 0.0% 30 to 45 minutes, 2.9% 45 to 60 minutes, 18.8% 60 minutes or more (2000)

BELLEVUE (city). Covers a land area of 0.975 square miles and a water area of 0.069 square miles. Located at 42.25° N. Lat.; 90.42° W. Long. Elevation is 617 feet.
History: Bellevue was the seat of Jackson County before Maquoketa obtained the privilege. It was first called Bell View in honor of one of the early settlers named Bell, who built his home on a bluff overlooking the town site.
Population: 2,350 (2000); Race: 99.7% White, 0.3% Black, 0.0% Asian, 0.0% American Indian and Alaska Native, 0.4% Hispanic of any race, 0.0% two or more races (2000); Density: 2,410.7 persons per square mile (2000); Age: 25.0% under 18, 21.9% over 64 (2000); Marriage status: 23.2% never married, 59.0% now married, 11.1% widowed, 6.7% divorced (2000); Foreign born: 0.5% (2000); Ancestry (includes multiple ancestries): 55.4% German, 11.7% Irish, 7.0% United States or American, 4.3% Luxemburger, 2.1% French (except Basque) (2000).
Economy: Single-family building permits issued: 7 (2001) / 4 (2000); Multi-family building permits issued: 0 (2001) / 0 (2000); Employment by occupation: 7.3% management, 10.7% professional, 16.3% services, 25.7% sales, 1.1% farming, 12.3% construction, 26.6% production (2000).
Income: Per capita income: $15,928 (2000); Median household income: $35,293 (2000); Poverty rate: 7.3% (2000).
Taxes: Total city taxes per capita: $252 (1997); City property taxes per capita: $188 (1997).
Education: High school graduation rate: 79.4% (2000); College graduation rate: 12.7% (2000).

School District(s)
Bellevue Community School District (PK-12)
2000 Enrollment: 659 319-872-4913
Housing: Homeownership rate: 77.9% (2000); Median home value: $85,700 (2000); Median rent: $284 per month (2000); Median age of housing: 50 years (2000).
Newspapers: The Bellevue Herald-Leader (1 x week)
Transportation: Commute to work: 89.9% car, 0.5% public transportation, 5.1% walk, 3.3% work from home (2000); Travel time to work: 52.1% less than 15 minutes, 12.1% 15 to 30 minutes, 21.1% 30 to 45 minutes, 8.8% 45 to 60 minutes, 6.0% 60 minutes or more (2000)
Additional Information Contacts
Bellevue Chamber of Commerce 563-872-5830

LA MOTTE (city). Covers a land area of 0.467 square miles and a water area of 0 square miles. Located at 42.29° N. Lat.; 90.62° W. Long. Elevation is 915 feet.
History: It is believed that La Motte was named for one of the town founders, Alexander La Motte.

Population: 272 (2000); Race: 100.0% White, 0.0% Black, 0.0% Asian, 0.0% American Indian and Alaska Native, 0.0% Hispanic of any race, 0.0% two or more races (2000); Density: 582.6 persons per square mile (2000); Age: 19.1% under 18, 18.3% over 64 (2000); Marriage status: 28.3% never married, 62.1% now married, 3.8% widowed, 5.8% divorced (2000); Foreign born: 1.4% (2000); Ancestry (includes multiple ancestries): 54.3% German, 25.2% Irish, 17.6% United States or American, 11.2% Luxemburger, 2.9% Polish (2000).
Economy: Single-family building permits issued: 0 (2001) / 0 (2000); Multi-family building permits issued: 0 (2001) / 0 (2000); Employment by occupation: 15.8% management, 13.3% professional, 7.9% services, 21.8% sales, 0.0% farming, 7.9% construction, 33.3% production (2000).
Income: Per capita income: $19,794 (2000); Median household income: $35,625 (2000); Poverty rate: 9.0% (2000).
Taxes: Total city taxes per capita: $178 (1997); City property taxes per capita: $119 (1997).
Education: High school graduation rate: 77.4% (2000); College graduation rate: 8.7% (2000).
Housing: Homeownership rate: 82.4% (2000); Median home value: $70,800 (2000); Median rent: $342 per month (2000); Median age of housing: 59 years (2000).
Transportation: Commute to work: 86.0% car, 1.8% public transportation, 6.1% walk, 3.7% work from home (2000); Travel time to work: 24.1% less than 15 minutes, 50.0% 15 to 30 minutes, 19.0% 30 to 45 minutes, 7.0% 45 to 60 minutes, 0.0% 60 minutes or more (2000)

MAQUOKETA (city). Covers a land area of 3.447 square miles and a water area of 0.030 square miles. Located at 42.06° N. Lat.; 90.66° W. Long. Elevation is 684 feet.
History: Maquoketa became the seat of Jackson County in 1873, when the county seat was transferred from the town of Andrew.
Population: 6,112 (2000); Race: 98.9% White, 0.1% Black, 0.0% Asian, 0.5% American Indian and Alaska Native, 0.4% Hispanic of any race, 0.4% two or more races (2000); Density: 1,773.3 persons per square mile (2000); Age: 24.1% under 18, 21.3% over 64 (2000); Marriage status: 25.1% never married, 51.0% now married, 11.8% widowed, 12.1% divorced (2000); Foreign born: 0.6% (2000); Ancestry (includes multiple ancestries): 37.5% German, 12.1% English, 12.0% Irish, 7.2% United States or American, 2.5% Other groups (2000).
Economy: Single-family building permits issued: 4 (2001) / 14 (2000); Multi-family building permits issued: 12 (2001) / 18 (2000); Employment by occupation: 8.5% management, 17.4% professional, 13.5% services, 25.3% sales, 0.8% farming, 11.2% construction, 23.2% production (2000).
Income: Per capita income: $16,360 (2000); Median household income: $28,984 (2000); Poverty rate: 12.3% (2000).
Taxes: Total city taxes per capita: $335 (2000); City property taxes per capita: $255 (2000).
Education: High school graduation rate: 80.8% (2000); College graduation rate: 14.5% (2000).

School District(s)

Maquoketa Community School District (PK-12)
2000 Enrollment: 1,706 319-652-4984
Housing: Homeownership rate: 67.0% (2000); Median home value: $68,800 (2000); Median rent: $303 per month (2000); Median age of housing: 41 years (2000).
Hospitals: Jackson County Public Hospital (61 beds)
Safety: Violent crime rate: 11.5 per 10,000 population; Property crime rate: 501.2 per 10,000 population (2001).
Newspapers: Maquoketa Sentinel-Press (2 x week)
Transportation: Commute to work: 87.3% car, 0.3% public transportation, 6.2% walk, 4.7% work from home (2000); Travel time to work: 64.2% less than 15 minutes, 12.7% 15 to 30 minutes, 9.2% 30 to 45 minutes, 10.4% 45 to 60 minutes, 3.6% 60 minutes or more (2000)
Additional Information Contacts
Jackson County Board of Realtors 563-652-2772
Maquoketa Chamber of Commerce 563-652-4602

MILES (city). Covers a land area of 1.147 square miles and a water area of 0 square miles. Located at 42.04° N. Lat.; 90.31° W. Long.
History: Miles was named after Forrest M. Miles, a member of a prominent family in the area.
Population: 462 (2000); Race: 98.3% White, 0.0% Black, 1.2% Asian, 0.0% American Indian and Alaska Native, 0.0% Hispanic of any race, 0.0% two or more races (2000); Density: 402.7 persons per square mile (2000); Age: 33.8% under 18, 15.6% over 64 (2000); Marriage status: 22.7% never married, 60.6% now married, 6.2% widowed, 10.5% divorced (2000); Foreign born: 1.2% (2000); Ancestry (includes multiple ancestries): 45.9% German, 10.8% English, 8.3% United States or American, 5.2% Irish, 2.7% Danish (2000).
Economy: Single-family building permits issued: 3 (2001) / 0 (2000); Multi-family building permits issued: 0 (2001) / 0 (2000); Employment by occupation: 10.6% management, 13.5% professional, 14.0% services, 19.8% sales, 1.0% farming, 7.7% construction, 33.3% production (2000).
Income: Per capita income: $17,005 (2000); Median household income: $33,036 (2000); Poverty rate: 10.1% (2000).
Taxes: Total city taxes per capita: $154 (1997); City property taxes per capita: $97 (1997).
Education: High school graduation rate: 90.7% (2000); College graduation rate: 12.0% (2000).

School District(s)

East Central Community School District (PK-12)
2000 Enrollment: 448 319-682-7510
Housing: Homeownership rate: 80.9% (2000); Median home value: $63,300 (2000); Median rent: $222 per month (2000); Median age of housing: 60+ years (2000).
Transportation: Commute to work: 94.6% car, 0.0% public transportation, 3.9% walk, 1.5% work from home (2000); Travel time to work: 37.6% less than 15 minutes, 19.8% 15 to 30 minutes, 30.7% 30 to 45 minutes, 5.0% 45 to 60 minutes, 6.9% 60 minutes or more (2000)

MONMOUTH (city). Covers a land area of 0.562 square miles and a water area of 0 square miles. Located at 42.07° N. Lat.; 90.88° W. Long.
History: Monmouth is believed to have been named after the famous Revolutionary War battle of 1778.
Population: 180 (2000); Race: 100.0% White, 0.0% Black, 0.0% Asian, 0.0% American Indian and Alaska Native, 5.7% Hispanic of any race, 0.0% two or more races (2000); Density: 320.5 persons per square mile (2000); Age: 32.8% under 18, 13.8% over 64 (2000); Marriage status: 26.2% never married, 47.7% now married, 8.5% widowed, 17.7% divorced (2000); Foreign born: 0.0% (2000); Ancestry (includes multiple ancestries): 58.6% German, 24.1% Other groups, 14.9% Irish, 12.6% United States or American, 4.6% Dutch (2000).
Economy: Employment by occupation: 8.6% management, 2.9% professional, 25.7% services, 12.9% sales, 2.9% farming, 12.9% construction, 34.3% production (2000).
Income: Per capita income: $10,671 (2000); Median household income: $25,714 (2000); Poverty rate: 7.5% (2000).
Taxes: Total city taxes per capita: $105 (1997); City property taxes per capita: $41 (1997).
Education: High school graduation rate: 65.7% (2000); College graduation rate: 0.0% (2000).
Housing: Homeownership rate: 72.5% (2000); Median home value: $23,600 (2000); Median rent: $271 per month (2000); Median age of housing: 60+ years (2000).
Transportation: Commute to work: 94.1% car, 0.0% public transportation, 2.9% walk, 2.9% work from home (2000); Travel time to work: 18.2% less than 15 minutes, 37.9% 15 to 30 minutes, 15.2% 30 to 45 minutes, 27.3% 45 to 60 minutes, 1.5% 60 minutes or more (2000)

PRESTON (city). Covers a land area of 0.986 square miles and a water area of 0 square miles. Located at 42.05° N. Lat.; 90.39° W. Long. Elevation is 660 feet.
History: Preston is believed to have been named for Col. I. M. Preston who was affiliated with the railroad in the area.
Population: 949 (2000); Race: 99.4% White, 0.0% Black, 0.4% Asian, 0.0% American Indian and Alaska Native, 0.8% Hispanic of any race, 0.2% two or more races (2000); Density: 962.2 persons per square mile (2000); Age: 23.1% under 18, 17.9% over 64 (2000); Marriage status: 25.4% never married, 58.2% now married, 12.2% widowed, 4.1% divorced (2000); Foreign born: 1.2% (2000); Ancestry (includes multiple ancestries): 47.5% German, 9.9% Irish, 7.5% United States or American, 4.0% English, 2.4% Swedish (2000).
Economy: Single-family building permits issued: 4 (2001) / 1 (2000); Multi-family building permits issued: 0 (2001) / 0 (2000); Employment by occupation: 13.3% management, 10.6% professional, 12.7% services, 22.7% sales, 0.4% farming, 10.4% construction, 29.9% production (2000).
Income: Per capita income: $17,639 (2000); Median household income: $35,909 (2000); Poverty rate: 6.8% (2000).
Taxes: Total city taxes per capita: $184 (1997); City property taxes per capita: $123 (1997).
Education: High school graduation rate: 76.0% (2000); College graduation rate: 10.1% (2000).

School District(s)

Preston Community School District (KG-12)
2000 Enrollment: 364 319-689-5822

Housing: Homeownership rate: 73.3% (2000); Median home value: $69,300 (2000); Median rent: $270 per month (2000); Median age of housing: 48 years (2000).

Newspapers: Preston Times (1 x week)

Transportation: Commute to work: 89.1% car, 0.0% public transportation, 7.6% walk, 3.3% work from home (2000); Travel time to work: 40.8% less than 15 minutes, 24.7% 15 to 30 minutes, 24.7% 30 to 45 minutes, 5.2% 45 to 60 minutes, 4.4% 60 minutes or more (2000)

SABULA (city). Covers a land area of 0.392 square miles and a water area of 0.975 square miles. Located at 42.06° N. Lat.; 90.17° W. Long.

History: Sabula was named in 1846 in honor of Mrs. Sabula Wood. Previously it had been called Carrolport, and then Charlestown.

Population: 670 (2000); Race: 99.4% White, 0.3% Black, 0.0% Asian, 0.0% American Indian and Alaska Native, 0.0% Hispanic of any race, 0.0% two or more races (2000); Density: 1,709.3 persons per square mile (2000); Age: 23.6% under 18, 21.7% over 64 (2000); Marriage status: 22.8% never married, 55.9% now married, 12.0% widowed, 9.3% divorced (2000); Foreign born: 0.3% (2000); Ancestry (includes multiple ancestries): 37.5% German, 9.7% United States or American, 8.7% English, 8.5% Irish, 5.1% French (except Basque) (2000).

Economy: Single-family building permits issued: 3 (2001) / 6 (2000); Multi-family building permits issued: 0 (2001) / 0 (2000); Employment by occupation: 7.1% management, 6.8% professional, 19.6% services, 22.5% sales, 1.4% farming, 6.4% construction, 36.1% production (2000).

Income: Per capita income: $16,901 (2000); Median household income: $30,192 (2000); Poverty rate: 14.4% (2000).

Taxes: Total city taxes per capita: $131 (1997); City property taxes per capita: $74 (1997).

Education: High school graduation rate: 76.6% (2000); College graduation rate: 7.0% (2000).

Housing: Homeownership rate: 75.1% (2000); Median home value: $64,200 (2000); Median rent: $255 per month (2000); Median age of housing: 60+ years (2000).

Transportation: Commute to work: 82.2% car, 0.0% public transportation, 14.9% walk, 1.1% work from home (2000); Travel time to work: 44.7% less than 15 minutes, 20.5% 15 to 30 minutes, 28.2% 30 to 45 minutes, 4.8% 45 to 60 minutes, 1.8% 60 minutes or more (2000)

SAINT DONATUS (city). Covers a land area of 0.365 square miles and a water area of 0 square miles. Located at 42.36° N. Lat.; 90.53° W. Long. Elevation is 674 feet.

History: St. Donatus was founded by a group of settlers from Luxembourg. It was originally known as Tetes de Morts (heads of the dead), named after the river of the same name. Father Michael Flaming, who came here in the early 1850's, so disliked the gruesome name that he changed it.

Population: 140 (2000); Race: 100.0% White, 0.0% Black, 0.0% Asian, 0.0% American Indian and Alaska Native, 0.0% Hispanic of any race, 0.0% two or more races (2000); Density: 383.6 persons per square mile (2000); Age: 27.4% under 18, 14.1% over 64 (2000); Marriage status: 24.3% never married, 65.0% now married, 2.9% widowed, 7.8% divorced (2000); Foreign born: 0.0% (2000); Ancestry (includes multiple ancestries): 60.7% German, 22.2% Irish, 21.5% Luxemburger, 5.2% Polish, 2.2% Dutch (2000).

Economy: Single-family building permits issued: 0 (2001) / 0 (2000); Multi-family building permits issued: 0 (2001) / 0 (2000); Employment by occupation: 13.8% management, 6.2% professional, 27.7% services, 24.6% sales, 0.0% farming, 6.2% construction, 21.5% production (2000).

Income: Per capita income: $15,369 (2000); Median household income: $39,750 (2000); Poverty rate: 0.7% (2000).

Education: High school graduation rate: 78.8% (2000); College graduation rate: 4.7% (2000).

Housing: Homeownership rate: 80.0% (2000); Median home value: $68,300 (2000); Median rent: $336 per month (2000); Median age of housing: 45 years (2000).

Transportation: Commute to work: 83.1% car, 0.0% public transportation, 6.2% walk, 10.8% work from home (2000); Travel time to work: 20.7% less than 15 minutes, 43.1% 15 to 30 minutes, 24.1% 30 to 45 minutes, 12.1% 45 to 60 minutes, 0.0% 60 minutes or more (2000)

SPRAGUEVILLE (city). Covers a land area of 0.665 square miles and a water area of 0 square miles. Located at 42.07° N. Lat.; 90.43° W. Long.

History: Spragueville was named for early resident William Sprague.

Population: 89 (2000); Race: 97.6% White, 0.0% Black, 0.0% Asian, 2.4% American Indian and Alaska Native, 6.1% Hispanic of any race, 0.0% two or more races (2000); Density: 133.8 persons per square mile (2000); Age: 26.8% under 18, 11.0% over 64 (2000); Marriage status: 22.6% never married, 50.0% now married, 17.7% widowed, 9.7% divorced (2000); Foreign born: 6.1% (2000); Ancestry (includes multiple ancestries): 50.0% German, 17.1% English, 9.8% Irish, 6.1% Other groups, 4.9% Luxemburger (2000).

Economy: Single-family building permits issued: 0 (2001) / 1 (2000); Multi-family building permits issued: 0 (2001) / 0 (2000); Employment by occupation: 11.1% management, 8.9% professional, 11.1% services, 15.6% sales, 0.0% farming, 8.9% construction, 44.4% production (2000).

Income: Per capita income: $14,906 (2000); Median household income: $28,750 (2000); Poverty rate: 15.9% (2000).

Taxes: Total city taxes per capita: $121 (1997); City property taxes per capita: $60 (1997).

Education: High school graduation rate: 60.0% (2000); College graduation rate: 3.6% (2000).

Housing: Homeownership rate: 73.5% (2000); Median home value: $65,000 (2000); Median rent: $306 per month (2000); Median age of housing: 60 years (2000).

Transportation: Commute to work: 80.0% car, 0.0% public transportation, 13.3% walk, 0.0% work from home (2000); Travel time to work: 24.4% less than 15 minutes, 26.7% 15 to 30 minutes, 28.9% 30 to 45 minutes, 0.0% 45 to 60 minutes, 20.0% 60 minutes or more (2000)

SPRINGBROOK (city). Covers a land area of 0.570 square miles and a water area of 0 square miles. Located at 42.16° N. Lat.; 90.48° W. Long. Elevation is 840 feet.

History: Springbrook was named in 1872 for its geographical features.

Population: 182 (2000); Race: 100.0% White, 0.0% Black, 0.0% Asian, 0.0% American Indian and Alaska Native, 0.0% Hispanic of any race, 0.0% two or more races (2000); Density: 319.2 persons per square mile (2000); Age: 26.3% under 18, 14.2% over 64 (2000); Marriage status: 29.6% never married, 66.4% now married, 1.3% widowed, 2.6% divorced (2000); Foreign born: 0.0% (2000); Ancestry (includes multiple ancestries): 47.4% German, 12.6% Luxemburger, 6.3% United States or American, 3.7% Irish, 2.1% Swedish (2000).

Economy: Single-family building permits issued: 1 (2001) / 0 (2000); Multi-family building permits issued: 0 (2001) / 0 (2000); Employment by occupation: 14.4% management, 5.8% professional, 13.5% services, 26.0% sales, 0.0% farming, 9.6% construction, 30.8% production (2000).

Income: Per capita income: $16,814 (2000); Median household income: $50,750 (2000); Poverty rate: 0.0% (2000).

Taxes: Total city taxes per capita: $157 (1997); City property taxes per capita: $94 (1997).

Education: High school graduation rate: 75.2% (2000); College graduation rate: 5.4% (2000).

Housing: Homeownership rate: 92.1% (2000); Median home value: $55,600 (2000); Median rent: $325 per month (2000); Median age of housing: 47 years (2000).

Transportation: Commute to work: 87.5% car, 0.0% public transportation, 12.5% walk, 0.0% work from home (2000); Travel time to work: 28.8% less than 15 minutes, 45.2% 15 to 30 minutes, 12.5% 30 to 45 minutes, 8.7% 45 to 60 minutes, 4.8% 60 minutes or more (2000)

Jasper County

Located in central Iowa; prairie area, drained by the Skunk and North Skunk Rivers. Covers a land area of 730.00 square miles, a water area of 2.90 square miles, and is located in the Central Time Zone. The county government was organized in 1846. County seat is Newton.

Weather Station: Newton — Elevation: 958 feet

	Jan	Feb	Mar	Apr	May	Jun	Jul	Aug	Sep	Oct	Nov	Dec
High	28	35	47	62	73	82	86	84	76	64	46	33
Low	11	17	27	39	50	60	64	62	53	42	29	17
Precip	1.0	1.1	2.3	3.3	4.6	4.3	4.0	4.2	3.8	2.9	2.3	1.1
Snow	7.4	6.4	4.4	1.5	tr	0.0	0.0	0.0	0.0	0.4	2.3	5.8

High and Low temperatures in degrees Fahrenheit; Precipitation and Snow in inches

Population: 37,213 (2000); Race: 97.4% White, 0.7% Black, 0.4% Asian, 0.2% American Indian and Alaska Native, 1.3% Hispanic of any race, 0.7% two or more races (2000); Density: 51.0 persons per square mile (2000); Age: 24.6% under 18, 16.0% over 64 (2000).

Religion: Five largest groups: 9.5% The United Methodist Church, 7.5% Catholic Church, 4.5% Christian Church (Disciples of Christ), 3.9% Christian Reformed Church in North America, 3.4% Reformed Church in America (2000).
Economy: Unemployment rate: 3.7% (11/2002); Total civilian labor force: 20,151 (11/2002); Leading industries: 36.1% manufacturing; 12.9% retail trade; 8.4% health care and social assistance (2000); Companies that employ more than 1,000 persons: 1 (2000); Companies that employ more than 100 persons: 14 (2000); Farms: 1,204 totaling 420,637 acres (1997); Minority business ownership rate: 0.0% (1997); Women business ownership rate: 25.6% (1997); Retail sales per capita: $6,492 (1997). Single-family building permits issued: 87 (2001) / 66 (2000); Multi-family building permits issued: 20 (2001) / 14 (2000).
Income: Per capita income: $19,622 (2000); Median household income: $41,683 (2000); Poverty rate: 6.5% (2000); Bankruptcy rate: 3.44% (2001).
Taxes: Total county taxes per capita: $251 (2000); County property taxes per capita: $243 (2000).
Education: High school graduation rate: 86.8% (2000); College graduation rate: 15.9% (2000).
Housing: Homeownership rate: 75.7% (2000); Median home value: $82,500 (2000); Median rent: $366 per month (2000); Median age of housing: 42 years (2000).
Health: Birth rate: 112.6 per 10,000 population (1998); Age adjusted death rate: 82.1 per 10,000 population (1999); Age adjusted cancer mortality rate: 208.9 deaths per 100,000 population (1999). Number of physicians: 4.3 per 10,000 population (1999); Number of hospital beds: 14.0 per 10,000 population (1999).
Elections: 2000 Presidential election results: 48.8% Gore, 48.9% Bush, 1.5% Nader, 0.4% Buchanan
National and State Parks: Kellogg State Game Management Area; Rock Creek State Park
Additional Information Contacts
Jasper County Government Offices 641-792-7016
Newton Board of Realtors 641-792-1454
Newton Chamber of Commerce 641-792-5545

Jasper County Communities

BAXTER (city). Covers a land area of 0.655 square miles and a water area of 0 square miles. Located at 41.82° N. Lat.; 93.15° W. Long. Elevation is 1,000 feet.
History: Baxter, originally known as Independence Centre, was named for postmaster Sidney Baxter Higgins.
Population: 1,052 (2000); Race: 99.6% White, 0.0% Black, 0.0% Asian, 0.2% American Indian and Alaska Native, 0.0% Hispanic of any race, 0.2% two or more races (2000); Density: 1,607.2 persons per square mile (2000); Age: 25.5% under 18, 19.0% over 64 (2000); Marriage status: 20.2% never married, 58.1% now married, 9.7% widowed, 12.0% divorced (2000); Foreign born: 1.0% (2000); Ancestry (includes multiple ancestries): 32.9% German, 16.9% English, 10.5% Irish, 9.9% United States or American, 5.2% Dutch (2000).
Economy: Single-family building permits issued: 2 (2001) / 6 (2000); Multi-family building permits issued: 0 (2001) / 0 (2000); Employment by occupation: 8.9% management, 10.5% professional, 17.4% services, 25.1% sales, 0.8% farming, 15.4% construction, 21.8% production (2000).
Income: Per capita income: $17,749 (2000); Median household income: $36,912 (2000); Poverty rate: 8.9% (2000).
Taxes: Total city taxes per capita: $238 (1997); City property taxes per capita: $233 (1997).
Education: High school graduation rate: 88.0% (2000); College graduation rate: 10.9% (2000).

School District(s)

Baxter Community School District (KG-12)
2000 Enrollment: 387 641-227-3102
Housing: Homeownership rate: 67.3% (2000); Median home value: $78,500 (2000); Median rent: $339 per month (2000); Median age of housing: 35 years (2000).
Transportation: Commute to work: 91.0% car, 0.0% public transportation, 6.4% walk, 2.6% work from home (2000); Travel time to work: 25.8% less than 15 minutes, 32.1% 15 to 30 minutes, 24.9% 30 to 45 minutes, 11.0% 45 to 60 minutes, 6.1% 60 minutes or more (2000)

COLFAX (city). Covers a land area of 1.362 square miles and a water area of 0.018 square miles. Located at 41.67° N. Lat.; 93.24° W. Long. Elevation is 791 feet.
History: Colfax was named in honor of Schuyler Colfax, Vice President of the United States during Grant's administration and passenger on the first train passing through the village. Colfax is the birthplace of James Norman Hall, author of "Mutiny on the Bounty."
Population: 2,223 (2000); Race: 98.1% White, 0.3% Black, 0.0% Asian, 0.6% American Indian and Alaska Native, 1.0% Hispanic of any race, 0.3% two or more races (2000); Density: 1,632.4 persons per square mile (2000); Age: 29.1% under 18, 11.8% over 64 (2000); Marriage status: 19.5% never married, 61.6% now married, 6.8% widowed, 12.1% divorced (2000); Foreign born: 0.3% (2000); Ancestry (includes multiple ancestries): 23.7% German, 14.8% Irish, 11.2% English, 9.5% United States or American, 8.1% Dutch (2000).
Economy: Single-family building permits issued: 2 (2001) / 0 (2000); Multi-family building permits issued: 0 (2001) / 0 (2000); Employment by occupation: 9.1% management, 11.1% professional, 15.2% services, 26.0% sales, 0.4% farming, 10.2% construction, 28.0% production (2000).
Income: Per capita income: $17,662 (2000); Median household income: $41,006 (2000); Poverty rate: 6.7% (2000).
Taxes: Total city taxes per capita: $161 (1997); City property taxes per capita: $152 (1997).
Education: High school graduation rate: 86.5% (2000); College graduation rate: 10.5% (2000).

School District(s)

Colfax-Mingo Community School District (PK-12)
2000 Enrollment: 917 515-674-3646
Housing: Homeownership rate: 77.0% (2000); Median home value: $72,300 (2000); Median rent: $382 per month (2000); Median age of housing: 58 years (2000).
Newspapers: Jasper County Tribune (1 x week)
Transportation: Commute to work: 87.6% car, 0.0% public transportation, 7.1% walk, 4.1% work from home (2000); Travel time to work: 27.3% less than 15 minutes, 33.5% 15 to 30 minutes, 28.1% 30 to 45 minutes, 6.7% 45 to 60 minutes, 4.4% 60 minutes or more (2000)

KELLOGG (city). Covers a land area of 0.364 square miles and a water area of 0 square miles. Located at 41.71° N. Lat.; 92.90° W. Long. Elevation is 844 feet.
History: Kellogg has had three names in its history — Jasper City, Kimball, and finally Kellogg in honor of Judge Abel Avery Kellogg. The town was originally laid out on the route of the Mississippi & Missouri River Railway.
Population: 606 (2000); Race: 97.6% White, 0.0% Black, 2.2% Asian, 0.1% American Indian and Alaska Native, 0.0% Hispanic of any race, 0.0% two or more races (2000); Density: 1,663.0 persons per square mile (2000); Age: 28.9% under 18, 12.6% over 64 (2000); Marriage status: 18.8% never married, 59.9% now married, 9.9% widowed, 11.4% divorced (2000); Foreign born: 1.9% (2000); Ancestry (includes multiple ancestries): 23.7% United States or American, 22.9% German, 9.7% Dutch, 9.4% Irish, 8.9% English (2000).
Economy: Employment by occupation: 8.0% management, 9.5% professional, 17.8% services, 16.1% sales, 0.0% farming, 11.2% construction, 37.4% production (2000).
Income: Per capita income: $17,161 (2000); Median household income: $37,000 (2000); Poverty rate: 6.0% (2000).
Taxes: Total city taxes per capita: $118 (1997); City property taxes per capita: $117 (1997).
Education: High school graduation rate: 80.3% (2000); College graduation rate: 8.6% (2000).
Housing: Homeownership rate: 78.4% (2000); Median home value: $70,500 (2000); Median rent: $375 per month (2000); Median age of housing: 38 years (2000).
Transportation: Commute to work: 93.9% car, 0.0% public transportation, 4.0% walk, 0.9% work from home (2000); Travel time to work: 35.3% less than 15 minutes, 50.1% 15 to 30 minutes, 9.6% 30 to 45 minutes, 1.7% 45 to 60 minutes, 3.2% 60 minutes or more (2000)

LAMBS GROVE (city). Covers a land area of 0.101 square miles and a water area of 0 square miles. Located at 41.70° N. Lat.; 93.07° W. Long.
Population: 225 (2000); Race: 100.0% White, 0.0% Black, 0.0% Asian, 0.0% American Indian and Alaska Native, 0.0% Hispanic of any race, 0.0% two or more races (2000); Density: 2,220.2 persons per square mile (2000); Age: 32.2% under 18, 8.2% over 64 (2000); Marriage status: 19.0% never married, 73.2% now married, 2.4% widowed, 5.4% divorced (2000); Foreign born: 0.0% (2000); Ancestry (includes multiple ancestries): 30.0% German, 22.3% English, 11.6% Dutch, 9.0% United States or American, 9.0% Irish (2000).

Economy: Single-family building permits issued: 0 (2001) / 0 (2000); Multi-family building permits issued: 0 (2001) / 0 (2000); Employment by occupation: 14.5% management, 28.2% professional, 13.7% services, 29.1% sales, 0.0% farming, 2.6% construction, 12.0% production (2000).
Income: Per capita income: $20,923 (2000); Median household income: $56,000 (2000); Poverty rate: 5.6% (2000).
Taxes: Total city taxes per capita: $158 (1997); City property taxes per capita: $158 (1997).
Education: High school graduation rate: 91.7% (2000); College graduation rate: 31.1% (2000).
Housing: Homeownership rate: 95.1% (2000); Median home value: $94,800 (2000); Median rent: $400 per month (2000); Median age of housing: 44 years (2000).
Transportation: Commute to work: 96.6% car, 0.0% public transportation, 0.0% walk, 0.0% work from home (2000); Travel time to work: 71.8% less than 15 minutes, 6.0% 15 to 30 minutes, 9.4% 30 to 45 minutes, 10.3% 45 to 60 minutes, 2.6% 60 minutes or more (2000)

LYNNVILLE (city). Covers a land area of 0.602 square miles and a water area of 0 square miles. Located at 41.57° N. Lat.; 92.78° W. Long.
History: Lynnville was named from its location in Lynn Grove Township.
Population: 366 (2000); Race: 100.0% White, 0.0% Black, 0.0% Asian, 0.0% American Indian and Alaska Native, 0.5% Hispanic of any race, 0.0% two or more races (2000); Density: 608.2 persons per square mile (2000); Age: 26.6% under 18, 16.7% over 64 (2000); Marriage status: 21.4% never married, 67.6% now married, 6.5% widowed, 4.5% divorced (2000); Foreign born: 0.5% (2000); Ancestry (includes multiple ancestries): 19.3% Dutch, 18.2% German, 12.5% United States or American, 10.2% Irish, 7.0% English (2000).
Economy: Single-family building permits issued: 2 (2001) / 2 (2000); Multi-family building permits issued: 0 (2001) / 0 (2000); Employment by occupation: 9.7% management, 11.1% professional, 14.0% services, 30.0% sales, 1.0% farming, 10.1% construction, 24.2% production (2000).
Income: Per capita income: $17,976 (2000); Median household income: $39,875 (2000); Poverty rate: 4.9% (2000).
Taxes: Total city taxes per capita: $118 (1997); City property taxes per capita: $115 (1997).
Education: High school graduation rate: 93.9% (2000); College graduation rate: 9.8% (2000).
Housing: Homeownership rate: 81.0% (2000); Median home value: $71,100 (2000); Median rent: $198 per month (2000); Median age of housing: 43 years (2000).
Transportation: Commute to work: 90.2% car, 0.0% public transportation, 6.9% walk, 2.9% work from home (2000); Travel time to work: 36.9% less than 15 minutes, 42.4% 15 to 30 minutes, 18.2% 30 to 45 minutes, 1.0% 45 to 60 minutes, 1.5% 60 minutes or more (2000)

MINGO (city). Covers a land area of 0.494 square miles and a water area of 0 square miles. Located at 41.76° N. Lat.; 93.28° W. Long.
History: Mingo was named after Mingo, Ohio.
Population: 269 (2000); Race: 99.2% White, 0.0% Black, 0.8% Asian, 0.0% American Indian and Alaska Native, 0.0% Hispanic of any race, 0.0% two or more races (2000); Density: 544.9 persons per square mile (2000); Age: 22.0% under 18, 14.6% over 64 (2000); Marriage status: 14.0% never married, 66.2% now married, 5.8% widowed, 14.0% divorced (2000); Foreign born: 0.8% (2000); Ancestry (includes multiple ancestries): 24.4% German, 20.1% English, 16.1% Irish, 9.1% Other groups, 8.7% United States or American (2000).
Economy: Employment by occupation: 9.3% management, 8.5% professional, 14.0% services, 31.0% sales, 1.6% farming, 10.1% construction, 25.6% production (2000).
Income: Per capita income: $18,834 (2000); Median household income: $40,341 (2000); Poverty rate: 3.9% (2000).
Taxes: Total city taxes per capita: $155 (1997); City property taxes per capita: $155 (1997).
Education: High school graduation rate: 90.8% (2000); College graduation rate: 12.1% (2000).
Housing: Homeownership rate: 81.9% (2000); Median home value: $81,500 (2000); Median rent: $388 per month (2000); Median age of housing: 29 years (2000).
Transportation: Commute to work: 89.3% car, 0.0% public transportation, 6.9% walk, 2.3% work from home (2000); Travel time to work: 24.2% less than 15 minutes, 31.3% 15 to 30 minutes, 27.3% 30 to 45 minutes, 11.7% 45 to 60 minutes, 5.5% 60 minutes or more (2000)

MONROE (city). Covers a land area of 1.693 square miles and a water area of 0 square miles. Located at 41.52° N. Lat.; 93.10° W. Long. Elevation is 922 feet.
History: Monroe was laid out by Adam Tool and recorded under the name of Tool's Point in 1851, but a year later its name was changed to Monroe, for President Monroe.
Population: 1,808 (2000); Race: 97.7% White, 0.2% Black, 0.3% Asian, 0.1% American Indian and Alaska Native, 0.3% Hispanic of any race, 1.4% two or more races (2000); Density: 1,067.6 persons per square mile (2000); Age: 25.1% under 18, 14.9% over 64 (2000); Marriage status: 18.2% never married, 63.8% now married, 7.8% widowed, 10.2% divorced (2000); Foreign born: 0.3% (2000); Ancestry (includes multiple ancestries): 23.8% German, 19.8% Dutch, 12.5% Irish, 12.4% English, 10.9% United States or American (2000).
Economy: Single-family building permits issued: 3 (2001) / 3 (2000); Multi-family building permits issued: 0 (2001) / 0 (2000); Employment by occupation: 12.0% management, 13.1% professional, 15.3% services, 26.5% sales, 0.5% farming, 8.6% construction, 23.9% production (2000).
Income: Per capita income: $18,518 (2000); Median household income: $39,837 (2000); Poverty rate: 5.6% (2000).
Taxes: Total city taxes per capita: $176 (1997); City property taxes per capita: $173 (1997).
Education: High school graduation rate: 85.0% (2000); College graduation rate: 12.9% (2000).
Housing: Homeownership rate: 77.9% (2000); Median home value: $75,700 (2000); Median rent: $332 per month (2000); Median age of housing: 41 years (2000).
Newspapers: Monroe Legacy (1 x week)
Transportation: Commute to work: 94.5% car, 0.0% public transportation, 2.5% walk, 2.4% work from home (2000); Travel time to work: 28.2% less than 15 minutes, 35.5% 15 to 30 minutes, 16.8% 30 to 45 minutes, 13.3% 45 to 60 minutes, 6.3% 60 minutes or more (2000)

NEWTON (city). Covers a land area of 10.257 square miles and a water area of 0 square miles. Located at 41.69° N. Lat.; 93.04° W. Long. Elevation is 944 feet.
History: Newton was incorporated in 1857 and named for a Revolutionary War soldier, Sergeant Newton. The washing machine industry began here in 1898. F. L. Maytag, who became the "Washing Machine King," worked here in the early part of the 20th century.
Population: 15,579 (2000); Race: 97.5% White, 0.4% Black, 0.3% Asian, 0.1% American Indian and Alaska Native, 1.6% Hispanic of any race, 0.8% two or more races (2000); Density: 1,518.9 persons per square mile (2000); Age: 23.5% under 18, 19.0% over 64 (2000); Marriage status: 19.9% never married, 59.4% now married, 10.1% widowed, 10.7% divorced (2000); Foreign born: 1.9% (2000); Ancestry (includes multiple ancestries): 27.5% German, 11.8% Irish, 10.4% United States or American, 10.1% English, 10.0% Dutch (2000).
Vital Statistics: Birth rate: 133.5 per 10,000 population (1998)
Economy: Single-family building permits issued: 25 (2001) / 14 (2000); Multi-family building permits issued: 20 (2001) / 14 (2000); Employment by occupation: 10.5% management, 18.2% professional, 12.5% services, 27.4% sales, 0.2% farming, 6.2% construction, 25.0% production (2000).
Income: Per capita income: $20,552 (2000); Median household income: $40,345 (2000); Poverty rate: 6.8% (2000).
Taxes: Total city taxes per capita: $473 (2000); City property taxes per capita: $439 (2000).
Education: High school graduation rate: 87.0% (2000); College graduation rate: 19.7% (2000).

School District(s)

Newton Community School District (PK-12)
2000 Enrollment: 3,529 641-792-5809
Newton Correctional Facility (N -N)
2000 Enrollment: n/a 515-791-1411

Housing: Homeownership rate: 69.0% (2000); Median home value: $78,700 (2000); Median rent: $375 per month (2000); Median age of housing: 43 years (2000).
Hospitals: Skiff Medical Center (68 beds)
Safety: Violent crime rate: 7.7 per 10,000 population; Property crime rate: 369.5 per 10,000 population (2001).
Newspapers: The Newton Daily News (6 x week)
Transportation: Commute to work: 92.2% car, 1.2% public transportation, 3.0% walk, 2.8% work from home (2000); Travel time to work: 73.6% less than 15 minutes, 9.4% 15 to 30 minutes, 8.5% 30 to 45 minutes, 5.7% 45 to 60 minutes, 2.8% 60 minutes or more (2000)

Airports: Newton Municipal
Additional Information Contacts
Newton Board of Realtors 641-792-1454
Newton Chamber of Commerce. 641-792-5545

OAKLAND ACRES (city). Covers a land area of 0.265 square miles and a water area of 0.022 square miles. Located at 41.71° N. Lat.; 92.82° W. Long.
Population: 166 (2000); Race: 86.5% White, 0.0% Black, 3.7% Asian, 0.0% American Indian and Alaska Native, 3.7% Hispanic of any race, 6.1% two or more races (2000); Density: 626.7 persons per square mile (2000); Age: 25.2% under 18, 8.6% over 64 (2000); Marriage status: 13.1% never married, 78.5% now married, 5.4% widowed, 3.1% divorced (2000); Foreign born: 6.7% (2000); Ancestry (includes multiple ancestries): 44.8% German, 13.5% Other groups, 11.7% Dutch, 11.7% Irish, 11.7% English (2000).
Economy: Corn; cattle, hogs, sheep. Single-family building permits issued: 0 (2001) / 0 (2000); Multi-family building permits issued: 0 (2001) / 0 (2000); Employment by occupation: 30.7% management, 25.3% professional, 12.0% services, 6.7% sales, 0.0% farming, 8.0% construction, 17.3% production (2000).
Income: Per capita income: $19,737 (2000); Median household income: $48,750 (2000); Poverty rate: 18.0% (2000).
Taxes: Total city taxes per capita: $124 (1997); City property taxes per capita: $124 (1997).
Education: High school graduation rate: 94.8% (2000); College graduation rate: 13.9% (2000).
Housing: Homeownership rate: 96.7% (2000); Median home value: $118,800 (2000); Median rent: $850 per month (2000); Median age of housing: 17 years (2000).
Transportation: Commute to work: 100.0% car, 0.0% public transportation, 0.0% walk, 0.0% work from home (2000); Travel time to work: 46.7% less than 15 minutes, 33.3% 15 to 30 minutes, 17.3% 30 to 45 minutes, 2.7% 45 to 60 minutes, 0.0% 60 minutes or more (2000)

PRAIRIE CITY (city). Covers a land area of 1.154 square miles and a water area of 0 square miles. Located at 41.59° N. Lat.; 93.23° W. Long. Elevation is 930 feet.
History: Prairie City was platted in 1856 by James A. Elliott, whose red brick house, built shortly after the Civil War, was opposite the village water tower.
Population: 1,365 (2000); Race: 97.4% White, 0.3% Black, 0.0% Asian, 0.4% American Indian and Alaska Native, 0.9% Hispanic of any race, 1.4% two or more races (2000); Density: 1,182.5 persons per square mile (2000); Age: 23.4% under 18, 19.8% over 64 (2000); Marriage status: 17.4% never married, 66.2% now married, 9.8% widowed, 6.7% divorced (2000); Foreign born: 0.9% (2000); Ancestry (includes multiple ancestries): 24.3% German, 16.6% Dutch, 15.8% Irish, 11.2% United States or American, 8.9% English (2000).
Economy: Single-family building permits issued: 5 (2001) / 5 (2000); Multi-family building permits issued: 0 (2001) / 0 (2000); Employment by occupation: 12.1% management, 15.7% professional, 15.1% services, 27.2% sales, 0.7% farming, 11.4% construction, 17.7% production (2000).
Income: Per capita income: $19,864 (2000); Median household income: $42,750 (2000); Poverty rate: 5.6% (2000).
Taxes: Total city taxes per capita: $197 (1997); City property taxes per capita: $195 (1997).
Education: High school graduation rate: 86.7% (2000); College graduation rate: 17.6% (2000).

School District(s)

Pcm Community School District (PK-12)
2000 Enrollment: 1,060 515-994-2685
Housing: Homeownership rate: 76.1% (2000); Median home value: $92,500 (2000); Median rent: $378 per month (2000); Median age of housing: 42 years (2000).
Newspapers: Prairie City News (1 x week)
Transportation: Commute to work: 94.2% car, 0.0% public transportation, 2.6% walk, 2.5% work from home (2000); Travel time to work: 22.2% less than 15 minutes, 24.1% 15 to 30 minutes, 45.3% 30 to 45 minutes, 7.1% 45 to 60 minutes, 1.3% 60 minutes or more (2000)

REASNOR (city). Covers a land area of 0.499 square miles and a water area of 0 square miles. Located at 41.57° N. Lat.; 93.02° W. Long. Elevation is 770 feet.
History: Reasnor was named for landowners Samuel and Mary Reasoner. The town was mapped out in 1877.
Population: 194 (2000); Race: 97.9% White, 2.1% Black, 0.0% Asian, 0.0% American Indian and Alaska Native, 0.0% Hispanic of any race, 0.0% two or more races (2000); Density: 388.5 persons per square mile (2000); Age: 22.9% under 18, 10.4% over 64 (2000); Marriage status: 23.0% never married, 57.8% now married, 5.6% widowed, 13.7% divorced (2000); Foreign born: 0.0% (2000); Ancestry (includes multiple ancestries): 21.4% German, 15.6% Dutch, 14.1% United States or American, 7.3% Irish, 4.2% Polish (2000).
Economy: Employment by occupation: 6.0% management, 10.0% professional, 13.0% services, 22.0% sales, 0.0% farming, 27.0% construction, 22.0% production (2000).
Income: Per capita income: $14,435 (2000); Median household income: $37,500 (2000); Poverty rate: 4.2% (2000).
Taxes: Total city taxes per capita: $94 (1997); City property taxes per capita: $94 (1997).
Education: High school graduation rate: 84.8% (2000); College graduation rate: 1.5% (2000).
Housing: Homeownership rate: 87.3% (2000); Median home value: $66,100 (2000); Median rent: $267 per month (2000); Median age of housing: 52 years (2000).
Transportation: Commute to work: 92.0% car, 0.0% public transportation, 2.0% walk, 4.0% work from home (2000); Travel time to work: 22.9% less than 15 minutes, 51.0% 15 to 30 minutes, 24.0% 30 to 45 minutes, 0.0% 45 to 60 minutes, 2.1% 60 minutes or more (2000)

SULLY (city). Covers a land area of 0.521 square miles and a water area of 0 square miles. Located at 41.57° N. Lat.; 92.84° W. Long.
History: Sully was named for Alfred Sully, who was a railroad executive, attorney and businessman.
Population: 904 (2000); Race: 99.2% White, 0.0% Black, 0.0% Asian, 0.3% American Indian and Alaska Native, 0.0% Hispanic of any race, 0.0% two or more races (2000); Density: 1,736.5 persons per square mile (2000); Age: 30.3% under 18, 19.9% over 64 (2000); Marriage status: 16.3% never married, 72.4% now married, 7.4% widowed, 3.9% divorced (2000); Foreign born: 1.4% (2000); Ancestry (includes multiple ancestries): 69.9% Dutch, 16.8% German, 7.5% English, 4.9% United States or American, 2.8% Irish (2000).
Economy: Single-family building permits issued: 0 (2001) / 1 (2000); Multi-family building permits issued: 0 (2001) / 0 (2000); Employment by occupation: 14.1% management, 10.4% professional, 10.0% services, 28.3% sales, 0.5% farming, 14.5% construction, 22.2% production (2000).
Income: Per capita income: $19,506 (2000); Median household income: $47,344 (2000); Poverty rate: 1.9% (2000).
Taxes: Total city taxes per capita: $196 (1997); City property taxes per capita: $195 (1997).
Education: High school graduation rate: 77.1% (2000); College graduation rate: 12.9% (2000).

School District(s)

Lynnville-Sully Community School District (KG-12)
2000 Enrollment: 550 641-594-4445
Housing: Homeownership rate: 86.8% (2000); Median home value: $81,800 (2000); Median rent: $329 per month (2000); Median age of housing: 34 years (2000).
Newspapers: Diamond Trail News (1 x week)
Transportation: Commute to work: 82.5% car, 0.0% public transportation, 10.2% walk, 6.1% work from home (2000); Travel time to work: 50.4% less than 15 minutes, 37.3% 15 to 30 minutes, 7.7% 30 to 45 minutes, 0.0% 45 to 60 minutes, 4.6% 60 minutes or more (2000)

VALERIA (city). Covers a land area of 0.044 square miles and a water area of 0 square miles. Located at 41.73° N. Lat.; 93.32° W. Long. Elevation is 855 feet.
History: Valeria was named for the daughter of W. H. Johnson, whose land was crossed by the railroad.
Population: 62 (2000); Race: 100.0% White, 0.0% Black, 0.0% Asian, 0.0% American Indian and Alaska Native, 0.0% Hispanic of any race, 0.0% two or more races (2000); Density: 1,394.9 persons per square mile (2000); Age: 21.7% under 18, 3.3% over 64 (2000); Marriage status: 10.2% never married, 67.3% now married, 4.1% widowed, 18.4% divorced (2000); Foreign born: 0.0% (2000); Ancestry (includes multiple ancestries): 71.7% United States or American, 3.3% Swedish, 3.3% English, 3.3% Dutch, 3.3% Scotch-Irish (2000).
Economy: Employment by occupation: 0.0% management, 0.0% professional, 14.8% services, 51.9% sales, 0.0% farming, 7.4% construction, 25.9% production (2000).

Income: Per capita income: $18,365 (2000); Median household income: $35,938 (2000); Poverty rate: 1.7% (2000).
Taxes: Total city taxes per capita: $54 (1997); City property taxes per capita: $54 (1997).
Education: High school graduation rate: 93.6% (2000); College graduation rate: 0.0% (2000).
Housing: Homeownership rate: 73.1% (2000); Median home value: $45,000 (2000); Median rent: $450 per month (2000); Median age of housing: 29 years (2000).
Transportation: Commute to work: 100.0% car, 0.0% public transportation, 0.0% walk, 0.0% work from home (2000); Travel time to work: 8.3% less than 15 minutes, 41.7% 15 to 30 minutes, 50.0% 30 to 45 minutes, 0.0% 45 to 60 minutes, 0.0% 60 minutes or more (2000)

Jefferson County

Located in southeastern Iowa; prairie area, drained by the Skunk River. Covers a land area of 435.30 square miles, a water area of 1.40 square miles, and is located in the Central Time Zone. The county government was organized in 1839. County seat is Fairfield.

Weather Station: Fairfield — Elevation: 738 feet

	Jan	Feb	Mar	Apr	May	Jun	Jul	Aug	Sep	Oct	Nov	Dec
High	30	37	49	63	74	83	87	85	77	65	48	35
Low	13	19	29	41	51	61	65	63	54	43	31	19
Precip	1.2	1.2	2.5	3.5	4.7	3.8	4.4	4.4	4.2	3.0	2.5	1.8
Snow	7.9	6.9	3.5	1.8	0.0	0.0	0.0	0.0	0.0	0.1	2.1	5.7

High and Low temperatures in degrees Fahrenheit; Precipitation and Snow in inches

Population: 16,181 (2000); Race: 96.1% White, 1.4% Black, 0.8% Asian, 0.3% American Indian and Alaska Native, 1.1% Hispanic of any race, 1.1% two or more races (2000); Density: 37.2 persons per square mile (2000); Age: 24.5% under 18, 13.7% over 64 (2000).
Religion: Five largest groups: 7.7% The United Methodist Church, 7.2% Catholic Church, 6.0% Christian Church (Disciples of Christ), 4.8% Evangelical Lutheran Church in America, 4.0% American Baptist Churches in the USA (2000).
Economy: Unemployment rate: 4.9% (11/2002); Total civilian labor force: 9,401 (11/2002); Leading industries: 22.1% manufacturing; 18.1% retail trade; 10.0% health care and social assistance (2000); Companies that employ more than 1,000 persons: 0 (2000); Companies that employ more than 100 persons: 12 (2000); Farms: 765 totaling 228,017 acres (1997); Minority business ownership rate: 0.0% (1997); Women business ownership rate: 19.3% (1997); Retail sales per capita: $16,363 (1997). Single-family building permits issued: 9 (2001) / 6 (2000); Multi-family building permits issued: 76 (2001) / 12 (2000).
Income: Per capita income: $19,579 (2000); Median household income: $33,851 (2000); Poverty rate: 10.9% (2000); Bankruptcy rate: 4.30% (2001).
Taxes: Total county taxes per capita: $203 (2000); County property taxes per capita: $195 (2000).
Education: High school graduation rate: 88.1% (2000); College graduation rate: 31.2% (2000).
Housing: Homeownership rate: 67.4% (2000); Median home value: $72,500 (2000); Median rent: $325 per month (2000); Median age of housing: 42 years (2000).
Health: Birth rate: 106.3 per 10,000 population (1998); Age adjusted death rate: 70.2 per 10,000 population (1999); Age adjusted cancer mortality rate: 209.5 deaths per 100,000 population (1999). Number of physicians: 11.1 per 10,000 population (1999); Number of hospital beds: 41.4 per 10,000 population (1999).
Elections: 2000 Presidential election results: 37.9% Gore, 43.0% Bush, 2.7% Nader, 0.6% Buchanan
National and State Parks: Woodthrush State Park
Additional Information Contacts
Jefferson County Government Offices 641-472-2851
Fairfield Chamber of Commerce 641-472-2111
Southeast Iowa Board of Realtors 641-472-2353

Jefferson County Communities

BATAVIA (city). Covers a land area of 0.592 square miles and a water area of 0 square miles. Located at 40.99° N. Lat.; 92.16° W. Long. Elevation is 731 feet.
History: Batavia was first called Greaseville in honor of one of the town's pioneers. The first cabin school, opened here in 1849, contained no windows, and for ventilation the taller boys would push aside the loose clapboards on the roof.
Population: 500 (2000); Race: 99.2% White, 0.0% Black, 0.0% Asian, 0.4% American Indian and Alaska Native, 0.8% Hispanic of any race, 0.0% two or more races (2000); Density: 844.6 persons per square mile (2000); Age: 21.5% under 18, 15.4% over 64 (2000); Marriage status: 18.3% never married, 64.5% now married, 7.5% widowed, 9.8% divorced (2000); Foreign born: 0.4% (2000); Ancestry (includes multiple ancestries): 22.3% German, 13.1% United States or American, 8.2% Irish, 6.4% English, 3.7% Dutch (2000).
Economy: Employment by occupation: 7.2% management, 11.8% professional, 12.9% services, 24.7% sales, 0.0% farming, 14.4% construction, 28.9% production (2000).
Income: Per capita income: $18,970 (2000); Median household income: $33,333 (2000); Poverty rate: 3.5% (2000).
Taxes: Total city taxes per capita: $66 (1997); City property taxes per capita: $63 (1997).
Education: High school graduation rate: 81.1% (2000); College graduation rate: 10.7% (2000).
Housing: Homeownership rate: 86.0% (2000); Median home value: $44,100 (2000); Median rent: $221 per month (2000); Median age of housing: 55 years (2000).
Transportation: Commute to work: 96.1% car, 0.0% public transportation, 0.0% walk, 1.9% work from home (2000); Travel time to work: 20.9% less than 15 minutes, 63.4% 15 to 30 minutes, 8.7% 30 to 45 minutes, 3.9% 45 to 60 minutes, 3.1% 60 minutes or more (2000)

FAIRFIELD (city). Covers a land area of 5.737 square miles and a water area of 0.134 square miles. Located at 41.00° N. Lat.; 91.96° W. Long. Elevation is 778 feet.
History: Fairfield was so named by its founders because of the natural beauty of the site. The first Iowa State Fair was held here in 1854.
Population: 9,509 (2000); Race: 95.0% White, 1.9% Black, 0.7% Asian, 0.5% American Indian and Alaska Native, 1.5% Hispanic of any race, 1.5% two or more races (2000); Density: 1,657.4 persons per square mile (2000); Age: 23.9% under 18, 13.6% over 64 (2000); Marriage status: 26.3% never married, 51.2% now married, 8.1% widowed, 14.5% divorced (2000); Foreign born: 5.4% (2000); Ancestry (includes multiple ancestries): 19.6% German, 13.6% English, 11.3% Irish, 8.8% Other groups, 8.2% United States or American (2000).
Economy: Single-family building permits issued: 9 (2001) / 6 (2000); Multi-family building permits issued: 76 (2001) / 12 (2000); Employment by occupation: 15.1% management, 23.2% professional, 14.5% services, 26.7% sales, 0.0% farming, 7.3% construction, 13.2% production (2000).
Income: Per capita income: $19,673 (2000); Median household income: $31,202 (2000); Poverty rate: 14.5% (2000).
Taxes: Total city taxes per capita: $428 (2000); City property taxes per capita: $325 (2000).
Education: High school graduation rate: 88.0% (2000); College graduation rate: 39.6% (2000).

School District(s)

Fairfield Community School District (PK-12)
2000 Enrollment: 2,050 641-472-2655

Four-year College(s)

Maharishi University of Management (Private, Not-for-profit)
2001 Enrollment: 806 515-472-7000
2001 Tuition: In-state $15,960; Out-of-state $15,960

Housing: Homeownership rate: 59.3% (2000); Median home value: $73,200 (2000); Median rent: $333 per month (2000); Median age of housing: 43 years (2000).
Hospitals: Jefferson County Hospital (67 beds)
Safety: Violent crime rate: 16.8 per 10,000 population; Property crime rate: 375.8 per 10,000 population (2001).
Newspapers: The Fairfield Ledger (5 x week)
Transportation: Commute to work: 82.8% car, 0.4% public transportation, 7.9% walk, 7.3% work from home (2000); Travel time to work: 82.5% less than 15 minutes, 7.6% 15 to 30 minutes, 5.9% 30 to 45 minutes, 2.1% 45 to 60 minutes, 1.9% 60 minutes or more (2000)
Airports: Fairfield Municipal
Additional Information Contacts
Fairfield Chamber of Commerce 641-472-2111
Southeast Iowa Board of Realtors 641-472-2353

LIBERTYVILLE (city). Covers a land area of 0.488 square miles and a water area of 0 square miles. Located at 40.95° N. Lat.; 92.04° W. Long. Elevation is 768 feet.

History: Libertyville was once known as Little Colony. It became Libertyville on July 4, 1842.
Population: 325 (2000); Race: 100.0% White, 0.0% Black, 0.0% Asian, 0.0% American Indian and Alaska Native, 0.0% Hispanic of any race, 0.0% two or more races (2000); Density: 665.4 persons per square mile (2000); Age: 29.8% under 18, 10.9% over 64 (2000); Marriage status: 14.8% never married, 67.4% now married, 5.9% widowed, 11.9% divorced (2000); Foreign born: 0.0% (2000); Ancestry (includes multiple ancestries): 27.6% German, 12.2% English, 9.6% United States or American, 5.8% Irish, 4.8% Scottish (2000).
Economy: Employment by occupation: 10.1% management, 8.9% professional, 23.8% services, 17.9% sales, 0.0% farming, 6.5% construction, 32.7% production (2000).
Income: Per capita income: $14,368 (2000); Median household income: $31,071 (2000); Poverty rate: 12.5% (2000).
Taxes: Total city taxes per capita: $97 (1997); City property taxes per capita: $93 (1997).
Education: High school graduation rate: 88.1% (2000); College graduation rate: 7.8% (2000).
Housing: Homeownership rate: 74.8% (2000); Median home value: $62,500 (2000); Median rent: $330 per month (2000); Median age of housing: 55 years (2000).
Transportation: Commute to work: 89.3% car, 0.0% public transportation, 3.6% walk, 6.0% work from home (2000); Travel time to work: 60.1% less than 15 minutes, 31.6% 15 to 30 minutes, 5.1% 30 to 45 minutes, 1.9% 45 to 60 minutes, 1.3% 60 minutes or more (2000)

LOCKRIDGE (city). Covers a land area of 0.730 square miles and a water area of 0 square miles. Located at 40.99° N. Lat.; 91.75° W. Long. Elevation is 732 feet.
History: Lockridge was settled in 1836 when Colonel W. G. Coop erected a cabin on the site as a trading post.
Population: 275 (2000); Race: 98.6% White, 0.0% Black, 0.0% Asian, 0.0% American Indian and Alaska Native, 1.4% Hispanic of any race, 0.0% two or more races (2000); Density: 376.8 persons per square mile (2000); Age: 36.2% under 18, 8.9% over 64 (2000); Marriage status: 16.8% never married, 55.9% now married, 6.9% widowed, 20.3% divorced (2000); Foreign born: 1.4% (2000); Ancestry (includes multiple ancestries): 28.7% German, 12.6% United States or American, 6.8% Swedish, 5.8% English, 5.8% Other groups (2000).
Economy: Employment by occupation: 6.0% management, 6.0% professional, 20.8% services, 10.1% sales, 2.7% farming, 14.8% construction, 39.6% production (2000).
Income: Per capita income: $14,347 (2000); Median household income: $31,250 (2000); Poverty rate: 9.6% (2000).
Taxes: Total city taxes per capita: $77 (1997); City property taxes per capita: $77 (1997).
Education: High school graduation rate: 82.9% (2000); College graduation rate: 4.7% (2000).
Housing: Homeownership rate: 79.8% (2000); Median home value: $33,800 (2000); Median rent: $281 per month (2000); Median age of housing: 55 years (2000).
Transportation: Commute to work: 84.2% car, 0.0% public transportation, 6.8% walk, 4.1% work from home (2000); Travel time to work: 22.9% less than 15 minutes, 62.9% 15 to 30 minutes, 8.6% 30 to 45 minutes, 0.0% 45 to 60 minutes, 5.7% 60 minutes or more (2000)

PACKWOOD (city). Covers a land area of 0.769 square miles and a water area of 0 square miles. Located at 41.13° N. Lat.; 92.08° W. Long. Elevation is 813 feet.
History: Packwood was named for its founder, Samuel Packwood.
Population: 223 (2000); Race: 96.7% White, 0.0% Black, 3.3% Asian, 0.0% American Indian and Alaska Native, 0.0% Hispanic of any race, 0.0% two or more races (2000); Density: 289.9 persons per square mile (2000); Age: 25.8% under 18, 25.0% over 64 (2000); Marriage status: 16.8% never married, 63.8% now married, 14.6% widowed, 4.9% divorced (2000); Foreign born: 2.5% (2000); Ancestry (includes multiple ancestries): 37.9% German, 25.4% Irish, 15.4% English, 11.7% United States or American, 6.3% Other groups (2000).
Economy: Employment by occupation: 7.3% management, 6.4% professional, 14.5% services, 29.1% sales, 0.0% farming, 10.9% construction, 31.8% production (2000).
Income: Per capita income: $17,081 (2000); Median household income: $32,000 (2000); Poverty rate: 0.8% (2000).
Taxes: Total city taxes per capita: $91 (1997); City property taxes per capita: $91 (1997).
Education: High school graduation rate: 80.1% (2000); College graduation rate: 7.8% (2000).

School District(s)
Pekin Community School District (PK-12)
2000 Enrollment: 812 319-695-3707
Housing: Homeownership rate: 67.6% (2000); Median home value: $54,400 (2000); Median rent: $213 per month (2000); Median age of housing: 42 years (2000).
Transportation: Commute to work: 94.3% car, 0.0% public transportation, 5.7% walk, 0.0% work from home (2000); Travel time to work: 24.8% less than 15 minutes, 61.0% 15 to 30 minutes, 14.3% 30 to 45 minutes, 0.0% 45 to 60 minutes, 0.0% 60 minutes or more (2000)

PLEASANT PLAIN (city). Covers a land area of 1.014 square miles and a water area of 0 square miles. Located at 41.14° N. Lat.; 91.86° W. Long. Elevation is 757 feet.
Population: 131 (2000); Race: 100.0% White, 0.0% Black, 0.0% Asian, 0.0% American Indian and Alaska Native, 0.0% Hispanic of any race, 0.0% two or more races (2000); Density: 129.2 persons per square mile (2000); Age: 17.5% under 18, 8.8% over 64 (2000); Marriage status: 18.6% never married, 72.2% now married, 7.2% widowed, 2.1% divorced (2000); Foreign born: 0.0% (2000); Ancestry (includes multiple ancestries): 34.2% German, 17.5% English, 13.2% Irish, 7.9% Polish, 7.0% Czech (2000).
Economy: In agricultural area. Employment by occupation: 6.0% management, 11.9% professional, 10.4% services, 26.9% sales, 3.0% farming, 9.0% construction, 32.8% production (2000).
Income: Per capita income: $14,282 (2000); Median household income: $28,125 (2000); Poverty rate: 25.0% (2000).
Taxes: Total city taxes per capita: $68 (1997); City property taxes per capita: $68 (1997).
Education: High school graduation rate: 95.3% (2000); College graduation rate: 11.6% (2000).
Housing: Homeownership rate: 70.2% (2000); Median home value: $60,000 (2000); Median rent: $275 per month (2000); Median age of housing: 41 years (2000).
Transportation: Commute to work: 95.2% car, 0.0% public transportation, 3.2% walk, 1.6% work from home (2000); Travel time to work: 9.7% less than 15 minutes, 67.7% 15 to 30 minutes, 12.9% 30 to 45 minutes, 9.7% 45 to 60 minutes, 0.0% 60 minutes or more (2000)

Johnson County

Located in eastern Iowa; prairie area, drained by the Iowa River. Covers a land area of 614.50 square miles, a water area of 8.90 square miles, and is located in the Central Time Zone. The county government was organized in 1837. County seat is Iowa City.

Johnson County is part of the Iowa City, IA MSA. The entire metro area includes: Johnson County

Weather Station: Iowa City — Elevation: 639 feet

	Jan	Feb	Mar	Apr	May	Jun	Jul	Aug	Sep	Oct	Nov	Dec
High	30	36	49	63	75	84	88	85	78	66	48	35
Low	13	19	30	41	52	62	66	64	55	44	31	20
Precip	1.1	1.1	2.5	3.7	4.5	4.8	4.5	4.9	3.7	2.8	2.4	1.5
Snow	8.0	5.3	3.7	1.9	tr	0.0	0.0	0.0	0.0	0.3	1.7	6.1

High and Low temperatures in degrees Fahrenheit; Precipitation and Snow in inches

Population: 111,006 (2000); Race: 90.3% White, 2.8% Black, 4.0% Asian, 0.2% American Indian and Alaska Native, 2.6% Hispanic of any race, 1.5% two or more races (2000); Density: 180.7 persons per square mile (2000); Age: 20.0% under 18, 7.5% over 64 (2000).
Religion: Five largest groups: 15.5% Catholic Church, 5.7% The United Methodist Church, 3.8% Evangelical Lutheran Church in America, 2.2% Presbyterian Church (U.S.A.), 1.4% Lutheran Church—Missouri Synod (2000).
Economy: Unemployment rate: 2.7% (11/2002); Total civilian labor force: 75,423 (11/2002); Leading industries: 24.6% health care and social assistance; 16.3% retail trade; 10.7% accommodation & food services (2000); Companies that employ more than 1,000 persons: 6 (2000); Companies that employ more than 100 persons: 64 (2000); Farms: 1,261 totaling 288,139 acres (1997); Minority business ownership rate: 3.6% (1997); Women business ownership rate: 28.5% (1997); Retail sales per capita: $9,722 (1997). Single-family building permits issued: 622 (2001) / 529 (2000); Multi-family building permits issued: 577 (2001) / 622 (2000).

Income: Per capita income: $22,220 (2000); Median household income: $40,060 (2000); Poverty rate: 15.0% (2000); Bankruptcy rate: 1.87% (2001).
Taxes: Total county taxes per capita: $170 (2000); County property taxes per capita: $165 (2000).
Education: High school graduation rate: 93.7% (2000); College graduation rate: 47.6% (2000).
Housing: Homeownership rate: 56.7% (2000); Median home value: $131,500 (2000); Median rent: $498 per month (2000); Median age of housing: 25 years (2000).
Health: Birth rate: 115.0 per 10,000 population (1998); Age adjusted death rate: 73.1 per 10,000 population (1999); Age adjusted cancer mortality rate: 208.0 deaths per 100,000 population (1999). Number of physicians: 125.3 per 10,000 population (1999); Number of hospital beds: 93.2 per 10,000 population (1999).
Elections: 2000 Presidential election results: 59.1% Gore, 33.9% Bush, 6.2% Nader, 0.2% Buchanan
National and State Parks: Hawkeye State Wildlife Area; Lake Macbride State Park; Swan Lake State Wildlife Area
Additional Information Contacts
Johnson County Government Offices 319-356-6000
Iowa City Area Association of Realtors.......... 319-338-6460
Iowa City Area Chamber 319-337-9637

Johnson County Communities

CORALVILLE (city). Covers a land area of 10.190 square miles and a water area of 0.040 square miles. Located at 41.68° N. Lat.; 91.58° W. Long. Elevation is 700 feet.
History: Coralville was named in 1866 when excavators, employed on water works, found formations of coral.
Population: 15,123 (2000); Race: 87.5% White, 4.5% Black, 4.3% Asian, 0.3% American Indian and Alaska Native, 4.2% Hispanic of any race, 1.9% two or more races (2000); Density: 1,484.1 persons per square mile (2000); Age: 22.1% under 18, 5.4% over 64 (2000); Marriage status: 38.5% never married, 48.2% now married, 3.4% widowed, 9.9% divorced (2000); Foreign born: 8.2% (2000); Ancestry (includes multiple ancestries): 31.1% German, 16.5% Irish, 14.3% Other groups, 10.8% English, 5.2% Norwegian (2000).
Vital Statistics: Birth rate: 162.0 per 10,000 population (1998)
Economy: Single-family building permits issued: 192 (2001) / 117 (2000); Multi-family building permits issued: 185 (2001) / 178 (2000); Employment by occupation: 14.0% management, 34.1% professional, 14.3% services, 25.1% sales, 0.0% farming, 5.7% construction, 6.7% production (2000).
Income: Per capita income: $23,283 (2000); Median household income: $38,080 (2000); Poverty rate: 10.1% (2000).
Taxes: Total city taxes per capita: $604 (2000); City property taxes per capita: $490 (2000).
Education: High school graduation rate: 96.3% (2000); College graduation rate: 51.8% (2000).
Housing: Homeownership rate: 49.0% (2000); Median home value: $127,200 (2000); Median rent: $500 per month (2000); Median age of housing: 19 years (2000).
Safety: Violent crime rate: 26.5 per 10,000 population; Property crime rate: 421.0 per 10,000 population (2001).
Transportation: Commute to work: 88.1% car, 6.2% public transportation, 1.9% walk, 2.5% work from home (2000); Travel time to work: 40.8% less than 15 minutes, 44.3% 15 to 30 minutes, 10.0% 30 to 45 minutes, 2.0% 45 to 60 minutes, 3.0% 60 minutes or more (2000)

HILLS (city). Aka Old Mans Creek Bridge. Covers a land area of 0.595 square miles and a water area of 0 square miles. Located at 41.55° N. Lat.; 91.53° W. Long. Elevation is 635 feet.
Population: 679 (2000); Race: 97.1% White, 0.0% Black, 1.8% Asian, 0.0% American Indian and Alaska Native, 0.7% Hispanic of any race, 0.4% two or more races (2000); Density: 1,140.9 persons per square mile (2000); Age: 22.5% under 18, 15.2% over 64 (2000); Marriage status: 20.3% never married, 57.9% now married, 9.9% widowed, 11.9% divorced (2000); Foreign born: 2.3% (2000); Ancestry (includes multiple ancestries): 44.3% German, 18.1% Irish, 10.5% English, 7.0% Czech, 6.7% Other groups (2000).
Economy: Single-family building permits issued: 1 (2001) / 1 (2000); Multi-family building permits issued: 0 (2001) / 0 (2000); Employment by occupation: 8.2% management, 19.9% professional, 17.1% services, 23.2% sales, 0.8% farming, 16.8% construction, 14.0% production (2000).
Income: Per capita income: $21,918 (2000); Median household income: $51,477 (2000); Poverty rate: 6.7% (2000).
Taxes: Total city taxes per capita: $154 (1997); City property taxes per capita: $152 (1997).
Education: High school graduation rate: 88.0% (2000); College graduation rate: 23.7% (2000).
Housing: Homeownership rate: 71.9% (2000); Median home value: $105,800 (2000); Median rent: $434 per month (2000); Median age of housing: 34 years (2000).
Transportation: Commute to work: 95.1% car, 0.0% public transportation, 2.6% walk, 1.3% work from home (2000); Travel time to work: 27.7% less than 15 minutes, 57.1% 15 to 30 minutes, 9.7% 30 to 45 minutes, 2.6% 45 to 60 minutes, 2.9% 60 minutes or more (2000)

IOWA CITY (city). Covers a land area of 24.163 square miles and a water area of 0.276 square miles. Located at 41.65° N. Lat.; 91.52° W. Long. Elevation is 654 feet.
History: Iowa City was the capital of Iowa until 1857. The city was incorporated in 1853. The first railroad company to lay tracks to the interior of Iowa set the goal of reaching Iowa City before January 1, 1856. Tracks were still 1,000 feet from the station at nine o'clock the night before. Prominent citizens toiled side by side with the railroad hands in zero degree weather to complete the task. For several years Iowa City was a railroad terminus, resulting in a large transient population from the East, the South, and Europe, most of them heading for the West.
Population: 62,220 (2000); Race: 87.2% White, 3.7% Black, 5.6% Asian, 0.2% American Indian and Alaska Native, 2.9% Hispanic of any race, 2.0% two or more races (2000); Density: 2,575.0 persons per square mile (2000); Age: 16.2% under 18, 7.2% over 64 (2000); Marriage status: 53.0% never married, 37.2% now married, 3.2% widowed, 6.7% divorced (2000); Foreign born: 8.2% (2000); Ancestry (includes multiple ancestries): 34.5% German, 17.4% Irish, 13.1% Other groups, 10.4% English, 5.2% Norwegian (2000).
Vital Statistics: Birth rate: 101.3 per 10,000 population (1998)
Economy: Unemployment rate: 2.9% (11/2002); Total civilian labor force: 46,306 (11/2002); Single-family building permits issued: 191 (2001) / 159 (2000); Multi-family building permits issued: 280 (2001) / 273 (2000); Employment by occupation: 8.9% management, 34.8% professional, 17.2% services, 27.0% sales, 0.2% farming, 4.2% construction, 7.8% production (2000).
Income: Per capita income: $20,269 (2000); Median household income: $34,977 (2000); Poverty rate: 21.7% (2000).
Taxes: Total city taxes per capita: $410 (2000); City property taxes per capita: $386 (2000).
Education: High school graduation rate: 94.8% (2000); College graduation rate: 55.9% (2000).

School District(s)
Iowa City Community School District (PK-12)
2000 Enrollment: 10,481 319-339-6800
Four-year College(s)
University of Iowa (Public)
2001 Enrollment: 28,768 319-335-3500
2001 Tuition: In-state $3,116; Out-of-state $11,544
Two-year College(s)
La James College of Hairstyling (Private, For-profit)
2001 Enrollment: 91 319-338-3926

Housing: Homeownership rate: 46.6% (2000); Median home value: $128,300 (2000); Median rent: $507 per month (2000); Median age of housing: 27 years (2000).
Hospitals: Mercy Hospital (218 beds); University of Iowa Hospitals and Clinics (1,103 beds); Veterans Affairs Medical Center
Safety: Violent crime rate: 41.7 per 10,000 population; Property crime rate: 239.1 per 10,000 population (2001).
Newspapers: Iowa City Gazette (7 x week); Iowa City Press-Citizen (7 x week); The Daily Iowan (5 x week)
Transportation: Commute to work: 71.2% car, 7.7% public transportation, 15.5% walk, 2.5% work from home (2000); Travel time to work: 51.4% less than 15 minutes, 36.4% 15 to 30 minutes, 8.1% 30 to 45 minutes, 2.1% 45 to 60 minutes, 1.9% 60 minutes or more (2000)
Airports: Iowa City Municipal
Additional Information Contacts
Iowa City Area Association of Realtors.................. 319-338-6460
Iowa City Area Chamber 319-337-9637

LONE TREE (city). Covers a land area of 0.988 square miles and a water area of 0 square miles. Located at 41.48° N. Lat.; 91.42° W. Long.
History: Lone Tree was named for a large white elm that could be seen for miles on the prairie by traveling pioneers.

Population: 1,151 (2000); Race: 98.4% White, 0.4% Black, 0.2% Asian, 0.0% American Indian and Alaska Native, 1.3% Hispanic of any race, 1.0% two or more races (2000); Density: 1,165.3 persons per square mile (2000); Age: 30.1% under 18, 11.3% over 64 (2000); Marriage status: 25.7% never married, 56.7% now married, 6.2% widowed, 11.3% divorced (2000); Foreign born: 0.3% (2000); Ancestry (includes multiple ancestries): 39.9% German, 17.0% Irish, 13.0% English, 9.7% United States or American, 9.5% Czech (2000).
Economy: Single-family building permits issued: 2 (2001) / 2 (2000); Multi-family building permits issued: 10 (2001) / 7 (2000); Employment by occupation: 7.1% management, 16.7% professional, 15.5% services, 25.1% sales, 0.6% farming, 16.3% construction, 18.6% production (2000).
Income: Per capita income: $18,990 (2000); Median household income: $42,431 (2000); Poverty rate: 7.8% (2000).
Taxes: Total city taxes per capita: $234 (1997); City property taxes per capita: $228 (1997).
Education: High school graduation rate: 90.2% (2000); College graduation rate: 16.4% (2000).

School District(s)

Lone Tree Community School District (KG-12)
2000 Enrollment: 470 319-629-4212
Housing: Homeownership rate: 78.8% (2000); Median home value: $92,900 (2000); Median rent: $408 per month (2000); Median age of housing: 38 years (2000).
Newspapers: Reporter (1 x week)
Transportation: Commute to work: 94.1% car, 0.0% public transportation, 3.6% walk, 1.5% work from home (2000); Travel time to work: 18.5% less than 15 minutes, 46.0% 15 to 30 minutes, 28.8% 30 to 45 minutes, 3.1% 45 to 60 minutes, 3.5% 60 minutes or more (2000)

NORTH LIBERTY (city). Covers a land area of 6.777 square miles and a water area of 0 square miles. Located at 41.74° N. Lat.; 91.60° W. Long. Elevation is 765 feet.
History: North Liberty was laid out in 1857.
Population: 5,367 (2000); Race: 96.2% White, 1.3% Black, 0.8% Asian, 0.0% American Indian and Alaska Native, 2.4% Hispanic of any race, 0.1% two or more races (2000); Density: 791.9 persons per square mile (2000); Age: 27.4% under 18, 3.6% over 64 (2000); Marriage status: 29.5% never married, 57.5% now married, 2.5% widowed, 10.5% divorced (2000); Foreign born: 1.9% (2000); Ancestry (includes multiple ancestries): 45.1% German, 15.9% Irish, 8.4% English, 8.0% United States or American, 6.3% Other groups (2000).
Economy: Single-family building permits issued: 97 (2001) / 88 (2000); Multi-family building permits issued: 35 (2001) / 112 (2000); Employment by occupation: 13.9% management, 24.2% professional, 13.3% services, 28.1% sales, 0.0% farming, 8.9% construction, 11.6% production (2000).
Income: Per capita income: $21,339 (2000); Median household income: $42,500 (2000); Poverty rate: 5.5% (2000).
Taxes: Total city taxes per capita: $355 (2000); City property taxes per capita: $316 (2000).
Education: High school graduation rate: 95.2% (2000); College graduation rate: 33.7% (2000).
Housing: Homeownership rate: 70.9% (2000); Median home value: $111,600 (2000); Median rent: $493 per month (2000); Median age of housing: 10 years (2000).
Safety: Violent crime rate: 11.2 per 10,000 population; Property crime rate: 119.4 per 10,000 population (2001).
Transportation: Commute to work: 96.9% car, 0.3% public transportation, 1.7% walk, 1.1% work from home (2000); Travel time to work: 32.6% less than 15 minutes, 49.1% 15 to 30 minutes, 14.7% 30 to 45 minutes, 1.3% 45 to 60 minutes, 2.3% 60 minutes or more (2000)

OXFORD (city). Covers a land area of 0.524 square miles and a water area of 0 square miles. Located at 41.72° N. Lat.; 91.79° W. Long. Elevation is 739 feet.
History: Oxford was named for Oxford, New York.
Population: 705 (2000); Race: 96.9% White, 0.0% Black, 2.2% Asian, 0.0% American Indian and Alaska Native, 0.3% Hispanic of any race, 0.6% two or more races (2000); Density: 1,346.3 persons per square mile (2000); Age: 25.9% under 18, 14.1% over 64 (2000); Marriage status: 27.7% never married, 57.4% now married, 8.4% widowed, 6.5% divorced (2000); Foreign born: 1.6% (2000); Ancestry (includes multiple ancestries): 29.3% German, 20.6% Irish, 14.5% United States or American, 8.4% Czech, 7.7% English (2000).
Economy: Single-family building permits issued: 1 (2001) / 1 (2000); Multi-family building permits issued: 0 (2001) / 0 (2000); Employment by occupation: 4.5% management, 15.6% professional, 22.2% services, 25.9% sales, 1.1% farming, 12.2% construction, 18.5% production (2000).
Income: Per capita income: $18,335 (2000); Median household income: $37,292 (2000); Poverty rate: 3.6% (2000).
Taxes: Total city taxes per capita: $219 (1997); City property taxes per capita: $216 (1997).
Education: High school graduation rate: 89.8% (2000); College graduation rate: 15.8% (2000).

School District(s)

Clear Creek-Amana Community School District (PK-12)
2000 Enrollment: 1,245 319-828-4510
Housing: Homeownership rate: 82.0% (2000); Median home value: $86,300 (2000); Median rent: $290 per month (2000); Median age of housing: 50 years (2000).
Transportation: Commute to work: 92.6% car, 0.0% public transportation, 4.3% walk, 2.3% work from home (2000); Travel time to work: 15.7% less than 15 minutes, 51.5% 15 to 30 minutes, 29.1% 30 to 45 minutes, 0.0% 45 to 60 minutes, 3.8% 60 minutes or more (2000)

SHUEYVILLE (city). Covers a land area of 1.492 square miles and a water area of 0 square miles. Located at 41.84° N. Lat.; 91.64° W. Long.
History: Shueyville was named for early settlers in the area.
Population: 250 (2000); Race: 97.4% White, 0.0% Black, 1.8% Asian, 0.0% American Indian and Alaska Native, 0.0% Hispanic of any race, 0.7% two or more races (2000); Density: 167.6 persons per square mile (2000); Age: 33.3% under 18, 8.8% over 64 (2000); Marriage status: 15.5% never married, 71.6% now married, 2.6% widowed, 10.3% divorced (2000); Foreign born: 4.0% (2000); Ancestry (includes multiple ancestries): 37.7% German, 15.8% Irish, 14.3% Czech, 8.4% English, 7.7% French (except Basque) (2000).
Economy: Single-family building permits issued: 6 (2001) / 5 (2000); Multi-family building permits issued: 0 (2001) / 0 (2000); Employment by occupation: 11.2% management, 21.7% professional, 13.2% services, 24.3% sales, 1.3% farming, 15.8% construction, 12.5% production (2000).
Income: Per capita income: $24,690 (2000); Median household income: $61,875 (2000); Poverty rate: 1.8% (2000).
Taxes: Total city taxes per capita: $161 (1997); City property taxes per capita: $152 (1997).
Education: High school graduation rate: 93.5% (2000); College graduation rate: 27.4% (2000).
Housing: Homeownership rate: 90.5% (2000); Median home value: $133,800 (2000); Median rent: $425 per month (2000); Median age of housing: 29 years (2000).
Transportation: Commute to work: 94.7% car, 0.0% public transportation, 1.3% walk, 3.9% work from home (2000); Travel time to work: 33.6% less than 15 minutes, 52.1% 15 to 30 minutes, 13.0% 30 to 45 minutes, 0.0% 45 to 60 minutes, 1.4% 60 minutes or more (2000)

SOLON (city). Covers a land area of 1.327 square miles and a water area of 0 square miles. Located at 41.80° N. Lat.; 91.49° W. Long. Elevation is 794 feet.
History: Solon was named in honor of an early resident's son.
Population: 1,177 (2000); Race: 99.4% White, 0.5% Black, 0.0% Asian, 0.0% American Indian and Alaska Native, 0.3% Hispanic of any race, 0.0% two or more races (2000); Density: 887.1 persons per square mile (2000); Age: 30.9% under 18, 17.2% over 64 (2000); Marriage status: 17.5% never married, 65.9% now married, 7.2% widowed, 9.3% divorced (2000); Foreign born: 0.1% (2000); Ancestry (includes multiple ancestries): 35.0% German, 14.8% Irish, 13.3% Czech, 4.9% Dutch, 4.9% United States or American (2000).
Economy: Single-family building permits issued: 22 (2001) / 8 (2000); Multi-family building permits issued: 0 (2001) / 0 (2000); Employment by occupation: 11.2% management, 25.3% professional, 14.8% services, 26.7% sales, 0.0% farming, 12.6% construction, 9.3% production (2000).
Income: Per capita income: $18,029 (2000); Median household income: $46,953 (2000); Poverty rate: 2.3% (2000).
Taxes: Total city taxes per capita: $251 (2000); City property taxes per capita: $248 (2000).
Education: High school graduation rate: 89.8% (2000); College graduation rate: 25.3% (2000).

School District(s)

Solon Community School District (KG-12)
2000 Enrollment: 1,045 319-624-3401
Housing: Homeownership rate: 78.4% (2000); Median home value: $114,500 (2000); Median rent: $453 per month (2000); Median age of housing: 32 years (2000).
Newspapers: Solon Economist (1 x week); North Liberty Leader (1 x week)

Transportation: Commute to work: 89.6% car, 0.0% public transportation, 6.7% walk, 3.3% work from home (2000); Travel time to work: 27.1% less than 15 minutes, 52.3% 15 to 30 minutes, 14.2% 30 to 45 minutes, 2.2% 45 to 60 minutes, 4.2% 60 minutes or more (2000)

SWISHER (city). Covers a land area of 0.459 square miles and a water area of 0 square miles. Located at 41.84° N. Lat.; 91.69° W. Long. Elevation is 793 feet.
History: Swisher was named for the owner of the original town site, Benjamin Swisher.
Population: 813 (2000); Race: 99.4% White, 0.2% Black, 0.4% Asian, 0.0% American Indian and Alaska Native, 0.1% Hispanic of any race, 0.0% two or more races (2000); Density: 1,769.6 persons per square mile (2000); Age: 27.1% under 18, 7.3% over 64 (2000); Marriage status: 20.0% never married, 67.6% now married, 4.5% widowed, 7.9% divorced (2000); Foreign born: 0.6% (2000); Ancestry (includes multiple ancestries): 46.7% German, 17.8% Czech, 17.5% Irish, 6.0% United States or American, 5.3% English (2000).
Economy: Single-family building permits issued: 5 (2001) / 3 (2000); Multi-family building permits issued: 0 (2001) / 0 (2000); Employment by occupation: 12.7% management, 19.3% professional, 10.4% services, 25.3% sales, 0.0% farming, 10.2% construction, 22.0% production (2000).
Income: Per capita income: $24,596 (2000); Median household income: $63,667 (2000); Poverty rate: 2.4% (2000).
Taxes: Total city taxes per capita: $148 (1997); City property taxes per capita: $144 (1997).
Education: High school graduation rate: 95.3% (2000); College graduation rate: 26.0% (2000).
Housing: Homeownership rate: 85.6% (2000); Median home value: $122,900 (2000); Median rent: $454 per month (2000); Median age of housing: 36 years (2000).
Transportation: Commute to work: 95.3% car, 0.0% public transportation, 1.0% walk, 2.7% work from home (2000); Travel time to work: 26.1% less than 15 minutes, 60.4% 15 to 30 minutes, 10.8% 30 to 45 minutes, 1.2% 45 to 60 minutes, 1.6% 60 minutes or more (2000)

TIFFIN (city). Covers a land area of 2.989 square miles and a water area of 0 square miles. Located at 41.70° N. Lat.; 91.66° W. Long. Elevation is 687 feet.
History: Tiffin was once part of the farm of Rolla Johnson, who named the place for his former home town of Tiffin, Ohio.
Population: 975 (2000); Race: 95.7% White, 0.9% Black, 1.8% Asian, 0.4% American Indian and Alaska Native, 1.0% Hispanic of any race, 0.4% two or more races (2000); Density: 326.2 persons per square mile (2000); Age: 25.3% under 18, 4.3% over 64 (2000); Marriage status: 27.2% never married, 55.2% now married, 3.9% widowed, 13.8% divorced (2000); Foreign born: 2.2% (2000); Ancestry (includes multiple ancestries): 41.0% German, 13.1% Irish, 7.6% English, 6.9% Other groups, 5.7% United States or American (2000).
Economy: Single-family building permits issued: 23 (2001) / 26 (2000); Multi-family building permits issued: 67 (2001) / 52 (2000); Employment by occupation: 13.1% management, 23.0% professional, 12.2% services, 29.8% sales, 0.0% farming, 9.7% construction, 12.1% production (2000).
Income: Per capita income: $20,222 (2000); Median household income: $42,381 (2000); Poverty rate: 4.3% (2000).
Taxes: Total city taxes per capita: $189 (1997); City property taxes per capita: $187 (1997).
Education: High school graduation rate: 96.2% (2000); College graduation rate: 30.4% (2000).
Housing: Homeownership rate: 67.3% (2000); Median home value: $114,500 (2000); Median rent: $465 per month (2000); Median age of housing: 5 years (2000).
Transportation: Commute to work: 95.5% car, 0.6% public transportation, 1.4% walk, 2.5% work from home (2000); Travel time to work: 32.8% less than 15 minutes, 52.5% 15 to 30 minutes, 10.3% 30 to 45 minutes, 1.1% 45 to 60 minutes, 3.3% 60 minutes or more (2000)

UNIVERSITY HEIGHTS (city). Covers a land area of 0.272 square miles and a water area of 0 square miles. Located at 41.65° N. Lat.; 91.55° W. Long. Elevation is 785 feet.
Population: 987 (2000); Race: 97.1% White, 0.7% Black, 0.2% Asian, 0.0% American Indian and Alaska Native, 1.9% Hispanic of any race, 1.9% two or more races (2000); Density: 3,626.3 persons per square mile (2000); Age: 18.3% under 18, 12.4% over 64 (2000); Marriage status: 35.2% never married, 53.5% now married, 4.3% widowed, 7.0% divorced (2000); Foreign born: 8.2% (2000); Ancestry (includes multiple ancestries): 33.4% German, 18.4% Irish, 14.1% English, 7.0% Other groups, 4.7% Norwegian (2000).
Economy: Single-family building permits issued: 0 (2001) / 2 (2000); Multi-family building permits issued: 0 (2001) / 0 (2000); Employment by occupation: 14.2% management, 48.5% professional, 9.0% services, 20.5% sales, 0.0% farming, 2.6% construction, 5.3% production (2000).
Income: Per capita income: $32,484 (2000); Median household income: $48,929 (2000); Poverty rate: 11.1% (2000).
Taxes: Total city taxes per capita: $307 (1997); City property taxes per capita: $299 (1997).
Education: High school graduation rate: 98.2% (2000); College graduation rate: 72.7% (2000).
Housing: Homeownership rate: 63.7% (2000); Median home value: $161,000 (2000); Median rent: $456 per month (2000); Median age of housing: 44 years (2000).
Transportation: Commute to work: 64.8% car, 5.0% public transportation, 22.7% walk, 1.6% work from home (2000); Travel time to work: 57.8% less than 15 minutes, 33.3% 15 to 30 minutes, 6.2% 30 to 45 minutes, 0.7% 45 to 60 minutes, 1.9% 60 minutes or more (2000)

Jones County

Located in eastern Iowa; prairie area, drained by the Wapsipinicon and Maquoketa Rivers. Covers a land area of 575.30 square miles, a water area of 1.40 square miles, and is located in the Central Time Zone. The county government was organized in 1837. County seat is Anamosa.

Weather Station: Anamosa 1 WNW — Elevation: 803 feet

	Jan	Feb	Mar	Apr	May	Jun	Jul	Aug	Sep	Oct	Nov	Dec
High	27	34	46	61	73	82	85	83	76	64	46	33
Low	9	15	26	37	47	57	61	59	50	39	28	16
Precip	1.2	1.3	2.4	3.5	4.2	4.3	4.2	4.4	3.5	2.5	2.5	1.5
Snow	7.4	4.7	3.4	1.3	0.0	0.0	0.0	0.0	0.0	0.1	2.0	5.7

High and Low temperatures in degrees Fahrenheit; Precipitation and Snow in inches

Population: 20,221 (2000); Race: 96.8% White, 1.7% Black, 0.3% Asian, 0.3% American Indian and Alaska Native, 1.3% Hispanic of any race, 0.8% two or more races (2000); Density: 35.1 persons per square mile (2000); Age: 24.2% under 18, 15.8% over 64 (2000).
Religion: Five largest groups: 30.7% Catholic Church, 17.2% Evangelical Lutheran Church in America, 7.0% The United Methodist Church, 5.9% United Church of Christ, 2.3% Presbyterian Church (U.S.A.) (2000).
Economy: Unemployment rate: 5.1% (11/2002); Total civilian labor force: 9,130 (11/2002); Leading industries: 21.4% manufacturing; 18.8% retail trade; 14.7% health care and social assistance (2000); Companies that employ more than 1,000 persons: 0 (2000); Companies that employ more than 100 persons: 7 (2000); Farms: 1,029 totaling 321,934 acres (1997); Minority business ownership rate: 0.0% (1997); Women business ownership rate: 21.9% (1997); Retail sales per capita: $6,113 (1997). Single-family building permits issued: 12 (2001) / 29 (2000); Multi-family building permits issued: 4 (2001) / 6 (2000).
Income: Per capita income: $17,816 (2000); Median household income: $37,449 (2000); Poverty rate: 8.6% (2000); Bankruptcy rate: 2.42% (2001).
Taxes: Total county taxes per capita: $193 (1997); County property taxes per capita: $185 (1997).
Education: High school graduation rate: 85.3% (2000); College graduation rate: 12.7% (2000).
Housing: Homeownership rate: 75.8% (2000); Median home value: $80,400 (2000); Median rent: $325 per month (2000); Median age of housing: 43 years (2000).
Health: Birth rate: 88.0 per 10,000 population (1998); Age adjusted death rate: 69.5 per 10,000 population (1999); Age adjusted cancer mortality rate: 189.4 deaths per 100,000 population (1999). Number of physicians: 3.5 per 10,000 population (1999); Number of hospital beds: 12.4 per 10,000 population (1999).
Elections: 2000 Presidential election results: 51.3% Gore, 46.0% Bush, 2.1% Nader, 0.3% Buchanan
National and State Parks: Chimney Rock Indian Bluffs State Game Mgt Ar; Indian Bluffs State Wildlife Management Area; Muskrat Slough State Game Management Area; Wapsipinicon State Park
Additional Information Contacts
Jones County Government Offices 319-462-2282
Anamosa Chamber of Commerce 319-462-4879
Monticello Chamber of Commerce 319-465-5626

Jones County Communities

ANAMOSA (city). Covers a land area of 2.239 square miles and a water area of 0.010 square miles. Located at 42.10° N. Lat.; 91.28° W. Long. Elevation is 829 feet.

History: Anamosa was first called Dartmouth, later Lexington; still later the name was changed to Anamosa (meaning "white fawn") for the daughter of a Winnebago chief. It is said that the girl fell in love with a young white engineer, and rather than marry the Indian her father had chosen, ended her life by jumping from a high bluff into the Maquoketa River.

Population: 5,494 (2000); Race: 90.7% White, 5.8% Black, 0.8% Asian, 0.8% American Indian and Alaska Native, 1.8% Hispanic of any race, 1.6% two or more races (2000); Density: 2,453.4 persons per square mile (2000); Age: 18.9% under 18, 15.0% over 64 (2000); Marriage status: 30.8% never married, 44.4% now married, 8.7% widowed, 16.1% divorced (2000); Foreign born: 2.0% (2000); Ancestry (includes multiple ancestries): 36.7% German, 15.4% Irish, 9.1% Other groups, 8.3% English, 6.4% United States or American (2000).

Economy: Single-family building permits issued: 5 (2001) / 9 (2000); Multi-family building permits issued: 4 (2001) / 6 (2000); Employment by occupation: 9.2% management, 17.2% professional, 15.3% services, 30.8% sales, 0.8% farming, 8.6% construction, 18.0% production (2000).

Income: Per capita income: $18,585 (2000); Median household income: $33,284 (2000); Poverty rate: 8.1% (2000).

Taxes: Total city taxes per capita: $162 (2000); City property taxes per capita: $159 (2000).

Education: High school graduation rate: 82.5% (2000); College graduation rate: 10.3% (2000).

School District(s)

Anamosa Community School District (PK-12)
2000 Enrollment: 1,294 319-462-4321

Anamosa State Penitentiary (N -N)
2000 Enrollment: n/a 319-462-3504

Housing: Homeownership rate: 69.2% (2000); Median home value: $78,300 (2000); Median rent: $333 per month (2000); Median age of housing: 38 years (2000).

Hospitals: Jones Regional Medical Center (38 beds)

Newspapers: The Anamosa Journal-Eureka (1 x week)

Transportation: Commute to work: 90.3% car, 0.0% public transportation, 6.2% walk, 3.0% work from home (2000); Travel time to work: 43.6% less than 15 minutes, 21.6% 15 to 30 minutes, 21.6% 30 to 45 minutes, 9.0% 45 to 60 minutes, 4.2% 60 minutes or more (2000)

Additional Information Contacts

Anamosa Chamber of Commerce 319-462-4879

CENTER JUNCTION (city). Covers a land area of 0.402 square miles and a water area of 0 square miles. Located at 42.11° N. Lat.; 91.08° W. Long.

History: Center Junction is the center, geographically, of Jones County.

Population: 131 (2000); Race: 100.0% White, 0.0% Black, 0.0% Asian, 0.0% American Indian and Alaska Native, 0.0% Hispanic of any race, 0.0% two or more races (2000); Density: 326.1 persons per square mile (2000); Age: 13.1% under 18, 18.9% over 64 (2000); Marriage status: 18.3% never married, 56.9% now married, 12.8% widowed, 11.9% divorced (2000); Foreign born: 1.6% (2000); Ancestry (includes multiple ancestries): 36.1% German, 11.5% United States or American, 5.7% Irish, 3.3% English, 1.6% Dutch (2000).

Economy: Single-family building permits issued: 0 (2001) / 0 (2000); Multi-family building permits issued: 0 (2001) / 0 (2000); Employment by occupation: 11.0% management, 0.0% professional, 4.1% services, 32.9% sales, 0.0% farming, 8.2% construction, 43.8% production (2000).

Income: Per capita income: $16,476 (2000); Median household income: $32,917 (2000); Poverty rate: 5.7% (2000).

Taxes: Total city taxes per capita: $119 (1997); City property taxes per capita: $65 (1997).

Education: High school graduation rate: 81.5% (2000); College graduation rate: 7.6% (2000).

Housing: Homeownership rate: 96.7% (2000); Median home value: $46,100 (2000); Median rent: $125 per month (2000); Median age of housing: 60+ years (2000).

Transportation: Commute to work: 100.0% car, 0.0% public transportation, 0.0% walk, 0.0% work from home (2000); Travel time to work: 13.5% less than 15 minutes, 70.3% 15 to 30 minutes, 2.7% 30 to 45 minutes, 8.1% 45 to 60 minutes, 5.4% 60 minutes or more (2000)

MARTELLE (city). Covers a land area of 0.329 square miles and a water area of 0 square miles. Located at 42.02° N. Lat.; 91.35° W. Long. Elevation is 908 feet.

History: Martelle was started by the Chicago, Milwaukee & St. Paul Railroad in 1872 and is believed to be named in honor of a railroad official.

Population: 280 (2000); Race: 99.3% White, 0.0% Black, 0.0% Asian, 0.0% American Indian and Alaska Native, 0.0% Hispanic of any race, 0.7% two or more races (2000); Density: 849.8 persons per square mile (2000); Age: 29.1% under 18, 14.7% over 64 (2000); Marriage status: 11.6% never married, 76.8% now married, 3.9% widowed, 7.7% divorced (2000); Foreign born: 0.0% (2000); Ancestry (includes multiple ancestries): 36.7% German, 13.7% United States or American, 13.3% Irish, 9.7% Czech, 6.5% English (2000).

Economy: Single-family building permits issued: 0 (2001) / 0 (2000); Multi-family building permits issued: 0 (2001) / 0 (2000); Employment by occupation: 8.3% management, 15.3% professional, 16.0% services, 24.3% sales, 0.7% farming, 17.4% construction, 18.1% production (2000).

Income: Per capita income: $20,134 (2000); Median household income: $47,500 (2000); Poverty rate: 2.9% (2000).

Taxes: Total city taxes per capita: $114 (1997); City property taxes per capita: $114 (1997).

Education: High school graduation rate: 87.6% (2000); College graduation rate: 8.1% (2000).

Housing: Homeownership rate: 84.8% (2000); Median home value: $58,900 (2000); Median rent: $380 per month (2000); Median age of housing: 46 years (2000).

Transportation: Commute to work: 91.0% car, 0.0% public transportation, 2.1% walk, 6.9% work from home (2000); Travel time to work: 14.2% less than 15 minutes, 35.8% 15 to 30 minutes, 41.0% 30 to 45 minutes, 4.5% 45 to 60 minutes, 4.5% 60 minutes or more (2000)

MONTICELLO (city). Covers a land area of 3.678 square miles and a water area of 0.023 square miles. Located at 42.23° N. Lat.; 91.18° W. Long. Elevation is 839 feet.

History: Daniel Varvel of Kentucky was the first settler of Monticello. His home also served as post office, and as headquarters for the men who laid out the Military Road, begun in 1839.

Population: 3,607 (2000); Race: 99.3% White, 0.2% Black, 0.2% Asian, 0.0% American Indian and Alaska Native, 2.4% Hispanic of any race, 0.3% two or more races (2000); Density: 980.8 persons per square mile (2000); Age: 23.2% under 18, 24.4% over 64 (2000); Marriage status: 20.0% never married, 55.5% now married, 14.1% widowed, 10.4% divorced (2000); Foreign born: 0.3% (2000); Ancestry (includes multiple ancestries): 53.4% German, 17.3% Irish, 6.4% English, 6.2% United States or American, 4.4% Other groups (2000).

Economy: Single-family building permits issued: 5 (2001) / 16 (2000); Multi-family building permits issued: 0 (2001) / 0 (2000); Employment by occupation: 8.0% management, 16.0% professional, 12.6% services, 26.1% sales, 1.2% farming, 8.6% construction, 27.5% production (2000).

Income: Per capita income: $16,699 (2000); Median household income: $34,932 (2000); Poverty rate: 7.2% (2000).

Taxes: Total city taxes per capita: $309 (1997); City property taxes per capita: $250 (1997).

Education: High school graduation rate: 81.1% (2000); College graduation rate: 15.0% (2000).

School District(s)

Monticello Community School District (PK-12)
2000 Enrollment: 1,102 319-465-5963

Housing: Homeownership rate: 68.5% (2000); Median home value: $78,200 (2000); Median rent: $323 per month (2000); Median age of housing: 40 years (2000).

Safety: Violent crime rate: 0.0 per 10,000 population; Property crime rate: 183.2 per 10,000 population (2001).

Newspapers: The Monticello Express (1 x week)

Transportation: Commute to work: 91.7% car, 0.0% public transportation, 3.5% walk, 3.9% work from home (2000); Travel time to work: 55.2% less than 15 minutes, 18.4% 15 to 30 minutes, 5.1% 30 to 45 minutes, 12.1% 45 to 60 minutes, 9.2% 60 minutes or more (2000)

Airports: Monticello Regional

Additional Information Contacts

Monticello Chamber of Commerce 319-465-5626

MORLEY (city). Covers a land area of 0.100 square miles and a water area of 0 square miles. Located at 42.00° N. Lat.; 91.24° W. Long.

History: Morley was once known as Viroqua. The name was changed in 1886 to honor a railroad official of the Chicago, Milwaukee & St. Paul Railroad.
Population: 88 (2000); Race: 100.0% White, 0.0% Black, 0.0% Asian, 0.0% American Indian and Alaska Native, 0.0% Hispanic of any race, 0.0% two or more races (2000); Density: 882.1 persons per square mile (2000); Age: 24.4% under 18, 13.4% over 64 (2000); Marriage status: 25.4% never married, 55.6% now married, 1.6% widowed, 17.5% divorced (2000); Foreign born: 0.0% (2000); Ancestry (includes multiple ancestries): 40.2% German, 9.8% English, 8.5% French (except Basque), 4.9% Scottish, 4.9% Irish (2000).
Economy: Employment by occupation: 8.9% management, 17.8% professional, 28.9% services, 11.1% sales, 0.0% farming, 15.6% construction, 17.8% production (2000).
Income: Per capita income: $22,167 (2000); Median household income: $44,375 (2000); Poverty rate: 4.9% (2000).
Taxes: Total city taxes per capita: $131 (1997); City property taxes per capita: $83 (1997).
Education: High school graduation rate: 81.5% (2000); College graduation rate: 11.1% (2000).
Housing: Homeownership rate: 71.4% (2000); Median home value: $48,800 (2000); Median rent: $442 per month (2000); Median age of housing: 60 years (2000).
Transportation: Commute to work: 93.3% car, 0.0% public transportation, 2.2% walk, 4.4% work from home (2000); Travel time to work: 7.0% less than 15 minutes, 34.9% 15 to 30 minutes, 51.2% 30 to 45 minutes, 4.7% 45 to 60 minutes, 2.3% 60 minutes or more (2000)

OLIN (city). Covers a land area of 0.994 square miles and a water area of 0.008 square miles. Located at 41.99° N. Lat.; 91.14° W. Long.
History: Olin has also been known as Elkford, Walnut Fork and Rome. The name Olin is in honor of Chicago, Milwaukee & St. Paul Railroad superintendent D. A. Olin.
Population: 716 (2000); Race: 98.8% White, 0.1% Black, 0.0% Asian, 0.0% American Indian and Alaska Native, 2.0% Hispanic of any race, 1.0% two or more races (2000); Density: 720.1 persons per square mile (2000); Age: 24.0% under 18, 18.4% over 64 (2000); Marriage status: 21.3% never married, 59.4% now married, 9.6% widowed, 9.7% divorced (2000); Foreign born: 0.6% (2000); Ancestry (includes multiple ancestries): 40.3% German, 10.7% Irish, 7.3% English, 6.9% Czech, 5.0% United States or American (2000).
Economy: Single-family building permits issued: 0 (2001) / 1 (2000); Multi-family building permits issued: 0 (2001) / 0 (2000); Employment by occupation: 6.0% management, 10.3% professional, 16.9% services, 23.6% sales, 0.9% farming, 11.8% construction, 30.5% production (2000).
Income: Per capita income: $14,809 (2000); Median household income: $33,906 (2000); Poverty rate: 11.2% (2000).
Taxes: Total city taxes per capita: $190 (1997); City property taxes per capita: $132 (1997).
Education: High school graduation rate: 83.4% (2000); College graduation rate: 4.3% (2000).

School District(s)

Olin Consolidated School District (PK-12)
2000 Enrollment: 323 319-484-2155
Housing: Homeownership rate: 78.7% (2000); Median home value: $65,500 (2000); Median rent: $294 per month (2000); Median age of housing: 60+ years (2000).
Transportation: Commute to work: 89.8% car, 0.0% public transportation, 9.0% walk, 1.2% work from home (2000); Travel time to work: 27.4% less than 15 minutes, 17.3% 15 to 30 minutes, 17.9% 30 to 45 minutes, 25.5% 45 to 60 minutes, 11.9% 60 minutes or more (2000)

ONSLOW (city). Covers a land area of 0.231 square miles and a water area of 0 square miles. Located at 42.10° N. Lat.; 91.01° W. Long. Elevation is 907 feet.
Population: 223 (2000); Race: 99.6% White, 0.0% Black, 0.0% Asian, 0.0% American Indian and Alaska Native, 0.0% Hispanic of any race, 0.4% two or more races (2000); Density: 965.4 persons per square mile (2000); Age: 34.7% under 18, 20.6% over 64 (2000); Marriage status: 22.7% never married, 56.9% now married, 9.9% widowed, 10.5% divorced (2000); Foreign born: 0.0% (2000); Ancestry (includes multiple ancestries): 22.2% German, 14.1% United States or American, 7.7% Norwegian, 5.6% Other groups, 5.6% Irish (2000).
Economy: In livestock and grain area; fertilizers; feeds. Single-family building permits issued: 0 (2001) / 0 (2000); Multi-family building permits issued: 0 (2001) / 0 (2000); Employment by occupation: 15.3% management, 7.2% professional, 16.2% services, 34.2% sales, 3.6% farming, 8.1% construction, 15.3% production (2000).
Income: Per capita income: $11,916 (2000); Median household income: $24,375 (2000); Poverty rate: 19.4% (2000).
Taxes: Total city taxes per capita: $151 (1997); City property taxes per capita: $100 (1997).
Education: High school graduation rate: 88.0% (2000); College graduation rate: 3.5% (2000).
Housing: Homeownership rate: 82.1% (2000); Median home value: $50,400 (2000); Median rent: $275 per month (2000); Median age of housing: 60+ years (2000).
Transportation: Commute to work: 97.3% car, 0.0% public transportation, 1.8% walk, 0.9% work from home (2000); Travel time to work: 32.7% less than 15 minutes, 14.5% 15 to 30 minutes, 19.1% 30 to 45 minutes, 18.2% 45 to 60 minutes, 15.5% 60 minutes or more (2000)

OXFORD JUNCTION (city). Covers a land area of 0.705 square miles and a water area of 0 square miles. Located at 41.98° N. Lat.; 90.95° W. Long. Elevation is 727 feet.
History: Oxford Junction was named for the intersection of rail lines of the Chicago, Milwaukee & St. Paul Railroad.
Population: 573 (2000); Race: 97.5% White, 0.0% Black, 0.2% Asian, 0.0% American Indian and Alaska Native, 0.0% Hispanic of any race, 2.4% two or more races (2000); Density: 813.3 persons per square mile (2000); Age: 27.4% under 18, 21.1% over 64 (2000); Marriage status: 22.4% never married, 57.6% now married, 11.1% widowed, 8.8% divorced (2000); Foreign born: 0.7% (2000); Ancestry (includes multiple ancestries): 43.2% German, 13.8% Irish, 11.8% Czech, 10.5% United States or American, 7.6% English (2000).
Economy: Single-family building permits issued: 0 (2001) / 0 (2000); Multi-family building permits issued: 0 (2001) / 0 (2000); Employment by occupation: 8.4% management, 8.8% professional, 24.0% services, 27.6% sales, 0.0% farming, 10.4% construction, 20.8% production (2000).
Income: Per capita income: $13,805 (2000); Median household income: $30,417 (2000); Poverty rate: 18.9% (2000).
Taxes: Total city taxes per capita: $157 (1997); City property taxes per capita: $115 (1997).
Education: High school graduation rate: 78.9% (2000); College graduation rate: 5.0% (2000).
Housing: Homeownership rate: 77.9% (2000); Median home value: $47,500 (2000); Median rent: $204 per month (2000); Median age of housing: 60+ years (2000).
Transportation: Commute to work: 82.3% car, 0.0% public transportation, 7.0% walk, 10.7% work from home (2000); Travel time to work: 25.3% less than 15 minutes, 18.4% 15 to 30 minutes, 32.3% 30 to 45 minutes, 6.5% 45 to 60 minutes, 17.5% 60 minutes or more (2000)

WYOMING (city). Covers a land area of 0.509 square miles and a water area of 0 square miles. Located at 42.05° N. Lat.; 91.00° W. Long. Elevation is 813 feet.
History: Wyoming was named after Wyoming County, New York.
Population: 626 (2000); Race: 97.7% White, 1.4% Black, 0.0% Asian, 0.9% American Indian and Alaska Native, 0.0% Hispanic of any race, 0.0% two or more races (2000); Density: 1,230.4 persons per square mile (2000); Age: 26.9% under 18, 20.9% over 64 (2000); Marriage status: 19.5% never married, 64.0% now married, 10.3% widowed, 6.2% divorced (2000); Foreign born: 0.2% (2000); Ancestry (includes multiple ancestries): 39.5% German, 10.5% Irish, 10.2% English, 9.7% United States or American, 2.7% Scotch-Irish (2000).
Economy: Single-family building permits issued: 2 (2001) / 3 (2000); Multi-family building permits issued: 0 (2001) / 0 (2000); Employment by occupation: 9.7% management, 10.7% professional, 14.2% services, 29.9% sales, 0.6% farming, 11.0% construction, 23.9% production (2000).
Income: Per capita income: $15,787 (2000); Median household income: $31,979 (2000); Poverty rate: 12.2% (2000).
Taxes: Total city taxes per capita: $195 (1997); City property taxes per capita: $143 (1997).
Education: High school graduation rate: 84.6% (2000); College graduation rate: 8.3% (2000).

School District(s)

Midland Community School District (PK-12)
2000 Enrollment: 742 319-488-2292
Housing: Homeownership rate: 77.7% (2000); Median home value: $55,300 (2000); Median rent: $257 per month (2000); Median age of housing: 59 years (2000).
Newspapers: Midland Times (1 x week)

Transportation: Commute to work: 88.5% car, 0.0% public transportation, 8.6% walk, 2.2% work from home (2000); Travel time to work: 39.5% less than 15 minutes, 28.1% 15 to 30 minutes, 11.8% 30 to 45 minutes, 10.8% 45 to 60 minutes, 9.8% 60 minutes or more (2000)

Keokuk County

Located in southeastern Iowa; prairie area, drained by the Skunk, North Skunk, and South Fork English Rivers. Covers a land area of 579.20 square miles, a water area of 0.70 square miles, and is located in the Central Time Zone. The county government was organized in 1837. County seat is Sigourney.

Weather Station: Sigourney — Elevation: 797 feet

	Jan	Feb	Mar	Apr	May	Jun	Jul	Aug	Sep	Oct	Nov	Dec
High	29	36	48	62	73	82	86	84	76	64	48	35
Low	12	17	28	39	51	61	65	63	54	42	30	18
Precip	1.1	1.0	2.4	3.6	4.3	4.0	4.1	4.4	3.9	2.8	2.6	1.3
Snow	7.4	6.3	2.8	2.1	tr	0.0	0.0	0.0	0.0	0.4	2.3	5.4

High and Low temperatures in degrees Fahrenheit; Precipitation and Snow in inches

Population: 11,400 (2000); Race: 98.9% White, 0.3% Black, 0.2% Asian, 0.1% American Indian and Alaska Native, 0.6% Hispanic of any race, 0.4% two or more races (2000); Density: 19.7 persons per square mile (2000); Age: 25.8% under 18, 20.2% over 64 (2000).

Religion: Five largest groups: 20.0% Catholic Church, 16.0% The United Methodist Church, 7.2% Christian Church (Disciples of Christ), 4.0% Presbyterian Church (U.S.A.), 2.7% Friends (Quakers) (2000).

Economy: Unemployment rate: 3.9% (11/2002); Total civilian labor force: 5,180 (11/2002); Leading industries: 23.8% retail trade; 19.4% health care and social assistance; 14.0% manufacturing (2000); Companies that employ more than 1,000 persons: 0 (2000); Companies that employ more than 100 persons: 0 (2000); Farms: 968 totaling 323,028 acres (1997); Minority business ownership rate: 0.0% (1997); Women business ownership rate: 15.9% (1997); Retail sales per capita: $8,202 (1997). Single-family building permits issued: 12 (2001) / 13 (2000); Multi-family building permits issued: 0 (2001) / 0 (2000).

Income: Per capita income: $17,120 (2000); Median household income: $34,025 (2000); Poverty rate: 10.1% (2000); Bankruptcy rate: 3.42% (2001).

Taxes: Total county taxes per capita: $307 (2000); County property taxes per capita: $298 (2000).

Education: High school graduation rate: 84.0% (2000); College graduation rate: 11.6% (2000).

Housing: Homeownership rate: 78.8% (2000); Median home value: $51,900 (2000); Median rent: $249 per month (2000); Median age of housing: 2000 years (2000).

Health: Birth rate: 124.6 per 10,000 population (1998); Age adjusted death rate: 66.8 per 10,000 population (1999); Age adjusted cancer mortality rate: 140.1 deaths per 100,000 population (1999). Number of physicians: 3.5 per 10,000 population (1999); Number of hospital beds: 21.9 per 10,000 population (1999).

Elections: 2000 Presidential election results: 44.1% Gore, 52.0% Bush, 2.0% Nader, 0.5% Buchanan

National and State Parks: Lake Darling State Park; Rubio State Access Area; South Skunk River State Wildlife Area; Spainer Br Skunk River State Wildlife Area

Additional Information Contacts

Keokuk County Government Offices.................... 641-622-2320
Sigourney Area Development 641-622-2288

Keokuk County Communities

DELTA (city). Covers a land area of 0.999 square miles and a water area of 0 square miles. Located at 41.32° N. Lat.; 92.32° W. Long.

History: Delta was laid out in a triangle shape, which led to its being named for the Greek letter "delta," represented by a triangle.

Population: 410 (2000); Race: 100.0% White, 0.0% Black, 0.0% Asian, 0.0% American Indian and Alaska Native, 0.0% Hispanic of any race, 0.0% two or more races (2000); Density: 410.6 persons per square mile (2000); Age: 29.8% under 18, 14.0% over 64 (2000); Marriage status: 17.9% never married, 55.3% now married, 13.2% widowed, 13.6% divorced (2000); Foreign born: 0.2% (2000); Ancestry (includes multiple ancestries): 18.2% United States or American, 17.9% German, 15.3% Irish, 8.0% Other groups, 7.7% English (2000).

Economy: Employment by occupation: 8.1% management, 4.3% professional, 23.0% services, 21.1% sales, 1.2% farming, 14.3% construction, 28.0% production (2000).

Income: Per capita income: $14,516 (2000); Median household income: $27,019 (2000); Poverty rate: 25.4% (2000).

Taxes: Total city taxes per capita: $62 (1997); City property taxes per capita: $60 (1997).

Education: High school graduation rate: 83.0% (2000); College graduation rate: 7.1% (2000).

Housing: Homeownership rate: 76.0% (2000); Median home value: $20,800 (2000); Median rent: $136 per month (2000); Median age of housing: 60+ years (2000).

Transportation: Commute to work: 87.7% car, 0.0% public transportation, 7.1% walk, 1.9% work from home (2000); Travel time to work: 25.0% less than 15 minutes, 23.0% 15 to 30 minutes, 23.0% 30 to 45 minutes, 19.7% 45 to 60 minutes, 9.2% 60 minutes or more (2000)

GIBSON (city). Covers a land area of 0.066 square miles and a water area of 0 square miles. Located at 41.48° N. Lat.; 92.39° W. Long.

History: Established in 1880, Gibson was first known as Nassau. The name was changed in 1903.

Population: 92 (2000); Race: 100.0% White, 0.0% Black, 0.0% Asian, 0.0% American Indian and Alaska Native, 0.0% Hispanic of any race, 0.0% two or more races (2000); Density: 1,389.9 persons per square mile (2000); Age: 38.1% under 18, 15.2% over 64 (2000); Marriage status: 15.4% never married, 63.1% now married, 9.2% widowed, 12.3% divorced (2000); Foreign born: 0.0% (2000); Ancestry (includes multiple ancestries): 27.6% United States or American, 26.7% German, 16.2% English, 5.7% Czech, 4.8% Scottish (2000).

Economy: Employment by occupation: 0.0% management, 27.9% professional, 14.0% services, 32.6% sales, 9.3% farming, 9.3% construction, 7.0% production (2000).

Income: Per capita income: $12,881 (2000); Median household income: $39,375 (2000); Poverty rate: 6.7% (2000).

Taxes: Total city taxes per capita: $45 (1997); City property taxes per capita: $45 (1997).

Education: High school graduation rate: 94.3% (2000); College graduation rate: 32.1% (2000).

Housing: Homeownership rate: 76.9% (2000); Median home value: $46,700 (2000); Median rent: $375 per month (2000); Median age of housing: 60+ years (2000).

Transportation: Commute to work: 100.0% car, 0.0% public transportation, 0.0% walk, 0.0% work from home (2000); Travel time to work: 32.6% less than 15 minutes, 25.6% 15 to 30 minutes, 32.6% 30 to 45 minutes, 4.7% 45 to 60 minutes, 4.7% 60 minutes or more (2000)

HARPER (city). Covers a land area of 0.088 square miles and a water area of 0 square miles. Located at 41.36° N. Lat.; 92.05° W. Long. Elevation is 810 feet.

Population: 134 (2000); Race: 100.0% White, 0.0% Black, 0.0% Asian, 0.0% American Indian and Alaska Native, 0.0% Hispanic of any race, 0.0% two or more races (2000); Density: 1,523.7 persons per square mile (2000); Age: 33.1% under 18, 16.2% over 64 (2000); Marriage status: 24.1% never married, 66.7% now married, 5.6% widowed, 3.7% divorced (2000); Foreign born: 0.0% (2000); Ancestry (includes multiple ancestries): 55.2% German, 32.5% Irish, 6.5% Norwegian, 4.5% Other groups, 3.9% Dutch (2000).

Economy: Feed milling. Employment by occupation: 12.3% management, 16.9% professional, 9.2% services, 15.4% sales, 4.6% farming, 3.1% construction, 38.5% production (2000).

Income: Per capita income: $12,620 (2000); Median household income: $37,875 (2000); Poverty rate: 4.5% (2000).

Taxes: Total city taxes per capita: $46 (1997); City property taxes per capita: $46 (1997).

Education: High school graduation rate: 83.5% (2000); College graduation rate: 11.3% (2000).

Housing: Homeownership rate: 72.7% (2000); Median home value: $45,000 (2000); Median rent: $304 per month (2000); Median age of housing: 60+ years (2000).

Transportation: Commute to work: 93.5% car, 0.0% public transportation, 3.2% walk, 3.2% work from home (2000); Travel time to work: 33.3% less than 15 minutes, 13.3% 15 to 30 minutes, 41.7% 30 to 45 minutes, 8.3% 45 to 60 minutes, 3.3% 60 minutes or more (2000)

HAYESVILLE (city). Covers a land area of 0.255 square miles and a water area of 0 square miles. Located at 41.26° N. Lat.; 92.24° W. Long. Elevation is 810 feet.

History: The land for the town of Hayesville was donated by Esther and Joel Winthrop Hayes, and the town was named for them.
Population: 64 (2000); Race: 100.0% White, 0.0% Black, 0.0% Asian, 0.0% American Indian and Alaska Native, 0.0% Hispanic of any race, 0.0% two or more races (2000); Density: 250.5 persons per square mile (2000); Age: 21.1% under 18, 15.5% over 64 (2000); Marriage status: 21.7% never married, 58.3% now married, 8.3% widowed, 11.7% divorced (2000); Foreign born: 0.0% (2000); Ancestry (includes multiple ancestries): 47.9% German, 12.7% English, 9.9% Dutch, 7.0% United States or American, 4.2% French (except Basque) (2000).
Economy: Employment by occupation: 5.0% management, 12.5% professional, 22.5% services, 22.5% sales, 0.0% farming, 10.0% construction, 27.5% production (2000).
Income: Per capita income: $15,973 (2000); Median household income: $38,125 (2000); Poverty rate: 0.0% (2000).
Taxes: Total city taxes per capita: $113 (1997); City property taxes per capita: $113 (1997).
Education: High school graduation rate: 72.3% (2000); College graduation rate: 8.5% (2000).
Housing: Homeownership rate: 90.0% (2000); Median home value: $27,900 (2000); Median rent: $125 per month (2000); Median age of housing: 58 years (2000).
Transportation: Commute to work: 86.5% car, 0.0% public transportation, 13.5% walk, 0.0% work from home (2000); Travel time to work: 45.9% less than 15 minutes, 27.0% 15 to 30 minutes, 10.8% 30 to 45 minutes, 10.8% 45 to 60 minutes, 5.4% 60 minutes or more (2000)

HEDRICK (city). Covers a land area of 1.541 square miles and a water area of 0 square miles. Located at 41.17° N. Lat.; 92.30° W. Long. Elevation is 794 feet.
History: Hedrick was once the site of the nationally known Hedrick One Mile Race Track. Thousands of people packed the amphitheater each day. The track was closed in 1902 or 1903.
Population: 837 (2000); Race: 98.7% White, 0.0% Black, 0.2% Asian, 0.1% American Indian and Alaska Native, 1.3% Hispanic of any race, 0.5% two or more races (2000); Density: 543.1 persons per square mile (2000); Age: 30.0% under 18, 14.5% over 64 (2000); Marriage status: 21.1% never married, 61.4% now married, 9.6% widowed, 7.8% divorced (2000); Foreign born: 0.2% (2000); Ancestry (includes multiple ancestries): 20.9% German, 12.8% Irish, 10.5% Other groups, 9.2% English, 9.1% United States or American (2000).
Economy: Single-family building permits issued: 2 (2001) / 5 (2000); Multi-family building permits issued: 0 (2001) / 0 (2000); Employment by occupation: 7.1% management, 12.6% professional, 17.5% services, 16.7% sales, 0.8% farming, 12.3% construction, 33.1% production (2000).
Income: Per capita income: $14,166 (2000); Median household income: $30,714 (2000); Poverty rate: 13.5% (2000).
Taxes: Total city taxes per capita: $118 (1997); City property taxes per capita: $118 (1997).
Education: High school graduation rate: 82.6% (2000); College graduation rate: 10.3% (2000).
Housing: Homeownership rate: 75.9% (2000); Median home value: $42,900 (2000); Median rent: $256 per month (2000); Median age of housing: 52 years (2000).
Transportation: Commute to work: 94.1% car, 0.0% public transportation, 4.2% walk, 1.7% work from home (2000); Travel time to work: 18.7% less than 15 minutes, 38.2% 15 to 30 minutes, 26.1% 30 to 45 minutes, 9.5% 45 to 60 minutes, 7.5% 60 minutes or more (2000)

KEOTA (city). Covers a land area of 0.626 square miles and a water area of 0 square miles. Located at 41.36° N. Lat.; 91.95° W. Long. Elevation is 800 feet.
History: In 1880, Keota was the site of the only glass works west of Cincinnati, Ohio.
Population: 1,025 (2000); Race: 99.7% White, 0.0% Black, 0.3% Asian, 0.0% American Indian and Alaska Native, 0.0% Hispanic of any race, 0.0% two or more races (2000); Density: 1,636.9 persons per square mile (2000); Age: 25.9% under 18, 20.9% over 64 (2000); Marriage status: 22.4% never married, 55.0% now married, 13.1% widowed, 9.5% divorced (2000); Foreign born: 0.7% (2000); Ancestry (includes multiple ancestries): 39.4% German, 18.0% United States or American, 12.7% Irish, 7.8% English, 5.1% Other groups (2000).
Economy: Single-family building permits issued: 2 (2001) / 0 (2000); Multi-family building permits issued: 0 (2001) / 0 (2000); Employment by occupation: 9.5% management, 16.4% professional, 16.8% services, 19.7% sales, 1.0% farming, 12.0% construction, 24.5% production (2000).
Income: Per capita income: $17,310 (2000); Median household income: $35,966 (2000); Poverty rate: 8.8% (2000).
Taxes: Total city taxes per capita: $193 (1997); City property taxes per capita: $192 (1997).
Education: High school graduation rate: 82.7% (2000); College graduation rate: 17.0% (2000).

School District(s)

Keota Community School District (PK-12)
2000 Enrollment: 404 641-636-2189

Housing: Homeownership rate: 83.4% (2000); Median home value: $61,000 (2000); Median rent: $334 per month (2000); Median age of housing: 59 years (2000).
Newspapers: The Keota Eagle (1 x week)
Transportation: Commute to work: 90.9% car, 0.4% public transportation, 6.1% walk, 1.7% work from home (2000); Travel time to work: 44.6% less than 15 minutes, 26.9% 15 to 30 minutes, 6.0% 30 to 45 minutes, 13.4% 45 to 60 minutes, 9.1% 60 minutes or more (2000)

KESWICK (city). Covers a land area of 0.438 square miles and a water area of 0 square miles. Located at 41.45° N. Lat.; 92.23° W. Long.
History: Keswick was platted in 1879. The name was suggested by an English immigrant, Mrs. Allan Cameron, Sr., after the town of Keswick, England.
Population: 295 (2000); Race: 100.0% White, 0.0% Black, 0.0% Asian, 0.0% American Indian and Alaska Native, 0.0% Hispanic of any race, 0.0% two or more races (2000); Density: 674.2 persons per square mile (2000); Age: 28.8% under 18, 19.5% over 64 (2000); Marriage status: 17.9% never married, 60.1% now married, 12.8% widowed, 9.2% divorced (2000); Foreign born: 0.0% (2000); Ancestry (includes multiple ancestries): 28.8% German, 11.6% Irish, 6.5% Norwegian, 5.1% United States or American, 5.1% French (except Basque) (2000).
Economy: Employment by occupation: 9.6% management, 16.8% professional, 16.8% services, 24.0% sales, 4.8% farming, 5.6% construction, 22.4% production (2000).
Income: Per capita income: $15,779 (2000); Median household income: $31,354 (2000); Poverty rate: 5.5% (2000).
Taxes: Total city taxes per capita: $65 (1997); City property taxes per capita: $62 (1997).
Education: High school graduation rate: 88.2% (2000); College graduation rate: 7.2% (2000).
Housing: Homeownership rate: 82.1% (2000); Median home value: $37,700 (2000); Median rent: $125 per month (2000); Median age of housing: 60+ years (2000).
Transportation: Commute to work: 93.6% car, 0.0% public transportation, 4.8% walk, 1.6% work from home (2000); Travel time to work: 35.0% less than 15 minutes, 20.3% 15 to 30 minutes, 22.8% 30 to 45 minutes, 9.8% 45 to 60 minutes, 12.2% 60 minutes or more (2000)

KINROSS (city). Covers a land area of 0.192 square miles and a water area of 0 square miles. Located at 41.45° N. Lat.; 91.98° W. Long.
History: There is some question as to the origin of the name of Kinross. It may have been named after John Kinross, a man reported to have been the town's first postmaster, or it may have originated from the Scottish word "kinross," meaning a market place and community center.
Population: 80 (2000); Race: 100.0% White, 0.0% Black, 0.0% Asian, 0.0% American Indian and Alaska Native, 0.0% Hispanic of any race, 0.0% two or more races (2000); Density: 416.5 persons per square mile (2000); Age: 26.7% under 18, 8.3% over 64 (2000); Marriage status: 13.0% never married, 56.5% now married, 10.9% widowed, 19.6% divorced (2000); Foreign born: 0.0% (2000); Ancestry (includes multiple ancestries): 43.3% German, 15.0% Dutch, 10.0% United States or American, 8.3% Irish, 6.7% English (2000).
Economy: Employment by occupation: 0.0% management, 17.6% professional, 44.1% services, 0.0% sales, 0.0% farming, 8.8% construction, 29.4% production (2000).
Income: Per capita income: $12,625 (2000); Median household income: $31,563 (2000); Poverty rate: 11.7% (2000).
Taxes: Total city taxes per capita: $33 (1997); City property taxes per capita: $33 (1997).
Education: High school graduation rate: 75.0% (2000); College graduation rate: 7.5% (2000).
Housing: Homeownership rate: 70.4% (2000); Median home value: $62,100 (2000); Median rent: $313 per month (2000); Median age of housing: 58 years (2000).
Transportation: Commute to work: 100.0% car, 0.0% public transportation, 0.0% walk, 0.0% work from home (2000); Travel time to work: 15.2% less

than 15 minutes, 27.3% 15 to 30 minutes, 42.4% 30 to 45 minutes, 15.2% 45 to 60 minutes, 0.0% 60 minutes or more (2000)

MARTINSBURG (city). Covers a land area of 0.378 square miles and a water area of 0 square miles. Located at 41.17° N. Lat.; 92.25° W. Long.
Population: 126 (2000); Race: 94.4% White, 0.0% Black, 0.0% Asian, 5.6% American Indian and Alaska Native, 0.0% Hispanic of any race, 0.0% two or more races (2000); Density: 333.4 persons per square mile (2000); Age: 9.5% under 18, 19.8% over 64 (2000); Marriage status: 14.9% never married, 69.3% now married, 8.8% widowed, 7.0% divorced (2000); Foreign born: 0.0% (2000); Ancestry (includes multiple ancestries): 18.3% German, 17.5% Irish, 15.1% United States or American, 11.1% Other groups, 4.8% English (2000).
Economy: Livestock; grain. Single-family building permits issued: 0 (2001) / 0 (2000); Multi-family building permits issued: 0 (2001) / 0 (2000); Employment by occupation: 2.8% management, 8.5% professional, 23.9% services, 16.9% sales, 7.0% farming, 14.1% construction, 26.8% production (2000).
Income: Per capita income: $17,807 (2000); Median household income: $35,625 (2000); Poverty rate: 1.6% (2000).
Taxes: Total city taxes per capita: $60 (1997); City property taxes per capita: $60 (1997).
Education: High school graduation rate: 76.7% (2000); College graduation rate: 1.9% (2000).
Housing: Homeownership rate: 94.1% (2000); Median home value: $43,300 (2000); Median rent: $125 per month (2000); Median age of housing: 59 years (2000).
Transportation: Commute to work: 97.1% car, 0.0% public transportation, 0.0% walk, 0.0% work from home (2000); Travel time to work: 16.2% less than 15 minutes, 32.4% 15 to 30 minutes, 30.9% 30 to 45 minutes, 8.8% 45 to 60 minutes, 11.8% 60 minutes or more (2000)

OLLIE (city). Covers a land area of 0.999 square miles and a water area of 0 square miles. Located at 41.19° N. Lat.; 92.09° W. Long. Elevation is 782 feet.
History: The town of Ollie was named in honor of the daughter of local landowners Margaret and William Fye.
Population: 224 (2000); Race: 98.5% White, 0.0% Black, 0.0% Asian, 0.0% American Indian and Alaska Native, 0.0% Hispanic of any race, 1.5% two or more races (2000); Density: 224.2 persons per square mile (2000); Age: 22.4% under 18, 25.4% over 64 (2000); Marriage status: 24.4% never married, 55.2% now married, 10.5% widowed, 9.9% divorced (2000); Foreign born: 1.0% (2000); Ancestry (includes multiple ancestries): 44.9% German, 13.7% Irish, 7.8% English, 7.8% Dutch, 4.9% United States or American (2000).
Economy: Employment by occupation: 15.8% management, 4.2% professional, 13.7% services, 25.3% sales, 2.1% farming, 17.9% construction, 21.1% production (2000).
Income: Per capita income: $15,100 (2000); Median household income: $30,000 (2000); Poverty rate: 7.3% (2000).
Taxes: Total city taxes per capita: $60 (1997); City property taxes per capita: $60 (1997).
Education: High school graduation rate: 89.7% (2000); College graduation rate: 3.2% (2000).
Housing: Homeownership rate: 84.2% (2000); Median home value: $54,400 (2000); Median rent: $175 per month (2000); Median age of housing: 55 years (2000).
Transportation: Commute to work: 90.5% car, 0.0% public transportation, 4.2% walk, 5.3% work from home (2000); Travel time to work: 31.1% less than 15 minutes, 40.0% 15 to 30 minutes, 24.4% 30 to 45 minutes, 0.0% 45 to 60 minutes, 4.4% 60 minutes or more (2000)

RICHLAND (city). Covers a land area of 0.771 square miles and a water area of 0 square miles. Located at 41.18° N. Lat.; 91.99° W. Long.
History: Richland got its name from the richness of the soil in the area.
Population: 587 (2000); Race: 97.9% White, 0.0% Black, 0.0% Asian, 0.0% American Indian and Alaska Native, 2.2% Hispanic of any race, 2.1% two or more races (2000); Density: 761.6 persons per square mile (2000); Age: 31.4% under 18, 15.5% over 64 (2000); Marriage status: 22.0% never married, 59.6% now married, 7.3% widowed, 11.0% divorced (2000); Foreign born: 0.3% (2000); Ancestry (includes multiple ancestries): 27.4% German, 13.8% English, 11.4% United States or American, 8.7% Irish, 6.3% Other groups (2000).
Economy: Single-family building permits issued: 3 (2001) / 1 (2000); Multi-family building permits issued: 0 (2001) / 0 (2000); Employment by occupation: 10.6% management, 13.0% professional, 14.7% services, 24.3% sales, 4.1% farming, 11.3% construction, 21.9% production (2000).
Income: Per capita income: $14,726 (2000); Median household income: $32,813 (2000); Poverty rate: 16.8% (2000).
Taxes: Total city taxes per capita: $149 (1997); City property taxes per capita: $147 (1997).
Education: High school graduation rate: 81.5% (2000); College graduation rate: 12.5% (2000).
Housing: Homeownership rate: 77.8% (2000); Median home value: $70,000 (2000); Median rent: $357 per month (2000); Median age of housing: 46 years (2000).
Newspapers: Richland Plainsman-Clarion (1 x week)
Transportation: Commute to work: 91.2% car, 0.0% public transportation, 2.8% walk, 3.5% work from home (2000); Travel time to work: 20.0% less than 15 minutes, 62.2% 15 to 30 minutes, 10.2% 30 to 45 minutes, 3.3% 45 to 60 minutes, 4.4% 60 minutes or more (2000)

SIGOURNEY (city). Covers a land area of 2.174 square miles and a water area of 0 square miles. Located at 41.33° N. Lat.; 92.20° W. Long. Elevation is 790 feet.
History: Sigourney was named for Lydia Huntley Sigourney of Connecticut, author of many books. When she learned of the honor, she presented the town library with 50 volumes.
Population: 2,209 (2000); Race: 98.8% White, 0.0% Black, 0.5% Asian, 0.0% American Indian and Alaska Native, 1.0% Hispanic of any race, 0.5% two or more races (2000); Density: 1,016.3 persons per square mile (2000); Age: 24.8% under 18, 26.7% over 64 (2000); Marriage status: 17.8% never married, 57.4% now married, 17.1% widowed, 7.7% divorced (2000); Foreign born: 0.8% (2000); Ancestry (includes multiple ancestries): 38.5% German, 12.2% Irish, 10.9% English, 7.3% Other groups, 6.8% United States or American (2000).
Economy: Single-family building permits issued: 5 (2001) / 5 (2000); Multi-family building permits issued: 0 (2001) / 0 (2000); Employment by occupation: 10.4% management, 18.8% professional, 18.9% services, 21.5% sales, 1.8% farming, 11.4% construction, 17.0% production (2000).
Income: Per capita income: $17,218 (2000); Median household income: $29,803 (2000); Poverty rate: 10.8% (2000).
Taxes: Total city taxes per capita: $192 (1997); City property taxes per capita: $190 (1997).
Education: High school graduation rate: 81.7% (2000); College graduation rate: 13.9% (2000).

School District(s)

Sigourney Community School District (PK-12)
2000 Enrollment: 786 641-622-2025

Housing: Homeownership rate: 74.9% (2000); Median home value: $56,600 (2000); Median rent: $279 per month (2000); Median age of housing: 60+ years (2000).
Hospitals: Keokuk County Health Center (25 beds)
Newspapers: Keokuk County Chief (1 x month); The Sigourney News-Review (1 x week)
Transportation: Commute to work: 89.0% car, 0.0% public transportation, 9.3% walk, 1.4% work from home (2000); Travel time to work: 60.7% less than 15 minutes, 11.1% 15 to 30 minutes, 14.9% 30 to 45 minutes, 5.6% 45 to 60 minutes, 7.7% 60 minutes or more (2000)
Additional Information Contacts
Sigourney Area Development 641-622-2288

SOUTH ENGLISH (city). Covers a land area of 0.306 square miles and a water area of 0 square miles. Located at 41.45° N. Lat.; 92.09° W. Long. Elevation is 840 feet.
History: South English was mapped in 1855. Its name reflected its location on the south bank of the English River.
Population: 213 (2000); Race: 99.5% White, 0.0% Black, 0.0% Asian, 0.0% American Indian and Alaska Native, 0.0% Hispanic of any race, 0.5% two or more races (2000); Density: 695.2 persons per square mile (2000); Age: 20.4% under 18, 18.5% over 64 (2000); Marriage status: 14.7% never married, 60.9% now married, 16.3% widowed, 8.2% divorced (2000); Foreign born: 0.0% (2000); Ancestry (includes multiple ancestries): 32.7% German, 16.6% English, 13.7% United States or American, 8.1% Irish, 3.3% Dutch (2000).
Economy: Employment by occupation: 11.0% management, 7.6% professional, 14.4% services, 22.9% sales, 0.0% farming, 10.2% construction, 33.9% production (2000).
Income: Per capita income: $21,833 (2000); Median household income: $36,429 (2000); Poverty rate: 6.7% (2000).

Taxes: Total city taxes per capita: $74 (1997); City property taxes per capita: $70 (1997).
Education: High school graduation rate: 87.7% (2000); College graduation rate: 3.2% (2000).
Housing: Homeownership rate: 80.2% (2000); Median home value: $47,500 (2000); Median rent: $225 per month (2000); Median age of housing: 52 years (2000).
Transportation: Commute to work: 93.2% car, 0.0% public transportation, 1.7% walk, 3.4% work from home (2000); Travel time to work: 31.6% less than 15 minutes, 19.3% 15 to 30 minutes, 20.2% 30 to 45 minutes, 19.3% 45 to 60 minutes, 9.6% 60 minutes or more (2000)

THORNBURG (city). Covers a land area of 0.197 square miles and a water area of 0 square miles. Located at 41.45° N. Lat.; 92.33° W. Long. Elevation is 878 feet.
History: Thornburg began in 1879. The name was in memory of Major Thomas J. Thornburg.
Population: 84 (2000); Race: 100.0% White, 0.0% Black, 0.0% Asian, 0.0% American Indian and Alaska Native, 0.0% Hispanic of any race, 0.0% two or more races (2000); Density: 426.9 persons per square mile (2000); Age: 17.6% under 18, 4.7% over 64 (2000); Marriage status: 31.9% never married, 54.2% now married, 5.6% widowed, 8.3% divorced (2000); Foreign born: 0.0% (2000); Ancestry (includes multiple ancestries): 27.1% German, 9.4% French (except Basque), 9.4% United States or American, 9.4% English, 7.1% Pennsylvania German (2000).
Economy: Employment by occupation: 6.9% management, 20.7% professional, 15.5% services, 25.9% sales, 0.0% farming, 6.9% construction, 24.1% production (2000).
Income: Per capita income: $15,954 (2000); Median household income: $45,313 (2000); Poverty rate: 4.9% (2000).
Taxes: Total city taxes per capita: $65 (1997); City property taxes per capita: $65 (1997).
Education: High school graduation rate: 94.4% (2000); College graduation rate: 13.0% (2000).

School District(s)

Tri-County Community School District (PK-12)
2000 Enrollment: 355 641-634-2408

Housing: Homeownership rate: 80.6% (2000); Median home value: $27,500 (2000); Median rent: $238 per month (2000); Median age of housing: 56 years (2000).
Transportation: Commute to work: 87.9% car, 3.4% public transportation, 8.6% walk, 0.0% work from home (2000); Travel time to work: 20.7% less than 15 minutes, 17.2% 15 to 30 minutes, 25.9% 30 to 45 minutes, 19.0% 45 to 60 minutes, 17.2% 60 minutes or more (2000)

WEBSTER (city). Covers a land area of 0.300 square miles and a water area of 0 square miles. Located at 41.43° N. Lat.; 92.17° W. Long. Elevation is 858 feet.
History: Webster got its name in 1855. It is believed to have been named for a stagecoach line owner.
Population: 110 (2000); Race: 100.0% White, 0.0% Black, 0.0% Asian, 0.0% American Indian and Alaska Native, 0.0% Hispanic of any race, 0.0% two or more races (2000); Density: 367.0 persons per square mile (2000); Age: 24.5% under 18, 28.4% over 64 (2000); Marriage status: 24.1% never married, 64.4% now married, 6.9% widowed, 4.6% divorced (2000); Foreign born: 0.0% (2000); Ancestry (includes multiple ancestries): 42.2% German, 22.5% Irish, 12.7% United States or American, 5.9% English, 4.9% Dutch (2000).
Economy: Single-family building permits issued: 0 (2001) / 0 (2000); Multi-family building permits issued: 0 (2001) / 0 (2000); Employment by occupation: 8.7% management, 15.2% professional, 13.0% services, 23.9% sales, 0.0% farming, 17.4% construction, 21.7% production (2000).
Income: Per capita income: $18,519 (2000); Median household income: $38,958 (2000); Poverty rate: 3.9% (2000).
Taxes: Total city taxes per capita: $71 (1997); City property taxes per capita: $71 (1997).
Education: High school graduation rate: 94.4% (2000); College graduation rate: 0.0% (2000).
Housing: Homeownership rate: 95.6% (2000); Median home value: $32,500 (2000); Median rent: $175 per month (2000); Median age of housing: 60+ years (2000).
Transportation: Commute to work: 82.6% car, 0.0% public transportation, 17.4% walk, 0.0% work from home (2000); Travel time to work: 30.4% less than 15 minutes, 17.4% 15 to 30 minutes, 19.6% 30 to 45 minutes, 23.9% 45 to 60 minutes, 8.7% 60 minutes or more (2000)

WHAT CHEER (city). Covers a land area of 1.212 square miles and a water area of 0.017 square miles. Located at 41.40° N. Lat.; 92.35° W. Long. Elevation is 751 feet.
History: What Cheer was probably named by Major Joseph Andrews who was of Welsh origin. There were also many Welsh and English miners in the area. "What Cheer" was an English greeting meaning "Be of good cheer."
Population: 678 (2000); Race: 98.5% White, 0.0% Black, 0.0% Asian, 0.0% American Indian and Alaska Native, 2.1% Hispanic of any race, 0.0% two or more races (2000); Density: 559.4 persons per square mile (2000); Age: 22.6% under 18, 24.9% over 64 (2000); Marriage status: 20.5% never married, 53.9% now married, 10.2% widowed, 15.4% divorced (2000); Foreign born: 0.3% (2000); Ancestry (includes multiple ancestries): 22.8% United States or American, 16.4% German, 11.4% Irish, 7.4% English, 6.4% Other groups (2000).
Economy: Single-family building permits issued: 0 (2001) / 2 (2000); Multi-family building permits issued: 0 (2001) / 0 (2000); Employment by occupation: 6.5% management, 9.1% professional, 13.3% services, 19.8% sales, 1.1% farming, 15.2% construction, 35.0% production (2000).
Income: Per capita income: $16,613 (2000); Median household income: $27,292 (2000); Poverty rate: 11.2% (2000).
Taxes: Total city taxes per capita: $103 (1997); City property taxes per capita: $103 (1997).
Education: High school graduation rate: 73.8% (2000); College graduation rate: 6.7% (2000).
Housing: Homeownership rate: 84.4% (2000); Median home value: $23,900 (2000); Median rent: $206 per month (2000); Median age of housing: 60+ years (2000).
Transportation: Commute to work: 96.5% car, 0.0% public transportation, 1.9% walk, 0.8% work from home (2000); Travel time to work: 21.6% less than 15 minutes, 25.9% 15 to 30 minutes, 25.5% 30 to 45 minutes, 9.8% 45 to 60 minutes, 17.3% 60 minutes or more (2000)

Kossuth County

Located in northern Iowa; bounded on the north by Minnesota; prairie area, drained by the East Des Moines River. Covers a land area of 973.00 square miles, a water area of 1.40 square miles, and is located in the Central Time Zone. The county government was organized in 1851. County seat is Algona.

Weather Station: Algona 3 W — Elevation: 1,227 feet

	Jan	Feb	Mar	Apr	May	Jun	Jul	Aug	Sep	Oct	Nov	Dec
High	24	30	42	59	72	81	84	81	74	61	42	28
Low	6	13	25	36	48	58	62	59	51	39	25	12
Precip	0.7	0.7	1.9	3.1	3.8	4.8	4.1	3.6	3.0	2.3	1.8	0.8
Snow	9.0	6.3	6.2	2.1	0.0	0.0	0.0	0.0	0.0	0.2	4.6	7.4

High and Low temperatures in degrees Fahrenheit; Precipitation and Snow in inches

Weather Station: Swea City 1 NE — Elevation: 1,227 feet

	Jan	Feb	Mar	Apr	May	Jun	Jul	Aug	Sep	Oct	Nov	Dec
High	23	29	41	57	72	81	83	81	74	61	42	28
Low	5	11	24	35	48	58	61	59	50	38	25	11
Precip	0.8	0.7	1.9	3.0	3.9	4.3	4.1	4.1	2.9	2.3	1.8	0.8
Snow	9.9	6.1	6.5	1.6	tr	0.0	0.0	0.0	tr	0.4	5.3	8.0

High and Low temperatures in degrees Fahrenheit; Precipitation and Snow in inches

Population: 17,163 (2000); Race: 98.8% White, 0.2% Black, 0.2% Asian, 0.1% American Indian and Alaska Native, 0.9% Hispanic of any race, 0.5% two or more races (2000); Density: 17.6 persons per square mile (2000); Age: 25.7% under 18, 20.1% over 64 (2000).
Religion: Five largest groups: 34.3% Catholic Church, 14.6% Lutheran Church—Missouri Synod, 11.3% The United Methodist Church, 10.5% Evangelical Lutheran Church in America, 4.0% Presbyterian Church (U.S.A.) (2000).
Economy: Unemployment rate: 3.3% (11/2002); Total civilian labor force: 8,530 (11/2002); Leading industries: 24.9% manufacturing; 16.8% retail trade; 13.8% health care and social assistance (2000); Companies that employ more than 1,000 persons: 0 (2000); Companies that employ more than 100 persons: 7 (2000); Farms: 1,404 totaling 580,884 acres (1997); Minority business ownership rate: 0.0% (1997); Women business ownership rate: 15.7% (1997); Retail sales per capita: $8,501 (1997). Single-family building permits issued: 18 (2001) / 9 (2000); Multi-family building permits issued: 5 (2001) / 2 (2000).
Income: Per capita income: $16,598 (2000); Median household income: $34,562 (2000); Poverty rate: 10.2% (2000); Bankruptcy rate: 1.81% (2001).

Taxes: Total county taxes per capita: $302 (2000); County property taxes per capita: $296 (2000).
Education: High school graduation rate: 85.6% (2000); College graduation rate: 13.6% (2000).
Housing: Homeownership rate: 77.6% (2000); Median home value: $54,300 (2000); Median rent: $257 per month (2000); Median age of housing: 50 years (2000).
Health: Birth rate: 104.9 per 10,000 population (1998); Age adjusted death rate: 78.2 per 10,000 population (1999); Age adjusted cancer mortality rate: 193.9 deaths per 100,000 population (1999). Number of physicians: 4.7 per 10,000 population (1999); Number of hospital beds: 14.0 per 10,000 population (1999).
Elections: 2000 Presidential election results: 44.6% Gore, 52.0% Bush, 2.3% Nader, 0.5% Buchanan
National and State Parks: Ambrose A Call State Park; Ambrose A Call State Park; Buffalo Creek State Game Management Area; Goose Lake State Game Management Area; Iowa Lake Marsh State Game Management Area; Schwob Marsh State Game Management Area; State Line Marsh State Game Management Area; Stinson Prairie State Park; Union Slough National Wildlife Refuge
Additional Information Contacts
Kossuth County Government Offices 515-295-2718
Algona Chamber of Commerce 515-295-7021

Kossuth County Communities

ALGONA (city). Covers a land area of 4.487 square miles and a water area of 0.017 square miles. Located at 43.07° N. Lat.; 94.23° W. Long. Elevation is 1,209 feet.
History: The first settlers of Algona were Asa C. and Ambrose A. Call, who arrived in 1854. For some time the community was known as Call's Grove, but at the suggestion of Mrs. Asa Call the present name was adopted—a derivation of "Algonquin."
Population: 5,741 (2000); Race: 98.0% White, 0.2% Black, 0.5% Asian, 0.2% American Indian and Alaska Native, 1.2% Hispanic of any race, 0.9% two or more races (2000); Density: 1,279.4 persons per square mile (2000); Age: 24.3% under 18, 21.4% over 64 (2000); Marriage status: 21.4% never married, 57.7% now married, 13.3% widowed, 7.7% divorced (2000); Foreign born: 1.5% (2000); Ancestry (includes multiple ancestries): 51.1% German, 9.9% Norwegian, 9.7% Irish, 8.3% English, 5.7% United States or American (2000).
Economy: Single-family building permits issued: 12 (2001) / 5 (2000); Multi-family building permits issued: 5 (2001) / 2 (2000); Employment by occupation: 12.3% management, 16.7% professional, 18.5% services, 23.8% sales, 1.1% farming, 6.8% construction, 20.7% production (2000).
Income: Per capita income: $16,979 (2000); Median household income: $32,207 (2000); Poverty rate: 10.8% (2000).
Taxes: Total city taxes per capita: $282 (1997); City property taxes per capita: $271 (1997).
Education: High school graduation rate: 82.8% (2000); College graduation rate: 16.1% (2000).

School District(s)
Algona Community School District (PK-12)
2000 Enrollment: 1,398 515-295-3528
Housing: Homeownership rate: 74.1% (2000); Median home value: $68,800 (2000); Median rent: $312 per month (2000); Median age of housing: 45 years (2000).
Hospitals: Kossuth Regional Health Center (40 beds)
Safety: Violent crime rate: 12.2 per 10,000 population; Property crime rate: 254.6 per 10,000 population (2001).
Newspapers: The Algona Upper Des Moines (1 x week); Weekend Express (1 x week); The Reminder (1 x week)
Transportation: Commute to work: 92.5% car, 1.0% public transportation, 2.6% walk, 2.9% work from home (2000); Travel time to work: 73.2% less than 15 minutes, 13.1% 15 to 30 minutes, 6.5% 30 to 45 minutes, 3.7% 45 to 60 minutes, 3.5% 60 minutes or more (2000)
Airports: Algona Municipal
Additional Information Contacts
Algona Chamber of Commerce 515-295-7021

BANCROFT (city). Covers a land area of 0.544 square miles and a water area of 0 square miles. Located at 43.29° N. Lat.; 94.21° W. Long. Elevation is 1,189 feet.
History: Bancroft was platted in 1881 by the Western Town Lot Company and named in honor of historian George Bancroft, who acknowledged the honor by presenting the town with 50 books as the nucleus of a library.
Population: 808 (2000); Race: 99.4% White, 0.2% Black, 0.0% Asian, 0.0% American Indian and Alaska Native, 1.1% Hispanic of any race, 0.0% two or more races (2000); Density: 1,484.2 persons per square mile (2000); Age: 24.8% under 18, 27.6% over 64 (2000); Marriage status: 19.0% never married, 55.1% now married, 19.8% widowed, 6.0% divorced (2000); Foreign born: 0.5% (2000); Ancestry (includes multiple ancestries): 56.9% German, 22.4% Irish, 5.9% Norwegian, 4.3% Swedish, 3.2% French (except Basque) (2000).
Economy: Single-family building permits issued: 1 (2001) / 1 (2000); Multi-family building permits issued: 0 (2001) / 0 (2000); Employment by occupation: 10.7% management, 10.1% professional, 17.2% services, 22.6% sales, 3.0% farming, 11.6% construction, 24.9% production (2000).
Income: Per capita income: $15,312 (2000); Median household income: $31,055 (2000); Poverty rate: 12.7% (2000).
Taxes: Total city taxes per capita: $208 (1997); City property taxes per capita: $195 (1997).
Education: High school graduation rate: 83.2% (2000); College graduation rate: 6.9% (2000).
Housing: Homeownership rate: 79.2% (2000); Median home value: $47,600 (2000); Median rent: $199 per month (2000); Median age of housing: 45 years (2000).
Newspapers: The Bancroft Register (1 x week)
Transportation: Commute to work: 84.0% car, 0.0% public transportation, 8.4% walk, 6.9% work from home (2000); Travel time to work: 63.1% less than 15 minutes, 18.8% 15 to 30 minutes, 6.5% 30 to 45 minutes, 9.4% 45 to 60 minutes, 2.3% 60 minutes or more (2000)

BURT (city). Covers a land area of 0.430 square miles and a water area of 0 square miles. Located at 43.19° N. Lat.; 94.22° W. Long. Elevation is 1,169 feet.
History: Burt was founded in 1881 when the Chicago & North Western Railroad was built through northern Iowa. The site was named for Horace G. Burt, chief engineer of the railroad at that time.
Population: 556 (2000); Race: 100.0% White, 0.0% Black, 0.0% Asian, 0.0% American Indian and Alaska Native, 0.7% Hispanic of any race, 0.0% two or more races (2000); Density: 1,294.2 persons per square mile (2000); Age: 20.3% under 18, 19.0% over 64 (2000); Marriage status: 26.3% never married, 60.6% now married, 6.8% widowed, 6.4% divorced (2000); Foreign born: 0.7% (2000); Ancestry (includes multiple ancestries): 47.9% German, 10.1% Irish, 8.4% Norwegian, 5.9% English, 5.0% United States or American (2000).
Economy: Single-family building permits issued: 0 (2001) / 0 (2000); Multi-family building permits issued: 0 (2001) / 0 (2000); Employment by occupation: 10.2% management, 14.5% professional, 20.0% services, 13.3% sales, 0.0% farming, 11.0% construction, 31.0% production (2000).
Income: Per capita income: $15,727 (2000); Median household income: $29,625 (2000); Poverty rate: 17.1% (2000).
Taxes: Total city taxes per capita: $132 (1997); City property taxes per capita: $132 (1997).
Education: High school graduation rate: 76.5% (2000); College graduation rate: 8.7% (2000).

School District(s)
Burt Community School District (KG-12)
2000 Enrollment: 0 515-924-3211
Housing: Homeownership rate: 81.3% (2000); Median home value: $33,500 (2000); Median rent: $240 per month (2000); Median age of housing: 57 years (2000).
Transportation: Commute to work: 94.8% car, 0.0% public transportation, 3.2% walk, 2.0% work from home (2000); Travel time to work: 52.4% less than 15 minutes, 36.2% 15 to 30 minutes, 3.3% 30 to 45 minutes, 2.0% 45 to 60 minutes, 6.1% 60 minutes or more (2000)

FENTON (city). Covers a land area of 0.348 square miles and a water area of 0 square miles. Located at 43.21° N. Lat.; 94.42° W. Long. Elevation is 1,250 feet.
History: Fenton, established in 1899, carries the name of Reuben Eaton Fenton (1819-1885), a New York governor and U.S. Senator.
Population: 317 (2000); Race: 100.0% White, 0.0% Black, 0.0% Asian, 0.0% American Indian and Alaska Native, 0.0% Hispanic of any race, 0.0% two or more races (2000); Density: 909.7 persons per square mile (2000); Age: 21.9% under 18, 30.2% over 64 (2000); Marriage status: 9.5% never married, 65.2% now married, 19.4% widowed, 5.9% divorced (2000); Foreign born: 0.0% (2000); Ancestry (includes multiple ancestries): 58.5%

German, 16.1% Norwegian, 9.3% Irish, 6.8% French (except Basque), 6.8% United States or American (2000).
Economy: Single-family building permits issued: 0 (2001) / 0 (2000); Multi-family building permits issued: 0 (2001) / 0 (2000); Employment by occupation: 22.0% management, 15.2% professional, 12.1% services, 22.7% sales, 0.0% farming, 11.4% construction, 16.7% production (2000).
Income: Per capita income: $15,154 (2000); Median household income: $30,714 (2000); Poverty rate: 6.4% (2000).
Taxes: Total city taxes per capita: $126 (1997); City property taxes per capita: $123 (1997).
Education: High school graduation rate: 84.2% (2000); College graduation rate: 14.9% (2000).

School District(s)

Sentral Community School District (KG-12)
2000 Enrollment: 271 515-889-2261
Housing: Homeownership rate: 89.7% (2000); Median home value: $23,000 (2000); Median rent: $163 per month (2000); Median age of housing: 60+ years (2000).
Transportation: Commute to work: 93.0% car, 0.0% public transportation, 3.9% walk, 1.6% work from home (2000); Travel time to work: 34.6% less than 15 minutes, 48.0% 15 to 30 minutes, 7.1% 30 to 45 minutes, 6.3% 45 to 60 minutes, 3.9% 60 minutes or more (2000)

LAKOTA (city). Covers a land area of 0.191 square miles and a water area of 0 square miles. Located at 43.37° N. Lat.; 94.09° W. Long. Elevation is 1,128 feet.
History: Lakota was originally called Germania because of its predominantly German population, but was renamed during World War I.
Population: 255 (2000); Race: 99.2% White, 0.0% Black, 0.0% Asian, 0.0% American Indian and Alaska Native, 2.4% Hispanic of any race, 0.8% two or more races (2000); Density: 1,334.7 persons per square mile (2000); Age: 21.1% under 18, 25.9% over 64 (2000); Marriage status: 14.1% never married, 59.5% now married, 12.7% widowed, 13.7% divorced (2000); Foreign born: 1.6% (2000); Ancestry (includes multiple ancestries): 55.5% German, 12.6% Norwegian, 7.7% Swedish, 6.1% Irish, 4.5% Other groups (2000).
Economy: Employment by occupation: 8.6% management, 16.2% professional, 15.2% services, 22.9% sales, 0.0% farming, 12.4% construction, 24.8% production (2000).
Income: Per capita income: $18,572 (2000); Median household income: $27,917 (2000); Poverty rate: 19.4% (2000).
Taxes: Total city taxes per capita: $247 (1997); City property taxes per capita: $244 (1997).
Education: High school graduation rate: 74.9% (2000); College graduation rate: 7.3% (2000).
Housing: Homeownership rate: 85.7% (2000); Median home value: $25,400 (2000); Median rent: $211 per month (2000); Median age of housing: 49 years (2000).
Transportation: Commute to work: 81.9% car, 0.0% public transportation, 6.7% walk, 9.5% work from home (2000); Travel time to work: 35.8% less than 15 minutes, 21.1% 15 to 30 minutes, 33.7% 30 to 45 minutes, 9.5% 45 to 60 minutes, 0.0% 60 minutes or more (2000)

LEDYARD (city). Covers a land area of 0.328 square miles and a water area of 0 square miles. Located at 43.42° N. Lat.; 94.16° W. Long. Elevation is 1,173 feet.
History: Ledyard was platted by the Western Town Lot Company in 1884. A large part of the town site was at one time owned by William Larrabee, Governor of Iowa (1886-1890), who named the place for his native town in New England.
Population: 147 (2000); Race: 98.6% White, 0.0% Black, 0.0% Asian, 0.0% American Indian and Alaska Native, 0.0% Hispanic of any race, 1.4% two or more races (2000); Density: 448.4 persons per square mile (2000); Age: 20.1% under 18, 21.6% over 64 (2000); Marriage status: 19.8% never married, 61.2% now married, 9.5% widowed, 9.5% divorced (2000); Foreign born: 0.0% (2000); Ancestry (includes multiple ancestries): 57.6% German, 19.4% Irish, 12.2% Norwegian, 11.5% Dutch, 10.1% English (2000).
Economy: Single-family building permits issued: 0 (2001) / 0 (2000); Multi-family building permits issued: 0 (2001) / 0 (2000); Employment by occupation: 18.6% management, 22.9% professional, 11.4% services, 14.3% sales, 0.0% farming, 8.6% construction, 24.3% production (2000).
Income: Per capita income: $17,512 (2000); Median household income: $22,500 (2000); Poverty rate: 11.5% (2000).
Taxes: Total city taxes per capita: $222 (1997); City property taxes per capita: $222 (1997).
Education: High school graduation rate: 85.7% (2000); College graduation rate: 15.2% (2000).
Housing: Homeownership rate: 88.2% (2000); Median home value: $18,700 (2000); Median rent: $213 per month (2000); Median age of housing: 49 years (2000).
Transportation: Commute to work: 77.9% car, 0.0% public transportation, 10.3% walk, 8.8% work from home (2000); Travel time to work: 32.3% less than 15 minutes, 30.6% 15 to 30 minutes, 21.0% 30 to 45 minutes, 11.3% 45 to 60 minutes, 4.8% 60 minutes or more (2000)

LONE ROCK (city). Covers a land area of 0.115 square miles and a water area of 0 square miles. Located at 43.22° N. Lat.; 94.32° W. Long.
History: Lone Rock was named for a prominent rock found on the site of the town. The town was mapped in 1899.
Population: 157 (2000); Race: 100.0% White, 0.0% Black, 0.0% Asian, 0.0% American Indian and Alaska Native, 0.0% Hispanic of any race, 0.0% two or more races (2000); Density: 1,368.3 persons per square mile (2000); Age: 23.6% under 18, 37.8% over 64 (2000); Marriage status: 6.0% never married, 70.7% now married, 19.0% widowed, 4.3% divorced (2000); Foreign born: 1.4% (2000); Ancestry (includes multiple ancestries): 44.6% German, 10.1% Irish, 6.8% Swedish, 6.8% Scottish, 6.8% Other groups (2000).
Economy: Employment by occupation: 10.0% management, 36.7% professional, 10.0% services, 6.7% sales, 0.0% farming, 0.0% construction, 36.7% production (2000).
Income: Per capita income: $16,205 (2000); Median household income: $29,896 (2000); Poverty rate: 7.4% (2000).
Taxes: Total city taxes per capita: $110 (1997); City property taxes per capita: $104 (1997).
Education: High school graduation rate: 84.3% (2000); College graduation rate: 17.6% (2000).
Housing: Homeownership rate: 91.3% (2000); Median home value: $36,300 (2000); Median rent: $263 per month (2000); Median age of housing: 46 years (2000).
Transportation: Commute to work: 91.4% car, 0.0% public transportation, 0.0% walk, 5.2% work from home (2000); Travel time to work: 27.3% less than 15 minutes, 67.3% 15 to 30 minutes, 3.6% 30 to 45 minutes, 0.0% 45 to 60 minutes, 1.8% 60 minutes or more (2000)

LU VERNE (city). Aka Luverne. Covers a land area of 2.260 square miles and a water area of 0 square miles. Located at 42.91° N. Lat.; 94.08° W. Long. Elevation is 1,169 feet.
History: Lu Verne was named for Lu Verne, Minnesota.
Population: 299 (2000); Race: 99.3% White, 0.0% Black, 0.0% Asian, 0.7% American Indian and Alaska Native, 1.1% Hispanic of any race, 0.0% two or more races (2000); Density: 132.3 persons per square mile (2000); Age: 22.5% under 18, 23.2% over 64 (2000); Marriage status: 25.7% never married, 49.1% now married, 14.9% widowed, 10.4% divorced (2000); Foreign born: 0.0% (2000); Ancestry (includes multiple ancestries): 47.1% German, 15.9% Irish, 14.1% Norwegian, 9.4% United States or American, 8.7% Danish (2000).
Economy: Employment by occupation: 11.2% management, 21.6% professional, 11.2% services, 20.8% sales, 1.6% farming, 12.8% construction, 20.8% production (2000).
Income: Per capita income: $16,281 (2000); Median household income: $30,625 (2000); Poverty rate: 13.8% (2000).
Taxes: Total city taxes per capita: $152 (1997); City property taxes per capita: $152 (1997).
Education: High school graduation rate: 77.2% (2000); College graduation rate: 13.0% (2000).
Housing: Homeownership rate: 81.1% (2000); Median home value: $26,300 (2000); Median rent: $233 per month (2000); Median age of housing: 59 years (2000).
Transportation: Commute to work: 87.1% car, 0.0% public transportation, 7.8% walk, 5.2% work from home (2000); Travel time to work: 45.5% less than 15 minutes, 30.9% 15 to 30 minutes, 9.1% 30 to 45 minutes, 5.5% 45 to 60 minutes, 9.1% 60 minutes or more (2000)

SWEA CITY (city). Covers a land area of 0.737 square miles and a water area of 0 square miles. Located at 43.38° N. Lat.; 94.30° W. Long. Elevation is 1,181 feet.
History: Swea City, first called Reynolds, officially adopted its present name in 1893. It is derived from the Swedish word "Svea," which is the affectionate term for Sweden. Captain R. E. Jensen, general agent for American Emigrant Company, which owned thousands of acres in this vicinity, brought a group of Swedish emigrants to the town in 1870.

Population: 642 (2000); Race: 100.0% White, 0.0% Black, 0.0% Asian, 0.0% American Indian and Alaska Native, 1.6% Hispanic of any race, 0.0% two or more races (2000); Density: 871.5 persons per square mile (2000); Age: 25.7% under 18, 21.7% over 64 (2000); Marriage status: 23.0% never married, 54.5% now married, 13.4% widowed, 9.1% divorced (2000); Foreign born: 0.5% (2000); Ancestry (includes multiple ancestries): 49.6% German, 14.7% Norwegian, 9.9% Swedish, 9.6% Irish, 6.4% United States or American (2000).
Economy: Single-family building permits issued: 0 (2001) / 0 (2000); Multi-family building permits issued: 0 (2001) / 0 (2000); Employment by occupation: 13.5% management, 17.8% professional, 15.3% services, 21.8% sales, 0.7% farming, 7.6% construction, 23.3% production (2000).
Income: Per capita income: $14,937 (2000); Median household income: $28,250 (2000); Poverty rate: 12.9% (2000).
Taxes: Total city taxes per capita: $219 (1997); City property taxes per capita: $217 (1997).
Education: High school graduation rate: 80.1% (2000); College graduation rate: 14.9% (2000).

School District(s)

North Kossuth Community School District (PK-12)
2000 Enrollment: 439 515-272-4361
Housing: Homeownership rate: 77.9% (2000); Median home value: $30,900 (2000); Median rent: $223 per month (2000); Median age of housing: 53 years (2000).
Newspapers: Swea City Herald-Press (1 x week)
Transportation: Commute to work: 87.7% car, 0.7% public transportation, 8.9% walk, 2.2% work from home (2000); Travel time to work: 47.5% less than 15 minutes, 20.9% 15 to 30 minutes, 27.4% 30 to 45 minutes, 2.7% 45 to 60 minutes, 1.5% 60 minutes or more (2000)

TITONKA (city). Covers a land area of 0.279 square miles and a water area of 0 square miles. Located at 43.23° N. Lat.; 94.04° W. Long. Elevation is 1,156 feet.
History: Titonka is a Sioux word meaning "big house."
Population: 584 (2000); Race: 99.8% White, 0.0% Black, 0.0% Asian, 0.0% American Indian and Alaska Native, 0.5% Hispanic of any race, 0.2% two or more races (2000); Density: 2,092.2 persons per square mile (2000); Age: 23.8% under 18, 35.3% over 64 (2000); Marriage status: 19.3% never married, 58.5% now married, 17.5% widowed, 4.7% divorced (2000); Foreign born: 0.3% (2000); Ancestry (includes multiple ancestries): 59.1% German, 13.6% Norwegian, 7.3% Irish, 5.2% English, 4.3% French (except Basque) (2000).
Economy: Single-family building permits issued: 0 (2001) / 1 (2000); Multi-family building permits issued: 0 (2001) / 0 (2000); Employment by occupation: 6.9% management, 17.1% professional, 15.4% services, 21.5% sales, 2.4% farming, 9.8% construction, 26.8% production (2000).
Income: Per capita income: $16,594 (2000); Median household income: $35,147 (2000); Poverty rate: 5.8% (2000).
Taxes: Total city taxes per capita: $154 (1997); City property taxes per capita: $153 (1997).
Education: High school graduation rate: 79.8% (2000); College graduation rate: 13.1% (2000).

School District(s)

Titonka Consolidated School District (KG-12)
2000 Enrollment: 186 515-928-2717
Housing: Homeownership rate: 83.3% (2000); Median home value: $39,400 (2000); Median rent: $216 per month (2000); Median age of housing: 47 years (2000).
Newspapers: Titonka Topic (1 x week)
Transportation: Commute to work: 78.5% car, 0.0% public transportation, 14.9% walk, 4.5% work from home (2000); Travel time to work: 52.4% less than 15 minutes, 21.2% 15 to 30 minutes, 21.6% 30 to 45 minutes, 2.2% 45 to 60 minutes, 2.6% 60 minutes or more (2000)

WESLEY (city). Covers a land area of 0.576 square miles and a water area of 0 square miles. Located at 43.08° N. Lat.; 93.99° W. Long. Elevation is 1,257 feet.
History: Wesley was named in 1871 for one of the builders of the railroad station.
Population: 467 (2000); Race: 97.3% White, 0.0% Black, 0.0% Asian, 0.0% American Indian and Alaska Native, 1.1% Hispanic of any race, 1.9% two or more races (2000); Density: 811.4 persons per square mile (2000); Age: 28.1% under 18, 20.5% over 64 (2000); Marriage status: 16.6% never married, 66.2% now married, 11.0% widowed, 6.2% divorced (2000); Foreign born: 0.0% (2000); Ancestry (includes multiple ancestries): 50.0% German, 9.7% Irish, 6.3% Norwegian, 5.1% Other groups, 4.4% United States or American (2000).
Economy: Single-family building permits issued: 0 (2001) / 0 (2000); Multi-family building permits issued: 0 (2001) / 0 (2000); Employment by occupation: 11.8% management, 7.6% professional, 13.3% services, 24.2% sales, 0.5% farming, 10.4% construction, 32.2% production (2000).
Income: Per capita income: $19,225 (2000); Median household income: $39,688 (2000); Poverty rate: 11.0% (2000).
Taxes: Total city taxes per capita: $220 (1997); City property taxes per capita: $217 (1997).
Education: High school graduation rate: 83.5% (2000); College graduation rate: 8.6% (2000).

School District(s)

Corwith-Wesley Community School District (KG-12)
2000 Enrollment: 176 515-679-4450
Housing: Homeownership rate: 86.9% (2000); Median home value: $51,400 (2000); Median rent: $258 per month (2000); Median age of housing: 46 years (2000).
Transportation: Commute to work: 90.0% car, 0.0% public transportation, 1.4% walk, 4.8% work from home (2000); Travel time to work: 37.7% less than 15 minutes, 44.7% 15 to 30 minutes, 13.1% 30 to 45 minutes, 3.5% 45 to 60 minutes, 1.0% 60 minutes or more (2000)

WHITTEMORE (city). Covers a land area of 0.418 square miles and a water area of 0 square miles. Located at 43.06° N. Lat.; 94.42° W. Long. Elevation is 1,206 feet.
History: Whittemore was platted in 1878 by W. H. Ingham and L. H. Smith.
Population: 530 (2000); Race: 97.8% White, 0.0% Black, 0.0% Asian, 0.0% American Indian and Alaska Native, 0.7% Hispanic of any race, 1.5% two or more races (2000); Density: 1,268.3 persons per square mile (2000); Age: 29.7% under 18, 25.6% over 64 (2000); Marriage status: 26.0% never married, 57.5% now married, 12.5% widowed, 4.1% divorced (2000); Foreign born: 0.7% (2000); Ancestry (includes multiple ancestries): 52.5% German, 14.4% Irish, 9.2% Norwegian, 6.4% English, 6.1% United States or American (2000).
Economy: Single-family building permits issued: 0 (2001) / 0 (2000); Multi-family building permits issued: 0 (2001) / 0 (2000); Employment by occupation: 11.2% management, 4.0% professional, 29.0% services, 25.0% sales, 3.1% farming, 8.9% construction, 18.8% production (2000).
Income: Per capita income: $14,669 (2000); Median household income: $31,111 (2000); Poverty rate: 6.6% (2000).
Taxes: Total city taxes per capita: $198 (1997); City property taxes per capita: $195 (1997).
Education: High school graduation rate: 89.5% (2000); College graduation rate: 10.5% (2000).
Housing: Homeownership rate: 82.3% (2000); Median home value: $38,800 (2000); Median rent: $268 per month (2000); Median age of housing: 56 years (2000).
Transportation: Commute to work: 94.1% car, 0.0% public transportation, 2.3% walk, 2.7% work from home (2000); Travel time to work: 41.3% less than 15 minutes, 47.4% 15 to 30 minutes, 5.6% 30 to 45 minutes, 3.8% 45 to 60 minutes, 1.9% 60 minutes or more (2000)

Lee County

Located in southeastern Iowa; bounded on the northeast by the Skunk River, on the east by the Mississippi River and the Illinois border, and on the south by the Des Moines River and the Missouri border. Covers a land area of 517.40 square miles, a water area of 21.40 square miles, and is located in the Central Time Zone. The county government was organized in 1836. County seat is Fort Madison.

Weather Station: Fort Madison — Elevation: 528 feet

	Jan	Feb	Mar	Apr	May	Jun	Jul	Aug	Sep	Oct	Nov	Dec
High	32	37	49	62	73	82	87	84	77	65	49	37
Low	14	20	31	42	53	62	67	64	56	44	32	20
Precip	1.3	1.5	2.9	3.6	4.9	4.1	4.3	4.0	4.3	2.8	3.0	2.3
Snow	6.4	4.3	1.6	0.6	0.0	0.0	0.0	0.0	0.0	tr	0.7	4.5

High and Low temperatures in degrees Fahrenheit; Precipitation and Snow in inches

Weather Station: Keokuk — Elevation: 574 feet

	Jan	Feb	Mar	Apr	May	Jun	Jul	Aug	Sep	Oct	Nov	Dec
High	33	39	51	64	74	83	88	85	78	67	51	38
Low	16	21	31	43	53	63	67	65	57	45	33	22
Precip	1.3	1.4	2.7	3.6	5.5	3.7	3.9	3.5	4.3	3.1	3.0	2.0
Snow	7.3	5.0	2.5	1.0	0.0	0.0	0.0	0.0	0.0	tr	1.3	4.0

High and Low temperatures in degrees Fahrenheit; Precipitation and Snow in inches

Population: 38,052 (2000); Race: 94.2% White, 2.3% Black, 0.8% Asian, 0.3% American Indian and Alaska Native, 2.1% Hispanic of any race, 1.6% two or more races (2000); Density: 73.5 persons per square mile (2000); Age: 24.3% under 18, 16.5% over 64 (2000).
Religion: Five largest groups: 19.5% Catholic Church, 5.7% The United Methodist Church, 4.8% Christian Church (Disciples of Christ), 4.6% United Church of Christ, 3.7% American Baptist Churches in the USA (2000).
Economy: Unemployment rate: 7.0% (11/2002); Total civilian labor force: 17,809 (11/2002); Leading industries: 36.6% manufacturing; 13.7% retail trade; 12.6% health care and social assistance (2000); Companies that employ more than 1,000 persons: 1 (2000); Companies that employ more than 100 persons: 28 (2000); Farms: 861 totaling 256,685 acres (1997); Minority business ownership rate: 0.0% (1997); Women business ownership rate: 22.7% (1997); Retail sales per capita: $8,902 (1997). Single-family building permits issued: 18 (2001) / 14 (2000); Multi-family building permits issued: 4 (2001) / 30 (2000).
Income: Per capita income: $18,430 (2000); Median household income: $36,193 (2000); Poverty rate: 9.7% (2000); Bankruptcy rate: 5.34% (2001).
Taxes: Total county taxes per capita: $232 (2000); County property taxes per capita: $189 (2000).
Education: High school graduation rate: 83.6% (2000); College graduation rate: 12.5% (2000).
Housing: Homeownership rate: 75.5% (2000); Median home value: $60,300 (2000); Median rent: $288 per month (2000); Median age of housing: 48 years (2000).
Health: Birth rate: 118.3 per 10,000 population (1998); Age adjusted death rate: 94.6 per 10,000 population (1999); Age adjusted cancer mortality rate: 244.9 deaths per 100,000 population (1999). Air Quality Index: 100% good, 0% moderate, 0% unhealthy (percent of days in 2000). Number of physicians: 12.1 per 10,000 population (1999); Number of hospital beds: 46.0 per 10,000 population (1999).
Elections: 2000 Presidential election results: 58.1% Gore, 38.3% Bush, 2.0% Nader, 0.5% Buchanan
National and State Parks: Galland School State Park Preserve; Shimek State Forest

Additional Information Contacts

Lee County Government Offices 319-372-6557
Fort Madison Area Board of Realtors 319-372-7777
Fort Madison Chamber of Commerce 319-372-5471
Keokuk Board of Realtors 319-524-9510
Keokuk Chamber of Commerce 319-524-5055
Keokuk Convention Tourism 319-524-5599
Riverbend Regional Convention & Visitors Bureau 319-372-5472

Lee County Communities

ARGYLE (unincorporated postal area, zip code 52619). Covers a land area of 47.075 square miles and a water area of 0.039 square miles. Located at 40.54° N. Lat.; 91.57° W. Long. Elevation is 668 feet.
History: Argyle is named after the County of Argyle, Scotland.
Population: 862 (2000); Race: 100.0% White, 0.0% Black, 0.0% Asian, 0.0% American Indian and Alaska Native, 0.0% Hispanic of any race, 0.0% two or more races (2000); Density: 18.3 persons per square mile (2000); Age: 28.9% under 18, 10.8% over 64 (2000); Marriage status: 18.8% never married, 60.8% now married, 8.3% widowed, 12.1% divorced (2000); Foreign born: 0.0% (2000); Ancestry (includes multiple ancestries): 32.2% German, 29.6% United States or American, 15.9% English, 9.4% Irish, 7.1% Other groups (2000).
Economy: Employment by occupation: 16.3% management, 12.2% professional, 14.8% services, 15.8% sales, 0.0% farming, 6.6% construction, 34.2% production (2000).
Income: Per capita income: $14,372 (2000); Median household income: $35,337 (2000); Poverty rate: 17.5% (2000).
Education: High school graduation rate: 79.1% (2000); College graduation rate: 8.0% (2000).
Housing: Homeownership rate: 79.4% (2000); Median home value: $69,200 (2000); Median rent: $332 per month (2000); Median age of housing: 35 years (2000).
Transportation: Commute to work: 89.6% car, 0.0% public transportation, 0.0% walk, 7.3% work from home (2000); Travel time to work: 22.3% less than 15 minutes, 51.1% 15 to 30 minutes, 19.0% 30 to 45 minutes, 5.6% 45 to 60 minutes, 2.0% 60 minutes or more (2000)

DENMARK (unincorporated postal area, zip code 52624). Covers a land area of 0.180 square miles and a water area of 0 square miles. Located at 40.74° N. Lat.; 91.33° W. Long. Elevation is 718 feet.
History: The naming of Denmark is attributed to Jonathan Edwards of New Hampshire. It was probably named for the country of Denmark.
Population: 274 (2000); Race: 100.0% White, 0.0% Black, 0.0% Asian, 0.0% American Indian and Alaska Native, 0.0% Hispanic of any race, 0.0% two or more races (2000); Density: 1,520.0 persons per square mile (2000); Age: 31.5% under 18, 29.4% over 64 (2000); Marriage status: 17.0% never married, 67.0% now married, 5.7% widowed, 10.3% divorced (2000); Foreign born: 0.0% (2000); Ancestry (includes multiple ancestries): 46.0% German, 12.1% United States or American, 9.7% Other groups, 9.3% English, 6.0% Dutch (2000).
Economy: Employment by occupation: 0.0% management, 17.6% professional, 21.6% services, 8.8% sales, 10.8% farming, 14.7% construction, 26.5% production (2000).
Income: Per capita income: $17,290 (2000); Median household income: $32,083 (2000); Poverty rate: 4.6% (2000).
Education: High school graduation rate: 97.6% (2000); College graduation rate: 6.5% (2000).
Housing: Homeownership rate: 86.6% (2000); Median home value: $59,000 (2000); Median rent: $463 per month (2000); Median age of housing: 48 years (2000).
Transportation: Commute to work: 82.4% car, 0.0% public transportation, 4.9% walk, 0.0% work from home (2000); Travel time to work: 30.4% less than 15 minutes, 32.4% 15 to 30 minutes, 37.3% 30 to 45 minutes, 0.0% 45 to 60 minutes, 0.0% 60 minutes or more (2000)

DONNELLSON (city). Covers a land area of 0.797 square miles and a water area of 0 square miles. Located at 40.64° N. Lat.; 91.56° W. Long.
History: Donnellson was first surveyed in the spring of 1881 by H. A. Summers for Esten A. Donnell and others.
Population: 963 (2000); Race: 96.5% White, 2.3% Black, 0.0% Asian, 0.0% American Indian and Alaska Native, 3.1% Hispanic of any race, 0.5% two or more races (2000); Density: 1,208.8 persons per square mile (2000); Age: 24.3% under 18, 25.6% over 64 (2000); Marriage status: 16.8% never married, 65.0% now married, 10.6% widowed, 7.7% divorced (2000); Foreign born: 0.1% (2000); Ancestry (includes multiple ancestries): 39.3% German, 15.4% United States or American, 8.9% English, 6.6% Irish, 6.0% Other groups (2000).
Economy: Single-family building permits issued: 1 (2001) / 0 (2000); Multi-family building permits issued: 0 (2001) / 0 (2000); Employment by occupation: 7.2% management, 13.4% professional, 21.9% services, 23.3% sales, 0.7% farming, 12.0% construction, 21.5% production (2000).
Income: Per capita income: $18,336 (2000); Median household income: $36,316 (2000); Poverty rate: 3.6% (2000).
Taxes: Total city taxes per capita: $201 (1997); City property taxes per capita: $131 (1997).
Education: High school graduation rate: 84.9% (2000); College graduation rate: 10.7% (2000).

School District(s)

Central Lee Community School District (PK-12)
2000 Enrollment: 1,113 319-835-9510

Housing: Homeownership rate: 69.9% (2000); Median home value: $67,400 (2000); Median rent: $279 per month (2000); Median age of housing: 42 years (2000).
Transportation: Commute to work: 95.3% car, 0.0% public transportation, 2.3% walk, 2.3% work from home (2000); Travel time to work: 30.3% less than 15 minutes, 43.8% 15 to 30 minutes, 21.9% 30 to 45 minutes, 3.6% 45 to 60 minutes, 0.5% 60 minutes or more (2000)

FORT MADISON (city). Covers a land area of 9.214 square miles and a water area of 3.737 square miles. Located at 40.62° N. Lat.; 91.33° W. Long. Elevation is 522 feet.
History: Fort Madison was established as a government trading post in 1808.
Population: 10,715 (2000); Race: 92.4% White, 2.5% Black, 1.4% Asian, 0.1% American Indian and Alaska Native, 4.9% Hispanic of any race, 1.4% two or more races (2000); Density: 1,162.9 persons per square mile (2000); Age: 23.7% under 18, 18.0% over 64 (2000); Marriage status: 21.3% never married, 55.3% now married, 8.9% widowed, 14.5% divorced (2000); Foreign born: 2.3% (2000); Ancestry (includes multiple ancestries): 35.5% German, 12.7% United States or American, 12.1% Other groups, 11.7% Irish, 8.4% English (2000).
Vital Statistics: Birth rate: 138.1 per 10,000 population (1998)

Economy: Single-family building permits issued: 6 (2001) / 0 (2000); Multi-family building permits issued: 0 (2001) / 0 (2000); Employment by occupation: 8.5% management, 13.4% professional, 19.4% services, 20.5% sales, 1.8% farming, 9.4% construction, 27.0% production (2000).
Income: Per capita income: $18,124 (2000); Median household income: $34,318 (2000); Poverty rate: 12.2% (2000).
Taxes: Total city taxes per capita: $369 (1997); City property taxes per capita: $266 (1997).
Education: High school graduation rate: 85.1% (2000); College graduation rate: 14.7% (2000).

School District(s)

Fort Madison Community School District (PK-12)
2000 Enrollment: 2,606 319-372-7252
Iowa State Penitentiary (N -N)
2000 Enrollment: n/a 319-372-5432

Two-year College(s)

Bill Hill's College of Cosmetology (Private, For-profit)
2001 Enrollment: n/a 319-372-6248

Housing: Homeownership rate: 69.7% (2000); Median home value: $53,700 (2000); Median rent: $300 per month (2000); Median age of housing: 57 years (2000).
Hospitals: Ft. Madison Community Hospital (50 beds)
Safety: Violent crime rate: 14.0 per 10,000 population; Property crime rate: 442.9 per 10,000 population (2001).
Newspapers: The Daily Democrat (5 x week)
Transportation: Commute to work: 89.3% car, 0.3% public transportation, 6.2% walk, 3.1% work from home (2000); Travel time to work: 61.9% less than 15 minutes, 20.8% 15 to 30 minutes, 12.2% 30 to 45 minutes, 1.8% 45 to 60 minutes, 3.3% 60 minutes or more (2000); Amtrak: Service available.
Airports: Fort Madison Municipal
Additional Information Contacts
Fort Madison Area Board of Realtors 319-372-7777
Fort Madison Chamber of Commerce 319-372-5471
Riverbend Regional Convention & Visitors Bureau 319-372-5472

FRANKLIN (city). Covers a land area of 0.160 square miles and a water area of 0 square miles. Located at 40.66° N. Lat.; 91.51° W. Long.
History: Franklin, formerly Franklin Center, was named after Franklin, Tennessee.
Population: 136 (2000); Race: 100.0% White, 0.0% Black, 0.0% Asian, 0.0% American Indian and Alaska Native, 0.0% Hispanic of any race, 0.0% two or more races (2000); Density: 851.3 persons per square mile (2000); Age: 18.1% under 18, 12.6% over 64 (2000); Marriage status: 20.0% never married, 52.4% now married, 15.2% widowed, 12.4% divorced (2000); Foreign born: 0.0% (2000); Ancestry (includes multiple ancestries): 37.0% German, 21.3% United States or American, 7.9% English, 7.9% Irish, 3.9% Slovak (2000).
Economy: Single-family building permits issued: 0 (2001) / 0 (2000); Multi-family building permits issued: 0 (2001) / 0 (2000); Employment by occupation: 9.7% management, 11.3% professional, 12.9% services, 11.3% sales, 0.0% farming, 11.3% construction, 43.5% production (2000).
Income: Per capita income: $18,129 (2000); Median household income: $33,125 (2000); Poverty rate: 5.5% (2000).
Taxes: Total city taxes per capita: $114 (1997); City property taxes per capita: $44 (1997).
Education: High school graduation rate: 87.0% (2000); College graduation rate: 13.0% (2000).
Housing: Homeownership rate: 94.5% (2000); Median home value: $62,000 (2000); Median age of housing: 29 years (2000).
Transportation: Commute to work: 100.0% car, 0.0% public transportation, 0.0% walk, 0.0% work from home (2000); Travel time to work: 23.3% less than 15 minutes, 48.3% 15 to 30 minutes, 28.3% 30 to 45 minutes, 0.0% 45 to 60 minutes, 0.0% 60 minutes or more (2000)

HOUGHTON (city). Covers a land area of 0.302 square miles and a water area of 0 square miles. Located at 40.78° N. Lat.; 91.61° W. Long.
History: Houghton was named for landowner John Hough, who served as postmaster in the early days of the community.
Population: 130 (2000); Race: 100.0% White, 0.0% Black, 0.0% Asian, 0.0% American Indian and Alaska Native, 0.0% Hispanic of any race, 0.0% two or more races (2000); Density: 431.1 persons per square mile (2000); Age: 21.7% under 18, 19.4% over 64 (2000); Marriage status: 13.2% never married, 77.4% now married, 9.4% widowed, 0.0% divorced (2000); Foreign born: 0.0% (2000); Ancestry (includes multiple ancestries): 72.9% German, 7.0% Dutch, 6.2% Irish, 4.7% United States or American, 3.1% English (2000).
Economy: Single-family building permits issued: 1 (2001) / 1 (2000); Multi-family building permits issued: 0 (2001) / 0 (2000); Employment by occupation: 29.5% management, 11.5% professional, 5.1% services, 35.9% sales, 0.0% farming, 7.7% construction, 10.3% production (2000).
Income: Per capita income: $19,203 (2000); Median household income: $47,500 (2000); Poverty rate: 3.1% (2000).
Taxes: Total city taxes per capita: $266 (1997); City property taxes per capita: $266 (1997).
Education: High school graduation rate: 92.6% (2000); College graduation rate: 10.5% (2000).
Housing: Homeownership rate: 84.0% (2000); Median home value: $75,000 (2000); Median rent: $167 per month (2000); Median age of housing: 32 years (2000).
Transportation: Commute to work: 87.2% car, 0.0% public transportation, 6.4% walk, 6.4% work from home (2000); Travel time to work: 61.6% less than 15 minutes, 23.3% 15 to 30 minutes, 12.3% 30 to 45 minutes, 2.7% 45 to 60 minutes, 0.0% 60 minutes or more (2000)

KEOKUK (city). Covers a land area of 9.160 square miles and a water area of 1.419 square miles. Located at 40.40° N. Lat.; 91.39° W. Long. Elevation is 505 feet.
History: Keokuk was named after Chief Keokuk of the Sac tribe. The city was platted in 1837 by Isaac Galland, an agent of the New York Land Company. In the days before railroads, Keokuk was known as the "Gate City," not only for Iowa, but for the North and West as well, because of its position at the foot of the Des Moines rapids on the Mississippi River. The first medical college in Iowa was established here in 1850.
Population: 11,427 (2000); Race: 92.7% White, 4.1% Black, 0.8% Asian, 0.4% American Indian and Alaska Native, 0.2% Hispanic of any race, 1.9% two or more races (2000); Density: 1,247.5 persons per square mile (2000); Age: 25.5% under 18, 17.7% over 64 (2000); Marriage status: 23.4% never married, 53.5% now married, 10.6% widowed, 12.5% divorced (2000); Foreign born: 1.0% (2000); Ancestry (includes multiple ancestries): 24.1% German, 12.3% Irish, 10.4% Other groups, 10.0% United States or American, 8.3% English (2000).
Vital Statistics: Birth rate: 134.8 per 10,000 population (1998)
Economy: Single-family building permits issued: 5 (2001) / 6 (2000); Multi-family building permits issued: 4 (2001) / 28 (2000); Employment by occupation: 7.1% management, 16.2% professional, 16.4% services, 21.0% sales, 0.2% farming, 9.5% construction, 29.6% production (2000).
Income: Per capita income: $17,144 (2000); Median household income: $31,586 (2000); Poverty rate: 11.9% (2000).
Taxes: Total city taxes per capita: $498 (2000); City property taxes per capita: $360 (2000).
Education: High school graduation rate: 78.5% (2000); College graduation rate: 13.4% (2000).

School District(s)

Keokuk Community School District (PK-12)
2000 Enrollment: 2,266 319-524-1402

Two-year College(s)

Dayton School of Hair Design (Private, For-profit)
2001 Enrollment: 15 319-524-6445

Housing: Homeownership rate: 69.3% (2000); Median home value: $50,500 (2000); Median rent: $279 per month (2000); Median age of housing: 55 years (2000).
Hospitals: Keokuk Area Hospital (120 beds)
Safety: Violent crime rate: 98.1 per 10,000 population; Property crime rate: 565.9 per 10,000 population (2001).
Newspapers: Daily Gate City (5 x week)
Transportation: Commute to work: 93.5% car, 0.5% public transportation, 2.7% walk, 2.4% work from home (2000); Travel time to work: 69.8% less than 15 minutes, 19.2% 15 to 30 minutes, 5.7% 30 to 45 minutes, 3.0% 45 to 60 minutes, 2.3% 60 minutes or more (2000)
Airports: Keokuk Municipal
Additional Information Contacts
Keokuk Board of Realtors 319-524-9510
Keokuk Chamber of Commerce 319-524-5055
Keokuk Convention Tourism 319-524-5599

MONTROSE (city). Covers a land area of 1.123 square miles and a water area of 0.016 square miles. Located at 40.53° N. Lat.; 91.41° W. Long. Elevation is 530 feet.
History: Montrose is the site of one of the first permanent settlements in Iowa. It was laid out in 1837 by D. W. Kilbourne. The settlement was first known as Cut Nose, in honor of Indian Chief Cut Nose who lived nearby. It

was later called Mount of Roses, because of the many wild roses on the nearby hillsides. This was contracted to Montrose.
Population: 957 (2000); Race: 96.2% White, 0.2% Black, 0.3% Asian, 1.2% American Indian and Alaska Native, 1.7% Hispanic of any race, 2.1% two or more races (2000); Density: 852.1 persons per square mile (2000); Age: 26.7% under 18, 18.1% over 64 (2000); Marriage status: 21.3% never married, 55.8% now married, 10.4% widowed, 12.5% divorced (2000); Foreign born: 0.7% (2000); Ancestry (includes multiple ancestries): 37.9% German, 17.2% Irish, 12.1% Other groups, 11.5% English, 8.9% United States or American (2000).
Economy: Single-family building permits issued: 3 (2001) / 4 (2000); Multi-family building permits issued: 0 (2001) / 0 (2000); Employment by occupation: 6.2% management, 14.5% professional, 18.2% services, 19.5% sales, 0.7% farming, 8.7% construction, 32.2% production (2000).
Income: Per capita income: $17,010 (2000); Median household income: $35,341 (2000); Poverty rate: 8.9% (2000).
Taxes: Total city taxes per capita: $148 (1997); City property taxes per capita: $71 (1997).
Education: High school graduation rate: 84.1% (2000); College graduation rate: 9.0% (2000).
Housing: Homeownership rate: 78.3% (2000); Median home value: $59,600 (2000); Median rent: $257 per month (2000); Median age of housing: 36 years (2000).
Transportation: Commute to work: 96.3% car, 0.0% public transportation, 1.4% walk, 2.3% work from home (2000); Travel time to work: 33.3% less than 15 minutes, 53.9% 15 to 30 minutes, 7.7% 30 to 45 minutes, 2.6% 45 to 60 minutes, 2.6% 60 minutes or more (2000)

SAINT PAUL (city). Covers a land area of 0.378 square miles and a water area of 0 square miles. Located at 40.76° N. Lat.; 91.51° W. Long. Elevation is 700 feet.
Population: 118 (2000); Race: 100.0% White, 0.0% Black, 0.0% Asian, 0.0% American Indian and Alaska Native, 0.0% Hispanic of any race, 0.0% two or more races (2000); Density: 312.3 persons per square mile (2000); Age: 21.3% under 18, 16.5% over 64 (2000); Marriage status: 20.8% never married, 67.9% now married, 4.7% widowed, 6.6% divorced (2000); Foreign born: 0.0% (2000); Ancestry (includes multiple ancestries): 67.7% German, 16.5% Irish, 6.3% Czech, 5.5% United States or American, 3.9% Norwegian (2000).
Economy: Single-family building permits issued: 0 (2001) / 1 (2000); Multi-family building permits issued: 0 (2001) / 0 (2000); Employment by occupation: 5.4% management, 21.6% professional, 6.8% services, 20.3% sales, 0.0% farming, 20.3% construction, 25.7% production (2000).
Income: Per capita income: $20,312 (2000); Median household income: $45,313 (2000); Poverty rate: 3.9% (2000).
Education: High school graduation rate: 76.6% (2000); College graduation rate: 7.4% (2000).
Housing: Homeownership rate: 83.6% (2000); Median home value: $85,000 (2000); Median rent: $145 per month (2000); Median age of housing: 33 years (2000).
Transportation: Commute to work: 93.1% car, 0.0% public transportation, 2.8% walk, 4.2% work from home (2000); Travel time to work: 23.2% less than 15 minutes, 55.1% 15 to 30 minutes, 20.3% 30 to 45 minutes, 0.0% 45 to 60 minutes, 1.4% 60 minutes or more (2000)

WEST POINT (city). Covers a land area of 0.581 square miles and a water area of 0 square miles. Located at 40.71° N. Lat.; 91.45° W. Long. Elevation is 774 feet.
History: West Point was named by officers of Fort Des Moines. The officers agreed to purchase lots if allowed to name the town.
Population: 980 (2000); Race: 99.7% White, 0.0% Black, 0.0% Asian, 0.2% American Indian and Alaska Native, 0.1% Hispanic of any race, 0.0% two or more races (2000); Density: 1,687.8 persons per square mile (2000); Age: 21.4% under 18, 27.5% over 64 (2000); Marriage status: 18.7% never married, 57.5% now married, 15.3% widowed, 8.4% divorced (2000); Foreign born: 0.0% (2000); Ancestry (includes multiple ancestries): 54.7% German, 11.9% United States or American, 11.2% Irish, 4.0% English, 3.0% Other groups (2000).
Economy: Single-family building permits issued: 2 (2001) / 2 (2000); Multi-family building permits issued: 0 (2001) / 2 (2000); Employment by occupation: 11.4% management, 14.2% professional, 15.6% services, 24.2% sales, 1.6% farming, 11.4% construction, 21.4% production (2000).
Income: Per capita income: $27,289 (2000); Median household income: $38,409 (2000); Poverty rate: 4.4% (2000).
Taxes: Total city taxes per capita: $171 (1997); City property taxes per capita: $91 (1997).
Education: High school graduation rate: 81.1% (2000); College graduation rate: 12.8% (2000).
Housing: Homeownership rate: 78.6% (2000); Median home value: $79,000 (2000); Median rent: $271 per month (2000); Median age of housing: 35 years (2000).
Newspapers: Donnellson Star (1 x week)
Transportation: Commute to work: 92.0% car, 0.5% public transportation, 5.2% walk, 1.6% work from home (2000); Travel time to work: 36.6% less than 15 minutes, 32.3% 15 to 30 minutes, 23.7% 30 to 45 minutes, 5.5% 45 to 60 minutes, 1.9% 60 minutes or more (2000)

WEVER (unincorporated postal area, zip code 52658). Covers a land area of 45.581 square miles and a water area of 0.441 square miles. Located at 40.70° N. Lat.; 91.23° W. Long. Elevation is 540 feet.
History: Wever was platted in 1891. It owes its existence to a branch line of the Chicago, Burlington & Quincy Railroad.
Population: 1,113 (2000); Race: 99.6% White, 0.3% Black, 0.0% Asian, 0.0% American Indian and Alaska Native, 0.5% Hispanic of any race, 0.2% two or more races (2000); Density: 24.4 persons per square mile (2000); Age: 25.5% under 18, 11.6% over 64 (2000); Marriage status: 14.9% never married, 68.8% now married, 6.3% widowed, 10.0% divorced (2000); Foreign born: 0.0% (2000); Ancestry (includes multiple ancestries): 36.9% German, 17.4% Irish, 11.7% United States or American, 5.2% English, 2.4% Other groups (2000).
Economy: Employment by occupation: 7.3% management, 12.1% professional, 14.6% services, 19.7% sales, 5.9% farming, 12.0% construction, 28.4% production (2000).
Income: Per capita income: $23,583 (2000); Median household income: $51,466 (2000); Poverty rate: 4.0% (2000).
Education: High school graduation rate: 89.8% (2000); College graduation rate: 12.6% (2000).
Housing: Homeownership rate: 92.2% (2000); Median home value: $84,000 (2000); Median rent: $313 per month (2000); Median age of housing: 35 years (2000).
Transportation: Commute to work: 91.8% car, 2.2% public transportation, 0.0% walk, 6.1% work from home (2000); Travel time to work: 22.6% less than 15 minutes, 63.5% 15 to 30 minutes, 8.9% 30 to 45 minutes, 3.1% 45 to 60 minutes, 1.8% 60 minutes or more (2000)

Linn County

Located in eastern Iowa; prairie area, drained by the Cedar and Wapsipinicon Rivers. Covers a land area of 717.40 square miles, a water area of 7.10 square miles, and is located in the Central Time Zone. The county government was organized in 1837. County seat is Cedar Rapids.

Linn County is part of the Cedar Rapids, IA MSA. The entire metro area includes: Linn County

Weather Station: Cedar Rapids 1 — Elevation: 849 feet

	Jan	Feb	Mar	Apr	May	Jun	Jul	Aug	Sep	Oct	Nov	Dec
High	28	35	47	62	73	82	85	83	76	64	47	33
Low	11	17	27	39	50	60	64	62	53	42	29	17
Precip	1.1	1.1	2.2	3.4	4.6	4.7	4.6	4.7	3.9	2.6	2.5	1.5
Snow	8.1	6.1	4.3	2.4	tr	0.0	0.0	0.0	0.0	0.4	3.5	7.0

High and Low temperatures in degrees Fahrenheit; Precipitation and Snow in inches

Weather Station: Cedar Rapids Municipal Airport — Elevation: 839 feet

	Jan	Feb	Mar	Apr	May	Jun	Jul	Aug	Sep	Oct	Nov	Dec
High	26	32	45	60	72	81	85	82	74	62	46	32
Low	9	15	27	39	50	60	64	61	52	40	28	16
Precip	1.0	1.0	2.3	3.3	3.8	4.3	4.2	4.2	3.5	2.2	2.3	1.5
Snow	7.3	6.5	3.6	1.8	tr	tr	0.0	0.0	0.0	tr	2.9	7.1

High and Low temperatures in degrees Fahrenheit; Precipitation and Snow in inches

Population: 191,701 (2000); Race: 94.0% White, 2.4% Black, 1.4% Asian, 0.2% American Indian and Alaska Native, 1.5% Hispanic of any race, 1.5% two or more races (2000); Density: 267.2 persons per square mile (2000); Age: 25.2% under 18, 12.2% over 64 (2000).
Religion: Five largest groups: 23.2% Catholic Church, 7.4% The United Methodist Church, 5.6% Evangelical Lutheran Church in America, 3.2% Lutheran Church—Missouri Synod, 2.8% Presbyterian Church (U.S.A.) (2000).
Economy: Unemployment rate: 4.2% (11/2002); Total civilian labor force: 118,121 (11/2002); Leading industries: 17.2% manufacturing; 12.1% retail trade; 10.0% health care and social assistance (2000); Companies that employ

more than 1,000 persons: 11 (2000); Companies that employ more than 100 persons: 187 (2000); Farms: 1,480 totaling 339,227 acres (1997); Minority business ownership rate: 3.3% (1997); Women business ownership rate: 28.6% (1997); Retail sales per capita: $11,242 (1997). Single-family building permits issued: 860 (2001) / 850 (2000); Multi-family building permits issued: 701 (2001) / 829 (2000).
Income: Per capita income: $22,977 (2000); Median household income: $46,206 (2000); Poverty rate: 6.5% (2000); Bankruptcy rate: 3.68% (2001).
Taxes: Total county taxes per capita: $192 (2000); County property taxes per capita: $183 (2000).
Education: High school graduation rate: 90.6% (2000); College graduation rate: 27.7% (2000).
Housing: Homeownership rate: 72.7% (2000); Median home value: $99,400 (2000); Median rent: $435 per month (2000); Median age of housing: 33 years (2000).
Health: Birth rate: 137.5 per 10,000 population (1998); Age adjusted death rate: 78.6 per 10,000 population (1999); Age adjusted cancer mortality rate: 208.0 deaths per 100,000 population (1999). Air Quality Index: 88% good, 12% moderate, 0% unhealthy (percent of days in 2000). Number of physicians: 19.4 per 10,000 population (1999); Number of hospital beds: 39.1 per 10,000 population (1999).
Elections: 2000 Presidential election results: 53.1% Gore, 43.9% Bush, 2.3% Nader, 0.3% Buchanan
National and State Parks: Palisades-Kepler State Park
Additional Information Contacts
Linn County Government Offices 319-398-3421
Cedar Rapids Area Association of Realtors 319-363-9604
Cedar Rapids Chamber of Commerce 319-398-5317
Cedar Rapids Convention & Visitors Bureau 319-398-5009
Marion Chamber of Commerce 319-377-6316
Mt Vernon Chamber of Commerce 319-895-8214

Linn County Communities

ALBURNETT (city). Covers a land area of 0.860 square miles and a water area of 0 square miles. Located at 42.14° N. Lat.; 91.62° W. Long. Elevation is 891 feet.
History: Alburnett was laid out by Albert C. Burnett. The name is a combination of his first and last names.
Population: 559 (2000); Race: 98.1% White, 0.0% Black, 0.0% Asian, 0.0% American Indian and Alaska Native, 2.2% Hispanic of any race, 0.0% two or more races (2000); Density: 650.3 persons per square mile (2000); Age: 32.2% under 18, 8.6% over 64 (2000); Marriage status: 23.3% never married, 61.2% now married, 6.0% widowed, 9.5% divorced (2000); Foreign born: 0.0% (2000); Ancestry (includes multiple ancestries): 43.7% German, 13.4% Irish, 9.4% United States or American, 9.4% Czech, 9.1% English (2000).
Economy: Single-family building permits issued: 3 (2001) / 3 (2000); Multi-family building permits issued: 0 (2001) / 0 (2000); Employment by occupation: 11.7% management, 13.3% professional, 16.0% services, 26.7% sales, 1.7% farming, 17.0% construction, 13.7% production (2000).
Income: Per capita income: $19,815 (2000); Median household income: $54,464 (2000); Poverty rate: 4.8% (2000).
Taxes: Total city taxes per capita: $141 (1997); City property taxes per capita: $133 (1997).
Education: High school graduation rate: 86.0% (2000); College graduation rate: 18.3% (2000).

School District(s)
Alburnett Community School District (KG-12)
2000 Enrollment: 623 319-842-2261
Housing: Homeownership rate: 80.7% (2000); Median home value: $93,100 (2000); Median rent: $369 per month (2000); Median age of housing: 38 years (2000).
Transportation: Commute to work: 95.2% car, 0.0% public transportation, 3.4% walk, 1.4% work from home (2000); Travel time to work: 22.5% less than 15 minutes, 52.2% 15 to 30 minutes, 21.5% 30 to 45 minutes, 1.4% 45 to 60 minutes, 2.4% 60 minutes or more (2000)

BERTRAM (city). Covers a land area of 1.276 square miles and a water area of 0 square miles. Located at 41.95° N. Lat.; 91.53° W. Long. Elevation is 716 feet.
History: The first railroad through Linn County was promoted by Captain John Bertram, for whom the community of Bertram was named.
Population: 681 (2000); Race: 96.0% White, 3.6% Black, 0.0% Asian, 0.0% American Indian and Alaska Native, 0.5% Hispanic of any race, 0.4% two or more races (2000); Density: 533.5 persons per square mile (2000); Age: 19.8% under 18, 2.7% over 64 (2000); Marriage status: 68.3% never married, 28.9% now married, 1.7% widowed, 1.1% divorced (2000); Foreign born: 0.1% (2000); Ancestry (includes multiple ancestries): 24.0% German, 15.2% Irish, 11.5% English, 6.9% Other groups, 5.9% Czech (2000).
Economy: Single-family building permits issued: 2 (2001) / 1 (2000); Multi-family building permits issued: 0 (2001) / 0 (2000); Employment by occupation: 19.7% management, 15.7% professional, 9.8% services, 32.9% sales, 0.0% farming, 3.7% construction, 18.3% production (2000).
Income: Per capita income: $16,015 (2000); Median household income: $58,750 (2000); Poverty rate: 16.5% (2000).
Taxes: Total city taxes per capita: $535 (1997); City property taxes per capita: $152 (1997).
Education: High school graduation rate: 86.3% (2000); College graduation rate: 21.4% (2000).
Housing: Homeownership rate: 97.1% (2000); Median home value: $130,300 (2000); Median rent: $525 per month (2000); Median age of housing: 24 years (2000).
Transportation: Commute to work: 45.2% car, 0.0% public transportation, 48.8% walk, 6.0% work from home (2000); Travel time to work: 57.4% less than 15 minutes, 35.3% 15 to 30 minutes, 6.7% 30 to 45 minutes, 0.0% 45 to 60 minutes, 0.6% 60 minutes or more (2000)

CEDAR RAPIDS (city). Covers a land area of 63.137 square miles and a water area of 1.278 square miles. Located at 41.98° N. Lat.; 91.66° W. Long. Elevation is 727 feet.
History: Cedar Rapids was named for the swift rapids of the Cedar River. The city was originally settled by Czech immigrants.
Population: 120,758 (2000); Race: 92.1% White, 3.4% Black, 1.8% Asian, 0.3% American Indian and Alaska Native, 1.8% Hispanic of any race, 1.8% two or more races (2000); Density: 1,912.6 persons per square mile (2000); Age: 24.4% under 18, 13.1% over 64 (2000); Marriage status: 27.6% never married, 55.1% now married, 6.4% widowed, 10.8% divorced (2000); Foreign born: 3.3% (2000); Ancestry (includes multiple ancestries): 35.5% German, 17.1% Irish, 9.4% English, 9.4% Other groups, 6.6% Czech (2000).
Vital Statistics: Birth rate: 146.7 per 10,000 population (1998)
Economy: Unemployment rate: 4.5% (11/2002); Total civilian labor force: 75,885 (11/2002); Single-family building permits issued: 363 (2001) / 349 (2000); Multi-family building permits issued: 470 (2001) / 616 (2000); Employment by occupation: 12.9% management, 21.7% professional, 12.4% services, 30.2% sales, 0.2% farming, 7.3% construction, 15.3% production (2000).
Income: Per capita income: $22,589 (2000); Median household income: $43,704 (2000); Poverty rate: 7.5% (2000).
Taxes: Total city taxes per capita: $500 (2000); City property taxes per capita: $457 (2000).
Education: High school graduation rate: 90.1% (2000); College graduation rate: 28.4% (2000).

School District(s)
Cedar Rapids Community School District (PK-12)
2000 Enrollment: 17,780 319-398-2000
College Community School District (PK-12)
2000 Enrollment: 3,476 319-848-5201

Four-year College(s)
Coe College (Private, Not-for-profit, Presbyterian Church (USA))
2001 Enrollment: 1,311 319-399-8000
2001 Tuition: In-state $19,140; Out-of-state $19,140
Hamilton College-Main Campus (Private, For-profit)
2001 Enrollment: 450 319-363-0481
2001 Tuition: In-state $9,360; Out-of-state $9,360
Mount Mercy College (Private, Not-for-profit, Roman Catholic)
2001 Enrollment: 1,387 319-363-8213
2001 Tuition: In-state $14,560; Out-of-state $14,560
Saint Luke's Hospital Medical Technology Program (Private, Not-for-profit, United Methodist)
2001 Enrollment: 5 319-369-7309

Two-year College(s)
Capri College (Private, For-profit)
2001 Enrollment: 116 319-364-1541
American College of Hairstyling-Cedar Rapids (Private, For-profit)
2001 Enrollment: 10 319-362-1488
Kirkwood Community College (Public)
2001 Enrollment: 12,555 319-398-5411
2001 Tuition: In-state $2,190; Out-of-state $4,380
Saint Luke's Methodist Hospital School of Rad Techn (Private, Not-for-profit, United Methodist)

2001 Enrollment: 19 319-396-7097
2001 Tuition: In-state $1,000; Out-of-state $1,000
Housing: Homeownership rate: 69.1% (2000); Median home value: $95,200 (2000); Median rent: $447 per month (2000); Median age of housing: 36 years (2000).
Hospitals: Mercy Medical Center (365 beds); Saint Luke's Hospital (560 beds)
Safety: Violent crime rate: 33.7 per 10,000 population; Property crime rate: 585.8 per 10,000 population (2001).
Newspapers: The Gazette (7 x week)
Transportation: Commute to work: 93.0% car, 1.3% public transportation, 2.5% walk, 2.3% work from home (2000); Travel time to work: 49.2% less than 15 minutes, 39.3% 15 to 30 minutes, 7.2% 30 to 45 minutes, 1.8% 45 to 60 minutes, 2.4% 60 minutes or more (2000)
Airports: The Eastern Iowa (primary service/small hub)
Additional Information Contacts
Cedar Rapids Area Association of Realtors 319-363-9604
Cedar Rapids Chamber of Commerce 319-398-5317
Cedar Rapids Convention & Visitors Bureau 319-398-5009

CENTER POINT (city). Covers a land area of 2.405 square miles and a water area of 0 square miles. Located at 42.19° N. Lat.; 91.78° W. Long.
History: Center Point was settled in 1839 by Bartimeas McGonigle, and was then known as McGonigle's Point. The town was the "center point" between the Cedar Rapids and Waterloo mail routes.
Population: 2,007 (2000); Race: 98.2% White, 0.5% Black, 0.2% Asian, 0.0% American Indian and Alaska Native, 0.3% Hispanic of any race, 0.8% two or more races (2000); Density: 834.5 persons per square mile (2000); Age: 29.7% under 18, 9.8% over 64 (2000); Marriage status: 19.8% never married, 63.7% now married, 7.0% widowed, 9.5% divorced (2000); Foreign born: 0.6% (2000); Ancestry (includes multiple ancestries): 41.3% German, 13.8% Irish, 9.4% English, 8.2% Czech, 6.6% United States or American (2000).
Economy: Single-family building permits issued: 30 (2001) / 28 (2000); Multi-family building permits issued: 0 (2001) / 0 (2000); Employment by occupation: 8.7% management, 16.0% professional, 11.6% services, 30.5% sales, 0.2% farming, 14.6% construction, 18.4% production (2000).
Income: Per capita income: $19,527 (2000); Median household income: $48,352 (2000); Poverty rate: 4.6% (2000).
Taxes: Total city taxes per capita: $210 (1997); City property taxes per capita: $201 (1997).
Education: High school graduation rate: 90.5% (2000); College graduation rate: 15.3% (2000).

School District(s)
Center Point-Urbana Community School District (PK-12)
2000 Enrollment: 1,127 319-849-1102
Housing: Homeownership rate: 79.3% (2000); Median home value: $89,600 (2000); Median rent: $306 per month (2000); Median age of housing: 37 years (2000).
Transportation: Commute to work: 93.5% car, 0.0% public transportation, 3.1% walk, 3.4% work from home (2000); Travel time to work: 18.9% less than 15 minutes, 56.3% 15 to 30 minutes, 20.3% 30 to 45 minutes, 2.0% 45 to 60 minutes, 2.5% 60 minutes or more (2000)

CENTRAL CITY (city). Covers a land area of 0.888 square miles and a water area of 0.022 square miles. Located at 42.20° N. Lat.; 91.52° W. Long. Elevation is 837 feet.
History: The East Star Mill was erected near Central City on the banks of the Wapsipinicon River in 1863.
Population: 1,157 (2000); Race: 98.2% White, 0.0% Black, 0.0% Asian, 0.0% American Indian and Alaska Native, 0.7% Hispanic of any race, 1.8% two or more races (2000); Density: 1,303.2 persons per square mile (2000); Age: 25.4% under 18, 17.3% over 64 (2000); Marriage status: 18.9% never married, 59.4% now married, 11.5% widowed, 10.2% divorced (2000); Foreign born: 0.4% (2000); Ancestry (includes multiple ancestries): 31.0% German, 16.9% Irish, 13.7% English, 6.9% United States or American, 4.6% Czech (2000).
Economy: Single-family building permits issued: 6 (2001) / 8 (2000); Multi-family building permits issued: 6 (2001) / 0 (2000); Employment by occupation: 11.4% management, 12.7% professional, 19.2% services, 30.5% sales, 0.0% farming, 11.3% construction, 15.0% production (2000).
Income: Per capita income: $18,800 (2000); Median household income: $36,544 (2000); Poverty rate: 3.3% (2000).
Taxes: Total city taxes per capita: $159 (1997); City property taxes per capita: $153 (1997).
Education: High school graduation rate: 81.1% (2000); College graduation rate: 11.6% (2000).

School District(s)
Central City Community School District (PK-12)
2000 Enrollment: 500 319-438-6183
Housing: Homeownership rate: 75.8% (2000); Median home value: $78,400 (2000); Median rent: $265 per month (2000); Median age of housing: 47 years (2000).
Newspapers: Linn News-Letter (1 x week)
Transportation: Commute to work: 93.6% car, 0.4% public transportation, 3.5% walk, 2.5% work from home (2000); Travel time to work: 19.7% less than 15 minutes, 35.3% 15 to 30 minutes, 36.6% 30 to 45 minutes, 4.5% 45 to 60 minutes, 3.8% 60 minutes or more (2000)

COGGON (city). Covers a land area of 0.626 square miles and a water area of 0.020 square miles. Located at 42.27° N. Lat.; 91.53° W. Long. Elevation is 950 feet.
History: Coggon, first called Green's Mill and later Nugent, is near the now extinct village of Sodtown, whose buildings were made of sod blocks in the early days of settlement.
Population: 745 (2000); Race: 98.3% White, 0.4% Black, 0.0% Asian, 0.0% American Indian and Alaska Native, 0.0% Hispanic of any race, 1.1% two or more races (2000); Density: 1,190.3 persons per square mile (2000); Age: 29.8% under 18, 19.3% over 64 (2000); Marriage status: 16.4% never married, 63.4% now married, 10.4% widowed, 9.7% divorced (2000); Foreign born: 0.5% (2000); Ancestry (includes multiple ancestries): 41.4% German, 19.9% Irish, 9.2% English, 3.5% Other groups, 3.2% United States or American (2000).
Economy: Single-family building permits issued: 0 (2001) / 0 (2000); Multi-family building permits issued: 0 (2001) / 0 (2000); Employment by occupation: 8.9% management, 19.3% professional, 15.4% services, 20.1% sales, 0.0% farming, 13.1% construction, 23.2% production (2000).
Income: Per capita income: $19,871 (2000); Median household income: $45,000 (2000); Poverty rate: 6.2% (2000).
Taxes: Total city taxes per capita: $156 (1997); City property taxes per capita: $153 (1997).
Education: High school graduation rate: 88.7% (2000); College graduation rate: 13.8% (2000).
Housing: Homeownership rate: 82.9% (2000); Median home value: $77,400 (2000); Median rent: $345 per month (2000); Median age of housing: 56 years (2000).
Transportation: Commute to work: 92.9% car, 0.0% public transportation, 3.7% walk, 1.4% work from home (2000); Travel time to work: 20.9% less than 15 minutes, 17.7% 15 to 30 minutes, 48.4% 30 to 45 minutes, 5.2% 45 to 60 minutes, 7.8% 60 minutes or more (2000)

ELY (city). Covers a land area of 1.355 square miles and a water area of 0 square miles. Located at 41.87° N. Lat.; 91.58° W. Long. Elevation is 741 feet.
History: Dr. John F. Ely, who gave his name to the town, was responsible for the development of the land purchased by the Burlington, Cedar Rapids & Northern Railroad. Ely was treasurer of the Railroad at the time.
Population: 1,149 (2000); Race: 95.4% White, 0.3% Black, 1.4% Asian, 0.0% American Indian and Alaska Native, 1.9% Hispanic of any race, 2.8% two or more races (2000); Density: 848.1 persons per square mile (2000); Age: 29.0% under 18, 7.1% over 64 (2000); Marriage status: 24.6% never married, 65.1% now married, 4.1% widowed, 6.3% divorced (2000); Foreign born: 1.8% (2000); Ancestry (includes multiple ancestries): 41.1% German, 11.7% Irish, 11.3% Czech, 7.2% English, 7.0% United States or American (2000).
Economy: Single-family building permits issued: 22 (2001) / 25 (2000); Multi-family building permits issued: 0 (2001) / 0 (2000); Employment by occupation: 12.2% management, 18.8% professional, 12.9% services, 27.5% sales, 0.1% farming, 14.0% construction, 14.5% production (2000).
Income: Per capita income: $20,936 (2000); Median household income: $57,250 (2000); Poverty rate: 5.8% (2000).
Education: High school graduation rate: 92.5% (2000); College graduation rate: 26.1% (2000).
Housing: Homeownership rate: 71.4% (2000); Median home value: $122,800 (2000); Median rent: $537 per month (2000); Median age of housing: 9 years (2000).
Transportation: Commute to work: 93.6% car, 0.0% public transportation, 2.3% walk, 3.1% work from home (2000); Travel time to work: 26.5% less than 15 minutes, 56.1% 15 to 30 minutes, 11.3% 30 to 45 minutes, 2.0% 45 to 60 minutes, 4.2% 60 minutes or more (2000)

FAIRFAX (city). Covers a land area of 1.362 square miles and a water area of 0 square miles. Located at 41.92° N. Lat.; 91.78° W. Long. Elevation is 769 feet.
History: Fairfax was first called Vanderbilt, after early settler Jacob Vanderbilt, but later changed to Fairfax after Fairfax County, Virginia.
Population: 889 (2000); Race: 95.7% White, 0.6% Black, 0.7% Asian, 0.0% American Indian and Alaska Native, 0.9% Hispanic of any race, 3.0% two or more races (2000); Density: 652.7 persons per square mile (2000); Age: 33.9% under 18, 11.3% over 64 (2000); Marriage status: 21.5% never married, 65.8% now married, 3.7% widowed, 8.9% divorced (2000); Foreign born: 1.7% (2000); Ancestry (includes multiple ancestries): 41.2% German, 16.9% Irish, 12.6% English, 8.7% Czech, 5.3% Other groups (2000).
Economy: Single-family building permits issued: 34 (2001) / 41 (2000); Multi-family building permits issued: 24 (2001) / 8 (2000); Employment by occupation: 9.6% management, 19.1% professional, 11.5% services, 28.9% sales, 0.0% farming, 11.3% construction, 19.5% production (2000).
Income: Per capita income: $19,583 (2000); Median household income: $57,850 (2000); Poverty rate: 2.9% (2000).
Taxes: Total city taxes per capita: $207 (1997); City property taxes per capita: $205 (1997).
Education: High school graduation rate: 90.2% (2000); College graduation rate: 16.6% (2000).
Housing: Homeownership rate: 87.8% (2000); Median home value: $105,200 (2000); Median rent: $415 per month (2000); Median age of housing: 32 years (2000).
Transportation: Commute to work: 93.9% car, 0.0% public transportation, 3.5% walk, 2.6% work from home (2000); Travel time to work: 33.3% less than 15 minutes, 53.4% 15 to 30 minutes, 12.6% 30 to 45 minutes, 0.7% 45 to 60 minutes, 0.0% 60 minutes or more (2000)

HIAWATHA (city). Covers a land area of 3.533 square miles and a water area of 0 square miles. Located at 42.04° N. Lat.; 91.68° W. Long.
History: Hiawatha was named for the title character in the poem by Henry Wadsworth Longfellow ("Song of Hiawatha").
Population: 6,480 (2000); Race: 92.7% White, 1.6% Black, 2.2% Asian, 0.4% American Indian and Alaska Native, 2.7% Hispanic of any race, 1.7% two or more races (2000); Density: 1,834.3 persons per square mile (2000); Age: 22.8% under 18, 9.8% over 64 (2000); Marriage status: 29.1% never married, 52.7% now married, 4.2% widowed, 14.0% divorced (2000); Foreign born: 2.7% (2000); Ancestry (includes multiple ancestries): 33.8% German, 14.3% Irish, 10.0% English, 9.5% Other groups, 6.0% United States or American (2000).
Economy: Single-family building permits issued: 39 (2001) / 24 (2000); Multi-family building permits issued: 0 (2001) / 24 (2000); Employment by occupation: 14.6% management, 18.3% professional, 9.8% services, 34.2% sales, 0.0% farming, 8.3% construction, 14.9% production (2000).
Income: Per capita income: $22,664 (2000); Median household income: $40,799 (2000); Poverty rate: 4.5% (2000).
Taxes: Total city taxes per capita: $232 (1997); City property taxes per capita: $203 (1997).
Education: High school graduation rate: 90.4% (2000); College graduation rate: 24.0% (2000).
Housing: Homeownership rate: 60.9% (2000); Median home value: $112,000 (2000); Median rent: $443 per month (2000); Median age of housing: 23 years (2000).
Transportation: Commute to work: 94.7% car, 2.1% public transportation, 1.4% walk, 1.5% work from home (2000); Travel time to work: 55.0% less than 15 minutes, 35.7% 15 to 30 minutes, 6.2% 30 to 45 minutes, 1.6% 45 to 60 minutes, 1.6% 60 minutes or more (2000)

LISBON (city). Covers a land area of 2.114 square miles and a water area of 0 square miles. Located at 41.92° N. Lat.; 91.38° W. Long.
History: Lisbon was colonized in 1847 by 61 people from Pennsylvania including Christian Hersey, with his sons and grandsons and their families.
Population: 1,898 (2000); Race: 97.2% White, 0.4% Black, 0.3% Asian, 0.1% American Indian and Alaska Native, 0.3% Hispanic of any race, 2.0% two or more races (2000); Density: 897.8 persons per square mile (2000); Age: 33.9% under 18, 7.8% over 64 (2000); Marriage status: 22.9% never married, 64.8% now married, 4.3% widowed, 7.9% divorced (2000); Foreign born: 0.8% (2000); Ancestry (includes multiple ancestries): 41.8% German, 15.1% Irish, 12.8% English, 8.7% Czech, 5.3% Other groups (2000).
Economy: Single-family building permits issued: 6 (2001) / 15 (2000); Multi-family building permits issued: 6 (2001) / 6 (2000); Employment by occupation: 11.4% management, 18.1% professional, 17.1% services, 27.0% sales, 0.0% farming, 10.8% construction, 15.5% production (2000).
Income: Per capita income: $18,275 (2000); Median household income: $45,139 (2000); Poverty rate: 6.8% (2000).
Taxes: Total city taxes per capita: $286 (1997); City property taxes per capita: $278 (1997).
Education: High school graduation rate: 90.4% (2000); College graduation rate: 21.0% (2000).

School District(s)

Lisbon Community School District (PK-12)
2000 Enrollment: 601 319-455-2075

Housing: Homeownership rate: 73.8% (2000); Median home value: $93,500 (2000); Median rent: $358 per month (2000); Median age of housing: 41 years (2000).
Transportation: Commute to work: 91.7% car, 0.0% public transportation, 3.2% walk, 4.5% work from home (2000); Travel time to work: 27.0% less than 15 minutes, 38.6% 15 to 30 minutes, 28.8% 30 to 45 minutes, 3.1% 45 to 60 minutes, 2.4% 60 minutes or more (2000)

MARION (city). Covers a land area of 11.995 square miles and a water area of 0 square miles. Located at 42.03° N. Lat.; 91.59° W. Long. Elevation is 848 feet.
History: Marion was named in honor of Gen. Francis Marion, officer in the Revolutionary War. Because of its luxuriant growth of shade trees, it is often called Grove City.
Population: 26,294 (2000); Race: 96.7% White, 0.6% Black, 0.8% Asian, 0.3% American Indian and Alaska Native, 1.1% Hispanic of any race, 1.1% two or more races (2000); Density: 2,192.1 persons per square mile (2000); Age: 26.4% under 18, 11.2% over 64 (2000); Marriage status: 23.1% never married, 60.6% now married, 5.6% widowed, 10.7% divorced (2000); Foreign born: 1.6% (2000); Ancestry (includes multiple ancestries): 39.7% German, 16.6% Irish, 11.3% English, 6.0% Other groups, 5.8% Norwegian (2000).
Vital Statistics: Birth rate: 147.9 per 10,000 population (1998)
Economy: Single-family building permits issued: 189 (2001) / 180 (2000); Multi-family building permits issued: 187 (2001) / 163 (2000); Employment by occupation: 12.9% management, 22.2% professional, 13.8% services, 31.4% sales, 0.0% farming, 7.2% construction, 12.4% production (2000).
Income: Per capita income: $23,158 (2000); Median household income: $48,591 (2000); Poverty rate: 5.2% (2000).
Taxes: Total city taxes per capita: $319 (2000); City property taxes per capita: $287 (2000).
Education: High school graduation rate: 92.0% (2000); College graduation rate: 29.1% (2000).

School District(s)

Linn-Mar Community School District (PK-12)
2000 Enrollment: 4,679 319-377-7373
Marion Independent School District (PK-12)
2000 Enrollment: 1,849 319-377-4691

Housing: Homeownership rate: 78.1% (2000); Median home value: $105,200 (2000); Median rent: $397 per month (2000); Median age of housing: 27 years (2000).
Safety: Violent crime rate: 1.5 per 10,000 population; Property crime rate: 134.8 per 10,000 population (2001).
Newspapers: Marion Times (1 x week)
Transportation: Commute to work: 93.9% car, 1.4% public transportation, 0.8% walk, 3.1% work from home (2000); Travel time to work: 36.8% less than 15 minutes, 47.5% 15 to 30 minutes, 10.3% 30 to 45 minutes, 2.6% 45 to 60 minutes, 2.7% 60 minutes or more (2000)
Additional Information Contacts
Marion Chamber of Commerce 319-377-6316

MOUNT VERNON (city). Covers a land area of 3.484 square miles and a water area of 0.006 square miles. Located at 41.92° N. Lat.; 91.42° W. Long. Elevation is 843 feet.
History: Mount Vernon was named by Elder George Bowman, a Methodist circuit rider. It is said that in 1851 he stopped his horse on the crest of a long hill, and inspired by the beauty of the scene, knelt to consecrate the spot to Christian education.
Population: 3,390 (2000); Race: 97.3% White, 0.0% Black, 0.9% Asian, 0.5% American Indian and Alaska Native, 0.7% Hispanic of any race, 1.3% two or more races (2000); Density: 973.0 persons per square mile (2000); Age: 25.1% under 18, 9.6% over 64 (2000); Marriage status: 35.9% never married, 52.0% now married, 3.3% widowed, 8.8% divorced (2000); Foreign born: 2.3% (2000); Ancestry (includes multiple ancestries): 36.9% German, 16.7% Irish, 11.9% English, 5.8% Swedish, 5.5% Norwegian (2000).
Economy: Single-family building permits issued: 16 (2001) / 21 (2000); Multi-family building permits issued: 6 (2001) / 12 (2000); Employment by

occupation: 16.5% management, 25.5% professional, 13.4% services, 28.1% sales, 0.0% farming, 5.3% construction, 11.2% production (2000).
Income: Per capita income: $19,027 (2000); Median household income: $51,228 (2000); Poverty rate: 5.5% (2000).
Taxes: Total city taxes per capita: $264 (1997); City property taxes per capita: $257 (1997).
Education: High school graduation rate: 93.6% (2000); College graduation rate: 43.8% (2000).

School District(s)

Mount Vernon Community School District (KG-12)
2000 Enrollment: 1,158 319-895-8845

Four-year College(s)

Cornell College (Private, Not-for-profit, United Methodist)
2001 Enrollment: 986 319-895-4000
2001 Tuition: In-state $20,090; Out-of-state $20,090
Housing: Homeownership rate: 77.2% (2000); Median home value: $119,000 (2000); Median rent: $453 per month (2000); Median age of housing: 45 years (2000).
Newspapers: The Sun (1 x week)
Transportation: Commute to work: 73.3% car, 0.0% public transportation, 22.3% walk, 4.4% work from home (2000); Travel time to work: 51.1% less than 15 minutes, 29.3% 15 to 30 minutes, 14.8% 30 to 45 minutes, 1.1% 45 to 60 minutes, 3.7% 60 minutes or more (2000)
Additional Information Contacts
Mt Vernon Chamber of Commerce 319-895-8214

PALO (city). Covers a land area of 1.252 square miles and a water area of 0.002 square miles. Located at 42.06° N. Lat.; 91.79° W. Long. Elevation is 751 feet.
History: Palo was named just after the beginning of the Mexican War. The name is in remembrance of the first battle of that war, the Battle of Palo Alto.
Population: 614 (2000); Race: 99.1% White, 0.0% Black, 0.0% Asian, 0.0% American Indian and Alaska Native, 1.3% Hispanic of any race, 0.5% two or more races (2000); Density: 490.4 persons per square mile (2000); Age: 24.2% under 18, 6.8% over 64 (2000); Marriage status: 17.2% never married, 68.3% now married, 3.9% widowed, 10.6% divorced (2000); Foreign born: 0.8% (2000); Ancestry (includes multiple ancestries): 37.4% German, 18.6% Irish, 12.8% English, 12.2% United States or American, 9.6% Czech (2000).
Economy: Single-family building permits issued: 10 (2001) / 8 (2000); Multi-family building permits issued: 0 (2001) / 0 (2000); Employment by occupation: 10.3% management, 9.3% professional, 16.0% services, 28.4% sales, 0.0% farming, 12.4% construction, 23.5% production (2000).
Income: Per capita income: $21,429 (2000); Median household income: $53,558 (2000); Poverty rate: 4.6% (2000).
Taxes: Total city taxes per capita: $170 (1997); City property taxes per capita: $167 (1997).
Education: High school graduation rate: 91.6% (2000); College graduation rate: 10.3% (2000).
Housing: Homeownership rate: 89.2% (2000); Median home value: $96,900 (2000); Median rent: $416 per month (2000); Median age of housing: 28 years (2000).
Transportation: Commute to work: 94.6% car, 0.0% public transportation, 2.8% walk, 1.8% work from home (2000); Travel time to work: 21.3% less than 15 minutes, 65.3% 15 to 30 minutes, 10.0% 30 to 45 minutes, 1.6% 45 to 60 minutes, 1.8% 60 minutes or more (2000)

PRAIRIEBURG (city). Covers a land area of 0.455 square miles and a water area of 0 square miles. Located at 42.23° N. Lat.; 91.42° W. Long.
Population: 175 (2000); Race: 100.0% White, 0.0% Black, 0.0% Asian, 0.0% American Indian and Alaska Native, 0.0% Hispanic of any race, 0.0% two or more races (2000); Density: 384.8 persons per square mile (2000); Age: 27.1% under 18, 12.9% over 64 (2000); Marriage status: 18.0% never married, 59.0% now married, 9.0% widowed, 13.9% divorced (2000); Foreign born: 1.3% (2000); Ancestry (includes multiple ancestries): 44.5% German, 18.7% Irish, 14.2% Czech, 7.7% United States or American, 4.5% Italian (2000).
Economy: Single-family building permits issued: 0 (2001) / 0 (2000); Multi-family building permits issued: 0 (2001) / 0 (2000); Employment by occupation: 7.0% management, 4.2% professional, 25.4% services, 25.4% sales, 1.4% farming, 15.5% construction, 21.1% production (2000).
Income: Per capita income: $17,197 (2000); Median household income: $36,750 (2000); Poverty rate: 12.9% (2000).
Taxes: Total city taxes per capita: $63 (1997); City property taxes per capita: $63 (1997).
Education: High school graduation rate: 78.6% (2000); College graduation rate: 4.9% (2000).
Housing: Homeownership rate: 97.1% (2000); Median home value: $56,400 (2000); Median rent: $325 per month (2000); Median age of housing: 56 years (2000).
Transportation: Commute to work: 87.3% car, 2.8% public transportation, 2.8% walk, 4.2% work from home (2000); Travel time to work: 14.7% less than 15 minutes, 22.1% 15 to 30 minutes, 33.8% 30 to 45 minutes, 17.6% 45 to 60 minutes, 11.8% 60 minutes or more (2000)

ROBINS (city). Covers a land area of 3.824 square miles and a water area of 0 square miles. Located at 42.07° N. Lat.; 91.66° W. Long.
History: Robins was named for its first postmaster and storekeeper.
Population: 1,806 (2000); Race: 97.9% White, 0.0% Black, 0.6% Asian, 0.0% American Indian and Alaska Native, 1.8% Hispanic of any race, 0.9% two or more races (2000); Density: 472.3 persons per square mile (2000); Age: 35.9% under 18, 4.2% over 64 (2000); Marriage status: 18.1% never married, 75.0% now married, 2.1% widowed, 4.8% divorced (2000); Foreign born: 0.8% (2000); Ancestry (includes multiple ancestries): 43.6% German, 17.4% Irish, 13.7% English, 7.8% Norwegian, 6.9% United States or American (2000).
Economy: Single-family building permits issued: 36 (2001) / 33 (2000); Multi-family building permits issued: 0 (2001) / 0 (2000); Employment by occupation: 17.1% management, 33.1% professional, 7.7% services, 21.9% sales, 0.0% farming, 9.5% construction, 10.7% production (2000).
Income: Per capita income: $25,078 (2000); Median household income: $74,211 (2000); Poverty rate: 1.2% (2000).
Taxes: Total city taxes per capita: $200 (1997); City property taxes per capita: $192 (1997).
Education: High school graduation rate: 95.7% (2000); College graduation rate: 36.4% (2000).
Housing: Homeownership rate: 95.4% (2000); Median home value: $156,300 (2000); Median rent: $436 per month (2000); Median age of housing: 16 years (2000).
Transportation: Commute to work: 94.7% car, 0.4% public transportation, 0.2% walk, 4.3% work from home (2000); Travel time to work: 39.4% less than 15 minutes, 48.1% 15 to 30 minutes, 9.2% 30 to 45 minutes, 1.2% 45 to 60 minutes, 2.1% 60 minutes or more (2000)

SPRINGVILLE (city). Covers a land area of 0.743 square miles and a water area of 0 square miles. Located at 42.05° N. Lat.; 91.44° W. Long. Elevation is 846 feet.
History: Nathan Brown, a Revolutionary War veteran, and Mrs. Winans, a survivor of the Ft. Dearborn massacre, are buried in the Springville Cemetery.
Population: 1,091 (2000); Race: 99.0% White, 0.0% Black, 0.7% Asian, 0.2% American Indian and Alaska Native, 0.7% Hispanic of any race, 0.0% two or more races (2000); Density: 1,467.7 persons per square mile (2000); Age: 28.4% under 18, 11.6% over 64 (2000); Marriage status: 20.9% never married, 61.5% now married, 6.9% widowed, 10.8% divorced (2000); Foreign born: 1.3% (2000); Ancestry (includes multiple ancestries): 41.7% German, 17.6% Irish, 11.6% English, 6.8% Czech, 5.0% United States or American (2000).
Economy: Single-family building permits issued: 4 (2001) / 2 (2000); Multi-family building permits issued: 0 (2001) / 0 (2000); Employment by occupation: 11.4% management, 9.7% professional, 18.0% services, 27.2% sales, 0.3% farming, 13.8% construction, 19.6% production (2000).
Income: Per capita income: $18,429 (2000); Median household income: $44,567 (2000); Poverty rate: 5.1% (2000).
Taxes: Total city taxes per capita: $137 (1997); City property taxes per capita: $134 (1997).
Education: High school graduation rate: 90.1% (2000); College graduation rate: 16.3% (2000).

School District(s)

Springville Community School District (PK-12)
2000 Enrollment: 491 319-854-6197
Housing: Homeownership rate: 75.9% (2000); Median home value: $88,100 (2000); Median rent: $344 per month (2000); Median age of housing: 39 years (2000).
Transportation: Commute to work: 93.5% car, 0.0% public transportation, 2.7% walk, 3.5% work from home (2000); Travel time to work: 16.5% less than 15 minutes, 52.7% 15 to 30 minutes, 23.2% 30 to 45 minutes, 3.8% 45 to 60 minutes, 3.8% 60 minutes or more (2000)

TODDVILLE (unincorporated postal area, zip code 52341). Covers a land area of 11.507 square miles and a water area of 0.041 square miles. Located at 42.11° N. Lat.; 91.72° W. Long. Elevation is 780 feet.
History: Toddville was named for a local sawmill operator.

Population: 1,021 (2000); Race: 99.4% White, 0.2% Black, 0.0% Asian, 0.0% American Indian and Alaska Native, 0.4% Hispanic of any race, 0.0% two or more races (2000); Density: 88.7 persons per square mile (2000); Age: 20.8% under 18, 13.9% over 64 (2000); Marriage status: 22.4% never married, 60.7% now married, 5.7% widowed, 11.3% divorced (2000); Foreign born: 0.0% (2000); Ancestry (includes multiple ancestries): 38.6% German, 11.7% English, 9.2% Czech, 6.8% Irish, 6.4% Norwegian (2000).
Economy: Employment by occupation: 14.1% management, 17.1% professional, 13.9% services, 30.9% sales, 0.8% farming, 12.1% construction, 11.1% production (2000).
Income: Per capita income: $26,699 (2000); Median household income: $50,375 (2000); Poverty rate: 2.9% (2000).
Education: High school graduation rate: 92.3% (2000); College graduation rate: 18.3% (2000).
Housing: Homeownership rate: 93.2% (2000); Median home value: $134,600 (2000); Median rent: $318 per month (2000); Median age of housing: 27 years (2000).
Transportation: Commute to work: 92.8% car, 0.0% public transportation, 0.0% walk, 7.2% work from home (2000); Travel time to work: 21.5% less than 15 minutes, 71.0% 15 to 30 minutes, 3.9% 30 to 45 minutes, 0.8% 45 to 60 minutes, 2.8% 60 minutes or more (2000)

WALKER (city). Covers a land area of 0.703 square miles and a water area of 0 square miles. Located at 42.28° N. Lat.; 91.78° W. Long. Elevation is 890 feet.
History: Walker was named for W. W. Walker, an official of the Chicago, Rock Island & Pacific Railroad.
Population: 750 (2000); Race: 99.6% White, 0.0% Black, 0.0% Asian, 0.0% American Indian and Alaska Native, 0.7% Hispanic of any race, 0.4% two or more races (2000); Density: 1,066.1 persons per square mile (2000); Age: 33.2% under 18, 9.4% over 64 (2000); Marriage status: 24.0% never married, 63.9% now married, 6.4% widowed, 5.6% divorced (2000); Foreign born: 0.0% (2000); Ancestry (includes multiple ancestries): 44.4% German, 16.3% Irish, 11.6% English, 10.5% Czech, 7.3% United States or American (2000).
Economy: Single-family building permits issued: 2 (2001) / 2 (2000); Multi-family building permits issued: 0 (2001) / 0 (2000); Employment by occupation: 4.7% management, 12.4% professional, 20.8% services, 25.3% sales, 0.8% farming, 15.6% construction, 20.3% production (2000).
Income: Per capita income: $16,258 (2000); Median household income: $43,438 (2000); Poverty rate: 5.2% (2000).
Taxes: Total city taxes per capita: $132 (1997); City property taxes per capita: $129 (1997).
Education: High school graduation rate: 89.3% (2000); College graduation rate: 11.9% (2000).
Housing: Homeownership rate: 82.4% (2000); Median home value: $82,100 (2000); Median rent: $318 per month (2000); Median age of housing: 50 years (2000).
Transportation: Commute to work: 91.1% car, 0.0% public transportation, 2.4% walk, 5.1% work from home (2000); Travel time to work: 23.2% less than 15 minutes, 20.7% 15 to 30 minutes, 50.7% 30 to 45 minutes, 3.1% 45 to 60 minutes, 2.3% 60 minutes or more (2000)

Louisa County

Located in southeastern Iowa; bounded on the east by the Mississippi River and the Illinois border; prairie area, drained by the Iowa River. Covers a land area of 401.90 square miles, a water area of 15.70 square miles, and is located in the Central Time Zone. The county government was organized in 1836. County seat is Wapello.

Weather Station: Columbus Junction 2 SSW — Elevation: 669 feet

	Jan	Feb	Mar	Apr	May	Jun	Jul	Aug	Sep	Oct	Nov	Dec
High	30	36	49	63	74	83	87	84	77	65	48	35
Low	12	19	29	40	51	60	64	62	54	42	31	19
Precip	1.2	1.3	2.8	3.6	4.5	4.2	4.4	4.7	4.0	3.0	2.7	1.9
Snow	10.0	7.9	6.0	2.6	0.0	0.0	0.0	0.0	0.0	0.4	3.6	8.4

High and Low temperatures in degrees Fahrenheit; Precipitation and Snow in inches

Population: 12,183 (2000); Race: 93.9% White, 0.2% Black, 0.4% Asian, 0.1% American Indian and Alaska Native, 12.7% Hispanic of any race, 0.7% two or more races (2000); Density: 30.3 persons per square mile (2000); Age: 27.7% under 18, 13.9% over 64 (2000).
Religion: Five largest groups: 18.7% The United Methodist Church, 7.5% Catholic Church, 6.5% Presbyterian Church (U.S.A.), 3.5% Apostolic Christian Church of America, Inc., 1.0% Lutheran Church—Missouri Synod (2000).
Economy: Unemployment rate: 3.7% (11/2002); Total civilian labor force: 6,217 (11/2002); Leading industries: 50.8% manufacturing; 9.6% health care and social assistance; 7.6% retail trade (2000); Companies that employ more than 1,000 persons: 1 (2000); Companies that employ more than 100 persons: 2 (2000); Farms: 593 totaling 201,393 acres (1997); Minority business ownership rate: 0.0% (1997); Women business ownership rate: 23.2% (1997); Retail sales per capita: $3,844 (1997). Single-family building permits issued: 26 (2001) / 17 (2000); Multi-family building permits issued: 0 (2001) / 0 (2000).
Income: Per capita income: $17,644 (2000); Median household income: $39,086 (2000); Poverty rate: 9.3% (2000); Bankruptcy rate: 3.39% (2001).
Taxes: Total county taxes per capita: $259 (2000); County property taxes per capita: $258 (2000).
Education: High school graduation rate: 79.7% (2000); College graduation rate: 12.7% (2000).
Housing: Homeownership rate: 77.3% (2000); Median home value: $66,600 (2000); Median rent: $317 per month (2000); Median age of housing: 43 years (2000).
Health: Birth rate: 141.2 per 10,000 population (1998); Age adjusted death rate: 67.4 per 10,000 population (1999); Age adjusted cancer mortality rate: 156.2 deaths per 100,000 population (1999). Number of physicians: 1.6 per 10,000 population (1999); Number of hospital beds: n/a (1999).
Elections: 2000 Presidential election results: 49.5% Gore, 47.6% Bush, 1.8% Nader, 0.7% Buchanan
National and State Parks: Cone Marsh State Wildlife Management Area; Klum Lake State Game Mgt Area; Mark Twain National Wildlife Refuge
Additional Information Contacts
Louisa County Government Offices. 319-523-3371

Louisa County Communities

COLUMBUS CITY (city). Covers a land area of 0.233 square miles and a water area of 0 square miles. Located at 41.25° N. Lat.; 91.37° W. Long.
Population: 376 (2000); Race: 64.8% White, 0.0% Black, 0.5% Asian, 0.0% American Indian and Alaska Native, 44.3% Hispanic of any race, 2.5% two or more races (2000); Density: 1,613.4 persons per square mile (2000); Age: 37.7% under 18, 7.4% over 64 (2000); Marriage status: 20.0% never married, 64.1% now married, 5.9% widowed, 10.0% divorced (2000); Foreign born: 24.4% (2000); Ancestry (includes multiple ancestries): 39.2% Other groups, 12.3% German, 11.8% United States or American, 7.6% Irish, 6.4% English (2000).
Economy: Single-family building permits issued: 0 (2001) / 0 (2000); Multi-family building permits issued: 0 (2001) / 0 (2000); Employment by occupation: 7.0% management, 6.4% professional, 20.9% services, 23.3% sales, 0.0% farming, 16.3% construction, 26.2% production (2000).
Income: Per capita income: $12,468 (2000); Median household income: $32,188 (2000); Poverty rate: 5.2% (2000).
Taxes: Total city taxes per capita: $69 (1997); City property taxes per capita: $66 (1997).
Education: High school graduation rate: 73.0% (2000); College graduation rate: 4.4% (2000).
Housing: Homeownership rate: 87.4% (2000); Median home value: $61,400 (2000); Median rent: $289 per month (2000); Median age of housing: 33 years (2000).
Transportation: Commute to work: 92.0% car, 0.0% public transportation, 4.9% walk, 3.1% work from home (2000); Travel time to work: 46.2% less than 15 minutes, 15.2% 15 to 30 minutes, 24.1% 30 to 45 minutes, 10.1% 45 to 60 minutes, 4.4% 60 minutes or more (2000)

COLUMBUS JUNCTION (city). Covers a land area of 2.160 square miles and a water area of 0 square miles. Located at 41.27° N. Lat.; 91.36° W. Long. Elevation is 595 feet.
History: Columbus Junction was so named because it was a railroad junction near Columbus City.
Population: 1,900 (2000); Race: 86.0% White, 0.8% Black, 0.4% Asian, 0.0% American Indian and Alaska Native, 37.5% Hispanic of any race, 1.3% two or more races (2000); Density: 879.6 persons per square mile (2000); Age: 26.6% under 18, 15.4% over 64 (2000); Marriage status: 24.6% never married, 59.5% now married, 7.5% widowed, 8.3% divorced (2000); Foreign born: 21.7% (2000); Ancestry (includes multiple ancestries): 34.4% Other groups, 17.6% German, 11.1% United States or American, 7.9% English, 7.6% Irish (2000).
Economy: Single-family building permits issued: 5 (2001) / 0 (2000); Multi-family building permits issued: 0 (2001) / 0 (2000); Employment by

occupation: 7.2% management, 13.7% professional, 13.4% services, 19.8% sales, 0.2% farming, 9.0% construction, 36.6% production (2000).
Income: Per capita income: $16,314 (2000); Median household income: $33,167 (2000); Poverty rate: 11.2% (2000).
Taxes: Total city taxes per capita: $135 (1997); City property taxes per capita: $128 (1997).
Education: High school graduation rate: 74.4% (2000); College graduation rate: 16.7% (2000).

School District(s)

Columbus Community School District (PK-12)
2000 Enrollment: 1,052 319-728-2911
Housing: Homeownership rate: 61.7% (2000); Median home value: $69,400 (2000); Median rent: $306 per month (2000); Median age of housing: 39 years (2000).
Newspapers: The Columbus Gazette (1 x week)
Transportation: Commute to work: 96.2% car, 0.0% public transportation, 1.7% walk, 1.2% work from home (2000); Travel time to work: 45.4% less than 15 minutes, 20.1% 15 to 30 minutes, 19.5% 30 to 45 minutes, 10.8% 45 to 60 minutes, 4.3% 60 minutes or more (2000)

COTTER (city). Covers a land area of 0.234 square miles and a water area of 0 square miles. Located at 41.29° N. Lat.; 91.46° W. Long.
History: Cotter is named for Margaret E. Cotter, who laid out the town. It was first known as Cotterville.
Population: 48 (2000); Race: 77.4% White, 0.0% Black, 7.5% Asian, 0.0% American Indian and Alaska Native, 15.1% Hispanic of any race, 0.0% two or more races (2000); Density: 205.3 persons per square mile (2000); Age: 30.2% under 18, 7.5% over 64 (2000); Marriage status: 24.4% never married, 70.7% now married, 0.0% widowed, 4.9% divorced (2000); Foreign born: 22.6% (2000); Ancestry (includes multiple ancestries): 30.2% Other groups, 24.5% German, 15.1% Scotch-Irish, 9.4% Welsh, 7.5% United States or American (2000).
Economy: Employment by occupation: 22.2% management, 7.4% professional, 18.5% services, 14.8% sales, 7.4% farming, 7.4% construction, 22.2% production (2000).
Income: Per capita income: $13,879 (2000); Median household income: $41,250 (2000); Poverty rate: 18.9% (2000).
Education: High school graduation rate: 82.9% (2000); College graduation rate: 22.9% (2000).
Housing: Homeownership rate: 75.0% (2000); Median home value: $51,300 (2000); Median rent: $275 per month (2000); Median age of housing: 60+ years (2000).
Transportation: Commute to work: 100.0% car, 0.0% public transportation, 0.0% walk, 0.0% work from home (2000); Travel time to work: 8.7% less than 15 minutes, 39.1% 15 to 30 minutes, 17.4% 30 to 45 minutes, 26.1% 45 to 60 minutes, 8.7% 60 minutes or more (2000)

FREDONIA (city). Covers a land area of 0.153 square miles and a water area of 0 square miles. Located at 41.28° N. Lat.; 91.33° W. Long.
History: Fredonia was considered as a possible territorial capital of Iowa in 1839, but received three less votes than Iowa City.
Population: 251 (2000); Race: 85.2% White, 0.0% Black, 1.6% Asian, 0.0% American Indian and Alaska Native, 42.4% Hispanic of any race, 3.6% two or more races (2000); Density: 1,635.7 persons per square mile (2000); Age: 31.2% under 18, 9.6% over 64 (2000); Marriage status: 20.0% never married, 65.6% now married, 6.7% widowed, 7.8% divorced (2000); Foreign born: 25.6% (2000); Ancestry (includes multiple ancestries): 47.2% Other groups, 10.4% German, 3.2% Irish, 2.8% French (except Basque), 2.4% English (2000).
Economy: Employment by occupation: 8.4% management, 2.8% professional, 23.4% services, 9.3% sales, 0.0% farming, 13.1% construction, 43.0% production (2000).
Income: Per capita income: $15,380 (2000); Median household income: $30,250 (2000); Poverty rate: 6.8% (2000).
Taxes: Total city taxes per capita: $50 (1997); City property taxes per capita: $45 (1997).
Education: High school graduation rate: 69.3% (2000); College graduation rate: 2.7% (2000).
Housing: Homeownership rate: 84.7% (2000); Median home value: $46,800 (2000); Median rent: $354 per month (2000); Median age of housing: 33 years (2000).
Transportation: Commute to work: 100.0% car, 0.0% public transportation, 0.0% walk, 0.0% work from home (2000); Travel time to work: 32.7% less than 15 minutes, 14.0% 15 to 30 minutes, 18.7% 30 to 45 minutes, 15.9% 45 to 60 minutes, 18.7% 60 minutes or more (2000)

GRANDVIEW (city). Covers a land area of 0.194 square miles and a water area of 0 square miles. Located at 41.27° N. Lat.; 91.18° W. Long. Elevation is 700 feet.
History: Grandview was laid out by Alvin Clark and Robert Childers, who chose a spot where the view was grand.
Population: 600 (2000); Race: 94.9% White, 0.0% Black, 1.0% Asian, 0.2% American Indian and Alaska Native, 3.7% Hispanic of any race, 1.5% two or more races (2000); Density: 3,093.0 persons per square mile (2000); Age: 29.3% under 18, 9.2% over 64 (2000); Marriage status: 21.2% never married, 56.6% now married, 6.5% widowed, 15.8% divorced (2000); Foreign born: 1.7% (2000); Ancestry (includes multiple ancestries): 28.7% German, 10.7% Irish, 9.9% United States or American, 7.5% English, 7.3% Other groups (2000).
Economy: Single-family building permits issued: 5 (2001) / 0 (2000); Multi-family building permits issued: 0 (2001) / 0 (2000); Employment by occupation: 2.7% management, 11.0% professional, 21.3% services, 22.3% sales, 0.0% farming, 11.0% construction, 31.6% production (2000).
Income: Per capita income: $17,152 (2000); Median household income: $37,625 (2000); Poverty rate: 10.1% (2000).
Taxes: Total city taxes per capita: $68 (1997); City property taxes per capita: $66 (1997).
Education: High school graduation rate: 80.4% (2000); College graduation rate: 5.8% (2000).
Housing: Homeownership rate: 74.4% (2000); Median home value: $63,900 (2000); Median rent: $313 per month (2000); Median age of housing: 37 years (2000).
Transportation: Commute to work: 95.2% car, 0.0% public transportation, 1.7% walk, 2.7% work from home (2000); Travel time to work: 26.9% less than 15 minutes, 52.3% 15 to 30 minutes, 14.8% 30 to 45 minutes, 4.9% 45 to 60 minutes, 1.1% 60 minutes or more (2000)

LETTS (city). Covers a land area of 0.555 square miles and a water area of 0 square miles. Located at 41.32° N. Lat.; 91.23° W. Long. Elevation is 672 feet.
History: Letts was originally known as Ononwa. As there was another Iowa town called Onawa, mail to the two towns was continually interchanged. About the time it was decided to change the name of Ononwa to end the confusion, the Methodist Church needed a bell and fixtures costing about $600. A townsman, Madison Letts, announced that he would donate $100 if the congregation would supply the rest. In gratitude, presumably, the residents voted to rename the town Lettsville; however, the Post Office Department shortened the name to Letts.
Population: 392 (2000); Race: 95.9% White, 0.0% Black, 0.0% Asian, 0.3% American Indian and Alaska Native, 1.5% Hispanic of any race, 3.6% two or more races (2000); Density: 706.3 persons per square mile (2000); Age: 28.8% under 18, 14.0% over 64 (2000); Marriage status: 17.5% never married, 66.0% now married, 4.4% widowed, 12.1% divorced (2000); Foreign born: 0.5% (2000); Ancestry (includes multiple ancestries): 34.4% German, 16.8% United States or American, 9.4% Irish, 8.9% English, 4.8% Other groups (2000).
Economy: Employment by occupation: 3.5% management, 5.8% professional, 20.8% services, 15.6% sales, 0.0% farming, 11.0% construction, 43.4% production (2000).
Income: Per capita income: $17,285 (2000); Median household income: $37,188 (2000); Poverty rate: 7.1% (2000).
Taxes: Total city taxes per capita: $69 (1997); City property taxes per capita: $69 (1997).
Education: High school graduation rate: 83.3% (2000); College graduation rate: 7.3% (2000).

School District(s)

Louisa-Muscatine Community School District (PK-12)
2000 Enrollment: 964 319-726-3541
Housing: Homeownership rate: 79.3% (2000); Median home value: $64,700 (2000); Median rent: $336 per month (2000); Median age of housing: 60+ years (2000).
Transportation: Commute to work: 93.5% car, 1.2% public transportation, 1.8% walk, 2.4% work from home (2000); Travel time to work: 15.2% less than 15 minutes, 48.2% 15 to 30 minutes, 15.9% 30 to 45 minutes, 7.9% 45 to 60 minutes, 12.8% 60 minutes or more (2000)

MORNING SUN (city). Covers a land area of 0.779 square miles and a water area of 0 square miles. Located at 41.09° N. Lat.; 91.25° W. Long.
History: Morning Sun is believed to have been named by two men returning from an all-night hunt who were inspired by the rising sun.

Population: 872 (2000); Race: 98.6% White, 0.1% Black, 0.8% Asian, 0.0% American Indian and Alaska Native, 1.7% Hispanic of any race, 0.1% two or more races (2000); Density: 1,119.5 persons per square mile (2000); Age: 23.6% under 18, 20.6% over 64 (2000); Marriage status: 20.0% never married, 62.8% now married, 8.2% widowed, 9.0% divorced (2000); Foreign born: 1.1% (2000); Ancestry (includes multiple ancestries): 30.1% German, 11.0% Irish, 10.1% English, 7.1% United States or American, 5.4% Other groups (2000).
Economy: Single-family building permits issued: 1 (2001) / 0 (2000); Multi-family building permits issued: 0 (2001) / 0 (2000); Employment by occupation: 6.6% management, 13.6% professional, 15.6% services, 22.1% sales, 2.9% farming, 8.8% construction, 30.4% production (2000).
Income: Per capita income: $19,041 (2000); Median household income: $37,727 (2000); Poverty rate: 12.2% (2000).
Taxes: Total city taxes per capita: $98 (1997); City property taxes per capita: $94 (1997).
Education: High school graduation rate: 80.8% (2000); College graduation rate: 13.1% (2000).

School District(s)

Morning Sun Community School District (PK-12)
2000 Enrollment: 203 319-868-7701
Housing: Homeownership rate: 79.4% (2000); Median home value: $46,100 (2000); Median rent: $285 per month (2000); Median age of housing: 60+ years (2000).
Newspapers: Morning Sun News-Herald (1 x week)
Transportation: Commute to work: 93.8% car, 0.7% public transportation, 3.7% walk, 1.0% work from home (2000); Travel time to work: 38.8% less than 15 minutes, 26.1% 15 to 30 minutes, 26.1% 30 to 45 minutes, 5.0% 45 to 60 minutes, 4.0% 60 minutes or more (2000)

OAKVILLE (city). Covers a land area of 0.420 square miles and a water area of 0.005 square miles. Located at 41.09° N. Lat.; 91.04° W. Long. Elevation is 543 feet.
History: Allen Green came to Oakville in 1911 and bought many hundreds of acres of bottomland, most of it tillable. The marshland gave him a chance to study and photograph wildlife. He built a steel mesh fence around a 100-acre area he used as a refuge, and wintered ducks there on corn from his farm.
Population: 439 (2000); Race: 99.4% White, 0.0% Black, 0.0% Asian, 0.0% American Indian and Alaska Native, 0.6% Hispanic of any race, 0.0% two or more races (2000); Density: 1,044.8 persons per square mile (2000); Age: 31.4% under 18, 14.1% over 64 (2000); Marriage status: 13.2% never married, 60.5% now married, 7.8% widowed, 18.6% divorced (2000); Foreign born: 0.0% (2000); Ancestry (includes multiple ancestries): 22.4% German, 13.0% United States or American, 10.5% Irish, 6.8% Other groups, 4.9% English (2000).
Economy: Single-family building permits issued: 1 (2001) / 0 (2000); Multi-family building permits issued: 0 (2001) / 0 (2000); Employment by occupation: 7.1% management, 6.1% professional, 12.2% services, 14.2% sales, 2.0% farming, 19.3% construction, 39.1% production (2000).
Income: Per capita income: $13,276 (2000); Median household income: $29,018 (2000); Poverty rate: 7.7% (2000).
Taxes: Total city taxes per capita: $129 (1997); City property taxes per capita: $126 (1997).
Education: High school graduation rate: 75.7% (2000); College graduation rate: 6.6% (2000).
Housing: Homeownership rate: 77.7% (2000); Median home value: $43,500 (2000); Median rent: $237 per month (2000); Median age of housing: 46 years (2000).
Transportation: Commute to work: 95.4% car, 0.0% public transportation, 1.0% walk, 3.6% work from home (2000); Travel time to work: 16.4% less than 15 minutes, 35.4% 15 to 30 minutes, 30.2% 30 to 45 minutes, 7.4% 45 to 60 minutes, 10.6% 60 minutes or more (2000)

WAPELLO (city). Covers a land area of 1.258 square miles and a water area of 0.046 square miles. Located at 41.18° N. Lat.; 91.18° W. Long. Elevation is 588 feet.
History: Wapello was one of the four specially chartered towns in Iowa, the State legislature having issued its charter in 1856. It was named for Chief Wapello.
Population: 2,124 (2000); Race: 97.2% White, 0.0% Black, 0.2% Asian, 0.0% American Indian and Alaska Native, 7.1% Hispanic of any race, 0.2% two or more races (2000); Density: 1,688.3 persons per square mile (2000); Age: 25.2% under 18, 17.9% over 64 (2000); Marriage status: 19.3% never married, 60.7% now married, 9.9% widowed, 10.1% divorced (2000); Foreign born: 2.5% (2000); Ancestry (includes multiple ancestries): 29.6% German, 14.4% Irish, 12.4% Other groups, 10.4% English, 8.6% United States or American (2000).
Economy: Single-family building permits issued: 0 (2001) / 6 (2000); Multi-family building permits issued: 0 (2001) / 0 (2000); Employment by occupation: 8.6% management, 17.8% professional, 11.1% services, 20.9% sales, 0.8% farming, 14.5% construction, 26.2% production (2000).
Income: Per capita income: $17,947 (2000); Median household income: $37,556 (2000); Poverty rate: 14.3% (2000).
Taxes: Total city taxes per capita: $143 (1997); City property taxes per capita: $140 (1997).
Education: High school graduation rate: 79.4% (2000); College graduation rate: 14.0% (2000).

School District(s)

Wapello Community School District (KG-12)
2000 Enrollment: 744 319-523-3641
Housing: Homeownership rate: 75.3% (2000); Median home value: $66,800 (2000); Median rent: $354 per month (2000); Median age of housing: 52 years (2000).
Newspapers: Wapello Republican (1 x week); Iowa Valley Messenger (1 x week)
Transportation: Commute to work: 93.8% car, 0.0% public transportation, 2.9% walk, 3.3% work from home (2000); Travel time to work: 40.4% less than 15 minutes, 23.8% 15 to 30 minutes, 26.5% 30 to 45 minutes, 7.5% 45 to 60 minutes, 1.9% 60 minutes or more (2000)

Lucas County

Located in southern Iowa; prairie area, drained by the Chariton River and Whitebreast Creek. Covers a land area of 430.50 square miles, a water area of 3.60 square miles, and is located in the Central Time Zone. The county government was organized in 1846. County seat is Chariton.

Weather Station: Chariton 1 E — Elevation: 938 feet

	Jan	Feb	Mar	Apr	May	Jun	Jul	Aug	Sep	Oct	Nov	Dec
High	31	37	49	63	73	82	87	85	77	65	49	36
Low	11	16	27	38	49	58	63	61	52	40	29	17
Precip	0.9	1.1	2.3	3.6	4.7	4.5	4.8	4.2	4.4	3.0	2.4	1.2
Snow	7.3	6.1	4.0	2.0	tr	0.0	0.0	0.0	0.0	0.3	2.1	4.7

High and Low temperatures in degrees Fahrenheit; Precipitation and Snow in inches

Population: 9,422 (2000); Race: 98.5% White, 0.2% Black, 0.5% Asian, 0.1% American Indian and Alaska Native, 0.5% Hispanic of any race, 0.6% two or more races (2000); Density: 21.9 persons per square mile (2000); Age: 25.4% under 18, 19.3% over 64 (2000).
Religion: Five largest groups: 11.2% The United Methodist Church, 6.8% Catholic Church, 5.9% American Baptist Churches in the USA, 4.2% Evangelical Lutheran Church in America, 4.1% Christian Church (Disciples of Christ) (2000).
Economy: Unemployment rate: 4.3% (11/2002); Total civilian labor force: 4,452 (11/2002); Leading industries: 15.2% health care and social assistance; 14.5% retail trade; 9.5% manufacturing (2000); Companies that employ more than 1,000 persons: 0 (2000); Companies that employ more than 100 persons: 6 (2000); Farms: 706 totaling 227,160 acres (1997); Minority business ownership rate: 0.0% (1997); Women business ownership rate: 32.5% (1997); Retail sales per capita: $5,514 (1997). Single-family building permits issued: 6 (2001) / 1 (2000); Multi-family building permits issued: 0 (2001) / 0 (2000).
Income: Per capita income: $15,341 (2000); Median household income: $30,876 (2000); Poverty rate: 13.7% (2000); Bankruptcy rate: 2.52% (2001).
Taxes: Total county taxes per capita: $289 (2000); County property taxes per capita: $283 (2000).
Education: High school graduation rate: 79.1% (2000); College graduation rate: 11.1% (2000).
Housing: Homeownership rate: 78.4% (2000); Median home value: $50,900 (2000); Median rent: $260 per month (2000); Median age of housing: 52 years (2000).
Health: Birth rate: 122.1 per 10,000 population (1998); Age adjusted death rate: 81.8 per 10,000 population (1999); Age adjusted cancer mortality rate: 220.2 deaths per 100,000 population (1999). Number of physicians: 3.2 per 10,000 population (1999); Number of hospital beds: 23.3 per 10,000 population (1999).
Elections: 2000 Presidential election results: 45.0% Gore, 52.6% Bush, 1.5% Nader, 0.4% Buchanan
National and State Parks: Colyn State Wildlife Area; Rathbun State Wildlife Area; Red Haw State Park; Stephens State Forest
Additional Information Contacts

Lucas County Government Offices 641-774-2018
Chariton Chamber of Commerce 641-774-4059

Lucas County Communities

CHARITON (city). Covers a land area of 3.693 square miles and a water area of 0 square miles. Located at 41.01° N. Lat.; 93.30° W. Long. Elevation is 1,042 feet.
History: Chariton was first called Polk, then Chariton Point, and finally Chariton. Pioneers believed the name to be of Indian origin, signifying "a country rich with honey."
Population: 4,573 (2000); Race: 99.0% White, 0.0% Black, 0.6% Asian, 0.0% American Indian and Alaska Native, 0.7% Hispanic of any race, 0.3% two or more races (2000); Density: 1,238.2 persons per square mile (2000); Age: 24.9% under 18, 21.5% over 64 (2000); Marriage status: 19.6% never married, 56.0% now married, 12.8% widowed, 11.6% divorced (2000); Foreign born: 0.6% (2000); Ancestry (includes multiple ancestries): 24.3% German, 16.8% English, 15.2% Irish, 8.5% United States or American, 4.7% Other groups (2000).
Economy: Single-family building permits issued: 6 (2001) / 1 (2000); Multi-family building permits issued: 0 (2001) / 0 (2000); Employment by occupation: 7.1% management, 12.8% professional, 19.2% services, 23.8% sales, 1.4% farming, 9.3% construction, 26.4% production (2000).
Income: Per capita income: $15,553 (2000); Median household income: $27,844 (2000); Poverty rate: 12.7% (2000).
Taxes: Total city taxes per capita: $256 (1997); City property taxes per capita: $249 (1997).
Education: High school graduation rate: 78.2% (2000); College graduation rate: 12.3% (2000).

School District(s)

Chariton Community School District (KG-12)
2000 Enrollment: 1,393 641-774-5967
Housing: Homeownership rate: 71.6% (2000); Median home value: $50,400 (2000); Median rent: $265 per month (2000); Median age of housing: 57 years (2000).
Hospitals: Lucas County Health Center (56 beds)
Safety: Violent crime rate: 17.5 per 10,000 population; Property crime rate: 468.5 per 10,000 population (2001).
Newspapers: Chariton Herald-Patriot (2 x week); Chariton Leader (2 x week); Pennysaver (1 x week); Chariton Shopper (1 x week)
Transportation: Commute to work: 91.5% car, 0.3% public transportation, 4.6% walk, 2.1% work from home (2000); Travel time to work: 70.3% less than 15 minutes, 6.3% 15 to 30 minutes, 6.9% 30 to 45 minutes, 2.7% 45 to 60 minutes, 13.7% 60 minutes or more (2000)
Additional Information Contacts
Chariton Chamber of Commerce 641-774-4059

DERBY (city). Covers a land area of 0.263 square miles and a water area of 0 square miles. Located at 40.93° N. Lat.; 93.45° W. Long. Elevation is 1,094 feet.
History: The name of Derby has its roots in England. It may have been named for Derbyshire, England, or after an English family.
Population: 131 (2000); Race: 100.0% White, 0.0% Black, 0.0% Asian, 0.0% American Indian and Alaska Native, 0.0% Hispanic of any race, 0.0% two or more races (2000); Density: 497.6 persons per square mile (2000); Age: 27.3% under 18, 15.9% over 64 (2000); Marriage status: 20.2% never married, 58.7% now married, 9.6% widowed, 11.5% divorced (2000); Foreign born: 0.0% (2000); Ancestry (includes multiple ancestries): 36.4% United States or American, 18.2% Irish, 16.7% English, 5.3% Dutch, 4.5% Other groups (2000).
Economy: Employment by occupation: 0.0% management, 1.9% professional, 11.3% services, 22.6% sales, 0.0% farming, 11.3% construction, 52.8% production (2000).
Income: Per capita income: $10,605 (2000); Median household income: $26,667 (2000); Poverty rate: 4.5% (2000).
Taxes: Total city taxes per capita: $92 (2000); City property taxes per capita: $0 (2000).
Education: High school graduation rate: 69.0% (2000); College graduation rate: 2.4% (2000).
Housing: Homeownership rate: 94.4% (2000); Median home value: $28,800 (2000); Median rent: $225 per month (2000); Median age of housing: 60+ years (2000).
Transportation: Commute to work: 90.6% car, 0.0% public transportation, 0.0% walk, 0.0% work from home (2000); Travel time to work: 20.8% less than 15 minutes, 20.8% 15 to 30 minutes, 28.3% 30 to 45 minutes, 0.0% 45 to 60 minutes, 30.2% 60 minutes or more (2000)

LUCAS (city). Covers a land area of 0.967 square miles and a water area of 0.007 square miles. Located at 41.03° N. Lat.; 93.46° W. Long.
History: Lucas was named for Robert Lucas, first Territorial Governor of Iowa (1838-1841). John L. Lewis, president of the United Mine Workers of America, was born here.
Population: 243 (2000); Race: 99.2% White, 0.0% Black, 0.0% Asian, 0.0% American Indian and Alaska Native, 0.0% Hispanic of any race, 0.8% two or more races (2000); Density: 251.4 persons per square mile (2000); Age: 28.4% under 18, 7.2% over 64 (2000); Marriage status: 18.2% never married, 59.1% now married, 9.4% widowed, 13.3% divorced (2000); Foreign born: 0.0% (2000); Ancestry (includes multiple ancestries): 17.8% German, 15.7% United States or American, 12.3% Irish, 8.1% English, 6.8% Other groups (2000).
Economy: Employment by occupation: 1.8% management, 8.8% professional, 8.8% services, 37.7% sales, 0.0% farming, 9.6% construction, 33.3% production (2000).
Income: Per capita income: $13,145 (2000); Median household income: $31,250 (2000); Poverty rate: 10.6% (2000).
Taxes: Total city taxes per capita: $70 (1997); City property taxes per capita: $70 (1997).
Education: High school graduation rate: 76.1% (2000); College graduation rate: 5.8% (2000).
Housing: Homeownership rate: 89.6% (2000); Median home value: $20,000 (2000); Median rent: $188 per month (2000); Median age of housing: 60+ years (2000).
Transportation: Commute to work: 91.9% car, 0.0% public transportation, 3.6% walk, 0.9% work from home (2000); Travel time to work: 28.2% less than 15 minutes, 36.4% 15 to 30 minutes, 16.4% 30 to 45 minutes, 2.7% 45 to 60 minutes, 16.4% 60 minutes or more (2000)

RUSSELL (city). Covers a land area of 1.036 square miles and a water area of <.001 square miles. Located at 40.98° N. Lat.; 93.19° W. Long.
History: Russell was named for H. S. Russell who platted the town and was also trustee of the land.
Population: 559 (2000); Race: 98.1% White, 0.0% Black, 1.6% Asian, 0.0% American Indian and Alaska Native, 0.3% Hispanic of any race, 0.3% two or more races (2000); Density: 539.7 persons per square mile (2000); Age: 31.0% under 18, 19.1% over 64 (2000); Marriage status: 26.1% never married, 50.8% now married, 10.9% widowed, 12.2% divorced (2000); Foreign born: 1.6% (2000); Ancestry (includes multiple ancestries): 23.1% German, 11.9% Irish, 10.3% English, 9.8% United States or American, 7.9% Other groups (2000).
Economy: Employment by occupation: 4.5% management, 11.0% professional, 17.6% services, 24.1% sales, 0.0% farming, 17.6% construction, 25.3% production (2000).
Income: Per capita income: $13,093 (2000); Median household income: $28,125 (2000); Poverty rate: 23.6% (2000).
Taxes: Total city taxes per capita: $89 (1997); City property taxes per capita: $89 (1997).
Education: High school graduation rate: 80.0% (2000); College graduation rate: 6.1% (2000).

School District(s)

Russell Community School District (PK-12)
2000 Enrollment: 180 641-535-2404
Housing: Homeownership rate: 78.0% (2000); Median home value: $33,900 (2000); Median rent: $241 per month (2000); Median age of housing: 53 years (2000).
Transportation: Commute to work: 90.4% car, 0.8% public transportation, 2.5% walk, 4.2% work from home (2000); Travel time to work: 39.6% less than 15 minutes, 38.3% 15 to 30 minutes, 6.5% 30 to 45 minutes, 11.3% 45 to 60 minutes, 4.3% 60 minutes or more (2000)

WILLIAMSON (city). Aka Gunwald. Covers a land area of 0.319 square miles and a water area of 0 square miles. Located at 41.09° N. Lat.; 93.25° W. Long. Elevation is 1,023 feet.
History: Williamson was named for George E. Williamson who owned the land on which the town was laid out. He also donated land for the Chicago, Rock Island & Pacific Railroad.
Population: 163 (2000); Race: 96.5% White, 0.0% Black, 0.0% Asian, 0.0% American Indian and Alaska Native, 2.3% Hispanic of any race, 3.5% two or more races (2000); Density: 510.3 persons per square mile (2000); Age: 28.9% under 18, 18.5% over 64 (2000); Marriage status: 28.9% never married, 43.8% now married, 7.0% widowed, 20.3% divorced (2000);

Foreign born: 0.0% (2000); Ancestry (includes multiple ancestries): 22.5% German, 14.5% Irish, 5.2% Italian, 5.2% English, 4.0% Swedish (2000).
Economy: Single-family building permits issued: 0 (2001) / 0 (2000); Multi-family building permits issued: 0 (2001) / 0 (2000); Employment by occupation: 16.1% management, 8.9% professional, 19.6% services, 0.0% sales, 0.0% farming, 14.3% construction, 41.1% production (2000).
Income: Per capita income: $10,456 (2000); Median household income: $20,000 (2000); Poverty rate: 26.2% (2000).
Taxes: Total city taxes per capita: $64 (1997); City property taxes per capita: $64 (1997).
Education: High school graduation rate: 76.4% (2000); College graduation rate: 1.8% (2000).
Housing: Homeownership rate: 77.8% (2000); Median home value: $18,100 (2000); Median rent: $238 per month (2000); Median age of housing: 60+ years (2000).
Transportation: Commute to work: 89.3% car, 0.0% public transportation, 0.0% walk, 0.0% work from home (2000); Travel time to work: 23.2% less than 15 minutes, 25.0% 15 to 30 minutes, 32.1% 30 to 45 minutes, 3.6% 45 to 60 minutes, 16.1% 60 minutes or more (2000)

Lyon County

Located in northwestern Iowa; bounded on the north by Minnesota, and on the west by the Big Sioux River and the South Dakota border; prairie area, drained by the Rock and Little Rock Rivers. Covers a land area of 587.50 square miles, a water area of 0.10 square miles, and is located in the Central Time Zone. The county government was organized in 1851. County seat is Rock Rapids.

Weather Station: Rock Rapids Elevation: 1,348 feet

	Jan	Feb	Mar	Apr	May	Jun	Jul	Aug	Sep	Oct	Nov	Dec
High	24	31	42	59	72	81	86	83	75	62	42	29
Low	3	10	22	34	46	57	61	58	48	35	22	9
Precip	0.5	0.5	1.9	2.6	3.2	4.3	3.5	3.8	2.5	2.0	1.6	0.7
Snow	5.7	4.3	6.4	1.6	tr	0.0	0.0	0.0	tr	0.6	4.6	5.3

High and Low temperatures in degrees Fahrenheit; Precipitation and Snow in inches

Population: 11,763 (2000); Race: 99.2% White, 0.2% Black, 0.1% Asian, 0.0% American Indian and Alaska Native, 0.3% Hispanic of any race, 0.2% two or more races (2000); Density: 20.0 persons per square mile (2000); Age: 28.1% under 18, 18.7% over 64 (2000).
Religion: Five largest groups: 17.2% Reformed Church in America, 14.7% Evangelical Lutheran Church in America, 12.9% Catholic Church, 8.0% Christian Reformed Church in North America, 7.4% Presbyterian Church (U.S.A.) (2000).
Economy: Unemployment rate: 4.0% (11/2002); Total civilian labor force: 5,383 (11/2002); Leading industries: 18.9% retail trade; 16.4% health care and social assistance; 16.2% manufacturing (2000); Companies that employ more than 1,000 persons: 0 (2000); Companies that employ more than 100 persons: 2 (2000); Farms: 1,149 totaling 348,492 acres (1997); Minority business ownership rate: 0.0% (1997); Women business ownership rate: 17.6% (1997); Retail sales per capita: $5,332 (1997). Single-family building permits issued: 21 (2001) / 21 (2000); Multi-family building permits issued: 4 (2001) / 0 (2000).
Income: Per capita income: $16,081 (2000); Median household income: $36,878 (2000); Poverty rate: 7.0% (2000); Bankruptcy rate: 1.41% (2001).
Taxes: Total county taxes per capita: $200 (2000); County property taxes per capita: $197 (2000).
Education: High school graduation rate: 78.7% (2000); College graduation rate: 14.2% (2000).
Housing: Homeownership rate: 81.7% (2000); Median home value: $64,000 (2000); Median rent: $252 per month (2000); Median age of housing: 52 years (2000).
Health: Birth rate: 130.9 per 10,000 population (1998); Age adjusted death rate: 73.7 per 10,000 population (1999); Age adjusted cancer mortality rate: 163.1 deaths per 100,000 population (1999). Number of physicians: 2.6 per 10,000 population (1999); Number of hospital beds: 13.6 per 10,000 population (1999).
Elections: 2000 Presidential election results: 24.6% Gore, 73.3% Bush, 1.3% Nader, 0.5% Buchanan
National and State Parks: Gitchie Manitou State Preserve
Additional Information Contacts
Lyon County Government Offices 712-472-3713

Lyon County Communities

ALVORD (city). Covers a land area of 0.273 square miles and a water area of 0 square miles. Located at 43.34° N. Lat.; 96.30° W. Long. Elevation is 1,335 feet.
History: Alvord was founded by W. B. Park. The town was originally known as Park, but due to confusion with the names of other towns, it was changed to Alvord, named after W. B. Park's brother-in-law.
Population: 187 (2000); Race: 100.0% White, 0.0% Black, 0.0% Asian, 0.0% American Indian and Alaska Native, 0.0% Hispanic of any race, 0.0% two or more races (2000); Density: 684.8 persons per square mile (2000); Age: 25.1% under 18, 11.8% over 64 (2000); Marriage status: 18.1% never married, 75.6% now married, 5.0% widowed, 1.3% divorced (2000); Foreign born: 0.0% (2000); Ancestry (includes multiple ancestries): 46.8% Dutch, 37.4% German, 8.4% United States or American, 3.4% Norwegian, 2.5% Scandinavian (2000).
Economy: Employment by occupation: 7.8% management, 3.9% professional, 7.8% services, 22.7% sales, 0.0% farming, 21.1% construction, 36.7% production (2000).
Income: Per capita income: $17,300 (2000); Median household income: $38,750 (2000); Poverty rate: 2.0% (2000).
Taxes: Total city taxes per capita: $84 (1997); City property taxes per capita: $84 (1997).
Education: High school graduation rate: 83.9% (2000); College graduation rate: 8.8% (2000).
Housing: Homeownership rate: 90.9% (2000); Median home value: $39,300 (2000); Median rent: $275 per month (2000); Median age of housing: 60+ years (2000).
Transportation: Commute to work: 83.6% car, 0.0% public transportation, 6.3% walk, 5.5% work from home (2000); Travel time to work: 26.4% less than 15 minutes, 34.7% 15 to 30 minutes, 26.4% 30 to 45 minutes, 6.6% 45 to 60 minutes, 5.8% 60 minutes or more (2000)

DOON (city). Covers a land area of 0.577 square miles and a water area of 0 square miles. Located at 43.27° N. Lat.; 96.23° W. Long. Elevation is 1,300 feet.
History: H.D. Rice, who settled in this area in 1868, chose the name of Doon from the Robert Burns poem, "Bonnie Doon."
Population: 533 (2000); Race: 99.6% White, 0.0% Black, 0.0% Asian, 0.4% American Indian and Alaska Native, 0.0% Hispanic of any race, 0.0% two or more races (2000); Density: 924.1 persons per square mile (2000); Age: 30.0% under 18, 12.8% over 64 (2000); Marriage status: 22.9% never married, 66.0% now married, 7.0% widowed, 4.1% divorced (2000); Foreign born: 1.7% (2000); Ancestry (includes multiple ancestries): 75.2% Dutch, 27.5% German, 3.9% Norwegian, 1.7% Other groups, 1.5% United States or American (2000).
Economy: Single-family building permits issued: 2 (2001) / 1 (2000); Multi-family building permits issued: 0 (2001) / 0 (2000); Employment by occupation: 7.0% management, 8.0% professional, 16.6% services, 14.0% sales, 3.0% farming, 15.6% construction, 35.9% production (2000).
Income: Per capita income: $14,698 (2000); Median household income: $33,281 (2000); Poverty rate: 7.0% (2000).
Taxes: Total city taxes per capita: $131 (1997); City property taxes per capita: $119 (1997).
Education: High school graduation rate: 75.2% (2000); College graduation rate: 8.8% (2000).
Housing: Homeownership rate: 85.0% (2000); Median home value: $58,500 (2000); Median rent: $241 per month (2000); Median age of housing: 49 years (2000).
Newspapers: Doon Press (1 x week)
Transportation: Commute to work: 84.5% car, 0.7% public transportation, 9.5% walk, 4.7% work from home (2000); Travel time to work: 46.8% less than 15 minutes, 35.5% 15 to 30 minutes, 6.7% 30 to 45 minutes, 7.4% 45 to 60 minutes, 3.5% 60 minutes or more (2000)

GEORGE (city). Covers a land area of 2.391 square miles and a water area of 0 square miles. Located at 43.34° N. Lat.; 96.00° W. Long. Elevation is 1,377 feet.
History: George was established in 1887 as a station for the Illinois Central Railroad. It was named for the son of a railroad employee.
Population: 1,051 (2000); Race: 99.2% White, 0.0% Black, 0.0% Asian, 0.0% American Indian and Alaska Native, 0.0% Hispanic of any race, 0.4% two or more races (2000); Density: 439.5 persons per square mile (2000); Age: 18.2% under 18, 35.7% over 64 (2000); Marriage status: 14.1% never married, 63.7% now married, 18.4% widowed, 3.8% divorced (2000);

Foreign born: 0.5% (2000); Ancestry (includes multiple ancestries): 64.9% German, 21.3% Dutch, 5.5% Norwegian, 4.4% Irish, 4.3% English (2000).
Economy: Single-family building permits issued: 1 (2001) / 0 (2000); Multi-family building permits issued: 0 (2001) / 0 (2000); Employment by occupation: 10.4% management, 15.2% professional, 17.2% services, 19.4% sales, 0.4% farming, 6.8% construction, 30.6% production (2000).
Income: Per capita income: $16,733 (2000); Median household income: $30,375 (2000); Poverty rate: 8.2% (2000).
Taxes: Total city taxes per capita: $174 (1997); City property taxes per capita: $160 (1997).
Education: High school graduation rate: 68.7% (2000); College graduation rate: 16.1% (2000).

School District(s)

George Community School District (KG-12)
2000 Enrollment: 317 712-475-3311
Housing: Homeownership rate: 79.7% (2000); Median home value: $49,900 (2000); Median rent: $237 per month (2000); Median age of housing: 51 years (2000).
Newspapers: Lyon County News (1 x week)
Transportation: Commute to work: 88.0% car, 0.4% public transportation, 7.6% walk, 4.0% work from home (2000); Travel time to work: 56.4% less than 15 minutes, 28.1% 15 to 30 minutes, 9.7% 30 to 45 minutes, 2.8% 45 to 60 minutes, 3.0% 60 minutes or more (2000)

INWOOD (city). Covers a land area of 1.330 square miles and a water area of 0 square miles. Located at 43.30° N. Lat.; 96.43° W. Long. Elevation is 1,473 feet.
History: Inwood was known as Warren when settled in 1883, and was later called Pennington. When Jacob Rogers and his wife platted the town in 1891 they called it by its present name.
Population: 875 (2000); Race: 98.3% White, 0.5% Black, 0.0% Asian, 0.0% American Indian and Alaska Native, 0.8% Hispanic of any race, 0.9% two or more races (2000); Density: 658.0 persons per square mile (2000); Age: 25.8% under 18, 25.0% over 64 (2000); Marriage status: 20.7% never married, 62.2% now married, 12.9% widowed, 4.1% divorced (2000); Foreign born: 1.3% (2000); Ancestry (includes multiple ancestries): 36.3% Dutch, 26.9% German, 13.7% Norwegian, 9.0% Irish, 4.0% Danish (2000).
Economy: Single-family building permits issued: 4 (2001) / 4 (2000); Multi-family building permits issued: 0 (2001) / 0 (2000); Employment by occupation: 9.5% management, 24.6% professional, 13.6% services, 25.1% sales, 1.3% farming, 13.3% construction, 12.6% production (2000).
Income: Per capita income: $15,651 (2000); Median household income: $33,889 (2000); Poverty rate: 7.9% (2000).
Taxes: Total city taxes per capita: $199 (1997); City property taxes per capita: $186 (1997).
Education: High school graduation rate: 76.4% (2000); College graduation rate: 15.6% (2000).

School District(s)

West Lyon Community School District (KG-12)
2000 Enrollment: 803 712-753-4917
Housing: Homeownership rate: 81.9% (2000); Median home value: $71,400 (2000); Median rent: $250 per month (2000); Median age of housing: 42 years (2000).
Newspapers: West Lyon Herald (1 x week)
Transportation: Commute to work: 90.2% car, 1.0% public transportation, 6.0% walk, 1.5% work from home (2000); Travel time to work: 44.6% less than 15 minutes, 21.4% 15 to 30 minutes, 22.2% 30 to 45 minutes, 8.2% 45 to 60 minutes, 3.6% 60 minutes or more (2000)

LARCHWOOD (city). Covers a land area of 0.970 square miles and a water area of 0 square miles. Located at 43.45° N. Lat.; 96.43° W. Long. Elevation is 1,462 feet.
History: Larchwood was so named because of the many larches planted in the vicinity by J. W. Fell, who founded the community in 1870. He planted more than 100,000 fruit and forest trees on land adjoining the town plat.
Population: 788 (2000); Race: 98.7% White, 0.0% Black, 0.0% Asian, 0.3% American Indian and Alaska Native, 0.0% Hispanic of any race, 1.0% two or more races (2000); Density: 812.1 persons per square mile (2000); Age: 24.8% under 18, 18.9% over 64 (2000); Marriage status: 20.2% never married, 66.2% now married, 8.4% widowed, 5.1% divorced (2000); Foreign born: 1.1% (2000); Ancestry (includes multiple ancestries): 51.3% German, 21.8% Dutch, 17.3% Norwegian, 15.7% Irish, 5.3% Swedish (2000).
Economy: Single-family building permits issued: 2 (2001) / 4 (2000); Multi-family building permits issued: 4 (2001) / 0 (2000); Employment by occupation: 11.1% management, 14.1% professional, 12.7% services, 30.9% sales, 0.7% farming, 17.1% construction, 13.4% production (2000).
Income: Per capita income: $21,092 (2000); Median household income: $42,250 (2000); Poverty rate: 2.0% (2000).
Taxes: Total city taxes per capita: $91 (1997); City property taxes per capita: $86 (1997).
Education: High school graduation rate: 84.4% (2000); College graduation rate: 11.5% (2000).
Housing: Homeownership rate: 84.9% (2000); Median home value: $79,900 (2000); Median rent: $346 per month (2000); Median age of housing: 33 years (2000).
Transportation: Commute to work: 95.3% car, 0.0% public transportation, 0.9% walk, 2.8% work from home (2000); Travel time to work: 41.8% less than 15 minutes, 22.6% 15 to 30 minutes, 33.1% 30 to 45 minutes, 1.9% 45 to 60 minutes, 0.5% 60 minutes or more (2000)

LESTER (city). Covers a land area of 1.815 square miles and a water area of 0 square miles. Located at 43.43° N. Lat.; 96.33° W. Long.
Population: 251 (2000); Race: 100.0% White, 0.0% Black, 0.0% Asian, 0.0% American Indian and Alaska Native, 0.0% Hispanic of any race, 0.0% two or more races (2000); Density: 138.3 persons per square mile (2000); Age: 16.6% under 18, 23.7% over 64 (2000); Marriage status: 28.5% never married, 62.8% now married, 5.8% widowed, 2.9% divorced (2000); Foreign born: 0.0% (2000); Ancestry (includes multiple ancestries): 44.4% German, 34.4% Dutch, 16.2% Swiss, 11.2% Norwegian, 5.8% Swedish (2000).
Economy: Livestock, grain. Employment by occupation: 9.2% management, 12.8% professional, 17.7% services, 25.5% sales, 0.7% farming, 7.1% construction, 27.0% production (2000).
Income: Per capita income: $17,410 (2000); Median household income: $38,750 (2000); Poverty rate: 4.3% (2000).
Taxes: Total city taxes per capita: $117 (1997); City property taxes per capita: $101 (1997).
Education: High school graduation rate: 76.3% (2000); College graduation rate: 5.0% (2000).
Housing: Homeownership rate: 90.3% (2000); Median home value: $76,700 (2000); Median rent: $125 per month (2000); Median age of housing: 47 years (2000).
Transportation: Commute to work: 87.1% car, 0.0% public transportation, 7.9% walk, 3.6% work from home (2000); Travel time to work: 34.3% less than 15 minutes, 13.4% 15 to 30 minutes, 38.1% 30 to 45 minutes, 11.2% 45 to 60 minutes, 3.0% 60 minutes or more (2000)

LITTLE ROCK (city). Covers a land area of 0.779 square miles and a water area of 0 square miles. Located at 43.44° N. Lat.; 95.88° W. Long.
History: Little Rock was named by the Burlington, Cedar Rapids & Northern Railroad because of its location on the Little Rock River. The town was platted in 1884.
Population: 489 (2000); Race: 100.0% White, 0.0% Black, 0.0% Asian, 0.0% American Indian and Alaska Native, 0.0% Hispanic of any race, 0.0% two or more races (2000); Density: 627.9 persons per square mile (2000); Age: 26.3% under 18, 23.8% over 64 (2000); Marriage status: 16.5% never married, 70.6% now married, 10.5% widowed, 2.4% divorced (2000); Foreign born: 1.2% (2000); Ancestry (includes multiple ancestries): 59.8% German, 19.2% Dutch, 8.3% Irish, 5.0% English, 4.8% United States or American (2000).
Economy: Single-family building permits issued: 1 (2001) / 1 (2000); Multi-family building permits issued: 0 (2001) / 0 (2000); Employment by occupation: 8.1% management, 10.9% professional, 14.5% services, 21.3% sales, 0.0% farming, 12.7% construction, 32.6% production (2000).
Income: Per capita income: $15,514 (2000); Median household income: $31,667 (2000); Poverty rate: 9.6% (2000).
Taxes: Total city taxes per capita: $138 (1997); City property taxes per capita: $125 (1997).
Education: High school graduation rate: 70.0% (2000); College graduation rate: 11.7% (2000).

School District(s)

Little Rock Community School District (KG-12)
2000 Enrollment: 183 712-479-2771
Housing: Homeownership rate: 83.3% (2000); Median home value: $33,500 (2000); Median rent: $158 per month (2000); Median age of housing: 60+ years (2000).
Newspapers: Little Rock Free Lance (1 x week)
Transportation: Commute to work: 93.5% car, 0.0% public transportation, 6.5% walk, 0.0% work from home (2000); Travel time to work: 25.2% less than 15 minutes, 54.7% 15 to 30 minutes, 13.6% 30 to 45 minutes, 2.8% 45 to 60 minutes, 3.7% 60 minutes or more (2000)

ROCK RAPIDS (city). Covers a land area of 3.957 square miles and a water area of 0 square miles. Located at 43.42° N. Lat.; 96.16° W. Long. Elevation is 1,345 feet.
History: Rock Rapids takes its name from the rapids in the Rock River.
Population: 2,573 (2000); Race: 99.5% White, 0.2% Black, 0.3% Asian, 0.0% American Indian and Alaska Native, 0.0% Hispanic of any race, 0.0% two or more races (2000); Density: 650.2 persons per square mile (2000); Age: 22.8% under 18, 26.7% over 64 (2000); Marriage status: 17.7% never married, 64.8% now married, 12.8% widowed, 4.6% divorced (2000); Foreign born: 0.7% (2000); Ancestry (includes multiple ancestries): 46.8% German, 35.3% Dutch, 7.0% Irish, 6.9% Norwegian, 5.3% English (2000).
Economy: Single-family building permits issued: 3 (2001) / 6 (2000); Multi-family building permits issued: 0 (2001) / 0 (2000); Employment by occupation: 12.6% management, 18.0% professional, 13.4% services, 28.1% sales, 2.1% farming, 8.9% construction, 16.9% production (2000).
Income: Per capita income: $18,035 (2000); Median household income: $35,135 (2000); Poverty rate: 7.5% (2000).
Taxes: Total city taxes per capita: $243 (1997); City property taxes per capita: $229 (1997).
Education: High school graduation rate: 76.4% (2000); College graduation rate: 19.7% (2000).

School District(s)

Central Lyon Community School District (KG-12)
2000 Enrollment: 667 712-472-2664

Housing: Homeownership rate: 78.8% (2000); Median home value: $65,000 (2000); Median rent: $245 per month (2000); Median age of housing: 46 years (2000).
Hospitals: Merrill Pioneer Community Hospital (25 beds)
Safety: Violent crime rate: 3.9 per 10,000 population; Property crime rate: 182.9 per 10,000 population (2001).
Newspapers: The Lyon County Reporter (1 x week)
Transportation: Commute to work: 91.3% car, 0.8% public transportation, 4.2% walk, 3.4% work from home (2000); Travel time to work: 64.9% less than 15 minutes, 8.3% 15 to 30 minutes, 11.5% 30 to 45 minutes, 13.5% 45 to 60 minutes, 1.8% 60 minutes or more (2000)

Madison County

Located in south central Iowa; prairie area, drained by the North and Middle Rivers. Covers a land area of 561.10 square miles, a water area of 1.20 square miles, and is located in the Central Time Zone. The county government was organized in 1844. County seat is Winterset.

Weather Station: Winterset 2 NNW — Elevation: 1,069 feet

	Jan	Feb	Mar	Apr	May	Jun	Jul	Aug	Sep	Oct	Nov	Dec
High	30	36	48	62	73	82	86	84	76	64	47	35
Low	10	16	27	38	49	58	63	61	52	41	28	17
Precip	1.0	1.0	2.2	3.6	4.3	4.5	4.1	4.3	3.9	2.6	2.2	1.1
Snow	7.5	7.2	3.4	1.5	tr	0.0	0.0	0.0	0.0	0.4	3.0	5.8

High and Low temperatures in degrees Fahrenheit; Precipitation and Snow in inches

Population: 14,019 (2000); Race: 98.4% White, 0.1% Black, 0.4% Asian, 0.1% American Indian and Alaska Native, 0.6% Hispanic of any race, 0.9% two or more races (2000); Density: 25.0 persons per square mile (2000); Age: 27.0% under 18, 15.2% over 64 (2000).
Religion: Five largest groups: 12.5% The United Methodist Church, 8.0% Christian Church (Disciples of Christ), 6.6% Catholic Church, 3.5% Evangelical Lutheran Church in America, 2.6% Southern Baptist Convention (2000).
Economy: Unemployment rate: 3.4% (11/2002); Total civilian labor force: 7,754 (11/2002); Leading industries: 18.7% health care and social assistance; 18.5% retail trade; 17.4% manufacturing (2000); Companies that employ more than 1,000 persons: 0 (2000); Companies that employ more than 100 persons: 2 (2000); Farms: 986 totaling 316,579 acres (1997); Minority business ownership rate: 0.0% (1997); Women business ownership rate: 18.2% (1997); Retail sales per capita: $6,025 (1997). Single-family building permits issued: 100 (2001) / 92 (2000); Multi-family building permits issued: 2 (2001) / 11 (2000).
Income: Per capita income: $19,357 (2000); Median household income: $41,845 (2000); Poverty rate: 6.7% (2000); Bankruptcy rate: 4.64% (2001).
Taxes: Total county taxes per capita: $177 (2000); County property taxes per capita: $171 (2000).
Education: High school graduation rate: 87.6% (2000); College graduation rate: 14.4% (2000).
Housing: Homeownership rate: 78.0% (2000); Median home value: $87,700 (2000); Median rent: $358 per month (2000); Median age of housing: 47 years (2000).
Health: Birth rate: 117.7 per 10,000 population (1998); Age adjusted death rate: 82.3 per 10,000 population (1999); Age adjusted cancer mortality rate: 234.2 deaths per 100,000 population (1999). Number of physicians: 1.4 per 10,000 population (1999); Number of hospital beds: 22.1 per 10,000 population (1999).
Elections: 2000 Presidential election results: 44.4% Gore, 52.6% Bush, 1.8% Nader, 0.6% Buchanan
National and State Parks: Badger Creek State Recreation Area; Pammel State Park
Additional Information Contacts
Madison County Government Offices 515-462-3225
Winterset Chamber of Commerce 515-462-1185

Madison County Communities

BEVINGTON (city). Covers a land area of 0.269 square miles and a water area of 0 square miles. Located at 41.36° N. Lat.; 93.79° W. Long.
History: Bevington was named for a citizen of the area, but whether that was Ed Bevington, a clerk of the district court, or Dr. C.D. Bevington, of Winterset, is uncertain.
Population: 58 (2000); Race: 90.2% White, 0.0% Black, 0.0% Asian, 0.0% American Indian and Alaska Native, 0.0% Hispanic of any race, 9.8% two or more races (2000); Density: 215.4 persons per square mile (2000); Age: 13.7% under 18, 7.8% over 64 (2000); Marriage status: 10.6% never married, 61.7% now married, 0.0% widowed, 27.7% divorced (2000); Foreign born: 0.0% (2000); Ancestry (includes multiple ancestries): 29.4% German, 19.6% Irish, 15.7% Dutch, 13.7% Other groups, 9.8% English (2000).
Economy: Single-family building permits issued: 0 (2001) / 0 (2000); Multi-family building permits issued: 0 (2001) / 0 (2000); Employment by occupation: 6.5% management, 0.0% professional, 22.6% services, 29.0% sales, 3.2% farming, 19.4% construction, 19.4% production (2000).
Income: Per capita income: $16,592 (2000); Median household income: $31,875 (2000); Poverty rate: 3.9% (2000).
Taxes: Total city taxes per capita: $99 (1997); City property taxes per capita: $85 (1997).
Education: High school graduation rate: 88.6% (2000); College graduation rate: 8.6% (2000).
Housing: Homeownership rate: 84.6% (2000); Median home value: $65,000 (2000); Median rent: $300 per month (2000); Median age of housing: 30 years (2000).
Transportation: Commute to work: 87.1% car, 0.0% public transportation, 0.0% walk, 12.9% work from home (2000); Travel time to work: 18.5% less than 15 minutes, 51.9% 15 to 30 minutes, 29.6% 30 to 45 minutes, 0.0% 45 to 60 minutes, 0.0% 60 minutes or more (2000)

EARLHAM (city). Covers a land area of 0.971 square miles and a water area of 0 square miles. Located at 41.49° N. Lat.; 94.12° W. Long.
History: Earlham is said to be named for a Quaker college in Richmond, Indiana.
Population: 1,298 (2000); Race: 99.5% White, 0.3% Black, 0.0% Asian, 0.0% American Indian and Alaska Native, 1.1% Hispanic of any race, 0.0% two or more races (2000); Density: 1,336.9 persons per square mile (2000); Age: 25.7% under 18, 12.5% over 64 (2000); Marriage status: 20.4% never married, 61.3% now married, 8.5% widowed, 9.8% divorced (2000); Foreign born: 0.4% (2000); Ancestry (includes multiple ancestries): 27.8% German, 12.7% Irish, 11.8% English, 11.7% United States or American, 5.1% Dutch (2000).
Economy: Single-family building permits issued: 4 (2001) / 11 (2000); Multi-family building permits issued: 0 (2001) / 0 (2000); Employment by occupation: 11.9% management, 20.5% professional, 12.8% services, 22.3% sales, 1.3% farming, 10.9% construction, 20.3% production (2000).
Income: Per capita income: $20,659 (2000); Median household income: $42,917 (2000); Poverty rate: 3.8% (2000).
Taxes: Total city taxes per capita: $207 (1997); City property taxes per capita: $204 (1997).
Education: High school graduation rate: 90.0% (2000); College graduation rate: 17.8% (2000).

School District(s)

Earlham Community School District (KG-12)
2000 Enrollment: 548 515-758-2235

Housing: Homeownership rate: 78.5% (2000); Median home value: $91,400 (2000); Median rent: $311 per month (2000); Median age of housing: 37 years (2000).
Transportation: Commute to work: 91.1% car, 0.3% public transportation, 5.2% walk, 2.0% work from home (2000); Travel time to work: 26.8% less than 15 minutes, 26.4% 15 to 30 minutes, 35.3% 30 to 45 minutes, 7.9% 45 to 60 minutes, 3.7% 60 minutes or more (2000)

EAST PERU (city). Aka Peru. Covers a land area of 0.937 square miles and a water area of 0 square miles. Located at 41.22° N. Lat.; 93.92° W. Long. Elevation is 960 feet.
History: East Peru was named for its location about one mile southeast of the town of Peru.
Population: 153 (2000); Race: 96.3% White, 0.0% Black, 0.0% Asian, 0.0% American Indian and Alaska Native, 3.7% Hispanic of any race, 3.7% two or more races (2000); Density: 163.3 persons per square mile (2000); Age: 17.6% under 18, 14.7% over 64 (2000); Marriage status: 22.2% never married, 61.5% now married, 5.1% widowed, 11.1% divorced (2000); Foreign born: 0.0% (2000); Ancestry (includes multiple ancestries): 14.0% United States or American, 13.2% Other groups, 9.6% German, 9.6% Dutch, 8.8% Irish (2000).
Economy: Employment by occupation: 7.2% management, 14.5% professional, 14.5% services, 18.8% sales, 0.0% farming, 26.1% construction, 18.8% production (2000).
Income: Per capita income: $14,756 (2000); Median household income: $32,083 (2000); Poverty rate: 19.1% (2000).
Taxes: Total city taxes per capita: $56 (1997); City property taxes per capita: $56 (1997).
Education: High school graduation rate: 88.8% (2000); College graduation rate: 2.2% (2000).
Housing: Homeownership rate: 92.3% (2000); Median home value: $18,100 (2000); Median rent: $275 per month (2000); Median age of housing: 60+ years (2000).
Transportation: Commute to work: 92.5% car, 0.0% public transportation, 3.0% walk, 4.5% work from home (2000); Travel time to work: 15.6% less than 15 minutes, 34.4% 15 to 30 minutes, 15.6% 30 to 45 minutes, 34.4% 45 to 60 minutes, 0.0% 60 minutes or more (2000)

MACKSBURG (city). Covers a land area of 1.973 square miles and a water area of 0 square miles. Located at 41.21° N. Lat.; 94.18° W. Long. Elevation is 1,254 feet.
History: Macksburg was named in honor of one of the town founders and its first mayor, Dr. J. H. Mack.
Population: 142 (2000); Race: 97.3% White, 0.0% Black, 2.0% Asian, 0.0% American Indian and Alaska Native, 2.0% Hispanic of any race, 0.7% two or more races (2000); Density: 72.0 persons per square mile (2000); Age: 23.8% under 18, 21.1% over 64 (2000); Marriage status: 15.8% never married, 65.8% now married, 11.4% widowed, 7.0% divorced (2000); Foreign born: 2.0% (2000); Ancestry (includes multiple ancestries): 22.4% German, 15.6% English, 11.6% United States or American, 8.2% Irish, 7.5% Other groups (2000).
Economy: Employment by occupation: 18.3% management, 8.3% professional, 11.7% services, 26.7% sales, 0.0% farming, 11.7% construction, 23.3% production (2000).
Income: Per capita income: $14,080 (2000); Median household income: $31,500 (2000); Poverty rate: 5.6% (2000).
Taxes: Total city taxes per capita: $101 (1997); City property taxes per capita: $84 (1997).
Education: High school graduation rate: 78.8% (2000); College graduation rate: 7.1% (2000).
Housing: Homeownership rate: 85.2% (2000); Median home value: $29,600 (2000); Median rent: $325 per month (2000); Median age of housing: 59 years (2000).
Transportation: Commute to work: 82.8% car, 0.0% public transportation, 3.4% walk, 10.3% work from home (2000); Travel time to work: 30.8% less than 15 minutes, 23.1% 15 to 30 minutes, 26.9% 30 to 45 minutes, 11.5% 45 to 60 minutes, 7.7% 60 minutes or more (2000)

PATTERSON (city). Covers a land area of 0.198 square miles and a water area of 0 square miles. Located at 41.34° N. Lat.; 93.88° W. Long.
History: The town of Patterson was laid out by Alexander Pattison. The town would have been called Pattison if not for errors in recording the official name.
Population: 126 (2000); Race: 100.0% White, 0.0% Black, 0.0% Asian, 0.0% American Indian and Alaska Native, 0.0% Hispanic of any race, 0.0% two or more races (2000); Density: 635.1 persons per square mile (2000); Age: 18.1% under 18, 8.0% over 64 (2000); Marriage status: 19.5% never married, 58.4% now married, 8.8% widowed, 13.3% divorced (2000); Foreign born: 0.0% (2000); Ancestry (includes multiple ancestries): 18.1% German, 13.0% English, 10.9% Dutch, 8.7% Irish, 5.8% Other groups (2000).
Economy: Single-family building permits issued: 0 (2001) / 2 (2000); Multi-family building permits issued: 0 (2001) / 0 (2000); Employment by occupation: 12.2% management, 10.8% professional, 9.5% services, 33.8% sales, 0.0% farming, 13.5% construction, 20.3% production (2000).
Income: Per capita income: $21,457 (2000); Median household income: $47,500 (2000); Poverty rate: 1.4% (2000).
Taxes: Total city taxes per capita: $86 (1997); City property taxes per capita: $79 (1997).
Education: High school graduation rate: 84.2% (2000); College graduation rate: 7.9% (2000).
Housing: Homeownership rate: 90.6% (2000); Median home value: $45,000 (2000); Median rent: $425 per month (2000); Median age of housing: 27 years (2000).
Transportation: Commute to work: 95.9% car, 0.0% public transportation, 0.0% walk, 4.1% work from home (2000); Travel time to work: 32.4% less than 15 minutes, 26.8% 15 to 30 minutes, 26.8% 30 to 45 minutes, 5.6% 45 to 60 minutes, 8.5% 60 minutes or more (2000)

PERU (unincorporated postal area, zip code 50222). Aka East Peru. Covers a land area of 42.727 square miles and a water area of 0.007 square miles. Located at 41.22° N. Lat.; 93.96° W. Long.
Population: 577 (2000); Race: 99.0% White, 0.0% Black, 0.0% Asian, 0.0% American Indian and Alaska Native, 1.0% Hispanic of any race, 1.0% two or more races (2000); Density: 13.5 persons per square mile (2000); Age: 26.8% under 18, 14.3% over 64 (2000); Marriage status: 26.3% never married, 62.4% now married, 4.0% widowed, 7.3% divorced (2000); Foreign born: 0.0% (2000); Ancestry (includes multiple ancestries): 17.7% German, 11.7% Irish, 10.5% United States or American, 10.1% English, 6.8% Dutch (2000).
Economy: Employment by occupation: 27.0% management, 8.5% professional, 14.7% services, 18.9% sales, 0.0% farming, 15.4% construction, 15.4% production (2000).
Income: Per capita income: $17,265 (2000); Median household income: $41,250 (2000); Poverty rate: 9.5% (2000).
Education: High school graduation rate: 79.8% (2000); College graduation rate: 8.0% (2000).
Housing: Homeownership rate: 93.2% (2000); Median home value: $37,900 (2000); Median rent: $275 per month (2000); Median age of housing: 60+ years (2000).
Transportation: Commute to work: 77.4% car, 1.6% public transportation, 1.6% walk, 19.5% work from home (2000); Travel time to work: 13.0% less than 15 minutes, 30.4% 15 to 30 minutes, 16.4% 30 to 45 minutes, 31.4% 45 to 60 minutes, 8.7% 60 minutes or more (2000)

SAINT CHARLES (city). Covers a land area of 0.562 square miles and a water area of 0 square miles. Located at 41.28° N. Lat.; 93.80° W. Long. Elevation is 1,070 feet.
History: St. Charles was named for St. Charles, Missouri.
Population: 619 (2000); Race: 98.2% White, 0.0% Black, 0.3% Asian, 1.2% American Indian and Alaska Native, 0.3% Hispanic of any race, 0.3% two or more races (2000); Density: 1,101.6 persons per square mile (2000); Age: 29.1% under 18, 11.2% over 64 (2000); Marriage status: 19.1% never married, 67.5% now married, 5.6% widowed, 7.8% divorced (2000); Foreign born: 0.8% (2000); Ancestry (includes multiple ancestries): 26.8% German, 14.7% Irish, 14.7% United States or American, 14.2% English, 4.1% Other groups (2000).
Economy: Single-family building permits issued: 5 (2001) / 4 (2000); Multi-family building permits issued: 0 (2001) / 2 (2000); Employment by occupation: 16.9% management, 12.3% professional, 9.1% services, 34.1% sales, 1.0% farming, 12.7% construction, 14.0% production (2000).
Income: Per capita income: $18,708 (2000); Median household income: $42,333 (2000); Poverty rate: 4.0% (2000).
Education: High school graduation rate: 92.9% (2000); College graduation rate: 13.4% (2000).
Housing: Homeownership rate: 77.0% (2000); Median home value: $89,000 (2000); Median rent: $309 per month (2000); Median age of housing: 45 years (2000).
Transportation: Commute to work: 92.8% car, 0.0% public transportation, 4.2% walk, 2.9% work from home (2000); Travel time to work: 20.5% less than 15 minutes, 23.8% 15 to 30 minutes, 43.6% 30 to 45 minutes, 10.1% 45 to 60 minutes, 2.0% 60 minutes or more (2000)

TRURO (city). Aka Turro. Covers a land area of 0.987 square miles and a water area of 0 square miles. Located at 41.20° N. Lat.; 93.84° W. Long. Elevation is 1,082 feet.
History: Truro is thought to be named after Truro, England.
Population: 427 (2000); Race: 98.8% White, 0.0% Black, 0.0% Asian, 0.0% American Indian and Alaska Native, 0.0% Hispanic of any race, 1.2% two or more races (2000); Density: 432.6 persons per square mile (2000); Age: 35.8% under 18, 12.9% over 64 (2000); Marriage status: 16.6% never married, 65.4% now married, 7.8% widowed, 10.2% divorced (2000); Foreign born: 0.5% (2000); Ancestry (includes multiple ancestries): 20.4% German, 17.3% Irish, 17.1% English, 7.5% United States or American, 7.0% Swedish (2000).
Economy: Single-family building permits issued: 3 (2001) / 2 (2000); Multi-family building permits issued: 2 (2001) / 6 (2000); Employment by occupation: 5.1% management, 18.5% professional, 13.5% services, 29.8% sales, 0.0% farming, 20.8% construction, 12.4% production (2000).
Income: Per capita income: $15,021 (2000); Median household income: $33,750 (2000); Poverty rate: 10.3% (2000).
Taxes: Total city taxes per capita: $122 (1997); City property taxes per capita: $119 (1997).
Education: High school graduation rate: 84.8% (2000); College graduation rate: 11.3% (2000).

School District(s)

Interstate 35 Community School District (PK-12)
2000 Enrollment: 758 641-765-4291
Housing: Homeownership rate: 69.9% (2000); Median home value: $64,400 (2000); Median rent: $240 per month (2000); Median age of housing: 60+ years (2000).
Transportation: Commute to work: 95.5% car, 0.0% public transportation, 1.7% walk, 2.8% work from home (2000); Travel time to work: 18.6% less than 15 minutes, 12.2% 15 to 30 minutes, 45.9% 30 to 45 minutes, 15.7% 45 to 60 minutes, 7.6% 60 minutes or more (2000)

WINTERSET (city). Covers a land area of 3.511 square miles and a water area of 0 square miles. Located at 41.33° N. Lat.; 94.01° W. Long. Elevation is 1,118 feet.
History: Winterset was established on a divide between the Middle River and Cedar Creek in 1846. Independence and Summerset were suggested as names for the new town. One of the members of the commission, shivering with cold and slightly under the influence of whiskey, cried: "Summerset! You'd a damn sight better name it Winterset!"
Population: 4,768 (2000); Race: 98.8% White, 0.1% Black, 0.2% Asian, 0.0% American Indian and Alaska Native, 0.3% Hispanic of any race, 0.7% two or more races (2000); Density: 1,357.9 persons per square mile (2000); Age: 26.3% under 18, 20.6% over 64 (2000); Marriage status: 17.7% never married, 63.8% now married, 10.5% widowed, 8.1% divorced (2000); Foreign born: 0.4% (2000); Ancestry (includes multiple ancestries): 24.7% German, 18.2% Irish, 11.2% United States or American, 10.7% English, 3.7% Other groups (2000).
Economy: Single-family building permits issued: 26 (2001) / 17 (2000); Multi-family building permits issued: 0 (2001) / 3 (2000); Employment by occupation: 12.6% management, 18.1% professional, 14.4% services, 30.4% sales, 0.8% farming, 11.0% construction, 12.8% production (2000).
Income: Per capita income: $17,274 (2000); Median household income: $33,142 (2000); Poverty rate: 8.4% (2000).
Taxes: Total city taxes per capita: $284 (1997); City property taxes per capita: $280 (1997).
Education: High school graduation rate: 83.4% (2000); College graduation rate: 12.8% (2000).

School District(s)

Winterset Community School District (PK-12)
2000 Enrollment: 1,669 515-462-2718
Housing: Homeownership rate: 68.7% (2000); Median home value: $85,300 (2000); Median rent: $378 per month (2000); Median age of housing: 47 years (2000).
Hospitals: Madison County Memorial Hospital (31 beds)
Newspapers: Winterset Madisonian (1 x week); The Shopper (1 x week)
Transportation: Commute to work: 95.8% car, 0.0% public transportation, 1.6% walk, 2.2% work from home (2000); Travel time to work: 54.9% less than 15 minutes, 5.3% 15 to 30 minutes, 21.4% 30 to 45 minutes, 14.5% 45 to 60 minutes, 3.9% 60 minutes or more (2000)
Additional Information Contacts
Winterset Chamber of Commerce 515-462-1185

Mahaska County

Located in south central Iowa; prairie area, drained by the Des Moines, Skunk, and North Skunk Rivers. Covers a land area of 570.90 square miles, a water area of 2.50 square miles, and is located in the Central Time Zone. The county government was organized in 1843. County seat is Oskaloosa.

Weather Station: Oskaloosa — Elevation: 830 feet

	Jan	Feb	Mar	Apr	May	Jun	Jul	Aug	Sep	Oct	Nov	Dec
High	30	36	49	62	73	82	86	84	76	64	48	35
Low	11	18	28	39	51	60	64	62	53	41	29	18
Precip	1.1	1.2	2.2	3.5	4.6	4.3	4.3	4.6	4.0	3.1	2.8	1.4
Snow	7.3	7.0	3.3	1.9	0.0	0.0	0.0	0.0	0.0	0.1	2.2	5.8

High and Low temperatures in degrees Fahrenheit; Precipitation and Snow in inches

Population: 22,335 (2000); Race: 96.8% White, 0.3% Black, 1.0% Asian, 0.3% American Indian and Alaska Native, 1.3% Hispanic of any race, 1.0% two or more races (2000); Density: 39.1 persons per square mile (2000); Age: 25.7% under 18, 16.3% over 64 (2000).
Religion: Five largest groups: 10.1% The United Methodist Church, 6.4% Christian Reformed Church in North America, 5.7% Catholic Church, 4.8% Christian Church (Disciples of Christ), 4.1% Church of the Nazarene (2000).
Economy: Unemployment rate: 4.5% (11/2002); Total civilian labor force: 11,714 (11/2002); Leading industries: 19.7% retail trade; 18.1% manufacturing; 12.1% health care and social assistance (2000); Companies that employ more than 1,000 persons: 0 (2000); Companies that employ more than 100 persons: 8 (2000); Farms: 1,022 totaling 329,038 acres (1997); Minority business ownership rate: 0.0% (1997); Women business ownership rate: 22.4% (1997); Retail sales per capita: $8,746 (1997). Single-family building permits issued: 35 (2001) / 30 (2000); Multi-family building permits issued: 8 (2001) / 2 (2000).
Income: Per capita income: $18,232 (2000); Median household income: $37,314 (2000); Poverty rate: 9.8% (2000); Bankruptcy rate: 4.21% (2001).
Taxes: Total county taxes per capita: $332 (2000); County property taxes per capita: $295 (2000).
Education: High school graduation rate: 82.6% (2000); College graduation rate: 16.5% (2000).
Housing: Homeownership rate: 71.1% (2000); Median home value: $68,100 (2000); Median rent: $335 per month (2000); Median age of housing: 47 years (2000).
Health: Birth rate: 127.6 per 10,000 population (1998); Age adjusted death rate: 77.8 per 10,000 population (1999); Age adjusted cancer mortality rate: 196.5 deaths per 100,000 population (1999). Number of physicians: 6.3 per 10,000 population (1999); Number of hospital beds: 23.7 per 10,000 population (1999).
Elections: 2000 Presidential election results: 35.3% Gore, 62.6% Bush, 1.5% Nader, 0.3% Buchanan
National and State Parks: Hull State Game Management Area; Lake Keomah State Park
Additional Information Contacts
Mahaska County Government Offices 641-673-3469
Oskaloosa Board of Realtors 641-673-9465
Oskaloosa Chamber of Commerce 641-672-2591

Mahaska County Communities

BARNES CITY (city). Covers a land area of 0.598 square miles and a water area of 0 square miles. Located at 41.50° N. Lat.; 92.46° W. Long. Elevation is 910 feet.
History: Barnes City was incorporated in 1898 and named after a railroad official
Population: 201 (2000); Race: 94.8% White, 5.2% Black, 0.0% Asian, 0.0% American Indian and Alaska Native, 0.0% Hispanic of any race, 0.0% two or more races (2000); Density: 336.1 persons per square mile (2000); Age: 30.5% under 18, 16.2% over 64 (2000); Marriage status: 23.2% never married, 58.3% now married, 6.0% widowed, 12.6% divorced (2000); Foreign born: 0.0% (2000); Ancestry (includes multiple ancestries): 27.1% Irish, 21.0% United States or American, 20.0% German, 11.0% Other groups, 5.2% Dutch (2000).
Economy: Employment by occupation: 10.0% management, 4.0% professional, 19.0% services, 17.0% sales, 2.0% farming, 7.0% construction, 41.0% production (2000).
Income: Per capita income: $14,135 (2000); Median household income: $29,583 (2000); Poverty rate: 20.7% (2000).
Taxes: Total city taxes per capita: $142 (1997); City property taxes per capita: $90 (1997).

Education: High school graduation rate: 74.8% (2000); College graduation rate: 7.9% (2000).
Housing: Homeownership rate: 77.3% (2000); Median home value: $28,200 (2000); Median rent: $200 per month (2000); Median age of housing: 60+ years (2000).
Transportation: Commute to work: 82.5% car, 0.0% public transportation, 11.3% walk, 4.1% work from home (2000); Travel time to work: 29.0% less than 15 minutes, 26.9% 15 to 30 minutes, 20.4% 30 to 45 minutes, 12.9% 45 to 60 minutes, 10.8% 60 minutes or more (2000)

BEACON (city). Covers a land area of 1.007 square miles and a water area of 0 square miles. Located at 41.27° N. Lat.; 92.68° W. Long. Elevation is 735 feet.
History: Beacon, first known as Enterprise, was a Welsh community established in 1864.
Population: 518 (2000); Race: 97.8% White, 0.4% Black, 0.0% Asian, 1.8% American Indian and Alaska Native, 0.0% Hispanic of any race, 0.0% two or more races (2000); Density: 514.5 persons per square mile (2000); Age: 21.6% under 18, 12.1% over 64 (2000); Marriage status: 16.2% never married, 65.1% now married, 6.7% widowed, 12.1% divorced (2000); Foreign born: 0.0% (2000); Ancestry (includes multiple ancestries): 16.0% United States or American, 11.5% Dutch, 9.1% German, 8.1% English, 5.9% Irish (2000).
Economy: Employment by occupation: 3.3% management, 4.7% professional, 8.4% services, 24.5% sales, 0.0% farming, 13.5% construction, 45.6% production (2000).
Income: Per capita income: $16,972 (2000); Median household income: $32,000 (2000); Poverty rate: 8.8% (2000).
Taxes: Total city taxes per capita: $58 (1997); City property taxes per capita: $58 (1997).
Education: High school graduation rate: 76.4% (2000); College graduation rate: 2.8% (2000).
Housing: Homeownership rate: 88.0% (2000); Median home value: $52,900 (2000); Median rent: $403 per month (2000); Median age of housing: 26 years (2000).
Transportation: Commute to work: 93.8% car, 0.0% public transportation, 0.7% walk, 4.0% work from home (2000); Travel time to work: 41.1% less than 15 minutes, 41.1% 15 to 30 minutes, 10.6% 30 to 45 minutes, 4.6% 45 to 60 minutes, 2.7% 60 minutes or more (2000)

CEDAR (unincorporated postal area, zip code 52543). Covers a land area of 20.125 square miles and a water area of 0.008 square miles. Located at 41.21° N. Lat.; 92.52° W. Long.
History: R. W. Moore, who was named postmaster here in 1869, selected the name of Cedar for the town.
Population: 275 (2000); Race: 97.3% White, 0.0% Black, 2.7% Asian, 0.0% American Indian and Alaska Native, 0.0% Hispanic of any race, 0.0% two or more races (2000); Density: 13.7 persons per square mile (2000); Age: 27.6% under 18, 4.4% over 64 (2000); Marriage status: 13.1% never married, 80.8% now married, 3.1% widowed, 3.1% divorced (2000); Foreign born: 1.4% (2000); Ancestry (includes multiple ancestries): 24.5% Dutch, 17.7% English, 17.7% German, 13.9% Irish, 9.5% Other groups (2000).
Economy: Employment by occupation: 32.7% management, 6.3% professional, 6.9% services, 17.0% sales, 5.7% farming, 16.4% construction, 15.1% production (2000).
Income: Per capita income: $18,913 (2000); Median household income: $55,469 (2000); Poverty rate: 0.0% (2000).
Education: High school graduation rate: 89.1% (2000); College graduation rate: 15.9% (2000).
Housing: Homeownership rate: 89.4% (2000); Median home value: $61,000 (2000); Median age of housing: 47 years (2000).
Transportation: Commute to work: 91.2% car, 0.0% public transportation, 1.9% walk, 6.9% work from home (2000); Travel time to work: 37.8% less than 15 minutes, 39.9% 15 to 30 minutes, 14.9% 30 to 45 minutes, 4.7% 45 to 60 minutes, 2.7% 60 minutes or more (2000)

FREMONT (city). Covers a land area of 1.031 square miles and a water area of 0 square miles. Located at 41.21° N. Lat.; 92.43° W. Long. Elevation is 842 feet.
History: Fremont was founded in 1848 and named in honor of Gen. John C. Fremont.
Population: 704 (2000); Race: 98.0% White, 0.0% Black, 0.3% Asian, 0.4% American Indian and Alaska Native, 1.5% Hispanic of any race, 1.0% two or more races (2000); Density: 682.7 persons per square mile (2000); Age: 27.3% under 18, 17.8% over 64 (2000); Marriage status: 18.9% never married, 66.7% now married, 8.6% widowed, 5.9% divorced (2000); Foreign born: 1.5% (2000); Ancestry (includes multiple ancestries): 28.1% German, 12.3% Irish, 9.8% English, 9.5% Dutch, 6.0% United States or American (2000).
Economy: Employment by occupation: 9.8% management, 11.7% professional, 12.3% services, 19.9% sales, 2.5% farming, 11.7% construction, 32.2% production (2000).
Income: Per capita income: $16,925 (2000); Median household income: $39,583 (2000); Poverty rate: 8.9% (2000).
Taxes: Total city taxes per capita: $150 (1997); City property taxes per capita: $96 (1997).
Education: High school graduation rate: 80.5% (2000); College graduation rate: 12.5% (2000).

School District(s)

Fremont Community School District (PK-12)
2000 Enrollment: 130 641-933-4211
Housing: Homeownership rate: 83.5% (2000); Median home value: $56,700 (2000); Median rent: $311 per month (2000); Median age of housing: 42 years (2000).
Transportation: Commute to work: 94.6% car, 0.0% public transportation, 4.1% walk, 1.3% work from home (2000); Travel time to work: 19.9% less than 15 minutes, 53.4% 15 to 30 minutes, 14.5% 30 to 45 minutes, 6.1% 45 to 60 minutes, 6.1% 60 minutes or more (2000)

KEOMAH VILLAGE (city). Covers a land area of 0.029 square miles and a water area of 0 square miles. Located at 41.28° N. Lat.; 92.53° W. Long.
History: The name Keomah is a combination of the names of two surrounding counties, Keokuk and Mahaska.
Population: 97 (2000); Race: 100.0% White, 0.0% Black, 0.0% Asian, 0.0% American Indian and Alaska Native, 0.0% Hispanic of any race, 0.0% two or more races (2000); Density: 3,370.2 persons per square mile (2000); Age: 11.8% under 18, 11.8% over 64 (2000); Marriage status: 10.5% never married, 76.8% now married, 0.0% widowed, 12.6% divorced (2000); Foreign born: 0.0% (2000); Ancestry (includes multiple ancestries): 29.4% German, 21.6% Dutch, 20.6% Irish, 13.7% English, 5.9% Scottish (2000).
Economy: Single-family building permits issued: 0 (2001) / 0 (2000); Multi-family building permits issued: 0 (2001) / 0 (2000); Employment by occupation: 26.1% management, 7.2% professional, 7.2% services, 34.8% sales, 0.0% farming, 14.5% construction, 10.1% production (2000).
Income: Per capita income: $27,891 (2000); Median household income: $63,750 (2000); Poverty rate: 9.8% (2000).
Taxes: Total city taxes per capita: $155 (1997); City property taxes per capita: $107 (1997).
Education: High school graduation rate: 90.6% (2000); College graduation rate: 37.6% (2000).
Housing: Homeownership rate: 93.0% (2000); Median home value: $95,000 (2000); Median rent: $525 per month (2000); Median age of housing: 29 years (2000).
Transportation: Commute to work: 97.0% car, 0.0% public transportation, 0.0% walk, 3.0% work from home (2000); Travel time to work: 26.2% less than 15 minutes, 60.0% 15 to 30 minutes, 1.5% 30 to 45 minutes, 7.7% 45 to 60 minutes, 4.6% 60 minutes or more (2000)

LEIGHTON (city). Covers a land area of 0.076 square miles and a water area of 0 square miles. Located at 41.33° N. Lat.; 92.78° W. Long. Elevation is 769 feet.
History: Leighton was named for land prospector William C. Leighton.
Population: 153 (2000); Race: 100.0% White, 0.0% Black, 0.0% Asian, 0.0% American Indian and Alaska Native, 0.0% Hispanic of any race, 0.0% two or more races (2000); Density: 2,004.7 persons per square mile (2000); Age: 35.8% under 18, 14.2% over 64 (2000); Marriage status: 6.1% never married, 85.2% now married, 7.0% widowed, 1.7% divorced (2000); Foreign born: 0.0% (2000); Ancestry (includes multiple ancestries): 69.9% Dutch, 17.0% German, 9.7% English, 6.3% Irish, 6.3% United States or American (2000).
Economy: Employment by occupation: 10.5% management, 19.8% professional, 16.3% services, 18.6% sales, 7.0% farming, 0.0% construction, 27.9% production (2000).
Income: Per capita income: $16,294 (2000); Median household income: $46,667 (2000); Poverty rate: 0.0% (2000).
Taxes: Total city taxes per capita: $113 (1997); City property taxes per capita: $92 (1997).
Education: High school graduation rate: 80.0% (2000); College graduation rate: 9.1% (2000).

Housing: Homeownership rate: 84.7% (2000); Median home value: $77,300 (2000); Median rent: $175 per month (2000); Median age of housing: 50 years (2000).
Transportation: Commute to work: 81.4% car, 0.0% public transportation, 9.3% walk, 9.3% work from home (2000); Travel time to work: 55.1% less than 15 minutes, 44.9% 15 to 30 minutes, 0.0% 30 to 45 minutes, 0.0% 45 to 60 minutes, 0.0% 60 minutes or more (2000)

NEW SHARON (city). Covers a land area of 0.935 square miles and a water area of 0 square miles. Located at 41.46° N. Lat.; 92.65° W. Long. Elevation is 859 feet.
History: New Sharon, first called Sharon, later New Sharon to avoid confusion with a town of that name in Warren County, was largely a Quaker settlement in early days.
Population: 1,301 (2000); Race: 99.0% White, 0.0% Black, 0.4% Asian, 0.0% American Indian and Alaska Native, 1.2% Hispanic of any race, 0.5% two or more races (2000); Density: 1,390.9 persons per square mile (2000); Age: 21.8% under 18, 22.3% over 64 (2000); Marriage status: 19.5% never married, 63.0% now married, 10.5% widowed, 7.0% divorced (2000); Foreign born: 0.7% (2000); Ancestry (includes multiple ancestries): 18.8% German, 12.4% Dutch, 10.7% English, 9.6% Irish, 7.7% United States or American (2000).
Economy: Single-family building permits issued: 3 (2001) / 1 (2000); Multi-family building permits issued: 0 (2001) / 0 (2000); Employment by occupation: 10.0% management, 16.6% professional, 14.8% services, 25.5% sales, 0.8% farming, 10.0% construction, 22.2% production (2000).
Income: Per capita income: $17,280 (2000); Median household income: $36,125 (2000); Poverty rate: 10.0% (2000).
Taxes: Total city taxes per capita: $155 (1997); City property taxes per capita: $100 (1997).
Education: High school graduation rate: 85.7% (2000); College graduation rate: 14.5% (2000).

School District(s)

North Mahaska Community School District (PK-12)
2000 Enrollment: 591 641-637-2295
Housing: Homeownership rate: 73.8% (2000); Median home value: $66,000 (2000); Median rent: $239 per month (2000); Median age of housing: 42 years (2000).
Transportation: Commute to work: 92.8% car, 0.0% public transportation, 2.7% walk, 4.2% work from home (2000); Travel time to work: 32.5% less than 15 minutes, 42.9% 15 to 30 minutes, 15.2% 30 to 45 minutes, 4.0% 45 to 60 minutes, 5.4% 60 minutes or more (2000)

OSKALOOSA (city). Covers a land area of 6.863 square miles and a water area of 0.015 square miles. Located at 41.29° N. Lat.; 92.64° W. Long. Elevation is 1,132 feet.
History: Oskaloosa, first settled by Quakers in 1843, was later named for a wife of Chief Osceola.
Population: 10,938 (2000); Race: 95.7% White, 0.4% Black, 1.1% Asian, 0.5% American Indian and Alaska Native, 1.8% Hispanic of any race, 1.5% two or more races (2000); Density: 1,593.8 persons per square mile (2000); Age: 24.0% under 18, 17.7% over 64 (2000); Marriage status: 24.5% never married, 55.2% now married, 8.8% widowed, 11.5% divorced (2000); Foreign born: 2.2% (2000); Ancestry (includes multiple ancestries): 19.3% German, 14.4% Dutch, 11.2% Irish, 10.1% English, 8.6% United States or American (2000).
Vital Statistics: Birth rate: 146.3 per 10,000 population (1998)
Economy: Single-family building permits issued: 31 (2001) / 28 (2000); Multi-family building permits issued: 8 (2001) / 2 (2000); Employment by occupation: 11.4% management, 18.1% professional, 13.1% services, 23.5% sales, 0.7% farming, 8.5% construction, 24.8% production (2000).
Income: Per capita income: $18,721 (2000); Median household income: $34,490 (2000); Poverty rate: 13.7% (2000).
Taxes: Total city taxes per capita: $381 (2000); City property taxes per capita: $291 (2000).
Education: High school graduation rate: 81.2% (2000); College graduation rate: 19.2% (2000).

School District(s)

Oskaloosa Community School District (KG-12)
2000 Enrollment: 2,660 641-673-8345

Four-year College(s)

William Penn University (Private, Not-for-profit, Friends)
2001 Enrollment: 1,547 515-673-1001
2001 Tuition: In-state $12,900; Out-of-state $12,900
Housing: Homeownership rate: 63.4% (2000); Median home value: $65,700 (2000); Median rent: $357 per month (2000); Median age of housing: 50 years (2000).
Hospitals: Mahaska Health Partnership (53 beds)
Safety: Violent crime rate: 22.0 per 10,000 population; Property crime rate: 385.3 per 10,000 population (2001).
Newspapers: Oskaloosa Herald (6 x week); Oskaloosa Shopper (1 x week)
Transportation: Commute to work: 92.1% car, 0.0% public transportation, 2.3% walk, 3.5% work from home (2000); Travel time to work: 54.8% less than 15 minutes, 28.9% 15 to 30 minutes, 9.3% 30 to 45 minutes, 2.3% 45 to 60 minutes, 4.7% 60 minutes or more (2000)
Additional Information Contacts
Oskaloosa Board of Realtors 641-673-9465
Oskaloosa Chamber of Commerce 641-672-2591

ROSE HILL (city). Covers a land area of 0.136 square miles and a water area of 0 square miles. Located at 41.32° N. Lat.; 92.46° W. Long. Elevation is 822 feet.
History: Rose Hill was founded by James Ornabaum in 1875.
Population: 205 (2000); Race: 98.9% White, 0.0% Black, 0.0% Asian, 1.1% American Indian and Alaska Native, 0.0% Hispanic of any race, 0.0% two or more races (2000); Density: 1,501.9 persons per square mile (2000); Age: 24.7% under 18, 15.6% over 64 (2000); Marriage status: 15.5% never married, 57.4% now married, 7.4% widowed, 19.6% divorced (2000); Foreign born: 0.0% (2000); Ancestry (includes multiple ancestries): 25.3% Irish, 22.0% German, 16.1% English, 10.8% Dutch, 9.1% United States or American (2000).
Economy: Employment by occupation: 6.7% management, 1.3% professional, 13.3% services, 12.0% sales, 0.0% farming, 12.0% construction, 54.7% production (2000).
Income: Per capita income: $21,298 (2000); Median household income: $30,469 (2000); Poverty rate: 14.0% (2000).
Taxes: Total city taxes per capita: $103 (1997); City property taxes per capita: $51 (1997).
Education: High school graduation rate: 58.6% (2000); College graduation rate: 0.8% (2000).
Housing: Homeownership rate: 84.1% (2000); Median home value: $25,000 (2000); Median rent: $313 per month (2000); Median age of housing: 60+ years (2000).
Transportation: Commute to work: 100.0% car, 0.0% public transportation, 0.0% walk, 0.0% work from home (2000); Travel time to work: 10.8% less than 15 minutes, 62.2% 15 to 30 minutes, 6.8% 30 to 45 minutes, 17.6% 45 to 60 minutes, 2.7% 60 minutes or more (2000)

UNIVERSITY PARK (city). Covers a land area of 0.769 square miles and a water area of 0 square miles. Located at 41.28° N. Lat.; 92.61° W. Long.
History: Seat of Kletzing College.
Population: 536 (2000); Race: 97.0% White, 0.6% Black, 1.9% Asian, 0.6% American Indian and Alaska Native, 0.0% Hispanic of any race, 0.0% two or more races (2000); Density: 697.0 persons per square mile (2000); Age: 22.5% under 18, 17.8% over 64 (2000); Marriage status: 23.5% never married, 65.8% now married, 2.8% widowed, 7.9% divorced (2000); Foreign born: 3.0% (2000); Ancestry (includes multiple ancestries): 17.6% German, 13.7% English, 12.4% Other groups, 10.1% Dutch, 9.8% Irish (2000).
Economy: Single-family building permits issued: 1 (2001) / 1 (2000); Multi-family building permits issued: 0 (2001) / 0 (2000); Employment by occupation: 4.9% management, 9.8% professional, 29.8% services, 23.9% sales, 0.0% farming, 8.4% construction, 23.2% production (2000).
Income: Per capita income: $14,212 (2000); Median household income: $31,875 (2000); Poverty rate: 7.3% (2000).
Taxes: Total city taxes per capita: $119 (1997); City property taxes per capita: $67 (1997).
Education: High school graduation rate: 83.8% (2000); College graduation rate: 27.9% (2000).

Four-year College(s)

Vennard College (Private, Not-for-profit, Undenominational)
2001 Enrollment: 88 641-673-8391
2001 Tuition: In-state $6,580; Out-of-state $6,580
Housing: Homeownership rate: 63.6% (2000); Median home value: $59,500 (2000); Median rent: $356 per month (2000); Median age of housing: 49 years (2000).
Transportation: Commute to work: 80.0% car, 0.0% public transportation, 9.3% walk, 10.0% work from home (2000); Travel time to work: 52.0% less than 15 minutes, 25.8% 15 to 30 minutes, 11.9% 30 to 45 minutes, 2.4% 45 to 60 minutes, 7.9% 60 minutes or more (2000)

Marion County

Located in south central Iowa; prairie area, drained by the Skunk and Des Moines Rivers. Covers a land area of 554.20 square miles, a water area of 16.30 square miles, and is located in the Central Time Zone. The county government was organized in 1845. County seat is Knoxville.

Weather Station: Knoxville Elevation: 918 feet

	Jan	Feb	Mar	Apr	May	Jun	Jul	Aug	Sep	Oct	Nov	Dec
High	30	37	49	62	74	83	87	85	77	65	48	35
Low	12	18	29	41	52	61	66	63	55	43	30	18
Precip	0.9	1.1	2.0	3.9	4.5	4.2	4.2	4.3	3.8	2.8	2.2	1.2
Snow	6.4	5.9	2.7	1.1	tr	0.0	0.0	0.0	0.0	0.4	2.0	5.6

High and Low temperatures in degrees Fahrenheit; Precipitation and Snow in inches

Population: 32,052 (2000); Race: 97.5% White, 0.6% Black, 1.0% Asian, 0.1% American Indian and Alaska Native, 0.7% Hispanic of any race, 0.4% two or more races (2000); Density: 57.8 persons per square mile (2000); Age: 25.4% under 18, 16.0% over 64 (2000).
Religion: Five largest groups: 13.3% Reformed Church in America, 9.9% Christian Reformed Church in North America, 8.0% The United Methodist Church, 6.0% Catholic Church, 3.2% American Baptist Churches in the USA (2000).
Economy: Unemployment rate: 4.1% (11/2002); Total civilian labor force: 17,660 (11/2002); Leading industries: 47.0% manufacturing; 13.5% health care and social assistance; 9.2% retail trade (2000); Companies that employ more than 1,000 persons: 3 (2000); Companies that employ more than 100 persons: 17 (2000); Farms: 971 totaling 285,724 acres (1997); Minority business ownership rate: 0.0% (1997); Women business ownership rate: 29.3% (1997); Retail sales per capita: $7,813 (1997). Single-family building permits issued: 104 (2001) / 188 (2000); Multi-family building permits issued: 129 (2001) / 50 (2000).
Income: Per capita income: $18,717 (2000); Median household income: $42,401 (2000); Poverty rate: 7.6% (2000); Bankruptcy rate: 3.61% (2001).
Taxes: Total county taxes per capita: $179 (2000); County property taxes per capita: $174 (2000).
Education: High school graduation rate: 84.0% (2000); College graduation rate: 18.9% (2000).
Housing: Homeownership rate: 75.5% (2000); Median home value: $88,300 (2000); Median rent: $384 per month (2000); Median age of housing: 35 years (2000).
Health: Birth rate: 125.7 per 10,000 population (1998); Age adjusted death rate: 79.4 per 10,000 population (1999); Age adjusted cancer mortality rate: 168.0 deaths per 100,000 population (1999). Number of physicians: 7.8 per 10,000 population (1999); Number of hospital beds: 64.9 per 10,000 population (1999).
Elections: 2000 Presidential election results: 39.9% Gore, 58.0% Bush, 1.4% Nader, 0.3% Buchanan
National and State Parks: Pella State Game Management Area
Additional Information Contacts
Marion County Government Offices 515-828-2231
Knoxville Chamber of Commerce 641-828-7555
Marion County Board of Realtors 641-628-9840
Pella Chamber of Commerce 641-628-2626
Pleasantville Chamber of Commerce 515-848-3903

Marion County Communities

BUSSEY (city). Covers a land area of 0.331 square miles and a water area of 0 square miles. Located at 41.20° N. Lat.; 92.88° W. Long. Elevation is 873 feet.
Population: 450 (2000); Race: 95.8% White, 0.0% Black, 0.0% Asian, 0.0% American Indian and Alaska Native, 6.2% Hispanic of any race, 0.9% two or more races (2000); Density: 1,358.1 persons per square mile (2000); Age: 28.8% under 18, 14.9% over 64 (2000); Marriage status: 23.2% never married, 54.4% now married, 9.7% widowed, 12.6% divorced (2000); Foreign born: 1.3% (2000); Ancestry (includes multiple ancestries): 19.1% German, 16.0% Dutch, 13.6% Irish, 13.4% English, 8.1% Other groups (2000).
Economy: In livestock-raising area. Employment by occupation: 5.7% management, 12.3% professional, 13.7% services, 13.7% sales, 0.5% farming, 10.0% construction, 44.1% production (2000).
Income: Per capita income: $14,657 (2000); Median household income: $32,500 (2000); Poverty rate: 12.6% (2000).
Taxes: Total city taxes per capita: $103 (1997); City property taxes per capita: $99 (1997).
Education: High school graduation rate: 77.9% (2000); College graduation rate: 6.3% (2000).

School District(s)
Twin Cedars Community School District (PK-12)
2000 Enrollment: 572 641-944-5241
Housing: Homeownership rate: 78.7% (2000); Median home value: $42,800 (2000); Median rent: $243 per month (2000); Median age of housing: 60 years (2000).
Transportation: Commute to work: 96.6% car, 0.0% public transportation, 1.5% walk, 1.9% work from home (2000); Travel time to work: 12.4% less than 15 minutes, 26.7% 15 to 30 minutes, 45.5% 30 to 45 minutes, 9.9% 45 to 60 minutes, 5.4% 60 minutes or more (2000)

COLUMBIA (unincorporated postal area, zip code 50057). Covers a land area of 16.609 square miles and a water area of 0.014 square miles. Located at 41.18° N. Lat.; 93.16° W. Long. Elevation is 952 feet.
Population: 217 (2000); Race: 100.0% White, 0.0% Black, 0.0% Asian, 0.0% American Indian and Alaska Native, 0.0% Hispanic of any race, 0.0% two or more races (2000); Density: 13.1 persons per square mile (2000); Age: 28.8% under 18, 19.2% over 64 (2000); Marriage status: 15.2% never married, 69.1% now married, 9.1% widowed, 6.7% divorced (2000); Foreign born: 0.9% (2000); Ancestry (includes multiple ancestries): 34.5% German, 16.2% United States or American, 14.8% Irish, 10.0% Dutch, 7.4% Norwegian (2000).
Economy: Employment by occupation: 19.6% management, 8.7% professional, 18.5% services, 19.6% sales, 3.3% farming, 10.9% construction, 19.6% production (2000).
Income: Per capita income: $14,233 (2000); Median household income: $35,000 (2000); Poverty rate: 0.9% (2000).
Education: High school graduation rate: 80.8% (2000); College graduation rate: 4.0% (2000).
Housing: Homeownership rate: 88.2% (2000); Median home value: $38,900 (2000); Median age of housing: 60+ years (2000).
Transportation: Commute to work: 90.2% car, 0.0% public transportation, 3.3% walk, 4.3% work from home (2000); Travel time to work: 38.6% less than 15 minutes, 27.3% 15 to 30 minutes, 13.6% 30 to 45 minutes, 6.8% 45 to 60 minutes, 13.6% 60 minutes or more (2000)

DALLAS (unincorporated postal area, zip code 50062). Covers a land area of 31.891 square miles and a water area of 0.009 square miles. Located at 41.33° N. Lat.; 93.14° W. Long.
Population: 1,650 (2000); Race: 98.9% White, 0.4% Black, 0.2% Asian, 0.1% American Indian and Alaska Native, 0.4% Hispanic of any race, 0.4% two or more races (2000); Density: 51.7 persons per square mile (2000); Age: 26.9% under 18, 16.9% over 64 (2000); Marriage status: 19.7% never married, 61.8% now married, 8.7% widowed, 9.8% divorced (2000); Foreign born: 0.4% (2000); Ancestry (includes multiple ancestries): 24.2% German, 11.6% English, 8.3% Irish, 8.0% Dutch, 7.6% United States or American (2000).
Economy: Employment by occupation: 10.2% management, 11.2% professional, 13.6% services, 22.7% sales, 0.0% farming, 12.4% construction, 29.9% production (2000).
Income: Per capita income: $15,743 (2000); Median household income: $36,941 (2000); Poverty rate: 7.5% (2000).
Education: High school graduation rate: 76.9% (2000); College graduation rate: 5.7% (2000).
Housing: Homeownership rate: 87.2% (2000); Median home value: $53,800 (2000); Median rent: $268 per month (2000); Median age of housing: 60+ years (2000).
Transportation: Commute to work: 89.5% car, 0.0% public transportation, 1.4% walk, 8.3% work from home (2000); Travel time to work: 15.7% less than 15 minutes, 25.0% 15 to 30 minutes, 13.2% 30 to 45 minutes, 24.8% 45 to 60 minutes, 21.3% 60 minutes or more (2000)

HAMILTON (city). Covers a land area of 0.542 square miles and a water area of 0 square miles. Located at 41.17° N. Lat.; 92.90° W. Long.
History: Hamilton was settled in 1849 by a group of people from Hamilton County, Ohio, who used the name of their former home for their new town.
Population: 144 (2000); Race: 100.0% White, 0.0% Black, 0.0% Asian, 0.0% American Indian and Alaska Native, 0.0% Hispanic of any race, 0.0% two or more races (2000); Density: 265.7 persons per square mile (2000); Age: 25.9% under 18, 13.3% over 64 (2000); Marriage status: 29.7% never married, 51.4% now married, 8.1% widowed, 10.8% divorced (2000); Foreign born: 0.0% (2000); Ancestry (includes multiple ancestries): 20.7% Dutch, 18.5% United States or American, 18.5% German, 13.3% Irish, 8.9% French (except Basque) (2000).

Economy: Employment by occupation: 7.4% management, 3.7% professional, 9.3% services, 3.7% sales, 5.6% farming, 16.7% construction, 53.7% production (2000).
Income: Per capita income: $42,935 (2000); Median household income: $37,083 (2000); Poverty rate: 10.5% (2000).
Taxes: Total city taxes per capita: $32 (1997); City property taxes per capita: $32 (1997).
Education: High school graduation rate: 76.5% (2000); College graduation rate: 3.7% (2000).
Housing: Homeownership rate: 92.5% (2000); Median home value: $41,700 (2000); Median rent: <$100 per month (2000); Median age of housing: 38 years (2000).
Transportation: Commute to work: 96.3% car, 3.7% public transportation, 0.0% walk, 0.0% work from home (2000); Travel time to work: 7.4% less than 15 minutes, 37.0% 15 to 30 minutes, 40.7% 30 to 45 minutes, 0.0% 45 to 60 minutes, 14.8% 60 minutes or more (2000)

HARVEY (city). Covers a land area of 0.679 square miles and a water area of 0 square miles. Located at 41.31° N. Lat.; 92.92° W. Long.
Population: 277 (2000); Race: 98.9% White, 0.0% Black, 0.0% Asian, 0.7% American Indian and Alaska Native, 0.0% Hispanic of any race, 0.4% two or more races (2000); Density: 408.2 persons per square mile (2000); Age: 26.5% under 18, 10.3% over 64 (2000); Marriage status: 22.0% never married, 58.7% now married, 6.4% widowed, 12.8% divorced (2000); Foreign born: 0.0% (2000); Ancestry (includes multiple ancestries): 20.6% Dutch, 16.5% German, 12.9% United States or American, 11.8% Other groups, 11.4% Irish (2000).
Economy: Brick and tile plant. Limestone quarries, sand and gravel pits nearby. Employment by occupation: 1.6% management, 2.3% professional, 17.2% services, 18.0% sales, 3.1% farming, 15.6% construction, 42.2% production (2000).
Income: Per capita income: $12,770 (2000); Median household income: $34,688 (2000); Poverty rate: 19.2% (2000).
Taxes: Total city taxes per capita: $45 (1997); City property taxes per capita: $45 (1997).
Education: High school graduation rate: 63.2% (2000); College graduation rate: 2.3% (2000).
Housing: Homeownership rate: 73.6% (2000); Median home value: $49,300 (2000); Median rent: $238 per month (2000); Median age of housing: 27 years (2000).
Transportation: Commute to work: 96.8% car, 0.0% public transportation, 3.2% walk, 0.0% work from home (2000); Travel time to work: 12.1% less than 15 minutes, 71.0% 15 to 30 minutes, 12.1% 30 to 45 minutes, 0.0% 45 to 60 minutes, 4.8% 60 minutes or more (2000)

KNOXVILLE (city). Covers a land area of 4.427 square miles and a water area of 0 square miles. Located at 41.31° N. Lat.; 93.10° W. Long. Elevation is 910 feet.
History: Knoxville was founded in 1845 and named for General Henry Knox, an officer in the Revolutionary War, who later became Secretary of War and the first Secretary of the Navy.
Population: 7,731 (2000); Race: 97.0% White, 1.6% Black, 0.4% Asian, 0.2% American Indian and Alaska Native, 0.7% Hispanic of any race, 0.4% two or more races (2000); Density: 1,746.2 persons per square mile (2000); Age: 22.8% under 18, 21.5% over 64 (2000); Marriage status: 18.5% never married, 57.2% now married, 10.7% widowed, 13.5% divorced (2000); Foreign born: 1.4% (2000); Ancestry (includes multiple ancestries): 24.1% German, 15.3% Irish, 14.2% English, 10.1% Dutch, 8.3% United States or American (2000).
Economy: Single-family building permits issued: 10 (2001) / 15 (2000); Multi-family building permits issued: 31 (2001) / 0 (2000); Employment by occupation: 11.3% management, 14.9% professional, 17.3% services, 26.3% sales, 0.3% farming, 6.4% construction, 23.4% production (2000).
Income: Per capita income: $17,893 (2000); Median household income: $34,055 (2000); Poverty rate: 11.1% (2000).
Taxes: Total city taxes per capita: $236 (1997); City property taxes per capita: $225 (1997).
Education: High school graduation rate: 83.0% (2000); College graduation rate: 12.7% (2000).

School District(s)

Knoxville Community School District (PK-12)
2000 Enrollment: 2,124 641-842-6552

Housing: Homeownership rate: 69.6% (2000); Median home value: $72,900 (2000); Median rent: $358 per month (2000); Median age of housing: 42 years (2000).
Hospitals: Knoxville Area Community Hospital (59 beds); Veterans Affairs Central Iowa Health Care System (521 beds)
Newspapers: The Knoxville Journal-Express (1 x week); Reminder (1 x week)
Transportation: Commute to work: 92.9% car, 0.0% public transportation, 4.8% walk, 1.9% work from home (2000); Travel time to work: 53.0% less than 15 minutes, 25.4% 15 to 30 minutes, 7.9% 30 to 45 minutes, 6.3% 45 to 60 minutes, 7.4% 60 minutes or more (2000)

Additional Information Contacts

Knoxville Chamber of Commerce 641-828-7555
Marion County Board of Realtors 641-628-9840

MARYSVILLE (city). Covers a land area of 0.363 square miles and a water area of 0 square miles. Located at 41.18° N. Lat.; 92.95° W. Long.
History: Marysville was mapped in 1851 by Joseph Brobst. Mr. Brobst had five women in his family named Mary, which is believed to be the reason for the name.
Population: 54 (2000); Race: 100.0% White, 0.0% Black, 0.0% Asian, 0.0% American Indian and Alaska Native, 0.0% Hispanic of any race, 0.0% two or more races (2000); Density: 148.7 persons per square mile (2000); Age: 31.7% under 18, 6.3% over 64 (2000); Marriage status: 13.3% never married, 77.8% now married, 4.4% widowed, 4.4% divorced (2000); Foreign born: 0.0% (2000); Ancestry (includes multiple ancestries): 28.6% United States or American, 25.4% German, 15.9% Dutch, 11.1% French (except Basque), 6.3% Irish (2000).
Economy: Employment by occupation: 2.6% management, 10.5% professional, 10.5% services, 10.5% sales, 0.0% farming, 5.3% construction, 60.5% production (2000).
Income: Per capita income: $17,135 (2000); Median household income: $43,750 (2000); Poverty rate: 0.0% (2000).
Taxes: Total city taxes per capita: $27 (1997); City property taxes per capita: $27 (1997).
Education: High school graduation rate: 94.6% (2000); College graduation rate: 5.4% (2000).
Housing: Homeownership rate: 100.0% (2000); Median home value: $41,300 (2000); Median age of housing: 55 years (2000).
Transportation: Commute to work: 100.0% car, 0.0% public transportation, 0.0% walk, 0.0% work from home (2000); Travel time to work: 15.8% less than 15 minutes, 26.3% 15 to 30 minutes, 57.9% 30 to 45 minutes, 0.0% 45 to 60 minutes, 0.0% 60 minutes or more (2000)

MELCHER-DALLAS (city). Covers a land area of 1.001 square miles and a water area of 0 square miles. Located at 41.22° N. Lat.; 93.24° W. Long.
History: Melcher was incorporated with Dallas, Iowa, in 1986 to form this town. The name Melcher came from a railroad employee who died in a train collision in 1912. The name Dallas was in honor of the Vice President under James Polk (1845-1849), George Mifflin Dallas.
Population: 1,298 (2000); Race: 98.9% White, 0.2% Black, 0.2% Asian, 0.2% American Indian and Alaska Native, 0.5% Hispanic of any race, 0.5% two or more races (2000); Density: 1,297.1 persons per square mile (2000); Age: 27.9% under 18, 17.5% over 64 (2000); Marriage status: 20.8% never married, 58.7% now married, 9.5% widowed, 11.0% divorced (2000); Foreign born: 0.5% (2000); Ancestry (includes multiple ancestries): 23.0% German, 12.0% English, 8.4% Dutch, 8.4% Irish, 8.1% United States or American (2000).
Economy: Single-family building permits issued: 3 (2001) / 6 (2000); Multi-family building permits issued: 0 (2001) / 0 (2000); Employment by occupation: 7.3% management, 10.8% professional, 15.2% services, 21.2% sales, 0.0% farming, 13.2% construction, 32.2% production (2000).
Income: Per capita income: $15,600 (2000); Median household income: $36,207 (2000); Poverty rate: 8.2% (2000).
Taxes: Total city taxes per capita: $101 (1997); City property taxes per capita: $99 (1997).
Education: High school graduation rate: 75.5% (2000); College graduation rate: 5.0% (2000).

School District(s)

Melcher-Dallas Community School District (PK-12)
2000 Enrollment: 449 641-947-2321

Housing: Homeownership rate: 85.1% (2000); Median home value: $51,800 (2000); Median rent: $264 per month (2000); Median age of housing: 60+ years (2000).
Transportation: Commute to work: 93.6% car, 0.0% public transportation, 0.7% walk, 4.6% work from home (2000); Travel time to work: 13.7% less than 15 minutes, 25.5% 15 to 30 minutes, 14.7% 30 to 45 minutes, 23.4% 45 to 60 minutes, 22.8% 60 minutes or more (2000)

OTLEY (unincorporated postal area, zip code 50214). Covers a land area of 38.539 square miles and a water area of 0.020 square miles. Located at 41.45° N. Lat.; 93.07° W. Long. Elevation is 875 feet.
History: Otley was settled in 1867 because of the discovery of a vein of coal in that vicinity. It was named for a railroad official.
Population: 834 (2000); Race: 100.0% White, 0.0% Black, 0.0% Asian, 0.0% American Indian and Alaska Native, 0.0% Hispanic of any race, 0.0% two or more races (2000); Density: 21.6 persons per square mile (2000); Age: 24.9% under 18, 6.1% over 64 (2000); Marriage status: 24.1% never married, 63.4% now married, 2.8% widowed, 9.7% divorced (2000); Foreign born: 2.2% (2000); Ancestry (includes multiple ancestries): 46.6% Dutch, 20.2% German, 14.8% Irish, 11.1% English, 2.7% United States or American (2000).
Economy: Employment by occupation: 16.1% management, 10.8% professional, 11.5% services, 19.1% sales, 1.1% farming, 6.0% construction, 35.5% production (2000).
Income: Per capita income: $18,028 (2000); Median household income: $45,481 (2000); Poverty rate: 7.9% (2000).
Education: High school graduation rate: 87.6% (2000); College graduation rate: 10.4% (2000).
Housing: Homeownership rate: 88.2% (2000); Median home value: $97,100 (2000); Median rent: $325 per month (2000); Median age of housing: 34 years (2000).
Transportation: Commute to work: 91.0% car, 0.0% public transportation, 0.0% walk, 9.0% work from home (2000); Travel time to work: 41.0% less than 15 minutes, 33.2% 15 to 30 minutes, 8.0% 30 to 45 minutes, 8.3% 45 to 60 minutes, 9.5% 60 minutes or more (2000)

PELLA (city). Covers a land area of 6.840 square miles and a water area of 0 square miles. Located at 41.40° N. Lat.; 92.91° W. Long. Elevation is 877 feet.
History: Pella was named by Dutch settlers, more than 700 of whom, headed by Henry Peter Scholte, fled religious intolerance in their native country and came to Iowa in 1847. They adopted for a city seal the motto "In Deo Spes Nostra et Refugium" (In God is our hope and refuge).
Population: 9,832 (2000); Race: 96.5% White, 0.3% Black, 2.5% Asian, 0.2% American Indian and Alaska Native, 0.3% Hispanic of any race, 0.6% two or more races (2000); Density: 1,437.4 persons per square mile (2000); Age: 22.1% under 18, 18.5% over 64 (2000); Marriage status: 29.0% never married, 58.2% now married, 8.7% widowed, 4.1% divorced (2000); Foreign born: 3.1% (2000); Ancestry (includes multiple ancestries): 45.8% Dutch, 19.2% German, 8.4% English, 7.1% Irish, 5.2% Other groups (2000).
Economy: Single-family building permits issued: 19 (2001) / 40 (2000); Multi-family building permits issued: 98 (2001) / 50 (2000); Employment by occupation: 11.1% management, 22.9% professional, 15.4% services, 26.0% sales, 0.1% farming, 6.3% construction, 18.2% production (2000).
Income: Per capita income: $19,674 (2000); Median household income: $45,496 (2000); Poverty rate: 7.7% (2000).
Taxes: Total city taxes per capita: $301 (2000); City property taxes per capita: $272 (2000).
Education: High school graduation rate: 81.6% (2000); College graduation rate: 31.4% (2000).

School District(s)

Pella Community School District (PK-12)
2000 Enrollment: 2,132 641-628-1111

Four-year College(s)

Central College (Private, Not-for-profit, Reformed Church in America)
2001 Enrollment: 1,425 641-628-9000
2001 Tuition: In-state $15,598; Out-of-state $15,598

Housing: Homeownership rate: 67.3% (2000); Median home value: $117,900 (2000); Median rent: $456 per month (2000); Median age of housing: 32 years (2000).
Hospitals: Pella Regional Health Center (47 beds)
Safety: Violent crime rate: 26.5 per 10,000 population; Property crime rate: 187.4 per 10,000 population (2001).
Newspapers: Pella Chronicle (1 x week)
Transportation: Commute to work: 79.4% car, 1.6% public transportation, 13.7% walk, 3.2% work from home (2000); Travel time to work: 82.4% less than 15 minutes, 9.4% 15 to 30 minutes, 2.9% 30 to 45 minutes, 2.1% 45 to 60 minutes, 3.2% 60 minutes or more (2000)
Airports: Pella Municipal

Additional Information Contacts

Pella Chamber of Commerce 641-628-2626

PLEASANTVILLE (city). Covers a land area of 1.164 square miles and a water area of 0 square miles. Located at 41.38° N. Lat.; 93.26° W. Long. Elevation is 926 feet.
Population: 1,539 (2000); Race: 98.7% White, 0.0% Black, 0.5% Asian, 0.1% American Indian and Alaska Native, 1.3% Hispanic of any race, 0.5% two or more races (2000); Density: 1,322.4 persons per square mile (2000); Age: 29.3% under 18, 17.2% over 64 (2000); Marriage status: 20.5% never married, 57.1% now married, 10.8% widowed, 11.6% divorced (2000); Foreign born: 0.5% (2000); Ancestry (includes multiple ancestries): 18.2% German, 14.6% English, 10.6% United States or American, 10.3% Irish, 9.8% Dutch (2000).
Economy: In agricultural area; feed manufacturing. Single-family building permits issued: 4 (2001) / 5 (2000); Multi-family building permits issued: 0 (2001) / 0 (2000); Employment by occupation: 11.5% management, 20.4% professional, 11.7% services, 25.1% sales, 1.5% farming, 10.1% construction, 19.6% production (2000).
Income: Per capita income: $18,279 (2000); Median household income: $40,000 (2000); Poverty rate: 7.1% (2000).
Taxes: Total city taxes per capita: $126 (1997); City property taxes per capita: $122 (1997).
Education: High school graduation rate: 88.4% (2000); College graduation rate: 18.9% (2000).

School District(s)

Pleasantville Community School District (PK-12)
2000 Enrollment: 721 515-848-0555

Housing: Homeownership rate: 75.6% (2000); Median home value: $78,400 (2000); Median rent: $327 per month (2000); Median age of housing: 35 years (2000).
Newspapers: Marion County News (1 x week)
Transportation: Commute to work: 94.6% car, 0.0% public transportation, 3.0% walk, 2.1% work from home (2000); Travel time to work: 24.4% less than 15 minutes, 16.1% 15 to 30 minutes, 35.6% 30 to 45 minutes, 17.6% 45 to 60 minutes, 6.4% 60 minutes or more (2000)

Additional Information Contacts

Pleasantville Chamber of Commerce 515-848-3903

SWAN (city). Covers a land area of 0.647 square miles and a water area of 0 square miles. Located at 41.46° N. Lat.; 93.31° W. Long.
History: Swan was named for Swan Township in Ohio.
Population: 121 (2000); Race: 100.0% White, 0.0% Black, 0.0% Asian, 0.0% American Indian and Alaska Native, 0.0% Hispanic of any race, 0.0% two or more races (2000); Density: 187.0 persons per square mile (2000); Age: 29.3% under 18, 15.8% over 64 (2000); Marriage status: 23.7% never married, 61.9% now married, 3.1% widowed, 11.3% divorced (2000); Foreign born: 0.0% (2000); Ancestry (includes multiple ancestries): 33.8% German, 12.8% Danish, 10.5% United States or American, 7.5% Swedish, 6.8% English (2000).
Economy: Employment by occupation: 11.3% management, 14.5% professional, 17.7% services, 29.0% sales, 0.0% farming, 8.1% construction, 19.4% production (2000).
Income: Per capita income: $12,936 (2000); Median household income: $32,750 (2000); Poverty rate: 12.0% (2000).
Taxes: Total city taxes per capita: $47 (1997); City property taxes per capita: $47 (1997).
Education: High school graduation rate: 85.5% (2000); College graduation rate: 0.0% (2000).
Housing: Homeownership rate: 93.0% (2000); Median home value: $62,500 (2000); Median rent: $175 per month (2000); Median age of housing: 57 years (2000).
Transportation: Commute to work: 90.3% car, 0.0% public transportation, 0.0% walk, 9.7% work from home (2000); Travel time to work: 14.3% less than 15 minutes, 0.0% 15 to 30 minutes, 51.8% 30 to 45 minutes, 33.9% 45 to 60 minutes, 0.0% 60 minutes or more (2000)

TRACY (unincorporated postal area, zip code 50256). Covers a land area of 24.713 square miles and a water area of 0.044 square miles. Located at 41.27° N. Lat.; 92.90° W. Long. Elevation is 775 feet.
History: Tracy was mapped in 1875.
Population: 513 (2000); Race: 99.3% White, 0.0% Black, 0.0% Asian, 0.0% American Indian and Alaska Native, 0.0% Hispanic of any race, 0.7% two or more races (2000); Density: 20.8 persons per square mile (2000); Age: 18.5% under 18, 16.2% over 64 (2000); Marriage status: 19.9% never married, 70.2% now married, 8.3% widowed, 1.7% divorced (2000); Foreign born: 0.0% (2000); Ancestry (includes multiple ancestries): 25.1% German, 23.9%

Dutch, 8.4% Irish, 6.8% United States or American, 6.6% Other groups (2000).
Economy: Employment by occupation: 2.5% management, 17.6% professional, 18.4% services, 14.2% sales, 0.0% farming, 9.6% construction, 37.7% production (2000).
Income: Per capita income: $17,394 (2000); Median household income: $37,125 (2000); Poverty rate: 9.4% (2000).
Education: High school graduation rate: 78.5% (2000); College graduation rate: 8.7% (2000).
Housing: Homeownership rate: 79.6% (2000); Median home value: $49,200 (2000); Median rent: $245 per month (2000); Median age of housing: 60 years (2000).
Transportation: Commute to work: 93.3% car, 0.0% public transportation, 1.3% walk, 5.4% work from home (2000); Travel time to work: 12.8% less than 15 minutes, 44.2% 15 to 30 minutes, 27.9% 30 to 45 minutes, 4.0% 45 to 60 minutes, 11.1% 60 minutes or more (2000)

Marshall County

Located in central Iowa; prairie area, drained by the Iowa and North Skunk Rivers. Covers a land area of 572.30 square miles, a water area of 0.70 square miles, and is located in the Central Time Zone. The county government was organized in 1846. County seat is Marshalltown.

Weather Station: Marshalltown Elevation: 869 feet

	Jan	Feb	Mar	Apr	May	Jun	Jul	Aug	Sep	Oct	Nov	Dec
High	27	33	45	60	72	81	85	82	75	63	46	32
Low	7	14	26	37	49	59	63	59	50	38	26	14
Precip	0.9	1.0	2.5	3.3	4.3	5.3	4.4	4.9	3.7	2.8	2.2	1.2
Snow	7.6	6.4	4.9	1.2	tr	0.0	0.0	0.0	0.0	0.2	2.3	6.5

High and Low temperatures in degrees Fahrenheit; Precipitation and Snow in inches

Population: 39,311 (2000); Race: 90.0% White, 0.8% Black, 0.9% Asian, 0.2% American Indian and Alaska Native, 8.9% Hispanic of any race, 1.6% two or more races (2000); Density: 68.7 persons per square mile (2000); Age: 25.3% under 18, 16.6% over 64 (2000).
Religion: Five largest groups: 16.1% Catholic Church, 9.9% The United Methodist Church, 5.7% Evangelical Lutheran Church in America, 3.7% Lutheran Church—Missouri Synod, 3.5% Christian Church (Disciples of Christ) (2000).
Economy: Unemployment rate: 4.0% (11/2002); Total civilian labor force: 21,097 (11/2002); Leading industries: 33.0% manufacturing; 15.8% retail trade; 13.6% health care and social assistance (2000); Companies that employ more than 1,000 persons: 3 (2000); Companies that employ more than 100 persons: 20 (2000); Farms: 912 totaling 319,392 acres (1997); Minority business ownership rate: 0.0% (1997); Women business ownership rate: 23.7% (1997); Retail sales per capita: $8,249 (1997). Single-family building permits issued: 59 (2001) / 45 (2000); Multi-family building permits issued: 35 (2001) / 16 (2000).
Income: Per capita income: $19,176 (2000); Median household income: $38,268 (2000); Poverty rate: 10.2% (2000); Bankruptcy rate: 2.72% (2001).
Taxes: Total county taxes per capita: $218 (2000); County property taxes per capita: $211 (2000).
Education: High school graduation rate: 82.3% (2000); College graduation rate: 17.0% (2000).
Housing: Homeownership rate: 73.8% (2000); Median home value: $71,200 (2000); Median rent: $365 per month (2000); Median age of housing: 45 years (2000).
Health: Birth rate: 130.2 per 10,000 population (1998); Age adjusted death rate: 96.7 per 10,000 population (1999); Age adjusted cancer mortality rate: 241.4 deaths per 100,000 population (1999). Number of physicians: 12.2 per 10,000 population (1999); Number of hospital beds: 28.2 per 10,000 population (1999).
Elections: 2000 Presidential election results: 47.2% Gore, 49.9% Bush, 1.9% Nader, 0.4% Buchanan

Additional Information Contacts

Marshall County Government Offices 641-754-6330
Marshalltown Board of Realtors 641-753-6453
Marshalltown Chamber of Commerce 641-753-6645

Marshall County Communities

ALBION (city). Covers a land area of 0.592 square miles and a water area of 0 square miles. Located at 42.11° N. Lat.; 92.99° W. Long. Elevation is 929 feet.
History: Albion was platted in 1852 as Lafayette.
Population: 592 (2000); Race: 98.7% White, 0.0% Black, 1.3% Asian, 0.0% American Indian and Alaska Native, 2.1% Hispanic of any race, 0.0% two or more races (2000); Density: 999.7 persons per square mile (2000); Age: 28.5% under 18, 13.2% over 64 (2000); Marriage status: 21.1% never married, 61.3% now married, 5.3% widowed, 12.4% divorced (2000); Foreign born: 1.5% (2000); Ancestry (includes multiple ancestries): 27.1% United States or American, 27.1% German, 10.5% Irish, 9.5% English, 6.9% Other groups (2000).
Economy: Single-family building permits issued: 2 (2001) / 2 (2000); Multi-family building permits issued: 0 (2001) / 0 (2000); Employment by occupation: 5.9% management, 8.6% professional, 20.3% services, 27.9% sales, 1.4% farming, 9.7% construction, 26.2% production (2000).
Income: Per capita income: $14,770 (2000); Median household income: $36,875 (2000); Poverty rate: 15.9% (2000).
Taxes: Total city taxes per capita: $146 (1997); City property taxes per capita: $145 (1997).
Education: High school graduation rate: 80.4% (2000); College graduation rate: 7.2% (2000).
Housing: Homeownership rate: 86.9% (2000); Median home value: $52,000 (2000); Median rent: $346 per month (2000); Median age of housing: 43 years (2000).
Transportation: Commute to work: 96.5% car, 0.0% public transportation, 1.8% walk, 1.8% work from home (2000); Travel time to work: 13.9% less than 15 minutes, 71.1% 15 to 30 minutes, 10.0% 30 to 45 minutes, 1.8% 45 to 60 minutes, 3.2% 60 minutes or more (2000)

CLEMONS (city). Aka Clemons Grove. Covers a land area of 0.270 square miles and a water area of 0 square miles. Located at 42.11° N. Lat.; 93.15° W. Long.
History: The Clemons family founded the town in 1882, first calling it Clemons Grove.
Population: 148 (2000); Race: 100.0% White, 0.0% Black, 0.0% Asian, 0.0% American Indian and Alaska Native, 0.0% Hispanic of any race, 0.0% two or more races (2000); Density: 547.7 persons per square mile (2000); Age: 23.6% under 18, 8.3% over 64 (2000); Marriage status: 26.6% never married, 46.8% now married, 1.6% widowed, 25.0% divorced (2000); Foreign born: 1.4% (2000); Ancestry (includes multiple ancestries): 38.2% German, 9.0% United States or American, 7.6% Irish, 6.9% Norwegian, 5.6% English (2000).
Economy: Employment by occupation: 4.5% management, 14.6% professional, 19.1% services, 13.5% sales, 2.2% farming, 14.6% construction, 31.5% production (2000).
Income: Per capita income: $18,517 (2000); Median household income: $46,964 (2000); Poverty rate: 4.2% (2000).
Taxes: Total city taxes per capita: $79 (1997); City property taxes per capita: $79 (1997).
Education: High school graduation rate: 83.2% (2000); College graduation rate: 6.9% (2000).
Housing: Homeownership rate: 87.9% (2000); Median home value: $27,900 (2000); Median rent: $185 per month (2000); Median age of housing: 60+ years (2000).
Transportation: Commute to work: 96.6% car, 0.0% public transportation, 0.0% walk, 3.4% work from home (2000); Travel time to work: 26.7% less than 15 minutes, 30.2% 15 to 30 minutes, 38.4% 30 to 45 minutes, 2.3% 45 to 60 minutes, 2.3% 60 minutes or more (2000)

FERGUSON (city). Covers a land area of 0.249 square miles and a water area of 0 square miles. Located at 41.93° N. Lat.; 92.86° W. Long.
History: Ferguson, established as a railroad town, was named for an early settler.
Population: 126 (2000); Race: 95.7% White, 0.0% Black, 0.0% Asian, 0.7% American Indian and Alaska Native, 0.0% Hispanic of any race, 3.5% two or more races (2000); Density: 505.7 persons per square mile (2000); Age: 18.4% under 18, 9.2% over 64 (2000); Marriage status: 18.3% never married, 55.8% now married, 6.7% widowed, 19.2% divorced (2000); Foreign born: 0.0% (2000); Ancestry (includes multiple ancestries): 26.2% German, 9.9% United States or American, 9.2% Norwegian, 7.8% Irish, 6.4% Dutch (2000).
Economy: Employment by occupation: 2.2% management, 12.0% professional, 27.2% services, 17.4% sales, 3.3% farming, 18.5% construction, 19.6% production (2000).
Income: Per capita income: $22,777 (2000); Median household income: $40,893 (2000); Poverty rate: 4.3% (2000).
Taxes: Total city taxes per capita: $115 (1997); City property taxes per capita: $115 (1997).
Education: High school graduation rate: 86.5% (2000); College graduation rate: 7.2% (2000).

Housing: Homeownership rate: 73.3% (2000); Median home value: $26,900 (2000); Median rent: $306 per month (2000); Median age of housing: 56 years (2000).
Transportation: Commute to work: 95.7% car, 0.0% public transportation, 2.2% walk, 2.2% work from home (2000); Travel time to work: 11.1% less than 15 minutes, 61.1% 15 to 30 minutes, 21.1% 30 to 45 minutes, 2.2% 45 to 60 minutes, 4.4% 60 minutes or more (2000)

GILMAN (city). Covers a land area of 0.546 square miles and a water area of 0 square miles. Located at 41.88° N. Lat.; 92.78° W. Long. Elevation is 1,031 feet.
History: Gilman was a station on the Iowa Central Railroad.
Population: 600 (2000); Race: 97.9% White, 0.0% Black, 0.0% Asian, 0.0% American Indian and Alaska Native, 0.0% Hispanic of any race, 2.1% two or more races (2000); Density: 1,099.0 persons per square mile (2000); Age: 29.2% under 18, 13.6% over 64 (2000); Marriage status: 18.5% never married, 59.6% now married, 8.3% widowed, 13.6% divorced (2000); Foreign born: 0.5% (2000); Ancestry (includes multiple ancestries): 23.5% German, 15.8% Irish, 8.9% Norwegian, 7.5% United States or American, 5.8% English (2000).
Economy: Single-family building permits issued: 0 (2001) / 0 (2000); Multi-family building permits issued: 0 (2001) / 0 (2000); Employment by occupation: 5.6% management, 19.3% professional, 16.5% services, 27.4% sales, 1.1% farming, 10.2% construction, 20.0% production (2000).
Income: Per capita income: $15,070 (2000); Median household income: $33,523 (2000); Poverty rate: 12.7% (2000).
Taxes: Total city taxes per capita: $124 (1997); City property taxes per capita: $121 (1997).
Education: High school graduation rate: 86.1% (2000); College graduation rate: 12.1% (2000).

School District(s)

East Marshall Community School District (KG-12)
2000 Enrollment: 883 641-498-7481
Housing: Homeownership rate: 71.6% (2000); Median home value: $55,500 (2000); Median rent: $260 per month (2000); Median age of housing: 44 years (2000).
Transportation: Commute to work: 94.4% car, 0.0% public transportation, 2.5% walk, 2.1% work from home (2000); Travel time to work: 21.1% less than 15 minutes, 62.7% 15 to 30 minutes, 3.9% 30 to 45 minutes, 6.1% 45 to 60 minutes, 6.1% 60 minutes or more (2000)

HAVERHILL (city). Covers a land area of 0.130 square miles and a water area of 0 square miles. Located at 41.94° N. Lat.; 92.96° W. Long.
History: Haverhill was named either for Haverhill, England, or Haverhill, Massachusetts. "Haver" is a British term for oats.
Population: 170 (2000); Race: 100.0% White, 0.0% Black, 0.0% Asian, 0.0% American Indian and Alaska Native, 0.0% Hispanic of any race, 0.0% two or more races (2000); Density: 1,304.0 persons per square mile (2000); Age: 31.4% under 18, 11.0% over 64 (2000); Marriage status: 18.8% never married, 66.2% now married, 7.5% widowed, 7.5% divorced (2000); Foreign born: 0.0% (2000); Ancestry (includes multiple ancestries): 36.6% German, 11.6% English, 10.5% United States or American, 8.7% Czech, 6.4% Austrian (2000).
Economy: Single-family building permits issued: 1 (2001) / 0 (2000); Multi-family building permits issued: 0 (2001) / 0 (2000); Employment by occupation: 10.4% management, 14.6% professional, 17.7% services, 28.1% sales, 2.1% farming, 8.3% construction, 18.8% production (2000).
Income: Per capita income: $18,702 (2000); Median household income: $45,417 (2000); Poverty rate: 0.0% (2000).
Taxes: Total city taxes per capita: $120 (1997); City property taxes per capita: $113 (1997).
Education: High school graduation rate: 88.0% (2000); College graduation rate: 17.6% (2000).
Housing: Homeownership rate: 92.1% (2000); Median home value: $70,000 (2000); Median rent: $508 per month (2000); Median age of housing: 35 years (2000).
Transportation: Commute to work: 95.8% car, 0.0% public transportation, 4.2% walk, 0.0% work from home (2000); Travel time to work: 19.8% less than 15 minutes, 64.6% 15 to 30 minutes, 9.4% 30 to 45 minutes, 0.0% 45 to 60 minutes, 6.3% 60 minutes or more (2000)

LAUREL (city). Covers a land area of 0.252 square miles and a water area of 0 square miles. Located at 41.88° N. Lat.; 92.92° W. Long. Elevation is 1,034 feet.
Population: 266 (2000); Race: 94.1% White, 0.0% Black, 2.4% Asian, 2.8% American Indian and Alaska Native, 0.0% Hispanic of any race, 0.7% two or more races (2000); Density: 1,056.7 persons per square mile (2000); Age: 24.4% under 18, 17.1% over 64 (2000); Marriage status: 18.9% never married, 57.7% now married, 8.4% widowed, 15.0% divorced (2000); Foreign born: 2.8% (2000); Ancestry (includes multiple ancestries): 27.9% German, 15.0% Other groups, 10.1% Irish, 9.4% English, 5.6% United States or American (2000).
Economy: In agricultural area. Employment by occupation: 12.5% management, 6.6% professional, 21.7% services, 24.3% sales, 1.3% farming, 5.9% construction, 27.6% production (2000).
Income: Per capita income: $14,980 (2000); Median household income: $32,031 (2000); Poverty rate: 7.0% (2000).
Taxes: Total city taxes per capita: $107 (1997); City property taxes per capita: $107 (1997).
Education: High school graduation rate: 86.6% (2000); College graduation rate: 4.0% (2000).
Housing: Homeownership rate: 78.3% (2000); Median home value: $55,000 (2000); Median rent: $275 per month (2000); Median age of housing: 42 years (2000).
Transportation: Commute to work: 86.2% car, 0.0% public transportation, 7.9% walk, 3.9% work from home (2000); Travel time to work: 34.9% less than 15 minutes, 53.4% 15 to 30 minutes, 4.8% 30 to 45 minutes, 4.1% 45 to 60 minutes, 2.7% 60 minutes or more (2000)

LE GRAND (city). Covers a land area of 1.043 square miles and a water area of 0.007 square miles. Located at 42.00° N. Lat.; 92.77° W. Long. Elevation is 938 feet.
History: Le Grand was settled by Quakers and named for Le Grand Byington, an Iowa City politician.
Population: 883 (2000); Race: 96.7% White, 0.0% Black, 1.2% Asian, 1.3% American Indian and Alaska Native, 1.7% Hispanic of any race, 0.2% two or more races (2000); Density: 847.0 persons per square mile (2000); Age: 27.6% under 18, 13.3% over 64 (2000); Marriage status: 18.0% never married, 66.1% now married, 4.2% widowed, 11.7% divorced (2000); Foreign born: 1.7% (2000); Ancestry (includes multiple ancestries): 37.0% German, 18.2% Irish, 12.0% English, 6.8% United States or American, 6.8% Other groups (2000).
Economy: Single-family building permits issued: 2 (2001) / 0 (2000); Multi-family building permits issued: 0 (2001) / 0 (2000); Employment by occupation: 7.4% management, 17.5% professional, 16.7% services, 25.4% sales, 1.1% farming, 8.9% construction, 23.0% production (2000).
Income: Per capita income: $16,470 (2000); Median household income: $39,333 (2000); Poverty rate: 4.5% (2000).
Taxes: Total city taxes per capita: $120 (1997); City property taxes per capita: $118 (1997).
Education: High school graduation rate: 91.9% (2000); College graduation rate: 15.0% (2000).
Housing: Homeownership rate: 83.2% (2000); Median home value: $67,400 (2000); Median rent: $322 per month (2000); Median age of housing: 29 years (2000).
Transportation: Commute to work: 92.7% car, 0.0% public transportation, 3.6% walk, 3.0% work from home (2000); Travel time to work: 39.1% less than 15 minutes, 51.7% 15 to 30 minutes, 7.1% 30 to 45 minutes, 0.4% 45 to 60 minutes, 1.8% 60 minutes or more (2000)

LISCOMB (city). Covers a land area of 0.983 square miles and a water area of 0 square miles. Located at 42.19° N. Lat.; 93.00° W. Long. Elevation is 997 feet.
History: Liscomb was named for an employee of the Iowa Central Railroad.
Population: 272 (2000); Race: 93.0% White, 0.0% Black, 0.0% Asian, 1.1% American Indian and Alaska Native, 3.0% Hispanic of any race, 3.0% two or more races (2000); Density: 276.6 persons per square mile (2000); Age: 23.3% under 18, 14.4% over 64 (2000); Marriage status: 21.5% never married, 51.6% now married, 5.4% widowed, 21.5% divorced (2000); Foreign born: 1.1% (2000); Ancestry (includes multiple ancestries): 37.0% German, 23.7% United States or American, 15.2% Irish, 10.0% Dutch, 9.3% Other groups (2000).
Economy: Employment by occupation: 6.5% management, 10.9% professional, 24.6% services, 15.9% sales, 0.0% farming, 12.3% construction, 29.7% production (2000).
Income: Per capita income: $16,678 (2000); Median household income: $40,000 (2000); Poverty rate: 8.1% (2000).
Taxes: Total city taxes per capita: $89 (1997); City property taxes per capita: $89 (1997).
Education: High school graduation rate: 80.8% (2000); College graduation rate: 4.9% (2000).

Housing: Homeownership rate: 69.7% (2000); Median home value: $56,300 (2000); Median rent: $263 per month (2000); Median age of housing: 55 years (2000).
Transportation: Commute to work: 100.0% car, 0.0% public transportation, 0.0% walk, 0.0% work from home (2000); Travel time to work: 7.4% less than 15 minutes, 57.8% 15 to 30 minutes, 22.2% 30 to 45 minutes, 4.4% 45 to 60 minutes, 8.1% 60 minutes or more (2000)

MARSHALLTOWN (city). Covers a land area of 18.028 square miles and a water area of 0.018 square miles. Located at 42.04° N. Lat.; 92.91° W. Long. Elevation is 899 feet.
History: Marshalltown was named for Marshall, Michigan, by its first settler, Henry Anson, who arrived in 1851. The suffix "town" was added to avoid confusion with another town in the state. Marshalltown and Marietta fought bitterly for seven years over which town would become the county seat. In 1859, the Iowa Supreme Court decided in favor of Marshalltown.
Population: 26,009 (2000); Race: 86.4% White, 1.2% Black, 1.0% Asian, 0.2% American Indian and Alaska Native, 12.5% Hispanic of any race, 2.1% two or more races (2000); Density: 1,442.7 persons per square mile (2000); Age: 24.5% under 18, 18.0% over 64 (2000); Marriage status: 22.6% never married, 59.2% now married, 8.1% widowed, 10.1% divorced (2000); Foreign born: 9.2% (2000); Ancestry (includes multiple ancestries): 28.3% German, 16.2% Other groups, 11.9% English, 9.7% Irish, 7.1% United States or American (2000).
Vital Statistics: Birth rate: 136.5 per 10,000 population (1998)
Economy: Unemployment rate: 4.2% (11/2002); Total civilian labor force: 13,721 (11/2002); Single-family building permits issued: 31 (2001) / 11 (2000); Multi-family building permits issued: 8 (2001) / 12 (2000); Employment by occupation: 9.7% management, 17.2% professional, 17.1% services, 23.2% sales, 0.5% farming, 8.3% construction, 24.1% production (2000).
Income: Per capita income: $19,113 (2000); Median household income: $35,688 (2000); Poverty rate: 12.5% (2000).
Taxes: Total city taxes per capita: $377 (2000); City property taxes per capita: $332 (2000).
Education: High school graduation rate: 79.0% (2000); College graduation rate: 18.0% (2000).

School District(s)

Marshalltown Community School District (PK-12)
2000 Enrollment: 4,930 641-754-1000

Two-year College(s)

Iowa School of Beauty (Private, For-profit)
2001 Enrollment: 31 515-752-4223
Iowa Valley Community College District (Public)
2001 Enrollment: 2,036 515-752-4643
2001 Tuition: In-state $1,776; Out-of-state $3,552

Housing: Homeownership rate: 70.1% (2000); Median home value: $68,800 (2000); Median rent: $375 per month (2000); Median age of housing: 45 years (2000).
Hospitals: Marshalltown Medical & Surgical Center (176 beds)
Safety: Violent crime rate: 84.3 per 10,000 population; Property crime rate: 483.0 per 10,000 population (2001).
Newspapers: Times-Republican (7 x week)
Transportation: Commute to work: 93.3% car, 0.7% public transportation, 2.9% walk, 1.9% work from home (2000); Travel time to work: 72.2% less than 15 minutes, 16.9% 15 to 30 minutes, 4.3% 30 to 45 minutes, 2.2% 45 to 60 minutes, 4.3% 60 minutes or more (2000)
Airports: Marshalltown Municipal
Additional Information Contacts
Marshalltown Board of Realtors 641-753-6453
Marshalltown Chamber of Commerce 641-753-6645

MELBOURNE (city). Covers a land area of 0.566 square miles and a water area of 0 square miles. Located at 41.94° N. Lat.; 93.10° W. Long. Elevation is 1,041 feet.
History: Melbourne was named in honor of a Chicago Great Western Railroad employee.
Population: 794 (2000); Race: 99.7% White, 0.0% Black, 0.0% Asian, 0.3% American Indian and Alaska Native, 0.0% Hispanic of any race, 0.0% two or more races (2000); Density: 1,402.4 persons per square mile (2000); Age: 26.9% under 18, 10.7% over 64 (2000); Marriage status: 20.2% never married, 63.5% now married, 4.6% widowed, 11.7% divorced (2000); Foreign born: 0.5% (2000); Ancestry (includes multiple ancestries): 42.5% German, 15.0% Irish, 9.4% United States or American, 8.0% English, 5.1% Dutch (2000).
Economy: Single-family building permits issued: 0 (2001) / 0 (2000); Multi-family building permits issued: 0 (2001) / 0 (2000); Employment by occupation: 9.1% management, 14.4% professional, 13.5% services, 23.6% sales, 1.9% farming, 7.9% construction, 29.6% production (2000).
Income: Per capita income: $18,641 (2000); Median household income: $47,019 (2000); Poverty rate: 3.7% (2000).
Taxes: Total city taxes per capita: $136 (1997); City property taxes per capita: $132 (1997).
Education: High school graduation rate: 89.1% (2000); College graduation rate: 15.0% (2000).
Housing: Homeownership rate: 81.7% (2000); Median home value: $68,400 (2000); Median rent: $353 per month (2000); Median age of housing: 44 years (2000).
Transportation: Commute to work: 95.4% car, 0.0% public transportation, 0.2% walk, 4.4% work from home (2000); Travel time to work: 15.4% less than 15 minutes, 51.9% 15 to 30 minutes, 15.4% 30 to 45 minutes, 11.6% 45 to 60 minutes, 5.6% 60 minutes or more (2000)

RHODES (city). Aka Edenville. Covers a land area of 1.016 square miles and a water area of 0 square miles. Located at 41.92° N. Lat.; 93.18° W. Long.
History: Rhodes was once known as Edenville. The name was changed to honor C. B. Rhodes, a landowner and prominent citizen in the town's history.
Population: 294 (2000); Race: 100.0% White, 0.0% Black, 0.0% Asian, 0.0% American Indian and Alaska Native, 0.0% Hispanic of any race, 0.0% two or more races (2000); Density: 289.4 persons per square mile (2000); Age: 26.6% under 18, 14.2% over 64 (2000); Marriage status: 23.6% never married, 53.3% now married, 8.3% widowed, 14.8% divorced (2000); Foreign born: 1.0% (2000); Ancestry (includes multiple ancestries): 27.7% United States or American, 24.2% German, 14.2% Irish, 7.6% English, 4.8% Other groups (2000).
Economy: Employment by occupation: 15.4% management, 8.3% professional, 19.2% services, 14.1% sales, 2.6% farming, 12.8% construction, 27.6% production (2000).
Income: Per capita income: $16,376 (2000); Median household income: $33,750 (2000); Poverty rate: 11.6% (2000).
Taxes: Total city taxes per capita: $130 (1997); City property taxes per capita: $130 (1997).
Education: High school graduation rate: 83.2% (2000); College graduation rate: 2.1% (2000).
Housing: Homeownership rate: 82.6% (2000); Median home value: $55,000 (2000); Median rent: $239 per month (2000); Median age of housing: 60+ years (2000).
Transportation: Commute to work: 94.9% car, 0.0% public transportation, 0.0% walk, 5.1% work from home (2000); Travel time to work: 6.1% less than 15 minutes, 31.8% 15 to 30 minutes, 37.8% 30 to 45 minutes, 4.1% 45 to 60 minutes, 20.3% 60 minutes or more (2000)

SAINT ANTHONY (city). Covers a land area of 0.560 square miles and a water area of 0 square miles. Located at 42.12° N. Lat.; 93.19° W. Long.
History: St. Anthony was named for John Q. Saint and Anthony R. Pierce who laid out the town.
Population: 109 (2000); Race: 98.1% White, 0.0% Black, 0.0% Asian, 0.0% American Indian and Alaska Native, 1.9% Hispanic of any race, 0.0% two or more races (2000); Density: 194.5 persons per square mile (2000); Age: 24.3% under 18, 17.8% over 64 (2000); Marriage status: 15.3% never married, 69.4% now married, 7.1% widowed, 8.2% divorced (2000); Foreign born: 1.9% (2000); Ancestry (includes multiple ancestries): 15.9% German, 14.0% Norwegian, 8.4% Other groups, 6.5% French (except Basque), 5.6% Swiss (2000).
Economy: Employment by occupation: 11.3% management, 7.5% professional, 24.5% services, 15.1% sales, 0.0% farming, 15.1% construction, 26.4% production (2000).
Income: Per capita income: $15,218 (2000); Median household income: $30,625 (2000); Poverty rate: 13.1% (2000).
Education: High school graduation rate: 72.0% (2000); College graduation rate: 5.3% (2000).
Housing: Homeownership rate: 83.7% (2000); Median home value: $25,600 (2000); Median rent: $288 per month (2000); Median age of housing: 60+ years (2000).
Transportation: Commute to work: 94.3% car, 0.0% public transportation, 5.7% walk, 0.0% work from home (2000); Travel time to work: 15.1% less than 15 minutes, 24.5% 15 to 30 minutes, 54.7% 30 to 45 minutes, 1.9% 45 to 60 minutes, 3.8% 60 minutes or more (2000)

STATE CENTER (city). Covers a land area of 0.974 square miles and a water area of 0 square miles. Located at 42.01° N. Lat.; 93.16° W. Long. Elevation is 870 feet.

History: State Center was laid out by the John Blair Company in 1865, when the railroad reached this point. The name was suggested by the geographical position of the tract in the state.

Population: 1,349 (2000); Race: 96.7% White, 0.0% Black, 0.5% Asian, 0.0% American Indian and Alaska Native, 2.8% Hispanic of any race, 0.6% two or more races (2000); Density: 1,384.4 persons per square mile (2000); Age: 27.2% under 18, 19.5% over 64 (2000); Marriage status: 19.5% never married, 61.6% now married, 9.2% widowed, 9.8% divorced (2000); Foreign born: 1.4% (2000); Ancestry (includes multiple ancestries): 44.7% German, 9.6% Irish, 7.9% United States or American, 7.4% English, 7.0% Norwegian (2000).

Economy: Single-family building permits issued: 1 (2001) / 1 (2000); Multi-family building permits issued: 0 (2001) / 0 (2000); Employment by occupation: 12.3% management, 16.2% professional, 17.2% services, 22.5% sales, 0.6% farming, 9.9% construction, 21.4% production (2000).

Income: Per capita income: $17,744 (2000); Median household income: $35,766 (2000); Poverty rate: 8.7% (2000).

Taxes: Total city taxes per capita: $125 (1997); City property taxes per capita: $123 (1997).

Education: High school graduation rate: 89.9% (2000); College graduation rate: 15.0% (2000).

School District(s)

West Marshall Community School District (PK-12)
2000 Enrollment: 869 641-483-2660

Housing: Homeownership rate: 73.5% (2000); Median home value: $75,200 (2000); Median rent: $331 per month (2000); Median age of housing: 43 years (2000).

Newspapers: Enterprise-Record (1 x week)

Transportation: Commute to work: 94.3% car, 0.3% public transportation, 2.1% walk, 1.8% work from home (2000); Travel time to work: 26.4% less than 15 minutes, 39.9% 15 to 30 minutes, 20.9% 30 to 45 minutes, 5.6% 45 to 60 minutes, 7.1% 60 minutes or more (2000)

Mills County

Located in southwestern Iowa; bounded on the west by the Missouri River and the Nebraska border; prairie area, drained by the West Nishnabotna River. Covers a land area of 436.50 square miles, a water area of 3.10 square miles, and is located in the Central Time Zone. The county government was organized in 1851. County seat is Glenwood.

Weather Station: Glenwood 3 SW Elevation: 977 feet

	Jan	Feb	Mar	Apr	May	Jun	Jul	Aug	Sep	Oct	Nov	Dec
High	32	39	51	64	75	84	88	86	79	67	49	36
Low	11	17	28	39	50	60	65	62	53	40	28	17
Precip	0.7	0.8	2.2	3.4	4.9	4.6	4.5	3.8	3.5	2.3	1.8	1.0
Snow	6.4	5.5	4.0	0.7	tr	0.0	0.0	0.0	0.0	0.4	2.2	4.6

High and Low temperatures in degrees Fahrenheit; Precipitation and Snow in inches

Population: 14,547 (2000); Race: 98.0% White, 0.2% Black, 0.4% Asian, 0.3% American Indian and Alaska Native, 1.2% Hispanic of any race, 0.6% two or more races (2000); Density: 33.3 persons per square mile (2000); Age: 26.7% under 18, 12.6% over 64 (2000).

Religion: Five largest groups: 12.5% The United Methodist Church, 9.6% Catholic Church, 4.8% American Baptist Churches in the USA, 4.0% Evangelical Lutheran Church in America, 3.6% Lutheran Church—Missouri Synod (2000).

Economy: Unemployment rate: 2.7% (11/2002); Total civilian labor force: 6,484 (11/2002); Leading industries: 54.5% health care and social assistance; 11.7% retail trade; except pub other services (2000); Companies that employ more than 1,000 persons: 0 (2000); Companies that employ more than 100 persons: 3 (2000); Farms: 496 totaling 232,129 acres (1997); Minority business ownership rate: 0.0% (1997); Women business ownership rate: 23.7% (1997); Retail sales per capita: $3,684 (1997). Single-family building permits issued: 18 (2001) / 12 (2000); Multi-family building permits issued: 0 (2001) / 8 (2000).

Income: Per capita income: $18,736 (2000); Median household income: $42,428 (2000); Poverty rate: 8.3% (2000); Bankruptcy rate: 4.62% (2001).

Taxes: Total county taxes per capita: $275 (1997); County property taxes per capita: $269 (1997).

Education: High school graduation rate: 83.2% (2000); College graduation rate: 16.3% (2000).

Housing: Homeownership rate: 79.5% (2000); Median home value: $92,900 (2000); Median rent: $364 per month (2000); Median age of housing: 34 years (2000).

Health: Birth rate: 132.0 per 10,000 population (1998); Age adjusted death rate: 95.3 per 10,000 population (1999); Age adjusted cancer mortality rate: 178.9 deaths per 100,000 population (1999). Number of physicians: 6.2 per 10,000 population (1999); Number of hospital beds: 270.8 per 10,000 population (1999).

Elections: 2000 Presidential election results: 34.5% Gore, 62.3% Bush, 2.1% Nader, 0.4% Buchanan

National and State Parks: Viking Lake State Park; Willow Slough State Game Management Area

Additional Information Contacts

Mills County Government Offices 712-527-3146
Glenwood Chamber of Commerce 712-527-3298

Mills County Communities

EMERSON (city). Covers a land area of 0.251 square miles and a water area of 0 square miles. Located at 41.01° N. Lat.; 95.40° W. Long.

History: The railroad was the main cause for Emerson's existence.

Population: 480 (2000); Race: 100.0% White, 0.0% Black, 0.0% Asian, 0.0% American Indian and Alaska Native, 0.8% Hispanic of any race, 0.0% two or more races (2000); Density: 1,914.2 persons per square mile (2000); Age: 27.1% under 18, 15.1% over 64 (2000); Marriage status: 14.9% never married, 67.8% now married, 8.4% widowed, 8.9% divorced (2000); Foreign born: 0.4% (2000); Ancestry (includes multiple ancestries): 19.2% English, 16.9% German, 14.7% Irish, 5.7% Norwegian, 5.7% United States or American (2000).

Economy: Single-family building permits issued: 3 (2001) / 1 (2000); Multi-family building permits issued: 0 (2001) / 0 (2000); Employment by occupation: 7.9% management, 18.4% professional, 15.9% services, 24.3% sales, 2.1% farming, 13.4% construction, 18.0% production (2000).

Income: Per capita income: $15,807 (2000); Median household income: $31,583 (2000); Poverty rate: 11.2% (2000).

Taxes: Total city taxes per capita: $141 (1997); City property taxes per capita: $91 (1997).

Education: High school graduation rate: 88.4% (2000); College graduation rate: 9.3% (2000).

Housing: Homeownership rate: 89.3% (2000); Median home value: $49,200 (2000); Median rent: $239 per month (2000); Median age of housing: 60+ years (2000).

Transportation: Commute to work: 94.2% car, 0.0% public transportation, 3.3% walk, 1.7% work from home (2000); Travel time to work: 46.4% less than 15 minutes, 28.7% 15 to 30 minutes, 4.6% 30 to 45 minutes, 13.1% 45 to 60 minutes, 7.2% 60 minutes or more (2000)

GLENWOOD (city). Covers a land area of 2.591 square miles and a water area of 0.010 square miles. Located at 41.04° N. Lat.; 95.74° W. Long. Elevation is 1,037 feet.

History: Glenwood was formerly a Mormon settlement known as Rushville. When the Mormons left for Utah, the remaining residents called the village Coonsville in honor of Dr. Libeud Coons, the founder and first physician of the community, but the name was changed again in 1853.

Population: 5,358 (2000); Race: 98.7% White, 0.3% Black, 0.0% Asian, 0.4% American Indian and Alaska Native, 1.2% Hispanic of any race, 0.0% two or more races (2000); Density: 2,067.7 persons per square mile (2000); Age: 26.4% under 18, 12.5% over 64 (2000); Marriage status: 21.4% never married, 61.2% now married, 7.3% widowed, 10.1% divorced (2000); Foreign born: 0.5% (2000); Ancestry (includes multiple ancestries): 27.7% German, 14.9% Irish, 14.3% English, 5.2% United States or American, 3.8% Danish (2000).

Economy: Single-family building permits issued: 14 (2001) / 6 (2000); Multi-family building permits issued: 0 (2001) / 8 (2000); Employment by occupation: 8.6% management, 14.6% professional, 26.3% services, 25.9% sales, 0.4% farming, 10.9% construction, 13.2% production (2000).

Income: Per capita income: $15,790 (2000); Median household income: $39,682 (2000); Poverty rate: 9.5% (2000).

Taxes: Total city taxes per capita: $266 (1997); City property taxes per capita: $261 (1997).

Education: High school graduation rate: 75.0% (2000); College graduation rate: 13.0% (2000).

School District(s)

Glenwood Community School District (PK-12)
2000 Enrollment: 2,040 712-527-9034

Housing: Homeownership rate: 67.0% (2000); Median home value: $91,900 (2000); Median rent: $371 per month (2000); Median age of housing: 35 years (2000).
Safety: Violent crime rate: 5.6 per 10,000 population; Property crime rate: 242.9 per 10,000 population (2001).
Newspapers: The Opinion-Tribune (1 x week)
Transportation: Commute to work: 95.1% car, 0.0% public transportation, 1.7% walk, 1.9% work from home (2000); Travel time to work: 53.2% less than 15 minutes, 14.7% 15 to 30 minutes, 21.9% 30 to 45 minutes, 7.0% 45 to 60 minutes, 3.1% 60 minutes or more (2000)

Additional Information Contacts

Glenwood Chamber of Commerce....................... 712-527-3298

HASTINGS (city). Covers a land area of 0.406 square miles and a water area of 0 square miles. Located at 41.02° N. Lat.; 95.49° W. Long. Elevation is 999 feet.
History: Hastings was named for a railroad official. The town was owned, platted, and put on sale by the railroad company in 1872.
Population: 214 (2000); Race: 97.8% White, 0.0% Black, 0.0% Asian, 0.0% American Indian and Alaska Native, 3.6% Hispanic of any race, 0.0% two or more races (2000); Density: 527.2 persons per square mile (2000); Age: 31.4% under 18, 7.6% over 64 (2000); Marriage status: 28.9% never married, 54.1% now married, 5.7% widowed, 11.3% divorced (2000); Foreign born: 1.8% (2000); Ancestry (includes multiple ancestries): 36.3% German, 16.6% Irish, 13.0% Other groups, 10.8% United States or American, 5.4% French (except Basque) (2000).
Economy: Single-family building permits issued: 0 (2001) / 3 (2000); Multi-family building permits issued: 0 (2001) / 0 (2000); Employment by occupation: 5.8% management, 7.7% professional, 22.1% services, 20.2% sales, 0.0% farming, 18.3% construction, 26.0% production (2000).
Income: Per capita income: $13,174 (2000); Median household income: $35,625 (2000); Poverty rate: 25.8% (2000).
Taxes: Total city taxes per capita: $110 (1997); City property taxes per capita: $110 (1997).
Education: High school graduation rate: 71.3% (2000); College graduation rate: 3.7% (2000).

School District(s)

Nishna Valley Community School District (KG-12)
2000 Enrollment: 328 712-624-8696
Housing: Homeownership rate: 67.0% (2000); Median home value: $35,600 (2000); Median rent: $273 per month (2000); Median age of housing: 49 years (2000).
Transportation: Commute to work: 88.1% car, 0.0% public transportation, 2.0% walk, 4.0% work from home (2000); Travel time to work: 18.6% less than 15 minutes, 35.1% 15 to 30 minutes, 16.5% 30 to 45 minutes, 21.6% 45 to 60 minutes, 8.2% 60 minutes or more (2000)

HENDERSON (city). Covers a land area of 0.223 square miles and a water area of 0 square miles. Located at 41.13° N. Lat.; 95.43° W. Long.
History: Originally called Potter, Henderson was incorporated in 1893. The name may refer to Dave Henderson, who owned property in the area.
Population: 171 (2000); Race: 100.0% White, 0.0% Black, 0.0% Asian, 0.0% American Indian and Alaska Native, 0.0% Hispanic of any race, 0.0% two or more races (2000); Density: 765.1 persons per square mile (2000); Age: 20.4% under 18, 21.0% over 64 (2000); Marriage status: 17.9% never married, 66.4% now married, 8.2% widowed, 7.5% divorced (2000); Foreign born: 0.0% (2000); Ancestry (includes multiple ancestries): 32.5% German, 15.3% United States or American, 9.6% Irish, 8.3% English, 4.5% Scottish (2000).
Economy: Employment by occupation: 16.3% management, 6.5% professional, 4.3% services, 32.6% sales, 0.0% farming, 15.2% construction, 25.0% production (2000).
Income: Per capita income: $32,175 (2000); Median household income: $45,000 (2000); Poverty rate: 1.9% (2000).
Taxes: Total city taxes per capita: $96 (1997); City property taxes per capita: $73 (1997).
Education: High school graduation rate: 88.1% (2000); College graduation rate: 2.5% (2000).
Housing: Homeownership rate: 89.6% (2000); Median home value: $62,200 (2000); Median rent: $175 per month (2000); Median age of housing: 60+ years (2000).
Transportation: Commute to work: 95.7% car, 0.0% public transportation, 2.2% walk, 2.2% work from home (2000); Travel time to work: 18.9% less than 15 minutes, 15.6% 15 to 30 minutes, 18.9% 30 to 45 minutes, 23.3% 45 to 60 minutes, 23.3% 60 minutes or more (2000)

MALVERN (city). Covers a land area of 1.193 square miles and a water area of 0 square miles. Located at 41.00° N. Lat.; 95.58° W. Long. Elevation is 1,047 feet.
History: Malvern was founded in 1869, after the completion of the Burlington main line between Omaha and Chicago. The railroad company gave the town its name.
Population: 1,256 (2000); Race: 98.2% White, 0.0% Black, 0.8% Asian, 0.2% American Indian and Alaska Native, 0.4% Hispanic of any race, 0.8% two or more races (2000); Density: 1,053.1 persons per square mile (2000); Age: 27.3% under 18, 20.1% over 64 (2000); Marriage status: 18.0% never married, 60.6% now married, 11.1% widowed, 10.4% divorced (2000); Foreign born: 0.6% (2000); Ancestry (includes multiple ancestries): 24.7% German, 15.9% English, 11.3% United States or American, 9.2% Irish, 5.6% Dutch (2000).
Economy: Employment by occupation: 8.8% management, 20.4% professional, 19.3% services, 21.5% sales, 1.3% farming, 10.6% construction, 18.1% production (2000).
Income: Per capita income: $15,553 (2000); Median household income: $33,182 (2000); Poverty rate: 11.2% (2000).
Taxes: Total city taxes per capita: $275 (2000); City property taxes per capita: $212 (2000).
Education: High school graduation rate: 78.9% (2000); College graduation rate: 17.8% (2000).

School District(s)

Malvern Community School District (PK-12)
2000 Enrollment: 413 712-624-8700
Housing: Homeownership rate: 80.4% (2000); Median home value: $71,800 (2000); Median rent: $341 per month (2000); Median age of housing: 60 years (2000).
Newspapers: The Malvern Leader (1 x week)
Transportation: Commute to work: 91.1% car, 0.4% public transportation, 4.6% walk, 3.5% work from home (2000); Travel time to work: 26.5% less than 15 minutes, 24.8% 15 to 30 minutes, 25.3% 30 to 45 minutes, 18.8% 45 to 60 minutes, 4.6% 60 minutes or more (2000)

MINEOLA (unincorporated postal area, zip code 51554). Covers a land area of 2.191 square miles and a water area of 0 square miles. Located at 41.14° N. Lat.; 95.69° W. Long. Elevation is 1,025 feet.
History: The name of Mineola may have Sioux origins meaning "much water."
Population: 203 (2000); Race: 100.0% White, 0.0% Black, 0.0% Asian, 0.0% American Indian and Alaska Native, 0.0% Hispanic of any race, 0.0% two or more races (2000); Density: 92.6 persons per square mile (2000); Age: 33.0% under 18, 14.0% over 64 (2000); Marriage status: 16.4% never married, 64.8% now married, 14.5% widowed, 4.4% divorced (2000); Foreign born: 4.7% (2000); Ancestry (includes multiple ancestries): 58.1% German, 27.4% English, 8.4% Swedish, 6.0% Other groups, 3.3% French (except Basque) (2000).
Economy: Employment by occupation: 11.7% management, 5.4% professional, 37.8% services, 19.8% sales, 0.0% farming, 17.1% construction, 8.1% production (2000).
Income: Per capita income: $16,243 (2000); Median household income: $28,393 (2000); Poverty rate: 0.0% (2000).
Education: High school graduation rate: 96.1% (2000); College graduation rate: 7.1% (2000).
Housing: Homeownership rate: 91.2% (2000); Median home value: $87,500 (2000); Median rent: $425 per month (2000); Median age of housing: 60+ years (2000).
Transportation: Commute to work: 56.8% car, 0.0% public transportation, 17.1% walk, 26.1% work from home (2000); Travel time to work: 23.2% less than 15 minutes, 15.9% 15 to 30 minutes, 47.6% 30 to 45 minutes, 13.4% 45 to 60 minutes, 0.0% 60 minutes or more (2000)

PACIFIC JUNCTION (city). Covers a land area of 0.762 square miles and a water area of 0 square miles. Located at 41.01° N. Lat.; 95.80° W. Long.
History: A championship boxing match between Tom Allen and Ben Hogan was held in Pacific Junction in 1873 after the promoters were banned from Missouri, Kansas, and Nebraska.
Population: 507 (2000); Race: 97.4% White, 0.0% Black, 0.0% Asian, 0.0% American Indian and Alaska Native, 3.4% Hispanic of any race, 2.4% two or more races (2000); Density: 665.0 persons per square mile (2000); Age: 24.2% under 18, 17.3% over 64 (2000); Marriage status: 19.6% never married, 60.4% now married, 8.2% widowed, 11.9% divorced (2000); Foreign born: 0.6% (2000); Ancestry (includes multiple ancestries): 35.5%

German, 17.9% English, 14.9% Other groups, 13.5% Irish, 7.1% United States or American (2000).
Economy: Single-family building permits issued: 0 (2001) / 0 (2000); Multi-family building permits issued: 0 (2001) / 0 (2000); Employment by occupation: 10.7% management, 8.6% professional, 29.2% services, 20.2% sales, 0.0% farming, 12.4% construction, 18.9% production (2000).
Income: Per capita income: $15,103 (2000); Median household income: $36,563 (2000); Poverty rate: 7.6% (2000).
Taxes: Total city taxes per capita: $167 (1997); City property taxes per capita: $165 (1997).
Education: High school graduation rate: 76.8% (2000); College graduation rate: 3.2% (2000).
Housing: Homeownership rate: 89.3% (2000); Median home value: $61,000 (2000); Median rent: $375 per month (2000); Median age of housing: 29 years (2000).
Transportation: Commute to work: 94.7% car, 0.0% public transportation, 1.8% walk, 1.8% work from home (2000); Travel time to work: 33.5% less than 15 minutes, 26.3% 15 to 30 minutes, 31.7% 30 to 45 minutes, 5.8% 45 to 60 minutes, 2.7% 60 minutes or more (2000)

SILVER CITY (city). Covers a land area of 0.215 square miles and a water area of 0 square miles. Located at 41.11° N. Lat.; 95.63° W. Long. Elevation is 1,044 feet.
History: Silver City was named for its location on Silver Creek.
Population: 259 (2000); Race: 94.4% White, 0.0% Black, 0.7% Asian, 0.0% American Indian and Alaska Native, 0.0% Hispanic of any race, 4.9% two or more races (2000); Density: 1,202.7 persons per square mile (2000); Age: 25.5% under 18, 16.5% over 64 (2000); Marriage status: 17.9% never married, 67.0% now married, 9.0% widowed, 6.1% divorced (2000); Foreign born: 0.7% (2000); Ancestry (includes multiple ancestries): 40.8% German, 13.5% English, 8.6% United States or American, 8.6% Irish, 4.5% Danish (2000).
Economy: Single-family building permits issued: 1 (2001) / 2 (2000); Multi-family building permits issued: 0 (2001) / 0 (2000); Employment by occupation: 4.7% management, 16.5% professional, 19.7% services, 23.6% sales, 2.4% farming, 19.7% construction, 13.4% production (2000).
Income: Per capita income: $14,864 (2000); Median household income: $36,250 (2000); Poverty rate: 5.2% (2000).
Taxes: Total city taxes per capita: $102 (1997); City property taxes per capita: $102 (1997).
Education: High school graduation rate: 78.1% (2000); College graduation rate: 10.4% (2000).
Housing: Homeownership rate: 86.8% (2000); Median home value: $67,100 (2000); Median rent: $515 per month (2000); Median age of housing: 60+ years (2000).
Transportation: Commute to work: 92.7% car, 0.8% public transportation, 0.0% walk, 6.5% work from home (2000); Travel time to work: 2.6% less than 15 minutes, 56.5% 15 to 30 minutes, 33.9% 30 to 45 minutes, 3.5% 45 to 60 minutes, 3.5% 60 minutes or more (2000)

Mitchell County

Located in northern Iowa; bounded on the north by Minnesota; prairie area, drained by the Wapsipinicon, Cedar, and Little Cedar Rivers. Covers a land area of 468.90 square miles, a water area of 0.50 square miles, and is located in the Central Time Zone. The county government was organized in 1851. County seat is Osage.

Weather Station: Osage — Elevation: 1,167 feet

	Jan	Feb	Mar	Apr	May	Jun	Jul	Aug	Sep	Oct	Nov	Dec
High	23	30	42	58	71	80	83	81	73	61	42	28
Low	6	13	25	37	49	58	63	60	51	40	26	13
Precip	1.0	0.7	2.0	3.5	4.2	4.6	4.3	4.7	3.8	2.5	2.1	1.2
Snow	9.4	5.9	6.0	2.1	0.0	0.0	0.0	0.0	0.0	0.2	4.0	8.1

High and Low temperatures in degrees Fahrenheit; Precipitation and Snow in inches

Population: 10,874 (2000); Race: 99.8% White, 0.1% Black, 0.0% Asian, 0.1% American Indian and Alaska Native, 0.1% Hispanic of any race, 0.1% two or more races (2000); Density: 23.2 persons per square mile (2000); Age: 26.4% under 18, 21.5% over 64 (2000).
Religion: Five largest groups: 33.7% Catholic Church, 29.0% Evangelical Lutheran Church in America, 12.5% Lutheran Church—Missouri Synod, 7.8% The United Methodist Church, 2.8% United Church of Christ (2000).
Economy: Unemployment rate: 2.5% (11/2002); Total civilian labor force: 5,410 (11/2002); Leading industries: 31.3% manufacturing; 18.4% health care and social assistance; 14.9% retail trade (2000); Companies that employ more than 1,000 persons: 0 (2000); Companies that employ more than 100 persons: 7 (2000); Farms: 824 totaling 265,173 acres (1997); Minority business ownership rate: 0.0% (1997); Women business ownership rate: 17.5% (1997); Retail sales per capita: $6,403 (1997). Single-family building permits issued: 8 (2001) / 6 (2000); Multi-family building permits issued: 0 (2001) / 0 (2000).
Income: Per capita income: $16,809 (2000); Median household income: $34,843 (2000); Poverty rate: 10.7% (2000); Bankruptcy rate: 1.86% (2001).
Taxes: Total county taxes per capita: $308 (2000); County property taxes per capita: $276 (2000).
Education: High school graduation rate: 84.4% (2000); College graduation rate: 12.8% (2000).
Housing: Homeownership rate: 81.5% (2000); Median home value: $66,500 (2000); Median rent: $263 per month (2000); Median age of housing: 56 years (2000).
Health: Birth rate: 113.1 per 10,000 population (1998); Age adjusted death rate: 66.1 per 10,000 population (1999); Age adjusted cancer mortality rate: 166.1 deaths per 100,000 population (1999). Number of physicians: 2.8 per 10,000 population (1999); Number of hospital beds: 25.7 per 10,000 population (1999).
Elections: 2000 Presidential election results: 51.3% Gore, 46.3% Bush, 1.7% Nader, 0.5% Buchanan
National and State Parks: Pioneer State Park
Additional Information Contacts
Mitchell County Government Offices 515-732-5861
Osage Chamber of Commerce 641-732-3163

Mitchell County Communities

CARPENTER (city). Covers a land area of 0.160 square miles and a water area of 0 square miles. Located at 43.41° N. Lat.; 93.01° W. Long. Elevation is 1,192 feet.
History: Carpenter, established in 1871, was probably named after Cyrus C. Carpenter, a surveyor who later served as Governor of Iowa (1872-1876).
Population: 130 (2000); Race: 100.0% White, 0.0% Black, 0.0% Asian, 0.0% American Indian and Alaska Native, 0.0% Hispanic of any race, 0.0% two or more races (2000); Density: 813.9 persons per square mile (2000); Age: 26.3% under 18, 22.6% over 64 (2000); Marriage status: 13.3% never married, 57.1% now married, 17.3% widowed, 12.2% divorced (2000); Foreign born: 0.0% (2000); Ancestry (includes multiple ancestries): 61.7% German, 39.8% Norwegian, 2.3% English, 1.5% Czech, 1.5% Irish (2000).
Economy: Employment by occupation: 7.5% management, 15.1% professional, 15.1% services, 20.8% sales, 5.7% farming, 24.5% construction, 11.3% production (2000).
Income: Per capita income: $14,864 (2000); Median household income: $27,500 (2000); Poverty rate: 5.3% (2000).
Taxes: Total city taxes per capita: $143 (1997); City property taxes per capita: $86 (1997).
Education: High school graduation rate: 74.7% (2000); College graduation rate: 7.7% (2000).
Housing: Homeownership rate: 94.2% (2000); Median home value: $32,100 (2000); Median age of housing: 49 years (2000).
Transportation: Commute to work: 83.0% car, 0.0% public transportation, 13.2% walk, 3.8% work from home (2000); Travel time to work: 60.8% less than 15 minutes, 19.6% 15 to 30 minutes, 9.8% 30 to 45 minutes, 0.0% 45 to 60 minutes, 9.8% 60 minutes or more (2000)

LITTLE CEDAR (unincorporated postal area, zip code 50454). Covers a land area of 14.925 square miles and a water area of 0 square miles. Located at 43.38° N. Lat.; 92.72° W. Long.
History: It is believed that Little Cedar is named after the Little Cedar River on which it is located.
Population: 120 (2000); Race: 100.0% White, 0.0% Black, 0.0% Asian, 0.0% American Indian and Alaska Native, 0.0% Hispanic of any race, 0.0% two or more races (2000); Density: 8.0 persons per square mile (2000); Age: 12.3% under 18, 35.8% over 64 (2000); Marriage status: 5.4% never married, 64.5% now married, 0.0% widowed, 30.1% divorced (2000); Foreign born: 0.0% (2000); Ancestry (includes multiple ancestries): 46.2% German, 32.1% Norwegian, 17.0% European, 11.3% Czech, 8.5% French (except Basque) (2000).
Economy: Employment by occupation: 0.0% management, 0.0% professional, 14.7% services, 0.0% sales, 0.0% farming, 29.4% construction, 55.9% production (2000).
Income: Per capita income: $21,328 (2000); Median household income: $36,250 (2000); Poverty rate: 0.0% (2000).

Education: High school graduation rate: 89.8% (2000); College graduation rate: 0.0% (2000).
Housing: Homeownership rate: 85.4% (2000); Median home value: $43,000 (2000); Median rent: $275 per month (2000); Median age of housing: 60+ years (2000).
Transportation: Commute to work: 100.0% car, 0.0% public transportation, 0.0% walk, 0.0% work from home (2000); Travel time to work: 0.0% less than 15 minutes, 85.3% 15 to 30 minutes, 0.0% 30 to 45 minutes, 0.0% 45 to 60 minutes, 14.7% 60 minutes or more (2000)

MCINTIRE (city). Covers a land area of 1.016 square miles and a water area of 0 square miles. Located at 43.43° N. Lat.; 92.59° W. Long. Elevation is 1,279 feet.
History: McIntire was named for landowner John McIntire. The railroad right-of-way ran through his property.
Population: 173 (2000); Race: 100.0% White, 0.0% Black, 0.0% Asian, 0.0% American Indian and Alaska Native, 0.0% Hispanic of any race, 0.0% two or more races (2000); Density: 170.2 persons per square mile (2000); Age: 33.5% under 18, 18.8% over 64 (2000); Marriage status: 15.6% never married, 63.9% now married, 9.8% widowed, 10.7% divorced (2000); Foreign born: 1.8% (2000); Ancestry (includes multiple ancestries): 44.7% German, 21.2% Norwegian, 5.3% Irish, 2.4% French (except Basque), 1.8% Czech (2000).
Economy: Employment by occupation: 2.6% management, 5.2% professional, 15.6% services, 15.6% sales, 0.0% farming, 7.8% construction, 53.2% production (2000).
Income: Per capita income: $13,319 (2000); Median household income: $26,875 (2000); Poverty rate: 7.6% (2000).
Taxes: Total city taxes per capita: $106 (1997); City property taxes per capita: $99 (1997).
Education: High school graduation rate: 74.3% (2000); College graduation rate: 2.8% (2000).
Housing: Homeownership rate: 85.1% (2000); Median home value: $15,600 (2000); Median rent: $138 per month (2000); Median age of housing: 60+ years (2000).
Transportation: Commute to work: 74.0% car, 6.8% public transportation, 2.7% walk, 16.4% work from home (2000); Travel time to work: 39.3% less than 15 minutes, 29.5% 15 to 30 minutes, 9.8% 30 to 45 minutes, 8.2% 45 to 60 minutes, 13.1% 60 minutes or more (2000)

MITCHELL (city). Covers a land area of 0.550 square miles and a water area of 0 square miles. Located at 43.32° N. Lat.; 92.87° W. Long. Elevation is 1,180 feet.
History: Mitchell was named for the Irishman John Mitchell.
Population: 155 (2000); Race: 100.0% White, 0.0% Black, 0.0% Asian, 0.0% American Indian and Alaska Native, 0.0% Hispanic of any race, 0.0% two or more races (2000); Density: 281.7 persons per square mile (2000); Age: 19.5% under 18, 21.4% over 64 (2000); Marriage status: 27.5% never married, 50.0% now married, 10.9% widowed, 11.6% divorced (2000); Foreign born: 0.0% (2000); Ancestry (includes multiple ancestries): 41.5% German, 27.7% Norwegian, 13.2% Irish, 6.3% Dutch, 4.4% United States or American (2000).
Economy: Single-family building permits issued: 0 (2001) / 0 (2000); Multi-family building permits issued: 0 (2001) / 0 (2000); Employment by occupation: 12.2% management, 2.7% professional, 10.8% services, 23.0% sales, 5.4% farming, 14.9% construction, 31.1% production (2000).
Income: Per capita income: $15,768 (2000); Median household income: $27,000 (2000); Poverty rate: 12.6% (2000).
Taxes: Total city taxes per capita: $120 (1997); City property taxes per capita: $72 (1997).
Education: High school graduation rate: 82.6% (2000); College graduation rate: 0.0% (2000).
Housing: Homeownership rate: 91.5% (2000); Median home value: $49,300 (2000); Median rent: $125 per month (2000); Median age of housing: 56 years (2000).
Transportation: Commute to work: 87.8% car, 0.0% public transportation, 6.8% walk, 5.4% work from home (2000); Travel time to work: 40.0% less than 15 minutes, 42.9% 15 to 30 minutes, 8.6% 30 to 45 minutes, 4.3% 45 to 60 minutes, 4.3% 60 minutes or more (2000)

ORCHARD (city). Covers a land area of 0.088 square miles and a water area of 0 square miles. Located at 43.22° N. Lat.; 92.77° W. Long. Elevation is 1,090 feet.
History: Orchard was named after landowner Moses Orchard. The town was platted by the Illinois Central Railroad Company.
Population: 88 (2000); Race: 100.0% White, 0.0% Black, 0.0% Asian, 0.0% American Indian and Alaska Native, 0.0% Hispanic of any race, 0.0% two or more races (2000); Density: 994.7 persons per square mile (2000); Age: 30.4% under 18, 26.6% over 64 (2000); Marriage status: 23.2% never married, 58.0% now married, 2.9% widowed, 15.9% divorced (2000); Foreign born: 0.0% (2000); Ancestry (includes multiple ancestries): 20.3% German, 17.7% English, 12.7% Norwegian, 7.6% Irish, 7.6% Other groups (2000).
Economy: Employment by occupation: 0.0% management, 20.0% professional, 16.0% services, 32.0% sales, 0.0% farming, 16.0% construction, 16.0% production (2000).
Income: Per capita income: $10,148 (2000); Median household income: $19,583 (2000); Poverty rate: 25.3% (2000).
Taxes: Total city taxes per capita: $84 (1997); City property taxes per capita: $42 (1997).
Education: High school graduation rate: 65.5% (2000); College graduation rate: 10.9% (2000).
Housing: Homeownership rate: 100.0% (2000); Median home value: $47,500 (2000); Median age of housing: 60+ years (2000).
Transportation: Commute to work: 92.0% car, 0.0% public transportation, 0.0% walk, 0.0% work from home (2000); Travel time to work: 56.0% less than 15 minutes, 24.0% 15 to 30 minutes, 12.0% 30 to 45 minutes, 0.0% 45 to 60 minutes, 8.0% 60 minutes or more (2000)

OSAGE (city). Covers a land area of 2.090 square miles and a water area of 0 square miles. Located at 43.28° N. Lat.; 92.81° W. Long. Elevation is 1,169 feet.
History: Osage was first settled in 1853 by Hiram Hunt, and named Coral in 1854 for the daughter of Dr. A. H. Moore who first platted the town. This plat was never recorded, but on a later plat made by representatives of the banker, Orrin Sage, of Ware, Massachusetts, the town was called Osage (O. Sage) in his honor.
Population: 3,451 (2000); Race: 99.7% White, 0.0% Black, 0.0% Asian, 0.3% American Indian and Alaska Native, 0.0% Hispanic of any race, 0.0% two or more races (2000); Density: 1,650.8 persons per square mile (2000); Age: 23.1% under 18, 29.1% over 64 (2000); Marriage status: 20.3% never married, 58.9% now married, 12.9% widowed, 8.0% divorced (2000); Foreign born: 0.9% (2000); Ancestry (includes multiple ancestries): 45.3% German, 16.5% Norwegian, 11.1% Irish, 10.6% English, 4.2% French (except Basque) (2000).
Economy: Single-family building permits issued: 7 (2001) / 2 (2000); Multi-family building permits issued: 0 (2001) / 0 (2000); Employment by occupation: 11.4% management, 17.0% professional, 17.1% services, 18.4% sales, 0.9% farming, 12.4% construction, 22.8% production (2000).
Income: Per capita income: $17,366 (2000); Median household income: $30,676 (2000); Poverty rate: 7.7% (2000).
Taxes: Total city taxes per capita: $308 (1997); City property taxes per capita: $301 (1997).
Education: High school graduation rate: 86.8% (2000); College graduation rate: 15.7% (2000).

School District(s)

Osage Community School District (PK-12)
2000 Enrollment: 1,105 641-732-5381

Housing: Homeownership rate: 77.8% (2000); Median home value: $69,300 (2000); Median rent: $301 per month (2000); Median age of housing: 50 years (2000).
Hospitals: Mitchell County Regional Health Center (25 beds)
Newspapers: Mitchell County Press-News (1 x week)
Transportation: Commute to work: 89.3% car, 0.0% public transportation, 5.0% walk, 5.4% work from home (2000); Travel time to work: 62.4% less than 15 minutes, 13.3% 15 to 30 minutes, 14.3% 30 to 45 minutes, 5.8% 45 to 60 minutes, 4.2% 60 minutes or more (2000)
Additional Information Contacts
Osage Chamber of Commerce 641-732-3163

RICEVILLE (city). Covers a land area of 1.097 square miles and a water area of 0.010 square miles. Located at 43.36° N. Lat.; 92.55° W. Long.
History: Riceville was named for the pioneer Rice family.
Population: 840 (2000); Race: 99.8% White, 0.2% Black, 0.0% Asian, 0.0% American Indian and Alaska Native, 0.0% Hispanic of any race, 0.0% two or more races (2000); Density: 765.8 persons per square mile (2000); Age: 19.9% under 18, 31.1% over 64 (2000); Marriage status: 19.7% never married, 62.7% now married, 12.0% widowed, 5.7% divorced (2000); Foreign born: 0.4% (2000); Ancestry (includes multiple ancestries): 42.5% German, 14.3% Irish, 13.1% Norwegian, 8.3% English, 5.0% United States or American (2000).

Economy: Single-family building permits issued: 1 (2001) / 4 (2000); Multi-family building permits issued: 0 (2001) / 0 (2000); Employment by occupation: 9.2% management, 13.8% professional, 15.9% services, 19.2% sales, 3.5% farming, 7.3% construction, 31.1% production (2000).
Income: Per capita income: $20,661 (2000); Median household income: $30,982 (2000); Poverty rate: 4.1% (2000).
Taxes: Total city taxes per capita: $189 (1997); City property taxes per capita: $130 (1997).
Education: High school graduation rate: 77.3% (2000); College graduation rate: 12.4% (2000).

School District(s)

Riceville Community School District (KG-12)
2000 Enrollment: 453 641-985-2288

Housing: Homeownership rate: 75.4% (2000); Median home value: $48,500 (2000); Median rent: $220 per month (2000); Median age of housing: 55 years (2000).
Newspapers: Riceville Recorder (1 x week)
Transportation: Commute to work: 89.6% car, 1.6% public transportation, 5.7% walk, 3.0% work from home (2000); Travel time to work: 54.4% less than 15 minutes, 23.1% 15 to 30 minutes, 7.6% 30 to 45 minutes, 6.5% 45 to 60 minutes, 8.5% 60 minutes or more (2000)

SAINT ANSGAR (city). Covers a land area of 0.781 square miles and a water area of 0 square miles. Located at 43.37° N. Lat.; 92.92° W. Long. Elevation is 1,171 feet.
History: St. Ansgar was settled in 1853 by immigrants from Czechoslovakia.
Population: 1,031 (2000); Race: 99.3% White, 0.0% Black, 0.0% Asian, 0.0% American Indian and Alaska Native, 0.7% Hispanic of any race, 0.7% two or more races (2000); Density: 1,320.7 persons per square mile (2000); Age: 24.7% under 18, 27.8% over 64 (2000); Marriage status: 19.1% never married, 57.5% now married, 17.8% widowed, 5.6% divorced (2000); Foreign born: 0.5% (2000); Ancestry (includes multiple ancestries): 47.3% German, 22.8% Norwegian, 8.1% Irish, 7.8% English, 6.5% Danish (2000).
Economy: Single-family building permits issued: 0 (2001) / 0 (2000); Multi-family building permits issued: 0 (2001) / 0 (2000); Employment by occupation: 8.8% management, 22.8% professional, 13.1% services, 24.7% sales, 2.1% farming, 8.3% construction, 20.3% production (2000).
Income: Per capita income: $16,100 (2000); Median household income: $33,977 (2000); Poverty rate: 9.3% (2000).
Education: High school graduation rate: 79.9% (2000); College graduation rate: 19.8% (2000).

School District(s)

Saint Ansgar Community School District (KG-12)
2000 Enrollment: 766 641-736-4681

Housing: Homeownership rate: 82.0% (2000); Median home value: $73,900 (2000); Median rent: $293 per month (2000); Median age of housing: 58 years (2000).
Newspapers: St. Ansgar Enterprise Journal (1 x week)
Transportation: Commute to work: 81.3% car, 0.7% public transportation, 12.7% walk, 3.2% work from home (2000); Travel time to work: 57.0% less than 15 minutes, 22.7% 15 to 30 minutes, 12.4% 30 to 45 minutes, 3.6% 45 to 60 minutes, 4.3% 60 minutes or more (2000)

STACYVILLE (city). Covers a land area of 0.444 square miles and a water area of 0.024 square miles. Located at 43.43° N. Lat.; 92.78° W. Long. Elevation is 1,208 feet.
History: Stacyville was settled about 1850.
Population: 469 (2000); Race: 100.0% White, 0.0% Black, 0.0% Asian, 0.0% American Indian and Alaska Native, 0.0% Hispanic of any race, 0.0% two or more races (2000); Density: 1,055.9 persons per square mile (2000); Age: 18.0% under 18, 38.7% over 64 (2000); Marriage status: 20.7% never married, 65.7% now married, 8.6% widowed, 5.0% divorced (2000); Foreign born: 0.0% (2000); Ancestry (includes multiple ancestries): 53.8% German, 10.8% Norwegian, 9.0% Irish, 7.7% English, 4.4% United States or American (2000).
Economy: Employment by occupation: 8.7% management, 18.0% professional, 14.8% services, 24.0% sales, 4.9% farming, 10.4% construction, 19.1% production (2000).
Income: Per capita income: $16,831 (2000); Median household income: $31,544 (2000); Poverty rate: 6.6% (2000).
Taxes: Total city taxes per capita: $173 (1997); City property taxes per capita: $121 (1997).
Education: High school graduation rate: 79.3% (2000); College graduation rate: 8.5% (2000).

Housing: Homeownership rate: 83.3% (2000); Median home value: $52,000 (2000); Median rent: $193 per month (2000); Median age of housing: 54 years (2000).
Newspapers: Monitor Review (1 x week)
Transportation: Commute to work: 81.4% car, 0.0% public transportation, 13.7% walk, 4.9% work from home (2000); Travel time to work: 60.9% less than 15 minutes, 27.6% 15 to 30 minutes, 6.3% 30 to 45 minutes, 0.0% 45 to 60 minutes, 5.2% 60 minutes or more (2000)

Monona County

Located in western Iowa; bounded on the west by the Missouri River and the Nebraska border; prairie area, drained by the Little Sioux, Maple, and Soldier Rivers; includes several lakes. Covers a land area of 693.10 square miles, a water area of 5.70 square miles, and is located in the Central Time Zone. The county government was organized in 1851. County seat is Onawa.

Weather Station: Castana Experiment Farm — Elevation: 1,450 feet

	Jan	Feb	Mar	Apr	May	Jun	Jul	Aug	Sep	Oct	Nov	Dec
High	29	36	48	62	73	82	85	83	76	64	46	33
Low	10	16	26	38	49	59	63	61	52	41	27	16
Precip	0.6	0.5	2.2	3.3	4.3	4.2	4.1	3.7	3.4	2.5	1.5	0.8
Snow	7.0	5.7	6.3	2.1	tr	0.0	0.0	0.0	0.0	1.1	4.6	6.5

High and Low temperatures in degrees Fahrenheit; Precipitation and Snow in inches

Weather Station: Mapleton 2 — Elevation: 1,187 feet

	Jan	Feb	Mar	Apr	May	Jun	Jul	Aug	Sep	Oct	Nov	Dec
High	29	35	47	63	74	82	85	83	76	64	46	33
Low	10	16	26	38	49	59	63	62	52	40	27	15
Precip	0.7	0.7	2.1	3.2	4.2	4.2	3.9	3.5	3.0	2.3	1.5	0.9
Snow	7.2	6.5	5.7	1.5	tr	0.0	0.0	0.0	0.0	0.7	3.5	6.7

High and Low temperatures in degrees Fahrenheit; Precipitation and Snow in inches

Weather Station: Onawa 3 NW — Elevation: 1,059 feet

	Jan	Feb	Mar	Apr	May	Jun	Jul	Aug	Sep	Oct	Nov	Dec
High	30	36	49	64	74	84	87	84	77	65	47	34
Low	10	16	27	39	50	60	64	62	53	41	27	16
Precip	0.6	0.6	2.2	3.1	4.2	4.2	4.0	3.4	3.1	2.4	1.6	0.8
Snow	7.6	6.1	6.0	2.0	tr	0.0	0.0	0.0	0.0	0.7	3.7	6.2

High and Low temperatures in degrees Fahrenheit; Precipitation and Snow in inches

Population: 10,020 (2000); Race: 98.5% White, 0.0% Black, 0.1% Asian, 0.5% American Indian and Alaska Native, 0.4% Hispanic of any race, 0.8% two or more races (2000); Density: 14.5 persons per square mile (2000); Age: 23.3% under 18, 23.9% over 64 (2000).
Religion: Five largest groups: 10.8% Evangelical Lutheran Church in America, 10.5% Lutheran Church—Missouri Synod, 10.2% Catholic Church, 8.0% The United Methodist Church, 7.7% Christian Churches and Churches of Christ (2000).
Economy: Unemployment rate: 3.8% (11/2002); Total civilian labor force: 4,800 (11/2002); Leading industries: 27.3% health care and social assistance; 21.0% retail trade; 11.1% accommodation & food services (2000); Companies that employ more than 1,000 persons: 0 (2000); Companies that employ more than 100 persons: 3 (2000); Farms: 697 totaling 367,651 acres (1997); Minority business ownership rate: 0.0% (1997); Women business ownership rate: 54.4% (1997); Retail sales per capita: $9,406 (1997). Single-family building permits issued: 17 (2001) / 32 (2000); Multi-family building permits issued: 10 (2001) / 9 (2000).
Income: Per capita income: $17,477 (2000); Median household income: $33,235 (2000); Poverty rate: 9.4% (2000); Bankruptcy rate: 4.17% (2001).
Taxes: Total county taxes per capita: $318 (2000); County property taxes per capita: $289 (2000).
Education: High school graduation rate: 81.7% (2000); College graduation rate: 13.4% (2000).
Housing: Homeownership rate: 76.2% (2000); Median home value: $54,400 (2000); Median rent: $267 per month (2000); Median age of housing: 56 years (2000).
Health: Birth rate: 96.8 per 10,000 population (1998); Age adjusted death rate: 83.4 per 10,000 population (1999); Age adjusted cancer mortality rate: 148.4 deaths per 100,000 population (1999). Number of physicians: 11.0 per 10,000 population (1999); Number of hospital beds: 47.9 per 10,000 population (1999).
Elections: 2000 Presidential election results: 45.8% Gore, 50.5% Bush, 2.0% Nader, 1.1% Buchanan
National and State Parks: Badger Lake State Wildlife Management Area; Lewis and Clark State Park; Preparation Canyon State Park
Additional Information Contacts

Monona County Government Offices 712-423-1585
Onawa Chamber of Commerce 712-423-1801

Monona County Communities

BLENCOE (city). Covers a land area of 0.747 square miles and a water area of 0 square miles. Located at 41.93° N. Lat.; 96.08° W. Long. Elevation is 1,038 feet.
History: Blencoe was platted by the Missouri Valley Land Company in 1881. The name may reflect the former home of a settler from Canada.
Population: 231 (2000); Race: 98.3% White, 0.0% Black, 0.0% Asian, 0.0% American Indian and Alaska Native, 0.0% Hispanic of any race, 1.7% two or more races (2000); Density: 309.3 persons per square mile (2000); Age: 26.3% under 18, 33.5% over 64 (2000); Marriage status: 16.5% never married, 62.8% now married, 16.0% widowed, 4.8% divorced (2000); Foreign born: 0.8% (2000); Ancestry (includes multiple ancestries): 19.5% German, 12.7% United States or American, 12.3% Irish, 10.2% English, 7.6% Danish (2000).
Economy: Single-family building permits issued: 1 (2001) / 0 (2000); Multi-family building permits issued: 0 (2001) / 0 (2000); Employment by occupation: 13.3% management, 8.4% professional, 12.0% services, 22.9% sales, 0.0% farming, 13.3% construction, 30.1% production (2000).
Income: Per capita income: $13,841 (2000); Median household income: $25,556 (2000); Poverty rate: 7.6% (2000).
Taxes: Total city taxes per capita: $198 (1997); City property taxes per capita: $144 (1997).
Education: High school graduation rate: 82.5% (2000); College graduation rate: 6.0% (2000).
Housing: Homeownership rate: 81.1% (2000); Median home value: $39,200 (2000); Median rent: $209 per month (2000); Median age of housing: 51 years (2000).
Transportation: Commute to work: 86.4% car, 0.0% public transportation, 13.6% walk, 0.0% work from home (2000); Travel time to work: 63.0% less than 15 minutes, 21.0% 15 to 30 minutes, 9.9% 30 to 45 minutes, 1.2% 45 to 60 minutes, 4.9% 60 minutes or more (2000)

CASTANA (city). Covers a land area of 0.926 square miles and a water area of 0 square miles. Located at 42.07° N. Lat.; 95.90° W. Long. Elevation is 1,166 feet.
History: Castana was platted in 1886 by the Western Town Lot Company, in an area already settled. The early settlers gave the name of Castana to the community, perhaps referring to the Latin name for chestnut tree (Castanea pumila). The trees in the area were actually oaks rather than chestnuts.
Population: 178 (2000); Race: 95.8% White, 0.0% Black, 0.0% Asian, 4.2% American Indian and Alaska Native, 0.0% Hispanic of any race, 0.0% two or more races (2000); Density: 192.2 persons per square mile (2000); Age: 33.9% under 18, 15.6% over 64 (2000); Marriage status: 20.3% never married, 57.3% now married, 7.0% widowed, 15.4% divorced (2000); Foreign born: 0.0% (2000); Ancestry (includes multiple ancestries): 40.1% German, 34.9% Irish, 12.0% English, 8.9% United States or American, 6.8% Norwegian (2000).
Economy: Employment by occupation: 6.2% management, 12.3% professional, 18.5% services, 27.2% sales, 2.5% farming, 17.3% construction, 16.0% production (2000).
Income: Per capita income: $12,327 (2000); Median household income: $25,000 (2000); Poverty rate: 25.0% (2000).
Taxes: Total city taxes per capita: $161 (1997); City property taxes per capita: $106 (1997).
Education: High school graduation rate: 76.5% (2000); College graduation rate: 1.7% (2000).
Housing: Homeownership rate: 85.1% (2000); Median home value: $23,300 (2000); Median rent: $175 per month (2000); Median age of housing: 60+ years (2000).
Transportation: Commute to work: 84.0% car, 0.0% public transportation, 4.9% walk, 8.6% work from home (2000); Travel time to work: 31.1% less than 15 minutes, 35.1% 15 to 30 minutes, 24.3% 30 to 45 minutes, 2.7% 45 to 60 minutes, 6.8% 60 minutes or more (2000)

MAPLETON (city). Covers a land area of 1.607 square miles and a water area of 0 square miles. Located at 42.16° N. Lat.; 95.79° W. Long. Elevation is 1,157 feet.
History: Mapleton was named by the town's first settler, William H. Wilsey, because of a grove of maple trees along the nearby Maple River.
Population: 1,416 (2000); Race: 99.0% White, 0.2% Black, 0.0% Asian, 0.2% American Indian and Alaska Native, 0.2% Hispanic of any race, 0.6% two or more races (2000); Density: 881.1 persons per square mile (2000); Age: 17.5% under 18, 38.2% over 64 (2000); Marriage status: 15.2% never married, 56.4% now married, 23.5% widowed, 4.9% divorced (2000); Foreign born: 0.1% (2000); Ancestry (includes multiple ancestries): 42.0% German, 14.4% Irish, 8.5% English, 7.3% United States or American, 4.3% Norwegian (2000).
Economy: Single-family building permits issued: 0 (2001) / 1 (2000); Multi-family building permits issued: 0 (2001) / 3 (2000); Employment by occupation: 10.1% management, 15.3% professional, 19.9% services, 28.7% sales, 1.3% farming, 12.0% construction, 12.7% production (2000).
Income: Per capita income: $19,516 (2000); Median household income: $29,479 (2000); Poverty rate: 11.2% (2000).
Taxes: Total city taxes per capita: $245 (1997); City property taxes per capita: $182 (1997).
Education: High school graduation rate: 70.4% (2000); College graduation rate: 13.2% (2000).

School District(s)

Maple Valley Community School District (PK-12)
2000 Enrollment: 555 712-882-1315

Housing: Homeownership rate: 81.3% (2000); Median home value: $54,100 (2000); Median rent: $294 per month (2000); Median age of housing: 48 years (2000).
Newspapers: Schleswig Leader (1 x week); Mapleton Press (1 x week)
Transportation: Commute to work: 86.8% car, 0.7% public transportation, 8.9% walk, 2.5% work from home (2000); Travel time to work: 59.0% less than 15 minutes, 9.5% 15 to 30 minutes, 16.3% 30 to 45 minutes, 8.0% 45 to 60 minutes, 7.2% 60 minutes or more (2000)

MOORHEAD (city). Covers a land area of 0.312 square miles and a water area of 0 square miles. Located at 41.92° N. Lat.; 95.85° W. Long. Elevation is 1,200 feet.
History: Moorhead was named for early resident, J. B. Moorhead. The town was mapped in 1899 by the Western Town Lot Company.
Population: 232 (2000); Race: 97.8% White, 0.0% Black, 0.4% Asian, 0.0% American Indian and Alaska Native, 0.0% Hispanic of any race, 1.7% two or more races (2000); Density: 742.9 persons per square mile (2000); Age: 24.8% under 18, 23.5% over 64 (2000); Marriage status: 17.9% never married, 59.8% now married, 13.6% widowed, 8.7% divorced (2000); Foreign born: 0.4% (2000); Ancestry (includes multiple ancestries): 33.9% Norwegian, 33.0% German, 23.5% Irish, 16.1% Danish, 9.1% English (2000).
Economy: Single-family building permits issued: 0 (2001) / 0 (2000); Multi-family building permits issued: 0 (2001) / 0 (2000); Employment by occupation: 11.9% management, 19.5% professional, 19.5% services, 17.8% sales, 1.7% farming, 12.7% construction, 16.9% production (2000).
Income: Per capita income: $16,644 (2000); Median household income: $26,042 (2000); Poverty rate: 9.1% (2000).
Taxes: Total city taxes per capita: $162 (1997); City property taxes per capita: $104 (1997).
Education: High school graduation rate: 90.3% (2000); College graduation rate: 11.5% (2000).

School District(s)

East Monona Community School District (KG-12)
2000 Enrollment: 99 712-886-5232

Housing: Homeownership rate: 88.4% (2000); Median home value: $34,600 (2000); Median rent: $225 per month (2000); Median age of housing: 60+ years (2000).
Transportation: Commute to work: 86.4% car, 0.0% public transportation, 11.9% walk, 0.0% work from home (2000); Travel time to work: 48.3% less than 15 minutes, 21.2% 15 to 30 minutes, 11.9% 30 to 45 minutes, 1.7% 45 to 60 minutes, 16.9% 60 minutes or more (2000)

ONAWA (city). Covers a land area of 4.913 square miles and a water area of 0 square miles. Located at 42.02° N. Lat.; 96.09° W. Long. Elevation is 1,052 feet.
History: Onawa was mapped by the Monona County Land Company. The name may have been taken from the word Onaiweh found in the poem "Hiawatha's Wedding Feast."
Population: 3,091 (2000); Race: 97.9% White, 0.0% Black, 0.0% Asian, 0.0% American Indian and Alaska Native, 0.3% Hispanic of any race, 1.8% two or more races (2000); Density: 629.1 persons per square mile (2000); Age: 23.2% under 18, 25.4% over 64 (2000); Marriage status: 17.8% never married, 52.9% now married, 17.0% widowed, 12.3% divorced (2000); Foreign born: 0.6% (2000); Ancestry (includes multiple ancestries): 29.1% German, 24.8% Irish, 14.5% English, 8.1% Norwegian, 7.3% United States or American (2000).

Economy: Single-family building permits issued: 3 (2001) / 7 (2000); Multi-family building permits issued: 10 (2001) / 4 (2000); Employment by occupation: 8.3% management, 14.8% professional, 22.6% services, 24.5% sales, 0.9% farming, 12.8% construction, 16.1% production (2000).
Income: Per capita income: $17,928 (2000); Median household income: $34,796 (2000); Poverty rate: 6.3% (2000).
Taxes: Total city taxes per capita: $253 (1997); City property taxes per capita: $189 (1997).
Education: High school graduation rate: 81.1% (2000); College graduation rate: 15.0% (2000).

School District(s)

West Monona Community School District (PK-12)
2000 Enrollment: 716 712-423-2043
Housing: Homeownership rate: 73.1% (2000); Median home value: $61,200 (2000); Median rent: $290 per month (2000); Median age of housing: 46 years (2000).
Hospitals: Burgess Health Center (48 beds)
Safety: Violent crime rate: 9.7 per 10,000 population; Property crime rate: 178.1 per 10,000 population (2001).
Newspapers: The Onawa Sentinel (1 x week); Onawa Democrat (1 x week)
Transportation: Commute to work: 89.8% car, 0.0% public transportation, 6.1% walk, 2.9% work from home (2000); Travel time to work: 66.0% less than 15 minutes, 9.8% 15 to 30 minutes, 13.5% 30 to 45 minutes, 4.6% 45 to 60 minutes, 6.2% 60 minutes or more (2000)
Additional Information Contacts
Onawa Chamber of Commerce 712-423-1801

RODNEY (city). Covers a land area of 0.167 square miles and a water area of 0 square miles. Located at 42.20° N. Lat.; 95.95° W. Long. Elevation is 1,122 feet.
History: Rodney was platted in 1887 with the arrival of the Chicago, Milwaukee, & St. Paul Railroad.
Population: 74 (2000); Race: 98.6% White, 0.0% Black, 1.4% Asian, 0.0% American Indian and Alaska Native, 0.0% Hispanic of any race, 0.0% two or more races (2000); Density: 444.3 persons per square mile (2000); Age: 20.0% under 18, 24.3% over 64 (2000); Marriage status: 16.1% never married, 57.1% now married, 19.6% widowed, 7.1% divorced (2000); Foreign born: 2.9% (2000); Ancestry (includes multiple ancestries): 37.1% German, 37.1% Irish, 17.1% Danish, 12.9% French (except Basque), 8.6% United States or American (2000).
Economy: Employment by occupation: 9.4% management, 6.3% professional, 6.3% services, 37.5% sales, 9.4% farming, 12.5% construction, 18.8% production (2000).
Income: Per capita income: $15,254 (2000); Median household income: $26,250 (2000); Poverty rate: 5.7% (2000).
Taxes: Total city taxes per capita: $151 (1997); City property taxes per capita: $96 (1997).
Education: High school graduation rate: 73.1% (2000); College graduation rate: 3.8% (2000).
Housing: Homeownership rate: 88.6% (2000); Median home value: $18,100 (2000); Median rent: $200 per month (2000); Median age of housing: 60+ years (2000).
Transportation: Commute to work: 100.0% car, 0.0% public transportation, 0.0% walk, 0.0% work from home (2000); Travel time to work: 6.9% less than 15 minutes, 13.8% 15 to 30 minutes, 24.1% 30 to 45 minutes, 41.4% 45 to 60 minutes, 13.8% 60 minutes or more (2000)

SOLDIER (city). Covers a land area of 0.297 square miles and a water area of 0 square miles. Located at 41.98° N. Lat.; 95.78° W. Long. Elevation is 1,170 feet.
History: Soldier was named for the nearby Soldier River. The town was mapped in 1899 by the Western Town Lot Company.
Population: 207 (2000); Race: 97.5% White, 0.0% Black, 0.0% Asian, 2.5% American Indian and Alaska Native, 0.0% Hispanic of any race, 0.0% two or more races (2000); Density: 696.6 persons per square mile (2000); Age: 12.4% under 18, 35.8% over 64 (2000); Marriage status: 17.9% never married, 53.8% now married, 16.3% widowed, 12.0% divorced (2000); Foreign born: 1.0% (2000); Ancestry (includes multiple ancestries): 36.3% Norwegian, 18.4% German, 11.9% Irish, 11.4% English, 10.0% Other groups (2000).
Economy: Employment by occupation: 7.1% management, 16.3% professional, 20.4% services, 25.5% sales, 0.0% farming, 7.1% construction, 23.5% production (2000).
Income: Per capita income: $14,877 (2000); Median household income: $22,344 (2000); Poverty rate: 16.8% (2000).
Taxes: Total city taxes per capita: $127 (1997); City property taxes per capita: $69 (1997).
Education: High school graduation rate: 84.1% (2000); College graduation rate: 13.4% (2000).
Housing: Homeownership rate: 80.2% (2000); Median home value: $27,800 (2000); Median rent: $142 per month (2000); Median age of housing: 60+ years (2000).
Transportation: Commute to work: 92.9% car, 0.0% public transportation, 7.1% walk, 0.0% work from home (2000); Travel time to work: 40.8% less than 15 minutes, 32.7% 15 to 30 minutes, 7.1% 30 to 45 minutes, 7.1% 45 to 60 minutes, 12.2% 60 minutes or more (2000)

TURIN (city). Covers a land area of 0.084 square miles and a water area of 0 square miles. Located at 42.02° N. Lat.; 95.96° W. Long. Elevation is 1,054 feet.
History: Turin was named for Turin, Italy. The town was platted in 1887.
Population: 75 (2000); Race: 100.0% White, 0.0% Black, 0.0% Asian, 0.0% American Indian and Alaska Native, 0.0% Hispanic of any race, 0.0% two or more races (2000); Density: 892.4 persons per square mile (2000); Age: 21.6% under 18, 9.1% over 64 (2000); Marriage status: 17.6% never married, 62.2% now married, 5.4% widowed, 14.9% divorced (2000); Foreign born: 2.3% (2000); Ancestry (includes multiple ancestries): 26.1% German, 25.0% Danish, 22.7% Irish, 18.2% English, 11.4% Swedish (2000).
Economy: Employment by occupation: 11.1% management, 13.3% professional, 35.6% services, 2.2% sales, 15.6% farming, 11.1% construction, 11.1% production (2000).
Income: Per capita income: $15,094 (2000); Median household income: $23,750 (2000); Poverty rate: 21.6% (2000).
Taxes: Total city taxes per capita: $117 (1997); City property taxes per capita: $64 (1997).
Education: High school graduation rate: 83.6% (2000); College graduation rate: 14.8% (2000).
Housing: Homeownership rate: 68.4% (2000); Median home value: $19,000 (2000); Median rent: $288 per month (2000); Median age of housing: 54 years (2000).
Transportation: Commute to work: 100.0% car, 0.0% public transportation, 0.0% walk, 0.0% work from home (2000); Travel time to work: 42.6% less than 15 minutes, 19.1% 15 to 30 minutes, 12.8% 30 to 45 minutes, 0.0% 45 to 60 minutes, 25.5% 60 minutes or more (2000)

UTE (city). Covers a land area of 0.395 square miles and a water area of 0 square miles. Located at 42.05° N. Lat.; 95.70° W. Long. Elevation is 1,205 feet.
History: Ute was named for a branch of the Shoshone tribe.
Population: 378 (2000); Race: 100.0% White, 0.0% Black, 0.0% Asian, 0.0% American Indian and Alaska Native, 0.0% Hispanic of any race, 0.0% two or more races (2000); Density: 956.7 persons per square mile (2000); Age: 21.4% under 18, 32.9% over 64 (2000); Marriage status: 16.6% never married, 62.1% now married, 14.3% widowed, 7.0% divorced (2000); Foreign born: 0.0% (2000); Ancestry (includes multiple ancestries): 53.4% German, 18.4% Irish, 9.6% Norwegian, 7.9% United States or American, 7.4% English (2000).
Economy: Single-family building permits issued: 0 (2001) / 1 (2000); Multi-family building permits issued: 0 (2001) / 0 (2000); Employment by occupation: 8.5% management, 14.9% professional, 11.3% services, 24.8% sales, 1.4% farming, 16.3% construction, 22.7% production (2000).
Income: Per capita income: $16,650 (2000); Median household income: $30,875 (2000); Poverty rate: 9.9% (2000).
Education: High school graduation rate: 75.5% (2000); College graduation rate: 9.9% (2000).
Housing: Homeownership rate: 83.7% (2000); Median home value: $40,500 (2000); Median rent: $188 per month (2000); Median age of housing: 60+ years (2000).
Transportation: Commute to work: 92.1% car, 0.0% public transportation, 7.9% walk, 0.0% work from home (2000); Travel time to work: 37.4% less than 15 minutes, 23.7% 15 to 30 minutes, 22.3% 30 to 45 minutes, 6.5% 45 to 60 minutes, 10.1% 60 minutes or more (2000)

WHITING (city). Covers a land area of 1.003 square miles and a water area of 0 square miles. Located at 42.12° N. Lat.; 96.15° W. Long. Elevation is 1,061 feet.
History: The name Whiting may have been in honor of one of the town founders, William B. Whiting.
Population: 707 (2000); Race: 98.5% White, 0.1% Black, 0.0% Asian, 0.7% American Indian and Alaska Native, 1.6% Hispanic of any race, 0.6% two or more races (2000); Density: 705.1 persons per square mile (2000); Age:

27.9% under 18, 21.2% over 64 (2000); Marriage status: 21.3% never married, 55.8% now married, 12.9% widowed, 9.9% divorced (2000); Foreign born: 0.3% (2000); Ancestry (includes multiple ancestries): 35.3% German, 15.3% Irish, 13.7% United States or American, 8.9% English, 6.1% French (except Basque) (2000).
Economy: Single-family building permits issued: 2 (2001) / 2 (2000); Multi-family building permits issued: 0 (2001) / 2 (2000); Employment by occupation: 7.9% management, 17.7% professional, 13.1% services, 36.7% sales, 1.6% farming, 9.8% construction, 13.1% production (2000).
Income: Per capita income: $16,284 (2000); Median household income: $32,212 (2000); Poverty rate: 8.8% (2000).
Taxes: Total city taxes per capita: $238 (1997); City property taxes per capita: $182 (1997).
Education: High school graduation rate: 85.2% (2000); College graduation rate: 16.2% (2000).

School District(s)
Whiting Community School District (KG-12)
2000 Enrollment: 238 712-458-2468
Housing: Homeownership rate: 76.2% (2000); Median home value: $55,600 (2000); Median rent: $438 per month (2000); Median age of housing: 53 years (2000).
Transportation: Commute to work: 88.4% car, 0.0% public transportation, 6.6% walk, 5.0% work from home (2000); Travel time to work: 37.5% less than 15 minutes, 25.7% 15 to 30 minutes, 24.3% 30 to 45 minutes, 7.6% 45 to 60 minutes, 4.9% 60 minutes or more (2000)

Monroe County

Located in southern Iowa; prairie area. Covers a land area of 433.40 square miles, a water area of 0.70 square miles, and is located in the Central Time Zone. The county government was organized in 1843. County seat is Albia.

Weather Station: Albia 3 NNE Elevation: 879 feet

	Jan	Feb	Mar	Apr	May	Jun	Jul	Aug	Sep	Oct	Nov	Dec
High	32	38	50	63	73	82	87	85	77	65	49	36
Low	14	19	29	41	51	60	65	63	54	43	31	19
Precip	1.1	1.3	2.4	3.7	4.8	4.3	5.0	3.9	4.5	2.8	2.7	1.4
Snow	7.4	6.8	4.0	2.5	0.0	0.0	0.0	0.0	0.0	0.6	2.9	5.2

High and Low temperatures in degrees Fahrenheit; Precipitation and Snow in inches

Population: 8,016 (2000); Race: 98.0% White, 0.2% Black, 0.0% Asian, 0.8% American Indian and Alaska Native, 0.4% Hispanic of any race, 0.5% two or more races (2000); Density: 18.5 persons per square mile (2000); Age: 25.4% under 18, 19.6% over 64 (2000).
Religion: Five largest groups: 24.3% Catholic Church, 12.9% The United Methodist Church, 6.6% Christian Church (Disciples of Christ), 2.4% Evangelical Lutheran Church in America, 2.1% Christian Churches and Churches of Christ (2000).
Economy: Unemployment rate: 3.8% (11/2002); Total civilian labor force: 3,997 (11/2002); Leading industries: 37.7% manufacturing; 18.4% health care and social assistance; 15.4% retail trade (2000); Companies that employ more than 1,000 persons: 0 (2000); Companies that employ more than 100 persons: 2 (2000); Farms: 691 totaling 217,317 acres (1997); Minority business ownership rate: 0.0% (1997); Women business ownership rate: 24.7% (1997); Retail sales per capita: $6,400 (1997). Single-family building permits issued: 13 (2001) / 5 (2000); Multi-family building permits issued: 0 (2001) / 0 (2000).
Income: Per capita income: $17,155 (2000); Median household income: $34,877 (2000); Poverty rate: 9.0% (2000); Bankruptcy rate: 3.11% (2001).
Taxes: Total county taxes per capita: $394 (2000); County property taxes per capita: $387 (2000).
Education: High school graduation rate: 82.2% (2000); College graduation rate: 12.6% (2000).
Housing: Homeownership rate: 78.5% (2000); Median home value: $52,400 (2000); Median rent: $297 per month (2000); Median age of housing: 52 years (2000).
Health: Birth rate: 96.1 per 10,000 population (1998); Age adjusted death rate: 75.5 per 10,000 population (1999); Age adjusted cancer mortality rate: 166.7 (Unreliable figure as per CDC) deaths per 100,000 population (1999). Number of physicians: 1.2 per 10,000 population (1999); Number of hospital beds: 47.4 per 10,000 population (1999).
Elections: 2000 Presidential election results: 46.6% Gore, 51.0% Bush, 1.5% Nader, 0.6% Buchanan
National and State Parks: Cottonwood Pits State Game Management Area; La Hart State Public Hunting Area; Miami Lake State Game Management Area; Tyrone State Game Management Area

Additional Information Contacts
Monroe County Government Offices.................................. 641-932-7706
Albia Chamber of Commerce.. 641-932-5108
Albia Industrial Development 641-932-7233
Monroe County Tourism 641-932-3319
Rathbun Area Board of Realtors 641-932-7129

Monroe County Communities

ALBIA (city). Covers a land area of 3.128 square miles and a water area of 0 square miles. Located at 41.02° N. Lat.; 92.80° W. Long. Elevation is 959 feet.
History: Albia was first known as Princeton. Most of the early settlers came from Illinois, Indiana, and Ohio. Those who were foreign-born were chiefly natives of Germany, Scandinavia, and Ireland.
Population: 3,706 (2000); Race: 97.6% White, 0.4% Black, 0.0% Asian, 0.6% American Indian and Alaska Native, 0.8% Hispanic of any race, 0.6% two or more races (2000); Density: 1,184.8 persons per square mile (2000); Age: 25.0% under 18, 22.1% over 64 (2000); Marriage status: 19.5% never married, 54.9% now married, 12.8% widowed, 12.8% divorced (2000); Foreign born: 0.7% (2000); Ancestry (includes multiple ancestries): 20.1% Irish, 19.8% German, 14.0% English, 7.1% United States or American, 6.3% Dutch (2000).
Economy: Single-family building permits issued: 8 (2001) / 2 (2000); Multi-family building permits issued: 0 (2001) / 0 (2000); Employment by occupation: 8.7% management, 16.2% professional, 11.1% services, 25.7% sales, 2.2% farming, 10.9% construction, 25.3% production (2000).
Income: Per capita income: $16,843 (2000); Median household income: $31,728 (2000); Poverty rate: 9.2% (2000).
Taxes: Total city taxes per capita: $236 (2000); City property taxes per capita: $230 (2000).
Education: High school graduation rate: 81.6% (2000); College graduation rate: 12.5% (2000).

School District(s)
Albia Community School District (KG-12)
2000 Enrollment: 1,279 641-932-5165
Housing: Homeownership rate: 71.1% (2000); Median home value: $54,400 (2000); Median rent: $312 per month (2000); Median age of housing: 59 years (2000).
Hospitals: Monroe County Hospital (46 beds)
Transportation: Commute to work: 92.6% car, 0.0% public transportation, 4.4% walk, 2.2% work from home (2000); Travel time to work: 57.0% less than 15 minutes, 11.0% 15 to 30 minutes, 17.9% 30 to 45 minutes, 9.8% 45 to 60 minutes, 4.3% 60 minutes or more (2000)
Additional Information Contacts
Albia Chamber of Commerce.. 641-932-5108
Albia Industrial Development 641-932-7233
Monroe County Tourism 641-932-3319
Rathbun Area Board of Realtors 641-932-7129

LOVILIA (city). Covers a land area of 0.502 square miles and a water area of 0 square miles. Located at 41.13° N. Lat.; 92.90° W. Long. Elevation is 932 feet.
History: Lovilia was named in honor of a daughter of the owner of the general store when the town was founded.
Population: 583 (2000); Race: 99.7% White, 0.3% Black, 0.0% Asian, 0.0% American Indian and Alaska Native, 0.0% Hispanic of any race, 0.0% two or more races (2000); Density: 1,160.8 persons per square mile (2000); Age: 28.9% under 18, 12.1% over 64 (2000); Marriage status: 18.1% never married, 63.8% now married, 9.4% widowed, 8.7% divorced (2000); Foreign born: 0.0% (2000); Ancestry (includes multiple ancestries): 19.8% German, 15.8% English, 11.8% Irish, 9.7% Dutch, 9.4% United States or American (2000).
Economy: Single-family building permits issued: 1 (2001) / 1 (2000); Multi-family building permits issued: 0 (2001) / 0 (2000); Employment by occupation: 6.9% management, 12.6% professional, 13.8% services, 16.9% sales, 1.1% farming, 8.0% construction, 40.6% production (2000).
Income: Per capita income: $14,978 (2000); Median household income: $35,577 (2000); Poverty rate: 7.3% (2000).
Taxes: Total city taxes per capita: $117 (1997); City property taxes per capita: $115 (1997).
Education: High school graduation rate: 88.3% (2000); College graduation rate: 8.5% (2000).

Housing: Homeownership rate: 90.1% (2000); Median home value: $37,000 (2000); Median rent: $283 per month (2000); Median age of housing: 58 years (2000).
Transportation: Commute to work: 93.1% car, 0.0% public transportation, 3.4% walk, 1.9% work from home (2000); Travel time to work: 15.2% less than 15 minutes, 27.3% 15 to 30 minutes, 36.7% 30 to 45 minutes, 6.3% 45 to 60 minutes, 14.5% 60 minutes or more (2000)

MELROSE (city). Covers a land area of 0.846 square miles and a water area of 0 square miles. Located at 40.97° N. Lat.; 93.05° W. Long. Elevation is 871 feet.
History: Melrose was named for Melrose, Massachusetts, birthplace of early resident John P. Currier.
Population: 130 (2000); Race: 97.7% White, 0.0% Black, 0.0% Asian, 2.3% American Indian and Alaska Native, 0.0% Hispanic of any race, 0.0% two or more races (2000); Density: 153.7 persons per square mile (2000); Age: 19.5% under 18, 20.3% over 64 (2000); Marriage status: 31.9% never married, 45.7% now married, 9.5% widowed, 12.9% divorced (2000); Foreign born: 1.6% (2000); Ancestry (includes multiple ancestries): 48.4% Irish, 25.0% German, 10.2% Swedish, 10.2% Italian, 6.3% Other groups (2000).
Economy: Single-family building permits issued: 0 (2001) / 0 (2000); Multi-family building permits issued: 0 (2001) / 0 (2000); Employment by occupation: 5.1% management, 22.0% professional, 13.6% services, 30.5% sales, 0.0% farming, 8.5% construction, 20.3% production (2000).
Income: Per capita income: $15,507 (2000); Median household income: $34,583 (2000); Poverty rate: 21.1% (2000).
Taxes: Total city taxes per capita: $132 (1997); City property taxes per capita: $125 (1997).
Education: High school graduation rate: 82.4% (2000); College graduation rate: 12.1% (2000).
Housing: Homeownership rate: 83.3% (2000); Median home value: $39,000 (2000); Median rent: $350 per month (2000); Median age of housing: 60+ years (2000).
Transportation: Commute to work: 93.2% car, 0.0% public transportation, 6.8% walk, 0.0% work from home (2000); Travel time to work: 20.3% less than 15 minutes, 32.2% 15 to 30 minutes, 8.5% 30 to 45 minutes, 11.9% 45 to 60 minutes, 27.1% 60 minutes or more (2000)

Montgomery County

Located in southwestern Iowa; prairie area, drained by the East Nishnabotna, West Nodaway, and Tarkio Rivers. Covers a land area of 423.90 square miles, a water area of 0.90 square miles, and is located in the Central Time Zone. The county government was organized in 1851. County seat is Red Oak.

Weather Station: Red Oak Elevation: 1,040 feet

	Jan	Feb	Mar	Apr	May	Jun	Jul	Aug	Sep	Oct	Nov	Dec
High	32	39	51	65	75	85	88	86	79	66	49	37
Low	12	17	28	39	50	60	64	62	53	41	28	18
Precip	1.0	1.1	2.4	3.7	4.8	4.8	4.5	4.1	4.2	2.7	2.1	1.2
Snow	8.0	8.1	4.8	1.7	0.0	0.0	0.0	0.0	tr	0.6	3.1	6.1

High and Low temperatures in degrees Fahrenheit; Precipitation and Snow in inches

Population: 11,771 (2000); Race: 97.9% White, 0.0% Black, 0.3% Asian, 0.0% American Indian and Alaska Native, 1.3% Hispanic of any race, 0.4% two or more races (2000); Density: 27.8 persons per square mile (2000); Age: 24.7% under 18, 20.2% over 64 (2000).
Religion: Five largest groups: 13.4% The United Methodist Church, 13.1% Evangelical Lutheran Church in America, 6.8% Catholic Church, 4.3% Christian Church (Disciples of Christ), 4.3% Presbyterian Church (U.S.A.) (2000).
Economy: Unemployment rate: 5.1% (11/2002); Total civilian labor force: 5,919 (11/2002); Leading industries: 26.2% manufacturing; 16.5% health care and social assistance; 13.8% retail trade (2000); Companies that employ more than 1,000 persons: 0 (2000); Companies that employ more than 100 persons: 8 (2000); Farms: 577 totaling 242,650 acres (1997); Minority business ownership rate: 0.0% (1997); Women business ownership rate: 43.3% (1997); Retail sales per capita: $6,990 (1997). Single-family building permits issued: 15 (2001) / 9 (2000); Multi-family building permits issued: 0 (2001) / 0 (2000).
Income: Per capita income: $16,373 (2000); Median household income: $33,214 (2000); Poverty rate: 9.1% (2000); Bankruptcy rate: 3.39% (2001).
Taxes: Total county taxes per capita: $361 (2000); County property taxes per capita: $325 (2000).
Education: High school graduation rate: 81.8% (2000); College graduation rate: 12.9% (2000).
Housing: Homeownership rate: 73.2% (2000); Median home value: $55,900 (2000); Median rent: $294 per month (2000); Median age of housing: 58 years (2000).
Health: Birth rate: 129.1 per 10,000 population (1998); Age adjusted death rate: 80.8 per 10,000 population (1999); Age adjusted cancer mortality rate: 196.5 deaths per 100,000 population (1999). Number of physicians: 8.5 per 10,000 population (1999); Number of hospital beds: 34.0 per 10,000 population (1999).
Elections: 2000 Presidential election results: 34.1% Gore, 63.4% Bush, 1.6% Nader, 0.4% Buchanan

Additional Information Contacts
Montgomery County Government Offices................ 712-623-5127
Montgomery County Board of Realtors.................. 712-623-9575
Red Oak Chamber of Commerce........................ 712-623-4821

Montgomery County Communities

COBURG (city). Covers a land area of 0.290 square miles and a water area of 0 square miles. Located at 40.91° N. Lat.; 95.26° W. Long. Elevation is 1,004 feet.
History: The name of Coburg commemorates the German ancestry of the early settlers.
Population: 31 (2000); Race: 100.0% White, 0.0% Black, 0.0% Asian, 0.0% American Indian and Alaska Native, 0.0% Hispanic of any race, 0.0% two or more races (2000); Density: 106.9 persons per square mile (2000); Age: 54.3% under 18, 0.0% over 64 (2000); Marriage status: 0.0% never married, 68.8% now married, 0.0% widowed, 31.3% divorced (2000); Foreign born: 0.0% (2000); Ancestry (includes multiple ancestries): 14.3% United States or American, 11.4% Other groups, 11.4% German, 5.7% English (2000).
Economy: Employment by occupation: 15.4% management, 0.0% professional, 0.0% services, 7.7% sales, 0.0% farming, 0.0% construction, 76.9% production (2000).
Income: Per capita income: $10,329 (2000); Median household income: $33,750 (2000); Poverty rate: 21.2% (2000).
Taxes: Total city taxes per capita: $117 (1997); City property taxes per capita: $83 (1997).
Education: High school graduation rate: 75.0% (2000); College graduation rate: 0.0% (2000).
Housing: Homeownership rate: 80.0% (2000); Median home value: $52,500 (2000); Median rent: $475 per month (2000); Median age of housing: 60+ years (2000).
Transportation: Commute to work: 100.0% car, 0.0% public transportation, 0.0% walk, 0.0% work from home (2000); Travel time to work: 69.2% less than 15 minutes, 30.8% 15 to 30 minutes, 0.0% 30 to 45 minutes, 0.0% 45 to 60 minutes, 0.0% 60 minutes or more (2000)

ELLIOTT (city). Covers a land area of 0.410 square miles and a water area of 0 square miles. Located at 41.14° N. Lat.; 95.16° W. Long. Elevation is 1,075 feet.
History: Elliott took on the middle name of Charles Elliott Perkins, an officer of the Chicago, Burlington & Quincy Railroad.
Population: 402 (2000); Race: 98.7% White, 0.0% Black, 0.5% Asian, 0.0% American Indian and Alaska Native, 0.0% Hispanic of any race, 0.8% two or more races (2000); Density: 981.1 persons per square mile (2000); Age: 22.9% under 18, 20.9% over 64 (2000); Marriage status: 25.5% never married, 54.8% now married, 11.5% widowed, 8.2% divorced (2000); Foreign born: 0.5% (2000); Ancestry (includes multiple ancestries): 24.0% German, 16.8% English, 15.2% Irish, 13.7% Swedish, 7.7% United States or American (2000).
Economy: Single-family building permits issued: 0 (2001) / 0 (2000); Multi-family building permits issued: 0 (2001) / 0 (2000); Employment by occupation: 6.0% management, 14.7% professional, 8.7% services, 36.4% sales, 2.2% farming, 10.3% construction, 21.7% production (2000).
Income: Per capita income: $15,018 (2000); Median household income: $31,528 (2000); Poverty rate: 14.9% (2000).
Taxes: Total city taxes per capita: $162 (1997); City property taxes per capita: $123 (1997).
Education: High school graduation rate: 81.4% (2000); College graduation rate: 12.4% (2000).
Housing: Homeownership rate: 85.2% (2000); Median home value: $32,500 (2000); Median rent: $179 per month (2000); Median age of housing: 60+ years (2000).

Transportation: Commute to work: 93.4% car, 0.0% public transportation, 4.9% walk, 1.1% work from home (2000); Travel time to work: 26.0% less than 15 minutes, 55.2% 15 to 30 minutes, 9.9% 30 to 45 minutes, 4.4% 45 to 60 minutes, 4.4% 60 minutes or more (2000)

GRANT (city). Covers a land area of 0.743 square miles and a water area of 0.010 square miles. Located at 41.14° N. Lat.; 94.98° W. Long. Elevation is 1,130 feet.
History: Grant was platted in 1858 under the name of Milford. Later, when it was found that another Milford existed in Iowa, the name was changed to honor Ulysses S. Grant.
Population: 102 (2000); Race: 100.0% White, 0.0% Black, 0.0% Asian, 0.0% American Indian and Alaska Native, 0.0% Hispanic of any race, 0.0% two or more races (2000); Density: 137.3 persons per square mile (2000); Age: 15.3% under 18, 16.2% over 64 (2000); Marriage status: 22.3% never married, 60.2% now married, 10.7% widowed, 6.8% divorced (2000); Foreign born: 0.0% (2000); Ancestry (includes multiple ancestries): 31.5% German, 22.5% United States or American, 19.8% Swedish, 18.9% English, 8.1% French (except Basque) (2000).
Economy: Single-family building permits issued: 0 (2001) / 0 (2000); Multi-family building permits issued: 0 (2001) / 0 (2000); Employment by occupation: 8.9% management, 14.3% professional, 0.0% services, 12.5% sales, 8.9% farming, 12.5% construction, 42.9% production (2000).
Income: Per capita income: $16,461 (2000); Median household income: $21,806 (2000); Poverty rate: 10.8% (2000).
Taxes: Total city taxes per capita: $76 (1997); City property taxes per capita: $76 (1997).
Education: High school graduation rate: 84.1% (2000); College graduation rate: 10.2% (2000).
Housing: Homeownership rate: 86.5% (2000); Median home value: $34,400 (2000); Median rent: $208 per month (2000); Median age of housing: 60+ years (2000).
Transportation: Commute to work: 94.4% car, 0.0% public transportation, 5.6% walk, 0.0% work from home (2000); Travel time to work: 13.0% less than 15 minutes, 48.1% 15 to 30 minutes, 27.8% 30 to 45 minutes, 0.0% 45 to 60 minutes, 11.1% 60 minutes or more (2000)

RED OAK (city). Covers a land area of 3.678 square miles and a water area of 0.057 square miles. Located at 41.01° N. Lat.; 95.22° W. Long. Elevation is 1,077 feet.
History: Red Oak was so named because of the many red oak trees growing on the banks of a small creek nearby. It was founded by Alfred Hebard, and was known as Red Oak Junction until 1901.
Population: 6,197 (2000); Race: 96.7% White, 0.0% Black, 0.4% Asian, 0.0% American Indian and Alaska Native, 2.2% Hispanic of any race, 0.6% two or more races (2000); Density: 1,684.7 persons per square mile (2000); Age: 23.7% under 18, 21.0% over 64 (2000); Marriage status: 17.5% never married, 58.7% now married, 10.7% widowed, 13.0% divorced (2000); Foreign born: 2.0% (2000); Ancestry (includes multiple ancestries): 28.2% German, 13.9% Irish, 10.8% English, 10.1% United States or American, 9.9% Swedish (2000).
Economy: Single-family building permits issued: 5 (2001) / 2 (2000); Multi-family building permits issued: 0 (2001) / 0 (2000); Employment by occupation: 10.0% management, 12.8% professional, 17.7% services, 24.8% sales, 3.7% farming, 9.9% construction, 21.1% production (2000).
Income: Per capita income: $15,793 (2000); Median household income: $30,098 (2000); Poverty rate: 10.3% (2000).
Taxes: Total city taxes per capita: $480 (2000); City property taxes per capita: $405 (2000).
Education: High school graduation rate: 79.8% (2000); College graduation rate: 13.3% (2000).

School District(s)

Red Oak Community School District (PK-12)
2000 Enrollment: 1,313 712-623-6600
Housing: Homeownership rate: 68.9% (2000); Median home value: $57,300 (2000); Median rent: $314 per month (2000); Median age of housing: 51 years (2000).
Hospitals: Montgomery County Memorial Hospital (40 beds)
Safety: Violent crime rate: 21.0 per 10,000 population; Property crime rate: 407.1 per 10,000 population (2001).
Newspapers: The Red Oak Express (1 x week)
Transportation: Commute to work: 92.2% car, 0.5% public transportation, 3.2% walk, 3.5% work from home (2000); Travel time to work: 76.1% less than 15 minutes, 8.8% 15 to 30 minutes, 6.1% 30 to 45 minutes, 4.5% 45 to 60 minutes, 4.5% 60 minutes or more (2000)
Additional Information Contacts
Montgomery County Board of Realtors 712-623-9575
Red Oak Chamber of Commerce 712-623-4821

STANTON (city). Covers a land area of 0.888 square miles and a water area of 0 square miles. Located at 40.98° N. Lat.; 95.10° W. Long.
History: Stanton was first settled by a native of Sweden and originally called Homlstad for a town in Sweden.
Population: 714 (2000); Race: 99.0% White, 0.0% Black, 0.0% Asian, 0.0% American Indian and Alaska Native, 0.8% Hispanic of any race, 0.4% two or more races (2000); Density: 803.9 persons per square mile (2000); Age: 26.4% under 18, 22.7% over 64 (2000); Marriage status: 15.3% never married, 68.4% now married, 6.7% widowed, 9.6% divorced (2000); Foreign born: 0.5% (2000); Ancestry (includes multiple ancestries): 25.8% German, 21.0% Swedish, 12.4% Irish, 7.1% United States or American, 6.3% English (2000).
Economy: Single-family building permits issued: 4 (2001) / 2 (2000); Multi-family building permits issued: 0 (2001) / 0 (2000); Employment by occupation: 13.1% management, 10.3% professional, 13.7% services, 26.0% sales, 5.1% farming, 12.9% construction, 18.9% production (2000).
Income: Per capita income: $15,628 (2000); Median household income: $36,607 (2000); Poverty rate: 6.1% (2000).
Taxes: Total city taxes per capita: $148 (1997); City property taxes per capita: $110 (1997).
Education: High school graduation rate: 82.7% (2000); College graduation rate: 12.0% (2000).

School District(s)

Stanton Community School District (KG-12)
2000 Enrollment: 328 712-829-2162
Housing: Homeownership rate: 74.6% (2000); Median home value: $63,000 (2000); Median rent: $283 per month (2000); Median age of housing: 59 years (2000).
Transportation: Commute to work: 88.7% car, 0.0% public transportation, 7.0% walk, 3.2% work from home (2000); Travel time to work: 53.9% less than 15 minutes, 35.9% 15 to 30 minutes, 4.8% 30 to 45 minutes, 2.4% 45 to 60 minutes, 3.0% 60 minutes or more (2000)

VILLISCA (city). Covers a land area of 1.909 square miles and a water area of 0 square miles. Located at 40.92° N. Lat.; 94.97° W. Long. Elevation is 1,050 feet.
History: Villisca was first known as The Forks, because of its position between the Middle and West Nodaway Rivers.
Population: 1,344 (2000); Race: 98.5% White, 0.0% Black, 0.6% Asian, 0.0% American Indian and Alaska Native, 0.7% Hispanic of any race, 0.3% two or more races (2000); Density: 703.9 persons per square mile (2000); Age: 26.3% under 18, 24.6% over 64 (2000); Marriage status: 19.4% never married, 55.9% now married, 11.4% widowed, 13.3% divorced (2000); Foreign born: 0.9% (2000); Ancestry (includes multiple ancestries): 28.5% German, 13.4% Irish, 11.4% English, 10.3% Other groups, 9.3% United States or American (2000).
Economy: Single-family building permits issued: 3 (2001) / 1 (2000); Multi-family building permits issued: 0 (2001) / 0 (2000); Employment by occupation: 6.4% management, 14.2% professional, 20.3% services, 21.3% sales, 2.1% farming, 10.6% construction, 25.1% production (2000).
Income: Per capita income: $14,067 (2000); Median household income: $26,694 (2000); Poverty rate: 12.9% (2000).
Taxes: Total city taxes per capita: $173 (1997); City property taxes per capita: $129 (1997).
Education: High school graduation rate: 77.1% (2000); College graduation rate: 10.2% (2000).

School District(s)

Villisca Community School District (KG-12)
2000 Enrollment: 445 712-826-2542
Housing: Homeownership rate: 77.4% (2000); Median home value: $37,300 (2000); Median rent: $188 per month (2000); Median age of housing: 60+ years (2000).
Newspapers: Villisca Review/Stanton Viking (1 x week)
Transportation: Commute to work: 90.3% car, 0.0% public transportation, 5.0% walk, 3.7% work from home (2000); Travel time to work: 40.8% less than 15 minutes, 43.0% 15 to 30 minutes, 10.8% 30 to 45 minutes, 1.1% 45 to 60 minutes, 4.3% 60 minutes or more (2000)

Muscatine County

Located in southeastern Iowa; bounded on the southeast by the Mississippi River and the Illinois border; prairie area, drained by the Cedar River. Covers a land area of 438.70 square miles, a water area of 10.40 square miles, and is located in the Central Time Zone. The county government was organized in 1836. County seat is Muscatine.

Weather Station: Muscatine — Elevation: 547 feet

	Jan	Feb	Mar	Apr	May	Jun	Jul	Aug	Sep	Oct	Nov	Dec
High	30	37	49	63	74	83	86	84	77	65	48	35
Low	13	19	29	40	52	61	66	63	54	43	31	19
Precip	1.3	1.3	2.7	3.3	4.3	4.3	4.3	4.5	3.7	2.7	2.6	2.0
Snow	8.4	5.7	2.9	1.1	tr	0.0	0.0	0.0	0.0	0.2	2.0	6.2

High and Low temperatures in degrees Fahrenheit; Precipitation and Snow in inches

Population: 41,722 (2000); Race: 90.7% White, 0.8% Black, 0.7% Asian, 0.4% American Indian and Alaska Native, 11.9% Hispanic of any race, 1.5% two or more races (2000); Density: 95.1 persons per square mile (2000); Age: 26.9% under 18, 12.9% over 64 (2000).
Religion: Five largest groups: 12.4% Catholic Church, 8.9% The United Methodist Church, 5.9% Evangelical Lutheran Church in America, 3.1% Lutheran Church—Missouri Synod, 2.8% Christian Church (Disciples of Christ) (2000).
Economy: Unemployment rate: 3.7% (11/2002); Total civilian labor force: 21,915 (11/2002); Leading industries: 39.0% manufacturing; 12.0% retail trade; 8.1% health care and social assistance (2000); Companies that employ more than 1,000 persons: 0 (2000); Companies that employ more than 100 persons: 31 (2000); Farms: 783 totaling 219,001 acres (1997); Minority business ownership rate: 0.0% (1997); Women business ownership rate: 31.3% (1997); Retail sales per capita: $8,254 (1997). Single-family building permits issued: 100 (2001) / 111 (2000); Multi-family building permits issued: 26 (2001) / 0 (2000).
Income: Per capita income: $19,625 (2000); Median household income: $41,803 (2000); Poverty rate: 8.9% (2000); Bankruptcy rate: 4.72% (2001).
Taxes: Total county taxes per capita: $233 (2000); County property taxes per capita: $197 (2000).
Education: High school graduation rate: 80.3% (2000); College graduation rate: 17.2% (2000).
Housing: Homeownership rate: 75.4% (2000); Median home value: $84,700 (2000); Median rent: $368 per month (2000); Median age of housing: 41 years (2000).
Health: Birth rate: 147.2 per 10,000 population (1998); Age adjusted death rate: 84.1 per 10,000 population (1999); Age adjusted cancer mortality rate: 180.6 deaths per 100,000 population (1999). Air Quality Index: 97% good, 3% moderate, 0% unhealthy (percent of days in 2000). Number of physicians: 8.6 per 10,000 population (1999); Number of hospital beds: 15.8 per 10,000 population (1999).
Elections: 2000 Presidential election results: 50.1% Gore, 46.6% Bush, 2.3% Nader, 0.5% Buchanan
National and State Parks: Wiese Slough State Game Management Area; Wildcat Den State Park
Additional Information Contacts
Muscatine County Government Offices.................. 563-263-5317
Muscatine Board of Realtors.................. 563-263-4250
Muscatine Chamber of Commerce.................. 563-263-8895
Muscatine Convention & Visitors Bureau.................. 563-263-8895
West Liberty Chamber of Commerce.................. 319-627-4876

Muscatine County Communities

ATALISSA (city). Covers a land area of 0.134 square miles and a water area of 0 square miles. Located at 41.57° N. Lat.; 91.16° W. Long.
History: Atalissa was named after Atalissa, California, by Captain William Lundy, who promised to give a corner lot to the first child born in the town who was given the name Atalissa. Atalissa Davis received the lot.
Population: 283 (2000); Race: 100.0% White, 0.0% Black, 0.0% Asian, 0.0% American Indian and Alaska Native, 0.0% Hispanic of any race, 0.0% two or more races (2000); Density: 2,119.8 persons per square mile (2000); Age: 24.5% under 18, 12.4% over 64 (2000); Marriage status: 18.4% never married, 60.1% now married, 10.1% widowed, 11.4% divorced (2000); Foreign born: 0.0% (2000); Ancestry (includes multiple ancestries): 32.1% German, 13.1% United States or American, 6.9% Dutch, 5.9% Irish, 5.2% Other groups (2000).
Economy: Single-family building permits issued: 0 (2001) / 3 (2000); Multi-family building permits issued: 0 (2001) / 0 (2000); Employment by occupation: 6.1% management, 8.6% professional, 20.9% services, 14.7% sales, 1.2% farming, 11.7% construction, 36.8% production (2000).
Income: Per capita income: $20,269 (2000); Median household income: $31,875 (2000); Poverty rate: 9.4% (2000).
Taxes: Total city taxes per capita: $125 (1997); City property taxes per capita: $47 (1997).
Education: High school graduation rate: 75.7% (2000); College graduation rate: 6.5% (2000).
Housing: Homeownership rate: 81.7% (2000); Median home value: $58,000 (2000); Median rent: $365 per month (2000); Median age of housing: 60+ years (2000).
Transportation: Commute to work: 95.1% car, 0.0% public transportation, 0.0% walk, 1.8% work from home (2000); Travel time to work: 31.3% less than 15 minutes, 38.8% 15 to 30 minutes, 22.5% 30 to 45 minutes, 5.6% 45 to 60 minutes, 1.9% 60 minutes or more (2000)

CONESVILLE (city). Aka Cone. Covers a land area of 0.369 square miles and a water area of 0 square miles. Located at 41.37° N. Lat.; 91.35° W. Long. Elevation is 615 feet.
History: Conesville was named for Beebe S. Cone, a major landowner.
Population: 424 (2000); Race: 76.9% White, 0.0% Black, 0.0% Asian, 0.5% American Indian and Alaska Native, 64.4% Hispanic of any race, 3.0% two or more races (2000); Density: 1,147.7 persons per square mile (2000); Age: 40.3% under 18, 9.5% over 64 (2000); Marriage status: 19.8% never married, 62.9% now married, 4.2% widowed, 13.1% divorced (2000); Foreign born: 23.4% (2000); Ancestry (includes multiple ancestries): 60.6% Other groups, 9.5% German, 4.6% United States or American, 3.7% English, 2.1% Irish (2000).
Economy: Employment by occupation: 3.0% management, 6.0% professional, 18.6% services, 5.4% sales, 0.6% farming, 19.8% construction, 46.7% production (2000).
Income: Per capita income: $10,097 (2000); Median household income: $29,464 (2000); Poverty rate: 13.9% (2000).
Taxes: Total city taxes per capita: $141 (1997); City property taxes per capita: $70 (1997).
Education: High school graduation rate: 63.4% (2000); College graduation rate: 7.2% (2000).
Housing: Homeownership rate: 68.7% (2000); Median home value: $55,600 (2000); Median rent: $358 per month (2000); Median age of housing: 30 years (2000).
Transportation: Commute to work: 94.5% car, 0.0% public transportation, 4.3% walk, 0.0% work from home (2000); Travel time to work: 29.4% less than 15 minutes, 25.2% 15 to 30 minutes, 27.0% 30 to 45 minutes, 11.0% 45 to 60 minutes, 7.4% 60 minutes or more (2000)

FRUITLAND (city). Covers a land area of 1.800 square miles and a water area of 0 square miles. Located at 41.35° N. Lat.; 91.12° W. Long. Elevation is 552 feet.
History: Fruitland was first known as Island, because of its location on Muscatine Island, but was renamed as a result of the rapid growth of the fruit industry in the vicinity.
Population: 703 (2000); Race: 95.0% White, 1.1% Black, 0.3% Asian, 0.3% American Indian and Alaska Native, 3.2% Hispanic of any race, 1.1% two or more races (2000); Density: 390.6 persons per square mile (2000); Age: 27.1% under 18, 8.4% over 64 (2000); Marriage status: 23.0% never married, 61.8% now married, 4.8% widowed, 10.4% divorced (2000); Foreign born: 1.1% (2000); Ancestry (includes multiple ancestries): 39.0% German, 17.4% Irish, 12.3% United States or American, 7.9% Other groups, 6.8% English (2000).
Economy: Single-family building permits issued: 21 (2001) / 13 (2000); Multi-family building permits issued: 0 (2001) / 0 (2000); Employment by occupation: 9.0% management, 12.7% professional, 15.1% services, 20.5% sales, 2.4% farming, 14.9% construction, 25.4% production (2000).
Income: Per capita income: $20,270 (2000); Median household income: $57,250 (2000); Poverty rate: 2.4% (2000).
Taxes: Total city taxes per capita: $176 (1997); City property taxes per capita: $96 (1997).
Education: High school graduation rate: 86.2% (2000); College graduation rate: 13.6% (2000).
Housing: Homeownership rate: 93.9% (2000); Median home value: $114,700 (2000); Median rent: $463 per month (2000); Median age of housing: 16 years (2000).
Transportation: Commute to work: 96.3% car, 0.5% public transportation, 1.2% walk, 1.5% work from home (2000); Travel time to work: 41.1% less than 15 minutes, 45.9% 15 to 30 minutes, 6.7% 30 to 45 minutes, 1.7% 45 to 60 minutes, 4.5% 60 minutes or more (2000)

MOSCOW (unincorporated postal area, zip code 52760). Covers a land area of 25.065 square miles and a water area of 0.098 square miles. Located at 41.57° N. Lat.; 91.08° W. Long. Elevation is 654 feet.

History: Moscow was named for Moscow, Russia.
Population: 617 (2000); Race: 98.9% White, 0.0% Black, 0.0% Asian, 0.0% American Indian and Alaska Native, 0.0% Hispanic of any race, 1.1% two or more races (2000); Density: 24.6 persons per square mile (2000); Age: 29.6% under 18, 14.7% over 64 (2000); Marriage status: 21.4% never married, 64.0% now married, 7.4% widowed, 7.2% divorced (2000); Foreign born: 0.0% (2000); Ancestry (includes multiple ancestries): 57.0% German, 12.2% Irish, 9.9% English, 4.6% Polish, 3.2% Swedish (2000).
Economy: Employment by occupation: 12.5% management, 7.5% professional, 12.8% services, 24.9% sales, 2.0% farming, 11.1% construction, 29.2% production (2000).
Income: Per capita income: $16,430 (2000); Median household income: $37,083 (2000); Poverty rate: 7.6% (2000).
Education: High school graduation rate: 85.4% (2000); College graduation rate: 8.5% (2000).
Housing: Homeownership rate: 84.1% (2000); Median home value: $89,400 (2000); Median rent: $400 per month (2000); Median age of housing: 55 years (2000).
Transportation: Commute to work: 90.0% car, 0.0% public transportation, 2.3% walk, 7.7% work from home (2000); Travel time to work: 37.3% less than 15 minutes, 40.6% 15 to 30 minutes, 16.7% 30 to 45 minutes, 5.4% 45 to 60 minutes, 0.0% 60 minutes or more (2000)

MUSCATINE (city). Covers a land area of 16.836 square miles and a water area of 1.046 square miles. Located at 41.42° N. Lat.; 91.05° W. Long. Elevation is 585 feet.
History: Muscatine first came into existence as a trading post in 1833. In 1836, the site was surveyed and called Bloomington, after Bloomington, Indiana. The name was changed to Muscatine in 1849.
Population: 22,697 (2000); Race: 90.7% White, 1.3% Black, 0.4% Asian, 0.4% American Indian and Alaska Native, 12.6% Hispanic of any race, 1.2% two or more races (2000); Density: 1,348.1 persons per square mile (2000); Age: 26.3% under 18, 13.7% over 64 (2000); Marriage status: 23.9% never married, 57.2% now married, 7.1% widowed, 11.8% divorced (2000); Foreign born: 5.2% (2000); Ancestry (includes multiple ancestries): 30.6% German, 19.2% Other groups, 11.3% Irish, 9.1% English, 8.5% United States or American (2000).
Vital Statistics: Birth rate: 158.6 per 10,000 population (1998)
Economy: Single-family building permits issued: 23 (2001) / 22 (2000); Multi-family building permits issued: 26 (2001) / 0 (2000); Employment by occupation: 7.8% management, 16.8% professional, 18.5% services, 21.3% sales, 0.1% farming, 8.6% construction, 26.9% production (2000).
Income: Per capita income: $19,483 (2000); Median household income: $38,122 (2000); Poverty rate: 10.9% (2000).
Taxes: Total city taxes per capita: $488 (2000); City property taxes per capita: $360 (2000).
Education: High school graduation rate: 77.9% (2000); College graduation rate: 16.5% (2000).

School District(s)

Muscatine Community School District (PK-12)
2000 Enrollment: 5,420 319-263-7223

Housing: Homeownership rate: 70.3% (2000); Median home value: $77,100 (2000); Median rent: $378 per month (2000); Median age of housing: 47 years (2000).
Hospitals: Unity Health System (80 beds)
Safety: Violent crime rate: 86.0 per 10,000 population; Property crime rate: 418.1 per 10,000 population (2001).
Newspapers: Muscatine Journal (6 x week); Muskie Trading Post (1 x week)
Transportation: Commute to work: 92.0% car, 1.6% public transportation, 1.9% walk, 2.8% work from home (2000); Travel time to work: 63.0% less than 15 minutes, 23.6% 15 to 30 minutes, 7.2% 30 to 45 minutes, 3.5% 45 to 60 minutes, 2.6% 60 minutes or more (2000)
Airports: Muscatine Municipal

Additional Information Contacts

Muscatine Board of Realtors 563-263-4250
Muscatine Chamber of Commerce...................... 563-263-8895
Muscatine Convention & Visitors Bureau 563-263-8895

NICHOLS (city). Covers a land area of 0.233 square miles and a water area of 0 square miles. Located at 41.47° N. Lat.; 91.30° W. Long. Elevation is 638 feet.
History: Nichols was named in honor of Samuel Nichols, a landowner who donated right-of-way to the Burlington, Cedar Rapids & Northern Railroad.
Population: 374 (2000); Race: 86.4% White, 0.0% Black, 4.5% Asian, 0.0% American Indian and Alaska Native, 15.3% Hispanic of any race, 1.7% two or more races (2000); Density: 1,604.8 persons per square mile (2000); Age: 24.6% under 18, 12.1% over 64 (2000); Marriage status: 25.2% never married, 59.9% now married, 6.9% widowed, 8.0% divorced (2000); Foreign born: 11.0% (2000); Ancestry (includes multiple ancestries): 32.5% German, 19.8% Other groups, 11.3% English, 10.7% Irish, 5.9% Dutch (2000).
Economy: Single-family building permits issued: 0 (2001) / 0 (2000); Multi-family building permits issued: 0 (2001) / 0 (2000); Employment by occupation: 4.2% management, 9.6% professional, 13.3% services, 21.7% sales, 1.2% farming, 10.2% construction, 39.8% production (2000).
Income: Per capita income: $16,082 (2000); Median household income: $43,750 (2000); Poverty rate: 13.7% (2000).
Taxes: Total city taxes per capita: $171 (1997); City property taxes per capita: $94 (1997).
Education: High school graduation rate: 75.4% (2000); College graduation rate: 9.9% (2000).
Housing: Homeownership rate: 78.8% (2000); Median home value: $64,700 (2000); Median rent: $365 per month (2000); Median age of housing: 60+ years (2000).
Transportation: Commute to work: 94.4% car, 1.3% public transportation, 4.4% walk, 0.0% work from home (2000); Travel time to work: 19.4% less than 15 minutes, 48.8% 15 to 30 minutes, 20.0% 30 to 45 minutes, 6.3% 45 to 60 minutes, 5.6% 60 minutes or more (2000)

STOCKTON (city). Covers a land area of 0.110 square miles and a water area of 0 square miles. Located at 41.59° N. Lat.; 90.85° W. Long.
History: Stockton was named Fulton in 1855, but later, when a shipment of goods went by mistake to another Iowa town of that name, the name was changed.
Population: 182 (2000); Race: 98.9% White, 0.0% Black, 1.1% Asian, 0.0% American Indian and Alaska Native, 1.1% Hispanic of any race, 0.0% two or more races (2000); Density: 1,656.3 persons per square mile (2000); Age: 25.9% under 18, 9.8% over 64 (2000); Marriage status: 19.8% never married, 68.7% now married, 0.0% widowed, 11.5% divorced (2000); Foreign born: 2.3% (2000); Ancestry (includes multiple ancestries): 40.2% German, 20.1% Irish, 14.4% English, 9.2% United States or American, 6.9% Scottish (2000).
Economy: Single-family building permits issued: 0 (2001) / 0 (2000); Multi-family building permits issued: 0 (2001) / 0 (2000); Employment by occupation: 0.0% management, 3.6% professional, 8.3% services, 38.1% sales, 0.0% farming, 14.3% construction, 35.7% production (2000).
Income: Per capita income: $17,003 (2000); Median household income: $35,417 (2000); Poverty rate: 6.3% (2000).
Taxes: Total city taxes per capita: $165 (1997); City property taxes per capita: $90 (1997).
Education: High school graduation rate: 68.6% (2000); College graduation rate: 3.3% (2000).
Housing: Homeownership rate: 75.0% (2000); Median home value: $56,900 (2000); Median rent: $306 per month (2000); Median age of housing: 50 years (2000).
Transportation: Commute to work: 97.6% car, 0.0% public transportation, 2.4% walk, 0.0% work from home (2000); Travel time to work: 22.6% less than 15 minutes, 33.3% 15 to 30 minutes, 29.8% 30 to 45 minutes, 8.3% 45 to 60 minutes, 6.0% 60 minutes or more (2000)

WEST LIBERTY (city). Covers a land area of 1.560 square miles and a water area of 0 square miles. Located at 41.57° N. Lat.; 91.26° W. Long. Elevation is 673 feet.
History: West Liberty was originally known as the Wapsinonoc Settlement. Joseph Smith, the Morman leader, in 1836 considered this place for the site of the Mormon colony.
Population: 3,332 (2000); Race: 63.5% White, 0.5% Black, 3.9% Asian, 1.2% American Indian and Alaska Native, 42.4% Hispanic of any race, 6.2% two or more races (2000); Density: 2,136.4 persons per square mile (2000); Age: 29.5% under 18, 14.7% over 64 (2000); Marriage status: 21.3% never married, 62.2% now married, 8.7% widowed, 7.8% divorced (2000); Foreign born: 25.6% (2000); Ancestry (includes multiple ancestries): 48.9% Other groups, 21.3% German, 10.4% Irish, 6.1% English, 3.8% Dutch (2000).
Economy: Single-family building permits issued: 1 (2001) / 1 (2000); Multi-family building permits issued: 0 (2001) / 0 (2000); Employment by occupation: 9.1% management, 15.3% professional, 13.8% services, 18.5% sales, 0.5% farming, 5.2% construction, 37.6% production (2000).
Income: Per capita income: $15,420 (2000); Median household income: $37,925 (2000); Poverty rate: 7.3% (2000).
Taxes: Total city taxes per capita: $227 (1997); City property taxes per capita: $216 (1997).
Education: High school graduation rate: 68.0% (2000); College graduation rate: 14.5% (2000).

School District(s)

West Liberty Community School District (PK-12)
2000 Enrollment: 1,200 319-627-2116

Housing: Homeownership rate: 68.9% (2000); Median home value: $85,000 (2000); Median rent: $335 per month (2000); Median age of housing: 42 years (2000).
Newspapers: West Liberty Index (1 x week)
Transportation: Commute to work: 85.6% car, 0.0% public transportation, 10.1% walk, 3.1% work from home (2000); Travel time to work: 41.3% less than 15 minutes, 35.8% 15 to 30 minutes, 17.8% 30 to 45 minutes, 3.6% 45 to 60 minutes, 1.4% 60 minutes or more (2000)
Additional Information Contacts
West Liberty Chamber of Commerce 319-627-4876

WILTON (city). Aka Wilton Junction. Covers a land area of 1.874 square miles and a water area of 0 square miles. Located at 41.58° N. Lat.; 91.01° W. Long.
History: Wilton was named after Wilton, Maine.
Population: 2,829 (2000); Race: 98.2% White, 0.5% Black, 0.7% Asian, 0.0% American Indian and Alaska Native, 0.6% Hispanic of any race, 0.5% two or more races (2000); Density: 1,509.5 persons per square mile (2000); Age: 26.3% under 18, 15.6% over 64 (2000); Marriage status: 18.8% never married, 61.2% now married, 7.4% widowed, 12.6% divorced (2000); Foreign born: 1.9% (2000); Ancestry (includes multiple ancestries): 40.9% German, 12.6% English, 9.2% Irish, 7.5% United States or American, 5.3% Other groups (2000).
Economy: Single-family building permits issued: 9 (2001) / 8 (2000); Multi-family building permits issued: 0 (2001) / 0 (2000); Employment by occupation: 7.9% management, 16.7% professional, 15.1% services, 27.2% sales, 0.0% farming, 10.5% construction, 22.6% production (2000).
Income: Per capita income: $18,445 (2000); Median household income: $44,278 (2000); Poverty rate: 6.5% (2000).
Taxes: Total city taxes per capita: $422 (2000); City property taxes per capita: $332 (2000).
Education: High school graduation rate: 85.0% (2000); College graduation rate: 17.3% (2000).

School District(s)

Wilton Community School District (PK-12)
2000 Enrollment: 988 319-732-2035

Housing: Homeownership rate: 78.3% (2000); Median home value: $86,400 (2000); Median rent: $361 per month (2000); Median age of housing: 35 years (2000).
Newspapers: Wilton-Durant Advocate News (1 x week)
Transportation: Commute to work: 91.5% car, 0.5% public transportation, 5.1% walk, 1.4% work from home (2000); Travel time to work: 46.9% less than 15 minutes, 29.7% 15 to 30 minutes, 16.7% 30 to 45 minutes, 4.3% 45 to 60 minutes, 2.4% 60 minutes or more (2000)

O'Brien County

Located in northwestern Iowa; drained by the Little Sioux and Floyd Rivers. Covers a land area of 573.10 square miles, a water area of 0.20 square miles, and is located in the Central Time Zone. The county government was organized in 1851. County seat is Primghar.

Weather Station: Primghar — Elevation: 1,519 feet

	Jan	Feb	Mar	Apr	May	Jun	Jul	Aug	Sep	Oct	Nov	Dec
High	25	32	44	60	73	82	85	83	75	63	43	29
Low	6	13	24	36	49	58	62	60	51	39	25	12
Precip	0.7	0.5	1.9	3.0	3.6	4.9	4.4	4.2	2.7	2.1	1.5	0.7
Snow	7.2	3.7	6.5	1.0	0.0	0.0	0.0	0.0	0.0	0.3	3.9	6.5

High and Low temperatures in degrees Fahrenheit; Precipitation and Snow in inches

Weather Station: Sanborn — Elevation: 1,548 feet

	Jan	Feb	Mar	Apr	May	Jun	Jul	Aug	Sep	Oct	Nov	Dec
High	23	30	41	58	71	80	83	81	73	61	41	28
Low	4	11	22	34	47	57	62	59	50	37	23	10
Precip	0.7	0.6	1.8	2.8	3.6	4.3	3.6	3.9	2.9	2.0	1.6	0.7
Snow	8.6	6.3	8.1	2.5	tr	0.0	0.0	0.0	tr	0.6	5.9	8.0

High and Low temperatures in degrees Fahrenheit; Precipitation and Snow in inches

Weather Station: Sheldon — Elevation: 1,417 feet

	Jan	Feb	Mar	Apr	May	Jun	Jul	Aug	Sep	Oct	Nov	Dec
High	24	31	43	59	72	81	84	81	74	61	42	28
Low	5	12	23	35	47	57	61	59	49	37	23	10
Precip	0.8	0.6	2.2	3.0	3.5	4.5	3.8	3.9	2.7	2.1	1.6	0.8
Snow	7.9	5.2	8.2	2.5	tr	tr	0.0	tr	tr	0.8	5.5	7.2

High and Low temperatures in degrees Fahrenheit; Precipitation and Snow in inches

Population: 15,102 (2000); Race: 97.9% White, 0.3% Black, 0.3% Asian, 0.2% American Indian and Alaska Native, 1.7% Hispanic of any race, 0.5% two or more races (2000); Density: 26.4 persons per square mile (2000); Age: 24.9% under 18, 21.2% over 64 (2000).
Religion: Five largest groups: 15.3% The United Methodist Church, 15.0% Reformed Church in America, 14.8% Lutheran Church—Missouri Synod, 11.4% Catholic Church, 9.6% Christian Reformed Church in North America (2000).
Economy: Unemployment rate: 2.5% (11/2002); Total civilian labor force: 7,871 (11/2002); Leading industries: 22.1% health care and social assistance; 18.6% retail trade; 14.3% manufacturing (2000); Companies that employ more than 1,000 persons: 0 (2000); Companies that employ more than 100 persons: 9 (2000); Farms: 977 totaling 358,472 acres (1997); Minority business ownership rate: 0.0% (1997); Women business ownership rate: 16.1% (1997); Retail sales per capita: $11,314 (1997). Single-family building permits issued: 15 (2001) / 23 (2000); Multi-family building permits issued: 14 (2001) / 17 (2000).
Income: Per capita income: $17,281 (2000); Median household income: $35,758 (2000); Poverty rate: 7.3% (2000); Bankruptcy rate: 3.13% (2001).
Taxes: Total county taxes per capita: $183 (1997); County property taxes per capita: $157 (1997).
Education: High school graduation rate: 80.7% (2000); College graduation rate: 14.7% (2000).
Housing: Homeownership rate: 76.8% (2000); Median home value: $58,300 (2000); Median rent: $258 per month (2000); Median age of housing: 50 years (2000).
Health: Birth rate: 106.0 per 10,000 population (1998); Age adjusted death rate: 67.0 per 10,000 population (1999); Age adjusted cancer mortality rate: 149.9 deaths per 100,000 population (1999). Number of physicians: 6.0 per 10,000 population (1999); Number of hospital beds: 88.7 per 10,000 population (1999).
Elections: 2000 Presidential election results: 30.8% Gore, 66.4% Bush, 1.5% Nader, 0.8% Buchanan
National and State Parks: Indian Village State Park; Mill Creek State Park
Additional Information Contacts
O'Brien County Government Offices 712-757-3255
Sheldon Community Development 712-324-2813

O'Brien County Communities

ARCHER (city). Covers a land area of 0.096 square miles and a water area of 0 square miles. Located at 43.11° N. Lat.; 95.74° W. Long. Elevation is 1,468 feet.
History: Archer was named for John H. Archer, who owned the land on which the town was platted.
Population: 126 (2000); Race: 100.0% White, 0.0% Black, 0.0% Asian, 0.0% American Indian and Alaska Native, 0.0% Hispanic of any race, 0.0% two or more races (2000); Density: 1,317.1 persons per square mile (2000); Age: 18.1% under 18, 26.0% over 64 (2000); Marriage status: 19.1% never married, 74.5% now married, 2.7% widowed, 3.6% divorced (2000); Foreign born: 1.6% (2000); Ancestry (includes multiple ancestries): 46.5% German, 39.4% Dutch, 15.7% English, 5.5% United States or American, 2.4% Scotch-Irish (2000).
Economy: Employment by occupation: 7.9% management, 20.6% professional, 15.9% services, 9.5% sales, 4.8% farming, 11.1% construction, 30.2% production (2000).
Income: Per capita income: $15,958 (2000); Median household income: $34,688 (2000); Poverty rate: 1.6% (2000).
Taxes: Total city taxes per capita: $138 (1997); City property taxes per capita: $87 (1997).
Education: High school graduation rate: 88.6% (2000); College graduation rate: 8.0% (2000).
Housing: Homeownership rate: 92.7% (2000); Median home value: $34,600 (2000); Median rent: $225 per month (2000); Median age of housing: 52 years (2000).
Transportation: Commute to work: 86.4% car, 0.0% public transportation, 6.8% walk, 6.8% work from home (2000); Travel time to work: 41.8% less

than 15 minutes, 52.7% 15 to 30 minutes, 5.5% 30 to 45 minutes, 0.0% 45 to 60 minutes, 0.0% 60 minutes or more (2000)

CALUMET (city). Covers a land area of 0.264 square miles and a water area of 0 square miles. Located at 42.94° N. Lat.; 95.55° W. Long. Elevation is 1,433 feet.
History: Calumet once had a visitor who ate 21 plates of pancakes during an annual Pancake Day celebration.
Population: 181 (2000); Race: 91.0% White, 3.4% Black, 0.0% Asian, 0.0% American Indian and Alaska Native, 1.7% Hispanic of any race, 5.6% two or more races (2000); Density: 684.5 persons per square mile (2000); Age: 26.6% under 18, 13.6% over 64 (2000); Marriage status: 7.5% never married, 75.2% now married, 6.8% widowed, 10.5% divorced (2000); Foreign born: 0.6% (2000); Ancestry (includes multiple ancestries): 48.0% German, 9.6% English, 9.0% Dutch, 7.3% Norwegian, 4.5% Swedish (2000).
Economy: Single-family building permits issued: 0 (2001) / 0 (2000); Multi-family building permits issued: 0 (2001) / 0 (2000); Employment by occupation: 14.6% management, 13.5% professional, 6.7% services, 13.5% sales, 0.0% farming, 14.6% construction, 37.1% production (2000).
Income: Per capita income: $17,659 (2000); Median household income: $33,750 (2000); Poverty rate: 8.5% (2000).
Taxes: Total city taxes per capita: $160 (1997); City property taxes per capita: $115 (1997).
Education: High school graduation rate: 84.7% (2000); College graduation rate: 13.6% (2000).
Housing: Homeownership rate: 90.5% (2000); Median home value: $39,200 (2000); Median rent: $275 per month (2000); Median age of housing: 60+ years (2000).
Transportation: Commute to work: 91.0% car, 0.0% public transportation, 2.2% walk, 5.6% work from home (2000); Travel time to work: 36.9% less than 15 minutes, 26.2% 15 to 30 minutes, 13.1% 30 to 45 minutes, 8.3% 45 to 60 minutes, 15.5% 60 minutes or more (2000)

HARTLEY (city). Covers a land area of 1.276 square miles and a water area of 0 square miles. Located at 43.18° N. Lat.; 95.47° W. Long. Elevation is 1,462 feet.
History: Harltey was named for a railroad surveyor.
Population: 1,733 (2000); Race: 96.3% White, 1.3% Black, 0.8% Asian, 0.1% American Indian and Alaska Native, 3.6% Hispanic of any race, 1.2% two or more races (2000); Density: 1,358.2 persons per square mile (2000); Age: 24.1% under 18, 26.6% over 64 (2000); Marriage status: 20.1% never married, 58.3% now married, 14.5% widowed, 7.2% divorced (2000); Foreign born: 7.3% (2000); Ancestry (includes multiple ancestries): 46.9% German, 10.7% Dutch, 9.2% Irish, 7.2% Norwegian, 6.7% English (2000).
Economy: Single-family building permits issued: 1 (2001) / 2 (2000); Multi-family building permits issued: 0 (2001) / 2 (2000); Employment by occupation: 6.5% management, 14.6% professional, 17.1% services, 19.8% sales, 1.0% farming, 8.4% construction, 32.6% production (2000).
Income: Per capita income: $17,068 (2000); Median household income: $31,016 (2000); Poverty rate: 9.5% (2000).
Taxes: Total city taxes per capita: $224 (1997); City property taxes per capita: $222 (1997).
Education: High school graduation rate: 75.6% (2000); College graduation rate: 12.7% (2000).

School District(s)

Hartley-Melvin-Sanborn Community School District (KG-12)
2000 Enrollment: 885 712-728-2022
Housing: Homeownership rate: 77.1% (2000); Median home value: $48,500 (2000); Median rent: $276 per month (2000); Median age of housing: 49 years (2000).
Newspapers: Hartley Sentinel (1 x week)
Transportation: Commute to work: 86.5% car, 0.1% public transportation, 9.8% walk, 2.4% work from home (2000); Travel time to work: 59.0% less than 15 minutes, 23.4% 15 to 30 minutes, 11.3% 30 to 45 minutes, 2.5% 45 to 60 minutes, 3.8% 60 minutes or more (2000)

PAULLINA (city). Covers a land area of 0.545 square miles and a water area of 0 square miles. Located at 42.97° N. Lat.; 95.68° W. Long. Elevation is 1,408 feet.
History: Paullina was mapped in 1882 by the Western Town Lot Company. The town was named in honor of local landowners, the Paullin brothers, who deeded their land to the railroad for the town site.
Population: 1,124 (2000); Race: 98.6% White, 0.0% Black, 0.0% Asian, 0.0% American Indian and Alaska Native, 0.9% Hispanic of any race, 1.4% two or more races (2000); Density: 2,061.6 persons per square mile (2000); Age: 19.5% under 18, 31.6% over 64 (2000); Marriage status: 18.1% never married, 62.5% now married, 13.7% widowed, 5.7% divorced (2000); Foreign born: 0.8% (2000); Ancestry (includes multiple ancestries): 62.7% German, 8.4% Irish, 8.0% Dutch, 6.9% English, 5.7% United States or American (2000).
Economy: Single-family building permits issued: 0 (2001) / 0 (2000); Multi-family building permits issued: 0 (2001) / 0 (2000); Employment by occupation: 9.7% management, 16.3% professional, 18.9% services, 20.9% sales, 2.4% farming, 7.2% construction, 24.5% production (2000).
Income: Per capita income: $17,644 (2000); Median household income: $32,188 (2000); Poverty rate: 9.1% (2000).
Taxes: Total city taxes per capita: $236 (1997); City property taxes per capita: $182 (1997).
Education: High school graduation rate: 81.2% (2000); College graduation rate: 15.2% (2000).

School District(s)

South O'brien Community School District (KG-12)
2000 Enrollment: 812 712-448-2115
Housing: Homeownership rate: 85.9% (2000); Median home value: $51,900 (2000); Median rent: $221 per month (2000); Median age of housing: 51 years (2000).
Newspapers: Paullina Times (1 x week)
Transportation: Commute to work: 81.5% car, 0.0% public transportation, 12.0% walk, 6.1% work from home (2000); Travel time to work: 51.6% less than 15 minutes, 22.9% 15 to 30 minutes, 21.0% 30 to 45 minutes, 2.4% 45 to 60 minutes, 2.2% 60 minutes or more (2000)

PRIMGHAR (city). Covers a land area of 1.384 square miles and a water area of 0 square miles. Located at 43.08° N. Lat.; 95.62° W. Long. Elevation is 1,498 feet.
History: The name Primghar combines the first letters of the surnames of eight early settlers.
Population: 891 (2000); Race: 98.5% White, 0.0% Black, 1.1% Asian, 0.0% American Indian and Alaska Native, 0.0% Hispanic of any race, 0.3% two or more races (2000); Density: 643.9 persons per square mile (2000); Age: 21.7% under 18, 28.5% over 64 (2000); Marriage status: 19.2% never married, 55.7% now married, 14.4% widowed, 10.7% divorced (2000); Foreign born: 1.2% (2000); Ancestry (includes multiple ancestries): 35.5% German, 14.5% Dutch, 10.9% Irish, 9.9% Norwegian, 6.4% English (2000).
Economy: Single-family building permits issued: 1 (2001) / 1 (2000); Multi-family building permits issued: 0 (2001) / 0 (2000); Employment by occupation: 8.7% management, 18.2% professional, 17.3% services, 18.7% sales, 2.2% farming, 13.1% construction, 21.8% production (2000).
Income: Per capita income: $17,791 (2000); Median household income: $31,304 (2000); Poverty rate: 9.6% (2000).
Taxes: Total city taxes per capita: $223 (1997); City property taxes per capita: $191 (1997).
Education: High school graduation rate: 78.1% (2000); College graduation rate: 16.7% (2000).
Housing: Homeownership rate: 82.7% (2000); Median home value: $39,800 (2000); Median rent: $225 per month (2000); Median age of housing: 60+ years (2000).
Hospitals: Baum Harmon Mercy Hospital (14 beds)
Transportation: Commute to work: 87.1% car, 0.0% public transportation, 11.2% walk, 1.7% work from home (2000); Travel time to work: 50.6% less than 15 minutes, 26.3% 15 to 30 minutes, 12.0% 30 to 45 minutes, 4.1% 45 to 60 minutes, 7.0% 60 minutes or more (2000)

SANBORN (city). Covers a land area of 1.811 square miles and a water area of 0 square miles. Located at 43.18° N. Lat.; 95.65° W. Long.
History: Sanborn was founded in 1878 as a terminal for the Chicago, Milwaukee & St. Paul Railroad, and was platted in the same year by J. A. Stocum and John Lawler. It was named for George W. Sanborn, first superintendent of the Iowa and Dakota division of the railroad.
Population: 1,353 (2000); Race: 98.5% White, 0.0% Black, 0.2% Asian, 0.2% American Indian and Alaska Native, 1.1% Hispanic of any race, 0.3% two or more races (2000); Density: 747.1 persons per square mile (2000); Age: 24.1% under 18, 27.1% over 64 (2000); Marriage status: 15.8% never married, 63.8% now married, 15.9% widowed, 4.5% divorced (2000); Foreign born: 1.3% (2000); Ancestry (includes multiple ancestries): 40.2% Dutch, 33.8% German, 9.8% Irish, 5.4% English, 4.2% United States or American (2000).
Economy: Single-family building permits issued: 6 (2001) / 3 (2000); Multi-family building permits issued: 6 (2001) / 3 (2000); Employment by occupation: 8.2% management, 16.3% professional, 21.2% services, 19.3% sales, 0.5% farming, 10.6% construction, 23.9% production (2000).

Income: Per capita income: $18,189 (2000); Median household income: $34,250 (2000); Poverty rate: 4.8% (2000).
Taxes: Total city taxes per capita: $234 (1997); City property taxes per capita: $231 (1997).
Education: High school graduation rate: 74.3% (2000); College graduation rate: 11.7% (2000).
Housing: Homeownership rate: 80.5% (2000); Median home value: $61,700 (2000); Median rent: $219 per month (2000); Median age of housing: 43 years (2000).
Newspapers: The Sanborn Pioneer (1 x week)
Transportation: Commute to work: 84.4% car, 0.3% public transportation, 7.9% walk, 4.2% work from home (2000); Travel time to work: 68.1% less than 15 minutes, 20.2% 15 to 30 minutes, 7.7% 30 to 45 minutes, 2.4% 45 to 60 minutes, 1.7% 60 minutes or more (2000)

SHELDON (city). Covers a land area of 4.389 square miles and a water area of 0 square miles. Located at 43.18° N. Lat.; 95.84° W. Long. Elevation is 1,421 feet.
History: Sheldon was named for Israel Sheldon, superintendent of the land department of the Sioux City & St. Paul Railroad.
Population: 4,914 (2000); Race: 97.5% White, 0.0% Black, 0.3% Asian, 0.2% American Indian and Alaska Native, 2.9% Hispanic of any race, 0.4% two or more races (2000); Density: 1,119.6 persons per square mile (2000); Age: 23.2% under 18, 19.7% over 64 (2000); Marriage status: 21.4% never married, 62.1% now married, 9.8% widowed, 6.7% divorced (2000); Foreign born: 2.4% (2000); Ancestry (includes multiple ancestries): 37.2% German, 33.4% Dutch, 7.2% Irish, 6.6% Other groups, 5.9% English (2000).
Economy: Single-family building permits issued: 6 (2001) / 16 (2000); Multi-family building permits issued: 8 (2001) / 12 (2000); Employment by occupation: 6.3% management, 19.6% professional, 14.3% services, 21.7% sales, 2.7% farming, 10.1% construction, 25.4% production (2000).
Income: Per capita income: $18,254 (2000); Median household income: $34,058 (2000); Poverty rate: 7.6% (2000).
Taxes: Total city taxes per capita: $361 (1997); City property taxes per capita: $301 (1997).
Education: High school graduation rate: 78.0% (2000); College graduation rate: 17.1% (2000).

School District(s)

Sheldon Community School District (KG-12)
2000 Enrollment: 1,078 712-324-2504

Two-year College(s)

Northwest Iowa Community College (Public)
2001 Enrollment: 1,017 712-324-5061
2001 Tuition: In-state $1,980; Out-of-state $2,970

Housing: Homeownership rate: 70.0% (2000); Median home value: $79,600 (2000); Median rent: $276 per month (2000); Median age of housing: 39 years (2000).
Hospitals: Northwest Iowa Health Center (28 beds)
Safety: Violent crime rate: 0.0 per 10,000 population; Property crime rate: 173.2 per 10,000 population (2001).
Newspapers: The Sheldon Mail-Sun (1 x week); The Northwest Iowa Review (1 x week)
Transportation: Commute to work: 91.9% car, 1.6% public transportation, 3.3% walk, 2.0% work from home (2000); Travel time to work: 73.7% less than 15 minutes, 16.2% 15 to 30 minutes, 4.9% 30 to 45 minutes, 1.8% 45 to 60 minutes, 3.4% 60 minutes or more (2000)
Airports: Sheldon Municipal
Additional Information Contacts
Sheldon Community Development 712-324-2813

SUTHERLAND (city). Covers a land area of 0.873 square miles and a water area of 0 square miles. Located at 42.97° N. Lat.; 95.49° W. Long. Elevation is 1,424 feet.
History: Sutherland was platted by the Western Town Lot Company in 1882. The name may have been chosen in honor of a railroad investor.
Population: 707 (2000); Race: 98.0% White, 0.7% Black, 0.1% Asian, 0.0% American Indian and Alaska Native, 0.0% Hispanic of any race, 1.1% two or more races (2000); Density: 810.2 persons per square mile (2000); Age: 18.4% under 18, 29.4% over 64 (2000); Marriage status: 18.5% never married, 57.7% now married, 15.6% widowed, 8.2% divorced (2000); Foreign born: 0.6% (2000); Ancestry (includes multiple ancestries): 46.4% German, 9.6% Irish, 5.4% United States or American, 5.2% Polish, 5.0% English (2000).
Economy: Single-family building permits issued: 1 (2001) / 1 (2000); Multi-family building permits issued: 0 (2001) / 0 (2000); Employment by occupation: 8.0% management, 16.0% professional, 19.3% services, 20.3% sales, 1.7% farming, 17.3% construction, 17.3% production (2000).
Income: Per capita income: $16,345 (2000); Median household income: $31,985 (2000); Poverty rate: 3.9% (2000).
Taxes: Total city taxes per capita: $204 (1997); City property taxes per capita: $151 (1997).
Education: High school graduation rate: 81.6% (2000); College graduation rate: 9.5% (2000).
Housing: Homeownership rate: 87.9% (2000); Median home value: $36,300 (2000); Median rent: $200 per month (2000); Median age of housing: 59 years (2000).
Newspapers: Sutherland Courier (1 x week)
Transportation: Commute to work: 88.5% car, 2.0% public transportation, 3.4% walk, 4.1% work from home (2000); Travel time to work: 49.6% less than 15 minutes, 17.6% 15 to 30 minutes, 16.2% 30 to 45 minutes, 6.7% 45 to 60 minutes, 9.9% 60 minutes or more (2000)

Osceola County

Located in northwestern Iowa; bounded on the north by Minnesota; drained by the Ocheyedan River; includes the highest point in Iowa (1,675 ft), and Rush Lake. Covers a land area of 398.80 square miles, a water area of 0.70 square miles, and is located in the Central Time Zone. The county government was organized in 1851. County seat is Sibley.

Weather Station: Sibley 5 NNE — Elevation: 1,669 feet

	Jan	Feb	Mar	Apr	May	Jun	Jul	Aug	Sep	Oct	Nov	Dec
High	22	29	41	57	71	79	83	80	73	61	41	27
Low	3	10	21	33	45	56	60	57	48	36	22	9
Precip	0.6	0.5	2.0	2.9	3.4	4.3	3.4	4.2	3.0	1.9	1.4	0.7
Snow	7.6	4.6	8.1	3.2	tr	0.0	0.0	0.0	tr	1.0	5.8	6.9

High and Low temperatures in degrees Fahrenheit; Precipitation and Snow in inches

Population: 7,003 (2000); Race: 98.0% White, 0.4% Black, 0.1% Asian, 0.1% American Indian and Alaska Native, 1.9% Hispanic of any race, 0.7% two or more races (2000); Density: 17.6 persons per square mile (2000); Age: 26.0% under 18, 19.1% over 64 (2000).
Religion: Five largest groups: 15.2% Catholic Church, 12.1% Evangelical Lutheran Church in America, 11.7% Reformed Church in America, 10.1% Lutheran Church—Missouri Synod, 9.9% The United Methodist Church (2000).
Economy: Unemployment rate: 2.2% (11/2002); Total civilian labor force: 3,746 (11/2002); Leading industries: 29.5% manufacturing; 17.4% health care and social assistance; 9.8% retail trade (2000); Companies that employ more than 1,000 persons: 0 (2000); Companies that employ more than 100 persons: 3 (2000); Farms: 649 totaling 240,601 acres (1997); Minority business ownership rate: 0.0% (1997); Women business ownership rate: 22.0% (1997); Retail sales per capita: $4,537 (1997). Single-family building permits issued: 4 (2001) / 4 (2000); Multi-family building permits issued: 0 (2001) / 0 (2000).
Income: Per capita income: $16,463 (2000); Median household income: $34,274 (2000); Poverty rate: 7.0% (2000); Bankruptcy rate: 1.56% (2001).
Taxes: Total county taxes per capita: $280 (1997); County property taxes per capita: $275 (1997).
Education: High school graduation rate: 81.1% (2000); College graduation rate: 13.4% (2000).
Housing: Homeownership rate: 77.8% (2000); Median home value: $53,400 (2000); Median rent: $281 per month (2000); Median age of housing: 55 years (2000).
Health: Birth rate: 114.2 per 10,000 population (1998); Age adjusted death rate: 74.8 per 10,000 population (1999); Age adjusted cancer mortality rate: 136.9 (Unreliable figure as per CDC) deaths per 100,000 population (1999). Number of physicians: 20.0 per 10,000 population (1999); Number of hospital beds: 45.7 per 10,000 population (1999).
Elections: 2000 Presidential election results: 29.8% Gore, 67.4% Bush, 1.8% Nader, 0.5% Buchanan
National and State Parks: Ashton Pits State Public Hunting Area; Iowa Lake State Game Management Area; Rush Lake State Game Management Area
Additional Information Contacts
Osceola County Government Offices. 712-754-2241
Sibley Chamber of Commerce 712-754-3212

Osceola County Communities

ASHTON (city). Covers a land area of 1.005 square miles and a water area of 0.005 square miles. Located at 43.31° N. Lat.; 95.79° W. Long. Elevation is 1,449 feet.
History: Ashton, first called Gilman, was named in 1875 after the white ash trees found in the area.
Population: 461 (2000); Race: 98.5% White, 0.6% Black, 0.0% Asian, 0.0% American Indian and Alaska Native, 0.9% Hispanic of any race, 0.0% two or more races (2000); Density: 458.6 persons per square mile (2000); Age: 23.2% under 18, 18.6% over 64 (2000); Marriage status: 19.3% never married, 65.2% now married, 11.3% widowed, 4.1% divorced (2000); Foreign born: 1.3% (2000); Ancestry (includes multiple ancestries): 63.0% German, 14.3% Dutch, 9.1% Irish, 6.9% Norwegian, 5.0% United States or American (2000).
Economy: Single-family building permits issued: 0 (2001) / 1 (2000); Multi-family building permits issued: 0 (2001) / 0 (2000); Employment by occupation: 8.1% management, 8.1% professional, 12.7% services, 17.2% sales, 2.7% farming, 18.6% construction, 32.6% production (2000).
Income: Per capita income: $15,848 (2000); Median household income: $29,821 (2000); Poverty rate: 5.0% (2000).
Taxes: Total city taxes per capita: $221 (1997); City property taxes per capita: $219 (1997).
Education: High school graduation rate: 82.7% (2000); College graduation rate: 5.1% (2000).
Housing: Homeownership rate: 84.6% (2000); Median home value: $39,600 (2000); Median rent: $263 per month (2000); Median age of housing: 56 years (2000).
Transportation: Commute to work: 82.6% car, 0.0% public transportation, 11.5% walk, 4.1% work from home (2000); Travel time to work: 47.8% less than 15 minutes, 41.1% 15 to 30 minutes, 6.7% 30 to 45 minutes, 1.0% 45 to 60 minutes, 3.3% 60 minutes or more (2000)

HARRIS (city). Covers a land area of 0.792 square miles and a water area of 0 square miles. Located at 43.44° N. Lat.; 95.43° W. Long.
History: Harris was named for landowner H.W. Harris, who helped to lay out the town in 1889.
Population: 200 (2000); Race: 91.5% White, 0.0% Black, 0.0% Asian, 0.9% American Indian and Alaska Native, 7.5% Hispanic of any race, 0.0% two or more races (2000); Density: 252.6 persons per square mile (2000); Age: 25.8% under 18, 10.8% over 64 (2000); Marriage status: 27.6% never married, 56.3% now married, 5.2% widowed, 10.9% divorced (2000); Foreign born: 2.8% (2000); Ancestry (includes multiple ancestries): 39.0% German, 13.1% Dutch, 12.2% Other groups, 6.1% Irish, 3.8% Norwegian (2000).
Economy: Single-family building permits issued: 0 (2001) / 0 (2000); Multi-family building permits issued: 0 (2001) / 0 (2000); Employment by occupation: 6.7% management, 9.5% professional, 4.8% services, 21.9% sales, 3.8% farming, 12.4% construction, 41.0% production (2000).
Income: Per capita income: $15,788 (2000); Median household income: $35,625 (2000); Poverty rate: 14.1% (2000).
Taxes: Total city taxes per capita: $130 (1997); City property taxes per capita: $130 (1997).
Education: High school graduation rate: 75.9% (2000); College graduation rate: 6.4% (2000).
Housing: Homeownership rate: 68.9% (2000); Median home value: $28,300 (2000); Median rent: $288 per month (2000); Median age of housing: 54 years (2000).
Transportation: Commute to work: 92.3% car, 0.0% public transportation, 1.9% walk, 3.8% work from home (2000); Travel time to work: 17.0% less than 15 minutes, 47.0% 15 to 30 minutes, 34.0% 30 to 45 minutes, 0.0% 45 to 60 minutes, 2.0% 60 minutes or more (2000)

MAY CITY (unincorporated postal area, zip code 51349). Covers a land area of 0.265 square miles and a water area of 0.005 square miles. Located at 43.37° N. Lat.; 95.62° W. Long.
Population: 43 (2000); Race: 100.0% White, 0.0% Black, 0.0% Asian, 0.0% American Indian and Alaska Native, 0.0% Hispanic of any race, 0.0% two or more races (2000); Density: 162.3 persons per square mile (2000); Age: 0.0% under 18, 12.5% over 64 (2000); Marriage status: 0.0% never married, 87.5% now married, 12.5% widowed, 0.0% divorced (2000); Foreign born: 0.0% (2000); Ancestry (includes multiple ancestries): 40.0% German, 25.0% Swiss, 15.0% United States or American, 15.0% Other groups, 15.0% Irish (2000).
Economy: Employment by occupation: 0.0% management, 0.0% professional, 78.6% services, 0.0% sales, 0.0% farming, 21.4% construction, 0.0% production (2000).
Income: Per capita income: $15,335 (2000); Median household income: $19,625 (2000); Poverty rate: 0.0% (2000).
Education: High school graduation rate: 100.0% (2000); College graduation rate: 0.0% (2000).
Housing: Homeownership rate: 75.0% (2000); Median home value: $26,300 (2000); Median rent: $275 per month (2000); Median age of housing: 46 years (2000).
Transportation: Commute to work: 100.0% car, 0.0% public transportation, 0.0% walk, 0.0% work from home (2000); Travel time to work: 0.0% less than 15 minutes, 42.9% 15 to 30 minutes, 57.1% 30 to 45 minutes, 0.0% 45 to 60 minutes, 0.0% 60 minutes or more (2000)

MELVIN (city). Covers a land area of 0.173 square miles and a water area of 0 square miles. Located at 43.28° N. Lat.; 95.60° W. Long.
Population: 243 (2000); Race: 99.2% White, 0.0% Black, 0.0% Asian, 0.0% American Indian and Alaska Native, 0.8% Hispanic of any race, 0.0% two or more races (2000); Density: 1,403.5 persons per square mile (2000); Age: 16.1% under 18, 37.7% over 64 (2000); Marriage status: 16.1% never married, 64.5% now married, 15.2% widowed, 4.3% divorced (2000); Foreign born: 0.0% (2000); Ancestry (includes multiple ancestries): 64.0% German, 16.9% Dutch, 11.0% Irish, 5.1% Norwegian, 3.8% French (except Basque) (2000).
Economy: In livestock and grain area. Employment by occupation: 18.2% management, 2.7% professional, 14.5% services, 19.1% sales, 5.5% farming, 12.7% construction, 27.3% production (2000).
Income: Per capita income: $17,827 (2000); Median household income: $27,750 (2000); Poverty rate: 8.5% (2000).
Taxes: Total city taxes per capita: $107 (1997); City property taxes per capita: $107 (1997).
Education: High school graduation rate: 73.9% (2000); College graduation rate: 0.5% (2000).
Housing: Homeownership rate: 86.1% (2000); Median home value: $25,800 (2000); Median rent: $206 per month (2000); Median age of housing: 59 years (2000).
Transportation: Commute to work: 85.3% car, 1.8% public transportation, 10.1% walk, 2.8% work from home (2000); Travel time to work: 44.3% less than 15 minutes, 37.7% 15 to 30 minutes, 12.3% 30 to 45 minutes, 3.8% 45 to 60 minutes, 1.9% 60 minutes or more (2000)

OCHEYEDAN (city). Covers a land area of 1.163 square miles and a water area of 0 square miles. Located at 43.41° N. Lat.; 95.53° W. Long. Elevation is 1,551 feet.
History: Ocheyedan comes from an Indian word meaning "spot where they weep." Early settlers suffered extreme hardship during the severe winter of 1871-72. The only houses were sod huts or shacks, small and cold. Many people were lost during blizzards, and some froze to death.
Population: 536 (2000); Race: 99.6% White, 0.0% Black, 0.0% Asian, 0.0% American Indian and Alaska Native, 0.0% Hispanic of any race, 0.4% two or more races (2000); Density: 461.1 persons per square mile (2000); Age: 24.7% under 18, 23.8% over 64 (2000); Marriage status: 19.9% never married, 62.7% now married, 9.6% widowed, 7.8% divorced (2000); Foreign born: 1.3% (2000); Ancestry (includes multiple ancestries): 54.8% German, 19.8% Dutch, 6.6% Irish, 6.6% Norwegian, 4.9% United States or American (2000).
Economy: Single-family building permits issued: 0 (2001) / 0 (2000); Multi-family building permits issued: 0 (2001) / 0 (2000); Employment by occupation: 6.6% management, 11.6% professional, 19.8% services, 19.4% sales, 5.0% farming, 7.4% construction, 30.2% production (2000).
Income: Per capita income: $14,554 (2000); Median household income: $31,513 (2000); Poverty rate: 4.8% (2000).
Taxes: Total city taxes per capita: $181 (1997); City property taxes per capita: $181 (1997).
Education: High school graduation rate: 83.3% (2000); College graduation rate: 8.9% (2000).
Housing: Homeownership rate: 82.7% (2000); Median home value: $39,000 (2000); Median rent: $225 per month (2000); Median age of housing: 60+ years (2000).
Newspapers: The Ocheyedan Press-Melvin News (1 x week)
Transportation: Commute to work: 88.0% car, 0.0% public transportation, 10.0% walk, 2.1% work from home (2000); Travel time to work: 39.8% less than 15 minutes, 45.3% 15 to 30 minutes, 11.0% 30 to 45 minutes, 1.3% 45 to 60 minutes, 2.5% 60 minutes or more (2000)

SIBLEY (city). Covers a land area of 1.612 square miles and a water area of 0 square miles. Located at 43.40° N. Lat.; 95.74° W. Long. Elevation is 1,502 feet.

History: Sibley was named in 1872 in honor of General G. H. Sibley of Minnesota. Sibley was the home of William L. Harding, Governor of Iowa (1917-1921).
Population: 2,796 (2000); Race: 97.6% White, 0.9% Black, 0.0% Asian, 0.1% American Indian and Alaska Native, 3.0% Hispanic of any race, 0.8% two or more races (2000); Density: 1,734.7 persons per square mile (2000); Age: 23.3% under 18, 23.7% over 64 (2000); Marriage status: 20.6% never married, 59.8% now married, 13.9% widowed, 5.7% divorced (2000); Foreign born: 1.5% (2000); Ancestry (includes multiple ancestries): 51.8% German, 22.3% Dutch, 9.3% Irish, 5.8% Norwegian, 5.6% Other groups (2000).
Economy: Single-family building permits issued: 3 (2001) / 3 (2000); Multi-family building permits issued: 0 (2001) / 0 (2000); Employment by occupation: 11.0% management, 15.8% professional, 13.6% services, 20.9% sales, 2.4% farming, 10.0% construction, 26.3% production (2000).
Income: Per capita income: $16,845 (2000); Median household income: $33,173 (2000); Poverty rate: 4.8% (2000).
Taxes: Total city taxes per capita: $234 (1997); City property taxes per capita: $228 (1997).
Education: High school graduation rate: 78.2% (2000); College graduation rate: 15.0% (2000).

School District(s)

Sibley-Ocheyedan Community School District (KG-12)
2000 Enrollment: 964 712-754-2533

Housing: Homeownership rate: 74.5% (2000); Median home value: $59,300 (2000); Median rent: $300 per month (2000); Median age of housing: 48 years (2000).
Hospitals: Osceola Community Hospital (32 beds)
Newspapers: The Osceola County Gazette-Tribune (1 x week)
Transportation: Commute to work: 89.9% car, 0.0% public transportation, 7.0% walk, 1.6% work from home (2000); Travel time to work: 70.0% less than 15 minutes, 19.7% 15 to 30 minutes, 5.3% 30 to 45 minutes, 2.4% 45 to 60 minutes, 2.7% 60 minutes or more (2000)
Additional Information Contacts
Sibley Chamber of Commerce 712-754-3212

Page County

Located in southwestern Iowa; bounded on the south by Missouri; drained by the Nodaway, East Nodaway, Tarkio, and East Nishnabotna Rivers. Covers a land area of 534.80 square miles, a water area of 0.50 square miles, and is located in the Central Time Zone. The county government was organized in 1847. County seat is Clarinda.

Weather Station: Clarinda — Elevation: 977 feet

	Jan	Feb	Mar	Apr	May	Jun	Jul	Aug	Sep	Oct	Nov	Dec
High	31	38	50	63	73	83	87	85	77	65	48	36
Low	12	18	28	39	50	60	65	62	53	41	29	18
Precip	0.9	1.0	2.5	3.4	4.8	4.5	4.9	4.4	4.0	2.7	2.4	1.2
Snow	7.4	5.6	3.8	0.9	0.0	0.0	0.0	0.0	0.0	0.2	2.6	5.3

High and Low temperatures in degrees Fahrenheit; Precipitation and Snow in inches

Weather Station: Shenandoah — Elevation: 974 feet

	Jan	Feb	Mar	Apr	May	Jun	Jul	Aug	Sep	Oct	Nov	Dec
High	32	39	51	64	75	84	88	86	79	67	49	37
Low	13	19	29	40	51	61	65	63	54	42	29	19
Precip	0.8	0.9	2.3	3.4	4.5	4.5	4.5	3.7	3.6	2.6	2.1	1.1
Snow	7.0	5.7	3.5	1.2	0.0	0.0	0.0	0.0	0.0	0.4	1.7	4.9

High and Low temperatures in degrees Fahrenheit; Precipitation and Snow in inches

Population: 16,976 (2000); Race: 96.8% White, 1.3% Black, 0.5% Asian, 0.4% American Indian and Alaska Native, 1.4% Hispanic of any race, 0.5% two or more races (2000); Density: 31.7 persons per square mile (2000); Age: 23.3% under 18, 19.7% over 64 (2000).
Religion: Five largest groups: 12.4% The United Methodist Church, 9.6% Lutheran Church—Missouri Synod, 7.3% Evangelical Lutheran Church in America, 6.0% Presbyterian Church (U.S.A.), 5.1% Christian Church (Disciples of Christ) (2000).
Economy: Unemployment rate: 4.4% (11/2002); Total civilian labor force: 8,041 (11/2002); Leading industries: 38.0% manufacturing; 15.6% health care and social assistance; 14.4% retail trade (2000); Companies that employ more than 1,000 persons: 0 (2000); Companies that employ more than 100 persons: 10 (2000); Farms: 845 totaling 309,228 acres (1997); Minority business ownership rate: 0.0% (1997); Women business ownership rate: 17.7% (1997); Retail sales per capita: $8,573 (1997). Single-family building permits issued: 17 (2001) / 20 (2000); Multi-family building permits issued: 0 (2001) / 2 (2000).
Income: Per capita income: $16,670 (2000); Median household income: $35,466 (2000); Poverty rate: 12.5% (2000); Bankruptcy rate: 4.05% (2001).
Taxes: Total county taxes per capita: $206 (1997); County property taxes per capita: $172 (1997).
Education: High school graduation rate: 85.5% (2000); College graduation rate: 16.6% (2000).
Housing: Homeownership rate: 71.7% (2000); Median home value: $60,000 (2000); Median rent: $290 per month (2000); Median age of housing: 55 years (2000).
Health: Birth rate: 112.5 per 10,000 population (1998); Age adjusted death rate: 93.6 per 10,000 population (1999); Age adjusted cancer mortality rate: 164.5 deaths per 100,000 population (1999). Number of physicians: 10.0 per 10,000 population (1999); Number of hospital beds: 119.6 per 10,000 population (1999).
Elections: 2000 Presidential election results: 32.5% Gore, 65.0% Bush, 1.8% Nader, 0.3% Buchanan
Additional Information Contacts
Page County Government Offices 712-542-3219
Clarinda Chamber of Commerce 712-542-2166
Essex Chamber of Commerce 712-379-3485
Fremont Page Board of Realtors 712-246-1072
Shenandoah Chamber of Commerce 712-246-3260

Page County Communities

BLANCHARD (city). Covers a land area of 0.225 square miles and a water area of 0 square miles. Located at 40.58° N. Lat.; 95.22° W. Long. Elevation is 1,050 feet.
History: Blanchard was named for J.W. Blanchard, a Wabash Railroad official.
Population: 61 (2000); Race: 100.0% White, 0.0% Black, 0.0% Asian, 0.0% American Indian and Alaska Native, 0.0% Hispanic of any race, 0.0% two or more races (2000); Density: 270.9 persons per square mile (2000); Age: 25.7% under 18, 21.4% over 64 (2000); Marriage status: 35.1% never married, 43.9% now married, 12.3% widowed, 8.8% divorced (2000); Foreign born: 0.0% (2000); Ancestry (includes multiple ancestries): 24.3% German, 10.0% Other groups, 8.6% Irish, 7.1% Scottish, 5.7% Scotch-Irish (2000).
Economy: Employment by occupation: 0.0% management, 0.0% professional, 27.3% services, 6.1% sales, 0.0% farming, 15.2% construction, 51.5% production (2000).
Income: Per capita income: $15,226 (2000); Median household income: $37,917 (2000); Poverty rate: 5.7% (2000).
Taxes: Total city taxes per capita: $213 (2000); City property taxes per capita: $148 (2000).
Education: High school graduation rate: 88.4% (2000); College graduation rate: 0.0% (2000).
Housing: Homeownership rate: 93.9% (2000); Median home value: $12,500 (2000); Median age of housing: 60+ years (2000).
Transportation: Commute to work: 100.0% car, 0.0% public transportation, 0.0% walk, 0.0% work from home (2000); Travel time to work: 3.2% less than 15 minutes, 22.6% 15 to 30 minutes, 74.2% 30 to 45 minutes, 0.0% 45 to 60 minutes, 0.0% 60 minutes or more (2000)

BRADDYVILLE (city). Covers a land area of 0.531 square miles and a water area of 0 square miles. Located at 40.57° N. Lat.; 95.03° W. Long. Elevation is 990 feet.
History: Braddyville was named for James Braddy, who platted the village in 1878.
Population: 176 (2000); Race: 100.0% White, 0.0% Black, 0.0% Asian, 0.0% American Indian and Alaska Native, 0.0% Hispanic of any race, 0.0% two or more races (2000); Density: 331.7 persons per square mile (2000); Age: 22.7% under 18, 14.1% over 64 (2000); Marriage status: 19.4% never married, 59.7% now married, 6.0% widowed, 14.9% divorced (2000); Foreign born: 0.0% (2000); Ancestry (includes multiple ancestries): 28.2% German, 26.4% United States or American, 16.0% Irish, 7.4% English, 6.1% Dutch (2000).
Economy: Employment by occupation: 2.0% management, 8.0% professional, 15.0% services, 30.0% sales, 0.0% farming, 10.0% construction, 35.0% production (2000).
Income: Per capita income: $18,421 (2000); Median household income: $37,917 (2000); Poverty rate: 4.9% (2000).

Taxes: Total city taxes per capita: $84 (1997); City property taxes per capita: $44 (1997).
Education: High school graduation rate: 95.6% (2000); College graduation rate: 15.0% (2000).
Housing: Homeownership rate: 77.6% (2000); Median home value: $48,100 (2000); Median rent: $265 per month (2000); Median age of housing: 34 years (2000).
Transportation: Commute to work: 100.0% car, 0.0% public transportation, 0.0% walk, 0.0% work from home (2000); Travel time to work: 14.6% less than 15 minutes, 58.3% 15 to 30 minutes, 16.7% 30 to 45 minutes, 2.1% 45 to 60 minutes, 8.3% 60 minutes or more (2000)

CLARINDA (city). Covers a land area of 5.191 square miles and a water area of 0.033 square miles. Located at 40.73° N. Lat.; 95.03° W. Long. Elevation is 1,009 feet.
History: Clarinda, a stop on the Underground Railway, was named for Clarinda Buck, an early settler.
Population: 5,690 (2000); Race: 92.7% White, 3.8% Black, 1.5% Asian, 0.8% American Indian and Alaska Native, 1.5% Hispanic of any race, 0.8% two or more races (2000); Density: 1,096.1 persons per square mile (2000); Age: 23.1% under 18, 16.9% over 64 (2000); Marriage status: 26.6% never married, 53.5% now married, 7.9% widowed, 12.0% divorced (2000); Foreign born: 1.3% (2000); Ancestry (includes multiple ancestries): 23.7% German, 13.6% Irish, 10.9% English, 10.3% Other groups, 10.2% United States or American (2000).
Economy: Single-family building permits issued: 6 (2001) / 7 (2000); Multi-family building permits issued: 0 (2001) / 0 (2000); Employment by occupation: 9.7% management, 22.1% professional, 20.0% services, 20.1% sales, 1.4% farming, 5.5% construction, 21.3% production (2000).
Income: Per capita income: $15,136 (2000); Median household income: $35,871 (2000); Poverty rate: 16.3% (2000).
Taxes: Total city taxes per capita: $331 (2000); City property taxes per capita: $267 (2000).
Education: High school graduation rate: 85.1% (2000); College graduation rate: 15.8% (2000).

School District(s)

Clarinda Community School District (PK-12)
2000 Enrollment: 1,233 712-542-5165
Mental Health Institute School (N -N)
2000 Enrollment: n/a 712-542-2161

Housing: Homeownership rate: 67.9% (2000); Median home value: $68,300 (2000); Median rent: $296 per month (2000); Median age of housing: 50 years (2000).
Hospitals: Clarinda Mental Health Institute (234 beds); Clarinda Regional Health Center (47 beds)
Safety: Violent crime rate: 21.1 per 10,000 population; Property crime rate: 288.5 per 10,000 population (2001).
Newspapers: The Clarinda Herald-Journal (1 x week)
Transportation: Commute to work: 90.3% car, 0.4% public transportation, 5.6% walk, 3.4% work from home (2000); Travel time to work: 76.5% less than 15 minutes, 13.5% 15 to 30 minutes, 5.9% 30 to 45 minutes, 1.3% 45 to 60 minutes, 2.7% 60 minutes or more (2000)

Additional Information Contacts

Clarinda Chamber of Commerce 712-542-2166

COIN (city). Covers a land area of 0.802 square miles and a water area of 0 square miles. Located at 40.65° N. Lat.; 95.23° W. Long. Elevation is 1,030 feet.
History: A story about the founding of Coin tells of a man coming across a silver coin while digging a foundation for a house here. This was considered an omen of prosperity for the town.
Population: 252 (2000); Race: 100.0% White, 0.0% Black, 0.0% Asian, 0.0% American Indian and Alaska Native, 1.7% Hispanic of any race, 0.0% two or more races (2000); Density: 314.4 persons per square mile (2000); Age: 22.0% under 18, 19.5% over 64 (2000); Marriage status: 18.0% never married, 56.5% now married, 7.0% widowed, 18.5% divorced (2000); Foreign born: 0.0% (2000); Ancestry (includes multiple ancestries): 19.1% German, 11.2% Other groups, 10.4% English, 9.5% Irish, 7.5% Swedish (2000).
Economy: Single-family building permits issued: 0 (2001) / 0 (2000); Multi-family building permits issued: 0 (2001) / 0 (2000); Employment by occupation: 6.5% management, 11.3% professional, 14.5% services, 21.8% sales, 0.0% farming, 16.1% construction, 29.8% production (2000).
Income: Per capita income: $16,080 (2000); Median household income: $33,500 (2000); Poverty rate: 7.5% (2000).
Taxes: Total city taxes per capita: $98 (1997); City property taxes per capita: $64 (1997).
Education: High school graduation rate: 79.8% (2000); College graduation rate: 4.2% (2000).
Housing: Homeownership rate: 80.2% (2000); Median home value: $27,500 (2000); Median rent: $220 per month (2000); Median age of housing: 60+ years (2000).
Transportation: Commute to work: 91.8% car, 1.6% public transportation, 1.6% walk, 1.6% work from home (2000); Travel time to work: 16.7% less than 15 minutes, 39.2% 15 to 30 minutes, 35.8% 30 to 45 minutes, 1.7% 45 to 60 minutes, 6.7% 60 minutes or more (2000)

COLLEGE SPRINGS (city). Covers a land area of 1.110 square miles and a water area of 0 square miles. Located at 40.62° N. Lat.; 95.12° W. Long.
History: The town here was first known as Amity. The present name came from the fact that it was the site of Amity College, as well as the location of a year-round spring.
Population: 246 (2000); Race: 99.2% White, 0.0% Black, 0.0% Asian, 0.8% American Indian and Alaska Native, 2.0% Hispanic of any race, 0.0% two or more races (2000); Density: 221.6 persons per square mile (2000); Age: 21.9% under 18, 18.8% over 64 (2000); Marriage status: 13.6% never married, 74.8% now married, 6.5% widowed, 5.1% divorced (2000); Foreign born: 0.0% (2000); Ancestry (includes multiple ancestries): 28.1% German, 21.5% Irish, 16.0% English, 12.1% United States or American, 7.8% Other groups (2000).
Economy: Employment by occupation: 1.6% management, 20.9% professional, 27.9% services, 13.2% sales, 0.0% farming, 6.2% construction, 30.2% production (2000).
Income: Per capita income: $15,102 (2000); Median household income: $38,500 (2000); Poverty rate: 4.3% (2000).
Taxes: Total city taxes per capita: $121 (1997); City property taxes per capita: $82 (1997).
Education: High school graduation rate: 86.3% (2000); College graduation rate: 14.8% (2000).

School District(s)

South Page Community School District (PK-12)
2000 Enrollment: 375 712-582-3212

Housing: Homeownership rate: 93.7% (2000); Median home value: $38,800 (2000); Median rent: $225 per month (2000); Median age of housing: 60+ years (2000).
Transportation: Commute to work: 86.6% car, 0.0% public transportation, 4.7% walk, 7.1% work from home (2000); Travel time to work: 18.6% less than 15 minutes, 51.7% 15 to 30 minutes, 19.5% 30 to 45 minutes, 5.1% 45 to 60 minutes, 5.1% 60 minutes or more (2000)

ESSEX (city). Covers a land area of 1.507 square miles and a water area of 0 square miles. Located at 40.83° N. Lat.; 95.30° W. Long. Elevation is 992 feet.
History: An early settler, Robert Bruce Wood, was born in Essex County, Massachusetts, and his parents were from Essex County, England. The name of Essex probably reflects this connection.
Population: 884 (2000); Race: 98.1% White, 0.2% Black, 0.2% Asian, 0.5% American Indian and Alaska Native, 0.6% Hispanic of any race, 1.0% two or more races (2000); Density: 586.7 persons per square mile (2000); Age: 25.3% under 18, 17.3% over 64 (2000); Marriage status: 19.2% never married, 66.7% now married, 5.5% widowed, 8.6% divorced (2000); Foreign born: 0.8% (2000); Ancestry (includes multiple ancestries): 23.1% German, 20.2% Irish, 18.9% Swedish, 11.0% English, 10.2% United States or American (2000).
Economy: Single-family building permits issued: 2 (2001) / 2 (2000); Multi-family building permits issued: 0 (2001) / 0 (2000); Employment by occupation: 9.6% management, 12.4% professional, 15.5% services, 20.3% sales, 0.7% farming, 8.1% construction, 33.6% production (2000).
Income: Per capita income: $18,202 (2000); Median household income: $41,382 (2000); Poverty rate: 5.5% (2000).
Taxes: Total city taxes per capita: $181 (1997); City property taxes per capita: $134 (1997).
Education: High school graduation rate: 90.8% (2000); College graduation rate: 13.2% (2000).

School District(s)

Essex Community School District (KG-12)
2000 Enrollment: 295 712-379-3117

Housing: Homeownership rate: 74.6% (2000); Median home value: $48,300 (2000); Median rent: $222 per month (2000); Median age of housing: 53 years (2000).

Newspapers: The Essex Independent (1 x week)
Transportation: Commute to work: 96.3% car, 0.0% public transportation, 1.1% walk, 1.8% work from home (2000); Travel time to work: 51.4% less than 15 minutes, 39.0% 15 to 30 minutes, 5.4% 30 to 45 minutes, 1.9% 45 to 60 minutes, 2.3% 60 minutes or more (2000)
Additional Information Contacts
Essex Chamber of Commerce 712-379-3485

HEPBURN (city). Covers a land area of 0.060 square miles and a water area of 0 square miles. Located at 40.84° N. Lat.; 95.01° W. Long. Elevation is 1,016 feet.
History: Hepburn was named for Colonel William Peters Hepburn, who was a U.S. Representative from this district (1880-1886 and 1893-1909).
Population: 39 (2000); Race: 100.0% White, 0.0% Black, 0.0% Asian, 0.0% American Indian and Alaska Native, 0.0% Hispanic of any race, 0.0% two or more races (2000); Density: 654.1 persons per square mile (2000); Age: 0.0% under 18, 35.7% over 64 (2000); Marriage status: 17.9% never married, 60.7% now married, 10.7% widowed, 10.7% divorced (2000); Foreign born: 0.0% (2000); Ancestry (includes multiple ancestries): 14.3% Swedish, 10.7% German, 7.1% Italian, 3.6% English (2000).
Economy: Employment by occupation: 0.0% management, 0.0% professional, 18.2% services, 36.4% sales, 9.1% farming, 0.0% construction, 36.4% production (2000).
Income: Per capita income: $13,629 (2000); Median household income: $22,500 (2000); Poverty rate: 32.1% (2000).
Taxes: Total city taxes per capita: $24 (1997); City property taxes per capita: $24 (1997).
Education: High school graduation rate: 45.8% (2000); College graduation rate: 0.0% (2000).
Housing: Homeownership rate: 78.6% (2000); Median home value: $22,500 (2000); Median age of housing: 60+ years (2000).
Transportation: Commute to work: 100.0% car, 0.0% public transportation, 0.0% walk, 0.0% work from home (2000); Travel time to work: 63.6% less than 15 minutes, 36.4% 15 to 30 minutes, 0.0% 30 to 45 minutes, 0.0% 45 to 60 minutes, 0.0% 60 minutes or more (2000)

NORTHBORO (city). Covers a land area of 0.254 square miles and a water area of 0 square miles. Located at 40.60° N. Lat.; 95.29° W. Long.
History: Northboro was probably named for Northboro, Massachusetts, home to original landowners of the area.
Population: 60 (2000); Race: 100.0% White, 0.0% Black, 0.0% Asian, 0.0% American Indian and Alaska Native, 0.0% Hispanic of any race, 0.0% two or more races (2000); Density: 236.0 persons per square mile (2000); Age: 23.1% under 18, 20.0% over 64 (2000); Marriage status: 8.0% never married, 68.0% now married, 18.0% widowed, 6.0% divorced (2000); Foreign born: 3.1% (2000); Ancestry (includes multiple ancestries): 15.4% German, 12.3% Irish, 10.8% United States or American, 9.2% Swedish, 9.2% English (2000).
Economy: Employment by occupation: 22.6% management, 6.5% professional, 6.5% services, 9.7% sales, 0.0% farming, 3.2% construction, 51.6% production (2000).
Income: Per capita income: $15,360 (2000); Median household income: $35,536 (2000); Poverty rate: 1.5% (2000).
Taxes: Total city taxes per capita: $88 (1997); City property taxes per capita: $63 (1997).
Education: High school graduation rate: 86.4% (2000); College graduation rate: 9.1% (2000).
Housing: Homeownership rate: 88.5% (2000); Median home value: $25,600 (2000); Median rent: $175 per month (2000); Median age of housing: 60+ years (2000).
Transportation: Commute to work: 74.2% car, 6.5% public transportation, 16.1% walk, 3.2% work from home (2000); Travel time to work: 26.7% less than 15 minutes, 56.7% 15 to 30 minutes, 16.7% 30 to 45 minutes, 0.0% 45 to 60 minutes, 0.0% 60 minutes or more (2000)

SHAMBAUGH (city). Covers a land area of 0.371 square miles and a water area of 0 square miles. Located at 40.65° N. Lat.; 95.03° W. Long. Elevation is 973 feet.
History: Shambaugh was a Mennonite settlement platted by James Shambaugh in 1881.
Population: 188 (2000); Race: 96.3% White, 0.0% Black, 0.0% Asian, 3.7% American Indian and Alaska Native, 3.7% Hispanic of any race, 0.0% two or more races (2000); Density: 506.9 persons per square mile (2000); Age: 29.4% under 18, 19.8% over 64 (2000); Marriage status: 12.8% never married, 71.4% now married, 12.0% widowed, 3.8% divorced (2000); Foreign born: 3.7% (2000); Ancestry (includes multiple ancestries): 21.4% German, 17.6% United States or American, 12.3% Other groups, 11.8% English, 10.2% Irish (2000).
Economy: Employment by occupation: 4.2% management, 6.9% professional, 15.3% services, 18.1% sales, 0.0% farming, 8.3% construction, 47.2% production (2000).
Income: Per capita income: $15,089 (2000); Median household income: $40,375 (2000); Poverty rate: 4.3% (2000).
Taxes: Total city taxes per capita: $94 (1997); City property taxes per capita: $52 (1997).
Education: High school graduation rate: 92.2% (2000); College graduation rate: 14.8% (2000).
Housing: Homeownership rate: 97.4% (2000); Median home value: $40,300 (2000); Median rent: $275 per month (2000); Median age of housing: 41 years (2000).
Transportation: Commute to work: 97.2% car, 0.0% public transportation, 1.4% walk, 1.4% work from home (2000); Travel time to work: 59.2% less than 15 minutes, 18.3% 15 to 30 minutes, 12.7% 30 to 45 minutes, 4.2% 45 to 60 minutes, 5.6% 60 minutes or more (2000)

SHENANDOAH (city). Covers a land area of 3.467 square miles and a water area of 0 square miles. Located at 40.76° N. Lat.; 95.37° W. Long. Elevation is 974 feet.
History: Shenandoah was founded in 1870 when the railroad was completed through the county. Most of the first settlers were Mormons who came from a small settlement called Manti. Shenandoah received its name because of the similarity of the Nishnabotna River Valley, in which the town lies, to the Shenandoah Valley in Virginia.
Population: 5,546 (2000); Race: 98.8% White, 0.1% Black, 0.1% Asian, 0.0% American Indian and Alaska Native, 2.1% Hispanic of any race, 0.4% two or more races (2000); Density: 1,599.6 persons per square mile (2000); Age: 22.0% under 18, 24.9% over 64 (2000); Marriage status: 21.2% never married, 58.5% now married, 9.9% widowed, 10.4% divorced (2000); Foreign born: 1.0% (2000); Ancestry (includes multiple ancestries): 23.8% German, 17.4% Irish, 12.4% English, 9.1% United States or American, 7.0% Swedish (2000).
Economy: Single-family building permits issued: 2 (2001) / 5 (2000); Multi-family building permits issued: 0 (2001) / 2 (2000); Employment by occupation: 8.7% management, 15.9% professional, 17.2% services, 25.7% sales, 1.0% farming, 7.3% construction, 24.2% production (2000).
Income: Per capita income: $16,301 (2000); Median household income: $29,435 (2000); Poverty rate: 15.4% (2000).
Taxes: Total city taxes per capita: $428 (2000); City property taxes per capita: $337 (2000).
Education: High school graduation rate: 84.1% (2000); College graduation rate: 16.8% (2000).

School District(s)

Shenandoah Community School District (KG-12)
2000 Enrollment: 1,042 712-246-1581
Housing: Homeownership rate: 66.1% (2000); Median home value: $55,100 (2000); Median rent: $295 per month (2000); Median age of housing: 51 years (2000).
Hospitals: Shenandoah Memorial Hospital (44 beds)
Safety: Violent crime rate: 3.6 per 10,000 population; Property crime rate: 315.9 per 10,000 population (2001).
Newspapers: Valley News Today (5 x week); The Weekly Times (1 x week)
Transportation: Commute to work: 91.8% car, 0.2% public transportation, 4.8% walk, 2.9% work from home (2000); Travel time to work: 74.4% less than 15 minutes, 14.1% 15 to 30 minutes, 6.1% 30 to 45 minutes, 2.0% 45 to 60 minutes, 3.5% 60 minutes or more (2000)
Additional Information Contacts
Fremont Page Board of Realtors 712-246-1072
Shenandoah Chamber of Commerce 712-246-3260

YORKTOWN (city). Covers a land area of 0.276 square miles and a water area of 0 square miles. Located at 40.73° N. Lat.; 95.15° W. Long.
Population: 82 (2000); Race: 100.0% White, 0.0% Black, 0.0% Asian, 0.0% American Indian and Alaska Native, 0.0% Hispanic of any race, 0.0% two or more races (2000); Density: 297.2 persons per square mile (2000); Age: 24.5% under 18, 21.6% over 64 (2000); Marriage status: 16.9% never married, 66.2% now married, 14.3% widowed, 2.6% divorced (2000); Foreign born: 0.0% (2000); Ancestry (includes multiple ancestries): 42.2% German, 21.6% United States or American, 4.9% Irish, 3.9% English, 2.0% French (except Basque) (2000).
Economy: In agricultural region. Employment by occupation: 10.6% management, 12.8% professional, 23.4% services, 4.3% sales, 0.0% farming, 17.0% construction, 31.9% production (2000).

Income: Per capita income: $13,248 (2000); Median household income: $30,417 (2000); Poverty rate: 23.2% (2000).
Taxes: Total city taxes per capita: $109 (1997); City property taxes per capita: $69 (1997).
Education: High school graduation rate: 75.3% (2000); College graduation rate: 16.4% (2000).
Housing: Homeownership rate: 87.8% (2000); Median home value: $30,000 (2000); Median rent: $425 per month (2000); Median age of housing: 60+ years (2000).
Transportation: Commute to work: 89.4% car, 0.0% public transportation, 0.0% walk, 10.6% work from home (2000); Travel time to work: 66.7% less than 15 minutes, 33.3% 15 to 30 minutes, 0.0% 30 to 45 minutes, 0.0% 45 to 60 minutes, 0.0% 60 minutes or more (2000)

Palo Alto County

Located in northwestern Iowa; prairie area, drained by the West Des Moines River. Covers a land area of 563.80 square miles, a water area of 5.60 square miles, and is located in the Central Time Zone. The county government was organized in 1851. County seat is Emmetsburg.

Weather Station: Emmetsburg Elevation: 1,269 feet

	Jan	Feb	Mar	Apr	May	Jun	Jul	Aug	Sep	Oct	Nov	Dec
High	24	31	43	59	72	82	84	82	75	62	42	29
Low	6	13	24	36	49	58	62	60	51	38	25	12
Precip	0.8	0.6	2.1	3.2	3.7	4.6	4.1	4.2	2.8	2.3	1.9	0.9
Snow	8.0	5.4	6.4	2.2	tr	0.0	0.0	0.0	0.0	0.2	4.8	7.1

High and Low temperatures in degrees Fahrenheit; Precipitation and Snow in inches

Population: 10,147 (2000); Race: 99.1% White, 0.0% Black, 0.0% Asian, 0.1% American Indian and Alaska Native, 1.3% Hispanic of any race, 0.6% two or more races (2000); Density: 18.0 persons per square mile (2000); Age: 24.2% under 18, 21.4% over 64 (2000).
Religion: Five largest groups: 36.1% Catholic Church, 20.5% The United Methodist Church, 16.6% Evangelical Lutheran Church in America, 12.2% Lutheran Church—Missouri Synod, 5.0% Apostolic Christian Church of America, Inc. (2000).
Economy: Unemployment rate: 3.2% (11/2002); Total civilian labor force: 4,856 (11/2002); Leading industries: 23.1% retail trade; 21.3% health care and social assistance; 15.6% manufacturing (2000); Companies that employ more than 1,000 persons: 0 (2000); Companies that employ more than 100 persons: 2 (2000); Farms: 787 totaling 327,733 acres (1997); Minority business ownership rate: 0.0% (1997); Women business ownership rate: 22.0% (1997); Retail sales per capita: $7,480 (1997). Single-family building permits issued: 8 (2001) / 14 (2000); Multi-family building permits issued: 0 (2001) / 2 (2000).
Income: Per capita income: $17,733 (2000); Median household income: $32,409 (2000); Poverty rate: 10.6% (2000); Bankruptcy rate: 3.03% (2001).
Taxes: Total county taxes per capita: $345 (2000); County property taxes per capita: $334 (2000).
Education: High school graduation rate: 83.7% (2000); College graduation rate: 13.9% (2000).
Housing: Homeownership rate: 74.0% (2000); Median home value: $53,500 (2000); Median rent: $243 per month (2000); Median age of housing: 49 years (2000).
Health: Birth rate: 105.5 per 10,000 population (1998); Age adjusted death rate: 83.0 per 10,000 population (1999); Age adjusted cancer mortality rate: 286.6 deaths per 100,000 population (1999). Air Quality Index: 93% good, 7% moderate, 0% unhealthy (percent of days in 2000). Number of physicians: 4.9 per 10,000 population (1999); Number of hospital beds: 53.2 per 10,000 population (1999).
Elections: 2000 Presidential election results: 48.2% Gore, 48.5% Bush, 1.7% Nader, 0.8% Buchanan
National and State Parks: Blue Wing Marsh State Game Management Area; Fallow Marsh State Game Management Area; Five Island Lake State Game Management Area; Lost Island Lake State Park; Oppedahl State Game Management Area; Palo Alto State Wildlife Area Number One; Perkins Marsh State Game Management Area; Rush Lake State Wildlife Management Area; Virgin Lake State Game Management Area
Additional Information Contacts
Palo Alto County Government Offices 712-852-2924
Emmetsburg Chamber of Commerce.................... 712-852-2283
West Bend Chamber of Commerce 515-887-4721

Palo Alto County Communities

AYRSHIRE (city). Covers a land area of 0.208 square miles and a water area of 0 square miles. Located at 43.03° N. Lat.; 94.83° W. Long. Elevation is 1,293 feet.
History: Ayrshire was established in 1881.
Population: 202 (2000); Race: 92.5% White, 0.0% Black, 0.0% Asian, 0.0% American Indian and Alaska Native, 8.0% Hispanic of any race, 0.0% two or more races (2000); Density: 970.6 persons per square mile (2000); Age: 20.3% under 18, 15.0% over 64 (2000); Marriage status: 14.4% never married, 60.1% now married, 9.2% widowed, 16.3% divorced (2000); Foreign born: 0.0% (2000); Ancestry (includes multiple ancestries): 27.3% German, 13.9% Norwegian, 9.6% Swedish, 9.1% Other groups, 8.6% Irish (2000).
Economy: Single-family building permits issued: 0 (2001) / 0 (2000); Multi-family building permits issued: 0 (2001) / 0 (2000); Employment by occupation: 2.3% management, 8.0% professional, 29.9% services, 10.3% sales, 0.0% farming, 9.2% construction, 40.2% production (2000).
Income: Per capita income: $13,371 (2000); Median household income: $27,500 (2000); Poverty rate: 4.8% (2000).
Taxes: Total city taxes per capita: $94 (1997); City property taxes per capita: $88 (1997).
Education: High school graduation rate: 77.7% (2000); College graduation rate: 1.4% (2000).
Housing: Homeownership rate: 76.4% (2000); Median home value: $24,300 (2000); Median rent: $189 per month (2000); Median age of housing: 49 years (2000).
Transportation: Commute to work: 89.7% car, 0.0% public transportation, 4.6% walk, 5.7% work from home (2000); Travel time to work: 11.0% less than 15 minutes, 78.0% 15 to 30 minutes, 8.5% 30 to 45 minutes, 2.4% 45 to 60 minutes, 0.0% 60 minutes or more (2000)

CURLEW (city). Covers a land area of 0.758 square miles and a water area of 0 square miles. Located at 42.98° N. Lat.; 94.73° W. Long. Elevation is 1,222 feet.
History: Curlew was named by bird-watcher Charles E. Whitehead of the Des Moines & Fort Dodge Railroad, who noticed many curlews in the area.
Population: 62 (2000); Race: 100.0% White, 0.0% Black, 0.0% Asian, 0.0% American Indian and Alaska Native, 0.0% Hispanic of any race, 0.0% two or more races (2000); Density: 81.8 persons per square mile (2000); Age: 19.3% under 18, 38.6% over 64 (2000); Marriage status: 8.7% never married, 73.9% now married, 17.4% widowed, 0.0% divorced (2000); Foreign born: 0.0% (2000); Ancestry (includes multiple ancestries): 33.3% German, 14.0% Irish, 8.8% Scottish, 8.8% English, 8.8% Norwegian (2000).
Economy: Employment by occupation: 12.5% management, 8.3% professional, 16.7% services, 16.7% sales, 0.0% farming, 16.7% construction, 29.2% production (2000).
Income: Per capita income: $23,788 (2000); Median household income: $20,250 (2000); Poverty rate: 28.1% (2000).
Taxes: Total city taxes per capita: $57 (1997); City property taxes per capita: $57 (1997).
Education: High school graduation rate: 69.6% (2000); College graduation rate: 4.3% (2000).
Housing: Homeownership rate: 92.9% (2000); Median home value: $26,300 (2000); Median rent: <$100 per month (2000); Median age of housing: 60+ years (2000).
Transportation: Commute to work: 66.7% car, 0.0% public transportation, 9.5% walk, 23.8% work from home (2000); Travel time to work: 25.0% less than 15 minutes, 56.3% 15 to 30 minutes, 0.0% 30 to 45 minutes, 18.8% 45 to 60 minutes, 0.0% 60 minutes or more (2000)

CYLINDER (city). Covers a land area of 0.068 square miles and a water area of 0 square miles. Located at 43.08° N. Lat.; 94.55° W. Long. Elevation is 1,194 feet.
History: Cylinder takes its name from nearyby Cylinder Creek, which was so dubbed because when pioneers were trying to carry a heavy machine across the creek, a cylinder from it became detached and was lost in the water.
Population: 110 (2000); Race: 100.0% White, 0.0% Black, 0.0% Asian, 0.0% American Indian and Alaska Native, 0.0% Hispanic of any race, 0.0% two or more races (2000); Density: 1,625.1 persons per square mile (2000); Age: 28.3% under 18, 13.3% over 64 (2000); Marriage status: 9.5% never married, 79.8% now married, 8.3% widowed, 2.4% divorced (2000); Foreign born: 0.0% (2000); Ancestry (includes multiple ancestries): 44.2% German, 20.4% Norwegian, 10.6% Other groups, 9.7% Danish, 3.5% Irish (2000).

Economy: Single-family building permits issued: 0 (2001) / 0 (2000); Multi-family building permits issued: 0 (2001) / 0 (2000); Employment by occupation: 10.2% management, 16.3% professional, 18.4% services, 22.4% sales, 6.1% farming, 10.2% construction, 16.3% production (2000).
Income: Per capita income: $12,953 (2000); Median household income: $24,750 (2000); Poverty rate: 31.9% (2000).
Taxes: Total city taxes per capita: $133 (1997); City property taxes per capita: $133 (1997).
Education: High school graduation rate: 85.5% (2000); College graduation rate: 2.6% (2000).
Housing: Homeownership rate: 74.4% (2000); Median home value: $35,000 (2000); Median rent: $279 per month (2000); Median age of housing: 51 years (2000).
Transportation: Commute to work: 72.3% car, 0.0% public transportation, 27.7% walk, 0.0% work from home (2000); Travel time to work: 61.7% less than 15 minutes, 29.8% 15 to 30 minutes, 4.3% 30 to 45 minutes, 0.0% 45 to 60 minutes, 4.3% 60 minutes or more (2000)

EMMETSBURG (city). Covers a land area of 3.781 square miles and a water area of 0.164 square miles. Located at 43.11° N. Lat.; 94.68° W. Long. Elevation is 1,234 feet.
History: Emmetsburg was founded in 1856 by an Irish colony of seven families and two unmarried men.
Population: 3,958 (2000); Race: 99.1% White, 0.0% Black, 0.0% Asian, 0.2% American Indian and Alaska Native, 2.6% Hispanic of any race, 0.7% two or more races (2000); Density: 1,046.9 persons per square mile (2000); Age: 21.4% under 18, 22.6% over 64 (2000); Marriage status: 28.4% never married, 51.4% now married, 13.9% widowed, 6.2% divorced (2000); Foreign born: 1.0% (2000); Ancestry (includes multiple ancestries): 38.7% German, 16.2% Irish, 15.2% Norwegian, 7.7% English, 6.1% United States or American (2000).
Economy: Single-family building permits issued: 4 (2001) / 6 (2000); Multi-family building permits issued: 0 (2001) / 2 (2000); Employment by occupation: 13.3% management, 17.3% professional, 19.5% services, 19.9% sales, 1.9% farming, 11.8% construction, 16.3% production (2000).
Income: Per capita income: $17,599 (2000); Median household income: $31,520 (2000); Poverty rate: 13.1% (2000).
Taxes: Total city taxes per capita: $196 (1997); City property taxes per capita: $189 (1997).
Education: High school graduation rate: 81.0% (2000); College graduation rate: 15.9% (2000).

School District(s)

Emmetsburg Community School District (PK-12)
2000 Enrollment: 830 712-852-3201
Housing: Homeownership rate: 68.3% (2000); Median home value: $61,700 (2000); Median rent: $263 per month (2000); Median age of housing: 45 years (2000).
Hospitals: Palo Alto County Hospital (54 beds)
Newspapers: The Reporter (1 x week); The Democrat (1 x week); Palo Alto Reminder (1 x week)
Transportation: Commute to work: 89.3% car, 1.4% public transportation, 5.1% walk, 3.8% work from home (2000); Travel time to work: 80.6% less than 15 minutes, 7.4% 15 to 30 minutes, 8.8% 30 to 45 minutes, 1.7% 45 to 60 minutes, 1.5% 60 minutes or more (2000)
Additional Information Contacts
Emmetsburg Chamber of Commerce...................... 712-852-2283

GRAETTINGER (city). Covers a land area of 0.766 square miles and a water area of 0 square miles. Located at 43.23° N. Lat.; 94.75° W. Long. Elevation is 1,250 feet.
History: Graettinger was built on land owned by Dr. Graettinger.
Population: 900 (2000); Race: 99.0% White, 0.0% Black, 0.0% Asian, 0.7% American Indian and Alaska Native, 0.2% Hispanic of any race, 0.3% two or more races (2000); Density: 1,174.8 persons per square mile (2000); Age: 26.7% under 18, 18.2% over 64 (2000); Marriage status: 22.9% never married, 59.1% now married, 10.0% widowed, 7.9% divorced (2000); Foreign born: 0.4% (2000); Ancestry (includes multiple ancestries): 38.8% German, 18.1% Norwegian, 12.9% Irish, 9.3% English, 7.6% Danish (2000).
Economy: Single-family building permits issued: 3 (2001) / 5 (2000); Multi-family building permits issued: 0 (2001) / 0 (2000); Employment by occupation: 9.0% management, 19.4% professional, 17.8% services, 21.1% sales, 2.4% farming, 12.3% construction, 18.0% production (2000).
Income: Per capita income: $15,520 (2000); Median household income: $28,988 (2000); Poverty rate: 9.4% (2000).
Taxes: Total city taxes per capita: $243 (1997); City property taxes per capita: $239 (1997).
Education: High school graduation rate: 82.7% (2000); College graduation rate: 13.3% (2000).

School District(s)

Graettinger Community School District (KG-12)
2000 Enrollment: 296 712-859-3286
Housing: Homeownership rate: 78.2% (2000); Median home value: $42,600 (2000); Median rent: $218 per month (2000); Median age of housing: 49 years (2000).
Newspapers: Graettinger Times (1 x week)
Transportation: Commute to work: 86.9% car, 0.0% public transportation, 11.7% walk, 1.4% work from home (2000); Travel time to work: 42.1% less than 15 minutes, 37.8% 15 to 30 minutes, 11.6% 30 to 45 minutes, 3.9% 45 to 60 minutes, 4.6% 60 minutes or more (2000)

MALLARD (city). Covers a land area of 0.380 square miles and a water area of 0 square miles. Located at 42.93° N. Lat.; 94.68° W. Long. Elevation is 1,198 feet.
History: Mallard got its name for the plentiful hunting in the area. The name was given by Charles E. Whitehead, president of the Des Moines & Fort Dodge Railroad.
Population: 298 (2000); Race: 100.0% White, 0.0% Black, 0.0% Asian, 0.0% American Indian and Alaska Native, 0.0% Hispanic of any race, 0.0% two or more races (2000); Density: 783.6 persons per square mile (2000); Age: 25.7% under 18, 28.0% over 64 (2000); Marriage status: 20.9% never married, 59.0% now married, 13.1% widowed, 7.0% divorced (2000); Foreign born: 0.0% (2000); Ancestry (includes multiple ancestries): 45.6% German, 11.7% United States or American, 9.4% Irish, 7.8% English, 5.5% Danish (2000).
Economy: Employment by occupation: 10.1% management, 8.5% professional, 21.7% services, 12.4% sales, 0.0% farming, 7.8% construction, 39.5% production (2000).
Income: Per capita income: $16,451 (2000); Median household income: $28,056 (2000); Poverty rate: 12.1% (2000).
Taxes: Total city taxes per capita: $209 (1997); City property taxes per capita: $209 (1997).
Education: High school graduation rate: 82.2% (2000); College graduation rate: 5.1% (2000).

School District(s)

West Bend-Mallard Community School District (PK-12)
2000 Enrollment: 452 712-425-3451
Housing: Homeownership rate: 84.6% (2000); Median home value: $30,200 (2000); Median rent: $258 per month (2000); Median age of housing: 49 years (2000).
Transportation: Commute to work: 89.1% car, 0.0% public transportation, 8.5% walk, 0.0% work from home (2000); Travel time to work: 37.2% less than 15 minutes, 45.0% 15 to 30 minutes, 11.6% 30 to 45 minutes, 3.1% 45 to 60 minutes, 3.1% 60 minutes or more (2000)

RODMAN (city). Covers a land area of 0.166 square miles and a water area of 0 square miles. Located at 43.02° N. Lat.; 94.52° W. Long. Elevation is 1,193 feet.
History: Rodman was named for a landowner who donated the land for the town site.
Population: 56 (2000); Race: 100.0% White, 0.0% Black, 0.0% Asian, 0.0% American Indian and Alaska Native, 0.0% Hispanic of any race, 0.0% two or more races (2000); Density: 336.7 persons per square mile (2000); Age: 25.5% under 18, 10.6% over 64 (2000); Marriage status: 25.6% never married, 38.5% now married, 20.5% widowed, 15.4% divorced (2000); Foreign born: 0.0% (2000); Ancestry (includes multiple ancestries): 72.3% German, 27.7% English, 23.4% Irish, 4.3% Other groups, 4.3% Polish (2000).
Economy: Employment by occupation: 0.0% management, 10.7% professional, 25.0% services, 7.1% sales, 0.0% farming, 0.0% construction, 57.1% production (2000).
Income: Per capita income: $15,347 (2000); Median household income: $29,063 (2000); Poverty rate: 0.0% (2000).
Taxes: Total city taxes per capita: $170 (1997); City property taxes per capita: $170 (1997).
Education: High school graduation rate: 75.8% (2000); College graduation rate: 6.1% (2000).
Housing: Homeownership rate: 91.7% (2000); Median home value: $10,600 (2000); Median rent: $125 per month (2000); Median age of housing: 60+ years (2000).
Transportation: Commute to work: 78.6% car, 0.0% public transportation, 0.0% walk, 21.4% work from home (2000); Travel time to work: 9.1% less

than 15 minutes, 81.8% 15 to 30 minutes, 0.0% 30 to 45 minutes, 9.1% 45 to 60 minutes, 0.0% 60 minutes or more (2000)

RUTHVEN (city). Covers a land area of 0.421 square miles and a water area of 0 square miles. Located at 43.13° N. Lat.; 94.90° W. Long. Elevation is 1,413 feet.

History: Ruthven was named for three Ruthven brothers who were settlers. One of them, Alex Ruthven, was several times elected mayor of the village.

Population: 711 (2000); Race: 98.3% White, 0.0% Black, 0.0% Asian, 0.0% American Indian and Alaska Native, 0.7% Hispanic of any race, 1.7% two or more races (2000); Density: 1,688.3 persons per square mile (2000); Age: 18.5% under 18, 26.2% over 64 (2000); Marriage status: 23.5% never married, 51.5% now married, 16.4% widowed, 8.5% divorced (2000); Foreign born: 0.6% (2000); Ancestry (includes multiple ancestries): 32.0% German, 14.7% Irish, 11.4% English, 10.0% Norwegian, 7.8% Danish (2000).

Economy: Single-family building permits issued: 0 (2001) / 0 (2000); Multi-family building permits issued: 0 (2001) / 0 (2000); Employment by occupation: 6.5% management, 15.9% professional, 19.7% services, 26.2% sales, 0.0% farming, 9.4% construction, 22.3% production (2000).

Income: Per capita income: $17,079 (2000); Median household income: $31,027 (2000); Poverty rate: 9.0% (2000).

Taxes: Total city taxes per capita: $239 (1997); City property taxes per capita: $237 (1997).

Education: High school graduation rate: 85.6% (2000); College graduation rate: 12.6% (2000).

School District(s)

Ruthven-Ayrshire Community School District (KG-12)
2000 Enrollment: 282 712-837-5211

Housing: Homeownership rate: 79.6% (2000); Median home value: $42,700 (2000); Median rent: $190 per month (2000); Median age of housing: 51 years (2000).

Newspapers: Ruthven Zipcode (1 x week)

Transportation: Commute to work: 93.9% car, 0.0% public transportation, 4.9% walk, 1.3% work from home (2000); Travel time to work: 30.8% less than 15 minutes, 48.9% 15 to 30 minutes, 10.5% 30 to 45 minutes, 4.9% 45 to 60 minutes, 4.9% 60 minutes or more (2000)

WEST BEND (city). Covers a land area of 0.884 square miles and a water area of 0 square miles. Located at 42.95° N. Lat.; 94.44° W. Long. Elevation is 1,197 feet.

History: West Bend was so named because of its proximity to a large bend in the West Fork of the Des Moines River. Although the town was not established until 1880, the first settlers, William Carter and Jeremiah Evans, came to this region 25 years earlier. West Bend is the site of the Grotto of the Redemption, an imposing religious structure whose construction was begun by Father Paul M. Dobberstein in 1928.

Population: 834 (2000); Race: 98.2% White, 0.0% Black, 0.4% Asian, 0.0% American Indian and Alaska Native, 1.0% Hispanic of any race, 0.7% two or more races (2000); Density: 943.3 persons per square mile (2000); Age: 22.9% under 18, 32.4% over 64 (2000); Marriage status: 16.3% never married, 62.4% now married, 17.0% widowed, 4.3% divorced (2000); Foreign born: 1.3% (2000); Ancestry (includes multiple ancestries): 50.7% German, 9.2% Irish, 8.5% Swiss, 5.1% English, 4.5% Norwegian (2000).

Economy: Single-family building permits issued: 1 (2001) / 3 (2000); Multi-family building permits issued: 0 (2001) / 0 (2000); Employment by occupation: 12.0% management, 15.5% professional, 18.4% services, 21.6% sales, 2.6% farming, 11.1% construction, 19.0% production (2000).

Income: Per capita income: $18,804 (2000); Median household income: $31,711 (2000); Poverty rate: 6.9% (2000).

Taxes: Total city taxes per capita: $199 (1997); City property taxes per capita: $195 (1997).

Education: High school graduation rate: 73.9% (2000); College graduation rate: 11.1% (2000).

Housing: Homeownership rate: 89.8% (2000); Median home value: $49,300 (2000); Median rent: $200 per month (2000); Median age of housing: 46 years (2000).

Newspapers: West Bend Journal (1 x week)

Transportation: Commute to work: 89.4% car, 0.0% public transportation, 4.7% walk, 5.0% work from home (2000); Travel time to work: 64.2% less than 15 minutes, 15.1% 15 to 30 minutes, 12.7% 30 to 45 minutes, 3.1% 45 to 60 minutes, 4.9% 60 minutes or more (2000)

Additional Information Contacts

West Bend Chamber of Commerce 515-887-4721

Plymouth County

Located in northwestern Iowa; bounded on the west by the Big Sioux River and the South Dakota border; drained by the Floyd River and West Fork of the Little Sioux River. Covers a land area of 863.60 square miles, a water area of 0.40 square miles, and is located in the Central Time Zone. The county government was organized in 1851. County seat is Le Mars.

Weather Station: Le Mars — Elevation: 1,194 feet

	Jan	Feb	Mar	Apr	May	Jun	Jul	Aug	Sep	Oct	Nov	Dec
High	27	34	46	62	74	83	87	84	77	64	44	31
Low	7	14	24	36	49	59	63	61	51	38	25	13
Precip	0.6	0.5	2.0	2.7	3.4	3.9	3.3	3.3	2.7	2.0	1.4	0.7
Snow	6.9	4.5	6.1	1.5	0.0	0.0	0.0	tr	0.0	0.7	3.8	6.1

High and Low temperatures in degrees Fahrenheit; Precipitation and Snow in inches

Population: 24,849 (2000); Race: 98.5% White, 0.3% Black, 0.3% Asian, 0.1% American Indian and Alaska Native, 1.1% Hispanic of any race, 0.5% two or more races (2000); Density: 28.8 persons per square mile (2000); Age: 28.3% under 18, 15.9% over 64 (2000).

Religion: Five largest groups: 35.4% Catholic Church, 13.8% Evangelical Lutheran Church in America, 8.4% The United Methodist Church, 8.1% Lutheran Church—Missouri Synod, 2.1% Presbyterian Church (U.S.A.) (2000).

Economy: Unemployment rate: 3.4% (11/2002); Total civilian labor force: 12,832 (11/2002); Leading industries: 18.1% manufacturing; 15.6% wholesale trade; 12.2% retail trade (2000); Companies that employ more than 1,000 persons: 0 (2000); Companies that employ more than 100 persons: 14 (2000); Farms: 1,490 totaling 512,029 acres (1997); Minority business ownership rate: 0.0% (1997); Women business ownership rate: 15.0% (1997); Retail sales per capita: $7,895 (1997). Single-family building permits issued: 91 (2001) / 91 (2000); Multi-family building permits issued: 10 (2001) / 10 (2000).

Income: Per capita income: $19,442 (2000); Median household income: $41,638 (2000); Poverty rate: 6.0% (2000); Bankruptcy rate: 3.13% (2001).

Taxes: Total county taxes per capita: $193 (2000); County property taxes per capita: $183 (2000).

Education: High school graduation rate: 87.4% (2000); College graduation rate: 19.3% (2000).

Housing: Homeownership rate: 77.4% (2000); Median home value: $88,200 (2000); Median rent: $326 per month (2000); Median age of housing: 43 years (2000).

Health: Birth rate: 123.1 per 10,000 population (1998); Age adjusted death rate: 74.1 per 10,000 population (1999); Age adjusted cancer mortality rate: 187.9 deaths per 100,000 population (1999). Number of physicians: 5.6 per 10,000 population (1999); Number of hospital beds: 17.7 per 10,000 population (1999).

Elections: 2000 Presidential election results: 34.6% Gore, 61.2% Bush, 2.0% Nader, 1.4% Buchanan

National and State Parks: Five Ridge Prairie State Preserve

Additional Information Contacts

Plymouth County Government Offices 712-546-6100
Le Mars Chamber of Commerce 712-546-8821

Plymouth County Communities

AKRON (city). Covers a land area of 1.208 square miles and a water area of 0 square miles. Located at 42.82° N. Lat.; 96.55° W. Long. Elevation is 1,147 feet.

History: Akron was platted in 1871 by W. Sargeant, father of F. R. Sargeant who became president of the Chicago & North Western Railroad. The town's name was first Portlandville, but was changed in the belief that it was going to grow to the size of Akron, Ohio.

Population: 1,489 (2000); Race: 99.4% White, 0.0% Black, 0.0% Asian, 0.0% American Indian and Alaska Native, 0.5% Hispanic of any race, 0.6% two or more races (2000); Density: 1,232.4 persons per square mile (2000); Age: 23.7% under 18, 27.3% over 64 (2000); Marriage status: 18.4% never married, 61.6% now married, 12.1% widowed, 7.9% divorced (2000); Foreign born: 1.2% (2000); Ancestry (includes multiple ancestries): 43.2% German, 14.8% Irish, 10.5% English, 8.8% Norwegian, 6.7% United States or American (2000).

Economy: Single-family building permits issued: 7 (2001) / 6 (2000); Multi-family building permits issued: 0 (2001) / 0 (2000); Employment by occupation: 9.8% management, 13.5% professional, 17.1% services, 22.4% sales, 1.9% farming, 14.2% construction, 21.1% production (2000).

Income: Per capita income: $18,631 (2000); Median household income: $29,583 (2000); Poverty rate: 7.2% (2000).
Taxes: Total city taxes per capita: $190 (2000); City property taxes per capita: $187 (2000).
Education: High school graduation rate: 81.9% (2000); College graduation rate: 13.3% (2000).

School District(s)

Akron Westfield Community School District (KG-12)
2000 Enrollment: 689 712-568-2616
Greater Hoyt 61-4 (KG-12)
2000 Enrollment: 0 712-568-2616

Housing: Homeownership rate: 72.1% (2000); Median home value: $71,300 (2000); Median rent: $317 per month (2000); Median age of housing: 45 years (2000).
Newspapers: Akron Register-Tribune (1 x week)
Transportation: Commute to work: 90.2% car, 0.0% public transportation, 6.4% walk, 2.8% work from home (2000); Travel time to work: 43.7% less than 15 minutes, 20.5% 15 to 30 minutes, 23.9% 30 to 45 minutes, 8.4% 45 to 60 minutes, 3.5% 60 minutes or more (2000)

BRUNSVILLE (city). Covers a land area of 0.237 square miles and a water area of 0 square miles. Located at 42.80° N. Lat.; 96.26° W. Long. Elevation is 1,264 feet.
History: Brunsville was laid out in 1910 as a railroad station on the Chicago & North Western Railroad.
Population: 146 (2000); Race: 100.0% White, 0.0% Black, 0.0% Asian, 0.0% American Indian and Alaska Native, 0.0% Hispanic of any race, 0.0% two or more races (2000); Density: 616.4 persons per square mile (2000); Age: 17.9% under 18, 25.5% over 64 (2000); Marriage status: 9.0% never married, 76.2% now married, 11.5% widowed, 3.3% divorced (2000); Foreign born: 0.0% (2000); Ancestry (includes multiple ancestries): 64.8% German, 9.0% Dutch, 6.9% Irish, 5.5% United States or American, 5.5% English (2000).
Economy: Employment by occupation: 9.8% management, 11.0% professional, 12.2% services, 30.5% sales, 7.3% farming, 0.0% construction, 29.3% production (2000).
Income: Per capita income: $23,200 (2000); Median household income: $47,188 (2000); Poverty rate: 0.0% (2000).
Taxes: Total city taxes per capita: $90 (1997); City property taxes per capita: $83 (1997).
Education: High school graduation rate: 81.1% (2000); College graduation rate: 13.5% (2000).
Housing: Homeownership rate: 80.7% (2000); Median home value: $77,300 (2000); Median rent: $432 per month (2000); Median age of housing: 38 years (2000).
Transportation: Commute to work: 93.9% car, 0.0% public transportation, 3.7% walk, 2.4% work from home (2000); Travel time to work: 40.0% less than 15 minutes, 41.3% 15 to 30 minutes, 13.8% 30 to 45 minutes, 2.5% 45 to 60 minutes, 2.5% 60 minutes or more (2000)

CRAIG (city). Covers a land area of 0.094 square miles and a water area of 0 square miles. Located at 42.89° N. Lat.; 96.31° W. Long. Elevation is 1,419 feet.
History: The town of Craig was named for Wright L. Craig, an attorney for the Chicago & North Western Railroad.
Population: 102 (2000); Race: 100.0% White, 0.0% Black, 0.0% Asian, 0.0% American Indian and Alaska Native, 0.0% Hispanic of any race, 0.0% two or more races (2000); Density: 1,086.8 persons per square mile (2000); Age: 16.8% under 18, 16.8% over 64 (2000); Marriage status: 27.6% never married, 65.5% now married, 4.6% widowed, 2.3% divorced (2000); Foreign born: 0.0% (2000); Ancestry (includes multiple ancestries): 65.3% German, 10.9% Swedish, 7.9% French (except Basque), 6.9% Norwegian, 6.9% Irish (2000).
Economy: Employment by occupation: 13.8% management, 6.2% professional, 13.8% services, 23.1% sales, 1.5% farming, 12.3% construction, 29.2% production (2000).
Income: Per capita income: $17,239 (2000); Median household income: $32,917 (2000); Poverty rate: 0.0% (2000).
Taxes: Total city taxes per capita: $98 (1997); City property taxes per capita: $89 (1997).
Education: High school graduation rate: 83.1% (2000); College graduation rate: 5.2% (2000).
Housing: Homeownership rate: 80.5% (2000); Median home value: $45,000 (2000); Median rent: $175 per month (2000); Median age of housing: 60+ years (2000).
Transportation: Commute to work: 80.0% car, 0.0% public transportation, 13.8% walk, 0.0% work from home (2000); Travel time to work: 33.8% less than 15 minutes, 33.8% 15 to 30 minutes, 21.5% 30 to 45 minutes, 4.6% 45 to 60 minutes, 6.2% 60 minutes or more (2000)

HINTON (city). Covers a land area of 0.583 square miles and a water area of 0 square miles. Located at 42.62° N. Lat.; 96.29° W. Long. Elevation is 1,144 feet.
History: An early settler from West Virginia, named Hinton, named this community for himself.
Population: 808 (2000); Race: 97.5% White, 1.4% Black, 0.0% Asian, 0.0% American Indian and Alaska Native, 1.0% Hispanic of any race, 0.6% two or more races (2000); Density: 1,386.1 persons per square mile (2000); Age: 25.5% under 18, 14.7% over 64 (2000); Marriage status: 21.9% never married, 64.0% now married, 6.5% widowed, 7.6% divorced (2000); Foreign born: 0.9% (2000); Ancestry (includes multiple ancestries): 53.6% German, 12.7% Irish, 9.5% English, 7.2% French (except Basque), 6.7% Swedish (2000).
Economy: Single-family building permits issued: 2 (2001) / 9 (2000); Multi-family building permits issued: 0 (2001) / 0 (2000); Employment by occupation: 14.6% management, 18.9% professional, 13.1% services, 33.1% sales, 0.5% farming, 11.0% construction, 8.8% production (2000).
Income: Per capita income: $20,358 (2000); Median household income: $49,375 (2000); Poverty rate: 4.4% (2000).
Taxes: Total city taxes per capita: $224 (1997); City property taxes per capita: $223 (1997).
Education: High school graduation rate: 90.6% (2000); College graduation rate: 21.5% (2000).

School District(s)

Hinton Community School District (KG-12)
2000 Enrollment: 627 712-947-4329

Housing: Homeownership rate: 83.1% (2000); Median home value: $106,600 (2000); Median rent: $334 per month (2000); Median age of housing: 29 years (2000).
Transportation: Commute to work: 93.4% car, 0.0% public transportation, 2.9% walk, 3.6% work from home (2000); Travel time to work: 21.4% less than 15 minutes, 55.8% 15 to 30 minutes, 16.2% 30 to 45 minutes, 1.6% 45 to 60 minutes, 4.9% 60 minutes or more (2000)

KINGSLEY (city). Covers a land area of 1.602 square miles and a water area of 0 square miles. Located at 42.58° N. Lat.; 95.96° W. Long. Elevation is 1,237 feet.
History: Kingsley was named after an early landowner, Henry W. Kingsley. Mr. Kingsley sold his land to the Blair Town Lot and Land Company, which platted the town.
Population: 1,245 (2000); Race: 96.8% White, 0.9% Black, 0.6% Asian, 0.3% American Indian and Alaska Native, 1.3% Hispanic of any race, 1.4% two or more races (2000); Density: 777.3 persons per square mile (2000); Age: 25.6% under 18, 27.0% over 64 (2000); Marriage status: 18.1% never married, 64.1% now married, 11.5% widowed, 6.3% divorced (2000); Foreign born: 1.0% (2000); Ancestry (includes multiple ancestries): 47.2% German, 10.5% English, 9.7% Irish, 6.0% Norwegian, 5.5% Swedish (2000).
Economy: Single-family building permits issued: 3 (2001) / 7 (2000); Multi-family building permits issued: 0 (2001) / 0 (2000); Employment by occupation: 11.0% management, 22.5% professional, 13.6% services, 18.5% sales, 4.9% farming, 12.8% construction, 16.7% production (2000).
Income: Per capita income: $19,052 (2000); Median household income: $34,697 (2000); Poverty rate: 6.9% (2000).
Taxes: Total city taxes per capita: $181 (1997); City property taxes per capita: $174 (1997).
Education: High school graduation rate: 87.2% (2000); College graduation rate: 16.1% (2000).

School District(s)

Kingsley-Pierson Community School District (KG-12)
2000 Enrollment: 513 712-378-2861

Housing: Homeownership rate: 80.9% (2000); Median home value: $79,400 (2000); Median rent: $288 per month (2000); Median age of housing: 52 years (2000).
Newspapers: Kingsley News Times (1 x week)
Transportation: Commute to work: 90.8% car, 0.0% public transportation, 5.5% walk, 3.3% work from home (2000); Travel time to work: 45.6% less than 15 minutes, 10.9% 15 to 30 minutes, 30.2% 30 to 45 minutes, 8.2% 45 to 60 minutes, 5.2% 60 minutes or more (2000)

LE MARS (city). Covers a land area of 6.807 square miles and a water area of 0.009 square miles. Located at 42.78° N. Lat.; 96.16° W. Long. Elevation is 1,231 feet.
History: Le Mars was named for the first initials of six young women who visited the settlement in the early days—Lucy Underhill, Elizabeth Parsons, Mary Weare, Anna Blair, Rebecca Smith, and Sarah Reynolds.
Population: 9,237 (2000); Race: 98.2% White, 0.3% Black, 0.2% Asian, 0.1% American Indian and Alaska Native, 1.9% Hispanic of any race, 0.4% two or more races (2000); Density: 1,356.9 persons per square mile (2000); Age: 27.2% under 18, 16.4% over 64 (2000); Marriage status: 23.3% never married, 60.0% now married, 8.5% widowed, 8.2% divorced (2000); Foreign born: 1.6% (2000); Ancestry (includes multiple ancestries): 49.2% German, 12.7% Irish, 7.5% Dutch, 6.8% United States or American, 6.4% English (2000).
Economy: Single-family building permits issued: 33 (2001) / 21 (2000); Multi-family building permits issued: 10 (2001) / 10 (2000); Employment by occupation: 12.4% management, 15.7% professional, 16.1% services, 28.2% sales, 0.5% farming, 8.6% construction, 18.5% production (2000).
Income: Per capita income: $19,598 (2000); Median household income: $38,892 (2000); Poverty rate: 6.2% (2000).
Taxes: Total city taxes per capita: $353 (2000); City property taxes per capita: $340 (2000).
Education: High school graduation rate: 85.7% (2000); College graduation rate: 21.3% (2000).

School District(s)

Le Mars Community School District (PK-12)
2000 Enrollment: 2,232 712-546-4155

Two-year College(s)

Le Mars Beauty College (Private, For-profit)
2001 Enrollment: n/a 712-546-4195

Housing: Homeownership rate: 71.7% (2000); Median home value: $92,600 (2000); Median rent: $326 per month (2000); Median age of housing: 39 years (2000).
Hospitals: Floyd Valley Hospital (44 beds)
Safety: Violent crime rate: 15.2 per 10,000 population; Property crime rate: 295.9 per 10,000 population (2001).
Newspapers: Le Mars Daily Sentinel (5 x week)
Transportation: Commute to work: 92.9% car, 0.1% public transportation, 2.5% walk, 3.5% work from home (2000); Travel time to work: 68.8% less than 15 minutes, 9.5% 15 to 30 minutes, 14.0% 30 to 45 minutes, 5.4% 45 to 60 minutes, 2.3% 60 minutes or more (2000)
Airports: Le Mars Municipal
Additional Information Contacts
Le Mars Chamber of Commerce 712-546-8821

MERRILL (city). Covers a land area of 0.433 square miles and a water area of 0 square miles. Located at 42.72° N. Lat.; 96.25° W. Long. Elevation is 1,174 feet.
History: Merrill was platted in 1872 by the Sioux City & Iowa Falls Railroad, which was built through the region in 1869. Before the days of the grain elevators, the local grocer, William Frost, often received washtubs full of wheat in payment for his commodities.
Population: 754 (2000); Race: 98.4% White, 0.8% Black, 0.1% Asian, 0.0% American Indian and Alaska Native, 1.6% Hispanic of any race, 0.5% two or more races (2000); Density: 1,739.5 persons per square mile (2000); Age: 31.5% under 18, 18.5% over 64 (2000); Marriage status: 20.2% never married, 65.8% now married, 4.7% widowed, 9.3% divorced (2000); Foreign born: 0.4% (2000); Ancestry (includes multiple ancestries): 43.8% German, 11.5% Irish, 7.2% Dutch, 6.3% United States or American, 6.1% English (2000).
Economy: Single-family building permits issued: 2 (2001) / 2 (2000); Multi-family building permits issued: 0 (2001) / 0 (2000); Employment by occupation: 10.7% management, 17.3% professional, 13.4% services, 23.9% sales, 0.3% farming, 12.2% construction, 22.1% production (2000).
Income: Per capita income: $15,656 (2000); Median household income: $43,333 (2000); Poverty rate: 4.1% (2000).
Taxes: Total city taxes per capita: $194 (2000); City property taxes per capita: $131 (2000).
Education: High school graduation rate: 86.3% (2000); College graduation rate: 15.2% (2000).
Housing: Homeownership rate: 88.9% (2000); Median home value: $75,800 (2000); Median rent: $322 per month (2000); Median age of housing: 49 years (2000).
Transportation: Commute to work: 95.2% car, 0.0% public transportation, 1.5% walk, 2.7% work from home (2000); Travel time to work: 44.7% less than 15 minutes, 30.1% 15 to 30 minutes, 21.4% 30 to 45 minutes, 2.5% 45 to 60 minutes, 1.2% 60 minutes or more (2000)

OYENS (city). Covers a land area of 0.094 square miles and a water area of 0 square miles. Located at 42.81° N. Lat.; 96.05° W. Long.
Population: 132 (2000); Race: 100.0% White, 0.0% Black, 0.0% Asian, 0.0% American Indian and Alaska Native, 0.0% Hispanic of any race, 0.0% two or more races (2000); Density: 1,405.9 persons per square mile (2000); Age: 30.7% under 18, 6.5% over 64 (2000); Marriage status: 24.1% never married, 63.0% now married, 1.9% widowed, 11.1% divorced (2000); Foreign born: 0.0% (2000); Ancestry (includes multiple ancestries): 59.5% German, 13.1% Irish, 12.4% Danish, 9.8% Dutch, 5.2% French (except Basque) (2000).
Economy: In livestock area. Employment by occupation: 11.7% management, 8.5% professional, 12.8% services, 13.8% sales, 0.0% farming, 11.7% construction, 41.5% production (2000).
Income: Per capita income: $17,969 (2000); Median household income: $53,333 (2000); Poverty rate: 2.0% (2000).
Taxes: Total city taxes per capita: $163 (1997); City property taxes per capita: $163 (1997).
Education: High school graduation rate: 92.1% (2000); College graduation rate: 10.1% (2000).
Housing: Homeownership rate: 96.1% (2000); Median home value: $61,500 (2000); Median rent: $400 per month (2000); Median age of housing: 43 years (2000).
Transportation: Commute to work: 96.8% car, 0.0% public transportation, 3.2% walk, 0.0% work from home (2000); Travel time to work: 48.4% less than 15 minutes, 29.0% 15 to 30 minutes, 7.5% 30 to 45 minutes, 11.8% 45 to 60 minutes, 3.2% 60 minutes or more (2000)

REMSEN (city). Covers a land area of 1.065 square miles and a water area of 0 square miles. Located at 42.81° N. Lat.; 95.97° W. Long. Elevation is 1,324 feet.
History: Remsen was named for Remsen Smith, a Sioux City landowner. On July 4, 1936 a major fire started by fireworks caused $400,000 worth of damage.
Population: 1,762 (2000); Race: 100.0% White, 0.0% Black, 0.0% Asian, 0.0% American Indian and Alaska Native, 0.0% Hispanic of any race, 0.0% two or more races (2000); Density: 1,655.2 persons per square mile (2000); Age: 27.8% under 18, 25.6% over 64 (2000); Marriage status: 19.1% never married, 62.5% now married, 13.9% widowed, 4.5% divorced (2000); Foreign born: 0.7% (2000); Ancestry (includes multiple ancestries): 54.2% German, 16.3% Luxemburger, 9.5% Irish, 6.3% United States or American, 4.4% Dutch (2000).
Economy: Single-family building permits issued: 3 (2001) / 2 (2000); Multi-family building permits issued: 0 (2001) / 0 (2000); Employment by occupation: 9.4% management, 14.4% professional, 15.6% services, 22.3% sales, 2.1% farming, 11.9% construction, 24.3% production (2000).
Income: Per capita income: $17,465 (2000); Median household income: $37,950 (2000); Poverty rate: 5.7% (2000).
Taxes: Total city taxes per capita: $186 (1997); City property taxes per capita: $181 (1997).
Education: High school graduation rate: 81.5% (2000); College graduation rate: 14.5% (2000).

School District(s)

Remsen-Union Community School District (PK-12)
2000 Enrollment: 427 712-786-1101

Housing: Homeownership rate: 82.8% (2000); Median home value: $80,200 (2000); Median rent: $336 per month (2000); Median age of housing: 44 years (2000).
Newspapers: Remsen Bell-Enterprise (1 x week)
Transportation: Commute to work: 90.2% car, 0.4% public transportation, 6.1% walk, 2.7% work from home (2000); Travel time to work: 52.1% less than 15 minutes, 32.9% 15 to 30 minutes, 7.2% 30 to 45 minutes, 5.9% 45 to 60 minutes, 2.0% 60 minutes or more (2000)

STRUBLE (city). Covers a land area of 0.156 square miles and a water area of 0 square miles. Located at 42.89° N. Lat.; 96.19° W. Long.
History: Struble was named for an Iowa congressman, Isaac S. Struble.
Population: 85 (2000); Race: 88.5% White, 0.0% Black, 0.0% Asian, 0.0% American Indian and Alaska Native, 11.5% Hispanic of any race, 11.5% two or more races (2000); Density: 546.2 persons per square mile (2000); Age: 32.1% under 18, 2.6% over 64 (2000); Marriage status: 14.5% never married, 76.4% now married, 3.6% widowed, 5.5% divorced (2000); Foreign born: 6.4% (2000); Ancestry (includes multiple ancestries): 55.1% German, 34.6% Dutch, 9.0% Other groups, 7.7% Welsh, 7.7% Norwegian (2000).

Economy: Employment by occupation: 0.0% management, 4.3% professional, 12.8% services, 14.9% sales, 8.5% farming, 4.3% construction, 55.3% production (2000).
Income: Per capita income: $16,423 (2000); Median household income: $37,813 (2000); Poverty rate: 0.0% (2000).
Taxes: Total city taxes per capita: $42 (1997); City property taxes per capita: $42 (1997).
Education: High school graduation rate: 92.2% (2000); College graduation rate: 15.7% (2000).
Housing: Homeownership rate: 82.1% (2000); Median home value: $46,700 (2000); Median rent: $350 per month (2000); Median age of housing: 50 years (2000).
Transportation: Commute to work: 100.0% car, 0.0% public transportation, 0.0% walk, 0.0% work from home (2000); Travel time to work: 25.5% less than 15 minutes, 63.8% 15 to 30 minutes, 10.6% 30 to 45 minutes, 0.0% 45 to 60 minutes, 0.0% 60 minutes or more (2000)

WESTFIELD (city). Covers a land area of 0.131 square miles and a water area of 0 square miles. Located at 42.75° N. Lat.; 96.60° W. Long. Elevation is 1,133 feet.
Population: 189 (2000); Race: 94.3% White, 0.0% Black, 2.6% Asian, 0.0% American Indian and Alaska Native, 0.0% Hispanic of any race, 3.1% two or more races (2000); Density: 1,438.3 persons per square mile (2000); Age: 24.2% under 18, 13.9% over 64 (2000); Marriage status: 26.9% never married, 53.1% now married, 3.1% widowed, 16.9% divorced (2000); Foreign born: 3.6% (2000); Ancestry (includes multiple ancestries): 32.0% German, 20.1% Irish, 13.4% English, 7.2% Other groups, 6.7% Danish (2000).
Economy: Employment by occupation: 14.8% management, 2.3% professional, 20.5% services, 30.7% sales, 3.4% farming, 6.8% construction, 21.6% production (2000).
Income: Per capita income: $15,211 (2000); Median household income: $28,929 (2000); Poverty rate: 3.6% (2000).
Taxes: Total city taxes per capita: $50 (1997); City property taxes per capita: $50 (1997).
Education: High school graduation rate: 63.6% (2000); College graduation rate: 13.2% (2000).
Housing: Homeownership rate: 71.1% (2000); Median home value: $30,000 (2000); Median rent: $408 per month (2000); Median age of housing: 51 years (2000).
Transportation: Commute to work: 92.0% car, 0.0% public transportation, 8.0% walk, 0.0% work from home (2000); Travel time to work: 19.3% less than 15 minutes, 19.3% 15 to 30 minutes, 33.0% 30 to 45 minutes, 12.5% 45 to 60 minutes, 15.9% 60 minutes or more (2000)

Pocahontas County

Located in north central Iowa; prairie area. Covers a land area of 577.70 square miles, a water area of 1.40 square miles, and is located in the Central Time Zone. The county government was organized in 1851. County seat is Pocahontas.

Weather Station: Pocahontas — Elevation: 1,210 feet

	Jan	Feb	Mar	Apr	May	Jun	Jul	Aug	Sep	Oct	Nov	Dec
High	24	30	43	59	72	82	84	81	75	62	43	29
Low	5	11	23	35	48	58	61	58	49	37	24	11
Precip	0.9	0.7	2.2	3.2	3.9	4.5	4.2	4.6	3.3	2.2	1.8	0.9
Snow	7.6	5.8	6.6	1.7	tr	0.0	0.0	0.0	0.0	0.3	4.8	7.5

High and Low temperatures in degrees Fahrenheit; Precipitation and Snow in inches

Population: 8,662 (2000); Race: 99.5% White, 0.0% Black, 0.2% Asian, 0.0% American Indian and Alaska Native, 0.7% Hispanic of any race, 0.1% two or more races (2000); Density: 15.0 persons per square mile (2000); Age: 25.5% under 18, 21.7% over 64 (2000).
Religion: Five largest groups: 32.2% Catholic Church, 24.3% Evangelical Lutheran Church in America, 15.7% The United Methodist Church, 3.0% Presbyterian Church (U.S.A.), 2.4% Christian Church (Disciples of Christ) (2000).
Economy: Unemployment rate: 4.8% (11/2002); Total civilian labor force: 3,805 (11/2002); Leading industries: 30.3% manufacturing; 16.1% health care and social assistance; 14.1% retail trade (2000); Companies that employ more than 1,000 persons: 0 (2000); Companies that employ more than 100 persons: 2 (2000); Farms: 778 totaling 356,988 acres (1997); Minority business ownership rate: 0.0% (1997); Women business ownership rate: 17.8% (1997); Retail sales per capita: $4,918 (1997). Single-family building permits issued: 1 (2001) / 0 (2000); Multi-family building permits issued: 0 (2001) / 0 (2000).
Income: Per capita income: $17,006 (2000); Median household income: $33,362 (2000); Poverty rate: 9.1% (2000); Bankruptcy rate: 2.84% (2001).
Taxes: Total county taxes per capita: $346 (1997); County property taxes per capita: $336 (1997).
Education: High school graduation rate: 86.6% (2000); College graduation rate: 15.0% (2000).
Housing: Homeownership rate: 79.2% (2000); Median home value: $40,400 (2000); Median rent: $225 per month (2000); Median age of housing: 58 years (2000).
Health: Birth rate: 82.0 per 10,000 population (1998); Age adjusted death rate: 66.8 per 10,000 population (1999); Age adjusted cancer mortality rate: 141.6 deaths per 100,000 population (1999). Number of physicians: 3.5 per 10,000 population (1999); Number of hospital beds: 28.9 per 10,000 population (1999).
Elections: 2000 Presidential election results: 41.9% Gore, 54.1% Bush, 1.9% Nader, 1.2% Buchanan
National and State Parks: Kaslow Prairie State Preserve; Sunken Grove State Game Management Area
Additional Information Contacts
Pocahontas County Government Offices 712-335-3361

Pocahontas County Communities

FONDA (city). Covers a land area of 1.024 square miles and a water area of 0 square miles. Located at 42.58° N. Lat.; 94.84° W. Long. Elevation is 1,234 feet.
History: Fonda was first named Marvin in honor of Marvin Hewitt, a railroad official, but the post office was called Cedarville because of nearby Cedar Creek. The resulting confusion prompted the citizens to abandon both names and substitute Fonda, a name chosen because it was found in the United States post office directory only once.
Population: 648 (2000); Race: 98.6% White, 0.0% Black, 0.0% Asian, 0.2% American Indian and Alaska Native, 1.3% Hispanic of any race, 0.0% two or more races (2000); Density: 632.8 persons per square mile (2000); Age: 21.0% under 18, 31.0% over 64 (2000); Marriage status: 17.8% never married, 50.8% now married, 18.6% widowed, 12.8% divorced (2000); Foreign born: 1.1% (2000); Ancestry (includes multiple ancestries): 46.2% German, 21.9% Irish, 7.5% English, 6.2% United States or American, 4.8% Swedish (2000).
Economy: Single-family building permits issued: 0 (2001) / 0 (2000); Multi-family building permits issued: 0 (2001) / 0 (2000); Employment by occupation: 11.9% management, 13.0% professional, 29.1% services, 15.7% sales, 1.5% farming, 5.7% construction, 23.0% production (2000).
Income: Per capita income: $15,626 (2000); Median household income: $26,731 (2000); Poverty rate: 11.1% (2000).
Taxes: Total city taxes per capita: $164 (1997); City property taxes per capita: $160 (1997).
Education: High school graduation rate: 85.9% (2000); College graduation rate: 12.6% (2000).
Housing: Homeownership rate: 80.1% (2000); Median home value: $27,600 (2000); Median rent: $210 per month (2000); Median age of housing: 60+ years (2000).
Transportation: Commute to work: 88.3% car, 0.0% public transportation, 9.3% walk, 1.6% work from home (2000); Travel time to work: 46.6% less than 15 minutes, 28.9% 15 to 30 minutes, 15.4% 30 to 45 minutes, 5.9% 45 to 60 minutes, 3.2% 60 minutes or more (2000)

HAVELOCK (city). Covers a land area of 0.563 square miles and a water area of 0 square miles. Located at 42.83° N. Lat.; 94.70° W. Long.
History: Havelock was laid out in 1882, and named for British General Sir Henry Havelock.
Population: 177 (2000); Race: 95.3% White, 0.0% Black, 4.7% Asian, 0.0% American Indian and Alaska Native, 0.0% Hispanic of any race, 0.0% two or more races (2000); Density: 314.3 persons per square mile (2000); Age: 37.9% under 18, 19.4% over 64 (2000); Marriage status: 25.7% never married, 53.4% now married, 17.6% widowed, 3.4% divorced (2000); Foreign born: 2.8% (2000); Ancestry (includes multiple ancestries): 19.4% German, 17.5% Other groups, 13.3% Italian, 13.3% French (except Basque), 7.1% Norwegian (2000).
Economy: Single-family building permits issued: 0 (2001) / 0 (2000); Multi-family building permits issued: 0 (2001) / 0 (2000); Employment by occupation: 0.0% management, 16.0% professional, 10.7% services, 16.0% sales, 0.0% farming, 36.0% construction, 21.3% production (2000).

Income: Per capita income: $11,548 (2000); Median household income: $28,462 (2000); Poverty rate: 12.8% (2000).
Taxes: Total city taxes per capita: $118 (1997); City property taxes per capita: $113 (1997).
Education: High school graduation rate: 68.6% (2000); College graduation rate: 5.9% (2000).
Housing: Homeownership rate: 87.3% (2000); Median home value: $11,700 (2000); Median rent: $290 per month (2000); Median age of housing: 53 years (2000).
Transportation: Commute to work: 100.0% car, 0.0% public transportation, 0.0% walk, 0.0% work from home (2000); Travel time to work: 28.8% less than 15 minutes, 53.4% 15 to 30 minutes, 9.6% 30 to 45 minutes, 5.5% 45 to 60 minutes, 2.7% 60 minutes or more (2000)

LAURENS (city). Covers a land area of 0.738 square miles and a water area of 0 square miles. Located at 42.84° N. Lat.; 94.85° W. Long. Elevation is 1,312 feet.
History: Laurens is named in honor of French Huguenots Henry and John Laurens, famous during the Revolutionary War. The town was platted in 1882 by the Western Town Lot Company.
Population: 1,476 (2000); Race: 99.9% White, 0.0% Black, 0.0% Asian, 0.0% American Indian and Alaska Native, 1.5% Hispanic of any race, 0.0% two or more races (2000); Density: 1,999.4 persons per square mile (2000); Age: 23.8% under 18, 25.1% over 64 (2000); Marriage status: 17.1% never married, 59.1% now married, 14.8% widowed, 9.0% divorced (2000); Foreign born: 1.1% (2000); Ancestry (includes multiple ancestries): 37.9% German, 13.0% English, 11.5% Irish, 8.2% Dutch, 7.9% Norwegian (2000).
Economy: Single-family building permits issued: 0 (2001) / 0 (2000); Multi-family building permits issued: 0 (2001) / 0 (2000); Employment by occupation: 14.5% management, 14.1% professional, 15.0% services, 23.7% sales, 1.9% farming, 6.9% construction, 23.8% production (2000).
Income: Per capita income: $16,711 (2000); Median household income: $33,188 (2000); Poverty rate: 7.4% (2000).
Taxes: Total city taxes per capita: $208 (1997); City property taxes per capita: $206 (1997).
Education: High school graduation rate: 83.8% (2000); College graduation rate: 13.6% (2000).

School District(s)

Laurens-Marathon Community School District (KG-12)
2000 Enrollment: 488 712-845-4508

Housing: Homeownership rate: 78.5% (2000); Median home value: $47,500 (2000); Median rent: $237 per month (2000); Median age of housing: 50 years (2000).
Newspapers: Laurens Sun (1 x week); The Laurens Reminder (1 x week)
Transportation: Commute to work: 89.5% car, 0.0% public transportation, 8.1% walk, 2.4% work from home (2000); Travel time to work: 68.8% less than 15 minutes, 12.8% 15 to 30 minutes, 7.5% 30 to 45 minutes, 4.2% 45 to 60 minutes, 6.7% 60 minutes or more (2000)

PALMER (city). Covers a land area of 0.426 square miles and a water area of 0 square miles. Located at 42.63° N. Lat.; 94.60° W. Long. Elevation is 1,244 feet.
History: The town of Palmer was once called Hanson. The name was changed to Palmer to avoid confusion with the town of Manson.
Population: 214 (2000); Race: 98.2% White, 0.0% Black, 0.0% Asian, 0.9% American Indian and Alaska Native, 0.9% Hispanic of any race, 0.9% two or more races (2000); Density: 502.8 persons per square mile (2000); Age: 22.0% under 18, 25.2% over 64 (2000); Marriage status: 14.8% never married, 60.8% now married, 15.9% widowed, 8.5% divorced (2000); Foreign born: 2.3% (2000); Ancestry (includes multiple ancestries): 63.8% German, 8.3% Swedish, 7.8% Irish, 5.5% Other groups, 3.7% Danish (2000).
Economy: Single-family building permits issued: 0 (2001) / 0 (2000); Multi-family building permits issued: 0 (2001) / 0 (2000); Employment by occupation: 17.6% management, 6.6% professional, 18.7% services, 17.6% sales, 2.2% farming, 6.6% construction, 30.8% production (2000).
Income: Per capita income: $17,775 (2000); Median household income: $25,000 (2000); Poverty rate: 16.5% (2000).
Taxes: Total city taxes per capita: $130 (1997); City property taxes per capita: $126 (1997).
Education: High school graduation rate: 79.2% (2000); College graduation rate: 9.4% (2000).
Housing: Homeownership rate: 77.1% (2000); Median home value: $18,300 (2000); Median rent: $192 per month (2000); Median age of housing: 60+ years (2000).
Transportation: Commute to work: 81.6% car, 0.0% public transportation, 12.6% walk, 5.7% work from home (2000); Travel time to work: 41.5% less than 15 minutes, 34.1% 15 to 30 minutes, 17.1% 30 to 45 minutes, 2.4% 45 to 60 minutes, 4.9% 60 minutes or more (2000)

PLOVER (city). Covers a land area of 0.543 square miles and a water area of 0 square miles. Located at 42.87° N. Lat.; 94.62° W. Long. Elevation is 1,190 feet.
History: Plover was founded in 1882. The name was chosen by the president of the Des Moines & Fort Dodge Railroad, presumably because he enjoyed hunting the plover bird.
Population: 95 (2000); Race: 100.0% White, 0.0% Black, 0.0% Asian, 0.0% American Indian and Alaska Native, 0.0% Hispanic of any race, 0.0% two or more races (2000); Density: 174.8 persons per square mile (2000); Age: 16.3% under 18, 16.3% over 64 (2000); Marriage status: 19.0% never married, 58.2% now married, 12.7% widowed, 10.1% divorced (2000); Foreign born: 0.0% (2000); Ancestry (includes multiple ancestries): 31.5% English, 29.3% German, 14.1% Dutch, 8.7% Norwegian, 5.4% Irish (2000).
Economy: Employment by occupation: 10.7% management, 7.1% professional, 16.1% services, 28.6% sales, 0.0% farming, 17.9% construction, 19.6% production (2000).
Income: Per capita income: $15,241 (2000); Median household income: $29,306 (2000); Poverty rate: 15.2% (2000).
Taxes: Total city taxes per capita: $172 (1997); City property taxes per capita: $172 (1997).
Education: High school graduation rate: 91.5% (2000); College graduation rate: 5.6% (2000).
Housing: Homeownership rate: 74.5% (2000); Median home value: <$10,000 (2000); Median rent: $200 per month (2000); Median age of housing: 60+ years (2000).
Transportation: Commute to work: 83.9% car, 0.0% public transportation, 3.6% walk, 12.5% work from home (2000); Travel time to work: 30.6% less than 15 minutes, 53.1% 15 to 30 minutes, 8.2% 30 to 45 minutes, 8.2% 45 to 60 minutes, 0.0% 60 minutes or more (2000)

POCAHONTAS (city). Covers a land area of 1.859 square miles and a water area of 0 square miles. Located at 42.73° N. Lat.; 94.67° W. Long. Elevation is 1,222 feet.
History: Pocahontas was named in honor of the daughter of the Indian chief, Powhatan.
Population: 1,970 (2000); Race: 99.8% White, 0.0% Black, 0.2% Asian, 0.0% American Indian and Alaska Native, 0.0% Hispanic of any race, 0.0% two or more races (2000); Density: 1,059.8 persons per square mile (2000); Age: 23.6% under 18, 25.3% over 64 (2000); Marriage status: 16.5% never married, 58.4% now married, 16.8% widowed, 8.2% divorced (2000); Foreign born: 0.7% (2000); Ancestry (includes multiple ancestries): 39.8% German, 12.4% Irish, 8.8% English, 8.3% United States or American, 6.2% Swedish (2000).
Economy: Single-family building permits issued: 1 (2001) / 0 (2000); Multi-family building permits issued: 0 (2001) / 0 (2000); Employment by occupation: 10.8% management, 23.8% professional, 18.5% services, 20.9% sales, 2.4% farming, 11.2% construction, 12.5% production (2000).
Income: Per capita income: $17,556 (2000); Median household income: $30,865 (2000); Poverty rate: 9.1% (2000).
Taxes: Total city taxes per capita: $253 (1997); City property taxes per capita: $246 (1997).
Education: High school graduation rate: 85.5% (2000); College graduation rate: 20.6% (2000).

School District(s)

Pocahontas Area Community School District (PK-12)
2000 Enrollment: 839 712-335-4311

Housing: Homeownership rate: 82.9% (2000); Median home value: $48,700 (2000); Median rent: $257 per month (2000); Median age of housing: 41 years (2000).
Hospitals: Pocahontas Community Hospital (25 beds)
Newspapers: Pocahontas Record-Democrat (1 x week)
Transportation: Commute to work: 93.6% car, 0.0% public transportation, 2.0% walk, 3.2% work from home (2000); Travel time to work: 68.3% less than 15 minutes, 17.2% 15 to 30 minutes, 7.7% 30 to 45 minutes, 1.7% 45 to 60 minutes, 5.2% 60 minutes or more (2000)

ROLFE (city). Covers a land area of 1.048 square miles and a water area of 0 square miles. Located at 42.81° N. Lat.; 94.53° W. Long. Elevation is 1,160 feet.
History: Rolfe was named for Englishman John Rolfe, husband of Pocahontas. The town was mapped in 1859.
Population: 675 (2000); Race: 99.4% White, 0.0% Black, 0.0% Asian, 0.0% American Indian and Alaska Native, 1.9% Hispanic of any race, 0.0% two or

more races (2000); Density: 643.9 persons per square mile (2000); Age: 24.0% under 18, 26.4% over 64 (2000); Marriage status: 12.5% never married, 63.3% now married, 15.2% widowed, 8.9% divorced (2000); Foreign born: 0.7% (2000); Ancestry (includes multiple ancestries): 36.1% German, 11.9% Irish, 11.2% Norwegian, 9.5% English, 5.7% United States or American (2000).
Economy: Single-family building permits issued: 0 (2001) / 0 (2000); Multi-family building permits issued: 0 (2001) / 0 (2000); Employment by occupation: 9.1% management, 10.6% professional, 25.5% services, 20.8% sales, 4.7% farming, 6.2% construction, 23.0% production (2000).
Income: Per capita income: $12,426 (2000); Median household income: $24,861 (2000); Poverty rate: 12.5% (2000).
Taxes: Total city taxes per capita: $205 (1997); City property taxes per capita: $203 (1997).
Education: High school graduation rate: 76.8% (2000); College graduation rate: 8.1% (2000).
Housing: Homeownership rate: 79.1% (2000); Median home value: $25,100 (2000); Median rent: $219 per month (2000); Median age of housing: 60+ years (2000).
Transportation: Commute to work: 88.1% car, 0.0% public transportation, 6.7% walk, 4.1% work from home (2000); Travel time to work: 51.7% less than 15 minutes, 27.8% 15 to 30 minutes, 11.6% 30 to 45 minutes, 4.2% 45 to 60 minutes, 4.6% 60 minutes or more (2000)

VARINA (city). Covers a land area of 0.247 square miles and a water area of 0 square miles. Located at 42.66° N. Lat.; 94.89° W. Long. Elevation is 1,261 feet.
History: Varina was named for a town in Virginia.
Population: 90 (2000); Race: 100.0% White, 0.0% Black, 0.0% Asian, 0.0% American Indian and Alaska Native, 0.0% Hispanic of any race, 0.0% two or more races (2000); Density: 364.9 persons per square mile (2000); Age: 22.1% under 18, 18.3% over 64 (2000); Marriage status: 14.3% never married, 66.7% now married, 8.3% widowed, 10.7% divorced (2000); Foreign born: 1.9% (2000); Ancestry (includes multiple ancestries): 52.9% German, 20.2% Irish, 13.5% Swedish, 10.6% Danish, 7.7% United States or American (2000).
Economy: Employment by occupation: 10.3% management, 0.0% professional, 30.8% services, 0.0% sales, 0.0% farming, 15.4% construction, 43.6% production (2000).
Income: Per capita income: $13,611 (2000); Median household income: $35,469 (2000); Poverty rate: 12.0% (2000).
Taxes: Total city taxes per capita: $65 (1997); City property taxes per capita: $65 (1997).
Education: High school graduation rate: 82.1% (2000); College graduation rate: 5.1% (2000).
Housing: Homeownership rate: 92.3% (2000); Median home value: $25,000 (2000); Median rent: $175 per month (2000); Median age of housing: 60+ years (2000).
Transportation: Commute to work: 83.8% car, 0.0% public transportation, 10.8% walk, 5.4% work from home (2000); Travel time to work: 17.1% less than 15 minutes, 65.7% 15 to 30 minutes, 8.6% 30 to 45 minutes, 0.0% 45 to 60 minutes, 8.6% 60 minutes or more (2000)

Polk County

Located in central Iowa; prairie area, drained by the Des Moines, Raccoon, and Skunk Rivers. Covers a land area of 569.30 square miles, a water area of 22.60 square miles, and is located in the Central Time Zone. The county government was organized in 1846. County seat is Des Moines.

Polk County is part of the Des Moines, IA MSA. The entire metro area includes: Dallas County; Polk County; Warren County

Weather Station: Ankeny — Elevation: 938 feet

	Jan	Feb	Mar	Apr	May	Jun	Jul	Aug	Sep	Oct	Nov	Dec
High	28	34	47	61	72	81	86	83	76	63	46	33
Low	9	15	27	38	50	59	64	61	52	39	27	15
Precip	0.7	0.9	2.1	3.2	4.5	4.9	4.1	4.5	3.2	2.6	1.9	1.0
Snow	6.5	6.2	4.0	1.1	tr	0.0	0.0	0.0	tr	0.4	2.0	5.6

High and Low temperatures in degrees Fahrenheit; Precipitation and Snow in inches

Weather Station: Des Moines Airport — Elevation: 954 feet

	Jan	Feb	Mar	Apr	May	Jun	Jul	Aug	Sep	Oct	Nov	Dec
High	29	35	48	61	73	82	86	84	76	63	47	34
Low	12	18	29	40	52	61	66	64	55	42	30	18
Precip	1.0	1.2	2.3	3.6	4.3	4.4	4.1	4.6	3.3	2.8	2.1	1.3
Snow	8.5	7.9	4.3	2.7	tr	tr	tr	0.0	tr	0.4	4.3	7.4

High and Low temperatures in degrees Fahrenheit; Precipitation and Snow in inches

Population: 374,601 (2000); Race: 88.4% White, 4.7% Black, 2.4% Asian, 0.3% American Indian and Alaska Native, 4.4% Hispanic of any race, 1.9% two or more races (2000); Density: 657.9 persons per square mile (2000); Age: 25.6% under 18, 11.1% over 64 (2000).
Religion: Five largest groups: 15.5% Catholic Church, 6.3% Evangelical Lutheran Church in America, 5.3% The United Methodist Church, 2.6% Christian Church (Disciples of Christ), 2.6% Assemblies of God (2000).
Economy: Unemployment rate: 3.2% (11/2002); Total civilian labor force: 225,364 (11/2002); Leading industries: 16.3% finance & insurance; 12.5% retail trade; 11.7% health care and social assistance (2000); Companies that employ more than 1,000 persons: 16 (2000); Companies that employ more than 100 persons: 393 (2000); Farms: 800 totaling 225,623 acres (1997); Minority business ownership rate: 4.0% (1997); Women business ownership rate: 25.0% (1997); Retail sales per capita: $12,503 (1997). Single-family building permits issued: 2,282 (2001) / 2,028 (2000); Multi-family building permits issued: 907 (2001) / 342 (2000).
Income: Per capita income: $23,654 (2000); Median household income: $46,116 (2000); Poverty rate: 7.9% (2000); Bankruptcy rate: 4.83% (2001).
Taxes: Total county taxes per capita: $275 (2000); County property taxes per capita: $265 (2000).
Education: High school graduation rate: 88.3% (2000); College graduation rate: 29.7% (2000).
Housing: Homeownership rate: 68.8% (2000); Median home value: $103,100 (2000); Median rent: $502 per month (2000); Median age of housing: 32 years (2000).
Health: Birth rate: 157.5 per 10,000 population (1998); Age adjusted death rate: 81.5 per 10,000 population (1999); Infant mortality rate: 8.3 per 1,000 live births (1998); Age adjusted cancer mortality rate: 201.0 deaths per 100,000 population (1999). Air Quality Index: 93% good, 7% moderate, 0% unhealthy (percent of days in 2000). Number of physicians: 22.0 per 10,000 population (1999); Number of hospital beds: 49.9 per 10,000 population (1999).
Elections: 2000 Presidential election results: 51.5% Gore, 45.9% Bush, 1.9% Nader, 0.2% Buchanan
National and State Parks: Big Creek State Park; Margo Frankel Woods State Park; Walnut Woods State Park
Additional Information Contacts
Polk County Government Offices 515-286-3117
Altoona Chamber of Commerce. 515-967-3366
Ankeny Chamber of Commerce. 515-964-0685
Calhoun County Board of Realtors 515-453-1064
Des Moines Area Association of Realtors 515-453-1064
Des Moines Convention & Visitors Bureau. 515-286-4960
Greater Des Moines Partnership. 515-286-4950
Iowa Association of Realtors 515-453-1064
West Des Moines Chamber of Commerce 515-225-6009

Polk County Communities

ALLEMAN (city). Covers a land area of 2.481 square miles and a water area of 0 square miles. Located at 41.81° N. Lat.; 93.61° W. Long.
History: Alleman was named for John L. Alleman.
Population: 439 (2000); Race: 100.0% White, 0.0% Black, 0.0% Asian, 0.0% American Indian and Alaska Native, 0.9% Hispanic of any race, 0.0% two or more races (2000); Density: 176.9 persons per square mile (2000); Age: 30.7% under 18, 7.9% over 64 (2000); Marriage status: 16.7% never married, 78.9% now married, 0.9% widowed, 3.4% divorced (2000); Foreign born: 0.2% (2000); Ancestry (includes multiple ancestries): 39.3% German, 17.1% Irish, 11.3% United States or American, 11.1% English, 7.2% Norwegian (2000).
Economy: Single-family building permits issued: 0 (2001) / 0 (2000); Multi-family building permits issued: 0 (2001) / 0 (2000); Employment by occupation: 17.4% management, 26.0% professional, 8.7% services, 24.7% sales, 0.0% farming, 10.5% construction, 12.8% production (2000).
Income: Per capita income: $20,970 (2000); Median household income: $66,458 (2000); Poverty rate: 1.6% (2000).
Taxes: Total city taxes per capita: $215 (1997); City property taxes per capita: $210 (1997).

Education: High school graduation rate: 92.6% (2000); College graduation rate: 30.5% (2000).

School District(s)

North Polk Community School District (KG-12)
2000 Enrollment: 942 515-685-3014

Housing: Homeownership rate: 91.1% (2000); Median home value: $133,900 (2000); Median rent: $325 per month (2000); Median age of housing: 24 years (2000).

Transportation: Commute to work: 88.2% car, 0.0% public transportation, 8.6% walk, 3.2% work from home (2000); Travel time to work: 33.6% less than 15 minutes, 39.3% 15 to 30 minutes, 24.8% 30 to 45 minutes, 0.9% 45 to 60 minutes, 1.4% 60 minutes or more (2000)

ALTOONA (city). Covers a land area of 7.104 square miles and a water area of 0 square miles. Located at 41.65° N. Lat.; 93.47° W. Long.

History: Altoona, from the Latin word for "high," was so named because it was the site of the highest point on the Des Moines Valley Railroad. The town was previously known as Yant's Siding and Yant's Station.

Population: 10,345 (2000); Race: 95.7% White, 0.5% Black, 0.9% Asian, 0.0% American Indian and Alaska Native, 2.0% Hispanic of any race, 1.8% two or more races (2000); Density: 1,456.2 persons per square mile (2000); Age: 30.5% under 18, 8.0% over 64 (2000); Marriage status: 22.6% never married, 62.2% now married, 4.8% widowed, 10.5% divorced (2000); Foreign born: 1.8% (2000); Ancestry (includes multiple ancestries): 29.4% German, 13.4% Irish, 9.6% English, 7.2% Other groups, 7.2% United States or American (2000).

Economy: Single-family building permits issued: 154 (2001) / 74 (2000); Multi-family building permits issued: 78 (2001) / 0 (2000); Employment by occupation: 15.7% management, 18.2% professional, 12.2% services, 34.8% sales, 0.2% farming, 5.7% construction, 13.1% production (2000).

Income: Per capita income: $20,336 (2000); Median household income: $50,162 (2000); Poverty rate: 5.5% (2000).

Taxes: Total city taxes per capita: $484 (2000); City property taxes per capita: $343 (2000).

Education: High school graduation rate: 93.1% (2000); College graduation rate: 23.8% (2000).

Housing: Homeownership rate: 71.0% (2000); Median home value: $115,600 (2000); Median rent: $477 per month (2000); Median age of housing: 21 years (2000).

Safety: Violent crime rate: 15.5 per 10,000 population; Property crime rate: 466.4 per 10,000 population (2001).

Newspapers: The Altoona Herald Mitchellville Index (1 x week)

Transportation: Commute to work: 94.8% car, 1.2% public transportation, 0.6% walk, 2.9% work from home (2000); Travel time to work: 26.4% less than 15 minutes, 53.2% 15 to 30 minutes, 17.4% 30 to 45 minutes, 1.2% 45 to 60 minutes, 1.8% 60 minutes or more (2000)

Additional Information Contacts

Altoona Chamber of Commerce.......................... 515-967-3366

ANKENY (city). Covers a land area of 16.775 square miles and a water area of 0 square miles. Located at 41.72° N. Lat.; 93.60° W. Long. Elevation is 1,001 feet.

History: Ankeny was founded in 1895 by Col. J. F. Ankeny as a station on a narrow-gauge railroad.

Population: 27,117 (2000); Race: 96.9% White, 0.4% Black, 0.7% Asian, 0.0% American Indian and Alaska Native, 1.2% Hispanic of any race, 1.1% two or more races (2000); Density: 1,616.5 persons per square mile (2000); Age: 27.2% under 18, 7.9% over 64 (2000); Marriage status: 25.5% never married, 63.5% now married, 3.3% widowed, 7.7% divorced (2000); Foreign born: 3.0% (2000); Ancestry (includes multiple ancestries): 35.0% German, 14.6% Irish, 11.8% English, 7.3% Norwegian, 6.3% United States or American (2000).

Vital Statistics: Birth rate: 159.3 per 10,000 population (1998)

Economy: Unemployment rate: 1.7% (11/2002); Total civilian labor force: 13,988 (11/2002); Single-family building permits issued: 514 (2001) / 390 (2000); Multi-family building permits issued: 87 (2001) / 66 (2000); Employment by occupation: 18.1% management, 22.8% professional, 11.9% services, 32.4% sales, 0.2% farming, 5.2% construction, 9.3% production (2000).

Income: Per capita income: $25,143 (2000); Median household income: $55,162 (2000); Poverty rate: 4.0% (2000).

Taxes: Total city taxes per capita: $379 (2000); City property taxes per capita: $343 (2000).

Education: High school graduation rate: 95.5% (2000); College graduation rate: 39.1% (2000).

School District(s)

Ankeny Community School District (PK-12)
2000 Enrollment: 5,735 515-965-9600

Four-year College(s)

Faith Baptist Bible College and Theological Seminary (Private, Not-for-profit, Baptist)
2001 Enrollment: 487 515-964-0601
2001 Tuition: In-state $8,690; Out-of-state $8,690

Two-year College(s)

Des Moines Community College (Public)
2001 Enrollment: 11,886 515-964-6241

Housing: Homeownership rate: 71.7% (2000); Median home value: $128,600 (2000); Median rent: $525 per month (2000); Median age of housing: 20 years (2000).

Safety: Violent crime rate: 7.8 per 10,000 population; Property crime rate: 261.4 per 10,000 population (2001).

Transportation: Commute to work: 93.6% car, 1.8% public transportation, 1.2% walk, 3.2% work from home (2000); Travel time to work: 31.6% less than 15 minutes, 48.0% 15 to 30 minutes, 16.8% 30 to 45 minutes, 1.9% 45 to 60 minutes, 1.7% 60 minutes or more (2000)

Airports: Ankeny Regional

Additional Information Contacts

Ankeny Chamber of Commerce.............................. 515-964-0685

BONDURANT (city). Covers a land area of 4.784 square miles and a water area of 0.022 square miles. Located at 41.69° N. Lat.; 93.46° W. Long. Elevation is 964 feet.

History: Alexander C. Bondurant was the founder of the town of Bondurant. His land became the right-of-way for the railroad.

Population: 1,846 (2000); Race: 98.3% White, 0.0% Black, 0.1% Asian, 0.2% American Indian and Alaska Native, 1.2% Hispanic of any race, 1.2% two or more races (2000); Density: 385.9 persons per square mile (2000); Age: 31.4% under 18, 7.0% over 64 (2000); Marriage status: 17.7% never married, 66.1% now married, 5.0% widowed, 11.2% divorced (2000); Foreign born: 0.6% (2000); Ancestry (includes multiple ancestries): 29.7% German, 15.0% United States or American, 14.3% Irish, 11.3% English, 6.6% Norwegian (2000).

Economy: Single-family building permits issued: 23 (2001) / 23 (2000); Multi-family building permits issued: 0 (2001) / 0 (2000); Employment by occupation: 11.4% management, 17.8% professional, 13.6% services, 33.9% sales, 0.5% farming, 10.4% construction, 12.5% production (2000).

Income: Per capita income: $19,196 (2000); Median household income: $52,877 (2000); Poverty rate: 5.7% (2000).

Taxes: Total city taxes per capita: $317 (1997); City property taxes per capita: $297 (1997).

Education: High school graduation rate: 95.5% (2000); College graduation rate: 19.4% (2000).

School District(s)

Bondurant-Farrar Community School District (PK-12)
2000 Enrollment: 935 515-967-7819

Housing: Homeownership rate: 84.3% (2000); Median home value: $91,500 (2000); Median rent: $395 per month (2000); Median age of housing: 23 years (2000).

Transportation: Commute to work: 96.1% car, 0.3% public transportation, 1.7% walk, 1.9% work from home (2000); Travel time to work: 25.8% less than 15 minutes, 52.0% 15 to 30 minutes, 19.5% 30 to 45 minutes, 0.2% 45 to 60 minutes, 2.5% 60 minutes or more (2000)

CLIVE (city). Covers a land area of 7.227 square miles and a water area of 0.107 square miles. Located at 41.60° N. Lat.; 93.78° W. Long. Elevation is 848 feet.

History: The town of Clive may refer to British General Robert Clive, known as "Clive of India."

Population: 12,855 (2000); Race: 92.4% White, 0.7% Black, 2.5% Asian, 0.3% American Indian and Alaska Native, 2.0% Hispanic of any race, 2.2% two or more races (2000); Density: 1,778.7 persons per square mile (2000); Age: 29.0% under 18, 5.7% over 64 (2000); Marriage status: 19.8% never married, 71.1% now married, 2.5% widowed, 6.5% divorced (2000); Foreign born: 6.6% (2000); Ancestry (includes multiple ancestries): 32.1% German, 14.2% Irish, 12.6% English, 7.6% Other groups, 5.6% Norwegian (2000).

Economy: Single-family building permits issued: 106 (2001) / 86 (2000); Multi-family building permits issued: 0 (2001) / 15 (2000); Employment by occupation: 28.8% management, 24.2% professional, 10.2% services, 28.9% sales, 0.3% farming, 1.9% construction, 5.6% production (2000).

Income: Per capita income: $40,053 (2000); Median household income: $74,127 (2000); Poverty rate: 3.5% (2000).

Taxes: Total city taxes per capita: $611 (2000); City property taxes per capita: $500 (2000).
Education: High school graduation rate: 97.7% (2000); College graduation rate: 56.0% (2000).
Housing: Homeownership rate: 76.3% (2000); Median home value: $180,700 (2000); Median rent: $527 per month (2000); Median age of housing: 16 years (2000).
Safety: Violent crime rate: 12.5 per 10,000 population; Property crime rate: 334.9 per 10,000 population (2001).
Transportation: Commute to work: 93.8% car, 1.0% public transportation, 1.5% walk, 3.4% work from home (2000); Travel time to work: 39.7% less than 15 minutes, 49.5% 15 to 30 minutes, 8.7% 30 to 45 minutes, 0.7% 45 to 60 minutes, 1.4% 60 minutes or more (2000)
Additional Information Contacts
Calhoun County Board of Realtors 515-453-1064
Des Moines Area Association of Realtors 515-453-1064
Iowa Association of Realtors 515-453-1064

DES MOINES (city). Covers a land area of 75.796 square miles and a water area of 1.451 square miles. Located at 41.59° N. Lat.; 93.62° W. Long. Elevation is 805 feet.
History: Des Moines gets its name from the Des Moines River, which is believed to come from the French word for "middle," referring to the middle river between the Mississippi and Missouri Rivers. The city was originally a military garrison established in 1843, and known as Fort Des Moines. The word "Fort" was dropped with the adoption of the city charter in 1857. Des Moines became the state capital in 1858.
Population: 198,682 (2000); Race: 82.5% White, 7.8% Black, 3.2% Asian, 0.5% American Indian and Alaska Native, 6.5% Hispanic of any race, 2.6% two or more races (2000); Density: 2,621.3 persons per square mile (2000); Age: 24.7% under 18, 12.4% over 64 (2000); Marriage status: 28.2% never married, 52.6% now married, 6.5% widowed, 12.7% divorced (2000); Foreign born: 7.9% (2000); Ancestry (includes multiple ancestries): 21.5% German, 19.1% Other groups, 12.7% Irish, 9.3% English, 6.8% United States or American (2000).
Vital Statistics: Birth rate: 170.8 per 10,000 population (1998)
Economy: Unemployment rate: 4.1% (11/2002); Total civilian labor force: 128,567 (11/2002); Single-family building permits issued: 283 (2001) / 312 (2000); Multi-family building permits issued: 86 (2001) / 15 (2000); Employment by occupation: 12.1% management, 17.0% professional, 16.2% services, 31.1% sales, 0.2% farming, 9.4% construction, 14.0% production (2000).
Income: Per capita income: $19,467 (2000); Median household income: $38,408 (2000); Poverty rate: 11.4% (2000).
Taxes: Total city taxes per capita: $482 (2000); City property taxes per capita: $437 (2000).
Education: High school graduation rate: 83.0% (2000); College graduation rate: 21.8% (2000).

School District(s)

Des Moines Independent Community School District (PK-12)
2000 Enrollment: 32,435 515-242-7911
Saydel Community School District (PK-12)
2000 Enrollment: 1,508 515-288-8557

Four-year College(s)

Drake University (Private, Not-for-profit)
2001 Enrollment: 5,150 515-271-2011
2001 Tuition: In-state $17,580; Out-of-state $17,580
Grand View College (Private, Not-for-profit, Evangelical Lutheran Church)
2001 Enrollment: 1,402 515-263-2800
2001 Tuition: In-state $13,340; Out-of-state $13,340
Mercy College of Health Sciences (Private, Not-for-profit, Roman Catholic)
2001 Enrollment: 443 515-643-3180
2001 Tuition: In-state $8,900; Out-of-state $8,900
Des Moines University-Osteopathic Medical Center (Private, Not-for-profit)
2001 Enrollment: 1,177 515-271-1400
2001 Tuition: In-state $14,600; Out-of-state $14,600
Mercy College of Health Sciences-Sch of Cytotech (Private, Not-for-profit, Roman Catholic)
2001 Enrollment: n/a 515-247-4466

Two-year College(s)

American Institute of Business (Private, Not-for-profit)
2001 Enrollment: 887 515-244-4221
2001 Tuition: In-state $7,380; Out-of-state $7,380
Iowa Methodist Medical Center-School of Rad Techn (Private, Not-for-profit, Christian Methodist Episcopal)
2001 Enrollment: 13 515-241-6171
2001 Tuition: In-state $1,000; Out-of-state $1,000
American College of Hairstyling-Des Moines (Private, For-profit)
2001 Enrollment: 15 515-244-0971
Iowa School of Beauty (Private, For-profit)
2001 Enrollment: 83 515-278-9939
La James College of Hairstyling (Private, For-profit)
2001 Enrollment: 112 515-278-2208
Vatterott College (Private, For-profit)
2001 Enrollment: 162 515-255-2220
2001 Tuition: In-state $6,884; Out-of-state $6,884
Housing: Homeownership rate: 64.7% (2000); Median home value: $81,100 (2000); Median rent: $468 per month (2000); Median age of housing: 45 years (2000).
Hospitals: Broadlawns Medical Center (200 beds); Des Moines General Hospital (226 beds); Iowa Lutheran Hospital (465 beds); Iowa Methodist Medical Center (674 beds); Mercy Hospital Center - DES Moines (673 beds); Veterans Affairs Central Iowa Health Care System (327 beds)
Safety: Violent crime rate: 37.8 per 10,000 population; Property crime rate: 597.6 per 10,000 population (2001).
Newspapers: Sunday Des Moines Register - Johnson County Edition; The Des Moines Register (7 x week); Cityview (1 x month); Western Express (1 x week); North Central Shopper (1 x week); Northwest Shopper (1 x week); Northeast Shopper (1 x week); Valley Shopper (1 x week); Central Shopper (1 x week); Lee Town Shopper (1 x week); South Des Moines Press Citizen (1 x week); Ankeny Press Citizen (1 x week)
Transportation: Commute to work: 91.4% car, 2.5% public transportation, 2.9% walk, 2.3% work from home (2000); Travel time to work: 38.9% less than 15 minutes, 47.7% 15 to 30 minutes, 9.4% 30 to 45 minutes, 2.0% 45 to 60 minutes, 2.0% 60 minutes or more (2000)
Airports: Des Moines International (primary service/small hub)
Additional Information Contacts
Des Moines Convention & Visitors Bureau.................. 515-286-4960
Greater Des Moines Partnership........................... 515-286-4950

ELKHART (city). Covers a land area of 1.182 square miles and a water area of 0 square miles. Located at 41.79° N. Lat.; 93.52° W. Long. Elevation is 980 feet.
History: Early residents named Elkhart after their former home in Elkhart, Indiana.
Population: 362 (2000); Race: 100.0% White, 0.0% Black, 0.0% Asian, 0.0% American Indian and Alaska Native, 0.0% Hispanic of any race, 0.0% two or more races (2000); Density: 306.3 persons per square mile (2000); Age: 15.7% under 18, 22.0% over 64 (2000); Marriage status: 27.3% never married, 52.0% now married, 8.5% widowed, 12.2% divorced (2000); Foreign born: 0.0% (2000); Ancestry (includes multiple ancestries): 32.1% German, 15.7% Irish, 14.5% English, 9.1% Norwegian, 9.1% Other groups (2000).
Economy: Single-family building permits issued: 0 (2001) / 0 (2000); Multi-family building permits issued: 4 (2001) / 0 (2000); Employment by occupation: 8.0% management, 20.9% professional, 20.9% services, 22.7% sales, 0.0% farming, 14.7% construction, 12.9% production (2000).
Income: Per capita income: $20,397 (2000); Median household income: $33,000 (2000); Poverty rate: 4.7% (2000).
Taxes: Total city taxes per capita: $86 (1997); City property taxes per capita: $81 (1997).
Education: High school graduation rate: 90.4% (2000); College graduation rate: 19.2% (2000).
Housing: Homeownership rate: 66.2% (2000); Median home value: $75,000 (2000); Median rent: $244 per month (2000); Median age of housing: 37 years (2000).
Transportation: Commute to work: 92.5% car, 1.2% public transportation, 3.7% walk, 2.5% work from home (2000); Travel time to work: 16.6% less than 15 minutes, 46.5% 15 to 30 minutes, 30.6% 30 to 45 minutes, 5.1% 45 to 60 minutes, 1.3% 60 minutes or more (2000)

GRIMES (city). Covers a land area of 8.953 square miles and a water area of 0.027 square miles. Located at 41.68° N. Lat.; 93.78° W. Long. Elevation is 967 feet.
History: Grimes was named for James W. Grimes, Governor of Iowa (1854-1858).
Population: 5,098 (2000); Race: 97.4% White, 0.4% Black, 0.0% Asian, 0.0% American Indian and Alaska Native, 1.3% Hispanic of any race, 2.3% two or more races (2000); Density: 569.4 persons per square mile (2000); Age: 31.6% under 18, 5.9% over 64 (2000); Marriage status: 18.7% never married, 65.5% now married, 3.8% widowed, 12.1% divorced (2000);

Foreign born: 0.8% (2000); Ancestry (includes multiple ancestries): 36.6% German, 12.0% Irish, 10.1% English, 7.0% United States or American, 4.8% Other groups (2000).
Economy: Single-family building permits issued: 30 (2001) / 36 (2000); Multi-family building permits issued: 12 (2001) / 34 (2000); Employment by occupation: 19.5% management, 23.0% professional, 10.4% services, 31.4% sales, 0.3% farming, 7.6% construction, 7.8% production (2000).
Income: Per capita income: $23,712 (2000); Median household income: $56,275 (2000); Poverty rate: 3.3% (2000).
Taxes: Total city taxes per capita: $392 (1997); City property taxes per capita: $357 (1997).
Education: High school graduation rate: 95.9% (2000); College graduation rate: 31.7% (2000).
Housing: Homeownership rate: 80.7% (2000); Median home value: $119,500 (2000); Median rent: $467 per month (2000); Median age of housing: 9 years (2000).
Transportation: Commute to work: 93.6% car, 0.0% public transportation, 1.2% walk, 5.2% work from home (2000); Travel time to work: 29.9% less than 15 minutes, 52.5% 15 to 30 minutes, 13.7% 30 to 45 minutes, 1.7% 45 to 60 minutes, 2.2% 60 minutes or more (2000)

JOHNSTON (city). Covers a land area of 14.348 square miles and a water area of 1.141 square miles. Located at 41.67° N. Lat.; 93.70° W. Long.
History: Johnston (also called Johnston Station) was named for railroad superintendent John F. Johnston.
Population: 8,649 (2000); Race: 95.3% White, 1.0% Black, 2.8% Asian, 0.1% American Indian and Alaska Native, 0.5% Hispanic of any race, 0.6% two or more races (2000); Density: 602.8 persons per square mile (2000); Age: 29.7% under 18, 11.0% over 64 (2000); Marriage status: 20.1% never married, 67.5% now married, 5.3% widowed, 7.1% divorced (2000); Foreign born: 3.7% (2000); Ancestry (includes multiple ancestries): 38.3% German, 15.8% Irish, 13.0% English, 7.2% Other groups, 6.3% Norwegian (2000).
Economy: Single-family building permits issued: 306 (2001) / 208 (2000); Multi-family building permits issued: 32 (2001) / 0 (2000); Employment by occupation: 22.8% management, 26.5% professional, 7.8% services, 30.0% sales, 0.6% farming, 5.8% construction, 6.5% production (2000).
Income: Per capita income: $36,407 (2000); Median household income: $76,094 (2000); Poverty rate: 4.1% (2000).
Taxes: Total city taxes per capita: $559 (2000); City property taxes per capita: $486 (2000).
Education: High school graduation rate: 94.7% (2000); College graduation rate: 49.9% (2000).

School District(s)

Johnston Community School District (PK-12)
2000 Enrollment: 4,178 515-278-0470
Housing: Homeownership rate: 74.0% (2000); Median home value: $188,300 (2000); Median rent: $670 per month (2000); Median age of housing: 11 years (2000).
Transportation: Commute to work: 96.3% car, 0.4% public transportation, 0.9% walk, 2.0% work from home (2000); Travel time to work: 37.2% less than 15 minutes, 48.6% 15 to 30 minutes, 10.9% 30 to 45 minutes, 1.6% 45 to 60 minutes, 1.7% 60 minutes or more (2000)

MITCHELLVILLE (city). Covers a land area of 2.298 square miles and a water area of 0.004 square miles. Located at 41.66° N. Lat.; 93.36° W. Long.
History: Mitchellville was named for Thomas Mitchell, a hotel proprietor.
Population: 1,715 (2000); Race: 97.1% White, 0.2% Black, 0.6% Asian, 0.0% American Indian and Alaska Native, 0.7% Hispanic of any race, 1.2% two or more races (2000); Density: 746.4 persons per square mile (2000); Age: 29.3% under 18, 13.5% over 64 (2000); Marriage status: 22.0% never married, 58.6% now married, 6.4% widowed, 13.0% divorced (2000); Foreign born: 0.8% (2000); Ancestry (includes multiple ancestries): 28.5% German, 15.3% English, 14.1% Irish, 8.2% United States or American, 6.9% Other groups (2000).
Economy: Single-family building permits issued: 7 (2001) / 5 (2000); Multi-family building permits issued: 0 (2001) / 0 (2000); Employment by occupation: 12.6% management, 16.9% professional, 11.6% services, 30.3% sales, 0.2% farming, 12.1% construction, 16.2% production (2000).
Income: Per capita income: $18,572 (2000); Median household income: $45,250 (2000); Poverty rate: 4.6% (2000).
Taxes: Total city taxes per capita: $213 (1997); City property taxes per capita: $206 (1997).
Education: High school graduation rate: 86.7% (2000); College graduation rate: 15.5% (2000).

School District(s)

Iowa Correctional Institution for Women (N -N)
2000 Enrollment: n/a 515-967-4236
Housing: Homeownership rate: 72.0% (2000); Median home value: $94,500 (2000); Median rent: $360 per month (2000); Median age of housing: 36 years (2000).
Transportation: Commute to work: 94.0% car, 0.9% public transportation, 2.1% walk, 3.0% work from home (2000); Travel time to work: 23.9% less than 15 minutes, 44.9% 15 to 30 minutes, 26.9% 30 to 45 minutes, 2.3% 45 to 60 minutes, 2.0% 60 minutes or more (2000)

PLEASANT HILL (city). Aka Youngstown. Covers a land area of 7.835 square miles and a water area of 0.108 square miles. Located at 41.58° N. Lat.; 93.51° W. Long.
History: Pleasant Hill took its name from the local school district. It is believed to have been named based on the founders' feelings for the location.
Population: 5,070 (2000); Race: 96.0% White, 0.2% Black, 1.8% Asian, 1.0% American Indian and Alaska Native, 2.0% Hispanic of any race, 1.1% two or more races (2000); Density: 647.1 persons per square mile (2000); Age: 25.9% under 18, 9.3% over 64 (2000); Marriage status: 17.7% never married, 66.0% now married, 6.4% widowed, 10.0% divorced (2000); Foreign born: 2.2% (2000); Ancestry (includes multiple ancestries): 26.2% German, 17.8% English, 13.2% Irish, 8.2% Other groups, 6.6% United States or American (2000).
Economy: Single-family building permits issued: 93 (2001) / 70 (2000); Multi-family building permits issued: 38 (2001) / 0 (2000); Employment by occupation: 16.6% management, 21.2% professional, 11.7% services, 30.8% sales, 0.0% farming, 8.2% construction, 11.5% production (2000).
Income: Per capita income: $25,316 (2000); Median household income: $60,694 (2000); Poverty rate: 1.3% (2000).
Taxes: Total city taxes per capita: $460 (2000); City property taxes per capita: $433 (2000).
Education: High school graduation rate: 93.3% (2000); College graduation rate: 25.7% (2000).
Housing: Homeownership rate: 79.1% (2000); Median home value: $121,400 (2000); Median rent: $495 per month (2000); Median age of housing: 20 years (2000).
Safety: Violent crime rate: 23.7 per 10,000 population; Property crime rate: 300.1 per 10,000 population (2001).
Transportation: Commute to work: 95.8% car, 0.3% public transportation, 0.3% walk, 3.6% work from home (2000); Travel time to work: 19.7% less than 15 minutes, 61.7% 15 to 30 minutes, 13.1% 30 to 45 minutes, 3.3% 45 to 60 minutes, 2.2% 60 minutes or more (2000)

POLK CITY (city). Covers a land area of 2.718 square miles and a water area of 0.008 square miles. Located at 41.77° N. Lat.; 93.71° W. Long. Elevation is 889 feet.
History: Polk was named in honor of President James K. Polk (1845-1849).
Population: 2,344 (2000); Race: 97.3% White, 0.3% Black, 0.6% Asian, 0.0% American Indian and Alaska Native, 0.8% Hispanic of any race, 1.2% two or more races (2000); Density: 862.4 persons per square mile (2000); Age: 27.8% under 18, 7.0% over 64 (2000); Marriage status: 23.1% never married, 64.3% now married, 3.1% widowed, 9.4% divorced (2000); Foreign born: 1.4% (2000); Ancestry (includes multiple ancestries): 32.2% German, 13.4% Irish, 11.0% English, 7.3% Norwegian, 6.5% United States or American (2000).
Economy: Single-family building permits issued: 27 (2001) / 14 (2000); Multi-family building permits issued: 0 (2001) / 6 (2000); Employment by occupation: 17.0% management, 19.0% professional, 11.7% services, 27.8% sales, 0.0% farming, 11.6% construction, 12.8% production (2000).
Income: Per capita income: $23,476 (2000); Median household income: $58,000 (2000); Poverty rate: 2.4% (2000).
Taxes: Total city taxes per capita: $315 (1997); City property taxes per capita: $185 (1997).
Education: High school graduation rate: 90.7% (2000); College graduation rate: 26.3% (2000).
Housing: Homeownership rate: 81.0% (2000); Median home value: $109,400 (2000); Median rent: $486 per month (2000); Median age of housing: 24 years (2000).
Transportation: Commute to work: 94.7% car, 0.1% public transportation, 0.7% walk, 4.0% work from home (2000); Travel time to work: 16.5% less than 15 minutes, 51.1% 15 to 30 minutes, 29.0% 30 to 45 minutes, 1.5% 45 to 60 minutes, 1.9% 60 minutes or more (2000)

RUNNELLS (city). Covers a land area of 0.424 square miles and a water area of 0 square miles. Located at 41.51° N. Lat.; 93.35° W. Long. Elevation is 800 feet.
History: Runnells was named in honor of a Des Moines attorney, John S. Runnells. Mr. Runnells helped to plat the town.
Population: 352 (2000); Race: 96.9% White, 0.0% Black, 0.0% Asian, 0.6% American Indian and Alaska Native, 0.0% Hispanic of any race, 2.6% two or more races (2000); Density: 830.9 persons per square mile (2000); Age: 30.8% under 18, 12.3% over 64 (2000); Marriage status: 13.6% never married, 63.2% now married, 11.2% widowed, 12.0% divorced (2000); Foreign born: 0.3% (2000); Ancestry (includes multiple ancestries): 21.7% Irish, 21.4% German, 20.2% English, 9.4% Dutch, 8.3% French (except Basque) (2000).
Economy: Single-family building permits issued: 5 (2001) / 3 (2000); Multi-family building permits issued: 0 (2001) / 0 (2000); Employment by occupation: 11.6% management, 9.8% professional, 13.9% services, 39.3% sales, 0.0% farming, 10.4% construction, 15.0% production (2000).
Income: Per capita income: $17,643 (2000); Median household income: $41,250 (2000); Poverty rate: 2.8% (2000).
Taxes: Total city taxes per capita: $145 (1997); City property taxes per capita: $142 (1997).
Education: High school graduation rate: 93.6% (2000); College graduation rate: 4.5% (2000).

School District(s)

Southeast Polk Community School District (PK-12)
2000 Enrollment: 4,564 515-967-4294

Housing: Homeownership rate: 70.5% (2000); Median home value: $85,000 (2000); Median rent: $314 per month (2000); Median age of housing: 35 years (2000).
Transportation: Commute to work: 94.9% car, 0.0% public transportation, 2.3% walk, 2.9% work from home (2000); Travel time to work: 10.6% less than 15 minutes, 31.2% 15 to 30 minutes, 41.2% 30 to 45 minutes, 15.9% 45 to 60 minutes, 1.2% 60 minutes or more (2000)

SAYLORVILLE (CDP). Covers a land area of 8.349 square miles and a water area of 0 square miles. Located at 41.69° N. Lat.; 93.62° W. Long.
History: Saylorville was named for pioneer Thomas Saylor.
Population: 3,238 (2000); Race: 96.1% White, 1.4% Black, 1.5% Asian, 0.0% American Indian and Alaska Native, 1.3% Hispanic of any race, 0.5% two or more races (2000); Density: 387.8 persons per square mile (2000); Age: 23.0% under 18, 15.5% over 64 (2000); Marriage status: 16.5% never married, 75.7% now married, 2.3% widowed, 5.4% divorced (2000); Foreign born: 2.5% (2000); Ancestry (includes multiple ancestries): 33.0% German, 17.2% Irish, 13.1% English, 7.2% Dutch, 6.4% Swedish (2000).
Economy: Employment by occupation: 17.2% management, 19.7% professional, 11.0% services, 32.1% sales, 0.0% farming, 9.2% construction, 10.8% production (2000).
Income: Per capita income: $28,034 (2000); Median household income: $67,197 (2000); Poverty rate: 2.1% (2000).
Education: High school graduation rate: 87.5% (2000); College graduation rate: 27.3% (2000).
Housing: Homeownership rate: 90.1% (2000); Median home value: $136,100 (2000); Median rent: $454 per month (2000); Median age of housing: 32 years (2000).
Transportation: Commute to work: 91.3% car, 0.0% public transportation, 1.1% walk, 6.3% work from home (2000); Travel time to work: 33.2% less than 15 minutes, 53.5% 15 to 30 minutes, 8.1% 30 to 45 minutes, 1.9% 45 to 60 minutes, 3.3% 60 minutes or more (2000)

URBANDALE (city). Covers a land area of 20.694 square miles and a water area of 0.024 square miles. Located at 41.63° N. Lat.; 93.73° W. Long. Elevation is 965 feet.
History: Urbandale was the end of the interurban streetcar line, which may have been the source of its name.
Population: 29,072 (2000); Race: 94.9% White, 1.9% Black, 1.3% Asian, 0.3% American Indian and Alaska Native, 1.7% Hispanic of any race, 1.0% two or more races (2000); Density: 1,404.9 persons per square mile (2000); Age: 26.3% under 18, 10.5% over 64 (2000); Marriage status: 21.3% never married, 65.1% now married, 5.0% widowed, 8.6% divorced (2000); Foreign born: 4.1% (2000); Ancestry (includes multiple ancestries): 37.3% German, 15.4% Irish, 13.3% English, 7.0% Other groups, 5.7% Norwegian (2000).
Vital Statistics: Birth rate: 132.1 per 10,000 population (1998)
Economy: Unemployment rate: 1.8% (11/2002); Total civilian labor force: 17,448 (11/2002); Single-family building permits issued: 294 (2001) / 301 (2000); Multi-family building permits issued: 296 (2001) / 32 (2000); Employment by occupation: 21.4% management, 24.4% professional, 10.3% services, 31.8% sales, 0.1% farming, 4.7% construction, 7.3% production (2000).
Income: Per capita income: $29,021 (2000); Median household income: $59,744 (2000); Poverty rate: 3.7% (2000).
Taxes: Total city taxes per capita: $408 (2000); City property taxes per capita: $350 (2000).
Education: High school graduation rate: 96.2% (2000); College graduation rate: 43.7% (2000).

School District(s)

Urbandale Community School District (PK-12)
2000 Enrollment: 3,499 515-457-5000

Two-year College(s)

Hamilton College (Private, For-profit)
2001 Enrollment: 436 515-727-2100
2001 Tuition: In-state $12,480; Out-of-state $12,480

Housing: Homeownership rate: 77.5% (2000); Median home value: $133,100 (2000); Median rent: $574 per month (2000); Median age of housing: 21 years (2000).
Transportation: Commute to work: 93.6% car, 1.0% public transportation, 1.0% walk, 4.2% work from home (2000); Travel time to work: 37.0% less than 15 minutes, 51.4% 15 to 30 minutes, 7.4% 30 to 45 minutes, 1.4% 45 to 60 minutes, 2.8% 60 minutes or more (2000)

WEST DES MOINES (city). Aka Valley Junction. Covers a land area of 26.784 square miles and a water area of 0.790 square miles. Located at 41.57° N. Lat.; 93.75° W. Long. Elevation is 850 feet.
History: West Des Moines was originally named Valley Junction. The name was changed by popular vote in 1938.
Population: 46,403 (2000); Race: 92.9% White, 1.8% Black, 2.7% Asian, 0.3% American Indian and Alaska Native, 3.3% Hispanic of any race, 1.2% two or more races (2000); Density: 1,732.5 persons per square mile (2000); Age: 24.9% under 18, 9.6% over 64 (2000); Marriage status: 27.3% never married, 58.4% now married, 3.9% widowed, 10.3% divorced (2000); Foreign born: 5.4% (2000); Ancestry (includes multiple ancestries): 33.2% German, 15.4% Irish, 11.6% English, 9.7% Other groups, 5.8% Norwegian (2000).
Vital Statistics: Birth rate: 150.4 per 10,000 population (1998)
Economy: Unemployment rate: 2.3% (11/2002); Total civilian labor force: 23,184 (11/2002); Single-family building permits issued: 256 (2001) / 301 (2000); Multi-family building permits issued: 274 (2001) / 174 (2000); Employment by occupation: 23.5% management, 26.5% professional, 9.7% services, 30.4% sales, 0.1% farming, 4.3% construction, 5.5% production (2000).
Income: Per capita income: $31,405 (2000); Median household income: $54,139 (2000); Poverty rate: 4.5% (2000).
Taxes: Total city taxes per capita: $562 (2000); City property taxes per capita: $520 (2000).
Education: High school graduation rate: 96.3% (2000); College graduation rate: 48.5% (2000).

School District(s)

West Des Moines Community School District (PK-12)
2000 Enrollment: 8,606 515-226-2700

Housing: Homeownership rate: 62.2% (2000); Median home value: $140,600 (2000); Median rent: $601 per month (2000); Median age of housing: 16 years (2000).
Safety: Violent crime rate: 16.6 per 10,000 population; Property crime rate: 374.9 per 10,000 population (2001).
Transportation: Commute to work: 92.6% car, 2.0% public transportation, 1.2% walk, 3.7% work from home (2000); Travel time to work: 39.1% less than 15 minutes, 49.6% 15 to 30 minutes, 7.5% 30 to 45 minutes, 1.6% 45 to 60 minutes, 2.2% 60 minutes or more (2000)
Additional Information Contacts
West Des Moines Chamber of Commerce 515-225-6009

WINDSOR HEIGHTS (city). Covers a land area of 1.414 square miles and a water area of 0 square miles. Located at 41.60° N. Lat.; 93.71° W. Long.
Population: 4,805 (2000); Race: 95.5% White, 0.4% Black, 2.1% Asian, 0.0% American Indian and Alaska Native, 2.7% Hispanic of any race, 0.5% two or more races (2000); Density: 3,399.3 persons per square mile (2000); Age: 19.2% under 18, 20.7% over 64 (2000); Marriage status: 20.0% never married, 61.1% now married, 7.1% widowed, 11.9% divorced (2000); Foreign born: 4.2% (2000); Ancestry (includes multiple ancestries): 28.9% German, 18.9% Irish, 15.4% English, 8.7% Other groups, 4.9% United States or American (2000).

Economy: Single-family building permits issued: 1 (2001) / 0 (2000); Multi-family building permits issued: 0 (2001) / 0 (2000); Employment by occupation: 19.8% management, 25.4% professional, 14.9% services, 28.8% sales, 0.2% farming, 5.7% construction, 5.2% production (2000).
Income: Per capita income: $29,966 (2000); Median household income: $55,931 (2000); Poverty rate: 5.2% (2000).
Taxes: Total city taxes per capita: $532 (2000); City property taxes per capita: $509 (2000).
Education: High school graduation rate: 93.5% (2000); College graduation rate: 43.3% (2000).
Housing: Homeownership rate: 81.0% (2000); Median home value: $121,300 (2000); Median rent: $651 per month (2000); Median age of housing: 42 years (2000).
Safety: Violent crime rate: 16.7 per 10,000 population; Property crime rate: 352.1 per 10,000 population (2001).
Transportation: Commute to work: 92.6% car, 1.3% public transportation, 1.3% walk, 4.9% work from home (2000); Travel time to work: 43.7% less than 15 minutes, 48.3% 15 to 30 minutes, 2.5% 30 to 45 minutes, 3.4% 45 to 60 minutes, 2.1% 60 minutes or more (2000)

Pottawattamie County

Located in southwestern Iowa; bounded on the west by the Missouri River and the Nebraska border; prairie area, drained by the West and East Nishnabotna Rivers. Covers a land area of 954.30 square miles, a water area of 5.70 square miles, and is located in the Central Time Zone. The county government was organized in 1848. County seat is Council Bluffs.

Pottawattamie County is part of the Omaha, NE-IA MSA. The entire metro area includes: Pottawattamie County, IA; Cass County, NE; Douglas County, NE; Sarpy County, NE; Washington County, NE

Weather Station: Oakland 2 SW — Elevation: 1,167 feet

	Jan	Feb	Mar	Apr	May	Jun	Jul	Aug	Sep	Oct	Nov	Dec
High	30	36	49	63	73	83	86	83	77	65	47	34
Low	10	16	26	38	49	59	63	61	52	39	27	16
Precip	0.8	0.8	2.3	3.4	4.6	4.6	4.2	4.1	3.7	2.6	1.8	0.9
Snow	6.4	5.8	4.3	1.4	tr	0.0	0.0	0.0	tr	0.7	2.6	4.8

High and Low temperatures in degrees Fahrenheit; Precipitation and Snow in inches

Population: 87,704 (2000); Race: 96.0% White, 0.7% Black, 0.6% Asian, 0.3% American Indian and Alaska Native, 3.2% Hispanic of any race, 1.0% two or more races (2000); Density: 91.9 persons per square mile (2000); Age: 25.8% under 18, 13.8% over 64 (2000).
Religion: Five largest groups: 12.3% Catholic Church, 6.8% Evangelical Lutheran Church in America, 5.3% The United Methodist Church, 2.9% Christian Churches and Churches of Christ, 2.8% Lutheran Church—Missouri Synod (2000).
Economy: Unemployment rate: 3.5% (11/2002); Total civilian labor force: 50,304 (11/2002); Leading industries: 21.8% retail trade; 17.9% accommodation & food services; 13.6% manufacturing (2000); Companies that employ more than 1,000 persons: 3 (2000); Companies that employ more than 100 persons: 51 (2000); Farms: 1,325 totaling 536,704 acres (1997); Minority business ownership rate: 0.0% (1997); Women business ownership rate: 22.3% (1997); Retail sales per capita: $11,469 (1997). Single-family building permits issued: 351 (2001) / 295 (2000); Multi-family building permits issued: 114 (2001) / 368 (2000).
Income: Per capita income: $19,275 (2000); Median household income: $40,089 (2000); Poverty rate: 8.4% (2000); Bankruptcy rate: 5.46% (2001).
Taxes: Total county taxes per capita: $211 (2000); County property taxes per capita: $164 (2000).
Education: High school graduation rate: 84.0% (2000); College graduation rate: 15.0% (2000).
Housing: Homeownership rate: 71.1% (2000); Median home value: $84,900 (2000); Median rent: $449 per month (2000); Median age of housing: 42 years (2000).
Health: Birth rate: 132.6 per 10,000 population (1998); Age adjusted death rate: 88.0 per 10,000 population (1999); Age adjusted cancer mortality rate: 215.3 deaths per 100,000 population (1999). Air Quality Index: 96% good, 4% moderate, 0% unhealthy (percent of days in 2000). Number of physicians: 11.7 per 10,000 population (1999); Number of hospital beds: 36.6 per 10,000 population (1999).
Elections: 2000 Presidential election results: 42.7% Gore, 54.5% Bush, 2.0% Nader, 0.4% Buchanan
National and State Parks: Historic Council Bluffs State Historical Marker; Historic Council Bluffs State Historical Marker; Lake Manawa State Park; Wilson Island State Park
Additional Information Contacts
Pottawattamie County Government Offices. 712-328-5604
Council Bluffs Chamber of Commerce 712-325-1000
Southwest Iowa Association of Realtors 712-323-3478
Walnut Chamber of Commerce 712-784-2100

Pottawattamie County Communities

AVOCA (city). Covers a land area of 1.938 square miles and a water area of 0 square miles. Located at 41.47° N. Lat.; 95.33° W. Long. Elevation is 1,137 feet.
History: Avoca was first known as Pacific, and later as Botna. The town was renamed for the Avoca River in Ireland.
Population: 1,610 (2000); Race: 96.7% White, 0.7% Black, 0.1% Asian, 0.0% American Indian and Alaska Native, 1.3% Hispanic of any race, 2.3% two or more races (2000); Density: 830.6 persons per square mile (2000); Age: 22.4% under 18, 22.2% over 64 (2000); Marriage status: 17.3% never married, 64.1% now married, 10.2% widowed, 8.5% divorced (2000); Foreign born: 0.4% (2000); Ancestry (includes multiple ancestries): 42.1% German, 13.2% Irish, 12.3% Danish, 8.1% English, 6.7% Other groups (2000).
Economy: Single-family building permits issued: 2 (2001) / 7 (2000); Multi-family building permits issued: 2 (2001) / 0 (2000); Employment by occupation: 10.1% management, 18.7% professional, 16.3% services, 28.3% sales, 0.6% farming, 9.8% construction, 16.2% production (2000).
Income: Per capita income: $20,908 (2000); Median household income: $39,826 (2000); Poverty rate: 3.5% (2000).
Taxes: Total city taxes per capita: $325 (1997); City property taxes per capita: $235 (1997).
Education: High school graduation rate: 88.8% (2000); College graduation rate: 15.7% (2000).

School District(s)
A-H-S-T Community School District (PK-12)
2000 Enrollment: 651 712-343-6304
Housing: Homeownership rate: 75.9% (2000); Median home value: $73,000 (2000); Median rent: $295 per month (2000); Median age of housing: 60+ years (2000).
Newspapers: The Journal-Herald (1 x week); The Oakland Herald (1 x week)
Transportation: Commute to work: 93.1% car, 0.5% public transportation, 3.7% walk, 2.5% work from home (2000); Travel time to work: 46.0% less than 15 minutes, 15.2% 15 to 30 minutes, 9.7% 30 to 45 minutes, 15.6% 45 to 60 minutes, 13.4% 60 minutes or more (2000)

CARSON (city). Covers a land area of 0.523 square miles and a water area of 0 square miles. Located at 41.23° N. Lat.; 95.41° W. Long. Elevation is 1,066 feet.
History: A town was established in 1880 at the point where two railroad lines met, known then as Lash's Mill. The name of Carson refers to one of the officials of the railroad company.
Population: 668 (2000); Race: 98.9% White, 0.0% Black, 1.1% Asian, 0.0% American Indian and Alaska Native, 0.0% Hispanic of any race, 0.0% two or more races (2000); Density: 1,277.6 persons per square mile (2000); Age: 21.7% under 18, 20.2% over 64 (2000); Marriage status: 21.8% never married, 61.0% now married, 8.8% widowed, 8.3% divorced (2000); Foreign born: 1.4% (2000); Ancestry (includes multiple ancestries): 37.8% German, 20.1% English, 15.8% Irish, 10.7% United States or American, 4.9% Danish (2000).
Economy: Single-family building permits issued: 3 (2001) / 2 (2000); Multi-family building permits issued: 0 (2001) / 0 (2000); Employment by occupation: 6.6% management, 12.1% professional, 15.0% services, 36.9% sales, 1.7% farming, 14.1% construction, 13.5% production (2000).
Income: Per capita income: $18,831 (2000); Median household income: $41,719 (2000); Poverty rate: 8.0% (2000).
Taxes: Total city taxes per capita: $216 (1997); City property taxes per capita: $144 (1997).
Education: High school graduation rate: 86.4% (2000); College graduation rate: 12.6% (2000).

School District(s)
Riverside Community School District (PK-12)
2000 Enrollment: 747 712-484-2212

Housing: Homeownership rate: 86.3% (2000); Median home value: $82,000 (2000); Median rent: $302 per month (2000); Median age of housing: 48 years (2000).
Transportation: Commute to work: 94.7% car, 0.0% public transportation, 1.2% walk, 3.5% work from home (2000); Travel time to work: 33.6% less than 15 minutes, 12.1% 15 to 30 minutes, 34.2% 30 to 45 minutes, 16.1% 45 to 60 minutes, 3.9% 60 minutes or more (2000)

CARTER LAKE (city). Covers a land area of 1.805 square miles and a water area of 0.201 square miles. Located at 41.29° N. Lat.; 95.91° W. Long.
Population: 3,248 (2000); Race: 96.5% White, 0.0% Black, 2.3% Asian, 0.0% American Indian and Alaska Native, 2.2% Hispanic of any race, 1.1% two or more races (2000); Density: 1,799.7 persons per square mile (2000); Age: 24.9% under 18, 12.5% over 64 (2000); Marriage status: 22.0% never married, 58.1% now married, 8.2% widowed, 11.7% divorced (2000); Foreign born: 2.6% (2000); Ancestry (includes multiple ancestries): 30.8% German, 17.6% Irish, 11.6% English, 9.1% Other groups, 6.6% Italian (2000).
Economy: Nearly surrounded by city of Omaha on Nebraska side of river. Manufacturing: steel products. Single-family building permits issued: 19 (2001) / 19 (2000); Multi-family building permits issued: 0 (2001) / 2 (2000); Employment by occupation: 10.9% management, 8.5% professional, 18.6% services, 27.0% sales, 0.0% farming, 11.7% construction, 23.4% production (2000).
Income: Per capita income: $18,758 (2000); Median household income: $37,851 (2000); Poverty rate: 7.1% (2000).
Taxes: Total city taxes per capita: $288 (1997); City property taxes per capita: $198 (1997).
Education: High school graduation rate: 79.9% (2000); College graduation rate: 8.6% (2000).
Housing: Homeownership rate: 86.7% (2000); Median home value: $70,400 (2000); Median rent: $435 per month (2000); Median age of housing: 37 years (2000).
Transportation: Commute to work: 94.6% car, 0.0% public transportation, 2.0% walk, 2.3% work from home (2000); Travel time to work: 38.9% less than 15 minutes, 43.1% 15 to 30 minutes, 12.9% 30 to 45 minutes, 2.1% 45 to 60 minutes, 3.0% 60 minutes or more (2000)

COUNCIL BLUFFS (city). Covers a land area of 37.384 square miles and a water area of 2.263 square miles. Located at 41.25° N. Lat.; 95.86° W. Long. Elevation is 986 feet.
History: Council Bluffs was originally known as Hart's Bluff. In 1846, the first Mormons arrived and changed the name of the settlement first to Miller's Hollow, and then to Kanesville in honor of Thomas L. Kane, an Army officer who was friendly to them. In 1852, the Mormons followed Brigham Young's calling and left for Utah. The remaining members of the town then changed the name to Council Bluffs. The following year the town was incorporated.
Population: 58,268 (2000); Race: 95.0% White, 1.0% Black, 0.6% Asian, 0.4% American Indian and Alaska Native, 4.5% Hispanic of any race, 1.0% two or more races (2000); Density: 1,558.7 persons per square mile (2000); Age: 25.9% under 18, 13.4% over 64 (2000); Marriage status: 26.4% never married, 52.6% now married, 7.7% widowed, 13.4% divorced (2000); Foreign born: 2.6% (2000); Ancestry (includes multiple ancestries): 31.5% German, 17.2% Irish, 10.3% Other groups, 10.1% English, 6.0% United States or American (2000).
Vital Statistics: Birth rate: 147.8 per 10,000 population (1998)
Economy: Unemployment rate: 4.1% (11/2002); Total civilian labor force: 32,518 (11/2002); Single-family building permits issued: 201 (2001) / 156 (2000); Multi-family building permits issued: 108 (2001) / 366 (2000); Employment by occupation: 9.3% management, 14.2% professional, 17.0% services, 31.0% sales, 0.2% farming, 10.2% construction, 18.1% production (2000).
Income: Per capita income: $18,143 (2000); Median household income: $36,221 (2000); Poverty rate: 10.3% (2000).
Taxes: Total city taxes per capita: $621 (2000); City property taxes per capita: $403 (2000).
Education: High school graduation rate: 81.3% (2000); College graduation rate: 13.9% (2000).

School District(s)

Council Bluffs Community School District (PK-12)
2000 Enrollment: 11,014 712-328-6418
Iowa School for the Deaf (N -N)
2000 Enrollment: n/a 712-366-0571
Lewis Central Community School District (PK-12)
2000 Enrollment: 2,778 712-366-8202

Two-year College(s)

Iowa Western Community College (Public)
2001 Enrollment: 4,300 712-325-3200
2001 Tuition: In-state $2,310; Out-of-state $3,465
Jennie Edmundson Memorial Hospital-School of Rad Tech (Private, Not-for-profit, United Methodist)
2001 Enrollment: n/a 712-328-6746
EQ School of Hair Design (Private, For-profit)
2001 Enrollment: 45 712-328-2613

Housing: Homeownership rate: 65.1% (2000); Median home value: $78,200 (2000); Median rent: $463 per month (2000); Median age of housing: 43 years (2000).
Hospitals: Alegent Mercy Hospital (300 beds); Jennie Edmundson Memorial Hospital (255 beds)
Safety: Violent crime rate: 78.3 per 10,000 population; Property crime rate: 919.9 per 10,000 population (2001).
Newspapers: Council Bluffs Shopper's Bulletin (1 x week); Daily Nonpareil (7 x week)
Transportation: Commute to work: 94.4% car, 0.7% public transportation, 2.1% walk, 2.0% work from home (2000); Travel time to work: 40.2% less than 15 minutes, 45.3% 15 to 30 minutes, 10.8% 30 to 45 minutes, 1.4% 45 to 60 minutes, 2.4% 60 minutes or more (2000)
Airports: Council Bluffs Municipal
Additional Information Contacts
Council Bluffs Chamber of Commerce 712-325-1000
Southwest Iowa Association of Realtors 712-323-3478

CRESCENT (city). Covers a land area of 1.258 square miles and a water area of 0 square miles. Located at 41.36° N. Lat.; 95.85° W. Long.
History: Crescent was formerly known as Crescent City, a name suggested by the shape of the bluffs rising above the town site. Crescent was first settled by Mormans in 1856.
Population: 537 (2000); Race: 100.0% White, 0.0% Black, 0.0% Asian, 0.0% American Indian and Alaska Native, 0.0% Hispanic of any race, 0.0% two or more races (2000); Density: 426.9 persons per square mile (2000); Age: 21.3% under 18, 13.7% over 64 (2000); Marriage status: 16.8% never married, 69.5% now married, 6.5% widowed, 7.2% divorced (2000); Foreign born: 0.0% (2000); Ancestry (includes multiple ancestries): 40.6% German, 15.4% English, 10.3% Irish, 9.7% Danish, 6.5% French (except Basque) (2000).
Economy: Employment by occupation: 12.1% management, 13.0% professional, 15.8% services, 29.5% sales, 0.0% farming, 11.5% construction, 18.0% production (2000).
Income: Per capita income: $24,548 (2000); Median household income: $60,000 (2000); Poverty rate: 2.5% (2000).
Taxes: Total city taxes per capita: $104 (1997); City property taxes per capita: $19 (1997).
Education: High school graduation rate: 84.2% (2000); College graduation rate: 15.5% (2000).
Housing: Homeownership rate: 91.6% (2000); Median home value: $102,900 (2000); Median rent: $325 per month (2000); Median age of housing: 31 years (2000).
Transportation: Commute to work: 94.1% car, 0.0% public transportation, 2.5% walk, 3.4% work from home (2000); Travel time to work: 20.8% less than 15 minutes, 65.5% 15 to 30 minutes, 11.2% 30 to 45 minutes, 0.0% 45 to 60 minutes, 2.6% 60 minutes or more (2000)

HANCOCK (city). Covers a land area of 0.747 square miles and a water area of 0.025 square miles. Located at 41.39° N. Lat.; 95.36° W. Long. Elevation is 1,113 feet.
History: Hancock was platted in 1880 when the railroad was extended from Avoca, but settlers had arrived here in 1852.
Population: 207 (2000); Race: 98.3% White, 0.0% Black, 0.0% Asian, 0.0% American Indian and Alaska Native, 4.2% Hispanic of any race, 0.0% two or more races (2000); Density: 277.1 persons per square mile (2000); Age: 18.2% under 18, 12.3% over 64 (2000); Marriage status: 23.5% never married, 57.4% now married, 7.8% widowed, 11.3% divorced (2000); Foreign born: 1.7% (2000); Ancestry (includes multiple ancestries): 32.6% German, 14.8% United States or American, 11.4% Irish, 7.6% French (except Basque), 6.8% Danish (2000).
Economy: Employment by occupation: 9.9% management, 6.3% professional, 19.0% services, 21.1% sales, 0.0% farming, 12.7% construction, 31.0% production (2000).
Income: Per capita income: $17,200 (2000); Median household income: $33,056 (2000); Poverty rate: 2.5% (2000).

Taxes: Total city taxes per capita: $218 (1997); City property taxes per capita: $218 (1997).
Education: High school graduation rate: 89.2% (2000); College graduation rate: 13.9% (2000).
Housing: Homeownership rate: 79.4% (2000); Median home value: $46,500 (2000); Median rent: $213 per month (2000); Median age of housing: 60+ years (2000).
Transportation: Commute to work: 94.4% car, 0.0% public transportation, 4.2% walk, 1.4% work from home (2000); Travel time to work: 57.1% less than 15 minutes, 10.7% 15 to 30 minutes, 16.4% 30 to 45 minutes, 10.7% 45 to 60 minutes, 5.0% 60 minutes or more (2000)

HONEY CREEK (unincorporated postal area, zip code 51542). Covers a land area of 35.467 square miles and a water area of 0.047 square miles. Located at 41.42° N. Lat.; 95.84° W. Long.
History: Honey Creek, named for a nearby stream, was settled by Mormans who were members of the group driven out of Nauvoo, Illinois, in 1846.
Population: 916 (2000); Race: 98.5% White, 0.0% Black, 0.0% Asian, 0.0% American Indian and Alaska Native, 0.0% Hispanic of any race, 1.5% two or more races (2000); Density: 25.8 persons per square mile (2000); Age: 18.5% under 18, 10.1% over 64 (2000); Marriage status: 15.5% never married, 73.0% now married, 1.9% widowed, 9.5% divorced (2000); Foreign born: 0.0% (2000); Ancestry (includes multiple ancestries): 39.2% German, 18.8% English, 15.4% Irish, 9.1% Danish, 6.5% Other groups (2000).
Economy: Employment by occupation: 20.9% management, 17.4% professional, 9.2% services, 24.5% sales, 0.0% farming, 10.0% construction, 18.0% production (2000).
Income: Per capita income: $25,621 (2000); Median household income: $52,361 (2000); Poverty rate: 4.0% (2000).
Education: High school graduation rate: 91.2% (2000); College graduation rate: 20.5% (2000).
Housing: Homeownership rate: 90.8% (2000); Median home value: $141,600 (2000); Median rent: $234 per month (2000); Median age of housing: 25 years (2000).
Transportation: Commute to work: 95.8% car, 0.0% public transportation, 1.1% walk, 3.1% work from home (2000); Travel time to work: 11.9% less than 15 minutes, 49.4% 15 to 30 minutes, 33.8% 30 to 45 minutes, 2.4% 45 to 60 minutes, 2.6% 60 minutes or more (2000)

MACEDONIA (city). Covers a land area of 0.341 square miles and a water area of 0 square miles. Located at 41.19° N. Lat.; 95.42° W. Long. Elevation is 1,107 feet.
History: Macedonia was founded in 1880 along the old Pioneer Trail.
Population: 325 (2000); Race: 99.1% White, 0.0% Black, 0.0% Asian, 0.0% American Indian and Alaska Native, 0.3% Hispanic of any race, 0.9% two or more races (2000); Density: 951.9 persons per square mile (2000); Age: 30.9% under 18, 14.4% over 64 (2000); Marriage status: 29.3% never married, 54.8% now married, 6.5% widowed, 9.5% divorced (2000); Foreign born: 0.6% (2000); Ancestry (includes multiple ancestries): 27.6% German, 20.0% Irish, 19.1% English, 12.6% United States or American, 6.8% Polish (2000).
Economy: Single-family building permits issued: 0 (2001) / 2 (2000); Multi-family building permits issued: 0 (2001) / 0 (2000); Employment by occupation: 10.8% management, 18.7% professional, 15.1% services, 24.7% sales, 0.0% farming, 10.2% construction, 20.5% production (2000).
Income: Per capita income: $14,189 (2000); Median household income: $32,813 (2000); Poverty rate: 14.5% (2000).
Taxes: Total city taxes per capita: $210 (1997); City property taxes per capita: $122 (1997).
Education: High school graduation rate: 86.5% (2000); College graduation rate: 20.3% (2000).
Housing: Homeownership rate: 77.0% (2000); Median home value: $62,900 (2000); Median rent: $248 per month (2000); Median age of housing: 60+ years (2000).
Transportation: Commute to work: 95.1% car, 0.0% public transportation, 2.5% walk, 2.5% work from home (2000); Travel time to work: 19.6% less than 15 minutes, 12.7% 15 to 30 minutes, 37.3% 30 to 45 minutes, 21.5% 45 to 60 minutes, 8.9% 60 minutes or more (2000)

MCCLELLAND (city). Covers a land area of 0.161 square miles and a water area of 0 square miles. Located at 41.32° N. Lat.; 95.68° W. Long. Elevation is 1,245 feet.
History: McClelland was established in 1902 when the Chicago Great Western Railroad came through. Land for the town was provided by Henry McClelland.
Population: 129 (2000); Race: 100.0% White, 0.0% Black, 0.0% Asian, 0.0% American Indian and Alaska Native, 0.0% Hispanic of any race, 0.0% two or more races (2000); Density: 803.7 persons per square mile (2000); Age: 18.0% under 18, 5.5% over 64 (2000); Marriage status: 23.5% never married, 47.0% now married, 5.2% widowed, 24.3% divorced (2000); Foreign born: 0.0% (2000); Ancestry (includes multiple ancestries): 46.1% German, 17.2% English, 16.4% Irish, 14.8% Danish, 14.8% Swedish (2000).
Economy: Employment by occupation: 18.5% management, 9.9% professional, 8.6% services, 33.3% sales, 0.0% farming, 13.6% construction, 16.0% production (2000).
Income: Per capita income: $22,155 (2000); Median household income: $41,625 (2000); Poverty rate: 2.3% (2000).
Taxes: Total city taxes per capita: $150 (1997); City property taxes per capita: $75 (1997).
Education: High school graduation rate: 86.7% (2000); College graduation rate: 13.3% (2000).
Housing: Homeownership rate: 74.5% (2000); Median home value: $93,000 (2000); Median rent: $363 per month (2000); Median age of housing: 51 years (2000).
Transportation: Commute to work: 100.0% car, 0.0% public transportation, 0.0% walk, 0.0% work from home (2000); Travel time to work: 23.5% less than 15 minutes, 19.8% 15 to 30 minutes, 46.9% 30 to 45 minutes, 2.5% 45 to 60 minutes, 7.4% 60 minutes or more (2000)

MINDEN (city). Covers a land area of 0.352 square miles and a water area of 0 square miles. Located at 41.46° N. Lat.; 95.54° W. Long. Elevation is 1,185 feet.
History: Minden was named by German settlers for a town in their former homeland.
Population: 564 (2000); Race: 100.0% White, 0.0% Black, 0.0% Asian, 0.0% American Indian and Alaska Native, 0.0% Hispanic of any race, 0.0% two or more races (2000); Density: 1,603.3 persons per square mile (2000); Age: 26.5% under 18, 14.8% over 64 (2000); Marriage status: 21.2% never married, 62.3% now married, 8.7% widowed, 7.8% divorced (2000); Foreign born: 0.0% (2000); Ancestry (includes multiple ancestries): 54.3% German, 14.1% Irish, 9.0% English, 8.4% Danish, 5.3% Czech (2000).
Economy: Single-family building permits issued: 0 (2001) / 6 (2000); Multi-family building permits issued: 0 (2001) / 0 (2000); Employment by occupation: 13.0% management, 16.3% professional, 10.0% services, 30.6% sales, 0.0% farming, 11.3% construction, 18.9% production (2000).
Income: Per capita income: $19,048 (2000); Median household income: $42,054 (2000); Poverty rate: 5.9% (2000).
Taxes: Total city taxes per capita: $233 (1997); City property taxes per capita: $147 (1997).
Education: High school graduation rate: 87.4% (2000); College graduation rate: 19.7% (2000).
Housing: Homeownership rate: 81.3% (2000); Median home value: $97,000 (2000); Median rent: $228 per month (2000); Median age of housing: 38 years (2000).
Transportation: Commute to work: 98.7% car, 0.0% public transportation, 1.3% walk, 0.0% work from home (2000); Travel time to work: 23.6% less than 15 minutes, 21.5% 15 to 30 minutes, 30.3% 30 to 45 minutes, 16.5% 45 to 60 minutes, 8.1% 60 minutes or more (2000)

NEOLA (city). Covers a land area of 0.405 square miles and a water area of 0 square miles. Located at 41.45° N. Lat.; 95.61° W. Long. Elevation is 1,098 feet.
Population: 845 (2000); Race: 98.8% White, 0.2% Black, 0.0% Asian, 0.2% American Indian and Alaska Native, 0.2% Hispanic of any race, 0.7% two or more races (2000); Density: 2,087.9 persons per square mile (2000); Age: 30.1% under 18, 12.1% over 64 (2000); Marriage status: 26.3% never married, 59.6% now married, 6.4% widowed, 7.7% divorced (2000); Foreign born: 0.0% (2000); Ancestry (includes multiple ancestries): 50.1% German, 19.8% Irish, 10.5% English, 4.9% United States or American, 4.5% Danish (2000).
Economy: In corn, wheat, livestock area. Single-family building permits issued: 1 (2001) / 2 (2000); Multi-family building permits issued: 0 (2001) / 0 (2000); Employment by occupation: 8.7% management, 19.5% professional, 15.1% services, 26.4% sales, 1.6% farming, 12.2% construction, 16.5% production (2000).
Income: Per capita income: $17,737 (2000); Median household income: $47,500 (2000); Poverty rate: 7.3% (2000).
Taxes: Total city taxes per capita: $177 (1997); City property taxes per capita: $90 (1997).
Education: High school graduation rate: 93.2% (2000); College graduation rate: 13.2% (2000).

School District(s)

Tri-Center Community School District (PK-12)
2000 Enrollment: 805 712-485-2257

Housing: Homeownership rate: 76.0% (2000); Median home value: $86,500 (2000); Median rent: $364 per month (2000); Median age of housing: 60+ years (2000).

Newspapers: Gazette (1 x week)

Transportation: Commute to work: 94.9% car, 0.5% public transportation, 2.1% walk, 2.5% work from home (2000); Travel time to work: 23.5% less than 15 minutes, 25.1% 15 to 30 minutes, 36.0% 30 to 45 minutes, 11.8% 45 to 60 minutes, 3.6% 60 minutes or more (2000)

OAKLAND (city). Covers a land area of 1.507 square miles and a water area of 0.016 square miles. Located at 41.30° N. Lat.; 95.39° W. Long. Elevation is 1,103 feet.

History: Oakland was first known as Big Grove, because of the oak trees that grew in abundance around the site.

Population: 1,487 (2000); Race: 97.5% White, 0.9% Black, 0.3% Asian, 0.4% American Indian and Alaska Native, 0.1% Hispanic of any race, 0.9% two or more races (2000); Density: 986.7 persons per square mile (2000); Age: 24.6% under 18, 22.3% over 64 (2000); Marriage status: 18.3% never married, 63.8% now married, 10.2% widowed, 7.8% divorced (2000); Foreign born: 1.4% (2000); Ancestry (includes multiple ancestries): 32.9% German, 11.9% Irish, 9.9% English, 7.4% United States or American, 4.8% Other groups (2000).

Economy: Single-family building permits issued: 3 (2001) / 5 (2000); Multi-family building permits issued: 0 (2001) / 0 (2000); Employment by occupation: 15.0% management, 12.0% professional, 13.5% services, 24.6% sales, 1.0% farming, 13.3% construction, 20.5% production (2000).

Income: Per capita income: $19,205 (2000); Median household income: $37,961 (2000); Poverty rate: 6.1% (2000).

Taxes: Total city taxes per capita: $187 (1997); City property taxes per capita: $104 (1997).

Education: High school graduation rate: 86.9% (2000); College graduation rate: 13.0% (2000).

Housing: Homeownership rate: 80.4% (2000); Median home value: $76,800 (2000); Median rent: $351 per month (2000); Median age of housing: 51 years (2000).

Newspapers: The Herald (1 x week)

Transportation: Commute to work: 94.4% car, 0.0% public transportation, 2.6% walk, 2.6% work from home (2000); Travel time to work: 41.2% less than 15 minutes, 10.7% 15 to 30 minutes, 25.3% 30 to 45 minutes, 16.7% 45 to 60 minutes, 6.1% 60 minutes or more (2000)

TREYNOR (city). Covers a land area of 0.586 square miles and a water area of 0 square miles. Located at 41.23° N. Lat.; 95.60° W. Long. Elevation is 1,210 feet.

History: Treynor was named for the postmaster in Council Bluffs in hopes he would approve a post office for Treynor.

Population: 950 (2000); Race: 99.3% White, 0.0% Black, 0.5% Asian, 0.0% American Indian and Alaska Native, 0.0% Hispanic of any race, 0.2% two or more races (2000); Density: 1,620.1 persons per square mile (2000); Age: 30.0% under 18, 14.3% over 64 (2000); Marriage status: 16.9% never married, 64.9% now married, 11.2% widowed, 6.9% divorced (2000); Foreign born: 0.2% (2000); Ancestry (includes multiple ancestries): 54.3% German, 15.6% Irish, 11.2% English, 8.8% Danish, 5.3% United States or American (2000).

Economy: Single-family building permits issued: 1 (2001) / 1 (2000); Multi-family building permits issued: 0 (2001) / 0 (2000); Employment by occupation: 15.6% management, 16.5% professional, 10.1% services, 35.5% sales, 1.1% farming, 7.8% construction, 13.5% production (2000).

Income: Per capita income: $22,118 (2000); Median household income: $56,696 (2000); Poverty rate: 2.7% (2000).

Taxes: Total city taxes per capita: $286 (1997); City property taxes per capita: $232 (1997).

Education: High school graduation rate: 90.2% (2000); College graduation rate: 23.7% (2000).

School District(s)

Treynor Community School District (KG-12)
2000 Enrollment: 583 712-487-3414

Housing: Homeownership rate: 79.9% (2000); Median home value: $108,100 (2000); Median rent: $407 per month (2000); Median age of housing: 28 years (2000).

Transportation: Commute to work: 94.8% car, 0.0% public transportation, 1.0% walk, 4.2% work from home (2000); Travel time to work: 21.1% less than 15 minutes, 39.0% 15 to 30 minutes, 30.6% 30 to 45 minutes, 7.4% 45 to 60 minutes, 1.8% 60 minutes or more (2000)

UNDERWOOD (city). Covers a land area of 0.365 square miles and a water area of 0 square miles. Located at 41.38° N. Lat.; 95.67° W. Long.

History: Underwood is believed to be named for the Chicago, Milwaukee & St. Paul Railroad engineer who brought the first train to town.

Population: 688 (2000); Race: 99.3% White, 0.0% Black, 0.0% Asian, 0.7% American Indian and Alaska Native, 0.6% Hispanic of any race, 0.0% two or more races (2000); Density: 1,886.8 persons per square mile (2000); Age: 30.5% under 18, 14.8% over 64 (2000); Marriage status: 24.9% never married, 57.1% now married, 10.5% widowed, 7.6% divorced (2000); Foreign born: 0.9% (2000); Ancestry (includes multiple ancestries): 48.7% German, 16.4% Irish, 12.9% Danish, 10.1% English, 6.7% Norwegian (2000).

Economy: Single-family building permits issued: 10 (2001) / 5 (2000); Multi-family building permits issued: 4 (2001) / 0 (2000); Employment by occupation: 12.2% management, 17.1% professional, 16.3% services, 27.1% sales, 0.0% farming, 12.7% construction, 14.6% production (2000).

Income: Per capita income: $17,953 (2000); Median household income: $42,143 (2000); Poverty rate: 5.4% (2000).

Taxes: Total city taxes per capita: $289 (1997); City property taxes per capita: $279 (1997).

Education: High school graduation rate: 86.1% (2000); College graduation rate: 15.4% (2000).

School District(s)

Underwood Community School District (PK-12)
2000 Enrollment: 751 712-566-2332

Housing: Homeownership rate: 74.6% (2000); Median home value: $95,900 (2000); Median rent: $362 per month (2000); Median age of housing: 29 years (2000).

Transportation: Commute to work: 93.0% car, 0.0% public transportation, 3.1% walk, 3.3% work from home (2000); Travel time to work: 26.5% less than 15 minutes, 36.9% 15 to 30 minutes, 30.5% 30 to 45 minutes, 4.9% 45 to 60 minutes, 1.2% 60 minutes or more (2000)

WALNUT (city). Covers a land area of 2.144 square miles and a water area of 0 square miles. Located at 41.48° N. Lat.; 95.22° W. Long. Elevation is 1,293 feet.

History: Walnut was incorporated in 1877. It was named for trees on the nearby Walnut Creek.

Population: 778 (2000); Race: 98.5% White, 0.5% Black, 0.4% Asian, 0.4% American Indian and Alaska Native, 0.3% Hispanic of any race, 0.3% two or more races (2000); Density: 362.8 persons per square mile (2000); Age: 25.0% under 18, 19.7% over 64 (2000); Marriage status: 19.5% never married, 63.5% now married, 10.2% widowed, 6.8% divorced (2000); Foreign born: 1.3% (2000); Ancestry (includes multiple ancestries): 42.9% German, 13.2% Irish, 8.2% Danish, 6.9% English, 5.3% Other groups (2000).

Economy: Employment by occupation: 12.7% management, 10.3% professional, 20.6% services, 28.8% sales, 0.5% farming, 12.0% construction, 15.1% production (2000).

Income: Per capita income: $16,489 (2000); Median household income: $36,154 (2000); Poverty rate: 8.5% (2000).

Taxes: Total city taxes per capita: $226 (1997); City property taxes per capita: $140 (1997).

Education: High school graduation rate: 86.8% (2000); College graduation rate: 12.1% (2000).

School District(s)

Walnut Community School District (PK-12)
2000 Enrollment: 292 712-784-2251

Housing: Homeownership rate: 81.3% (2000); Median home value: $66,900 (2000); Median rent: $190 per month (2000); Median age of housing: 60+ years (2000).

Newspapers: The Walnut Bureau (1 x week)

Transportation: Commute to work: 86.2% car, 0.0% public transportation, 8.2% walk, 4.1% work from home (2000); Travel time to work: 51.5% less than 15 minutes, 21.7% 15 to 30 minutes, 5.8% 30 to 45 minutes, 4.8% 45 to 60 minutes, 16.2% 60 minutes or more (2000)

Additional Information Contacts

Walnut Chamber of Commerce 712-784-2100

Poweshiek County

Located in central Iowa; prairie area, drained by forks of the English River. Covers a land area of 585.00 square miles, a water area of 1.10 square miles, and is located in the Central Time Zone. The county government was organized in 1843. County seat is Montezuma.

Weather Station: Grinnell 3 SW — Elevation: 902 feet

	Jan	Feb	Mar	Apr	May	Jun	Jul	Aug	Sep	Oct	Nov	Dec
High	27	33	45	59	70	80	84	82	74	62	46	32
Low	7	13	24	35	46	56	61	58	49	37	26	14
Precip	1.2	1.3	2.5	3.6	4.4	4.5	4.1	4.6	3.7	2.9	2.4	1.4
Snow	8.3	6.7	4.1	1.6	tr	0.0	0.0	0.0	0.0	0.5	2.8	6.3

High and Low temperatures in degrees Fahrenheit; Precipitation and Snow in inches

Population: 18,815 (2000); Race: 97.0% White, 0.4% Black, 1.0% Asian, 0.3% American Indian and Alaska Native, 1.2% Hispanic of any race, 1.1% two or more races (2000); Density: 32.2 persons per square mile (2000); Age: 22.6% under 18, 17.6% over 64 (2000).
Religion: Five largest groups: 12.5% The United Methodist Church, 11.9% Catholic Church, 7.0% Christian Churches and Churches of Christ, 4.4% Evangelical Lutheran Church in America, 4.1% Presbyterian Church (U.S.A.) (2000).
Economy: Unemployment rate: 4.1% (11/2002); Total civilian labor force: 9,885 (11/2002); Leading industries: 20.3% manufacturing; 11.9% health care and social assistance; 10.9% retail trade (2000); Companies that employ more than 1,000 persons: 1 (2000); Companies that employ more than 100 persons: 16 (2000); Farms: 934 totaling 335,296 acres (1997); Minority business ownership rate: 0.0% (1997); Women business ownership rate: 17.9% (1997); Retail sales per capita: $10,065 (1997). Single-family building permits issued: 49 (2001) / 60 (2000); Multi-family building permits issued: 0 (2001) / 27 (2000).
Income: Per capita income: $18,629 (2000); Median household income: $37,836 (2000); Poverty rate: 9.8% (2000); Bankruptcy rate: 2.59% (2001).
Taxes: Total county taxes per capita: $181 (2000); County property taxes per capita: $174 (2000).
Education: High school graduation rate: 86.7% (2000); College graduation rate: 18.5% (2000).
Housing: Homeownership rate: 71.9% (2000); Median home value: $81,600 (2000); Median rent: $334 per month (2000); Median age of housing: 39 years (2000).
Health: Birth rate: 103.6 per 10,000 population (1998); Age adjusted death rate: 85.0 per 10,000 population (1999); Age adjusted cancer mortality rate: 212.0 deaths per 100,000 population (1999). Number of physicians: 12.2 per 10,000 population (1999); Number of hospital beds: 25.0 per 10,000 population (1999).
Elections: 2000 Presidential election results: 47.0% Gore, 49.0% Bush, 3.2% Nader, 0.4% Buchanan

Additional Information Contacts
Poweshiek County Government Offices 641-623-5443
Brooklyn Chamber of Commerce 641-522-5300
Grinnell Chamber of Commerce 641-236-6555
Poweshiek County Board of Realtors 641-236-7557

Poweshiek County Communities

BROOKLYN (city). Covers a land area of 1.196 square miles and a water area of 0 square miles. Located at 41.73° N. Lat.; 92.44° W. Long. Elevation is 848 feet.
History: Brooklyn was named because of its site between two creeks (or brooks). The original form of the name, Brookland, later became Brooklyn.
Population: 1,367 (2000); Race: 99.2% White, 0.1% Black, 0.0% Asian, 0.0% American Indian and Alaska Native, 0.5% Hispanic of any race, 0.7% two or more races (2000); Density: 1,142.8 persons per square mile (2000); Age: 23.3% under 18, 23.5% over 64 (2000); Marriage status: 25.4% never married, 51.9% now married, 10.9% widowed, 11.8% divorced (2000); Foreign born: 0.3% (2000); Ancestry (includes multiple ancestries): 38.9% German, 17.4% Irish, 6.8% English, 5.8% Belgian, 5.7% United States or American (2000).
Economy: Single-family building permits issued: 7 (2001) / 2 (2000); Multi-family building permits issued: 0 (2001) / 8 (2000); Employment by occupation: 6.2% management, 13.0% professional, 13.5% services, 28.6% sales, 0.1% farming, 11.9% construction, 26.7% production (2000).
Income: Per capita income: $18,315 (2000); Median household income: $34,583 (2000); Poverty rate: 6.2% (2000).
Taxes: Total city taxes per capita: $195 (1997); City property taxes per capita: $193 (1997).
Education: High school graduation rate: 84.7% (2000); College graduation rate: 13.7% (2000).

School District(s)
Brooklyn-Guernsey-Malcom Community School District (PK-12)
2000 Enrollment: 666 641-522-7058
Housing: Homeownership rate: 70.4% (2000); Median home value: $69,400 (2000); Median rent: $331 per month (2000); Median age of housing: 48 years (2000).
Newspapers: Brooklyn Chronicle (1 x week)
Transportation: Commute to work: 89.2% car, 0.0% public transportation, 5.0% walk, 4.1% work from home (2000); Travel time to work: 50.3% less than 15 minutes, 32.1% 15 to 30 minutes, 11.1% 30 to 45 minutes, 2.8% 45 to 60 minutes, 3.6% 60 minutes or more (2000)

Additional Information Contacts
Brooklyn Chamber of Commerce 641-522-5300

DEEP RIVER (city). Covers a land area of 0.423 square miles and a water area of 0 square miles. Located at 41.58° N. Lat.; 92.37° W. Long. Elevation is 862 feet.
History: Deep River was originally settled by people of Irish descent.
Population: 288 (2000); Race: 100.0% White, 0.0% Black, 0.0% Asian, 0.0% American Indian and Alaska Native, 0.0% Hispanic of any race, 0.0% two or more races (2000); Density: 681.1 persons per square mile (2000); Age: 29.5% under 18, 13.2% over 64 (2000); Marriage status: 14.3% never married, 65.2% now married, 12.1% widowed, 8.5% divorced (2000); Foreign born: 0.0% (2000); Ancestry (includes multiple ancestries): 37.1% German, 14.6% Irish, 7.3% Dutch, 7.0% United States or American, 5.3% French (except Basque) (2000).
Economy: Employment by occupation: 7.9% management, 3.3% professional, 18.4% services, 15.1% sales, 2.6% farming, 17.8% construction, 34.9% production (2000).
Income: Per capita income: $16,437 (2000); Median household income: $33,438 (2000); Poverty rate: 5.6% (2000).
Taxes: Total city taxes per capita: $71 (1997); City property taxes per capita: $71 (1997).
Education: High school graduation rate: 83.2% (2000); College graduation rate: 4.6% (2000).
Housing: Homeownership rate: 82.0% (2000); Median home value: $40,300 (2000); Median rent: $232 per month (2000); Median age of housing: 60+ years (2000).
Transportation: Commute to work: 90.7% car, 0.0% public transportation, 4.6% walk, 4.6% work from home (2000); Travel time to work: 27.1% less than 15 minutes, 34.0% 15 to 30 minutes, 20.1% 30 to 45 minutes, 8.3% 45 to 60 minutes, 10.4% 60 minutes or more (2000)

GRINNELL (city). Covers a land area of 4.987 square miles and a water area of 0.036 square miles. Located at 41.74° N. Lat.; 92.72° W. Long. Elevation is 1,011 feet.
History: When Josiah Bushnell Grinnell, a Congregational minister in New York City, went to Horace Greeley for advice, Greeley made his much-quoted statement: "Go west, young man, go west and grow up with the country!" In 1854, Grinnell, accompanied by Dr. Thomas Holyoke of Scarsport, Maine, and the Rev. Homer Hamlin of Hudson, Ohio, came west and founded the settlement that became Grinnell.
Population: 9,105 (2000); Race: 95.4% White, 0.7% Black, 1.6% Asian, 0.5% American Indian and Alaska Native, 1.6% Hispanic of any race, 1.6% two or more races (2000); Density: 1,825.7 persons per square mile (2000); Age: 20.6% under 18, 18.2% over 64 (2000); Marriage status: 33.9% never married, 47.3% now married, 8.8% widowed, 10.0% divorced (2000); Foreign born: 2.9% (2000); Ancestry (includes multiple ancestries): 27.0% German, 15.1% Irish, 14.1% English, 8.7% United States or American, 6.9% Other groups (2000).
Economy: Single-family building permits issued: 9 (2001) / 17 (2000); Multi-family building permits issued: 0 (2001) / 19 (2000); Employment by occupation: 12.8% management, 20.6% professional, 20.1% services, 21.5% sales, 0.2% farming, 5.4% construction, 19.5% production (2000).
Income: Per capita income: $17,939 (2000); Median household income: $35,625 (2000); Poverty rate: 13.3% (2000).
Taxes: Total city taxes per capita: $316 (2000); City property taxes per capita: $296 (2000).
Education: High school graduation rate: 85.4% (2000); College graduation rate: 24.2% (2000).

School District(s)
Grinnell-Newburg Community School District (PK-12)
2000 Enrollment: 1,797 641-236-2700

Four-year College(s)

Grinnell College (Private, Not-for-profit)
2001 Enrollment: 1,338 641-269-4000
2001 Tuition: In-state $21,700; Out-of-state $21,700

Housing: Homeownership rate: 65.4% (2000); Median home value: $88,200 (2000); Median rent: $357 per month (2000); Median age of housing: 44 years (2000).
Hospitals: Grinnell Regional Medical Center (81 beds)
Safety: Violent crime rate: 19.8 per 10,000 population; Property crime rate: 282.6 per 10,000 population (2001).
Newspapers: Grinnell Herald-Register (2 x week)
Transportation: Commute to work: 74.9% car, 0.2% public transportation, 19.3% walk, 2.1% work from home (2000); Travel time to work: 80.1% less than 15 minutes, 9.4% 15 to 30 minutes, 4.2% 30 to 45 minutes, 2.7% 45 to 60 minutes, 3.6% 60 minutes or more (2000)
Additional Information Contacts
Grinnell Chamber of Commerce 641-236-6555
Poweshiek County Board of Realtors 641-236-7557

GUERNSEY (city). Covers a land area of 0.184 square miles and a water area of 0 square miles. Located at 41.65° N. Lat.; 92.34° W. Long. Elevation is 834 feet.
History: Guernsey was settled by migrants from Guernsey County, Ohio, who transferred the name of their former home.
Population: 70 (2000); Race: 98.1% White, 0.0% Black, 0.0% Asian, 0.0% American Indian and Alaska Native, 1.9% Hispanic of any race, 0.0% two or more races (2000); Density: 379.8 persons per square mile (2000); Age: 13.5% under 18, 11.5% over 64 (2000); Marriage status: 24.4% never married, 62.2% now married, 8.9% widowed, 4.4% divorced (2000); Foreign born: 1.9% (2000); Ancestry (includes multiple ancestries): 40.4% German, 15.4% Belgian, 13.5% United States or American, 9.6% Irish, 3.8% French (except Basque) (2000).
Economy: Employment by occupation: 5.9% management, 5.9% professional, 29.4% services, 20.6% sales, 0.0% farming, 8.8% construction, 29.4% production (2000).
Income: Per capita income: $17,727 (2000); Median household income: $36,250 (2000); Poverty rate: 0.0% (2000).
Taxes: Total city taxes per capita: $130 (1997); City property taxes per capita: $130 (1997).
Education: High school graduation rate: 82.1% (2000); College graduation rate: 5.1% (2000).
Housing: Homeownership rate: 77.8% (2000); Median home value: $72,500 (2000); Median rent: $175 per month (2000); Median age of housing: 60+ years (2000).
Transportation: Commute to work: 100.0% car, 0.0% public transportation, 0.0% walk, 0.0% work from home (2000); Travel time to work: 23.5% less than 15 minutes, 38.2% 15 to 30 minutes, 17.6% 30 to 45 minutes, 11.8% 45 to 60 minutes, 8.8% 60 minutes or more (2000)

HARTWICK (city). Covers a land area of 0.130 square miles and a water area of 0 square miles. Located at 41.78° N. Lat.; 92.34° W. Long. Elevation is 955 feet.
History: Hartwick was established as a station for the Chicago & North Western Railroad, and named by the railroad company.
Population: 83 (2000); Race: 100.0% White, 0.0% Black, 0.0% Asian, 0.0% American Indian and Alaska Native, 0.0% Hispanic of any race, 0.0% two or more races (2000); Density: 640.7 persons per square mile (2000); Age: 11.0% under 18, 28.8% over 64 (2000); Marriage status: 17.6% never married, 63.2% now married, 11.8% widowed, 7.4% divorced (2000); Foreign born: 0.0% (2000); Ancestry (includes multiple ancestries): 38.4% German, 19.2% United States or American, 9.6% English, 9.6% French (except Basque), 5.5% Norwegian (2000).
Economy: Employment by occupation: 0.0% management, 4.9% professional, 26.8% services, 22.0% sales, 9.8% farming, 7.3% construction, 29.3% production (2000).
Income: Per capita income: $18,830 (2000); Median household income: $36,250 (2000); Poverty rate: 2.7% (2000).
Taxes: Total city taxes per capita: $97 (1997); City property taxes per capita: $97 (1997).
Education: High school graduation rate: 83.9% (2000); College graduation rate: 10.7% (2000).
Housing: Homeownership rate: 94.3% (2000); Median home value: $54,100 (2000); Median rent: $375 per month (2000); Median age of housing: 60+ years (2000).
Transportation: Commute to work: 82.9% car, 0.0% public transportation, 14.6% walk, 0.0% work from home (2000); Travel time to work: 39.0% less than 15 minutes, 29.3% 15 to 30 minutes, 17.1% 30 to 45 minutes, 0.0% 45 to 60 minutes, 14.6% 60 minutes or more (2000)

MALCOM (city). Covers a land area of 0.612 square miles and a water area of 0 square miles. Located at 41.70° N. Lat.; 92.55° W. Long. Elevation is 892 feet.
History: The railroad established a station in Malcom in 1863. The town is believed to be named for a railroad surveyor.
Population: 352 (2000); Race: 100.0% White, 0.0% Black, 0.0% Asian, 0.0% American Indian and Alaska Native, 0.0% Hispanic of any race, 0.0% two or more races (2000); Density: 575.6 persons per square mile (2000); Age: 24.9% under 18, 15.6% over 64 (2000); Marriage status: 22.9% never married, 59.2% now married, 5.6% widowed, 12.3% divorced (2000); Foreign born: 0.0% (2000); Ancestry (includes multiple ancestries): 33.2% German, 13.1% Irish, 9.5% French (except Basque), 6.4% United States or American, 6.4% English (2000).
Economy: Single-family building permits issued: 1 (2001) / 0 (2000); Multi-family building permits issued: 0 (2001) / 0 (2000); Employment by occupation: 7.4% management, 7.4% professional, 16.7% services, 21.6% sales, 4.4% farming, 13.2% construction, 29.4% production (2000).
Income: Per capita income: $17,059 (2000); Median household income: $39,167 (2000); Poverty rate: 9.3% (2000).
Taxes: Total city taxes per capita: $130 (1997); City property taxes per capita: $128 (1997).
Education: High school graduation rate: 89.6% (2000); College graduation rate: 7.1% (2000).
Housing: Homeownership rate: 76.9% (2000); Median home value: $55,000 (2000); Median rent: $297 per month (2000); Median age of housing: 49 years (2000).
Transportation: Commute to work: 87.3% car, 0.0% public transportation, 1.0% walk, 9.8% work from home (2000); Travel time to work: 40.8% less than 15 minutes, 38.6% 15 to 30 minutes, 7.1% 30 to 45 minutes, 4.3% 45 to 60 minutes, 9.2% 60 minutes or more (2000)

MONTEZUMA (city). Covers a land area of 2.454 square miles and a water area of 0.013 square miles. Located at 41.58° N. Lat.; 92.52° W. Long. Elevation is 958 feet.
History: Montezuma was named in honor of the Aztec emperor of Mexico (1502-1520), whose romantic history caught the fancy of the town's early pioneers.
Population: 1,440 (2000); Race: 98.3% White, 0.0% Black, 1.0% Asian, 0.4% American Indian and Alaska Native, 1.0% Hispanic of any race, 0.3% two or more races (2000); Density: 586.9 persons per square mile (2000); Age: 23.3% under 18, 22.6% over 64 (2000); Marriage status: 19.7% never married, 58.5% now married, 11.1% widowed, 10.7% divorced (2000); Foreign born: 0.9% (2000); Ancestry (includes multiple ancestries): 23.2% German, 13.8% Irish, 10.3% United States or American, 9.3% English, 8.8% Dutch (2000).
Economy: Single-family building permits issued: 4 (2001) / 3 (2000); Multi-family building permits issued: 0 (2001) / 0 (2000); Employment by occupation: 10.1% management, 13.0% professional, 15.0% services, 25.7% sales, 1.9% farming, 10.5% construction, 23.8% production (2000).
Income: Per capita income: $17,806 (2000); Median household income: $35,820 (2000); Poverty rate: 6.4% (2000).
Taxes: Total city taxes per capita: $194 (1997); City property taxes per capita: $189 (1997).
Education: High school graduation rate: 85.9% (2000); College graduation rate: 13.5% (2000).

School District(s)

Montezuma Community School District (PK-12)
2000 Enrollment: 612 641-623-5121

Housing: Homeownership rate: 65.1% (2000); Median home value: $73,800 (2000); Median rent: $297 per month (2000); Median age of housing: 48 years (2000).
Newspapers: The Montezuma Republican (1 x week)
Transportation: Commute to work: 85.9% car, 0.3% public transportation, 6.4% walk, 5.0% work from home (2000); Travel time to work: 62.2% less than 15 minutes, 18.0% 15 to 30 minutes, 11.6% 30 to 45 minutes, 3.7% 45 to 60 minutes, 4.6% 60 minutes or more (2000)

SEARSBORO (city). Covers a land area of 0.395 square miles and a water area of 0 square miles. Located at 41.58° N. Lat.; 92.70° W. Long. Elevation is 806 feet.
History: Searsboro was platted by, and named for, R. Sears.
Population: 155 (2000); Race: 100.0% White, 0.0% Black, 0.0% Asian, 0.0% American Indian and Alaska Native, 0.0% Hispanic of any race, 0.0%

two or more races (2000); Density: 392.4 persons per square mile (2000); Age: 22.2% under 18, 22.2% over 64 (2000); Marriage status: 29.5% never married, 48.1% now married, 7.8% widowed, 14.7% divorced (2000); Foreign born: 0.0% (2000); Ancestry (includes multiple ancestries): 27.5% German, 11.8% English, 11.1% French (except Basque), 11.1% Dutch, 10.5% Scotch-Irish (2000).
Economy: Employment by occupation: 1.4% management, 5.5% professional, 20.5% services, 34.2% sales, 0.0% farming, 8.2% construction, 30.1% production (2000).
Income: Per capita income: $11,958 (2000); Median household income: $25,795 (2000); Poverty rate: 5.2% (2000).
Taxes: Total city taxes per capita: $121 (1997); City property taxes per capita: $115 (1997).
Education: High school graduation rate: 72.3% (2000); College graduation rate: 4.0% (2000).
Housing: Homeownership rate: 76.5% (2000); Median home value: $37,100 (2000); Median rent: $175 per month (2000); Median age of housing: 46 years (2000).
Transportation: Commute to work: 100.0% car, 0.0% public transportation, 0.0% walk, 0.0% work from home (2000); Travel time to work: 6.1% less than 15 minutes, 84.8% 15 to 30 minutes, 3.0% 30 to 45 minutes, 6.1% 45 to 60 minutes, 0.0% 60 minutes or more (2000)

Ringgold County

Located in southern Iowa; bounded on the south by Missouri; prairie area, drained by the Little Platte and Grand Rivers. Covers a land area of 537.70 square miles, a water area of 1.30 square miles, and is located in the Central Time Zone. The county government was organized in 1855. County seat is Mount Ayr.

Weather Station: Beaconsfield — Elevation: 1,197 feet

	Jan	Feb	Mar	Apr	May	Jun	Jul	Aug	Sep	Oct	Nov	Dec
High	30	37	49	62	72	81	86	84	76	64	48	35
Low	12	18	28	39	50	59	64	62	53	41	29	18
Precip	0.8	1.0	2.4	3.5	4.6	4.2	4.5	3.9	4.4	3.0	2.3	1.1
Snow	6.2	5.0	3.4	1.3	tr	0.0	0.0	0.0	0.0	0.5	2.4	5.3

High and Low temperatures in degrees Fahrenheit; Precipitation and Snow in inches

Weather Station: Mount Ayr 4 SW — Elevation: 1,240 feet

	Jan	Feb	Mar	Apr	May	Jun	Jul	Aug	Sep	Oct	Nov	Dec
High	31	37	49	62	72	81	85	83	76	65	48	36
Low	12	17	28	39	50	60	65	62	54	42	29	19
Precip	0.8	1.1	2.3	3.1	4.5	4.3	4.8	4.3	3.9	2.9	2.3	1.3
Snow	4.7	4.6	3.0	1.1	tr	0.0	0.0	0.0	0.0	0.4	1.2	3.6

High and Low temperatures in degrees Fahrenheit; Precipitation and Snow in inches

Population: 5,469 (2000); Race: 98.8% White, 0.1% Black, 0.3% Asian, 0.4% American Indian and Alaska Native, 0.3% Hispanic of any race, 0.3% two or more races (2000); Density: 10.2 persons per square mile (2000); Age: 24.0% under 18, 24.1% over 64 (2000).
Religion: Five largest groups: 18.3% The United Methodist Church, 13.8% Christian Church (Disciples of Christ), 4.2% American Baptist Churches in the USA, 3.3% Catholic Church, 3.0% Presbyterian Church (U.S.A.) (2000).
Economy: Unemployment rate: 3.0% (11/2002); Total civilian labor force: 2,661 (11/2002); Leading industries: 26.8% health care and social assistance; 20.7% manufacturing; 19.5% retail trade (2000); Companies that employ more than 1,000 persons: 0 (2000); Companies that employ more than 100 persons: 1 (2000); Farms: 671 totaling 263,753 acres (1997); Minority business ownership rate: 0.0% (1997); Women business ownership rate: 21.5% (1997); Retail sales per capita: $7,117 (1997). Single-family building permits issued: 8 (2001) / 3 (2000); Multi-family building permits issued: 0 (2001) / 0 (2000).
Income: Per capita income: $15,023 (2000); Median household income: $29,110 (2000); Poverty rate: 14.3% (2000); Bankruptcy rate: 2.98% (2001).
Taxes: Total county taxes per capita: $398 (1997); County property taxes per capita: $398 (1997).
Education: High school graduation rate: 82.8% (2000); College graduation rate: 13.4% (2000).
Housing: Homeownership rate: 75.5% (2000); Median home value: $45,000 (2000); Median rent: $231 per month (2000); Median age of housing: 51 years (2000).
Health: Birth rate: 85.9 per 10,000 population (1998); Age adjusted death rate: 82.5 per 10,000 population (1999); Age adjusted cancer mortality rate: 211.8 deaths per 100,000 population (1999). Number of physicians: 5.5 per 10,000 population (1999); Number of hospital beds: 65.8 per 10,000 population (1999).
Elections: 2000 Presidential election results: 46.3% Gore, 50.9% Bush, 1.8% Nader, 0.4% Buchanan
National and State Parks: Mount Ayr State Wildlife Area; Ringgold State Wildlife Area
Additional Information Contacts
Ringgold County Government Offices. 515-464-3234

Ringgold County Communities

BEACONSFIELD (city). Covers a land area of 0.722 square miles and a water area of 0 square miles. Located at 40.80° N. Lat.; 94.05° W. Long.
History: Beaconsfield was named for Lord Beaconsfield of England. The town was named by Pete McCavett, a relative of the Lord.
Population: 11 (2000); Race: 100.0% White, 0.0% Black, 0.0% Asian, 0.0% American Indian and Alaska Native, 0.0% Hispanic of any race, 0.0% two or more races (2000); Density: 15.2 persons per square mile (2000); Age: 0.0% under 18, 100.0% over 64 (2000); Marriage status: 0.0% never married, 80.0% now married, 20.0% widowed, 0.0% divorced (2000); Foreign born: 0.0% (2000); Ancestry (includes multiple ancestries): 30.0% English, 20.0% United States or American, 20.0% Irish, 10.0% German (2000).
Economy: Employment by occupation: 100.0% management, 0.0% professional, 0.0% services, 0.0% sales, 0.0% farming, 0.0% construction, 0.0% production (2000).
Income: Per capita income: $5,990 (2000); Median household income: $10,833 (2000); Poverty rate: 20.0% (2000).
Taxes: Total city taxes per capita: $34 (1997); City property taxes per capita: $34 (1997).
Education: High school graduation rate: 60.0% (2000); College graduation rate: 0.0% (2000).
Housing: Homeownership rate: 75.0% (2000); Median home value: $55,000 (2000); Median age of housing: 25 years (2000).
Transportation: Commute to work: 0.0% car, 0.0% public transportation, 100.0% walk, 0.0% work from home (2000); Travel time to work: 100.0% less than 15 minutes, 0.0% 15 to 30 minutes, 0.0% 30 to 45 minutes, 0.0% 45 to 60 minutes, 0.0% 60 minutes or more (2000)

BENTON (city). Covers a land area of 0.669 square miles and a water area of 0 square miles. Located at 40.70° N. Lat.; 94.35° W. Long. Elevation is 1,059 feet.
Population: 40 (2000); Race: 100.0% White, 0.0% Black, 0.0% Asian, 0.0% American Indian and Alaska Native, 0.0% Hispanic of any race, 0.0% two or more races (2000); Density: 59.8 persons per square mile (2000); Age: 3.2% under 18, 29.0% over 64 (2000); Marriage status: 13.3% never married, 76.7% now married, 0.0% widowed, 10.0% divorced (2000); Foreign born: 0.0% (2000); Ancestry (includes multiple ancestries): 35.5% Irish, 22.6% Scotch-Irish, 19.4% Dutch, 16.1% English, 6.5% Polish (2000).
Economy: Employment by occupation: 13.6% management, 22.7% professional, 31.8% services, 9.1% sales, 0.0% farming, 13.6% construction, 9.1% production (2000).
Income: Per capita income: $15,752 (2000); Median household income: $26,250 (2000); Poverty rate: 0.0% (2000).
Taxes: Total city taxes per capita: $385 (1997); City property taxes per capita: $385 (1997).
Education: High school graduation rate: 85.2% (2000); College graduation rate: 11.1% (2000).
Housing: Homeownership rate: 87.5% (2000); Median home value: $18,300 (2000); Median rent: $125 per month (2000); Median age of housing: 57 years (2000).
Transportation: Commute to work: 94.1% car, 0.0% public transportation, 5.9% walk, 0.0% work from home (2000); Travel time to work: 64.7% less than 15 minutes, 11.8% 15 to 30 minutes, 11.8% 30 to 45 minutes, 11.8% 45 to 60 minutes, 0.0% 60 minutes or more (2000)

DELPHOS (city). Covers a land area of 0.223 square miles and a water area of 0 square miles. Located at 40.66° N. Lat.; 94.34° W. Long.
History: After first being caled Borneo, Delphos was named Delphi, after the oracle in Greek history. The form of the name was changed to Delphos, which has the same meaning of "brother," because of a duplication with another Iowa place name.
Population: 25 (2000); Race: 100.0% White, 0.0% Black, 0.0% Asian, 0.0% American Indian and Alaska Native, 0.0% Hispanic of any race, 0.0% two or more races (2000); Density: 112.1 persons per square mile (2000); Age: 29.2% under 18, 12.5% over 64 (2000); Marriage status: 21.1% never

married, 78.9% now married, 0.0% widowed, 0.0% divorced (2000); Foreign born: 0.0% (2000); Ancestry (includes multiple ancestries): 50.0% United States or American (2000).
Economy: Employment by occupation: 28.6% management, 21.4% professional, 0.0% services, 14.3% sales, 7.1% farming, 14.3% construction, 14.3% production (2000).
Income: Per capita income: $13,925 (2000); Median household income: $33,125 (2000); Poverty rate: 0.0% (2000).
Taxes: Total city taxes per capita: $43 (1997); City property taxes per capita: $43 (1997).
Education: High school graduation rate: 93.3% (2000); College graduation rate: 0.0% (2000).
Housing: Homeownership rate: 100.0% (2000); Median home value: $23,800 (2000); Median age of housing: 60+ years (2000).
Transportation: Commute to work: 85.7% car, 0.0% public transportation, 0.0% walk, 14.3% work from home (2000); Travel time to work: 66.7% less than 15 minutes, 33.3% 15 to 30 minutes, 0.0% 30 to 45 minutes, 0.0% 45 to 60 minutes, 0.0% 60 minutes or more (2000)

DIAGONAL (city). Covers a land area of 0.908 square miles and a water area of 0 square miles. Located at 40.80° N. Lat.; 94.34° W. Long. Elevation is 1,089 feet.
History: Diagonal takes its name from the shortline railroad route from the northeast to the southwest of the state, called the Diagonal. The town was laid out in 1889 and named by surveyor Josiah Lateer.
Population: 312 (2000); Race: 99.7% White, 0.3% Black, 0.0% Asian, 0.0% American Indian and Alaska Native, 0.0% Hispanic of any race, 0.0% two or more races (2000); Density: 343.5 persons per square mile (2000); Age: 25.0% under 18, 14.8% over 64 (2000); Marriage status: 22.9% never married, 57.4% now married, 7.2% widowed, 12.4% divorced (2000); Foreign born: 1.0% (2000); Ancestry (includes multiple ancestries): 20.7% German, 18.8% Irish, 7.9% English, 7.2% United States or American, 5.9% Czech (2000).
Economy: Employment by occupation: 9.7% management, 9.0% professional, 7.6% services, 30.6% sales, 2.8% farming, 13.9% construction, 26.4% production (2000).
Income: Per capita income: $16,601 (2000); Median household income: $24,063 (2000); Poverty rate: 15.8% (2000).
Taxes: Total city taxes per capita: $101 (1997); City property taxes per capita: $101 (1997).
Education: High school graduation rate: 82.4% (2000); College graduation rate: 6.7% (2000).

School District(s)

Diagonal Community School District (PK-12)
2000 Enrollment: 109 641-734-5331

Housing: Homeownership rate: 77.5% (2000); Median home value: $19,700 (2000); Median rent: $207 per month (2000); Median age of housing: 60+ years (2000).
Newspapers: The Diagonal Progress (1 x week)
Transportation: Commute to work: 94.4% car, 0.0% public transportation, 5.6% walk, 0.0% work from home (2000); Travel time to work: 29.9% less than 15 minutes, 49.3% 15 to 30 minutes, 9.0% 30 to 45 minutes, 0.0% 45 to 60 minutes, 11.8% 60 minutes or more (2000)

ELLSTON (city). Covers a land area of 0.223 square miles and a water area of 0 square miles. Located at 40.84° N. Lat.; 94.10° W. Long. Elevation is 1,214 feet.
Population: 57 (2000); Race: 100.0% White, 0.0% Black, 0.0% Asian, 0.0% American Indian and Alaska Native, 0.0% Hispanic of any race, 0.0% two or more races (2000); Density: 255.5 persons per square mile (2000); Age: 26.3% under 18, 0.0% over 64 (2000); Marriage status: 23.0% never married, 57.4% now married, 0.0% widowed, 19.7% divorced (2000); Foreign born: 0.0% (2000); Ancestry (includes multiple ancestries): 71.3% German, 17.5% French (except Basque), 15.0% Dutch, 12.5% Irish, 12.5% Scottish (2000).
Economy: Livestock, grain. Employment by occupation: 23.1% management, 7.7% professional, 7.7% services, 15.4% sales, 9.6% farming, 23.1% construction, 13.5% production (2000).
Income: Per capita income: $10,345 (2000); Median household income: $35,625 (2000); Poverty rate: 17.5% (2000).
Taxes: Total city taxes per capita: $68 (1997); City property taxes per capita: $68 (1997).
Education: High school graduation rate: 95.8% (2000); College graduation rate: 10.4% (2000).
Housing: Homeownership rate: 88.5% (2000); Median home value: $13,200 (2000); Median age of housing: 60+ years (2000).
Transportation: Commute to work: 78.8% car, 0.0% public transportation, 7.7% walk, 3.8% work from home (2000); Travel time to work: 52.0% less than 15 minutes, 22.0% 15 to 30 minutes, 12.0% 30 to 45 minutes, 10.0% 45 to 60 minutes, 4.0% 60 minutes or more (2000)

KELLERTON (city). Covers a land area of 0.665 square miles and a water area of 0 square miles. Located at 40.71° N. Lat.; 94.05° W. Long. Elevation is 1,197 feet.
History: Kellerton was named for Judge Isaac W. Keller of Mount Ayr.
Population: 372 (2000); Race: 98.0% White, 0.6% Black, 0.0% Asian, 0.6% American Indian and Alaska Native, 0.0% Hispanic of any race, 0.9% two or more races (2000); Density: 559.2 persons per square mile (2000); Age: 34.6% under 18, 11.8% over 64 (2000); Marriage status: 28.7% never married, 50.7% now married, 9.6% widowed, 11.0% divorced (2000); Foreign born: 0.0% (2000); Ancestry (includes multiple ancestries): 17.9% German, 11.5% English, 9.8% Other groups, 7.8% Irish, 7.8% United States or American (2000).
Economy: Employment by occupation: 10.1% management, 13.8% professional, 14.5% services, 20.8% sales, 1.3% farming, 15.7% construction, 23.9% production (2000).
Income: Per capita income: $11,442 (2000); Median household income: $29,000 (2000); Poverty rate: 20.6% (2000).
Taxes: Total city taxes per capita: $75 (1997); City property taxes per capita: $75 (1997).
Education: High school graduation rate: 79.2% (2000); College graduation rate: 5.6% (2000).
Housing: Homeownership rate: 68.0% (2000); Median home value: $25,600 (2000); Median rent: $194 per month (2000); Median age of housing: 56 years (2000).
Transportation: Commute to work: 93.6% car, 0.0% public transportation, 1.9% walk, 4.5% work from home (2000); Travel time to work: 32.9% less than 15 minutes, 36.2% 15 to 30 minutes, 16.1% 30 to 45 minutes, 0.0% 45 to 60 minutes, 14.8% 60 minutes or more (2000)

MALOY (city). Covers a land area of 0.621 square miles and a water area of 0 square miles. Located at 40.67° N. Lat.; 94.41° W. Long. Elevation is 1,120 feet.
History: Maloy was also known as Foxtown and Delphi. The name was changed to Maloy in honor of David Maloy, a prominent local landowner and cattleman.
Population: 28 (2000); Race: 100.0% White, 0.0% Black, 0.0% Asian, 0.0% American Indian and Alaska Native, 0.0% Hispanic of any race, 0.0% two or more races (2000); Density: 45.1 persons per square mile (2000); Age: 42.9% under 18, 9.5% over 64 (2000); Marriage status: 41.2% never married, 41.2% now married, 11.8% widowed, 5.9% divorced (2000); Foreign born: 0.0% (2000); Ancestry (includes multiple ancestries): 14.3% Irish, 14.3% English, 9.5% Scottish, 9.5% United States or American, 4.8% Other groups (2000).
Economy: Employment by occupation: 10.0% management, 10.0% professional, 20.0% services, 40.0% sales, 0.0% farming, 0.0% construction, 20.0% production (2000).
Income: Per capita income: $10,386 (2000); Median household income: $36,250 (2000); Poverty rate: 42.9% (2000).
Taxes: Total city taxes per capita: $57 (1997); City property taxes per capita: $57 (1997).
Education: High school graduation rate: 100.0% (2000); College graduation rate: 75.0% (2000).
Housing: Homeownership rate: 81.8% (2000); Median home value: $21,700 (2000); Median age of housing: 60+ years (2000).
Transportation: Commute to work: 70.0% car, 0.0% public transportation, 10.0% walk, 20.0% work from home (2000); Travel time to work: 25.0% less than 15 minutes, 25.0% 15 to 30 minutes, 50.0% 30 to 45 minutes, 0.0% 45 to 60 minutes, 0.0% 60 minutes or more (2000)

MOUNT AYR (city). Covers a land area of 2.530 square miles and a water area of 0.006 square miles. Located at 40.71° N. Lat.; 94.23° W. Long. Elevation is 1,232 feet.
History: The name Mount Ayr indicated it was the highest point of land in the area and also honored Ayr, Scotland.
Population: 1,822 (2000); Race: 98.3% White, 0.1% Black, 0.4% Asian, 0.4% American Indian and Alaska Native, 0.8% Hispanic of any race, 0.3% two or more races (2000); Density: 720.2 persons per square mile (2000); Age: 22.5% under 18, 31.0% over 64 (2000); Marriage status: 14.8% never married, 63.3% now married, 13.6% widowed, 8.3% divorced (2000); Foreign born: 0.6% (2000); Ancestry (includes multiple ancestries): 16.2% German, 14.4% United States or American, 10.8% English, 9.0% Irish, 5.3% Other groups (2000).

Economy: Single-family building permits issued: 8 (2001) / 3 (2000); Multi-family building permits issued: 0 (2001) / 0 (2000); Employment by occupation: 9.1% management, 19.6% professional, 19.9% services, 19.5% sales, 2.6% farming, 13.1% construction, 16.2% production (2000).
Income: Per capita income: $14,444 (2000); Median household income: $26,893 (2000); Poverty rate: 13.1% (2000).
Taxes: Total city taxes per capita: $239 (1997); City property taxes per capita: $236 (1997).
Education: High school graduation rate: 81.4% (2000); College graduation rate: 16.6% (2000).

School District(s)

Mount Ayr Community School District (PK-12)
2000 Enrollment: 831 641-464-0500
Housing: Homeownership rate: 68.9% (2000); Median home value: $52,300 (2000); Median rent: $238 per month (2000); Median age of housing: 45 years (2000).
Hospitals: Ringgold County Hospital (40 beds)
Newspapers: Mount Ayr Record-News (1 x week)
Transportation: Commute to work: 91.3% car, 0.4% public transportation, 5.6% walk, 2.1% work from home (2000); Travel time to work: 68.7% less than 15 minutes, 11.0% 15 to 30 minutes, 9.5% 30 to 45 minutes, 2.8% 45 to 60 minutes, 8.0% 60 minutes or more (2000)

REDDING (city). Covers a land area of 1.005 square miles and a water area of 0 square miles. Located at 40.60° N. Lat.; 94.38° W. Long. Elevation is 1,130 feet.
History: Redding had a post office in 1856 but the town was not founded until 1880 when the Chicago, Burlington & Quincy Railroad was built through the section. The railroad company bought and sold 200 acres of land as town lots.
Population: 78 (2000); Race: 100.0% White, 0.0% Black, 0.0% Asian, 0.0% American Indian and Alaska Native, 0.0% Hispanic of any race, 0.0% two or more races (2000); Density: 77.6 persons per square mile (2000); Age: 22.1% under 18, 17.4% over 64 (2000); Marriage status: 20.0% never married, 48.6% now married, 22.9% widowed, 8.6% divorced (2000); Foreign born: 0.0% (2000); Ancestry (includes multiple ancestries): 22.1% German, 14.0% English, 12.8% United States or American, 10.5% Other groups, 5.8% Dutch (2000).
Economy: Employment by occupation: 0.0% management, 21.7% professional, 17.4% services, 17.4% sales, 8.7% farming, 26.1% construction, 8.7% production (2000).
Income: Per capita income: $10,144 (2000); Median household income: $13,750 (2000); Poverty rate: 30.2% (2000).
Taxes: Total city taxes per capita: $25 (1997); City property taxes per capita: $25 (1997).
Education: High school graduation rate: 73.4% (2000); College graduation rate: 10.9% (2000).
Housing: Homeownership rate: 94.3% (2000); Median home value: $18,300 (2000); Median age of housing: 60+ years (2000).
Transportation: Commute to work: 91.3% car, 0.0% public transportation, 8.7% walk, 0.0% work from home (2000); Travel time to work: 17.4% less than 15 minutes, 47.8% 15 to 30 minutes, 8.7% 30 to 45 minutes, 26.1% 45 to 60 minutes, 0.0% 60 minutes or more (2000)

TINGLEY (city). Covers a land area of 0.674 square miles and a water area of 0 square miles. Located at 40.85° N. Lat.; 94.19° W. Long. Elevation is 1,251 feet.
History: Tingley is believed to have been named for railroad surveyor, Major Richard Tingley.
Population: 171 (2000); Race: 98.2% White, 0.0% Black, 0.0% Asian, 0.0% American Indian and Alaska Native, 0.0% Hispanic of any race, 1.8% two or more races (2000); Density: 253.6 persons per square mile (2000); Age: 22.0% under 18, 25.0% over 64 (2000); Marriage status: 17.4% never married, 49.7% now married, 20.8% widowed, 12.1% divorced (2000); Foreign born: 0.0% (2000); Ancestry (includes multiple ancestries): 19.6% United States or American, 15.5% English, 13.1% German, 6.0% Irish, 6.0% Dutch (2000).
Economy: Employment by occupation: 12.3% management, 10.8% professional, 16.9% services, 18.5% sales, 10.8% farming, 7.7% construction, 23.1% production (2000).
Income: Per capita income: $14,475 (2000); Median household income: $22,321 (2000); Poverty rate: 10.1% (2000).
Taxes: Total city taxes per capita: $67 (1997); City property taxes per capita: $67 (1997).
Education: High school graduation rate: 73.0% (2000); College graduation rate: 12.7% (2000).
Housing: Homeownership rate: 68.9% (2000); Median home value: $22,500 (2000); Median rent: $317 per month (2000); Median age of housing: 60+ years (2000).
Transportation: Commute to work: 92.3% car, 0.0% public transportation, 0.0% walk, 3.1% work from home (2000); Travel time to work: 33.3% less than 15 minutes, 30.2% 15 to 30 minutes, 23.8% 30 to 45 minutes, 7.9% 45 to 60 minutes, 4.8% 60 minutes or more (2000)

Sac County

Located in western Iowa; prairie area, drained by the Raccoon and Boyer Rivers. Covers a land area of 575.80 square miles, a water area of 2.60 square miles, and is located in the Central Time Zone. The county government was organized in 1851. County seat is Sac City.

Weather Station: Sac City — Elevation: 1,197 feet

	Jan	Feb	Mar	Apr	May	Jun	Jul	Aug	Sep	Oct	Nov	Dec
High	26	33	44	60	72	81	85	82	75	62	44	31
Low	7	13	24	36	47	57	62	60	50	38	25	14
Precip	0.8	0.8	2.5	3.4	4.3	4.7	4.0	3.8	3.4	2.5	1.8	1.1
Snow	6.8	6.0	5.9	1.7	tr	0.0	0.0	0.0	tr	0.4	2.9	7.0

High and Low temperatures in degrees Fahrenheit; Precipitation and Snow in inches

Population: 11,529 (2000); Race: 97.9% White, 0.3% Black, 0.3% Asian, 0.1% American Indian and Alaska Native, 0.8% Hispanic of any race, 1.1% two or more races (2000); Density: 20.0 persons per square mile (2000); Age: 24.1% under 18, 22.7% over 64 (2000).
Religion: Five largest groups: 22.6% Catholic Church, 22.2% Lutheran Church—Missouri Synod, 15.2% The United Methodist Church, 7.8% Presbyterian Church (U.S.A.), 7.1% Evangelical Lutheran Church in America (2000).
Economy: Unemployment rate: 2.8% (11/2002); Total civilian labor force: 6,091 (11/2002); Leading industries: 25.0% health care and social assistance; 19.3% retail trade; 8.5% manufacturing (2000); Companies that employ more than 1,000 persons: 0 (2000); Companies that employ more than 100 persons: 2 (2000); Farms: 813 totaling 344,949 acres (1997); Minority business ownership rate: 0.0% (1997); Women business ownership rate: 28.8% (1997); Retail sales per capita: $7,022 (1997). Single-family building permits issued: 8 (2001) / 14 (2000); Multi-family building permits issued: 0 (2001) / 0 (2000).
Income: Per capita income: $16,902 (2000); Median household income: $32,874 (2000); Poverty rate: 9.9% (2000); Bankruptcy rate: 1.60% (2001).
Taxes: Total county taxes per capita: $296 (1997); County property taxes per capita: $296 (1997).
Education: High school graduation rate: 84.2% (2000); College graduation rate: 13.6% (2000).
Housing: Homeownership rate: 76.8% (2000); Median home value: $50,000 (2000); Median rent: $229 per month (2000); Median age of housing: 54 years (2000).
Health: Birth rate: 98.0 per 10,000 population (1998); Age adjusted death rate: 82.9 per 10,000 population (1999); Age adjusted cancer mortality rate: 195.2 deaths per 100,000 population (1999). Number of physicians: 4.3 per 10,000 population (1999); Number of hospital beds: 46.8 per 10,000 population (1999).
Elections: 2000 Presidential election results: 41.7% Gore, 55.2% Bush, 1.9% Nader, 0.9% Buchanan
National and State Parks: Black Hawk Lake State Game Management Area; Black Hawk Lake State Recreation Area; Black Hawk Marsh State Game Management Area; Kiowa Marsh State Public Hunting Area
Additional Information Contacts
Sac County Government Offices 712-662-7401
Sac City Chamber of Commerce 712-662-7316

Sac County Communities

AUBURN (city). Covers a land area of 0.485 square miles and a water area of 0 square miles. Located at 42.25° N. Lat.; 94.87° W. Long. Elevation is 1,220 feet.
History: Auburn was platted by the Western Town Lot Company and named for Auburn, New York.
Population: 296 (2000); Race: 99.4% White, 0.0% Black, 0.0% Asian, 0.0% American Indian and Alaska Native, 0.0% Hispanic of any race, 0.6% two or more races (2000); Density: 609.9 persons per square mile (2000); Age: 23.9% under 18, 21.7% over 64 (2000); Marriage status: 24.1% never married, 58.6% now married, 10.0% widowed, 7.2% divorced (2000);

Foreign born: 1.0% (2000); Ancestry (includes multiple ancestries): 53.2% German, 16.6% Irish, 7.0% English, 5.1% Swedish, 4.5% Austrian (2000).
Economy: Employment by occupation: 13.2% management, 15.8% professional, 17.8% services, 25.0% sales, 2.6% farming, 8.6% construction, 17.1% production (2000).
Income: Per capita income: $20,494 (2000); Median household income: $42,500 (2000); Poverty rate: 4.5% (2000).
Taxes: Total city taxes per capita: $74 (1997); City property taxes per capita: $71 (1997).
Education: High school graduation rate: 80.7% (2000); College graduation rate: 12.7% (2000).
Housing: Homeownership rate: 81.1% (2000); Median home value: $45,900 (2000); Median rent: $238 per month (2000); Median age of housing: 60+ years (2000).
Newspapers: Auburn Enterprise & Tri-County Special (1 x week)
Transportation: Commute to work: 90.1% car, 0.0% public transportation, 3.3% walk, 3.3% work from home (2000); Travel time to work: 42.9% less than 15 minutes, 41.5% 15 to 30 minutes, 8.2% 30 to 45 minutes, 2.7% 45 to 60 minutes, 4.8% 60 minutes or more (2000)

EARLY (city). Covers a land area of 0.395 square miles and a water area of 0 square miles. Located at 42.46° N. Lat.; 95.15° W. Long.
History: Early was named for D. C. Early, a pioneer, and was settled in the late 1870's.
Population: 605 (2000); Race: 95.3% White, 0.3% Black, 0.0% Asian, 0.7% American Indian and Alaska Native, 4.0% Hispanic of any race, 0.2% two or more races (2000); Density: 1,532.3 persons per square mile (2000); Age: 30.8% under 18, 17.6% over 64 (2000); Marriage status: 19.6% never married, 61.7% now married, 9.0% widowed, 9.7% divorced (2000); Foreign born: 3.7% (2000); Ancestry (includes multiple ancestries): 51.6% German, 15.0% Irish, 10.0% English, 8.7% United States or American, 7.2% Other groups (2000).
Economy: Single-family building permits issued: 0 (2001) / 0 (2000); Multi-family building permits issued: 0 (2001) / 0 (2000); Employment by occupation: 6.2% management, 15.4% professional, 13.5% services, 21.2% sales, 3.1% farming, 11.6% construction, 29.0% production (2000).
Income: Per capita income: $14,317 (2000); Median household income: $30,972 (2000); Poverty rate: 12.1% (2000).
Taxes: Total city taxes per capita: $142 (1997); City property taxes per capita: $138 (1997).
Education: High school graduation rate: 84.2% (2000); College graduation rate: 11.9% (2000).
Housing: Homeownership rate: 77.0% (2000); Median home value: $41,300 (2000); Median rent: $186 per month (2000); Median age of housing: 54 years (2000).
Transportation: Commute to work: 96.0% car, 0.0% public transportation, 1.6% walk, 2.4% work from home (2000); Travel time to work: 27.1% less than 15 minutes, 51.4% 15 to 30 minutes, 12.6% 30 to 45 minutes, 3.2% 45 to 60 minutes, 5.7% 60 minutes or more (2000)

LAKE VIEW (city). Covers a land area of 1.835 square miles and a water area of 0.280 square miles. Located at 42.30° N. Lat.; 95.04° W. Long. Elevation is 1,270 feet.
History: Lake View was once known as Fletcher, after an early settler. The town was renamed because of its location at the head of Wall Lake.
Population: 1,278 (2000); Race: 98.9% White, 0.0% Black, 0.2% Asian, 0.0% American Indian and Alaska Native, 0.0% Hispanic of any race, 0.9% two or more races (2000); Density: 696.4 persons per square mile (2000); Age: 23.2% under 18, 29.0% over 64 (2000); Marriage status: 15.3% never married, 60.3% now married, 15.2% widowed, 9.2% divorced (2000); Foreign born: 0.6% (2000); Ancestry (includes multiple ancestries): 57.2% German, 7.9% Irish, 7.3% United States or American, 6.1% English, 4.3% Swedish (2000).
Economy: Single-family building permits issued: 6 (2001) / 1 (2000); Multi-family building permits issued: 0 (2001) / 0 (2000); Employment by occupation: 6.7% management, 9.5% professional, 23.9% services, 24.5% sales, 2.2% farming, 14.3% construction, 18.9% production (2000).
Income: Per capita income: $15,857 (2000); Median household income: $26,691 (2000); Poverty rate: 13.3% (2000).
Taxes: Total city taxes per capita: $224 (1997); City property taxes per capita: $182 (1997).
Education: High school graduation rate: 80.6% (2000); College graduation rate: 8.9% (2000).

School District(s)

Wall Lake View Auburn Community School District (PK-12)
2000 Enrollment: 676 712-664-5000

Housing: Homeownership rate: 73.7% (2000); Median home value: $64,600 (2000); Median rent: $258 per month (2000); Median age of housing: 41 years (2000).
Newspapers: Lake View Resort (1 x week)
Transportation: Commute to work: 90.0% car, 0.4% public transportation, 4.7% walk, 3.8% work from home (2000); Travel time to work: 61.6% less than 15 minutes, 19.2% 15 to 30 minutes, 14.1% 30 to 45 minutes, 2.2% 45 to 60 minutes, 2.9% 60 minutes or more (2000)

LYTTON (city). Covers a land area of 0.192 square miles and a water area of 0 square miles. Located at 42.42° N. Lat.; 94.85° W. Long.
History: Lytton was established in 1899 and named for Lord Bulwer-Lytton, a British author.
Population: 305 (2000); Race: 100.0% White, 0.0% Black, 0.0% Asian, 0.0% American Indian and Alaska Native, 0.0% Hispanic of any race, 0.0% two or more races (2000); Density: 1,591.3 persons per square mile (2000); Age: 26.4% under 18, 17.1% over 64 (2000); Marriage status: 27.6% never married, 44.7% now married, 13.6% widowed, 14.0% divorced (2000); Foreign born: 0.0% (2000); Ancestry (includes multiple ancestries): 46.8% German, 9.7% English, 9.4% Irish, 7.4% Norwegian, 6.7% United States or American (2000).
Economy: Single-family building permits issued: 0 (2001) / 0 (2000); Multi-family building permits issued: 0 (2001) / 0 (2000); Employment by occupation: 14.1% management, 16.7% professional, 14.7% services, 14.1% sales, 1.9% farming, 9.6% construction, 28.8% production (2000).
Income: Per capita income: $14,650 (2000); Median household income: $29,844 (2000); Poverty rate: 8.4% (2000).
Taxes: Total city taxes per capita: $161 (1997); City property taxes per capita: $161 (1997).
Education: High school graduation rate: 93.8% (2000); College graduation rate: 16.0% (2000).
Housing: Homeownership rate: 66.4% (2000); Median home value: $20,800 (2000); Median rent: $232 per month (2000); Median age of housing: 57 years (2000).
Transportation: Commute to work: 82.2% car, 1.3% public transportation, 9.9% walk, 6.6% work from home (2000); Travel time to work: 62.7% less than 15 minutes, 16.2% 15 to 30 minutes, 14.1% 30 to 45 minutes, 7.0% 45 to 60 minutes, 0.0% 60 minutes or more (2000)

NEMAHA (city). Covers a land area of 0.160 square miles and a water area of 0 square miles. Located at 42.51° N. Lat.; 95.08° W. Long. Elevation is 1,318 feet.
History: The town of Nemaha is named after the Nemaha River.
Population: 102 (2000); Race: 100.0% White, 0.0% Black, 0.0% Asian, 0.0% American Indian and Alaska Native, 0.0% Hispanic of any race, 0.0% two or more races (2000); Density: 637.4 persons per square mile (2000); Age: 23.2% under 18, 13.7% over 64 (2000); Marriage status: 23.8% never married, 56.3% now married, 10.0% widowed, 10.0% divorced (2000); Foreign born: 0.0% (2000); Ancestry (includes multiple ancestries): 44.2% German, 13.7% Irish, 10.5% United States or American, 10.5% English, 8.4% Dutch (2000).
Economy: Employment by occupation: 8.8% management, 8.8% professional, 22.8% services, 22.8% sales, 0.0% farming, 8.8% construction, 28.1% production (2000).
Income: Per capita income: $11,997 (2000); Median household income: $27,708 (2000); Poverty rate: 9.5% (2000).
Taxes: Total city taxes per capita: $58 (1997); City property taxes per capita: $58 (1997).
Education: High school graduation rate: 79.0% (2000); College graduation rate: 27.4% (2000).
Housing: Homeownership rate: 93.2% (2000); Median home value: $22,000 (2000); Median age of housing: 60+ years (2000).
Transportation: Commute to work: 89.5% car, 0.0% public transportation, 10.5% walk, 0.0% work from home (2000); Travel time to work: 33.3% less than 15 minutes, 43.9% 15 to 30 minutes, 12.3% 30 to 45 minutes, 7.0% 45 to 60 minutes, 3.5% 60 minutes or more (2000)

ODEBOLT (city). Covers a land area of 1.046 square miles and a water area of 0 square miles. Located at 42.31° N. Lat.; 95.25° W. Long. Elevation is 1,377 feet.
History: In 1911, Odebolt produced $400,000 worth of popcorn.
Population: 1,153 (2000); Race: 99.0% White, 0.0% Black, 0.2% Asian, 0.0% American Indian and Alaska Native, 0.2% Hispanic of any race, 0.8% two or more races (2000); Density: 1,102.7 persons per square mile (2000); Age: 23.0% under 18, 30.6% over 64 (2000); Marriage status: 19.1% never married, 60.0% now married, 15.5% widowed, 5.5% divorced (2000);

Foreign born: 0.4% (2000); Ancestry (includes multiple ancestries): 45.4% German, 12.3% United States or American, 7.9% Swedish, 7.6% Irish, 6.0% English (2000).
Economy: Single-family building permits issued: 0 (2001) / 2 (2000); Multi-family building permits issued: 0 (2001) / 0 (2000); Employment by occupation: 6.6% management, 13.4% professional, 20.0% services, 25.2% sales, 2.0% farming, 9.4% construction, 23.4% production (2000).
Income: Per capita income: $15,971 (2000); Median household income: $30,208 (2000); Poverty rate: 9.5% (2000).
Taxes: Total city taxes per capita: $146 (1997); City property taxes per capita: $144 (1997).
Education: High school graduation rate: 81.6% (2000); College graduation rate: 13.8% (2000).

School District(s)

Odebolt-Arthur Community School District (KG-12)
2000 Enrollment: 435 712-668-2289
Housing: Homeownership rate: 81.6% (2000); Median home value: $43,400 (2000); Median rent: $234 per month (2000); Median age of housing: 56 years (2000).
Transportation: Commute to work: 88.5% car, 0.0% public transportation, 4.3% walk, 6.8% work from home (2000); Travel time to work: 51.3% less than 15 minutes, 29.4% 15 to 30 minutes, 13.1% 30 to 45 minutes, 3.5% 45 to 60 minutes, 2.7% 60 minutes or more (2000)

SAC CITY (city). Covers a land area of 4.902 square miles and a water area of 0.007 square miles. Located at 42.42° N. Lat.; 94.99° W. Long. Elevation is 1,196 feet.
History: Sac City was named for an Indian tribe.
Population: 2,368 (2000); Race: 95.9% White, 1.3% Black, 0.7% Asian, 0.0% American Indian and Alaska Native, 0.0% Hispanic of any race, 2.2% two or more races (2000); Density: 483.0 persons per square mile (2000); Age: 18.0% under 18, 29.4% over 64 (2000); Marriage status: 21.2% never married, 53.7% now married, 16.2% widowed, 8.9% divorced (2000); Foreign born: 1.4% (2000); Ancestry (includes multiple ancestries): 41.4% German, 11.7% Irish, 11.1% English, 5.8% United States or American, 5.6% Swedish (2000).
Economy: Single-family building permits issued: 0 (2001) / 3 (2000); Multi-family building permits issued: 0 (2001) / 0 (2000); Employment by occupation: 11.5% management, 14.8% professional, 23.9% services, 23.5% sales, 0.8% farming, 8.3% construction, 17.2% production (2000).
Income: Per capita income: $17,229 (2000); Median household income: $30,300 (2000); Poverty rate: 13.6% (2000).
Taxes: Total city taxes per capita: $224 (1997); City property taxes per capita: $223 (1997).
Education: High school graduation rate: 78.6% (2000); College graduation rate: 14.1% (2000).

School District(s)

Sac Community School District (PK-12)
2000 Enrollment: 576 712-662-7030
Housing: Homeownership rate: 73.4% (2000); Median home value: $46,600 (2000); Median rent: $229 per month (2000); Median age of housing: 52 years (2000).
Hospitals: Loring Hospital (33 beds)
Newspapers: The Sac Sun (1 x week)
Transportation: Commute to work: 86.4% car, 0.9% public transportation, 8.0% walk, 4.4% work from home (2000); Travel time to work: 71.4% less than 15 minutes, 11.0% 15 to 30 minutes, 11.4% 30 to 45 minutes, 3.7% 45 to 60 minutes, 2.4% 60 minutes or more (2000)
Additional Information Contacts
Sac City Chamber of Commrece 712-662-7316

SCHALLER (city). Covers a land area of 1.258 square miles and a water area of 0 square miles. Located at 42.49° N. Lat.; 95.29° W. Long. Elevation is 1,410 feet.
History: Schaller was named for the landowner of the town site, Phillip Schaller.
Population: 779 (2000); Race: 94.5% White, 0.0% Black, 1.7% Asian, 0.5% American Indian and Alaska Native, 6.7% Hispanic of any race, 1.4% two or more races (2000); Density: 619.4 persons per square mile (2000); Age: 25.3% under 18, 20.4% over 64 (2000); Marriage status: 20.0% never married, 62.0% now married, 10.1% widowed, 7.9% divorced (2000); Foreign born: 5.2% (2000); Ancestry (includes multiple ancestries): 49.1% German, 11.9% Irish, 8.4% Other groups, 6.9% English, 6.2% United States or American (2000).
Economy: Employment by occupation: 10.8% management, 8.4% professional, 15.4% services, 17.3% sales, 0.5% farming, 17.1% construction, 30.4% production (2000).
Income: Per capita income: $15,520 (2000); Median household income: $33,365 (2000); Poverty rate: 5.0% (2000).
Taxes: Total city taxes per capita: $170 (1997); City property taxes per capita: $169 (1997).
Education: High school graduation rate: 88.1% (2000); College graduation rate: 14.7% (2000).

School District(s)

Schaller-Crestland Community School District (KG-12)
2000 Enrollment: 507 712-275-4267
Housing: Homeownership rate: 85.4% (2000); Median home value: $46,000 (2000); Median rent: $278 per month (2000); Median age of housing: 56 years (2000).
Newspapers: The Schaller Herald (1 x week)
Transportation: Commute to work: 82.0% car, 0.0% public transportation, 9.3% walk, 8.2% work from home (2000); Travel time to work: 49.0% less than 15 minutes, 43.0% 15 to 30 minutes, 2.1% 30 to 45 minutes, 3.0% 45 to 60 minutes, 3.0% 60 minutes or more (2000)

WALL LAKE (city). Covers a land area of 1.084 square miles and a water area of 0 square miles. Located at 42.27° N. Lat.; 95.09° W. Long. Elevation is 1,233 feet.
History: Wall Lake was mapped in 1877 by the Blair Land Company. The town was named for a nearby lake.
Population: 841 (2000); Race: 98.1% White, 0.0% Black, 0.0% Asian, 0.0% American Indian and Alaska Native, 0.2% Hispanic of any race, 1.9% two or more races (2000); Density: 776.2 persons per square mile (2000); Age: 24.6% under 18, 25.4% over 64 (2000); Marriage status: 21.4% never married, 60.9% now married, 12.0% widowed, 5.6% divorced (2000); Foreign born: 1.2% (2000); Ancestry (includes multiple ancestries): 53.5% German, 5.7% Irish, 5.5% United States or American, 4.6% English, 4.5% Other groups (2000).
Economy: Single-family building permits issued: 2 (2001) / 8 (2000); Multi-family building permits issued: 0 (2001) / 0 (2000); Employment by occupation: 11.0% management, 10.2% professional, 16.4% services, 28.2% sales, 1.3% farming, 9.4% construction, 23.6% production (2000).
Income: Per capita income: $15,390 (2000); Median household income: $33,125 (2000); Poverty rate: 11.0% (2000).
Taxes: Total city taxes per capita: $84 (1997); City property taxes per capita: $80 (1997).
Education: High school graduation rate: 79.4% (2000); College graduation rate: 10.4% (2000).
Housing: Homeownership rate: 86.7% (2000); Median home value: $53,700 (2000); Median rent: $225 per month (2000); Median age of housing: 52 years (2000).
Transportation: Commute to work: 90.7% car, 0.0% public transportation, 6.5% walk, 2.7% work from home (2000); Travel time to work: 62.2% less than 15 minutes, 16.8% 15 to 30 minutes, 14.6% 30 to 45 minutes, 2.0% 45 to 60 minutes, 4.5% 60 minutes or more (2000)

Scott County

Located in eastern Iowa; bounded on the east and south by the Mississippi River and the Illinois border, and on the north by the Sapsipinicon River. Covers a land area of 457.90 square miles, a water area of 10.20 square miles, and is located in the Central Time Zone. The county government was organized in 1837. County seat is Davenport.

Scott County is part of the Davenport-Moline-Rock Island, IA-IL MSA. The entire metro area includes: Henry County, IL; Rock Island County, IL; Scott County, IA

Weather Station: Le Claire Lock & Dam 14 — Elevation: 574 feet

	Jan	Feb	Mar	Apr	May	Jun	Jul	Aug	Sep	Oct	Nov	Dec
High	29	34	46	60	72	81	85	83	75	63	47	34
Low	12	18	29	41	52	62	67	64	56	44	31	19
Precip	1.1	1.3	2.4	3.2	3.9	4.6	3.6	4.4	3.2	2.5	2.4	2.0
Snow	na	3.3	1.9	0.7	0.0	0.0	0.0	0.0	0.0	tr	0.2	2.5

High and Low temperatures in degrees Fahrenheit; Precipitation and Snow in inches

Population: 158,668 (2000); Race: 88.6% White, 6.0% Black, 1.4% Asian, 0.4% American Indian and Alaska Native, 4.0% Hispanic of any race, 1.9% two or more races (2000); Density: 346.5 persons per square mile (2000); Age: 26.3% under 18, 11.9% over 64 (2000).

Religion: Five largest groups: 20.9% Catholic Church, 8.5% Evangelical Lutheran Church in America, 3.4% Lutheran Church—Missouri Synod, 3.3% The United Methodist Church, 2.4% Presbyterian Church (U.S.A.) (2000).
Economy: Unemployment rate: 3.7% (11/2002); Total civilian labor force: 86,410 (11/2002); Leading industries: 16.0% manufacturing; 14.7% retail trade; 12.3% accommodation & food services (2000); Companies that employ more than 1,000 persons: 5 (2000); Companies that employ more than 100 persons: 128 (2000); Farms: 799 totaling 225,248 acres (1997); Minority business ownership rate: 5.8% (1997); Women business ownership rate: 26.3% (1997); Retail sales per capita: $11,610 (1997). Single-family building permits issued: 486 (2001) / 474 (2000); Multi-family building permits issued: 198 (2001) / 227 (2000).
Income: Per capita income: $21,310 (2000); Median household income: $42,701 (2000); Poverty rate: 10.5% (2000); Bankruptcy rate: 4.43% (2001).
Taxes: Total county taxes per capita: $152 (2000); County property taxes per capita: $122 (2000).
Education: High school graduation rate: 86.3% (2000); College graduation rate: 24.9% (2000).
Housing: Homeownership rate: 70.5% (2000); Median home value: $92,400 (2000); Median rent: $410 per month (2000); Median age of housing: 35 years (2000).
Health: Birth rate: 147.5 per 10,000 population (1998); Age adjusted death rate: 91.7 per 10,000 population (1999); Age adjusted cancer mortality rate: 221.1 deaths per 100,000 population (1999). Air Quality Index: 79% good, 21% moderate, 0% unhealthy (percent of days in 2000). Number of physicians: 21.6 per 10,000 population (1999); Number of hospital beds: 34.5 per 10,000 population (1999).
Elections: 2000 Presidential election results: 50.8% Gore, 46.5% Bush, 2.0% Nader, 0.4% Buchanan
National and State Parks: Princeton State Wildlife Management Area
Additional Information Contacts
Scott County Government Offices 563-326-8611
Bettendorf Chamber of Commerce 563-355-4753
Davenport Chamber of Commerce. 563-322-1706
Eldridge Economic Development 563-285-9965
Eldridte N Scott Chamber of Commerce 563-285-9965
Greater Davenport Board of Realtors. 563-386-6030

Scott County Communities

BETTENDORF (city). Covers a land area of 21.236 square miles and a water area of 1.138 square miles. Located at 41.55° N. Lat.; 90.49° W. Long. Elevation is 565 feet.
History: Bettendorf was known as Gilbert Town until 1902, when the Bettendorf Company, manufacturer of railroad equipment, moved its plant here. The town was renamed to honor the company's president, W. P. Bettendorf.
Population: 31,275 (2000); Race: 95.3% White, 1.5% Black, 1.4% Asian, 0.2% American Indian and Alaska Native, 2.6% Hispanic of any race, 1.0% two or more races (2000); Density: 1,472.8 persons per square mile (2000); Age: 26.4% under 18, 12.2% over 64 (2000); Marriage status: 21.0% never married, 63.6% now married, 6.2% widowed, 9.1% divorced (2000); Foreign born: 2.9% (2000); Ancestry (includes multiple ancestries): 37.4% German, 17.9% Irish, 10.6% English, 8.8% Other groups, 6.5% United States or American (2000).
Vital Statistics: Birth rate: 71.9 per 10,000 population (1998)
Economy: Unemployment rate: 2.6% (11/2002); Total civilian labor force: 17,193 (11/2002); Single-family building permits issued: 144 (2001) / 143 (2000); Multi-family building permits issued: 12 (2001) / 12 (2000); Employment by occupation: 19.7% management, 22.5% professional, 12.2% services, 27.9% sales, 0.1% farming, 6.1% construction, 11.5% production (2000).
Income: Per capita income: $28,053 (2000); Median household income: $54,217 (2000); Poverty rate: 4.8% (2000).
Taxes: Total city taxes per capita: $652 (2000); City property taxes per capita: $418 (2000).
Education: High school graduation rate: 92.6% (2000); College graduation rate: 38.8% (2000).

School District(s)

Bettendorf Community School District (PK-12)
2000 Enrollment: 4,462 319-359-3681
Housing: Homeownership rate: 77.1% (2000); Median home value: $118,400 (2000); Median rent: $472 per month (2000); Median age of housing: 28 years (2000).
Safety: Violent crime rate: 33.0 per 10,000 population; Property crime rate: 232.1 per 10,000 population (2001).
Transportation: Commute to work: 94.8% car, 0.4% public transportation, 1.2% walk, 3.0% work from home (2000); Travel time to work: 40.5% less than 15 minutes, 49.4% 15 to 30 minutes, 5.9% 30 to 45 minutes, 1.6% 45 to 60 minutes, 2.6% 60 minutes or more (2000)
Additional Information Contacts
Bettendorf Chamber of Commerce 563-355-4753

BLUE GRASS (city). Covers a land area of 2.694 square miles and a water area of 0 square miles. Located at 41.51° N. Lat.; 90.76° W. Long.
History: Blue Grass got its name because of the quantity of blue grass in the area.
Population: 1,169 (2000); Race: 97.4% White, 0.7% Black, 0.3% Asian, 0.3% American Indian and Alaska Native, 0.8% Hispanic of any race, 0.9% two or more races (2000); Density: 434.0 persons per square mile (2000); Age: 24.7% under 18, 8.0% over 64 (2000); Marriage status: 25.2% never married, 57.7% now married, 5.0% widowed, 12.1% divorced (2000); Foreign born: 1.6% (2000); Ancestry (includes multiple ancestries): 46.6% German, 15.1% Irish, 7.5% Other groups, 6.9% United States or American, 6.2% English (2000).
Economy: Single-family building permits issued: 5 (2001) / 3 (2000); Multi-family building permits issued: 0 (2001) / 0 (2000); Employment by occupation: 10.3% management, 11.2% professional, 16.2% services, 23.6% sales, 0.0% farming, 12.0% construction, 26.7% production (2000).
Income: Per capita income: $20,811 (2000); Median household income: $51,923 (2000); Poverty rate: 4.9% (2000).
Taxes: Total city taxes per capita: $328 (1997); City property taxes per capita: $205 (1997).
Education: High school graduation rate: 90.3% (2000); College graduation rate: 12.5% (2000).
Housing: Homeownership rate: 84.6% (2000); Median home value: $90,600 (2000); Median rent: $461 per month (2000); Median age of housing: 33 years (2000).
Transportation: Commute to work: 92.8% car, 0.0% public transportation, 1.7% walk, 5.1% work from home (2000); Travel time to work: 20.7% less than 15 minutes, 54.9% 15 to 30 minutes, 19.6% 30 to 45 minutes, 1.3% 45 to 60 minutes, 3.5% 60 minutes or more (2000)

BUFFALO (city). Covers a land area of 6.017 square miles and a water area of 0.033 square miles. Located at 41.45° N. Lat.; 90.72° W. Long. Elevation is 559 feet.
History: Buffalo is near the point where Clark's ferry brought many early settlers into the Iowa Territory in the late 1830's. Clam scows once dotted the streams, and barges delivered the shells to factories along the river.
Population: 1,321 (2000); Race: 96.7% White, 0.2% Black, 0.2% Asian, 0.6% American Indian and Alaska Native, 4.7% Hispanic of any race, 0.2% two or more races (2000); Density: 219.5 persons per square mile (2000); Age: 25.3% under 18, 13.6% over 64 (2000); Marriage status: 21.0% never married, 60.9% now married, 7.4% widowed, 10.7% divorced (2000); Foreign born: 0.9% (2000); Ancestry (includes multiple ancestries): 27.1% German, 16.4% Irish, 15.4% Other groups, 8.1% United States or American, 7.3% English (2000).
Economy: Single-family building permits issued: 0 (2001) / 3 (2000); Multi-family building permits issued: 0 (2001) / 0 (2000); Employment by occupation: 6.5% management, 9.1% professional, 16.1% services, 25.5% sales, 0.0% farming, 14.3% construction, 28.6% production (2000).
Income: Per capita income: $21,957 (2000); Median household income: $44,250 (2000); Poverty rate: 5.9% (2000).
Taxes: Total city taxes per capita: $459 (1997); City property taxes per capita: $336 (1997).
Education: High school graduation rate: 79.6% (2000); College graduation rate: 9.0% (2000).
Housing: Homeownership rate: 72.9% (2000); Median home value: $74,100 (2000); Median rent: $398 per month (2000); Median age of housing: 48 years (2000).
Transportation: Commute to work: 94.5% car, 0.0% public transportation, 2.0% walk, 3.5% work from home (2000); Travel time to work: 24.1% less than 15 minutes, 48.1% 15 to 30 minutes, 19.5% 30 to 45 minutes, 3.9% 45 to 60 minutes, 4.3% 60 minutes or more (2000)

DAVENPORT (city). Covers a land area of 62.791 square miles and a water area of 2.150 square miles. Located at 41.54° N. Lat.; 90.59° W. Long. Elevation is 559 feet.
History: Davenport was named for Colonel George Davenport, an Englishman who served in the United States Army. Davenport was the first

city in Iowa to have railroad service, and it was here that the first train crossed the Mississippi River in 1856. Dred Scott based his famous fight for freedom upon his residence in Davenport.
Population: 98,359 (2000); Race: 83.9% White, 9.1% Black, 1.8% Asian, 0.6% American Indian and Alaska Native, 5.2% Hispanic of any race, 2.6% two or more races (2000); Density: 1,566.5 persons per square mile (2000); Age: 25.9% under 18, 12.3% over 64 (2000); Marriage status: 29.6% never married, 52.2% now married, 6.6% widowed, 11.6% divorced (2000); Foreign born: 3.7% (2000); Ancestry (includes multiple ancestries): 32.9% German, 19.0% Other groups, 14.9% Irish, 7.9% English, 5.8% United States or American (2000).
Vital Statistics: Birth rate: 166.2 per 10,000 population (1998)
Economy: Unemployment rate: 4.4% (11/2002); Total civilian labor force: 52,891 (11/2002); Single-family building permits issued: 208 (2001) / 196 (2000); Multi-family building permits issued: 90 (2001) / 131 (2000); Employment by occupation: 10.8% management, 17.9% professional, 17.4% services, 28.4% sales, 0.1% farming, 7.7% construction, 17.7% production (2000).
Income: Per capita income: $18,828 (2000); Median household income: $37,242 (2000); Poverty rate: 14.1% (2000).
Taxes: Total city taxes per capita: $486 (2000); City property taxes per capita: $381 (2000).
Education: High school graduation rate: 83.4% (2000); College graduation rate: 21.5% (2000).

School District(s)

Davenport Community School District (PK-12)
2000 Enrollment: 16,874 319-336-5000

Four-year College(s)

Hamilton Technical College (Private, For-profit)
2001 Enrollment: 391 319-386-3570
2001 Tuition: In-state $6,300; Out-of-state $6,300
Marycrest International University (Private, Not-for-profit)
2001 Enrollment: 666 563-326-9512
2001 Tuition: In-state $13,400; Out-of-state $13,400
Palmer College of Chiropractic (Private, Not-for-profit)
2001 Enrollment: 1,727 563-884-5000
2001 Tuition: In-state $4,665; Out-of-state $4,665
Saint Ambrose University (Private, Not-for-profit, Roman Catholic)
2001 Enrollment: 3,291 563-333-6000
2001 Tuition: In-state $14,654; Out-of-state $14,654

Two-year College(s)

Eastern Iowa Community College District (Public)
2001 Enrollment: 6,331 563-336-3309
2001 Tuition: In-state $2,160; Out-of-state $3,240
La James College of Hairstyling (Private, For-profit)
2001 Enrollment: 35 319-386-7700
Capri College (Private, For-profit)
2001 Enrollment: 104 563-388-6642
Quest College (Private, For-profit)
2001 Enrollment: 745 563-355-3500
2001 Tuition: In-state $9,360; Out-of-state $9,360
Davenport Barber Styling College (Private, For-profit)
2001 Enrollment: 34 319-391-9950

Housing: Homeownership rate: 65.1% (2000); Median home value: $80,200 (2000); Median rent: $400 per month (2000); Median age of housing: 41 years (2000).
Hospitals: Davenport Medical Center (150 beds); Genesis Medical Center (502 beds)
Safety: Violent crime rate: 151.6 per 10,000 population; Property crime rate: 774.3 per 10,000 population (2001).
Newspapers: Quad-City Times (7 x week); Bettendorf News (1 x week); The Catholic Messenger (1 x week)
Transportation: Commute to work: 93.3% car, 1.1% public transportation, 2.2% walk, 2.5% work from home (2000); Travel time to work: 44.9% less than 15 minutes, 42.7% 15 to 30 minutes, 6.9% 30 to 45 minutes, 2.5% 45 to 60 minutes, 3.0% 60 minutes or more (2000); Amtrak: Service available.
Airports: Davenport Municipal

Additional Information Contacts

Davenport Chamber of Commerce 563-322-1706
Greater Davenport Board of Realtors 563-386-6030

DIXON (city). Covers a land area of 0.147 square miles and a water area of 0 square miles. Located at 41.74° N. Lat.; 90.78° W. Long. Elevation is 676 feet.
History: Dixon's name reflects the name of the man who ordered the platting of the town, variously reported as Dickenson and Dickinson.
Population: 276 (2000); Race: 97.1% White, 2.2% Black, 0.0% Asian, 0.0% American Indian and Alaska Native, 0.0% Hispanic of any race, 0.7% two or more races (2000); Density: 1,881.7 persons per square mile (2000); Age: 31.6% under 18, 12.0% over 64 (2000); Marriage status: 23.5% never married, 62.3% now married, 4.4% widowed, 9.8% divorced (2000); Foreign born: 0.0% (2000); Ancestry (includes multiple ancestries): 47.3% German, 16.4% English, 5.8% Irish, 5.5% Other groups, 5.1% United States or American (2000).
Economy: Employment by occupation: 7.0% management, 6.2% professional, 14.7% services, 27.1% sales, 0.0% farming, 17.1% construction, 27.9% production (2000).
Income: Per capita income: $14,826 (2000); Median household income: $37,292 (2000); Poverty rate: 5.1% (2000).
Taxes: Total city taxes per capita: $213 (1997); City property taxes per capita: $100 (1997).
Education: High school graduation rate: 84.8% (2000); College graduation rate: 5.5% (2000).
Housing: Homeownership rate: 73.0% (2000); Median home value: $70,300 (2000); Median rent: $393 per month (2000); Median age of housing: 60+ years (2000).
Transportation: Commute to work: 98.4% car, 0.0% public transportation, 0.0% walk, 1.6% work from home (2000); Travel time to work: 26.0% less than 15 minutes, 23.6% 15 to 30 minutes, 37.0% 30 to 45 minutes, 5.5% 45 to 60 minutes, 7.9% 60 minutes or more (2000)

DONAHUE (city). Covers a land area of 0.337 square miles and a water area of 0 square miles. Located at 41.69° N. Lat.; 90.67° W. Long. Elevation is 700 feet.
History: Michael Donahue, who was honored in the naming of Donahue, was the president of the Davenport Water Works and a mayor of Davenport, Iowa.
Population: 293 (2000); Race: 99.3% White, 0.0% Black, 0.0% Asian, 0.0% American Indian and Alaska Native, 1.8% Hispanic of any race, 0.7% two or more races (2000); Density: 870.6 persons per square mile (2000); Age: 29.0% under 18, 9.2% over 64 (2000); Marriage status: 17.2% never married, 71.3% now married, 4.3% widowed, 7.2% divorced (2000); Foreign born: 0.0% (2000); Ancestry (includes multiple ancestries): 62.5% German, 5.7% English, 4.9% Danish, 3.9% Belgian, 3.5% Dutch (2000).
Economy: Employment by occupation: 10.1% management, 11.5% professional, 7.4% services, 31.1% sales, 1.4% farming, 20.9% construction, 17.6% production (2000).
Income: Per capita income: $24,895 (2000); Median household income: $56,250 (2000); Poverty rate: 11.0% (2000).
Taxes: Total city taxes per capita: $190 (1997); City property taxes per capita: $81 (1997).
Education: High school graduation rate: 91.5% (2000); College graduation rate: 12.2% (2000).
Housing: Homeownership rate: 99.0% (2000); Median home value: $90,500 (2000); Median rent: $325 per month (2000); Median age of housing: 32 years (2000).
Transportation: Commute to work: 91.1% car, 0.0% public transportation, 4.1% walk, 4.8% work from home (2000); Travel time to work: 25.2% less than 15 minutes, 42.4% 15 to 30 minutes, 18.0% 30 to 45 minutes, 1.4% 45 to 60 minutes, 12.9% 60 minutes or more (2000)

ELDRIDGE (city). Covers a land area of 9.402 square miles and a water area of 0 square miles. Located at 41.64° N. Lat.; 90.58° W. Long. Elevation is 794 feet.
History: Originally called Eldridge Junction, the town of Eldridge is named for its founder, Jacob M. Eldridge, a realtor from Davenport.
Population: 4,159 (2000); Race: 97.0% White, 0.3% Black, 1.2% Asian, 0.0% American Indian and Alaska Native, 1.6% Hispanic of any race, 0.6% two or more races (2000); Density: 442.4 persons per square mile (2000); Age: 31.9% under 18, 7.2% over 64 (2000); Marriage status: 21.9% never married, 66.2% now married, 4.6% widowed, 7.3% divorced (2000); Foreign born: 1.4% (2000); Ancestry (includes multiple ancestries): 52.4% German, 13.7% Irish, 11.4% English, 5.5% United States or American, 5.1% Norwegian (2000).
Economy: Single-family building permits issued: 30 (2001) / 36 (2000); Multi-family building permits issued: 96 (2001) / 84 (2000); Employment by occupation: 14.1% management, 19.0% professional, 9.6% services, 28.8% sales, 0.5% farming, 9.5% construction, 18.6% production (2000).
Income: Per capita income: $21,514 (2000); Median household income: $54,167 (2000); Poverty rate: 4.5% (2000).
Taxes: Total city taxes per capita: $382 (2000); City property taxes per capita: $257 (2000).

Education: High school graduation rate: 92.4% (2000); College graduation rate: 33.1% (2000).

School District(s)

North Scott Community School District (PK-12)
2000 Enrollment: 3,007 319-285-9081

Housing: Homeownership rate: 78.3% (2000); Median home value: $131,900 (2000); Median rent: $427 per month (2000); Median age of housing: 25 years (2000).

Safety: Violent crime rate: 4.8 per 10,000 population; Property crime rate: 575.2 per 10,000 population (2001).

Newspapers: North Scott Press (1 x week)

Transportation: Commute to work: 95.0% car, 0.0% public transportation, 0.7% walk, 4.0% work from home (2000); Travel time to work: 35.7% less than 15 minutes, 45.7% 15 to 30 minutes, 13.2% 30 to 45 minutes, 1.9% 45 to 60 minutes, 3.5% 60 minutes or more (2000)

Additional Information Contacts

Eldridge Economic Development 563-285-9965
Eldridte N Scott Chamber of Commerce 563-285-9965

LE CLAIRE (city).

Covers a land area of 4.187 square miles and a water area of 0.198 square miles. Located at 41.59° N. Lat.; 90.35° W. Long. Elevation is 580 feet.

History: Le Claire was the boyhood home of William F. (Buffalo Bill) Cody. William, one of five children, was born in 1846, on what was then known as the John S. Wilson farm.

Population: 2,847 (2000); Race: 98.2% White, 0.0% Black, 0.0% Asian, 0.4% American Indian and Alaska Native, 1.7% Hispanic of any race, 1.3% two or more races (2000); Density: 680.0 persons per square mile (2000); Age: 24.5% under 18, 10.7% over 64 (2000); Marriage status: 20.9% never married, 60.5% now married, 3.9% widowed, 14.7% divorced (2000); Foreign born: 0.5% (2000); Ancestry (includes multiple ancestries): 39.8% German, 17.7% Irish, 8.9% United States or American, 8.0% English, 6.2% Other groups (2000).

Economy: Employment by occupation: 10.9% management, 15.7% professional, 17.9% services, 24.4% sales, 0.0% farming, 12.6% construction, 18.6% production (2000).

Income: Per capita income: $21,243 (2000); Median household income: $45,644 (2000); Poverty rate: 5.1% (2000).

Taxes: Total city taxes per capita: $355 (1997); City property taxes per capita: $297 (1997).

Education: High school graduation rate: 90.8% (2000); College graduation rate: 20.3% (2000).

Housing: Homeownership rate: 79.0% (2000); Median home value: $89,600 (2000); Median rent: $346 per month (2000); Median age of housing: 38 years (2000).

Transportation: Commute to work: 91.7% car, 0.0% public transportation, 5.3% walk, 2.8% work from home (2000); Travel time to work: 20.8% less than 15 minutes, 59.7% 15 to 30 minutes, 16.9% 30 to 45 minutes, 1.2% 45 to 60 minutes, 1.3% 60 minutes or more (2000)

LONG GROVE (city).

Covers a land area of 0.844 square miles and a water area of 0 square miles. Located at 41.69° N. Lat.; 90.58° W. Long.

History: Long Grove was named for Schultz's Grove, a large tract of timber that was standing here when the town was settled. In 1838 Alex and James Brownlie built cabins of logs and boards in the east end of the grove. The stagecoaches on the Davenport-De Witt line regularly stopped here.

Population: 597 (2000); Race: 98.3% White, 0.0% Black, 1.5% Asian, 0.0% American Indian and Alaska Native, 0.2% Hispanic of any race, 0.0% two or more races (2000); Density: 707.2 persons per square mile (2000); Age: 35.9% under 18, 4.2% over 64 (2000); Marriage status: 28.1% never married, 64.9% now married, 1.4% widowed, 5.7% divorced (2000); Foreign born: 1.7% (2000); Ancestry (includes multiple ancestries): 52.3% German, 19.1% Irish, 11.0% English, 6.9% Norwegian, 6.9% United States or American (2000).

Economy: Single-family building permits issued: 9 (2001) / 0 (2000); Multi-family building permits issued: 0 (2001) / 0 (2000); Employment by occupation: 10.5% management, 23.5% professional, 21.4% services, 14.2% sales, 1.2% farming, 13.0% construction, 16.3% production (2000).

Income: Per capita income: $23,041 (2000); Median household income: $65,250 (2000); Poverty rate: 2.1% (2000).

Taxes: Total city taxes per capita: $288 (1997); City property taxes per capita: $150 (1997).

Education: High school graduation rate: 93.7% (2000); College graduation rate: 30.9% (2000).

Housing: Homeownership rate: 98.0% (2000); Median home value: $142,300 (2000); Median rent: $525 per month (2000); Median age of housing: 25 years (2000).

Transportation: Commute to work: 96.0% car, 1.5% public transportation, 1.2% walk, 1.2% work from home (2000); Travel time to work: 30.1% less than 15 minutes, 48.8% 15 to 30 minutes, 13.7% 30 to 45 minutes, 4.3% 45 to 60 minutes, 3.1% 60 minutes or more (2000)

MAYSVILLE (city).

Aka Amity. Covers a land area of 0.272 square miles and a water area of 0 square miles. Located at 41.64° N. Lat.; 90.71° W. Long.

History: Maysville was the first town and the first post office in the county. A two-story stone schoolhouse was built in 1856.

Population: 163 (2000); Race: 100.0% White, 0.0% Black, 0.0% Asian, 0.0% American Indian and Alaska Native, 0.6% Hispanic of any race, 0.0% two or more races (2000); Density: 598.7 persons per square mile (2000); Age: 25.9% under 18, 8.4% over 64 (2000); Marriage status: 29.5% never married, 61.2% now married, 2.3% widowed, 7.0% divorced (2000); Foreign born: 0.0% (2000); Ancestry (includes multiple ancestries): 41.6% German, 22.9% United States or American, 19.3% Irish, 9.0% Dutch, 5.4% English (2000).

Economy: Single-family building permits issued: 0 (2001) / 1 (2000); Multi-family building permits issued: 0 (2001) / 0 (2000); Employment by occupation: 20.2% management, 0.0% professional, 16.0% services, 21.3% sales, 0.0% farming, 22.3% construction, 20.2% production (2000).

Income: Per capita income: $23,404 (2000); Median household income: $52,500 (2000); Poverty rate: 1.8% (2000).

Taxes: Total city taxes per capita: $171 (1997); City property taxes per capita: $171 (1997).

Education: High school graduation rate: 85.7% (2000); College graduation rate: 17.3% (2000).

Housing: Homeownership rate: 93.3% (2000); Median home value: $92,500 (2000); Median rent: $375 per month (2000); Median age of housing: 40 years (2000).

Transportation: Commute to work: 96.8% car, 0.0% public transportation, 0.0% walk, 3.2% work from home (2000); Travel time to work: 24.2% less than 15 minutes, 42.9% 15 to 30 minutes, 27.5% 30 to 45 minutes, 5.5% 45 to 60 minutes, 0.0% 60 minutes or more (2000)

MCCAUSLAND (city).

Covers a land area of 0.534 square miles and a water area of 0.023 square miles. Located at 41.74° N. Lat.; 90.44° W. Long.

History: McCausland was named for grocery store owner Tom McCausland.

Population: 299 (2000); Race: 97.8% White, 0.0% Black, 0.0% Asian, 0.0% American Indian and Alaska Native, 0.0% Hispanic of any race, 2.2% two or more races (2000); Density: 559.5 persons per square mile (2000); Age: 22.1% under 18, 12.2% over 64 (2000); Marriage status: 20.3% never married, 63.1% now married, 8.8% widowed, 7.8% divorced (2000); Foreign born: 0.0% (2000); Ancestry (includes multiple ancestries): 53.9% German, 17.3% Irish, 15.5% English, 5.9% Other groups, 3.7% Swedish (2000).

Economy: Employment by occupation: 12.8% management, 10.9% professional, 15.4% services, 23.1% sales, 0.0% farming, 17.9% construction, 19.9% production (2000).

Income: Per capita income: $22,426 (2000); Median household income: $34,531 (2000); Poverty rate: 6.3% (2000).

Taxes: Total city taxes per capita: $195 (1997); City property taxes per capita: $83 (1997).

Education: High school graduation rate: 77.9% (2000); College graduation rate: 16.0% (2000).

Housing: Homeownership rate: 89.1% (2000); Median home value: $79,000 (2000); Median rent: $330 per month (2000); Median age of housing: 35 years (2000).

Transportation: Commute to work: 94.7% car, 0.0% public transportation, 2.7% walk, 1.3% work from home (2000); Travel time to work: 23.6% less than 15 minutes, 50.7% 15 to 30 minutes, 23.0% 30 to 45 minutes, 2.7% 45 to 60 minutes, 0.0% 60 minutes or more (2000)

NEW LIBERTY (city).

Covers a land area of 0.095 square miles and a water area of 0 square miles. Located at 41.71° N. Lat.; 90.87° W. Long.

History: The town of New Liberty was founded with the arrival of the Burlington, Cedar Rapids & Northern Railroad.

Population: 121 (2000); Race: 100.0% White, 0.0% Black, 0.0% Asian, 0.0% American Indian and Alaska Native, 0.0% Hispanic of any race, 0.0% two or more races (2000); Density: 1,275.5 persons per square mile (2000); Age: 31.3% under 18, 20.6% over 64 (2000); Marriage status: 18.8% never married, 65.6% now married, 5.2% widowed, 10.4% divorced (2000); Foreign born: 0.0% (2000); Ancestry (includes multiple ancestries): 33.6%

German, 6.9% United States or American, 4.6% Irish, 4.6% European, 2.3% Norwegian (2000).
Economy: Employment by occupation: 20.7% management, 3.4% professional, 17.2% services, 22.4% sales, 0.0% farming, 15.5% construction, 20.7% production (2000).
Income: Per capita income: $18,195 (2000); Median household income: $50,625 (2000); Poverty rate: 19.5% (2000).
Taxes: Total city taxes per capita: $115 (1997); City property taxes per capita: $20 (1997).
Education: High school graduation rate: 71.8% (2000); College graduation rate: 2.4% (2000).
Housing: Homeownership rate: 76.1% (2000); Median home value: $55,000 (2000); Median rent: $508 per month (2000); Median age of housing: 60+ years (2000).
Transportation: Commute to work: 83.9% car, 3.6% public transportation, 10.7% walk, 1.8% work from home (2000); Travel time to work: 20.0% less than 15 minutes, 27.3% 15 to 30 minutes, 45.5% 30 to 45 minutes, 0.0% 45 to 60 minutes, 7.3% 60 minutes or more (2000)

PANORAMA PARK (city). Covers a land area of 0.068 square miles and a water area of 0 square miles. Located at 41.55° N. Lat.; 90.45° W. Long.
Population: 111 (2000); Race: 98.5% White, 0.0% Black, 1.5% Asian, 0.0% American Indian and Alaska Native, 0.0% Hispanic of any race, 0.0% two or more races (2000); Density: 1,638.2 persons per square mile (2000); Age: 23.7% under 18, 17.6% over 64 (2000); Marriage status: 16.2% never married, 62.9% now married, 14.3% widowed, 6.7% divorced (2000); Foreign born: 1.5% (2000); Ancestry (includes multiple ancestries): 54.2% German, 17.6% Irish, 13.0% United States or American, 10.7% Swedish, 8.4% English (2000).
Economy: Single-family building permits issued: 1 (2001) / 0 (2000); Multi-family building permits issued: 0 (2001) / 0 (2000); Employment by occupation: 7.4% management, 5.6% professional, 11.1% services, 14.8% sales, 0.0% farming, 13.0% construction, 48.1% production (2000).
Income: Per capita income: $17,062 (2000); Median household income: $38,125 (2000); Poverty rate: 0.0% (2000).
Taxes: Total city taxes per capita: $208 (1997); City property taxes per capita: $104 (1997).
Education: High school graduation rate: 80.0% (2000); College graduation rate: 4.4% (2000).
Housing: Homeownership rate: 78.2% (2000); Median home value: $76,900 (2000); Median rent: $400 per month (2000); Median age of housing: 37 years (2000).
Transportation: Commute to work: 92.6% car, 7.4% public transportation, 0.0% walk, 0.0% work from home (2000); Travel time to work: 22.2% less than 15 minutes, 51.9% 15 to 30 minutes, 13.0% 30 to 45 minutes, 0.0% 45 to 60 minutes, 13.0% 60 minutes or more (2000)

PARK VIEW (CDP). Covers a land area of 1.081 square miles and a water area of 0 square miles. Located at 41.69° N. Lat.; 90.54° W. Long.
Population: 2,169 (2000); Race: 94.4% White, 1.3% Black, 1.0% Asian, 0.0% American Indian and Alaska Native, 1.2% Hispanic of any race, 1.8% two or more races (2000); Density: 2,006.5 persons per square mile (2000); Age: 35.8% under 18, 3.6% over 64 (2000); Marriage status: 22.3% never married, 68.0% now married, 1.5% widowed, 8.1% divorced (2000); Foreign born: 1.9% (2000); Ancestry (includes multiple ancestries): 31.8% German, 13.5% Irish, 10.4% Other groups, 9.2% United States or American, 6.9% English (2000).
Economy: Employment by occupation: 10.5% management, 17.0% professional, 11.9% services, 29.4% sales, 1.4% farming, 5.6% construction, 24.3% production (2000).
Income: Per capita income: $18,649 (2000); Median household income: $51,000 (2000); Poverty rate: 1.0% (2000).
Education: High school graduation rate: 91.7% (2000); College graduation rate: 24.0% (2000).
Housing: Homeownership rate: 64.7% (2000); Median home value: $119,700 (2000); Median rent: $473 per month (2000); Median age of housing: 24 years (2000).
Transportation: Commute to work: 98.4% car, 0.0% public transportation, 0.3% walk, 1.3% work from home (2000); Travel time to work: 19.9% less than 15 minutes, 56.1% 15 to 30 minutes, 20.1% 30 to 45 minutes, 2.2% 45 to 60 minutes, 1.7% 60 minutes or more (2000)

PRINCETON (city). Covers a land area of 2.554 square miles and a water area of 0 square miles. Located at 41.67° N. Lat.; 90.34° W. Long. Elevation is 597 feet.
Population: 946 (2000); Race: 94.9% White, 0.6% Black, 0.0% Asian, 0.2% American Indian and Alaska Native, 2.5% Hispanic of any race, 3.0% two or more races (2000); Density: 370.5 persons per square mile (2000); Age: 28.6% under 18, 9.8% over 64 (2000); Marriage status: 22.5% never married, 59.4% now married, 7.4% widowed, 10.7% divorced (2000); Foreign born: 0.6% (2000); Ancestry (includes multiple ancestries): 42.5% German, 20.4% Irish, 13.1% Other groups, 11.3% English, 5.2% United States or American (2000).
Economy: Single-family building permits issued: 0 (2001) / 1 (2000); Multi-family building permits issued: 0 (2001) / 0 (2000); Employment by occupation: 8.4% management, 10.8% professional, 20.5% services, 21.5% sales, 0.4% farming, 10.6% construction, 27.8% production (2000).
Income: Per capita income: $18,678 (2000); Median household income: $44,833 (2000); Poverty rate: 6.0% (2000).
Taxes: Total city taxes per capita: $209 (1997); City property taxes per capita: $100 (1997).
Education: High school graduation rate: 88.3% (2000); College graduation rate: 12.4% (2000).
Housing: Homeownership rate: 86.1% (2000); Median home value: $94,200 (2000); Median rent: $356 per month (2000); Median age of housing: 35 years (2000).
Transportation: Commute to work: 93.4% car, 0.0% public transportation, 2.0% walk, 3.4% work from home (2000); Travel time to work: 18.6% less than 15 minutes, 40.4% 15 to 30 minutes, 35.7% 30 to 45 minutes, 2.1% 45 to 60 minutes, 3.3% 60 minutes or more (2000)

RIVERDALE (city). Covers a land area of 1.788 square miles and a water area of 0.390 square miles. Located at 41.53° N. Lat.; 90.46° W. Long.
Population: 656 (2000); Race: 97.9% White, 0.0% Black, 0.0% Asian, 0.0% American Indian and Alaska Native, 1.3% Hispanic of any race, 1.1% two or more races (2000); Density: 366.8 persons per square mile (2000); Age: 24.7% under 18, 20.5% over 64 (2000); Marriage status: 21.6% never married, 60.1% now married, 6.9% widowed, 11.5% divorced (2000); Foreign born: 0.3% (2000); Ancestry (includes multiple ancestries): 31.5% German, 15.7% English, 13.6% United States or American, 12.7% Irish, 3.2% French (except Basque) (2000).
Economy: Employment by occupation: 12.9% management, 21.2% professional, 14.1% services, 21.2% sales, 0.0% farming, 14.1% construction, 16.5% production (2000).
Income: Per capita income: $19,074 (2000); Median household income: $32,656 (2000); Poverty rate: 16.7% (2000).
Taxes: Total city taxes per capita: $797 (1997); City property taxes per capita: $599 (1997).
Education: High school graduation rate: 81.9% (2000); College graduation rate: 25.2% (2000).
Housing: Homeownership rate: 75.0% (2000); Median home value: $138,000 (2000); Median rent: $323 per month (2000); Median age of housing: 37 years (2000).
Transportation: Commute to work: 92.9% car, 3.5% public transportation, 0.0% walk, 2.0% work from home (2000); Travel time to work: 41.6% less than 15 minutes, 46.4% 15 to 30 minutes, 2.0% 30 to 45 minutes, 5.2% 45 to 60 minutes, 4.8% 60 minutes or more (2000)

WALCOTT (city). Covers a land area of 2.960 square miles and a water area of 0.025 square miles. Located at 41.59° N. Lat.; 90.77° W. Long. Elevation is 740 feet.
History: Walcott was established in 1853, and did not have a serious crime committed in the town until 1936, when $200 in stamps were stolen.
Population: 1,528 (2000); Race: 98.5% White, 0.0% Black, 0.5% Asian, 0.3% American Indian and Alaska Native, 0.1% Hispanic of any race, 0.7% two or more races (2000); Density: 516.2 persons per square mile (2000); Age: 26.2% under 18, 12.8% over 64 (2000); Marriage status: 21.4% never married, 62.5% now married, 4.5% widowed, 11.6% divorced (2000); Foreign born: 0.7% (2000); Ancestry (includes multiple ancestries): 51.5% German, 13.5% Irish, 6.6% English, 6.3% United States or American, 3.3% Other groups (2000).
Economy: Single-family building permits issued: 4 (2001) / 3 (2000); Multi-family building permits issued: 0 (2001) / 0 (2000); Employment by occupation: 12.7% management, 13.5% professional, 17.3% services, 24.2% sales, 0.6% farming, 12.6% construction, 19.0% production (2000).
Income: Per capita income: $20,018 (2000); Median household income: $45,281 (2000); Poverty rate: 7.0% (2000).
Taxes: Total city taxes per capita: $575 (2000); City property taxes per capita: $433 (2000).
Education: High school graduation rate: 86.9% (2000); College graduation rate: 16.8% (2000).

Housing: Homeownership rate: 78.0% (2000); Median home value: $96,900 (2000); Median rent: $353 per month (2000); Median age of housing: 30 years (2000).
Transportation: Commute to work: 94.4% car, 0.0% public transportation, 2.3% walk, 2.4% work from home (2000); Travel time to work: 31.5% less than 15 minutes, 44.9% 15 to 30 minutes, 18.5% 30 to 45 minutes, 1.5% 45 to 60 minutes, 3.6% 60 minutes or more (2000)

Shelby County

Located in western Iowa; prairie area, drained by the West Nishnabotna River. Covers a land area of 590.80 square miles, a water area of 0.50 square miles, and is located in the Central Time Zone. The county government was organized in 1851. County seat is Harlan.

Weather Station: Harlan Elevation: 1,207 feet

	Jan	Feb	Mar	Apr	May	Jun	Jul	Aug	Sep	Oct	Nov	Dec
High	29	36	48	62	73	83	85	83	75	63	46	33
Low	10	17	27	38	50	60	64	62	53	40	28	16
Precip	0.8	0.7	2.2	3.3	4.3	4.3	4.1	3.7	4.6	2.8	1.8	1.0
Snow	7.6	6.5	5.3	1.6	tr	tr	tr	0.0	tr	0.9	3.1	6.2

High and Low temperatures in degrees Fahrenheit; Precipitation and Snow in inches

Population: 13,173 (2000); Race: 98.8% White, 0.1% Black, 0.3% Asian, 0.0% American Indian and Alaska Native, 0.7% Hispanic of any race, 0.5% two or more races (2000); Density: 22.3 persons per square mile (2000); Age: 26.3% under 18, 20.5% over 64 (2000).
Religion: Five largest groups: 32.6% Catholic Church, 18.9% Evangelical Lutheran Church in America, 12.1% The United Methodist Church, 4.3% American Baptist Churches in the USA, 2.0% Christian Churches and Churches of Christ (2000).
Economy: Unemployment rate: 2.8% (11/2002); Total civilian labor force: 7,145 (11/2002); Leading industries: 20.3% health care and social assistance; 15.3% retail trade; 11.1% information (2000); Companies that employ more than 1,000 persons: 0 (2000); Companies that employ more than 100 persons: 7 (2000); Farms: 921 totaling 342,366 acres (1997); Minority business ownership rate: 0.0% (1997); Women business ownership rate: 14.5% (1997); Retail sales per capita: $8,984 (1997). Single-family building permits issued: 25 (2001) / 29 (2000); Multi-family building permits issued: 0 (2001) / 0 (2000).
Income: Per capita income: $16,969 (2000); Median household income: $37,442 (2000); Poverty rate: 6.0% (2000); Bankruptcy rate: 1.46% (2001).
Taxes: Total county taxes per capita: $356 (2000); County property taxes per capita: $337 (2000).
Education: High school graduation rate: 86.6% (2000); College graduation rate: 15.3% (2000).
Housing: Homeownership rate: 77.1% (2000); Median home value: $73,800 (2000); Median rent: $293 per month (2000); Median age of housing: 52 years (2000).
Health: Birth rate: 107.8 per 10,000 population (1998); Age adjusted death rate: 72.8 per 10,000 population (1999); Age adjusted cancer mortality rate: 186.3 deaths per 100,000 population (1999). Number of physicians: 4.6 per 10,000 population (1999); Number of hospital beds: 39.5 per 10,000 population (1999).
Elections: 2000 Presidential election results: 36.3% Gore, 60.8% Bush, 1.9% Nader, 0.6% Buchanan
National and State Parks: Prairie Rose State Park
Additional Information Contacts
Shelby County Government Offices 712-755-3831
Harlan Chamber of Commerce. 712-755-2114
West Central Iowa Board of Realtors. 712-755-5446

Shelby County Communities

DEFIANCE (city). Covers a land area of 0.398 square miles and a water area of 0 square miles. Located at 41.82° N. Lat.; 95.34° W. Long. Elevation is 1,283 feet.
Population: 346 (2000); Race: 92.7% White, 0.0% Black, 0.0% Asian, 0.0% American Indian and Alaska Native, 5.9% Hispanic of any race, 1.4% two or more races (2000); Density: 868.9 persons per square mile (2000); Age: 36.3% under 18, 13.4% over 64 (2000); Marriage status: 21.5% never married, 69.5% now married, 3.9% widowed, 5.1% divorced (2000); Foreign born: 1.7% (2000); Ancestry (includes multiple ancestries): 62.8% German, 13.4% Irish, 7.0% Other groups, 5.3% Dutch, 4.5% French (except Basque) (2000).
Economy: In agricultural area. Single-family building permits issued: 0 (2001) / 1 (2000); Multi-family building permits issued: 0 (2001) / 0 (2000); Employment by occupation: 9.3% management, 9.3% professional, 13.2% services, 33.8% sales, 0.0% farming, 19.2% construction, 15.2% production (2000).
Income: Per capita income: $12,492 (2000); Median household income: $36,875 (2000); Poverty rate: 7.0% (2000).
Taxes: Total city taxes per capita: $98 (1997); City property taxes per capita: $94 (1997).
Education: High school graduation rate: 89.1% (2000); College graduation rate: 5.2% (2000).
Housing: Homeownership rate: 85.0% (2000); Median home value: $57,000 (2000); Median rent: $257 per month (2000); Median age of housing: 57 years (2000).
Transportation: Commute to work: 90.5% car, 0.0% public transportation, 5.4% walk, 2.7% work from home (2000); Travel time to work: 32.6% less than 15 minutes, 52.8% 15 to 30 minutes, 11.1% 30 to 45 minutes, 0.0% 45 to 60 minutes, 3.5% 60 minutes or more (2000)

EARLING (city). Covers a land area of 0.610 square miles and a water area of 0 square miles. Located at 41.77° N. Lat.; 95.41° W. Long. Elevation is 1,408 feet.
History: Earling, first called Marathon, was named for H.B. Earling, president of the Chicago, Milwaukee & St. Paul Railroad.
Population: 471 (2000); Race: 99.1% White, 0.0% Black, 0.0% Asian, 0.9% American Indian and Alaska Native, 0.2% Hispanic of any race, 0.0% two or more races (2000); Density: 772.3 persons per square mile (2000); Age: 14.6% under 18, 36.5% over 64 (2000); Marriage status: 26.2% never married, 57.0% now married, 10.7% widowed, 6.1% divorced (2000); Foreign born: 0.0% (2000); Ancestry (includes multiple ancestries): 55.0% German, 8.1% Other groups, 8.1% Irish, 3.5% Danish, 2.8% United States or American (2000).
Economy: Employment by occupation: 11.3% management, 10.4% professional, 21.3% services, 19.9% sales, 3.6% farming, 12.2% construction, 21.3% production (2000).
Income: Per capita income: $15,866 (2000); Median household income: $29,702 (2000); Poverty rate: 7.5% (2000).
Taxes: Total city taxes per capita: $150 (1997); City property taxes per capita: $148 (1997).
Education: High school graduation rate: 79.1% (2000); College graduation rate: 8.4% (2000).
Housing: Homeownership rate: 81.9% (2000); Median home value: $57,700 (2000); Median rent: $208 per month (2000); Median age of housing: 43 years (2000).
Transportation: Commute to work: 93.5% car, 0.5% public transportation, 0.9% walk, 3.7% work from home (2000); Travel time to work: 35.3% less than 15 minutes, 42.0% 15 to 30 minutes, 9.7% 30 to 45 minutes, 4.8% 45 to 60 minutes, 8.2% 60 minutes or more (2000)

ELK HORN (city). Covers a land area of 0.768 square miles and a water area of 0 square miles. Located at 41.59° N. Lat.; 95.06° W. Long. Elevation is 1,363 feet.
Population: 649 (2000); Race: 98.9% White, 0.0% Black, 0.5% Asian, 0.0% American Indian and Alaska Native, 0.6% Hispanic of any race, 0.6% two or more races (2000); Density: 844.6 persons per square mile (2000); Age: 21.5% under 18, 41.8% over 64 (2000); Marriage status: 14.3% never married, 56.2% now married, 23.2% widowed, 6.3% divorced (2000); Foreign born: 3.2% (2000); Ancestry (includes multiple ancestries): 42.9% Danish, 22.7% German, 8.5% English, 8.3% Irish, 5.9% United States or American (2000).
Economy: In agricultural area: grain, meal. Elk Horn and neighboring Kimballton (Audubon co.) are known as Danish Villages. Single-family building permits issued: 1 (2001) / 1 (2000); Multi-family building permits issued: 0 (2001) / 0 (2000); Employment by occupation: 13.5% management, 16.8% professional, 22.5% services, 25.4% sales, 0.0% farming, 7.8% construction, 13.9% production (2000).
Income: Per capita income: $15,412 (2000); Median household income: $33,333 (2000); Poverty rate: 2.7% (2000).
Taxes: Total city taxes per capita: $194 (1997); City property taxes per capita: $191 (1997).
Education: High school graduation rate: 78.7% (2000); College graduation rate: 13.2% (2000).

School District(s)

Elk Horn-Kimballton Community School District (PK-12)
2000 Enrollment: 334 712-764-4616

Housing: Homeownership rate: 83.5% (2000); Median home value: $64,000 (2000); Median rent: $199 per month (2000); Median age of housing: 53 years (2000).
Newspapers: The Danish Villages Voice (1 x week)
Transportation: Commute to work: 80.3% car, 0.0% public transportation, 14.8% walk, 4.9% work from home (2000); Travel time to work: 55.6% less than 15 minutes, 29.7% 15 to 30 minutes, 10.8% 30 to 45 minutes, 3.0% 45 to 60 minutes, 0.9% 60 minutes or more (2000)

HARLAN (city). Covers a land area of 4.366 square miles and a water area of 0 square miles. Located at 41.65° N. Lat.; 95.32° W. Long. Elevation is 1,250 feet.
History: Harlan was settled in 1858 and named for James Harlan, whose only daughter married Robert T. Lincoln, son of the President.
Population: 5,282 (2000); Race: 98.9% White, 0.0% Black, 0.5% Asian, 0.0% American Indian and Alaska Native, 0.4% Hispanic of any race, 0.6% two or more races (2000); Density: 1,209.8 persons per square mile (2000); Age: 25.7% under 18, 21.6% over 64 (2000); Marriage status: 18.0% never married, 64.4% now married, 9.8% widowed, 7.8% divorced (2000); Foreign born: 0.4% (2000); Ancestry (includes multiple ancestries): 48.7% German, 13.7% Danish, 12.6% Irish, 7.6% English, 5.1% United States or American (2000).
Economy: Single-family building permits issued: 11 (2001) / 20 (2000); Multi-family building permits issued: 0 (2001) / 0 (2000); Employment by occupation: 12.4% management, 13.4% professional, 14.3% services, 29.2% sales, 2.0% farming, 9.5% construction, 19.2% production (2000).
Income: Per capita income: $17,514 (2000); Median household income: $35,899 (2000); Poverty rate: 7.0% (2000).
Taxes: Total city taxes per capita: $313 (2000); City property taxes per capita: $305 (2000).
Education: High school graduation rate: 85.4% (2000); College graduation rate: 18.4% (2000).

School District(s)

Harlan Community School District (KG-12)
2000 Enrollment: 1,691 712-755-2152

Housing: Homeownership rate: 75.1% (2000); Median home value: $75,600 (2000); Median rent: $322 per month (2000); Median age of housing: 43 years (2000).
Hospitals: Shelby County Myrtue Memorial Hospital (52 beds)
Newspapers: Rocket (1 x week); Penny Saver (1 x week); Harlan Tribune (1 x week); Harlan News-Advertiser (1 x week)
Transportation: Commute to work: 87.8% car, 0.2% public transportation, 5.4% walk, 5.6% work from home (2000); Travel time to work: 70.9% less than 15 minutes, 12.1% 15 to 30 minutes, 7.3% 30 to 45 minutes, 2.8% 45 to 60 minutes, 6.9% 60 minutes or more (2000)

Additional Information Contacts

Harlan Chamber of Commerce. 712-755-2114
West Central Iowa Board of Realtors. 712-755-5446

IRWIN (city). Covers a land area of 0.596 square miles and a water area of 0 square miles. Located at 41.79° N. Lat.; 95.20° W. Long. Elevation is 1,264 feet.
History: The owner of the site of Irwin, established in 1881, was E.W. Irwin, who gave his name to the town.
Population: 372 (2000); Race: 98.9% White, 0.0% Black, 0.0% Asian, 0.0% American Indian and Alaska Native, 4.9% Hispanic of any race, 1.1% two or more races (2000); Density: 624.4 persons per square mile (2000); Age: 17.5% under 18, 25.6% over 64 (2000); Marriage status: 21.5% never married, 64.4% now married, 9.9% widowed, 4.2% divorced (2000); Foreign born: 0.3% (2000); Ancestry (includes multiple ancestries): 40.5% German, 14.4% Norwegian, 12.9% Danish, 8.9% Irish, 6.9% Other groups (2000).
Economy: Single-family building permits issued: 3 (2001) / 1 (2000); Multi-family building permits issued: 0 (2001) / 0 (2000); Employment by occupation: 15.9% management, 9.7% professional, 15.3% services, 25.6% sales, 1.1% farming, 15.9% construction, 16.5% production (2000).
Income: Per capita income: $15,429 (2000); Median household income: $30,417 (2000); Poverty rate: 9.8% (2000).
Taxes: Total city taxes per capita: $112 (1997); City property taxes per capita: $112 (1997).
Education: High school graduation rate: 86.7% (2000); College graduation rate: 14.9% (2000).
Housing: Homeownership rate: 80.4% (2000); Median home value: $42,500 (2000); Median rent: $173 per month (2000); Median age of housing: 53 years (2000).
Transportation: Commute to work: 89.1% car, 0.0% public transportation, 9.8% walk, 1.1% work from home (2000); Travel time to work: 43.0% less than 15 minutes, 38.4% 15 to 30 minutes, 16.3% 30 to 45 minutes, 0.0% 45 to 60 minutes, 2.3% 60 minutes or more (2000)

KIRKMAN (city). Covers a land area of 0.285 square miles and a water area of 0 square miles. Located at 41.72° N. Lat.; 95.26° W. Long. Elevation is 1,235 feet.
History: Kirkman was named for the Chicago & North Western Railroad official, M. M. Kirkman. The town was laid out in 1880 by the Western Town Lot Company.
Population: 76 (2000); Race: 97.5% White, 0.0% Black, 0.0% Asian, 0.0% American Indian and Alaska Native, 2.5% Hispanic of any race, 0.0% two or more races (2000); Density: 266.3 persons per square mile (2000); Age: 29.6% under 18, 16.0% over 64 (2000); Marriage status: 38.2% never married, 55.9% now married, 0.0% widowed, 5.9% divorced (2000); Foreign born: 2.5% (2000); Ancestry (includes multiple ancestries): 30.9% United States or American, 23.5% German, 13.6% Danish, 8.6% Irish, 4.9% English (2000).
Economy: Employment by occupation: 0.0% management, 7.0% professional, 4.7% services, 30.2% sales, 0.0% farming, 27.9% construction, 30.2% production (2000).
Income: Per capita income: $16,941 (2000); Median household income: $49,375 (2000); Poverty rate: 11.8% (2000).
Taxes: Total city taxes per capita: $53 (1997); City property taxes per capita: $53 (1997).
Education: High school graduation rate: 74.5% (2000); College graduation rate: 0.0% (2000).
Housing: Homeownership rate: 77.8% (2000); Median home value: $40,000 (2000); Median rent: $133 per month (2000); Median age of housing: 60+ years (2000).
Transportation: Commute to work: 100.0% car, 0.0% public transportation, 0.0% walk, 0.0% work from home (2000); Travel time to work: 9.8% less than 15 minutes, 63.4% 15 to 30 minutes, 14.6% 30 to 45 minutes, 0.0% 45 to 60 minutes, 12.2% 60 minutes or more (2000)

PANAMA (city). Covers a land area of 0.285 square miles and a water area of 0 square miles. Located at 41.72° N. Lat.; 95.47° W. Long. Elevation is 1,325 feet.
History: The town of Panama was once known as Crandallville. The origin of the name of Panama is not recorded.
Population: 212 (2000); Race: 98.6% White, 0.0% Black, 0.0% Asian, 0.0% American Indian and Alaska Native, 0.0% Hispanic of any race, 1.4% two or more races (2000); Density: 745.0 persons per square mile (2000); Age: 19.9% under 18, 19.9% over 64 (2000); Marriage status: 25.8% never married, 60.4% now married, 12.6% widowed, 1.1% divorced (2000); Foreign born: 0.0% (2000); Ancestry (includes multiple ancestries): 64.8% German, 8.8% Irish, 6.0% United States or American, 5.6% English, 4.6% Polish (2000).
Economy: Single-family building permits issued: 2 (2001) / 1 (2000); Multi-family building permits issued: 0 (2001) / 0 (2000); Employment by occupation: 8.8% management, 15.8% professional, 11.4% services, 32.5% sales, 0.0% farming, 12.3% construction, 19.3% production (2000).
Income: Per capita income: $20,078 (2000); Median household income: $37,917 (2000); Poverty rate: 5.6% (2000).
Taxes: Total city taxes per capita: $177 (1997); City property taxes per capita: $172 (1997).
Education: High school graduation rate: 85.8% (2000); College graduation rate: 9.7% (2000).
Housing: Homeownership rate: 90.2% (2000); Median home value: $62,500 (2000); Median rent: $238 per month (2000); Median age of housing: 44 years (2000).
Transportation: Commute to work: 81.3% car, 0.0% public transportation, 17.0% walk, 1.8% work from home (2000); Travel time to work: 45.5% less than 15 minutes, 30.0% 15 to 30 minutes, 8.2% 30 to 45 minutes, 8.2% 45 to 60 minutes, 8.2% 60 minutes or more (2000)

PORTSMOUTH (city). Covers a land area of 0.273 square miles and a water area of 0 square miles. Located at 41.65° N. Lat.; 95.52° W. Long. Elevation is 1,237 feet.
Population: 225 (2000); Race: 100.0% White, 0.0% Black, 0.0% Asian, 0.0% American Indian and Alaska Native, 0.0% Hispanic of any race, 0.0% two or more races (2000); Density: 823.5 persons per square mile (2000); Age: 34.0% under 18, 18.0% over 64 (2000); Marriage status: 35.3% never married, 48.4% now married, 9.5% widowed, 6.8% divorced (2000); Foreign born: 0.0% (2000); Ancestry (includes multiple ancestries): 54.5% German, 7.0% United States or American, 6.6% Irish, 6.1% Danish, 3.3% Russian (2000).

Economy: Single-family building permits issued: 0 (2001) / 1 (2000); Multi-family building permits issued: 0 (2001) / 0 (2000); Employment by occupation: 10.3% management, 11.2% professional, 24.3% services, 23.4% sales, 0.0% farming, 16.8% construction, 14.0% production (2000).
Income: Per capita income: $15,473 (2000); Median household income: $28,000 (2000); Poverty rate: 14.8% (2000).
Taxes: Total city taxes per capita: $137 (1997); City property taxes per capita: $137 (1997).
Education: High school graduation rate: 86.6% (2000); College graduation rate: 7.7% (2000).
Housing: Homeownership rate: 84.8% (2000); Median home value: $60,700 (2000); Median rent: $231 per month (2000); Median age of housing: 56 years (2000).
Transportation: Commute to work: 80.8% car, 0.0% public transportation, 14.4% walk, 4.8% work from home (2000); Travel time to work: 32.3% less than 15 minutes, 17.2% 15 to 30 minutes, 11.1% 30 to 45 minutes, 22.2% 45 to 60 minutes, 17.2% 60 minutes or more (2000)

SHELBY (city). Covers a land area of 1.637 square miles and a water area of 0 square miles. Located at 41.51° N. Lat.; 95.45° W. Long. Elevation is 1,338 feet.
History: Shelby was named after the Revolutionary War officer, General Isaac Shelby.
Population: 696 (2000); Race: 96.5% White, 0.0% Black, 0.3% Asian, 0.1% American Indian and Alaska Native, 2.0% Hispanic of any race, 2.8% two or more races (2000); Density: 425.2 persons per square mile (2000); Age: 27.7% under 18, 14.3% over 64 (2000); Marriage status: 17.7% never married, 66.5% now married, 7.3% widowed, 8.4% divorced (2000); Foreign born: 0.6% (2000); Ancestry (includes multiple ancestries): 42.8% German, 13.3% Irish, 10.5% Danish, 8.1% United States or American, 8.1% English (2000).
Economy: Single-family building permits issued: 1 (2001) / 1 (2000); Multi-family building permits issued: 0 (2001) / 0 (2000); Employment by occupation: 10.3% management, 14.2% professional, 15.4% services, 28.4% sales, 2.7% farming, 14.5% construction, 14.5% production (2000).
Income: Per capita income: $14,720 (2000); Median household income: $31,250 (2000); Poverty rate: 13.0% (2000).
Taxes: Total city taxes per capita: $99 (1997); City property taxes per capita: $97 (1997).
Education: High school graduation rate: 90.6% (2000); College graduation rate: 12.1% (2000).
Housing: Homeownership rate: 80.6% (2000); Median home value: $73,400 (2000); Median rent: $282 per month (2000); Median age of housing: 60+ years (2000).
Transportation: Commute to work: 94.8% car, 0.0% public transportation, 2.8% walk, 1.5% work from home (2000); Travel time to work: 30.8% less than 15 minutes, 21.8% 15 to 30 minutes, 16.5% 30 to 45 minutes, 24.6% 45 to 60 minutes, 6.2% 60 minutes or more (2000)

TENNANT (city). Covers a land area of 0.714 square miles and a water area of 0 square miles. Located at 41.59° N. Lat.; 95.44° W. Long. Elevation is 1,382 feet.
History: Tennant was founded in 1903. The town was named for Englishman George Tennant, an investor with the Chicago Great Western Railway.
Population: 73 (2000); Race: 96.7% White, 0.0% Black, 3.3% Asian, 0.0% American Indian and Alaska Native, 0.0% Hispanic of any race, 0.0% two or more races (2000); Density: 102.3 persons per square mile (2000); Age: 10.0% under 18, 41.7% over 64 (2000); Marriage status: 3.6% never married, 75.0% now married, 5.4% widowed, 16.1% divorced (2000); Foreign born: 3.3% (2000); Ancestry (includes multiple ancestries): 28.3% German, 20.0% United States or American, 13.3% Danish, 6.7% English, 3.3% Scottish (2000).
Economy: Employment by occupation: 10.3% management, 0.0% professional, 20.7% services, 24.1% sales, 0.0% farming, 17.2% construction, 27.6% production (2000).
Income: Per capita income: $18,982 (2000); Median household income: $32,321 (2000); Poverty rate: 1.7% (2000).
Taxes: Total city taxes per capita: $52 (1997); City property taxes per capita: $52 (1997).
Education: High school graduation rate: 85.2% (2000); College graduation rate: 13.0% (2000).
Housing: Homeownership rate: 93.3% (2000); Median home value: $50,000 (2000); Median age of housing: 48 years (2000).
Transportation: Commute to work: 55.2% car, 0.0% public transportation, 13.8% walk, 31.0% work from home (2000); Travel time to work: 30.0% less than 15 minutes, 50.0% 15 to 30 minutes, 20.0% 30 to 45 minutes, 0.0% 45 to 60 minutes, 0.0% 60 minutes or more (2000)

WESTPHALIA (city). Covers a land area of 0.091 square miles and a water area of 0 square miles. Located at 41.71° N. Lat.; 95.39° W. Long. Elevation is 1,402 feet.
History: Westphalia was named for a German province.
Population: 160 (2000); Race: 98.6% White, 0.0% Black, 0.0% Asian, 0.0% American Indian and Alaska Native, 0.0% Hispanic of any race, 1.4% two or more races (2000); Density: 1,761.4 persons per square mile (2000); Age: 30.1% under 18, 16.8% over 64 (2000); Marriage status: 17.5% never married, 63.1% now married, 14.6% widowed, 4.9% divorced (2000); Foreign born: 0.0% (2000); Ancestry (includes multiple ancestries): 79.7% German, 8.4% English, 8.4% Danish, 7.0% Austrian, 6.3% Other groups (2000).
Economy: Single-family building permits issued: 1 (2001) / 1 (2000); Multi-family building permits issued: 0 (2001) / 0 (2000); Employment by occupation: 9.7% management, 6.5% professional, 14.5% services, 38.7% sales, 0.0% farming, 11.3% construction, 19.4% production (2000).
Income: Per capita income: $17,066 (2000); Median household income: $35,938 (2000); Poverty rate: 11.2% (2000).
Taxes: Total city taxes per capita: $88 (1997); City property taxes per capita: $80 (1997).
Education: High school graduation rate: 91.3% (2000); College graduation rate: 13.0% (2000).
Housing: Homeownership rate: 82.5% (2000); Median home value: $53,000 (2000); Median rent: $188 per month (2000); Median age of housing: 55 years (2000).
Transportation: Commute to work: 95.2% car, 0.0% public transportation, 0.0% walk, 1.6% work from home (2000); Travel time to work: 44.3% less than 15 minutes, 21.3% 15 to 30 minutes, 11.5% 30 to 45 minutes, 0.0% 45 to 60 minutes, 23.0% 60 minutes or more (2000)

Sioux County

Located in northwestern Iowa; bounded on the west by the Big Sioux River and the South Dakota border; drained by the Rock, Floyd, and West Branch Floyd Rivers. Covers a land area of 767.90 square miles, a water area of 0.70 square miles, and is located in the Central Time Zone. The county government was organized in 1851. County seat is Orange City.

Weather Station: Hawarden Elevation: 1,187 feet

	Jan	Feb	Mar	Apr	May	Jun	Jul	Aug	Sep	Oct	Nov	Dec
High	26	33	45	61	73	82	85	83	75	63	43	31
Low	6	13	24	36	48	58	63	61	50	37	24	11
Precip	0.5	0.6	2.0	2.9	3.6	3.7	3.6	3.1	2.8	2.0	1.6	0.7
Snow	6.2	4.9	6.0	1.8	0.0	0.0	0.0	0.0	0.0	1.1	6.0	6.9

High and Low temperatures in degrees Fahrenheit; Precipitation and Snow in inches

Weather Station: Sioux Center 2 SE Elevation: 1,358 feet

	Jan	Feb	Mar	Apr	May	Jun	Jul	Aug	Sep	Oct	Nov	Dec
High	25	33	45	61	74	83	85	83	76	64	43	30
Low	6	13	24	36	48	58	62	59	50	38	24	12
Precip	0.7	0.7	2.1	2.9	3.5	4.5	3.8	3.3	2.8	2.2	1.6	0.8
Snow	7.5	5.6	7.9	2.8	tr	0.0	0.0	0.0	tr	1.1	6.0	6.8

High and Low temperatures in degrees Fahrenheit; Precipitation and Snow in inches

Population: 31,589 (2000); Race: 97.3% White, 0.3% Black, 0.6% Asian, 0.1% American Indian and Alaska Native, 2.1% Hispanic of any race, 0.6% two or more races (2000); Density: 41.1 persons per square mile (2000); Age: 27.2% under 18, 15.0% over 64 (2000).
Religion: Five largest groups: 35.7% Reformed Church in America, 28.9% Christian Reformed Church in North America, 7.7% Catholic Church, 5.2% Evangelical Lutheran Church in America, 5.0% Netherlands Reformed Congregations (2000).
Economy: Unemployment rate: 2.5% (11/2002); Total civilian labor force: 18,607 (11/2002); Leading industries: 32.8% manufacturing; 11.5% retail trade; 10.0% health care and social assistance (2000); Companies that employ more than 1,000 persons: 1 (2000); Companies that employ more than 100 persons: 24 (2000); Farms: 1,752 totaling 493,556 acres (1997); Minority business ownership rate: 0.0% (1997); Women business ownership rate: 21.0% (1997); Retail sales per capita: $9,113 (1997). Single-family building permits issued: 77 (2001) / 78 (2000); Multi-family building permits issued: 3 (2001) / 55 (2000).
Income: Per capita income: $16,532 (2000); Median household income: $40,536 (2000); Poverty rate: 6.4% (2000); Bankruptcy rate: 1.33% (2001).

Taxes: Total county taxes per capita: $152 (2000); County property taxes per capita: $118 (2000).
Education: High school graduation rate: 80.4% (2000); College graduation rate: 19.8% (2000).
Housing: Homeownership rate: 80.4% (2000); Median home value: $84,700 (2000); Median rent: $317 per month (2000); Median age of housing: 40 years (2000).
Health: Birth rate: 126.6 per 10,000 population (1998); Age adjusted death rate: 60.2 per 10,000 population (1999); Age adjusted cancer mortality rate: 158.5 deaths per 100,000 population (1999). Number of physicians: 7.6 per 10,000 population (1999); Number of hospital beds: 108.9 per 10,000 population (1999).
Elections: 2000 Presidential election results: 14.6% Gore, 83.3% Bush, 1.1% Nader, 0.6% Buchanan
National and State Parks: Oak Grove State Park
Additional Information Contacts
Sioux County Government Offices 712-737-2216
Hawarden Chamber of Commerce 712-551-2233
North West Iowa Board of Realtors 712-722-4466
Orange City Chamber of Commerce 712-737-4510
Rock Valley Chamber of Commerce 712-476-9300
Sioux Center Chamber of Commerce 712-722-3457

Sioux County Communities

ALTON (city). Covers a land area of 1.489 square miles and a water area of 0 square miles. Located at 42.98° N. Lat.; 96.01° W. Long. Elevation is 1,299 feet.
History: Alton was originally settled by natives of Holland. It was first named East Orange, and later Orange City, in honor of William the Silent, Prince of Orange. The present name is for both Alton, Illinois, and Alton, New Hampshire.
Population: 1,095 (2000); Race: 99.5% White, 0.0% Black, 0.3% Asian, 0.0% American Indian and Alaska Native, 0.2% Hispanic of any race, 0.2% two or more races (2000); Density: 735.3 persons per square mile (2000); Age: 26.4% under 18, 13.6% over 64 (2000); Marriage status: 22.8% never married, 66.0% now married, 6.1% widowed, 5.1% divorced (2000); Foreign born: 0.9% (2000); Ancestry (includes multiple ancestries): 39.7% German, 33.8% Dutch, 10.6% Luxemburger, 7.7% Irish, 4.4% United States or American (2000).
Economy: Single-family building permits issued: 1 (2001) / 1 (2000); Multi-family building permits issued: 0 (2001) / 0 (2000); Employment by occupation: 8.8% management, 13.4% professional, 18.8% services, 19.1% sales, 0.3% farming, 14.2% construction, 25.4% production (2000).
Income: Per capita income: $16,663 (2000); Median household income: $39,911 (2000); Poverty rate: 4.2% (2000).
Taxes: Total city taxes per capita: $230 (1997); City property taxes per capita: $171 (1997).
Education: High school graduation rate: 87.1% (2000); College graduation rate: 17.7% (2000).
Housing: Homeownership rate: 77.9% (2000); Median home value: $73,600 (2000); Median rent: $285 per month (2000); Median age of housing: 45 years (2000).
Transportation: Commute to work: 91.6% car, 0.0% public transportation, 5.2% walk, 2.8% work from home (2000); Travel time to work: 72.0% less than 15 minutes, 17.6% 15 to 30 minutes, 6.3% 30 to 45 minutes, 0.3% 45 to 60 minutes, 3.7% 60 minutes or more (2000)

BOYDEN (city). Covers a land area of 0.348 square miles and a water area of 0 square miles. Located at 43.19° N. Lat.; 96.00° W. Long. Elevation is 1,424 feet.
History: Boyden was orginally a Chicago, Milwaukee & St. Paul Railroad station known as Sheridan, but was renamed in 1889.
Population: 672 (2000); Race: 95.6% White, 0.3% Black, 0.0% Asian, 1.1% American Indian and Alaska Native, 2.7% Hispanic of any race, 0.3% two or more races (2000); Density: 1,932.9 persons per square mile (2000); Age: 21.2% under 18, 18.5% over 64 (2000); Marriage status: 19.5% never married, 69.7% now married, 8.6% widowed, 2.2% divorced (2000); Foreign born: 3.0% (2000); Ancestry (includes multiple ancestries): 54.0% Dutch, 36.1% German, 5.5% United States or American, 4.1% Other groups, 3.5% Swedish (2000).
Economy: Single-family building permits issued: 0 (2001) / 2 (2000); Multi-family building permits issued: 0 (2001) / 0 (2000); Employment by occupation: 10.8% management, 12.4% professional, 14.2% services, 21.1% sales, 3.1% farming, 8.8% construction, 29.6% production (2000).
Income: Per capita income: $17,323 (2000); Median household income: $39,688 (2000); Poverty rate: 5.3% (2000).
Taxes: Total city taxes per capita: $187 (1997); City property taxes per capita: $135 (1997).
Education: High school graduation rate: 78.8% (2000); College graduation rate: 8.8% (2000).
Housing: Homeownership rate: 84.8% (2000); Median home value: $66,500 (2000); Median rent: $268 per month (2000); Median age of housing: 39 years (2000).
Transportation: Commute to work: 85.2% car, 0.0% public transportation, 10.6% walk, 2.3% work from home (2000); Travel time to work: 58.0% less than 15 minutes, 33.0% 15 to 30 minutes, 2.4% 30 to 45 minutes, 1.6% 45 to 60 minutes, 5.1% 60 minutes or more (2000)

CHATSWORTH (city). Covers a land area of 0.487 square miles and a water area of 0 square miles. Located at 42.91° N. Lat.; 96.51° W. Long. Elevation is 1,162 feet.
History: Chatsworth was founded by the Chicago, Milwaukee & St. Paul Railroad, and named by the railroad company.
Population: 89 (2000); Race: 100.0% White, 0.0% Black, 0.0% Asian, 0.0% American Indian and Alaska Native, 0.0% Hispanic of any race, 0.0% two or more races (2000); Density: 182.7 persons per square mile (2000); Age: 32.1% under 18, 23.8% over 64 (2000); Marriage status: 22.1% never married, 50.0% now married, 7.4% widowed, 20.6% divorced (2000); Foreign born: 0.0% (2000); Ancestry (includes multiple ancestries): 34.5% German, 16.7% Irish, 9.5% Dutch, 8.3% Norwegian, 6.0% United States or American (2000).
Economy: Employment by occupation: 6.1% management, 0.0% professional, 18.2% services, 15.2% sales, 0.0% farming, 15.2% construction, 45.5% production (2000).
Income: Per capita income: $12,673 (2000); Median household income: $18,333 (2000); Poverty rate: 38.1% (2000).
Taxes: Total city taxes per capita: $77 (1997); City property taxes per capita: $48 (1997).
Education: High school graduation rate: 58.9% (2000); College graduation rate: 0.0% (2000).
Housing: Homeownership rate: 97.1% (2000); Median home value: $25,500 (2000); Median rent: $125 per month (2000); Median age of housing: 60+ years (2000).
Transportation: Commute to work: 100.0% car, 0.0% public transportation, 0.0% walk, 0.0% work from home (2000); Travel time to work: 81.8% less than 15 minutes, 12.1% 15 to 30 minutes, 6.1% 30 to 45 minutes, 0.0% 45 to 60 minutes, 0.0% 60 minutes or more (2000)

GRANVILLE (city). Covers a land area of 0.290 square miles and a water area of 0 square miles. Located at 42.98° N. Lat.; 95.87° W. Long.
History: Granville was platted in 1882 under that name, but the Chicago & North Western Railroad station name was spelled Grenville. The name came from British navigator Sir Richard Grenville, a 16th century explorer of the east coast of North America.
Population: 325 (2000); Race: 100.0% White, 0.0% Black, 0.0% Asian, 0.0% American Indian and Alaska Native, 0.0% Hispanic of any race, 0.0% two or more races (2000); Density: 1,121.6 persons per square mile (2000); Age: 30.4% under 18, 16.6% over 64 (2000); Marriage status: 24.5% never married, 57.5% now married, 11.2% widowed, 6.9% divorced (2000); Foreign born: 0.0% (2000); Ancestry (includes multiple ancestries): 59.8% German, 12.8% Dutch, 9.5% Irish, 7.8% Luxemburger, 5.1% French (except Basque) (2000).
Economy: Single-family building permits issued: 0 (2001) / 2 (2000); Multi-family building permits issued: 0 (2001) / 0 (2000); Employment by occupation: 13.1% management, 10.3% professional, 18.6% services, 15.2% sales, 2.8% farming, 13.8% construction, 26.2% production (2000).
Income: Per capita income: $15,352 (2000); Median household income: $33,000 (2000); Poverty rate: 14.9% (2000).
Taxes: Total city taxes per capita: $191 (1997); City property taxes per capita: $134 (1997).
Education: High school graduation rate: 78.5% (2000); College graduation rate: 13.1% (2000).
Housing: Homeownership rate: 82.4% (2000); Median home value: $52,300 (2000); Median rent: $225 per month (2000); Median age of housing: 46 years (2000).
Transportation: Commute to work: 89.5% car, 0.0% public transportation, 5.6% walk, 1.4% work from home (2000); Travel time to work: 41.1% less than 15 minutes, 49.6% 15 to 30 minutes, 7.8% 30 to 45 minutes, 1.4% 45 to 60 minutes, 0.0% 60 minutes or more (2000)

HAWARDEN (city). Covers a land area of 2.880 square miles and a water area of 0.128 square miles. Located at 43.00° N. Lat.; 96.48° W. Long. Elevation is 1,181 feet.
History: Hawarden was laid out in 1882, and named for Hawarden in Flint County, Wales, the home of British statesman William E. Gladstone.
Population: 2,478 (2000); Race: 94.6% White, 0.0% Black, 0.6% Asian, 0.0% American Indian and Alaska Native, 5.7% Hispanic of any race, 0.9% two or more races (2000); Density: 860.6 persons per square mile (2000); Age: 26.0% under 18, 21.7% over 64 (2000); Marriage status: 19.5% never married, 60.1% now married, 10.5% widowed, 9.9% divorced (2000); Foreign born: 4.1% (2000); Ancestry (includes multiple ancestries): 30.1% German, 17.2% Dutch, 9.2% Norwegian, 8.8% Irish, 8.0% English (2000).
Economy: Single-family building permits issued: 1 (2001) / 1 (2000); Multi-family building permits issued: 0 (2001) / 0 (2000); Employment by occupation: 12.9% management, 14.5% professional, 17.3% services, 18.0% sales, 1.8% farming, 8.2% construction, 27.3% production (2000).
Income: Per capita income: $17,459 (2000); Median household income: $34,360 (2000); Poverty rate: 6.6% (2000).
Taxes: Total city taxes per capita: $279 (1997); City property taxes per capita: $211 (1997).
Education: High school graduation rate: 75.7% (2000); College graduation rate: 14.7% (2000).

School District(s)

Greater Scott 61-5 (KG-12)
2000 Enrollment: 0 712-551-1461
West Sioux Community School District (PK-12)
2000 Enrollment: 761 712-551-1461

Housing: Homeownership rate: 77.5% (2000); Median home value: $59,600 (2000); Median rent: $300 per month (2000); Median age of housing: 45 years (2000).
Hospitals: Hawarden Community Hospital (27 beds)
Safety: Violent crime rate: 12.1 per 10,000 population; Property crime rate: 40.4 per 10,000 population (2001).
Newspapers: The Independent (1 x week); The Advertiser (1 x week)
Transportation: Commute to work: 92.8% car, 0.0% public transportation, 3.6% walk, 3.7% work from home (2000); Travel time to work: 69.2% less than 15 minutes, 14.5% 15 to 30 minutes, 8.1% 30 to 45 minutes, 4.7% 45 to 60 minutes, 3.4% 60 minutes or more (2000)

Additional Information Contacts

Hawarden Chamber of Commerce 712-551-2233

HOSPERS (city). Covers a land area of 0.471 square miles and a water area of 0 square miles. Located at 43.07° N. Lat.; 95.90° W. Long. Elevation is 1,343 feet.
History: Hospers is named for an early settler in Sioux County, Henry Hospers, who was a banker and the mayor of Pella.
Population: 672 (2000); Race: 97.3% White, 0.0% Black, 0.0% Asian, 1.9% American Indian and Alaska Native, 0.3% Hispanic of any race, 0.6% two or more races (2000); Density: 1,427.7 persons per square mile (2000); Age: 28.9% under 18, 15.6% over 64 (2000); Marriage status: 22.7% never married, 64.7% now married, 6.5% widowed, 6.1% divorced (2000); Foreign born: 0.4% (2000); Ancestry (includes multiple ancestries): 43.7% Dutch, 30.6% German, 8.7% Irish, 8.4% United States or American, 3.9% Other groups (2000).
Economy: Single-family building permits issued: 1 (2001) / 1 (2000); Multi-family building permits issued: 0 (2001) / 0 (2000); Employment by occupation: 13.9% management, 13.1% professional, 16.7% services, 21.7% sales, 1.1% farming, 10.3% construction, 23.1% production (2000).
Income: Per capita income: $17,851 (2000); Median household income: $37,083 (2000); Poverty rate: 6.4% (2000).
Taxes: Total city taxes per capita: $159 (1997); City property taxes per capita: $137 (1997).
Education: High school graduation rate: 81.7% (2000); College graduation rate: 10.9% (2000).
Housing: Homeownership rate: 82.8% (2000); Median home value: $67,200 (2000); Median rent: $305 per month (2000); Median age of housing: 41 years (2000).
Newspapers: Northwest Iowa Peach (1 x week); Siouxland Press (1 x week)
Transportation: Commute to work: 88.2% car, 0.0% public transportation, 6.5% walk, 4.8% work from home (2000); Travel time to work: 53.0% less than 15 minutes, 40.5% 15 to 30 minutes, 3.8% 30 to 45 minutes, 0.0% 45 to 60 minutes, 2.7% 60 minutes or more (2000)

HULL (city). Covers a land area of 1.196 square miles and a water area of 0 square miles. Located at 43.19° N. Lat.; 96.13° W. Long.
History: Hull was originally a Dutch community called Pattersonville. Its present name was adopted in 1882 when the town was organized.
Population: 1,960 (2000); Race: 91.5% White, 0.4% Black, 1.2% Asian, 0.0% American Indian and Alaska Native, 7.2% Hispanic of any race, 1.1% two or more races (2000); Density: 1,638.4 persons per square mile (2000); Age: 30.3% under 18, 18.3% over 64 (2000); Marriage status: 17.4% never married, 72.2% now married, 8.1% widowed, 2.2% divorced (2000); Foreign born: 5.6% (2000); Ancestry (includes multiple ancestries): 66.1% Dutch, 13.9% German, 9.7% Other groups, 5.0% United States or American, 1.8% Norwegian (2000).
Economy: Single-family building permits issued: 23 (2001) / 8 (2000); Multi-family building permits issued: 0 (2001) / 0 (2000); Employment by occupation: 11.7% management, 15.2% professional, 16.5% services, 19.6% sales, 1.5% farming, 11.4% construction, 24.1% production (2000).
Income: Per capita income: $16,153 (2000); Median household income: $38,269 (2000); Poverty rate: 8.2% (2000).
Taxes: Total city taxes per capita: $287 (1997); City property taxes per capita: $231 (1997).
Education: High school graduation rate: 76.7% (2000); College graduation rate: 15.8% (2000).

School District(s)

Boyden-Hull Community School District (KG-12)
2000 Enrollment: 571 712-439-2711

Housing: Homeownership rate: 85.4% (2000); Median home value: $75,200 (2000); Median rent: $294 per month (2000); Median age of housing: 40 years (2000).
Newspapers: The Sioux County Index-Reporter (1 x week)
Transportation: Commute to work: 86.4% car, 0.8% public transportation, 5.5% walk, 5.5% work from home (2000); Travel time to work: 63.3% less than 15 minutes, 31.0% 15 to 30 minutes, 3.9% 30 to 45 minutes, 0.2% 45 to 60 minutes, 1.7% 60 minutes or more (2000)

IRETON (city). Covers a land area of 1.006 square miles and a water area of 0 square miles. Located at 42.97° N. Lat.; 96.31° W. Long. Elevation is 1,373 feet.
History: Ireton was laid out in 1882, and named for General Henry Ireton (1610-1651), who was the son-in-law of Oliver Cromwell.
Population: 585 (2000); Race: 100.0% White, 0.0% Black, 0.0% Asian, 0.0% American Indian and Alaska Native, 0.3% Hispanic of any race, 0.0% two or more races (2000); Density: 581.4 persons per square mile (2000); Age: 22.0% under 18, 21.3% over 64 (2000); Marriage status: 21.0% never married, 65.2% now married, 8.0% widowed, 5.8% divorced (2000); Foreign born: 0.3% (2000); Ancestry (includes multiple ancestries): 46.1% Dutch, 28.6% German, 7.1% Irish, 6.4% United States or American, 4.3% Norwegian (2000).
Economy: Single-family building permits issued: 0 (2001) / 0 (2000); Multi-family building permits issued: 0 (2001) / 0 (2000); Employment by occupation: 6.6% management, 7.3% professional, 12.3% services, 35.4% sales, 1.7% farming, 14.6% construction, 22.2% production (2000).
Income: Per capita income: $16,879 (2000); Median household income: $36,250 (2000); Poverty rate: 1.0% (2000).
Taxes: Total city taxes per capita: $235 (1997); City property taxes per capita: $180 (1997).
Education: High school graduation rate: 76.5% (2000); College graduation rate: 8.3% (2000).
Housing: Homeownership rate: 85.0% (2000); Median home value: $65,200 (2000); Median rent: $316 per month (2000); Median age of housing: 46 years (2000).
Transportation: Commute to work: 90.3% car, 0.0% public transportation, 6.3% walk, 2.7% work from home (2000); Travel time to work: 42.8% less than 15 minutes, 43.2% 15 to 30 minutes, 7.5% 30 to 45 minutes, 3.4% 45 to 60 minutes, 3.1% 60 minutes or more (2000)

MATLOCK (city). Covers a land area of 0.378 square miles and a water area of 0 square miles. Located at 43.24° N. Lat.; 95.93° W. Long. Elevation is 1,395 feet.
History: Matlock was named for Matlock, England, by English immigrant Robert Allen.
Population: 83 (2000); Race: 95.1% White, 0.0% Black, 4.9% Asian, 0.0% American Indian and Alaska Native, 0.0% Hispanic of any race, 0.0% two or more races (2000); Density: 219.6 persons per square mile (2000); Age: 28.4% under 18, 4.9% over 64 (2000); Marriage status: 17.7% never married, 79.0% now married, 0.0% widowed, 3.2% divorced (2000); Foreign born: 7.4% (2000); Ancestry (includes multiple ancestries): 44.4% Dutch, 33.3% German, 17.3% United States or American, 11.1% Irish, 8.6% Other groups (2000).

Economy: Employment by occupation: 10.0% management, 6.0% professional, 10.0% services, 14.0% sales, 4.0% farming, 10.0% construction, 46.0% production (2000).
Income: Per capita income: $17,448 (2000); Median household income: $36,750 (2000); Poverty rate: 11.1% (2000).
Taxes: Total city taxes per capita: $217 (1997); City property taxes per capita: $163 (1997).
Education: High school graduation rate: 87.3% (2000); College graduation rate: 7.3% (2000).
Housing: Homeownership rate: 90.6% (2000); Median home value: $43,800 (2000); Median rent: $275 per month (2000); Median age of housing: 58 years (2000).
Transportation: Commute to work: 74.0% car, 0.0% public transportation, 22.0% walk, 4.0% work from home (2000); Travel time to work: 62.5% less than 15 minutes, 14.6% 15 to 30 minutes, 22.9% 30 to 45 minutes, 0.0% 45 to 60 minutes, 0.0% 60 minutes or more (2000)

MAURICE (city). Covers a land area of 0.539 square miles and a water area of 0.006 square miles. Located at 42.96° N. Lat.; 96.18° W. Long.
History: Maurice was named for Count Maurice of Nassau, Prince of Orange and son of William the Silent.
Population: 254 (2000); Race: 100.0% White, 0.0% Black, 0.0% Asian, 0.0% American Indian and Alaska Native, 0.0% Hispanic of any race, 0.0% two or more races (2000); Density: 471.0 persons per square mile (2000); Age: 27.0% under 18, 12.7% over 64 (2000); Marriage status: 14.1% never married, 80.2% now married, 2.1% widowed, 3.6% divorced (2000); Foreign born: 0.0% (2000); Ancestry (includes multiple ancestries): 76.2% Dutch, 13.1% German, 2.4% English, 2.0% Other groups, 1.6% United States or American (2000).
Economy: Single-family building permits issued: 1 (2001) / 1 (2000); Multi-family building permits issued: 0 (2001) / 0 (2000); Employment by occupation: 8.2% management, 7.5% professional, 21.8% services, 23.8% sales, 0.7% farming, 12.2% construction, 25.9% production (2000).
Income: Per capita income: $15,455 (2000); Median household income: $41,591 (2000); Poverty rate: 0.0% (2000).
Taxes: Total city taxes per capita: $202 (1997); City property taxes per capita: $154 (1997).
Education: High school graduation rate: 89.9% (2000); College graduation rate: 10.8% (2000).
Housing: Homeownership rate: 84.7% (2000); Median home value: $63,300 (2000); Median rent: $344 per month (2000); Median age of housing: 60+ years (2000).
Transportation: Commute to work: 89.7% car, 0.0% public transportation, 3.4% walk, 4.8% work from home (2000); Travel time to work: 45.7% less than 15 minutes, 44.2% 15 to 30 minutes, 8.0% 30 to 45 minutes, 0.0% 45 to 60 minutes, 2.2% 60 minutes or more (2000)

ORANGE CITY (city). Covers a land area of 3.087 square miles and a water area of 0 square miles. Located at 43.00° N. Lat.; 96.05° W. Long. Elevation is 1,412 feet.
History: Orange City, a Dutch town founded by Henry Hospers in 1869, was named for Prince William of Orange.
Population: 5,582 (2000); Race: 97.4% White, 1.2% Black, 0.7% Asian, 0.0% American Indian and Alaska Native, 0.2% Hispanic of any race, 0.4% two or more races (2000); Density: 1,808.5 persons per square mile (2000); Age: 22.9% under 18, 16.0% over 64 (2000); Marriage status: 34.9% never married, 57.3% now married, 5.8% widowed, 2.0% divorced (2000); Foreign born: 2.2% (2000); Ancestry (includes multiple ancestries): 52.7% Dutch, 23.2% German, 5.8% Norwegian, 4.8% United States or American, 4.8% Irish (2000).
Economy: Single-family building permits issued: 11 (2001) / 16 (2000); Multi-family building permits issued: 0 (2001) / 4 (2000); Employment by occupation: 11.9% management, 21.0% professional, 18.4% services, 28.3% sales, 0.6% farming, 6.7% construction, 13.1% production (2000).
Income: Per capita income: $17,413 (2000); Median household income: $39,721 (2000); Poverty rate: 4.8% (2000).
Taxes: Total city taxes per capita: $291 (2000); City property taxes per capita: $229 (2000).
Education: High school graduation rate: 83.6% (2000); College graduation rate: 31.4% (2000).

School District(s)

Moc-Floyd Valley Community School District (PK-12)
2000 Enrollment: 1,403 712-737-4873

Four-year College(s)

Northwestern College (Private, Not-for-profit, Reformed Church in America)
2001 Enrollment: 1,287 712-737-7000
2001 Tuition: In-state $13,750; Out-of-state $13,750
Housing: Homeownership rate: 79.8% (2000); Median home value: $99,200 (2000); Median rent: $350 per month (2000); Median age of housing: 36 years (2000).
Hospitals: Orange City Health System (63 beds)
Newspapers: Sioux County Capital-Democrat (1 x week)
Transportation: Commute to work: 77.5% car, 0.4% public transportation, 18.7% walk, 2.2% work from home (2000); Travel time to work: 82.1% less than 15 minutes, 12.4% 15 to 30 minutes, 2.1% 30 to 45 minutes, 1.3% 45 to 60 minutes, 2.3% 60 minutes or more (2000)
Additional Information Contacts
Orange City Chamber of Commerce 712-737-4510

ROCK VALLEY (city). Covers a land area of 1.689 square miles and a water area of 0.052 square miles. Located at 43.20° N. Lat.; 96.29° W. Long. Elevation is 1,255 feet.
History: Rock Valley was named for its location in the Rock River Valley.
Population: 2,702 (2000); Race: 98.4% White, 0.0% Black, 0.4% Asian, 0.0% American Indian and Alaska Native, 0.9% Hispanic of any race, 1.2% two or more races (2000); Density: 1,599.9 persons per square mile (2000); Age: 23.4% under 18, 21.9% over 64 (2000); Marriage status: 20.4% never married, 66.2% now married, 8.9% widowed, 4.5% divorced (2000); Foreign born: 2.6% (2000); Ancestry (includes multiple ancestries): 65.4% Dutch, 13.0% German, 5.0% United States or American, 4.6% Norwegian, 3.9% Irish (2000).
Economy: Single-family building permits issued: 8 (2001) / 8 (2000); Multi-family building permits issued: 0 (2001) / 0 (2000); Employment by occupation: 9.0% management, 19.6% professional, 15.3% services, 21.0% sales, 1.2% farming, 9.3% construction, 24.6% production (2000).
Income: Per capita income: $19,660 (2000); Median household income: $36,967 (2000); Poverty rate: 4.1% (2000).
Taxes: Total city taxes per capita: $316 (1997); City property taxes per capita: $281 (1997).
Education: High school graduation rate: 73.5% (2000); College graduation rate: 17.8% (2000).

School District(s)

Rock Valley Community School District (PK-12)
2000 Enrollment: 576 712-476-2125
Housing: Homeownership rate: 80.1% (2000); Median home value: $77,600 (2000); Median rent: $305 per month (2000); Median age of housing: 33 years (2000).
Hospitals: Hegg Memorial Hospital (123 beds)
Newspapers: Rock Valley Bee (1 x week)
Transportation: Commute to work: 86.8% car, 1.3% public transportation, 8.5% walk, 2.0% work from home (2000); Travel time to work: 72.4% less than 15 minutes, 14.7% 15 to 30 minutes, 6.3% 30 to 45 minutes, 1.2% 45 to 60 minutes, 5.4% 60 minutes or more (2000)
Additional Information Contacts
Rock Valley Chamber of Commerce 712-476-9300

SIOUX CENTER (city). Covers a land area of 5.288 square miles and a water area of 0 square miles. Located at 43.07° N. Lat.; 96.17° W. Long. Elevation is 1,450 feet.
History: In 1935, the Farmers Mutual Co-operative Creamery of Sioux Center sold almost 3,000,000 pounds of butter.
Population: 6,002 (2000); Race: 95.1% White, 0.3% Black, 1.2% Asian, 0.4% American Indian and Alaska Native, 4.3% Hispanic of any race, 1.5% two or more races (2000); Density: 1,134.9 persons per square mile (2000); Age: 22.8% under 18, 14.5% over 64 (2000); Marriage status: 40.2% never married, 51.7% now married, 6.4% widowed, 1.7% divorced (2000); Foreign born: 6.3% (2000); Ancestry (includes multiple ancestries): 70.5% Dutch, 13.3% German, 7.7% Other groups, 2.7% United States or American, 2.2% Irish (2000).
Economy: Single-family building permits issued: 28 (2001) / 35 (2000); Multi-family building permits issued: 0 (2001) / 48 (2000); Employment by occupation: 11.7% management, 19.8% professional, 18.7% services, 21.5% sales, 3.6% farming, 8.4% construction, 16.2% production (2000).
Income: Per capita income: $16,912 (2000); Median household income: $42,775 (2000); Poverty rate: 7.1% (2000).
Taxes: Total city taxes per capita: $375 (2000); City property taxes per capita: $306 (2000).
Education: High school graduation rate: 79.5% (2000); College graduation rate: 27.8% (2000).

School District(s)

Sioux Center Community School District (KG-12)
2000 Enrollment: 945 712-722-2981

Four-year College(s)

Dordt College (Private, Not-for-profit, Christian Reformed Church)
2001 Enrollment: 1,460 712-722-6000
2001 Tuition: In-state $13,950; Out-of-state $13,950

Housing: Homeownership rate: 76.3% (2000); Median home value: $106,200 (2000); Median rent: $342 per month (2000); Median age of housing: 30 years (2000).
Hospitals: Sioux Center Community Hospital (90 beds)
Newspapers: Sioux Center Shopper (1 x week); Sioux Center News (1 x week)
Transportation: Commute to work: 74.0% car, 0.1% public transportation, 20.3% walk, 3.8% work from home (2000); Travel time to work: 80.5% less than 15 minutes, 13.4% 15 to 30 minutes, 2.4% 30 to 45 minutes, 0.9% 45 to 60 minutes, 2.8% 60 minutes or more (2000)
Airports: Sioux Center Municipal
Additional Information Contacts
North West Iowa Board of Realtors 712-722-4466
Sioux Center Chamber of Commerce 712-722-3457

Story County

Located in central Iowa; prairie area, drained by the Skunk River. Covers a land area of 572.90 square miles, a water area of 0.80 square miles, and is located in the Central Time Zone. The county government was organized in 1846. County seat is Nevada.

Weather Station: Colo — Elevation: 997 feet

	Jan	Feb	Mar	Apr	May	Jun	Jul	Aug	Sep	Oct	Nov	Dec
High	25	32	44	59	71	80	84	81	74	62	44	31
Low	7	13	25	36	48	58	63	60	51	38	26	14
Precip	0.9	0.9	2.1	3.2	4.4	5.2	4.9	4.7	3.3	2.6	2.0	1.1
Snow	6.7	5.4	4.7	1.6	0.0	0.0	0.0	0.0	0.0	0.4	2.8	6.3

High and Low temperatures in degrees Fahrenheit; Precipitation and Snow in inches

Population: 79,981 (2000); Race: 91.1% White, 1.9% Black, 4.5% Asian, 0.3% American Indian and Alaska Native, 1.7% Hispanic of any race, 1.3% two or more races (2000); Density: 139.6 persons per square mile (2000); Age: 19.0% under 18, 9.7% over 64 (2000).
Religion: Five largest groups: 14.2% Evangelical Lutheran Church in America, 11.6% Catholic Church, 7.9% The United Methodist Church, 2.0% Lutheran Church—Missouri Synod, 1.8% Presbyterian Church (U.S.A.) (2000).
Economy: Unemployment rate: 2.7% (11/2002); Total civilian labor force: 48,310 (11/2002); Leading industries: 17.1% retail trade; 15.8% health care and social assistance; 14.7% accommodation & food services (2000); Companies that employ more than 1,000 persons: 1 (2000); Companies that employ more than 100 persons: 41 (2000); Farms: 946 totaling 340,885 acres (1997); Minority business ownership rate: 2.1% (1997); Women business ownership rate: 32.0% (1997); Retail sales per capita: $8,426 (1997). Single-family building permits issued: 242 (2001) / 254 (2000); Multi-family building permits issued: 258 (2001) / 420 (2000).
Income: Per capita income: $19,949 (2000); Median household income: $40,442 (2000); Poverty rate: 14.1% (2000); Bankruptcy rate: 2.62% (2001).
Taxes: Total county taxes per capita: $174 (2000); County property taxes per capita: $156 (2000).
Education: High school graduation rate: 93.5% (2000); College graduation rate: 44.5% (2000).
Housing: Homeownership rate: 58.3% (2000); Median home value: $115,800 (2000); Median rent: $504 per month (2000); Median age of housing: 29 years (2000).
Health: Birth rate: 107.7 per 10,000 population (1998); Age adjusted death rate: 66.5 per 10,000 population (1999); Age adjusted cancer mortality rate: 168.0 deaths per 100,000 population (1999). Air Quality Index: 96% good, 4% moderate, 0% unhealthy (percent of days in 2000). Number of physicians: 18.1 per 10,000 population (1999); Number of hospital beds: 46.3 per 10,000 population (1999).
Elections: 2000 Presidential election results: 49.4% Gore, 45.9% Bush, 3.7% Nader, 0.3% Buchanan
National and State Parks: Doolittle Prairie State Preserve
Additional Information Contacts
Story County Government Offices 515-382-7200
Ames Chamber of Commerce 515-232-2310
Central Iowa Board of Realtors 515-296-4680
Nevada Chamber of Commerce 515-382-6538
Story City Chamber of Commerce 515-733-4214

Story County Communities

AMES (city). Covers a land area of 21.567 square miles and a water area of 0.017 square miles. Located at 42.02° N. Lat.; 93.63° W. Long. Elevation is 922 feet.
History: When Mrs. Cynthia Duff bought the farmland occupying the future town site of Ames in 1864, no one knew she was buying it for John I. Blair, who planned to build a depot for the Cedar Rapids and Missouri Railroad. The town was named for Oakes Ames, one of the proprietors of the railroad. Until 1866, Ames was known as College Farm, because it was adjacent to the land purchased for the State Agricultural College.
Population: 50,731 (2000); Race: 87.3% White, 2.7% Black, 6.9% Asian, 0.3% American Indian and Alaska Native, 2.2% Hispanic of any race, 1.7% two or more races (2000); Density: 2,352.3 persons per square mile (2000); Age: 14.6% under 18, 7.4% over 64 (2000); Marriage status: 54.4% never married, 38.1% now married, 2.9% widowed, 4.6% divorced (2000); Foreign born: 10.3% (2000); Ancestry (includes multiple ancestries): 33.5% German, 12.8% Other groups, 11.4% Irish, 10.2% English, 8.6% Norwegian (2000).
Vital Statistics: Birth rate: 97.2 per 10,000 population (1998)
Economy: Unemployment rate: 3.0% (11/2002); Total civilian labor force: 31,138 (11/2002); Single-family building permits issued: 133 (2001) / 141 (2000); Multi-family building permits issued: 157 (2001) / 400 (2000); Employment by occupation: 10.3% management, 37.0% professional, 15.6% services, 24.5% sales, 1.2% farming, 4.7% construction, 6.7% production (2000).
Income: Per capita income: $18,881 (2000); Median household income: $36,042 (2000); Poverty rate: 20.4% (2000).
Taxes: Total city taxes per capita: $322 (2000); City property taxes per capita: $250 (2000).
Education: High school graduation rate: 95.3% (2000); College graduation rate: 58.6% (2000).

School District(s)

Ames Community School District (PK-12)
2000 Enrollment: 4,751 515-239-3700

Four-year College(s)

Iowa State University (Public)
2001 Enrollment: 27,823 515-294-5836
2001 Tuition: In-state $3,116; Out-of-state $10,450

Two-year College(s)

Professional Cosmetology Institute (Private, For-profit)
2001 Enrollment: 119 515-232-7250

Housing: Homeownership rate: 46.1% (2000); Median home value: $130,900 (2000); Median rent: $532 per month (2000); Median age of housing: 27 years (2000).
Hospitals: Mary Greeley Medical Center (220 beds)
Safety: Violent crime rate: 19.1 per 10,000 population; Property crime rate: 272.9 per 10,000 population (2001).
Newspapers: The Daily Tribune (6 x week); Story County Advertiser (1 x week); Iowa State Daily (5 x week)
Transportation: Commute to work: 74.5% car, 6.1% public transportation, 13.2% walk, 3.2% work from home (2000); Travel time to work: 63.4% less than 15 minutes, 24.1% 15 to 30 minutes, 6.0% 30 to 45 minutes, 4.4% 45 to 60 minutes, 2.0% 60 minutes or more (2000)
Airports: Ames Municipal
Additional Information Contacts
Ames Chamber of Commerce 515-232-2310
Central Iowa Board of Realtors 515-296-4680

CAMBRIDGE (city). Covers a land area of 1.031 square miles and a water area of 0.001 square miles. Located at 41.89° N. Lat.; 93.53° W. Long. Elevation is 861 feet.
History: The name of Cambridge may reflect an early settler, W.G. Cambridge, or Cambridge, England.
Population: 819 (2000); Race: 95.5% White, 0.2% Black, 1.1% Asian, 0.7% American Indian and Alaska Native, 1.8% Hispanic of any race, 2.2% two or more races (2000); Density: 794.5 persons per square mile (2000); Age: 27.3% under 18, 9.8% over 64 (2000); Marriage status: 25.2% never married, 60.1% now married, 5.7% widowed, 9.0% divorced (2000); Foreign born: 2.0% (2000); Ancestry (includes multiple ancestries): 34.3% German, 11.3% English, 10.4% Norwegian, 10.2% Irish, 9.4% United States or American (2000).
Economy: Single-family building permits issued: 2 (2001) / 2 (2000); Multi-family building permits issued: 0 (2001) / 0 (2000); Employment by

occupation: 11.6% management, 16.8% professional, 10.8% services, 31.2% sales, 0.0% farming, 11.2% construction, 18.5% production (2000).
Income: Per capita income: $18,524 (2000); Median household income: $42,059 (2000); Poverty rate: 8.6% (2000).
Taxes: Total city taxes per capita: $189 (1997); City property taxes per capita: $106 (1997).
Education: High school graduation rate: 91.4% (2000); College graduation rate: 17.2% (2000).
Housing: Homeownership rate: 87.5% (2000); Median home value: $83,800 (2000); Median rent: $400 per month (2000); Median age of housing: 37 years (2000).
Transportation: Commute to work: 96.3% car, 0.4% public transportation, 1.3% walk, 1.9% work from home (2000); Travel time to work: 11.7% less than 15 minutes, 51.4% 15 to 30 minutes, 27.4% 30 to 45 minutes, 4.4% 45 to 60 minutes, 5.1% 60 minutes or more (2000)

COLLINS (city). Covers a land area of 0.492 square miles and a water area of 0 square miles. Located at 41.90° N. Lat.; 93.30° W. Long. Elevation is 1,005 feet.
History: After beginning as Plum Center, named after storekeeper James Plumb, the town name was changed to Collins Center and then to Collins, probably in memory of the New York home of other early residents.
Population: 499 (2000); Race: 100.0% White, 0.0% Black, 0.0% Asian, 0.0% American Indian and Alaska Native, 0.8% Hispanic of any race, 0.0% two or more races (2000); Density: 1,013.9 persons per square mile (2000); Age: 24.7% under 18, 23.5% over 64 (2000); Marriage status: 17.2% never married, 63.8% now married, 10.2% widowed, 8.9% divorced (2000); Foreign born: 0.8% (2000); Ancestry (includes multiple ancestries): 18.9% German, 18.1% English, 11.6% Irish, 8.4% United States or American, 5.2% Norwegian (2000).
Economy: Single-family building permits issued: 0 (2001) / 0 (2000); Multi-family building permits issued: 0 (2001) / 0 (2000); Employment by occupation: 12.6% management, 11.7% professional, 15.7% services, 30.0% sales, 0.0% farming, 7.6% construction, 22.4% production (2000).
Income: Per capita income: $20,284 (2000); Median household income: $37,917 (2000); Poverty rate: 5.0% (2000).
Taxes: Total city taxes per capita: $200 (1997); City property taxes per capita: $113 (1997).
Education: High school graduation rate: 85.2% (2000); College graduation rate: 7.0% (2000).
Housing: Homeownership rate: 72.0% (2000); Median home value: $56,300 (2000); Median rent: $322 per month (2000); Median age of housing: 55 years (2000).
Transportation: Commute to work: 92.4% car, 0.0% public transportation, 4.5% walk, 3.1% work from home (2000); Travel time to work: 16.2% less than 15 minutes, 15.3% 15 to 30 minutes, 52.8% 30 to 45 minutes, 10.2% 45 to 60 minutes, 5.6% 60 minutes or more (2000)

COLO (city). Covers a land area of 0.774 square miles and a water area of 0 square miles. Located at 42.01° N. Lat.; 93.31° W. Long.
History: Colo was the first railroad station in the county. John Blair, a railroad official, named the town for his dog, Colo, who had been crushed near here by a construction train.
Population: 868 (2000); Race: 95.7% White, 2.5% Black, 0.0% Asian, 0.2% American Indian and Alaska Native, 0.8% Hispanic of any race, 1.3% two or more races (2000); Density: 1,121.9 persons per square mile (2000); Age: 28.4% under 18, 16.8% over 64 (2000); Marriage status: 20.2% never married, 68.7% now married, 5.6% widowed, 5.5% divorced (2000); Foreign born: 0.0% (2000); Ancestry (includes multiple ancestries): 30.9% German, 15.1% United States or American, 12.7% Irish, 12.7% English, 10.4% Norwegian (2000).
Economy: Single-family building permits issued: 3 (2001) / 0 (2000); Multi-family building permits issued: 0 (2001) / 0 (2000); Employment by occupation: 9.1% management, 19.6% professional, 16.5% services, 25.4% sales, 1.6% farming, 15.6% construction, 12.2% production (2000).
Income: Per capita income: $19,173 (2000); Median household income: $41,711 (2000); Poverty rate: 5.6% (2000).
Taxes: Total city taxes per capita: $214 (1997); City property taxes per capita: $129 (1997).
Education: High school graduation rate: 93.7% (2000); College graduation rate: 21.6% (2000).
Housing: Homeownership rate: 81.7% (2000); Median home value: $72,200 (2000); Median rent: $336 per month (2000); Median age of housing: 46 years (2000).
Transportation: Commute to work: 90.7% car, 0.0% public transportation, 4.1% walk, 4.6% work from home (2000); Travel time to work: 24.3% less than 15 minutes, 48.0% 15 to 30 minutes, 15.5% 30 to 45 minutes, 9.3% 45 to 60 minutes, 2.9% 60 minutes or more (2000)

GILBERT (city). Covers a land area of 0.826 square miles and a water area of 0 square miles. Located at 42.10° N. Lat.; 93.64° W. Long. Elevation is 998 feet.
History: George Gilbert owned the land on which Gilbert was established. The name may also have come from an early postmaster, Hezekiah Gilbert.
Population: 987 (2000); Race: 95.6% White, 0.7% Black, 1.8% Asian, 0.0% American Indian and Alaska Native, 1.7% Hispanic of any race, 1.9% two or more races (2000); Density: 1,195.6 persons per square mile (2000); Age: 32.2% under 18, 3.4% over 64 (2000); Marriage status: 27.3% never married, 64.8% now married, 2.8% widowed, 5.1% divorced (2000); Foreign born: 2.5% (2000); Ancestry (includes multiple ancestries): 38.2% German, 19.3% Norwegian, 10.8% Irish, 9.1% English, 8.8% United States or American (2000).
Economy: Single-family building permits issued: 7 (2001) / 7 (2000); Multi-family building permits issued: 0 (2001) / 0 (2000); Employment by occupation: 9.9% management, 27.4% professional, 13.9% services, 25.7% sales, 0.3% farming, 9.7% construction, 13.0% production (2000).
Income: Per capita income: $19,741 (2000); Median household income: $56,406 (2000); Poverty rate: 2.4% (2000).
Taxes: Total city taxes per capita: $256 (1997); City property taxes per capita: $163 (1997).
Education: High school graduation rate: 94.0% (2000); College graduation rate: 39.5% (2000).

School District(s)

Gilbert Community School District (KG-12)
2000 Enrollment: 967 515-232-3740
Housing: Homeownership rate: 72.3% (2000); Median home value: $114,600 (2000); Median rent: $463 per month (2000); Median age of housing: 27 years (2000).
Transportation: Commute to work: 96.5% car, 0.0% public transportation, 1.2% walk, 1.9% work from home (2000); Travel time to work: 32.6% less than 15 minutes, 53.3% 15 to 30 minutes, 4.1% 30 to 45 minutes, 2.7% 45 to 60 minutes, 7.3% 60 minutes or more (2000)

HUXLEY (city). Covers a land area of 1.134 square miles and a water area of 0 square miles. Located at 41.89° N. Lat.; 93.60° W. Long. Elevation is 1,035 feet.
History: Huxley was platted by a group of Norwegians in 1882.
Population: 2,316 (2000); Race: 97.1% White, 1.3% Black, 0.0% Asian, 0.4% American Indian and Alaska Native, 1.1% Hispanic of any race, 1.0% two or more races (2000); Density: 2,042.9 persons per square mile (2000); Age: 26.7% under 18, 8.8% over 64 (2000); Marriage status: 23.2% never married, 60.8% now married, 8.0% widowed, 8.0% divorced (2000); Foreign born: 1.2% (2000); Ancestry (includes multiple ancestries): 36.4% German, 19.8% Norwegian, 12.9% Irish, 11.7% English, 6.7% Other groups (2000).
Economy: Single-family building permits issued: 16 (2001) / 16 (2000); Multi-family building permits issued: 34 (2001) / 0 (2000); Employment by occupation: 10.5% management, 23.6% professional, 13.8% services, 27.4% sales, 0.2% farming, 9.3% construction, 15.1% production (2000).
Income: Per capita income: $20,172 (2000); Median household income: $48,068 (2000); Poverty rate: 6.8% (2000).
Taxes: Total city taxes per capita: $447 (1997); City property taxes per capita: $356 (1997).
Education: High school graduation rate: 90.9% (2000); College graduation rate: 32.5% (2000).

School District(s)

Ballard Community School District (KG-12)
2000 Enrollment: 1,300 515-597-2811
Housing: Homeownership rate: 75.9% (2000); Median home value: $111,400 (2000); Median rent: $446 per month (2000); Median age of housing: 25 years (2000).
Transportation: Commute to work: 96.4% car, 0.0% public transportation, 1.2% walk, 1.7% work from home (2000); Travel time to work: 22.9% less than 15 minutes, 48.6% 15 to 30 minutes, 24.4% 30 to 45 minutes, 1.5% 45 to 60 minutes, 2.6% 60 minutes or more (2000)

KELLEY (city). Covers a land area of 0.280 square miles and a water area of 0 square miles. Located at 41.95° N. Lat.; 93.66° W. Long. Elevation is 1,033 feet.
History: Kelley was named for the original owner of the town site, J. T. Kelly. Postal authorities added the additional 'e'.
Population: 300 (2000); Race: 100.0% White, 0.0% Black, 0.0% Asian, 0.0% American Indian and Alaska Native, 0.0% Hispanic of any race, 0.0%

two or more races (2000); Density: 1,072.7 persons per square mile (2000); Age: 31.9% under 18, 3.3% over 64 (2000); Marriage status: 24.0% never married, 62.7% now married, 0.4% widowed, 12.9% divorced (2000); Foreign born: 0.0% (2000); Ancestry (includes multiple ancestries): 47.5% German, 31.6% Irish, 12.3% Norwegian, 10.6% English, 5.0% Welsh (2000).
Economy: Single-family building permits issued: 2 (2001) / 0 (2000); Multi-family building permits issued: 0 (2001) / 0 (2000); Employment by occupation: 13.3% management, 17.7% professional, 19.9% services, 27.6% sales, 1.1% farming, 8.8% construction, 11.6% production (2000).
Income: Per capita income: $17,574 (2000); Median household income: $54,375 (2000); Poverty rate: 1.0% (2000).
Taxes: Total city taxes per capita: $211 (1997); City property taxes per capita: $118 (1997).
Education: High school graduation rate: 91.4% (2000); College graduation rate: 16.1% (2000).
Housing: Homeownership rate: 72.1% (2000); Median home value: $85,500 (2000); Median rent: $406 per month (2000); Median age of housing: 40 years (2000).
Transportation: Commute to work: 94.5% car, 0.0% public transportation, 3.9% walk, 1.7% work from home (2000); Travel time to work: 29.8% less than 15 minutes, 59.0% 15 to 30 minutes, 5.6% 30 to 45 minutes, 2.2% 45 to 60 minutes, 3.4% 60 minutes or more (2000)

MAXWELL (city). Covers a land area of 1.146 square miles and a water area of 0 square miles. Located at 41.89° N. Lat.; 93.39° W. Long.
History: Maxwell was incorporated in 1883 and named for pioneer and early merchant Joseph Warren Maxwell.
Population: 807 (2000); Race: 99.7% White, 0.0% Black, 0.3% Asian, 0.0% American Indian and Alaska Native, 0.0% Hispanic of any race, 0.0% two or more races (2000); Density: 703.9 persons per square mile (2000); Age: 29.6% under 18, 16.3% over 64 (2000); Marriage status: 18.0% never married, 60.6% now married, 11.3% widowed, 10.1% divorced (2000); Foreign born: 0.5% (2000); Ancestry (includes multiple ancestries): 31.1% German, 18.8% English, 10.7% Norwegian, 7.8% Irish, 4.6% Scottish (2000).
Economy: Single-family building permits issued: 2 (2001) / 3 (2000); Multi-family building permits issued: 0 (2001) / 0 (2000); Employment by occupation: 8.2% management, 16.5% professional, 10.9% services, 31.5% sales, 1.0% farming, 11.6% construction, 20.3% production (2000).
Income: Per capita income: $19,069 (2000); Median household income: $43,125 (2000); Poverty rate: 3.9% (2000).
Taxes: Total city taxes per capita: $218 (1997); City property taxes per capita: $130 (1997).
Education: High school graduation rate: 86.0% (2000); College graduation rate: 13.2% (2000).

School District(s)

Collins-Maxwell Community School District (KG-12)
2000 Enrollment: 529 515-387-1115
Housing: Homeownership rate: 79.0% (2000); Median home value: $74,500 (2000); Median rent: $371 per month (2000); Median age of housing: 60+ years (2000).
Transportation: Commute to work: 93.1% car, 0.7% public transportation, 2.2% walk, 3.4% work from home (2000); Travel time to work: 19.6% less than 15 minutes, 37.8% 15 to 30 minutes, 35.5% 30 to 45 minutes, 6.4% 45 to 60 minutes, 0.8% 60 minutes or more (2000)

MCCALLSBURG (city). Covers a land area of 0.530 square miles and a water area of 0 square miles. Located at 42.16° N. Lat.; 93.39° W. Long. Elevation is 1,089 feet.
History: There are different stories on how McCallsburg got its name. One source indicates that the name was in honor of T. C. McCall, a prominent early settler, and that the name was drawn from a hat in order to resolve a dispute over appropriate names.
Population: 318 (2000); Race: 98.7% White, 0.0% Black, 0.0% Asian, 0.0% American Indian and Alaska Native, 0.7% Hispanic of any race, 0.7% two or more races (2000); Density: 600.2 persons per square mile (2000); Age: 26.5% under 18, 22.9% over 64 (2000); Marriage status: 19.7% never married, 63.1% now married, 10.0% widowed, 7.2% divorced (2000); Foreign born: 0.0% (2000); Ancestry (includes multiple ancestries): 33.0% Norwegian, 27.5% German, 11.1% English, 8.8% Irish, 6.2% United States or American (2000).
Economy: Single-family building permits issued: 1 (2001) / 1 (2000); Multi-family building permits issued: 0 (2001) / 0 (2000); Employment by occupation: 10.7% management, 5.0% professional, 20.0% services, 28.6% sales, 5.0% farming, 16.4% construction, 14.3% production (2000).
Income: Per capita income: $16,135 (2000); Median household income: $35,250 (2000); Poverty rate: 9.2% (2000).
Taxes: Total city taxes per capita: $257 (1997); City property taxes per capita: $164 (1997).
Education: High school graduation rate: 84.7% (2000); College graduation rate: 7.2% (2000).

School District(s)

Colo-Nesco Community School District (KG-12)
2000 Enrollment: 589 515-434-2302
Housing: Homeownership rate: 75.6% (2000); Median home value: $70,500 (2000); Median rent: $238 per month (2000); Median age of housing: 49 years (2000).
Transportation: Commute to work: 94.3% car, 0.0% public transportation, 0.0% walk, 5.7% work from home (2000); Travel time to work: 16.5% less than 15 minutes, 42.9% 15 to 30 minutes, 34.6% 30 to 45 minutes, 3.0% 45 to 60 minutes, 3.0% 60 minutes or more (2000)

NEVADA (city). Covers a land area of 4.175 square miles and a water area of 0.013 square miles. Located at 42.01° N. Lat.; 93.45° W. Long. Elevation is 1,003 feet.
History: Nevada was established in 1853. Thrift, a settler, named the village for his daughter, Sierra Nevada, who had been named for the California mountain range.
Population: 6,658 (2000); Race: 97.2% White, 0.6% Black, 0.6% Asian, 0.1% American Indian and Alaska Native, 0.3% Hispanic of any race, 1.3% two or more races (2000); Density: 1,594.7 persons per square mile (2000); Age: 24.7% under 18, 14.0% over 64 (2000); Marriage status: 23.9% never married, 55.9% now married, 8.0% widowed, 12.1% divorced (2000); Foreign born: 1.4% (2000); Ancestry (includes multiple ancestries): 31.8% German, 11.7% Norwegian, 11.5% Irish, 8.6% English, 6.9% United States or American (2000).
Economy: Single-family building permits issued: 12 (2001) / 12 (2000); Multi-family building permits issued: 3 (2001) / 18 (2000); Employment by occupation: 12.1% management, 20.0% professional, 17.4% services, 25.5% sales, 0.0% farming, 8.7% construction, 16.3% production (2000).
Income: Per capita income: $20,392 (2000); Median household income: $42,527 (2000); Poverty rate: 5.6% (2000).
Taxes: Total city taxes per capita: $388 (1997); City property taxes per capita: $291 (1997).
Education: High school graduation rate: 88.2% (2000); College graduation rate: 22.7% (2000).

School District(s)

Nevada Community School District (PK-12)
2000 Enrollment: 1,614 515-382-2783
Housing: Homeownership rate: 71.0% (2000); Median home value: $91,100 (2000); Median rent: $401 per month (2000); Median age of housing: 35 years (2000).
Hospitals: Story County Hospital (122 beds)
Safety: Violent crime rate: 21.0 per 10,000 population; Property crime rate: 321.8 per 10,000 population (2001).
Newspapers: Nevada Journal (1 x week); Money Saver (1 x week)
Transportation: Commute to work: 90.9% car, 0.4% public transportation, 5.8% walk, 2.1% work from home (2000); Travel time to work: 46.3% less than 15 minutes, 36.3% 15 to 30 minutes, 8.6% 30 to 45 minutes, 6.7% 45 to 60 minutes, 2.2% 60 minutes or more (2000)

Additional Information Contacts

Nevada Chamber of Commerce 515-382-6538

ROLAND (city). Covers a land area of 1.083 square miles and a water area of 0 square miles. Located at 42.16° N. Lat.; 93.50° W. Long. Elevation is 1,028 feet.
Population: 1,324 (2000); Race: 98.0% White, 0.0% Black, 0.2% Asian, 0.0% American Indian and Alaska Native, 1.6% Hispanic of any race, 1.7% two or more races (2000); Density: 1,223.0 persons per square mile (2000); Age: 35.4% under 18, 10.3% over 64 (2000); Marriage status: 19.4% never married, 68.1% now married, 5.1% widowed, 7.4% divorced (2000); Foreign born: 1.4% (2000); Ancestry (includes multiple ancestries): 33.8% German, 32.6% Norwegian, 13.1% Irish, 7.1% English, 5.0% Other groups (2000).
Economy: Single-family building permits issued: 3 (2001) / 3 (2000); Multi-family building permits issued: 0 (2001) / 0 (2000); Employment by occupation: 12.2% management, 25.5% professional, 16.4% services, 21.5% sales, 0.3% farming, 10.4% construction, 13.6% production (2000).
Income: Per capita income: $18,165 (2000); Median household income: $47,461 (2000); Poverty rate: 4.3% (2000).
Taxes: Total city taxes per capita: $250 (1997); City property taxes per capita: $163 (1997).
Education: High school graduation rate: 95.3% (2000); College graduation rate: 29.4% (2000).

Housing: Homeownership rate: 87.2% (2000); Median home value: $97,700 (2000); Median rent: $355 per month (2000); Median age of housing: 39 years (2000).
Transportation: Commute to work: 92.5% car, 0.2% public transportation, 3.6% walk, 3.5% work from home (2000); Travel time to work: 34.7% less than 15 minutes, 47.0% 15 to 30 minutes, 9.3% 30 to 45 minutes, 5.4% 45 to 60 minutes, 3.6% 60 minutes or more (2000)

SHELDAHL (city). Covers a land area of 0.843 square miles and a water area of 0 square miles. Located at 41.86° N. Lat.; 93.69° W. Long.
History: Sheldahl was named by and for the Rev. D. Kjaldahl. Because of the difficulty of pronouncing it, the name was Anglicized.
Population: 336 (2000); Race: 99.4% White, 0.0% Black, 0.6% Asian, 0.0% American Indian and Alaska Native, 0.0% Hispanic of any race, 0.0% two or more races (2000); Density: 398.5 persons per square mile (2000); Age: 29.6% under 18, 10.5% over 64 (2000); Marriage status: 25.6% never married, 70.3% now married, 1.5% widowed, 2.6% divorced (2000); Foreign born: 2.0% (2000); Ancestry (includes multiple ancestries): 31.9% German, 18.2% English, 13.4% Norwegian, 11.7% Irish, 5.4% Danish (2000).
Economy: Single-family building permits issued: 1 (2001) / 0 (2000); Multi-family building permits issued: 0 (2001) / 0 (2000); Employment by occupation: 10.3% management, 11.3% professional, 10.8% services, 32.5% sales, 1.0% farming, 20.1% construction, 13.9% production (2000).
Income: Per capita income: $17,811 (2000); Median household income: $48,393 (2000); Poverty rate: 3.4% (2000).
Education: High school graduation rate: 88.7% (2000); College graduation rate: 14.0% (2000).
Housing: Homeownership rate: 98.4% (2000); Median home value: $73,800 (2000); Median rent: $325 per month (2000); Median age of housing: 45 years (2000).
Transportation: Commute to work: 95.9% car, 0.0% public transportation, 1.5% walk, 2.6% work from home (2000); Travel time to work: 12.2% less than 15 minutes, 33.3% 15 to 30 minutes, 41.3% 30 to 45 minutes, 6.9% 45 to 60 minutes, 6.3% 60 minutes or more (2000)

SLATER (city). Covers a land area of 1.235 square miles and a water area of 0 square miles. Located at 41.88° N. Lat.; 93.68° W. Long.
History: Slater is believed to have been named in honor of landowner Michael Slater on whose land the town was established.
Population: 1,306 (2000); Race: 99.2% White, 0.2% Black, 0.0% Asian, 0.0% American Indian and Alaska Native, 0.6% Hispanic of any race, 0.5% two or more races (2000); Density: 1,057.6 persons per square mile (2000); Age: 27.2% under 18, 13.6% over 64 (2000); Marriage status: 18.4% never married, 64.7% now married, 8.0% widowed, 8.8% divorced (2000); Foreign born: 1.4% (2000); Ancestry (includes multiple ancestries): 34.7% German, 22.5% Norwegian, 11.4% Irish, 9.4% English, 5.5% United States or American (2000).
Economy: Single-family building permits issued: 8 (2001) / 9 (2000); Multi-family building permits issued: 2 (2001) / 2 (2000); Employment by occupation: 14.9% management, 23.5% professional, 11.6% services, 30.2% sales, 0.3% farming, 8.2% construction, 11.5% production (2000).
Income: Per capita income: $20,647 (2000); Median household income: $45,417 (2000); Poverty rate: 2.0% (2000).
Taxes: Total city taxes per capita: $288 (1997); City property taxes per capita: $200 (1997).
Education: High school graduation rate: 93.6% (2000); College graduation rate: 25.0% (2000).
Housing: Homeownership rate: 79.5% (2000); Median home value: $96,300 (2000); Median rent: $402 per month (2000); Median age of housing: 36 years (2000).
Newspapers: The Tri-County Times (1 x week)
Transportation: Commute to work: 96.6% car, 0.0% public transportation, 1.1% walk, 2.1% work from home (2000); Travel time to work: 22.4% less than 15 minutes, 45.7% 15 to 30 minutes, 25.2% 30 to 45 minutes, 3.2% 45 to 60 minutes, 3.5% 60 minutes or more (2000)

STORY CITY (city). Covers a land area of 2.420 square miles and a water area of 0.002 square miles. Located at 42.18° N. Lat.; 93.59° W. Long. Elevation is 1,011 feet.
History: From 1855, when the town was platted, until the Civil War, the place was a Hoosier settlement known as Fairview. Anticipating the arrival of the railroad, a group of settlers platted Story City adjacent to Fairview in 1878. Later the two towns were incorporated as one.
Population: 3,228 (2000); Race: 99.0% White, 0.0% Black, 0.2% Asian, 0.8% American Indian and Alaska Native, 0.0% Hispanic of any race, 0.0% two or more races (2000); Density: 1,334.1 persons per square mile (2000); Age: 22.5% under 18, 24.0% over 64 (2000); Marriage status: 18.7% never married, 58.7% now married, 12.0% widowed, 10.7% divorced (2000); Foreign born: 0.2% (2000); Ancestry (includes multiple ancestries): 33.9% Norwegian, 33.7% German, 10.0% English, 9.0% Irish, 5.2% Swedish (2000).
Economy: Single-family building permits issued: 9 (2001) / 9 (2000); Multi-family building permits issued: 62 (2001) / 0 (2000); Employment by occupation: 14.4% management, 10.8% professional, 18.7% services, 32.8% sales, 0.0% farming, 10.5% construction, 12.9% production (2000).
Income: Per capita income: $20,345 (2000); Median household income: $41,275 (2000); Poverty rate: 6.4% (2000).
Taxes: Total city taxes per capita: $528 (2000); City property taxes per capita: $416 (2000).
Education: High school graduation rate: 91.6% (2000); College graduation rate: 27.1% (2000).

School District(s)

Roland-Story Community School District (PK-12)
2000 Enrollment: 1,173 515-733-4301
Housing: Homeownership rate: 67.1% (2000); Median home value: $93,800 (2000); Median rent: $416 per month (2000); Median age of housing: 33 years (2000).
Safety: Violent crime rate: 3.1 per 10,000 population; Property crime rate: 58.9 per 10,000 population (2001).
Newspapers: The Story City Herald (1 x week); Story City Reminder (1 x week)
Transportation: Commute to work: 90.1% car, 2.2% public transportation, 4.3% walk, 2.8% work from home (2000); Travel time to work: 47.6% less than 15 minutes, 35.5% 15 to 30 minutes, 13.0% 30 to 45 minutes, 1.8% 45 to 60 minutes, 2.1% 60 minutes or more (2000)
Additional Information Contacts
Story City Chamber of Commerce. 515-733-4214

ZEARING (city). Covers a land area of 0.745 square miles and a water area of 0 square miles. Located at 42.16° N. Lat.; 93.29° W. Long.
History: Zearing was named Ashhurst in 1882, but Major Zearing, a doctor in Chicago who was visiting the town, promised to build an Evangelical Church if the town was named for him.
Population: 617 (2000); Race: 98.7% White, 0.0% Black, 0.0% Asian, 0.5% American Indian and Alaska Native, 2.4% Hispanic of any race, 0.3% two or more races (2000); Density: 828.4 persons per square mile (2000); Age: 27.0% under 18, 15.2% over 64 (2000); Marriage status: 23.1% never married, 58.4% now married, 9.9% widowed, 8.7% divorced (2000); Foreign born: 0.0% (2000); Ancestry (includes multiple ancestries): 40.8% German, 16.3% Norwegian, 14.9% English, 10.0% Irish, 8.0% United States or American (2000).
Economy: Single-family building permits issued: 1 (2001) / 3 (2000); Multi-family building permits issued: 0 (2001) / 0 (2000); Employment by occupation: 8.7% management, 13.0% professional, 20.3% services, 22.9% sales, 2.3% farming, 16.2% construction, 16.5% production (2000).
Income: Per capita income: $14,615 (2000); Median household income: $37,614 (2000); Poverty rate: 3.2% (2000).
Taxes: Total city taxes per capita: $216 (1997); City property taxes per capita: $129 (1997).
Education: High school graduation rate: 91.0% (2000); College graduation rate: 10.4% (2000).
Housing: Homeownership rate: 83.9% (2000); Median home value: $62,200 (2000); Median rent: $273 per month (2000); Median age of housing: 48 years (2000).
Transportation: Commute to work: 91.6% car, 0.0% public transportation, 4.2% walk, 3.6% work from home (2000); Travel time to work: 37.8% less than 15 minutes, 21.1% 15 to 30 minutes, 33.1% 30 to 45 minutes, 5.6% 45 to 60 minutes, 2.5% 60 minutes or more (2000)

Tama County

Located in central Iowa; drained by the Iowa River. Covers a land area of 721.30 square miles, a water area of 1.10 square miles, and is located in the Central Time Zone. The county government was organized in 1843. County seat is Toledo.

Weather Station: Toledo Elevation: 918 feet

	Jan	Feb	Mar	Apr	May	Jun	Jul	Aug	Sep	Oct	Nov	Dec
High	26	33	45	59	71	81	85	83	75	63	46	32
Low	8	14	25	36	48	58	62	60	50	39	27	14
Precip	1.0	1.0	2.4	3.4	4.7	5.0	4.3	4.6	3.6	2.7	2.2	1.2
Snow	8.3	5.4	4.2	1.3	0.0	0.0	0.0	0.0	0.0	0.3	2.3	6.3

High and Low temperatures in degrees Fahrenheit; Precipitation and Snow in inches

Population: 18,103 (2000); Race: 90.5% White, 0.1% Black, 0.5% Asian, 5.8% American Indian and Alaska Native, 3.2% Hispanic of any race, 1.1% two or more races (2000); Density: 25.1 persons per square mile (2000); Age: 26.6% under 18, 18.7% over 64 (2000).
Religion: Five largest groups: 17.0% Catholic Church, 16.4% The United Methodist Church, 7.1% Evangelical Lutheran Church in America, 5.5% United Church of Christ, 2.5% Presbyterian Church (U.S.A.) (2000).
Economy: Unemployment rate: 4.4% (11/2002); Total civilian labor force: 8,370 (11/2002); Leading industries: 15.6% retail trade; 12.1% health care and social assistance; 10.4% manufacturing (2000); Companies that employ more than 1,000 persons: 1 (2000); Companies that employ more than 100 persons: 4 (2000); Farms: 1,152 totaling 396,220 acres (1997); Minority business ownership rate: 0.0% (1997); Women business ownership rate: 23.0% (1997); Retail sales per capita: $5,133 (1997). Single-family building permits issued: 32 (2001) / 40 (2000); Multi-family building permits issued: 0 (2001) / 13 (2000).
Income: Per capita income: $17,097 (2000); Median household income: $37,419 (2000); Poverty rate: 10.5% (2000); Bankruptcy rate: 3.30% (2001).
Taxes: Total county taxes per capita: $241 (2000); County property taxes per capita: $233 (2000).
Education: High school graduation rate: 84.2% (2000); College graduation rate: 12.9% (2000).
Housing: Homeownership rate: 77.6% (2000); Median home value: $64,200 (2000); Median rent: $305 per month (2000); Median age of housing: 57 years (2000).
Health: Birth rate: 122.6 per 10,000 population (1998); Age adjusted death rate: 78.6 per 10,000 population (1999); Age adjusted cancer mortality rate: 166.2 deaths per 100,000 population (1999). Number of physicians: 2.2 per 10,000 population (1999); Number of hospital beds: n/a (1999).
Elections: 2000 Presidential election results: 48.7% Gore, 48.5% Bush, 1.9% Nader, 0.4% Buchanan
National and State Parks: Otter Creek Marsh State Wildlife Refuge; T F Clark State Park; Union Grove State Park
Additional Information Contacts
Tama County Government Offices 641-484-3980
Tama County Board of Realtors 641-476-4949
Toledo Community Development 641-484-4193

Tama County Communities

BUCKINGHAM (unincorporated postal area, zip code 50612). Covers a land area of 23.377 square miles and a water area of 0.064 square miles. Located at 42.27° N. Lat.; 92.39° W. Long. Elevation is 894 feet.
History: Buckingham may have been named for William A. Buckingham, Governor of Connecticut (1858-1866) and senator (1869-1875), or for Buckinghamshire in England.
Population: 413 (2000); Race: 100.0% White, 0.0% Black, 0.0% Asian, 0.0% American Indian and Alaska Native, 0.0% Hispanic of any race, 0.0% two or more races (2000); Density: 17.7 persons per square mile (2000); Age: 13.5% under 18, 13.2% over 64 (2000); Marriage status: 18.0% never married, 75.5% now married, 4.1% widowed, 2.4% divorced (2000); Foreign born: 0.0% (2000); Ancestry (includes multiple ancestries): 56.2% German, 21.2% Irish, 11.7% English, 3.9% French Canadian, 3.9% Czech (2000).
Economy: Employment by occupation: 22.2% management, 27.0% professional, 7.7% services, 29.4% sales, 5.2% farming, 2.0% construction, 6.5% production (2000).
Income: Per capita income: $26,337 (2000); Median household income: $55,375 (2000); Poverty rate: 13.0% (2000).
Education: High school graduation rate: 94.6% (2000); College graduation rate: 42.4% (2000).
Housing: Homeownership rate: 74.5% (2000); Median home value: $110,700 (2000); Median rent: $245 per month (2000); Median age of housing: 40 years (2000).
Transportation: Commute to work: 90.3% car, 0.0% public transportation, 3.8% walk, 5.9% work from home (2000); Travel time to work: 20.5% less than 15 minutes, 52.7% 15 to 30 minutes, 26.8% 30 to 45 minutes, 0.0% 45 to 60 minutes, 0.0% 60 minutes or more (2000)

CHELSEA (city). Covers a land area of 1.012 square miles and a water area of 0 square miles. Located at 41.92° N. Lat.; 92.39° W. Long. Elevation is 792 feet.
History: Chelsea, founded by John I. Blair, was first known as Otter Creek Station. In 1864 it became Chelsea, referring to the former home in Massachusetts of one of the original land-owners, S.G. Breese.
Population: 287 (2000); Race: 91.4% White, 0.0% Black, 0.0% Asian, 0.0% American Indian and Alaska Native, 22.6% Hispanic of any race, 0.0% two or more races (2000); Density: 283.6 persons per square mile (2000); Age: 38.7% under 18, 15.1% over 64 (2000); Marriage status: 27.8% never married, 52.6% now married, 8.2% widowed, 11.3% divorced (2000); Foreign born: 6.5% (2000); Ancestry (includes multiple ancestries): 21.9% German, 20.2% Czech, 15.1% Other groups, 11.0% United States or American, 5.1% Irish (2000).
Economy: Single-family building permits issued: 0 (2001) / 0 (2000); Multi-family building permits issued: 0 (2001) / 0 (2000); Employment by occupation: 6.3% management, 1.8% professional, 16.2% services, 14.4% sales, 7.2% farming, 18.9% construction, 35.1% production (2000).
Income: Per capita income: $13,608 (2000); Median household income: $30,625 (2000); Poverty rate: 19.5% (2000).
Taxes: Total city taxes per capita: $263 (1997); City property taxes per capita: $260 (1997).
Education: High school graduation rate: 77.9% (2000); College graduation rate: 6.4% (2000).
Housing: Homeownership rate: 82.4% (2000); Median home value: $30,700 (2000); Median rent: $275 per month (2000); Median age of housing: 60+ years (2000).
Transportation: Commute to work: 89.2% car, 0.0% public transportation, 6.3% walk, 4.5% work from home (2000); Travel time to work: 34.0% less than 15 minutes, 33.0% 15 to 30 minutes, 11.3% 30 to 45 minutes, 1.9% 45 to 60 minutes, 19.8% 60 minutes or more (2000)

CLUTIER (city). Covers a land area of 0.762 square miles and a water area of 0 square miles. Located at 42.07° N. Lat.; 92.40° W. Long. Elevation is 861 feet.
History: The name of Clutier comes from the surname of early residents of the area.
Population: 229 (2000); Race: 95.8% White, 0.0% Black, 0.0% Asian, 0.0% American Indian and Alaska Native, 0.0% Hispanic of any race, 0.0% two or more races (2000); Density: 300.4 persons per square mile (2000); Age: 23.8% under 18, 29.7% over 64 (2000); Marriage status: 16.3% never married, 61.6% now married, 16.8% widowed, 5.3% divorced (2000); Foreign born: 0.8% (2000); Ancestry (includes multiple ancestries): 38.9% Czech, 26.4% German, 7.9% Czechoslovakian, 7.9% Irish, 5.0% Norwegian (2000).
Economy: Employment by occupation: 6.3% management, 7.4% professional, 18.9% services, 21.1% sales, 3.2% farming, 17.9% construction, 25.3% production (2000).
Income: Per capita income: $14,092 (2000); Median household income: $27,344 (2000); Poverty rate: 12.6% (2000).
Taxes: Total city taxes per capita: $127 (1997); City property taxes per capita: $118 (1997).
Education: High school graduation rate: 75.1% (2000); College graduation rate: 6.9% (2000).
Housing: Homeownership rate: 86.4% (2000); Median home value: $39,600 (2000); Median rent: $200 per month (2000); Median age of housing: 60+ years (2000).
Transportation: Commute to work: 92.4% car, 0.0% public transportation, 7.6% walk, 0.0% work from home (2000); Travel time to work: 26.1% less than 15 minutes, 31.5% 15 to 30 minutes, 29.3% 30 to 45 minutes, 6.5% 45 to 60 minutes, 6.5% 60 minutes or more (2000)

DYSART (city). Covers a land area of 1.259 square miles and a water area of 0 square miles. Located at 42.16° N. Lat.; 92.30° W. Long.
History: Joseph Dysart, at various times a state senator from Tama and Benton counties and lieutenant governor of Iowa, is honored in the name of Dysart.
Population: 1,303 (2000); Race: 99.5% White, 0.0% Black, 0.3% Asian, 0.0% American Indian and Alaska Native, 0.8% Hispanic of any race, 0.2% two or more races (2000); Density: 1,034.5 persons per square mile (2000); Age: 25.8% under 18, 24.2% over 64 (2000); Marriage status: 14.4% never married, 67.3% now married, 11.8% widowed, 6.5% divorced (2000); Foreign born: 0.7% (2000); Ancestry (includes multiple ancestries): 48.9% German, 15.5% Irish, 9.2% English, 8.8% United States or American, 6.7% Czech (2000).

Economy: Single-family building permits issued: 7 (2001) / 3 (2000); Multi-family building permits issued: 0 (2001) / 4 (2000); Employment by occupation: 12.0% management, 19.1% professional, 12.7% services, 27.1% sales, 1.2% farming, 11.2% construction, 16.6% production (2000).
Income: Per capita income: $20,203 (2000); Median household income: $40,857 (2000); Poverty rate: 6.8% (2000).
Taxes: Total city taxes per capita: $251 (1997); City property taxes per capita: $248 (1997).
Education: High school graduation rate: 86.4% (2000); College graduation rate: 17.4% (2000).
Housing: Homeownership rate: 80.3% (2000); Median home value: $75,000 (2000); Median rent: $337 per month (2000); Median age of housing: 52 years (2000).
Newspapers: The Dysart Reporter (1 x week)
Transportation: Commute to work: 88.8% car, 0.0% public transportation, 5.7% walk, 4.4% work from home (2000); Travel time to work: 38.2% less than 15 minutes, 24.4% 15 to 30 minutes, 22.5% 30 to 45 minutes, 8.6% 45 to 60 minutes, 6.3% 60 minutes or more (2000)
Additional Information Contacts
Tama County Board of Realtors........................... 641-476-4949

ELBERON (city). Covers a land area of 0.656 square miles and a water area of 0 square miles. Located at 42.00° N. Lat.; 92.31° W. Long. Elevation is 836 feet.
History: Elberon was named in 1882 for Elberon, New Jersey, the town where President Garfield was assassinated in 1881.
Population: 245 (2000); Race: 98.6% White, 0.0% Black, 0.0% Asian, 0.0% American Indian and Alaska Native, 0.0% Hispanic of any race, 1.4% two or more races (2000); Density: 373.6 persons per square mile (2000); Age: 42.7% under 18, 6.1% over 64 (2000); Marriage status: 28.4% never married, 60.3% now married, 5.7% widowed, 5.7% divorced (2000); Foreign born: 0.0% (2000); Ancestry (includes multiple ancestries): 44.6% German, 14.1% Czech, 9.9% Irish, 8.9% United States or American, 3.8% European (2000).
Economy: Employment by occupation: 5.8% management, 8.7% professional, 14.4% services, 22.1% sales, 1.9% farming, 12.5% construction, 34.6% production (2000).
Income: Per capita income: $12,440 (2000); Median household income: $38,594 (2000); Poverty rate: 15.5% (2000).
Taxes: Total city taxes per capita: $107 (1997); City property taxes per capita: $92 (1997).
Education: High school graduation rate: 88.9% (2000); College graduation rate: 5.1% (2000).
Housing: Homeownership rate: 81.8% (2000); Median home value: $48,800 (2000); Median rent: $254 per month (2000); Median age of housing: 60+ years (2000).
Transportation: Commute to work: 98.0% car, 0.0% public transportation, 2.0% walk, 0.0% work from home (2000); Travel time to work: 31.7% less than 15 minutes, 20.8% 15 to 30 minutes, 9.9% 30 to 45 minutes, 35.6% 45 to 60 minutes, 2.0% 60 minutes or more (2000)

GARWIN (city). Covers a land area of 1.002 square miles and a water area of 0 square miles. Located at 42.09° N. Lat.; 92.67° W. Long. Elevation is 797 feet.
History: Garvin may have been named for an early resident, or for an employee of the Chicago & North Western Railroad.
Population: 565 (2000); Race: 98.3% White, 1.0% Black, 0.0% Asian, 0.0% American Indian and Alaska Native, 1.2% Hispanic of any race, 0.0% two or more races (2000); Density: 564.0 persons per square mile (2000); Age: 28.6% under 18, 12.8% over 64 (2000); Marriage status: 21.4% never married, 58.6% now married, 7.2% widowed, 12.7% divorced (2000); Foreign born: 0.3% (2000); Ancestry (includes multiple ancestries): 37.9% German, 12.5% Irish, 9.8% English, 8.2% United States or American, 6.9% Czech (2000).
Economy: Single-family building permits issued: 1 (2001) / 1 (2000); Multi-family building permits issued: 0 (2001) / 0 (2000); Employment by occupation: 10.4% management, 11.3% professional, 23.9% services, 22.0% sales, 1.0% farming, 12.0% construction, 19.4% production (2000).
Income: Per capita income: $16,660 (2000); Median household income: $38,269 (2000); Poverty rate: 5.2% (2000).
Taxes: Total city taxes per capita: $173 (1997); City property taxes per capita: $169 (1997).
Education: High school graduation rate: 85.4% (2000); College graduation rate: 7.7% (2000).

School District(s)

Gmg Community School District (KG-12)
2000 Enrollment: 431 641-499-2239

Housing: Homeownership rate: 81.1% (2000); Median home value: $51,100 (2000); Median rent: $272 per month (2000); Median age of housing: 55 years (2000).
Transportation: Commute to work: 93.3% car, 0.0% public transportation, 3.0% walk, 3.7% work from home (2000); Travel time to work: 22.1% less than 15 minutes, 54.0% 15 to 30 minutes, 16.6% 30 to 45 minutes, 2.1% 45 to 60 minutes, 5.2% 60 minutes or more (2000)

GLADBROOK (city). Covers a land area of 0.697 square miles and a water area of 0 square miles. Located at 42.18° N. Lat.; 92.71° W. Long. Elevation is 950 feet.
History: Local legend tells of W.F. Johnston and Leander Clark, who were laying out the site for a town, consulting with officials of the Chicago & North Western Railroad about a name for the place. They told the official that the thing that made them happiest about the location was that there was a brook, and the railroad official suggested the name of Gladbrook.
Population: 1,015 (2000); Race: 98.6% White, 0.0% Black, 0.0% Asian, 0.8% American Indian and Alaska Native, 0.0% Hispanic of any race, 0.6% two or more races (2000); Density: 1,456.9 persons per square mile (2000); Age: 24.4% under 18, 26.7% over 64 (2000); Marriage status: 16.6% never married, 61.3% now married, 10.5% widowed, 11.6% divorced (2000); Foreign born: 0.8% (2000); Ancestry (includes multiple ancestries): 47.0% German, 13.7% Irish, 9.1% Norwegian, 7.3% English, 3.7% Other groups (2000).
Economy: Single-family building permits issued: 0 (2001) / 1 (2000); Multi-family building permits issued: 0 (2001) / 4 (2000); Employment by occupation: 9.4% management, 18.8% professional, 18.2% services, 23.5% sales, 0.6% farming, 8.8% construction, 20.7% production (2000).
Income: Per capita income: $18,484 (2000); Median household income: $38,167 (2000); Poverty rate: 6.3% (2000).
Taxes: Total city taxes per capita: $293 (1997); City property taxes per capita: $289 (1997).
Education: High school graduation rate: 82.7% (2000); College graduation rate: 18.0% (2000).
Housing: Homeownership rate: 83.7% (2000); Median home value: $57,400 (2000); Median rent: $261 per month (2000); Median age of housing: 55 years (2000).
Newspapers: Northern-Sun Print (1 x week)
Transportation: Commute to work: 90.6% car, 0.0% public transportation, 7.0% walk, 2.0% work from home (2000); Travel time to work: 37.2% less than 15 minutes, 36.7% 15 to 30 minutes, 17.8% 30 to 45 minutes, 5.1% 45 to 60 minutes, 3.1% 60 minutes or more (2000)

LINCOLN (city). Covers a land area of 0.459 square miles and a water area of 0 square miles. Located at 42.26° N. Lat.; 92.69° W. Long. Elevation is 1,060 feet.
History: Lincoln was founded on land owned by the Spencer family. The town had several names. The present name was put in use after World War I.
Population: 182 (2000); Race: 95.4% White, 0.0% Black, 0.0% Asian, 0.0% American Indian and Alaska Native, 2.6% Hispanic of any race, 2.0% two or more races (2000); Density: 396.3 persons per square mile (2000); Age: 30.6% under 18, 14.3% over 64 (2000); Marriage status: 21.8% never married, 67.3% now married, 6.1% widowed, 4.8% divorced (2000); Foreign born: 2.6% (2000); Ancestry (includes multiple ancestries): 49.0% German, 17.3% Norwegian, 9.2% Irish, 7.1% English, 6.6% Other groups (2000).
Economy: Single-family building permits issued: 0 (2001) / 0 (2000); Multi-family building permits issued: 0 (2001) / 0 (2000); Employment by occupation: 9.3% management, 2.1% professional, 26.8% services, 26.8% sales, 0.0% farming, 14.4% construction, 20.6% production (2000).
Income: Per capita income: $14,313 (2000); Median household income: $33,750 (2000); Poverty rate: 15.5% (2000).
Taxes: Total city taxes per capita: $137 (2000); City property taxes per capita: $132 (2000).
Education: High school graduation rate: 82.4% (2000); College graduation rate: 10.1% (2000).
Housing: Homeownership rate: 84.8% (2000); Median home value: $35,900 (2000); Median rent: $281 per month (2000); Median age of housing: 57 years (2000).
Transportation: Commute to work: 83.5% car, 0.0% public transportation, 12.4% walk, 4.1% work from home (2000); Travel time to work: 55.9% less than 15 minutes, 23.7% 15 to 30 minutes, 9.7% 30 to 45 minutes, 10.8% 45 to 60 minutes, 0.0% 60 minutes or more (2000)

MONTOUR (city). Covers a land area of 0.452 square miles and a water area of 0 square miles. Located at 41.98° N. Lat.; 92.71° W. Long. Elevation is 850 feet.

History: Montour dates back to 1855, when the settlements of Indian Town and Oxford were combined.
Population: 285 (2000); Race: 97.0% White, 0.0% Black, 0.0% Asian, 1.3% American Indian and Alaska Native, 0.4% Hispanic of any race, 1.3% two or more races (2000); Density: 630.0 persons per square mile (2000); Age: 21.7% under 18, 18.3% over 64 (2000); Marriage status: 12.8% never married, 72.8% now married, 2.6% widowed, 11.8% divorced (2000); Foreign born: 0.9% (2000); Ancestry (includes multiple ancestries): 31.5% German, 25.5% Irish, 13.2% English, 10.6% Czech, 8.9% Norwegian (2000).
Economy: Employment by occupation: 8.5% management, 15.4% professional, 25.4% services, 10.0% sales, 0.0% farming, 11.5% construction, 29.2% production (2000).
Income: Per capita income: $16,786 (2000); Median household income: $40,000 (2000); Poverty rate: 4.7% (2000).
Taxes: Total city taxes per capita: $61 (1997); City property taxes per capita: $61 (1997).
Education: High school graduation rate: 70.8% (2000); College graduation rate: 2.3% (2000).
Housing: Homeownership rate: 80.4% (2000); Median home value: $41,700 (2000); Median rent: $304 per month (2000); Median age of housing: 57 years (2000).
Transportation: Commute to work: 91.4% car, 0.0% public transportation, 8.6% walk, 0.0% work from home (2000); Travel time to work: 27.3% less than 15 minutes, 54.7% 15 to 30 minutes, 14.1% 30 to 45 minutes, 0.0% 45 to 60 minutes, 3.9% 60 minutes or more (2000)

TAMA (city). Covers a land area of 3.017 square miles and a water area of 0.148 square miles. Located at 41.96° N. Lat.; 92.57° W. Long. Elevation is 820 feet.
History: Tama, named in memory of the a Fox chief, Taimah, was called Iuka when it was platted in 1862.
Population: 2,731 (2000); Race: 84.6% White, 0.3% Black, 1.4% Asian, 2.8% American Indian and Alaska Native, 11.3% Hispanic of any race, 2.2% two or more races (2000); Density: 905.1 persons per square mile (2000); Age: 27.2% under 18, 18.7% over 64 (2000); Marriage status: 17.1% never married, 65.6% now married, 9.4% widowed, 8.0% divorced (2000); Foreign born: 6.2% (2000); Ancestry (includes multiple ancestries): 24.0% German, 16.2% Other groups, 13.7% Irish, 9.8% English, 9.3% Czech (2000).
Economy: Single-family building permits issued: 1 (2001) / 1 (2000); Multi-family building permits issued: 0 (2001) / 0 (2000); Employment by occupation: 6.8% management, 12.8% professional, 25.5% services, 21.4% sales, 0.7% farming, 9.6% construction, 23.2% production (2000).
Income: Per capita income: $16,676 (2000); Median household income: $35,531 (2000); Poverty rate: 12.3% (2000).
Taxes: Total city taxes per capita: $220 (1997); City property taxes per capita: $214 (1997).
Education: High school graduation rate: 84.6% (2000); College graduation rate: 10.5% (2000).

School District(s)

South Tama County Community School District (PK-12)
2000 Enrollment: 1,740 641-484-4811
Housing: Homeownership rate: 70.5% (2000); Median home value: $58,400 (2000); Median rent: $359 per month (2000); Median age of housing: 59 years (2000).
Newspapers: Toledo Chronicle (1 x week); The Tama News-Herald (1 x week); Tama County Shopper (1 x week)
Transportation: Commute to work: 92.1% car, 0.2% public transportation, 4.1% walk, 1.7% work from home (2000); Travel time to work: 59.8% less than 15 minutes, 16.7% 15 to 30 minutes, 13.9% 30 to 45 minutes, 2.8% 45 to 60 minutes, 6.9% 60 minutes or more (2000)

TOLEDO (city). Covers a land area of 2.296 square miles and a water area of 0 square miles. Located at 41.99° N. Lat.; 92.57° W. Long. Elevation is 852 feet.
History: Toledo was named for Toledo, Ohio.
Population: 2,539 (2000); Race: 90.8% White, 0.0% Black, 0.0% Asian, 6.1% American Indian and Alaska Native, 3.7% Hispanic of any race, 1.6% two or more races (2000); Density: 1,105.9 persons per square mile (2000); Age: 28.2% under 18, 19.7% over 64 (2000); Marriage status: 27.1% never married, 50.0% now married, 12.1% widowed, 10.7% divorced (2000); Foreign born: 2.2% (2000); Ancestry (includes multiple ancestries): 31.6% German, 14.7% Irish, 11.6% Czech, 10.2% English, 9.2% Other groups (2000).
Economy: Single-family building permits issued: 4 (2001) / 5 (2000); Multi-family building permits issued: 0 (2001) / 0 (2000); Employment by occupation: 3.4% management, 14.1% professional, 28.6% services, 26.6% sales, 0.4% farming, 11.3% construction, 15.6% production (2000).
Income: Per capita income: $16,293 (2000); Median household income: $33,750 (2000); Poverty rate: 11.0% (2000).
Taxes: Total city taxes per capita: $320 (1997); City property taxes per capita: $313 (1997).
Education: High school graduation rate: 80.2% (2000); College graduation rate: 11.4% (2000).

School District(s)

Iowa Juvenile Home Herbert Hoover School (N -N)
2000 Enrollment: n/a 515-484-2560
Housing: Homeownership rate: 65.2% (2000); Median home value: $61,900 (2000); Median rent: $325 per month (2000); Median age of housing: 50 years (2000).
Transportation: Commute to work: 92.9% car, 0.0% public transportation, 4.8% walk, 2.3% work from home (2000); Travel time to work: 64.5% less than 15 minutes, 19.6% 15 to 30 minutes, 9.6% 30 to 45 minutes, 2.3% 45 to 60 minutes, 4.0% 60 minutes or more (2000)
Additional Information Contacts
Toledo Community Development 641-484-4193

TRAER (city). Covers a land area of 1.102 square miles and a water area of 0 square miles. Located at 42.19° N. Lat.; 92.46° W. Long. Elevation is 916 feet.
History: Traer was the birthplace (1882) of Margaret Wilson, who won the Pulitzer Prize in 1924 with her first novel, "The Able McLaughlins."
Population: 1,594 (2000); Race: 99.0% White, 0.2% Black, 0.0% Asian, 0.0% American Indian and Alaska Native, 0.8% Hispanic of any race, 0.8% two or more races (2000); Density: 1,446.4 persons per square mile (2000); Age: 21.2% under 18, 29.1% over 64 (2000); Marriage status: 18.5% never married, 61.2% now married, 13.0% widowed, 7.4% divorced (2000); Foreign born: 0.2% (2000); Ancestry (includes multiple ancestries): 37.2% German, 9.3% Irish, 8.3% English, 8.2% Czech, 5.1% United States or American (2000).
Economy: Single-family building permits issued: 6 (2001) / 6 (2000); Multi-family building permits issued: 0 (2001) / 5 (2000); Employment by occupation: 8.7% management, 15.7% professional, 16.2% services, 27.9% sales, 0.7% farming, 8.7% construction, 22.1% production (2000).
Income: Per capita income: $17,811 (2000); Median household income: $35,329 (2000); Poverty rate: 7.0% (2000).
Taxes: Total city taxes per capita: $244 (1997); City property taxes per capita: $240 (1997).
Education: High school graduation rate: 87.7% (2000); College graduation rate: 15.0% (2000).

School District(s)

North Tama County Community School District (KG-12)
2000 Enrollment: 534 319-478-2265
Housing: Homeownership rate: 80.4% (2000); Median home value: $68,400 (2000); Median rent: $323 per month (2000); Median age of housing: 55 years (2000).
Newspapers: The Traer Star-Clipper (1 x week)
Transportation: Commute to work: 87.8% car, 0.0% public transportation, 6.5% walk, 4.0% work from home (2000); Travel time to work: 49.3% less than 15 minutes, 13.5% 15 to 30 minutes, 29.7% 30 to 45 minutes, 4.0% 45 to 60 minutes, 3.6% 60 minutes or more (2000)

VINING (city). Covers a land area of 0.576 square miles and a water area of 0 square miles. Located at 41.99° N. Lat.; 92.38° W. Long.
History: Vining was established in 1881 by the Chicago, Milwaukee & St. Paul Railroad.
Population: 70 (2000); Race: 100.0% White, 0.0% Black, 0.0% Asian, 0.0% American Indian and Alaska Native, 0.0% Hispanic of any race, 0.0% two or more races (2000); Density: 121.4 persons per square mile (2000); Age: 28.7% under 18, 8.8% over 64 (2000); Marriage status: 18.3% never married, 75.0% now married, 3.3% widowed, 3.3% divorced (2000); Foreign born: 0.0% (2000); Ancestry (includes multiple ancestries): 43.8% Czech, 30.0% German, 12.5% Irish, 6.3% English, 6.3% Danish (2000).
Economy: Employment by occupation: 4.0% management, 8.0% professional, 14.0% services, 22.0% sales, 6.0% farming, 16.0% construction, 30.0% production (2000).
Income: Per capita income: $17,458 (2000); Median household income: $42,917 (2000); Poverty rate: 2.5% (2000).
Taxes: Total city taxes per capita: $65 (1997); City property taxes per capita: $65 (1997).
Education: High school graduation rate: 86.3% (2000); College graduation rate: 0.0% (2000).

Housing: Homeownership rate: 77.4% (2000); Median home value: $31,900 (2000); Median rent: $363 per month (2000); Median age of housing: 60+ years (2000).
Transportation: Commute to work: 85.4% car, 0.0% public transportation, 0.0% walk, 14.6% work from home (2000); Travel time to work: 12.2% less than 15 minutes, 36.6% 15 to 30 minutes, 9.8% 30 to 45 minutes, 19.5% 45 to 60 minutes, 22.0% 60 minutes or more (2000)

Taylor County

Located in southwestern Iowa; bounded on the south by Missouri; drained by the One Hundred and Two, Little Platte, and East Nodaway Rivers. Covers a land area of 534.00 square miles, a water area of 0.90 square miles, and is located in the Central Time Zone. The county government was organized in 1847. County seat is Bedford.

Weather Station: Bedford — Elevation: 1,131 feet

	Jan	Feb	Mar	Apr	May	Jun	Jul	Aug	Sep	Oct	Nov	Dec
High	31	39	51	63	73	83	87	85	77	65	49	36
Low	12	18	29	40	51	60	65	63	54	42	30	18
Precip	1.0	1.0	2.3	3.3	4.9	4.4	5.1	4.0	3.9	3.0	2.4	1.1
Snow	6.4	5.7	3.9	1.7	0.0	0.0	0.0	0.0	0.0	0.2	2.2	4.6

High and Low temperatures in degrees Fahrenheit; Precipitation and Snow in inches

Population: 6,958 (2000); Race: 97.7% White, 0.0% Black, 0.3% Asian, 0.3% American Indian and Alaska Native, 3.6% Hispanic of any race, 0.4% two or more races (2000); Density: 13.0 persons per square mile (2000); Age: 24.0% under 18, 22.1% over 64 (2000).
Religion: Five largest groups: 19.8% The United Methodist Church, 10.2% American Baptist Churches in the USA, 8.1% Christian Church (Disciples of Christ), 5.9% Christian Churches and Churches of Christ, 4.4% Presbyterian Church (U.S.A.) (2000).
Economy: Unemployment rate: 3.3% (11/2002); Total civilian labor force: 3,345 (11/2002); Leading industries: 30.3% manufacturing; 18.0% retail trade; 11.7% transportation & warehousing (2000); Companies that employ more than 1,000 persons: 0 (2000); Companies that employ more than 100 persons: 1 (2000); Farms: 746 totaling 291,497 acres (1997); Minority business ownership rate: 0.0% (1997); Women business ownership rate: 33.6% (1997); Retail sales per capita: $3,477 (1997). Single-family building permits issued: 6 (2001) / 7 (2000); Multi-family building permits issued: 0 (2001) / 0 (2000).
Income: Per capita income: $15,082 (2000); Median household income: $31,297 (2000); Poverty rate: 12.1% (2000); Bankruptcy rate: 2.63% (2001).
Taxes: Total county taxes per capita: $207 (1997); County property taxes per capita: $200 (1997).
Education: High school graduation rate: 83.3% (2000); College graduation rate: 12.0% (2000).
Housing: Homeownership rate: 76.6% (2000); Median home value: $37,900 (2000); Median rent: $231 per month (2000); Median age of housing: 2000 years (2000).
Health: Birth rate: 96.3 per 10,000 population (1998); Age adjusted death rate: 82.8 per 10,000 population (1999); Age adjusted cancer mortality rate: 158.8 (Unreliable figure as per CDC) deaths per 100,000 population (1999). Number of physicians: n/a (1999); Number of hospital beds: n/a (1999).
Elections: 2000 Presidential election results: 40.3% Gore, 57.2% Bush, 1.5% Nader, 0.4% Buchanan
National and State Parks: Lake of Three Fires State Park
Additional Information Contacts
Taylor County Government Offices. 712-523-2280
Bedford Chamber of Commerce 712-523-2234
Lenox Chamber of Commerce. 641-333-4272

Taylor County Communities

ATHELSTAN (city). Covers a land area of 0.130 square miles and a water area of 0 square miles. Located at 40.57° N. Lat.; 94.54° W. Long.
History: Athelstan was established in 1887 by the St. Paul & Kansas City Railroad.
Population: 18 (2000); Race: 94.7% White, 0.0% Black, 0.0% Asian, 0.0% American Indian and Alaska Native, 5.3% Hispanic of any race, 5.3% two or more races (2000); Density: 138.8 persons per square mile (2000); Age: 0.0% under 18, 52.6% over 64 (2000); Marriage status: 10.5% never married, 57.9% now married, 15.8% widowed, 15.8% divorced (2000); Foreign born: 0.0% (2000); Ancestry (includes multiple ancestries): 26.3% Other groups, 26.3% English, 21.1% Irish, 15.8% United States or American, 10.5% Swedish (2000).
Economy: Employment by occupation: 0.0% management, 0.0% professional, 0.0% services, 100.0% sales, 0.0% farming, 0.0% construction, 0.0% production (2000).
Income: Per capita income: $13,737 (2000); Median household income: $23,750 (2000); Poverty rate: 31.6% (2000).
Taxes: Total city taxes per capita: $31 (1997); City property taxes per capita: $31 (1997).
Education: High school graduation rate: 31.6% (2000); College graduation rate: 0.0% (2000).
Housing: Homeownership rate: 83.3% (2000); Median home value: <$10,000 (2000); Median rent: $175 per month (2000); Median age of housing: 60+ years (2000).
Transportation: Commute to work: 100.0% car, 0.0% public transportation, 0.0% walk, 0.0% work from home (2000); Travel time to work: 0.0% less than 15 minutes, 0.0% 15 to 30 minutes, 100.0% 30 to 45 minutes, 0.0% 45 to 60 minutes, 0.0% 60 minutes or more (2000)

BEDFORD (city). Covers a land area of 1.608 square miles and a water area of 0 square miles. Located at 40.66° N. Lat.; 94.72° W. Long. Elevation is 1,098 feet.
History: Bedford was named for Bedford, England.
Population: 1,620 (2000); Race: 98.2% White, 0.0% Black, 0.0% Asian, 0.0% American Indian and Alaska Native, 1.4% Hispanic of any race, 0.5% two or more races (2000); Density: 1,007.2 persons per square mile (2000); Age: 23.9% under 18, 25.8% over 64 (2000); Marriage status: 16.9% never married, 58.2% now married, 14.5% widowed, 10.4% divorced (2000); Foreign born: 0.1% (2000); Ancestry (includes multiple ancestries): 23.2% German, 15.6% English, 14.5% Irish, 9.2% United States or American, 7.9% Other groups (2000).
Economy: Single-family building permits issued: 4 (2001) / 4 (2000); Multi-family building permits issued: 0 (2001) / 0 (2000); Employment by occupation: 9.3% management, 9.6% professional, 22.0% services, 19.5% sales, 1.5% farming, 7.6% construction, 30.6% production (2000).
Income: Per capita income: $14,313 (2000); Median household income: $28,125 (2000); Poverty rate: 13.7% (2000).
Taxes: Total city taxes per capita: $120 (1997); City property taxes per capita: $117 (1997).
Education: High school graduation rate: 84.6% (2000); College graduation rate: 10.9% (2000).

School District(s)
Bedford Community School District (KG-12)
2000 Enrollment: 646 712-523-2656
Housing: Homeownership rate: 77.4% (2000); Median home value: $38,500 (2000); Median rent: $226 per month (2000); Median age of housing: 59 years (2000).
Newspapers: The Bedford Times-Press (1 x week); Double Time (1 x week)
Transportation: Commute to work: 87.3% car, 0.0% public transportation, 4.6% walk, 7.8% work from home (2000); Travel time to work: 54.4% less than 15 minutes, 16.4% 15 to 30 minutes, 20.5% 30 to 45 minutes, 5.9% 45 to 60 minutes, 2.7% 60 minutes or more (2000)
Additional Information Contacts
Bedford Chamber of Commerce 712-523-2234

BLOCKTON (city). Covers a land area of 0.647 square miles and a water area of 0 square miles. Located at 40.61° N. Lat.; 94.47° W. Long. Elevation is 1,081 feet.
History: Blockton was first known as Mormon Town. The name was later changed to recognize Willard T. Block, a stockholder in the Chicago, St. Paul & Kansas City Railroad, who had donated the land for the town.
Population: 192 (2000); Race: 97.3% White, 0.0% Black, 2.7% Asian, 0.0% American Indian and Alaska Native, 0.0% Hispanic of any race, 0.0% two or more races (2000); Density: 296.7 persons per square mile (2000); Age: 31.0% under 18, 23.5% over 64 (2000); Marriage status: 13.3% never married, 65.9% now married, 14.8% widowed, 5.9% divorced (2000); Foreign born: 2.7% (2000); Ancestry (includes multiple ancestries): 14.4% German, 11.8% Irish, 11.2% United States or American, 4.3% English, 3.7% Other groups (2000).
Economy: Employment by occupation: 8.5% management, 13.6% professional, 23.7% services, 11.9% sales, 3.4% farming, 8.5% construction, 30.5% production (2000).
Income: Per capita income: $15,413 (2000); Median household income: $22,917 (2000); Poverty rate: 20.0% (2000).
Taxes: Total city taxes per capita: $73 (1997); City property taxes per capita: $73 (1997).
Education: High school graduation rate: 73.8% (2000); College graduation rate: 0.8% (2000).

Housing: Homeownership rate: 74.4% (2000); Median home value: $19,200 (2000); Median rent: $195 per month (2000); Median age of housing: 60+ years (2000).
Transportation: Commute to work: 94.6% car, 0.0% public transportation, 1.8% walk, 3.6% work from home (2000); Travel time to work: 25.9% less than 15 minutes, 35.2% 15 to 30 minutes, 16.7% 30 to 45 minutes, 22.2% 45 to 60 minutes, 0.0% 60 minutes or more (2000)

CLEARFIELD (city). Covers a land area of 0.808 square miles and a water area of 0 square miles. Located at 40.80° N. Lat.; 94.47° W. Long. Elevation is 1,250 feet.
History: Clearfield was settled by emigrants from Clearfield County, Pennsylvania, who brought the name of their community with them.
Population: 371 (2000); Race: 100.0% White, 0.0% Black, 0.0% Asian, 0.0% American Indian and Alaska Native, 0.0% Hispanic of any race, 0.0% two or more races (2000); Density: 459.2 persons per square mile (2000); Age: 15.0% under 18, 32.7% over 64 (2000); Marriage status: 17.1% never married, 57.5% now married, 18.9% widowed, 6.5% divorced (2000); Foreign born: 0.0% (2000); Ancestry (includes multiple ancestries): 19.8% English, 14.5% German, 9.1% Irish, 5.6% Swedish, 5.1% Scottish (2000).
Economy: Single-family building permits issued: 2 (2001) / 2 (2000); Multi-family building permits issued: 0 (2001) / 0 (2000); Employment by occupation: 6.4% management, 10.2% professional, 15.3% services, 21.7% sales, 4.5% farming, 21.0% construction, 21.0% production (2000).
Income: Per capita income: $13,810 (2000); Median household income: $23,203 (2000); Poverty rate: 10.7% (2000).
Taxes: Total city taxes per capita: $77 (1997); City property taxes per capita: $75 (1997).
Education: High school graduation rate: 88.9% (2000); College graduation rate: 12.5% (2000).

School District(s)

Clearfield Community School District (PK-12)
2000 Enrollment: 49 641-336-2353
Housing: Homeownership rate: 72.4% (2000); Median home value: $24,100 (2000); Median rent: $212 per month (2000); Median age of housing: 60+ years (2000).
Transportation: Commute to work: 82.8% car, 0.0% public transportation, 14.6% walk, 2.6% work from home (2000); Travel time to work: 53.7% less than 15 minutes, 19.7% 15 to 30 minutes, 14.3% 30 to 45 minutes, 4.1% 45 to 60 minutes, 8.2% 60 minutes or more (2000)

CONWAY (city). Covers a land area of 0.222 square miles and a water area of 0 square miles. Located at 40.74° N. Lat.; 94.62° W. Long.
History: The town of Conway (originally spelled Conwa) was laid out about 1870 for the Chicago, Burlington & Quincy Railroad. The present spelling of the name is credited to newspaper editor Johnny Scott.
Population: 63 (2000); Race: 100.0% White, 0.0% Black, 0.0% Asian, 0.0% American Indian and Alaska Native, 0.0% Hispanic of any race, 0.0% two or more races (2000); Density: 283.6 persons per square mile (2000); Age: 32.0% under 18, 2.0% over 64 (2000); Marriage status: 25.0% never married, 42.5% now married, 7.5% widowed, 25.0% divorced (2000); Foreign born: 0.0% (2000); Ancestry (includes multiple ancestries): 36.0% German, 20.0% United States or American, 12.0% Swiss, 12.0% Swedish, 8.0% Other groups (2000).
Economy: Employment by occupation: 0.0% management, 22.2% professional, 25.9% services, 14.8% sales, 0.0% farming, 14.8% construction, 22.2% production (2000).
Income: Per capita income: $11,780 (2000); Median household income: $31,250 (2000); Poverty rate: 28.0% (2000).
Taxes: Total city taxes per capita: $33 (1997); City property taxes per capita: $33 (1997).
Education: High school graduation rate: 89.3% (2000); College graduation rate: 14.3% (2000).
Housing: Homeownership rate: 70.0% (2000); Median home value: $32,500 (2000); Median age of housing: 52 years (2000).
Transportation: Commute to work: 88.9% car, 0.0% public transportation, 11.1% walk, 0.0% work from home (2000); Travel time to work: 18.5% less than 15 minutes, 37.0% 15 to 30 minutes, 22.2% 30 to 45 minutes, 22.2% 45 to 60 minutes, 0.0% 60 minutes or more (2000)

GRAVITY (city). Covers a land area of 0.299 square miles and a water area of 0 square miles. Located at 40.75° N. Lat.; 94.74° W. Long. Elevation is 1,149 feet.
History: Local legend says that Gravity received its name because it was the "center of gravity" for trading in Washington Township.
Population: 218 (2000); Race: 99.6% White, 0.0% Black, 0.4% Asian, 0.0% American Indian and Alaska Native, 3.5% Hispanic of any race, 0.0% two or more races (2000); Density: 729.6 persons per square mile (2000); Age: 22.6% under 18, 24.8% over 64 (2000); Marriage status: 14.4% never married, 68.4% now married, 9.6% widowed, 7.5% divorced (2000); Foreign born: 0.4% (2000); Ancestry (includes multiple ancestries): 18.6% German, 12.8% United States or American, 12.4% English, 8.4% Irish, 6.6% Other groups (2000).
Economy: Employment by occupation: 4.5% management, 12.4% professional, 20.2% services, 13.5% sales, 1.1% farming, 11.2% construction, 37.1% production (2000).
Income: Per capita income: $13,312 (2000); Median household income: $25,000 (2000); Poverty rate: 18.1% (2000).
Taxes: Total city taxes per capita: $18 (1997); City property taxes per capita: $18 (1997).
Education: High school graduation rate: 80.4% (2000); College graduation rate: 7.4% (2000).
Housing: Homeownership rate: 94.3% (2000); Median home value: $22,300 (2000); Median rent: $175 per month (2000); Median age of housing: 60+ years (2000).
Transportation: Commute to work: 94.4% car, 0.0% public transportation, 3.4% walk, 2.2% work from home (2000); Travel time to work: 20.7% less than 15 minutes, 51.7% 15 to 30 minutes, 25.3% 30 to 45 minutes, 0.0% 45 to 60 minutes, 2.3% 60 minutes or more (2000)

LENOX (city). Covers a land area of 1.976 square miles and a water area of 0.072 square miles. Located at 40.88° N. Lat.; 94.56° W. Long. Elevation is 1,293 feet.
History: Lenox was originally called Summit. The name was changed in honor of the daughter of a railroad official of the Chicago, Burlington & Quincy Railroad.
Population: 1,401 (2000); Race: 92.3% White, 0.0% Black, 0.8% Asian, 1.4% American Indian and Alaska Native, 15.3% Hispanic of any race, 0.6% two or more races (2000); Density: 709.0 persons per square mile (2000); Age: 23.0% under 18, 22.4% over 64 (2000); Marriage status: 23.9% never married, 55.5% now married, 10.5% widowed, 10.1% divorced (2000); Foreign born: 9.1% (2000); Ancestry (includes multiple ancestries): 21.1% German, 19.9% Other groups, 10.7% English, 9.5% Irish, 5.1% United States or American (2000).
Economy: Single-family building permits issued: 0 (2001) / 1 (2000); Multi-family building permits issued: 0 (2001) / 0 (2000); Employment by occupation: 9.7% management, 11.1% professional, 18.4% services, 18.4% sales, 2.4% farming, 7.1% construction, 32.8% production (2000).
Income: Per capita income: $14,299 (2000); Median household income: $29,958 (2000); Poverty rate: 14.2% (2000).
Taxes: Total city taxes per capita: $194 (1997); City property taxes per capita: $193 (1997).
Education: High school graduation rate: 74.3% (2000); College graduation rate: 10.9% (2000).

School District(s)

Lenox Community School District (KG-12)
2000 Enrollment: 412 641-333-2244
Housing: Homeownership rate: 68.4% (2000); Median home value: $46,400 (2000); Median rent: $249 per month (2000); Median age of housing: 47 years (2000).
Newspapers: Lenox Time-Table (1 x week)
Transportation: Commute to work: 89.2% car, 0.0% public transportation, 5.8% walk, 2.8% work from home (2000); Travel time to work: 65.9% less than 15 minutes, 19.5% 15 to 30 minutes, 9.1% 30 to 45 minutes, 1.5% 45 to 60 minutes, 3.9% 60 minutes or more (2000)
Additional Information Contacts
Lenox Chamber of Commerce 641-333-4272

NEW MARKET (city). Covers a land area of 0.439 square miles and a water area of 0 square miles. Located at 40.73° N. Lat.; 94.90° W. Long. Elevation is 1,153 feet.
History: New Market sprang up along the railroad when a large vein of coal was found nearby.
Population: 456 (2000); Race: 98.5% White, 0.0% Black, 0.0% Asian, 0.0% American Indian and Alaska Native, 1.1% Hispanic of any race, 0.9% two or more races (2000); Density: 1,038.7 persons per square mile (2000); Age: 24.4% under 18, 24.0% over 64 (2000); Marriage status: 17.0% never married, 59.1% now married, 10.4% widowed, 13.5% divorced (2000); Foreign born: 0.0% (2000); Ancestry (includes multiple ancestries): 31.7% German, 14.8% English, 11.0% Irish, 9.3% Other groups, 6.8% United States or American (2000).

Economy: Employment by occupation: 3.3% management, 14.6% professional, 21.1% services, 17.8% sales, 2.8% farming, 8.0% construction, 32.4% production (2000).
Income: Per capita income: $15,381 (2000); Median household income: $31,771 (2000); Poverty rate: 14.2% (2000).
Taxes: Total city taxes per capita: $59 (1997); City property taxes per capita: $57 (1997).
Education: High school graduation rate: 88.4% (2000); College graduation rate: 9.6% (2000).

School District(s)

New Market Community School District (KG-12)
2000 Enrollment: 118 712-585-3222

Housing: Homeownership rate: 79.1% (2000); Median home value: $37,800 (2000); Median rent: $290 per month (2000); Median age of housing: 60+ years (2000).
Transportation: Commute to work: 96.7% car, 0.0% public transportation, 1.4% walk, 1.9% work from home (2000); Travel time to work: 47.4% less than 15 minutes, 31.6% 15 to 30 minutes, 13.9% 30 to 45 minutes, 2.4% 45 to 60 minutes, 4.8% 60 minutes or more (2000)

SHARPSBURG (city). Covers a land area of 0.363 square miles and a water area of 0.007 square miles. Located at 40.80° N. Lat.; 94.64° W. Long. Elevation is 1,270 feet.
History: Sharpsburg was named for the original owner of the town site, Thomas H. Sharp.
Population: 98 (2000); Race: 98.2% White, 0.0% Black, 0.0% Asian, 0.0% American Indian and Alaska Native, 0.0% Hispanic of any race, 1.8% two or more races (2000); Density: 270.2 persons per square mile (2000); Age: 31.5% under 18, 23.4% over 64 (2000); Marriage status: 26.5% never married, 51.8% now married, 12.0% widowed, 9.6% divorced (2000); Foreign born: 0.0% (2000); Ancestry (includes multiple ancestries): 28.8% Irish, 12.6% German, 9.0% Swedish, 8.1% English, 8.1% United States or American (2000).
Economy: Single-family building permits issued: 0 (2001) / 0 (2000); Multi-family building permits issued: 0 (2001) / 0 (2000); Employment by occupation: 5.6% management, 11.1% professional, 11.1% services, 19.4% sales, 5.6% farming, 11.1% construction, 36.1% production (2000).
Income: Per capita income: $8,779 (2000); Median household income: $26,042 (2000); Poverty rate: 14.4% (2000).
Taxes: Total city taxes per capita: $55 (1997); City property taxes per capita: $55 (1997).
Education: High school graduation rate: 70.6% (2000); College graduation rate: 11.8% (2000).
Housing: Homeownership rate: 80.5% (2000); Median home value: $13,800 (2000); Median rent: $150 per month (2000); Median age of housing: 60+ years (2000).
Transportation: Commute to work: 94.4% car, 0.0% public transportation, 0.0% walk, 5.6% work from home (2000); Travel time to work: 52.9% less than 15 minutes, 17.6% 15 to 30 minutes, 5.9% 30 to 45 minutes, 14.7% 45 to 60 minutes, 8.8% 60 minutes or more (2000)

Union County

Located in southern Iowa; prairie area, drained by the Little Platte, Grand, and Thompson Rivers. Covers a land area of 424.40 square miles, a water area of 1.60 square miles, and is located in the Central Time Zone. The county government was organized in 1851. County seat is Creston.

Weather Station: Creston 2 SW — Elevation: 1,318 feet

	Jan	Feb	Mar	Apr	May	Jun	Jul	Aug	Sep	Oct	Nov	Dec
High	30	37	49	62	73	82	86	84	77	64	47	35
Low	12	18	28	39	50	60	64	62	53	42	29	17
Precip	0.8	1.0	2.1	3.4	4.6	4.2	4.3	3.9	4.2	2.6	2.3	1.0
Snow	6.6	na	3.3	1.1	0.0	0.0	0.0	0.0	0.0	0.4	2.6	na

High and Low temperatures in degrees Fahrenheit; Precipitation and Snow in inches

Population: 12,309 (2000); Race: 98.0% White, 0.1% Black, 0.4% Asian, 0.0% American Indian and Alaska Native, 0.7% Hispanic of any race, 1.2% two or more races (2000); Density: 29.0 persons per square mile (2000); Age: 23.4% under 18, 18.7% over 64 (2000).
Religion: Five largest groups: 12.0% Catholic Church, 10.5% Christian Church (Disciples of Christ), 10.4% The United Methodist Church, 5.0% United Church of Christ, 4.8% General Association of Regular Baptist Churches (2000).
Economy: Unemployment rate: 4.7% (11/2002); Total civilian labor force: 6,881 (11/2002); Leading industries: 19.5% health care and social assistance; 19.1% manufacturing; 17.2% retail trade (2000); Companies that employ more than 1,000 persons: 0 (2000); Companies that employ more than 100 persons: 9 (2000); Farms: 671 totaling 225,134 acres (1997); Minority business ownership rate: 0.0% (1997); Women business ownership rate: 10.9% (1997); Retail sales per capita: $9,167 (1997). Single-family building permits issued: 10 (2001) / 17 (2000); Multi-family building permits issued: 3 (2001) / 0 (2000).
Income: Per capita income: $16,690 (2000); Median household income: $31,905 (2000); Poverty rate: 11.4% (2000); Bankruptcy rate: 2.67% (2001).
Taxes: Total county taxes per capita: $265 (2000); County property taxes per capita: $257 (2000).
Education: High school graduation rate: 87.3% (2000); College graduation rate: 14.7% (2000).
Housing: Homeownership rate: 72.0% (2000); Median home value: $55,600 (2000); Median rent: $273 per month (2000); Median age of housing: 53 years (2000).
Health: Birth rate: 126.7 per 10,000 population (1998); Age adjusted death rate: 87.2 per 10,000 population (1999); Age adjusted cancer mortality rate: 204.1 deaths per 100,000 population (1999). Number of physicians: 7.3 per 10,000 population (1999); Number of hospital beds: 39.8 per 10,000 population (1999).
Elections: 2000 Presidential election results: 44.3% Gore, 52.3% Bush, 1.9% Nader, 0.8% Buchanan
National and State Parks: Green Valley State Park
Additional Information Contacts
Union County Government Offices 515-782-7918
Bluegrass Board of Realtors.......................... 641-782-8516
Creston Chamber of Commerce.......................... 641-782-7021

Union County Communities

AFTON (city). Covers a land area of 0.984 square miles and a water area of 0 square miles. Located at 41.02° N. Lat.; 94.19° W. Long. Elevation is 1,198 feet.
History: Afton was selected as the seat of Union County in 1855. After the Chicago, Burlington & Quincy Railroad was built through the county in 1869, the seat was moved to Creston. Mrs. James Baker, an early resident, suggested this name for the village because of her fondness for the Scottish song, "Flow Gently Sweet Afton."
Population: 917 (2000); Race: 98.4% White, 0.0% Black, 0.3% Asian, 0.0% American Indian and Alaska Native, 2.9% Hispanic of any race, 0.2% two or more races (2000); Density: 931.7 persons per square mile (2000); Age: 27.5% under 18, 18.9% over 64 (2000); Marriage status: 23.3% never married, 56.9% now married, 9.7% widowed, 10.1% divorced (2000); Foreign born: 1.7% (2000); Ancestry (includes multiple ancestries): 24.1% German, 12.5% Irish, 9.0% United States or American, 7.6% English, 4.9% Other groups (2000).
Economy: Single-family building permits issued: 1 (2001) / 2 (2000); Multi-family building permits issued: 0 (2001) / 0 (2000); Employment by occupation: 7.2% management, 11.0% professional, 23.8% services, 20.9% sales, 1.1% farming, 8.3% construction, 27.6% production (2000).
Income: Per capita income: $12,920 (2000); Median household income: $28,281 (2000); Poverty rate: 19.4% (2000).
Taxes: Total city taxes per capita: $108 (1997); City property taxes per capita: $105 (1997).
Education: High school graduation rate: 83.6% (2000); College graduation rate: 9.7% (2000).

School District(s)

East Union Community School District (KG-12)
2000 Enrollment: 535 641-347-5215

Housing: Homeownership rate: 67.9% (2000); Median home value: $45,000 (2000); Median rent: $198 per month (2000); Median age of housing: 39 years (2000).
Newspapers: Afton Star-Enterprise (1 x week)
Transportation: Commute to work: 90.3% car, 2.5% public transportation, 5.3% walk, 1.8% work from home (2000); Travel time to work: 38.9% less than 15 minutes, 43.8% 15 to 30 minutes, 11.0% 30 to 45 minutes, 2.1% 45 to 60 minutes, 4.2% 60 minutes or more (2000)

ARISPE (city). Covers a land area of 0.519 square miles and a water area of 0 square miles. Located at 40.94° N. Lat.; 94.21° W. Long. Elevation is 1,267 feet.
History: Arispe was named by Burr Forbes, a settler, for one of his friends.
Population: 89 (2000); Race: 100.0% White, 0.0% Black, 0.0% Asian, 0.0% American Indian and Alaska Native, 0.0% Hispanic of any race, 0.0% two or

more races (2000); Density: 171.6 persons per square mile (2000); Age: 15.6% under 18, 37.7% over 64 (2000); Marriage status: 14.7% never married, 64.7% now married, 11.8% widowed, 8.8% divorced (2000); Foreign born: 0.0% (2000); Ancestry (includes multiple ancestries): 32.5% United States or American, 28.6% German, 14.3% English, 13.0% Irish, 10.4% Danish (2000).
Economy: Employment by occupation: 13.9% management, 5.6% professional, 11.1% services, 19.4% sales, 0.0% farming, 22.2% construction, 27.8% production (2000).
Income: Per capita income: $11,999 (2000); Median household income: $25,000 (2000); Poverty rate: 11.7% (2000).
Taxes: Total city taxes per capita: $54 (1997); City property taxes per capita: $54 (1997).
Education: High school graduation rate: 88.3% (2000); College graduation rate: 3.3% (2000).
Housing: Homeownership rate: 92.5% (2000); Median home value: $17,500 (2000); Median age of housing: 60+ years (2000).
Transportation: Commute to work: 86.1% car, 0.0% public transportation, 2.8% walk, 0.0% work from home (2000); Travel time to work: 50.0% less than 15 minutes, 16.7% 15 to 30 minutes, 8.3% 30 to 45 minutes, 19.4% 45 to 60 minutes, 5.6% 60 minutes or more (2000)

CRESTON (city). Covers a land area of 5.078 square miles and a water area of 0.051 square miles. Located at 41.05° N. Lat.; 94.36° W. Long. Elevation is 1,320 feet.
History: Creston was named divisional headquarters of the Chicago, Burlington & Quincy Railroad in 1869. In early days, Creston had trouble maintaining an adequate water supply.
Population: 7,597 (2000); Race: 98.4% White, 0.1% Black, 0.4% Asian, 0.0% American Indian and Alaska Native, 0.7% Hispanic of any race, 0.9% two or more races (2000); Density: 1,496.2 persons per square mile (2000); Age: 22.9% under 18, 20.2% over 64 (2000); Marriage status: 22.2% never married, 55.9% now married, 11.6% widowed, 10.3% divorced (2000); Foreign born: 1.2% (2000); Ancestry (includes multiple ancestries): 23.9% German, 12.4% Irish, 12.0% United States or American, 10.7% English, 4.6% Other groups (2000).
Economy: Single-family building permits issued: 9 (2001) / 15 (2000); Multi-family building permits issued: 3 (2001) / 0 (2000); Employment by occupation: 9.7% management, 15.0% professional, 17.1% services, 23.5% sales, 0.9% farming, 10.3% construction, 23.5% production (2000).
Income: Per capita income: $16,411 (2000); Median household income: $29,831 (2000); Poverty rate: 11.5% (2000).
Taxes: Total city taxes per capita: $244 (1997); City property taxes per capita: $241 (1997).
Education: High school graduation rate: 86.8% (2000); College graduation rate: 14.8% (2000).

School District(s)

Creston Community School District (PK-12)
2000 Enrollment: 1,598 641-782-7028

Two-year College(s)

Southwestern Community College (Public)
2001 Enrollment: 1,198 641-782-7081
2001 Tuition: In-state $2,144; Out-of-state $3,216

Housing: Homeownership rate: 67.1% (2000); Median home value: $57,700 (2000); Median rent: $279 per month (2000); Median age of housing: 52 years (2000).
Hospitals: Greater Community Hospital (80 beds)
Newspapers: Creston News-Advertiser (5 x week)
Transportation: Commute to work: 91.9% car, 2.3% public transportation, 3.4% walk, 1.7% work from home (2000); Travel time to work: 78.8% less than 15 minutes, 9.8% 15 to 30 minutes, 5.2% 30 to 45 minutes, 1.7% 45 to 60 minutes, 4.4% 60 minutes or more (2000); Amtrak: Service available.

Additional Information Contacts

Bluegrass Board of Realtors. 641-782-8516
Creston Chamber of Commerce 641-782-7021

CROMWELL (city). Covers a land area of 0.288 square miles and a water area of 0 square miles. Located at 41.04° N. Lat.; 94.46° W. Long.
Population: 120 (2000); Race: 100.0% White, 0.0% Black, 0.0% Asian, 0.0% American Indian and Alaska Native, 0.0% Hispanic of any race, 0.0% two or more races (2000); Density: 416.6 persons per square mile (2000); Age: 28.2% under 18, 13.5% over 64 (2000); Marriage status: 21.0% never married, 63.7% now married, 10.5% widowed, 4.8% divorced (2000); Foreign born: 0.0% (2000); Ancestry (includes multiple ancestries): 15.4% German, 9.0% Irish, 7.7% United States or American, 4.5% Norwegian, 3.2% Welsh (2000).
Economy: Livestock; grain. Employment by occupation: 6.5% management, 17.7% professional, 11.3% services, 22.6% sales, 0.0% farming, 16.1% construction, 25.8% production (2000).
Income: Per capita income: $12,190 (2000); Median household income: $35,000 (2000); Poverty rate: 42.9% (2000).
Taxes: Total city taxes per capita: $75 (1997); City property taxes per capita: $75 (1997).
Education: High school graduation rate: 83.7% (2000); College graduation rate: 4.3% (2000).
Housing: Homeownership rate: 89.6% (2000); Median home value: $33,400 (2000); Median rent: $242 per month (2000); Median age of housing: 60+ years (2000).
Transportation: Commute to work: 96.8% car, 0.0% public transportation, 3.2% walk, 0.0% work from home (2000); Travel time to work: 38.7% less than 15 minutes, 40.3% 15 to 30 minutes, 3.2% 30 to 45 minutes, 3.2% 45 to 60 minutes, 14.5% 60 minutes or more (2000)

KENT (city). Covers a land area of 0.259 square miles and a water area of 0 square miles. Located at 40.95° N. Lat.; 94.45° W. Long.
History: Kent was named for an Ohio jeweler, A. Kent, who owned a farm near the town site.
Population: 52 (2000); Race: 100.0% White, 0.0% Black, 0.0% Asian, 0.0% American Indian and Alaska Native, 0.0% Hispanic of any race, 0.0% two or more races (2000); Density: 201.1 persons per square mile (2000); Age: 22.0% under 18, 4.9% over 64 (2000); Marriage status: 17.6% never married, 41.2% now married, 5.9% widowed, 35.3% divorced (2000); Foreign born: 0.0% (2000); Ancestry (includes multiple ancestries): 9.8% United States or American, 7.3% Irish, 7.3% Belgian, 2.4% German (2000).
Economy: Employment by occupation: 9.5% management, 28.6% professional, 0.0% services, 19.0% sales, 0.0% farming, 19.0% construction, 23.8% production (2000).
Income: Per capita income: $13,529 (2000); Median household income: $27,917 (2000); Poverty rate: 17.1% (2000).
Taxes: Total city taxes per capita: $61 (1997); City property taxes per capita: $61 (1997).
Education: High school graduation rate: 86.7% (2000); College graduation rate: 0.0% (2000).
Housing: Homeownership rate: 85.0% (2000); Median home value: $25,400 (2000); Median rent: $225 per month (2000); Median age of housing: 60+ years (2000).
Transportation: Commute to work: 100.0% car, 0.0% public transportation, 0.0% walk, 0.0% work from home (2000); Travel time to work: 15.0% less than 15 minutes, 45.0% 15 to 30 minutes, 30.0% 30 to 45 minutes, 0.0% 45 to 60 minutes, 10.0% 60 minutes or more (2000)

LORIMOR (city). Covers a land area of 0.405 square miles and a water area of 0 square miles. Located at 41.12° N. Lat.; 94.05° W. Long. Elevation is 1,227 feet.
History: Lorimor was founded and named by Josiah Lorimor in 1877.
Population: 427 (2000); Race: 96.9% White, 0.0% Black, 1.4% Asian, 0.0% American Indian and Alaska Native, 0.0% Hispanic of any race, 1.7% two or more races (2000); Density: 1,055.2 persons per square mile (2000); Age: 29.5% under 18, 16.3% over 64 (2000); Marriage status: 16.9% never married, 63.5% now married, 10.4% widowed, 9.1% divorced (2000); Foreign born: 0.2% (2000); Ancestry (includes multiple ancestries): 21.6% United States or American, 14.9% German, 12.7% Irish, 12.5% English, 12.0% Other groups (2000).
Economy: Employment by occupation: 8.5% management, 0.7% professional, 15.5% services, 20.4% sales, 0.0% farming, 27.5% construction, 27.5% production (2000).
Income: Per capita income: $12,713 (2000); Median household income: $28,636 (2000); Poverty rate: 18.9% (2000).
Taxes: Total city taxes per capita: $85 (1997); City property taxes per capita: $85 (1997).
Education: High school graduation rate: 78.4% (2000); College graduation rate: 3.3% (2000).
Housing: Homeownership rate: 75.4% (2000); Median home value: $29,100 (2000); Median rent: $331 per month (2000); Median age of housing: 60+ years (2000).
Transportation: Commute to work: 95.8% car, 0.0% public transportation, 1.4% walk, 1.4% work from home (2000); Travel time to work: 13.6% less than 15 minutes, 25.0% 15 to 30 minutes, 25.7% 30 to 45 minutes, 11.4% 45 to 60 minutes, 24.3% 60 minutes or more (2000)

SHANNON CITY (city). Covers a land area of 0.149 square miles and a water area of 0 square miles. Located at 40.90° N. Lat.; 94.26° W. Long.

Population: 70 (2000); Race: 92.4% White, 0.0% Black, 5.1% Asian, 0.0% American Indian and Alaska Native, 0.0% Hispanic of any race, 2.5% two or more races (2000); Density: 470.6 persons per square mile (2000); Age: 31.6% under 18, 5.1% over 64 (2000); Marriage status: 32.8% never married, 45.9% now married, 8.2% widowed, 13.1% divorced (2000); Foreign born: 0.0% (2000); Ancestry (includes multiple ancestries): 30.4% United States or American, 21.5% Other groups, 11.4% Irish, 5.1% Pennsylvania German, 3.8% Dutch (2000).
Economy: Employment by occupation: 0.0% management, 9.4% professional, 6.3% services, 15.6% sales, 6.3% farming, 25.0% construction, 37.5% production (2000).
Income: Per capita income: $10,554 (2000); Median household income: $19,583 (2000); Poverty rate: 17.7% (2000).
Taxes: Total city taxes per capita: $31 (1997); City property taxes per capita: $21 (1997).
Education: High school graduation rate: 83.3% (2000); College graduation rate: 2.1% (2000).
Housing: Homeownership rate: 61.5% (2000); Median home value: $15,800 (2000); Median rent: $178 per month (2000); Median age of housing: 60+ years (2000).
Transportation: Commute to work: 93.8% car, 0.0% public transportation, 6.3% walk, 0.0% work from home (2000); Travel time to work: 12.5% less than 15 minutes, 46.9% 15 to 30 minutes, 21.9% 30 to 45 minutes, 12.5% 45 to 60 minutes, 6.3% 60 minutes or more (2000)

THAYER (city). Covers a land area of 0.098 square miles and a water area of 0 square miles. Located at 41.02° N. Lat.; 94.05° W. Long. Elevation is 1,107 feet.
Population: 66 (2000); Race: 100.0% White, 0.0% Black, 0.0% Asian, 0.0% American Indian and Alaska Native, 0.0% Hispanic of any race, 0.0% two or more races (2000); Density: 672.7 persons per square mile (2000); Age: 15.9% under 18, 12.7% over 64 (2000); Marriage status: 20.8% never married, 52.8% now married, 15.1% widowed, 11.3% divorced (2000); Foreign born: 0.0% (2000); Ancestry (includes multiple ancestries): 19.0% United States or American, 9.5% English, 9.5% German, 7.9% Scottish, 7.9% Italian (2000).
Economy: Livestock, grain. Employment by occupation: 0.0% management, 8.8% professional, 26.5% services, 11.8% sales, 0.0% farming, 2.9% construction, 50.0% production (2000).
Income: Per capita income: $13,705 (2000); Median household income: $31,250 (2000); Poverty rate: 6.3% (2000).
Taxes: Total city taxes per capita: $418 (1997); City property taxes per capita: $418 (1997).
Education: High school graduation rate: 69.8% (2000); College graduation rate: 0.0% (2000).
Housing: Homeownership rate: 92.6% (2000); Median home value: $12,500 (2000); Median age of housing: 60+ years (2000).
Transportation: Commute to work: 85.3% car, 0.0% public transportation, 5.9% walk, 0.0% work from home (2000); Travel time to work: 5.9% less than 15 minutes, 47.1% 15 to 30 minutes, 38.2% 30 to 45 minutes, 0.0% 45 to 60 minutes, 8.8% 60 minutes or more (2000)

Van Buren County

Located in southeastern Iowa; bounded on the south by Missouri; prairie area, drained by the Des Moines and Fox Rivers. Covers a land area of 484.80 square miles, a water area of 5.70 square miles, and is located in the Central Time Zone. The county government was organized in 1836. County seat is Keosauqua.

Weather Station: Keosauqua — Elevation: 623 feet

	Jan	Feb	Mar	Apr	May	Jun	Jul	Aug	Sep	Oct	Nov	Dec
High	33	39	52	65	75	84	88	86	79	67	50	37
Low	14	19	30	40	50	60	65	62	54	42	31	20
Precip	1.4	1.3	2.7	3.7	4.9	4.4	4.9	4.0	4.1	2.9	2.9	2.0
Snow	7.7	6.0	3.2	1.7	0.0	0.0	0.0	0.0	0.0	tr	2.0	6.0

High and Low temperatures in degrees Fahrenheit; Precipitation and Snow in inches

Population: 7,809 (2000); Race: 99.1% White, 0.1% Black, 0.2% Asian, 0.1% American Indian and Alaska Native, 0.2% Hispanic of any race, 0.4% two or more races (2000); Density: 16.1 persons per square mile (2000); Age: 24.7% under 18, 18.9% over 64 (2000).
Religion: Five largest groups: 18.5% The United Methodist Church, 5.2% Christian Churches and Churches of Christ, 3.7% Presbyterian Church (U.S.A.), 3.5% Catholic Church, 2.5% Old Order Amish Church (2000).
Economy: Unemployment rate: 5.8% (11/2002); Total civilian labor force: 4,059 (11/2002); Leading industries: 44.8% manufacturing; 19.9% health care and social assistance; 10.1% retail trade (2000); Companies that employ more than 1,000 persons: 0 (2000); Companies that employ more than 100 persons: 3 (2000); Farms: 807 totaling 257,227 acres (1997); Minority business ownership rate: 0.0% (1997); Women business ownership rate: 0.0% (1997); Retail sales per capita: $2,529 (1997). Single-family building permits issued: 3 (2001) / 6 (2000); Multi-family building permits issued: 0 (2001) / 0 (2000).
Income: Per capita income: $15,748 (2000); Median household income: $31,094 (2000); Poverty rate: 12.7% (2000); Bankruptcy rate: 4.68% (2001).
Taxes: Total county taxes per capita: $149 (2000); County property taxes per capita: $142 (2000).
Education: High school graduation rate: 82.7% (2000); College graduation rate: 11.8% (2000).
Housing: Homeownership rate: 79.3% (2000); Median home value: $43,100 (2000); Median rent: $221 per month (2000); Median age of housing: 53 years (2000).
Health: Birth rate: 137.0 per 10,000 population (1998); Age adjusted death rate: 87.7 per 10,000 population (1999); Age adjusted cancer mortality rate: 151.5 (Unreliable figure as per CDC) deaths per 100,000 population (1999). Air Quality Index: 85% good, 15% moderate, 0% unhealthy (percent of days in 2000). Number of physicians: 3.8 per 10,000 population (1999); Number of hospital beds: 26.9 per 10,000 population (1999).
Elections: 2000 Presidential election results: 40.4% Gore, 56.6% Bush, 1.4% Nader, 1.0% Buchanan
National and State Parks: Lacey-Keosauqua State Park
Additional Information Contacts
Van Buren County Government Offices 319-293-3129

Van Buren County Communities

BIRMINGHAM (city). Covers a land area of 1.051 square miles and a water area of 0.003 square miles. Located at 40.87° N. Lat.; 91.94° W. Long. Elevation is 750 feet.
History: Birmingham was named for the city of Birmingham in England.
Population: 423 (2000); Race: 98.8% White, 0.7% Black, 0.0% Asian, 0.0% American Indian and Alaska Native, 0.0% Hispanic of any race, 0.5% two or more races (2000); Density: 402.5 persons per square mile (2000); Age: 21.3% under 18, 18.1% over 64 (2000); Marriage status: 17.1% never married, 61.8% now married, 9.8% widowed, 11.3% divorced (2000); Foreign born: 0.0% (2000); Ancestry (includes multiple ancestries): 25.2% United States or American, 18.1% German, 6.4% English, 4.2% Dutch, 4.0% Other groups (2000).
Economy: Employment by occupation: 11.8% management, 12.8% professional, 12.3% services, 28.9% sales, 0.0% farming, 11.4% construction, 22.7% production (2000).
Income: Per capita income: $15,554 (2000); Median household income: $31,406 (2000); Poverty rate: 8.8% (2000).
Taxes: Total city taxes per capita: $81 (1997); City property taxes per capita: $79 (1997).
Education: High school graduation rate: 86.8% (2000); College graduation rate: 10.1% (2000).
Housing: Homeownership rate: 86.4% (2000); Median home value: $46,500 (2000); Median rent: $281 per month (2000); Median age of housing: 56 years (2000).
Transportation: Commute to work: 96.7% car, 0.0% public transportation, 2.4% walk, 1.0% work from home (2000); Travel time to work: 26.1% less than 15 minutes, 50.2% 15 to 30 minutes, 15.0% 30 to 45 minutes, 3.4% 45 to 60 minutes, 5.3% 60 minutes or more (2000)

BONAPARTE (city). Covers a land area of 0.365 square miles and a water area of 0 square miles. Located at 40.70° N. Lat.; 91.80° W. Long. Elevation is 554 feet.
History: Before 1841, Bonaparte was known as Meeks Mills. William Meek, one of the town's founders, asked that the name be changed to Bonaparte because of his admiration of Napoleon.
Population: 458 (2000); Race: 99.6% White, 0.0% Black, 0.0% Asian, 0.0% American Indian and Alaska Native, 0.4% Hispanic of any race, 0.4% two or more races (2000); Density: 1,254.2 persons per square mile (2000); Age: 27.3% under 18, 16.4% over 64 (2000); Marriage status: 27.3% never married, 52.4% now married, 9.5% widowed, 10.9% divorced (2000); Foreign born: 0.7% (2000); Ancestry (includes multiple ancestries): 20.7% German, 15.1% United States or American, 12.7% English, 11.6% Irish, 5.7% Other groups (2000).

Economy: Single-family building permits issued: 0 (2001) / 2 (2000); Multi-family building permits issued: 0 (2001) / 0 (2000); Employment by occupation: 8.4% management, 8.8% professional, 14.9% services, 16.3% sales, 0.0% farming, 9.3% construction, 42.3% production (2000).
Income: Per capita income: $12,479 (2000); Median household income: $28,438 (2000); Poverty rate: 15.9% (2000).
Taxes: Total city taxes per capita: $117 (1997); City property taxes per capita: $113 (1997).
Education: High school graduation rate: 79.9% (2000); College graduation rate: 6.0% (2000).

School District(s)

Harmony Community School District (KG-12)
2000 Enrollment: 523 319-592-3600

Housing: Homeownership rate: 71.2% (2000); Median home value: $34,300 (2000); Median rent: $228 per month (2000); Median age of housing: 60+ years (2000).
Transportation: Commute to work: 88.1% car, 0.0% public transportation, 6.7% walk, 2.9% work from home (2000); Travel time to work: 34.8% less than 15 minutes, 18.6% 15 to 30 minutes, 25.0% 30 to 45 minutes, 13.7% 45 to 60 minutes, 7.8% 60 minutes or more (2000)

CANTRIL (city). Covers a land area of 0.506 square miles and a water area of 0 square miles. Located at 40.64° N. Lat.; 92.06° W. Long. Elevation is 760 feet.
History: Cantril was named for L. W. Cantril, the town's first store proprietor.
Population: 257 (2000); Race: 95.4% White, 0.0% Black, 0.0% Asian, 1.9% American Indian and Alaska Native, 3.1% Hispanic of any race, 1.9% two or more races (2000); Density: 507.5 persons per square mile (2000); Age: 23.2% under 18, 22.0% over 64 (2000); Marriage status: 18.5% never married, 55.1% now married, 11.7% widowed, 14.6% divorced (2000); Foreign born: 0.8% (2000); Ancestry (includes multiple ancestries): 29.3% United States or American, 15.1% German, 10.8% English, 10.0% Other groups, 9.3% Irish (2000).
Economy: Employment by occupation: 7.6% management, 10.5% professional, 12.4% services, 17.1% sales, 0.0% farming, 12.4% construction, 40.0% production (2000).
Income: Per capita income: $12,488 (2000); Median household income: $22,917 (2000); Poverty rate: 22.0% (2000).
Taxes: Total city taxes per capita: $130 (1997); City property taxes per capita: $130 (1997).
Education: High school graduation rate: 78.9% (2000); College graduation rate: 6.4% (2000).

School District(s)

Fox Valley Community School District (KG-12)
2000 Enrollment: 188 319-397-2374

Housing: Homeownership rate: 79.8% (2000); Median home value: $34,600 (2000); Median rent: $178 per month (2000); Median age of housing: 60+ years (2000).
Transportation: Commute to work: 93.2% car, 0.0% public transportation, 0.0% walk, 6.8% work from home (2000); Travel time to work: 26.0% less than 15 minutes, 41.7% 15 to 30 minutes, 14.6% 30 to 45 minutes, 12.5% 45 to 60 minutes, 5.2% 60 minutes or more (2000)

DOUDS (CDP). Covers a land area of 2.208 square miles and a water area of 0.091 square miles. Located at 40.84° N. Lat.; 92.08° W. Long. Elevation is 610 feet.
History: Eliah and David Doud were brothers who owned land along the Chicago, Rock Island & Pacific Railroad in Van Buren County. Douds was named for them.
Population: 165 (2000); Race: 100.0% White, 0.0% Black, 0.0% Asian, 0.0% American Indian and Alaska Native, 0.0% Hispanic of any race, 0.0% two or more races (2000); Density: 74.7 persons per square mile (2000); Age: 17.3% under 18, 35.1% over 64 (2000); Marriage status: 11.8% never married, 54.9% now married, 29.4% widowed, 3.9% divorced (2000); Foreign born: 0.0% (2000); Ancestry (includes multiple ancestries): 31.9% German, 29.2% United States or American, 24.9% Irish, 13.0% English, 7.0% Dutch (2000).
Economy: Employment by occupation: 17.3% management, 17.3% professional, 9.3% services, 30.7% sales, 0.0% farming, 25.3% construction, 0.0% production (2000).
Income: Per capita income: $17,428 (2000); Median household income: $25,893 (2000); Poverty rate: 16.8% (2000).
Education: High school graduation rate: 73.8% (2000); College graduation rate: 29.8% (2000).
Housing: Homeownership rate: 67.3% (2000); Median home value: $41,900 (2000); Median rent: $105 per month (2000); Median age of housing: 35 years (2000).
Transportation: Commute to work: 100.0% car, 0.0% public transportation, 0.0% walk, 0.0% work from home (2000); Travel time to work: 49.3% less than 15 minutes, 50.7% 15 to 30 minutes, 0.0% 30 to 45 minutes, 0.0% 45 to 60 minutes, 0.0% 60 minutes or more (2000)

FARMINGTON (city). Covers a land area of 0.472 square miles and a water area of 0 square miles. Located at 40.64° N. Lat.; 91.73° W. Long. Elevation is 569 feet.
History: Farmington was platted in 1839.
Population: 756 (2000); Race: 99.5% White, 0.0% Black, 0.3% Asian, 0.0% American Indian and Alaska Native, 0.0% Hispanic of any race, 0.3% two or more races (2000); Density: 1,602.4 persons per square mile (2000); Age: 26.6% under 18, 21.1% over 64 (2000); Marriage status: 22.0% never married, 52.5% now married, 15.9% widowed, 9.5% divorced (2000); Foreign born: 0.5% (2000); Ancestry (includes multiple ancestries): 23.6% United States or American, 18.1% German, 11.5% Irish, 9.5% English, 6.2% Other groups (2000).
Economy: Single-family building permits issued: 0 (2001) / 0 (2000); Multi-family building permits issued: 0 (2001) / 0 (2000); Employment by occupation: 8.5% management, 13.3% professional, 24.2% services, 15.7% sales, 0.6% farming, 7.9% construction, 29.9% production (2000).
Income: Per capita income: $13,591 (2000); Median household income: $26,354 (2000); Poverty rate: 12.8% (2000).
Taxes: Total city taxes per capita: $124 (1997); City property taxes per capita: $123 (1997).
Education: High school graduation rate: 87.1% (2000); College graduation rate: 8.4% (2000).
Housing: Homeownership rate: 73.5% (2000); Median home value: $39,900 (2000); Median rent: $200 per month (2000); Median age of housing: 60+ years (2000).
Newspapers: Van Buren County Leader-Record (1 x week)
Transportation: Commute to work: 94.2% car, 0.0% public transportation, 2.4% walk, 2.4% work from home (2000); Travel time to work: 33.0% less than 15 minutes, 25.2% 15 to 30 minutes, 26.5% 30 to 45 minutes, 10.0% 45 to 60 minutes, 5.3% 60 minutes or more (2000)

KEOSAUQUA (city). Covers a land area of 1.463 square miles and a water area of 0.118 square miles. Located at 40.73° N. Lat.; 91.96° W. Long. Elevation is 664 feet.
History: Keosauqua was settled in 1836. The name comes from an Indian word meaning "great bend." The town became involved in a boundry dispute between Iowa and Missouri, settled in favor of Iowa by the U.S. Supreme Court in 1849.
Population: 1,066 (2000); Race: 99.5% White, 0.3% Black, 0.2% Asian, 0.0% American Indian and Alaska Native, 0.0% Hispanic of any race, 0.0% two or more races (2000); Density: 728.7 persons per square mile (2000); Age: 21.7% under 18, 29.4% over 64 (2000); Marriage status: 19.1% never married, 52.2% now married, 16.2% widowed, 12.5% divorced (2000); Foreign born: 0.9% (2000); Ancestry (includes multiple ancestries): 22.3% German, 18.2% United States or American, 13.9% English, 7.3% Irish, 3.9% French (except Basque) (2000).
Economy: Single-family building permits issued: 3 (2001) / 4 (2000); Multi-family building permits issued: 0 (2001) / 0 (2000); Employment by occupation: 9.7% management, 17.7% professional, 16.8% services, 21.1% sales, 0.2% farming, 8.3% construction, 26.2% production (2000).
Income: Per capita income: $16,097 (2000); Median household income: $27,833 (2000); Poverty rate: 12.1% (2000).
Taxes: Total city taxes per capita: $132 (1997); City property taxes per capita: $129 (1997).
Education: High school graduation rate: 86.8% (2000); College graduation rate: 14.5% (2000).

School District(s)

Van Buren Community School District (KG-12)
2000 Enrollment: 665 319-293-3334

Housing: Homeownership rate: 69.6% (2000); Median home value: $57,800 (2000); Median rent: $217 per month (2000); Median age of housing: 44 years (2000).
Hospitals: Van Buren County Hospital
Newspapers: Van Buren Register (1 x week)
Transportation: Commute to work: 89.3% car, 0.0% public transportation, 8.9% walk, 1.4% work from home (2000); Travel time to work: 68.3% less than 15 minutes, 10.6% 15 to 30 minutes, 13.0% 30 to 45 minutes, 4.3% 45 to 60 minutes, 3.8% 60 minutes or more (2000)

LEANDO (CDP). Covers a land area of 1.971 square miles and a water area of 0.094 square miles. Located at 40.83° N. Lat.; 92.08° W. Long.
Population: 135 (2000); Race: 100.0% White, 0.0% Black, 0.0% Asian, 0.0% American Indian and Alaska Native, 0.0% Hispanic of any race, 0.0% two or more races (2000); Density: 68.5 persons per square mile (2000); Age: 9.1% under 18, 29.5% over 64 (2000); Marriage status: 0.0% never married, 78.8% now married, 0.0% widowed, 21.3% divorced (2000); Foreign born: 0.0% (2000); Ancestry (includes multiple ancestries): 38.6% United States or American, 13.6% German, 6.8% English, 6.8% French (except Basque) (2000).
Economy: Employment by occupation: 0.0% management, 0.0% professional, 9.3% services, 25.6% sales, 0.0% farming, 11.6% construction, 53.5% production (2000).
Income: Per capita income: $17,097 (2000); Median household income: $36,875 (2000); Poverty rate: 5.7% (2000).
Education: High school graduation rate: 76.3% (2000); College graduation rate: 0.0% (2000).
Housing: Homeownership rate: 90.2% (2000); Median home value: $31,700 (2000); Median rent: $275 per month (2000); Median age of housing: 60+ years (2000).
Transportation: Commute to work: 81.4% car, 0.0% public transportation, 0.0% walk, 18.6% work from home (2000); Travel time to work: 0.0% less than 15 minutes, 54.3% 15 to 30 minutes, 34.3% 30 to 45 minutes, 11.4% 45 to 60 minutes, 0.0% 60 minutes or more (2000)

MILTON (city). Covers a land area of 2.505 square miles and a water area of 0.004 square miles. Located at 40.67° N. Lat.; 92.16° W. Long.
History: Milton, named for the poet John Milton, was settled in 1847.
Population: 550 (2000); Race: 98.3% White, 1.0% Black, 0.0% Asian, 0.4% American Indian and Alaska Native, 0.0% Hispanic of any race, 0.4% two or more races (2000); Density: 219.6 persons per square mile (2000); Age: 23.8% under 18, 25.7% over 64 (2000); Marriage status: 15.7% never married, 67.2% now married, 8.9% widowed, 8.2% divorced (2000); Foreign born: 0.4% (2000); Ancestry (includes multiple ancestries): 19.3% German, 16.1% United States or American, 13.3% English, 8.3% Irish, 7.9% Other groups (2000).
Economy: Employment by occupation: 8.1% management, 11.1% professional, 13.1% services, 20.2% sales, 2.5% farming, 13.1% construction, 31.8% production (2000).
Income: Per capita income: $12,696 (2000); Median household income: $25,938 (2000); Poverty rate: 12.0% (2000).
Taxes: Total city taxes per capita: $80 (2000); City property taxes per capita: $78 (2000).
Education: High school graduation rate: 73.6% (2000); College graduation rate: 8.6% (2000).
Housing: Homeownership rate: 83.1% (2000); Median home value: $27,100 (2000); Median rent: $182 per month (2000); Median age of housing: 60+ years (2000).
Transportation: Commute to work: 90.0% car, 0.0% public transportation, 4.2% walk, 3.2% work from home (2000); Travel time to work: 29.9% less than 15 minutes, 21.2% 15 to 30 minutes, 18.5% 30 to 45 minutes, 15.8% 45 to 60 minutes, 14.7% 60 minutes or more (2000)

MOUNT STERLING (city). Covers a land area of 0.400 square miles and a water area of 0 square miles. Located at 40.61° N. Lat.; 91.93° W. Long. Elevation is 655 feet.
History: Mount Sterling has also been known as Dogtown, Wood's Mills and Union Corner. The name Mount Sterling indicated its high elevation and its "sterling" location.
Population: 40 (2000); Race: 100.0% White, 0.0% Black, 0.0% Asian, 0.0% American Indian and Alaska Native, 0.0% Hispanic of any race, 0.0% two or more races (2000); Density: 100.0 persons per square mile (2000); Age: 31.1% under 18, 3.3% over 64 (2000); Marriage status: 39.2% never married, 56.9% now married, 0.0% widowed, 3.9% divorced (2000); Foreign born: 0.0% (2000); Ancestry (includes multiple ancestries): 4.9% United States or American, 3.3% Irish, 3.3% Scotch-Irish, 3.3% Hungarian, 3.3% German (2000).
Economy: Employment by occupation: 13.3% management, 0.0% professional, 30.0% services, 6.7% sales, 0.0% farming, 10.0% construction, 40.0% production (2000).
Income: Per capita income: $10,072 (2000); Median household income: $31,250 (2000); Poverty rate: 3.3% (2000).
Taxes: Total city taxes per capita: $35 (1997); City property taxes per capita: $35 (1997).
Education: High school graduation rate: 76.2% (2000); College graduation rate: 9.5% (2000).
Housing: Homeownership rate: 100.0% (2000); Median home value: $18,300 (2000); Median age of housing: 60+ years (2000).
Transportation: Commute to work: 100.0% car, 0.0% public transportation, 0.0% walk, 0.0% work from home (2000); Travel time to work: 23.3% less than 15 minutes, 23.3% 15 to 30 minutes, 43.3% 30 to 45 minutes, 10.0% 45 to 60 minutes, 0.0% 60 minutes or more (2000)

SELMA (unincorporated postal area, zip code 52588). Covers a land area of 24.343 square miles and a water area of 0.921 square miles. Located at 40.87° N. Lat.; 92.13° W. Long. Elevation is 655 feet.
History: Selma is believed to be named after Selma, Alabama. The town was also once known as Stumptown and Hickory.
Population: 375 (2000); Race: 100.0% White, 0.0% Black, 0.0% Asian, 0.0% American Indian and Alaska Native, 0.0% Hispanic of any race, 0.0% two or more races (2000); Density: 15.4 persons per square mile (2000); Age: 24.8% under 18, 21.6% over 64 (2000); Marriage status: 14.1% never married, 65.0% now married, 13.5% widowed, 7.5% divorced (2000); Foreign born: 0.0% (2000); Ancestry (includes multiple ancestries): 28.1% United States or American, 15.1% German, 13.9% Irish, 13.2% English, 9.9% Scotch-Irish (2000).
Economy: Employment by occupation: 29.3% management, 15.6% professional, 10.2% services, 22.9% sales, 3.4% farming, 7.8% construction, 10.7% production (2000).
Income: Per capita income: $13,392 (2000); Median household income: $21,250 (2000); Poverty rate: 7.7% (2000).
Education: High school graduation rate: 85.2% (2000); College graduation rate: 13.1% (2000).
Housing: Homeownership rate: 78.9% (2000); Median home value: $51,900 (2000); Median rent: $105 per month (2000); Median age of housing: 43 years (2000).
Transportation: Commute to work: 69.8% car, 0.0% public transportation, 0.0% walk, 30.2% work from home (2000); Travel time to work: 14.4% less than 15 minutes, 48.2% 15 to 30 minutes, 28.8% 30 to 45 minutes, 0.0% 45 to 60 minutes, 8.6% 60 minutes or more (2000)

STOCKPORT (city). Covers a land area of 1.027 square miles and a water area of 0 square miles. Located at 40.85° N. Lat.; 91.83° W. Long. Elevation is 754 feet.
History: It is believed that Stockport was named after Stockport, England.
Population: 284 (2000); Race: 98.6% White, 0.0% Black, 0.0% Asian, 0.0% American Indian and Alaska Native, 0.7% Hispanic of any race, 1.4% two or more races (2000); Density: 276.4 persons per square mile (2000); Age: 27.9% under 18, 12.0% over 64 (2000); Marriage status: 21.7% never married, 58.5% now married, 7.1% widowed, 12.7% divorced (2000); Foreign born: 0.0% (2000); Ancestry (includes multiple ancestries): 24.0% German, 14.5% United States or American, 9.2% Irish, 8.5% English, 4.2% French (except Basque) (2000).
Economy: Employment by occupation: 6.7% management, 7.4% professional, 23.7% services, 12.6% sales, 1.5% farming, 18.5% construction, 29.6% production (2000).
Income: Per capita income: $13,389 (2000); Median household income: $28,438 (2000); Poverty rate: 10.2% (2000).
Taxes: Total city taxes per capita: $98 (1997); City property taxes per capita: $98 (1997).
Education: High school graduation rate: 83.4% (2000); College graduation rate: 9.9% (2000).
Housing: Homeownership rate: 77.6% (2000); Median home value: $30,000 (2000); Median rent: $250 per month (2000); Median age of housing: 60+ years (2000).
Transportation: Commute to work: 87.7% car, 0.0% public transportation, 10.0% walk, 2.3% work from home (2000); Travel time to work: 25.2% less than 15 minutes, 45.7% 15 to 30 minutes, 22.0% 30 to 45 minutes, 1.6% 45 to 60 minutes, 5.5% 60 minutes or more (2000)

Wapello County

Located in southeastern Iowa; prairie area, drained by the Des Moines River. Covers a land area of 431.80 square miles, a water area of 4.20 square miles, and is located in the Central Time Zone. The county government was organized in 1843. County seat is Ottumwa.

Weather Station: Ottumwa Industrial Airport Elevation: 839 feet

	Jan	Feb	Mar	Apr	May	Jun	Jul	Aug	Sep	Oct	Nov	Dec
High	30	36	48	61	73	82	86	84	76	64	48	35
Low	13	19	30	41	53	62	67	64	55	43	31	19
Precip	1.0	1.1	2.4	3.3	4.5	4.3	4.4	4.2	4.0	2.8	2.4	1.4
Snow	7.1	5.8	3.7	2.0	tr	tr	tr	tr	tr	0.4	1.9	5.7

High and Low temperatures in degrees Fahrenheit; Precipitation and Snow in inches

Population: 36,051 (2000); Race: 96.1% White, 1.0% Black, 0.6% Asian, 0.1% American Indian and Alaska Native, 2.4% Hispanic of any race, 1.0% two or more races (2000); Density: 83.5 persons per square mile (2000); Age: 23.2% under 18, 17.8% over 64 (2000).
Religion: Five largest groups: 8.7% Catholic Church, 7.1% The United Methodist Church, 5.7% Christian Church (Disciples of Christ), 2.4% Evangelical Lutheran Church in America, 2.3% Assemblies of God (2000).
Economy: Unemployment rate: 5.1% (11/2002); Total civilian labor force: 18,528 (11/2002); Leading industries: 22.8% manufacturing; 18.6% retail trade; 17.7% health care and social assistance (2000); Companies that employ more than 1,000 persons: 1 (2000); Companies that employ more than 100 persons: 14 (2000); Farms: 781 totaling 208,213 acres (1997); Minority business ownership rate: 0.0% (1997); Women business ownership rate: 23.6% (1997); Retail sales per capita: $9,325 (1997). Single-family building permits issued: 48 (2001) / 53 (2000); Multi-family building permits issued: 14 (2001) / 0 (2000).
Income: Per capita income: $16,500 (2000); Median household income: $32,188 (2000); Poverty rate: 13.2% (2000); Bankruptcy rate: 5.45% (2001).
Taxes: Total county taxes per capita: $261 (2000); County property taxes per capita: $260 (2000).
Education: High school graduation rate: 81.5% (2000); College graduation rate: 14.6% (2000).
Housing: Homeownership rate: 75.6% (2000); Median home value: $50,100 (2000); Median rent: $340 per month (2000); Median age of housing: 50 years (2000).
Health: Birth rate: 108.5 per 10,000 population (1998); Age adjusted death rate: 91.8 per 10,000 population (1999); Age adjusted cancer mortality rate: 201.8 deaths per 100,000 population (1999). Number of physicians: 19.4 per 10,000 population (1999); Number of hospital beds: 24.1 per 10,000 population (1999).
Elections: 2000 Presidential election results: 55.2% Gore, 41.7% Bush, 2.1% Nader, 0.4% Buchanan
Additional Information Contacts
Wapello County Government Offices 641-683-0020
Ottumwa Board of Realtors 641-683-3235
Ottumwa Chamber of Commerce. 641-682-3465

Wapello County Communities

AGENCY (city). Aka Agency City. Covers a land area of 0.579 square miles and a water area of 0 square miles. Located at 40.99° N. Lat.; 92.30° W. Long.
History: Agency, called Agency City until 1883, was established in 1838 as an Indian Agency, following the Treaty of 1837, when the Sac and Fox Indians, with the agent, Joseph M. Street, selected the site on which was built an immense council house.
Population: 622 (2000); Race: 98.3% White, 0.0% Black, 0.9% Asian, 0.0% American Indian and Alaska Native, 0.0% Hispanic of any race, 0.8% two or more races (2000); Density: 1,074.6 persons per square mile (2000); Age: 23.2% under 18, 23.7% over 64 (2000); Marriage status: 14.0% never married, 64.3% now married, 12.7% widowed, 9.0% divorced (2000); Foreign born: 0.6% (2000); Ancestry (includes multiple ancestries): 22.6% German, 16.4% United States or American, 11.3% Irish, 10.2% English, 7.0% Norwegian (2000).
Economy: Single-family building permits issued: 7 (2001) / 3 (2000); Multi-family building permits issued: 0 (2001) / 0 (2000); Employment by occupation: 8.7% management, 12.5% professional, 12.5% services, 29.4% sales, 2.1% farming, 13.1% construction, 21.8% production (2000).
Income: Per capita income: $16,896 (2000); Median household income: $36,912 (2000); Poverty rate: 5.3% (2000).
Taxes: Total city taxes per capita: $106 (1997); City property taxes per capita: $101 (1997).
Education: High school graduation rate: 88.9% (2000); College graduation rate: 7.4% (2000).
Housing: Homeownership rate: 81.7% (2000); Median home value: $62,500 (2000); Median rent: $259 per month (2000); Median age of housing: 46 years (2000).
Transportation: Commute to work: 95.1% car, 1.4% public transportation, 1.1% walk, 2.5% work from home (2000); Travel time to work: 27.9% less than 15 minutes, 55.1% 15 to 30 minutes, 8.7% 30 to 45 minutes, 4.0% 45 to 60 minutes, 4.3% 60 minutes or more (2000)

BLAKESBURG (city). Covers a land area of 0.265 square miles and a water area of 0 square miles. Located at 40.96° N. Lat.; 92.63° W. Long. Elevation is 912 feet.
History: Blakesburg was named for Theophilus Blake, who donated the land for the site in 1852.
Population: 374 (2000); Race: 97.4% White, 0.0% Black, 0.0% Asian, 1.1% American Indian and Alaska Native, 0.0% Hispanic of any race, 1.6% two or more races (2000); Density: 1,408.9 persons per square mile (2000); Age: 22.1% under 18, 13.2% over 64 (2000); Marriage status: 28.3% never married, 48.4% now married, 9.5% widowed, 13.8% divorced (2000); Foreign born: 1.6% (2000); Ancestry (includes multiple ancestries): 20.0% German, 12.9% Irish, 11.8% Dutch, 9.5% Other groups, 7.9% English (2000).
Economy: Single-family building permits issued: 0 (2001) / 0 (2000); Multi-family building permits issued: 0 (2001) / 0 (2000); Employment by occupation: 5.9% management, 10.3% professional, 17.6% services, 27.0% sales, 1.0% farming, 8.3% construction, 29.9% production (2000).
Income: Per capita income: $13,962 (2000); Median household income: $28,500 (2000); Poverty rate: 14.3% (2000).
Taxes: Total city taxes per capita: $149 (1997); City property taxes per capita: $146 (1997).
Education: High school graduation rate: 84.3% (2000); College graduation rate: 11.8% (2000).
Housing: Homeownership rate: 74.4% (2000); Median home value: $37,500 (2000); Median rent: $241 per month (2000); Median age of housing: 58 years (2000).
Transportation: Commute to work: 96.6% car, 0.0% public transportation, 2.9% walk, 0.5% work from home (2000); Travel time to work: 10.3% less than 15 minutes, 51.7% 15 to 30 minutes, 27.1% 30 to 45 minutes, 3.9% 45 to 60 minutes, 6.9% 60 minutes or more (2000)

CHILLICOTHE (city). Covers a land area of 0.227 square miles and a water area of 0.006 square miles. Located at 41.08° N. Lat.; 92.52° W. Long. Elevation is 660 feet.
History: Chillicothe was settled by emigrants from Chillicothe, Ohio, who brought their town name with them. The word is Shawnee in origin.
Population: 90 (2000); Race: 97.5% White, 0.0% Black, 0.0% Asian, 0.0% American Indian and Alaska Native, 0.0% Hispanic of any race, 2.5% two or more races (2000); Density: 395.7 persons per square mile (2000); Age: 22.5% under 18, 13.8% over 64 (2000); Marriage status: 18.2% never married, 51.5% now married, 4.5% widowed, 25.8% divorced (2000); Foreign born: 0.0% (2000); Ancestry (includes multiple ancestries): 21.3% German, 13.8% Irish, 12.5% Dutch, 12.5% English, 5.0% Slavic (2000).
Economy: Employment by occupation: 12.8% management, 10.6% professional, 19.1% services, 8.5% sales, 0.0% farming, 4.3% construction, 44.7% production (2000).
Income: Per capita income: $19,075 (2000); Median household income: $30,781 (2000); Poverty rate: 13.8% (2000).
Taxes: Total city taxes per capita: $100 (2000); City property taxes per capita: $89 (2000).
Education: High school graduation rate: 90.6% (2000); College graduation rate: 13.2% (2000).
Housing: Homeownership rate: 84.4% (2000); Median home value: $53,900 (2000); Median rent: $408 per month (2000); Median age of housing: 39 years (2000).
Transportation: Commute to work: 93.6% car, 0.0% public transportation, 6.4% walk, 0.0% work from home (2000); Travel time to work: 48.9% less than 15 minutes, 48.9% 15 to 30 minutes, 0.0% 30 to 45 minutes, 2.1% 45 to 60 minutes, 0.0% 60 minutes or more (2000)

EDDYVILLE (city). Covers a land area of 1.184 square miles and a water area of 0 square miles. Located at 41.15° N. Lat.; 92.63° W. Long.
History: In 1840 Jabish P. Eddy was given a permit to open a fur trading post at Chief Hard Fish's village on the Des Moines River. The post eventually became Eddyville.
Population: 1,064 (2000); Race: 99.1% White, 0.0% Black, 0.1% Asian, 0.2% American Indian and Alaska Native, 0.7% Hispanic of any race, 0.3% two or more races (2000); Density: 898.9 persons per square mile (2000); Age: 25.2% under 18, 14.2% over 64 (2000); Marriage status: 25.6% never married, 54.4% now married, 9.3% widowed, 10.7% divorced (2000); Foreign born: 0.5% (2000); Ancestry (includes multiple ancestries): 21.9%

German, 13.2% Irish, 10.6% Dutch, 10.5% United States or American, 7.3% English (2000).
Economy: Single-family building permits issued: 2 (2001) / 3 (2000); Multi-family building permits issued: 2 (2001) / 0 (2000); Employment by occupation: 9.1% management, 11.8% professional, 14.6% services, 16.3% sales, 0.4% farming, 12.4% construction, 35.3% production (2000).
Income: Per capita income: $16,354 (2000); Median household income: $32,446 (2000); Poverty rate: 12.0% (2000).
Taxes: Total city taxes per capita: $245 (2000); City property taxes per capita: $204 (2000).
Education: High school graduation rate: 80.3% (2000); College graduation rate: 8.7% (2000).

School District(s)

Eddyville-Blakesburg Community School District (PK-12)
2000 Enrollment: 927 641-969-4226

Housing: Homeownership rate: 71.6% (2000); Median home value: $53,700 (2000); Median rent: $270 per month (2000); Median age of housing: 29 years (2000).
Newspapers: Eddyville Tribune (1 x week)
Transportation: Commute to work: 95.2% car, 0.0% public transportation, 1.8% walk, 2.2% work from home (2000); Travel time to work: 36.6% less than 15 minutes, 33.3% 15 to 30 minutes, 23.8% 30 to 45 minutes, 3.9% 45 to 60 minutes, 2.5% 60 minutes or more (2000)

ELDON (city). Covers a land area of 1.129 square miles and a water area of 0.007 square miles. Located at 40.91° N. Lat.; 92.22° W. Long. Elevation is 630 feet.
History: At one time known simultaneously as Oakland Crossing, Williamsburg, and Eldon, the town took its permanent name from a visiting Englishman, Lord Eldon, who was particularly appreciative of the beauty of the spot.
Population: 998 (2000); Race: 97.8% White, 0.0% Black, 0.0% Asian, 0.0% American Indian and Alaska Native, 1.4% Hispanic of any race, 1.9% two or more races (2000); Density: 884.3 persons per square mile (2000); Age: 26.0% under 18, 16.8% over 64 (2000); Marriage status: 14.9% never married, 58.7% now married, 10.2% widowed, 16.2% divorced (2000); Foreign born: 0.9% (2000); Ancestry (includes multiple ancestries): 24.5% German, 17.0% Irish, 13.8% English, 8.2% Other groups, 7.6% Dutch (2000).
Economy: Single-family building permits issued: 3 (2001) / 3 (2000); Multi-family building permits issued: 0 (2001) / 0 (2000); Employment by occupation: 4.2% management, 10.4% professional, 15.5% services, 24.1% sales, 1.2% farming, 13.9% construction, 30.8% production (2000).
Income: Per capita income: $14,495 (2000); Median household income: $26,950 (2000); Poverty rate: 15.5% (2000).
Taxes: Total city taxes per capita: $106 (1997); City property taxes per capita: $102 (1997).
Education: High school graduation rate: 79.1% (2000); College graduation rate: 5.6% (2000).

School District(s)

Cardinal Community School District (PK-12)
2000 Enrollment: 648 641-652-7531

Housing: Homeownership rate: 81.9% (2000); Median home value: $30,800 (2000); Median rent: $202 per month (2000); Median age of housing: 60+ years (2000).
Transportation: Commute to work: 92.6% car, 0.0% public transportation, 2.9% walk, 4.0% work from home (2000); Travel time to work: 22.1% less than 15 minutes, 38.2% 15 to 30 minutes, 30.5% 30 to 45 minutes, 1.7% 45 to 60 minutes, 7.4% 60 minutes or more (2000)

KIRKVILLE (city). Covers a land area of 0.554 square miles and a water area of 0 square miles. Located at 41.14° N. Lat.; 92.50° W. Long.
History: Kirkville was founded by William Bayliss and John Hill, two Englishmen who left England in 1840 to seek their fortunes.
Population: 214 (2000); Race: 100.0% White, 0.0% Black, 0.0% Asian, 0.0% American Indian and Alaska Native, 0.0% Hispanic of any race, 0.0% two or more races (2000); Density: 386.2 persons per square mile (2000); Age: 27.5% under 18, 7.4% over 64 (2000); Marriage status: 22.6% never married, 64.5% now married, 5.8% widowed, 7.1% divorced (2000); Foreign born: 0.0% (2000); Ancestry (includes multiple ancestries): 27.9% United States or American, 22.5% German, 13.7% English, 12.7% Irish, 5.4% Other groups (2000).
Economy: Employment by occupation: 6.1% management, 11.1% professional, 12.1% services, 21.2% sales, 4.0% farming, 13.1% construction, 32.3% production (2000).
Income: Per capita income: $14,366 (2000); Median household income: $31,354 (2000); Poverty rate: 8.5% (2000).
Taxes: Total city taxes per capita: $71 (1997); City property taxes per capita: $71 (1997).
Education: High school graduation rate: 87.7% (2000); College graduation rate: 10.0% (2000).
Housing: Homeownership rate: 91.5% (2000); Median home value: $63,000 (2000); Median rent: $463 per month (2000); Median age of housing: 38 years (2000).
Transportation: Commute to work: 92.9% car, 0.0% public transportation, 0.0% walk, 0.0% work from home (2000); Travel time to work: 10.1% less than 15 minutes, 52.5% 15 to 30 minutes, 30.3% 30 to 45 minutes, 7.1% 45 to 60 minutes, 0.0% 60 minutes or more (2000)

OTTUMWA (city). Covers a land area of 15.799 square miles and a water area of 0.674 square miles. Located at 41.01° N. Lat.; 92.41° W. Long. Elevation is 649 feet.
History: Ottumwa, originally known as Louisville, comes from an Indian word meaning "rippling waters." The town was promoted in 1842 by the Appanoose Rapids and Milling Company. One of the first bridges to span the Des Moines River was constructed here in 1860.
Population: 24,998 (2000); Race: 95.2% White, 1.4% Black, 0.7% Asian, 0.1% American Indian and Alaska Native, 3.1% Hispanic of any race, 1.2% two or more races (2000); Density: 1,582.2 persons per square mile (2000); Age: 22.9% under 18, 19.2% over 64 (2000); Marriage status: 23.7% never married, 53.8% now married, 9.3% widowed, 13.2% divorced (2000); Foreign born: 2.3% (2000); Ancestry (includes multiple ancestries): 19.1% German, 12.4% English, 12.4% Irish, 10.8% United States or American, 9.9% Other groups (2000).
Vital Statistics: Birth rate: 111.2 per 10,000 population (1998)
Economy: Unemployment rate: 5.9% (11/2002); Total civilian labor force: 12,343 (11/2002); Single-family building permits issued: 8 (2001) / 14 (2000); Multi-family building permits issued: 12 (2001) / 0 (2000); Employment by occupation: 8.3% management, 16.0% professional, 19.4% services, 22.3% sales, 0.5% farming, 9.0% construction, 24.4% production (2000).
Income: Per capita income: $16,040 (2000); Median household income: $30,174 (2000); Poverty rate: 15.2% (2000).
Taxes: Total city taxes per capita: $450 (2000); City property taxes per capita: $348 (2000).
Education: High school graduation rate: 79.9% (2000); College graduation rate: 15.4% (2000).

School District(s)

Ottumwa Community School District (PK-12)
2000 Enrollment: 5,019 641-684-6596

Two-year College(s)

Indian Hills Community College (Public)
2001 Enrollment: 3,926 515-683-5111
2001 Tuition: In-state $2,070; Out-of-state $3,120
Iowa School of Beauty (Private, For-profit)
2001 Enrollment: 38 515-684-6504

Housing: Homeownership rate: 71.6% (2000); Median home value: $47,900 (2000); Median rent: $351 per month (2000); Median age of housing: 54 years (2000).
Hospitals: Ottumwa Regional Health Center (235 beds)
Safety: Violent crime rate: 65.3 per 10,000 population; Property crime rate: 549.4 per 10,000 population (2001).
Newspapers: The Ottumwa Courier (6 x week); Wapello Shopper (1 x week)
Transportation: Commute to work: 93.1% car, 1.4% public transportation, 1.9% walk, 2.3% work from home (2000); Travel time to work: 63.7% less than 15 minutes, 20.7% 15 to 30 minutes, 7.6% 30 to 45 minutes, 3.5% 45 to 60 minutes, 4.6% 60 minutes or more (2000); Amtrak: Service available.
Airports: Ottumwa Industrial

Additional Information Contacts

Ottumwa Board of Realtors 641-683-3235
Ottumwa Chamber of Commerce. 641-682-3465

Warren County

Located in south central Iowa; prairie area, drained by the North, South, and Middle Rivers. Covers a land area of 571.60 square miles, a water area of 1.60 square miles, and is located in the Central Time Zone. The county government was organized in 1846. County seat is Indianola.

Warren County is part of the Des Moines, IA MSA. The entire metro area includes: Dallas County; Polk County; Warren County

Weather Station: Indianola Elevation: 938 feet

	Jan	Feb	Mar	Apr	May	Jun	Jul	Aug	Sep	Oct	Nov	Dec
High	31	37	49	63	73	82	86	85	77	65	48	35
Low	11	17	28	39	50	59	64	61	52	40	28	17
Precip	1.0	1.1	2.2	3.7	4.7	4.4	4.2	3.7	3.8	3.0	2.1	1.2
Snow	6.9	6.7	2.8	1.3	tr	0.0	0.0	0.0	0.0	0.4	2.6	4.5

High and Low temperatures in degrees Fahrenheit; Precipitation and Snow in inches

Population: 40,671 (2000); Race: 97.9% White, 0.2% Black, 0.5% Asian, 0.3% American Indian and Alaska Native, 1.1% Hispanic of any race, 0.8% two or more races (2000); Density: 71.1 persons per square mile (2000); Age: 27.0% under 18, 11.8% over 64 (2000).
Religion: Five largest groups: 11.7% The United Methodist Church, 9.6% Catholic Church, 3.6% Evangelical Lutheran Church in America, 2.5% Christian Church (Disciples of Christ), 2.3% Presbyterian Church (U.S.A.) (2000).
Economy: Unemployment rate: 2.8% (11/2002); Total civilian labor force: 24,472 (11/2002); Leading industries: 22.8% retail trade; 14.3% health care and social assistance; 12.2% construction (2000); Companies that employ more than 1,000 persons: 0 (2000); Companies that employ more than 100 persons: 6 (2000); Farms: 1,214 totaling 299,835 acres (1997); Minority business ownership rate: 0.0% (1997); Women business ownership rate: 37.7% (1997); Retail sales per capita: $6,154 (1997). Single-family building permits issued: 180 (2001) / 154 (2000); Multi-family building permits issued: 8 (2001) / 210 (2000).
Income: Per capita income: $20,558 (2000); Median household income: $50,349 (2000); Poverty rate: 5.1% (2000); Bankruptcy rate: 3.62% (2001).
Taxes: Total county taxes per capita: $148 (2000); County property taxes per capita: $142 (2000).
Education: High school graduation rate: 90.0% (2000); College graduation rate: 21.2% (2000).
Housing: Homeownership rate: 79.9% (2000); Median home value: $102,000 (2000); Median rent: $421 per month (2000); Median age of housing: 28 years (2000).
Health: Birth rate: 123.9 per 10,000 population (1998); Age adjusted death rate: 78.7 per 10,000 population (1999); Age adjusted cancer mortality rate: 158.4 deaths per 100,000 population (1999). Air Quality Index: 97% good, 3% moderate, 0% unhealthy (percent of days in 2000). Number of physicians: 2.0 per 10,000 population (1999); Number of hospital beds: n/a (1999).
Elections: 2000 Presidential election results: 48.5% Gore, 49.0% Bush, 1.9% Nader, 0.3% Buchanan
National and State Parks: Banner Mine State Wildlife Mgt Area; Hooper State Game Area; Lake Ahquabi State Park; Lake Ahquabi State Park
Additional Information Contacts
Warren County Government Offices 515-961-1028
Indianola Chamber of Commerce 515-961-6269
Norwalk Chamber of Commerce 515-981-0619

Warren County Communities

ACKWORTH (city). Covers a land area of 0.298 square miles and a water area of 0 square miles. Located at 41.36° N. Lat.; 93.47° W. Long.
History: Ackworth was named for Ackworth, England. In 1869 a Friends' academy was established here and $1,000 was sent from Ackworth, England, for books.
Population: 85 (2000); Race: 94.8% White, 0.0% Black, 0.0% Asian, 2.6% American Indian and Alaska Native, 0.0% Hispanic of any race, 0.0% two or more races (2000); Density: 284.8 persons per square mile (2000); Age: 19.5% under 18, 22.1% over 64 (2000); Marriage status: 17.2% never married, 71.9% now married, 10.9% widowed, 0.0% divorced (2000); Foreign born: 0.0% (2000); Ancestry (includes multiple ancestries): 35.1% English, 35.1% Irish, 29.9% German, 10.4% Dutch, 2.6% Welsh (2000).
Economy: Single-family building permits issued: 1 (2001) / 6 (2000); Multi-family building permits issued: 0 (2001) / 0 (2000); Employment by occupation: 12.5% management, 8.3% professional, 22.9% services, 27.1% sales, 0.0% farming, 16.7% construction, 12.5% production (2000).
Income: Per capita income: $17,478 (2000); Median household income: $32,500 (2000); Poverty rate: 6.5% (2000).
Taxes: Total city taxes per capita: $62 (1997); City property taxes per capita: $62 (1997).
Education: High school graduation rate: 96.6% (2000); College graduation rate: 0.0% (2000).
Housing: Homeownership rate: 93.3% (2000); Median home value: $60,000 (2000); Median rent: $275 per month (2000); Median age of housing: 55 years (2000).
Transportation: Commute to work: 93.5% car, 0.0% public transportation, 0.0% walk, 6.5% work from home (2000); Travel time to work: 27.9% less than 15 minutes, 34.9% 15 to 30 minutes, 23.3% 30 to 45 minutes, 9.3% 45 to 60 minutes, 4.7% 60 minutes or more (2000)

CARLISLE (city). Covers a land area of 4.329 square miles and a water area of 0 square miles. Located at 41.50° N. Lat.; 93.49° W. Long. Elevation is 784 feet.
History: Carlisle was founded by Jeremiah Church and Daniel Moore, and named for Church's former home of Carlisle, Pennsylvania.
Population: 3,497 (2000); Race: 97.9% White, 0.4% Black, 1.0% Asian, 0.0% American Indian and Alaska Native, 0.6% Hispanic of any race, 0.7% two or more races (2000); Density: 807.8 persons per square mile (2000); Age: 27.1% under 18, 13.5% over 64 (2000); Marriage status: 17.6% never married, 66.2% now married, 6.5% widowed, 9.7% divorced (2000); Foreign born: 1.6% (2000); Ancestry (includes multiple ancestries): 26.3% German, 15.2% Irish, 12.7% English, 9.8% United States or American, 7.1% Dutch (2000).
Economy: Single-family building permits issued: 6 (2001) / 6 (2000); Multi-family building permits issued: 0 (2001) / 0 (2000); Employment by occupation: 14.4% management, 17.0% professional, 10.5% services, 31.0% sales, 0.0% farming, 11.1% construction, 15.9% production (2000).
Income: Per capita income: $19,467 (2000); Median household income: $47,528 (2000); Poverty rate: 3.3% (2000).
Taxes: Total city taxes per capita: $184 (1997); City property taxes per capita: $173 (1997).
Education: High school graduation rate: 82.4% (2000); College graduation rate: 21.8% (2000).

School District(s)

Carlisle Community School District (PK-12)
2000 Enrollment: 1,246 515-989-3589
Housing: Homeownership rate: 78.4% (2000); Median home value: $96,300 (2000); Median rent: $399 per month (2000); Median age of housing: 30 years (2000).
Safety: Violent crime rate: 11.5 per 10,000 population; Property crime rate: 177.5 per 10,000 population (2001).
Newspapers: The Carlisle Citizen (1 x week)
Transportation: Commute to work: 94.1% car, 0.4% public transportation, 1.5% walk, 3.3% work from home (2000); Travel time to work: 16.2% less than 15 minutes, 42.1% 15 to 30 minutes, 32.5% 30 to 45 minutes, 5.0% 45 to 60 minutes, 4.1% 60 minutes or more (2000)

CUMMING (city). Covers a land area of 2.107 square miles and a water area of 0 square miles. Located at 41.48° N. Lat.; 93.76° W. Long.
History: Local legend tells of a construction worker who, when asked how work was progressing on buildings in the town, answered, "It's cumming," thus giving name to the town of Cumming. Cumming was founded in 1888 by Frazer Callison.
Population: 162 (2000); Race: 100.0% White, 0.0% Black, 0.0% Asian, 0.0% American Indian and Alaska Native, 0.0% Hispanic of any race, 0.0% two or more races (2000); Density: 76.9 persons per square mile (2000); Age: 15.3% under 18, 12.3% over 64 (2000); Marriage status: 9.4% never married, 72.5% now married, 2.9% widowed, 15.2% divorced (2000); Foreign born: 1.2% (2000); Ancestry (includes multiple ancestries): 24.5% Irish, 12.9% German, 11.0% United States or American, 6.1% Other groups, 6.1% English (2000).
Economy: Single-family building permits issued: 4 (2001) / 6 (2000); Multi-family building permits issued: 0 (2001) / 0 (2000); Employment by occupation: 23.1% management, 13.2% professional, 11.0% services, 29.7% sales, 0.0% farming, 3.3% construction, 19.8% production (2000).
Income: Per capita income: $23,575 (2000); Median household income: $52,813 (2000); Poverty rate: 0.0% (2000).
Taxes: Total city taxes per capita: $168 (1997); City property taxes per capita: $161 (1997).
Education: High school graduation rate: 97.7% (2000); College graduation rate: 17.4% (2000).
Housing: Homeownership rate: 85.5% (2000); Median home value: $91,300 (2000); Median rent: $450 per month (2000); Median age of housing: 60 years (2000).
Transportation: Commute to work: 93.4% car, 0.0% public transportation, 2.2% walk, 4.4% work from home (2000); Travel time to work: 19.5% less than 15 minutes, 52.9% 15 to 30 minutes, 27.6% 30 to 45 minutes, 0.0% 45 to 60 minutes, 0.0% 60 minutes or more (2000)

HARTFORD (city). Covers a land area of 0.974 square miles and a water area of 0 square miles. Located at 41.46° N. Lat.; 93.40° W. Long. Elevation is 815 feet.
History: Hartford was located at a ford on the Middle River. The town was founded by John D. Hartman, and named for him.
Population: 759 (2000); Race: 96.1% White, 0.0% Black, 0.0% Asian, 2.7% American Indian and Alaska Native, 3.2% Hispanic of any race, 0.1% two or more races (2000); Density: 778.9 persons per square mile (2000); Age: 26.8% under 18, 7.7% over 64 (2000); Marriage status: 19.9% never married, 61.9% now married, 5.3% widowed, 12.9% divorced (2000); Foreign born: 0.4% (2000); Ancestry (includes multiple ancestries): 19.5% German, 15.2% United States or American, 13.7% Irish, 11.5% English, 7.3% Other groups (2000).
Economy: Single-family building permits issued: 2 (2001) / 2 (2000); Multi-family building permits issued: 0 (2001) / 0 (2000); Employment by occupation: 10.7% management, 9.0% professional, 16.1% services, 28.7% sales, 0.0% farming, 15.9% construction, 19.7% production (2000).
Income: Per capita income: $18,141 (2000); Median household income: $39,539 (2000); Poverty rate: 4.7% (2000).
Taxes: Total city taxes per capita: $170 (1997); City property taxes per capita: $166 (1997).
Education: High school graduation rate: 82.8% (2000); College graduation rate: 7.4% (2000).
Housing: Homeownership rate: 98.5% (2000); Median home value: $78,600 (2000); Median rent: $425 per month (2000); Median age of housing: 29 years (2000).
Transportation: Commute to work: 95.9% car, 0.0% public transportation, 1.0% walk, 2.4% work from home (2000); Travel time to work: 13.3% less than 15 minutes, 27.1% 15 to 30 minutes, 41.9% 30 to 45 minutes, 15.8% 45 to 60 minutes, 2.0% 60 minutes or more (2000)

INDIANOLA (city). Covers a land area of 9.188 square miles and a water area of 0 square miles. Located at 41.36° N. Lat.; 93.56° W. Long. Elevation is 966 feet.
History: Indianola was selected as county seat when Warren County was organized in 1849. It is said that the surveyors of the town were discussing a suitable name for it while eating lunch. One man had his food wrapped in a newspaper. As the men read the paper before discarding it they noticed an item from a Texas town called Indianola. The name pleased them and they selected it for the town.
Population: 12,998 (2000); Race: 97.7% White, 0.2% Black, 0.5% Asian, 0.3% American Indian and Alaska Native, 0.6% Hispanic of any race, 1.0% two or more races (2000); Density: 1,414.7 persons per square mile (2000); Age: 23.8% under 18, 15.4% over 64 (2000); Marriage status: 27.1% never married, 55.8% now married, 7.8% widowed, 9.3% divorced (2000); Foreign born: 1.3% (2000); Ancestry (includes multiple ancestries): 28.1% German, 13.4% English, 12.2% United States or American, 12.1% Irish, 4.9% Other groups (2000).
Vital Statistics: Birth rate: 133.1 per 10,000 population (1998)
Economy: Single-family building permits issued: 72 (2001) / 53 (2000); Multi-family building permits issued: 8 (2001) / 18 (2000); Employment by occupation: 12.4% management, 18.9% professional, 16.6% services, 31.0% sales, 0.3% farming, 9.8% construction, 11.0% production (2000).
Income: Per capita income: $19,574 (2000); Median household income: $43,725 (2000); Poverty rate: 7.2% (2000).
Taxes: Total city taxes per capita: $237 (2000); City property taxes per capita: $218 (2000).
Education: High school graduation rate: 90.8% (2000); College graduation rate: 27.0% (2000).

School District(s)

Indianola Community School District (PK-12)
2000 Enrollment: 3,224 515-961-9500

Four-year College(s)

Simpson College (Private, Not-for-profit, United Methodist)
2001 Enrollment: 1,816 515-961-6251
2001 Tuition: In-state $15,766; Out-of-state $15,766
Housing: Homeownership rate: 66.1% (2000); Median home value: $103,700 (2000); Median rent: $433 per month (2000); Median age of housing: 30 years (2000).
Safety: Violent crime rate: 5.4 per 10,000 population; Property crime rate: 286.5 per 10,000 population (2001).
Newspapers: The Record Herald/Indianola Tribune (1 x week)
Transportation: Commute to work: 88.5% car, 0.6% public transportation, 6.2% walk, 3.6% work from home (2000); Travel time to work: 43.1% less than 15 minutes, 14.7% 15 to 30 minutes, 33.2% 30 to 45 minutes, 6.7% 45 to 60 minutes, 2.2% 60 minutes or more (2000)
Additional Information Contacts
Indianola Chamber of Commerce 515-961-6269

LACONA (city). Covers a land area of 0.362 square miles and a water area of 0 square miles. Located at 41.18° N. Lat.; 93.38° W. Long. Elevation is 822 feet.
History: The name Lacona is believed to be taken from the name of nearby Lake Ona.
Population: 360 (2000); Race: 100.0% White, 0.0% Black, 0.0% Asian, 0.0% American Indian and Alaska Native, 0.0% Hispanic of any race, 0.0% two or more races (2000); Density: 993.2 persons per square mile (2000); Age: 18.9% under 18, 15.9% over 64 (2000); Marriage status: 22.8% never married, 63.6% now married, 7.6% widowed, 6.0% divorced (2000); Foreign born: 0.0% (2000); Ancestry (includes multiple ancestries): 36.5% German, 18.4% United States or American, 9.7% English, 9.2% Irish, 5.3% French (except Basque) (2000).
Economy: Single-family building permits issued: 1 (2001) / 0 (2000); Multi-family building permits issued: 0 (2001) / 0 (2000); Employment by occupation: 12.8% management, 13.3% professional, 14.3% services, 24.5% sales, 2.0% farming, 8.2% construction, 25.0% production (2000).
Income: Per capita income: $17,897 (2000); Median household income: $39,375 (2000); Poverty rate: 7.0% (2000).
Taxes: Total city taxes per capita: $161 (1997); City property taxes per capita: $161 (1997).
Education: High school graduation rate: 79.9% (2000); College graduation rate: 12.3% (2000).
Housing: Homeownership rate: 73.2% (2000); Median home value: $58,800 (2000); Median rent: $230 per month (2000); Median age of housing: 60+ years (2000).
Transportation: Commute to work: 91.1% car, 0.0% public transportation, 6.8% walk, 2.1% work from home (2000); Travel time to work: 20.9% less than 15 minutes, 18.2% 15 to 30 minutes, 19.8% 30 to 45 minutes, 12.3% 45 to 60 minutes, 28.9% 60 minutes or more (2000)

LIBERTY CENTER (unincorporated postal area, zip code 50145). Covers a land area of 0.027 square miles and a water area of 0 square miles. Located at 41.20° N. Lat.; 93.50° W. Long.
History: Liberty Center is believed to be named as a result of high patriotic feelings during the Civil War.
Population: 26 (2000); Race: 100.0% White, 0.0% Black, 0.0% Asian, 0.0% American Indian and Alaska Native, 0.0% Hispanic of any race, 0.0% two or more races (2000); Density: 946.9 persons per square mile (2000); Age: 0.0% under 18, 0.0% over 64 (2000); Marriage status: 45.5% never married, 0.0% now married, 0.0% widowed, 54.5% divorced (2000); Foreign born: 0.0% (2000); Ancestry (includes multiple ancestries): 45.5% United States or American (2000).
Economy: Employment by occupation: 0.0% management, 0.0% professional, 54.5% services, 0.0% sales, 0.0% farming, 0.0% construction, 45.5% production (2000).
Income: Per capita income: $18,318 (2000); Median household income: $17,292 (2000); Poverty rate: 0.0% (2000).
Education: High school graduation rate: 100.0% (2000); College graduation rate: 54.5% (2000).

School District(s)

Southeast Warren Community School District (PK-12)
2000 Enrollment: 597 641-466-3510
Housing: Homeownership rate: 0.0% (2000); Median rent: $225 per month (2000); Median age of housing: 60+ years (2000).
Transportation: Commute to work: 100.0% car, 0.0% public transportation, 0.0% walk, 0.0% work from home (2000); Travel time to work: 0.0% less than 15 minutes, 100.0% 15 to 30 minutes, 0.0% 30 to 45 minutes, 0.0% 45 to 60 minutes, 0.0% 60 minutes or more (2000)

MARTENSDALE (city). Covers a land area of 0.378 square miles and a water area of 0 square miles. Located at 41.37° N. Lat.; 93.74° W. Long. Elevation is 840 feet.
History: Martensdale was established at the junction of the Chicago, Rock Island & Pacific and Chicago Great Western Railroads as a shipping point for the surrounding farms.
Population: 467 (2000); Race: 97.8% White, 0.4% Black, 0.0% Asian, 0.0% American Indian and Alaska Native, 0.9% Hispanic of any race, 1.7% two or more races (2000); Density: 1,236.3 persons per square mile (2000); Age: 31.0% under 18, 13.1% over 64 (2000); Marriage status: 23.4% never married, 59.7% now married, 5.6% widowed, 11.3% divorced (2000);

Foreign born: 1.3% (2000); Ancestry (includes multiple ancestries): 26.9% German, 11.4% Irish, 7.8% Other groups, 6.7% English, 6.3% United States or American (2000).
Economy: Single-family building permits issued: 1 (2001) / 1 (2000); Multi-family building permits issued: 0 (2001) / 0 (2000); Employment by occupation: 11.7% management, 11.7% professional, 12.6% services, 29.6% sales, 0.0% farming, 10.3% construction, 24.2% production (2000).
Income: Per capita income: $16,638 (2000); Median household income: $41,250 (2000); Poverty rate: 4.5% (2000).
Taxes: Total city taxes per capita: $106 (1997); City property taxes per capita: $104 (1997).
Education: High school graduation rate: 88.4% (2000); College graduation rate: 11.6% (2000).

School District(s)

Martensdale-Saint Marys Community School District (KG-12)
2000 Enrollment: 509 641-764-2466
Housing: Homeownership rate: 76.2% (2000); Median home value: $84,000 (2000); Median rent: $356 per month (2000); Median age of housing: 35 years (2000).
Transportation: Commute to work: 96.1% car, 0.0% public transportation, 0.0% walk, 3.9% work from home (2000); Travel time to work: 13.6% less than 15 minutes, 44.3% 15 to 30 minutes, 30.8% 30 to 45 minutes, 5.9% 45 to 60 minutes, 5.4% 60 minutes or more (2000)

MILO (city). Covers a land area of 0.620 square miles and a water area of 0 square miles. Located at 41.28° N. Lat.; 93.44° W. Long. Elevation is 972 feet.
History: Milo was named by an employee named Mallory of the Chicago, Burlington & Quincy Railroad.
Population: 839 (2000); Race: 99.8% White, 0.2% Black, 0.0% Asian, 0.0% American Indian and Alaska Native, 0.1% Hispanic of any race, 0.0% two or more races (2000); Density: 1,353.2 persons per square mile (2000); Age: 31.2% under 18, 13.2% over 64 (2000); Marriage status: 17.9% never married, 70.0% now married, 5.2% widowed, 6.9% divorced (2000); Foreign born: 1.2% (2000); Ancestry (includes multiple ancestries): 23.6% German, 17.8% United States or American, 13.1% English, 8.4% Irish, 5.1% Other groups (2000).
Economy: Single-family building permits issued: 1 (2001) / 0 (2000); Multi-family building permits issued: 0 (2001) / 0 (2000); Employment by occupation: 11.0% management, 16.1% professional, 17.3% services, 25.4% sales, 0.5% farming, 9.8% construction, 20.0% production (2000).
Income: Per capita income: $16,263 (2000); Median household income: $41,927 (2000); Poverty rate: 6.2% (2000).
Taxes: Total city taxes per capita: $104 (1997); City property taxes per capita: $103 (1997).
Education: High school graduation rate: 90.2% (2000); College graduation rate: 11.0% (2000).
Housing: Homeownership rate: 82.6% (2000); Median home value: $78,600 (2000); Median rent: $194 per month (2000); Median age of housing: 36 years (2000).
Transportation: Commute to work: 90.6% car, 1.5% public transportation, 2.5% walk, 4.0% work from home (2000); Travel time to work: 9.5% less than 15 minutes, 28.6% 15 to 30 minutes, 17.8% 30 to 45 minutes, 31.2% 45 to 60 minutes, 12.9% 60 minutes or more (2000)

NEW VIRGINIA (city). Covers a land area of 0.461 square miles and a water area of 0 square miles. Located at 41.18° N. Lat.; 93.73° W. Long. Elevation is 1,047 feet.
History: New Virginia was named for Virginia and West Virginia by the settlers who arrived from that area.
Population: 469 (2000); Race: 98.5% White, 0.0% Black, 0.0% Asian, 0.0% American Indian and Alaska Native, 0.2% Hispanic of any race, 1.3% two or more races (2000); Density: 1,017.5 persons per square mile (2000); Age: 21.9% under 18, 15.7% over 64 (2000); Marriage status: 16.8% never married, 65.5% now married, 11.0% widowed, 6.8% divorced (2000); Foreign born: 0.0% (2000); Ancestry (includes multiple ancestries): 34.9% German, 17.1% Irish, 15.4% United States or American, 11.7% English, 5.8% Scottish (2000).
Economy: Single-family building permits issued: 2 (2001) / 2 (2000); Multi-family building permits issued: 0 (2001) / 0 (2000); Employment by occupation: 9.5% management, 8.4% professional, 8.0% services, 41.2% sales, 0.0% farming, 19.1% construction, 13.7% production (2000).
Income: Per capita income: $20,803 (2000); Median household income: $38,750 (2000); Poverty rate: 9.9% (2000).
Taxes: Total city taxes per capita: $82 (1997); City property taxes per capita: $80 (1997).
Education: High school graduation rate: 90.8% (2000); College graduation rate: 7.4% (2000).
Housing: Homeownership rate: 80.8% (2000); Median home value: $74,800 (2000); Median rent: $323 per month (2000); Median age of housing: 40 years (2000).
Transportation: Commute to work: 94.9% car, 0.0% public transportation, 3.5% walk, 1.6% work from home (2000); Travel time to work: 15.9% less than 15 minutes, 18.3% 15 to 30 minutes, 31.3% 30 to 45 minutes, 25.4% 45 to 60 minutes, 9.1% 60 minutes or more (2000)

NORWALK (city). Covers a land area of 6.561 square miles and a water area of 0.215 square miles. Located at 41.48° N. Lat.; 93.67° W. Long. Elevation is 896 feet.
History: In 1855 Norwalk was named in honor of Norwalk, Ohio. The town was originally known as Pyra.
Population: 6,884 (2000); Race: 97.8% White, 0.4% Black, 0.2% Asian, 0.2% American Indian and Alaska Native, 2.1% Hispanic of any race, 0.8% two or more races (2000); Density: 1,049.2 persons per square mile (2000); Age: 31.7% under 18, 7.1% over 64 (2000); Marriage status: 21.2% never married, 64.3% now married, 4.4% widowed, 10.2% divorced (2000); Foreign born: 1.2% (2000); Ancestry (includes multiple ancestries): 33.6% German, 14.4% Irish, 12.9% English, 6.8% United States or American, 5.5% Norwegian (2000).
Economy: Single-family building permits issued: 24 (2001) / 15 (2000); Multi-family building permits issued: 0 (2001) / 192 (2000); Employment by occupation: 16.0% management, 20.1% professional, 12.9% services, 31.3% sales, 0.0% farming, 8.3% construction, 11.3% production (2000).
Income: Per capita income: $21,895 (2000); Median household income: $58,933 (2000); Poverty rate: 2.4% (2000).
Taxes: Total city taxes per capita: $171 (1997); City property taxes per capita: $166 (1997).
Education: High school graduation rate: 93.8% (2000); College graduation rate: 25.1% (2000).

School District(s)

Norwalk Community School District (PK-12)
2000 Enrollment: 2,179 515-981-0676
Housing: Homeownership rate: 83.2% (2000); Median home value: $103,500 (2000); Median rent: $468 per month (2000); Median age of housing: 23 years (2000).
Safety: Violent crime rate: 8.7 per 10,000 population; Property crime rate: 155.6 per 10,000 population (2001).
Newspapers: North Warren Town and County News (1 x week)
Transportation: Commute to work: 94.5% car, 0.1% public transportation, 0.6% walk, 4.6% work from home (2000); Travel time to work: 22.0% less than 15 minutes, 57.7% 15 to 30 minutes, 15.9% 30 to 45 minutes, 1.2% 45 to 60 minutes, 3.1% 60 minutes or more (2000)
Additional Information Contacts
Norwalk Chamber of Commerce 515-981-0619

PROLE (unincorporated postal area, zip code 50229). Covers a land area of 39.691 square miles and a water area of 0.031 square miles. Located at 41.38° N. Lat.; 93.77° W. Long.
History: Prole was named for Albert Westren Prole, a local pharmacist. Mr. Prole was also a strong supporter of the arrival of the Des Moines, Osceola & Southern Railroad.
Population: 898 (2000); Race: 97.5% White, 0.0% Black, 2.0% Asian, 0.0% American Indian and Alaska Native, 0.0% Hispanic of any race, 0.6% two or more races (2000); Density: 22.6 persons per square mile (2000); Age: 34.2% under 18, 7.9% over 64 (2000); Marriage status: 17.5% never married, 73.2% now married, 3.4% widowed, 5.9% divorced (2000); Foreign born: 1.3% (2000); Ancestry (includes multiple ancestries): 25.3% German, 24.3% Irish, 10.3% Other groups, 7.3% English, 7.3% United States or American (2000).
Economy: Employment by occupation: 14.1% management, 15.0% professional, 6.4% services, 24.4% sales, 0.4% farming, 19.9% construction, 19.7% production (2000).
Income: Per capita income: $19,877 (2000); Median household income: $56,667 (2000); Poverty rate: 5.4% (2000).
Education: High school graduation rate: 88.8% (2000); College graduation rate: 8.4% (2000).
Housing: Homeownership rate: 88.3% (2000); Median home value: $121,300 (2000); Median rent: $335 per month (2000); Median age of housing: 28 years (2000).
Transportation: Commute to work: 90.7% car, 0.0% public transportation, 2.4% walk, 6.1% work from home (2000); Travel time to work: 14.5% less than 15 minutes, 34.8% 15 to 30 minutes, 41.2% 30 to 45 minutes, 6.2% 45 to 60 minutes, 3.2% 60 minutes or more (2000)

SAINT MARYS (city). Covers a land area of 0.138 square miles and a water area of 0 square miles. Located at 41.30° N. Lat.; 93.73° W. Long. Elevation is 1,033 feet.
History: St. Marys was named for the Catholic church in town.
Population: 134 (2000); Race: 100.0% White, 0.0% Black, 0.0% Asian, 0.0% American Indian and Alaska Native, 3.4% Hispanic of any race, 0.0% two or more races (2000); Density: 968.3 persons per square mile (2000); Age: 29.7% under 18, 9.3% over 64 (2000); Marriage status: 19.1% never married, 66.3% now married, 6.7% widowed, 7.9% divorced (2000); Foreign born: 0.0% (2000); Ancestry (includes multiple ancestries): 52.5% German, 25.4% Irish, 11.9% United States or American, 11.9% English, 5.9% Italian (2000).
Economy: Single-family building permits issued: 0 (2001) / 0 (2000); Multi-family building permits issued: 0 (2001) / 0 (2000); Employment by occupation: 8.9% management, 14.3% professional, 3.6% services, 30.4% sales, 0.0% farming, 19.6% construction, 23.2% production (2000).
Income: Per capita income: $16,747 (2000); Median household income: $38,750 (2000); Poverty rate: 0.0% (2000).
Education: High school graduation rate: 100.0% (2000); College graduation rate: 17.3% (2000).
Housing: Homeownership rate: 90.2% (2000); Median home value: $85,000 (2000); Median rent: $450 per month (2000); Median age of housing: 39 years (2000).
Transportation: Commute to work: 93.0% car, 0.0% public transportation, 7.0% walk, 0.0% work from home (2000); Travel time to work: 19.3% less than 15 minutes, 17.5% 15 to 30 minutes, 35.1% 30 to 45 minutes, 24.6% 45 to 60 minutes, 3.5% 60 minutes or more (2000)

SANDYVILLE (city). Covers a land area of 0.510 square miles and a water area of 0 square miles. Located at 41.37° N. Lat.; 93.38° W. Long.
History: Sandyville was platted in 1851.
Population: 61 (2000); Race: 100.0% White, 0.0% Black, 0.0% Asian, 0.0% American Indian and Alaska Native, 0.0% Hispanic of any race, 0.0% two or more races (2000); Density: 119.6 persons per square mile (2000); Age: 11.5% under 18, 11.5% over 64 (2000); Marriage status: 21.1% never married, 71.9% now married, 7.0% widowed, 0.0% divorced (2000); Foreign born: 0.0% (2000); Ancestry (includes multiple ancestries): 18.0% German, 18.0% United States or American, 8.2% English, 4.9% Irish, 4.9% Other groups (2000).
Economy: Employment by occupation: 16.2% management, 8.1% professional, 0.0% services, 35.1% sales, 0.0% farming, 32.4% construction, 8.1% production (2000).
Income: Per capita income: $20,028 (2000); Median household income: $31,667 (2000); Poverty rate: 0.0% (2000).
Taxes: Total city taxes per capita: $65 (1997); City property taxes per capita: $65 (1997).
Education: High school graduation rate: 70.6% (2000); College graduation rate: 0.0% (2000).
Housing: Homeownership rate: 90.3% (2000); Median home value: $46,700 (2000); Median age of housing: 60+ years (2000).
Transportation: Commute to work: 100.0% car, 0.0% public transportation, 0.0% walk, 0.0% work from home (2000); Travel time to work: 18.9% less than 15 minutes, 8.1% 15 to 30 minutes, 40.5% 30 to 45 minutes, 8.1% 45 to 60 minutes, 24.3% 60 minutes or more (2000)

SPRING HILL (city). Covers a land area of 0.119 square miles and a water area of 0 square miles. Located at 41.41° N. Lat.; 93.64° W. Long. Elevation is 817 feet.
History: Spring Hill derived its name from its location on a hill with a spring.
Population: 92 (2000); Race: 100.0% White, 0.0% Black, 0.0% Asian, 0.0% American Indian and Alaska Native, 0.0% Hispanic of any race, 0.0% two or more races (2000); Density: 773.4 persons per square mile (2000); Age: 36.0% under 18, 8.0% over 64 (2000); Marriage status: 23.6% never married, 45.5% now married, 7.3% widowed, 23.6% divorced (2000); Foreign born: 0.0% (2000); Ancestry (includes multiple ancestries): 44.0% German, 8.0% Irish, 8.0% Swedish, 8.0% United States or American, 6.7% French Canadian (2000).
Economy: Employment by occupation: 0.0% management, 6.5% professional, 12.9% services, 45.2% sales, 0.0% farming, 16.1% construction, 19.4% production (2000).
Income: Per capita income: $11,671 (2000); Median household income: $33,750 (2000); Poverty rate: 10.7% (2000).
Taxes: Total city taxes per capita: $33 (1997); City property taxes per capita: $33 (1997).
Education: High school graduation rate: 66.7% (2000); College graduation rate: 0.0% (2000).
Housing: Homeownership rate: 96.6% (2000); Median home value: $51,400 (2000); Median age of housing: 57 years (2000).
Transportation: Commute to work: 90.3% car, 0.0% public transportation, 0.0% walk, 0.0% work from home (2000); Travel time to work: 3.2% less than 15 minutes, 38.7% 15 to 30 minutes, 35.5% 30 to 45 minutes, 22.6% 45 to 60 minutes, 0.0% 60 minutes or more (2000)

Washington County

Located in southeastern Iowa; prairie area, drained by the Skunk and English Rivers. Covers a land area of 568.70 square miles, a water area of 2.10 square miles, and is located in the Central Time Zone. The county government was organized in 1837. County seat is Washington.

Weather Station: Washington — Elevation: 754 feet

	Jan	Feb	Mar	Apr	May	Jun	Jul	Aug	Sep	Oct	Nov	Dec
High	30	37	50	64	75	84	88	85	78	66	49	35
Low	13	19	30	41	52	61	66	63	55	43	31	20
Precip	1.2	1.1	2.3	3.0	4.4	4.2	4.2	4.1	3.9	2.6	2.3	1.7
Snow	7.4	4.9	2.5	1.3	tr	0.0	0.0	0.0	0.0	0.2	1.4	5.1

High and Low temperatures in degrees Fahrenheit; Precipitation and Snow in inches

Population: 20,670 (2000); Race: 97.0% White, 0.4% Black, 0.1% Asian, 0.1% American Indian and Alaska Native, 2.7% Hispanic of any race, 0.9% two or more races (2000); Density: 36.3 persons per square mile (2000); Age: 26.1% under 18, 17.8% over 64 (2000).
Religion: Five largest groups: 14.0% Catholic Church, 12.0% The United Methodist Church, 5.9% Presbyterian Church (U.S.A.), 5.2% Mennonite Church USA, 3.2% American Baptist Churches in the USA (2000).
Economy: Unemployment rate: 2.5% (11/2002); Total civilian labor force: 11,754 (11/2002); Leading industries: 21.1% manufacturing; 19.5% health care and social assistance; 19.2% retail trade (2000); Companies that employ more than 1,000 persons: 0 (2000); Companies that employ more than 100 persons: 11 (2000); Farms: 1,061 totaling 317,699 acres (1997); Minority business ownership rate: 0.0% (1997); Women business ownership rate: 19.3% (1997); Retail sales per capita: $7,451 (1997). Single-family building permits issued: 36 (2001) / 54 (2000); Multi-family building permits issued: 11 (2001) / 0 (2000).
Income: Per capita income: $18,221 (2000); Median household income: $39,103 (2000); Poverty rate: 7.6% (2000); Bankruptcy rate: 2.90% (2001).
Taxes: Total county taxes per capita: $217 (2000); County property taxes per capita: $215 (2000).
Education: High school graduation rate: 82.5% (2000); College graduation rate: 16.4% (2000).
Housing: Homeownership rate: 75.3% (2000); Median home value: $83,600 (2000); Median rent: $334 per month (2000); Median age of housing: 49 years (2000).
Health: Birth rate: 137.9 per 10,000 population (1998); Age adjusted death rate: 70.7 per 10,000 population (1999); Age adjusted cancer mortality rate: 165.0 deaths per 100,000 population (1999). Number of physicians: 5.8 per 10,000 population (1999); Number of hospital beds: 44.0 per 10,000 population (1999).
Elections: 2000 Presidential election results: 43.2% Gore, 53.1% Bush, 2.7% Nader, 0.5% Buchanan

Additional Information Contacts
Washington County Government Offices 319-653-7717
English River Board of Realtors 319-653-9800
Kalona Chamber of Commerce 319-656-2660
Washington Chamber of Commerce 319-653-3272

Washington County Communities

AINSWORTH (city). Covers a land area of 0.379 square miles and a water area of 0 square miles. Located at 41.29° N. Lat.; 91.55° W. Long. Elevation is 700 feet.
History: Ainsworth was laid out by D. H. Ainsworth in 1858.
Population: 524 (2000); Race: 92.2% White, 0.0% Black, 0.0% Asian, 0.7% American Indian and Alaska Native, 10.4% Hispanic of any race, 0.2% two or more races (2000); Density: 1,381.0 persons per square mile (2000); Age: 33.5% under 18, 9.2% over 64 (2000); Marriage status: 13.7% never married, 71.6% now married, 5.8% widowed, 8.9% divorced (2000); Foreign born: 9.1% (2000); Ancestry (includes multiple ancestries): 34.2% German, 15.7% Irish, 12.0% Other groups, 7.6% English, 7.4% United States or American (2000).

Economy: Employment by occupation: 6.4% management, 11.0% professional, 17.3% services, 15.5% sales, 0.7% farming, 8.5% construction, 40.6% production (2000).
Income: Per capita income: $15,627 (2000); Median household income: $41,071 (2000); Poverty rate: 10.0% (2000).
Taxes: Total city taxes per capita: $52 (1997); City property taxes per capita: $50 (1997).
Education: High school graduation rate: 81.8% (2000); College graduation rate: 10.9% (2000).
Housing: Homeownership rate: 77.5% (2000); Median home value: $70,000 (2000); Median rent: $292 per month (2000); Median age of housing: 48 years (2000).
Transportation: Commute to work: 91.4% car, 0.0% public transportation, 1.8% walk, 5.7% work from home (2000); Travel time to work: 35.2% less than 15 minutes, 17.4% 15 to 30 minutes, 33.7% 30 to 45 minutes, 7.6% 45 to 60 minutes, 6.1% 60 minutes or more (2000)

BRIGHTON (city). Covers a land area of 0.719 square miles and a water area of 0 square miles. Located at 41.17° N. Lat.; 91.82° W. Long. Elevation is 748 feet.
History: Brighton shares its name with cities in several eastern and mid-western states, perhaps reflecting the westward movement of settlers.
Population: 687 (2000); Race: 97.8% White, 0.0% Black, 0.6% Asian, 0.0% American Indian and Alaska Native, 0.0% Hispanic of any race, 1.6% two or more races (2000); Density: 955.3 persons per square mile (2000); Age: 23.5% under 18, 16.2% over 64 (2000); Marriage status: 18.2% never married, 58.8% now married, 10.7% widowed, 12.3% divorced (2000); Foreign born: 0.7% (2000); Ancestry (includes multiple ancestries): 37.2% German, 12.1% Irish, 10.8% English, 9.2% United States or American, 8.1% Dutch (2000).
Economy: Single-family building permits issued: 0 (2001) / 3 (2000); Multi-family building permits issued: 0 (2001) / 0 (2000); Employment by occupation: 10.7% management, 6.1% professional, 15.9% services, 21.6% sales, 0.9% farming, 14.9% construction, 29.9% production (2000).
Income: Per capita income: $15,140 (2000); Median household income: $30,139 (2000); Poverty rate: 14.1% (2000).
Taxes: Total city taxes per capita: $85 (1997); City property taxes per capita: $84 (1997).
Education: High school graduation rate: 77.9% (2000); College graduation rate: 7.5% (2000).
Housing: Homeownership rate: 76.3% (2000); Median home value: $41,900 (2000); Median rent: $294 per month (2000); Median age of housing: 56 years (2000).
Transportation: Commute to work: 90.5% car, 0.0% public transportation, 4.9% walk, 4.0% work from home (2000); Travel time to work: 26.3% less than 15 minutes, 50.5% 15 to 30 minutes, 15.9% 30 to 45 minutes, 2.2% 45 to 60 minutes, 5.1% 60 minutes or more (2000)

CRAWFORDSVILLE (city). Covers a land area of 0.367 square miles and a water area of 0 square miles. Located at 41.21° N. Lat.; 91.53° W. Long. Elevation is 700 feet.
History: Crawfordsville, the oldest town in Washington County, was first named Nealtown, for J. W. Neal and his brothers who laid out the town site. Later, as a partial inducement to secure the services of a physician, Dr. Crawford, they changed the name to Crawfordsville.
Population: 295 (2000); Race: 90.7% White, 2.3% Black, 0.0% Asian, 0.0% American Indian and Alaska Native, 6.6% Hispanic of any race, 0.3% two or more races (2000); Density: 803.0 persons per square mile (2000); Age: 23.3% under 18, 21.9% over 64 (2000); Marriage status: 26.5% never married, 55.7% now married, 7.9% widowed, 9.9% divorced (2000); Foreign born: 1.3% (2000); Ancestry (includes multiple ancestries): 23.6% German, 19.6% Irish, 13.0% Other groups, 7.6% English, 6.3% United States or American (2000).
Economy: Employment by occupation: 12.0% management, 5.1% professional, 10.8% services, 29.7% sales, 1.3% farming, 13.9% construction, 27.2% production (2000).
Income: Per capita income: $17,238 (2000); Median household income: $39,063 (2000); Poverty rate: 2.0% (2000).
Taxes: Total city taxes per capita: $69 (1997); City property taxes per capita: $69 (1997).
Education: High school graduation rate: 86.6% (2000); College graduation rate: 11.1% (2000).
Housing: Homeownership rate: 85.8% (2000); Median home value: $53,500 (2000); Median rent: $350 per month (2000); Median age of housing: 60+ years (2000).
Transportation: Commute to work: 91.1% car, 0.0% public transportation, 7.6% walk, 1.3% work from home (2000); Travel time to work: 21.8% less than 15 minutes, 30.8% 15 to 30 minutes, 29.5% 30 to 45 minutes, 10.3% 45 to 60 minutes, 7.7% 60 minutes or more (2000)

KALONA (city). Covers a land area of 2.047 square miles and a water area of 0 square miles. Located at 41.48° N. Lat.; 91.70° W. Long. Elevation is 661 feet.
History: Kalona was the location of Myers' shorthorn breeding service, and was earlier known as Bulltown. When a railroad station was established, Myers himself suggested naming it Myersville or Kalona (the name of one of his prize bulls).
Population: 2,293 (2000); Race: 97.9% White, 0.4% Black, 0.1% Asian, 0.4% American Indian and Alaska Native, 1.9% Hispanic of any race, 0.8% two or more races (2000); Density: 1,119.9 persons per square mile (2000); Age: 24.3% under 18, 25.7% over 64 (2000); Marriage status: 20.1% never married, 66.9% now married, 7.8% widowed, 5.1% divorced (2000); Foreign born: 2.5% (2000); Ancestry (includes multiple ancestries): 43.4% German, 10.2% Irish, 9.7% United States or American, 5.9% English, 4.5% Swiss (2000).
Economy: Single-family building permits issued: 10 (2001) / 14 (2000); Multi-family building permits issued: 6 (2001) / 0 (2000); Employment by occupation: 10.0% management, 22.9% professional, 11.7% services, 25.4% sales, 0.4% farming, 11.2% construction, 18.4% production (2000).
Income: Per capita income: $22,474 (2000); Median household income: $33,750 (2000); Poverty rate: 6.7% (2000).
Taxes: Total city taxes per capita: $262 (1997); City property taxes per capita: $260 (1997).
Education: High school graduation rate: 72.8% (2000); College graduation rate: 16.2% (2000).
Housing: Homeownership rate: 73.2% (2000); Median home value: $99,400 (2000); Median rent: $350 per month (2000); Median age of housing: 29 years (2000).
Newspapers: Kalona News (1 x week)
Transportation: Commute to work: 89.6% car, 0.5% public transportation, 3.0% walk, 5.1% work from home (2000); Travel time to work: 41.3% less than 15 minutes, 19.6% 15 to 30 minutes, 28.5% 30 to 45 minutes, 7.8% 45 to 60 minutes, 2.8% 60 minutes or more (2000)
Additional Information Contacts
Kalona Chamber of Commerce 319-656-2660

RIVERSIDE (city). Covers a land area of 1.007 square miles and a water area of 0 square miles. Located at 41.48° N. Lat.; 91.57° W. Long. Elevation is 641 feet.
History: Riverside was named for its location on the English River.
Population: 928 (2000); Race: 99.1% White, 0.0% Black, 0.2% Asian, 0.1% American Indian and Alaska Native, 0.6% Hispanic of any race, 0.6% two or more races (2000); Density: 921.6 persons per square mile (2000); Age: 28.9% under 18, 9.4% over 64 (2000); Marriage status: 22.8% never married, 61.5% now married, 7.0% widowed, 8.7% divorced (2000); Foreign born: 0.5% (2000); Ancestry (includes multiple ancestries): 40.3% German, 14.9% Irish, 11.9% United States or American, 7.0% English, 5.0% Other groups (2000).
Economy: Single-family building permits issued: 4 (2001) / 4 (2000); Multi-family building permits issued: 3 (2001) / 0 (2000); Employment by occupation: 11.7% management, 17.0% professional, 13.9% services, 32.4% sales, 0.6% farming, 11.9% construction, 12.6% production (2000).
Income: Per capita income: $17,744 (2000); Median household income: $41,080 (2000); Poverty rate: 2.6% (2000).
Taxes: Total city taxes per capita: $223 (1997); City property taxes per capita: $219 (1997).
Education: High school graduation rate: 90.3% (2000); College graduation rate: 21.0% (2000).

School District(s)

Highland Community School District (KG-12)
2000 Enrollment: 614 319-648-3822
Housing: Homeownership rate: 72.7% (2000); Median home value: $92,000 (2000); Median rent: $332 per month (2000); Median age of housing: 37 years (2000).
Newspapers: Riverside Current (1 x week)
Transportation: Commute to work: 95.6% car, 0.0% public transportation, 2.2% walk, 1.5% work from home (2000); Travel time to work: 15.4% less than 15 minutes, 58.3% 15 to 30 minutes, 20.8% 30 to 45 minutes, 3.6% 45 to 60 minutes, 1.9% 60 minutes or more (2000)

WASHINGTON (city). Covers a land area of 4.846 square miles and a water area of 0.002 square miles. Located at 41.30° N. Lat.; 91.68° W. Long. Elevation is 746 feet.

History: Washington was the home of Smith Wildman Brookhart, U.S. Senator from Iowa (1922-1925; 1927-1933).

Population: 7,047 (2000); Race: 94.7% White, 0.5% Black, 0.0% Asian, 0.0% American Indian and Alaska Native, 5.1% Hispanic of any race, 1.5% two or more races (2000); Density: 1,454.3 persons per square mile (2000); Age: 22.5% under 18, 23.7% over 64 (2000); Marriage status: 20.3% never married, 57.4% now married, 12.2% widowed, 10.0% divorced (2000); Foreign born: 2.1% (2000); Ancestry (includes multiple ancestries): 29.8% German, 10.2% Irish, 9.7% Other groups, 9.4% English, 8.0% United States or American (2000).

Economy: Single-family building permits issued: 22 (2001) / 33 (2000); Multi-family building permits issued: 2 (2001) / 0 (2000); Employment by occupation: 10.9% management, 15.8% professional, 16.5% services, 25.1% sales, 0.8% farming, 10.3% construction, 20.6% production (2000).

Income: Per capita income: $18,145 (2000); Median household income: $36,067 (2000); Poverty rate: 9.3% (2000).

Taxes: Total city taxes per capita: $247 (1997); City property taxes per capita: $240 (1997).

Education: High school graduation rate: 84.9% (2000); College graduation rate: 16.6% (2000).

School District(s)

Washington Community School District (PK-12)
2000 Enrollment: 1,721 319-653-6543

Housing: Homeownership rate: 70.5% (2000); Median home value: $79,200 (2000); Median rent: $343 per month (2000); Median age of housing: 55 years (2000).

Hospitals: Washington County Hospital (91 beds)

Safety: Violent crime rate: 45.5 per 10,000 population; Property crime rate: 163.4 per 10,000 population (2001).

Newspapers: The Washington Evening Journal (5 x week)

Transportation: Commute to work: 90.0% car, 0.7% public transportation, 4.6% walk, 3.9% work from home (2000); Travel time to work: 62.8% less than 15 minutes, 12.6% 15 to 30 minutes, 12.3% 30 to 45 minutes, 7.8% 45 to 60 minutes, 4.6% 60 minutes or more (2000)

Additional Information Contacts

English River Board of Realtors 319-653-9800
Washington Chamber of Commerce 319-653-3272

WELLMAN (city). Covers a land area of 0.981 square miles and a water area of 0 square miles. Located at 41.46° N. Lat.; 91.83° W. Long. Elevation is 698 feet.

History: Wellman was named for Joseph Wellman, a local settler who sold his land for development of the town.

Population: 1,393 (2000); Race: 97.2% White, 0.4% Black, 0.1% Asian, 0.4% American Indian and Alaska Native, 2.4% Hispanic of any race, 1.7% two or more races (2000); Density: 1,419.6 persons per square mile (2000); Age: 26.3% under 18, 24.5% over 64 (2000); Marriage status: 19.0% never married, 59.1% now married, 11.6% widowed, 10.2% divorced (2000); Foreign born: 0.6% (2000); Ancestry (includes multiple ancestries): 40.4% German, 10.0% United States or American, 8.3% Irish, 8.0% English, 5.9% Other groups (2000).

Economy: Employment by occupation: 7.3% management, 17.7% professional, 20.8% services, 23.8% sales, 0.9% farming, 11.4% construction, 18.1% production (2000).

Income: Per capita income: $17,430 (2000); Median household income: $37,083 (2000); Poverty rate: 7.3% (2000).

Taxes: Total city taxes per capita: $164 (1997); City property taxes per capita: $160 (1997).

Education: High school graduation rate: 79.3% (2000); College graduation rate: 18.9% (2000).

School District(s)

Mid-Prairie Community School District (PK-12)
2000 Enrollment: 1,205 319-646-6093

Housing: Homeownership rate: 77.5% (2000); Median home value: $73,000 (2000); Median rent: $313 per month (2000); Median age of housing: 42 years (2000).

Newspapers: The Wellman Advance (1 x week)

Transportation: Commute to work: 86.9% car, 0.6% public transportation, 6.5% walk, 5.3% work from home (2000); Travel time to work: 35.4% less than 15 minutes, 14.8% 15 to 30 minutes, 32.3% 30 to 45 minutes, 15.0% 45 to 60 minutes, 2.5% 60 minutes or more (2000)

WEST CHESTER (city). Covers a land area of 0.253 square miles and a water area of 0 square miles. Located at 41.33° N. Lat.; 91.81° W. Long. Elevation is 780 feet.

History: West Chester was named for an employee of the Chicago, Rock Island & Pacific Railroad, Charles Fox Chester.

Population: 159 (2000); Race: 100.0% White, 0.0% Black, 0.0% Asian, 0.0% American Indian and Alaska Native, 0.0% Hispanic of any race, 0.0% two or more races (2000); Density: 629.0 persons per square mile (2000); Age: 15.5% under 18, 10.8% over 64 (2000); Marriage status: 15.2% never married, 47.7% now married, 6.8% widowed, 30.3% divorced (2000); Foreign born: 0.0% (2000); Ancestry (includes multiple ancestries): 21.6% German, 12.8% Irish, 11.5% French (except Basque), 10.1% United States or American, 9.5% English (2000).

Economy: Employment by occupation: 17.2% management, 4.0% professional, 16.2% services, 25.3% sales, 2.0% farming, 2.0% construction, 33.3% production (2000).

Income: Per capita income: $22,609 (2000); Median household income: $37,500 (2000); Poverty rate: 6.8% (2000).

Taxes: Total city taxes per capita: $69 (1997); City property taxes per capita: $69 (1997).

Education: High school graduation rate: 76.1% (2000); College graduation rate: 4.6% (2000).

Housing: Homeownership rate: 85.1% (2000); Median home value: $40,000 (2000); Median rent: $188 per month (2000); Median age of housing: 60+ years (2000).

Transportation: Commute to work: 93.9% car, 0.0% public transportation, 4.0% walk, 0.0% work from home (2000); Travel time to work: 22.2% less than 15 minutes, 45.5% 15 to 30 minutes, 12.1% 30 to 45 minutes, 6.1% 45 to 60 minutes, 14.1% 60 minutes or more (2000)

Wayne County

Located in southern Iowa; prairie area, bounded on the south by Missouri; drained by a branch of the Chariton River. Covers a land area of 525.60 square miles, a water area of 1.50 square miles, and is located in the Central Time Zone. The county government was organized in 1846. County seat is Corydon.

Population: 6,730 (2000); Race: 98.5% White, 0.4% Black, 0.4% Asian, 0.1% American Indian and Alaska Native, 0.6% Hispanic of any race, 0.5% two or more races (2000); Density: 12.8 persons per square mile (2000); Age: 23.8% under 18, 23.6% over 64 (2000).

Religion: Five largest groups: 19.7% The United Methodist Church, 6.3% Christian Church (Disciples of Christ), 6.0% American Baptist Churches in the USA, 4.2% Southern Baptist Convention, 3.9% Assemblies of God (2000).

Economy: Unemployment rate: 3.9% (11/2002); Total civilian labor force: 2,958 (11/2002); Leading industries: 29.4% manufacturing; 23.7% health care and social assistance; 16.6% retail trade (2000); Companies that employ more than 1,000 persons: 0 (2000); Companies that employ more than 100 persons: 2 (2000); Farms: 729 totaling 286,412 acres (1997); Minority business ownership rate: 0.0% (1997); Women business ownership rate: 22.3% (1997); Retail sales per capita: $4,663 (1997). Single-family building permits issued: 1 (2001) / 2 (2000); Multi-family building permits issued: 0 (2001) / 2 (2000).

Income: Per capita income: $15,613 (2000); Median household income: $29,380 (2000); Poverty rate: 14.0% (2000); Bankruptcy rate: 4.09% (2001).

Taxes: Total county taxes per capita: $167 (1997); County property taxes per capita: $162 (1997).

Education: High school graduation rate: 83.9% (2000); College graduation rate: 12.1% (2000).

Housing: Homeownership rate: 79.5% (2000); Median home value: $35,600 (2000); Median rent: $217 per month (2000); Median age of housing: 54 years (2000).

Health: Birth rate: 83.2 per 10,000 population (1998); Age adjusted death rate: 80.8 per 10,000 population (1999); Age adjusted cancer mortality rate: 272.5 deaths per 100,000 population (1999). Number of physicians: 4.5 per 10,000 population (1999); Number of hospital beds: 41.6 per 10,000 population (1999).

Elections: 2000 Presidential election results: 43.0% Gore, 55.2% Bush, 1.0% Nader, 0.4% Buchanan

National and State Parks: Bob White State Park

Additional Information Contacts

Wayne County Government Offices 515-872-2221
Corydon Chamber of Commerce 641-872-1338

Wayne County Communities

ALLERTON (city). Covers a land area of 1.140 square miles and a water area of 0 square miles. Located at 40.70° N. Lat.; 93.36° W. Long. Elevation is 1,103 feet.
History: Allertown, originally known as Aller Town, was named after railroad magnate Judge H. M. Aller.
Population: 559 (2000); Race: 99.6% White, 0.0% Black, 0.0% Asian, 0.0% American Indian and Alaska Native, 1.8% Hispanic of any race, 0.4% two or more races (2000); Density: 490.4 persons per square mile (2000); Age: 33.2% under 18, 14.5% over 64 (2000); Marriage status: 22.3% never married, 57.4% now married, 12.7% widowed, 7.6% divorced (2000); Foreign born: 0.4% (2000); Ancestry (includes multiple ancestries): 17.8% United States or American, 13.4% English, 12.3% German, 6.0% Irish, 6.0% Dutch (2000).
Economy: Employment by occupation: 7.2% management, 16.7% professional, 14.9% services, 16.7% sales, 0.9% farming, 6.8% construction, 36.7% production (2000).
Income: Per capita income: $12,218 (2000); Median household income: $28,929 (2000); Poverty rate: 18.5% (2000).
Taxes: Total city taxes per capita: $266 (1997); City property taxes per capita: $266 (1997).
Education: High school graduation rate: 81.3% (2000); College graduation rate: 7.0% (2000).
Housing: Homeownership rate: 80.8% (2000); Median home value: $28,000 (2000); Median rent: $163 per month (2000); Median age of housing: 59 years (2000).
Transportation: Commute to work: 91.3% car, 0.0% public transportation, 4.6% walk, 3.2% work from home (2000); Travel time to work: 60.7% less than 15 minutes, 14.7% 15 to 30 minutes, 9.0% 30 to 45 minutes, 10.0% 45 to 60 minutes, 5.7% 60 minutes or more (2000)

CLIO (city). Covers a land area of 0.743 square miles and a water area of 0 square miles. Located at 40.63° N. Lat.; 93.45° W. Long. Elevation is 1,117 feet.
History: The town of Clio was named for the Greek muse of history.
Population: 91 (2000); Race: 100.0% White, 0.0% Black, 0.0% Asian, 0.0% American Indian and Alaska Native, 1.7% Hispanic of any race, 0.0% two or more races (2000); Density: 122.4 persons per square mile (2000); Age: 43.3% under 18, 14.2% over 64 (2000); Marriage status: 36.1% never married, 53.6% now married, 4.1% widowed, 6.2% divorced (2000); Foreign born: 0.0% (2000); Ancestry (includes multiple ancestries): 24.2% German, 20.8% Other groups, 12.5% Scotch-Irish, 10.8% English, 8.3% Canadian (2000).
Economy: Employment by occupation: 23.9% management, 15.2% professional, 13.0% services, 21.7% sales, 0.0% farming, 10.9% construction, 15.2% production (2000).
Income: Per capita income: $14,362 (2000); Median household income: $42,813 (2000); Poverty rate: 10.8% (2000).
Taxes: Total city taxes per capita: $49 (1997); City property taxes per capita: $49 (1997).
Education: High school graduation rate: 73.8% (2000); College graduation rate: 24.6% (2000).
Housing: Homeownership rate: 92.5% (2000); Median home value: $18,800 (2000); Median age of housing: 60+ years (2000).
Transportation: Commute to work: 95.7% car, 0.0% public transportation, 4.3% walk, 0.0% work from home (2000); Travel time to work: 52.2% less than 15 minutes, 26.1% 15 to 30 minutes, 0.0% 30 to 45 minutes, 15.2% 45 to 60 minutes, 6.5% 60 minutes or more (2000)

CORYDON (city). Covers a land area of 1.390 square miles and a water area of 0 square miles. Located at 40.75° N. Lat.; 93.31° W. Long. Elevation is 1,105 feet.
History: Corydon was formerly called Springfield.
Population: 1,591 (2000); Race: 99.6% White, 0.0% Black, 0.3% Asian, 0.0% American Indian and Alaska Native, 0.3% Hispanic of any race, 0.1% two or more races (2000); Density: 1,144.3 persons per square mile (2000); Age: 22.2% under 18, 27.4% over 64 (2000); Marriage status: 18.1% never married, 56.7% now married, 15.6% widowed, 9.6% divorced (2000); Foreign born: 0.4% (2000); Ancestry (includes multiple ancestries): 20.3% German, 15.1% English, 14.2% Irish, 10.3% United States or American, 5.3% Dutch (2000).
Economy: Single-family building permits issued: 1 (2001) / 2 (2000); Multi-family building permits issued: 0 (2001) / 2 (2000); Employment by occupation: 11.4% management, 18.1% professional, 19.2% services, 24.4% sales, 0.6% farming, 9.1% construction, 17.3% production (2000).
Income: Per capita income: $17,496 (2000); Median household income: $28,542 (2000); Poverty rate: 12.1% (2000).
Taxes: Total city taxes per capita: $237 (1997); City property taxes per capita: $235 (1997).
Education: High school graduation rate: 83.8% (2000); College graduation rate: 16.9% (2000).

School District(s)

Wayne Community School District (KG-12)
2000 Enrollment: 679 641-872-1220
Housing: Homeownership rate: 73.5% (2000); Median home value: $46,400 (2000); Median rent: $227 per month (2000); Median age of housing: 51 years (2000).
Hospitals: Wayne County Hospital (28 beds)
Newspapers: Times Republican (1 x week)
Transportation: Commute to work: 86.6% car, 0.0% public transportation, 8.6% walk, 3.0% work from home (2000); Travel time to work: 65.9% less than 15 minutes, 15.0% 15 to 30 minutes, 7.3% 30 to 45 minutes, 3.4% 45 to 60 minutes, 8.5% 60 minutes or more (2000)
Additional Information Contacts
Corydon Chamber of Commerce 641-872-1338

HUMESTON (city). Covers a land area of 0.630 square miles and a water area of 0.011 square miles. Located at 40.86° N. Lat.; 93.49° W. Long. Elevation is 1,104 feet.
History: Humeston, established in 1872, was named for Alva Humeston, a railroad official who was active in promoting the extension of the railroad through the town.
Population: 543 (2000); Race: 97.7% White, 0.0% Black, 0.6% Asian, 1.4% American Indian and Alaska Native, 0.8% Hispanic of any race, 0.4% two or more races (2000); Density: 862.5 persons per square mile (2000); Age: 21.6% under 18, 25.1% over 64 (2000); Marriage status: 18.5% never married, 57.6% now married, 14.9% widowed, 9.1% divorced (2000); Foreign born: 1.2% (2000); Ancestry (includes multiple ancestries): 23.2% German, 19.5% English, 14.8% Irish, 10.1% United States or American, 8.4% Other groups (2000).
Economy: Employment by occupation: 5.5% management, 12.7% professional, 15.0% services, 24.1% sales, 0.5% farming, 15.5% construction, 26.8% production (2000).
Income: Per capita income: $15,617 (2000); Median household income: $22,917 (2000); Poverty rate: 21.4% (2000).
Taxes: Total city taxes per capita: $122 (1997); City property taxes per capita: $106 (1997).
Education: High school graduation rate: 88.8% (2000); College graduation rate: 7.6% (2000).

School District(s)

Mormon Trail Community School District (PK-12)
2000 Enrollment: 323 641-877-2521
Housing: Homeownership rate: 75.3% (2000); Median home value: $33,200 (2000); Median rent: $192 per month (2000); Median age of housing: 51 years (2000).
Transportation: Commute to work: 81.4% car, 0.0% public transportation, 3.2% walk, 10.9% work from home (2000); Travel time to work: 35.7% less than 15 minutes, 21.4% 15 to 30 minutes, 32.1% 30 to 45 minutes, 4.6% 45 to 60 minutes, 6.1% 60 minutes or more (2000)

LINEVILLE (city). Covers a land area of 0.909 square miles and a water area of 0 square miles. Located at 40.58° N. Lat.; 93.52° W. Long.
History: Lineville was so named because it lies partly in Iowa and partly in Missouri. In 1851 a pioneer merchant of the town built a store, half in Missouri and half in Iowa. In the Iowa part he sold clothing and groceries, and in the Missouri part he dispensed liquor, operating within the law in both states.
Population: 273 (2000); Race: 100.0% White, 0.0% Black, 0.0% Asian, 0.0% American Indian and Alaska Native, 0.0% Hispanic of any race, 0.0% two or more races (2000); Density: 300.5 persons per square mile (2000); Age: 28.1% under 18, 22.9% over 64 (2000); Marriage status: 17.3% never married, 60.0% now married, 14.2% widowed, 8.4% divorced (2000); Foreign born: 0.0% (2000); Ancestry (includes multiple ancestries): 22.9% Irish, 16.3% United States or American, 12.2% English, 11.1% German, 2.8% Norwegian (2000).
Economy: Employment by occupation: 17.8% management, 12.1% professional, 17.8% services, 15.9% sales, 3.7% farming, 10.3% construction, 22.4% production (2000).

Income: Per capita income: $18,414 (2000); Median household income: $30,625 (2000); Poverty rate: 24.0% (2000).
Taxes: Total city taxes per capita: $65 (1997); City property taxes per capita: $65 (1997).
Education: High school graduation rate: 73.7% (2000); College graduation rate: 7.7% (2000).

School District(s)

Lineville-Clio Community School District (PK-12)
2000 Enrollment: 101 641-876-5345

Housing: Homeownership rate: 80.0% (2000); Median home value: $31,700 (2000); Median rent: $197 per month (2000); Median age of housing: 42 years (2000).
Transportation: Commute to work: 84.9% car, 0.0% public transportation, 0.9% walk, 12.3% work from home (2000); Travel time to work: 28.0% less than 15 minutes, 12.9% 15 to 30 minutes, 36.6% 30 to 45 minutes, 3.2% 45 to 60 minutes, 19.4% 60 minutes or more (2000)

MILLERTON (city). Covers a land area of 0.209 square miles and a water area of 0 square miles. Located at 40.84° N. Lat.; 93.30° W. Long. Elevation is 1,072 feet.
History: Millerton was named for its founder George Miller.
Population: 48 (2000); Race: 100.0% White, 0.0% Black, 0.0% Asian, 0.0% American Indian and Alaska Native, 0.0% Hispanic of any race, 0.0% two or more races (2000); Density: 230.1 persons per square mile (2000); Age: 32.7% under 18, 21.2% over 64 (2000); Marriage status: 18.4% never married, 55.3% now married, 21.1% widowed, 5.3% divorced (2000); Foreign born: 0.0% (2000); Ancestry (includes multiple ancestries): 26.9% United States or American, 15.4% English, 3.8% Scottish, 3.8% Dutch, 1.9% Swedish (2000).
Economy: Employment by occupation: 15.8% management, 10.5% professional, 0.0% services, 26.3% sales, 0.0% farming, 21.1% construction, 26.3% production (2000).
Income: Per capita income: $10,650 (2000); Median household income: $19,286 (2000); Poverty rate: 0.0% (2000).
Taxes: Total city taxes per capita: $91 (1997); City property taxes per capita: $91 (1997).
Education: High school graduation rate: 79.4% (2000); College graduation rate: 0.0% (2000).
Housing: Homeownership rate: 76.0% (2000); Median home value: $29,500 (2000); Median age of housing: 60+ years (2000).
Transportation: Commute to work: 100.0% car, 0.0% public transportation, 0.0% walk, 0.0% work from home (2000); Travel time to work: 15.8% less than 15 minutes, 36.8% 15 to 30 minutes, 26.3% 30 to 45 minutes, 0.0% 45 to 60 minutes, 21.1% 60 minutes or more (2000)

PROMISE CITY (city). Covers a land area of 0.187 square miles and a water area of 0.002 square miles. Located at 40.74° N. Lat.; 93.14° W. Long. Elevation is 1,065 feet.
History: Promise City received its name from the Mormons who had a camp here.
Population: 105 (2000); Race: 100.0% White, 0.0% Black, 0.0% Asian, 0.0% American Indian and Alaska Native, 1.9% Hispanic of any race, 0.0% two or more races (2000); Density: 561.6 persons per square mile (2000); Age: 24.3% under 18, 28.2% over 64 (2000); Marriage status: 9.6% never married, 60.2% now married, 13.3% widowed, 16.9% divorced (2000); Foreign born: 0.0% (2000); Ancestry (includes multiple ancestries): 19.4% Irish, 15.5% German, 13.6% United States or American, 8.7% European, 5.8% Other groups (2000).
Economy: Employment by occupation: 9.8% management, 9.8% professional, 17.1% services, 19.5% sales, 0.0% farming, 9.8% construction, 34.1% production (2000).
Income: Per capita income: $10,637 (2000); Median household income: $17,917 (2000); Poverty rate: 19.8% (2000).
Taxes: Total city taxes per capita: $46 (1997); City property taxes per capita: $46 (1997).
Education: High school graduation rate: 70.7% (2000); College graduation rate: 2.7% (2000).
Housing: Homeownership rate: 92.2% (2000); Median home value: $22,900 (2000); Median rent: $375 per month (2000); Median age of housing: 60+ years (2000).
Transportation: Commute to work: 89.7% car, 0.0% public transportation, 10.3% walk, 0.0% work from home (2000); Travel time to work: 43.6% less than 15 minutes, 43.6% 15 to 30 minutes, 0.0% 30 to 45 minutes, 0.0% 45 to 60 minutes, 12.8% 60 minutes or more (2000)

SEYMOUR (city). Covers a land area of 2.351 square miles and a water area of 0.004 square miles. Located at 40.68° N. Lat.; 93.12° W. Long. Elevation is 1,074 feet.
History: Seymour is believed to be named after a railroad engineer.
Population: 810 (2000); Race: 95.0% White, 0.0% Black, 1.8% Asian, 0.0% American Indian and Alaska Native, 2.3% Hispanic of any race, 1.6% two or more races (2000); Density: 344.5 persons per square mile (2000); Age: 23.6% under 18, 26.4% over 64 (2000); Marriage status: 17.4% never married, 63.9% now married, 9.3% widowed, 9.5% divorced (2000); Foreign born: 2.7% (2000); Ancestry (includes multiple ancestries): 17.0% German, 16.0% English, 14.8% Irish, 9.2% Other groups, 8.7% United States or American (2000).
Economy: Single-family building permits issued: 0 (2001) / 0 (2000); Multi-family building permits issued: 0 (2001) / 0 (2000); Employment by occupation: 6.2% management, 12.4% professional, 18.5% services, 22.4% sales, 3.5% farming, 10.0% construction, 27.1% production (2000).
Income: Per capita income: $13,581 (2000); Median household income: $26,172 (2000); Poverty rate: 22.0% (2000).
Taxes: Total city taxes per capita: $136 (1997); City property taxes per capita: $133 (1997).
Education: High school graduation rate: 78.2% (2000); College graduation rate: 14.3% (2000).

School District(s)

Seymour Community School District (PK-12)
2000 Enrollment: 431 641-898-2291

Housing: Homeownership rate: 76.6% (2000); Median home value: $24,800 (2000); Median rent: $229 per month (2000); Median age of housing: 60+ years (2000).
Newspapers: Seymour Herald (1 x week)
Transportation: Commute to work: 90.5% car, 0.0% public transportation, 2.7% walk, 6.2% work from home (2000); Travel time to work: 36.1% less than 15 minutes, 35.1% 15 to 30 minutes, 14.9% 30 to 45 minutes, 7.6% 45 to 60 minutes, 6.3% 60 minutes or more (2000)

Webster County

Located in central Iowa; prairie area, drained by the Des Moines River. Covers a land area of 715.20 square miles, a water area of 2.80 square miles, and is located in the Central Time Zone. The county government was organized in 1853. County seat is Fort Dodge.

Weather Station: Fort Dodge Elevation: 1,112 feet

	Jan	Feb	Mar	Apr	May	Jun	Jul	Aug	Sep	Oct	Nov	Dec
High	26	32	45	60	72	82	85	82	75	62	44	30
Low	7	13	25	36	49	58	63	60	51	39	26	13
Precip	0.9	0.8	2.3	3.5	4.4	5.1	4.4	4.3	3.4	2.5	1.9	1.1
Snow	8.6	7.1	6.2	2.0	0.0	0.0	0.0	0.0	0.0	0.2	4.5	7.6

High and Low temperatures in degrees Fahrenheit; Precipitation and Snow in inches

Population: 40,235 (2000); Race: 93.6% White, 2.8% Black, 1.0% Asian, 0.3% American Indian and Alaska Native, 2.0% Hispanic of any race, 1.4% two or more races (2000); Density: 56.3 persons per square mile (2000); Age: 24.5% under 18, 17.4% over 64 (2000).
Religion: Five largest groups: 17.8% Catholic Church, 12.5% Evangelical Lutheran Church in America, 9.6% The United Methodist Church, 8.8% Lutheran Church—Missouri Synod, 2.6% Presbyterian Church (U.S.A.) (2000).
Economy: Unemployment rate: 3.5% (11/2002); Total civilian labor force: 22,331 (11/2002); Leading industries: 20.0% retail trade; 17.7% health care and social assistance; 13.5% manufacturing (2000); Companies that employ more than 1,000 persons: 0 (2000); Companies that employ more than 100 persons: 22 (2000); Farms: 937 totaling 412,641 acres (1997); Minority business ownership rate: 0.0% (1997); Women business ownership rate: 24.4% (1997); Retail sales per capita: $11,338 (1997). Single-family building permits issued: 71 (2001) / 72 (2000); Multi-family building permits issued: 18 (2001) / 10 (2000).
Income: Per capita income: $17,857 (2000); Median household income: $35,334 (2000); Poverty rate: 10.0% (2000); Bankruptcy rate: 4.20% (2001).
Taxes: Total county taxes per capita: $203 (2000); County property taxes per capita: $197 (2000).
Education: High school graduation rate: 84.2% (2000); College graduation rate: 16.9% (2000).
Housing: Homeownership rate: 71.2% (2000); Median home value: $66,000 (2000); Median rent: $325 per month (2000); Median age of housing: 49 years (2000).

Health: Birth rate: 127.5 per 10,000 population (1998); Age adjusted death rate: 89.1 per 10,000 population (1999); Age adjusted cancer mortality rate: 200.0 deaths per 100,000 population (1999). Number of physicians: 15.9 per 10,000 population (1999); Number of hospital beds: 37.5 per 10,000 population (1999).
Elections: 2000 Presidential election results: 49.7% Gore, 47.9% Bush, 1.7% Nader, 0.4% Buchanan
National and State Parks: Brushy Creek State Park; Dolliver Memorial State Park; Lizard Creek State Recreation Area; Woodmans Hollow State Park
Additional Information Contacts
Webster County Government Offices 515-573-7175
Fort Dodge Board of Realtors 515-576-5703
Fort Dodge Chamber of Commerce 515-955-5500
Fort Dodge Convention & Visitors Bureau 515-573-4282
Webster County Industrial Development 515-955-7788

Webster County Communities

BADGER (city). Covers a land area of 1.691 square miles and a water area of 0 square miles. Located at 42.61° N. Lat.; 94.14° W. Long. Elevation is 1,156 feet.
Population: 610 (2000); Race: 99.3% White, 0.0% Black, 0.4% Asian, 0.0% American Indian and Alaska Native, 0.7% Hispanic of any race, 0.3% two or more races (2000); Density: 360.7 persons per square mile (2000); Age: 37.9% under 18, 11.5% over 64 (2000); Marriage status: 21.1% never married, 66.3% now married, 6.2% widowed, 6.4% divorced (2000); Foreign born: 0.1% (2000); Ancestry (includes multiple ancestries): 30.4% German, 20.2% Norwegian, 13.1% United States or American, 8.6% Other groups, 7.2% Irish (2000).
Economy: Livestock, grain. Single-family building permits issued: 0 (2001) / 0 (2000); Multi-family building permits issued: 0 (2001) / 0 (2000); Employment by occupation: 9.5% management, 15.2% professional, 16.2% services, 26.7% sales, 0.0% farming, 10.5% construction, 21.9% production (2000).
Income: Per capita income: $15,573 (2000); Median household income: $41,250 (2000); Poverty rate: 7.8% (2000).
Taxes: Total city taxes per capita: $142 (1997); City property taxes per capita: $142 (1997).
Education: High school graduation rate: 81.5% (2000); College graduation rate: 10.5% (2000).
Housing: Homeownership rate: 79.5% (2000); Median home value: $72,500 (2000); Median rent: $238 per month (2000); Median age of housing: 35 years (2000).
Transportation: Commute to work: 93.9% car, 0.0% public transportation, 1.9% walk, 3.9% work from home (2000); Travel time to work: 28.9% less than 15 minutes, 59.1% 15 to 30 minutes, 3.0% 30 to 45 minutes, 2.0% 45 to 60 minutes, 7.0% 60 minutes or more (2000)

BARNUM (city). Covers a land area of 0.317 square miles and a water area of 0 square miles. Located at 42.50° N. Lat.; 94.36° W. Long.
History: Barnum was settled at the time of the construction of the Iowa Falls-Sioux City Railroad through the region.
Population: 195 (2000); Race: 100.0% White, 0.0% Black, 0.0% Asian, 0.0% American Indian and Alaska Native, 1.0% Hispanic of any race, 0.0% two or more races (2000); Density: 615.9 persons per square mile (2000); Age: 41.3% under 18, 3.6% over 64 (2000); Marriage status: 28.3% never married, 59.8% now married, 0.0% widowed, 11.8% divorced (2000); Foreign born: 0.0% (2000); Ancestry (includes multiple ancestries): 50.5% German, 20.9% Irish, 9.7% United States or American, 6.1% English, 4.1% Polish (2000).
Economy: Single-family building permits issued: 2 (2001) / 1 (2000); Multi-family building permits issued: 0 (2001) / 0 (2000); Employment by occupation: 6.9% management, 8.0% professional, 32.2% services, 11.5% sales, 2.3% farming, 6.9% construction, 32.2% production (2000).
Income: Per capita income: $12,252 (2000); Median household income: $40,000 (2000); Poverty rate: 9.7% (2000).
Taxes: Total city taxes per capita: $169 (1997); City property taxes per capita: $169 (1997).
Education: High school graduation rate: 82.9% (2000); College graduation rate: 11.4% (2000).
Housing: Homeownership rate: 80.3% (2000); Median home value: $49,600 (2000); Median rent: $225 per month (2000); Median age of housing: 33 years (2000).
Transportation: Commute to work: 95.3% car, 0.0% public transportation, 2.4% walk, 2.4% work from home (2000); Travel time to work: 19.3% less than 15 minutes, 57.8% 15 to 30 minutes, 10.8% 30 to 45 minutes, 9.6% 45 to 60 minutes, 2.4% 60 minutes or more (2000)

BURNSIDE (unincorporated postal area, zip code 50521). Covers a land area of 0.997 square miles and a water area of 0 square miles. Located at 42.34° N. Lat.; 94.10° W. Long. Elevation is 1,137 feet.
History: Burnside, originally called Hesperion, was renamed in 1882 when the railroad was extended through it. The new name honors General Ambrose E. Burnside, a Civil War leader in the Union Army, and was suggested by a railroad conductor who had served under Burnside.
Population: 96 (2000); Race: 96.8% White, 0.0% Black, 3.2% Asian, 0.0% American Indian and Alaska Native, 0.0% Hispanic of any race, 0.0% two or more races (2000); Density: 96.3 persons per square mile (2000); Age: 21.5% under 18, 38.7% over 64 (2000); Marriage status: 10.5% never married, 57.9% now married, 14.5% widowed, 17.1% divorced (2000); Foreign born: 5.4% (2000); Ancestry (includes multiple ancestries): 18.3% English, 18.3% German, 11.8% Swedish, 7.5% Irish, 7.5% Scottish (2000).
Economy: Employment by occupation: 16.0% management, 8.0% professional, 0.0% services, 40.0% sales, 0.0% farming, 12.0% construction, 24.0% production (2000).
Income: Per capita income: $22,251 (2000); Median household income: $35,893 (2000); Poverty rate: 15.1% (2000).
Education: High school graduation rate: 91.8% (2000); College graduation rate: 19.2% (2000).

School District(s)

Southeast Webster Community School District (PK-12)
2000 Enrollment: 585 515-359-2235
Housing: Homeownership rate: 80.4% (2000); Median home value: $52,000 (2000); Median rent: $163 per month (2000); Median age of housing: 43 years (2000).
Transportation: Commute to work: 100.0% car, 0.0% public transportation, 0.0% walk, 0.0% work from home (2000); Travel time to work: 0.0% less than 15 minutes, 64.0% 15 to 30 minutes, 16.0% 30 to 45 minutes, 16.0% 45 to 60 minutes, 4.0% 60 minutes or more (2000)

CALLENDER (city). Covers a land area of 0.510 square miles and a water area of 0 square miles. Located at 42.36° N. Lat.; 94.29° W. Long. Elevation is 1,151 feet.
History: Callender was founded by Agnes and James Callender. Though first called Kesho, the name of the town was changed to honor the Callenders.
Population: 424 (2000); Race: 98.3% White, 1.0% Black, 0.0% Asian, 0.2% American Indian and Alaska Native, 2.6% Hispanic of any race, 0.0% two or more races (2000); Density: 830.8 persons per square mile (2000); Age: 28.8% under 18, 18.1% over 64 (2000); Marriage status: 24.8% never married, 56.4% now married, 8.5% widowed, 10.3% divorced (2000); Foreign born: 0.0% (2000); Ancestry (includes multiple ancestries): 30.5% German, 19.8% Norwegian, 18.8% Irish, 10.2% English, 6.9% United States or American (2000).
Economy: Single-family building permits issued: 0 (2001) / 0 (2000); Multi-family building permits issued: 3 (2001) / 4 (2000); Employment by occupation: 8.9% management, 10.1% professional, 21.3% services, 28.4% sales, 5.3% farming, 12.4% construction, 13.6% production (2000).
Income: Per capita income: $14,411 (2000); Median household income: $33,906 (2000); Poverty rate: 11.0% (2000).
Taxes: Total city taxes per capita: $151 (1997); City property taxes per capita: $151 (1997).
Education: High school graduation rate: 85.8% (2000); College graduation rate: 9.1% (2000).
Housing: Homeownership rate: 69.6% (2000); Median home value: $50,000 (2000); Median rent: $228 per month (2000); Median age of housing: 57 years (2000).
Transportation: Commute to work: 91.4% car, 0.0% public transportation, 5.6% walk, 3.1% work from home (2000); Travel time to work: 31.2% less than 15 minutes, 47.1% 15 to 30 minutes, 13.4% 30 to 45 minutes, 3.2% 45 to 60 minutes, 5.1% 60 minutes or more (2000)

CLARE (city). Covers a land area of 0.507 square miles and a water area of 0 square miles. Located at 42.58° N. Lat.; 94.34° W. Long. Elevation is 1,194 feet.
History: The name of Clare, first used when the town was "christened," comes from Clare, Ireland.
Population: 190 (2000); Race: 98.4% White, 0.0% Black, 0.0% Asian, 0.0% American Indian and Alaska Native, 0.0% Hispanic of any race, 1.6% two or more races (2000); Density: 374.4 persons per square mile (2000); Age:

26.9% under 18, 19.2% over 64 (2000); Marriage status: 23.9% never married, 47.9% now married, 11.3% widowed, 16.9% divorced (2000); Foreign born: 0.0% (2000); Ancestry (includes multiple ancestries): 39.6% German, 17.6% Irish, 12.6% Swedish, 12.1% Norwegian, 8.8% Czech (2000).
Economy: Single-family building permits issued: 0 (2001) / 0 (2000); Multi-family building permits issued: 0 (2001) / 0 (2000); Employment by occupation: 3.8% management, 11.3% professional, 12.5% services, 40.0% sales, 5.0% farming, 7.5% construction, 20.0% production (2000).
Income: Per capita income: $13,838 (2000); Median household income: $24,500 (2000); Poverty rate: 6.0% (2000).
Taxes: Total city taxes per capita: $304 (1997); City property taxes per capita: $298 (1997).
Education: High school graduation rate: 73.9% (2000); College graduation rate: 6.1% (2000).
Housing: Homeownership rate: 83.1% (2000); Median home value: $61,300 (2000); Median rent: $300 per month (2000); Median age of housing: 48 years (2000).
Transportation: Commute to work: 85.0% car, 0.0% public transportation, 12.5% walk, 2.5% work from home (2000); Travel time to work: 33.3% less than 15 minutes, 53.8% 15 to 30 minutes, 10.3% 30 to 45 minutes, 2.6% 45 to 60 minutes, 0.0% 60 minutes or more (2000)

COALVILLE (CDP). Covers a land area of 2.162 square miles and a water area of <.001 square miles. Located at 42.44° N. Lat.; 94.12° W. Long.
Population: 591 (2000); Race: 100.0% White, 0.0% Black, 0.0% Asian, 0.0% American Indian and Alaska Native, 1.0% Hispanic of any race, 0.0% two or more races (2000); Density: 273.4 persons per square mile (2000); Age: 29.1% under 18, 14.6% over 64 (2000); Marriage status: 21.7% never married, 62.6% now married, 8.1% widowed, 7.6% divorced (2000); Foreign born: 2.1% (2000); Ancestry (includes multiple ancestries): 40.5% German, 20.9% Norwegian, 12.6% English, 8.1% Irish, 7.6% French (except Basque) (2000).
Economy: Employment by occupation: 1.9% management, 11.2% professional, 14.2% services, 30.7% sales, 0.0% farming, 22.7% construction, 19.3% production (2000).
Income: Per capita income: $17,178 (2000); Median household income: $43,750 (2000); Poverty rate: 2.6% (2000).
Education: High school graduation rate: 85.1% (2000); College graduation rate: 9.2% (2000).
Housing: Homeownership rate: 91.4% (2000); Median home value: $63,500 (2000); Median rent: $200 per month (2000); Median age of housing: 33 years (2000).
Transportation: Commute to work: 95.9% car, 0.0% public transportation, 2.2% walk, 1.9% work from home (2000); Travel time to work: 22.9% less than 15 minutes, 67.9% 15 to 30 minutes, 2.2% 30 to 45 minutes, 2.0% 45 to 60 minutes, 5.0% 60 minutes or more (2000)

DAYTON (city). Covers a land area of 0.832 square miles and a water area of 0 square miles. Located at 42.26° N. Lat.; 94.06° W. Long.
History: Dayton (originally called West Dayton) was established as a station at a railroad crossing, and was named after Dayton, Ohio.
Population: 884 (2000); Race: 97.1% White, 0.0% Black, 1.0% Asian, 0.3% American Indian and Alaska Native, 0.0% Hispanic of any race, 1.2% two or more races (2000); Density: 1,062.8 persons per square mile (2000); Age: 25.2% under 18, 26.8% over 64 (2000); Marriage status: 18.0% never married, 57.9% now married, 13.8% widowed, 10.4% divorced (2000); Foreign born: 1.3% (2000); Ancestry (includes multiple ancestries): 26.4% German, 16.2% Swedish, 10.4% Irish, 9.5% English, 9.4% Norwegian (2000).
Economy: Single-family building permits issued: 1 (2001) / 2 (2000); Multi-family building permits issued: 0 (2001) / 0 (2000); Employment by occupation: 15.1% management, 14.0% professional, 15.7% services, 24.9% sales, 1.7% farming, 11.8% construction, 16.8% production (2000).
Income: Per capita income: $15,714 (2000); Median household income: $33,864 (2000); Poverty rate: 11.5% (2000).
Taxes: Total city taxes per capita: $322 (1997); City property taxes per capita: $229 (1997).
Education: High school graduation rate: 82.6% (2000); College graduation rate: 8.4% (2000).
Housing: Homeownership rate: 78.0% (2000); Median home value: $49,400 (2000); Median rent: $195 per month (2000); Median age of housing: 54 years (2000).
Newspapers: Dayton Review (1 x week)
Transportation: Commute to work: 89.2% car, 0.0% public transportation, 7.3% walk, 3.2% work from home (2000); Travel time to work: 41.6% less than 15 minutes, 17.2% 15 to 30 minutes, 30.1% 30 to 45 minutes, 3.3% 45 to 60 minutes, 7.8% 60 minutes or more (2000)

DUNCOMBE (city). Covers a land area of 1.967 square miles and a water area of 0 square miles. Located at 42.47° N. Lat.; 93.99° W. Long. Elevation is 1,108 feet.
History: The land on which the town of Duncombe was situated was originally owned by John F. Duncombe, for whom the town was named.
Population: 474 (2000); Race: 94.6% White, 0.4% Black, 1.0% Asian, 1.4% American Indian and Alaska Native, 1.2% Hispanic of any race, 2.5% two or more races (2000); Density: 241.0 persons per square mile (2000); Age: 30.2% under 18, 13.9% over 64 (2000); Marriage status: 18.3% never married, 59.2% now married, 10.1% widowed, 12.4% divorced (2000); Foreign born: 1.7% (2000); Ancestry (includes multiple ancestries): 24.2% German, 16.8% Irish, 14.1% Norwegian, 7.5% Other groups, 6.4% Swedish (2000).
Economy: Single-family building permits issued: 1 (2001) / 0 (2000); Multi-family building permits issued: 0 (2001) / 0 (2000); Employment by occupation: 7.6% management, 7.1% professional, 17.3% services, 21.3% sales, 0.0% farming, 6.7% construction, 40.0% production (2000).
Income: Per capita income: $14,915 (2000); Median household income: $34,750 (2000); Poverty rate: 7.7% (2000).
Taxes: Total city taxes per capita: $224 (1997); City property taxes per capita: $219 (1997).
Education: High school graduation rate: 83.7% (2000); College graduation rate: 9.5% (2000).
Housing: Homeownership rate: 73.3% (2000); Median home value: $51,400 (2000); Median rent: $266 per month (2000); Median age of housing: 39 years (2000).
Transportation: Commute to work: 93.3% car, 0.9% public transportation, 4.5% walk, 1.3% work from home (2000); Travel time to work: 37.6% less than 15 minutes, 50.7% 15 to 30 minutes, 5.4% 30 to 45 minutes, 1.8% 45 to 60 minutes, 4.5% 60 minutes or more (2000)

FORT DODGE (city). Covers a land area of 14.562 square miles and a water area of 0.277 square miles. Located at 42.50° N. Lat.; 94.18° W. Long. Elevation is 1,011 feet.
History: In 1850, the Federal Government established a fort here known as Fort Clarke. Its name was changed in 1851 to Fort Dodge, in honor of U.S. Senator Henry Dodge of Wisconsin. The fort was abandoned in 1853. William Williams purchased the barracks and fort site in 1854, and laid out the town of Fort Dodge.
Population: 25,136 (2000); Race: 93.0% White, 3.2% Black, 1.0% Asian, 0.1% American Indian and Alaska Native, 2.6% Hispanic of any race, 1.3% two or more races (2000); Density: 1,726.1 persons per square mile (2000); Age: 24.3% under 18, 18.6% over 64 (2000); Marriage status: 26.1% never married, 52.1% now married, 10.7% widowed, 11.1% divorced (2000); Foreign born: 2.3% (2000); Ancestry (includes multiple ancestries): 32.4% German, 14.7% Irish, 9.6% Norwegian, 9.5% Other groups, 7.0% English (2000).
Vital Statistics: Birth rate: 150.8 per 10,000 population (1998)
Economy: Unemployment rate: 3.7% (11/2002); Total civilian labor force: 14,333 (11/2002); Single-family building permits issued: 34 (2001) / 30 (2000); Multi-family building permits issued: 15 (2001) / 6 (2000); Employment by occupation: 9.5% management, 18.8% professional, 17.7% services, 26.7% sales, 0.6% farming, 7.4% construction, 19.3% production (2000).
Income: Per capita income: $18,018 (2000); Median household income: $33,361 (2000); Poverty rate: 11.6% (2000).
Taxes: Total city taxes per capita: $375 (2000); City property taxes per capita: $353 (2000).
Education: High school graduation rate: 83.8% (2000); College graduation rate: 19.4% (2000).

School District(s)

Fort Dodge Community School District (KG-12)
2000 Enrollment: 4,208 515-576-1161

Two-year College(s)

Iowa Central Community College (Public)
2001 Enrollment: 4,567 515-576-7201
2001 Tuition: In-state $2,070; Out-of-state $3,105
La James College of Hairstyling and Cosmetology (Private, For-profit)
2001 Enrollment: 45 515-576-3119

Housing: Homeownership rate: 66.3% (2000); Median home value: $65,600 (2000); Median rent: $338 per month (2000); Median age of housing: 48 years (2000).
Hospitals: Trinity Regional Medical Center (200 beds)

Safety: Violent crime rate: 65.7 per 10,000 population; Property crime rate: 759.1 per 10,000 population (2001).
Newspapers: The Messenger (6 x week)
Transportation: Commute to work: 95.2% car, 0.6% public transportation, 2.1% walk, 1.4% work from home (2000); Travel time to work: 71.2% less than 15 minutes, 20.0% 15 to 30 minutes, 5.0% 30 to 45 minutes, 1.6% 45 to 60 minutes, 2.2% 60 minutes or more (2000)
Airports: Fort Dodge Regional (commercial service)
Additional Information Contacts
Fort Dodge Board of Realtors 515-576-5703
Fort Dodge Chamber of Commerce 515-955-5500
Fort Dodge Convention & Visitors Bureau 515-573-4282
Webster County Industrial Development 515-955-7788

GOWRIE (city). Covers a land area of 1.463 square miles and a water area of 0 square miles. Located at 42.28° N. Lat.; 94.29° W. Long. Elevation is 1,137 feet.
History: Gowrie is named after Gowrie, Scotland, by a railroad stockholder who had come from Scotland.
Population: 1,038 (2000); Race: 97.1% White, 0.0% Black, 0.0% Asian, 1.4% American Indian and Alaska Native, 0.8% Hispanic of any race, 1.2% two or more races (2000); Density: 709.4 persons per square mile (2000); Age: 25.6% under 18, 27.1% over 64 (2000); Marriage status: 19.7% never married, 58.5% now married, 14.0% widowed, 7.9% divorced (2000); Foreign born: 0.5% (2000); Ancestry (includes multiple ancestries): 32.5% German, 22.7% Swedish, 11.6% Irish, 8.8% Norwegian, 8.0% English (2000).
Economy: Single-family building permits issued: 5 (2001) / 11 (2000); Multi-family building permits issued: 0 (2001) / 0 (2000); Employment by occupation: 10.6% management, 19.1% professional, 16.8% services, 25.3% sales, 0.5% farming, 10.3% construction, 17.5% production (2000).
Income: Per capita income: $17,348 (2000); Median household income: $36,136 (2000); Poverty rate: 6.2% (2000).
Taxes: Total city taxes per capita: $209 (1997); City property taxes per capita: $207 (1997).
Education: High school graduation rate: 88.7% (2000); College graduation rate: 16.6% (2000).

School District(s)
Prairie Valley Community School District (PK-12)
2000 Enrollment: 855 515-352-3173
Housing: Homeownership rate: 75.3% (2000); Median home value: $62,600 (2000); Median rent: $238 per month (2000); Median age of housing: 55 years (2000).
Newspapers: The Gowrie News (1 x week)
Transportation: Commute to work: 93.2% car, 0.0% public transportation, 4.0% walk, 2.8% work from home (2000); Travel time to work: 45.7% less than 15 minutes, 17.9% 15 to 30 minutes, 28.0% 30 to 45 minutes, 3.9% 45 to 60 minutes, 4.6% 60 minutes or more (2000)

HARCOURT (city). Covers a land area of 0.574 square miles and a water area of 0 square miles. Located at 42.26° N. Lat.; 94.17° W. Long. Elevation is 1,174 feet.
History: Harcourt, platted in 1881, is said to be named for a British statesman of that name.
Population: 340 (2000); Race: 100.0% White, 0.0% Black, 0.0% Asian, 0.0% American Indian and Alaska Native, 1.8% Hispanic of any race, 0.0% two or more races (2000); Density: 592.5 persons per square mile (2000); Age: 23.3% under 18, 20.2% over 64 (2000); Marriage status: 22.6% never married, 54.4% now married, 17.4% widowed, 5.6% divorced (2000); Foreign born: 0.0% (2000); Ancestry (includes multiple ancestries): 24.8% German, 18.7% Swedish, 14.5% Irish, 13.6% Norwegian, 10.6% Other groups (2000).
Economy: Single-family building permits issued: 1 (2001) / 0 (2000); Multi-family building permits issued: 0 (2001) / 0 (2000); Employment by occupation: 5.3% management, 19.2% professional, 13.2% services, 33.1% sales, 1.3% farming, 10.6% construction, 17.2% production (2000).
Income: Per capita income: $22,461 (2000); Median household income: $37,212 (2000); Poverty rate: 3.3% (2000).
Taxes: Total city taxes per capita: $107 (1997); City property taxes per capita: $107 (1997).
Education: High school graduation rate: 92.1% (2000); College graduation rate: 14.0% (2000).
Housing: Homeownership rate: 70.5% (2000); Median home value: $38,900 (2000); Median rent: $185 per month (2000); Median age of housing: 54 years (2000).
Transportation: Commute to work: 91.3% car, 0.0% public transportation, 4.0% walk, 2.7% work from home (2000); Travel time to work: 31.7% less than 15 minutes, 40.7% 15 to 30 minutes, 18.6% 30 to 45 minutes, 3.4% 45 to 60 minutes, 5.5% 60 minutes or more (2000)

LEHIGH (city). Covers a land area of 2.077 square miles and a water area of 0.060 square miles. Located at 42.35° N. Lat.; 94.05° W. Long. Elevation is 956 feet.
History: Lehigh was settled in the early 1850's. It was originally known as Slabtown, because of the log slabs with which settlers built shacks along the river. In 1870 this name was abandoned for Tyson's Mill. Oliver Tyson was one of Lehigh's prominent settlers. Still later it was called Vesper, for a town in Pennsylvania, but this was changed to its present name, also in honor of a Pennsylvania town, the former home of a considerable number of the settlers.
Population: 497 (2000); Race: 98.0% White, 0.0% Black, 0.0% Asian, 0.0% American Indian and Alaska Native, 0.0% Hispanic of any race, 2.0% two or more races (2000); Density: 239.3 persons per square mile (2000); Age: 25.0% under 18, 20.6% over 64 (2000); Marriage status: 18.8% never married, 57.0% now married, 9.0% widowed, 15.1% divorced (2000); Foreign born: 0.0% (2000); Ancestry (includes multiple ancestries): 29.8% German, 14.9% Irish, 11.1% Norwegian, 10.3% Swedish, 6.9% English (2000).
Economy: Employment by occupation: 9.3% management, 10.6% professional, 12.3% services, 14.8% sales, 1.3% farming, 16.1% construction, 35.6% production (2000).
Income: Per capita income: $13,816 (2000); Median household income: $25,227 (2000); Poverty rate: 14.9% (2000).
Taxes: Total city taxes per capita: $126 (1997); City property taxes per capita: $122 (1997).
Education: High school graduation rate: 78.7% (2000); College graduation rate: 11.1% (2000).
Housing: Homeownership rate: 81.0% (2000); Median home value: $35,500 (2000); Median rent: $235 per month (2000); Median age of housing: 58 years (2000).
Transportation: Commute to work: 94.1% car, 0.0% public transportation, 1.7% walk, 3.4% work from home (2000); Travel time to work: 19.3% less than 15 minutes, 45.2% 15 to 30 minutes, 28.1% 30 to 45 minutes, 3.9% 45 to 60 minutes, 3.5% 60 minutes or more (2000)

MOORLAND (city). Covers a land area of 1.000 square miles and a water area of 0 square miles. Located at 42.44° N. Lat.; 94.29° W. Long. Elevation is 1,152 feet.
History: The name Moorland was chosen to reflect the local region's geography.
Population: 197 (2000); Race: 98.6% White, 0.0% Black, 0.0% Asian, 0.0% American Indian and Alaska Native, 7.6% Hispanic of any race, 0.0% two or more races (2000); Density: 197.1 persons per square mile (2000); Age: 31.3% under 18, 11.4% over 64 (2000); Marriage status: 19.5% never married, 64.3% now married, 7.1% widowed, 9.1% divorced (2000); Foreign born: 0.0% (2000); Ancestry (includes multiple ancestries): 36.5% German, 14.2% Irish, 12.8% Norwegian, 12.3% Swedish, 8.1% Other groups (2000).
Economy: Single-family building permits issued: 0 (2001) / 0 (2000); Multi-family building permits issued: 0 (2001) / 0 (2000); Employment by occupation: 9.0% management, 19.0% professional, 9.0% services, 22.0% sales, 0.0% farming, 10.0% construction, 31.0% production (2000).
Income: Per capita income: $16,051 (2000); Median household income: $43,750 (2000); Poverty rate: 6.6% (2000).
Taxes: Total city taxes per capita: $112 (1997); City property taxes per capita: $112 (1997).
Education: High school graduation rate: 84.4% (2000); College graduation rate: 14.1% (2000).
Housing: Homeownership rate: 96.1% (2000); Median home value: $50,000 (2000); Median age of housing: 60+ years (2000).
Transportation: Commute to work: 93.1% car, 0.0% public transportation, 1.0% walk, 4.0% work from home (2000); Travel time to work: 20.6% less than 15 minutes, 61.9% 15 to 30 minutes, 8.2% 30 to 45 minutes, 4.1% 45 to 60 minutes, 5.2% 60 minutes or more (2000)

OTHO (city). Covers a land area of 0.446 square miles and a water area of 0 square miles. Located at 42.42° N. Lat.; 94.15° W. Long. Elevation is 1,132 feet.
History: Otho was named for King Otho I of Germany.
Population: 571 (2000); Race: 96.7% White, 0.0% Black, 0.0% Asian, 0.9% American Indian and Alaska Native, 1.2% Hispanic of any race, 2.2% two or more races (2000); Density: 1,281.2 persons per square mile (2000); Age: 30.2% under 18, 13.5% over 64 (2000); Marriage status: 17.6% never

married, 58.6% now married, 9.0% widowed, 14.8% divorced (2000); Foreign born: 0.7% (2000); Ancestry (includes multiple ancestries): 36.1% German, 16.4% Irish, 13.1% United States or American, 9.0% English, 8.6% Other groups (2000).
Economy: Employment by occupation: 6.9% management, 13.0% professional, 18.8% services, 22.0% sales, 1.4% farming, 11.9% construction, 26.0% production (2000).
Income: Per capita income: $14,907 (2000); Median household income: $34,318 (2000); Poverty rate: 9.5% (2000).
Taxes: Total city taxes per capita: $79 (1997); City property taxes per capita: $77 (1997).
Education: High school graduation rate: 80.8% (2000); College graduation rate: 5.0% (2000).
Housing: Homeownership rate: 73.9% (2000); Median home value: $46,000 (2000); Median rent: $257 per month (2000); Median age of housing: 41 years (2000).
Transportation: Commute to work: 94.5% car, 0.0% public transportation, 1.1% walk, 2.9% work from home (2000); Travel time to work: 44.2% less than 15 minutes, 44.2% 15 to 30 minutes, 7.9% 30 to 45 minutes, 1.9% 45 to 60 minutes, 1.9% 60 minutes or more (2000)

VINCENT (city). Covers a land area of 0.223 square miles and a water area of 0 square miles. Located at 42.59° N. Lat.; 94.01° W. Long. Elevation is 1,139 feet.
History: The town of Vincent was named for Vincent Webb, a gypsum pioneer.
Population: 158 (2000); Race: 100.0% White, 0.0% Black, 0.0% Asian, 0.0% American Indian and Alaska Native, 0.0% Hispanic of any race, 0.0% two or more races (2000); Density: 708.5 persons per square mile (2000); Age: 27.6% under 18, 12.4% over 64 (2000); Marriage status: 18.9% never married, 67.6% now married, 9.9% widowed, 3.6% divorced (2000); Foreign born: 0.0% (2000); Ancestry (includes multiple ancestries): 51.7% German, 22.1% Norwegian, 16.6% Irish, 13.1% Swedish, 5.5% Dutch (2000).
Economy: Single-family building permits issued: 0 (2001) / 0 (2000); Multi-family building permits issued: 0 (2001) / 0 (2000); Employment by occupation: 14.1% management, 7.8% professional, 21.9% services, 12.5% sales, 0.0% farming, 12.5% construction, 31.3% production (2000).
Income: Per capita income: $16,341 (2000); Median household income: $32,500 (2000); Poverty rate: 6.2% (2000).
Taxes: Total city taxes per capita: $306 (1997); City property taxes per capita: $306 (1997).
Education: High school graduation rate: 83.2% (2000); College graduation rate: 6.9% (2000).
Housing: Homeownership rate: 90.8% (2000); Median home value: $49,200 (2000); Median rent: $225 per month (2000); Median age of housing: 43 years (2000).
Transportation: Commute to work: 92.4% car, 0.0% public transportation, 6.1% walk, 1.5% work from home (2000); Travel time to work: 23.1% less than 15 minutes, 58.5% 15 to 30 minutes, 12.3% 30 to 45 minutes, 0.0% 45 to 60 minutes, 6.2% 60 minutes or more (2000)

Winnebago County

Located in northern Iowa; prairie area, bounded on the north by Minnesota. Covers a land area of 400.50 square miles, a water area of 1.10 square miles, and is located in the Central Time Zone. The county government was organized in 1847. County seat is Forest City.

Weather Station: Forest City 2 NNE Elevation: 1,299 feet

	Jan	Feb	Mar	Apr	May	Jun	Jul	Aug	Sep	Oct	Nov	Dec
High	23	29	42	58	71	80	83	80	73	61	41	28
Low	4	11	24	36	48	58	62	59	50	38	24	12
Precip	0.9	0.7	2.0	3.3	3.8	4.6	4.3	4.5	3.0	2.4	1.6	1.0
Snow	10.6	6.3	6.0	2.2	tr	0.0	0.0	0.0	0.0	0.2	4.8	8.9

High and Low temperatures in degrees Fahrenheit; Precipitation and Snow in inches

Population: 11,723 (2000); Race: 97.6% White, 0.1% Black, 0.3% Asian, 0.2% American Indian and Alaska Native, 2.3% Hispanic of any race, 0.5% two or more races (2000); Density: 29.3 persons per square mile (2000); Age: 23.9% under 18, 18.9% over 64 (2000).
Religion: Five largest groups: 52.4% Evangelical Lutheran Church in America, 11.9% The United Methodist Church, 9.9% Catholic Church, 3.3% Reformed Church in America, 3.2% Baptist General Conference (2000).
Economy: Unemployment rate: 2.8% (11/2002); Total civilian labor force: 6,679 (11/2002); Leading industries: 59.2% manufacturing; 7.2% health care and social assistance; 7.0% retail trade (2000); Companies that employ more than 1,000 persons: 1 (2000); Companies that employ more than 100 persons: 10 (2000); Farms: 607 totaling 241,600 acres (1997); Minority business ownership rate: 0.0% (1997); Women business ownership rate: 9.7% (1997); Retail sales per capita: $6,767 (1997). Single-family building permits issued: 9 (2001) / 16 (2000); Multi-family building permits issued: 0 (2001) / 16 (2000).
Income: Per capita income: $18,494 (2000); Median household income: $38,381 (2000); Poverty rate: 8.4% (2000); Bankruptcy rate: 2.98% (2001).
Taxes: Total county taxes per capita: $214 (1997); County property taxes per capita: $205 (1997).
Education: High school graduation rate: 87.3% (2000); College graduation rate: 16.5% (2000).
Housing: Homeownership rate: 76.1% (2000); Median home value: $61,200 (2000); Median rent: $269 per month (2000); Median age of housing: 45 years (2000).
Health: Birth rate: 108.3 per 10,000 population (1998); Age adjusted death rate: 90.1 per 10,000 population (1999); Age adjusted cancer mortality rate: 258.7 deaths per 100,000 population (1999). Number of physicians: 2.6 per 10,000 population (1999); Number of hospital beds: n/a (1999).
Elections: 2000 Presidential election results: 48.7% Gore, 48.2% Bush, 2.1% Nader, 0.5% Buchanan
National and State Parks: Harmon Lake State Game Management Area; Myre Slough State Game Management Area; Rice Lake State Park
Additional Information Contacts
Winnebago County Government Offices 641-585-3412
Lake Mills Chamber of Commerce 641-592-5253

Winnebago County Communities

BUFFALO CENTER (city). Covers a land area of 1.095 square miles and a water area of 0 square miles. Located at 43.38° N. Lat.; 93.94° W. Long. Elevation is 1,183 feet.
History: The first consolidated school in the state was organized in Buffalo Center in 1896. The people were determined to better the educational opportunities of their children and took turns in conveying them to and from the schoolhouse.
Population: 963 (2000); Race: 98.2% White, 0.0% Black, 0.2% Asian, 0.0% American Indian and Alaska Native, 1.7% Hispanic of any race, 0.4% two or more races (2000); Density: 879.3 persons per square mile (2000); Age: 19.9% under 18, 38.3% over 64 (2000); Marriage status: 14.8% never married, 61.5% now married, 17.9% widowed, 5.8% divorced (2000); Foreign born: 1.3% (2000); Ancestry (includes multiple ancestries): 54.4% German, 22.2% Norwegian, 7.4% English, 6.5% Irish, 4.5% Dutch (2000).
Economy: Single-family building permits issued: 0 (2001) / 0 (2000); Multi-family building permits issued: 0 (2001) / 0 (2000); Employment by occupation: 7.7% management, 13.8% professional, 16.9% services, 26.2% sales, 1.0% farming, 8.7% construction, 25.6% production (2000).
Income: Per capita income: $17,944 (2000); Median household income: $30,694 (2000); Poverty rate: 9.0% (2000).
Taxes: Total city taxes per capita: $205 (1997); City property taxes per capita: $203 (1997).
Education: High school graduation rate: 78.6% (2000); College graduation rate: 11.3% (2000).

School District(s)

North Iowa Community School District (PK-12)
2000 Enrollment: 591 641-562-2921
Housing: Homeownership rate: 86.4% (2000); Median home value: $36,800 (2000); Median rent: $227 per month (2000); Median age of housing: 51 years (2000).
Newspapers: Tribune (1 x week)
Transportation: Commute to work: 85.2% car, 0.0% public transportation, 11.7% walk, 3.1% work from home (2000); Travel time to work: 60.2% less than 15 minutes, 12.6% 15 to 30 minutes, 18.7% 30 to 45 minutes, 4.5% 45 to 60 minutes, 4.0% 60 minutes or more (2000)

FOREST CITY (city). Covers a land area of 4.155 square miles and a water area of 0 square miles. Located at 43.26° N. Lat.; 93.64° W. Long. Elevation is 1,251 feet.
History: Forest City, platted in 1856, was named by an early settler, Judge Robert Clark, who appreciated the fine timberland near the site. Rudolph M. Anderson, Arctic explorer, spent his boyhood here.
Population: 4,362 (2000); Race: 95.8% White, 0.4% Black, 0.6% Asian, 0.3% American Indian and Alaska Native, 4.7% Hispanic of any race, 0.6% two or more races (2000); Density: 1,049.7 persons per square mile (2000); Age: 24.2% under 18, 14.4% over 64 (2000); Marriage status: 29.9% never

married, 54.7% now married, 5.9% widowed, 9.4% divorced (2000); Foreign born: 4.3% (2000); Ancestry (includes multiple ancestries): 39.4% German, 31.9% Norwegian, 8.2% Irish, 7.8% English, 6.0% Other groups (2000).
Economy: Single-family building permits issued: 4 (2001) / 7 (2000); Multi-family building permits issued: 0 (2001) / 16 (2000); Employment by occupation: 10.3% management, 16.0% professional, 16.8% services, 14.8% sales, 3.5% farming, 9.5% construction, 29.1% production (2000).
Income: Per capita income: $18,285 (2000); Median household income: $40,031 (2000); Poverty rate: 9.7% (2000).
Taxes: Total city taxes per capita: $253 (1997); City property taxes per capita: $252 (1997).
Education: High school graduation rate: 85.9% (2000); College graduation rate: 22.2% (2000).

School District(s)

Forest City Community School District (PK-12)
2000 Enrollment: 1,476 641-585-2323

Four-year College(s)

Waldorf College (Private, Not-for-profit, Evangelical Lutheran Church)
2001 Enrollment: 642 641-585-8130
2001 Tuition: In-state $13,708; Out-of-state $13,708
Housing: Homeownership rate: 71.9% (2000); Median home value: $65,800 (2000); Median rent: $296 per month (2000); Median age of housing: 38 years (2000).
Safety: Violent crime rate: 9.2 per 10,000 population; Property crime rate: 43.6 per 10,000 population (2001).
Newspapers: The Forest City Summit (1 x week)
Transportation: Commute to work: 87.3% car, 0.2% public transportation, 9.6% walk, 2.1% work from home (2000); Travel time to work: 82.0% less than 15 minutes, 9.6% 15 to 30 minutes, 5.0% 30 to 45 minutes, 1.5% 45 to 60 minutes, 1.9% 60 minutes or more (2000)
Airports: Forest City Municipal

LAKE MILLS (city). Covers a land area of 2.605 square miles and a water area of 0.014 square miles. Located at 43.41° N. Lat.; 93.53° W. Long.
History: Lake Mills, first known as Slauchville, later as Saylorville, received its present name when a mill was built nearby on the edge of a small lake.
Population: 2,140 (2000); Race: 98.7% White, 0.0% Black, 0.0% Asian, 0.4% American Indian and Alaska Native, 2.4% Hispanic of any race, 0.2% two or more races (2000); Density: 821.6 persons per square mile (2000); Age: 22.5% under 18, 23.2% over 64 (2000); Marriage status: 20.0% never married, 57.2% now married, 14.4% widowed, 8.3% divorced (2000); Foreign born: 1.6% (2000); Ancestry (includes multiple ancestries): 50.4% Norwegian, 34.9% German, 10.0% Irish, 4.2% Swedish, 3.5% Other groups (2000).
Economy: Single-family building permits issued: 2 (2001) / 8 (2000); Multi-family building permits issued: 0 (2001) / 0 (2000); Employment by occupation: 9.2% management, 14.0% professional, 11.4% services, 20.7% sales, 0.2% farming, 8.5% construction, 36.0% production (2000).
Income: Per capita income: $19,155 (2000); Median household income: $33,723 (2000); Poverty rate: 8.9% (2000).
Taxes: Total city taxes per capita: $296 (1997); City property taxes per capita: $293 (1997).
Education: High school graduation rate: 87.5% (2000); College graduation rate: 12.9% (2000).

School District(s)

Lake Mills Community School District (PK-12)
2000 Enrollment: 741 641-592-0881
Housing: Homeownership rate: 68.6% (2000); Median home value: $73,900 (2000); Median rent: $271 per month (2000); Median age of housing: 37 years (2000).
Newspapers: Lake Mills Graphic (1 x week)
Transportation: Commute to work: 91.9% car, 0.0% public transportation, 5.6% walk, 2.1% work from home (2000); Travel time to work: 71.2% less than 15 minutes, 18.6% 15 to 30 minutes, 7.2% 30 to 45 minutes, 2.2% 45 to 60 minutes, 0.8% 60 minutes or more (2000)
Additional Information Contacts
Lake Mills Chamber of Commerce 641-592-5253

LELAND (city). Covers a land area of 1.534 square miles and a water area of 0.026 square miles. Located at 43.33° N. Lat.; 93.63° W. Long. Elevation is 1,217 feet.
History: Leland was named in 1882 for the town's first postmaster, J. D. Leland.
Population: 258 (2000); Race: 97.2% White, 0.0% Black, 1.2% Asian, 1.6% American Indian and Alaska Native, 3.6% Hispanic of any race, 0.0% two or more races (2000); Density: 168.2 persons per square mile (2000); Age: 24.3% under 18, 8.8% over 64 (2000); Marriage status: 23.7% never married, 60.1% now married, 7.6% widowed, 8.6% divorced (2000); Foreign born: 1.2% (2000); Ancestry (includes multiple ancestries): 42.2% German, 35.9% Norwegian, 12.0% Irish, 10.0% English, 8.8% Other groups (2000).
Economy: Single-family building permits issued: 2 (2001) / 0 (2000); Multi-family building permits issued: 0 (2001) / 0 (2000); Employment by occupation: 5.6% management, 1.4% professional, 21.1% services, 18.3% sales, 0.0% farming, 12.7% construction, 40.8% production (2000).
Income: Per capita income: $16,175 (2000); Median household income: $35,000 (2000); Poverty rate: 7.2% (2000).
Taxes: Total city taxes per capita: $86 (1997); City property taxes per capita: $86 (1997).
Education: High school graduation rate: 90.5% (2000); College graduation rate: 1.8% (2000).
Housing: Homeownership rate: 75.2% (2000); Median home value: $52,600 (2000); Median rent: $313 per month (2000); Median age of housing: 44 years (2000).
Transportation: Commute to work: 90.1% car, 0.0% public transportation, 4.2% walk, 4.9% work from home (2000); Travel time to work: 67.4% less than 15 minutes, 25.2% 15 to 30 minutes, 3.7% 30 to 45 minutes, 1.5% 45 to 60 minutes, 2.2% 60 minutes or more (2000)

RAKE (city). Covers a land area of 1.008 square miles and a water area of 0 square miles. Located at 43.48° N. Lat.; 93.91° W. Long.
History: Rake was named for early prominent citizen A. A. Rake.
Population: 227 (2000); Race: 94.4% White, 0.0% Black, 0.0% Asian, 0.0% American Indian and Alaska Native, 8.4% Hispanic of any race, 0.0% two or more races (2000); Density: 225.3 persons per square mile (2000); Age: 25.9% under 18, 24.3% over 64 (2000); Marriage status: 26.7% never married, 48.2% now married, 18.8% widowed, 6.3% divorced (2000); Foreign born: 2.0% (2000); Ancestry (includes multiple ancestries): 31.5% Norwegian, 30.7% German, 17.5% United States or American, 5.6% Other groups, 4.4% Irish (2000).
Economy: Single-family building permits issued: 0 (2001) / 0 (2000); Multi-family building permits issued: 0 (2001) / 0 (2000); Employment by occupation: 1.8% management, 3.6% professional, 10.7% services, 25.9% sales, 3.6% farming, 25.0% construction, 29.5% production (2000).
Income: Per capita income: $15,816 (2000); Median household income: $24,375 (2000); Poverty rate: 13.1% (2000).
Taxes: Total city taxes per capita: $171 (1997); City property taxes per capita: $171 (1997).
Education: High school graduation rate: 77.3% (2000); College graduation rate: 3.1% (2000).
Housing: Homeownership rate: 82.3% (2000); Median home value: $18,000 (2000); Median rent: $264 per month (2000); Median age of housing: 59 years (2000).
Transportation: Commute to work: 78.6% car, 1.8% public transportation, 15.2% walk, 4.5% work from home (2000); Travel time to work: 32.7% less than 15 minutes, 38.3% 15 to 30 minutes, 13.1% 30 to 45 minutes, 12.1% 45 to 60 minutes, 3.7% 60 minutes or more (2000)

SCARVILLE (city). Covers a land area of 0.097 square miles and a water area of 0 square miles. Located at 43.47° N. Lat.; 93.61° W. Long. Elevation is 1,250 feet.
History: Scarville was named for Ole Scar, who owned much of the land in this vicinity when the town was established.
Population: 97 (2000); Race: 100.0% White, 0.0% Black, 0.0% Asian, 0.0% American Indian and Alaska Native, 0.0% Hispanic of any race, 0.0% two or more races (2000); Density: 997.4 persons per square mile (2000); Age: 29.4% under 18, 14.7% over 64 (2000); Marriage status: 24.0% never married, 66.7% now married, 6.7% widowed, 2.7% divorced (2000); Foreign born: 0.0% (2000); Ancestry (includes multiple ancestries): 59.8% Norwegian, 39.2% German, 11.8% Irish, 10.8% Northern European, 4.9% Swedish (2000).
Economy: Employment by occupation: 15.9% management, 20.5% professional, 13.6% services, 13.6% sales, 0.0% farming, 0.0% construction, 36.4% production (2000).
Income: Per capita income: $18,949 (2000); Median household income: $40,139 (2000); Poverty rate: 6.9% (2000).
Taxes: Total city taxes per capita: $99 (1997); City property taxes per capita: $88 (1997).
Education: High school graduation rate: 82.5% (2000); College graduation rate: 7.9% (2000).
Housing: Homeownership rate: 94.6% (2000); Median home value: $28,000 (2000); Median age of housing: 60+ years (2000).

Transportation: Commute to work: 83.7% car, 0.0% public transportation, 11.6% walk, 4.7% work from home (2000); Travel time to work: 34.1% less than 15 minutes, 51.2% 15 to 30 minutes, 7.3% 30 to 45 minutes, 7.3% 45 to 60 minutes, 0.0% 60 minutes or more (2000)

THOMPSON (city). Covers a land area of 0.875 square miles and a water area of 0 square miles. Located at 43.37° N. Lat.; 93.77° W. Long. Elevation is 1,259 feet.
History: Thompson was founded in 1890.
Population: 596 (2000); Race: 98.4% White, 0.0% Black, 0.0% Asian, 0.0% American Indian and Alaska Native, 1.6% Hispanic of any race, 1.1% two or more races (2000); Density: 681.3 persons per square mile (2000); Age: 23.8% under 18, 22.5% over 64 (2000); Marriage status: 23.5% never married, 56.9% now married, 9.2% widowed, 10.4% divorced (2000); Foreign born: 0.2% (2000); Ancestry (includes multiple ancestries): 45.7% Norwegian, 38.9% German, 7.2% Irish, 6.3% Dutch, 5.3% English (2000).
Economy: Single-family building permits issued: 1 (2001) / 1 (2000); Multi-family building permits issued: 0 (2001) / 0 (2000); Employment by occupation: 5.3% management, 7.2% professional, 14.1% services, 21.9% sales, 1.3% farming, 8.1% construction, 42.2% production (2000).
Income: Per capita income: $18,919 (2000); Median household income: $32,868 (2000); Poverty rate: 9.6% (2000).
Taxes: Total city taxes per capita: $184 (1997); City property taxes per capita: $184 (1997).
Education: High school graduation rate: 84.8% (2000); College graduation rate: 11.1% (2000).
Housing: Homeownership rate: 76.9% (2000); Median home value: $34,600 (2000); Median rent: $189 per month (2000); Median age of housing: 51 years (2000).
Newspapers: The Thompson Courier and Rake Register (1 x week)
Transportation: Commute to work: 86.9% car, 0.0% public transportation, 8.0% walk, 5.1% work from home (2000); Travel time to work: 33.9% less than 15 minutes, 53.4% 15 to 30 minutes, 8.1% 30 to 45 minutes, 2.3% 45 to 60 minutes, 2.3% 60 minutes or more (2000)

Winneshiek County

Located in northeastern Iowa; bounded on the north by Minnesota; drained by the Upper Iowa and Turkey Rivers. Covers a land area of 689.60 square miles, a water area of 0.30 square miles, and is located in the Central Time Zone. The county government was organized in 1847. County seat is Decorah.

Weather Station: Decorah — Elevation: 859 feet

	Jan	Feb	Mar	Apr	May	Jun	Jul	Aug	Sep	Oct	Nov	Dec
High	24	30	43	58	71	80	83	81	73	61	43	29
Low	6	12	24	36	48	57	61	59	51	39	26	13
Precip	0.9	0.8	1.9	3.7	3.8	4.4	4.2	4.4	3.6	2.4	2.2	1.1
Snow	10.6	7.4	6.3	1.7	tr	0.0	0.0	0.0	0.0	0.2	4.6	8.6

High and Low temperatures in degrees Fahrenheit; Precipitation and Snow in inches

Population: 21,310 (2000); Race: 97.6% White, 0.7% Black, 0.9% Asian, 0.0% American Indian and Alaska Native, 0.8% Hispanic of any race, 0.6% two or more races (2000); Density: 30.9 persons per square mile (2000); Age: 22.7% under 18, 15.8% over 64 (2000).
Religion: Five largest groups: 45.0% Evangelical Lutheran Church in America, 39.7% Catholic Church, 4.1% The United Methodist Church, 1.0% Friends (Quakers), 0.7% Baptist General Conference (2000).
Economy: Unemployment rate: 3.7% (11/2002); Total civilian labor force: 12,570 (11/2002); Leading industries: 19.8% manufacturing; 14.0% health care and social assistance; 11.6% retail trade (2000); Companies that employ more than 1,000 persons: 1 (2000); Companies that employ more than 100 persons: 14 (2000); Farms: 1,450 totaling 360,778 acres (1997); Minority business ownership rate: 0.0% (1997); Women business ownership rate: 21.3% (1997); Retail sales per capita: $8,645 (1997). Single-family building permits issued: 69 (2001) / 60 (2000); Multi-family building permits issued: 12 (2001) / 20 (2000).
Income: Per capita income: $17,047 (2000); Median household income: $38,908 (2000); Poverty rate: 8.0% (2000); Bankruptcy rate: 0.76% (2001).
Taxes: Total county taxes per capita: $211 (2000); County property taxes per capita: $162 (2000).
Education: High school graduation rate: 84.1% (2000); College graduation rate: 20.5% (2000).
Housing: Homeownership rate: 73.6% (2000); Median home value: $86,000 (2000); Median rent: $310 per month (2000); Median age of housing: 52 years (2000).
Health: Birth rate: 97.6 per 10,000 population (1998); Age adjusted death rate: 67.8 per 10,000 population (1999); Age adjusted cancer mortality rate: 213.8 deaths per 100,000 population (1999). Number of physicians: 10.3 per 10,000 population (1999); Number of hospital beds: 38.9 per 10,000 population (1999).
Elections: 2000 Presidential election results: 46.1% Gore, 49.4% Bush, 3.6% Nader, 0.5% Buchanan
National and State Parks: Bluffton Fir Stand State Preserve; Cardinal Marsh State Wildlife Area; Cold Water Springs State Wildlife Area; Falcon Springs State Wildlife Area; Fort Atkinson State Preserve; Malanaphy Springs State Preserve; Saint James Lutheran Church State Preserve; Siewers Spring State Park
Additional Information Contacts
Winneshiek County Government Offices 563-382-5085
Decorah Chamber of Commerce 563-382-3990
Northeast Iowa Board of Realtors 563-532-3881

Winneshiek County Communities

CALMAR (city). Covers a land area of 1.051 square miles and a water area of 0 square miles. Located at 43.18° N. Lat.; 91.86° W. Long. Elevation is 1,262 feet.
History: Calmar, a town of Czech descent, was an important division point on the Chicago, Milwaukee & St. Paul Railroad.
Population: 1,058 (2000); Race: 99.6% White, 0.0% Black, 0.0% Asian, 0.4% American Indian and Alaska Native, 0.0% Hispanic of any race, 0.0% two or more races (2000); Density: 1,006.8 persons per square mile (2000); Age: 22.1% under 18, 15.4% over 64 (2000); Marriage status: 31.6% never married, 53.3% now married, 8.4% widowed, 6.8% divorced (2000); Foreign born: 0.9% (2000); Ancestry (includes multiple ancestries): 55.6% German, 20.0% Norwegian, 14.6% Czech, 10.9% Irish, 4.4% English (2000).
Economy: Single-family building permits issued: 3 (2001) / 2 (2000); Multi-family building permits issued: 0 (2001) / 12 (2000); Employment by occupation: 11.9% management, 17.5% professional, 12.6% services, 26.5% sales, 2.9% farming, 10.2% construction, 18.5% production (2000).
Income: Per capita income: $17,958 (2000); Median household income: $36,250 (2000); Poverty rate: 9.6% (2000).
Taxes: Total city taxes per capita: $218 (1997); City property taxes per capita: $151 (1997).
Education: High school graduation rate: 82.7% (2000); College graduation rate: 18.3% (2000).

School District(s)
South Winneshiek Community School District (PK-12)
2000 Enrollment: 707 319-562-3269
Two-year College(s)
Northeast Iowa Community College-Calmar (Public)
2001 Enrollment: 3,615 563-562-3263
2001 Tuition: In-state $2,496; Out-of-state $2,496

Housing: Homeownership rate: 69.7% (2000); Median home value: $67,800 (2000); Median rent: $317 per month (2000); Median age of housing: 50 years (2000).
Newspapers: Calmar Courier (1 x week); Calmar Courier Plus (1 x week)
Transportation: Commute to work: 89.4% car, 0.0% public transportation, 6.3% walk, 2.9% work from home (2000); Travel time to work: 41.2% less than 15 minutes, 46.3% 15 to 30 minutes, 7.7% 30 to 45 minutes, 2.1% 45 to 60 minutes, 2.6% 60 minutes or more (2000)

CASTALIA (city). Covers a land area of 0.720 square miles and a water area of 0 square miles. Located at 43.11° N. Lat.; 91.67° W. Long. Elevation is 1,240 feet.
History: Castalia lies on the route of the old Military Trail, between Fort Crawford, Wisconsin, and Fort Atkinson, Iowa. According to an old story, the village was known as Rattletrap owing to the loquacity of the wife of the first settler, Hamilton Campbell, who, it is believed, came here in 1848.
Population: 175 (2000); Race: 95.3% White, 0.0% Black, 0.0% Asian, 0.0% American Indian and Alaska Native, 4.7% Hispanic of any race, 0.0% two or more races (2000); Density: 243.0 persons per square mile (2000); Age: 16.0% under 18, 12.4% over 64 (2000); Marriage status: 22.9% never married, 53.5% now married, 4.9% widowed, 18.8% divorced (2000); Foreign born: 2.4% (2000); Ancestry (includes multiple ancestries): 46.2% German, 16.0% Norwegian, 15.4% English, 9.5% Irish, 8.3% Scotch-Irish (2000).
Economy: Employment by occupation: 14.7% management, 12.6% professional, 9.5% services, 22.1% sales, 4.2% farming, 10.5% construction, 26.3% production (2000).

Income: Per capita income: $17,228 (2000); Median household income: $30,417 (2000); Poverty rate: 15.4% (2000).
Taxes: Total city taxes per capita: $125 (1997); City property taxes per capita: $68 (1997).
Education: High school graduation rate: 80.2% (2000); College graduation rate: 14.5% (2000).
Housing: Homeownership rate: 74.1% (2000); Median home value: $39,600 (2000); Median rent: $233 per month (2000); Median age of housing: 60+ years (2000).
Transportation: Commute to work: 95.7% car, 0.0% public transportation, 4.3% walk, 0.0% work from home (2000); Travel time to work: 34.8% less than 15 minutes, 37.0% 15 to 30 minutes, 28.3% 30 to 45 minutes, 0.0% 45 to 60 minutes, 0.0% 60 minutes or more (2000)

DECORAH (city). Covers a land area of 6.405 square miles and a water area of 0.025 square miles. Located at 43.30° N. Lat.; 91.79° W. Long. Elevation is 862 feet.
History: Decorah was named for Chief Waukon Decorah, who aided the settlers during the Black Hawk War.
Population: 8,172 (2000); Race: 95.0% White, 1.7% Black, 2.0% Asian, 0.0% American Indian and Alaska Native, 1.4% Hispanic of any race, 1.0% two or more races (2000); Density: 1,275.9 persons per square mile (2000); Age: 14.1% under 18, 19.6% over 64 (2000); Marriage status: 43.3% never married, 43.7% now married, 8.1% widowed, 4.9% divorced (2000); Foreign born: 4.2% (2000); Ancestry (includes multiple ancestries): 37.9% German, 34.4% Norwegian, 10.4% Irish, 9.1% English, 5.4% Other groups (2000).
Economy: Single-family building permits issued: 15 (2001) / 21 (2000); Multi-family building permits issued: 8 (2001) / 8 (2000); Employment by occupation: 12.7% management, 26.3% professional, 20.5% services, 23.5% sales, 0.3% farming, 5.7% construction, 11.1% production (2000).
Income: Per capita income: $16,351 (2000); Median household income: $37,485 (2000); Poverty rate: 8.0% (2000).
Taxes: Total city taxes per capita: $349 (2000); City property taxes per capita: $252 (2000).
Education: High school graduation rate: 84.7% (2000); College graduation rate: 30.6% (2000).

School District(s)

Decorah Community School District (PK-12)
2000 Enrollment: 1,745 319-382-4208
North Winneshiek Community School District (PK-12)
2000 Enrollment: 354 319-735-5411

Four-year College(s)

Luther College (Private, Not-for-profit, Evangelical Lutheran Church)
2001 Enrollment: 2,575 319-387-2000
2001 Tuition: In-state $19,325; Out-of-state $19,325

Housing: Homeownership rate: 63.8% (2000); Median home value: $96,000 (2000); Median rent: $353 per month (2000); Median age of housing: 45 years (2000).
Hospitals: Winneshiek County Memorial Hospital (83 beds)
Newspapers: Decorah Public Opinion (1 x week); Decorah Journal (2 x week)
Transportation: Commute to work: 65.5% car, 0.0% public transportation, 30.0% walk, 3.1% work from home (2000); Travel time to work: 79.9% less than 15 minutes, 11.9% 15 to 30 minutes, 3.4% 30 to 45 minutes, 1.1% 45 to 60 minutes, 3.8% 60 minutes or more (2000)
Airports: Decorah Municipal
Additional Information Contacts
Decorah Chamber of Commerce 563-382-3990

FORT ATKINSON (city). Covers a land area of 0.313 square miles and a water area of 0 square miles. Located at 43.14° N. Lat.; 91.93° W. Long. Elevation is 1,021 feet.
History: Fort Atkinson was initially inhabited largely by people of Czechoslovakian descent. The Fort was built by the Federal Government in 1840 to protect the Winnebago from the Sac and Fox and the Sioux.
Population: 389 (2000); Race: 99.5% White, 0.0% Black, 0.0% Asian, 0.5% American Indian and Alaska Native, 0.5% Hispanic of any race, 0.0% two or more races (2000); Density: 1,240.9 persons per square mile (2000); Age: 31.1% under 18, 18.1% over 64 (2000); Marriage status: 20.1% never married, 69.6% now married, 6.5% widowed, 3.8% divorced (2000); Foreign born: 0.8% (2000); Ancestry (includes multiple ancestries): 57.4% German, 21.7% Czech, 13.5% Norwegian, 6.1% Irish, 5.1% United States or American (2000).
Economy: Single-family building permits issued: 1 (2001) / 1 (2000); Multi-family building permits issued: 0 (2001) / 0 (2000); Employment by occupation: 3.9% management, 5.2% professional, 17.0% services, 24.2% sales, 3.3% farming, 16.3% construction, 30.1% production (2000).
Income: Per capita income: $14,702 (2000); Median household income: $34,205 (2000); Poverty rate: 12.7% (2000).
Taxes: Total city taxes per capita: $153 (1997); City property taxes per capita: $91 (1997).
Education: High school graduation rate: 78.1% (2000); College graduation rate: 8.7% (2000).
Housing: Homeownership rate: 85.2% (2000); Median home value: $70,300 (2000); Median rent: $267 per month (2000); Median age of housing: 41 years (2000).
Transportation: Commute to work: 85.0% car, 0.0% public transportation, 13.1% walk, 2.0% work from home (2000); Travel time to work: 51.3% less than 15 minutes, 29.3% 15 to 30 minutes, 12.0% 30 to 45 minutes, 0.0% 45 to 60 minutes, 7.3% 60 minutes or more (2000)

JACKSON JUNCTION (city). Covers a land area of 6.007 square miles and a water area of 0 square miles. Located at 43.10° N. Lat.; 92.04° W. Long. Elevation is 1,169 feet.
History: The Jack family, who were early settlers in this area, gave their name to Jackson Junction, a station on the Chicago, Milwaukee & St. Paul Railroad.
Population: 60 (2000); Race: 98.5% White, 0.0% Black, 1.5% Asian, 0.0% American Indian and Alaska Native, 0.0% Hispanic of any race, 0.0% two or more races (2000); Density: 10.0 persons per square mile (2000); Age: 32.4% under 18, 11.8% over 64 (2000); Marriage status: 32.0% never married, 54.0% now married, 4.0% widowed, 10.0% divorced (2000); Foreign born: 1.5% (2000); Ancestry (includes multiple ancestries): 38.2% German, 33.8% Czech, 19.1% Swedish, 16.2% Irish, 2.9% English (2000).
Economy: Employment by occupation: 39.0% management, 4.9% professional, 4.9% services, 7.3% sales, 14.6% farming, 17.1% construction, 12.2% production (2000).
Income: Per capita income: $15,825 (2000); Median household income: $31,875 (2000); Poverty rate: 4.4% (2000).
Taxes: Total city taxes per capita: $133 (1997); City property taxes per capita: $72 (1997).
Education: High school graduation rate: 88.4% (2000); College graduation rate: 2.3% (2000).
Housing: Homeownership rate: 75.0% (2000); Median home value: $101,800 (2000); Median rent: $175 per month (2000); Median age of housing: 55 years (2000).
Transportation: Commute to work: 68.3% car, 0.0% public transportation, 9.8% walk, 22.0% work from home (2000); Travel time to work: 56.3% less than 15 minutes, 18.8% 15 to 30 minutes, 25.0% 30 to 45 minutes, 0.0% 45 to 60 minutes, 0.0% 60 minutes or more (2000)

OSSIAN (city). Covers a land area of 1.095 square miles and a water area of 0 square miles. Located at 43.14° N. Lat.; 91.76° W. Long. Elevation is 1,271 feet.
History: Ossian was named for the Irish poet, Ossian, and for the town's first settler, John Ossian Porter, a native of Pennsylvania.
Population: 853 (2000); Race: 100.0% White, 0.0% Black, 0.0% Asian, 0.0% American Indian and Alaska Native, 0.2% Hispanic of any race, 0.0% two or more races (2000); Density: 778.7 persons per square mile (2000); Age: 26.8% under 18, 21.3% over 64 (2000); Marriage status: 16.6% never married, 62.4% now married, 15.6% widowed, 5.3% divorced (2000); Foreign born: 0.0% (2000); Ancestry (includes multiple ancestries): 73.1% German, 21.4% Norwegian, 7.5% Irish, 4.8% Czech, 4.2% French (except Basque) (2000).
Economy: Single-family building permits issued: 3 (2001) / 3 (2000); Multi-family building permits issued: 0 (2001) / 0 (2000); Employment by occupation: 13.2% management, 15.0% professional, 21.0% services, 23.8% sales, 1.8% farming, 9.0% construction, 16.2% production (2000).
Income: Per capita income: $16,490 (2000); Median household income: $38,214 (2000); Poverty rate: 5.8% (2000).
Taxes: Total city taxes per capita: $213 (1997); City property taxes per capita: $144 (1997).
Education: High school graduation rate: 77.7% (2000); College graduation rate: 10.7% (2000).
Housing: Homeownership rate: 79.6% (2000); Median home value: $68,300 (2000); Median rent: $301 per month (2000); Median age of housing: 56 years (2000).
Newspapers: Ossian Bee (1 x week)
Transportation: Commute to work: 82.7% car, 0.0% public transportation, 11.4% walk, 5.4% work from home (2000); Travel time to work: 50.1% less

than 15 minutes, 38.5% 15 to 30 minutes, 5.7% 30 to 45 minutes, 3.5% 45 to 60 minutes, 2.2% 60 minutes or more (2000)
Additional Information Contacts
Northeast Iowa Board of Realtors 563-532-3881

RIDGEWAY (city). Covers a land area of 1.061 square miles and a water area of 0 square miles. Located at 43.29° N. Lat.; 91.98° W. Long. Elevation is 1,209 feet.
Population: 293 (2000); Race: 99.3% White, 0.7% Black, 0.0% Asian, 0.0% American Indian and Alaska Native, 0.0% Hispanic of any race, 0.0% two or more races (2000); Density: 276.0 persons per square mile (2000); Age: 23.6% under 18, 17.5% over 64 (2000); Marriage status: 22.5% never married, 59.3% now married, 9.1% widowed, 9.1% divorced (2000); Foreign born: 0.0% (2000); Ancestry (includes multiple ancestries): 50.0% Norwegian, 46.2% German, 20.2% Irish, 11.6% Czech, 4.8% English (2000).
Economy: In agricultural area. Single-family building permits issued: 0 (2001) / 1 (2000); Multi-family building permits issued: 0 (2001) / 0 (2000); Employment by occupation: 3.0% management, 13.2% professional, 19.2% services, 24.6% sales, 4.8% farming, 15.6% construction, 19.8% production (2000).
Income: Per capita income: $15,206 (2000); Median household income: $33,750 (2000); Poverty rate: 8.2% (2000).
Taxes: Total city taxes per capita: $105 (1997); City property taxes per capita: $44 (1997).
Education: High school graduation rate: 85.9% (2000); College graduation rate: 12.0% (2000).
Housing: Homeownership rate: 78.0% (2000); Median home value: $55,800 (2000); Median rent: $213 per month (2000); Median age of housing: 59 years (2000).
Transportation: Commute to work: 92.8% car, 0.0% public transportation, 5.4% walk, 1.8% work from home (2000); Travel time to work: 39.0% less than 15 minutes, 54.9% 15 to 30 minutes, 3.7% 30 to 45 minutes, 0.0% 45 to 60 minutes, 2.4% 60 minutes or more (2000)

SPILLVILLE (city). Covers a land area of 0.419 square miles and a water area of 0.008 square miles. Located at 43.20° N. Lat.; 91.95° W. Long.
History: Spillville is where Antonin Dvorak, the Bohemian composer, spent the summer of 1893. Along the banks of the quiet Turkey River, Dvorak is said to have found inspiration for many beautiful melodies he used in his later works.
Population: 386 (2000); Race: 98.4% White, 0.0% Black, 0.0% Asian, 0.5% American Indian and Alaska Native, 1.1% Hispanic of any race, 0.5% two or more races (2000); Density: 920.8 persons per square mile (2000); Age: 24.5% under 18, 20.7% over 64 (2000); Marriage status: 17.9% never married, 67.5% now married, 8.6% widowed, 6.0% divorced (2000); Foreign born: 0.5% (2000); Ancestry (includes multiple ancestries): 56.6% German, 44.4% Czech, 11.4% Norwegian, 6.6% United States or American, 4.0% Irish (2000).
Economy: Single-family building permits issued: 2 (2001) / 1 (2000); Multi-family building permits issued: 4 (2001) / 0 (2000); Employment by occupation: 9.2% management, 15.4% professional, 11.8% services, 25.1% sales, 2.1% farming, 10.3% construction, 26.2% production (2000).
Income: Per capita income: $15,674 (2000); Median household income: $32,500 (2000); Poverty rate: 6.9% (2000).
Taxes: Total city taxes per capita: $156 (1997); City property taxes per capita: $93 (1997).
Education: High school graduation rate: 74.9% (2000); College graduation rate: 7.6% (2000).
Housing: Homeownership rate: 86.0% (2000); Median home value: $61,100 (2000); Median rent: $175 per month (2000); Median age of housing: 60+ years (2000).
Transportation: Commute to work: 90.3% car, 0.0% public transportation, 6.2% walk, 2.6% work from home (2000); Travel time to work: 31.6% less than 15 minutes, 54.2% 15 to 30 minutes, 9.5% 30 to 45 minutes, 0.0% 45 to 60 minutes, 4.7% 60 minutes or more (2000)

Woodbury County

Located in western Iowa; bounded partly on the west by the Big Sioux River and the South Dakota border, and partly by the Missouri River and the Nebraska border; drained by the Little Sioux River. Covers a land area of 872.60 square miles, a water area of 4.80 square miles, and is located in the Central Time Zone. The county government was organized in 1851. County seat is Sioux City.

Woodbury County is part of the Sioux City, IA-NE MSA. The entire metro area includes: Woodbury County, IA; Dakota County, NE

Weather Station: Sioux City Municipal Airport Elevation: 1,092 feet

	Jan	Feb	Mar	Apr	May	Jun	Jul	Aug	Sep	Oct	Nov	Dec
High	28	34	47	61	73	82	86	83	76	63	45	32
Low	9	16	26	38	50	59	64	62	52	39	26	14
Precip	0.6	0.6	2.0	2.8	3.7	3.5	3.3	2.9	2.6	2.1	1.4	0.7
Snow	6.3	5.5	6.3	1.7	tr	tr	tr	0.0	tr	1.0	4.3	5.9

High and Low temperatures in degrees Fahrenheit; Precipitation and Snow in inches

Population: 103,877 (2000); Race: 87.6% White, 2.0% Black, 2.3% Asian, 1.6% American Indian and Alaska Native, 9.0% Hispanic of any race, 1.9% two or more races (2000); Density: 119.0 persons per square mile (2000); Age: 27.3% under 18, 13.4% over 64 (2000).
Religion: Five largest groups: 20.7% Catholic Church, 8.9% Evangelical Lutheran Church in America, 8.0% The United Methodist Church, 5.1% Lutheran Church—Missouri Synod, 2.2% Presbyterian Church (U.S.A.) (2000).
Economy: Unemployment rate: 3.8% (11/2002); Total civilian labor force: 55,878 (11/2002); Leading industries: 16.0% retail trade; 15.8% health care and social assistance; 14.2% manufacturing (2000); Companies that employ more than 1,000 persons: 4 (2000); Companies that employ more than 100 persons: 74 (2000); Farms: 1,306 totaling 497,241 acres (1997); Minority business ownership rate: 2.8% (1997); Women business ownership rate: 30.0% (1997); Retail sales per capita: $11,226 (1997). Single-family building permits issued: 191 (2001) / 186 (2000); Multi-family building permits issued: 60 (2001) / 18 (2000).
Income: Per capita income: $18,771 (2000); Median household income: $38,509 (2000); Poverty rate: 10.3% (2000); Bankruptcy rate: 5.20% (2001).
Taxes: Total county taxes per capita: $164 (2000); County property taxes per capita: $147 (2000).
Education: High school graduation rate: 81.4% (2000); College graduation rate: 18.9% (2000).
Housing: Homeownership rate: 68.6% (2000); Median home value: $76,400 (2000); Median rent: $407 per month (2000); Median age of housing: 47 years (2000).
Health: Birth rate: 160.2 per 10,000 population (1998); Age adjusted death rate: 82.6 per 10,000 population (1999); Age adjusted cancer mortality rate: 201.2 deaths per 100,000 population (1999). Air Quality Index: 94% good, 6% moderate, 0% unhealthy (percent of days in 2000). Number of physicians: 21.1 per 10,000 population (1999); Number of hospital beds: 45.1 per 10,000 population (1999).
Elections: 2000 Presidential election results: 46.7% Gore, 49.8% Bush, 2.1% Nader, 1.1% Buchanan
National and State Parks: Bigelow State Park; Stone State Park
Additional Information Contacts
Woodbury County Government Offices 712-279-6525
Greater Sioux City Board of Realtors 712-255-8810
Siouxland Chamber of Commerce 712-255-7903

Woodbury County Communities

ANTHON (city). Covers a land area of 0.713 square miles and a water area of 0 square miles. Located at 42.38° N. Lat.; 95.86° W. Long. Elevation is 1,119 feet.
History: Anthon, incorporated in 1890, was named after J. C. Anthon, an engineer with the Illinois Central Railroad.
Population: 649 (2000); Race: 98.7% White, 0.0% Black, 0.3% Asian, 1.0% American Indian and Alaska Native, 1.6% Hispanic of any race, 0.0% two or more races (2000); Density: 909.7 persons per square mile (2000); Age: 23.5% under 18, 29.0% over 64 (2000); Marriage status: 23.1% never married, 54.3% now married, 12.2% widowed, 10.4% divorced (2000); Foreign born: 0.8% (2000); Ancestry (includes multiple ancestries): 41.9% German, 21.4% Irish, 7.2% United States or American, 6.7% English, 5.3% Other groups (2000).
Economy: Single-family building permits issued: 0 (2001) / 2 (2000); Multi-family building permits issued: 0 (2001) / 0 (2000); Employment by occupation: 3.9% management, 18.9% professional, 20.4% services, 31.4% sales, 0.0% farming, 11.8% construction, 13.6% production (2000).
Income: Per capita income: $19,228 (2000); Median household income: $26,364 (2000); Poverty rate: 6.9% (2000).
Taxes: Total city taxes per capita: $208 (1997); City property taxes per capita: $106 (1997).
Education: High school graduation rate: 78.3% (2000); College graduation rate: 13.8% (2000).

School District(s)

Anthon-Oto Community School District (KG-12)
2000 Enrollment: 350 712-373-5246

Housing: Homeownership rate: 83.5% (2000); Median home value: $49,000 (2000); Median rent: $263 per month (2000); Median age of housing: 60+ years (2000).

Newspapers: Anthon Herald (1 x week)

Transportation: Commute to work: 91.8% car, 0.7% public transportation, 5.3% walk, 2.1% work from home (2000); Travel time to work: 30.9% less than 15 minutes, 12.7% 15 to 30 minutes, 28.4% 30 to 45 minutes, 21.5% 45 to 60 minutes, 6.5% 60 minutes or more (2000)

BRONSON (city). Covers a land area of 0.326 square miles and a water area of 0 square miles. Located at 42.40° N. Lat.; 96.21° W. Long.

History: Bronson was established in 1901 by the Chicago & North Western Railroad, and named for Ira D. Bronson, an early resident.

Population: 269 (2000); Race: 99.3% White, 0.0% Black, 0.0% Asian, 0.0% American Indian and Alaska Native, 0.7% Hispanic of any race, 0.0% two or more races (2000); Density: 825.0 persons per square mile (2000); Age: 33.6% under 18, 4.0% over 64 (2000); Marriage status: 23.3% never married, 63.4% now married, 4.0% widowed, 9.4% divorced (2000); Foreign born: 0.7% (2000); Ancestry (includes multiple ancestries): 51.6% German, 10.1% English, 7.2% Irish, 5.8% Swedish, 4.7% Dutch (2000).

Economy: Single-family building permits issued: 0 (2001) / 3 (2000); Multi-family building permits issued: 0 (2001) / 0 (2000); Employment by occupation: 8.8% management, 9.4% professional, 17.5% services, 32.2% sales, 0.0% farming, 13.5% construction, 18.7% production (2000).

Income: Per capita income: $19,086 (2000); Median household income: $52,727 (2000); Poverty rate: 0.4% (2000).

Taxes: Total city taxes per capita: $191 (1997); City property taxes per capita: $100 (1997).

Education: High school graduation rate: 87.7% (2000); College graduation rate: 15.4% (2000).

Housing: Homeownership rate: 83.3% (2000); Median home value: $80,500 (2000); Median rent: $450 per month (2000); Median age of housing: 51 years (2000).

Transportation: Commute to work: 93.1% car, 0.0% public transportation, 4.6% walk, 2.3% work from home (2000); Travel time to work: 16.0% less than 15 minutes, 58.0% 15 to 30 minutes, 25.4% 30 to 45 minutes, 0.0% 45 to 60 minutes, 0.6% 60 minutes or more (2000)

CORRECTIONVILLE (city). Covers a land area of 0.573 square miles and a water area of 0 square miles. Located at 42.47° N. Lat.; 95.78° W. Long. Elevation is 1,129 feet.

History: Correctionville was so named by surveyors because the town lies on a "correction line" established for verification and correction of land surveying.

Population: 851 (2000); Race: 99.0% White, 0.0% Black, 0.0% Asian, 0.2% American Indian and Alaska Native, 3.8% Hispanic of any race, 0.7% two or more races (2000); Density: 1,484.5 persons per square mile (2000); Age: 25.0% under 18, 26.7% over 64 (2000); Marriage status: 18.5% never married, 55.2% now married, 16.2% widowed, 10.1% divorced (2000); Foreign born: 1.1% (2000); Ancestry (includes multiple ancestries): 40.9% German, 12.4% United States or American, 11.9% Irish, 11.0% English, 5.4% Other groups (2000).

Economy: Single-family building permits issued: 2 (2001) / 4 (2000); Multi-family building permits issued: 9 (2001) / 0 (2000); Employment by occupation: 13.8% management, 14.7% professional, 12.6% services, 24.0% sales, 0.0% farming, 19.5% construction, 15.6% production (2000).

Income: Per capita income: $16,074 (2000); Median household income: $24,615 (2000); Poverty rate: 17.4% (2000).

Taxes: Total city taxes per capita: $180 (1997); City property taxes per capita: $85 (1997).

Education: High school graduation rate: 75.5% (2000); College graduation rate: 9.8% (2000).

School District(s)

River Valley Community School District (PK-12)
2000 Enrollment: 526 712-372-4420

Housing: Homeownership rate: 78.8% (2000); Median home value: $50,800 (2000); Median rent: $243 per month (2000); Median age of housing: 57 years (2000).

Newspapers: Correctionville News (1 x week)

Transportation: Commute to work: 91.9% car, 0.0% public transportation, 3.9% walk, 2.7% work from home (2000); Travel time to work: 35.9% less than 15 minutes, 13.3% 15 to 30 minutes, 21.4% 30 to 45 minutes, 21.7% 45 to 60 minutes, 7.7% 60 minutes or more (2000)

CUSHING (city). Covers a land area of 0.319 square miles and a water area of 0 square miles. Located at 42.46° N. Lat.; 95.67° W. Long. Elevation is 1,327 feet.

History: First called Penrose, Cushing got its present name from the Blair Town Lot and Land Company, who named it after L. Cushing Kimball of Boston, Massachusetts.

Population: 246 (2000); Race: 100.0% White, 0.0% Black, 0.0% Asian, 0.0% American Indian and Alaska Native, 0.8% Hispanic of any race, 0.0% two or more races (2000); Density: 771.9 persons per square mile (2000); Age: 28.9% under 18, 15.8% over 64 (2000); Marriage status: 11.6% never married, 66.8% now married, 11.6% widowed, 10.0% divorced (2000); Foreign born: 0.0% (2000); Ancestry (includes multiple ancestries): 53.0% German, 11.9% Irish, 8.3% Norwegian, 6.3% United States or American, 5.5% Swedish (2000).

Economy: Single-family building permits issued: 0 (2001) / 0 (2000); Multi-family building permits issued: 0 (2001) / 0 (2000); Employment by occupation: 16.2% management, 14.0% professional, 15.4% services, 19.1% sales, 2.2% farming, 6.6% construction, 26.5% production (2000).

Income: Per capita income: $18,408 (2000); Median household income: $37,500 (2000); Poverty rate: 6.7% (2000).

Taxes: Total city taxes per capita: $176 (1997); City property taxes per capita: $80 (1997).

Education: High school graduation rate: 90.6% (2000); College graduation rate: 25.3% (2000).

Housing: Homeownership rate: 87.9% (2000); Median home value: $30,000 (2000); Median rent: $206 per month (2000); Median age of housing: 60+ years (2000).

Transportation: Commute to work: 93.3% car, 1.5% public transportation, 1.5% walk, 3.7% work from home (2000); Travel time to work: 30.2% less than 15 minutes, 34.9% 15 to 30 minutes, 8.5% 30 to 45 minutes, 21.7% 45 to 60 minutes, 4.7% 60 minutes or more (2000)

DANBURY (city). Covers a land area of 0.409 square miles and a water area of 0 square miles. Located at 42.23° N. Lat.; 95.72° W. Long. Elevation is 1,307 feet.

History: Danbury was established by Daniel Thomas, and named for him.

Population: 384 (2000); Race: 97.0% White, 0.0% Black, 2.5% Asian, 0.0% American Indian and Alaska Native, 0.0% Hispanic of any race, 0.5% two or more races (2000); Density: 938.8 persons per square mile (2000); Age: 21.0% under 18, 23.2% over 64 (2000); Marriage status: 12.1% never married, 63.4% now married, 15.8% widowed, 8.7% divorced (2000); Foreign born: 1.4% (2000); Ancestry (includes multiple ancestries): 40.6% German, 15.3% Irish, 12.8% United States or American, 6.5% Dutch, 6.0% English (2000).

Economy: Single-family building permits issued: 0 (2001) / 1 (2000); Multi-family building permits issued: 0 (2001) / 0 (2000); Employment by occupation: 20.4% management, 16.7% professional, 14.8% services, 22.2% sales, 1.2% farming, 5.6% construction, 19.1% production (2000).

Income: Per capita income: $21,801 (2000); Median household income: $33,409 (2000); Poverty rate: 9.3% (2000).

Taxes: Total city taxes per capita: $177 (1997); City property taxes per capita: $75 (1997).

Education: High school graduation rate: 81.4% (2000); College graduation rate: 11.3% (2000).

Housing: Homeownership rate: 88.5% (2000); Median home value: $43,500 (2000); Median rent: $200 per month (2000); Median age of housing: 58 years (2000).

Transportation: Commute to work: 91.1% car, 0.0% public transportation, 7.0% walk, 1.9% work from home (2000); Travel time to work: 46.8% less than 15 minutes, 11.7% 15 to 30 minutes, 12.3% 30 to 45 minutes, 6.5% 45 to 60 minutes, 22.7% 60 minutes or more (2000)

HORNICK (city). Covers a land area of 0.257 square miles and a water area of 0.005 square miles. Located at 42.23° N. Lat.; 96.09° W. Long. Elevation is 1,067 feet.

History: Hornick was established as a railroad town in 1887, and named for landowner John Hornick of Sioux City.

Population: 253 (2000); Race: 97.4% White, 0.7% Black, 0.0% Asian, 0.0% American Indian and Alaska Native, 0.0% Hispanic of any race, 1.9% two or more races (2000); Density: 984.4 persons per square mile (2000); Age: 29.4% under 18, 17.1% over 64 (2000); Marriage status: 23.8% never married, 55.9% now married, 10.9% widowed, 9.4% divorced (2000); Foreign born: 1.5% (2000); Ancestry (includes multiple ancestries): 43.1% German, 11.5% Irish, 9.3% English, 6.7% Norwegian, 5.6% United States or American (2000).

Economy: Single-family building permits issued: 0 (2001) / 0 (2000); Multi-family building permits issued: 0 (2001) / 0 (2000); Employment by occupation: 6.3% management, 18.3% professional, 20.4% services, 23.9% sales, 1.4% farming, 8.5% construction, 21.1% production (2000).
Income: Per capita income: $15,246 (2000); Median household income: $28,958 (2000); Poverty rate: 8.9% (2000).
Taxes: Total city taxes per capita: $195 (1997); City property taxes per capita: $100 (1997).
Education: High school graduation rate: 88.1% (2000); College graduation rate: 11.9% (2000).
Housing: Homeownership rate: 98.1% (2000); Median home value: $61,800 (2000); Median rent: $325 per month (2000); Median age of housing: 58 years (2000).
Transportation: Commute to work: 87.3% car, 0.0% public transportation, 7.0% walk, 4.9% work from home (2000); Travel time to work: 17.8% less than 15 minutes, 25.2% 15 to 30 minutes, 44.4% 30 to 45 minutes, 7.4% 45 to 60 minutes, 5.2% 60 minutes or more (2000)

LAWTON (city). Covers a land area of 0.508 square miles and a water area of 0 square miles. Located at 42.47° N. Lat.; 96.18° W. Long. Elevation is 1,179 feet.
History: Lawton was named for John Law, on whose farm the town was founded. In early days a settlement of Winebenarians, a religious sect that observed foot-washing as a ceremony, was established near the town.
Population: 697 (2000); Race: 98.8% White, 0.0% Black, 0.7% Asian, 0.0% American Indian and Alaska Native, 0.7% Hispanic of any race, 0.6% two or more races (2000); Density: 1,372.3 persons per square mile (2000); Age: 30.7% under 18, 11.2% over 64 (2000); Marriage status: 19.3% never married, 72.9% now married, 3.2% widowed, 4.5% divorced (2000); Foreign born: 1.4% (2000); Ancestry (includes multiple ancestries): 55.0% German, 14.5% Irish, 6.3% Swedish, 5.6% Dutch, 5.5% English (2000).
Economy: Single-family building permits issued: 3 (2001) / 2 (2000); Multi-family building permits issued: 0 (2001) / 0 (2000); Employment by occupation: 14.2% management, 21.4% professional, 6.9% services, 28.8% sales, 0.0% farming, 11.6% construction, 17.2% production (2000).
Income: Per capita income: $18,432 (2000); Median household income: $52,917 (2000); Poverty rate: 6.8% (2000).
Taxes: Total city taxes per capita: $217 (1997); City property taxes per capita: $130 (1997).
Education: High school graduation rate: 92.9% (2000); College graduation rate: 25.6% (2000).

School District(s)

Lawton-Bronson Community School District (PK-12)
2000 Enrollment: 630 712-944-5183
Housing: Homeownership rate: 87.0% (2000); Median home value: $103,800 (2000); Median rent: $400 per month (2000); Median age of housing: 33 years (2000).
Transportation: Commute to work: 94.2% car, 0.0% public transportation, 3.7% walk, 2.1% work from home (2000); Travel time to work: 21.8% less than 15 minutes, 63.9% 15 to 30 minutes, 12.9% 30 to 45 minutes, 0.5% 45 to 60 minutes, 0.8% 60 minutes or more (2000)

MOVILLE (city). Covers a land area of 0.887 square miles and a water area of 0 square miles. Located at 42.48° N. Lat.; 96.07° W. Long. Elevation is 1,180 feet.
History: Moville was named for Moville, Ireland, home town of the first postmaster. In 1890, the town's postmaster received the following dispatch from the U.S. Post Office Department: "Sir: Complaint has reached the Department that the mail carrier on route No. 27637, from Moville to Sioux City, Iowa frequently stops on lower Fourth Street for a glass of beer and a game of billiards, which causes him to fail to connect with the train at Moville. You will please see that this is corrected at once, and that the mails on this route are hereafter carried on schedule time."
Population: 1,583 (2000); Race: 99.0% White, 0.1% Black, 0.2% Asian, 0.0% American Indian and Alaska Native, 0.8% Hispanic of any race, 0.4% two or more races (2000); Density: 1,785.1 persons per square mile (2000); Age: 30.1% under 18, 15.5% over 64 (2000); Marriage status: 19.4% never married, 65.1% now married, 8.2% widowed, 7.3% divorced (2000); Foreign born: 0.8% (2000); Ancestry (includes multiple ancestries): 44.1% German, 16.3% Irish, 12.6% English, 5.5% United States or American, 4.9% Norwegian (2000).
Economy: Single-family building permits issued: 16 (2001) / 16 (2000); Multi-family building permits issued: 0 (2001) / 0 (2000); Employment by occupation: 11.5% management, 20.2% professional, 12.8% services, 28.4% sales, 0.6% farming, 9.1% construction, 17.3% production (2000).
Income: Per capita income: $19,578 (2000); Median household income: $42,222 (2000); Poverty rate: 7.1% (2000).
Taxes: Total city taxes per capita: $192 (1997); City property taxes per capita: $114 (1997).
Education: High school graduation rate: 91.1% (2000); College graduation rate: 19.0% (2000).

School District(s)

Woodbury Central Community School District (PK-12)
2000 Enrollment: 700 712-873-3128
Housing: Homeownership rate: 78.0% (2000); Median home value: $88,000 (2000); Median rent: $253 per month (2000); Median age of housing: 41 years (2000).
Newspapers: Moville Record (1 x week)
Transportation: Commute to work: 91.4% car, 0.7% public transportation, 4.7% walk, 2.9% work from home (2000); Travel time to work: 32.4% less than 15 minutes, 38.5% 15 to 30 minutes, 24.3% 30 to 45 minutes, 1.9% 45 to 60 minutes, 2.8% 60 minutes or more (2000)

OTO (city). Covers a land area of 0.262 square miles and a water area of 0 square miles. Located at 42.28° N. Lat.; 95.89° W. Long. Elevation is 1,095 feet.
History: Oto was founded in 1883.
Population: 145 (2000); Race: 100.0% White, 0.0% Black, 0.0% Asian, 0.0% American Indian and Alaska Native, 0.0% Hispanic of any race, 0.0% two or more races (2000); Density: 552.7 persons per square mile (2000); Age: 39.9% under 18, 12.6% over 64 (2000); Marriage status: 31.2% never married, 57.0% now married, 5.4% widowed, 6.5% divorced (2000); Foreign born: 2.1% (2000); Ancestry (includes multiple ancestries): 40.6% German, 28.7% Irish, 13.3% Canadian, 7.0% Dutch, 5.6% English (2000).
Economy: Employment by occupation: 0.0% management, 0.0% professional, 18.0% services, 8.0% sales, 0.0% farming, 30.0% construction, 44.0% production (2000).
Income: Per capita income: $9,237 (2000); Median household income: $22,857 (2000); Poverty rate: 21.3% (2000).
Education: High school graduation rate: 71.4% (2000); College graduation rate: 6.5% (2000).
Housing: Homeownership rate: 56.6% (2000); Median home value: $33,300 (2000); Median rent: $250 per month (2000); Median age of housing: 59 years (2000).
Transportation: Commute to work: 96.0% car, 0.0% public transportation, 4.0% walk, 0.0% work from home (2000); Travel time to work: 14.0% less than 15 minutes, 18.0% 15 to 30 minutes, 26.0% 30 to 45 minutes, 34.0% 45 to 60 minutes, 8.0% 60 minutes or more (2000)

PIERSON (city). Covers a land area of 0.490 square miles and a water area of 0 square miles. Located at 42.54° N. Lat.; 95.86° W. Long. Elevation is 1,268 feet.
History: Pierson may have been named in honor of an early settler, Andrew Pierson.
Population: 371 (2000); Race: 98.6% White, 0.0% Black, 0.0% Asian, 0.0% American Indian and Alaska Native, 0.6% Hispanic of any race, 1.1% two or more races (2000); Density: 757.3 persons per square mile (2000); Age: 27.7% under 18, 17.4% over 64 (2000); Marriage status: 19.4% never married, 63.1% now married, 9.3% widowed, 8.2% divorced (2000); Foreign born: 0.9% (2000); Ancestry (includes multiple ancestries): 45.4% German, 17.7% English, 8.9% Other groups, 7.7% Irish, 6.6% Danish (2000).
Economy: Single-family building permits issued: 0 (2001) / 1 (2000); Multi-family building permits issued: 0 (2001) / 0 (2000); Employment by occupation: 6.4% management, 17.0% professional, 14.0% services, 22.8% sales, 0.0% farming, 18.1% construction, 21.6% production (2000).
Income: Per capita income: $15,945 (2000); Median household income: $35,278 (2000); Poverty rate: 6.3% (2000).
Taxes: Total city taxes per capita: $235 (1997); City property taxes per capita: $131 (1997).
Education: High school graduation rate: 85.6% (2000); College graduation rate: 14.0% (2000).
Housing: Homeownership rate: 84.9% (2000); Median home value: $47,000 (2000); Median rent: $175 per month (2000); Median age of housing: 60+ years (2000).
Transportation: Commute to work: 88.6% car, 1.2% public transportation, 8.4% walk, 1.2% work from home (2000); Travel time to work: 24.8% less than 15 minutes, 4.2% 15 to 30 minutes, 44.8% 30 to 45 minutes, 21.8% 45 to 60 minutes, 4.2% 60 minutes or more (2000)

SALIX (city). Covers a land area of 0.667 square miles and a water area of 0.013 square miles. Located at 42.30° N. Lat.; 96.28° W. Long. Elevation is 1,083 feet.
History: Salix was incorporated in 1893. The town name was derived from the name of the willow trees in the area.
Population: 370 (2000); Race: 100.0% White, 0.0% Black, 0.0% Asian, 0.0% American Indian and Alaska Native, 0.0% Hispanic of any race, 0.0% two or more races (2000); Density: 554.4 persons per square mile (2000); Age: 26.5% under 18, 23.6% over 64 (2000); Marriage status: 15.9% never married, 60.0% now married, 8.1% widowed, 15.9% divorced (2000); Foreign born: 0.5% (2000); Ancestry (includes multiple ancestries): 28.1% German, 17.1% French (except Basque), 14.8% Irish, 8.6% United States or American, 6.5% Norwegian (2000).
Economy: Single-family building permits issued: 1 (2001) / 0 (2000); Multi-family building permits issued: 0 (2001) / 0 (2000); Employment by occupation: 10.1% management, 14.8% professional, 21.3% services, 18.3% sales, 0.0% farming, 14.2% construction, 21.3% production (2000).
Income: Per capita income: $15,242 (2000); Median household income: $27,396 (2000); Poverty rate: 9.4% (2000).
Taxes: Total city taxes per capita: $180 (1997); City property taxes per capita: $87 (1997).
Education: High school graduation rate: 83.4% (2000); College graduation rate: 10.3% (2000).
Housing: Homeownership rate: 79.4% (2000); Median home value: $62,800 (2000); Median rent: $316 per month (2000); Median age of housing: 50 years (2000).
Transportation: Commute to work: 93.9% car, 0.0% public transportation, 1.2% walk, 4.9% work from home (2000); Travel time to work: 27.7% less than 15 minutes, 54.2% 15 to 30 minutes, 7.7% 30 to 45 minutes, 9.7% 45 to 60 minutes, 0.6% 60 minutes or more (2000)

SERGEANT BLUFF (city). Covers a land area of 1.990 square miles and a water area of 0 square miles. Located at 42.40° N. Lat.; 96.35° W. Long. Elevation is 1,092 feet.
History: Sergeant Bluff was named in honor of a member of the Lewis and Clark party buried here below a high bluff.
Population: 3,321 (2000); Race: 92.9% White, 1.5% Black, 2.0% Asian, 1.7% American Indian and Alaska Native, 0.5% Hispanic of any race, 1.8% two or more races (2000); Density: 1,668.7 persons per square mile (2000); Age: 33.3% under 18, 6.9% over 64 (2000); Marriage status: 27.0% never married, 59.1% now married, 4.0% widowed, 9.9% divorced (2000); Foreign born: 1.7% (2000); Ancestry (includes multiple ancestries): 42.3% German, 14.3% Irish, 10.2% English, 8.2% Other groups, 5.9% United States or American (2000).
Economy: Single-family building permits issued: 50 (2001) / 32 (2000); Multi-family building permits issued: 0 (2001) / 0 (2000); Employment by occupation: 10.5% management, 19.0% professional, 15.9% services, 34.5% sales, 0.5% farming, 7.6% construction, 11.9% production (2000).
Income: Per capita income: $19,320 (2000); Median household income: $46,630 (2000); Poverty rate: 5.5% (2000).
Taxes: Total city taxes per capita: $247 (2000); City property taxes per capita: $149 (2000).
Education: High school graduation rate: 90.6% (2000); College graduation rate: 21.2% (2000).

School District(s)

Sergeant Bluff-Luton Community School District (PK-12)
2000 Enrollment: 1,269 712-943-4338
Housing: Homeownership rate: 71.0% (2000); Median home value: $122,400 (2000); Median rent: $516 per month (2000); Median age of housing: 28 years (2000).
Safety: Violent crime rate: 21.1 per 10,000 population; Property crime rate: 313.5 per 10,000 population (2001).
Newspapers: Sergeant Bluff Advocate (1 x week)
Transportation: Commute to work: 93.7% car, 0.2% public transportation, 2.6% walk, 3.1% work from home (2000); Travel time to work: 51.7% less than 15 minutes, 42.0% 15 to 30 minutes, 4.1% 30 to 45 minutes, 0.2% 45 to 60 minutes, 2.0% 60 minutes or more (2000)

SIOUX CITY (city). Covers a land area of 54.801 square miles and a water area of 1.147 square miles. Located at 42.49° N. Lat.; 96.39° W. Long. Elevation is 1,117 feet.
History: Sioux City, named after the Sioux Indians, was founded in 1854 by John K. Cooke.
Population: 85,013 (2000); Race: 85.5% White, 2.4% Black, 2.6% Asian, 1.9% American Indian and Alaska Native, 10.8% Hispanic of any race, 2.2% two or more races (2000); Density: 1,551.3 persons per square mile (2000); Age: 27.0% under 18, 13.3% over 64 (2000); Marriage status: 28.2% never married, 53.7% now married, 7.6% widowed, 10.5% divorced (2000); Foreign born: 8.6% (2000); Ancestry (includes multiple ancestries): 31.1% German, 18.7% Other groups, 14.9% Irish, 8.2% English, 6.4% Norwegian (2000).
Vital Statistics: Birth rate: 167.3 per 10,000 population (1998)
Economy: Unemployment rate: 4.2% (11/2002); Total civilian labor force: 46,049 (11/2002); Single-family building permits issued: 79 (2001) / 80 (2000); Multi-family building permits issued: 51 (2001) / 18 (2000); Employment by occupation: 9.6% management, 17.5% professional, 16.6% services, 27.2% sales, 0.3% farming, 8.3% construction, 20.5% production (2000).
Income: Per capita income: $18,666 (2000); Median household income: $37,429 (2000); Poverty rate: 11.2% (2000).
Taxes: Total city taxes per capita: $535 (2000); City property taxes per capita: $387 (2000).
Education: High school graduation rate: 79.7% (2000); College graduation rate: 19.0% (2000).

School District(s)

Sioux City Community School District (PK-12)
2000 Enrollment: 14,318 712-279-6667

Four-year College(s)

Briar Cliff College (Private, Not-for-profit, Roman Catholic)
2001 Enrollment: 969 712-279-5321
2001 Tuition: In-state $14,220; Out-of-state $14,220
Mercy Medical Center School of Medical Technology (Private, Not-for-profit, Roman Catholic)
2001 Enrollment: n/a 712-279-2371
Morningside College (Private, Not-for-profit, United Methodist)
2001 Enrollment: 996 712-274-5000
2001 Tuition: In-state $13,930; Out-of-state $13,930

Two-year College(s)

Saint Luke's College of Nursing and Health Sciences (Private, Not-for-profit, Other Protestant)
2001 Enrollment: 106 712-279-3149
2001 Tuition: In-state $4,612; Out-of-state $4,612
Western Iowa Tech Community College (Public)
2001 Enrollment: 4,920 712-274-6400
2001 Tuition: In-state $2,220; Out-of-state $3,990
Saint Luke's Regional Medical Center-School of Med Tec (Private, Not-for-profit, Other Protestant)
2001 Enrollment: n/a 712-279-3164
Housing: Homeownership rate: 66.3% (2000); Median home value: $74,800 (2000); Median rent: $412 per month (2000); Median age of housing: 47 years (2000).
Hospitals: Mercy Medical Center (483 beds); Saint Luke's Regional Medical Center (353 beds)
Safety: Violent crime rate: 61.8 per 10,000 population; Property crime rate: 585.6 per 10,000 population (2001).
Newspapers: The Globe (1 x week); Sioux City Journal (7 x week)
Transportation: Commute to work: 92.7% car, 1.2% public transportation, 2.9% walk, 2.2% work from home (2000); Travel time to work: 44.3% less than 15 minutes, 46.5% 15 to 30 minutes, 5.3% 30 to 45 minutes, 1.1% 45 to 60 minutes, 2.8% 60 minutes or more (2000)
Airports: Sioux Gateway/Col. Bud Day Field (primary service)
Additional Information Contacts
Greater Sioux City Board of Realtors 712-255-8810
Siouxland Chamber of Commerce 712-255-7903

SLOAN (city). Covers a land area of 0.465 square miles and a water area of 0 square miles. Located at 42.23° N. Lat.; 96.22° W. Long. Elevation is 176 feet.
History: Sloan was named for New York railroad executive Samuel Sloan.
Population: 1,032 (2000); Race: 95.5% White, 0.0% Black, 0.4% Asian, 1.1% American Indian and Alaska Native, 3.1% Hispanic of any race, 1.8% two or more races (2000); Density: 2,217.4 persons per square mile (2000); Age: 27.9% under 18, 16.5% over 64 (2000); Marriage status: 18.4% never married, 59.9% now married, 10.9% widowed, 10.8% divorced (2000); Foreign born: 1.5% (2000); Ancestry (includes multiple ancestries): 35.7% German, 17.2% Irish, 12.9% English, 10.3% Norwegian, 7.7% Swedish (2000).
Economy: Single-family building permits issued: 1 (2001) / 3 (2000); Multi-family building permits issued: 0 (2001) / 0 (2000); Employment by occupation: 12.3% management, 16.9% professional, 13.8% services, 31.5% sales, 0.8% farming, 9.5% construction, 15.2% production (2000).

Income: Per capita income: $17,310 (2000); Median household income: $38,026 (2000); Poverty rate: 6.6% (2000).
Taxes: Total city taxes per capita: $218 (1997); City property taxes per capita: $124 (1997).
Education: High school graduation rate: 94.0% (2000); College graduation rate: 18.3% (2000).

School District(s)

Westwood Community School District (PK-12)
2000 Enrollment: 742 712-428-3355
Housing: Homeownership rate: 72.4% (2000); Median home value: $82,200 (2000); Median rent: $305 per month (2000); Median age of housing: 30 years (2000).
Transportation: Commute to work: 93.1% car, 0.0% public transportation, 2.9% walk, 2.7% work from home (2000); Travel time to work: 31.4% less than 15 minutes, 40.8% 15 to 30 minutes, 23.3% 30 to 45 minutes, 1.1% 45 to 60 minutes, 3.4% 60 minutes or more (2000)

SMITHLAND (city). Covers a land area of 0.361 square miles and a water area of 0 square miles. Located at 42.22° N. Lat.; 95.93° W. Long. Elevation is 1,090 feet.
History: Smithland was first known as White's Settlement.
Population: 221 (2000); Race: 99.1% White, 0.0% Black, 0.0% Asian, 0.0% American Indian and Alaska Native, 0.0% Hispanic of any race, 0.9% two or more races (2000); Density: 613.0 persons per square mile (2000); Age: 19.5% under 18, 30.0% over 64 (2000); Marriage status: 12.9% never married, 68.0% now married, 7.3% widowed, 11.8% divorced (2000); Foreign born: 0.9% (2000); Ancestry (includes multiple ancestries): 43.2% German, 18.2% Irish, 11.4% English, 5.9% Danish, 4.1% Swedish (2000).
Economy: Employment by occupation: 9.1% management, 2.3% professional, 13.6% services, 31.8% sales, 1.1% farming, 28.4% construction, 13.6% production (2000).
Income: Per capita income: $14,722 (2000); Median household income: $31,406 (2000); Poverty rate: 6.4% (2000).
Taxes: Total city taxes per capita: $127 (1997); City property taxes per capita: $119 (1997).
Education: High school graduation rate: 70.1% (2000); College graduation rate: 3.9% (2000).
Housing: Homeownership rate: 89.0% (2000); Median home value: $42,100 (2000); Median rent: $200 per month (2000); Median age of housing: 48 years (2000).
Transportation: Commute to work: 87.2% car, 0.0% public transportation, 9.3% walk, 3.5% work from home (2000); Travel time to work: 16.9% less than 15 minutes, 30.1% 15 to 30 minutes, 28.9% 30 to 45 minutes, 21.7% 45 to 60 minutes, 2.4% 60 minutes or more (2000)

Worth County

Located in northern Iowa; prairie area, bounded on the north by Minnesota; drained by Shell Rock River. Covers a land area of 400.00 square miles, a water area of 1.70 square miles, and is located in the Central Time Zone. The county government was organized in 1851. County seat is Northwood.

Weather Station: Northwood Elevation: 1,187 feet

	Jan	Feb	Mar	Apr	May	Jun	Jul	Aug	Sep	Oct	Nov	Dec
High	22	29	41	57	71	80	83	81	73	60	41	27
Low	4	11	23	35	48	58	62	59	50	38	24	11
Precip	0.9	0.7	2.1	3.2	4.0	4.3	4.4	4.8	3.4	2.4	1.9	1.1
Snow	9.8	6.2	5.8	2.1	0.0	0.0	0.0	0.0	0.0	0.3	4.9	9.5

High and Low temperatures in degrees Fahrenheit; Precipitation and Snow in inches

Population: 7,909 (2000); Race: 97.5% White, 0.3% Black, 0.3% Asian, 0.3% American Indian and Alaska Native, 1.1% Hispanic of any race, 1.1% two or more races (2000); Density: 19.8 persons per square mile (2000); Age: 24.1% under 18, 19.4% over 64 (2000).
Religion: Five largest groups: 53.7% Evangelical Lutheran Church in America, 11.4% The United Methodist Church, 4.6% Catholic Church, 3.0% Christian Churches and Churches of Christ, 1.7% Southern Baptist Convention (2000).
Economy: Unemployment rate: 4.5% (11/2002); Total civilian labor force: 4,166 (11/2002); Leading industries: 32.8% manufacturing; 14.0% health care and social assistance; 13.6% retail trade (2000); Companies that employ more than 1,000 persons: 0 (2000); Companies that employ more than 100 persons: 3 (2000); Farms: 608 totaling 227,898 acres (1997); Minority business ownership rate: 0.0% (1997); Women business ownership rate: 0.0% (1997); Retail sales per capita: $3,701 (1997). Single-family building permits issued: 8 (2001) / 7 (2000); Multi-family building permits issued: 0 (2001) / 0 (2000).
Income: Per capita income: $16,952 (2000); Median household income: $36,444 (2000); Poverty rate: 8.3% (2000); Bankruptcy rate: 2.61% (2001).
Taxes: Total county taxes per capita: $291 (2000); County property taxes per capita: $290 (2000).
Education: High school graduation rate: 86.0% (2000); College graduation rate: 12.7% (2000).
Housing: Homeownership rate: 79.0% (2000); Median home value: $55,900 (2000); Median rent: $263 per month (2000); Median age of housing: 59 years (2000).
Health: Birth rate: 118.9 per 10,000 population (1998); Age adjusted death rate: 90.4 per 10,000 population (1999); Age adjusted cancer mortality rate: 182.6 deaths per 100,000 population (1999). Number of physicians: 2.5 per 10,000 population (1999); Number of hospital beds: n/a (1999).
Elections: 2000 Presidential election results: 55.1% Gore, 41.4% Bush, 2.3% Nader, 0.5% Buchanan
National and State Parks: Brights Lake State Game Management Area; Elk Creek Marsh State Game Management Area; Rice Lake State Game Management Area; Silver Lake State Game Management Area
Additional Information Contacts
Worth County Government Offices 641-324-2316

Worth County Communities

FERTILE (city). Covers a land area of 0.940 square miles and a water area of 0 square miles. Located at 43.26° N. Lat.; 93.42° W. Long. Elevation is 1,180 feet.
History: Fertile was founded in 1869 by William Rhodes.
Population: 360 (2000); Race: 95.5% White, 0.5% Black, 0.0% Asian, 0.8% American Indian and Alaska Native, 3.7% Hispanic of any race, 0.0% two or more races (2000); Density: 382.9 persons per square mile (2000); Age: 22.1% under 18, 20.5% over 64 (2000); Marriage status: 18.6% never married, 63.5% now married, 8.7% widowed, 9.3% divorced (2000); Foreign born: 0.0% (2000); Ancestry (includes multiple ancestries): 41.0% German, 35.9% Norwegian, 9.3% English, 4.5% Irish, 4.3% Other groups (2000).
Economy: Single-family building permits issued: 0 (2001) / 3 (2000); Multi-family building permits issued: 0 (2001) / 0 (2000); Employment by occupation: 5.9% management, 7.5% professional, 11.8% services, 31.6% sales, 1.6% farming, 15.0% construction, 26.7% production (2000).
Income: Per capita income: $14,464 (2000); Median household income: $33,558 (2000); Poverty rate: 9.3% (2000).
Taxes: Total city taxes per capita: $85 (1997); City property taxes per capita: $77 (1997).
Education: High school graduation rate: 82.0% (2000); College graduation rate: 9.4% (2000).
Housing: Homeownership rate: 87.4% (2000); Median home value: $48,800 (2000); Median rent: $256 per month (2000); Median age of housing: 52 years (2000).
Transportation: Commute to work: 94.1% car, 0.0% public transportation, 3.8% walk, 1.1% work from home (2000); Travel time to work: 17.9% less than 15 minutes, 57.6% 15 to 30 minutes, 17.4% 30 to 45 minutes, 1.1% 45 to 60 minutes, 6.0% 60 minutes or more (2000)

GRAFTON (city). Covers a land area of 0.324 square miles and a water area of 0 square miles. Located at 43.32° N. Lat.; 93.07° W. Long. Elevation is 1,130 feet.
History: Grafton was established in 1878 by the Chicago, Milwaukee & St. Paul Railroad.
Population: 290 (2000); Race: 97.3% White, 1.0% Black, 0.0% Asian, 0.0% American Indian and Alaska Native, 0.0% Hispanic of any race, 1.7% two or more races (2000); Density: 895.8 persons per square mile (2000); Age: 27.6% under 18, 22.1% over 64 (2000); Marriage status: 24.1% never married, 58.8% now married, 9.2% widowed, 7.9% divorced (2000); Foreign born: 0.7% (2000); Ancestry (includes multiple ancestries): 70.4% German, 15.0% Norwegian, 3.7% Russian, 3.7% Irish, 3.1% French (except Basque) (2000).
Economy: Employment by occupation: 13.2% management, 7.9% professional, 17.9% services, 23.2% sales, 0.0% farming, 19.2% construction, 18.5% production (2000).
Income: Per capita income: $14,201 (2000); Median household income: $28,594 (2000); Poverty rate: 5.8% (2000).
Taxes: Total city taxes per capita: $92 (1997); City property taxes per capita: $82 (1997).

Education: High school graduation rate: 84.3% (2000); College graduation rate: 11.2% (2000).
Housing: Homeownership rate: 76.4% (2000); Median home value: $42,100 (2000); Median rent: $225 per month (2000); Median age of housing: 60+ years (2000).
Transportation: Commute to work: 94.0% car, 0.0% public transportation, 3.3% walk, 2.6% work from home (2000); Travel time to work: 21.1% less than 15 minutes, 40.8% 15 to 30 minutes, 27.2% 30 to 45 minutes, 6.1% 45 to 60 minutes, 4.8% 60 minutes or more (2000)

HANLONTOWN (city). Covers a land area of 0.971 square miles and a water area of 0 square miles. Located at 43.28° N. Lat.; 93.37° W. Long.
History: Hanlontown carries the name of Frank James Hanlon, who owned the land on which the town was sited.
Population: 229 (2000); Race: 99.1% White, 0.0% Black, 0.9% Asian, 0.0% American Indian and Alaska Native, 2.3% Hispanic of any race, 0.0% two or more races (2000); Density: 235.9 persons per square mile (2000); Age: 25.9% under 18, 12.3% over 64 (2000); Marriage status: 11.4% never married, 76.5% now married, 9.0% widowed, 3.0% divorced (2000); Foreign born: 1.8% (2000); Ancestry (includes multiple ancestries): 47.7% Norwegian, 42.7% German, 8.6% English, 7.7% Dutch, 5.9% Other groups (2000).
Economy: Employment by occupation: 7.6% management, 9.3% professional, 11.9% services, 26.3% sales, 0.0% farming, 11.9% construction, 33.1% production (2000).
Income: Per capita income: $17,320 (2000); Median household income: $35,000 (2000); Poverty rate: 2.7% (2000).
Taxes: Total city taxes per capita: $109 (1997); City property taxes per capita: $99 (1997).
Education: High school graduation rate: 88.7% (2000); College graduation rate: 7.9% (2000).
Housing: Homeownership rate: 83.1% (2000); Median home value: $45,000 (2000); Median rent: $311 per month (2000); Median age of housing: 50 years (2000).
Transportation: Commute to work: 94.8% car, 0.0% public transportation, 3.4% walk, 0.0% work from home (2000); Travel time to work: 16.4% less than 15 minutes, 45.7% 15 to 30 minutes, 23.3% 30 to 45 minutes, 1.7% 45 to 60 minutes, 12.9% 60 minutes or more (2000)

JOICE (city). Covers a land area of 1.002 square miles and a water area of 0 square miles. Located at 43.36° N. Lat.; 93.45° W. Long. Elevation is 1,261 feet.
History: Joice was named for P.M. Joice, a banker who had invested in the town.
Population: 231 (2000); Race: 98.6% White, 0.0% Black, 0.0% Asian, 1.4% American Indian and Alaska Native, 0.0% Hispanic of any race, 0.0% two or more races (2000); Density: 230.5 persons per square mile (2000); Age: 23.9% under 18, 9.6% over 64 (2000); Marriage status: 15.5% never married, 59.6% now married, 6.8% widowed, 18.0% divorced (2000); Foreign born: 0.0% (2000); Ancestry (includes multiple ancestries): 48.3% Norwegian, 31.1% German, 11.0% Irish, 6.7% Dutch, 4.3% Swedish (2000).
Economy: Employment by occupation: 8.3% management, 12.5% professional, 11.7% services, 17.5% sales, 0.0% farming, 10.0% construction, 40.0% production (2000).
Income: Per capita income: $17,530 (2000); Median household income: $39,375 (2000); Poverty rate: 13.0% (2000).
Taxes: Total city taxes per capita: $119 (1997); City property taxes per capita: $111 (1997).
Education: High school graduation rate: 94.9% (2000); College graduation rate: 12.5% (2000).
Housing: Homeownership rate: 88.3% (2000); Median home value: $44,100 (2000); Median rent: $196 per month (2000); Median age of housing: 49 years (2000).
Transportation: Commute to work: 94.0% car, 0.0% public transportation, 2.6% walk, 3.4% work from home (2000); Travel time to work: 39.3% less than 15 minutes, 37.5% 15 to 30 minutes, 20.5% 30 to 45 minutes, 2.7% 45 to 60 minutes, 0.0% 60 minutes or more (2000)

KENSETT (city). Covers a land area of 1.526 square miles and a water area of 0 square miles. Located at 43.35° N. Lat.; 93.20° W. Long. Elevation is 1,225 feet.
History: Kensett was named for an official of the Iowa Central Railroad, Thomas Kensett.
Population: 280 (2000); Race: 100.0% White, 0.0% Black, 0.0% Asian, 0.0% American Indian and Alaska Native, 0.0% Hispanic of any race, 0.0% two or more races (2000); Density: 183.5 persons per square mile (2000); Age: 15.8% under 18, 18.4% over 64 (2000); Marriage status: 18.8% never married, 60.7% now married, 11.3% widowed, 9.2% divorced (2000); Foreign born: 0.0% (2000); Ancestry (includes multiple ancestries): 44.5% Norwegian, 33.8% German, 8.1% English, 8.1% Irish, 4.0% Dutch (2000).
Economy: Single-family building permits issued: 2 (2001) / 0 (2000); Multi-family building permits issued: 0 (2001) / 0 (2000); Employment by occupation: 7.1% management, 9.0% professional, 23.7% services, 17.9% sales, 1.3% farming, 4.5% construction, 36.5% production (2000).
Income: Per capita income: $15,601 (2000); Median household income: $30,500 (2000); Poverty rate: 17.2% (2000).
Taxes: Total city taxes per capita: $153 (1997); City property taxes per capita: $139 (1997).
Education: High school graduation rate: 78.2% (2000); College graduation rate: 11.4% (2000).
Housing: Homeownership rate: 91.3% (2000); Median home value: $40,500 (2000); Median rent: $181 per month (2000); Median age of housing: 60+ years (2000).
Transportation: Commute to work: 92.3% car, 0.0% public transportation, 5.1% walk, 2.6% work from home (2000); Travel time to work: 28.3% less than 15 minutes, 36.8% 15 to 30 minutes, 31.6% 30 to 45 minutes, 1.3% 45 to 60 minutes, 2.0% 60 minutes or more (2000)

MANLY (city). Covers a land area of 1.438 square miles and a water area of 0 square miles. Located at 43.28° N. Lat.; 93.20° W. Long. Elevation is 1,198 feet.
History: Manly was named for a freight agent of the Iowa Central Railroad, J. C. Manly.
Population: 1,342 (2000); Race: 95.4% White, 1.3% Black, 0.7% Asian, 0.7% American Indian and Alaska Native, 2.3% Hispanic of any race, 1.4% two or more races (2000); Density: 933.2 persons per square mile (2000); Age: 25.5% under 18, 19.1% over 64 (2000); Marriage status: 16.7% never married, 60.9% now married, 11.6% widowed, 10.9% divorced (2000); Foreign born: 2.1% (2000); Ancestry (includes multiple ancestries): 39.1% German, 20.4% Norwegian, 16.8% Irish, 9.1% English, 6.5% Other groups (2000).
Economy: Single-family building permits issued: 3 (2001) / 2 (2000); Multi-family building permits issued: 0 (2001) / 0 (2000); Employment by occupation: 8.4% management, 13.9% professional, 13.6% services, 27.9% sales, 0.7% farming, 11.3% construction, 24.2% production (2000).
Income: Per capita income: $15,808 (2000); Median household income: $33,603 (2000); Poverty rate: 7.9% (2000).
Taxes: Total city taxes per capita: $183 (1997); City property taxes per capita: $177 (1997).
Education: High school graduation rate: 85.8% (2000); College graduation rate: 16.1% (2000).

School District(s)

North Central Community School District (KG-12)
2000 Enrollment: 579 641-454-2211

Housing: Homeownership rate: 77.0% (2000); Median home value: $51,000 (2000); Median rent: $280 per month (2000); Median age of housing: 53 years (2000).
Newspapers: Manly Signal (1 x week)
Transportation: Commute to work: 91.3% car, 0.0% public transportation, 5.2% walk, 1.6% work from home (2000); Travel time to work: 27.3% less than 15 minutes, 53.6% 15 to 30 minutes, 13.6% 30 to 45 minutes, 2.3% 45 to 60 minutes, 3.2% 60 minutes or more (2000)

NORTHWOOD (city). Covers a land area of 3.781 square miles and a water area of 0 square miles. Located at 43.44° N. Lat.; 93.21° W. Long. Elevation is 1,222 feet.
History: Northwood was largely settled by Norwegians; the first arrival was Gilbrand Nellum in 1853.
Population: 2,050 (2000); Race: 96.1% White, 0.0% Black, 0.7% Asian, 0.0% American Indian and Alaska Native, 1.7% Hispanic of any race, 2.1% two or more races (2000); Density: 542.2 persons per square mile (2000); Age: 20.1% under 18, 26.5% over 64 (2000); Marriage status: 20.0% never married, 53.2% now married, 16.4% widowed, 10.5% divorced (2000); Foreign born: 2.0% (2000); Ancestry (includes multiple ancestries): 40.8% Norwegian, 35.9% German, 6.2% Danish, 5.8% Irish, 4.7% Other groups (2000).
Economy: Single-family building permits issued: 3 (2001) / 2 (2000); Multi-family building permits issued: 0 (2001) / 0 (2000); Employment by occupation: 10.2% management, 11.6% professional, 14.5% services, 25.4% sales, 0.9% farming, 10.6% construction, 26.7% production (2000).
Income: Per capita income: $18,167 (2000); Median household income: $33,030 (2000); Poverty rate: 7.9% (2000).

Taxes: Total city taxes per capita: $413 (1997); City property taxes per capita: $410 (1997).
Education: High school graduation rate: 83.1% (2000); College graduation rate: 14.4% (2000).

School District(s)

Northwood-Kensett Community School District (KG-12)
2000 Enrollment: 560 641-324-2021
Housing: Homeownership rate: 72.0% (2000); Median home value: $57,200 (2000); Median rent: $259 per month (2000); Median age of housing: 51 years (2000).
Newspapers: The Northwood Anchor (1 x week)
Transportation: Commute to work: 88.1% car, 1.4% public transportation, 5.3% walk, 3.7% work from home (2000); Travel time to work: 57.1% less than 15 minutes, 20.0% 15 to 30 minutes, 13.5% 30 to 45 minutes, 4.6% 45 to 60 minutes, 4.9% 60 minutes or more (2000)

Wright County

Located in north central Iowa; prairie area, drained by the Iowa and Boone Rivers. Covers a land area of 580.70 square miles, a water area of 1.80 square miles, and is located in the Central Time Zone. The county government was organized in 1851. County seat is Clarion.

Weather Station: Clarion Elevation: 1,187 feet

	Jan	Feb	Mar	Apr	May	Jun	Jul	Aug	Sep	Oct	Nov	Dec
High	23	30	42	58	71	80	83	81	74	61	43	28
Low	4	11	23	35	48	58	61	59	49	37	24	11
Precip	0.7	0.7	2.0	3.3	4.2	5.1	4.2	4.1	3.2	2.5	1.9	1.0
Snow	8.4	5.6	6.0	1.9	tr	0.0	0.0	0.0	tr	0.2	3.6	7.2

High and Low temperatures in degrees Fahrenheit; Precipitation and Snow in inches

Population: 14,334 (2000); Race: 95.7% White, 0.2% Black, 0.2% Asian, 0.2% American Indian and Alaska Native, 4.6% Hispanic of any race, 0.4% two or more races (2000); Density: 24.7 persons per square mile (2000); Age: 24.5% under 18, 21.1% over 64 (2000).
Religion: Five largest groups: 23.9% Evangelical Lutheran Church in America, 16.5% The United Methodist Church, 16.2% Catholic Church, 6.1% United Church of Christ, 3.0% Presbyterian Church (U.S.A.) (2000).
Economy: Unemployment rate: 3.5% (11/2002); Total civilian labor force: 7,193 (11/2002); Leading industries: 27.1% manufacturing; 14.4% health care and social assistance; 12.8% retail trade (2000); Companies that employ more than 1,000 persons: 0 (2000); Companies that employ more than 100 persons: 7 (2000); Farms: 717 totaling 349,675 acres (1997); Minority business ownership rate: 0.0% (1997); Women business ownership rate: 21.5% (1997); Retail sales per capita: $5,228 (1997). Single-family building permits issued: 17 (2001) / 12 (2000); Multi-family building permits issued: 8 (2001) / 0 (2000).
Income: Per capita income: $18,247 (2000); Median household income: $36,197 (2000); Poverty rate: 7.0% (2000); Bankruptcy rate: 3.81% (2001).
Taxes: Total county taxes per capita: $401 (2000); County property taxes per capita: $391 (2000).
Education: High school graduation rate: 84.4% (2000); College graduation rate: 13.5% (2000).
Housing: Homeownership rate: 74.1% (2000); Median home value: $52,500 (2000); Median rent: $283 per month (2000); Median age of housing: 50 years (2000).
Health: Birth rate: 104.0 per 10,000 population (1998); Age adjusted death rate: 79.0 per 10,000 population (1999); Age adjusted cancer mortality rate: 169.2 deaths per 100,000 population (1999). Number of physicians: 7.7 per 10,000 population (1999); Number of hospital beds: 32.8 per 10,000 population (1999).
Elections: 2000 Presidential election results: 44.1% Gore, 53.4% Bush, 1.7% Nader, 0.3% Buchanan
National and State Parks: Lake Cornelia State Game Management Area
Additional Information Contacts
Wright County Government Offices 515-532-3262
Belmond Chamber of Commerce 641-444-3937
Clarion Chamber of Commerce 515-532-2256
Eagle Grove Chamber of Commerce 515-448-4821

Wright County Communities

BELMOND (city). Covers a land area of 2.854 square miles and a water area of 0 square miles. Located at 42.84° N. Lat.; 93.61° W. Long. Elevation is 1,184 feet.
History: Belmond is the oldest town in Wright County. It was named by the young men and women of the settlement in honor of the attractive daughter, Belle, of Mr. and Mrs. Dumond, first settlers here (Belle and Dumond being combined).
Population: 2,560 (2000); Race: 94.2% White, 0.0% Black, 0.3% Asian, 0.9% American Indian and Alaska Native, 6.3% Hispanic of any race, 0.7% two or more races (2000); Density: 896.9 persons per square mile (2000); Age: 22.1% under 18, 24.4% over 64 (2000); Marriage status: 20.3% never married, 57.1% now married, 13.7% widowed, 8.8% divorced (2000); Foreign born: 5.3% (2000); Ancestry (includes multiple ancestries): 39.4% German, 21.1% Norwegian, 8.7% English, 7.9% Irish, 7.7% Other groups (2000).
Economy: Single-family building permits issued: 3 (2001) / 2 (2000); Multi-family building permits issued: 2 (2001) / 0 (2000); Employment by occupation: 11.2% management, 17.7% professional, 14.9% services, 17.0% sales, 3.3% farming, 8.5% construction, 27.3% production (2000).
Income: Per capita income: $17,317 (2000); Median household income: $32,841 (2000); Poverty rate: 5.7% (2000).
Taxes: Total city taxes per capita: $331 (1997); City property taxes per capita: $323 (1997).
Education: High school graduation rate: 82.3% (2000); College graduation rate: 12.5% (2000).

School District(s)

Belmond-Klemme Community School District (PK-12)
2000 Enrollment: 885 641-444-3930
Housing: Homeownership rate: 72.7% (2000); Median home value: $62,800 (2000); Median rent: $264 per month (2000); Median age of housing: 37 years (2000).
Hospitals: Belmond Medical Center (23 beds)
Newspapers: The Belmond Independent (1 x week)
Transportation: Commute to work: 90.2% car, 0.0% public transportation, 5.1% walk, 2.6% work from home (2000); Travel time to work: 65.7% less than 15 minutes, 17.9% 15 to 30 minutes, 8.7% 30 to 45 minutes, 2.2% 45 to 60 minutes, 5.5% 60 minutes or more (2000)
Additional Information Contacts
Belmond Chamber of Commerce 641-444-3937

CLARION (city). Covers a land area of 2.744 square miles and a water area of 0 square miles. Located at 42.73° N. Lat.; 93.73° W. Long. Elevation is 1,168 feet.
History: Clarion is the only county seat in Iowa that is in the exact center of the county. Incorporated in 1881, the town was named for Clarion, Pennsylvania.
Population: 2,968 (2000); Race: 92.3% White, 0.0% Black, 0.0% Asian, 0.0% American Indian and Alaska Native, 9.7% Hispanic of any race, 0.2% two or more races (2000); Density: 1,081.6 persons per square mile (2000); Age: 22.9% under 18, 22.7% over 64 (2000); Marriage status: 18.6% never married, 61.9% now married, 12.4% widowed, 7.1% divorced (2000); Foreign born: 6.6% (2000); Ancestry (includes multiple ancestries): 32.2% German, 13.2% Norwegian, 11.9% Other groups, 10.8% English, 8.6% United States or American (2000).
Economy: Single-family building permits issued: 8 (2001) / 2 (2000); Multi-family building permits issued: 0 (2001) / 0 (2000); Employment by occupation: 12.6% management, 15.9% professional, 15.6% services, 25.6% sales, 2.7% farming, 7.7% construction, 19.9% production (2000).
Income: Per capita income: $18,431 (2000); Median household income: $37,026 (2000); Poverty rate: 9.9% (2000).
Taxes: Total city taxes per capita: $300 (2000); City property taxes per capita: $293 (2000).
Education: High school graduation rate: 83.3% (2000); College graduation rate: 16.6% (2000).

School District(s)

Clarion-Goldfield Community School District (PK-12)
2000 Enrollment: 953 515-532-3423
Housing: Homeownership rate: 72.3% (2000); Median home value: $57,900 (2000); Median rent: $275 per month (2000); Median age of housing: 49 years (2000).
Hospitals: Wright Medical Center (25 beds)
Newspapers: Wright County Monitor (1 x week); Clarion Reminder (1 x week)
Transportation: Commute to work: 90.8% car, 0.3% public transportation, 4.7% walk, 3.9% work from home (2000); Travel time to work: 69.5% less than 15 minutes, 17.9% 15 to 30 minutes, 5.1% 30 to 45 minutes, 3.9% 45 to 60 minutes, 3.6% 60 minutes or more (2000)
Additional Information Contacts
Clarion Chamber of Commerce 515-532-2256

DOWS (city). Covers a land area of 0.778 square miles and a water area of 0.026 square miles. Located at 42.65° N. Lat.; 93.50° W. Long.
History: The settlement of Dows, platted in 1881, was originally called Otisville. It was later named after railroad contractor Stephen L. Dows of Cedar Rapids.
Population: 675 (2000); Race: 88.9% White, 2.2% Black, 2.2% Asian, 0.0% American Indian and Alaska Native, 10.8% Hispanic of any race, 0.0% two or more races (2000); Density: 867.3 persons per square mile (2000); Age: 17.5% under 18, 27.2% over 64 (2000); Marriage status: 26.1% never married, 48.6% now married, 18.2% widowed, 7.1% divorced (2000); Foreign born: 4.5% (2000); Ancestry (includes multiple ancestries): 43.7% German, 14.2% Other groups, 10.5% Norwegian, 9.0% English, 7.1% Irish (2000).
Economy: Single-family building permits issued: 0 (2001) / 0 (2000); Multi-family building permits issued: 0 (2001) / 0 (2000); Employment by occupation: 9.0% management, 12.5% professional, 21.9% services, 12.2% sales, 9.0% farming, 13.9% construction, 21.5% production (2000).
Income: Per capita income: $15,109 (2000); Median household income: $26,141 (2000); Poverty rate: 7.7% (2000).
Taxes: Total city taxes per capita: $184 (2000); City property taxes per capita: $164 (2000).
Education: High school graduation rate: 78.0% (2000); College graduation rate: 8.9% (2000).

School District(s)

Dows Community School District (KG-12)
2000 Enrollment: 171 515-852-4164

Housing: Homeownership rate: 77.5% (2000); Median home value: $31,100 (2000); Median rent: $259 per month (2000); Median age of housing: 57 years (2000).
Newspapers: The Dows Advocate (1 x week)
Transportation: Commute to work: 91.5% car, 0.0% public transportation, 3.9% walk, 2.1% work from home (2000); Travel time to work: 36.0% less than 15 minutes, 38.8% 15 to 30 minutes, 14.0% 30 to 45 minutes, 6.8% 45 to 60 minutes, 4.3% 60 minutes or more (2000)

EAGLE GROVE (city). Covers a land area of 3.965 square miles and a water area of 0 square miles. Located at 42.66° N. Lat.; 93.90° W. Long. Elevation is 1,115 feet.
History: Eagle Grove was first known either as Eagle Grove Junction or as Eagle Tree, for the eagle nests in the trees there. It was platted in 1881 by the Western Town Lot Company for the railroad. The name was changed to Eagle Grove by the postal authorities.
Population: 3,712 (2000); Race: 98.1% White, 0.4% Black, 0.2% Asian, 0.0% American Indian and Alaska Native, 1.2% Hispanic of any race, 0.1% two or more races (2000); Density: 936.1 persons per square mile (2000); Age: 25.7% under 18, 20.2% over 64 (2000); Marriage status: 19.1% never married, 58.8% now married, 11.9% widowed, 10.2% divorced (2000); Foreign born: 0.7% (2000); Ancestry (includes multiple ancestries): 34.2% German, 22.9% Norwegian, 13.3% Irish, 10.5% English, 6.3% French (except Basque) (2000).
Economy: Single-family building permits issued: 3 (2001) / 2 (2000); Multi-family building permits issued: 6 (2001) / 0 (2000); Employment by occupation: 9.3% management, 16.2% professional, 17.6% services, 18.7% sales, 0.0% farming, 10.5% construction, 27.7% production (2000).
Income: Per capita income: $20,563 (2000); Median household income: $35,505 (2000); Poverty rate: 5.7% (2000).
Taxes: Total city taxes per capita: $243 (1997); City property taxes per capita: $236 (1997).
Education: High school graduation rate: 82.8% (2000); College graduation rate: 14.4% (2000).

School District(s)

Eagle Grove Community School District (KG-12)
2000 Enrollment: 925 515-448-4749

Housing: Homeownership rate: 73.5% (2000); Median home value: $44,200 (2000); Median rent: $313 per month (2000); Median age of housing: 57 years (2000).
Safety: Violent crime rate: 10.8 per 10,000 population; Property crime rate: 169.9 per 10,000 population (2001).
Newspapers: Eagle Grove Eagle (1 x week); Wright County Shopper's Guide (1 x week)
Transportation: Commute to work: 88.3% car, 1.4% public transportation, 4.9% walk, 2.8% work from home (2000); Travel time to work: 62.9% less than 15 minutes, 22.0% 15 to 30 minutes, 9.7% 30 to 45 minutes, 1.7% 45 to 60 minutes, 3.7% 60 minutes or more (2000)
Additional Information Contacts
Eagle Grove Chamber of Commerce 515-448-4821

GALT (city). Covers a land area of 0.538 square miles and a water area of 0 square miles. Located at 42.69° N. Lat.; 93.60° W. Long. Elevation is 1,212 feet.
History: Galt, platted in 1881, was originally known as Norwich, and later as Galtville, probably after an early resident.
Population: 30 (2000); Race: 100.0% White, 0.0% Black, 0.0% Asian, 0.0% American Indian and Alaska Native, 0.0% Hispanic of any race, 0.0% two or more races (2000); Density: 55.8 persons per square mile (2000); Age: 10.7% under 18, 28.6% over 64 (2000); Marriage status: 10.7% never married, 82.1% now married, 7.1% widowed, 0.0% divorced (2000); Foreign born: 0.0% (2000); Ancestry (includes multiple ancestries): 53.6% English, 35.7% German, 21.4% Norwegian, 7.1% Danish, 3.6% United States or American (2000).
Economy: Employment by occupation: 29.2% management, 8.3% professional, 0.0% services, 12.5% sales, 12.5% farming, 8.3% construction, 29.2% production (2000).
Income: Per capita income: $15,668 (2000); Median household income: $30,625 (2000); Poverty rate: 0.0% (2000).
Taxes: Total city taxes per capita: $116 (1997); City property taxes per capita: $116 (1997).
Education: High school graduation rate: 76.0% (2000); College graduation rate: 0.0% (2000).
Housing: Homeownership rate: 100.0% (2000); Median home value: $34,400 (2000); Median age of housing: 47 years (2000).
Transportation: Commute to work: 83.3% car, 0.0% public transportation, 8.3% walk, 8.3% work from home (2000); Travel time to work: 54.5% less than 15 minutes, 45.5% 15 to 30 minutes, 0.0% 30 to 45 minutes, 0.0% 45 to 60 minutes, 0.0% 60 minutes or more (2000)

GOLDFIELD (city). Covers a land area of 1.021 square miles and a water area of 0 square miles. Located at 42.73° N. Lat.; 93.92° W. Long. Elevation is 1,130 feet.
History: Early residents wanted to name their town for Major Minter Brassfield, who had lived there in 1853, but they thought that "gold" would sound better than "brass," so chose the name of Goldfield.
Population: 680 (2000); Race: 100.0% White, 0.0% Black, 0.0% Asian, 0.0% American Indian and Alaska Native, 0.6% Hispanic of any race, 0.0% two or more races (2000); Density: 666.0 persons per square mile (2000); Age: 19.3% under 18, 28.7% over 64 (2000); Marriage status: 18.0% never married, 62.6% now married, 10.9% widowed, 8.6% divorced (2000); Foreign born: 0.0% (2000); Ancestry (includes multiple ancestries): 34.9% German, 22.7% Norwegian, 11.3% English, 10.1% Irish, 6.4% Scottish (2000).
Economy: Single-family building permits issued: 0 (2001) / 0 (2000); Multi-family building permits issued: 0 (2001) / 0 (2000); Employment by occupation: 12.1% management, 10.2% professional, 15.1% services, 23.3% sales, 0.7% farming, 7.9% construction, 30.8% production (2000).
Income: Per capita income: $16,983 (2000); Median household income: $32,411 (2000); Poverty rate: 7.2% (2000).
Taxes: Total city taxes per capita: $261 (1997); City property taxes per capita: $258 (1997).
Education: High school graduation rate: 87.4% (2000); College graduation rate: 7.6% (2000).
Housing: Homeownership rate: 83.8% (2000); Median home value: $38,300 (2000); Median rent: $272 per month (2000); Median age of housing: 47 years (2000).
Transportation: Commute to work: 87.6% car, 0.0% public transportation, 4.7% walk, 6.4% work from home (2000); Travel time to work: 56.8% less than 15 minutes, 27.9% 15 to 30 minutes, 9.6% 30 to 45 minutes, 2.1% 45 to 60 minutes, 3.6% 60 minutes or more (2000)

ROWAN (city). Covers a land area of 0.563 square miles and a water area of 0 square miles. Located at 42.74° N. Lat.; 93.55° W. Long. Elevation is 1,203 feet.
History: Rowan was named for an early family of the area, the Robert Rowen family. The variation in spelling was made to avoid confusion with another town called Bowen.
Population: 218 (2000); Race: 100.0% White, 0.0% Black, 0.0% Asian, 0.0% American Indian and Alaska Native, 0.0% Hispanic of any race, 0.0% two or more races (2000); Density: 387.4 persons per square mile (2000); Age: 25.1% under 18, 27.5% over 64 (2000); Marriage status: 6.3% never married, 66.9% now married, 15.6% widowed, 11.3% divorced (2000); Foreign born: 0.0% (2000); Ancestry (includes multiple ancestries): 23.7%

German, 10.1% United States or American, 9.2% English, 7.2% Welsh, 6.8% Irish (2000).
Economy: Employment by occupation: 5.8% management, 10.5% professional, 12.8% services, 17.4% sales, 2.3% farming, 11.6% construction, 39.5% production (2000).
Income: Per capita income: $13,077 (2000); Median household income: $25,000 (2000); Poverty rate: 6.3% (2000).
Taxes: Total city taxes per capita: $126 (1997); City property taxes per capita: $126 (1997).
Education: High school graduation rate: 91.4% (2000); College graduation rate: 4.6% (2000).
Housing: Homeownership rate: 84.9% (2000); Median home value: $25,300 (2000); Median rent: $264 per month (2000); Median age of housing: 60+ years (2000).
Transportation: Commute to work: 85.7% car, 0.0% public transportation, 6.0% walk, 6.0% work from home (2000); Travel time to work: 41.8% less than 15 minutes, 38.0% 15 to 30 minutes, 5.1% 30 to 45 minutes, 2.5% 45 to 60 minutes, 12.7% 60 minutes or more (2000)

WOOLSTOCK (city). Covers a land area of 1.032 square miles and a water area of 0 square miles. Located at 42.56° N. Lat.; 93.84° W. Long. Elevation is 1,090 feet.
History: Woolstock was platted in 1881 by the Western Town Lot Company. It may have been named for the large number of sheep grazing on the land that would become the town site.
Population: 204 (2000); Race: 95.2% White, 0.0% Black, 0.0% Asian, 0.0% American Indian and Alaska Native, 0.5% Hispanic of any race, 4.3% two or more races (2000); Density: 197.7 persons per square mile (2000); Age: 15.0% under 18, 21.3% over 64 (2000); Marriage status: 16.0% never married, 63.0% now married, 11.0% widowed, 9.9% divorced (2000); Foreign born: 0.5% (2000); Ancestry (includes multiple ancestries): 38.2% German, 18.4% Norwegian, 15.5% Irish, 15.5% French (except Basque), 5.8% United States or American (2000).
Economy: Employment by occupation: 9.3% management, 4.7% professional, 5.6% services, 18.7% sales, 1.9% farming, 7.5% construction, 52.3% production (2000).
Income: Per capita income: $20,599 (2000); Median household income: $34,479 (2000); Poverty rate: 4.9% (2000).
Taxes: Total city taxes per capita: $157 (1997); City property taxes per capita: $157 (1997).
Education: High school graduation rate: 79.0% (2000); College graduation rate: 1.9% (2000).
Housing: Homeownership rate: 83.8% (2000); Median home value: $40,500 (2000); Median rent: $194 per month (2000); Median age of housing: 54 years (2000).
Transportation: Commute to work: 100.0% car, 0.0% public transportation, 0.0% walk, 0.0% work from home (2000); Travel time to work: 42.5% less than 15 minutes, 50.9% 15 to 30 minutes, 2.8% 30 to 45 minutes, 1.9% 45 to 60 minutes, 1.9% 60 minutes or more (2000)

Michigan

The Wolverine State

MICHIGAN –Metropolitan Areas, Counties, and Central Cities

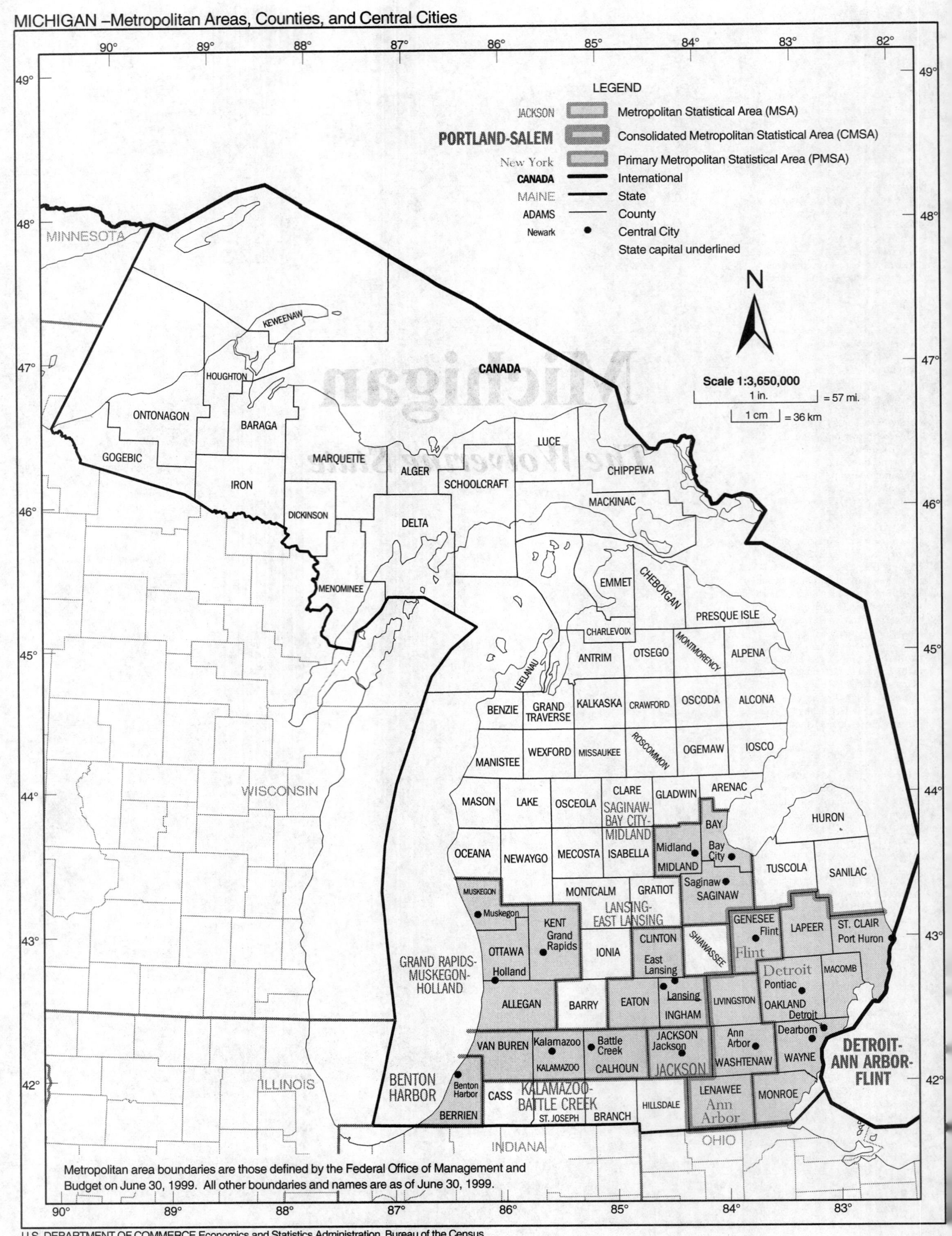

Metropolitan area boundaries are those defined by the Federal Office of Management and Budget on June 30, 1999. All other boundaries and names are as of June 30, 1999.

CDP = Census Designated Place

H

I

CDP = Census Designated Place

J

K

L

M

N

O

P

Q

R

S

CDP = Census Designated Place

T

U

V

W

CDP = Census Designated Place

Y

Z

Alcona County

Located in northeast Michigan; bounded on the east by Lake Huron; includes Hubbard Lake, and part of Huron National Forest. Covers a land area of 674.40 square miles, a water area of 1,116.10 square miles, and is located in the Eastern Time Zone. The county government was organized in 1840. County seat is Harrisville.
Population: 11,719 (2000); Race: 97.7% White, 0.2% Black, 0.2% Asian, 0.6% American Indian and Alaska Native, 0.9% Hispanic of any race, 1.1% two or more races (2000); Density: 17.4 persons per square mile (2000); Age: 19.2% under 18, 24.5% over 64 (2000).
Religion: Five largest groups: 9.1% Catholic Church, 3.2% The United Methodist Church, 2.1% Evangelical Lutheran Church in America, 2.0% Presbyterian Church (U.S.A.), 1.7% American Baptist Churches in the USA (2000).
Economy: Unemployment rate: 8.7% (11/2002); Total civilian labor force: 4,554 (11/2002); Leading industries: 23.0% retail trade; 21.4% manufacturing; 17.5% health care and social assistance (2000); Companies that employ more than 1,000 persons: 0 (2000); Companies that employ more than 100 persons: 0 (2000); Farms: 207 totaling 43,383 acres (1997); Minority business ownership rate: 0.0% (1997); Women business ownership rate: 36.8% (1997); Retail sales per capita: $4,561 (1997). Single-family building permits issued: 129 (2001) / 135 (2000); Multi-family building permits issued: 0 (2001) / 0 (2000).
Income: Per capita income: $17,653 (2000); Median household income: $31,362 (2000); Poverty rate: 12.6% (2000); Bankruptcy rate: 4.52% (2001).
Taxes: Total county taxes per capita: $198 (1997); County property taxes per capita: $197 (1997).
Education: High school graduation rate: 79.7% (2000); College graduation rate: 10.9% (2000).
Housing: Homeownership rate: 89.5% (2000); Median home value: $83,700 (2000); Median rent: $322 per month (2000); Median age of housing: 30 years (2000).
Health: Birth rate: 75.1 per 10,000 population (1998); Age adjusted death rate: 94.9 per 10,000 population (1999); Age adjusted cancer mortality rate: 239.7 deaths per 100,000 population (1999). Number of physicians: 3.4 per 10,000 population (1999); Number of hospital beds: n/a (1999).
Elections: 2000 Presidential election results: 45.0% Gore, 52.6% Bush, 2.1% Nader, 0.1% Buchanan
National and State Parks: Alpena State Forest; Harrisville State Park; Sturgeon Point State Park
Additional Information Contacts
Alcona County Government Offices 517-724-6807
Curtis Chamber of Commerce 906-586-3700
Harrisville Chamber of Commerce 989-724-5107

Alcona County Communities

ALCONA (township). Covers a land area of 57.627 square miles and a water area of 8.771 square miles. Located at 44.78° N. Lat.; 83.44° W. Long.
Population: 1,089 (2000); Race: 97.0% White, 0.0% Black, 0.0% Asian, 1.4% American Indian and Alaska Native, 1.2% Hispanic of any race, 1.5% two or more races (2000); Density: 18.9 persons per square mile (2000); Age: 16.3% under 18, 33.4% over 64 (2000); Marriage status: 9.6% never married, 74.6% now married, 8.1% widowed, 7.7% divorced (2000); Foreign born: 0.7% (2000); Ancestry (includes multiple ancestries): 25.9% German, 17.3% English, 11.6% Polish, 11.5% French (except Basque), 6.9% Irish (2000).
Economy: Employment by occupation: 14.3% management, 21.6% professional, 16.9% services, 19.3% sales, 0.3% farming, 15.6% construction, 12.0% production (2000).
Income: Per capita income: $20,160 (2000); Median household income: $34,125 (2000); Poverty rate: 8.7% (2000).
Taxes: Total city taxes per capita: $254 (1997); City property taxes per capita: $252 (1997).
Education: High school graduation rate: 87.4% (2000); College graduation rate: 21.5% (2000).
Housing: Homeownership rate: 92.4% (2000); Median home value: $112,100 (2000); Median rent: $338 per month (2000); Median age of housing: 30 years (2000).
Transportation: Commute to work: 93.1% car, 0.7% public transportation, 0.7% walk, 4.8% work from home (2000); Travel time to work: 25.7% less than 15 minutes, 34.1% 15 to 30 minutes, 29.0% 30 to 45 minutes, 2.9% 45 to 60 minutes, 8.3% 60 minutes or more (2000)

BARTON CITY (unincorporated postal area, zip code 48705). Covers a land area of 112.535 square miles and a water area of 0.631 square miles. Located at 44.70° N. Lat.; 83.63° W. Long.
History: Barton City was first called Mud Lake, for its location on that lake. When a town was laid out in 1912, it was named for resident Frank Barton.
Population: 584 (2000); Race: 98.0% White, 0.0% Black, 0.0% Asian, 0.7% American Indian and Alaska Native, 1.4% Hispanic of any race, 0.9% two or more races (2000); Density: 5.2 persons per square mile (2000); Age: 18.9% under 18, 23.4% over 64 (2000); Marriage status: 18.9% never married, 62.0% now married, 8.6% widowed, 10.5% divorced (2000); Foreign born: 0.9% (2000); Ancestry (includes multiple ancestries): 25.2% German, 10.8% Other groups, 10.6% English, 9.4% Polish, 7.2% Irish (2000).
Economy: Employment by occupation: 6.5% management, 11.3% professional, 22.0% services, 15.5% sales, 0.0% farming, 20.8% construction, 23.8% production (2000).
Income: Per capita income: $15,860 (2000); Median household income: $26,477 (2000); Poverty rate: 21.0% (2000).
Education: High school graduation rate: 70.4% (2000); College graduation rate: 5.6% (2000).
Housing: Homeownership rate: 93.6% (2000); Median home value: $56,900 (2000); Median rent: $425 per month (2000); Median age of housing: 30 years (2000).
Transportation: Commute to work: 97.6% car, 0.0% public transportation, 1.2% walk, 1.2% work from home (2000); Travel time to work: 5.5% less than 15 minutes, 45.7% 15 to 30 minutes, 17.1% 30 to 45 minutes, 23.2% 45 to 60 minutes, 8.5% 60 minutes or more (2000)

BLACK RIVER (unincorporated postal area, zip code 48721). Covers a land area of 27.575 square miles and a water area of 0.004 square miles. Located at 44.79° N. Lat.; 83.32° W. Long. Elevation is 590 feet.
History: Black River began as a fishing camp in 1849. It was later settled by French trappers and fishermen, and became the headquarters of the Alger, Smith & Company lumber operations.
Population: 485 (2000); Race: 95.8% White, 0.0% Black, 0.0% Asian, 2.4% American Indian and Alaska Native, 2.6% Hispanic of any race, 1.8% two or more races (2000); Density: 17.6 persons per square mile (2000); Age: 25.5% under 18, 13.5% over 64 (2000); Marriage status: 16.1% never married, 68.1% now married, 4.4% widowed, 11.4% divorced (2000); Foreign born: 0.0% (2000); Ancestry (includes multiple ancestries): 25.7% German, 19.7% French (except Basque), 15.1% Polish, 12.7% English, 9.6% Irish (2000).
Economy: Employment by occupation: 13.0% management, 15.3% professional, 23.7% services, 16.4% sales, 0.6% farming, 22.0% construction, 9.0% production (2000).
Income: Per capita income: $19,023 (2000); Median household income: $34,750 (2000); Poverty rate: 13.5% (2000).
Education: High school graduation rate: 85.3% (2000); College graduation rate: 16.4% (2000).
Housing: Homeownership rate: 90.9% (2000); Median home value: $133,300 (2000); Median rent: $330 per month (2000); Median age of housing: 28 years (2000).
Transportation: Commute to work: 90.6% car, 0.0% public transportation, 1.2% walk, 8.2% work from home (2000); Travel time to work: 30.8% less than 15 minutes, 26.3% 15 to 30 minutes, 31.4% 30 to 45 minutes, 1.9% 45 to 60 minutes, 9.6% 60 minutes or more (2000)

CALEDONIA (township). Covers a land area of 67.411 square miles and a water area of 5.097 square miles. Located at 44.82° N. Lat.; 83.61° W. Long.
Population: 1,203 (2000); Race: 99.8% White, 0.0% Black, 0.0% Asian, 0.0% American Indian and Alaska Native, 0.3% Hispanic of any race, 0.2% two or more races (2000); Density: 17.8 persons per square mile (2000); Age: 16.3% under 18, 23.5% over 64 (2000); Marriage status: 16.7% never married, 65.8% now married, 9.2% widowed, 8.3% divorced (2000); Foreign born: 0.3% (2000); Ancestry (includes multiple ancestries): 26.4% German, 12.5% English, 10.8% French (except Basque), 9.7% Irish, 8.9% Polish (2000).
Economy: Employment by occupation: 8.5% management, 12.5% professional, 18.7% services, 20.8% sales, 1.2% farming, 16.6% construction, 21.7% production (2000).
Income: Per capita income: $19,051 (2000); Median household income: $36,000 (2000); Poverty rate: 13.6% (2000).
Taxes: Total city taxes per capita: $229 (2000); City property taxes per capita: $227 (2000).
Education: High school graduation rate: 80.9% (2000); College graduation rate: 11.8% (2000).

Housing: Homeownership rate: 92.1% (2000); Median home value: $111,100 (2000); Median rent: $311 per month (2000); Median age of housing: 31 years (2000).
Transportation: Commute to work: 84.4% car, 0.0% public transportation, 1.4% walk, 10.6% work from home (2000); Travel time to work: 23.5% less than 15 minutes, 27.2% 15 to 30 minutes, 36.9% 30 to 45 minutes, 7.1% 45 to 60 minutes, 5.3% 60 minutes or more (2000)

CURRAN (unincorporated postal area, zip code 48728). Covers a land area of 111.924 square miles and a water area of 1.158 square miles. Located at 44.74° N. Lat.; 83.83° W. Long.
History: Curran began as a lumber camp in the mid-1870's, and by 1886 a village had grown up around it. The Loud & Sons Lumber Company ran a narrow gauge railroad through Curran in 1890.
Population: 307 (2000); Race: 98.2% White, 0.0% Black, 0.0% Asian, 0.0% American Indian and Alaska Native, 1.4% Hispanic of any race, 1.8% two or more races (2000); Density: 2.7 persons per square mile (2000); Age: 7.0% under 18, 31.3% over 64 (2000); Marriage status: 13.0% never married, 63.3% now married, 14.1% widowed, 9.6% divorced (2000); Foreign born: 4.2% (2000); Ancestry (includes multiple ancestries): 36.3% German, 11.3% English, 10.2% Irish, 8.5% Polish, 7.4% French (except Basque) (2000).
Economy: Employment by occupation: 12.3% management, 11.1% professional, 14.8% services, 23.5% sales, 4.9% farming, 11.1% construction, 22.2% production (2000).
Income: Per capita income: $22,167 (2000); Median household income: $29,844 (2000); Poverty rate: 12.2% (2000).
Education: High school graduation rate: 78.3% (2000); College graduation rate: 5.9% (2000).
Housing: Homeownership rate: 98.7% (2000); Median home value: $68,600 (2000); Median rent: $125 per month (2000); Median age of housing: 28 years (2000).
Transportation: Commute to work: 87.0% car, 0.0% public transportation, 0.0% walk, 10.4% work from home (2000); Travel time to work: 2.9% less than 15 minutes, 56.5% 15 to 30 minutes, 24.6% 30 to 45 minutes, 4.3% 45 to 60 minutes, 11.6% 60 minutes or more (2000)

CURTIS (township). Covers a land area of 68.269 square miles and a water area of 2.378 square miles. Located at 44.55° N. Lat.; 83.76° W. Long.
Population: 1,378 (2000); Race: 98.8% White, 0.0% Black, 0.0% Asian, 0.0% American Indian and Alaska Native, 0.4% Hispanic of any race, 1.2% two or more races (2000); Density: 20.2 persons per square mile (2000); Age: 20.7% under 18, 24.3% over 64 (2000); Marriage status: 12.1% never married, 67.5% now married, 8.6% widowed, 11.8% divorced (2000); Foreign born: 0.9% (2000); Ancestry (includes multiple ancestries): 22.9% German, 17.7% English, 15.6% Irish, 9.2% United States or American, 8.4% French (except Basque) (2000).
Economy: Employment by occupation: 6.3% management, 10.3% professional, 18.1% services, 27.0% sales, 2.3% farming, 15.1% construction, 20.9% production (2000).
Income: Per capita income: $15,457 (2000); Median household income: $27,048 (2000); Poverty rate: 15.1% (2000).
Taxes: Total city taxes per capita: $84 (1997); City property taxes per capita: $82 (1997).
Education: High school graduation rate: 72.7% (2000); College graduation rate: 5.0% (2000).
Housing: Homeownership rate: 90.6% (2000); Median home value: $68,100 (2000); Median rent: $315 per month (2000); Median age of housing: 27 years (2000).
Transportation: Commute to work: 89.0% car, 0.0% public transportation, 3.7% walk, 7.3% work from home (2000); Travel time to work: 29.9% less than 15 minutes, 19.2% 15 to 30 minutes, 25.9% 30 to 45 minutes, 10.7% 45 to 60 minutes, 14.4% 60 minutes or more (2000)
Additional Information Contacts
Curtis Chamber of Commerce 906-586-3700

GLENNIE (unincorporated postal area, zip code 48737). Covers a land area of 119.456 square miles and a water area of 1.295 square miles. Located at 44.54° N. Lat.; 83.71° W. Long. Elevation is 993 feet.
History: Glennie grew up around a station of the Detroit & Mackinaw Railroad in the late 1880's.
Population: 1,345 (2000); Race: 97.0% White, 0.0% Black, 0.0% Asian, 1.0% American Indian and Alaska Native, 0.3% Hispanic of any race, 2.1% two or more races (2000); Density: 11.3 persons per square mile (2000); Age: 19.0% under 18, 27.1% over 64 (2000); Marriage status: 12.9% never married, 66.2% now married, 10.2% widowed, 10.7% divorced (2000); Foreign born: 0.3% (2000); Ancestry (includes multiple ancestries): 21.8% German, 18.2% English, 16.0% Irish, 9.3% United States or American, 6.7% French (except Basque) (2000).
Economy: Employment by occupation: 6.5% management, 10.7% professional, 20.1% services, 24.7% sales, 2.1% farming, 15.4% construction, 20.6% production (2000).
Income: Per capita income: $15,946 (2000); Median household income: $26,782 (2000); Poverty rate: 13.4% (2000).
Education: High school graduation rate: 70.2% (2000); College graduation rate: 5.6% (2000).
Housing: Homeownership rate: 91.3% (2000); Median home value: $65,700 (2000); Median rent: $318 per month (2000); Median age of housing: 28 years (2000).
Transportation: Commute to work: 88.8% car, 0.0% public transportation, 4.4% walk, 6.8% work from home (2000); Travel time to work: 31.1% less than 15 minutes, 13.8% 15 to 30 minutes, 30.8% 30 to 45 minutes, 12.0% 45 to 60 minutes, 12.3% 60 minutes or more (2000)

GREENBUSH (township). Covers a land area of 24.919 square miles and a water area of 1.218 square miles. Located at 44.55° N. Lat.; 83.33° W. Long.
Population: 1,499 (2000); Race: 98.3% White, 0.6% Black, 0.0% Asian, 0.3% American Indian and Alaska Native, 0.7% Hispanic of any race, 0.9% two or more races (2000); Density: 60.2 persons per square mile (2000); Age: 17.8% under 18, 27.8% over 64 (2000); Marriage status: 13.3% never married, 70.7% now married, 9.0% widowed, 7.0% divorced (2000); Foreign born: 0.6% (2000); Ancestry (includes multiple ancestries): 27.3% German, 15.5% English, 11.4% Irish, 9.2% United States or American, 9.1% Polish (2000).
Economy: Employment by occupation: 15.7% management, 9.6% professional, 16.9% services, 21.3% sales, 0.8% farming, 16.1% construction, 19.5% production (2000).
Income: Per capita income: $18,248 (2000); Median household income: $32,823 (2000); Poverty rate: 11.1% (2000).
Taxes: Total city taxes per capita: $68 (1997); City property taxes per capita: $68 (1997).
Education: High school graduation rate: 82.4% (2000); College graduation rate: 12.5% (2000).
Housing: Homeownership rate: 90.7% (2000); Median home value: $100,400 (2000); Median rent: $400 per month (2000); Median age of housing: 34 years (2000).
Transportation: Commute to work: 92.6% car, 0.0% public transportation, 1.2% walk, 6.2% work from home (2000); Travel time to work: 18.0% less than 15 minutes, 55.4% 15 to 30 minutes, 13.1% 30 to 45 minutes, 6.0% 45 to 60 minutes, 7.5% 60 minutes or more (2000)

GUSTIN (township). Covers a land area of 35.694 square miles and a water area of 0.150 square miles. Located at 44.64° N. Lat.; 83.44° W. Long.
Population: 832 (2000); Race: 98.9% White, 0.0% Black, 0.0% Asian, 0.2% American Indian and Alaska Native, 0.4% Hispanic of any race, 0.8% two or more races (2000); Density: 23.3 persons per square mile (2000); Age: 20.9% under 18, 20.7% over 64 (2000); Marriage status: 17.2% never married, 62.6% now married, 9.9% widowed, 10.3% divorced (2000); Foreign born: 0.9% (2000); Ancestry (includes multiple ancestries): 19.6% German, 15.0% English, 10.7% United States or American, 10.6% Irish, 9.1% French (except Basque) (2000).
Economy: Employment by occupation: 6.4% management, 12.8% professional, 24.3% services, 23.3% sales, 3.2% farming, 11.8% construction, 18.2% production (2000).
Income: Per capita income: $19,848 (2000); Median household income: $27,350 (2000); Poverty rate: 15.0% (2000).
Taxes: Total city taxes per capita: $68 (1997); City property taxes per capita: $67 (1997).
Education: High school graduation rate: 78.3% (2000); College graduation rate: 6.4% (2000).
Housing: Homeownership rate: 80.6% (2000); Median home value: $65,200 (2000); Median rent: $297 per month (2000); Median age of housing: 29 years (2000).
Transportation: Commute to work: 86.7% car, 0.0% public transportation, 1.3% walk, 10.6% work from home (2000); Travel time to work: 41.3% less than 15 minutes, 31.2% 15 to 30 minutes, 11.5% 30 to 45 minutes, 11.9% 45 to 60 minutes, 4.1% 60 minutes or more (2000)

HARRISVILLE (city). Covers a land area of 0.618 square miles and a water area of 0 square miles. Located at 44.65° N. Lat.; 83.29° W. Long. Elevation is 623 feet.

History: Harrisville, established in 1854 as Davison's Mills on the shores of Lake Huron, grew as a fishing village, particularly popular during the summer months.
Population: 514 (2000); Race: 96.2% White, 1.4% Black, 0.5% Asian, 0.0% American Indian and Alaska Native, 1.2% Hispanic of any race, 1.9% two or more races (2000); Density: 831.2 persons per square mile (2000); Age: 13.7% under 18, 31.5% over 64 (2000); Marriage status: 19.1% never married, 59.4% now married, 13.7% widowed, 7.8% divorced (2000); Foreign born: 3.2% (2000); Ancestry (includes multiple ancestries): 22.9% English, 19.5% German, 15.2% Irish, 7.2% French (except Basque), 5.8% United States or American (2000).
Economy: Employment by occupation: 7.5% management, 23.0% professional, 26.1% services, 23.6% sales, 0.0% farming, 7.5% construction, 12.4% production (2000).
Income: Per capita income: $16,983 (2000); Median household income: $27,500 (2000); Poverty rate: 13.6% (2000).
Taxes: Total city taxes per capita: $217 (1997); City property taxes per capita: $217 (1997).
Education: High school graduation rate: 77.8% (2000); College graduation rate: 11.6% (2000).
Housing: Homeownership rate: 64.9% (2000); Median home value: $79,400 (2000); Median rent: $287 per month (2000); Median age of housing: 42 years (2000).
Newspapers: Alcona County Review (1 x week)
Transportation: Commute to work: 91.9% car, 0.0% public transportation, 4.4% walk, 3.8% work from home (2000); Travel time to work: 48.7% less than 15 minutes, 33.8% 15 to 30 minutes, 10.4% 30 to 45 minutes, 4.5% 45 to 60 minutes, 2.6% 60 minutes or more (2000)
Additional Information Contacts
Harrisville Chamber of Commerce 989-724-5107

HARRISVILLE (township). Covers a land area of 30.224 square miles and a water area of 0.035 square miles. Located at 44.65° N. Lat.; 83.33° W. Long. Elevation is 623 feet.
History: Harrisville Township was organized in 1860 and named for Benjamin Harris and his sons, Levi O. and Henry H. Harris, who had purchased the mill here from Crosier Davison.
Population: 1,411 (2000); Race: 97.4% White, 0.0% Black, 1.1% Asian, 0.0% American Indian and Alaska Native, 0.8% Hispanic of any race, 1.0% two or more races (2000); Density: 46.7 persons per square mile (2000); Age: 21.3% under 18, 22.4% over 64 (2000); Marriage status: 17.0% never married, 66.6% now married, 9.0% widowed, 7.4% divorced (2000); Foreign born: 2.7% (2000); Ancestry (includes multiple ancestries): 21.0% German, 16.7% English, 12.0% Irish, 7.3% Other groups, 7.2% United States or American (2000).
Economy: Employment by occupation: 14.9% management, 14.9% professional, 19.2% services, 22.5% sales, 2.1% farming, 10.5% construction, 15.8% production (2000).
Income: Per capita income: $15,907 (2000); Median household income: $35,074 (2000); Poverty rate: 9.9% (2000).
Taxes: Total city taxes per capita: $26 (1997); City property taxes per capita: $24 (1997).
Education: High school graduation rate: 84.0% (2000); College graduation rate: 13.5% (2000).
Housing: Homeownership rate: 91.2% (2000); Median home value: $89,400 (2000); Median rent: $342 per month (2000); Median age of housing: 28 years (2000).
Transportation: Commute to work: 85.1% car, 0.0% public transportation, 2.5% walk, 11.6% work from home (2000); Travel time to work: 40.2% less than 15 minutes, 28.8% 15 to 30 minutes, 16.9% 30 to 45 minutes, 7.6% 45 to 60 minutes, 6.4% 60 minutes or more (2000)

HAWES (township). Covers a land area of 70.011 square miles and a water area of 1.445 square miles. Located at 44.71° N. Lat.; 83.50° W. Long.
Population: 1,167 (2000); Race: 99.7% White, 0.1% Black, 0.0% Asian, 0.2% American Indian and Alaska Native, 0.0% Hispanic of any race, 0.0% two or more races (2000); Density: 16.7 persons per square mile (2000); Age: 20.1% under 18, 21.1% over 64 (2000); Marriage status: 18.2% never married, 60.6% now married, 9.2% widowed, 11.9% divorced (2000); Foreign born: 1.1% (2000); Ancestry (includes multiple ancestries): 25.4% German, 12.9% Irish, 12.7% Polish, 11.8% English, 9.9% French (except Basque) (2000).
Economy: Employment by occupation: 9.7% management, 16.5% professional, 14.9% services, 24.1% sales, 1.7% farming, 12.5% construction, 20.6% production (2000).
Income: Per capita income: $16,332 (2000); Median household income: $28,938 (2000); Poverty rate: 12.2% (2000).
Taxes: Total city taxes per capita: $32 (1997); City property taxes per capita: $32 (1997).
Education: High school graduation rate: 79.4% (2000); College graduation rate: 9.3% (2000).
Housing: Homeownership rate: 92.3% (2000); Median home value: $74,500 (2000); Median rent: $375 per month (2000); Median age of housing: 31 years (2000).
Transportation: Commute to work: 94.0% car, 0.0% public transportation, 2.2% walk, 3.2% work from home (2000); Travel time to work: 37.4% less than 15 minutes, 28.1% 15 to 30 minutes, 17.3% 30 to 45 minutes, 10.1% 45 to 60 minutes, 7.2% 60 minutes or more (2000)

HAYNES (township). Covers a land area of 34.950 square miles and a water area of 0.144 square miles. Located at 44.73° N. Lat.; 83.32° W. Long.
Population: 724 (2000); Race: 97.7% White, 0.0% Black, 0.0% Asian, 0.3% American Indian and Alaska Native, 0.9% Hispanic of any race, 1.4% two or more races (2000); Density: 20.7 persons per square mile (2000); Age: 17.4% under 18, 22.9% over 64 (2000); Marriage status: 16.9% never married, 65.6% now married, 6.5% widowed, 10.9% divorced (2000); Foreign born: 2.3% (2000); Ancestry (includes multiple ancestries): 23.4% German, 18.8% English, 13.7% Irish, 10.8% French (except Basque), 10.8% Polish (2000).
Economy: Single-family building permits issued: 10 (2001) / 10 (2000); Multi-family building permits issued: 0 (2001) / 0 (2000); Employment by occupation: 8.0% management, 12.2% professional, 22.9% services, 24.8% sales, 1.1% farming, 11.5% construction, 19.5% production (2000).
Income: Per capita income: $20,279 (2000); Median household income: $34,896 (2000); Poverty rate: 6.9% (2000).
Taxes: Total city taxes per capita: $78 (1997); City property taxes per capita: $78 (1997).
Education: High school graduation rate: 83.0% (2000); College graduation rate: 17.0% (2000).
Housing: Homeownership rate: 93.5% (2000); Median home value: $99,500 (2000); Median rent: $375 per month (2000); Median age of housing: 27 years (2000).
Transportation: Commute to work: 93.8% car, 0.8% public transportation, 0.4% walk, 4.2% work from home (2000); Travel time to work: 39.0% less than 15 minutes, 24.5% 15 to 30 minutes, 21.3% 30 to 45 minutes, 11.6% 45 to 60 minutes, 3.6% 60 minutes or more (2000)

HUBBARD LAKE (CDP). Covers a land area of 8.855 square miles and a water area of 13.652 square miles. Located at 44.82° N. Lat.; 83.55° W. Long.
Population: 993 (2000); Race: 99.1% White, 0.0% Black, 0.0% Asian, 0.0% American Indian and Alaska Native, 0.0% Hispanic of any race, 0.9% two or more races (2000); Density: 112.1 persons per square mile (2000); Age: 7.7% under 18, 36.7% over 64 (2000); Marriage status: 13.0% never married, 70.2% now married, 10.3% widowed, 6.5% divorced (2000); Foreign born: 1.2% (2000); Ancestry (includes multiple ancestries): 30.0% German, 16.1% English, 11.6% Irish, 11.1% Polish, 10.4% French (except Basque) (2000).
Economy: Employment by occupation: 8.9% management, 27.4% professional, 15.6% services, 19.3% sales, 0.0% farming, 11.1% construction, 17.8% production (2000).
Income: Per capita income: $24,550 (2000); Median household income: $38,611 (2000); Poverty rate: 7.0% (2000).
Education: High school graduation rate: 84.7% (2000); College graduation rate: 19.2% (2000).
Housing: Homeownership rate: 94.5% (2000); Median home value: $137,800 (2000); Median rent: $338 per month (2000); Median age of housing: 35 years (2000).
Transportation: Commute to work: 79.5% car, 0.8% public transportation, 1.9% walk, 14.1% work from home (2000); Travel time to work: 16.8% less than 15 minutes, 35.4% 15 to 30 minutes, 37.6% 30 to 45 minutes, 5.3% 45 to 60 minutes, 4.9% 60 minutes or more (2000)

LINCOLN (village). Covers a land area of 0.767 square miles and a water area of 0.217 square miles. Located at 44.68° N. Lat.; 83.41° W. Long.
History: Lincoln grew up around a lumber mill in 1885. It was incorporated as a village in 1907.
Population: 364 (2000); Race: 98.4% White, 0.0% Black, 0.0% Asian, 0.5% American Indian and Alaska Native, 0.0% Hispanic of any race, 1.1% two or more races (2000); Density: 474.8 persons per square mile (2000); Age: 23.9% under 18, 24.1% over 64 (2000); Marriage status: 12.8% never married, 53.4% now married, 16.6% widowed, 17.2% divorced (2000); Foreign born: 0.0% (2000); Ancestry (includes multiple ancestries): 18.6%

German, 16.2% Irish, 14.3% United States or American, 14.3% English, 11.4% French (except Basque) (2000).
Economy: Employment by occupation: 8.0% management, 19.7% professional, 15.3% services, 23.4% sales, 1.5% farming, 10.2% construction, 21.9% production (2000).
Income: Per capita income: $16,860 (2000); Median household income: $24,464 (2000); Poverty rate: 15.7% (2000).
Taxes: Total city taxes per capita: $104 (1997); City property taxes per capita: $104 (1997).
Education: High school graduation rate: 75.5% (2000); College graduation rate: 9.0% (2000).

School District(s)

Alcona Community Schools (KG-12)
2000 Enrollment: 1,045 517-736-6212
Housing: Homeownership rate: 75.0% (2000); Median home value: $63,800 (2000); Median rent: $294 per month (2000); Median age of housing: 44 years (2000).
Transportation: Commute to work: 89.6% car, 0.0% public transportation, 8.1% walk, 2.2% work from home (2000); Travel time to work: 52.3% less than 15 minutes, 22.7% 15 to 30 minutes, 6.1% 30 to 45 minutes, 12.1% 45 to 60 minutes, 6.8% 60 minutes or more (2000)

LOST LAKE WOODS (CDP). Covers a land area of 5.001 square miles and a water area of 0.138 square miles. Located at 44.77° N. Lat.; 83.42° W. Long.
Population: 339 (2000); Race: 98.8% White, 0.0% Black, 0.0% Asian, 1.2% American Indian and Alaska Native, 0.0% Hispanic of any race, 0.0% two or more races (2000); Density: 67.8 persons per square mile (2000); Age: 5.3% under 18, 56.9% over 64 (2000); Marriage status: 1.8% never married, 81.2% now married, 11.1% widowed, 5.8% divorced (2000); Foreign born: 1.8% (2000); Ancestry (includes multiple ancestries): 27.7% German, 22.7% English, 9.1% Irish, 8.6% French (except Basque), 8.0% Scotch-Irish (2000).
Economy: Employment by occupation: 12.3% management, 21.5% professional, 15.4% services, 32.3% sales, 0.0% farming, 6.2% construction, 12.3% production (2000).
Income: Per capita income: $22,546 (2000); Median household income: $32,361 (2000); Poverty rate: 3.8% (2000).
Education: High school graduation rate: 89.4% (2000); College graduation rate: 24.3% (2000).
Housing: Homeownership rate: 98.4% (2000); Median home value: $87,900 (2000); Median age of housing: 27 years (2000).
Transportation: Commute to work: 95.2% car, 0.0% public transportation, 0.0% walk, 4.8% work from home (2000); Travel time to work: 28.3% less than 15 minutes, 46.7% 15 to 30 minutes, 16.7% 30 to 45 minutes, 3.3% 45 to 60 minutes, 5.0% 60 minutes or more (2000)

MIKADO (township). Covers a land area of 71.334 square miles and a water area of 0.083 square miles. Located at 44.56° N. Lat.; 83.52° W. Long. Elevation is 647 feet.
Population: 1,043 (2000); Race: 95.2% White, 0.0% Black, 0.6% Asian, 2.3% American Indian and Alaska Native, 1.5% Hispanic of any race, 1.5% two or more races (2000); Density: 14.6 persons per square mile (2000); Age: 25.7% under 18, 17.1% over 64 (2000); Marriage status: 17.1% never married, 65.4% now married, 7.0% widowed, 10.6% divorced (2000); Foreign born: 3.2% (2000); Ancestry (includes multiple ancestries): 24.0% German, 12.5% Irish, 10.8% French (except Basque), 9.4% English, 8.4% Other groups (2000).
Economy: Employment by occupation: 8.9% management, 10.7% professional, 15.4% services, 28.9% sales, 1.6% farming, 14.1% construction, 20.6% production (2000).
Income: Per capita income: $16,886 (2000); Median household income: $31,713 (2000); Poverty rate: 14.2% (2000).
Taxes: Total city taxes per capita: $93 (1997); City property taxes per capita: $93 (1997).
Education: High school graduation rate: 75.4% (2000); College graduation rate: 5.1% (2000).
Housing: Homeownership rate: 88.0% (2000); Median home value: $72,000 (2000); Median rent: $295 per month (2000); Median age of housing: 34 years (2000).
Transportation: Commute to work: 96.3% car, 0.0% public transportation, 1.6% walk, 1.9% work from home (2000); Travel time to work: 19.1% less than 15 minutes, 54.0% 15 to 30 minutes, 16.3% 30 to 45 minutes, 4.4% 45 to 60 minutes, 6.3% 60 minutes or more (2000)

MILLEN (township). Covers a land area of 70.609 square miles and a water area of 0.606 square miles. Located at 44.64° N. Lat.; 83.63° W. Long.
Population: 463 (2000); Race: 90.7% White, 0.0% Black, 0.0% Asian, 5.8% American Indian and Alaska Native, 5.3% Hispanic of any race, 3.5% two or more races (2000); Density: 6.6 persons per square mile (2000); Age: 23.6% under 18, 22.2% over 64 (2000); Marriage status: 22.3% never married, 60.6% now married, 7.5% widowed, 9.5% divorced (2000); Foreign born: 1.2% (2000); Ancestry (includes multiple ancestries): 22.2% German, 12.3% English, 11.6% Other groups, 8.6% United States or American, 5.8% Polish (2000).
Economy: Employment by occupation: 4.5% management, 8.3% professional, 16.7% services, 20.5% sales, 1.3% farming, 14.1% construction, 34.6% production (2000).
Income: Per capita income: $14,475 (2000); Median household income: $26,932 (2000); Poverty rate: 21.4% (2000).
Taxes: Total city taxes per capita: $22 (1997); City property taxes per capita: $22 (1997).
Education: High school graduation rate: 71.7% (2000); College graduation rate: 5.9% (2000).
Housing: Homeownership rate: 92.8% (2000); Median home value: $54,300 (2000); Median rent: $235 per month (2000); Median age of housing: 33 years (2000).
Transportation: Commute to work: 91.0% car, 0.0% public transportation, 1.3% walk, 7.7% work from home (2000); Travel time to work: 3.5% less than 15 minutes, 50.7% 15 to 30 minutes, 16.0% 30 to 45 minutes, 22.2% 45 to 60 minutes, 7.6% 60 minutes or more (2000)

MITCHELL (township). Covers a land area of 142.768 square miles and a water area of 0.907 square miles. Located at 44.71° N. Lat.; 83.79° W. Long.
Population: 396 (2000); Race: 96.6% White, 0.0% Black, 0.0% Asian, 0.0% American Indian and Alaska Native, 0.5% Hispanic of any race, 2.8% two or more races (2000); Density: 2.8 persons per square mile (2000); Age: 11.4% under 18, 32.0% over 64 (2000); Marriage status: 11.0% never married, 66.6% now married, 13.9% widowed, 8.5% divorced (2000); Foreign born: 3.1% (2000); Ancestry (includes multiple ancestries): 28.7% German, 13.4% Irish, 9.8% English, 9.3% French (except Basque), 6.5% Polish (2000).
Economy: Employment by occupation: 14.3% management, 14.3% professional, 22.0% services, 14.3% sales, 4.4% farming, 14.3% construction, 16.5% production (2000).
Income: Per capita income: $18,739 (2000); Median household income: $26,875 (2000); Poverty rate: 16.5% (2000).
Taxes: Total city taxes per capita: $16 (1997); City property taxes per capita: $16 (1997).
Education: High school graduation rate: 74.9% (2000); College graduation rate: 5.0% (2000).
Housing: Homeownership rate: 97.0% (2000); Median home value: $70,400 (2000); Median rent: $300 per month (2000); Median age of housing: 27 years (2000).
Transportation: Commute to work: 88.5% car, 0.0% public transportation, 0.0% walk, 9.2% work from home (2000); Travel time to work: 7.6% less than 15 minutes, 49.4% 15 to 30 minutes, 21.5% 30 to 45 minutes, 10.1% 45 to 60 minutes, 11.4% 60 minutes or more (2000)

SPRUCE (unincorporated postal area, zip code 48762). Covers a land area of 55.433 square miles and a water area of 0.225 square miles. Located at 44.82° N. Lat.; 83.50° W. Long.
History: A post office was established in Spruce in 1898, with sawmill owner Don A. Hecox as the postmaster.
Population: 1,329 (2000); Race: 99.5% White, 0.1% Black, 0.0% Asian, 0.0% American Indian and Alaska Native, 0.3% Hispanic of any race, 0.4% two or more races (2000); Density: 24.0 persons per square mile (2000); Age: 20.0% under 18, 20.5% over 64 (2000); Marriage status: 15.4% never married, 65.7% now married, 10.1% widowed, 8.8% divorced (2000); Foreign born: 1.1% (2000); Ancestry (includes multiple ancestries): 27.2% German, 14.4% English, 12.5% French (except Basque), 11.7% Polish, 11.1% Irish (2000).
Economy: Employment by occupation: 6.3% management, 21.5% professional, 12.9% services, 25.9% sales, 0.6% farming, 13.8% construction, 19.0% production (2000).
Income: Per capita income: $17,435 (2000); Median household income: $34,423 (2000); Poverty rate: 11.4% (2000).
Education: High school graduation rate: 82.8% (2000); College graduation rate: 12.7% (2000).
Housing: Homeownership rate: 92.1% (2000); Median home value: $89,900 (2000); Median rent: $329 per month (2000); Median age of housing: 33 years (2000).

Transportation: Commute to work: 92.0% car, 0.4% public transportation, 1.0% walk, 6.0% work from home (2000); Travel time to work: 22.9% less than 15 minutes, 35.0% 15 to 30 minutes, 30.3% 30 to 45 minutes, 4.2% 45 to 60 minutes, 7.6% 60 minutes or more (2000)

Alger County

Located in northern Michigan, on the Upper Peninsula; bounded on the north by Lake Superior; includes part of Hiawatha National Forest. Covers a land area of 917.80 square miles, a water area of 4,131.20 square miles, and is located in the Eastern Time Zone. The county government was organized in 1885. County seat is Munising.

Weather Station: Grand Marais 2 E Elevation: 623 feet

	Jan	Feb	Mar	Apr	May	Jun	Jul	Aug	Sep	Oct	Nov	Dec
High	25	28	37	49	62	71	76	76	67	55	41	30
Low	10	11	17	28	37	46	51	52	46	36	27	17
Precip	2.3	1.2	1.4	1.4	2.6	2.9	3.0	2.9	3.6	3.1	2.4	2.2
Snow	47.9	27.9	16.1	5.0	0.4	0.0	0.0	0.0	tr	0.7	13.0	39.4

High and Low temperatures in degrees Fahrenheit; Precipitation and Snow in inches

Population: 9,862 (2000); Race: 87.5% White, 5.8% Black, 0.4% Asian, 4.1% American Indian and Alaska Native, 0.8% Hispanic of any race, 2.1% two or more races (2000); Density: 10.7 persons per square mile (2000); Age: 20.4% under 18, 17.1% over 64 (2000).
Religion: Five largest groups: 31.9% Catholic Church, 8.5% Evangelical Lutheran Church in America, 5.5% Lutheran Church—Missouri Synod, 2.1% The United Methodist Church, 1.8% The Association of Free Lutheran Congregations (2000).
Economy: Unemployment rate: 5.9% (11/2002); Total civilian labor force: 4,247 (11/2002); Leading industries: 31.5% manufacturing; 16.8% accommodation & food services; 13.6% retail trade (2000); Companies that employ more than 1,000 persons: 0 (2000); Companies that employ more than 100 persons: 3 (2000); Farms: 60 totaling 16,029 acres (1997); Minority business ownership rate: 0.0% (1997); Women business ownership rate: 31.9% (1997); Retail sales per capita: $3,712 (1997). Single-family building permits issued: 59 (2001) / 91 (2000); Multi-family building permits issued: 0 (2001) / 0 (2000).
Income: Per capita income: $18,210 (2000); Median household income: $35,892 (2000); Poverty rate: 10.3% (2000); Bankruptcy rate: 2.47% (2001).
Taxes: Total county taxes per capita: $112 (1997); County property taxes per capita: $107 (1997).
Education: High school graduation rate: 81.5% (2000); College graduation rate: 14.7% (2000).
Housing: Homeownership rate: 82.4% (2000); Median home value: $75,900 (2000); Median rent: $317 per month (2000); Median age of housing: 32 years (2000).
Health: Birth rate: 85.2 per 10,000 population (1998); Age adjusted death rate: 91.1 per 10,000 population (1999); Age adjusted cancer mortality rate: 164.4 deaths per 100,000 population (1999). Number of physicians: 13.2 per 10,000 population (1999); Number of hospital beds: 40.6 per 10,000 population (1999).
Elections: 2000 Presidential election results: 47.4% Gore, 49.1% Bush, 2.9% Nader, 0.1% Buchanan
National and State Parks: Escanaba River State Forest; Pictured Rocks National Lakeshore
Additional Information Contacts
Alger County Government Offices 906-387-2076
Grand Marais Chamber of Commerce 906-494-2447
Munising Chamber of Commerce 906-387-2138

Alger County Communities

AU TRAIN (township). Covers a land area of 142.053 square miles and a water area of 23.449 square miles. Located at 46.35° N. Lat.; 86.75° W. Long. Elevation is 612 feet.
Population: 1,172 (2000); Race: 91.3% White, 0.0% Black, 0.0% Asian, 6.6% American Indian and Alaska Native, 0.0% Hispanic of any race, 2.1% two or more races (2000); Density: 8.3 persons per square mile (2000); Age: 20.8% under 18, 14.2% over 64 (2000); Marriage status: 19.7% never married, 64.3% now married, 4.7% widowed, 11.2% divorced (2000); Foreign born: 1.3% (2000); Ancestry (includes multiple ancestries): 21.3% German, 16.3% French (except Basque), 13.1% English, 11.6% Finnish, 8.8% Irish (2000).
Economy: Timber; fishing. Employment by occupation: 7.8% management, 14.4% professional, 20.0% services, 23.4% sales, 0.8% farming, 17.5% construction, 16.2% production (2000).
Income: Per capita income: $18,751 (2000); Median household income: $40,331 (2000); Poverty rate: 10.2% (2000).
Taxes: Total city taxes per capita: $94 (1997); City property taxes per capita: $94 (1997).
Education: High school graduation rate: 87.9% (2000); College graduation rate: 16.1% (2000).
Housing: Homeownership rate: 87.2% (2000); Median home value: $103,900 (2000); Median rent: $321 per month (2000); Median age of housing: 28 years (2000).
Transportation: Commute to work: 91.3% car, 1.7% public transportation, 2.3% walk, 3.9% work from home (2000); Travel time to work: 29.3% less than 15 minutes, 46.5% 15 to 30 minutes, 12.3% 30 to 45 minutes, 4.4% 45 to 60 minutes, 7.5% 60 minutes or more (2000)

BURT (township). Covers a land area of 230.947 square miles and a water area of 27.149 square miles. Located at 46.60° N. Lat.; 86.05° W. Long.
Population: 480 (2000); Race: 95.7% White, 0.0% Black, 0.0% Asian, 1.1% American Indian and Alaska Native, 0.7% Hispanic of any race, 3.2% two or more races (2000); Density: 2.1 persons per square mile (2000); Age: 14.9% under 18, 32.1% over 64 (2000); Marriage status: 17.2% never married, 65.7% now married, 9.0% widowed, 8.2% divorced (2000); Foreign born: 2.0% (2000); Ancestry (includes multiple ancestries): 27.5% German, 16.0% English, 14.4% Irish, 11.5% French (except Basque), 8.8% Polish (2000).
Economy: Employment by occupation: 18.2% management, 16.8% professional, 21.9% services, 32.1% sales, 0.0% farming, 5.8% construction, 5.1% production (2000).
Income: Per capita income: $18,008 (2000); Median household income: $27,500 (2000); Poverty rate: 7.2% (2000).
Taxes: Total city taxes per capita: $106 (1997); City property taxes per capita: $106 (1997).
Education: High school graduation rate: 87.4% (2000); College graduation rate: 19.9% (2000).
Housing: Homeownership rate: 87.6% (2000); Median home value: $72,200 (2000); Median rent: $264 per month (2000); Median age of housing: 27 years (2000).
Transportation: Commute to work: 73.7% car, 0.0% public transportation, 13.5% walk, 12.8% work from home (2000); Travel time to work: 90.5% less than 15 minutes, 3.4% 15 to 30 minutes, 4.3% 30 to 45 minutes, 0.0% 45 to 60 minutes, 1.7% 60 minutes or more (2000)

CHATHAM (village). Covers a land area of 2.637 square miles and a water area of 0.017 square miles. Located at 46.34° N. Lat.; 86.92° W. Long. Elevation is 867 feet.
History: Chatham was founded by James Finn in 1896 as a lumber camp. It was named for Chatham, Ontario. The Michigan Agricultural Experiment Station was established in Chatham in the late 1890's, as an extension of the Michigan State College of Agriculture.
Population: 231 (2000); Race: 94.0% White, 0.0% Black, 0.0% Asian, 6.0% American Indian and Alaska Native, 0.0% Hispanic of any race, 0.0% two or more races (2000); Density: 87.6 persons per square mile (2000); Age: 20.5% under 18, 16.3% over 64 (2000); Marriage status: 24.0% never married, 62.8% now married, 7.7% widowed, 5.5% divorced (2000); Foreign born: 0.9% (2000); Ancestry (includes multiple ancestries): 57.2% Finnish, 14.4% German, 11.6% Swedish, 9.8% French (except Basque), 8.8% Other groups (2000).
Economy: Employment by occupation: 3.2% management, 12.6% professional, 18.9% services, 27.4% sales, 2.1% farming, 14.7% construction, 21.1% production (2000).
Income: Per capita income: $14,266 (2000); Median household income: $31,406 (2000); Poverty rate: 8.4% (2000).
Taxes: Total city taxes per capita: $66 (1997); City property taxes per capita: $66 (1997).
Education: High school graduation rate: 85.1% (2000); College graduation rate: 8.5% (2000).
Housing: Homeownership rate: 84.8% (2000); Median home value: $60,800 (2000); Median rent: $288 per month (2000); Median age of housing: 51 years (2000).
Transportation: Commute to work: 80.0% car, 4.2% public transportation, 11.6% walk, 4.2% work from home (2000); Travel time to work: 44.0% less than 15 minutes, 18.7% 15 to 30 minutes, 20.9% 30 to 45 minutes, 14.3% 45 to 60 minutes, 2.2% 60 minutes or more (2000)

DEERTON (unincorporated postal area, zip code 49822). Covers a land area of 33.898 square miles and a water area of 0.241 square miles. Located at 46.47° N. Lat.; 87.06° W. Long. Elevation is 716 feet.
Population: 164 (2000); Race: 98.1% White, 0.0% Black, 0.0% Asian, 0.0% American Indian and Alaska Native, 0.0% Hispanic of any race, 1.9% two or more races (2000); Density: 4.8 persons per square mile (2000); Age: 27.4% under 18, 14.9% over 64 (2000); Marriage status: 20.5% never married, 61.4% now married, 6.6% widowed, 11.4% divorced (2000); Foreign born: 0.0% (2000); Ancestry (includes multiple ancestries): 25.1% French (except Basque), 22.3% Italian, 18.1% German, 7.9% Polish, 7.4% English (2000).
Economy: Employment by occupation: 24.4% management, 19.8% professional, 25.6% services, 11.6% sales, 0.0% farming, 5.8% construction, 12.8% production (2000).
Income: Per capita income: $17,158 (2000); Median household income: $34,821 (2000); Poverty rate: 8.9% (2000).
Education: High school graduation rate: 86.7% (2000); College graduation rate: 27.3% (2000).

School District(s)

Autrain-Onota Public Schools (PK-06)
2000 Enrollment: 34 906-343-6632
Housing: Homeownership rate: 95.3% (2000); Median home value: $83,000 (2000); Median rent: $225 per month (2000); Median age of housing: 27 years (2000).
Transportation: Commute to work: 90.7% car, 0.0% public transportation, 0.0% walk, 9.3% work from home (2000); Travel time to work: 25.6% less than 15 minutes, 53.8% 15 to 30 minutes, 17.9% 30 to 45 minutes, 2.6% 45 to 60 minutes, 0.0% 60 minutes or more (2000)

EBEN JUNCTION (unincorporated postal area, zip code 49825). Aka Eben. Covers a land area of 12.716 square miles and a water area of 0 square miles. Located at 46.36° N. Lat.; 86.98° W. Long.
History: Many of the early residents of Eben Junction were from Finland, and the first houses reflected a Finnish architectural style.
Population: 214 (2000); Race: 95.8% White, 0.0% Black, 0.0% Asian, 1.0% American Indian and Alaska Native, 3.1% Hispanic of any race, 0.0% two or more races (2000); Density: 16.8 persons per square mile (2000); Age: 26.0% under 18, 18.8% over 64 (2000); Marriage status: 18.4% never married, 71.4% now married, 4.8% widowed, 5.4% divorced (2000); Foreign born: 2.1% (2000); Ancestry (includes multiple ancestries): 47.4% Finnish, 19.8% German, 10.9% French Canadian, 10.9% English, 7.8% United States or American (2000).
Economy: Employment by occupation: 10.8% management, 20.3% professional, 27.0% services, 16.2% sales, 0.0% farming, 12.2% construction, 13.5% production (2000).
Income: Per capita income: $17,188 (2000); Median household income: $38,750 (2000); Poverty rate: 20.3% (2000).
Education: High school graduation rate: 98.5% (2000); College graduation rate: 20.5% (2000).

School District(s)

Superior Central Schools (KG-12)
2000 Enrollment: 401 906-439-5531
Housing: Homeownership rate: 85.4% (2000); Median home value: $56,000 (2000); Median rent: $342 per month (2000); Median age of housing: 36 years (2000).
Transportation: Commute to work: 82.4% car, 0.0% public transportation, 5.4% walk, 9.5% work from home (2000); Travel time to work: 17.9% less than 15 minutes, 20.9% 15 to 30 minutes, 37.3% 30 to 45 minutes, 23.9% 45 to 60 minutes, 0.0% 60 minutes or more (2000)

GRAND ISLAND (township). Covers a land area of 22.382 square miles and a water area of 26.614 square miles. Located at 46.48° N. Lat.; 86.67° W. Long.
History: Grand Island had a few settlers in the 1840's. Much of the land was owned by the Cleveland-Cliffs Iron Company, which conducted logging operations here. A lighthouse was built in 1856 on the northwest tip of the island, to help ships navigate on Lake Superior.
Population: 45 (2000); Race: 92.3% White, 0.0% Black, 2.6% Asian, 5.1% American Indian and Alaska Native, 0.0% Hispanic of any race, 0.0% two or more races (2000); Density: 2.0 persons per square mile (2000); Age: 12.8% under 18, 20.5% over 64 (2000); Marriage status: 8.8% never married, 73.5% now married, 5.9% widowed, 11.8% divorced (2000); Foreign born: 2.6% (2000); Ancestry (includes multiple ancestries): 17.9% Other groups, 17.9% Finnish, 12.8% English, 10.3% German, 5.1% French (except Basque) (2000).
Economy: Employment by occupation: 19.0% management, 33.3% professional, 14.3% services, 33.3% sales, 0.0% farming, 0.0% construction, 0.0% production (2000).
Income: Per capita income: $33,892 (2000); Median household income: $76,094 (2000); Poverty rate: 2.6% (2000).
Taxes: Total city taxes per capita: $33 (1997); City property taxes per capita: $33 (1997).
Education: High school graduation rate: 94.1% (2000); College graduation rate: 26.5% (2000).
Housing: Homeownership rate: 100.0% (2000); Median home value: $162,500 (2000); Median age of housing: 36 years (2000).
Transportation: Commute to work: 100.0% car, 0.0% public transportation, 0.0% walk, 0.0% work from home (2000); Travel time to work: 76.2% less than 15 minutes, 19.0% 15 to 30 minutes, 0.0% 30 to 45 minutes, 4.8% 45 to 60 minutes, 0.0% 60 minutes or more (2000)

GRAND MARAIS (unincorporated postal area, zip code 49839). Covers a land area of 23.038 square miles and a water area of 0.128 square miles. Located at 46.65° N. Lat.; 85.95° W. Long. Elevation is 650 feet.
History: Grand Marais developed as a commercial fishing center with its harbor on Lake Superior. The Endress Fish Company was established here in 1872.
Population: 433 (2000); Race: 95.4% White, 0.0% Black, 0.0% Asian, 1.2% American Indian and Alaska Native, 0.7% Hispanic of any race, 3.4% two or more races (2000); Density: 18.8 persons per square mile (2000); Age: 15.8% under 18, 33.3% over 64 (2000); Marriage status: 18.6% never married, 65.2% now married, 8.9% widowed, 7.3% divorced (2000); Foreign born: 2.2% (2000); Ancestry (includes multiple ancestries): 27.3% German, 15.1% Irish, 15.1% English, 11.2% French (except Basque), 9.0% Polish (2000).
Economy: Employment by occupation: 19.8% management, 18.3% professional, 23.8% services, 28.6% sales, 0.0% farming, 6.3% construction, 3.2% production (2000).
Income: Per capita income: $17,491 (2000); Median household income: $27,614 (2000); Poverty rate: 6.8% (2000).
Education: High school graduation rate: 88.7% (2000); College graduation rate: 21.8% (2000).

School District(s)

Burt Township School District (KG-12)
2000 Enrollment: 86 906-494-2543
Housing: Homeownership rate: 86.2% (2000); Median home value: $70,600 (2000); Median rent: $264 per month (2000); Median age of housing: 28 years (2000).
Newspapers: Great Lakes Pilot (1 x month)
Transportation: Commute to work: 73.8% car, 0.0% public transportation, 12.3% walk, 13.9% work from home (2000); Travel time to work: 92.4% less than 15 minutes, 3.8% 15 to 30 minutes, 1.9% 30 to 45 minutes, 0.0% 45 to 60 minutes, 1.9% 60 minutes or more (2000)

Additional Information Contacts

Grand Marais Chamber of Commerce 906-494-2447

LIMESTONE (township). Covers a land area of 74.556 square miles and a water area of 0.496 square miles. Located at 46.22° N. Lat.; 87.01° W. Long. Elevation is 912 feet.
History: Limestone Township was first settled in 1889. It was named for the limestone bed of Johnson Creek, which runs through it.
Population: 407 (2000); Race: 98.5% White, 0.0% Black, 0.0% Asian, 1.2% American Indian and Alaska Native, 0.2% Hispanic of any race, 0.2% two or more races (2000); Density: 5.5 persons per square mile (2000); Age: 23.5% under 18, 14.4% over 64 (2000); Marriage status: 13.3% never married, 72.3% now married, 6.5% widowed, 8.0% divorced (2000); Foreign born: 0.0% (2000); Ancestry (includes multiple ancestries): 18.6% German, 16.6% Finnish, 13.7% United States or American, 12.2% Polish, 9.0% French (except Basque) (2000).
Economy: Employment by occupation: 4.9% management, 27.2% professional, 14.2% services, 17.9% sales, 4.3% farming, 12.3% construction, 19.1% production (2000).
Income: Per capita income: $15,384 (2000); Median household income: $35,938 (2000); Poverty rate: 9.0% (2000).
Taxes: Total city taxes per capita: $22 (1997); City property taxes per capita: $22 (1997).
Education: High school graduation rate: 83.5% (2000); College graduation rate: 13.9% (2000).
Housing: Homeownership rate: 91.0% (2000); Median home value: $62,200 (2000); Median age of housing: 31 years (2000).
Transportation: Commute to work: 94.9% car, 0.6% public transportation, 0.6% walk, 3.2% work from home (2000); Travel time to work: 20.5% less

than 15 minutes, 26.5% 15 to 30 minutes, 29.1% 30 to 45 minutes, 16.6% 45 to 60 minutes, 7.3% 60 minutes or more (2000)

MATHIAS (township). Covers a land area of 71.023 square miles and a water area of 1.055 square miles. Located at 46.18° N. Lat.; 86.86° W. Long.
Population: 571 (2000); Race: 98.8% White, 0.0% Black, 0.9% Asian, 0.4% American Indian and Alaska Native, 0.0% Hispanic of any race, 0.0% two or more races (2000); Density: 8.0 persons per square mile (2000); Age: 19.0% under 18, 22.6% over 64 (2000); Marriage status: 20.1% never married, 57.4% now married, 12.6% widowed, 9.9% divorced (2000); Foreign born: 2.1% (2000); Ancestry (includes multiple ancestries): 30.2% Finnish, 16.9% German, 10.1% French (except Basque), 8.5% English, 8.2% Irish (2000).
Economy: Employment by occupation: 15.4% management, 18.1% professional, 11.8% services, 16.3% sales, 3.6% farming, 13.6% construction, 21.3% production (2000).
Income: Per capita income: $16,135 (2000); Median household income: $25,167 (2000); Poverty rate: 20.4% (2000).
Taxes: Total city taxes per capita: $37 (1997); City property taxes per capita: $37 (1997).
Education: High school graduation rate: 79.0% (2000); College graduation rate: 11.5% (2000).
Housing: Homeownership rate: 92.5% (2000); Median home value: $50,000 (2000); Median rent: $325 per month (2000); Median age of housing: 31 years (2000).
Transportation: Commute to work: 88.1% car, 0.0% public transportation, 6.0% walk, 5.0% work from home (2000); Travel time to work: 27.1% less than 15 minutes, 17.9% 15 to 30 minutes, 27.1% 30 to 45 minutes, 22.2% 45 to 60 minutes, 5.8% 60 minutes or more (2000)

MUNISING (city). Covers a land area of 5.357 square miles and a water area of 3.778 square miles. Located at 46.41° N. Lat.; 86.64° W. Long. Elevation is 626 feet.
History: Munising's name came from the Ojibway name for Grand Island, which was Gitchi-Menesing. A town was mapped out in the 1850's by a group of land speculators, but not until the 1870's did the town become a reality. Iron furnaces were the first industry, followed by a tannery and sawmills. Munising was incorporated as a village in 1897 and as a city in 1919.
Population: 2,539 (2000); Race: 92.5% White, 0.0% Black, 0.6% Asian, 5.1% American Indian and Alaska Native, 0.5% Hispanic of any race, 1.8% two or more races (2000); Density: 474.0 persons per square mile (2000); Age: 20.5% under 18, 25.9% over 64 (2000); Marriage status: 21.1% never married, 53.4% now married, 15.6% widowed, 10.0% divorced (2000); Foreign born: 0.6% (2000); Ancestry (includes multiple ancestries): 14.7% French (except Basque), 14.3% German, 13.5% Finnish, 12.1% Irish, 10.8% Polish (2000).
Economy: Employment by occupation: 10.8% management, 16.9% professional, 29.3% services, 22.0% sales, 2.2% farming, 5.8% construction, 13.0% production (2000).
Income: Per capita income: $19,779 (2000); Median household income: $33,899 (2000); Poverty rate: 11.4% (2000).
Taxes: Total city taxes per capita: $355 (1997); City property taxes per capita: $350 (1997).
Education: High school graduation rate: 81.8% (2000); College graduation rate: 18.9% (2000).

School District(s)

Munising Public Schools (KG-12)
2000 Enrollment: 1,038 906-387-2251
Housing: Homeownership rate: 64.9% (2000); Median home value: $66,500 (2000); Median rent: $331 per month (2000); Median age of housing: 53 years (2000).
Hospitals: Munising Memorial Hospital (40 beds)
Safety: Violent crime rate: 0.0 per 10,000 population; Property crime rate: 74.5 per 10,000 population (2001).
Newspapers: The Munising News (1 x week)
Transportation: Commute to work: 79.9% car, 1.5% public transportation, 13.5% walk, 3.7% work from home (2000); Travel time to work: 79.2% less than 15 minutes, 9.1% 15 to 30 minutes, 0.7% 30 to 45 minutes, 5.5% 45 to 60 minutes, 5.5% 60 minutes or more (2000)

Additional Information Contacts

Munising Chamber of Commerce 906-387-2138

MUNISING (township). Covers a land area of 202.596 square miles and a water area of 15.107 square miles. Located at 46.33° N. Lat.; 86.57° W. Long. Elevation is 626 feet.
History: Incorporated as village 1897, as city 1916.
Population: 3,125 (2000); Race: 73.4% White, 18.0% Black, 0.5% Asian, 4.5% American Indian and Alaska Native, 1.3% Hispanic of any race, 3.1% two or more races (2000); Density: 15.4 persons per square mile (2000); Age: 21.0% under 18, 8.3% over 64 (2000); Marriage status: 32.4% never married, 58.0% now married, 3.2% widowed, 6.4% divorced (2000); Foreign born: 0.9% (2000); Ancestry (includes multiple ancestries): 25.5% Other groups, 12.1% German, 9.9% French (except Basque), 9.1% Irish, 8.5% English (2000).
Economy: Lumbering and agriculture in area. Manufacturing: paper and wood products, including log homes; fisheries. Headquarters for Pictured Rocks National Lakeshore to Northeast; Hiawatha National Forest to West, South, and East. Employment by occupation: 8.8% management, 13.0% professional, 21.8% services, 21.0% sales, 2.4% farming, 10.3% construction, 22.8% production (2000).
Income: Per capita income: $17,448 (2000); Median household income: $40,946 (2000); Poverty rate: 7.8% (2000).
Taxes: Total city taxes per capita: $18 (1997); City property taxes per capita: $18 (1997).
Education: High school graduation rate: 77.2% (2000); College graduation rate: 8.3% (2000).
Housing: Homeownership rate: 91.5% (2000); Median home value: $84,100 (2000); Median rent: $280 per month (2000); Median age of housing: 25 years (2000).
Transportation: Commute to work: 93.1% car, 0.9% public transportation, 2.6% walk, 2.8% work from home (2000); Travel time to work: 56.9% less than 15 minutes, 33.3% 15 to 30 minutes, 2.2% 30 to 45 minutes, 2.3% 45 to 60 minutes, 5.2% 60 minutes or more (2000)

ONOTA (township). Covers a land area of 87.991 square miles and a water area of 8.136 square miles. Located at 46.47° N. Lat.; 86.99° W. Long.
Population: 310 (2000); Race: 97.7% White, 0.0% Black, 0.0% Asian, 0.0% American Indian and Alaska Native, 0.0% Hispanic of any race, 2.3% two or more races (2000); Density: 3.5 persons per square mile (2000); Age: 14.1% under 18, 21.2% over 64 (2000); Marriage status: 16.5% never married, 72.1% now married, 4.0% widowed, 7.4% divorced (2000); Foreign born: 0.0% (2000); Ancestry (includes multiple ancestries): 22.2% German, 12.7% Finnish, 10.5% English, 9.8% Irish, 8.5% Polish (2000).
Economy: Employment by occupation: 22.5% management, 24.6% professional, 17.6% services, 16.9% sales, 1.4% farming, 5.6% construction, 11.3% production (2000).
Income: Per capita income: $24,267 (2000); Median household income: $38,750 (2000); Poverty rate: 7.5% (2000).
Taxes: Total city taxes per capita: $362 (1997); City property taxes per capita: $362 (1997).
Education: High school graduation rate: 89.4% (2000); College graduation rate: 30.6% (2000).
Housing: Homeownership rate: 94.5% (2000); Median home value: $117,900 (2000); Median rent: $225 per month (2000); Median age of housing: 27 years (2000).
Transportation: Commute to work: 90.6% car, 0.0% public transportation, 0.0% walk, 9.4% work from home (2000); Travel time to work: 27.2% less than 15 minutes, 36.8% 15 to 30 minutes, 20.0% 30 to 45 minutes, 11.2% 45 to 60 minutes, 4.8% 60 minutes or more (2000)

ROCK RIVER (township). Covers a land area of 80.927 square miles and a water area of 0.080 square miles. Located at 46.35° N. Lat.; 86.96° W. Long. Elevation is 614 feet.
Population: 1,213 (2000); Race: 95.3% White, 0.0% Black, 0.0% Asian, 3.1% American Indian and Alaska Native, 1.5% Hispanic of any race, 1.1% two or more races (2000); Density: 15.0 persons per square mile (2000); Age: 21.9% under 18, 16.2% over 64 (2000); Marriage status: 20.5% never married, 64.3% now married, 8.7% widowed, 6.6% divorced (2000); Foreign born: 1.3% (2000); Ancestry (includes multiple ancestries): 38.1% Finnish, 13.1% German, 8.7% French (except Basque), 8.2% English, 7.2% Polish (2000).
Economy: Employment by occupation: 7.6% management, 12.5% professional, 22.6% services, 22.8% sales, 2.7% farming, 14.4% construction, 17.5% production (2000).
Income: Per capita income: $16,360 (2000); Median household income: $32,619 (2000); Poverty rate: 10.8% (2000).
Taxes: Total city taxes per capita: $27 (1997); City property taxes per capita: $27 (1997).
Education: High school graduation rate: 81.4% (2000); College graduation rate: 15.5% (2000).

Housing: Homeownership rate: 87.2% (2000); Median home value: $60,600 (2000); Median rent: $298 per month (2000); Median age of housing: 33 years (2000).
Transportation: Commute to work: 90.8% car, 0.8% public transportation, 3.3% walk, 4.4% work from home (2000); Travel time to work: 26.1% less than 15 minutes, 23.5% 15 to 30 minutes, 29.9% 30 to 45 minutes, 15.1% 45 to 60 minutes, 5.4% 60 minutes or more (2000)

RUMELY (unincorporated postal area, zip code 49826). Covers a land area of 1.364 square miles and a water area of 0 square miles. Located at 46.36° N. Lat.; 86.99° W. Long.
History: Rumely was named for a settler who came here in the early 1870's.
Population: 38 (2000); Race: 100.0% White, 0.0% Black, 0.0% Asian, 0.0% American Indian and Alaska Native, 0.0% Hispanic of any race, 0.0% two or more races (2000); Density: 27.9 persons per square mile (2000); Age: 28.1% under 18, 18.8% over 64 (2000); Marriage status: 16.0% never married, 72.0% now married, 0.0% widowed, 12.0% divorced (2000); Foreign born: 0.0% (2000); Ancestry (includes multiple ancestries): 31.3% Finnish, 21.9% Irish, 21.9% Polish, 21.9% English, 15.6% Other groups (2000).
Economy: Employment by occupation: 0.0% management, 20.0% professional, 30.0% services, 0.0% sales, 0.0% farming, 50.0% construction, 0.0% production (2000).
Income: Per capita income: $13,822 (2000); Median household income: $34,375 (2000); Poverty rate: 3.1% (2000).
Education: High school graduation rate: 87.0% (2000); College graduation rate: 13.0% (2000).
Housing: Homeownership rate: 100.0% (2000); Median home value: $55,000 (2000); Median age of housing: 19 years (2000).
Transportation: Commute to work: 100.0% car, 0.0% public transportation, 0.0% walk, 0.0% work from home (2000); Travel time to work: 0.0% less than 15 minutes, 30.0% 15 to 30 minutes, 50.0% 30 to 45 minutes, 0.0% 45 to 60 minutes, 20.0% 60 minutes or more (2000)

SHINGLETON (unincorporated postal area, zip code 49884). Covers a land area of 109.131 square miles and a water area of 1.067 square miles. Located at 46.40° N. Lat.; 86.43° W. Long. Elevation is 821 feet.
History: Shingleton was named for a shingle mill that operated here in the early 1880's. When the Detroit, Mackinaw & Marquette Railroad built a station here in 1882, they named it Jeromeville for David H. Jerome, the governor of Michigan at that time. The name was changed to Shingleton in 1887.
Population: 942 (2000); Race: 71.5% White, 18.1% Black, 0.7% Asian, 4.8% American Indian and Alaska Native, 2.7% Hispanic of any race, 3.4% two or more races (2000); Density: 8.6 persons per square mile (2000); Age: 16.9% under 18, 8.5% over 64 (2000); Marriage status: 28.0% never married, 60.8% now married, 2.9% widowed, 8.3% divorced (2000); Foreign born: 1.4% (2000); Ancestry (includes multiple ancestries): 27.3% Other groups, 10.3% German, 7.7% Irish, 7.4% French (except Basque), 7.4% United States or American (2000).
Economy: Employment by occupation: 5.9% management, 5.5% professional, 21.7% services, 19.5% sales, 1.8% farming, 14.7% construction, 30.9% production (2000).
Income: Per capita income: $18,598 (2000); Median household income: $34,615 (2000); Poverty rate: 14.1% (2000).
Education: High school graduation rate: 72.6% (2000); College graduation rate: 3.3% (2000).
Housing: Homeownership rate: 91.7% (2000); Median home value: $57,900 (2000); Median rent: $275 per month (2000); Median age of housing: 24 years (2000).
Transportation: Commute to work: 88.8% car, 1.1% public transportation, 5.2% walk, 3.0% work from home (2000); Travel time to work: 37.7% less than 15 minutes, 55.8% 15 to 30 minutes, 2.7% 30 to 45 minutes, 1.5% 45 to 60 minutes, 2.3% 60 minutes or more (2000)

TRENARY (unincorporated postal area, zip code 49891). Covers a land area of 111.009 square miles and a water area of 0.063 square miles. Located at 46.22° N. Lat.; 87.01° W. Long. Elevation is 851 feet.
Population: 944 (2000); Race: 96.9% White, 0.0% Black, 0.5% Asian, 2.0% American Indian and Alaska Native, 1.4% Hispanic of any race, 0.5% two or more races (2000); Density: 8.5 persons per square mile (2000); Age: 21.8% under 18, 19.5% over 64 (2000); Marriage status: 17.2% never married, 62.8% now married, 9.3% widowed, 10.6% divorced (2000); Foreign born: 1.6% (2000); Ancestry (includes multiple ancestries): 31.9% Finnish, 16.0% German, 8.9% Polish, 8.6% English, 7.4% French (except Basque) (2000).
Economy: Employment by occupation: 8.9% management, 15.8% professional, 18.9% services, 19.2% sales, 2.5% farming, 13.1% construction, 21.7% production (2000).
Income: Per capita income: $16,224 (2000); Median household income: $28,641 (2000); Poverty rate: 14.0% (2000).
Education: High school graduation rate: 79.2% (2000); College graduation rate: 14.0% (2000).
Housing: Homeownership rate: 89.0% (2000); Median home value: $55,900 (2000); Median rent: $294 per month (2000); Median age of housing: 36 years (2000).
Transportation: Commute to work: 91.8% car, 0.3% public transportation, 4.0% walk, 3.1% work from home (2000); Travel time to work: 22.0% less than 15 minutes, 17.9% 15 to 30 minutes, 29.9% 30 to 45 minutes, 22.6% 45 to 60 minutes, 7.6% 60 minutes or more (2000)

WETMORE (unincorporated postal area, zip code 49895). Covers a land area of 181.112 square miles and a water area of 6.030 square miles. Located at 46.19° N. Lat.; 86.64° W. Long. Elevation is 872 feet.
Population: 663 (2000); Race: 88.5% White, 0.0% Black, 0.0% Asian, 6.2% American Indian and Alaska Native, 2.4% Hispanic of any race, 5.0% two or more races (2000); Density: 3.7 persons per square mile (2000); Age: 23.1% under 18, 17.8% over 64 (2000); Marriage status: 17.4% never married, 67.1% now married, 5.9% widowed, 9.6% divorced (2000); Foreign born: 0.5% (2000); Ancestry (includes multiple ancestries): 17.5% German, 15.2% Other groups, 15.2% French (except Basque), 10.7% English, 10.4% Polish (2000).
Economy: Employment by occupation: 6.1% management, 12.6% professional, 27.9% services, 15.6% sales, 4.2% farming, 12.6% construction, 21.0% production (2000).
Income: Per capita income: $18,494 (2000); Median household income: $38,750 (2000); Poverty rate: 8.7% (2000).
Education: High school graduation rate: 83.7% (2000); College graduation rate: 13.0% (2000).
Housing: Homeownership rate: 90.0% (2000); Median home value: $94,800 (2000); Median rent: $267 per month (2000); Median age of housing: 31 years (2000).
Transportation: Commute to work: 92.6% car, 2.3% public transportation, 0.0% walk, 5.1% work from home (2000); Travel time to work: 38.9% less than 15 minutes, 41.8% 15 to 30 minutes, 4.5% 30 to 45 minutes, 5.3% 45 to 60 minutes, 9.4% 60 minutes or more (2000)

Allegan County

Located in southwestern Michigan; bounded on the west by Lake Michigan. Covers a land area of 827.50 square miles, a water area of 1,005.80 square miles, and is located in the Eastern Time Zone. The county government was organized in 1831. County seat is Allegan.

Allegan County is part of the Grand Rapids-Muskegon-Holland, MI MSA. The entire metro area includes: Allegan County; Kent County; Muskegon County; Ottawa County

Weather Station: Allegan 5 NE — Elevation: 748 feet

	Jan	Feb	Mar	Apr	May	Jun	Jul	Aug	Sep	Oct	Nov	Dec
High	31	34	44	58	70	79	83	81	73	61	47	35
Low	15	16	24	35	45	54	59	57	50	39	31	21
Precip	2.9	1.8	2.7	3.4	3.4	4.1	3.6	3.9	4.2	3.0	3.7	3.1
Snow	26.7	15.2	8.4	2.0	tr	0.0	0.0	0.0	0.0	0.4	7.3	21.7

High and Low temperatures in degrees Fahrenheit; Precipitation and Snow in inches

Population: 105,665 (2000); Race: 93.1% White, 1.4% Black, 0.6% Asian, 0.5% American Indian and Alaska Native, 6.0% Hispanic of any race, 1.4% two or more races (2000); Density: 127.7 persons per square mile (2000); Age: 28.7% under 18, 11.1% over 64 (2000).
Religion: Five largest groups: 11.3% Catholic Church, 9.6% Christian Reformed Church in North America, 4.2% Reformed Church in America, 3.1% The United Methodist Church, 1.1% The Wesleyan Church (2000).
Economy: Unemployment rate: 5.1% (11/2002); Total civilian labor force: 59,118 (11/2002); Leading industries: 45.8% manufacturing; 10.9% retail trade; 7.3% health care and social assistance (2000); Companies that employ more than 1,000 persons: 3 (2000); Companies that employ more than 100 persons: 53 (2000); Farms: 1,337 totaling 236,936 acres (1997); Minority business ownership rate: 2.8% (1997); Women business ownership rate: 23.9% (1997); Retail sales per capita: $6,389 (1997). Single-family building permits issued: 644 (2001) / 642 (2000); Multi-family building permits issued: 156 (2001) / 47 (2000).

Income: Per capita income: $19,918 (2000); Median household income: $45,813 (2000); Poverty rate: 7.3% (2000); Bankruptcy rate: 4.08% (2001).
Taxes: Total county taxes per capita: $146 (2000); County property taxes per capita: $141 (2000).
Education: High school graduation rate: 82.3% (2000); College graduation rate: 15.8% (2000).
Housing: Homeownership rate: 82.9% (2000); Median home value: $115,500 (2000); Median rent: $441 per month (2000); Median age of housing: 27 years (2000).
Health: Birth rate: 132.1 per 10,000 population (1998); Age adjusted death rate: 92.6 per 10,000 population (1999); Age adjusted cancer mortality rate: 240.2 deaths per 100,000 population (1999). Air Quality Index: 65% good, 35% moderate, 0% unhealthy (percent of days in 2000). Number of physicians: 5.4 per 10,000 population (1999); Number of hospital beds: 6.0 per 10,000 population (1999).
Elections: 2000 Presidential election results: 34.5% Gore, 62.8% Bush, 2.1% Nader, 0.0% Buchanan
National and State Parks: Allegan State Forest; Saugatuck Dunes State Park
Additional Information Contacts
Allegan County Government Offices. 616-673-0205
Allegan Chamber of Commerce. 616-673-2479
Fennville Chamber of Commerce 616-561-5550
Otsego Chamber of Commerce 616-694-6880
Plainwell Chamber of Commerce 616-685-8877
Wayland Chamber of Commerce. 616-792-9246

Allegan County Communities

ALLEGAN (city). Covers a land area of 3.807 square miles and a water area of 0.510 square miles. Located at 42.52° N. Lat.; 85.85° W. Long. Elevation is 658 feet.
History: Allegan was settled in 1833. It was incorporated as a village in 1838 and as a city in 1907. The name was chosen by Henry Rowe Schoolcraft for the Alleghen tribe.
Population: 4,838 (2000); Race: 91.2% White, 4.6% Black, 0.2% Asian, 0.1% American Indian and Alaska Native, 3.3% Hispanic of any race, 1.3% two or more races (2000); Density: 1,270.9 persons per square mile (2000); Age: 26.8% under 18, 15.3% over 64 (2000); Marriage status: 28.3% never married, 48.1% now married, 8.4% widowed, 15.3% divorced (2000); Foreign born: 0.8% (2000); Ancestry (includes multiple ancestries): 19.2% German, 12.5% English, 12.3% Irish, 10.7% Other groups, 9.6% United States or American (2000).
Economy: Single-family building permits issued: 2 (2001) / 2 (2000); Multi-family building permits issued: 21 (2001) / 30 (2000); Employment by occupation: 7.5% management, 14.5% professional, 20.3% services, 20.4% sales, 0.0% farming, 8.4% construction, 28.8% production (2000).
Income: Per capita income: $17,075 (2000); Median household income: $39,539 (2000); Poverty rate: 13.5% (2000).
Taxes: Total city taxes per capita: $424 (1997); City property taxes per capita: $421 (1997).
Education: High school graduation rate: 81.1% (2000); College graduation rate: 14.4% (2000).

School District(s)

Allegan Public Schools (PK-12)
2000 Enrollment: 3,028 616-673-5431
Housing: Homeownership rate: 63.1% (2000); Median home value: $87,700 (2000); Median rent: $409 per month (2000); Median age of housing: 57 years (2000).
Hospitals: Allegan General Hospital (63 beds)
Safety: Violent crime rate: 127.5 per 10,000 population; Property crime rate: 329.0 per 10,000 population (2001).
Newspapers: Quad City Flashes Shoppers Guide (1 x week); Lakeshore Flashes Shopping Guide (1 x week); Allegan Flashes Shopping Guide (1 x week); The Allegan County News (1 x week); Holland Flashes Community Shopper (1 x week)
Transportation: Commute to work: 89.5% car, 0.8% public transportation, 1.4% walk, 5.6% work from home (2000); Travel time to work: 52.4% less than 15 minutes, 18.8% 15 to 30 minutes, 17.0% 30 to 45 minutes, 8.1% 45 to 60 minutes, 3.7% 60 minutes or more (2000)
Additional Information Contacts
Allegan Chamber of Commerce. 616-673-2479

ALLEGAN (township). Covers a land area of 30.429 square miles and a water area of 1.439 square miles. Located at 42.54° N. Lat.; 85.84° W. Long. Elevation is 658 feet.
History: Settled 1834, incorporated as city 1907.
Population: 4,050 (2000); Race: 96.0% White, 0.3% Black, 0.0% Asian, 1.4% American Indian and Alaska Native, 2.6% Hispanic of any race, 1.0% two or more races (2000); Density: 133.1 persons per square mile (2000); Age: 26.6% under 18, 14.8% over 64 (2000); Marriage status: 20.0% never married, 60.7% now married, 6.3% widowed, 13.0% divorced (2000); Foreign born: 1.0% (2000); Ancestry (includes multiple ancestries): 22.9% German, 16.0% English, 13.0% Dutch, 11.6% Irish, 10.1% Other groups (2000).
Economy: In farming area: livestock, dairy products, poultry, oats, corn, fruit. Manufactures pharmaceuticals, wood products, furniture, electric products, fabricated pipe; publishing industry. Single-family building permits issued: 43 (2001) / 42 (2000); Multi-family building permits issued: 0 (2001) / 0 (2000); Employment by occupation: 11.2% management, 13.3% professional, 14.8% services, 23.1% sales, 1.3% farming, 8.3% construction, 28.2% production (2000).
Income: Per capita income: $18,545 (2000); Median household income: $40,760 (2000); Poverty rate: 8.1% (2000).
Taxes: Total city taxes per capita: $49 (1997); City property taxes per capita: $41 (1997).
Education: High school graduation rate: 84.4% (2000); College graduation rate: 14.5% (2000).
Housing: Homeownership rate: 89.6% (2000); Median home value: $106,300 (2000); Median rent: $384 per month (2000); Median age of housing: 32 years (2000).
Transportation: Commute to work: 96.4% car, 0.0% public transportation, 1.2% walk, 2.4% work from home (2000); Travel time to work: 49.5% less than 15 minutes, 19.4% 15 to 30 minutes, 18.1% 30 to 45 minutes, 8.3% 45 to 60 minutes, 4.6% 60 minutes or more (2000)

CASCO (township). Covers a land area of 38.869 square miles and a water area of 0 square miles. Located at 42.47° N. Lat.; 86.20° W. Long.
Population: 3,019 (2000); Race: 89.6% White, 5.1% Black, 1.0% Asian, 0.2% American Indian and Alaska Native, 10.3% Hispanic of any race, 0.3% two or more races (2000); Density: 77.7 persons per square mile (2000); Age: 26.3% under 18, 12.9% over 64 (2000); Marriage status: 21.3% never married, 63.8% now married, 6.7% widowed, 8.2% divorced (2000); Foreign born: 5.4% (2000); Ancestry (includes multiple ancestries): 23.5% German, 18.0% Other groups, 15.2% United States or American, 14.4% English, 7.8% Irish (2000).
Economy: Employment by occupation: 12.2% management, 15.4% professional, 13.6% services, 18.3% sales, 5.8% farming, 14.3% construction, 20.3% production (2000).
Income: Per capita income: $22,356 (2000); Median household income: $45,043 (2000); Poverty rate: 8.5% (2000).
Taxes: Total city taxes per capita: $127 (1997); City property taxes per capita: $120 (1997).
Education: High school graduation rate: 83.4% (2000); College graduation rate: 19.7% (2000).
Housing: Homeownership rate: 86.4% (2000); Median home value: $112,800 (2000); Median rent: $416 per month (2000); Median age of housing: 28 years (2000).
Transportation: Commute to work: 89.9% car, 0.4% public transportation, 3.7% walk, 4.6% work from home (2000); Travel time to work: 28.2% less than 15 minutes, 40.8% 15 to 30 minutes, 18.7% 30 to 45 minutes, 5.5% 45 to 60 minutes, 6.7% 60 minutes or more (2000)

CHESHIRE (township). Covers a land area of 34.948 square miles and a water area of 1.066 square miles. Located at 42.45° N. Lat.; 85.95° W. Long.
History: Cheshire Township was organized in 1851 around four sawmill villages.
Population: 2,335 (2000); Race: 93.5% White, 3.0% Black, 0.3% Asian, 0.7% American Indian and Alaska Native, 0.0% Hispanic of any race, 2.5% two or more races (2000); Density: 66.8 persons per square mile (2000); Age: 28.9% under 18, 11.1% over 64 (2000); Marriage status: 18.5% never married, 64.2% now married, 4.2% widowed, 13.1% divorced (2000); Foreign born: 1.1% (2000); Ancestry (includes multiple ancestries): 21.2% German, 11.9% English, 11.6% Irish, 10.2% Dutch, 10.0% Other groups (2000).
Economy: Single-family building permits issued: 17 (2001) / 5 (2000); Multi-family building permits issued: 0 (2001) / 0 (2000); Employment by

occupation: 8.6% management, 14.6% professional, 15.0% services, 18.4% sales, 1.3% farming, 10.7% construction, 31.3% production (2000).
Income: Per capita income: $16,350 (2000); Median household income: $40,405 (2000); Poverty rate: 9.4% (2000).
Taxes: Total city taxes per capita: $14 (1997); City property taxes per capita: $5 (1997).
Education: High school graduation rate: 76.1% (2000); College graduation rate: 14.1% (2000).
Housing: Homeownership rate: 88.8% (2000); Median home value: $91,400 (2000); Median rent: $390 per month (2000); Median age of housing: 28 years (2000).
Transportation: Commute to work: 96.6% car, 0.0% public transportation, 1.6% walk, 1.7% work from home (2000); Travel time to work: 17.2% less than 15 minutes, 42.6% 15 to 30 minutes, 20.4% 30 to 45 minutes, 13.2% 45 to 60 minutes, 6.6% 60 minutes or more (2000)

CLYDE (township). Covers a land area of 34.976 square miles and a water area of 0.619 square miles. Located at 42.55° N. Lat.; 86.07° W. Long.
History: Clyde Township was organized in 1859 and named for Clyde, New York, the former home of its first supervisor.
Population: 2,104 (2000); Race: 80.0% White, 1.4% Black, 0.5% Asian, 0.6% American Indian and Alaska Native, 31.2% Hispanic of any race, 1.2% two or more races (2000); Density: 60.2 persons per square mile (2000); Age: 30.1% under 18, 7.9% over 64 (2000); Marriage status: 18.8% never married, 65.4% now married, 4.6% widowed, 11.2% divorced (2000); Foreign born: 11.5% (2000); Ancestry (includes multiple ancestries): 37.0% Other groups, 14.6% Dutch, 11.4% German, 9.3% Irish, 7.4% English (2000).
Economy: Employment by occupation: 6.0% management, 8.2% professional, 12.3% services, 15.2% sales, 2.7% farming, 12.4% construction, 43.3% production (2000).
Income: Per capita income: $15,986 (2000); Median household income: $42,717 (2000); Poverty rate: 9.5% (2000).
Taxes: Total city taxes per capita: $72 (1997); City property taxes per capita: $71 (1997).
Education: High school graduation rate: 69.1% (2000); College graduation rate: 7.0% (2000).
Housing: Homeownership rate: 87.6% (2000); Median home value: $92,800 (2000); Median rent: $391 per month (2000); Median age of housing: 27 years (2000).
Transportation: Commute to work: 96.7% car, 0.1% public transportation, 0.2% walk, 2.2% work from home (2000); Travel time to work: 20.5% less than 15 minutes, 38.6% 15 to 30 minutes, 29.1% 30 to 45 minutes, 7.2% 45 to 60 minutes, 4.6% 60 minutes or more (2000)

DORR (township). Covers a land area of 36.155 square miles and a water area of 0.019 square miles. Located at 42.73° N. Lat.; 85.71° W. Long.
Population: 6,579 (2000); Race: 97.2% White, 0.4% Black, 0.3% Asian, 0.4% American Indian and Alaska Native, 2.5% Hispanic of any race, 1.0% two or more races (2000); Density: 182.0 persons per square mile (2000); Age: 33.6% under 18, 5.4% over 64 (2000); Marriage status: 23.2% never married, 68.6% now married, 2.9% widowed, 5.3% divorced (2000); Foreign born: 1.4% (2000); Ancestry (includes multiple ancestries): 26.9% Dutch, 24.8% German, 11.9% Irish, 9.7% United States or American, 9.5% Polish (2000).
Economy: Single-family building permits issued: 60 (2001) / 57 (2000); Multi-family building permits issued: 0 (2001) / 0 (2000); Employment by occupation: 14.0% management, 12.2% professional, 6.9% services, 24.6% sales, 0.7% farming, 13.9% construction, 27.8% production (2000).
Income: Per capita income: $18,756 (2000); Median household income: $60,446 (2000); Poverty rate: 5.1% (2000).
Taxes: Total city taxes per capita: $64 (1997); City property taxes per capita: $52 (1997).
Education: High school graduation rate: 87.7% (2000); College graduation rate: 12.3% (2000).
Housing: Homeownership rate: 94.5% (2000); Median home value: $122,300 (2000); Median rent: $467 per month (2000); Median age of housing: 21 years (2000).
Transportation: Commute to work: 95.4% car, 0.0% public transportation, 0.0% walk, 4.3% work from home (2000); Travel time to work: 12.0% less than 15 minutes, 52.7% 15 to 30 minutes, 28.1% 30 to 45 minutes, 4.2% 45 to 60 minutes, 2.9% 60 minutes or more (2000)

DOUGLAS (village). Covers a land area of 1.755 square miles and a water area of 0.129 square miles. Located at 42.64° N. Lat.; 86.20° W. Long.
History: Douglas grew around an art colony.
Population: 1,214 (2000); Race: 98.2% White, 0.2% Black, 0.0% Asian, 0.0% American Indian and Alaska Native, 1.7% Hispanic of any race, 0.7% two or more races (2000); Density: 691.6 persons per square mile (2000); Age: 18.9% under 18, 23.1% over 64 (2000); Marriage status: 23.9% never married, 48.3% now married, 11.6% widowed, 16.1% divorced (2000); Foreign born: 1.8% (2000); Ancestry (includes multiple ancestries): 21.0% German, 15.0% English, 14.5% Irish, 11.8% Dutch, 7.5% Polish (2000).
Economy: Employment by occupation: 12.2% management, 15.0% professional, 19.2% services, 25.5% sales, 0.0% farming, 7.3% construction, 20.7% production (2000).
Income: Per capita income: $26,517 (2000); Median household income: $41,250 (2000); Poverty rate: 10.3% (2000).
Taxes: Total city taxes per capita: $702 (1997); City property taxes per capita: $698 (1997).
Education: High school graduation rate: 85.3% (2000); College graduation rate: 27.4% (2000).

School District(s)
Saugatuck Public Schools (PK-12)
2000 Enrollment: 718 616-857-1444
Housing: Homeownership rate: 70.8% (2000); Median home value: $175,000 (2000); Median rent: $501 per month (2000); Median age of housing: 27 years (2000).
Safety: Violent crime rate: 48.0 per 10,000 population; Property crime rate: 436.5 per 10,000 population (2001).
Transportation: Commute to work: 88.5% car, 1.7% public transportation, 2.7% walk, 7.1% work from home (2000); Travel time to work: 37.5% less than 15 minutes, 38.8% 15 to 30 minutes, 10.9% 30 to 45 minutes, 3.3% 45 to 60 minutes, 9.5% 60 minutes or more (2000)

FENNVILLE (city). Covers a land area of 1.058 square miles and a water area of 0.020 square miles. Located at 42.59° N. Lat.; 86.10° W. Long. Elevation is 664 feet.
Population: 1,459 (2000); Race: 72.0% White, 4.5% Black, 0.0% Asian, 1.1% American Indian and Alaska Native, 29.4% Hispanic of any race, 2.5% two or more races (2000); Density: 1,378.4 persons per square mile (2000); Age: 35.2% under 18, 7.4% over 64 (2000); Marriage status: 24.3% never married, 58.5% now married, 7.1% widowed, 10.1% divorced (2000); Foreign born: 9.5% (2000); Ancestry (includes multiple ancestries): 38.0% Other groups, 11.7% German, 9.3% English, 8.9% Irish, 8.1% Dutch (2000).
Economy: In fruit-growing and dairying area. Manufacturing: food processing, automotive parts. Employment by occupation: 6.1% management, 7.1% professional, 21.3% services, 15.2% sales, 1.7% farming, 7.3% construction, 41.3% production (2000).
Income: Per capita income: $16,127 (2000); Median household income: $39,013 (2000); Poverty rate: 12.2% (2000).
Taxes: Total city taxes per capita: $244 (1997); City property taxes per capita: $241 (1997).
Education: High school graduation rate: 76.3% (2000); College graduation rate: 8.6% (2000).

School District(s)
Discovery Elementary School (KG-06)
2000 Enrollment: 97 616-895-3029
Fennville Public Schools (KG-12)
2000 Enrollment: 1,637 616-561-7331
Housing: Homeownership rate: 74.1% (2000); Median home value: $88,000 (2000); Median rent: $418 per month (2000); Median age of housing: 20 years (2000).
Transportation: Commute to work: 93.7% car, 0.0% public transportation, 4.1% walk, 1.5% work from home (2000); Travel time to work: 24.0% less than 15 minutes, 46.9% 15 to 30 minutes, 22.7% 30 to 45 minutes, 3.0% 45 to 60 minutes, 3.5% 60 minutes or more (2000)
Additional Information Contacts
Fennville Chamber of Commerce 616-561-5550

FILLMORE (township). Covers a land area of 28.572 square miles and a water area of 0.010 square miles. Located at 42.72° N. Lat.; 86.06° W. Long.
Population: 2,756 (2000); Race: 91.1% White, 1.4% Black, 1.9% Asian, 0.2% American Indian and Alaska Native, 6.2% Hispanic of any race, 2.6% two or more races (2000); Density: 96.5 persons per square mile (2000); Age: 31.5% under 18, 8.3% over 64 (2000); Marriage status: 24.3% never married, 64.4% now married, 4.2% widowed, 7.1% divorced (2000); Foreign born: 2.7% (2000); Ancestry (includes multiple ancestries): 45.4% Dutch, 18.4% German, 10.3% Other groups, 5.7% United States or American, 5.1% Irish (2000).
Economy: Single-family building permits issued: 9 (2001) / 7 (2000); Multi-family building permits issued: 0 (2001) / 0 (2000); Employment by

occupation: 10.7% management, 11.5% professional, 15.5% services, 20.5% sales, 3.9% farming, 14.6% construction, 23.4% production (2000).
Income: Per capita income: $20,166 (2000); Median household income: $52,969 (2000); Poverty rate: 5.4% (2000).
Taxes: Total city taxes per capita: $97 (1997); City property taxes per capita: $88 (1997).
Education: High school graduation rate: 75.8% (2000); College graduation rate: 13.9% (2000).
Housing: Homeownership rate: 86.9% (2000); Median home value: $127,200 (2000); Median rent: $475 per month (2000); Median age of housing: 31 years (2000).
Transportation: Commute to work: 93.5% car, 0.0% public transportation, 1.3% walk, 4.8% work from home (2000); Travel time to work: 49.1% less than 15 minutes, 36.6% 15 to 30 minutes, 7.3% 30 to 45 minutes, 4.2% 45 to 60 minutes, 2.8% 60 minutes or more (2000)

GANGES (township). Covers a land area of 32.457 square miles and a water area of 0.227 square miles. Located at 42.54° N. Lat.; 86.19° W. Long. Elevation is 661 feet.
Population: 2,524 (2000); Race: 91.8% White, 0.0% Black, 0.2% Asian, 0.4% American Indian and Alaska Native, 13.7% Hispanic of any race, 0.8% two or more races (2000); Density: 77.8 persons per square mile (2000); Age: 23.7% under 18, 14.1% over 64 (2000); Marriage status: 25.8% never married, 58.0% now married, 5.8% widowed, 10.4% divorced (2000); Foreign born: 4.2% (2000); Ancestry (includes multiple ancestries): 19.7% German, 16.3% Other groups, 15.1% English, 14.9% Irish, 13.0% Dutch (2000).
Economy: Single-family building permits issued: 30 (2001) / 33 (2000); Multi-family building permits issued: 0 (2001) / 0 (2000); Employment by occupation: 9.1% management, 13.4% professional, 13.4% services, 24.3% sales, 5.7% farming, 7.8% construction, 26.4% production (2000).
Income: Per capita income: $22,753 (2000); Median household income: $47,143 (2000); Poverty rate: 5.9% (2000).
Taxes: Total city taxes per capita: $131 (1997); City property taxes per capita: $115 (1997).
Education: High school graduation rate: 82.0% (2000); College graduation rate: 22.5% (2000).
Housing: Homeownership rate: 88.5% (2000); Median home value: $122,100 (2000); Median rent: $377 per month (2000); Median age of housing: 34 years (2000).
Transportation: Commute to work: 86.6% car, 1.0% public transportation, 1.9% walk, 8.8% work from home (2000); Travel time to work: 21.7% less than 15 minutes, 40.1% 15 to 30 minutes, 25.3% 30 to 45 minutes, 6.6% 45 to 60 minutes, 6.2% 60 minutes or more (2000)

GUNPLAIN (township). Covers a land area of 34.148 square miles and a water area of 0.277 square miles. Located at 42.46° N. Lat.; 85.61° W. Long.
Population: 5,637 (2000); Race: 96.1% White, 0.6% Black, 0.7% Asian, 0.4% American Indian and Alaska Native, 0.2% Hispanic of any race, 2.1% two or more races (2000); Density: 165.1 persons per square mile (2000); Age: 26.2% under 18, 9.5% over 64 (2000); Marriage status: 17.2% never married, 69.1% now married, 4.9% widowed, 8.7% divorced (2000); Foreign born: 1.4% (2000); Ancestry (includes multiple ancestries): 24.9% German, 17.0% Dutch, 16.6% English, 14.0% Irish, 7.6% Other groups (2000).
Economy: Single-family building permits issued: 53 (2001) / 53 (2000); Multi-family building permits issued: 0 (2001) / 0 (2000); Employment by occupation: 16.0% management, 18.0% professional, 13.7% services, 23.6% sales, 0.5% farming, 6.8% construction, 21.4% production (2000).
Income: Per capita income: $22,941 (2000); Median household income: $53,495 (2000); Poverty rate: 7.8% (2000).
Taxes: Total city taxes per capita: $34 (1997); City property taxes per capita: $28 (1997).
Education: High school graduation rate: 86.9% (2000); College graduation rate: 24.4% (2000).
Housing: Homeownership rate: 90.8% (2000); Median home value: $131,100 (2000); Median rent: $439 per month (2000); Median age of housing: 24 years (2000).
Transportation: Commute to work: 93.9% car, 0.0% public transportation, 0.5% walk, 4.9% work from home (2000); Travel time to work: 25.0% less than 15 minutes, 40.1% 15 to 30 minutes, 22.1% 30 to 45 minutes, 7.9% 45 to 60 minutes, 4.9% 60 minutes or more (2000)

HAMILTON (unincorporated postal area, zip code 49419). Covers a land area of 69.130 square miles and a water area of 0.169 square miles. Located at 42.68° N. Lat.; 85.99° W. Long. Elevation is 643 feet.
History: Hamilton was first called Rabbit River, for its location on that river. The name was changed in 1870.
Population: 6,479 (2000); Race: 96.7% White, 0.0% Black, 1.2% Asian, 0.0% American Indian and Alaska Native, 2.1% Hispanic of any race, 0.7% two or more races (2000); Density: 93.7 persons per square mile (2000); Age: 31.1% under 18, 6.1% over 64 (2000); Marriage status: 19.2% never married, 73.3% now married, 2.4% widowed, 5.0% divorced (2000); Foreign born: 2.2% (2000); Ancestry (includes multiple ancestries): 51.3% Dutch, 18.7% German, 6.9% United States or American, 6.4% Other groups, 6.0% Irish (2000).
Economy: Employment by occupation: 10.3% management, 11.2% professional, 11.3% services, 23.6% sales, 2.1% farming, 13.8% construction, 27.7% production (2000).
Income: Per capita income: $20,396 (2000); Median household income: $55,426 (2000); Poverty rate: 3.6% (2000).
Education: High school graduation rate: 86.0% (2000); College graduation rate: 14.1% (2000).

School District(s)

Hamilton Community Schools (KG-12)
2000 Enrollment: 2,351 616-751-5148
Housing: Homeownership rate: 91.0% (2000); Median home value: $140,900 (2000); Median rent: $448 per month (2000); Median age of housing: 21 years (2000).
Transportation: Commute to work: 96.2% car, 0.0% public transportation, 0.9% walk, 2.7% work from home (2000); Travel time to work: 23.1% less than 15 minutes, 54.1% 15 to 30 minutes, 14.8% 30 to 45 minutes, 4.5% 45 to 60 minutes, 3.4% 60 minutes or more (2000)

HEATH (township). Covers a land area of 35.478 square miles and a water area of 0.441 square miles. Located at 42.64° N. Lat.; 85.96° W. Long.
Population: 3,100 (2000); Race: 97.5% White, 0.1% Black, 0.9% Asian, 0.0% American Indian and Alaska Native, 2.6% Hispanic of any race, 1.0% two or more races (2000); Density: 87.4 persons per square mile (2000); Age: 32.3% under 18, 5.1% over 64 (2000); Marriage status: 19.7% never married, 70.9% now married, 2.8% widowed, 6.5% divorced (2000); Foreign born: 2.8% (2000); Ancestry (includes multiple ancestries): 42.1% Dutch, 16.7% German, 9.5% United States or American, 7.5% Other groups, 6.2% English (2000).
Economy: Single-family building permits issued: 35 (2001) / 31 (2000); Multi-family building permits issued: 0 (2001) / 0 (2000); Employment by occupation: 10.9% management, 11.4% professional, 10.6% services, 18.9% sales, 0.6% farming, 15.7% construction, 31.9% production (2000).
Income: Per capita income: $20,248 (2000); Median household income: $54,545 (2000); Poverty rate: 3.8% (2000).
Taxes: Total city taxes per capita: $72 (1997); City property taxes per capita: $60 (1997).
Education: High school graduation rate: 86.0% (2000); College graduation rate: 15.1% (2000).
Housing: Homeownership rate: 89.7% (2000); Median home value: $137,500 (2000); Median rent: $446 per month (2000); Median age of housing: 16 years (2000).
Transportation: Commute to work: 98.4% car, 0.0% public transportation, 0.1% walk, 1.5% work from home (2000); Travel time to work: 23.1% less than 15 minutes, 52.1% 15 to 30 minutes, 14.9% 30 to 45 minutes, 5.9% 45 to 60 minutes, 4.0% 60 minutes or more (2000)

HOPKINS (village). Covers a land area of 0.521 square miles and a water area of 0 square miles. Located at 42.62° N. Lat.; 85.76° W. Long. Elevation is 704 feet.
History: Hopkins grew up around the railroad station which was named Hopkins Station in 1874. The village was platted by John Hoffmaster.
Population: 592 (2000); Race: 93.1% White, 0.0% Black, 0.0% Asian, 2.5% American Indian and Alaska Native, 3.4% Hispanic of any race, 3.2% two or more races (2000); Density: 1,137.1 persons per square mile (2000); Age: 28.4% under 18, 13.8% over 64 (2000); Marriage status: 31.2% never married, 50.6% now married, 5.6% widowed, 12.6% divorced (2000); Foreign born: 2.4% (2000); Ancestry (includes multiple ancestries): 38.3% German, 13.8% Dutch, 13.8% Irish, 11.8% English, 8.6% Other groups (2000).
Economy: Single-family building permits issued: 0 (2001) / 0 (2000); Multi-family building permits issued: 0 (2001) / 0 (2000); Employment by occupation: 5.6% management, 7.9% professional, 14.9% services, 31.0% sales, 2.3% farming, 7.9% construction, 30.4% production (2000).
Income: Per capita income: $16,667 (2000); Median household income: $38,462 (2000); Poverty rate: 8.9% (2000).

Taxes: Total city taxes per capita: $92 (1997); City property taxes per capita: $85 (1997).
Education: High school graduation rate: 82.2% (2000); College graduation rate: 10.5% (2000).

School District(s)

Hopkins Public Schools (KG-12)
2000 Enrollment: 1,402 616-793-7261

Housing: Homeownership rate: 81.3% (2000); Median home value: $87,300 (2000); Median rent: $404 per month (2000); Median age of housing: 60+ years (2000).
Transportation: Commute to work: 92.2% car, 0.0% public transportation, 3.7% walk, 3.0% work from home (2000); Travel time to work: 26.1% less than 15 minutes, 32.4% 15 to 30 minutes, 30.3% 30 to 45 minutes, 9.1% 45 to 60 minutes, 2.1% 60 minutes or more (2000)

HOPKINS (township). Covers a land area of 35.841 square miles and a water area of 0.188 square miles. Located at 42.63° N. Lat.; 85.72° W. Long. Elevation is 704 feet.
Population: 2,671 (2000); Race: 92.4% White, 0.2% Black, 0.0% Asian, 2.1% American Indian and Alaska Native, 4.7% Hispanic of any race, 1.1% two or more races (2000); Density: 74.5 persons per square mile (2000); Age: 32.0% under 18, 10.4% over 64 (2000); Marriage status: 24.7% never married, 61.9% now married, 4.3% widowed, 9.1% divorced (2000); Foreign born: 3.1% (2000); Ancestry (includes multiple ancestries): 29.0% German, 22.6% Dutch, 12.0% Polish, 8.8% English, 7.8% Irish (2000).
Economy: In farm area. Manufacturing: trash compactors. Single-family building permits issued: 6 (2001) / 7 (2000); Multi-family building permits issued: 0 (2001) / 0 (2000); Employment by occupation: 9.6% management, 9.1% professional, 14.1% services, 20.9% sales, 1.6% farming, 12.6% construction, 32.1% production (2000).
Income: Per capita income: $17,220 (2000); Median household income: $46,296 (2000); Poverty rate: 4.7% (2000).
Taxes: Total city taxes per capita: $50 (1997); City property taxes per capita: $50 (1997).
Education: High school graduation rate: 83.6% (2000); College graduation rate: 8.3% (2000).
Housing: Homeownership rate: 87.4% (2000); Median home value: $102,000 (2000); Median rent: $408 per month (2000); Median age of housing: 44 years (2000).
Transportation: Commute to work: 89.3% car, 0.0% public transportation, 3.1% walk, 6.6% work from home (2000); Travel time to work: 25.6% less than 15 minutes, 31.2% 15 to 30 minutes, 28.2% 30 to 45 minutes, 10.9% 45 to 60 minutes, 4.2% 60 minutes or more (2000)

LAKETOWN (township). Covers a land area of 21.627 square miles and a water area of 0.075 square miles. Located at 42.72° N. Lat.; 86.16° W. Long.
Population: 5,561 (2000); Race: 96.2% White, 0.6% Black, 0.0% Asian, 0.1% American Indian and Alaska Native, 4.7% Hispanic of any race, 1.0% two or more races (2000); Density: 257.1 persons per square mile (2000); Age: 26.4% under 18, 11.1% over 64 (2000); Marriage status: 20.1% never married, 69.9% now married, 4.5% widowed, 5.5% divorced (2000); Foreign born: 1.5% (2000); Ancestry (includes multiple ancestries): 46.3% Dutch, 19.3% German, 8.1% Other groups, 7.6% English, 6.4% Irish (2000).
Economy: Single-family building permits issued: 38 (2001) / 35 (2000); Multi-family building permits issued: 11 (2001) / 7 (2000); Employment by occupation: 16.8% management, 21.8% professional, 10.4% services, 23.5% sales, 1.0% farming, 10.7% construction, 15.8% production (2000).
Income: Per capita income: $29,377 (2000); Median household income: $60,893 (2000); Poverty rate: 2.8% (2000).
Taxes: Total city taxes per capita: $120 (1997); City property taxes per capita: $109 (1997).
Education: High school graduation rate: 91.2% (2000); College graduation rate: 31.0% (2000).
Housing: Homeownership rate: 85.3% (2000); Median home value: $158,800 (2000); Median rent: $526 per month (2000); Median age of housing: 20 years (2000).
Transportation: Commute to work: 94.6% car, 0.0% public transportation, 0.7% walk, 4.7% work from home (2000); Travel time to work: 38.8% less than 15 minutes, 48.5% 15 to 30 minutes, 5.5% 30 to 45 minutes, 3.8% 45 to 60 minutes, 3.3% 60 minutes or more (2000)

LEE (township). Covers a land area of 35.331 square miles and a water area of 0.776 square miles. Located at 42.46° N. Lat.; 86.07° W. Long.
Population: 4,114 (2000); Race: 72.5% White, 7.4% Black, 0.4% Asian, 1.6% American Indian and Alaska Native, 22.2% Hispanic of any race, 3.4% two or more races (2000); Density: 116.4 persons per square mile (2000); Age: 34.0% under 18, 6.9% over 64 (2000); Marriage status: 27.1% never married, 53.9% now married, 4.4% widowed, 14.6% divorced (2000); Foreign born: 11.6% (2000); Ancestry (includes multiple ancestries): 33.0% Other groups, 10.7% German, 8.9% United States or American, 8.8% Irish, 6.1% Dutch (2000).
Economy: Single-family building permits issued: 6 (2001) / 6 (2000); Multi-family building permits issued: 0 (2001) / 0 (2000); Employment by occupation: 6.7% management, 5.5% professional, 15.2% services, 13.7% sales, 7.8% farming, 10.5% construction, 40.5% production (2000).
Income: Per capita income: $11,836 (2000); Median household income: $30,875 (2000); Poverty rate: 21.1% (2000).
Education: High school graduation rate: 63.8% (2000); College graduation rate: 3.6% (2000).
Housing: Homeownership rate: 70.5% (2000); Median home value: $75,400 (2000); Median rent: $352 per month (2000); Median age of housing: 27 years (2000).
Transportation: Commute to work: 95.8% car, 0.3% public transportation, 0.7% walk, 1.9% work from home (2000); Travel time to work: 14.0% less than 15 minutes, 43.4% 15 to 30 minutes, 28.0% 30 to 45 minutes, 10.2% 45 to 60 minutes, 4.5% 60 minutes or more (2000)

LEIGHTON (township). Covers a land area of 34.881 square miles and a water area of 0.641 square miles. Located at 42.72° N. Lat.; 85.61° W. Long.
Population: 3,652 (2000); Race: 99.7% White, 0.0% Black, 0.2% Asian, 0.0% American Indian and Alaska Native, 0.8% Hispanic of any race, 0.1% two or more races (2000); Density: 104.7 persons per square mile (2000); Age: 31.1% under 18, 7.9% over 64 (2000); Marriage status: 22.9% never married, 69.2% now married, 1.7% widowed, 6.2% divorced (2000); Foreign born: 1.5% (2000); Ancestry (includes multiple ancestries): 35.4% Dutch, 21.2% German, 11.5% United States or American, 10.8% Irish, 9.1% English (2000).
Economy: Single-family building permits issued: 36 (2001) / 41 (2000); Multi-family building permits issued: 0 (2001) / 0 (2000); Employment by occupation: 14.2% management, 14.9% professional, 6.2% services, 23.2% sales, 2.3% farming, 15.4% construction, 23.9% production (2000).
Income: Per capita income: $18,736 (2000); Median household income: $51,743 (2000); Poverty rate: 5.3% (2000).
Taxes: Total city taxes per capita: $131 (1997); City property taxes per capita: $123 (1997).
Education: High school graduation rate: 88.4% (2000); College graduation rate: 11.1% (2000).
Housing: Homeownership rate: 88.3% (2000); Median home value: $113,400 (2000); Median rent: $525 per month (2000); Median age of housing: 39 years (2000).
Transportation: Commute to work: 92.8% car, 0.0% public transportation, 1.2% walk, 5.7% work from home (2000); Travel time to work: 26.6% less than 15 minutes, 38.0% 15 to 30 minutes, 28.7% 30 to 45 minutes, 5.7% 45 to 60 minutes, 0.9% 60 minutes or more (2000)

MANLIUS (township). Covers a land area of 35.363 square miles and a water area of 0.577 square miles. Located at 42.64° N. Lat.; 86.07° W. Long.
Population: 2,634 (2000); Race: 93.6% White, 1.3% Black, 0.5% Asian, 0.2% American Indian and Alaska Native, 10.5% Hispanic of any race, 1.1% two or more races (2000); Density: 74.5 persons per square mile (2000); Age: 32.5% under 18, 6.6% over 64 (2000); Marriage status: 19.0% never married, 70.6% now married, 3.1% widowed, 7.2% divorced (2000); Foreign born: 3.7% (2000); Ancestry (includes multiple ancestries): 38.7% Dutch, 23.6% German, 15.5% Other groups, 11.6% Irish, 6.3% English (2000).
Economy: Employment by occupation: 7.5% management, 13.8% professional, 13.5% services, 21.3% sales, 1.7% farming, 15.9% construction, 26.3% production (2000).
Income: Per capita income: $19,009 (2000); Median household income: $51,653 (2000); Poverty rate: 4.0% (2000).
Taxes: Total city taxes per capita: $127 (1997); City property taxes per capita: $126 (1997).
Education: High school graduation rate: 83.4% (2000); College graduation rate: 17.7% (2000).
Housing: Homeownership rate: 90.5% (2000); Median home value: $140,200 (2000); Median rent: $420 per month (2000); Median age of housing: 15 years (2000).
Transportation: Commute to work: 95.4% car, 0.0% public transportation, 1.2% walk, 3.1% work from home (2000); Travel time to work: 19.0% less than 15 minutes, 57.4% 15 to 30 minutes, 15.8% 30 to 45 minutes, 3.9% 45 to 60 minutes, 3.8% 60 minutes or more (2000)

MARTIN (village). Covers a land area of 0.875 square miles and a water area of 0 square miles. Located at 42.53° N. Lat.; 85.63° W. Long. Elevation is 832 feet.
Population: 435 (2000); Race: 93.6% White, 0.9% Black, 0.0% Asian, 0.4% American Indian and Alaska Native, 4.0% Hispanic of any race, 0.2% two or more races (2000); Density: 497.3 persons per square mile (2000); Age: 28.9% under 18, 13.5% over 64 (2000); Marriage status: 22.1% never married, 62.8% now married, 4.4% widowed, 10.8% divorced (2000); Foreign born: 5.1% (2000); Ancestry (includes multiple ancestries): 21.0% German, 18.1% Dutch, 12.1% English, 9.7% French (except Basque), 9.1% Other groups (2000).
Economy: Single-family building permits issued: 0 (2001) / 0 (2000); Multi-family building permits issued: 0 (2001) / 0 (2000); Employment by occupation: 5.4% management, 13.1% professional, 19.0% services, 22.2% sales, 3.6% farming, 13.1% construction, 23.5% production (2000).
Income: Per capita income: $16,238 (2000); Median household income: $41,389 (2000); Poverty rate: 9.6% (2000).
Taxes: Total city taxes per capita: $135 (1997); City property taxes per capita: $135 (1997).
Education: High school graduation rate: 79.7% (2000); College graduation rate: 18.1% (2000).

School District(s)

Martin Public Schools (KG-12)
2000 Enrollment: 755 616-672-7194
Housing: Homeownership rate: 69.3% (2000); Median home value: $90,300 (2000); Median rent: $364 per month (2000); Median age of housing: 52 years (2000).
Transportation: Commute to work: 89.4% car, 0.0% public transportation, 6.9% walk, 1.8% work from home (2000); Travel time to work: 38.5% less than 15 minutes, 31.9% 15 to 30 minutes, 21.1% 30 to 45 minutes, 5.2% 45 to 60 minutes, 3.3% 60 minutes or more (2000)

MARTIN (township). Covers a land area of 35.650 square miles and a water area of 0.304 square miles. Located at 42.54° N. Lat.; 85.59° W. Long. Elevation is 832 feet.
Population: 2,514 (2000); Race: 96.0% White, 0.2% Black, 0.7% Asian, 0.2% American Indian and Alaska Native, 3.4% Hispanic of any race, 1.2% two or more races (2000); Density: 70.5 persons per square mile (2000); Age: 29.1% under 18, 11.8% over 64 (2000); Marriage status: 21.4% never married, 64.0% now married, 4.6% widowed, 10.0% divorced (2000); Foreign born: 2.5% (2000); Ancestry (includes multiple ancestries): 25.9% Dutch, 18.8% German, 11.4% English, 11.1% United States or American, 9.5% Irish (2000).
Economy: Manufacturing: plastic products. Single-family building permits issued: 16 (2001) / 13 (2000); Multi-family building permits issued: 0 (2001) / 0 (2000); Employment by occupation: 6.3% management, 11.9% professional, 14.5% services, 19.4% sales, 5.9% farming, 13.7% construction, 28.4% production (2000).
Income: Per capita income: $17,233 (2000); Median household income: $40,565 (2000); Poverty rate: 8.4% (2000).
Taxes: Total city taxes per capita: $70 (1997); City property taxes per capita: $67 (1997).
Education: High school graduation rate: 81.1% (2000); College graduation rate: 8.7% (2000).
Housing: Homeownership rate: 83.2% (2000); Median home value: $101,100 (2000); Median rent: $390 per month (2000); Median age of housing: 38 years (2000).
Transportation: Commute to work: 92.3% car, 0.0% public transportation, 4.8% walk, 2.0% work from home (2000); Travel time to work: 31.7% less than 15 minutes, 34.9% 15 to 30 minutes, 22.5% 30 to 45 minutes, 7.7% 45 to 60 minutes, 3.3% 60 minutes or more (2000)

MONTEREY (township). Covers a land area of 35.728 square miles and a water area of 0.246 square miles. Located at 42.63° N. Lat.; 85.83° W. Long.
Population: 2,065 (2000); Race: 94.5% White, 0.4% Black, 0.3% Asian, 1.9% American Indian and Alaska Native, 2.4% Hispanic of any race, 1.5% two or more races (2000); Density: 57.8 persons per square mile (2000); Age: 31.7% under 18, 6.9% over 64 (2000); Marriage status: 23.6% never married, 62.8% now married, 5.1% widowed, 8.5% divorced (2000); Foreign born: 1.5% (2000); Ancestry (includes multiple ancestries): 27.2% German, 21.1% Dutch, 9.6% Irish, 8.5% English, 7.8% Other groups (2000).
Economy: Single-family building permits issued: 10 (2001) / 10 (2000); Multi-family building permits issued: 12 (2001) / 6 (2000); Employment by occupation: 15.4% management, 9.5% professional, 10.8% services, 18.8% sales, 2.9% farming, 12.7% construction, 29.9% production (2000).
Income: Per capita income: $18,718 (2000); Median household income: $48,750 (2000); Poverty rate: 4.8% (2000).
Taxes: Total city taxes per capita: $101 (1997); City property taxes per capita: $99 (1997).
Education: High school graduation rate: 81.7% (2000); College graduation rate: 11.7% (2000).
Housing: Homeownership rate: 90.2% (2000); Median home value: $106,700 (2000); Median rent: $519 per month (2000); Median age of housing: 23 years (2000).
Transportation: Commute to work: 89.9% car, 0.2% public transportation, 4.6% walk, 5.0% work from home (2000); Travel time to work: 20.2% less than 15 minutes, 31.5% 15 to 30 minutes, 33.4% 30 to 45 minutes, 10.1% 45 to 60 minutes, 4.8% 60 minutes or more (2000)

OTSEGO (city). Covers a land area of 1.995 square miles and a water area of 0.077 square miles. Located at 42.45° N. Lat.; 85.69° W. Long. Elevation is 721 feet.
History: Otsego grew up around its paper mills, with rapids on the Kalamazoo River generating power for the paper companies.
Population: 3,933 (2000); Race: 96.7% White, 0.8% Black, 0.7% Asian, 0.8% American Indian and Alaska Native, 0.5% Hispanic of any race, 0.8% two or more races (2000); Density: 1,971.2 persons per square mile (2000); Age: 26.8% under 18, 16.0% over 64 (2000); Marriage status: 22.0% never married, 54.4% now married, 8.4% widowed, 15.2% divorced (2000); Foreign born: 0.9% (2000); Ancestry (includes multiple ancestries): 23.1% German, 15.2% English, 12.1% Irish, 12.0% Dutch, 7.9% United States or American (2000).
Economy: Single-family building permits issued: 23 (2001) / 21 (2000); Multi-family building permits issued: 0 (2001) / 0 (2000); Employment by occupation: 8.5% management, 11.3% professional, 11.4% services, 23.6% sales, 0.6% farming, 12.6% construction, 32.1% production (2000).
Income: Per capita income: $17,521 (2000); Median household income: $37,525 (2000); Poverty rate: 6.9% (2000).
Taxes: Total city taxes per capita: $252 (1997); City property taxes per capita: $242 (1997).
Education: High school graduation rate: 84.3% (2000); College graduation rate: 9.2% (2000).

School District(s)

Otsego Public Schools (KG-12)
2000 Enrollment: 2,422 616-694-5131
Housing: Homeownership rate: 68.7% (2000); Median home value: $88,200 (2000); Median rent: $425 per month (2000); Median age of housing: 52 years (2000).
Safety: Violent crime rate: 30.3 per 10,000 population; Property crime rate: 359.1 per 10,000 population (2001).
Transportation: Commute to work: 92.3% car, 0.3% public transportation, 2.1% walk, 4.1% work from home (2000); Travel time to work: 44.9% less than 15 minutes, 29.8% 15 to 30 minutes, 14.9% 30 to 45 minutes, 5.0% 45 to 60 minutes, 5.4% 60 minutes or more (2000)
Additional Information Contacts
Otsego Chamber of Commerce 616-694-6880

OTSEGO (township). Covers a land area of 33.290 square miles and a water area of 0.602 square miles. Located at 42.46° N. Lat.; 85.71° W. Long. Elevation is 721 feet.
History: Settled 1832; incorporated as village 1865, as city 1918.
Population: 4,854 (2000); Race: 95.2% White, 0.8% Black, 0.5% Asian, 0.3% American Indian and Alaska Native, 0.4% Hispanic of any race, 3.1% two or more races (2000); Density: 145.8 persons per square mile (2000); Age: 28.4% under 18, 7.2% over 64 (2000); Marriage status: 21.9% never married, 64.2% now married, 4.4% widowed, 9.4% divorced (2000); Foreign born: 0.8% (2000); Ancestry (includes multiple ancestries): 25.0% German, 17.5% Dutch, 15.8% English, 11.4% Irish, 10.7% United States or American (2000).
Economy: In agricultural area. Manufacturing: plastic, paper and metal products; machinery. Single-family building permits issued: 31 (2001) / 30 (2000); Multi-family building permits issued: 0 (2001) / 0 (2000); Employment by occupation: 8.4% management, 13.4% professional, 13.7% services, 25.5% sales, 0.0% farming, 10.0% construction, 29.1% production (2000).
Income: Per capita income: $20,546 (2000); Median household income: $48,654 (2000); Poverty rate: 4.6% (2000).
Taxes: Total city taxes per capita: $48 (1997); City property taxes per capita: $41 (1997).

Education: High school graduation rate: 84.8% (2000); College graduation rate: 14.8% (2000).
Housing: Homeownership rate: 89.5% (2000); Median home value: $112,500 (2000); Median rent: $478 per month (2000); Median age of housing: 27 years (2000).
Transportation: Commute to work: 94.3% car, 0.0% public transportation, 0.9% walk, 3.8% work from home (2000); Travel time to work: 33.3% less than 15 minutes, 31.8% 15 to 30 minutes, 23.6% 30 to 45 minutes, 5.9% 45 to 60 minutes, 5.4% 60 minutes or more (2000)

OVERISEL (township). Covers a land area of 35.809 square miles and a water area of 0.005 square miles. Located at 42.71° N. Lat.; 85.96° W. Long.
Population: 2,594 (2000); Race: 94.5% White, 0.1% Black, 0.6% Asian, 0.0% American Indian and Alaska Native, 4.6% Hispanic of any race, 1.6% two or more races (2000); Density: 72.4 persons per square mile (2000); Age: 31.2% under 18, 9.4% over 64 (2000); Marriage status: 20.7% never married, 72.4% now married, 4.0% widowed, 2.9% divorced (2000); Foreign born: 1.0% (2000); Ancestry (includes multiple ancestries): 62.4% Dutch, 12.5% German, 7.3% Other groups, 3.9% United States or American, 3.0% Irish (2000).
Economy: Single-family building permits issued: 10 (2001) / 14 (2000); Multi-family building permits issued: 0 (2001) / 0 (2000); Employment by occupation: 9.9% management, 9.9% professional, 12.4% services, 24.6% sales, 4.5% farming, 12.8% construction, 26.0% production (2000).
Income: Per capita income: $18,831 (2000); Median household income: $52,857 (2000); Poverty rate: 2.3% (2000).
Taxes: Total city taxes per capita: $231 (2000); City property taxes per capita: $225 (2000).
Education: High school graduation rate: 83.5% (2000); College graduation rate: 11.8% (2000).
Housing: Homeownership rate: 88.4% (2000); Median home value: $129,800 (2000); Median rent: $534 per month (2000); Median age of housing: 36 years (2000).
Transportation: Commute to work: 92.5% car, 0.0% public transportation, 2.2% walk, 5.4% work from home (2000); Travel time to work: 35.2% less than 15 minutes, 51.5% 15 to 30 minutes, 8.5% 30 to 45 minutes, 2.2% 45 to 60 minutes, 2.7% 60 minutes or more (2000)

PLAINWELL (city). Covers a land area of 2.072 square miles and a water area of 0.087 square miles. Located at 42.44° N. Lat.; 85.64° W. Long. Elevation is 750 feet.
History: Plainwell, first settled in the early 1830's on the Kalamazoo River, developed around a paper mill, and later an office-equipment factory, and some canning plants.
Population: 3,933 (2000); Race: 96.9% White, 0.0% Black, 0.6% Asian, 0.0% American Indian and Alaska Native, 2.6% Hispanic of any race, 2.0% two or more races (2000); Density: 1,897.9 persons per square mile (2000); Age: 28.5% under 18, 16.0% over 64 (2000); Marriage status: 25.1% never married, 55.1% now married, 8.5% widowed, 11.3% divorced (2000); Foreign born: 1.6% (2000); Ancestry (includes multiple ancestries): 20.7% German, 19.1% English, 16.4% Dutch, 10.8% Irish, 8.6% United States or American (2000).
Economy: Single-family building permits issued: 0 (2001) / 15 (2000); Multi-family building permits issued: 4 (2001) / 2 (2000); Employment by occupation: 10.3% management, 12.4% professional, 16.6% services, 26.6% sales, 0.7% farming, 9.5% construction, 23.9% production (2000).
Income: Per capita income: $16,982 (2000); Median household income: $39,590 (2000); Poverty rate: 6.1% (2000).
Taxes: Total city taxes per capita: $326 (1997); City property taxes per capita: $321 (1997).
Education: High school graduation rate: 79.5% (2000); College graduation rate: 18.0% (2000).

School District(s)

Plainwell Community Schools (PK-12)
2000 Enrollment: 2,755 616-685-5823

Housing: Homeownership rate: 70.6% (2000); Median home value: $97,500 (2000); Median rent: $449 per month (2000); Median age of housing: 46 years (2000).
Hospitals: Borgess-Pipp Health Center (43 beds)
Safety: Violent crime rate: 32.9 per 10,000 population; Property crime rate: 419.8 per 10,000 population (2001).
Newspapers: Union Enterprise (1 x week)
Transportation: Commute to work: 90.8% car, 0.0% public transportation, 5.1% walk, 2.6% work from home (2000); Travel time to work: 34.5% less than 15 minutes, 41.6% 15 to 30 minutes, 17.2% 30 to 45 minutes, 4.5% 45 to 60 minutes, 2.1% 60 minutes or more (2000)

Additional Information Contacts
Plainwell Chamber of Commerce 616-685-8877

PULLMAN (unincorporated postal area, zip code 49450). Covers a land area of 32.850 square miles and a water area of 0.330 square miles. Located at 42.48° N. Lat.; 86.07° W. Long. Elevation is 651 feet.
History: Pullman grew up around a sawmill built in 1870 by the Clement brothers. When the Chicago & Western Michigan Railroad put a station here, they called it Hoppertown. The town was renamed in 1901, probably for George Pullman who invented the railroad sleeping car.
Population: 3,348 (2000); Race: 71.7% White, 7.6% Black, 0.8% Asian, 1.6% American Indian and Alaska Native, 26.3% Hispanic of any race, 3.0% two or more races (2000); Density: 101.9 persons per square mile (2000); Age: 33.9% under 18, 7.0% over 64 (2000); Marriage status: 26.6% never married, 55.4% now married, 4.7% widowed, 13.4% divorced (2000); Foreign born: 14.9% (2000); Ancestry (includes multiple ancestries): 36.9% Other groups, 11.3% German, 9.5% Irish, 9.3% United States or American, 7.0% Dutch (2000).
Economy: Employment by occupation: 8.1% management, 5.3% professional, 15.2% services, 12.5% sales, 9.8% farming, 12.1% construction, 37.0% production (2000).
Income: Per capita income: $12,303 (2000); Median household income: $33,261 (2000); Poverty rate: 17.0% (2000).
Education: High school graduation rate: 62.7% (2000); College graduation rate: 3.7% (2000).
Housing: Homeownership rate: 72.4% (2000); Median home value: $74,900 (2000); Median rent: $353 per month (2000); Median age of housing: 27 years (2000).
Transportation: Commute to work: 95.9% car, 0.0% public transportation, 0.9% walk, 1.6% work from home (2000); Travel time to work: 14.5% less than 15 minutes, 40.7% 15 to 30 minutes, 27.6% 30 to 45 minutes, 11.9% 45 to 60 minutes, 5.3% 60 minutes or more (2000)

SALEM (township). Covers a land area of 35.768 square miles and a water area of 0.267 square miles. Located at 42.71° N. Lat.; 85.83° W. Long.
Population: 3,486 (2000); Race: 96.6% White, 0.0% Black, 0.0% Asian, 1.4% American Indian and Alaska Native, 1.6% Hispanic of any race, 1.3% two or more races (2000); Density: 97.5 persons per square mile (2000); Age: 31.4% under 18, 8.1% over 64 (2000); Marriage status: 20.7% never married, 69.4% now married, 2.9% widowed, 7.0% divorced (2000); Foreign born: 1.3% (2000); Ancestry (includes multiple ancestries): 33.6% Dutch, 25.0% German, 9.5% Polish, 7.8% Irish, 6.9% English (2000).
Economy: Single-family building permits issued: 14 (2001) / 13 (2000); Multi-family building permits issued: 0 (2001) / 0 (2000); Employment by occupation: 9.1% management, 9.2% professional, 12.0% services, 21.6% sales, 1.5% farming, 17.4% construction, 29.1% production (2000).
Income: Per capita income: $19,620 (2000); Median household income: $48,203 (2000); Poverty rate: 3.3% (2000).
Taxes: Total city taxes per capita: $124 (1997); City property taxes per capita: $107 (1997).
Education: High school graduation rate: 79.1% (2000); College graduation rate: 8.4% (2000).
Housing: Homeownership rate: 92.1% (2000); Median home value: $120,600 (2000); Median rent: $402 per month (2000); Median age of housing: 20 years (2000).
Transportation: Commute to work: 93.7% car, 0.0% public transportation, 2.8% walk, 3.4% work from home (2000); Travel time to work: 17.0% less than 15 minutes, 44.2% 15 to 30 minutes, 29.1% 30 to 45 minutes, 5.6% 45 to 60 minutes, 4.1% 60 minutes or more (2000)

SAUGATUCK (city). Covers a land area of 1.192 square miles and a water area of 0.260 square miles. Located at 42.65° N. Lat.; 86.20° W. Long. Elevation is 656 feet.
History: Saugatuck was first settled in the 1830's and developed as an art colony, attracting landscape painters to the Lake Michigan dunes region. James Fenimore Cooper spent time here. The name is the Pottawattomi term for the mouth of a river.
Population: 1,065 (2000); Race: 97.7% White, 1.2% Black, 0.4% Asian, 0.2% American Indian and Alaska Native, 2.5% Hispanic of any race, 0.0% two or more races (2000); Density: 893.6 persons per square mile (2000); Age: 18.4% under 18, 17.0% over 64 (2000); Marriage status: 31.0% never married, 48.4% now married, 8.4% widowed, 12.2% divorced (2000); Foreign born: 3.0% (2000); Ancestry (includes multiple ancestries): 23.3% German, 17.0% English, 16.8% Irish, 13.9% Dutch, 6.5% Polish (2000).

Economy: Employment by occupation: 19.7% management, 19.2% professional, 14.3% services, 26.1% sales, 0.6% farming, 6.8% construction, 13.2% production (2000).
Income: Per capita income: $34,382 (2000); Median household income: $44,318 (2000); Poverty rate: 11.5% (2000).
Taxes: Total city taxes per capita: $966 (1997); City property taxes per capita: $959 (1997).
Education: High school graduation rate: 94.1% (2000); College graduation rate: 41.7% (2000).
Housing: Homeownership rate: 64.4% (2000); Median home value: $184,400 (2000); Median rent: $412 per month (2000); Median age of housing: 43 years (2000).
Newspapers: The Commercial Record (1 x week)
Transportation: Commute to work: 78.0% car, 2.6% public transportation, 10.5% walk, 7.8% work from home (2000); Travel time to work: 41.0% less than 15 minutes, 40.3% 15 to 30 minutes, 8.4% 30 to 45 minutes, 3.0% 45 to 60 minutes, 7.4% 60 minutes or more (2000)

SAUGATUCK (township). Covers a land area of 25.255 square miles and a water area of 0.932 square miles. Located at 42.64° N. Lat.; 86.19° W. Long. Elevation is 656 feet.
Population: 3,590 (2000); Race: 96.7% White, 0.1% Black, 0.0% Asian, 0.7% American Indian and Alaska Native, 6.7% Hispanic of any race, 0.7% two or more races (2000); Density: 142.2 persons per square mile (2000); Age: 20.5% under 18, 17.7% over 64 (2000); Marriage status: 21.0% never married, 54.8% now married, 9.3% widowed, 14.9% divorced (2000); Foreign born: 2.2% (2000); Ancestry (includes multiple ancestries): 23.0% German, 18.0% Dutch, 13.4% English, 12.6% Irish, 10.6% Other groups (2000).
Economy: Manufacturing: boats, frozen pies, tools. Resort; Bed and breakfast. Area contains large sand dunes. Single-family building permits issued: 50 (2001) / 49 (2000); Multi-family building permits issued: 0 (2001) / 2 (2000); Employment by occupation: 11.7% management, 14.3% professional, 13.4% services, 26.4% sales, 0.0% farming, 9.5% construction, 24.7% production (2000).
Income: Per capita income: $30,056 (2000); Median household income: $43,771 (2000); Poverty rate: 7.9% (2000).
Taxes: Total city taxes per capita: $166 (1997); City property taxes per capita: $150 (1997).
Education: High school graduation rate: 85.7% (2000); College graduation rate: 23.2% (2000).
Housing: Homeownership rate: 81.1% (2000); Median home value: $161,700 (2000); Median rent: $506 per month (2000); Median age of housing: 24 years (2000).
Transportation: Commute to work: 89.5% car, 0.5% public transportation, 0.9% walk, 9.1% work from home (2000); Travel time to work: 34.1% less than 15 minutes, 45.4% 15 to 30 minutes, 12.7% 30 to 45 minutes, 2.2% 45 to 60 minutes, 5.6% 60 minutes or more (2000)

SHELBYVILLE (unincorporated postal area, zip code 49344). Covers a land area of 30.216 square miles and a water area of 0.648 square miles. Located at 42.58° N. Lat.; 85.58° W. Long. Elevation is 831 feet.
History: Shelbyville grew up around a station of the Grand Rapids & Indiana Railroad in 1870, and was named for the station agent, a Mr. Shelby.
Population: 3,314 (2000); Race: 96.4% White, 0.0% Black, 0.5% Asian, 0.0% American Indian and Alaska Native, 1.7% Hispanic of any race, 1.8% two or more races (2000); Density: 109.7 persons per square mile (2000); Age: 25.5% under 18, 15.4% over 64 (2000); Marriage status: 17.6% never married, 66.1% now married, 5.7% widowed, 10.6% divorced (2000); Foreign born: 1.0% (2000); Ancestry (includes multiple ancestries): 20.0% German, 16.3% Dutch, 12.2% English, 10.1% Irish, 9.6% United States or American (2000).
Economy: Employment by occupation: 8.2% management, 13.2% professional, 12.6% services, 24.3% sales, 1.9% farming, 16.4% construction, 23.4% production (2000).
Income: Per capita income: $19,622 (2000); Median household income: $41,591 (2000); Poverty rate: 4.3% (2000).
Education: High school graduation rate: 77.3% (2000); College graduation rate: 9.2% (2000).
Housing: Homeownership rate: 85.7% (2000); Median home value: $128,100 (2000); Median rent: $465 per month (2000); Median age of housing: 30 years (2000).
Transportation: Commute to work: 96.0% car, 0.0% public transportation, 1.9% walk, 1.8% work from home (2000); Travel time to work: 16.4% less than 15 minutes, 25.3% 15 to 30 minutes, 36.2% 30 to 45 minutes, 17.0% 45 to 60 minutes, 5.1% 60 minutes or more (2000)

TROWBRIDGE (township). Covers a land area of 34.703 square miles and a water area of 1.113 square miles. Located at 42.47° N. Lat.; 85.82° W. Long.
Population: 2,519 (2000); Race: 96.1% White, 1.1% Black, 0.0% Asian, 0.6% American Indian and Alaska Native, 1.3% Hispanic of any race, 1.6% two or more races (2000); Density: 72.6 persons per square mile (2000); Age: 24.9% under 18, 10.2% over 64 (2000); Marriage status: 16.3% never married, 66.8% now married, 3.6% widowed, 13.3% divorced (2000); Foreign born: 1.0% (2000); Ancestry (includes multiple ancestries): 20.4% German, 13.1% Other groups, 12.4% English, 11.9% Dutch, 11.4% Irish (2000).
Economy: Single-family building permits issued: 0 (2001) / 0 (2000); Multi-family building permits issued: 0 (2001) / 0 (2000); Employment by occupation: 10.0% management, 11.3% professional, 11.2% services, 20.8% sales, 2.4% farming, 10.0% construction, 34.4% production (2000).
Income: Per capita income: $20,137 (2000); Median household income: $40,476 (2000); Poverty rate: 8.1% (2000).
Taxes: Total city taxes per capita: $33 (1997); City property taxes per capita: $31 (1997).
Education: High school graduation rate: 83.8% (2000); College graduation rate: 10.8% (2000).
Housing: Homeownership rate: 85.4% (2000); Median home value: $101,200 (2000); Median rent: $434 per month (2000); Median age of housing: 26 years (2000).
Transportation: Commute to work: 91.6% car, 0.0% public transportation, 1.9% walk, 5.9% work from home (2000); Travel time to work: 30.9% less than 15 minutes, 31.6% 15 to 30 minutes, 20.0% 30 to 45 minutes, 11.2% 45 to 60 minutes, 6.3% 60 minutes or more (2000)

VALLEY (township). Covers a land area of 32.948 square miles and a water area of 3.043 square miles. Located at 42.55° N. Lat.; 85.95° W. Long.
Population: 1,831 (2000); Race: 94.4% White, 2.2% Black, 0.0% Asian, 0.9% American Indian and Alaska Native, 2.2% Hispanic of any race, 0.9% two or more races (2000); Density: 55.6 persons per square mile (2000); Age: 25.9% under 18, 9.7% over 64 (2000); Marriage status: 18.2% never married, 66.6% now married, 4.2% widowed, 11.0% divorced (2000); Foreign born: 2.1% (2000); Ancestry (includes multiple ancestries): 21.6% German, 16.2% Dutch, 11.7% Irish, 9.5% English, 9.1% Other groups (2000).
Economy: Employment by occupation: 8.0% management, 14.2% professional, 11.1% services, 18.2% sales, 1.1% farming, 12.9% construction, 34.5% production (2000).
Income: Per capita income: $21,990 (2000); Median household income: $48,672 (2000); Poverty rate: 6.2% (2000).
Taxes: Total city taxes per capita: $60 (1997); City property taxes per capita: $60 (1997).
Education: High school graduation rate: 82.6% (2000); College graduation rate: 15.8% (2000).
Housing: Homeownership rate: 89.4% (2000); Median home value: $116,400 (2000); Median rent: $404 per month (2000); Median age of housing: 14 years (2000).
Transportation: Commute to work: 95.2% car, 0.0% public transportation, 0.2% walk, 3.5% work from home (2000); Travel time to work: 24.3% less than 15 minutes, 28.9% 15 to 30 minutes, 30.0% 30 to 45 minutes, 9.7% 45 to 60 minutes, 7.1% 60 minutes or more (2000)

WATSON (township). Aka Watson Corners. Covers a land area of 35.431 square miles and a water area of 0.679 square miles. Located at 42.55° N. Lat.; 85.72° W. Long. Elevation is 812 feet.
Population: 2,086 (2000); Race: 98.9% White, 0.1% Black, 0.0% Asian, 0.6% American Indian and Alaska Native, 1.9% Hispanic of any race, 0.1% two or more races (2000); Density: 58.9 persons per square mile (2000); Age: 30.7% under 18, 7.6% over 64 (2000); Marriage status: 21.7% never married, 65.5% now married, 3.8% widowed, 9.0% divorced (2000); Foreign born: 0.5% (2000); Ancestry (includes multiple ancestries): 23.5% German, 16.1% Dutch, 14.4% English, 10.8% Irish, 10.8% United States or American (2000).
Economy: Employment by occupation: 8.9% management, 10.4% professional, 11.9% services, 18.9% sales, 1.5% farming, 13.2% construction, 35.2% production (2000).
Income: Per capita income: $18,095 (2000); Median household income: $49,070 (2000); Poverty rate: 8.4% (2000).
Taxes: Total city taxes per capita: $32 (1997); City property taxes per capita: $31 (1997).
Education: High school graduation rate: 83.8% (2000); College graduation rate: 10.5% (2000).

Housing: Homeownership rate: 91.5% (2000); Median home value: $110,100 (2000); Median rent: $363 per month (2000); Median age of housing: 28 years (2000).
Transportation: Commute to work: 95.2% car, 0.0% public transportation, 0.2% walk, 3.8% work from home (2000); Travel time to work: 22.7% less than 15 minutes, 36.6% 15 to 30 minutes, 23.7% 30 to 45 minutes, 10.3% 45 to 60 minutes, 6.6% 60 minutes or more (2000)

WAYLAND (city). Covers a land area of 2.888 square miles and a water area of 0.042 square miles. Located at 42.67° N. Lat.; 85.64° W. Long. Elevation is 748 feet.
History: Wayland developed as a center for a dairy area, with a Pet Milk Company processing plant located here.
Population: 3,939 (2000); Race: 96.5% White, 0.0% Black, 0.0% Asian, 0.0% American Indian and Alaska Native, 4.3% Hispanic of any race, 1.2% two or more races (2000); Density: 1,363.8 persons per square mile (2000); Age: 30.9% under 18, 11.0% over 64 (2000); Marriage status: 20.4% never married, 62.8% now married, 7.3% widowed, 9.5% divorced (2000); Foreign born: 1.4% (2000); Ancestry (includes multiple ancestries): 25.6% German, 21.8% Dutch, 10.1% Other groups, 10.0% Polish, 9.2% Irish (2000).
Economy: Employment by occupation: 5.2% management, 12.3% professional, 12.5% services, 29.3% sales, 0.0% farming, 12.0% construction, 28.8% production (2000).
Income: Per capita income: $18,077 (2000); Median household income: $41,852 (2000); Poverty rate: 7.9% (2000).
Taxes: Total city taxes per capita: $202 (1997); City property taxes per capita: $200 (1997).
Education: High school graduation rate: 82.3% (2000); College graduation rate: 11.7% (2000).

School District(s)

Wayland Union Schools (PK-12)
2000 Enrollment: 3,223 616-792-2181
Housing: Homeownership rate: 70.6% (2000); Median home value: $99,500 (2000); Median rent: $458 per month (2000); Median age of housing: 18 years (2000).
Safety: Violent crime rate: 7.6 per 10,000 population; Property crime rate: 207.1 per 10,000 population (2001).
Newspapers: Penasee Globe (1 x week)
Transportation: Commute to work: 94.5% car, 0.9% public transportation, 0.5% walk, 3.4% work from home (2000); Travel time to work: 27.7% less than 15 minutes, 33.6% 15 to 30 minutes, 28.9% 30 to 45 minutes, 7.3% 45 to 60 minutes, 2.5% 60 minutes or more (2000)
Additional Information Contacts
Wayland Chamber of Commerce 616-792-9246

WAYLAND (township). Covers a land area of 32.738 square miles and a water area of 0.762 square miles. Located at 42.62° N. Lat.; 85.61° W. Long. Elevation is 748 feet.
History: Settled 1836, incorporated 1858.
Population: 3,013 (2000); Race: 96.3% White, 0.0% Black, 0.5% Asian, 0.6% American Indian and Alaska Native, 1.8% Hispanic of any race, 1.4% two or more races (2000); Density: 92.0 persons per square mile (2000); Age: 28.3% under 18, 8.8% over 64 (2000); Marriage status: 24.1% never married, 63.7% now married, 4.4% widowed, 7.8% divorced (2000); Foreign born: 0.7% (2000); Ancestry (includes multiple ancestries): 28.8% German, 20.2% Dutch, 12.5% Irish, 12.3% English, 7.0% Other groups (2000).
Economy: In farm area: cucumbers, apples, corn, hay; poultry. Manufacturing includes auto test equipment, tool and die. Yankee Springs State Recreation Area to Southeast. Single-family building permits issued: 27 (2001) / 25 (2000); Multi-family building permits issued: 0 (2001) / 0 (2000); Employment by occupation: 8.7% management, 14.4% professional, 13.8% services, 21.5% sales, 0.7% farming, 12.4% construction, 28.4% production (2000).
Income: Per capita income: $18,870 (2000); Median household income: $46,853 (2000); Poverty rate: 2.8% (2000).
Taxes: Total city taxes per capita: $22 (1997); City property taxes per capita: $22 (1997).
Education: High school graduation rate: 82.1% (2000); College graduation rate: 14.5% (2000).
Housing: Homeownership rate: 90.9% (2000); Median home value: $118,500 (2000); Median rent: $442 per month (2000); Median age of housing: 27 years (2000).
Transportation: Commute to work: 95.8% car, 0.0% public transportation, 0.0% walk, 3.5% work from home (2000); Travel time to work: 19.0% less than 15 minutes, 32.7% 15 to 30 minutes, 32.9% 30 to 45 minutes, 9.6% 45 to 60 minutes, 5.8% 60 minutes or more (2000)

Alpena County

Located in northeastern Michigan; bounded on the east by Lake Huron. Covers a land area of 574.20 square miles, a water area of 1,120.80 square miles, and is located in the Eastern Time Zone. The county government was organized in 1840. County seat is Alpena.

Weather Station: Alpena Phelps Collins Airport — Elevation: 688 feet

	Jan	Feb	Mar	Apr	May	Jun	Jul	Aug	Sep	Oct	Nov	Dec
High	27	29	38	52	65	75	80	77	68	56	43	32
Low	10	10	19	30	40	49	55	53	46	36	28	18
Precip	1.8	1.3	2.2	2.3	2.6	2.5	3.3	3.5	2.8	2.4	2.1	1.9
Snow	22.3	16.0	13.6	5.7	0.3	0.0	tr	tr	tr	0.4	8.6	20.2

High and Low temperatures in degrees Fahrenheit; Precipitation and Snow in inches

Weather Station: Alpena Wastewater Plant — Elevation: 587 feet

	Jan	Feb	Mar	Apr	May	Jun	Jul	Aug	Sep	Oct	Nov	Dec
High	27	29	37	49	61	71	77	76	68	55	43	33
Low	12	13	22	33	44	53	59	58	50	40	30	20
Precip	1.7	1.3	1.9	2.1	2.8	2.6	3.3	3.4	3.2	2.5	2.0	1.9
Snow	16.0	10.8	9.6	2.0	0.2	0.0	0.0	0.0	0.0	0.2	4.8	12.7

High and Low temperatures in degrees Fahrenheit; Precipitation and Snow in inches

Population: 31,314 (2000); Race: 97.7% White, 0.4% Black, 0.4% Asian, 0.7% American Indian and Alaska Native, 0.4% Hispanic of any race, 0.8% two or more races (2000); Density: 54.5 persons per square mile (2000); Age: 23.7% under 18, 17.1% over 64 (2000).
Religion: Five largest groups: 43.5% Catholic Church, 11.0% Evangelical Lutheran Church in America, 8.1% Lutheran Church—Missouri Synod, 2.5% The United Methodist Church, 1.4% Episcopal Church (2000).
Economy: Unemployment rate: 7.0% (11/2002); Total civilian labor force: 16,435 (11/2002); Leading industries: 22.6% manufacturing; 21.5% health care and social assistance; 14.2% retail trade (2000); Companies that employ more than 1,000 persons: 0 (2000); Companies that employ more than 100 persons: 14 (2000); Farms: 412 totaling 78,047 acres (1997); Minority business ownership rate: 0.0% (1997); Women business ownership rate: 17.2% (1997); Retail sales per capita: $9,429 (1997). Single-family building permits issued: 97 (2001) / 90 (2000); Multi-family building permits issued: 0 (2001) / 0 (2000).
Income: Per capita income: $17,566 (2000); Median household income: $34,177 (2000); Poverty rate: 10.5% (2000); Bankruptcy rate: 2.82% (2001).
Taxes: Total county taxes per capita: $161 (2000); County property taxes per capita: $160 (2000).
Education: High school graduation rate: 83.1% (2000); College graduation rate: 13.2% (2000).
Housing: Homeownership rate: 79.3% (2000); Median home value: $78,100 (2000); Median rent: $325 per month (2000); Median age of housing: 36 years (2000).
Health: Birth rate: 108.9 per 10,000 population (1998); Age adjusted death rate: 97.9 per 10,000 population (1999); Age adjusted cancer mortality rate: 178.4 deaths per 100,000 population (1999). Number of physicians: 19.2 per 10,000 population (1999); Number of hospital beds: 39.6 per 10,000 population (1999).
Elections: 2000 Presidential election results: 49.9% Gore, 47.9% Bush, 1.9% Nader, 0.0% Buchanan
National and State Parks: Alpena State Forest; Alpena State Park; Thunder Bay River State Forest
Additional Information Contacts
Alpena County Government Offices 989-356-0115
Alpena Alcona Presque Isle Board of Realtors 989-356-3772
Alpena Chamber of Commerce 989-354-4181

Alpena County Communities

ALPENA (city). Covers a land area of 8.380 square miles and a water area of 0.697 square miles. Located at 45.06° N. Lat.; 83.44° W. Long. Elevation is 591 feet.
History: The first settler came to Alpena in 1835, but the village was laid out in 1856 by several men from Detroit. They first called it Fremont, for General John C. Fremont, but the post office used the name of Alpena (Indian origin, meaning "partridge") when it was established in 1857. Daniel Carter was the first resident of the new town, followed by G.N. Fletcher who built a store and boarding house. Soon there were many lumber and shingle mills in Alpena. After 1900, limestone quarrying was begun.
Population: 11,304 (2000); Race: 96.5% White, 0.8% Black, 0.6% Asian, 0.8% American Indian and Alaska Native, 0.1% Hispanic of any race, 1.1%

two or more races (2000); Density: 1,348.9 persons per square mile (2000); Age: 23.8% under 18, 18.7% over 64 (2000); Marriage status: 25.0% never married, 50.9% now married, 11.6% widowed, 12.6% divorced (2000); Foreign born: 1.3% (2000); Ancestry (includes multiple ancestries): 26.6% Polish, 25.0% German, 14.2% French (except Basque), 9.5% English, 7.7% Irish (2000).
Vital Statistics: Birth rate: 115.9 per 10,000 population (1998)
Economy: Single-family building permits issued: 3 (2001) / 9 (2000); Multi-family building permits issued: 0 (2001) / 0 (2000); Employment by occupation: 7.9% management, 23.6% professional, 22.1% services, 23.6% sales, 0.5% farming, 6.8% construction, 15.5% production (2000).
Income: Per capita income: $17,476 (2000); Median household income: $30,353 (2000); Poverty rate: 13.5% (2000).
Taxes: Total city taxes per capita: $372 (2000); City property taxes per capita: $366 (2000).
Education: High school graduation rate: 84.0% (2000); College graduation rate: 14.5% (2000).

School District(s)

Alpena Public Schools (KG-12)
2000 Enrollment: 5,391 517-356-4863

Two-year College(s)

Alpena Community College (Public)
2001 Enrollment: 1,933 517-356-9021
2001 Tuition: In-state $2,580; Out-of-state $3,450
Housing: Homeownership rate: 67.4% (2000); Median home value: $70,600 (2000); Median rent: $324 per month (2000); Median age of housing: 51 years (2000).
Hospitals: Alpena General Hospital (124 beds)
Safety: Violent crime rate: 25.5 per 10,000 population; Property crime rate: 358.1 per 10,000 population (2001).
Newspapers: The Alpena News (6 x week); Presque Isle Star (1 x week); Alpena Star (1 x week)
Transportation: Commute to work: 90.2% car, 0.6% public transportation, 4.3% walk, 3.8% work from home (2000); Travel time to work: 76.1% less than 15 minutes, 15.8% 15 to 30 minutes, 4.1% 30 to 45 minutes, 0.7% 45 to 60 minutes, 3.3% 60 minutes or more (2000)
Airports: Alpena County Regional (primary service)
Additional Information Contacts
Alpena Alcona Presque Isle Board of Realtors 989-356-3772
Alpena Chamber of Commerce 989-354-4181

ALPENA (township). Covers a land area of 105.025 square miles and a water area of 36.405 square miles. Located at 45.08° N. Lat.; 83.44° W. Long. Elevation is 591 feet.
History: When Alpena Township was surveyed in 1839, land was offered to anyone in the survey party in lieu of wages, but there were no takers. The area was desolate cedar swamp.
Population: 9,788 (2000); Race: 98.5% White, 0.0% Black, 0.4% Asian, 0.6% American Indian and Alaska Native, 0.4% Hispanic of any race, 0.5% two or more races (2000); Density: 93.2 persons per square mile (2000); Age: 21.2% under 18, 17.9% over 64 (2000); Marriage status: 21.7% never married, 61.0% now married, 8.3% widowed, 9.0% divorced (2000); Foreign born: 1.4% (2000); Ancestry (includes multiple ancestries): 30.7% German, 25.7% Polish, 12.0% French (except Basque), 8.7% English, 8.0% Irish (2000).
Economy: Single-family building permits issued: 42 (2001) / 30 (2000); Multi-family building permits issued: 0 (2001) / 0 (2000); Employment by occupation: 7.7% management, 16.2% professional, 16.5% services, 28.4% sales, 0.8% farming, 11.1% construction, 19.3% production (2000).
Income: Per capita income: $18,779 (2000); Median household income: $39,889 (2000); Poverty rate: 8.2% (2000).
Taxes: Total city taxes per capita: $75 (2000); City property taxes per capita: $61 (2000).
Education: High school graduation rate: 85.1% (2000); College graduation rate: 14.8% (2000).
Housing: Homeownership rate: 84.0% (2000); Median home value: $88,200 (2000); Median rent: $327 per month (2000); Median age of housing: 31 years (2000).
Transportation: Commute to work: 94.4% car, 0.3% public transportation, 1.3% walk, 2.8% work from home (2000); Travel time to work: 55.8% less than 15 minutes, 37.2% 15 to 30 minutes, 3.5% 30 to 45 minutes, 1.2% 45 to 60 minutes, 2.3% 60 minutes or more (2000)
Airports: Alpena County Regional (primary service)

GREEN (township). Covers a land area of 71.373 square miles and a water area of 8.731 square miles. Located at 45.02° N. Lat.; 83.78° W. Long.
Population: 1,205 (2000); Race: 96.4% White, 0.7% Black, 0.2% Asian, 0.0% American Indian and Alaska Native, 0.6% Hispanic of any race, 2.7% two or more races (2000); Density: 16.9 persons per square mile (2000); Age: 24.1% under 18, 17.0% over 64 (2000); Marriage status: 18.2% never married, 67.7% now married, 6.7% widowed, 7.4% divorced (2000); Foreign born: 0.9% (2000); Ancestry (includes multiple ancestries): 24.1% German, 13.9% English, 12.6% French (except Basque), 12.1% Polish, 7.4% Irish (2000).
Economy: Employment by occupation: 9.2% management, 15.4% professional, 14.2% services, 21.4% sales, 3.0% farming, 15.2% construction, 21.6% production (2000).
Income: Per capita income: $16,454 (2000); Median household income: $34,271 (2000); Poverty rate: 7.2% (2000).
Taxes: Total city taxes per capita: $50 (1997); City property taxes per capita: $41 (1997).
Education: High school graduation rate: 82.5% (2000); College graduation rate: 9.6% (2000).
Housing: Homeownership rate: 91.5% (2000); Median home value: $75,200 (2000); Median rent: $319 per month (2000); Median age of housing: 27 years (2000).
Transportation: Commute to work: 90.6% car, 1.4% public transportation, 2.1% walk, 5.3% work from home (2000); Travel time to work: 21.3% less than 15 minutes, 38.4% 15 to 30 minutes, 31.9% 30 to 45 minutes, 2.6% 45 to 60 minutes, 5.9% 60 minutes or more (2000)

HERRON (unincorporated postal area, zip code 49744). Covers a land area of 32.271 square miles and a water area of 0.016 square miles. Located at 44.99° N. Lat.; 83.65° W. Long.
History: Herron was founded in 1920 by Fred Herron, for whom it was named.
Population: 778 (2000); Race: 96.2% White, 0.9% Black, 0.0% Asian, 0.5% American Indian and Alaska Native, 0.0% Hispanic of any race, 2.4% two or more races (2000); Density: 24.1 persons per square mile (2000); Age: 29.8% under 18, 12.7% over 64 (2000); Marriage status: 19.7% never married, 71.2% now married, 3.8% widowed, 5.3% divorced (2000); Foreign born: 0.4% (2000); Ancestry (includes multiple ancestries): 33.5% German, 21.7% Polish, 13.1% French (except Basque), 7.9% English, 6.6% United States or American (2000).
Economy: Employment by occupation: 10.1% management, 17.7% professional, 17.7% services, 21.4% sales, 2.0% farming, 12.4% construction, 18.6% production (2000).
Income: Per capita income: $16,923 (2000); Median household income: $37,625 (2000); Poverty rate: 3.0% (2000).
Education: High school graduation rate: 77.3% (2000); College graduation rate: 10.5% (2000).
Housing: Homeownership rate: 84.5% (2000); Median home value: $75,000 (2000); Median rent: $331 per month (2000); Median age of housing: 32 years (2000).
Transportation: Commute to work: 88.1% car, 0.0% public transportation, 1.7% walk, 9.7% work from home (2000); Travel time to work: 17.9% less than 15 minutes, 67.6% 15 to 30 minutes, 9.7% 30 to 45 minutes, 1.3% 45 to 60 minutes, 3.5% 60 minutes or more (2000)

LACHINE (unincorporated postal area, zip code 49753). Covers a land area of 181.612 square miles and a water area of 1.495 square miles. Located at 44.99° N. Lat.; 83.79° W. Long. Elevation is 734 feet.
History: Lachine was founded as a station of the Detroit & Mackinaw Railway in 1909, and named by a railroad conductor who came from Lachine, Quebec.
Population: 2,227 (2000); Race: 97.7% White, 0.4% Black, 0.1% Asian, 0.3% American Indian and Alaska Native, 0.4% Hispanic of any race, 1.6% two or more races (2000); Density: 12.3 persons per square mile (2000); Age: 24.6% under 18, 17.3% over 64 (2000); Marriage status: 17.1% never married, 67.9% now married, 6.8% widowed, 8.2% divorced (2000); Foreign born: 0.8% (2000); Ancestry (includes multiple ancestries): 27.0% German, 16.6% Polish, 13.5% French (except Basque), 11.0% English, 8.5% Irish (2000).
Economy: Employment by occupation: 12.1% management, 13.3% professional, 15.3% services, 22.9% sales, 2.1% farming, 11.5% construction, 22.9% production (2000).
Income: Per capita income: $17,050 (2000); Median household income: $33,849 (2000); Poverty rate: 6.8% (2000).
Education: High school graduation rate: 80.9% (2000); College graduation rate: 9.4% (2000).

Housing: Homeownership rate: 90.9% (2000); Median home value: $72,500 (2000); Median rent: $313 per month (2000); Median age of housing: 28 years (2000).
Transportation: Commute to work: 90.9% car, 0.6% public transportation, 1.3% walk, 6.5% work from home (2000); Travel time to work: 15.1% less than 15 minutes, 45.8% 15 to 30 minutes, 29.8% 30 to 45 minutes, 3.8% 45 to 60 minutes, 5.6% 60 minutes or more (2000)

LONG RAPIDS (township). Covers a land area of 54.659 square miles and a water area of 0.011 square miles. Located at 45.13° N. Lat.; 83.70° W. Long. Elevation is 726 feet.
History: Long Rapids Township was organized in 1871 and named for the rapids on the Thunder Bay River, which traversed the township. A village grew up around a sawmill founded by Albert Merrill, and known for a time as Merrillsville.
Population: 1,019 (2000); Race: 99.0% White, 0.0% Black, 0.0% Asian, 0.6% American Indian and Alaska Native, 0.0% Hispanic of any race, 0.4% two or more races (2000); Density: 18.6 persons per square mile (2000); Age: 24.1% under 18, 14.7% over 64 (2000); Marriage status: 19.6% never married, 65.4% now married, 7.2% widowed, 7.9% divorced (2000); Foreign born: 0.8% (2000); Ancestry (includes multiple ancestries): 25.9% German, 23.9% Polish, 11.3% French (except Basque), 8.6% English, 8.5% Norwegian (2000).
Economy: Employment by occupation: 12.8% management, 11.0% professional, 15.3% services, 26.0% sales, 2.9% farming, 10.3% construction, 21.7% production (2000).
Income: Per capita income: $16,829 (2000); Median household income: $36,083 (2000); Poverty rate: 5.0% (2000).
Taxes: Total city taxes per capita: $32 (1997); City property taxes per capita: $25 (1997).
Education: High school graduation rate: 80.9% (2000); College graduation rate: 11.3% (2000).
Housing: Homeownership rate: 92.4% (2000); Median home value: $67,400 (2000); Median rent: $314 per month (2000); Median age of housing: 28 years (2000).
Transportation: Commute to work: 90.9% car, 0.0% public transportation, 1.2% walk, 6.4% work from home (2000); Travel time to work: 16.0% less than 15 minutes, 47.1% 15 to 30 minutes, 29.1% 30 to 45 minutes, 4.0% 45 to 60 minutes, 3.8% 60 minutes or more (2000)

MAPLE RIDGE (township). Covers a land area of 51.928 square miles and a water area of 1.926 square miles. Located at 45.12° N. Lat.; 83.57° W. Long.
Population: 1,715 (2000); Race: 98.7% White, 0.3% Black, 0.1% Asian, 0.9% American Indian and Alaska Native, 0.4% Hispanic of any race, 0.0% two or more races (2000); Density: 33.0 persons per square mile (2000); Age: 27.9% under 18, 13.1% over 64 (2000); Marriage status: 19.3% never married, 65.1% now married, 4.8% widowed, 10.8% divorced (2000); Foreign born: 0.3% (2000); Ancestry (includes multiple ancestries): 28.0% Polish, 25.7% German, 10.2% French (except Basque), 9.3% Irish, 8.0% English (2000).
Economy: Single-family building permits issued: 3 (2001) / 3 (2000); Multi-family building permits issued: 0 (2001) / 0 (2000); Employment by occupation: 11.6% management, 18.3% professional, 15.4% services, 20.2% sales, 0.5% farming, 10.1% construction, 23.9% production (2000).
Income: Per capita income: $16,024 (2000); Median household income: $35,871 (2000); Poverty rate: 12.2% (2000).
Taxes: Total city taxes per capita: $27 (1997); City property taxes per capita: $22 (1997).
Education: High school graduation rate: 81.7% (2000); College graduation rate: 10.8% (2000).
Housing: Homeownership rate: 92.3% (2000); Median home value: $78,200 (2000); Median rent: $335 per month (2000); Median age of housing: 28 years (2000).
Transportation: Commute to work: 90.4% car, 0.3% public transportation, 1.5% walk, 6.1% work from home (2000); Travel time to work: 24.5% less than 15 minutes, 60.7% 15 to 30 minutes, 11.1% 30 to 45 minutes, 1.5% 45 to 60 minutes, 2.2% 60 minutes or more (2000)

OSSINEKE (township). Covers a land area of 106.033 square miles and a water area of 1.238 square miles. Located at 44.91° N. Lat.; 83.72° W. Long. Elevation is 604 feet.
Population: 1,761 (2000); Race: 99.1% White, 0.3% Black, 0.2% Asian, 0.2% American Indian and Alaska Native, 0.5% Hispanic of any race, 0.2% two or more races (2000); Density: 16.6 persons per square mile (2000); Age: 25.3% under 18, 15.2% over 64 (2000); Marriage status: 17.1% never married, 69.9% now married, 4.6% widowed, 8.4% divorced (2000); Foreign born: 0.6% (2000); Ancestry (includes multiple ancestries): 35.0% German, 11.4% French (except Basque), 10.2% Polish, 8.9% English, 7.9% Irish (2000).
Economy: Michigan Islands National Wildlife Refuge to East Southeast. Employment by occupation: 10.6% management, 14.6% professional, 17.6% services, 23.4% sales, 1.4% farming, 13.7% construction, 18.7% production (2000).
Income: Per capita income: $16,473 (2000); Median household income: $34,375 (2000); Poverty rate: 10.8% (2000).
Taxes: Total city taxes per capita: $61 (1997); City property taxes per capita: $53 (1997).
Education: High school graduation rate: 76.5% (2000); College graduation rate: 10.5% (2000).
Housing: Homeownership rate: 89.9% (2000); Median home value: $73,600 (2000); Median rent: $315 per month (2000); Median age of housing: 28 years (2000).
Transportation: Commute to work: 91.3% car, 0.3% public transportation, 0.6% walk, 6.6% work from home (2000); Travel time to work: 11.3% less than 15 minutes, 37.9% 15 to 30 minutes, 36.5% 30 to 45 minutes, 7.7% 45 to 60 minutes, 6.6% 60 minutes or more (2000)

SANBORN (township). Covers a land area of 43.841 square miles and a water area of 5.888 square miles. Located at 44.91° N. Lat.; 83.44° W. Long.
Population: 2,152 (2000); Race: 98.5% White, 0.2% Black, 0.2% Asian, 0.8% American Indian and Alaska Native, 1.0% Hispanic of any race, 0.2% two or more races (2000); Density: 49.1 persons per square mile (2000); Age: 23.7% under 18, 14.3% over 64 (2000); Marriage status: 23.0% never married, 57.9% now married, 11.0% widowed, 8.0% divorced (2000); Foreign born: 1.4% (2000); Ancestry (includes multiple ancestries): 30.8% German, 20.9% Polish, 16.1% French (except Basque), 11.0% Irish, 8.0% English (2000).
Economy: Employment by occupation: 7.9% management, 16.5% professional, 13.7% services, 25.6% sales, 2.1% farming, 13.6% construction, 20.5% production (2000).
Income: Per capita income: $16,867 (2000); Median household income: $35,000 (2000); Poverty rate: 14.2% (2000).
Taxes: Total city taxes per capita: $21 (1997); City property taxes per capita: $17 (1997).
Education: High school graduation rate: 80.2% (2000); College graduation rate: 9.7% (2000).
Housing: Homeownership rate: 84.0% (2000); Median home value: $77,500 (2000); Median rent: $320 per month (2000); Median age of housing: 36 years (2000).
Transportation: Commute to work: 92.8% car, 0.0% public transportation, 1.7% walk, 3.6% work from home (2000); Travel time to work: 25.9% less than 15 minutes, 49.8% 15 to 30 minutes, 15.9% 30 to 45 minutes, 3.4% 45 to 60 minutes, 4.9% 60 minutes or more (2000)

WELLINGTON (township). Covers a land area of 53.394 square miles and a water area of 0 square miles. Located at 45.13° N. Lat.; 83.80° W. Long.
Population: 296 (2000); Race: 95.6% White, 0.0% Black, 0.0% Asian, 1.5% American Indian and Alaska Native, 0.0% Hispanic of any race, 2.9% two or more races (2000); Density: 5.5 persons per square mile (2000); Age: 29.5% under 18, 17.1% over 64 (2000); Marriage status: 13.9% never married, 72.1% now married, 9.0% widowed, 5.0% divorced (2000); Foreign born: 0.0% (2000); Ancestry (includes multiple ancestries): 39.6% German, 17.1% Polish, 15.6% Irish, 7.3% United States or American, 6.9% Other groups (2000).
Economy: Employment by occupation: 22.9% management, 15.2% professional, 13.3% services, 7.6% sales, 5.7% farming, 14.3% construction, 21.0% production (2000).
Income: Per capita income: $13,513 (2000); Median household income: $28,393 (2000); Poverty rate: 12.0% (2000).
Taxes: Total city taxes per capita: $47 (1997); City property taxes per capita: $47 (1997).
Education: High school graduation rate: 77.3% (2000); College graduation rate: 8.0% (2000).
Housing: Homeownership rate: 87.0% (2000); Median home value: $60,000 (2000); Median rent: $325 per month (2000); Median age of housing: 31 years (2000).
Transportation: Commute to work: 90.5% car, 0.0% public transportation, 0.0% walk, 5.7% work from home (2000); Travel time to work: 19.2% less than 15 minutes, 36.4% 15 to 30 minutes, 25.3% 30 to 45 minutes, 7.1% 45 to 60 minutes, 12.1% 60 minutes or more (2000)

WILSON (township). Covers a land area of 79.517 square miles and a water area of 0.248 square miles. Located at 45.00° N. Lat.; 83.62° W. Long.
Population: 2,074 (2000); Race: 97.4% White, 0.5% Black, 0.0% Asian, 0.3% American Indian and Alaska Native, 1.2% Hispanic of any race, 1.7% two or more races (2000); Density: 26.1 persons per square mile (2000); Age: 28.7% under 18, 13.9% over 64 (2000); Marriage status: 20.7% never married, 66.6% now married, 4.7% widowed, 8.0% divorced (2000); Foreign born: 0.6% (2000); Ancestry (includes multiple ancestries): 33.4% German, 18.3% Polish, 11.9% French (except Basque), 7.9% Irish, 7.6% English (2000).
Economy: Employment by occupation: 9.1% management, 15.9% professional, 17.1% services, 24.5% sales, 2.0% farming, 12.4% construction, 19.0% production (2000).
Income: Per capita income: $16,758 (2000); Median household income: $37,198 (2000); Poverty rate: 5.4% (2000).
Taxes: Total city taxes per capita: $20 (1997); City property taxes per capita: $20 (1997).
Education: High school graduation rate: 79.7% (2000); College graduation rate: 9.1% (2000).
Housing: Homeownership rate: 89.5% (2000); Median home value: $76,400 (2000); Median rent: $327 per month (2000); Median age of housing: 29 years (2000).
Transportation: Commute to work: 89.3% car, 0.2% public transportation, 1.6% walk, 8.7% work from home (2000); Travel time to work: 16.9% less than 15 minutes, 66.1% 15 to 30 minutes, 11.9% 30 to 45 minutes, 0.9% 45 to 60 minutes, 4.2% 60 minutes or more (2000)

Antrim County

Located in northwestern Michigan; bounded on the west by Grand Traverse Bay; includes Torch Lake. Covers a land area of 476.90 square miles, a water area of 125.00 square miles, and is located in the Eastern Time Zone. The county government was organized in 1840. County seat is Bellaire.
Population: 23,110 (2000); Race: 97.2% White, 0.2% Black, 0.2% Asian, 1.0% American Indian and Alaska Native, 0.9% Hispanic of any race, 1.1% two or more races (2000); Density: 48.5 persons per square mile (2000); Age: 24.4% under 18, 17.6% over 64 (2000).
Religion: Five largest groups: 5.6% Catholic Church, 3.7% The United Methodist Church, 3.2% Presbyterian Church (U.S.A.), 2.5% Christian Reformed Church in North America, 1.6% The Wesleyan Church (2000).
Economy: Unemployment rate: 7.9% (11/2002); Total civilian labor force: 10,461 (11/2002); Leading industries: 27.4% manufacturing; 12.9% professional, scientific & technical services; 12.2% retail trade (2000); Companies that employ more than 1,000 persons: 0 (2000); Companies that employ more than 100 persons: 6 (2000); Farms: 261 totaling 55,166 acres (1997); Minority business ownership rate: 0.0% (1997); Women business ownership rate: 31.7% (1997); Retail sales per capita: $5,079 (1997). Single-family building permits issued: 250 (2001) / 308 (2000); Multi-family building permits issued: 4 (2001) / 0 (2000).
Income: Per capita income: $19,485 (2000); Median household income: $38,107 (2000); Poverty rate: 9.0% (2000); Bankruptcy rate: 3.57% (2001).
Taxes: Total county taxes per capita: $224 (1997); County property taxes per capita: $202 (1997).
Education: High school graduation rate: 84.6% (2000); College graduation rate: 19.4% (2000).
Housing: Homeownership rate: 85.0% (2000); Median home value: $110,000 (2000); Median rent: $384 per month (2000); Median age of housing: 25 years (2000).
Health: Birth rate: 100.8 per 10,000 population (1998); Age adjusted death rate: 88.1 per 10,000 population (1999); Age adjusted cancer mortality rate: 218.3 deaths per 100,000 population (1999). Number of physicians: 5.2 per 10,000 population (1999); Number of hospital beds: n/a (1999).
Elections: 2000 Presidential election results: 37.6% Gore, 58.9% Bush, 2.7% Nader, 0.2% Buchanan
National and State Parks: Petobego State Game Area
Additional Information Contacts
Antrim County Government Offices 231-533-6353
Bellaire Chamber of Commerce. 231-533-6023
Cemtral Lake Chamber of Commerce 231-544-3322
Elk Rapids Chamber of Commerce 231-264-8202
Mancelona Area Chamber of Commerce. 231-587-5500

Antrim County Communities

ALDEN (unincorporated postal area, zip code 49612). Covers a land area of 28.147 square miles and a water area of 0.178 square miles. Located at 44.87° N. Lat.; 85.24° W. Long. Elevation is 604 feet.
History: Alden began in 1868, when F.J. Lewis built a store here and a settlement grew up around it. First called Noble, and then Spencer Creek, when the Pere Marquette Railroad arrived in 1891 the name was changed to honor William Alden Smith, a railroad official.
Population: 1,101 (2000); Race: 95.7% White, 0.0% Black, 0.5% Asian, 2.8% American Indian and Alaska Native, 1.2% Hispanic of any race, 1.1% two or more races (2000); Density: 39.1 persons per square mile (2000); Age: 21.3% under 18, 17.9% over 64 (2000); Marriage status: 19.3% never married, 64.2% now married, 7.7% widowed, 8.7% divorced (2000); Foreign born: 1.1% (2000); Ancestry (includes multiple ancestries): 17.9% German, 14.4% English, 11.2% Irish, 8.9% Other groups, 7.3% United States or American (2000).
Economy: Employment by occupation: 11.3% management, 11.5% professional, 20.8% services, 26.9% sales, 0.4% farming, 14.4% construction, 14.8% production (2000).
Income: Per capita income: $20,902 (2000); Median household income: $36,375 (2000); Poverty rate: 9.6% (2000).
Education: High school graduation rate: 86.1% (2000); College graduation rate: 21.0% (2000).
Housing: Homeownership rate: 87.0% (2000); Median home value: $108,200 (2000); Median rent: $321 per month (2000); Median age of housing: 27 years (2000).
Transportation: Commute to work: 88.4% car, 1.1% public transportation, 1.3% walk, 7.9% work from home (2000); Travel time to work: 23.1% less than 15 minutes, 44.8% 15 to 30 minutes, 17.2% 30 to 45 minutes, 7.7% 45 to 60 minutes, 7.2% 60 minutes or more (2000)

BANKS (township). Covers a land area of 45.002 square miles and a water area of 6.228 square miles. Located at 45.16° N. Lat.; 85.29° W. Long.
Population: 1,813 (2000); Race: 97.2% White, 0.2% Black, 0.6% Asian, 0.4% American Indian and Alaska Native, 0.0% Hispanic of any race, 1.2% two or more races (2000); Density: 40.3 persons per square mile (2000); Age: 27.9% under 18, 13.8% over 64 (2000); Marriage status: 16.8% never married, 67.7% now married, 5.9% widowed, 9.6% divorced (2000); Foreign born: 1.2% (2000); Ancestry (includes multiple ancestries): 23.0% German, 19.9% Dutch, 10.5% English, 8.3% Irish, 7.5% United States or American (2000).
Economy: Employment by occupation: 9.9% management, 16.6% professional, 15.9% services, 20.2% sales, 1.7% farming, 16.9% construction, 18.6% production (2000).
Income: Per capita income: $17,378 (2000); Median household income: $41,500 (2000); Poverty rate: 7.2% (2000).
Taxes: Total city taxes per capita: $92 (1997); City property taxes per capita: $91 (1997).
Education: High school graduation rate: 87.0% (2000); College graduation rate: 19.3% (2000).
Housing: Homeownership rate: 88.7% (2000); Median home value: $94,800 (2000); Median rent: $393 per month (2000); Median age of housing: 33 years (2000).
Transportation: Commute to work: 89.4% car, 0.0% public transportation, 2.0% walk, 7.7% work from home (2000); Travel time to work: 32.9% less than 15 minutes, 43.3% 15 to 30 minutes, 11.5% 30 to 45 minutes, 6.7% 45 to 60 minutes, 5.5% 60 minutes or more (2000)

BELLAIRE (village). Covers a land area of 1.830 square miles and a water area of 0.118 square miles. Located at 44.97° N. Lat.; 85.20° W. Long. Elevation is 616 feet.
History: The site of Bellaire was chosen to be the seat of Elk Rapids County in 1879. The town was established on land belonging to Ambrose E. Palmer, who named it for the clear, pure air.
Population: 1,164 (2000); Race: 98.1% White, 0.3% Black, 0.5% Asian, 0.0% American Indian and Alaska Native, 2.4% Hispanic of any race, 1.1% two or more races (2000); Density: 636.1 persons per square mile (2000); Age: 23.9% under 18, 14.8% over 64 (2000); Marriage status: 17.7% never married, 62.0% now married, 5.2% widowed, 15.1% divorced (2000); Foreign born: 1.9% (2000); Ancestry (includes multiple ancestries): 26.0% German, 18.9% English, 13.7% Irish, 9.5% United States or American, 5.5% Other groups (2000).

Economy: Employment by occupation: 14.4% management, 16.3% professional, 17.2% services, 27.9% sales, 0.0% farming, 5.9% construction, 18.3% production (2000).
Income: Per capita income: $18,327 (2000); Median household income: $32,243 (2000); Poverty rate: 5.5% (2000).
Taxes: Total city taxes per capita: $278 (1997); City property taxes per capita: $277 (1997).
Education: High school graduation rate: 87.8% (2000); College graduation rate: 18.7% (2000).

School District(s)

Bellaire Public Schools (KG-12)
2000 Enrollment: 646 231-533-8141
Housing: Homeownership rate: 72.2% (2000); Median home value: $90,400 (2000); Median rent: $349 per month (2000); Median age of housing: 37 years (2000).
Safety: Violent crime rate: 0.0 per 10,000 population; Property crime rate: 94.0 per 10,000 population (2001).
Newspapers: Antrim County News (1 x week); Penny Stretcher (1 x week)
Transportation: Commute to work: 84.7% car, 0.9% public transportation, 5.3% walk, 7.4% work from home (2000); Travel time to work: 57.9% less than 15 minutes, 18.2% 15 to 30 minutes, 13.7% 30 to 45 minutes, 7.4% 45 to 60 minutes, 2.9% 60 minutes or more (2000)
Airports: Antrim County
Additional Information Contacts
Bellaire Chamber of Commerce. 231-533-6023

CENTRAL LAKE (village). Covers a land area of 1.048 square miles and a water area of 0.163 square miles. Located at 45.06° N. Lat.; 85.26° W. Long. Elevation is 635 feet.
History: The village of Central Lake was platted in 1883. The railroad came through in 1892, and in 1895 the village was incorporated.
Population: 990 (2000); Race: 95.9% White, 0.2% Black, 0.0% Asian, 2.4% American Indian and Alaska Native, 0.2% Hispanic of any race, 1.5% two or more races (2000); Density: 944.8 persons per square mile (2000); Age: 25.0% under 18, 16.7% over 64 (2000); Marriage status: 22.7% never married, 57.9% now married, 8.1% widowed, 11.3% divorced (2000); Foreign born: 1.0% (2000); Ancestry (includes multiple ancestries): 20.5% German, 15.7% Irish, 11.5% English, 7.2% United States or American, 7.1% Polish (2000).
Economy: Employment by occupation: 10.0% management, 11.8% professional, 14.0% services, 22.6% sales, 1.8% farming, 12.0% construction, 27.9% production (2000).
Income: Per capita income: $18,133 (2000); Median household income: $38,173 (2000); Poverty rate: 12.2% (2000).
Taxes: Total city taxes per capita: $149 (1997); City property taxes per capita: $149 (1997).
Education: High school graduation rate: 84.5% (2000); College graduation rate: 12.0% (2000).

School District(s)

Central Lake Public Schools (KG-12)
2000 Enrollment: 493 231-544-3141
Housing: Homeownership rate: 73.9% (2000); Median home value: $77,000 (2000); Median rent: $360 per month (2000); Median age of housing: 38 years (2000).
Transportation: Commute to work: 88.9% car, 0.0% public transportation, 6.3% walk, 4.8% work from home (2000); Travel time to work: 46.7% less than 15 minutes, 31.4% 15 to 30 minutes, 11.2% 30 to 45 minutes, 5.7% 45 to 60 minutes, 5.0% 60 minutes or more (2000)
Additional Information Contacts
Cemtral Lake Chamber of Commerce 231-544-3322

CENTRAL LAKE (township). Covers a land area of 27.593 square miles and a water area of 3.701 square miles. Located at 45.07° N. Lat.; 85.26° W. Long. Elevation is 635 feet.
Population: 2,254 (2000); Race: 96.8% White, 0.1% Black, 0.1% Asian, 1.5% American Indian and Alaska Native, 0.2% Hispanic of any race, 1.4% two or more races (2000); Density: 81.7 persons per square mile (2000); Age: 22.4% under 18, 18.3% over 64 (2000); Marriage status: 18.6% never married, 65.3% now married, 7.1% widowed, 9.0% divorced (2000); Foreign born: 1.5% (2000); Ancestry (includes multiple ancestries): 20.5% German, 15.8% English, 13.1% Irish, 8.9% Dutch, 6.5% United States or American (2000).
Economy: In agricultural area: corn, potatoes. Manufacturing: steel stampings, bullet proof vests, electrical motor protectors. Employment by occupation: 11.9% management, 15.6% professional, 13.7% services, 19.1% sales, 1.0% farming, 13.2% construction, 25.4% production (2000).
Income: Per capita income: $19,040 (2000); Median household income: $38,750 (2000); Poverty rate: 8.6% (2000).
Taxes: Total city taxes per capita: $160 (1997); City property taxes per capita: $160 (1997).
Education: High school graduation rate: 86.2% (2000); College graduation rate: 17.0% (2000).
Housing: Homeownership rate: 83.3% (2000); Median home value: $93,000 (2000); Median rent: $362 per month (2000); Median age of housing: 30 years (2000).
Transportation: Commute to work: 89.8% car, 0.5% public transportation, 4.6% walk, 5.1% work from home (2000); Travel time to work: 42.9% less than 15 minutes, 34.6% 15 to 30 minutes, 10.3% 30 to 45 minutes, 5.8% 45 to 60 minutes, 6.4% 60 minutes or more (2000)

CHESTONIA (township). Covers a land area of 35.528 square miles and a water area of 0.012 square miles. Located at 44.97° N. Lat.; 85.03° W. Long. Elevation is 638 feet.
History: Chestonia Township was organized in 1874 with Thomas R. Van Wert as the first supervisor and postmster.
Population: 546 (2000); Race: 95.4% White, 0.4% Black, 0.0% Asian, 1.5% American Indian and Alaska Native, 0.0% Hispanic of any race, 2.7% two or more races (2000); Density: 15.4 persons per square mile (2000); Age: 31.6% under 18, 9.1% over 64 (2000); Marriage status: 22.5% never married, 57.0% now married, 4.6% widowed, 15.9% divorced (2000); Foreign born: 1.1% (2000); Ancestry (includes multiple ancestries): 18.8% German, 10.8% United States or American, 10.6% English, 8.2% Irish, 4.6% French (except Basque) (2000).
Economy: Employment by occupation: 6.5% management, 10.2% professional, 18.5% services, 21.8% sales, 1.4% farming, 16.2% construction, 25.5% production (2000).
Income: Per capita income: $13,094 (2000); Median household income: $37,344 (2000); Poverty rate: 12.2% (2000).
Taxes: Total city taxes per capita: $61 (1997); City property taxes per capita: $61 (1997).
Education: High school graduation rate: 74.8% (2000); College graduation rate: 11.9% (2000).
Housing: Homeownership rate: 85.3% (2000); Median home value: $76,000 (2000); Median rent: $425 per month (2000); Median age of housing: 24 years (2000).
Transportation: Commute to work: 87.7% car, 1.9% public transportation, 2.8% walk, 4.7% work from home (2000); Travel time to work: 18.4% less than 15 minutes, 38.3% 15 to 30 minutes, 22.9% 30 to 45 minutes, 5.0% 45 to 60 minutes, 15.4% 60 minutes or more (2000)

CUSTER (township). Covers a land area of 34.742 square miles and a water area of 0.442 square miles. Located at 44.92° N. Lat.; 85.15° W. Long.
Population: 988 (2000); Race: 98.9% White, 0.0% Black, 0.0% Asian, 1.0% American Indian and Alaska Native, 0.3% Hispanic of any race, 0.2% two or more races (2000); Density: 28.4 persons per square mile (2000); Age: 24.2% under 18, 12.7% over 64 (2000); Marriage status: 19.5% never married, 67.6% now married, 5.2% widowed, 7.8% divorced (2000); Foreign born: 0.2% (2000); Ancestry (includes multiple ancestries): 26.9% German, 15.3% English, 11.2% United States or American, 10.8% Polish, 7.5% Irish (2000).
Economy: Employment by occupation: 9.4% management, 12.5% professional, 19.1% services, 22.0% sales, 0.8% farming, 17.0% construction, 19.3% production (2000).
Income: Per capita income: $19,643 (2000); Median household income: $41,645 (2000); Poverty rate: 6.3% (2000).
Taxes: Total city taxes per capita: $299 (1997); City property taxes per capita: $299 (1997).
Education: High school graduation rate: 84.7% (2000); College graduation rate: 17.1% (2000).
Housing: Homeownership rate: 89.1% (2000); Median home value: $114,300 (2000); Median rent: $394 per month (2000); Median age of housing: 21 years (2000).
Transportation: Commute to work: 91.2% car, 0.2% public transportation, 2.1% walk, 5.8% work from home (2000); Travel time to work: 49.6% less than 15 minutes, 27.3% 15 to 30 minutes, 6.8% 30 to 45 minutes, 7.9% 45 to 60 minutes, 8.5% 60 minutes or more (2000)

ECHO (township). Covers a land area of 34.862 square miles and a water area of 0.479 square miles. Located at 45.08° N. Lat.; 85.15° W. Long.
Population: 928 (2000); Race: 98.0% White, 0.0% Black, 0.0% Asian, 0.7% American Indian and Alaska Native, 0.0% Hispanic of any race, 1.3% two or more races (2000); Density: 26.6 persons per square mile (2000); Age: 28.5% under 18, 14.0% over 64 (2000); Marriage status: 15.5% never married,

71.3% now married, 7.2% widowed, 6.0% divorced (2000); Foreign born: 0.3% (2000); Ancestry (includes multiple ancestries): 21.1% German, 14.8% United States or American, 12.2% English, 9.0% Irish, 7.4% French (except Basque) (2000).
Economy: Employment by occupation: 7.5% management, 7.2% professional, 19.3% services, 15.2% sales, 1.5% farming, 14.9% construction, 34.4% production (2000).
Income: Per capita income: $15,427 (2000); Median household income: $36,406 (2000); Poverty rate: 8.6% (2000).
Taxes: Total city taxes per capita: $17 (1997); City property taxes per capita: $17 (1997).
Education: High school graduation rate: 72.4% (2000); College graduation rate: 9.8% (2000).
Housing: Homeownership rate: 90.0% (2000); Median home value: $88,700 (2000); Median rent: $429 per month (2000); Median age of housing: 27 years (2000).
Transportation: Commute to work: 97.9% car, 0.3% public transportation, 0.0% walk, 1.8% work from home (2000); Travel time to work: 23.1% less than 15 minutes, 43.8% 15 to 30 minutes, 18.3% 30 to 45 minutes, 9.0% 45 to 60 minutes, 5.8% 60 minutes or more (2000)

ELK RAPIDS (village). Covers a land area of 1.676 square miles and a water area of 0.348 square miles. Located at 44.89° N. Lat.; 85.41° W. Long. Elevation is 587 feet.
History: Elk Rapids was settled in 1852 around a sawmill operated by power from the Elk River. A charcoal iron furnace and a chemical plant were also built here, but the area later became a summer resort village.
Population: 1,700 (2000); Race: 98.6% White, 0.0% Black, 0.0% Asian, 0.1% American Indian and Alaska Native, 2.1% Hispanic of any race, 1.1% two or more races (2000); Density: 1,014.3 persons per square mile (2000); Age: 25.5% under 18, 20.4% over 64 (2000); Marriage status: 19.2% never married, 58.3% now married, 11.7% widowed, 10.8% divorced (2000); Foreign born: 2.0% (2000); Ancestry (includes multiple ancestries): 28.9% German, 20.5% English, 15.7% Irish, 7.3% French (except Basque), 5.9% Polish (2000).
Economy: Employment by occupation: 11.9% management, 19.7% professional, 15.9% services, 26.4% sales, 0.9% farming, 9.4% construction, 15.8% production (2000).
Income: Per capita income: $19,735 (2000); Median household income: $31,382 (2000); Poverty rate: 8.2% (2000).
Taxes: Total city taxes per capita: $364 (1997); City property taxes per capita: $352 (1997).
Education: High school graduation rate: 91.2% (2000); College graduation rate: 28.4% (2000).

School District(s)

Elk Rapids Schools (PK-12)
2000 Enrollment: 1,542 231-264-8692
Housing: Homeownership rate: 72.6% (2000); Median home value: $136,900 (2000); Median rent: $401 per month (2000); Median age of housing: 34 years (2000).
Safety: Violent crime rate: 0.0 per 10,000 population; Property crime rate: 339.4 per 10,000 population (2001).
Newspapers: The Town Meeting (1 x week)
Transportation: Commute to work: 88.4% car, 1.4% public transportation, 4.4% walk, 5.0% work from home (2000); Travel time to work: 41.3% less than 15 minutes, 28.1% 15 to 30 minutes, 23.4% 30 to 45 minutes, 3.8% 45 to 60 minutes, 3.3% 60 minutes or more (2000)
Additional Information Contacts
Elk Rapids Chamber of Commerce 231-264-8202

ELK RAPIDS (township). Covers a land area of 7.114 square miles and a water area of 3.822 square miles. Located at 44.90° N. Lat.; 85.40° W. Long. Elevation is 587 feet.
Population: 2,741 (2000); Race: 98.3% White, 0.2% Black, 0.3% Asian, 0.2% American Indian and Alaska Native, 2.1% Hispanic of any race, 0.8% two or more races (2000); Density: 385.3 persons per square mile (2000); Age: 21.3% under 18, 23.0% over 64 (2000); Marriage status: 17.7% never married, 63.3% now married, 10.2% widowed, 8.9% divorced (2000); Foreign born: 2.8% (2000); Ancestry (includes multiple ancestries): 28.2% German, 20.1% English, 15.8% Irish, 7.0% Polish, 6.5% French (except Basque) (2000).
Economy: Agriculture: potatoes, beans, cherries. Manufacturing: fruit products, cutting tools. Resort. Employment by occupation: 13.0% management, 19.6% professional, 15.0% services, 27.7% sales, 0.6% farming, 10.6% construction, 13.6% production (2000).
Income: Per capita income: $21,970 (2000); Median household income: $36,250 (2000); Poverty rate: 7.6% (2000).
Taxes: Total city taxes per capita: $108 (1997); City property taxes per capita: $107 (1997).
Education: High school graduation rate: 92.4% (2000); College graduation rate: 29.7% (2000).
Housing: Homeownership rate: 77.8% (2000); Median home value: $168,600 (2000); Median rent: $415 per month (2000); Median age of housing: 26 years (2000).
Transportation: Commute to work: 89.3% car, 0.9% public transportation, 4.0% walk, 5.1% work from home (2000); Travel time to work: 38.3% less than 15 minutes, 28.0% 15 to 30 minutes, 26.1% 30 to 45 minutes, 4.3% 45 to 60 minutes, 3.2% 60 minutes or more (2000)

ELLSWORTH (village). Covers a land area of 0.740 square miles and a water area of 0.083 square miles. Located at 45.16° N. Lat.; 85.24° W. Long. Elevation is 621 feet.
Population: 483 (2000); Race: 98.3% White, 0.0% Black, 0.0% Asian, 0.0% American Indian and Alaska Native, 0.0% Hispanic of any race, 0.8% two or more races (2000); Density: 652.9 persons per square mile (2000); Age: 29.0% under 18, 8.9% over 64 (2000); Marriage status: 21.8% never married, 64.0% now married, 6.1% widowed, 8.1% divorced (2000); Foreign born: 0.0% (2000); Ancestry (includes multiple ancestries): 36.2% Dutch, 22.9% German, 7.0% English, 5.9% Irish, 3.8% Polish (2000).
Economy: In resort and farm area. Manufacturing: wooden pallets. Employment by occupation: 13.9% management, 16.8% professional, 21.0% services, 15.5% sales, 2.9% farming, 11.3% construction, 18.5% production (2000).
Income: Per capita income: $16,781 (2000); Median household income: $38,125 (2000); Poverty rate: 7.3% (2000).
Taxes: Total city taxes per capita: $126 (1997); City property taxes per capita: $126 (1997).
Education: High school graduation rate: 89.4% (2000); College graduation rate: 16.4% (2000).

School District(s)

Ellsworth Community Schools (KG-12)
2000 Enrollment: 258 231-588-2544
Housing: Homeownership rate: 78.2% (2000); Median home value: $84,700 (2000); Median rent: $363 per month (2000); Median age of housing: 46 years (2000).
Transportation: Commute to work: 87.9% car, 0.0% public transportation, 3.9% walk, 8.2% work from home (2000); Travel time to work: 44.6% less than 15 minutes, 37.6% 15 to 30 minutes, 11.3% 30 to 45 minutes, 2.3% 45 to 60 minutes, 4.2% 60 minutes or more (2000)

FOREST HOME (township). Covers a land area of 24.254 square miles and a water area of 9.287 square miles. Located at 44.98° N. Lat.; 85.25° W. Long.
Population: 1,858 (2000); Race: 98.6% White, 0.2% Black, 0.3% Asian, 0.2% American Indian and Alaska Native, 1.2% Hispanic of any race, 0.5% two or more races (2000); Density: 76.6 persons per square mile (2000); Age: 20.5% under 18, 22.0% over 64 (2000); Marriage status: 15.9% never married, 68.2% now married, 8.0% widowed, 7.8% divorced (2000); Foreign born: 1.5% (2000); Ancestry (includes multiple ancestries): 26.6% German, 23.1% English, 13.8% Irish, 7.9% United States or American, 6.8% Polish (2000).
Economy: Employment by occupation: 11.0% management, 18.1% professional, 17.8% services, 27.1% sales, 0.5% farming, 9.5% construction, 16.0% production (2000).
Income: Per capita income: $24,319 (2000); Median household income: $40,980 (2000); Poverty rate: 5.0% (2000).
Taxes: Total city taxes per capita: $239 (1997); City property taxes per capita: $236 (1997).
Education: High school graduation rate: 91.3% (2000); College graduation rate: 27.3% (2000).
Housing: Homeownership rate: 90.7% (2000); Median home value: $129,000 (2000); Median rent: $484 per month (2000); Median age of housing: 29 years (2000).
Transportation: Commute to work: 93.5% car, 0.0% public transportation, 1.9% walk, 4.0% work from home (2000); Travel time to work: 53.5% less than 15 minutes, 19.7% 15 to 30 minutes, 12.8% 30 to 45 minutes, 6.0% 45 to 60 minutes, 8.1% 60 minutes or more (2000)

HELENA (township). Covers a land area of 16.260 square miles and a water area of 6.854 square miles. Located at 44.89° N. Lat.; 85.26° W. Long.

Population: 878 (2000); Race: 95.5% White, 0.0% Black, 0.6% Asian, 2.1% American Indian and Alaska Native, 0.0% Hispanic of any race, 1.8% two or more races (2000); Density: 54.0 persons per square mile (2000); Age: 17.6% under 18, 24.6% over 64 (2000); Marriage status: 14.2% never married, 68.9% now married, 7.4% widowed, 9.5% divorced (2000); Foreign born: 1.8% (2000); Ancestry (includes multiple ancestries): 23.1% German, 19.2% English, 12.5% Irish, 6.9% United States or American, 6.1% Polish (2000).
Economy: Employment by occupation: 13.5% management, 14.8% professional, 18.2% services, 27.4% sales, 0.0% farming, 12.7% construction, 13.5% production (2000).
Income: Per capita income: $24,948 (2000); Median household income: $40,096 (2000); Poverty rate: 6.9% (2000).
Taxes: Total city taxes per capita: $114 (1997); City property taxes per capita: $114 (1997).
Education: High school graduation rate: 89.3% (2000); College graduation rate: 28.9% (2000).
Housing: Homeownership rate: 89.6% (2000); Median home value: $131,300 (2000); Median rent: $324 per month (2000); Median age of housing: 27 years (2000).
Transportation: Commute to work: 85.9% car, 0.0% public transportation, 3.3% walk, 10.3% work from home (2000); Travel time to work: 27.5% less than 15 minutes, 45.3% 15 to 30 minutes, 11.8% 30 to 45 minutes, 7.9% 45 to 60 minutes, 7.6% 60 minutes or more (2000)

JORDAN (township). Covers a land area of 35.324 square miles and a water area of 0.074 square miles. Located at 45.07° N. Lat.; 85.05° W. Long.
Population: 875 (2000); Race: 96.8% White, 0.0% Black, 0.0% Asian, 1.0% American Indian and Alaska Native, 0.6% Hispanic of any race, 2.1% two or more races (2000); Density: 24.8 persons per square mile (2000); Age: 25.7% under 18, 10.0% over 64 (2000); Marriage status: 24.4% never married, 59.3% now married, 3.4% widowed, 12.9% divorced (2000); Foreign born: 1.0% (2000); Ancestry (includes multiple ancestries): 17.1% German, 13.4% Irish, 11.8% United States or American, 9.6% English, 7.1% Polish (2000).
Economy: Employment by occupation: 7.3% management, 14.9% professional, 19.9% services, 19.1% sales, 1.6% farming, 10.7% construction, 26.4% production (2000).
Income: Per capita income: $16,420 (2000); Median household income: $38,229 (2000); Poverty rate: 12.9% (2000).
Taxes: Total city taxes per capita: $48 (1997); City property taxes per capita: $48 (1997).
Education: High school graduation rate: 82.1% (2000); College graduation rate: 12.1% (2000).
Housing: Homeownership rate: 88.9% (2000); Median home value: $86,300 (2000); Median rent: $400 per month (2000); Median age of housing: 20 years (2000).
Transportation: Commute to work: 94.1% car, 0.5% public transportation, 1.1% walk, 3.5% work from home (2000); Travel time to work: 20.7% less than 15 minutes, 42.4% 15 to 30 minutes, 28.4% 30 to 45 minutes, 5.8% 45 to 60 minutes, 2.8% 60 minutes or more (2000)

KEARNEY (township). Covers a land area of 34.245 square miles and a water area of 0.938 square miles. Located at 44.97° N. Lat.; 85.17° W. Long.
Population: 1,764 (2000); Race: 97.7% White, 0.4% Black, 0.0% Asian, 0.3% American Indian and Alaska Native, 0.8% Hispanic of any race, 0.9% two or more races (2000); Density: 51.5 persons per square mile (2000); Age: 23.0% under 18, 22.7% over 64 (2000); Marriage status: 17.3% never married, 65.1% now married, 6.5% widowed, 11.2% divorced (2000); Foreign born: 1.6% (2000); Ancestry (includes multiple ancestries): 24.6% German, 16.9% English, 14.0% Irish, 7.0% United States or American, 6.0% Dutch (2000).
Economy: Employment by occupation: 15.6% management, 11.9% professional, 19.2% services, 23.2% sales, 0.0% farming, 8.9% construction, 21.2% production (2000).
Income: Per capita income: $19,106 (2000); Median household income: $36,058 (2000); Poverty rate: 8.1% (2000).
Taxes: Total city taxes per capita: $166 (1997); City property taxes per capita: $165 (1997).
Education: High school graduation rate: 80.7% (2000); College graduation rate: 16.3% (2000).
Housing: Homeownership rate: 77.9% (2000); Median home value: $90,200 (2000); Median rent: $350 per month (2000); Median age of housing: 27 years (2000).
Transportation: Commute to work: 87.4% car, 0.7% public transportation, 4.3% walk, 6.0% work from home (2000); Travel time to work: 50.5% less than 15 minutes, 25.2% 15 to 30 minutes, 10.0% 30 to 45 minutes, 9.2% 45 to 60 minutes, 5.2% 60 minutes or more (2000)

KEWADIN (unincorporated postal area, zip code 49648). Covers a land area of 28.109 square miles and a water area of 0.240 square miles. Located at 45.00° N. Lat.; 85.36° W. Long. Elevation is 609 feet.
History: Kewadin was named for Chief Kewaydin ("northwest wind"), who once lived here. A post office was established in 1883.
Population: 2,026 (2000); Race: 95.8% White, 1.0% Black, 0.4% Asian, 1.1% American Indian and Alaska Native, 2.2% Hispanic of any race, 0.6% two or more races (2000); Density: 72.1 persons per square mile (2000); Age: 21.9% under 18, 19.8% over 64 (2000); Marriage status: 16.1% never married, 71.8% now married, 6.1% widowed, 6.0% divorced (2000); Foreign born: 1.7% (2000); Ancestry (includes multiple ancestries): 23.1% German, 16.4% English, 15.5% Irish, 6.7% Polish, 6.7% French (except Basque) (2000).
Economy: Employment by occupation: 15.7% management, 10.5% professional, 17.8% services, 28.3% sales, 2.1% farming, 11.6% construction, 14.0% production (2000).
Income: Per capita income: $24,640 (2000); Median household income: $43,750 (2000); Poverty rate: 7.5% (2000).
Education: High school graduation rate: 90.6% (2000); College graduation rate: 31.6% (2000).
Housing: Homeownership rate: 91.0% (2000); Median home value: $207,500 (2000); Median rent: $421 per month (2000); Median age of housing: 20 years (2000).
Transportation: Commute to work: 87.9% car, 0.4% public transportation, 2.5% walk, 8.9% work from home (2000); Travel time to work: 29.7% less than 15 minutes, 27.6% 15 to 30 minutes, 24.3% 30 to 45 minutes, 13.3% 45 to 60 minutes, 5.0% 60 minutes or more (2000)

MANCELONA (village). Covers a land area of 0.991 square miles and a water area of 0 square miles. Located at 44.90° N. Lat.; 85.06° W. Long. Elevation is 1,112 feet.
History: Mancelona grew up as a residential area for workers at the Antrim Iron Company furnace and sawmill, founded in 1882.
Population: 1,408 (2000); Race: 95.3% White, 0.6% Black, 0.0% Asian, 1.4% American Indian and Alaska Native, 2.0% Hispanic of any race, 2.7% two or more races (2000); Density: 1,420.7 persons per square mile (2000); Age: 29.2% under 18, 11.4% over 64 (2000); Marriage status: 24.8% never married, 53.6% now married, 6.9% widowed, 14.7% divorced (2000); Foreign born: 1.4% (2000); Ancestry (includes multiple ancestries): 26.9% German, 16.1% Irish, 15.4% English, 9.8% Other groups, 8.8% French (except Basque) (2000).
Economy: Employment by occupation: 6.3% management, 10.4% professional, 24.5% services, 16.6% sales, 0.5% farming, 13.4% construction, 28.2% production (2000).
Income: Per capita income: $12,391 (2000); Median household income: $29,583 (2000); Poverty rate: 17.4% (2000).
Taxes: Total city taxes per capita: $151 (1997); City property taxes per capita: $151 (1997).
Education: High school graduation rate: 74.0% (2000); College graduation rate: 6.3% (2000).

School District(s)

Concord Academy:Antrim (KG-09)
2000 Enrollment: 146 906-635-2211
Mancelona Public Schools (KG-12)
2000 Enrollment: 1,067 231-587-9764

Housing: Homeownership rate: 72.2% (2000); Median home value: $59,500 (2000); Median rent: $370 per month (2000); Median age of housing: 46 years (2000).
Safety: Violent crime rate: 35.3 per 10,000 population; Property crime rate: 388.7 per 10,000 population (2001).
Transportation: Commute to work: 87.9% car, 1.1% public transportation, 5.1% walk, 3.8% work from home (2000); Travel time to work: 48.2% less than 15 minutes, 29.2% 15 to 30 minutes, 12.8% 30 to 45 minutes, 7.5% 45 to 60 minutes, 2.3% 60 minutes or more (2000); Amtrak: Service available.
Additional Information Contacts
Mancelona Area Chamber of Commerce.................. 231-587-5500

MANCELONA (township). Covers a land area of 71.374 square miles and a water area of 0.257 square miles. Located at 44.91° N. Lat.; 84.99° W. Long. Elevation is 1,112 feet.
History: Incorporated 1889.
Population: 4,100 (2000); Race: 96.8% White, 0.2% Black, 0.0% Asian, 1.7% American Indian and Alaska Native, 1.0% Hispanic of any race, 1.3% two or more races (2000); Density: 57.4 persons per square mile (2000); Age: 29.0% under 18, 12.2% over 64 (2000); Marriage status: 22.6% never

married, 56.4% now married, 7.6% widowed, 13.3% divorced (2000); Foreign born: 1.4% (2000); Ancestry (includes multiple ancestries): 22.5% German, 16.8% Irish, 13.6% English, 10.3% French (except Basque), 8.9% United States or American (2000).
Economy: In dairy and agricultural area: livestock; cherries, apples; dairy. Manufacturing: transportation equipment, metal stampings, storage tanks, wood products. Schuss Mt. and Shanty Creek ski areas to Northwest. Employment by occupation: 5.0% management, 9.6% professional, 21.2% services, 18.5% sales, 0.2% farming, 13.4% construction, 32.2% production (2000).
Income: Per capita income: $13,574 (2000); Median household income: $30,858 (2000); Poverty rate: 15.7% (2000).
Taxes: Total city taxes per capita: $59 (1997); City property taxes per capita: $59 (1997).
Education: High school graduation rate: 72.0% (2000); College graduation rate: 4.5% (2000).
Housing: Homeownership rate: 79.9% (2000); Median home value: $63,800 (2000); Median rent: $379 per month (2000); Median age of housing: 24 years (2000).
Transportation: Commute to work: 91.6% car, 0.4% public transportation, 2.3% walk, 4.6% work from home (2000); Travel time to work: 40.5% less than 15 minutes, 31.6% 15 to 30 minutes, 18.4% 30 to 45 minutes, 5.4% 45 to 60 minutes, 4.1% 60 minutes or more (2000); Amtrak: Service available.

MILTON (township). Covers a land area of 25.837 square miles and a water area of 17.818 square miles. Located at 44.91° N. Lat.; 85.34° W. Long.
Population: 2,072 (2000); Race: 96.8% White, 0.0% Black, 0.5% Asian, 1.3% American Indian and Alaska Native, 2.1% Hispanic of any race, 0.5% two or more races (2000); Density: 80.2 persons per square mile (2000); Age: 22.5% under 18, 19.0% over 64 (2000); Marriage status: 16.3% never married, 70.3% now married, 6.9% widowed, 6.5% divorced (2000); Foreign born: 1.4% (2000); Ancestry (includes multiple ancestries): 23.7% German, 18.8% English, 15.8% Irish, 8.1% French (except Basque), 6.8% Polish (2000).
Economy: Employment by occupation: 11.9% management, 16.6% professional, 15.8% services, 28.7% sales, 0.3% farming, 12.8% construction, 13.8% production (2000).
Income: Per capita income: $26,817 (2000); Median household income: $44,890 (2000); Poverty rate: 5.0% (2000).
Taxes: Total city taxes per capita: $184 (1997); City property taxes per capita: $176 (1997).
Education: High school graduation rate: 91.3% (2000); College graduation rate: 28.6% (2000).
Housing: Homeownership rate: 92.7% (2000); Median home value: $177,700 (2000); Median rent: $425 per month (2000); Median age of housing: 24 years (2000).
Transportation: Commute to work: 88.8% car, 0.1% public transportation, 2.4% walk, 7.7% work from home (2000); Travel time to work: 27.2% less than 15 minutes, 31.6% 15 to 30 minutes, 22.0% 30 to 45 minutes, 12.2% 45 to 60 minutes, 6.9% 60 minutes or more (2000)

STAR (township). Covers a land area of 34.194 square miles and a water area of 0.066 square miles. Located at 44.96° N. Lat.; 84.90° W. Long.
Population: 745 (2000); Race: 94.9% White, 0.0% Black, 0.0% Asian, 3.3% American Indian and Alaska Native, 1.4% Hispanic of any race, 1.1% two or more races (2000); Density: 21.8 persons per square mile (2000); Age: 24.7% under 18, 14.4% over 64 (2000); Marriage status: 16.7% never married, 69.3% now married, 6.4% widowed, 7.6% divorced (2000); Foreign born: 0.9% (2000); Ancestry (includes multiple ancestries): 19.5% German, 13.6% English, 12.3% Irish, 10.9% Other groups, 10.0% Polish (2000).
Economy: Employment by occupation: 6.7% management, 13.7% professional, 10.8% services, 22.3% sales, 1.9% farming, 15.3% construction, 29.3% production (2000).
Income: Per capita income: $17,896 (2000); Median household income: $37,500 (2000); Poverty rate: 6.7% (2000).
Taxes: Total city taxes per capita: $41 (1997); City property taxes per capita: $38 (1997).
Education: High school graduation rate: 81.1% (2000); College graduation rate: 9.8% (2000).
Housing: Homeownership rate: 83.1% (2000); Median home value: $80,000 (2000); Median rent: $357 per month (2000); Median age of housing: 17 years (2000).
Transportation: Commute to work: 96.0% car, 0.0% public transportation, 2.0% walk, 2.0% work from home (2000); Travel time to work: 19.3% less than 15 minutes, 52.7% 15 to 30 minutes, 19.3% 30 to 45 minutes, 2.4% 45 to 60 minutes, 6.4% 60 minutes or more (2000)

TORCH LAKE (township). Covers a land area of 15.192 square miles and a water area of 5.932 square miles. Located at 45.06° N. Lat.; 85.35° W. Long. Elevation is 620 feet.
History: Torch Lake got its name from the native custom of spearing fish at night by the light of torches.
Population: 1,159 (2000); Race: 97.0% White, 1.4% Black, 0.0% Asian, 0.5% American Indian and Alaska Native, 1.2% Hispanic of any race, 0.3% two or more races (2000); Density: 76.3 persons per square mile (2000); Age: 20.3% under 18, 27.0% over 64 (2000); Marriage status: 11.7% never married, 75.9% now married, 5.7% widowed, 6.7% divorced (2000); Foreign born: 2.4% (2000); Ancestry (includes multiple ancestries): 23.1% German, 20.6% English, 13.7% Irish, 6.8% United States or American, 6.5% Polish (2000).
Economy: Employment by occupation: 20.2% management, 18.4% professional, 15.9% services, 20.2% sales, 3.8% farming, 11.8% construction, 9.8% production (2000).
Income: Per capita income: $24,984 (2000); Median household income: $43,816 (2000); Poverty rate: 9.4% (2000).
Taxes: Total city taxes per capita: $224 (1997); City property taxes per capita: $220 (1997).
Education: High school graduation rate: 92.5% (2000); College graduation rate: 36.8% (2000).
Housing: Homeownership rate: 90.3% (2000); Median home value: $215,200 (2000); Median rent: $450 per month (2000); Median age of housing: 22 years (2000).
Transportation: Commute to work: 91.0% car, 0.5% public transportation, 1.5% walk, 6.9% work from home (2000); Travel time to work: 26.6% less than 15 minutes, 33.0% 15 to 30 minutes, 16.8% 30 to 45 minutes, 14.8% 45 to 60 minutes, 8.8% 60 minutes or more (2000)

WARNER (township). Covers a land area of 35.416 square miles and a water area of 0.169 square miles. Located at 45.07° N. Lat.; 84.91° W. Long.
Population: 389 (2000); Race: 94.0% White, 0.5% Black, 0.0% Asian, 0.0% American Indian and Alaska Native, 1.6% Hispanic of any race, 5.5% two or more races (2000); Density: 11.0 persons per square mile (2000); Age: 30.9% under 18, 11.2% over 64 (2000); Marriage status: 20.4% never married, 57.7% now married, 6.0% widowed, 15.8% divorced (2000); Foreign born: 1.3% (2000); Ancestry (includes multiple ancestries): 33.2% Polish, 17.1% German, 10.9% English, 7.5% Irish, 5.7% Other groups (2000).
Economy: Employment by occupation: 9.4% management, 12.0% professional, 13.0% services, 22.9% sales, 3.1% farming, 13.5% construction, 26.0% production (2000).
Income: Per capita income: $14,948 (2000); Median household income: $35,357 (2000); Poverty rate: 8.6% (2000).
Taxes: Total city taxes per capita: $153 (1997); City property taxes per capita: $153 (1997).
Education: High school graduation rate: 84.1% (2000); College graduation rate: 8.4% (2000).
Housing: Homeownership rate: 88.3% (2000); Median home value: $85,000 (2000); Median rent: $481 per month (2000); Median age of housing: 24 years (2000).
Transportation: Commute to work: 92.0% car, 0.0% public transportation, 3.2% walk, 3.2% work from home (2000); Travel time to work: 31.9% less than 15 minutes, 47.8% 15 to 30 minutes, 12.6% 30 to 45 minutes, 7.7% 45 to 60 minutes, 0.0% 60 minutes or more (2000)

Arenac County

Located in eastern Michigan; bounded on the southeast by Saginaw Bay. Covers a land area of 366.80 square miles, a water area of 314.00 square miles, and is located in the Eastern Time Zone. The county government was organized in 1883. County seat is Standish.
Population: 17,269 (2000); Race: 95.2% White, 1.8% Black, 0.4% Asian, 0.8% American Indian and Alaska Native, 1.3% Hispanic of any race, 1.4% two or more races (2000); Density: 47.1 persons per square mile (2000); Age: 23.2% under 18, 16.5% over 64 (2000).
Religion: Five largest groups: 17.9% Catholic Church, 4.7% The United Methodist Church, 3.8% Lutheran Church—Missouri Synod, 1.7% The Wesleyan Church, 1.5% Evangelical Lutheran Church in America (2000).
Economy: Unemployment rate: 8.9% (11/2002); Total civilian labor force: 7,194 (11/2002); Leading industries: 21.3% health care and social assistance; 17.3% administration, support, waste management, remediation services;

14.9% retail trade (2000); Companies that employ more than 1,000 persons: 0 (2000); Companies that employ more than 100 persons: 9 (2000); Farms: 325 totaling 86,240 acres (1997); Minority business ownership rate: 0.0% (1997); Women business ownership rate: 22.9% (1997); Retail sales per capita: $7,815 (1997). Single-family building permits issued: 68 (2001) / 81 (2000); Multi-family building permits issued: 0 (2001) / 0 (2000).
Income: Per capita income: $16,300 (2000); Median household income: $32,805 (2000); Poverty rate: 13.9% (2000); Bankruptcy rate: 2.51% (2001).
Taxes: Total county taxes per capita: $149 (2000); County property taxes per capita: $146 (2000).
Education: High school graduation rate: 76.8% (2000); College graduation rate: 9.1% (2000).
Housing: Homeownership rate: 84.3% (2000); Median home value: $77,700 (2000); Median rent: $317 per month (2000); Median age of housing: 29 years (2000).
Health: Birth rate: 105.4 per 10,000 population (1998); Age adjusted death rate: 89.8 per 10,000 population (1999); Age adjusted cancer mortality rate: 220.5 deaths per 100,000 population (1999). Number of physicians: 9.3 per 10,000 population (1999); Number of hospital beds: 40.0 per 10,000 population (1999).
Elections: 2000 Presidential election results: 50.7% Gore, 47.1% Bush, 1.6% Nader, 0.1% Buchanan

Additional Information Contacts
Arenac County Government Offices 989-846-6188
Au Gres Chamber of Commerce 989-876-6688
Standish Area Chamber of Commerce 989-846-7867
Standish Chamber of Commerce 989-846-7867

Arenac County Communities

ADAMS (township). Covers a land area of 35.675 square miles and a water area of 0.077 square miles. Located at 44.03° N. Lat.; 84.08° W. Long.
Population: 550 (2000); Race: 96.4% White, 0.0% Black, 1.2% Asian, 1.2% American Indian and Alaska Native, 0.3% Hispanic of any race, 1.2% two or more races (2000); Density: 15.4 persons per square mile (2000); Age: 29.9% under 18, 10.4% over 64 (2000); Marriage status: 20.0% never married, 65.2% now married, 5.9% widowed, 8.9% divorced (2000); Foreign born: 1.4% (2000); Ancestry (includes multiple ancestries): 19.4% German, 13.4% United States or American, 12.8% French (except Basque), 12.2% English, 10.4% Polish (2000).
Economy: Employment by occupation: 7.8% management, 12.5% professional, 20.7% services, 22.7% sales, 2.0% farming, 16.4% construction, 18.0% production (2000).
Income: Per capita income: $14,776 (2000); Median household income: $36,346 (2000); Poverty rate: 15.4% (2000).
Taxes: Total city taxes per capita: $40 (1997); City property taxes per capita: $40 (1997).
Education: High school graduation rate: 79.3% (2000); College graduation rate: 9.8% (2000).
Housing: Homeownership rate: 96.0% (2000); Median home value: $73,600 (2000); Median rent: $275 per month (2000); Median age of housing: 29 years (2000).
Transportation: Commute to work: 89.6% car, 0.0% public transportation, 0.0% walk, 9.6% work from home (2000); Travel time to work: 33.0% less than 15 minutes, 39.2% 15 to 30 minutes, 16.7% 30 to 45 minutes, 7.5% 45 to 60 minutes, 3.5% 60 minutes or more (2000)

ALGER (unincorporated postal area, zip code 48610). Covers a land area of 104.831 square miles and a water area of 0.987 square miles. Located at 44.14° N. Lat.; 84.14° W. Long. Elevation is 784 feet.
History: Alger grew up around a railroad junction in 1883. It was named for Governor Russell A. Alger.
Population: 3,452 (2000); Race: 96.3% White, 0.1% Black, 0.2% Asian, 0.8% American Indian and Alaska Native, 1.1% Hispanic of any race, 2.3% two or more races (2000); Density: 32.9 persons per square mile (2000); Age: 22.0% under 18, 19.0% over 64 (2000); Marriage status: 19.4% never married, 62.0% now married, 7.4% widowed, 11.3% divorced (2000); Foreign born: 1.0% (2000); Ancestry (includes multiple ancestries): 25.6% German, 12.5% English, 11.4% Irish, 9.9% Polish, 8.0% Other groups (2000).
Economy: Employment by occupation: 7.4% management, 10.3% professional, 24.8% services, 21.3% sales, 0.9% farming, 12.4% construction, 22.9% production (2000).
Income: Per capita income: $14,703 (2000); Median household income: $27,756 (2000); Poverty rate: 15.3% (2000).
Education: High school graduation rate: 70.0% (2000); College graduation rate: 6.3% (2000).
Housing: Homeownership rate: 89.9% (2000); Median home value: $73,400 (2000); Median rent: $321 per month (2000); Median age of housing: 27 years (2000).
Transportation: Commute to work: 93.3% car, 0.0% public transportation, 2.8% walk, 3.3% work from home (2000); Travel time to work: 24.7% less than 15 minutes, 40.2% 15 to 30 minutes, 17.3% 30 to 45 minutes, 7.6% 45 to 60 minutes, 10.2% 60 minutes or more (2000)

ARENAC (township). Covers a land area of 36.579 square miles and a water area of 1.390 square miles. Located at 44.02° N. Lat.; 83.85° W. Long.
Population: 992 (2000); Race: 98.4% White, 0.0% Black, 0.0% Asian, 1.1% American Indian and Alaska Native, 1.1% Hispanic of any race, 0.4% two or more races (2000); Density: 27.1 persons per square mile (2000); Age: 22.3% under 18, 17.0% over 64 (2000); Marriage status: 25.1% never married, 57.6% now married, 8.2% widowed, 9.1% divorced (2000); Foreign born: 0.3% (2000); Ancestry (includes multiple ancestries): 16.8% Polish, 16.1% German, 11.4% United States or American, 11.3% French (except Basque), 8.2% English (2000).
Economy: Single-family building permits issued: 0 (2001) / 0 (2000); Multi-family building permits issued: 0 (2001) / 0 (2000); Employment by occupation: 7.4% management, 15.7% professional, 18.1% services, 22.3% sales, 2.5% farming, 13.5% construction, 20.6% production (2000).
Income: Per capita income: $16,673 (2000); Median household income: $35,417 (2000); Poverty rate: 12.4% (2000).
Taxes: Total city taxes per capita: $17 (1997); City property taxes per capita: $15 (1997).
Education: High school graduation rate: 79.3% (2000); College graduation rate: 9.2% (2000).
Housing: Homeownership rate: 87.3% (2000); Median home value: $65,200 (2000); Median rent: $330 per month (2000); Median age of housing: 28 years (2000).
Transportation: Commute to work: 96.3% car, 0.2% public transportation, 1.0% walk, 1.7% work from home (2000); Travel time to work: 32.1% less than 15 minutes, 26.5% 15 to 30 minutes, 10.9% 30 to 45 minutes, 10.1% 45 to 60 minutes, 20.5% 60 minutes or more (2000)

AU GRES (city). Covers a land area of 2.284 square miles and a water area of 0.092 square miles. Located at 44.04° N. Lat.; 83.68° W. Long. Elevation is 589 feet.
History: Au Gres was settled by construction workers who came to work on the Saginaw-Au Sable State Road about 1862. The name of Au Gres refers to the "gritty stone" in the area, and was given to Point Au Gres by early French explorers. Au Gres was incorporated as a city in 1905.
Population: 1,028 (2000); Race: 93.9% White, 0.6% Black, 0.9% Asian, 2.0% American Indian and Alaska Native, 0.4% Hispanic of any race, 2.5% two or more races (2000); Density: 450.1 persons per square mile (2000); Age: 21.0% under 18, 20.7% over 64 (2000); Marriage status: 21.4% never married, 57.9% now married, 10.6% widowed, 10.2% divorced (2000); Foreign born: 2.3% (2000); Ancestry (includes multiple ancestries): 29.7% German, 10.5% French (except Basque), 9.3% United States or American, 9.1% Other groups, 8.5% English (2000).
Economy: Employment by occupation: 11.8% management, 11.0% professional, 18.7% services, 26.9% sales, 0.5% farming, 11.5% construction, 19.7% production (2000).
Income: Per capita income: $15,229 (2000); Median household income: $24,511 (2000); Poverty rate: 17.5% (2000).
Taxes: Total city taxes per capita: $796 (1997); City property taxes per capita: $793 (1997).
Education: High school graduation rate: 75.4% (2000); College graduation rate: 9.3% (2000).

School District(s)
Au Gres-Sims School District (KG-12)
2000 Enrollment: 535 517-876-7150

Housing: Homeownership rate: 64.3% (2000); Median home value: $83,200 (2000); Median rent: $298 per month (2000); Median age of housing: 24 years (2000).
Transportation: Commute to work: 86.8% car, 0.5% public transportation, 7.4% walk, 4.5% work from home (2000); Travel time to work: 48.3% less than 15 minutes, 21.3% 15 to 30 minutes, 7.7% 30 to 45 minutes, 11.6% 45 to 60 minutes, 11.0% 60 minutes or more (2000)

Additional Information Contacts
Au Gres Chamber of Commerce 989-876-6688

AU GRES (township). Covers a land area of 33.879 square miles and a water area of 5.005 square miles. Located at 44.04° N. Lat.; 83.72° W. Long. Elevation is 589 feet.
Population: 1,007 (2000); Race: 98.6% White, 0.0% Black, 0.1% Asian, 0.4% American Indian and Alaska Native, 0.0% Hispanic of any race, 0.9% two or more races (2000); Density: 29.7 persons per square mile (2000); Age: 20.7% under 18, 18.8% over 64 (2000); Marriage status: 13.7% never married, 68.4% now married, 8.9% widowed, 8.9% divorced (2000); Foreign born: 0.2% (2000); Ancestry (includes multiple ancestries): 25.8% German, 20.3% French (except Basque), 11.4% English, 11.0% Polish, 9.6% Irish (2000).
Economy: Farming. Resort. Manufacturing: light and heavy machinery, metal stampings, foundry equipment. Single-family building permits issued: 3 (2001) / 3 (2000); Multi-family building permits issued: 0 (2001) / 0 (2000); Employment by occupation: 8.9% management, 9.9% professional, 11.0% services, 30.1% sales, 1.0% farming, 17.5% construction, 21.5% production (2000).
Income: Per capita income: $18,049 (2000); Median household income: $34,141 (2000); Poverty rate: 9.4% (2000).
Taxes: Total city taxes per capita: $90 (1997); City property taxes per capita: $86 (1997).
Education: High school graduation rate: 77.7% (2000); College graduation rate: 7.9% (2000).
Housing: Homeownership rate: 93.6% (2000); Median home value: $95,200 (2000); Median rent: $339 per month (2000); Median age of housing: 25 years (2000).
Transportation: Commute to work: 95.9% car, 0.0% public transportation, 0.5% walk, 2.7% work from home (2000); Travel time to work: 33.9% less than 15 minutes, 31.4% 15 to 30 minutes, 13.6% 30 to 45 minutes, 4.7% 45 to 60 minutes, 16.4% 60 minutes or more (2000)

CLAYTON (township). Covers a land area of 32.088 square miles and a water area of 0 square miles. Located at 44.13° N. Lat.; 83.99° W. Long.
Population: 1,101 (2000); Race: 99.2% White, 0.0% Black, 0.0% Asian, 0.5% American Indian and Alaska Native, 0.5% Hispanic of any race, 0.4% two or more races (2000); Density: 34.3 persons per square mile (2000); Age: 26.1% under 18, 11.7% over 64 (2000); Marriage status: 27.0% never married, 57.8% now married, 5.8% widowed, 9.4% divorced (2000); Foreign born: 0.0% (2000); Ancestry (includes multiple ancestries): 22.1% German, 18.4% French (except Basque), 14.7% Polish, 11.4% Irish, 9.6% English (2000).
Economy: Employment by occupation: 6.4% management, 12.1% professional, 19.0% services, 19.4% sales, 3.1% farming, 12.8% construction, 27.3% production (2000).
Income: Per capita income: $14,494 (2000); Median household income: $32,500 (2000); Poverty rate: 14.7% (2000).
Taxes: Total city taxes per capita: $45 (1997); City property taxes per capita: $45 (1997).
Education: High school graduation rate: 75.5% (2000); College graduation rate: 6.2% (2000).
Housing: Homeownership rate: 84.0% (2000); Median home value: $67,100 (2000); Median rent: $321 per month (2000); Median age of housing: 28 years (2000).
Transportation: Commute to work: 93.8% car, 0.0% public transportation, 1.2% walk, 5.0% work from home (2000); Travel time to work: 18.5% less than 15 minutes, 39.6% 15 to 30 minutes, 17.3% 30 to 45 minutes, 6.3% 45 to 60 minutes, 18.3% 60 minutes or more (2000)

DEEP RIVER (township). Covers a land area of 35.355 square miles and a water area of 0.064 square miles. Located at 44.03° N. Lat.; 83.99° W. Long.
Population: 2,244 (2000); Race: 96.5% White, 0.0% Black, 0.3% Asian, 1.5% American Indian and Alaska Native, 2.5% Hispanic of any race, 1.7% two or more races (2000); Density: 63.5 persons per square mile (2000); Age: 25.7% under 18, 16.2% over 64 (2000); Marriage status: 22.3% never married, 64.8% now married, 5.7% widowed, 7.2% divorced (2000); Foreign born: 1.6% (2000); Ancestry (includes multiple ancestries): 29.5% German, 21.1% Polish, 11.0% French (except Basque), 9.4% English, 9.2% Irish (2000).
Economy: Single-family building permits issued: 9 (2001) / 9 (2000); Multi-family building permits issued: 0 (2001) / 0 (2000); Employment by occupation: 7.8% management, 15.9% professional, 19.4% services, 25.2% sales, 1.6% farming, 11.9% construction, 18.2% production (2000).
Income: Per capita income: $16,945 (2000); Median household income: $37,457 (2000); Poverty rate: 12.1% (2000).
Taxes: Total city taxes per capita: $40 (1997); City property taxes per capita: $40 (1997).
Education: High school graduation rate: 79.4% (2000); College graduation rate: 10.5% (2000).
Housing: Homeownership rate: 88.4% (2000); Median home value: $70,900 (2000); Median rent: $351 per month (2000); Median age of housing: 28 years (2000).
Transportation: Commute to work: 94.1% car, 0.4% public transportation, 0.4% walk, 4.5% work from home (2000); Travel time to work: 39.1% less than 15 minutes, 25.1% 15 to 30 minutes, 11.6% 30 to 45 minutes, 15.9% 45 to 60 minutes, 8.3% 60 minutes or more (2000)

LINCOLN (township). Covers a land area of 20.968 square miles and a water area of 0.051 square miles. Located at 43.96° N. Lat.; 83.99° W. Long.
Population: 1,522 (2000); Race: 76.3% White, 18.6% Black, 0.2% Asian, 0.8% American Indian and Alaska Native, 2.1% Hispanic of any race, 3.4% two or more races (2000); Density: 72.6 persons per square mile (2000); Age: 16.5% under 18, 9.7% over 64 (2000); Marriage status: 38.4% never married, 49.4% now married, 3.2% widowed, 9.0% divorced (2000); Foreign born: 1.0% (2000); Ancestry (includes multiple ancestries): 23.3% German, 12.2% Other groups, 11.7% French (except Basque), 11.6% Polish, 8.1% Irish (2000).
Economy: Employment by occupation: 9.0% management, 12.7% professional, 14.6% services, 28.2% sales, 0.4% farming, 11.9% construction, 23.2% production (2000).
Income: Per capita income: $13,796 (2000); Median household income: $35,982 (2000); Poverty rate: 19.7% (2000).
Taxes: Total city taxes per capita: $17 (1997); City property taxes per capita: $17 (1997).
Education: High school graduation rate: 65.6% (2000); College graduation rate: 4.1% (2000).
Housing: Homeownership rate: 87.2% (2000); Median home value: $76,800 (2000); Median rent: $313 per month (2000); Median age of housing: 27 years (2000).
Transportation: Commute to work: 92.5% car, 0.0% public transportation, 1.7% walk, 3.9% work from home (2000); Travel time to work: 44.1% less than 15 minutes, 17.0% 15 to 30 minutes, 17.4% 30 to 45 minutes, 12.5% 45 to 60 minutes, 8.9% 60 minutes or more (2000)

MASON (township). Covers a land area of 32.099 square miles and a water area of 0 square miles. Located at 44.12° N. Lat.; 83.85° W. Long.
Population: 994 (2000); Race: 94.2% White, 0.5% Black, 0.0% Asian, 1.5% American Indian and Alaska Native, 1.6% Hispanic of any race, 2.6% two or more races (2000); Density: 31.0 persons per square mile (2000); Age: 30.1% under 18, 11.2% over 64 (2000); Marriage status: 25.3% never married, 54.2% now married, 7.5% widowed, 13.0% divorced (2000); Foreign born: 0.8% (2000); Ancestry (includes multiple ancestries): 25.4% German, 10.6% English, 9.7% Other groups, 9.5% United States or American, 9.2% Polish (2000).
Economy: Employment by occupation: 8.1% management, 12.5% professional, 23.2% services, 17.7% sales, 2.6% farming, 7.5% construction, 28.4% production (2000).
Income: Per capita income: $12,991 (2000); Median household income: $30,357 (2000); Poverty rate: 17.0% (2000).
Taxes: Total city taxes per capita: $14 (1997); City property taxes per capita: $14 (1997).
Education: High school graduation rate: 74.1% (2000); College graduation rate: 4.0% (2000).
Housing: Homeownership rate: 89.3% (2000); Median home value: $51,900 (2000); Median rent: $313 per month (2000); Median age of housing: 28 years (2000).
Transportation: Commute to work: 94.1% car, 0.6% public transportation, 1.2% walk, 3.0% work from home (2000); Travel time to work: 19.6% less than 15 minutes, 33.3% 15 to 30 minutes, 16.8% 30 to 45 minutes, 15.6% 45 to 60 minutes, 14.7% 60 minutes or more (2000)

MOFFATT (township). Covers a land area of 31.665 square miles and a water area of 0.405 square miles. Located at 44.11° N. Lat.; 84.08° W. Long.
Population: 1,121 (2000); Race: 98.2% White, 0.2% Black, 0.0% Asian, 0.4% American Indian and Alaska Native, 0.0% Hispanic of any race, 1.2% two or more races (2000); Density: 35.4 persons per square mile (2000); Age: 22.7% under 18, 20.4% over 64 (2000); Marriage status: 17.6% never married, 63.2% now married, 8.8% widowed, 10.5% divorced (2000); Foreign born: 0.7% (2000); Ancestry (includes multiple ancestries): 27.2% German, 15.2% Polish, 12.0% Irish, 11.1% English, 9.6% French (except Basque) (2000).

Economy: Single-family building permits issued: 3 (2001) / n/a (2000); Multi-family building permits issued: 0 (2001) / n/a (2000); Employment by occupation: 11.1% management, 11.3% professional, 23.4% services, 21.1% sales, 1.5% farming, 12.6% construction, 19.0% production (2000).
Income: Per capita income: $16,058 (2000); Median household income: $32,250 (2000); Poverty rate: 9.5% (2000).
Taxes: Total city taxes per capita: $188 (1997); City property taxes per capita: $176 (1997).
Education: High school graduation rate: 77.5% (2000); College graduation rate: 7.4% (2000).
Housing: Homeownership rate: 89.8% (2000); Median home value: $91,700 (2000); Median rent: $296 per month (2000); Median age of housing: 21 years (2000).
Transportation: Commute to work: 93.2% car, 0.0% public transportation, 2.6% walk, 3.7% work from home (2000); Travel time to work: 22.9% less than 15 minutes, 48.5% 15 to 30 minutes, 10.1% 30 to 45 minutes, 8.4% 45 to 60 minutes, 10.1% 60 minutes or more (2000)

OMER (city). Covers a land area of 1.238 square miles and a water area of 0 square miles. Located at 44.04° N. Lat.; 83.85° W. Long. Elevation is 611 feet.
History: Omer was settled in 1873 and incorporated as a city in 1903. The Rifle River provided good fishing.
Population: 337 (2000); Race: 95.8% White, 0.0% Black, 0.0% Asian, 0.9% American Indian and Alaska Native, 0.3% Hispanic of any race, 3.3% two or more races (2000); Density: 272.2 persons per square mile (2000); Age: 22.7% under 18, 21.5% over 64 (2000); Marriage status: 25.1% never married, 55.8% now married, 10.2% widowed, 8.8% divorced (2000); Foreign born: 0.0% (2000); Ancestry (includes multiple ancestries): 26.3% German, 21.5% French (except Basque), 14.9% Polish, 11.6% Irish, 10.1% English (2000).
Economy: Single-family building permits issued: 0 (2001) / 0 (2000); Multi-family building permits issued: 0 (2001) / 0 (2000); Employment by occupation: 10.2% management, 7.0% professional, 26.1% services, 17.2% sales, 3.2% farming, 17.8% construction, 18.5% production (2000).
Income: Per capita income: $16,755 (2000); Median household income: $28,125 (2000); Poverty rate: 15.2% (2000).
Taxes: Total city taxes per capita: $149 (1997); City property taxes per capita: $149 (1997).
Education: High school graduation rate: 66.8% (2000); College graduation rate: 3.5% (2000).
Housing: Homeownership rate: 90.1% (2000); Median home value: $65,000 (2000); Median rent: $375 per month (2000); Median age of housing: 35 years (2000).
Transportation: Commute to work: 93.3% car, 0.0% public transportation, 4.0% walk, 2.0% work from home (2000); Travel time to work: 30.1% less than 15 minutes, 23.3% 15 to 30 minutes, 16.4% 30 to 45 minutes, 13.0% 45 to 60 minutes, 17.1% 60 minutes or more (2000)

SIMS (township). Covers a land area of 11.529 square miles and a water area of 32.164 square miles. Located at 44.06° N. Lat.; 83.62° W. Long.
Population: 1,091 (2000); Race: 98.2% White, 0.2% Black, 0.4% Asian, 0.7% American Indian and Alaska Native, 0.5% Hispanic of any race, 0.4% two or more races (2000); Density: 94.6 persons per square mile (2000); Age: 16.1% under 18, 24.8% over 64 (2000); Marriage status: 13.0% never married, 67.4% now married, 9.3% widowed, 10.3% divorced (2000); Foreign born: 1.7% (2000); Ancestry (includes multiple ancestries): 31.3% German, 13.8% English, 11.1% French (except Basque), 9.7% Polish, 9.0% United States or American (2000).
Economy: Single-family building permits issued: 7 (2001) / 11 (2000); Multi-family building permits issued: 0 (2001) / 0 (2000); Employment by occupation: 15.9% management, 13.2% professional, 15.3% services, 21.5% sales, 0.5% farming, 12.6% construction, 21.0% production (2000).
Income: Per capita income: $25,135 (2000); Median household income: $35,703 (2000); Poverty rate: 9.6% (2000).
Taxes: Total city taxes per capita: $131 (1997); City property taxes per capita: $128 (1997).
Education: High school graduation rate: 85.7% (2000); College graduation rate: 15.9% (2000).
Housing: Homeownership rate: 92.5% (2000); Median home value: $116,900 (2000); Median rent: $353 per month (2000); Median age of housing: 30 years (2000).
Transportation: Commute to work: 93.9% car, 0.0% public transportation, 0.3% walk, 5.8% work from home (2000); Travel time to work: 37.3% less than 15 minutes, 21.6% 15 to 30 minutes, 19.2% 30 to 45 minutes, 3.8% 45 to 60 minutes, 18.0% 60 minutes or more (2000)

STANDISH (city). Covers a land area of 2.142 square miles and a water area of 0 square miles. Located at 43.98° N. Lat.; 83.95° W. Long. Elevation is 631 feet.
History: Standish was named for John D. Standish of Detroit, who built a mill here in 1871. Standish developed as a shipping and trading center for a farming area that produced sugar beets and dairy products.
Population: 1,581 (2000); Race: 95.4% White, 0.3% Black, 1.8% Asian, 0.4% American Indian and Alaska Native, 1.6% Hispanic of any race, 1.6% two or more races (2000); Density: 738.1 persons per square mile (2000); Age: 25.7% under 18, 18.2% over 64 (2000); Marriage status: 24.3% never married, 50.6% now married, 11.6% widowed, 13.5% divorced (2000); Foreign born: 1.3% (2000); Ancestry (includes multiple ancestries): 22.4% German, 15.0% Polish, 11.1% English, 9.7% Irish, 9.5% French (except Basque) (2000).
Economy: Employment by occupation: 9.4% management, 18.1% professional, 24.5% services, 20.8% sales, 1.2% farming, 6.7% construction, 19.2% production (2000).
Income: Per capita income: $13,608 (2000); Median household income: $22,212 (2000); Poverty rate: 19.1% (2000).
Taxes: Total city taxes per capita: $304 (1997); City property taxes per capita: $303 (1997).
Education: High school graduation rate: 75.7% (2000); College graduation rate: 14.2% (2000).

School District(s)

Standish-Sterling Community Scho (KG-12)
2000 Enrollment: 1,976 517-846-4526

Housing: Homeownership rate: 57.8% (2000); Median home value: $66,500 (2000); Median rent: $291 per month (2000); Median age of housing: 41 years (2000).
Hospitals: Standish Community Hospital (77 beds)
Newspapers: Arenac County Independent (1 x week)
Transportation: Commute to work: 90.2% car, 0.0% public transportation, 5.5% walk, 4.0% work from home (2000); Travel time to work: 61.9% less than 15 minutes, 11.4% 15 to 30 minutes, 9.1% 30 to 45 minutes, 11.0% 45 to 60 minutes, 6.6% 60 minutes or more (2000)

Additional Information Contacts

Standish Area Chamber of Commerce 989-846-7867
Standish Chamber of Commerce 989-846-7867

STANDISH (township). Covers a land area of 27.662 square miles and a water area of 2.874 square miles. Located at 43.95° N. Lat.; 83.90° W. Long. Elevation is 631 feet.
History: Incorporated as city 1903.
Population: 2,026 (2000); Race: 97.2% White, 0.6% Black, 0.2% Asian, 0.8% American Indian and Alaska Native, 1.6% Hispanic of any race, 0.6% two or more races (2000); Density: 73.2 persons per square mile (2000); Age: 23.8% under 18, 13.4% over 64 (2000); Marriage status: 20.7% never married, 63.4% now married, 7.1% widowed, 8.8% divorced (2000); Foreign born: 0.9% (2000); Ancestry (includes multiple ancestries): 23.6% German, 19.4% French (except Basque), 17.2% Polish, 12.7% Irish, 7.6% United States or American (2000).
Economy: Trade and shipping center for farm area. Manufacturing of fire sprinklers, machinery. Recreation. Employment by occupation: 5.2% management, 12.9% professional, 16.8% services, 26.8% sales, 1.9% farming, 14.6% construction, 21.9% production (2000).
Income: Per capita income: $17,252 (2000); Median household income: $36,894 (2000); Poverty rate: 11.5% (2000).
Taxes: Total city taxes per capita: $12 (1997); City property taxes per capita: $11 (1997).
Education: High school graduation rate: 79.4% (2000); College graduation rate: 9.2% (2000).
Housing: Homeownership rate: 87.6% (2000); Median home value: $82,300 (2000); Median rent: $330 per month (2000); Median age of housing: 30 years (2000).
Transportation: Commute to work: 95.6% car, 0.0% public transportation, 0.8% walk, 3.7% work from home (2000); Travel time to work: 43.0% less than 15 minutes, 17.6% 15 to 30 minutes, 13.3% 30 to 45 minutes, 13.3% 45 to 60 minutes, 12.8% 60 minutes or more (2000)

STERLING (village). Covers a land area of 1.002 square miles and a water area of 0 square miles. Located at 44.03° N. Lat.; 84.02° W. Long. Elevation is 759 feet.
History: Sterling grew up around a sawmill built in 1871, and a railroad station established in 1872. It was named for lumberman William C. Sterling.

Population: 533 (2000); Race: 97.0% White, 0.0% Black, 0.0% Asian, 0.4% American Indian and Alaska Native, 0.7% Hispanic of any race, 2.6% two or more races (2000); Density: 532.2 persons per square mile (2000); Age: 22.4% under 18, 27.7% over 64 (2000); Marriage status: 19.9% never married, 68.4% now married, 4.2% widowed, 7.6% divorced (2000); Foreign born: 0.4% (2000); Ancestry (includes multiple ancestries): 31.2% German, 12.5% Irish, 12.5% Polish, 11.8% French (except Basque), 11.0% United States or American (2000).
Economy: Employment by occupation: 8.1% management, 10.7% professional, 22.8% services, 24.4% sales, 2.5% farming, 14.2% construction, 17.3% production (2000).
Income: Per capita income: $14,181 (2000); Median household income: $34,583 (2000); Poverty rate: 9.8% (2000).
Taxes: Total city taxes per capita: $47 (1997); City property taxes per capita: $47 (1997).
Education: High school graduation rate: 81.3% (2000); College graduation rate: 8.6% (2000).
Housing: Homeownership rate: 81.7% (2000); Median home value: $58,200 (2000); Median rent: $356 per month (2000); Median age of housing: 43 years (2000).
Transportation: Commute to work: 93.7% car, 0.0% public transportation, 2.1% walk, 4.2% work from home (2000); Travel time to work: 47.0% less than 15 minutes, 23.0% 15 to 30 minutes, 3.3% 30 to 45 minutes, 14.8% 45 to 60 minutes, 12.0% 60 minutes or more (2000)

TURNER (village). Covers a land area of 1.021 square miles and a water area of 0 square miles. Located at 44.14° N. Lat.; 83.78° W. Long. Elevation is 636 feet.
Population: 139 (2000); Race: 100.0% White, 0.0% Black, 0.0% Asian, 0.0% American Indian and Alaska Native, 0.0% Hispanic of any race, 0.0% two or more races (2000); Density: 136.1 persons per square mile (2000); Age: 33.7% under 18, 11.5% over 64 (2000); Marriage status: 28.2% never married, 47.1% now married, 12.9% widowed, 11.8% divorced (2000); Foreign born: 0.0% (2000); Ancestry (includes multiple ancestries): 35.6% Other groups, 14.4% Irish, 13.5% French Canadian, 11.5% French (except Basque), 8.7% German (2000).
Economy: Employment by occupation: 6.7% management, 0.0% professional, 50.0% services, 16.7% sales, 0.0% farming, 6.7% construction, 20.0% production (2000).
Income: Per capita income: $9,406 (2000); Median household income: $22,813 (2000); Poverty rate: 34.6% (2000).
Taxes: Total city taxes per capita: $53 (1997); City property taxes per capita: $53 (1997).
Education: High school graduation rate: 87.7% (2000); College graduation rate: 0.0% (2000).
Housing: Homeownership rate: 85.0% (2000); Median home value: $38,800 (2000); Median rent: $325 per month (2000); Median age of housing: 46 years (2000).
Transportation: Commute to work: 90.0% car, 0.0% public transportation, 0.0% walk, 10.0% work from home (2000); Travel time to work: 0.0% less than 15 minutes, 37.0% 15 to 30 minutes, 40.7% 30 to 45 minutes, 7.4% 45 to 60 minutes, 14.8% 60 minutes or more (2000)

TURNER (township). Covers a land area of 32.362 square miles and a water area of 0 square miles. Located at 44.12° N. Lat.; 83.75° W. Long. Elevation is 636 feet.
Population: 642 (2000); Race: 97.4% White, 0.0% Black, 1.2% Asian, 0.0% American Indian and Alaska Native, 1.8% Hispanic of any race, 1.4% two or more races (2000); Density: 19.8 persons per square mile (2000); Age: 27.5% under 18, 15.8% over 64 (2000); Marriage status: 24.1% never married, 62.3% now married, 5.7% widowed, 8.0% divorced (2000); Foreign born: 0.8% (2000); Ancestry (includes multiple ancestries): 21.0% German, 14.1% French (except Basque), 11.7% United States or American, 10.4% English, 10.2% Other groups (2000).
Economy: In farm area; gypsum refining. Employment by occupation: 16.0% management, 8.4% professional, 14.3% services, 19.8% sales, 3.4% farming, 8.4% construction, 29.5% production (2000).
Income: Per capita income: $13,416 (2000); Median household income: $35,104 (2000); Poverty rate: 21.1% (2000).
Taxes: Total city taxes per capita: $24 (1997); City property taxes per capita: $24 (1997).
Education: High school graduation rate: 76.6% (2000); College graduation rate: 3.9% (2000).
Housing: Homeownership rate: 84.3% (2000); Median home value: $60,400 (2000); Median rent: $350 per month (2000); Median age of housing: 39 years (2000).
Transportation: Commute to work: 89.7% car, 0.0% public transportation, 1.7% walk, 8.6% work from home (2000); Travel time to work: 29.7% less than 15 minutes, 37.7% 15 to 30 minutes, 15.1% 30 to 45 minutes, 6.1% 45 to 60 minutes, 11.3% 60 minutes or more (2000)

TWINING (village). Covers a land area of 0.958 square miles and a water area of 0 square miles. Located at 44.11° N. Lat.; 83.80° W. Long.
Population: 192 (2000); Race: 95.6% White, 0.0% Black, 0.0% Asian, 0.0% American Indian and Alaska Native, 4.4% Hispanic of any race, 2.5% two or more races (2000); Density: 200.4 persons per square mile (2000); Age: 24.4% under 18, 10.0% over 64 (2000); Marriage status: 24.8% never married, 54.3% now married, 8.5% widowed, 12.4% divorced (2000); Foreign born: 1.9% (2000); Ancestry (includes multiple ancestries): 23.8% United States or American, 19.4% German, 8.8% Irish, 5.6% Other groups, 5.6% French (except Basque) (2000).
Economy: In farm area. Employment by occupation: 19.6% management, 10.7% professional, 21.4% services, 17.9% sales, 0.0% farming, 5.4% construction, 25.0% production (2000).
Income: Per capita income: $13,744 (2000); Median household income: $31,875 (2000); Poverty rate: 25.9% (2000).
Taxes: Total city taxes per capita: $111 (1997); City property taxes per capita: $111 (1997).
Education: High school graduation rate: 69.0% (2000); College graduation rate: 1.8% (2000).

School District(s)

Arenac Eastern School District (KG-12)
2000 Enrollment: 435 517-867-4234

Housing: Homeownership rate: 84.3% (2000); Median home value: $41,700 (2000); Median rent: $325 per month (2000); Median age of housing: 47 years (2000).
Transportation: Commute to work: 92.9% car, 0.0% public transportation, 7.1% walk, 0.0% work from home (2000); Travel time to work: 44.6% less than 15 minutes, 25.0% 15 to 30 minutes, 8.9% 30 to 45 minutes, 12.5% 45 to 60 minutes, 8.9% 60 minutes or more (2000)

WHITNEY (township). Covers a land area of 31.319 square miles and a water area of 16.333 square miles. Located at 44.11° N. Lat.; 83.60° W. Long.
Population: 1,033 (2000); Race: 99.1% White, 0.0% Black, 0.0% Asian, 0.0% American Indian and Alaska Native, 1.3% Hispanic of any race, 0.2% two or more races (2000); Density: 33.0 persons per square mile (2000); Age: 19.4% under 18, 23.5% over 64 (2000); Marriage status: 14.4% never married, 73.2% now married, 7.1% widowed, 5.3% divorced (2000); Foreign born: 2.1% (2000); Ancestry (includes multiple ancestries): 29.6% German, 11.8% French (except Basque), 11.7% English, 10.1% Polish, 9.8% Irish (2000).
Economy: Single-family building permits issued: 3 (2001) / 3 (2000); Multi-family building permits issued: 0 (2001) / 0 (2000); Employment by occupation: 10.2% management, 15.4% professional, 18.6% services, 26.2% sales, 1.2% farming, 15.1% construction, 13.4% production (2000).
Income: Per capita income: $18,326 (2000); Median household income: $32,989 (2000); Poverty rate: 10.9% (2000).
Taxes: Total city taxes per capita: $88 (1997); City property taxes per capita: $80 (1997).
Education: High school graduation rate: 76.1% (2000); College graduation rate: 11.7% (2000).
Housing: Homeownership rate: 87.6% (2000); Median home value: $100,800 (2000); Median rent: $320 per month (2000); Median age of housing: 40 years (2000).
Transportation: Commute to work: 94.6% car, 0.0% public transportation, 1.8% walk, 3.0% work from home (2000); Travel time to work: 30.7% less than 15 minutes, 35.6% 15 to 30 minutes, 15.3% 30 to 45 minutes, 8.3% 45 to 60 minutes, 10.1% 60 minutes or more (2000)

Baraga County

Located in northwestern Michigan, on the Upper Peninsula; partly bounded on the north by Keweenaw and Huron Bays. Covers a land area of 904.00 square miles, a water area of 164.80 square miles, and is located in the Eastern Time Zone. The county government was organized in 1875. County seat is L'Anse.

Weather Station: Alberta Ford — Elevation: 1,309 feet

	Jan	Feb	Mar	Apr	May	Jun	Jul	Aug	Sep	Oct	Nov	Dec
High	22	27	37	51	66	74	79	76	67	55	38	26
Low	3	4	14	27	39	48	54	53	45	35	23	10
Precip	1.7	1.3	2.2	2.2	3.5	3.4	4.0	3.9	3.8	3.2	2.9	1.9
Snow	34.9	23.2	22.7	8.9	0.9	0.0	0.0	0.0	tr	3.7	22.4	30.3

High and Low temperatures in degrees Fahrenheit; Precipitation and Snow in inches

Weather Station: Herman — Elevation: 1,738 feet

	Jan	Feb	Mar	Apr	May	Jun	Jul	Aug	Sep	Oct	Nov	Dec
High	20	26	36	50	65	73	77	74	65	53	36	25
Low	3	5	14	26	38	47	52	51	43	34	22	10
Precip	2.4	1.6	2.7	2.3	3.6	3.6	4.3	4.1	4.2	3.6	3.3	2.6
Snow	55.0	34.0	35.9	14.9	3.5	tr	0.0	0.0	0.2	8.5	34.6	49.3

High and Low temperatures in degrees Fahrenheit; Precipitation and Snow in inches

Population: 8,746 (2000); Race: 78.4% White, 4.4% Black, 0.3% Asian, 12.1% American Indian and Alaska Native, 1.0% Hispanic of any race, 4.6% two or more races (2000); Density: 9.7 persons per square mile (2000); Age: 22.8% under 18, 16.3% over 64 (2000).
Religion: Five largest groups: 28.3% Catholic Church, 19.0% Evangelical Lutheran Church in America, 3.1% Lutheran Church—Missouri Synod, 2.7% The United Methodist Church, 1.4% The Church of Jesus Christ of Latter-day Saints (2000).
Economy: Unemployment rate: 7.2% (11/2002); Total civilian labor force: 4,081 (11/2002); Leading industries: 33.4% manufacturing; 19.2% health care and social assistance; 15.3% retail trade (2000); Companies that employ more than 1,000 persons: 0 (2000); Companies that employ more than 100 persons: 3 (2000); Farms: 54 totaling 14,988 acres (1997); Minority business ownership rate: 0.0% (1997); Women business ownership rate: 0.0% (1997); Retail sales per capita: $5,774 (1997). Single-family building permits issued: 43 (2001) / 51 (2000); Multi-family building permits issued: 0 (2001) / 7 (2000).
Income: Per capita income: $15,860 (2000); Median household income: $33,673 (2000); Poverty rate: 11.1% (2000); Bankruptcy rate: 1.95% (2001).
Taxes: Total county taxes per capita: $137 (1997); County property taxes per capita: $134 (1997).
Education: High school graduation rate: 80.6% (2000); College graduation rate: 10.9% (2000).
Housing: Homeownership rate: 77.7% (2000); Median home value: $67,100 (2000); Median rent: $256 per month (2000); Median age of housing: 35 years (2000).
Health: Birth rate: 114.3 per 10,000 population (1998); Age adjusted death rate: 113.8 per 10,000 population (1999); Age adjusted cancer mortality rate: 227.9 deaths per 100,000 population (1999). Number of physicians: 4.6 per 10,000 population (1999); Number of hospital beds: 59.5 per 10,000 population (1999).
Elections: 2000 Presidential election results: 41.3% Gore, 54.1% Bush, 4.2% Nader, 0.0% Buchanan
Additional Information Contacts
Baraga County Government Offices 906-524-6183

Baraga County Communities

ARVON (township). Covers a land area of 124.605 square miles and a water area of 6.696 square miles. Located at 46.82° N. Lat.; 88.16° W. Long.
Population: 482 (2000); Race: 95.2% White, 0.0% Black, 0.0% Asian, 3.4% American Indian and Alaska Native, 0.0% Hispanic of any race, 1.5% two or more races (2000); Density: 3.9 persons per square mile (2000); Age: 12.8% under 18, 28.6% over 64 (2000); Marriage status: 10.8% never married, 62.5% now married, 10.8% widowed, 15.9% divorced (2000); Foreign born: 0.0% (2000); Ancestry (includes multiple ancestries): 23.7% Swedish, 18.2% German, 15.7% Finnish, 10.9% French (except Basque), 8.2% Irish (2000).
Economy: Single-family building permits issued: 8 (2001) / 14 (2000); Multi-family building permits issued: 0 (2001) / 0 (2000); Employment by occupation: 5.9% management, 20.7% professional, 21.5% services, 17.0% sales, 1.5% farming, 8.1% construction, 25.2% production (2000).
Income: Per capita income: $19,800 (2000); Median household income: $31,705 (2000); Poverty rate: 8.0% (2000).
Taxes: Total city taxes per capita: $115 (1997); City property taxes per capita: $115 (1997).
Education: High school graduation rate: 86.0% (2000); College graduation rate: 16.9% (2000).
Housing: Homeownership rate: 92.2% (2000); Median home value: $85,000 (2000); Median rent: $225 per month (2000); Median age of housing: 30 years (2000).
Transportation: Commute to work: 92.3% car, 0.0% public transportation, 0.0% walk, 7.7% work from home (2000); Travel time to work: 23.3% less than 15 minutes, 42.5% 15 to 30 minutes, 20.0% 30 to 45 minutes, 5.8% 45 to 60 minutes, 8.3% 60 minutes or more (2000)

BARAGA (village). Covers a land area of 2.256 square miles and a water area of 0.025 square miles. Located at 46.77° N. Lat.; 88.48° W. Long. Elevation is 614 feet.
History: Baraga was named for Father Frederic Baraga, who founded a mission here in 1843. The village was incorporated in 1891, and became a summer resort area.
Population: 1,285 (2000); Race: 69.3% White, 0.2% Black, 0.0% Asian, 24.1% American Indian and Alaska Native, 0.5% Hispanic of any race, 6.0% two or more races (2000); Density: 569.6 persons per square mile (2000); Age: 25.8% under 18, 19.2% over 64 (2000); Marriage status: 29.2% never married, 45.5% now married, 14.9% widowed, 10.5% divorced (2000); Foreign born: 0.4% (2000); Ancestry (includes multiple ancestries): 24.5% Finnish, 23.9% Other groups, 12.5% French (except Basque), 12.1% German, 7.9% French Canadian (2000).
Economy: Single-family building permits issued: 18 (2001) / 22 (2000); Multi-family building permits issued: 0 (2001) / 0 (2000); Employment by occupation: 9.6% management, 8.3% professional, 33.5% services, 24.6% sales, 1.0% farming, 5.8% construction, 17.3% production (2000).
Income: Per capita income: $14,795 (2000); Median household income: $26,290 (2000); Poverty rate: 15.6% (2000).
Taxes: Total city taxes per capita: $110 (1997); City property taxes per capita: $110 (1997).
Education: High school graduation rate: 77.6% (2000); College graduation rate: 8.9% (2000).

School District(s)

Baraga Area Schools (KG-12)
2000 Enrollment: 607 906-353-6664
Housing: Homeownership rate: 51.1% (2000); Median home value: $63,500 (2000); Median rent: $204 per month (2000); Median age of housing: 29 years (2000).
Transportation: Commute to work: 90.2% car, 1.2% public transportation, 5.9% walk, 1.6% work from home (2000); Travel time to work: 75.6% less than 15 minutes, 14.9% 15 to 30 minutes, 3.6% 30 to 45 minutes, 1.4% 45 to 60 minutes, 4.6% 60 minutes or more (2000)

BARAGA (township). Covers a land area of 185.641 square miles and a water area of 1.646 square miles. Located at 46.76° N. Lat.; 88.55° W. Long. Elevation is 614 feet.
History: Hanka Homestead, 1896 Finnish restored homestead. Native American relics found in vicinity.
Population: 3,542 (2000); Race: 65.9% White, 10.9% Black, 0.7% Asian, 15.0% American Indian and Alaska Native, 1.1% Hispanic of any race, 7.3% two or more races (2000); Density: 19.1 persons per square mile (2000); Age: 23.7% under 18, 12.8% over 64 (2000); Marriage status: 39.3% never married, 42.3% now married, 9.6% widowed, 8.8% divorced (2000); Foreign born: 0.9% (2000); Ancestry (includes multiple ancestries): 26.1% Finnish, 20.3% Other groups, 11.9% French (except Basque), 11.3% German, 5.2% French Canadian (2000).
Economy: Manufacturing: railroad ties, materials-handling equipment. Resort; fishing. Employment by occupation: 9.4% management, 14.4% professional, 27.4% services, 21.4% sales, 2.0% farming, 7.1% construction, 18.4% production (2000).
Income: Per capita income: $14,550 (2000); Median household income: $32,639 (2000); Poverty rate: 11.8% (2000).
Taxes: Total city taxes per capita: $33 (1997); City property taxes per capita: $33 (1997).
Education: High school graduation rate: 80.7% (2000); College graduation rate: 11.5% (2000).
Housing: Homeownership rate: 73.0% (2000); Median home value: $68,100 (2000); Median rent: $207 per month (2000); Median age of housing: 31 years (2000).
Transportation: Commute to work: 89.3% car, 0.7% public transportation, 3.4% walk, 4.7% work from home (2000); Travel time to work: 59.3% less than 15 minutes, 30.5% 15 to 30 minutes, 5.4% 30 to 45 minutes, 0.9% 45 to 60 minutes, 3.8% 60 minutes or more (2000)

COVINGTON (township). Covers a land area of 193.188 square miles and a water area of 3.196 square miles. Located at 46.53° N. Lat.; 88.52° W. Long. Elevation is 1,601 feet.

History: Covington was first settled by French Canadians. It was named by John Lyons, the first postmaster, after his former home in Covington, Kentucky.
Population: 569 (2000); Race: 98.5% White, 0.0% Black, 0.0% Asian, 1.0% American Indian and Alaska Native, 0.8% Hispanic of any race, 0.5% two or more races (2000); Density: 2.9 persons per square mile (2000); Age: 18.8% under 18, 23.3% over 64 (2000); Marriage status: 18.3% never married, 63.0% now married, 13.0% widowed, 5.7% divorced (2000); Foreign born: 0.3% (2000); Ancestry (includes multiple ancestries): 60.4% Finnish, 8.5% French (except Basque), 7.6% German, 4.9% Irish, 4.9% Swedish (2000).
Economy: Single-family building permits issued: 5 (2001) / 4 (2000); Multi-family building permits issued: 0 (2001) / 0 (2000); Employment by occupation: 5.2% management, 5.7% professional, 21.0% services, 19.2% sales, 4.8% farming, 12.7% construction, 31.4% production (2000).
Income: Per capita income: $16,297 (2000); Median household income: $37,344 (2000); Poverty rate: 11.6% (2000).
Taxes: Total city taxes per capita: $57 (1997); City property taxes per capita: $53 (1997).
Education: High school graduation rate: 70.8% (2000); College graduation rate: 4.9% (2000).
Housing: Homeownership rate: 89.9% (2000); Median home value: $47,000 (2000); Median rent: $342 per month (2000); Median age of housing: 60+ years (2000).
Transportation: Commute to work: 96.9% car, 0.0% public transportation, 0.4% walk, 0.9% work from home (2000); Travel time to work: 31.5% less than 15 minutes, 27.5% 15 to 30 minutes, 10.8% 30 to 45 minutes, 2.7% 45 to 60 minutes, 27.5% 60 minutes or more (2000)

L'ANSE (village). Covers a land area of 2.564 square miles and a water area of 0.010 square miles. Located at 46.75° N. Lat.; 88.44° W. Long. Elevation is 682 feet.
History: L'Anse grew up on a site that had been a campground for French explorers, trappers, and missionaries. The village was platted in 1871 when the Marquette, Houghton & Ontonagon Railroad arrived.
Population: 2,107 (2000); Race: 91.4% White, 0.2% Black, 0.0% Asian, 4.2% American Indian and Alaska Native, 1.1% Hispanic of any race, 4.1% two or more races (2000); Density: 821.9 persons per square mile (2000); Age: 23.5% under 18, 21.5% over 64 (2000); Marriage status: 23.3% never married, 55.7% now married, 10.4% widowed, 10.6% divorced (2000); Foreign born: 0.9% (2000); Ancestry (includes multiple ancestries): 26.4% Finnish, 15.5% French (except Basque), 15.3% German, 9.3% English, 8.5% Norwegian (2000).
Economy: Single-family building permits issued: 4 (2001) / 2 (2000); Multi-family building permits issued: 0 (2001) / 0 (2000); Employment by occupation: 4.4% management, 14.3% professional, 26.4% services, 26.7% sales, 1.2% farming, 6.7% construction, 20.2% production (2000).
Income: Per capita income: $15,857 (2000); Median household income: $31,406 (2000); Poverty rate: 11.0% (2000).
Taxes: Total city taxes per capita: $229 (1997); City property taxes per capita: $229 (1997).
Education: High school graduation rate: 80.5% (2000); College graduation rate: 10.6% (2000).

School District(s)

L'anse Area Schools (KG-12)
2000 Enrollment: 792 906-524-6121

Housing: Homeownership rate: 71.1% (2000); Median home value: $61,000 (2000); Median rent: $300 per month (2000); Median age of housing: 52 years (2000).
Newspapers: L'Anse Sentinel (1 x week)
Transportation: Commute to work: 87.8% car, 0.6% public transportation, 8.1% walk, 2.5% work from home (2000); Travel time to work: 74.9% less than 15 minutes, 13.3% 15 to 30 minutes, 5.6% 30 to 45 minutes, 3.0% 45 to 60 minutes, 3.2% 60 minutes or more (2000)

L'ANSE (township). Covers a land area of 248.681 square miles and a water area of 20.280 square miles. Located at 46.72° N. Lat.; 88.37° W. Long. Elevation is 682 feet.
Population: 3,926 (2000); Race: 83.6% White, 0.1% Black, 0.0% Asian, 12.7% American Indian and Alaska Native, 0.9% Hispanic of any race, 3.5% two or more races (2000); Density: 15.8 persons per square mile (2000); Age: 23.9% under 18, 17.0% over 64 (2000); Marriage status: 23.3% never married, 57.0% now married, 10.2% widowed, 9.4% divorced (2000); Foreign born: 0.7% (2000); Ancestry (includes multiple ancestries): 25.8% Finnish, 15.9% French (except Basque), 14.0% Other groups, 13.9% German, 7.5% English (2000).
Economy: Single-family building permits issued: 5 (2001) / 7 (2000); Multi-family building permits issued: 0 (2001) / 7 (2000); Employment by occupation: 4.4% management, 17.0% professional, 23.8% services, 23.9% sales, 1.9% farming, 10.0% construction, 19.0% production (2000).
Income: Per capita income: $16,455 (2000); Median household income: $33,750 (2000); Poverty rate: 11.0% (2000).
Education: High school graduation rate: 81.0% (2000); College graduation rate: 10.6% (2000).
Housing: Homeownership rate: 76.6% (2000); Median home value: $66,800 (2000); Median rent: $291 per month (2000); Median age of housing: 38 years (2000).
Transportation: Commute to work: 90.0% car, 0.3% public transportation, 5.0% walk, 4.1% work from home (2000); Travel time to work: 61.7% less than 15 minutes, 25.0% 15 to 30 minutes, 5.9% 30 to 45 minutes, 2.8% 45 to 60 minutes, 4.6% 60 minutes or more (2000)

LANSE (unincorporated postal area, zip code 49946). Covers a land area of 151.571 square miles and a water area of 0.394 square miles. Located at 46.74° N. Lat.; 88.44° W. Long.
Population: 4,148 (2000); Race: 83.9% White, 0.1% Black, 0.0% Asian, 12.5% American Indian and Alaska Native, 0.9% Hispanic of any race, 3.4% two or more races (2000); Density: 27.4 persons per square mile (2000); Age: 23.4% under 18, 17.6% over 64 (2000); Marriage status: 22.7% never married, 58.0% now married, 9.9% widowed, 9.3% divorced (2000); Foreign born: 0.7% (2000); Ancestry (includes multiple ancestries): 25.2% Finnish, 15.7% French (except Basque), 14.2% German, 13.8% Other groups, 7.5% English (2000).
Economy: Employment by occupation: 4.5% management, 17.3% professional, 23.4% services, 23.8% sales, 1.9% farming, 9.8% construction, 19.2% production (2000).
Income: Per capita income: $16,553 (2000); Median household income: $33,670 (2000); Poverty rate: 11.0% (2000).
Education: High school graduation rate: 81.5% (2000); College graduation rate: 11.0% (2000).
Housing: Homeownership rate: 77.2% (2000); Median home value: $67,800 (2000); Median rent: $288 per month (2000); Median age of housing: 36 years (2000).
Hospitals: Baraga County Memorial Hospital (52 beds)
Transportation: Commute to work: 90.4% car, 0.3% public transportation, 4.8% walk, 3.9% work from home (2000); Travel time to work: 60.3% less than 15 minutes, 25.8% 15 to 30 minutes, 6.2% 30 to 45 minutes, 2.8% 45 to 60 minutes, 4.9% 60 minutes or more (2000)

PELKIE (unincorporated postal area, zip code 49958). Covers a land area of 108.677 square miles and a water area of 0.014 square miles. Located at 46.83° N. Lat.; 88.65° W. Long. Elevation is 672 feet.
History: Pelkie was originally called King's Landing. It was settled by French Canadian lumbermen about 1885.
Population: 1,286 (2000); Race: 95.5% White, 0.0% Black, 0.0% Asian, 2.8% American Indian and Alaska Native, 0.0% Hispanic of any race, 1.7% two or more races (2000); Density: 11.8 persons per square mile (2000); Age: 24.8% under 18, 21.0% over 64 (2000); Marriage status: 20.3% never married, 54.7% now married, 13.7% widowed, 11.3% divorced (2000); Foreign born: 0.2% (2000); Ancestry (includes multiple ancestries): 52.7% Finnish, 14.7% German, 11.2% French (except Basque), 6.1% Swedish, 4.8% English (2000).
Economy: Employment by occupation: 16.6% management, 18.9% professional, 15.7% services, 17.2% sales, 4.1% farming, 14.0% construction, 13.5% production (2000).
Income: Per capita income: $17,377 (2000); Median household income: $34,375 (2000); Poverty rate: 5.7% (2000).
Education: High school graduation rate: 80.7% (2000); College graduation rate: 17.9% (2000).
Housing: Homeownership rate: 93.9% (2000); Median home value: $65,000 (2000); Median rent: $188 per month (2000); Median age of housing: 43 years (2000).
Transportation: Commute to work: 89.9% car, 0.0% public transportation, 1.9% walk, 7.1% work from home (2000); Travel time to work: 14.6% less than 15 minutes, 49.0% 15 to 30 minutes, 22.0% 30 to 45 minutes, 7.8% 45 to 60 minutes, 6.6% 60 minutes or more (2000)

SKANEE (unincorporated postal area, zip code 49962). Covers a land area of 40.280 square miles and a water area of 0.077 square miles. Located at 46.87° N. Lat.; 88.17° W. Long. Elevation is 747 feet.
History: Skanee was first settled by fishermen who appreciated its protected harbor. Later, Swedish lumbermen worked here, towing their pine logs in

long rafts across Keweenaw Bay and up the Portage River. When the timber was gone, Skanee turned to farming, growing apples and potatoes for market. Skanee was named for the province of Skane in Sweden.
Population: 248 (2000); Race: 99.0% White, 0.0% Black, 0.0% Asian, 0.0% American Indian and Alaska Native, 0.0% Hispanic of any race, 1.0% two or more races (2000); Density: 6.2 persons per square mile (2000); Age: 10.1% under 18, 30.4% over 64 (2000); Marriage status: 11.6% never married, 46.8% now married, 17.4% widowed, 24.2% divorced (2000); Foreign born: 0.0% (2000); Ancestry (includes multiple ancestries): 39.6% Swedish, 17.9% German, 17.4% Finnish, 11.6% French (except Basque), 9.2% Norwegian (2000).
Economy: Employment by occupation: 3.1% management, 16.9% professional, 24.6% services, 9.2% sales, 3.1% farming, 13.8% construction, 29.2% production (2000).
Income: Per capita income: $21,407 (2000); Median household income: $28,750 (2000); Poverty rate: 7.2% (2000).
Education: High school graduation rate: 84.5% (2000); College graduation rate: 16.6% (2000).

School District(s)

Arvon Township School District (KG-06)
2000 Enrollment: 13 906-524-7336

Housing: Homeownership rate: 94.7% (2000); Median home value: $58,600 (2000); Median rent: $275 per month (2000); Median age of housing: 37 years (2000).
Transportation: Commute to work: 90.0% car, 0.0% public transportation, 0.0% walk, 10.0% work from home (2000); Travel time to work: 18.5% less than 15 minutes, 38.9% 15 to 30 minutes, 29.6% 30 to 45 minutes, 9.3% 45 to 60 minutes, 3.7% 60 minutes or more (2000)

SPURR (township). Covers a land area of 151.883 square miles and a water area of 7.324 square miles. Located at 46.54° N. Lat.; 88.18° W. Long.
Population: 227 (2000); Race: 99.1% White, 0.0% Black, 0.0% Asian, 0.0% American Indian and Alaska Native, 0.9% Hispanic of any race, 0.0% two or more races (2000); Density: 1.5 persons per square mile (2000); Age: 16.6% under 18, 15.6% over 64 (2000); Marriage status: 15.8% never married, 70.7% now married, 6.5% widowed, 7.1% divorced (2000); Foreign born: 1.9% (2000); Ancestry (includes multiple ancestries): 37.4% Finnish, 19.9% German, 10.4% Irish, 10.4% English, 6.6% Polish (2000).
Economy: Single-family building permits issued: 3 (2001) / 2 (2000); Multi-family building permits issued: 0 (2001) / 0 (2000); Employment by occupation: 7.9% management, 3.4% professional, 22.5% services, 30.3% sales, 0.0% farming, 21.3% construction, 14.6% production (2000).
Income: Per capita income: $17,316 (2000); Median household income: $36,667 (2000); Poverty rate: 7.6% (2000).
Taxes: Total city taxes per capita: $301 (1997); City property taxes per capita: $301 (1997).
Education: High school graduation rate: 87.6% (2000); College graduation rate: 13.0% (2000).
Housing: Homeownership rate: 90.1% (2000); Median home value: $82,500 (2000); Median rent: $225 per month (2000); Median age of housing: 31 years (2000).
Transportation: Commute to work: 90.7% car, 0.0% public transportation, 7.0% walk, 2.3% work from home (2000); Travel time to work: 25.0% less than 15 minutes, 10.7% 15 to 30 minutes, 26.2% 30 to 45 minutes, 28.6% 45 to 60 minutes, 9.5% 60 minutes or more (2000)

WATTON (unincorporated postal area, zip code 49970). Covers a land area of 49.696 square miles and a water area of 0.036 square miles. Located at 46.53° N. Lat.; 88.60° W. Long.
Population: 360 (2000); Race: 100.0% White, 0.0% Black, 0.0% Asian, 0.0% American Indian and Alaska Native, 1.3% Hispanic of any race, 0.0% two or more races (2000); Density: 7.2 persons per square mile (2000); Age: 18.0% under 18, 27.2% over 64 (2000); Marriage status: 16.1% never married, 63.6% now married, 16.8% widowed, 3.5% divorced (2000); Foreign born: 0.0% (2000); Ancestry (includes multiple ancestries): 64.8% Finnish, 8.2% German, 5.8% French (except Basque), 4.5% Irish, 4.2% Dutch (2000).
Economy: Employment by occupation: 5.8% management, 3.6% professional, 21.6% services, 18.7% sales, 2.9% farming, 14.4% construction, 33.1% production (2000).
Income: Per capita income: $15,521 (2000); Median household income: $37,969 (2000); Poverty rate: 17.0% (2000).
Education: High school graduation rate: 62.0% (2000); College graduation rate: 5.1% (2000).
Housing: Homeownership rate: 89.4% (2000); Median home value: $47,300 (2000); Median rent: $375 per month (2000); Median age of housing: 60+ years (2000).
Transportation: Commute to work: 100.0% car, 0.0% public transportation, 0.0% walk, 0.0% work from home (2000); Travel time to work: 36.8% less than 15 minutes, 18.4% 15 to 30 minutes, 12.5% 30 to 45 minutes, 1.5% 45 to 60 minutes, 30.9% 60 minutes or more (2000)

Barry County

Located in southwestern Michigan; drained by the Thornapple River. Covers a land area of 556.10 square miles, a water area of 20.80 square miles, and is located in the Eastern Time Zone. The county government was organized in 1829. County seat is Hastings.

Weather Station: Hastings — Elevation: 816 feet

	Jan	Feb	Mar	Apr	May	Jun	Jul	Aug	Sep	Oct	Nov	Dec
High	30	34	44	58	70	79	83	81	73	61	47	35
Low	14	15	24	35	45	55	59	57	49	38	30	20
Precip	2.0	1.5	2.5	3.3	2.9	4.0	3.2	3.7	3.9	3.0	3.0	2.4
Snow	17.4	10.4	7.4	2.3	tr	0.0	0.0	0.0	0.0	0.5	4.9	12.9

High and Low temperatures in degrees Fahrenheit; Precipitation and Snow in inches

Population: 56,755 (2000); Race: 97.1% White, 0.4% Black, 0.2% Asian, 0.5% American Indian and Alaska Native, 1.2% Hispanic of any race, 1.2% two or more races (2000); Density: 102.1 persons per square mile (2000); Age: 27.2% under 18, 11.7% over 64 (2000).
Religion: Five largest groups: 6.7% Catholic Church, 4.3% The United Methodist Church, 1.6% General Association of Regular Baptist Churches, 1.4% Reformed Church in America, 1.1% Evangelical Lutheran Church in America (2000).
Economy: Unemployment rate: 3.9% (11/2002); Total civilian labor force: 33,944 (11/2002); Leading industries: 30.9% manufacturing; 16.4% retail trade; 9.5% health care and social assistance (2000); Companies that employ more than 1,000 persons: 1 (2000); Companies that employ more than 100 persons: 16 (2000); Farms: 881 totaling 164,815 acres (1997); Minority business ownership rate: 0.0% (1997); Women business ownership rate: 32.7% (1997); Retail sales per capita: $4,832 (1997). Single-family building permits issued: 342 (2001) / 319 (2000); Multi-family building permits issued: 0 (2001) / 12 (2000).
Income: Per capita income: $20,636 (2000); Median household income: $46,820 (2000); Poverty rate: 5.5% (2000); Bankruptcy rate: 4.18% (2001).
Taxes: Total county taxes per capita: $112 (1997); County property taxes per capita: $108 (1997).
Education: High school graduation rate: 86.8% (2000); College graduation rate: 14.7% (2000).
Housing: Homeownership rate: 85.9% (2000); Median home value: $107,100 (2000); Median rent: $422 per month (2000); Median age of housing: 32 years (2000).
Health: Birth rate: 119.5 per 10,000 population (1998); Age adjusted death rate: 87.8 per 10,000 population (1999); Age adjusted cancer mortality rate: 207.2 deaths per 100,000 population (1999). Number of physicians: 7.8 per 10,000 population (1999); Number of hospital beds: 15.5 per 10,000 population (1999).
Elections: 2000 Presidential election results: 37.2% Gore, 59.9% Bush, 2.3% Nader, 0.1% Buchanan
National and State Parks: Barry State Game Area; Middleville State Game Area

Additional Information Contacts

Barry County Government Offices 616-948-4810
Barry Co. Area Chamber of Commerce.................... 616-945-2454
Delton Area Business Association.......................... 616-623-5511

Barry County Communities

ASSYRIA (township). Covers a land area of 36.049 square miles and a water area of 0.311 square miles. Located at 42.45° N. Lat.; 85.14° W. Long.
Population: 1,912 (2000); Race: 97.6% White, 0.8% Black, 0.4% Asian, 0.0% American Indian and Alaska Native, 0.6% Hispanic of any race, 0.5% two or more races (2000); Density: 53.0 persons per square mile (2000); Age: 23.6% under 18, 11.3% over 64 (2000); Marriage status: 18.2% never married, 70.2% now married, 4.0% widowed, 7.6% divorced (2000); Foreign born: 0.4% (2000); Ancestry (includes multiple ancestries): 24.3% German, 17.3% English, 13.8% Irish, 7.6% United States or American, 6.6% French (except Basque) (2000).

Economy: Employment by occupation: 12.4% management, 11.4% professional, 9.3% services, 23.6% sales, 1.2% farming, 12.8% construction, 29.4% production (2000).
Income: Per capita income: $20,908 (2000); Median household income: $50,192 (2000); Poverty rate: 2.8% (2000).
Taxes: Total city taxes per capita: $19 (1997); City property taxes per capita: $19 (1997).
Education: High school graduation rate: 87.4% (2000); College graduation rate: 11.3% (2000).
Housing: Homeownership rate: 92.2% (2000); Median home value: $97,500 (2000); Median rent: $378 per month (2000); Median age of housing: 32 years (2000).
Transportation: Commute to work: 93.5% car, 0.0% public transportation, 0.0% walk, 6.5% work from home (2000); Travel time to work: 9.2% less than 15 minutes, 45.4% 15 to 30 minutes, 30.8% 30 to 45 minutes, 10.5% 45 to 60 minutes, 4.2% 60 minutes or more (2000)

BALTIMORE (township). Covers a land area of 35.425 square miles and a water area of 0.746 square miles. Located at 42.55° N. Lat.; 85.24° W. Long.
History: Baltimore Township was named for their former home by settlers who had come from Maryland.
Population: 1,845 (2000); Race: 96.8% White, 0.0% Black, 0.6% Asian, 0.4% American Indian and Alaska Native, 1.1% Hispanic of any race, 2.0% two or more races (2000); Density: 52.1 persons per square mile (2000); Age: 23.2% under 18, 15.2% over 64 (2000); Marriage status: 26.4% never married, 63.5% now married, 4.3% widowed, 5.9% divorced (2000); Foreign born: 1.5% (2000); Ancestry (includes multiple ancestries): 18.9% English, 17.9% German, 11.2% United States or American, 11.1% Other groups, 7.9% Irish (2000).
Economy: Employment by occupation: 10.8% management, 8.8% professional, 12.4% services, 23.0% sales, 0.4% farming, 14.4% construction, 30.3% production (2000).
Income: Per capita income: $20,405 (2000); Median household income: $45,761 (2000); Poverty rate: 9.8% (2000).
Taxes: Total city taxes per capita: $15 (1997); City property taxes per capita: $15 (1997).
Education: High school graduation rate: 82.6% (2000); College graduation rate: 7.2% (2000).
Housing: Homeownership rate: 90.3% (2000); Median home value: $99,000 (2000); Median rent: $398 per month (2000); Median age of housing: 30 years (2000).
Transportation: Commute to work: 90.8% car, 0.6% public transportation, 0.6% walk, 7.5% work from home (2000); Travel time to work: 13.5% less than 15 minutes, 48.0% 15 to 30 minutes, 14.0% 30 to 45 minutes, 17.8% 45 to 60 minutes, 6.8% 60 minutes or more (2000)

BARRY (township). Covers a land area of 34.804 square miles and a water area of 1.726 square miles. Located at 42.46° N. Lat.; 85.37° W. Long.
Population: 3,489 (2000); Race: 97.9% White, 1.2% Black, 0.0% Asian, 0.3% American Indian and Alaska Native, 0.5% Hispanic of any race, 0.5% two or more races (2000); Density: 100.2 persons per square mile (2000); Age: 25.9% under 18, 12.6% over 64 (2000); Marriage status: 19.1% never married, 69.7% now married, 3.2% widowed, 8.0% divorced (2000); Foreign born: 0.0% (2000); Ancestry (includes multiple ancestries): 17.8% English, 17.8% German, 14.8% Irish, 10.4% Dutch, 5.7% United States or American (2000).
Economy: Employment by occupation: 16.8% management, 14.1% professional, 12.7% services, 23.5% sales, 0.7% farming, 9.9% construction, 22.3% production (2000).
Income: Per capita income: $22,370 (2000); Median household income: $45,339 (2000); Poverty rate: 5.5% (2000).
Taxes: Total city taxes per capita: $69 (1997); City property taxes per capita: $69 (1997).
Education: High school graduation rate: 87.4% (2000); College graduation rate: 13.5% (2000).
Housing: Homeownership rate: 88.2% (2000); Median home value: $97,200 (2000); Median rent: $463 per month (2000); Median age of housing: 40 years (2000).
Transportation: Commute to work: 91.1% car, 0.0% public transportation, 0.9% walk, 8.0% work from home (2000); Travel time to work: 20.4% less than 15 minutes, 30.0% 15 to 30 minutes, 37.2% 30 to 45 minutes, 11.5% 45 to 60 minutes, 0.9% 60 minutes or more (2000)

CARLTON (township). Covers a land area of 35.150 square miles and a water area of 0.459 square miles. Located at 42.73° N. Lat.; 85.25° W. Long. Elevation is 832 feet.
Population: 2,331 (2000); Race: 98.1% White, 0.9% Black, 0.0% Asian, 0.2% American Indian and Alaska Native, 1.5% Hispanic of any race, 0.8% two or more races (2000); Density: 66.3 persons per square mile (2000); Age: 28.2% under 18, 11.0% over 64 (2000); Marriage status: 19.3% never married, 65.0% now married, 5.6% widowed, 10.2% divorced (2000); Foreign born: 0.5% (2000); Ancestry (includes multiple ancestries): 20.3% German, 16.4% English, 12.0% Irish, 9.4% Dutch, 8.6% United States or American (2000).
Economy: Employment by occupation: 10.3% management, 12.9% professional, 10.7% services, 20.5% sales, 1.1% farming, 13.5% construction, 30.9% production (2000).
Income: Per capita income: $20,226 (2000); Median household income: $46,359 (2000); Poverty rate: 6.6% (2000).
Taxes: Total city taxes per capita: $38 (1997); City property taxes per capita: $37 (1997).
Education: High school graduation rate: 86.7% (2000); College graduation rate: 11.0% (2000).
Housing: Homeownership rate: 91.6% (2000); Median home value: $100,600 (2000); Median rent: $520 per month (2000); Median age of housing: 32 years (2000).
Transportation: Commute to work: 93.7% car, 0.2% public transportation, 0.9% walk, 4.5% work from home (2000); Travel time to work: 26.4% less than 15 minutes, 32.8% 15 to 30 minutes, 18.7% 30 to 45 minutes, 16.7% 45 to 60 minutes, 5.4% 60 minutes or more (2000)

CASTLETON (township). Covers a land area of 35.147 square miles and a water area of 0.597 square miles. Located at 42.62° N. Lat.; 85.12° W. Long.
Population: 3,475 (2000); Race: 97.3% White, 0.2% Black, 0.0% Asian, 0.7% American Indian and Alaska Native, 0.9% Hispanic of any race, 1.7% two or more races (2000); Density: 98.9 persons per square mile (2000); Age: 27.2% under 18, 12.3% over 64 (2000); Marriage status: 22.0% never married, 58.8% now married, 7.3% widowed, 11.9% divorced (2000); Foreign born: 0.9% (2000); Ancestry (includes multiple ancestries): 17.0% German, 13.6% English, 13.5% Irish, 7.6% Other groups, 6.1% United States or American (2000).
Economy: Employment by occupation: 9.2% management, 11.5% professional, 11.8% services, 17.9% sales, 1.2% farming, 11.9% construction, 36.5% production (2000).
Income: Per capita income: $16,534 (2000); Median household income: $33,929 (2000); Poverty rate: 9.1% (2000).
Taxes: Total city taxes per capita: $28 (1997); City property taxes per capita: $28 (1997).
Education: High school graduation rate: 79.5% (2000); College graduation rate: 11.4% (2000).
Housing: Homeownership rate: 79.2% (2000); Median home value: $78,400 (2000); Median rent: $341 per month (2000); Median age of housing: 46 years (2000).
Transportation: Commute to work: 93.2% car, 0.1% public transportation, 3.1% walk, 3.2% work from home (2000); Travel time to work: 19.8% less than 15 minutes, 30.7% 15 to 30 minutes, 22.4% 30 to 45 minutes, 13.7% 45 to 60 minutes, 13.5% 60 minutes or more (2000)

DELTON (unincorporated postal area, zip code 49046). Covers a land area of 79.614 square miles and a water area of 6.311 square miles. Located at 42.50° N. Lat.; 85.39° W. Long.
Population: 7,421 (2000); Race: 96.7% White, 1.0% Black, 0.1% Asian, 0.5% American Indian and Alaska Native, 1.2% Hispanic of any race, 1.4% two or more races (2000); Density: 93.2 persons per square mile (2000); Age: 24.6% under 18, 12.9% over 64 (2000); Marriage status: 22.3% never married, 64.3% now married, 6.0% widowed, 7.4% divorced (2000); Foreign born: 0.6% (2000); Ancestry (includes multiple ancestries): 17.9% German, 17.3% English, 14.4% Dutch, 10.2% Irish, 9.8% United States or American (2000).
Economy: Employment by occupation: 13.2% management, 16.5% professional, 11.3% services, 21.0% sales, 1.3% farming, 13.0% construction, 23.8% production (2000).
Income: Per capita income: $19,218 (2000); Median household income: $43,348 (2000); Poverty rate: 6.2% (2000).
Education: High school graduation rate: 85.4% (2000); College graduation rate: 10.1% (2000).

School District(s)

Delton-Kellogg School District (KG-12)
2000 Enrollment: 2,160 616-623-9246

Housing: Homeownership rate: 85.1% (2000); Median home value: $98,600 (2000); Median rent: $451 per month (2000); Median age of housing: 35 years (2000).

Transportation: Commute to work: 91.0% car, 0.0% public transportation, 1.6% walk, 6.6% work from home (2000); Travel time to work: 16.3% less than 15 minutes, 33.3% 15 to 30 minutes, 34.5% 30 to 45 minutes, 12.0% 45 to 60 minutes, 3.8% 60 minutes or more (2000)

Additional Information Contacts

Delton Area Business Association 616-623-5511

DOWLING (unincorporated postal area, zip code 49050). Covers a land area of 25.858 square miles and a water area of 0.807 square miles. Located at 42.50° N. Lat.; 85.24° W. Long. Elevation is 956 feet.

Population: 1,562 (2000); Race: 97.6% White, 0.8% Black, 0.0% Asian, 1.0% American Indian and Alaska Native, 0.3% Hispanic of any race, 0.7% two or more races (2000); Density: 60.4 persons per square mile (2000); Age: 23.9% under 18, 10.8% over 64 (2000); Marriage status: 24.0% never married, 66.1% now married, 4.0% widowed, 5.9% divorced (2000); Foreign born: 0.3% (2000); Ancestry (includes multiple ancestries): 14.9% English, 13.2% German, 10.1% United States or American, 8.0% Other groups, 7.1% European (2000).

Economy: Employment by occupation: 10.5% management, 21.7% professional, 9.1% services, 16.7% sales, 0.0% farming, 8.2% construction, 33.8% production (2000).

Income: Per capita income: $21,725 (2000); Median household income: $51,406 (2000); Poverty rate: 6.7% (2000).

Education: High school graduation rate: 92.5% (2000); College graduation rate: 11.4% (2000).

Housing: Homeownership rate: 84.7% (2000); Median home value: $104,600 (2000); Median rent: $433 per month (2000); Median age of housing: 29 years (2000).

Transportation: Commute to work: 90.2% car, 0.0% public transportation, 2.8% walk, 7.0% work from home (2000); Travel time to work: 7.1% less than 15 minutes, 38.1% 15 to 30 minutes, 33.0% 30 to 45 minutes, 13.8% 45 to 60 minutes, 8.1% 60 minutes or more (2000)

FREEPORT (village). Covers a land area of 0.771 square miles and a water area of 0 square miles. Located at 42.76° N. Lat.; 85.31° W. Long. Elevation is 806 feet.

Population: 444 (2000); Race: 93.5% White, 1.0% Black, 0.0% Asian, 0.0% American Indian and Alaska Native, 0.0% Hispanic of any race, 5.1% two or more races (2000); Density: 575.8 persons per square mile (2000); Age: 23.4% under 18, 9.2% over 64 (2000); Marriage status: 30.8% never married, 52.8% now married, 3.2% widowed, 13.2% divorced (2000); Foreign born: 0.5% (2000); Ancestry (includes multiple ancestries): 31.8% German, 15.9% Dutch, 12.5% English, 11.3% Other groups, 11.1% Irish (2000).

Economy: In agricultural area. Manufacturing: lumber, trimming dies. Employment by occupation: 5.6% management, 6.8% professional, 9.4% services, 21.4% sales, 1.3% farming, 14.1% construction, 41.5% production (2000).

Income: Per capita income: $18,684 (2000); Median household income: $42,708 (2000); Poverty rate: 0.7% (2000).

Taxes: Total city taxes per capita: $80 (1997); City property taxes per capita: $80 (1997).

Education: High school graduation rate: 89.3% (2000); College graduation rate: 3.6% (2000).

Housing: Homeownership rate: 80.5% (2000); Median home value: $79,400 (2000); Median rent: $463 per month (2000); Median age of housing: 60+ years (2000).

Transportation: Commute to work: 92.0% car, 0.0% public transportation, 2.7% walk, 5.3% work from home (2000); Travel time to work: 17.3% less than 15 minutes, 38.3% 15 to 30 minutes, 32.2% 30 to 45 minutes, 7.0% 45 to 60 minutes, 5.1% 60 minutes or more (2000)

HASTINGS (city). Covers a land area of 5.243 square miles and a water area of 0.022 square miles. Located at 42.64° N. Lat.; 85.28° W. Long. Elevation is 810 feet.

History: Hastings was settled in 1836 when a group of promoters purchased the land from Eurotas P. Hastings with the promise that the town would be the county seat, and it was so named in 1841. Hastings was incorporated as a village in 1855 and as a city in 1871.

Population: 7,095 (2000); Race: 97.1% White, 0.2% Black, 0.3% Asian, 0.7% American Indian and Alaska Native, 1.8% Hispanic of any race, 0.1% two or more races (2000); Density: 1,353.3 persons per square mile (2000); Age: 27.6% under 18, 14.7% over 64 (2000); Marriage status: 19.4% never married, 60.2% now married, 8.8% widowed, 11.6% divorced (2000); Foreign born: 1.4% (2000); Ancestry (includes multiple ancestries): 22.5% German, 15.8% English, 12.7% Irish, 9.1% United States or American, 6.5% Other groups (2000).

Economy: In agricultural area. Manufacturing: transportation equipment, machinery, rubber products, fire-fighting apparatus, crossbows; publishing. Resort. Airport to West. Employment by occupation: 11.4% management, 16.2% professional, 9.8% services, 26.8% sales, 0.2% farming, 9.2% construction, 26.4% production (2000).

Income: Per capita income: $18,042 (2000); Median household income: $39,033 (2000); Poverty rate: 8.1% (2000).

Taxes: Total city taxes per capita: $281 (1997); City property taxes per capita: $281 (1997).

Education: High school graduation rate: 86.4% (2000); College graduation rate: 19.1% (2000).

School District(s)

Hastings Area School District (KG-12)
2000 Enrollment: 3,278 616-948-4400

Housing: Homeownership rate: 67.8% (2000); Median home value: $89,500 (2000); Median rent: $412 per month (2000); Median age of housing: 48 years (2000).

Hospitals: Pennock Hospital (89 beds)

Safety: Violent crime rate: 16.8 per 10,000 population; Property crime rate: 267.8 per 10,000 population (2001).

Newspapers: Weekender (1 x week); Sun and News (1 x week); Maple Valley News (1 x week); Lakewood News (1 x week); The Hastings Reminder (1 x week); The Hastings Banner (1 x week)

Transportation: Commute to work: 92.4% car, 0.0% public transportation, 4.0% walk, 3.4% work from home (2000); Travel time to work: 52.8% less than 15 minutes, 15.6% 15 to 30 minutes, 13.4% 30 to 45 minutes, 10.7% 45 to 60 minutes, 7.5% 60 minutes or more (2000)

Additional Information Contacts

Barry Co. Area Chamber of Commerce 616-945-2454

HASTINGS CHARTER (township). Covers a land area of 30.172 square miles and a water area of 0.378 square miles. Located at 42.62° N. Lat.; 85.24° W. Long. Elevation is 777 feet.

Population: 2,930 (2000); Race: 98.0% White, 0.0% Black, 0.4% Asian, 0.0% American Indian and Alaska Native, 0.0% Hispanic of any race, 1.6% two or more races (2000); Density: 97.1 persons per square mile (2000); Age: 24.0% under 18, 18.3% over 64 (2000); Marriage status: 17.6% never married, 64.0% now married, 9.4% widowed, 9.0% divorced (2000); Foreign born: 0.0% (2000); Ancestry (includes multiple ancestries): 23.1% German, 13.2% Irish, 10.4% English, 7.2% United States or American, 6.1% Dutch (2000).

Economy: Employment by occupation: 10.9% management, 18.8% professional, 14.0% services, 25.1% sales, 0.7% farming, 10.4% construction, 20.0% production (2000).

Income: Per capita income: $22,492 (2000); Median household income: $51,316 (2000); Poverty rate: 3.6% (2000).

Taxes: Total city taxes per capita: $13 (1997); City property taxes per capita: $13 (1997).

Education: High school graduation rate: 85.9% (2000); College graduation rate: 14.5% (2000).

Housing: Homeownership rate: 94.4% (2000); Median home value: $106,900 (2000); Median rent: $261 per month (2000); Median age of housing: 32 years (2000).

Transportation: Commute to work: 95.5% car, 0.0% public transportation, 0.0% walk, 4.5% work from home (2000); Travel time to work: 39.2% less than 15 minutes, 19.8% 15 to 30 minutes, 22.4% 30 to 45 minutes, 12.9% 45 to 60 minutes, 5.7% 60 minutes or more (2000)

HICKORY CORNERS (unincorporated postal area, zip code 49060). Covers a land area of 22.067 square miles and a water area of 0.972 square miles. Located at 42.42° N. Lat.; 85.40° W. Long. Elevation is 967 feet.

History: A schoolhouse was built in 1837 near a large hickory tree, giving the spot the name of Hickory Corners. A community grew up around the school.

Population: 2,086 (2000); Race: 97.6% White, 0.6% Black, 0.4% Asian, 0.2% American Indian and Alaska Native, 0.3% Hispanic of any race, 0.3% two or more races (2000); Density: 94.5 persons per square mile (2000); Age: 20.8% under 18, 10.9% over 64 (2000); Marriage status: 16.8% never married, 73.2% now married, 3.1% widowed, 7.0% divorced (2000); Foreign born: 1.3% (2000); Ancestry (includes multiple ancestries): 17.9% German,

17.8% English, 17.1% Irish, 7.8% United States or American, 7.3% Dutch (2000).
Economy: Employment by occupation: 23.0% management, 15.3% professional, 15.2% services, 22.3% sales, 0.6% farming, 6.8% construction, 16.8% production (2000).
Income: Per capita income: $36,299 (2000); Median household income: $61,201 (2000); Poverty rate: 2.6% (2000).
Education: High school graduation rate: 93.4% (2000); College graduation rate: 31.2% (2000).
Housing: Homeownership rate: 84.5% (2000); Median home value: $133,200 (2000); Median rent: $387 per month (2000); Median age of housing: 43 years (2000).
Transportation: Commute to work: 95.3% car, 0.0% public transportation, 1.2% walk, 2.7% work from home (2000); Travel time to work: 23.9% less than 15 minutes, 35.5% 15 to 30 minutes, 31.0% 30 to 45 minutes, 5.4% 45 to 60 minutes, 4.2% 60 minutes or more (2000)

HOPE (township). Covers a land area of 32.605 square miles and a water area of 3.480 square miles. Located at 42.55° N. Lat.; 85.37° W. Long.
Population: 3,283 (2000); Race: 95.7% White, 0.3% Black, 0.2% Asian, 1.2% American Indian and Alaska Native, 1.8% Hispanic of any race, 1.9% two or more races (2000); Density: 100.7 persons per square mile (2000); Age: 26.3% under 18, 10.5% over 64 (2000); Marriage status: 22.6% never married, 64.6% now married, 5.2% widowed, 7.6% divorced (2000); Foreign born: 1.4% (2000); Ancestry (includes multiple ancestries): 17.1% Dutch, 16.4% German, 15.4% English, 10.8% Irish, 8.7% United States or American (2000).
Economy: Single-family building permits issued: 30 (2001) / 26 (2000); Multi-family building permits issued: 0 (2001) / 0 (2000); Employment by occupation: 10.9% management, 15.9% professional, 15.6% services, 20.8% sales, 1.7% farming, 12.5% construction, 22.6% production (2000).
Income: Per capita income: $19,399 (2000); Median household income: $41,983 (2000); Poverty rate: 6.8% (2000).
Taxes: Total city taxes per capita: $50 (1997); City property taxes per capita: $40 (1997).
Education: High school graduation rate: 87.9% (2000); College graduation rate: 14.8% (2000).
Housing: Homeownership rate: 83.0% (2000); Median home value: $108,300 (2000); Median rent: $421 per month (2000); Median age of housing: 33 years (2000).
Transportation: Commute to work: 92.8% car, 0.0% public transportation, 1.0% walk, 4.6% work from home (2000); Travel time to work: 16.2% less than 15 minutes, 36.7% 15 to 30 minutes, 31.7% 30 to 45 minutes, 10.0% 45 to 60 minutes, 5.3% 60 minutes or more (2000)

IRVING (township). Covers a land area of 35.888 square miles and a water area of 0.156 square miles. Located at 42.72° N. Lat.; 85.34° W. Long. Elevation is 752 feet.
History: Irving Township was settled about 1850 and developed around a dam and sawmill built by L.B. Hills. The township was named for American writer Washington Irving.
Population: 2,682 (2000); Race: 98.4% White, 0.1% Black, 0.2% Asian, 0.0% American Indian and Alaska Native, 0.0% Hispanic of any race, 1.1% two or more races (2000); Density: 74.7 persons per square mile (2000); Age: 31.8% under 18, 6.7% over 64 (2000); Marriage status: 22.4% never married, 67.5% now married, 2.8% widowed, 7.3% divorced (2000); Foreign born: 0.6% (2000); Ancestry (includes multiple ancestries): 24.5% German, 16.7% Dutch, 12.3% Irish, 11.9% English, 9.1% United States or American (2000).
Economy: Employment by occupation: 6.9% management, 12.7% professional, 12.4% services, 25.0% sales, 0.5% farming, 12.3% construction, 30.2% production (2000).
Income: Per capita income: $17,523 (2000); Median household income: $50,532 (2000); Poverty rate: 1.9% (2000).
Taxes: Total city taxes per capita: $17 (1997); City property taxes per capita: $17 (1997).
Education: High school graduation rate: 89.1% (2000); College graduation rate: 10.3% (2000).
Housing: Homeownership rate: 91.9% (2000); Median home value: $112,400 (2000); Median rent: $459 per month (2000); Median age of housing: 19 years (2000).
Transportation: Commute to work: 94.8% car, 0.0% public transportation, 1.0% walk, 4.1% work from home (2000); Travel time to work: 19.2% less than 15 minutes, 35.6% 15 to 30 minutes, 31.9% 30 to 45 minutes, 8.6% 45 to 60 minutes, 4.8% 60 minutes or more (2000)

JOHNSTOWN (township). Covers a land area of 35.250 square miles and a water area of 1.352 square miles. Located at 42.46° N. Lat.; 85.25° W. Long.
History: Johnstown Township was organized in 1838 and named for John Mott, a Quaker preacher who planned to found a colony here. His plans changed, but the name remained.
Population: 3,067 (2000); Race: 97.0% White, 0.8% Black, 0.0% Asian, 0.4% American Indian and Alaska Native, 1.1% Hispanic of any race, 1.9% two or more races (2000); Density: 87.0 persons per square mile (2000); Age: 23.7% under 18, 11.6% over 64 (2000); Marriage status: 19.4% never married, 68.1% now married, 5.0% widowed, 7.4% divorced (2000); Foreign born: 0.3% (2000); Ancestry (includes multiple ancestries): 19.4% German, 14.9% United States or American, 14.6% English, 5.8% Other groups, 5.5% French (except Basque) (2000).
Economy: Employment by occupation: 15.6% management, 20.2% professional, 10.0% services, 14.8% sales, 0.9% farming, 10.4% construction, 28.2% production (2000).
Income: Per capita income: $22,153 (2000); Median household income: $50,216 (2000); Poverty rate: 4.5% (2000).
Taxes: Total city taxes per capita: $45 (1997); City property taxes per capita: $45 (1997).
Education: High school graduation rate: 89.9% (2000); College graduation rate: 13.4% (2000).
Housing: Homeownership rate: 90.6% (2000); Median home value: $115,500 (2000); Median rent: $483 per month (2000); Median age of housing: 37 years (2000).
Transportation: Commute to work: 93.7% car, 0.0% public transportation, 1.7% walk, 4.6% work from home (2000); Travel time to work: 3.5% less than 15 minutes, 51.5% 15 to 30 minutes, 28.3% 30 to 45 minutes, 9.3% 45 to 60 minutes, 7.3% 60 minutes or more (2000)

MAPLE GROVE (township). Covers a land area of 35.910 square miles and a water area of 0.044 square miles. Located at 42.55° N. Lat.; 85.13° W. Long.
Population: 1,471 (2000); Race: 98.1% White, 0.0% Black, 0.5% Asian, 0.0% American Indian and Alaska Native, 0.3% Hispanic of any race, 1.1% two or more races (2000); Density: 41.0 persons per square mile (2000); Age: 30.7% under 18, 9.2% over 64 (2000); Marriage status: 19.0% never married, 70.2% now married, 4.9% widowed, 5.9% divorced (2000); Foreign born: 0.8% (2000); Ancestry (includes multiple ancestries): 20.7% German, 16.8% English, 12.0% United States or American, 10.2% Irish, 8.8% Dutch (2000).
Economy: Employment by occupation: 6.6% management, 16.7% professional, 10.0% services, 22.7% sales, 1.0% farming, 12.7% construction, 30.4% production (2000).
Income: Per capita income: $18,512 (2000); Median household income: $51,200 (2000); Poverty rate: 5.8% (2000).
Taxes: Total city taxes per capita: $28 (1997); City property taxes per capita: $28 (1997).
Education: High school graduation rate: 86.2% (2000); College graduation rate: 11.9% (2000).
Housing: Homeownership rate: 93.2% (2000); Median home value: $95,600 (2000); Median rent: $420 per month (2000); Median age of housing: 45 years (2000).
Transportation: Commute to work: 89.1% car, 0.0% public transportation, 5.3% walk, 5.7% work from home (2000); Travel time to work: 21.3% less than 15 minutes, 31.4% 15 to 30 minutes, 23.2% 30 to 45 minutes, 14.4% 45 to 60 minutes, 9.8% 60 minutes or more (2000)

MIDDLEVILLE (village). Covers a land area of 2.071 square miles and a water area of 0.073 square miles. Located at 42.71° N. Lat.; 85.46° W. Long. Elevation is 726 feet.
Population: 2,721 (2000); Race: 95.4% White, 0.0% Black, 0.2% Asian, 0.9% American Indian and Alaska Native, 3.6% Hispanic of any race, 1.5% two or more races (2000); Density: 1,313.7 persons per square mile (2000); Age: 33.1% under 18, 9.8% over 64 (2000); Marriage status: 21.8% never married, 59.5% now married, 4.7% widowed, 14.0% divorced (2000); Foreign born: 2.9% (2000); Ancestry (includes multiple ancestries): 26.0% German, 15.6% Dutch, 15.3% Irish, 15.0% English, 10.4% Other groups (2000).
Economy: In farm area. Manufacturing: clothing, machinery, transportation equipment, metal fabrication. Middleville Ski Area to North; Yankee Springs State Recreational Area to Southwest. Employment by occupation: 7.5% management, 15.5% professional, 14.6% services, 23.7% sales, 1.0% farming, 9.0% construction, 28.6% production (2000).

Income: Per capita income: $17,005 (2000); Median household income: $41,947 (2000); Poverty rate: 4.5% (2000).
Taxes: Total city taxes per capita: $188 (1997); City property taxes per capita: $186 (1997).
Education: High school graduation rate: 85.1% (2000); College graduation rate: 11.1% (2000).

School District(s)

Thornapple Kellogg School District (PK-12)
2000 Enrollment: 2,804 616-795-3313

Housing: Homeownership rate: 77.9% (2000); Median home value: $92,900 (2000); Median rent: $393 per month (2000); Median age of housing: 28 years (2000).
Transportation: Commute to work: 95.7% car, 0.2% public transportation, 3.5% walk, 0.7% work from home (2000); Travel time to work: 29.3% less than 15 minutes, 38.8% 15 to 30 minutes, 25.2% 30 to 45 minutes, 3.9% 45 to 60 minutes, 2.8% 60 minutes or more (2000)

NASHVILLE (village). Covers a land area of 2.098 square miles and a water area of 0.091 square miles. Located at 42.60° N. Lat.; 85.09° W. Long. Elevation is 820 feet.
History: Plotted 1865, incorporated 1869.
Population: 1,684 (2000); Race: 98.0% White, 0.1% Black, 0.0% Asian, 0.6% American Indian and Alaska Native, 1.4% Hispanic of any race, 1.2% two or more races (2000); Density: 802.8 persons per square mile (2000); Age: 30.2% under 18, 12.4% over 64 (2000); Marriage status: 24.9% never married, 54.6% now married, 7.4% widowed, 13.2% divorced (2000); Foreign born: 0.5% (2000); Ancestry (includes multiple ancestries): 19.2% German, 16.5% English, 11.7% Irish, 7.6% United States or American, 6.9% Other groups (2000).
Economy: In agricultural area. Manufacturing: tool and die. Employment by occupation: 5.8% management, 9.2% professional, 14.2% services, 21.7% sales, 0.0% farming, 11.6% construction, 37.6% production (2000).
Income: Per capita income: $14,147 (2000); Median household income: $32,857 (2000); Poverty rate: 10.6% (2000).
Taxes: Total city taxes per capita: $127 (1997); City property taxes per capita: $125 (1997).
Education: High school graduation rate: 79.1% (2000); College graduation rate: 9.2% (2000).
Housing: Homeownership rate: 68.2% (2000); Median home value: $72,300 (2000); Median rent: $335 per month (2000); Median age of housing: 60+ years (2000).
Safety: Violent crime rate: 53.2 per 10,000 population; Property crime rate: 177.2 per 10,000 population (2001).
Transportation: Commute to work: 92.7% car, 0.3% public transportation, 5.9% walk, 0.4% work from home (2000); Travel time to work: 23.4% less than 15 minutes, 27.3% 15 to 30 minutes, 23.9% 30 to 45 minutes, 15.4% 45 to 60 minutes, 10.0% 60 minutes or more (2000)

ORANGEVILLE (township). Covers a land area of 33.580 square miles and a water area of 2.029 square miles. Located at 42.56° N. Lat.; 85.50° W. Long. Elevation is 777 feet.
Population: 3,321 (2000); Race: 96.4% White, 0.6% Black, 0.2% Asian, 0.3% American Indian and Alaska Native, 1.8% Hispanic of any race, 1.6% two or more races (2000); Density: 98.9 persons per square mile (2000); Age: 26.7% under 18, 13.0% over 64 (2000); Marriage status: 18.9% never married, 66.7% now married, 5.1% widowed, 9.3% divorced (2000); Foreign born: 0.0% (2000); Ancestry (includes multiple ancestries): 20.1% German, 12.8% English, 12.2% Dutch, 10.7% United States or American, 10.2% Irish (2000).
Economy: Employment by occupation: 10.1% management, 16.7% professional, 14.6% services, 21.4% sales, 1.7% farming, 13.9% construction, 21.7% production (2000).
Income: Per capita income: $20,709 (2000); Median household income: $44,348 (2000); Poverty rate: 7.1% (2000).
Taxes: Total city taxes per capita: $53 (2000); City property taxes per capita: $53 (2000).
Education: High school graduation rate: 76.2% (2000); College graduation rate: 10.9% (2000).
Housing: Homeownership rate: 87.1% (2000); Median home value: $112,100 (2000); Median rent: $453 per month (2000); Median age of housing: 25 years (2000).
Transportation: Commute to work: 93.2% car, 0.0% public transportation, 3.2% walk, 3.5% work from home (2000); Travel time to work: 11.5% less than 15 minutes, 28.7% 15 to 30 minutes, 38.8% 30 to 45 minutes, 13.8% 45 to 60 minutes, 7.2% 60 minutes or more (2000)

PRAIRIEVILLE (township). Covers a land area of 33.299 square miles and a water area of 3.295 square miles. Located at 42.47° N. Lat.; 85.48° W. Long.
History: Prairieville Township was organized in 1841. It was first called Spalding, for an early settler, but was renamed in 1843. The village of Prairieville formed around a tavern operated in 1837 by Hiram Lucas.
Population: 3,175 (2000); Race: 98.4% White, 0.3% Black, 0.0% Asian, 0.9% American Indian and Alaska Native, 1.1% Hispanic of any race, 0.3% two or more races (2000); Density: 95.3 persons per square mile (2000); Age: 24.6% under 18, 11.0% over 64 (2000); Marriage status: 17.3% never married, 67.2% now married, 6.7% widowed, 8.8% divorced (2000); Foreign born: 0.6% (2000); Ancestry (includes multiple ancestries): 24.7% German, 16.2% English, 15.3% Dutch, 11.5% United States or American, 8.4% Irish (2000).
Economy: Single-family building permits issued: 25 (2001) / 19 (2000); Multi-family building permits issued: 0 (2001) / 12 (2000); Employment by occupation: 20.0% management, 15.9% professional, 11.5% services, 20.5% sales, 1.5% farming, 10.6% construction, 20.0% production (2000).
Income: Per capita income: $22,838 (2000); Median household income: $51,071 (2000); Poverty rate: 2.9% (2000).
Taxes: Total city taxes per capita: $137 (2000); City property taxes per capita: $129 (2000).
Education: High school graduation rate: 89.3% (2000); College graduation rate: 18.4% (2000).
Housing: Homeownership rate: 88.7% (2000); Median home value: $132,400 (2000); Median rent: $463 per month (2000); Median age of housing: 31 years (2000).
Safety: Violent crime rate: 15.7 per 10,000 population; Property crime rate: 103.4 per 10,000 population (2001).
Transportation: Commute to work: 91.8% car, 0.0% public transportation, 0.9% walk, 6.8% work from home (2000); Travel time to work: 13.5% less than 15 minutes, 32.8% 15 to 30 minutes, 39.0% 30 to 45 minutes, 8.7% 45 to 60 minutes, 6.0% 60 minutes or more (2000)

RUTLAND CHARTER (township). Covers a land area of 35.185 square miles and a water area of 0.952 square miles. Located at 42.64° N. Lat.; 85.35° W. Long.
Population: 3,646 (2000); Race: 97.3% White, 0.2% Black, 0.4% Asian, 0.5% American Indian and Alaska Native, 0.4% Hispanic of any race, 1.3% two or more races (2000); Density: 103.6 persons per square mile (2000); Age: 28.3% under 18, 10.3% over 64 (2000); Marriage status: 18.4% never married, 67.4% now married, 3.9% widowed, 10.3% divorced (2000); Foreign born: 0.4% (2000); Ancestry (includes multiple ancestries): 25.2% German, 15.2% Irish, 11.8% English, 7.4% Dutch, 7.4% Other groups (2000).
Economy: Single-family building permits issued: 28 (2001) / 34 (2000); Multi-family building permits issued: 0 (2001) / 0 (2000); Employment by occupation: 10.0% management, 19.8% professional, 6.0% services, 30.0% sales, 0.4% farming, 10.4% construction, 23.3% production (2000).
Income: Per capita income: $23,141 (2000); Median household income: $52,065 (2000); Poverty rate: 3.9% (2000).
Taxes: Total city taxes per capita: $57 (1997); City property taxes per capita: $50 (1997).
Education: High school graduation rate: 91.0% (2000); College graduation rate: 21.2% (2000).
Housing: Homeownership rate: 91.6% (2000); Median home value: $114,500 (2000); Median rent: $452 per month (2000); Median age of housing: 26 years (2000).
Transportation: Commute to work: 95.7% car, 0.4% public transportation, 0.4% walk, 3.4% work from home (2000); Travel time to work: 35.5% less than 15 minutes, 23.2% 15 to 30 minutes, 25.2% 30 to 45 minutes, 8.0% 45 to 60 minutes, 8.1% 60 minutes or more (2000)

THORNAPPLE (township). Covers a land area of 35.508 square miles and a water area of 0.364 square miles. Located at 42.72° N. Lat.; 85.48° W. Long.
Population: 6,685 (2000); Race: 96.1% White, 0.0% Black, 0.4% Asian, 0.6% American Indian and Alaska Native, 2.2% Hispanic of any race, 2.0% two or more races (2000); Density: 188.3 persons per square mile (2000); Age: 31.9% under 18, 7.6% over 64 (2000); Marriage status: 21.1% never married, 65.1% now married, 3.9% widowed, 9.9% divorced (2000); Foreign born: 1.7% (2000); Ancestry (includes multiple ancestries): 26.3% German, 23.3% Dutch, 13.3% English, 13.2% Irish, 8.6% Other groups (2000).

Economy: Employment by occupation: 9.2% management, 17.7% professional, 11.3% services, 24.9% sales, 0.4% farming, 9.7% construction, 26.9% production (2000).
Income: Per capita income: $20,782 (2000); Median household income: $53,333 (2000); Poverty rate: 4.9% (2000).
Taxes: Total city taxes per capita: $38 (2000); City property taxes per capita: $38 (2000).
Education: High school graduation rate: 90.9% (2000); College graduation rate: 16.5% (2000).
Housing: Homeownership rate: 87.4% (2000); Median home value: $119,900 (2000); Median rent: $451 per month (2000); Median age of housing: 23 years (2000).
Transportation: Commute to work: 95.5% car, 0.1% public transportation, 1.7% walk, 2.6% work from home (2000); Travel time to work: 26.4% less than 15 minutes, 38.9% 15 to 30 minutes, 27.1% 30 to 45 minutes, 5.6% 45 to 60 minutes, 2.0% 60 minutes or more (2000)

WOODLAND (village). Covers a land area of 0.798 square miles and a water area of 0 square miles. Located at 42.72° N. Lat.; 85.13° W. Long. Elevation is 875 feet.
Population: 495 (2000); Race: 98.6% White, 0.4% Black, 0.0% Asian, 0.6% American Indian and Alaska Native, 2.8% Hispanic of any race, 0.0% two or more races (2000); Density: 620.4 persons per square mile (2000); Age: 28.7% under 18, 9.6% over 64 (2000); Marriage status: 21.5% never married, 62.7% now married, 4.5% widowed, 11.3% divorced (2000); Foreign born: 1.0% (2000); Ancestry (includes multiple ancestries): 28.7% German, 15.3% English, 13.9% Irish, 8.6% Other groups, 6.9% Dutch (2000).
Economy: Employment by occupation: 9.8% management, 10.7% professional, 15.1% services, 22.2% sales, 1.8% farming, 14.7% construction, 25.8% production (2000).
Income: Per capita income: $14,908 (2000); Median household income: $32,222 (2000); Poverty rate: 15.4% (2000).
Taxes: Total city taxes per capita: $102 (1997); City property taxes per capita: $102 (1997).
Education: High school graduation rate: 81.2% (2000); College graduation rate: 9.4% (2000).
Housing: Homeownership rate: 74.9% (2000); Median home value: $80,000 (2000); Median rent: $258 per month (2000); Median age of housing: 60+ years (2000).
Transportation: Commute to work: 95.6% car, 0.0% public transportation, 3.5% walk, 0.9% work from home (2000); Travel time to work: 19.6% less than 15 minutes, 31.6% 15 to 30 minutes, 26.2% 30 to 45 minutes, 15.1% 45 to 60 minutes, 7.6% 60 minutes or more (2000)

WOODLAND (township). Covers a land area of 35.429 square miles and a water area of 0.525 square miles. Located at 42.73° N. Lat.; 85.12° W. Long. Elevation is 875 feet.
Population: 2,129 (2000); Race: 97.7% White, 0.3% Black, 0.1% Asian, 0.1% American Indian and Alaska Native, 1.4% Hispanic of any race, 1.1% two or more races (2000); Density: 60.1 persons per square mile (2000); Age: 26.7% under 18, 12.4% over 64 (2000); Marriage status: 20.3% never married, 65.3% now married, 5.8% widowed, 8.6% divorced (2000); Foreign born: 1.6% (2000); Ancestry (includes multiple ancestries): 32.3% German, 15.5% English, 14.0% Irish, 10.0% United States or American, 7.0% Other groups (2000).
Economy: In farm area. Employment by occupation: 13.0% management, 15.6% professional, 12.9% services, 20.4% sales, 2.0% farming, 15.3% construction, 20.9% production (2000).
Income: Per capita income: $19,787 (2000); Median household income: $38,920 (2000); Poverty rate: 6.6% (2000).
Taxes: Total city taxes per capita: $49 (1997); City property taxes per capita: $49 (1997).
Education: High school graduation rate: 84.4% (2000); College graduation rate: 13.7% (2000).
Housing: Homeownership rate: 85.6% (2000); Median home value: $97,400 (2000); Median rent: $279 per month (2000); Median age of housing: 48 years (2000).
Transportation: Commute to work: 90.4% car, 0.0% public transportation, 2.5% walk, 5.9% work from home (2000); Travel time to work: 27.0% less than 15 minutes, 27.2% 15 to 30 minutes, 23.1% 30 to 45 minutes, 18.0% 45 to 60 minutes, 4.7% 60 minutes or more (2000)

YANKEE SPRINGS (township). Covers a land area of 31.490 square miles and a water area of 4.330 square miles. Located at 42.63° N. Lat.; 85.51° W. Long.
Population: 4,219 (2000); Race: 96.1% White, 0.4% Black, 0.0% Asian, 1.5% American Indian and Alaska Native, 0.4% Hispanic of any race, 1.6% two or more races (2000); Density: 134.0 persons per square mile (2000); Age: 25.6% under 18, 11.4% over 64 (2000); Marriage status: 18.8% never married, 66.9% now married, 4.1% widowed, 10.3% divorced (2000); Foreign born: 0.6% (2000); Ancestry (includes multiple ancestries): 24.8% German, 23.4% Dutch, 13.7% English, 10.2% Irish, 9.2% United States or American (2000).
Economy: Employment by occupation: 14.3% management, 13.6% professional, 8.7% services, 31.2% sales, 0.5% farming, 11.8% construction, 19.9% production (2000).
Income: Per capita income: $25,100 (2000); Median household income: $52,661 (2000); Poverty rate: 2.5% (2000).
Taxes: Total city taxes per capita: $59 (1997); City property taxes per capita: $43 (1997).
Education: High school graduation rate: 88.9% (2000); College graduation rate: 15.8% (2000).
Housing: Homeownership rate: 91.2% (2000); Median home value: $185,300 (2000); Median rent: $617 per month (2000); Median age of housing: 20 years (2000).
Transportation: Commute to work: 97.2% car, 0.0% public transportation, 0.0% walk, 2.8% work from home (2000); Travel time to work: 16.0% less than 15 minutes, 33.0% 15 to 30 minutes, 32.6% 30 to 45 minutes, 12.4% 45 to 60 minutes, 6.0% 60 minutes or more (2000)

Bay County

Located in eastern Michigan; bounded on the east by Saginaw Bay and drained by the Saginaw River. Covers a land area of 444.20 square miles, a water area of 186.70 square miles, and is located in the Eastern Time Zone. The county government was organized in 1857. County seat is Bay City.

Bay County is part of the Saginaw-Bay City-Midland, MI MSA. The entire metro area includes: Bay County; Midland County; Saginaw County

Population: 110,157 (2000); Race: 94.9% White, 1.2% Black, 0.6% Asian, 0.5% American Indian and Alaska Native, 3.8% Hispanic of any race, 1.6% two or more races (2000); Density: 248.0 persons per square mile (2000); Age: 24.3% under 18, 14.7% over 64 (2000).
Religion: Five largest groups: 36.2% Catholic Church, 11.2% Lutheran Church—Missouri Synod, 3.0% Wisconsin Evangelical Lutheran Synod, 2.0% The United Methodist Church, 1.5% Presbyterian Church (U.S.A.) (2000).
Economy: Unemployment rate: 5.7% (11/2002); Total civilian labor force: 54,564 (11/2002); Leading industries: 19.8% retail trade; 17.0% manufacturing; 15.1% health care and social assistance (2000); Companies that employ more than 1,000 persons: 3 (2000); Companies that employ more than 100 persons: 50 (2000); Farms: 730 totaling 175,931 acres (1997); Minority business ownership rate: 4.8% (1997); Women business ownership rate: 29.5% (1997); Retail sales per capita: $9,980 (1997). Single-family building permits issued: 329 (2001) / 248 (2000); Multi-family building permits issued: 36 (2001) / 26 (2000).
Income: Per capita income: $19,698 (2000); Median household income: $38,646 (2000); Poverty rate: 9.7% (2000); Bankruptcy rate: 4.52% (2001).
Taxes: Total county taxes per capita: $177 (2000); County property taxes per capita: $171 (2000).
Education: High school graduation rate: 82.4% (2000); College graduation rate: 14.2% (2000).
Housing: Homeownership rate: 79.3% (2000); Median home value: $84,900 (2000); Median rent: $378 per month (2000); Median age of housing: 42 years (2000).
Health: Birth rate: 121.7 per 10,000 population (1998); Age adjusted death rate: 90.4 per 10,000 population (1999); Age adjusted cancer mortality rate: 205.4 deaths per 100,000 population (1999). Number of physicians: 13.3 per 10,000 population (1999); Number of hospital beds: 30.2 per 10,000 population (1999).
Elections: 2000 Presidential election results: 54.7% Gore, 42.9% Bush, 1.9% Nader, 0.1% Buchanan
National and State Parks: Bay City State Park; Tobico Marsh State Game Area
Additional Information Contacts
Bay County Government Offices 989-686-4610
Auburn Area Chamber of Commerce 989-662-4001
Auburn Chamber of Commerce 989-662-4001
Bay Area Chamber of Commerce 989-893-4567

Bay Area Convention & Visitors Bureau. 989-893-1222
Realtor Association of Bay County 989-892-8541

Bay County Communities

AUBURN (city). Covers a land area of 1.020 square miles and a water area of 0 square miles. Located at 43.60° N. Lat.; 84.07° W. Long. Elevation is 617 feet.

History: Auburn was settled by John Gaffney from Ireland in 1854. The village that grew up was first called Skinner, but was renamed Auburn in 1877, the name having been chosen from the first lines of Oliver Goldsmith's poem "The Deserted Village." Auburn was incorporated as a city in 1947.

Population: 2,011 (2000); Race: 96.4% White, 0.2% Black, 0.2% Asian, 1.0% American Indian and Alaska Native, 3.2% Hispanic of any race, 1.8% two or more races (2000); Density: 1,971.6 persons per square mile (2000); Age: 26.1% under 18, 14.1% over 64 (2000); Marriage status: 25.0% never married, 55.7% now married, 8.3% widowed, 10.9% divorced (2000); Foreign born: 0.8% (2000); Ancestry (includes multiple ancestries): 34.6% German, 24.0% Polish, 13.3% Irish, 13.0% French (except Basque), 10.9% English (2000).

Economy: Single-family building permits issued: 4 (2001) / 0 (2000); Multi-family building permits issued: 0 (2001) / 2 (2000); Employment by occupation: 13.3% management, 20.5% professional, 15.7% services, 29.9% sales, 0.0% farming, 8.6% construction, 11.9% production (2000).

Income: Per capita income: $20,941 (2000); Median household income: $42,014 (2000); Poverty rate: 6.4% (2000).

Taxes: Total city taxes per capita: $217 (1997); City property taxes per capita: $206 (1997).

Education: High school graduation rate: 87.9% (2000); College graduation rate: 20.6% (2000).

Housing: Homeownership rate: 67.3% (2000); Median home value: $100,300 (2000); Median rent: $389 per month (2000); Median age of housing: 30 years (2000).

Safety: Violent crime rate: 0.0 per 10,000 population; Property crime rate: 103.9 per 10,000 population (2001).

Transportation: Commute to work: 95.3% car, 0.5% public transportation, 2.7% walk, 1.4% work from home (2000); Travel time to work: 29.0% less than 15 minutes, 51.9% 15 to 30 minutes, 11.3% 30 to 45 minutes, 3.4% 45 to 60 minutes, 4.4% 60 minutes or more (2000)

Additional Information Contacts
Auburn Area Chamber of Commerce 989-662-4001
Auburn Chamber of Commerce 989-662-4001

BANGOR (township). Covers a land area of 13.888 square miles and a water area of 8.013 square miles. Located at 43.63° N. Lat.; 83.90° W. Long.

Population: 15,547 (2000); Race: 96.8% White, 0.8% Black, 0.6% Asian, 0.3% American Indian and Alaska Native, 2.6% Hispanic of any race, 0.9% two or more races (2000); Density: 1,119.4 persons per square mile (2000); Age: 23.3% under 18, 14.8% over 64 (2000); Marriage status: 23.8% never married, 58.1% now married, 7.9% widowed, 10.1% divorced (2000); Foreign born: 1.7% (2000); Ancestry (includes multiple ancestries): 32.0% German, 19.2% Polish, 16.2% French (except Basque), 11.0% Irish, 8.7% English (2000).

Vital Statistics: Birth rate: 83.0 per 10,000 population (1998)

Economy: Single-family building permits issued: 23 (2001) / 22 (2000); Multi-family building permits issued: 0 (2001) / 0 (2000); Employment by occupation: 9.8% management, 17.3% professional, 16.8% services, 29.3% sales, 0.3% farming, 11.6% construction, 15.0% production (2000).

Income: Per capita income: $21,723 (2000); Median household income: $42,358 (2000); Poverty rate: 7.2% (2000).

Taxes: Total city taxes per capita: $184 (2000); City property taxes per capita: $167 (2000).

Education: High school graduation rate: 83.2% (2000); College graduation rate: 15.8% (2000).

Housing: Homeownership rate: 80.8% (2000); Median home value: $96,100 (2000); Median rent: $397 per month (2000); Median age of housing: 36 years (2000).

Transportation: Commute to work: 97.2% car, 0.5% public transportation, 0.3% walk, 2.0% work from home (2000); Travel time to work: 38.0% less than 15 minutes, 40.2% 15 to 30 minutes, 13.7% 30 to 45 minutes, 2.5% 45 to 60 minutes, 5.7% 60 minutes or more (2000)

BAY CITY (city). Covers a land area of 10.409 square miles and a water area of 0.919 square miles. Located at 43.59° N. Lat.; 83.88° W. Long. Elevation is 594 feet.

History: Several small communities sprang up in the 1830's near the mouth of the Saginaw River on Lake Huron. The Tromble brothers, Joseph and Mader, built the first permanent frame house in 1836. The villages took the names of Lower Saginaw, Portsmouth, Wenona, Salzburg, and Banks. This was lumber country, and by 1872 there were 36 sawmills operating in the area, regulating the life of the towns. In the 1860's, Lower Saginaw had annexed several of the nearby settlements and changed its name to Bay City, to distinguish it from the earlier established Saginaw upstream. The villages on the west bank merged as West Bay City. In 1903, Bay City and West Bay City were consolidated as Bay City. When the lumber industry declined in the early 1900's, Bay City turned to soft-coal mining, commercial fishing, and beet sugar.

Population: 36,817 (2000); Race: 90.7% White, 2.7% Black, 0.6% Asian, 0.9% American Indian and Alaska Native, 6.7% Hispanic of any race, 2.6% two or more races (2000); Density: 3,537.1 persons per square mile (2000); Age: 25.4% under 18, 14.2% over 64 (2000); Marriage status: 29.5% never married, 49.3% now married, 9.0% widowed, 12.2% divorced (2000); Foreign born: 1.4% (2000); Ancestry (includes multiple ancestries): 27.5% German, 21.6% Polish, 13.2% Other groups, 12.5% Irish, 12.0% French (except Basque) (2000).

Vital Statistics: Birth rate: 165.1 per 10,000 population (1998)

Economy: Unemployment rate: 7.6% (11/2002); Total civilian labor force: 17,913 (11/2002); Single-family building permits issued: 5 (2001) / 3 (2000); Multi-family building permits issued: 0 (2001) / 0 (2000); Employment by occupation: 7.9% management, 16.9% professional, 18.8% services, 27.5% sales, 0.4% farming, 9.7% construction, 18.7% production (2000).

Income: Per capita income: $16,550 (2000); Median household income: $30,425 (2000); Poverty rate: 14.6% (2000).

Taxes: Total city taxes per capita: $348 (2000); City property taxes per capita: $331 (2000).

Education: High school graduation rate: 80.8% (2000); College graduation rate: 12.8% (2000).

School District(s)

Bangor Township Schools (KG-12)
2000 Enrollment: 2,568 517-684-8121
Bay City School District (KG-12)
2000 Enrollment: 9,997 517-686-9700
Bay County Psa (KG-06)
2000 Enrollment: 0 989-684-6484

Housing: Homeownership rate: 69.5% (2000); Median home value: $65,700 (2000); Median rent: $356 per month (2000); Median age of housing: 60+ years (2000).

Hospitals: Bay Medical Center (441 beds)

Safety: Violent crime rate: 59.4 per 10,000 population; Property crime rate: 387.2 per 10,000 population (2001).

Newspapers: The Bay City Times (7 x week); Bay City Democrat & Bay County Legal News (1 x week)

Transportation: Commute to work: 91.9% car, 1.1% public transportation, 3.0% walk, 2.9% work from home (2000); Travel time to work: 47.3% less than 15 minutes, 33.3% 15 to 30 minutes, 12.3% 30 to 45 minutes, 2.6% 45 to 60 minutes, 4.5% 60 minutes or more (2000)

Airports: James Clements Municipal

Additional Information Contacts
Bay Area Chamber of Commerce 989-893-4567
Bay Area Convention & Visitors Bureau. 989-893-1222
Realtor Association of Bay County 989-892-8541

BEAVER (township). Covers a land area of 35.383 square miles and a water area of 0 square miles. Located at 43.69° N. Lat.; 84.09° W. Long. Elevation is 631 feet.

Population: 2,806 (2000); Race: 98.8% White, 0.1% Black, 0.2% Asian, 0.1% American Indian and Alaska Native, 1.1% Hispanic of any race, 0.6% two or more races (2000); Density: 79.3 persons per square mile (2000); Age: 25.2% under 18, 11.5% over 64 (2000); Marriage status: 23.2% never married, 65.7% now married, 5.7% widowed, 5.4% divorced (2000); Foreign born: 0.7% (2000); Ancestry (includes multiple ancestries): 38.1% German, 24.3% Polish, 14.3% French (except Basque), 10.7% English, 10.4% Irish (2000).

Economy: Single-family building permits issued: 18 (2001) / 17 (2000); Multi-family building permits issued: 0 (2001) / 0 (2000); Employment by occupation: 10.9% management, 14.6% professional, 14.5% services, 26.1% sales, 0.6% farming, 12.5% construction, 20.8% production (2000).

Income: Per capita income: $19,654 (2000); Median household income: $51,546 (2000); Poverty rate: 5.4% (2000).

Taxes: Total city taxes per capita: $121 (1997); City property taxes per capita: $114 (1997).

Education: High school graduation rate: 84.0% (2000); College graduation rate: 10.9% (2000).
Housing: Homeownership rate: 93.1% (2000); Median home value: $93,900 (2000); Median rent: $455 per month (2000); Median age of housing: 30 years (2000).
Transportation: Commute to work: 95.8% car, 0.0% public transportation, 1.8% walk, 2.2% work from home (2000); Travel time to work: 13.5% less than 15 minutes, 50.6% 15 to 30 minutes, 24.8% 30 to 45 minutes, 5.9% 45 to 60 minutes, 5.2% 60 minutes or more (2000)

ESSEXVILLE (city). Covers a land area of 1.209 square miles and a water area of 0.166 square miles. Located at 43.61° N. Lat.; 83.84° W. Long. Elevation is 590 feet.
History: Essexville developed around a beet-sugar refinery, one of the first in the state. In the early 1900's, the economy changed to commercial fishing, and cement manufacturing.
Population: 3,766 (2000); Race: 95.8% White, 0.3% Black, 0.0% Asian, 0.9% American Indian and Alaska Native, 2.9% Hispanic of any race, 1.4% two or more races (2000); Density: 3,114.3 persons per square mile (2000); Age: 24.9% under 18, 16.4% over 64 (2000); Marriage status: 22.1% never married, 59.0% now married, 9.9% widowed, 9.0% divorced (2000); Foreign born: 0.6% (2000); Ancestry (includes multiple ancestries): 27.8% German, 22.5% Polish, 16.0% Irish, 15.4% French (except Basque), 11.6% English (2000).
Economy: Single-family building permits issued: 0 (2001) / 1 (2000); Multi-family building permits issued: 0 (2001) / 0 (2000); Employment by occupation: 10.2% management, 16.4% professional, 17.9% services, 33.9% sales, 0.0% farming, 7.4% construction, 14.1% production (2000).
Income: Per capita income: $25,060 (2000); Median household income: $43,750 (2000); Poverty rate: 4.4% (2000).
Taxes: Total city taxes per capita: $249 (1997); City property taxes per capita: $235 (1997).
Education: High school graduation rate: 89.6% (2000); College graduation rate: 21.6% (2000).

School District(s)

Bay-Arenac Community High School (09-12)
2000 Enrollment: 121 517-686-4410
Essexville-Hampton Public School (KG-12)
2000 Enrollment: 1,892 517-894-9700

Housing: Homeownership rate: 90.8% (2000); Median home value: $88,400 (2000); Median rent: $493 per month (2000); Median age of housing: 48 years (2000).
Safety: Violent crime rate: 7.9 per 10,000 population; Property crime rate: 264.1 per 10,000 population (2001).
Transportation: Commute to work: 95.9% car, 1.0% public transportation, 0.8% walk, 1.4% work from home (2000); Travel time to work: 56.9% less than 15 minutes, 26.4% 15 to 30 minutes, 9.2% 30 to 45 minutes, 3.7% 45 to 60 minutes, 3.9% 60 minutes or more (2000)

FRANKENLUST (township). Covers a land area of 22.796 square miles and a water area of 0.321 square miles. Located at 43.55° N. Lat.; 83.95° W. Long.
Population: 2,530 (2000); Race: 95.1% White, 0.4% Black, 2.6% Asian, 0.1% American Indian and Alaska Native, 0.4% Hispanic of any race, 1.7% two or more races (2000); Density: 111.0 persons per square mile (2000); Age: 21.5% under 18, 16.3% over 64 (2000); Marriage status: 20.4% never married, 65.7% now married, 5.7% widowed, 8.2% divorced (2000); Foreign born: 3.9% (2000); Ancestry (includes multiple ancestries): 48.3% German, 16.4% Polish, 9.9% Irish, 9.7% English, 9.1% French (except Basque) (2000).
Economy: Single-family building permits issued: 49 (2001) / 26 (2000); Multi-family building permits issued: 0 (2001) / 12 (2000); Employment by occupation: 15.3% management, 23.9% professional, 9.0% services, 30.1% sales, 0.0% farming, 8.5% construction, 13.2% production (2000).
Income: Per capita income: $27,204 (2000); Median household income: $52,161 (2000); Poverty rate: 3.2% (2000).
Taxes: Total city taxes per capita: $81 (1997); City property taxes per capita: $63 (1997).
Education: High school graduation rate: 85.8% (2000); College graduation rate: 29.1% (2000).
Housing: Homeownership rate: 87.0% (2000); Median home value: $129,300 (2000); Median rent: $457 per month (2000); Median age of housing: 28 years (2000).
Transportation: Commute to work: 96.0% car, 0.0% public transportation, 0.3% walk, 3.5% work from home (2000); Travel time to work: 27.1% less than 15 minutes, 56.1% 15 to 30 minutes, 8.3% 30 to 45 minutes, 3.5% 45 to 60 minutes, 5.1% 60 minutes or more (2000)

FRASER (township). Covers a land area of 32.322 square miles and a water area of 5.886 square miles. Located at 43.78° N. Lat.; 83.97° W. Long.
Population: 3,375 (2000); Race: 96.2% White, 0.6% Black, 0.0% Asian, 0.0% American Indian and Alaska Native, 2.2% Hispanic of any race, 2.8% two or more races (2000); Density: 104.4 persons per square mile (2000); Age: 24.0% under 18, 12.1% over 64 (2000); Marriage status: 22.8% never married, 65.2% now married, 6.1% widowed, 6.0% divorced (2000); Foreign born: 0.6% (2000); Ancestry (includes multiple ancestries): 25.5% German, 24.0% Polish, 23.1% French (except Basque), 7.1% Other groups, 7.1% Irish (2000).
Economy: Single-family building permits issued: 9 (2001) / 7 (2000); Multi-family building permits issued: 0 (2001) / 0 (2000); Employment by occupation: 8.8% management, 12.2% professional, 14.9% services, 27.2% sales, 0.3% farming, 10.1% construction, 26.5% production (2000).
Income: Per capita income: $18,721 (2000); Median household income: $41,581 (2000); Poverty rate: 9.2% (2000).
Taxes: Total city taxes per capita: $31 (1997); City property taxes per capita: $22 (1997).
Education: High school graduation rate: 81.2% (2000); College graduation rate: 8.1% (2000).
Housing: Homeownership rate: 93.2% (2000); Median home value: $84,400 (2000); Median rent: $345 per month (2000); Median age of housing: 30 years (2000).
Transportation: Commute to work: 91.6% car, 0.3% public transportation, 1.8% walk, 4.3% work from home (2000); Travel time to work: 26.7% less than 15 minutes, 33.0% 15 to 30 minutes, 27.3% 30 to 45 minutes, 7.2% 45 to 60 minutes, 5.8% 60 minutes or more (2000)

GARFIELD (township). Covers a land area of 35.672 square miles and a water area of 0.020 square miles. Located at 43.79° N. Lat.; 84.09° W. Long.
History: Garfield Township was organized in 1887 and named for President James A. Garfield.
Population: 1,775 (2000); Race: 99.2% White, 0.0% Black, 0.0% Asian, 0.2% American Indian and Alaska Native, 2.3% Hispanic of any race, 0.6% two or more races (2000); Density: 49.8 persons per square mile (2000); Age: 26.0% under 18, 7.7% over 64 (2000); Marriage status: 24.0% never married, 62.1% now married, 5.2% widowed, 8.7% divorced (2000); Foreign born: 1.0% (2000); Ancestry (includes multiple ancestries): 30.4% German, 22.4% Polish, 18.9% French (except Basque), 9.0% English, 7.5% Irish (2000).
Economy: Single-family building permits issued: 13 (2001) / 8 (2000); Multi-family building permits issued: 0 (2001) / 0 (2000); Employment by occupation: 7.8% management, 9.7% professional, 16.5% services, 22.8% sales, 0.6% farming, 18.9% construction, 23.7% production (2000).
Income: Per capita income: $17,306 (2000); Median household income: $44,044 (2000); Poverty rate: 10.5% (2000).
Taxes: Total city taxes per capita: $47 (1997); City property taxes per capita: $46 (1997).
Education: High school graduation rate: 80.6% (2000); College graduation rate: 8.2% (2000).
Housing: Homeownership rate: 94.7% (2000); Median home value: $84,200 (2000); Median rent: $388 per month (2000); Median age of housing: 26 years (2000).
Transportation: Commute to work: 97.8% car, 0.0% public transportation, 0.6% walk, 1.5% work from home (2000); Travel time to work: 9.5% less than 15 minutes, 38.9% 15 to 30 minutes, 36.6% 30 to 45 minutes, 11.0% 45 to 60 minutes, 4.0% 60 minutes or more (2000)

GIBSON (township). Covers a land area of 35.673 square miles and a water area of 0.004 square miles. Located at 43.96° N. Lat.; 84.09° W. Long.
Population: 1,245 (2000); Race: 98.3% White, 0.0% Black, 0.0% Asian, 0.0% American Indian and Alaska Native, 10.5% Hispanic of any race, 0.8% two or more races (2000); Density: 34.9 persons per square mile (2000); Age: 30.6% under 18, 9.7% over 64 (2000); Marriage status: 22.7% never married, 64.7% now married, 5.8% widowed, 6.8% divorced (2000); Foreign born: 5.3% (2000); Ancestry (includes multiple ancestries): 25.2% German, 18.8% French (except Basque), 17.0% Other groups, 14.7% Polish, 8.8% Irish (2000).
Economy: Single-family building permits issued: 13 (2001) / 5 (2000); Multi-family building permits issued: 0 (2001) / 0 (2000); Employment by occupation: 11.1% management, 12.5% professional, 14.6% services, 16.8% sales, 6.0% farming, 16.6% construction, 22.4% production (2000).
Income: Per capita income: $14,969 (2000); Median household income: $35,978 (2000); Poverty rate: 12.5% (2000).

Taxes: Total city taxes per capita: $67 (1997); City property taxes per capita: $67 (1997).
Education: High school graduation rate: 71.3% (2000); College graduation rate: 3.9% (2000).
Housing: Homeownership rate: 93.2% (2000); Median home value: $67,000 (2000); Median rent: $325 per month (2000); Median age of housing: 28 years (2000).
Transportation: Commute to work: 90.3% car, 0.0% public transportation, 3.9% walk, 4.9% work from home (2000); Travel time to work: 18.9% less than 15 minutes, 36.2% 15 to 30 minutes, 22.3% 30 to 45 minutes, 12.1% 45 to 60 minutes, 10.4% 60 minutes or more (2000)

HAMPTON (township). Covers a land area of 27.051 square miles and a water area of 5.467 square miles. Located at 43.60° N. Lat.; 83.80° W. Long.
Population: 9,902 (2000); Race: 96.5% White, 1.0% Black, 0.8% Asian, 0.0% American Indian and Alaska Native, 2.5% Hispanic of any race, 1.4% two or more races (2000); Density: 366.0 persons per square mile (2000); Age: 22.5% under 18, 17.7% over 64 (2000); Marriage status: 24.8% never married, 57.2% now married, 9.3% widowed, 8.7% divorced (2000); Foreign born: 1.6% (2000); Ancestry (includes multiple ancestries): 28.7% German, 18.0% Polish, 16.3% French (except Basque), 9.1% Irish, 8.9% English (2000).
Economy: Single-family building permits issued: 41 (2001) / 32 (2000); Multi-family building permits issued: 2 (2001) / 0 (2000); Employment by occupation: 13.1% management, 20.6% professional, 16.0% services, 25.3% sales, 0.2% farming, 7.8% construction, 17.1% production (2000).
Income: Per capita income: $20,857 (2000); Median household income: $34,579 (2000); Poverty rate: 11.1% (2000).
Taxes: Total city taxes per capita: $246 (2000); City property taxes per capita: $226 (2000).
Education: High school graduation rate: 83.4% (2000); College graduation rate: 16.2% (2000).
Housing: Homeownership rate: 62.8% (2000); Median home value: $112,100 (2000); Median rent: $424 per month (2000); Median age of housing: 28 years (2000).
Safety: Violent crime rate: 5.0 per 10,000 population; Property crime rate: 364.7 per 10,000 population (2001).
Transportation: Commute to work: 96.0% car, 1.0% public transportation, 1.6% walk, 1.2% work from home (2000); Travel time to work: 37.0% less than 15 minutes, 38.2% 15 to 30 minutes, 16.5% 30 to 45 minutes, 3.2% 45 to 60 minutes, 5.1% 60 minutes or more (2000)

KAWKAWLIN (township). Covers a land area of 32.668 square miles and a water area of 8.845 square miles. Located at 43.69° N. Lat.; 83.97° W. Long. Elevation is 594 feet.
History: Kawkawlin developed around the water powered mill of James Fraser and the steam powered mill of Frederick A. Kaiser.
Population: 5,104 (2000); Race: 96.3% White, 0.1% Black, 1.5% Asian, 0.7% American Indian and Alaska Native, 2.6% Hispanic of any race, 1.2% two or more races (2000); Density: 156.2 persons per square mile (2000); Age: 24.3% under 18, 13.2% over 64 (2000); Marriage status: 22.4% never married, 63.4% now married, 6.7% widowed, 7.5% divorced (2000); Foreign born: 1.1% (2000); Ancestry (includes multiple ancestries): 31.1% German, 24.1% Polish, 19.2% French (except Basque), 10.6% Irish, 7.6% English (2000).
Economy: Single-family building permits issued: 26 (2001) / 10 (2000); Multi-family building permits issued: 0 (2001) / 0 (2000); Employment by occupation: 8.4% management, 15.8% professional, 17.1% services, 24.3% sales, 0.2% farming, 11.6% construction, 22.8% production (2000).
Income: Per capita income: $20,648 (2000); Median household income: $43,951 (2000); Poverty rate: 4.9% (2000).
Taxes: Total city taxes per capita: $37 (1997); City property taxes per capita: $28 (1997).
Education: High school graduation rate: 83.7% (2000); College graduation rate: 11.7% (2000).
Housing: Homeownership rate: 90.3% (2000); Median home value: $98,300 (2000); Median rent: $372 per month (2000); Median age of housing: 29 years (2000).
Transportation: Commute to work: 92.8% car, 0.0% public transportation, 1.4% walk, 5.2% work from home (2000); Travel time to work: 19.3% less than 15 minutes, 53.7% 15 to 30 minutes, 19.7% 30 to 45 minutes, 0.6% 45 to 60 minutes, 6.6% 60 minutes or more (2000)

LINWOOD (unincorporated postal area, zip code 48634). Covers a land area of 48.046 square miles and a water area of 0.108 square miles. Located at 43.74° N. Lat.; 84.01° W. Long. Elevation is 587 feet.
History: Linwood was established in 1872 as a station on the Mackinaw division of the Michigan Central Railroad, which was first called Terry's Station.
Population: 4,684 (2000); Race: 95.2% White, 0.4% Black, 1.1% Asian, 0.7% American Indian and Alaska Native, 3.6% Hispanic of any race, 2.4% two or more races (2000); Density: 97.5 persons per square mile (2000); Age: 26.1% under 18, 11.2% over 64 (2000); Marriage status: 24.5% never married, 63.5% now married, 5.5% widowed, 6.5% divorced (2000); Foreign born: 1.2% (2000); Ancestry (includes multiple ancestries): 26.8% German, 25.1% Polish, 20.6% French (except Basque), 8.6% English, 8.3% French Canadian (2000).
Economy: Employment by occupation: 7.5% management, 15.0% professional, 15.8% services, 23.9% sales, 0.6% farming, 10.4% construction, 26.6% production (2000).
Income: Per capita income: $18,831 (2000); Median household income: $43,534 (2000); Poverty rate: 7.7% (2000).
Education: High school graduation rate: 82.6% (2000); College graduation rate: 9.3% (2000).
Housing: Homeownership rate: 90.7% (2000); Median home value: $89,900 (2000); Median rent: $333 per month (2000); Median age of housing: 32 years (2000).
Transportation: Commute to work: 93.5% car, 0.0% public transportation, 1.6% walk, 4.2% work from home (2000); Travel time to work: 20.2% less than 15 minutes, 44.8% 15 to 30 minutes, 24.3% 30 to 45 minutes, 5.2% 45 to 60 minutes, 5.5% 60 minutes or more (2000)

MERRITT (township). Covers a land area of 31.742 square miles and a water area of 0 square miles. Located at 43.51° N. Lat.; 83.74° W. Long.
Population: 1,510 (2000); Race: 98.4% White, 0.0% Black, 0.2% Asian, 0.0% American Indian and Alaska Native, 7.3% Hispanic of any race, 0.0% two or more races (2000); Density: 47.6 persons per square mile (2000); Age: 25.9% under 18, 15.0% over 64 (2000); Marriage status: 21.7% never married, 66.5% now married, 6.2% widowed, 5.7% divorced (2000); Foreign born: 4.0% (2000); Ancestry (includes multiple ancestries): 44.7% German, 21.3% Polish, 12.7% Irish, 11.9% French (except Basque), 8.6% Other groups (2000).
Economy: Single-family building permits issued: 6 (2001) / 5 (2000); Multi-family building permits issued: 0 (2001) / 0 (2000); Employment by occupation: 8.7% management, 13.4% professional, 14.0% services, 29.7% sales, 1.3% farming, 10.9% construction, 22.1% production (2000).
Income: Per capita income: $19,420 (2000); Median household income: $44,861 (2000); Poverty rate: 5.4% (2000).
Taxes: Total city taxes per capita: $98 (1997); City property taxes per capita: $96 (1997).
Education: High school graduation rate: 78.0% (2000); College graduation rate: 9.6% (2000).
Housing: Homeownership rate: 91.9% (2000); Median home value: $89,600 (2000); Median rent: $338 per month (2000); Median age of housing: 45 years (2000).
Transportation: Commute to work: 95.4% car, 0.7% public transportation, 1.5% walk, 2.1% work from home (2000); Travel time to work: 25.6% less than 15 minutes, 44.0% 15 to 30 minutes, 21.4% 30 to 45 minutes, 3.0% 45 to 60 minutes, 6.0% 60 minutes or more (2000)

MONITOR (township). Covers a land area of 36.992 square miles and a water area of 0.007 square miles. Located at 43.61° N. Lat.; 83.96° W. Long.
Population: 10,037 (2000); Race: 97.7% White, 0.7% Black, 0.5% Asian, 0.2% American Indian and Alaska Native, 1.1% Hispanic of any race, 0.7% two or more races (2000); Density: 271.3 persons per square mile (2000); Age: 21.3% under 18, 19.3% over 64 (2000); Marriage status: 19.0% never married, 65.2% now married, 7.7% widowed, 8.1% divorced (2000); Foreign born: 1.1% (2000); Ancestry (includes multiple ancestries): 39.2% German, 22.4% Polish, 12.5% French (except Basque), 10.1% Irish, 9.1% English (2000).
Economy: Single-family building permits issued: 43 (2001) / 42 (2000); Multi-family building permits issued: 34 (2001) / 12 (2000); Employment by occupation: 10.2% management, 22.4% professional, 14.0% services, 27.2% sales, 0.0% farming, 12.6% construction, 13.7% production (2000).
Income: Per capita income: $23,644 (2000); Median household income: $50,106 (2000); Poverty rate: 5.5% (2000).
Taxes: Total city taxes per capita: $60 (1997); City property taxes per capita: $48 (1997).
Education: High school graduation rate: 84.2% (2000); College graduation rate: 17.6% (2000).

Housing: Homeownership rate: 93.2% (2000); Median home value: $115,800 (2000); Median rent: $419 per month (2000); Median age of housing: 33 years (2000).
Transportation: Commute to work: 97.1% car, 0.3% public transportation, 0.6% walk, 1.7% work from home (2000); Travel time to work: 33.9% less than 15 minutes, 50.1% 15 to 30 minutes, 8.3% 30 to 45 minutes, 2.9% 45 to 60 minutes, 4.8% 60 minutes or more (2000)

MOUNT FOREST (township). Covers a land area of 36.006 square miles and a water area of 0 square miles. Located at 43.86° N. Lat.; 84.09° W. Long.
Population: 1,405 (2000); Race: 98.4% White, 0.1% Black, 0.0% Asian, 0.7% American Indian and Alaska Native, 1.1% Hispanic of any race, 0.8% two or more races (2000); Density: 39.0 persons per square mile (2000); Age: 25.9% under 18, 9.3% over 64 (2000); Marriage status: 21.1% never married, 65.2% now married, 7.1% widowed, 6.7% divorced (2000); Foreign born: 0.1% (2000); Ancestry (includes multiple ancestries): 27.9% German, 25.2% Polish, 16.0% French (except Basque), 9.4% United States or American, 7.7% Irish (2000).
Economy: Single-family building permits issued: 24 (2001) / 24 (2000); Multi-family building permits issued: 0 (2001) / 0 (2000); Employment by occupation: 6.7% management, 12.0% professional, 11.3% services, 23.9% sales, 1.2% farming, 16.5% construction, 28.4% production (2000).
Income: Per capita income: $17,627 (2000); Median household income: $38,125 (2000); Poverty rate: 8.7% (2000).
Taxes: Total city taxes per capita: $59 (1997); City property taxes per capita: $58 (1997).
Education: High school graduation rate: 78.4% (2000); College graduation rate: 6.4% (2000).
Housing: Homeownership rate: 93.7% (2000); Median home value: $82,000 (2000); Median rent: $294 per month (2000); Median age of housing: 26 years (2000).
Transportation: Commute to work: 95.2% car, 0.0% public transportation, 1.1% walk, 3.7% work from home (2000); Travel time to work: 12.2% less than 15 minutes, 32.2% 15 to 30 minutes, 35.6% 30 to 45 minutes, 13.9% 45 to 60 minutes, 6.1% 60 minutes or more (2000)

MUNGER (unincorporated postal area, zip code 48747). Covers a land area of 32.058 square miles and a water area of 0 square miles. Located at 43.52° N. Lat.; 83.76° W. Long. Elevation is 596 feet.
Population: 1,542 (2000); Race: 97.7% White, 0.7% Black, 0.2% Asian, 0.1% American Indian and Alaska Native, 7.0% Hispanic of any race, 0.0% two or more races (2000); Density: 48.1 persons per square mile (2000); Age: 23.7% under 18, 16.1% over 64 (2000); Marriage status: 22.0% never married, 65.9% now married, 6.7% widowed, 5.4% divorced (2000); Foreign born: 4.0% (2000); Ancestry (includes multiple ancestries): 43.5% German, 22.3% Polish, 13.3% Irish, 9.8% French (except Basque), 9.5% English (2000).
Economy: Employment by occupation: 7.6% management, 16.0% professional, 12.9% services, 27.9% sales, 1.3% farming, 10.3% construction, 23.9% production (2000).
Income: Per capita income: $19,262 (2000); Median household income: $42,500 (2000); Poverty rate: 6.7% (2000).
Education: High school graduation rate: 75.9% (2000); College graduation rate: 11.4% (2000).
Housing: Homeownership rate: 93.9% (2000); Median home value: $81,900 (2000); Median rent: $325 per month (2000); Median age of housing: 47 years (2000).
Transportation: Commute to work: 93.6% car, 0.7% public transportation, 1.6% walk, 3.8% work from home (2000); Travel time to work: 25.4% less than 15 minutes, 45.4% 15 to 30 minutes, 20.9% 30 to 45 minutes, 2.5% 45 to 60 minutes, 5.7% 60 minutes or more (2000)

PINCONNING (city). Covers a land area of 0.869 square miles and a water area of 0 square miles. Located at 43.85° N. Lat.; 83.96° W. Long. Elevation is 596 feet.
History: The name of Pinconning is of Indian origin, meaning "place of the potato." The community was settled in 1866 and was an important rail center in logging days. Later it became a trading center in an area of sugar beets, chicory, and beans. Old maps show the Pinconning River as the Potato River.
Population: 1,386 (2000); Race: 97.9% White, 0.0% Black, 0.1% Asian, 0.4% American Indian and Alaska Native, 3.0% Hispanic of any race, 1.1% two or more races (2000); Density: 1,594.9 persons per square mile (2000); Age: 25.1% under 18, 20.4% over 64 (2000); Marriage status: 24.8% never married, 47.2% now married, 12.9% widowed, 15.1% divorced (2000); Foreign born: 0.3% (2000); Ancestry (includes multiple ancestries): 23.4% French (except Basque), 22.2% German, 18.4% Polish, 9.7% English, 9.7% Irish (2000).
Economy: Single-family building permits issued: 0 (2001) / 2 (2000); Multi-family building permits issued: 0 (2001) / 0 (2000); Employment by occupation: 5.5% management, 11.0% professional, 21.0% services, 21.6% sales, 0.0% farming, 13.5% construction, 27.5% production (2000).
Income: Per capita income: $16,210 (2000); Median household income: $27,188 (2000); Poverty rate: 15.9% (2000).
Taxes: Total city taxes per capita: $255 (1997); City property taxes per capita: $255 (1997).
Education: High school graduation rate: 78.0% (2000); College graduation rate: 9.0% (2000).

School District(s)

Pinconning Area Schools (PK-12)
2000 Enrollment: 2,106 517-879-4556

Housing: Homeownership rate: 70.5% (2000); Median home value: $65,100 (2000); Median rent: $281 per month (2000); Median age of housing: 37 years (2000).
Safety: Violent crime rate: 7.2 per 10,000 population; Property crime rate: 373.3 per 10,000 population (2001).
Newspapers: Pinconning Journal (1 x week)
Transportation: Commute to work: 86.6% car, 2.2% public transportation, 5.1% walk, 4.5% work from home (2000); Travel time to work: 40.0% less than 15 minutes, 18.2% 15 to 30 minutes, 20.8% 30 to 45 minutes, 11.4% 45 to 60 minutes, 9.5% 60 minutes or more (2000)

PINCONNING (township). Covers a land area of 36.565 square miles and a water area of 5.351 square miles. Located at 43.86° N. Lat.; 83.96° W. Long. Elevation is 596 feet.
History: Settled c.1866; incorporated as village 1877, as city 1931.
Population: 2,608 (2000); Race: 95.4% White, 0.0% Black, 0.1% Asian, 1.8% American Indian and Alaska Native, 1.9% Hispanic of any race, 1.4% two or more races (2000); Density: 71.3 persons per square mile (2000); Age: 24.3% under 18, 12.2% over 64 (2000); Marriage status: 23.9% never married, 63.1% now married, 5.1% widowed, 7.9% divorced (2000); Foreign born: 1.2% (2000); Ancestry (includes multiple ancestries): 29.5% German, 24.5% Polish, 23.8% French (except Basque), 8.0% Irish, 7.2% English (2000).
Economy: Agricultural trade center: sugar beets, grains, beans, cucumbers, soybeans, corn; livestock; food processing. Light manufacturing. Summer resort. Arenac County Saginaw Project, on Indian reservation, to Northeast. Single-family building permits issued: 2 (2001) / 6 (2000); Multi-family building permits issued: 0 (2001) / 0 (2000); Employment by occupation: 7.0% management, 10.2% professional, 18.5% services, 25.8% sales, 1.8% farming, 16.2% construction, 20.4% production (2000).
Income: Per capita income: $19,163 (2000); Median household income: $43,021 (2000); Poverty rate: 7.9% (2000).
Taxes: Total city taxes per capita: $57 (1997); City property taxes per capita: $50 (1997).
Education: High school graduation rate: 78.3% (2000); College graduation rate: 6.2% (2000).
Housing: Homeownership rate: 89.1% (2000); Median home value: $81,500 (2000); Median rent: $367 per month (2000); Median age of housing: 30 years (2000).
Transportation: Commute to work: 95.1% car, 0.0% public transportation, 1.0% walk, 2.1% work from home (2000); Travel time to work: 36.6% less than 15 minutes, 22.7% 15 to 30 minutes, 25.8% 30 to 45 minutes, 9.7% 45 to 60 minutes, 5.3% 60 minutes or more (2000)

PORTSMOUTH (township). Covers a land area of 19.999 square miles and a water area of 0.101 square miles. Located at 43.55° N. Lat.; 83.85° W. Long.
Population: 3,619 (2000); Race: 96.1% White, 1.4% Black, 0.0% Asian, 0.2% American Indian and Alaska Native, 1.7% Hispanic of any race, 2.0% two or more races (2000); Density: 181.0 persons per square mile (2000); Age: 23.4% under 18, 14.1% over 64 (2000); Marriage status: 21.6% never married, 64.9% now married, 5.7% widowed, 7.7% divorced (2000); Foreign born: 1.0% (2000); Ancestry (includes multiple ancestries): 35.0% Polish, 33.0% German, 8.9% French (except Basque), 8.5% Irish, 4.9% English (2000).
Economy: Single-family building permits issued: 8 (2001) / 15 (2000); Multi-family building permits issued: 0 (2001) / 0 (2000); Employment by occupation: 6.7% management, 13.9% professional, 23.0% services, 23.8% sales, 0.0% farming, 12.3% construction, 20.4% production (2000).
Income: Per capita income: $19,337 (2000); Median household income: $45,500 (2000); Poverty rate: 8.2% (2000).

Taxes: Total city taxes per capita: $52 (1997); City property taxes per capita: $43 (1997).
Education: High school graduation rate: 80.0% (2000); College graduation rate: 8.4% (2000).
Housing: Homeownership rate: 94.5% (2000); Median home value: $93,700 (2000); Median rent: $371 per month (2000); Median age of housing: 38 years (2000).
Transportation: Commute to work: 96.0% car, 0.0% public transportation, 0.0% walk, 4.0% work from home (2000); Travel time to work: 36.2% less than 15 minutes, 45.5% 15 to 30 minutes, 11.5% 30 to 45 minutes, 1.7% 45 to 60 minutes, 5.1% 60 minutes or more (2000)

WILLIAMS (township). Covers a land area of 33.543 square miles and a water area of 0.044 square miles. Located at 43.60° N. Lat.; 84.11° W. Long.
Population: 4,492 (2000); Race: 99.0% White, 0.0% Black, 0.0% Asian, 0.0% American Indian and Alaska Native, 2.1% Hispanic of any race, 0.0% two or more races (2000); Density: 133.9 persons per square mile (2000); Age: 27.5% under 18, 10.8% over 64 (2000); Marriage status: 22.9% never married, 65.1% now married, 5.0% widowed, 7.0% divorced (2000); Foreign born: 0.7% (2000); Ancestry (includes multiple ancestries): 41.6% German, 20.6% Polish, 11.8% French (except Basque), 9.3% English, 7.3% Irish (2000).
Economy: Single-family building permits issued: 45 (2001) / 23 (2000); Multi-family building permits issued: 0 (2001) / 0 (2000); Employment by occupation: 15.1% management, 19.6% professional, 11.9% services, 24.5% sales, 0.6% farming, 13.0% construction, 15.3% production (2000).
Income: Per capita income: $22,262 (2000); Median household income: $54,766 (2000); Poverty rate: 4.8% (2000).
Taxes: Total city taxes per capita: $162 (1997); City property taxes per capita: $151 (1997).
Education: High school graduation rate: 85.5% (2000); College graduation rate: 18.2% (2000).
Housing: Homeownership rate: 97.3% (2000); Median home value: $99,800 (2000); Median rent: $333 per month (2000); Median age of housing: 32 years (2000).
Transportation: Commute to work: 95.5% car, 0.1% public transportation, 0.0% walk, 4.4% work from home (2000); Travel time to work: 29.5% less than 15 minutes, 47.3% 15 to 30 minutes, 18.6% 30 to 45 minutes, 2.9% 45 to 60 minutes, 1.7% 60 minutes or more (2000)

Benzie County

Located in northwestern Michigan; bounded on the west by Lake Michigan; includes Crystal, Platte, and other lakes. Covers a land area of 321.30 square miles, a water area of 538.30 square miles, and is located in the Eastern Time Zone. The county government was organized in 1863. County seat is Beulah.

Weather Station: Frankfort — Elevation: 718 feet

	Jan	Feb	Mar	Apr	May	Jun	Jul	Aug	Sep	Oct	Nov	Dec
High	28	30	39	51	64	73	77	75	68	57	44	33
Low	17	18	24	34	44	52	58	59	52	42	32	22
Precip	2.8	2.0	2.4	2.6	2.7	3.2	3.0	3.4	4.2	3.3	3.0	2.8
Snow	37.4	22.0	14.7	4.4	0.2	0.0	0.0	0.0	tr	0.5	9.0	27.5

High and Low temperatures in degrees Fahrenheit; Precipitation and Snow in inches

Population: 15,998 (2000); Race: 96.1% White, 0.2% Black, 0.1% Asian, 1.9% American Indian and Alaska Native, 1.7% Hispanic of any race, 1.2% two or more races (2000); Density: 49.8 persons per square mile (2000); Age: 23.3% under 18, 17.5% over 64 (2000).
Religion: Five largest groups: 5.3% The United Methodist Church, 4.1% Catholic Church, 3.9% Evangelical Lutheran Church in America, 3.0% United Church of Christ, 1.8% The Church of Jesus Christ of Latter-day Saints (2000).
Economy: Unemployment rate: 6.8% (11/2002); Total civilian labor force: 8,066 (11/2002); Leading industries: 26.6% accommodation & food services; 17.6% retail trade; 13.3% manufacturing (2000); Companies that employ more than 1,000 persons: 0 (2000); Companies that employ more than 100 persons: 4 (2000); Farms: 140 totaling 22,556 acres (1997); Minority business ownership rate: 0.0% (1997); Women business ownership rate: 22.6% (1997); Retail sales per capita: $7,307 (1997). Single-family building permits issued: 274 (2001) / 250 (2000); Multi-family building permits issued: 0 (2001) / 0 (2000).
Income: Per capita income: $18,524 (2000); Median household income: $37,350 (2000); Poverty rate: 7.0% (2000); Bankruptcy rate: 3.58% (2001).
Taxes: Total county taxes per capita: $237 (1997); County property taxes per capita: $219 (1997).
Education: High school graduation rate: 85.4% (2000); College graduation rate: 20.0% (2000).
Housing: Homeownership rate: 85.8% (2000); Median home value: $107,400 (2000); Median rent: $403 per month (2000); Median age of housing: 27 years (2000).
Health: Birth rate: 114.4 per 10,000 population (1998); Age adjusted death rate: 83.4 per 10,000 population (1999); Age adjusted cancer mortality rate: 227.0 deaths per 100,000 population (1999). Air Quality Index: 70% good, 29% moderate, 1% unhealthy (percent of days in 2000). Number of physicians: 11.3 per 10,000 population (1999); Number of hospital beds: 30.0 per 10,000 population (1999).
Elections: 2000 Presidential election results: 43.9% Gore, 51.7% Bush, 3.9% Nader, 0.0% Buchanan
National and State Parks: Betsie River State Game Refuge; Pere Marquette State Forest
Additional Information Contacts
Benzie County Government Offices 231-882-9671
Benzie Chamber of Commerce 231-882-5801
Benzie County Board of Realtors 231-352-9870
Frankfort Chamber of Commerce 231-352-7251

Benzie County Communities

ALMIRA (township). Covers a land area of 33.805 square miles and a water area of 2.221 square miles. Located at 44.72° N. Lat.; 85.85° W. Long.
History: Almira Township was named for Almira Burrell who had come here from New York in 1863.
Population: 2,811 (2000); Race: 98.0% White, 0.1% Black, 0.0% Asian, 0.8% American Indian and Alaska Native, 0.1% Hispanic of any race, 1.1% two or more races (2000); Density: 83.2 persons per square mile (2000); Age: 28.4% under 18, 10.1% over 64 (2000); Marriage status: 19.9% never married, 67.4% now married, 3.9% widowed, 8.8% divorced (2000); Foreign born: 1.4% (2000); Ancestry (includes multiple ancestries): 31.9% German, 13.8% English, 12.3% Irish, 10.5% Polish, 7.7% French (except Basque) (2000).
Economy: Employment by occupation: 9.1% management, 15.9% professional, 18.0% services, 28.4% sales, 0.5% farming, 14.6% construction, 13.7% production (2000).
Income: Per capita income: $20,137 (2000); Median household income: $46,389 (2000); Poverty rate: 4.0% (2000).
Taxes: Total city taxes per capita: $122 (1997); City property taxes per capita: $120 (1997).
Education: High school graduation rate: 90.3% (2000); College graduation rate: 22.1% (2000).
Housing: Homeownership rate: 91.8% (2000); Median home value: $118,000 (2000); Median rent: $504 per month (2000); Median age of housing: 15 years (2000).
Transportation: Commute to work: 94.1% car, 0.9% public transportation, 1.9% walk, 2.9% work from home (2000); Travel time to work: 13.1% less than 15 minutes, 48.4% 15 to 30 minutes, 27.7% 30 to 45 minutes, 7.0% 45 to 60 minutes, 3.9% 60 minutes or more (2000)

BENZONIA (village). Covers a land area of 1.063 square miles and a water area of 0 square miles. Located at 44.61° N. Lat.; 86.10° W. Long.
History: Benzonia was platted in 1857 by a Congregational minister, Reverend Charles E. Bailey, who wanted to establish a Christian institution. The college closed in 1918.
Population: 519 (2000); Race: 93.0% White, 0.0% Black, 0.0% Asian, 3.6% American Indian and Alaska Native, 2.8% Hispanic of any race, 0.8% two or more races (2000); Density: 488.2 persons per square mile (2000); Age: 20.3% under 18, 24.1% over 64 (2000); Marriage status: 19.4% never married, 53.4% now married, 11.6% widowed, 15.5% divorced (2000); Foreign born: 1.3% (2000); Ancestry (includes multiple ancestries): 26.7% German, 15.2% English, 8.3% Other groups, 8.1% Irish, 6.6% French (except Basque) (2000).
Economy: Single-family building permits issued: n/a (2001) / 0 (2000); Multi-family building permits issued: n/a (2001) / 0 (2000); Employment by occupation: 7.5% management, 12.1% professional, 21.6% services, 25.1% sales, 0.0% farming, 10.1% construction, 23.6% production (2000).
Income: Per capita income: $15,515 (2000); Median household income: $28,650 (2000); Poverty rate: 10.1% (2000).
Taxes: Total city taxes per capita: $224 (1997); City property taxes per capita: $214 (1997).
Education: High school graduation rate: 83.8% (2000); College graduation rate: 17.5% (2000).

School District(s)

Benzie County Central Schools (KG-12)
2000 Enrollment: 1,953 231-882-9654

Housing: Homeownership rate: 84.3% (2000); Median home value: $88,000 (2000); Median rent: $378 per month (2000); Median age of housing: 43 years (2000).
Transportation: Commute to work: 84.8% car, 0.0% public transportation, 7.6% walk, 5.1% work from home (2000); Travel time to work: 57.8% less than 15 minutes, 21.9% 15 to 30 minutes, 5.3% 30 to 45 minutes, 9.1% 45 to 60 minutes, 5.9% 60 minutes or more (2000)

Additional Information Contacts

Benzie Chamber of Commerce 231-882-5801

BENZONIA (township). Covers a land area of 28.284 square miles and a water area of 5.706 square miles. Located at 44.63° N. Lat.; 86.09° W. Long.
Population: 2,839 (2000); Race: 94.8% White, 0.0% Black, 0.1% Asian, 3.2% American Indian and Alaska Native, 2.8% Hispanic of any race, 0.7% two or more races (2000); Density: 100.4 persons per square mile (2000); Age: 20.3% under 18, 23.1% over 64 (2000); Marriage status: 21.1% never married, 59.1% now married, 9.4% widowed, 10.4% divorced (2000); Foreign born: 2.4% (2000); Ancestry (includes multiple ancestries): 23.7% German, 17.0% English, 11.4% Irish, 6.5% United States or American, 6.3% French (except Basque) (2000).
Economy: In agricultural area: corn, beans. Manufacturing: motor vehicle parts. Employment by occupation: 9.9% management, 14.9% professional, 20.2% services, 24.7% sales, 0.9% farming, 12.3% construction, 17.2% production (2000).
Income: Per capita income: $18,720 (2000); Median household income: $32,837 (2000); Poverty rate: 7.0% (2000).
Taxes: Total city taxes per capita: $70 (1997); City property taxes per capita: $70 (1997).
Education: High school graduation rate: 86.6% (2000); College graduation rate: 20.3% (2000).
Housing: Homeownership rate: 82.5% (2000); Median home value: $120,400 (2000); Median rent: $404 per month (2000); Median age of housing: 37 years (2000).
Transportation: Commute to work: 88.3% car, 1.1% public transportation, 4.4% walk, 5.6% work from home (2000); Travel time to work: 53.5% less than 15 minutes, 20.1% 15 to 30 minutes, 11.7% 30 to 45 minutes, 9.7% 45 to 60 minutes, 5.0% 60 minutes or more (2000)

BEULAH (village). Covers a land area of 0.455 square miles and a water area of 0 square miles. Located at 44.63° N. Lat.; 86.09° W. Long. Elevation is 595 feet.
History: Beulah, established on Crystal Lake about 1880, became the business center for the nearby tourist region. Smelt runs, the result of fish planted in Crystal Lake in 1912, attracted many sportsmen. The village was named by its founder, Reverend Charles E. Bailey, for the land of Beulah mentioned in Isaiah 62:4.
Population: 363 (2000); Race: 97.5% White, 0.0% Black, 0.0% Asian, 0.6% American Indian and Alaska Native, 2.0% Hispanic of any race, 0.6% two or more races (2000); Density: 798.2 persons per square mile (2000); Age: 13.8% under 18, 23.7% over 64 (2000); Marriage status: 28.5% never married, 43.3% now married, 14.6% widowed, 13.6% divorced (2000); Foreign born: 1.4% (2000); Ancestry (includes multiple ancestries): 29.7% German, 16.4% English, 15.3% Irish, 7.1% Polish, 6.8% United States or American (2000).
Economy: Employment by occupation: 12.0% management, 23.4% professional, 19.4% services, 25.1% sales, 1.1% farming, 9.1% construction, 9.7% production (2000).
Income: Per capita income: $22,389 (2000); Median household income: $31,250 (2000); Poverty rate: 17.2% (2000).
Taxes: Total city taxes per capita: $364 (1997); City property taxes per capita: $356 (1997).
Education: High school graduation rate: 91.5% (2000); College graduation rate: 24.3% (2000).
Housing: Homeownership rate: 60.7% (2000); Median home value: $94,700 (2000); Median rent: $367 per month (2000); Median age of housing: 51 years (2000).
Transportation: Commute to work: 79.3% car, 3.0% public transportation, 12.4% walk, 5.3% work from home (2000); Travel time to work: 54.4% less than 15 minutes, 13.8% 15 to 30 minutes, 15.0% 30 to 45 minutes, 8.1% 45 to 60 minutes, 8.8% 60 minutes or more (2000)

BLAINE (township). Covers a land area of 19.428 square miles and a water area of 1.550 square miles. Located at 44.56° N. Lat.; 86.19° W. Long.
Population: 491 (2000); Race: 98.5% White, 0.0% Black, 0.0% Asian, 0.0% American Indian and Alaska Native, 2.4% Hispanic of any race, 1.5% two or more races (2000); Density: 25.3 persons per square mile (2000); Age: 16.5% under 18, 19.3% over 64 (2000); Marriage status: 13.2% never married, 69.0% now married, 6.1% widowed, 11.7% divorced (2000); Foreign born: 2.6% (2000); Ancestry (includes multiple ancestries): 25.8% German, 16.3% English, 10.6% United States or American, 8.9% French (except Basque), 8.7% Polish (2000).
Economy: Employment by occupation: 16.9% management, 20.2% professional, 4.2% services, 25.8% sales, 4.7% farming, 16.0% construction, 12.2% production (2000).
Income: Per capita income: $21,465 (2000); Median household income: $42,500 (2000); Poverty rate: 4.3% (2000).
Taxes: Total city taxes per capita: $86 (1997); City property taxes per capita: $86 (1997).
Education: High school graduation rate: 90.6% (2000); College graduation rate: 23.7% (2000).
Housing: Homeownership rate: 90.1% (2000); Median home value: $100,000 (2000); Median rent: $325 per month (2000); Median age of housing: 40 years (2000).
Transportation: Commute to work: 89.6% car, 0.0% public transportation, 3.3% walk, 4.7% work from home (2000); Travel time to work: 29.9% less than 15 minutes, 36.3% 15 to 30 minutes, 9.0% 30 to 45 minutes, 12.4% 45 to 60 minutes, 12.4% 60 minutes or more (2000)

COLFAX (township). Covers a land area of 35.769 square miles and a water area of 0.141 square miles. Located at 44.55° N. Lat.; 85.87° W. Long.
Population: 585 (2000); Race: 92.6% White, 0.5% Black, 0.0% Asian, 2.3% American Indian and Alaska Native, 1.4% Hispanic of any race, 1.9% two or more races (2000); Density: 16.4 persons per square mile (2000); Age: 28.8% under 18, 10.7% over 64 (2000); Marriage status: 19.4% never married, 66.9% now married, 3.0% widowed, 10.6% divorced (2000); Foreign born: 0.4% (2000); Ancestry (includes multiple ancestries): 20.9% German, 13.5% English, 12.8% Dutch, 9.7% Other groups, 5.8% Irish (2000).
Economy: Employment by occupation: 5.7% management, 6.0% professional, 23.0% services, 20.4% sales, 0.0% farming, 20.8% construction, 24.2% production (2000).
Income: Per capita income: $14,812 (2000); Median household income: $37,250 (2000); Poverty rate: 6.9% (2000).
Taxes: Total city taxes per capita: $31 (1997); City property taxes per capita: $31 (1997).
Education: High school graduation rate: 79.5% (2000); College graduation rate: 8.1% (2000).
Housing: Homeownership rate: 93.2% (2000); Median home value: $80,500 (2000); Median rent: $363 per month (2000); Median age of housing: 21 years (2000).
Transportation: Commute to work: 94.3% car, 0.0% public transportation, 0.0% walk, 3.4% work from home (2000); Travel time to work: 16.2% less than 15 minutes, 23.7% 15 to 30 minutes, 39.5% 30 to 45 minutes, 9.1% 45 to 60 minutes, 11.5% 60 minutes or more (2000)

CRYSTAL LAKE (township). Covers a land area of 12.821 square miles and a water area of 4.247 square miles. Located at 44.64° N. Lat.; 86.21° W. Long.
Population: 960 (2000); Race: 98.9% White, 0.0% Black, 0.2% Asian, 0.4% American Indian and Alaska Native, 0.0% Hispanic of any race, 0.5% two or more races (2000); Density: 74.9 persons per square mile (2000); Age: 21.6% under 18, 21.3% over 64 (2000); Marriage status: 15.8% never married, 69.9% now married, 6.9% widowed, 7.4% divorced (2000); Foreign born: 2.1% (2000); Ancestry (includes multiple ancestries): 29.2% German, 15.3% English, 11.5% Irish, 7.0% United States or American, 5.6% Dutch (2000).
Economy: Employment by occupation: 10.0% management, 19.1% professional, 21.5% services, 25.4% sales, 0.0% farming, 10.3% construction, 13.6% production (2000).
Income: Per capita income: $20,987 (2000); Median household income: $36,528 (2000); Poverty rate: 5.3% (2000).
Taxes: Total city taxes per capita: $125 (1997); City property taxes per capita: $123 (1997).
Education: High school graduation rate: 88.9% (2000); College graduation rate: 31.5% (2000).
Housing: Homeownership rate: 81.9% (2000); Median home value: $134,800 (2000); Median rent: $400 per month (2000); Median age of housing: 42 years (2000).
Transportation: Commute to work: 93.8% car, 0.2% public transportation, 0.7% walk, 5.3% work from home (2000); Travel time to work: 64.7% less

than 15 minutes, 15.7% 15 to 30 minutes, 8.4% 30 to 45 minutes, 6.3% 45 to 60 minutes, 4.8% 60 minutes or more (2000)

ELBERTA (village). Covers a land area of 0.746 square miles and a water area of 0.232 square miles. Located at 44.61° N. Lat.; 86.22° W. Long. Elevation is 579 feet.
History: Elberta grew around a charcoal-iron industry. When that closed, the town lagged until car-ferry service was begun from here to Manitowoc, Wisconsin, and to points in Upper Michigan.
Population: 457 (2000); Race: 95.8% White, 0.0% Black, 0.0% Asian, 1.8% American Indian and Alaska Native, 3.4% Hispanic of any race, 1.8% two or more races (2000); Density: 612.9 persons per square mile (2000); Age: 32.4% under 18, 11.9% over 64 (2000); Marriage status: 21.2% never married, 56.0% now married, 6.0% widowed, 16.8% divorced (2000); Foreign born: 0.0% (2000); Ancestry (includes multiple ancestries): 28.4% German, 15.1% Other groups, 14.7% Irish, 11.9% English, 4.8% French (except Basque) (2000).
Economy: Employment by occupation: 7.6% management, 14.6% professional, 29.8% services, 11.6% sales, 1.0% farming, 13.1% construction, 22.2% production (2000).
Income: Per capita income: $13,594 (2000); Median household income: $28,403 (2000); Poverty rate: 10.7% (2000).
Taxes: Total city taxes per capita: $133 (1997); City property taxes per capita: $131 (1997).
Education: High school graduation rate: 75.6% (2000); College graduation rate: 9.9% (2000).
Housing: Homeownership rate: 76.8% (2000); Median home value: $72,800 (2000); Median rent: $473 per month (2000); Median age of housing: 60+ years (2000).
Transportation: Commute to work: 81.3% car, 0.0% public transportation, 8.6% walk, 4.0% work from home (2000); Travel time to work: 53.7% less than 15 minutes, 17.9% 15 to 30 minutes, 4.7% 30 to 45 minutes, 5.3% 45 to 60 minutes, 18.4% 60 minutes or more (2000)

FRANKFORT (city). Covers a land area of 1.395 square miles and a water area of 0.192 square miles. Located at 44.63° N. Lat.; 86.23° W. Long. Elevation is 600 feet.
History: Frankfort was established on the hills overlooking Betsie Lake and the Betsie River, where docks accommodated the commercial fishing boats.
Population: 1,513 (2000); Race: 94.3% White, 0.9% Black, 0.3% Asian, 3.0% American Indian and Alaska Native, 1.9% Hispanic of any race, 1.1% two or more races (2000); Density: 1,084.4 persons per square mile (2000); Age: 17.2% under 18, 32.4% over 64 (2000); Marriage status: 18.8% never married, 54.5% now married, 16.5% widowed, 10.1% divorced (2000); Foreign born: 1.6% (2000); Ancestry (includes multiple ancestries): 24.3% German, 18.1% English, 11.6% Irish, 10.5% Norwegian, 9.0% Other groups (2000).
Economy: Single-family building permits issued: n/a (2001) / 0 (2000); Multi-family building permits issued: n/a (2001) / 0 (2000); Employment by occupation: 9.2% management, 22.8% professional, 19.6% services, 21.3% sales, 1.2% farming, 12.8% construction, 13.1% production (2000).
Income: Per capita income: $20,132 (2000); Median household income: $33,821 (2000); Poverty rate: 10.2% (2000).
Taxes: Total city taxes per capita: $462 (2000); City property taxes per capita: $461 (2000).
Education: High school graduation rate: 85.0% (2000); College graduation rate: 28.5% (2000).

School District(s)

Frankfort-Elberta Area Schools (KG-12)
2000 Enrollment: 593 231-352-4641

Housing: Homeownership rate: 70.6% (2000); Median home value: $101,900 (2000); Median rent: $363 per month (2000); Median age of housing: 48 years (2000).
Hospitals: Paul Oliver Memorial Hospital (48 beds)
Safety: Violent crime rate: 0.0 per 10,000 population; Property crime rate: 486.5 per 10,000 population (2001).
Newspapers: The Benzie County Record-Patriot (1 x week)
Transportation: Commute to work: 86.3% car, 0.0% public transportation, 7.7% walk, 4.4% work from home (2000); Travel time to work: 60.1% less than 15 minutes, 19.0% 15 to 30 minutes, 6.4% 30 to 45 minutes, 7.5% 45 to 60 minutes, 7.0% 60 minutes or more (2000)

Additional Information Contacts

Benzie County Board of Realtors........................ 231-352-9870
Frankfort Chamber of Commerce 231-352-7251

GILMORE (township). Covers a land area of 7.251 square miles and a water area of 0.232 square miles. Located at 44.60° N. Lat.; 86.21° W. Long.
Population: 850 (2000); Race: 96.5% White, 0.0% Black, 0.0% Asian, 1.0% American Indian and Alaska Native, 3.2% Hispanic of any race, 1.1% two or more races (2000); Density: 117.2 persons per square mile (2000); Age: 29.5% under 18, 13.5% over 64 (2000); Marriage status: 18.4% never married, 63.4% now married, 5.2% widowed, 13.0% divorced (2000); Foreign born: 0.2% (2000); Ancestry (includes multiple ancestries): 26.8% German, 15.1% Irish, 13.3% English, 10.0% Other groups, 7.8% United States or American (2000).
Economy: Employment by occupation: 9.2% management, 18.1% professional, 22.5% services, 18.3% sales, 0.6% farming, 11.9% construction, 19.4% production (2000).
Income: Per capita income: $14,999 (2000); Median household income: $29,712 (2000); Poverty rate: 9.1% (2000).
Taxes: Total city taxes per capita: $27 (1997); City property taxes per capita: $27 (1997).
Education: High school graduation rate: 82.2% (2000); College graduation rate: 14.8% (2000).
Housing: Homeownership rate: 83.4% (2000); Median home value: $84,300 (2000); Median rent: $463 per month (2000); Median age of housing: 41 years (2000).
Transportation: Commute to work: 86.8% car, 0.0% public transportation, 5.4% walk, 3.9% work from home (2000); Travel time to work: 52.5% less than 15 minutes, 21.4% 15 to 30 minutes, 5.0% 30 to 45 minutes, 8.2% 45 to 60 minutes, 12.9% 60 minutes or more (2000)

HOMESTEAD (township). Covers a land area of 30.235 square miles and a water area of 0 square miles. Located at 44.65° N. Lat.; 85.98° W. Long.
Population: 2,078 (2000); Race: 95.4% White, 0.0% Black, 0.2% Asian, 2.5% American Indian and Alaska Native, 0.9% Hispanic of any race, 1.4% two or more races (2000); Density: 68.7 persons per square mile (2000); Age: 24.5% under 18, 12.7% over 64 (2000); Marriage status: 16.7% never married, 62.4% now married, 8.2% widowed, 12.8% divorced (2000); Foreign born: 1.5% (2000); Ancestry (includes multiple ancestries): 23.8% German, 12.9% English, 11.5% Irish, 7.3% Other groups, 6.4% Polish (2000).
Economy: Employment by occupation: 8.4% management, 11.3% professional, 20.8% services, 24.1% sales, 0.6% farming, 14.5% construction, 20.2% production (2000).
Income: Per capita income: $15,387 (2000); Median household income: $35,833 (2000); Poverty rate: 8.0% (2000).
Taxes: Total city taxes per capita: $34 (1997); City property taxes per capita: $33 (1997).
Education: High school graduation rate: 81.1% (2000); College graduation rate: 11.7% (2000).
Housing: Homeownership rate: 90.4% (2000); Median home value: $85,800 (2000); Median rent: $403 per month (2000); Median age of housing: 24 years (2000).
Transportation: Commute to work: 92.8% car, 0.9% public transportation, 2.7% walk, 3.2% work from home (2000); Travel time to work: 28.8% less than 15 minutes, 30.4% 15 to 30 minutes, 26.5% 30 to 45 minutes, 7.0% 45 to 60 minutes, 7.4% 60 minutes or more (2000)

HONOR (village). Covers a land area of 0.551 square miles and a water area of 0 square miles. Located at 44.66° N. Lat.; 86.02° W. Long. Elevation is 605 feet.
History: Honor was founded in 1895 on the Platte River when the Guelph Patent Cask Company was established here. It was named for the daughter of the company's general manager.
Population: 299 (2000); Race: 90.8% White, 0.0% Black, 0.0% Asian, 5.0% American Indian and Alaska Native, 2.1% Hispanic of any race, 4.3% two or more races (2000); Density: 543.1 persons per square mile (2000); Age: 20.9% under 18, 18.1% over 64 (2000); Marriage status: 17.0% never married, 47.7% now married, 14.5% widowed, 20.9% divorced (2000); Foreign born: 1.4% (2000); Ancestry (includes multiple ancestries): 19.5% Irish, 17.7% German, 14.5% French (except Basque), 11.0% English, 10.6% Other groups (2000).
Economy: Employment by occupation: 14.1% management, 10.2% professional, 22.7% services, 25.0% sales, 0.0% farming, 12.5% construction, 15.6% production (2000).
Income: Per capita income: $14,274 (2000); Median household income: $32,917 (2000); Poverty rate: 11.9% (2000).

Taxes: Total city taxes per capita: $161 (2000); City property taxes per capita: $157 (2000).
Education: High school graduation rate: 79.1% (2000); College graduation rate: 12.2% (2000).
Housing: Homeownership rate: 79.5% (2000); Median home value: $70,000 (2000); Median rent: $413 per month (2000); Median age of housing: 37 years (2000).
Newspapers: Advisor Community Weekly (1 x week)
Transportation: Commute to work: 96.1% car, 0.0% public transportation, 1.6% walk, 1.6% work from home (2000); Travel time to work: 35.7% less than 15 minutes, 25.4% 15 to 30 minutes, 19.0% 30 to 45 minutes, 4.0% 45 to 60 minutes, 15.9% 60 minutes or more (2000)

INLAND (township). Covers a land area of 35.830 square miles and a water area of 0.372 square miles. Located at 44.66° N. Lat.; 85.88° W. Long.
Population: 1,587 (2000); Race: 95.9% White, 0.1% Black, 0.1% Asian, 1.7% American Indian and Alaska Native, 1.9% Hispanic of any race, 1.7% two or more races (2000); Density: 44.3 persons per square mile (2000); Age: 25.6% under 18, 9.1% over 64 (2000); Marriage status: 22.2% never married, 59.3% now married, 4.9% widowed, 13.7% divorced (2000); Foreign born: 1.3% (2000); Ancestry (includes multiple ancestries): 26.6% German, 13.8% English, 13.4% Irish, 8.1% French (except Basque), 7.5% Polish (2000).
Economy: Employment by occupation: 5.1% management, 10.2% professional, 18.8% services, 26.0% sales, 0.2% farming, 17.2% construction, 22.5% production (2000).
Income: Per capita income: $15,935 (2000); Median household income: $38,125 (2000); Poverty rate: 7.8% (2000).
Taxes: Total city taxes per capita: $20 (1997); City property taxes per capita: $18 (1997).
Education: High school graduation rate: 83.1% (2000); College graduation rate: 9.9% (2000).
Housing: Homeownership rate: 86.5% (2000); Median home value: $103,000 (2000); Median rent: $388 per month (2000); Median age of housing: 18 years (2000).
Transportation: Commute to work: 94.9% car, 0.2% public transportation, 0.2% walk, 2.7% work from home (2000); Travel time to work: 13.6% less than 15 minutes, 44.7% 15 to 30 minutes, 32.6% 30 to 45 minutes, 4.7% 45 to 60 minutes, 4.5% 60 minutes or more (2000)

JOYFIELD (township). Covers a land area of 20.008 square miles and a water area of 0 square miles. Located at 44.56° N. Lat.; 86.09° W. Long.
Population: 777 (2000); Race: 96.4% White, 0.4% Black, 0.0% Asian, 1.1% American Indian and Alaska Native, 4.5% Hispanic of any race, 1.0% two or more races (2000); Density: 38.8 persons per square mile (2000); Age: 27.9% under 18, 12.2% over 64 (2000); Marriage status: 12.0% never married, 72.9% now married, 5.0% widowed, 10.0% divorced (2000); Foreign born: 3.1% (2000); Ancestry (includes multiple ancestries): 22.8% German, 11.2% English, 9.0% Irish, 8.8% French (except Basque), 7.7% Other groups (2000).
Economy: Employment by occupation: 8.6% management, 10.4% professional, 23.9% services, 23.1% sales, 0.6% farming, 13.3% construction, 20.2% production (2000).
Income: Per capita income: $14,692 (2000); Median household income: $36,029 (2000); Poverty rate: 9.5% (2000).
Taxes: Total city taxes per capita: $20 (1997); City property taxes per capita: $20 (1997).
Education: High school graduation rate: 77.9% (2000); College graduation rate: 8.0% (2000).
Housing: Homeownership rate: 90.5% (2000); Median home value: $91,600 (2000); Median rent: $403 per month (2000); Median age of housing: 24 years (2000).
Transportation: Commute to work: 95.2% car, 0.0% public transportation, 0.6% walk, 3.0% work from home (2000); Travel time to work: 36.3% less than 15 minutes, 28.6% 15 to 30 minutes, 13.8% 30 to 45 minutes, 11.4% 45 to 60 minutes, 9.8% 60 minutes or more (2000)

LAKE (township). Covers a land area of 23.669 square miles and a water area of 11.468 square miles. Located at 44.69° N. Lat.; 86.13° W. Long.
Population: 635 (2000); Race: 99.0% White, 0.3% Black, 0.3% Asian, 0.0% American Indian and Alaska Native, 0.0% Hispanic of any race, 0.3% two or more races (2000); Density: 26.8 persons per square mile (2000); Age: 9.1% under 18, 40.9% over 64 (2000); Marriage status: 8.5% never married, 78.0% now married, 8.7% widowed, 4.9% divorced (2000); Foreign born: 2.2% (2000); Ancestry (includes multiple ancestries): 27.8% German, 26.2% English, 10.9% Irish, 8.6% Polish, 8.0% Dutch (2000).
Economy: Employment by occupation: 19.3% management, 31.8% professional, 4.2% services, 28.6% sales, 0.0% farming, 5.7% construction, 10.4% production (2000).
Income: Per capita income: $31,021 (2000); Median household income: $46,979 (2000); Poverty rate: 2.6% (2000).
Taxes: Total city taxes per capita: $173 (1997); City property taxes per capita: $171 (1997).
Education: High school graduation rate: 94.7% (2000); College graduation rate: 48.2% (2000).
Housing: Homeownership rate: 90.4% (2000); Median home value: $230,500 (2000); Median rent: $500 per month (2000); Median age of housing: 29 years (2000).
Transportation: Commute to work: 87.6% car, 0.0% public transportation, 1.1% walk, 10.2% work from home (2000); Travel time to work: 28.7% less than 15 minutes, 48.5% 15 to 30 minutes, 10.2% 30 to 45 minutes, 4.2% 45 to 60 minutes, 8.4% 60 minutes or more (2000)

LAKE ANN (village). Covers a land area of 0.436 square miles and a water area of 0.033 square miles. Located at 44.72° N. Lat.; 85.84° W. Long. Elevation is 887 feet.
History: Both the lake and the village of Lake Ann were named for the wife of A.P. Wheelock, the first settler here in 1862.
Population: 276 (2000); Race: 96.8% White, 0.0% Black, 0.0% Asian, 1.6% American Indian and Alaska Native, 0.6% Hispanic of any race, 1.6% two or more races (2000); Density: 632.9 persons per square mile (2000); Age: 23.9% under 18, 15.9% over 64 (2000); Marriage status: 27.3% never married, 60.0% now married, 3.8% widowed, 8.8% divorced (2000); Foreign born: 0.0% (2000); Ancestry (includes multiple ancestries): 29.3% German, 20.7% English, 11.5% Other groups, 8.6% French Canadian, 6.7% Scottish (2000).
Economy: Employment by occupation: 8.6% management, 13.0% professional, 17.3% services, 34.6% sales, 3.1% farming, 11.1% construction, 12.3% production (2000).
Income: Per capita income: $17,387 (2000); Median household income: $42,917 (2000); Poverty rate: 4.8% (2000).
Education: High school graduation rate: 89.9% (2000); College graduation rate: 20.7% (2000).
Housing: Homeownership rate: 78.0% (2000); Median home value: $129,200 (2000); Median rent: $506 per month (2000); Median age of housing: 32 years (2000).
Transportation: Commute to work: 82.7% car, 0.0% public transportation, 4.7% walk, 10.7% work from home (2000); Travel time to work: 19.4% less than 15 minutes, 47.0% 15 to 30 minutes, 14.9% 30 to 45 minutes, 9.7% 45 to 60 minutes, 9.0% 60 minutes or more (2000)

PLATTE (township). Covers a land area of 36.216 square miles and a water area of 0.160 square miles. Located at 44.73° N. Lat.; 86.00° W. Long.
Population: 342 (2000); Race: 95.4% White, 0.0% Black, 0.0% Asian, 1.7% American Indian and Alaska Native, 2.3% Hispanic of any race, 2.3% two or more races (2000); Density: 9.4 persons per square mile (2000); Age: 22.0% under 18, 11.3% over 64 (2000); Marriage status: 20.3% never married, 66.5% now married, 3.6% widowed, 9.6% divorced (2000); Foreign born: 1.4% (2000); Ancestry (includes multiple ancestries): 26.9% German, 13.6% English, 11.0% Irish, 9.2% United States or American, 6.1% French Canadian (2000).
Economy: Employment by occupation: 9.5% management, 13.4% professional, 16.8% services, 14.0% sales, 6.1% farming, 21.2% construction, 19.0% production (2000).
Income: Per capita income: $18,499 (2000); Median household income: $36,979 (2000); Poverty rate: 6.1% (2000).
Taxes: Total city taxes per capita: $23 (1997); City property taxes per capita: $23 (1997).
Education: High school graduation rate: 87.7% (2000); College graduation rate: 19.8% (2000).
Housing: Homeownership rate: 91.9% (2000); Median home value: $100,000 (2000); Median age of housing: 21 years (2000).
Transportation: Commute to work: 82.5% car, 1.1% public transportation, 5.6% walk, 10.7% work from home (2000); Travel time to work: 27.8% less than 15 minutes, 34.2% 15 to 30 minutes, 15.8% 30 to 45 minutes, 15.8% 45 to 60 minutes, 6.3% 60 minutes or more (2000)

THOMPSONVILLE (village). Covers a land area of 1.006 square miles and a water area of 0 square miles. Located at 44.52° N. Lat.; 85.94° W. Long. Elevation is 793 feet.
Population: 457 (2000); Race: 91.7% White, 0.0% Black, 0.0% Asian, 4.0% American Indian and Alaska Native, 2.6% Hispanic of any race, 3.4% two or

more races (2000); Density: 454.5 persons per square mile (2000); Age: 28.1% under 18, 13.8% over 64 (2000); Marriage status: 28.7% never married, 49.0% now married, 7.1% widowed, 15.2% divorced (2000); Foreign born: 0.8% (2000); Ancestry (includes multiple ancestries): 26.7% German, 15.4% English, 13.2% Other groups, 10.7% Dutch, 10.7% Irish (2000).
Economy: Crystal Mt. Ski Area to West. Employment by occupation: 4.6% management, 3.8% professional, 33.3% services, 14.8% sales, 0.0% farming, 13.1% construction, 30.4% production (2000).
Income: Per capita income: $12,104 (2000); Median household income: $29,125 (2000); Poverty rate: 13.3% (2000).
Taxes: Total city taxes per capita: $55 (2000); City property taxes per capita: $50 (2000).
Education: High school graduation rate: 65.9% (2000); College graduation rate: 5.0% (2000).
Housing: Homeownership rate: 83.3% (2000); Median home value: $55,000 (2000); Median rent: $368 per month (2000); Median age of housing: 42 years (2000).
Transportation: Commute to work: 89.5% car, 0.0% public transportation, 3.4% walk, 7.2% work from home (2000); Travel time to work: 25.5% less than 15 minutes, 24.5% 15 to 30 minutes, 33.6% 30 to 45 minutes, 9.1% 45 to 60 minutes, 7.3% 60 minutes or more (2000)

WELDON (township). Covers a land area of 36.601 square miles and a water area of 0.025 square miles. Located at 44.55° N. Lat.; 85.98° W. Long. Elevation is 833 feet.
Population: 530 (2000); Race: 93.0% White, 0.0% Black, 0.0% Asian, 3.3% American Indian and Alaska Native, 3.3% Hispanic of any race, 2.4% two or more races (2000); Density: 14.5 persons per square mile (2000); Age: 21.2% under 18, 18.1% over 64 (2000); Marriage status: 22.4% never married, 55.4% now married, 7.1% widowed, 15.1% divorced (2000); Foreign born: 1.1% (2000); Ancestry (includes multiple ancestries): 27.3% German, 18.5% English, 13.4% Irish, 11.5% Other groups, 7.0% United States or American (2000).
Economy: Employment by occupation: 10.9% management, 11.6% professional, 24.3% services, 13.9% sales, 0.0% farming, 10.1% construction, 29.2% production (2000).
Income: Per capita income: $17,725 (2000); Median household income: $33,125 (2000); Poverty rate: 12.6% (2000).
Taxes: Total city taxes per capita: $99 (1997); City property taxes per capita: $99 (1997).
Education: High school graduation rate: 71.4% (2000); College graduation rate: 10.9% (2000).
Housing: Homeownership rate: 84.1% (2000); Median home value: $71,000 (2000); Median rent: $375 per month (2000); Median age of housing: 18 years (2000).
Transportation: Commute to work: 87.3% car, 0.0% public transportation, 5.4% walk, 7.3% work from home (2000); Travel time to work: 28.2% less than 15 minutes, 23.7% 15 to 30 minutes, 29.5% 30 to 45 minutes, 13.3% 45 to 60 minutes, 5.4% 60 minutes or more (2000)

Berrien County

Located in southwestern Michigan; bounded on the south by Indiana, and on the west by Lake Michigan. Covers a land area of 571.00 square miles, a water area of 1,010.40 square miles, and is located in the Eastern Time Zone. The county government was organized in 1829. County seat is St. Joseph.

Berrien County is part of the Benton Harbor, MI MSA. The entire metro area includes: Berrien County

Weather Station: Benton Harbor Ross Field — Elevation: 626 feet

	Jan	Feb	Mar	Apr	May	Jun	Jul	Aug	Sep	Oct	Nov	Dec
High	32	36	46	58	69	79	83	81	74	63	49	37
Low	18	19	27	37	46	56	61	59	52	42	32	23
Precip	2.1	1.6	2.5	3.7	3.3	3.5	3.3	3.5	4.2	3.1	3.3	2.7
Snow	26.2	18.8	7.9	1.1	tr	0.0	0.0	0.0	tr	0.4	3.6	19.9

High and Low temperatures in degrees Fahrenheit; Precipitation and Snow in inches

Weather Station: Eau Claire 4 NE — Elevation: 869 feet

	Jan	Feb	Mar	Apr	May	Jun	Jul	Aug	Sep	Oct	Nov	Dec
High	31	35	46	59	71	80	84	81	74	62	48	36
Low	17	20	28	38	49	58	63	62	54	44	33	23
Precip	2.0	1.6	2.6	3.4	3.4	3.5	3.4	3.7	3.8	3.1	3.3	2.7
Snow	25.9	15.1	8.4	1.8	tr	0.0	0.0	0.0	0.0	0.4	7.6	21.6

High and Low temperatures in degrees Fahrenheit; Precipitation and Snow in inches

Population: 162,453 (2000); Race: 79.6% White, 16.0% Black, 1.0% Asian, 0.5% American Indian and Alaska Native, 2.8% Hispanic of any race, 1.7% two or more races (2000); Density: 284.5 persons per square mile (2000); Age: 25.9% under 18, 14.5% over 64 (2000).
Religion: Five largest groups: 15.6% Catholic Church, 5.5% Lutheran Church—Missouri Synod, 5.5% Seventh-day Adventist Church, 3.1% The United Methodist Church, 2.5% Wisconsin Evangelical Lutheran Synod (2000).
Economy: Unemployment rate: 4.9% (11/2002); Total civilian labor force: 83,964 (11/2002); Leading industries: 26.6% manufacturing; 13.1% retail trade; 13.0% health care and social assistance (2000); Companies that employ more than 1,000 persons: 5 (2000); Companies that employ more than 100 persons: 92 (2000); Farms: 1,182 totaling 173,958 acres (1997); Minority business ownership rate: 7.5% (1997); Women business ownership rate: 28.2% (1997); Retail sales per capita: $8,121 (1997). Single-family building permits issued: 522 (2001) / 485 (2000); Multi-family building permits issued: 22 (2001) / 22 (2000).
Income: Per capita income: $19,952 (2000); Median household income: $38,567 (2000); Poverty rate: 12.7% (2000); Bankruptcy rate: 5.67% (2001).
Taxes: Total county taxes per capita: $158 (2000); County property taxes per capita: $152 (2000).
Education: High school graduation rate: 81.9% (2000); College graduation rate: 19.6% (2000).
Housing: Homeownership rate: 72.2% (2000); Median home value: $94,700 (2000); Median rent: $403 per month (2000); Median age of housing: 40 years (2000).
Health: Birth rate: 131.8 per 10,000 population (1998); Age adjusted death rate: 95.7 per 10,000 population (1999); Age adjusted cancer mortality rate: 221.7 deaths per 100,000 population (1999). Air Quality Index: 63% good, 36% moderate, 1% unhealthy (percent of days in 2000). Number of physicians: 15.8 per 10,000 population (1999); Number of hospital beds: 25.6 per 10,000 population (1999).
Elections: 2000 Presidential election results: 43.2% Gore, 54.7% Bush, 1.8% Nader, 0.0% Buchanan
National and State Parks: Warren Dunes State Park; Warren Woods State Park
Additional Information Contacts
Berrien County Government Offices 616-983-7111
Berrien Springs Chamber of Commerce 616-471-9680
Bridgman Area Chamber of Commerce. 616-465-4413
Buchanan Area Chamber of Commerce. 616-695-3291
Coloma Area Chamber of Commerce 616-468-9160
Coloma Area Chmber of Commerce 616-468-9160
Lakeshore Chamber of Commerce. 616-429-1170
New Buffalo Chamber of Commerce. 616-469-5409
Niles Chamber of Commerce. 616-687-7293
Southwestern Michigan Association of Realtors 616-983-6375
St. Joseph Chamber of Commerce 616-982-0032

Berrien County Communities

BAINBRIDGE (township). Covers a land area of 35.160 square miles and a water area of 0.271 square miles. Located at 42.10° N. Lat.; 86.29° W. Long.
History: Bainbridge Township was surveyed in 1830 and named for the former home in New York of Jehiel Enos, who was responsible for the survey.
Population: 3,132 (2000); Race: 95.9% White, 0.3% Black, 0.0% Asian, 0.4% American Indian and Alaska Native, 12.8% Hispanic of any race, 0.9% two or more races (2000); Density: 89.1 persons per square mile (2000); Age: 24.2% under 18, 13.8% over 64 (2000); Marriage status: 21.8% never married, 64.1% now married, 6.3% widowed, 7.8% divorced (2000); Foreign born: 10.0% (2000); Ancestry (includes multiple ancestries): 28.6% German, 19.8% Other groups, 10.2% English, 8.6% United States or American, 7.2% Irish (2000).
Economy: Single-family building permits issued: 18 (2001) / 18 (2000); Multi-family building permits issued: 0 (2001) / 0 (2000); Employment by occupation: 14.7% management, 11.8% professional, 8.8% services, 20.1% sales, 9.0% farming, 12.1% construction, 23.5% production (2000).
Income: Per capita income: $17,854 (2000); Median household income: $38,750 (2000); Poverty rate: 12.5% (2000).
Taxes: Total city taxes per capita: $18 (1997); City property taxes per capita: $12 (1997).
Education: High school graduation rate: 76.0% (2000); College graduation rate: 12.2% (2000).

Housing: Homeownership rate: 85.6% (2000); Median home value: $90,300 (2000); Median rent: $390 per month (2000); Median age of housing: 38 years (2000).
Transportation: Commute to work: 92.2% car, 0.6% public transportation, 2.5% walk, 4.5% work from home (2000); Travel time to work: 31.4% less than 15 minutes, 47.2% 15 to 30 minutes, 16.5% 30 to 45 minutes, 3.3% 45 to 60 minutes, 1.6% 60 minutes or more (2000)

BARODA (village). Covers a land area of 0.639 square miles and a water area of 0 square miles. Located at 41.95° N. Lat.; 86.48° W. Long.
History: Baroda was named for a city in India. It was incorporated as a village in 1907.
Population: 858 (2000); Race: 97.3% White, 0.0% Black, 1.2% Asian, 0.0% American Indian and Alaska Native, 0.9% Hispanic of any race, 1.5% two or more races (2000); Density: 1,343.2 persons per square mile (2000); Age: 28.6% under 18, 14.0% over 64 (2000); Marriage status: 19.2% never married, 60.1% now married, 7.7% widowed, 13.0% divorced (2000); Foreign born: 2.3% (2000); Ancestry (includes multiple ancestries): 39.8% German, 17.8% Irish, 8.2% United States or American, 7.2% English, 5.1% Polish (2000).
Economy: Single-family building permits issued: 0 (2001) / 4 (2000); Multi-family building permits issued: 0 (2001) / 0 (2000); Employment by occupation: 7.5% management, 17.7% professional, 16.3% services, 18.9% sales, 0.0% farming, 11.7% construction, 28.0% production (2000).
Income: Per capita income: $16,412 (2000); Median household income: $36,250 (2000); Poverty rate: 7.9% (2000).
Taxes: Total city taxes per capita: $144 (1997); City property taxes per capita: $139 (1997).
Education: High school graduation rate: 78.9% (2000); College graduation rate: 7.9% (2000).
Housing: Homeownership rate: 79.4% (2000); Median home value: $94,200 (2000); Median rent: $483 per month (2000); Median age of housing: 24 years (2000).
Transportation: Commute to work: 89.6% car, 0.0% public transportation, 4.2% walk, 1.9% work from home (2000); Travel time to work: 38.1% less than 15 minutes, 44.8% 15 to 30 minutes, 8.2% 30 to 45 minutes, 3.4% 45 to 60 minutes, 5.5% 60 minutes or more (2000)

BARODA (township). Covers a land area of 17.798 square miles and a water area of 0.035 square miles. Located at 41.94° N. Lat.; 86.48° W. Long.
Population: 2,880 (2000); Race: 98.2% White, 0.1% Black, 0.3% Asian, 0.0% American Indian and Alaska Native, 1.3% Hispanic of any race, 0.5% two or more races (2000); Density: 161.8 persons per square mile (2000); Age: 26.6% under 18, 12.7% over 64 (2000); Marriage status: 20.2% never married, 65.2% now married, 6.4% widowed, 8.2% divorced (2000); Foreign born: 2.8% (2000); Ancestry (includes multiple ancestries): 41.8% German, 11.1% Irish, 8.3% English, 8.1% United States or American, 5.9% Other groups (2000).
Economy: In orchard and farm area. Manufacturing: building materials, fabricated metal products. Single-family building permits issued: 9 (2001) / 6 (2000); Multi-family building permits issued: 0 (2001) / 0 (2000); Employment by occupation: 12.3% management, 13.7% professional, 12.9% services, 23.9% sales, 0.7% farming, 9.7% construction, 26.8% production (2000).
Income: Per capita income: $21,837 (2000); Median household income: $44,219 (2000); Poverty rate: 4.7% (2000).
Taxes: Total city taxes per capita: $123 (1997); City property taxes per capita: $118 (1997).
Education: High school graduation rate: 83.1% (2000); College graduation rate: 12.9% (2000).
Housing: Homeownership rate: 85.4% (2000); Median home value: $109,700 (2000); Median rent: $459 per month (2000); Median age of housing: 29 years (2000).
Transportation: Commute to work: 91.0% car, 0.0% public transportation, 1.5% walk, 5.9% work from home (2000); Travel time to work: 36.6% less than 15 minutes, 46.6% 15 to 30 minutes, 11.4% 30 to 45 minutes, 2.6% 45 to 60 minutes, 2.8% 60 minutes or more (2000)

BENTON CHARTER (township). Covers a land area of 32.571 square miles and a water area of 0.096 square miles. Located at 42.11° N. Lat.; 86.41° W. Long.
Population: 16,404 (2000); Race: 42.5% White, 53.4% Black, 0.6% Asian, 0.4% American Indian and Alaska Native, 3.3% Hispanic of any race, 1.0% two or more races (2000); Density: 503.6 persons per square mile (2000); Age: 30.2% under 18, 13.6% over 64 (2000); Marriage status: 33.4% never married, 44.1% now married, 9.5% widowed, 13.0% divorced (2000); Foreign born: 2.5% (2000); Ancestry (includes multiple ancestries): 52.2% Other groups, 10.6% German, 6.0% Irish, 4.3% United States or American, 3.2% English (2000).
Economy: Employment by occupation: 7.3% management, 10.5% professional, 17.6% services, 24.3% sales, 1.4% farming, 6.8% construction, 32.0% production (2000).
Income: Per capita income: $14,137 (2000); Median household income: $25,942 (2000); Poverty rate: 27.7% (2000).
Taxes: Total city taxes per capita: $223 (2000); City property taxes per capita: $209 (2000).
Education: High school graduation rate: 66.4% (2000); College graduation rate: 9.0% (2000).
Housing: Homeownership rate: 56.7% (2000); Median home value: $64,400 (2000); Median rent: $371 per month (2000); Median age of housing: 39 years (2000).
Transportation: Commute to work: 93.4% car, 1.0% public transportation, 1.6% walk, 3.0% work from home (2000); Travel time to work: 43.8% less than 15 minutes, 41.4% 15 to 30 minutes, 8.5% 30 to 45 minutes, 1.9% 45 to 60 minutes, 4.4% 60 minutes or more (2000)

BENTON HARBOR (city). Covers a land area of 4.392 square miles and a water area of 0.084 square miles. Located at 42.11° N. Lat.; 86.44° W. Long. Elevation is 596 feet.
History: Benton Harbor was founded slightly after its neighboring city, St. Joseph, by settlers who preferred the less expensive, marshier land on the other side of the river. The fruit orchards that surrounded the early town were said to be started by Johnny Appleseed, but many pioneers brought young fruit trees with them from New York that contributed to southwestern Michigan's fruit industry. Benton Harbor grew larger than its earlier neighbor. In 1903 it attracted Benjamin Franklin Purnell, known as King Ben, who established a colony of the Israelite House of David here.
Population: 11,182 (2000); Race: 6.9% White, 91.7% Black, 0.1% Asian, 0.2% American Indian and Alaska Native, 0.6% Hispanic of any race, 0.9% two or more races (2000); Density: 2,545.7 persons per square mile (2000); Age: 39.0% under 18, 8.3% over 64 (2000); Marriage status: 48.6% never married, 32.7% now married, 6.5% widowed, 12.2% divorced (2000); Foreign born: 0.3% (2000); Ancestry (includes multiple ancestries): 76.2% Other groups, 4.2% African, 1.9% United States or American, 1.7% German, 0.9% Italian (2000).
Vital Statistics: Birth rate: 310.3 per 10,000 population (1998)
Economy: Single-family building permits issued: 7 (2001) / 3 (2000); Multi-family building permits issued: 0 (2001) / 0 (2000); Employment by occupation: 3.7% management, 6.1% professional, 27.6% services, 23.4% sales, 0.6% farming, 5.3% construction, 33.3% production (2000).
Income: Per capita income: $8,965 (2000); Median household income: $17,471 (2000); Poverty rate: 42.6% (2000).
Taxes: Total city taxes per capita: $302 (1997); City property taxes per capita: $293 (1997).
Education: High school graduation rate: 60.5% (2000); College graduation rate: 4.2% (2000).

School District(s)

Benton Harbor Area Schools (PK-12)
2000 Enrollment: 5,171 616-927-0600
Benton Harbor Charter School (KG-12)
2000 Enrollment: 570 231-591-5802
Countryside Charter School (PK-11)
2000 Enrollment: 466 517-774-2100

Two-year College(s)

Lake Michigan College (Public)
2001 Enrollment: 3,384 616-927-3571
2001 Tuition: In-state $1,830; Out-of-state $2,130

Housing: Homeownership rate: 37.8% (2000); Median home value: $38,700 (2000); Median rent: $353 per month (2000); Median age of housing: 49 years (2000).
Safety: Violent crime rate: 258.0 per 10,000 population; Property crime rate: 613.8 per 10,000 population (2001).
Transportation: Commute to work: 85.7% car, 4.0% public transportation, 4.7% walk, 3.1% work from home (2000); Travel time to work: 51.7% less than 15 minutes, 33.8% 15 to 30 minutes, 9.3% 30 to 45 minutes, 1.5% 45 to 60 minutes, 3.8% 60 minutes or more (2000); Amtrak: Service available.
Airports: Southwest Michigan Regional

BENTON HEIGHTS (CDP). Covers a land area of 3.844 square miles and a water area of 0 square miles. Located at 42.11° N. Lat.; 86.41° W. Long.

History: Benton Heights was called Euclid Center until the name was changed by the residents in 1957.
Population: 5,458 (2000); Race: 28.1% White, 67.9% Black, 0.7% Asian, 0.6% American Indian and Alaska Native, 0.8% Hispanic of any race, 1.7% two or more races (2000); Density: 1,419.8 persons per square mile (2000); Age: 36.2% under 18, 14.5% over 64 (2000); Marriage status: 38.3% never married, 40.3% now married, 10.9% widowed, 10.6% divorced (2000); Foreign born: 1.1% (2000); Ancestry (includes multiple ancestries): 66.1% Other groups, 3.9% German, 3.6% United States or American, 3.0% Irish, 2.8% African (2000).
Economy: Employment by occupation: 2.5% management, 6.3% professional, 22.8% services, 22.7% sales, 0.6% farming, 8.6% construction, 36.5% production (2000).
Income: Per capita income: $9,959 (2000); Median household income: $19,651 (2000); Poverty rate: 38.0% (2000).
Education: High school graduation rate: 56.8% (2000); College graduation rate: 4.4% (2000).
Housing: Homeownership rate: 47.2% (2000); Median home value: $38,700 (2000); Median rent: $358 per month (2000); Median age of housing: 43 years (2000).
Transportation: Commute to work: 91.4% car, 1.5% public transportation, 2.5% walk, 2.8% work from home (2000); Travel time to work: 39.9% less than 15 minutes, 44.0% 15 to 30 minutes, 10.9% 30 to 45 minutes, 3.1% 45 to 60 minutes, 2.2% 60 minutes or more (2000)

BERRIEN (township). Covers a land area of 35.308 square miles and a water area of 1.426 square miles. Located at 41.95° N. Lat.; 86.28° W. Long.
History: Berrien Township was named for John M. Berrien, attorney general under President Andrew Jackson.
Population: 5,075 (2000); Race: 87.8% White, 5.5% Black, 1.6% Asian, 0.5% American Indian and Alaska Native, 6.8% Hispanic of any race, 2.0% two or more races (2000); Density: 143.7 persons per square mile (2000); Age: 26.8% under 18, 13.1% over 64 (2000); Marriage status: 22.7% never married, 64.4% now married, 4.6% widowed, 8.4% divorced (2000); Foreign born: 8.9% (2000); Ancestry (includes multiple ancestries): 26.7% German, 14.0% Other groups, 11.4% English, 10.3% Irish, 9.9% United States or American (2000).
Economy: Single-family building permits issued: 43 (2001) / 25 (2000); Multi-family building permits issued: 0 (2001) / 0 (2000); Employment by occupation: 10.6% management, 22.6% professional, 12.5% services, 21.3% sales, 4.6% farming, 10.1% construction, 18.2% production (2000).
Income: Per capita income: $18,448 (2000); Median household income: $46,293 (2000); Poverty rate: 7.9% (2000).
Taxes: Total city taxes per capita: $14 (1997); City property taxes per capita: $11 (1997).
Education: High school graduation rate: 80.4% (2000); College graduation rate: 23.3% (2000).
Housing: Homeownership rate: 83.7% (2000); Median home value: $115,100 (2000); Median rent: $413 per month (2000); Median age of housing: 29 years (2000).
Transportation: Commute to work: 90.0% car, 0.4% public transportation, 1.7% walk, 6.6% work from home (2000); Travel time to work: 31.8% less than 15 minutes, 39.7% 15 to 30 minutes, 20.1% 30 to 45 minutes, 4.3% 45 to 60 minutes, 4.1% 60 minutes or more (2000)

BERRIEN CENTER (unincorporated postal area, zip code 49102). Covers a land area of 16.942 square miles and a water area of 0.499 square miles. Located at 41.94° N. Lat.; 86.26° W. Long.
History: Berrien Center was settled about 1828. A post office was established here in 1857.
Population: 1,493 (2000); Race: 87.4% White, 8.9% Black, 0.5% Asian, 1.4% American Indian and Alaska Native, 3.6% Hispanic of any race, 0.6% two or more races (2000); Density: 88.1 persons per square mile (2000); Age: 26.3% under 18, 18.6% over 64 (2000); Marriage status: 24.2% never married, 63.3% now married, 5.9% widowed, 6.6% divorced (2000); Foreign born: 4.8% (2000); Ancestry (includes multiple ancestries): 26.2% German, 11.0% United States or American, 10.6% English, 8.7% Irish, 7.5% Other groups (2000).
Economy: Employment by occupation: 12.1% management, 16.8% professional, 12.1% services, 24.8% sales, 6.9% farming, 11.6% construction, 15.8% production (2000).
Income: Per capita income: $14,022 (2000); Median household income: $42,202 (2000); Poverty rate: 9.8% (2000).
Education: High school graduation rate: 69.6% (2000); College graduation rate: 19.1% (2000).
Housing: Homeownership rate: 82.7% (2000); Median home value: $111,500 (2000); Median rent: $440 per month (2000); Median age of housing: 37 years (2000).
Transportation: Commute to work: 86.3% car, 1.0% public transportation, 3.4% walk, 8.2% work from home (2000); Travel time to work: 38.7% less than 15 minutes, 37.1% 15 to 30 minutes, 14.8% 30 to 45 minutes, 3.7% 45 to 60 minutes, 5.8% 60 minutes or more (2000)

BERRIEN SPRINGS (village). Covers a land area of 0.904 square miles and a water area of 0.073 square miles. Located at 41.94° N. Lat.; 86.33° W. Long. Elevation is 671 feet.
History: Settlers came to Berrien Springs in 1829, to a site first called Wolf's Prairie. The village was platted in 1831, and named for John M. Berrien, attorney general under President Andrew Jackson, and for the many springs in the area.
Population: 1,862 (2000); Race: 77.5% White, 12.4% Black, 3.9% Asian, 0.3% American Indian and Alaska Native, 3.6% Hispanic of any race, 3.0% two or more races (2000); Density: 2,059.6 persons per square mile (2000); Age: 24.0% under 18, 14.4% over 64 (2000); Marriage status: 31.8% never married, 49.7% now married, 8.4% widowed, 10.1% divorced (2000); Foreign born: 13.8% (2000); Ancestry (includes multiple ancestries): 23.8% German, 16.5% Other groups, 8.3% Irish, 7.2% United States or American, 6.8% English (2000).
Economy: Single-family building permits issued: 0 (2001) / 0 (2000); Multi-family building permits issued: 0 (2001) / 0 (2000); Employment by occupation: 8.0% management, 23.8% professional, 22.9% services, 23.1% sales, 0.0% farming, 6.6% construction, 15.5% production (2000).
Income: Per capita income: $16,093 (2000); Median household income: $32,396 (2000); Poverty rate: 17.5% (2000).
Taxes: Total city taxes per capita: $418 (1997); City property taxes per capita: $417 (1997).
Education: High school graduation rate: 83.7% (2000); College graduation rate: 28.9% (2000).

School District(s)

Berrien Springs Public Schools (PK-12)
2000 Enrollment: 1,521 616-471-2891

Four-year College(s)

Andrews University (Private, Not-for-profit, Sevent Day Adventists Church)
2001 Enrollment: 2,721 800-253-2874
2001 Tuition: In-state $13,350; Out-of-state $13,350

Housing: Homeownership rate: 69.8% (2000); Median home value: $82,300 (2000); Median rent: $381 per month (2000); Median age of housing: 50 years (2000).
Safety: Violent crime rate: 12.1 per 10,000 population; Property crime rate: 237.5 per 10,000 population (2001).
Newspapers: Journal Era (1 x week)
Transportation: Commute to work: 86.6% car, 0.9% public transportation, 8.1% walk, 2.1% work from home (2000); Travel time to work: 48.5% less than 15 minutes, 26.5% 15 to 30 minutes, 17.4% 30 to 45 minutes, 4.1% 45 to 60 minutes, 3.4% 60 minutes or more (2000)
Additional Information Contacts
Berrien Springs Chamber of Commerce 616-471-9680

BERTRAND (township). Covers a land area of 34.540 square miles and a water area of 0.476 square miles. Located at 41.78° N. Lat.; 86.36° W. Long. Elevation is 726 feet.
History: Bertrand Township was named for Joseph Bertrand, a French-Canadian who operated a trading post here in the early 1800's.
Population: 2,380 (2000); Race: 97.5% White, 0.0% Black, 0.6% Asian, 0.2% American Indian and Alaska Native, 0.7% Hispanic of any race, 1.5% two or more races (2000); Density: 68.9 persons per square mile (2000); Age: 23.6% under 18, 13.6% over 64 (2000); Marriage status: 18.7% never married, 67.3% now married, 5.5% widowed, 8.5% divorced (2000); Foreign born: 0.7% (2000); Ancestry (includes multiple ancestries): 34.7% German, 12.3% Irish, 11.8% Polish, 10.6% English, 8.7% Dutch (2000).
Economy: Single-family building permits issued: 19 (2001) / 20 (2000); Multi-family building permits issued: 0 (2001) / 0 (2000); Employment by occupation: 13.1% management, 16.2% professional, 12.2% services, 21.7% sales, 0.0% farming, 12.4% construction, 24.3% production (2000).
Income: Per capita income: $22,130 (2000); Median household income: $55,183 (2000); Poverty rate: 3.9% (2000).
Taxes: Total city taxes per capita: $62 (1997); City property taxes per capita: $50 (1997).
Education: High school graduation rate: 88.2% (2000); College graduation rate: 18.7% (2000).

Housing: Homeownership rate: 92.1% (2000); Median home value: $100,000 (2000); Median rent: $346 per month (2000); Median age of housing: 41 years (2000).
Transportation: Commute to work: 89.4% car, 0.2% public transportation, 0.5% walk, 6.6% work from home (2000); Travel time to work: 32.4% less than 15 minutes, 47.3% 15 to 30 minutes, 14.1% 30 to 45 minutes, 3.2% 45 to 60 minutes, 3.1% 60 minutes or more (2000)

BRIDGMAN (city). Covers a land area of 2.927 square miles and a water area of 0 square miles. Located at 41.94° N. Lat.; 86.56° W. Long. Elevation is 629 feet.
History: Bridgman grew as the location of plant nurseries, shipping plants to many locations in the United States and Canada. The village was named in 1870 for George C. Bridgman, owner of a lumber company. After uniting with nearby Charlotteville, Bridgman was incorporated as a village in 1927 and as a city in 1949.
Population: 2,428 (2000); Race: 95.5% White, 1.6% Black, 0.7% Asian, 0.2% American Indian and Alaska Native, 1.8% Hispanic of any race, 1.1% two or more races (2000); Density: 829.4 persons per square mile (2000); Age: 22.2% under 18, 17.1% over 64 (2000); Marriage status: 20.6% never married, 58.3% now married, 10.7% widowed, 10.3% divorced (2000); Foreign born: 3.1% (2000); Ancestry (includes multiple ancestries): 34.1% German, 11.2% English, 10.6% Irish, 8.5% Other groups, 6.9% Polish (2000).
Economy: Single-family building permits issued: 13 (2001) / 8 (2000); Multi-family building permits issued: 0 (2001) / 0 (2000); Employment by occupation: 11.2% management, 21.2% professional, 16.1% services, 25.5% sales, 0.4% farming, 7.0% construction, 18.6% production (2000).
Income: Per capita income: $25,405 (2000); Median household income: $48,292 (2000); Poverty rate: 6.9% (2000).
Taxes: Total city taxes per capita: $479 (1997); City property taxes per capita: $460 (1997).
Education: High school graduation rate: 87.8% (2000); College graduation rate: 26.4% (2000).

School District(s)

Bridgman Public Schools (KG-12)
2000 Enrollment: 1,042 616-465-5432

Housing: Homeownership rate: 64.0% (2000); Median home value: $122,600 (2000); Median rent: $424 per month (2000); Median age of housing: 29 years (2000).
Safety: Violent crime rate: 20.5 per 10,000 population; Property crime rate: 151.6 per 10,000 population (2001).
Transportation: Commute to work: 92.9% car, 1.0% public transportation, 4.1% walk, 1.6% work from home (2000); Travel time to work: 44.9% less than 15 minutes, 39.1% 15 to 30 minutes, 7.6% 30 to 45 minutes, 1.6% 45 to 60 minutes, 6.8% 60 minutes or more (2000)
Additional Information Contacts
Bridgman Area Chamber of Commerce 616-465-4413

BUCHANAN (city). Covers a land area of 2.400 square miles and a water area of 0.067 square miles. Located at 41.82° N. Lat.; 86.36° W. Long. Elevation is 732 feet.
History: Buchanan was once known as McCoy's Creek, settled by John Hatfield and Russell McCoy in 1834. It was later named for James Buchanan, who became the 15th U.S. president.
Population: 4,681 (2000); Race: 85.2% White, 11.6% Black, 0.3% Asian, 0.8% American Indian and Alaska Native, 1.9% Hispanic of any race, 1.4% two or more races (2000); Density: 1,950.8 persons per square mile (2000); Age: 27.5% under 18, 13.2% over 64 (2000); Marriage status: 26.5% never married, 52.9% now married, 9.5% widowed, 11.1% divorced (2000); Foreign born: 3.0% (2000); Ancestry (includes multiple ancestries): 25.9% German, 17.0% United States or American, 15.2% Other groups, 12.4% Irish, 9.6% English (2000).
Economy: Single-family building permits issued: 4 (2001) / 7 (2000); Multi-family building permits issued: 0 (2001) / 0 (2000); Employment by occupation: 6.4% management, 15.0% professional, 15.1% services, 29.0% sales, 0.0% farming, 11.0% construction, 23.4% production (2000).
Income: Per capita income: $16,600 (2000); Median household income: $34,244 (2000); Poverty rate: 12.4% (2000).
Taxes: Total city taxes per capita: $244 (1997); City property taxes per capita: $234 (1997).
Education: High school graduation rate: 79.8% (2000); College graduation rate: 13.6% (2000).

School District(s)

Buchanan Community Schools (PK-12)
2000 Enrollment: 1,697 616-695-8401

Housing: Homeownership rate: 62.8% (2000); Median home value: $69,300 (2000); Median rent: $358 per month (2000); Median age of housing: 47 years (2000).
Newspapers: Berrien County Record (1 x week)
Transportation: Commute to work: 92.5% car, 0.8% public transportation, 1.5% walk, 3.3% work from home (2000); Travel time to work: 39.4% less than 15 minutes, 31.3% 15 to 30 minutes, 17.2% 30 to 45 minutes, 5.7% 45 to 60 minutes, 6.3% 60 minutes or more (2000)
Additional Information Contacts
Buchanan Area Chamber of Commerce 616-695-3291

BUCHANAN (township). Covers a land area of 32.279 square miles and a water area of 0.945 square miles. Located at 41.84° N. Lat.; 86.39° W. Long. Elevation is 732 feet.
History: Buchanan Township was named for President James Buchanan.
Population: 3,510 (2000); Race: 98.6% White, 0.0% Black, 0.0% Asian, 1.0% American Indian and Alaska Native, 0.2% Hispanic of any race, 0.2% two or more races (2000); Density: 108.7 persons per square mile (2000); Age: 23.1% under 18, 14.7% over 64 (2000); Marriage status: 19.6% never married, 64.2% now married, 7.2% widowed, 9.0% divorced (2000); Foreign born: 1.1% (2000); Ancestry (includes multiple ancestries): 28.3% German, 12.7% Irish, 11.3% English, 9.7% Other groups, 9.1% United States or American (2000).
Economy: Single-family building permits issued: 28 (2001) / 22 (2000); Multi-family building permits issued: 0 (2001) / 0 (2000); Employment by occupation: 11.1% management, 15.4% professional, 11.8% services, 23.2% sales, 0.0% farming, 13.5% construction, 25.0% production (2000).
Income: Per capita income: $19,572 (2000); Median household income: $40,503 (2000); Poverty rate: 5.2% (2000).
Taxes: Total city taxes per capita: $32 (1997); City property taxes per capita: $21 (1997).
Education: High school graduation rate: 87.7% (2000); College graduation rate: 15.9% (2000).
Housing: Homeownership rate: 94.3% (2000); Median home value: $95,000 (2000); Median rent: $346 per month (2000); Median age of housing: 32 years (2000).
Transportation: Commute to work: 92.7% car, 0.0% public transportation, 1.0% walk, 6.2% work from home (2000); Travel time to work: 26.4% less than 15 minutes, 35.7% 15 to 30 minutes, 21.9% 30 to 45 minutes, 7.0% 45 to 60 minutes, 9.0% 60 minutes or more (2000)

CHIKAMING (township). Covers a land area of 22.058 square miles and a water area of 0.057 square miles. Located at 41.86° N. Lat.; 86.63° W. Long.
History: Chickaming Township was organized in 1856. The name is of Indian origin meaning "lake."
Population: 3,678 (2000); Race: 95.6% White, 3.2% Black, 0.2% Asian, 0.2% American Indian and Alaska Native, 0.4% Hispanic of any race, 0.8% two or more races (2000); Density: 166.7 persons per square mile (2000); Age: 19.3% under 18, 22.1% over 64 (2000); Marriage status: 16.8% never married, 65.2% now married, 6.2% widowed, 11.8% divorced (2000); Foreign born: 2.9% (2000); Ancestry (includes multiple ancestries): 34.4% German, 12.7% Irish, 10.4% English, 9.7% Swedish, 8.4% Polish (2000).
Economy: Single-family building permits issued: 27 (2001) / 23 (2000); Multi-family building permits issued: 0 (2001) / 0 (2000); Employment by occupation: 18.4% management, 17.8% professional, 18.5% services, 21.8% sales, 0.0% farming, 9.4% construction, 14.1% production (2000).
Income: Per capita income: $30,868 (2000); Median household income: $47,778 (2000); Poverty rate: 3.8% (2000).
Taxes: Total city taxes per capita: $146 (1997); City property taxes per capita: $133 (1997).
Education: High school graduation rate: 87.8% (2000); College graduation rate: 27.4% (2000).
Housing: Homeownership rate: 87.7% (2000); Median home value: $162,200 (2000); Median rent: $512 per month (2000); Median age of housing: 49 years (2000).
Safety: Violent crime rate: 16.2 per 10,000 population; Property crime rate: 216.4 per 10,000 population (2001).
Transportation: Commute to work: 87.8% car, 1.4% public transportation, 5.5% walk, 4.6% work from home (2000); Travel time to work: 41.0% less than 15 minutes, 31.7% 15 to 30 minutes, 14.3% 30 to 45 minutes, 3.7% 45 to 60 minutes, 9.4% 60 minutes or more (2000)

COLOMA (city). Covers a land area of 0.903 square miles and a water area of 0 square miles. Located at 42.18° N. Lat.; 86.30° W. Long. Elevation is 649 feet.

History: Coloma was settled by Stephen R. Gilson, who platted the village in 1855 and named it for the town in California where he had once lived. Coloma developed as a canning center.
Population: 1,595 (2000); Race: 96.9% White, 0.7% Black, 0.2% Asian, 0.2% American Indian and Alaska Native, 0.9% Hispanic of any race, 1.6% two or more races (2000); Density: 1,766.9 persons per square mile (2000); Age: 29.7% under 18, 11.5% over 64 (2000); Marriage status: 22.5% never married, 57.1% now married, 7.5% widowed, 12.8% divorced (2000); Foreign born: 1.5% (2000); Ancestry (includes multiple ancestries): 27.6% German, 16.2% Irish, 13.2% English, 11.9% United States or American, 7.4% Other groups (2000).
Economy: In fruit-growing region. Manufacturing: prepared foods, fabricated metal products, paper products, steel. Two miles inland from Lake Michigan (resort). Single-family building permits issued: 0 (2001) / 0 (2000); Multi-family building permits issued: 0 (2001) / 0 (2000); Employment by occupation: 7.6% management, 19.2% professional, 13.9% services, 25.7% sales, 0.5% farming, 8.1% construction, 24.9% production (2000).
Income: Per capita income: $17,714 (2000); Median household income: $38,882 (2000); Poverty rate: 8.9% (2000).
Taxes: Total city taxes per capita: $252 (1997); City property taxes per capita: $245 (1997).
Education: High school graduation rate: 83.0% (2000); College graduation rate: 15.6% (2000).

School District(s)

Coloma Community Schools (PK-12)
2000 Enrollment: 2,147 616-468-2424
Housing: Homeownership rate: 73.4% (2000); Median home value: $79,500 (2000); Median rent: $432 per month (2000); Median age of housing: 45 years (2000).
Safety: Violent crime rate: 15.3 per 10,000 population; Property crime rate: 219.3 per 10,000 population (2001).
Transportation: Commute to work: 95.4% car, 0.0% public transportation, 3.0% walk, 1.5% work from home (2000); Travel time to work: 36.4% less than 15 minutes, 49.6% 15 to 30 minutes, 8.3% 30 to 45 minutes, 3.0% 45 to 60 minutes, 2.7% 60 minutes or more (2000)

Additional Information Contacts

Coloma Area Chamber of Commerce 616-468-9160
Coloma Area Chmber of Commerce 616-468-9160

COLOMA CHARTER (township). Covers a land area of 18.221 square miles and a water area of 0.822 square miles. Located at 42.20° N. Lat.; 86.29° W. Long. Elevation is 649 feet.
Population: 5,217 (2000); Race: 95.5% White, 0.7% Black, 2.2% Asian, 0.4% American Indian and Alaska Native, 2.1% Hispanic of any race, 0.9% two or more races (2000); Density: 286.3 persons per square mile (2000); Age: 23.4% under 18, 15.0% over 64 (2000); Marriage status: 19.6% never married, 64.3% now married, 7.1% widowed, 9.0% divorced (2000); Foreign born: 2.5% (2000); Ancestry (includes multiple ancestries): 26.4% German, 15.6% Irish, 11.7% United States or American, 11.5% Other groups, 11.5% English (2000).
Economy: Single-family building permits issued: 24 (2001) / 20 (2000); Multi-family building permits issued: 0 (2001) / 0 (2000); Employment by occupation: 8.2% management, 17.7% professional, 14.4% services, 24.2% sales, 1.4% farming, 11.5% construction, 22.7% production (2000).
Income: Per capita income: $20,377 (2000); Median household income: $40,029 (2000); Poverty rate: 5.4% (2000).
Taxes: Total city taxes per capita: $164 (2000); City property taxes per capita: $153 (2000).
Education: High school graduation rate: 83.2% (2000); College graduation rate: 13.1% (2000).
Housing: Homeownership rate: 83.9% (2000); Median home value: $95,400 (2000); Median rent: $463 per month (2000); Median age of housing: 35 years (2000).
Transportation: Commute to work: 94.9% car, 0.2% public transportation, 2.1% walk, 1.9% work from home (2000); Travel time to work: 28.7% less than 15 minutes, 50.6% 15 to 30 minutes, 13.0% 30 to 45 minutes, 2.9% 45 to 60 minutes, 4.8% 60 minutes or more (2000)

EAU CLAIRE (village). Covers a land area of 0.727 square miles and a water area of 0 square miles. Located at 41.98° N. Lat.; 86.30° W. Long. Elevation is 718 feet.
Population: 656 (2000); Race: 92.4% White, 2.7% Black, 1.0% Asian, 0.9% American Indian and Alaska Native, 11.8% Hispanic of any race, 0.3% two or more races (2000); Density: 902.4 persons per square mile (2000); Age: 29.5% under 18, 9.8% over 64 (2000); Marriage status: 29.8% never married, 52.3% now married, 5.4% widowed, 12.5% divorced (2000); Foreign born: 8.0% (2000); Ancestry (includes multiple ancestries): 26.5% German, 17.4% Other groups, 15.1% United States or American, 9.2% Irish, 6.9% Dutch (2000).
Economy: Manufacturing: machining, fruit juices, zinc and lead castings. Single-family building permits issued: 4 (2001) / 0 (2000); Multi-family building permits issued: 0 (2001) / 0 (2000); Employment by occupation: 8.6% management, 12.5% professional, 15.0% services, 22.6% sales, 6.1% farming, 15.0% construction, 20.1% production (2000).
Income: Per capita income: $15,668 (2000); Median household income: $38,750 (2000); Poverty rate: 10.3% (2000).
Taxes: Total city taxes per capita: $390 (1997); City property taxes per capita: $371 (1997).
Education: High school graduation rate: 80.7% (2000); College graduation rate: 9.7% (2000).

School District(s)

Eau Claire Public Schools (KG-12)
2000 Enrollment: 922 616-461-6947
Housing: Homeownership rate: 71.4% (2000); Median home value: $73,600 (2000); Median rent: $493 per month (2000); Median age of housing: 45 years (2000).
Safety: Violent crime rate: 45.5 per 10,000 population; Property crime rate: 424.9 per 10,000 population (2001).
Newspapers: Twin City Trade Lines Shopper's Guide (1 x week); Central County Trade Lines Shopper's Guide (1 x week)
Transportation: Commute to work: 95.1% car, 0.0% public transportation, 2.3% walk, 1.2% work from home (2000); Travel time to work: 34.3% less than 15 minutes, 46.0% 15 to 30 minutes, 13.8% 30 to 45 minutes, 3.8% 45 to 60 minutes, 2.1% 60 minutes or more (2000)

FAIR PLAIN (CDP). Covers a land area of 4.208 square miles and a water area of 0.237 square miles. Located at 42.08° N. Lat.; 86.45° W. Long. Elevation is 626 feet.
Population: 7,828 (2000); Race: 48.5% White, 48.5% Black, 0.9% Asian, 0.5% American Indian and Alaska Native, 1.3% Hispanic of any race, 1.2% two or more races (2000); Density: 1,860.2 persons per square mile (2000); Age: 24.9% under 18, 13.4% over 64 (2000); Marriage status: 29.5% never married, 50.3% now married, 8.3% widowed, 11.8% divorced (2000); Foreign born: 2.6% (2000); Ancestry (includes multiple ancestries): 45.5% Other groups, 15.3% German, 7.4% Irish, 5.0% English, 4.8% United States or American (2000).
Economy: Residential suburb of St. Joseph and Benton Harbor. Employment by occupation: 10.0% management, 19.9% professional, 14.4% services, 21.2% sales, 0.5% farming, 5.4% construction, 28.5% production (2000).
Income: Per capita income: $20,344 (2000); Median household income: $37,154 (2000); Poverty rate: 16.0% (2000).
Education: High school graduation rate: 80.1% (2000); College graduation rate: 18.0% (2000).
Housing: Homeownership rate: 69.9% (2000); Median home value: $81,900 (2000); Median rent: $419 per month (2000); Median age of housing: 43 years (2000).
Transportation: Commute to work: 95.7% car, 0.6% public transportation, 1.2% walk, 1.5% work from home (2000); Travel time to work: 56.4% less than 15 minutes, 32.7% 15 to 30 minutes, 6.1% 30 to 45 minutes, 1.7% 45 to 60 minutes, 3.0% 60 minutes or more (2000)

GALIEN (village). Covers a land area of 0.446 square miles and a water area of 0 square miles. Located at 41.80° N. Lat.; 86.49° W. Long. Elevation is 679 feet.
History: Galien was settled in 1854 when George A. Blakeslee bought the mill here and built a store, which also served as the post office with Blakeslee as postmaster. The village was named for the nearby river, which had been named for Rene Brehant de Galinee, a priest who mapped the area in the 1670's.
Population: 593 (2000); Race: 95.4% White, 0.0% Black, 2.1% Asian, 0.0% American Indian and Alaska Native, 0.3% Hispanic of any race, 2.6% two or more races (2000); Density: 1,329.9 persons per square mile (2000); Age: 33.0% under 18, 12.0% over 64 (2000); Marriage status: 23.5% never married, 56.9% now married, 6.4% widowed, 13.3% divorced (2000); Foreign born: 2.1% (2000); Ancestry (includes multiple ancestries): 31.2% German, 14.5% United States or American, 10.8% Irish, 10.3% English, 9.5% Polish (2000).
Economy: Single-family building permits issued: 0 (2001) / 0 (2000); Multi-family building permits issued: 0 (2001) / 0 (2000); Employment by occupation: 8.2% management, 17.0% professional, 16.0% services, 22.0% sales, 2.8% farming, 5.0% construction, 29.1% production (2000).

Income: Per capita income: $15,739 (2000); Median household income: $35,250 (2000); Poverty rate: 14.3% (2000).
Taxes: Total city taxes per capita: $97 (1997); City property taxes per capita: $95 (1997).
Education: High school graduation rate: 84.1% (2000); College graduation rate: 6.8% (2000).

School District(s)

Galien Township School District (KG-12)
2000 Enrollment: 377 616-545-3364
Housing: Homeownership rate: 79.0% (2000); Median home value: $70,200 (2000); Median rent: $379 per month (2000); Median age of housing: 53 years (2000).
Transportation: Commute to work: 92.4% car, 0.0% public transportation, 5.4% walk, 1.4% work from home (2000); Travel time to work: 21.9% less than 15 minutes, 42.7% 15 to 30 minutes, 24.1% 30 to 45 minutes, 7.3% 45 to 60 minutes, 4.0% 60 minutes or more (2000)

GALIEN (township). Covers a land area of 22.058 square miles and a water area of 0.039 square miles. Located at 41.79° N. Lat.; 86.51° W. Long. Elevation is 679 feet.
Population: 1,611 (2000); Race: 96.1% White, 0.4% Black, 0.9% Asian, 0.2% American Indian and Alaska Native, 0.7% Hispanic of any race, 1.8% two or more races (2000); Density: 73.0 persons per square mile (2000); Age: 25.1% under 18, 12.1% over 64 (2000); Marriage status: 22.6% never married, 59.8% now married, 6.8% widowed, 10.8% divorced (2000); Foreign born: 2.0% (2000); Ancestry (includes multiple ancestries): 32.2% German, 16.0% United States or American, 12.5% Irish, 8.5% English, 7.9% Other groups (2000).
Economy: In agricultural area: grain, fruit, peppermint, honey; dairy products; poultry. Manufacturing: wood products. Single-family building permits issued: 9 (2001) / 9 (2000); Multi-family building permits issued: 0 (2001) / 0 (2000); Employment by occupation: 7.9% management, 13.5% professional, 14.2% services, 24.2% sales, 1.3% farming, 12.0% construction, 26.8% production (2000).
Income: Per capita income: $17,850 (2000); Median household income: $37,434 (2000); Poverty rate: 7.7% (2000).
Taxes: Total city taxes per capita: $32 (1997); City property taxes per capita: $31 (1997).
Education: High school graduation rate: 83.9% (2000); College graduation rate: 9.4% (2000).
Housing: Homeownership rate: 84.8% (2000); Median home value: $77,100 (2000); Median rent: $371 per month (2000); Median age of housing: 44 years (2000).
Transportation: Commute to work: 93.7% car, 0.9% public transportation, 1.9% walk, 2.8% work from home (2000); Travel time to work: 19.5% less than 15 minutes, 40.4% 15 to 30 minutes, 25.6% 30 to 45 minutes, 10.9% 45 to 60 minutes, 3.6% 60 minutes or more (2000)

GRAND BEACH (village). Covers a land area of 0.858 square miles and a water area of 0 square miles. Located at 41.77° N. Lat.; 86.79° W. Long.
History: Grand Beach developed as a resort on Lake Michigan. It was incorporated as a village in 1934.
Population: 221 (2000); Race: 98.2% White, 1.8% Black, 0.0% Asian, 0.0% American Indian and Alaska Native, 0.0% Hispanic of any race, 0.0% two or more races (2000); Density: 257.6 persons per square mile (2000); Age: 14.1% under 18, 26.4% over 64 (2000); Marriage status: 17.4% never married, 72.3% now married, 8.2% widowed, 2.1% divorced (2000); Foreign born: 2.6% (2000); Ancestry (includes multiple ancestries): 30.8% German, 21.6% Irish, 14.5% Polish, 10.1% French (except Basque), 10.1% English (2000).
Economy: Single-family building permits issued: 11 (2001) / 5 (2000); Multi-family building permits issued: 0 (2001) / 0 (2000); Employment by occupation: 25.5% management, 40.4% professional, 5.3% services, 22.3% sales, 0.0% farming, 4.3% construction, 2.1% production (2000).
Income: Per capita income: $51,788 (2000); Median household income: $61,875 (2000); Poverty rate: 1.8% (2000).
Taxes: Total city taxes per capita: $1,830 (1997); City property taxes per capita: $1,730 (1997).
Education: High school graduation rate: 93.2% (2000); College graduation rate: 54.2% (2000).
Housing: Homeownership rate: 91.1% (2000); Median home value: $278,100 (2000); Median rent: $875 per month (2000); Median age of housing: 42 years (2000).
Safety: Violent crime rate: 0.0 per 10,000 population; Property crime rate: 450.5 per 10,000 population (2001).

Transportation: Commute to work: 84.4% car, 5.6% public transportation, 0.0% walk, 10.0% work from home (2000); Travel time to work: 37.0% less than 15 minutes, 25.9% 15 to 30 minutes, 7.4% 30 to 45 minutes, 4.9% 45 to 60 minutes, 24.7% 60 minutes or more (2000)

HAGAR (township). Covers a land area of 18.579 square miles and a water area of 0.112 square miles. Located at 42.20° N. Lat.; 86.38° W. Long.
History: Hagar Township was named for William S. Hagar, whose son-in-law had been instrumental in the organizing of the township.
Population: 3,964 (2000); Race: 95.4% White, 1.2% Black, 0.0% Asian, 0.2% American Indian and Alaska Native, 3.3% Hispanic of any race, 1.2% two or more races (2000); Density: 213.4 persons per square mile (2000); Age: 23.8% under 18, 12.6% over 64 (2000); Marriage status: 22.5% never married, 59.4% now married, 6.5% widowed, 11.6% divorced (2000); Foreign born: 1.6% (2000); Ancestry (includes multiple ancestries): 23.3% German, 14.9% Irish, 10.1% Other groups, 9.8% English, 7.4% Italian (2000).
Economy: Single-family building permits issued: 19 (2001) / 13 (2000); Multi-family building permits issued: 0 (2001) / 0 (2000); Employment by occupation: 9.4% management, 12.7% professional, 13.6% services, 24.9% sales, 0.1% farming, 14.5% construction, 24.9% production (2000).
Income: Per capita income: $19,710 (2000); Median household income: $38,614 (2000); Poverty rate: 8.0% (2000).
Taxes: Total city taxes per capita: $61 (1997); City property taxes per capita: $54 (1997).
Education: High school graduation rate: 84.7% (2000); College graduation rate: 12.8% (2000).
Housing: Homeownership rate: 71.5% (2000); Median home value: $89,300 (2000); Median rent: $447 per month (2000); Median age of housing: 43 years (2000).
Transportation: Commute to work: 97.5% car, 0.0% public transportation, 0.0% walk, 2.5% work from home (2000); Travel time to work: 28.8% less than 15 minutes, 53.4% 15 to 30 minutes, 10.7% 30 to 45 minutes, 3.4% 45 to 60 minutes, 3.7% 60 minutes or more (2000)

LAKE CHARTER (township). Covers a land area of 18.695 square miles and a water area of 0 square miles. Located at 41.93° N. Lat.; 86.54° W. Long.
Population: 3,148 (2000); Race: 97.3% White, 0.9% Black, 0.2% Asian, 1.3% American Indian and Alaska Native, 0.4% Hispanic of any race, 0.0% two or more races (2000); Density: 168.4 persons per square mile (2000); Age: 25.4% under 18, 15.9% over 64 (2000); Marriage status: 20.1% never married, 61.4% now married, 10.2% widowed, 8.4% divorced (2000); Foreign born: 2.3% (2000); Ancestry (includes multiple ancestries): 45.1% German, 14.8% Irish, 10.3% English, 7.5% French (except Basque), 6.7% Polish (2000).
Economy: Single-family building permits issued: 13 (2001) / 13 (2000); Multi-family building permits issued: 0 (2001) / 0 (2000); Employment by occupation: 16.2% management, 13.9% professional, 14.4% services, 24.1% sales, 0.5% farming, 9.0% construction, 21.9% production (2000).
Income: Per capita income: $21,666 (2000); Median household income: $49,764 (2000); Poverty rate: 8.7% (2000).
Taxes: Total city taxes per capita: $889 (2000); City property taxes per capita: $881 (2000).
Education: High school graduation rate: 83.6% (2000); College graduation rate: 12.9% (2000).
Housing: Homeownership rate: 92.3% (2000); Median home value: $122,700 (2000); Median rent: $414 per month (2000); Median age of housing: 30 years (2000).
Transportation: Commute to work: 95.6% car, 0.0% public transportation, 0.5% walk, 3.9% work from home (2000); Travel time to work: 40.4% less than 15 minutes, 42.8% 15 to 30 minutes, 7.3% 30 to 45 minutes, 3.7% 45 to 60 minutes, 5.8% 60 minutes or more (2000)

LAKE MICHIGAN BEACH (CDP). Aka Hagar Shores. Covers a land area of 3.837 square miles and a water area of 0.079 square miles. Located at 42.21° N. Lat.; 86.37° W. Long.
Population: 1,509 (2000); Race: 97.1% White, 0.0% Black, 0.0% Asian, 0.4% American Indian and Alaska Native, 4.8% Hispanic of any race, 0.6% two or more races (2000); Density: 393.2 persons per square mile (2000); Age: 20.5% under 18, 18.8% over 64 (2000); Marriage status: 21.5% never married, 59.9% now married, 8.5% widowed, 10.0% divorced (2000); Foreign born: 1.3% (2000); Ancestry (includes multiple ancestries): 21.3% German, 16.5% Irish, 13.6% Other groups, 11.2% English, 6.7% Italian (2000).

Economy: Employment by occupation: 9.2% management, 13.8% professional, 15.6% services, 20.9% sales, 0.0% farming, 11.2% construction, 29.4% production (2000).
Income: Per capita income: $20,253 (2000); Median household income: $33,150 (2000); Poverty rate: 7.7% (2000).
Education: High school graduation rate: 85.7% (2000); College graduation rate: 10.7% (2000).
Housing: Homeownership rate: 72.6% (2000); Median home value: $83,100 (2000); Median rent: $420 per month (2000); Median age of housing: 48 years (2000).
Transportation: Commute to work: 98.9% car, 0.0% public transportation, 0.0% walk, 1.1% work from home (2000); Travel time to work: 22.1% less than 15 minutes, 58.2% 15 to 30 minutes, 13.3% 30 to 45 minutes, 1.1% 45 to 60 minutes, 5.3% 60 minutes or more (2000)

LAKESIDE (unincorporated postal area, zip code 49116). Covers a land area of 0.997 square miles and a water area of 0 square miles. Located at 41.84° N. Lat.; 86.67° W. Long.
History: Lakeside began as a lumber town when the three Wilkinson brothers built a sawmill here in 1854. Lakeside later became a resort.
Population: 250 (2000); Race: 83.9% White, 14.5% Black, 0.0% Asian, 0.0% American Indian and Alaska Native, 0.0% Hispanic of any race, 1.6% two or more races (2000); Density: 250.9 persons per square mile (2000); Age: 22.2% under 18, 37.3% over 64 (2000); Marriage status: 3.3% never married, 91.3% now married, 5.4% widowed, 0.0% divorced (2000); Foreign born: 4.2% (2000); Ancestry (includes multiple ancestries): 36.0% German, 15.1% English, 12.5% Polish, 9.3% Irish, 6.4% Scottish (2000).
Economy: Employment by occupation: 49.1% management, 20.9% professional, 10.9% services, 19.1% sales, 0.0% farming, 0.0% construction, 0.0% production (2000).
Income: Per capita income: $39,409 (2000); Median household income: $64,167 (2000); Poverty rate: 0.0% (2000).
Education: High school graduation rate: 93.5% (2000); College graduation rate: 46.3% (2000).
Housing: Homeownership rate: 90.6% (2000); Median home value: $345,500 (2000); Median rent: $454 per month (2000); Median age of housing: 55 years (2000).
Transportation: Commute to work: 68.2% car, 5.5% public transportation, 5.5% walk, 20.9% work from home (2000); Travel time to work: 13.8% less than 15 minutes, 34.5% 15 to 30 minutes, 0.0% 30 to 45 minutes, 26.4% 45 to 60 minutes, 25.3% 60 minutes or more (2000)

LINCOLN CHARTER (township). Covers a land area of 17.928 square miles and a water area of 0.236 square miles. Located at 42.02° N. Lat.; 86.50° W. Long.
Population: 13,952 (2000); Race: 95.7% White, 0.8% Black, 1.3% Asian, 0.3% American Indian and Alaska Native, 0.8% Hispanic of any race, 1.3% two or more races (2000); Density: 778.2 persons per square mile (2000); Age: 25.7% under 18, 13.0% over 64 (2000); Marriage status: 19.0% never married, 67.1% now married, 5.8% widowed, 8.2% divorced (2000); Foreign born: 4.2% (2000); Ancestry (includes multiple ancestries): 39.9% German, 13.4% English, 11.5% Irish, 6.9% Other groups, 6.3% United States or American (2000).
Economy: Single-family building permits issued: 67 (2001) / 65 (2000); Multi-family building permits issued: 4 (2001) / 0 (2000); Employment by occupation: 15.8% management, 26.5% professional, 13.5% services, 24.0% sales, 0.5% farming, 6.4% construction, 13.3% production (2000).
Income: Per capita income: $27,559 (2000); Median household income: $53,718 (2000); Poverty rate: 2.7% (2000).
Taxes: Total city taxes per capita: $114 (2000); City property taxes per capita: $97 (2000).
Education: High school graduation rate: 88.6% (2000); College graduation rate: 31.0% (2000).
Housing: Homeownership rate: 79.6% (2000); Median home value: $133,400 (2000); Median rent: $515 per month (2000); Median age of housing: 28 years (2000).
Transportation: Commute to work: 96.0% car, 0.5% public transportation, 1.0% walk, 2.2% work from home (2000); Travel time to work: 45.8% less than 15 minutes, 41.6% 15 to 30 minutes, 6.0% 30 to 45 minutes, 2.4% 45 to 60 minutes, 4.3% 60 minutes or more (2000)

MICHIANA (village). Covers a land area of 0.391 square miles and a water area of 0 square miles. Located at 41.76° N. Lat.; 86.81° W. Long.
Population: 200 (2000); Race: 98.4% White, 0.0% Black, 0.0% Asian, 0.0% American Indian and Alaska Native, 0.0% Hispanic of any race, 1.6% two or more races (2000); Density: 512.0 persons per square mile (2000); Age: 14.7% under 18, 28.8% over 64 (2000); Marriage status: 19.6% never married, 59.5% now married, 3.1% widowed, 17.8% divorced (2000); Foreign born: 7.6% (2000); Ancestry (includes multiple ancestries): 29.3% Irish, 28.8% German, 13.0% English, 10.9% Italian, 8.7% Lithuanian (2000).
Economy: Single-family building permits issued: 2 (2001) / 4 (2000); Multi-family building permits issued: 0 (2001) / 0 (2000); Employment by occupation: 18.0% management, 40.0% professional, 6.0% services, 28.0% sales, 0.0% farming, 5.0% construction, 3.0% production (2000).
Income: Per capita income: $63,558 (2000); Median household income: $75,984 (2000); Poverty rate: 1.1% (2000).
Taxes: Total city taxes per capita: $1,853 (1997); City property taxes per capita: $1,729 (1997).
Education: High school graduation rate: 98.1% (2000); College graduation rate: 64.5% (2000).
Housing: Homeownership rate: 96.7% (2000); Median home value: $231,900 (2000); Median rent: $675 per month (2000); Median age of housing: 42 years (2000).
Safety: Violent crime rate: 0.0 per 10,000 population; Property crime rate: 348.3 per 10,000 population (2001).
Transportation: Commute to work: 71.1% car, 12.4% public transportation, 2.1% walk, 14.4% work from home (2000); Travel time to work: 37.3% less than 15 minutes, 24.1% 15 to 30 minutes, 9.6% 30 to 45 minutes, 7.2% 45 to 60 minutes, 21.7% 60 minutes or more (2000)

NEW BUFFALO (city). Covers a land area of 2.416 square miles and a water area of 0.051 square miles. Located at 41.79° N. Lat.; 86.74° W. Long. Elevation is 590 feet.
History: New Buffalo was settled in 1835. A number of summer camps were established in the area.
Population: 2,200 (2000); Race: 97.0% White, 0.5% Black, 0.1% Asian, 1.0% American Indian and Alaska Native, 1.6% Hispanic of any race, 0.8% two or more races (2000); Density: 910.4 persons per square mile (2000); Age: 20.4% under 18, 17.8% over 64 (2000); Marriage status: 24.2% never married, 55.2% now married, 7.9% widowed, 12.7% divorced (2000); Foreign born: 3.1% (2000); Ancestry (includes multiple ancestries): 31.6% German, 14.6% Irish, 11.8% Polish, 10.3% English, 8.5% Other groups (2000).
Economy: Single-family building permits issued: 6 (2001) / 3 (2000); Multi-family building permits issued: 0 (2001) / 0 (2000); Employment by occupation: 9.8% management, 11.1% professional, 19.4% services, 24.7% sales, 0.0% farming, 17.0% construction, 17.9% production (2000).
Income: Per capita income: $24,440 (2000); Median household income: $41,658 (2000); Poverty rate: 6.2% (2000).
Taxes: Total city taxes per capita: $490 (1997); City property taxes per capita: $479 (1997).
Education: High school graduation rate: 84.1% (2000); College graduation rate: 17.3% (2000).

School District(s)

New Buffalo Area Schools (KG-12)
2000 Enrollment: 628 616-469-2211

Housing: Homeownership rate: 71.3% (2000); Median home value: $103,000 (2000); Median rent: $426 per month (2000); Median age of housing: 36 years (2000).
Safety: Violent crime rate: 0.0 per 10,000 population; Property crime rate: 542.5 per 10,000 population (2001).
Newspapers: Harbor Country News (1 x week); The Buffalo Times (1 x week)
Transportation: Commute to work: 89.2% car, 0.2% public transportation, 6.2% walk, 3.3% work from home (2000); Travel time to work: 46.0% less than 15 minutes, 27.8% 15 to 30 minutes, 14.5% 30 to 45 minutes, 5.6% 45 to 60 minutes, 6.1% 60 minutes or more (2000); Amtrak: Service available.
Additional Information Contacts
New Buffalo Chamber of Commerce. 616-469-5409

NEW BUFFALO (township). Covers a land area of 20.253 square miles and a water area of 0.010 square miles. Located at 41.78° N. Lat.; 86.75° W. Long. Elevation is 590 feet.
History: Settled 1835, incorporated 1936.
Population: 2,468 (2000); Race: 94.3% White, 3.0% Black, 0.1% Asian, 0.6% American Indian and Alaska Native, 1.3% Hispanic of any race, 1.5% two or more races (2000); Density: 121.9 persons per square mile (2000); Age: 18.2% under 18, 21.8% over 64 (2000); Marriage status: 17.6% never married, 65.3% now married, 8.4% widowed, 8.7% divorced (2000); Foreign born: 4.9% (2000); Ancestry (includes multiple ancestries): 26.6% German, 18.6% Irish, 13.1% English, 10.6% Polish, 7.9% Other groups (2000).

Economy: In orchard and farm area: fruits, vegetables. Manufacturing: steel castings, plastic products, air compressors; resorts. Railroad junction to Northeast. Single-family building permits issued: 23 (2001) / 29 (2000); Multi-family building permits issued: 0 (2001) / 0 (2000); Employment by occupation: 19.3% management, 20.7% professional, 10.5% services, 24.0% sales, 0.0% farming, 12.6% construction, 13.0% production (2000).
Income: Per capita income: $33,587 (2000); Median household income: $46,991 (2000); Poverty rate: 6.3% (2000).
Taxes: Total city taxes per capita: $99 (1997); City property taxes per capita: $71 (1997).
Education: High school graduation rate: 84.8% (2000); College graduation rate: 30.5% (2000).
Housing: Homeownership rate: 86.5% (2000); Median home value: $169,500 (2000); Median rent: $394 per month (2000); Median age of housing: 37 years (2000).
Transportation: Commute to work: 88.9% car, 1.9% public transportation, 2.0% walk, 6.6% work from home (2000); Travel time to work: 41.2% less than 15 minutes, 27.6% 15 to 30 minutes, 10.9% 30 to 45 minutes, 7.0% 45 to 60 minutes, 13.3% 60 minutes or more (2000); Amtrak: Service available.

NILES (city). Covers a land area of 5.785 square miles and a water area of 0.139 square miles. Located at 41.83° N. Lat.; 86.25° W. Long. Elevation is 658 feet.
History: Niles was an early stopping place on the stagecoach route between Detroit and Chicago. Prominent people who came from Niles are Montgomery Ward, who founded the department store and mail order chain, the Dodge brothers, who made automobiles, and writer Ring Lardner.
Population: 12,204 (2000); Race: 81.7% White, 11.5% Black, 0.4% Asian, 0.8% American Indian and Alaska Native, 3.6% Hispanic of any race, 4.1% two or more races (2000); Density: 2,109.5 persons per square mile (2000); Age: 26.6% under 18, 15.9% over 64 (2000); Marriage status: 25.2% never married, 50.6% now married, 9.7% widowed, 14.5% divorced (2000); Foreign born: 2.5% (2000); Ancestry (includes multiple ancestries): 23.7% German, 19.6% Other groups, 12.5% Irish, 9.3% English, 7.6% United States or American (2000).
Vital Statistics: Birth rate: 217.1 per 10,000 population (1998)
Economy: Single-family building permits issued: 5 (2001) / 9 (2000); Multi-family building permits issued: 0 (2001) / 0 (2000); Employment by occupation: 8.8% management, 15.2% professional, 16.9% services, 23.9% sales, 0.2% farming, 8.0% construction, 26.9% production (2000).
Income: Per capita income: $16,584 (2000); Median household income: $31,208 (2000); Poverty rate: 13.6% (2000).
Taxes: Total city taxes per capita: $236 (2000); City property taxes per capita: $225 (2000).
Education: High school graduation rate: 83.5% (2000); College graduation rate: 14.3% (2000).

School District(s)

Brandywine Public School District (KG-12)
2000 Enrollment: 1,657 616-684-7150
Niles Community School District (KG-12)
2000 Enrollment: 4,068 616-683-0732

Housing: Homeownership rate: 59.4% (2000); Median home value: $69,600 (2000); Median rent: $377 per month (2000); Median age of housing: 52 years (2000).
Hospitals: Niles Lakeland Medical Center (106 beds)
Safety: Violent crime rate: 49.7 per 10,000 population; Property crime rate: 591.0 per 10,000 population (2001).
Newspapers: The Niles Daily Star (6 x week); Edwardsburg Argus (1 x week); The Leader (1 x week); Cassopolis Vigilant (1 x week)
Transportation: Commute to work: 95.5% car, 0.1% public transportation, 2.1% walk, 1.7% work from home (2000); Travel time to work: 40.5% less than 15 minutes, 33.3% 15 to 30 minutes, 18.3% 30 to 45 minutes, 3.4% 45 to 60 minutes, 4.4% 60 minutes or more (2000); Amtrak: Service available.
Additional Information Contacts
Niles Chamber of Commerce 616-687-7293

NILES (township). Covers a land area of 37.689 square miles and a water area of 0.793 square miles. Located at 41.81° N. Lat.; 86.26° W. Long. Elevation is 658 feet.
History: It was the site of a Jesuit Mission (1690) and of Fort St. Joseph, built by the French (1697). The fort fell to the British (1761), to the Native Americans (Pontiac's Rebellion, 1763), and to the Spanish and Native Americans (1780, 1781). Permanent settlement began in 1827, and as a station on the stagecoach route between Detroit and Chicago, Niles grew as a commercial and industrial center. Ring Lardner was born here. Incorporated 1829.
Population: 13,325 (2000); Race: 93.3% White, 3.3% Black, 0.1% Asian, 0.4% American Indian and Alaska Native, 1.8% Hispanic of any race, 1.8% two or more races (2000); Density: 353.5 persons per square mile (2000); Age: 25.0% under 18, 16.1% over 64 (2000); Marriage status: 24.6% never married, 57.1% now married, 7.6% widowed, 10.7% divorced (2000); Foreign born: 3.3% (2000); Ancestry (includes multiple ancestries): 30.2% German, 13.1% Irish, 12.3% Other groups, 10.4% English, 9.8% United States or American (2000).
Economy: In a farm and fruit area. Manufacturing includes paper products, transportation equipment, fabricated metal products and machinery. Single-family building permits issued: 34 (2001) / 35 (2000); Multi-family building permits issued: 18 (2001) / 14 (2000); Employment by occupation: 8.8% management, 13.0% professional, 15.7% services, 25.4% sales, 0.8% farming, 11.1% construction, 25.2% production (2000).
Income: Per capita income: $18,249 (2000); Median household income: $37,794 (2000); Poverty rate: 9.0% (2000).
Taxes: Total city taxes per capita: $71 (1997); City property taxes per capita: $66 (1997).
Education: High school graduation rate: 82.4% (2000); College graduation rate: 12.6% (2000).
Housing: Homeownership rate: 84.1% (2000); Median home value: $80,000 (2000); Median rent: $420 per month (2000); Median age of housing: 39 years (2000).
Transportation: Commute to work: 95.7% car, 0.2% public transportation, 1.1% walk, 2.3% work from home (2000); Travel time to work: 35.5% less than 15 minutes, 38.6% 15 to 30 minutes, 18.4% 30 to 45 minutes, 3.5% 45 to 60 minutes, 4.0% 60 minutes or more (2000); Amtrak: Service available.

ORONOKO CHARTER (township). Covers a land area of 32.537 square miles and a water area of 0.835 square miles. Located at 41.94° N. Lat.; 86.36° W. Long.
Population: 9,843 (2000); Race: 65.5% White, 17.5% Black, 6.0% Asian, 0.6% American Indian and Alaska Native, 8.1% Hispanic of any race, 5.0% two or more races (2000); Density: 302.5 persons per square mile (2000); Age: 21.9% under 18, 11.8% over 64 (2000); Marriage status: 37.0% never married, 50.8% now married, 5.9% widowed, 6.3% divorced (2000); Foreign born: 28.2% (2000); Ancestry (includes multiple ancestries): 23.1% Other groups, 21.0% German, 8.7% English, 6.3% United States or American, 5.8% Irish (2000).
Economy: Single-family building permits issued: 7 (2001) / 12 (2000); Multi-family building permits issued: 0 (2001) / 0 (2000); Employment by occupation: 8.2% management, 32.6% professional, 17.6% services, 23.8% sales, 1.3% farming, 5.8% construction, 10.7% production (2000).
Income: Per capita income: $16,904 (2000); Median household income: $35,980 (2000); Poverty rate: 18.3% (2000).
Taxes: Total city taxes per capita: $18 (1997); City property taxes per capita: $16 (1997).
Education: High school graduation rate: 88.4% (2000); College graduation rate: 43.3% (2000).
Housing: Homeownership rate: 55.4% (2000); Median home value: $111,600 (2000); Median rent: $450 per month (2000); Median age of housing: 33 years (2000).
Transportation: Commute to work: 78.3% car, 0.8% public transportation, 15.8% walk, 3.1% work from home (2000); Travel time to work: 54.8% less than 15 minutes, 28.0% 15 to 30 minutes, 11.9% 30 to 45 minutes, 3.6% 45 to 60 minutes, 1.7% 60 minutes or more (2000)

PAW PAW LAKE (CDP). Covers a land area of 5.242 square miles and a water area of 1.524 square miles. Located at 42.21° N. Lat.; 86.27° W. Long. Elevation is 630 feet.
History: The summer resort of Paw Paw Lake was opened in the 1850's. The operator of the hotel, Wiliam A. Baker, became the first postmaster in 1901.
Population: 3,944 (2000); Race: 96.5% White, 0.2% Black, 1.6% Asian, 0.4% American Indian and Alaska Native, 1.8% Hispanic of any race, 0.9% two or more races (2000); Density: 752.4 persons per square mile (2000); Age: 20.0% under 18, 18.1% over 64 (2000); Marriage status: 21.8% never married, 60.5% now married, 8.2% widowed, 9.5% divorced (2000); Foreign born: 3.3% (2000); Ancestry (includes multiple ancestries): 25.9% German, 15.8% Irish, 11.3% English, 10.6% United States or American, 10.6% Other groups (2000).
Economy: Employment by occupation: 8.0% management, 14.8% professional, 17.8% services, 21.3% sales, 0.8% farming, 13.3% construction, 24.1% production (2000).
Income: Per capita income: $21,003 (2000); Median household income: $38,216 (2000); Poverty rate: 6.6% (2000).

Education: High school graduation rate: 82.7% (2000); College graduation rate: 12.3% (2000).
Housing: Homeownership rate: 79.4% (2000); Median home value: $89,000 (2000); Median rent: $456 per month (2000); Median age of housing: 42 years (2000).
Transportation: Commute to work: 93.5% car, 0.2% public transportation, 2.5% walk, 2.3% work from home (2000); Travel time to work: 25.8% less than 15 minutes, 52.0% 15 to 30 minutes, 13.1% 30 to 45 minutes, 4.6% 45 to 60 minutes, 4.4% 60 minutes or more (2000)

PIPESTONE (township). Covers a land area of 35.651 square miles and a water area of 0.237 square miles. Located at 42.02° N. Lat.; 86.29° W. Long.
Population: 2,474 (2000); Race: 88.3% White, 4.6% Black, 0.5% Asian, 1.2% American Indian and Alaska Native, 11.4% Hispanic of any race, 2.3% two or more races (2000); Density: 69.4 persons per square mile (2000); Age: 26.4% under 18, 12.5% over 64 (2000); Marriage status: 24.4% never married, 61.4% now married, 5.9% widowed, 8.2% divorced (2000); Foreign born: 6.9% (2000); Ancestry (includes multiple ancestries): 31.3% German, 18.4% Other groups, 12.7% United States or American, 11.2% Irish, 8.0% English (2000).
Economy: Single-family building permits issued: 25 (2001) / 11 (2000); Multi-family building permits issued: 0 (2001) / 0 (2000); Employment by occupation: 10.8% management, 12.7% professional, 12.2% services, 20.8% sales, 4.9% farming, 15.1% construction, 23.5% production (2000).
Income: Per capita income: $16,423 (2000); Median household income: $41,440 (2000); Poverty rate: 11.6% (2000).
Taxes: Total city taxes per capita: $19 (1997); City property taxes per capita: $14 (1997).
Education: High school graduation rate: 74.0% (2000); College graduation rate: 10.1% (2000).
Housing: Homeownership rate: 83.5% (2000); Median home value: $89,800 (2000); Median rent: $420 per month (2000); Median age of housing: 40 years (2000).
Transportation: Commute to work: 89.7% car, 0.2% public transportation, 2.4% walk, 6.6% work from home (2000); Travel time to work: 28.9% less than 15 minutes, 47.6% 15 to 30 minutes, 12.6% 30 to 45 minutes, 6.6% 45 to 60 minutes, 4.3% 60 minutes or more (2000)

ROYALTON (township). Covers a land area of 18.069 square miles and a water area of 0.444 square miles. Located at 42.03° N. Lat.; 86.43° W. Long.
History: Royalton was settled in the early 1830's by John Pike and his family from Fort Royal, South Carolina.
Population: 3,888 (2000); Race: 94.1% White, 2.3% Black, 1.2% Asian, 0.6% American Indian and Alaska Native, 2.4% Hispanic of any race, 1.7% two or more races (2000); Density: 215.2 persons per square mile (2000); Age: 28.6% under 18, 13.9% over 64 (2000); Marriage status: 17.1% never married, 70.5% now married, 6.7% widowed, 5.7% divorced (2000); Foreign born: 4.2% (2000); Ancestry (includes multiple ancestries): 38.7% German, 12.6% Other groups, 12.0% Irish, 11.6% English, 6.2% Polish (2000).
Economy: Single-family building permits issued: 24 (2001) / 24 (2000); Multi-family building permits issued: 0 (2001) / 0 (2000); Employment by occupation: 19.0% management, 23.2% professional, 9.8% services, 26.3% sales, 0.7% farming, 6.6% construction, 14.5% production (2000).
Income: Per capita income: $26,926 (2000); Median household income: $69,375 (2000); Poverty rate: 9.4% (2000).
Taxes: Total city taxes per capita: $83 (1997); City property taxes per capita: $61 (1997).
Education: High school graduation rate: 88.9% (2000); College graduation rate: 35.8% (2000).
Housing: Homeownership rate: 91.7% (2000); Median home value: $172,700 (2000); Median rent: $629 per month (2000); Median age of housing: 27 years (2000).
Transportation: Commute to work: 94.2% car, 1.1% public transportation, 1.7% walk, 2.1% work from home (2000); Travel time to work: 45.7% less than 15 minutes, 37.4% 15 to 30 minutes, 8.7% 30 to 45 minutes, 3.7% 45 to 60 minutes, 4.5% 60 minutes or more (2000)

SAINT JOSEPH (city). Covers a land area of 3.431 square miles and a water area of 2.546 square miles. Located at 42.09° N. Lat.; 86.48° W. Long. Elevation is 591 feet.
History: St. Joseph was preceded by the town of Newburyport, founded in 1831 at the mouth of the St. Joseph River. The constantly shifting sands won out over the residents, who abandoned the site in five years and moved farther up the hills onto the site of St. Joseph. St. Joseph was incorporated as a village in 1836. The town grew slowly, some of the settlers choosing to locate across the river where they established the town that became Benton Harbor. Rivalry between the two towns was bitter until around 1900. Later the two became so homogeneous that only residents knew exactly where the boundary lines were.
Population: 8,789 (2000); Race: 90.6% White, 5.3% Black, 1.8% Asian, 0.6% American Indian and Alaska Native, 1.0% Hispanic of any race, 1.0% two or more races (2000); Density: 2,561.3 persons per square mile (2000); Age: 19.1% under 18, 17.8% over 64 (2000); Marriage status: 30.4% never married, 45.2% now married, 10.1% widowed, 14.3% divorced (2000); Foreign born: 5.4% (2000); Ancestry (includes multiple ancestries): 36.4% German, 15.4% English, 15.1% Irish, 10.5% Other groups, 7.1% Polish (2000).
Economy: Single-family building permits issued: 14 (2001) / 19 (2000); Multi-family building permits issued: 0 (2001) / 0 (2000); Employment by occupation: 12.7% management, 27.0% professional, 13.7% services, 25.6% sales, 0.2% farming, 6.4% construction, 14.3% production (2000).
Income: Per capita income: $24,949 (2000); Median household income: $37,032 (2000); Poverty rate: 6.6% (2000).
Education: High school graduation rate: 89.7% (2000); College graduation rate: 32.3% (2000).

School District(s)

Saint Joseph Public Schools (PK-12)
2000 Enrollment: 2,783 616-982-4621
Housing: Homeownership rate: 57.9% (2000); Median home value: $100,000 (2000); Median rent: $463 per month (2000); Median age of housing: 53 years (2000).
Hospitals: Lakeland Medical Center (300 beds)
Safety: Violent crime rate: 19.2 per 10,000 population; Property crime rate: 442.6 per 10,000 population (2001).
Newspapers: The Herald-Palladium (7 x week)
Transportation: Commute to work: 92.5% car, 0.0% public transportation, 3.6% walk, 3.0% work from home (2000); Travel time to work: 61.2% less than 15 minutes, 26.6% 15 to 30 minutes, 6.4% 30 to 45 minutes, 2.2% 45 to 60 minutes, 3.6% 60 minutes or more (2000); Amtrak: Service available.
Additional Information Contacts
Southwestern Michigan Association of Realtors 616-983-6375
St. Joseph Chamber of Commerce 616-982-0032

SAINT JOSEPH CHARTER (township). Covers a land area of 6.663 square miles and a water area of 0.305 square miles. Located at 42.07° N. Lat.; 86.47° W. Long.
Population: 10,042 (2000); Race: 85.7% White, 11.3% Black, 1.5% Asian, 0.1% American Indian and Alaska Native, 2.0% Hispanic of any race, 1.1% two or more races (2000); Density: 1,507.1 persons per square mile (2000); Age: 23.6% under 18, 19.0% over 64 (2000); Marriage status: 17.2% never married, 68.5% now married, 6.7% widowed, 7.6% divorced (2000); Foreign born: 4.7% (2000); Ancestry (includes multiple ancestries): 30.8% German, 16.7% Other groups, 11.5% English, 10.7% Irish, 5.6% Italian (2000).
Economy: Single-family building permits issued: 37 (2001) / 45 (2000); Multi-family building permits issued: 0 (2001) / 0 (2000); Employment by occupation: 17.8% management, 28.2% professional, 11.3% services, 23.1% sales, 0.0% farming, 6.0% construction, 13.7% production (2000).
Income: Per capita income: $28,095 (2000); Median household income: $54,158 (2000); Poverty rate: 3.7% (2000).
Education: High school graduation rate: 89.8% (2000); College graduation rate: 32.7% (2000).
Housing: Homeownership rate: 89.2% (2000); Median home value: $113,500 (2000); Median rent: $602 per month (2000); Median age of housing: 36 years (2000).
Safety: Violent crime rate: 16.8 per 10,000 population; Property crime rate: 255.6 per 10,000 population (2001).
Transportation: Commute to work: 94.6% car, 0.1% public transportation, 0.7% walk, 3.6% work from home (2000); Travel time to work: 57.3% less than 15 minutes, 32.6% 15 to 30 minutes, 4.6% 30 to 45 minutes, 2.5% 45 to 60 minutes, 3.0% 60 minutes or more (2000)

SAWYER (unincorporated postal area, zip code 49125). Covers a land area of 15.093 square miles and a water area of 0.027 square miles. Located at 41.89° N. Lat.; 86.59° W. Long. Elevation is 654 feet.
History: Sawyer began as a station on the Chicago & Western Michigan Railroad called Troy. It was renamed in 1854 for Silas Sawyer, who operated a mill here.
Population: 2,578 (2000); Race: 98.0% White, 0.0% Black, 0.3% Asian, 0.3% American Indian and Alaska Native, 0.3% Hispanic of any race, 1.2% two or more races (2000); Density: 170.8 persons per square mile (2000);

Age: 26.2% under 18, 17.9% over 64 (2000); Marriage status: 22.5% never married, 58.6% now married, 5.9% widowed, 13.0% divorced (2000); Foreign born: 1.8% (2000); Ancestry (includes multiple ancestries): 39.1% German, 12.5% Irish, 11.5% Swedish, 11.1% English, 9.5% Polish (2000).
Economy: Employment by occupation: 13.3% management, 15.4% professional, 18.9% services, 21.6% sales, 0.0% farming, 10.1% construction, 20.7% production (2000).
Income: Per capita income: $26,907 (2000); Median household income: $43,883 (2000); Poverty rate: 6.3% (2000).
Education: High school graduation rate: 84.1% (2000); College graduation rate: 16.9% (2000).
Housing: Homeownership rate: 79.3% (2000); Median home value: $119,100 (2000); Median rent: $507 per month (2000); Median age of housing: 51 years (2000).
Transportation: Commute to work: 92.3% car, 0.4% public transportation, 3.0% walk, 3.3% work from home (2000); Travel time to work: 40.1% less than 15 minutes, 35.9% 15 to 30 minutes, 18.1% 30 to 45 minutes, 0.0% 45 to 60 minutes, 5.9% 60 minutes or more (2000)

SHOREHAM (village). Covers a land area of 0.571 square miles and a water area of 0 square miles. Located at 42.06° N. Lat.; 86.50° W. Long. Elevation is 645 feet.
History: The village of Shoreham was founded by William Ducker, an early resident here who wanted to keep the area residential. He named the village for its location along the shore of Lake Michigan.
Population: 860 (2000); Race: 93.1% White, 0.5% Black, 4.4% Asian, 1.0% American Indian and Alaska Native, 0.8% Hispanic of any race, 0.2% two or more races (2000); Density: 1,505.8 persons per square mile (2000); Age: 19.5% under 18, 23.1% over 64 (2000); Marriage status: 16.7% never married, 59.1% now married, 9.9% widowed, 14.2% divorced (2000); Foreign born: 5.5% (2000); Ancestry (includes multiple ancestries): 30.4% German, 16.5% English, 11.9% Irish, 7.8% Other groups, 7.3% Italian (2000).
Economy: Employment by occupation: 22.4% management, 28.8% professional, 9.0% services, 22.4% sales, 0.0% farming, 4.0% construction, 13.3% production (2000).
Income: Per capita income: $32,449 (2000); Median household income: $51,333 (2000); Poverty rate: 5.5% (2000).
Taxes: Total city taxes per capita: $21 (1997); City property taxes per capita: $21 (1997).
Education: High school graduation rate: 91.2% (2000); College graduation rate: 38.8% (2000).
Housing: Homeownership rate: 56.7% (2000); Median home value: $142,000 (2000); Median rent: $664 per month (2000); Median age of housing: 25 years (2000).
Transportation: Commute to work: 97.1% car, 0.0% public transportation, 0.0% walk, 2.9% work from home (2000); Travel time to work: 64.0% less than 15 minutes, 24.1% 15 to 30 minutes, 5.2% 30 to 45 minutes, 3.7% 45 to 60 minutes, 3.0% 60 minutes or more (2000)

SHOREWOOD-TOWER HILLS-HARBERT (CDP). Covers a land area of 4.537 square miles and a water area of 0.019 square miles. Located at 41.88° N. Lat.; 86.61° W. Long.
Population: 1,619 (2000); Race: 97.4% White, 1.3% Black, 0.0% Asian, 0.4% American Indian and Alaska Native, 0.4% Hispanic of any race, 0.9% two or more races (2000); Density: 356.9 persons per square mile (2000); Age: 20.8% under 18, 25.2% over 64 (2000); Marriage status: 19.9% never married, 57.9% now married, 6.2% widowed, 16.0% divorced (2000); Foreign born: 2.4% (2000); Ancestry (includes multiple ancestries): 34.0% German, 17.5% Swedish, 12.4% English, 11.4% Irish, 6.6% Polish (2000).
Economy: Employment by occupation: 18.7% management, 22.8% professional, 15.6% services, 21.8% sales, 0.0% farming, 10.4% construction, 10.6% production (2000).
Income: Per capita income: $36,219 (2000); Median household income: $47,708 (2000); Poverty rate: 4.5% (2000).
Education: High school graduation rate: 89.5% (2000); College graduation rate: 26.8% (2000).
Housing: Homeownership rate: 83.6% (2000); Median home value: $166,700 (2000); Median rent: $552 per month (2000); Median age of housing: 50 years (2000).
Transportation: Commute to work: 91.2% car, 0.8% public transportation, 5.0% walk, 3.0% work from home (2000); Travel time to work: 46.4% less than 15 minutes, 31.2% 15 to 30 minutes, 15.5% 30 to 45 minutes, 0.7% 45 to 60 minutes, 6.2% 60 minutes or more (2000)

SODUS (township). Covers a land area of 19.529 square miles and a water area of 0.536 square miles. Located at 42.04° N. Lat.; 86.38° W. Long. Elevation is 672 feet.
History: The Sodus area was settled in the mid-1830's by William H. and David Rector. Sodus Township was separated out in 1859 and named by Rector for his home town of Sodus, New York.
Population: 2,139 (2000); Race: 86.4% White, 6.5% Black, 0.1% Asian, 0.6% American Indian and Alaska Native, 8.5% Hispanic of any race, 2.7% two or more races (2000); Density: 109.5 persons per square mile (2000); Age: 22.5% under 18, 17.0% over 64 (2000); Marriage status: 20.2% never married, 61.1% now married, 7.9% widowed, 10.9% divorced (2000); Foreign born: 5.2% (2000); Ancestry (includes multiple ancestries): 29.9% German, 14.6% Other groups, 12.9% United States or American, 11.5% Irish, 8.8% English (2000).
Economy: Single-family building permits issued: 5 (2001) / 6 (2000); Multi-family building permits issued: 0 (2001) / 0 (2000); Employment by occupation: 9.0% management, 12.7% professional, 14.7% services, 22.9% sales, 6.8% farming, 11.9% construction, 22.0% production (2000).
Income: Per capita income: $17,646 (2000); Median household income: $33,804 (2000); Poverty rate: 13.6% (2000).
Taxes: Total city taxes per capita: $87 (1997); City property taxes per capita: $79 (1997).
Education: High school graduation rate: 76.4% (2000); College graduation rate: 12.0% (2000).

School District(s)

Sodus Township School District #5 (KG-08)
2000 Enrollment: 70 616-925-6757
Housing: Homeownership rate: 87.5% (2000); Median home value: $89,200 (2000); Median rent: $368 per month (2000); Median age of housing: 30 years (2000).
Transportation: Commute to work: 93.3% car, 1.3% public transportation, 1.4% walk, 4.0% work from home (2000); Travel time to work: 37.6% less than 15 minutes, 49.8% 15 to 30 minutes, 8.2% 30 to 45 minutes, 3.0% 45 to 60 minutes, 1.5% 60 minutes or more (2000)

STEVENSVILLE (village). Covers a land area of 1.032 square miles and a water area of 0 square miles. Located at 42.01° N. Lat.; 86.52° W. Long. Elevation is 635 feet.
History: Stevensville was named for Thomas Stevens, who donated right-of-way land to the railroad and platted the village.
Population: 1,191 (2000); Race: 96.3% White, 0.0% Black, 0.8% Asian, 0.4% American Indian and Alaska Native, 0.5% Hispanic of any race, 2.3% two or more races (2000); Density: 1,153.9 persons per square mile (2000); Age: 21.3% under 18, 17.0% over 64 (2000); Marriage status: 19.2% never married, 64.7% now married, 8.0% widowed, 8.2% divorced (2000); Foreign born: 2.4% (2000); Ancestry (includes multiple ancestries): 39.6% German, 16.3% Irish, 10.8% English, 8.0% Other groups, 7.1% Polish (2000).
Economy: Single-family building permits issued: 2 (2001) / 2 (2000); Multi-family building permits issued: 0 (2001) / 0 (2000); Employment by occupation: 11.7% management, 23.4% professional, 11.4% services, 27.5% sales, 0.0% farming, 10.5% construction, 15.5% production (2000).
Income: Per capita income: $23,228 (2000); Median household income: $42,569 (2000); Poverty rate: 1.5% (2000).
Taxes: Total city taxes per capita: $187 (1997); City property taxes per capita: $180 (1997).
Education: High school graduation rate: 85.6% (2000); College graduation rate: 22.1% (2000).

School District(s)

Lakeshore School District (Berri (KG-12)
2000 Enrollment: 2,889 616-428-1400
Housing: Homeownership rate: 67.7% (2000); Median home value: $102,600 (2000); Median rent: $486 per month (2000); Median age of housing: 32 years (2000).
Transportation: Commute to work: 94.6% car, 0.0% public transportation, 2.5% walk, 2.9% work from home (2000); Travel time to work: 46.1% less than 15 minutes, 42.3% 15 to 30 minutes, 7.1% 30 to 45 minutes, 1.7% 45 to 60 minutes, 2.8% 60 minutes or more (2000)
Additional Information Contacts
Lakeshore Chamber of Commerce.......................... 616-429-1170

THREE OAKS (village). Covers a land area of 0.983 square miles and a water area of 0 square miles. Located at 41.80° N. Lat.; 86.61° W. Long. Elevation is 679 feet.
History: The village of Three Oaks was founded by Henry Chamberlain, who named it for the three trees that stood near the post office.

Population: 1,829 (2000); Race: 95.1% White, 0.9% Black, 0.0% Asian, 1.0% American Indian and Alaska Native, 1.2% Hispanic of any race, 2.0% two or more races (2000); Density: 1,861.4 persons per square mile (2000); Age: 27.2% under 18, 11.4% over 64 (2000); Marriage status: 24.9% never married, 53.4% now married, 8.0% widowed, 13.7% divorced (2000); Foreign born: 1.9% (2000); Ancestry (includes multiple ancestries): 32.9% German, 17.7% Irish, 11.4% Other groups, 10.2% Polish, 9.5% English (2000).
Economy: Employment by occupation: 9.2% management, 11.9% professional, 20.9% services, 22.4% sales, 0.2% farming, 12.1% construction, 23.3% production (2000).
Income: Per capita income: $16,361 (2000); Median household income: $34,120 (2000); Poverty rate: 11.7% (2000).
Taxes: Total city taxes per capita: $204 (1997); City property taxes per capita: $204 (1997).
Education: High school graduation rate: 80.7% (2000); College graduation rate: 10.5% (2000).

School District(s)

River Valley School District (PK-12)
2000 Enrollment: 1,194 616-756-9541
Housing: Homeownership rate: 71.1% (2000); Median home value: $80,200 (2000); Median rent: $394 per month (2000); Median age of housing: 56 years (2000).
Safety: Violent crime rate: 10.9 per 10,000 population; Property crime rate: 299.1 per 10,000 population (2001).
Newspapers: The Other Side of the Lake; Southcounty Gazette and Shopper (1 x week)
Transportation: Commute to work: 91.1% car, 0.5% public transportation, 4.0% walk, 3.9% work from home (2000); Travel time to work: 31.9% less than 15 minutes, 37.6% 15 to 30 minutes, 18.0% 30 to 45 minutes, 5.0% 45 to 60 minutes, 7.6% 60 minutes or more (2000)

THREE OAKS (township). Covers a land area of 23.394 square miles and a water area of 0.068 square miles. Located at 41.79° N. Lat.; 86.61° W. Long. Elevation is 679 feet.
History: Has museum containing Native American and historic relics. Settled 1850, incorporated 1867.
Population: 2,949 (2000); Race: 95.5% White, 0.6% Black, 0.0% Asian, 0.6% American Indian and Alaska Native, 1.9% Hispanic of any race, 2.5% two or more races (2000); Density: 126.1 persons per square mile (2000); Age: 25.4% under 18, 14.0% over 64 (2000); Marriage status: 23.9% never married, 56.5% now married, 7.5% widowed, 12.1% divorced (2000); Foreign born: 1.8% (2000); Ancestry (includes multiple ancestries): 31.9% German, 17.5% Irish, 10.3% Other groups, 9.2% English, 8.3% United States or American (2000).
Economy: In area growing fruit, corn, grains, wheat, tomatoes. Hogs. Manufacturing includes plastic moldings, hardware packaging. Single-family building permits issued: 6 (2001) / 5 (2000); Multi-family building permits issued: 0 (2001) / 0 (2000); Employment by occupation: 11.1% management, 10.9% professional, 19.9% services, 22.5% sales, 0.7% farming, 13.6% construction, 21.3% production (2000).
Income: Per capita income: $17,901 (2000); Median household income: $36,989 (2000); Poverty rate: 9.9% (2000).
Taxes: Total city taxes per capita: $69 (1997); City property taxes per capita: $68 (1997).
Education: High school graduation rate: 82.2% (2000); College graduation rate: 9.6% (2000).
Housing: Homeownership rate: 79.9% (2000); Median home value: $86,400 (2000); Median rent: $390 per month (2000); Median age of housing: 50 years (2000).
Transportation: Commute to work: 90.9% car, 0.6% public transportation, 3.3% walk, 3.6% work from home (2000); Travel time to work: 39.2% less than 15 minutes, 35.3% 15 to 30 minutes, 15.1% 30 to 45 minutes, 3.5% 45 to 60 minutes, 6.8% 60 minutes or more (2000)

UNION PIER (unincorporated postal area, zip code 49129). Covers a land area of 4.739 square miles and a water area of 0.005 square miles. Located at 41.82° N. Lat.; 86.69° W. Long.
Population: 727 (2000); Race: 89.8% White, 9.1% Black, 0.0% Asian, 0.8% American Indian and Alaska Native, 1.1% Hispanic of any race, 0.0% two or more races (2000); Density: 153.4 persons per square mile (2000); Age: 17.5% under 18, 23.3% over 64 (2000); Marriage status: 14.5% never married, 67.9% now married, 8.6% widowed, 8.9% divorced (2000); Foreign born: 9.6% (2000); Ancestry (includes multiple ancestries): 25.6% German, 21.2% Irish, 11.6% Other groups, 10.5% English, 9.0% Lithuanian (2000).
Economy: Employment by occupation: 20.2% management, 15.7% professional, 14.3% services, 22.2% sales, 0.0% farming, 11.5% construction, 16.0% production (2000).
Income: Per capita income: $30,849 (2000); Median household income: $51,406 (2000); Poverty rate: 6.2% (2000).
Education: High school graduation rate: 83.3% (2000); College graduation rate: 32.2% (2000).
Housing: Homeownership rate: 88.3% (2000); Median home value: $152,100 (2000); Median rent: $463 per month (2000); Median age of housing: 51 years (2000).
Transportation: Commute to work: 91.6% car, 1.4% public transportation, 1.4% walk, 5.5% work from home (2000); Travel time to work: 36.3% less than 15 minutes, 27.7% 15 to 30 minutes, 14.6% 30 to 45 minutes, 2.4% 45 to 60 minutes, 18.9% 60 minutes or more (2000)

WATERVLIET (city). Covers a land area of 1.232 square miles and a water area of 0 square miles. Located at 42.18° N. Lat.; 86.26° W. Long.
History: Watervliet was settled in the early 1830's and named for the rapids that were once evident in the Paw Paw River.
Population: 1,843 (2000); Race: 95.7% White, 0.0% Black, 3.2% Asian, 0.1% American Indian and Alaska Native, 1.0% Hispanic of any race, 1.0% two or more races (2000); Density: 1,495.9 persons per square mile (2000); Age: 31.6% under 18, 14.5% over 64 (2000); Marriage status: 23.1% never married, 54.2% now married, 9.0% widowed, 13.7% divorced (2000); Foreign born: 3.1% (2000); Ancestry (includes multiple ancestries): 22.7% German, 16.5% Other groups, 15.6% Irish, 10.6% English, 8.4% United States or American (2000).
Economy: Single-family building permits issued: 2 (2001) / 2 (2000); Multi-family building permits issued: 0 (2001) / 0 (2000); Employment by occupation: 5.0% management, 12.9% professional, 17.8% services, 30.6% sales, 0.0% farming, 9.4% construction, 24.3% production (2000).
Income: Per capita income: $16,691 (2000); Median household income: $38,681 (2000); Poverty rate: 6.9% (2000).
Taxes: Total city taxes per capita: $231 (1997); City property taxes per capita: $223 (1997).
Education: High school graduation rate: 78.2% (2000); College graduation rate: 8.7% (2000).

School District(s)

Watervliet School District (KG-12)
2000 Enrollment: 1,300 616-463-5566
Housing: Homeownership rate: 68.9% (2000); Median home value: $72,400 (2000); Median rent: $399 per month (2000); Median age of housing: 48 years (2000).
Hospitals: Community Hospital (70 beds)
Safety: Violent crime rate: 32.4 per 10,000 population; Property crime rate: 496.5 per 10,000 population (2001).
Newspapers: Tri-City Record (1 x week)
Transportation: Commute to work: 95.2% car, 0.0% public transportation, 2.7% walk, 0.7% work from home (2000); Travel time to work: 37.0% less than 15 minutes, 42.1% 15 to 30 minutes, 14.7% 30 to 45 minutes, 2.9% 45 to 60 minutes, 3.4% 60 minutes or more (2000)

WATERVLIET (township). Covers a land area of 13.642 square miles and a water area of 0.807 square miles. Located at 42.20° N. Lat.; 86.25° W. Long.
History: Settled in 1830s; incorporated as village 1891, as city 1925.
Population: 3,392 (2000); Race: 95.7% White, 0.8% Black, 0.1% Asian, 0.7% American Indian and Alaska Native, 3.5% Hispanic of any race, 0.8% two or more races (2000); Density: 248.7 persons per square mile (2000); Age: 23.7% under 18, 14.7% over 64 (2000); Marriage status: 19.7% never married, 60.3% now married, 7.4% widowed, 12.6% divorced (2000); Foreign born: 2.2% (2000); Ancestry (includes multiple ancestries): 32.2% German, 16.2% Irish, 10.8% Other groups, 9.1% English, 7.5% Italian (2000).
Economy: In orchard and farm area; poultry. Paw Paw Lake resort is just North. Manufacturing of paper products, brushes. Single-family building permits issued: 15 (2001) / 18 (2000); Multi-family building permits issued: 0 (2001) / 8 (2000); Employment by occupation: 9.1% management, 11.3% professional, 14.8% services, 25.6% sales, 1.0% farming, 11.6% construction, 26.5% production (2000).
Income: Per capita income: $22,134 (2000); Median household income: $39,152 (2000); Poverty rate: 10.5% (2000).
Taxes: Total city taxes per capita: $88 (1997); City property taxes per capita: $78 (1997).
Education: High school graduation rate: 85.6% (2000); College graduation rate: 8.7% (2000).

Housing: Homeownership rate: 78.7% (2000); Median home value: $89,800 (2000); Median rent: $428 per month (2000); Median age of housing: 36 years (2000).
Transportation: Commute to work: 93.4% car, 0.2% public transportation, 2.2% walk, 2.2% work from home (2000); Travel time to work: 29.0% less than 15 minutes, 50.8% 15 to 30 minutes, 12.7% 30 to 45 minutes, 3.8% 45 to 60 minutes, 3.7% 60 minutes or more (2000)

WEESAW (township). Covers a land area of 35.528 square miles and a water area of 0.096 square miles. Located at 41.86° N. Lat.; 86.52° W. Long.
Population: 2,065 (2000); Race: 96.0% White, 0.0% Black, 0.0% Asian, 1.2% American Indian and Alaska Native, 1.3% Hispanic of any race, 1.2% two or more races (2000); Density: 58.1 persons per square mile (2000); Age: 24.3% under 18, 13.6% over 64 (2000); Marriage status: 21.9% never married, 63.4% now married, 6.6% widowed, 8.1% divorced (2000); Foreign born: 1.7% (2000); Ancestry (includes multiple ancestries): 40.0% German, 12.9% Irish, 12.8% English, 8.3% Polish, 8.2% Other groups (2000).
Economy: Employment by occupation: 11.1% management, 13.4% professional, 15.7% services, 18.4% sales, 1.9% farming, 11.2% construction, 28.3% production (2000).
Income: Per capita income: $18,159 (2000); Median household income: $41,434 (2000); Poverty rate: 6.6% (2000).
Taxes: Total city taxes per capita: $115 (2000); City property taxes per capita: $113 (2000).
Education: High school graduation rate: 78.6% (2000); College graduation rate: 7.9% (2000).
Housing: Homeownership rate: 87.0% (2000); Median home value: $92,600 (2000); Median rent: $403 per month (2000); Median age of housing: 51 years (2000).
Transportation: Commute to work: 90.6% car, 0.0% public transportation, 1.3% walk, 6.1% work from home (2000); Travel time to work: 25.1% less than 15 minutes, 47.0% 15 to 30 minutes, 19.5% 30 to 45 minutes, 1.5% 45 to 60 minutes, 6.8% 60 minutes or more (2000)

Branch County

Located in southern Michigan; bounded on the south by Indiana. Covers a land area of 507.40 square miles, a water area of 12.10 square miles, and is located in the Eastern Time Zone. The county government was organized in 1829. County seat is Coldwater.

Weather Station: Coldwater State School — Elevation: 980 feet

	Jan	Feb	Mar	Apr	May	Jun	Jul	Aug	Sep	Oct	Nov	Dec
High	30	34	44	57	70	79	82	80	73	61	46	35
Low	14	17	25	36	47	56	60	58	50	40	31	21
Precip	1.8	1.7	2.5	3.2	3.7	3.6	4.0	3.9	3.5	2.8	2.7	2.4
Snow	16.2	10.3	7.9	1.9	tr	0.0	0.0	0.0	tr	0.6	5.2	13.5

High and Low temperatures in degrees Fahrenheit; Precipitation and Snow in inches

Population: 45,787 (2000); Race: 93.4% White, 2.2% Black, 0.5% Asian, 0.4% American Indian and Alaska Native, 2.9% Hispanic of any race, 2.0% two or more races (2000); Density: 90.2 persons per square mile (2000); Age: 25.6% under 18, 13.0% over 64 (2000).
Religion: Five largest groups: 14.0% Catholic Church, 2.5% The United Methodist Church, 1.8% American Baptist Churches in the USA, 1.6% Lutheran Church—Missouri Synod, 1.4% Old Order Amish Church (2000).
Economy: Unemployment rate: 5.0% (11/2002); Total civilian labor force: 25,393 (11/2002); Leading industries: 32.0% manufacturing; 15.7% retail trade; 12.0% health care and social assistance (2000); Companies that employ more than 1,000 persons: 0 (2000); Companies that employ more than 100 persons: 22 (2000); Farms: 980 totaling 234,076 acres (1997); Minority business ownership rate: 0.0% (1997); Women business ownership rate: 19.3% (1997); Retail sales per capita: $7,342 (1997). Single-family building permits issued: 101 (2001) / 123 (2000); Multi-family building permits issued: 180 (2001) / 0 (2000).
Income: Per capita income: $17,552 (2000); Median household income: $38,760 (2000); Poverty rate: 9.3% (2000); Bankruptcy rate: 5.14% (2001).
Taxes: Total county taxes per capita: $122 (2000); County property taxes per capita: $107 (2000).
Education: High school graduation rate: 80.0% (2000); College graduation rate: 10.6% (2000).
Housing: Homeownership rate: 78.9% (2000); Median home value: $85,000 (2000); Median rent: $396 per month (2000); Median age of housing: 38 years (2000).
Health: Birth rate: 121.2 per 10,000 population (1998); Age adjusted death rate: 86.6 per 10,000 population (1999); Age adjusted cancer mortality rate: 136.3 deaths per 100,000 population (1999). Number of physicians: 8.1 per 10,000 population (1999); Number of hospital beds: 21.0 per 10,000 population (1999).
Elections: 2000 Presidential election results: 42.4% Gore, 55.4% Bush, 1.8% Nader, 0.0% Buchanan
Additional Information Contacts
Branch County Government Offices 517-279-4300
Branch County Board of Realtors 517-278-3192
Coldwater Chamber of Commerce. 517-278-5985

Branch County Communities

ALGANSEE (township). Covers a land area of 35.564 square miles and a water area of 0.537 square miles. Located at 41.86° N. Lat.; 84.89° W. Long.
Population: 2,061 (2000); Race: 99.6% White, 0.0% Black, 0.0% Asian, 0.0% American Indian and Alaska Native, 0.5% Hispanic of any race, 0.4% two or more races (2000); Density: 58.0 persons per square mile (2000); Age: 27.1% under 18, 13.6% over 64 (2000); Marriage status: 21.7% never married, 63.4% now married, 6.4% widowed, 8.5% divorced (2000); Foreign born: 0.9% (2000); Ancestry (includes multiple ancestries): 31.5% German, 16.2% English, 11.9% Irish, 11.2% United States or American, 6.8% French (except Basque) (2000).
Economy: Employment by occupation: 8.6% management, 14.1% professional, 8.1% services, 24.2% sales, 0.6% farming, 9.0% construction, 35.4% production (2000).
Income: Per capita income: $18,299 (2000); Median household income: $42,794 (2000); Poverty rate: 7.7% (2000).
Taxes: Total city taxes per capita: $22 (1997); City property taxes per capita: $21 (1997).
Education: High school graduation rate: 83.9% (2000); College graduation rate: 9.1% (2000).
Housing: Homeownership rate: 89.4% (2000); Median home value: $111,600 (2000); Median rent: $441 per month (2000); Median age of housing: 31 years (2000).
Transportation: Commute to work: 91.0% car, 1.2% public transportation, 1.2% walk, 4.8% work from home (2000); Travel time to work: 18.5% less than 15 minutes, 57.9% 15 to 30 minutes, 13.3% 30 to 45 minutes, 1.2% 45 to 60 minutes, 9.2% 60 minutes or more (2000)

BATAVIA (township). Aka Batavia Station. Covers a land area of 35.741 square miles and a water area of 0.413 square miles. Located at 41.93° N. Lat.; 85.10° W. Long.
History: Batavia was named after Batavia, New York.
Population: 1,546 (2000); Race: 97.4% White, 0.5% Black, 0.1% Asian, 0.4% American Indian and Alaska Native, 0.6% Hispanic of any race, 1.3% two or more races (2000); Density: 43.3 persons per square mile (2000); Age: 23.6% under 18, 14.9% over 64 (2000); Marriage status: 23.1% never married, 58.9% now married, 6.8% widowed, 11.2% divorced (2000); Foreign born: 0.3% (2000); Ancestry (includes multiple ancestries): 26.6% German, 17.6% English, 13.6% Irish, 10.1% Polish, 9.0% United States or American (2000).
Economy: Employment by occupation: 8.0% management, 11.5% professional, 10.0% services, 23.5% sales, 1.5% farming, 10.0% construction, 35.4% production (2000).
Income: Per capita income: $18,526 (2000); Median household income: $41,351 (2000); Poverty rate: 9.4% (2000).
Taxes: Total city taxes per capita: $17 (1997); City property taxes per capita: $17 (1997).
Education: High school graduation rate: 80.7% (2000); College graduation rate: 6.5% (2000).
Housing: Homeownership rate: 81.0% (2000); Median home value: $84,100 (2000); Median rent: $385 per month (2000); Median age of housing: 39 years (2000).
Transportation: Commute to work: 94.7% car, 0.5% public transportation, 0.3% walk, 3.9% work from home (2000); Travel time to work: 35.6% less than 15 minutes, 40.5% 15 to 30 minutes, 13.2% 30 to 45 minutes, 5.2% 45 to 60 minutes, 5.5% 60 minutes or more (2000)

BETHEL (township). Covers a land area of 35.907 square miles and a water area of 0.177 square miles. Located at 41.85° N. Lat.; 85.12° W. Long. Elevation is 997 feet.
History: The name of Bethel is Old Testament Hebrew meaning "House of the Lord." The area was settled in 1830.
Population: 1,421 (2000); Race: 91.5% White, 0.1% Black, 0.0% Asian, 0.9% American Indian and Alaska Native, 9.9% Hispanic of any race, 0.8%

two or more races (2000); Density: 39.6 persons per square mile (2000); Age: 27.4% under 18, 9.5% over 64 (2000); Marriage status: 24.8% never married, 60.4% now married, 6.2% widowed, 8.6% divorced (2000); Foreign born: 4.4% (2000); Ancestry (includes multiple ancestries): 19.1% German, 12.5% English, 9.5% Other groups, 9.3% Polish, 8.2% United States or American (2000).
Economy: Employment by occupation: 13.6% management, 10.7% professional, 9.7% services, 17.5% sales, 4.0% farming, 11.6% construction, 32.9% production (2000).
Income: Per capita income: $16,252 (2000); Median household income: $40,400 (2000); Poverty rate: 10.2% (2000).
Taxes: Total city taxes per capita: $16 (1997); City property taxes per capita: $14 (1997).
Education: High school graduation rate: 77.0% (2000); College graduation rate: 6.9% (2000).
Housing: Homeownership rate: 86.4% (2000); Median home value: $78,000 (2000); Median rent: $373 per month (2000); Median age of housing: 34 years (2000).
Transportation: Commute to work: 86.7% car, 0.3% public transportation, 2.2% walk, 10.1% work from home (2000); Travel time to work: 23.8% less than 15 minutes, 43.7% 15 to 30 minutes, 19.4% 30 to 45 minutes, 7.3% 45 to 60 minutes, 5.8% 60 minutes or more (2000)

BRONSON (city). Covers a land area of 1.356 square miles and a water area of 0 square miles. Located at 41.87° N. Lat.; 85.19° W. Long. Elevation is 916 feet.
History: Jabez Bronson built a hunting lodge and tavern here in 1828. When the settlement was asked to serve as the first seat of Branch County, Bronson was the law and his tavern was the court. The village grew in the 1870's with the arrival of many Polish immigrants, attracted by the fertile land.
Population: 2,421 (2000); Race: 90.1% White, 0.0% Black, 0.8% Asian, 0.2% American Indian and Alaska Native, 9.8% Hispanic of any race, 1.7% two or more races (2000); Density: 1,784.8 persons per square mile (2000); Age: 30.1% under 18, 14.9% over 64 (2000); Marriage status: 25.3% never married, 54.2% now married, 8.1% widowed, 12.3% divorced (2000); Foreign born: 7.8% (2000); Ancestry (includes multiple ancestries): 18.8% German, 17.1% Other groups, 13.7% Polish, 10.6% Irish, 7.1% United States or American (2000).
Economy: Employment by occupation: 7.1% management, 10.6% professional, 12.8% services, 20.7% sales, 1.7% farming, 9.9% construction, 37.2% production (2000).
Income: Per capita income: $17,023 (2000); Median household income: $32,035 (2000); Poverty rate: 12.7% (2000).
Taxes: Total city taxes per capita: $187 (1997); City property taxes per capita: $184 (1997).
Education: High school graduation rate: 69.3% (2000); College graduation rate: 7.3% (2000).

School District(s)

Bronson Community School District (KG-12)
2000 Enrollment: 1,372 517-369-3257
Housing: Homeownership rate: 67.7% (2000); Median home value: $65,300 (2000); Median rent: $370 per month (2000); Median age of housing: 50 years (2000).
Safety: Violent crime rate: 12.3 per 10,000 population; Property crime rate: 386.2 per 10,000 population (2001).
Newspapers: The Bronson Journal (1 x week)
Transportation: Commute to work: 94.7% car, 0.2% public transportation, 3.7% walk, 0.6% work from home (2000); Travel time to work: 27.6% less than 15 minutes, 50.5% 15 to 30 minutes, 14.8% 30 to 45 minutes, 3.8% 45 to 60 minutes, 3.3% 60 minutes or more (2000)

BRONSON (township). Covers a land area of 34.739 square miles and a water area of 0.025 square miles. Located at 41.85° N. Lat.; 85.23° W. Long. Elevation is 916 feet.
History: Bronson Township was first called Prairie River, but was renamed by the state legislature in 1837 for Jabez B. Bronson.
Population: 1,358 (2000); Race: 96.2% White, 0.0% Black, 0.0% Asian, 0.8% American Indian and Alaska Native, 4.3% Hispanic of any race, 0.5% two or more races (2000); Density: 39.1 persons per square mile (2000); Age: 30.6% under 18, 12.3% over 64 (2000); Marriage status: 21.7% never married, 61.9% now married, 5.6% widowed, 10.7% divorced (2000); Foreign born: 1.2% (2000); Ancestry (includes multiple ancestries): 23.7% German, 18.9% Polish, 13.6% United States or American, 10.0% Other groups, 9.5% Irish (2000).
Economy: Employment by occupation: 7.6% management, 10.8% professional, 8.9% services, 22.6% sales, 2.6% farming, 10.8% construction, 36.8% production (2000).
Income: Per capita income: $16,223 (2000); Median household income: $41,202 (2000); Poverty rate: 5.1% (2000).
Taxes: Total city taxes per capita: $19 (1997); City property taxes per capita: $18 (1997).
Education: High school graduation rate: 77.5% (2000); College graduation rate: 6.5% (2000).
Housing: Homeownership rate: 82.8% (2000); Median home value: $93,900 (2000); Median rent: $322 per month (2000); Median age of housing: 38 years (2000).
Transportation: Commute to work: 92.5% car, 0.5% public transportation, 1.2% walk, 3.2% work from home (2000); Travel time to work: 32.0% less than 15 minutes, 48.8% 15 to 30 minutes, 11.0% 30 to 45 minutes, 3.7% 45 to 60 minutes, 4.6% 60 minutes or more (2000)

BUTLER (township). Covers a land area of 35.639 square miles and a water area of 0.117 square miles. Located at 42.02° N. Lat.; 84.87° W. Long. Elevation is 1,014 feet.
History: Butler Township was organized in 1838 and named for Butler, New York, the former home of many early residents.
Population: 1,362 (2000); Race: 97.9% White, 0.7% Black, 0.0% Asian, 0.4% American Indian and Alaska Native, 0.1% Hispanic of any race, 1.0% two or more races (2000); Density: 38.2 persons per square mile (2000); Age: 34.6% under 18, 9.2% over 64 (2000); Marriage status: 23.3% never married, 62.9% now married, 6.3% widowed, 7.5% divorced (2000); Foreign born: 0.4% (2000); Ancestry (includes multiple ancestries): 24.2% German, 22.4% United States or American, 10.2% English, 6.9% Irish, 5.2% Other groups (2000).
Economy: Employment by occupation: 11.8% management, 10.5% professional, 12.3% services, 21.1% sales, 1.8% farming, 12.1% construction, 30.6% production (2000).
Income: Per capita income: $14,731 (2000); Median household income: $38,631 (2000); Poverty rate: 9.7% (2000).
Taxes: Total city taxes per capita: $17 (1997); City property taxes per capita: $17 (1997).
Education: High school graduation rate: 73.2% (2000); College graduation rate: 8.7% (2000).
Housing: Homeownership rate: 89.1% (2000); Median home value: $79,800 (2000); Median rent: $350 per month (2000); Median age of housing: 43 years (2000).
Transportation: Commute to work: 87.8% car, 0.3% public transportation, 1.0% walk, 8.7% work from home (2000); Travel time to work: 27.2% less than 15 minutes, 46.0% 15 to 30 minutes, 13.1% 30 to 45 minutes, 6.5% 45 to 60 minutes, 7.2% 60 minutes or more (2000)

CALIFORNIA (township). Covers a land area of 21.257 square miles and a water area of 0.044 square miles. Located at 41.78° N. Lat.; 84.88° W. Long. Elevation is 1,060 feet.
History: California Township was settled in 1835 by Israel R. Hall and his family. The settlement that grew up around him was called Hall's Corners after Joseph Hall, who operated a general store here.
Population: 909 (2000); Race: 93.9% White, 0.0% Black, 0.0% Asian, 0.6% American Indian and Alaska Native, 1.9% Hispanic of any race, 5.5% two or more races (2000); Density: 42.8 persons per square mile (2000); Age: 43.9% under 18, 8.3% over 64 (2000); Marriage status: 22.0% never married, 66.2% now married, 5.3% widowed, 6.5% divorced (2000); Foreign born: 1.3% (2000); Ancestry (includes multiple ancestries): 36.9% German, 8.2% English, 8.0% United States or American, 5.8% Irish, 5.6% Pennsylvania German (2000).
Economy: Employment by occupation: 10.8% management, 7.6% professional, 13.6% services, 16.7% sales, 4.5% farming, 10.2% construction, 36.5% production (2000).
Income: Per capita income: $11,341 (2000); Median household income: $34,545 (2000); Poverty rate: 31.8% (2000).
Taxes: Total city taxes per capita: $27 (1997); City property taxes per capita: $27 (1997).
Education: High school graduation rate: 59.7% (2000); College graduation rate: 4.5% (2000).
Housing: Homeownership rate: 84.9% (2000); Median home value: $63,900 (2000); Median rent: $429 per month (2000); Median age of housing: 60+ years (2000).
Transportation: Commute to work: 84.3% car, 0.0% public transportation, 0.3% walk, 7.1% work from home (2000); Travel time to work: 23.7% less

than 15 minutes, 46.8% 15 to 30 minutes, 14.5% 30 to 45 minutes, 7.7% 45 to 60 minutes, 7.4% 60 minutes or more (2000)

COLDWATER (city). Covers a land area of 8.126 square miles and a water area of 0.221 square miles. Located at 41.94° N. Lat.; 85.00° W. Long. Elevation is 969 feet.
History: Coldwater grew up at the place where the Chicago Turnpike crossed the Coldwater River. A village was platted here in 1832, incorporated in 1837, and chartered as a city in 1861. Coldwater was an active and very successful station on the Underground Railroad, claiming that no slave was ever captured in the vicinity of Coldwater.
Population: 12,697 (2000); Race: 85.4% White, 7.4% Black, 1.1% Asian, 0.8% American Indian and Alaska Native, 4.4% Hispanic of any race, 3.7% two or more races (2000); Density: 1,562.5 persons per square mile (2000); Age: 22.5% under 18, 11.4% over 64 (2000); Marriage status: 27.2% never married, 49.6% now married, 7.0% widowed, 16.2% divorced (2000); Foreign born: 4.9% (2000); Ancestry (includes multiple ancestries): 19.4% German, 15.9% Other groups, 9.7% English, 8.7% Irish, 7.4% United States or American (2000).
Economy: Single-family building permits issued: 42 (2001) / 18 (2000); Multi-family building permits issued: 180 (2001) / 0 (2000); Employment by occupation: 8.6% management, 14.6% professional, 17.8% services, 20.9% sales, 1.1% farming, 6.6% construction, 30.4% production (2000).
Income: Per capita income: $15,833 (2000); Median household income: $33,913 (2000); Poverty rate: 9.6% (2000).
Taxes: Total city taxes per capita: $231 (2000); City property taxes per capita: $214 (2000).
Education: High school graduation rate: 78.5% (2000); College graduation rate: 11.1% (2000).

School District(s)

Coldwater Community Schools (KG-12)
2000 Enrollment: 3,330 517-279-5910
Pansophia Academy (KG-12)
2000 Enrollment: 200 517-774-2100

Housing: Homeownership rate: 67.2% (2000); Median home value: $77,800 (2000); Median rent: $415 per month (2000); Median age of housing: 47 years (2000).
Hospitals: Community Health Center of Branch County (96 beds)
Safety: Violent crime rate: 33.7 per 10,000 population; Property crime rate: 414.4 per 10,000 population (2001).
Newspapers: The Daily Reporter (6 x week); The Extra (1 x week)
Transportation: Commute to work: 89.1% car, 0.2% public transportation, 5.1% walk, 3.9% work from home (2000); Travel time to work: 64.2% less than 15 minutes, 21.1% 15 to 30 minutes, 8.5% 30 to 45 minutes, 3.2% 45 to 60 minutes, 2.9% 60 minutes or more (2000)

Additional Information Contacts

Branch County Board of Realtors 517-278-3192
Coldwater Chamber of Commerce 517-278-5985

COLDWATER (township). Covers a land area of 27.388 square miles and a water area of 1.140 square miles. Located at 41.95° N. Lat.; 85.00° W. Long. Elevation is 969 feet.
History: Settled 1830; incorporated as village in 1837, as city in 1861.
Population: 3,678 (2000); Race: 95.6% White, 0.0% Black, 1.0% Asian, 0.1% American Indian and Alaska Native, 1.4% Hispanic of any race, 2.5% two or more races (2000); Density: 134.3 persons per square mile (2000); Age: 24.0% under 18, 19.0% over 64 (2000); Marriage status: 19.4% never married, 60.6% now married, 6.9% widowed, 13.1% divorced (2000); Foreign born: 3.0% (2000); Ancestry (includes multiple ancestries): 27.8% German, 15.3% English, 14.1% Irish, 10.7% United States or American, 7.2% Other groups (2000).
Economy: Trade center in grain-growing, livestock, and dairying area. Manufacturing: chemicals, consumer products, furniture, machinery, prepared foods, publishing. Aiport. Employment by occupation: 13.9% management, 15.6% professional, 12.1% services, 22.5% sales, 0.0% farming, 8.2% construction, 27.7% production (2000).
Income: Per capita income: $21,247 (2000); Median household income: $44,360 (2000); Poverty rate: 3.4% (2000).
Taxes: Total city taxes per capita: $24 (1997); City property taxes per capita: $21 (1997).
Education: High school graduation rate: 85.6% (2000); College graduation rate: 18.2% (2000).
Housing: Homeownership rate: 85.1% (2000); Median home value: $104,800 (2000); Median rent: $403 per month (2000); Median age of housing: 31 years (2000).
Transportation: Commute to work: 94.4% car, 1.4% public transportation, 0.7% walk, 3.2% work from home (2000); Travel time to work: 58.0% less than 15 minutes, 27.1% 15 to 30 minutes, 7.9% 30 to 45 minutes, 5.3% 45 to 60 minutes, 1.6% 60 minutes or more (2000)

GILEAD (township). Aka Gilead Lake. Covers a land area of 21.066 square miles and a water area of 0.347 square miles. Located at 41.78° N. Lat.; 85.10° W. Long.
Population: 753 (2000); Race: 89.4% White, 0.0% Black, 0.0% Asian, 0.8% American Indian and Alaska Native, 10.1% Hispanic of any race, 0.4% two or more races (2000); Density: 35.7 persons per square mile (2000); Age: 24.0% under 18, 12.2% over 64 (2000); Marriage status: 22.7% never married, 61.7% now married, 6.2% widowed, 9.4% divorced (2000); Foreign born: 0.4% (2000); Ancestry (includes multiple ancestries): 24.0% German, 13.0% English, 12.5% Irish, 9.5% United States or American, 8.7% Polish (2000).
Economy: Employment by occupation: 11.9% management, 14.4% professional, 15.7% services, 17.5% sales, 6.6% farming, 6.8% construction, 27.1% production (2000).
Income: Per capita income: $17,256 (2000); Median household income: $37,000 (2000); Poverty rate: 18.2% (2000).
Taxes: Total city taxes per capita: $19 (1997); City property taxes per capita: $19 (1997).
Education: High school graduation rate: 79.3% (2000); College graduation rate: 16.1% (2000).
Housing: Homeownership rate: 76.1% (2000); Median home value: $100,000 (2000); Median rent: $442 per month (2000); Median age of housing: 40 years (2000).
Transportation: Commute to work: 81.8% car, 0.0% public transportation, 1.3% walk, 15.6% work from home (2000); Travel time to work: 34.0% less than 15 minutes, 37.4% 15 to 30 minutes, 18.8% 30 to 45 minutes, 1.5% 45 to 60 minutes, 8.2% 60 minutes or more (2000)

GIRARD (township). Covers a land area of 35.239 square miles and a water area of 0.997 square miles. Located at 42.02° N. Lat.; 85.01° W. Long.
Population: 1,916 (2000); Race: 98.1% White, 0.3% Black, 0.0% Asian, 0.2% American Indian and Alaska Native, 1.4% Hispanic of any race, 1.1% two or more races (2000); Density: 54.4 persons per square mile (2000); Age: 19.2% under 18, 12.2% over 64 (2000); Marriage status: 18.3% never married, 65.5% now married, 6.1% widowed, 10.1% divorced (2000); Foreign born: 0.5% (2000); Ancestry (includes multiple ancestries): 25.8% German, 16.8% English, 12.4% United States or American, 9.3% Irish, 7.0% Other groups (2000).
Economy: Employment by occupation: 10.6% management, 9.4% professional, 16.3% services, 26.3% sales, 0.5% farming, 8.9% construction, 28.1% production (2000).
Income: Per capita income: $21,016 (2000); Median household income: $43,173 (2000); Poverty rate: 6.6% (2000).
Taxes: Total city taxes per capita: $19 (1997); City property taxes per capita: $19 (1997).
Education: High school graduation rate: 81.8% (2000); College graduation rate: 11.1% (2000).
Housing: Homeownership rate: 88.3% (2000); Median home value: $99,300 (2000); Median rent: $379 per month (2000); Median age of housing: 37 years (2000).
Transportation: Commute to work: 94.5% car, 0.2% public transportation, 0.7% walk, 3.8% work from home (2000); Travel time to work: 35.1% less than 15 minutes, 44.7% 15 to 30 minutes, 11.5% 30 to 45 minutes, 4.5% 45 to 60 minutes, 4.2% 60 minutes or more (2000)

KINDERHOOK (township). Covers a land area of 19.473 square miles and a water area of 1.842 square miles. Located at 41.78° N. Lat.; 85.00° W. Long. Elevation is 1,003 feet.
History: Kinderhook Township was named to honor President Martin Van Buren, who had been born in Kinderhook, New York.
Population: 1,614 (2000); Race: 97.5% White, 0.9% Black, 0.1% Asian, 0.2% American Indian and Alaska Native, 0.4% Hispanic of any race, 1.1% two or more races (2000); Density: 82.9 persons per square mile (2000); Age: 23.6% under 18, 13.1% over 64 (2000); Marriage status: 16.0% never married, 69.3% now married, 4.7% widowed, 10.0% divorced (2000); Foreign born: 1.5% (2000); Ancestry (includes multiple ancestries): 30.1% German, 12.4% English, 10.5% United States or American, 9.5% Irish, 7.2% Other groups (2000).
Economy: Employment by occupation: 14.6% management, 7.8% professional, 12.9% services, 22.3% sales, 1.1% farming, 13.5% construction, 27.9% production (2000).

Income: Per capita income: $21,801 (2000); Median household income: $45,903 (2000); Poverty rate: 5.1% (2000).
Taxes: Total city taxes per capita: $47 (1997); City property taxes per capita: $42 (1997).
Education: High school graduation rate: 85.8% (2000); College graduation rate: 13.0% (2000).
Housing: Homeownership rate: 89.5% (2000); Median home value: $150,000 (2000); Median rent: $392 per month (2000); Median age of housing: 30 years (2000).
Transportation: Commute to work: 94.2% car, 0.0% public transportation, 0.2% walk, 5.2% work from home (2000); Travel time to work: 18.0% less than 15 minutes, 57.1% 15 to 30 minutes, 10.0% 30 to 45 minutes, 9.9% 45 to 60 minutes, 5.1% 60 minutes or more (2000)

MATTESON (township). Covers a land area of 35.813 square miles and a water area of 0.476 square miles. Located at 41.93° N. Lat.; 85.23° W. Long.
Population: 1,285 (2000); Race: 98.4% White, 0.2% Black, 0.0% Asian, 0.2% American Indian and Alaska Native, 1.9% Hispanic of any race, 0.8% two or more races (2000); Density: 35.9 persons per square mile (2000); Age: 26.3% under 18, 13.6% over 64 (2000); Marriage status: 18.1% never married, 62.8% now married, 7.7% widowed, 11.5% divorced (2000); Foreign born: 1.7% (2000); Ancestry (includes multiple ancestries): 23.4% German, 11.5% Polish, 9.9% English, 9.6% United States or American, 9.5% Irish (2000).
Economy: Employment by occupation: 8.7% management, 11.5% professional, 8.3% services, 20.5% sales, 1.2% farming, 9.4% construction, 40.3% production (2000).
Income: Per capita income: $19,626 (2000); Median household income: $42,500 (2000); Poverty rate: 7.9% (2000).
Taxes: Total city taxes per capita: $22 (1997); City property taxes per capita: $22 (1997).
Education: High school graduation rate: 84.0% (2000); College graduation rate: 8.6% (2000).
Housing: Homeownership rate: 87.4% (2000); Median home value: $86,600 (2000); Median rent: $383 per month (2000); Median age of housing: 37 years (2000).
Transportation: Commute to work: 93.0% car, 0.7% public transportation, 1.6% walk, 2.3% work from home (2000); Travel time to work: 25.9% less than 15 minutes, 42.3% 15 to 30 minutes, 15.8% 30 to 45 minutes, 6.3% 45 to 60 minutes, 9.7% 60 minutes or more (2000)

NOBLE (township). Covers a land area of 20.959 square miles and a water area of 0.341 square miles. Located at 41.78° N. Lat.; 85.24° W. Long.
Population: 518 (2000); Race: 98.8% White, 0.0% Black, 0.0% Asian, 0.0% American Indian and Alaska Native, 0.0% Hispanic of any race, 1.2% two or more races (2000); Density: 24.7 persons per square mile (2000); Age: 30.2% under 18, 9.1% over 64 (2000); Marriage status: 21.9% never married, 66.1% now married, 3.6% widowed, 8.3% divorced (2000); Foreign born: 1.4% (2000); Ancestry (includes multiple ancestries): 32.7% German, 11.5% Irish, 11.1% English, 7.1% Polish, 6.2% French (except Basque) (2000).
Economy: Employment by occupation: 13.5% management, 11.9% professional, 6.0% services, 19.8% sales, 4.4% farming, 13.1% construction, 31.3% production (2000).
Income: Per capita income: $14,885 (2000); Median household income: $40,625 (2000); Poverty rate: 15.8% (2000).
Taxes: Total city taxes per capita: $18 (1997); City property taxes per capita: $18 (1997).
Education: High school graduation rate: 71.4% (2000); College graduation rate: 7.1% (2000).
Housing: Homeownership rate: 85.2% (2000); Median home value: $75,000 (2000); Median rent: $306 per month (2000); Median age of housing: 32 years (2000).
Transportation: Commute to work: 82.5% car, 1.2% public transportation, 1.6% walk, 11.8% work from home (2000); Travel time to work: 31.8% less than 15 minutes, 41.9% 15 to 30 minutes, 11.5% 30 to 45 minutes, 4.1% 45 to 60 minutes, 10.6% 60 minutes or more (2000)

OVID (township). Covers a land area of 33.257 square miles and a water area of 2.921 square miles. Located at 41.85° N. Lat.; 84.99° W. Long.
Population: 2,432 (2000); Race: 98.1% White, 0.0% Black, 0.9% Asian, 0.5% American Indian and Alaska Native, 0.4% Hispanic of any race, 0.3% two or more races (2000); Density: 73.1 persons per square mile (2000); Age: 19.5% under 18, 20.2% over 64 (2000); Marriage status: 17.7% never married, 65.9% now married, 6.7% widowed, 9.6% divorced (2000); Foreign born: 1.1% (2000); Ancestry (includes multiple ancestries): 30.4% German, 16.3% English, 10.2% United States or American, 9.6% Irish, 8.1% Other groups (2000).
Economy: Employment by occupation: 10.2% management, 15.5% professional, 12.0% services, 27.1% sales, 1.0% farming, 12.2% construction, 22.0% production (2000).
Income: Per capita income: $21,942 (2000); Median household income: $44,593 (2000); Poverty rate: 3.1% (2000).
Taxes: Total city taxes per capita: $46 (1997); City property taxes per capita: $40 (1997).
Education: High school graduation rate: 83.4% (2000); College graduation rate: 15.3% (2000).
Housing: Homeownership rate: 90.4% (2000); Median home value: $114,400 (2000); Median rent: $454 per month (2000); Median age of housing: 30 years (2000).
Transportation: Commute to work: 93.4% car, 0.3% public transportation, 1.1% walk, 4.0% work from home (2000); Travel time to work: 23.0% less than 15 minutes, 53.7% 15 to 30 minutes, 12.3% 30 to 45 minutes, 3.5% 45 to 60 minutes, 7.5% 60 minutes or more (2000)

QUINCY (village). Covers a land area of 1.282 square miles and a water area of <.001 square miles. Located at 41.94° N. Lat.; 84.88° W. Long. Elevation is 1,017 feet.
History: A flour mill built in Quincy in 1863 became a cereal-foods and milling plant, the mainstay of the early economy, along with a Portland cement plant which used local clay.
Population: 1,701 (2000); Race: 96.0% White, 0.9% Black, 0.5% Asian, 0.0% American Indian and Alaska Native, 1.6% Hispanic of any race, 1.8% two or more races (2000); Density: 1,327.0 persons per square mile (2000); Age: 31.2% under 18, 12.0% over 64 (2000); Marriage status: 23.8% never married, 53.7% now married, 6.5% widowed, 16.0% divorced (2000); Foreign born: 1.5% (2000); Ancestry (includes multiple ancestries): 26.6% German, 10.8% English, 10.4% United States or American, 8.9% Irish, 8.9% Other groups (2000).
Economy: Employment by occupation: 11.0% management, 11.7% professional, 18.9% services, 19.8% sales, 0.8% farming, 8.3% construction, 29.5% production (2000).
Income: Per capita income: $15,951 (2000); Median household income: $35,987 (2000); Poverty rate: 10.6% (2000).
Taxes: Total city taxes per capita: $180 (1997); City property taxes per capita: $171 (1997).
Education: High school graduation rate: 84.6% (2000); College graduation rate: 7.8% (2000).

School District(s)

Quincy Community School District (PK-12)
2000 Enrollment: 1,446 517-639-7141
Housing: Homeownership rate: 63.8% (2000); Median home value: $68,600 (2000); Median rent: $364 per month (2000); Median age of housing: 60+ years (2000).
Transportation: Commute to work: 85.4% car, 0.5% public transportation, 9.1% walk, 3.8% work from home (2000); Travel time to work: 41.4% less than 15 minutes, 37.3% 15 to 30 minutes, 11.1% 30 to 45 minutes, 2.1% 45 to 60 minutes, 8.0% 60 minutes or more (2000)

QUINCY (township). Covers a land area of 35.307 square miles and a water area of 0.966 square miles. Located at 41.93° N. Lat.; 84.89° W. Long. Elevation is 1,017 feet.
History: The first settler came to Quincy in 1830. Quincy Township was separated from Coldwater in 1836, and named for Quincy, Massachusetts, the former home of one of the settlers.
Population: 4,411 (2000); Race: 98.1% White, 0.4% Black, 0.2% Asian, 0.0% American Indian and Alaska Native, 1.0% Hispanic of any race, 1.0% two or more races (2000); Density: 124.9 persons per square mile (2000); Age: 29.0% under 18, 11.2% over 64 (2000); Marriage status: 20.9% never married, 60.1% now married, 6.3% widowed, 12.6% divorced (2000); Foreign born: 0.7% (2000); Ancestry (includes multiple ancestries): 28.3% German, 11.3% English, 9.0% Irish, 8.4% United States or American, 6.8% Other groups (2000).
Economy: Employment by occupation: 11.2% management, 12.5% professional, 14.8% services, 21.4% sales, 1.8% farming, 8.4% construction, 29.9% production (2000).
Income: Per capita income: $17,667 (2000); Median household income: $41,823 (2000); Poverty rate: 10.9% (2000).
Taxes: Total city taxes per capita: $21 (1997); City property taxes per capita: $16 (1997).
Education: High school graduation rate: 86.2% (2000); College graduation rate: 10.1% (2000).

Housing: Homeownership rate: 78.6% (2000); Median home value: $85,400 (2000); Median rent: $375 per month (2000); Median age of housing: 41 years (2000).
Transportation: Commute to work: 91.3% car, 0.2% public transportation, 3.6% walk, 3.7% work from home (2000); Travel time to work: 35.4% less than 15 minutes, 41.3% 15 to 30 minutes, 12.4% 30 to 45 minutes, 4.5% 45 to 60 minutes, 6.4% 60 minutes or more (2000)

SHERWOOD (village). Covers a land area of 1.010 square miles and a water area of 0 square miles. Located at 42.00° N. Lat.; 85.24° W. Long. Elevation is 883 feet.
History: When Sherwood was founded on land belonging to E.F. Hazen in 1832, it was called Hazenville. The name was changed in 1839 to Sherwood for Sherwood Forest in England, the former home of early settler Alexander E. Tomlinson.
Population: 324 (2000); Race: 98.4% White, 0.0% Black, 0.0% Asian, 0.0% American Indian and Alaska Native, 0.6% Hispanic of any race, 1.6% two or more races (2000); Density: 320.8 persons per square mile (2000); Age: 28.7% under 18, 7.6% over 64 (2000); Marriage status: 28.0% never married, 58.9% now married, 4.2% widowed, 8.9% divorced (2000); Foreign born: 1.0% (2000); Ancestry (includes multiple ancestries): 23.9% United States or American, 12.7% German, 7.0% Dutch, 6.7% Other groups, 6.7% Irish (2000).
Economy: Employment by occupation: 4.3% management, 11.1% professional, 19.8% services, 13.0% sales, 0.0% farming, 10.5% construction, 41.4% production (2000).
Income: Per capita income: $16,101 (2000); Median household income: $39,844 (2000); Poverty rate: 10.6% (2000).
Taxes: Total city taxes per capita: $33 (1997); City property taxes per capita: $33 (1997).
Education: High school graduation rate: 79.3% (2000); College graduation rate: 1.0% (2000).
Housing: Homeownership rate: 77.6% (2000); Median home value: $56,500 (2000); Median rent: $365 per month (2000); Median age of housing: 60+ years (2000).
Transportation: Commute to work: 96.8% car, 0.0% public transportation, 0.0% walk, 1.3% work from home (2000); Travel time to work: 21.8% less than 15 minutes, 32.7% 15 to 30 minutes, 26.9% 30 to 45 minutes, 11.5% 45 to 60 minutes, 7.1% 60 minutes or more (2000)

SHERWOOD (township). Covers a land area of 34.871 square miles and a water area of 1.232 square miles. Located at 42.02° N. Lat.; 85.23° W. Long. Elevation is 883 feet.
Population: 2,284 (2000); Race: 97.4% White, 0.3% Black, 0.0% Asian, 0.0% American Indian and Alaska Native, 0.1% Hispanic of any race, 2.2% two or more races (2000); Density: 65.5 persons per square mile (2000); Age: 26.4% under 18, 11.7% over 64 (2000); Marriage status: 20.3% never married, 63.2% now married, 4.6% widowed, 11.9% divorced (2000); Foreign born: 0.3% (2000); Ancestry (includes multiple ancestries): 18.0% German, 10.0% English, 9.6% Irish, 9.6% United States or American, 9.2% Other groups (2000).
Economy: In farm area. Employment by occupation: 9.9% management, 8.0% professional, 11.5% services, 19.7% sales, 0.9% farming, 9.9% construction, 40.2% production (2000).
Income: Per capita income: $15,560 (2000); Median household income: $34,231 (2000); Poverty rate: 11.4% (2000).
Taxes: Total city taxes per capita: $14 (1997); City property taxes per capita: $14 (1997).
Education: High school graduation rate: 76.4% (2000); College graduation rate: 5.6% (2000).
Housing: Homeownership rate: 78.1% (2000); Median home value: $77,100 (2000); Median rent: $369 per month (2000); Median age of housing: 39 years (2000).
Transportation: Commute to work: 93.2% car, 0.3% public transportation, 1.2% walk, 3.5% work from home (2000); Travel time to work: 15.1% less than 15 minutes, 30.9% 15 to 30 minutes, 32.6% 30 to 45 minutes, 10.5% 45 to 60 minutes, 10.9% 60 minutes or more (2000)

UNION (township). Covers a land area of 35.712 square miles and a water area of 0.283 square miles. Located at 42.05° N. Lat.; 85.12° W. Long.
Population: 3,121 (2000); Race: 97.3% White, 0.2% Black, 0.1% Asian, 0.6% American Indian and Alaska Native, 1.3% Hispanic of any race, 1.6% two or more races (2000); Density: 87.4 persons per square mile (2000); Age: 27.5% under 18, 13.5% over 64 (2000); Marriage status: 23.7% never married, 57.5% now married, 6.9% widowed, 11.9% divorced (2000); Foreign born: 0.5% (2000); Ancestry (includes multiple ancestries): 23.3% German, 13.8% United States or American, 12.2% Irish, 10.4% English, 9.1% Other groups (2000).
Economy: Employment by occupation: 8.9% management, 11.6% professional, 14.9% services, 23.1% sales, 0.4% farming, 9.1% construction, 32.1% production (2000).
Income: Per capita income: $17,203 (2000); Median household income: $36,990 (2000); Poverty rate: 10.7% (2000).
Taxes: Total city taxes per capita: $22 (1997); City property taxes per capita: $22 (1997).
Education: High school graduation rate: 79.9% (2000); College graduation rate: 9.0% (2000).
Housing: Homeownership rate: 77.8% (2000); Median home value: $75,700 (2000); Median rent: $361 per month (2000); Median age of housing: 55 years (2000).
Transportation: Commute to work: 92.5% car, 0.4% public transportation, 2.1% walk, 4.7% work from home (2000); Travel time to work: 28.7% less than 15 minutes, 43.7% 15 to 30 minutes, 18.7% 30 to 45 minutes, 5.1% 45 to 60 minutes, 3.8% 60 minutes or more (2000)

UNION CITY (village). Covers a land area of 1.474 square miles and a water area of 0.009 square miles. Located at 42.06° N. Lat.; 85.13° W. Long.
History: Union City was named for the junction of the Coldwater and St. Joseph Rivers at this point. The village was a station on the Underground Railroad, helping slaves to freedom. Industries in the early 1900's included creamery products and dried milk processing.
Population: 1,804 (2000); Race: 96.2% White, 0.4% Black, 0.2% Asian, 0.3% American Indian and Alaska Native, 0.7% Hispanic of any race, 2.7% two or more races (2000); Density: 1,223.7 persons per square mile (2000); Age: 29.2% under 18, 11.8% over 64 (2000); Marriage status: 27.1% never married, 51.2% now married, 7.6% widowed, 14.1% divorced (2000); Foreign born: 0.9% (2000); Ancestry (includes multiple ancestries): 22.0% German, 12.3% United States or American, 11.6% Irish, 10.8% English, 9.4% Other groups (2000).
Economy: Employment by occupation: 7.9% management, 13.7% professional, 14.1% services, 22.5% sales, 0.2% farming, 7.4% construction, 34.1% production (2000).
Income: Per capita income: $15,101 (2000); Median household income: $37,065 (2000); Poverty rate: 11.7% (2000).
Taxes: Total city taxes per capita: $111 (1997); City property taxes per capita: $109 (1997).
Education: High school graduation rate: 81.0% (2000); College graduation rate: 11.1% (2000).

School District(s)

Union City Community Schools (PK-12)
2000 Enrollment: 1,330 517-741-8091

Housing: Homeownership rate: 70.7% (2000); Median home value: $68,000 (2000); Median rent: $370 per month (2000); Median age of housing: 60+ years (2000).
Safety: Violent crime rate: 38.6 per 10,000 population; Property crime rate: 380.4 per 10,000 population (2001).
Newspapers: Register-Tribune (1 x week)
Transportation: Commute to work: 90.5% car, 0.7% public transportation, 3.4% walk, 5.0% work from home (2000); Travel time to work: 32.9% less than 15 minutes, 38.7% 15 to 30 minutes, 19.3% 30 to 45 minutes, 4.8% 45 to 60 minutes, 4.2% 60 minutes or more (2000)

Calhoun County

Located in southern Michigan; drained by the Kalamazoo and St. Joseph Rivers. Covers a land area of 708.70 square miles, a water area of 9.70 square miles, and is located in the Eastern Time Zone. The county government was organized in 1829. County seat is Marshall.

Calhoun County is part of the Kalamazoo-Battle Creek, MI MSA. The entire metro area includes: Calhoun County; Kalamazoo County; Van Buren County

Weather Station: Battle Creek — Elevation: 954 feet

	Jan	Feb	Mar	Apr	May	Jun	Jul	Aug	Sep	Oct	Nov	Dec
High	31	35	45	59	71	80	83	81	73	61	47	35
Low	15	17	26	36	46	56	60	58	51	40	31	21
Precip	1.6	1.5	2.5	3.3	3.3	3.4	3.5	3.6	3.8	3.0	3.0	2.5
Snow	14.5	9.7	6.1	2.2	tr	0.0	0.0	0.0	tr	0.4	5.5	13.3

High and Low temperatures in degrees Fahrenheit; Precipitation and Snow in inches

Population: 137,985 (2000); Race: 83.9% White, 10.7% Black, 1.1% Asian, 0.7% American Indian and Alaska Native, 3.2% Hispanic of any race, 2.3% two or more races (2000); Density: 194.7 persons per square mile (2000); Age: 25.9% under 18, 13.8% over 64 (2000).
Religion: Five largest groups: 9.0% Catholic Church, 4.3% The Wesleyan Church, 3.0% The United Methodist Church, 2.5% Lutheran Church—Missouri Synod, 1.8% Presbyterian Church (U.S.A.) (2000).
Economy: Unemployment rate: 5.7% (11/2002); Total civilian labor force: 71,259 (11/2002); Leading industries: 26.4% manufacturing; 14.6% health care and social assistance; 13.0% retail trade (2000); Companies that employ more than 1,000 persons: 7 (2000); Companies that employ more than 100 persons: 106 (2000); Farms: 1,085 totaling 243,151 acres (1997); Minority business ownership rate: 6.9% (1997); Women business ownership rate: 26.9% (1997); Retail sales per capita: $8,884 (1997). Single-family building permits issued: 316 (2001) / 368 (2000); Multi-family building permits issued: 96 (2001) / 115 (2000).
Income: Per capita income: $19,230 (2000); Median household income: $38,918 (2000); Poverty rate: 11.3% (2000); Bankruptcy rate: 5.04% (2001).
Taxes: Total county taxes per capita: $139 (2000); County property taxes per capita: $129 (2000).
Education: High school graduation rate: 83.2% (2000); College graduation rate: 16.0% (2000).
Housing: Homeownership rate: 73.0% (2000); Median home value: $81,000 (2000); Median rent: $414 per month (2000); Median age of housing: 42 years (2000).
Health: Birth rate: 134.8 per 10,000 population (1998); Age adjusted death rate: 100.3 per 10,000 population (1999); Age adjusted cancer mortality rate: 230.5 deaths per 100,000 population (1999). Air Quality Index: 100% good, 0% moderate, 0% unhealthy (percent of days in 2000). Number of physicians: 14.5 per 10,000 population (1999); Number of hospital beds: 61.7 per 10,000 population (1999).
Elections: 2000 Presidential election results: 49.6% Gore, 47.7% Bush, 2.1% Nader, 0.1% Buchanan
Additional Information Contacts
Calhoun County Government Offices 616-781-0730
Albion Chamber of Commerce 517-629-5533
Battle Creek Area Association of Realtors.......................... 616-962-5193
Battle Creek Chamber of Commerce 616-962-4076
Marshall Chamber of Commerce 616-781-5163

Calhoun County Communities

ALBION (city). Covers a land area of 4.460 square miles and a water area of 0.038 square miles. Located at 42.24° N. Lat.; 84.75° W. Long. Elevation is 959 feet.
History: Albion developed as an industrial city, taking its name from the Albion Company grist mill established in 1835 by Jesse Crowell, who had formerly lived in Albion, New York. The village was platted by Crowell in 1836, incorporated as a village in 1855, and as a city in 1885.
Population: 9,144 (2000); Race: 61.9% White, 31.4% Black, 0.4% Asian, 1.1% American Indian and Alaska Native, 4.8% Hispanic of any race, 3.6% two or more races (2000); Density: 2,050.2 persons per square mile (2000); Age: 25.6% under 18, 13.6% over 64 (2000); Marriage status: 36.6% never married, 43.6% now married, 8.5% widowed, 11.3% divorced (2000); Foreign born: 1.9% (2000); Ancestry (includes multiple ancestries): 37.3% Other groups, 14.2% German, 8.5% Irish, 7.7% English, 5.0% United States or American (2000).
Vital Statistics: Birth rate: 152.0 per 10,000 population (1998)
Economy: Single-family building permits issued: 11 (2001) / 11 (2000); Multi-family building permits issued: 0 (2001) / 0 (2000); Employment by occupation: 6.1% management, 21.0% professional, 19.7% services, 23.4% sales, 0.2% farming, 5.0% construction, 24.5% production (2000).
Income: Per capita income: $14,165 (2000); Median household income: $30,245 (2000); Poverty rate: 20.0% (2000).
Taxes: Total city taxes per capita: $257 (1997); City property taxes per capita: $134 (1997).
Education: High school graduation rate: 82.8% (2000); College graduation rate: 15.5% (2000).

School District(s)

Albion Public Schools (PK-12)
2000 Enrollment: 2,010 517-629-9166

Four-year College(s)

Albion College (Private, Not-for-profit, United Methodist)
2001 Enrollment: 1,546 517-629-1000
2001 Tuition: In-state $19,390; Out-of-state $19,390

Housing: Homeownership rate: 59.1% (2000); Median home value: $60,300 (2000); Median rent: $357 per month (2000); Median age of housing: 56 years (2000).
Hospitals: Trillium Hospital (89 beds)
Safety: Violent crime rate: 139.3 per 10,000 population; Property crime rate: 662.5 per 10,000 population (2001).
Newspapers: Albion Recorder (6 x week); The Pennysaver (1 x week)
Transportation: Commute to work: 76.7% car, 1.3% public transportation, 17.3% walk, 3.0% work from home (2000); Travel time to work: 60.5% less than 15 minutes, 24.7% 15 to 30 minutes, 8.3% 30 to 45 minutes, 4.0% 45 to 60 minutes, 2.4% 60 minutes or more (2000); Amtrak: Service available.
Additional Information Contacts
Albion Chamber of Commerce 517-629-5533

ALBION (township). Covers a land area of 32.752 square miles and a water area of 0.280 square miles. Located at 42.19° N. Lat.; 84.76° W. Long. Elevation is 959 feet.
Population: 1,200 (2000); Race: 94.6% White, 2.5% Black, 0.3% Asian, 0.5% American Indian and Alaska Native, 3.5% Hispanic of any race, 1.8% two or more races (2000); Density: 36.6 persons per square mile (2000); Age: 25.4% under 18, 15.2% over 64 (2000); Marriage status: 19.1% never married, 66.0% now married, 5.5% widowed, 9.3% divorced (2000); Foreign born: 1.3% (2000); Ancestry (includes multiple ancestries): 20.6% German, 14.3% English, 11.8% Other groups, 9.7% United States or American, 8.6% Irish (2000).
Economy: Agricultural area: corn, wheat, soybeans, onions, apples; hogs, cattle, poultry. Manufactures construction materials, industrial products. Single-family building permits issued: 8 (2001) / 8 (2000); Multi-family building permits issued: 0 (2001) / 0 (2000); Employment by occupation: 14.9% management, 16.2% professional, 11.7% services, 17.7% sales, 1.1% farming, 11.7% construction, 26.8% production (2000).
Income: Per capita income: $16,849 (2000); Median household income: $40,625 (2000); Poverty rate: 8.8% (2000).
Taxes: Total city taxes per capita: $42 (1997); City property taxes per capita: $27 (1997).
Education: High school graduation rate: 84.5% (2000); College graduation rate: 13.0% (2000).
Housing: Homeownership rate: 85.3% (2000); Median home value: $89,000 (2000); Median rent: $377 per month (2000); Median age of housing: 42 years (2000).
Transportation: Commute to work: 92.8% car, 1.0% public transportation, 1.3% walk, 4.2% work from home (2000); Travel time to work: 41.1% less than 15 minutes, 33.3% 15 to 30 minutes, 13.3% 30 to 45 minutes, 4.6% 45 to 60 minutes, 7.7% 60 minutes or more (2000); Amtrak: Service available.

ATHENS (village). Covers a land area of 0.996 square miles and a water area of 0 square miles. Located at 42.08° N. Lat.; 85.23° W. Long. Elevation is 896 feet.
History: Athens was settled in 1831 along the Nottawaseepe River. In 1854, William Simons built a store here, and in 1860 the village was platted. Athens was named for Athens, New York, from which many of its early residents had come.
Population: 1,111 (2000); Race: 96.8% White, 0.8% Black, 0.0% Asian, 1.8% American Indian and Alaska Native, 1.3% Hispanic of any race, 0.0% two or more races (2000); Density: 1,115.7 persons per square mile (2000); Age: 31.9% under 18, 13.1% over 64 (2000); Marriage status: 20.5% never married, 63.5% now married, 6.8% widowed, 9.2% divorced (2000); Foreign born: 1.0% (2000); Ancestry (includes multiple ancestries): 20.3% German, 19.9% United States or American, 15.2% English, 10.3% Other groups, 7.7% Irish (2000).
Economy: Single-family building permits issued: 1 (2001) / 1 (2000); Multi-family building permits issued: 0 (2001) / 0 (2000); Employment by occupation: 7.1% management, 11.8% professional, 15.0% services, 24.7% sales, 0.0% farming, 9.3% construction, 32.0% production (2000).
Income: Per capita income: $16,409 (2000); Median household income: $42,083 (2000); Poverty rate: 5.3% (2000).
Taxes: Total city taxes per capita: $141 (1997); City property taxes per capita: $138 (1997).
Education: High school graduation rate: 88.8% (2000); College graduation rate: 10.9% (2000).

School District(s)

Athens Area Schools (KG-12)
2000 Enrollment: 899 616-729-5427

Housing: Homeownership rate: 79.8% (2000); Median home value: $78,300 (2000); Median rent: $384 per month (2000); Median age of housing: 49 years (2000).

Transportation: Commute to work: 94.7% car, 1.0% public transportation, 3.7% walk, 0.6% work from home (2000); Travel time to work: 25.3% less than 15 minutes, 33.5% 15 to 30 minutes, 30.0% 30 to 45 minutes, 4.5% 45 to 60 minutes, 6.6% 60 minutes or more (2000)

ATHENS (township). Covers a land area of 36.148 square miles and a water area of 0 square miles. Located at 42.10° N. Lat.; 85.23° W. Long. Elevation is 896 feet.
Population: 2,571 (2000); Race: 97.1% White, 0.4% Black, 0.0% Asian, 1.5% American Indian and Alaska Native, 1.3% Hispanic of any race, 0.6% two or more races (2000); Density: 71.1 persons per square mile (2000); Age: 27.9% under 18, 14.5% over 64 (2000); Marriage status: 20.1% never married, 62.3% now married, 7.3% widowed, 10.3% divorced (2000); Foreign born: 1.3% (2000); Ancestry (includes multiple ancestries): 17.9% United States or American, 17.2% German, 16.3% English, 8.2% Irish, 6.4% Other groups (2000).
Economy: In orchard and farm area. Employment by occupation: 7.0% management, 13.6% professional, 11.3% services, 26.8% sales, 0.3% farming, 14.3% construction, 26.8% production (2000).
Income: Per capita income: $18,864 (2000); Median household income: $43,929 (2000); Poverty rate: 5.2% (2000).
Taxes: Total city taxes per capita: $37 (1997); City property taxes per capita: $37 (1997).
Education: High school graduation rate: 87.7% (2000); College graduation rate: 9.5% (2000).
Housing: Homeownership rate: 85.6% (2000); Median home value: $82,700 (2000); Median rent: $362 per month (2000); Median age of housing: 39 years (2000).
Transportation: Commute to work: 95.2% car, 0.4% public transportation, 2.4% walk, 1.8% work from home (2000); Travel time to work: 19.4% less than 15 minutes, 39.8% 15 to 30 minutes, 28.3% 30 to 45 minutes, 6.0% 45 to 60 minutes, 6.5% 60 minutes or more (2000)

BATTLE CREEK (city). Covers a land area of 42.829 square miles and a water area of 0.842 square miles. Located at 42.31° N. Lat.; 85.20° W. Long. Elevation is 819 feet.
History: Battle Creek was called Milton when it was first settled in 1831 by Samuel Guernsey of New York. When the post office was established in 1833, the community was renamed for the nearby creek, where a small battle between some individuals had taken place in 1825. Battle Creek's character was shaped in 1855 when Captain Joseph Bates moved the headquarters of the Seventh Day Adventist Church here. The church's emphasis on health reforms led to the founding of the Western Health Reform Institute, renamed the Battle Creek Sanitarium when Dr. John Harvey Kellogg took charge of it in 1876. Among other medical innovations, Kellogg perfected methods and machines for processing foods which resulted in new cereal and nut-food products. C.W. Post, who benefited from treatment at the sanitarium in 1891, established La Vita Inn in Battle Creek and began to serve a warm cereal drink, marketed as Postum. Later, the Kellogg and Post cereal factories were major employers in Battle Creek.
Population: 53,364 (2000); Race: 74.0% White, 18.0% Black, 1.8% Asian, 0.9% American Indian and Alaska Native, 4.5% Hispanic of any race, 3.2% two or more races (2000); Density: 1,246.0 persons per square mile (2000); Age: 27.1% under 18, 13.7% over 64 (2000); Marriage status: 27.9% never married, 49.5% now married, 8.2% widowed, 14.3% divorced (2000); Foreign born: 3.4% (2000); Ancestry (includes multiple ancestries): 21.6% Other groups, 15.7% German, 11.5% English, 8.9% United States or American, 8.7% Irish (2000).
Vital Statistics: Birth rate: 191.5 per 10,000 population (1998)
Economy: Unemployment rate: 6.6% (11/2002); Total civilian labor force: 26,854 (11/2002); Single-family building permits issued: 77 (2001) / 99 (2000); Multi-family building permits issued: 96 (2001) / 115 (2000); Employment by occupation: 11.7% management, 15.0% professional, 18.4% services, 25.5% sales, 0.1% farming, 6.6% construction, 22.8% production (2000).
Income: Per capita income: $18,424 (2000); Median household income: $35,491 (2000); Poverty rate: 14.4% (2000).
Taxes: Total city taxes per capita: $760 (2000); City property taxes per capita: $506 (2000).
Education: High school graduation rate: 82.4% (2000); College graduation rate: 17.2% (2000).

School District(s)

Arbor Academy (KG-04)
2000 Enrollment: 110 616-895-3029
Battle Creek Public Schools (PK-12)
2000 Enrollment: 8,004 616-965-9500
Harper Creek Community Schools (KG-12)
2000 Enrollment: 2,591 616-979-1136
Lakeview School District (Calhoun) (PK-12)
2000 Enrollment: 3,315 616-965-3080
Pennfield School District (KG-12)
2000 Enrollment: 1,747 616-961-9781

Two-year College(s)

Kellogg Community College (Public)
2001 Enrollment: 5,886 616-965-3931
2001 Tuition: In-state $2,709; Out-of-state $4,149

Housing: Homeownership rate: 65.9% (2000); Median home value: $71,000 (2000); Median rent: $419 per month (2000); Median age of housing: 46 years (2000).
Hospitals: Battle Creek Health System (315 beds); Fieldstone Center of Battle Creek Health System (80 beds); Southwest Rehab Hospital (30 beds); Veterans Affairs Medical Center (473 beds)
Safety: Violent crime rate: 162.4 per 10,000 population; Property crime rate: 814.2 per 10,000 population (2001).
Newspapers: South Central Michigan Senior Times (1 x month); Senior Times of Greater Branch County (1 x month); Battle Creek Enquirer (7 x week); Battle Creek Shopper News (1 x week); Barry County Senior Exchange (1 x month); Scene Magazine (1 x month)
Transportation: Commute to work: 93.1% car, 1.7% public transportation, 2.1% walk, 2.2% work from home (2000); Travel time to work: 47.4% less than 15 minutes, 37.8% 15 to 30 minutes, 7.8% 30 to 45 minutes, 3.3% 45 to 60 minutes, 3.7% 60 minutes or more (2000); Amtrak: Service available.
Airports: W K Kellogg
Additional Information Contacts
Battle Creek Area Association of Realtors. 616-962-5193
Battle Creek Chamber of Commerce 616-962-4076

BEDFORD (township). Covers a land area of 29.370 square miles and a water area of 0.416 square miles. Located at 42.37° N. Lat.; 85.23° W. Long.
History: Bedford was named by Josiah Gilbert for his former home in Bedford, Westchester County, New York. Stagecoaches traveling between Grand Rapids and Battle Creek passed through Bedford.
Population: 9,517 (2000); Race: 85.0% White, 11.5% Black, 0.2% Asian, 0.8% American Indian and Alaska Native, 1.4% Hispanic of any race, 1.8% two or more races (2000); Density: 324.0 persons per square mile (2000); Age: 24.3% under 18, 14.5% over 64 (2000); Marriage status: 18.9% never married, 60.7% now married, 7.6% widowed, 12.8% divorced (2000); Foreign born: 1.7% (2000); Ancestry (includes multiple ancestries): 18.5% German, 14.7% English, 14.5% Other groups, 9.4% Irish, 8.5% United States or American (2000).
Economy: Unemployment rate: 3.5% (11/2002); Total civilian labor force: 13,779 (11/2002); Single-family building permits issued: 25 (2001) / 32 (2000); Multi-family building permits issued: 0 (2001) / 0 (2000); Employment by occupation: 10.7% management, 15.1% professional, 16.9% services, 22.9% sales, 0.8% farming, 9.3% construction, 24.2% production (2000).
Income: Per capita income: $20,303 (2000); Median household income: $44,462 (2000); Poverty rate: 5.8% (2000).
Taxes: Total city taxes per capita: $44 (1997); City property taxes per capita: $37 (1997).
Education: High school graduation rate: 80.3% (2000); College graduation rate: 12.3% (2000).
Housing: Homeownership rate: 90.2% (2000); Median home value: $79,400 (2000); Median rent: $432 per month (2000); Median age of housing: 40 years (2000).
Safety: Violent crime rate: 53.3 per 10,000 population; Property crime rate: 359.6 per 10,000 population (2001).
Transportation: Commute to work: 95.6% car, 0.7% public transportation, 1.0% walk, 2.6% work from home (2000); Travel time to work: 33.1% less than 15 minutes, 47.5% 15 to 30 minutes, 12.4% 30 to 45 minutes, 4.1% 45 to 60 minutes, 2.9% 60 minutes or more (2000)

BROWNLEE PARK (CDP). Covers a land area of 1.994 square miles and a water area of 0.014 square miles. Located at 42.32° N. Lat.; 85.14° W. Long.
Population: 2,588 (2000); Race: 94.0% White, 0.6% Black, 0.0% Asian, 0.2% American Indian and Alaska Native, 4.7% Hispanic of any race, 2.9% two or more races (2000); Density: 1,297.7 persons per square mile (2000); Age: 23.0% under 18, 15.0% over 64 (2000); Marriage status: 22.6% never married, 52.4% now married, 8.0% widowed, 16.9% divorced (2000); Foreign born: 0.6% (2000); Ancestry (includes multiple ancestries): 16.6%

Other groups, 13.9% German, 13.2% United States or American, 10.3% Irish, 6.7% English (2000).
Economy: Suburb of Battle Creek. Employment by occupation: 6.2% management, 3.3% professional, 22.6% services, 25.0% sales, 0.0% farming, 15.6% construction, 27.4% production (2000).
Income: Per capita income: $17,026 (2000); Median household income: $26,694 (2000); Poverty rate: 19.0% (2000).
Education: High school graduation rate: 59.2% (2000); College graduation rate: 0.6% (2000).
Housing: Homeownership rate: 77.8% (2000); Median home value: $42,200 (2000); Median rent: $363 per month (2000); Median age of housing: 43 years (2000).
Transportation: Commute to work: 91.9% car, 3.3% public transportation, 0.8% walk, 0.3% work from home (2000); Travel time to work: 35.1% less than 15 minutes, 49.4% 15 to 30 minutes, 9.0% 30 to 45 minutes, 2.2% 45 to 60 minutes, 4.3% 60 minutes or more (2000)

BURLINGTON (village). Covers a land area of 0.737 square miles and a water area of 0 square miles. Located at 42.10° N. Lat.; 85.08° W. Long. Elevation is 923 feet.
History: Burlington was founded in 1833 by William and Ansel Adams. The village as well as the township was named for a gunboat used in the War of 1812.
Population: 405 (2000); Race: 97.3% White, 1.1% Black, 0.0% Asian, 1.1% American Indian and Alaska Native, 0.0% Hispanic of any race, 0.4% two or more races (2000); Density: 549.3 persons per square mile (2000); Age: 31.1% under 18, 8.9% over 64 (2000); Marriage status: 27.0% never married, 61.0% now married, 5.2% widowed, 6.7% divorced (2000); Foreign born: 0.7% (2000); Ancestry (includes multiple ancestries): 12.8% United States or American, 10.1% English, 9.2% Other groups, 7.8% German, 7.4% Irish (2000).
Economy: Employment by occupation: 3.2% management, 7.5% professional, 10.2% services, 16.6% sales, 1.6% farming, 11.8% construction, 49.2% production (2000).
Income: Per capita income: $23,240 (2000); Median household income: $32,857 (2000); Poverty rate: 15.2% (2000).
Taxes: Total city taxes per capita: $70 (1997); City property taxes per capita: $67 (1997).
Education: High school graduation rate: 80.4% (2000); College graduation rate: 3.8% (2000).
Housing: Homeownership rate: 88.5% (2000); Median home value: $62,300 (2000); Median rent: $361 per month (2000); Median age of housing: 60+ years (2000).
Transportation: Commute to work: 96.2% car, 0.0% public transportation, 0.0% walk, 3.8% work from home (2000); Travel time to work: 24.7% less than 15 minutes, 42.1% 15 to 30 minutes, 23.6% 30 to 45 minutes, 6.2% 45 to 60 minutes, 3.4% 60 minutes or more (2000)

BURLINGTON (township). Covers a land area of 35.869 square miles and a water area of 0.254 square miles. Located at 42.10° N. Lat.; 85.12° W. Long. Elevation is 923 feet.
History: Burlington Township was named for the gunboat "Burlington" which saw duty on the Great Lakes during the War of 1812.
Population: 1,929 (2000); Race: 98.2% White, 0.5% Black, 0.4% Asian, 0.5% American Indian and Alaska Native, 0.9% Hispanic of any race, 0.5% two or more races (2000); Density: 53.8 persons per square mile (2000); Age: 24.4% under 18, 12.8% over 64 (2000); Marriage status: 19.2% never married, 65.2% now married, 5.6% widowed, 10.1% divorced (2000); Foreign born: 0.9% (2000); Ancestry (includes multiple ancestries): 19.4% German, 17.3% English, 10.6% United States or American, 8.3% Irish, 8.2% Other groups (2000).
Economy: Single-family building permits issued: 3 (2001) / 4 (2000); Multi-family building permits issued: 0 (2001) / 0 (2000); Employment by occupation: 8.6% management, 14.1% professional, 11.5% services, 17.5% sales, 0.9% farming, 9.3% construction, 38.1% production (2000).
Income: Per capita income: $20,960 (2000); Median household income: $42,778 (2000); Poverty rate: 12.1% (2000).
Taxes: Total city taxes per capita: $18 (1997); City property taxes per capita: $13 (1997).
Education: High school graduation rate: 82.0% (2000); College graduation rate: 8.5% (2000).
Housing: Homeownership rate: 86.6% (2000); Median home value: $77,100 (2000); Median rent: $334 per month (2000); Median age of housing: 42 years (2000).
Transportation: Commute to work: 93.5% car, 0.0% public transportation, 0.0% walk, 4.4% work from home (2000); Travel time to work: 17.7% less than 15 minutes, 37.1% 15 to 30 minutes, 29.2% 30 to 45 minutes, 10.9% 45 to 60 minutes, 5.2% 60 minutes or more (2000)

CERESCO (unincorporated postal area, zip code 49033). Covers a land area of 31.243 square miles and a water area of 0.230 square miles. Located at 42.24° N. Lat.; 85.09° W. Long.
History: Ceresco grew up around a sawmill and a stone flour mill built in 1838 on the Kalamazoo River. The name came from the Roman goddess of agriculture.
Population: 1,638 (2000); Race: 99.4% White, 0.0% Black, 0.1% Asian, 0.0% American Indian and Alaska Native, 0.3% Hispanic of any race, 0.3% two or more races (2000); Density: 52.4 persons per square mile (2000); Age: 25.4% under 18, 10.9% over 64 (2000); Marriage status: 12.5% never married, 73.1% now married, 3.5% widowed, 11.0% divorced (2000); Foreign born: 1.2% (2000); Ancestry (includes multiple ancestries): 30.6% German, 16.1% English, 11.5% Irish, 8.0% United States or American, 6.2% Other groups (2000).
Economy: Employment by occupation: 10.2% management, 14.2% professional, 13.4% services, 26.0% sales, 2.0% farming, 7.6% construction, 26.6% production (2000).
Income: Per capita income: $21,726 (2000); Median household income: $52,700 (2000); Poverty rate: 9.0% (2000).
Education: High school graduation rate: 91.0% (2000); College graduation rate: 14.9% (2000).
Housing: Homeownership rate: 90.4% (2000); Median home value: $113,300 (2000); Median rent: $413 per month (2000); Median age of housing: 38 years (2000).
Transportation: Commute to work: 98.1% car, 0.0% public transportation, 1.0% walk, 0.9% work from home (2000); Travel time to work: 21.9% less than 15 minutes, 58.6% 15 to 30 minutes, 13.3% 30 to 45 minutes, 3.5% 45 to 60 minutes, 2.6% 60 minutes or more (2000)

CLARENCE (township). Covers a land area of 32.736 square miles and a water area of 1.460 square miles. Located at 42.38° N. Lat.; 84.78° W. Long.
History: Clarence Township was first settled in 1836, and organized in 1838.
Population: 2,032 (2000); Race: 96.0% White, 0.4% Black, 0.0% Asian, 1.3% American Indian and Alaska Native, 0.0% Hispanic of any race, 2.3% two or more races (2000); Density: 62.1 persons per square mile (2000); Age: 23.5% under 18, 13.6% over 64 (2000); Marriage status: 18.0% never married, 65.0% now married, 6.6% widowed, 10.3% divorced (2000); Foreign born: 0.9% (2000); Ancestry (includes multiple ancestries): 21.9% German, 16.0% English, 11.5% United States or American, 10.6% Irish, 9.0% Other groups (2000).
Economy: Single-family building permits issued: 8 (2001) / 8 (2000); Multi-family building permits issued: 0 (2001) / 0 (2000); Employment by occupation: 10.5% management, 8.0% professional, 19.8% services, 19.5% sales, 0.5% farming, 9.6% construction, 32.0% production (2000).
Income: Per capita income: $18,713 (2000); Median household income: $40,700 (2000); Poverty rate: 14.9% (2000).
Taxes: Total city taxes per capita: $32 (1997); City property taxes per capita: $25 (1997).
Education: High school graduation rate: 80.6% (2000); College graduation rate: 8.8% (2000).
Housing: Homeownership rate: 84.0% (2000); Median home value: $104,200 (2000); Median rent: $354 per month (2000); Median age of housing: 31 years (2000).
Transportation: Commute to work: 94.2% car, 0.0% public transportation, 0.7% walk, 5.1% work from home (2000); Travel time to work: 15.6% less than 15 minutes, 40.4% 15 to 30 minutes, 17.5% 30 to 45 minutes, 16.1% 45 to 60 minutes, 10.5% 60 minutes or more (2000)

CLARENDON (township). Covers a land area of 35.637 square miles and a water area of 0.080 square miles. Located at 42.12° N. Lat.; 84.88° W. Long. Elevation is 97 feet.
History: Many of the early residents in Clarendon Township had come from Clarendon, New York.
Population: 1,114 (2000); Race: 98.6% White, 0.2% Black, 0.2% Asian, 0.2% American Indian and Alaska Native, 1.4% Hispanic of any race, 0.7% two or more races (2000); Density: 31.3 persons per square mile (2000); Age: 28.3% under 18, 9.6% over 64 (2000); Marriage status: 24.9% never married, 61.9% now married, 4.0% widowed, 9.3% divorced (2000); Foreign born: 0.9% (2000); Ancestry (includes multiple ancestries): 20.3% German, 16.1% English, 13.9% United States or American, 8.1% Other groups, 7.7% Irish (2000).

Economy: Employment by occupation: 10.1% management, 11.2% professional, 14.1% services, 21.9% sales, 0.4% farming, 8.5% construction, 33.7% production (2000).
Income: Per capita income: $18,247 (2000); Median household income: $44,750 (2000); Poverty rate: 8.0% (2000).
Taxes: Total city taxes per capita: $23 (1997); City property taxes per capita: $23 (1997).
Education: High school graduation rate: 81.2% (2000); College graduation rate: 7.9% (2000).
Housing: Homeownership rate: 87.3% (2000); Median home value: $78,600 (2000); Median rent: $378 per month (2000); Median age of housing: 41 years (2000).
Transportation: Commute to work: 96.0% car, 0.0% public transportation, 1.4% walk, 2.6% work from home (2000); Travel time to work: 28.0% less than 15 minutes, 41.4% 15 to 30 minutes, 16.9% 30 to 45 minutes, 5.7% 45 to 60 minutes, 8.0% 60 minutes or more (2000)

CONVIS (township). Covers a land area of 35.304 square miles and a water area of 1.131 square miles. Located at 42.38° N. Lat.; 84.99° W. Long.
Population: 1,666 (2000); Race: 98.2% White, 0.0% Black, 0.8% Asian, 0.0% American Indian and Alaska Native, 2.4% Hispanic of any race, 0.9% two or more races (2000); Density: 47.2 persons per square mile (2000); Age: 25.4% under 18, 11.8% over 64 (2000); Marriage status: 21.4% never married, 62.8% now married, 5.8% widowed, 9.9% divorced (2000); Foreign born: 2.0% (2000); Ancestry (includes multiple ancestries): 20.1% German, 17.3% English, 17.1% United States or American, 7.6% Irish, 6.2% Other groups (2000).
Economy: Single-family building permits issued: 8 (2001) / 4 (2000); Multi-family building permits issued: 0 (2001) / 0 (2000); Employment by occupation: 15.0% management, 10.5% professional, 13.0% services, 22.4% sales, 0.7% farming, 12.1% construction, 26.4% production (2000).
Income: Per capita income: $18,870 (2000); Median household income: $42,222 (2000); Poverty rate: 7.4% (2000).
Taxes: Total city taxes per capita: $19 (1997); City property taxes per capita: $12 (1997).
Education: High school graduation rate: 81.2% (2000); College graduation rate: 9.6% (2000).
Housing: Homeownership rate: 91.4% (2000); Median home value: $89,300 (2000); Median rent: $446 per month (2000); Median age of housing: 33 years (2000).
Transportation: Commute to work: 95.4% car, 0.0% public transportation, 0.0% walk, 4.6% work from home (2000); Travel time to work: 22.2% less than 15 minutes, 44.3% 15 to 30 minutes, 21.3% 30 to 45 minutes, 9.4% 45 to 60 minutes, 2.8% 60 minutes or more (2000)

EAST LEROY (unincorporated postal area, zip code 49051). Covers a land area of 36.144 square miles and a water area of 0.163 square miles. Located at 42.18° N. Lat.; 85.24° W. Long. Elevation is 921 feet.
Population: 2,296 (2000); Race: 97.4% White, 0.0% Black, 0.8% Asian, 0.0% American Indian and Alaska Native, 3.1% Hispanic of any race, 1.0% two or more races (2000); Density: 63.5 persons per square mile (2000); Age: 22.6% under 18, 15.1% over 64 (2000); Marriage status: 15.3% never married, 65.6% now married, 4.9% widowed, 14.2% divorced (2000); Foreign born: 2.3% (2000); Ancestry (includes multiple ancestries): 27.4% German, 15.0% English, 9.3% Irish, 8.5% Other groups, 7.0% United States or American (2000).
Economy: Employment by occupation: 9.7% management, 21.2% professional, 10.1% services, 20.6% sales, 0.8% farming, 17.1% construction, 20.4% production (2000).
Income: Per capita income: $20,515 (2000); Median household income: $51,726 (2000); Poverty rate: 7.1% (2000).
Education: High school graduation rate: 86.2% (2000); College graduation rate: 12.6% (2000).
Housing: Homeownership rate: 92.5% (2000); Median home value: $99,700 (2000); Median rent: $403 per month (2000); Median age of housing: 34 years (2000).
Transportation: Commute to work: 97.1% car, 0.0% public transportation, 0.7% walk, 1.6% work from home (2000); Travel time to work: 19.6% less than 15 minutes, 53.7% 15 to 30 minutes, 17.5% 30 to 45 minutes, 3.1% 45 to 60 minutes, 6.1% 60 minutes or more (2000)

ECKFORD (township). Covers a land area of 35.435 square miles and a water area of 0.240 square miles. Located at 42.20° N. Lat.; 84.89° W. Long. Elevation is 953 feet.
Population: 1,282 (2000); Race: 98.6% White, 0.1% Black, 0.0% Asian, 0.3% American Indian and Alaska Native, 0.5% Hispanic of any race, 1.0% two or more races (2000); Density: 36.2 persons per square mile (2000); Age: 26.4% under 18, 12.8% over 64 (2000); Marriage status: 17.7% never married, 71.5% now married, 4.4% widowed, 6.4% divorced (2000); Foreign born: 0.9% (2000); Ancestry (includes multiple ancestries): 30.3% German, 20.0% English, 14.3% United States or American, 11.3% Irish, 4.6% French (except Basque) (2000).
Economy: Single-family building permits issued: 8 (2001) / 11 (2000); Multi-family building permits issued: 0 (2001) / 0 (2000); Employment by occupation: 14.6% management, 15.9% professional, 12.3% services, 26.7% sales, 0.7% farming, 6.7% construction, 23.1% production (2000).
Income: Per capita income: $19,835 (2000); Median household income: $48,382 (2000); Poverty rate: 5.9% (2000).
Taxes: Total city taxes per capita: $33 (1997); City property taxes per capita: $28 (1997).
Education: High school graduation rate: 87.6% (2000); College graduation rate: 15.0% (2000).
Housing: Homeownership rate: 89.6% (2000); Median home value: $93,400 (2000); Median rent: $420 per month (2000); Median age of housing: 48 years (2000).
Transportation: Commute to work: 89.6% car, 0.4% public transportation, 2.1% walk, 6.4% work from home (2000); Travel time to work: 38.7% less than 15 minutes, 40.6% 15 to 30 minutes, 10.3% 30 to 45 minutes, 4.8% 45 to 60 minutes, 5.6% 60 minutes or more (2000)

EMMETT (township). Covers a land area of 32.260 square miles and a water area of 0.208 square miles. Located at 42.29° N. Lat.; 85.13° W. Long.
Population: 11,979 (2000); Race: 94.0% White, 1.3% Black, 1.5% Asian, 0.1% American Indian and Alaska Native, 2.4% Hispanic of any race, 1.7% two or more races (2000); Density: 371.3 persons per square mile (2000); Age: 23.9% under 18, 13.4% over 64 (2000); Marriage status: 21.7% never married, 60.3% now married, 6.0% widowed, 12.0% divorced (2000); Foreign born: 2.7% (2000); Ancestry (includes multiple ancestries): 20.9% German, 11.9% English, 11.1% Other groups, 10.9% Irish, 9.8% United States or American (2000).
Economy: Single-family building permits issued: 49 (2001) / 40 (2000); Multi-family building permits issued: 0 (2001) / 0 (2000); Employment by occupation: 12.0% management, 13.7% professional, 13.5% services, 25.4% sales, 0.4% farming, 13.1% construction, 21.9% production (2000).
Income: Per capita income: $22,608 (2000); Median household income: $42,868 (2000); Poverty rate: 8.8% (2000).
Taxes: Total city taxes per capita: $87 (2000); City property taxes per capita: $72 (2000).
Education: High school graduation rate: 81.2% (2000); College graduation rate: 16.3% (2000).
Housing: Homeownership rate: 73.4% (2000); Median home value: $95,600 (2000); Median rent: $502 per month (2000); Median age of housing: 34 years (2000).
Safety: Violent crime rate: 70.6 per 10,000 population; Property crime rate: 546.4 per 10,000 population (2001).
Transportation: Commute to work: 95.6% car, 0.8% public transportation, 0.8% walk, 2.0% work from home (2000); Travel time to work: 36.2% less than 15 minutes, 45.9% 15 to 30 minutes, 9.6% 30 to 45 minutes, 2.8% 45 to 60 minutes, 5.5% 60 minutes or more (2000)

FREDONIA (township). Covers a land area of 34.158 square miles and a water area of 0.850 square miles. Located at 42.19° N. Lat.; 85.00° W. Long.
Population: 1,723 (2000); Race: 95.2% White, 0.2% Black, 0.1% Asian, 2.2% American Indian and Alaska Native, 1.3% Hispanic of any race, 1.7% two or more races (2000); Density: 50.4 persons per square mile (2000); Age: 22.5% under 18, 14.7% over 64 (2000); Marriage status: 20.8% never married, 62.4% now married, 6.6% widowed, 10.2% divorced (2000); Foreign born: 0.3% (2000); Ancestry (includes multiple ancestries): 26.1% German, 18.9% English, 8.8% Irish, 8.6% Other groups, 7.1% United States or American (2000).
Economy: Single-family building permits issued: 4 (2001) / 4 (2000); Multi-family building permits issued: 0 (2001) / 0 (2000); Employment by occupation: 13.0% management, 14.7% professional, 12.5% services, 24.1% sales, 0.4% farming, 8.4% construction, 27.0% production (2000).
Income: Per capita income: $21,354 (2000); Median household income: $46,635 (2000); Poverty rate: 7.8% (2000).
Taxes: Total city taxes per capita: $22 (1997); City property taxes per capita: $13 (1997).
Education: High school graduation rate: 84.3% (2000); College graduation rate: 14.4% (2000).

Housing: Homeownership rate: 88.3% (2000); Median home value: $101,300 (2000); Median rent: $434 per month (2000); Median age of housing: 35 years (2000).
Transportation: Commute to work: 95.1% car, 0.0% public transportation, 1.2% walk, 2.3% work from home (2000); Travel time to work: 33.4% less than 15 minutes, 35.9% 15 to 30 minutes, 20.9% 30 to 45 minutes, 7.0% 45 to 60 minutes, 2.8% 60 minutes or more (2000)

HOMER (village). Covers a land area of 1.423 square miles and a water area of 0.028 square miles. Located at 42.14° N. Lat.; 84.80° W. Long. Elevation is 994 feet.
History: Homer was founded by Milton Barney, who built a sawmill and a grist mill here, and opened a store and an inn in the early 1830's. The village was first called Barneyville, but was later renamed for its township. Homer grew up on the burr oak plains, and became known for making products of wood and grains.
Population: 1,851 (2000); Race: 97.3% White, 0.1% Black, 0.0% Asian, 0.7% American Indian and Alaska Native, 3.5% Hispanic of any race, 0.5% two or more races (2000); Density: 1,300.6 persons per square mile (2000); Age: 30.9% under 18, 9.6% over 64 (2000); Marriage status: 27.7% never married, 51.7% now married, 7.6% widowed, 13.1% divorced (2000); Foreign born: 0.8% (2000); Ancestry (includes multiple ancestries): 19.1% United States or American, 18.2% German, 13.1% Irish, 11.1% Other groups, 10.4% English (2000).
Economy: Employment by occupation: 6.3% management, 8.9% professional, 17.2% services, 17.8% sales, 1.2% farming, 9.1% construction, 39.6% production (2000).
Income: Per capita income: $16,394 (2000); Median household income: $35,542 (2000); Poverty rate: 11.5% (2000).
Taxes: Total city taxes per capita: $159 (1997); City property taxes per capita: $157 (1997).
Education: High school graduation rate: 82.5% (2000); College graduation rate: 6.3% (2000).

School District(s)

Homer Community Schools (KG-12)
2000 Enrollment: 1,132 517-568-4461
Housing: Homeownership rate: 71.2% (2000); Median home value: $67,700 (2000); Median rent: $281 per month (2000); Median age of housing: 47 years (2000).
Safety: Violent crime rate: 48.4 per 10,000 population; Property crime rate: 279.4 per 10,000 population (2001).
Newspapers: The Homer Index (1 x week)
Transportation: Commute to work: 89.3% car, 0.0% public transportation, 6.9% walk, 2.9% work from home (2000); Travel time to work: 36.3% less than 15 minutes, 39.4% 15 to 30 minutes, 17.8% 30 to 45 minutes, 3.4% 45 to 60 minutes, 3.1% 60 minutes or more (2000)

HOMER (township). Covers a land area of 35.716 square miles and a water area of 0.436 square miles. Located at 42.12° N. Lat.; 84.79° W. Long. Elevation is 994 feet.
History: Homer Township was organized in 1834 and named for Homer, New York, at the request of residents who had come from New York.
Population: 3,010 (2000); Race: 96.6% White, 0.1% Black, 0.0% Asian, 1.2% American Indian and Alaska Native, 2.7% Hispanic of any race, 0.8% two or more races (2000); Density: 84.3 persons per square mile (2000); Age: 29.8% under 18, 10.9% over 64 (2000); Marriage status: 26.2% never married, 55.1% now married, 6.8% widowed, 11.9% divorced (2000); Foreign born: 0.5% (2000); Ancestry (includes multiple ancestries): 21.6% German, 17.4% United States or American, 11.6% Other groups, 11.0% Irish, 10.1% English (2000).
Economy: Single-family building permits issued: 4 (2001) / 10 (2000); Multi-family building permits issued: 0 (2001) / 0 (2000); Employment by occupation: 9.1% management, 9.3% professional, 13.9% services, 14.4% sales, 1.6% farming, 10.2% construction, 41.4% production (2000).
Income: Per capita income: $16,686 (2000); Median household income: $36,250 (2000); Poverty rate: 14.6% (2000).
Taxes: Total city taxes per capita: $16 (1997); City property taxes per capita: $14 (1997).
Education: High school graduation rate: 79.0% (2000); College graduation rate: 6.7% (2000).
Housing: Homeownership rate: 76.3% (2000); Median home value: $66,800 (2000); Median rent: $310 per month (2000); Median age of housing: 40 years (2000).
Transportation: Commute to work: 86.0% car, 0.0% public transportation, 5.4% walk, 7.1% work from home (2000); Travel time to work: 35.5% less than 15 minutes, 38.5% 15 to 30 minutes, 17.7% 30 to 45 minutes, 4.6% 45 to 60 minutes, 3.7% 60 minutes or more (2000)

LEE (township). Covers a land area of 36.262 square miles and a water area of 0.140 square miles. Located at 42.37° N. Lat.; 84.90° W. Long.
Population: 1,257 (2000); Race: 95.5% White, 0.0% Black, 0.0% Asian, 0.2% American Indian and Alaska Native, 2.9% Hispanic of any race, 1.8% two or more races (2000); Density: 34.7 persons per square mile (2000); Age: 30.2% under 18, 7.9% over 64 (2000); Marriage status: 26.7% never married, 60.7% now married, 4.4% widowed, 8.1% divorced (2000); Foreign born: 0.6% (2000); Ancestry (includes multiple ancestries): 20.6% German, 15.0% United States or American, 12.1% English, 8.4% Irish, 8.1% Other groups (2000).
Economy: Single-family building permits issued: 3 (2001) / 3 (2000); Multi-family building permits issued: 0 (2001) / 0 (2000); Employment by occupation: 12.0% management, 10.5% professional, 12.1% services, 22.3% sales, 1.5% farming, 11.6% construction, 30.0% production (2000).
Income: Per capita income: $19,445 (2000); Median household income: $45,592 (2000); Poverty rate: 10.3% (2000).
Education: High school graduation rate: 80.6% (2000); College graduation rate: 10.0% (2000).
Housing: Homeownership rate: 82.5% (2000); Median home value: $79,300 (2000); Median rent: $387 per month (2000); Median age of housing: 34 years (2000).
Transportation: Commute to work: 94.4% car, 0.0% public transportation, 0.7% walk, 4.9% work from home (2000); Travel time to work: 20.2% less than 15 minutes, 46.2% 15 to 30 minutes, 18.5% 30 to 45 minutes, 11.4% 45 to 60 minutes, 3.7% 60 minutes or more (2000)

LEROY (township). Covers a land area of 35.929 square miles and a water area of 0.431 square miles. Located at 42.20° N. Lat.; 85.23° W. Long.
Population: 3,240 (2000); Race: 97.6% White, 0.0% Black, 0.8% Asian, 0.0% American Indian and Alaska Native, 3.2% Hispanic of any race, 0.5% two or more races (2000); Density: 90.2 persons per square mile (2000); Age: 26.8% under 18, 12.6% over 64 (2000); Marriage status: 21.4% never married, 61.8% now married, 4.7% widowed, 12.1% divorced (2000); Foreign born: 1.6% (2000); Ancestry (includes multiple ancestries): 31.0% German, 12.8% Irish, 12.7% English, 11.2% United States or American, 8.3% Other groups (2000).
Economy: Single-family building permits issued: 32 (2001) / 26 (2000); Multi-family building permits issued: 0 (2001) / 0 (2000); Employment by occupation: 9.1% management, 21.2% professional, 13.4% services, 24.0% sales, 0.4% farming, 11.5% construction, 20.5% production (2000).
Income: Per capita income: $22,799 (2000); Median household income: $52,361 (2000); Poverty rate: 8.6% (2000).
Taxes: Total city taxes per capita: $25 (1997); City property taxes per capita: $15 (1997).
Education: High school graduation rate: 83.4% (2000); College graduation rate: 17.8% (2000).

School District(s)

Pine River Area Schools (KG-12)
2000 Enrollment: 1,374 231-829-3141
Housing: Homeownership rate: 92.6% (2000); Median home value: $110,900 (2000); Median rent: $356 per month (2000); Median age of housing: 36 years (2000).
Transportation: Commute to work: 99.3% car, 0.0% public transportation, 0.5% walk, 0.3% work from home (2000); Travel time to work: 28.4% less than 15 minutes, 50.5% 15 to 30 minutes, 14.1% 30 to 45 minutes, 2.5% 45 to 60 minutes, 4.5% 60 minutes or more (2000)

LEVEL PARK-OAK PARK (CDP). Covers a land area of 5.322 square miles and a water area of 0 square miles. Located at 42.36° N. Lat.; 85.25° W. Long.
Population: 3,605 (2000); Race: 91.5% White, 3.6% Black, 0.0% Asian, 1.6% American Indian and Alaska Native, 2.3% Hispanic of any race, 1.8% two or more races (2000); Density: 677.3 persons per square mile (2000); Age: 27.4% under 18, 12.5% over 64 (2000); Marriage status: 18.6% never married, 65.8% now married, 7.0% widowed, 8.6% divorced (2000); Foreign born: 2.1% (2000); Ancestry (includes multiple ancestries): 18.9% German, 15.8% English, 11.2% Other groups, 8.7% United States or American, 7.8% Irish (2000).
Economy: Employment by occupation: 8.4% management, 16.4% professional, 16.2% services, 22.8% sales, 1.1% farming, 12.1% construction, 23.0% production (2000).
Income: Per capita income: $18,983 (2000); Median household income: $42,388 (2000); Poverty rate: 7.0% (2000).

Education: High school graduation rate: 79.2% (2000); College graduation rate: 11.0% (2000).
Housing: Homeownership rate: 93.2% (2000); Median home value: $81,200 (2000); Median rent: $440 per month (2000); Median age of housing: 43 years (2000).
Transportation: Commute to work: 95.3% car, 0.0% public transportation, 1.8% walk, 2.9% work from home (2000); Travel time to work: 33.8% less than 15 minutes, 47.0% 15 to 30 minutes, 11.5% 30 to 45 minutes, 4.6% 45 to 60 minutes, 3.1% 60 minutes or more (2000)

MARENGO (township). Covers a land area of 35.204 square miles and a water area of 0.531 square miles. Located at 42.28° N. Lat.; 84.89° W. Long. Elevation is 925 feet.
Population: 2,131 (2000); Race: 98.3% White, 0.0% Black, 0.1% Asian, 0.0% American Indian and Alaska Native, 3.9% Hispanic of any race, 0.8% two or more races (2000); Density: 60.5 persons per square mile (2000); Age: 27.0% under 18, 11.0% over 64 (2000); Marriage status: 19.3% never married, 72.5% now married, 3.6% widowed, 4.6% divorced (2000); Foreign born: 0.0% (2000); Ancestry (includes multiple ancestries): 22.4% German, 14.9% English, 13.6% Irish, 13.3% United States or American, 8.5% Other groups (2000).
Economy: Single-family building permits issued: 10 (2001) / 12 (2000); Multi-family building permits issued: 0 (2001) / 0 (2000); Employment by occupation: 11.4% management, 14.2% professional, 12.8% services, 28.2% sales, 0.8% farming, 11.1% construction, 21.5% production (2000).
Income: Per capita income: $18,550 (2000); Median household income: $50,473 (2000); Poverty rate: 8.0% (2000).
Taxes: Total city taxes per capita: $23 (1997); City property taxes per capita: $14 (1997).
Education: High school graduation rate: 90.7% (2000); College graduation rate: 12.9% (2000).
Housing: Homeownership rate: 89.4% (2000); Median home value: $110,000 (2000); Median rent: $283 per month (2000); Median age of housing: 35 years (2000).
Transportation: Commute to work: 96.4% car, 0.0% public transportation, 0.3% walk, 2.4% work from home (2000); Travel time to work: 45.4% less than 15 minutes, 30.3% 15 to 30 minutes, 18.1% 30 to 45 minutes, 4.1% 45 to 60 minutes, 2.1% 60 minutes or more (2000)

MARSHALL (city). Covers a land area of 5.917 square miles and a water area of 0.176 square miles. Located at 42.27° N. Lat.; 84.96° W. Long. Elevation is 916 feet.
History: Marshall was settled in 1830 and named for U.S. Chief Justice John Marshall. An event that led to the passage of the New Fugitive Slave Bill of 1850 occurred in Marshall in 1846, when resident Adam Crosswhite, a slave who had escaped from Kentucky and had lived in Marshall for two years, was seized by slavehunters. The town not only freed Crosswhite and his family and sent them on to Canada on the Underground Railroad, but arrested those who had tried to take the Crosswhites. Marshall is also known as the place where John D. Pierce and Isaac E. Crary designed the Michigan State public school system.
Population: 7,459 (2000); Race: 96.2% White, 0.1% Black, 0.4% Asian, 0.9% American Indian and Alaska Native, 2.6% Hispanic of any race, 1.9% two or more races (2000); Density: 1,260.7 persons per square mile (2000); Age: 24.5% under 18, 18.9% over 64 (2000); Marriage status: 21.4% never married, 59.4% now married, 9.7% widowed, 9.6% divorced (2000); Foreign born: 1.8% (2000); Ancestry (includes multiple ancestries): 26.1% German, 17.8% English, 14.7% Irish, 9.7% United States or American, 7.0% Other groups (2000).
Economy: Single-family building permits issued: 6 (2001) / 10 (2000); Multi-family building permits issued: 0 (2001) / 0 (2000); Employment by occupation: 15.3% management, 27.0% professional, 14.3% services, 20.7% sales, 0.0% farming, 7.3% construction, 15.4% production (2000).
Income: Per capita income: $22,101 (2000); Median household income: $41,171 (2000); Poverty rate: 5.0% (2000).
Taxes: Total city taxes per capita: $488 (2000); City property taxes per capita: $480 (2000).
Education: High school graduation rate: 87.3% (2000); College graduation rate: 29.8% (2000).

School District(s)

Mar Lee School District (KG-08)
2000 Enrollment: 272 616-781-5412
Marshall Academy (KG-06)
2000 Enrollment: 83 616-781-6330
Marshall Public Schools (KG-12)
2000 Enrollment: 2,534 616-781-1256

Housing: Homeownership rate: 66.9% (2000); Median home value: $102,200 (2000); Median rent: $465 per month (2000); Median age of housing: 47 years (2000).
Hospitals: Oaklawn Hospital (94 beds)
Safety: Violent crime rate: 22.7 per 10,000 population; Property crime rate: 470.8 per 10,000 population (2001).
Newspapers: The Marshall Chronicle (6 x week); Marshall Ad-Visor (1 x week); Community Ad-Visor (1 x week)
Transportation: Commute to work: 91.3% car, 0.2% public transportation, 4.3% walk, 3.7% work from home (2000); Travel time to work: 44.8% less than 15 minutes, 31.0% 15 to 30 minutes, 15.9% 30 to 45 minutes, 5.1% 45 to 60 minutes, 3.3% 60 minutes or more (2000)
Additional Information Contacts
Marshall Chamber of Commerce 616-781-5163

MARSHALL (township). Covers a land area of 31.189 square miles and a water area of 0.436 square miles. Located at 42.28° N. Lat.; 85.00° W. Long. Elevation is 916 feet.
History: Historical homes. Settled 1831; incorporated as village 1836, as city 1859.
Population: 2,922 (2000); Race: 98.6% White, 0.5% Black, 0.3% Asian, 0.2% American Indian and Alaska Native, 1.1% Hispanic of any race, 0.1% two or more races (2000); Density: 93.7 persons per square mile (2000); Age: 24.4% under 18, 11.3% over 64 (2000); Marriage status: 19.0% never married, 68.9% now married, 5.3% widowed, 6.8% divorced (2000); Foreign born: 2.1% (2000); Ancestry (includes multiple ancestries): 29.6% German, 17.5% English, 11.0% Irish, 7.1% United States or American, 6.9% Other groups (2000).
Economy: In farm area: livestock, poultry; grain. Manufacturing: plastic products, transportation equipment, foods, fabricated metal products, chemicals; vehicle-component testing laboratory. Single-family building permits issued: 12 (2001) / 10 (2000); Multi-family building permits issued: 0 (2001) / 0 (2000); Employment by occupation: 15.5% management, 20.2% professional, 12.4% services, 29.1% sales, 1.2% farming, 7.7% construction, 14.0% production (2000).
Income: Per capita income: $25,163 (2000); Median household income: $56,563 (2000); Poverty rate: 5.0% (2000).
Taxes: Total city taxes per capita: $46 (1997); City property taxes per capita: $32 (1997).
Education: High school graduation rate: 93.9% (2000); College graduation rate: 27.9% (2000).
Housing: Homeownership rate: 91.1% (2000); Median home value: $137,100 (2000); Median rent: $461 per month (2000); Median age of housing: 33 years (2000).
Transportation: Commute to work: 91.4% car, 0.0% public transportation, 0.9% walk, 7.4% work from home (2000); Travel time to work: 43.7% less than 15 minutes, 32.2% 15 to 30 minutes, 14.6% 30 to 45 minutes, 5.6% 45 to 60 minutes, 3.8% 60 minutes or more (2000)

NEWTON (township). Covers a land area of 35.936 square miles and a water area of 0.345 square miles. Located at 42.20° N. Lat.; 85.12° W. Long.
Population: 2,493 (2000); Race: 98.8% White, 0.0% Black, 0.4% Asian, 0.5% American Indian and Alaska Native, 0.8% Hispanic of any race, 0.3% two or more races (2000); Density: 69.4 persons per square mile (2000); Age: 21.1% under 18, 14.8% over 64 (2000); Marriage status: 13.4% never married, 72.3% now married, 5.7% widowed, 8.7% divorced (2000); Foreign born: 1.4% (2000); Ancestry (includes multiple ancestries): 29.3% German, 19.2% English, 11.0% Irish, 8.6% United States or American, 7.0% Dutch (2000).
Economy: Single-family building permits issued: 8 (2001) / 15 (2000); Multi-family building permits issued: 0 (2001) / 0 (2000); Employment by occupation: 12.9% management, 14.4% professional, 11.2% services, 28.8% sales, 0.9% farming, 8.4% construction, 23.4% production (2000).
Income: Per capita income: $23,569 (2000); Median household income: $48,568 (2000); Poverty rate: 5.4% (2000).
Taxes: Total city taxes per capita: $41 (1997); City property taxes per capita: $16 (1997).
Education: High school graduation rate: 92.1% (2000); College graduation rate: 16.6% (2000).
Housing: Homeownership rate: 95.7% (2000); Median home value: $141,600 (2000); Median rent: $331 per month (2000); Median age of housing: 23 years (2000).
Transportation: Commute to work: 96.4% car, 0.0% public transportation, 0.0% walk, 3.0% work from home (2000); Travel time to work: 22.4% less than 15 minutes, 53.3% 15 to 30 minutes, 14.5% 30 to 45 minutes, 6.5% 45 to 60 minutes, 3.3% 60 minutes or more (2000)

PENNFIELD CHARTER (township). Covers a land area of 34.776 square miles and a water area of 0.340 square miles. Located at 42.36° N. Lat.; 85.14° W. Long.
Population: 8,913 (2000); Race: 92.1% White, 5.0% Black, 0.5% Asian, 0.4% American Indian and Alaska Native, 1.9% Hispanic of any race, 0.9% two or more races (2000); Density: 256.3 persons per square mile (2000); Age: 26.5% under 18, 12.6% over 64 (2000); Marriage status: 23.5% never married, 59.8% now married, 6.2% widowed, 10.6% divorced (2000); Foreign born: 1.1% (2000); Ancestry (includes multiple ancestries): 22.1% German, 15.0% English, 12.3% Irish, 11.5% Other groups, 10.7% United States or American (2000).
Economy: Single-family building permits issued: 15 (2001) / 22 (2000); Multi-family building permits issued: 0 (2001) / 0 (2000); Employment by occupation: 10.3% management, 17.8% professional, 16.9% services, 26.7% sales, 0.1% farming, 7.9% construction, 20.3% production (2000).
Income: Per capita income: $20,846 (2000); Median household income: $44,277 (2000); Poverty rate: 7.3% (2000).
Taxes: Total city taxes per capita: $92 (2000); City property taxes per capita: $81 (2000).
Education: High school graduation rate: 87.0% (2000); College graduation rate: 16.9% (2000).
Housing: Homeownership rate: 78.3% (2000); Median home value: $91,000 (2000); Median rent: $431 per month (2000); Median age of housing: 37 years (2000).
Safety: Violent crime rate: 42.4 per 10,000 population; Property crime rate: 473.2 per 10,000 population (2001).
Transportation: Commute to work: 94.6% car, 1.1% public transportation, 1.1% walk, 2.8% work from home (2000); Travel time to work: 35.6% less than 15 minutes, 46.4% 15 to 30 minutes, 9.4% 30 to 45 minutes, 4.9% 45 to 60 minutes, 3.6% 60 minutes or more (2000)

SHERIDAN (township). Covers a land area of 31.440 square miles and a water area of 0.366 square miles. Located at 42.28° N. Lat.; 84.76° W. Long.
History: Sheridan was settled in the early 1830's, and the township was organized in 1836.
Population: 2,116 (2000); Race: 88.7% White, 7.0% Black, 0.3% Asian, 0.9% American Indian and Alaska Native, 4.6% Hispanic of any race, 2.3% two or more races (2000); Density: 67.3 persons per square mile (2000); Age: 30.2% under 18, 16.5% over 64 (2000); Marriage status: 22.2% never married, 62.4% now married, 7.4% widowed, 8.0% divorced (2000); Foreign born: 1.0% (2000); Ancestry (includes multiple ancestries): 19.6% German, 15.0% English, 9.1% Irish, 8.8% Other groups, 6.9% United States or American (2000).
Economy: Single-family building permits issued: 10 (2001) / 8 (2000); Multi-family building permits issued: 0 (2001) / 0 (2000); Employment by occupation: 7.7% management, 14.9% professional, 17.7% services, 19.5% sales, 1.0% farming, 11.3% construction, 27.9% production (2000).
Income: Per capita income: $14,886 (2000); Median household income: $32,075 (2000); Poverty rate: 11.3% (2000).
Taxes: Total city taxes per capita: $72 (1997); City property taxes per capita: $65 (1997).
Education: High school graduation rate: 78.8% (2000); College graduation rate: 8.3% (2000).
Housing: Homeownership rate: 81.0% (2000); Median home value: $77,300 (2000); Median rent: $356 per month (2000); Median age of housing: 38 years (2000).
Transportation: Commute to work: 94.6% car, 0.0% public transportation, 2.1% walk, 1.5% work from home (2000); Travel time to work: 39.6% less than 15 minutes, 36.0% 15 to 30 minutes, 11.8% 30 to 45 minutes, 4.4% 45 to 60 minutes, 8.1% 60 minutes or more (2000)

SPRINGFIELD (city). Covers a land area of 3.717 square miles and a water area of 0.031 square miles. Located at 42.32° N. Lat.; 85.23° W. Long.
History: First platted as Merrill Park, the name was changed to Springfield for Springfield, Illinois, former home of C.W. Post.
Population: 5,189 (2000); Race: 85.9% White, 7.1% Black, 2.0% Asian, 0.7% American Indian and Alaska Native, 1.8% Hispanic of any race, 3.9% two or more races (2000); Density: 1,395.9 persons per square mile (2000); Age: 21.6% under 18, 15.4% over 64 (2000); Marriage status: 29.0% never married, 48.9% now married, 5.7% widowed, 16.5% divorced (2000); Foreign born: 3.9% (2000); Ancestry (includes multiple ancestries): 16.0% Other groups, 14.8% German, 11.3% United States or American, 10.6% English, 9.4% Irish (2000).
Economy: Single-family building permits issued: 14 (2001) / 30 (2000); Multi-family building permits issued: 0 (2001) / 0 (2000); Employment by occupation: 8.4% management, 8.4% professional, 17.4% services, 21.6% sales, 0.3% farming, 11.2% construction, 32.8% production (2000).
Income: Per capita income: $15,413 (2000); Median household income: $29,790 (2000); Poverty rate: 13.0% (2000).
Taxes: Total city taxes per capita: $191 (1997); City property taxes per capita: $182 (1997).
Education: High school graduation rate: 79.9% (2000); College graduation rate: 8.6% (2000).

School District(s)

Endeavor Charter Academy (KG-07)
2000 Enrollment: 537 616-895-3029

Housing: Homeownership rate: 55.6% (2000); Median home value: $61,000 (2000); Median rent: $404 per month (2000); Median age of housing: 34 years (2000).
Safety: Violent crime rate: 47.9 per 10,000 population; Property crime rate: 471.6 per 10,000 population (2001).
Transportation: Commute to work: 96.9% car, 0.7% public transportation, 1.2% walk, 0.7% work from home (2000); Travel time to work: 55.5% less than 15 minutes, 32.3% 15 to 30 minutes, 8.0% 30 to 45 minutes, 1.2% 45 to 60 minutes, 2.9% 60 minutes or more (2000)

TEKONSHA (village). Covers a land area of 0.689 square miles and a water area of 0 square miles. Located at 42.09° N. Lat.; 84.98° W. Long. Elevation is 947 feet.
History: Tekonsha was settled in 1832 and named for a Potawatomi chief, Tekonquasha (1768-1825).
Population: 712 (2000); Race: 98.1% White, 0.0% Black, 0.0% Asian, 0.3% American Indian and Alaska Native, 2.0% Hispanic of any race, 1.6% two or more races (2000); Density: 1,033.0 persons per square mile (2000); Age: 24.4% under 18, 12.4% over 64 (2000); Marriage status: 22.2% never married, 55.8% now married, 9.7% widowed, 12.4% divorced (2000); Foreign born: 0.0% (2000); Ancestry (includes multiple ancestries): 22.3% German, 14.6% English, 8.2% United States or American, 5.5% Irish, 4.0% Other groups (2000).
Economy: Single-family building permits issued: 0 (2001) / 0 (2000); Multi-family building permits issued: 0 (2001) / 0 (2000); Employment by occupation: 6.6% management, 14.6% professional, 16.1% services, 16.9% sales, 2.0% farming, 4.6% construction, 39.1% production (2000).
Income: Per capita income: $18,531 (2000); Median household income: $39,917 (2000); Poverty rate: 7.1% (2000).
Taxes: Total city taxes per capita: $92 (1997); City property taxes per capita: $91 (1997).
Education: High school graduation rate: 84.1% (2000); College graduation rate: 7.6% (2000).

School District(s)

Tekonsha Community Schools (KG-12)
2000 Enrollment: 403 517-767-4121

Housing: Homeownership rate: 77.0% (2000); Median home value: $78,700 (2000); Median rent: $391 per month (2000); Median age of housing: 59 years (2000).
Transportation: Commute to work: 89.8% car, 0.0% public transportation, 4.7% walk, 3.4% work from home (2000); Travel time to work: 33.3% less than 15 minutes, 40.1% 15 to 30 minutes, 17.3% 30 to 45 minutes, 5.7% 45 to 60 minutes, 3.5% 60 minutes or more (2000)

TEKONSHA (township). Covers a land area of 35.671 square miles and a water area of 0.696 square miles. Located at 42.09° N. Lat.; 84.99° W. Long. Elevation is 947 feet.
Population: 1,734 (2000); Race: 98.6% White, 0.0% Black, 0.0% Asian, 0.2% American Indian and Alaska Native, 1.2% Hispanic of any race, 1.2% two or more races (2000); Density: 48.6 persons per square mile (2000); Age: 25.9% under 18, 11.4% over 64 (2000); Marriage status: 21.4% never married, 57.6% now married, 8.2% widowed, 12.8% divorced (2000); Foreign born: 0.6% (2000); Ancestry (includes multiple ancestries): 22.9% German, 14.8% English, 9.1% United States or American, 5.7% Irish, 5.5% Other groups (2000).
Economy: In farm area; food processing; manufacturing of motor vehicle parts. Employment by occupation: 10.2% management, 14.7% professional, 12.3% services, 17.7% sales, 1.7% farming, 7.7% construction, 35.7% production (2000).
Income: Per capita income: $18,604 (2000); Median household income: $42,121 (2000); Poverty rate: 7.5% (2000).
Taxes: Total city taxes per capita: $14 (1997); City property taxes per capita: $14 (1997).
Education: High school graduation rate: 81.6% (2000); College graduation rate: 7.7% (2000).

Housing: Homeownership rate: 77.7% (2000); Median home value: $82,100 (2000); Median rent: $402 per month (2000); Median age of housing: 46 years (2000).
Transportation: Commute to work: 90.9% car, 0.0% public transportation, 2.1% walk, 5.3% work from home (2000); Travel time to work: 29.6% less than 15 minutes, 41.2% 15 to 30 minutes, 17.2% 30 to 45 minutes, 7.5% 45 to 60 minutes, 4.5% 60 minutes or more (2000)

Cass County

Located in southwestern Michigan; bounded on the south by Indiana; drained by the St. Joseph River and Short Dowagiac Creek. Covers a land area of 492.20 square miles, a water area of 16.30 square miles, and is located in the Eastern Time Zone. The county government was organized in 1829. County seat is Cassopolis.

Weather Station: Dowagiac 1 W Elevation: 738 feet

	Jan	Feb	Mar	Apr	May	Jun	Jul	Aug	Sep	Oct	Nov	Dec
High	31	35	46	58	71	80	84	81	74	62	48	37
Low	14	17	26	36	46	56	60	58	50	40	31	21
Precip	2.7	2.0	2.7	3.6	3.6	3.7	3.8	3.9	4.1	3.6	3.4	3.1
Snow	21.3	12.7	6.2	1.3	tr	0.0	0.0	0.0	0.0	tr	6.0	16.7

High and Low temperatures in degrees Fahrenheit; Precipitation and Snow in inches

Population: 51,104 (2000); Race: 89.6% White, 5.5% Black, 0.6% Asian, 0.8% American Indian and Alaska Native, 2.3% Hispanic of any race, 2.4% two or more races (2000); Density: 103.8 persons per square mile (2000); Age: 25.6% under 18, 13.6% over 64 (2000).
Religion: Five largest groups: 15.6% Catholic Church, 3.0% The United Methodist Church, 1.0% Wisconsin Evangelical Lutheran Synod, 0.8% Seventh-day Adventist Church, 0.7% Christian Churches and Churches of Christ (2000).
Economy: Unemployment rate: 3.9% (11/2002); Total civilian labor force: 27,366 (11/2002); Leading industries: 41.0% manufacturing; 12.0% retail trade; 9.8% health care and social assistance (2000); Companies that employ more than 1,000 persons: 0 (2000); Companies that employ more than 100 persons: 14 (2000); Farms: 700 totaling 176,831 acres (1997); Minority business ownership rate: 8.1% (1997); Women business ownership rate: 31.3% (1997); Retail sales per capita: $3,191 (1997). Single-family building permits issued: 291 (2001) / 314 (2000); Multi-family building permits issued: 14 (2001) / 8 (2000).
Income: Per capita income: $19,474 (2000); Median household income: $41,264 (2000); Poverty rate: 9.9% (2000); Bankruptcy rate: 5.14% (2001).
Taxes: Total county taxes per capita: $126 (1997); County property taxes per capita: $124 (1997).
Education: High school graduation rate: 80.4% (2000); College graduation rate: 12.1% (2000).
Housing: Homeownership rate: 81.9% (2000); Median home value: $91,800 (2000); Median rent: $387 per month (2000); Median age of housing: 36 years (2000).
Health: Birth rate: 113.3 per 10,000 population (1998); Age adjusted death rate: 89.2 per 10,000 population (1999); Age adjusted cancer mortality rate: 249.3 deaths per 100,000 population (1999). Air Quality Index: 63% good, 36% moderate, 1% unhealthy (percent of days in 2000). Number of physicians: 2.2 per 10,000 population (1999); Number of hospital beds: 7.8 per 10,000 population (1999).
Elections: 2000 Presidential election results: 44.4% Gore, 53.2% Bush, 1.9% Nader, 0.0% Buchanan
Additional Information Contacts
Cass County Government Offices 616-445-8621
Cassopolis-Vandalia Chamber 616-445-5538

Cass County Communities

CALVIN (township). Covers a land area of 34.424 square miles and a water area of 1.139 square miles. Located at 41.85° N. Lat.; 85.94° W. Long.
History: Calvin Township was organized in 1835 and named for Calvin Britain, the territorial representative for the county at that time.
Population: 2,041 (2000); Race: 68.7% White, 22.7% Black, 2.6% Asian, 0.2% American Indian and Alaska Native, 1.1% Hispanic of any race, 4.8% two or more races (2000); Density: 59.3 persons per square mile (2000); Age: 25.4% under 18, 11.7% over 64 (2000); Marriage status: 20.1% never married, 60.7% now married, 7.3% widowed, 11.9% divorced (2000); Foreign born: 5.0% (2000); Ancestry (includes multiple ancestries): 33.5% Other groups, 16.5% German, 10.8% United States or American, 8.2% Irish, 6.4% English (2000).
Economy: Single-family building permits issued: 25 (2001) / 17 (2000); Multi-family building permits issued: 0 (2001) / 0 (2000); Employment by occupation: 8.1% management, 11.1% professional, 10.7% services, 21.8% sales, 1.3% farming, 13.0% construction, 34.1% production (2000).
Income: Per capita income: $21,387 (2000); Median household income: $42,171 (2000); Poverty rate: 16.1% (2000).
Taxes: Total city taxes per capita: $27 (1997); City property taxes per capita: $21 (1997).
Education: High school graduation rate: 74.6% (2000); College graduation rate: 10.2% (2000).
Housing: Homeownership rate: 79.7% (2000); Median home value: $110,400 (2000); Median rent: $356 per month (2000); Median age of housing: 25 years (2000).
Transportation: Commute to work: 94.8% car, 0.3% public transportation, 0.0% walk, 4.0% work from home (2000); Travel time to work: 14.5% less than 15 minutes, 46.4% 15 to 30 minutes, 24.2% 30 to 45 minutes, 8.0% 45 to 60 minutes, 6.8% 60 minutes or more (2000)

CASSOPOLIS (village). Covers a land area of 1.750 square miles and a water area of 0.179 square miles. Located at 41.91° N. Lat.; 86.00° W. Long. Elevation is 902 feet.
History: Cassopolis was settled in 1829 and named for territorial governor Lewis Cass.
Population: 1,740 (2000); Race: 54.5% White, 31.7% Black, 3.7% Asian, 1.1% American Indian and Alaska Native, 1.7% Hispanic of any race, 8.6% two or more races (2000); Density: 994.1 persons per square mile (2000); Age: 29.5% under 18, 11.5% over 64 (2000); Marriage status: 28.0% never married, 48.2% now married, 9.6% widowed, 14.2% divorced (2000); Foreign born: 4.4% (2000); Ancestry (includes multiple ancestries): 41.3% Other groups, 15.5% German, 8.7% Irish, 7.8% United States or American, 6.6% English (2000).
Economy: Single-family building permits issued: 1 (2001) / 2 (2000); Multi-family building permits issued: 0 (2001) / 0 (2000); Employment by occupation: 5.1% management, 13.9% professional, 19.4% services, 20.2% sales, 0.0% farming, 8.8% construction, 32.5% production (2000).
Income: Per capita income: $14,359 (2000); Median household income: $28,696 (2000); Poverty rate: 13.9% (2000).
Taxes: Total city taxes per capita: $234 (1997); City property taxes per capita: $230 (1997).
Education: High school graduation rate: 78.6% (2000); College graduation rate: 10.9% (2000).

School District(s)

Cassopolis Public Schools (KG-12)
2000 Enrollment: 1,401 616-445-0503
Housing: Homeownership rate: 57.9% (2000); Median home value: $59,400 (2000); Median rent: $335 per month (2000); Median age of housing: 50 years (2000).
Transportation: Commute to work: 89.7% car, 1.1% public transportation, 4.6% walk, 2.9% work from home (2000); Travel time to work: 31.5% less than 15 minutes, 32.6% 15 to 30 minutes, 21.9% 30 to 45 minutes, 9.1% 45 to 60 minutes, 4.9% 60 minutes or more (2000)
Additional Information Contacts
Cassopolis-Vandalia Chamber 616-445-5538

DOWAGIAC (city). Covers a land area of 4.016 square miles and a water area of 0.028 square miles. Located at 41.98° N. Lat.; 86.10° W. Long. Elevation is 772 feet.
History: The city of Dowagiac grew up around the stove manufacturing industry, begun in the 1850's.
Population: 6,147 (2000); Race: 78.0% White, 13.8% Black, 1.4% Asian, 2.0% American Indian and Alaska Native, 2.8% Hispanic of any race, 3.7% two or more races (2000); Density: 1,530.8 persons per square mile (2000); Age: 28.7% under 18, 14.6% over 64 (2000); Marriage status: 25.1% never married, 47.3% now married, 10.6% widowed, 17.0% divorced (2000); Foreign born: 2.9% (2000); Ancestry (includes multiple ancestries): 22.9% Other groups, 20.9% German, 11.6% Irish, 8.9% English, 7.9% Dutch (2000).
Economy: Single-family building permits issued: 13 (2001) / 14 (2000); Multi-family building permits issued: 0 (2001) / 0 (2000); Employment by occupation: 7.5% management, 12.6% professional, 17.0% services, 23.2% sales, 0.6% farming, 10.8% construction, 28.3% production (2000).
Income: Per capita income: $16,659 (2000); Median household income: $29,926 (2000); Poverty rate: 17.8% (2000).
Taxes: Total city taxes per capita: $217 (1997); City property taxes per capita: $208 (1997).

Education: High school graduation rate: 77.1% (2000); College graduation rate: 12.0% (2000).

School District(s)

Dowagiac Union School District (KG-12)
2000 Enrollment: 2,869 616-782-4402

Two-year College(s)

Southwestern Michigan College (Public)
2001 Enrollment: 3,172 616-782-1000
2001 Tuition: In-state $2,015; Out-of-state $2,635

Housing: Homeownership rate: 61.0% (2000); Median home value: $62,600 (2000); Median rent: $352 per month (2000); Median age of housing: 53 years (2000).
Hospitals: Borgess-Lee Memorial Hospital (74 beds)
Safety: Violent crime rate: 74.4 per 10,000 population; Property crime rate: 721.8 per 10,000 population (2001).
Newspapers: Dowagiac Daily News (5 x week)
Transportation: Commute to work: 91.4% car, 0.0% public transportation, 3.7% walk, 3.9% work from home (2000); Travel time to work: 53.1% less than 15 minutes, 22.5% 15 to 30 minutes, 15.4% 30 to 45 minutes, 6.7% 45 to 60 minutes, 2.3% 60 minutes or more (2000); Amtrak: Service available.

EDWARDSBURG (village). Covers a land area of 0.922 square miles and a water area of 0.086 square miles. Located at 41.79° N. Lat.; 86.08° W. Long. Elevation is 829 feet.
Population: 1,147 (2000); Race: 95.5% White, 0.1% Black, 0.7% Asian, 2.2% American Indian and Alaska Native, 0.2% Hispanic of any race, 1.5% two or more races (2000); Density: 1,244.3 persons per square mile (2000); Age: 25.8% under 18, 14.2% over 64 (2000); Marriage status: 24.1% never married, 51.2% now married, 7.6% widowed, 17.0% divorced (2000); Foreign born: 1.9% (2000); Ancestry (includes multiple ancestries): 25.3% German, 12.1% United States or American, 11.5% Irish, 10.8% Other groups, 8.9% English (2000).
Economy: In farm and lake area. Manufacturing: tool and die, van conversions, wood cabinets, R.V. bathtubs. Single-family building permits issued: 1 (2001) / 0 (2000); Multi-family building permits issued: 0 (2001) / 0 (2000); Employment by occupation: 5.4% management, 11.4% professional, 10.7% services, 23.1% sales, 0.5% farming, 10.8% construction, 38.1% production (2000).
Income: Per capita income: $18,842 (2000); Median household income: $33,359 (2000); Poverty rate: 11.3% (2000).
Taxes: Total city taxes per capita: $113 (1997); City property taxes per capita: $109 (1997).
Education: High school graduation rate: 81.9% (2000); College graduation rate: 11.0% (2000).

School District(s)

Edwardsburg Public Schools (KG-12)
2000 Enrollment: 2,147 616-663-1053

Housing: Homeownership rate: 72.4% (2000); Median home value: $77,400 (2000); Median rent: $421 per month (2000); Median age of housing: 36 years (2000).
Transportation: Commute to work: 92.6% car, 0.7% public transportation, 2.2% walk, 2.9% work from home (2000); Travel time to work: 33.3% less than 15 minutes, 43.9% 15 to 30 minutes, 16.9% 30 to 45 minutes, 3.7% 45 to 60 minutes, 2.0% 60 minutes or more (2000)

HOWARD (township). Covers a land area of 34.829 square miles and a water area of 0.550 square miles. Located at 41.85° N. Lat.; 86.17° W. Long.
Population: 6,309 (2000); Race: 95.0% White, 3.2% Black, 0.0% Asian, 0.1% American Indian and Alaska Native, 1.6% Hispanic of any race, 1.3% two or more races (2000); Density: 181.1 persons per square mile (2000); Age: 22.8% under 18, 13.9% over 64 (2000); Marriage status: 18.2% never married, 63.0% now married, 7.3% widowed, 11.4% divorced (2000); Foreign born: 1.0% (2000); Ancestry (includes multiple ancestries): 29.2% German, 11.3% Irish, 11.2% English, 10.6% Other groups, 9.2% United States or American (2000).
Economy: Single-family building permits issued: 35 (2001) / 35 (2000); Multi-family building permits issued: 0 (2001) / 0 (2000); Employment by occupation: 10.7% management, 12.8% professional, 13.3% services, 23.9% sales, 0.1% farming, 12.9% construction, 26.3% production (2000).
Income: Per capita income: $19,429 (2000); Median household income: $41,477 (2000); Poverty rate: 7.0% (2000).
Taxes: Total city taxes per capita: $25 (1997); City property taxes per capita: $16 (1997).
Education: High school graduation rate: 80.6% (2000); College graduation rate: 10.9% (2000).
Housing: Homeownership rate: 90.2% (2000); Median home value: $90,400 (2000); Median rent: $428 per month (2000); Median age of housing: 35 years (2000).
Safety: Violent crime rate: 3.2 per 10,000 population; Property crime rate: 110.4 per 10,000 population (2001).
Transportation: Commute to work: 95.9% car, 0.7% public transportation, 1.0% walk, 2.3% work from home (2000); Travel time to work: 31.5% less than 15 minutes, 39.0% 15 to 30 minutes, 19.2% 30 to 45 minutes, 4.0% 45 to 60 minutes, 6.3% 60 minutes or more (2000)

JEFFERSON (township). Covers a land area of 35.004 square miles and a water area of 0.982 square miles. Located at 41.85° N. Lat.; 86.04° W. Long.
Population: 2,401 (2000); Race: 92.8% White, 4.5% Black, 0.6% Asian, 0.0% American Indian and Alaska Native, 0.3% Hispanic of any race, 1.9% two or more races (2000); Density: 68.6 persons per square mile (2000); Age: 24.6% under 18, 14.3% over 64 (2000); Marriage status: 22.8% never married, 57.5% now married, 8.5% widowed, 11.2% divorced (2000); Foreign born: 1.0% (2000); Ancestry (includes multiple ancestries): 27.5% German, 16.7% Irish, 12.0% English, 11.7% United States or American, 11.2% Other groups (2000).
Economy: Single-family building permits issued: 26 (2001) / 48 (2000); Multi-family building permits issued: 0 (2001) / 0 (2000); Employment by occupation: 14.3% management, 10.6% professional, 9.6% services, 23.7% sales, 1.1% farming, 12.5% construction, 28.1% production (2000).
Income: Per capita income: $20,161 (2000); Median household income: $43,633 (2000); Poverty rate: 12.2% (2000).
Taxes: Total city taxes per capita: $39 (1997); City property taxes per capita: $36 (1997).
Education: High school graduation rate: 80.9% (2000); College graduation rate: 13.2% (2000).
Housing: Homeownership rate: 85.7% (2000); Median home value: $90,000 (2000); Median rent: $436 per month (2000); Median age of housing: 26 years (2000).
Transportation: Commute to work: 94.7% car, 0.4% public transportation, 0.6% walk, 4.3% work from home (2000); Travel time to work: 19.1% less than 15 minutes, 41.2% 15 to 30 minutes, 25.8% 30 to 45 minutes, 10.2% 45 to 60 minutes, 3.6% 60 minutes or more (2000)

JONES (unincorporated postal area, zip code 49061). Covers a land area of 37.360 square miles and a water area of 1.211 square miles. Located at 41.87° N. Lat.; 85.81° W. Long.
History: The community of Jones was platted in 1875 on land owned by William D. Jones, and named for him.
Population: 1,634 (2000); Race: 93.1% White, 1.8% Black, 0.6% Asian, 0.0% American Indian and Alaska Native, 3.0% Hispanic of any race, 3.8% two or more races (2000); Density: 43.7 persons per square mile (2000); Age: 26.2% under 18, 8.7% over 64 (2000); Marriage status: 20.9% never married, 64.3% now married, 4.1% widowed, 10.8% divorced (2000); Foreign born: 1.5% (2000); Ancestry (includes multiple ancestries): 26.2% German, 13.0% Other groups, 12.6% English, 11.5% Irish, 9.8% United States or American (2000).
Economy: Employment by occupation: 13.7% management, 9.7% professional, 14.5% services, 20.5% sales, 2.4% farming, 11.1% construction, 28.2% production (2000).
Income: Per capita income: $21,898 (2000); Median household income: $51,719 (2000); Poverty rate: 11.1% (2000).
Education: High school graduation rate: 77.9% (2000); College graduation rate: 9.7% (2000).
Housing: Homeownership rate: 80.7% (2000); Median home value: $78,300 (2000); Median rent: $333 per month (2000); Median age of housing: 41 years (2000).
Transportation: Commute to work: 90.7% car, 0.0% public transportation, 3.6% walk, 5.2% work from home (2000); Travel time to work: 20.6% less than 15 minutes, 46.5% 15 to 30 minutes, 20.9% 30 to 45 minutes, 6.4% 45 to 60 minutes, 5.6% 60 minutes or more (2000)

LA GRANGE (township). Covers a land area of 33.525 square miles and a water area of 1.235 square miles. Located at 41.93° N. Lat.; 86.02° W. Long.
History: La Grange Township was organized in 1829 and named for General LaFayette's home in France. Settlements were made around a sawmill built here in 1829, and a grist mill built in 1832.
Population: 3,340 (2000); Race: 71.4% White, 18.7% Black, 2.0% Asian, 0.8% American Indian and Alaska Native, 3.2% Hispanic of any race, 5.0% two or more races (2000); Density: 99.6 persons per square mile (2000); Age:

26.2% under 18, 14.7% over 64 (2000); Marriage status: 22.4% never married, 59.5% now married, 7.5% widowed, 10.6% divorced (2000); Foreign born: 3.5% (2000); Ancestry (includes multiple ancestries): 27.6% Other groups, 19.4% German, 9.4% Irish, 9.0% English, 8.5% United States or American (2000).
Economy: Single-family building permits issued: 6 (2001) / 6 (2000); Multi-family building permits issued: 0 (2001) / 0 (2000); Employment by occupation: 6.5% management, 16.7% professional, 16.7% services, 20.9% sales, 0.0% farming, 10.7% construction, 28.5% production (2000).
Income: Per capita income: $17,221 (2000); Median household income: $35,566 (2000); Poverty rate: 10.6% (2000).
Taxes: Total city taxes per capita: $27 (1997); City property taxes per capita: $26 (1997).
Education: High school graduation rate: 80.7% (2000); College graduation rate: 13.4% (2000).
Housing: Homeownership rate: 73.0% (2000); Median home value: $75,600 (2000); Median rent: $335 per month (2000); Median age of housing: 45 years (2000).
Transportation: Commute to work: 93.3% car, 0.6% public transportation, 2.3% walk, 2.9% work from home (2000); Travel time to work: 35.6% less than 15 minutes, 28.8% 15 to 30 minutes, 22.3% 30 to 45 minutes, 8.6% 45 to 60 minutes, 4.6% 60 minutes or more (2000)

MARCELLUS (village). Covers a land area of 0.676 square miles and a water area of 0.009 square miles. Located at 42.02° N. Lat.; 85.81° W. Long. Elevation is 889 feet.
Population: 1,162 (2000); Race: 97.9% White, 0.8% Black, 0.0% Asian, 0.0% American Indian and Alaska Native, 0.0% Hispanic of any race, 1.4% two or more races (2000); Density: 1,719.3 persons per square mile (2000); Age: 30.0% under 18, 12.5% over 64 (2000); Marriage status: 21.0% never married, 59.0% now married, 7.4% widowed, 12.7% divorced (2000); Foreign born: 0.4% (2000); Ancestry (includes multiple ancestries): 23.3% German, 17.9% English, 16.3% Irish, 10.9% United States or American, 8.6% Other groups (2000).
Economy: Single-family building permits issued: 0 (2001) / 2 (2000); Multi-family building permits issued: 0 (2001) / 0 (2000); Employment by occupation: 6.9% management, 11.5% professional, 15.5% services, 21.5% sales, 1.3% farming, 8.4% construction, 35.1% production (2000).
Income: Per capita income: $16,296 (2000); Median household income: $38,958 (2000); Poverty rate: 11.7% (2000).
Taxes: Total city taxes per capita: $111 (1997); City property taxes per capita: $111 (1997).
Education: High school graduation rate: 78.8% (2000); College graduation rate: 8.6% (2000).

School District(s)

Marcellus Community Schools (KG-12)
2000 Enrollment: 1,070 616-646-7655

Housing: Homeownership rate: 81.3% (2000); Median home value: $64,400 (2000); Median rent: $367 per month (2000); Median age of housing: 60+ years (2000).
Safety: Violent crime rate: 17.1 per 10,000 population; Property crime rate: 479.5 per 10,000 population (2001).
Newspapers: Marcellus News (1 x week)
Transportation: Commute to work: 92.6% car, 0.2% public transportation, 2.6% walk, 2.9% work from home (2000); Travel time to work: 18.8% less than 15 minutes, 23.5% 15 to 30 minutes, 32.4% 30 to 45 minutes, 11.8% 45 to 60 minutes, 13.5% 60 minutes or more (2000)

MARCELLUS (township). Covers a land area of 33.330 square miles and a water area of 1.483 square miles. Located at 42.02° N. Lat.; 85.81° W. Long. Elevation is 889 feet.
History: Incorporated 1879.
Population: 2,712 (2000); Race: 97.2% White, 0.7% Black, 0.0% Asian, 0.2% American Indian and Alaska Native, 0.9% Hispanic of any race, 1.6% two or more races (2000); Density: 81.4 persons per square mile (2000); Age: 27.1% under 18, 12.8% over 64 (2000); Marriage status: 22.4% never married, 58.3% now married, 6.4% widowed, 12.9% divorced (2000); Foreign born: 0.7% (2000); Ancestry (includes multiple ancestries): 25.2% German, 16.6% English, 14.0% Irish, 9.4% United States or American, 8.7% Other groups (2000).
Economy: In farm and lake resort area. Manufacturing: logging, machining. Single-family building permits issued: 6 (2001) / 7 (2000); Multi-family building permits issued: 0 (2001) / 0 (2000); Employment by occupation: 9.7% management, 10.9% professional, 12.3% services, 21.2% sales, 1.9% farming, 12.4% construction, 31.6% production (2000).
Income: Per capita income: $17,442 (2000); Median household income: $39,306 (2000); Poverty rate: 12.1% (2000).
Taxes: Total city taxes per capita: $48 (1997); City property taxes per capita: $46 (1997).
Education: High school graduation rate: 80.1% (2000); College graduation rate: 9.9% (2000).
Housing: Homeownership rate: 81.8% (2000); Median home value: $73,700 (2000); Median rent: $354 per month (2000); Median age of housing: 44 years (2000).
Transportation: Commute to work: 92.1% car, 0.2% public transportation, 1.4% walk, 4.8% work from home (2000); Travel time to work: 17.3% less than 15 minutes, 28.0% 15 to 30 minutes, 30.4% 30 to 45 minutes, 13.6% 45 to 60 minutes, 10.7% 60 minutes or more (2000)

MASON (township). Covers a land area of 20.268 square miles and a water area of 0.289 square miles. Located at 41.78° N. Lat.; 85.94° W. Long.
Population: 2,514 (2000); Race: 97.5% White, 0.0% Black, 0.9% Asian, 0.0% American Indian and Alaska Native, 0.4% Hispanic of any race, 1.0% two or more races (2000); Density: 124.0 persons per square mile (2000); Age: 25.5% under 18, 11.1% over 64 (2000); Marriage status: 18.6% never married, 61.3% now married, 4.6% widowed, 15.6% divorced (2000); Foreign born: 2.3% (2000); Ancestry (includes multiple ancestries): 29.8% German, 15.0% Irish, 10.7% Other groups, 9.8% United States or American, 9.0% English (2000).
Economy: Single-family building permits issued: 22 (2001) / 27 (2000); Multi-family building permits issued: 12 (2001) / 8 (2000); Employment by occupation: 12.6% management, 6.6% professional, 12.3% services, 20.2% sales, 0.0% farming, 8.3% construction, 40.0% production (2000).
Income: Per capita income: $19,497 (2000); Median household income: $41,902 (2000); Poverty rate: 6.9% (2000).
Taxes: Total city taxes per capita: $17 (1997); City property taxes per capita: $11 (1997).
Education: High school graduation rate: 75.1% (2000); College graduation rate: 7.5% (2000).
Housing: Homeownership rate: 80.5% (2000); Median home value: $98,300 (2000); Median rent: $454 per month (2000); Median age of housing: 25 years (2000).
Transportation: Commute to work: 95.2% car, 0.0% public transportation, 2.2% walk, 2.5% work from home (2000); Travel time to work: 25.3% less than 15 minutes, 49.2% 15 to 30 minutes, 20.5% 30 to 45 minutes, 3.4% 45 to 60 minutes, 1.7% 60 minutes or more (2000)

MILTON (township). Covers a land area of 21.267 square miles and a water area of 0.154 square miles. Located at 41.78° N. Lat.; 86.18° W. Long.
Population: 2,646 (2000); Race: 94.5% White, 1.6% Black, 0.7% Asian, 0.9% American Indian and Alaska Native, 2.3% Hispanic of any race, 1.2% two or more races (2000); Density: 124.4 persons per square mile (2000); Age: 24.7% under 18, 12.4% over 64 (2000); Marriage status: 18.7% never married, 69.7% now married, 4.6% widowed, 7.0% divorced (2000); Foreign born: 2.0% (2000); Ancestry (includes multiple ancestries): 28.2% German, 15.5% Irish, 14.9% English, 10.2% Other groups, 9.2% United States or American (2000).
Economy: Single-family building permits issued: 32 (2001) / 31 (2000); Multi-family building permits issued: 2 (2001) / 0 (2000); Employment by occupation: 12.7% management, 19.2% professional, 10.7% services, 22.3% sales, 0.8% farming, 15.0% construction, 19.3% production (2000).
Income: Per capita income: $23,168 (2000); Median household income: $53,750 (2000); Poverty rate: 6.6% (2000).
Taxes: Total city taxes per capita: $21 (1997); City property taxes per capita: $18 (1997).
Education: High school graduation rate: 86.9% (2000); College graduation rate: 18.1% (2000).
Housing: Homeownership rate: 96.4% (2000); Median home value: $106,500 (2000); Median rent: $517 per month (2000); Median age of housing: 29 years (2000).
Transportation: Commute to work: 95.5% car, 0.0% public transportation, 0.3% walk, 3.8% work from home (2000); Travel time to work: 27.1% less than 15 minutes, 44.6% 15 to 30 minutes, 19.9% 30 to 45 minutes, 5.1% 45 to 60 minutes, 3.3% 60 minutes or more (2000)

NEWBERG (township). Covers a land area of 34.591 square miles and a water area of 0.917 square miles. Located at 41.93° N. Lat.; 85.80° W. Long.
Population: 1,703 (2000); Race: 96.0% White, 1.1% Black, 0.6% Asian, 0.0% American Indian and Alaska Native, 2.7% Hispanic of any race, 2.4% two or more races (2000); Density: 49.2 persons per square mile (2000); Age: 26.5% under 18, 12.7% over 64 (2000); Marriage status: 21.6% never

married, 63.4% now married, 6.9% widowed, 8.2% divorced (2000); Foreign born: 1.1% (2000); Ancestry (includes multiple ancestries): 26.2% German, 12.2% English, 11.7% Other groups, 8.4% United States or American, 6.4% Irish (2000).
Economy: Employment by occupation: 7.8% management, 10.7% professional, 14.8% services, 17.1% sales, 2.9% farming, 11.5% construction, 35.2% production (2000).
Income: Per capita income: $18,078 (2000); Median household income: $43,466 (2000); Poverty rate: 10.7% (2000).
Taxes: Total city taxes per capita: $55 (1997); City property taxes per capita: $54 (1997).
Education: High school graduation rate: 79.1% (2000); College graduation rate: 7.1% (2000).
Housing: Homeownership rate: 83.8% (2000); Median home value: $77,100 (2000); Median rent: $405 per month (2000); Median age of housing: 40 years (2000).
Transportation: Commute to work: 91.3% car, 0.0% public transportation, 3.5% walk, 3.9% work from home (2000); Travel time to work: 27.0% less than 15 minutes, 38.7% 15 to 30 minutes, 21.9% 30 to 45 minutes, 6.7% 45 to 60 minutes, 5.6% 60 minutes or more (2000)

ONTWA (township). Covers a land area of 19.526 square miles and a water area of 1.452 square miles. Located at 41.79° N. Lat.; 86.05° W. Long.
Population: 5,865 (2000); Race: 97.4% White, 0.1% Black, 0.1% Asian, 0.8% American Indian and Alaska Native, 0.1% Hispanic of any race, 1.6% two or more races (2000); Density: 300.4 persons per square mile (2000); Age: 25.5% under 18, 13.6% over 64 (2000); Marriage status: 20.8% never married, 60.9% now married, 6.1% widowed, 12.2% divorced (2000); Foreign born: 1.0% (2000); Ancestry (includes multiple ancestries): 29.5% German, 14.3% Irish, 13.9% English, 9.3% United States or American, 6.9% Other groups (2000).
Economy: Single-family building permits issued: 26 (2001) / 24 (2000); Multi-family building permits issued: 0 (2001) / 0 (2000); Employment by occupation: 11.0% management, 11.6% professional, 11.5% services, 26.3% sales, 0.4% farming, 10.7% construction, 28.5% production (2000).
Income: Per capita income: $21,691 (2000); Median household income: $43,488 (2000); Poverty rate: 5.7% (2000).
Taxes: Total city taxes per capita: $28 (1997); City property taxes per capita: $20 (1997).
Education: High school graduation rate: 81.9% (2000); College graduation rate: 13.7% (2000).
Housing: Homeownership rate: 86.3% (2000); Median home value: $103,200 (2000); Median rent: $435 per month (2000); Median age of housing: 34 years (2000).
Safety: Violent crime rate: 17.0 per 10,000 population; Property crime rate: 322.3 per 10,000 population (2001).
Transportation: Commute to work: 94.7% car, 0.1% public transportation, 1.7% walk, 2.7% work from home (2000); Travel time to work: 27.8% less than 15 minutes, 45.5% 15 to 30 minutes, 18.5% 30 to 45 minutes, 4.0% 45 to 60 minutes, 4.2% 60 minutes or more (2000)

PENN (township). Covers a land area of 33.654 square miles and a water area of 1.765 square miles. Located at 41.93° N. Lat.; 85.92° W. Long. Elevation is 900 feet.
History: Penn Township was organized in 1829 and named for William Penn by its first settlers, who were Quakers from Pennsylvania.
Population: 1,902 (2000); Race: 80.9% White, 14.4% Black, 1.1% Asian, 0.6% American Indian and Alaska Native, 0.3% Hispanic of any race, 2.9% two or more races (2000); Density: 56.5 persons per square mile (2000); Age: 25.6% under 18, 15.7% over 64 (2000); Marriage status: 22.2% never married, 63.0% now married, 5.0% widowed, 9.8% divorced (2000); Foreign born: 2.2% (2000); Ancestry (includes multiple ancestries): 25.3% German, 20.9% Other groups, 12.7% English, 10.9% Irish, 5.7% United States or American (2000).
Economy: Employment by occupation: 10.8% management, 14.9% professional, 12.8% services, 24.7% sales, 0.8% farming, 9.4% construction, 26.6% production (2000).
Income: Per capita income: $19,462 (2000); Median household income: $38,375 (2000); Poverty rate: 13.6% (2000).
Taxes: Total city taxes per capita: $52 (1997); City property taxes per capita: $47 (1997).
Education: High school graduation rate: 82.3% (2000); College graduation rate: 17.4% (2000).
Housing: Homeownership rate: 81.2% (2000); Median home value: $110,100 (2000); Median rent: $408 per month (2000); Median age of housing: 40 years (2000).
Transportation: Commute to work: 95.1% car, 0.0% public transportation, 1.0% walk, 3.6% work from home (2000); Travel time to work: 24.8% less than 15 minutes, 31.1% 15 to 30 minutes, 28.2% 30 to 45 minutes, 9.3% 45 to 60 minutes, 6.4% 60 minutes or more (2000)

POKAGON (township). Covers a land area of 34.556 square miles and a water area of 0.070 square miles. Located at 41.94° N. Lat.; 86.17° W. Long.
Population: 2,199 (2000); Race: 86.2% White, 7.1% Black, 0.7% Asian, 0.6% American Indian and Alaska Native, 5.2% Hispanic of any race, 3.6% two or more races (2000); Density: 63.6 persons per square mile (2000); Age: 24.6% under 18, 16.1% over 64 (2000); Marriage status: 20.1% never married, 66.4% now married, 5.7% widowed, 7.7% divorced (2000); Foreign born: 1.3% (2000); Ancestry (includes multiple ancestries): 26.5% German, 16.2% Other groups, 11.2% Irish, 8.3% United States or American, 7.8% English (2000).
Economy: Single-family building permits issued: 12 (2001) / 12 (2000); Multi-family building permits issued: 0 (2001) / 0 (2000); Employment by occupation: 9.0% management, 13.3% professional, 11.5% services, 19.9% sales, 5.5% farming, 12.2% construction, 28.6% production (2000).
Income: Per capita income: $18,215 (2000); Median household income: $38,850 (2000); Poverty rate: 8.3% (2000).
Taxes: Total city taxes per capita: $50 (1997); City property taxes per capita: $46 (1997).
Education: High school graduation rate: 75.0% (2000); College graduation rate: 8.8% (2000).
Housing: Homeownership rate: 86.9% (2000); Median home value: $84,200 (2000); Median rent: $415 per month (2000); Median age of housing: 39 years (2000).
Transportation: Commute to work: 90.3% car, 0.9% public transportation, 3.3% walk, 4.6% work from home (2000); Travel time to work: 34.3% less than 15 minutes, 38.5% 15 to 30 minutes, 15.2% 30 to 45 minutes, 6.7% 45 to 60 minutes, 5.4% 60 minutes or more (2000)

PORTER (township). Covers a land area of 51.741 square miles and a water area of 2.947 square miles. Located at 41.81° N. Lat.; 85.82° W. Long.
History: Porter Township was organized in 1833 and named for George B. Porter, governor of Michigan.
Population: 3,794 (2000); Race: 96.4% White, 0.2% Black, 0.0% Asian, 1.4% American Indian and Alaska Native, 0.5% Hispanic of any race, 2.1% two or more races (2000); Density: 73.3 persons per square mile (2000); Age: 23.3% under 18, 13.0% over 64 (2000); Marriage status: 17.5% never married, 67.0% now married, 6.4% widowed, 9.2% divorced (2000); Foreign born: 0.9% (2000); Ancestry (includes multiple ancestries): 34.1% German, 14.3% Irish, 14.0% English, 7.8% Other groups, 5.4% United States or American (2000).
Economy: Single-family building permits issued: 39 (2001) / 31 (2000); Multi-family building permits issued: 0 (2001) / 0 (2000); Employment by occupation: 14.5% management, 11.8% professional, 10.0% services, 25.4% sales, 0.0% farming, 10.3% construction, 28.0% production (2000).
Income: Per capita income: $24,026 (2000); Median household income: $51,320 (2000); Poverty rate: 6.2% (2000).
Taxes: Total city taxes per capita: $38 (1997); City property taxes per capita: $26 (1997).
Education: High school graduation rate: 81.5% (2000); College graduation rate: 11.9% (2000).
Housing: Homeownership rate: 84.2% (2000); Median home value: $130,700 (2000); Median rent: $438 per month (2000); Median age of housing: 33 years (2000).
Transportation: Commute to work: 92.8% car, 0.0% public transportation, 2.7% walk, 4.5% work from home (2000); Travel time to work: 16.4% less than 15 minutes, 49.6% 15 to 30 minutes, 22.6% 30 to 45 minutes, 7.7% 45 to 60 minutes, 3.7% 60 minutes or more (2000)

SILVER CREEK (township). Covers a land area of 32.173 square miles and a water area of 2.070 square miles. Located at 42.02° N. Lat.; 86.17° W. Long.
History: Silver Creek Township was organized in 1837. Silver Creek got its name from the silvery look to the marl bottom of the lake from which it runs.
Population: 3,491 (2000); Race: 92.0% White, 0.3% Black, 0.0% Asian, 1.3% American Indian and Alaska Native, 10.8% Hispanic of any race, 2.6% two or more races (2000); Density: 108.5 persons per square mile (2000); Age: 25.3% under 18, 18.2% over 64 (2000); Marriage status: 14.6% never married, 69.2% now married, 7.1% widowed, 9.1% divorced (2000); Foreign born: 4.3% (2000); Ancestry (includes multiple ancestries): 29.6% German, 16.1% Irish, 15.9% Other groups, 10.1% English, 6.9% Dutch (2000).

Economy: Single-family building permits issued: 32 (2001) / 31 (2000); Multi-family building permits issued: 0 (2001) / 0 (2000); Employment by occupation: 11.2% management, 10.4% professional, 12.1% services, 28.7% sales, 1.9% farming, 11.6% construction, 24.1% production (2000).
Income: Per capita income: $18,866 (2000); Median household income: $42,572 (2000); Poverty rate: 10.1% (2000).
Taxes: Total city taxes per capita: $37 (1997); City property taxes per capita: $37 (1997).
Education: High school graduation rate: 86.1% (2000); College graduation rate: 15.9% (2000).
Housing: Homeownership rate: 83.0% (2000); Median home value: $120,600 (2000); Median rent: $533 per month (2000); Median age of housing: 35 years (2000).
Transportation: Commute to work: 90.7% car, 0.0% public transportation, 2.6% walk, 6.6% work from home (2000); Travel time to work: 34.8% less than 15 minutes, 24.3% 15 to 30 minutes, 27.5% 30 to 45 minutes, 7.6% 45 to 60 minutes, 5.8% 60 minutes or more (2000)

UNION (unincorporated postal area, zip code 49130). Covers a land area of 6.837 square miles and a water area of 0.574 square miles. Located at 41.78° N. Lat.; 85.83° W. Long.
History: Union grew up as a trading center around a crossroads on Baldwin's Prairie.
Population: 1,301 (2000); Race: 97.2% White, 0.0% Black, 0.0% Asian, 1.6% American Indian and Alaska Native, 0.0% Hispanic of any race, 1.3% two or more races (2000); Density: 190.3 persons per square mile (2000); Age: 24.2% under 18, 15.1% over 64 (2000); Marriage status: 11.2% never married, 76.1% now married, 8.1% widowed, 4.7% divorced (2000); Foreign born: 1.6% (2000); Ancestry (includes multiple ancestries): 40.1% German, 20.3% English, 8.7% Irish, 7.7% Other groups, 5.3% Swiss (2000).
Economy: Employment by occupation: 17.4% management, 13.0% professional, 6.9% services, 30.7% sales, 0.0% farming, 10.2% construction, 21.7% production (2000).
Income: Per capita income: $26,647 (2000); Median household income: $55,000 (2000); Poverty rate: 4.7% (2000).
Education: High school graduation rate: 85.1% (2000); College graduation rate: 14.1% (2000).
Housing: Homeownership rate: 90.2% (2000); Median home value: $163,400 (2000); Median rent: $400 per month (2000); Median age of housing: 35 years (2000).
Transportation: Commute to work: 94.8% car, 0.0% public transportation, 1.5% walk, 3.7% work from home (2000); Travel time to work: 20.5% less than 15 minutes, 48.7% 15 to 30 minutes, 23.4% 30 to 45 minutes, 6.5% 45 to 60 minutes, 1.0% 60 minutes or more (2000)

VANDALIA (village). Covers a land area of 0.992 square miles and a water area of 0 square miles. Located at 41.91° N. Lat.; 85.91° W. Long. Elevation is 877 feet.
Population: 429 (2000); Race: 28.5% White, 58.3% Black, 3.0% Asian, 0.0% American Indian and Alaska Native, 0.0% Hispanic of any race, 9.5% two or more races (2000); Density: 432.5 persons per square mile (2000); Age: 37.7% under 18, 12.0% over 64 (2000); Marriage status: 33.3% never married, 46.7% now married, 5.5% widowed, 14.4% divorced (2000); Foreign born: 3.9% (2000); Ancestry (includes multiple ancestries): 68.5% Other groups, 4.4% German, 2.3% Polish, 2.3% English, 2.1% French (except Basque) (2000).
Economy: In farm area. Swiss Valley Ski Area to East. Employment by occupation: 1.3% management, 7.0% professional, 19.6% services, 25.3% sales, 0.0% farming, 3.8% construction, 43.0% production (2000).
Income: Per capita income: $11,394 (2000); Median household income: $30,417 (2000); Poverty rate: 14.7% (2000).
Taxes: Total city taxes per capita: $74 (1997); City property taxes per capita: $74 (1997).
Education: High school graduation rate: 70.2% (2000); College graduation rate: 3.3% (2000).
Housing: Homeownership rate: 68.5% (2000); Median home value: $50,700 (2000); Median rent: $363 per month (2000); Median age of housing: 52 years (2000).
Transportation: Commute to work: 98.7% car, 0.0% public transportation, 1.3% walk, 0.0% work from home (2000); Travel time to work: 20.3% less than 15 minutes, 38.6% 15 to 30 minutes, 32.9% 30 to 45 minutes, 7.0% 45 to 60 minutes, 1.3% 60 minutes or more (2000)

VOLINIA (township). Covers a land area of 34.367 square miles and a water area of 0.690 square miles. Located at 42.02° N. Lat.; 85.93° W. Long. Elevation is 865 feet.
Population: 1,174 (2000); Race: 95.2% White, 2.3% Black, 0.0% Asian, 0.0% American Indian and Alaska Native, 0.7% Hispanic of any race, 2.5% two or more races (2000); Density: 34.2 persons per square mile (2000); Age: 29.4% under 18, 10.7% over 64 (2000); Marriage status: 22.5% never married, 66.0% now married, 5.4% widowed, 6.1% divorced (2000); Foreign born: 0.6% (2000); Ancestry (includes multiple ancestries): 27.9% German, 16.0% English, 15.7% Irish, 10.7% United States or American, 9.3% Other groups (2000).
Economy: Single-family building permits issued: 6 (2001) / 5 (2000); Multi-family building permits issued: 0 (2001) / 0 (2000); Employment by occupation: 9.5% management, 14.1% professional, 11.9% services, 21.0% sales, 1.1% farming, 13.9% construction, 28.4% production (2000).
Income: Per capita income: $17,375 (2000); Median household income: $38,900 (2000); Poverty rate: 3.5% (2000).
Taxes: Total city taxes per capita: $40 (1997); City property taxes per capita: $38 (1997).
Education: High school graduation rate: 85.4% (2000); College graduation rate: 11.8% (2000).
Housing: Homeownership rate: 81.5% (2000); Median home value: $93,700 (2000); Median rent: $369 per month (2000); Median age of housing: 40 years (2000).
Transportation: Commute to work: 89.6% car, 0.0% public transportation, 1.7% walk, 6.8% work from home (2000); Travel time to work: 22.3% less than 15 minutes, 31.8% 15 to 30 minutes, 23.3% 30 to 45 minutes, 14.0% 45 to 60 minutes, 8.7% 60 minutes or more (2000)

WAYNE (township). Covers a land area of 34.271 square miles and a water area of 0.514 square miles. Located at 42.02° N. Lat.; 86.04° W. Long.
Population: 2,861 (2000); Race: 92.6% White, 1.1% Black, 0.3% Asian, 1.2% American Indian and Alaska Native, 3.3% Hispanic of any race, 1.7% two or more races (2000); Density: 83.5 persons per square mile (2000); Age: 27.0% under 18, 8.0% over 64 (2000); Marriage status: 25.2% never married, 60.0% now married, 3.7% widowed, 11.1% divorced (2000); Foreign born: 1.0% (2000); Ancestry (includes multiple ancestries): 28.9% German, 14.5% Irish, 13.5% Other groups, 10.9% English, 9.1% United States or American (2000).
Economy: Single-family building permits issued: 9 (2001) / 22 (2000); Multi-family building permits issued: 0 (2001) / 0 (2000); Employment by occupation: 5.2% management, 12.8% professional, 16.2% services, 23.9% sales, 2.0% farming, 13.5% construction, 26.5% production (2000).
Income: Per capita income: $17,621 (2000); Median household income: $42,816 (2000); Poverty rate: 10.8% (2000).
Taxes: Total city taxes per capita: $28 (1997); City property taxes per capita: $24 (1997).
Education: High school graduation rate: 79.5% (2000); College graduation rate: 8.0% (2000).
Housing: Homeownership rate: 89.3% (2000); Median home value: $81,700 (2000); Median rent: $366 per month (2000); Median age of housing: 34 years (2000).
Transportation: Commute to work: 90.6% car, 1.8% public transportation, 3.8% walk, 3.2% work from home (2000); Travel time to work: 32.5% less than 15 minutes, 31.0% 15 to 30 minutes, 17.0% 30 to 45 minutes, 9.9% 45 to 60 minutes, 9.6% 60 minutes or more (2000)

Charlevoix County

Located in northwestern Michigan; bounded on the northwest by Lake Michigan; drained by the Boyne and Jordan Rivers; includes the Beaver Islands, and Charlevoix and Walloon Lakes. Covers a land area of 416.80 square miles, a water area of 973.90 square miles, and is located in the Eastern Time Zone. The county government was organized in 1869. County seat is Charlevoix.

Weather Station: Boyne Falls — Elevation: 734 feet

	Jan	Feb	Mar	Apr	May	Jun	Jul	Aug	Sep	Oct	Nov	Dec
High	28	31	41	56	70	78	82	80	71	59	44	32
Low	11	11	19	31	41	50	55	54	47	38	29	19
Precip	2.4	1.4	2.0	2.3	2.6	2.6	3.2	3.6	4.1	3.4	2.9	2.5
Snow	33.6	19.9	12.4	4.6	0.4	0.0	0.0	0.0	tr	0.9	14.3	30.2

High and Low temperatures in degrees Fahrenheit; Precipitation and Snow in inches

Weather Station: East Jordan Elevation: 587 feet

	Jan	Feb	Mar	Apr	May	Jun	Jul	Aug	Sep	Oct	Nov	Dec
High	28	32	41	55	69	77	81	79	71	59	45	34
Low	13	11	19	31	41	49	55	53	47	38	29	20
Precip	2.1	1.2	1.6	2.4	2.6	2.7	3.1	3.5	4.2	3.6	2.8	2.4
Snow	33.9	18.0	10.2	2.5	0.2	0.0	0.0	0.0	0.0	0.4	10.0	29.6

High and Low temperatures in degrees Fahrenheit; Precipitation and Snow in inches

Weather Station: Saint James 2 S Beaver Island Elevation: 669 feet

	Jan	Feb	Mar	Apr	May	Jun	Jul	Aug	Sep	Oct	Nov	Dec
High	26	27	36	48	62	71	76	74	67	55	42	32
Low	14	12	20	31	41	50	57	57	50	40	31	22
Precip	2.4	1.2	2.1	2.5	2.8	2.6	2.7	3.1	3.7	3.2	2.6	2.2
Snow	28.0	15.6	12.2	4.4	0.2	0.0	0.0	0.0	tr	tr	6.3	19.6

High and Low temperatures in degrees Fahrenheit; Precipitation and Snow in inches

Population: 26,090 (2000); Race: 96.4% White, 0.2% Black, 0.2% Asian, 1.5% American Indian and Alaska Native, 1.0% Hispanic of any race, 1.1% two or more races (2000); Density: 62.6 persons per square mile (2000); Age: 26.0% under 18, 14.8% over 64 (2000).

Religion: Five largest groups: 20.0% Catholic Church, 3.2% Reformed Church in America, 3.0% The United Methodist Church, 2.4% United Church of Christ, 2.3% Lutheran Church—Missouri Synod (2000).

Economy: Unemployment rate: 6.8% (11/2002); Total civilian labor force: 13,464 (11/2002); Leading industries: 29.9% manufacturing; 14.8% accommodation & food services; 13.7% retail trade (2000); Companies that employ more than 1,000 persons: 0 (2000); Companies that employ more than 100 persons: 17 (2000); Farms: 188 totaling 31,077 acres (1997); Minority business ownership rate: 3.7% (1997); Women business ownership rate: 18.7% (1997); Retail sales per capita: $8,414 (1997). Single-family building permits issued: 436 (2001) / 371 (2000); Multi-family building permits issued: 0 (2001) / 0 (2000).

Income: Per capita income: $20,130 (2000); Median household income: $39,788 (2000); Poverty rate: 8.0% (2000); Bankruptcy rate: 2.33% (2001).

Taxes: Total county taxes per capita: $214 (1997); County property taxes per capita: $195 (1997).

Education: High school graduation rate: 86.0% (2000); College graduation rate: 19.8% (2000).

Housing: Homeownership rate: 81.2% (2000); Median home value: $112,700 (2000); Median rent: $409 per month (2000); Median age of housing: 27 years (2000).

Health: Birth rate: 124.6 per 10,000 population (1998); Age adjusted death rate: 81.9 per 10,000 population (1999); Age adjusted cancer mortality rate: 180.6 deaths per 100,000 population (1999). Number of physicians: 12.6 per 10,000 population (1999); Number of hospital beds: 12.6 per 10,000 population (1999).

Elections: 2000 Presidential election results: 39.7% Gore, 56.2% Bush, 3.4% Nader, 0.1% Buchanan

National and State Parks: Michigan Islands National Wildlife Refuge; Young State Park

Additional Information Contacts

Charlevoix County Government Offices 231-547-7200
Antrim Charlevoix Kalkaska Association of Realtors 231-237-6394
Beaver Island Chamber of Commerce 231-448-2505
Boyne City Chamber of Commerce 231-582-6222
Charlevoix Chamber of Commerce 231-547-2101
Charlevoix Convention Bureau 231-547-3003
East Jordan Area Chamber of Commerce 231-536-7351

Charlevoix County Communities

BAY (township). Covers a land area of 15.533 square miles and a water area of 3.318 square miles. Located at 45.29° N. Lat.; 85.07° W. Long.

Population: 1,068 (2000); Race: 98.9% White, 0.0% Black, 0.6% Asian, 0.4% American Indian and Alaska Native, 0.0% Hispanic of any race, 0.2% two or more races (2000); Density: 68.8 persons per square mile (2000); Age: 25.2% under 18, 16.2% over 64 (2000); Marriage status: 19.0% never married, 70.9% now married, 3.8% widowed, 6.3% divorced (2000); Foreign born: 1.6% (2000); Ancestry (includes multiple ancestries): 23.1% German, 14.2% English, 11.1% Irish, 9.2% United States or American, 8.6% Polish (2000).

Economy: Employment by occupation: 15.5% management, 19.2% professional, 17.2% services, 21.5% sales, 1.9% farming, 13.6% construction, 11.1% production (2000).

Income: Per capita income: $25,594 (2000); Median household income: $48,462 (2000); Poverty rate: 4.9% (2000).

Education: High school graduation rate: 89.1% (2000); College graduation rate: 29.8% (2000).

Housing: Homeownership rate: 91.5% (2000); Median home value: $180,900 (2000); Median rent: $440 per month (2000); Median age of housing: 21 years (2000).

Transportation: Commute to work: 90.0% car, 0.4% public transportation, 2.3% walk, 6.8% work from home (2000); Travel time to work: 24.4% less than 15 minutes, 51.6% 15 to 30 minutes, 13.0% 30 to 45 minutes, 2.7% 45 to 60 minutes, 8.2% 60 minutes or more (2000)

BEAVER ISLAND (unincorporated postal area, zip code 49782). Covers a land area of 72.445 square miles and a water area of 1.834 square miles. Located at 45.66° N. Lat.; 85.54° W. Long.

Population: 551 (2000); Race: 98.0% White, 0.0% Black, 0.0% Asian, 1.3% American Indian and Alaska Native, 0.0% Hispanic of any race, 0.7% two or more races (2000); Density: 7.6 persons per square mile (2000); Age: 18.8% under 18, 23.5% over 64 (2000); Marriage status: 19.8% never married, 58.6% now married, 8.2% widowed, 13.3% divorced (2000); Foreign born: 0.6% (2000); Ancestry (includes multiple ancestries): 35.7% Irish, 18.2% English, 17.8% German, 12.9% Polish, 10.8% French (except Basque) (2000).

Economy: Employment by occupation: 9.0% management, 15.2% professional, 12.7% services, 29.9% sales, 0.8% farming, 19.3% construction, 13.1% production (2000).

Income: Per capita income: $25,097 (2000); Median household income: $31,447 (2000); Poverty rate: 7.2% (2000).

Education: High school graduation rate: 88.1% (2000); College graduation rate: 24.5% (2000).

School District(s)

Beaver Island Community School (KG-12)
2000 Enrollment: 91 231-448-2744

Housing: Homeownership rate: 90.6% (2000); Median home value: $137,500 (2000); Median rent: $463 per month (2000); Median age of housing: 21 years (2000).

Transportation: Commute to work: 78.8% car, 0.0% public transportation, 8.7% walk, 6.6% work from home (2000); Travel time to work: 80.0% less than 15 minutes, 13.8% 15 to 30 minutes, 4.0% 30 to 45 minutes, 1.3% 45 to 60 minutes, 0.9% 60 minutes or more (2000)

Airports: Beaver Island

Additional Information Contacts

Beaver Island Chamber of Commerce 231-448-2505

BOYNE CITY (city). Covers a land area of 3.907 square miles and a water area of 1.323 square miles. Located at 45.21° N. Lat.; 85.01° W. Long. Elevation is 706 feet.

History: Boyne City developed along Lake Charlevoix as an area of summer homes and cottages. In the mid-1800's it was the site of a sawmill, and a charcoal foundry. In the 1900's, the tourist trade became the principal source of revenue, with the smelt run in the river in the spring attracting many visitors. The Boyne River, near which the city was established, was named for a river in Ireland.

Population: 3,503 (2000); Race: 97.1% White, 0.0% Black, 0.2% Asian, 1.4% American Indian and Alaska Native, 0.7% Hispanic of any race, 0.9% two or more races (2000); Density: 896.7 persons per square mile (2000); Age: 26.3% under 18, 16.0% over 64 (2000); Marriage status: 22.0% never married, 56.3% now married, 6.5% widowed, 15.2% divorced (2000); Foreign born: 1.7% (2000); Ancestry (includes multiple ancestries): 24.0% German, 15.3% English, 13.4% Irish, 9.1% United States or American, 8.5% Polish (2000).

Economy: Employment by occupation: 11.3% management, 18.5% professional, 17.5% services, 20.7% sales, 0.7% farming, 12.1% construction, 19.1% production (2000).

Income: Per capita income: $19,030 (2000); Median household income: $35,819 (2000); Poverty rate: 11.8% (2000).

Taxes: Total city taxes per capita: $454 (1997); City property taxes per capita: $454 (1997).

Education: High school graduation rate: 87.4% (2000); College graduation rate: 19.2% (2000).

School District(s)

Boyne City Public Schools (KG-12)
2000 Enrollment: 1,354 231-582-6503

Concord Academy: Boyne (KG-12)
2000 Enrollment: 250 517-774-2100

Housing: Homeownership rate: 77.0% (2000); Median home value: $94,200 (2000); Median rent: $441 per month (2000); Median age of housing: 31 years (2000).

Safety: Violent crime rate: 19.9 per 10,000 population; Property crime rate: 440.2 per 10,000 population (2001).
Newspapers: The Citizen (1 x week)
Transportation: Commute to work: 93.4% car, 1.1% public transportation, 2.7% walk, 2.5% work from home (2000); Travel time to work: 43.6% less than 15 minutes, 31.1% 15 to 30 minutes, 17.6% 30 to 45 minutes, 4.0% 45 to 60 minutes, 3.7% 60 minutes or more (2000); Amtrak: Service available.
Additional Information Contacts
Boyne City Chamber of Commerce 231-582-6222

BOYNE FALLS (village). Covers a land area of 0.547 square miles and a water area of 0.008 square miles. Located at 45.16° N. Lat.; 84.91° W. Long. Elevation is 706 feet.
History: Boyne Falls was established when the Grand Rapids & Indiana Railroad arrived here in 1874. It was incorporated as a village in 1893, and named for the falls on the nearby Boyne River.
Population: 370 (2000); Race: 97.5% White, 1.4% Black, 0.0% Asian, 1.1% American Indian and Alaska Native, 0.0% Hispanic of any race, 0.0% two or more races (2000); Density: 675.9 persons per square mile (2000); Age: 24.2% under 18, 15.6% over 64 (2000); Marriage status: 33.4% never married, 46.5% now married, 7.0% widowed, 13.0% divorced (2000); Foreign born: 0.6% (2000); Ancestry (includes multiple ancestries): 21.1% Polish, 18.3% German, 7.8% Italian, 7.8% English, 7.8% Irish (2000).
Economy: Employment by occupation: 5.2% management, 6.9% professional, 23.6% services, 23.0% sales, 2.3% farming, 13.8% construction, 25.3% production (2000).
Income: Per capita income: $15,027 (2000); Median household income: $32,143 (2000); Poverty rate: 10.3% (2000).
Taxes: Total city taxes per capita: $110 (1997); City property taxes per capita: $107 (1997).
Education: High school graduation rate: 72.9% (2000); College graduation rate: 8.9% (2000).

School District(s)

Boyne Falls Public School District (KG-12)
2000 Enrollment: 310 231-549-2211
Housing: Homeownership rate: 74.1% (2000); Median home value: $74,700 (2000); Median rent: $420 per month (2000); Median age of housing: 37 years (2000).
Transportation: Commute to work: 88.0% car, 0.0% public transportation, 0.0% walk, 10.2% work from home (2000); Travel time to work: 46.3% less than 15 minutes, 26.2% 15 to 30 minutes, 19.5% 30 to 45 minutes, 4.7% 45 to 60 minutes, 3.4% 60 minutes or more (2000); Amtrak: Service available.

BOYNE VALLEY (township). Covers a land area of 35.136 square miles and a water area of 0.542 square miles. Located at 45.16° N. Lat.; 84.91° W. Long.
Population: 1,215 (2000); Race: 98.0% White, 0.4% Black, 0.0% Asian, 1.6% American Indian and Alaska Native, 0.0% Hispanic of any race, 0.0% two or more races (2000); Density: 34.6 persons per square mile (2000); Age: 27.1% under 18, 13.8% over 64 (2000); Marriage status: 23.8% never married, 58.4% now married, 6.8% widowed, 11.0% divorced (2000); Foreign born: 0.4% (2000); Ancestry (includes multiple ancestries): 23.5% Polish, 21.7% German, 10.4% Irish, 9.0% English, 5.8% United States or American (2000).
Economy: Employment by occupation: 9.1% management, 12.7% professional, 17.2% services, 19.0% sales, 1.8% farming, 13.2% construction, 26.9% production (2000).
Income: Per capita income: $16,805 (2000); Median household income: $38,167 (2000); Poverty rate: 6.4% (2000).
Taxes: Total city taxes per capita: $146 (1997); City property taxes per capita: $146 (1997).
Education: High school graduation rate: 78.2% (2000); College graduation rate: 10.6% (2000).
Housing: Homeownership rate: 81.9% (2000); Median home value: $90,800 (2000); Median rent: $411 per month (2000); Median age of housing: 28 years (2000).
Transportation: Commute to work: 93.2% car, 0.9% public transportation, 0.2% walk, 5.3% work from home (2000); Travel time to work: 44.5% less than 15 minutes, 34.2% 15 to 30 minutes, 14.8% 30 to 45 minutes, 3.2% 45 to 60 minutes, 3.2% 60 minutes or more (2000)

CHANDLER (township). Covers a land area of 35.636 square miles and a water area of 0.009 square miles. Located at 45.23° N. Lat.; 84.78° W. Long.
Population: 230 (2000); Race: 99.2% White, 0.0% Black, 0.8% Asian, 0.0% American Indian and Alaska Native, 0.8% Hispanic of any race, 0.0% two or more races (2000); Density: 6.5 persons per square mile (2000); Age: 27.5% under 18, 9.6% over 64 (2000); Marriage status: 20.1% never married, 71.7% now married, 1.1% widowed, 7.1% divorced (2000); Foreign born: 4.2% (2000); Ancestry (includes multiple ancestries): 20.4% German, 17.9% English, 15.8% Polish, 5.0% United States or American, 4.2% Irish (2000).
Economy: Employment by occupation: 6.5% management, 12.9% professional, 19.4% services, 20.2% sales, 0.0% farming, 25.0% construction, 16.1% production (2000).
Income: Per capita income: $24,855 (2000); Median household income: $43,750 (2000); Poverty rate: 4.3% (2000).
Taxes: Total city taxes per capita: $163 (1997); City property taxes per capita: $163 (1997).
Education: High school graduation rate: 76.1% (2000); College graduation rate: 14.2% (2000).
Housing: Homeownership rate: 94.5% (2000); Median home value: $85,000 (2000); Median rent: $325 per month (2000); Median age of housing: 32 years (2000).
Transportation: Commute to work: 96.7% car, 0.0% public transportation, 1.7% walk, 1.7% work from home (2000); Travel time to work: 5.1% less than 15 minutes, 68.6% 15 to 30 minutes, 21.2% 30 to 45 minutes, 1.7% 45 to 60 minutes, 3.4% 60 minutes or more (2000)

CHARLEVOIX (city). Covers a land area of 2.043 square miles and a water area of 0.103 square miles. Located at 45.31° N. Lat.; 85.25° W. Long. Elevation is 592 feet.
History: The first settlement here was called Pine River, and was the scene of a skirmish in 1853 between mainland settlers and those on Beaver Island. When the river was dredged between Round Lake and Lake Michigan, Charlevoix became a busy port of entry. Much lumber was shipped from here between 1876 and 1925. Charlevoix, which later became a popular resort, was named for the French explorer, Pierre Francois Xavier de Charlevoix.
Population: 2,994 (2000); Race: 94.8% White, 0.7% Black, 0.8% Asian, 1.9% American Indian and Alaska Native, 0.6% Hispanic of any race, 1.3% two or more races (2000); Density: 1,465.8 persons per square mile (2000); Age: 21.7% under 18, 19.1% over 64 (2000); Marriage status: 21.4% never married, 55.3% now married, 7.7% widowed, 15.6% divorced (2000); Foreign born: 1.5% (2000); Ancestry (includes multiple ancestries): 17.8% German, 15.8% English, 15.5% Irish, 8.4% United States or American, 8.4% Dutch (2000).
Economy: Employment by occupation: 10.3% management, 13.2% professional, 20.5% services, 28.5% sales, 0.0% farming, 14.5% construction, 13.0% production (2000).
Income: Per capita income: $21,319 (2000); Median household income: $35,284 (2000); Poverty rate: 9.5% (2000).
Taxes: Total city taxes per capita: $804 (2000); City property taxes per capita: $804 (2000).
Education: High school graduation rate: 88.0% (2000); College graduation rate: 22.7% (2000).

School District(s)

Charlevoix Public Schools (KG-12)
2000 Enrollment: 1,426 231-547-3200
Northwest Academy (06-12)
2000 Enrollment: 74 517-695-5325
Housing: Homeownership rate: 60.8% (2000); Median home value: $113,400 (2000); Median rent: $392 per month (2000); Median age of housing: 44 years (2000).
Hospitals: Charlevoix Area Hospital (50 beds)
Newspapers: Charlevoix Courier (1 x week)
Transportation: Commute to work: 86.7% car, 0.0% public transportation, 8.4% walk, 1.7% work from home (2000); Travel time to work: 65.8% less than 15 minutes, 18.9% 15 to 30 minutes, 9.0% 30 to 45 minutes, 1.7% 45 to 60 minutes, 4.5% 60 minutes or more (2000)
Airports: Charlevoix Municipal (primary service)
Additional Information Contacts
Antrim Charlevoix Kalkaska Association of Realtors 231-237-6394
Charlevoix Chamber of Commerce 231-547-2101
Charlevoix Convention Bureau 231-547-3003

CHARLEVOIX (township). Covers a land area of 5.990 square miles and a water area of 6.128 square miles. Located at 45.32° N. Lat.; 85.25° W. Long. Elevation is 592 feet.
History: Settled 1852; Incorporated as village 1879, as city 1905.
Population: 1,697 (2000); Race: 95.3% White, 0.5% Black, 0.6% Asian, 2.4% American Indian and Alaska Native, 2.4% Hispanic of any race, 0.7% two or more races (2000); Density: 283.3 persons per square mile (2000); Age: 27.0% under 18, 15.7% over 64 (2000); Marriage status: 18.9% never

married, 65.2% now married, 6.4% widowed, 9.5% divorced (2000); Foreign born: 1.9% (2000); Ancestry (includes multiple ancestries): 21.9% German, 15.6% English, 15.4% Irish, 8.3% Polish, 8.2% Dutch (2000).
Economy: Agriculture includes potatoes, seed. Manufacturing includes candles, transportation equipment, store display racks, pollution control systems. Resort. Employment by occupation: 16.4% management, 29.9% professional, 8.9% services, 20.1% sales, 0.7% farming, 9.1% construction, 14.9% production (2000).
Income: Per capita income: $22,835 (2000); Median household income: $45,758 (2000); Poverty rate: 4.7% (2000).
Taxes: Total city taxes per capita: $213 (2000); City property taxes per capita: $213 (2000).
Education: High school graduation rate: 91.1% (2000); College graduation rate: 33.4% (2000).
Housing: Homeownership rate: 88.3% (2000); Median home value: $167,800 (2000); Median rent: $420 per month (2000); Median age of housing: 15 years (2000).
Transportation: Commute to work: 94.5% car, 0.0% public transportation, 1.0% walk, 3.3% work from home (2000); Travel time to work: 64.7% less than 15 minutes, 20.1% 15 to 30 minutes, 9.9% 30 to 45 minutes, 2.7% 45 to 60 minutes, 2.7% 60 minutes or more (2000)
Airports: Charlevoix Municipal (primary service)

EAST JORDAN (city). Covers a land area of 3.062 square miles and a water area of 0.901 square miles. Located at 45.15° N. Lat.; 85.12° W. Long. Elevation is 660 feet.
History: East Jordan was originally two settlements, East Jordan and South Arm, connected by a bridge across the Jordan River. The two were incorporated as one village in 1887 and as a city in 1911. First lumber and then canning and a creamery supported the East Jordan economy.
Population: 2,507 (2000); Race: 95.1% White, 0.2% Black, 0.0% Asian, 1.2% American Indian and Alaska Native, 2.5% Hispanic of any race, 1.9% two or more races (2000); Density: 818.7 persons per square mile (2000); Age: 30.4% under 18, 14.0% over 64 (2000); Marriage status: 23.4% never married, 55.7% now married, 6.9% widowed, 13.9% divorced (2000); Foreign born: 1.3% (2000); Ancestry (includes multiple ancestries): 19.3% German, 15.4% Irish, 12.1% English, 8.9% United States or American, 8.7% Other groups (2000).
Economy: Employment by occupation: 7.5% management, 11.3% professional, 21.0% services, 20.4% sales, 0.8% farming, 9.3% construction, 29.7% production (2000).
Income: Per capita income: $14,920 (2000); Median household income: $35,924 (2000); Poverty rate: 10.6% (2000).
Taxes: Total city taxes per capita: $293 (1997); City property taxes per capita: $293 (1997).
Education: High school graduation rate: 76.4% (2000); College graduation rate: 9.4% (2000).

School District(s)

East Jordan Public Schools (KG-12)
2000 Enrollment: 1,282 231-536-3131

Housing: Homeownership rate: 70.5% (2000); Median home value: $76,000 (2000); Median rent: $405 per month (2000); Median age of housing: 36 years (2000).
Safety: Violent crime rate: 35.7 per 10,000 population; Property crime rate: 436.5 per 10,000 population (2001).
Transportation: Commute to work: 91.2% car, 0.9% public transportation, 4.0% walk, 2.9% work from home (2000); Travel time to work: 52.4% less than 15 minutes, 27.7% 15 to 30 minutes, 12.2% 30 to 45 minutes, 3.7% 45 to 60 minutes, 4.1% 60 minutes or more (2000)
Additional Information Contacts
East Jordan Area Chamber of Commerce 231-536-7351

EVANGELINE (township). Covers a land area of 10.994 square miles and a water area of 3.729 square miles. Located at 45.25° N. Lat.; 85.02° W. Long.
Population: 773 (2000); Race: 98.1% White, 0.0% Black, 0.0% Asian, 1.0% American Indian and Alaska Native, 0.0% Hispanic of any race, 0.9% two or more races (2000); Density: 70.3 persons per square mile (2000); Age: 24.9% under 18, 14.0% over 64 (2000); Marriage status: 19.4% never married, 67.1% now married, 6.0% widowed, 7.6% divorced (2000); Foreign born: 1.0% (2000); Ancestry (includes multiple ancestries): 21.2% German, 17.6% English, 10.9% United States or American, 9.9% Polish, 8.9% Irish (2000).
Economy: Employment by occupation: 15.7% management, 16.0% professional, 15.5% services, 24.5% sales, 0.0% farming, 17.0% construction, 11.3% production (2000).
Income: Per capita income: $28,279 (2000); Median household income: $46,250 (2000); Poverty rate: 4.4% (2000).
Taxes: Total city taxes per capita: $99 (1997); City property taxes per capita: $99 (1997).
Education: High school graduation rate: 91.1% (2000); College graduation rate: 27.4% (2000).
Housing: Homeownership rate: 91.7% (2000); Median home value: $134,400 (2000); Median rent: $433 per month (2000); Median age of housing: 26 years (2000).
Transportation: Commute to work: 91.4% car, 0.5% public transportation, 0.0% walk, 8.1% work from home (2000); Travel time to work: 42.7% less than 15 minutes, 31.3% 15 to 30 minutes, 16.0% 30 to 45 minutes, 7.4% 45 to 60 minutes, 2.6% 60 minutes or more (2000)

EVELINE (township). Covers a land area of 26.043 square miles and a water area of 10.721 square miles. Located at 45.23° N. Lat.; 85.15° W. Long.
Population: 1,560 (2000); Race: 95.5% White, 0.1% Black, 0.3% Asian, 1.8% American Indian and Alaska Native, 2.3% Hispanic of any race, 0.4% two or more races (2000); Density: 59.9 persons per square mile (2000); Age: 22.3% under 18, 18.3% over 64 (2000); Marriage status: 16.9% never married, 68.4% now married, 6.3% widowed, 8.3% divorced (2000); Foreign born: 1.1% (2000); Ancestry (includes multiple ancestries): 22.7% German, 15.3% English, 13.7% Irish, 10.1% United States or American, 6.1% Other groups (2000).
Economy: Employment by occupation: 15.5% management, 17.6% professional, 14.1% services, 23.1% sales, 0.4% farming, 12.6% construction, 16.7% production (2000).
Income: Per capita income: $22,440 (2000); Median household income: $46,250 (2000); Poverty rate: 9.4% (2000).
Taxes: Total city taxes per capita: $194 (1997); City property taxes per capita: $191 (1997).
Education: High school graduation rate: 89.0% (2000); College graduation rate: 24.6% (2000).
Housing: Homeownership rate: 89.6% (2000); Median home value: $172,900 (2000); Median rent: $425 per month (2000); Median age of housing: 27 years (2000).
Transportation: Commute to work: 93.4% car, 0.0% public transportation, 1.0% walk, 5.0% work from home (2000); Travel time to work: 37.8% less than 15 minutes, 40.6% 15 to 30 minutes, 11.5% 30 to 45 minutes, 4.4% 45 to 60 minutes, 5.6% 60 minutes or more (2000)

HAYES (township). Covers a land area of 30.097 square miles and a water area of 13.144 square miles. Located at 45.32° N. Lat.; 85.14° W. Long.
Population: 1,893 (2000); Race: 96.6% White, 0.2% Black, 0.0% Asian, 1.6% American Indian and Alaska Native, 0.2% Hispanic of any race, 1.5% two or more races (2000); Density: 62.9 persons per square mile (2000); Age: 22.9% under 18, 13.3% over 64 (2000); Marriage status: 15.7% never married, 68.9% now married, 4.7% widowed, 10.7% divorced (2000); Foreign born: 1.1% (2000); Ancestry (includes multiple ancestries): 29.0% German, 17.2% English, 12.3% Irish, 7.5% Polish, 7.3% French (except Basque) (2000).
Economy: Employment by occupation: 13.7% management, 19.7% professional, 13.5% services, 23.4% sales, 0.2% farming, 13.7% construction, 15.7% production (2000).
Income: Per capita income: $25,512 (2000); Median household income: $50,478 (2000); Poverty rate: 6.2% (2000).
Taxes: Total city taxes per capita: $142 (1997); City property taxes per capita: $141 (1997).
Education: High school graduation rate: 92.1% (2000); College graduation rate: 21.8% (2000).
Housing: Homeownership rate: 94.0% (2000); Median home value: $122,800 (2000); Median rent: $414 per month (2000); Median age of housing: 16 years (2000).
Transportation: Commute to work: 94.1% car, 0.9% public transportation, 0.1% walk, 4.2% work from home (2000); Travel time to work: 27.0% less than 15 minutes, 57.8% 15 to 30 minutes, 8.7% 30 to 45 minutes, 2.3% 45 to 60 minutes, 4.1% 60 minutes or more (2000)

HUDSON (township). Covers a land area of 34.435 square miles and a water area of 1.102 square miles. Located at 45.15° N. Lat.; 84.79° W. Long.
Population: 639 (2000); Race: 96.8% White, 0.3% Black, 0.0% Asian, 1.2% American Indian and Alaska Native, 0.7% Hispanic of any race, 1.4% two or more races (2000); Density: 18.6 persons per square mile (2000); Age: 26.5% under 18, 11.4% over 64 (2000); Marriage status: 15.0% never married, 68.6% now married, 4.5% widowed, 11.9% divorced (2000); Foreign born:

2.6% (2000); Ancestry (includes multiple ancestries): 32.3% German, 12.6% Polish, 10.2% English, 9.5% Irish, 5.8% United States or American (2000).
Economy: Employment by occupation: 5.3% management, 13.4% professional, 23.7% services, 18.7% sales, 1.9% farming, 18.7% construction, 18.3% production (2000).
Income: Per capita income: $15,138 (2000); Median household income: $34,318 (2000); Poverty rate: 11.4% (2000).
Taxes: Total city taxes per capita: $124 (1997); City property taxes per capita: $122 (1997).
Education: High school graduation rate: 80.4% (2000); College graduation rate: 16.9% (2000).
Housing: Homeownership rate: 94.6% (2000); Median home value: $113,600 (2000); Median rent: $350 per month (2000); Median age of housing: 24 years (2000).
Transportation: Commute to work: 87.2% car, 5.4% public transportation, 1.2% walk, 6.2% work from home (2000); Travel time to work: 17.0% less than 15 minutes, 37.8% 15 to 30 minutes, 30.3% 30 to 45 minutes, 5.4% 45 to 60 minutes, 9.5% 60 minutes or more (2000)

MARION (township). Covers a land area of 25.626 square miles and a water area of 0.867 square miles. Located at 45.25° N. Lat.; 85.24° W. Long.
Population: 1,492 (2000); Race: 96.3% White, 0.0% Black, 0.0% Asian, 1.1% American Indian and Alaska Native, 2.3% Hispanic of any race, 1.7% two or more races (2000); Density: 58.2 persons per square mile (2000); Age: 31.8% under 18, 8.4% over 64 (2000); Marriage status: 20.0% never married, 65.9% now married, 5.1% widowed, 9.0% divorced (2000); Foreign born: 1.9% (2000); Ancestry (includes multiple ancestries): 24.6% German, 13.0% Irish, 12.4% English, 11.3% Dutch, 7.7% French (except Basque) (2000).
Economy: Employment by occupation: 8.2% management, 17.1% professional, 18.3% services, 24.5% sales, 2.2% farming, 12.6% construction, 17.1% production (2000).
Income: Per capita income: $16,854 (2000); Median household income: $40,694 (2000); Poverty rate: 6.8% (2000).
Taxes: Total city taxes per capita: $72 (1997); City property taxes per capita: $70 (1997).
Education: High school graduation rate: 84.5% (2000); College graduation rate: 17.6% (2000).
Housing: Homeownership rate: 86.7% (2000); Median home value: $117,500 (2000); Median rent: $410 per month (2000); Median age of housing: 21 years (2000).
Transportation: Commute to work: 90.1% car, 0.0% public transportation, 2.8% walk, 6.5% work from home (2000); Travel time to work: 52.0% less than 15 minutes, 33.9% 15 to 30 minutes, 10.5% 30 to 45 minutes, 1.6% 45 to 60 minutes, 2.0% 60 minutes or more (2000)

MELROSE (township). Covers a land area of 32.915 square miles and a water area of 2.013 square miles. Located at 45.25° N. Lat.; 84.92° W. Long.
Population: 1,388 (2000); Race: 97.6% White, 0.0% Black, 0.0% Asian, 0.8% American Indian and Alaska Native, 0.3% Hispanic of any race, 1.3% two or more races (2000); Density: 42.2 persons per square mile (2000); Age: 28.0% under 18, 12.6% over 64 (2000); Marriage status: 19.7% never married, 66.8% now married, 4.6% widowed, 8.9% divorced (2000); Foreign born: 1.2% (2000); Ancestry (includes multiple ancestries): 20.1% German, 13.5% English, 10.6% Irish, 8.7% Polish, 8.0% United States or American (2000).
Economy: Employment by occupation: 8.4% management, 13.3% professional, 21.4% services, 24.9% sales, 0.6% farming, 16.7% construction, 14.7% production (2000).
Income: Per capita income: $20,426 (2000); Median household income: $41,000 (2000); Poverty rate: 8.2% (2000).
Taxes: Total city taxes per capita: $125 (1997); City property taxes per capita: $125 (1997).
Education: High school graduation rate: 86.8% (2000); College graduation rate: 21.3% (2000).
Housing: Homeownership rate: 83.3% (2000); Median home value: $101,600 (2000); Median rent: $432 per month (2000); Median age of housing: 26 years (2000).
Transportation: Commute to work: 90.9% car, 0.3% public transportation, 0.7% walk, 7.1% work from home (2000); Travel time to work: 26.4% less than 15 minutes, 56.6% 15 to 30 minutes, 9.7% 30 to 45 minutes, 1.9% 45 to 60 minutes, 5.4% 60 minutes or more (2000)

NORWOOD (township). Covers a land area of 18.189 square miles and a water area of 6.202 square miles. Located at 45.24° N. Lat.; 85.34° W. Long.
Population: 714 (2000); Race: 98.3% White, 0.0% Black, 0.6% Asian, 1.2% American Indian and Alaska Native, 0.0% Hispanic of any race, 0.0% two or more races (2000); Density: 39.3 persons per square mile (2000); Age: 23.0% under 18, 18.6% over 64 (2000); Marriage status: 16.8% never married, 71.3% now married, 5.7% widowed, 6.1% divorced (2000); Foreign born: 2.2% (2000); Ancestry (includes multiple ancestries): 25.8% German, 23.5% English, 13.8% Dutch, 10.6% Polish, 10.3% Irish (2000).
Economy: Employment by occupation: 12.5% management, 24.8% professional, 10.3% services, 23.8% sales, 0.6% farming, 15.4% construction, 12.5% production (2000).
Income: Per capita income: $23,802 (2000); Median household income: $50,500 (2000); Poverty rate: 3.8% (2000).
Taxes: Total city taxes per capita: $124 (1997); City property taxes per capita: $117 (1997).
Education: High school graduation rate: 91.1% (2000); College graduation rate: 28.0% (2000).
Housing: Homeownership rate: 90.9% (2000); Median home value: $135,300 (2000); Median rent: $338 per month (2000); Median age of housing: 25 years (2000).
Transportation: Commute to work: 90.9% car, 1.3% public transportation, 0.6% walk, 6.5% work from home (2000); Travel time to work: 26.0% less than 15 minutes, 43.6% 15 to 30 minutes, 15.9% 30 to 45 minutes, 5.9% 45 to 60 minutes, 8.7% 60 minutes or more (2000)

PEAINE (township). Covers a land area of 52.446 square miles and a water area of 20.593 square miles. Located at 45.67° N. Lat.; 85.56° W. Long.
Population: 244 (2000); Race: 97.1% White, 0.0% Black, 0.0% Asian, 1.0% American Indian and Alaska Native, 0.0% Hispanic of any race, 1.9% two or more races (2000); Density: 4.7 persons per square mile (2000); Age: 5.3% under 18, 24.4% over 64 (2000); Marriage status: 19.0% never married, 57.0% now married, 4.0% widowed, 20.0% divorced (2000); Foreign born: 0.0% (2000); Ancestry (includes multiple ancestries): 29.7% Irish, 21.5% German, 19.6% English, 10.0% United States or American, 7.7% Swedish (2000).
Economy: Employment by occupation: 8.0% management, 26.0% professional, 10.0% services, 21.0% sales, 2.0% farming, 22.0% construction, 11.0% production (2000).
Income: Per capita income: $33,091 (2000); Median household income: $29,167 (2000); Poverty rate: 8.2% (2000).
Taxes: Total city taxes per capita: $1,272 (1997); City property taxes per capita: $1,252 (1997).
Education: High school graduation rate: 92.0% (2000); College graduation rate: 28.3% (2000).
Housing: Homeownership rate: 93.9% (2000); Median home value: $115,200 (2000); Median rent: $375 per month (2000); Median age of housing: 21 years (2000).
Transportation: Commute to work: 83.5% car, 0.0% public transportation, 2.1% walk, 9.3% work from home (2000); Travel time to work: 59.1% less than 15 minutes, 27.3% 15 to 30 minutes, 8.0% 30 to 45 minutes, 3.4% 45 to 60 minutes, 2.3% 60 minutes or more (2000)

SAINT JAMES (township). Covers a land area of 19.999 square miles and a water area of 296.025 square miles. Located at 45.75° N. Lat.; 85.54° W. Long. Elevation is 590 feet.
History: St. James, on Beaver Island, was first inhabited by ancient mound builders. The island was called Isle du Castor by French adventurers in the 1600's and 1700's. A Mormon colony was established here in 1848, led by James Jesse Strang, known as King Strang. The colonists were forced to leave after Strang's death in 1856. Irish fishermen later rebuilt the town of St. James and reclaimed the farm lands, encouraging other Irish immigrants to settle here.
Population: 307 (2000); Race: 98.5% White, 0.0% Black, 0.0% Asian, 1.5% American Indian and Alaska Native, 0.0% Hispanic of any race, 0.0% two or more races (2000); Density: 15.4 persons per square mile (2000); Age: 27.2% under 18, 23.0% over 64 (2000); Marriage status: 20.4% never married, 59.9% now married, 11.3% widowed, 8.4% divorced (2000); Foreign born: 0.9% (2000); Ancestry (includes multiple ancestries): 39.4% Irish, 17.3% English, 17.0% Polish, 15.5% German, 14.0% French (except Basque) (2000).
Economy: Employment by occupation: 9.7% management, 7.6% professional, 14.6% services, 36.1% sales, 0.0% farming, 17.4% construction, 14.6% production (2000).
Income: Per capita income: $20,109 (2000); Median household income: $33,182 (2000); Poverty rate: 6.6% (2000).
Education: High school graduation rate: 85.0% (2000); College graduation rate: 21.4% (2000).

Housing: Homeownership rate: 87.8% (2000); Median home value: $151,900 (2000); Median rent: $488 per month (2000); Median age of housing: 20 years (2000).
Transportation: Commute to work: 75.7% car, 0.0% public transportation, 13.2% walk, 4.9% work from home (2000); Travel time to work: 93.4% less than 15 minutes, 5.1% 15 to 30 minutes, 1.5% 30 to 45 minutes, 0.0% 45 to 60 minutes, 0.0% 60 minutes or more (2000)

SOUTH ARM (township). Covers a land area of 30.720 square miles and a water area of 1.933 square miles. Located at 45.16° N. Lat.; 85.15° W. Long.
History: South Arm was named for its location on the south arm of Pine Lake (later called Lake Charlevoix). A general store was opened here in the early 1870's.
Population: 1,844 (2000); Race: 96.2% White, 0.0% Black, 0.3% Asian, 1.9% American Indian and Alaska Native, 2.1% Hispanic of any race, 0.5% two or more races (2000); Density: 60.0 persons per square mile (2000); Age: 25.1% under 18, 17.2% over 64 (2000); Marriage status: 16.0% never married, 68.5% now married, 9.0% widowed, 6.5% divorced (2000); Foreign born: 1.1% (2000); Ancestry (includes multiple ancestries): 24.5% German, 12.9% English, 10.3% United States or American, 9.7% Irish, 6.5% Other groups (2000).
Economy: Employment by occupation: 12.0% management, 12.0% professional, 16.3% services, 21.4% sales, 0.3% farming, 15.6% construction, 22.5% production (2000).
Income: Per capita income: $17,554 (2000); Median household income: $42,159 (2000); Poverty rate: 4.8% (2000).
Taxes: Total city taxes per capita: $22 (1997); City property taxes per capita: $22 (1997).
Education: High school graduation rate: 81.1% (2000); College graduation rate: 13.1% (2000).
Housing: Homeownership rate: 90.5% (2000); Median home value: $117,400 (2000); Median rent: $370 per month (2000); Median age of housing: 29 years (2000).
Transportation: Commute to work: 93.4% car, 0.8% public transportation, 0.3% walk, 3.1% work from home (2000); Travel time to work: 36.4% less than 15 minutes, 34.6% 15 to 30 minutes, 16.8% 30 to 45 minutes, 7.0% 45 to 60 minutes, 5.2% 60 minutes or more (2000)

WILSON (township). Covers a land area of 34.069 square miles and a water area of 0.358 square miles. Located at 45.15° N. Lat.; 85.03° W. Long.
Population: 2,022 (2000); Race: 96.1% White, 0.0% Black, 0.1% Asian, 1.8% American Indian and Alaska Native, 0.3% Hispanic of any race, 1.5% two or more races (2000); Density: 59.4 persons per square mile (2000); Age: 29.0% under 18, 8.1% over 64 (2000); Marriage status: 25.5% never married, 58.6% now married, 5.1% widowed, 10.9% divorced (2000); Foreign born: 0.7% (2000); Ancestry (includes multiple ancestries): 25.5% German, 12.9% Irish, 11.7% English, 10.2% United States or American, 6.9% Polish (2000).
Economy: Employment by occupation: 8.8% management, 10.3% professional, 17.2% services, 23.4% sales, 0.2% farming, 18.0% construction, 22.1% production (2000).
Income: Per capita income: $16,691 (2000); Median household income: $38,030 (2000); Poverty rate: 8.0% (2000).
Taxes: Total city taxes per capita: $45 (1997); City property taxes per capita: $43 (1997).
Education: High school graduation rate: 85.2% (2000); College graduation rate: 11.8% (2000).
Housing: Homeownership rate: 77.8% (2000); Median home value: $108,600 (2000); Median rent: $327 per month (2000); Median age of housing: 19 years (2000).
Transportation: Commute to work: 94.0% car, 0.2% public transportation, 0.9% walk, 4.1% work from home (2000); Travel time to work: 43.6% less than 15 minutes, 30.9% 15 to 30 minutes, 18.5% 30 to 45 minutes, 3.6% 45 to 60 minutes, 3.4% 60 minutes or more (2000)

Cheboygan County

Located in northern Michigan; bounded on the north by the Straits of Mackinac; drained by the Cheboygan, Black, and Sturgeon Rivers. Covers a land area of 715.60 square miles, a water area of 169.60 square miles, and is located in the Eastern Time Zone. The county government was organized in 1840. County seat is Cheboygan.

Weather Station: Cheboygan Elevation: 587 feet

	Jan	Feb	Mar	Apr	May	Jun	Jul	Aug	Sep	Oct	Nov	Dec
High	26	29	37	49	63	72	78	76	68	56	43	32
Low	9	9	17	30	41	51	57	56	48	38	29	18
Precip	1.7	1.2	1.9	2.5	2.6	2.5	3.3	3.0	3.9	2.9	2.4	2.2
Snow	26.5	16.0	11.7	3.7	tr	0.0	0.0	0.0	0.0	tr	7.7	23.6

High and Low temperatures in degrees Fahrenheit; Precipitation and Snow in inches

Population: 26,448 (2000); Race: 94.8% White, 0.2% Black, 0.3% Asian, 2.9% American Indian and Alaska Native, 0.8% Hispanic of any race, 1.6% two or more races (2000); Density: 37.0 persons per square mile (2000); Age: 23.6% under 18, 17.9% over 64 (2000).
Religion: Five largest groups: 21.2% Catholic Church, 3.2% The United Methodist Church, 3.0% Evangelical Lutheran Church in America, 1.5% Episcopal Church, 1.5% Assemblies of God (2000).
Economy: Unemployment rate: 10.6% (11/2002); Total civilian labor force: 12,274 (11/2002); Leading industries: 22.1% retail trade; 16.5% health care and social assistance; 15.7% construction (2000); Companies that employ more than 1,000 persons: 0 (2000); Companies that employ more than 100 persons: 10 (2000); Farms: 210 totaling 50,582 acres (1997); Minority business ownership rate: 0.0% (1997); Women business ownership rate: 20.5% (1997); Retail sales per capita: $10,834 (1997). Single-family building permits issued: 208 (2001) / 240 (2000); Multi-family building permits issued: 6 (2001) / 14 (2000).
Income: Per capita income: $18,088 (2000); Median household income: $33,417 (2000); Poverty rate: 12.2% (2000); Bankruptcy rate: 2.62% (2001).
Taxes: Total county taxes per capita: $135 (1997); County property taxes per capita: $124 (1997).
Education: High school graduation rate: 81.9% (2000); College graduation rate: 13.9% (2000).
Housing: Homeownership rate: 82.8% (2000); Median home value: $94,500 (2000); Median rent: $368 per month (2000); Median age of housing: 27 years (2000).
Health: Birth rate: 113.1 per 10,000 population (1998); Age adjusted death rate: 89.7 per 10,000 population (1999); Age adjusted cancer mortality rate: 211.5 deaths per 100,000 population (1999). Number of physicians: 5.3 per 10,000 population (1999); Number of hospital beds: 34.8 per 10,000 population (1999).
Elections: 2000 Presidential election results: 43.5% Gore, 54.0% Bush, 2.0% Nader, 0.1% Buchanan
National and State Parks: Aloha State Park; Black Lake State Forest; Burt Lake State Park; Michilimackinac State Park
Additional Information Contacts
Cheboygan County Government Offices 231-627-8808
Cheboygan Chamber of Commerce 231-627-7183
Indian River Chamber of Commerce 231-238-9325

Cheboygan County Communities

AFTON (unincorporated postal area, zip code 49705). Covers a land area of 66.522 square miles and a water area of 0.165 square miles. Located at 45.35° N. Lat.; 84.47° W. Long.
History: Afton began as a lumber camp in 1887. When a post office was established in 1905 it was named Ellisville, but the name was changed at the request of a resident who fancied that the nearby Pigeon River looked like the Afton River in Scotland.
Population: 921 (2000); Race: 96.5% White, 0.3% Black, 0.3% Asian, 0.3% American Indian and Alaska Native, 0.3% Hispanic of any race, 2.2% two or more races (2000); Density: 13.8 persons per square mile (2000); Age: 27.5% under 18, 12.6% over 64 (2000); Marriage status: 23.9% never married, 62.1% now married, 6.2% widowed, 7.8% divorced (2000); Foreign born: 0.8% (2000); Ancestry (includes multiple ancestries): 14.6% German, 12.1% United States or American, 11.8% English, 10.9% Other groups, 7.5% Irish (2000).
Economy: Employment by occupation: 6.4% management, 9.9% professional, 25.1% services, 14.9% sales, 0.0% farming, 18.2% construction, 25.4% production (2000).
Income: Per capita income: $14,846 (2000); Median household income: $32,434 (2000); Poverty rate: 12.2% (2000).
Education: High school graduation rate: 79.6% (2000); College graduation rate: 8.4% (2000).
Housing: Homeownership rate: 86.7% (2000); Median home value: $61,500 (2000); Median rent: $356 per month (2000); Median age of housing: 27 years (2000).
Transportation: Commute to work: 94.3% car, 0.3% public transportation, 1.7% walk, 2.9% work from home (2000); Travel time to work: 26.2% less

than 15 minutes, 25.3% 15 to 30 minutes, 17.4% 30 to 45 minutes, 23.5% 45 to 60 minutes, 7.6% 60 minutes or more (2000)

ALOHA (township). Covers a land area of 29.387 square miles and a water area of 2.895 square miles. Located at 45.51° N. Lat.; 84.42° W. Long.
Population: 1,041 (2000); Race: 95.3% White, 0.0% Black, 0.0% Asian, 2.5% American Indian and Alaska Native, 0.2% Hispanic of any race, 2.2% two or more races (2000); Density: 35.4 persons per square mile (2000); Age: 23.7% under 18, 18.6% over 64 (2000); Marriage status: 19.3% never married, 66.6% now married, 7.4% widowed, 6.7% divorced (2000); Foreign born: 0.7% (2000); Ancestry (includes multiple ancestries): 21.0% German, 12.0% English, 11.8% Irish, 11.3% Polish, 11.3% French (except Basque) (2000).
Economy: Employment by occupation: 14.2% management, 10.5% professional, 24.4% services, 22.7% sales, 0.5% farming, 12.0% construction, 15.7% production (2000).
Income: Per capita income: $18,656 (2000); Median household income: $34,853 (2000); Poverty rate: 13.9% (2000).
Taxes: Total city taxes per capita: $38 (1997); City property taxes per capita: $38 (1997).
Education: High school graduation rate: 80.3% (2000); College graduation rate: 16.9% (2000).
Housing: Homeownership rate: 90.6% (2000); Median home value: $118,800 (2000); Median rent: $417 per month (2000); Median age of housing: 24 years (2000).
Transportation: Commute to work: 92.8% car, 1.0% public transportation, 2.3% walk, 3.3% work from home (2000); Travel time to work: 14.4% less than 15 minutes, 58.0% 15 to 30 minutes, 11.7% 30 to 45 minutes, 5.6% 45 to 60 minutes, 10.4% 60 minutes or more (2000)

BEAUGRAND (township). Covers a land area of 23.859 square miles and a water area of 0.057 square miles. Located at 45.66° N. Lat.; 84.54° W. Long.
History: Beaugrand Township was named for an early settler, Oliver Beaugrand. Settlement began here about 1852.
Population: 1,157 (2000); Race: 93.3% White, 0.0% Black, 0.3% Asian, 2.4% American Indian and Alaska Native, 0.8% Hispanic of any race, 4.0% two or more races (2000); Density: 48.5 persons per square mile (2000); Age: 20.8% under 18, 18.2% over 64 (2000); Marriage status: 19.5% never married, 61.8% now married, 8.3% widowed, 10.4% divorced (2000); Foreign born: 1.5% (2000); Ancestry (includes multiple ancestries): 26.7% German, 17.0% French (except Basque), 12.6% English, 11.5% Polish, 9.8% Other groups (2000).
Economy: Employment by occupation: 11.4% management, 10.5% professional, 21.7% services, 29.1% sales, 0.4% farming, 12.4% construction, 14.5% production (2000).
Income: Per capita income: $20,244 (2000); Median household income: $34,792 (2000); Poverty rate: 9.5% (2000).
Taxes: Total city taxes per capita: $41 (1997); City property taxes per capita: $37 (1997).
Education: High school graduation rate: 84.1% (2000); College graduation rate: 13.1% (2000).
Housing: Homeownership rate: 89.6% (2000); Median home value: $104,700 (2000); Median rent: $409 per month (2000); Median age of housing: 26 years (2000).
Transportation: Commute to work: 95.8% car, 0.0% public transportation, 1.7% walk, 2.3% work from home (2000); Travel time to work: 46.2% less than 15 minutes, 35.4% 15 to 30 minutes, 8.6% 30 to 45 minutes, 5.6% 45 to 60 minutes, 4.1% 60 minutes or more (2000)

BENTON (township). Covers a land area of 58.700 square miles and a water area of 3.762 square miles. Located at 45.60° N. Lat.; 84.41° W. Long.
Population: 3,080 (2000); Race: 95.1% White, 0.0% Black, 0.1% Asian, 2.9% American Indian and Alaska Native, 0.9% Hispanic of any race, 1.7% two or more races (2000); Density: 52.5 persons per square mile (2000); Age: 23.2% under 18, 16.0% over 64 (2000); Marriage status: 20.3% never married, 64.9% now married, 6.7% widowed, 8.1% divorced (2000); Foreign born: 1.0% (2000); Ancestry (includes multiple ancestries): 26.9% German, 15.9% French (except Basque), 11.4% Irish, 11.3% English, 9.7% Polish (2000).
Economy: Employment by occupation: 11.3% management, 15.7% professional, 16.1% services, 28.1% sales, 0.5% farming, 12.9% construction, 15.4% production (2000).
Income: Per capita income: $21,130 (2000); Median household income: $37,818 (2000); Poverty rate: 8.8% (2000).
Taxes: Total city taxes per capita: $25 (1997); City property taxes per capita: $25 (1997).
Education: High school graduation rate: 85.3% (2000); College graduation rate: 17.9% (2000).
Housing: Homeownership rate: 93.8% (2000); Median home value: $108,300 (2000); Median rent: $379 per month (2000); Median age of housing: 22 years (2000).
Transportation: Commute to work: 92.9% car, 0.5% public transportation, 1.6% walk, 4.2% work from home (2000); Travel time to work: 45.4% less than 15 minutes, 35.2% 15 to 30 minutes, 8.8% 30 to 45 minutes, 6.6% 45 to 60 minutes, 4.0% 60 minutes or more (2000)

BURT (township). Covers a land area of 19.686 square miles and a water area of 15.430 square miles. Located at 45.49° N. Lat.; 84.69° W. Long.
Population: 654 (2000); Race: 94.2% White, 0.0% Black, 0.0% Asian, 3.2% American Indian and Alaska Native, 0.0% Hispanic of any race, 2.1% two or more races (2000); Density: 33.2 persons per square mile (2000); Age: 14.2% under 18, 32.1% over 64 (2000); Marriage status: 15.1% never married, 66.5% now married, 10.7% widowed, 7.7% divorced (2000); Foreign born: 2.4% (2000); Ancestry (includes multiple ancestries): 28.9% German, 16.3% English, 11.6% Polish, 9.3% Irish, 6.8% French (except Basque) (2000).
Economy: Employment by occupation: 10.2% management, 24.1% professional, 9.0% services, 34.7% sales, 3.3% farming, 10.6% construction, 8.2% production (2000).
Income: Per capita income: $28,059 (2000); Median household income: $38,816 (2000); Poverty rate: 4.0% (2000).
Taxes: Total city taxes per capita: $85 (1997); City property taxes per capita: $83 (1997).
Education: High school graduation rate: 90.5% (2000); College graduation rate: 24.5% (2000).
Housing: Homeownership rate: 96.8% (2000); Median home value: $163,500 (2000); Median rent: $388 per month (2000); Median age of housing: 21 years (2000).
Transportation: Commute to work: 89.8% car, 0.0% public transportation, 2.5% walk, 7.6% work from home (2000); Travel time to work: 19.7% less than 15 minutes, 41.3% 15 to 30 minutes, 22.5% 30 to 45 minutes, 8.7% 45 to 60 minutes, 7.8% 60 minutes or more (2000)

CHEBOYGAN (city). Covers a land area of 6.793 square miles and a water area of 0.192 square miles. Located at 45.64° N. Lat.; 84.47° W. Long. Elevation is 598 feet.
History: Cheboygan was established in 1844 on the Cheboygan River where it empties into Lake Huron. It developed as an important lumbering center in the late 1800's. When the timber was depleted, the land was used for fruit orchards.
Population: 5,295 (2000); Race: 91.4% White, 0.1% Black, 0.8% Asian, 6.1% American Indian and Alaska Native, 1.3% Hispanic of any race, 1.0% two or more races (2000); Density: 779.5 persons per square mile (2000); Age: 25.8% under 18, 18.1% over 64 (2000); Marriage status: 24.2% never married, 55.6% now married, 8.1% widowed, 12.0% divorced (2000); Foreign born: 1.6% (2000); Ancestry (includes multiple ancestries): 18.3% German, 14.1% Irish, 13.1% French (except Basque), 11.1% Other groups, 8.0% English (2000).
Economy: Employment by occupation: 9.7% management, 13.0% professional, 28.0% services, 26.3% sales, 0.7% farming, 10.2% construction, 12.2% production (2000).
Income: Per capita income: $14,318 (2000); Median household income: $25,033 (2000); Poverty rate: 19.9% (2000).
Taxes: Total city taxes per capita: $263 (1997); City property taxes per capita: $262 (1997).
Education: High school graduation rate: 76.6% (2000); College graduation rate: 11.0% (2000).

School District(s)

Cheboygan Area Schools (KG-12)
2000 Enrollment: 2,307 231-627-4436

Housing: Homeownership rate: 61.5% (2000); Median home value: $68,800 (2000); Median rent: $358 per month (2000); Median age of housing: 51 years (2000).
Hospitals: Cheboygan Memorial Hospital (129 beds)
Safety: Violent crime rate: 11.3 per 10,000 population; Property crime rate: 402.0 per 10,000 population (2001).
Newspapers: Cheboygan Daily Tribune (5 x week); Straits Area Star (1 x week)
Transportation: Commute to work: 90.0% car, 0.2% public transportation, 3.2% walk, 6.0% work from home (2000); Travel time to work: 72.6% less

than 15 minutes, 13.6% 15 to 30 minutes, 6.4% 30 to 45 minutes, 1.8% 45 to 60 minutes, 5.6% 60 minutes or more (2000)
Airports: Cheboygan County; Hoffman's Black Mountain Aerodrome
Additional Information Contacts
Cheboygan Chamber of Commerce 231-627-7183

ELLIS (township). Covers a land area of 35.573 square miles and a water area of 0.046 square miles. Located at 45.32° N. Lat.; 84.55° W. Long.
Population: 519 (2000); Race: 97.7% White, 0.6% Black, 0.0% Asian, 0.8% American Indian and Alaska Native, 1.7% Hispanic of any race, 0.4% two or more races (2000); Density: 14.6 persons per square mile (2000); Age: 27.0% under 18, 11.2% over 64 (2000); Marriage status: 15.7% never married, 69.6% now married, 5.5% widowed, 9.2% divorced (2000); Foreign born: 0.8% (2000); Ancestry (includes multiple ancestries): 27.2% German, 11.8% French (except Basque), 11.2% English, 10.6% Irish, 10.2% United States or American (2000).
Economy: Employment by occupation: 6.3% management, 8.9% professional, 15.7% services, 19.9% sales, 1.0% farming, 22.5% construction, 25.7% production (2000).
Income: Per capita income: $15,525 (2000); Median household income: $31,131 (2000); Poverty rate: 13.3% (2000).
Taxes: Total city taxes per capita: $102 (1997); City property taxes per capita: $102 (1997).
Education: High school graduation rate: 84.9% (2000); College graduation rate: 9.1% (2000).
Housing: Homeownership rate: 93.1% (2000); Median home value: $58,000 (2000); Median rent: $288 per month (2000); Median age of housing: 24 years (2000).
Transportation: Commute to work: 94.6% car, 0.0% public transportation, 1.6% walk, 3.8% work from home (2000); Travel time to work: 20.8% less than 15 minutes, 27.0% 15 to 30 minutes, 21.9% 30 to 45 minutes, 20.8% 45 to 60 minutes, 9.6% 60 minutes or more (2000)

FOREST (township). Covers a land area of 68.742 square miles and a water area of 0.893 square miles. Located at 45.32° N. Lat.; 84.30° W. Long.
Population: 1,080 (2000); Race: 97.9% White, 0.5% Black, 0.0% Asian, 0.4% American Indian and Alaska Native, 0.2% Hispanic of any race, 1.0% two or more races (2000); Density: 15.7 persons per square mile (2000); Age: 24.2% under 18, 17.3% over 64 (2000); Marriage status: 21.1% never married, 59.2% now married, 8.1% widowed, 11.5% divorced (2000); Foreign born: 0.8% (2000); Ancestry (includes multiple ancestries): 21.1% German, 12.5% United States or American, 12.4% English, 10.5% Irish, 7.6% Other groups (2000).
Economy: Employment by occupation: 4.4% management, 10.7% professional, 20.4% services, 19.5% sales, 1.2% farming, 11.8% construction, 32.0% production (2000).
Income: Per capita income: $15,373 (2000); Median household income: $28,424 (2000); Poverty rate: 17.5% (2000).
Taxes: Total city taxes per capita: $35 (1997); City property taxes per capita: $35 (1997).
Education: High school graduation rate: 73.6% (2000); College graduation rate: 4.8% (2000).
Housing: Homeownership rate: 85.3% (2000); Median home value: $65,500 (2000); Median rent: $343 per month (2000); Median age of housing: 25 years (2000).
Transportation: Commute to work: 95.4% car, 0.0% public transportation, 1.2% walk, 3.4% work from home (2000); Travel time to work: 40.4% less than 15 minutes, 20.5% 15 to 30 minutes, 11.4% 30 to 45 minutes, 11.0% 45 to 60 minutes, 16.7% 60 minutes or more (2000)

GRANT (township). Covers a land area of 48.760 square miles and a water area of 9.180 square miles. Located at 45.51° N. Lat.; 84.31° W. Long.
Population: 947 (2000); Race: 95.1% White, 0.9% Black, 0.0% Asian, 1.9% American Indian and Alaska Native, 0.0% Hispanic of any race, 2.1% two or more races (2000); Density: 19.4 persons per square mile (2000); Age: 20.0% under 18, 25.3% over 64 (2000); Marriage status: 12.0% never married, 73.1% now married, 7.7% widowed, 7.3% divorced (2000); Foreign born: 0.8% (2000); Ancestry (includes multiple ancestries): 27.1% German, 12.8% English, 12.0% French (except Basque), 9.7% Irish, 8.0% United States or American (2000).
Economy: Employment by occupation: 10.1% management, 11.4% professional, 15.0% services, 30.3% sales, 0.7% farming, 16.6% construction, 16.0% production (2000).
Income: Per capita income: $15,865 (2000); Median household income: $32,000 (2000); Poverty rate: 11.0% (2000).
Taxes: Total city taxes per capita: $62 (1997); City property taxes per capita: $62 (1997).
Education: High school graduation rate: 78.9% (2000); College graduation rate: 10.9% (2000).
Housing: Homeownership rate: 87.3% (2000); Median home value: $112,000 (2000); Median rent: $375 per month (2000); Median age of housing: 29 years (2000).
Transportation: Commute to work: 91.5% car, 0.0% public transportation, 2.0% walk, 4.9% work from home (2000); Travel time to work: 11.0% less than 15 minutes, 50.0% 15 to 30 minutes, 20.5% 30 to 45 minutes, 7.2% 45 to 60 minutes, 11.3% 60 minutes or more (2000)

HEBRON (township). Covers a land area of 34.063 square miles and a water area of 0.713 square miles. Located at 45.67° N. Lat.; 84.68° W. Long.
Population: 303 (2000); Race: 89.3% White, 0.0% Black, 0.0% Asian, 4.9% American Indian and Alaska Native, 2.6% Hispanic of any race, 5.8% two or more races (2000); Density: 8.9 persons per square mile (2000); Age: 27.8% under 18, 7.8% over 64 (2000); Marriage status: 19.7% never married, 59.5% now married, 6.1% widowed, 14.8% divorced (2000); Foreign born: 0.6% (2000); Ancestry (includes multiple ancestries): 21.7% German, 13.3% Other groups, 11.9% French (except Basque), 9.3% English, 7.5% Irish (2000).
Economy: Employment by occupation: 16.1% management, 14.2% professional, 16.1% services, 22.6% sales, 0.0% farming, 13.5% construction, 17.4% production (2000).
Income: Per capita income: $15,737 (2000); Median household income: $36,875 (2000); Poverty rate: 12.0% (2000).
Taxes: Total city taxes per capita: $5 (1997); City property taxes per capita: $5 (1997).
Education: High school graduation rate: 79.4% (2000); College graduation rate: 9.0% (2000).
Housing: Homeownership rate: 90.7% (2000); Median home value: $111,100 (2000); Median rent: $375 per month (2000); Median age of housing: 16 years (2000).
Transportation: Commute to work: 95.6% car, 0.0% public transportation, 0.0% walk, 4.4% work from home (2000); Travel time to work: 23.7% less than 15 minutes, 60.3% 15 to 30 minutes, 4.6% 30 to 45 minutes, 9.9% 45 to 60 minutes, 1.5% 60 minutes or more (2000)

INDIAN RIVER (CDP). Covers a land area of 12.841 square miles and a water area of 7.488 square miles. Located at 45.41° N. Lat.; 84.62° W. Long. Elevation is 616 feet.
History: The village of Indian River was founded in 1878 by Floyd E. Martin, who named it for the river here. Indian River grew as a popular summer recreation center.
Population: 2,008 (2000); Race: 98.0% White, 0.3% Black, 0.0% Asian, 0.8% American Indian and Alaska Native, 1.7% Hispanic of any race, 0.4% two or more races (2000); Density: 156.4 persons per square mile (2000); Age: 20.0% under 18, 24.2% over 64 (2000); Marriage status: 17.0% never married, 66.7% now married, 8.7% widowed, 7.6% divorced (2000); Foreign born: 2.5% (2000); Ancestry (includes multiple ancestries): 26.6% German, 15.7% English, 11.6% Irish, 8.5% French (except Basque), 8.0% Polish (2000).
Economy: Employment by occupation: 13.3% management, 19.0% professional, 21.2% services, 23.5% sales, 0.5% farming, 11.8% construction, 10.7% production (2000).
Income: Per capita income: $20,191 (2000); Median household income: $34,854 (2000); Poverty rate: 7.1% (2000).
Education: High school graduation rate: 86.6% (2000); College graduation rate: 17.8% (2000).

School District(s)

Inland Lakes Schools (KG-12)
2000 Enrollment: 1,099 231-238-6868
Housing: Homeownership rate: 80.8% (2000); Median home value: $122,300 (2000); Median rent: $302 per month (2000); Median age of housing: 24 years (2000).
Newspapers: Straitsland Resorter (1 x week)
Transportation: Commute to work: 90.8% car, 0.4% public transportation, 4.2% walk, 3.3% work from home (2000); Travel time to work: 39.8% less than 15 minutes, 23.3% 15 to 30 minutes, 28.1% 30 to 45 minutes, 3.7% 45 to 60 minutes, 5.1% 60 minutes or more (2000)
Additional Information Contacts
Indian River Chamber of Commerce 231-238-9325

INVERNESS (township). Covers a land area of 33.927 square miles and a water area of 3.267 square miles. Located at 45.59° N. Lat.; 84.51° W. Long.

Population: 2,278 (2000); Race: 96.1% White, 0.0% Black, 0.0% Asian, 2.4% American Indian and Alaska Native, 0.0% Hispanic of any race, 1.4% two or more races (2000); Density: 67.1 persons per square mile (2000); Age: 25.0% under 18, 15.6% over 64 (2000); Marriage status: 19.0% never married, 64.2% now married, 5.3% widowed, 11.5% divorced (2000); Foreign born: 0.5% (2000); Ancestry (includes multiple ancestries): 24.7% German, 18.1% French (except Basque), 16.1% Polish, 9.9% Irish, 8.4% English (2000).
Economy: Employment by occupation: 7.7% management, 13.1% professional, 19.9% services, 30.6% sales, 1.0% farming, 13.1% construction, 14.5% production (2000).
Income: Per capita income: $21,921 (2000); Median household income: $37,121 (2000); Poverty rate: 7.9% (2000).
Taxes: Total city taxes per capita: $58 (1997); City property taxes per capita: $58 (1997).
Education: High school graduation rate: 82.6% (2000); College graduation rate: 17.4% (2000).
Housing: Homeownership rate: 86.9% (2000); Median home value: $95,300 (2000); Median rent: $396 per month (2000); Median age of housing: 30 years (2000).
Transportation: Commute to work: 93.0% car, 0.8% public transportation, 1.8% walk, 4.2% work from home (2000); Travel time to work: 47.8% less than 15 minutes, 35.6% 15 to 30 minutes, 5.9% 30 to 45 minutes, 6.9% 45 to 60 minutes, 3.8% 60 minutes or more (2000)

KOEHLER (township). Covers a land area of 43.536 square miles and a water area of 2.223 square miles. Located at 45.42° N. Lat.; 84.52° W. Long.
Population: 1,168 (2000); Race: 97.0% White, 0.0% Black, 0.5% Asian, 0.8% American Indian and Alaska Native, 2.6% Hispanic of any race, 1.7% two or more races (2000); Density: 26.8 persons per square mile (2000); Age: 22.8% under 18, 16.6% over 64 (2000); Marriage status: 17.6% never married, 71.2% now married, 4.3% widowed, 7.0% divorced (2000); Foreign born: 1.2% (2000); Ancestry (includes multiple ancestries): 16.8% German, 13.8% English, 12.3% United States or American, 10.4% Irish, 10.0% Other groups (2000).
Economy: Employment by occupation: 10.5% management, 14.9% professional, 23.5% services, 18.9% sales, 0.4% farming, 13.2% construction, 18.5% production (2000).
Income: Per capita income: $16,072 (2000); Median household income: $31,509 (2000); Poverty rate: 14.4% (2000).
Taxes: Total city taxes per capita: $49 (1997); City property taxes per capita: $49 (1997).
Education: High school graduation rate: 79.9% (2000); College graduation rate: 11.2% (2000).
Housing: Homeownership rate: 87.8% (2000); Median home value: $101,800 (2000); Median rent: $375 per month (2000); Median age of housing: 26 years (2000).
Transportation: Commute to work: 94.3% car, 0.0% public transportation, 1.6% walk, 3.0% work from home (2000); Travel time to work: 35.8% less than 15 minutes, 24.5% 15 to 30 minutes, 20.0% 30 to 45 minutes, 15.6% 45 to 60 minutes, 4.0% 60 minutes or more (2000)

MACKINAW (township). Covers a land area of 11.448 square miles and a water area of 1.008 square miles. Located at 45.76° N. Lat.; 84.70° W. Long.
Population: 576 (2000); Race: 89.8% White, 0.0% Black, 2.6% Asian, 2.6% American Indian and Alaska Native, 0.0% Hispanic of any race, 5.0% two or more races (2000); Density: 50.3 persons per square mile (2000); Age: 24.1% under 18, 19.8% over 64 (2000); Marriage status: 18.1% never married, 61.9% now married, 8.4% widowed, 11.6% divorced (2000); Foreign born: 1.7% (2000); Ancestry (includes multiple ancestries): 24.7% German, 12.0% Irish, 11.1% English, 8.5% Other groups, 8.3% French (except Basque) (2000).
Economy: Employment by occupation: 13.7% management, 20.6% professional, 20.0% services, 25.1% sales, 0.0% farming, 8.6% construction, 12.0% production (2000).
Income: Per capita income: $20,766 (2000); Median household income: $38,500 (2000); Poverty rate: 9.6% (2000).
Taxes: Total city taxes per capita: $87 (1997); City property taxes per capita: $87 (1997).
Education: High school graduation rate: 91.3% (2000); College graduation rate: 21.9% (2000).
Housing: Homeownership rate: 76.2% (2000); Median home value: $119,200 (2000); Median rent: $347 per month (2000); Median age of housing: 34 years (2000).
Transportation: Commute to work: 80.0% car, 0.0% public transportation, 4.6% walk, 14.3% work from home (2000); Travel time to work: 53.3% less than 15 minutes, 32.7% 15 to 30 minutes, 2.7% 30 to 45 minutes, 10.0% 45 to 60 minutes, 1.3% 60 minutes or more (2000)

MENTOR (township). Covers a land area of 35.778 square miles and a water area of 0.074 square miles. Located at 45.34° N. Lat.; 84.66° W. Long.
Population: 781 (2000); Race: 95.8% White, 0.0% Black, 0.0% Asian, 1.4% American Indian and Alaska Native, 0.7% Hispanic of any race, 2.5% two or more races (2000); Density: 21.8 persons per square mile (2000); Age: 22.3% under 18, 15.8% over 64 (2000); Marriage status: 18.0% never married, 64.5% now married, 8.1% widowed, 9.3% divorced (2000); Foreign born: 0.4% (2000); Ancestry (includes multiple ancestries): 33.1% German, 18.0% English, 10.9% Polish, 8.6% Irish, 6.5% Italian (2000).
Economy: Employment by occupation: 7.7% management, 10.4% professional, 22.3% services, 22.0% sales, 1.1% farming, 14.0% construction, 22.5% production (2000).
Income: Per capita income: $15,888 (2000); Median household income: $32,750 (2000); Poverty rate: 14.1% (2000).
Taxes: Total city taxes per capita: $25 (1997); City property taxes per capita: $25 (1997).
Education: High school graduation rate: 80.4% (2000); College graduation rate: 11.8% (2000).
Housing: Homeownership rate: 89.0% (2000); Median home value: $91,300 (2000); Median rent: $375 per month (2000); Median age of housing: 23 years (2000).
Transportation: Commute to work: 93.2% car, 0.0% public transportation, 0.3% walk, 4.5% work from home (2000); Travel time to work: 33.0% less than 15 minutes, 15.9% 15 to 30 minutes, 33.0% 30 to 45 minutes, 7.1% 45 to 60 minutes, 10.9% 60 minutes or more (2000)

MULLETT (township). Covers a land area of 19.037 square miles and a water area of 16.661 square miles. Located at 45.50° N. Lat.; 84.56° W. Long.
Population: 1,284 (2000); Race: 93.5% White, 0.5% Black, 0.0% Asian, 3.3% American Indian and Alaska Native, 0.0% Hispanic of any race, 2.6% two or more races (2000); Density: 67.4 persons per square mile (2000); Age: 20.6% under 18, 21.2% over 64 (2000); Marriage status: 19.9% never married, 59.8% now married, 9.5% widowed, 10.7% divorced (2000); Foreign born: 1.1% (2000); Ancestry (includes multiple ancestries): 20.9% German, 16.1% English, 14.0% Irish, 10.4% Polish, 7.9% French (except Basque) (2000).
Economy: Employment by occupation: 8.8% management, 15.0% professional, 20.3% services, 26.9% sales, 0.8% farming, 11.5% construction, 16.8% production (2000).
Income: Per capita income: $18,758 (2000); Median household income: $33,438 (2000); Poverty rate: 9.4% (2000).
Taxes: Total city taxes per capita: $187 (1997); City property taxes per capita: $187 (1997).
Education: High school graduation rate: 84.5% (2000); College graduation rate: 14.9% (2000).
Housing: Homeownership rate: 86.3% (2000); Median home value: $95,000 (2000); Median rent: $383 per month (2000); Median age of housing: 32 years (2000).
Transportation: Commute to work: 94.4% car, 0.0% public transportation, 1.8% walk, 3.6% work from home (2000); Travel time to work: 19.3% less than 15 minutes, 50.4% 15 to 30 minutes, 15.6% 30 to 45 minutes, 13.1% 45 to 60 minutes, 1.7% 60 minutes or more (2000)

MUNRO (township). Covers a land area of 28.502 square miles and a water area of 6.720 square miles. Located at 45.59° N. Lat.; 84.68° W. Long.
Population: 679 (2000); Race: 97.8% White, 0.0% Black, 0.0% Asian, 1.1% American Indian and Alaska Native, 0.0% Hispanic of any race, 1.1% two or more races (2000); Density: 23.8 persons per square mile (2000); Age: 20.1% under 18, 15.6% over 64 (2000); Marriage status: 20.2% never married, 67.6% now married, 4.9% widowed, 7.3% divorced (2000); Foreign born: 0.5% (2000); Ancestry (includes multiple ancestries): 25.3% German, 14.9% Irish, 14.9% English, 13.5% Polish, 7.2% Other groups (2000).
Economy: Employment by occupation: 9.5% management, 13.6% professional, 15.0% services, 21.2% sales, 2.2% farming, 13.6% construction, 24.9% production (2000).
Income: Per capita income: $22,658 (2000); Median household income: $37,500 (2000); Poverty rate: 8.7% (2000).
Taxes: Total city taxes per capita: $43 (1997); City property taxes per capita: $43 (1997).

Education: High school graduation rate: 88.8% (2000); College graduation rate: 16.2% (2000).
Housing: Homeownership rate: 91.3% (2000); Median home value: $119,200 (2000); Median rent: $488 per month (2000); Median age of housing: 25 years (2000).
Transportation: Commute to work: 93.7% car, 0.0% public transportation, 2.4% walk, 3.9% work from home (2000); Travel time to work: 19.7% less than 15 minutes, 56.6% 15 to 30 minutes, 13.1% 30 to 45 minutes, 4.5% 45 to 60 minutes, 6.1% 60 minutes or more (2000)

NUNDA (township). Covers a land area of 70.275 square miles and a water area of 1.113 square miles. Located at 45.24° N. Lat.; 84.53° W. Long.
Population: 925 (2000); Race: 96.4% White, 0.3% Black, 0.4% Asian, 1.1% American Indian and Alaska Native, 0.5% Hispanic of any race, 1.8% two or more races (2000); Density: 13.2 persons per square mile (2000); Age: 28.5% under 18, 13.9% over 64 (2000); Marriage status: 23.2% never married, 56.9% now married, 8.6% widowed, 11.4% divorced (2000); Foreign born: 0.7% (2000); Ancestry (includes multiple ancestries): 24.7% German, 16.9% English, 14.8% Irish, 9.3% Other groups, 7.9% French (except Basque) (2000).
Economy: Employment by occupation: 7.3% management, 9.2% professional, 17.1% services, 17.1% sales, 0.8% farming, 21.4% construction, 27.1% production (2000).
Income: Per capita income: $12,802 (2000); Median household income: $28,036 (2000); Poverty rate: 14.0% (2000).
Taxes: Total city taxes per capita: $47 (1997); City property taxes per capita: $47 (1997).
Education: High school graduation rate: 79.0% (2000); College graduation rate: 5.4% (2000).
Housing: Homeownership rate: 86.5% (2000); Median home value: $76,000 (2000); Median rent: $333 per month (2000); Median age of housing: 24 years (2000).
Transportation: Commute to work: 91.5% car, 1.6% public transportation, 0.8% walk, 5.2% work from home (2000); Travel time to work: 15.6% less than 15 minutes, 29.1% 15 to 30 minutes, 28.0% 30 to 45 minutes, 16.4% 45 to 60 minutes, 11.0% 60 minutes or more (2000)

TOWER (unincorporated postal area, zip code 49792). Covers a land area of 0.046 square miles and a water area of 0 square miles. Located at 45.35° N. Lat.; 84.30° W. Long. Elevation is 741 feet.
Population: 69 (2000); Race: 95.2% White, 0.0% Black, 0.0% Asian, 0.0% American Indian and Alaska Native, 0.0% Hispanic of any race, 4.8% two or more races (2000); Density: 1,500.1 persons per square mile (2000); Age: 34.9% under 18, 19.0% over 64 (2000); Marriage status: 17.1% never married, 41.5% now married, 29.3% widowed, 12.2% divorced (2000); Foreign born: 0.0% (2000); Ancestry (includes multiple ancestries): 27.0% Other groups, 20.6% German, 7.9% French (except Basque), 4.8% French Canadian, 4.8% Hungarian (2000).
Economy: Employment by occupation: 26.3% management, 0.0% professional, 15.8% services, 0.0% sales, 0.0% farming, 10.5% construction, 47.4% production (2000).
Income: Per capita income: $6,770 (2000); Median household income: $14,375 (2000); Poverty rate: 30.2% (2000).
Education: High school graduation rate: 77.1% (2000); College graduation rate: 0.0% (2000).
Housing: Homeownership rate: 91.7% (2000); Median home value: $35,500 (2000); Median rent: $275 per month (2000); Median age of housing: 36 years (2000).
Transportation: Commute to work: 73.7% car, 0.0% public transportation, 10.5% walk, 15.8% work from home (2000); Travel time to work: 37.5% less than 15 minutes, 0.0% 15 to 30 minutes, 18.8% 30 to 45 minutes, 31.3% 45 to 60 minutes, 12.5% 60 minutes or more (2000)

TUSCARORA (township). Covers a land area of 29.449 square miles and a water area of 12.534 square miles. Located at 45.41° N. Lat.; 84.63° W. Long.
Population: 3,091 (2000); Race: 97.3% White, 0.3% Black, 0.1% Asian, 1.7% American Indian and Alaska Native, 1.1% Hispanic of any race, 0.3% two or more races (2000); Density: 105.0 persons per square mile (2000); Age: 22.0% under 18, 20.4% over 64 (2000); Marriage status: 19.3% never married, 64.4% now married, 8.9% widowed, 7.5% divorced (2000); Foreign born: 2.0% (2000); Ancestry (includes multiple ancestries): 28.9% German, 16.1% English, 11.7% Irish, 7.8% French (except Basque), 7.2% Polish (2000).
Economy: Employment by occupation: 10.8% management, 18.3% professional, 19.0% services, 27.2% sales, 0.6% farming, 11.4% construction, 12.7% production (2000).
Income: Per capita income: $20,609 (2000); Median household income: $36,091 (2000); Poverty rate: 7.5% (2000).
Taxes: Total city taxes per capita: $244 (2000); City property taxes per capita: $244 (2000).
Education: High school graduation rate: 87.2% (2000); College graduation rate: 18.8% (2000).
Housing: Homeownership rate: 82.5% (2000); Median home value: $114,600 (2000); Median rent: $323 per month (2000); Median age of housing: 24 years (2000).
Safety: Violent crime rate: 9.7 per 10,000 population; Property crime rate: 177.0 per 10,000 population (2001).
Transportation: Commute to work: 91.0% car, 0.2% public transportation, 4.3% walk, 3.7% work from home (2000); Travel time to work: 34.3% less than 15 minutes, 29.8% 15 to 30 minutes, 28.1% 30 to 45 minutes, 2.4% 45 to 60 minutes, 5.3% 60 minutes or more (2000)

WALKER (township). Covers a land area of 34.271 square miles and a water area of 0.333 square miles. Located at 45.32° N. Lat.; 84.41° W. Long.
Population: 292 (2000); Race: 98.2% White, 0.0% Black, 0.0% Asian, 0.0% American Indian and Alaska Native, 0.0% Hispanic of any race, 1.8% two or more races (2000); Density: 8.5 persons per square mile (2000); Age: 22.3% under 18, 15.8% over 64 (2000); Marriage status: 23.3% never married, 55.1% now married, 10.1% widowed, 11.5% divorced (2000); Foreign born: 0.4% (2000); Ancestry (includes multiple ancestries): 12.1% United States or American, 10.3% English, 10.3% German, 7.0% Polish, 5.9% French (except Basque) (2000).
Economy: Employment by occupation: 8.9% management, 6.5% professional, 22.0% services, 20.3% sales, 0.0% farming, 13.0% construction, 29.3% production (2000).
Income: Per capita income: $16,833 (2000); Median household income: $39,286 (2000); Poverty rate: 6.2% (2000).
Taxes: Total city taxes per capita: $14 (1997); City property taxes per capita: $14 (1997).
Education: High school graduation rate: 82.6% (2000); College graduation rate: 6.2% (2000).
Housing: Homeownership rate: 87.3% (2000); Median home value: $75,700 (2000); Median rent: $338 per month (2000); Median age of housing: 25 years (2000).
Transportation: Commute to work: 95.8% car, 0.8% public transportation, 1.7% walk, 1.7% work from home (2000); Travel time to work: 28.0% less than 15 minutes, 27.1% 15 to 30 minutes, 24.6% 30 to 45 minutes, 9.3% 45 to 60 minutes, 11.0% 60 minutes or more (2000)

WAVERLY (township). Covers a land area of 48.107 square miles and a water area of 5.069 square miles. Located at 45.41° N. Lat.; 84.32° W. Long.
Population: 472 (2000); Race: 100.0% White, 0.0% Black, 0.0% Asian, 0.0% American Indian and Alaska Native, 0.0% Hispanic of any race, 0.0% two or more races (2000); Density: 9.8 persons per square mile (2000); Age: 25.1% under 18, 20.5% over 64 (2000); Marriage status: 15.5% never married, 73.9% now married, 7.1% widowed, 3.5% divorced (2000); Foreign born: 2.8% (2000); Ancestry (includes multiple ancestries): 23.1% Irish, 20.9% German, 13.1% English, 9.4% Polish, 8.9% French (except Basque) (2000).
Economy: Employment by occupation: 9.7% management, 8.4% professional, 19.5% services, 25.3% sales, 1.3% farming, 12.3% construction, 23.4% production (2000).
Income: Per capita income: $17,085 (2000); Median household income: $31,875 (2000); Poverty rate: 11.6% (2000).
Taxes: Total city taxes per capita: $100 (1997); City property taxes per capita: $100 (1997).
Education: High school graduation rate: 76.5% (2000); College graduation rate: 11.1% (2000).
Housing: Homeownership rate: 95.7% (2000); Median home value: $99,100 (2000); Median rent: $663 per month (2000); Median age of housing: 39 years (2000).
Transportation: Commute to work: 87.2% car, 1.3% public transportation, 2.7% walk, 6.0% work from home (2000); Travel time to work: 27.1% less than 15 minutes, 14.3% 15 to 30 minutes, 17.9% 30 to 45 minutes, 16.4% 45 to 60 minutes, 24.3% 60 minutes or more (2000)

WILMOT (township). Covers a land area of 35.705 square miles and a water area of 0.140 square miles. Located at 45.24° N. Lat.; 84.66° W. Long.

Population: 826 (2000); Race: 94.8% White, 0.0% Black, 0.4% Asian, 4.1% American Indian and Alaska Native, 1.2% Hispanic of any race, 0.7% two or more races (2000); Density: 23.1 persons per square mile (2000); Age: 28.4% under 18, 9.7% over 64 (2000); Marriage status: 18.3% never married, 64.8% now married, 4.9% widowed, 12.1% divorced (2000); Foreign born: 1.8% (2000); Ancestry (includes multiple ancestries): 18.9% German, 13.3% English, 12.1% Other groups, 12.0% Irish, 11.3% French (except Basque) (2000).
Economy: Employment by occupation: 5.5% management, 8.7% professional, 14.0% services, 18.0% sales, 0.0% farming, 23.0% construction, 30.8% production (2000).
Income: Per capita income: $13,625 (2000); Median household income: $32,500 (2000); Poverty rate: 14.7% (2000).
Taxes: Total city taxes per capita: $17 (1997); City property taxes per capita: $17 (1997).
Education: High school graduation rate: 74.3% (2000); College graduation rate: 6.1% (2000).
Housing: Homeownership rate: 85.2% (2000); Median home value: $77,500 (2000); Median rent: $378 per month (2000); Median age of housing: 24 years (2000).
Transportation: Commute to work: 94.6% car, 0.0% public transportation, 0.9% walk, 4.5% work from home (2000); Travel time to work: 23.5% less than 15 minutes, 31.0% 15 to 30 minutes, 32.0% 30 to 45 minutes, 8.2% 45 to 60 minutes, 5.3% 60 minutes or more (2000)

WOLVERINE (village). Covers a land area of 0.890 square miles and a water area of 0 square miles. Located at 45.27° N. Lat.; 84.60° W. Long. Elevation is 773 feet.
History: Wolverine was settled as a sawmill center, and later grew as a resort area.
Population: 359 (2000); Race: 96.3% White, 0.0% Black, 0.0% Asian, 1.5% American Indian and Alaska Native, 0.2% Hispanic of any race, 2.2% two or more races (2000); Density: 403.5 persons per square mile (2000); Age: 36.9% under 18, 11.0% over 64 (2000); Marriage status: 33.6% never married, 43.0% now married, 6.3% widowed, 17.1% divorced (2000); Foreign born: 0.7% (2000); Ancestry (includes multiple ancestries): 26.4% German, 16.7% Irish, 15.0% Other groups, 11.0% English, 9.5% United States or American (2000).
Economy: Employment by occupation: 6.3% management, 6.3% professional, 24.4% services, 13.4% sales, 0.8% farming, 18.1% construction, 30.7% production (2000).
Income: Per capita income: $9,612 (2000); Median household income: $22,813 (2000); Poverty rate: 20.4% (2000).
Taxes: Total city taxes per capita: $126 (1997); City property taxes per capita: $126 (1997).
Education: High school graduation rate: 80.2% (2000); College graduation rate: 3.8% (2000).

School District(s)

Wolverine Community Schools (KG-12)
2000 Enrollment: 306 231-525-8201

Housing: Homeownership rate: 77.1% (2000); Median home value: $52,800 (2000); Median rent: $350 per month (2000); Median age of housing: 44 years (2000).
Transportation: Commute to work: 86.6% car, 4.7% public transportation, 2.4% walk, 4.7% work from home (2000); Travel time to work: 22.3% less than 15 minutes, 32.2% 15 to 30 minutes, 33.1% 30 to 45 minutes, 9.9% 45 to 60 minutes, 2.5% 60 minutes or more (2000)

Chippewa County

Located in northwestern Michigan on the Upper Peninsula; bounded on the east by St. Marys River, on the north by Whitefish Bay, and on the south by Lake Huron; includes Sugar, Neebish, and Drummond Islands, and part of Marquette National Forest. Covers a land area of 1,561.10 square miles, a water area of 1,136.90 square miles, and is located in the Eastern Time Zone. The county government was organized in 1826. County seat is Sault Ste. Marie.

Weather Station: Detour Village — Elevation: 593 feet

	Jan	Feb	Mar	Apr	May	Jun	Jul	Aug	Sep	Oct	Nov	Dec
High	24	26	35	47	61	70	76	75	65	54	42	31
Low	8	8	17	30	41	50	57	57	49	39	30	17
Precip	1.9	1.2	2.2	2.3	2.6	2.6	3.2	3.0	4.0	2.7	2.4	2.0
Snow	19.1	13.2	13.1	3.6	tr	0.0	0.0	0.0	0.0	tr	5.1	15.6

High and Low temperatures in degrees Fahrenheit; Precipitation and Snow in inches

Weather Station: Sault Ste Marie Sanderson Field — Elevation: 715 feet

	Jan	Feb	Mar	Apr	May	Jun	Jul	Aug	Sep	Oct	Nov	Dec
High	21	24	33	48	63	71	76	74	65	53	39	27
Low	5	6	15	29	39	46	52	52	45	36	26	13
Precip	2.6	1.6	2.3	2.6	2.7	2.9	3.2	3.5	3.9	3.4	3.4	3.0
Snow	34.9	19.3	15.0	7.3	0.3	0.0	tr	tr	tr	2.4	16.2	35.8

High and Low temperatures in degrees Fahrenheit; Precipitation and Snow in inches

Weather Station: Whitefish Point — Elevation: 603 feet

	Jan	Feb	Mar	Apr	May	Jun	Jul	Aug	Sep	Oct	Nov	Dec
High	24	26	34	45	57	66	72	72	65	53	40	29
Low	11	9	16	28	37	45	51	54	48	39	29	18
Precip	3.1	1.9	2.0	2.1	2.8	3.0	3.3	3.4	3.3	3.2	3.0	3.2
Snow	40.8	22.2	14.0	4.8	tr	0.0	0.0	0.0	tr	0.9	12.9	37.1

High and Low temperatures in degrees Fahrenheit; Precipitation and Snow in inches

Population: 38,543 (2000); Race: 75.8% White, 5.3% Black, 0.6% Asian, 13.3% American Indian and Alaska Native, 1.6% Hispanic of any race, 4.7% two or more races (2000); Density: 24.7 persons per square mile (2000); Age: 21.3% under 18, 12.7% over 64 (2000).
Religion: Five largest groups: 18.9% Catholic Church, 2.5% Presbyterian Church (U.S.A.), 2.2% The United Methodist Church, 1.7% Southern Baptist Convention, 1.7% Evangelical Lutheran Church in America (2000).
Economy: Unemployment rate: 6.3% (11/2002); Total civilian labor force: 17,667 (11/2002); Leading industries: 17.8% retail trade; 13.9% health care and social assistance; 13.1% accommodation & food services (2000); Companies that employ more than 1,000 persons: 1 (2000); Companies that employ more than 100 persons: 8 (2000); Farms: 319 totaling 98,979 acres (1997); Minority business ownership rate: 4.7% (1997); Women business ownership rate: 23.6% (1997); Retail sales per capita: $7,673 (1997). Single-family building permits issued: 220 (2001) / 199 (2000); Multi-family building permits issued: 26 (2001) / 0 (2000).
Income: Per capita income: $15,858 (2000); Median household income: $34,464 (2000); Poverty rate: 12.8% (2000); Bankruptcy rate: 2.80% (2001).
Taxes: Total county taxes per capita: $130 (2000); County property taxes per capita: $127 (2000).
Education: High school graduation rate: 82.4% (2000); College graduation rate: 15.0% (2000).
Housing: Homeownership rate: 74.0% (2000); Median home value: $77,300 (2000); Median rent: $365 per month (2000); Median age of housing: 32 years (2000).
Health: Birth rate: 102.2 per 10,000 population (1998); Age adjusted death rate: 85.3 per 10,000 population (1999); Age adjusted cancer mortality rate: 232.0 deaths per 100,000 population (1999). Number of physicians: 8.3 per 10,000 population (1999); Number of hospital beds: 22.3 per 10,000 population (1999).
Elections: 2000 Presidential election results: 44.4% Gore, 52.4% Bush, 2.5% Nader, 0.0% Buchanan
National and State Parks: Brimley State Park; De Tour State Park; Munuscong State Forest; Tahquamenon Falls State Park
Additional Information Contacts
Chippewa County Government Offices 906-635-6300
De Tour Village Chamber of Commerce 906-297-5987
Drummond Island Chamber of Commerce 906-493-5245
Eastern Upper Peninsula Board of Realtors 906-632-7336
Sault Ste Marie Chamber of Commerce. 906-632-3301

Chippewa County Communities

BARBEAU (unincorporated postal area, zip code 49710). Covers a land area of 44.953 square miles and a water area of 0.036 square miles. Located at 46.27° N. Lat.; 84.17° W. Long. Elevation is 656 feet.
History: Barbeau was named for an early settler, Peter B. Barbeau. The community began in 1877 when Thomas Henderson homesteaded here. A post office was established in 1883.
Population: 436 (2000); Race: 88.9% White, 0.4% Black, 0.0% Asian, 7.1% American Indian and Alaska Native, 0.7% Hispanic of any race, 3.6% two or more races (2000); Density: 9.7 persons per square mile (2000); Age: 19.8% under 18, 24.4% over 64 (2000); Marriage status: 11.2% never married, 70.1% now married, 5.6% widowed, 13.1% divorced (2000); Foreign born: 1.8% (2000); Ancestry (includes multiple ancestries): 20.0% English, 14.9% Other groups, 14.7% German, 14.7% French (except Basque), 10.0% Irish (2000).
Economy: Employment by occupation: 12.3% management, 21.0% professional, 16.7% services, 22.2% sales, 0.0% farming, 12.3% construction, 15.4% production (2000).

Income: Per capita income: $16,538 (2000); Median household income: $29,063 (2000); Poverty rate: 16.1% (2000).
Education: High school graduation rate: 75.6% (2000); College graduation rate: 17.2% (2000).
Housing: Homeownership rate: 89.7% (2000); Median home value: $82,200 (2000); Median rent: $385 per month (2000); Median age of housing: 34 years (2000).
Transportation: Commute to work: 89.0% car, 0.0% public transportation, 3.9% walk, 7.1% work from home (2000); Travel time to work: 21.5% less than 15 minutes, 38.9% 15 to 30 minutes, 37.5% 30 to 45 minutes, 1.4% 45 to 60 minutes, 0.7% 60 minutes or more (2000)

BAY MILLS (township). Covers a land area of 64.683 square miles and a water area of 33.241 square miles. Located at 46.45° N. Lat.; 84.68° W. Long. Elevation is 605 feet.
Population: 1,214 (2000); Race: 42.3% White, 0.2% Black, 0.0% Asian, 51.7% American Indian and Alaska Native, 0.0% Hispanic of any race, 5.5% two or more races (2000); Density: 18.8 persons per square mile (2000); Age: 28.8% under 18, 12.6% over 64 (2000); Marriage status: 25.5% never married, 58.0% now married, 4.6% widowed, 11.9% divorced (2000); Foreign born: 3.1% (2000); Ancestry (includes multiple ancestries): 51.7% Other groups, 6.7% German, 6.6% French (except Basque), 6.5% Irish, 6.2% English (2000).
Economy: Employment by occupation: 9.8% management, 16.8% professional, 29.2% services, 22.6% sales, 1.9% farming, 14.0% construction, 5.7% production (2000).
Income: Per capita income: $18,285 (2000); Median household income: $35,875 (2000); Poverty rate: 11.8% (2000).
Taxes: Total city taxes per capita: $19 (2000); City property taxes per capita: $19 (2000).
Education: High school graduation rate: 83.9% (2000); College graduation rate: 16.4% (2000).
Housing: Homeownership rate: 83.5% (2000); Median home value: $90,000 (2000); Median rent: $289 per month (2000); Median age of housing: 22 years (2000).
Transportation: Commute to work: 92.0% car, 2.5% public transportation, 1.9% walk, 1.9% work from home (2000); Travel time to work: 57.5% less than 15 minutes, 19.2% 15 to 30 minutes, 16.1% 30 to 45 minutes, 3.9% 45 to 60 minutes, 3.3% 60 minutes or more (2000)

BRUCE (township). Covers a land area of 87.405 square miles and a water area of 3.269 square miles. Located at 46.33° N. Lat.; 84.31° W. Long.
History: Bruce Township was named for Lord Bruce of the Shetland Islands, a friend of early settler Andrew J. Smith.
Population: 1,940 (2000); Race: 84.2% White, 0.2% Black, 0.1% Asian, 11.4% American Indian and Alaska Native, 1.1% Hispanic of any race, 3.7% two or more races (2000); Density: 22.2 persons per square mile (2000); Age: 27.5% under 18, 12.3% over 64 (2000); Marriage status: 18.3% never married, 67.2% now married, 5.2% widowed, 9.3% divorced (2000); Foreign born: 2.3% (2000); Ancestry (includes multiple ancestries): 17.0% German, 16.2% English, 14.0% Other groups, 13.5% French (except Basque), 13.4% Irish (2000).
Economy: Employment by occupation: 9.1% management, 15.2% professional, 21.2% services, 28.7% sales, 0.7% farming, 13.6% construction, 11.4% production (2000).
Income: Per capita income: $16,666 (2000); Median household income: $39,207 (2000); Poverty rate: 7.8% (2000).
Taxes: Total city taxes per capita: $22 (1997); City property taxes per capita: $22 (1997).
Education: High school graduation rate: 81.5% (2000); College graduation rate: 14.4% (2000).
Housing: Homeownership rate: 91.0% (2000); Median home value: $88,200 (2000); Median rent: $393 per month (2000); Median age of housing: 25 years (2000).
Transportation: Commute to work: 92.5% car, 0.6% public transportation, 1.8% walk, 4.7% work from home (2000); Travel time to work: 17.3% less than 15 minutes, 63.2% 15 to 30 minutes, 15.2% 30 to 45 minutes, 1.2% 45 to 60 minutes, 3.1% 60 minutes or more (2000)

CHIPPEWA (township). Covers a land area of 94.896 square miles and a water area of 0.589 square miles. Located at 46.33° N. Lat.; 84.99° W. Long.
Population: 238 (2000); Race: 91.1% White, 0.0% Black, 0.0% Asian, 7.0% American Indian and Alaska Native, 4.2% Hispanic of any race, 0.9% two or more races (2000); Density: 2.5 persons per square mile (2000); Age: 35.7% under 18, 14.1% over 64 (2000); Marriage status: 24.7% never married, 53.1% now married, 6.2% widowed, 16.0% divorced (2000); Foreign born: 1.9% (2000); Ancestry (includes multiple ancestries): 31.5% German, 10.3% Other groups, 9.9% Dutch, 7.5% English, 6.6% United States or American (2000).
Economy: Hiawatha National Forest to West. Employment by occupation: 9.7% management, 2.8% professional, 27.8% services, 26.4% sales, 0.0% farming, 18.1% construction, 15.3% production (2000).
Income: Per capita income: $12,433 (2000); Median household income: $32,500 (2000); Poverty rate: 13.2% (2000).
Taxes: Total city taxes per capita: $25 (1997); City property taxes per capita: $25 (1997).
Education: High school graduation rate: 72.6% (2000); College graduation rate: 12.1% (2000).
Housing: Homeownership rate: 78.9% (2000); Median home value: $83,800 (2000); Median rent: $263 per month (2000); Median age of housing: 26 years (2000).
Transportation: Commute to work: 74.3% car, 0.0% public transportation, 11.4% walk, 11.4% work from home (2000); Travel time to work: 25.8% less than 15 minutes, 0.0% 15 to 30 minutes, 50.0% 30 to 45 minutes, 17.7% 45 to 60 minutes, 6.5% 60 minutes or more (2000)

DAFTER (township). Covers a land area of 47.837 square miles and a water area of 0.053 square miles. Located at 46.36° N. Lat.; 84.44° W. Long. Elevation is 695 feet.
Population: 1,304 (2000); Race: 84.9% White, 0.2% Black, 0.2% Asian, 9.7% American Indian and Alaska Native, 0.2% Hispanic of any race, 4.6% two or more races (2000); Density: 27.3 persons per square mile (2000); Age: 27.5% under 18, 10.3% over 64 (2000); Marriage status: 22.5% never married, 62.9% now married, 4.3% widowed, 10.3% divorced (2000); Foreign born: 3.0% (2000); Ancestry (includes multiple ancestries): 17.7% German, 15.8% English, 13.0% Other groups, 12.8% Irish, 10.1% French (except Basque) (2000).
Economy: Employment by occupation: 9.6% management, 14.0% professional, 33.1% services, 19.3% sales, 1.6% farming, 10.2% construction, 12.2% production (2000).
Income: Per capita income: $17,713 (2000); Median household income: $42,452 (2000); Poverty rate: 8.0% (2000).
Taxes: Total city taxes per capita: $27 (1997); City property taxes per capita: $27 (1997).
Education: High school graduation rate: 85.8% (2000); College graduation rate: 13.6% (2000).
Housing: Homeownership rate: 87.7% (2000); Median home value: $67,900 (2000); Median rent: $365 per month (2000); Median age of housing: 28 years (2000).
Transportation: Commute to work: 94.1% car, 0.6% public transportation, 1.9% walk, 3.3% work from home (2000); Travel time to work: 21.8% less than 15 minutes, 65.8% 15 to 30 minutes, 7.1% 30 to 45 minutes, 1.8% 45 to 60 minutes, 3.5% 60 minutes or more (2000)

DE TOUR VILLAGE (village). Aka De Tour. Covers a land area of 3.560 square miles and a water area of 4.846 square miles. Located at 45.99° N. Lat.; 83.90° W. Long. Elevation is 613 feet.
Population: 421 (2000); Race: 82.4% White, 0.0% Black, 1.6% Asian, 12.0% American Indian and Alaska Native, 0.0% Hispanic of any race, 4.0% two or more races (2000); Density: 118.2 persons per square mile (2000); Age: 12.3% under 18, 28.3% over 64 (2000); Marriage status: 15.4% never married, 54.3% now married, 13.9% widowed, 16.3% divorced (2000); Foreign born: 3.5% (2000); Ancestry (includes multiple ancestries): 18.4% English, 13.6% German, 12.0% Other groups, 11.7% Irish, 10.7% Polish (2000).
Economy: Lighthouse here. Fueling point for commercial shipping; resort. Employment by occupation: 11.3% management, 17.0% professional, 22.0% services, 15.6% sales, 2.8% farming, 19.9% construction, 11.3% production (2000).
Income: Per capita income: $19,967 (2000); Median household income: $31,250 (2000); Poverty rate: 10.4% (2000).
Taxes: Total city taxes per capita: $236 (1997); City property taxes per capita: $236 (1997).
Education: High school graduation rate: 85.5% (2000); College graduation rate: 16.4% (2000).
Housing: Homeownership rate: 81.7% (2000); Median home value: $114,800 (2000); Median rent: $284 per month (2000); Median age of housing: 35 years (2000).
Transportation: Commute to work: 82.5% car, 1.5% public transportation, 12.4% walk, 3.6% work from home (2000); Travel time to work: 61.4% less than 15 minutes, 12.1% 15 to 30 minutes, 15.9% 30 to 45 minutes, 4.5% 45 to 60 minutes, 6.1% 60 minutes or more (2000)

Additional Information Contacts
De Tour Village Chamber of Commerce 906-297-5987

DETOUR (township). Covers a land area of 48.848 square miles and a water area of 26.597 square miles. Located at 45.99° N. Lat.; 83.96° W. Long.
History: The township was first called Warren, for Ebenezer Warren, the postmaster. The name change to Detour reflects the French Canadian heritage of the early settlers, and the sharp turns that ships had to make to enter St. Mary's River.
Population: 894 (2000); Race: 83.2% White, 0.0% Black, 0.7% Asian, 11.3% American Indian and Alaska Native, 0.4% Hispanic of any race, 4.8% two or more races (2000); Density: 18.3 persons per square mile (2000); Age: 14.4% under 18, 25.6% over 64 (2000); Marriage status: 17.8% never married, 59.1% now married, 11.0% widowed, 12.1% divorced (2000); Foreign born: 2.7% (2000); Ancestry (includes multiple ancestries): 16.0% English, 15.9% German, 12.6% Other groups, 11.1% Polish, 10.4% French (except Basque) (2000).
Economy: Employment by occupation: 8.1% management, 17.6% professional, 20.3% services, 14.9% sales, 2.0% farming, 17.2% construction, 19.9% production (2000).
Income: Per capita income: $19,984 (2000); Median household income: $36,500 (2000); Poverty rate: 6.0% (2000).
Taxes: Total city taxes per capita: $111 (1997); City property taxes per capita: $111 (1997).
Education: High school graduation rate: 85.4% (2000); College graduation rate: 16.4% (2000).
Housing: Homeownership rate: 88.6% (2000); Median home value: $104,200 (2000); Median rent: $294 per month (2000); Median age of housing: 27 years (2000).
Transportation: Commute to work: 82.4% car, 1.7% public transportation, 10.3% walk, 5.5% work from home (2000); Travel time to work: 52.2% less than 15 minutes, 13.9% 15 to 30 minutes, 13.5% 30 to 45 minutes, 10.2% 45 to 60 minutes, 10.2% 60 minutes or more (2000)

DRUMMOND (township). Covers a land area of 129.065 square miles and a water area of 119.927 square miles. Located at 45.99° N. Lat.; 83.75° W. Long. Elevation is 619 feet.
History: Drummond Island, township, and village were named for Sir Gordon Drummond, a British commander who built a fort here after the War of 1812. Stone quarries were opened in Drummond in the late 1870's to furnish stone for the first lock at Sault Ste. Marie.
Population: 992 (2000); Race: 90.5% White, 0.0% Black, 0.0% Asian, 5.8% American Indian and Alaska Native, 0.8% Hispanic of any race, 3.4% two or more races (2000); Density: 7.7 persons per square mile (2000); Age: 18.5% under 18, 22.1% over 64 (2000); Marriage status: 14.5% never married, 66.3% now married, 9.0% widowed, 10.2% divorced (2000); Foreign born: 1.0% (2000); Ancestry (includes multiple ancestries): 21.5% German, 15.8% English, 9.2% Irish, 8.1% Polish, 7.8% United States or American (2000).
Economy: Employment by occupation: 11.3% management, 13.5% professional, 18.4% services, 23.3% sales, 0.9% farming, 22.7% construction, 9.8% production (2000).
Income: Per capita income: $21,963 (2000); Median household income: $36,131 (2000); Poverty rate: 9.0% (2000).
Taxes: Total city taxes per capita: $319 (1997); City property taxes per capita: $319 (1997).
Education: High school graduation rate: 85.2% (2000); College graduation rate: 17.0% (2000).
Housing: Homeownership rate: 90.3% (2000); Median home value: $113,200 (2000); Median rent: $288 per month (2000); Median age of housing: 21 years (2000).
Transportation: Commute to work: 89.4% car, 0.0% public transportation, 2.2% walk, 6.5% work from home (2000); Travel time to work: 51.2% less than 15 minutes, 21.9% 15 to 30 minutes, 13.3% 30 to 45 minutes, 1.0% 45 to 60 minutes, 12.6% 60 minutes or more (2000)
Additional Information Contacts
Drummond Island Chamber of Commerce 906-493-5245

ECKERMAN (unincorporated postal area, zip code 49728). Covers a land area of 169.322 square miles and a water area of 1.181 square miles. Located at 46.35° N. Lat.; 84.99° W. Long. Elevation is 778 feet.
History: Eckerman began as a supply depot for logging camps.
Population: 331 (2000); Race: 90.8% White, 0.0% Black, 0.0% Asian, 7.2% American Indian and Alaska Native, 3.0% Hispanic of any race, 1.3% two or more races (2000); Density: 2.0 persons per square mile (2000); Age: 30.2% under 18, 18.0% over 64 (2000); Marriage status: 17.9% never married, 64.2% now married, 4.2% widowed, 13.8% divorced (2000); Foreign born: 2.0% (2000); Ancestry (includes multiple ancestries): 27.9% German, 11.1% English, 9.2% Dutch, 8.9% Irish, 7.2% Other groups (2000).
Economy: Employment by occupation: 8.2% management, 10.2% professional, 25.5% services, 27.6% sales, 3.1% farming, 13.3% construction, 12.2% production (2000).
Income: Per capita income: $13,788 (2000); Median household income: $31,389 (2000); Poverty rate: 11.4% (2000).
Education: High school graduation rate: 79.4% (2000); College graduation rate: 14.6% (2000).
Housing: Homeownership rate: 84.9% (2000); Median home value: $89,200 (2000); Median rent: $275 per month (2000); Median age of housing: 28 years (2000).
Transportation: Commute to work: 74.0% car, 0.0% public transportation, 8.3% walk, 15.6% work from home (2000); Travel time to work: 32.1% less than 15 minutes, 13.6% 15 to 30 minutes, 35.8% 30 to 45 minutes, 13.6% 45 to 60 minutes, 4.9% 60 minutes or more (2000)

GOETZVILLE (unincorporated postal area, zip code 49736). Covers a land area of 65.810 square miles and a water area of 0.332 square miles. Located at 46.06° N. Lat.; 84.15° W. Long. Elevation is 752 feet.
History: Goetzville was named for the Goetz family, who settled here in 1882. The name of the post office was first Gatesville, but was changed in 1917 to Goetzville.
Population: 599 (2000); Race: 92.3% White, 0.0% Black, 0.0% Asian, 2.5% American Indian and Alaska Native, 0.9% Hispanic of any race, 4.8% two or more races (2000); Density: 9.1 persons per square mile (2000); Age: 12.8% under 18, 27.0% over 64 (2000); Marriage status: 17.0% never married, 60.5% now married, 12.5% widowed, 10.0% divorced (2000); Foreign born: 1.4% (2000); Ancestry (includes multiple ancestries): 29.9% Polish, 15.7% German, 14.8% English, 7.8% French (except Basque), 6.8% Irish (2000).
Economy: Employment by occupation: 8.4% management, 15.7% professional, 15.2% services, 18.5% sales, 3.4% farming, 16.9% construction, 21.9% production (2000).
Income: Per capita income: $19,599 (2000); Median household income: $28,375 (2000); Poverty rate: 12.3% (2000).
Education: High school graduation rate: 74.5% (2000); College graduation rate: 8.2% (2000).
Housing: Homeownership rate: 94.4% (2000); Median home value: $76,900 (2000); Median rent: $308 per month (2000); Median age of housing: 28 years (2000).
Transportation: Commute to work: 84.7% car, 0.0% public transportation, 4.5% walk, 10.7% work from home (2000); Travel time to work: 25.3% less than 15 minutes, 24.7% 15 to 30 minutes, 25.9% 30 to 45 minutes, 15.2% 45 to 60 minutes, 8.9% 60 minutes or more (2000)

HULBERT (township). Covers a land area of 71.056 square miles and a water area of 0.721 square miles. Located at 46.32° N. Lat.; 85.16° W. Long. Elevation is 726 feet.
Population: 211 (2000); Race: 89.2% White, 0.0% Black, 0.0% Asian, 7.8% American Indian and Alaska Native, 0.0% Hispanic of any race, 2.9% two or more races (2000); Density: 3.0 persons per square mile (2000); Age: 18.1% under 18, 21.1% over 64 (2000); Marriage status: 23.7% never married, 57.4% now married, 8.3% widowed, 10.7% divorced (2000); Foreign born: 0.0% (2000); Ancestry (includes multiple ancestries): 18.6% German, 13.2% Other groups, 9.3% Polish, 8.3% French (except Basque), 7.8% Dutch (2000).
Economy: Employment by occupation: 9.3% management, 8.0% professional, 41.3% services, 13.3% sales, 0.0% farming, 6.7% construction, 21.3% production (2000).
Income: Per capita income: $13,624 (2000); Median household income: $24,286 (2000); Poverty rate: 25.5% (2000).
Taxes: Total city taxes per capita: $43 (1997); City property taxes per capita: $43 (1997).
Education: High school graduation rate: 66.9% (2000); College graduation rate: 8.4% (2000).
Housing: Homeownership rate: 84.9% (2000); Median home value: $72,500 (2000); Median rent: $315 per month (2000); Median age of housing: 26 years (2000).
Transportation: Commute to work: 72.7% car, 0.0% public transportation, 10.4% walk, 16.9% work from home (2000); Travel time to work: 26.6% less than 15 minutes, 34.4% 15 to 30 minutes, 14.1% 30 to 45 minutes, 4.7% 45 to 60 minutes, 20.3% 60 minutes or more (2000)

KINROSS CHARTER (township). Covers a land area of 120.074 square miles and a water area of 0.888 square miles. Located at 46.28° N. Lat.; 84.57° W. Long. Elevation is 778 feet.
History: Kinross Township was named for Kinross, Scotland, by Scoth-Irish settlers.
Population: 5,922 (2000); Race: 64.7% White, 16.0% Black, 0.7% Asian, 11.3% American Indian and Alaska Native, 3.2% Hispanic of any race, 6.5% two or more races (2000); Density: 49.3 persons per square mile (2000); Age: 20.3% under 18, 4.0% over 64 (2000); Marriage status: 35.4% never married, 44.1% now married, 2.2% widowed, 18.3% divorced (2000); Foreign born: 2.2% (2000); Ancestry (includes multiple ancestries): 24.7% Other groups, 15.7% German, 10.5% Irish, 8.9% English, 6.8% French (except Basque) (2000).
Economy: Employment by occupation: 10.1% management, 13.4% professional, 34.0% services, 24.7% sales, 0.8% farming, 6.7% construction, 10.3% production (2000).
Income: Per capita income: $14,003 (2000); Median household income: $36,525 (2000); Poverty rate: 16.4% (2000).
Taxes: Total city taxes per capita: $37 (2000); City property taxes per capita: $37 (2000).
Education: High school graduation rate: 83.4% (2000); College graduation rate: 11.1% (2000).
Housing: Homeownership rate: 53.2% (2000); Median home value: $72,600 (2000); Median rent: $385 per month (2000); Median age of housing: 36 years (2000).
Safety: Violent crime rate: 16.8 per 10,000 population; Property crime rate: 63.8 per 10,000 population (2001).
Transportation: Commute to work: 94.5% car, 1.3% public transportation, 0.7% walk, 2.9% work from home (2000); Travel time to work: 38.2% less than 15 minutes, 34.3% 15 to 30 minutes, 20.5% 30 to 45 minutes, 3.9% 45 to 60 minutes, 3.1% 60 minutes or more (2000)

PARADISE (unincorporated postal area, zip code 49768). Aka Tahquamenon. Covers a land area of 172.635 square miles and a water area of 3.579 square miles. Located at 46.66° N. Lat.; 85.09° W. Long. Elevation is 615 feet.
History: Paradise was founded in 1925 by Ed LeDuc, and named by a promoter who wanted people to appreciate the scenery and abundance of fish and game.
Population: 445 (2000); Race: 95.6% White, 0.0% Black, 0.0% Asian, 0.6% American Indian and Alaska Native, 1.0% Hispanic of any race, 3.4% two or more races (2000); Density: 2.6 persons per square mile (2000); Age: 14.5% under 18, 26.6% over 64 (2000); Marriage status: 11.8% never married, 70.5% now married, 8.6% widowed, 9.1% divorced (2000); Foreign born: 1.0% (2000); Ancestry (includes multiple ancestries): 24.1% German, 17.2% English, 14.9% Irish, 6.7% French (except Basque), 6.5% United States or American (2000).
Economy: Employment by occupation: 14.9% management, 15.7% professional, 21.6% services, 22.4% sales, 1.5% farming, 15.7% construction, 8.2% production (2000).
Income: Per capita income: $18,791 (2000); Median household income: $30,556 (2000); Poverty rate: 14.0% (2000).
Education: High school graduation rate: 86.2% (2000); College graduation rate: 13.6% (2000).

School District(s)

Whitefish Township Schools (KG-12)
2000 Enrollment: 79 906-492-3353
Housing: Homeownership rate: 91.5% (2000); Median home value: $86,800 (2000); Median rent: $364 per month (2000); Median age of housing: 25 years (2000).
Transportation: Commute to work: 88.4% car, 0.0% public transportation, 3.9% walk, 7.8% work from home (2000); Travel time to work: 52.9% less than 15 minutes, 21.0% 15 to 30 minutes, 1.7% 30 to 45 minutes, 4.2% 45 to 60 minutes, 20.2% 60 minutes or more (2000)

PICKFORD (township). Covers a land area of 108.436 square miles and a water area of 11.038 square miles. Located at 46.18° N. Lat.; 84.35° W. Long. Elevation is 616 feet.
History: Pickford Township was named for Charles W. Pickford, the first settler here in 1877.
Population: 1,584 (2000); Race: 90.9% White, 0.1% Black, 0.4% Asian, 6.4% American Indian and Alaska Native, 0.5% Hispanic of any race, 2.2% two or more races (2000); Density: 14.6 persons per square mile (2000); Age: 25.1% under 18, 15.0% over 64 (2000); Marriage status: 16.7% never married, 71.3% now married, 5.8% widowed, 6.2% divorced (2000); Foreign born: 1.4% (2000); Ancestry (includes multiple ancestries): 21.3% English, 16.9% German, 8.8% Irish, 8.6% Polish, 7.9% Other groups (2000).
Economy: Employment by occupation: 10.6% management, 13.8% professional, 23.4% services, 23.4% sales, 1.0% farming, 14.2% construction, 13.6% production (2000).
Income: Per capita income: $16,320 (2000); Median household income: $40,850 (2000); Poverty rate: 6.6% (2000).
Taxes: Total city taxes per capita: $58 (1997); City property taxes per capita: $58 (1997).
Education: High school graduation rate: 86.4% (2000); College graduation rate: 11.9% (2000).

School District(s)

Pickford Public Schools (KG-12)
2000 Enrollment: 471 906-647-6285
Housing: Homeownership rate: 90.1% (2000); Median home value: $80,000 (2000); Median rent: $358 per month (2000); Median age of housing: 31 years (2000).
Transportation: Commute to work: 86.9% car, 0.0% public transportation, 5.8% walk, 6.4% work from home (2000); Travel time to work: 35.7% less than 15 minutes, 31.4% 15 to 30 minutes, 25.1% 30 to 45 minutes, 2.7% 45 to 60 minutes, 5.1% 60 minutes or more (2000)

RABER (township). Covers a land area of 98.048 square miles and a water area of 45.002 square miles. Located at 46.06° N. Lat.; 84.15° W. Long. Elevation is 594 feet.
History: Settlement began in the late 1870's in Raber, which was named for Mueller M. Raber, a lumberman who lived in that area.
Population: 670 (2000); Race: 92.5% White, 0.0% Black, 0.0% Asian, 2.5% American Indian and Alaska Native, 0.8% Hispanic of any race, 4.3% two or more races (2000); Density: 6.8 persons per square mile (2000); Age: 12.6% under 18, 28.2% over 64 (2000); Marriage status: 14.7% never married, 60.8% now married, 13.1% widowed, 11.4% divorced (2000); Foreign born: 1.0% (2000); Ancestry (includes multiple ancestries): 28.3% Polish, 16.4% German, 15.3% English, 7.8% Irish, 7.0% French (except Basque) (2000).
Economy: Employment by occupation: 7.0% management, 18.2% professional, 16.0% services, 20.9% sales, 2.1% farming, 14.4% construction, 21.4% production (2000).
Income: Per capita income: $18,956 (2000); Median household income: $27,589 (2000); Poverty rate: 11.5% (2000).
Taxes: Total city taxes per capita: $98 (1997); City property taxes per capita: $98 (1997).
Education: High school graduation rate: 75.5% (2000); College graduation rate: 8.7% (2000).
Housing: Homeownership rate: 95.7% (2000); Median home value: $83,100 (2000); Median rent: $308 per month (2000); Median age of housing: 27 years (2000).
Transportation: Commute to work: 86.6% car, 0.0% public transportation, 4.3% walk, 9.1% work from home (2000); Travel time to work: 25.4% less than 15 minutes, 23.7% 15 to 30 minutes, 25.4% 30 to 45 minutes, 16.0% 45 to 60 minutes, 9.5% 60 minutes or more (2000)

RUDYARD (township). Covers a land area of 89.901 square miles and a water area of 0.164 square miles. Located at 46.21° N. Lat.; 84.63° W. Long. Elevation is 687 feet.
History: Rudyard was named in 1896 by Fred D. Underwood, general manager of the Baltimore & Ohio Railroad, for Rudyard Kipling, the English poet and author. In acknowledgment of the honor, Kipling sent a photograph with a poem on the back written about Michigan. Rudyard was established in dense forests and on swampy land, but became farming land.
Population: 1,315 (2000); Race: 89.0% White, 0.0% Black, 0.8% Asian, 6.0% American Indian and Alaska Native, 1.1% Hispanic of any race, 4.1% two or more races (2000); Density: 14.6 persons per square mile (2000); Age: 29.5% under 18, 11.0% over 64 (2000); Marriage status: 25.3% never married, 59.7% now married, 6.1% widowed, 8.8% divorced (2000); Foreign born: 2.0% (2000); Ancestry (includes multiple ancestries): 21.2% German, 15.3% Finnish, 12.2% Irish, 11.0% Other groups, 10.2% English (2000).
Economy: Employment by occupation: 8.3% management, 15.3% professional, 30.5% services, 17.9% sales, 1.3% farming, 12.9% construction, 13.9% production (2000).
Income: Per capita income: $15,941 (2000); Median household income: $37,000 (2000); Poverty rate: 8.0% (2000).
Taxes: Total city taxes per capita: $84 (1997); City property taxes per capita: $83 (1997).
Education: High school graduation rate: 88.9% (2000); College graduation rate: 12.9% (2000).

School District(s)

Rudyard Area Schools (KG-12)
2000 Enrollment: 1,155 906-478-3771

Housing: Homeownership rate: 87.5% (2000); Median home value: $59,700 (2000); Median rent: $355 per month (2000); Median age of housing: 36 years (2000).
Transportation: Commute to work: 93.7% car, 0.0% public transportation, 3.2% walk, 3.1% work from home (2000); Travel time to work: 40.2% less than 15 minutes, 29.6% 15 to 30 minutes, 20.4% 30 to 45 minutes, 5.4% 45 to 60 minutes, 4.4% 60 minutes or more (2000)

SAULT SAINTE MARIE (city). Covers a land area of 14.818 square miles and a water area of 5.379 square miles. Located at 46.48° N. Lat.; 84.35° W. Long. Elevation is 613 feet.
History: Sault Ste. Marie, described by Henry Clay as the "remotest settlement in the United States, if not in the moon," was the first permanent settlement in Michigan. Etienne Brule, sent by Champlain to find a Northwest Passage, landed here in 1618. In 1668 the Jesuits built a mission at the Soo, as it was called. After more than two hundred years of French and British reign, the Soo came under American rule with the building of Fort Brady in 1823. The first canal and lock were built in 1855, and replaced by the improved Weitzel Lock in 1881. Poe Lock was added in 1896. Both the American Sault Ste. Marie and its Canadian counterpart of the same name, across the St. Marys River, attract many tourists.
Population: 16,542 (2000); Race: 74.0% White, 6.5% Black, 0.8% Asian, 13.8% American Indian and Alaska Native, 2.1% Hispanic of any race, 4.6% two or more races (2000); Density: 1,116.3 persons per square mile (2000); Age: 19.4% under 18, 12.6% over 64 (2000); Marriage status: 37.7% never married, 42.9% now married, 7.3% widowed, 12.1% divorced (2000); Foreign born: 4.1% (2000); Ancestry (includes multiple ancestries): 18.6% Other groups, 16.7% German, 13.5% Irish, 9.9% English, 9.2% French (except Basque) (2000).
Vital Statistics: Birth rate: 108.2 per 10,000 population (1998)
Economy: Single-family building permits issued: 13 (2001) / 5 (2000); Multi-family building permits issued: 0 (2001) / 0 (2000); Employment by occupation: 10.2% management, 18.4% professional, 28.8% services, 26.7% sales, 0.1% farming, 6.7% construction, 9.1% production (2000).
Income: Per capita income: $14,460 (2000); Median household income: $29,652 (2000); Poverty rate: 17.5% (2000).
Taxes: Total city taxes per capita: $285 (1997); City property taxes per capita: $279 (1997).
Education: High school graduation rate: 80.6% (2000); College graduation rate: 16.9% (2000).

School District(s)

Bahweting Anishnabe Psa (KG-08)
2000 Enrollment: 182 906-227-2920
Sault Ste. Marie Area Schools (KG-12)
2000 Enrollment: 3,127 906-635-6609

Four-year College(s)

Lake Superior State University (Public)
2001 Enrollment: 3,142 906-632-6841
2001 Tuition: In-state $4,128; Out-of-state $8,106

Housing: Homeownership rate: 61.9% (2000); Median home value: $67,700 (2000); Median rent: $357 per month (2000); Median age of housing: 47 years (2000).
Hospitals: Chippewa County War Memorial Hospital (133 beds)
Safety: Violent crime rate: 27.1 per 10,000 population; Property crime rate: 305.5 per 10,000 population (2001).
Newspapers: The Evening News (6 x week)
Transportation: Commute to work: 85.3% car, 2.7% public transportation, 7.7% walk, 2.7% work from home (2000); Travel time to work: 73.1% less than 15 minutes, 17.7% 15 to 30 minutes, 6.0% 30 to 45 minutes, 0.6% 45 to 60 minutes, 2.6% 60 minutes or more (2000)
Airports: Chippewa County International (primary service); Sault Ste Marie Municipal/Sanderson Fiel (primary service)
Additional Information Contacts
Eastern Upper Peninsula Board of Realtors 906-632-7336
Sault Ste Marie Chamber of Commerce 906-632-3301

SOO (township). Covers a land area of 50.168 square miles and a water area of 17.757 square miles. Located at 46.42° N. Lat.; 84.31° W. Long.
Population: 2,652 (2000); Race: 83.9% White, 0.1% Black, 0.0% Asian, 11.2% American Indian and Alaska Native, 0.5% Hispanic of any race, 4.9% two or more races (2000); Density: 52.9 persons per square mile (2000); Age: 22.1% under 18, 16.5% over 64 (2000); Marriage status: 21.1% never married, 65.5% now married, 6.2% widowed, 7.3% divorced (2000); Foreign born: 3.2% (2000); Ancestry (includes multiple ancestries): 17.4% English, 16.6% German, 15.4% Irish, 12.0% Other groups, 10.3% French (except Basque) (2000).
Economy: Single-family building permits issued: 0 (2001) / 0 (2000); Multi-family building permits issued: 0 (2001) / 0 (2000); Employment by occupation: 8.5% management, 17.5% professional, 28.1% services, 26.7% sales, 0.3% farming, 7.5% construction, 11.4% production (2000).
Income: Per capita income: $20,625 (2000); Median household income: $42,917 (2000); Poverty rate: 4.4% (2000).
Education: High school graduation rate: 84.6% (2000); College graduation rate: 18.9% (2000).
Housing: Homeownership rate: 83.5% (2000); Median home value: $98,300 (2000); Median rent: $437 per month (2000); Median age of housing: 26 years (2000).
Transportation: Commute to work: 93.7% car, 1.5% public transportation, 0.8% walk, 3.6% work from home (2000); Travel time to work: 46.6% less than 15 minutes, 39.4% 15 to 30 minutes, 7.0% 30 to 45 minutes, 1.6% 45 to 60 minutes, 5.5% 60 minutes or more (2000)

SUGAR ISLAND (township). Covers a land area of 49.445 square miles and a water area of 27.002 square miles. Located at 46.46° N. Lat.; 84.20° W. Long.
History: Boundary disputes between England and America kept the ownership of Sugar Island in question from 1783 to 1842, when it was placed in U.S. territory by the Webster Ashburton Treaty.
Population: 683 (2000); Race: 66.0% White, 0.0% Black, 0.0% Asian, 28.9% American Indian and Alaska Native, 0.0% Hispanic of any race, 5.1% two or more races (2000); Density: 13.8 persons per square mile (2000); Age: 19.5% under 18, 15.2% over 64 (2000); Marriage status: 17.1% never married, 67.0% now married, 6.2% widowed, 9.8% divorced (2000); Foreign born: 2.3% (2000); Ancestry (includes multiple ancestries): 28.9% Other groups, 17.6% German, 12.0% English, 9.1% Irish, 7.0% French (except Basque) (2000).
Economy: Employment by occupation: 9.5% management, 13.6% professional, 21.6% services, 25.0% sales, 0.0% farming, 12.9% construction, 17.4% production (2000).
Income: Per capita income: $16,076 (2000); Median household income: $34,000 (2000); Poverty rate: 10.9% (2000).
Taxes: Total city taxes per capita: $189 (1997); City property taxes per capita: $189 (1997).
Education: High school graduation rate: 81.4% (2000); College graduation rate: 9.1% (2000).
Housing: Homeownership rate: 92.5% (2000); Median home value: $98,700 (2000); Median rent: $388 per month (2000); Median age of housing: 36 years (2000).
Transportation: Commute to work: 92.9% car, 3.7% public transportation, 0.0% walk, 2.6% work from home (2000); Travel time to work: 9.6% less than 15 minutes, 29.6% 15 to 30 minutes, 38.8% 30 to 45 minutes, 11.9% 45 to 60 minutes, 10.0% 60 minutes or more (2000)

SUPERIOR (township). Covers a land area of 103.165 square miles and a water area of 1.492 square miles. Located at 46.37° N. Lat.; 84.65° W. Long.
Population: 1,329 (2000); Race: 71.9% White, 0.1% Black, 0.6% Asian, 21.9% American Indian and Alaska Native, 0.5% Hispanic of any race, 5.4% two or more races (2000); Density: 12.9 persons per square mile (2000); Age: 27.1% under 18, 11.3% over 64 (2000); Marriage status: 26.6% never married, 60.7% now married, 4.6% widowed, 8.1% divorced (2000); Foreign born: 2.2% (2000); Ancestry (includes multiple ancestries): 27.1% Other groups, 18.2% German, 11.4% English, 11.4% Irish, 10.0% French (except Basque) (2000).
Economy: Employment by occupation: 7.1% management, 18.4% professional, 29.9% services, 23.7% sales, 1.4% farming, 6.4% construction, 13.2% production (2000).
Income: Per capita income: $17,260 (2000); Median household income: $39,375 (2000); Poverty rate: 5.7% (2000).
Taxes: Total city taxes per capita: $58 (1997); City property taxes per capita: $58 (1997).
Education: High school graduation rate: 84.7% (2000); College graduation rate: 16.4% (2000).
Housing: Homeownership rate: 88.2% (2000); Median home value: $68,400 (2000); Median rent: $406 per month (2000); Median age of housing: 26 years (2000).
Transportation: Commute to work: 90.9% car, 1.2% public transportation, 4.9% walk, 1.2% work from home (2000); Travel time to work: 43.4% less than 15 minutes, 39.5% 15 to 30 minutes, 11.2% 30 to 45 minutes, 2.6% 45 to 60 minutes, 3.2% 60 minutes or more (2000)

TROUT LAKE (township). Covers a land area of 141.709 square miles and a water area of 1.926 square miles. Located at 46.19° N. Lat.; 84.96° W. Long. Elevation is 850 feet.
History: The Trout Lake area was settled in 1881 at a railway junction, and became a trading center for lumber camps.
Population: 465 (2000); Race: 91.6% White, 0.0% Black, 0.9% Asian, 5.4% American Indian and Alaska Native, 0.0% Hispanic of any race, 2.1% two or more races (2000); Density: 3.3 persons per square mile (2000); Age: 21.2% under 18, 25.3% over 64 (2000); Marriage status: 15.2% never married, 65.2% now married, 12.4% widowed, 7.2% divorced (2000); Foreign born: 1.3% (2000); Ancestry (includes multiple ancestries): 31.7% German, 17.3% English, 11.8% Polish, 11.6% Irish, 9.9% French (except Basque) (2000).
Economy: Employment by occupation: 3.3% management, 7.9% professional, 40.1% services, 20.4% sales, 3.3% farming, 7.2% construction, 17.8% production (2000).
Income: Per capita income: $15,221 (2000); Median household income: $28,571 (2000); Poverty rate: 12.8% (2000).
Taxes: Total city taxes per capita: $83 (1997); City property taxes per capita: $83 (1997).
Education: High school graduation rate: 76.8% (2000); College graduation rate: 12.2% (2000).
Housing: Homeownership rate: 90.6% (2000); Median home value: $79,600 (2000); Median rent: $263 per month (2000); Median age of housing: 26 years (2000).
Transportation: Commute to work: 89.9% car, 0.0% public transportation, 4.7% walk, 5.4% work from home (2000); Travel time to work: 27.1% less than 15 minutes, 2.1% 15 to 30 minutes, 36.4% 30 to 45 minutes, 23.6% 45 to 60 minutes, 10.7% 60 minutes or more (2000)

WHITEFISH (township). Covers a land area of 241.508 square miles and a water area of 51.947 square miles. Located at 46.62° N. Lat.; 85.09° W. Long.
Population: 588 (2000); Race: 93.5% White, 0.0% Black, 0.0% Asian, 3.4% American Indian and Alaska Native, 0.8% Hispanic of any race, 2.9% two or more races (2000); Density: 2.4 persons per square mile (2000); Age: 13.9% under 18, 26.8% over 64 (2000); Marriage status: 11.4% never married, 72.4% now married, 6.9% widowed, 9.3% divorced (2000); Foreign born: 1.1% (2000); Ancestry (includes multiple ancestries): 22.0% German, 16.6% English, 14.4% Irish, 6.2% Other groups, 5.9% United States or American (2000).
Economy: Employment by occupation: 11.7% management, 16.1% professional, 21.7% services, 27.2% sales, 2.8% farming, 13.9% construction, 6.7% production (2000).
Income: Per capita income: $18,154 (2000); Median household income: $29,432 (2000); Poverty rate: 12.5% (2000).
Taxes: Total city taxes per capita: $98 (1997); City property taxes per capita: $98 (1997).
Education: High school graduation rate: 83.2% (2000); College graduation rate: 14.3% (2000).
Housing: Homeownership rate: 91.5% (2000); Median home value: $90,700 (2000); Median rent: $355 per month (2000); Median age of housing: 26 years (2000).
Transportation: Commute to work: 87.4% car, 0.0% public transportation, 2.9% walk, 9.7% work from home (2000); Travel time to work: 50.6% less than 15 minutes, 27.2% 15 to 30 minutes, 2.5% 30 to 45 minutes, 4.4% 45 to 60 minutes, 15.2% 60 minutes or more (2000)

Clare County

Located in central Michigan; drained by the Muskegon, Tobacco, and Small Cedar Rivers. Covers a land area of 566.80 square miles, a water area of 8.40 square miles, and is located in the Eastern Time Zone. The county government was organized in 1840. County seat is Harrison.
Population: 31,252 (2000); Race: 97.3% White, 0.3% Black, 0.3% Asian, 0.6% American Indian and Alaska Native, 1.1% Hispanic of any race, 1.3% two or more races (2000); Density: 55.1 persons per square mile (2000); Age: 24.5% under 18, 17.3% over 64 (2000).
Religion: Five largest groups: 6.9% Catholic Church, 2.0% The United Methodist Church, 1.6% Lutheran Church—Missouri Synod, 1.5% United Church of Christ, 1.2% Church of the Nazarene (2000).
Economy: Unemployment rate: 7.8% (11/2002); Total civilian labor force: 11,017 (11/2002); Leading industries: 23.2% retail trade; 17.2% manufacturing; 16.9% health care and social assistance (2000); Companies that employ more than 1,000 persons: 0 (2000); Companies that employ more than 100 persons: 8 (2000); Farms: 350 totaling 62,831 acres (1997); Minority business ownership rate: 0.0% (1997); Women business ownership rate: 23.7% (1997); Retail sales per capita: $7,517 (1997). Single-family building permits issued: 142 (2001) / 146 (2000); Multi-family building permits issued: 14 (2001) / 14 (2000).
Income: Per capita income: $15,922 (2000); Median household income: $28,845 (2000); Poverty rate: 16.0% (2000); Bankruptcy rate: 6.62% (2001).
Taxes: Total county taxes per capita: $117 (2000); County property taxes per capita: $108 (2000).
Education: High school graduation rate: 76.1% (2000); College graduation rate: 8.8% (2000).
Housing: Homeownership rate: 82.2% (2000); Median home value: $70,500 (2000); Median rent: $324 per month (2000); Median age of housing: 29 years (2000).
Health: Birth rate: 106.9 per 10,000 population (1998); Age adjusted death rate: 113.3 per 10,000 population (1999); Age adjusted cancer mortality rate: 237.9 deaths per 100,000 population (1999). Number of physicians: 5.8 per 10,000 population (1999); Number of hospital beds: 20.5 per 10,000 population (1999).
Elections: 2000 Presidential election results: 49.9% Gore, 47.1% Bush, 2.1% Nader, 0.0% Buchanan
National and State Parks: Wilson State Park
Additional Information Contacts
Clare County Government Offices. 989-539-7131
Clare Chamber of Commerce. 989-386-2442
Clare County Convention & Visitors Bureau. 989-386-6400
Harrison Chamber of Commerce 989-539-6011

Clare County Communities

ARTHUR (township). Covers a land area of 36.078 square miles and a water area of 0.121 square miles. Located at 43.95° N. Lat.; 84.67° W. Long.
Population: 667 (2000); Race: 98.4% White, 0.3% Black, 0.0% Asian, 1.1% American Indian and Alaska Native, 0.0% Hispanic of any race, 0.0% two or more races (2000); Density: 18.5 persons per square mile (2000); Age: 30.7% under 18, 13.5% over 64 (2000); Marriage status: 21.3% never married, 68.9% now married, 4.3% widowed, 5.5% divorced (2000); Foreign born: 0.5% (2000); Ancestry (includes multiple ancestries): 22.8% German, 13.6% English, 11.2% Irish, 9.3% United States or American, 4.9% Other groups (2000).
Economy: Employment by occupation: 15.4% management, 14.8% professional, 11.9% services, 22.3% sales, 6.0% farming, 12.3% construction, 17.3% production (2000).
Income: Per capita income: $18,380 (2000); Median household income: $39,148 (2000); Poverty rate: 8.5% (2000).
Taxes: Total city taxes per capita: $53 (1997); City property taxes per capita: $53 (1997).
Education: High school graduation rate: 81.6% (2000); College graduation rate: 9.9% (2000).
Housing: Homeownership rate: 86.1% (2000); Median home value: $72,800 (2000); Median rent: $415 per month (2000); Median age of housing: 28 years (2000).
Transportation: Commute to work: 88.0% car, 0.0% public transportation, 2.6% walk, 8.7% work from home (2000); Travel time to work: 18.4% less than 15 minutes, 50.7% 15 to 30 minutes, 15.2% 30 to 45 minutes, 5.7% 45 to 60 minutes, 9.9% 60 minutes or more (2000)

CLARE (city). Covers a land area of 3.121 square miles and a water area of 0.094 square miles. Located at 43.82° N. Lat.; 84.76° W. Long. Elevation is 841 feet.
History: Clare was platted in 1870 when the Flint and Pere Marquette Railway was built, and named for County Clare in Ireland. It was incorporated as a village in 1879. Industries in the early 1900's included the manufacture of house trailers, highway equipment, and cheese. In 1930, oil and gas fields near the town added to the economic growth.
Population: 3,173 (2000); Race: 95.6% White, 0.2% Black, 1.3% Asian, 0.7% American Indian and Alaska Native, 1.5% Hispanic of any race, 2.2% two or more races (2000); Density: 1,016.7 persons per square mile (2000); Age: 24.4% under 18, 20.5% over 64 (2000); Marriage status: 24.1% never married, 47.5% now married, 12.2% widowed, 16.2% divorced (2000); Foreign born: 2.0% (2000); Ancestry (includes multiple ancestries): 28.0% German, 18.2% English, 14.5% Irish, 7.7% French (except Basque), 7.6% Other groups (2000).
Economy: Single-family building permits issued: 8 (2001) / 3 (2000); Multi-family building permits issued: 4 (2001) / 4 (2000); Employment by

occupation: 9.1% management, 21.2% professional, 18.5% services, 25.1% sales, 0.0% farming, 8.5% construction, 17.5% production (2000).
Income: Per capita income: $18,006 (2000); Median household income: $27,299 (2000); Poverty rate: 16.0% (2000).
Taxes: Total city taxes per capita: $277 (1997); City property taxes per capita: $273 (1997).
Education: High school graduation rate: 81.2% (2000); College graduation rate: 16.7% (2000).

School District(s)

Clare Public Schools (KG-12)
2000 Enrollment: 1,627 517-386-9945
Housing: Homeownership rate: 52.5% (2000); Median home value: $78,500 (2000); Median rent: $307 per month (2000); Median age of housing: 34 years (2000).
Hospitals: MidMichigan Medical Center Clare (64 beds)
Safety: Violent crime rate: 40.8 per 10,000 population; Property crime rate: 705.3 per 10,000 population (2001).
Newspapers: The Clare Sentinel (1 x week); Clare County Review (1 x week)
Transportation: Commute to work: 89.7% car, 1.4% public transportation, 4.7% walk, 3.7% work from home (2000); Travel time to work: 48.7% less than 15 minutes, 31.2% 15 to 30 minutes, 13.7% 30 to 45 minutes, 3.3% 45 to 60 minutes, 3.1% 60 minutes or more (2000)
Additional Information Contacts
Clare Chamber of Commerce. 989-386-2442
Clare County Convention & Visitors Bureau. 989-386-6400

FARWELL (village). Covers a land area of 1.378 square miles and a water area of 0.032 square miles. Located at 43.83° N. Lat.; 84.86° W. Long. Elevation is 933 feet.
History: Farwell came into existence when the Flint and Pere Marquette Railway was built through the area in 1870. For a time in the early 1900's, the Portland Cement Company had a plant here, using marl deposits from Littlefield Lake in the manufacture of cement.
Population: 855 (2000); Race: 95.2% White, 0.8% Black, 0.0% Asian, 2.3% American Indian and Alaska Native, 0.5% Hispanic of any race, 1.7% two or more races (2000); Density: 620.5 persons per square mile (2000); Age: 23.8% under 18, 20.7% over 64 (2000); Marriage status: 27.0% never married, 45.7% now married, 12.9% widowed, 14.3% divorced (2000); Foreign born: 0.6% (2000); Ancestry (includes multiple ancestries): 17.2% German, 14.4% Irish, 14.2% United States or American, 9.4% English, 5.7% French (except Basque) (2000).
Economy: Employment by occupation: 3.2% management, 13.8% professional, 25.7% services, 23.2% sales, 0.0% farming, 9.5% construction, 24.6% production (2000).
Income: Per capita income: $19,870 (2000); Median household income: $24,583 (2000); Poverty rate: 13.3% (2000).
Taxes: Total city taxes per capita: $139 (1997); City property taxes per capita: $139 (1997).
Education: High school graduation rate: 75.4% (2000); College graduation rate: 6.6% (2000).

School District(s)

Farwell Area Schools (KG-12)
2000 Enrollment: 1,650 517-588-9917
Housing: Homeownership rate: 66.9% (2000); Median home value: $63,300 (2000); Median rent: $256 per month (2000); Median age of housing: 30 years (2000).
Transportation: Commute to work: 90.3% car, 2.0% public transportation, 5.1% walk, 2.6% work from home (2000); Travel time to work: 46.2% less than 15 minutes, 19.9% 15 to 30 minutes, 24.6% 30 to 45 minutes, 3.5% 45 to 60 minutes, 5.8% 60 minutes or more (2000)

FRANKLIN (township). Covers a land area of 35.398 square miles and a water area of 0.125 square miles. Located at 44.12° N. Lat.; 84.65° W. Long.
Population: 809 (2000); Race: 98.4% White, 0.0% Black, 0.0% Asian, 0.0% American Indian and Alaska Native, 0.9% Hispanic of any race, 1.4% two or more races (2000); Density: 22.9 persons per square mile (2000); Age: 24.6% under 18, 12.5% over 64 (2000); Marriage status: 21.8% never married, 57.5% now married, 5.4% widowed, 15.4% divorced (2000); Foreign born: 0.2% (2000); Ancestry (includes multiple ancestries): 20.2% German, 15.4% English, 15.4% United States or American, 8.9% Other groups, 8.7% Irish (2000).
Economy: Employment by occupation: 3.7% management, 11.6% professional, 19.3% services, 23.9% sales, 0.7% farming, 20.6% construction, 20.3% production (2000).
Income: Per capita income: $12,353 (2000); Median household income: $25,598 (2000); Poverty rate: 19.6% (2000).
Taxes: Total city taxes per capita: $67 (1997); City property taxes per capita: $67 (1997).
Education: High school graduation rate: 72.6% (2000); College graduation rate: 5.3% (2000).
Housing: Homeownership rate: 89.1% (2000); Median home value: $46,300 (2000); Median rent: $342 per month (2000); Median age of housing: 26 years (2000).
Transportation: Commute to work: 94.1% car, 0.0% public transportation, 1.7% walk, 3.5% work from home (2000); Travel time to work: 16.9% less than 15 minutes, 32.4% 15 to 30 minutes, 29.9% 30 to 45 minutes, 9.4% 45 to 60 minutes, 11.5% 60 minutes or more (2000)

FREEMAN (township). Covers a land area of 34.573 square miles and a water area of 1.087 square miles. Located at 43.94° N. Lat.; 85.02° W. Long.
Population: 1,118 (2000); Race: 97.5% White, 0.0% Black, 0.0% Asian, 1.5% American Indian and Alaska Native, 1.8% Hispanic of any race, 1.0% two or more races (2000); Density: 32.3 persons per square mile (2000); Age: 23.2% under 18, 20.9% over 64 (2000); Marriage status: 14.3% never married, 66.6% now married, 6.8% widowed, 12.3% divorced (2000); Foreign born: 0.4% (2000); Ancestry (includes multiple ancestries): 24.8% German, 15.1% Irish, 13.6% English, 9.6% French (except Basque), 9.1% Other groups (2000).
Economy: Single-family building permits issued: 17 (2001) / 23 (2000); Multi-family building permits issued: 0 (2001) / 0 (2000); Employment by occupation: 10.4% management, 9.9% professional, 14.1% services, 22.5% sales, 1.1% farming, 12.1% construction, 29.9% production (2000).
Income: Per capita income: $14,624 (2000); Median household income: $30,398 (2000); Poverty rate: 13.0% (2000).
Taxes: Total city taxes per capita: $148 (1997); City property taxes per capita: $135 (1997).
Education: High school graduation rate: 76.4% (2000); College graduation rate: 6.3% (2000).
Housing: Homeownership rate: 90.6% (2000); Median home value: $83,700 (2000); Median rent: $371 per month (2000); Median age of housing: 15 years (2000).
Transportation: Commute to work: 97.1% car, 0.0% public transportation, 1.2% walk, 1.8% work from home (2000); Travel time to work: 11.4% less than 15 minutes, 32.7% 15 to 30 minutes, 26.1% 30 to 45 minutes, 20.7% 45 to 60 minutes, 9.0% 60 minutes or more (2000)

FROST (township). Covers a land area of 35.032 square miles and a water area of 0.428 square miles. Located at 44.10° N. Lat.; 84.78° W. Long.
Population: 1,159 (2000); Race: 97.2% White, 0.3% Black, 0.1% Asian, 0.3% American Indian and Alaska Native, 1.5% Hispanic of any race, 2.1% two or more races (2000); Density: 33.1 persons per square mile (2000); Age: 18.4% under 18, 21.4% over 64 (2000); Marriage status: 13.6% never married, 62.1% now married, 9.9% widowed, 14.5% divorced (2000); Foreign born: 1.9% (2000); Ancestry (includes multiple ancestries): 19.7% German, 12.2% English, 11.5% Irish, 11.2% United States or American, 6.1% Other groups (2000).
Economy: Employment by occupation: 6.6% management, 14.3% professional, 16.9% services, 20.9% sales, 2.0% farming, 20.1% construction, 19.2% production (2000).
Income: Per capita income: $16,387 (2000); Median household income: $27,243 (2000); Poverty rate: 16.9% (2000).
Taxes: Total city taxes per capita: $23 (1997); City property taxes per capita: $23 (1997).
Education: High school graduation rate: 75.5% (2000); College graduation rate: 6.5% (2000).
Housing: Homeownership rate: 89.3% (2000); Median home value: $81,900 (2000); Median rent: $308 per month (2000); Median age of housing: 28 years (2000).
Safety: Violent crime rate: 0.0 per 10,000 population; Property crime rate: 120.2 per 10,000 population (2001).
Transportation: Commute to work: 93.2% car, 0.6% public transportation, 1.8% walk, 3.9% work from home (2000); Travel time to work: 23.5% less than 15 minutes, 35.6% 15 to 30 minutes, 19.5% 30 to 45 minutes, 10.2% 45 to 60 minutes, 11.1% 60 minutes or more (2000)

GARFIELD (township). Covers a land area of 33.385 square miles and a water area of 2.305 square miles. Located at 43.85° N. Lat.; 85.03° W. Long.
Population: 1,968 (2000); Race: 98.0% White, 0.0% Black, 0.1% Asian, 0.3% American Indian and Alaska Native, 0.8% Hispanic of any race, 1.4% two or more races (2000); Density: 58.9 persons per square mile (2000); Age:

21.7% under 18, 20.2% over 64 (2000); Marriage status: 16.6% never married, 62.6% now married, 8.0% widowed, 12.7% divorced (2000); Foreign born: 2.0% (2000); Ancestry (includes multiple ancestries): 25.5% German, 14.0% English, 12.5% Irish, 12.2% United States or American, 6.1% Other groups (2000).
Economy: Employment by occupation: 7.0% management, 13.5% professional, 19.0% services, 19.8% sales, 1.1% farming, 10.0% construction, 29.6% production (2000).
Income: Per capita income: $17,209 (2000); Median household income: $29,038 (2000); Poverty rate: 12.7% (2000).
Taxes: Total city taxes per capita: $59 (1997); City property taxes per capita: $58 (1997).
Education: High school graduation rate: 77.4% (2000); College graduation rate: 9.3% (2000).
Housing: Homeownership rate: 86.8% (2000); Median home value: $80,400 (2000); Median rent: $342 per month (2000); Median age of housing: 27 years (2000).
Transportation: Commute to work: 94.8% car, 0.4% public transportation, 2.2% walk, 2.2% work from home (2000); Travel time to work: 21.1% less than 15 minutes, 30.3% 15 to 30 minutes, 25.0% 30 to 45 minutes, 14.6% 45 to 60 minutes, 9.1% 60 minutes or more (2000)

GRANT (township). Covers a land area of 33.222 square miles and a water area of 0.378 square miles. Located at 43.85° N. Lat.; 84.79° W. Long.
Population: 3,034 (2000); Race: 97.9% White, 0.2% Black, 0.1% Asian, 0.5% American Indian and Alaska Native, 0.4% Hispanic of any race, 1.3% two or more races (2000); Density: 91.3 persons per square mile (2000); Age: 24.9% under 18, 14.2% over 64 (2000); Marriage status: 19.6% never married, 65.1% now married, 6.3% widowed, 9.0% divorced (2000); Foreign born: 1.2% (2000); Ancestry (includes multiple ancestries): 28.1% German, 14.1% English, 9.7% Irish, 5.8% Dutch, 5.4% Other groups (2000).
Economy: Employment by occupation: 9.9% management, 14.9% professional, 16.5% services, 22.5% sales, 0.3% farming, 13.4% construction, 22.5% production (2000).
Income: Per capita income: $17,597 (2000); Median household income: $35,245 (2000); Poverty rate: 11.1% (2000).
Taxes: Total city taxes per capita: $55 (1997); City property taxes per capita: $48 (1997).
Education: High school graduation rate: 80.8% (2000); College graduation rate: 13.4% (2000).
Housing: Homeownership rate: 89.0% (2000); Median home value: $87,700 (2000); Median rent: $341 per month (2000); Median age of housing: 26 years (2000).
Transportation: Commute to work: 91.5% car, 0.0% public transportation, 1.2% walk, 6.8% work from home (2000); Travel time to work: 40.1% less than 15 minutes, 27.8% 15 to 30 minutes, 19.6% 30 to 45 minutes, 5.9% 45 to 60 minutes, 6.5% 60 minutes or more (2000)

GREENWOOD (township). Covers a land area of 35.160 square miles and a water area of 0.291 square miles. Located at 44.02° N. Lat.; 84.92° W. Long.
Population: 1,059 (2000); Race: 98.5% White, 0.0% Black, 0.4% Asian, 0.3% American Indian and Alaska Native, 0.5% Hispanic of any race, 0.5% two or more races (2000); Density: 30.1 persons per square mile (2000); Age: 22.8% under 18, 16.5% over 64 (2000); Marriage status: 14.8% never married, 67.6% now married, 6.8% widowed, 10.8% divorced (2000); Foreign born: 1.2% (2000); Ancestry (includes multiple ancestries): 22.0% German, 16.7% English, 11.2% Irish, 9.7% United States or American, 6.3% French (except Basque) (2000).
Economy: Employment by occupation: 6.2% management, 11.4% professional, 19.8% services, 22.8% sales, 1.7% farming, 14.1% construction, 24.0% production (2000).
Income: Per capita income: $17,283 (2000); Median household income: $32,228 (2000); Poverty rate: 16.0% (2000).
Taxes: Total city taxes per capita: $147 (1997); City property taxes per capita: $147 (1997).
Education: High school graduation rate: 76.8% (2000); College graduation rate: 4.7% (2000).
Housing: Homeownership rate: 90.9% (2000); Median home value: $65,000 (2000); Median rent: $295 per month (2000); Median age of housing: 24 years (2000).
Transportation: Commute to work: 97.4% car, 0.0% public transportation, 0.0% walk, 2.6% work from home (2000); Travel time to work: 30.9% less than 15 minutes, 31.9% 15 to 30 minutes, 16.0% 30 to 45 minutes, 12.3% 45 to 60 minutes, 8.9% 60 minutes or more (2000)

HAMILTON (township). Covers a land area of 35.921 square miles and a water area of 0.481 square miles. Located at 44.03° N. Lat.; 84.68° W. Long.
History: Hamilton Township was subdivided from Hayes Township in 1885.
Population: 1,988 (2000); Race: 97.0% White, 0.2% Black, 1.0% Asian, 0.2% American Indian and Alaska Native, 1.4% Hispanic of any race, 1.5% two or more races (2000); Density: 55.3 persons per square mile (2000); Age: 24.7% under 18, 17.4% over 64 (2000); Marriage status: 18.7% never married, 62.7% now married, 7.6% widowed, 11.0% divorced (2000); Foreign born: 2.4% (2000); Ancestry (includes multiple ancestries): 20.9% German, 16.0% United States or American, 12.2% English, 11.7% Irish, 7.2% Other groups (2000).
Economy: Single-family building permits issued: 12 (2001) / 12 (2000); Multi-family building permits issued: 0 (2001) / 0 (2000); Employment by occupation: 8.1% management, 14.3% professional, 22.1% services, 19.4% sales, 0.3% farming, 13.9% construction, 21.8% production (2000).
Income: Per capita income: $13,433 (2000); Median household income: $26,221 (2000); Poverty rate: 23.3% (2000).
Taxes: Total city taxes per capita: $36 (1997); City property taxes per capita: $32 (1997).
Education: High school graduation rate: 74.3% (2000); College graduation rate: 5.4% (2000).
Housing: Homeownership rate: 91.1% (2000); Median home value: $54,700 (2000); Median rent: $358 per month (2000); Median age of housing: 32 years (2000).
Transportation: Commute to work: 95.7% car, 0.3% public transportation, 0.3% walk, 3.1% work from home (2000); Travel time to work: 21.2% less than 15 minutes, 41.6% 15 to 30 minutes, 17.3% 30 to 45 minutes, 9.8% 45 to 60 minutes, 10.2% 60 minutes or more (2000)

HARRISON (city). Covers a land area of 3.742 square miles and a water area of 0.279 square miles. Located at 44.02° N. Lat.; 84.80° W. Long. Elevation is 1,186 feet.
History: Harrison was founded in 1879 as the seat of Clare County when the courthouse at Farwell was destroyed by fire. The new city was platted by the Pere Marquette Railway and named for President William Henry Harrison. Harrison became the center of a resort area offering hunting and fishing.
Population: 2,108 (2000); Race: 94.9% White, 1.1% Black, 0.0% Asian, 0.7% American Indian and Alaska Native, 2.0% Hispanic of any race, 2.6% two or more races (2000); Density: 563.3 persons per square mile (2000); Age: 22.6% under 18, 18.2% over 64 (2000); Marriage status: 24.4% never married, 51.5% now married, 11.3% widowed, 12.8% divorced (2000); Foreign born: 0.8% (2000); Ancestry (includes multiple ancestries): 19.5% German, 12.4% English, 11.2% Irish, 10.4% Other groups, 9.3% United States or American (2000).
Economy: Employment by occupation: 11.1% management, 15.8% professional, 21.5% services, 25.4% sales, 0.3% farming, 8.9% construction, 17.1% production (2000).
Income: Per capita income: $15,443 (2000); Median household income: $26,392 (2000); Poverty rate: 18.5% (2000).
Taxes: Total city taxes per capita: $192 (1997); City property taxes per capita: $189 (1997).
Education: High school graduation rate: 79.0% (2000); College graduation rate: 12.8% (2000).

School District(s)

Bark River-Harris School District (KG-12)
2000 Enrollment: 622 906-466-9981

Two-year College(s)

Mid-Michigan Community College (Public)
2001 Enrollment: 2,411 517-386-6622
2001 Tuition: In-state $2,728; Out-of-state $3,906

Housing: Homeownership rate: 65.5% (2000); Median home value: $82,100 (2000); Median rent: $301 per month (2000); Median age of housing: 36 years (2000).
Newspapers: Clare County Cleaver (1 x week)
Transportation: Commute to work: 91.8% car, 0.0% public transportation, 4.0% walk, 2.5% work from home (2000); Travel time to work: 51.6% less than 15 minutes, 19.8% 15 to 30 minutes, 14.2% 30 to 45 minutes, 6.2% 45 to 60 minutes, 8.3% 60 minutes or more (2000)

Additional Information Contacts

Harrison Chamber of Commerce 989-539-6011

HATTON (township). Covers a land area of 35.967 square miles and a water area of 0.212 square miles. Located at 43.94° N. Lat.; 84.77° W. Long. Elevation is 1,000 feet.

Population: 923 (2000); Race: 97.1% White, 0.0% Black, 0.4% Asian, 0.5% American Indian and Alaska Native, 0.6% Hispanic of any race, 2.1% two or more races (2000); Density: 25.7 persons per square mile (2000); Age: 28.5% under 18, 13.0% over 64 (2000); Marriage status: 21.7% never married, 63.7% now married, 6.6% widowed, 8.0% divorced (2000); Foreign born: 0.4% (2000); Ancestry (includes multiple ancestries): 30.9% German, 14.6% Irish, 13.2% English, 7.7% French (except Basque), 6.9% Other groups (2000).
Economy: Employment by occupation: 10.1% management, 20.0% professional, 12.8% services, 24.3% sales, 0.0% farming, 18.4% construction, 14.4% production (2000).
Income: Per capita income: $15,848 (2000); Median household income: $30,461 (2000); Poverty rate: 11.3% (2000).
Taxes: Total city taxes per capita: $16 (1997); City property taxes per capita: $14 (1997).
Education: High school graduation rate: 80.9% (2000); College graduation rate: 13.0% (2000).
Housing: Homeownership rate: 87.7% (2000); Median home value: $75,000 (2000); Median rent: $350 per month (2000); Median age of housing: 25 years (2000).
Transportation: Commute to work: 93.6% car, 0.6% public transportation, 1.1% walk, 4.7% work from home (2000); Travel time to work: 34.0% less than 15 minutes, 37.2% 15 to 30 minutes, 13.4% 30 to 45 minutes, 6.4% 45 to 60 minutes, 9.0% 60 minutes or more (2000)

HAYES (township). Covers a land area of 31.452 square miles and a water area of 0.700 square miles. Located at 44.04° N. Lat.; 84.78° W. Long.
Population: 4,916 (2000); Race: 98.2% White, 0.3% Black, 0.2% Asian, 0.4% American Indian and Alaska Native, 0.8% Hispanic of any race, 0.8% two or more races (2000); Density: 156.3 persons per square mile (2000); Age: 25.6% under 18, 16.5% over 64 (2000); Marriage status: 17.8% never married, 61.0% now married, 9.3% widowed, 11.9% divorced (2000); Foreign born: 0.3% (2000); Ancestry (includes multiple ancestries): 22.4% German, 13.1% English, 12.4% Irish, 8.6% United States or American, 7.4% Polish (2000).
Economy: Employment by occupation: 5.8% management, 12.9% professional, 24.3% services, 25.1% sales, 0.7% farming, 11.9% construction, 19.2% production (2000).
Income: Per capita income: $14,394 (2000); Median household income: $26,495 (2000); Poverty rate: 20.3% (2000).
Taxes: Total city taxes per capita: $108 (1997); City property taxes per capita: $107 (1997).
Education: High school graduation rate: 71.3% (2000); College graduation rate: 5.8% (2000).
Housing: Homeownership rate: 87.4% (2000); Median home value: $44,500 (2000); Median rent: $324 per month (2000); Median age of housing: 33 years (2000).
Transportation: Commute to work: 94.5% car, 0.6% public transportation, 2.0% walk, 1.0% work from home (2000); Travel time to work: 36.7% less than 15 minutes, 23.2% 15 to 30 minutes, 20.5% 30 to 45 minutes, 8.4% 45 to 60 minutes, 11.3% 60 minutes or more (2000)

LAKE (unincorporated postal area, zip code 48632). Covers a land area of 128.395 square miles and a water area of 4.176 square miles. Located at 43.86° N. Lat.; 85.00° W. Long.
History: Lake began in 1877 as a depot on the Pere Marquette Railroad. The first post office here was called Crooked Lake, but the name was later shortened to Lake.
Population: 5,159 (2000); Race: 97.7% White, 0.1% Black, 0.1% Asian, 0.7% American Indian and Alaska Native, 1.2% Hispanic of any race, 1.2% two or more races (2000); Density: 40.2 persons per square mile (2000); Age: 21.4% under 18, 20.1% over 64 (2000); Marriage status: 15.8% never married, 64.3% now married, 7.9% widowed, 12.0% divorced (2000); Foreign born: 1.5% (2000); Ancestry (includes multiple ancestries): 24.2% German, 14.3% English, 12.7% Irish, 9.5% United States or American, 7.1% French (except Basque) (2000).
Economy: Employment by occupation: 9.8% management, 12.4% professional, 16.9% services, 19.6% sales, 1.2% farming, 11.0% construction, 29.1% production (2000).
Income: Per capita income: $16,282 (2000); Median household income: $29,209 (2000); Poverty rate: 11.0% (2000).
Education: High school graduation rate: 75.9% (2000); College graduation rate: 8.0% (2000).
Housing: Homeownership rate: 89.2% (2000); Median home value: $77,400 (2000); Median rent: $336 per month (2000); Median age of housing: 25 years (2000).
Transportation: Commute to work: 93.9% car, 0.4% public transportation, 1.7% walk, 3.7% work from home (2000); Travel time to work: 15.0% less than 15 minutes, 30.4% 15 to 30 minutes, 29.2% 30 to 45 minutes, 13.1% 45 to 60 minutes, 12.3% 60 minutes or more (2000)

LINCOLN (township). Covers a land area of 35.200 square miles and a water area of 0.735 square miles. Located at 43.94° N. Lat.; 84.92° W. Long.
Population: 1,758 (2000); Race: 96.8% White, 1.0% Black, 0.2% Asian, 0.6% American Indian and Alaska Native, 1.8% Hispanic of any race, 1.1% two or more races (2000); Density: 49.9 persons per square mile (2000); Age: 20.6% under 18, 20.9% over 64 (2000); Marriage status: 13.4% never married, 65.0% now married, 9.2% widowed, 12.4% divorced (2000); Foreign born: 2.2% (2000); Ancestry (includes multiple ancestries): 21.3% German, 14.3% English, 13.3% Irish, 9.0% Other groups, 7.0% United States or American (2000).
Economy: Single-family building permits issued: 36 (2001) / 36 (2000); Multi-family building permits issued: 0 (2001) / 0 (2000); Employment by occupation: 11.8% management, 9.0% professional, 18.6% services, 23.8% sales, 0.8% farming, 14.1% construction, 21.8% production (2000).
Income: Per capita income: $18,146 (2000); Median household income: $32,279 (2000); Poverty rate: 11.1% (2000).
Taxes: Total city taxes per capita: $173 (1997); City property taxes per capita: $165 (1997).
Education: High school graduation rate: 78.0% (2000); College graduation rate: 7.8% (2000).
Housing: Homeownership rate: 92.0% (2000); Median home value: $81,500 (2000); Median rent: $375 per month (2000); Median age of housing: 27 years (2000).
Transportation: Commute to work: 95.3% car, 0.7% public transportation, 1.4% walk, 2.6% work from home (2000); Travel time to work: 12.7% less than 15 minutes, 34.9% 15 to 30 minutes, 20.5% 30 to 45 minutes, 9.1% 45 to 60 minutes, 22.8% 60 minutes or more (2000)

REDDING (township). Covers a land area of 35.282 square miles and a water area of 0.041 square miles. Located at 44.03° N. Lat.; 85.03° W. Long.
Population: 526 (2000); Race: 98.1% White, 0.0% Black, 0.4% Asian, 0.0% American Indian and Alaska Native, 0.0% Hispanic of any race, 1.5% two or more races (2000); Density: 14.9 persons per square mile (2000); Age: 22.2% under 18, 14.6% over 64 (2000); Marriage status: 24.1% never married, 57.3% now married, 6.8% widowed, 11.8% divorced (2000); Foreign born: 0.8% (2000); Ancestry (includes multiple ancestries): 21.6% German, 14.0% United States or American, 11.2% Irish, 9.1% English, 7.6% Other groups (2000).
Economy: Employment by occupation: 7.2% management, 10.6% professional, 16.7% services, 15.6% sales, 0.0% farming, 18.9% construction, 31.1% production (2000).
Income: Per capita income: $14,687 (2000); Median household income: $24,438 (2000); Poverty rate: 19.4% (2000).
Taxes: Total city taxes per capita: $66 (1997); City property taxes per capita: $66 (1997).
Education: High school graduation rate: 61.9% (2000); College graduation rate: 3.2% (2000).
Housing: Homeownership rate: 85.3% (2000); Median home value: $49,600 (2000); Median rent: $325 per month (2000); Median age of housing: 24 years (2000).
Transportation: Commute to work: 92.6% car, 1.1% public transportation, 1.7% walk, 1.7% work from home (2000); Travel time to work: 7.6% less than 15 minutes, 26.7% 15 to 30 minutes, 22.7% 30 to 45 minutes, 19.2% 45 to 60 minutes, 23.8% 60 minutes or more (2000)

SHERIDAN (township). Covers a land area of 36.331 square miles and a water area of 0.206 square miles. Located at 43.86° N. Lat.; 84.67° W. Long.
Population: 1,588 (2000); Race: 97.8% White, 0.0% Black, 0.6% Asian, 0.6% American Indian and Alaska Native, 0.3% Hispanic of any race, 0.9% two or more races (2000); Density: 43.7 persons per square mile (2000); Age: 37.1% under 18, 7.9% over 64 (2000); Marriage status: 26.8% never married, 57.6% now married, 5.9% widowed, 9.7% divorced (2000); Foreign born: 0.5% (2000); Ancestry (includes multiple ancestries): 28.4% German, 16.1% United States or American, 7.8% English, 7.3% Irish, 6.8% Other groups (2000).
Economy: Employment by occupation: 15.5% management, 12.2% professional, 12.1% services, 21.1% sales, 7.1% farming, 12.4% construction, 19.6% production (2000).
Income: Per capita income: $12,163 (2000); Median household income: $32,069 (2000); Poverty rate: 22.2% (2000).

Taxes: Total city taxes per capita: $1 (1997); City property taxes per capita: $1 (1997).
Education: High school graduation rate: 69.3% (2000); College graduation rate: 9.3% (2000).
Housing: Homeownership rate: 80.6% (2000); Median home value: $78,500 (2000); Median rent: $296 per month (2000); Median age of housing: 26 years (2000).
Transportation: Commute to work: 78.7% car, 0.0% public transportation, 5.4% walk, 13.6% work from home (2000); Travel time to work: 29.6% less than 15 minutes, 36.4% 15 to 30 minutes, 16.2% 30 to 45 minutes, 9.4% 45 to 60 minutes, 8.4% 60 minutes or more (2000)

SUMMERFIELD (township). Covers a land area of 35.637 square miles and a water area of 0.254 square miles. Located at 44.12° N. Lat.; 84.91° W. Long.
Population: 453 (2000); Race: 98.6% White, 0.0% Black, 0.0% Asian, 0.9% American Indian and Alaska Native, 0.5% Hispanic of any race, 0.5% two or more races (2000); Density: 12.7 persons per square mile (2000); Age: 15.4% under 18, 24.1% over 64 (2000); Marriage status: 13.6% never married, 59.3% now married, 11.2% widowed, 15.9% divorced (2000); Foreign born: 1.6% (2000); Ancestry (includes multiple ancestries): 20.6% German, 17.3% United States or American, 13.3% English, 10.5% Irish, 7.5% Other groups (2000).
Economy: Employment by occupation: 6.7% management, 5.9% professional, 28.9% services, 16.3% sales, 0.0% farming, 14.1% construction, 28.1% production (2000).
Income: Per capita income: $15,912 (2000); Median household income: $21,250 (2000); Poverty rate: 19.3% (2000).
Taxes: Total city taxes per capita: $188 (1997); City property taxes per capita: $186 (1997).
Education: High school graduation rate: 66.9% (2000); College graduation rate: 3.2% (2000).
Housing: Homeownership rate: 89.8% (2000); Median home value: $50,500 (2000); Median rent: $338 per month (2000); Median age of housing: 30 years (2000).
Transportation: Commute to work: 87.1% car, 1.6% public transportation, 3.2% walk, 8.1% work from home (2000); Travel time to work: 17.5% less than 15 minutes, 35.1% 15 to 30 minutes, 21.9% 30 to 45 minutes, 14.9% 45 to 60 minutes, 10.5% 60 minutes or more (2000)

SURREY (township). Covers a land area of 35.270 square miles and a water area of 0.590 square miles. Located at 43.85° N. Lat.; 84.88° W. Long.
History: Surrey was settled in 1866 by the Wilkins family, and was named after Surrey in England.
Population: 3,555 (2000); Race: 97.2% White, 0.5% Black, 0.0% Asian, 1.3% American Indian and Alaska Native, 1.8% Hispanic of any race, 1.0% two or more races (2000); Density: 100.8 persons per square mile (2000); Age: 22.7% under 18, 18.9% over 64 (2000); Marriage status: 21.4% never married, 57.1% now married, 10.3% widowed, 11.3% divorced (2000); Foreign born: 0.5% (2000); Ancestry (includes multiple ancestries): 19.0% German, 12.2% English, 11.3% United States or American, 11.1% Irish, 7.6% French (except Basque) (2000).
Economy: Employment by occupation: 7.5% management, 10.3% professional, 21.3% services, 24.9% sales, 0.5% farming, 11.0% construction, 24.5% production (2000).
Income: Per capita income: $17,027 (2000); Median household income: $28,350 (2000); Poverty rate: 11.0% (2000).
Taxes: Total city taxes per capita: $74 (1997); City property taxes per capita: $73 (1997).
Education: High school graduation rate: 76.9% (2000); College graduation rate: 7.1% (2000).
Housing: Homeownership rate: 82.7% (2000); Median home value: $72,200 (2000); Median rent: $339 per month (2000); Median age of housing: 27 years (2000).
Transportation: Commute to work: 94.8% car, 0.9% public transportation, 1.6% walk, 2.5% work from home (2000); Travel time to work: 39.0% less than 15 minutes, 23.0% 15 to 30 minutes, 25.2% 30 to 45 minutes, 5.1% 45 to 60 minutes, 7.7% 60 minutes or more (2000)

WINTERFIELD (township). Covers a land area of 36.581 square miles and a water area of 0.095 square miles. Located at 44.10° N. Lat.; 85.01° W. Long.
Population: 483 (2000); Race: 98.8% White, 0.0% Black, 0.0% Asian, 1.2% American Indian and Alaska Native, 0.0% Hispanic of any race, 0.0% two or more races (2000); Density: 13.2 persons per square mile (2000); Age: 28.1% under 18, 14.3% over 64 (2000); Marriage status: 22.9% never married, 60.1% now married, 5.4% widowed, 11.6% divorced (2000); Foreign born: 0.0% (2000); Ancestry (includes multiple ancestries): 20.3% English, 18.2% German, 9.6% Dutch, 8.2% French (except Basque), 8.0% Irish (2000).
Economy: Employment by occupation: 9.9% management, 9.3% professional, 16.0% services, 17.3% sales, 1.2% farming, 11.1% construction, 35.2% production (2000).
Income: Per capita income: $14,322 (2000); Median household income: $26,953 (2000); Poverty rate: 22.5% (2000).
Taxes: Total city taxes per capita: $83 (1997); City property taxes per capita: $80 (1997).
Education: High school graduation rate: 74.5% (2000); College graduation rate: 3.6% (2000).
Housing: Homeownership rate: 83.8% (2000); Median home value: $68,000 (2000); Median rent: $342 per month (2000); Median age of housing: 27 years (2000).
Transportation: Commute to work: 96.3% car, 0.0% public transportation, 0.0% walk, 3.8% work from home (2000); Travel time to work: 25.3% less than 15 minutes, 18.8% 15 to 30 minutes, 37.0% 30 to 45 minutes, 5.2% 45 to 60 minutes, 13.6% 60 minutes or more (2000)

Clinton County

Located in south central Michigan; drained by the Maple, Lookingglass, and Grand Rivers. Covers a land area of 571.50 square miles, a water area of 3.10 square miles, and is located in the Eastern Time Zone. The county government was organized in 1831. County seat is St. Johns.

Clinton County is part of the Lansing-East Lansing, MI MSA. The entire metro area includes: Clinton County; Eaton County; Ingham County

Weather Station: Lansing Capital City Airport — Elevation: 839 feet

	Jan	Feb	Mar	Apr	May	Jun	Jul	Aug	Sep	Oct	Nov	Dec
High	29	32	43	57	69	78	82	80	72	60	46	34
Low	14	15	24	35	45	55	59	57	49	39	30	20
Precip	1.6	1.4	2.4	3.1	2.6	3.6	2.7	3.5	3.4	2.4	2.7	2.2
Snow	14.3	10.7	8.8	3.0	tr	tr	0.0	0.0	tr	0.4	4.7	13.0

High and Low temperatures in degrees Fahrenheit; Precipitation and Snow in inches

Weather Station: Saint Johns — Elevation: 741 feet

	Jan	Feb	Mar	Apr	May	Jun	Jul	Aug	Sep	Oct	Nov	Dec
High	30	33	44	58	71	79	84	81	74	61	47	35
Low	14	16	25	35	46	55	60	58	50	40	30	21
Precip	1.7	1.4	2.3	3.2	2.9	3.4	3.0	3.7	3.8	3.0	2.6	1.9
Snow	13.7	9.2	7.1	2.2	tr	0.0	0.0	0.0	0.0	0.2	2.9	10.0

High and Low temperatures in degrees Fahrenheit; Precipitation and Snow in inches

Population: 64,753 (2000); Race: 96.2% White, 0.4% Black, 0.6% Asian, 0.6% American Indian and Alaska Native, 2.8% Hispanic of any race, 1.3% two or more races (2000); Density: 113.3 persons per square mile (2000); Age: 28.1% under 18, 10.8% over 64 (2000).
Religion: Five largest groups: 24.9% Catholic Church, 4.3% The United Methodist Church, 2.4% Lutheran Church—Missouri Synod, 1.6% Christian Churches and Churches of Christ, 0.9% General Association of Regular Baptist Churches (2000).
Economy: Unemployment rate: 3.0% (11/2002); Total civilian labor force: 35,084 (11/2002); Leading industries: 22.3% manufacturing; 16.9% retail trade; 11.3% administration, support, waste management, remediation services (2000); Companies that employ more than 1,000 persons: 0 (2000); Companies that employ more than 100 persons: 16 (2000); Farms: 1,123 totaling 243,850 acres (1997); Minority business ownership rate: 2.3% (1997); Women business ownership rate: 33.6% (1997); Retail sales per capita: $6,779 (1997). Single-family building permits issued: 485 (2001) / 430 (2000); Multi-family building permits issued: 737 (2001) / 250 (2000).
Income: Per capita income: $22,913 (2000); Median household income: $52,806 (2000); Poverty rate: 4.6% (2000); Bankruptcy rate: 2.82% (2001).
Taxes: Total county taxes per capita: $118 (2000); County property taxes per capita: $110 (2000).
Education: High school graduation rate: 89.2% (2000); College graduation rate: 21.2% (2000).
Housing: Homeownership rate: 85.2% (2000); Median home value: $120,500 (2000); Median rent: $436 per month (2000); Median age of housing: 30 years (2000).
Health: Birth rate: 124.2 per 10,000 population (1998); Age adjusted death rate: 87.0 per 10,000 population (1999); Age adjusted cancer mortality rate: 220.5 deaths per 100,000 population (1999). Air Quality Index: 68% good, 32% moderate, 0% unhealthy (percent of days in 2000). Number of

physicians: 4.5 per 10,000 population (1999); Number of hospital beds: 4.3 per 10,000 population (1999).
Elections: 2000 Presidential election results: 41.6% Gore, 56.1% Bush, 1.9% Nader, 0.0% Buchanan
National and State Parks: Maple River State Game Area; Rose Lake State Wildlife Research Area; Sleepy Hollow State Park
Additional Information Contacts
Clinton County Government Offices 989-224-5120

Clinton County Communities

BATH (township). Covers a land area of 36.146 square miles and a water area of 0.512 square miles. Located at 42.80° N. Lat.; 84.42° W. Long. Elevation is 877 feet.
History: Bath Township was named in 1836 by Canadian Ira Cushman after Bath, England.
Population: 7,541 (2000); Race: 94.3% White, 0.3% Black, 1.2% Asian, 0.3% American Indian and Alaska Native, 3.7% Hispanic of any race, 2.6% two or more races (2000); Density: 208.6 persons per square mile (2000); Age: 28.5% under 18, 7.7% over 64 (2000); Marriage status: 22.5% never married, 62.7% now married, 4.1% widowed, 10.7% divorced (2000); Foreign born: 1.9% (2000); Ancestry (includes multiple ancestries): 24.3% German, 15.0% English, 11.7% Irish, 9.9% United States or American, 9.8% Other groups (2000).
Economy: Single-family building permits issued: 81 (2001) / 9 (2000); Multi-family building permits issued: 632 (2001) / 0 (2000); Employment by occupation: 12.0% management, 18.0% professional, 14.8% services, 26.4% sales, 0.6% farming, 10.2% construction, 17.8% production (2000).
Income: Per capita income: $24,675 (2000); Median household income: $53,881 (2000); Poverty rate: 4.5% (2000).
Taxes: Total city taxes per capita: $99 (1997); City property taxes per capita: $96 (1997).
Education: High school graduation rate: 90.2% (2000); College graduation rate: 26.9% (2000).

School District(s)

Bath Community Schools (KG-12)
2000 Enrollment: 991 517-641-6721
Housing: Homeownership rate: 88.5% (2000); Median home value: $123,000 (2000); Median rent: $434 per month (2000); Median age of housing: 24 years (2000).
Transportation: Commute to work: 92.9% car, 0.4% public transportation, 2.7% walk, 3.4% work from home (2000); Travel time to work: 20.0% less than 15 minutes, 54.5% 15 to 30 minutes, 13.3% 30 to 45 minutes, 3.8% 45 to 60 minutes, 8.4% 60 minutes or more (2000)

BENGAL (township). Covers a land area of 36.520 square miles and a water area of 0 square miles. Located at 42.98° N. Lat.; 84.67° W. Long.
Population: 1,174 (2000); Race: 95.0% White, 0.0% Black, 1.3% Asian, 0.8% American Indian and Alaska Native, 3.5% Hispanic of any race, 1.0% two or more races (2000); Density: 32.1 persons per square mile (2000); Age: 34.3% under 18, 8.8% over 64 (2000); Marriage status: 20.7% never married, 71.5% now married, 3.6% widowed, 4.2% divorced (2000); Foreign born: 1.9% (2000); Ancestry (includes multiple ancestries): 49.1% German, 12.1% English, 9.5% Irish, 8.0% United States or American, 4.5% Other groups (2000).
Economy: Employment by occupation: 11.2% management, 11.9% professional, 17.0% services, 25.5% sales, 1.9% farming, 12.6% construction, 19.9% production (2000).
Income: Per capita income: $20,917 (2000); Median household income: $60,673 (2000); Poverty rate: 4.2% (2000).
Taxes: Total city taxes per capita: $67 (1997); City property taxes per capita: $67 (1997).
Education: High school graduation rate: 90.8% (2000); College graduation rate: 11.4% (2000).
Housing: Homeownership rate: 90.7% (2000); Median home value: $125,600 (2000); Median rent: $563 per month (2000); Median age of housing: 53 years (2000).
Transportation: Commute to work: 91.6% car, 0.0% public transportation, 3.3% walk, 4.8% work from home (2000); Travel time to work: 24.5% less than 15 minutes, 28.3% 15 to 30 minutes, 35.9% 30 to 45 minutes, 6.0% 45 to 60 minutes, 5.2% 60 minutes or more (2000)

BINGHAM (township). Covers a land area of 32.344 square miles and a water area of 0.014 square miles. Located at 42.98° N. Lat.; 84.54° W. Long.
History: Bingham Township was named for Governor Kingsley S. Bingham.
Population: 2,776 (2000); Race: 96.8% White, 0.0% Black, 0.2% Asian, 0.7% American Indian and Alaska Native, 3.8% Hispanic of any race, 0.7% two or more races (2000); Density: 85.8 persons per square mile (2000); Age: 25.7% under 18, 17.2% over 64 (2000); Marriage status: 21.5% never married, 57.7% now married, 9.4% widowed, 11.3% divorced (2000); Foreign born: 0.4% (2000); Ancestry (includes multiple ancestries): 42.3% German, 11.4% English, 10.5% Irish, 6.6% Other groups, 5.2% Italian (2000).
Economy: Employment by occupation: 9.4% management, 17.5% professional, 14.2% services, 21.3% sales, 1.7% farming, 12.4% construction, 23.5% production (2000).
Income: Per capita income: $18,047 (2000); Median household income: $52,853 (2000); Poverty rate: 5.5% (2000).
Taxes: Total city taxes per capita: $24 (1997); City property taxes per capita: $24 (1997).
Education: High school graduation rate: 90.2% (2000); College graduation rate: 16.3% (2000).
Housing: Homeownership rate: 91.5% (2000); Median home value: $120,800 (2000); Median rent: $409 per month (2000); Median age of housing: 27 years (2000).
Transportation: Commute to work: 90.7% car, 0.2% public transportation, 2.4% walk, 6.8% work from home (2000); Travel time to work: 32.0% less than 15 minutes, 28.0% 15 to 30 minutes, 27.4% 30 to 45 minutes, 6.0% 45 to 60 minutes, 6.6% 60 minutes or more (2000)

DALLAS (township). Covers a land area of 36.574 square miles and a water area of 0 square miles. Located at 42.99° N. Lat.; 84.76° W. Long.
Population: 2,323 (2000); Race: 99.1% White, 0.2% Black, 0.0% Asian, 0.2% American Indian and Alaska Native, 0.9% Hispanic of any race, 0.4% two or more races (2000); Density: 63.5 persons per square mile (2000); Age: 30.6% under 18, 11.6% over 64 (2000); Marriage status: 27.0% never married, 64.0% now married, 6.0% widowed, 3.0% divorced (2000); Foreign born: 0.2% (2000); Ancestry (includes multiple ancestries): 68.6% German, 6.6% Irish, 6.2% United States or American, 3.9% English, 1.9% Polish (2000).
Economy: Employment by occupation: 13.2% management, 11.9% professional, 13.4% services, 25.7% sales, 3.8% farming, 13.4% construction, 18.6% production (2000).
Income: Per capita income: $18,085 (2000); Median household income: $50,156 (2000); Poverty rate: 3.3% (2000).
Taxes: Total city taxes per capita: $43 (1997); City property taxes per capita: $43 (1997).
Education: High school graduation rate: 84.4% (2000); College graduation rate: 11.3% (2000).
Housing: Homeownership rate: 86.8% (2000); Median home value: $113,600 (2000); Median rent: $350 per month (2000); Median age of housing: 50 years (2000).
Transportation: Commute to work: 89.6% car, 0.2% public transportation, 3.5% walk, 6.1% work from home (2000); Travel time to work: 25.6% less than 15 minutes, 23.9% 15 to 30 minutes, 37.9% 30 to 45 minutes, 8.8% 45 to 60 minutes, 3.7% 60 minutes or more (2000)

DE WITT (city). Covers a land area of 2.865 square miles and a water area of 0.109 square miles. Located at 42.83° N. Lat.; 84.57° W. Long.
Population: 4,702 (2000); Race: 96.7% White, 0.6% Black, 0.0% Asian, 0.0% American Indian and Alaska Native, 2.0% Hispanic of any race, 2.4% two or more races (2000); Density: 1,641.3 persons per square mile (2000); Age: 31.7% under 18, 5.7% over 64 (2000); Marriage status: 21.3% never married, 64.7% now married, 4.1% widowed, 9.9% divorced (2000); Foreign born: 1.4% (2000); Ancestry (includes multiple ancestries): 31.5% German, 13.4% English, 13.3% Irish, 8.6% Other groups, 7.1% Scottish (2000).
Economy: Employment by occupation: 22.3% management, 19.6% professional, 12.5% services, 29.7% sales, 0.0% farming, 6.2% construction, 9.6% production (2000).
Income: Per capita income: $26,997 (2000); Median household income: $69,174 (2000); Poverty rate: 4.3% (2000).
Taxes: Total city taxes per capita: $257 (1997); City property taxes per capita: $244 (1997).
Education: High school graduation rate: 96.4% (2000); College graduation rate: 37.3% (2000).

School District(s)

Dewitt Public Schools (KG-12)
2000 Enrollment: 2,655 517-669-2260
Housing: Homeownership rate: 78.7% (2000); Median home value: $147,300 (2000); Median rent: $487 per month (2000); Median age of housing: 23 years (2000).

Safety: Violent crime rate: 2.1 per 10,000 population; Property crime rate: 65.6 per 10,000 population (2001).
Transportation: Commute to work: 96.2% car, 0.4% public transportation, 0.0% walk, 3.4% work from home (2000); Travel time to work: 21.8% less than 15 minutes, 59.3% 15 to 30 minutes, 13.6% 30 to 45 minutes, 2.6% 45 to 60 minutes, 2.7% 60 minutes or more (2000)

DE WITT (township). Covers a land area of 31.662 square miles and a water area of 0.042 square miles. Located at 42.80° N. Lat.; 84.53° W. Long.
Population: 12,143 (2000); Race: 93.7% White, 0.9% Black, 0.3% Asian, 2.2% American Indian and Alaska Native, 4.4% Hispanic of any race, 1.5% two or more races (2000); Density: 383.5 persons per square mile (2000); Age: 25.5% under 18, 12.7% over 64 (2000); Marriage status: 21.0% never married, 62.8% now married, 5.7% widowed, 10.5% divorced (2000); Foreign born: 1.5% (2000); Ancestry (includes multiple ancestries): 30.6% German, 14.9% English, 14.6% Irish, 9.9% Other groups, 8.3% United States or American (2000).
Economy: In agricultural area. Capital City Airport to Southwest. Employment by occupation: 16.2% management, 19.6% professional, 13.1% services, 29.6% sales, 0.3% farming, 8.3% construction, 12.8% production (2000).
Income: Per capita income: $24,624 (2000); Median household income: $49,782 (2000); Poverty rate: 5.4% (2000).
Education: High school graduation rate: 88.1% (2000); College graduation rate: 24.6% (2000).
Housing: Homeownership rate: 83.5% (2000); Median home value: $125,300 (2000); Median rent: $462 per month (2000); Median age of housing: 27 years (2000).
Safety: Violent crime rate: 22.1 per 10,000 population; Property crime rate: 281.0 per 10,000 population (2001).
Transportation: Commute to work: 95.7% car, 0.2% public transportation, 1.0% walk, 2.9% work from home (2000); Travel time to work: 26.2% less than 15 minutes, 57.8% 15 to 30 minutes, 7.8% 30 to 45 minutes, 3.0% 45 to 60 minutes, 5.1% 60 minutes or more (2000)

DUPLAIN (township). Covers a land area of 35.313 square miles and a water area of 0.104 square miles. Located at 43.08° N. Lat.; 84.42° W. Long.
Population: 2,329 (2000); Race: 97.9% White, 0.0% Black, 0.2% Asian, 0.1% American Indian and Alaska Native, 3.0% Hispanic of any race, 0.2% two or more races (2000); Density: 66.0 persons per square mile (2000); Age: 27.5% under 18, 14.4% over 64 (2000); Marriage status: 18.8% never married, 65.4% now married, 7.4% widowed, 8.4% divorced (2000); Foreign born: 1.0% (2000); Ancestry (includes multiple ancestries): 25.1% German, 16.4% English, 8.2% Irish, 7.3% United States or American, 6.1% Czech (2000).
Economy: Employment by occupation: 10.1% management, 10.9% professional, 14.1% services, 21.7% sales, 4.2% farming, 10.0% construction, 29.0% production (2000).
Income: Per capita income: $16,888 (2000); Median household income: $39,968 (2000); Poverty rate: 7.5% (2000).
Taxes: Total city taxes per capita: $14 (1997); City property taxes per capita: $14 (1997).
Education: High school graduation rate: 84.9% (2000); College graduation rate: 9.4% (2000).
Housing: Homeownership rate: 81.3% (2000); Median home value: $86,900 (2000); Median rent: $380 per month (2000); Median age of housing: 56 years (2000).
Transportation: Commute to work: 91.5% car, 0.0% public transportation, 3.5% walk, 4.9% work from home (2000); Travel time to work: 36.6% less than 15 minutes, 24.6% 15 to 30 minutes, 20.7% 30 to 45 minutes, 11.3% 45 to 60 minutes, 6.7% 60 minutes or more (2000)

EAGLE (village). Covers a land area of 0.123 square miles and a water area of 0 square miles. Located at 42.80° N. Lat.; 84.79° W. Long.
Population: 130 (2000); Race: 100.0% White, 0.0% Black, 0.0% Asian, 0.0% American Indian and Alaska Native, 0.0% Hispanic of any race, 0.0% two or more races (2000); Density: 1,061.2 persons per square mile (2000); Age: 24.8% under 18, 12.9% over 64 (2000); Marriage status: 17.5% never married, 72.5% now married, 5.0% widowed, 5.0% divorced (2000); Foreign born: 0.0% (2000); Ancestry (includes multiple ancestries): 32.7% German, 9.9% United States or American, 6.9% Irish, 5.9% Polish, 5.0% Other groups (2000).
Economy: Employment by occupation: 17.4% management, 6.5% professional, 13.0% services, 19.6% sales, 0.0% farming, 34.8% construction, 8.7% production (2000).
Income: Per capita income: $19,332 (2000); Median household income: $41,667 (2000); Poverty rate: 2.0% (2000).
Taxes: Total city taxes per capita: $64 (1997); City property taxes per capita: $64 (1997).
Education: High school graduation rate: 74.3% (2000); College graduation rate: 2.7% (2000).
Housing: Homeownership rate: 95.5% (2000); Median home value: $86,800 (2000); Median rent: $425 per month (2000); Median age of housing: 60+ years (2000).
Transportation: Commute to work: 95.0% car, 0.0% public transportation, 0.0% walk, 5.0% work from home (2000); Travel time to work: 2.6% less than 15 minutes, 68.4% 15 to 30 minutes, 10.5% 30 to 45 minutes, 0.0% 45 to 60 minutes, 18.4% 60 minutes or more (2000)

EAGLE (township). Covers a land area of 35.082 square miles and a water area of 0.355 square miles. Located at 42.81° N. Lat.; 84.78° W. Long.
Population: 2,332 (2000); Race: 96.6% White, 0.2% Black, 0.4% Asian, 0.1% American Indian and Alaska Native, 3.5% Hispanic of any race, 1.4% two or more races (2000); Density: 66.5 persons per square mile (2000); Age: 24.4% under 18, 12.5% over 64 (2000); Marriage status: 16.5% never married, 72.6% now married, 4.4% widowed, 6.4% divorced (2000); Foreign born: 1.6% (2000); Ancestry (includes multiple ancestries): 37.3% German, 13.4% English, 10.0% Irish, 8.0% Other groups, 6.1% United States or American (2000).
Economy: Employment by occupation: 18.8% management, 20.1% professional, 9.4% services, 21.9% sales, 1.5% farming, 15.8% construction, 12.5% production (2000).
Income: Per capita income: $32,160 (2000); Median household income: $61,129 (2000); Poverty rate: 1.0% (2000).
Taxes: Total city taxes per capita: $49 (1997); City property taxes per capita: $49 (1997).
Education: High school graduation rate: 91.6% (2000); College graduation rate: 24.2% (2000).
Housing: Homeownership rate: 93.5% (2000); Median home value: $142,900 (2000); Median rent: $335 per month (2000); Median age of housing: 28 years (2000).
Transportation: Commute to work: 95.5% car, 0.0% public transportation, 0.9% walk, 3.2% work from home (2000); Travel time to work: 16.3% less than 15 minutes, 52.8% 15 to 30 minutes, 20.0% 30 to 45 minutes, 4.3% 45 to 60 minutes, 6.5% 60 minutes or more (2000)

ELSIE (village). Covers a land area of 1.224 square miles and a water area of 0.008 square miles. Located at 43.08° N. Lat.; 84.39° W. Long. Elevation is 716 feet.
Population: 1,055 (2000); Race: 98.5% White, 0.0% Black, 0.0% Asian, 0.0% American Indian and Alaska Native, 1.9% Hispanic of any race, 0.1% two or more races (2000); Density: 861.9 persons per square mile (2000); Age: 26.3% under 18, 19.0% over 64 (2000); Marriage status: 17.8% never married, 61.0% now married, 9.6% widowed, 11.6% divorced (2000); Foreign born: 0.6% (2000); Ancestry (includes multiple ancestries): 25.5% German, 17.1% English, 9.5% Irish, 8.6% United States or American, 7.4% French (except Basque) (2000).
Economy: In farm area: dairy products; grain, sugar beets. Manufacturing: seat tracks. Employment by occupation: 6.4% management, 11.8% professional, 18.9% services, 20.2% sales, 2.4% farming, 4.9% construction, 35.3% production (2000).
Income: Per capita income: $15,809 (2000); Median household income: $36,635 (2000); Poverty rate: 11.6% (2000).
Taxes: Total city taxes per capita: $221 (1997); City property taxes per capita: $216 (1997).
Education: High school graduation rate: 84.4% (2000); College graduation rate: 8.0% (2000).

School District(s)

Ovid-Elsie Area Schools (KG-12)
2000 Enrollment: 1,772 517-834-2271

Housing: Homeownership rate: 76.6% (2000); Median home value: $77,600 (2000); Median rent: $391 per month (2000); Median age of housing: 60 years (2000).
Safety: Violent crime rate: 9.4 per 10,000 population; Property crime rate: 94.3 per 10,000 population (2001).
Transportation: Commute to work: 92.1% car, 0.0% public transportation, 5.7% walk, 2.3% work from home (2000); Travel time to work: 42.2% less than 15 minutes, 25.1% 15 to 30 minutes, 13.9% 30 to 45 minutes, 11.4% 45 to 60 minutes, 7.4% 60 minutes or more (2000)

ESSEX (township). Covers a land area of 35.591 square miles and a water area of 0 square miles. Located at 43.08° N. Lat.; 84.67° W. Long.
Population: 1,812 (2000); Race: 99.2% White, 0.0% Black, 0.0% Asian, 0.3% American Indian and Alaska Native, 1.8% Hispanic of any race, 0.2% two or more races (2000); Density: 50.9 persons per square mile (2000); Age: 30.5% under 18, 9.5% over 64 (2000); Marriage status: 21.5% never married, 66.1% now married, 4.9% widowed, 7.5% divorced (2000); Foreign born: 0.4% (2000); Ancestry (includes multiple ancestries): 30.1% German, 14.5% English, 9.9% Irish, 9.0% European, 8.4% United States or American (2000).
Economy: Employment by occupation: 11.2% management, 11.9% professional, 16.9% services, 22.9% sales, 3.3% farming, 14.6% construction, 19.1% production (2000).
Income: Per capita income: $18,075 (2000); Median household income: $47,647 (2000); Poverty rate: 5.6% (2000).
Taxes: Total city taxes per capita: $17 (1997); City property taxes per capita: $17 (1997).
Education: High school graduation rate: 88.2% (2000); College graduation rate: 9.2% (2000).
Housing: Homeownership rate: 88.8% (2000); Median home value: $88,800 (2000); Median rent: $402 per month (2000); Median age of housing: 43 years (2000).
Transportation: Commute to work: 90.8% car, 0.0% public transportation, 2.0% walk, 6.4% work from home (2000); Travel time to work: 18.0% less than 15 minutes, 32.3% 15 to 30 minutes, 27.3% 30 to 45 minutes, 12.2% 45 to 60 minutes, 10.2% 60 minutes or more (2000)

FOWLER (village). Covers a land area of 1.295 square miles and a water area of 0 square miles. Located at 43.00° N. Lat.; 84.74° W. Long. Elevation is 743 feet.
Population: 1,136 (2000); Race: 99.0% White, 0.4% Black, 0.0% Asian, 0.1% American Indian and Alaska Native, 0.8% Hispanic of any race, 0.4% two or more races (2000); Density: 877.0 persons per square mile (2000); Age: 28.3% under 18, 15.8% over 64 (2000); Marriage status: 24.6% never married, 64.4% now married, 7.3% widowed, 3.7% divorced (2000); Foreign born: 0.4% (2000); Ancestry (includes multiple ancestries): 63.2% German, 8.2% United States or American, 6.6% Irish, 3.1% English, 2.4% Polish (2000).
Economy: Farm area. Employment by occupation: 14.1% management, 10.3% professional, 14.3% services, 25.4% sales, 3.9% farming, 12.0% construction, 20.0% production (2000).
Income: Per capita income: $18,123 (2000); Median household income: $42,171 (2000); Poverty rate: 4.0% (2000).
Taxes: Total city taxes per capita: $133 (1997); City property taxes per capita: $133 (1997).
Education: High school graduation rate: 81.4% (2000); College graduation rate: 10.5% (2000).

School District(s)

Fowler Public Schools (KG-12)
2000 Enrollment: 507 517-593-2296
Housing: Homeownership rate: 82.8% (2000); Median home value: $105,400 (2000); Median rent: $342 per month (2000); Median age of housing: 42 years (2000).
Transportation: Commute to work: 89.8% car, 0.4% public transportation, 3.1% walk, 5.3% work from home (2000); Travel time to work: 26.1% less than 15 minutes, 24.1% 15 to 30 minutes, 39.6% 30 to 45 minutes, 6.6% 45 to 60 minutes, 3.5% 60 minutes or more (2000)

GREENBUSH (township). Covers a land area of 35.237 square miles and a water area of 0.242 square miles. Located at 43.06° N. Lat.; 84.53° W. Long.
Population: 2,115 (2000); Race: 99.2% White, 0.0% Black, 0.0% Asian, 0.0% American Indian and Alaska Native, 1.5% Hispanic of any race, 0.6% two or more races (2000); Density: 60.0 persons per square mile (2000); Age: 26.5% under 18, 10.9% over 64 (2000); Marriage status: 20.2% never married, 68.1% now married, 5.0% widowed, 6.7% divorced (2000); Foreign born: 0.3% (2000); Ancestry (includes multiple ancestries): 36.4% German, 15.1% English, 9.5% Irish, 9.0% European, 8.9% United States or American (2000).
Economy: Employment by occupation: 8.5% management, 14.0% professional, 10.4% services, 28.3% sales, 2.3% farming, 15.1% construction, 21.5% production (2000).
Income: Per capita income: $21,453 (2000); Median household income: $53,021 (2000); Poverty rate: 3.3% (2000).
Taxes: Total city taxes per capita: $22 (1997); City property taxes per capita: $22 (1997).
Education: High school graduation rate: 87.0% (2000); College graduation rate: 12.3% (2000).
Housing: Homeownership rate: 91.8% (2000); Median home value: $117,600 (2000); Median rent: $407 per month (2000); Median age of housing: 35 years (2000).
Transportation: Commute to work: 93.4% car, 0.8% public transportation, 1.3% walk, 3.5% work from home (2000); Travel time to work: 26.8% less than 15 minutes, 26.8% 15 to 30 minutes, 31.3% 30 to 45 minutes, 10.7% 45 to 60 minutes, 4.5% 60 minutes or more (2000)

LEBANON (township). Covers a land area of 35.398 square miles and a water area of 0.017 square miles. Located at 43.07° N. Lat.; 84.79° W. Long.
Population: 705 (2000); Race: 98.1% White, 0.0% Black, 0.9% Asian, 0.0% American Indian and Alaska Native, 1.2% Hispanic of any race, 1.0% two or more races (2000); Density: 19.9 persons per square mile (2000); Age: 34.6% under 18, 9.2% over 64 (2000); Marriage status: 22.9% never married, 67.5% now married, 3.9% widowed, 5.7% divorced (2000); Foreign born: 0.9% (2000); Ancestry (includes multiple ancestries): 44.4% German, 10.8% Irish, 9.6% English, 7.9% United States or American, 7.3% European (2000).
Economy: Employment by occupation: 14.1% management, 8.6% professional, 10.8% services, 26.0% sales, 3.7% farming, 12.6% construction, 24.2% production (2000).
Income: Per capita income: $16,640 (2000); Median household income: $52,500 (2000); Poverty rate: 7.4% (2000).
Taxes: Total city taxes per capita: $35 (1997); City property taxes per capita: $35 (1997).
Education: High school graduation rate: 82.8% (2000); College graduation rate: 7.5% (2000).
Housing: Homeownership rate: 89.0% (2000); Median home value: $88,300 (2000); Median rent: $375 per month (2000); Median age of housing: 60+ years (2000).
Transportation: Commute to work: 89.5% car, 1.9% public transportation, 0.7% walk, 7.9% work from home (2000); Travel time to work: 17.1% less than 15 minutes, 26.0% 15 to 30 minutes, 29.3% 30 to 45 minutes, 18.7% 45 to 60 minutes, 8.9% 60 minutes or more (2000)

MAPLE RAPIDS (village). Covers a land area of 1.410 square miles and a water area of 0 square miles. Located at 43.10° N. Lat.; 84.69° W. Long.
Population: 643 (2000); Race: 99.0% White, 0.0% Black, 0.0% Asian, 0.8% American Indian and Alaska Native, 0.5% Hispanic of any race, 0.2% two or more races (2000); Density: 456.0 persons per square mile (2000); Age: 29.6% under 18, 11.6% over 64 (2000); Marriage status: 18.7% never married, 61.3% now married, 7.3% widowed, 12.7% divorced (2000); Foreign born: 0.3% (2000); Ancestry (includes multiple ancestries): 30.9% German, 16.2% English, 13.7% European, 8.7% Irish, 8.4% United States or American (2000).
Economy: In farm area. Employment by occupation: 4.2% management, 7.2% professional, 22.4% services, 25.9% sales, 4.2% farming, 16.3% construction, 19.8% production (2000).
Income: Per capita income: $14,190 (2000); Median household income: $33,036 (2000); Poverty rate: 14.6% (2000).
Taxes: Total city taxes per capita: $105 (1997); City property taxes per capita: $104 (1997).
Education: High school graduation rate: 81.9% (2000); College graduation rate: 3.8% (2000).
Housing: Homeownership rate: 84.8% (2000); Median home value: $77,400 (2000); Median rent: $331 per month (2000); Median age of housing: 60+ years (2000).
Transportation: Commute to work: 95.7% car, 0.0% public transportation, 0.8% walk, 2.7% work from home (2000); Travel time to work: 20.5% less than 15 minutes, 35.3% 15 to 30 minutes, 18.1% 30 to 45 minutes, 12.9% 45 to 60 minutes, 13.3% 60 minutes or more (2000)

OLIVE (township). Covers a land area of 35.665 square miles and a water area of 0.124 square miles. Located at 42.89° N. Lat.; 84.53° W. Long.
Population: 2,322 (2000); Race: 94.6% White, 0.9% Black, 2.2% Asian, 0.3% American Indian and Alaska Native, 1.4% Hispanic of any race, 1.4% two or more races (2000); Density: 65.1 persons per square mile (2000); Age: 26.7% under 18, 11.3% over 64 (2000); Marriage status: 18.3% never married, 68.7% now married, 6.4% widowed, 6.7% divorced (2000); Foreign born: 1.9% (2000); Ancestry (includes multiple ancestries): 35.1% German, 20.1% English, 16.2% Irish, 8.3% Other groups, 8.0% Polish (2000).
Economy: Employment by occupation: 14.1% management, 23.0% professional, 10.6% services, 19.9% sales, 2.5% farming, 12.3% construction, 17.6% production (2000).

Income: Per capita income: $23,253 (2000); Median household income: $58,571 (2000); Poverty rate: 4.1% (2000).
Taxes: Total city taxes per capita: $22 (1997); City property taxes per capita: $22 (1997).
Education: High school graduation rate: 88.6% (2000); College graduation rate: 21.2% (2000).
Housing: Homeownership rate: 93.2% (2000); Median home value: $124,100 (2000); Median rent: $441 per month (2000); Median age of housing: 28 years (2000).
Transportation: Commute to work: 93.6% car, 0.0% public transportation, 0.9% walk, 5.3% work from home (2000); Travel time to work: 22.5% less than 15 minutes, 51.8% 15 to 30 minutes, 18.5% 30 to 45 minutes, 2.1% 45 to 60 minutes, 5.0% 60 minutes or more (2000)

OVID (village). Covers a land area of 0.926 square miles and a water area of 0 square miles. Located at 43.00° N. Lat.; 84.37° W. Long. Elevation is 733 feet.
Population: 1,514 (2000); Race: 97.4% White, 0.0% Black, 0.0% Asian, 0.2% American Indian and Alaska Native, 4.9% Hispanic of any race, 1.1% two or more races (2000); Density: 1,634.9 persons per square mile (2000); Age: 27.7% under 18, 10.6% over 64 (2000); Marriage status: 24.4% never married, 55.0% now married, 4.5% widowed, 16.1% divorced (2000); Foreign born: 0.5% (2000); Ancestry (includes multiple ancestries): 25.0% German, 16.4% English, 13.1% Irish, 10.9% Other groups, 8.9% United States or American (2000).
Economy: Employment by occupation: 2.8% management, 11.4% professional, 19.4% services, 27.9% sales, 1.7% farming, 10.4% construction, 26.4% production (2000).
Income: Per capita income: $15,324 (2000); Median household income: $33,333 (2000); Poverty rate: 11.5% (2000).
Taxes: Total city taxes per capita: $246 (1997); City property taxes per capita: $244 (1997).
Education: High school graduation rate: 83.9% (2000); College graduation rate: 11.0% (2000).
Housing: Homeownership rate: 75.1% (2000); Median home value: $80,300 (2000); Median rent: $430 per month (2000); Median age of housing: 60+ years (2000).
Safety: Violent crime rate: 6.6 per 10,000 population; Property crime rate: 164.3 per 10,000 population (2001).
Transportation: Commute to work: 92.1% car, 0.0% public transportation, 3.4% walk, 2.8% work from home (2000); Travel time to work: 25.4% less than 15 minutes, 35.8% 15 to 30 minutes, 24.6% 30 to 45 minutes, 9.2% 45 to 60 minutes, 5.0% 60 minutes or more (2000)

OVID (township). Covers a land area of 35.848 square miles and a water area of 0.113 square miles. Located at 42.99° N. Lat.; 84.40° W. Long. Elevation is 733 feet.
History: Plotted 1857; incorporated 1869.
Population: 3,490 (2000); Race: 98.1% White, 0.1% Black, 0.0% Asian, 0.2% American Indian and Alaska Native, 2.9% Hispanic of any race, 0.8% two or more races (2000); Density: 97.4 persons per square mile (2000); Age: 28.5% under 18, 13.1% over 64 (2000); Marriage status: 22.9% never married, 58.9% now married, 7.6% widowed, 10.6% divorced (2000); Foreign born: 0.6% (2000); Ancestry (includes multiple ancestries): 25.1% German, 15.0% English, 11.1% Other groups, 9.8% Irish, 8.3% United States or American (2000).
Economy: In agricultural area. Manufacturing: metal-forming equipment, dairy products. Employment by occupation: 6.0% management, 15.4% professional, 14.3% services, 28.0% sales, 1.0% farming, 9.2% construction, 26.1% production (2000).
Income: Per capita income: $17,602 (2000); Median household income: $42,250 (2000); Poverty rate: 6.6% (2000).
Taxes: Total city taxes per capita: $17 (1997); City property taxes per capita: $17 (1997).
Education: High school graduation rate: 82.3% (2000); College graduation rate: 9.5% (2000).
Housing: Homeownership rate: 85.1% (2000); Median home value: $88,700 (2000); Median rent: $418 per month (2000); Median age of housing: 52 years (2000).
Transportation: Commute to work: 89.0% car, 0.0% public transportation, 3.4% walk, 5.8% work from home (2000); Travel time to work: 26.4% less than 15 minutes, 33.1% 15 to 30 minutes, 25.4% 30 to 45 minutes, 9.0% 45 to 60 minutes, 6.2% 60 minutes or more (2000)

RILEY (township). Covers a land area of 35.663 square miles and a water area of 0 square miles. Located at 42.90° N. Lat.; 84.67° W. Long. Elevation is 750 feet.
History: Riley Township was organized in 1841, after settlers had come to the area a few years earlier.
Population: 1,767 (2000); Race: 97.4% White, 0.0% Black, 0.2% Asian, 0.2% American Indian and Alaska Native, 1.8% Hispanic of any race, 1.5% two or more races (2000); Density: 49.5 persons per square mile (2000); Age: 29.2% under 18, 8.4% over 64 (2000); Marriage status: 19.4% never married, 71.0% now married, 2.8% widowed, 6.8% divorced (2000); Foreign born: 0.2% (2000); Ancestry (includes multiple ancestries): 46.4% German, 13.2% English, 9.3% Irish, 5.4% Polish, 4.8% United States or American (2000).
Economy: Employment by occupation: 13.8% management, 15.3% professional, 11.6% services, 29.2% sales, 1.5% farming, 12.8% construction, 15.8% production (2000).
Income: Per capita income: $21,682 (2000); Median household income: $61,375 (2000); Poverty rate: 3.7% (2000).
Taxes: Total city taxes per capita: $41 (1997); City property taxes per capita: $41 (1997).
Education: High school graduation rate: 91.7% (2000); College graduation rate: 18.2% (2000).
Housing: Homeownership rate: 94.9% (2000); Median home value: $124,800 (2000); Median rent: $433 per month (2000); Median age of housing: 30 years (2000).
Transportation: Commute to work: 92.7% car, 0.2% public transportation, 1.9% walk, 4.4% work from home (2000); Travel time to work: 12.0% less than 15 minutes, 55.8% 15 to 30 minutes, 26.4% 30 to 45 minutes, 2.4% 45 to 60 minutes, 3.3% 60 minutes or more (2000)

SAINT JOHNS (city). Covers a land area of 3.921 square miles and a water area of 0 square miles. Located at 43.00° N. Lat.; 84.55° W. Long. Elevation is 794 feet.
History: St. Johns was laid out in 1853 by John Swegles, a surveyor for the Detroit & Milwaukee Railroad. The town was named for him, with the "Saint" added by Reverend C.A. Lamb, a Baptist minister. St. Johns was incorporated as a village in 1857 and as a city in 1904.
Population: 7,485 (2000); Race: 96.1% White, 0.2% Black, 1.6% Asian, 0.1% American Indian and Alaska Native, 3.2% Hispanic of any race, 1.0% two or more races (2000); Density: 1,909.1 persons per square mile (2000); Age: 27.3% under 18, 13.7% over 64 (2000); Marriage status: 23.4% never married, 58.4% now married, 7.8% widowed, 10.4% divorced (2000); Foreign born: 1.8% (2000); Ancestry (includes multiple ancestries): 36.8% German, 12.9% English, 11.5% Irish, 8.3% Other groups, 7.6% United States or American (2000).
Economy: Single-family building permits issued: 32 (2001) / 19 (2000); Multi-family building permits issued: 2 (2001) / 36 (2000); Employment by occupation: 11.5% management, 15.7% professional, 16.4% services, 29.9% sales, 0.1% farming, 8.2% construction, 18.2% production (2000).
Income: Per capita income: $21,611 (2000); Median household income: $41,713 (2000); Poverty rate: 6.5% (2000).
Education: High school graduation rate: 88.4% (2000); College graduation rate: 19.9% (2000).

School District(s)

Saint Johns Public Schools (KG-12)
2000 Enrollment: 3,361 517-227-4050

Housing: Homeownership rate: 67.7% (2000); Median home value: $99,500 (2000); Median rent: $447 per month (2000); Median age of housing: 43 years (2000).
Hospitals: Clinton Memorial Hospital (28 beds)
Safety: Violent crime rate: 12.0 per 10,000 population; Property crime rate: 200.7 per 10,000 population (2001).
Newspapers: Saint Johns Reminder (1 x week); Clinton County News (1 x week)
Transportation: Commute to work: 92.4% car, 0.5% public transportation, 2.8% walk, 4.4% work from home (2000); Travel time to work: 45.1% less than 15 minutes, 22.2% 15 to 30 minutes, 27.7% 30 to 45 minutes, 2.0% 45 to 60 minutes, 3.0% 60 minutes or more (2000)

VICTOR (township). Covers a land area of 34.561 square miles and a water area of 1.404 square miles. Located at 42.89° N. Lat.; 84.42° W. Long.
Population: 3,275 (2000); Race: 97.2% White, 1.1% Black, 0.0% Asian, 0.1% American Indian and Alaska Native, 0.6% Hispanic of any race, 1.1% two or more races (2000); Density: 94.8 persons per square mile (2000); Age: 29.1% under 18, 7.1% over 64 (2000); Marriage status: 18.6% never married, 69.7% now married, 3.8% widowed, 8.0% divorced (2000); Foreign born:

0.5% (2000); Ancestry (includes multiple ancestries): 28.5% German, 20.6% English, 14.2% Irish, 11.0% United States or American, 5.9% French (except Basque) (2000).
Economy: Employment by occupation: 13.2% management, 15.7% professional, 12.6% services, 24.3% sales, 0.3% farming, 17.5% construction, 16.4% production (2000).
Income: Per capita income: $24,353 (2000); Median household income: $59,375 (2000); Poverty rate: 2.0% (2000).
Taxes: Total city taxes per capita: $24 (1997); City property taxes per capita: $23 (1997).
Education: High school graduation rate: 91.3% (2000); College graduation rate: 21.9% (2000).
Housing: Homeownership rate: 95.5% (2000); Median home value: $126,100 (2000); Median rent: $471 per month (2000); Median age of housing: 24 years (2000).
Transportation: Commute to work: 94.4% car, 0.2% public transportation, 0.4% walk, 4.9% work from home (2000); Travel time to work: 9.3% less than 15 minutes, 45.4% 15 to 30 minutes, 34.4% 30 to 45 minutes, 4.1% 45 to 60 minutes, 6.8% 60 minutes or more (2000)

WATERTOWN (township). Covers a land area of 35.728 square miles and a water area of 0.050 square miles. Located at 42.80° N. Lat.; 84.65° W. Long.
Population: 4,162 (2000); Race: 97.2% White, 0.3% Black, 0.4% Asian, 0.2% American Indian and Alaska Native, 2.1% Hispanic of any race, 0.9% two or more races (2000); Density: 116.5 persons per square mile (2000); Age: 27.5% under 18, 6.7% over 64 (2000); Marriage status: 21.3% never married, 69.4% now married, 3.2% widowed, 6.0% divorced (2000); Foreign born: 0.8% (2000); Ancestry (includes multiple ancestries): 34.0% German, 13.6% English, 12.3% Irish, 9.3% United States or American, 6.2% Dutch (2000).
Economy: Single-family building permits issued: 31 (2001) / 39 (2000); Multi-family building permits issued: 0 (2001) / 0 (2000); Employment by occupation: 18.2% management, 17.6% professional, 12.2% services, 28.3% sales, 1.5% farming, 8.3% construction, 14.0% production (2000).
Income: Per capita income: $26,631 (2000); Median household income: $67,034 (2000); Poverty rate: 2.2% (2000).
Taxes: Total city taxes per capita: $135 (1997); City property taxes per capita: $131 (1997).
Education: High school graduation rate: 93.4% (2000); College graduation rate: 28.2% (2000).
Housing: Homeownership rate: 94.9% (2000); Median home value: $144,900 (2000); Median rent: $492 per month (2000); Median age of housing: 28 years (2000).
Transportation: Commute to work: 92.2% car, 0.2% public transportation, 2.0% walk, 4.4% work from home (2000); Travel time to work: 20.3% less than 15 minutes, 65.3% 15 to 30 minutes, 9.9% 30 to 45 minutes, 0.7% 45 to 60 minutes, 3.9% 60 minutes or more (2000)

WESTPHALIA (village). Covers a land area of 1.144 square miles and a water area of 0 square miles. Located at 42.92° N. Lat.; 84.79° W. Long. Elevation is 761 feet.
History: Westphalia was settled in 1836 by immigrants from Westphalia, Germany. The site was chosen by a priest, who established a parish for German-speaking Roman Catholics.
Population: 876 (2000); Race: 99.9% White, 0.0% Black, 0.0% Asian, 0.1% American Indian and Alaska Native, 0.0% Hispanic of any race, 0.0% two or more races (2000); Density: 765.7 persons per square mile (2000); Age: 29.4% under 18, 16.6% over 64 (2000); Marriage status: 20.4% never married, 71.3% now married, 5.6% widowed, 2.7% divorced (2000); Foreign born: 0.0% (2000); Ancestry (includes multiple ancestries): 70.1% German, 5.6% Irish, 5.4% United States or American, 3.7% English, 1.7% Dutch (2000).
Economy: Employment by occupation: 12.6% management, 14.6% professional, 13.1% services, 28.8% sales, 2.3% farming, 11.6% construction, 16.9% production (2000).
Income: Per capita income: $20,112 (2000); Median household income: $52,500 (2000); Poverty rate: 4.2% (2000).
Taxes: Total city taxes per capita: $154 (2000); City property taxes per capita: $152 (2000).
Education: High school graduation rate: 85.5% (2000); College graduation rate: 11.6% (2000).
Housing: Homeownership rate: 83.2% (2000); Median home value: $118,800 (2000); Median rent: $339 per month (2000); Median age of housing: 37 years (2000).
Transportation: Commute to work: 93.2% car, 0.0% public transportation, 3.8% walk, 3.0% work from home (2000); Travel time to work: 21.1% less than 15 minutes, 29.9% 15 to 30 minutes, 43.2% 30 to 45 minutes, 1.8% 45 to 60 minutes, 3.9% 60 minutes or more (2000)

WESTPHALIA (township). Covers a land area of 35.525 square miles and a water area of 0.030 square miles. Located at 42.89° N. Lat.; 84.77° W. Long. Elevation is 761 feet.
Population: 2,257 (2000); Race: 99.4% White, 0.0% Black, 0.0% Asian, 0.2% American Indian and Alaska Native, 0.4% Hispanic of any race, 0.2% two or more races (2000); Density: 63.5 persons per square mile (2000); Age: 33.8% under 18, 10.2% over 64 (2000); Marriage status: 24.3% never married, 69.5% now married, 3.3% widowed, 3.0% divorced (2000); Foreign born: 0.9% (2000); Ancestry (includes multiple ancestries): 65.6% German, 7.0% United States or American, 5.4% Irish, 3.9% English, 2.4% Other groups (2000).
Economy: In farm area. Employment by occupation: 17.0% management, 11.8% professional, 11.2% services, 26.4% sales, 1.8% farming, 16.1% construction, 15.6% production (2000).
Income: Per capita income: $19,491 (2000); Median household income: $58,966 (2000); Poverty rate: 2.6% (2000).
Taxes: Total city taxes per capita: $50 (1997); City property taxes per capita: $50 (1997).
Education: High school graduation rate: 87.7% (2000); College graduation rate: 12.7% (2000).
Housing: Homeownership rate: 89.8% (2000); Median home value: $124,900 (2000); Median rent: $342 per month (2000); Median age of housing: 37 years (2000).
Transportation: Commute to work: 91.8% car, 0.2% public transportation, 2.6% walk, 5.3% work from home (2000); Travel time to work: 22.1% less than 15 minutes, 31.8% 15 to 30 minutes, 38.4% 30 to 45 minutes, 4.1% 45 to 60 minutes, 3.7% 60 minutes or more (2000)

Crawford County

Located in north central Michigan; drained by the North, Middle, and South Branches of the Au Sable River; includes part of Huron National Forest. Covers a land area of 558.10 square miles, a water area of 5.30 square miles, and is located in the Eastern Time Zone. The county government was organized in 1818. County seat is Grayling.

Weather Station: Grayling Elevation: 1,138 feet

	Jan	Feb	Mar	Apr	May	Jun	Jul	Aug	Sep	Oct	Nov	Dec
High	25	28	38	53	67	76	80	78	69	56	42	31
Low	7	6	15	28	39	49	53	51	43	34	25	15
Precip	1.7	1.3	2.0	2.7	3.1	3.4	3.8	3.8	4.1	3.5	2.5	1.8
Snow	31.5	19.6	15.1	3.9	0.1	0.0	0.0	0.0	0.0	0.9	11.0	24.4

High and Low temperatures in degrees Fahrenheit; Precipitation and Snow in inches

Population: 14,273 (2000); Race: 96.1% White, 1.6% Black, 0.7% Asian, 0.7% American Indian and Alaska Native, 1.2% Hispanic of any race, 0.7% two or more races (2000); Density: 25.6 persons per square mile (2000); Age: 24.4% under 18, 16.6% over 64 (2000).
Religion: Five largest groups: 10.1% Catholic Church, 3.4% The United Methodist Church, 2.4% Lutheran Church—Missouri Synod, 1.3% The Church of Jesus Christ of Latter-day Saints, 1.1% Evangelical Lutheran Church in America (2000).
Economy: Unemployment rate: 6.9% (11/2002); Total civilian labor force: 5,341 (11/2002); Leading industries: 25.2% health care and social assistance; 19.2% retail trade; 15.3% accommodation & food services (2000); Companies that employ more than 1,000 persons: 0 (2000); Companies that employ more than 100 persons: 5 (2000); Farms: 27 totaling 2,568 acres (1997); Minority business ownership rate: 0.0% (1997); Women business ownership rate: 19.6% (1997); Retail sales per capita: $8,340 (1997). Single-family building permits issued: 87 (2001) / 100 (2000); Multi-family building permits issued: 0 (2001) / 0 (2000).
Income: Per capita income: $16,903 (2000); Median household income: $33,364 (2000); Poverty rate: 12.7% (2000); Bankruptcy rate: 3.86% (2001).
Taxes: Total county taxes per capita: $219 (1997); County property taxes per capita: $208 (1997).
Education: High school graduation rate: 80.8% (2000); College graduation rate: 12.9% (2000).
Housing: Homeownership rate: 82.8% (2000); Median home value: $79,500 (2000); Median rent: $372 per month (2000); Median age of housing: 27 years (2000).

Health: Birth rate: 98.8 per 10,000 population (1998); Age adjusted death rate: 88.4 per 10,000 population (1999); Age adjusted cancer mortality rate: 200.8 deaths per 100,000 population (1999). Number of physicians: 11.9 per 10,000 population (1999); Number of hospital beds: 51.8 per 10,000 population (1999).
Elections: 2000 Presidential election results: 43.8% Gore, 52.6% Bush, 2.8% Nader, 0.4% Buchanan
National and State Parks: Au Sable State Forest; Hanson State Game Refuge; Hartwick Pines State Park; Higgins Lake State Forest
Additional Information Contacts
Crawford County Government Offices 989-348-2841
Grayling Chamber of Commerce 989-348-2921

Crawford County Communities

BEAVER CREEK (township). Covers a land area of 71.416 square miles and a water area of 0.081 square miles. Located at 44.54° N. Lat.; 84.73° W. Long.
Population: 1,486 (2000); Race: 96.4% White, 0.3% Black, 0.7% Asian, 0.9% American Indian and Alaska Native, 0.9% Hispanic of any race, 1.4% two or more races (2000); Density: 20.8 persons per square mile (2000); Age: 22.5% under 18, 15.1% over 64 (2000); Marriage status: 18.3% never married, 65.7% now married, 5.4% widowed, 10.6% divorced (2000); Foreign born: 2.9% (2000); Ancestry (includes multiple ancestries): 28.3% German, 13.5% Irish, 11.3% English, 7.9% Polish, 7.4% United States or American (2000).
Economy: Employment by occupation: 11.4% management, 11.3% professional, 20.0% services, 24.9% sales, 0.7% farming, 13.0% construction, 18.7% production (2000).
Income: Per capita income: $18,388 (2000); Median household income: $36,613 (2000); Poverty rate: 9.7% (2000).
Taxes: Total city taxes per capita: $43 (1997); City property taxes per capita: $43 (1997).
Education: High school graduation rate: 75.1% (2000); College graduation rate: 10.0% (2000).
Housing: Homeownership rate: 90.1% (2000); Median home value: $68,600 (2000); Median rent: $358 per month (2000); Median age of housing: 26 years (2000).
Transportation: Commute to work: 97.1% car, 0.6% public transportation, 0.0% walk, 1.8% work from home (2000); Travel time to work: 39.7% less than 15 minutes, 40.9% 15 to 30 minutes, 11.2% 30 to 45 minutes, 0.3% 45 to 60 minutes, 7.8% 60 minutes or more (2000)

FREDERIC (township). Covers a land area of 71.988 square miles and a water area of 0.148 square miles. Located at 44.76° N. Lat.; 84.77° W. Long. Elevation is 1,205 feet.
Population: 1,401 (2000); Race: 98.2% White, 0.0% Black, 0.1% Asian, 0.9% American Indian and Alaska Native, 0.0% Hispanic of any race, 0.9% two or more races (2000); Density: 19.5 persons per square mile (2000); Age: 25.1% under 18, 16.6% over 64 (2000); Marriage status: 22.0% never married, 56.1% now married, 9.1% widowed, 12.8% divorced (2000); Foreign born: 1.2% (2000); Ancestry (includes multiple ancestries): 23.6% German, 12.8% Irish, 11.7% English, 8.0% French (except Basque), 7.3% United States or American (2000).
Economy: Employment by occupation: 8.9% management, 11.3% professional, 22.7% services, 23.4% sales, 1.6% farming, 12.2% construction, 19.9% production (2000).
Income: Per capita income: $15,273 (2000); Median household income: $31,923 (2000); Poverty rate: 12.1% (2000).
Taxes: Total city taxes per capita: $106 (1997); City property taxes per capita: $106 (1997).
Education: High school graduation rate: 76.0% (2000); College graduation rate: 11.4% (2000).
Housing: Homeownership rate: 85.6% (2000); Median home value: $71,200 (2000); Median rent: $375 per month (2000); Median age of housing: 26 years (2000).
Transportation: Commute to work: 91.4% car, 2.7% public transportation, 2.7% walk, 2.7% work from home (2000); Travel time to work: 28.5% less than 15 minutes, 41.5% 15 to 30 minutes, 20.0% 30 to 45 minutes, 4.8% 45 to 60 minutes, 5.2% 60 minutes or more (2000)

GRAYLING (city). Covers a land area of 2.008 square miles and a water area of 0 square miles. Located at 44.66° N. Lat.; 84.71° W. Long. Elevation is 1,137 feet.
History: Grayling was named for the Michigan grayling fish, until 1884 a popular game fish in the Au Sable River. The grayling disappeared in the 1880's, and brook trout were planted in the Au Sable River.
Population: 1,952 (2000); Race: 94.4% White, 0.7% Black, 2.1% Asian, 1.0% American Indian and Alaska Native, 2.6% Hispanic of any race, 1.6% two or more races (2000); Density: 972.1 persons per square mile (2000); Age: 28.2% under 18, 20.1% over 64 (2000); Marriage status: 23.5% never married, 45.7% now married, 14.3% widowed, 16.5% divorced (2000); Foreign born: 1.0% (2000); Ancestry (includes multiple ancestries): 20.8% German, 12.6% English, 11.6% Irish, 8.2% Other groups, 6.9% United States or American (2000).
Economy: Employment by occupation: 8.2% management, 13.7% professional, 28.2% services, 26.7% sales, 0.5% farming, 7.2% construction, 15.4% production (2000).
Income: Per capita income: $13,089 (2000); Median household income: $24,250 (2000); Poverty rate: 21.8% (2000).
Taxes: Total city taxes per capita: $438 (1997); City property taxes per capita: $435 (1997).
Education: High school graduation rate: 78.5% (2000); College graduation rate: 12.1% (2000).

School District(s)

Crawford Ausable Schools (KG-12)
2000 Enrollment: 2,168 517-348-7641
Housing: Homeownership rate: 55.0% (2000); Median home value: $62,400 (2000); Median rent: $310 per month (2000); Median age of housing: 44 years (2000).
Hospitals: Mercy Hospital (130 beds)
Safety: Violent crime rate: 35.7 per 10,000 population; Property crime rate: 504.6 per 10,000 population (2001).
Newspapers: Crawford County Avalanche (1 x week)
Transportation: Commute to work: 85.3% car, 0.0% public transportation, 7.6% walk, 6.4% work from home (2000); Travel time to work: 74.0% less than 15 minutes, 10.4% 15 to 30 minutes, 9.9% 30 to 45 minutes, 1.9% 45 to 60 minutes, 3.9% 60 minutes or more (2000)
Additional Information Contacts
Grayling Chamber of Commerce 989-348-2921

GRAYLING (township). Covers a land area of 171.079 square miles and a water area of 3.725 square miles. Located at 44.67° N. Lat.; 84.64° W. Long. Elevation is 1,137 feet.
History: Incorporated as village 1903, as city 1934.
Population: 6,516 (2000); Race: 94.9% White, 3.2% Black, 0.7% Asian, 0.5% American Indian and Alaska Native, 1.3% Hispanic of any race, 0.4% two or more races (2000); Density: 38.1 persons per square mile (2000); Age: 24.9% under 18, 14.7% over 64 (2000); Marriage status: 18.9% never married, 64.4% now married, 5.6% widowed, 11.0% divorced (2000); Foreign born: 0.7% (2000); Ancestry (includes multiple ancestries): 26.5% German, 13.3% English, 12.6% Irish, 8.5% Polish, 8.2% Other groups (2000).
Economy: Resort area (winter-sports and canoeing center); timber and farm area; lumber milling. A National Guard training camp, camp Grayling, to West; state fish hatchery to North. Sky ski area to South; Huron National Forest to Southeast. Single-family building permits issued: 45 (2001) / 43 (2000); Multi-family building permits issued: 0 (2001) / 0 (2000); Employment by occupation: 7.3% management, 18.8% professional, 21.0% services, 24.9% sales, 1.1% farming, 11.0% construction, 15.9% production (2000).
Income: Per capita income: $17,355 (2000); Median household income: $34,690 (2000); Poverty rate: 11.7% (2000).
Taxes: Total city taxes per capita: $27 (1997); City property taxes per capita: $20 (1997).
Education: High school graduation rate: 86.1% (2000); College graduation rate: 14.7% (2000).
Housing: Homeownership rate: 84.7% (2000); Median home value: $86,500 (2000); Median rent: $430 per month (2000); Median age of housing: 26 years (2000).
Transportation: Commute to work: 95.6% car, 0.1% public transportation, 0.9% walk, 3.0% work from home (2000); Travel time to work: 56.0% less than 15 minutes, 21.4% 15 to 30 minutes, 12.7% 30 to 45 minutes, 4.4% 45 to 60 minutes, 5.5% 60 minutes or more (2000)

LOVELLS (township). Covers a land area of 100.995 square miles and a water area of 0.763 square miles. Located at 44.78° N. Lat.; 84.45° W. Long. Elevation is 1,162 feet.
Population: 578 (2000); Race: 98.4% White, 0.2% Black, 1.5% Asian, 0.0% American Indian and Alaska Native, 0.2% Hispanic of any race, 0.0% two or

more races (2000); Density: 5.7 persons per square mile (2000); Age: 17.1% under 18, 29.2% over 64 (2000); Marriage status: 13.9% never married, 65.6% now married, 9.1% widowed, 11.4% divorced (2000); Foreign born: 2.4% (2000); Ancestry (includes multiple ancestries): 23.2% German, 20.7% English, 11.6% French (except Basque), 9.8% Irish, 7.1% Polish (2000).
Economy: Employment by occupation: 10.7% management, 16.1% professional, 15.5% services, 32.1% sales, 1.2% farming, 10.1% construction, 14.3% production (2000).
Income: Per capita income: $21,401 (2000); Median household income: $31,023 (2000); Poverty rate: 7.6% (2000).
Taxes: Total city taxes per capita: $222 (1997); City property taxes per capita: $222 (1997).
Education: High school graduation rate: 80.0% (2000); College graduation rate: 11.8% (2000).
Housing: Homeownership rate: 94.0% (2000); Median home value: $75,800 (2000); Median rent: $400 per month (2000); Median age of housing: 28 years (2000).
Transportation: Commute to work: 89.8% car, 0.0% public transportation, 1.8% walk, 8.4% work from home (2000); Travel time to work: 21.7% less than 15 minutes, 25.0% 15 to 30 minutes, 33.6% 30 to 45 minutes, 6.6% 45 to 60 minutes, 13.2% 60 minutes or more (2000)

MAPLE FOREST (township). Covers a land area of 35.261 square miles and a water area of 0.281 square miles. Located at 44.82° N. Lat.; 84.67° W. Long.
Population: 498 (2000); Race: 96.2% White, 0.0% Black, 0.4% Asian, 2.1% American Indian and Alaska Native, 0.8% Hispanic of any race, 1.3% two or more races (2000); Density: 14.1 persons per square mile (2000); Age: 21.1% under 18, 15.0% over 64 (2000); Marriage status: 16.6% never married, 69.7% now married, 5.3% widowed, 8.5% divorced (2000); Foreign born: 1.1% (2000); Ancestry (includes multiple ancestries): 29.1% German, 12.8% United States or American, 10.7% Irish, 9.9% English, 7.0% Polish (2000).
Economy: Employment by occupation: 9.2% management, 10.5% professional, 21.0% services, 25.6% sales, 0.8% farming, 18.1% construction, 14.7% production (2000).
Income: Per capita income: $21,507 (2000); Median household income: $38,235 (2000); Poverty rate: 7.6% (2000).
Taxes: Total city taxes per capita: $72 (1997); City property taxes per capita: $72 (1997).
Education: High school graduation rate: 70.0% (2000); College graduation rate: 11.5% (2000).
Housing: Homeownership rate: 92.3% (2000); Median home value: $93,800 (2000); Median rent: $325 per month (2000); Median age of housing: 22 years (2000).
Transportation: Commute to work: 91.4% car, 0.0% public transportation, 0.9% walk, 7.8% work from home (2000); Travel time to work: 23.8% less than 15 minutes, 55.1% 15 to 30 minutes, 10.3% 30 to 45 minutes, 6.1% 45 to 60 minutes, 4.7% 60 minutes or more (2000)

SOUTH BRANCH (township). Covers a land area of 105.375 square miles and a water area of 0.252 square miles. Located at 44.57° N. Lat.; 84.50° W. Long.
Population: 1,842 (2000); Race: 99.7% White, 0.0% Black, 0.0% Asian, 0.1% American Indian and Alaska Native, 0.7% Hispanic of any race, 0.2% two or more races (2000); Density: 17.5 persons per square mile (2000); Age: 22.7% under 18, 17.2% over 64 (2000); Marriage status: 16.0% never married, 68.2% now married, 7.4% widowed, 8.4% divorced (2000); Foreign born: 2.1% (2000); Ancestry (includes multiple ancestries): 20.3% German, 15.4% English, 13.7% Irish, 9.6% French (except Basque), 9.5% Polish (2000).
Economy: Employment by occupation: 6.6% management, 19.7% professional, 14.2% services, 20.6% sales, 0.8% farming, 13.2% construction, 24.9% production (2000).
Income: Per capita income: $16,763 (2000); Median household income: $34,537 (2000); Poverty rate: 12.5% (2000).
Taxes: Total city taxes per capita: $117 (1997); City property taxes per capita: $117 (1997).
Education: High school graduation rate: 76.9% (2000); College graduation rate: 12.1% (2000).
Housing: Homeownership rate: 93.3% (2000); Median home value: $84,500 (2000); Median rent: $325 per month (2000); Median age of housing: 26 years (2000).
Transportation: Commute to work: 96.4% car, 0.7% public transportation, 0.0% walk, 2.4% work from home (2000); Travel time to work: 38.3% less than 15 minutes, 30.5% 15 to 30 minutes, 15.6% 30 to 45 minutes, 8.3% 45 to 60 minutes, 7.3% 60 minutes or more (2000)

Delta County

Located in northwestern Michigan, on the Upper Peninsula; bounded on the south by Lake Michigan; drained by the Ford, Escanaba, Whitefish, and Days Rivers; includes part of Hiawatha National Forest. Covers a land area of 1,170.00 square miles, a water area of 821.60 square miles, and is located in the Eastern Time Zone. The county government was organized in 1843. County seat is Escanaba.

Weather Station: Fayette 4 SW — Elevation: 744 feet

	Jan	Feb	Mar	Apr	May	Jun	Jul	Aug	Sep	Oct	Nov	Dec
High	24	27	36	48	61	70	75	74	66	55	41	30
Low	10	12	21	31	41	51	58	58	51	41	30	18
Precip	1.5	1.0	2.1	2.3	2.8	2.6	2.9	3.5	3.3	2.8	2.4	1.8
Snow	15.7	9.8	9.6	2.6	tr	0.0	0.0	0.0	0.0	0.2	na	13.5

High and Low temperatures in degrees Fahrenheit; Precipitation and Snow in inches

Population: 38,520 (2000); Race: 95.5% White, 0.1% Black, 0.3% Asian, 2.7% American Indian and Alaska Native, 0.4% Hispanic of any race, 1.3% two or more races (2000); Density: 32.9 persons per square mile (2000); Age: 23.8% under 18, 17.1% over 64 (2000).
Religion: Five largest groups: 53.3% Catholic Church, 11.2% Evangelical Lutheran Church in America, 3.0% The United Methodist Church, 1.6% Wisconsin Evangelical Lutheran Synod, 1.5% Baptist General Conference (2000).
Economy: Unemployment rate: 6.0% (11/2002); Total civilian labor force: 19,603 (11/2002); Leading industries: 20.7% manufacturing; 18.6% retail trade; 12.5% health care and social assistance (2000); Companies that employ more than 1,000 persons: 1 (2000); Companies that employ more than 100 persons: 16 (2000); Farms: 253 totaling 70,232 acres (1997); Minority business ownership rate: 0.0% (1997); Women business ownership rate: 26.1% (1997); Retail sales per capita: $9,766 (1997). Single-family building permits issued: 181 (2001) / 180 (2000); Multi-family building permits issued: 88 (2001) / 57 (2000).
Income: Per capita income: $18,667 (2000); Median household income: $35,511 (2000); Poverty rate: 9.5% (2000); Bankruptcy rate: 2.64% (2001).
Taxes: Total county taxes per capita: $110 (1997); County property taxes per capita: $108 (1997).
Education: High school graduation rate: 86.1% (2000); College graduation rate: 17.1% (2000).
Housing: Homeownership rate: 79.6% (2000); Median home value: $80,000 (2000); Median rent: $323 per month (2000); Median age of housing: 39 years (2000).
Health: Birth rate: 112.9 per 10,000 population (1998); Age adjusted death rate: 83.3 per 10,000 population (1999); Age adjusted cancer mortality rate: 212.6 deaths per 100,000 population (1999). Air Quality Index: 100% good, 0% moderate, 0% unhealthy (percent of days in 2000). Number of physicians: 12.7 per 10,000 population (1999); Number of hospital beds: 17.1 per 10,000 population (1999).
Elections: 2000 Presidential election results: 46.0% Gore, 51.2% Bush, 2.3% Nader, 0.1% Buchanan
National and State Parks: Hiawatha National Forest; Manistique River State Forest
Additional Information Contacts
Delta County Government Offices 906-789-5100
Bays De Noc Convention Bureau 906-789-7862
Escanaba Chamber of Commerce 906-786-2192

Delta County Communities

BALDWIN (township). Covers a land area of 83.771 square miles and a water area of 0.426 square miles. Located at 45.97° N. Lat.; 87.10° W. Long.
History: Baldwin Township was named in 1873 for C.S. Baldwin, a railroad superintendent.
Population: 748 (2000); Race: 95.5% White, 0.0% Black, 0.4% Asian, 1.2% American Indian and Alaska Native, 0.6% Hispanic of any race, 2.3% two or more races (2000); Density: 8.9 persons per square mile (2000); Age: 22.0% under 18, 14.0% over 64 (2000); Marriage status: 20.9% never married, 65.7% now married, 8.1% widowed, 5.3% divorced (2000); Foreign born: 0.3% (2000); Ancestry (includes multiple ancestries): 20.0% French (except Basque), 19.6% German, 14.8% Swedish, 11.2% Irish, 8.5% Finnish (2000).
Economy: Employment by occupation: 8.2% management, 13.2% professional, 15.0% services, 22.6% sales, 2.2% farming, 12.9% construction, 26.0% production (2000).
Income: Per capita income: $17,532 (2000); Median household income: $35,917 (2000); Poverty rate: 3.9% (2000).

Taxes: Total city taxes per capita: $104 (1997); City property taxes per capita: $104 (1997).
Education: High school graduation rate: 83.3% (2000); College graduation rate: 8.1% (2000).
Housing: Homeownership rate: 95.0% (2000); Median home value: $64,000 (2000); Median rent: $288 per month (2000); Median age of housing: 27 years (2000).
Transportation: Commute to work: 86.0% car, 2.6% public transportation, 2.6% walk, 6.5% work from home (2000); Travel time to work: 10.1% less than 15 minutes, 41.3% 15 to 30 minutes, 29.5% 30 to 45 minutes, 2.1% 45 to 60 minutes, 17.0% 60 minutes or more (2000)

BARK RIVER (township). Covers a land area of 45.587 square miles and a water area of 0.057 square miles. Located at 45.72° N. Lat.; 87.29° W. Long. Elevation is 744 feet.
History: Bark River was named by railway engineers for the quantities of birch bark floating in the river. The village of Bark River was established in 1871 as a station on the Chicago & Northwestern Railway.
Population: 1,650 (2000); Race: 94.4% White, 0.1% Black, 0.6% Asian, 2.8% American Indian and Alaska Native, 0.2% Hispanic of any race, 1.5% two or more races (2000); Density: 36.2 persons per square mile (2000); Age: 27.0% under 18, 10.0% over 64 (2000); Marriage status: 23.5% never married, 66.4% now married, 4.2% widowed, 6.0% divorced (2000); Foreign born: 1.2% (2000); Ancestry (includes multiple ancestries): 26.2% German, 20.1% French (except Basque), 14.3% Swedish, 12.5% Polish, 11.6% French Canadian (2000).
Economy: Employment by occupation: 11.9% management, 13.9% professional, 15.3% services, 23.1% sales, 2.4% farming, 9.9% construction, 23.4% production (2000).
Income: Per capita income: $16,649 (2000); Median household income: $41,477 (2000); Poverty rate: 5.8% (2000).
Taxes: Total city taxes per capita: $21 (1997); City property taxes per capita: $21 (1997).
Education: High school graduation rate: 87.1% (2000); College graduation rate: 13.3% (2000).
Housing: Homeownership rate: 87.4% (2000); Median home value: $71,400 (2000); Median rent: $311 per month (2000); Median age of housing: 35 years (2000).
Transportation: Commute to work: 95.0% car, 0.0% public transportation, 2.6% walk, 2.4% work from home (2000); Travel time to work: 30.7% less than 15 minutes, 55.3% 15 to 30 minutes, 7.6% 30 to 45 minutes, 1.8% 45 to 60 minutes, 4.7% 60 minutes or more (2000)

BAY DE NOC (township). Covers a land area of 67.484 square miles and a water area of 23.573 square miles. Located at 45.77° N. Lat.; 86.92° W. Long.
History: Bay de Noc Township was named for the Noquet Indians who once owned the land.
Population: 329 (2000); Race: 99.7% White, 0.0% Black, 0.0% Asian, 0.0% American Indian and Alaska Native, 0.3% Hispanic of any race, 0.3% two or more races (2000); Density: 4.9 persons per square mile (2000); Age: 13.7% under 18, 22.8% over 64 (2000); Marriage status: 13.4% never married, 71.0% now married, 6.4% widowed, 9.1% divorced (2000); Foreign born: 0.5% (2000); Ancestry (includes multiple ancestries): 22.0% Swedish, 20.6% German, 13.1% French (except Basque), 11.8% Norwegian, 8.6% English (2000).
Economy: Employment by occupation: 5.6% management, 19.4% professional, 18.8% services, 19.4% sales, 0.7% farming, 16.0% construction, 20.1% production (2000).
Income: Per capita income: $24,472 (2000); Median household income: $33,571 (2000); Poverty rate: 7.0% (2000).
Taxes: Total city taxes per capita: $79 (1997); City property taxes per capita: $79 (1997).
Education: High school graduation rate: 85.9% (2000); College graduation rate: 17.7% (2000).
Housing: Homeownership rate: 96.3% (2000); Median home value: $130,200 (2000); Median age of housing: 35 years (2000).
Transportation: Commute to work: 91.0% car, 1.4% public transportation, 1.4% walk, 6.3% work from home (2000); Travel time to work: 11.1% less than 15 minutes, 6.7% 15 to 30 minutes, 51.1% 30 to 45 minutes, 24.4% 45 to 60 minutes, 6.7% 60 minutes or more (2000)

BRAMPTON (township). Covers a land area of 23.715 square miles and a water area of 1.876 square miles. Located at 45.90° N. Lat.; 87.04° W. Long.
History: Promoters for the Chicago & Northwestern Railroad, trying to interest investors in the area, named it Brampton after the city in England.
Population: 1,090 (2000); Race: 97.1% White, 0.0% Black, 0.6% Asian, 1.6% American Indian and Alaska Native, 0.2% Hispanic of any race, 0.8% two or more races (2000); Density: 46.0 persons per square mile (2000); Age: 22.4% under 18, 13.4% over 64 (2000); Marriage status: 18.3% never married, 68.3% now married, 6.2% widowed, 7.1% divorced (2000); Foreign born: 0.6% (2000); Ancestry (includes multiple ancestries): 18.1% German, 16.0% French (except Basque), 15.9% Swedish, 8.9% United States or American, 8.1% English (2000).
Economy: Employment by occupation: 8.6% management, 20.3% professional, 16.6% services, 27.0% sales, 1.1% farming, 9.4% construction, 17.0% production (2000).
Income: Per capita income: $18,893 (2000); Median household income: $45,441 (2000); Poverty rate: 6.3% (2000).
Taxes: Total city taxes per capita: $18 (1997); City property taxes per capita: $18 (1997).
Education: High school graduation rate: 85.2% (2000); College graduation rate: 17.2% (2000).
Housing: Homeownership rate: 92.6% (2000); Median home value: $95,000 (2000); Median rent: $342 per month (2000); Median age of housing: 26 years (2000).
Transportation: Commute to work: 92.5% car, 0.8% public transportation, 0.4% walk, 4.5% work from home (2000); Travel time to work: 32.2% less than 15 minutes, 54.0% 15 to 30 minutes, 7.8% 30 to 45 minutes, 1.8% 45 to 60 minutes, 4.1% 60 minutes or more (2000)

CORNELL (township). Covers a land area of 59.763 square miles and a water area of 0.426 square miles. Located at 45.90° N. Lat.; 87.27° W. Long. Elevation is 817 feet.
History: The township and village of Cornell were named for Cornell University, the alma mater of one of the town's founder, George H. Mashek.
Population: 557 (2000); Race: 99.3% White, 0.0% Black, 0.7% Asian, 0.0% American Indian and Alaska Native, 2.5% Hispanic of any race, 0.0% two or more races (2000); Density: 9.3 persons per square mile (2000); Age: 21.8% under 18, 16.7% over 64 (2000); Marriage status: 15.6% never married, 72.6% now married, 3.1% widowed, 8.8% divorced (2000); Foreign born: 1.6% (2000); Ancestry (includes multiple ancestries): 20.5% German, 15.4% Swedish, 12.9% French (except Basque), 12.0% Finnish, 9.6% French Canadian (2000).
Economy: Employment by occupation: 7.9% management, 8.3% professional, 18.9% services, 17.7% sales, 6.0% farming, 17.0% construction, 24.2% production (2000).
Income: Per capita income: $18,334 (2000); Median household income: $41,528 (2000); Poverty rate: 5.9% (2000).
Taxes: Total city taxes per capita: $23 (1997); City property taxes per capita: $23 (1997).
Education: High school graduation rate: 81.3% (2000); College graduation rate: 9.0% (2000).
Housing: Homeownership rate: 94.2% (2000); Median home value: $84,500 (2000); Median age of housing: 29 years (2000).
Transportation: Commute to work: 93.5% car, 0.0% public transportation, 1.2% walk, 4.6% work from home (2000); Travel time to work: 8.9% less than 15 minutes, 60.1% 15 to 30 minutes, 25.4% 30 to 45 minutes, 0.0% 45 to 60 minutes, 5.6% 60 minutes or more (2000)

ENSIGN (township). Covers a land area of 58.968 square miles and a water area of 6.819 square miles. Located at 45.87° N. Lat.; 86.89° W. Long. Elevation is 711 feet.
Population: 780 (2000); Race: 97.0% White, 0.0% Black, 0.0% Asian, 1.9% American Indian and Alaska Native, 0.0% Hispanic of any race, 1.0% two or more races (2000); Density: 13.2 persons per square mile (2000); Age: 21.6% under 18, 19.3% over 64 (2000); Marriage status: 17.6% never married, 68.9% now married, 4.8% widowed, 8.7% divorced (2000); Foreign born: 0.0% (2000); Ancestry (includes multiple ancestries): 25.0% Swedish, 19.0% German, 13.7% French (except Basque), 12.2% English, 11.5% Irish (2000).
Economy: Employment by occupation: 10.1% management, 17.9% professional, 9.8% services, 19.7% sales, 3.2% farming, 14.5% construction, 24.9% production (2000).
Income: Per capita income: $25,546 (2000); Median household income: $39,375 (2000); Poverty rate: 4.1% (2000).
Taxes: Total city taxes per capita: $42 (1997); City property taxes per capita: $42 (1997).
Education: High school graduation rate: 83.0% (2000); College graduation rate: 22.0% (2000).

Housing: Homeownership rate: 95.2% (2000); Median home value: $107,100 (2000); Median rent: $350 per month (2000); Median age of housing: 27 years (2000).
Transportation: Commute to work: 95.3% car, 0.0% public transportation, 1.2% walk, 2.1% work from home (2000); Travel time to work: 17.9% less than 15 minutes, 35.8% 15 to 30 minutes, 29.1% 30 to 45 minutes, 6.4% 45 to 60 minutes, 10.9% 60 minutes or more (2000)

ESCANABA (city). Covers a land area of 12.655 square miles and a water area of 3.851 square miles. Located at 45.74° N. Lat.; 87.07° W. Long. Elevation is 598 feet.
History: Escanaba became an important iron-ore shipping port in 1863, when the first dock was constructed by the railroad. Commercial fishing was also a part of the early economy of Escanaba.
Population: 13,140 (2000); Race: 95.9% White, 0.1% Black, 0.0% Asian, 3.0% American Indian and Alaska Native, 0.7% Hispanic of any race, 0.8% two or more races (2000); Density: 1,038.3 persons per square mile (2000); Age: 22.6% under 18, 21.4% over 64 (2000); Marriage status: 25.4% never married, 53.4% now married, 10.2% widowed, 11.0% divorced (2000); Foreign born: 0.9% (2000); Ancestry (includes multiple ancestries): 21.4% German, 20.2% French (except Basque), 11.1% Swedish, 10.6% French Canadian, 9.2% Irish (2000).
Vital Statistics: Birth rate: 137.8 per 10,000 population (1998)
Economy: Single-family building permits issued: 0 (2001) / 0 (2000); Multi-family building permits issued: 0 (2001) / 0 (2000); Employment by occupation: 8.4% management, 17.2% professional, 22.5% services, 24.1% sales, 0.6% farming, 7.7% construction, 19.4% production (2000).
Income: Per capita income: $17,589 (2000); Median household income: $29,125 (2000); Poverty rate: 13.8% (2000).
Taxes: Total city taxes per capita: $262 (2000); City property taxes per capita: $261 (2000).
Education: High school graduation rate: 86.2% (2000); College graduation rate: 19.5% (2000).

School District(s)

Escanaba Area Public Schools (KG-12)
2000 Enrollment: 3,369 906-786-5411

Two-year College(s)

Bay De Noc Community College (Public)
2001 Enrollment: 2,198 906-786-5802
2001 Tuition: In-state $2,528; Out-of-state $3,968

Housing: Homeownership rate: 64.3% (2000); Median home value: $75,800 (2000); Median rent: $320 per month (2000); Median age of housing: 55 years (2000).
Hospitals: Saint Francis Hospital (110 beds)
Newspapers: The Daily Press (6 x week)
Transportation: Commute to work: 92.9% car, 1.6% public transportation, 3.0% walk, 1.8% work from home (2000); Travel time to work: 71.7% less than 15 minutes, 18.8% 15 to 30 minutes, 3.5% 30 to 45 minutes, 1.4% 45 to 60 minutes, 4.6% 60 minutes or more (2000); Amtrak: Service available.
Airports: Delta County (primary service)
Additional Information Contacts
Bays De Noc Convention Bureau 906-789-7862
Escanaba Chamber of Commerce 906-786-2192

ESCANABA (township). Covers a land area of 59.572 square miles and a water area of 0.749 square miles. Located at 45.83° N. Lat.; 87.11° W. Long. Elevation is 598 feet.
History: Settled 1852; Incorporated 1883.
Population: 3,587 (2000); Race: 94.8% White, 0.1% Black, 0.2% Asian, 3.3% American Indian and Alaska Native, 0.0% Hispanic of any race, 1.5% two or more races (2000); Density: 60.2 persons per square mile (2000); Age: 27.5% under 18, 8.9% over 64 (2000); Marriage status: 19.1% never married, 68.5% now married, 3.5% widowed, 8.9% divorced (2000); Foreign born: 0.2% (2000); Ancestry (includes multiple ancestries): 18.7% French (except Basque), 18.6% German, 15.9% French Canadian, 10.1% Swedish, 7.4% Irish (2000).
Economy: A railroad and manufacturing center for soft drinks, automotive parts and concrete products. It stores and exports coal and petrochemicals from its harbor. Lumber and lumber by- products are the chief economic mainstay. Employment by occupation: 13.7% management, 14.7% professional, 15.4% services, 23.4% sales, 1.2% farming, 13.8% construction, 17.7% production (2000).
Income: Per capita income: $18,454 (2000); Median household income: $44,730 (2000); Poverty rate: 4.2% (2000).
Taxes: Total city taxes per capita: $13 (1997); City property taxes per capita: $13 (1997).
Education: High school graduation rate: 90.9% (2000); College graduation rate: 15.6% (2000).
Housing: Homeownership rate: 94.2% (2000); Median home value: $95,500 (2000); Median rent: $322 per month (2000); Median age of housing: 24 years (2000).
Transportation: Commute to work: 96.6% car, 0.0% public transportation, 2.1% walk, 0.7% work from home (2000); Travel time to work: 42.5% less than 15 minutes, 45.7% 15 to 30 minutes, 5.8% 30 to 45 minutes, 1.0% 45 to 60 minutes, 5.1% 60 minutes or more (2000); Amtrak: Service available.
Airports: Delta County (primary service)

FAIRBANKS (township). Covers a land area of 47.188 square miles and a water area of 252.039 square miles. Located at 45.68° N. Lat.; 86.65° W. Long.
Population: 321 (2000); Race: 89.0% White, 0.0% Black, 0.0% Asian, 4.7% American Indian and Alaska Native, 0.0% Hispanic of any race, 6.3% two or more races (2000); Density: 6.8 persons per square mile (2000); Age: 15.8% under 18, 20.5% over 64 (2000); Marriage status: 24.3% never married, 57.4% now married, 10.2% widowed, 8.1% divorced (2000); Foreign born: 0.6% (2000); Ancestry (includes multiple ancestries): 35.0% French (except Basque), 23.7% German, 14.8% Irish, 12.9% Other groups, 6.3% Swedish (2000).
Economy: Employment by occupation: 19.1% management, 6.1% professional, 22.6% services, 4.3% sales, 17.4% farming, 11.3% construction, 19.1% production (2000).
Income: Per capita income: $15,327 (2000); Median household income: $24,643 (2000); Poverty rate: 12.3% (2000).
Taxes: Total city taxes per capita: $57 (1997); City property taxes per capita: $57 (1997).
Education: High school graduation rate: 77.5% (2000); College graduation rate: 10.0% (2000).
Housing: Homeownership rate: 87.1% (2000); Median home value: $68,900 (2000); Median rent: $250 per month (2000); Median age of housing: 30 years (2000).
Transportation: Commute to work: 76.8% car, 0.0% public transportation, 6.3% walk, 14.3% work from home (2000); Travel time to work: 26.0% less than 15 minutes, 30.2% 15 to 30 minutes, 10.4% 30 to 45 minutes, 18.8% 45 to 60 minutes, 14.6% 60 minutes or more (2000)

FORD RIVER (township). Covers a land area of 64.812 square miles and a water area of 0.454 square miles. Located at 45.66° N. Lat.; 87.17° W. Long. Elevation is 591 feet.
History: Ford River Township was named for Thomas Ford, a governor of Illinois and an explorer of the Upper Peninsula in the 1840's. Ford wrote a history of Michigan in which he described the river.
Population: 2,241 (2000); Race: 95.8% White, 0.0% Black, 0.6% Asian, 2.2% American Indian and Alaska Native, 0.3% Hispanic of any race, 1.1% two or more races (2000); Density: 34.6 persons per square mile (2000); Age: 21.4% under 18, 18.1% over 64 (2000); Marriage status: 22.3% never married, 64.8% now married, 6.4% widowed, 6.5% divorced (2000); Foreign born: 1.2% (2000); Ancestry (includes multiple ancestries): 19.3% German, 17.8% Swedish, 15.6% French (except Basque), 12.6% Irish, 8.7% English (2000).
Economy: Employment by occupation: 9.5% management, 16.0% professional, 15.1% services, 22.8% sales, 0.5% farming, 12.2% construction, 23.9% production (2000).
Income: Per capita income: $25,299 (2000); Median household income: $42,260 (2000); Poverty rate: 5.2% (2000).
Taxes: Total city taxes per capita: $17 (1997); City property taxes per capita: $16 (1997).
Education: High school graduation rate: 84.8% (2000); College graduation rate: 18.1% (2000).
Housing: Homeownership rate: 87.1% (2000); Median home value: $97,300 (2000); Median rent: $379 per month (2000); Median age of housing: 29 years (2000).
Transportation: Commute to work: 95.6% car, 0.0% public transportation, 0.2% walk, 2.6% work from home (2000); Travel time to work: 27.3% less than 15 minutes, 56.3% 15 to 30 minutes, 8.1% 30 to 45 minutes, 1.9% 45 to 60 minutes, 6.4% 60 minutes or more (2000)

GARDEN (village). Covers a land area of 0.848 square miles and a water area of 0.170 square miles. Located at 45.77° N. Lat.; 86.55° W. Long. Elevation is 618 feet.
History: Garden was established on the peninsula that creates Big Bay de Noc from a corner of Lake Michigan. Philomen Thompson built a cabin here

in 1850, and was joined by other settlers of French ancestry. The village was incorporated in 1886.
Population: 240 (2000); Race: 79.0% White, 0.0% Black, 0.0% Asian, 9.2% American Indian and Alaska Native, 0.0% Hispanic of any race, 11.8% two or more races (2000); Density: 283.1 persons per square mile (2000); Age: 25.6% under 18, 22.3% over 64 (2000); Marriage status: 15.3% never married, 63.7% now married, 12.1% widowed, 8.9% divorced (2000); Foreign born: 0.0% (2000); Ancestry (includes multiple ancestries): 25.2% French (except Basque), 16.0% Other groups, 15.5% German, 13.0% French Canadian, 8.8% Irish (2000).
Economy: Employment by occupation: 8.3% management, 8.3% professional, 17.9% services, 23.8% sales, 2.4% farming, 19.0% construction, 20.2% production (2000).
Income: Per capita income: $16,605 (2000); Median household income: $36,250 (2000); Poverty rate: 7.6% (2000).
Taxes: Total city taxes per capita: $63 (1997); City property taxes per capita: $63 (1997).
Education: High school graduation rate: 81.3% (2000); College graduation rate: 8.0% (2000).
Housing: Homeownership rate: 85.8% (2000); Median home value: $56,100 (2000); Median rent: $263 per month (2000); Median age of housing: 54 years (2000).
Transportation: Commute to work: 75.6% car, 0.0% public transportation, 4.9% walk, 14.6% work from home (2000); Travel time to work: 28.6% less than 15 minutes, 21.4% 15 to 30 minutes, 25.7% 30 to 45 minutes, 10.0% 45 to 60 minutes, 14.3% 60 minutes or more (2000)

GARDEN (township). Covers a land area of 159.922 square miles and a water area of 24.464 square miles. Located at 45.96° N. Lat.; 86.53° W. Long. Elevation is 618 feet.
History: Garden Township was named for the good soil that made it a garden spot on the Upper Peninsula.
Population: 817 (2000); Race: 87.8% White, 0.0% Black, 0.0% Asian, 6.2% American Indian and Alaska Native, 0.3% Hispanic of any race, 6.0% two or more races (2000); Density: 5.1 persons per square mile (2000); Age: 23.4% under 18, 18.4% over 64 (2000); Marriage status: 14.9% never married, 70.3% now married, 7.2% widowed, 7.5% divorced (2000); Foreign born: 0.3% (2000); Ancestry (includes multiple ancestries): 19.8% German, 19.3% French (except Basque), 12.9% Irish, 11.9% Other groups, 11.8% French Canadian (2000).
Economy: Employment by occupation: 11.9% management, 11.5% professional, 12.9% services, 20.3% sales, 3.5% farming, 14.7% construction, 25.2% production (2000).
Income: Per capita income: $20,445 (2000); Median household income: $37,083 (2000); Poverty rate: 9.1% (2000).
Taxes: Total city taxes per capita: $79 (1997); City property taxes per capita: $79 (1997).
Education: High school graduation rate: 79.2% (2000); College graduation rate: 12.5% (2000).
Housing: Homeownership rate: 95.0% (2000); Median home value: $80,300 (2000); Median rent: $269 per month (2000); Median age of housing: 35 years (2000).
Transportation: Commute to work: 88.1% car, 0.0% public transportation, 4.2% walk, 5.8% work from home (2000); Travel time to work: 21.2% less than 15 minutes, 28.6% 15 to 30 minutes, 26.9% 30 to 45 minutes, 11.8% 45 to 60 minutes, 11.4% 60 minutes or more (2000)

GLADSTONE (city). Covers a land area of 4.957 square miles and a water area of 2.929 square miles. Located at 45.84° N. Lat.; 87.03° W. Long. Elevation is 601 feet.
History: Gladstone was founded in 1887 as a railroad shipping center for grain shipments. The city was incorporated in 1889. A cooperage company was founded here in 1892 and expanded into the making of hardwood flooring. Gladstone was named for William E. Gladstone, British prime minister.
Population: 5,032 (2000); Race: 95.2% White, 0.1% Black, 1.0% Asian, 1.7% American Indian and Alaska Native, 0.0% Hispanic of any race, 2.0% two or more races (2000); Density: 1,015.2 persons per square mile (2000); Age: 25.2% under 18, 19.7% over 64 (2000); Marriage status: 21.7% never married, 57.5% now married, 11.4% widowed, 9.3% divorced (2000); Foreign born: 2.2% (2000); Ancestry (includes multiple ancestries): 21.3% German, 18.8% French (except Basque), 14.0% Swedish, 10.1% French Canadian, 9.7% Irish (2000).
Economy: Single-family building permits issued: 21 (2001) / 20 (2000); Multi-family building permits issued: 80 (2001) / 57 (2000); Employment by occupation: 6.7% management, 24.0% professional, 17.8% services, 22.9% sales, 0.8% farming, 8.1% construction, 19.7% production (2000).
Income: Per capita income: $17,973 (2000); Median household income: $34,328 (2000); Poverty rate: 10.2% (2000).
Taxes: Total city taxes per capita: $200 (1997); City property taxes per capita: $198 (1997).
Education: High school graduation rate: 87.3% (2000); College graduation rate: 21.3% (2000).

School District(s)

Gladstone Area Schools (KG-12)
2000 Enrollment: 1,825 906-428-2417

Housing: Homeownership rate: 79.5% (2000); Median home value: $68,500 (2000); Median rent: $335 per month (2000); Median age of housing: 46 years (2000).
Safety: Violent crime rate: 21.7 per 10,000 population; Property crime rate: 258.9 per 10,000 population (2001).
Transportation: Commute to work: 93.2% car, 0.3% public transportation, 3.3% walk, 2.3% work from home (2000); Travel time to work: 47.2% less than 15 minutes, 41.3% 15 to 30 minutes, 6.4% 30 to 45 minutes, 2.0% 45 to 60 minutes, 3.1% 60 minutes or more (2000)

MAPLE RIDGE (township). Covers a land area of 108.231 square miles and a water area of 0 square miles. Located at 46.09° N. Lat.; 87.14° W. Long.
Population: 808 (2000); Race: 97.0% White, 0.0% Black, 1.2% Asian, 0.5% American Indian and Alaska Native, 0.5% Hispanic of any race, 1.3% two or more races (2000); Density: 7.5 persons per square mile (2000); Age: 23.4% under 18, 13.2% over 64 (2000); Marriage status: 23.1% never married, 63.0% now married, 5.6% widowed, 8.4% divorced (2000); Foreign born: 0.2% (2000); Ancestry (includes multiple ancestries): 23.2% German, 22.3% Finnish, 14.0% Swedish, 11.4% French (except Basque), 11.3% French Canadian (2000).
Economy: Employment by occupation: 10.4% management, 13.0% professional, 14.6% services, 19.7% sales, 6.6% farming, 10.1% construction, 25.5% production (2000).
Income: Per capita income: $17,664 (2000); Median household income: $36,050 (2000); Poverty rate: 13.0% (2000).
Taxes: Total city taxes per capita: $18 (1997); City property taxes per capita: $18 (1997).
Education: High school graduation rate: 86.7% (2000); College graduation rate: 13.5% (2000).
Housing: Homeownership rate: 86.9% (2000); Median home value: $52,800 (2000); Median rent: $225 per month (2000); Median age of housing: 46 years (2000).
Transportation: Commute to work: 88.7% car, 1.1% public transportation, 2.8% walk, 6.1% work from home (2000); Travel time to work: 22.0% less than 15 minutes, 18.2% 15 to 30 minutes, 40.8% 30 to 45 minutes, 10.0% 45 to 60 minutes, 9.1% 60 minutes or more (2000)

MASONVILLE (township). Covers a land area of 167.671 square miles and a water area of 2.738 square miles. Located at 45.98° N. Lat.; 86.91° W. Long.
History: Masonville was the site of the first sawmill in Delta County, built in 1847 by Darius Clark.
Population: 1,877 (2000); Race: 94.3% White, 0.0% Black, 0.0% Asian, 3.8% American Indian and Alaska Native, 0.5% Hispanic of any race, 1.9% two or more races (2000); Density: 11.2 persons per square mile (2000); Age: 23.2% under 18, 15.5% over 64 (2000); Marriage status: 20.3% never married, 61.5% now married, 7.8% widowed, 10.5% divorced (2000); Foreign born: 0.6% (2000); Ancestry (includes multiple ancestries): 27.5% German, 16.1% Swedish, 15.8% French (except Basque), 10.1% Irish, 8.6% English (2000).
Economy: Single-family building permits issued: 20 (2001) / 19 (2000); Multi-family building permits issued: 0 (2001) / 0 (2000); Employment by occupation: 8.6% management, 17.1% professional, 14.6% services, 20.7% sales, 1.6% farming, 15.5% construction, 21.9% production (2000).
Income: Per capita income: $18,375 (2000); Median household income: $35,887 (2000); Poverty rate: 9.8% (2000).
Taxes: Total city taxes per capita: $22 (1997); City property taxes per capita: $21 (1997).
Education: High school graduation rate: 85.4% (2000); College graduation rate: 14.9% (2000).
Housing: Homeownership rate: 85.6% (2000); Median home value: $85,000 (2000); Median rent: $283 per month (2000); Median age of housing: 34 years (2000).

Transportation: Commute to work: 92.5% car, 0.5% public transportation, 3.6% walk, 3.0% work from home (2000); Travel time to work: 27.3% less than 15 minutes, 47.2% 15 to 30 minutes, 18.0% 30 to 45 minutes, 2.1% 45 to 60 minutes, 5.4% 60 minutes or more (2000)

NAHMA (township). Covers a land area of 166.238 square miles and a water area of 22.632 square miles. Located at 46.01° N. Lat.; 86.70° W. Long. Elevation is 580 feet.

History: The name of Nahma is of Indian origin meaning "sturgeon." The town, located at the mouth of the Sturgeon River, developed as a sawmill village.

Population: 499 (2000); Race: 91.3% White, 0.0% Black, 0.0% Asian, 3.9% American Indian and Alaska Native, 0.0% Hispanic of any race, 4.7% two or more races (2000); Density: 3.0 persons per square mile (2000); Age: 17.8% under 18, 33.3% over 64 (2000); Marriage status: 14.2% never married, 71.2% now married, 8.6% widowed, 6.1% divorced (2000); Foreign born: 1.2% (2000); Ancestry (includes multiple ancestries): 19.7% French (except Basque), 17.4% German, 16.0% French Canadian, 9.1% Swedish, 8.3% English (2000).

Economy: Employment by occupation: 8.4% management, 7.1% professional, 26.0% services, 14.9% sales, 3.9% farming, 18.8% construction, 20.8% production (2000).

Income: Per capita income: $16,981 (2000); Median household income: $28,077 (2000); Poverty rate: 12.6% (2000).

Taxes: Total city taxes per capita: $57 (1997); City property taxes per capita: $57 (1997).

Education: High school graduation rate: 79.1% (2000); College graduation rate: 4.0% (2000).

Housing: Homeownership rate: 91.3% (2000); Median home value: $57,300 (2000); Median rent: $338 per month (2000); Median age of housing: 33 years (2000).

Transportation: Commute to work: 90.7% car, 0.0% public transportation, 1.3% walk, 6.7% work from home (2000); Travel time to work: 13.6% less than 15 minutes, 14.3% 15 to 30 minutes, 46.4% 30 to 45 minutes, 15.7% 45 to 60 minutes, 10.0% 60 minutes or more (2000)

RAPID RIVER (unincorporated postal area, zip code 49878). Covers a land area of 364.734 square miles and a water area of 2.785 square miles. Located at 45.92° N. Lat.; 86.90° W. Long. Elevation is 591 feet.

History: Logging began in Rapid River in 1847, and at the peak of the lumber period, there were twelve mills here. The village was platted in 1887.

Population: 3,918 (2000); Race: 95.4% White, 0.0% Black, 0.0% Asian, 2.7% American Indian and Alaska Native, 0.4% Hispanic of any race, 1.8% two or more races (2000); Density: 10.7 persons per square mile (2000); Age: 21.4% under 18, 17.9% over 64 (2000); Marriage status: 18.6% never married, 65.8% now married, 6.9% widowed, 8.7% divorced (2000); Foreign born: 0.7% (2000); Ancestry (includes multiple ancestries): 22.7% German, 17.4% Swedish, 16.1% French (except Basque), 9.8% Irish, 9.1% English (2000).

Economy: Employment by occupation: 8.5% management, 17.3% professional, 15.3% services, 19.5% sales, 2.0% farming, 15.9% construction, 21.6% production (2000).

Income: Per capita income: $20,172 (2000); Median household income: $36,196 (2000); Poverty rate: 8.6% (2000).

Education: High school graduation rate: 83.6% (2000); College graduation rate: 14.9% (2000).

School District(s)

Rapid River Public Schools (KG-12)
2000 Enrollment: 504 906-474-6424

Housing: Homeownership rate: 90.3% (2000); Median home value: $91,600 (2000); Median rent: $309 per month (2000); Median age of housing: 31 years (2000).

Transportation: Commute to work: 93.0% car, 0.6% public transportation, 2.4% walk, 3.2% work from home (2000); Travel time to work: 21.2% less than 15 minutes, 37.3% 15 to 30 minutes, 26.9% 30 to 45 minutes, 6.5% 45 to 60 minutes, 8.1% 60 minutes or more (2000)

ROCK (unincorporated postal area, zip code 49880). Covers a land area of 235.783 square miles and a water area of 0.081 square miles. Located at 46.08° N. Lat.; 87.20° W. Long. Elevation is 959 feet.

History: Rock grew as a stagecoach stop on the Marquette route until 1865, when the Chicago & Northwestern Railway arrived. The first industry here was cutting timber for the charcoal kilns. When the kilns closed in 1873, Rock residents turned to farming and poultry raising. Many of the early residents of Rock were of Finnish ancestry.

Population: 1,214 (2000); Race: 97.1% White, 0.2% Black, 1.1% Asian, 0.7% American Indian and Alaska Native, 0.3% Hispanic of any race, 1.1% two or more races (2000); Density: 5.1 persons per square mile (2000); Age: 25.1% under 18, 13.0% over 64 (2000); Marriage status: 23.4% never married, 62.3% now married, 6.3% widowed, 8.0% divorced (2000); Foreign born: 0.3% (2000); Ancestry (includes multiple ancestries): 23.6% Finnish, 19.7% German, 14.6% Swedish, 12.3% French (except Basque), 10.0% Irish (2000).

Economy: Employment by occupation: 11.1% management, 12.6% professional, 16.4% services, 19.3% sales, 5.9% farming, 8.2% construction, 26.4% production (2000).

Income: Per capita income: $14,995 (2000); Median household income: $34,013 (2000); Poverty rate: 11.4% (2000).

Education: High school graduation rate: 85.4% (2000); College graduation rate: 10.3% (2000).

School District(s)

Mid Peninsula School District (KG-12)
2000 Enrollment: 313 906-359-4387

Housing: Homeownership rate: 88.3% (2000); Median home value: $53,500 (2000); Median rent: $213 per month (2000); Median age of housing: 36 years (2000).

Transportation: Commute to work: 87.8% car, 1.2% public transportation, 2.8% walk, 6.7% work from home (2000); Travel time to work: 19.4% less than 15 minutes, 20.9% 15 to 30 minutes, 36.5% 30 to 45 minutes, 12.4% 45 to 60 minutes, 10.8% 60 minutes or more (2000)

WELLS (township). Covers a land area of 39.489 square miles and a water area of 0.346 square miles. Located at 45.77° N. Lat.; 87.11° W. Long. Elevation is 632 feet.

Population: 5,044 (2000); Race: 96.3% White, 0.2% Black, 0.0% Asian, 2.6% American Indian and Alaska Native, 0.5% Hispanic of any race, 0.5% two or more races (2000); Density: 127.7 persons per square mile (2000); Age: 26.4% under 18, 10.8% over 64 (2000); Marriage status: 21.5% never married, 67.4% now married, 4.2% widowed, 6.9% divorced (2000); Foreign born: 1.0% (2000); Ancestry (includes multiple ancestries): 22.8% French (except Basque), 21.3% German, 13.7% Swedish, 11.0% French Canadian, 8.8% Irish (2000).

Economy: Hiawatha National Forest to East. Employment by occupation: 7.3% management, 11.4% professional, 17.1% services, 27.5% sales, 1.1% farming, 11.7% construction, 23.8% production (2000).

Income: Per capita income: $19,012 (2000); Median household income: $48,065 (2000); Poverty rate: 6.4% (2000).

Taxes: Total city taxes per capita: $12 (1997); City property taxes per capita: $12 (1997).

Education: High school graduation rate: 86.4% (2000); College graduation rate: 14.0% (2000).

Housing: Homeownership rate: 90.7% (2000); Median home value: $86,500 (2000); Median rent: $337 per month (2000); Median age of housing: 27 years (2000).

Transportation: Commute to work: 94.3% car, 0.4% public transportation, 1.7% walk, 3.0% work from home (2000); Travel time to work: 60.1% less than 15 minutes, 30.9% 15 to 30 minutes, 2.3% 30 to 45 minutes, 1.1% 45 to 60 minutes, 5.6% 60 minutes or more (2000)

Dickinson County

Located in northwestern Michigan on the Upper Peninsula; bounded on the southwest by Wisconsin; drained by the Menominee, Ford, and Escanaba Rivers. Covers a land area of 766.30 square miles, a water area of 10.80 square miles, and is located in the Central Time Zone. The county government was organized in 1891. County seat is Iron Mountain.

Weather Station: Iron Mountain-Kingsford WWTP Elevation: 1,059 feet

	Jan	Feb	Mar	Apr	May	Jun	Jul	Aug	Sep	Oct	Nov	Dec
High	23	29	39	53	68	76	80	78	68	56	40	28
Low	1	6	16	29	41	50	56	54	45	35	23	10
Precip	1.4	0.9	1.7	2.2	3.2	3.4	3.6	3.7	3.6	2.8	2.0	1.5
Snow	16.9	9.0	11.3	4.2	0.8	0.0	0.0	0.0	tr	0.3	6.4	15.5

High and Low temperatures in degrees Fahrenheit; Precipitation and Snow in inches

Population: 27,472 (2000); Race: 97.9% White, 0.2% Black, 0.6% Asian, 0.4% American Indian and Alaska Native, 0.5% Hispanic of any race, 0.7% two or more races (2000); Density: 35.8 persons per square mile (2000); Age: 25.1% under 18, 18.1% over 64 (2000).

Religion: Five largest groups: 52.6% Catholic Church, 11.5% Evangelical Lutheran Church in America, 3.9% The United Methodist Church, 2.4%

Presbyterian Church (U.S.A.), 2.2% The Evangelical Covenant Church (2000).
Economy: Unemployment rate: 4.9% (11/2002); Total civilian labor force: 14,493 (11/2002); Leading industries: 18.2% manufacturing; 16.9% retail trade; 16.2% construction (2000); Companies that employ more than 1,000 persons: 0 (2000); Companies that employ more than 100 persons: 19 (2000); Farms: 116 totaling 28,298 acres (1997); Minority business ownership rate: 0.0% (1997); Women business ownership rate: 24.4% (1997); Retail sales per capita: $11,663 (1997). Single-family building permits issued: 76 (2001) / 104 (2000); Multi-family building permits issued: 0 (2001) / 2 (2000).
Income: Per capita income: $18,516 (2000); Median household income: $34,825 (2000); Poverty rate: 9.1% (2000); Bankruptcy rate: 2.40% (2001).
Taxes: Total county taxes per capita: $167 (1997); County property taxes per capita: $165 (1997).
Education: High school graduation rate: 88.8% (2000); College graduation rate: 16.7% (2000).
Housing: Homeownership rate: 80.1% (2000); Median home value: $64,600 (2000); Median rent: $347 per month (2000); Median age of housing: 41 years (2000).
Health: Birth rate: 106.3 per 10,000 population (1998); Age adjusted death rate: 83.2 per 10,000 population (1999); Age adjusted cancer mortality rate: 188.0 deaths per 100,000 population (1999). Number of physicians: 19.7 per 10,000 population (1999); Number of hospital beds: 61.9 per 10,000 population (1999).
Elections: 2000 Presidential election results: 43.1% Gore, 54.0% Bush, 2.4% Nader, 0.1% Buchanan
National and State Parks: Sturgeon River State Forest
Additional Information Contacts
Dickinson County Government Offices 906-774-2573
Dickinson County Area Chamber 906-774-2002

Dickinson County Communities

BREEN (township). Covers a land area of 87.860 square miles and a water area of 0.411 square miles. Located at 45.96° N. Lat.; 87.72° W. Long.
Population: 479 (2000); Race: 100.0% White, 0.0% Black, 0.0% Asian, 0.0% American Indian and Alaska Native, 0.0% Hispanic of any race, 0.0% two or more races (2000); Density: 5.5 persons per square mile (2000); Age: 19.7% under 18, 20.7% over 64 (2000); Marriage status: 18.5% never married, 68.5% now married, 6.9% widowed, 6.2% divorced (2000); Foreign born: 0.0% (2000); Ancestry (includes multiple ancestries): 36.3% Swedish, 25.4% German, 19.4% French (except Basque), 8.5% Belgian, 7.9% Finnish (2000).
Economy: Employment by occupation: 9.2% management, 16.4% professional, 14.4% services, 19.5% sales, 11.3% farming, 11.3% construction, 17.9% production (2000).
Income: Per capita income: $14,497 (2000); Median household income: $30,313 (2000); Poverty rate: 13.5% (2000).
Taxes: Total city taxes per capita: $40 (1997); City property taxes per capita: $40 (1997).
Education: High school graduation rate: 86.4% (2000); College graduation rate: 8.9% (2000).
Housing: Homeownership rate: 87.8% (2000); Median home value: $63,200 (2000); Median rent: $121 per month (2000); Median age of housing: 32 years (2000).
Transportation: Commute to work: 90.7% car, 0.0% public transportation, 1.0% walk, 7.3% work from home (2000); Travel time to work: 17.9% less than 15 minutes, 13.4% 15 to 30 minutes, 31.8% 30 to 45 minutes, 30.2% 45 to 60 minutes, 6.7% 60 minutes or more (2000)

BREITUNG (township). Covers a land area of 65.060 square miles and a water area of 3.207 square miles. Located at 45.80° N. Lat.; 88.03° W. Long.
Population: 5,930 (2000); Race: 98.9% White, 0.0% Black, 0.8% Asian, 0.0% American Indian and Alaska Native, 0.0% Hispanic of any race, 0.2% two or more races (2000); Density: 91.1 persons per square mile (2000); Age: 24.4% under 18, 18.3% over 64 (2000); Marriage status: 17.3% never married, 67.4% now married, 7.4% widowed, 7.9% divorced (2000); Foreign born: 1.1% (2000); Ancestry (includes multiple ancestries): 25.2% German, 18.4% Swedish, 16.2% Italian, 11.6% French (except Basque), 10.9% English (2000).
Economy: Employment by occupation: 10.8% management, 19.0% professional, 13.9% services, 28.9% sales, 0.7% farming, 10.2% construction, 16.5% production (2000).
Income: Per capita income: $18,920 (2000); Median household income: $39,820 (2000); Poverty rate: 4.6% (2000).
Taxes: Total city taxes per capita: $130 (1997); City property taxes per capita: $129 (1997).
Education: High school graduation rate: 92.1% (2000); College graduation rate: 17.4% (2000).
Housing: Homeownership rate: 95.2% (2000); Median home value: $84,000 (2000); Median rent: $369 per month (2000); Median age of housing: 22 years (2000).
Transportation: Commute to work: 97.1% car, 0.3% public transportation, 1.4% walk, 1.0% work from home (2000); Travel time to work: 57.3% less than 15 minutes, 35.1% 15 to 30 minutes, 3.0% 30 to 45 minutes, 1.3% 45 to 60 minutes, 3.3% 60 minutes or more (2000)

CHANNING (unincorporated postal area, zip code 49815). Covers a land area of 106.012 square miles and a water area of 1.772 square miles. Located at 46.18° N. Lat.; 88.04° W. Long. Elevation is 1,397 feet.
History: Channing grew up around a railroad junction called Ford Siding.
Population: 544 (2000); Race: 99.3% White, 0.0% Black, 0.4% Asian, 0.4% American Indian and Alaska Native, 0.0% Hispanic of any race, 0.0% two or more races (2000); Density: 5.1 persons per square mile (2000); Age: 26.1% under 18, 19.6% over 64 (2000); Marriage status: 19.7% never married, 59.4% now married, 12.7% widowed, 8.2% divorced (2000); Foreign born: 1.3% (2000); Ancestry (includes multiple ancestries): 25.5% German, 12.9% French (except Basque), 12.0% Irish, 11.3% English, 10.5% Swedish (2000).
Economy: Employment by occupation: 5.2% management, 21.9% professional, 15.1% services, 24.0% sales, 2.1% farming, 13.5% construction, 18.2% production (2000).
Income: Per capita income: $14,927 (2000); Median household income: $31,364 (2000); Poverty rate: 17.2% (2000).
Education: High school graduation rate: 85.2% (2000); College graduation rate: 14.3% (2000).
Housing: Homeownership rate: 94.8% (2000); Median home value: $50,400 (2000); Median rent: $300 per month (2000); Median age of housing: 34 years (2000).
Transportation: Commute to work: 94.2% car, 0.0% public transportation, 0.0% walk, 5.8% work from home (2000); Travel time to work: 22.5% less than 15 minutes, 24.2% 15 to 30 minutes, 38.2% 30 to 45 minutes, 6.2% 45 to 60 minutes, 9.0% 60 minutes or more (2000)

FELCH (township). Covers a land area of 143.077 square miles and a water area of 0.676 square miles. Located at 46.08° N. Lat.; 87.87° W. Long. Elevation is 1,172 feet.
Population: 726 (2000); Race: 97.7% White, 0.0% Black, 0.3% Asian, 0.4% American Indian and Alaska Native, 0.0% Hispanic of any race, 1.0% two or more races (2000); Density: 5.1 persons per square mile (2000); Age: 26.1% under 18, 11.2% over 64 (2000); Marriage status: 23.1% never married, 60.2% now married, 6.7% widowed, 10.0% divorced (2000); Foreign born: 0.7% (2000); Ancestry (includes multiple ancestries): 34.1% Swedish, 22.0% Finnish, 20.4% German, 10.9% French (except Basque), 9.7% Italian (2000).
Economy: Employment by occupation: 6.6% management, 14.9% professional, 14.0% services, 16.3% sales, 5.4% farming, 20.1% construction, 22.6% production (2000).
Income: Per capita income: $16,096 (2000); Median household income: $36,667 (2000); Poverty rate: 8.1% (2000).
Taxes: Total city taxes per capita: $249 (1997); City property taxes per capita: $249 (1997).
Education: High school graduation rate: 88.3% (2000); College graduation rate: 10.7% (2000).

School District(s)
North Dickinson County Schools (KG-12)
2000 Enrollment: 425 906-542-9281
Housing: Homeownership rate: 87.8% (2000); Median home value: $67,500 (2000); Median rent: $266 per month (2000); Median age of housing: 25 years (2000).
Transportation: Commute to work: 91.8% car, 0.9% public transportation, 3.6% walk, 3.6% work from home (2000); Travel time to work: 25.4% less than 15 minutes, 27.6% 15 to 30 minutes, 31.3% 30 to 45 minutes, 8.5% 45 to 60 minutes, 7.2% 60 minutes or more (2000)

FOSTER CITY (unincorporated postal area, zip code 49834). Covers a land area of 59.343 square miles and a water area of 0.375 square miles. Located at 45.94° N. Lat.; 87.77° W. Long. Elevation is 1,029 feet.
Population: 279 (2000); Race: 98.1% White, 0.0% Black, 0.0% Asian, 0.0% American Indian and Alaska Native, 0.0% Hispanic of any race, 1.9% two or more races (2000); Density: 4.7 persons per square mile (2000); Age: 22.6% under 18, 16.3% over 64 (2000); Marriage status: 20.3% never married, 58.9% now married, 13.0% widowed, 7.7% divorced (2000); Foreign born:

0.0% (2000); Ancestry (includes multiple ancestries): 41.2% Swedish, 20.6% German, 17.1% French (except Basque), 12.1% Belgian, 8.9% Finnish (2000).
Economy: Employment by occupation: 5.8% management, 14.4% professional, 20.2% services, 18.3% sales, 13.5% farming, 8.7% construction, 19.2% production (2000).
Income: Per capita income: $13,496 (2000); Median household income: $27,143 (2000); Poverty rate: 18.3% (2000).
Education: High school graduation rate: 84.7% (2000); College graduation rate: 6.8% (2000).
Housing: Homeownership rate: 79.2% (2000); Median home value: $73,800 (2000); Median rent: $113 per month (2000); Median age of housing: 36 years (2000).
Transportation: Commute to work: 92.2% car, 0.0% public transportation, 3.9% walk, 2.0% work from home (2000); Travel time to work: 21.0% less than 15 minutes, 22.0% 15 to 30 minutes, 25.0% 30 to 45 minutes, 29.0% 45 to 60 minutes, 3.0% 60 minutes or more (2000)

IRON MOUNTAIN (city). Covers a land area of 7.199 square miles and a water area of 0.603 square miles. Located at 45.82° N. Lat.; 88.06° W. Long. Elevation is 1,138 feet.
History: Iron Mountain was named for the nearby bluff that was stratified with iron ore. The city developed as a manufacturing and distribution point for the Menominee Range district, which produced hematite. Mining declined here in the 1930's.
Population: 8,154 (2000); Race: 96.9% White, 0.6% Black, 1.1% Asian, 0.1% American Indian and Alaska Native, 0.7% Hispanic of any race, 0.9% two or more races (2000); Density: 1,132.6 persons per square mile (2000); Age: 25.1% under 18, 18.9% over 64 (2000); Marriage status: 21.1% never married, 58.5% now married, 10.0% widowed, 10.4% divorced (2000); Foreign born: 1.7% (2000); Ancestry (includes multiple ancestries): 20.5% German, 19.7% Italian, 14.3% English, 13.7% Swedish, 13.2% French (except Basque) (2000).
Economy: Employment by occupation: 10.5% management, 17.7% professional, 19.0% services, 29.5% sales, 0.0% farming, 8.9% construction, 14.5% production (2000).
Income: Per capita income: $19,918 (2000); Median household income: $32,526 (2000); Poverty rate: 10.6% (2000).
Taxes: Total city taxes per capita: $390 (1997); City property taxes per capita: $387 (1997).
Education: High school graduation rate: 87.3% (2000); College graduation rate: 18.5% (2000).

School District(s)

Iron Mountain Public Schools (PK-12)
2000 Enrollment: 1,495 906-779-2600
Housing: Homeownership rate: 72.0% (2000); Median home value: $62,400 (2000); Median rent: $340 per month (2000); Median age of housing: 59 years (2000).
Hospitals: Dickinson County Healthcare System (96 beds); Veterans Affairs Medical Center (57 beds)
Safety: Violent crime rate: 12.2 per 10,000 population; Property crime rate: 316.0 per 10,000 population (2001).
Newspapers: The Daily News (6 x week)
Transportation: Commute to work: 89.6% car, 0.0% public transportation, 6.8% walk, 2.3% work from home (2000); Travel time to work: 78.3% less than 15 minutes, 15.7% 15 to 30 minutes, 2.0% 30 to 45 minutes, 0.8% 45 to 60 minutes, 3.2% 60 minutes or more (2000)
Airports: Ford (commercial service)
Additional Information Contacts
Dickinson County Area Chamber 906-774-2002

KINGSFORD (city). Covers a land area of 4.314 square miles and a water area of 0.213 square miles. Located at 45.80° N. Lat.; 88.08° W. Long. Elevation is 1,113 feet.
History: Kingsford was planned around the Ford Motor Company plant, and was named for a Ford Company official, Edward G. Kingsford. Kingsford was incorporated as a village in 1924 and as a city in 1947. Ford's holdings here included a sawmill, a chemical plant, a hydroelectric plant on the Menominee River, and several plants that made wood parts for the cars.
Population: 5,549 (2000); Race: 97.7% White, 0.0% Black, 0.3% Asian, 0.9% American Indian and Alaska Native, 0.6% Hispanic of any race, 0.9% two or more races (2000); Density: 1,286.2 persons per square mile (2000); Age: 25.5% under 18, 19.6% over 64 (2000); Marriage status: 20.0% never married, 58.1% now married, 11.9% widowed, 9.9% divorced (2000); Foreign born: 0.7% (2000); Ancestry (includes multiple ancestries): 25.2% German, 16.6% Swedish, 16.6% Italian, 13.0% French (except Basque), 10.4% English (2000).
Economy: Employment by occupation: 9.3% management, 22.2% professional, 16.9% services, 24.5% sales, 0.4% farming, 9.8% construction, 17.0% production (2000).
Income: Per capita income: $17,615 (2000); Median household income: $33,165 (2000); Poverty rate: 10.4% (2000).
Taxes: Total city taxes per capita: $274 (1997); City property taxes per capita: $274 (1997).
Education: High school graduation rate: 90.4% (2000); College graduation rate: 18.6% (2000).

School District(s)

Breitung Township Schools (KG-12)
2000 Enrollment: 2,160 906-779-2650
Housing: Homeownership rate: 72.1% (2000); Median home value: $59,200 (2000); Median rent: $365 per month (2000); Median age of housing: 46 years (2000).
Safety: Violent crime rate: 3.6 per 10,000 population; Property crime rate: 261.7 per 10,000 population (2001).
Transportation: Commute to work: 96.9% car, 0.0% public transportation, 0.4% walk, 1.4% work from home (2000); Travel time to work: 72.9% less than 15 minutes, 18.8% 15 to 30 minutes, 3.0% 30 to 45 minutes, 1.9% 45 to 60 minutes, 3.3% 60 minutes or more (2000)

NORWAY (city). Covers a land area of 8.817 square miles and a water area of 0.053 square miles. Located at 45.78° N. Lat.; 87.90° W. Long. Elevation is 944 feet.
History: Norway came into existence because of the Vulcan hematite vein, where mining began in 1877.
Population: 2,959 (2000); Race: 97.0% White, 0.1% Black, 0.0% Asian, 1.1% American Indian and Alaska Native, 1.5% Hispanic of any race, 1.1% two or more races (2000); Density: 335.6 persons per square mile (2000); Age: 26.2% under 18, 17.8% over 64 (2000); Marriage status: 23.2% never married, 56.4% now married, 10.4% widowed, 10.0% divorced (2000); Foreign born: 0.9% (2000); Ancestry (includes multiple ancestries): 19.9% German, 19.8% Italian, 13.0% French (except Basque), 11.9% Swedish, 10.7% Polish (2000).
Economy: Employment by occupation: 8.6% management, 14.9% professional, 16.6% services, 24.8% sales, 0.6% farming, 12.0% construction, 22.5% production (2000).
Income: Per capita income: $17,681 (2000); Median household income: $31,059 (2000); Poverty rate: 10.8% (2000).
Taxes: Total city taxes per capita: $266 (1997); City property taxes per capita: $265 (1997).
Education: High school graduation rate: 86.1% (2000); College graduation rate: 12.6% (2000).

School District(s)

Norway-Vulcan Area Schools (PK-12)
2000 Enrollment: 1,045 906-563-9552
Housing: Homeownership rate: 75.7% (2000); Median home value: $53,800 (2000); Median rent: $345 per month (2000); Median age of housing: 58 years (2000).
Safety: Violent crime rate: 3.4 per 10,000 population; Property crime rate: 191.6 per 10,000 population (2001).
Newspapers: Norway Current (1 x week)
Transportation: Commute to work: 92.8% car, 0.4% public transportation, 3.6% walk, 2.8% work from home (2000); Travel time to work: 45.7% less than 15 minutes, 43.7% 15 to 30 minutes, 4.9% 30 to 45 minutes, 1.8% 45 to 60 minutes, 3.8% 60 minutes or more (2000)

NORWAY (township). Covers a land area of 89.291 square miles and a water area of 1.608 square miles. Located at 45.82° N. Lat.; 87.88° W. Long. Elevation is 944 feet.
History: Norway Spring, artesian spring created in 1903 by 1,904 foot drill-hole made in search of iron deposits. Settled c.1879, incorporated 1891.
Population: 1,639 (2000); Race: 99.6% White, 0.0% Black, 0.2% Asian, 0.0% American Indian and Alaska Native, 0.3% Hispanic of any race, 0.1% two or more races (2000); Density: 18.4 persons per square mile (2000); Age: 24.7% under 18, 15.7% over 64 (2000); Marriage status: 23.0% never married, 62.1% now married, 7.7% widowed, 7.1% divorced (2000); Foreign born: 0.3% (2000); Ancestry (includes multiple ancestries): 22.3% German, 20.1% Italian, 15.2% Polish, 12.0% French (except Basque), 10.8% Swedish (2000).
Economy: In lumbering and farming region: potatoes; cattle. Manufacturing: printing, transportation equipment. Iron Mt. Iron Mine is here (tourist attraction). Vulcan U.S.A. Ski Area to East. Trout hatchery nearby.

Employment by occupation: 10.5% management, 14.3% professional, 17.4% services, 23.0% sales, 0.9% farming, 8.5% construction, 25.4% production (2000).
Income: Per capita income: $19,938 (2000); Median household income: $40,000 (2000); Poverty rate: 8.2% (2000).
Taxes: Total city taxes per capita: $57 (1997); City property taxes per capita: $57 (1997).
Education: High school graduation rate: 86.9% (2000); College graduation rate: 15.8% (2000).
Housing: Homeownership rate: 87.4% (2000); Median home value: $88,000 (2000); Median rent: $353 per month (2000); Median age of housing: 29 years (2000).
Transportation: Commute to work: 94.2% car, 0.0% public transportation, 1.2% walk, 3.8% work from home (2000); Travel time to work: 44.4% less than 15 minutes, 42.8% 15 to 30 minutes, 7.8% 30 to 45 minutes, 2.6% 45 to 60 minutes, 2.4% 60 minutes or more (2000)

QUINNESEC (CDP). Covers a land area of 1.131 square miles and a water area of 0.061 square miles. Located at 45.80° N. Lat.; 87.99° W. Long.
History: Quinnesec developed as a mining town in the Menominee Range, with ore being extracted here as early as 1873.
Population: 1,187 (2000); Race: 100.0% White, 0.0% Black, 0.0% Asian, 0.0% American Indian and Alaska Native, 0.0% Hispanic of any race, 0.0% two or more races (2000); Density: 1,049.2 persons per square mile (2000); Age: 26.3% under 18, 12.0% over 64 (2000); Marriage status: 21.2% never married, 65.8% now married, 4.4% widowed, 8.6% divorced (2000); Foreign born: 0.0% (2000); Ancestry (includes multiple ancestries): 23.0% German, 18.5% Italian, 14.7% Swedish, 11.9% Finnish, 11.4% French (except Basque) (2000).
Economy: Employment by occupation: 5.7% management, 14.1% professional, 15.5% services, 21.6% sales, 1.1% farming, 20.8% construction, 21.2% production (2000).
Income: Per capita income: $17,139 (2000); Median household income: $41,957 (2000); Poverty rate: 2.7% (2000).
Education: High school graduation rate: 91.0% (2000); College graduation rate: 9.5% (2000).
Housing: Homeownership rate: 98.1% (2000); Median home value: $65,400 (2000); Median age of housing: 27 years (2000).
Transportation: Commute to work: 97.8% car, 1.3% public transportation, 0.0% walk, 0.9% work from home (2000); Travel time to work: 72.7% less than 15 minutes, 17.2% 15 to 30 minutes, 3.5% 30 to 45 minutes, 0.0% 45 to 60 minutes, 6.6% 60 minutes or more (2000)

SAGOLA (township). Covers a land area of 160.315 square miles and a water area of 2.527 square miles. Located at 46.13° N. Lat.; 88.05° W. Long. Elevation is 1,436 feet.
History: Sagola grew around the Sagola Lumber Company operation, begun in the 1880's. The name comes from the Indian word for welcome.
Population: 1,169 (2000); Race: 98.7% White, 0.0% Black, 0.2% Asian, 0.9% American Indian and Alaska Native, 0.0% Hispanic of any race, 0.2% two or more races (2000); Density: 7.3 persons per square mile (2000); Age: 27.1% under 18, 15.5% over 64 (2000); Marriage status: 19.1% never married, 63.3% now married, 9.7% widowed, 7.9% divorced (2000); Foreign born: 0.8% (2000); Ancestry (includes multiple ancestries): 26.3% German, 12.7% Swedish, 11.7% Irish, 11.1% French (except Basque), 8.9% English (2000).
Economy: Employment by occupation: 8.0% management, 15.5% professional, 17.0% services, 24.3% sales, 2.5% farming, 16.0% construction, 16.8% production (2000).
Income: Per capita income: $15,531 (2000); Median household income: $33,333 (2000); Poverty rate: 12.1% (2000).
Taxes: Total city taxes per capita: $64 (1997); City property taxes per capita: $63 (1997).
Education: High school graduation rate: 84.2% (2000); College graduation rate: 11.9% (2000).
Housing: Homeownership rate: 92.6% (2000); Median home value: $56,200 (2000); Median rent: $300 per month (2000); Median age of housing: 29 years (2000).
Transportation: Commute to work: 93.5% car, 0.0% public transportation, 0.4% walk, 5.3% work from home (2000); Travel time to work: 23.3% less than 15 minutes, 35.7% 15 to 30 minutes, 31.7% 30 to 45 minutes, 3.3% 45 to 60 minutes, 6.0% 60 minutes or more (2000)

VULCAN (unincorporated postal area, zip code 49892). Covers a land area of 150.724 square miles and a water area of 1.409 square miles. Located at 45.75° N. Lat.; 87.78° W. Long. Elevation is 932 feet.
History: Blue hematite was found in the Vulcan area in 1874, and mining operations began. The community grew when the railroad arrived in 1877.
Population: 2,046 (2000); Race: 99.4% White, 0.1% Black, 0.0% Asian, 0.1% American Indian and Alaska Native, 0.2% Hispanic of any race, 0.3% two or more races (2000); Density: 13.6 persons per square mile (2000); Age: 25.2% under 18, 13.9% over 64 (2000); Marriage status: 22.1% never married, 62.5% now married, 7.9% widowed, 7.5% divorced (2000); Foreign born: 0.3% (2000); Ancestry (includes multiple ancestries): 24.8% German, 18.8% Italian, 14.2% Polish, 11.6% French (except Basque), 9.8% Irish (2000).
Economy: Employment by occupation: 8.9% management, 12.5% professional, 18.5% services, 23.6% sales, 0.9% farming, 9.9% construction, 25.7% production (2000).
Income: Per capita income: $17,568 (2000); Median household income: $38,393 (2000); Poverty rate: 8.3% (2000).
Education: High school graduation rate: 87.0% (2000); College graduation rate: 13.2% (2000).
Housing: Homeownership rate: 87.7% (2000); Median home value: $72,500 (2000); Median rent: $342 per month (2000); Median age of housing: 34 years (2000).
Transportation: Commute to work: 95.1% car, 0.0% public transportation, 0.6% walk, 3.6% work from home (2000); Travel time to work: 31.3% less than 15 minutes, 48.7% 15 to 30 minutes, 13.6% 30 to 45 minutes, 4.1% 45 to 60 minutes, 2.4% 60 minutes or more (2000)

WAUCEDAH (township). Covers a land area of 88.942 square miles and a water area of 1.094 square miles. Located at 45.81° N. Lat.; 87.77° W. Long. Elevation is 900 feet.
Population: 800 (2000); Race: 99.1% White, 0.6% Black, 0.0% Asian, 0.0% American Indian and Alaska Native, 0.2% Hispanic of any race, 0.2% two or more races (2000); Density: 9.0 persons per square mile (2000); Age: 25.6% under 18, 11.0% over 64 (2000); Marriage status: 17.3% never married, 68.1% now married, 7.0% widowed, 7.6% divorced (2000); Foreign born: 0.0% (2000); Ancestry (includes multiple ancestries): 26.3% German, 22.3% Italian, 11.6% French (except Basque), 11.3% Irish, 11.2% Polish (2000).
Economy: Employment by occupation: 10.4% management, 13.6% professional, 15.2% services, 28.8% sales, 0.5% farming, 12.9% construction, 18.7% production (2000).
Income: Per capita income: $17,706 (2000); Median household income: $40,400 (2000); Poverty rate: 6.0% (2000).
Taxes: Total city taxes per capita: $27 (1997); City property taxes per capita: $27 (1997).
Education: High school graduation rate: 89.2% (2000); College graduation rate: 14.0% (2000).
Housing: Homeownership rate: 92.0% (2000); Median home value: $87,900 (2000); Median rent: $313 per month (2000); Median age of housing: 34 years (2000).
Transportation: Commute to work: 93.7% car, 0.0% public transportation, 1.2% walk, 4.0% work from home (2000); Travel time to work: 26.2% less than 15 minutes, 53.5% 15 to 30 minutes, 12.8% 30 to 45 minutes, 5.1% 45 to 60 minutes, 2.4% 60 minutes or more (2000)

WEST BRANCH (township). Covers a land area of 111.461 square miles and a water area of 0.387 square miles. Located at 46.14° N. Lat.; 87.72° W. Long.
Population: 67 (2000); Race: 90.0% White, 0.0% Black, 0.0% Asian, 10.0% American Indian and Alaska Native, 0.0% Hispanic of any race, 0.0% two or more races (2000); Density: 0.6 persons per square mile (2000); Age: 10.0% under 18, 28.6% over 64 (2000); Marriage status: 20.0% never married, 55.4% now married, 15.4% widowed, 9.2% divorced (2000); Foreign born: 5.7% (2000); Ancestry (includes multiple ancestries): 15.7% Finnish, 14.3% English, 14.3% German, 12.9% Polish, 11.4% Swedish (2000).
Economy: Employment by occupation: 20.5% management, 5.1% professional, 33.3% services, 5.1% sales, 5.1% farming, 10.3% construction, 20.5% production (2000).
Income: Per capita income: $12,286 (2000); Median household income: $21,875 (2000); Poverty rate: 11.4% (2000).
Taxes: Total city taxes per capita: $138 (1997); City property taxes per capita: $138 (1997).
Education: High school graduation rate: 83.1% (2000); College graduation rate: 6.8% (2000).
Housing: Homeownership rate: 81.8% (2000); Median home value: $23,800 (2000); Median rent: $325 per month (2000); Median age of housing: 44 years (2000).
Transportation: Commute to work: 62.2% car, 0.0% public transportation, 0.0% walk, 37.8% work from home (2000); Travel time to work: 21.7% less

than 15 minutes, 34.8% 15 to 30 minutes, 17.4% 30 to 45 minutes, 8.7% 45 to 60 minutes, 17.4% 60 minutes or more (2000)

Eaton County

Located in south central Michigan; drained by the Grand and Thornapple Rivers. Covers a land area of 576.40 square miles, a water area of 2.60 square miles, and is located in the Eastern Time Zone. The county government was organized in 1837. County seat is Charlotte.

Eaton County is part of the Lansing-East Lansing, MI MSA. The entire metro area includes: Clinton County; Eaton County; Ingham County

Weather Station: Charlotte — Elevation: 898 feet

	Jan	Feb	Mar	Apr	May	Jun	Jul	Aug	Sep	Oct	Nov	Dec
High	29	33	43	56	69	78	82	80	73	60	46	35
Low	13	14	23	34	45	54	58	56	48	38	29	19
Precip	1.7	1.3	2.4	3.3	3.1	3.5	3.2	3.8	3.8	2.9	2.8	2.3
Snow	14.1	8.8	7.5	2.2	tr	0.0	0.0	0.0	0.0	0.4	3.5	11.3

High and Low temperatures in degrees Fahrenheit; Precipitation and Snow in inches

Population: 103,655 (2000); Race: 90.0% White, 5.0% Black, 1.2% Asian, 0.4% American Indian and Alaska Native, 3.1% Hispanic of any race, 2.2% two or more races (2000); Density: 179.8 persons per square mile (2000); Age: 26.1% under 18, 11.3% over 64 (2000).
Religion: Five largest groups: 8.2% Assemblies of God, 7.6% Catholic Church, 3.5% The United Methodist Church, 1.2% United Church of Christ, 1.1% Church of the Nazarene (2000).
Economy: Unemployment rate: 3.2% (11/2002); Total civilian labor force: 57,230 (11/2002); Leading industries: 22.4% manufacturing; 20.0% retail trade; 9.3% accommodation & food services (2000); Companies that employ more than 1,000 persons: 1 (2000); Companies that employ more than 100 persons: 50 (2000); Farms: 1,062 totaling 231,870 acres (1997); Minority business ownership rate: 4.4% (1997); Women business ownership rate: 34.1% (1997); Retail sales per capita: $8,954 (1997). Single-family building permits issued: 491 (2001) / 519 (2000); Multi-family building permits issued: 62 (2001) / 130 (2000).
Income: Per capita income: $22,411 (2000); Median household income: $49,588 (2000); Poverty rate: 5.8% (2000); Bankruptcy rate: 4.49% (2001).
Taxes: Total county taxes per capita: $155 (2000); County property taxes per capita: $140 (2000).
Education: High school graduation rate: 89.5% (2000); College graduation rate: 21.7% (2000).
Housing: Homeownership rate: 74.1% (2000); Median home value: $113,700 (2000); Median rent: $504 per month (2000); Median age of housing: 28 years (2000).
Health: Birth rate: 114.3 per 10,000 population (1998); Age adjusted death rate: 87.6 per 10,000 population (1999); Age adjusted cancer mortality rate: 219.3 deaths per 100,000 population (1999). Number of physicians: 6.0 per 10,000 population (1999); Number of hospital beds: 5.3 per 10,000 population (1999).
Elections: 2000 Presidential election results: 47.1% Gore, 50.3% Bush, 2.0% Nader, 0.0% Buchanan

Additional Information Contacts

Eaton County Government Offices 517-543-7500
Charlotte Chamber of Commerce. 517-543-0400
Eaton Rapids Chamber of Commerce 517-663-6480
Grand Ledge Chamber of Commerce 517-627-2383

Eaton County Communities

BELLEVUE (village). Covers a land area of 0.990 square miles and a water area of 0.062 square miles. Located at 42.44° N. Lat.; 85.01° W. Long. Elevation is 866 feet.
History: Bellevue, laid out in 1835, served as the seat of Eaton County from 1838 to 1840. The name was first spelled Bellvue; the extra "e" was added in 1841.
Population: 1,365 (2000); Race: 96.9% White, 0.1% Black, 0.6% Asian, 0.1% American Indian and Alaska Native, 1.5% Hispanic of any race, 1.8% two or more races (2000); Density: 1,378.7 persons per square mile (2000); Age: 28.1% under 18, 15.6% over 64 (2000); Marriage status: 24.6% never married, 53.6% now married, 9.1% widowed, 12.6% divorced (2000); Foreign born: 2.2% (2000); Ancestry (includes multiple ancestries): 25.0% German, 15.9% English, 12.6% Irish, 9.3% Other groups, 8.3% United States or American (2000).
Economy: Employment by occupation: 8.1% management, 14.7% professional, 18.4% services, 21.7% sales, 0.0% farming, 12.2% construction, 24.9% production (2000).
Income: Per capita income: $16,245 (2000); Median household income: $37,292 (2000); Poverty rate: 7.8% (2000).
Taxes: Total city taxes per capita: $115 (1997); City property taxes per capita: $112 (1997).
Education: High school graduation rate: 86.3% (2000); College graduation rate: 11.1% (2000).

School District(s)

Bellevue Community Schools (KG-12)
2000 Enrollment: 1,005 616-763-9432

Housing: Homeownership rate: 76.6% (2000); Median home value: $74,400 (2000); Median rent: $412 per month (2000); Median age of housing: 60 years (2000).
Transportation: Commute to work: 92.2% car, 0.0% public transportation, 4.5% walk, 2.6% work from home (2000); Travel time to work: 23.6% less than 15 minutes, 36.3% 15 to 30 minutes, 29.6% 30 to 45 minutes, 9.0% 45 to 60 minutes, 1.5% 60 minutes or more (2000)

BELLEVUE (township). Covers a land area of 36.374 square miles and a water area of 0.198 square miles. Located at 42.44° N. Lat.; 85.01° W. Long. Elevation is 866 feet.
History: Settled 1830; incorporated 1867.
Population: 3,144 (2000); Race: 98.1% White, 0.1% Black, 0.3% Asian, 0.1% American Indian and Alaska Native, 1.1% Hispanic of any race, 1.1% two or more races (2000); Density: 86.4 persons per square mile (2000); Age: 26.8% under 18, 12.5% over 64 (2000); Marriage status: 21.2% never married, 62.6% now married, 7.2% widowed, 9.1% divorced (2000); Foreign born: 1.2% (2000); Ancestry (includes multiple ancestries): 27.1% German, 14.6% English, 14.3% Irish, 10.2% United States or American, 8.0% Other groups (2000).
Economy: In farm area: grain, corn, beans. Cement manufacturing, crushed limestone. Employment by occupation: 8.8% management, 11.6% professional, 13.7% services, 25.7% sales, 0.1% farming, 14.7% construction, 25.4% production (2000).
Income: Per capita income: $17,586 (2000); Median household income: $43,393 (2000); Poverty rate: 6.1% (2000).
Taxes: Total city taxes per capita: $25 (1997); City property taxes per capita: $25 (1997).
Education: High school graduation rate: 89.0% (2000); College graduation rate: 8.8% (2000).
Housing: Homeownership rate: 86.4% (2000); Median home value: $82,100 (2000); Median rent: $408 per month (2000); Median age of housing: 43 years (2000).
Transportation: Commute to work: 93.9% car, 0.3% public transportation, 2.8% walk, 2.4% work from home (2000); Travel time to work: 20.4% less than 15 minutes, 36.6% 15 to 30 minutes, 28.5% 30 to 45 minutes, 10.1% 45 to 60 minutes, 4.3% 60 minutes or more (2000)

BENTON (township). Covers a land area of 33.729 square miles and a water area of 0 square miles. Located at 42.63° N. Lat.; 84.76° W. Long.
Population: 2,712 (2000); Race: 97.2% White, 0.7% Black, 0.1% Asian, 0.3% American Indian and Alaska Native, 3.1% Hispanic of any race, 0.9% two or more races (2000); Density: 80.4 persons per square mile (2000); Age: 24.9% under 18, 8.8% over 64 (2000); Marriage status: 20.1% never married, 63.9% now married, 5.6% widowed, 10.4% divorced (2000); Foreign born: 0.5% (2000); Ancestry (includes multiple ancestries): 24.2% German, 14.9% English, 10.1% United States or American, 9.1% Other groups, 8.4% Irish (2000).
Economy: Employment by occupation: 11.0% management, 18.3% professional, 9.0% services, 26.6% sales, 1.7% farming, 12.8% construction, 20.6% production (2000).
Income: Per capita income: $23,990 (2000); Median household income: $56,815 (2000); Poverty rate: 2.0% (2000).
Taxes: Total city taxes per capita: $19 (1997); City property taxes per capita: $19 (1997).
Education: High school graduation rate: 90.4% (2000); College graduation rate: 16.5% (2000).
Housing: Homeownership rate: 92.4% (2000); Median home value: $119,000 (2000); Median rent: $409 per month (2000); Median age of housing: 27 years (2000).
Transportation: Commute to work: 94.8% car, 0.0% public transportation, 0.5% walk, 3.2% work from home (2000); Travel time to work: 21.8% less than 15 minutes, 51.1% 15 to 30 minutes, 21.6% 30 to 45 minutes, 1.6% 45 to 60 minutes, 3.8% 60 minutes or more (2000)

BROOKFIELD (township). Covers a land area of 35.907 square miles and a water area of 0.314 square miles. Located at 42.46° N. Lat.; 84.77° W. Long. Elevation is 928 feet.
History: Brookfield Township was organized in 1841.
Population: 1,429 (2000); Race: 98.7% White, 0.0% Black, 0.0% Asian, 0.5% American Indian and Alaska Native, 3.0% Hispanic of any race, 0.7% two or more races (2000); Density: 39.8 persons per square mile (2000); Age: 27.2% under 18, 11.8% over 64 (2000); Marriage status: 19.5% never married, 66.6% now married, 3.9% widowed, 10.0% divorced (2000); Foreign born: 0.3% (2000); Ancestry (includes multiple ancestries): 27.3% German, 15.0% English, 13.2% United States or American, 11.1% Irish, 5.7% Other groups (2000).
Economy: Employment by occupation: 16.8% management, 11.6% professional, 10.9% services, 23.9% sales, 0.3% farming, 12.7% construction, 23.9% production (2000).
Income: Per capita income: $19,720 (2000); Median household income: $47,604 (2000); Poverty rate: 6.1% (2000).
Taxes: Total city taxes per capita: $20 (1997); City property taxes per capita: $20 (1997).
Education: High school graduation rate: 84.6% (2000); College graduation rate: 10.1% (2000).
Housing: Homeownership rate: 90.0% (2000); Median home value: $105,600 (2000); Median rent: $411 per month (2000); Median age of housing: 34 years (2000).
Transportation: Commute to work: 93.2% car, 0.3% public transportation, 0.4% walk, 5.4% work from home (2000); Travel time to work: 18.3% less than 15 minutes, 30.8% 15 to 30 minutes, 34.6% 30 to 45 minutes, 10.9% 45 to 60 minutes, 5.4% 60 minutes or more (2000)

CARMEL (township). Covers a land area of 34.123 square miles and a water area of 0.028 square miles. Located at 42.53° N. Lat.; 84.88° W. Long.
Population: 2,626 (2000); Race: 94.7% White, 0.0% Black, 0.1% Asian, 0.4% American Indian and Alaska Native, 4.1% Hispanic of any race, 2.7% two or more races (2000); Density: 77.0 persons per square mile (2000); Age: 26.7% under 18, 7.9% over 64 (2000); Marriage status: 20.2% never married, 69.6% now married, 4.2% widowed, 5.9% divorced (2000); Foreign born: 1.2% (2000); Ancestry (includes multiple ancestries): 25.8% German, 15.4% English, 12.4% United States or American, 10.5% Irish, 9.4% Other groups (2000).
Economy: Employment by occupation: 8.2% management, 16.3% professional, 11.2% services, 27.2% sales, 0.6% farming, 14.7% construction, 21.8% production (2000).
Income: Per capita income: $21,176 (2000); Median household income: $53,229 (2000); Poverty rate: 3.6% (2000).
Taxes: Total city taxes per capita: $19 (1997); City property taxes per capita: $17 (1997).
Education: High school graduation rate: 88.9% (2000); College graduation rate: 15.3% (2000).
Housing: Homeownership rate: 90.6% (2000); Median home value: $123,500 (2000); Median rent: $503 per month (2000); Median age of housing: 25 years (2000).
Transportation: Commute to work: 94.4% car, 0.0% public transportation, 0.0% walk, 5.2% work from home (2000); Travel time to work: 29.2% less than 15 minutes, 29.2% 15 to 30 minutes, 24.1% 30 to 45 minutes, 11.1% 45 to 60 minutes, 6.4% 60 minutes or more (2000)

CHARLOTTE (city). Covers a land area of 5.976 square miles and a water area of 0.012 square miles. Located at 42.56° N. Lat.; 84.83° W. Long. Elevation is 917 feet.
History: Charlotte was founded in the 1830's and named for the wife of one of the founders. Incorporated as a village in 1863 and as a city in 1871, Charlotte developed as a distribution center for maple sugar products.
Population: 8,389 (2000); Race: 96.0% White, 0.1% Black, 0.4% Asian, 0.5% American Indian and Alaska Native, 3.0% Hispanic of any race, 1.9% two or more races (2000); Density: 1,403.8 persons per square mile (2000); Age: 26.9% under 18, 14.3% over 64 (2000); Marriage status: 24.6% never married, 52.9% now married, 9.4% widowed, 13.1% divorced (2000); Foreign born: 1.5% (2000); Ancestry (includes multiple ancestries): 22.0% German, 13.6% English, 12.4% United States or American, 9.4% Other groups, 8.6% Irish (2000).
Economy: Single-family building permits issued: 30 (2001) / 42 (2000); Multi-family building permits issued: 20 (2001) / 4 (2000); Employment by occupation: 8.3% management, 16.9% professional, 14.3% services, 29.2% sales, 0.2% farming, 8.6% construction, 22.5% production (2000).
Income: Per capita income: $18,066 (2000); Median household income: $37,473 (2000); Poverty rate: 10.0% (2000).
Taxes: Total city taxes per capita: $239 (1997); City property taxes per capita: $232 (1997).
Education: High school graduation rate: 85.0% (2000); College graduation rate: 18.7% (2000).

School District(s)

Charlotte Public Schools (PK-12)
2000 Enrollment: 3,303 517-543-2810

Housing: Homeownership rate: 67.4% (2000); Median home value: $83,700 (2000); Median rent: $397 per month (2000); Median age of housing: 49 years (2000).
Hospitals: Hayes-Green-Beach Memorial Hospital (45 beds)
Safety: Violent crime rate: 30.8 per 10,000 population; Property crime rate: 328.5 per 10,000 population (2001).
Newspapers: Charlotte Shopping Guide (1 x week); De Witt Bath Review (1 x week); Eaton County News (1 x week)
Transportation: Commute to work: 90.7% car, 1.7% public transportation, 4.3% walk, 2.2% work from home (2000); Travel time to work: 42.8% less than 15 minutes, 28.9% 15 to 30 minutes, 20.1% 30 to 45 minutes, 3.7% 45 to 60 minutes, 4.5% 60 minutes or more (2000)
Additional Information Contacts
Charlotte Chamber of Commerce. 517-543-0400

CHESTER (township). Covers a land area of 36.130 square miles and a water area of 0.008 square miles. Located at 42.64° N. Lat.; 84.90° W. Long.
Population: 1,778 (2000); Race: 98.4% White, 0.0% Black, 0.4% Asian, 0.1% American Indian and Alaska Native, 1.2% Hispanic of any race, 1.0% two or more races (2000); Density: 49.2 persons per square mile (2000); Age: 26.7% under 18, 11.6% over 64 (2000); Marriage status: 18.9% never married, 68.2% now married, 5.3% widowed, 7.6% divorced (2000); Foreign born: 0.4% (2000); Ancestry (includes multiple ancestries): 28.6% German, 17.2% English, 11.6% United States or American, 10.0% Irish, 5.3% French (except Basque) (2000).
Economy: Employment by occupation: 8.4% management, 15.4% professional, 10.7% services, 28.7% sales, 1.5% farming, 12.2% construction, 23.1% production (2000).
Income: Per capita income: $21,588 (2000); Median household income: $52,438 (2000); Poverty rate: 5.3% (2000).
Taxes: Total city taxes per capita: $15 (1997); City property taxes per capita: $15 (1997).
Education: High school graduation rate: 87.7% (2000); College graduation rate: 11.6% (2000).
Housing: Homeownership rate: 89.4% (2000); Median home value: $107,200 (2000); Median rent: $343 per month (2000); Median age of housing: 39 years (2000).
Transportation: Commute to work: 91.4% car, 0.5% public transportation, 0.8% walk, 6.9% work from home (2000); Travel time to work: 21.1% less than 15 minutes, 35.5% 15 to 30 minutes, 29.1% 30 to 45 minutes, 7.6% 45 to 60 minutes, 6.7% 60 minutes or more (2000)

DELTA CHARTER (township). Covers a land area of 34.528 square miles and a water area of 0.457 square miles. Located at 42.73° N. Lat.; 84.64° W. Long.
Population: 29,682 (2000); Race: 84.6% White, 7.8% Black, 2.4% Asian, 0.2% American Indian and Alaska Native, 3.6% Hispanic of any race, 3.2% two or more races (2000); Density: 859.6 persons per square mile (2000); Age: 22.8% under 18, 13.1% over 64 (2000); Marriage status: 25.1% never married, 58.3% now married, 6.4% widowed, 10.2% divorced (2000); Foreign born: 4.0% (2000); Ancestry (includes multiple ancestries): 27.0% German, 16.6% Other groups, 15.4% English, 14.1% Irish, 5.4% Polish (2000).
Vital Statistics: Birth rate: 109.8 per 10,000 population (1998)
Economy: Unemployment rate: 2.3% (11/2002); Total civilian labor force: 17,498 (11/2002); Single-family building permits issued: 129 (2001) / 154 (2000); Multi-family building permits issued: 40 (2001) / 124 (2000); Employment by occupation: 17.0% management, 23.4% professional, 13.3% services, 29.0% sales, 0.1% farming, 5.8% construction, 11.3% production (2000).
Income: Per capita income: $27,048 (2000); Median household income: $52,711 (2000); Poverty rate: 5.0% (2000).
Taxes: Total city taxes per capita: $186 (2000); City property taxes per capita: $156 (2000).
Education: High school graduation rate: 93.2% (2000); College graduation rate: 33.7% (2000).

Housing: Homeownership rate: 64.2% (2000); Median home value: $133,800 (2000); Median rent: $574 per month (2000); Median age of housing: 24 years (2000).
Transportation: Commute to work: 94.3% car, 0.6% public transportation, 1.6% walk, 2.9% work from home (2000); Travel time to work: 42.8% less than 15 minutes, 44.6% 15 to 30 minutes, 5.3% 30 to 45 minutes, 2.6% 45 to 60 minutes, 4.6% 60 minutes or more (2000)

DIMONDALE (village). Covers a land area of 0.970 square miles and a water area of 0 square miles. Located at 42.64° N. Lat.; 84.64° W. Long.
Population: 1,342 (2000); Race: 95.3% White, 0.6% Black, 0.2% Asian, 1.4% American Indian and Alaska Native, 3.3% Hispanic of any race, 1.6% two or more races (2000); Density: 1,383.5 persons per square mile (2000); Age: 30.7% under 18, 9.4% over 64 (2000); Marriage status: 22.8% never married, 64.4% now married, 4.3% widowed, 8.4% divorced (2000); Foreign born: 0.6% (2000); Ancestry (includes multiple ancestries): 24.4% German, 19.7% English, 16.3% Irish, 9.9% Other groups, 8.2% Dutch (2000).
Economy: In farm area; light manufacturing. Employment by occupation: 16.3% management, 16.1% professional, 14.8% services, 31.6% sales, 0.2% farming, 6.2% construction, 14.9% production (2000).
Income: Per capita income: $23,611 (2000); Median household income: $57,917 (2000); Poverty rate: 3.7% (2000).
Taxes: Total city taxes per capita: $103 (1997); City property taxes per capita: $99 (1997).
Education: High school graduation rate: 93.1% (2000); College graduation rate: 23.7% (2000).
Housing: Homeownership rate: 87.3% (2000); Median home value: $117,400 (2000); Median rent: $497 per month (2000); Median age of housing: 42 years (2000).
Transportation: Commute to work: 95.3% car, 0.0% public transportation, 1.7% walk, 3.0% work from home (2000); Travel time to work: 26.8% less than 15 minutes, 59.6% 15 to 30 minutes, 6.9% 30 to 45 minutes, 3.0% 45 to 60 minutes, 3.7% 60 minutes or more (2000)

EATON (township). Covers a land area of 32.585 square miles and a water area of 0.023 square miles. Located at 42.56° N. Lat.; 84.77° W. Long.
Population: 4,278 (2000); Race: 97.0% White, 1.1% Black, 0.6% Asian, 0.0% American Indian and Alaska Native, 1.9% Hispanic of any race, 0.8% two or more races (2000); Density: 131.3 persons per square mile (2000); Age: 27.1% under 18, 9.3% over 64 (2000); Marriage status: 19.8% never married, 67.4% now married, 2.8% widowed, 9.9% divorced (2000); Foreign born: 1.2% (2000); Ancestry (includes multiple ancestries): 30.3% German, 18.0% English, 13.2% United States or American, 12.1% Irish, 7.2% Dutch (2000).
Economy: Employment by occupation: 14.2% management, 12.4% professional, 13.9% services, 30.6% sales, 0.0% farming, 9.4% construction, 19.5% production (2000).
Income: Per capita income: $23,379 (2000); Median household income: $55,518 (2000); Poverty rate: 3.9% (2000).
Taxes: Total city taxes per capita: $33 (1997); City property taxes per capita: $33 (1997).
Education: High school graduation rate: 91.2% (2000); College graduation rate: 19.4% (2000).
Housing: Homeownership rate: 93.0% (2000); Median home value: $113,300 (2000); Median rent: $508 per month (2000); Median age of housing: 24 years (2000).
Transportation: Commute to work: 93.8% car, 0.6% public transportation, 0.6% walk, 4.2% work from home (2000); Travel time to work: 30.5% less than 15 minutes, 38.0% 15 to 30 minutes, 21.4% 30 to 45 minutes, 6.4% 45 to 60 minutes, 3.7% 60 minutes or more (2000)

EATON RAPIDS (city). Covers a land area of 3.380 square miles and a water area of 0.110 square miles. Located at 42.50° N. Lat.; 84.65° W. Long. Elevation is 871 feet.
History: Eaton Rapids grew up around woolen mills, powered by water from the Grand River. The city was established as the center for a large sheep raising area.
Population: 5,330 (2000); Race: 96.2% White, 0.3% Black, 0.0% Asian, 1.2% American Indian and Alaska Native, 3.3% Hispanic of any race, 0.7% two or more races (2000); Density: 1,576.8 persons per square mile (2000); Age: 30.0% under 18, 11.2% over 64 (2000); Marriage status: 23.2% never married, 52.9% now married, 9.0% widowed, 15.0% divorced (2000); Foreign born: 0.5% (2000); Ancestry (includes multiple ancestries): 21.5% German, 16.0% English, 10.9% United States or American, 9.1% Irish, 8.5% Other groups (2000).
Economy: Single-family building permits issued: 11 (2001) / 14 (2000); Multi-family building permits issued: 0 (2001) / 2 (2000); Employment by occupation: 9.6% management, 15.2% professional, 15.6% services, 25.3% sales, 0.0% farming, 10.8% construction, 23.5% production (2000).
Income: Per capita income: $18,446 (2000); Median household income: $39,769 (2000); Poverty rate: 5.9% (2000).
Taxes: Total city taxes per capita: $214 (1997); City property taxes per capita: $202 (1997).
Education: High school graduation rate: 86.8% (2000); College graduation rate: 16.3% (2000).

School District(s)

Eaton Rapids Public Schools (PK-12)
2000 Enrollment: 3,270 517-663-8155
Island City Academy (KG-11)
2000 Enrollment: 195 517-774-2100

Housing: Homeownership rate: 68.4% (2000); Median home value: $90,900 (2000); Median rent: $404 per month (2000); Median age of housing: 46 years (2000).
Hospitals: Eaton Rapids Community Hospital (41 beds)
Safety: Violent crime rate: 29.9 per 10,000 population; Property crime rate: 235.2 per 10,000 population (2001).
Transportation: Commute to work: 94.6% car, 0.0% public transportation, 2.2% walk, 2.7% work from home (2000); Travel time to work: 30.7% less than 15 minutes, 25.2% 15 to 30 minutes, 35.8% 30 to 45 minutes, 5.1% 45 to 60 minutes, 3.1% 60 minutes or more (2000)
Additional Information Contacts
Eaton Rapids Chamber of Commerce 517-663-6480

EATON RAPIDS (township). Covers a land area of 34.112 square miles and a water area of 0.202 square miles. Located at 42.55° N. Lat.; 84.65° W. Long. Elevation is 871 feet.
History: Settled 1837; incorporated as village 1871, as city 1881.
Population: 3,821 (2000); Race: 95.7% White, 0.4% Black, 0.3% Asian, 0.6% American Indian and Alaska Native, 2.3% Hispanic of any race, 1.8% two or more races (2000); Density: 112.0 persons per square mile (2000); Age: 27.7% under 18, 8.4% over 64 (2000); Marriage status: 20.7% never married, 68.4% now married, 2.7% widowed, 8.3% divorced (2000); Foreign born: 0.5% (2000); Ancestry (includes multiple ancestries): 24.5% German, 17.5% English, 13.3% United States or American, 10.4% Irish, 8.8% Other groups (2000).
Economy: In sheep-raising area. Manufacturing: woolen goods, metal parts, food products; dairy, poultry. Manufacturing: plastic compounds and adhesives, small engine parts, corrugated packing. Mineral springs. Employment by occupation: 14.0% management, 12.9% professional, 14.4% services, 24.5% sales, 0.8% farming, 15.1% construction, 18.4% production (2000).
Income: Per capita income: $21,000 (2000); Median household income: $56,599 (2000); Poverty rate: 3.2% (2000).
Taxes: Total city taxes per capita: $23 (1997); City property taxes per capita: $22 (1997).
Education: High school graduation rate: 85.7% (2000); College graduation rate: 13.9% (2000).
Housing: Homeownership rate: 92.9% (2000); Median home value: $124,900 (2000); Median rent: $449 per month (2000); Median age of housing: 23 years (2000).
Transportation: Commute to work: 94.7% car, 2.0% public transportation, 0.6% walk, 2.7% work from home (2000); Travel time to work: 23.2% less than 15 minutes, 45.3% 15 to 30 minutes, 17.6% 30 to 45 minutes, 7.9% 45 to 60 minutes, 5.9% 60 minutes or more (2000)

GRAND LEDGE (city). Covers a land area of 3.553 square miles and a water area of 0.084 square miles. Located at 42.75° N. Lat.; 84.74° W. Long. Elevation is 849 feet.
History: Grand Ledge was named for the sandstone ledges that overhang the river in this area. The sandstone furnished material for the tile and clay product factories of the city.
Population: 7,813 (2000); Race: 96.2% White, 0.7% Black, 0.5% Asian, 0.3% American Indian and Alaska Native, 2.1% Hispanic of any race, 1.4% two or more races (2000); Density: 2,199.2 persons per square mile (2000); Age: 26.7% under 18, 10.7% over 64 (2000); Marriage status: 23.9% never married, 54.8% now married, 5.3% widowed, 15.9% divorced (2000); Foreign born: 1.4% (2000); Ancestry (includes multiple ancestries): 29.5% German, 15.8% English, 13.6% Irish, 8.3% United States or American, 7.6% Other groups (2000).
Economy: Single-family building permits issued: 26 (2001) / 25 (2000); Multi-family building permits issued: 0 (2001) / 0 (2000); Employment by

occupation: 12.0% management, 18.6% professional, 12.8% services, 28.6% sales, 0.0% farming, 11.0% construction, 16.9% production (2000).
Income: Per capita income: $22,438 (2000); Median household income: $47,043 (2000); Poverty rate: 9.3% (2000).
Taxes: Total city taxes per capita: $281 (1997); City property taxes per capita: $273 (1997).
Education: High school graduation rate: 88.3% (2000); College graduation rate: 24.7% (2000).

School District(s)

Grand Ledge Public Schools (PK-12)
2000 Enrollment: 5,280 517-627-3241
Oneida Township School District #3 (KG-05)
2000 Enrollment: 20 517-543-5500

Housing: Homeownership rate: 66.2% (2000); Median home value: $105,500 (2000); Median rent: $481 per month (2000); Median age of housing: 33 years (2000).
Safety: Violent crime rate: 8.9 per 10,000 population; Property crime rate: 203.7 per 10,000 population (2001).
Newspapers: Portland Review & Observer (1 x week); Grand Ledge Independent (1 x week); Delta-Waverly News Herald (1 x week)
Transportation: Commute to work: 93.2% car, 0.8% public transportation, 2.2% walk, 3.2% work from home (2000); Travel time to work: 26.5% less than 15 minutes, 50.5% 15 to 30 minutes, 15.5% 30 to 45 minutes, 3.0% 45 to 60 minutes, 4.5% 60 minutes or more (2000)

Additional Information Contacts

Grand Ledge Chamber of Commerce 517-627-2383

HAMLIN (township). Covers a land area of 34.299 square miles and a water area of 0.159 square miles. Located at 42.47° N. Lat.; 84.66° W. Long.
History: Hamlin Township was set off from Eaton Rapids Township in 1869 by the legislature. It was named for Samuel Hamlin who had built a road through the northwestern part of the county.
Population: 2,953 (2000); Race: 98.5% White, 0.1% Black, 0.0% Asian, 0.0% American Indian and Alaska Native, 1.1% Hispanic of any race, 0.9% two or more races (2000); Density: 86.1 persons per square mile (2000); Age: 31.2% under 18, 8.0% over 64 (2000); Marriage status: 19.9% never married, 69.9% now married, 2.7% widowed, 7.5% divorced (2000); Foreign born: 1.1% (2000); Ancestry (includes multiple ancestries): 28.0% German, 15.5% English, 14.7% Irish, 8.8% United States or American, 8.7% Other groups (2000).
Economy: Employment by occupation: 13.3% management, 12.1% professional, 10.3% services, 25.7% sales, 1.0% farming, 14.3% construction, 23.3% production (2000).
Income: Per capita income: $23,931 (2000); Median household income: $57,473 (2000); Poverty rate: 2.6% (2000).
Taxes: Total city taxes per capita: $21 (1997); City property taxes per capita: $21 (1997).
Education: High school graduation rate: 89.2% (2000); College graduation rate: 15.9% (2000).
Housing: Homeownership rate: 91.1% (2000); Median home value: $110,300 (2000); Median rent: $597 per month (2000); Median age of housing: 20 years (2000).
Transportation: Commute to work: 94.9% car, 0.4% public transportation, 2.2% walk, 2.4% work from home (2000); Travel time to work: 28.2% less than 15 minutes, 24.0% 15 to 30 minutes, 37.5% 30 to 45 minutes, 6.4% 45 to 60 minutes, 3.9% 60 minutes or more (2000)

KALAMO (township). Covers a land area of 36.640 square miles and a water area of 0.121 square miles. Located at 42.55° N. Lat.; 85.00° W. Long.
Population: 1,742 (2000); Race: 98.0% White, 0.3% Black, 0.0% Asian, 0.2% American Indian and Alaska Native, 1.4% Hispanic of any race, 0.9% two or more races (2000); Density: 47.5 persons per square mile (2000); Age: 27.0% under 18, 9.8% over 64 (2000); Marriage status: 20.6% never married, 65.1% now married, 5.4% widowed, 8.9% divorced (2000); Foreign born: 0.2% (2000); Ancestry (includes multiple ancestries): 24.8% German, 17.6% English, 12.8% Irish, 7.2% United States or American, 6.3% Dutch (2000).
Economy: Employment by occupation: 9.3% management, 9.2% professional, 10.7% services, 21.3% sales, 1.0% farming, 15.7% construction, 32.8% production (2000).
Income: Per capita income: $17,934 (2000); Median household income: $46,927 (2000); Poverty rate: 5.3% (2000).
Taxes: Total city taxes per capita: $21 (1997); City property taxes per capita: $21 (1997).
Education: High school graduation rate: 83.3% (2000); College graduation rate: 8.2% (2000).
Housing: Homeownership rate: 92.9% (2000); Median home value: $99,500 (2000); Median rent: $436 per month (2000); Median age of housing: 36 years (2000).
Transportation: Commute to work: 91.2% car, 1.3% public transportation, 1.9% walk, 4.2% work from home (2000); Travel time to work: 17.7% less than 15 minutes, 33.7% 15 to 30 minutes, 27.8% 30 to 45 minutes, 12.7% 45 to 60 minutes, 8.2% 60 minutes or more (2000)

MULLIKEN (village). Covers a land area of 1.043 square miles and a water area of 0 square miles. Located at 42.76° N. Lat.; 84.89° W. Long.
Population: 557 (2000); Race: 93.7% White, 1.4% Black, 0.0% Asian, 2.3% American Indian and Alaska Native, 3.8% Hispanic of any race, 2.5% two or more races (2000); Density: 534.2 persons per square mile (2000); Age: 29.1% under 18, 7.4% over 64 (2000); Marriage status: 28.8% never married, 54.0% now married, 5.7% widowed, 11.4% divorced (2000); Foreign born: 2.2% (2000); Ancestry (includes multiple ancestries): 28.9% German, 15.7% English, 11.0% United States or American, 10.5% Irish, 7.4% Other groups (2000).
Economy: In farm area. Manufacturing: metal fabrication. Employment by occupation: 11.4% management, 9.7% professional, 13.4% services, 20.7% sales, 0.0% farming, 13.4% construction, 31.4% production (2000).
Income: Per capita income: $18,181 (2000); Median household income: $50,391 (2000); Poverty rate: 3.6% (2000).
Taxes: Total city taxes per capita: $63 (1997); City property taxes per capita: $63 (1997).
Education: High school graduation rate: 85.8% (2000); College graduation rate: 8.9% (2000).

School District(s)

Roxand School District #12 (KG-08)
2000 Enrollment: 8 517-543-5500

Housing: Homeownership rate: 92.1% (2000); Median home value: $84,700 (2000); Median rent: $431 per month (2000); Median age of housing: 48 years (2000).
Transportation: Commute to work: 97.9% car, 1.4% public transportation, 0.0% walk, 0.7% work from home (2000); Travel time to work: 11.7% less than 15 minutes, 36.0% 15 to 30 minutes, 39.2% 30 to 45 minutes, 8.1% 45 to 60 minutes, 4.9% 60 minutes or more (2000)

OLIVET (city). Aka Ainger. Covers a land area of 1.013 square miles and a water area of 0 square miles. Located at 42.44° N. Lat.; 84.92° W. Long. Elevation is 885 feet.
History: Olivet College was founded in Olivet in 1844 by the Congregational Church. The site was chosen by Reverend John Shiperd, the founder of Oberlin College in Ohio, who got lost in the woods here and decided this must be the place to locate a new college.
Population: 1,758 (2000); Race: 83.0% White, 10.9% Black, 1.5% Asian, 0.7% American Indian and Alaska Native, 1.5% Hispanic of any race, 2.3% two or more races (2000); Density: 1,735.0 persons per square mile (2000); Age: 21.0% under 18, 4.0% over 64 (2000); Marriage status: 43.3% never married, 43.1% now married, 3.2% widowed, 10.5% divorced (2000); Foreign born: 4.1% (2000); Ancestry (includes multiple ancestries): 23.5% German, 12.0% English, 9.0% United States or American, 8.2% Other groups, 5.7% Irish (2000).
Economy: Employment by occupation: 10.7% management, 19.0% professional, 18.7% services, 23.3% sales, 0.4% farming, 7.3% construction, 20.6% production (2000).
Income: Per capita income: $11,682 (2000); Median household income: $34,474 (2000); Poverty rate: 10.7% (2000).
Taxes: Total city taxes per capita: $85 (1997); City property taxes per capita: $78 (1997).
Education: High school graduation rate: 91.2% (2000); College graduation rate: 24.0% (2000).

School District(s)

Olivet Community Schools (KG-12)
2000 Enrollment: 1,314 616-749-9129

Four-year College(s)

Olivet College (Private, Not-for-profit, United Church of Christ)
2001 Enrollment: 834 616-749-7000
2001 Tuition: In-state $13,982; Out-of-state $13,982

Housing: Homeownership rate: 44.8% (2000); Median home value: $87,400 (2000); Median rent: $374 per month (2000); Median age of housing: 50 years (2000).
Transportation: Commute to work: 77.1% car, 0.3% public transportation, 20.5% walk, 1.8% work from home (2000); Travel time to work: 38.9% less than 15 minutes, 33.2% 15 to 30 minutes, 20.3% 30 to 45 minutes, 5.0% 45 to 60 minutes, 2.6% 60 minutes or more (2000)

ONEIDA CHARTER (township). Covers a land area of 32.520 square miles and a water area of 0.093 square miles. Located at 42.72° N. Lat.; 84.76° W. Long.
Population: 3,703 (2000); Race: 98.4% White, 0.0% Black, 0.3% Asian, 1.1% American Indian and Alaska Native, 1.9% Hispanic of any race, 0.0% two or more races (2000); Density: 113.9 persons per square mile (2000); Age: 26.2% under 18, 12.3% over 64 (2000); Marriage status: 18.2% never married, 70.8% now married, 6.0% widowed, 5.0% divorced (2000); Foreign born: 1.8% (2000); Ancestry (includes multiple ancestries): 32.8% German, 16.2% English, 15.7% Irish, 9.3% United States or American, 5.9% Dutch (2000).
Economy: Single-family building permits issued: 29 (2001) / 30 (2000); Multi-family building permits issued: 0 (2001) / 0 (2000); Employment by occupation: 14.0% management, 20.7% professional, 12.3% services, 23.3% sales, 0.0% farming, 11.6% construction, 18.2% production (2000).
Income: Per capita income: $26,787 (2000); Median household income: $63,750 (2000); Poverty rate: 2.7% (2000).
Taxes: Total city taxes per capita: $52 (1997); City property taxes per capita: $44 (1997).
Education: High school graduation rate: 93.8% (2000); College graduation rate: 20.4% (2000).
Housing: Homeownership rate: 90.1% (2000); Median home value: $135,600 (2000); Median rent: $1,648 per month (2000); Median age of housing: 29 years (2000).
Transportation: Commute to work: 94.1% car, 0.0% public transportation, 2.1% walk, 3.6% work from home (2000); Travel time to work: 27.8% less than 15 minutes, 52.0% 15 to 30 minutes, 13.2% 30 to 45 minutes, 2.4% 45 to 60 minutes, 4.5% 60 minutes or more (2000)

POTTERVILLE (city). Covers a land area of 1.840 square miles and a water area of 0.006 square miles. Located at 42.62° N. Lat.; 84.74° W. Long. Elevation is 904 feet.
History: Linus Potter and his family settled here in 1844. The eldest son, George, built a sawmill and a boarding house that later became a hotel. Pottervile developed as the center of an area known for its purebred sheep, cattle, and Percheron horses.
Population: 2,168 (2000); Race: 94.9% White, 0.8% Black, 0.4% Asian, 0.3% American Indian and Alaska Native, 3.3% Hispanic of any race, 2.3% two or more races (2000); Density: 1,178.3 persons per square mile (2000); Age: 32.8% under 18, 6.2% over 64 (2000); Marriage status: 23.2% never married, 60.3% now married, 4.5% widowed, 11.9% divorced (2000); Foreign born: 0.9% (2000); Ancestry (includes multiple ancestries): 26.5% German, 14.0% English, 13.0% Irish, 12.2% United States or American, 8.6% Other groups (2000).
Economy: Employment by occupation: 6.6% management, 14.1% professional, 16.1% services, 30.3% sales, 1.1% farming, 11.0% construction, 20.8% production (2000).
Income: Per capita income: $17,880 (2000); Median household income: $42,292 (2000); Poverty rate: 5.9% (2000).
Taxes: Total city taxes per capita: $241 (1997); City property taxes per capita: $239 (1997).
Education: High school graduation rate: 87.9% (2000); College graduation rate: 9.2% (2000).

School District(s)

Potterville Public Schools (PK-12)
2000 Enrollment: 831 517-645-2662
Housing: Homeownership rate: 74.6% (2000); Median home value: $88,100 (2000); Median rent: $382 per month (2000); Median age of housing: 24 years (2000).
Safety: Violent crime rate: 18.4 per 10,000 population; Property crime rate: 234.1 per 10,000 population (2001).
Transportation: Commute to work: 94.8% car, 0.4% public transportation, 1.2% walk, 2.8% work from home (2000); Travel time to work: 23.1% less than 15 minutes, 51.1% 15 to 30 minutes, 17.8% 30 to 45 minutes, 4.1% 45 to 60 minutes, 3.8% 60 minutes or more (2000)

ROXAND (township). Covers a land area of 36.487 square miles and a water area of 0.025 square miles. Located at 42.73° N. Lat.; 84.90° W. Long.
History: Roxand was settled in the 1830's. It was named for a woman, Roxana, an early settler here. The "a" became a "d" through a clerk's error.
Population: 1,903 (2000); Race: 96.5% White, 0.4% Black, 0.0% Asian, 1.0% American Indian and Alaska Native, 2.7% Hispanic of any race, 1.6% two or more races (2000); Density: 52.2 persons per square mile (2000); Age: 27.4% under 18, 11.2% over 64 (2000); Marriage status: 24.1% never married, 62.0% now married, 4.2% widowed, 9.7% divorced (2000); Foreign born: 1.7% (2000); Ancestry (includes multiple ancestries): 29.4% German, 15.0% English, 11.4% United States or American, 9.2% Irish, 6.9% Other groups (2000).
Economy: Employment by occupation: 13.5% management, 8.4% professional, 14.0% services, 22.7% sales, 0.6% farming, 15.4% construction, 25.4% production (2000).
Income: Per capita income: $19,491 (2000); Median household income: $51,216 (2000); Poverty rate: 4.1% (2000).
Taxes: Total city taxes per capita: $49 (1997); City property taxes per capita: $49 (1997).
Education: High school graduation rate: 85.6% (2000); College graduation rate: 8.3% (2000).
Housing: Homeownership rate: 90.0% (2000); Median home value: $89,100 (2000); Median rent: $456 per month (2000); Median age of housing: 46 years (2000).
Transportation: Commute to work: 95.5% car, 0.9% public transportation, 0.7% walk, 2.6% work from home (2000); Travel time to work: 11.9% less than 15 minutes, 42.2% 15 to 30 minutes, 33.5% 30 to 45 minutes, 5.9% 45 to 60 minutes, 6.5% 60 minutes or more (2000)

SUNFIELD (village). Covers a land area of 0.643 square miles and a water area of 0 square miles. Located at 42.76° N. Lat.; 84.99° W. Long. Elevation is 866 feet.
History: The village of Sunfield was laid out by land speculators and was named for the township.
Population: 591 (2000); Race: 96.6% White, 0.0% Black, 0.0% Asian, 0.0% American Indian and Alaska Native, 2.2% Hispanic of any race, 3.1% two or more races (2000); Density: 919.8 persons per square mile (2000); Age: 29.2% under 18, 13.7% over 64 (2000); Marriage status: 20.1% never married, 55.0% now married, 9.4% widowed, 15.5% divorced (2000); Foreign born: 0.5% (2000); Ancestry (includes multiple ancestries): 24.8% German, 17.4% English, 13.0% Irish, 7.9% Other groups, 7.7% United States or American (2000).
Economy: Employment by occupation: 11.0% management, 13.2% professional, 10.3% services, 29.5% sales, 0.0% farming, 9.6% construction, 26.3% production (2000).
Income: Per capita income: $18,779 (2000); Median household income: $41,607 (2000); Poverty rate: 4.0% (2000).
Taxes: Total city taxes per capita: $123 (1997); City property taxes per capita: $120 (1997).
Education: High school graduation rate: 85.2% (2000); College graduation rate: 10.0% (2000).
Housing: Homeownership rate: 77.0% (2000); Median home value: $82,900 (2000); Median rent: $460 per month (2000); Median age of housing: 37 years (2000).
Newspapers: Sunfield Sentinel (1 x week)
Transportation: Commute to work: 92.1% car, 0.0% public transportation, 2.5% walk, 5.4% work from home (2000); Travel time to work: 17.9% less than 15 minutes, 29.4% 15 to 30 minutes, 33.6% 30 to 45 minutes, 9.2% 45 to 60 minutes, 9.9% 60 minutes or more (2000)

SUNFIELD (township). Covers a land area of 36.035 square miles and a water area of 0.324 square miles. Located at 42.72° N. Lat.; 85.01° W. Long. Elevation is 866 feet.
Population: 2,177 (2000); Race: 98.3% White, 0.0% Black, 0.0% Asian, 0.0% American Indian and Alaska Native, 3.0% Hispanic of any race, 1.6% two or more races (2000); Density: 60.4 persons per square mile (2000); Age: 26.8% under 18, 11.4% over 64 (2000); Marriage status: 22.9% never married, 62.9% now married, 4.5% widowed, 9.7% divorced (2000); Foreign born: 0.5% (2000); Ancestry (includes multiple ancestries): 28.5% German, 14.1% English, 12.0% Irish, 9.0% Dutch, 7.6% Other groups (2000).
Economy: In farm area. Employment by occupation: 10.7% management, 13.8% professional, 13.9% services, 21.9% sales, 1.9% farming, 14.5% construction, 23.2% production (2000).
Income: Per capita income: $19,291 (2000); Median household income: $50,104 (2000); Poverty rate: 4.2% (2000).
Taxes: Total city taxes per capita: $19 (1997); City property taxes per capita: $19 (1997).
Education: High school graduation rate: 88.2% (2000); College graduation rate: 9.3% (2000).
Housing: Homeownership rate: 85.2% (2000); Median home value: $93,000 (2000); Median rent: $454 per month (2000); Median age of housing: 38 years (2000).
Transportation: Commute to work: 91.0% car, 0.4% public transportation, 2.3% walk, 6.4% work from home (2000); Travel time to work: 19.4% less

than 15 minutes, 24.9% 15 to 30 minutes, 33.3% 30 to 45 minutes, 12.5% 45 to 60 minutes, 9.9% 60 minutes or more (2000)

VERMONTVILLE (village). Covers a land area of 1.210 square miles and a water area of 0 square miles. Located at 42.62° N. Lat.; 85.02° W. Long. Elevation is 928 feet.
History: Vermontville was settled in 1836 by a group from Vermont, who brought the maple sugar industry with them.
Population: 789 (2000); Race: 93.3% White, 0.0% Black, 1.0% Asian, 1.2% American Indian and Alaska Native, 1.9% Hispanic of any race, 4.5% two or more races (2000); Density: 651.8 persons per square mile (2000); Age: 31.3% under 18, 11.5% over 64 (2000); Marriage status: 20.7% never married, 59.4% now married, 10.1% widowed, 9.9% divorced (2000); Foreign born: 1.5% (2000); Ancestry (includes multiple ancestries): 23.2% German, 14.8% English, 10.5% Irish, 10.5% United States or American, 9.8% Other groups (2000).
Economy: Employment by occupation: 7.7% management, 19.2% professional, 11.2% services, 27.2% sales, 1.3% farming, 7.0% construction, 26.5% production (2000).
Income: Per capita income: $17,582 (2000); Median household income: $40,441 (2000); Poverty rate: 9.7% (2000).
Taxes: Total city taxes per capita: $120 (1997); City property taxes per capita: $120 (1997).
Education: High school graduation rate: 84.5% (2000); College graduation rate: 10.1% (2000).

School District(s)

Maple Valley Schools (PK-12)
2000 Enrollment: 1,693 517-852-9699
Housing: Homeownership rate: 80.9% (2000); Median home value: $77,300 (2000); Median rent: $379 per month (2000); Median age of housing: 60+ years (2000).
Transportation: Commute to work: 92.1% car, 1.3% public transportation, 2.6% walk, 3.9% work from home (2000); Travel time to work: 15.4% less than 15 minutes, 23.3% 15 to 30 minutes, 32.5% 30 to 45 minutes, 22.3% 45 to 60 minutes, 6.5% 60 minutes or more (2000)

VERMONTVILLE (township). Covers a land area of 36.318 square miles and a water area of 0.077 square miles. Located at 42.63° N. Lat.; 85.01° W. Long. Elevation is 928 feet.
Population: 2,100 (2000); Race: 96.9% White, 0.0% Black, 0.3% Asian, 0.4% American Indian and Alaska Native, 2.1% Hispanic of any race, 2.2% two or more races (2000); Density: 57.8 persons per square mile (2000); Age: 30.5% under 18, 9.9% over 64 (2000); Marriage status: 19.3% never married, 63.2% now married, 7.9% widowed, 9.5% divorced (2000); Foreign born: 1.1% (2000); Ancestry (includes multiple ancestries): 26.5% German, 15.9% English, 10.4% United States or American, 9.7% Irish, 7.0% Other groups (2000).
Economy: In farm area. Manufacturing of magnetic recording labels. Employment by occupation: 9.9% management, 17.7% professional, 12.3% services, 20.8% sales, 0.6% farming, 13.0% construction, 25.7% production (2000).
Income: Per capita income: $17,998 (2000); Median household income: $45,848 (2000); Poverty rate: 7.0% (2000).
Taxes: Total city taxes per capita: $21 (1997); City property taxes per capita: $21 (1997).
Education: High school graduation rate: 85.3% (2000); College graduation rate: 10.2% (2000).
Housing: Homeownership rate: 88.1% (2000); Median home value: $85,800 (2000); Median rent: $406 per month (2000); Median age of housing: 35 years (2000).
Transportation: Commute to work: 91.0% car, 1.1% public transportation, 2.3% walk, 5.2% work from home (2000); Travel time to work: 18.7% less than 15 minutes, 27.7% 15 to 30 minutes, 31.2% 30 to 45 minutes, 14.9% 45 to 60 minutes, 7.5% 60 minutes or more (2000)

WALTON (township). Covers a land area of 35.210 square miles and a water area of 0.196 square miles. Located at 42.47° N. Lat.; 84.90° W. Long.
Population: 2,011 (2000); Race: 98.0% White, 0.5% Black, 0.3% Asian, 0.6% American Indian and Alaska Native, 1.0% Hispanic of any race, 0.3% two or more races (2000); Density: 57.1 persons per square mile (2000); Age: 29.1% under 18, 8.7% over 64 (2000); Marriage status: 17.8% never married, 69.1% now married, 4.8% widowed, 8.3% divorced (2000); Foreign born: 0.8% (2000); Ancestry (includes multiple ancestries): 25.5% German, 14.7% English, 12.5% United States or American, 9.9% Irish, 6.7% Other groups (2000).
Economy: Employment by occupation: 11.4% management, 13.2% professional, 14.9% services, 21.1% sales, 0.2% farming, 13.5% construction, 25.6% production (2000).
Income: Per capita income: $20,034 (2000); Median household income: $50,571 (2000); Poverty rate: 3.1% (2000).
Taxes: Total city taxes per capita: $16 (1997); City property taxes per capita: $16 (1997).
Education: High school graduation rate: 89.4% (2000); College graduation rate: 12.4% (2000).
Housing: Homeownership rate: 90.0% (2000); Median home value: $97,600 (2000); Median rent: $433 per month (2000); Median age of housing: 28 years (2000).
Transportation: Commute to work: 94.0% car, 0.0% public transportation, 0.6% walk, 4.4% work from home (2000); Travel time to work: 23.0% less than 15 minutes, 36.2% 15 to 30 minutes, 28.1% 30 to 45 minutes, 8.2% 45 to 60 minutes, 4.4% 60 minutes or more (2000)

WAVERLY (CDP). Covers a land area of 5.692 square miles and a water area of <.001 square miles. Located at 42.73° N. Lat.; 84.62° W. Long.
Population: 16,194 (2000); Race: 80.0% White, 10.6% Black, 3.0% Asian, 0.1% American Indian and Alaska Native, 4.3% Hispanic of any race, 4.3% two or more races (2000); Density: 2,845.1 persons per square mile (2000); Age: 23.4% under 18, 12.7% over 64 (2000); Marriage status: 26.8% never married, 55.7% now married, 6.7% widowed, 10.9% divorced (2000); Foreign born: 4.4% (2000); Ancestry (includes multiple ancestries): 25.0% German, 20.1% Other groups, 15.1% English, 13.5% Irish, 5.7% Polish (2000).
Economy: Employment by occupation: 14.9% management, 24.9% professional, 12.6% services, 30.3% sales, 0.1% farming, 5.2% construction, 12.1% production (2000).
Income: Per capita income: $26,867 (2000); Median household income: $51,148 (2000); Poverty rate: 5.8% (2000).
Education: High school graduation rate: 92.7% (2000); College graduation rate: 34.4% (2000).
Housing: Homeownership rate: 60.9% (2000); Median home value: $127,800 (2000); Median rent: $533 per month (2000); Median age of housing: 27 years (2000).
Transportation: Commute to work: 94.2% car, 0.8% public transportation, 2.0% walk, 2.5% work from home (2000); Travel time to work: 46.4% less than 15 minutes, 42.8% 15 to 30 minutes, 4.6% 30 to 45 minutes, 1.8% 45 to 60 minutes, 4.3% 60 minutes or more (2000)

WINDSOR CHARTER (township). Covers a land area of 34.907 square miles and a water area of 0.168 square miles. Located at 42.64° N. Lat.; 84.65° W. Long.
Population: 7,340 (2000); Race: 91.2% White, 2.1% Black, 1.2% Asian, 0.7% American Indian and Alaska Native, 4.6% Hispanic of any race, 2.9% two or more races (2000); Density: 210.3 persons per square mile (2000); Age: 24.1% under 18, 15.3% over 64 (2000); Marriage status: 18.9% never married, 64.4% now married, 8.9% widowed, 7.8% divorced (2000); Foreign born: 1.6% (2000); Ancestry (includes multiple ancestries): 23.6% German, 17.5% English, 12.2% Irish, 12.1% Other groups, 8.2% United States or American (2000).
Economy: Employment by occupation: 14.4% management, 16.4% professional, 10.4% services, 31.3% sales, 0.0% farming, 10.5% construction, 17.0% production (2000).
Income: Per capita income: $23,912 (2000); Median household income: $57,793 (2000); Poverty rate: 3.3% (2000).
Taxes: Total city taxes per capita: $50 (2000); City property taxes per capita: $47 (2000).
Education: High school graduation rate: 89.4% (2000); College graduation rate: 20.9% (2000).
Housing: Homeownership rate: 94.5% (2000); Median home value: $133,700 (2000); Median rent: $503 per month (2000); Median age of housing: 26 years (2000).
Transportation: Commute to work: 95.7% car, 0.1% public transportation, 1.0% walk, 3.3% work from home (2000); Travel time to work: 21.8% less than 15 minutes, 62.6% 15 to 30 minutes, 8.8% 30 to 45 minutes, 2.8% 45 to 60 minutes, 4.0% 60 minutes or more (2000)

Emmet County

Located in northwestern Michigan; bounded on the west by Little Traverse Bay and Lake Michigan, and on the north by the Straits of Mackinac; drained by the Maple River. Covers a land area of 467.80 square miles, a water area of 414.40 square miles, and is located in the Eastern Time Zone. The county government was organized in 1853. County seat is Petoskey.

Weather Station: Cross Village Elevation: 741 feet

	Jan	Feb	Mar	Apr	May	Jun	Jul	Aug	Sep	Oct	Nov	Dec
High	27	29	39	52	65	72	77	76	68	57	43	32
Low	12	11	19	31	41	50	57	57	50	41	31	21
Precip	1.8	1.1	1.9	2.4	2.4	2.5	2.2	3.3	3.5	2.8	2.4	2.0
Snow	23.7	15.4	11.0	4.3	0.2	0.0	0.0	0.0	tr	0.3	5.4	18.0

High and Low temperatures in degrees Fahrenheit; Precipitation and Snow in inches

Weather Station: Pellston Emmet County Airport Elevation: 711 feet

	Jan	Feb	Mar	Apr	May	Jun	Jul	Aug	Sep	Oct	Nov	Dec
High	26	28	37	51	66	75	79	77	68	56	42	31
Low	8	7	17	30	40	49	55	53	46	36	28	17
Precip	2.4	1.6	2.3	2.6	2.7	2.5	2.8	3.2	4.1	3.3	3.0	2.5
Snow	34.2	20.4	13.5	5.4	0.3	0.0	tr	tr	tr	0.8	12.2	28.1

High and Low temperatures in degrees Fahrenheit; Precipitation and Snow in inches

Weather Station: Petoskey Elevation: 606 feet

	Jan	Feb	Mar	Apr	May	Jun	Jul	Aug	Sep	Oct	Nov	Dec
High	27	29	38	50	62	71	76	75	68	57	44	33
Low	14	13	21	32	42	52	59	58	51	41	32	22
Precip	2.1	1.2	2.0	2.5	2.7	2.7	3.2	3.4	3.8	3.2	2.5	2.2
Snow	39.7	21.9	12.1	4.1	0.2	0.0	0.0	0.0	tr	0.4	10.6	31.6

High and Low temperatures in degrees Fahrenheit; Precipitation and Snow in inches

Population: 31,437 (2000); Race: 94.7% White, 0.4% Black, 0.2% Asian, 3.4% American Indian and Alaska Native, 0.8% Hispanic of any race, 1.2% two or more races (2000); Density: 67.2 persons per square mile (2000); Age: 25.3% under 18, 14.3% over 64 (2000).
Religion: Five largest groups: 23.4% Catholic Church, 3.3% The United Methodist Church, 3.3% Presbyterian Church (U.S.A.), 1.7% Lutheran Church—Missouri Synod, 1.5% Christian Church (Disciples of Christ) (2000).
Economy: Unemployment rate: 7.2% (11/2002); Total civilian labor force: 18,454 (11/2002); Leading industries: 17.8% retail trade; 17.0% health care and social assistance; 16.3% accommodation & food services (2000); Companies that employ more than 1,000 persons: 1 (2000); Companies that employ more than 100 persons: 22 (2000); Farms: 207 totaling 40,115 acres (1997); Minority business ownership rate: 0.0% (1997); Women business ownership rate: 19.7% (1997); Retail sales per capita: $14,277 (1997). Single-family building permits issued: 235 (2001) / 378 (2000); Multi-family building permits issued: 170 (2001) / 114 (2000).
Income: Per capita income: $21,070 (2000); Median household income: $40,222 (2000); Poverty rate: 7.4% (2000); Bankruptcy rate: 2.77% (2001).
Taxes: Total county taxes per capita: $263 (2000); County property taxes per capita: $231 (2000).
Education: High school graduation rate: 89.0% (2000); College graduation rate: 26.2% (2000).
Housing: Homeownership rate: 75.5% (2000); Median home value: $131,500 (2000); Median rent: $449 per month (2000); Median age of housing: 25 years (2000).
Health: Birth rate: 118.3 per 10,000 population (1998); Age adjusted death rate: 86.4 per 10,000 population (1999); Age adjusted cancer mortality rate: 181.6 deaths per 100,000 population (1999). Number of physicians: 42.3 per 10,000 population (1999); Number of hospital beds: 84.3 per 10,000 population (1999).
Elections: 2000 Presidential election results: 37.1% Gore, 58.5% Bush, 3.6% Nader, 0.1% Buchanan
National and State Parks: Fort Michilimackinac State Park; Hardwood State Forest; Wilderness State Park
Additional Information Contacts
Emmet County Government Offices 231-348-1744
Boyne Country Convention & Visitors Bureau 231-348-2755
Emmet Association of Realtors 231-347-0700
Harbor Springs Chamber of Commerce 231-526-7999
Mackinaw City Chamber of Commerce 231-436-5574
Petoskey Chamber of Commerce 231-347-4150

Emmet County Communities

ALANSON (village). Covers a land area of 0.972 square miles and a water area of 0.043 square miles. Located at 45.44° N. Lat.; 84.78° W. Long. Elevation is 615 feet.
History: Alanson was settled in 1875. First called Hinman, it was later named for Alanson Cook, a railroad official with the Grand Rapids & Indiana. The village was incorporated in 1905.
Population: 785 (2000); Race: 90.3% White, 0.0% Black, 1.1% Asian, 5.1% American Indian and Alaska Native, 0.3% Hispanic of any race, 3.2% two or more races (2000); Density: 807.8 persons per square mile (2000); Age: 30.2% under 18, 10.2% over 64 (2000); Marriage status: 16.9% never married, 63.8% now married, 7.0% widowed, 12.4% divorced (2000); Foreign born: 2.9% (2000); Ancestry (includes multiple ancestries): 22.4% German, 13.5% Irish, 13.4% Other groups, 12.2% English, 9.6% United States or American (2000).
Economy: Employment by occupation: 11.3% management, 12.8% professional, 19.2% services, 24.4% sales, 0.5% farming, 13.1% construction, 18.7% production (2000).
Income: Per capita income: $20,703 (2000); Median household income: $33,125 (2000); Poverty rate: 8.1% (2000).
Taxes: Total city taxes per capita: $135 (1997); City property taxes per capita: $135 (1997).
Education: High school graduation rate: 86.2% (2000); College graduation rate: 12.1% (2000).

School District(s)

Littlefield Public Schools (KG-12)
2000 Enrollment: 489 231-548-2261
Housing: Homeownership rate: 72.2% (2000); Median home value: $82,400 (2000); Median rent: $428 per month (2000); Median age of housing: 22 years (2000).
Transportation: Commute to work: 93.6% car, 0.3% public transportation, 3.4% walk, 2.1% work from home (2000); Travel time to work: 15.3% less than 15 minutes, 56.6% 15 to 30 minutes, 17.6% 30 to 45 minutes, 6.6% 45 to 60 minutes, 3.9% 60 minutes or more (2000)

BEAR CREEK (township). Covers a land area of 39.604 square miles and a water area of 6.170 square miles. Located at 45.37° N. Lat.; 84.92° W. Long.
Population: 5,269 (2000); Race: 96.6% White, 0.4% Black, 0.2% Asian, 1.8% American Indian and Alaska Native, 0.5% Hispanic of any race, 0.9% two or more races (2000); Density: 133.0 persons per square mile (2000); Age: 28.2% under 18, 12.5% over 64 (2000); Marriage status: 21.3% never married, 62.1% now married, 7.7% widowed, 8.9% divorced (2000); Foreign born: 0.9% (2000); Ancestry (includes multiple ancestries): 30.8% German, 14.9% Irish, 14.4% English, 11.5% Polish, 6.3% Other groups (2000).
Economy: Single-family building permits issued: 37 (2001) / 62 (2000); Multi-family building permits issued: 124 (2001) / 49 (2000); Employment by occupation: 12.2% management, 23.2% professional, 16.2% services, 22.7% sales, 0.8% farming, 13.3% construction, 11.6% production (2000).
Income: Per capita income: $22,534 (2000); Median household income: $44,129 (2000); Poverty rate: 5.0% (2000).
Taxes: Total city taxes per capita: $93 (1997); City property taxes per capita: $78 (1997).
Education: High school graduation rate: 90.8% (2000); College graduation rate: 31.5% (2000).
Housing: Homeownership rate: 79.0% (2000); Median home value: $148,100 (2000); Median rent: $576 per month (2000); Median age of housing: 20 years (2000).
Transportation: Commute to work: 91.1% car, 0.0% public transportation, 3.6% walk, 5.1% work from home (2000); Travel time to work: 46.4% less than 15 minutes, 41.1% 15 to 30 minutes, 7.4% 30 to 45 minutes, 3.1% 45 to 60 minutes, 1.9% 60 minutes or more (2000)

BLISS (township). Covers a land area of 43.935 square miles and a water area of 2.306 square miles. Located at 45.69° N. Lat.; 84.92° W. Long.
History: Bliss Township was named for Aaron T. Bliss, a lumberman who became a governor of Michigan.
Population: 572 (2000); Race: 90.6% White, 0.0% Black, 0.0% Asian, 6.5% American Indian and Alaska Native, 0.0% Hispanic of any race, 2.8% two or more races (2000); Density: 13.0 persons per square mile (2000); Age: 27.8% under 18, 9.4% over 64 (2000); Marriage status: 20.1% never married, 65.4% now married, 6.5% widowed, 8.0% divorced (2000); Foreign born: 5.2% (2000); Ancestry (includes multiple ancestries): 32.4% German, 22.1% Irish, 12.0% English, 8.7% Other groups, 7.2% United States or American (2000).
Economy: Employment by occupation: 13.1% management, 17.4% professional, 16.5% services, 19.1% sales, 0.0% farming, 17.8% construction, 16.1% production (2000).
Income: Per capita income: $17,094 (2000); Median household income: $36,339 (2000); Poverty rate: 5.5% (2000).

Taxes: Total city taxes per capita: $36 (1997); City property taxes per capita: $36 (1997).
Education: High school graduation rate: 87.5% (2000); College graduation rate: 16.6% (2000).
Housing: Homeownership rate: 91.1% (2000); Median home value: $90,000 (2000); Median rent: $283 per month (2000); Median age of housing: 26 years (2000).
Transportation: Commute to work: 86.5% car, 0.0% public transportation, 2.2% walk, 11.2% work from home (2000); Travel time to work: 11.1% less than 15 minutes, 27.3% 15 to 30 minutes, 33.8% 30 to 45 minutes, 20.7% 45 to 60 minutes, 7.1% 60 minutes or more (2000)

BRUTUS (unincorporated postal area, zip code 49716). Covers a land area of 28.299 square miles and a water area of 0.072 square miles. Located at 45.51° N. Lat.; 84.72° W. Long. Elevation is 680 feet.
History: Brutus was a stop on the stagecoach line in 1874. A Mennonite settlement was founded near Brutus in the 1870's. The community was named for Brutus, New York, the home of one of the early settlers.
Population: 834 (2000); Race: 92.7% White, 0.0% Black, 0.0% Asian, 6.3% American Indian and Alaska Native, 0.0% Hispanic of any race, 1.0% two or more races (2000); Density: 29.5 persons per square mile (2000); Age: 25.3% under 18, 14.8% over 64 (2000); Marriage status: 20.4% never married, 65.4% now married, 6.6% widowed, 7.6% divorced (2000); Foreign born: 0.0% (2000); Ancestry (includes multiple ancestries): 24.9% German, 10.5% Polish, 9.8% English, 8.4% Other groups, 8.2% Irish (2000).
Economy: Employment by occupation: 7.8% management, 14.6% professional, 17.4% services, 28.6% sales, 1.4% farming, 19.0% construction, 11.2% production (2000).
Income: Per capita income: $22,254 (2000); Median household income: $43,214 (2000); Poverty rate: 7.4% (2000).
Education: High school graduation rate: 91.1% (2000); College graduation rate: 20.3% (2000).
Housing: Homeownership rate: 88.6% (2000); Median home value: $113,000 (2000); Median rent: $350 per month (2000); Median age of housing: 24 years (2000).
Transportation: Commute to work: 94.9% car, 0.0% public transportation, 0.7% walk, 3.7% work from home (2000); Travel time to work: 19.1% less than 15 minutes, 39.5% 15 to 30 minutes, 33.5% 30 to 45 minutes, 2.4% 45 to 60 minutes, 5.5% 60 minutes or more (2000)

CARP LAKE (township). Covers a land area of 32.359 square miles and a water area of 2.778 square miles. Located at 45.68° N. Lat.; 84.78° W. Long.
Population: 807 (2000); Race: 91.3% White, 0.5% Black, 1.1% Asian, 4.8% American Indian and Alaska Native, 0.5% Hispanic of any race, 2.0% two or more races (2000); Density: 24.9 persons per square mile (2000); Age: 22.2% under 18, 13.9% over 64 (2000); Marriage status: 18.7% never married, 61.9% now married, 7.3% widowed, 12.1% divorced (2000); Foreign born: 1.0% (2000); Ancestry (includes multiple ancestries): 22.8% German, 15.5% English, 13.9% Irish, 13.6% United States or American, 8.4% Other groups (2000).
Economy: Resort Area. Employment by occupation: 10.6% management, 13.2% professional, 21.8% services, 23.4% sales, 0.7% farming, 13.9% construction, 16.5% production (2000).
Income: Per capita income: $18,667 (2000); Median household income: $34,750 (2000); Poverty rate: 7.9% (2000).
Taxes: Total city taxes per capita: $107 (1997); City property taxes per capita: $107 (1997).
Education: High school graduation rate: 84.3% (2000); College graduation rate: 14.2% (2000).
Housing: Homeownership rate: 84.5% (2000); Median home value: $74,000 (2000); Median rent: $388 per month (2000); Median age of housing: 41 years (2000).
Transportation: Commute to work: 97.3% car, 0.0% public transportation, 1.0% walk, 1.7% work from home (2000); Travel time to work: 25.9% less than 15 minutes, 33.2% 15 to 30 minutes, 24.5% 30 to 45 minutes, 14.0% 45 to 60 minutes, 2.4% 60 minutes or more (2000)

CENTER (township). Covers a land area of 34.364 square miles and a water area of 0.926 square miles. Located at 45.59° N. Lat.; 84.92° W. Long.
Population: 499 (2000); Race: 94.4% White, 0.0% Black, 0.4% Asian, 3.2% American Indian and Alaska Native, 3.2% Hispanic of any race, 2.1% two or more races (2000); Density: 14.5 persons per square mile (2000); Age: 31.3% under 18, 13.1% over 64 (2000); Marriage status: 28.3% never married, 60.5% now married, 3.3% widowed, 7.9% divorced (2000); Foreign born: 1.5% (2000); Ancestry (includes multiple ancestries): 30.0% German, 18.2% Polish, 17.2% Irish, 10.7% English, 6.6% Other groups (2000).
Economy: Employment by occupation: 9.5% management, 21.0% professional, 26.2% services, 20.0% sales, 0.0% farming, 14.8% construction, 8.6% production (2000).
Income: Per capita income: $16,201 (2000); Median household income: $38,333 (2000); Poverty rate: 6.9% (2000).
Taxes: Total city taxes per capita: $16 (1997); City property taxes per capita: $16 (1997).
Education: High school graduation rate: 82.2% (2000); College graduation rate: 16.3% (2000).
Housing: Homeownership rate: 91.5% (2000); Median home value: $92,200 (2000); Median rent: $325 per month (2000); Median age of housing: 40 years (2000).
Transportation: Commute to work: 88.5% car, 4.3% public transportation, 1.0% walk, 6.3% work from home (2000); Travel time to work: 13.8% less than 15 minutes, 44.1% 15 to 30 minutes, 29.7% 30 to 45 minutes, 5.1% 45 to 60 minutes, 7.2% 60 minutes or more (2000)

CROSS VILLAGE (township). Covers a land area of 10.024 square miles and a water area of 0.207 square miles. Located at 45.64° N. Lat.; 85.01° W. Long. Elevation is 689 feet.
History: The cross for which Cross Village was named may have been placed here by Father Marquette. The area was known as La Croix (French, the cross) in the early 1800's, and was given its present name in 1875.
Population: 294 (2000); Race: 82.1% White, 0.0% Black, 0.0% Asian, 12.0% American Indian and Alaska Native, 1.8% Hispanic of any race, 5.8% two or more races (2000); Density: 29.3 persons per square mile (2000); Age: 15.3% under 18, 15.7% over 64 (2000); Marriage status: 28.6% never married, 57.1% now married, 4.9% widowed, 9.4% divorced (2000); Foreign born: 0.7% (2000); Ancestry (includes multiple ancestries): 21.9% Other groups, 21.5% German, 21.2% Polish, 13.9% English, 13.1% Irish (2000).
Economy: Employment by occupation: 12.4% management, 24.0% professional, 26.4% services, 19.4% sales, 0.0% farming, 10.9% construction, 7.0% production (2000).
Income: Per capita income: $32,535 (2000); Median household income: $46,364 (2000); Poverty rate: 20.0% (2000).
Taxes: Total city taxes per capita: $124 (1997); City property taxes per capita: $124 (1997).
Education: High school graduation rate: 84.8% (2000); College graduation rate: 28.3% (2000).
Housing: Homeownership rate: 92.3% (2000); Median home value: $131,300 (2000); Median rent: $175 per month (2000); Median age of housing: 22 years (2000).
Transportation: Commute to work: 96.9% car, 0.0% public transportation, 0.0% walk, 3.1% work from home (2000); Travel time to work: 24.0% less than 15 minutes, 26.4% 15 to 30 minutes, 34.4% 30 to 45 minutes, 13.6% 45 to 60 minutes, 1.6% 60 minutes or more (2000)

FRIENDSHIP (township). Covers a land area of 31.395 square miles and a water area of 0.005 square miles. Located at 45.51° N. Lat.; 85.04° W. Long.
Population: 844 (2000); Race: 95.0% White, 0.5% Black, 0.0% Asian, 2.8% American Indian and Alaska Native, 0.0% Hispanic of any race, 1.7% two or more races (2000); Density: 26.9 persons per square mile (2000); Age: 25.4% under 18, 10.9% over 64 (2000); Marriage status: 21.8% never married, 67.9% now married, 3.7% widowed, 6.6% divorced (2000); Foreign born: 1.5% (2000); Ancestry (includes multiple ancestries): 25.3% German, 20.9% English, 14.7% Irish, 13.4% Polish, 6.6% French (except Basque) (2000).
Economy: Employment by occupation: 13.8% management, 19.0% professional, 22.0% services, 26.4% sales, 1.6% farming, 10.6% construction, 6.7% production (2000).
Income: Per capita income: $22,324 (2000); Median household income: $46,000 (2000); Poverty rate: 6.0% (2000).
Taxes: Total city taxes per capita: $89 (1997); City property taxes per capita: $89 (1997).
Education: High school graduation rate: 93.2% (2000); College graduation rate: 31.2% (2000).
Housing: Homeownership rate: 87.5% (2000); Median home value: $134,600 (2000); Median rent: $472 per month (2000); Median age of housing: 21 years (2000).
Transportation: Commute to work: 94.5% car, 0.0% public transportation, 0.5% walk, 5.0% work from home (2000); Travel time to work: 23.5% less than 15 minutes, 49.3% 15 to 30 minutes, 21.8% 30 to 45 minutes, 2.3% 45 to 60 minutes, 3.3% 60 minutes or more (2000)

HARBOR SPRINGS (city). Covers a land area of 1.296 square miles and a water area of 0 square miles. Located at 45.43° N. Lat.; 84.99° W. Long. Elevation is 650 feet.
History: The Mission of the Holy Childhood of Jesus was founded here in 1827 by Father Peter de Jean. The town of Harbor Springs was settled in the 1870's as a lumber and fishing center, but later became dependent on the summer vacationers for its revenue.
Population: 1,567 (2000); Race: 90.3% White, 0.7% Black, 0.0% Asian, 7.5% American Indian and Alaska Native, 0.2% Hispanic of any race, 1.5% two or more races (2000); Density: 1,208.9 persons per square mile (2000); Age: 20.2% under 18, 24.2% over 64 (2000); Marriage status: 19.8% never married, 52.0% now married, 13.5% widowed, 14.7% divorced (2000); Foreign born: 1.2% (2000); Ancestry (includes multiple ancestries): 17.4% German, 16.2% English, 14.1% Irish, 8.6% Other groups, 7.4% French (except Basque) (2000).
Economy: Employment by occupation: 11.3% management, 19.4% professional, 19.3% services, 29.6% sales, 0.9% farming, 11.8% construction, 7.7% production (2000).
Income: Per capita income: $21,876 (2000); Median household income: $35,341 (2000); Poverty rate: 6.8% (2000).
Taxes: Total city taxes per capita: $528 (1997); City property taxes per capita: $523 (1997).
Education: High school graduation rate: 88.3% (2000); College graduation rate: 33.4% (2000).

School District(s)

Harbor Springs School District (KG-12)
2000 Enrollment: 1,079 231-526-2801

Four-year College(s)

Black Forest Hall (Private, Not-for-profit)
2001 Enrollment: n/a 616-526-7066

Housing: Homeownership rate: 70.0% (2000); Median home value: $151,600 (2000); Median rent: $463 per month (2000); Median age of housing: 49 years (2000).
Safety: Violent crime rate: 12.7 per 10,000 population; Property crime rate: 171.4 per 10,000 population (2001).
Newspapers: Harbor Light (1 x week)
Transportation: Commute to work: 89.0% car, 0.0% public transportation, 6.0% walk, 4.9% work from home (2000); Travel time to work: 50.0% less than 15 minutes, 33.5% 15 to 30 minutes, 9.3% 30 to 45 minutes, 2.8% 45 to 60 minutes, 4.4% 60 minutes or more (2000)
Airports: Harbor Springs
Additional Information Contacts
Harbor Springs Chamber of Commerce 231-526-7999

LEVERING (unincorporated postal area, zip code 49755). Covers a land area of 108.272 square miles and a water area of 1.148 square miles. Located at 45.63° N. Lat.; 84.79° W. Long. Elevation is 756 feet.
History: Levering was founded in 1882 as a station on the Grand Rapids & Indiana Railroad, and was named for Joshua Levering. It developed as a shipping point for farm produce.
Population: 2,040 (2000); Race: 93.3% White, 0.1% Black, 0.6% Asian, 3.3% American Indian and Alaska Native, 0.2% Hispanic of any race, 2.7% two or more races (2000); Density: 18.8 persons per square mile (2000); Age: 24.7% under 18, 12.5% over 64 (2000); Marriage status: 19.8% never married, 63.0% now married, 7.0% widowed, 10.1% divorced (2000); Foreign born: 1.6% (2000); Ancestry (includes multiple ancestries): 27.8% German, 17.0% Irish, 11.9% English, 8.8% United States or American, 7.4% Other groups (2000).
Economy: Employment by occupation: 9.8% management, 17.8% professional, 20.7% services, 17.6% sales, 1.0% farming, 17.9% construction, 15.3% production (2000).
Income: Per capita income: $18,966 (2000); Median household income: $36,375 (2000); Poverty rate: 6.5% (2000).
Education: High school graduation rate: 85.1% (2000); College graduation rate: 15.1% (2000).
Housing: Homeownership rate: 88.6% (2000); Median home value: $90,800 (2000); Median rent: $356 per month (2000); Median age of housing: 28 years (2000).
Transportation: Commute to work: 90.8% car, 0.0% public transportation, 1.5% walk, 7.2% work from home (2000); Travel time to work: 14.7% less than 15 minutes, 33.4% 15 to 30 minutes, 32.3% 30 to 45 minutes, 12.7% 45 to 60 minutes, 6.9% 60 minutes or more (2000)

LITTLE TRAVERSE (township). Covers a land area of 18.015 square miles and a water area of 2.367 square miles. Located at 45.43° N. Lat.; 84.92° W. Long.
Population: 2,426 (2000); Race: 97.2% White, 0.4% Black, 0.0% Asian, 1.9% American Indian and Alaska Native, 0.5% Hispanic of any race, 0.3% two or more races (2000); Density: 134.7 persons per square mile (2000); Age: 24.5% under 18, 14.2% over 64 (2000); Marriage status: 17.7% never married, 66.4% now married, 5.4% widowed, 10.6% divorced (2000); Foreign born: 0.0% (2000); Ancestry (includes multiple ancestries): 26.4% German, 14.7% English, 14.5% Irish, 9.2% Polish, 6.7% Dutch (2000).
Economy: Employment by occupation: 14.8% management, 15.8% professional, 17.4% services, 31.8% sales, 0.5% farming, 8.6% construction, 11.1% production (2000).
Income: Per capita income: $20,830 (2000); Median household income: $41,228 (2000); Poverty rate: 6.1% (2000).
Taxes: Total city taxes per capita: $64 (1997); City property taxes per capita: $63 (1997).
Education: High school graduation rate: 91.5% (2000); College graduation rate: 27.1% (2000).
Housing: Homeownership rate: 78.5% (2000); Median home value: $163,800 (2000); Median rent: $448 per month (2000); Median age of housing: 23 years (2000).
Transportation: Commute to work: 92.0% car, 0.6% public transportation, 1.1% walk, 4.9% work from home (2000); Travel time to work: 48.8% less than 15 minutes, 39.5% 15 to 30 minutes, 7.4% 30 to 45 minutes, 2.2% 45 to 60 minutes, 2.0% 60 minutes or more (2000)

LITTLEFIELD (township). Covers a land area of 21.724 square miles and a water area of 2.805 square miles. Located at 45.43° N. Lat.; 84.79° W. Long.
Population: 2,783 (2000); Race: 94.6% White, 0.0% Black, 1.1% Asian, 3.3% American Indian and Alaska Native, 0.1% Hispanic of any race, 0.9% two or more races (2000); Density: 128.1 persons per square mile (2000); Age: 25.5% under 18, 10.5% over 64 (2000); Marriage status: 19.6% never married, 61.0% now married, 5.1% widowed, 14.4% divorced (2000); Foreign born: 2.0% (2000); Ancestry (includes multiple ancestries): 21.5% German, 13.1% Irish, 10.2% English, 9.1% United States or American, 7.3% Other groups (2000).
Economy: Employment by occupation: 7.5% management, 13.9% professional, 18.3% services, 27.6% sales, 0.8% farming, 14.8% construction, 17.1% production (2000).
Income: Per capita income: $18,737 (2000); Median household income: $37,694 (2000); Poverty rate: 6.2% (2000).
Taxes: Total city taxes per capita: $39 (1997); City property taxes per capita: $39 (1997).
Education: High school graduation rate: 85.8% (2000); College graduation rate: 12.8% (2000).
Housing: Homeownership rate: 80.5% (2000); Median home value: $90,700 (2000); Median rent: $420 per month (2000); Median age of housing: 23 years (2000).
Transportation: Commute to work: 93.9% car, 0.1% public transportation, 1.8% walk, 4.0% work from home (2000); Travel time to work: 22.3% less than 15 minutes, 54.5% 15 to 30 minutes, 17.5% 30 to 45 minutes, 4.4% 45 to 60 minutes, 1.3% 60 minutes or more (2000)

MACKINAW CITY (village). Covers a land area of 3.364 square miles and a water area of 4.212 square miles. Located at 45.78° N. Lat.; 84.73° W. Long.
History: Mackinaw City grew as a gateway to the Upper Peninsula for tourists and vacationers. There was a fort here in the mid-1700's, called Fort Michilimackinac, as were several forts in the area. Built by the French, the fort was taken over by the British in 1761, who moved it to Mackinac Island in 1780.
Population: 859 (2000); Race: 92.6% White, 0.0% Black, 1.7% Asian, 3.7% American Indian and Alaska Native, 0.2% Hispanic of any race, 2.1% two or more races (2000); Density: 255.3 persons per square mile (2000); Age: 22.9% under 18, 16.2% over 64 (2000); Marriage status: 19.6% never married, 58.8% now married, 7.2% widowed, 14.4% divorced (2000); Foreign born: 2.9% (2000); Ancestry (includes multiple ancestries): 22.9% German, 16.2% Irish, 10.0% English, 8.9% French (except Basque), 8.7% Other groups (2000).
Economy: Employment by occupation: 13.9% management, 15.8% professional, 25.6% services, 24.7% sales, 0.0% farming, 12.0% construction, 7.9% production (2000).

Income: Per capita income: $18,725 (2000); Median household income: $37,031 (2000); Poverty rate: 9.7% (2000).
Education: High school graduation rate: 88.9% (2000); College graduation rate: 21.3% (2000).

School District(s)

Mackinaw City Public Schools (PK-12)
2000 Enrollment: 233 231-436-8211

Housing: Homeownership rate: 73.3% (2000); Median home value: $119,100 (2000); Median rent: $318 per month (2000); Median age of housing: 37 years (2000).
Safety: Violent crime rate: 0.0 per 10,000 population; Property crime rate: 1,018.5 per 10,000 population (2001).
Transportation: Commute to work: 86.9% car, 0.0% public transportation, 4.5% walk, 7.3% work from home (2000); Travel time to work: 55.2% less than 15 minutes, 19.3% 15 to 30 minutes, 7.9% 30 to 45 minutes, 11.7% 45 to 60 minutes, 5.9% 60 minutes or more (2000); Amtrak: Service available.

Additional Information Contacts

Mackinaw City Chamber of Commerce. 231-436-5574

MAPLE RIVER (township). Covers a land area of 35.310 square miles and a water area of 0.170 square miles. Located at 45.51° N. Lat.; 84.78° W. Long.
Population: 1,232 (2000); Race: 94.1% White, 0.0% Black, 0.0% Asian, 4.8% American Indian and Alaska Native, 1.1% Hispanic of any race, 1.2% two or more races (2000); Density: 34.9 persons per square mile (2000); Age: 28.4% under 18, 10.4% over 64 (2000); Marriage status: 24.6% never married, 62.9% now married, 2.9% widowed, 9.6% divorced (2000); Foreign born: 0.4% (2000); Ancestry (includes multiple ancestries): 27.7% German, 9.6% Irish, 8.4% Polish, 8.1% English, 7.8% Other groups (2000).
Economy: Employment by occupation: 6.1% management, 9.6% professional, 21.4% services, 27.1% sales, 0.8% farming, 20.6% construction, 14.3% production (2000).
Income: Per capita income: $16,765 (2000); Median household income: $40,270 (2000); Poverty rate: 5.9% (2000).
Taxes: Total city taxes per capita: $21 (1997); City property taxes per capita: $21 (1997).
Education: High school graduation rate: 89.3% (2000); College graduation rate: 13.5% (2000).
Housing: Homeownership rate: 85.9% (2000); Median home value: $105,300 (2000); Median rent: $391 per month (2000); Median age of housing: 22 years (2000).
Transportation: Commute to work: 93.6% car, 0.0% public transportation, 1.6% walk, 4.3% work from home (2000); Travel time to work: 21.3% less than 15 minutes, 46.0% 15 to 30 minutes, 27.0% 30 to 45 minutes, 2.2% 45 to 60 minutes, 3.5% 60 minutes or more (2000)

MCKINLEY (township). Covers a land area of 35.229 square miles and a water area of 0.061 square miles. Located at 45.58° N. Lat.; 84.78° W. Long.
Population: 1,269 (2000); Race: 90.9% White, 0.1% Black, 0.0% Asian, 5.6% American Indian and Alaska Native, 0.6% Hispanic of any race, 3.4% two or more races (2000); Density: 36.0 persons per square mile (2000); Age: 30.7% under 18, 11.6% over 64 (2000); Marriage status: 23.4% never married, 54.8% now married, 7.3% widowed, 14.5% divorced (2000); Foreign born: 0.1% (2000); Ancestry (includes multiple ancestries): 17.3% German, 12.3% Irish, 10.0% English, 9.3% United States or American, 8.5% Other groups (2000).
Economy: Employment by occupation: 7.4% management, 11.0% professional, 24.7% services, 24.1% sales, 0.0% farming, 15.0% construction, 17.8% production (2000).
Income: Per capita income: $13,907 (2000); Median household income: $32,961 (2000); Poverty rate: 13.9% (2000).
Taxes: Total city taxes per capita: $19 (1997); City property taxes per capita: $19 (1997).
Education: High school graduation rate: 80.1% (2000); College graduation rate: 7.6% (2000).
Housing: Homeownership rate: 81.5% (2000); Median home value: $68,200 (2000); Median rent: $416 per month (2000); Median age of housing: 35 years (2000).
Transportation: Commute to work: 91.9% car, 0.0% public transportation, 2.6% walk, 4.7% work from home (2000); Travel time to work: 20.0% less than 15 minutes, 27.6% 15 to 30 minutes, 39.3% 30 to 45 minutes, 8.3% 45 to 60 minutes, 4.7% 60 minutes or more (2000)

PELLSTON (village). Covers a land area of 1.914 square miles and a water area of 0 square miles. Located at 45.55° N. Lat.; 84.78° W. Long. Elevation is 702 feet.
History: Pellston was platted in 1882 by William H. Pells, who named the town for himself. Pellston grew up around a large lumber mill and a station on the Grand Rapids & Indiana Railroad. It was incorporated as a village in 1907.
Population: 771 (2000); Race: 91.0% White, 0.1% Black, 0.0% Asian, 7.7% American Indian and Alaska Native, 1.1% Hispanic of any race, 1.2% two or more races (2000); Density: 402.8 persons per square mile (2000); Age: 32.7% under 18, 9.2% over 64 (2000); Marriage status: 24.5% never married, 55.4% now married, 5.0% widowed, 15.1% divorced (2000); Foreign born: 0.1% (2000); Ancestry (includes multiple ancestries): 17.5% German, 12.7% Irish, 10.6% Other groups, 9.8% English, 7.6% French (except Basque) (2000).
Economy: Employment by occupation: 8.1% management, 12.5% professional, 21.9% services, 27.2% sales, 0.0% farming, 13.1% construction, 17.2% production (2000).
Income: Per capita income: $13,047 (2000); Median household income: $37,292 (2000); Poverty rate: 13.7% (2000).
Taxes: Total city taxes per capita: $101 (1997); City property taxes per capita: $101 (1997).
Education: High school graduation rate: 85.6% (2000); College graduation rate: 8.2% (2000).

School District(s)

Pellston Public Schools (KG-12)
2000 Enrollment: 792 231-539-8682

Housing: Homeownership rate: 79.8% (2000); Median home value: $71,600 (2000); Median rent: $455 per month (2000); Median age of housing: 34 years (2000).
Transportation: Commute to work: 96.8% car, 0.0% public transportation, 1.9% walk, 1.3% work from home (2000); Travel time to work: 21.2% less than 15 minutes, 31.3% 15 to 30 minutes, 37.5% 30 to 45 minutes, 8.8% 45 to 60 minutes, 1.3% 60 minutes or more (2000); Amtrak: Service available.
Airports: Pellston Regional Airport of Emmet Count (primary service)

PETOSKEY (city). Covers a land area of 5.021 square miles and a water area of 0.205 square miles. Located at 45.36° N. Lat.; 84.96° W. Long. Elevation is 786 feet.
History: Petoskey was established on Little Traverse Bay, and named for Chief Bidasiga (Rising Sun), who owned this land when the Presbyterians founded a mission in 1852.
Population: 6,080 (2000); Race: 94.6% White, 0.0% Black, 0.0% Asian, 4.0% American Indian and Alaska Native, 1.5% Hispanic of any race, 1.2% two or more races (2000); Density: 1,210.9 persons per square mile (2000); Age: 22.6% under 18, 19.0% over 64 (2000); Marriage status: 29.3% never married, 49.1% now married, 7.9% widowed, 13.6% divorced (2000); Foreign born: 3.5% (2000); Ancestry (includes multiple ancestries): 23.1% German, 14.4% English, 14.4% Irish, 9.7% Other groups, 9.2% Polish (2000).
Economy: Single-family building permits issued: 17 (2001) / 29 (2000); Multi-family building permits issued: 46 (2001) / 27 (2000); Employment by occupation: 10.2% management, 24.2% professional, 19.8% services, 28.1% sales, 0.0% farming, 7.3% construction, 10.4% production (2000).
Income: Per capita income: $20,259 (2000); Median household income: $33,657 (2000); Poverty rate: 12.0% (2000).
Taxes: Total city taxes per capita: $737 (2000); City property taxes per capita: $726 (2000).
Education: High school graduation rate: 87.1% (2000); College graduation rate: 31.0% (2000).

School District(s)

Concord Academy - Petoskey (KG-12)
2000 Enrollment: 288 517-774-2100
Public Schools of Petoskey (KG-12)
2000 Enrollment: 3,020 231-348-0160

Two-year College(s)

North Central Michigan College (Public)
2001 Enrollment: 2,248 231-348-6602
2001 Tuition: In-state $2,256; Out-of-state $2,790

Housing: Homeownership rate: 50.8% (2000); Median home value: $120,700 (2000); Median rent: $421 per month (2000); Median age of housing: 43 years (2000).
Hospitals: Northern Michigan Hospital (299 beds)
Safety: Violent crime rate: 22.9 per 10,000 population; Property crime rate: 265.1 per 10,000 population (2001).
Newspapers: Petoskey News-Review (5 x week); The AD-vertiser (1 x week); Charlevoix County Star (1 x week); Petoskey Star (1 x week)
Transportation: Commute to work: 84.7% car, 0.0% public transportation, 11.4% walk, 3.4% work from home (2000); Travel time to work: 70.4% less

than 15 minutes, 20.1% 15 to 30 minutes, 4.5% 30 to 45 minutes, 1.4% 45 to 60 minutes, 3.6% 60 minutes or more (2000); Amtrak: Service available.

Additional Information Contacts

Boyne Country Convention & Visitors Bureau 231-348-2755
Emmet Association of Realtors 231-347-0700
Petoskey Chamber of Commerce 231-347-4150

PLEASANTVIEW (township). Covers a land area of 35.682 square miles and a water area of 0.014 square miles. Located at 45.50° N. Lat.; 84.92° W. Long.
History: Pleasant View Township was organized in 1876.
Population: 943 (2000); Race: 87.4% White, 7.4% Black, 0.7% Asian, 1.3% American Indian and Alaska Native, 1.6% Hispanic of any race, 2.3% two or more races (2000); Density: 26.4 persons per square mile (2000); Age: 21.6% under 18, 8.9% over 64 (2000); Marriage status: 19.9% never married, 67.0% now married, 2.7% widowed, 10.5% divorced (2000); Foreign born: 1.9% (2000); Ancestry (includes multiple ancestries): 20.2% German, 9.5% English, 8.9% Other groups, 8.1% Irish, 5.8% United States or American (2000).
Economy: Employment by occupation: 18.9% management, 13.2% professional, 20.8% services, 21.1% sales, 0.0% farming, 12.1% construction, 13.9% production (2000).
Income: Per capita income: $20,332 (2000); Median household income: $42,333 (2000); Poverty rate: 4.5% (2000).
Taxes: Total city taxes per capita: $152 (1997); City property taxes per capita: $147 (1997).
Education: High school graduation rate: 92.1% (2000); College graduation rate: 22.6% (2000).
Housing: Homeownership rate: 85.6% (2000); Median home value: $144,400 (2000); Median rent: $425 per month (2000); Median age of housing: 11 years (2000).
Transportation: Commute to work: 90.9% car, 0.0% public transportation, 1.1% walk, 7.2% work from home (2000); Travel time to work: 34.6% less than 15 minutes, 49.9% 15 to 30 minutes, 7.8% 30 to 45 minutes, 4.6% 45 to 60 minutes, 3.2% 60 minutes or more (2000)

READMOND (township). Covers a land area of 30.989 square miles and a water area of 0 square miles. Located at 45.57° N. Lat.; 85.03° W. Long.
Population: 493 (2000); Race: 95.5% White, 0.0% Black, 0.0% Asian, 1.4% American Indian and Alaska Native, 1.4% Hispanic of any race, 3.2% two or more races (2000); Density: 15.9 persons per square mile (2000); Age: 24.5% under 18, 12.8% over 64 (2000); Marriage status: 20.4% never married, 68.7% now married, 4.5% widowed, 6.5% divorced (2000); Foreign born: 1.2% (2000); Ancestry (includes multiple ancestries): 31.2% German, 14.6% Irish, 13.6% Polish, 10.7% English, 7.7% French (except Basque) (2000).
Economy: Employment by occupation: 13.9% management, 12.3% professional, 21.0% services, 19.8% sales, 0.0% farming, 22.2% construction, 10.7% production (2000).
Income: Per capita income: $20,270 (2000); Median household income: $40,114 (2000); Poverty rate: 6.4% (2000).
Taxes: Total city taxes per capita: $157 (1997); City property taxes per capita: $157 (1997).
Education: High school graduation rate: 91.4% (2000); College graduation rate: 34.1% (2000).
Housing: Homeownership rate: 86.5% (2000); Median home value: $158,700 (2000); Median rent: $417 per month (2000); Median age of housing: 26 years (2000).
Transportation: Commute to work: 92.9% car, 0.0% public transportation, 2.4% walk, 4.0% work from home (2000); Travel time to work: 9.1% less than 15 minutes, 44.2% 15 to 30 minutes, 28.1% 30 to 45 minutes, 11.2% 45 to 60 minutes, 7.4% 60 minutes or more (2000)

RESORT (township). Covers a land area of 19.111 square miles and a water area of 2.426 square miles. Located at 45.33° N. Lat.; 85.01° W. Long.
Population: 2,479 (2000); Race: 96.7% White, 0.2% Black, 0.2% Asian, 2.3% American Indian and Alaska Native, 0.4% Hispanic of any race, 0.3% two or more races (2000); Density: 129.7 persons per square mile (2000); Age: 27.8% under 18, 11.3% over 64 (2000); Marriage status: 19.4% never married, 69.0% now married, 3.7% widowed, 7.9% divorced (2000); Foreign born: 1.4% (2000); Ancestry (includes multiple ancestries): 32.8% German, 11.2% Irish, 10.4% Polish, 10.2% English, 7.9% Dutch (2000).
Economy: Employment by occupation: 13.3% management, 21.7% professional, 13.2% services, 28.7% sales, 0.3% farming, 12.6% construction, 10.2% production (2000).
Income: Per capita income: $25,080 (2000); Median household income: $52,772 (2000); Poverty rate: 3.4% (2000).
Taxes: Total city taxes per capita: $75 (1997); City property taxes per capita: $75 (1997).
Education: High school graduation rate: 92.0% (2000); College graduation rate: 27.7% (2000).
Housing: Homeownership rate: 89.6% (2000); Median home value: $160,700 (2000); Median rent: $524 per month (2000); Median age of housing: 21 years (2000).
Transportation: Commute to work: 92.1% car, 0.7% public transportation, 0.2% walk, 5.7% work from home (2000); Travel time to work: 50.6% less than 15 minutes, 37.5% 15 to 30 minutes, 5.1% 30 to 45 minutes, 2.6% 45 to 60 minutes, 4.2% 60 minutes or more (2000)

SPRINGVALE (township). Covers a land area of 44.702 square miles and a water area of 2.381 square miles. Located at 45.35° N. Lat.; 84.79° W. Long.
Population: 1,727 (2000); Race: 95.7% White, 0.0% Black, 0.2% Asian, 2.8% American Indian and Alaska Native, 1.1% Hispanic of any race, 1.1% two or more races (2000); Density: 38.6 persons per square mile (2000); Age: 28.6% under 18, 10.1% over 64 (2000); Marriage status: 20.0% never married, 64.4% now married, 4.0% widowed, 11.6% divorced (2000); Foreign born: 0.9% (2000); Ancestry (includes multiple ancestries): 27.6% German, 14.9% Irish, 9.9% English, 9.1% Polish, 7.7% United States or American (2000).
Economy: Employment by occupation: 11.5% management, 15.8% professional, 17.2% services, 29.1% sales, 0.9% farming, 11.8% construction, 13.6% production (2000).
Income: Per capita income: $19,640 (2000); Median household income: $44,148 (2000); Poverty rate: 8.2% (2000).
Taxes: Total city taxes per capita: $43 (1997); City property taxes per capita: $43 (1997).
Education: High school graduation rate: 89.2% (2000); College graduation rate: 18.3% (2000).
Housing: Homeownership rate: 84.3% (2000); Median home value: $127,300 (2000); Median rent: $520 per month (2000); Median age of housing: 25 years (2000).
Transportation: Commute to work: 92.3% car, 0.6% public transportation, 0.6% walk, 6.1% work from home (2000); Travel time to work: 18.1% less than 15 minutes, 62.9% 15 to 30 minutes, 14.7% 30 to 45 minutes, 2.6% 45 to 60 minutes, 1.7% 60 minutes or more (2000)

WAWATAM (township). Covers a land area of 15.723 square miles and a water area of 4.640 square miles. Located at 45.77° N. Lat.; 84.76° W. Long.
Population: 705 (2000); Race: 95.7% White, 0.3% Black, 0.0% Asian, 3.6% American Indian and Alaska Native, 0.3% Hispanic of any race, 0.4% two or more races (2000); Density: 44.8 persons per square mile (2000); Age: 20.6% under 18, 19.9% over 64 (2000); Marriage status: 17.5% never married, 60.1% now married, 8.1% widowed, 14.2% divorced (2000); Foreign born: 2.1% (2000); Ancestry (includes multiple ancestries): 25.0% German, 18.1% Irish, 12.4% French (except Basque), 11.8% English, 8.2% Polish (2000).
Economy: Employment by occupation: 14.1% management, 12.6% professional, 27.8% services, 23.5% sales, 0.0% farming, 15.5% construction, 6.5% production (2000).
Income: Per capita income: $19,525 (2000); Median household income: $35,909 (2000); Poverty rate: 7.5% (2000).
Taxes: Total city taxes per capita: $79 (1997); City property taxes per capita: $79 (1997).
Education: High school graduation rate: 88.9% (2000); College graduation rate: 22.7% (2000).
Housing: Homeownership rate: 78.2% (2000); Median home value: $133,500 (2000); Median rent: $305 per month (2000); Median age of housing: 31 years (2000).
Transportation: Commute to work: 89.8% car, 0.7% public transportation, 2.9% walk, 5.1% work from home (2000); Travel time to work: 56.2% less than 15 minutes, 14.6% 15 to 30 minutes, 11.2% 30 to 45 minutes, 10.4% 45 to 60 minutes, 7.7% 60 minutes or more (2000)

WEST TRAVERSE (township). Covers a land area of 13.336 square miles and a water area of 0.028 square miles. Located at 45.45° N. Lat.; 85.02° W. Long.
Population: 1,448 (2000); Race: 97.2% White, 0.3% Black, 0.3% Asian, 1.7% American Indian and Alaska Native, 0.9% Hispanic of any race, 0.5% two or more races (2000); Density: 108.6 persons per square mile (2000); Age: 24.0% under 18, 16.7% over 64 (2000); Marriage status: 16.5% never married, 72.9% now married, 5.2% widowed, 5.4% divorced (2000); Foreign born: 3.2% (2000); Ancestry (includes multiple ancestries): 25.5% German,

17.7% English, 14.9% Irish, 8.7% Polish, 6.8% United States or American (2000).
Economy: Employment by occupation: 16.7% management, 20.7% professional, 14.0% services, 30.1% sales, 0.0% farming, 10.8% construction, 7.7% production (2000).
Income: Per capita income: $31,136 (2000); Median household income: $64,167 (2000); Poverty rate: 4.5% (2000).
Taxes: Total city taxes per capita: $174 (1997); City property taxes per capita: $166 (1997).
Education: High school graduation rate: 95.5% (2000); College graduation rate: 43.4% (2000).
Housing: Homeownership rate: 91.3% (2000); Median home value: $228,800 (2000); Median rent: $579 per month (2000); Median age of housing: 15 years (2000).
Transportation: Commute to work: 91.7% car, 0.0% public transportation, 1.7% walk, 5.1% work from home (2000); Travel time to work: 45.5% less than 15 minutes, 35.4% 15 to 30 minutes, 10.4% 30 to 45 minutes, 2.6% 45 to 60 minutes, 6.2% 60 minutes or more (2000)

Genesee County

Located in southeast central Michigan; drained by the Flint and Shiawassee Rivers. Covers a land area of 639.60 square miles, a water area of 9.70 square miles, and is located in the Eastern Time Zone. The county government was organized in 1835. County seat is Flint.

Genesee County is part of the Flint, MI PMSA. The entire metro area includes: Genesee County

Weather Station: Flint Bishop Airport Elevation: 764 feet

	Jan	Feb	Mar	Apr	May	Jun	Jul	Aug	Sep	Oct	Nov	Dec
High	29	32	43	56	69	78	82	80	72	60	46	34
Low	15	17	25	36	46	55	60	58	51	40	32	21
Precip	1.6	1.3	2.3	3.1	2.6	3.1	3.0	3.4	3.7	2.4	2.7	2.1
Snow	13.0	9.4	8.0	2.7	tr	tr	tr	tr	tr	0.3	3.5	11.2

High and Low temperatures in degrees Fahrenheit; Precipitation and Snow in inches

Population: 436,141 (2000); Race: 75.2% White, 20.1% Black, 0.7% Asian, 0.6% American Indian and Alaska Native, 2.3% Hispanic of any race, 2.4% two or more races (2000); Density: 681.9 persons per square mile (2000); Age: 27.4% under 18, 11.6% over 64 (2000).
Religion: Five largest groups: 14.9% Catholic Church, 2.5% The United Methodist Church, 2.3% Lutheran Church—Missouri Synod, 2.1% Southern Baptist Convention, 1.6% Independent, Non-Charismatic Churches (2000).
Economy: Unemployment rate: 7.4% (11/2002); Total civilian labor force: 184,075 (11/2002); Leading industries: 16.7% manufacturing; 16.7% retail trade; 14.2% health care and social assistance (2000); Companies that employ more than 1,000 persons: 17 (2000); Companies that employ more than 100 persons: 212 (2000); Farms: 796 totaling 117,968 acres (1997); Minority business ownership rate: 9.0% (1997); Women business ownership rate: 29.8% (1997); Retail sales per capita: $10,386 (1997). Single-family building permits issued: 1,864 (2001) / 1,746 (2000); Multi-family building permits issued: 1,589 (2001) / 578 (2000).
Income: Per capita income: $20,883 (2000); Median household income: $41,951 (2000); Poverty rate: 13.1% (2000); Bankruptcy rate: 5.86% (2001).
Taxes: Total county taxes per capita: $116 (2000); County property taxes per capita: $110 (2000).
Education: High school graduation rate: 83.1% (2000); College graduation rate: 16.2% (2000).
Housing: Homeownership rate: 73.2% (2000); Median home value: $95,000 (2000); Median rent: $413 per month (2000); Median age of housing: 36 years (2000).
Health: Birth rate: 146.7 per 10,000 population (1998); Age adjusted death rate: 97.0 per 10,000 population (1999); Infant mortality rate: 11.7 per 1,000 live births (1998); Age adjusted cancer mortality rate: 223.0 deaths per 100,000 population (1999). Air Quality Index: 77% good, 23% moderate, 0% unhealthy (percent of days in 2000). Number of physicians: 20.9 per 10,000 population (1999); Number of hospital beds: 29.3 per 10,000 population (1999).
Elections: 2000 Presidential election results: 62.8% Gore, 34.9% Bush, 1.9% Nader, 0.0% Buchanan

Additional Information Contacts

Genesee County Government Offices 810-257-3282
Clio Chamber of Commerce 810-686-4480
Davison Chamber of Commerce 810-653-6266
Fenton Chamber of Commerce 810-629-5447
Flint Area Association of Realtors 810-767-6330
Flint Area Convention & Visitors Bureau 810-232-8900
Flint Chamber of Commerce 810-232-7101
Flushing Chamber of Commerce 810-659-4141
Grand Blanc Chamber of Commerce 810-695-4222
Swartz Creek Chamber of Commerce 810-635-9643

Genesee County Communities

ARGENTINE (township). Covers a land area of 35.125 square miles and a water area of 1.210 square miles. Located at 42.81° N. Lat.; 83.86° W. Long.
Population: 6,521 (2000); Race: 98.3% White, 1.2% Black, 0.1% Asian, 0.2% American Indian and Alaska Native, 0.7% Hispanic of any race, 0.0% two or more races (2000); Density: 185.7 persons per square mile (2000); Age: 29.1% under 18, 8.0% over 64 (2000); Marriage status: 19.3% never married, 69.8% now married, 1.9% widowed, 9.0% divorced (2000); Foreign born: 1.3% (2000); Ancestry (includes multiple ancestries): 21.4% German, 17.3% Irish, 14.8% English, 10.4% Polish, 8.6% French (except Basque) (2000).
Economy: Single-family building permits issued: 46 (2001) / 68 (2000); Multi-family building permits issued: 0 (2001) / 0 (2000); Employment by occupation: 11.7% management, 18.2% professional, 11.3% services, 20.9% sales, 0.0% farming, 16.9% construction, 21.0% production (2000).
Income: Per capita income: $24,343 (2000); Median household income: $60,641 (2000); Poverty rate: 2.2% (2000).
Taxes: Total city taxes per capita: $33 (1997); City property taxes per capita: $24 (1997).
Education: High school graduation rate: 91.3% (2000); College graduation rate: 18.1% (2000).
Housing: Homeownership rate: 91.4% (2000); Median home value: $151,200 (2000); Median rent: $561 per month (2000); Median age of housing: 25 years (2000).
Safety: Violent crime rate: 10.7 per 10,000 population; Property crime rate: 167.8 per 10,000 population (2001).
Transportation: Commute to work: 97.1% car, 0.0% public transportation, 0.6% walk, 2.3% work from home (2000); Travel time to work: 16.6% less than 15 minutes, 31.4% 15 to 30 minutes, 24.6% 30 to 45 minutes, 12.2% 45 to 60 minutes, 15.3% 60 minutes or more (2000)

ATLAS (township). Covers a land area of 35.372 square miles and a water area of 0.604 square miles. Located at 42.92° N. Lat.; 83.50° W. Long. Elevation is 846 feet.
Population: 7,257 (2000); Race: 97.0% White, 0.2% Black, 0.7% Asian, 0.3% American Indian and Alaska Native, 1.4% Hispanic of any race, 1.6% two or more races (2000); Density: 205.2 persons per square mile (2000); Age: 29.9% under 18, 6.8% over 64 (2000); Marriage status: 20.1% never married, 69.0% now married, 3.5% widowed, 7.3% divorced (2000); Foreign born: 2.7% (2000); Ancestry (includes multiple ancestries): 23.8% German, 16.6% English, 13.3% Irish, 8.2% United States or American, 7.2% Polish (2000).
Economy: Single-family building permits issued: 29 (2001) / 63 (2000); Multi-family building permits issued: 0 (2001) / 0 (2000); Employment by occupation: 12.6% management, 22.2% professional, 13.8% services, 22.0% sales, 0.2% farming, 11.6% construction, 17.6% production (2000).
Income: Per capita income: $27,960 (2000); Median household income: $73,720 (2000); Poverty rate: 4.0% (2000).
Taxes: Total city taxes per capita: $58 (1997); City property taxes per capita: $51 (1997).
Education: High school graduation rate: 94.0% (2000); College graduation rate: 25.5% (2000).
Housing: Homeownership rate: 94.8% (2000); Median home value: $164,200 (2000); Median rent: $401 per month (2000); Median age of housing: 23 years (2000).
Transportation: Commute to work: 98.1% car, 0.0% public transportation, 0.7% walk, 0.9% work from home (2000); Travel time to work: 18.4% less than 15 minutes, 35.4% 15 to 30 minutes, 23.7% 30 to 45 minutes, 13.2% 45 to 60 minutes, 9.2% 60 minutes or more (2000)

BEECHER (CDP). Covers a land area of 5.923 square miles and a water area of 0 square miles. Located at 43.08° N. Lat.; 83.70° W. Long. Elevation is 800 feet.
Population: 12,793 (2000); Race: 28.0% White, 66.0% Black, 0.1% Asian, 0.4% American Indian and Alaska Native, 3.8% Hispanic of any race, 3.6% two or more races (2000); Density: 2,159.8 persons per square mile (2000);

Age: 34.6% under 18, 9.6% over 64 (2000); Marriage status: 41.1% never married, 36.8% now married, 7.2% widowed, 14.9% divorced (2000); Foreign born: 0.8% (2000); Ancestry (includes multiple ancestries): 62.0% Other groups, 3.2% German, 3.1% English, 3.0% United States or American, 2.4% African (2000).
Economy: Employment by occupation: 4.4% management, 7.9% professional, 25.6% services, 22.0% sales, 0.4% farming, 8.0% construction, 31.7% production (2000).
Income: Per capita income: $13,484 (2000); Median household income: $25,925 (2000); Poverty rate: 30.3% (2000).
Education: High school graduation rate: 68.6% (2000); College graduation rate: 3.9% (2000).
Housing: Homeownership rate: 62.5% (2000); Median home value: $38,400 (2000); Median rent: $389 per month (2000); Median age of housing: 40 years (2000).
Transportation: Commute to work: 91.3% car, 2.7% public transportation, 2.0% walk, 2.5% work from home (2000); Travel time to work: 24.7% less than 15 minutes, 45.9% 15 to 30 minutes, 12.0% 30 to 45 minutes, 9.1% 45 to 60 minutes, 8.3% 60 minutes or more (2000)

BURTON (city). Covers a land area of 23.472 square miles and a water area of 0 square miles. Located at 42.99° N. Lat.; 83.63° W. Long. Elevation is 774 feet.
Population: 30,308 (2000); Race: 92.5% White, 3.2% Black, 0.9% Asian, 0.8% American Indian and Alaska Native, 2.7% Hispanic of any race, 1.9% two or more races (2000); Density: 1,291.3 persons per square mile (2000); Age: 27.4% under 18, 11.2% over 64 (2000); Marriage status: 24.7% never married, 56.1% now married, 6.9% widowed, 12.3% divorced (2000); Foreign born: 2.2% (2000); Ancestry (includes multiple ancestries): 17.9% German, 12.2% Irish, 11.7% English, 11.5% Other groups, 11.2% United States or American (2000).
Vital Statistics: Birth rate: 137.3 per 10,000 population (1998)
Economy: Unemployment rate: 8.3% (11/2002); Total civilian labor force: 11,696 (11/2002); Single-family building permits issued: 124 (2001) / 122 (2000); Multi-family building permits issued: 0 (2001) / 0 (2000); Employment by occupation: 8.6% management, 14.0% professional, 16.4% services, 23.9% sales, 0.1% farming, 14.0% construction, 23.1% production (2000).
Income: Per capita income: $20,548 (2000); Median household income: $44,050 (2000); Poverty rate: 8.7% (2000).
Taxes: Total city taxes per capita: $154 (1997); City property taxes per capita: $139 (1997).
Education: High school graduation rate: 81.9% (2000); College graduation rate: 11.2% (2000).

School District(s)

Atherton Community Schools (KG-12)
2000 Enrollment: 1,096 810-591-9182
Bendle Public Schools (KG-12)
2000 Enrollment: 1,469 810-591-2501
Bentley Community Schools (PK-12)
2000 Enrollment: 1,148 810-591-9100
Burton Glen Charter Academy (KG-06)
2000 Enrollment: 395 810-744-2300

Housing: Homeownership rate: 80.7% (2000); Median home value: $84,500 (2000); Median rent: $409 per month (2000); Median age of housing: 40 years (2000).
Safety: Violent crime rate: 43.3 per 10,000 population; Property crime rate: 655.8 per 10,000 population (2001).
Transportation: Commute to work: 96.1% car, 0.4% public transportation, 1.2% walk, 1.8% work from home (2000); Travel time to work: 33.2% less than 15 minutes, 40.6% 15 to 30 minutes, 9.5% 30 to 45 minutes, 7.3% 45 to 60 minutes, 9.4% 60 minutes or more (2000)

CLAYTON (township). Covers a land area of 34.250 square miles and a water area of 0 square miles. Located at 42.99° N. Lat.; 83.87° W. Long.
Population: 7,546 (2000); Race: 94.6% White, 1.1% Black, 0.4% Asian, 0.5% American Indian and Alaska Native, 2.4% Hispanic of any race, 2.2% two or more races (2000); Density: 220.3 persons per square mile (2000); Age: 26.3% under 18, 10.6% over 64 (2000); Marriage status: 18.8% never married, 68.2% now married, 4.8% widowed, 8.2% divorced (2000); Foreign born: 3.1% (2000); Ancestry (includes multiple ancestries): 22.1% German, 13.2% English, 12.8% Irish, 8.5% Polish, 7.7% United States or American (2000).
Economy: Single-family building permits issued: 55 (2001) / 61 (2000); Multi-family building permits issued: 0 (2001) / 0 (2000); Employment by occupation: 12.1% management, 17.6% professional, 12.3% services, 26.3% sales, 0.2% farming, 12.4% construction, 19.0% production (2000).
Income: Per capita income: $23,445 (2000); Median household income: $53,062 (2000); Poverty rate: 5.2% (2000).
Taxes: Total city taxes per capita: $58 (2000); City property taxes per capita: $42 (2000).
Education: High school graduation rate: 89.4% (2000); College graduation rate: 18.1% (2000).
Housing: Homeownership rate: 91.0% (2000); Median home value: $119,900 (2000); Median rent: $560 per month (2000); Median age of housing: 25 years (2000).
Transportation: Commute to work: 96.0% car, 0.0% public transportation, 0.9% walk, 2.3% work from home (2000); Travel time to work: 26.6% less than 15 minutes, 47.1% 15 to 30 minutes, 11.6% 30 to 45 minutes, 7.0% 45 to 60 minutes, 7.8% 60 minutes or more (2000)

CLIO (city). Covers a land area of 1.177 square miles and a water area of 0 square miles. Located at 43.17° N. Lat.; 83.73° W. Long. Elevation is 720 feet.
History: A sawmill was built here in 1837, and the village grew with the arrival of the Pere Marquette Railroad in 1861. Clio was incorporated as a village in 1873 and as a city in 1928.
Population: 2,483 (2000); Race: 96.7% White, 0.3% Black, 0.2% Asian, 0.3% American Indian and Alaska Native, 0.8% Hispanic of any race, 1.4% two or more races (2000); Density: 2,109.8 persons per square mile (2000); Age: 24.2% under 18, 13.7% over 64 (2000); Marriage status: 31.1% never married, 48.5% now married, 5.8% widowed, 14.6% divorced (2000); Foreign born: 0.4% (2000); Ancestry (includes multiple ancestries): 19.3% German, 14.9% United States or American, 13.4% English, 11.5% Other groups, 10.6% Irish (2000).
Economy: Single-family building permits issued: 8 (2001) / 11 (2000); Multi-family building permits issued: 90 (2001) / 0 (2000); Employment by occupation: 7.5% management, 15.7% professional, 14.9% services, 33.0% sales, 0.4% farming, 9.1% construction, 19.3% production (2000).
Income: Per capita income: $19,727 (2000); Median household income: $35,859 (2000); Poverty rate: 7.9% (2000).
Taxes: Total city taxes per capita: $186 (1997); City property taxes per capita: $179 (1997).
Education: High school graduation rate: 86.5% (2000); College graduation rate: 14.8% (2000).

School District(s)

Clio Area School District (KG-12)
2000 Enrollment: 3,594 810-591-0502

Housing: Homeownership rate: 56.9% (2000); Median home value: $89,900 (2000); Median rent: $395 per month (2000); Median age of housing: 42 years (2000).
Safety: Violent crime rate: 20.0 per 10,000 population; Property crime rate: 540.9 per 10,000 population (2001).
Newspapers: Birch Run/Bridgeport Herald (1 x week); The Flint-Genesee County Legal News (1 x week); Mount Morris' Gilo Herald (1 x week)
Transportation: Commute to work: 94.1% car, 0.0% public transportation, 2.6% walk, 2.3% work from home (2000); Travel time to work: 32.1% less than 15 minutes, 35.0% 15 to 30 minutes, 18.7% 30 to 45 minutes, 5.1% 45 to 60 minutes, 9.0% 60 minutes or more (2000)

Additional Information Contacts

Clio Chamber of Commerce........................ 810-686-4480

DAVISON (city). Covers a land area of 1.782 square miles and a water area of 0 square miles. Located at 43.03° N. Lat.; 83.51° W. Long. Elevation is 799 feet.
History: Davison developed as a service center for the surrounding farming area, and a residential center for workers employed in Flint factories.
Population: 5,536 (2000); Race: 97.2% White, 0.6% Black, 0.3% Asian, 0.2% American Indian and Alaska Native, 2.4% Hispanic of any race, 1.0% two or more races (2000); Density: 3,106.3 persons per square mile (2000); Age: 23.9% under 18, 17.3% over 64 (2000); Marriage status: 22.2% never married, 50.4% now married, 10.8% widowed, 16.6% divorced (2000); Foreign born: 2.4% (2000); Ancestry (includes multiple ancestries): 26.9% German, 18.2% Irish, 16.3% English, 8.3% Other groups, 7.3% Polish (2000).
Economy: Single-family building permits issued: 11 (2001) / 18 (2000); Multi-family building permits issued: 0 (2001) / 0 (2000); Employment by occupation: 11.4% management, 22.2% professional, 16.6% services, 25.8% sales, 0.0% farming, 8.0% construction, 16.1% production (2000).
Income: Per capita income: $24,449 (2000); Median household income: $37,482 (2000); Poverty rate: 6.7% (2000).

Taxes: Total city taxes per capita: $211 (1997); City property taxes per capita: $207 (1997).
Education: High school graduation rate: 83.7% (2000); College graduation rate: 22.2% (2000).

School District(s)

Davison Community Schools (KG-12)
2000 Enrollment: 5,274 810-658-5001

Housing: Homeownership rate: 56.1% (2000); Median home value: $100,000 (2000); Median rent: $439 per month (2000); Median age of housing: 35 years (2000).
Safety: Violent crime rate: 14.4 per 10,000 population; Property crime rate: 237.2 per 10,000 population (2001).
Newspapers: The Davison Index (1 x week)
Transportation: Commute to work: 95.3% car, 0.8% public transportation, 1.9% walk, 1.6% work from home (2000); Travel time to work: 27.5% less than 15 minutes, 42.7% 15 to 30 minutes, 11.7% 30 to 45 minutes, 6.9% 45 to 60 minutes, 11.2% 60 minutes or more (2000)

Additional Information Contacts

Davison Chamber of Commerce 810-653-6266

DAVISON (township). Covers a land area of 33.492 square miles and a water area of 0.225 square miles. Located at 43.01° N. Lat.; 83.52° W. Long. Elevation is 799 feet.
History: Settled 1836; incorporated as village 1889, as city 1939.
Population: 17,722 (2000); Race: 94.3% White, 1.7% Black, 0.9% Asian, 0.4% American Indian and Alaska Native, 2.2% Hispanic of any race, 2.0% two or more races (2000); Density: 529.1 persons per square mile (2000); Age: 24.4% under 18, 10.8% over 64 (2000); Marriage status: 26.9% never married, 56.9% now married, 4.8% widowed, 11.4% divorced (2000); Foreign born: 3.0% (2000); Ancestry (includes multiple ancestries): 23.7% German, 15.6% Irish, 14.0% English, 10.1% Other groups, 8.1% United States or American (2000).
Economy: In agricultural area. Manufacturing: machinery, printing and publishing. Has Rosemoor Park, with race track. Single-family building permits issued: 145 (2001) / 94 (2000); Multi-family building permits issued: 19 (2001) / 62 (2000); Employment by occupation: 10.2% management, 21.4% professional, 13.8% services, 23.4% sales, 0.1% farming, 11.7% construction, 19.5% production (2000).
Income: Per capita income: $23,595 (2000); Median household income: $45,417 (2000); Poverty rate: 6.3% (2000).
Taxes: Total city taxes per capita: $128 (2000); City property taxes per capita: $117 (2000).
Education: High school graduation rate: 90.3% (2000); College graduation rate: 19.4% (2000).
Housing: Homeownership rate: 66.4% (2000); Median home value: $126,900 (2000); Median rent: $437 per month (2000); Median age of housing: 22 years (2000).
Safety: Violent crime rate: 13.5 per 10,000 population; Property crime rate: 275.6 per 10,000 population (2001).
Transportation: Commute to work: 97.8% car, 0.0% public transportation, 0.1% walk, 1.6% work from home (2000); Travel time to work: 25.0% less than 15 minutes, 47.2% 15 to 30 minutes, 11.1% 30 to 45 minutes, 6.9% 45 to 60 minutes, 9.8% 60 minutes or more (2000)

FENTON (city). Covers a land area of 6.562 square miles and a water area of 0.319 square miles. Located at 42.79° N. Lat.; 83.71° W. Long. Elevation is 907 feet.
History: Fenton developed around a cement plant, utilizing marl taken from the many nearby lakes.
Population: 10,582 (2000); Race: 96.6% White, 0.7% Black, 0.7% Asian, 0.7% American Indian and Alaska Native, 2.2% Hispanic of any race, 1.1% two or more races (2000); Density: 1,612.5 persons per square mile (2000); Age: 25.7% under 18, 13.4% over 64 (2000); Marriage status: 24.7% never married, 56.4% now married, 7.7% widowed, 11.2% divorced (2000); Foreign born: 2.2% (2000); Ancestry (includes multiple ancestries): 19.9% German, 14.7% English, 13.8% Irish, 7.2% Other groups, 7.0% French (except Basque) (2000).
Economy: Single-family building permits issued: 29 (2001) / 71 (2000); Multi-family building permits issued: 402 (2001) / 136 (2000); Employment by occupation: 11.3% management, 22.9% professional, 14.2% services, 23.7% sales, 0.1% farming, 12.2% construction, 15.5% production (2000).
Income: Per capita income: $22,435 (2000); Median household income: $47,400 (2000); Poverty rate: 6.2% (2000).
Taxes: Total city taxes per capita: $257 (1997); City property taxes per capita: $237 (1997).
Education: High school graduation rate: 87.5% (2000); College graduation rate: 22.4% (2000).

School District(s)

Fenton Area Public Schools (PK-12)
2000 Enrollment: 3,450 810-591-2268
Lake Fenton Community Schools (KG-12)
2000 Enrollment: 1,437 810-591-1004

Housing: Homeownership rate: 66.4% (2000); Median home value: $124,200 (2000); Median rent: $549 per month (2000); Median age of housing: 27 years (2000).
Safety: Violent crime rate: 14.1 per 10,000 population; Property crime rate: 297.0 per 10,000 population (2001).
Transportation: Commute to work: 96.1% car, 0.0% public transportation, 1.2% walk, 1.7% work from home (2000); Travel time to work: 26.9% less than 15 minutes, 31.9% 15 to 30 minutes, 17.6% 30 to 45 minutes, 11.6% 45 to 60 minutes, 12.0% 60 minutes or more (2000)

Additional Information Contacts

Fenton Chamber of Commerce 810-629-5447

FENTON (township). Covers a land area of 23.873 square miles and a water area of 3.659 square miles. Located at 42.82° N. Lat.; 83.74° W. Long. Elevation is 907 feet.
History: Settled 1834, incorporated 1863.
Population: 12,968 (2000); Race: 97.5% White, 0.4% Black, 1.0% Asian, 0.5% American Indian and Alaska Native, 1.1% Hispanic of any race, 0.4% two or more races (2000); Density: 543.2 persons per square mile (2000); Age: 25.2% under 18, 9.3% over 64 (2000); Marriage status: 19.4% never married, 67.2% now married, 4.3% widowed, 9.1% divorced (2000); Foreign born: 1.8% (2000); Ancestry (includes multiple ancestries): 23.0% German, 16.0% Irish, 15.1% English, 9.2% United States or American, 9.0% Polish (2000).
Economy: In agricultural area: dairy products; livestock; apples, grain. Manufacturing: plastic and rubber products, motor vehicle parts, insulated glass. Single-family building permits issued: 171 (2001) / 229 (2000); Multi-family building permits issued: 0 (2001) / 4 (2000); Employment by occupation: 14.6% management, 23.5% professional, 9.3% services, 27.3% sales, 0.1% farming, 9.7% construction, 15.4% production (2000).
Income: Per capita income: $31,560 (2000); Median household income: $71,094 (2000); Poverty rate: 3.4% (2000).
Taxes: Total city taxes per capita: $85 (1997); City property taxes per capita: $73 (1997).
Education: High school graduation rate: 92.6% (2000); College graduation rate: 32.6% (2000).
Housing: Homeownership rate: 94.2% (2000); Median home value: $184,100 (2000); Median rent: $579 per month (2000); Median age of housing: 24 years (2000).
Transportation: Commute to work: 96.9% car, 0.2% public transportation, 0.5% walk, 2.4% work from home (2000); Travel time to work: 23.9% less than 15 minutes, 36.6% 15 to 30 minutes, 15.4% 30 to 45 minutes, 12.1% 45 to 60 minutes, 11.9% 60 minutes or more (2000)

FLINT (city). Covers a land area of 33.633 square miles and a water area of 0.430 square miles. Located at 43.02° N. Lat.; 83.69° W. Long. Elevation is 712 feet.
History: Jacob Smith settled on the site of Flint after negotiating a treaty with the local tribes in 1819. Others joined him, including John Todd in 1830, who operated a tavern and a ferry across the Flint River. When Michigan became a state in 1837, Flint was a village of 300 and the seat of Genesee County. The early lumbering industry led to the manufacture of two-wheeled carts, which later gave way to carriage shops. Flint was ready in 1904 for the founding of the Buick Motor Company, which added engines to Flint's carriages. Pioneers in Flint's automobile industry were C.W. Nash, Walter P. Chrysler, and William C. Durant.
Population: 124,943 (2000); Race: 41.6% White, 52.4% Black, 0.3% Asian, 0.9% American Indian and Alaska Native, 3.0% Hispanic of any race, 3.6% two or more races (2000); Density: 3,714.9 persons per square mile (2000); Age: 30.6% under 18, 10.5% over 64 (2000); Marriage status: 39.0% never married, 39.2% now married, 7.2% widowed, 14.6% divorced (2000); Foreign born: 1.5% (2000); Ancestry (includes multiple ancestries): 50.6% Other groups, 7.9% German, 5.6% Irish, 4.9% English, 4.3% United States or American (2000).
Vital Statistics: Birth rate: 225.5 per 10,000 population (1998)
Economy: Unemployment rate: 12.8% (11/2002); Total civilian labor force: 51,300 (11/2002); Single-family building permits issued: 29 (2001) / 63 (2000); Multi-family building permits issued: 0 (2001) / 8 (2000); Employment by occupation: 6.7% management, 14.3% professional, 23.7%

services, 22.4% sales, 0.1% farming, 8.2% construction, 24.6% production (2000).
Income: Per capita income: $15,733 (2000); Median household income: $28,015 (2000); Poverty rate: 26.4% (2000).
Taxes: Total city taxes per capita: $412 (2000); City property taxes per capita: $398 (2000).
Education: High school graduation rate: 74.5% (2000); College graduation rate: 11.3% (2000).

School District(s)

Academy of Flint (KG-07)
2000 Enrollment: 431 517-774-2100
Beecher Community School District (KG-12)
2000 Enrollment: 2,231 810-591-4731
Carman-Ainsworth Community Schoo (KG-12)
2000 Enrollment: 5,237 810-591-3205
Center Academy (KG-07)
2000 Enrollment: 303 517-774-2100
Flint City School District (PK-12)
2000 Enrollment: 22,532 810-760-1249
International Academy of Flint (KG-09)
2000 Enrollment: 698 517-774-2100
Kearsley Community Schools (KG-12)
2000 Enrollment: 3,905 810-591-9830
Linden Charter Academy (KG-07)
2000 Enrollment: 516 517-774-2100
Northridge Academy (KG-08)
2000 Enrollment: 292 231-591-5802
Questar Academy (KG-07)
2000 Enrollment: 87 517-774-2100
Westwood Heights Schools (KG-12)
2000 Enrollment: 1,093 810-591-0870

Four-year College(s)

Baker College of Flint (Private, Not-for-profit)
2001 Enrollment: 4,399 810-767-7600
2001 Tuition: In-state $5,600; Out-of-state $5,600
Flint Bible Institute (Private, Not-for-profit, Undenominational)
2001 Enrollment: n/a 313-232-6770
Kettering University (Private, Not-for-profit)
2001 Enrollment: 3,346 800-955-4464
2001 Tuition: In-state $18,500; Out-of-state $18,500
University of Michigan-Flint (Public)
2001 Enrollment: 6,397 810-762-3000
2001 Tuition: In-state $4,135; Out-of-state $8,271
United Bible Institute of United Theological Seminary (Private, Not-for-profit, Baptist)
2001 Enrollment: n/a 313-787-2564
Baker College Center for Graduate Studies (Private, Not-for-profit)
2001 Enrollment: 1,785 810-766-4390
2001 Tuition: In-state $7,440; Out-of-state $7,440
Baker College Corporate Services (Private, Not-for-profit)
2001 Enrollment: 897 810-766-4242
2001 Tuition: In-state $7,440; Out-of-state $7,440

Two-year College(s)

Mott Community College (Public)
2001 Enrollment: 9,019 810-762-0200
2001 Tuition: In-state $4,501; Out-of-state $6,003
Flint Institute of Barbering (Private, For-profit)
2001 Enrollment: 36 810-232-4711
Hurley Medical Center-School of Radiologic Tech (Public)
2001 Enrollment: n/a 810-257-9835

Housing: Homeownership rate: 58.9% (2000); Median home value: $49,700 (2000); Median rent: $374 per month (2000); Median age of housing: 47 years (2000).
Hospitals: Hurley Medical Center
Safety: Violent crime rate: 159.9 per 10,000 population; Property crime rate: 712.9 per 10,000 population (2001).
Newspapers: The Swartz Creek News (1 x week); The Flint Journal (7 x week); Fenton Press; The Clio Messenger; Flint Township News (1 x week); The Suburban News (1 x week); The Flushing Observer; The Davison Flagstaff (1 x week); The Grand Blanc News (1 x week); Flint Township/Swartz Creek Advance (2 x week); Flint Enquirer (1 x week)
Transportation: Commute to work: 90.8% car, 4.0% public transportation, 2.4% walk, 1.9% work from home (2000); Travel time to work: 36.7% less than 15 minutes, 36.6% 15 to 30 minutes, 10.6% 30 to 45 minutes, 7.3% 45 to 60 minutes, 8.7% 60 minutes or more (2000); Amtrak: Service available.
Airports: Bishop International (primary service)

Additional Information Contacts
Flint Area Association of Realtors 810-767-6330
Flint Area Convention & Visitors Bureau 810-232-8900
Flint Chamber of Commerce 810-232-7101

FLINT (township). Covers a land area of 23.635 square miles and a water area of 0 square miles. Located at 42.99° N. Lat.; 83.75° W. Long. Elevation is 712 feet.
Population: 33,691 (2000); Race: 77.3% White, 15.4% Black, 2.2% Asian, 0.7% American Indian and Alaska Native, 2.4% Hispanic of any race, 3.4% two or more races (2000); Density: 1,425.5 persons per square mile (2000); Age: 24.4% under 18, 16.1% over 64 (2000); Marriage status: 26.2% never married, 51.6% now married, 8.5% widowed, 13.7% divorced (2000); Foreign born: 4.7% (2000); Ancestry (includes multiple ancestries): 23.1% Other groups, 16.5% German, 12.4% English, 10.7% Irish, 6.3% United States or American (2000).
Vital Statistics: Birth rate: 102.4 per 10,000 population (1998)
Economy: Unemployment rate: 4.7% (11/2002); Total civilian labor force: 15,411 (11/2002); Single-family building permits issued: 60 (2001) / 98 (2000); Multi-family building permits issued: 0 (2001) / 0 (2000); Employment by occupation: 8.9% management, 19.7% professional, 16.0% services, 26.0% sales, 0.1% farming, 10.2% construction, 19.2% production (2000).
Income: Per capita income: $22,216 (2000); Median household income: $39,718 (2000); Poverty rate: 10.4% (2000).
Taxes: Total city taxes per capita: $51 (2000); City property taxes per capita: $35 (2000).
Education: High school graduation rate: 84.5% (2000); College graduation rate: 17.5% (2000).
Housing: Homeownership rate: 68.6% (2000); Median home value: $98,600 (2000); Median rent: $459 per month (2000); Median age of housing: 32 years (2000).
Hospitals: McLaren Regional Medical Center (467 beds)
Safety: Violent crime rate: 69.7 per 10,000 population; Property crime rate: 785.4 per 10,000 population (2001).
Transportation: Commute to work: 94.8% car, 0.7% public transportation, 1.3% walk, 2.6% work from home (2000); Travel time to work: 35.7% less than 15 minutes, 42.4% 15 to 30 minutes, 8.7% 30 to 45 minutes, 6.3% 45 to 60 minutes, 6.8% 60 minutes or more (2000); Amtrak: Service available.

FLUSHING (city). Covers a land area of 4.310 square miles and a water area of 0.036 square miles. Located at 43.06° N. Lat.; 83.84° W. Long. Elevation is 728 feet.
Population: 8,348 (2000); Race: 96.1% White, 1.2% Black, 0.5% Asian, 0.3% American Indian and Alaska Native, 1.1% Hispanic of any race, 1.1% two or more races (2000); Density: 1,936.7 persons per square mile (2000); Age: 22.8% under 18, 19.5% over 64 (2000); Marriage status: 22.0% never married, 59.2% now married, 7.4% widowed, 11.4% divorced (2000); Foreign born: 2.2% (2000); Ancestry (includes multiple ancestries): 26.8% German, 19.9% English, 18.8% Irish, 8.0% Polish, 6.5% Other groups (2000).
Economy: Single-family building permits issued: 19 (2001) / 12 (2000); Multi-family building permits issued: 4 (2001) / 6 (2000); Employment by occupation: 16.0% management, 24.4% professional, 13.5% services, 26.5% sales, 0.0% farming, 7.4% construction, 12.2% production (2000).
Income: Per capita income: $24,697 (2000); Median household income: $54,010 (2000); Poverty rate: 4.7% (2000).
Taxes: Total city taxes per capita: $213 (1997); City property taxes per capita: $206 (1997).
Education: High school graduation rate: 88.8% (2000); College graduation rate: 28.1% (2000).

School District(s)

Flushing Community Schools (PK-12)
2000 Enrollment: 4,323 810-591-0600

Housing: Homeownership rate: 78.3% (2000); Median home value: $122,500 (2000); Median rent: $427 per month (2000); Median age of housing: 32 years (2000).
Safety: Violent crime rate: 13.1 per 10,000 population; Property crime rate: 174.0 per 10,000 population (2001).
Newspapers: Catholic Times (1 x week)
Transportation: Commute to work: 94.5% car, 0.1% public transportation, 1.8% walk, 3.3% work from home (2000); Travel time to work: 27.1% less than 15 minutes, 45.2% 15 to 30 minutes, 14.0% 30 to 45 minutes, 5.3% 45 to 60 minutes, 8.4% 60 minutes or more (2000)

Additional Information Contacts
Flushing Chamber of Commerce 810-659-4141

FLUSHING (township). Covers a land area of 30.852 square miles and a water area of 0.155 square miles. Located at 43.09° N. Lat.; 83.85° W. Long. Elevation is 728 feet.
History: Indian mounds nearby. Settled 1833, incorporated 1877.
Population: 10,230 (2000); Race: 96.5% White, 0.9% Black, 0.5% Asian, 0.3% American Indian and Alaska Native, 1.4% Hispanic of any race, 1.5% two or more races (2000); Density: 331.6 persons per square mile (2000); Age: 26.5% under 18, 11.6% over 64 (2000); Marriage status: 20.1% never married, 68.0% now married, 5.1% widowed, 6.8% divorced (2000); Foreign born: 2.2% (2000); Ancestry (includes multiple ancestries): 22.9% German, 14.4% English, 13.4% Irish, 12.6% Polish, 7.5% Other groups (2000).
Economy: In agricultural area: dairy products; grain, beans, apples; flour milling; light manufacturing. Single-family building permits issued: 63 (2001) / 51 (2000); Multi-family building permits issued: 4 (2001) / 22 (2000); Employment by occupation: 14.7% management, 21.9% professional, 9.3% services, 28.0% sales, 0.0% farming, 11.0% construction, 15.1% production (2000).
Income: Per capita income: $26,102 (2000); Median household income: $60,946 (2000); Poverty rate: 2.2% (2000).
Taxes: Total city taxes per capita: $99 (1997); City property taxes per capita: $61 (1997).
Education: High school graduation rate: 91.4% (2000); College graduation rate: 21.9% (2000).
Housing: Homeownership rate: 96.0% (2000); Median home value: $135,500 (2000); Median rent: $447 per month (2000); Median age of housing: 27 years (2000).
Safety: Violent crime rate: 6.8 per 10,000 population; Property crime rate: 117.7 per 10,000 population (2001).
Transportation: Commute to work: 96.2% car, 0.0% public transportation, 0.8% walk, 2.3% work from home (2000); Travel time to work: 20.0% less than 15 minutes, 46.3% 15 to 30 minutes, 20.1% 30 to 45 minutes, 4.9% 45 to 60 minutes, 8.7% 60 minutes or more (2000)

FOREST (township). Covers a land area of 35.777 square miles and a water area of 0.340 square miles. Located at 43.17° N. Lat.; 83.51° W. Long.
Population: 4,738 (2000); Race: 97.5% White, 0.0% Black, 0.1% Asian, 0.7% American Indian and Alaska Native, 1.0% Hispanic of any race, 0.9% two or more races (2000); Density: 132.4 persons per square mile (2000); Age: 25.2% under 18, 9.1% over 64 (2000); Marriage status: 21.2% never married, 66.2% now married, 4.7% widowed, 8.0% divorced (2000); Foreign born: 0.5% (2000); Ancestry (includes multiple ancestries): 21.9% German, 12.2% English, 11.4% Irish, 9.3% United States or American, 7.9% French (except Basque) (2000).
Economy: Single-family building permits issued: 24 (2001) / 29 (2000); Multi-family building permits issued: 0 (2001) / 0 (2000); Employment by occupation: 5.4% management, 13.4% professional, 14.9% services, 22.7% sales, 0.2% farming, 14.4% construction, 29.0% production (2000).
Income: Per capita income: $20,773 (2000); Median household income: $51,235 (2000); Poverty rate: 3.0% (2000).
Taxes: Total city taxes per capita: $64 (1997); City property taxes per capita: $63 (1997).
Education: High school graduation rate: 86.7% (2000); College graduation rate: 6.8% (2000).
Housing: Homeownership rate: 91.0% (2000); Median home value: $110,600 (2000); Median rent: $405 per month (2000); Median age of housing: 28 years (2000).
Transportation: Commute to work: 93.6% car, 0.3% public transportation, 1.3% walk, 4.5% work from home (2000); Travel time to work: 13.7% less than 15 minutes, 29.1% 15 to 30 minutes, 33.9% 30 to 45 minutes, 12.7% 45 to 60 minutes, 10.7% 60 minutes or more (2000)

GAINES (village). Covers a land area of 0.304 square miles and a water area of 0 square miles. Located at 42.87° N. Lat.; 83.91° W. Long.
History: The area was settled in the 1830's, but the village of Gaines began when the railroad depot was built in 1856.
Population: 366 (2000); Race: 93.3% White, 0.0% Black, 0.0% Asian, 0.0% American Indian and Alaska Native, 3.1% Hispanic of any race, 5.2% two or more races (2000); Density: 1,205.5 persons per square mile (2000); Age: 23.0% under 18, 14.0% over 64 (2000); Marriage status: 22.8% never married, 56.4% now married, 7.8% widowed, 13.0% divorced (2000); Foreign born: 0.0% (2000); Ancestry (includes multiple ancestries): 24.5% German, 15.8% English, 14.7% United States or American, 10.9% Other groups, 10.9% Irish (2000).
Economy: Employment by occupation: 10.6% management, 9.6% professional, 14.9% services, 23.9% sales, 0.0% farming, 14.4% construction, 26.6% production (2000).
Income: Per capita income: $19,790 (2000); Median household income: $44,375 (2000); Poverty rate: 10.3% (2000).
Taxes: Total city taxes per capita: $97 (1997); City property taxes per capita: $93 (1997).
Education: High school graduation rate: 84.5% (2000); College graduation rate: 5.3% (2000).
Housing: Homeownership rate: 77.2% (2000); Median home value: $88,700 (2000); Median rent: $400 per month (2000); Median age of housing: 55 years (2000).
Transportation: Commute to work: 92.4% car, 0.0% public transportation, 2.7% walk, 4.9% work from home (2000); Travel time to work: 10.8% less than 15 minutes, 38.6% 15 to 30 minutes, 34.1% 30 to 45 minutes, 11.9% 45 to 60 minutes, 4.5% 60 minutes or more (2000)

GAINES (township). Covers a land area of 35.210 square miles and a water area of 0.069 square miles. Located at 42.91° N. Lat.; 83.88° W. Long.
History: Gaines Township was organized in 1842 and named for General E.P. Gaines, a friend of an early settler.
Population: 6,491 (2000); Race: 97.0% White, 0.0% Black, 0.2% Asian, 0.0% American Indian and Alaska Native, 2.2% Hispanic of any race, 2.1% two or more races (2000); Density: 184.4 persons per square mile (2000); Age: 26.3% under 18, 7.0% over 64 (2000); Marriage status: 23.9% never married, 63.0% now married, 4.8% widowed, 8.3% divorced (2000); Foreign born: 1.2% (2000); Ancestry (includes multiple ancestries): 25.2% German, 16.7% English, 15.1% Irish, 9.3% United States or American, 6.8% Other groups (2000).
Economy: Single-family building permits issued: 46 (2001) / 47 (2000); Multi-family building permits issued: 0 (2001) / 0 (2000); Employment by occupation: 8.3% management, 15.9% professional, 11.0% services, 28.0% sales, 0.0% farming, 13.0% construction, 23.9% production (2000).
Income: Per capita income: $24,816 (2000); Median household income: $66,289 (2000); Poverty rate: 3.6% (2000).
Taxes: Total city taxes per capita: $27 (1997); City property taxes per capita: $18 (1997).
Education: High school graduation rate: 92.2% (2000); College graduation rate: 16.8% (2000).
Housing: Homeownership rate: 94.1% (2000); Median home value: $127,000 (2000); Median rent: $483 per month (2000); Median age of housing: 25 years (2000).
Transportation: Commute to work: 97.1% car, 0.0% public transportation, 0.3% walk, 2.3% work from home (2000); Travel time to work: 18.2% less than 15 minutes, 48.8% 15 to 30 minutes, 17.9% 30 to 45 minutes, 6.3% 45 to 60 minutes, 8.9% 60 minutes or more (2000)

GENESEE (township). Covers a land area of 29.393 square miles and a water area of 0.991 square miles. Located at 43.09° N. Lat.; 83.64° W. Long. Elevation is 750 feet.
Population: 24,125 (2000); Race: 87.2% White, 9.2% Black, 0.2% Asian, 0.5% American Indian and Alaska Native, 2.7% Hispanic of any race, 1.8% two or more races (2000); Density: 820.8 persons per square mile (2000); Age: 28.0% under 18, 12.6% over 64 (2000); Marriage status: 24.1% never married, 55.3% now married, 6.9% widowed, 13.7% divorced (2000); Foreign born: 1.3% (2000); Ancestry (includes multiple ancestries): 19.3% German, 18.6% Other groups, 12.9% Irish, 10.7% English, 8.1% United States or American (2000).
Economy: Single-family building permits issued: 39 (2001) / 41 (2000); Multi-family building permits issued: 0 (2001) / 144 (2000); Employment by occupation: 7.8% management, 12.3% professional, 16.1% services, 22.9% sales, 0.1% farming, 14.2% construction, 26.6% production (2000).
Income: Per capita income: $18,306 (2000); Median household income: $39,440 (2000); Poverty rate: 12.8% (2000).
Taxes: Total city taxes per capita: $46 (2000); City property taxes per capita: $39 (2000).
Education: High school graduation rate: 79.8% (2000); College graduation rate: 7.1% (2000).

School District(s)

Genesee School District (PK-12)
2000 Enrollment: 986 810-591-1650
Housing: Homeownership rate: 87.2% (2000); Median home value: $90,100 (2000); Median rent: $378 per month (2000); Median age of housing: 34 years (2000).
Safety: Violent crime rate: 64.7 per 10,000 population; Property crime rate: 388.4 per 10,000 population (2001).

Transportation: Commute to work: 96.5% car, 0.5% public transportation, 1.3% walk, 1.5% work from home (2000); Travel time to work: 24.1% less than 15 minutes, 46.7% 15 to 30 minutes, 12.7% 30 to 45 minutes, 6.8% 45 to 60 minutes, 9.8% 60 minutes or more (2000)

GOODRICH (village). Covers a land area of 2.348 square miles and a water area of 0.040 square miles. Located at 42.91° N. Lat.; 83.50° W. Long. Elevation is 894 feet.
History: Goodrich was settled in 1835 by the Goodrich brothers (Enos, Moses, and Levi) and their families. The village was first called Atlas, but renamed Goodrich when Reuben Goodrich became the postmaster in 1849.
Population: 1,353 (2000); Race: 97.9% White, 0.6% Black, 0.0% Asian, 0.0% American Indian and Alaska Native, 1.6% Hispanic of any race, 1.5% two or more races (2000); Density: 576.3 persons per square mile (2000); Age: 29.8% under 18, 8.5% over 64 (2000); Marriage status: 19.3% never married, 68.3% now married, 3.6% widowed, 8.8% divorced (2000); Foreign born: 1.9% (2000); Ancestry (includes multiple ancestries): 24.3% German, 15.3% English, 14.7% Irish, 7.3% Polish, 6.0% French (except Basque) (2000).
Economy: Single-family building permits issued: 24 (2001) / 11 (2000); Multi-family building permits issued: 0 (2001) / 0 (2000); Employment by occupation: 15.5% management, 18.9% professional, 11.1% services, 28.6% sales, 0.3% farming, 9.3% construction, 16.4% production (2000).
Income: Per capita income: $26,089 (2000); Median household income: $65,089 (2000); Poverty rate: 2.7% (2000).
Taxes: Total city taxes per capita: $213 (1997); City property taxes per capita: $196 (1997).
Education: High school graduation rate: 93.1% (2000); College graduation rate: 27.1% (2000).

School District(s)

Goodrich Area Schools (KG-12)
2000 Enrollment: 1,922 810-591-2250

Housing: Homeownership rate: 85.7% (2000); Median home value: $152,100 (2000); Median rent: $413 per month (2000); Median age of housing: 25 years (2000).
Transportation: Commute to work: 96.3% car, 0.0% public transportation, 1.5% walk, 1.2% work from home (2000); Travel time to work: 20.9% less than 15 minutes, 24.4% 15 to 30 minutes, 26.6% 30 to 45 minutes, 14.7% 45 to 60 minutes, 13.4% 60 minutes or more (2000)

GRAND BLANC (city). Covers a land area of 3.751 square miles and a water area of 0.010 square miles. Located at 42.92° N. Lat.; 83.62° W. Long. Elevation is 839 feet.
History: Grand Blanc took its name from the nickname given to a fur trader named Fisher, who with Antoine Campau established a post here. Fisher was a large man, known as Le Grand Blanc (French, "the big white"). Settlement began here in the 1820's; Rufus Stevens opened a trading post in 1826.
Population: 8,242 (2000); Race: 89.1% White, 5.9% Black, 3.0% Asian, 0.1% American Indian and Alaska Native, 0.8% Hispanic of any race, 1.4% two or more races (2000); Density: 2,197.3 persons per square mile (2000); Age: 23.9% under 18, 14.7% over 64 (2000); Marriage status: 24.9% never married, 55.7% now married, 7.7% widowed, 11.7% divorced (2000); Foreign born: 5.3% (2000); Ancestry (includes multiple ancestries): 25.3% German, 16.8% Irish, 13.9% Other groups, 13.4% English, 8.2% Polish (2000).
Economy: Single-family building permits issued: 10 (2001) / 8 (2000); Multi-family building permits issued: 0 (2001) / 0 (2000); Employment by occupation: 17.2% management, 29.7% professional, 11.5% services, 25.3% sales, 0.3% farming, 5.6% construction, 10.4% production (2000).
Income: Per capita income: $32,622 (2000); Median household income: $54,099 (2000); Poverty rate: 5.5% (2000).
Taxes: Total city taxes per capita: $287 (1997); City property taxes per capita: $277 (1997).
Education: High school graduation rate: 94.1% (2000); College graduation rate: 40.8% (2000).

School District(s)

Grand Blanc Academy (KG-08)
2000 Enrollment: 415 313-487-2420
Grand Blanc Community Schools (KG-12)
2000 Enrollment: 6,261 810-591-6000
Woodland Park Academy (KG-08)
2000 Enrollment: 356 517-774-2100

Housing: Homeownership rate: 59.2% (2000); Median home value: $148,500 (2000); Median rent: $490 per month (2000); Median age of housing: 28 years (2000).
Hospitals: Genesys Regional Medical Center (379 beds)
Safety: Violent crime rate: 16.9 per 10,000 population; Property crime rate: 357.3 per 10,000 population (2001).
Transportation: Commute to work: 94.1% car, 1.2% public transportation, 1.7% walk, 2.6% work from home (2000); Travel time to work: 27.2% less than 15 minutes, 42.2% 15 to 30 minutes, 11.9% 30 to 45 minutes, 9.7% 45 to 60 minutes, 9.0% 60 minutes or more (2000)
Additional Information Contacts
Grand Blanc Chamber of Commerce 810-695-4222

GRAND BLANC (township). Covers a land area of 32.614 square miles and a water area of 0.122 square miles. Located at 42.93° N. Lat.; 83.64° W. Long. Elevation is 839 feet.
History: Settled 1823, incorporated 1930.
Population: 29,827 (2000); Race: 87.9% White, 6.9% Black, 2.0% Asian, 0.5% American Indian and Alaska Native, 2.3% Hispanic of any race, 1.8% two or more races (2000); Density: 914.5 persons per square mile (2000); Age: 25.6% under 18, 10.5% over 64 (2000); Marriage status: 22.5% never married, 63.0% now married, 4.8% widowed, 9.7% divorced (2000); Foreign born: 3.8% (2000); Ancestry (includes multiple ancestries): 22.5% German, 14.6% Other groups, 14.6% English, 14.3% Irish, 8.0% United States or American (2000).
Vital Statistics: Birth rate: 86.5 per 10,000 population (1998)
Economy: In agricultural area: livestock; soybeans, apples, grain, beans; dairy products. Manufacturing: transportation equipment, concrete blocks, environmental testing equipment, chemicals. Unemployment rate: 3.5% (11/2002); Total civilian labor force: 13,267 (11/2002); Single-family building permits issued: 410 (2001) / 291 (2000); Multi-family building permits issued: 704 (2001) / 48 (2000); Employment by occupation: 14.8% management, 25.0% professional, 10.8% services, 24.4% sales, 0.1% farming, 8.2% construction, 16.6% production (2000).
Income: Per capita income: $27,510 (2000); Median household income: $59,858 (2000); Poverty rate: 4.2% (2000).
Taxes: Total city taxes per capita: $47 (2000); City property taxes per capita: $17 (2000).
Education: High school graduation rate: 92.1% (2000); College graduation rate: 30.7% (2000).
Housing: Homeownership rate: 73.9% (2000); Median home value: $134,900 (2000); Median rent: $536 per month (2000); Median age of housing: 26 years (2000).
Safety: Violent crime rate: 18.0 per 10,000 population; Property crime rate: 283.8 per 10,000 population (2001).
Transportation: Commute to work: 97.7% car, 0.1% public transportation, 0.2% walk, 1.8% work from home (2000); Travel time to work: 29.0% less than 15 minutes, 38.7% 15 to 30 minutes, 12.7% 30 to 45 minutes, 9.8% 45 to 60 minutes, 9.9% 60 minutes or more (2000)

LAKE FENTON (CDP). Covers a land area of 5.514 square miles and a water area of 1.674 square miles. Located at 42.84° N. Lat.; 83.70° W. Long.
Population: 4,876 (2000); Race: 97.0% White, 0.6% Black, 0.8% Asian, 1.0% American Indian and Alaska Native, 1.4% Hispanic of any race, 0.6% two or more races (2000); Density: 884.3 persons per square mile (2000); Age: 23.3% under 18, 11.3% over 64 (2000); Marriage status: 20.6% never married, 63.0% now married, 5.3% widowed, 11.1% divorced (2000); Foreign born: 1.4% (2000); Ancestry (includes multiple ancestries): 23.3% German, 16.1% Irish, 13.1% English, 10.0% United States or American, 9.9% Polish (2000).
Economy: Employment by occupation: 17.2% management, 24.2% professional, 9.7% services, 29.4% sales, 0.0% farming, 5.0% construction, 14.5% production (2000).
Income: Per capita income: $32,717 (2000); Median household income: $67,885 (2000); Poverty rate: 3.2% (2000).
Education: High school graduation rate: 93.7% (2000); College graduation rate: 37.4% (2000).
Housing: Homeownership rate: 92.9% (2000); Median home value: $207,200 (2000); Median rent: $601 per month (2000); Median age of housing: 28 years (2000).
Transportation: Commute to work: 97.8% car, 0.3% public transportation, 0.4% walk, 1.5% work from home (2000); Travel time to work: 24.5% less than 15 minutes, 37.2% 15 to 30 minutes, 14.4% 30 to 45 minutes, 13.7% 45 to 60 minutes, 10.2% 60 minutes or more (2000)

LINDEN (city). Covers a land area of 2.389 square miles and a water area of 0.034 square miles. Located at 42.81° N. Lat.; 83.78° W. Long. Elevation is 872 feet.
History: Linden was settled in 1835 by Richard and Perry Lamb. It was incorporated as a village in 1871.

Population: 2,861 (2000); Race: 97.9% White, 0.1% Black, 0.8% Asian, 0.6% American Indian and Alaska Native, 1.0% Hispanic of any race, 0.6% two or more races (2000); Density: 1,197.5 persons per square mile (2000); Age: 24.7% under 18, 16.6% over 64 (2000); Marriage status: 20.6% never married, 62.3% now married, 7.9% widowed, 9.2% divorced (2000); Foreign born: 2.1% (2000); Ancestry (includes multiple ancestries): 20.3% German, 16.6% English, 16.6% Irish, 8.8% Other groups, 7.4% Polish (2000).
Economy: Single-family building permits issued: 68 (2001) / 32 (2000); Multi-family building permits issued: 0 (2001) / 0 (2000); Employment by occupation: 13.8% management, 20.7% professional, 10.6% services, 25.6% sales, 0.0% farming, 16.1% construction, 13.1% production (2000).
Income: Per capita income: $23,620 (2000); Median household income: $50,932 (2000); Poverty rate: 4.6% (2000).
Taxes: Total city taxes per capita: $222 (1997); City property taxes per capita: $209 (1997).
Education: High school graduation rate: 90.4% (2000); College graduation rate: 20.3% (2000).

School District(s)

Linden Community Schools (KG-12)
2000 Enrollment: 2,822 810-591-7821

Housing: Homeownership rate: 81.2% (2000); Median home value: $129,400 (2000); Median rent: $506 per month (2000); Median age of housing: 24 years (2000).
Safety: Violent crime rate: 3.5 per 10,000 population; Property crime rate: 132.1 per 10,000 population (2001).
Transportation: Commute to work: 94.3% car, 0.1% public transportation, 1.8% walk, 3.4% work from home (2000); Travel time to work: 24.8% less than 15 minutes, 29.6% 15 to 30 minutes, 22.7% 30 to 45 minutes, 13.3% 45 to 60 minutes, 9.6% 60 minutes or more (2000)

MONTROSE (city). Covers a land area of 0.913 square miles and a water area of 0 square miles. Located at 43.17° N. Lat.; 83.89° W. Long. Elevation is 670 feet.
Population: 1,619 (2000); Race: 97.2% White, 0.7% Black, 0.5% Asian, 0.4% American Indian and Alaska Native, 1.7% Hispanic of any race, 1.0% two or more races (2000); Density: 1,773.7 persons per square mile (2000); Age: 27.5% under 18, 12.2% over 64 (2000); Marriage status: 23.1% never married, 58.3% now married, 7.5% widowed, 11.1% divorced (2000); Foreign born: 0.7% (2000); Ancestry (includes multiple ancestries): 21.9% German, 14.5% English, 9.2% Irish, 8.6% United States or American, 8.0% Other groups (2000).
Economy: Single-family building permits issued: 0 (2001) / 0 (2000); Multi-family building permits issued: 0 (2001) / 0 (2000); Employment by occupation: 7.9% management, 9.8% professional, 14.8% services, 31.3% sales, 0.3% farming, 10.9% construction, 25.0% production (2000).
Income: Per capita income: $17,056 (2000); Median household income: $36,667 (2000); Poverty rate: 7.8% (2000).
Taxes: Total city taxes per capita: $171 (1997); City property taxes per capita: $165 (1997).
Education: High school graduation rate: 84.1% (2000); College graduation rate: 8.3% (2000).

School District(s)

Montrose Community Schools (PK-12)
2000 Enrollment: 1,657 810-591-7267

Housing: Homeownership rate: 70.7% (2000); Median home value: $80,300 (2000); Median rent: $340 per month (2000); Median age of housing: 44 years (2000).
Transportation: Commute to work: 93.0% car, 0.0% public transportation, 4.1% walk, 2.2% work from home (2000); Travel time to work: 26.5% less than 15 minutes, 25.1% 15 to 30 minutes, 30.9% 30 to 45 minutes, 8.7% 45 to 60 minutes, 8.7% 60 minutes or more (2000)

MONTROSE (township). Covers a land area of 34.429 square miles and a water area of 0.184 square miles. Located at 43.16° N. Lat.; 83.86° W. Long. Elevation is 670 feet.
Population: 6,336 (2000); Race: 95.7% White, 1.5% Black, 0.1% Asian, 0.3% American Indian and Alaska Native, 3.3% Hispanic of any race, 1.5% two or more races (2000); Density: 184.0 persons per square mile (2000); Age: 29.2% under 18, 10.3% over 64 (2000); Marriage status: 23.7% never married, 60.5% now married, 5.4% widowed, 10.4% divorced (2000); Foreign born: 0.7% (2000); Ancestry (includes multiple ancestries): 25.1% German, 13.3% United States or American, 12.0% Other groups, 10.3% Irish, 9.6% English (2000).
Economy: In farm area; lumber. Single-family building permits issued: 32 (2001) / 28 (2000); Multi-family building permits issued: 0 (2001) / 0 (2000); Employment by occupation: 5.5% management, 11.5% professional, 21.0% services, 20.7% sales, 0.5% farming, 10.9% construction, 29.8% production (2000).
Income: Per capita income: $19,725 (2000); Median household income: $51,502 (2000); Poverty rate: 11.7% (2000).
Taxes: Total city taxes per capita: $58 (2000); City property taxes per capita: $54 (2000).
Education: High school graduation rate: 79.2% (2000); College graduation rate: 10.5% (2000).
Housing: Homeownership rate: 92.6% (2000); Median home value: $93,100 (2000); Median rent: $441 per month (2000); Median age of housing: 28 years (2000).
Safety: Violent crime rate: 11.0 per 10,000 population; Property crime rate: 131.9 per 10,000 population (2001).
Transportation: Commute to work: 93.8% car, 0.2% public transportation, 0.3% walk, 5.4% work from home (2000); Travel time to work: 20.2% less than 15 minutes, 32.3% 15 to 30 minutes, 31.0% 30 to 45 minutes, 5.4% 45 to 60 minutes, 11.0% 60 minutes or more (2000)

MOUNT MORRIS (city). Covers a land area of 1.201 square miles and a water area of 0 square miles. Located at 43.12° N. Lat.; 83.69° W. Long. Elevation is 794 feet.
History: Mount Morris developed as a residential center for workers employed in Flint's industrial plants.
Population: 3,194 (2000); Race: 95.0% White, 3.8% Black, 0.0% Asian, 0.2% American Indian and Alaska Native, 1.6% Hispanic of any race, 0.1% two or more races (2000); Density: 2,660.0 persons per square mile (2000); Age: 25.9% under 18, 11.7% over 64 (2000); Marriage status: 30.4% never married, 48.5% now married, 7.9% widowed, 13.2% divorced (2000); Foreign born: 1.8% (2000); Ancestry (includes multiple ancestries): 21.8% German, 13.1% Irish, 10.9% English, 10.2% Other groups, 9.9% United States or American (2000).
Economy: Single-family building permits issued: 8 (2001) / 3 (2000); Multi-family building permits issued: 120 (2001) / 0 (2000); Employment by occupation: 3.8% management, 14.9% professional, 18.5% services, 27.2% sales, 0.0% farming, 12.3% construction, 23.3% production (2000).
Income: Per capita income: $19,132 (2000); Median household income: $32,617 (2000); Poverty rate: 14.5% (2000).
Taxes: Total city taxes per capita: $166 (1997); City property taxes per capita: $165 (1997).
Education: High school graduation rate: 79.3% (2000); College graduation rate: 6.2% (2000).

School District(s)

Mount Morris Consolidated Schools (KG-12)
2000 Enrollment: 3,098 810-591-8760

Housing: Homeownership rate: 62.6% (2000); Median home value: $67,000 (2000); Median rent: $438 per month (2000); Median age of housing: 45 years (2000).
Safety: Violent crime rate: 43.6 per 10,000 population; Property crime rate: 383.1 per 10,000 population (2001).
Transportation: Commute to work: 98.0% car, 0.0% public transportation, 0.3% walk, 1.6% work from home (2000); Travel time to work: 27.7% less than 15 minutes, 44.0% 15 to 30 minutes, 12.6% 30 to 45 minutes, 8.1% 45 to 60 minutes, 7.5% 60 minutes or more (2000)

MOUNT MORRIS (township). Covers a land area of 31.435 square miles and a water area of 0.036 square miles. Located at 43.08° N. Lat.; 83.74° W. Long. Elevation is 794 feet.
History: Settled 1842; incorporated as village 1867, as city 1930.
Population: 23,725 (2000); Race: 54.1% White, 40.3% Black, 0.1% Asian, 0.4% American Indian and Alaska Native, 2.2% Hispanic of any race, 4.1% two or more races (2000); Density: 754.7 persons per square mile (2000); Age: 30.1% under 18, 11.7% over 64 (2000); Marriage status: 32.7% never married, 47.2% now married, 7.2% widowed, 12.9% divorced (2000); Foreign born: 1.7% (2000); Ancestry (includes multiple ancestries): 40.2% Other groups, 10.0% German, 7.0% English, 6.7% Irish, 5.6% United States or American (2000).
Vital Statistics: Birth rate: 81.8 per 10,000 population (1998)
Economy: In farm area: grain, potatoes; dairy products. Manufacturing: packaging, machining. Unemployment rate: 9.7% (11/2002); Total civilian labor force: 9,860 (11/2002); Single-family building permits issued: 20 (2001) / 14 (2000); Multi-family building permits issued: 246 (2001) / 4 (2000); Employment by occupation: 7.3% management, 9.9% professional, 18.7% services, 24.1% sales, 0.4% farming, 11.5% construction, 28.1% production (2000).
Income: Per capita income: $17,161 (2000); Median household income: $36,069 (2000); Poverty rate: 18.3% (2000).

Taxes: Total city taxes per capita: $195 (2000); City property taxes per capita: $186 (2000).
Education: High school graduation rate: 77.7% (2000); College graduation rate: 8.2% (2000).
Housing: Homeownership rate: 77.2% (2000); Median home value: $68,800 (2000); Median rent: $407 per month (2000); Median age of housing: 37 years (2000).
Safety: Violent crime rate: 80.5 per 10,000 population; Property crime rate: 568.6 per 10,000 population (2001).
Transportation: Commute to work: 95.4% car, 1.0% public transportation, 0.9% walk, 1.4% work from home (2000); Travel time to work: 24.3% less than 15 minutes, 46.3% 15 to 30 minutes, 12.9% 30 to 45 minutes, 8.4% 45 to 60 minutes, 8.2% 60 minutes or more (2000)

MUNDY (township). Covers a land area of 35.981 square miles and a water area of 0.097 square miles. Located at 42.92° N. Lat.; 83.74° W. Long.
Population: 12,191 (2000); Race: 95.5% White, 1.3% Black, 0.6% Asian, 0.5% American Indian and Alaska Native, 2.2% Hispanic of any race, 0.9% two or more races (2000); Density: 338.8 persons per square mile (2000); Age: 22.6% under 18, 13.1% over 64 (2000); Marriage status: 20.3% never married, 64.9% now married, 5.3% widowed, 9.6% divorced (2000); Foreign born: 2.0% (2000); Ancestry (includes multiple ancestries): 22.0% German, 14.6% Irish, 14.1% English, 10.1% Other groups, 8.2% United States or American (2000).
Economy: Single-family building permits issued: 172 (2001) / 83 (2000); Multi-family building permits issued: 0 (2001) / 140 (2000); Employment by occupation: 8.2% management, 20.4% professional, 14.1% services, 26.6% sales, 0.3% farming, 11.5% construction, 18.9% production (2000).
Income: Per capita income: $23,581 (2000); Median household income: $53,948 (2000); Poverty rate: 3.7% (2000).
Taxes: Total city taxes per capita: $164 (1997); City property taxes per capita: $131 (1997).
Education: High school graduation rate: 88.5% (2000); College graduation rate: 17.9% (2000).
Housing: Homeownership rate: 87.9% (2000); Median home value: $122,100 (2000); Median rent: $509 per month (2000); Median age of housing: 26 years (2000).
Safety: Violent crime rate: 10.6 per 10,000 population; Property crime rate: 473.3 per 10,000 population (2001).
Transportation: Commute to work: 97.4% car, 0.1% public transportation, 0.4% walk, 1.8% work from home (2000); Travel time to work: 27.8% less than 15 minutes, 44.7% 15 to 30 minutes, 11.0% 30 to 45 minutes, 7.2% 45 to 60 minutes, 9.2% 60 minutes or more (2000)

OTISVILLE (village). Covers a land area of 0.883 square miles and a water area of 0.086 square miles. Located at 43.16° N. Lat.; 83.52° W. Long. Elevation is 812 feet.
Population: 882 (2000); Race: 94.2% White, 0.0% Black, 0.4% Asian, 0.6% American Indian and Alaska Native, 2.2% Hispanic of any race, 2.2% two or more races (2000); Density: 999.1 persons per square mile (2000); Age: 28.6% under 18, 7.8% over 64 (2000); Marriage status: 21.9% never married, 62.2% now married, 6.0% widowed, 9.9% divorced (2000); Foreign born: 0.8% (2000); Ancestry (includes multiple ancestries): 17.7% German, 11.0% Irish, 10.7% United States or American, 8.9% French (except Basque), 8.9% English (2000).
Economy: In farm area. Manufacturing: fishing tackle. Single-family building permits issued: 2 (2001) / 0 (2000); Multi-family building permits issued: 0 (2001) / 0 (2000); Employment by occupation: 4.7% management, 7.0% professional, 19.1% services, 27.0% sales, 0.0% farming, 12.8% construction, 29.5% production (2000).
Income: Per capita income: $17,540 (2000); Median household income: $40,341 (2000); Poverty rate: 6.0% (2000).
Taxes: Total city taxes per capita: $211 (1997); City property taxes per capita: $204 (1997).
Education: High school graduation rate: 82.5% (2000); College graduation rate: 7.6% (2000).

School District(s)

Lakeville Community Schools (KG-12)
2000 Enrollment: 2,117 810-591-6525
Housing: Homeownership rate: 82.1% (2000); Median home value: $79,300 (2000); Median rent: $388 per month (2000); Median age of housing: 42 years (2000).
Transportation: Commute to work: 94.3% car, 0.0% public transportation, 3.8% walk, 1.4% work from home (2000); Travel time to work: 20.6% less than 15 minutes, 23.0% 15 to 30 minutes, 33.7% 30 to 45 minutes, 9.6% 45 to 60 minutes, 13.2% 60 minutes or more (2000)

RICHFIELD (township). Covers a land area of 35.300 square miles and a water area of 1.073 square miles. Located at 43.09° N. Lat.; 83.52° W. Long.
Population: 8,170 (2000); Race: 93.5% White, 2.7% Black, 0.2% Asian, 0.8% American Indian and Alaska Native, 1.5% Hispanic of any race, 2.2% two or more races (2000); Density: 231.4 persons per square mile (2000); Age: 26.5% under 18, 9.8% over 64 (2000); Marriage status: 21.9% never married, 64.0% now married, 4.6% widowed, 9.5% divorced (2000); Foreign born: 0.6% (2000); Ancestry (includes multiple ancestries): 22.5% German, 12.8% Irish, 11.4% Other groups, 11.1% English, 8.9% Polish (2000).
Economy: Single-family building permits issued: 62 (2001) / 60 (2000); Multi-family building permits issued: 0 (2001) / 0 (2000); Employment by occupation: 8.4% management, 16.8% professional, 14.2% services, 21.7% sales, 0.0% farming, 13.4% construction, 25.5% production (2000).
Income: Per capita income: $21,177 (2000); Median household income: $51,265 (2000); Poverty rate: 5.3% (2000).
Taxes: Total city taxes per capita: $92 (1997); City property taxes per capita: $80 (1997).
Education: High school graduation rate: 86.4% (2000); College graduation rate: 13.5% (2000).
Housing: Homeownership rate: 95.8% (2000); Median home value: $115,500 (2000); Median rent: $483 per month (2000); Median age of housing: 24 years (2000).
Safety: Violent crime rate: 12.2 per 10,000 population; Property crime rate: 278.8 per 10,000 population (2001).
Transportation: Commute to work: 95.9% car, 0.1% public transportation, 0.7% walk, 2.7% work from home (2000); Travel time to work: 20.4% less than 15 minutes, 41.8% 15 to 30 minutes, 17.5% 30 to 45 minutes, 9.0% 45 to 60 minutes, 11.3% 60 minutes or more (2000)

SWARTZ CREEK (city). Covers a land area of 4.019 square miles and a water area of 0 square miles. Located at 42.95° N. Lat.; 83.83° W. Long. Elevation is 779 feet.
History: First called Miller Settlement for Adam Miller, who came here in 1836, the town was named Swartz Creek in 1843. The earliest residents were German immigrants.
Population: 5,102 (2000); Race: 93.8% White, 1.2% Black, 0.3% Asian, 0.4% American Indian and Alaska Native, 1.5% Hispanic of any race, 2.3% two or more races (2000); Density: 1,269.6 persons per square mile (2000); Age: 22.3% under 18, 16.7% over 64 (2000); Marriage status: 24.7% never married, 54.6% now married, 7.9% widowed, 12.8% divorced (2000); Foreign born: 1.1% (2000); Ancestry (includes multiple ancestries): 20.7% German, 16.2% English, 12.9% Irish, 10.0% United States or American, 7.5% Other groups (2000).
Economy: Single-family building permits issued: 46 (2001) / 44 (2000); Multi-family building permits issued: 0 (2001) / 0 (2000); Employment by occupation: 8.1% management, 18.4% professional, 18.9% services, 26.7% sales, 0.0% farming, 8.4% construction, 19.5% production (2000).
Income: Per capita income: $22,046 (2000); Median household income: $42,112 (2000); Poverty rate: 6.5% (2000).
Taxes: Total city taxes per capita: $211 (1997); City property taxes per capita: $200 (1997).
Education: High school graduation rate: 89.8% (2000); College graduation rate: 15.8% (2000).

School District(s)

Swartz Creek Community Schools (KG-12)
2000 Enrollment: 4,031 810-591-2300
Housing: Homeownership rate: 74.1% (2000); Median home value: $112,400 (2000); Median rent: $444 per month (2000); Median age of housing: 32 years (2000).
Safety: Violent crime rate: 15.6 per 10,000 population; Property crime rate: 434.8 per 10,000 population (2001).
Transportation: Commute to work: 95.2% car, 1.4% public transportation, 1.4% walk, 1.7% work from home (2000); Travel time to work: 31.8% less than 15 minutes, 42.6% 15 to 30 minutes, 9.9% 30 to 45 minutes, 5.9% 45 to 60 minutes, 9.7% 60 minutes or more (2000)
Additional Information Contacts
Swartz Creek Chamber of Commerce 810-635-9643

THETFORD (township). Covers a land area of 34.685 square miles and a water area of 0.066 square miles. Located at 43.16° N. Lat.; 83.63° W. Long.
Population: 8,277 (2000); Race: 94.5% White, 2.2% Black, 0.3% Asian, 1.1% American Indian and Alaska Native, 2.7% Hispanic of any race, 1.2% two or more races (2000); Density: 238.6 persons per square mile (2000); Age: 26.6% under 18, 8.0% over 64 (2000); Marriage status: 23.1% never

married, 62.2% now married, 4.5% widowed, 10.2% divorced (2000); Foreign born: 0.9% (2000); Ancestry (includes multiple ancestries): 18.2% German, 14.6% Irish, 12.4% Other groups, 12.2% English, 10.0% United States or American (2000).
Economy: Single-family building permits issued: 16 (2001) / 24 (2000); Multi-family building permits issued: 0 (2001) / 0 (2000); Employment by occupation: 8.9% management, 12.3% professional, 14.5% services, 24.5% sales, 0.4% farming, 12.7% construction, 26.7% production (2000).
Income: Per capita income: $21,057 (2000); Median household income: $47,175 (2000); Poverty rate: 7.4% (2000).
Taxes: Total city taxes per capita: $25 (2000); City property taxes per capita: $19 (2000).
Education: High school graduation rate: 82.4% (2000); College graduation rate: 9.4% (2000).
Housing: Homeownership rate: 89.0% (2000); Median home value: $102,100 (2000); Median rent: $365 per month (2000); Median age of housing: 28 years (2000).
Transportation: Commute to work: 95.9% car, 0.6% public transportation, 0.5% walk, 2.1% work from home (2000); Travel time to work: 18.1% less than 15 minutes, 42.7% 15 to 30 minutes, 22.9% 30 to 45 minutes, 6.0% 45 to 60 minutes, 10.3% 60 minutes or more (2000)

VIENNA (township). Covers a land area of 35.009 square miles and a water area of 0.041 square miles. Located at 43.17° N. Lat.; 83.74° W. Long.
Population: 13,108 (2000); Race: 96.2% White, 0.9% Black, 0.3% Asian, 0.4% American Indian and Alaska Native, 1.2% Hispanic of any race, 1.1% two or more races (2000); Density: 374.4 persons per square mile (2000); Age: 24.5% under 18, 11.8% over 64 (2000); Marriage status: 23.5% never married, 59.3% now married, 6.9% widowed, 10.3% divorced (2000); Foreign born: 1.6% (2000); Ancestry (includes multiple ancestries): 20.7% German, 14.7% Irish, 12.4% English, 10.1% United States or American, 8.4% French (except Basque) (2000).
Economy: Single-family building permits issued: 96 (2001) / 70 (2000); Multi-family building permits issued: 0 (2001) / 4 (2000); Employment by occupation: 8.8% management, 12.4% professional, 14.9% services, 27.1% sales, 0.1% farming, 13.9% construction, 22.9% production (2000).
Income: Per capita income: $21,711 (2000); Median household income: $46,863 (2000); Poverty rate: 8.3% (2000).
Taxes: Total city taxes per capita: $57 (1997); City property taxes per capita: $52 (1997).
Education: High school graduation rate: 82.5% (2000); College graduation rate: 11.7% (2000).
Housing: Homeownership rate: 84.0% (2000); Median home value: $109,500 (2000); Median rent: $441 per month (2000); Median age of housing: 29 years (2000).
Transportation: Commute to work: 95.6% car, 1.0% public transportation, 0.6% walk, 1.7% work from home (2000); Travel time to work: 25.7% less than 15 minutes, 41.7% 15 to 30 minutes, 18.4% 30 to 45 minutes, 6.1% 45 to 60 minutes, 8.1% 60 minutes or more (2000)

Gladwin County

Located in east central Michigan; drained by the Tittabawassee and Tobacco Rivers; includes many small lakes. Covers a land area of 506.80 square miles, a water area of 9.60 square miles, and is located in the Eastern Time Zone. The county government was organized in 1855. County seat is Gladwin.

Weather Station: Gladwin — Elevation: 774 feet

	Jan	Feb	Mar	Apr	May	Jun	Jul	Aug	Sep	Oct	Nov	Dec
High	28	32	42	56	70	79	83	80	72	60	45	34
Low	10	12	21	32	43	52	56	55	47	36	28	19
Precip	1.9	1.3	2.3	2.5	2.8	3.2	3.0	3.6	3.5	2.7	2.5	2.1
Snow	15.0	9.2	9.0	1.9	tr	0.0	0.0	0.0	0.0	0.3	4.0	10.8

High and Low temperatures in degrees Fahrenheit; Precipitation and Snow in inches

Population: 26,023 (2000); Race: 97.8% White, 0.1% Black, 0.1% Asian, 0.5% American Indian and Alaska Native, 0.9% Hispanic of any race, 1.2% two or more races (2000); Density: 51.3 persons per square mile (2000); Age: 23.2% under 18, 18.3% over 64 (2000).
Religion: Five largest groups: 7.2% Catholic Church, 2.7% Evangelical Lutheran Church in America, 2.6% The United Methodist Church, 2.1% Lutheran Church—Missouri Synod, 1.2% Community of Christ (2000).
Economy: Unemployment rate: 7.5% (11/2002); Total civilian labor force: 9,340 (11/2002); Leading industries: 30.6% manufacturing; 20.7% retail trade; 10.9% health care and social assistance (2000); Companies that employ more than 1,000 persons: 0 (2000); Companies that employ more than 100 persons: 6 (2000); Farms: 424 totaling 68,036 acres (1997); Minority business ownership rate: 0.0% (1997); Women business ownership rate: 29.2% (1997); Retail sales per capita: $6,139 (1997). Single-family building permits issued: 274 (2001) / 266 (2000); Multi-family building permits issued: 0 (2001) / 0 (2000).
Income: Per capita income: $16,614 (2000); Median household income: $32,019 (2000); Poverty rate: 13.8% (2000); Bankruptcy rate: 4.99% (2001).
Taxes: Total county taxes per capita: $171 (1997); County property taxes per capita: $160 (1997).
Education: High school graduation rate: 78.3% (2000); College graduation rate: 9.2% (2000).
Housing: Homeownership rate: 85.6% (2000); Median home value: $86,800 (2000); Median rent: $312 per month (2000); Median age of housing: 27 years (2000).
Health: Birth rate: 101.8 per 10,000 population (1998); Age adjusted death rate: 91.2 per 10,000 population (1999); Age adjusted cancer mortality rate: 213.6 deaths per 100,000 population (1999). Number of physicians: 4.2 per 10,000 population (1999); Number of hospital beds: 16.1 per 10,000 population (1999).
Elections: 2000 Presidential election results: 47.9% Gore, 49.4% Bush, 2.0% Nader, 0.0% Buchanan
National and State Parks: Gladwin State Park
Additional Information Contacts
Gladwin County Government Offices 989-426-4821
Clare Gladwin Board of Realtors 989-246-0714
Gladwin County Chamber 989-426-5451

Gladwin County Communities

BEAVERTON (city). Covers a land area of 1.087 square miles and a water area of 0.220 square miles. Located at 43.88° N. Lat.; 84.48° W. Long. Elevation is 711 feet.
History: Beaverton was settled by lumbermen about 1863. It later developed as a farming center, and was incorporated as a village in 1901 and as a city in 1903. First known as Grand Forks for its location at the forks of the Tobacco and Cedar Rivers, it was later named for Beaverton, Ontario, the former home of settler Donald Gunn Ross.
Population: 1,106 (2000); Race: 97.3% White, 0.9% Black, 0.0% Asian, 0.0% American Indian and Alaska Native, 0.3% Hispanic of any race, 1.8% two or more races (2000); Density: 1,017.6 persons per square mile (2000); Age: 27.9% under 18, 18.7% over 64 (2000); Marriage status: 22.7% never married, 51.4% now married, 12.6% widowed, 13.4% divorced (2000); Foreign born: 0.5% (2000); Ancestry (includes multiple ancestries): 23.8% German, 13.5% English, 12.2% Irish, 8.6% United States or American, 6.9% French (except Basque) (2000).
Economy: Employment by occupation: 10.8% management, 12.7% professional, 26.4% services, 16.6% sales, 0.0% farming, 8.4% construction, 25.0% production (2000).
Income: Per capita income: $12,125 (2000); Median household income: $20,625 (2000); Poverty rate: 21.9% (2000).
Taxes: Total city taxes per capita: $161 (1997); City property taxes per capita: $159 (1997).
Education: High school graduation rate: 80.9% (2000); College graduation rate: 7.0% (2000).

School District(s)

Beaverton Rural Schools (KG-12)
2000 Enrollment: 1,810 517-246-3000
Creative Learning Academy of Sci (KG-08)
2000 Enrollment: 38 517-790-4000

Housing: Homeownership rate: 54.1% (2000); Median home value: $65,000 (2000); Median rent: $293 per month (2000); Median age of housing: 30 years (2000).
Transportation: Commute to work: 92.2% car, 0.0% public transportation, 5.5% walk, 1.3% work from home (2000); Travel time to work: 43.1% less than 15 minutes, 24.6% 15 to 30 minutes, 17.5% 30 to 45 minutes, 9.1% 45 to 60 minutes, 5.6% 60 minutes or more (2000)

BEAVERTON (township). Covers a land area of 35.421 square miles and a water area of 0.138 square miles. Located at 43.86° N. Lat.; 84.52° W. Long. Elevation is 711 feet.
Population: 1,815 (2000); Race: 97.6% White, 0.0% Black, 0.2% Asian, 1.0% American Indian and Alaska Native, 0.1% Hispanic of any race, 1.2% two or more races (2000); Density: 51.2 persons per square mile (2000); Age: 28.4% under 18, 11.0% over 64 (2000); Marriage status: 18.1% never married, 66.7% now married, 4.6% widowed, 10.7% divorced (2000);

Foreign born: 0.3% (2000); Ancestry (includes multiple ancestries): 26.9% German, 11.8% English, 10.4% Irish, 7.2% United States or American, 7.1% Other groups (2000).
Economy: In farm area: livestock; grain. Manufacturing: rubber products, insulation. Employment by occupation: 7.0% management, 12.0% professional, 13.5% services, 22.7% sales, 2.2% farming, 15.3% construction, 27.4% production (2000).
Income: Per capita income: $15,370 (2000); Median household income: $36,823 (2000); Poverty rate: 12.9% (2000).
Taxes: Total city taxes per capita: $34 (1997); City property taxes per capita: $33 (1997).
Education: High school graduation rate: 79.8% (2000); College graduation rate: 8.1% (2000).
Housing: Homeownership rate: 87.9% (2000); Median home value: $80,500 (2000); Median rent: $332 per month (2000); Median age of housing: 23 years (2000).
Transportation: Commute to work: 86.6% car, 0.5% public transportation, 5.3% walk, 5.1% work from home (2000); Travel time to work: 39.5% less than 15 minutes, 22.7% 15 to 30 minutes, 24.0% 30 to 45 minutes, 8.4% 45 to 60 minutes, 5.4% 60 minutes or more (2000)

BENTLEY (township). Covers a land area of 35.707 square miles and a water area of 0.131 square miles. Located at 43.86° N. Lat.; 84.19° W. Long.
History: Bentley Township was named for Murray Bentley, a storekeeper and first supervisor of the township.
Population: 859 (2000); Race: 98.0% White, 0.0% Black, 0.0% Asian, 0.9% American Indian and Alaska Native, 0.4% Hispanic of any race, 1.1% two or more races (2000); Density: 24.1 persons per square mile (2000); Age: 28.4% under 18, 11.7% over 64 (2000); Marriage status: 24.6% never married, 60.7% now married, 5.1% widowed, 9.5% divorced (2000); Foreign born: 0.4% (2000); Ancestry (includes multiple ancestries): 29.8% German, 14.5% Polish, 14.5% French (except Basque), 8.5% Irish, 8.2% United States or American (2000).
Economy: Employment by occupation: 8.6% management, 14.5% professional, 16.4% services, 27.6% sales, 0.0% farming, 15.8% construction, 17.2% production (2000).
Income: Per capita income: $15,074 (2000); Median household income: $37,125 (2000); Poverty rate: 16.1% (2000).
Taxes: Total city taxes per capita: $35 (1997); City property taxes per capita: $35 (1997).
Education: High school graduation rate: 76.6% (2000); College graduation rate: 4.0% (2000).
Housing: Homeownership rate: 92.8% (2000); Median home value: $72,100 (2000); Median rent: $363 per month (2000); Median age of housing: 26 years (2000).
Transportation: Commute to work: 96.2% car, 0.0% public transportation, 1.1% walk, 2.7% work from home (2000); Travel time to work: 9.2% less than 15 minutes, 29.0% 15 to 30 minutes, 41.2% 30 to 45 minutes, 17.3% 45 to 60 minutes, 3.3% 60 minutes or more (2000)

BILLINGS (township). Covers a land area of 21.721 square miles and a water area of 1.427 square miles. Located at 43.87° N. Lat.; 84.32° W. Long. Elevation is 706 feet.
Population: 2,715 (2000); Race: 97.7% White, 0.0% Black, 0.3% Asian, 0.5% American Indian and Alaska Native, 1.0% Hispanic of any race, 0.7% two or more races (2000); Density: 125.0 persons per square mile (2000); Age: 19.0% under 18, 19.8% over 64 (2000); Marriage status: 15.3% never married, 63.4% now married, 9.5% widowed, 11.9% divorced (2000); Foreign born: 1.1% (2000); Ancestry (includes multiple ancestries): 26.6% German, 10.6% Irish, 9.8% English, 8.0% United States or American, 7.5% French (except Basque) (2000).
Economy: Employment by occupation: 11.0% management, 7.7% professional, 13.9% services, 25.7% sales, 0.7% farming, 16.6% construction, 24.3% production (2000).
Income: Per capita income: $17,999 (2000); Median household income: $31,677 (2000); Poverty rate: 12.4% (2000).
Taxes: Total city taxes per capita: $48 (1997); City property taxes per capita: $45 (1997).
Education: High school graduation rate: 77.2% (2000); College graduation rate: 6.5% (2000).
Housing: Homeownership rate: 89.4% (2000); Median home value: $94,400 (2000); Median rent: $323 per month (2000); Median age of housing: 27 years (2000).
Transportation: Commute to work: 94.5% car, 0.9% public transportation, 0.0% walk, 4.6% work from home (2000); Travel time to work: 6.5% less than 15 minutes, 28.9% 15 to 30 minutes, 28.5% 30 to 45 minutes, 14.8% 45 to 60 minutes, 21.3% 60 minutes or more (2000)

BOURRET (township). Covers a land area of 32.371 square miles and a water area of 0.382 square miles. Located at 44.11° N. Lat.; 84.26° W. Long.
Population: 471 (2000); Race: 97.3% White, 0.0% Black, 0.0% Asian, 0.9% American Indian and Alaska Native, 0.0% Hispanic of any race, 1.8% two or more races (2000); Density: 14.6 persons per square mile (2000); Age: 14.4% under 18, 23.1% over 64 (2000); Marriage status: 14.4% never married, 64.0% now married, 7.1% widowed, 14.6% divorced (2000); Foreign born: 2.0% (2000); Ancestry (includes multiple ancestries): 16.6% German, 12.6% Irish, 12.1% Other groups, 9.9% English, 8.1% Polish (2000).
Economy: Employment by occupation: 9.0% management, 16.2% professional, 14.4% services, 27.0% sales, 0.0% farming, 16.2% construction, 17.1% production (2000).
Income: Per capita income: $16,094 (2000); Median household income: $26,103 (2000); Poverty rate: 20.9% (2000).
Taxes: Total city taxes per capita: $125 (1997); City property taxes per capita: $125 (1997).
Education: High school graduation rate: 64.6% (2000); College graduation rate: 7.9% (2000).
Housing: Homeownership rate: 91.6% (2000); Median home value: $76,300 (2000); Median rent: $238 per month (2000); Median age of housing: 32 years (2000).
Transportation: Commute to work: 83.8% car, 0.0% public transportation, 7.6% walk, 8.6% work from home (2000); Travel time to work: 18.8% less than 15 minutes, 54.2% 15 to 30 minutes, 15.6% 30 to 45 minutes, 2.1% 45 to 60 minutes, 9.4% 60 minutes or more (2000)

BUCKEYE (township). Covers a land area of 34.626 square miles and a water area of 0.003 square miles. Located at 43.94° N. Lat.; 84.42° W. Long.
Population: 1,333 (2000); Race: 97.4% White, 0.0% Black, 0.3% Asian, 0.1% American Indian and Alaska Native, 0.0% Hispanic of any race, 2.2% two or more races (2000); Density: 38.5 persons per square mile (2000); Age: 28.0% under 18, 11.4% over 64 (2000); Marriage status: 21.2% never married, 61.5% now married, 7.8% widowed, 9.5% divorced (2000); Foreign born: 1.2% (2000); Ancestry (includes multiple ancestries): 22.1% German, 13.0% Irish, 9.1% English, 8.8% United States or American, 7.5% Other groups (2000).
Economy: Employment by occupation: 6.5% management, 6.1% professional, 19.1% services, 26.5% sales, 0.9% farming, 12.5% construction, 28.3% production (2000).
Income: Per capita income: $13,709 (2000); Median household income: $31,591 (2000); Poverty rate: 17.3% (2000).
Taxes: Total city taxes per capita: $74 (1997); City property taxes per capita: $74 (1997).
Education: High school graduation rate: 73.7% (2000); College graduation rate: 3.5% (2000).
Housing: Homeownership rate: 85.7% (2000); Median home value: $60,500 (2000); Median rent: $292 per month (2000); Median age of housing: 25 years (2000).
Transportation: Commute to work: 92.3% car, 0.0% public transportation, 1.1% walk, 5.0% work from home (2000); Travel time to work: 40.2% less than 15 minutes, 21.0% 15 to 30 minutes, 21.4% 30 to 45 minutes, 7.0% 45 to 60 minutes, 10.5% 60 minutes or more (2000)

BUTMAN (township). Covers a land area of 34.056 square miles and a water area of 1.602 square miles. Located at 44.11° N. Lat.; 84.44° W. Long. Elevation is 958 feet.
History: Butman Township was organized in 1883 and named for Myron Butman, a businessman from Saginaw. The Lovell P. Sherman family of Rhode Island had settled here in 1878.
Population: 1,947 (2000); Race: 98.1% White, 0.0% Black, 0.2% Asian, 0.7% American Indian and Alaska Native, 0.6% Hispanic of any race, 0.5% two or more races (2000); Density: 57.2 persons per square mile (2000); Age: 14.8% under 18, 27.3% over 64 (2000); Marriage status: 12.8% never married, 75.3% now married, 5.1% widowed, 6.8% divorced (2000); Foreign born: 2.4% (2000); Ancestry (includes multiple ancestries): 29.7% German, 17.1% English, 12.3% Irish, 7.1% United States or American, 6.8% Polish (2000).
Economy: Employment by occupation: 9.7% management, 14.8% professional, 11.6% services, 28.2% sales, 2.4% farming, 14.3% construction, 18.9% production (2000).
Income: Per capita income: $21,332 (2000); Median household income: $36,510 (2000); Poverty rate: 7.4% (2000).

Taxes: Total city taxes per capita: $102 (1997); City property taxes per capita: $99 (1997).
Education: High school graduation rate: 85.9% (2000); College graduation rate: 14.7% (2000).
Housing: Homeownership rate: 95.3% (2000); Median home value: $132,500 (2000); Median rent: $300 per month (2000); Median age of housing: 13 years (2000).
Transportation: Commute to work: 89.2% car, 0.0% public transportation, 1.4% walk, 8.7% work from home (2000); Travel time to work: 17.4% less than 15 minutes, 42.4% 15 to 30 minutes, 17.6% 30 to 45 minutes, 5.6% 45 to 60 minutes, 17.0% 60 minutes or more (2000)

CLEMENT (township). Covers a land area of 20.150 square miles and a water area of 0.792 square miles. Located at 44.10° N. Lat.; 84.33° W. Long.
Population: 994 (2000); Race: 95.2% White, 0.5% Black, 0.0% Asian, 1.7% American Indian and Alaska Native, 1.1% Hispanic of any race, 1.6% two or more races (2000); Density: 49.3 persons per square mile (2000); Age: 16.1% under 18, 28.0% over 64 (2000); Marriage status: 9.7% never married, 70.6% now married, 9.8% widowed, 9.8% divorced (2000); Foreign born: 2.2% (2000); Ancestry (includes multiple ancestries): 29.2% German, 16.1% Irish, 10.5% English, 9.8% French (except Basque), 7.8% Polish (2000).
Economy: Employment by occupation: 7.7% management, 10.9% professional, 17.6% services, 23.2% sales, 2.8% farming, 13.0% construction, 24.6% production (2000).
Income: Per capita income: $18,329 (2000); Median household income: $29,286 (2000); Poverty rate: 13.7% (2000).
Taxes: Total city taxes per capita: $190 (1997); City property taxes per capita: $185 (1997).
Education: High school graduation rate: 72.8% (2000); College graduation rate: 4.5% (2000).
Housing: Homeownership rate: 93.8% (2000); Median home value: $86,600 (2000); Median rent: $308 per month (2000); Median age of housing: 36 years (2000).
Transportation: Commute to work: 89.7% car, 2.6% public transportation, 0.4% walk, 5.5% work from home (2000); Travel time to work: 13.2% less than 15 minutes, 42.2% 15 to 30 minutes, 17.8% 30 to 45 minutes, 11.6% 45 to 60 minutes, 15.1% 60 minutes or more (2000)

GLADWIN (city). Covers a land area of 2.865 square miles and a water area of 0 square miles. Located at 43.98° N. Lat.; 84.49° W. Long. Elevation is 786 feet.
History: The community of Gladwin was established in the early 1870's by lumbermen. First called Cedar, it soon took the name of the county, which had been named for Major Henry Gladwin, British commander at Detroit.
Population: 3,001 (2000); Race: 97.7% White, 0.0% Black, 0.0% Asian, 0.4% American Indian and Alaska Native, 1.0% Hispanic of any race, 1.9% two or more races (2000); Density: 1,047.5 persons per square mile (2000); Age: 24.7% under 18, 22.4% over 64 (2000); Marriage status: 19.2% never married, 60.3% now married, 10.9% widowed, 9.6% divorced (2000); Foreign born: 1.8% (2000); Ancestry (includes multiple ancestries): 26.0% German, 13.7% English, 12.4% Irish, 6.8% French (except Basque), 6.7% United States or American (2000).
Economy: Employment by occupation: 8.7% management, 23.4% professional, 14.6% services, 27.0% sales, 0.3% farming, 10.9% construction, 15.0% production (2000).
Income: Per capita income: $16,370 (2000); Median household income: $29,598 (2000); Poverty rate: 11.7% (2000).
Taxes: Total city taxes per capita: $319 (1997); City property taxes per capita: $315 (1997).
Education: High school graduation rate: 80.8% (2000); College graduation rate: 16.3% (2000).

School District(s)

Gladwin Community Schools (KG-12)
2000 Enrollment: 2,065 517-426-9255
Housing: Homeownership rate: 62.9% (2000); Median home value: $74,900 (2000); Median rent: $318 per month (2000); Median age of housing: 34 years (2000).
Hospitals: Mid Michigan Medical Center - Gladwin (42 beds)
Safety: Violent crime rate: 19.9 per 10,000 population; Property crime rate: 500.5 per 10,000 population (2001).
Newspapers: Gladwin County Record and Beaverton Clarion (1 x week)
Transportation: Commute to work: 90.3% car, 0.2% public transportation, 3.8% walk, 4.2% work from home (2000); Travel time to work: 62.6% less than 15 minutes, 16.9% 15 to 30 minutes, 4.8% 30 to 45 minutes, 8.9% 45 to 60 minutes, 6.7% 60 minutes or more (2000)
Additional Information Contacts
Clare Gladwin Board of Realtors 989-246-0714
Gladwin County Chamber 989-426-5451

GLADWIN (township). Covers a land area of 35.280 square miles and a water area of 0.022 square miles. Located at 44.02° N. Lat.; 84.41° W. Long. Elevation is 786 feet.
History: Settled 1865; incorporated as village 1885, as city 1893.
Population: 1,044 (2000); Race: 98.2% White, 0.2% Black, 0.0% Asian, 0.0% American Indian and Alaska Native, 0.9% Hispanic of any race, 0.8% two or more races (2000); Density: 29.6 persons per square mile (2000); Age: 33.9% under 18, 11.0% over 64 (2000); Marriage status: 20.2% never married, 67.4% now married, 5.2% widowed, 7.2% divorced (2000); Foreign born: 1.2% (2000); Ancestry (includes multiple ancestries): 32.9% German, 10.1% Irish, 9.6% United States or American, 8.1% English, 7.5% Other groups (2000).
Economy: In livestock and dairy area; apples; light manufacturing. District office of Michigan Conservation Department to South. Recreation. Municipal airport. Employment by occupation: 14.4% management, 7.9% professional, 17.1% services, 24.3% sales, 4.5% farming, 13.6% construction, 18.1% production (2000).
Income: Per capita income: $14,659 (2000); Median household income: $35,441 (2000); Poverty rate: 26.1% (2000).
Taxes: Total city taxes per capita: $22 (1997); City property taxes per capita: $22 (1997).
Education: High school graduation rate: 71.6% (2000); College graduation rate: 8.0% (2000).
Housing: Homeownership rate: 90.2% (2000); Median home value: $72,500 (2000); Median rent: $325 per month (2000); Median age of housing: 29 years (2000).
Transportation: Commute to work: 83.3% car, 0.0% public transportation, 0.5% walk, 12.9% work from home (2000); Travel time to work: 39.0% less than 15 minutes, 22.7% 15 to 30 minutes, 9.9% 30 to 45 minutes, 12.2% 45 to 60 minutes, 16.3% 60 minutes or more (2000)

GRIM (township). Covers a land area of 70.713 square miles and a water area of 0.716 square miles. Located at 43.98° N. Lat.; 84.23° W. Long.
Population: 129 (2000); Race: 100.0% White, 0.0% Black, 0.0% Asian, 0.0% American Indian and Alaska Native, 0.0% Hispanic of any race, 0.0% two or more races (2000); Density: 1.8 persons per square mile (2000); Age: 26.1% under 18, 11.7% over 64 (2000); Marriage status: 8.0% never married, 60.9% now married, 5.7% widowed, 25.3% divorced (2000); Foreign born: 0.0% (2000); Ancestry (includes multiple ancestries): 27.9% German, 18.9% Polish, 15.3% Irish, 12.6% French (except Basque), 10.8% English (2000).
Economy: Employment by occupation: 5.9% management, 11.8% professional, 0.0% services, 32.4% sales, 0.0% farming, 26.5% construction, 23.5% production (2000).
Income: Per capita income: $24,326 (2000); Median household income: $27,000 (2000); Poverty rate: 27.5% (2000).
Taxes: Total city taxes per capita: $325 (1997); City property taxes per capita: $325 (1997).
Education: High school graduation rate: 79.7% (2000); College graduation rate: 10.1% (2000).
Housing: Homeownership rate: 85.1% (2000); Median home value: $45,000 (2000); Median rent: $275 per month (2000); Median age of housing: 29 years (2000).
Transportation: Commute to work: 100.0% car, 0.0% public transportation, 0.0% walk, 0.0% work from home (2000); Travel time to work: 22.6% less than 15 minutes, 25.8% 15 to 30 minutes, 6.5% 30 to 45 minutes, 32.3% 45 to 60 minutes, 12.9% 60 minutes or more (2000)

GROUT (township). Covers a land area of 34.704 square miles and a water area of 0.143 square miles. Located at 43.94° N. Lat.; 84.55° W. Long.
History: Grout Township was settled in 1863 by Benjamin Teeple, but Willard Grout had filed the first homestead claim here, and the township was named for him. Grout became the postmaster in 1874.
Population: 1,869 (2000); Race: 99.2% White, 0.0% Black, 0.0% Asian, 0.2% American Indian and Alaska Native, 0.6% Hispanic of any race, 0.6% two or more races (2000); Density: 53.9 persons per square mile (2000); Age: 25.0% under 18, 14.2% over 64 (2000); Marriage status: 24.0% never married, 63.4% now married, 5.4% widowed, 7.2% divorced (2000); Foreign born: 0.7% (2000); Ancestry (includes multiple ancestries): 25.4% German, 12.2% English, 10.4% Irish, 9.1% United States or American, 7.9% French (except Basque) (2000).
Economy: Employment by occupation: 12.8% management, 12.3% professional, 11.6% services, 25.2% sales, 1.8% farming, 12.9% construction, 23.4% production (2000).

Income: Per capita income: $15,438 (2000); Median household income: $34,808 (2000); Poverty rate: 12.3% (2000).
Taxes: Total city taxes per capita: $21 (1997); City property taxes per capita: $21 (1997).
Education: High school graduation rate: 76.8% (2000); College graduation rate: 9.2% (2000).
Housing: Homeownership rate: 86.8% (2000); Median home value: $75,700 (2000); Median rent: $284 per month (2000); Median age of housing: 25 years (2000).
Transportation: Commute to work: 83.5% car, 1.8% public transportation, 4.1% walk, 9.1% work from home (2000); Travel time to work: 46.5% less than 15 minutes, 24.7% 15 to 30 minutes, 13.2% 30 to 45 minutes, 6.0% 45 to 60 minutes, 9.6% 60 minutes or more (2000)

HAY (township). Covers a land area of 22.237 square miles and a water area of 0.447 square miles. Located at 43.96° N. Lat.; 84.33° W. Long.
Population: 1,402 (2000); Race: 99.3% White, 0.0% Black, 0.0% Asian, 0.5% American Indian and Alaska Native, 1.1% Hispanic of any race, 0.2% two or more races (2000); Density: 63.0 persons per square mile (2000); Age: 24.6% under 18, 17.9% over 64 (2000); Marriage status: 18.5% never married, 59.4% now married, 9.6% widowed, 12.5% divorced (2000); Foreign born: 1.2% (2000); Ancestry (includes multiple ancestries): 21.3% German, 15.0% English, 9.8% Irish, 9.0% Polish, 8.9% United States or American (2000).
Economy: Employment by occupation: 7.4% management, 8.8% professional, 20.6% services, 22.6% sales, 0.0% farming, 17.1% construction, 23.6% production (2000).
Income: Per capita income: $13,322 (2000); Median household income: $24,444 (2000); Poverty rate: 19.1% (2000).
Education: High school graduation rate: 70.2% (2000); College graduation rate: 2.4% (2000).
Housing: Homeownership rate: 92.8% (2000); Median home value: $74,600 (2000); Median rent: $316 per month (2000); Median age of housing: 30 years (2000).
Transportation: Commute to work: 96.2% car, 0.5% public transportation, 0.0% walk, 1.7% work from home (2000); Travel time to work: 21.0% less than 15 minutes, 33.0% 15 to 30 minutes, 17.8% 30 to 45 minutes, 12.5% 45 to 60 minutes, 15.6% 60 minutes or more (2000)

RHODES (unincorporated postal area, zip code 48652). Covers a land area of 45.313 square miles and a water area of 0.133 square miles. Located at 43.86° N. Lat.; 84.19° W. Long.
History: Rhodes grew up around a station of the Michigan Central Railroad. It was named for Murray Bentley Rhodes, a lumberman who founded the village and became its postmaster in 1889.
Population: 1,520 (2000); Race: 98.1% White, 0.0% Black, 0.0% Asian, 1.1% American Indian and Alaska Native, 0.3% Hispanic of any race, 0.8% two or more races (2000); Density: 33.5 persons per square mile (2000); Age: 27.7% under 18, 10.6% over 64 (2000); Marriage status: 23.2% never married, 61.8% now married, 6.3% widowed, 8.6% divorced (2000); Foreign born: 0.4% (2000); Ancestry (includes multiple ancestries): 32.4% German, 15.1% French (except Basque), 15.1% Polish, 10.1% Irish, 6.9% United States or American (2000).
Economy: Employment by occupation: 8.4% management, 12.9% professional, 15.1% services, 26.0% sales, 0.3% farming, 16.6% construction, 20.7% production (2000).
Income: Per capita income: $16,198 (2000); Median household income: $37,717 (2000); Poverty rate: 13.6% (2000).
Education: High school graduation rate: 74.9% (2000); College graduation rate: 5.6% (2000).
Housing: Homeownership rate: 93.9% (2000); Median home value: $76,800 (2000); Median rent: $371 per month (2000); Median age of housing: 25 years (2000).
Transportation: Commute to work: 96.3% car, 0.0% public transportation, 1.1% walk, 2.6% work from home (2000); Travel time to work: 7.8% less than 15 minutes, 32.6% 15 to 30 minutes, 38.9% 30 to 45 minutes, 15.4% 45 to 60 minutes, 5.3% 60 minutes or more (2000)

SAGE (township). Covers a land area of 34.530 square miles and a water area of 0.903 square miles. Located at 44.02° N. Lat.; 84.54° W. Long.
Population: 2,617 (2000); Race: 96.7% White, 0.0% Black, 0.5% Asian, 0.7% American Indian and Alaska Native, 0.3% Hispanic of any race, 2.0% two or more races (2000); Density: 75.8 persons per square mile (2000); Age: 25.6% under 18, 18.3% over 64 (2000); Marriage status: 17.9% never married, 67.7% now married, 7.5% widowed, 6.9% divorced (2000); Foreign born: 1.1% (2000); Ancestry (includes multiple ancestries): 25.0% German, 14.7% Irish, 10.7% English, 8.0% Polish, 7.5% United States or American (2000).
Economy: Employment by occupation: 10.4% management, 17.6% professional, 18.4% services, 19.8% sales, 2.2% farming, 11.6% construction, 19.9% production (2000).
Income: Per capita income: $15,470 (2000); Median household income: $33,173 (2000); Poverty rate: 12.2% (2000).
Taxes: Total city taxes per capita: $18 (2000); City property taxes per capita: $16 (2000).
Education: High school graduation rate: 77.4% (2000); College graduation rate: 10.8% (2000).
Housing: Homeownership rate: 89.5% (2000); Median home value: $87,900 (2000); Median rent: $338 per month (2000); Median age of housing: 28 years (2000).
Transportation: Commute to work: 91.6% car, 0.2% public transportation, 0.5% walk, 6.5% work from home (2000); Travel time to work: 40.8% less than 15 minutes, 29.8% 15 to 30 minutes, 9.9% 30 to 45 minutes, 8.4% 45 to 60 minutes, 11.1% 60 minutes or more (2000)

SECORD (township). Covers a land area of 22.471 square miles and a water area of 0.934 square miles. Located at 44.04° N. Lat.; 84.33° W. Long. Elevation is 739 feet.
History: Marcel Secord settled here in the early 1860's, where he operated a boarding house for lumbermen.
Population: 1,140 (2000); Race: 98.6% White, 0.2% Black, 0.0% Asian, 0.5% American Indian and Alaska Native, 0.7% Hispanic of any race, 0.4% two or more races (2000); Density: 50.7 persons per square mile (2000); Age: 13.5% under 18, 27.1% over 64 (2000); Marriage status: 12.3% never married, 68.3% now married, 8.9% widowed, 10.5% divorced (2000); Foreign born: 1.7% (2000); Ancestry (includes multiple ancestries): 27.4% German, 13.7% English, 11.8% Irish, 9.6% Polish, 7.9% French (except Basque) (2000).
Economy: Employment by occupation: 8.5% management, 15.4% professional, 18.1% services, 24.7% sales, 0.5% farming, 12.1% construction, 20.6% production (2000).
Income: Per capita income: $18,542 (2000); Median household income: $30,500 (2000); Poverty rate: 16.1% (2000).
Taxes: Total city taxes per capita: $104 (1997); City property taxes per capita: $97 (1997).
Education: High school graduation rate: 75.8% (2000); College graduation rate: 6.6% (2000).
Housing: Homeownership rate: 93.0% (2000); Median home value: $108,400 (2000); Median rent: $310 per month (2000); Median age of housing: 27 years (2000).
Transportation: Commute to work: 90.2% car, 0.6% public transportation, 2.3% walk, 6.3% work from home (2000); Travel time to work: 18.2% less than 15 minutes, 43.4% 15 to 30 minutes, 16.6% 30 to 45 minutes, 7.7% 45 to 60 minutes, 14.2% 60 minutes or more (2000)

SHERMAN (township). Covers a land area of 34.858 square miles and a water area of 0.460 square miles. Located at 44.11° N. Lat.; 84.55° W. Long.
Population: 1,029 (2000); Race: 96.1% White, 0.2% Black, 0.8% Asian, 0.2% American Indian and Alaska Native, 0.9% Hispanic of any race, 2.4% two or more races (2000); Density: 29.5 persons per square mile (2000); Age: 22.3% under 18, 16.1% over 64 (2000); Marriage status: 19.8% never married, 64.8% now married, 5.4% widowed, 9.9% divorced (2000); Foreign born: 1.9% (2000); Ancestry (includes multiple ancestries): 28.1% German, 14.8% English, 12.5% United States or American, 11.3% Irish, 7.4% Other groups (2000).
Economy: Employment by occupation: 8.7% management, 20.0% professional, 16.3% services, 16.0% sales, 2.0% farming, 14.3% construction, 22.7% production (2000).
Income: Per capita income: $15,386 (2000); Median household income: $30,508 (2000); Poverty rate: 14.9% (2000).
Taxes: Total city taxes per capita: $17 (1997); City property taxes per capita: $17 (1997).
Education: High school graduation rate: 76.2% (2000); College graduation rate: 10.4% (2000).
Housing: Homeownership rate: 87.0% (2000); Median home value: $50,800 (2000); Median rent: $278 per month (2000); Median age of housing: 31 years (2000).
Transportation: Commute to work: 91.6% car, 0.0% public transportation, 1.0% walk, 6.6% work from home (2000); Travel time to work: 18.7% less than 15 minutes, 42.5% 15 to 30 minutes, 20.1% 30 to 45 minutes, 4.1% 45 to 60 minutes, 14.6% 60 minutes or more (2000)

TOBACCO (township). Covers a land area of 34.009 square miles and a water area of 1.310 square miles. Located at 43.86° N. Lat.; 84.42° W. Long.
Population: 2,552 (2000); Race: 99.2% White, 0.2% Black, 0.0% Asian, 0.1% American Indian and Alaska Native, 3.1% Hispanic of any race, 0.2% two or more races (2000); Density: 75.0 persons per square mile (2000); Age: 22.4% under 18, 15.2% over 64 (2000); Marriage status: 16.7% never married, 69.4% now married, 7.6% widowed, 6.3% divorced (2000); Foreign born: 1.0% (2000); Ancestry (includes multiple ancestries): 25.9% German, 13.0% English, 10.4% Irish, 9.1% United States or American, 8.6% Other groups (2000).
Economy: Employment by occupation: 11.7% management, 17.3% professional, 14.3% services, 22.9% sales, 0.9% farming, 15.1% construction, 17.8% production (2000).
Income: Per capita income: $20,037 (2000); Median household income: $40,813 (2000); Poverty rate: 8.7% (2000).
Taxes: Total city taxes per capita: $51 (1997); City property taxes per capita: $51 (1997).
Education: High school graduation rate: 86.3% (2000); College graduation rate: 10.8% (2000).
Housing: Homeownership rate: 91.5% (2000); Median home value: $108,600 (2000); Median rent: $313 per month (2000); Median age of housing: 25 years (2000).
Transportation: Commute to work: 95.0% car, 0.0% public transportation, 1.4% walk, 3.0% work from home (2000); Travel time to work: 21.1% less than 15 minutes, 24.6% 15 to 30 minutes, 27.5% 30 to 45 minutes, 12.6% 45 to 60 minutes, 14.2% 60 minutes or more (2000)

Gogebic County

Located in northwestern Michigan on the Upper Peninsula; bounded on the northwest by Lake Superior, and on the south and southwest by Wisconsin; drained by the Montreal, Presque Isle, and Ontonagon Rivers; includes part of Ottawa National Forest, and many small lakes and waterfalls. Covers a land area of 1,101.90 square miles, a water area of 374.60 square miles, and is located in the Central Time Zone. The county government was organized in 1881. County seat is Bessemer.

Weather Station: Ironwood — Elevation: 1,427 feet

	Jan	Feb	Mar	Apr	May	Jun	Jul	Aug	Sep	Oct	Nov	Dec
High	19	26	35	50	64	73	77	75	65	53	37	25
Low	-0	3	14	28	40	50	54	52	44	34	21	8
Precip	2.1	1.2	2.0	2.1	3.1	4.0	4.0	3.7	3.9	3.5	3.0	2.1
Snow	45.6	24.3	22.2	9.6	2.1	0.0	0.0	0.0	0.3	5.2	27.5	40.3

High and Low temperatures in degrees Fahrenheit; Precipitation and Snow in inches

Population: 17,370 (2000); Race: 94.3% White, 1.8% Black, 0.2% Asian, 1.9% American Indian and Alaska Native, 0.8% Hispanic of any race, 1.5% two or more races (2000); Density: 15.8 persons per square mile (2000); Age: 20.5% under 18, 22.6% over 64 (2000).
Religion: Five largest groups: 32.1% Catholic Church, 18.6% Evangelical Lutheran Church in America, 6.2% Lutheran Church—Missouri Synod, 1.6% The United Methodist Church, 1.3% General Association of Regular Baptist Churches (2000).
Economy: Unemployment rate: 6.9% (11/2002); Total civilian labor force: 8,290 (11/2002); Leading industries: 26.0% accommodation & food services; 18.5% retail trade; 15.5% health care and social assistance (2000); Companies that employ more than 1,000 persons: 0 (2000); Companies that employ more than 100 persons: 8 (2000); Farms: 48 totaling 4,197 acres (1997); Minority business ownership rate: 0.0% (1997); Women business ownership rate: 33.3% (1997); Retail sales per capita: $7,704 (1997). Single-family building permits issued: 53 (2001) / 46 (2000); Multi-family building permits issued: 0 (2001) / 0 (2000).
Income: Per capita income: $16,169 (2000); Median household income: $27,405 (2000); Poverty rate: 14.4% (2000); Bankruptcy rate: 3.11% (2001).
Taxes: Total county taxes per capita: $134 (1997); County property taxes per capita: $133 (1997).
Education: High school graduation rate: 85.5% (2000); College graduation rate: 15.8% (2000).
Housing: Homeownership rate: 78.7% (2000); Median home value: $39,700 (2000); Median rent: $268 per month (2000); Median age of housing: 53 years (2000).
Health: Birth rate: 89.8 per 10,000 population (1998); Age adjusted death rate: 92.6 per 10,000 population (1999); Age adjusted cancer mortality rate: 247.2 deaths per 100,000 population (1999). Number of physicians: 10.9 per 10,000 population (1999); Number of hospital beds: 31.1 per 10,000 population (1999).
Elections: 2000 Presidential election results: 48.8% Gore, 47.1% Bush, 3.4% Nader, 0.3% Buchanan
National and State Parks: Gogebic Lake State Park
Additional Information Contacts
Gogebic County Government Offices 906-667-0411
Bessemer Chamber of Commerce 906-663-4542
Ironwood Chamber of Commerce 906-932-1122
Western Upper Peninsula Conv 906-932-4850

Gogebic County Communities

BESSEMER (city). Covers a land area of 5.467 square miles and a water area of 0 square miles. Located at 46.47° N. Lat.; 90.05° W. Long. Elevation is 1,432 feet.
History: Bessemer was established at a point where a copper lode to the north and an iron lode to the south met. Bessemer experienced rapid growth in the 1890's, when the expansion of the railroads created a wide market for Bessemer steel rails. The city was named for Sir Henry Bessemer (1813-1898), who devised the smelting process that made his name well-known.
Population: 2,148 (2000); Race: 96.5% White, 0.0% Black, 0.2% Asian, 1.4% American Indian and Alaska Native, 0.4% Hispanic of any race, 2.0% two or more races (2000); Density: 392.9 persons per square mile (2000); Age: 24.2% under 18, 21.4% over 64 (2000); Marriage status: 25.4% never married, 55.4% now married, 9.5% widowed, 9.7% divorced (2000); Foreign born: 1.6% (2000); Ancestry (includes multiple ancestries): 23.9% Italian, 23.0% Finnish, 18.2% German, 14.8% Polish, 9.9% Swedish (2000).
Economy: Single-family building permits issued: 1 (2001) / 0 (2000); Multi-family building permits issued: 0 (2001) / 0 (2000); Employment by occupation: 10.1% management, 16.2% professional, 20.9% services, 20.2% sales, 2.0% farming, 11.0% construction, 19.6% production (2000).
Income: Per capita income: $17,499 (2000); Median household income: $27,639 (2000); Poverty rate: 12.1% (2000).
Taxes: Total city taxes per capita: $175 (1997); City property taxes per capita: $174 (1997).
Education: High school graduation rate: 86.6% (2000); College graduation rate: 17.3% (2000).

School District(s)

Bessemer Area School District (PK-12)
2000 Enrollment: 553 906-667-0802
Housing: Homeownership rate: 73.7% (2000); Median home value: $39,100 (2000); Median rent: $259 per month (2000); Median age of housing: 60+ years (2000).
Transportation: Commute to work: 88.2% car, 0.3% public transportation, 6.0% walk, 4.6% work from home (2000); Travel time to work: 67.4% less than 15 minutes, 19.2% 15 to 30 minutes, 4.5% 30 to 45 minutes, 3.6% 45 to 60 minutes, 5.3% 60 minutes or more (2000)
Additional Information Contacts
Bessemer Chamber of Commerce 906-663-4542

BESSEMER (township). Covers a land area of 113.844 square miles and a water area of 1.557 square miles. Located at 46.42° N. Lat.; 89.99° W. Long. Elevation is 1,432 feet.
History: Bessemer Township was named for Sir Henry Bessemer (1813-1898), a British metallurgist whose name became associated with the Bessemer process for making steel by blasting compressed air through molten iron.
Population: 1,270 (2000); Race: 97.5% White, 0.0% Black, 0.2% Asian, 1.0% American Indian and Alaska Native, 0.0% Hispanic of any race, 1.3% two or more races (2000); Density: 11.2 persons per square mile (2000); Age: 18.3% under 18, 22.8% over 64 (2000); Marriage status: 23.9% never married, 56.7% now married, 11.9% widowed, 7.6% divorced (2000); Foreign born: 1.5% (2000); Ancestry (includes multiple ancestries): 29.1% Finnish, 17.0% Italian, 16.5% German, 13.0% Swedish, 10.4% English (2000).
Economy: Single-family building permits issued: 5 (2001) / 5 (2000); Multi-family building permits issued: 0 (2001) / 0 (2000); Employment by occupation: 6.4% management, 19.9% professional, 18.2% services, 24.2% sales, 1.7% farming, 10.4% construction, 19.1% production (2000).
Income: Per capita income: $18,917 (2000); Median household income: $27,000 (2000); Poverty rate: 8.9% (2000).
Taxes: Total city taxes per capita: $140 (1997); City property taxes per capita: $137 (1997).

Education: High school graduation rate: 88.6% (2000); College graduation rate: 14.1% (2000).
Housing: Homeownership rate: 90.1% (2000); Median home value: $31,400 (2000); Median rent: $277 per month (2000); Median age of housing: 56 years (2000).
Transportation: Commute to work: 92.5% car, 0.4% public transportation, 1.5% walk, 5.2% work from home (2000); Travel time to work: 56.8% less than 15 minutes, 27.3% 15 to 30 minutes, 5.7% 30 to 45 minutes, 5.1% 45 to 60 minutes, 5.3% 60 minutes or more (2000)

ERWIN (township). Covers a land area of 47.207 square miles and a water area of 0.950 square miles. Located at 46.39° N. Lat.; 90.08° W. Long.
Population: 357 (2000); Race: 100.0% White, 0.0% Black, 0.0% Asian, 0.0% American Indian and Alaska Native, 0.0% Hispanic of any race, 0.0% two or more races (2000); Density: 7.6 persons per square mile (2000); Age: 25.5% under 18, 16.3% over 64 (2000); Marriage status: 22.3% never married, 62.4% now married, 6.1% widowed, 9.2% divorced (2000); Foreign born: 1.3% (2000); Ancestry (includes multiple ancestries): 37.6% Finnish, 18.2% Italian, 16.6% German, 10.8% Swedish, 9.7% Polish (2000).
Economy: Employment by occupation: 11.9% management, 16.7% professional, 17.3% services, 25.0% sales, 2.4% farming, 12.5% construction, 14.3% production (2000).
Income: Per capita income: $14,014 (2000); Median household income: $31,071 (2000); Poverty rate: 7.4% (2000).
Taxes: Total city taxes per capita: $69 (1997); City property taxes per capita: $67 (1997).
Education: High school graduation rate: 87.9% (2000); College graduation rate: 14.8% (2000).
Housing: Homeownership rate: 97.4% (2000); Median home value: $49,400 (2000); Median age of housing: 54 years (2000).
Transportation: Commute to work: 91.5% car, 1.2% public transportation, 1.2% walk, 6.1% work from home (2000); Travel time to work: 47.7% less than 15 minutes, 38.7% 15 to 30 minutes, 1.9% 30 to 45 minutes, 3.2% 45 to 60 minutes, 8.4% 60 minutes or more (2000)

IRONWOOD (city). Covers a land area of 6.553 square miles and a water area of 0 square miles. Located at 46.45° N. Lat.; 90.15° W. Long. Elevation is 1,503 feet.
History: Lumbering and mining both contributed to the development of Ironwood, the central city of the mining area that included Bessemer, Ramsay, and Wakefield. Iron ore was discovered in 1884 in this area, and the railroad line was extended in 1885 to tap the new resources. Ironwood was platted by the railroad in 1885, incorporated as a village in 1887, and chartered as a city in 1889. Ironwood was named for James R. Wood, known as "Iron" Wood.
Population: 6,293 (2000); Race: 97.4% White, 0.2% Black, 0.1% Asian, 0.0% American Indian and Alaska Native, 0.3% Hispanic of any race, 2.2% two or more races (2000); Density: 960.3 persons per square mile (2000); Age: 22.3% under 18, 24.4% over 64 (2000); Marriage status: 24.0% never married, 52.6% now married, 12.2% widowed, 11.2% divorced (2000); Foreign born: 1.3% (2000); Ancestry (includes multiple ancestries): 24.7% Finnish, 17.0% German, 14.8% Italian, 12.6% Polish, 10.4% English (2000).
Economy: Single-family building permits issued: 2 (2001) / 1 (2000); Multi-family building permits issued: 0 (2001) / 0 (2000); Employment by occupation: 9.0% management, 17.1% professional, 19.6% services, 22.7% sales, 0.2% farming, 10.7% construction, 20.6% production (2000).
Income: Per capita income: $14,131 (2000); Median household income: $23,502 (2000); Poverty rate: 18.5% (2000).
Taxes: Total city taxes per capita: $214 (1997); City property taxes per capita: $209 (1997).
Education: High school graduation rate: 86.2% (2000); College graduation rate: 16.3% (2000).

School District(s)

Ironwood Area Schools (KG-12)
2000 Enrollment: 1,275 906-932-0200

Two-year College(s)

Gogebic Community College (Public)
2001 Enrollment: 1,170 906-932-4231
2001 Tuition: In-state $2,015; Out-of-state $2,790

Housing: Homeownership rate: 71.7% (2000); Median home value: $35,500 (2000); Median rent: $293 per month (2000); Median age of housing: 60+ years (2000).
Hospitals: Grand View Hospital (54 beds)
Safety: Violent crime rate: 11.1 per 10,000 population; Property crime rate: 129.6 per 10,000 population (2001).
Newspapers: Daily Globe (6 x week); North Country Sun (1 x week)
Transportation: Commute to work: 90.5% car, 0.6% public transportation, 7.6% walk, 1.2% work from home (2000); Travel time to work: 70.7% less than 15 minutes, 16.1% 15 to 30 minutes, 4.6% 30 to 45 minutes, 4.0% 45 to 60 minutes, 4.6% 60 minutes or more (2000)

Additional Information Contacts

Ironwood Chamber of Commerce 906-932-1122
Western Upper Peninsula Conv 906-932-4850

IRONWOOD (township). Covers a land area of 175.417 square miles and a water area of 13.402 square miles. Located at 46.54° N. Lat.; 90.14° W. Long. Elevation is 1,503 feet.
History: Founded 1885, Incorporated 1889.
Population: 2,330 (2000); Race: 98.8% White, 0.3% Black, 0.2% Asian, 0.6% American Indian and Alaska Native, 0.5% Hispanic of any race, 0.2% two or more races (2000); Density: 13.3 persons per square mile (2000); Age: 20.5% under 18, 20.7% over 64 (2000); Marriage status: 20.7% never married, 64.8% now married, 7.7% widowed, 6.8% divorced (2000); Foreign born: 0.8% (2000); Ancestry (includes multiple ancestries): 33.1% Finnish, 14.9% Italian, 14.3% German, 12.3% Swedish, 9.9% English (2000).
Economy: Trade center for Gogebic Range region. Manufacturing includes sportswear, publishing, plastic molding, concrete blocks, canvas products. Lumbering. Dairy and vegetable farming. Resort for winter sports. Single-family building permits issued: 12 (2001) / 8 (2000); Multi-family building permits issued: 0 (2001) / 0 (2000); Employment by occupation: 11.7% management, 16.9% professional, 18.9% services, 26.5% sales, 1.3% farming, 10.0% construction, 14.7% production (2000).
Income: Per capita income: $18,702 (2000); Median household income: $36,053 (2000); Poverty rate: 10.5% (2000).
Taxes: Total city taxes per capita: $90 (1997); City property taxes per capita: $88 (1997).
Education: High school graduation rate: 91.0% (2000); College graduation rate: 21.4% (2000).
Housing: Homeownership rate: 84.9% (2000); Median home value: $70,300 (2000); Median rent: $243 per month (2000); Median age of housing: 37 years (2000).
Transportation: Commute to work: 95.0% car, 0.6% public transportation, 0.7% walk, 3.8% work from home (2000); Travel time to work: 51.9% less than 15 minutes, 35.2% 15 to 30 minutes, 5.2% 30 to 45 minutes, 3.1% 45 to 60 minutes, 4.5% 60 minutes or more (2000)

MARENISCO (township). Covers a land area of 310.854 square miles and a water area of 15.033 square miles. Located at 46.36° N. Lat.; 89.59° W. Long. Elevation is 1,515 feet.
Population: 1,051 (2000); Race: 67.7% White, 26.1% Black, 0.5% Asian, 0.8% American Indian and Alaska Native, 6.4% Hispanic of any race, 1.3% two or more races (2000); Density: 3.4 persons per square mile (2000); Age: 13.4% under 18, 10.0% over 64 (2000); Marriage status: 17.9% never married, 74.7% now married, 3.4% widowed, 4.0% divorced (2000); Foreign born: 0.3% (2000); Ancestry (includes multiple ancestries): 16.2% German, 7.7% Finnish, 7.2% Irish, 5.8% English, 5.7% United States or American (2000).
Economy: In lumbering and agricultural area. Manufacturing: wood products. Single-family building permits issued: 2 (2001) / 2 (2000); Multi-family building permits issued: 0 (2001) / 0 (2000); Employment by occupation: 13.2% management, 9.6% professional, 31.6% services, 13.6% sales, 5.2% farming, 7.2% construction, 19.6% production (2000).
Income: Per capita income: $13,156 (2000); Median household income: $33,438 (2000); Poverty rate: 9.6% (2000).
Taxes: Total city taxes per capita: $228 (1997); City property taxes per capita: $225 (1997).
Education: High school graduation rate: 81.7% (2000); College graduation rate: 9.0% (2000).

School District(s)

Marenisco School District (KG-12)
2000 Enrollment: 101 906-787-2288

Housing: Homeownership rate: 90.9% (2000); Median home value: $55,900 (2000); Median rent: $294 per month (2000); Median age of housing: 36 years (2000).
Transportation: Commute to work: 88.3% car, 0.0% public transportation, 4.4% walk, 7.3% work from home (2000); Travel time to work: 33.9% less than 15 minutes, 16.5% 15 to 30 minutes, 29.6% 30 to 45 minutes, 9.1% 45 to 60 minutes, 10.9% 60 minutes or more (2000)

WAKEFIELD (city). Covers a land area of 7.972 square miles and a water area of 0.548 square miles. Located at 46.47° N. Lat.; 89.93° W. Long. Elevation is 1,550 feet.

History: Wakefield grew up, literally, around several mines which were located within the boundaries of the city. The village was named for George M. Wakefield, a mine owner, who platted it in 1886. Wakefield was incorporated as a city in 1919.
Population: 2,085 (2000); Race: 98.1% White, 0.1% Black, 0.5% Asian, 0.4% American Indian and Alaska Native, 0.0% Hispanic of any race, 0.9% two or more races (2000); Density: 261.5 persons per square mile (2000); Age: 15.3% under 18, 32.0% over 64 (2000); Marriage status: 21.2% never married, 58.6% now married, 14.5% widowed, 5.6% divorced (2000); Foreign born: 1.7% (2000); Ancestry (includes multiple ancestries): 28.6% Finnish, 12.1% German, 11.6% Italian, 10.1% Irish, 9.4% Swedish (2000).
Economy: Single-family building permits issued: 2 (2001) / 2 (2000); Multi-family building permits issued: 0 (2001) / 0 (2000); Employment by occupation: 10.2% management, 14.8% professional, 26.9% services, 17.3% sales, 2.5% farming, 15.7% construction, 12.6% production (2000).
Income: Per capita income: $17,036 (2000); Median household income: $25,368 (2000); Poverty rate: 12.2% (2000).
Taxes: Total city taxes per capita: $114 (1997); City property taxes per capita: $114 (1997).
Education: High school graduation rate: 80.8% (2000); College graduation rate: 11.0% (2000).

School District(s)

Wakefield School District (PK-12)
2000 Enrollment: 292 906-224-9421

Housing: Homeownership rate: 82.2% (2000); Median home value: $35,000 (2000); Median rent: $217 per month (2000); Median age of housing: 60+ years (2000).
Newspapers: Wakefield News (1 x week)
Transportation: Commute to work: 89.9% car, 0.6% public transportation, 6.8% walk, 2.8% work from home (2000); Travel time to work: 50.6% less than 15 minutes, 27.4% 15 to 30 minutes, 6.6% 30 to 45 minutes, 7.4% 45 to 60 minutes, 8.0% 60 minutes or more (2000)

WAKEFIELD (township). Covers a land area of 179.781 square miles and a water area of 0.980 square miles. Located at 46.53° N. Lat.; 89.87° W. Long. Elevation is 1,550 feet.
History: Settled 1866; incorporated as village 1887, as city 1919.
Population: 364 (2000); Race: 99.0% White, 0.0% Black, 0.0% Asian, 0.0% American Indian and Alaska Native, 0.3% Hispanic of any race, 1.0% two or more races (2000); Density: 2.0 persons per square mile (2000); Age: 20.0% under 18, 16.2% over 64 (2000); Marriage status: 24.3% never married, 61.8% now married, 6.8% widowed, 7.1% divorced (2000); Foreign born: 0.0% (2000); Ancestry (includes multiple ancestries): 32.2% Finnish, 19.7% German, 11.9% Irish, 9.6% Polish, 5.8% Italian (2000).
Economy: Cattle; forage crops; sawmilling. Manufacturing of wood products; resort. Single-family building permits issued: 3 (2001) / 1 (2000); Multi-family building permits issued: 0 (2001) / 0 (2000); Employment by occupation: 4.7% management, 18.0% professional, 24.4% services, 23.8% sales, 0.0% farming, 8.7% construction, 20.3% production (2000).
Income: Per capita income: $17,400 (2000); Median household income: $31,875 (2000); Poverty rate: 9.4% (2000).
Taxes: Total city taxes per capita: $473 (1997); City property taxes per capita: $469 (1997).
Education: High school graduation rate: 83.1% (2000); College graduation rate: 19.6% (2000).
Housing: Homeownership rate: 87.5% (2000); Median home value: $65,000 (2000); Median rent: $225 per month (2000); Median age of housing: 27 years (2000).
Transportation: Commute to work: 90.6% car, 0.0% public transportation, 3.5% walk, 5.9% work from home (2000); Travel time to work: 34.4% less than 15 minutes, 46.9% 15 to 30 minutes, 15.6% 30 to 45 minutes, 0.0% 45 to 60 minutes, 3.1% 60 minutes or more (2000)

WATERSMEET (township). Covers a land area of 254.765 square miles and a water area of 23.051 square miles. Located at 46.25° N. Lat.; 89.26° W. Long. Elevation is 1,598 feet.
History: Watersmeet was named for the junction of the middle branch of the Ontonagon River and Duck Creek, which was the apex of three watersheds, water draining to Lake Superior on the north, to Lake Michigan on the east, and to the Mississippi Valley on the south.
Population: 1,472 (2000); Race: 78.8% White, 0.8% Black, 0.6% Asian, 17.6% American Indian and Alaska Native, 1.6% Hispanic of any race, 1.2% two or more races (2000); Density: 5.8 persons per square mile (2000); Age: 20.6% under 18, 19.0% over 64 (2000); Marriage status: 20.8% never married, 63.0% now married, 7.2% widowed, 9.0% divorced (2000); Foreign born: 1.4% (2000); Ancestry (includes multiple ancestries): 20.1% German, 19.2% Other groups, 8.7% Polish, 8.7% Irish, 7.8% English (2000).
Economy: Single-family building permits issued: 26 (2001) / 27 (2000); Multi-family building permits issued: 0 (2001) / 0 (2000); Employment by occupation: 10.5% management, 13.2% professional, 27.1% services, 19.4% sales, 2.2% farming, 14.6% construction, 13.0% production (2000).
Income: Per capita income: $17,874 (2000); Median household income: $32,019 (2000); Poverty rate: 19.8% (2000).
Taxes: Total city taxes per capita: $269 (1997); City property taxes per capita: $262 (1997).
Education: High school graduation rate: 78.8% (2000); College graduation rate: 15.4% (2000).

School District(s)

Watersmeet Township School District (KG-12)
2000 Enrollment: 207 906-358-4504

Housing: Homeownership rate: 80.6% (2000); Median home value: $77,100 (2000); Median rent: $310 per month (2000); Median age of housing: 26 years (2000).
Transportation: Commute to work: 81.8% car, 0.4% public transportation, 9.9% walk, 5.9% work from home (2000); Travel time to work: 62.7% less than 15 minutes, 22.7% 15 to 30 minutes, 8.4% 30 to 45 minutes, 4.9% 45 to 60 minutes, 1.3% 60 minutes or more (2000)

Grand Traverse County

Located in northwestern Michigan; drained by the Boardman and Betsie Rivers; includes Traverse Bay in the north, and Green, Duck, and Long Lakes. Covers a land area of 465.10 square miles, a water area of 136.10 square miles, and is located in the Eastern Time Zone. The county government was organized in 1851. County seat is Traverse City.

Weather Station: Traverse City Cherry Capital — Elevation: 620 feet

	Jan	Feb	Mar	Apr	May	Jun	Jul	Aug	Sep	Oct	Nov	Dec
High	27	29	39	53	67	77	81	79	70	58	43	32
Low	14	12	21	32	42	52	58	57	50	40	30	21
Precip	3.0	1.8	2.0	2.6	2.3	3.2	3.2	3.4	3.8	3.0	2.8	2.7
Snow	30.8	19.1	10.4	2.7	0.1	tr	0.0	0.0	tr	0.4	9.2	24.1

High and Low temperatures in degrees Fahrenheit; Precipitation and Snow in inches

Population: 77,654 (2000); Race: 96.2% White, 0.5% Black, 0.4% Asian, 1.2% American Indian and Alaska Native, 1.2% Hispanic of any race, 1.3% two or more races (2000); Density: 167.0 persons per square mile (2000); Age: 25.4% under 18, 13.1% over 64 (2000).
Religion: Five largest groups: 23.5% Catholic Church, 3.7% The United Methodist Church, 3.0% Lutheran Church—Missouri Synod, 2.2% Evangelical Lutheran Church in America, 2.0% United Church of Christ (2000).
Economy: Unemployment rate: 4.5% (11/2002); Total civilian labor force: 46,222 (11/2002); Leading industries: 18.6% retail trade; 14.9% health care and social assistance; 14.8% manufacturing (2000); Companies that employ more than 1,000 persons: 2 (2000); Companies that employ more than 100 persons: 52 (2000); Farms: 413 totaling 61,767 acres (1997); Minority business ownership rate: 2.3% (1997); Women business ownership rate: 25.0% (1997); Retail sales per capita: $16,916 (1997). Single-family building permits issued: 533 (2001) / 604 (2000); Multi-family building permits issued: 105 (2001) / 375 (2000).
Income: Per capita income: $22,111 (2000); Median household income: $43,169 (2000); Poverty rate: 5.9% (2000); Bankruptcy rate: 3.64% (2001).
Taxes: Total county taxes per capita: $201 (2000); County property taxes per capita: $176 (2000).
Education: High school graduation rate: 89.3% (2000); College graduation rate: 26.1% (2000).
Housing: Homeownership rate: 77.3% (2000); Median home value: $130,400 (2000); Median rent: $554 per month (2000); Median age of housing: 23 years (2000).
Health: Birth rate: 119.8 per 10,000 population (1998); Age adjusted death rate: 77.2 per 10,000 population (1999); Age adjusted cancer mortality rate: 178.5 deaths per 100,000 population (1999). Number of physicians: 35.3 per 10,000 population (1999); Number of hospital beds: 47.4 per 10,000 population (1999).
Elections: 2000 Presidential election results: 37.6% Gore, 58.5% Bush, 3.3% Nader, 0.1% Buchanan
National and State Parks: Interlochen State Park; Traverse City State Park
Additional Information Contacts
Grand Traverse County Government Offices 231-922-4700
Interlochen Chamber of Commerce 231-276-7141

Kingsley Area Chamber of Commerce 231-263-5678
Paradise Chamber of Commerce 906-492-3219
Traverse Area Association of Realtors.................... 231-947-2050
Traverse City Chamber of Commerce 231-947-5075
Traverse City Convention Bureau 231-947-1120

Grand Traverse County Communities

ACME (township). Covers a land area of 25.175 square miles and a water area of 0.157 square miles. Located at 44.78° N. Lat.; 85.47° W. Long.
Population: 4,332 (2000); Race: 96.1% White, 0.0% Black, 0.0% Asian, 0.3% American Indian and Alaska Native, 1.4% Hispanic of any race, 3.0% two or more races (2000); Density: 172.1 persons per square mile (2000); Age: 24.4% under 18, 13.4% over 64 (2000); Marriage status: 20.2% never married, 65.5% now married, 5.9% widowed, 8.4% divorced (2000); Foreign born: 4.3% (2000); Ancestry (includes multiple ancestries): 27.4% German, 14.2% English, 10.8% Polish, 10.2% Irish, 5.4% United States or American (2000).
Economy: Employment by occupation: 19.0% management, 19.4% professional, 15.3% services, 30.2% sales, 1.8% farming, 8.5% construction, 5.8% production (2000).
Income: Per capita income: $24,219 (2000); Median household income: $50,425 (2000); Poverty rate: 6.5% (2000).
Taxes: Total city taxes per capita: $133 (1997); City property taxes per capita: $129 (1997).
Education: High school graduation rate: 91.0% (2000); College graduation rate: 35.8% (2000).
Housing: Homeownership rate: 80.3% (2000); Median home value: $148,900 (2000); Median rent: $624 per month (2000); Median age of housing: 17 years (2000).
Transportation: Commute to work: 89.6% car, 1.6% public transportation, 2.4% walk, 6.1% work from home (2000); Travel time to work: 34.3% less than 15 minutes, 49.8% 15 to 30 minutes, 10.6% 30 to 45 minutes, 2.2% 45 to 60 minutes, 3.0% 60 minutes or more (2000)

BLAIR (township). Covers a land area of 35.615 square miles and a water area of 0.336 square miles. Located at 44.65° N. Lat.; 85.64° W. Long.
Population: 6,448 (2000); Race: 93.6% White, 1.0% Black, 0.4% Asian, 1.7% American Indian and Alaska Native, 1.1% Hispanic of any race, 2.7% two or more races (2000); Density: 181.0 persons per square mile (2000); Age: 30.7% under 18, 6.5% over 64 (2000); Marriage status: 26.1% never married, 53.8% now married, 3.2% widowed, 16.9% divorced (2000); Foreign born: 1.7% (2000); Ancestry (includes multiple ancestries): 27.4% German, 11.0% Irish, 8.5% English, 7.8% Polish, 7.0% United States or American (2000).
Economy: Employment by occupation: 8.9% management, 12.1% professional, 21.8% services, 26.1% sales, 0.0% farming, 12.5% construction, 18.7% production (2000).
Income: Per capita income: $14,745 (2000); Median household income: $40,125 (2000); Poverty rate: 11.0% (2000).
Taxes: Total city taxes per capita: $86 (2000); City property taxes per capita: $78 (2000).
Education: High school graduation rate: 81.5% (2000); College graduation rate: 9.8% (2000).
Housing: Homeownership rate: 83.5% (2000); Median home value: $100,100 (2000); Median rent: $461 per month (2000); Median age of housing: 20 years (2000).
Transportation: Commute to work: 94.7% car, 0.4% public transportation, 0.2% walk, 3.2% work from home (2000); Travel time to work: 23.9% less than 15 minutes, 55.1% 15 to 30 minutes, 11.3% 30 to 45 minutes, 4.5% 45 to 60 minutes, 5.2% 60 minutes or more (2000)

EAST BAY (township). Covers a land area of 39.905 square miles and a water area of 2.440 square miles. Located at 44.70° N. Lat.; 85.52° W. Long.
Population: 9,919 (2000); Race: 97.3% White, 0.4% Black, 0.4% Asian, 0.7% American Indian and Alaska Native, 1.2% Hispanic of any race, 0.8% two or more races (2000); Density: 248.6 persons per square mile (2000); Age: 28.0% under 18, 8.1% over 64 (2000); Marriage status: 23.3% never married, 64.2% now married, 4.0% widowed, 8.5% divorced (2000); Foreign born: 1.7% (2000); Ancestry (includes multiple ancestries): 27.9% German, 12.4% English, 11.8% Irish, 8.3% United States or American, 8.3% Polish (2000).
Economy: Employment by occupation: 11.8% management, 18.6% professional, 15.1% services, 29.6% sales, 0.2% farming, 12.7% construction, 12.0% production (2000).
Income: Per capita income: $21,427 (2000); Median household income: $47,569 (2000); Poverty rate: 3.3% (2000).
Taxes: Total city taxes per capita: $59 (1997); City property taxes per capita: $52 (1997).
Education: High school graduation rate: 90.7% (2000); College graduation rate: 27.4% (2000).
Housing: Homeownership rate: 83.5% (2000); Median home value: $121,600 (2000); Median rent: $577 per month (2000); Median age of housing: 21 years (2000).
Transportation: Commute to work: 91.3% car, 0.6% public transportation, 1.1% walk, 6.1% work from home (2000); Travel time to work: 31.9% less than 15 minutes, 52.3% 15 to 30 minutes, 8.2% 30 to 45 minutes, 2.6% 45 to 60 minutes, 5.1% 60 minutes or more (2000)

FIFE LAKE (village). Covers a land area of 0.737 square miles and a water area of 0.466 square miles. Located at 44.57° N. Lat.; 85.35° W. Long. Elevation is 1,038 feet.
Population: 466 (2000); Race: 90.8% White, 0.0% Black, 0.0% Asian, 2.2% American Indian and Alaska Native, 2.9% Hispanic of any race, 6.9% two or more races (2000); Density: 632.1 persons per square mile (2000); Age: 30.5% under 18, 10.6% over 64 (2000); Marriage status: 21.3% never married, 59.1% now married, 8.7% widowed, 10.9% divorced (2000); Foreign born: 0.4% (2000); Ancestry (includes multiple ancestries): 23.6% German, 17.7% United States or American, 13.2% Other groups, 13.2% English, 11.6% Irish (2000).
Economy: Employment by occupation: 7.6% management, 8.0% professional, 21.3% services, 27.7% sales, 0.0% farming, 13.3% construction, 22.1% production (2000).
Income: Per capita income: $19,024 (2000); Median household income: $32,361 (2000); Poverty rate: 13.8% (2000).
Taxes: Total city taxes per capita: $147 (1997); City property taxes per capita: $145 (1997).
Education: High school graduation rate: 84.7% (2000); College graduation rate: 10.1% (2000).

School District(s)

Forest Area Community Schools (KG-12)
2000 Enrollment: 854 231-369-4191

Housing: Homeownership rate: 80.8% (2000); Median home value: $74,500 (2000); Median rent: $431 per month (2000); Median age of housing: 44 years (2000).
Transportation: Commute to work: 89.5% car, 0.8% public transportation, 2.5% walk, 4.2% work from home (2000); Travel time to work: 20.5% less than 15 minutes, 28.4% 15 to 30 minutes, 40.2% 30 to 45 minutes, 5.2% 45 to 60 minutes, 5.7% 60 minutes or more (2000)

FIFE LAKE (township). Covers a land area of 34.390 square miles and a water area of 1.559 square miles. Located at 44.55° N. Lat.; 85.38° W. Long. Elevation is 1,038 feet.
Population: 1,517 (2000); Race: 89.2% White, 4.9% Black, 0.0% Asian, 2.6% American Indian and Alaska Native, 2.3% Hispanic of any race, 2.7% two or more races (2000); Density: 44.1 persons per square mile (2000); Age: 23.5% under 18, 13.0% over 64 (2000); Marriage status: 22.8% never married, 63.4% now married, 5.7% widowed, 8.1% divorced (2000); Foreign born: 1.2% (2000); Ancestry (includes multiple ancestries): 22.2% German, 11.7% United States or American, 11.1% Other groups, 10.0% Irish, 9.7% English (2000).
Economy: Resort; manufacturing. Employment by occupation: 6.4% management, 10.3% professional, 20.8% services, 27.5% sales, 0.0% farming, 13.4% construction, 21.7% production (2000).
Income: Per capita income: $18,739 (2000); Median household income: $36,667 (2000); Poverty rate: 8.7% (2000).
Taxes: Total city taxes per capita: $43 (1997); City property taxes per capita: $41 (1997).
Education: High school graduation rate: 80.5% (2000); College graduation rate: 12.2% (2000).
Housing: Homeownership rate: 85.8% (2000); Median home value: $81,900 (2000); Median rent: $410 per month (2000); Median age of housing: 29 years (2000).
Transportation: Commute to work: 94.2% car, 0.3% public transportation, 1.5% walk, 2.1% work from home (2000); Travel time to work: 16.6% less than 15 minutes, 28.5% 15 to 30 minutes, 42.2% 30 to 45 minutes, 7.4% 45 to 60 minutes, 5.3% 60 minutes or more (2000)

GARFIELD (township). Covers a land area of 26.694 square miles and a water area of 0.980 square miles. Located at 44.72° N. Lat.; 85.64° W. Long.

History: Garfield Township was organized in 1882 and named for President James A. Garfield, who had just been assassinated.
Population: 13,840 (2000); Race: 95.9% White, 0.4% Black, 0.1% Asian, 2.2% American Indian and Alaska Native, 1.0% Hispanic of any race, 1.2% two or more races (2000); Density: 518.5 persons per square mile (2000); Age: 21.3% under 18, 20.5% over 64 (2000); Marriage status: 21.6% never married, 55.4% now married, 9.5% widowed, 13.5% divorced (2000); Foreign born: 2.6% (2000); Ancestry (includes multiple ancestries): 25.9% German, 15.5% English, 14.3% Irish, 7.7% Polish, 7.3% United States or American (2000).
Economy: Single-family building permits issued: 109 (2001) / 122 (2000); Multi-family building permits issued: 62 (2001) / 355 (2000); Employment by occupation: 11.8% management, 17.3% professional, 16.9% services, 30.0% sales, 0.3% farming, 10.8% construction, 13.0% production (2000).
Income: Per capita income: $22,142 (2000); Median household income: $37,472 (2000); Poverty rate: 6.0% (2000).
Taxes: Total city taxes per capita: $141 (1997); City property taxes per capita: $115 (1997).
Education: High school graduation rate: 87.7% (2000); College graduation rate: 21.3% (2000).
Housing: Homeownership rate: 72.4% (2000); Median home value: $135,700 (2000); Median rent: $555 per month (2000); Median age of housing: 17 years (2000).
Transportation: Commute to work: 94.3% car, 0.8% public transportation, 1.1% walk, 2.9% work from home (2000); Travel time to work: 55.6% less than 15 minutes, 33.7% 15 to 30 minutes, 6.3% 30 to 45 minutes, 2.0% 45 to 60 minutes, 2.5% 60 minutes or more (2000)

GRANT (township). Covers a land area of 35.447 square miles and a water area of 0.642 square miles. Located at 44.57° N. Lat.; 85.77° W. Long.
History: Grant Township was organized in 1866 and named for General Ulysses S. Grant.
Population: 947 (2000); Race: 96.3% White, 0.0% Black, 0.2% Asian, 1.2% American Indian and Alaska Native, 1.5% Hispanic of any race, 1.1% two or more races (2000); Density: 26.7 persons per square mile (2000); Age: 26.5% under 18, 13.0% over 64 (2000); Marriage status: 17.7% never married, 68.0% now married, 5.4% widowed, 8.9% divorced (2000); Foreign born: 0.4% (2000); Ancestry (includes multiple ancestries): 30.9% German, 13.2% English, 11.6% United States or American, 9.0% Other groups, 8.5% Irish (2000).
Economy: Employment by occupation: 11.2% management, 14.1% professional, 13.8% services, 28.8% sales, 0.0% farming, 14.5% construction, 17.6% production (2000).
Income: Per capita income: $17,282 (2000); Median household income: $37,269 (2000); Poverty rate: 6.3% (2000).
Taxes: Total city taxes per capita: $28 (1997); City property taxes per capita: $28 (1997).
Education: High school graduation rate: 81.8% (2000); College graduation rate: 11.3% (2000).
Housing: Homeownership rate: 91.3% (2000); Median home value: $108,700 (2000); Median rent: $400 per month (2000); Median age of housing: 28 years (2000).
Transportation: Commute to work: 92.0% car, 0.0% public transportation, 0.5% walk, 6.6% work from home (2000); Travel time to work: 13.4% less than 15 minutes, 40.3% 15 to 30 minutes, 32.5% 30 to 45 minutes, 7.6% 45 to 60 minutes, 6.1% 60 minutes or more (2000)

GRAWN (unincorporated postal area, zip code 49637). Covers a land area of 22.211 square miles and a water area of 0.202 square miles. Located at 44.64° N. Lat.; 85.70° W. Long.
History: The village here was first named Blackwood for James R. Blackwood, who owned much of the land that was platted. When the Pere Marquette Railroad built a station here, they called it Grawn Station. Grawn was first a lumber town, and then a shipping center for potatoes and other produce.
Population: 2,429 (2000); Race: 95.8% White, 0.0% Black, 0.0% Asian, 1.5% American Indian and Alaska Native, 0.6% Hispanic of any race, 2.6% two or more races (2000); Density: 109.4 persons per square mile (2000); Age: 28.4% under 18, 10.5% over 64 (2000); Marriage status: 19.4% never married, 64.2% now married, 3.5% widowed, 12.9% divorced (2000); Foreign born: 0.7% (2000); Ancestry (includes multiple ancestries): 37.3% German, 15.1% Irish, 11.5% English, 9.0% Polish, 8.0% French (except Basque) (2000).
Economy: Employment by occupation: 10.9% management, 14.5% professional, 20.3% services, 27.2% sales, 0.0% farming, 8.2% construction, 18.9% production (2000).
Income: Per capita income: $17,399 (2000); Median household income: $43,085 (2000); Poverty rate: 5.3% (2000).
Education: High school graduation rate: 85.0% (2000); College graduation rate: 14.8% (2000).
Housing: Homeownership rate: 86.7% (2000); Median home value: $102,200 (2000); Median rent: $462 per month (2000); Median age of housing: 22 years (2000).
Transportation: Commute to work: 95.2% car, 0.0% public transportation, 2.3% walk, 1.6% work from home (2000); Travel time to work: 24.7% less than 15 minutes, 55.2% 15 to 30 minutes, 8.8% 30 to 45 minutes, 3.2% 45 to 60 minutes, 8.1% 60 minutes or more (2000)

GREEN LAKE (township). Covers a land area of 29.394 square miles and a water area of 6.941 square miles. Located at 44.64° N. Lat.; 85.76° W. Long.
Population: 5,009 (2000); Race: 96.2% White, 0.0% Black, 0.0% Asian, 2.2% American Indian and Alaska Native, 0.6% Hispanic of any race, 1.1% two or more races (2000); Density: 170.4 persons per square mile (2000); Age: 28.9% under 18, 10.4% over 64 (2000); Marriage status: 21.2% never married, 65.4% now married, 2.9% widowed, 10.5% divorced (2000); Foreign born: 2.0% (2000); Ancestry (includes multiple ancestries): 30.9% German, 15.2% Irish, 14.0% English, 9.4% Polish, 6.9% United States or American (2000).
Economy: Single-family building permits issued: 0 (2001) / 76 (2000); Multi-family building permits issued: 0 (2001) / 0 (2000); Employment by occupation: 10.1% management, 18.8% professional, 18.1% services, 25.7% sales, 0.2% farming, 12.4% construction, 14.7% production (2000).
Income: Per capita income: $19,594 (2000); Median household income: $45,884 (2000); Poverty rate: 4.5% (2000).
Taxes: Total city taxes per capita: $42 (1997); City property taxes per capita: $20 (1997).
Education: High school graduation rate: 90.8% (2000); College graduation rate: 20.4% (2000).
Housing: Homeownership rate: 85.9% (2000); Median home value: $114,300 (2000); Median rent: $489 per month (2000); Median age of housing: 20 years (2000).
Transportation: Commute to work: 94.1% car, 0.0% public transportation, 1.6% walk, 4.0% work from home (2000); Travel time to work: 21.1% less than 15 minutes, 52.6% 15 to 30 minutes, 16.2% 30 to 45 minutes, 3.4% 45 to 60 minutes, 6.7% 60 minutes or more (2000)

INTERLOCHEN (unincorporated postal area, zip code 49643). Covers a land area of 56.921 square miles and a water area of 4.198 square miles. Located at 44.63° N. Lat.; 85.80° W. Long. Elevation is 841 feet.
History: The National High School Orchestra and Band Camp, a nonprofit summer school of music for high-school students, was established in 1927 at Interlochen, midway between Lake Wahbekaness and Lake Wahbekanetta.
Population: 5,002 (2000); Race: 96.5% White, 0.0% Black, 0.0% Asian, 1.7% American Indian and Alaska Native, 0.9% Hispanic of any race, 1.2% two or more races (2000); Density: 87.9 persons per square mile (2000); Age: 26.7% under 18, 10.3% over 64 (2000); Marriage status: 23.7% never married, 59.6% now married, 3.9% widowed, 12.9% divorced (2000); Foreign born: 2.1% (2000); Ancestry (includes multiple ancestries): 28.2% German, 15.5% Irish, 13.1% English, 8.8% Polish, 6.3% United States or American (2000).
Economy: Employment by occupation: 7.5% management, 17.0% professional, 18.7% services, 24.5% sales, 0.3% farming, 15.8% construction, 16.2% production (2000).
Income: Per capita income: $18,978 (2000); Median household income: $41,406 (2000); Poverty rate: 5.4% (2000).
Education: High school graduation rate: 87.4% (2000); College graduation rate: 17.3% (2000).
Housing: Homeownership rate: 84.1% (2000); Median home value: $109,400 (2000); Median rent: $463 per month (2000); Median age of housing: 20 years (2000).
Transportation: Commute to work: 93.7% car, 0.0% public transportation, 0.5% walk, 4.9% work from home (2000); Travel time to work: 17.3% less than 15 minutes, 49.3% 15 to 30 minutes, 24.4% 30 to 45 minutes, 4.3% 45 to 60 minutes, 4.8% 60 minutes or more (2000)
Additional Information Contacts
Interlochen Chamber of Commerce 231-276-7141

KINGSLEY (village). Covers a land area of 1.109 square miles and a water area of 0 square miles. Located at 44.58° N. Lat.; 85.53° W. Long. Elevation is 996 feet.

History: The village of Kingsley was laid out on land belonging to Judson W. Kingsley, and called Kingsley Station when the Grand Rapids & Indiana Railroad built a depot here in 1874.
Population: 1,469 (2000); Race: 97.1% White, 0.3% Black, 0.0% Asian, 1.0% American Indian and Alaska Native, 1.2% Hispanic of any race, 0.3% two or more races (2000); Density: 1,324.8 persons per square mile (2000); Age: 32.6% under 18, 9.5% over 64 (2000); Marriage status: 21.4% never married, 56.7% now married, 6.8% widowed, 15.1% divorced (2000); Foreign born: 0.7% (2000); Ancestry (includes multiple ancestries): 29.0% German, 11.5% English, 10.4% Irish, 7.0% Other groups, 5.9% Dutch (2000).
Economy: Employment by occupation: 8.5% management, 8.9% professional, 20.6% services, 27.6% sales, 0.0% farming, 13.1% construction, 21.3% production (2000).
Income: Per capita income: $14,945 (2000); Median household income: $32,614 (2000); Poverty rate: 9.7% (2000).
Taxes: Total city taxes per capita: $112 (1997); City property taxes per capita: $110 (1997).
Education: High school graduation rate: 84.9% (2000); College graduation rate: 10.7% (2000).

School District(s)

Kingsley Area Schools (KG-12)
2000 Enrollment: 1,308 231-263-5262

Housing: Homeownership rate: 79.4% (2000); Median home value: $100,300 (2000); Median rent: $407 per month (2000); Median age of housing: 13 years (2000).
Transportation: Commute to work: 93.0% car, 0.0% public transportation, 4.6% walk, 2.2% work from home (2000); Travel time to work: 13.2% less than 15 minutes, 57.6% 15 to 30 minutes, 21.2% 30 to 45 minutes, 1.1% 45 to 60 minutes, 7.0% 60 minutes or more (2000)
Additional Information Contacts
Kingsley Area Chamber of Commerce 231-263-5678

LONG LAKE (township). Covers a land area of 30.112 square miles and a water area of 5.527 square miles. Located at 44.73° N. Lat.; 85.76° W. Long.
History: Long Lake Township was organized in 1867. The Hannah, Lay & Company built a sawmill here in 1871.
Population: 7,648 (2000); Race: 96.9% White, 0.1% Black, 0.5% Asian, 1.0% American Indian and Alaska Native, 0.7% Hispanic of any race, 1.6% two or more races (2000); Density: 254.0 persons per square mile (2000); Age: 28.5% under 18, 8.5% over 64 (2000); Marriage status: 22.5% never married, 66.1% now married, 2.9% widowed, 8.5% divorced (2000); Foreign born: 1.4% (2000); Ancestry (includes multiple ancestries): 28.9% German, 13.7% English, 10.8% Irish, 9.3% Polish, 6.3% French (except Basque) (2000).
Economy: Employment by occupation: 13.4% management, 19.8% professional, 18.1% services, 27.8% sales, 0.0% farming, 10.2% construction, 10.8% production (2000).
Income: Per capita income: $21,943 (2000); Median household income: $48,826 (2000); Poverty rate: 3.0% (2000).
Taxes: Total city taxes per capita: $31 (1997); City property taxes per capita: $25 (1997).
Education: High school graduation rate: 94.6% (2000); College graduation rate: 29.0% (2000).
Housing: Homeownership rate: 84.2% (2000); Median home value: $132,500 (2000); Median rent: $574 per month (2000); Median age of housing: 17 years (2000).
Transportation: Commute to work: 95.5% car, 0.6% public transportation, 0.3% walk, 3.3% work from home (2000); Travel time to work: 23.9% less than 15 minutes, 59.6% 15 to 30 minutes, 10.8% 30 to 45 minutes, 2.2% 45 to 60 minutes, 3.4% 60 minutes or more (2000)

MAYFIELD (township). Covers a land area of 35.897 square miles and a water area of 0.162 square miles. Located at 44.54° N. Lat.; 85.65° W. Long. Elevation is 842 feet.
Population: 1,271 (2000); Race: 97.6% White, 0.0% Black, 0.0% Asian, 0.3% American Indian and Alaska Native, 2.1% Hispanic of any race, 2.1% two or more races (2000); Density: 35.4 persons per square mile (2000); Age: 28.4% under 18, 9.6% over 64 (2000); Marriage status: 25.7% never married, 62.4% now married, 4.1% widowed, 7.8% divorced (2000); Foreign born: 1.0% (2000); Ancestry (includes multiple ancestries): 38.8% German, 11.8% English, 8.7% French (except Basque), 7.6% Irish, 6.2% United States or American (2000).
Economy: Employment by occupation: 9.0% management, 11.4% professional, 15.4% services, 26.9% sales, 1.6% farming, 14.6% construction, 21.2% production (2000).
Income: Per capita income: $15,755 (2000); Median household income: $40,820 (2000); Poverty rate: 8.4% (2000).
Taxes: Total city taxes per capita: $22 (1997); City property taxes per capita: $21 (1997).
Education: High school graduation rate: 86.6% (2000); College graduation rate: 9.5% (2000).
Housing: Homeownership rate: 83.9% (2000); Median home value: $93,500 (2000); Median rent: $458 per month (2000); Median age of housing: 23 years (2000).
Transportation: Commute to work: 92.7% car, 0.0% public transportation, 1.1% walk, 5.2% work from home (2000); Travel time to work: 13.1% less than 15 minutes, 47.6% 15 to 30 minutes, 32.3% 30 to 45 minutes, 2.7% 45 to 60 minutes, 4.3% 60 minutes or more (2000)

PARADISE (township). Covers a land area of 52.877 square miles and a water area of 0.075 square miles. Located at 44.59° N. Lat.; 85.52° W. Long.
Population: 4,191 (2000); Race: 97.5% White, 0.3% Black, 0.0% Asian, 1.2% American Indian and Alaska Native, 0.6% Hispanic of any race, 0.5% two or more races (2000); Density: 79.3 persons per square mile (2000); Age: 33.4% under 18, 7.0% over 64 (2000); Marriage status: 22.1% never married, 62.0% now married, 4.4% widowed, 11.6% divorced (2000); Foreign born: 0.5% (2000); Ancestry (includes multiple ancestries): 32.1% German, 13.0% Irish, 10.7% English, 6.9% Dutch, 6.4% Polish (2000).
Economy: Employment by occupation: 7.2% management, 12.0% professional, 17.6% services, 25.5% sales, 0.3% farming, 14.7% construction, 22.7% production (2000).
Income: Per capita income: $16,507 (2000); Median household income: $44,776 (2000); Poverty rate: 5.2% (2000).
Taxes: Total city taxes per capita: $20 (1997); City property taxes per capita: $17 (1997).
Education: High school graduation rate: 86.3% (2000); College graduation rate: 11.6% (2000).
Housing: Homeownership rate: 86.3% (2000); Median home value: $103,800 (2000); Median rent: $442 per month (2000); Median age of housing: 13 years (2000).
Transportation: Commute to work: 92.9% car, 0.0% public transportation, 2.6% walk, 3.9% work from home (2000); Travel time to work: 12.5% less than 15 minutes, 54.6% 15 to 30 minutes, 23.7% 30 to 45 minutes, 4.2% 45 to 60 minutes, 5.0% 60 minutes or more (2000)
Additional Information Contacts
Paradise Chamber of Commerce 906-492-3219

PENINSULA (township). Covers a land area of 27.861 square miles and a water area of 3.978 square miles. Located at 44.87° N. Lat.; 85.53° W. Long.
Population: 5,265 (2000); Race: 97.8% White, 0.0% Black, 0.4% Asian, 0.0% American Indian and Alaska Native, 2.9% Hispanic of any race, 0.7% two or more races (2000); Density: 189.0 persons per square mile (2000); Age: 23.2% under 18, 20.0% over 64 (2000); Marriage status: 15.5% never married, 73.8% now married, 6.5% widowed, 4.3% divorced (2000); Foreign born: 2.9% (2000); Ancestry (includes multiple ancestries): 30.3% German, 18.9% English, 15.6% Irish, 8.3% Polish, 6.6% French (except Basque) (2000).
Economy: Employment by occupation: 21.1% management, 34.8% professional, 10.3% services, 26.1% sales, 1.2% farming, 3.4% construction, 3.1% production (2000).
Income: Per capita income: $40,753 (2000); Median household income: $66,019 (2000); Poverty rate: 2.3% (2000).
Taxes: Total city taxes per capita: $178 (2000); City property taxes per capita: $175 (2000).
Education: High school graduation rate: 96.6% (2000); College graduation rate: 53.2% (2000).
Housing: Homeownership rate: 89.6% (2000); Median home value: $246,600 (2000); Median rent: $486 per month (2000); Median age of housing: 23 years (2000).
Transportation: Commute to work: 89.2% car, 0.5% public transportation, 2.1% walk, 7.5% work from home (2000); Travel time to work: 30.8% less than 15 minutes, 47.0% 15 to 30 minutes, 13.9% 30 to 45 minutes, 2.1% 45 to 60 minutes, 6.2% 60 minutes or more (2000)

TRAVERSE CITY (city). Covers a land area of 8.406 square miles and a water area of 0.297 square miles. Located at 44.76° N. Lat.; 85.61° W. Long. Elevation is 599 feet.

History: Traverse City began in 1847 when the Boardmans, father and son, purchased land and built a mill near the mouth of Mill Creek. Other mills soon followed, and Traverse City was incorporated in 1895. Apples were the first commercial crop in Traverse City after the lumber mills closed, but it soon became known as the cherry capital of the state. The Traverse City Canning Company was established in 1907 to can cherries.
Population: 14,532 (2000); Race: 95.9% White, 0.8% Black, 1.0% Asian, 0.9% American Indian and Alaska Native, 1.2% Hispanic of any race, 1.0% two or more races (2000); Density: 1,728.7 persons per square mile (2000); Age: 20.2% under 18, 15.7% over 64 (2000); Marriage status: 28.2% never married, 49.9% now married, 7.2% widowed, 14.8% divorced (2000); Foreign born: 2.7% (2000); Ancestry (includes multiple ancestries): 25.8% German, 16.4% Irish, 16.0% English, 8.9% Polish, 7.6% Other groups (2000).
Economy: Single-family building permits issued: 0 (2001) / 0 (2000); Multi-family building permits issued: 0 (2001) / 0 (2000); Employment by occupation: 13.5% management, 20.6% professional, 18.0% services, 28.2% sales, 0.5% farming, 8.3% construction, 10.9% production (2000).
Income: Per capita income: $22,247 (2000); Median household income: $37,330 (2000); Poverty rate: 8.4% (2000).
Taxes: Total city taxes per capita: $457 (2000); City property taxes per capita: $444 (2000).
Education: High school graduation rate: 88.7% (2000); College graduation rate: 31.2% (2000).

School District(s)

Grand Traverse Academy (KG-06)
2000 Enrollment: 0 231-995-0665
Traverse Bay Community School (KG-08)
2000 Enrollment: 172 517-790-4000
Traverse City Area Public School (KG-12)
2000 Enrollment: 10,958 231-933-1727

Two-year College(s)

Northwestern Michigan College (Public)
2001 Enrollment: 4,251 616-922-1000
2001 Tuition: In-state $2,984; Out-of-state $3,392

Housing: Homeownership rate: 59.0% (2000); Median home value: $124,600 (2000); Median rent: $563 per month (2000); Median age of housing: 47 years (2000).
Hospitals: Munson Medical Center (368 beds)
Safety: Violent crime rate: 24.6 per 10,000 population; Property crime rate: 489.4 per 10,000 population (2001).
Newspapers: Northern Express Weekly (1 x week); The Business News (1 x month); The Grand Traverse Herald (1 x week); Traverse City Record-Eagle (7 x week); Preview Community Weekly (1 x week)
Transportation: Commute to work: 86.1% car, 1.2% public transportation, 6.0% walk, 4.0% work from home (2000); Travel time to work: 62.0% less than 15 minutes, 26.3% 15 to 30 minutes, 5.9% 30 to 45 minutes, 1.6% 45 to 60 minutes, 4.2% 60 minutes or more (2000); Amtrak: Service available.
Airports: Cherry Capital (primary service)

Additional Information Contacts

Traverse Area Association of Realtors 231-947-2050
Traverse City Chamber of Commerce 231-947-5075
Traverse City Convention Bureau 231-947-1120

UNION (township). Covers a land area of 35.818 square miles and a water area of 0.170 square miles. Located at 44.64° N. Lat.; 85.39° W. Long.
Population: 417 (2000); Race: 99.3% White, 0.0% Black, 0.0% Asian, 0.7% American Indian and Alaska Native, 0.0% Hispanic of any race, 0.0% two or more races (2000); Density: 11.6 persons per square mile (2000); Age: 30.4% under 18, 4.6% over 64 (2000); Marriage status: 22.4% never married, 63.0% now married, 3.9% widowed, 10.7% divorced (2000); Foreign born: 0.0% (2000); Ancestry (includes multiple ancestries): 23.6% English, 20.0% German, 7.5% French (except Basque), 7.5% Polish, 5.4% Scotch-Irish (2000).
Economy: Employment by occupation: 14.0% management, 23.3% professional, 10.2% services, 22.8% sales, 0.0% farming, 14.0% construction, 15.8% production (2000).
Income: Per capita income: $19,016 (2000); Median household income: $51,250 (2000); Poverty rate: 11.0% (2000).
Taxes: Total city taxes per capita: $51 (1997); City property taxes per capita: $51 (1997).
Education: High school graduation rate: 93.2% (2000); College graduation rate: 26.3% (2000).
Housing: Homeownership rate: 95.3% (2000); Median home value: $134,100 (2000); Median rent: $417 per month (2000); Median age of housing: 23 years (2000).
Transportation: Commute to work: 96.6% car, 0.0% public transportation, 0.0% walk, 2.4% work from home (2000); Travel time to work: 9.4% less than 15 minutes, 46.3% 15 to 30 minutes, 31.5% 30 to 45 minutes, 3.9% 45 to 60 minutes, 8.9% 60 minutes or more (2000)

WHITEWATER (township). Covers a land area of 47.823 square miles and a water area of 5.770 square miles. Located at 44.75° N. Lat.; 85.39° W. Long.
Population: 2,467 (2000); Race: 98.2% White, 0.1% Black, 0.7% Asian, 0.2% American Indian and Alaska Native, 1.3% Hispanic of any race, 0.7% two or more races (2000); Density: 51.6 persons per square mile (2000); Age: 28.0% under 18, 11.7% over 64 (2000); Marriage status: 19.6% never married, 67.2% now married, 3.2% widowed, 10.0% divorced (2000); Foreign born: 2.0% (2000); Ancestry (includes multiple ancestries): 29.7% German, 18.0% English, 13.1% Irish, 7.6% United States or American, 6.0% Polish (2000).
Economy: Employment by occupation: 13.1% management, 17.9% professional, 13.4% services, 25.0% sales, 0.5% farming, 13.4% construction, 16.6% production (2000).
Income: Per capita income: $21,890 (2000); Median household income: $49,572 (2000); Poverty rate: 4.9% (2000).
Taxes: Total city taxes per capita: $102 (2000); City property taxes per capita: $101 (2000).
Education: High school graduation rate: 90.6% (2000); College graduation rate: 22.8% (2000).
Housing: Homeownership rate: 90.1% (2000); Median home value: $137,000 (2000); Median rent: $446 per month (2000); Median age of housing: 22 years (2000).
Transportation: Commute to work: 91.7% car, 0.4% public transportation, 1.6% walk, 5.2% work from home (2000); Travel time to work: 18.2% less than 15 minutes, 47.2% 15 to 30 minutes, 27.4% 30 to 45 minutes, 2.3% 45 to 60 minutes, 4.8% 60 minutes or more (2000)

WILLIAMSBURG (unincorporated postal area, zip code 49690). Covers a land area of 81.996 square miles and a water area of 5.761 square miles. Located at 44.77° N. Lat.; 85.41° W. Long. Elevation is 732 feet.
Population: 6,682 (2000); Race: 96.8% White, 0.2% Black, 0.5% Asian, 0.2% American Indian and Alaska Native, 1.8% Hispanic of any race, 1.8% two or more races (2000); Density: 81.5 persons per square mile (2000); Age: 24.3% under 18, 14.3% over 64 (2000); Marriage status: 19.5% never married, 67.2% now married, 4.9% widowed, 8.3% divorced (2000); Foreign born: 3.4% (2000); Ancestry (includes multiple ancestries): 26.2% German, 16.7% English, 11.3% Irish, 9.8% Polish, 6.0% United States or American (2000).
Economy: Employment by occupation: 16.0% management, 19.8% professional, 12.4% services, 29.8% sales, 1.4% farming, 10.9% construction, 9.7% production (2000).
Income: Per capita income: $23,599 (2000); Median household income: $49,289 (2000); Poverty rate: 6.2% (2000).
Education: High school graduation rate: 90.9% (2000); College graduation rate: 30.6% (2000).
Housing: Homeownership rate: 83.0% (2000); Median home value: $149,500 (2000); Median rent: $614 per month (2000); Median age of housing: 18 years (2000).
Transportation: Commute to work: 90.9% car, 1.2% public transportation, 2.2% walk, 5.2% work from home (2000); Travel time to work: 28.2% less than 15 minutes, 46.3% 15 to 30 minutes, 18.9% 30 to 45 minutes, 2.0% 45 to 60 minutes, 4.6% 60 minutes or more (2000)

Gratiot County

Located in central Michigan; drained by the Maple, Pine, and Bad Rivers. Covers a land area of 570.10 square miles, a water area of 1.50 square miles, and is located in the Eastern Time Zone. The county government was organized in 1855. County seat is Ithaca.

Weather Station: Alma — Elevation: 757 feet

	Jan	Feb	Mar	Apr	May	Jun	Jul	Aug	Sep	Oct	Nov	Dec
High	29	32	42	56	70	79	83	81	72	60	45	34
Low	13	15	23	34	45	54	59	57	49	38	29	20
Precip	1.8	1.4	2.4	2.9	2.8	3.1	2.7	3.8	3.8	2.8	2.7	2.1
Snow	11.2	7.3	7.2	2.1	tr	0.0	0.0	0.0	0.0	0.3	3.3	8.8

High and Low temperatures in degrees Fahrenheit; Precipitation and Snow in inches

Population: 42,285 (2000); Race: 91.9% White, 3.9% Black, 0.4% Asian, 0.5% American Indian and Alaska Native, 4.3% Hispanic of any race, 1.5%

two or more races (2000); Density: 74.2 persons per square mile (2000); Age: 23.8% under 18, 13.5% over 64 (2000).
Religion: Five largest groups: 10.1% Catholic Church, 4.6% The United Methodist Church, 3.2% Christian Churches and Churches of Christ, 1.8% Presbyterian Church (U.S.A.), 1.8% Lutheran Church—Missouri Synod (2000).
Economy: Unemployment rate: 4.9% (11/2002); Total civilian labor force: 20,285 (11/2002); Leading industries: 23.3% manufacturing; 21.7% health care and social assistance; 13.9% retail trade (2000); Companies that employ more than 1,000 persons: 0 (2000); Companies that employ more than 100 persons: 18 (2000); Farms: 873 totaling 276,833 acres (1997); Minority business ownership rate: 0.0% (1997); Women business ownership rate: 22.9% (1997); Retail sales per capita: $7,399 (1997). Single-family building permits issued: 63 (2001) / 62 (2000); Multi-family building permits issued: 2 (2001) / 50 (2000).
Income: Per capita income: $17,118 (2000); Median household income: $37,262 (2000); Poverty rate: 10.3% (2000); Bankruptcy rate: 4.10% (2001).
Taxes: Total county taxes per capita: $94 (2000); County property taxes per capita: $88 (2000).
Education: High school graduation rate: 83.5% (2000); College graduation rate: 12.9% (2000).
Housing: Homeownership rate: 77.5% (2000); Median home value: $75,300 (2000); Median rent: $349 per month (2000); Median age of housing: 40 years (2000).
Health: Birth rate: 119.7 per 10,000 population (1998); Age adjusted death rate: 90.2 per 10,000 population (1999); Age adjusted cancer mortality rate: 199.4 deaths per 100,000 population (1999). Number of physicians: 13.2 per 10,000 population (1999); Number of hospital beds: 30.0 per 10,000 population (1999).
Elections: 2000 Presidential election results: 43.1% Gore, 54.8% Bush, 1.8% Nader, 0.1% Buchanan
Additional Information Contacts
Gratiot County Government Offices 989-875-5215
Alma Chamber of Commerce. 989-463-5525

Gratiot County Communities

ALMA (city). Covers a land area of 5.362 square miles and a water area of 0.102 square miles. Located at 43.37° N. Lat.; 84.65° W. Long. Elevation is 736 feet.
History: Alma was settled in 1853 by General Ralph Ely, who built a sawmill here and platted the village in 1856. First called Elyton, the name was changed to Alma by a Mr. Gargett when he platted an addition to the town. Alma was incorporated as a village in 1872 and as a city in 1905.
Population: 9,275 (2000); Race: 92.7% White, 0.9% Black, 0.7% Asian, 0.6% American Indian and Alaska Native, 6.3% Hispanic of any race, 2.0% two or more races (2000); Density: 1,729.7 persons per square mile (2000); Age: 21.6% under 18, 17.1% over 64 (2000); Marriage status: 34.9% never married, 43.8% now married, 11.3% widowed, 9.9% divorced (2000); Foreign born: 2.0% (2000); Ancestry (includes multiple ancestries): 23.7% German, 14.1% English, 11.4% Other groups, 10.7% Irish, 9.6% United States or American (2000).
Economy: Single-family building permits issued: 3 (2001) / 7 (2000); Multi-family building permits issued: 0 (2001) / 48 (2000); Employment by occupation: 10.6% management, 20.0% professional, 20.0% services, 25.1% sales, 0.1% farming, 7.1% construction, 17.2% production (2000).
Income: Per capita income: $18,218 (2000); Median household income: $33,536 (2000); Poverty rate: 11.6% (2000).
Taxes: Total city taxes per capita: $264 (1997); City property taxes per capita: $256 (1997).
Education: High school graduation rate: 84.3% (2000); College graduation rate: 20.2% (2000).

School District(s)

Alma Public Schools (PK-12)
2000 Enrollment: 2,480 517-463-3111

Four-year College(s)

Alma College (Private, Not-for-profit, Presbyterian Church (USA))
2001 Enrollment: 1,371 517-463-7111
2001 Tuition: In-state $16,442; Out-of-state $16,442
Housing: Homeownership rate: 62.6% (2000); Median home value: $72,500 (2000); Median rent: $353 per month (2000); Median age of housing: 42 years (2000).
Hospitals: Gratiot Health System (142 beds)
Safety: Violent crime rate: 2.1 per 10,000 population; Property crime rate: 305.7 per 10,000 population (2001).
Transportation: Commute to work: 84.3% car, 0.2% public transportation, 10.7% walk, 2.6% work from home (2000); Travel time to work: 64.4% less than 15 minutes, 21.7% 15 to 30 minutes, 5.4% 30 to 45 minutes, 2.1% 45 to 60 minutes, 6.3% 60 minutes or more (2000)
Airports: Gratiot Community
Additional Information Contacts
Alma Chamber of Commerce. 989-463-5525

ARCADA (township). Covers a land area of 32.539 square miles and a water area of 0.164 square miles. Located at 43.34° N. Lat.; 84.67° W. Long.
Population: 1,708 (2000); Race: 96.9% White, 0.0% Black, 0.0% Asian, 0.0% American Indian and Alaska Native, 3.7% Hispanic of any race, 2.2% two or more races (2000); Density: 52.5 persons per square mile (2000); Age: 27.0% under 18, 14.2% over 64 (2000); Marriage status: 19.1% never married, 68.5% now married, 7.7% widowed, 4.7% divorced (2000); Foreign born: 0.0% (2000); Ancestry (includes multiple ancestries): 26.6% German, 15.6% United States or American, 13.1% English, 11.5% Irish, 7.4% Other groups (2000).
Economy: Employment by occupation: 11.0% management, 17.0% professional, 18.3% services, 21.0% sales, 0.8% farming, 11.6% construction, 20.3% production (2000).
Income: Per capita income: $20,781 (2000); Median household income: $44,097 (2000); Poverty rate: 7.5% (2000).
Taxes: Total city taxes per capita: $33 (1997); City property taxes per capita: $32 (1997).
Education: High school graduation rate: 90.5% (2000); College graduation rate: 18.5% (2000).
Housing: Homeownership rate: 88.6% (2000); Median home value: $88,000 (2000); Median rent: $400 per month (2000); Median age of housing: 35 years (2000).
Transportation: Commute to work: 94.8% car, 0.0% public transportation, 1.9% walk, 3.3% work from home (2000); Travel time to work: 48.9% less than 15 minutes, 28.4% 15 to 30 minutes, 6.9% 30 to 45 minutes, 5.2% 45 to 60 minutes, 10.6% 60 minutes or more (2000)

ASHLEY (village). Covers a land area of 0.645 square miles and a water area of 0 square miles. Located at 43.18° N. Lat.; 84.47° W. Long. Elevation is 671 feet.
History: Ashley was laid out in 1883, and incorporated as a village in 1887. It was named for John M. Ashley, who was responsible for the railroad branch being built to the town.
Population: 526 (2000); Race: 97.7% White, 0.0% Black, 0.5% Asian, 0.0% American Indian and Alaska Native, 1.4% Hispanic of any race, 1.7% two or more races (2000); Density: 815.9 persons per square mile (2000); Age: 25.4% under 18, 19.0% over 64 (2000); Marriage status: 21.7% never married, 56.7% now married, 12.9% widowed, 8.7% divorced (2000); Foreign born: 0.9% (2000); Ancestry (includes multiple ancestries): 19.9% German, 14.3% English, 11.0% United States or American, 5.7% Other groups, 5.7% Irish (2000).
Economy: Employment by occupation: 8.5% management, 11.1% professional, 19.1% services, 18.7% sales, 2.6% farming, 11.9% construction, 28.1% production (2000).
Income: Per capita income: $15,714 (2000); Median household income: $32,917 (2000); Poverty rate: 14.1% (2000).
Taxes: Total city taxes per capita: $89 (1997); City property taxes per capita: $89 (1997).
Education: High school graduation rate: 72.4% (2000); College graduation rate: 7.3% (2000).

School District(s)

Ashley Community Schools (KG-12)
2000 Enrollment: 384 517-847-4000
Housing: Homeownership rate: 81.5% (2000); Median home value: $64,700 (2000); Median rent: $318 per month (2000); Median age of housing: 41 years (2000).
Transportation: Commute to work: 97.0% car, 0.0% public transportation, 3.0% walk, 0.0% work from home (2000); Travel time to work: 22.7% less than 15 minutes, 23.6% 15 to 30 minutes, 20.2% 30 to 45 minutes, 22.3% 45 to 60 minutes, 11.2% 60 minutes or more (2000)

BANNISTER (unincorporated postal area, zip code 48807). Covers a land area of 25.868 square miles and a water area of 0 square miles. Located at 43.14° N. Lat.; 84.41° W. Long.
Population: 920 (2000); Race: 98.6% White, 0.0% Black, 0.2% Asian, 0.3% American Indian and Alaska Native, 2.7% Hispanic of any race, 0.1% two or more races (2000); Density: 35.6 persons per square mile (2000); Age: 23.9% under 18, 12.7% over 64 (2000); Marriage status: 21.7% never married,

63.3% now married, 8.1% widowed, 6.9% divorced (2000); Foreign born: 1.5% (2000); Ancestry (includes multiple ancestries): 25.2% German, 14.8% English, 10.2% Czech, 9.8% United States or American, 6.4% Slovak (2000).
Economy: Employment by occupation: 6.5% management, 7.6% professional, 12.0% services, 14.4% sales, 2.1% farming, 15.7% construction, 41.8% production (2000).
Income: Per capita income: $19,412 (2000); Median household income: $35,441 (2000); Poverty rate: 13.5% (2000).
Education: High school graduation rate: 81.0% (2000); College graduation rate: 6.2% (2000).
Housing: Homeownership rate: 83.3% (2000); Median home value: $76,800 (2000); Median rent: $330 per month (2000); Median age of housing: 34 years (2000).
Transportation: Commute to work: 89.1% car, 0.5% public transportation, 2.4% walk, 6.7% work from home (2000); Travel time to work: 17.7% less than 15 minutes, 31.4% 15 to 30 minutes, 19.7% 30 to 45 minutes, 20.0% 45 to 60 minutes, 11.1% 60 minutes or more (2000)

BETHANY (township). Covers a land area of 35.188 square miles and a water area of 0.009 square miles. Located at 43.42° N. Lat.; 84.54° W. Long.
History: Bethany Township was organized in 1858, and named for a Lutheran mission, called Bethanien, that had been founded here in 1847.
Population: 3,492 (2000); Race: 64.8% White, 28.7% Black, 0.6% Asian, 1.7% American Indian and Alaska Native, 4.1% Hispanic of any race, 2.9% two or more races (2000); Density: 99.2 persons per square mile (2000); Age: 11.1% under 18, 5.4% over 64 (2000); Marriage status: 46.8% never married, 33.6% now married, 3.8% widowed, 15.7% divorced (2000); Foreign born: 1.1% (2000); Ancestry (includes multiple ancestries): 24.3% Other groups, 15.0% German, 7.8% English, 6.9% Irish, 4.9% United States or American (2000).
Economy: Employment by occupation: 9.5% management, 19.5% professional, 16.4% services, 20.6% sales, 2.6% farming, 10.4% construction, 20.9% production (2000).
Income: Per capita income: $15,177 (2000); Median household income: $43,177 (2000); Poverty rate: 7.6% (2000).
Taxes: Total city taxes per capita: $20 (1997); City property taxes per capita: $20 (1997).
Education: High school graduation rate: 79.2% (2000); College graduation rate: 8.5% (2000).
Housing: Homeownership rate: 87.3% (2000); Median home value: $85,400 (2000); Median rent: $332 per month (2000); Median age of housing: 39 years (2000).
Transportation: Commute to work: 92.8% car, 0.0% public transportation, 1.2% walk, 5.4% work from home (2000); Travel time to work: 43.7% less than 15 minutes, 35.1% 15 to 30 minutes, 12.9% 30 to 45 minutes, 3.4% 45 to 60 minutes, 4.8% 60 minutes or more (2000)

BRECKENRIDGE (village). Covers a land area of 1.056 square miles and a water area of 0 square miles. Located at 43.40° N. Lat.; 84.47° W. Long. Elevation is 726 feet.
History: Breckenridge grew up in 1872 around a station of the Pere Marquette Railroad. The village was named for Daniel W. and Justin A. Breckenridge, who owned a mill here.
Population: 1,339 (2000); Race: 94.2% White, 0.6% Black, 0.5% Asian, 0.0% American Indian and Alaska Native, 4.9% Hispanic of any race, 1.6% two or more races (2000); Density: 1,268.4 persons per square mile (2000); Age: 30.4% under 18, 10.0% over 64 (2000); Marriage status: 25.7% never married, 54.8% now married, 7.0% widowed, 12.5% divorced (2000); Foreign born: 0.6% (2000); Ancestry (includes multiple ancestries): 28.9% German, 11.5% United States or American, 11.4% Other groups, 9.7% English, 7.7% Irish (2000).
Economy: Employment by occupation: 9.8% management, 15.2% professional, 18.6% services, 24.1% sales, 0.3% farming, 7.7% construction, 24.4% production (2000).
Income: Per capita income: $16,204 (2000); Median household income: $36,200 (2000); Poverty rate: 8.3% (2000).
Taxes: Total city taxes per capita: $185 (1997); City property taxes per capita: $183 (1997).
Education: High school graduation rate: 87.2% (2000); College graduation rate: 14.0% (2000).

School District(s)

Breckenridge Community Schools (KG-12)
2000 Enrollment: 1,128 517-842-3182

Housing: Homeownership rate: 73.6% (2000); Median home value: $68,400 (2000); Median rent: $296 per month (2000); Median age of housing: 43 years (2000).
Safety: Violent crime rate: 7.4 per 10,000 population; Property crime rate: 118.9 per 10,000 population (2001).
Transportation: Commute to work: 93.2% car, 0.0% public transportation, 4.0% walk, 2.4% work from home (2000); Travel time to work: 34.3% less than 15 minutes, 31.6% 15 to 30 minutes, 21.2% 30 to 45 minutes, 7.9% 45 to 60 minutes, 5.0% 60 minutes or more (2000)

ELBA (township). Covers a land area of 35.124 square miles and a water area of 0 square miles. Located at 43.16° N. Lat.; 84.43° W. Long.
Population: 1,394 (2000); Race: 97.3% White, 0.1% Black, 0.3% Asian, 0.4% American Indian and Alaska Native, 2.7% Hispanic of any race, 1.4% two or more races (2000); Density: 39.7 persons per square mile (2000); Age: 25.1% under 18, 17.1% over 64 (2000); Marriage status: 20.9% never married, 62.7% now married, 10.7% widowed, 5.8% divorced (2000); Foreign born: 1.2% (2000); Ancestry (includes multiple ancestries): 20.7% German, 15.1% English, 12.6% United States or American, 8.1% Czech, 6.6% Slovak (2000).
Economy: Employment by occupation: 10.2% management, 8.8% professional, 14.4% services, 18.2% sales, 3.0% farming, 12.4% construction, 33.1% production (2000).
Income: Per capita income: $18,323 (2000); Median household income: $35,650 (2000); Poverty rate: 13.4% (2000).
Taxes: Total city taxes per capita: $50 (1997); City property taxes per capita: $48 (1997).
Education: High school graduation rate: 77.6% (2000); College graduation rate: 7.0% (2000).
Housing: Homeownership rate: 83.9% (2000); Median home value: $71,400 (2000); Median rent: $316 per month (2000); Median age of housing: 42 years (2000).
Transportation: Commute to work: 90.5% car, 0.3% public transportation, 3.2% walk, 4.9% work from home (2000); Travel time to work: 22.5% less than 15 minutes, 27.1% 15 to 30 minutes, 17.6% 30 to 45 minutes, 21.3% 45 to 60 minutes, 11.4% 60 minutes or more (2000)

ELWELL (unincorporated postal area, zip code 48832). Covers a land area of 23.227 square miles and a water area of 0 square miles. Located at 43.41° N. Lat.; 84.77° W. Long. Elevation is 775 feet.
Population: 1,434 (2000); Race: 99.2% White, 0.3% Black, 0.0% Asian, 0.0% American Indian and Alaska Native, 1.1% Hispanic of any race, 0.3% two or more races (2000); Density: 61.7 persons per square mile (2000); Age: 29.1% under 18, 11.2% over 64 (2000); Marriage status: 18.0% never married, 69.9% now married, 2.8% widowed, 9.3% divorced (2000); Foreign born: 0.1% (2000); Ancestry (includes multiple ancestries): 27.3% German, 17.5% English, 13.8% United States or American, 8.0% Irish, 8.0% Other groups (2000).
Economy: Employment by occupation: 11.5% management, 12.7% professional, 22.3% services, 23.5% sales, 0.5% farming, 14.1% construction, 15.5% production (2000).
Income: Per capita income: $16,307 (2000); Median household income: $43,068 (2000); Poverty rate: 10.6% (2000).
Education: High school graduation rate: 85.0% (2000); College graduation rate: 12.2% (2000).
Housing: Homeownership rate: 87.8% (2000); Median home value: $89,600 (2000); Median rent: $378 per month (2000); Median age of housing: 25 years (2000).
Transportation: Commute to work: 96.5% car, 0.0% public transportation, 0.6% walk, 2.9% work from home (2000); Travel time to work: 18.7% less than 15 minutes, 54.3% 15 to 30 minutes, 15.2% 30 to 45 minutes, 2.1% 45 to 60 minutes, 9.7% 60 minutes or more (2000)

EMERSON (township). Covers a land area of 35.202 square miles and a water area of 0 square miles. Located at 43.34° N. Lat.; 84.55° W. Long.
Population: 966 (2000); Race: 98.3% White, 0.0% Black, 0.0% Asian, 0.0% American Indian and Alaska Native, 3.3% Hispanic of any race, 0.0% two or more races (2000); Density: 27.4 persons per square mile (2000); Age: 26.8% under 18, 14.4% over 64 (2000); Marriage status: 17.2% never married, 69.6% now married, 4.6% widowed, 8.6% divorced (2000); Foreign born: 1.0% (2000); Ancestry (includes multiple ancestries): 31.6% German, 14.8% English, 12.4% United States or American, 10.1% Irish, 5.6% French (except Basque) (2000).
Economy: Employment by occupation: 11.1% management, 13.6% professional, 15.4% services, 23.4% sales, 3.5% farming, 9.4% construction, 23.6% production (2000).
Income: Per capita income: $18,159 (2000); Median household income: $45,054 (2000); Poverty rate: 12.0% (2000).

Taxes: Total city taxes per capita: $47 (1997); City property taxes per capita: $47 (1997).
Education: High school graduation rate: 86.3% (2000); College graduation rate: 11.6% (2000).
Housing: Homeownership rate: 82.7% (2000); Median home value: $78,800 (2000); Median rent: $363 per month (2000); Median age of housing: 45 years (2000).
Transportation: Commute to work: 94.3% car, 0.0% public transportation, 0.8% walk, 4.9% work from home (2000); Travel time to work: 47.9% less than 15 minutes, 30.2% 15 to 30 minutes, 11.8% 30 to 45 minutes, 6.0% 45 to 60 minutes, 4.2% 60 minutes or more (2000)

FULTON (township). Covers a land area of 35.203 square miles and a water area of 0.560 square miles. Located at 43.16° N. Lat.; 84.67° W. Long.
Population: 2,413 (2000); Race: 96.7% White, 0.0% Black, 0.0% Asian, 0.2% American Indian and Alaska Native, 3.2% Hispanic of any race, 1.2% two or more races (2000); Density: 68.5 persons per square mile (2000); Age: 26.8% under 18, 13.3% over 64 (2000); Marriage status: 21.9% never married, 64.1% now married, 5.6% widowed, 8.3% divorced (2000); Foreign born: 0.7% (2000); Ancestry (includes multiple ancestries): 27.7% German, 16.4% English, 14.5% United States or American, 10.1% Irish, 6.9% Other groups (2000).
Economy: Employment by occupation: 7.8% management, 14.5% professional, 14.9% services, 23.4% sales, 3.6% farming, 10.8% construction, 25.0% production (2000).
Income: Per capita income: $19,101 (2000); Median household income: $41,667 (2000); Poverty rate: 10.8% (2000).
Taxes: Total city taxes per capita: $19 (1997); City property taxes per capita: $19 (1997).
Education: High school graduation rate: 87.7% (2000); College graduation rate: 12.6% (2000).
Housing: Homeownership rate: 84.9% (2000); Median home value: $89,500 (2000); Median rent: $373 per month (2000); Median age of housing: 36 years (2000).
Transportation: Commute to work: 94.5% car, 0.0% public transportation, 0.6% walk, 3.3% work from home (2000); Travel time to work: 18.3% less than 15 minutes, 24.1% 15 to 30 minutes, 26.0% 30 to 45 minutes, 16.4% 45 to 60 minutes, 15.1% 60 minutes or more (2000)

HAMILTON (township). Covers a land area of 34.849 square miles and a water area of 0.071 square miles. Located at 43.25° N. Lat.; 84.44° W. Long.
Population: 491 (2000); Race: 95.1% White, 0.0% Black, 0.4% Asian, 0.9% American Indian and Alaska Native, 2.0% Hispanic of any race, 2.2% two or more races (2000); Density: 14.1 persons per square mile (2000); Age: 21.8% under 18, 14.9% over 64 (2000); Marriage status: 25.1% never married, 59.7% now married, 6.1% widowed, 9.1% divorced (2000); Foreign born: 1.3% (2000); Ancestry (includes multiple ancestries): 20.4% United States or American, 18.0% German, 14.9% English, 11.1% Irish, 5.3% Polish (2000).
Economy: Employment by occupation: 11.4% management, 8.6% professional, 20.0% services, 20.5% sales, 0.5% farming, 11.4% construction, 27.6% production (2000).
Income: Per capita income: $18,715 (2000); Median household income: $46,607 (2000); Poverty rate: 3.1% (2000).
Taxes: Total city taxes per capita: $24 (1997); City property taxes per capita: $24 (1997).
Education: High school graduation rate: 81.2% (2000); College graduation rate: 6.5% (2000).
Housing: Homeownership rate: 86.4% (2000); Median home value: $60,000 (2000); Median rent: $375 per month (2000); Median age of housing: 38 years (2000).
Transportation: Commute to work: 96.6% car, 0.0% public transportation, 0.0% walk, 3.4% work from home (2000); Travel time to work: 12.6% less than 15 minutes, 42.4% 15 to 30 minutes, 16.2% 30 to 45 minutes, 17.2% 45 to 60 minutes, 11.6% 60 minutes or more (2000)

ITHACA (city). Covers a land area of 4.077 square miles and a water area of 0 square miles. Located at 43.29° N. Lat.; 84.60° W. Long. Elevation is 747 feet.
History: Ithaca was settled in the 1850's and developed as the center of a farming community. First called Gratiot Center, it was renamed in 1857 for Ithaca, New York. The economy was boosted in the 1920's by the discovery of oil in the county.
Population: 3,098 (2000); Race: 97.7% White, 0.0% Black, 0.1% Asian, 0.5% American Indian and Alaska Native, 5.9% Hispanic of any race, 1.2% two or more races (2000); Density: 759.9 persons per square mile (2000); Age: 27.4% under 18, 14.2% over 64 (2000); Marriage status: 24.9% never married, 56.7% now married, 8.8% widowed, 9.6% divorced (2000); Foreign born: 1.1% (2000); Ancestry (includes multiple ancestries): 25.5% German, 16.5% English, 15.0% United States or American, 7.8% Irish, 7.3% Other groups (2000).
Economy: Single-family building permits issued: 11 (2001) / 2 (2000); Multi-family building permits issued: 0 (2001) / 0 (2000); Employment by occupation: 9.4% management, 11.1% professional, 17.1% services, 22.7% sales, 1.9% farming, 8.8% construction, 29.0% production (2000).
Income: Per capita income: $17,291 (2000); Median household income: $35,045 (2000); Poverty rate: 11.5% (2000).
Taxes: Total city taxes per capita: $199 (1997); City property taxes per capita: $194 (1997).
Education: High school graduation rate: 82.1% (2000); College graduation rate: 12.6% (2000).

School District(s)

Ithaca Public Schools (KG-12)
2000 Enrollment: 1,549 517-875-3700
Housing: Homeownership rate: 71.9% (2000); Median home value: $72,700 (2000); Median rent: $364 per month (2000); Median age of housing: 46 years (2000).
Newspapers: Gratiot County Herald (1 x week)
Transportation: Commute to work: 92.8% car, 0.0% public transportation, 4.3% walk, 2.7% work from home (2000); Travel time to work: 39.9% less than 15 minutes, 40.4% 15 to 30 minutes, 10.1% 30 to 45 minutes, 4.5% 45 to 60 minutes, 5.1% 60 minutes or more (2000)

LAFAYETTE (township). Covers a land area of 36.023 square miles and a water area of 0 square miles. Located at 43.33° N. Lat.; 84.42° W. Long.
Population: 656 (2000); Race: 96.5% White, 0.0% Black, 0.0% Asian, 0.2% American Indian and Alaska Native, 4.6% Hispanic of any race, 0.3% two or more races (2000); Density: 18.2 persons per square mile (2000); Age: 26.5% under 18, 13.9% over 64 (2000); Marriage status: 20.8% never married, 64.2% now married, 7.1% widowed, 7.9% divorced (2000); Foreign born: 0.8% (2000); Ancestry (includes multiple ancestries): 32.8% German, 16.4% United States or American, 15.9% English, 8.2% Irish, 6.6% French (except Basque) (2000).
Economy: Employment by occupation: 13.3% management, 13.3% professional, 12.9% services, 24.8% sales, 2.2% farming, 14.0% construction, 19.4% production (2000).
Income: Per capita income: $17,203 (2000); Median household income: $43,229 (2000); Poverty rate: 6.0% (2000).
Taxes: Total city taxes per capita: $88 (1997); City property taxes per capita: $88 (1997).
Education: High school graduation rate: 90.5% (2000); College graduation rate: 11.7% (2000).
Housing: Homeownership rate: 84.7% (2000); Median home value: $76,000 (2000); Median rent: $329 per month (2000); Median age of housing: 58 years (2000).
Transportation: Commute to work: 94.0% car, 0.0% public transportation, 0.4% walk, 5.6% work from home (2000); Travel time to work: 19.1% less than 15 minutes, 35.5% 15 to 30 minutes, 25.9% 30 to 45 minutes, 17.1% 45 to 60 minutes, 2.4% 60 minutes or more (2000)

MIDDLETON (unincorporated postal area, zip code 48856). Covers a land area of 27.552 square miles and a water area of 0 square miles. Located at 43.19° N. Lat.; 84.73° W. Long.
Population: 937 (2000); Race: 99.6% White, 0.0% Black, 0.0% Asian, 0.0% American Indian and Alaska Native, 2.9% Hispanic of any race, 0.4% two or more races (2000); Density: 34.0 persons per square mile (2000); Age: 31.9% under 18, 13.8% over 64 (2000); Marriage status: 22.7% never married, 64.1% now married, 4.1% widowed, 9.0% divorced (2000); Foreign born: 0.2% (2000); Ancestry (includes multiple ancestries): 25.8% German, 19.2% United States or American, 14.7% English, 7.1% Irish, 5.3% Other groups (2000).
Economy: Employment by occupation: 14.7% management, 15.6% professional, 17.3% services, 13.0% sales, 6.0% farming, 12.5% construction, 20.9% production (2000).
Income: Per capita income: $18,440 (2000); Median household income: $37,563 (2000); Poverty rate: 13.7% (2000).
Education: High school graduation rate: 81.6% (2000); College graduation rate: 11.6% (2000).

School District(s)

Fulton Schools (PK-12)
2000 Enrollment: 987 517-236-7300

Housing: Homeownership rate: 77.1% (2000); Median home value: $71,800 (2000); Median rent: $370 per month (2000); Median age of housing: 60+ years (2000).
Transportation: Commute to work: 88.1% car, 0.0% public transportation, 2.4% walk, 8.3% work from home (2000); Travel time to work: 31.8% less than 15 minutes, 22.0% 15 to 30 minutes, 24.7% 30 to 45 minutes, 11.4% 45 to 60 minutes, 10.1% 60 minutes or more (2000)

NEW HAVEN (township). Covers a land area of 35.526 square miles and a water area of 0.076 square miles. Located at 43.24° N. Lat.; 84.77° W. Long.
Population: 1,016 (2000); Race: 99.0% White, 0.0% Black, 0.2% Asian, 0.0% American Indian and Alaska Native, 1.4% Hispanic of any race, 0.8% two or more races (2000); Density: 28.6 persons per square mile (2000); Age: 28.9% under 18, 13.3% over 64 (2000); Marriage status: 19.6% never married, 65.2% now married, 8.4% widowed, 6.8% divorced (2000); Foreign born: 0.9% (2000); Ancestry (includes multiple ancestries): 26.6% German, 18.7% United States or American, 14.9% English, 7.1% Irish, 6.2% Other groups (2000).
Economy: Employment by occupation: 15.6% management, 14.7% professional, 14.5% services, 16.0% sales, 3.4% farming, 12.2% construction, 23.7% production (2000).
Income: Per capita income: $16,085 (2000); Median household income: $39,048 (2000); Poverty rate: 13.4% (2000).
Taxes: Total city taxes per capita: $21 (1997); City property taxes per capita: $21 (1997).
Education: High school graduation rate: 79.9% (2000); College graduation rate: 9.7% (2000).
Housing: Homeownership rate: 89.5% (2000); Median home value: $87,100 (2000); Median rent: $367 per month (2000); Median age of housing: 42 years (2000).
Transportation: Commute to work: 90.0% car, 0.0% public transportation, 3.1% walk, 6.6% work from home (2000); Travel time to work: 26.2% less than 15 minutes, 39.3% 15 to 30 minutes, 15.0% 30 to 45 minutes, 7.2% 45 to 60 minutes, 12.4% 60 minutes or more (2000)

NEWARK (township). Covers a land area of 34.411 square miles and a water area of 0 square miles. Located at 43.23° N. Lat.; 84.66° W. Long. Elevation is 751 feet.
Population: 1,149 (2000); Race: 98.5% White, 0.2% Black, 0.0% Asian, 0.0% American Indian and Alaska Native, 1.2% Hispanic of any race, 0.9% two or more races (2000); Density: 33.4 persons per square mile (2000); Age: 28.6% under 18, 12.5% over 64 (2000); Marriage status: 22.5% never married, 62.9% now married, 6.4% widowed, 8.2% divorced (2000); Foreign born: 1.2% (2000); Ancestry (includes multiple ancestries): 33.0% German, 12.4% United States or American, 12.3% English, 7.4% Irish, 6.2% Other groups (2000).
Economy: Employment by occupation: 11.0% management, 11.2% professional, 15.7% services, 17.0% sales, 8.0% farming, 13.8% construction, 23.3% production (2000).
Income: Per capita income: $17,269 (2000); Median household income: $44,659 (2000); Poverty rate: 3.2% (2000).
Taxes: Total city taxes per capita: $21 (1997); City property taxes per capita: $21 (1997).
Education: High school graduation rate: 80.0% (2000); College graduation rate: 8.6% (2000).
Housing: Homeownership rate: 78.1% (2000); Median home value: $90,800 (2000); Median rent: $308 per month (2000); Median age of housing: 43 years (2000).
Transportation: Commute to work: 86.5% car, 0.0% public transportation, 2.3% walk, 9.0% work from home (2000); Travel time to work: 37.7% less than 15 minutes, 29.7% 15 to 30 minutes, 12.4% 30 to 45 minutes, 8.0% 45 to 60 minutes, 12.2% 60 minutes or more (2000)

NORTH SHADE (township). Covers a land area of 35.608 square miles and a water area of 0.008 square miles. Located at 43.16° N. Lat.; 84.76° W. Long.
Population: 706 (2000); Race: 98.3% White, 0.0% Black, 0.0% Asian, 0.3% American Indian and Alaska Native, 1.6% Hispanic of any race, 0.9% two or more races (2000); Density: 19.8 persons per square mile (2000); Age: 33.6% under 18, 12.7% over 64 (2000); Marriage status: 16.4% never married, 70.5% now married, 4.0% widowed, 9.1% divorced (2000); Foreign born: 0.9% (2000); Ancestry (includes multiple ancestries): 28.3% German, 17.4% United States or American, 14.4% English, 8.1% Irish, 6.0% Dutch (2000).
Economy: Employment by occupation: 16.4% management, 14.8% professional, 18.6% services, 18.2% sales, 2.8% farming, 10.1% construction, 19.2% production (2000).
Income: Per capita income: $19,583 (2000); Median household income: $43,000 (2000); Poverty rate: 3.8% (2000).
Taxes: Total city taxes per capita: $24 (1997); City property taxes per capita: $24 (1997).
Education: High school graduation rate: 88.8% (2000); College graduation rate: 13.6% (2000).
Housing: Homeownership rate: 87.9% (2000); Median home value: $84,300 (2000); Median rent: $381 per month (2000); Median age of housing: 60+ years (2000).
Transportation: Commute to work: 85.3% car, 0.0% public transportation, 0.6% walk, 13.4% work from home (2000); Travel time to work: 35.4% less than 15 minutes, 23.2% 15 to 30 minutes, 19.9% 30 to 45 minutes, 9.6% 45 to 60 minutes, 11.8% 60 minutes or more (2000)

NORTH STAR (township). Aka Northstar. Covers a land area of 34.526 square miles and a water area of 0.040 square miles. Located at 43.24° N. Lat.; 84.54° W. Long. Elevation is 717 feet.
Population: 996 (2000); Race: 97.3% White, 0.1% Black, 0.0% Asian, 0.5% American Indian and Alaska Native, 1.5% Hispanic of any race, 1.2% two or more races (2000); Density: 28.8 persons per square mile (2000); Age: 24.3% under 18, 15.7% over 64 (2000); Marriage status: 21.9% never married, 67.3% now married, 5.3% widowed, 5.5% divorced (2000); Foreign born: 0.9% (2000); Ancestry (includes multiple ancestries): 22.3% German, 16.4% English, 15.8% United States or American, 11.7% Irish, 6.3% Other groups (2000).
Economy: Employment by occupation: 10.7% management, 12.4% professional, 14.3% services, 24.2% sales, 1.9% farming, 7.6% construction, 29.0% production (2000).
Income: Per capita income: $19,246 (2000); Median household income: $38,750 (2000); Poverty rate: 12.2% (2000).
Taxes: Total city taxes per capita: $35 (1997); City property taxes per capita: $35 (1997).
Education: High school graduation rate: 82.7% (2000); College graduation rate: 9.8% (2000).
Housing: Homeownership rate: 84.8% (2000); Median home value: $72,500 (2000); Median rent: $361 per month (2000); Median age of housing: 54 years (2000).
Transportation: Commute to work: 90.1% car, 0.0% public transportation, 3.9% walk, 4.7% work from home (2000); Travel time to work: 28.2% less than 15 minutes, 42.9% 15 to 30 minutes, 13.7% 30 to 45 minutes, 10.3% 45 to 60 minutes, 4.9% 60 minutes or more (2000)

PERRINTON (village). Covers a land area of 0.628 square miles and a water area of 0 square miles. Located at 43.18° N. Lat.; 84.68° W. Long.
History: Perrinton was established when the Toledo, Saginaw & Muskegon Railroad was built through here in 1886. The Perrin for whom it was named was the head of a law firm that had interests in the land here.
Population: 439 (2000); Race: 94.6% White, 0.0% Black, 0.0% Asian, 0.0% American Indian and Alaska Native, 2.7% Hispanic of any race, 2.7% two or more races (2000); Density: 699.4 persons per square mile (2000); Age: 25.9% under 18, 11.3% over 64 (2000); Marriage status: 27.0% never married, 51.3% now married, 6.8% widowed, 14.8% divorced (2000); Foreign born: 0.0% (2000); Ancestry (includes multiple ancestries): 28.6% German, 18.4% United States or American, 8.8% Other groups, 8.8% English, 7.5% Irish (2000).
Economy: Employment by occupation: 0.5% management, 6.2% professional, 29.4% services, 26.8% sales, 2.6% farming, 9.8% construction, 24.7% production (2000).
Income: Per capita income: $16,988 (2000); Median household income: $34,500 (2000); Poverty rate: 14.4% (2000).
Taxes: Total city taxes per capita: $74 (1997); City property taxes per capita: $74 (1997).
Education: High school graduation rate: 87.3% (2000); College graduation rate: 5.5% (2000).
Housing: Homeownership rate: 74.0% (2000); Median home value: $57,000 (2000); Median rent: $365 per month (2000); Median age of housing: 41 years (2000).
Transportation: Commute to work: 90.1% car, 0.0% public transportation, 1.6% walk, 5.2% work from home (2000); Travel time to work: 27.5% less than 15 minutes, 31.9% 15 to 30 minutes, 18.1% 30 to 45 minutes, 12.1% 45 to 60 minutes, 10.4% 60 minutes or more (2000)

PINE RIVER (township). Covers a land area of 30.711 square miles and a water area of 0.092 square miles. Located at 43.41° N. Lat.; 84.66° W. Long.
Population: 2,451 (2000); Race: 95.1% White, 0.5% Black, 1.7% Asian, 0.6% American Indian and Alaska Native, 1.6% Hispanic of any race, 1.7% two or more races (2000); Density: 79.8 persons per square mile (2000); Age: 26.7% under 18, 15.3% over 64 (2000); Marriage status: 18.2% never married, 64.6% now married, 7.2% widowed, 10.0% divorced (2000); Foreign born: 2.4% (2000); Ancestry (includes multiple ancestries): 29.1% German, 12.5% United States or American, 10.7% Irish, 9.8% English, 8.0% Other groups (2000).
Economy: Employment by occupation: 10.2% management, 13.9% professional, 23.4% services, 24.3% sales, 0.3% farming, 7.6% construction, 20.3% production (2000).
Income: Per capita income: $16,504 (2000); Median household income: $36,615 (2000); Poverty rate: 6.3% (2000).
Taxes: Total city taxes per capita: $64 (1997); City property taxes per capita: $61 (1997).
Education: High school graduation rate: 85.4% (2000); College graduation rate: 13.2% (2000).
Housing: Homeownership rate: 90.0% (2000); Median home value: $87,600 (2000); Median rent: $367 per month (2000); Median age of housing: 30 years (2000).
Transportation: Commute to work: 92.0% car, 0.0% public transportation, 1.5% walk, 6.0% work from home (2000); Travel time to work: 55.3% less than 15 minutes, 29.8% 15 to 30 minutes, 3.7% 30 to 45 minutes, 1.8% 45 to 60 minutes, 9.4% 60 minutes or more (2000)

RIVERDALE (unincorporated postal area, zip code 48877). Covers a land area of 39.228 square miles and a water area of 0.236 square miles. Located at 43.40° N. Lat.; 84.84° W. Long.
History: Riverdale was founded in 1874 by Arthur G. Newton, who named it for its location on the Pine River.
Population: 2,477 (2000); Race: 96.6% White, 0.0% Black, 0.0% Asian, 0.3% American Indian and Alaska Native, 1.9% Hispanic of any race, 2.3% two or more races (2000); Density: 63.1 persons per square mile (2000); Age: 30.0% under 18, 9.7% over 64 (2000); Marriage status: 25.9% never married, 58.8% now married, 3.5% widowed, 11.8% divorced (2000); Foreign born: 1.1% (2000); Ancestry (includes multiple ancestries): 26.6% German, 15.5% United States or American, 15.0% English, 9.2% Other groups, 8.0% Irish (2000).
Economy: Employment by occupation: 6.9% management, 13.1% professional, 22.9% services, 19.6% sales, 1.7% farming, 7.9% construction, 27.8% production (2000).
Income: Per capita income: $15,309 (2000); Median household income: $36,818 (2000); Poverty rate: 12.8% (2000).
Education: High school graduation rate: 81.4% (2000); College graduation rate: 8.0% (2000).
Housing: Homeownership rate: 83.8% (2000); Median home value: $66,600 (2000); Median rent: $328 per month (2000); Median age of housing: 27 years (2000).
Transportation: Commute to work: 92.2% car, 0.0% public transportation, 1.1% walk, 6.1% work from home (2000); Travel time to work: 16.7% less than 15 minutes, 59.8% 15 to 30 minutes, 13.2% 30 to 45 minutes, 3.1% 45 to 60 minutes, 7.2% 60 minutes or more (2000)

SAINT LOUIS (city). Covers a land area of 2.865 square miles and a water area of 0.156 square miles. Located at 43.40° N. Lat.; 84.61° W. Long. Elevation is 740 feet.
History: St. Louis was settled in 1853 around a sawmill. First called Pine River, it was consolidated with a nearby settlement called St. Louis in 1865. St. Louis later grew as a spa and health resort when the therapeutic value of its water was discovered. The mineral baths were especially sought by those suffering from rheumatism.
Population: 4,494 (2000); Race: 82.8% White, 11.6% Black, 0.6% Asian, 0.8% American Indian and Alaska Native, 7.3% Hispanic of any race, 1.1% two or more races (2000); Density: 1,568.4 persons per square mile (2000); Age: 19.3% under 18, 12.0% over 64 (2000); Marriage status: 35.5% never married, 45.1% now married, 5.6% widowed, 13.8% divorced (2000); Foreign born: 1.3% (2000); Ancestry (includes multiple ancestries): 20.1% Other groups, 19.2% German, 11.6% English, 9.2% United States or American, 9.0% Irish (2000).
Economy: Single-family building permits issued: 4 (2001) / 4 (2000); Multi-family building permits issued: 2 (2001) / 2 (2000); Employment by occupation: 6.4% management, 14.6% professional, 24.3% services, 24.0% sales, 1.2% farming, 7.2% construction, 22.3% production (2000).
Income: Per capita income: $14,196 (2000); Median household income: $31,122 (2000); Poverty rate: 15.9% (2000).
Education: High school graduation rate: 82.5% (2000); College graduation rate: 12.8% (2000).

School District(s)

Saint Louis Public Schools (KG-12)
2000 Enrollment: 1,294 517-681-2545
Housing: Homeownership rate: 69.6% (2000); Median home value: $63,100 (2000); Median rent: $328 per month (2000); Median age of housing: 44 years (2000).
Safety: Violent crime rate: 28.8 per 10,000 population; Property crime rate: 278.9 per 10,000 population (2001).
Transportation: Commute to work: 92.8% car, 0.0% public transportation, 2.6% walk, 2.9% work from home (2000); Travel time to work: 64.6% less than 15 minutes, 20.9% 15 to 30 minutes, 5.8% 30 to 45 minutes, 3.8% 45 to 60 minutes, 4.9% 60 minutes or more (2000)

SEVILLE (township). Covers a land area of 35.742 square miles and a water area of 0.132 square miles. Located at 43.41° N. Lat.; 84.79° W. Long.
History: Seville Township was organized in 1856, the first settler in the area having arrived the previous year.
Population: 2,375 (2000); Race: 99.0% White, 0.2% Black, 0.0% Asian, 0.0% American Indian and Alaska Native, 0.9% Hispanic of any race, 0.7% two or more races (2000); Density: 66.4 persons per square mile (2000); Age: 28.5% under 18, 11.3% over 64 (2000); Marriage status: 21.5% never married, 63.5% now married, 3.1% widowed, 11.9% divorced (2000); Foreign born: 0.0% (2000); Ancestry (includes multiple ancestries): 28.5% German, 17.6% United States or American, 15.2% English, 7.1% Irish, 6.7% Other groups (2000).
Economy: Employment by occupation: 10.5% management, 13.7% professional, 22.0% services, 21.0% sales, 1.1% farming, 11.3% construction, 20.5% production (2000).
Income: Per capita income: $16,400 (2000); Median household income: $40,809 (2000); Poverty rate: 12.8% (2000).
Taxes: Total city taxes per capita: $12 (1997); City property taxes per capita: $12 (1997).
Education: High school graduation rate: 84.0% (2000); College graduation rate: 10.4% (2000).
Housing: Homeownership rate: 87.4% (2000); Median home value: $83,800 (2000); Median rent: $374 per month (2000); Median age of housing: 27 years (2000).
Transportation: Commute to work: 94.8% car, 0.0% public transportation, 0.7% walk, 4.5% work from home (2000); Travel time to work: 19.0% less than 15 minutes, 59.6% 15 to 30 minutes, 12.8% 30 to 45 minutes, 1.5% 45 to 60 minutes, 7.2% 60 minutes or more (2000)

SUMNER (township). Covers a land area of 35.895 square miles and a water area of 0.036 square miles. Located at 43.32° N. Lat.; 84.79° W. Long. Elevation is 764 feet.
History: Sumner Township was organized in 1855 and named for pioneer settler Charles Sumner. For a time the village here was called Belltown, for its principal landowner, and later Stover, for its first storekeeper.
Population: 1,911 (2000); Race: 96.5% White, 0.2% Black, 0.0% Asian, 0.4% American Indian and Alaska Native, 2.7% Hispanic of any race, 1.9% two or more races (2000); Density: 53.2 persons per square mile (2000); Age: 26.9% under 18, 11.7% over 64 (2000); Marriage status: 24.6% never married, 61.3% now married, 4.3% widowed, 9.8% divorced (2000); Foreign born: 1.0% (2000); Ancestry (includes multiple ancestries): 22.7% United States or American, 20.5% German, 15.2% English, 8.9% Other groups, 6.4% Irish (2000).
Economy: Employment by occupation: 9.0% management, 12.2% professional, 20.5% services, 19.6% sales, 2.0% farming, 10.0% construction, 26.8% production (2000).
Income: Per capita income: $16,034 (2000); Median household income: $38,309 (2000); Poverty rate: 9.6% (2000).
Taxes: Total city taxes per capita: $34 (1997); City property taxes per capita: $34 (1997).
Education: High school graduation rate: 78.5% (2000); College graduation rate: 7.5% (2000).
Housing: Homeownership rate: 82.3% (2000); Median home value: $69,200 (2000); Median rent: $339 per month (2000); Median age of housing: 33 years (2000).
Transportation: Commute to work: 91.0% car, 0.0% public transportation, 1.3% walk, 5.8% work from home (2000); Travel time to work: 14.5% less

than 15 minutes, 50.2% 15 to 30 minutes, 16.5% 30 to 45 minutes, 8.5% 45 to 60 minutes, 10.2% 60 minutes or more (2000)

WASHINGTON (township). Covers a land area of 35.441 square miles and a water area of 0.035 square miles. Located at 43.15° N. Lat.; 84.53° W. Long.
Population: 909 (2000); Race: 98.4% White, 0.0% Black, 0.0% Asian, 0.5% American Indian and Alaska Native, 2.0% Hispanic of any race, 0.0% two or more races (2000); Density: 25.6 persons per square mile (2000); Age: 24.6% under 18, 12.4% over 64 (2000); Marriage status: 19.4% never married, 68.8% now married, 6.0% widowed, 5.8% divorced (2000); Foreign born: 1.2% (2000); Ancestry (includes multiple ancestries): 27.1% German, 21.0% United States or American, 13.8% English, 9.4% Irish, 5.4% French (except Basque) (2000).
Economy: Employment by occupation: 10.6% management, 13.0% professional, 11.6% services, 21.1% sales, 3.0% farming, 8.6% construction, 32.2% production (2000).
Income: Per capita income: $16,859 (2000); Median household income: $40,958 (2000); Poverty rate: 4.2% (2000).
Taxes: Total city taxes per capita: $21 (1997); City property taxes per capita: $21 (1997).
Education: High school graduation rate: 84.5% (2000); College graduation rate: 6.2% (2000).
Housing: Homeownership rate: 81.9% (2000); Median home value: $80,600 (2000); Median rent: $315 per month (2000); Median age of housing: 52 years (2000).
Transportation: Commute to work: 92.2% car, 0.0% public transportation, 1.7% walk, 5.4% work from home (2000); Travel time to work: 18.5% less than 15 minutes, 37.4% 15 to 30 minutes, 21.7% 30 to 45 minutes, 13.0% 45 to 60 minutes, 9.5% 60 minutes or more (2000)

WHEELER (township). Covers a land area of 35.836 square miles and a water area of 0 square miles. Located at 43.41° N. Lat.; 84.44° W. Long.
Population: 2,785 (2000); Race: 94.8% White, 0.3% Black, 0.2% Asian, 0.1% American Indian and Alaska Native, 5.2% Hispanic of any race, 1.4% two or more races (2000); Density: 77.7 persons per square mile (2000); Age: 27.9% under 18, 12.0% over 64 (2000); Marriage status: 20.6% never married, 63.0% now married, 6.2% widowed, 10.2% divorced (2000); Foreign born: 0.7% (2000); Ancestry (includes multiple ancestries): 28.2% German, 11.8% English, 9.7% Other groups, 9.0% United States or American, 5.9% Irish (2000).
Economy: Employment by occupation: 8.2% management, 15.6% professional, 19.0% services, 20.7% sales, 0.5% farming, 10.5% construction, 25.5% production (2000).
Income: Per capita income: $16,006 (2000); Median household income: $35,688 (2000); Poverty rate: 7.2% (2000).
Taxes: Total city taxes per capita: $20 (1997); City property taxes per capita: $20 (1997).
Education: High school graduation rate: 85.8% (2000); College graduation rate: 11.5% (2000).
Housing: Homeownership rate: 82.1% (2000); Median home value: $68,400 (2000); Median rent: $313 per month (2000); Median age of housing: 44 years (2000).
Transportation: Commute to work: 94.6% car, 0.0% public transportation, 2.8% walk, 2.3% work from home (2000); Travel time to work: 29.6% less than 15 minutes, 32.3% 15 to 30 minutes, 25.1% 30 to 45 minutes, 6.4% 45 to 60 minutes, 6.6% 60 minutes or more (2000)

Hillsdale County

Located in southern Michigan; bounded on the south by Ohio; drained by headstreams of the Kalamazoo and St. Joseph Rivers; includes many small lakes. Covers a land area of 598.80 square miles, a water area of 8.30 square miles, and is located in the Eastern Time Zone. The county government was organized in 1835. County seat is Hillsdale.

Weather Station: Hillsdale — Elevation: 1,079 feet

	Jan	Feb	Mar	Apr	May	Jun	Jul	Aug	Sep	Oct	Nov	Dec
High	30	34	44	57	69	78	82	80	73	61	47	35
Low	13	15	25	35	46	55	59	57	49	39	30	20
Precip	2.1	1.8	2.9	3.3	3.7	4.2	3.7	3.6	3.7	2.8	3.0	2.6
Snow	14.8	10.7	7.4	1.6	tr	0.0	0.0	0.0	0.0	0.3	4.5	12.0

High and Low temperatures in degrees Fahrenheit; Precipitation and Snow in inches

Population: 46,527 (2000); Race: 97.7% White, 0.5% Black, 0.4% Asian, 0.3% American Indian and Alaska Native, 1.1% Hispanic of any race, 0.9% two or more races (2000); Density: 77.7 persons per square mile (2000); Age: 26.3% under 18, 13.3% over 64 (2000).
Religion: Five largest groups: 6.2% Catholic Church, 2.9% The United Methodist Church, 1.6% American Baptist Churches in the USA, 1.6% Presbyterian Church (U.S.A.), 1.4% General Association of Regular Baptist Churches (2000).
Economy: Unemployment rate: 4.7% (11/2002); Total civilian labor force: 25,063 (11/2002); Leading industries: 46.1% manufacturing; 10.8% retail trade; 8.9% health care and social assistance (2000); Companies that employ more than 1,000 persons: 0 (2000); Companies that employ more than 100 persons: 29 (2000); Farms: 1,236 totaling 257,469 acres (1997); Minority business ownership rate: 0.0% (1997); Women business ownership rate: 23.9% (1997); Retail sales per capita: $5,513 (1997). Single-family building permits issued: 249 (2001) / 263 (2000); Multi-family building permits issued: 52 (2001) / 68 (2000).
Income: Per capita income: $18,255 (2000); Median household income: $40,396 (2000); Poverty rate: 8.2% (2000); Bankruptcy rate: 4.12% (2001).
Taxes: Total county taxes per capita: $113 (2000); County property taxes per capita: $107 (2000).
Education: High school graduation rate: 83.1% (2000); College graduation rate: 12.0% (2000).
Housing: Homeownership rate: 79.9% (2000); Median home value: $85,800 (2000); Median rent: $359 per month (2000); Median age of housing: 38 years (2000).
Health: Birth rate: 124.9 per 10,000 population (1998); Age adjusted death rate: 93.3 per 10,000 population (1999); Age adjusted cancer mortality rate: 243.3 deaths per 100,000 population (1999). Number of physicians: 8.0 per 10,000 population (1999); Number of hospital beds: 15.7 per 10,000 population (1999).
Elections: 2000 Presidential election results: 37.2% Gore, 60.0% Bush, 2.1% Nader, 0.1% Buchanan
National and State Parks: Pittsford State Game Area
Additional Information Contacts
Hillsdale County Government Offices 517-437-3391
Hillsdale Chamber of Commerce 517-439-4341
Hillsdale County Board of Realtors 517-439-1770

Hillsdale County Communities

ADAMS (township). Covers a land area of 35.725 square miles and a water area of 0.355 square miles. Located at 41.93° N. Lat.; 84.54° W. Long.
History: Adams became a township in 1836, being separated out from Moscow Township. It was named for Henry P. Adams, an early settler.
Population: 2,498 (2000); Race: 99.1% White, 0.8% Black, 0.0% Asian, 0.0% American Indian and Alaska Native, 1.2% Hispanic of any race, 0.0% two or more races (2000); Density: 69.9 persons per square mile (2000); Age: 27.0% under 18, 13.5% over 64 (2000); Marriage status: 18.1% never married, 66.0% now married, 5.9% widowed, 10.0% divorced (2000); Foreign born: 0.4% (2000); Ancestry (includes multiple ancestries): 22.0% German, 13.5% Irish, 11.8% English, 9.9% Other groups, 7.7% United States or American (2000).
Economy: In agricultural area. Manufacturing of screw machine products, metal stampings. Employment by occupation: 8.1% management, 12.1% professional, 13.5% services, 21.0% sales, 1.3% farming, 13.6% construction, 30.4% production (2000).
Income: Per capita income: $19,821 (2000); Median household income: $42,708 (2000); Poverty rate: 5.4% (2000).
Taxes: Total city taxes per capita: $27 (1997); City property taxes per capita: $26 (1997).
Education: High school graduation rate: 84.2% (2000); College graduation rate: 11.9% (2000).
Housing: Homeownership rate: 85.8% (2000); Median home value: $84,500 (2000); Median rent: $367 per month (2000); Median age of housing: 34 years (2000).
Transportation: Commute to work: 93.0% car, 0.0% public transportation, 1.6% walk, 4.9% work from home (2000); Travel time to work: 34.3% less than 15 minutes, 38.2% 15 to 30 minutes, 16.5% 30 to 45 minutes, 6.1% 45 to 60 minutes, 4.9% 60 minutes or more (2000)

ALLEN (village). Covers a land area of 0.153 square miles and a water area of 0 square miles. Located at 41.95° N. Lat.; 84.76° W. Long. Elevation is 1,054 feet.
History: Allen was settled by Captain Moses Allen and his family in 1827.
Population: 225 (2000); Race: 100.0% White, 0.0% Black, 0.0% Asian, 0.0% American Indian and Alaska Native, 0.0% Hispanic of any race, 0.0%

two or more races (2000); Density: 1,470.7 persons per square mile (2000); Age: 27.6% under 18, 16.1% over 64 (2000); Marriage status: 19.9% never married, 62.2% now married, 7.1% widowed, 10.9% divorced (2000); Foreign born: 1.0% (2000); Ancestry (includes multiple ancestries): 24.1% German, 14.6% English, 13.1% United States or American, 5.5% Polish, 5.5% Scottish (2000).
Economy: Employment by occupation: 4.9% management, 1.0% professional, 16.5% services, 30.1% sales, 0.0% farming, 5.8% construction, 41.7% production (2000).
Income: Per capita income: $14,251 (2000); Median household income: $42,344 (2000); Poverty rate: 5.5% (2000).
Taxes: Total city taxes per capita: $14 (1997); City property taxes per capita: $14 (1997).
Education: High school graduation rate: 77.3% (2000); College graduation rate: 3.9% (2000).
Housing: Homeownership rate: 86.7% (2000); Median home value: $77,200 (2000); Median rent: $425 per month (2000); Median age of housing: 60+ years (2000).
Transportation: Commute to work: 93.9% car, 0.0% public transportation, 3.0% walk, 3.0% work from home (2000); Travel time to work: 32.3% less than 15 minutes, 58.3% 15 to 30 minutes, 5.2% 30 to 45 minutes, 2.1% 45 to 60 minutes, 2.1% 60 minutes or more (2000)

ALLEN (township). Covers a land area of 36.102 square miles and a water area of 0.188 square miles. Located at 41.95° N. Lat.; 84.77° W. Long. Elevation is 1,054 feet.
Population: 1,631 (2000); Race: 99.0% White, 0.0% Black, 0.2% Asian, 0.4% American Indian and Alaska Native, 1.0% Hispanic of any race, 0.4% two or more races (2000); Density: 45.2 persons per square mile (2000); Age: 29.7% under 18, 10.6% over 64 (2000); Marriage status: 19.6% never married, 65.3% now married, 5.9% widowed, 9.1% divorced (2000); Foreign born: 1.1% (2000); Ancestry (includes multiple ancestries): 26.4% German, 14.0% English, 12.9% United States or American, 7.4% Irish, 5.5% Polish (2000).
Economy: Employment by occupation: 10.6% management, 11.2% professional, 9.8% services, 22.8% sales, 2.2% farming, 9.5% construction, 33.8% production (2000).
Income: Per capita income: $17,734 (2000); Median household income: $44,213 (2000); Poverty rate: 7.4% (2000).
Taxes: Total city taxes per capita: $13 (1997); City property taxes per capita: $13 (1997).
Education: High school graduation rate: 88.3% (2000); College graduation rate: 10.6% (2000).
Housing: Homeownership rate: 84.6% (2000); Median home value: $87,600 (2000); Median rent: $378 per month (2000); Median age of housing: 42 years (2000).
Transportation: Commute to work: 93.7% car, 0.0% public transportation, 1.9% walk, 4.0% work from home (2000); Travel time to work: 33.5% less than 15 minutes, 45.9% 15 to 30 minutes, 9.3% 30 to 45 minutes, 2.4% 45 to 60 minutes, 8.9% 60 minutes or more (2000)

AMBOY (township). Covers a land area of 29.963 square miles and a water area of 0.662 square miles. Located at 41.71° N. Lat.; 84.60° W. Long.
History: Amboy Township was separated from Rowland in 1850.
Population: 1,224 (2000); Race: 98.4% White, 0.0% Black, 0.6% Asian, 0.2% American Indian and Alaska Native, 0.8% Hispanic of any race, 0.9% two or more races (2000); Density: 40.8 persons per square mile (2000); Age: 24.7% under 18, 12.8% over 64 (2000); Marriage status: 20.3% never married, 68.3% now married, 3.8% widowed, 7.5% divorced (2000); Foreign born: 1.5% (2000); Ancestry (includes multiple ancestries): 28.1% German, 13.3% United States or American, 12.0% English, 11.6% Irish, 7.7% Other groups (2000).
Economy: Employment by occupation: 8.2% management, 15.6% professional, 16.3% services, 21.4% sales, 1.4% farming, 8.6% construction, 28.5% production (2000).
Income: Per capita income: $20,578 (2000); Median household income: $42,250 (2000); Poverty rate: 10.7% (2000).
Taxes: Total city taxes per capita: $24 (1997); City property taxes per capita: $24 (1997).
Education: High school graduation rate: 81.0% (2000); College graduation rate: 11.7% (2000).
Housing: Homeownership rate: 89.3% (2000); Median home value: $140,800 (2000); Median rent: $369 per month (2000); Median age of housing: 21 years (2000).
Transportation: Commute to work: 93.1% car, 0.0% public transportation, 1.2% walk, 5.6% work from home (2000); Travel time to work: 13.2% less than 15 minutes, 32.0% 15 to 30 minutes, 32.6% 30 to 45 minutes, 8.6% 45 to 60 minutes, 13.6% 60 minutes or more (2000)

CAMBRIA (township). Covers a land area of 34.898 square miles and a water area of 1.281 square miles. Located at 41.86° N. Lat.; 84.65° W. Long.
History: Cambria Township was established in 1841 by the Willits brothers (Moses, Barron, and Jonathan) and named for their former home of Cambria, New York.
Population: 2,546 (2000); Race: 98.7% White, 0.2% Black, 0.0% Asian, 0.0% American Indian and Alaska Native, 0.7% Hispanic of any race, 1.0% two or more races (2000); Density: 73.0 persons per square mile (2000); Age: 25.4% under 18, 14.3% over 64 (2000); Marriage status: 18.6% never married, 63.5% now married, 6.8% widowed, 11.1% divorced (2000); Foreign born: 0.7% (2000); Ancestry (includes multiple ancestries): 28.9% German, 12.6% English, 11.5% United States or American, 9.6% Irish, 8.0% Other groups (2000).
Economy: Employment by occupation: 12.0% management, 14.3% professional, 13.2% services, 19.8% sales, 0.8% farming, 8.5% construction, 31.5% production (2000).
Income: Per capita income: $20,109 (2000); Median household income: $40,889 (2000); Poverty rate: 8.2% (2000).
Taxes: Total city taxes per capita: $19 (1997); City property taxes per capita: $19 (1997).
Education: High school graduation rate: 83.6% (2000); College graduation rate: 11.8% (2000).
Housing: Homeownership rate: 81.2% (2000); Median home value: $96,800 (2000); Median rent: $369 per month (2000); Median age of housing: 39 years (2000).
Transportation: Commute to work: 95.3% car, 0.0% public transportation, 1.2% walk, 3.1% work from home (2000); Travel time to work: 36.2% less than 15 minutes, 39.4% 15 to 30 minutes, 14.4% 30 to 45 minutes, 4.2% 45 to 60 minutes, 5.9% 60 minutes or more (2000)

CAMDEN (village). Covers a land area of 0.844 square miles and a water area of 0 square miles. Located at 41.75° N. Lat.; 84.75° W. Long.
History: Camden grew up around the sawmills built in the late 1830's. It was incorporated as a village in 1899, and named for Camden, New York.
Population: 550 (2000); Race: 95.8% White, 0.0% Black, 0.0% Asian, 0.0% American Indian and Alaska Native, 0.0% Hispanic of any race, 4.2% two or more races (2000); Density: 651.5 persons per square mile (2000); Age: 34.7% under 18, 9.7% over 64 (2000); Marriage status: 24.3% never married, 49.0% now married, 10.7% widowed, 16.0% divorced (2000); Foreign born: 0.0% (2000); Ancestry (includes multiple ancestries): 25.5% German, 16.5% Other groups, 12.8% Irish, 11.0% United States or American, 10.8% English (2000).
Economy: Employment by occupation: 2.0% management, 12.4% professional, 14.7% services, 17.9% sales, 0.8% farming, 6.4% construction, 45.8% production (2000).
Income: Per capita income: $13,846 (2000); Median household income: $34,028 (2000); Poverty rate: 12.1% (2000).
Taxes: Total city taxes per capita: $119 (1997); City property taxes per capita: $119 (1997).
Education: High school graduation rate: 77.2% (2000); College graduation rate: 6.6% (2000).

School District(s)

Camden-Frontier Schools (KG-12)
2000 Enrollment: 689 517-368-5991

Housing: Homeownership rate: 70.2% (2000); Median home value: $60,800 (2000); Median rent: $350 per month (2000); Median age of housing: 55 years (2000).
Newspapers: The Farmer's Advance (1 x week)
Transportation: Commute to work: 83.4% car, 0.8% public transportation, 11.3% walk, 2.0% work from home (2000); Travel time to work: 26.0% less than 15 minutes, 37.6% 15 to 30 minutes, 22.7% 30 to 45 minutes, 6.2% 45 to 60 minutes, 7.4% 60 minutes or more (2000)

CAMDEN (township). Covers a land area of 42.396 square miles and a water area of 0.210 square miles. Located at 41.77° N. Lat.; 84.77° W. Long.
History: Camden Township was named for Camden, New York, the name being suggested by Easton T. Chester who had lived there previously.
Population: 2,088 (2000); Race: 97.3% White, 0.1% Black, 0.1% Asian, 0.0% American Indian and Alaska Native, 0.5% Hispanic of any race, 2.4% two or more races (2000); Density: 49.2 persons per square mile (2000); Age: 31.3% under 18, 11.9% over 64 (2000); Marriage status: 21.2% never married, 61.2% now married, 7.0% widowed, 10.5% divorced (2000); Foreign born: 0.5% (2000); Ancestry (includes multiple ancestries): 30.6%

German, 12.0% English, 10.8% United States or American, 9.6% Other groups, 8.5% Irish (2000).
Economy: Employment by occupation: 8.6% management, 8.6% professional, 13.5% services, 17.4% sales, 1.5% farming, 9.9% construction, 40.6% production (2000).
Income: Per capita income: $17,882 (2000); Median household income: $37,386 (2000); Poverty rate: 15.0% (2000).
Taxes: Total city taxes per capita: $59 (1997); City property taxes per capita: $57 (1997).
Education: High school graduation rate: 75.3% (2000); College graduation rate: 6.7% (2000).
Housing: Homeownership rate: 79.8% (2000); Median home value: $68,200 (2000); Median rent: $339 per month (2000); Median age of housing: 54 years (2000).
Transportation: Commute to work: 87.8% car, 0.9% public transportation, 3.9% walk, 6.3% work from home (2000); Travel time to work: 20.7% less than 15 minutes, 44.1% 15 to 30 minutes, 23.1% 30 to 45 minutes, 4.2% 45 to 60 minutes, 7.9% 60 minutes or more (2000)

FAYETTE (township). Covers a land area of 23.140 square miles and a water area of 0.228 square miles. Located at 41.97° N. Lat.; 84.66° W. Long.
Population: 3,350 (2000); Race: 97.0% White, 1.5% Black, 0.6% Asian, 0.1% American Indian and Alaska Native, 1.7% Hispanic of any race, 0.5% two or more races (2000); Density: 144.8 persons per square mile (2000); Age: 28.1% under 18, 13.8% over 64 (2000); Marriage status: 19.7% never married, 62.3% now married, 6.9% widowed, 11.2% divorced (2000); Foreign born: 0.9% (2000); Ancestry (includes multiple ancestries): 20.4% German, 16.5% English, 12.7% United States or American, 9.9% Irish, 7.2% Other groups (2000).
Economy: Employment by occupation: 9.5% management, 12.1% professional, 15.0% services, 21.0% sales, 0.8% farming, 8.7% construction, 32.8% production (2000).
Income: Per capita income: $17,629 (2000); Median household income: $38,974 (2000); Poverty rate: 7.3% (2000).
Taxes: Total city taxes per capita: $25 (1997); City property taxes per capita: $24 (1997).
Education: High school graduation rate: 85.6% (2000); College graduation rate: 11.2% (2000).
Housing: Homeownership rate: 79.3% (2000); Median home value: $85,500 (2000); Median rent: $323 per month (2000); Median age of housing: 42 years (2000).
Transportation: Commute to work: 91.2% car, 0.6% public transportation, 3.1% walk, 3.8% work from home (2000); Travel time to work: 57.1% less than 15 minutes, 26.8% 15 to 30 minutes, 9.6% 30 to 45 minutes, 2.9% 45 to 60 minutes, 3.7% 60 minutes or more (2000)

HILLSDALE (city). Covers a land area of 5.318 square miles and a water area of 0.240 square miles. Located at 41.92° N. Lat.; 84.63° W. Long. Elevation is 1,090 feet.
History: Hillsdale was settled in 1834 by Jeremiah Arnold. In the 1840's, the railroad built a station here, the Free Will Baptist organization founded a college, and Hillsdale was made the seat of Hillsdale County.
Population: 8,233 (2000); Race: 96.8% White, 0.8% Black, 0.7% Asian, 0.6% American Indian and Alaska Native, 1.4% Hispanic of any race, 1.0% two or more races (2000); Density: 1,548.2 persons per square mile (2000); Age: 22.8% under 18, 13.9% over 64 (2000); Marriage status: 34.3% never married, 48.0% now married, 7.6% widowed, 10.1% divorced (2000); Foreign born: 1.9% (2000); Ancestry (includes multiple ancestries): 26.9% German, 14.5% Irish, 12.1% English, 8.5% Other groups, 8.5% United States or American (2000).
Economy: Single-family building permits issued: 4 (2001) / 2 (2000); Multi-family building permits issued: 52 (2001) / 50 (2000); Employment by occupation: 9.1% management, 15.4% professional, 15.3% services, 23.0% sales, 0.7% farming, 6.7% construction, 29.9% production (2000).
Income: Per capita income: $16,062 (2000); Median household income: $34,695 (2000); Poverty rate: 10.3% (2000).
Taxes: Total city taxes per capita: $269 (2000); City property taxes per capita: $261 (2000).
Education: High school graduation rate: 82.6% (2000); College graduation rate: 16.0% (2000).

School District(s)

Hillsdale Community Schools (PK-12)
2000 Enrollment: 1,908 517-437-4401
Sauk Trail Academy (PK-08)
2000 Enrollment: 129 517-437-0990
Will Carleton Academy (KG-08)
2000 Enrollment: 164 517-437-0990

Four-year College(s)

Hillsdale College (Private, Not-for-profit)
2001 Enrollment: n/a 517-437-7341
Housing: Homeownership rate: 57.1% (2000); Median home value: $71,800 (2000); Median rent: $346 per month (2000); Median age of housing: 51 years (2000).
Hospitals: Hillsdale Community Health Center (65 beds)
Safety: Violent crime rate: 29.0 per 10,000 population; Property crime rate: 302.1 per 10,000 population (2001).
Newspapers: The Hillsdale Daily News (6 x week); Hillsdale County Sampler (1 x week)
Transportation: Commute to work: 83.9% car, 0.4% public transportation, 11.4% walk, 3.3% work from home (2000); Travel time to work: 59.2% less than 15 minutes, 26.1% 15 to 30 minutes, 7.4% 30 to 45 minutes, 3.9% 45 to 60 minutes, 3.3% 60 minutes or more (2000)
Additional Information Contacts
Hillsdale Chamber of Commerce 517-439-4341
Hillsdale County Board of Realtors 517-439-1770

HILLSDALE (township). Covers a land area of 12.634 square miles and a water area of 0.531 square miles. Located at 41.92° N. Lat.; 84.65° W. Long. Elevation is 1,090 feet.
History: Seat of Hillsdale College, with 60-acre Slayton Arboretum. Native American mounds nearby. Settled 1834; incorporated as village 1847, as city 1869.
Population: 1,965 (2000); Race: 94.7% White, 2.3% Black, 1.6% Asian, 0.5% American Indian and Alaska Native, 0.0% Hispanic of any race, 0.9% two or more races (2000); Density: 155.5 persons per square mile (2000); Age: 24.6% under 18, 12.0% over 64 (2000); Marriage status: 19.3% never married, 71.3% now married, 5.2% widowed, 4.2% divorced (2000); Foreign born: 3.5% (2000); Ancestry (includes multiple ancestries): 28.8% German, 16.0% English, 13.0% Irish, 7.9% United States or American, 6.1% Other groups (2000).
Economy: Trade and manufacturing center: transportation equipment, textiles; food processing. Employment by occupation: 12.0% management, 16.0% professional, 14.4% services, 20.5% sales, 0.5% farming, 9.8% construction, 26.8% production (2000).
Income: Per capita income: $22,396 (2000); Median household income: $50,357 (2000); Poverty rate: 4.2% (2000).
Taxes: Total city taxes per capita: $16 (1997); City property taxes per capita: $16 (1997).
Education: High school graduation rate: 87.2% (2000); College graduation rate: 22.8% (2000).
Housing: Homeownership rate: 91.2% (2000); Median home value: $116,700 (2000); Median rent: $379 per month (2000); Median age of housing: 29 years (2000).
Transportation: Commute to work: 91.0% car, 0.0% public transportation, 2.9% walk, 3.7% work from home (2000); Travel time to work: 64.1% less than 15 minutes, 18.6% 15 to 30 minutes, 8.3% 30 to 45 minutes, 5.7% 45 to 60 minutes, 3.3% 60 minutes or more (2000)

JEFFERSON (township). Covers a land area of 35.619 square miles and a water area of 0.517 square miles. Located at 41.86° N. Lat.; 84.54° W. Long.
History: Jefferson Township was set off from Moscow Township in 1837, when it was named Florida. In 1849 the name was changed to Jefferson.
Population: 3,141 (2000); Race: 98.5% White, 0.0% Black, 0.5% Asian, 0.0% American Indian and Alaska Native, 1.6% Hispanic of any race, 1.0% two or more races (2000); Density: 88.2 persons per square mile (2000); Age: 25.5% under 18, 14.1% over 64 (2000); Marriage status: 21.0% never married, 61.7% now married, 6.1% widowed, 11.2% divorced (2000); Foreign born: 0.4% (2000); Ancestry (includes multiple ancestries): 23.8% German, 11.4% English, 10.8% Irish, 10.1% United States or American, 6.8% Other groups (2000).
Economy: Employment by occupation: 9.6% management, 10.9% professional, 15.3% services, 13.8% sales, 0.9% farming, 8.0% construction, 41.4% production (2000).
Income: Per capita income: $17,484 (2000); Median household income: $43,750 (2000); Poverty rate: 5.3% (2000).
Taxes: Total city taxes per capita: $12 (1997); City property taxes per capita: $11 (1997).
Education: High school graduation rate: 83.1% (2000); College graduation rate: 9.4% (2000).

Housing: Homeownership rate: 86.3% (2000); Median home value: $86,400 (2000); Median rent: $368 per month (2000); Median age of housing: 37 years (2000).
Transportation: Commute to work: 96.4% car, 0.0% public transportation, 1.0% walk, 2.2% work from home (2000); Travel time to work: 23.7% less than 15 minutes, 41.7% 15 to 30 minutes, 16.8% 30 to 45 minutes, 9.9% 45 to 60 minutes, 7.9% 60 minutes or more (2000)

JEROME (unincorporated postal area, zip code 49249). Covers a land area of 33.809 square miles and a water area of 1.711 square miles. Located at 42.04° N. Lat.; 84.44° W. Long.
History: Jerome was laid out by Jerome Smith in 1871, when the railroad arrived. Smith, the first station agent and the first postmaster, named the town for himself.
Population: 3,575 (2000); Race: 98.6% White, 0.6% Black, 0.0% Asian, 0.3% American Indian and Alaska Native, 1.5% Hispanic of any race, 0.3% two or more races (2000); Density: 105.7 persons per square mile (2000); Age: 22.3% under 18, 14.4% over 64 (2000); Marriage status: 14.0% never married, 71.3% now married, 4.3% widowed, 10.5% divorced (2000); Foreign born: 1.0% (2000); Ancestry (includes multiple ancestries): 22.9% German, 18.0% English, 10.2% Irish, 10.1% United States or American, 8.4% Polish (2000).
Economy: Employment by occupation: 12.9% management, 16.8% professional, 12.5% services, 23.1% sales, 0.1% farming, 11.2% construction, 23.4% production (2000).
Income: Per capita income: $24,850 (2000); Median household income: $49,844 (2000); Poverty rate: 3.6% (2000).
Education: High school graduation rate: 83.1% (2000); College graduation rate: 15.7% (2000).
Housing: Homeownership rate: 91.2% (2000); Median home value: $138,400 (2000); Median rent: $423 per month (2000); Median age of housing: 25 years (2000).
Transportation: Commute to work: 94.6% car, 0.0% public transportation, 0.4% walk, 4.1% work from home (2000); Travel time to work: 12.2% less than 15 minutes, 36.0% 15 to 30 minutes, 27.3% 30 to 45 minutes, 6.2% 45 to 60 minutes, 18.3% 60 minutes or more (2000)

JONESVILLE (village). Covers a land area of 2.728 square miles and a water area of 0.030 square miles. Located at 41.98° N. Lat.; 84.66° W. Long.
History: Jonesville was settled in 1829 at a place where the St. Joseph River could be forded. The village was platted by Benaiah Jones in 1831 and named for him.
Population: 2,337 (2000); Race: 95.9% White, 2.1% Black, 0.7% Asian, 0.1% American Indian and Alaska Native, 1.8% Hispanic of any race, 0.7% two or more races (2000); Density: 856.7 persons per square mile (2000); Age: 29.2% under 18, 14.0% over 64 (2000); Marriage status: 22.8% never married, 56.5% now married, 8.8% widowed, 11.9% divorced (2000); Foreign born: 0.9% (2000); Ancestry (includes multiple ancestries): 18.3% German, 16.6% English, 12.9% United States or American, 10.7% Irish, 8.7% Other groups (2000).
Economy: Employment by occupation: 10.2% management, 12.0% professional, 16.6% services, 22.9% sales, 0.5% farming, 6.7% construction, 31.1% production (2000).
Income: Per capita income: $15,877 (2000); Median household income: $35,223 (2000); Poverty rate: 9.9% (2000).
Taxes: Total city taxes per capita: $312 (1997); City property taxes per capita: $311 (1997).
Education: High school graduation rate: 86.4% (2000); College graduation rate: 11.6% (2000).

School District(s)

Jonesville Community Schools (PK-12)
2000 Enrollment: 1,303 517-849-9075
Housing: Homeownership rate: 75.6% (2000); Median home value: $80,300 (2000); Median rent: $323 per month (2000); Median age of housing: 47 years (2000).
Safety: Violent crime rate: 46.8 per 10,000 population; Property crime rate: 417.2 per 10,000 population (2001).
Newspapers: Tip Off Shopping Guide (1 x week); Jonesville Independent (1 x week)
Transportation: Commute to work: 90.4% car, 0.6% public transportation, 3.5% walk, 4.8% work from home (2000); Travel time to work: 57.7% less than 15 minutes, 26.9% 15 to 30 minutes, 8.0% 30 to 45 minutes, 2.4% 45 to 60 minutes, 4.9% 60 minutes or more (2000)

LITCHFIELD (city). Covers a land area of 2.394 square miles and a water area of 0 square miles. Located at 42.04° N. Lat.; 84.75° W. Long. Elevation is 1,014 feet.
History: Litchfield was settled in 1834 and platted as Smithville in 1836. It was later named Litchfield for the town of that name in Connecticut, the former home of some of the early residents.
Population: 1,458 (2000); Race: 97.4% White, 0.5% Black, 0.1% Asian, 0.1% American Indian and Alaska Native, 2.1% Hispanic of any race, 1.6% two or more races (2000); Density: 608.9 persons per square mile (2000); Age: 24.6% under 18, 20.0% over 64 (2000); Marriage status: 22.2% never married, 58.9% now married, 8.0% widowed, 11.0% divorced (2000); Foreign born: 0.2% (2000); Ancestry (includes multiple ancestries): 24.2% German, 15.5% Irish, 11.5% United States or American, 9.8% English, 8.7% Other groups (2000).
Economy: Employment by occupation: 9.8% management, 10.7% professional, 14.3% services, 17.2% sales, 1.9% farming, 9.5% construction, 36.6% production (2000).
Income: Per capita income: $17,362 (2000); Median household income: $39,292 (2000); Poverty rate: 10.3% (2000).
Taxes: Total city taxes per capita: $472 (1997); City property taxes per capita: $468 (1997).
Education: High school graduation rate: 80.2% (2000); College graduation rate: 9.9% (2000).

School District(s)

Litchfield Community Schools (KG-12)
2000 Enrollment: 594 517-542-2388
Housing: Homeownership rate: 63.7% (2000); Median home value: $75,500 (2000); Median rent: $358 per month (2000); Median age of housing: 41 years (2000).
Safety: Violent crime rate: 47.7 per 10,000 population; Property crime rate: 893.6 per 10,000 population (2001).
Transportation: Commute to work: 92.7% car, 0.3% public transportation, 3.4% walk, 1.8% work from home (2000); Travel time to work: 52.7% less than 15 minutes, 30.3% 15 to 30 minutes, 7.3% 30 to 45 minutes, 4.4% 45 to 60 minutes, 5.3% 60 minutes or more (2000)

LITCHFIELD (township). Covers a land area of 33.113 square miles and a water area of 0.017 square miles. Located at 42.02° N. Lat.; 84.76° W. Long. Elevation is 1,014 feet.
Population: 969 (2000); Race: 97.9% White, 0.5% Black, 0.0% Asian, 0.6% American Indian and Alaska Native, 1.2% Hispanic of any race, 0.9% two or more races (2000); Density: 29.3 persons per square mile (2000); Age: 26.2% under 18, 11.4% over 64 (2000); Marriage status: 19.2% never married, 65.8% now married, 5.7% widowed, 9.3% divorced (2000); Foreign born: 0.8% (2000); Ancestry (includes multiple ancestries): 21.4% German, 18.3% English, 12.5% Irish, 9.0% United States or American, 7.6% Other groups (2000).
Economy: Agriculture includes poultry; farming; dairy. Manufacturing includes apparel, transportation equipment, metal products. Employment by occupation: 10.7% management, 10.9% professional, 11.6% services, 17.3% sales, 2.9% farming, 15.2% construction, 31.4% production (2000).
Income: Per capita income: $17,625 (2000); Median household income: $42,153 (2000); Poverty rate: 9.5% (2000).
Taxes: Total city taxes per capita: $32 (1997); City property taxes per capita: $32 (1997).
Education: High school graduation rate: 88.5% (2000); College graduation rate: 8.0% (2000).
Housing: Homeownership rate: 88.5% (2000); Median home value: $85,900 (2000); Median rent: $421 per month (2000); Median age of housing: 42 years (2000).
Transportation: Commute to work: 92.6% car, 0.4% public transportation, 0.8% walk, 5.7% work from home (2000); Travel time to work: 45.0% less than 15 minutes, 30.6% 15 to 30 minutes, 13.7% 30 to 45 minutes, 3.8% 45 to 60 minutes, 6.8% 60 minutes or more (2000)

MONTGOMERY (village). Covers a land area of 0.984 square miles and a water area of 0.003 square miles. Located at 41.77° N. Lat.; 84.80° W. Long. Elevation is 1,043 feet.
Population: 386 (2000); Race: 99.5% White, 0.0% Black, 0.0% Asian, 0.0% American Indian and Alaska Native, 2.4% Hispanic of any race, 0.5% two or more races (2000); Density: 392.3 persons per square mile (2000); Age: 33.5% under 18, 13.9% over 64 (2000); Marriage status: 25.1% never married, 56.7% now married, 5.5% widowed, 12.7% divorced (2000); Foreign born: 0.0% (2000); Ancestry (includes multiple ancestries): 23.7%

German, 17.0% United States or American, 7.4% Other groups, 6.9% Irish, 6.2% English (2000).
Economy: In farm area; egg processing; manufacturing of auto parts. Employment by occupation: 4.9% management, 3.3% professional, 19.2% services, 13.2% sales, 0.0% farming, 8.8% construction, 50.5% production (2000).
Income: Per capita income: $14,975 (2000); Median household income: $42,500 (2000); Poverty rate: 13.9% (2000).
Taxes: Total city taxes per capita: $47 (1997); City property taxes per capita: $47 (1997).
Education: High school graduation rate: 71.0% (2000); College graduation rate: 2.0% (2000).
Housing: Homeownership rate: 76.1% (2000); Median home value: $54,700 (2000); Median rent: $375 per month (2000); Median age of housing: 60+ years (2000).
Transportation: Commute to work: 92.1% car, 3.4% public transportation, 0.0% walk, 2.8% work from home (2000); Travel time to work: 12.8% less than 15 minutes, 43.6% 15 to 30 minutes, 30.8% 30 to 45 minutes, 6.4% 45 to 60 minutes, 6.4% 60 minutes or more (2000)

MOSCOW (township). Covers a land area of 35.151 square miles and a water area of 0.277 square miles. Located at 42.03° N. Lat.; 84.52° W. Long.
History: In the Moscow area, stagecoach drivers forded the Kalamazoo River, then a river of some size. A log tavern erected at the ford in 1831 was replaced about 1850 by the Moscow Tavern.
Population: 1,445 (2000); Race: 97.9% White, 0.3% Black, 0.0% Asian, 0.5% American Indian and Alaska Native, 0.3% Hispanic of any race, 1.3% two or more races (2000); Density: 41.1 persons per square mile (2000); Age: 27.8% under 18, 11.1% over 64 (2000); Marriage status: 18.3% never married, 65.1% now married, 6.1% widowed, 10.5% divorced (2000); Foreign born: 0.3% (2000); Ancestry (includes multiple ancestries): 29.0% German, 19.9% English, 8.3% Irish, 7.8% United States or American, 7.3% Polish (2000).
Economy: Employment by occupation: 13.3% management, 5.8% professional, 11.4% services, 20.8% sales, 2.9% farming, 9.2% construction, 36.6% production (2000).
Income: Per capita income: $18,682 (2000); Median household income: $44,740 (2000); Poverty rate: 4.2% (2000).
Taxes: Total city taxes per capita: $16 (1997); City property taxes per capita: $16 (1997).
Education: High school graduation rate: 85.2% (2000); College graduation rate: 9.5% (2000).
Housing: Homeownership rate: 86.6% (2000); Median home value: $87,500 (2000); Median rent: $415 per month (2000); Median age of housing: 29 years (2000).
Transportation: Commute to work: 92.3% car, 0.0% public transportation, 0.6% walk, 6.3% work from home (2000); Travel time to work: 21.8% less than 15 minutes, 44.4% 15 to 30 minutes, 24.1% 30 to 45 minutes, 3.8% 45 to 60 minutes, 6.0% 60 minutes or more (2000)

NORTH ADAMS (village). Covers a land area of 0.527 square miles and a water area of 0 square miles. Located at 41.97° N. Lat.; 84.52° W. Long. Elevation is 1,196 feet.
Population: 514 (2000); Race: 99.2% White, 0.4% Black, 0.0% Asian, 0.0% American Indian and Alaska Native, 3.4% Hispanic of any race, 0.0% two or more races (2000); Density: 974.5 persons per square mile (2000); Age: 23.8% under 18, 17.2% over 64 (2000); Marriage status: 23.1% never married, 59.2% now married, 6.8% widowed, 11.0% divorced (2000); Foreign born: 0.9% (2000); Ancestry (includes multiple ancestries): 20.2% German, 11.1% Irish, 10.9% Other groups, 10.2% United States or American, 9.6% English (2000).
Economy: Employment by occupation: 7.5% management, 10.1% professional, 14.6% services, 21.3% sales, 2.6% farming, 1.9% construction, 42.2% production (2000).
Income: Per capita income: $19,850 (2000); Median household income: $38,523 (2000); Poverty rate: 3.2% (2000).
Taxes: Total city taxes per capita: $117 (1997); City property taxes per capita: $117 (1997).
Education: High school graduation rate: 88.1% (2000); College graduation rate: 9.0% (2000).

School District(s)

North Adams-Jerome Schools (KG-12)
2000 Enrollment: 566 517-287-4214
Housing: Homeownership rate: 74.1% (2000); Median home value: $64,300 (2000); Median rent: $363 per month (2000); Median age of housing: 60+ years (2000).
Transportation: Commute to work: 91.5% car, 0.0% public transportation, 4.3% walk, 4.3% work from home (2000); Travel time to work: 27.5% less than 15 minutes, 47.4% 15 to 30 minutes, 16.6% 30 to 45 minutes, 4.9% 45 to 60 minutes, 3.6% 60 minutes or more (2000)

OSSEO (unincorporated postal area, zip code 49266). Covers a land area of 43.292 square miles and a water area of 0.677 square miles. Located at 41.84° N. Lat.; 84.55° W. Long. Elevation is 1,104 feet.
Population: 2,973 (2000); Race: 98.4% White, 0.1% Black, 0.5% Asian, 0.0% American Indian and Alaska Native, 1.5% Hispanic of any race, 1.0% two or more races (2000); Density: 68.7 persons per square mile (2000); Age: 28.5% under 18, 11.6% over 64 (2000); Marriage status: 19.4% never married, 63.5% now married, 6.0% widowed, 11.2% divorced (2000); Foreign born: 0.8% (2000); Ancestry (includes multiple ancestries): 25.4% German, 11.3% Irish, 10.8% English, 8.2% United States or American, 7.6% Other groups (2000).
Economy: Employment by occupation: 9.7% management, 13.3% professional, 13.2% services, 18.9% sales, 1.7% farming, 7.9% construction, 35.2% production (2000).
Income: Per capita income: $17,355 (2000); Median household income: $44,975 (2000); Poverty rate: 5.7% (2000).
Education: High school graduation rate: 82.2% (2000); College graduation rate: 11.1% (2000).
Housing: Homeownership rate: 86.4% (2000); Median home value: $87,300 (2000); Median rent: $377 per month (2000); Median age of housing: 38 years (2000).
Transportation: Commute to work: 92.6% car, 0.0% public transportation, 1.3% walk, 4.9% work from home (2000); Travel time to work: 26.6% less than 15 minutes, 43.0% 15 to 30 minutes, 15.8% 30 to 45 minutes, 9.1% 45 to 60 minutes, 5.4% 60 minutes or more (2000)

PITTSFORD (township). Covers a land area of 35.479 square miles and a water area of 0.151 square miles. Located at 41.86° N. Lat.; 84.42° W. Long.
Population: 1,600 (2000); Race: 97.5% White, 0.0% Black, 0.4% Asian, 0.3% American Indian and Alaska Native, 2.2% Hispanic of any race, 0.3% two or more races (2000); Density: 45.1 persons per square mile (2000); Age: 26.1% under 18, 12.7% over 64 (2000); Marriage status: 20.5% never married, 66.5% now married, 4.8% widowed, 8.2% divorced (2000); Foreign born: 1.1% (2000); Ancestry (includes multiple ancestries): 28.0% German, 13.3% English, 8.9% United States or American, 8.0% Irish, 5.7% Other groups (2000).
Economy: Employment by occupation: 9.4% management, 15.2% professional, 12.4% services, 21.9% sales, 0.1% farming, 9.4% construction, 31.6% production (2000).
Income: Per capita income: $19,852 (2000); Median household income: $44,539 (2000); Poverty rate: 3.7% (2000).
Taxes: Total city taxes per capita: $12 (1997); City property taxes per capita: $12 (1997).
Education: High school graduation rate: 85.4% (2000); College graduation rate: 11.2% (2000).

School District(s)

Pittsford Area Schools (KG-12)
2000 Enrollment: 769 517-523-3481
Housing: Homeownership rate: 89.2% (2000); Median home value: $80,800 (2000); Median rent: $344 per month (2000); Median age of housing: 47 years (2000).
Transportation: Commute to work: 94.5% car, 0.0% public transportation, 1.9% walk, 3.1% work from home (2000); Travel time to work: 27.7% less than 15 minutes, 34.6% 15 to 30 minutes, 23.4% 30 to 45 minutes, 9.1% 45 to 60 minutes, 5.1% 60 minutes or more (2000)

RANSOM (township). Covers a land area of 30.147 square miles and a water area of 0.064 square miles. Located at 41.77° N. Lat.; 84.53° W. Long.
Population: 982 (2000); Race: 99.8% White, 0.2% Black, 0.0% Asian, 0.0% American Indian and Alaska Native, 0.1% Hispanic of any race, 0.0% two or more races (2000); Density: 32.6 persons per square mile (2000); Age: 31.2% under 18, 9.6% over 64 (2000); Marriage status: 23.1% never married, 66.3% now married, 3.8% widowed, 6.8% divorced (2000); Foreign born: 1.0% (2000); Ancestry (includes multiple ancestries): 23.7% German, 12.9% United States or American, 9.3% Irish, 5.9% English, 5.1% Other groups (2000).
Economy: Employment by occupation: 13.6% management, 11.9% professional, 10.3% services, 18.8% sales, 4.4% farming, 9.4% construction, 31.6% production (2000).

Income: Per capita income: $15,904 (2000); Median household income: $40,069 (2000); Poverty rate: 13.4% (2000).
Taxes: Total city taxes per capita: $13 (1997); City property taxes per capita: $13 (1997).
Education: High school graduation rate: 83.1% (2000); College graduation rate: 10.6% (2000).
Housing: Homeownership rate: 86.8% (2000); Median home value: $61,100 (2000); Median rent: $425 per month (2000); Median age of housing: 57 years (2000).
Transportation: Commute to work: 82.0% car, 0.0% public transportation, 1.7% walk, 14.1% work from home (2000); Travel time to work: 11.3% less than 15 minutes, 47.4% 15 to 30 minutes, 26.2% 30 to 45 minutes, 7.8% 45 to 60 minutes, 7.3% 60 minutes or more (2000)

READING (city). Covers a land area of 0.976 square miles and a water area of 0 square miles. Located at 41.83° N. Lat.; 84.74° W. Long. Elevation is 1,208 feet.
History: Reading was first called Basswood Corners for a group of seven basswood trees near the four corners of the village, as it was laid out. It became Reading in 1840, named after its township. Reading grew around a sawmill built in 1852, and a railroad station established in 1869. It was incorporated as a village in 1873, and as a city in 1934.
Population: 1,134 (2000); Race: 98.6% White, 0.0% Black, 0.2% Asian, 0.4% American Indian and Alaska Native, 0.9% Hispanic of any race, 0.1% two or more races (2000); Density: 1,162.3 persons per square mile (2000); Age: 34.2% under 18, 9.8% over 64 (2000); Marriage status: 22.7% never married, 59.6% now married, 5.8% widowed, 11.9% divorced (2000); Foreign born: 0.5% (2000); Ancestry (includes multiple ancestries): 28.6% German, 10.3% Other groups, 9.3% Irish, 8.9% English, 6.4% United States or American (2000).
Economy: Employment by occupation: 6.4% management, 10.8% professional, 13.5% services, 21.0% sales, 0.4% farming, 6.9% construction, 41.0% production (2000).
Income: Per capita income: $15,300 (2000); Median household income: $33,750 (2000); Poverty rate: 11.8% (2000).
Taxes: Total city taxes per capita: $82 (1997); City property taxes per capita: $82 (1997).
Education: High school graduation rate: 84.9% (2000); College graduation rate: 7.9% (2000).

School District(s)

Reading Community Schools (KG-12)
2000 Enrollment: 1,061 517-283-2166
Housing: Homeownership rate: 76.1% (2000); Median home value: $56,700 (2000); Median rent: $373 per month (2000); Median age of housing: 60+ years (2000).
Safety: Violent crime rate: 35.1 per 10,000 population; Property crime rate: 236.8 per 10,000 population (2001).
Transportation: Commute to work: 87.4% car, 0.0% public transportation, 9.2% walk, 2.6% work from home (2000); Travel time to work: 32.9% less than 15 minutes, 52.9% 15 to 30 minutes, 8.7% 30 to 45 minutes, 2.3% 45 to 60 minutes, 3.1% 60 minutes or more (2000)

READING (township). Covers a land area of 34.077 square miles and a water area of 0.989 square miles. Located at 41.86° N. Lat.; 84.77° W. Long. Elevation is 1,208 feet.
History: Settled 1840; incorporated as village 1873; as city 1934.
Population: 1,781 (2000); Race: 96.6% White, 0.5% Black, 0.2% Asian, 0.0% American Indian and Alaska Native, 1.4% Hispanic of any race, 1.6% two or more races (2000); Density: 52.3 persons per square mile (2000); Age: 22.8% under 18, 16.9% over 64 (2000); Marriage status: 17.2% never married, 69.2% now married, 5.7% widowed, 8.0% divorced (2000); Foreign born: 0.6% (2000); Ancestry (includes multiple ancestries): 28.4% German, 16.5% English, 11.5% Irish, 10.2% United States or American, 7.9% Other groups (2000).
Economy: Livestock; agriculture. Manufacturing: air-conditioning hoses and tubes. Employment by occupation: 8.7% management, 14.9% professional, 10.7% services, 21.1% sales, 2.4% farming, 7.3% construction, 35.0% production (2000).
Income: Per capita income: $19,625 (2000); Median household income: $40,938 (2000); Poverty rate: 8.8% (2000).
Taxes: Total city taxes per capita: $34 (1997); City property taxes per capita: $32 (1997).
Education: High school graduation rate: 85.5% (2000); College graduation rate: 13.3% (2000).
Housing: Homeownership rate: 88.1% (2000); Median home value: $95,900 (2000); Median rent: $385 per month (2000); Median age of housing: 33 years (2000).
Transportation: Commute to work: 93.0% car, 0.1% public transportation, 1.5% walk, 4.2% work from home (2000); Travel time to work: 18.8% less than 15 minutes, 50.3% 15 to 30 minutes, 17.1% 30 to 45 minutes, 7.5% 45 to 60 minutes, 6.3% 60 minutes or more (2000)

SCIPIO (township). Covers a land area of 29.320 square miles and a water area of 0.226 square miles. Located at 42.03° N. Lat.; 84.66° W. Long.
History: Scipio Township was organized in 1836.
Population: 1,822 (2000); Race: 97.5% White, 0.4% Black, 0.0% Asian, 1.3% American Indian and Alaska Native, 0.2% Hispanic of any race, 0.6% two or more races (2000); Density: 62.1 persons per square mile (2000); Age: 30.9% under 18, 9.0% over 64 (2000); Marriage status: 23.0% never married, 62.8% now married, 5.8% widowed, 8.4% divorced (2000); Foreign born: 0.3% (2000); Ancestry (includes multiple ancestries): 21.1% German, 13.2% English, 12.3% Irish, 12.2% United States or American, 11.3% Other groups (2000).
Economy: Employment by occupation: 10.5% management, 9.5% professional, 13.5% services, 19.4% sales, 2.0% farming, 12.2% construction, 32.8% production (2000).
Income: Per capita income: $17,427 (2000); Median household income: $42,361 (2000); Poverty rate: 8.6% (2000).
Taxes: Total city taxes per capita: $15 (1997); City property taxes per capita: $15 (1997).
Education: High school graduation rate: 81.5% (2000); College graduation rate: 5.5% (2000).
Housing: Homeownership rate: 82.4% (2000); Median home value: $75,300 (2000); Median rent: $381 per month (2000); Median age of housing: 26 years (2000).
Transportation: Commute to work: 94.5% car, 0.1% public transportation, 0.5% walk, 4.4% work from home (2000); Travel time to work: 34.1% less than 15 minutes, 42.4% 15 to 30 minutes, 12.5% 30 to 45 minutes, 6.4% 45 to 60 minutes, 4.6% 60 minutes or more (2000)

SOMERSET (township). Covers a land area of 33.358 square miles and a water area of 2.184 square miles. Located at 42.05° N. Lat.; 84.41° W. Long.
History: Somerset was settled in the early 1830's, when it was known as Wheatland. Somerset Township was organized later and named for Somerset in New York.
Population: 4,277 (2000); Race: 98.9% White, 0.5% Black, 0.2% Asian, 0.2% American Indian and Alaska Native, 1.6% Hispanic of any race, 0.0% two or more races (2000); Density: 128.2 persons per square mile (2000); Age: 22.7% under 18, 14.9% over 64 (2000); Marriage status: 14.6% never married, 69.7% now married, 5.7% widowed, 10.0% divorced (2000); Foreign born: 1.9% (2000); Ancestry (includes multiple ancestries): 22.4% German, 14.9% English, 10.8% United States or American, 10.7% Irish, 8.2% Polish (2000).
Economy: Single-family building permits issued: 47 (2001) / 52 (2000); Multi-family building permits issued: 0 (2001) / 0 (2000); Employment by occupation: 13.7% management, 20.1% professional, 10.9% services, 22.4% sales, 0.2% farming, 9.9% construction, 22.8% production (2000).
Income: Per capita income: $22,462 (2000); Median household income: $48,529 (2000); Poverty rate: 4.0% (2000).
Taxes: Total city taxes per capita: $61 (1997); City property taxes per capita: $55 (1997).
Education: High school graduation rate: 83.3% (2000); College graduation rate: 16.2% (2000).
Housing: Homeownership rate: 93.6% (2000); Median home value: $146,300 (2000); Median rent: $425 per month (2000); Median age of housing: 23 years (2000).
Safety: Violent crime rate: 27.9 per 10,000 population; Property crime rate: 216.3 per 10,000 population (2001).
Transportation: Commute to work: 96.1% car, 0.0% public transportation, 0.6% walk, 2.7% work from home (2000); Travel time to work: 12.7% less than 15 minutes, 32.5% 15 to 30 minutes, 27.5% 30 to 45 minutes, 7.0% 45 to 60 minutes, 20.3% 60 minutes or more (2000)

SOMERSET CENTER (unincorporated postal area, zip code 49282). Covers a land area of 4.100 square miles and a water area of 0.058 square miles. Located at 42.05° N. Lat.; 84.39° W. Long.
Population: 785 (2000); Race: 98.7% White, 0.0% Black, 0.9% Asian, 0.0% American Indian and Alaska Native, 1.6% Hispanic of any race, 0.0% two or more races (2000); Density: 191.5 persons per square mile (2000); Age: 26.0% under 18, 19.5% over 64 (2000); Marriage status: 22.1% never

married, 58.1% now married, 12.3% widowed, 7.5% divorced (2000); Foreign born: 4.0% (2000); Ancestry (includes multiple ancestries): 24.6% German, 15.4% English, 10.4% Irish, 7.9% Polish, 7.4% Dutch (2000).
Economy: Employment by occupation: 7.2% management, 20.1% professional, 13.8% services, 24.0% sales, 1.0% farming, 4.6% construction, 29.3% production (2000).
Income: Per capita income: $16,235 (2000); Median household income: $33,913 (2000); Poverty rate: 7.0% (2000).
Education: High school graduation rate: 77.3% (2000); College graduation rate: 7.6% (2000).
Housing: Homeownership rate: 96.8% (2000); Median home value: $136,300 (2000); Median rent: $425 per month (2000); Median age of housing: 17 years (2000).
Transportation: Commute to work: 98.3% car, 0.0% public transportation, 1.7% walk, 0.0% work from home (2000); Travel time to work: 16.2% less than 15 minutes, 38.4% 15 to 30 minutes, 21.5% 30 to 45 minutes, 9.4% 45 to 60 minutes, 14.5% 60 minutes or more (2000)

WALDRON (village). Covers a land area of 1.025 square miles and a water area of 0 square miles. Located at 41.72° N. Lat.; 84.41° W. Long. Elevation is 900 feet.
Population: 590 (2000); Race: 98.3% White, 0.0% Black, 0.3% Asian, 0.3% American Indian and Alaska Native, 0.0% Hispanic of any race, 1.0% two or more races (2000); Density: 575.6 persons per square mile (2000); Age: 30.2% under 18, 11.8% over 64 (2000); Marriage status: 25.6% never married, 54.0% now married, 8.9% widowed, 11.6% divorced (2000); Foreign born: 0.3% (2000); Ancestry (includes multiple ancestries): 18.4% German, 12.3% United States or American, 9.1% Irish, 8.5% Other groups, 8.3% English (2000).
Economy: In livestock and grain region. Sheet metal fabricating. Employment by occupation: 3.4% management, 8.8% professional, 13.0% services, 18.3% sales, 2.3% farming, 8.0% construction, 46.2% production (2000).
Income: Per capita income: $15,083 (2000); Median household income: $30,417 (2000); Poverty rate: 16.4% (2000).
Taxes: Total city taxes per capita: $82 (1997); City property taxes per capita: $82 (1997).
Education: High school graduation rate: 77.4% (2000); College graduation rate: 3.8% (2000).

School District(s)

Waldron Area Schools (KG-12)
2000 Enrollment: 476 517-286-6251

Housing: Homeownership rate: 72.8% (2000); Median home value: $58,100 (2000); Median rent: $286 per month (2000); Median age of housing: 59 years (2000).
Transportation: Commute to work: 92.2% car, 0.8% public transportation, 4.3% walk, 2.7% work from home (2000); Travel time to work: 26.6% less than 15 minutes, 23.8% 15 to 30 minutes, 27.4% 30 to 45 minutes, 8.1% 45 to 60 minutes, 14.1% 60 minutes or more (2000)

WHEATLAND (township). Covers a land area of 35.634 square miles and a water area of 0.019 square miles. Located at 41.94° N. Lat.; 84.40° W. Long. Elevation is 1,102 feet.
Population: 1,258 (2000); Race: 97.8% White, 0.0% Black, 0.0% Asian, 0.0% American Indian and Alaska Native, 1.0% Hispanic of any race, 1.8% two or more races (2000); Density: 35.3 persons per square mile (2000); Age: 26.8% under 18, 13.3% over 64 (2000); Marriage status: 17.8% never married, 70.2% now married, 5.2% widowed, 6.8% divorced (2000); Foreign born: 1.0% (2000); Ancestry (includes multiple ancestries): 28.0% German, 12.8% English, 12.1% United States or American, 7.8% Irish, 5.8% Other groups (2000).
Economy: Employment by occupation: 10.3% management, 12.9% professional, 9.8% services, 20.6% sales, 2.2% farming, 13.9% construction, 30.2% production (2000).
Income: Per capita income: $18,026 (2000); Median household income: $40,000 (2000); Poverty rate: 6.3% (2000).
Taxes: Total city taxes per capita: $14 (1997); City property taxes per capita: $14 (1997).
Education: High school graduation rate: 82.4% (2000); College graduation rate: 8.1% (2000).
Housing: Homeownership rate: 86.2% (2000); Median home value: $79,700 (2000); Median rent: $406 per month (2000); Median age of housing: 42 years (2000).
Transportation: Commute to work: 93.2% car, 0.0% public transportation, 0.2% walk, 6.6% work from home (2000); Travel time to work: 21.5% less than 15 minutes, 33.4% 15 to 30 minutes, 27.2% 30 to 45 minutes, 7.3% 45 to 60 minutes, 10.6% 60 minutes or more (2000)

WOODBRIDGE (township). Covers a land area of 30.076 square miles and a water area of 0.007 square miles. Located at 41.78° N. Lat.; 84.65° W. Long.
Population: 1,337 (2000); Race: 96.2% White, 0.0% Black, 0.5% Asian, 0.7% American Indian and Alaska Native, 0.8% Hispanic of any race, 2.4% two or more races (2000); Density: 44.5 persons per square mile (2000); Age: 35.0% under 18, 10.6% over 64 (2000); Marriage status: 24.3% never married, 64.6% now married, 4.3% widowed, 6.8% divorced (2000); Foreign born: 1.3% (2000); Ancestry (includes multiple ancestries): 28.0% German, 9.2% Other groups, 9.1% English, 9.0% Irish, 6.0% United States or American (2000).
Economy: Employment by occupation: 9.6% management, 8.3% professional, 15.2% services, 13.5% sales, 4.2% farming, 11.7% construction, 37.5% production (2000).
Income: Per capita income: $14,088 (2000); Median household income: $35,294 (2000); Poverty rate: 13.3% (2000).
Taxes: Total city taxes per capita: $11 (1997); City property taxes per capita: $11 (1997).
Education: High school graduation rate: 76.1% (2000); College graduation rate: 7.4% (2000).
Housing: Homeownership rate: 84.0% (2000); Median home value: $75,800 (2000); Median rent: $403 per month (2000); Median age of housing: 57 years (2000).
Transportation: Commute to work: 88.8% car, 0.0% public transportation, 1.0% walk, 9.8% work from home (2000); Travel time to work: 12.9% less than 15 minutes, 41.0% 15 to 30 minutes, 25.7% 30 to 45 minutes, 6.8% 45 to 60 minutes, 13.7% 60 minutes or more (2000)

WRIGHT (township). Covers a land area of 43.323 square miles and a water area of 0.150 square miles. Located at 41.76° N. Lat.; 84.41° W. Long.
Population: 1,788 (2000); Race: 97.3% White, 0.0% Black, 0.2% Asian, 1.2% American Indian and Alaska Native, 0.3% Hispanic of any race, 1.3% two or more races (2000); Density: 41.3 persons per square mile (2000); Age: 28.3% under 18, 12.9% over 64 (2000); Marriage status: 22.2% never married, 62.6% now married, 7.0% widowed, 8.1% divorced (2000); Foreign born: 0.7% (2000); Ancestry (includes multiple ancestries): 23.9% German, 11.5% United States or American, 9.4% English, 9.2% Other groups, 6.7% Irish (2000).
Economy: Employment by occupation: 8.6% management, 7.5% professional, 12.8% services, 17.5% sales, 1.9% farming, 12.2% construction, 39.4% production (2000).
Income: Per capita income: $16,235 (2000); Median household income: $36,591 (2000); Poverty rate: 12.6% (2000).
Taxes: Total city taxes per capita: $16 (1997); City property taxes per capita: $16 (1997).
Education: High school graduation rate: 77.7% (2000); College graduation rate: 7.5% (2000).
Housing: Homeownership rate: 85.0% (2000); Median home value: $68,800 (2000); Median rent: $308 per month (2000); Median age of housing: 60+ years (2000).
Transportation: Commute to work: 88.8% car, 0.3% public transportation, 2.3% walk, 7.7% work from home (2000); Travel time to work: 26.8% less than 15 minutes, 24.9% 15 to 30 minutes, 28.0% 30 to 45 minutes, 10.9% 45 to 60 minutes, 9.4% 60 minutes or more (2000)

Houghton County

Located in northwestern Michigan, on the Upper Peninsula; includes part of the Keweenaw Peninsula, extending into Lake Superior; partly bounded on the southeast by Keweenaw Bay; drained by the Ontonagon and Sturgeon Rivers. Covers a land area of 1,011.70 square miles, a water area of 489.80 square miles, and is located in the Eastern Time Zone. The county government was organized in 1845. County seat is Houghton.

Weather Station: Hancock Houghton Co. Airport Elevation: 1,072 feet

	Jan	Feb	Mar	Apr	May	Jun	Jul	Aug	Sep	Oct	Nov	Dec
High	21	24	32	46	61	71	76	73	63	51	36	26
Low	9	9	18	30	41	50	56	56	47	37	26	15
Precip	4.2	2.3	2.4	1.7	2.6	2.9	3.1	2.7	3.3	2.6	2.9	3.5
Snow	70.5	34.2	23.7	7.7	1.1	tr	tr	tr	0.1	3.8	23.8	57.7

High and Low temperatures in degrees Fahrenheit; Precipitation and Snow in inches

Population: 36,016 (2000); Race: 95.6% White, 1.1% Black, 1.4% Asian, 0.6% American Indian and Alaska Native, 0.7% Hispanic of any race, 1.1% two or more races (2000); Density: 35.6 persons per square mile (2000); Age: 21.9% under 18, 15.5% over 64 (2000).
Religion: Five largest groups: 27.2% Catholic Church, 9.4% Evangelical Lutheran Church in America, 3.5% The United Methodist Church, 1.8% Lutheran Church—Missouri Synod, 1.3% Assemblies of God (2000).
Economy: Unemployment rate: 4.7% (11/2002); Total civilian labor force: 17,105 (11/2002); Leading industries: 24.1% health care and social assistance; 21.1% retail trade; 12.7% accommodation & food services (2000); Companies that employ more than 1,000 persons: 0 (2000); Companies that employ more than 100 persons: 11 (2000); Farms: 128 totaling 23,126 acres (1997); Minority business ownership rate: 0.0% (1997); Women business ownership rate: 35.0% (1997); Retail sales per capita: $7,337 (1997). Single-family building permits issued: 129 (2001) / 116 (2000); Multi-family building permits issued: 4 (2001) / 6 (2000).
Income: Per capita income: $15,078 (2000); Median household income: $28,817 (2000); Poverty rate: 16.8% (2000); Bankruptcy rate: 1.58% (2001).
Taxes: Total county taxes per capita: $78 (2000); County property taxes per capita: $71 (2000).
Education: High school graduation rate: 84.6% (2000); College graduation rate: 23.0% (2000).
Housing: Homeownership rate: 71.5% (2000); Median home value: $54,800 (2000); Median rent: $316 per month (2000); Median age of housing: 58 years (2000).
Health: Birth rate: 101.6 per 10,000 population (1998); Age adjusted death rate: 110.0 per 10,000 population (1999); Age adjusted cancer mortality rate: 230.6 deaths per 100,000 population (1999). Number of physicians: 13.9 per 10,000 population (1999); Number of hospital beds: 28.3 per 10,000 population (1999).
Elections: 2000 Presidential election results: 40.0% Gore, 55.5% Bush, 3.6% Nader, 0.1% Buchanan
National and State Parks: Baraga State Forest; Keweenaw National Historical Park; McLain State Park
Additional Information Contacts
Houghton County Government Offices 906-482-1150
Calumet Chamber of Commerce 906-337-4579
Houghton Chamber of Commerce 906-482-5240

Houghton County Communities

ADAMS (township). Covers a land area of 47.248 square miles and a water area of 0.476 square miles. Located at 47.05° N. Lat.; 88.66° W. Long.
Population: 2,747 (2000); Race: 93.4% White, 4.0% Black, 0.3% Asian, 0.6% American Indian and Alaska Native, 1.0% Hispanic of any race, 0.9% two or more races (2000); Density: 58.1 persons per square mile (2000); Age: 25.0% under 18, 14.3% over 64 (2000); Marriage status: 36.1% never married, 46.9% now married, 7.6% widowed, 9.5% divorced (2000); Foreign born: 1.0% (2000); Ancestry (includes multiple ancestries): 44.6% Finnish, 11.1% German, 9.7% English, 8.8% Italian, 7.4% Swedish (2000).
Economy: Employment by occupation: 8.7% management, 14.2% professional, 22.8% services, 24.5% sales, 0.6% farming, 12.0% construction, 17.1% production (2000).
Income: Per capita income: $12,741 (2000); Median household income: $28,776 (2000); Poverty rate: 11.9% (2000).
Taxes: Total city taxes per capita: $18 (1997); City property taxes per capita: $18 (1997).
Education: High school graduation rate: 80.8% (2000); College graduation rate: 11.3% (2000).
Housing: Homeownership rate: 83.5% (2000); Median home value: $37,400 (2000); Median rent: $302 per month (2000); Median age of housing: 60+ years (2000).
Transportation: Commute to work: 95.4% car, 0.2% public transportation, 1.9% walk, 2.1% work from home (2000); Travel time to work: 50.6% less than 15 minutes, 38.6% 15 to 30 minutes, 8.1% 30 to 45 minutes, 2.0% 45 to 60 minutes, 0.7% 60 minutes or more (2000)

ATLANTIC MINE (unincorporated postal area, zip code 49905). Aka Atlantic. Covers a land area of 77.676 square miles and a water area of 0.213 square miles. Located at 47.10° N. Lat.; 88.71° W. Long.
History: The village of Atlantic Mine grew up around the Atlantic Mining Company's stamping works, which operated here until 1911. A post office was established in 1876.
Population: 1,613 (2000); Race: 98.1% White, 0.4% Black, 0.4% Asian, 0.0% American Indian and Alaska Native, 0.4% Hispanic of any race, 0.8% two or more races (2000); Density: 20.8 persons per square mile (2000); Age: 38.3% under 18, 9.3% over 64 (2000); Marriage status: 32.3% never married, 53.0% now married, 5.6% widowed, 9.2% divorced (2000); Foreign born: 1.4% (2000); Ancestry (includes multiple ancestries): 54.2% Finnish, 11.9% Swedish, 10.6% German, 8.0% English, 6.2% Irish (2000).
Economy: Employment by occupation: 7.6% management, 21.6% professional, 18.1% services, 26.2% sales, 1.3% farming, 10.1% construction, 15.1% production (2000).
Income: Per capita income: $12,308 (2000); Median household income: $36,518 (2000); Poverty rate: 10.5% (2000).
Education: High school graduation rate: 84.9% (2000); College graduation rate: 21.0% (2000).

School District(s)

Stanton Township Public Schools (PK-08)
2000 Enrollment: 138 906-482-2797
Housing: Homeownership rate: 88.8% (2000); Median home value: $46,300 (2000); Median rent: $344 per month (2000); Median age of housing: 58 years (2000).
Transportation: Commute to work: 96.8% car, 0.3% public transportation, 0.3% walk, 2.4% work from home (2000); Travel time to work: 44.4% less than 15 minutes, 43.5% 15 to 30 minutes, 10.3% 30 to 45 minutes, 0.0% 45 to 60 minutes, 1.8% 60 minutes or more (2000)

CALUMET (village). Covers a land area of 0.194 square miles and a water area of 0 square miles. Located at 47.24° N. Lat.; 88.45° W. Long. Elevation is 1,208 feet.
History: Calumet developed as a company town for the Calumet and Hecla Consolidated Copper Company, formed in 1871 from the consolidation of two smaller companies. The name of Calumet refers to the clay stone bowl of a peace pipe.
Population: 879 (2000); Race: 97.5% White, 0.0% Black, 0.0% Asian, 0.0% American Indian and Alaska Native, 2.7% Hispanic of any race, 1.2% two or more races (2000); Density: 4,524.2 persons per square mile (2000); Age: 21.0% under 18, 14.4% over 64 (2000); Marriage status: 44.1% never married, 29.5% now married, 12.6% widowed, 13.9% divorced (2000); Foreign born: 0.3% (2000); Ancestry (includes multiple ancestries): 29.3% Finnish, 15.5% German, 8.9% Irish, 8.1% Italian, 8.1% French (except Basque) (2000).
Economy: Single-family building permits issued: 0 (2001) / 0 (2000); Multi-family building permits issued: 0 (2001) / 0 (2000); Employment by occupation: 10.5% management, 16.9% professional, 19.7% services, 28.3% sales, 1.6% farming, 7.0% construction, 15.9% production (2000).
Income: Per capita income: $12,111 (2000); Median household income: $17,404 (2000); Poverty rate: 35.0% (2000).
Taxes: Total city taxes per capita: $176 (1997); City property taxes per capita: $175 (1997).
Education: High school graduation rate: 76.1% (2000); College graduation rate: 13.3% (2000).

School District(s)

Public Schools of Calumet (KG-12)
2000 Enrollment: 1,665 906-337-0311
Housing: Homeownership rate: 31.4% (2000); Median home value: $46,300 (2000); Median rent: $247 per month (2000); Median age of housing: 60+ years (2000).
Safety: Violent crime rate: 0.0 per 10,000 population; Property crime rate: 113.1 per 10,000 population (2001).
Transportation: Commute to work: 66.1% car, 1.6% public transportation, 26.8% walk, 4.8% work from home (2000); Travel time to work: 63.4% less than 15 minutes, 27.5% 15 to 30 minutes, 6.7% 30 to 45 minutes, 2.3% 45 to 60 minutes, 0.0% 60 minutes or more (2000)
Additional Information Contacts
Calumet Chamber of Commerce 906-337-4579

CALUMET (township). Covers a land area of 33.250 square miles and a water area of 0.066 square miles. Located at 47.24° N. Lat.; 88.44° W. Long. Elevation is 1,208 feet.
History: Village grew after development of Calumet and Hecla copper mine here in 1860s. Incorporated 1875 as Red Jacket, renamed 1929.
Population: 6,997 (2000); Race: 98.7% White, 0.0% Black, 0.2% Asian, 0.3% American Indian and Alaska Native, 1.2% Hispanic of any race, 0.5% two or more races (2000); Density: 210.4 persons per square mile (2000); Age: 25.1% under 18, 20.5% over 64 (2000); Marriage status: 27.5% never married, 50.9% now married, 11.4% widowed, 10.1% divorced (2000); Foreign born: 1.0% (2000); Ancestry (includes multiple ancestries): 40.0% Finnish, 14.8% German, 9.7% Italian, 9.7% French (except Basque), 9.1% English (2000).

Economy: Dairy; cattle farming; lumbering. Manufacturing: printed circuit boards. Resort. Employment by occupation: 9.0% management, 21.2% professional, 21.5% services, 26.0% sales, 0.7% farming, 8.0% construction, 13.7% production (2000).
Income: Per capita income: $14,711 (2000); Median household income: $24,928 (2000); Poverty rate: 17.6% (2000).
Taxes: Total city taxes per capita: $13 (1997); City property taxes per capita: $13 (1997).
Education: High school graduation rate: 81.2% (2000); College graduation rate: 18.4% (2000).
Housing: Homeownership rate: 76.8% (2000); Median home value: $42,600 (2000); Median rent: $271 per month (2000); Median age of housing: 60+ years (2000).
Transportation: Commute to work: 84.5% car, 1.4% public transportation, 9.1% walk, 4.2% work from home (2000); Travel time to work: 52.0% less than 15 minutes, 33.9% 15 to 30 minutes, 8.4% 30 to 45 minutes, 2.6% 45 to 60 minutes, 3.1% 60 minutes or more (2000)

CHASSELL (township). Covers a land area of 48.742 square miles and a water area of 3.189 square miles. Located at 47.01° N. Lat.; 88.52° W. Long.
History: Chassell was named for its founder, a French farmer named John Chassell.
Population: 1,822 (2000); Race: 97.7% White, 0.0% Black, 0.0% Asian, 1.5% American Indian and Alaska Native, 0.0% Hispanic of any race, 0.8% two or more races (2000); Density: 37.4 persons per square mile (2000); Age: 26.5% under 18, 16.1% over 64 (2000); Marriage status: 20.0% never married, 66.6% now married, 6.0% widowed, 7.4% divorced (2000); Foreign born: 0.5% (2000); Ancestry (includes multiple ancestries): 51.5% Finnish, 12.8% German, 7.2% English, 7.0% French (except Basque), 5.0% Irish (2000).
Economy: Employment by occupation: 11.2% management, 17.7% professional, 18.9% services, 27.0% sales, 0.1% farming, 14.5% construction, 10.6% production (2000).
Income: Per capita income: $18,133 (2000); Median household income: $38,333 (2000); Poverty rate: 6.9% (2000).
Taxes: Total city taxes per capita: $48 (1997); City property taxes per capita: $46 (1997).
Education: High school graduation rate: 87.9% (2000); College graduation rate: 22.3% (2000).

School District(s)

Chassell Township School District (KG-12)
2000 Enrollment: 334 906-523-4691

Housing: Homeownership rate: 86.6% (2000); Median home value: $73,000 (2000); Median rent: $315 per month (2000); Median age of housing: 40 years (2000).
Transportation: Commute to work: 93.7% car, 0.0% public transportation, 1.2% walk, 5.1% work from home (2000); Travel time to work: 29.4% less than 15 minutes, 55.3% 15 to 30 minutes, 13.1% 30 to 45 minutes, 0.5% 45 to 60 minutes, 1.7% 60 minutes or more (2000)

COPPER CITY (village). Covers a land area of 0.084 square miles and a water area of 0 square miles. Located at 47.28° N. Lat.; 88.38° W. Long. Elevation is 877 feet.
History: Copper City was established as a station on the rail line, in a copper mining region. It was incorporated in 1917.
Population: 205 (2000); Race: 99.0% White, 0.0% Black, 0.0% Asian, 1.0% American Indian and Alaska Native, 0.0% Hispanic of any race, 0.0% two or more races (2000); Density: 2,426.8 persons per square mile (2000); Age: 29.0% under 18, 19.5% over 64 (2000); Marriage status: 17.5% never married, 68.2% now married, 6.5% widowed, 7.8% divorced (2000); Foreign born: 1.0% (2000); Ancestry (includes multiple ancestries): 57.0% Finnish, 13.5% German, 11.0% English, 7.0% United States or American, 6.5% Irish (2000).
Economy: Employment by occupation: 7.7% management, 17.9% professional, 16.7% services, 24.4% sales, 2.6% farming, 2.6% construction, 28.2% production (2000).
Income: Per capita income: $12,281 (2000); Median household income: $24,500 (2000); Poverty rate: 24.5% (2000).
Taxes: Total city taxes per capita: $70 (1997); City property taxes per capita: $70 (1997).
Education: High school graduation rate: 77.0% (2000); College graduation rate: 13.7% (2000).
Housing: Homeownership rate: 84.3% (2000); Median home value: $35,000 (2000); Median rent: $342 per month (2000); Median age of housing: 60+ years (2000).
Transportation: Commute to work: 93.2% car, 0.0% public transportation, 6.8% walk, 0.0% work from home (2000); Travel time to work: 47.9% less than 15 minutes, 27.4% 15 to 30 minutes, 20.5% 30 to 45 minutes, 4.1% 45 to 60 minutes, 0.0% 60 minutes or more (2000)

DODGEVILLE (unincorporated postal area, zip code 49921). Covers a land area of 2.973 square miles and a water area of 0 square miles. Located at 47.09° N. Lat.; 88.57° W. Long.
History: In former copper-mining area.
Population: 413 (2000); Race: 97.2% White, 0.0% Black, 0.0% Asian, 1.0% American Indian and Alaska Native, 0.0% Hispanic of any race, 1.8% two or more races (2000); Density: 138.9 persons per square mile (2000); Age: 26.7% under 18, 10.3% over 64 (2000); Marriage status: 24.5% never married, 56.6% now married, 9.1% widowed, 9.8% divorced (2000); Foreign born: 0.0% (2000); Ancestry (includes multiple ancestries): 45.1% Finnish, 15.1% French (except Basque), 7.7% French Canadian, 7.4% German, 6.4% Croatian (2000).
Economy: Employment by occupation: 0.0% management, 11.5% professional, 24.8% services, 41.4% sales, 0.0% farming, 0.0% construction, 22.3% production (2000).
Income: Per capita income: $12,488 (2000); Median household income: $27,614 (2000); Poverty rate: 3.3% (2000).
Education: High school graduation rate: 94.4% (2000); College graduation rate: 5.6% (2000).
Housing: Homeownership rate: 78.5% (2000); Median home value: $46,800 (2000); Median rent: $345 per month (2000); Median age of housing: 60+ years (2000).
Transportation: Commute to work: 89.8% car, 0.0% public transportation, 0.0% walk, 10.2% work from home (2000); Travel time to work: 79.4% less than 15 minutes, 12.1% 15 to 30 minutes, 8.5% 30 to 45 minutes, 0.0% 45 to 60 minutes, 0.0% 60 minutes or more (2000)

DUNCAN (township). Covers a land area of 176.475 square miles and a water area of 1.106 square miles. Located at 46.49° N. Lat.; 88.83° W. Long.
Population: 280 (2000); Race: 94.5% White, 0.7% Black, 2.6% Asian, 0.7% American Indian and Alaska Native, 1.5% Hispanic of any race, 1.5% two or more races (2000); Density: 1.6 persons per square mile (2000); Age: 17.9% under 18, 24.1% over 64 (2000); Marriage status: 13.2% never married, 62.8% now married, 9.0% widowed, 15.0% divorced (2000); Foreign born: 2.9% (2000); Ancestry (includes multiple ancestries): 22.6% Finnish, 15.0% English, 15.0% French (except Basque), 13.5% Irish, 9.1% Swedish (2000).
Economy: Single-family building permits issued: 5 (2001) / 0 (2000); Multi-family building permits issued: 0 (2001) / 0 (2000); Employment by occupation: 8.4% management, 12.0% professional, 24.1% services, 13.3% sales, 2.4% farming, 12.0% construction, 27.7% production (2000).
Income: Per capita income: $13,484 (2000); Median household income: $27,625 (2000); Poverty rate: 17.9% (2000).
Taxes: Total city taxes per capita: $46 (1997); City property taxes per capita: $46 (1997).
Education: High school graduation rate: 72.6% (2000); College graduation rate: 10.6% (2000).
Housing: Homeownership rate: 85.5% (2000); Median home value: $41,200 (2000); Median rent: $208 per month (2000); Median age of housing: 40 years (2000).
Transportation: Commute to work: 85.9% car, 0.0% public transportation, 5.1% walk, 5.1% work from home (2000); Travel time to work: 39.2% less than 15 minutes, 20.3% 15 to 30 minutes, 23.0% 30 to 45 minutes, 10.8% 45 to 60 minutes, 6.8% 60 minutes or more (2000)

ELM RIVER (township). Covers a land area of 91.349 square miles and a water area of 1.924 square miles. Located at 46.89° N. Lat.; 88.85° W. Long.
Population: 169 (2000); Race: 100.0% White, 0.0% Black, 0.0% Asian, 0.0% American Indian and Alaska Native, 0.0% Hispanic of any race, 0.0% two or more races (2000); Density: 1.9 persons per square mile (2000); Age: 18.7% under 18, 20.6% over 64 (2000); Marriage status: 20.8% never married, 67.7% now married, 6.2% widowed, 5.4% divorced (2000); Foreign born: 0.0% (2000); Ancestry (includes multiple ancestries): 47.1% Finnish, 25.2% Irish, 12.3% German, 8.4% English, 7.1% Swedish (2000).
Economy: Employment by occupation: 18.9% management, 3.8% professional, 22.6% services, 35.8% sales, 0.0% farming, 7.5% construction, 11.3% production (2000).
Income: Per capita income: $15,024 (2000); Median household income: $27,813 (2000); Poverty rate: 15.0% (2000).
Taxes: Total city taxes per capita: $213 (1997); City property taxes per capita: $213 (1997).

Education: High school graduation rate: 83.8% (2000); College graduation rate: 10.3% (2000).
Housing: Homeownership rate: 93.9% (2000); Median home value: $71,000 (2000); Median rent: $300 per month (2000); Median age of housing: 41 years (2000).
Transportation: Commute to work: 80.4% car, 0.0% public transportation, 15.7% walk, 3.9% work from home (2000); Travel time to work: 38.8% less than 15 minutes, 22.4% 15 to 30 minutes, 14.3% 30 to 45 minutes, 20.4% 45 to 60 minutes, 4.1% 60 minutes or more (2000)

FRANKLIN (township). Covers a land area of 20.012 square miles and a water area of 0.689 square miles. Located at 47.15° N. Lat.; 88.54° W. Long.
Population: 1,320 (2000); Race: 99.1% White, 0.0% Black, 0.1% Asian, 0.5% American Indian and Alaska Native, 0.4% Hispanic of any race, 0.3% two or more races (2000); Density: 66.0 persons per square mile (2000); Age: 29.6% under 18, 13.2% over 64 (2000); Marriage status: 25.9% never married, 57.2% now married, 6.7% widowed, 10.3% divorced (2000); Foreign born: 1.2% (2000); Ancestry (includes multiple ancestries): 52.5% Finnish, 16.4% German, 10.4% English, 9.3% French (except Basque), 6.9% Irish (2000).
Economy: Employment by occupation: 7.0% management, 21.1% professional, 21.6% services, 25.4% sales, 0.0% farming, 11.8% construction, 13.1% production (2000).
Income: Per capita income: $14,866 (2000); Median household income: $31,176 (2000); Poverty rate: 11.6% (2000).
Taxes: Total city taxes per capita: $43 (1997); City property taxes per capita: $41 (1997).
Education: High school graduation rate: 86.9% (2000); College graduation rate: 18.0% (2000).
Housing: Homeownership rate: 86.5% (2000); Median home value: $49,700 (2000); Median rent: $331 per month (2000); Median age of housing: 60+ years (2000).
Transportation: Commute to work: 94.7% car, 0.7% public transportation, 2.5% walk, 2.1% work from home (2000); Travel time to work: 61.1% less than 15 minutes, 27.4% 15 to 30 minutes, 5.0% 30 to 45 minutes, 2.0% 45 to 60 minutes, 4.5% 60 minutes or more (2000)

HANCOCK (city). Covers a land area of 2.502 square miles and a water area of 0.349 square miles. Located at 47.13° N. Lat.; 88.59° W. Long. Elevation is 686 feet.
History: Hancock was named for the patriot John Hancock, a signer of the Declaration of Independence. It developed as a copper mining center, with the Quincy Copper Mine opening in 1848. Suomi College was founded here in 1899 by the Finnish Evangelical Lutheran Church.
Population: 4,323 (2000); Race: 96.2% White, 0.4% Black, 1.0% Asian, 1.9% American Indian and Alaska Native, 0.1% Hispanic of any race, 0.6% two or more races (2000); Density: 1,727.5 persons per square mile (2000); Age: 18.9% under 18, 20.3% over 64 (2000); Marriage status: 31.4% never married, 47.0% now married, 10.7% widowed, 10.9% divorced (2000); Foreign born: 2.3% (2000); Ancestry (includes multiple ancestries): 32.3% Finnish, 21.9% German, 11.4% English, 7.1% French (except Basque), 7.0% Irish (2000).
Economy: Single-family building permits issued: 11 (2001) / 7 (2000); Multi-family building permits issued: 0 (2001) / 4 (2000); Employment by occupation: 11.4% management, 32.1% professional, 17.8% services, 25.6% sales, 0.5% farming, 5.5% construction, 7.1% production (2000).
Income: Per capita income: $16,669 (2000); Median household income: $28,118 (2000); Poverty rate: 14.4% (2000).
Taxes: Total city taxes per capita: $145 (1997); City property taxes per capita: $145 (1997).
Education: High school graduation rate: 82.1% (2000); College graduation rate: 27.7% (2000).

School District(s)

Hancock Public Schools (KG-12)
2000 Enrollment: 984 906-487-9205

Four-year College(s)

Finlandia University (Private, Not-for-profit, Evangelical Lutheran Church)
2001 Enrollment: 418 906-482-5300
2001 Tuition: In-state $11,575; Out-of-state $11,575

Housing: Homeownership rate: 58.3% (2000); Median home value: $66,700 (2000); Median rent: $338 per month (2000); Median age of housing: 60+ years (2000).
Hospitals: Portage Health System (74 beds)
Safety: Violent crime rate: 6.9 per 10,000 population; Property crime rate: 158.8 per 10,000 population (2001).
Newspapers: The Finnish American Reporter (1 x month)
Transportation: Commute to work: 91.1% car, 0.5% public transportation, 5.7% walk, 1.2% work from home (2000); Travel time to work: 71.7% less than 15 minutes, 21.5% 15 to 30 minutes, 3.2% 30 to 45 minutes, 1.1% 45 to 60 minutes, 2.4% 60 minutes or more (2000)
Airports: Houghton County Memorial (primary service)

HANCOCK (township). Covers a land area of 15.914 square miles and a water area of 0.982 square miles. Located at 47.21° N. Lat.; 88.58° W. Long. Elevation is 686 feet.
History: Seat of Suomi College. Historic Arcadian Copper Mines (tours). Plotted 1859; incorporated as village 1875, as city 1903.
Population: 408 (2000); Race: 97.7% White, 0.0% Black, 0.0% Asian, 0.0% American Indian and Alaska Native, 0.5% Hispanic of any race, 1.8% two or more races (2000); Density: 25.6 persons per square mile (2000); Age: 23.8% under 18, 18.2% over 64 (2000); Marriage status: 21.7% never married, 65.5% now married, 6.5% widowed, 6.2% divorced (2000); Foreign born: 0.5% (2000); Ancestry (includes multiple ancestries): 46.3% Finnish, 10.6% German, 10.4% Irish, 7.6% English, 5.1% Danish (2000).
Economy: Light manufacturing; meat processing. Tourism; resort. Lift bridge connects it to Houghton. Houghton County Airport to Northeast. Employment by occupation: 12.1% management, 17.6% professional, 16.4% services, 30.3% sales, 0.0% farming, 14.5% construction, 9.1% production (2000).
Income: Per capita income: $20,707 (2000); Median household income: $42,083 (2000); Poverty rate: 8.4% (2000).
Taxes: Total city taxes per capita: $71 (1997); City property taxes per capita: $71 (1997).
Education: High school graduation rate: 85.3% (2000); College graduation rate: 29.3% (2000).
Housing: Homeownership rate: 90.3% (2000); Median home value: $94,300 (2000); Median rent: $200 per month (2000); Median age of housing: 32 years (2000).
Transportation: Commute to work: 98.8% car, 0.0% public transportation, 0.0% walk, 1.3% work from home (2000); Travel time to work: 28.5% less than 15 minutes, 58.2% 15 to 30 minutes, 9.5% 30 to 45 minutes, 1.3% 45 to 60 minutes, 2.5% 60 minutes or more (2000)
Airports: Houghton County Memorial (primary service)

HOUGHTON (city). Covers a land area of 4.313 square miles and a water area of 0.248 square miles. Located at 47.11° N. Lat.; 88.56° W. Long. Elevation is 607 feet.
History: Houghton was founded in 1852 and named for Douglass Houghton, a geologist. The town became a copper center, and later a governmental and business center. The Michigan College of Mining and Technology was founded here.
Population: 7,010 (2000); Race: 88.2% White, 3.2% Black, 5.5% Asian, 0.3% American Indian and Alaska Native, 1.4% Hispanic of any race, 2.4% two or more races (2000); Density: 1,625.5 persons per square mile (2000); Age: 12.2% under 18, 6.9% over 64 (2000); Marriage status: 67.2% never married, 25.5% now married, 4.3% widowed, 3.0% divorced (2000); Foreign born: 8.4% (2000); Ancestry (includes multiple ancestries): 25.3% German, 12.5% Finnish, 11.3% English, 11.1% Irish, 10.0% Other groups (2000).
Economy: Single-family building permits issued: 14 (2001) / 29 (2000); Multi-family building permits issued: 4 (2001) / 0 (2000); Employment by occupation: 8.8% management, 33.9% professional, 23.8% services, 25.2% sales, 1.2% farming, 3.9% construction, 3.2% production (2000).
Income: Per capita income: $11,750 (2000); Median household income: $21,186 (2000); Poverty rate: 36.9% (2000).
Taxes: Total city taxes per capita: $202 (1997); City property taxes per capita: $200 (1997).
Education: High school graduation rate: 92.2% (2000); College graduation rate: 45.5% (2000).

School District(s)

Houghton-Portage Township School (KG-12)
2000 Enrollment: 1,297 906-482-0451

Four-year College(s)

Michigan Technological University (Public)
2001 Enrollment: 6,603 906-487-1885
2001 Tuition: In-state $5,028; Out-of-state $12,306

Housing: Homeownership rate: 35.8% (2000); Median home value: $92,700 (2000); Median rent: $336 per month (2000); Median age of housing: 38 years (2000).
Safety: Violent crime rate: 0.0 per 10,000 population; Property crime rate: 105.0 per 10,000 population (2001).
Newspapers: The Daily Mining Gazette (6 x week); Copper Nugget (1 x week)

Transportation: Commute to work: 55.2% car, 2.0% public transportation, 37.0% walk, 4.4% work from home (2000); Travel time to work: 81.6% less than 15 minutes, 14.7% 15 to 30 minutes, 2.5% 30 to 45 minutes, 0.4% 45 to 60 minutes, 0.9% 60 minutes or more (2000)

Additional Information Contacts

Houghton Chamber of Commerce 906-482-5240

HUBBELL (CDP). Covers a land area of 1.866 square miles and a water area of 0.010 square miles. Located at 47.17° N. Lat.; 88.43° W. Long. Elevation is 735 feet.

History: The community of Hubbell, which began with a sawmill, developed around the Calumet and Hecla Smelting Works.

Population: 1,105 (2000); Race: 98.0% White, 0.2% Black, 0.0% Asian, 0.3% American Indian and Alaska Native, 0.8% Hispanic of any race, 1.3% two or more races (2000); Density: 592.2 persons per square mile (2000); Age: 22.7% under 18, 20.5% over 64 (2000); Marriage status: 23.3% never married, 50.4% now married, 14.8% widowed, 11.4% divorced (2000); Foreign born: 1.6% (2000); Ancestry (includes multiple ancestries): 25.4% Finnish, 23.2% French (except Basque), 16.3% German, 10.8% English, 10.7% French Canadian (2000).

Economy: Employment by occupation: 5.5% management, 14.5% professional, 33.7% services, 27.0% sales, 0.4% farming, 8.6% construction, 10.4% production (2000).

Income: Per capita income: $19,260 (2000); Median household income: $29,612 (2000); Poverty rate: 13.1% (2000).

Education: High school graduation rate: 80.8% (2000); College graduation rate: 12.3% (2000).

Housing: Homeownership rate: 86.3% (2000); Median home value: $37,900 (2000); Median rent: $287 per month (2000); Median age of housing: 60+ years (2000).

Transportation: Commute to work: 90.1% car, 0.0% public transportation, 3.2% walk, 6.7% work from home (2000); Travel time to work: 34.8% less than 15 minutes, 52.3% 15 to 30 minutes, 5.2% 30 to 45 minutes, 2.4% 45 to 60 minutes, 5.4% 60 minutes or more (2000)

LAIRD (township). Covers a land area of 188.072 square miles and a water area of 1.313 square miles. Located at 46.71° N. Lat.; 88.79° W. Long.

Population: 634 (2000); Race: 98.0% White, 0.0% Black, 0.0% Asian, 1.2% American Indian and Alaska Native, 0.0% Hispanic of any race, 0.8% two or more races (2000); Density: 3.4 persons per square mile (2000); Age: 28.6% under 18, 14.0% over 64 (2000); Marriage status: 19.3% never married, 63.1% now married, 7.0% widowed, 10.6% divorced (2000); Foreign born: 0.5% (2000); Ancestry (includes multiple ancestries): 52.3% Finnish, 17.5% German, 11.9% French (except Basque), 5.5% Swedish, 4.7% English (2000).

Economy: Employment by occupation: 11.5% management, 11.9% professional, 20.5% services, 19.4% sales, 2.2% farming, 19.4% construction, 15.1% production (2000).

Income: Per capita income: $14,728 (2000); Median household income: $33,333 (2000); Poverty rate: 8.5% (2000).

Taxes: Total city taxes per capita: $68 (1997); City property taxes per capita: $68 (1997).

Education: High school graduation rate: 86.4% (2000); College graduation rate: 8.6% (2000).

Housing: Homeownership rate: 93.8% (2000); Median home value: $60,800 (2000); Median rent: $200 per month (2000); Median age of housing: 38 years (2000).

Transportation: Commute to work: 89.5% car, 0.0% public transportation, 2.2% walk, 8.3% work from home (2000); Travel time to work: 14.2% less than 15 minutes, 41.9% 15 to 30 minutes, 26.5% 30 to 45 minutes, 14.2% 45 to 60 minutes, 3.2% 60 minutes or more (2000)

LAKE LINDEN (village). Covers a land area of 0.656 square miles and a water area of 0.109 square miles. Located at 47.19° N. Lat.; 88.40° W. Long. Elevation is 609 feet.

History: First settled in 1851, the community of Lake Linden grew up around the Calumet and Hecla Stamping Mills located here in 1867. The town was named for the linden trees that lined the lake shore.

Population: 1,081 (2000); Race: 97.3% White, 0.3% Black, 0.9% Asian, 0.0% American Indian and Alaska Native, 0.6% Hispanic of any race, 1.5% two or more races (2000); Density: 1,646.8 persons per square mile (2000); Age: 23.6% under 18, 22.7% over 64 (2000); Marriage status: 24.4% never married, 54.1% now married, 12.2% widowed, 9.2% divorced (2000); Foreign born: 0.6% (2000); Ancestry (includes multiple ancestries): 25.9% French (except Basque), 25.5% Finnish, 19.4% German, 14.7% French Canadian, 13.8% English (2000).

Economy: Employment by occupation: 8.2% management, 16.9% professional, 25.8% services, 26.4% sales, 0.0% farming, 8.7% construction, 14.0% production (2000).

Income: Per capita income: $14,189 (2000); Median household income: $24,234 (2000); Poverty rate: 17.8% (2000).

Taxes: Total city taxes per capita: $81 (1997); City property taxes per capita: $81 (1997).

Education: High school graduation rate: 81.1% (2000); College graduation rate: 13.4% (2000).

School District(s)

Lake Linden-Hubbell School District (KG-12)
2000 Enrollment: 585 906-296-6211

Housing: Homeownership rate: 68.6% (2000); Median home value: $42,400 (2000); Median rent: $244 per month (2000); Median age of housing: 60+ years (2000).

Safety: Violent crime rate: 0.0 per 10,000 population; Property crime rate: 101.2 per 10,000 population (2001).

Transportation: Commute to work: 90.7% car, 0.0% public transportation, 6.3% walk, 1.9% work from home (2000); Travel time to work: 34.7% less than 15 minutes, 54.5% 15 to 30 minutes, 7.5% 30 to 45 minutes, 2.6% 45 to 60 minutes, 0.7% 60 minutes or more (2000)

LAURIUM (village). Covers a land area of 0.672 square miles and a water area of 0 square miles. Located at 47.23° N. Lat.; 88.44° W. Long. Elevation is 1,246 feet.

History: Laurium was platted by the Laurium Mining Company and developed as a residential area for workers in Calumet. Notre Dame University football player George Gipp was a native of Laurium.

Population: 2,126 (2000); Race: 98.4% White, 0.1% Black, 0.1% Asian, 0.3% American Indian and Alaska Native, 1.1% Hispanic of any race, 0.9% two or more races (2000); Density: 3,163.7 persons per square mile (2000); Age: 29.1% under 18, 17.8% over 64 (2000); Marriage status: 24.2% never married, 52.1% now married, 11.6% widowed, 12.1% divorced (2000); Foreign born: 0.6% (2000); Ancestry (includes multiple ancestries): 38.6% Finnish, 16.5% German, 10.8% English, 10.7% Italian, 10.2% French (except Basque) (2000).

Economy: Employment by occupation: 9.8% management, 26.2% professional, 19.0% services, 24.9% sales, 0.6% farming, 5.1% construction, 14.5% production (2000).

Income: Per capita income: $16,686 (2000); Median household income: $30,404 (2000); Poverty rate: 12.4% (2000).

Taxes: Total city taxes per capita: $119 (1997); City property taxes per capita: $119 (1997).

Education: High school graduation rate: 86.3% (2000); College graduation rate: 21.2% (2000).

Housing: Homeownership rate: 75.6% (2000); Median home value: $50,600 (2000); Median rent: $272 per month (2000); Median age of housing: 60+ years (2000).

Hospitals: Keweenaw Memorial Medical Center (49 beds)

Safety: Violent crime rate: 32.8 per 10,000 population; Property crime rate: 126.3 per 10,000 population (2001).

Transportation: Commute to work: 90.3% car, 0.6% public transportation, 5.0% walk, 3.9% work from home (2000); Travel time to work: 53.7% less than 15 minutes, 35.6% 15 to 30 minutes, 8.0% 30 to 45 minutes, 1.3% 45 to 60 minutes, 1.3% 60 minutes or more (2000)

NISULA (unincorporated postal area, zip code 49952). Covers a land area of 11.636 square miles and a water area of 0.022 square miles. Located at 46.76° N. Lat.; 88.84° W. Long. Elevation is 1,050 feet.

Population: 73 (2000); Race: 100.0% White, 0.0% Black, 0.0% Asian, 0.0% American Indian and Alaska Native, 0.0% Hispanic of any race, 0.0% two or more races (2000); Density: 6.3 persons per square mile (2000); Age: 18.5% under 18, 17.3% over 64 (2000); Marriage status: 20.6% never married, 72.1% now married, 0.0% widowed, 7.4% divorced (2000); Foreign born: 0.0% (2000); Ancestry (includes multiple ancestries): 53.1% Finnish, 16.0% German, 6.2% United States or American, 6.2% English, 6.2% French (except Basque) (2000).

Economy: Employment by occupation: 16.7% management, 0.0% professional, 25.0% services, 30.6% sales, 0.0% farming, 8.3% construction, 19.4% production (2000).

Income: Per capita income: $14,216 (2000); Median household income: $29,375 (2000); Poverty rate: 11.1% (2000).

Education: High school graduation rate: 92.7% (2000); College graduation rate: 0.0% (2000).

Housing: Homeownership rate: 100.0% (2000); Median home value: $63,800 (2000); Median age of housing: 36 years (2000).

Transportation: Commute to work: 91.7% car, 0.0% public transportation, 0.0% walk, 8.3% work from home (2000); Travel time to work: 18.2% less than 15 minutes, 30.3% 15 to 30 minutes, 45.5% 30 to 45 minutes, 6.1% 45 to 60 minutes, 0.0% 60 minutes or more (2000)

OSCEOLA (township). Covers a land area of 24.836 square miles and a water area of 1.137 square miles. Located at 47.18° N. Lat.; 88.47° W. Long.
History: Osceola grew up around the Osceola Mine, a unit of the Calumet and Hecla Consolidated Copper Company.
Population: 1,908 (2000); Race: 97.7% White, 0.3% Black, 0.3% Asian, 0.2% American Indian and Alaska Native, 0.8% Hispanic of any race, 1.6% two or more races (2000); Density: 76.8 persons per square mile (2000); Age: 23.1% under 18, 15.5% over 64 (2000); Marriage status: 24.0% never married, 60.7% now married, 6.2% widowed, 9.1% divorced (2000); Foreign born: 0.9% (2000); Ancestry (includes multiple ancestries): 39.2% Finnish, 21.6% German, 12.5% English, 11.6% French (except Basque), 7.5% Swedish (2000).
Economy: Employment by occupation: 10.6% management, 17.5% professional, 26.4% services, 24.4% sales, 0.2% farming, 9.9% construction, 10.9% production (2000).
Income: Per capita income: $15,727 (2000); Median household income: $31,278 (2000); Poverty rate: 11.5% (2000).
Taxes: Total city taxes per capita: $19 (1997); City property taxes per capita: $19 (1997).
Education: High school graduation rate: 85.6% (2000); College graduation rate: 17.3% (2000).
Housing: Homeownership rate: 82.9% (2000); Median home value: $46,100 (2000); Median rent: $291 per month (2000); Median age of housing: 60+ years (2000).
Transportation: Commute to work: 94.9% car, 0.0% public transportation, 2.5% walk, 2.3% work from home (2000); Travel time to work: 45.6% less than 15 minutes, 44.3% 15 to 30 minutes, 3.7% 30 to 45 minutes, 3.0% 45 to 60 minutes, 3.4% 60 minutes or more (2000)

PORTAGE (township). Covers a land area of 112.615 square miles and a water area of 3.946 square miles. Located at 47.01° N. Lat.; 88.60° W. Long.
Population: 3,156 (2000); Race: 96.5% White, 0.6% Black, 0.9% Asian, 0.8% American Indian and Alaska Native, 0.0% Hispanic of any race, 1.3% two or more races (2000); Density: 28.0 persons per square mile (2000); Age: 22.0% under 18, 15.5% over 64 (2000); Marriage status: 28.9% never married, 52.8% now married, 8.4% widowed, 9.9% divorced (2000); Foreign born: 2.1% (2000); Ancestry (includes multiple ancestries): 34.7% Finnish, 20.5% German, 9.8% French (except Basque), 9.5% English, 7.2% Italian (2000).
Economy: Single-family building permits issued: 7 (2001) / 10 (2000); Multi-family building permits issued: 0 (2001) / 0 (2000); Employment by occupation: 11.5% management, 29.0% professional, 16.5% services, 24.5% sales, 0.8% farming, 7.1% construction, 10.6% production (2000).
Income: Per capita income: $17,655 (2000); Median household income: $33,080 (2000); Poverty rate: 14.2% (2000).
Taxes: Total city taxes per capita: $46 (2000); City property taxes per capita: $43 (2000).
Education: High school graduation rate: 86.5% (2000); College graduation rate: 29.3% (2000).
Housing: Homeownership rate: 78.3% (2000); Median home value: $68,500 (2000); Median rent: $358 per month (2000); Median age of housing: 37 years (2000).
Transportation: Commute to work: 90.3% car, 0.0% public transportation, 2.8% walk, 5.4% work from home (2000); Travel time to work: 58.6% less than 15 minutes, 29.9% 15 to 30 minutes, 7.3% 30 to 45 minutes, 0.5% 45 to 60 minutes, 3.7% 60 minutes or more (2000)

QUINCY (township). Covers a land area of 3.826 square miles and a water area of 0 square miles. Located at 47.14° N. Lat.; 88.58° W. Long.
Population: 251 (2000); Race: 100.0% White, 0.0% Black, 0.0% Asian, 0.0% American Indian and Alaska Native, 0.0% Hispanic of any race, 0.0% two or more races (2000); Density: 65.6 persons per square mile (2000); Age: 29.2% under 18, 11.4% over 64 (2000); Marriage status: 25.1% never married, 58.6% now married, 8.9% widowed, 7.4% divorced (2000); Foreign born: 5.5% (2000); Ancestry (includes multiple ancestries): 39.1% Finnish, 9.2% German, 9.2% Polish, 9.2% Swedish, 7.4% French (except Basque) (2000).
Economy: Employment by occupation: 7.3% management, 26.4% professional, 27.3% services, 23.6% sales, 0.0% farming, 5.5% construction, 10.0% production (2000).
Income: Per capita income: $19,591 (2000); Median household income: $28,750 (2000); Poverty rate: 19.6% (2000).
Taxes: Total city taxes per capita: $26 (1997); City property taxes per capita: $26 (1997).
Education: High school graduation rate: 84.9% (2000); College graduation rate: 26.4% (2000).
Housing: Homeownership rate: 71.0% (2000); Median home value: $75,600 (2000); Median rent: $283 per month (2000); Median age of housing: 60+ years (2000).
Transportation: Commute to work: 81.4% car, 2.9% public transportation, 3.9% walk, 7.8% work from home (2000); Travel time to work: 52.1% less than 15 minutes, 40.4% 15 to 30 minutes, 2.1% 30 to 45 minutes, 3.2% 45 to 60 minutes, 2.1% 60 minutes or more (2000)

SCHOOLCRAFT (township). Covers a land area of 40.091 square miles and a water area of 0.682 square miles. Located at 47.20° N. Lat.; 88.39° W. Long.
Population: 1,863 (2000); Race: 98.4% White, 0.2% Black, 0.5% Asian, 0.0% American Indian and Alaska Native, 0.4% Hispanic of any race, 0.9% two or more races (2000); Density: 46.5 persons per square mile (2000); Age: 26.3% under 18, 17.7% over 64 (2000); Marriage status: 23.1% never married, 60.2% now married, 9.1% widowed, 7.6% divorced (2000); Foreign born: 0.5% (2000); Ancestry (includes multiple ancestries): 26.8% Finnish, 23.5% French (except Basque), 17.9% German, 11.6% French Canadian, 11.6% English (2000).
Economy: Employment by occupation: 11.3% management, 17.3% professional, 24.9% services, 24.8% sales, 0.0% farming, 11.2% construction, 10.4% production (2000).
Income: Per capita income: $14,472 (2000); Median household income: $27,440 (2000); Poverty rate: 13.7% (2000).
Taxes: Total city taxes per capita: $28 (1997); City property taxes per capita: $28 (1997).
Education: High school graduation rate: 82.3% (2000); College graduation rate: 16.1% (2000).
Housing: Homeownership rate: 77.9% (2000); Median home value: $42,500 (2000); Median rent: $255 per month (2000); Median age of housing: 60+ years (2000).
Transportation: Commute to work: 92.0% car, 0.0% public transportation, 5.0% walk, 2.4% work from home (2000); Travel time to work: 32.8% less than 15 minutes, 50.3% 15 to 30 minutes, 13.3% 30 to 45 minutes, 1.7% 45 to 60 minutes, 1.9% 60 minutes or more (2000)

SOUTH RANGE (village). Covers a land area of 0.399 square miles and a water area of 0 square miles. Located at 47.07° N. Lat.; 88.64° W. Long. Elevation is 1,140 feet.
History: South Range was founded by the Whealkate Mining Company in 1902, and grew as an ore-shipping point on the Copper Range Railroad. Many of the early residents of South Range were of Italian heritage.
Population: 727 (2000); Race: 98.3% White, 0.0% Black, 0.0% Asian, 1.5% American Indian and Alaska Native, 0.3% Hispanic of any race, 0.0% two or more races (2000); Density: 1,821.1 persons per square mile (2000); Age: 18.7% under 18, 22.0% over 64 (2000); Marriage status: 28.8% never married, 48.6% now married, 11.4% widowed, 11.1% divorced (2000); Foreign born: 0.3% (2000); Ancestry (includes multiple ancestries): 45.6% Finnish, 13.7% Italian, 11.3% English, 10.4% German, 6.9% French (except Basque) (2000).
Economy: Employment by occupation: 8.3% management, 13.5% professional, 23.2% services, 30.0% sales, 0.6% farming, 14.1% construction, 10.4% production (2000).
Income: Per capita income: $15,611 (2000); Median household income: $26,250 (2000); Poverty rate: 13.7% (2000).
Taxes: Total city taxes per capita: $130 (1997); City property taxes per capita: $126 (1997).
Education: High school graduation rate: 81.6% (2000); College graduation rate: 12.7% (2000).
Housing: Homeownership rate: 74.1% (2000); Median home value: $42,000 (2000); Median rent: $247 per month (2000); Median age of housing: 60+ years (2000).
Transportation: Commute to work: 92.5% car, 0.0% public transportation, 5.6% walk, 0.9% work from home (2000); Travel time to work: 60.1% less than 15 minutes, 28.3% 15 to 30 minutes, 6.0% 30 to 45 minutes, 4.1% 45 to 60 minutes, 1.6% 60 minutes or more (2000)

STANTON (township). Covers a land area of 122.329 square miles and a water area of 1.240 square miles. Located at 47.08° N. Lat.; 88.78° W. Long.

Population: 1,268 (2000); Race: 98.8% White, 0.2% Black, 0.0% Asian, 0.0% American Indian and Alaska Native, 1.1% Hispanic of any race, 0.6% two or more races (2000); Density: 10.4 persons per square mile (2000); Age: 32.3% under 18, 12.7% over 64 (2000); Marriage status: 25.2% never married, 61.8% now married, 4.2% widowed, 8.8% divorced (2000); Foreign born: 1.1% (2000); Ancestry (includes multiple ancestries): 55.1% Finnish, 10.9% German, 8.4% English, 6.1% Irish, 4.8% French (except Basque) (2000).
Economy: Single-family building permits issued: 12 (2001) / 10 (2000); Multi-family building permits issued: 0 (2001) / 0 (2000); Employment by occupation: 12.8% management, 25.1% professional, 16.6% services, 20.9% sales, 1.7% farming, 10.1% construction, 12.8% production (2000).
Income: Per capita income: $16,338 (2000); Median household income: $38,200 (2000); Poverty rate: 7.1% (2000).
Taxes: Total city taxes per capita: $29 (1997); City property taxes per capita: $28 (1997).
Education: High school graduation rate: 89.3% (2000); College graduation rate: 24.7% (2000).
Housing: Homeownership rate: 82.5% (2000); Median home value: $74,700 (2000); Median rent: $263 per month (2000); Median age of housing: 39 years (2000).
Transportation: Commute to work: 95.2% car, 0.0% public transportation, 0.4% walk, 4.4% work from home (2000); Travel time to work: 24.6% less than 15 minutes, 54.1% 15 to 30 minutes, 17.4% 30 to 45 minutes, 0.7% 45 to 60 minutes, 3.3% 60 minutes or more (2000)

TOIVOLA (unincorporated postal area, zip code 49965). Covers a land area of 105.459 square miles and a water area of 0.817 square miles. Located at 47.00° N. Lat.; 88.88° W. Long. Elevation is 1,275 feet.
History: Toivola was settled by people of Finnish ancestry. Formerly a logging camp, it became a farming area.
Population: 437 (2000); Race: 100.0% White, 0.0% Black, 0.0% Asian, 0.0% American Indian and Alaska Native, 0.5% Hispanic of any race, 0.0% two or more races (2000); Density: 4.1 persons per square mile (2000); Age: 15.5% under 18, 20.0% over 64 (2000); Marriage status: 24.1% never married, 61.7% now married, 6.4% widowed, 7.8% divorced (2000); Foreign born: 0.5% (2000); Ancestry (includes multiple ancestries): 59.8% Finnish, 12.8% Irish, 8.8% English, 8.5% German, 6.0% Italian (2000).
Economy: Employment by occupation: 12.6% management, 7.3% professional, 25.2% services, 26.5% sales, 1.3% farming, 5.3% construction, 21.9% production (2000).
Income: Per capita income: $16,040 (2000); Median household income: $22,109 (2000); Poverty rate: 15.1% (2000).
Education: High school graduation rate: 82.1% (2000); College graduation rate: 12.3% (2000).

School District(s)

Elm River Township School District (KG-08)
2000 Enrollment: 9 906-288-3751
Housing: Homeownership rate: 81.8% (2000); Median home value: $48,300 (2000); Median rent: $245 per month (2000); Median age of housing: 44 years (2000).
Transportation: Commute to work: 88.5% car, 0.0% public transportation, 6.8% walk, 4.7% work from home (2000); Travel time to work: 21.3% less than 15 minutes, 22.7% 15 to 30 minutes, 38.3% 30 to 45 minutes, 15.6% 45 to 60 minutes, 2.1% 60 minutes or more (2000)

TORCH LAKE (township). Covers a land area of 80.145 square miles and a water area of 12.858 square miles. Located at 47.12° N. Lat.; 88.40° W. Long.
Population: 1,860 (2000); Race: 98.8% White, 0.1% Black, 0.2% Asian, 0.0% American Indian and Alaska Native, 0.2% Hispanic of any race, 0.7% two or more races (2000); Density: 23.2 persons per square mile (2000); Age: 23.8% under 18, 19.2% over 64 (2000); Marriage status: 20.9% never married, 59.6% now married, 11.0% widowed, 8.5% divorced (2000); Foreign born: 1.4% (2000); Ancestry (includes multiple ancestries): 28.6% Finnish, 20.3% French (except Basque), 18.4% German, 9.9% English, 9.6% Italian (2000).
Economy: Employment by occupation: 10.5% management, 18.5% professional, 22.9% services, 28.2% sales, 0.2% farming, 9.4% construction, 10.3% production (2000).
Income: Per capita income: $19,158 (2000); Median household income: $35,893 (2000); Poverty rate: 9.8% (2000).
Taxes: Total city taxes per capita: $31 (1997); City property taxes per capita: $31 (1997).
Education: High school graduation rate: 86.1% (2000); College graduation rate: 17.8% (2000).
Housing: Homeownership rate: 87.6% (2000); Median home value: $72,600 (2000); Median rent: $290 per month (2000); Median age of housing: 35 years (2000).
Transportation: Commute to work: 89.9% car, 0.0% public transportation, 2.9% walk, 6.8% work from home (2000); Travel time to work: 28.5% less than 15 minutes, 50.1% 15 to 30 minutes, 15.0% 30 to 45 minutes, 2.2% 45 to 60 minutes, 4.3% 60 minutes or more (2000)

Huron County

Located in eastern Michigan, at the tip of the Thumb; bounded on the east and north by Lake Huron, and on the west by Saginaw Bay; drained by headwaters of the Cass and by Pigeon and Willow Rivers. Covers a land area of 836.50 square miles, a water area of 1,300.00 square miles, and is located in the Eastern Time Zone. The county government was organized in 1840. County seat is Bad Axe.

Weather Station: Bad Axe Elevation: 711 feet

	Jan	Feb	Mar	Apr	May	Jun	Jul	Aug	Sep	Oct	Nov	Dec
High	28	30	40	53	67	76	81	79	71	59	45	33
Low	14	15	23	33	44	53	58	56	50	40	31	21
Precip	1.9	1.6	2.4	2.8	2.7	2.8	3.1	3.6	3.8	2.6	2.8	2.1
Snow	13.0	9.3	9.9	3.0	tr	0.0	0.0	0.0	tr	0.6	5.0	10.9

High and Low temperatures in degrees Fahrenheit; Precipitation and Snow in inches

Weather Station: Harbor Beach 1 SSE Elevation: 597 feet

	Jan	Feb	Mar	Apr	May	Jun	Jul	Aug	Sep	Oct	Nov	Dec
High	29	31	39	50	63	72	78	77	70	58	45	34
Low	14	15	24	34	44	53	59	58	51	41	31	22
Precip	2.7	2.0	2.5	2.8	2.8	2.6	3.0	3.5	4.0	2.7	3.1	2.7
Snow	na	12.8	10.6	3.1	0.2	0.0	0.0	0.0	tr	0.2	3.8	15.9

High and Low temperatures in degrees Fahrenheit; Precipitation and Snow in inches

Population: 36,079 (2000); Race: 97.9% White, 0.2% Black, 0.3% Asian, 0.4% American Indian and Alaska Native, 1.4% Hispanic of any race, 1.0% two or more races (2000); Density: 43.1 persons per square mile (2000); Age: 24.3% under 18, 19.5% over 64 (2000).
Religion: Five largest groups: 40.4% Catholic Church, 13.8% Lutheran Church—Missouri Synod, 7.3% The United Methodist Church, 2.4% Wisconsin Evangelical Lutheran Synod, 1.7% Evangelical Lutheran Church in America (2000).
Economy: Unemployment rate: 7.5% (11/2002); Total civilian labor force: 18,279 (11/2002); Leading industries: 37.1% manufacturing; 14.9% retail trade; 13.9% health care and social assistance (2000); Companies that employ more than 1,000 persons: 0 (2000); Companies that employ more than 100 persons: 21 (2000); Farms: 1,184 totaling 424,122 acres (1997); Minority business ownership rate: 0.0% (1997); Women business ownership rate: 26.0% (1997); Retail sales per capita: $7,441 (1997). Single-family building permits issued: 162 (2001) / 206 (2000); Multi-family building permits issued: 10 (2001) / 0 (2000).
Income: Per capita income: $17,851 (2000); Median household income: $35,315 (2000); Poverty rate: 10.2% (2000); Bankruptcy rate: 3.18% (2001).
Taxes: Total county taxes per capita: $228 (2000); County property taxes per capita: $212 (2000).
Education: High school graduation rate: 78.3% (2000); College graduation rate: 10.9% (2000).
Housing: Homeownership rate: 83.5% (2000); Median home value: $78,000 (2000); Median rent: $322 per month (2000); Median age of housing: 38 years (2000).
Health: Birth rate: 107.0 per 10,000 population (1998); Age adjusted death rate: 95.1 per 10,000 population (1999); Age adjusted cancer mortality rate: 206.0 deaths per 100,000 population (1999). Air Quality Index: 67% good, 32% moderate, 1% unhealthy (percent of days in 2000). Number of physicians: 8.9 per 10,000 population (1999); Number of hospital beds: 46.3 per 10,000 population (1999).
Elections: 2000 Presidential election results: 42.9% Gore, 55.4% Bush, 1.4% Nader, 0.0% Buchanan
National and State Parks: Albert E Sleeper State Park; Port Crescent State Park; Wild Fowl Bay State Park
Additional Information Contacts
Huron County Government Offices 989-269-8242
Bay Port Chamber of Commerce 989-453-0109
Caseville Chamber of Commerce. 989-856-3818
Harbor Beach Chamber of Commerce 989-479-6477
Port Austin Chamber of Commerce 989-738-7600

Huron County Communities

BAD AXE (city). Covers a land area of 2.141 square miles and a water area of 0 square miles. Located at 43.80° N. Lat.; 83.00° W. Long. Elevation is 765 feet.

History: Local legend says that Bad Axe received its unusual name from a broken axe found on the site when it was surveyed. For a time, mail was delivered to Bad Axe if it had the sketch of a broken axe on the envelope. The village was planned in 1873, incorporated as a village in 1885 and as a city in 1905. For a time in the early 1900's it was known as Huron, but the residents voted back in the name of Bad Axe.

Population: 3,462 (2000); Race: 97.4% White, 0.3% Black, 0.2% Asian, 0.7% American Indian and Alaska Native, 1.0% Hispanic of any race, 1.1% two or more races (2000); Density: 1,617.3 persons per square mile (2000); Age: 24.2% under 18, 19.0% over 64 (2000); Marriage status: 25.9% never married, 52.1% now married, 10.7% widowed, 11.4% divorced (2000); Foreign born: 2.0% (2000); Ancestry (includes multiple ancestries): 31.2% German, 18.2% Polish, 14.1% English, 13.4% Irish, 8.7% French (except Basque) (2000).

Economy: Employment by occupation: 10.3% management, 21.0% professional, 14.4% services, 24.7% sales, 0.8% farming, 6.3% construction, 22.6% production (2000).

Income: Per capita income: $17,465 (2000); Median household income: $32,125 (2000); Poverty rate: 14.1% (2000).

Taxes: Total city taxes per capita: $375 (1997); City property taxes per capita: $372 (1997).

Education: High school graduation rate: 76.7% (2000); College graduation rate: 16.4% (2000).

School District(s)

Bad Axe Public Schools (KG-12)
2000 Enrollment: 1,417 517-269-9938
Bloomfield Township School District #7f (KG-08)
2000 Enrollment: 15 517-269-6406
Church School District (KG-08)
2000 Enrollment: 26 517-269-6406
Colfax Township School District 1F (KG-08)
2000 Enrollment: 12 517-269-6406
Sigel Township School District #3f (KG-08)
2000 Enrollment: 21 517-269-6406
Verona Township School District #1f (KG-08)
2000 Enrollment: 24 517-269-6406

Housing: Homeownership rate: 68.1% (2000); Median home value: $70,800 (2000); Median rent: $316 per month (2000); Median age of housing: 47 years (2000).

Safety: Violent crime rate: 23.0 per 10,000 population; Property crime rate: 474.1 per 10,000 population (2001).

Newspapers: The Huron Daily Tribune (6 x week)

Transportation: Commute to work: 92.9% car, 1.3% public transportation, 3.3% walk, 0.9% work from home (2000); Travel time to work: 64.1% less than 15 minutes, 24.7% 15 to 30 minutes, 5.5% 30 to 45 minutes, 2.3% 45 to 60 minutes, 3.4% 60 minutes or more (2000)

BAY PORT (unincorporated postal area, zip code 48720). Covers a land area of 32.496 square miles and a water area of 0 square miles. Located at 43.83° N. Lat.; 83.34° W. Long. Elevation is 597 feet.

History: First a lumber town, Bay Port later depended on commercial fishing for its revenue. Its location on Wild Fowl Bay, a nook off Saginaw Bay, gave it a scenic setting.

Population: 1,218 (2000); Race: 97.7% White, 0.1% Black, 0.8% Asian, 0.3% American Indian and Alaska Native, 1.7% Hispanic of any race, 0.7% two or more races (2000); Density: 37.5 persons per square mile (2000); Age: 26.9% under 18, 14.8% over 64 (2000); Marriage status: 22.0% never married, 59.5% now married, 7.2% widowed, 11.3% divorced (2000); Foreign born: 2.0% (2000); Ancestry (includes multiple ancestries): 54.1% German, 8.5% English, 7.8% Irish, 7.8% French (except Basque), 6.4% Polish (2000).

Economy: Employment by occupation: 10.9% management, 7.8% professional, 16.0% services, 16.8% sales, 2.3% farming, 14.5% construction, 31.7% production (2000).

Income: Per capita income: $15,999 (2000); Median household income: $35,655 (2000); Poverty rate: 10.9% (2000).

Education: High school graduation rate: 79.6% (2000); College graduation rate: 9.4% (2000).

Housing: Homeownership rate: 85.9% (2000); Median home value: $65,000 (2000); Median rent: $313 per month (2000); Median age of housing: 59 years (2000).

Transportation: Commute to work: 90.4% car, 0.8% public transportation, 4.4% walk, 4.1% work from home (2000); Travel time to work: 52.6% less than 15 minutes, 27.1% 15 to 30 minutes, 11.1% 30 to 45 minutes, 2.3% 45 to 60 minutes, 6.9% 60 minutes or more (2000)

Additional Information Contacts

Bay Port Chamber of Commerce 989-453-0109

BINGHAM (township). Covers a land area of 35.877 square miles and a water area of 0 square miles. Located at 43.71° N. Lat.; 82.93° W. Long.

History: Bingham Township was organized in 1863 and named for Governor Kingsley S. Bingham.

Population: 1,751 (2000); Race: 99.0% White, 0.0% Black, 0.2% Asian, 0.0% American Indian and Alaska Native, 0.4% Hispanic of any race, 0.8% two or more races (2000); Density: 48.8 persons per square mile (2000); Age: 27.7% under 18, 14.9% over 64 (2000); Marriage status: 20.4% never married, 65.1% now married, 8.4% widowed, 6.1% divorced (2000); Foreign born: 1.2% (2000); Ancestry (includes multiple ancestries): 40.0% Polish, 37.9% German, 7.1% English, 5.9% Irish, 5.0% French (except Basque) (2000).

Economy: Employment by occupation: 12.5% management, 13.1% professional, 14.1% services, 19.7% sales, 1.5% farming, 12.1% construction, 27.1% production (2000).

Income: Per capita income: $17,916 (2000); Median household income: $37,102 (2000); Poverty rate: 10.5% (2000).

Taxes: Total city taxes per capita: $76 (1997); City property taxes per capita: $76 (1997).

Education: High school graduation rate: 78.8% (2000); College graduation rate: 10.1% (2000).

Housing: Homeownership rate: 86.3% (2000); Median home value: $77,800 (2000); Median rent: $294 per month (2000); Median age of housing: 36 years (2000).

Transportation: Commute to work: 91.8% car, 0.1% public transportation, 2.9% walk, 4.5% work from home (2000); Travel time to work: 40.5% less than 15 minutes, 35.8% 15 to 30 minutes, 14.4% 30 to 45 minutes, 1.9% 45 to 60 minutes, 7.4% 60 minutes or more (2000)

BLOOMFIELD (township). Covers a land area of 35.954 square miles and a water area of 0.046 square miles. Located at 43.89° N. Lat.; 82.83° W. Long.

Population: 535 (2000); Race: 99.8% White, 0.0% Black, 0.0% Asian, 0.0% American Indian and Alaska Native, 0.0% Hispanic of any race, 0.2% two or more races (2000); Density: 14.9 persons per square mile (2000); Age: 24.0% under 18, 18.2% over 64 (2000); Marriage status: 21.1% never married, 66.5% now married, 6.2% widowed, 6.2% divorced (2000); Foreign born: 0.4% (2000); Ancestry (includes multiple ancestries): 55.5% German, 19.1% Polish, 9.0% United States or American, 8.2% English, 7.0% Irish (2000).

Economy: Employment by occupation: 21.9% management, 7.6% professional, 10.7% services, 15.6% sales, 4.9% farming, 9.4% construction, 29.9% production (2000).

Income: Per capita income: $16,996 (2000); Median household income: $40,000 (2000); Poverty rate: 6.7% (2000).

Taxes: Total city taxes per capita: $155 (1997); City property taxes per capita: $155 (1997).

Education: High school graduation rate: 73.7% (2000); College graduation rate: 7.3% (2000).

Housing: Homeownership rate: 96.3% (2000); Median home value: $74,600 (2000); Median rent: $375 per month (2000); Median age of housing: 60 years (2000).

Transportation: Commute to work: 79.9% car, 1.3% public transportation, 6.7% walk, 12.1% work from home (2000); Travel time to work: 28.9% less than 15 minutes, 34.0% 15 to 30 minutes, 26.4% 30 to 45 minutes, 3.6% 45 to 60 minutes, 7.1% 60 minutes or more (2000)

BROOKFIELD (township). Covers a land area of 35.528 square miles and a water area of 0 square miles. Located at 43.73° N. Lat.; 83.28° W. Long.

History: Brookfield Township was first settled by A.H. Burton, whose home was the location of the first township election in 1868. He named the township for his former home in New York.

Population: 914 (2000); Race: 98.8% White, 0.0% Black, 0.4% Asian, 0.2% American Indian and Alaska Native, 8.3% Hispanic of any race, 0.5% two or more races (2000); Density: 25.7 persons per square mile (2000); Age: 24.1% under 18, 18.0% over 64 (2000); Marriage status: 27.4% never married,

57.7% now married, 6.2% widowed, 8.7% divorced (2000); Foreign born: 6.3% (2000); Ancestry (includes multiple ancestries): 44.2% German, 10.9% English, 10.5% Other groups, 9.6% Polish, 8.4% United States or American (2000).
Economy: Employment by occupation: 8.8% management, 7.7% professional, 17.6% services, 18.1% sales, 3.2% farming, 8.2% construction, 36.4% production (2000).
Income: Per capita income: $14,737 (2000); Median household income: $32,656 (2000); Poverty rate: 14.3% (2000).
Taxes: Total city taxes per capita: $158 (1997); City property taxes per capita: $156 (1997).
Education: High school graduation rate: 70.7% (2000); College graduation rate: 4.2% (2000).
Housing: Homeownership rate: 82.4% (2000); Median home value: $58,800 (2000); Median rent: $310 per month (2000); Median age of housing: 54 years (2000).
Transportation: Commute to work: 82.7% car, 0.0% public transportation, 4.8% walk, 12.4% work from home (2000); Travel time to work: 26.4% less than 15 minutes, 37.7% 15 to 30 minutes, 18.3% 30 to 45 minutes, 10.1% 45 to 60 minutes, 7.5% 60 minutes or more (2000)

CASEVILLE (village). Covers a land area of 1.141 square miles and a water area of 0 square miles. Located at 43.94° N. Lat.; 83.27° W. Long. Elevation is 587 feet.
History: Caseville was first settled in 1836, when it was known as Pigeon River Settlement. Once an industrial center with lake and rail shipping facilities for its salt and iron works, Caseville later became a tourist village, drawing vacationers to the shores of Saginaw Bay.
Population: 888 (2000); Race: 95.6% White, 0.8% Black, 0.0% Asian, 1.4% American Indian and Alaska Native, 0.8% Hispanic of any race, 2.2% two or more races (2000); Density: 778.4 persons per square mile (2000); Age: 16.2% under 18, 28.4% over 64 (2000); Marriage status: 21.1% never married, 51.9% now married, 14.4% widowed, 12.6% divorced (2000); Foreign born: 1.6% (2000); Ancestry (includes multiple ancestries): 29.9% German, 14.0% Irish, 13.9% English, 11.1% Polish, 6.7% Other groups (2000).
Economy: Employment by occupation: 12.9% management, 16.9% professional, 20.0% services, 19.7% sales, 0.0% farming, 12.3% construction, 18.2% production (2000).
Income: Per capita income: $20,501 (2000); Median household income: $27,065 (2000); Poverty rate: 13.5% (2000).
Taxes: Total city taxes per capita: $341 (1997); City property taxes per capita: $330 (1997).
Education: High school graduation rate: 80.4% (2000); College graduation rate: 10.5% (2000).

School District(s)

Caseville Public Schools (KG-12)
2000 Enrollment: 296 517-856-2940
Housing: Homeownership rate: 72.2% (2000); Median home value: $82,200 (2000); Median rent: $316 per month (2000); Median age of housing: 29 years (2000).
Safety: Violent crime rate: 0.0 per 10,000 population; Property crime rate: 369.5 per 10,000 population (2001).
Transportation: Commute to work: 92.6% car, 1.2% public transportation, 2.8% walk, 3.4% work from home (2000); Travel time to work: 42.3% less than 15 minutes, 29.2% 15 to 30 minutes, 12.8% 30 to 45 minutes, 5.4% 45 to 60 minutes, 10.3% 60 minutes or more (2000)
Additional Information Contacts
Caseville Chamber of Commerce. 989-856-3818

CASEVILLE (township). Covers a land area of 13.925 square miles and a water area of 0.279 square miles. Located at 43.92° N. Lat.; 83.29° W. Long. Elevation is 587 feet.
History: Caseville Township was named for Leonard Case, who owned land in the area.
Population: 2,723 (2000); Race: 96.9% White, 0.3% Black, 0.2% Asian, 0.5% American Indian and Alaska Native, 0.6% Hispanic of any race, 1.8% two or more races (2000); Density: 195.5 persons per square mile (2000); Age: 16.5% under 18, 28.3% over 64 (2000); Marriage status: 16.8% never married, 64.3% now married, 9.8% widowed, 9.1% divorced (2000); Foreign born: 2.7% (2000); Ancestry (includes multiple ancestries): 30.9% German, 15.2% English, 13.5% Irish, 12.8% Polish, 6.3% French (except Basque) (2000).
Economy: Single-family building permits issued: 14 (2001) / 28 (2000); Multi-family building permits issued: 10 (2001) / 0 (2000); Employment by occupation: 13.3% management, 18.8% professional, 15.0% services, 21.4% sales, 0.2% farming, 11.9% construction, 19.4% production (2000).
Income: Per capita income: $24,128 (2000); Median household income: $35,558 (2000); Poverty rate: 8.6% (2000).
Taxes: Total city taxes per capita: $134 (1997); City property taxes per capita: $124 (1997).
Education: High school graduation rate: 83.1% (2000); College graduation rate: 16.0% (2000).
Housing: Homeownership rate: 85.2% (2000); Median home value: $119,500 (2000); Median rent: $322 per month (2000); Median age of housing: 25 years (2000).
Transportation: Commute to work: 92.9% car, 1.2% public transportation, 2.2% walk, 3.4% work from home (2000); Travel time to work: 40.5% less than 15 minutes, 30.3% 15 to 30 minutes, 14.6% 30 to 45 minutes, 5.5% 45 to 60 minutes, 9.1% 60 minutes or more (2000)

CHANDLER (township). Covers a land area of 35.339 square miles and a water area of 0 square miles. Located at 43.88° N. Lat.; 83.17° W. Long.
History: Chandler Township was organized in 1880 and named for Zachariah Chandler, a U.S. senator from Michigan.
Population: 501 (2000); Race: 95.9% White, 0.2% Black, 1.3% Asian, 0.9% American Indian and Alaska Native, 0.6% Hispanic of any race, 1.1% two or more races (2000); Density: 14.2 persons per square mile (2000); Age: 27.7% under 18, 14.9% over 64 (2000); Marriage status: 20.7% never married, 63.4% now married, 5.0% widowed, 10.9% divorced (2000); Foreign born: 0.9% (2000); Ancestry (includes multiple ancestries): 40.9% German, 12.8% English, 10.9% Irish, 10.4% Polish, 8.3% Other groups (2000).
Economy: Employment by occupation: 19.6% management, 11.0% professional, 11.9% services, 15.1% sales, 4.6% farming, 10.0% construction, 27.9% production (2000).
Income: Per capita income: $16,540 (2000); Median household income: $40,938 (2000); Poverty rate: 6.6% (2000).
Taxes: Total city taxes per capita: $398 (1997); City property taxes per capita: $398 (1997).
Education: High school graduation rate: 81.1% (2000); College graduation rate: 9.4% (2000).
Housing: Homeownership rate: 89.5% (2000); Median home value: $85,400 (2000); Median rent: $483 per month (2000); Median age of housing: 48 years (2000).
Transportation: Commute to work: 91.2% car, 0.9% public transportation, 0.5% walk, 7.4% work from home (2000); Travel time to work: 39.3% less than 15 minutes, 45.8% 15 to 30 minutes, 10.0% 30 to 45 minutes, 3.0% 45 to 60 minutes, 2.0% 60 minutes or more (2000)

COLFAX (township). Covers a land area of 34.915 square miles and a water area of 0.034 square miles. Located at 43.80° N. Lat.; 83.05° W. Long.
Population: 1,954 (2000); Race: 97.1% White, 0.2% Black, 0.2% Asian, 0.2% American Indian and Alaska Native, 0.9% Hispanic of any race, 1.6% two or more races (2000); Density: 56.0 persons per square mile (2000); Age: 24.4% under 18, 18.6% over 64 (2000); Marriage status: 18.6% never married, 64.1% now married, 9.8% widowed, 7.4% divorced (2000); Foreign born: 0.9% (2000); Ancestry (includes multiple ancestries): 40.6% German, 16.9% Polish, 11.8% United States or American, 9.4% Irish, 7.2% French (except Basque) (2000).
Economy: Employment by occupation: 11.5% management, 12.2% professional, 15.0% services, 28.3% sales, 2.1% farming, 8.0% construction, 23.0% production (2000).
Income: Per capita income: $19,237 (2000); Median household income: $42,727 (2000); Poverty rate: 3.3% (2000).
Taxes: Total city taxes per capita: $79 (1997); City property taxes per capita: $79 (1997).
Education: High school graduation rate: 80.4% (2000); College graduation rate: 8.7% (2000).
Housing: Homeownership rate: 85.3% (2000); Median home value: $88,700 (2000); Median rent: $370 per month (2000); Median age of housing: 27 years (2000).
Transportation: Commute to work: 92.9% car, 0.0% public transportation, 3.1% walk, 2.5% work from home (2000); Travel time to work: 64.3% less than 15 minutes, 26.1% 15 to 30 minutes, 4.1% 30 to 45 minutes, 1.1% 45 to 60 minutes, 4.4% 60 minutes or more (2000)

DWIGHT (township). Covers a land area of 35.679 square miles and a water area of 0.019 square miles. Located at 43.97° N. Lat.; 82.95° W. Long.
Population: 930 (2000); Race: 99.5% White, 0.0% Black, 0.5% Asian, 0.0% American Indian and Alaska Native, 0.0% Hispanic of any race, 0.0% two or more races (2000); Density: 26.1 persons per square mile (2000); Age: 29.4%

under 18, 16.6% over 64 (2000); Marriage status: 22.1% never married, 62.2% now married, 8.0% widowed, 7.7% divorced (2000); Foreign born: 1.2% (2000); Ancestry (includes multiple ancestries): 39.4% Polish, 38.3% German, 10.4% Irish, 6.3% English, 5.8% Other groups (2000).
Economy: Employment by occupation: 14.4% management, 9.0% professional, 17.7% services, 18.5% sales, 3.6% farming, 6.4% construction, 30.3% production (2000).
Income: Per capita income: $14,598 (2000); Median household income: $35,000 (2000); Poverty rate: 11.1% (2000).
Taxes: Total city taxes per capita: $84 (1997); City property taxes per capita: $84 (1997).
Education: High school graduation rate: 75.1% (2000); College graduation rate: 6.1% (2000).
Housing: Homeownership rate: 83.3% (2000); Median home value: $64,800 (2000); Median rent: $309 per month (2000); Median age of housing: 51 years (2000).
Transportation: Commute to work: 87.5% car, 0.0% public transportation, 2.9% walk, 8.1% work from home (2000); Travel time to work: 32.7% less than 15 minutes, 41.5% 15 to 30 minutes, 20.2% 30 to 45 minutes, 3.4% 45 to 60 minutes, 2.3% 60 minutes or more (2000)

ELKTON (village). Covers a land area of 0.991 square miles and a water area of 0 square miles. Located at 43.81° N. Lat.; 83.18° W. Long. Elevation is 647 feet.
Population: 863 (2000); Race: 94.5% White, 0.6% Black, 0.7% Asian, 0.0% American Indian and Alaska Native, 2.5% Hispanic of any race, 3.8% two or more races (2000); Density: 870.6 persons per square mile (2000); Age: 27.7% under 18, 18.0% over 64 (2000); Marriage status: 26.6% never married, 52.2% now married, 10.1% widowed, 11.0% divorced (2000); Foreign born: 0.8% (2000); Ancestry (includes multiple ancestries): 42.2% German, 11.9% Polish, 10.5% Other groups, 8.8% French (except Basque), 8.5% Irish (2000).
Economy: In agricultural area; dairy products. Manufacturing: metal stampings. Employment by occupation: 5.0% management, 9.1% professional, 20.9% services, 27.5% sales, 0.5% farming, 10.8% construction, 26.2% production (2000).
Income: Per capita income: $14,490 (2000); Median household income: $28,859 (2000); Poverty rate: 15.2% (2000).
Taxes: Total city taxes per capita: $221 (1997); City property taxes per capita: $221 (1997).
Education: High school graduation rate: 71.9% (2000); College graduation rate: 5.1% (2000).
Housing: Homeownership rate: 73.7% (2000); Median home value: $64,000 (2000); Median rent: $305 per month (2000); Median age of housing: 46 years (2000).
Safety: Violent crime rate: 0.0 per 10,000 population; Property crime rate: 414.7 per 10,000 population (2001).
Transportation: Commute to work: 81.7% car, 0.0% public transportation, 12.7% walk, 2.0% work from home (2000); Travel time to work: 58.3% less than 15 minutes, 29.8% 15 to 30 minutes, 7.3% 30 to 45 minutes, 1.0% 45 to 60 minutes, 3.6% 60 minutes or more (2000)

FAIRHAVEN (township). Covers a land area of 21.084 square miles and a water area of 36.948 square miles. Located at 43.80° N. Lat.; 83.40° W. Long.
Population: 1,259 (2000); Race: 96.8% White, 0.1% Black, 0.4% Asian, 0.3% American Indian and Alaska Native, 2.9% Hispanic of any race, 1.3% two or more races (2000); Density: 59.7 persons per square mile (2000); Age: 23.9% under 18, 17.4% over 64 (2000); Marriage status: 22.4% never married, 56.9% now married, 9.2% widowed, 11.6% divorced (2000); Foreign born: 1.3% (2000); Ancestry (includes multiple ancestries): 51.4% German, 11.3% Irish, 10.0% English, 7.7% French (except Basque), 7.6% United States or American (2000).
Economy: Employment by occupation: 8.1% management, 9.0% professional, 17.6% services, 18.0% sales, 2.4% farming, 14.2% construction, 30.7% production (2000).
Income: Per capita income: $16,689 (2000); Median household income: $33,500 (2000); Poverty rate: 11.0% (2000).
Taxes: Total city taxes per capita: $153 (2000); City property taxes per capita: $149 (2000).
Education: High school graduation rate: 78.3% (2000); College graduation rate: 9.8% (2000).
Housing: Homeownership rate: 86.1% (2000); Median home value: $68,700 (2000); Median rent: $327 per month (2000); Median age of housing: 45 years (2000).
Transportation: Commute to work: 89.1% car, 0.9% public transportation, 5.7% walk, 4.0% work from home (2000); Travel time to work: 44.5% less than 15 minutes, 27.8% 15 to 30 minutes, 16.2% 30 to 45 minutes, 3.6% 45 to 60 minutes, 7.9% 60 minutes or more (2000)

FILION (unincorporated postal area, zip code 48432). Covers a land area of 38.211 square miles and a water area of 0.006 square miles. Located at 43.89° N. Lat.; 83.01° W. Long.
History: Filion was founded in 1861 by a group of French Canadians. The village was an early producer of honey, with the David Running Apiary established here.
Population: 794 (2000); Race: 98.9% White, 0.0% Black, 0.6% Asian, 0.0% American Indian and Alaska Native, 0.0% Hispanic of any race, 0.5% two or more races (2000); Density: 20.8 persons per square mile (2000); Age: 23.9% under 18, 16.9% over 64 (2000); Marriage status: 23.8% never married, 61.8% now married, 8.4% widowed, 5.9% divorced (2000); Foreign born: 0.9% (2000); Ancestry (includes multiple ancestries): 39.4% German, 33.6% Polish, 9.7% Irish, 8.8% French (except Basque), 7.3% English (2000).
Economy: Employment by occupation: 10.0% management, 10.0% professional, 13.7% services, 20.5% sales, 4.2% farming, 10.3% construction, 31.3% production (2000).
Income: Per capita income: $15,714 (2000); Median household income: $35,903 (2000); Poverty rate: 8.5% (2000).
Education: High school graduation rate: 71.8% (2000); College graduation rate: 6.7% (2000).
Housing: Homeownership rate: 90.7% (2000); Median home value: $64,400 (2000); Median rent: $292 per month (2000); Median age of housing: 46 years (2000).
Transportation: Commute to work: 85.8% car, 3.0% public transportation, 2.4% walk, 8.9% work from home (2000); Travel time to work: 27.4% less than 15 minutes, 50.1% 15 to 30 minutes, 14.5% 30 to 45 minutes, 4.4% 45 to 60 minutes, 3.5% 60 minutes or more (2000)

GORE (township). Covers a land area of 6.768 square miles and a water area of 0.084 square miles. Located at 43.96° N. Lat.; 82.75° W. Long.
History: Gore Township was organized in 1862 and named for the triangular shape formed by its boundaries.
Population: 139 (2000); Race: 89.9% White, 0.0% Black, 0.0% Asian, 0.0% American Indian and Alaska Native, 0.0% Hispanic of any race, 10.1% two or more races (2000); Density: 20.5 persons per square mile (2000); Age: 22.3% under 18, 20.1% over 64 (2000); Marriage status: 16.1% never married, 67.9% now married, 9.8% widowed, 6.3% divorced (2000); Foreign born: 0.0% (2000); Ancestry (includes multiple ancestries): 51.8% German, 18.0% Polish, 18.0% English, 10.8% Greek, 6.5% French (except Basque) (2000).
Economy: Employment by occupation: 6.1% management, 24.5% professional, 0.0% services, 28.6% sales, 10.2% farming, 4.1% construction, 26.5% production (2000).
Income: Per capita income: $19,401 (2000); Median household income: $25,625 (2000); Poverty rate: 16.5% (2000).
Taxes: Total city taxes per capita: $163 (1997); City property taxes per capita: $163 (1997).
Education: High school graduation rate: 73.6% (2000); College graduation rate: 15.1% (2000).
Housing: Homeownership rate: 97.0% (2000); Median home value: $86,100 (2000); Median age of housing: 22 years (2000).
Transportation: Commute to work: 87.8% car, 0.0% public transportation, 0.0% walk, 12.2% work from home (2000); Travel time to work: 51.2% less than 15 minutes, 30.2% 15 to 30 minutes, 7.0% 30 to 45 minutes, 11.6% 45 to 60 minutes, 0.0% 60 minutes or more (2000)

GRANT (township). Covers a land area of 35.430 square miles and a water area of 0.047 square miles. Located at 43.72° N. Lat.; 83.18° W. Long.
History: Grant Township was first settled by Levin Williamson in 1863. The township was organized in 1867 and named for General Ulysses S. Grant.
Population: 833 (2000); Race: 95.8% White, 1.8% Black, 0.0% Asian, 0.0% American Indian and Alaska Native, 1.4% Hispanic of any race, 1.9% two or more races (2000); Density: 23.5 persons per square mile (2000); Age: 28.8% under 18, 12.6% over 64 (2000); Marriage status: 19.9% never married, 64.2% now married, 6.4% widowed, 9.5% divorced (2000); Foreign born: 1.2% (2000); Ancestry (includes multiple ancestries): 31.6% German, 14.5% Polish, 12.0% English, 9.6% Irish, 7.4% Other groups (2000).
Economy: Employment by occupation: 10.6% management, 6.9% professional, 15.8% services, 16.6% sales, 1.2% farming, 9.9% construction, 38.9% production (2000).

Income: Per capita income: $17,615 (2000); Median household income: $40,536 (2000); Poverty rate: 10.3% (2000).
Taxes: Total city taxes per capita: $81 (1997); City property taxes per capita: $81 (1997).
Education: High school graduation rate: 78.6% (2000); College graduation rate: 7.2% (2000).
Housing: Homeownership rate: 87.7% (2000); Median home value: $71,000 (2000); Median rent: $372 per month (2000); Median age of housing: 40 years (2000).
Transportation: Commute to work: 92.3% car, 0.8% public transportation, 1.0% walk, 6.0% work from home (2000); Travel time to work: 17.3% less than 15 minutes, 52.9% 15 to 30 minutes, 11.2% 30 to 45 minutes, 8.5% 45 to 60 minutes, 10.1% 60 minutes or more (2000)

HARBOR BEACH (city). Covers a land area of 1.773 square miles and a water area of 0.080 square miles. Located at 43.84° N. Lat.; 82.65° W. Long. Elevation is 610 feet.
History: Harbor Beach was founded in 1837. Earlier names of Barnettsville and Sand Beach were replaced in 1889 with Harbor Beach. Harbor Beach had an unusual early industry in the making of counterfeit money, both U.S. currency and Mexican dollars being made here and distributed in large quantities. Later, the town became a resort and commercial fishing center.
Population: 1,837 (2000); Race: 98.2% White, 0.0% Black, 0.8% Asian, 0.0% American Indian and Alaska Native, 1.3% Hispanic of any race, 0.6% two or more races (2000); Density: 1,036.3 persons per square mile (2000); Age: 25.4% under 18, 22.7% over 64 (2000); Marriage status: 22.2% never married, 57.3% now married, 11.6% widowed, 8.9% divorced (2000); Foreign born: 1.7% (2000); Ancestry (includes multiple ancestries): 42.0% German, 19.9% Polish, 7.9% United States or American, 7.9% Irish, 6.8% English (2000).
Economy: Employment by occupation: 7.6% management, 15.6% professional, 10.5% services, 25.5% sales, 1.0% farming, 8.9% construction, 30.8% production (2000).
Income: Per capita income: $14,917 (2000); Median household income: $29,469 (2000); Poverty rate: 15.1% (2000).
Taxes: Total city taxes per capita: $402 (1997); City property taxes per capita: $401 (1997).
Education: High school graduation rate: 75.2% (2000); College graduation rate: 10.4% (2000).

School District(s)

Harbor Beach Community Schools (KG-12)
2000 Enrollment: 794 517-479-3261
Sigel Township School District #4f (KG-08)
2000 Enrollment: 27 517-269-6406
Sigel Township School District #6 (KG-08)
2000 Enrollment: 19 517-269-2406

Housing: Homeownership rate: 76.1% (2000); Median home value: $66,600 (2000); Median rent: $336 per month (2000); Median age of housing: 57 years (2000).
Hospitals: Harbor Beach Community Hospital (61 beds)
Safety: Violent crime rate: 0.0 per 10,000 population; Property crime rate: 216.6 per 10,000 population (2001).
Newspapers: The Harbor Beach Times (1 x week)
Transportation: Commute to work: 80.1% car, 1.0% public transportation, 15.6% walk, 1.2% work from home (2000); Travel time to work: 64.7% less than 15 minutes, 15.7% 15 to 30 minutes, 9.7% 30 to 45 minutes, 5.2% 45 to 60 minutes, 4.7% 60 minutes or more (2000)
Additional Information Contacts
Harbor Beach Chamber of Commerce 989-479-6477

HUME (township). Covers a land area of 30.016 square miles and a water area of 0.030 square miles. Located at 43.97° N. Lat.; 83.07° W. Long.
History: Hume Township was organized in 1860 and named for Walter Hume, who had come from Canada to settle here in 1844.
Population: 801 (2000); Race: 98.5% White, 0.0% Black, 0.0% Asian, 0.4% American Indian and Alaska Native, 0.6% Hispanic of any race, 1.1% two or more races (2000); Density: 26.7 persons per square mile (2000); Age: 17.6% under 18, 22.7% over 64 (2000); Marriage status: 18.7% never married, 64.1% now married, 9.6% widowed, 7.6% divorced (2000); Foreign born: 1.0% (2000); Ancestry (includes multiple ancestries): 36.1% Polish, 31.9% German, 9.3% Irish, 8.5% English, 8.2% French (except Basque) (2000).
Economy: Employment by occupation: 18.1% management, 9.1% professional, 16.0% services, 13.3% sales, 1.2% farming, 9.1% construction, 33.2% production (2000).
Income: Per capita income: $18,810 (2000); Median household income: $33,047 (2000); Poverty rate: 9.2% (2000).
Taxes: Total city taxes per capita: $119 (1997); City property taxes per capita: $119 (1997).
Education: High school graduation rate: 78.5% (2000); College graduation rate: 14.6% (2000).
Housing: Homeownership rate: 90.2% (2000); Median home value: $90,500 (2000); Median rent: $275 per month (2000); Median age of housing: 34 years (2000).
Transportation: Commute to work: 85.5% car, 0.0% public transportation, 4.6% walk, 8.3% work from home (2000); Travel time to work: 24.2% less than 15 minutes, 44.8% 15 to 30 minutes, 18.2% 30 to 45 minutes, 7.1% 45 to 60 minutes, 5.7% 60 minutes or more (2000)

HURON (township). Covers a land area of 33.611 square miles and a water area of 0 square miles. Located at 43.98° N. Lat.; 82.83° W. Long.
Population: 423 (2000); Race: 98.0% White, 0.0% Black, 0.0% Asian, 0.0% American Indian and Alaska Native, 0.0% Hispanic of any race, 2.0% two or more races (2000); Density: 12.6 persons per square mile (2000); Age: 18.4% under 18, 27.6% over 64 (2000); Marriage status: 15.5% never married, 73.8% now married, 6.0% widowed, 4.7% divorced (2000); Foreign born: 0.4% (2000); Ancestry (includes multiple ancestries): 47.9% German, 24.7% Polish, 13.3% English, 7.2% French (except Basque), 5.4% Irish (2000).
Economy: Employment by occupation: 14.4% management, 13.8% professional, 6.3% services, 21.3% sales, 5.7% farming, 15.5% construction, 23.0% production (2000).
Income: Per capita income: $19,725 (2000); Median household income: $33,250 (2000); Poverty rate: 11.0% (2000).
Taxes: Total city taxes per capita: $247 (1997); City property taxes per capita: $244 (1997).
Education: High school graduation rate: 79.2% (2000); College graduation rate: 9.6% (2000).
Housing: Homeownership rate: 90.8% (2000); Median home value: $80,500 (2000); Median rent: $313 per month (2000); Median age of housing: 29 years (2000).
Safety: Violent crime rate: 15.9 per 10,000 population; Property crime rate: 227.4 per 10,000 population (2001).
Transportation: Commute to work: 90.8% car, 1.2% public transportation, 6.9% walk, 1.2% work from home (2000); Travel time to work: 28.7% less than 15 minutes, 29.2% 15 to 30 minutes, 28.1% 30 to 45 minutes, 9.9% 45 to 60 minutes, 4.1% 60 minutes or more (2000)

KINDE (village). Covers a land area of 1.007 square miles and a water area of 0 square miles. Located at 43.93° N. Lat.; 82.99° W. Long. Elevation is 704 feet.
History: Kinde was established as a station on the Port Huron & Northwestern Railroad in 1884, and was named for storekeeper John Kinde. Many of the early residents of Kinde were of Polish ancestry. The village grew as the center of a farming area.
Population: 534 (2000); Race: 97.8% White, 0.4% Black, 0.0% Asian, 0.0% American Indian and Alaska Native, 0.4% Hispanic of any race, 1.9% two or more races (2000); Density: 530.2 persons per square mile (2000); Age: 25.5% under 18, 16.9% over 64 (2000); Marriage status: 23.8% never married, 57.9% now married, 7.1% widowed, 11.2% divorced (2000); Foreign born: 0.6% (2000); Ancestry (includes multiple ancestries): 34.8% German, 30.0% Polish, 14.2% Irish, 11.4% English, 7.1% Other groups (2000).
Economy: Employment by occupation: 6.9% management, 11.3% professional, 21.6% services, 18.1% sales, 1.0% farming, 8.3% construction, 32.8% production (2000).
Income: Per capita income: $12,623 (2000); Median household income: $29,125 (2000); Poverty rate: 14.6% (2000).
Taxes: Total city taxes per capita: $172 (1997); City property taxes per capita: $172 (1997).
Education: High school graduation rate: 76.2% (2000); College graduation rate: 6.4% (2000).

School District(s)

North Huron School District (KG-12)
2000 Enrollment: 634 517-874-4100

Housing: Homeownership rate: 82.8% (2000); Median home value: $46,800 (2000); Median rent: $308 per month (2000); Median age of housing: 53 years (2000).
Transportation: Commute to work: 89.1% car, 0.0% public transportation, 4.5% walk, 4.5% work from home (2000); Travel time to work: 28.1% less than 15 minutes, 50.0% 15 to 30 minutes, 12.0% 30 to 45 minutes, 3.1% 45 to 60 minutes, 6.8% 60 minutes or more (2000)

LAKE (township). Covers a land area of 19.188 square miles and a water area of 1.547 square miles. Located at 43.95° N. Lat.; 83.19° W. Long.
Population: 996 (2000); Race: 98.3% White, 0.0% Black, 0.0% Asian, 1.3% American Indian and Alaska Native, 2.4% Hispanic of any race, 0.4% two or more races (2000); Density: 51.9 persons per square mile (2000); Age: 13.7% under 18, 35.9% over 64 (2000); Marriage status: 12.4% never married, 66.6% now married, 13.2% widowed, 7.8% divorced (2000); Foreign born: 2.7% (2000); Ancestry (includes multiple ancestries): 28.4% German, 17.4% Polish, 12.3% English, 10.9% Irish, 9.6% French (except Basque) (2000).
Economy: Single-family building permits issued: 21 (2001) / 16 (2000); Multi-family building permits issued: 0 (2001) / 0 (2000); Employment by occupation: 16.3% management, 15.9% professional, 12.2% services, 22.5% sales, 0.9% farming, 14.1% construction, 18.1% production (2000).
Income: Per capita income: $20,364 (2000); Median household income: $32,708 (2000); Poverty rate: 10.0% (2000).
Taxes: Total city taxes per capita: $119 (1997); City property taxes per capita: $106 (1997).
Education: High school graduation rate: 83.5% (2000); College graduation rate: 12.1% (2000).
Housing: Homeownership rate: 93.5% (2000); Median home value: $100,300 (2000); Median rent: $375 per month (2000); Median age of housing: 35 years (2000).
Transportation: Commute to work: 98.1% car, 0.0% public transportation, 1.0% walk, 1.0% work from home (2000); Travel time to work: 27.4% less than 15 minutes, 39.7% 15 to 30 minutes, 20.3% 30 to 45 minutes, 1.0% 45 to 60 minutes, 11.6% 60 minutes or more (2000)

LINCOLN (township). Covers a land area of 35.757 square miles and a water area of 0.016 square miles. Located at 43.90° N. Lat.; 82.95° W. Long.
History: Lincoln Township was organized in 1877 and named for Abraham Lincoln.
Population: 873 (2000); Race: 98.1% White, 0.2% Black, 0.6% Asian, 0.0% American Indian and Alaska Native, 0.2% Hispanic of any race, 1.1% two or more races (2000); Density: 24.4 persons per square mile (2000); Age: 24.2% under 18, 15.2% over 64 (2000); Marriage status: 22.3% never married, 66.1% now married, 6.8% widowed, 4.9% divorced (2000); Foreign born: 0.8% (2000); Ancestry (includes multiple ancestries): 42.5% Polish, 32.7% German, 8.7% English, 7.5% French (except Basque), 7.0% Irish (2000).
Economy: Employment by occupation: 10.8% management, 11.3% professional, 12.3% services, 25.7% sales, 2.4% farming, 12.3% construction, 25.2% production (2000).
Income: Per capita income: $16,145 (2000); Median household income: $36,250 (2000); Poverty rate: 10.4% (2000).
Taxes: Total city taxes per capita: $101 (1997); City property taxes per capita: $101 (1997).
Education: High school graduation rate: 76.2% (2000); College graduation rate: 10.3% (2000).
Housing: Homeownership rate: 91.1% (2000); Median home value: $61,100 (2000); Median rent: $400 per month (2000); Median age of housing: 44 years (2000).
Transportation: Commute to work: 85.3% car, 2.7% public transportation, 2.9% walk, 9.1% work from home (2000); Travel time to work: 31.3% less than 15 minutes, 47.2% 15 to 30 minutes, 11.9% 30 to 45 minutes, 5.1% 45 to 60 minutes, 4.6% 60 minutes or more (2000)

MCKINLEY (township). Covers a land area of 20.344 square miles and a water area of 0.346 square miles. Located at 43.87° N. Lat.; 83.30° W. Long.
Population: 503 (2000); Race: 96.3% White, 1.4% Black, 0.2% Asian, 0.4% American Indian and Alaska Native, 1.2% Hispanic of any race, 1.6% two or more races (2000); Density: 24.7 persons per square mile (2000); Age: 20.7% under 18, 19.1% over 64 (2000); Marriage status: 17.1% never married, 69.3% now married, 5.9% widowed, 7.8% divorced (2000); Foreign born: 0.8% (2000); Ancestry (includes multiple ancestries): 45.5% German, 8.3% Irish, 7.5% United States or American, 6.3% Polish, 6.3% English (2000).
Economy: Employment by occupation: 11.8% management, 13.9% professional, 15.6% services, 21.5% sales, 3.0% farming, 9.7% construction, 24.5% production (2000).
Income: Per capita income: $17,453 (2000); Median household income: $37,212 (2000); Poverty rate: 5.3% (2000).
Taxes: Total city taxes per capita: $183 (1997); City property taxes per capita: $183 (1997).
Education: High school graduation rate: 79.2% (2000); College graduation rate: 8.8% (2000).
Housing: Homeownership rate: 87.8% (2000); Median home value: $90,900 (2000); Median rent: $331 per month (2000); Median age of housing: 44 years (2000).
Transportation: Commute to work: 88.4% car, 0.9% public transportation, 3.0% walk, 7.7% work from home (2000); Travel time to work: 67.4% less than 15 minutes, 16.7% 15 to 30 minutes, 4.7% 30 to 45 minutes, 1.9% 45 to 60 minutes, 9.3% 60 minutes or more (2000)

MEADE (township). Covers a land area of 35.689 square miles and a water area of 0 square miles. Located at 43.89° N. Lat.; 83.06° W. Long.
Population: 799 (2000); Race: 99.5% White, 0.0% Black, 0.0% Asian, 0.0% American Indian and Alaska Native, 0.0% Hispanic of any race, 0.5% two or more races (2000); Density: 22.4 persons per square mile (2000); Age: 23.9% under 18, 17.8% over 64 (2000); Marriage status: 23.3% never married, 61.1% now married, 8.6% widowed, 7.0% divorced (2000); Foreign born: 0.4% (2000); Ancestry (includes multiple ancestries): 42.0% German, 18.9% Polish, 11.4% Irish, 11.0% English, 9.3% French (except Basque) (2000).
Economy: Employment by occupation: 11.4% management, 12.2% professional, 14.5% services, 20.2% sales, 5.7% farming, 7.3% construction, 28.8% production (2000).
Income: Per capita income: $17,126 (2000); Median household income: $39,750 (2000); Poverty rate: 6.6% (2000).
Taxes: Total city taxes per capita: $123 (1997); City property taxes per capita: $122 (1997).
Education: High school graduation rate: 78.0% (2000); College graduation rate: 5.9% (2000).
Housing: Homeownership rate: 88.3% (2000); Median home value: $65,800 (2000); Median rent: $350 per month (2000); Median age of housing: 41 years (2000).
Transportation: Commute to work: 93.7% car, 0.0% public transportation, 1.1% walk, 4.8% work from home (2000); Travel time to work: 31.4% less than 15 minutes, 45.8% 15 to 30 minutes, 14.4% 30 to 45 minutes, 3.6% 45 to 60 minutes, 4.7% 60 minutes or more (2000)

OLIVER (township). Covers a land area of 35.305 square miles and a water area of 0.045 square miles. Located at 43.81° N. Lat.; 83.18° W. Long.
Population: 1,626 (2000); Race: 96.0% White, 0.4% Black, 0.5% Asian, 0.0% American Indian and Alaska Native, 4.6% Hispanic of any race, 2.6% two or more races (2000); Density: 46.1 persons per square mile (2000); Age: 27.9% under 18, 15.5% over 64 (2000); Marriage status: 24.8% never married, 57.4% now married, 8.8% widowed, 8.9% divorced (2000); Foreign born: 0.9% (2000); Ancestry (includes multiple ancestries): 41.1% German, 13.1% United States or American, 10.9% Polish, 8.8% Other groups, 7.5% Irish (2000).
Economy: Employment by occupation: 8.2% management, 12.2% professional, 17.9% services, 23.5% sales, 2.7% farming, 11.6% construction, 23.9% production (2000).
Income: Per capita income: $15,482 (2000); Median household income: $32,315 (2000); Poverty rate: 16.0% (2000).
Taxes: Total city taxes per capita: $126 (1997); City property taxes per capita: $126 (1997).
Education: High school graduation rate: 74.8% (2000); College graduation rate: 9.0% (2000).
Housing: Homeownership rate: 79.3% (2000); Median home value: $67,900 (2000); Median rent: $294 per month (2000); Median age of housing: 48 years (2000).
Transportation: Commute to work: 85.8% car, 0.0% public transportation, 7.2% walk, 4.0% work from home (2000); Travel time to work: 50.2% less than 15 minutes, 33.7% 15 to 30 minutes, 10.2% 30 to 45 minutes, 1.4% 45 to 60 minutes, 4.4% 60 minutes or more (2000)

OWENDALE (village). Covers a land area of 0.743 square miles and a water area of 0 square miles. Located at 43.72° N. Lat.; 83.26° W. Long. Elevation is 643 feet.
Population: 296 (2000); Race: 98.8% White, 0.0% Black, 0.6% Asian, 0.0% American Indian and Alaska Native, 13.6% Hispanic of any race, 0.6% two or more races (2000); Density: 398.2 persons per square mile (2000); Age: 27.9% under 18, 10.5% over 64 (2000); Marriage status: 34.3% never married, 52.2% now married, 3.2% widowed, 10.4% divorced (2000); Foreign born: 9.9% (2000); Ancestry (includes multiple ancestries): 32.2% German, 15.8% Other groups, 12.4% English, 11.1% United States or American, 8.7% Irish (2000).
Economy: Employment by occupation: 2.5% management, 6.6% professional, 19.7% services, 23.0% sales, 3.3% farming, 8.2% construction, 36.9% production (2000).

Income: Per capita income: $11,985 (2000); Median household income: $29,861 (2000); Poverty rate: 19.8% (2000).
Taxes: Total city taxes per capita: $117 (1997); City property taxes per capita: $117 (1997).
Education: High school graduation rate: 70.4% (2000); College graduation rate: 0.6% (2000).

School District(s)

Owendale-Gagetown Area Schools (KG-12)
2000 Enrollment: 286 517-678-4261

Housing: Homeownership rate: 78.4% (2000); Median home value: $46,100 (2000); Median rent: $335 per month (2000); Median age of housing: 54 years (2000).
Transportation: Commute to work: 89.0% car, 0.0% public transportation, 2.9% walk, 8.1% work from home (2000); Travel time to work: 34.4% less than 15 minutes, 32.8% 15 to 30 minutes, 18.4% 30 to 45 minutes, 9.6% 45 to 60 minutes, 4.8% 60 minutes or more (2000)

PARIS (township). Covers a land area of 36.121 square miles and a water area of 0 square miles. Located at 43.73° N. Lat.; 82.80° W. Long.
Population: 557 (2000); Race: 98.6% White, 0.5% Black, 0.0% Asian, 0.0% American Indian and Alaska Native, 0.0% Hispanic of any race, 0.9% two or more races (2000); Density: 15.4 persons per square mile (2000); Age: 34.7% under 18, 12.5% over 64 (2000); Marriage status: 21.3% never married, 65.9% now married, 7.6% widowed, 5.1% divorced (2000); Foreign born: 0.0% (2000); Ancestry (includes multiple ancestries): 49.6% Polish, 41.6% German, 6.3% Irish, 4.2% United States or American, 3.9% English (2000).
Economy: Employment by occupation: 21.6% management, 6.2% professional, 7.9% services, 16.2% sales, 3.7% farming, 10.8% construction, 33.6% production (2000).
Income: Per capita income: $14,714 (2000); Median household income: $32,321 (2000); Poverty rate: 13.8% (2000).
Taxes: Total city taxes per capita: $110 (1997); City property taxes per capita: $110 (1997).
Education: High school graduation rate: 77.8% (2000); College graduation rate: 5.0% (2000).

School District(s)

Big Jackson School District (KG-06)
2000 Enrollment: 42 231-796-8947

Housing: Homeownership rate: 86.7% (2000); Median home value: $68,300 (2000); Median rent: $269 per month (2000); Median age of housing: 58 years (2000).
Transportation: Commute to work: 80.3% car, 0.0% public transportation, 3.4% walk, 15.4% work from home (2000); Travel time to work: 34.3% less than 15 minutes, 33.8% 15 to 30 minutes, 13.6% 30 to 45 minutes, 12.6% 45 to 60 minutes, 5.6% 60 minutes or more (2000)

PIGEON (village). Covers a land area of 0.824 square miles and a water area of 0 square miles. Located at 43.83° N. Lat.; 83.27° W. Long. Elevation is 610 feet.
History: Pigeon was founded in 1888, and named for the nearby Pigeon River, where many wild pigeons were seen.
Population: 1,207 (2000); Race: 97.0% White, 0.2% Black, 0.0% Asian, 0.4% American Indian and Alaska Native, 2.2% Hispanic of any race, 1.2% two or more races (2000); Density: 1,464.2 persons per square mile (2000); Age: 21.5% under 18, 25.1% over 64 (2000); Marriage status: 21.2% never married, 63.6% now married, 9.9% widowed, 5.3% divorced (2000); Foreign born: 1.9% (2000); Ancestry (includes multiple ancestries): 49.8% German, 9.5% Irish, 8.6% United States or American, 7.6% French (except Basque), 6.3% Polish (2000).
Economy: Employment by occupation: 8.9% management, 16.3% professional, 15.4% services, 25.5% sales, 2.0% farming, 8.9% construction, 23.0% production (2000).
Income: Per capita income: $17,142 (2000); Median household income: $33,618 (2000); Poverty rate: 6.4% (2000).
Taxes: Total city taxes per capita: $193 (1997); City property taxes per capita: $190 (1997).
Education: High school graduation rate: 76.2% (2000); College graduation rate: 11.5% (2000).

School District(s)

Laker Schools (KG-12)
2000 Enrollment: 1,217 517-453-2097

Housing: Homeownership rate: 76.1% (2000); Median home value: $69,100 (2000); Median rent: $344 per month (2000); Median age of housing: 47 years (2000).
Hospitals: Scheurer Hospital (47 beds)
Transportation: Commute to work: 88.2% car, 2.0% public transportation, 6.0% walk, 2.2% work from home (2000); Travel time to work: 63.8% less than 15 minutes, 27.0% 15 to 30 minutes, 3.3% 30 to 45 minutes, 0.9% 45 to 60 minutes, 5.0% 60 minutes or more (2000)

POINTE AUX BARQUES (township). Covers a land area of 1.328 square miles and a water area of 0.282 square miles. Located at 44.06° N. Lat.; 82.95° W. Long.
History: At the tip of Michigan's "thumb," Pointe Aux Barques is believed to be named for the large rocks off shore, which resemble the prows of ships. The area became a resort center, and the location of estates owned by wealthy Detroit families.
Population: 10 (2000); Race: 100.0% White, 0.0% Black, 0.0% Asian, 0.0% American Indian and Alaska Native, 0.0% Hispanic of any race, 0.0% two or more races (2000); Density: 7.5 persons per square mile (2000); Age: 41.7% under 18, 16.7% over 64 (2000); Marriage status: 42.9% never married, 0.0% now married, 0.0% widowed, 57.1% divorced (2000); Foreign born: 0.0% (2000); Ancestry (includes multiple ancestries): 58.3% German, 41.7% English, 33.3% Belgian, 25.0% French (except Basque), 16.7% Scottish (2000).
Economy: Employment by occupation: 0.0% management, 0.0% professional, 0.0% services, 0.0% sales, 0.0% farming, 100.0% construction, 0.0% production (2000).
Income: Per capita income: $9,400 (2000); Median household income: $23,750 (2000); Poverty rate: 0.0% (2000).
Education: High school graduation rate: 100.0% (2000); College graduation rate: 28.6% (2000).
Housing: Homeownership rate: 40.0% (2000); Median home value: $85,000 (2000); Median age of housing: 57 years (2000).
Transportation: Commute to work: 0.0% car, 0.0% public transportation, 100.0% walk, 0.0% work from home (2000); Travel time to work: 100.0% less than 15 minutes, 0.0% 15 to 30 minutes, 0.0% 30 to 45 minutes, 0.0% 45 to 60 minutes, 0.0% 60 minutes or more (2000)

PORT AUSTIN (village). Covers a land area of 1.004 square miles and a water area of 0.002 square miles. Located at 44.04° N. Lat.; 82.99° W. Long. Elevation is 604 feet.
History: The first "settler" in Port Austin was reportedly a fugitive from Canada, who hid in a cove on the shore here in 1837. Others found the hideaway a good place to live, and the village of Port Austin grew up. It became a resort center.
Population: 737 (2000); Race: 97.6% White, 0.0% Black, 0.0% Asian, 0.4% American Indian and Alaska Native, 0.3% Hispanic of any race, 2.0% two or more races (2000); Density: 733.7 persons per square mile (2000); Age: 16.1% under 18, 31.8% over 64 (2000); Marriage status: 23.0% never married, 49.1% now married, 16.2% widowed, 11.7% divorced (2000); Foreign born: 1.7% (2000); Ancestry (includes multiple ancestries): 28.6% Polish, 25.6% German, 15.1% Irish, 12.3% English, 9.8% French (except Basque) (2000).
Economy: Employment by occupation: 7.4% management, 13.1% professional, 14.8% services, 28.6% sales, 1.1% farming, 9.9% construction, 25.1% production (2000).
Income: Per capita income: $18,480 (2000); Median household income: $29,643 (2000); Poverty rate: 14.3% (2000).
Taxes: Total city taxes per capita: $316 (1997); City property taxes per capita: $316 (1997).
Education: High school graduation rate: 76.3% (2000); College graduation rate: 16.7% (2000).
Housing: Homeownership rate: 77.0% (2000); Median home value: $87,100 (2000); Median rent: $294 per month (2000); Median age of housing: 39 years (2000).
Safety: Violent crime rate: 13.5 per 10,000 population; Property crime rate: 391.4 per 10,000 population (2001).
Transportation: Commute to work: 87.8% car, 0.0% public transportation, 9.4% walk, 1.4% work from home (2000); Travel time to work: 49.3% less than 15 minutes, 17.9% 15 to 30 minutes, 28.5% 30 to 45 minutes, 2.2% 45 to 60 minutes, 2.2% 60 minutes or more (2000)

Additional Information Contacts

Port Austin Chamber of Commerce 989-738-7600

PORT AUSTIN (township). Covers a land area of 16.404 square miles and a water area of 0.262 square miles. Located at 44.04° N. Lat.; 82.94° W. Long. Elevation is 604 feet.
History: Grindstone City to East, with 6-ft-diameter grindstones on beach produced at nearby quarries in pioneer days. Port Crescent State Park to West has petroglyphs in sandstone outcrops.

Population: 1,591 (2000); Race: 98.7% White, 0.0% Black, 0.0% Asian, 0.3% American Indian and Alaska Native, 0.3% Hispanic of any race, 1.0% two or more races (2000); Density: 97.0 persons per square mile (2000); Age: 16.0% under 18, 28.6% over 64 (2000); Marriage status: 18.5% never married, 60.7% now married, 10.9% widowed, 9.9% divorced (2000); Foreign born: 1.3% (2000); Ancestry (includes multiple ancestries): 29.7% Polish, 26.1% German, 12.6% English, 12.2% Irish, 9.2% French (except Basque) (2000).
Economy: Manufacturing: hand tools, thread rolling. Employment by occupation: 12.7% management, 11.5% professional, 10.8% services, 24.5% sales, 1.3% farming, 11.0% construction, 28.2% production (2000).
Income: Per capita income: $19,219 (2000); Median household income: $32,841 (2000); Poverty rate: 12.9% (2000).
Taxes: Total city taxes per capita: $158 (1997); City property taxes per capita: $155 (1997).
Education: High school graduation rate: 76.6% (2000); College graduation rate: 15.7% (2000).
Housing: Homeownership rate: 85.7% (2000); Median home value: $95,800 (2000); Median rent: $307 per month (2000); Median age of housing: 32 years (2000).
Transportation: Commute to work: 89.0% car, 0.0% public transportation, 4.7% walk, 4.9% work from home (2000); Travel time to work: 42.2% less than 15 minutes, 19.0% 15 to 30 minutes, 29.4% 30 to 45 minutes, 4.4% 45 to 60 minutes, 5.0% 60 minutes or more (2000)

PORT HOPE (village). Covers a land area of 1.004 square miles and a water area of 0 square miles. Located at 43.94° N. Lat.; 82.71° W. Long. Elevation is 606 feet.
History: Port Hope was supposedly named in 1855 by sailors whose ship had been wrecked on the rocks off shore. The village grew up around a lumber mill built in 1858. Port Hope later became a summer home location for vacationers.
Population: 310 (2000); Race: 99.3% White, 0.0% Black, 0.0% Asian, 0.0% American Indian and Alaska Native, 0.0% Hispanic of any race, 0.7% two or more races (2000); Density: 308.7 persons per square mile (2000); Age: 16.2% under 18, 29.2% over 64 (2000); Marriage status: 19.0% never married, 63.3% now married, 7.7% widowed, 10.1% divorced (2000); Foreign born: 0.0% (2000); Ancestry (includes multiple ancestries): 38.7% German, 18.0% English, 13.4% Irish, 12.0% Polish, 12.0% Scottish (2000).
Economy: Employment by occupation: 3.5% management, 5.3% professional, 15.8% services, 24.6% sales, 0.0% farming, 9.6% construction, 41.2% production (2000).
Income: Per capita income: $16,428 (2000); Median household income: $31,071 (2000); Poverty rate: 4.6% (2000).
Taxes: Total city taxes per capita: $221 (1997); City property taxes per capita: $221 (1997).
Education: High school graduation rate: 76.4% (2000); College graduation rate: 8.6% (2000).

School District(s)

Port Hope Community Schools (KG-12)
2000 Enrollment: 146 517-428-4151

Housing: Homeownership rate: 89.3% (2000); Median home value: $64,300 (2000); Median rent: $388 per month (2000); Median age of housing: 49 years (2000).
Transportation: Commute to work: 73.9% car, 6.3% public transportation, 12.6% walk, 7.2% work from home (2000); Travel time to work: 47.6% less than 15 minutes, 13.6% 15 to 30 minutes, 28.2% 30 to 45 minutes, 10.7% 45 to 60 minutes, 0.0% 60 minutes or more (2000)

RUBICON (township). Covers a land area of 23.734 square miles and a water area of 0.023 square miles. Located at 43.91° N. Lat.; 82.71° W. Long.
Population: 778 (2000); Race: 98.8% White, 0.0% Black, 0.3% Asian, 0.5% American Indian and Alaska Native, 0.0% Hispanic of any race, 0.3% two or more races (2000); Density: 32.8 persons per square mile (2000); Age: 23.3% under 18, 22.0% over 64 (2000); Marriage status: 16.9% never married, 68.4% now married, 6.6% widowed, 8.1% divorced (2000); Foreign born: 0.7% (2000); Ancestry (includes multiple ancestries): 50.9% German, 16.6% Polish, 10.5% English, 8.4% Irish, 5.5% Scottish (2000).
Economy: Employment by occupation: 10.0% management, 7.3% professional, 13.5% services, 23.9% sales, 4.8% farming, 8.3% construction, 32.2% production (2000).
Income: Per capita income: $16,012 (2000); Median household income: $33,359 (2000); Poverty rate: 4.6% (2000).
Taxes: Total city taxes per capita: $185 (1997); City property taxes per capita: $185 (1997).
Education: High school graduation rate: 77.9% (2000); College graduation rate: 7.4% (2000).
Housing: Homeownership rate: 89.1% (2000); Median home value: $76,800 (2000); Median rent: $320 per month (2000); Median age of housing: 41 years (2000).
Transportation: Commute to work: 82.1% car, 3.6% public transportation, 7.1% walk, 7.1% work from home (2000); Travel time to work: 41.9% less than 15 minutes, 20.4% 15 to 30 minutes, 22.3% 30 to 45 minutes, 10.4% 45 to 60 minutes, 5.0% 60 minutes or more (2000)

RUTH (unincorporated postal area, zip code 48470). Covers a land area of 41.227 square miles and a water area of 0 square miles. Located at 43.73° N. Lat.; 82.75° W. Long. Elevation is 754 feet.
History: Ruth was first known as German Settlement for its residents who came from Baden and Westphalia in Germany. The name of Ruth was chosen in 1880 for Michael Ruth, who donated land for the railroad depot.
Population: 921 (2000); Race: 98.3% White, 0.3% Black, 0.0% Asian, 0.9% American Indian and Alaska Native, 1.1% Hispanic of any race, 0.5% two or more races (2000); Density: 22.3 persons per square mile (2000); Age: 32.3% under 18, 15.4% over 64 (2000); Marriage status: 20.6% never married, 65.6% now married, 9.9% widowed, 3.9% divorced (2000); Foreign born: 0.2% (2000); Ancestry (includes multiple ancestries): 53.4% German, 37.0% Polish, 10.7% Irish, 5.0% English, 4.4% United States or American (2000).
Economy: Employment by occupation: 15.6% management, 8.7% professional, 12.6% services, 14.6% sales, 6.9% farming, 8.7% construction, 32.9% production (2000).
Income: Per capita income: $15,137 (2000); Median household income: $36,528 (2000); Poverty rate: 6.3% (2000).
Education: High school graduation rate: 73.3% (2000); College graduation rate: 3.4% (2000).
Housing: Homeownership rate: 90.9% (2000); Median home value: $63,900 (2000); Median rent: $300 per month (2000); Median age of housing: 47 years (2000).
Transportation: Commute to work: 82.3% car, 0.5% public transportation, 4.1% walk, 11.1% work from home (2000); Travel time to work: 30.8% less than 15 minutes, 35.6% 15 to 30 minutes, 19.9% 30 to 45 minutes, 8.0% 45 to 60 minutes, 5.7% 60 minutes or more (2000)

SAND BEACH (township). Covers a land area of 36.419 square miles and a water area of 0.226 square miles. Located at 43.82° N. Lat.; 82.67° W. Long.
Population: 1,470 (2000); Race: 97.5% White, 0.0% Black, 0.8% Asian, 0.6% American Indian and Alaska Native, 0.2% Hispanic of any race, 1.0% two or more races (2000); Density: 40.4 persons per square mile (2000); Age: 27.6% under 18, 19.4% over 64 (2000); Marriage status: 19.0% never married, 67.2% now married, 9.5% widowed, 4.3% divorced (2000); Foreign born: 1.5% (2000); Ancestry (includes multiple ancestries): 57.4% German, 24.9% Polish, 7.8% Irish, 7.4% English, 6.5% French (except Basque) (2000).
Economy: Employment by occupation: 17.2% management, 16.4% professional, 10.3% services, 20.4% sales, 2.6% farming, 6.2% construction, 26.8% production (2000).
Income: Per capita income: $17,476 (2000); Median household income: $38,250 (2000); Poverty rate: 6.2% (2000).
Taxes: Total city taxes per capita: $113 (1997); City property taxes per capita: $112 (1997).
Education: High school graduation rate: 75.7% (2000); College graduation rate: 10.1% (2000).
Housing: Homeownership rate: 82.0% (2000); Median home value: $97,400 (2000); Median rent: $224 per month (2000); Median age of housing: 36 years (2000).
Transportation: Commute to work: 85.5% car, 0.0% public transportation, 4.7% walk, 9.5% work from home (2000); Travel time to work: 59.0% less than 15 minutes, 18.8% 15 to 30 minutes, 15.1% 30 to 45 minutes, 3.5% 45 to 60 minutes, 3.5% 60 minutes or more (2000)

SEBEWAING (village). Covers a land area of 1.602 square miles and a water area of 0.070 square miles. Located at 43.73° N. Lat.; 83.44° W. Long. Elevation is 585 feet.
History: Commercial fishing has been important to Sebewaing, situated at the mouth of the Sebewaing River on Saginaw Bay. Early industries also included a beet sugar refinery, a brewery, and a plant that manufactured fish-net anchors.
Population: 1,974 (2000); Race: 98.6% White, 0.0% Black, 0.2% Asian, 0.2% American Indian and Alaska Native, 4.7% Hispanic of any race, 0.4% two or more races (2000); Density: 1,232.4 persons per square mile (2000);

Age: 22.9% under 18, 19.9% over 64 (2000); Marriage status: 21.7% never married, 53.2% now married, 13.1% widowed, 12.0% divorced (2000); Foreign born: 0.7% (2000); Ancestry (includes multiple ancestries): 51.2% German, 12.7% English, 9.3% Polish, 7.2% United States or American, 6.0% Other groups (2000).
Economy: Employment by occupation: 10.3% management, 12.3% professional, 18.8% services, 18.3% sales, 1.7% farming, 6.9% construction, 31.6% production (2000).
Income: Per capita income: $16,894 (2000); Median household income: $32,721 (2000); Poverty rate: 17.5% (2000).
Taxes: Total city taxes per capita: $290 (1997); City property taxes per capita: $287 (1997).
Education: High school graduation rate: 74.8% (2000); College graduation rate: 10.6% (2000).

School District(s)

Unionville-Sebewaing Area School (KG-12)
2000 Enrollment: 903 517-883-2360
Housing: Homeownership rate: 75.1% (2000); Median home value: $67,200 (2000); Median rent: $357 per month (2000); Median age of housing: 50 years (2000).
Newspapers: The Blade & Progress Newsweekly (1 x week)
Transportation: Commute to work: 92.4% car, 0.0% public transportation, 5.6% walk, 2.0% work from home (2000); Travel time to work: 48.5% less than 15 minutes, 21.3% 15 to 30 minutes, 17.2% 30 to 45 minutes, 4.3% 45 to 60 minutes, 8.7% 60 minutes or more (2000)

SEBEWAING (township). Covers a land area of 32.594 square miles and a water area of 0.226 square miles. Located at 43.72° N. Lat.; 83.43° W. Long. Elevation is 585 feet.
History: Sebewaing was settled by a group led by Reverend John F.J. Auch, a Luthern minister from Ann Arbor, who came in 1845. The name is of Indian origin, meaning "crooked creek."
Population: 2,944 (2000); Race: 99.0% White, 0.0% Black, 0.1% Asian, 0.1% American Indian and Alaska Native, 3.6% Hispanic of any race, 0.3% two or more races (2000); Density: 90.3 persons per square mile (2000); Age: 23.9% under 18, 18.5% over 64 (2000); Marriage status: 20.2% never married, 57.8% now married, 11.1% widowed, 10.9% divorced (2000); Foreign born: 1.0% (2000); Ancestry (includes multiple ancestries): 55.4% German, 10.4% English, 8.8% Polish, 6.2% United States or American, 5.8% Irish (2000).
Economy: Single-family building permits issued: 5 (2001) / 3 (2000); Multi-family building permits issued: 0 (2001) / 0 (2000); Employment by occupation: 13.8% management, 13.3% professional, 13.5% services, 20.6% sales, 2.9% farming, 9.1% construction, 26.7% production (2000).
Income: Per capita income: $17,787 (2000); Median household income: $34,275 (2000); Poverty rate: 13.9% (2000).
Taxes: Total city taxes per capita: $144 (1997); City property taxes per capita: $144 (1997).
Education: High school graduation rate: 80.9% (2000); College graduation rate: 10.0% (2000).
Housing: Homeownership rate: 79.6% (2000); Median home value: $69,200 (2000); Median rent: $352 per month (2000); Median age of housing: 48 years (2000).
Transportation: Commute to work: 92.2% car, 0.0% public transportation, 3.7% walk, 4.1% work from home (2000); Travel time to work: 46.1% less than 15 minutes, 22.6% 15 to 30 minutes, 16.9% 30 to 45 minutes, 6.6% 45 to 60 minutes, 7.9% 60 minutes or more (2000)

SHERIDAN (township). Covers a land area of 36.169 square miles and a water area of 0 square miles. Located at 43.71° N. Lat.; 83.06° W. Long.
History: John McIntosh settled in Sheridan in 1859 and became its first supervisor when the township was organized in 1866. Sheridan was named for General Philip H. Sheridan.
Population: 736 (2000); Race: 98.0% White, 0.0% Black, 0.0% Asian, 0.0% American Indian and Alaska Native, 0.0% Hispanic of any race, 2.0% two or more races (2000); Density: 20.3 persons per square mile (2000); Age: 29.1% under 18, 11.7% over 64 (2000); Marriage status: 23.5% never married, 64.6% now married, 4.4% widowed, 7.5% divorced (2000); Foreign born: 0.8% (2000); Ancestry (includes multiple ancestries): 39.1% German, 32.2% Polish, 7.9% Irish, 7.9% English, 6.5% United States or American (2000).
Economy: Employment by occupation: 15.6% management, 12.2% professional, 15.6% services, 18.1% sales, 3.4% farming, 7.4% construction, 27.8% production (2000).
Income: Per capita income: $19,065 (2000); Median household income: $39,850 (2000); Poverty rate: 6.5% (2000).
Taxes: Total city taxes per capita: $96 (1997); City property taxes per capita: $96 (1997).
Education: High school graduation rate: 83.2% (2000); College graduation rate: 7.1% (2000).
Housing: Homeownership rate: 89.0% (2000); Median home value: $83,800 (2000); Median rent: $350 per month (2000); Median age of housing: 43 years (2000).
Transportation: Commute to work: 85.7% car, 0.0% public transportation, 4.6% walk, 9.7% work from home (2000); Travel time to work: 38.1% less than 15 minutes, 44.8% 15 to 30 minutes, 13.3% 30 to 45 minutes, 0.6% 45 to 60 minutes, 3.2% 60 minutes or more (2000)

SHERMAN (township). Covers a land area of 44.145 square miles and a water area of 0.009 square miles. Located at 43.73° N. Lat.; 82.67° W. Long.
Population: 1,165 (2000); Race: 99.4% White, 0.0% Black, 0.0% Asian, 0.2% American Indian and Alaska Native, 1.0% Hispanic of any race, 0.3% two or more races (2000); Density: 26.4 persons per square mile (2000); Age: 28.3% under 18, 15.6% over 64 (2000); Marriage status: 18.7% never married, 67.2% now married, 8.8% widowed, 5.3% divorced (2000); Foreign born: 0.9% (2000); Ancestry (includes multiple ancestries): 61.3% German, 28.1% Polish, 8.3% Irish, 4.5% English, 4.1% United States or American (2000).
Economy: Employment by occupation: 19.4% management, 9.8% professional, 12.4% services, 18.8% sales, 6.4% farming, 9.6% construction, 23.7% production (2000).
Income: Per capita income: $15,013 (2000); Median household income: $32,875 (2000); Poverty rate: 6.3% (2000).
Taxes: Total city taxes per capita: $165 (1997); City property taxes per capita: $165 (1997).
Education: High school graduation rate: 71.9% (2000); College graduation rate: 4.4% (2000).
Housing: Homeownership rate: 91.2% (2000); Median home value: $79,700 (2000); Median rent: $281 per month (2000); Median age of housing: 38 years (2000).
Transportation: Commute to work: 79.3% car, 0.4% public transportation, 5.6% walk, 13.3% work from home (2000); Travel time to work: 31.5% less than 15 minutes, 31.9% 15 to 30 minutes, 27.7% 30 to 45 minutes, 3.1% 45 to 60 minutes, 5.8% 60 minutes or more (2000)

SIGEL (township). Covers a land area of 35.777 square miles and a water area of 0.006 square miles. Located at 43.81° N. Lat.; 82.80° W. Long.
History: Sigel Township was organized in 1863 and named (though spelled differently) for General Franz Seigel who served during the Civil War.
Population: 576 (2000); Race: 97.5% White, 0.0% Black, 0.0% Asian, 1.8% American Indian and Alaska Native, 0.3% Hispanic of any race, 0.7% two or more races (2000); Density: 16.1 persons per square mile (2000); Age: 35.4% under 18, 10.3% over 64 (2000); Marriage status: 24.3% never married, 65.5% now married, 5.3% widowed, 4.9% divorced (2000); Foreign born: 0.5% (2000); Ancestry (includes multiple ancestries): 54.2% German, 37.9% Polish, 11.6% Irish, 4.8% Other groups, 4.5% French (except Basque) (2000).
Economy: Employment by occupation: 23.3% management, 10.9% professional, 11.7% services, 12.8% sales, 2.7% farming, 10.1% construction, 28.4% production (2000).
Income: Per capita income: $16,264 (2000); Median household income: $41,442 (2000); Poverty rate: 7.8% (2000).
Taxes: Total city taxes per capita: $134 (1997); City property taxes per capita: $134 (1997).
Education: High school graduation rate: 82.0% (2000); College graduation rate: 6.7% (2000).
Housing: Homeownership rate: 85.0% (2000); Median home value: $69,100 (2000); Median rent: $275 per month (2000); Median age of housing: 44 years (2000).
Transportation: Commute to work: 79.6% car, 0.0% public transportation, 2.0% walk, 18.4% work from home (2000); Travel time to work: 24.0% less than 15 minutes, 54.3% 15 to 30 minutes, 15.4% 30 to 45 minutes, 1.4% 45 to 60 minutes, 4.8% 60 minutes or more (2000)

UBLY (village). Covers a land area of 0.883 square miles and a water area of 0 square miles. Located at 43.71° N. Lat.; 82.93° W. Long. Elevation is 789 feet.
Population: 873 (2000); Race: 98.6% White, 0.0% Black, 0.0% Asian, 0.0% American Indian and Alaska Native, 0.8% Hispanic of any race, 1.4% two or more races (2000); Density: 989.0 persons per square mile (2000); Age: 25.1% under 18, 16.8% over 64 (2000); Marriage status: 21.9% never married, 58.9% now married, 11.6% widowed, 7.5% divorced (2000); Foreign born: 0.5% (2000); Ancestry (includes multiple ancestries): 38.9%

Polish, 34.8% German, 5.0% Irish, 4.9% United States or American, 4.9% English (2000).
Economy: In farm area: grain, potatoes, beans; livestock. Meat processing. Employment by occupation: 11.3% management, 13.5% professional, 14.8% services, 20.6% sales, 1.3% farming, 15.0% construction, 23.6% production (2000).
Income: Per capita income: $18,140 (2000); Median household income: $35,729 (2000); Poverty rate: 12.7% (2000).
Taxes: Total city taxes per capita: $193 (1997); City property taxes per capita: $187 (1997).
Education: High school graduation rate: 77.5% (2000); College graduation rate: 9.1% (2000).

School District(s)

Ubly Community Schools (KG-12)
2000 Enrollment: 907 517-658-8202
Housing: Homeownership rate: 82.0% (2000); Median home value: $75,200 (2000); Median rent: $302 per month (2000); Median age of housing: 41 years (2000).
Safety: Violent crime rate: 0.0 per 10,000 population; Property crime rate: 136.7 per 10,000 population (2001).
Transportation: Commute to work: 91.4% car, 0.3% public transportation, 4.9% walk, 2.6% work from home (2000); Travel time to work: 33.1% less than 15 minutes, 43.5% 15 to 30 minutes, 13.6% 30 to 45 minutes, 2.1% 45 to 60 minutes, 7.7% 60 minutes or more (2000)

VERONA (township). Aka Verona Mills. Covers a land area of 34.132 square miles and a water area of 0.048 square miles. Located at 43.81° N. Lat.; 82.95° W. Long. Elevation is 803 feet.
Population: 1,349 (2000); Race: 97.4% White, 0.0% Black, 0.3% Asian, 1.3% American Indian and Alaska Native, 1.0% Hispanic of any race, 0.5% two or more races (2000); Density: 39.5 persons per square mile (2000); Age: 27.8% under 18, 12.4% over 64 (2000); Marriage status: 21.9% never married, 64.5% now married, 5.0% widowed, 8.7% divorced (2000); Foreign born: 0.4% (2000); Ancestry (includes multiple ancestries): 46.2% German, 32.9% Polish, 8.3% English, 8.0% Irish, 7.0% French (except Basque) (2000).
Economy: Employment by occupation: 12.1% management, 13.8% professional, 15.9% services, 20.6% sales, 0.6% farming, 12.6% construction, 24.4% production (2000).
Income: Per capita income: $20,854 (2000); Median household income: $44,028 (2000); Poverty rate: 7.8% (2000).
Taxes: Total city taxes per capita: $111 (1997); City property taxes per capita: $109 (1997).
Education: High school graduation rate: 80.6% (2000); College graduation rate: 12.8% (2000).
Housing: Homeownership rate: 91.2% (2000); Median home value: $84,400 (2000); Median rent: $300 per month (2000); Median age of housing: 27 years (2000).
Transportation: Commute to work: 92.4% car, 0.9% public transportation, 1.3% walk, 4.2% work from home (2000); Travel time to work: 62.9% less than 15 minutes, 22.4% 15 to 30 minutes, 7.2% 30 to 45 minutes, 3.3% 45 to 60 minutes, 4.2% 60 minutes or more (2000)

WINSOR (township). Covers a land area of 35.372 square miles and a water area of 0.041 square miles. Located at 43.81° N. Lat.; 83.28° W. Long.
Population: 2,044 (2000); Race: 97.7% White, 0.1% Black, 0.2% Asian, 0.5% American Indian and Alaska Native, 1.9% Hispanic of any race, 0.7% two or more races (2000); Density: 57.8 persons per square mile (2000); Age: 25.6% under 18, 20.3% over 64 (2000); Marriage status: 21.8% never married, 64.4% now married, 8.6% widowed, 5.2% divorced (2000); Foreign born: 1.4% (2000); Ancestry (includes multiple ancestries): 55.5% German, 9.7% Irish, 7.6% French (except Basque), 6.6% United States or American, 6.1% English (2000).
Economy: Employment by occupation: 13.8% management, 13.3% professional, 15.5% services, 22.6% sales, 1.9% farming, 10.5% construction, 22.4% production (2000).
Income: Per capita income: $17,122 (2000); Median household income: $37,222 (2000); Poverty rate: 7.2% (2000).
Taxes: Total city taxes per capita: $119 (1997); City property taxes per capita: $119 (1997).
Education: High school graduation rate: 78.2% (2000); College graduation rate: 12.0% (2000).
Housing: Homeownership rate: 80.2% (2000); Median home value: $70,600 (2000); Median rent: $338 per month (2000); Median age of housing: 54 years (2000).
Transportation: Commute to work: 87.7% car, 1.1% public transportation, 6.0% walk, 4.2% work from home (2000); Travel time to work: 63.5% less than 15 minutes, 25.7% 15 to 30 minutes, 4.3% 30 to 45 minutes, 1.6% 45 to 60 minutes, 4.8% 60 minutes or more (2000)

Ingham County

Located in south central Michigan; drained by the Grand and Red Cedar Rivers. Covers a land area of 559.20 square miles, a water area of 1.80 square miles, and is located in the Eastern Time Zone. The county government was organized in 1838. County seat is Mason.

Ingham County is part of the Lansing-East Lansing, MI MSA. The entire metro area includes: Clinton County; Eaton County; Ingham County

Weather Station: East Lansing 4 S — Elevation: 879 feet

	Jan	Feb	Mar	Apr	May	Jun	Jul	Aug	Sep	Oct	Nov	Dec
High	29	32	43	56	69	78	82	80	73	60	46	34
Low	14	15	24	35	46	55	59	57	49	39	30	20
Precip	1.5	1.4	2.2	3.3	2.6	3.2	3.1	3.3	3.4	2.5	2.6	2.0
Snow	11.3	8.1	5.1	1.4	0.0	0.0	0.0	0.0	0.0	0.2	2.2	9.0

High and Low temperatures in degrees Fahrenheit; Precipitation and Snow in inches

Population: 279,320 (2000); Race: 79.4% White, 10.7% Black, 3.6% Asian, 0.6% American Indian and Alaska Native, 5.7% Hispanic of any race, 3.2% two or more races (2000); Density: 499.5 persons per square mile (2000); Age: 23.4% under 18, 9.4% over 64 (2000).
Religion: Five largest groups: 17.8% Catholic Church, 2.6% The United Methodist Church, 1.6% Evangelical Lutheran Church in America, 1.5% United Church of Christ, 1.4% Presbyterian Church (U.S.A.) (2000).
Economy: Unemployment rate: 3.6% (11/2002); Total civilian labor force: 156,134 (11/2002); Leading industries: 14.5% retail trade; 14.0% health care and social assistance; 12.4% manufacturing (2000); Companies that employ more than 1,000 persons: 8 (2000); Companies that employ more than 100 persons: 182 (2000); Farms: 827 totaling 190,405 acres (1997); Minority business ownership rate: 9.1% (1997); Women business ownership rate: 27.3% (1997); Retail sales per capita: $10,424 (1997). Single-family building permits issued: 666 (2001) / 712 (2000); Multi-family building permits issued: 28 (2001) / 275 (2000).
Income: Per capita income: $21,079 (2000); Median household income: $40,774 (2000); Poverty rate: 14.6% (2000); Bankruptcy rate: 4.19% (2001).
Taxes: Total county taxes per capita: $144 (2000); County property taxes per capita: $140 (2000).
Education: High school graduation rate: 88.1% (2000); College graduation rate: 33.0% (2000).
Housing: Homeownership rate: 60.7% (2000); Median home value: $98,400 (2000); Median rent: $489 per month (2000); Median age of housing: 35 years (2000).
Health: Birth rate: 135.2 per 10,000 population (1998); Age adjusted death rate: 81.2 per 10,000 population (1999); Infant mortality rate: 7.2 per 1,000 live births (1998); Age adjusted cancer mortality rate: 175.1 deaths per 100,000 population (1999). Air Quality Index: 71% good, 29% moderate, 0% unhealthy (percent of days in 2000). Number of physicians: 29.6 per 10,000 population (1999); Number of hospital beds: 38.1 per 10,000 population (1999).
Elections: 2000 Presidential election results: 57.4% Gore, 39.2% Bush, 2.7% Nader, 0.0% Buchanan

Additional Information Contacts

Ingham County Government Offices 517-676-7200
Greater Lansing Association of Realtors 517-323-4090
Greater Lansing Hispanic Chamber 517-334-9233
Lansing Chamber of Commerce. 517-372-2278
Mason Chamber of Commerce. 517-676-1046
Michigan Association of Realtors 517-372-8890
Williamston Chamber of Commerce 517-655-1549

Ingham County Communities

ALAIEDON (township). Covers a land area of 35.540 square miles and a water area of 0.048 square miles. Located at 42.64° N. Lat.; 84.42° W. Long.
History: Many of the early residents of Alaiedon were German immigrants, and the community was first called German Settlement. The township was formed in 1842.
Population: 3,498 (2000); Race: 89.8% White, 5.5% Black, 0.0% Asian, 0.4% American Indian and Alaska Native, 3.3% Hispanic of any race, 2.3% two or more races (2000); Density: 98.4 persons per square mile (2000); Age:

21.9% under 18, 11.1% over 64 (2000); Marriage status: 28.3% never married, 60.8% now married, 5.8% widowed, 5.1% divorced (2000); Foreign born: 1.4% (2000); Ancestry (includes multiple ancestries): 21.3% German, 17.7% English, 11.0% Irish, 7.2% United States or American, 5.3% Other groups (2000).
Economy: Single-family building permits issued: 5 (2001) / 2 (2000); Multi-family building permits issued: 0 (2001) / 0 (2000); Employment by occupation: 17.8% management, 24.9% professional, 11.7% services, 26.3% sales, 1.0% farming, 8.2% construction, 10.1% production (2000).
Income: Per capita income: $24,048 (2000); Median household income: $64,680 (2000); Poverty rate: 5.2% (2000).
Taxes: Total city taxes per capita: $59 (1997); City property taxes per capita: $34 (1997).
Education: High school graduation rate: 90.0% (2000); College graduation rate: 32.2% (2000).
Housing: Homeownership rate: 90.2% (2000); Median home value: $143,400 (2000); Median rent: $588 per month (2000); Median age of housing: 37 years (2000).
Transportation: Commute to work: 90.8% car, 1.4% public transportation, 1.0% walk, 6.1% work from home (2000); Travel time to work: 27.7% less than 15 minutes, 52.9% 15 to 30 minutes, 13.3% 30 to 45 minutes, 1.4% 45 to 60 minutes, 4.6% 60 minutes or more (2000)

AURELIUS (township). Covers a land area of 36.501 square miles and a water area of 0.001 square miles. Located at 42.55° N. Lat.; 84.54° W. Long.
History: Aurelius Township was named by early settler Elijah Woodworth for his former home in Cayuga County, New York.
Population: 3,318 (2000); Race: 97.2% White, 1.0% Black, 0.1% Asian, 0.3% American Indian and Alaska Native, 3.8% Hispanic of any race, 1.2% two or more races (2000); Density: 90.9 persons per square mile (2000); Age: 29.7% under 18, 7.1% over 64 (2000); Marriage status: 20.0% never married, 69.6% now married, 3.0% widowed, 7.5% divorced (2000); Foreign born: 1.0% (2000); Ancestry (includes multiple ancestries): 32.5% German, 21.7% English, 12.6% Irish, 9.7% Other groups, 8.7% United States or American (2000).
Economy: Single-family building permits issued: 30 (2001) / 19 (2000); Multi-family building permits issued: 0 (2001) / 0 (2000); Employment by occupation: 13.0% management, 20.0% professional, 10.9% services, 29.2% sales, 1.3% farming, 11.8% construction, 13.8% production (2000).
Income: Per capita income: $22,983 (2000); Median household income: $62,750 (2000); Poverty rate: 3.9% (2000).
Taxes: Total city taxes per capita: $33 (1997); City property taxes per capita: $25 (1997).
Education: High school graduation rate: 90.7% (2000); College graduation rate: 22.8% (2000).
Housing: Homeownership rate: 94.3% (2000); Median home value: $123,900 (2000); Median rent: $480 per month (2000); Median age of housing: 25 years (2000).
Transportation: Commute to work: 93.3% car, 0.0% public transportation, 0.5% walk, 6.2% work from home (2000); Travel time to work: 22.5% less than 15 minutes, 51.7% 15 to 30 minutes, 19.6% 30 to 45 minutes, 2.7% 45 to 60 minutes, 3.5% 60 minutes or more (2000)

BUNKER HILL (township). Covers a land area of 32.962 square miles and a water area of 0.003 square miles. Located at 42.46° N. Lat.; 84.32° W. Long. Elevation is 946 feet.
History: Bunker Hill Township was organized in 1839, and was probably named for Adam Bunker, an early settler here.
Population: 1,979 (2000); Race: 98.3% White, 0.0% Black, 0.2% Asian, 0.3% American Indian and Alaska Native, 1.8% Hispanic of any race, 1.0% two or more races (2000); Density: 60.0 persons per square mile (2000); Age: 28.3% under 18, 7.9% over 64 (2000); Marriage status: 21.1% never married, 67.4% now married, 3.3% widowed, 8.2% divorced (2000); Foreign born: 0.6% (2000); Ancestry (includes multiple ancestries): 26.1% German, 16.7% English, 14.0% Irish, 9.8% United States or American, 7.4% Other groups (2000).
Economy: Single-family building permits issued: 15 (2001) / 10 (2000); Multi-family building permits issued: 0 (2001) / 0 (2000); Employment by occupation: 10.5% management, 12.6% professional, 14.5% services, 22.3% sales, 1.1% farming, 14.3% construction, 24.7% production (2000).
Income: Per capita income: $19,474 (2000); Median household income: $49,345 (2000); Poverty rate: 5.8% (2000).
Taxes: Total city taxes per capita: $356 (1997); City property taxes per capita: $356 (1997).
Education: High school graduation rate: 81.8% (2000); College graduation rate: 9.5% (2000).
Housing: Homeownership rate: 91.1% (2000); Median home value: $112,200 (2000); Median rent: $406 per month (2000); Median age of housing: 26 years (2000).
Transportation: Commute to work: 93.8% car, 0.0% public transportation, 0.9% walk, 5.2% work from home (2000); Travel time to work: 12.5% less than 15 minutes, 30.2% 15 to 30 minutes, 34.5% 30 to 45 minutes, 14.1% 45 to 60 minutes, 8.7% 60 minutes or more (2000)

DANSVILLE (village). Covers a land area of 1.000 square miles and a water area of 0 square miles. Located at 42.55° N. Lat.; 84.30° W. Long. Elevation is 976 feet.
Population: 429 (2000); Race: 95.1% White, 0.4% Black, 0.0% Asian, 0.4% American Indian and Alaska Native, 4.7% Hispanic of any race, 0.7% two or more races (2000); Density: 429.0 persons per square mile (2000); Age: 31.2% under 18, 6.3% over 64 (2000); Marriage status: 23.1% never married, 59.7% now married, 4.6% widowed, 12.6% divorced (2000); Foreign born: 0.0% (2000); Ancestry (includes multiple ancestries): 26.1% German, 15.1% Irish, 14.2% English, 13.0% Other groups, 5.8% United States or American (2000).
Economy: In agricultural area. Single-family building permits issued: 2 (2001) / 2 (2000); Multi-family building permits issued: 0 (2001) / 0 (2000); Employment by occupation: 11.0% management, 12.3% professional, 16.0% services, 24.7% sales, 0.0% farming, 16.0% construction, 20.1% production (2000).
Income: Per capita income: $16,951 (2000); Median household income: $48,214 (2000); Poverty rate: 4.3% (2000).
Taxes: Total city taxes per capita: $98 (1997); City property taxes per capita: $93 (1997).
Education: High school graduation rate: 88.9% (2000); College graduation rate: 10.7% (2000).

School District(s)

Dansville Schools (KG-12)
2000 Enrollment: 853 517-623-6120
Housing: Homeownership rate: 89.2% (2000); Median home value: $93,300 (2000); Median rent: $386 per month (2000); Median age of housing: 60+ years (2000).
Transportation: Commute to work: 86.3% car, 1.0% public transportation, 4.9% walk, 4.4% work from home (2000); Travel time to work: 23.0% less than 15 minutes, 28.6% 15 to 30 minutes, 33.2% 30 to 45 minutes, 5.6% 45 to 60 minutes, 9.7% 60 minutes or more (2000)

DELHI CHARTER (township). Covers a land area of 28.815 square miles and a water area of 0.145 square miles. Located at 42.64° N. Lat.; 84.53° W. Long.
Population: 22,569 (2000); Race: 92.6% White, 2.1% Black, 1.2% Asian, 0.8% American Indian and Alaska Native, 3.3% Hispanic of any race, 2.5% two or more races (2000); Density: 783.2 persons per square mile (2000); Age: 29.1% under 18, 10.0% over 64 (2000); Marriage status: 23.6% never married, 59.7% now married, 5.2% widowed, 11.5% divorced (2000); Foreign born: 2.8% (2000); Ancestry (includes multiple ancestries): 26.2% German, 15.6% English, 13.3% Irish, 10.6% Other groups, 6.7% United States or American (2000).
Economy: Single-family building permits issued: 147 (2001) / 205 (2000); Multi-family building permits issued: 4 (2001) / 24 (2000); Employment by occupation: 15.6% management, 20.7% professional, 13.7% services, 27.5% sales, 0.1% farming, 8.9% construction, 13.5% production (2000).
Income: Per capita income: $23,485 (2000); Median household income: $50,922 (2000); Poverty rate: 5.2% (2000).
Taxes: Total city taxes per capita: $125 (2000); City property taxes per capita: $102 (2000).
Education: High school graduation rate: 90.1% (2000); College graduation rate: 26.0% (2000).
Housing: Homeownership rate: 78.4% (2000); Median home value: $124,700 (2000); Median rent: $503 per month (2000); Median age of housing: 24 years (2000).
Transportation: Commute to work: 93.8% car, 1.3% public transportation, 1.0% walk, 3.3% work from home (2000); Travel time to work: 30.5% less than 15 minutes, 52.0% 15 to 30 minutes, 9.7% 30 to 45 minutes, 2.1% 45 to 60 minutes, 5.7% 60 minutes or more (2000)

EAST LANSING (city). Covers a land area of 11.247 square miles and a water area of 0.009 square miles. Located at 42.74° N. Lat.; 84.48° W. Long. Elevation is 870 feet.
History: In 1849, D. Robert Burcham bought land and settled on the site that became East Lansing. This was the location of the first agricultural college in the United States, authorized by the state in 1855 and opened in 1857 as the

Michigan Agricultural College (later Michigan State College of Agriculture and Applied Science). When East Lansing was granted a city charter in 1907, the residents favored College Park as a name, but the post office insisted on East Lansing.
Population: 46,525 (2000); Race: 80.6% White, 7.2% Black, 8.2% Asian, 0.6% American Indian and Alaska Native, 3.0% Hispanic of any race, 2.2% two or more races (2000); Density: 4,136.6 persons per square mile (2000); Age: 9.2% under 18, 6.1% over 64 (2000); Marriage status: 68.1% never married, 25.1% now married, 2.6% widowed, 4.2% divorced (2000); Foreign born: 11.7% (2000); Ancestry (includes multiple ancestries): 20.7% German, 19.5% Other groups, 12.2% Irish, 10.1% English, 8.4% Polish (2000).
Vital Statistics: Birth rate: 63.2 per 10,000 population (1998)
Economy: Unemployment rate: 4.1% (11/2002); Total civilian labor force: 29,494 (11/2002); Single-family building permits issued: 19 (2001) / 17 (2000); Multi-family building permits issued: 0 (2001) / 0 (2000); Employment by occupation: 10.1% management, 34.5% professional, 20.8% services, 27.3% sales, 0.4% farming, 2.6% construction, 4.3% production (2000).
Income: Per capita income: $16,333 (2000); Median household income: $28,217 (2000); Poverty rate: 34.8% (2000).
Taxes: Total city taxes per capita: $279 (2000); City property taxes per capita: $254 (2000).
Education: High school graduation rate: 96.9% (2000); College graduation rate: 70.4% (2000).

School District(s)

East Lansing School District (PK-12)
2000 Enrollment: 3,603 517-333-7424

Four-year College(s)

Michigan State University-Detroit College of Law (Private, Not-for-profit)
2001 Enrollment: 780 517-432-6800
Michigan State University (Public)
2001 Enrollment: 44,227 517-355-1855
2001 Tuition: In-state $5,257; Out-of-state $13,560

Housing: Homeownership rate: 32.2% (2000); Median home value: $144,300 (2000); Median rent: $536 per month (2000); Median age of housing: 33 years (2000).
Safety: Violent crime rate: 43.0 per 10,000 population; Property crime rate: 336.1 per 10,000 population (2001).
Newspapers: The State News (5 x week)
Transportation: Commute to work: 68.5% car, 4.3% public transportation, 21.4% walk, 2.6% work from home (2000); Travel time to work: 56.7% less than 15 minutes, 34.0% 15 to 30 minutes, 4.6% 30 to 45 minutes, 1.6% 45 to 60 minutes, 3.2% 60 minutes or more (2000); Amtrak: Service available.

EDGEMONT PARK (CDP). Covers a land area of 0.848 square miles and a water area of 0 square miles. Located at 42.74° N. Lat.; 84.59° W. Long.
Population: 2,442 (2000); Race: 84.4% White, 10.2% Black, 0.8% Asian, 0.0% American Indian and Alaska Native, 6.3% Hispanic of any race, 1.5% two or more races (2000); Density: 2,881.1 persons per square mile (2000); Age: 22.9% under 18, 19.7% over 64 (2000); Marriage status: 25.7% never married, 56.3% now married, 7.0% widowed, 11.0% divorced (2000); Foreign born: 2.4% (2000); Ancestry (includes multiple ancestries): 24.9% German, 19.2% Other groups, 15.4% English, 13.1% Irish, 9.8% United States or American (2000).
Economy: Employment by occupation: 15.9% management, 19.3% professional, 13.0% services, 29.9% sales, 0.0% farming, 7.5% construction, 14.3% production (2000).
Income: Per capita income: $23,981 (2000); Median household income: $43,173 (2000); Poverty rate: 5.5% (2000).
Education: High school graduation rate: 92.0% (2000); College graduation rate: 27.5% (2000).
Housing: Homeownership rate: 71.9% (2000); Median home value: $95,800 (2000); Median rent: $437 per month (2000); Median age of housing: 42 years (2000).
Transportation: Commute to work: 92.1% car, 3.5% public transportation, 1.4% walk, 3.0% work from home (2000); Travel time to work: 44.9% less than 15 minutes, 42.0% 15 to 30 minutes, 3.6% 30 to 45 minutes, 1.1% 45 to 60 minutes, 8.4% 60 minutes or more (2000)

HASLETT (CDP). Covers a land area of 8.328 square miles and a water area of 0.746 square miles. Located at 42.75° N. Lat.; 84.40° W. Long.
Population: 11,283 (2000); Race: 92.4% White, 1.9% Black, 2.3% Asian, 0.7% American Indian and Alaska Native, 2.3% Hispanic of any race, 2.0% two or more races (2000); Density: 1,354.8 persons per square mile (2000); Age: 23.5% under 18, 11.8% over 64 (2000); Marriage status: 26.1% never married, 54.1% now married, 5.8% widowed, 13.9% divorced (2000); Foreign born: 4.6% (2000); Ancestry (includes multiple ancestries): 28.7% German, 15.5% Irish, 14.3% English, 9.8% Other groups, 8.0% Polish (2000).
Economy: Manufacturing: metal finishing. Employment by occupation: 17.0% management, 34.5% professional, 13.5% services, 23.3% sales, 0.1% farming, 4.4% construction, 7.2% production (2000).
Income: Per capita income: $28,686 (2000); Median household income: $50,679 (2000); Poverty rate: 7.1% (2000).
Education: High school graduation rate: 93.2% (2000); College graduation rate: 47.5% (2000).

School District(s)

Haslett Public Schools (KG-12)
2000 Enrollment: 2,906 517-339-8242

Housing: Homeownership rate: 60.0% (2000); Median home value: $143,900 (2000); Median rent: $535 per month (2000); Median age of housing: 24 years (2000).
Newspapers: Lansing Community Newspaper (1 x week); Towne Courier (1 x week); Williamston Enterprise (1 x week)
Transportation: Commute to work: 95.0% car, 0.7% public transportation, 0.5% walk, 3.2% work from home (2000); Travel time to work: 29.9% less than 15 minutes, 49.9% 15 to 30 minutes, 11.2% 30 to 45 minutes, 3.4% 45 to 60 minutes, 5.6% 60 minutes or more (2000)

HOLT (CDP). Covers a land area of 4.313 square miles and a water area of 0.022 square miles. Located at 42.63° N. Lat.; 84.52° W. Long. Elevation is 885 feet.
History: The first settlement was made here in 1837, and was known as Delhi or Delhi Center, for the township. It was renamed Holt by the post office in 1860 for John Holt, postmaster general.
Population: 11,315 (2000); Race: 92.6% White, 2.3% Black, 0.8% Asian, 1.2% American Indian and Alaska Native, 3.4% Hispanic of any race, 2.3% two or more races (2000); Density: 2,623.2 persons per square mile (2000); Age: 28.8% under 18, 8.0% over 64 (2000); Marriage status: 27.3% never married, 53.5% now married, 4.3% widowed, 14.8% divorced (2000); Foreign born: 3.1% (2000); Ancestry (includes multiple ancestries): 24.6% German, 15.6% English, 13.7% Irish, 11.9% Other groups, 6.8% United States or American (2000).
Economy: Employment by occupation: 12.7% management, 20.5% professional, 14.0% services, 28.0% sales, 0.0% farming, 9.3% construction, 15.5% production (2000).
Income: Per capita income: $21,733 (2000); Median household income: $44,382 (2000); Poverty rate: 6.7% (2000).
Education: High school graduation rate: 90.6% (2000); College graduation rate: 24.1% (2000).

School District(s)

Holt Public Schools (KG-12)
2000 Enrollment: 5,324 517-694-5715

Housing: Homeownership rate: 67.2% (2000); Median home value: $103,700 (2000); Median rent: $489 per month (2000); Median age of housing: 28 years (2000).
Transportation: Commute to work: 92.3% car, 2.3% public transportation, 1.3% walk, 3.6% work from home (2000); Travel time to work: 28.5% less than 15 minutes, 51.8% 15 to 30 minutes, 11.8% 30 to 45 minutes, 2.8% 45 to 60 minutes, 5.1% 60 minutes or more (2000)

INGHAM (township). Covers a land area of 32.650 square miles and a water area of 0.027 square miles. Located at 42.55° N. Lat.; 84.30° W. Long.
History: Ingham Township was named for Samuel D. Ingham, who served as secretary of the treasury under President Andrew Jackson.
Population: 2,061 (2000); Race: 97.0% White, 0.2% Black, 0.0% Asian, 0.6% American Indian and Alaska Native, 1.8% Hispanic of any race, 0.7% two or more races (2000); Density: 63.1 persons per square mile (2000); Age: 27.1% under 18, 9.5% over 64 (2000); Marriage status: 21.6% never married, 66.1% now married, 3.8% widowed, 8.5% divorced (2000); Foreign born: 0.7% (2000); Ancestry (includes multiple ancestries): 28.0% German, 16.0% English, 14.5% Irish, 8.7% Other groups, 7.7% United States or American (2000).
Economy: Single-family building permits issued: 14 (2001) / 14 (2000); Multi-family building permits issued: 0 (2001) / 0 (2000); Employment by occupation: 13.0% management, 16.0% professional, 13.9% services, 24.4% sales, 0.9% farming, 15.6% construction, 16.3% production (2000).
Income: Per capita income: $21,348 (2000); Median household income: $56,741 (2000); Poverty rate: 3.3% (2000).
Taxes: Total city taxes per capita: $23 (1997); City property taxes per capita: $17 (1997).

Education: High school graduation rate: 88.3% (2000); College graduation rate: 14.9% (2000).
Housing: Homeownership rate: 93.1% (2000); Median home value: $114,400 (2000); Median rent: $378 per month (2000); Median age of housing: 29 years (2000).
Transportation: Commute to work: 93.3% car, 0.3% public transportation, 1.6% walk, 3.9% work from home (2000); Travel time to work: 16.5% less than 15 minutes, 35.0% 15 to 30 minutes, 33.4% 30 to 45 minutes, 6.3% 45 to 60 minutes, 8.8% 60 minutes or more (2000)

LANSING (city). Covers a land area of 35.048 square miles and a water area of 0.196 square miles. Located at 42.71° N. Lat.; 84.55° W. Long. Elevation is 828 feet.
History: When Lansing was chosen as the state capital in 1847, it had only one log house and a sawmill. The few families here had come from Lansing, New York, and named their settlement after their former home, which had been named for Chancellor John Lansing of New York. Though its choice as capital seemed a joke, the community arose to the honor and erected a capitol building the same year. Lansing was incorporated as a city in 1859. Industrial development came after 1871, when the railroads connected the city with the rest of the state. Ransom E. Olds, automobile pioneer, brought Lansing into the auto manufacturing scene in the early 1900's.
Population: 119,128 (2000); Race: 65.3% White, 21.6% Black, 2.7% Asian, 0.8% American Indian and Alaska Native, 9.9% Hispanic of any race, 5.0% two or more races (2000); Density: 3,399.0 persons per square mile (2000); Age: 26.7% under 18, 9.8% over 64 (2000); Marriage status: 36.0% never married, 43.7% now married, 5.6% widowed, 14.7% divorced (2000); Foreign born: 5.9% (2000); Ancestry (includes multiple ancestries): 34.2% Other groups, 17.0% German, 9.3% English, 9.2% Irish, 4.9% United States or American (2000).
Vital Statistics: Birth rate: 191.6 per 10,000 population (1998)
Economy: Unemployment rate: 4.6% (11/2002); Total civilian labor force: 67,856 (11/2002); Single-family building permits issued: 48 (2001) / 36 (2000); Multi-family building permits issued: 6 (2001) / 170 (2000); Employment by occupation: 9.6% management, 18.2% professional, 18.9% services, 28.8% sales, 0.2% farming, 8.3% construction, 15.9% production (2000).
Income: Per capita income: $17,924 (2000); Median household income: $34,833 (2000); Poverty rate: 16.9% (2000).
Taxes: Total city taxes per capita: $542 (2000); City property taxes per capita: $297 (2000).
Education: High school graduation rate: 82.4% (2000); College graduation rate: 21.2% (2000).

School District(s)

Community Health Agency (UG-UG)
2000 Enrollment: 0 517-335-0256
Department of Corrections (UG-UG)
2000 Enrollment: 0 517-335-4927
Department of Education (UG-UG)
2000 Enrollment: 0 313-257-1414
Family Independence Agency (UG-UG)
2000 Enrollment: 0 517-373-2048
Lansing Public School District (PK-12)
2000 Enrollment: 17,610 517-325-6007
Waverly Community Schools (KG-12)
2000 Enrollment: 3,365 517-321-7265

Four-year College(s)

Davenport University-Western Region-Lansing (Private, Not-for-profit)
2001 Enrollment: 1,209 517-484-2600
2001 Tuition: In-state $8,586; Out-of-state $8,586
Great Lakes Christian College (Private, Not-for-profit, Christian Churches and Churches of Christ)
2001 Enrollment: 220 517-321-0242
2001 Tuition: In-state $6,656; Out-of-state $6,656
Thomas M Cooley Law School (Private, Not-for-profit)
2001 Enrollment: 1,819 517-371-5140

Two-year College(s)

The Education Institute-American Hotel and Motel Association (Private, Not-for-profit)
2001 Enrollment: n/a 517-353-5500
Lansing Community College (Public)
2001 Enrollment: 17,358 517-483-1957
2001 Tuition: In-state $1,896; Out-of-state $2,592

Housing: Homeownership rate: 57.4% (2000); Median home value: $73,500 (2000); Median rent: $454 per month (2000); Median age of housing: 42 years (2000).
Hospitals: Michigan Capital Medical Center-Greenlawn Campus (448 beds); Sparrow Hospital (502 beds); Saint Lawrence Hospital
Safety: Violent crime rate: 113.0 per 10,000 population; Property crime rate: 489.2 per 10,000 population (2001).
Newspapers: Lansing State Journal (7 x week)
Transportation: Commute to work: 91.5% car, 2.7% public transportation, 2.4% walk, 2.5% work from home (2000); Travel time to work: 40.7% less than 15 minutes, 43.2% 15 to 30 minutes, 8.1% 30 to 45 minutes, 2.9% 45 to 60 minutes, 5.1% 60 minutes or more (2000)
Airports: Capital City (primary service)
Additional Information Contacts
Greater Lansing Association of Realtors 517-323-4090
Greater Lansing Hispanic Chamber 517-334-9233
Lansing Chamber of Commerce. 517-372-2278
Michigan Association of Realtors 517-372-8890

LANSING CHARTER (township). Covers a land area of 4.949 square miles and a water area of 0.101 square miles. Located at 42.75° N. Lat.; 84.52° W. Long. Elevation is 828 feet.
History: Lansing Township was organized in 1841 and named for Lansing, New York, the former home of an early resident. The New York town had been named for John Lansing, a Revolutionary War hero.
Population: 8,458 (2000); Race: 81.8% White, 10.0% Black, 2.5% Asian, 0.1% American Indian and Alaska Native, 6.8% Hispanic of any race, 2.4% two or more races (2000); Density: 1,709.0 persons per square mile (2000); Age: 20.5% under 18, 13.8% over 64 (2000); Marriage status: 34.9% never married, 46.6% now married, 5.8% widowed, 12.7% divorced (2000); Foreign born: 4.5% (2000); Ancestry (includes multiple ancestries): 24.8% German, 20.8% Other groups, 13.1% English, 11.6% Irish, 6.5% United States or American (2000).
Economy: Single-family building permits issued: 4 (2001) / 3 (2000); Multi-family building permits issued: 0 (2001) / 0 (2000); Employment by occupation: 13.3% management, 22.1% professional, 14.0% services, 28.9% sales, 0.2% farming, 6.7% construction, 14.7% production (2000).
Income: Per capita income: $22,885 (2000); Median household income: $41,017 (2000); Poverty rate: 7.5% (2000).
Taxes: Total city taxes per capita: $273 (2000); City property taxes per capita: $264 (2000).
Education: High school graduation rate: 90.0% (2000); College graduation rate: 29.2% (2000).
Housing: Homeownership rate: 53.2% (2000); Median home value: $90,800 (2000); Median rent: $482 per month (2000); Median age of housing: 40 years (2000).
Safety: Violent crime rate: 54.1 per 10,000 population; Property crime rate: 475.1 per 10,000 population (2001).
Transportation: Commute to work: 93.2% car, 2.3% public transportation, 2.1% walk, 2.0% work from home (2000); Travel time to work: 50.7% less than 15 minutes, 37.9% 15 to 30 minutes, 5.0% 30 to 45 minutes, 1.9% 45 to 60 minutes, 4.4% 60 minutes or more (2000)

LEROY (township). Covers a land area of 34.208 square miles and a water area of 0.011 square miles. Located at 42.66° N. Lat.; 84.19° W. Long.
Population: 3,653 (2000); Race: 96.6% White, 0.5% Black, 0.2% Asian, 0.3% American Indian and Alaska Native, 1.5% Hispanic of any race, 1.5% two or more races (2000); Density: 106.8 persons per square mile (2000); Age: 28.9% under 18, 9.1% over 64 (2000); Marriage status: 20.9% never married, 62.9% now married, 5.4% widowed, 10.8% divorced (2000); Foreign born: 1.0% (2000); Ancestry (includes multiple ancestries): 27.9% German, 17.4% English, 10.9% Irish, 8.4% United States or American, 6.4% Other groups (2000).
Economy: Single-family building permits issued: 8 (2001) / 15 (2000); Multi-family building permits issued: 0 (2001) / 0 (2000); Employment by occupation: 8.7% management, 19.5% professional, 15.7% services, 23.5% sales, 0.8% farming, 12.0% construction, 19.9% production (2000).
Income: Per capita income: $19,552 (2000); Median household income: $45,234 (2000); Poverty rate: 8.0% (2000).
Taxes: Total city taxes per capita: $32 (1997); City property taxes per capita: $28 (1997).
Education: High school graduation rate: 88.8% (2000); College graduation rate: 18.6% (2000).
Housing: Homeownership rate: 87.0% (2000); Median home value: $124,000 (2000); Median rent: $447 per month (2000); Median age of housing: 28 years (2000).
Transportation: Commute to work: 93.1% car, 0.5% public transportation, 2.2% walk, 3.6% work from home (2000); Travel time to work: 25.2% less

than 15 minutes, 37.0% 15 to 30 minutes, 26.0% 30 to 45 minutes, 6.3% 45 to 60 minutes, 5.5% 60 minutes or more (2000)

LESLIE (city). Covers a land area of 1.331 square miles and a water area of 0 square miles. Located at 42.45° N. Lat.; 84.43° W. Long. Elevation is 935 feet.
History: Leslie was settled in 1836 as the center of a farming area. In North Leslie, an ancient burial mound revealed a human skull and thigh bone of very large dimensions.
Population: 2,044 (2000); Race: 96.3% White, 0.0% Black, 0.4% Asian, 0.0% American Indian and Alaska Native, 1.6% Hispanic of any race, 1.9% two or more races (2000); Density: 1,535.6 persons per square mile (2000); Age: 31.5% under 18, 7.9% over 64 (2000); Marriage status: 24.7% never married, 56.3% now married, 5.6% widowed, 13.4% divorced (2000); Foreign born: 0.5% (2000); Ancestry (includes multiple ancestries): 20.5% German, 17.3% United States or American, 13.7% English, 10.7% Other groups, 10.5% Irish (2000).
Economy: Single-family building permits issued: 5 (2001) / 0 (2000); Multi-family building permits issued: 0 (2001) / 0 (2000); Employment by occupation: 9.3% management, 13.3% professional, 17.5% services, 23.9% sales, 0.0% farming, 10.1% construction, 25.9% production (2000).
Income: Per capita income: $18,124 (2000); Median household income: $42,700 (2000); Poverty rate: 7.5% (2000).
Taxes: Total city taxes per capita: $316 (1997); City property taxes per capita: $311 (1997).
Education: High school graduation rate: 87.7% (2000); College graduation rate: 9.4% (2000).

School District(s)

Leslie Public Schools (KG-12)
2000 Enrollment: 1,392 517-589-8200
White Pine Academy (KG-08)
2000 Enrollment: 137 517-249-4623

Housing: Homeownership rate: 76.2% (2000); Median home value: $83,000 (2000); Median rent: $373 per month (2000); Median age of housing: 55 years (2000).
Safety: Violent crime rate: 14.6 per 10,000 population; Property crime rate: 506.1 per 10,000 population (2001).
Newspapers: Leslie Local Independent (1 x week)
Transportation: Commute to work: 93.0% car, 1.7% public transportation, 4.1% walk, 0.8% work from home (2000); Travel time to work: 26.1% less than 15 minutes, 38.7% 15 to 30 minutes, 22.0% 30 to 45 minutes, 7.3% 45 to 60 minutes, 6.0% 60 minutes or more (2000)

LESLIE (township). Covers a land area of 34.999 square miles and a water area of 0.052 square miles. Located at 42.46° N. Lat.; 84.42° W. Long. Elevation is 935 feet.
History: Settled 1836, incorporated 1869.
Population: 2,327 (2000); Race: 99.0% White, 0.1% Black, 0.1% Asian, 0.0% American Indian and Alaska Native, 0.4% Hispanic of any race, 0.6% two or more races (2000); Density: 66.5 persons per square mile (2000); Age: 24.8% under 18, 10.3% over 64 (2000); Marriage status: 21.4% never married, 63.5% now married, 5.1% widowed, 10.0% divorced (2000); Foreign born: 0.7% (2000); Ancestry (includes multiple ancestries): 27.6% German, 20.0% English, 12.3% Irish, 10.3% United States or American, 4.1% French (except Basque) (2000).
Economy: In agricultural area: livestock; dairy; grain, apples, corn, soybeans; light manufacturing. Single-family building permits issued: 16 (2001) / 17 (2000); Multi-family building permits issued: 0 (2001) / 0 (2000); Employment by occupation: 11.9% management, 12.2% professional, 13.4% services, 27.7% sales, 0.9% farming, 11.4% construction, 22.6% production (2000).
Income: Per capita income: $23,179 (2000); Median household income: $55,476 (2000); Poverty rate: 6.7% (2000).
Taxes: Total city taxes per capita: $63 (1997); City property taxes per capita: $57 (1997).
Education: High school graduation rate: 89.5% (2000); College graduation rate: 11.7% (2000).
Housing: Homeownership rate: 88.7% (2000); Median home value: $122,500 (2000); Median rent: $486 per month (2000); Median age of housing: 27 years (2000).
Transportation: Commute to work: 93.7% car, 0.0% public transportation, 0.5% walk, 5.3% work from home (2000); Travel time to work: 25.3% less than 15 minutes, 33.1% 15 to 30 minutes, 28.5% 30 to 45 minutes, 6.1% 45 to 60 minutes, 7.1% 60 minutes or more (2000)

LOCKE (township). Covers a land area of 36.049 square miles and a water area of 0.011 square miles. Located at 42.73° N. Lat.; 84.20° W. Long.
Population: 1,671 (2000); Race: 97.2% White, 0.3% Black, 0.8% Asian, 1.4% American Indian and Alaska Native, 1.3% Hispanic of any race, 0.2% two or more races (2000); Density: 46.4 persons per square mile (2000); Age: 27.9% under 18, 8.3% over 64 (2000); Marriage status: 20.0% never married, 69.6% now married, 3.4% widowed, 7.0% divorced (2000); Foreign born: 1.7% (2000); Ancestry (includes multiple ancestries): 27.9% German, 16.4% English, 11.3% Irish, 7.9% Other groups, 5.6% Dutch (2000).
Economy: Single-family building permits issued: 13 (2001) / 18 (2000); Multi-family building permits issued: 0 (2001) / 0 (2000); Employment by occupation: 15.3% management, 18.1% professional, 16.1% services, 19.5% sales, 1.9% farming, 14.3% construction, 14.7% production (2000).
Income: Per capita income: $23,149 (2000); Median household income: $58,188 (2000); Poverty rate: 4.1% (2000).
Taxes: Total city taxes per capita: $35 (1997); City property taxes per capita: $24 (1997).
Education: High school graduation rate: 92.3% (2000); College graduation rate: 19.8% (2000).
Housing: Homeownership rate: 89.1% (2000); Median home value: $135,400 (2000); Median rent: $500 per month (2000); Median age of housing: 39 years (2000).
Transportation: Commute to work: 93.9% car, 0.8% public transportation, 0.8% walk, 4.2% work from home (2000); Travel time to work: 18.9% less than 15 minutes, 34.4% 15 to 30 minutes, 30.5% 30 to 45 minutes, 8.6% 45 to 60 minutes, 7.5% 60 minutes or more (2000)

MASON (city). Covers a land area of 4.578 square miles and a water area of 0 square miles. Located at 42.58° N. Lat.; 84.44° W. Long. Elevation is 902 feet.
History: Mason was settled in 1836 at the junction of two trails. It became the seat of Ingham County in 1840.
Population: 6,714 (2000); Race: 96.1% White, 0.2% Black, 1.8% Asian, 0.1% American Indian and Alaska Native, 2.8% Hispanic of any race, 1.2% two or more races (2000); Density: 1,466.6 persons per square mile (2000); Age: 25.1% under 18, 14.4% over 64 (2000); Marriage status: 25.3% never married, 55.3% now married, 6.8% widowed, 12.7% divorced (2000); Foreign born: 3.4% (2000); Ancestry (includes multiple ancestries): 28.3% German, 19.2% English, 12.6% Irish, 8.6% Other groups, 6.4% United States or American (2000).
Economy: Single-family building permits issued: 56 (2001) / 40 (2000); Multi-family building permits issued: 6 (2001) / 34 (2000); Employment by occupation: 10.6% management, 20.6% professional, 13.9% services, 30.5% sales, 0.3% farming, 6.7% construction, 17.4% production (2000).
Income: Per capita income: $20,866 (2000); Median household income: $41,790 (2000); Poverty rate: 4.1% (2000).
Taxes: Total city taxes per capita: $290 (1997); City property taxes per capita: $273 (1997).
Education: High school graduation rate: 89.4% (2000); College graduation rate: 26.3% (2000).

School District(s)

Mason Public Schools (Ingham) (PK-12)
2000 Enrollment: 3,271 517-676-2484

Housing: Homeownership rate: 63.5% (2000); Median home value: $113,300 (2000); Median rent: $503 per month (2000); Median age of housing: 34 years (2000).
Safety: Violent crime rate: 16.3 per 10,000 population; Property crime rate: 426.7 per 10,000 population (2001).
Newspapers: Holt Community News (1 x week); Ingham County Community News (1 x week)
Transportation: Commute to work: 92.7% car, 0.4% public transportation, 3.0% walk, 3.5% work from home (2000); Travel time to work: 30.5% less than 15 minutes, 49.2% 15 to 30 minutes, 13.5% 30 to 45 minutes, 2.1% 45 to 60 minutes, 4.8% 60 minutes or more (2000)
Additional Information Contacts
Mason Chamber of Commerce. 517-676-1046

MERIDIAN CHARTER (township). Covers a land area of 31.015 square miles and a water area of 0.771 square miles. Located at 42.73° N. Lat.; 84.42° W. Long.
Population: 39,116 (2000); Race: 86.9% White, 3.7% Black, 6.3% Asian, 0.4% American Indian and Alaska Native, 2.2% Hispanic of any race, 2.1% two or more races (2000); Density: 1,261.2 persons per square mile (2000); Age: 23.7% under 18, 9.8% over 64 (2000); Marriage status: 30.2% never married, 55.5% now married, 4.3% widowed, 9.9% divorced (2000); Foreign

born: 8.7% (2000); Ancestry (includes multiple ancestries): 25.8% German, 15.4% English, 15.4% Other groups, 13.0% Irish, 6.9% Polish (2000).
Vital Statistics: Birth rate: 92.3 per 10,000 population (1998)
Economy: Unemployment rate: 1.7% (11/2002); Total civilian labor force: 21,224 (11/2002); Single-family building permits issued: 112 (2001) / 157 (2000); Multi-family building permits issued: 2 (2001) / 12 (2000); Employment by occupation: 18.3% management, 37.7% professional, 11.1% services, 23.5% sales, 0.1% farming, 3.2% construction, 6.1% production (2000).
Income: Per capita income: $32,190 (2000); Median household income: $55,203 (2000); Poverty rate: 9.4% (2000).
Taxes: Total city taxes per capita: $211 (2000); City property taxes per capita: $201 (2000).
Education: High school graduation rate: 95.6% (2000); College graduation rate: 59.9% (2000).
Housing: Homeownership rate: 62.0% (2000); Median home value: $165,600 (2000); Median rent: $585 per month (2000); Median age of housing: 23 years (2000).
Safety: Violent crime rate: 12.7 per 10,000 population; Property crime rate: 331.9 per 10,000 population (2001).
Transportation: Commute to work: 93.5% car, 1.1% public transportation, 1.3% walk, 3.5% work from home (2000); Travel time to work: 35.8% less than 15 minutes, 47.4% 15 to 30 minutes, 8.3% 30 to 45 minutes, 2.5% 45 to 60 minutes, 5.9% 60 minutes or more (2000)

OKEMOS (CDP). Covers a land area of 16.806 square miles and a water area of 0.025 square miles. Located at 42.71° N. Lat.; 84.42° W. Long. Elevation is 839 feet.
Population: 22,805 (2000); Race: 84.8% White, 3.9% Black, 8.4% Asian, 0.1% American Indian and Alaska Native, 1.9% Hispanic of any race, 2.1% two or more races (2000); Density: 1,356.9 persons per square mile (2000); Age: 24.0% under 18, 9.3% over 64 (2000); Marriage status: 31.0% never married, 57.5% now married, 3.5% widowed, 8.0% divorced (2000); Foreign born: 10.3% (2000); Ancestry (includes multiple ancestries): 25.0% German, 16.8% Other groups, 16.3% English, 11.7% Irish, 6.7% Polish (2000).
Economy: Employment by occupation: 19.3% management, 40.1% professional, 9.6% services, 23.6% sales, 0.1% farming, 2.7% construction, 4.6% production (2000).
Income: Per capita income: $33,401 (2000); Median household income: $62,810 (2000); Poverty rate: 9.6% (2000).
Education: High school graduation rate: 97.0% (2000); College graduation rate: 66.8% (2000).

School District(s)

Okemos Public Schools (PK-12)
2000 Enrollment: 4,200 517-349-9460
Housing: Homeownership rate: 64.7% (2000); Median home value: $176,000 (2000); Median rent: $624 per month (2000); Median age of housing: 23 years (2000).
Transportation: Commute to work: 92.6% car, 1.3% public transportation, 1.5% walk, 4.1% work from home (2000); Travel time to work: 38.2% less than 15 minutes, 45.9% 15 to 30 minutes, 7.9% 30 to 45 minutes, 2.2% 45 to 60 minutes, 5.8% 60 minutes or more (2000)

ONONDAGA (township). Covers a land area of 36.524 square miles and a water area of 0.026 square miles. Located at 42.45° N. Lat.; 84.55° W. Long.
Population: 2,958 (2000); Race: 96.4% White, 0.3% Black, 0.2% Asian, 0.0% American Indian and Alaska Native, 2.2% Hispanic of any race, 1.5% two or more races (2000); Density: 81.0 persons per square mile (2000); Age: 29.6% under 18, 8.0% over 64 (2000); Marriage status: 23.9% never married, 62.3% now married, 2.8% widowed, 11.0% divorced (2000); Foreign born: 1.2% (2000); Ancestry (includes multiple ancestries): 19.7% German, 15.9% English, 12.7% Irish, 10.3% United States or American, 4.6% Other groups (2000).
Economy: Single-family building permits issued: 23 (2001) / 28 (2000); Multi-family building permits issued: 0 (2001) / 0 (2000); Employment by occupation: 11.0% management, 9.8% professional, 13.3% services, 26.9% sales, 3.2% farming, 16.1% construction, 19.8% production (2000).
Income: Per capita income: $18,981 (2000); Median household income: $52,216 (2000); Poverty rate: 9.0% (2000).
Taxes: Total city taxes per capita: $38 (2000); City property taxes per capita: $23 (2000).
Education: High school graduation rate: 89.6% (2000); College graduation rate: 10.5% (2000).
Housing: Homeownership rate: 87.9% (2000); Median home value: $110,200 (2000); Median rent: $473 per month (2000); Median age of housing: 28 years (2000).
Transportation: Commute to work: 95.0% car, 0.0% public transportation, 1.6% walk, 3.4% work from home (2000); Travel time to work: 11.5% less than 15 minutes, 34.5% 15 to 30 minutes, 43.7% 30 to 45 minutes, 5.5% 45 to 60 minutes, 4.9% 60 minutes or more (2000)

STOCKBRIDGE (village). Covers a land area of 1.455 square miles and a water area of 0.013 square miles. Located at 42.44° N. Lat.; 84.17° W. Long. Elevation is 944 feet.
History: Stockbridge was settled in 1835 by Herman Lowe. The village was first called Pekin by Elijah Smith, who platted it and named it for his former home in New York. The name was later changed to that of the township.
Population: 1,260 (2000); Race: 98.0% White, 0.0% Black, 0.0% Asian, 0.5% American Indian and Alaska Native, 0.5% Hispanic of any race, 1.1% two or more races (2000); Density: 866.1 persons per square mile (2000); Age: 27.3% under 18, 16.3% over 64 (2000); Marriage status: 21.6% never married, 52.1% now married, 12.6% widowed, 13.7% divorced (2000); Foreign born: 1.6% (2000); Ancestry (includes multiple ancestries): 27.9% German, 22.0% English, 14.8% Irish, 7.8% Other groups, 5.2% Polish (2000).
Economy: Employment by occupation: 12.1% management, 16.9% professional, 15.5% services, 21.5% sales, 0.0% farming, 11.4% construction, 22.5% production (2000).
Income: Per capita income: $17,614 (2000); Median household income: $38,456 (2000); Poverty rate: 11.6% (2000).
Taxes: Total city taxes per capita: $320 (1997); City property taxes per capita: $318 (1997).
Education: High school graduation rate: 80.6% (2000); College graduation rate: 18.5% (2000).

School District(s)

Stockbridge Community Schools (KG-12)
2000 Enrollment: 1,777 517-851-7188
Housing: Homeownership rate: 66.4% (2000); Median home value: $120,600 (2000); Median rent: $392 per month (2000); Median age of housing: 54 years (2000).
Newspapers: The Town Crier (1 x week)
Transportation: Commute to work: 90.6% car, 0.0% public transportation, 5.6% walk, 3.3% work from home (2000); Travel time to work: 20.6% less than 15 minutes, 18.7% 15 to 30 minutes, 29.8% 30 to 45 minutes, 19.7% 45 to 60 minutes, 11.2% 60 minutes or more (2000)

STOCKBRIDGE (township). Covers a land area of 35.646 square miles and a water area of 0.260 square miles. Located at 42.45° N. Lat.; 84.19° W. Long. Elevation is 944 feet.
Population: 3,435 (2000); Race: 96.2% White, 0.2% Black, 0.3% Asian, 0.6% American Indian and Alaska Native, 1.4% Hispanic of any race, 2.1% two or more races (2000); Density: 96.4 persons per square mile (2000); Age: 27.6% under 18, 11.5% over 64 (2000); Marriage status: 20.3% never married, 62.8% now married, 7.7% widowed, 9.2% divorced (2000); Foreign born: 1.5% (2000); Ancestry (includes multiple ancestries): 24.4% German, 17.5% English, 14.9% Irish, 8.4% Other groups, 7.7% United States or American (2000).
Economy: In farm area: dairy products; grain, soybeans; poultry. Manufacturing: machinery; machining. Single-family building permits issued: 47 (2001) / 32 (2000); Multi-family building permits issued: 0 (2001) / 0 (2000); Employment by occupation: 9.9% management, 17.9% professional, 15.1% services, 19.1% sales, 0.2% farming, 12.2% construction, 25.7% production (2000).
Income: Per capita income: $22,014 (2000); Median household income: $44,295 (2000); Poverty rate: 9.4% (2000).
Taxes: Total city taxes per capita: $25 (1997); City property taxes per capita: $20 (1997).
Education: High school graduation rate: 83.2% (2000); College graduation rate: 15.4% (2000).
Housing: Homeownership rate: 80.4% (2000); Median home value: $131,700 (2000); Median rent: $414 per month (2000); Median age of housing: 34 years (2000).
Transportation: Commute to work: 92.6% car, 0.3% public transportation, 2.9% walk, 3.7% work from home (2000); Travel time to work: 21.4% less than 15 minutes, 19.8% 15 to 30 minutes, 26.3% 30 to 45 minutes, 20.4% 45 to 60 minutes, 12.1% 60 minutes or more (2000)

VEVAY (township). Covers a land area of 32.175 square miles and a water area of 0.023 square miles. Located at 42.55° N. Lat.; 84.42° W. Long.

Population: 3,614 (2000); Race: 96.2% White, 0.5% Black, 0.3% Asian, 0.5% American Indian and Alaska Native, 1.7% Hispanic of any race, 1.1% two or more races (2000); Density: 112.3 persons per square mile (2000); Age: 27.8% under 18, 7.3% over 64 (2000); Marriage status: 23.0% never married, 64.4% now married, 3.8% widowed, 8.8% divorced (2000); Foreign born: 0.6% (2000); Ancestry (includes multiple ancestries): 31.6% German, 21.8% English, 11.5% Irish, 11.2% United States or American, 7.9% Other groups (2000).
Economy: Single-family building permits issued: 15 (2001) / 17 (2000); Multi-family building permits issued: 0 (2001) / 0 (2000); Employment by occupation: 13.3% management, 16.6% professional, 18.0% services, 28.3% sales, 0.2% farming, 9.1% construction, 14.4% production (2000).
Income: Per capita income: $21,488 (2000); Median household income: $56,324 (2000); Poverty rate: 2.3% (2000).
Taxes: Total city taxes per capita: $28 (1997); City property taxes per capita: $25 (1997).
Education: High school graduation rate: 91.7% (2000); College graduation rate: 19.9% (2000).
Housing: Homeownership rate: 92.9% (2000); Median home value: $137,900 (2000); Median rent: $436 per month (2000); Median age of housing: 24 years (2000).
Transportation: Commute to work: 93.6% car, 0.4% public transportation, 1.5% walk, 4.2% work from home (2000); Travel time to work: 28.9% less than 15 minutes, 44.7% 15 to 30 minutes, 18.0% 30 to 45 minutes, 2.5% 45 to 60 minutes, 5.8% 60 minutes or more (2000)

WEBBERVILLE (village). Covers a land area of 1.245 square miles and a water area of 0 square miles. Located at 42.66° N. Lat.; 84.17° W. Long.
Population: 1,503 (2000); Race: 95.9% White, 0.7% Black, 0.4% Asian, 0.0% American Indian and Alaska Native, 1.9% Hispanic of any race, 1.6% two or more races (2000); Density: 1,207.0 persons per square mile (2000); Age: 32.5% under 18, 7.4% over 64 (2000); Marriage status: 23.0% never married, 56.2% now married, 5.0% widowed, 15.7% divorced (2000); Foreign born: 1.0% (2000); Ancestry (includes multiple ancestries): 22.5% German, 15.0% English, 13.2% Irish, 10.2% United States or American, 6.3% Other groups (2000).
Economy: In farm area. Single-family building permits issued: 5 (2001) / 5 (2000); Multi-family building permits issued: 0 (2001) / 0 (2000); Employment by occupation: 7.1% management, 11.9% professional, 15.4% services, 27.9% sales, 0.1% farming, 13.0% construction, 24.5% production (2000).
Income: Per capita income: $17,663 (2000); Median household income: $45,388 (2000); Poverty rate: 5.5% (2000).
Taxes: Total city taxes per capita: $154 (1997); City property taxes per capita: $143 (1997).
Education: High school graduation rate: 90.3% (2000); College graduation rate: 11.0% (2000).

School District(s)

Webberville Community Schools (KG-12)
2000 Enrollment: 700 517-521-3422

Housing: Homeownership rate: 80.2% (2000); Median home value: $105,800 (2000); Median rent: $554 per month (2000); Median age of housing: 31 years (2000).
Transportation: Commute to work: 93.1% car, 1.2% public transportation, 2.0% walk, 3.3% work from home (2000); Travel time to work: 25.1% less than 15 minutes, 39.7% 15 to 30 minutes, 20.9% 30 to 45 minutes, 8.1% 45 to 60 minutes, 6.2% 60 minutes or more (2000)

WHEATFIELD (township). Covers a land area of 29.071 square miles and a water area of 0.004 square miles. Located at 42.64° N. Lat.; 84.31° W. Long.
Population: 1,641 (2000); Race: 95.7% White, 1.1% Black, 2.0% Asian, 0.1% American Indian and Alaska Native, 0.9% Hispanic of any race, 0.9% two or more races (2000); Density: 56.4 persons per square mile (2000); Age: 25.8% under 18, 10.4% over 64 (2000); Marriage status: 20.3% never married, 68.2% now married, 4.3% widowed, 7.2% divorced (2000); Foreign born: 2.5% (2000); Ancestry (includes multiple ancestries): 28.8% German, 21.5% English, 12.0% Irish, 7.0% United States or American, 6.0% Dutch (2000).
Economy: Single-family building permits issued: 5 (2001) / 7 (2000); Multi-family building permits issued: 0 (2001) / 0 (2000); Employment by occupation: 21.6% management, 22.4% professional, 10.4% services, 22.4% sales, 1.4% farming, 10.9% construction, 10.8% production (2000).
Income: Per capita income: $26,540 (2000); Median household income: $63,636 (2000); Poverty rate: 2.1% (2000).
Taxes: Total city taxes per capita: $39 (2000); City property taxes per capita: $24 (2000).
Education: High school graduation rate: 93.2% (2000); College graduation rate: 32.6% (2000).
Housing: Homeownership rate: 92.5% (2000); Median home value: $150,600 (2000); Median rent: $575 per month (2000); Median age of housing: 28 years (2000).
Transportation: Commute to work: 89.7% car, 0.6% public transportation, 1.4% walk, 7.6% work from home (2000); Travel time to work: 22.8% less than 15 minutes, 52.7% 15 to 30 minutes, 18.3% 30 to 45 minutes, 2.4% 45 to 60 minutes, 3.7% 60 minutes or more (2000)

WHITE OAK (township). Covers a land area of 36.481 square miles and a water area of 0.017 square miles. Located at 42.55° N. Lat.; 84.20° W. Long.
Population: 1,177 (2000); Race: 95.3% White, 0.5% Black, 0.4% Asian, 1.7% American Indian and Alaska Native, 1.8% Hispanic of any race, 1.0% two or more races (2000); Density: 32.3 persons per square mile (2000); Age: 25.9% under 18, 8.7% over 64 (2000); Marriage status: 25.5% never married, 60.3% now married, 5.2% widowed, 8.9% divorced (2000); Foreign born: 1.3% (2000); Ancestry (includes multiple ancestries): 30.5% German, 20.2% English, 11.5% Other groups, 11.4% Irish, 5.9% French (except Basque) (2000).
Economy: Single-family building permits issued: 12 (2001) / 12 (2000); Multi-family building permits issued: 0 (2001) / 0 (2000); Employment by occupation: 12.6% management, 15.2% professional, 13.0% services, 23.4% sales, 1.0% farming, 14.0% construction, 20.9% production (2000).
Income: Per capita income: $21,670 (2000); Median household income: $53,594 (2000); Poverty rate: 4.5% (2000).
Taxes: Total city taxes per capita: $32 (1997); City property taxes per capita: $30 (1997).
Education: High school graduation rate: 87.1% (2000); College graduation rate: 12.3% (2000).
Housing: Homeownership rate: 88.6% (2000); Median home value: $125,600 (2000); Median rent: $430 per month (2000); Median age of housing: 39 years (2000).
Transportation: Commute to work: 95.5% car, 0.3% public transportation, 0.9% walk, 1.7% work from home (2000); Travel time to work: 17.4% less than 15 minutes, 28.3% 15 to 30 minutes, 34.6% 30 to 45 minutes, 10.2% 45 to 60 minutes, 9.5% 60 minutes or more (2000)

WILLIAMSTON (city). Covers a land area of 2.547 square miles and a water area of 0.026 square miles. Located at 42.68° N. Lat.; 84.28° W. Long. Elevation is 883 feet.
History: Williamston developed in an area where large clay pits contained layers of soft coal. Both clay and coal have been mined commercially.
Population: 3,441 (2000); Race: 97.1% White, 0.0% Black, 0.0% Asian, 0.2% American Indian and Alaska Native, 3.0% Hispanic of any race, 1.6% two or more races (2000); Density: 1,351.2 persons per square mile (2000); Age: 26.3% under 18, 13.3% over 64 (2000); Marriage status: 22.5% never married, 56.0% now married, 8.9% widowed, 12.7% divorced (2000); Foreign born: 2.5% (2000); Ancestry (includes multiple ancestries): 29.9% German, 13.8% English, 12.2% Irish, 8.7% Other groups, 5.5% Polish (2000).
Economy: Single-family building permits issued: 37 (2001) / 33 (2000); Multi-family building permits issued: 10 (2001) / 35 (2000); Employment by occupation: 11.1% management, 23.9% professional, 9.1% services, 30.9% sales, 0.3% farming, 10.0% construction, 14.8% production (2000).
Income: Per capita income: $22,798 (2000); Median household income: $39,727 (2000); Poverty rate: 8.2% (2000).
Taxes: Total city taxes per capita: $578 (1997); City property taxes per capita: $576 (1997).
Education: High school graduation rate: 90.5% (2000); College graduation rate: 30.7% (2000).

School District(s)

Williamston Community Schools (KG-12)
2000 Enrollment: 1,982 517-655-4361

Housing: Homeownership rate: 65.2% (2000); Median home value: $114,600 (2000); Median rent: $451 per month (2000); Median age of housing: 40 years (2000).
Safety: Violent crime rate: 11.6 per 10,000 population; Property crime rate: 187.9 per 10,000 population (2001).
Transportation: Commute to work: 95.5% car, 0.8% public transportation, 1.4% walk, 1.8% work from home (2000); Travel time to work: 26.3% less than 15 minutes, 46.7% 15 to 30 minutes, 16.4% 30 to 45 minutes, 3.8% 45 to 60 minutes, 6.8% 60 minutes or more (2000)

Additional Information Contacts
Williamston Chamber of Commerce 517-655-1549

WILLIAMSTOWN (township). Covers a land area of 29.414 square miles and a water area of 0.027 square miles. Located at 42.72° N. Lat.; 84.31° W. Long.
Population: 4,834 (2000); Race: 97.2% White, 1.0% Black, 0.4% Asian, 0.1% American Indian and Alaska Native, 0.9% Hispanic of any race, 0.7% two or more races (2000); Density: 164.3 persons per square mile (2000); Age: 30.1% under 18, 8.3% over 64 (2000); Marriage status: 17.2% never married, 72.6% now married, 4.0% widowed, 6.2% divorced (2000); Foreign born: 2.1% (2000); Ancestry (includes multiple ancestries): 29.7% German, 19.7% English, 14.7% Irish, 7.6% Polish, 5.5% Other groups (2000).
Economy: Single-family building permits issued: 28 (2001) / 23 (2000); Multi-family building permits issued: 0 (2001) / 0 (2000); Employment by occupation: 19.0% management, 33.0% professional, 8.8% services, 24.9% sales, 0.2% farming, 5.9% construction, 8.2% production (2000).
Income: Per capita income: $30,710 (2000); Median household income: $79,778 (2000); Poverty rate: 2.0% (2000).
Taxes: Total city taxes per capita: $34 (1997); City property taxes per capita: $23 (1997).
Education: High school graduation rate: 96.3% (2000); College graduation rate: 50.4% (2000).
Housing: Homeownership rate: 94.5% (2000); Median home value: $152,400 (2000); Median rent: $442 per month (2000); Median age of housing: 27 years (2000).
Transportation: Commute to work: 96.3% car, 0.3% public transportation, 0.4% walk, 3.0% work from home (2000); Travel time to work: 20.2% less than 15 minutes, 48.5% 15 to 30 minutes, 22.1% 30 to 45 minutes, 2.4% 45 to 60 minutes, 6.7% 60 minutes or more (2000)

Ionia County

Located in south central Michigan; crossed by the Grand River; drained by the Flat, Lookingglass, and Maple Rivers. Covers a land area of 573.20 square miles, a water area of 7.00 square miles, and is located in the Eastern Time Zone. The county government was organized in 1837. County seat is Ionia.

Weather Station: Ionia 2 SSW — Elevation: 803 feet

	Jan	Feb	Mar	Apr	May	Jun	Jul	Aug	Sep	Oct	Nov	Dec
High	29	33	44	57	71	80	84	81	73	61	46	34
Low	13	15	23	34	45	54	59	57	49	38	30	20
Precip	2.1	1.8	2.8	3.1	3.1	3.5	2.9	4.2	3.9	3.0	2.9	2.5
Snow	14.5	9.4	8.1	1.8	tr	0.0	0.0	0.0	0.0	0.3	4.1	12.9

High and Low temperatures in degrees Fahrenheit; Precipitation and Snow in inches

Population: 61,518 (2000); Race: 92.1% White, 4.5% Black, 0.4% Asian, 0.4% American Indian and Alaska Native, 2.4% Hispanic of any race, 1.6% two or more races (2000); Density: 107.3 persons per square mile (2000); Age: 26.9% under 18, 10.0% over 64 (2000).
Religion: Five largest groups: 22.5% Catholic Church, 2.9% The United Methodist Church, 1.4% Lutheran Church—Missouri Synod, 1.2% General Association of Regular Baptist Churches, 0.9% Christian Reformed Church in North America (2000).
Economy: Unemployment rate: 5.3% (11/2002); Total civilian labor force: 28,801 (11/2002); Leading industries: 30.3% manufacturing; 19.0% retail trade; 10.1% health care and social assistance (2000); Companies that employ more than 1,000 persons: 0 (2000); Companies that employ more than 100 persons: 14 (2000); Farms: 1,004 totaling 236,652 acres (1997); Minority business ownership rate: 2.8% (1997); Women business ownership rate: 32.3% (1997); Retail sales per capita: $5,014 (1997). Single-family building permits issued: 226 (2001) / 370 (2000); Multi-family building permits issued: 72 (2001) / 54 (2000).
Income: Per capita income: $17,451 (2000); Median household income: $43,074 (2000); Poverty rate: 8.7% (2000); Bankruptcy rate: 3.73% (2001).
Taxes: Total county taxes per capita: $80 (2000); County property taxes per capita: $71 (2000).
Education: High school graduation rate: 83.4% (2000); College graduation rate: 10.8% (2000).
Housing: Homeownership rate: 80.1% (2000); Median home value: $94,400 (2000); Median rent: $394 per month (2000); Median age of housing: 36 years (2000).
Health: Birth rate: 133.5 per 10,000 population (1998); Age adjusted death rate: 80.8 per 10,000 population (1999); Age adjusted cancer mortality rate: 177.8 deaths per 100,000 population (1999). Number of physicians: 3.1 per 10,000 population (1999); Number of hospital beds: 9.1 per 10,000 population (1999).
Elections: 2000 Presidential election results: 39.6% Gore, 58.1% Bush, 1.8% Nader, 0.1% Buchanan
National and State Parks: Ionia State Recreation Area; Lowell State Game Area; Portland State Game Area
Additional Information Contacts
Ionia County Government Offices 616-527-5322
Belding Chamber of Commerce 616-794-2210
Ionia Chamber of Commerce 616-527-2560
Ionia County Board of Realtors 616-527-9101
Lake Odessa Chamber of Commerce 616-374-0766
Portland Chamber of Commerce 517-647-2100

Ionia County Communities

BELDING (city). Covers a land area of 4.716 square miles and a water area of 0.156 square miles. Located at 43.09° N. Lat.; 85.23° W. Long. Elevation is 774 feet.
History: Belding was first known as Broas Rapids for Charles Broas, who settled on the site in 1839. Later it was named Patterson's Mills, when Lucius Patterson bought an interest in the Broas mill property. In 1864, the Belding brothers founded a silk mill here. The mill was purchased in 1928 by a group of New York bankers, who abandoned the enterprise when the economic depression hit the country. The citizens of Belding later reopened the mill.
Population: 5,877 (2000); Race: 98.2% White, 0.0% Black, 0.3% Asian, 0.7% American Indian and Alaska Native, 1.9% Hispanic of any race, 0.5% two or more races (2000); Density: 1,246.1 persons per square mile (2000); Age: 30.5% under 18, 14.1% over 64 (2000); Marriage status: 25.6% never married, 52.4% now married, 8.7% widowed, 13.3% divorced (2000); Foreign born: 0.8% (2000); Ancestry (includes multiple ancestries): 25.8% German, 12.0% Irish, 10.9% English, 10.7% United States or American, 7.2% Dutch (2000).
Economy: Single-family building permits issued: 16 (2001) / 8 (2000); Multi-family building permits issued: 0 (2001) / 2 (2000); Employment by occupation: 9.4% management, 10.6% professional, 17.7% services, 20.5% sales, 1.3% farming, 10.4% construction, 30.0% production (2000).
Income: Per capita income: $14,779 (2000); Median household income: $32,878 (2000); Poverty rate: 16.3% (2000).
Taxes: Total city taxes per capita: $188 (1997); City property taxes per capita: $182 (1997).
Education: High school graduation rate: 74.7% (2000); College graduation rate: 8.8% (2000).

School District(s)
Belding Area School District (KG-12)
2000 Enrollment: 2,576 616-794-4444
Grattan Academy (KG-08)
2000 Enrollment: 89 517-790-4000

Housing: Homeownership rate: 66.4% (2000); Median home value: $86,300 (2000); Median rent: $361 per month (2000); Median age of housing: 44 years (2000).
Safety: Violent crime rate: 57.5 per 10,000 population; Property crime rate: 443.5 per 10,000 population (2001).
Transportation: Commute to work: 91.9% car, 0.5% public transportation, 3.2% walk, 1.8% work from home (2000); Travel time to work: 35.2% less than 15 minutes, 24.4% 15 to 30 minutes, 21.4% 30 to 45 minutes, 9.8% 45 to 60 minutes, 9.3% 60 minutes or more (2000)
Additional Information Contacts
Belding Chamber of Commerce 616-794-2210

BERLIN (township). Covers a land area of 41.618 square miles and a water area of 0.271 square miles. Located at 42.90° N. Lat.; 85.12° W. Long.
History: Berlin Township was organized in 1839.
Population: 2,787 (2000); Race: 80.3% White, 15.2% Black, 0.9% Asian, 1.0% American Indian and Alaska Native, 2.0% Hispanic of any race, 2.0% two or more races (2000); Density: 67.0 persons per square mile (2000); Age: 17.3% under 18, 8.7% over 64 (2000); Marriage status: 28.1% never married, 51.0% now married, 4.8% widowed, 16.1% divorced (2000); Foreign born: 1.9% (2000); Ancestry (includes multiple ancestries): 21.2% German, 15.2% Other groups, 13.5% United States or American, 11.1% English, 8.3% Irish (2000).
Economy: Employment by occupation: 12.0% management, 15.4% professional, 17.7% services, 25.8% sales, 0.7% farming, 9.8% construction, 18.6% production (2000).

Income: Per capita income: $16,780 (2000); Median household income: $48,158 (2000); Poverty rate: 5.9% (2000).
Taxes: Total city taxes per capita: $39 (1997); City property taxes per capita: $39 (1997).
Education: High school graduation rate: 85.5% (2000); College graduation rate: 11.4% (2000).
Housing: Homeownership rate: 92.2% (2000); Median home value: $114,000 (2000); Median rent: $492 per month (2000); Median age of housing: 33 years (2000).
Transportation: Commute to work: 93.2% car, 0.0% public transportation, 0.7% walk, 5.4% work from home (2000); Travel time to work: 33.8% less than 15 minutes, 24.2% 15 to 30 minutes, 25.2% 30 to 45 minutes, 11.1% 45 to 60 minutes, 5.8% 60 minutes or more (2000)

BOSTON (township). Covers a land area of 34.979 square miles and a water area of 0.897 square miles. Located at 42.90° N. Lat.; 85.24° W. Long.
History: Boston Township was named by its early settlers who had come from New England.
Population: 4,961 (2000); Race: 98.8% White, 0.3% Black, 0.2% Asian, 0.1% American Indian and Alaska Native, 1.1% Hispanic of any race, 0.5% two or more races (2000); Density: 141.8 persons per square mile (2000); Age: 27.8% under 18, 12.1% over 64 (2000); Marriage status: 21.6% never married, 62.4% now married, 6.6% widowed, 9.5% divorced (2000); Foreign born: 1.0% (2000); Ancestry (includes multiple ancestries): 23.9% German, 14.2% English, 12.6% Irish, 12.0% United States or American, 12.0% Dutch (2000).
Economy: Employment by occupation: 8.4% management, 13.9% professional, 16.4% services, 23.0% sales, 0.0% farming, 12.5% construction, 25.8% production (2000).
Income: Per capita income: $18,836 (2000); Median household income: $43,172 (2000); Poverty rate: 6.7% (2000).
Taxes: Total city taxes per capita: $14 (1997); City property taxes per capita: $13 (1997).
Education: High school graduation rate: 84.1% (2000); College graduation rate: 11.7% (2000).
Housing: Homeownership rate: 79.3% (2000); Median home value: $113,500 (2000); Median rent: $363 per month (2000); Median age of housing: 26 years (2000).
Transportation: Commute to work: 94.5% car, 0.1% public transportation, 1.4% walk, 3.7% work from home (2000); Travel time to work: 17.4% less than 15 minutes, 35.5% 15 to 30 minutes, 31.1% 30 to 45 minutes, 9.7% 45 to 60 minutes, 6.3% 60 minutes or more (2000)

CAMPBELL (township). Covers a land area of 35.756 square miles and a water area of 0.147 square miles. Located at 42.82° N. Lat.; 85.25° W. Long.
History: Campbell Township was named for Jeremiah and Martin Campbell, Irish immigrants who settled here in 1840. The township was organized in 1849.
Population: 2,243 (2000); Race: 99.0% White, 0.5% Black, 0.0% Asian, 0.1% American Indian and Alaska Native, 1.7% Hispanic of any race, 0.2% two or more races (2000); Density: 62.7 persons per square mile (2000); Age: 30.5% under 18, 7.9% over 64 (2000); Marriage status: 22.4% never married, 65.1% now married, 4.7% widowed, 7.8% divorced (2000); Foreign born: 0.6% (2000); Ancestry (includes multiple ancestries): 23.5% German, 17.0% United States or American, 12.4% English, 11.6% Dutch, 8.3% Irish (2000).
Economy: Employment by occupation: 14.5% management, 9.9% professional, 12.7% services, 24.3% sales, 1.7% farming, 10.6% construction, 26.2% production (2000).
Income: Per capita income: $20,122 (2000); Median household income: $50,370 (2000); Poverty rate: 6.2% (2000).
Taxes: Total city taxes per capita: $70 (2000); City property taxes per capita: $70 (2000).
Education: High school graduation rate: 89.1% (2000); College graduation rate: 12.9% (2000).
Housing: Homeownership rate: 89.5% (2000); Median home value: $98,400 (2000); Median rent: $383 per month (2000); Median age of housing: 37 years (2000).
Transportation: Commute to work: 89.4% car, 0.3% public transportation, 3.3% walk, 5.8% work from home (2000); Travel time to work: 15.3% less than 15 minutes, 33.7% 15 to 30 minutes, 29.6% 30 to 45 minutes, 14.3% 45 to 60 minutes, 7.1% 60 minutes or more (2000)

CLARKSVILLE (village). Covers a land area of 0.507 square miles and a water area of 0 square miles. Located at 42.84° N. Lat.; 85.24° W. Long. Elevation is 826 feet.
History: Clarksville was settled in 1840 by two brothers who had immigrated from Ireland. First called Skipperville, the village was renamed in 1875 for Clark L. Howard, who opened a store here and secured a post office.
Population: 317 (2000); Race: 97.9% White, 0.0% Black, 0.0% Asian, 0.0% American Indian and Alaska Native, 1.4% Hispanic of any race, 1.4% two or more races (2000); Density: 625.3 persons per square mile (2000); Age: 25.5% under 18, 14.8% over 64 (2000); Marriage status: 23.5% never married, 56.2% now married, 7.1% widowed, 13.3% divorced (2000); Foreign born: 0.3% (2000); Ancestry (includes multiple ancestries): 19.7% United States or American, 18.6% German, 11.7% Dutch, 9.0% English, 7.6% Irish (2000).
Economy: Employment by occupation: 13.3% management, 8.9% professional, 14.8% services, 31.1% sales, 0.0% farming, 4.4% construction, 27.4% production (2000).
Income: Per capita income: $16,066 (2000); Median household income: $35,313 (2000); Poverty rate: 8.6% (2000).
Taxes: Total city taxes per capita: $96 (1997); City property taxes per capita: $96 (1997).
Education: High school graduation rate: 88.8% (2000); College graduation rate: 8.7% (2000).
Housing: Homeownership rate: 69.2% (2000); Median home value: $82,900 (2000); Median rent: $258 per month (2000); Median age of housing: 60+ years (2000).
Transportation: Commute to work: 83.0% car, 2.2% public transportation, 10.4% walk, 4.4% work from home (2000); Travel time to work: 16.3% less than 15 minutes, 43.4% 15 to 30 minutes, 28.7% 30 to 45 minutes, 7.0% 45 to 60 minutes, 4.7% 60 minutes or more (2000)

DANBY (township). Covers a land area of 35.310 square miles and a water area of 0.805 square miles. Located at 42.80° N. Lat.; 84.88° W. Long.
Population: 2,696 (2000); Race: 98.1% White, 0.0% Black, 1.2% Asian, 0.0% American Indian and Alaska Native, 0.2% Hispanic of any race, 0.3% two or more races (2000); Density: 76.4 persons per square mile (2000); Age: 30.3% under 18, 9.7% over 64 (2000); Marriage status: 23.7% never married, 66.8% now married, 2.3% widowed, 7.2% divorced (2000); Foreign born: 0.8% (2000); Ancestry (includes multiple ancestries): 38.3% German, 16.7% English, 10.4% Irish, 7.4% United States or American, 5.1% Other groups (2000).
Economy: Employment by occupation: 12.2% management, 15.1% professional, 14.1% services, 22.2% sales, 0.7% farming, 15.0% construction, 20.7% production (2000).
Income: Per capita income: $21,574 (2000); Median household income: $55,662 (2000); Poverty rate: 0.9% (2000).
Taxes: Total city taxes per capita: $30 (1997); City property taxes per capita: $30 (1997).
Education: High school graduation rate: 87.2% (2000); College graduation rate: 14.4% (2000).
Housing: Homeownership rate: 93.0% (2000); Median home value: $132,600 (2000); Median rent: $400 per month (2000); Median age of housing: 27 years (2000).
Transportation: Commute to work: 93.2% car, 0.0% public transportation, 1.5% walk, 5.2% work from home (2000); Travel time to work: 20.3% less than 15 minutes, 34.1% 15 to 30 minutes, 35.4% 30 to 45 minutes, 6.2% 45 to 60 minutes, 3.9% 60 minutes or more (2000)

EASTON (township). Covers a land area of 28.416 square miles and a water area of 0.167 square miles. Located at 42.99° N. Lat.; 85.12° W. Long.
Population: 2,835 (2000); Race: 96.8% White, 0.0% Black, 0.8% Asian, 0.0% American Indian and Alaska Native, 1.5% Hispanic of any race, 1.6% two or more races (2000); Density: 99.8 persons per square mile (2000); Age: 25.7% under 18, 15.0% over 64 (2000); Marriage status: 18.9% never married, 60.6% now married, 8.0% widowed, 12.6% divorced (2000); Foreign born: 0.6% (2000); Ancestry (includes multiple ancestries): 20.6% German, 15.4% English, 11.8% United States or American, 11.2% Irish, 5.6% Other groups (2000).
Economy: Employment by occupation: 7.7% management, 9.5% professional, 13.6% services, 22.1% sales, 1.7% farming, 15.7% construction, 29.8% production (2000).
Income: Per capita income: $19,942 (2000); Median household income: $40,493 (2000); Poverty rate: 9.7% (2000).
Taxes: Total city taxes per capita: $7 (1997); City property taxes per capita: $7 (1997).
Education: High school graduation rate: 84.8% (2000); College graduation rate: 6.6% (2000).

Housing: Homeownership rate: 83.7% (2000); Median home value: $88,600 (2000); Median rent: $400 per month (2000); Median age of housing: 33 years (2000).
Transportation: Commute to work: 96.3% car, 0.4% public transportation, 0.7% walk, 2.2% work from home (2000); Travel time to work: 33.9% less than 15 minutes, 28.7% 15 to 30 minutes, 16.6% 30 to 45 minutes, 13.1% 45 to 60 minutes, 7.7% 60 minutes or more (2000)

HUBBARDSTON (village). Covers a land area of 1.575 square miles and a water area of 0.052 square miles. Located at 43.09° N. Lat.; 84.84° W. Long.
History: Hubbardston began in 1865 when a town was laid out around a dam and sawmill built in the early 1850's by Joseph Brown. The town was named for Thomas Hubbard, one of the men who platted it.
Population: 394 (2000); Race: 95.3% White, 0.0% Black, 0.0% Asian, 0.8% American Indian and Alaska Native, 2.1% Hispanic of any race, 3.9% two or more races (2000); Density: 250.2 persons per square mile (2000); Age: 31.5% under 18, 13.4% over 64 (2000); Marriage status: 21.8% never married, 60.0% now married, 4.6% widowed, 13.6% divorced (2000); Foreign born: 0.0% (2000); Ancestry (includes multiple ancestries): 23.5% Irish, 21.4% United States or American, 11.4% German, 10.1% Other groups, 3.1% English (2000).
Economy: Employment by occupation: 3.0% management, 3.7% professional, 18.5% services, 22.2% sales, 1.5% farming, 13.3% construction, 37.8% production (2000).
Income: Per capita income: $12,690 (2000); Median household income: $36,458 (2000); Poverty rate: 11.5% (2000).
Taxes: Total city taxes per capita: $51 (1997); City property taxes per capita: $49 (1997).
Education: High school graduation rate: 70.1% (2000); College graduation rate: 1.6% (2000).
Housing: Homeownership rate: 83.7% (2000); Median home value: $71,300 (2000); Median rent: $355 per month (2000); Median age of housing: 60+ years (2000).
Transportation: Commute to work: 91.5% car, 3.8% public transportation, 3.8% walk, 0.8% work from home (2000); Travel time to work: 20.9% less than 15 minutes, 34.1% 15 to 30 minutes, 13.2% 30 to 45 minutes, 24.0% 45 to 60 minutes, 7.8% 60 minutes or more (2000)

IONIA (city). Covers a land area of 5.043 square miles and a water area of 0.163 square miles. Located at 42.98° N. Lat.; 85.06° W. Long. Elevation is 660 feet.
History: Ionia was established in 1833 by settlers who purchased wigwams and fields of corn, melons, and squash from the native inhabitants. Named for the county, which had been named for the ancient Greek province, the town became a shipping point for beans, as well as a producer of furniture, pottery, and flour.
Population: 10,569 (2000); Race: 70.9% White, 21.2% Black, 0.6% Asian, 0.9% American Indian and Alaska Native, 5.5% Hispanic of any race, 3.8% two or more races (2000); Density: 2,095.9 persons per square mile (2000); Age: 18.6% under 18, 6.9% over 64 (2000); Marriage status: 42.1% never married, 43.8% now married, 4.9% widowed, 9.2% divorced (2000); Foreign born: 2.6% (2000); Ancestry (includes multiple ancestries): 20.7% Other groups, 15.8% German, 8.7% Irish, 7.7% English, 5.9% United States or American (2000).
Economy: Single-family building permits issued: 7 (2001) / 5 (2000); Multi-family building permits issued: 56 (2001) / 0 (2000); Employment by occupation: 6.8% management, 14.3% professional, 18.0% services, 24.3% sales, 0.5% farming, 9.2% construction, 26.9% production (2000).
Income: Per capita income: $12,157 (2000); Median household income: $38,289 (2000); Poverty rate: 15.8% (2000).
Taxes: Total city taxes per capita: $297 (1997); City property taxes per capita: $294 (1997).
Education: High school graduation rate: 79.6% (2000); College graduation rate: 9.2% (2000).

School District(s)

Berlin Township School District #3 (KG-08)
2000 Enrollment: 18 616-527-4900
Easton Township School District #6 (KG-06)
2000 Enrollment: 34 616-527-4900
Ionia Public Schools (PK-12)
2000 Enrollment: 3,359 616-527-9280
Ionia Township School District #2 (KG-05)
2000 Enrollment: 25 616-527-4900

Housing: Homeownership rate: 60.5% (2000); Median home value: $77,400 (2000); Median rent: $387 per month (2000); Median age of housing: 58 years (2000).
Hospitals: Ionia County Memorial Hospital (77 beds)
Safety: Violent crime rate: 26.4 per 10,000 population; Property crime rate: 293.6 per 10,000 population (2001).
Newspapers: Sentinel-Standard (6 x week)
Transportation: Commute to work: 93.0% car, 0.3% public transportation, 3.3% walk, 2.4% work from home (2000); Travel time to work: 52.5% less than 15 minutes, 18.0% 15 to 30 minutes, 11.2% 30 to 45 minutes, 11.1% 45 to 60 minutes, 7.3% 60 minutes or more (2000)
Additional Information Contacts
Ionia Chamber of Commerce 616-527-2560
Ionia County Board of Realtors 616-527-9101

IONIA (township). Covers a land area of 33.672 square miles and a water area of 0.401 square miles. Located at 42.99° N. Lat.; 85.03° W. Long. Elevation is 660 feet.
History: Settled 1833; incorporated as village 1865, as city 1873.
Population: 3,669 (2000); Race: 97.7% White, 0.1% Black, 0.4% Asian, 0.1% American Indian and Alaska Native, 1.5% Hispanic of any race, 1.0% two or more races (2000); Density: 109.0 persons per square mile (2000); Age: 27.7% under 18, 10.8% over 64 (2000); Marriage status: 24.0% never married, 61.2% now married, 5.1% widowed, 9.7% divorced (2000); Foreign born: 1.0% (2000); Ancestry (includes multiple ancestries): 25.0% German, 15.7% English, 12.9% United States or American, 12.6% Irish, 7.4% Other groups (2000).
Economy: Poultry. Agriculture: grain, fruit. Manufacturing: furniture, food processing, motor-vehicle parts, fabricated metal products, printing; ships beans. Airport. Has a state reformatory and a state mental hospital. Employment by occupation: 6.0% management, 12.9% professional, 19.2% services, 22.3% sales, 1.2% farming, 8.3% construction, 30.1% production (2000).
Income: Per capita income: $17,985 (2000); Median household income: $44,659 (2000); Poverty rate: 6.9% (2000).
Taxes: Total city taxes per capita: $25 (1997); City property taxes per capita: $25 (1997).
Education: High school graduation rate: 82.3% (2000); College graduation rate: 10.6% (2000).
Housing: Homeownership rate: 90.3% (2000); Median home value: $87,300 (2000); Median rent: $418 per month (2000); Median age of housing: 25 years (2000).
Transportation: Commute to work: 94.5% car, 0.1% public transportation, 0.5% walk, 3.9% work from home (2000); Travel time to work: 40.6% less than 15 minutes, 23.6% 15 to 30 minutes, 12.3% 30 to 45 minutes, 14.1% 45 to 60 minutes, 9.5% 60 minutes or more (2000)

KEENE (township). Covers a land area of 35.713 square miles and a water area of 0.275 square miles. Located at 42.98° N. Lat.; 85.26° W. Long.
History: Keene Township was organized in 1842 and named for Keene, New Hampshire, the former home of early settler Edward Butterfield.
Population: 1,660 (2000); Race: 97.1% White, 0.0% Black, 0.0% Asian, 0.2% American Indian and Alaska Native, 2.5% Hispanic of any race, 2.6% two or more races (2000); Density: 46.5 persons per square mile (2000); Age: 33.5% under 18, 7.1% over 64 (2000); Marriage status: 22.4% never married, 69.4% now married, 1.8% widowed, 6.4% divorced (2000); Foreign born: 1.5% (2000); Ancestry (includes multiple ancestries): 25.3% German, 11.1% Dutch, 10.8% United States or American, 10.4% Irish, 9.9% English (2000).
Economy: Employment by occupation: 12.5% management, 9.9% professional, 12.6% services, 23.6% sales, 3.3% farming, 14.6% construction, 23.4% production (2000).
Income: Per capita income: $18,017 (2000); Median household income: $50,114 (2000); Poverty rate: 5.8% (2000).
Taxes: Total city taxes per capita: $13 (1997); City property taxes per capita: $12 (1997).
Education: High school graduation rate: 87.7% (2000); College graduation rate: 7.3% (2000).
Housing: Homeownership rate: 92.4% (2000); Median home value: $116,500 (2000); Median rent: $360 per month (2000); Median age of housing: 23 years (2000).
Transportation: Commute to work: 93.1% car, 0.0% public transportation, 2.1% walk, 4.8% work from home (2000); Travel time to work: 22.5% less than 15 minutes, 37.0% 15 to 30 minutes, 26.9% 30 to 45 minutes, 9.2% 45 to 60 minutes, 4.4% 60 minutes or more (2000)

LAKE ODESSA (village). Covers a land area of 0.821 square miles and a water area of 0 square miles. Located at 42.78° N. Lat.; 85.13° W. Long. Elevation is 877 feet.
History: Lake Odessa was founded on the shores of both Jordan and Tupper Lakes in 1887, and named for the Russian city.
Population: 2,272 (2000); Race: 92.0% White, 0.3% Black, 0.9% Asian, 0.9% American Indian and Alaska Native, 6.8% Hispanic of any race, 1.9% two or more races (2000); Density: 2,767.8 persons per square mile (2000); Age: 32.1% under 18, 13.5% over 64 (2000); Marriage status: 27.4% never married, 51.0% now married, 8.6% widowed, 13.0% divorced (2000); Foreign born: 1.6% (2000); Ancestry (includes multiple ancestries): 25.2% German, 15.5% United States or American, 15.4% English, 12.0% Other groups, 10.5% Irish (2000).
Economy: Employment by occupation: 8.6% management, 16.0% professional, 14.7% services, 20.4% sales, 0.3% farming, 13.1% construction, 26.9% production (2000).
Income: Per capita income: $19,822 (2000); Median household income: $34,896 (2000); Poverty rate: 8.8% (2000).
Taxes: Total city taxes per capita: $150 (1997); City property taxes per capita: $147 (1997).
Education: High school graduation rate: 82.5% (2000); College graduation rate: 12.2% (2000).

School District(s)

Lakewood Public Schools (PK-12)
2000 Enrollment: 2,742 616-374-8043
Housing: Homeownership rate: 70.6% (2000); Median home value: $83,400 (2000); Median rent: $372 per month (2000); Median age of housing: 50 years (2000).
Safety: Violent crime rate: 21.9 per 10,000 population; Property crime rate: 345.9 per 10,000 population (2001).
Transportation: Commute to work: 93.2% car, 0.0% public transportation, 4.1% walk, 2.1% work from home (2000); Travel time to work: 32.0% less than 15 minutes, 18.4% 15 to 30 minutes, 28.3% 30 to 45 minutes, 14.9% 45 to 60 minutes, 6.4% 60 minutes or more (2000)
Additional Information Contacts
Lake Odessa Chamber of Commerce. 616-374-0766

LYONS (village). Covers a land area of 1.217 square miles and a water area of 0.110 square miles. Located at 42.98° N. Lat.; 84.94° W. Long.
History: This site was owned by Lucius Lyon, who platted it in 1836 with the thought that it would become an important town. Lyons was incorporated as a village in 1859.
Population: 726 (2000); Race: 95.6% White, 0.6% Black, 0.0% Asian, 0.0% American Indian and Alaska Native, 3.0% Hispanic of any race, 3.6% two or more races (2000); Density: 596.7 persons per square mile (2000); Age: 24.5% under 18, 9.7% over 64 (2000); Marriage status: 23.8% never married, 54.3% now married, 5.6% widowed, 16.3% divorced (2000); Foreign born: 0.4% (2000); Ancestry (includes multiple ancestries): 30.2% German, 17.6% Irish, 17.2% English, 9.8% United States or American, 8.7% Other groups (2000).
Economy: Employment by occupation: 7.0% management, 10.6% professional, 14.4% services, 17.9% sales, 0.0% farming, 10.9% construction, 39.3% production (2000).
Income: Per capita income: $18,629 (2000); Median household income: $39,191 (2000); Poverty rate: 9.0% (2000).
Taxes: Total city taxes per capita: $100 (1997); City property taxes per capita: $100 (1997).
Education: High school graduation rate: 76.5% (2000); College graduation rate: 3.9% (2000).
Housing: Homeownership rate: 81.2% (2000); Median home value: $74,100 (2000); Median rent: $373 per month (2000); Median age of housing: 46 years (2000).
Transportation: Commute to work: 93.5% car, 0.0% public transportation, 1.8% walk, 2.4% work from home (2000); Travel time to work: 15.2% less than 15 minutes, 43.3% 15 to 30 minutes, 20.7% 30 to 45 minutes, 15.9% 45 to 60 minutes, 4.9% 60 minutes or more (2000)

LYONS (township). Covers a land area of 36.234 square miles and a water area of 0.715 square miles. Located at 42.99° N. Lat.; 84.91° W. Long.
History: Lyons Township was organized in 1837 when it was called Maple. It was renamed Lyons in 1840.
Population: 3,446 (2000); Race: 97.2% White, 0.1% Black, 0.0% Asian, 0.2% American Indian and Alaska Native, 1.9% Hispanic of any race, 2.1% two or more races (2000); Density: 95.1 persons per square mile (2000); Age: 29.9% under 18, 10.9% over 64 (2000); Marriage status: 22.9% never married, 59.5% now married, 6.3% widowed, 11.3% divorced (2000); Foreign born: 0.1% (2000); Ancestry (includes multiple ancestries): 38.9% German, 13.2% English, 13.1% Irish, 12.9% United States or American, 6.8% Other groups (2000).
Economy: Employment by occupation: 8.1% management, 10.4% professional, 17.2% services, 21.8% sales, 0.9% farming, 12.2% construction, 29.3% production (2000).
Income: Per capita income: $16,578 (2000); Median household income: $38,750 (2000); Poverty rate: 8.7% (2000).
Taxes: Total city taxes per capita: $29 (1997); City property taxes per capita: $29 (1997).
Education: High school graduation rate: 82.2% (2000); College graduation rate: 6.1% (2000).
Housing: Homeownership rate: 82.6% (2000); Median home value: $84,000 (2000); Median rent: $338 per month (2000); Median age of housing: 36 years (2000).
Transportation: Commute to work: 91.7% car, 0.3% public transportation, 1.2% walk, 6.3% work from home (2000); Travel time to work: 18.3% less than 15 minutes, 40.2% 15 to 30 minutes, 17.2% 30 to 45 minutes, 18.8% 45 to 60 minutes, 5.5% 60 minutes or more (2000)

MUIR (village). Covers a land area of 0.763 square miles and a water area of 0.007 square miles. Located at 42.99° N. Lat.; 84.94° W. Long. Elevation is 655 feet.
Population: 634 (2000); Race: 94.9% White, 0.0% Black, 0.0% Asian, 0.0% American Indian and Alaska Native, 2.5% Hispanic of any race, 3.1% two or more races (2000); Density: 830.5 persons per square mile (2000); Age: 31.4% under 18, 9.3% over 64 (2000); Marriage status: 26.9% never married, 47.1% now married, 11.3% widowed, 14.7% divorced (2000); Foreign born: 0.3% (2000); Ancestry (includes multiple ancestries): 25.2% German, 16.4% United States or American, 12.2% Irish, 11.3% English, 9.9% Other groups (2000).
Economy: In farm area. Employment by occupation: 4.4% management, 9.5% professional, 20.7% services, 16.4% sales, 1.1% farming, 12.4% construction, 35.6% production (2000).
Income: Per capita income: $13,938 (2000); Median household income: $30,096 (2000); Poverty rate: 15.8% (2000).
Taxes: Total city taxes per capita: $122 (1997); City property taxes per capita: $122 (1997).
Education: High school graduation rate: 83.1% (2000); College graduation rate: 3.8% (2000).
Housing: Homeownership rate: 69.2% (2000); Median home value: $74,200 (2000); Median rent: $341 per month (2000); Median age of housing: 35 years (2000).
Transportation: Commute to work: 94.8% car, 0.0% public transportation, 3.7% walk, 1.5% work from home (2000); Travel time to work: 26.6% less than 15 minutes, 33.7% 15 to 30 minutes, 15.0% 30 to 45 minutes, 17.6% 45 to 60 minutes, 7.1% 60 minutes or more (2000)

NORTH PLAINS (township). Covers a land area of 35.893 square miles and a water area of 0.058 square miles. Located at 43.08° N. Lat.; 84.88° W. Long.
Population: 1,366 (2000); Race: 96.0% White, 0.0% Black, 0.0% Asian, 1.2% American Indian and Alaska Native, 2.1% Hispanic of any race, 1.9% two or more races (2000); Density: 38.1 persons per square mile (2000); Age: 29.8% under 18, 8.5% over 64 (2000); Marriage status: 24.2% never married, 59.3% now married, 5.6% widowed, 10.9% divorced (2000); Foreign born: 1.0% (2000); Ancestry (includes multiple ancestries): 20.9% German, 20.5% Irish, 12.0% United States or American, 10.1% Other groups, 7.5% English (2000).
Economy: Employment by occupation: 6.7% management, 8.4% professional, 18.9% services, 19.2% sales, 4.4% farming, 14.0% construction, 28.3% production (2000).
Income: Per capita income: $15,946 (2000); Median household income: $39,833 (2000); Poverty rate: 11.3% (2000).
Taxes: Total city taxes per capita: $13 (1997); City property taxes per capita: $13 (1997).
Education: High school graduation rate: 76.5% (2000); College graduation rate: 2.8% (2000).
Housing: Homeownership rate: 87.0% (2000); Median home value: $78,300 (2000); Median rent: $357 per month (2000); Median age of housing: 40 years (2000).
Transportation: Commute to work: 91.5% car, 1.5% public transportation, 2.7% walk, 3.9% work from home (2000); Travel time to work: 16.9% less than 15 minutes, 37.1% 15 to 30 minutes, 17.2% 30 to 45 minutes, 18.3% 45 to 60 minutes, 10.5% 60 minutes or more (2000)

ODESSA (township). Covers a land area of 35.768 square miles and a water area of 0.449 square miles. Located at 42.79° N. Lat.; 85.13° W. Long.
Population: 4,036 (2000); Race: 93.8% White, 0.4% Black, 0.8% Asian, 0.5% American Indian and Alaska Native, 4.4% Hispanic of any race, 2.0% two or more races (2000); Density: 112.8 persons per square mile (2000); Age: 30.2% under 18, 12.0% over 64 (2000); Marriage status: 26.2% never married, 59.0% now married, 6.0% widowed, 8.8% divorced (2000); Foreign born: 1.3% (2000); Ancestry (includes multiple ancestries): 28.4% German, 15.0% English, 11.9% United States or American, 9.3% Other groups, 8.4% Dutch (2000).
Economy: Employment by occupation: 10.4% management, 14.0% professional, 12.2% services, 20.9% sales, 1.0% farming, 15.8% construction, 25.7% production (2000).
Income: Per capita income: $19,505 (2000); Median household income: $40,625 (2000); Poverty rate: 5.7% (2000).
Taxes: Total city taxes per capita: $42 (1997); City property taxes per capita: $42 (1997).
Education: High school graduation rate: 86.3% (2000); College graduation rate: 12.8% (2000).
Housing: Homeownership rate: 77.3% (2000); Median home value: $93,300 (2000); Median rent: $377 per month (2000); Median age of housing: 46 years (2000).
Transportation: Commute to work: 91.7% car, 0.0% public transportation, 3.9% walk, 3.9% work from home (2000); Travel time to work: 28.8% less than 15 minutes, 19.4% 15 to 30 minutes, 26.3% 30 to 45 minutes, 16.9% 45 to 60 minutes, 8.6% 60 minutes or more (2000)

ORANGE (township). Covers a land area of 36.004 square miles and a water area of 0.028 square miles. Located at 42.90° N. Lat.; 85.02° W. Long.
Population: 1,040 (2000); Race: 96.3% White, 0.2% Black, 0.0% Asian, 0.6% American Indian and Alaska Native, 0.8% Hispanic of any race, 0.9% two or more races (2000); Density: 28.9 persons per square mile (2000); Age: 29.3% under 18, 9.5% over 64 (2000); Marriage status: 21.2% never married, 65.2% now married, 5.6% widowed, 8.0% divorced (2000); Foreign born: 0.4% (2000); Ancestry (includes multiple ancestries): 34.8% German, 16.8% English, 11.6% Irish, 7.2% United States or American, 5.2% Other groups (2000).
Economy: Employment by occupation: 17.2% management, 8.0% professional, 15.1% services, 24.0% sales, 1.5% farming, 10.5% construction, 23.8% production (2000).
Income: Per capita income: $18,188 (2000); Median household income: $50,217 (2000); Poverty rate: 6.2% (2000).
Taxes: Total city taxes per capita: $25 (1997); City property taxes per capita: $25 (1997).
Education: High school graduation rate: 90.7% (2000); College graduation rate: 10.2% (2000).
Housing: Homeownership rate: 89.2% (2000); Median home value: $99,000 (2000); Median rent: $360 per month (2000); Median age of housing: 40 years (2000).
Transportation: Commute to work: 87.5% car, 0.4% public transportation, 1.8% walk, 9.7% work from home (2000); Travel time to work: 31.8% less than 15 minutes, 32.9% 15 to 30 minutes, 21.7% 30 to 45 minutes, 9.3% 45 to 60 minutes, 4.3% 60 minutes or more (2000)

ORLEANS (township). Covers a land area of 35.511 square miles and a water area of 0.724 square miles. Located at 43.08° N. Lat.; 85.12° W. Long.
Population: 2,736 (2000); Race: 97.9% White, 0.0% Black, 0.0% Asian, 0.0% American Indian and Alaska Native, 1.2% Hispanic of any race, 1.8% two or more races (2000); Density: 77.0 persons per square mile (2000); Age: 29.7% under 18, 9.1% over 64 (2000); Marriage status: 23.9% never married, 60.2% now married, 5.1% widowed, 10.7% divorced (2000); Foreign born: 0.4% (2000); Ancestry (includes multiple ancestries): 22.0% German, 14.9% United States or American, 13.3% English, 10.9% Irish, 8.0% Other groups (2000).
Economy: Employment by occupation: 7.6% management, 10.9% professional, 19.0% services, 16.7% sales, 1.4% farming, 11.3% construction, 33.2% production (2000).
Income: Per capita income: $17,425 (2000); Median household income: $42,665 (2000); Poverty rate: 8.5% (2000).
Taxes: Total city taxes per capita: $12 (1997); City property taxes per capita: $11 (1997).
Education: High school graduation rate: 78.3% (2000); College graduation rate: 8.8% (2000).
Housing: Homeownership rate: 82.4% (2000); Median home value: $95,200 (2000); Median rent: $413 per month (2000); Median age of housing: 30 years (2000).
Transportation: Commute to work: 97.2% car, 0.0% public transportation, 0.2% walk, 2.1% work from home (2000); Travel time to work: 13.9% less than 15 minutes, 32.3% 15 to 30 minutes, 22.3% 30 to 45 minutes, 13.9% 45 to 60 minutes, 17.5% 60 minutes or more (2000)

OTISCO (township). Covers a land area of 31.589 square miles and a water area of 0.412 square miles. Located at 43.07° N. Lat.; 85.24° W. Long.
Population: 2,243 (2000); Race: 97.7% White, 0.0% Black, 0.0% Asian, 0.6% American Indian and Alaska Native, 1.7% Hispanic of any race, 0.0% two or more races (2000); Density: 71.0 persons per square mile (2000); Age: 28.8% under 18, 7.0% over 64 (2000); Marriage status: 24.4% never married, 63.3% now married, 4.3% widowed, 8.0% divorced (2000); Foreign born: 1.0% (2000); Ancestry (includes multiple ancestries): 25.6% German, 15.2% English, 13.5% Irish, 8.1% French (except Basque), 7.9% Dutch (2000).
Economy: Employment by occupation: 11.8% management, 11.1% professional, 11.4% services, 25.1% sales, 1.8% farming, 14.3% construction, 24.6% production (2000).
Income: Per capita income: $21,674 (2000); Median household income: $45,042 (2000); Poverty rate: 8.3% (2000).
Taxes: Total city taxes per capita: $60 (1997); City property taxes per capita: $59 (1997).
Education: High school graduation rate: 85.5% (2000); College graduation rate: 15.8% (2000).
Housing: Homeownership rate: 90.7% (2000); Median home value: $97,800 (2000); Median rent: $458 per month (2000); Median age of housing: 28 years (2000).
Transportation: Commute to work: 95.3% car, 0.0% public transportation, 0.5% walk, 2.6% work from home (2000); Travel time to work: 34.4% less than 15 minutes, 27.5% 15 to 30 minutes, 15.2% 30 to 45 minutes, 12.7% 45 to 60 minutes, 10.2% 60 minutes or more (2000)

PEWAMO (village). Covers a land area of 1.019 square miles and a water area of 0 square miles. Located at 43.00° N. Lat.; 84.84° W. Long.
History: Pewamo began in 1857 as a station on the Detroit & Milwaukee Railroad, and was founded as a village in 1859.
Population: 560 (2000); Race: 98.8% White, 0.0% Black, 0.0% Asian, 1.2% American Indian and Alaska Native, 0.0% Hispanic of any race, 0.0% two or more races (2000); Density: 549.7 persons per square mile (2000); Age: 32.5% under 18, 13.7% over 64 (2000); Marriage status: 18.7% never married, 68.9% now married, 6.3% widowed, 6.1% divorced (2000); Foreign born: 0.0% (2000); Ancestry (includes multiple ancestries): 64.2% German, 7.8% United States or American, 6.8% Irish, 6.6% English, 3.1% Italian (2000).
Economy: Employment by occupation: 9.9% management, 9.4% professional, 15.0% services, 28.2% sales, 0.0% farming, 10.8% construction, 26.8% production (2000).
Income: Per capita income: $14,776 (2000); Median household income: $39,500 (2000); Poverty rate: 3.3% (2000).
Taxes: Total city taxes per capita: $133 (1997); City property taxes per capita: $131 (1997).
Education: High school graduation rate: 85.5% (2000); College graduation rate: 7.7% (2000).

School District(s)

Pewamo-Westphalia Community Schools (PK-12)
2000 Enrollment: 682 517-587-5110

Housing: Homeownership rate: 82.8% (2000); Median home value: $87,300 (2000); Median rent: $317 per month (2000); Median age of housing: 57 years (2000).
Transportation: Commute to work: 95.6% car, 0.0% public transportation, 0.0% walk, 4.4% work from home (2000); Travel time to work: 17.3% less than 15 minutes, 34.0% 15 to 30 minutes, 24.9% 30 to 45 minutes, 19.3% 45 to 60 minutes, 4.6% 60 minutes or more (2000)

PORTLAND (city). Covers a land area of 2.402 square miles and a water area of 0.120 square miles. Located at 42.86° N. Lat.; 84.90° W. Long. Elevation is 717 feet.
History: Portland was established in the 1830's at the junction of the Looking Glass and Grand Rivers, and became an industrial center and a shipping point for farm produce.
Population: 3,789 (2000); Race: 98.8% White, 0.3% Black, 0.1% Asian, 0.0% American Indian and Alaska Native, 0.2% Hispanic of any race, 0.7% two or more races (2000); Density: 1,577.7 persons per square mile (2000); Age: 28.4% under 18, 11.0% over 64 (2000); Marriage status: 20.7% never

married, 59.9% now married, 8.0% widowed, 11.5% divorced (2000); Foreign born: 0.2% (2000); Ancestry (includes multiple ancestries): 42.1% German, 15.2% Irish, 11.9% English, 8.5% United States or American, 6.9% Dutch (2000).
Economy: Single-family building permits issued: 0 (2001) / 1 (2000); Multi-family building permits issued: 0 (2001) / 32 (2000); Employment by occupation: 12.4% management, 17.0% professional, 14.2% services, 29.0% sales, 0.0% farming, 9.6% construction, 17.8% production (2000).
Income: Per capita income: $20,028 (2000); Median household income: $45,656 (2000); Poverty rate: 6.6% (2000).
Taxes: Total city taxes per capita: $350 (1997); City property taxes per capita: $338 (1997).
Education: High school graduation rate: 91.3% (2000); College graduation rate: 17.2% (2000).

School District(s)

Portland Public School District (PK-12)
2000 Enrollment: 1,989 517-647-4161

Housing: Homeownership rate: 74.5% (2000); Median home value: $104,300 (2000); Median rent: $446 per month (2000); Median age of housing: 47 years (2000).
Safety: Violent crime rate: 7.9 per 10,000 population; Property crime rate: 231.0 per 10,000 population (2001).
Transportation: Commute to work: 94.0% car, 0.0% public transportation, 2.5% walk, 3.0% work from home (2000); Travel time to work: 27.7% less than 15 minutes, 29.7% 15 to 30 minutes, 33.9% 30 to 45 minutes, 5.7% 45 to 60 minutes, 3.0% 60 minutes or more (2000)

Additional Information Contacts

Portland Chamber of Commerce 517-647-2100

PORTLAND (township). Covers a land area of 32.444 square miles and a water area of 1.068 square miles. Located at 42.88° N. Lat.; 84.91° W. Long. Elevation is 717 feet.
Population: 2,460 (2000); Race: 97.8% White, 0.0% Black, 0.0% Asian, 0.7% American Indian and Alaska Native, 2.0% Hispanic of any race, 0.3% two or more races (2000); Density: 75.8 persons per square mile (2000); Age: 30.5% under 18, 8.1% over 64 (2000); Marriage status: 22.0% never married, 69.7% now married, 2.8% widowed, 5.5% divorced (2000); Foreign born: 1.5% (2000); Ancestry (includes multiple ancestries): 49.7% German, 10.3% English, 9.3% Irish, 6.4% United States or American, 5.8% Dutch (2000).
Economy: Agricultural area: corn, wheat, soybeans, apples, green beans; poultry, cattle, hogs; dairying. Manufacturing: building materials, feeds, transportation equipment, fabricated metal products, chemicals. Employment by occupation: 13.9% management, 13.1% professional, 11.5% services, 32.1% sales, 0.9% farming, 11.1% construction, 17.5% production (2000).
Income: Per capita income: $23,792 (2000); Median household income: $59,700 (2000); Poverty rate: 3.6% (2000).
Taxes: Total city taxes per capita: $33 (1997); City property taxes per capita: $32 (1997).
Education: High school graduation rate: 88.9% (2000); College graduation rate: 18.8% (2000).
Housing: Homeownership rate: 90.8% (2000); Median home value: $128,900 (2000); Median rent: $464 per month (2000); Median age of housing: 27 years (2000).
Transportation: Commute to work: 92.5% car, 0.0% public transportation, 0.8% walk, 6.1% work from home (2000); Travel time to work: 36.1% less than 15 minutes, 25.2% 15 to 30 minutes, 25.6% 30 to 45 minutes, 8.5% 45 to 60 minutes, 4.6% 60 minutes or more (2000)

RONALD (township). Covers a land area of 36.330 square miles and a water area of 0.155 square miles. Located at 43.08° N. Lat.; 85.00° W. Long.
Population: 1,903 (2000); Race: 95.9% White, 0.5% Black, 0.0% Asian, 0.3% American Indian and Alaska Native, 3.6% Hispanic of any race, 1.8% two or more races (2000); Density: 52.4 persons per square mile (2000); Age: 29.0% under 18, 9.8% over 64 (2000); Marriage status: 25.2% never married, 59.3% now married, 4.7% widowed, 10.8% divorced (2000); Foreign born: 1.0% (2000); Ancestry (includes multiple ancestries): 27.8% German, 18.8% English, 10.4% United States or American, 10.1% Other groups, 9.8% Irish (2000).
Economy: Employment by occupation: 11.8% management, 11.6% professional, 15.3% services, 20.1% sales, 2.9% farming, 8.9% construction, 29.4% production (2000).
Income: Per capita income: $17,826 (2000); Median household income: $45,952 (2000); Poverty rate: 9.8% (2000).
Taxes: Total city taxes per capita: $18 (1997); City property taxes per capita: $18 (1997).
Education: High school graduation rate: 83.0% (2000); College graduation rate: 8.9% (2000).
Housing: Homeownership rate: 89.2% (2000); Median home value: $88,200 (2000); Median rent: $419 per month (2000); Median age of housing: 29 years (2000).
Transportation: Commute to work: 92.0% car, 0.0% public transportation, 2.5% walk, 4.7% work from home (2000); Travel time to work: 14.6% less than 15 minutes, 46.2% 15 to 30 minutes, 12.5% 30 to 45 minutes, 13.2% 45 to 60 minutes, 13.4% 60 minutes or more (2000)

SARANAC (village). Covers a land area of 1.161 square miles and a water area of 0.054 square miles. Located at 42.93° N. Lat.; 85.21° W. Long. Elevation is 644 feet.
History: The village of Saranac was laid out in the 1830's and named for the resort town in New York, hoping to attract more settlers from New York.
Population: 1,326 (2000); Race: 98.9% White, 0.0% Black, 0.3% Asian, 0.0% American Indian and Alaska Native, 1.1% Hispanic of any race, 0.4% two or more races (2000); Density: 1,142.1 persons per square mile (2000); Age: 27.1% under 18, 17.7% over 64 (2000); Marriage status: 24.2% never married, 52.5% now married, 9.2% widowed, 14.1% divorced (2000); Foreign born: 0.9% (2000); Ancestry (includes multiple ancestries): 20.5% German, 19.1% English, 17.4% United States or American, 11.1% Irish, 8.6% Dutch (2000).
Economy: Employment by occupation: 6.8% management, 14.1% professional, 18.5% services, 22.9% sales, 0.0% farming, 11.3% construction, 26.4% production (2000).
Income: Per capita income: $15,867 (2000); Median household income: $31,350 (2000); Poverty rate: 11.3% (2000).
Taxes: Total city taxes per capita: $133 (1997); City property taxes per capita: $126 (1997).
Education: High school graduation rate: 85.5% (2000); College graduation rate: 11.5% (2000).

School District(s)

Saranac Community Schools (KG-12)
2000 Enrollment: 1,222 616-642-9102

Housing: Homeownership rate: 61.8% (2000); Median home value: $92,700 (2000); Median rent: $282 per month (2000); Median age of housing: 41 years (2000).
Transportation: Commute to work: 91.2% car, 0.3% public transportation, 3.1% walk, 5.1% work from home (2000); Travel time to work: 33.8% less than 15 minutes, 26.7% 15 to 30 minutes, 25.5% 30 to 45 minutes, 9.1% 45 to 60 minutes, 4.8% 60 minutes or more (2000)

SEBEWA (township). Covers a land area of 35.816 square miles and a water area of 0.008 square miles. Located at 42.81° N. Lat.; 85.01° W. Long.
History: Sebewa Township was organized in 1845 and named for Sebewa ("little river") Creek. The first permanent settlements in the area were made in the 1830's.
Population: 1,202 (2000); Race: 98.8% White, 0.0% Black, 0.0% Asian, 0.4% American Indian and Alaska Native, 1.1% Hispanic of any race, 0.4% two or more races (2000); Density: 33.6 persons per square mile (2000); Age: 30.1% under 18, 10.6% over 64 (2000); Marriage status: 22.7% never married, 67.2% now married, 3.8% widowed, 6.3% divorced (2000); Foreign born: 0.4% (2000); Ancestry (includes multiple ancestries): 28.3% German, 14.6% United States or American, 11.9% English, 11.0% Irish, 6.9% Dutch (2000).
Economy: Employment by occupation: 9.4% management, 9.7% professional, 13.9% services, 27.6% sales, 0.8% farming, 10.7% construction, 27.9% production (2000).
Income: Per capita income: $17,774 (2000); Median household income: $47,065 (2000); Poverty rate: 6.1% (2000).
Taxes: Total city taxes per capita: $65 (1997); City property taxes per capita: $65 (1997).
Education: High school graduation rate: 86.7% (2000); College graduation rate: 7.1% (2000).
Housing: Homeownership rate: 90.4% (2000); Median home value: $91,200 (2000); Median rent: $396 per month (2000); Median age of housing: 51 years (2000).
Transportation: Commute to work: 92.2% car, 0.7% public transportation, 2.0% walk, 4.9% work from home (2000); Travel time to work: 18.3% less than 15 minutes, 28.4% 15 to 30 minutes, 34.3% 30 to 45 minutes, 9.7% 45 to 60 minutes, 9.3% 60 minutes or more (2000)

Iosco County

Located in northeastern Michigan; bounded on the east by Lake Huron; drained by the Au Sable, Au Gres, and Tawas Rivers; includes part of Huron National Forest, and Tawas and Van Ettan Lakes. Covers a land area of 549.10 square miles, a water area of 1,341.70 square miles, and is located in the Eastern Time Zone. The county government was organized in 1840. County seat is Tawas City.

Weather Station: East Tawas Elevation: 583 feet

	Jan	Feb	Mar	Apr	May	Jun	Jul	Aug	Sep	Oct	Nov	Dec
High	29	31	40	52	66	75	80	78	70	58	45	34
Low	11	12	21	32	43	52	57	56	48	38	29	19
Precip	2.1	1.3	2.1	2.6	2.7	3.1	2.9	3.3	3.4	2.6	2.5	2.0
Snow	17.9	11.9	9.9	2.5	0.1	0.0	0.0	0.0	tr	tr	3.3	10.5

High and Low temperatures in degrees Fahrenheit; Precipitation and Snow in inches

Weather Station: Hale Loud Dam Elevation: 813 feet

	Jan	Feb	Mar	Apr	May	Jun	Jul	Aug	Sep	Oct	Nov	Dec
High	28	31	41	55	68	76	81	78	70	58	44	33
Low	9	10	19	31	42	51	57	55	48	37	28	18
Precip	1.7	1.1	1.8	2.2	2.4	3.0	3.2	3.5	3.3	2.5	2.3	1.7
Snow	13.9	8.3	7.6	1.6	0.2	0.0	0.0	0.0	tr	tr	3.4	8.7

High and Low temperatures in degrees Fahrenheit; Precipitation and Snow in inches

Population: 27,339 (2000); Race: 96.7% White, 0.5% Black, 0.2% Asian, 0.7% American Indian and Alaska Native, 0.8% Hispanic of any race, 1.7% two or more races (2000); Density: 49.8 persons per square mile (2000); Age: 22.3% under 18, 21.5% over 64 (2000).

Religion: Five largest groups: 19.5% Catholic Church, 6.1% Lutheran Church—Missouri Synod, 5.8% The United Methodist Church, 2.3% Southern Baptist Convention, 2.2% Wisconsin Evangelical Lutheran Synod (2000).

Economy: Unemployment rate: 8.5% (11/2002); Total civilian labor force: 10,601 (11/2002); Leading industries: 24.1% retail trade; 16.7% accommodation & food services; 14.4% manufacturing (2000); Companies that employ more than 1,000 persons: 0 (2000); Companies that employ more than 100 persons: 5 (2000); Farms: 238 totaling 42,667 acres (1997); Minority business ownership rate: 0.0% (1997); Women business ownership rate: 12.9% (1997); Retail sales per capita: $8,772 (1997). Single-family building permits issued: 165 (2001) / 161 (2000); Multi-family building permits issued: 2 (2001) / 0 (2000).

Income: Per capita income: $17,115 (2000); Median household income: $31,321 (2000); Poverty rate: 12.7% (2000); Bankruptcy rate: 3.92% (2001).

Taxes: Total county taxes per capita: $133 (1997); County property taxes per capita: $124 (1997).

Education: High school graduation rate: 77.9% (2000); College graduation rate: 11.3% (2000).

Housing: Homeownership rate: 82.0% (2000); Median home value: $77,100 (2000); Median rent: $352 per month (2000); Median age of housing: 34 years (2000).

Health: Birth rate: 105.7 per 10,000 population (1998); Age adjusted death rate: 91.2 per 10,000 population (1999); Age adjusted cancer mortality rate: 254.9 deaths per 100,000 population (1999). Number of physicians: 6.6 per 10,000 population (1999); Number of hospital beds: 17.9 per 10,000 population (1999).

Elections: 2000 Presidential election results: 49.2% Gore, 48.0% Bush, 2.3% Nader, 0.1% Buchanan

National and State Parks: Huron National Forest; Tawas Point State Park; Tuttle Marsh National Wildlife Area

Additional Information Contacts

Iosco County Government Offices 517-362-4212
Northeastern Michigan Board of Realtors 989-728-5165
Oscoda Chamber of Commerce 989-739-7322
Tawas Area Chamber of Commerce 989-362-8643
Whittemore Chamber of Commerce 989-756-5231

Iosco County Communities

ALABASTER (township). Covers a land area of 22.145 square miles and a water area of 0 square miles. Located at 44.20° N. Lat.; 83.56° W. Long. Elevation is 603 feet.

History: Alabaster rock had been quarried here for some 25 years before the township was formed in 1866. The U.S. Gypsum Company used the docks here to ship gypsum from its mine.

Population: 503 (2000); Race: 97.2% White, 0.0% Black, 1.3% Asian, 0.0% American Indian and Alaska Native, 0.8% Hispanic of any race, 1.1% two or more races (2000); Density: 22.7 persons per square mile (2000); Age: 14.0% under 18, 25.4% over 64 (2000); Marriage status: 13.4% never married, 70.2% now married, 5.8% widowed, 10.6% divorced (2000); Foreign born: 1.7% (2000); Ancestry (includes multiple ancestries): 35.2% German, 22.5% English, 10.2% Irish, 8.0% French (except Basque), 7.6% Polish (2000).

Economy: Employment by occupation: 12.2% management, 20.0% professional, 12.2% services, 35.7% sales, 0.0% farming, 7.4% construction, 12.6% production (2000).

Income: Per capita income: $23,384 (2000); Median household income: $44,000 (2000); Poverty rate: 6.1% (2000).

Taxes: Total city taxes per capita: $405 (1997); City property taxes per capita: $402 (1997).

Education: High school graduation rate: 78.6% (2000); College graduation rate: 19.0% (2000).

Housing: Homeownership rate: 92.2% (2000); Median home value: $144,400 (2000); Median rent: $470 per month (2000); Median age of housing: 38 years (2000).

Transportation: Commute to work: 90.2% car, 1.8% public transportation, 1.3% walk, 5.8% work from home (2000); Travel time to work: 36.8% less than 15 minutes, 31.1% 15 to 30 minutes, 17.5% 30 to 45 minutes, 8.0% 45 to 60 minutes, 6.6% 60 minutes or more (2000)

AU SABLE (township). Covers a land area of 20.609 square miles and a water area of 0.520 square miles. Located at 44.39° N. Lat.; 83.34° W. Long.

History: A village was platted here in 1849 by Curtis Emerson and James Eldridge. Incorporated as a village in 1872 and as a city in 1889, Au Sable relinquished its city charter in 1931 and became a township. The name is French for "sandy."

Population: 2,230 (2000); Race: 96.6% White, 1.4% Black, 0.0% Asian, 0.0% American Indian and Alaska Native, 1.2% Hispanic of any race, 2.0% two or more races (2000); Density: 108.2 persons per square mile (2000); Age: 24.4% under 18, 16.8% over 64 (2000); Marriage status: 21.0% never married, 59.5% now married, 6.6% widowed, 13.0% divorced (2000); Foreign born: 1.2% (2000); Ancestry (includes multiple ancestries): 22.8% German, 18.7% English, 17.2% Irish, 15.1% French (except Basque), 9.4% Other groups (2000).

Economy: Employment by occupation: 7.8% management, 11.0% professional, 18.1% services, 23.5% sales, 0.5% farming, 13.1% construction, 26.1% production (2000).

Income: Per capita income: $20,025 (2000); Median household income: $34,570 (2000); Poverty rate: 12.3% (2000).

Taxes: Total city taxes per capita: $176 (1997); City property taxes per capita: $175 (1997).

Education: High school graduation rate: 82.5% (2000); College graduation rate: 10.9% (2000).

Housing: Homeownership rate: 83.5% (2000); Median home value: $67,200 (2000); Median rent: $340 per month (2000); Median age of housing: 32 years (2000).

Transportation: Commute to work: 93.6% car, 1.3% public transportation, 0.3% walk, 4.0% work from home (2000); Travel time to work: 50.9% less than 15 minutes, 26.7% 15 to 30 minutes, 8.6% 30 to 45 minutes, 5.2% 45 to 60 minutes, 8.6% 60 minutes or more (2000)

BALDWIN (township). Covers a land area of 28.422 square miles and a water area of 2.880 square miles. Located at 44.32° N. Lat.; 83.45° W. Long.

Population: 1,726 (2000); Race: 96.6% White, 0.0% Black, 0.2% Asian, 2.5% American Indian and Alaska Native, 0.1% Hispanic of any race, 0.7% two or more races (2000); Density: 60.7 persons per square mile (2000); Age: 19.6% under 18, 22.5% over 64 (2000); Marriage status: 15.0% never married, 62.2% now married, 8.9% widowed, 13.9% divorced (2000); Foreign born: 1.1% (2000); Ancestry (includes multiple ancestries): 27.0% German, 19.0% Irish, 11.8% Polish, 10.5% English, 7.7% United States or American (2000).

Economy: Employment by occupation: 9.9% management, 19.5% professional, 18.6% services, 20.6% sales, 0.0% farming, 11.5% construction, 20.0% production (2000).

Income: Per capita income: $17,367 (2000); Median household income: $29,783 (2000); Poverty rate: 9.2% (2000).

Taxes: Total city taxes per capita: $198 (1997); City property taxes per capita: $197 (1997).

Education: High school graduation rate: 84.0% (2000); College graduation rate: 13.2% (2000).

Housing: Homeownership rate: 85.8% (2000); Median home value: $91,300 (2000); Median rent: $355 per month (2000); Median age of housing: 40 years (2000).
Transportation: Commute to work: 95.9% car, 0.0% public transportation, 1.3% walk, 2.4% work from home (2000); Travel time to work: 49.4% less than 15 minutes, 35.2% 15 to 30 minutes, 8.0% 30 to 45 minutes, 1.8% 45 to 60 minutes, 5.6% 60 minutes or more (2000)

BURLEIGH (township). Covers a land area of 34.714 square miles and a water area of 0.012 square miles. Located at 44.20° N. Lat.; 83.82° W. Long.
Population: 775 (2000); Race: 97.5% White, 0.0% Black, 0.0% Asian, 1.1% American Indian and Alaska Native, 0.7% Hispanic of any race, 1.2% two or more races (2000); Density: 22.3 persons per square mile (2000); Age: 19.1% under 18, 17.6% over 64 (2000); Marriage status: 17.8% never married, 64.8% now married, 6.0% widowed, 11.4% divorced (2000); Foreign born: 0.3% (2000); Ancestry (includes multiple ancestries): 17.9% German, 13.4% English, 10.8% United States or American, 8.7% Irish, 8.0% French (except Basque) (2000).
Economy: Employment by occupation: 12.3% management, 9.9% professional, 12.0% services, 18.3% sales, 5.6% farming, 17.6% construction, 24.3% production (2000).
Income: Per capita income: $15,726 (2000); Median household income: $33,542 (2000); Poverty rate: 11.7% (2000).
Taxes: Total city taxes per capita: $69 (1997); City property taxes per capita: $69 (1997).
Education: High school graduation rate: 75.4% (2000); College graduation rate: 7.1% (2000).
Housing: Homeownership rate: 90.1% (2000); Median home value: $62,400 (2000); Median rent: $270 per month (2000); Median age of housing: 36 years (2000).
Transportation: Commute to work: 90.9% car, 0.0% public transportation, 1.4% walk, 7.2% work from home (2000); Travel time to work: 25.8% less than 15 minutes, 34.8% 15 to 30 minutes, 24.6% 30 to 45 minutes, 3.1% 45 to 60 minutes, 11.7% 60 minutes or more (2000)

EAST TAWAS (city). Aka East Tawas-Tawas City. Covers a land area of 2.876 square miles and a water area of 0.454 square miles. Located at 44.28° N. Lat.; 83.48° W. Long. Elevation is 689 feet.
History: East Tawas developed at the mouth of the Tawas River, where it emptied into Tawas Bay on Lake Huron. A twin with the city of Tawas, East Tawas grew with the lumber industry. Later, tourism provided a source of revenue, with the shops of the Detroit & Mackinac Railroad located here.
Population: 2,951 (2000); Race: 98.2% White, 0.0% Black, 0.2% Asian, 0.4% American Indian and Alaska Native, 0.6% Hispanic of any race, 1.0% two or more races (2000); Density: 1,026.0 persons per square mile (2000); Age: 22.7% under 18, 27.6% over 64 (2000); Marriage status: 15.0% never married, 55.7% now married, 14.7% widowed, 14.5% divorced (2000); Foreign born: 1.2% (2000); Ancestry (includes multiple ancestries): 27.9% German, 13.2% English, 12.6% Irish, 10.9% French (except Basque), 9.3% Polish (2000).
Economy: Employment by occupation: 11.9% management, 18.1% professional, 17.0% services, 25.2% sales, 0.0% farming, 10.6% construction, 17.2% production (2000).
Income: Per capita income: $17,168 (2000); Median household income: $30,229 (2000); Poverty rate: 10.2% (2000).
Taxes: Total city taxes per capita: $407 (1997); City property taxes per capita: $405 (1997).
Education: High school graduation rate: 81.7% (2000); College graduation rate: 19.4% (2000).
Housing: Homeownership rate: 68.8% (2000); Median home value: $78,400 (2000); Median rent: $371 per month (2000); Median age of housing: 37 years (2000).
Safety: Violent crime rate: 40.4 per 10,000 population; Property crime rate: 610.0 per 10,000 population (2001).
Newspapers: Iosco County News Herald (1 x week)
Transportation: Commute to work: 94.2% car, 0.4% public transportation, 2.0% walk, 3.4% work from home (2000); Travel time to work: 67.6% less than 15 minutes, 21.5% 15 to 30 minutes, 6.3% 30 to 45 minutes, 0.0% 45 to 60 minutes, 4.7% 60 minutes or more (2000)

GRANT (township). Covers a land area of 34.930 square miles and a water area of 0.551 square miles. Located at 44.31° N. Lat.; 83.68° W. Long.
Population: 1,560 (2000); Race: 99.1% White, 0.2% Black, 0.1% Asian, 0.1% American Indian and Alaska Native, 0.6% Hispanic of any race, 0.3% two or more races (2000); Density: 44.7 persons per square mile (2000); Age: 19.7% under 18, 21.6% over 64 (2000); Marriage status: 15.6% never married, 63.5% now married, 8.6% widowed, 12.3% divorced (2000); Foreign born: 0.3% (2000); Ancestry (includes multiple ancestries): 30.7% German, 12.9% Irish, 11.8% English, 8.4% French (except Basque), 7.5% Polish (2000).
Economy: Employment by occupation: 8.1% management, 11.5% professional, 19.7% services, 22.0% sales, 0.7% farming, 14.7% construction, 23.3% production (2000).
Income: Per capita income: $16,708 (2000); Median household income: $27,625 (2000); Poverty rate: 15.0% (2000).
Taxes: Total city taxes per capita: $106 (1997); City property taxes per capita: $106 (1997).
Education: High school graduation rate: 77.1% (2000); College graduation rate: 8.2% (2000).
Housing: Homeownership rate: 91.5% (2000); Median home value: $75,500 (2000); Median rent: $290 per month (2000); Median age of housing: 34 years (2000).
Transportation: Commute to work: 92.0% car, 0.0% public transportation, 2.4% walk, 4.7% work from home (2000); Travel time to work: 15.6% less than 15 minutes, 52.1% 15 to 30 minutes, 12.9% 30 to 45 minutes, 6.8% 45 to 60 minutes, 12.5% 60 minutes or more (2000)

HALE (unincorporated postal area, zip code 48739). Covers a land area of 102.957 square miles and a water area of 3.500 square miles. Located at 44.37° N. Lat.; 83.83° W. Long. Elevation is 643 feet.
History: Hale began as a lumber camp established by C.D. Hale about 1880.
Population: 4,615 (2000); Race: 96.1% White, 0.3% Black, 0.0% Asian, 0.6% American Indian and Alaska Native, 0.7% Hispanic of any race, 2.6% two or more races (2000); Density: 44.8 persons per square mile (2000); Age: 19.8% under 18, 24.6% over 64 (2000); Marriage status: 14.9% never married, 63.1% now married, 10.2% widowed, 11.8% divorced (2000); Foreign born: 0.5% (2000); Ancestry (includes multiple ancestries): 24.1% German, 14.1% English, 11.5% Irish, 8.6% French (except Basque), 8.4% United States or American (2000).
Economy: Employment by occupation: 10.2% management, 11.6% professional, 17.4% services, 22.3% sales, 0.6% farming, 12.9% construction, 25.0% production (2000).
Income: Per capita income: $16,761 (2000); Median household income: $28,979 (2000); Poverty rate: 15.4% (2000).
Education: High school graduation rate: 69.6% (2000); College graduation rate: 7.5% (2000).

School District(s)

Hale Area Schools (KG-12)
2000 Enrollment: 817 517-728-7661
Housing: Homeownership rate: 88.7% (2000); Median home value: $80,600 (2000); Median rent: $297 per month (2000); Median age of housing: 34 years (2000).
Transportation: Commute to work: 91.1% car, 0.0% public transportation, 1.8% walk, 5.8% work from home (2000); Travel time to work: 42.5% less than 15 minutes, 17.0% 15 to 30 minutes, 20.7% 30 to 45 minutes, 12.6% 45 to 60 minutes, 7.2% 60 minutes or more (2000)
Additional Information Contacts
Northeastern Michigan Board of Realtors 989-728-5165

LONG LAKE (unincorporated postal area, zip code 48743). Covers a land area of 1.185 square miles and a water area of 0.062 square miles. Located at 44.44° N. Lat.; 83.87° W. Long. Elevation is 918 feet.
History: The shape of the lake influenced the name of the post office, Ellake, that was established here in 1902, as well as the name of the railroad station, Long Lake, established in 1894.
Population: 25 (2000); Race: 100.0% White, 0.0% Black, 0.0% Asian, 0.0% American Indian and Alaska Native, 0.0% Hispanic of any race, 0.0% two or more races (2000); Density: 21.1 persons per square mile (2000); Age: 0.0% under 18, 61.5% over 64 (2000); Marriage status: 38.5% never married, 42.3% now married, 19.2% widowed, 0.0% divorced (2000); Foreign born: 0.0% (2000); Ancestry (includes multiple ancestries): 38.5% English (2000).
Economy: Employment by occupation: 0.0% management, 0.0% professional, 0.0% services, 0.0% sales, 0.0% farming, 50.0% construction, 50.0% production (2000).
Income: Per capita income: $14,896 (2000); Median household income: $28,750 (2000); Poverty rate: 0.0% (2000).
Education: High school graduation rate: 19.2% (2000); College graduation rate: 0.0% (2000).
Housing: Homeownership rate: 100.0% (2000); Median home value: $94,200 (2000); Median age of housing: 29 years (2000).
Transportation: Commute to work: 100.0% car, 0.0% public transportation, 0.0% walk, 0.0% work from home (2000); Travel time to work: 0.0% less

than 15 minutes, 50.0% 15 to 30 minutes, 0.0% 30 to 45 minutes, 50.0% 45 to 60 minutes, 0.0% 60 minutes or more (2000)

NATIONAL CITY (unincorporated postal area, zip code 48748). Covers a land area of 49.120 square miles and a water area of 1.284 square miles. Located at 44.32° N. Lat.; 83.66° W. Long. Elevation is 674 feet.
Population: 1,776 (2000); Race: 97.8% White, 0.2% Black, 0.1% Asian, 0.3% American Indian and Alaska Native, 1.1% Hispanic of any race, 1.1% two or more races (2000); Density: 36.2 persons per square mile (2000); Age: 18.6% under 18, 23.3% over 64 (2000); Marriage status: 14.6% never married, 68.1% now married, 8.6% widowed, 8.7% divorced (2000); Foreign born: 1.4% (2000); Ancestry (includes multiple ancestries): 27.6% German, 12.5% Irish, 11.7% English, 8.9% French (except Basque), 8.9% Polish (2000).
Economy: Gypsum quarrying and processing. Employment by occupation: 8.7% management, 17.1% professional, 16.3% services, 24.5% sales, 0.7% farming, 12.9% construction, 19.7% production (2000).
Income: Per capita income: $19,010 (2000); Median household income: $30,068 (2000); Poverty rate: 14.8% (2000).
Education: High school graduation rate: 80.0% (2000); College graduation rate: 9.9% (2000).
Housing: Homeownership rate: 93.3% (2000); Median home value: $83,400 (2000); Median rent: $308 per month (2000); Median age of housing: 34 years (2000).
Transportation: Commute to work: 94.0% car, 0.0% public transportation, 1.2% walk, 4.5% work from home (2000); Travel time to work: 16.0% less than 15 minutes, 51.3% 15 to 30 minutes, 11.9% 30 to 45 minutes, 5.4% 45 to 60 minutes, 15.5% 60 minutes or more (2000)

OSCODA (township). Covers a land area of 121.758 square miles and a water area of 9.367 square miles. Located at 44.46° N. Lat.; 83.45° W. Long.
Population: 7,248 (2000); Race: 95.6% White, 0.8% Black, 0.0% Asian, 0.8% American Indian and Alaska Native, 0.4% Hispanic of any race, 2.5% two or more races (2000); Density: 59.5 persons per square mile (2000); Age: 24.7% under 18, 18.1% over 64 (2000); Marriage status: 19.3% never married, 60.5% now married, 8.6% widowed, 11.7% divorced (2000); Foreign born: 2.1% (2000); Ancestry (includes multiple ancestries): 24.4% German, 16.2% English, 13.9% Irish, 9.0% Polish, 7.5% Other groups (2000).
Economy: Trade center for resort and farm area: potatoes; cattle; fisheries. Manufacturing: transportation equipment, vinyl floor coverings. Paul B. Wurstmith Air Force Base to Northwest. Employment by occupation: 6.5% management, 10.8% professional, 22.0% services, 28.4% sales, 0.0% farming, 14.8% construction, 17.5% production (2000).
Income: Per capita income: $16,312 (2000); Median household income: $31,250 (2000); Poverty rate: 13.4% (2000).
Taxes: Total city taxes per capita: $147 (2000); City property taxes per capita: $147 (2000).
Education: High school graduation rate: 80.3% (2000); College graduation rate: 11.0% (2000).

School District(s)

Oscoda Area Schools (KG-12)
2000 Enrollment: 2,161 517-739-2033

Housing: Homeownership rate: 76.5% (2000); Median home value: $77,300 (2000); Median rent: $360 per month (2000); Median age of housing: 33 years (2000).
Safety: Violent crime rate: 19.2 per 10,000 population; Property crime rate: 391.2 per 10,000 population (2001).
Newspapers: Oscoda Press (1 x week)
Transportation: Commute to work: 94.0% car, 0.0% public transportation, 1.9% walk, 2.2% work from home (2000); Travel time to work: 53.5% less than 15 minutes, 28.2% 15 to 30 minutes, 10.5% 30 to 45 minutes, 2.1% 45 to 60 minutes, 5.8% 60 minutes or more (2000)

Additional Information Contacts

Oscoda Chamber of Commerce 989-739-7322

PLAINFIELD (township). Covers a land area of 103.772 square miles and a water area of 3.827 square miles. Located at 44.40° N. Lat.; 83.78° W. Long.
Population: 4,292 (2000); Race: 96.0% White, 0.3% Black, 0.0% Asian, 0.7% American Indian and Alaska Native, 0.9% Hispanic of any race, 2.7% two or more races (2000); Density: 41.4 persons per square mile (2000); Age: 19.3% under 18, 26.3% over 64 (2000); Marriage status: 14.6% never married, 63.0% now married, 10.5% widowed, 11.9% divorced (2000); Foreign born: 0.5% (2000); Ancestry (includes multiple ancestries): 21.2% German, 14.0% English, 11.7% Irish, 9.0% French (except Basque), 8.5% United States or American (2000).
Economy: Unemployment rate: 3.6% (11/2002); Total civilian labor force: 17,772 (11/2002); Single-family building permits issued: 33 (2001) / 46 (2000); Multi-family building permits issued: 0 (2001) / 0 (2000); Employment by occupation: 10.7% management, 11.4% professional, 17.5% services, 21.9% sales, 0.3% farming, 10.8% construction, 27.4% production (2000).
Income: Per capita income: $17,720 (2000); Median household income: $29,220 (2000); Poverty rate: 15.3% (2000).
Taxes: Total city taxes per capita: $102 (1997); City property taxes per capita: $86 (1997).
Education: High school graduation rate: 68.5% (2000); College graduation rate: 7.3% (2000).
Housing: Homeownership rate: 88.4% (2000); Median home value: $82,900 (2000); Median rent: $283 per month (2000); Median age of housing: 33 years (2000).
Transportation: Commute to work: 91.8% car, 0.0% public transportation, 1.4% walk, 5.8% work from home (2000); Travel time to work: 41.9% less than 15 minutes, 14.5% 15 to 30 minutes, 24.0% 30 to 45 minutes, 13.7% 45 to 60 minutes, 5.9% 60 minutes or more (2000)

RENO (township). Covers a land area of 35.351 square miles and a water area of 0.054 square miles. Located at 44.28° N. Lat.; 83.81° W. Long.
Population: 656 (2000); Race: 97.8% White, 0.5% Black, 0.3% Asian, 0.3% American Indian and Alaska Native, 0.3% Hispanic of any race, 0.8% two or more races (2000); Density: 18.6 persons per square mile (2000); Age: 24.8% under 18, 12.8% over 64 (2000); Marriage status: 16.8% never married, 64.6% now married, 6.1% widowed, 12.6% divorced (2000); Foreign born: 1.3% (2000); Ancestry (includes multiple ancestries): 28.4% German, 14.7% United States or American, 12.0% Irish, 11.8% English, 7.5% Polish (2000).
Economy: Employment by occupation: 14.1% management, 11.0% professional, 9.9% services, 19.8% sales, 3.0% farming, 17.1% construction, 25.1% production (2000).
Income: Per capita income: $14,682 (2000); Median household income: $32,019 (2000); Poverty rate: 25.2% (2000).
Taxes: Total city taxes per capita: $35 (1997); City property taxes per capita: $35 (1997).
Education: High school graduation rate: 72.3% (2000); College graduation rate: 6.9% (2000).
Housing: Homeownership rate: 86.9% (2000); Median home value: $67,800 (2000); Median rent: $283 per month (2000); Median age of housing: 25 years (2000).
Transportation: Commute to work: 86.7% car, 0.8% public transportation, 3.4% walk, 4.9% work from home (2000); Travel time to work: 30.8% less than 15 minutes, 36.8% 15 to 30 minutes, 14.0% 30 to 45 minutes, 5.2% 45 to 60 minutes, 13.2% 60 minutes or more (2000)

SHERMAN (township). Covers a land area of 35.915 square miles and a water area of 0 square miles. Located at 44.20° N. Lat.; 83.71° W. Long.
Population: 493 (2000); Race: 95.6% White, 1.1% Black, 0.0% Asian, 0.6% American Indian and Alaska Native, 3.2% Hispanic of any race, 1.3% two or more races (2000); Density: 13.7 persons per square mile (2000); Age: 21.3% under 18, 18.8% over 64 (2000); Marriage status: 19.1% never married, 65.6% now married, 7.4% widowed, 7.9% divorced (2000); Foreign born: 2.3% (2000); Ancestry (includes multiple ancestries): 25.3% German, 13.9% French (except Basque), 10.3% English, 9.9% United States or American, 8.4% Irish (2000).
Economy: Employment by occupation: 12.2% management, 8.8% professional, 16.0% services, 22.7% sales, 0.0% farming, 13.8% construction, 26.5% production (2000).
Income: Per capita income: $18,432 (2000); Median household income: $40,547 (2000); Poverty rate: 10.8% (2000).
Taxes: Total city taxes per capita: $31 (1997); City property taxes per capita: $31 (1997).
Education: High school graduation rate: 78.5% (2000); College graduation rate: 8.4% (2000).
Housing: Homeownership rate: 93.8% (2000); Median home value: $75,900 (2000); Median rent: $325 per month (2000); Median age of housing: 28 years (2000).
Transportation: Commute to work: 90.9% car, 0.0% public transportation, 2.3% walk, 5.7% work from home (2000); Travel time to work: 22.3% less than 15 minutes, 40.4% 15 to 30 minutes, 12.7% 30 to 45 minutes, 10.2% 45 to 60 minutes, 14.5% 60 minutes or more (2000)

TAWAS (township). Covers a land area of 33.443 square miles and a water area of 0.004 square miles. Located at 44.28° N. Lat.; 83.57° W. Long.
Population: 1,684 (2000); Race: 96.3% White, 0.2% Black, 1.1% Asian, 1.4% American Indian and Alaska Native, 0.4% Hispanic of any race, 1.0% two or more races (2000); Density: 50.4 persons per square mile (2000); Age: 24.5% under 18, 19.5% over 64 (2000); Marriage status: 17.9% never married, 69.2% now married, 4.4% widowed, 8.6% divorced (2000); Foreign born: 1.4% (2000); Ancestry (includes multiple ancestries): 35.1% German, 16.5% English, 12.0% Irish, 11.1% Polish, 8.8% French (except Basque) (2000).
Economy: Employment by occupation: 6.3% management, 14.1% professional, 15.7% services, 23.5% sales, 1.0% farming, 12.3% construction, 27.1% production (2000).
Income: Per capita income: $16,632 (2000); Median household income: $37,941 (2000); Poverty rate: 8.2% (2000).
Taxes: Total city taxes per capita: $51 (1997); City property taxes per capita: $50 (1997).
Education: High school graduation rate: 83.0% (2000); College graduation rate: 11.8% (2000).
Housing: Homeownership rate: 92.8% (2000); Median home value: $76,900 (2000); Median rent: $403 per month (2000); Median age of housing: 30 years (2000).
Transportation: Commute to work: 95.9% car, 0.0% public transportation, 1.7% walk, 1.8% work from home (2000); Travel time to work: 55.1% less than 15 minutes, 27.0% 15 to 30 minutes, 10.5% 30 to 45 minutes, 2.0% 45 to 60 minutes, 5.3% 60 minutes or more (2000)

TAWAS CITY (city). Covers a land area of 1.707 square miles and a water area of 0.439 square miles. Located at 44.27° N. Lat.; 83.52° W. Long. Elevation is 587 feet.
History: Tawas City, a twin with East Tawas, both located on Tawas Bay of Lake Huron, developed an early dependence on tourism for its source of revenue. The Tawas City Perch Festival was originated in 1936 to exploit the popularity of perch fishing in Tawas Bay.
Population: 2,005 (2000); Race: 96.8% White, 0.4% Black, 0.1% Asian, 0.6% American Indian and Alaska Native, 1.5% Hispanic of any race, 1.3% two or more races (2000); Density: 1,174.4 persons per square mile (2000); Age: 21.2% under 18, 26.6% over 64 (2000); Marriage status: 20.6% never married, 50.6% now married, 18.1% widowed, 10.7% divorced (2000); Foreign born: 1.0% (2000); Ancestry (includes multiple ancestries): 20.4% German, 11.4% Irish, 11.3% English, 9.2% United States or American, 8.7% Polish (2000).
Economy: Employment by occupation: 12.4% management, 14.8% professional, 16.0% services, 21.6% sales, 0.0% farming, 13.3% construction, 21.8% production (2000).
Income: Per capita income: $16,061 (2000); Median household income: $32,813 (2000); Poverty rate: 9.6% (2000).
Taxes: Total city taxes per capita: $493 (1997); City property taxes per capita: $493 (1997).
Education: High school graduation rate: 74.3% (2000); College graduation rate: 12.1% (2000).

School District(s)

Sunrise Education Center (KG-06)
2000 Enrollment: 31 517-249-4623
Tawas Area Schools (KG-12)
2000 Enrollment: 1,730 517-362-4481

Housing: Homeownership rate: 77.7% (2000); Median home value: $69,200 (2000); Median rent: $367 per month (2000); Median age of housing: 36 years (2000).
Transportation: Commute to work: 93.6% car, 0.8% public transportation, 2.5% walk, 2.1% work from home (2000); Travel time to work: 60.9% less than 15 minutes, 18.8% 15 to 30 minutes, 14.7% 30 to 45 minutes, 1.3% 45 to 60 minutes, 4.4% 60 minutes or more (2000)
Additional Information Contacts
Tawas Area Chamber of Commerce 989-362-8643

WHITTEMORE (city). Covers a land area of 0.985 square miles and a water area of 0 square miles. Located at 44.23° N. Lat.; 83.80° W. Long. Elevation is 776 feet.
Population: 476 (2000); Race: 98.2% White, 0.0% Black, 0.0% Asian, 1.4% American Indian and Alaska Native, 2.6% Hispanic of any race, 0.4% two or more races (2000); Density: 483.1 persons per square mile (2000); Age: 31.2% under 18, 16.7% over 64 (2000); Marriage status: 24.7% never married, 47.1% now married, 15.4% widowed, 12.8% divorced (2000); Foreign born: 1.6% (2000); Ancestry (includes multiple ancestries): 18.5% German, 17.7% English, 15.9% Irish, 9.7% French (except Basque), 8.9% Other groups (2000).
Economy: In farm area; manufacturing; tool and die. Employment by occupation: 3.3% management, 13.7% professional, 24.6% services, 20.8% sales, 1.1% farming, 10.9% construction, 25.7% production (2000).
Income: Per capita income: $12,175 (2000); Median household income: $22,500 (2000); Poverty rate: 24.6% (2000).
Taxes: Total city taxes per capita: $80 (1997); City property taxes per capita: $80 (1997).
Education: High school graduation rate: 69.3% (2000); College graduation rate: 5.9% (2000).

School District(s)

Whittemore-Prescott Area Schools (KG-12)
2000 Enrollment: 1,451 517-756-2500

Housing: Homeownership rate: 69.4% (2000); Median home value: $51,400 (2000); Median rent: $271 per month (2000); Median age of housing: 47 years (2000).
Transportation: Commute to work: 90.7% car, 0.0% public transportation, 4.9% walk, 2.2% work from home (2000); Travel time to work: 33.0% less than 15 minutes, 28.5% 15 to 30 minutes, 27.9% 30 to 45 minutes, 1.7% 45 to 60 minutes, 8.9% 60 minutes or more (2000)
Additional Information Contacts
Whittemore Chamber of Commerce 989-756-5231

WILBER (township). Covers a land area of 72.484 square miles and a water area of 0.209 square miles. Located at 44.38° N. Lat.; 83.55° W. Long. Elevation is 659 feet.
Population: 740 (2000); Race: 97.8% White, 0.1% Black, 0.0% Asian, 0.3% American Indian and Alaska Native, 1.7% Hispanic of any race, 0.9% two or more races (2000); Density: 10.2 persons per square mile (2000); Age: 20.1% under 18, 19.3% over 64 (2000); Marriage status: 15.8% never married, 66.9% now married, 5.4% widowed, 12.0% divorced (2000); Foreign born: 0.3% (2000); Ancestry (includes multiple ancestries): 33.3% German, 16.3% Irish, 12.5% United States or American, 11.2% English, 9.1% Polish (2000).
Economy: Employment by occupation: 8.2% management, 17.5% professional, 10.0% services, 27.9% sales, 0.7% farming, 15.6% construction, 20.1% production (2000).
Income: Per capita income: $18,224 (2000); Median household income: $36,786 (2000); Poverty rate: 9.4% (2000).
Taxes: Total city taxes per capita: $155 (1997); City property taxes per capita: $155 (1997).
Education: High school graduation rate: 81.5% (2000); College graduation rate: 11.1% (2000).
Housing: Homeownership rate: 93.1% (2000); Median home value: $81,000 (2000); Median rent: $475 per month (2000); Median age of housing: 31 years (2000).
Transportation: Commute to work: 93.0% car, 0.0% public transportation, 0.0% walk, 6.6% work from home (2000); Travel time to work: 14.9% less than 15 minutes, 55.6% 15 to 30 minutes, 12.0% 30 to 45 minutes, 5.4% 45 to 60 minutes, 12.0% 60 minutes or more (2000)

Iron County

Located in northwestern Michigan, on the Upper Peninsula; bounded on the south by Wisconsin; drained by the Brule, Michigamme, Paint, and Iron Rivers; includes part of Ottawa National Forest, the Menominee range, and many small lakes. Covers a land area of 1,166.40 square miles, a water area of 44.70 square miles, and is located in the Central Time Zone. The county government was organized in 1885. County seat is Crystal Falls.

Weather Station: Stambaugh 2 SSE Elevation: 1,558 feet

	Jan	Feb	Mar	Apr	May	Jun	Jul	Aug	Sep	Oct	Nov	Dec
High	21	27	37	52	66	74	78	76	66	54	38	26
Low	-2	1	12	26	37	46	51	49	41	32	20	7
Precip	1.1	0.8	1.6	2.2	3.3	3.6	4.0	3.7	3.9	2.9	2.1	1.4
Snow	17.8	10.6	12.6	5.7	0.8	0.0	0.0	tr	tr	1.8	10.2	17.1

High and Low temperatures in degrees Fahrenheit; Precipitation and Snow in inches

Population: 13,138 (2000); Race: 96.4% White, 0.9% Black, 0.2% Asian, 1.1% American Indian and Alaska Native, 0.8% Hispanic of any race, 1.2% two or more races (2000); Density: 11.3 persons per square mile (2000); Age: 20.6% under 18, 25.1% over 64 (2000).
Religion: Five largest groups: 36.0% Catholic Church, 13.8% Evangelical Lutheran Church in America, 2.6% The United Methodist Church, 2.0% The Evangelical Covenant Church, 1.6% Lutheran Church—Missouri Synod (2000).

Economy: Unemployment rate: 5.5% (11/2002); Total civilian labor force: 5,280 (11/2002); Leading industries: 22.6% health care and social assistance; 18.9% retail trade; 12.1% accommodation & food services (2000); Companies that employ more than 1,000 persons: 0 (2000); Companies that employ more than 100 persons: 4 (2000); Farms: 86 totaling 23,823 acres (1997); Minority business ownership rate: 0.0% (1997); Women business ownership rate: 19.6% (1997); Retail sales per capita: $7,141 (1997). Single-family building permits issued: 79 (2001) / 50 (2000); Multi-family building permits issued: 0 (2001) / 0 (2000).
Income: Per capita income: $16,506 (2000); Median household income: $28,560 (2000); Poverty rate: 11.3% (2000); Bankruptcy rate: 2.18% (2001).
Taxes: Total county taxes per capita: $191 (1997); County property taxes per capita: $189 (1997).
Education: High school graduation rate: 84.8% (2000); College graduation rate: 13.7% (2000).
Housing: Homeownership rate: 82.5% (2000); Median home value: $47,500 (2000); Median rent: $262 per month (2000); Median age of housing: 46 years (2000).
Health: Birth rate: 86.0 per 10,000 population (1998); Age adjusted death rate: 103.1 per 10,000 population (1999); Age adjusted cancer mortality rate: 172.5 deaths per 100,000 population (1999). Number of physicians: 10.7 per 10,000 population (1999); Number of hospital beds: 62.4 per 10,000 population (1999).
Elections: 2000 Presidential election results: 48.7% Gore, 48.0% Bush, 2.6% Nader, 0.0% Buchanan
National and State Parks: Iron Range State Forest
Additional Information Contacts
Iron County Government Offices. 906-875-3301
Iron County Chamber of Commerce 906-265-3822

Iron County Communities

ALPHA (village). Covers a land area of 0.940 square miles and a water area of 0.053 square miles. Located at 46.04° N. Lat.; 88.37° W. Long. Elevation is 1,500 feet.
History: The settlement at Alpha grew up around the Mastodon Mine, opened in 1881. First called Mastodon, the village was incorporated as Alpha in 1914.
Population: 198 (2000); Race: 100.0% White, 0.0% Black, 0.0% Asian, 0.0% American Indian and Alaska Native, 0.0% Hispanic of any race, 0.0% two or more races (2000); Density: 210.6 persons per square mile (2000); Age: 23.5% under 18, 28.0% over 64 (2000); Marriage status: 21.5% never married, 42.3% now married, 21.5% widowed, 14.7% divorced (2000); Foreign born: 1.0% (2000); Ancestry (includes multiple ancestries): 25.5% Finnish, 24.5% German, 17.0% Polish, 12.5% Irish, 12.0% Italian (2000).
Economy: Employment by occupation: 5.2% management, 24.1% professional, 29.3% services, 22.4% sales, 0.0% farming, 3.4% construction, 15.5% production (2000).
Income: Per capita income: $12,084 (2000); Median household income: $21,750 (2000); Poverty rate: 11.0% (2000).
Taxes: Total city taxes per capita: $123 (1997); City property taxes per capita: $123 (1997).
Education: High school graduation rate: 86.2% (2000); College graduation rate: 8.7% (2000).
Housing: Homeownership rate: 89.1% (2000); Median home value: $29,600 (2000); Median rent: $250 per month (2000); Median age of housing: 60+ years (2000).
Transportation: Commute to work: 91.4% car, 0.0% public transportation, 5.2% walk, 0.0% work from home (2000); Travel time to work: 53.4% less than 15 minutes, 15.5% 15 to 30 minutes, 24.1% 30 to 45 minutes, 3.4% 45 to 60 minutes, 3.4% 60 minutes or more (2000)

BATES (township). Covers a land area of 125.395 square miles and a water area of 5.901 square miles. Located at 46.27° N. Lat.; 88.63° W. Long.
Population: 1,021 (2000); Race: 97.5% White, 0.0% Black, 0.0% Asian, 1.8% American Indian and Alaska Native, 1.0% Hispanic of any race, 0.8% two or more races (2000); Density: 8.1 persons per square mile (2000); Age: 21.5% under 18, 21.4% over 64 (2000); Marriage status: 20.8% never married, 62.8% now married, 8.2% widowed, 8.2% divorced (2000); Foreign born: 1.4% (2000); Ancestry (includes multiple ancestries): 18.4% German, 18.2% Swedish, 15.6% Polish, 11.8% Italian, 11.4% English (2000).
Economy: Employment by occupation: 10.3% management, 10.3% professional, 22.1% services, 27.0% sales, 2.8% farming, 13.6% construction, 13.8% production (2000).
Income: Per capita income: $19,194 (2000); Median household income: $31,983 (2000); Poverty rate: 7.1% (2000).
Taxes: Total city taxes per capita: $104 (1997); City property taxes per capita: $104 (1997).
Education: High school graduation rate: 86.3% (2000); College graduation rate: 13.1% (2000).
Housing: Homeownership rate: 92.6% (2000); Median home value: $66,700 (2000); Median rent: $250 per month (2000); Median age of housing: 31 years (2000).
Transportation: Commute to work: 95.5% car, 0.5% public transportation, 1.2% walk, 1.9% work from home (2000); Travel time to work: 49.4% less than 15 minutes, 28.5% 15 to 30 minutes, 6.8% 30 to 45 minutes, 6.8% 45 to 60 minutes, 8.5% 60 minutes or more (2000)

CASPIAN (city). Covers a land area of 1.408 square miles and a water area of 0 square miles. Located at 46.06° N. Lat.; 88.62° W. Long. Elevation is 1,492 feet.
History: The Chicago & Northwestern Railroad built a branch line station here in 1884. The village was platted in 1908 by the Veroner Mining Company to provide housing for employees in the Caspian, Baltic, and Fogarty mines.
Population: 997 (2000); Race: 98.2% White, 0.0% Black, 0.0% Asian, 1.1% American Indian and Alaska Native, 0.3% Hispanic of any race, 0.4% two or more races (2000); Density: 707.9 persons per square mile (2000); Age: 25.2% under 18, 25.6% over 64 (2000); Marriage status: 17.7% never married, 56.4% now married, 12.7% widowed, 13.2% divorced (2000); Foreign born: 2.5% (2000); Ancestry (includes multiple ancestries): 27.3% Italian, 20.6% German, 13.4% Polish, 11.8% Swedish, 11.3% Finnish (2000).
Economy: Employment by occupation: 5.5% management, 7.4% professional, 24.0% services, 30.1% sales, 2.9% farming, 11.3% construction, 18.7% production (2000).
Income: Per capita income: $14,544 (2000); Median household income: $24,524 (2000); Poverty rate: 18.3% (2000).
Taxes: Total city taxes per capita: $142 (1997); City property taxes per capita: $142 (1997).
Education: High school graduation rate: 87.6% (2000); College graduation rate: 9.8% (2000).
Housing: Homeownership rate: 76.5% (2000); Median home value: $35,100 (2000); Median rent: $259 per month (2000); Median age of housing: 60 years (2000).
Transportation: Commute to work: 96.0% car, 0.5% public transportation, 1.1% walk, 1.6% work from home (2000); Travel time to work: 65.1% less than 15 minutes, 22.3% 15 to 30 minutes, 4.1% 30 to 45 minutes, 3.5% 45 to 60 minutes, 4.9% 60 minutes or more (2000)

CRYSTAL FALLS (city). Covers a land area of 3.376 square miles and a water area of 0.192 square miles. Located at 46.09° N. Lat.; 88.33° W. Long. Elevation is 1,517 feet.
History: Crystal Falls, named for a cascade on the Paint River, was first a lumber village but grew with the development of the Bristol Mine which opened in 1882.
Population: 1,791 (2000); Race: 98.5% White, 0.2% Black, 0.1% Asian, 0.5% American Indian and Alaska Native, 1.2% Hispanic of any race, 0.4% two or more races (2000); Density: 530.6 persons per square mile (2000); Age: 23.6% under 18, 28.8% over 64 (2000); Marriage status: 20.8% never married, 54.6% now married, 13.7% widowed, 10.9% divorced (2000); Foreign born: 1.9% (2000); Ancestry (includes multiple ancestries): 20.4% Finnish, 15.9% German, 15.0% Swedish, 14.8% Italian, 11.9% English (2000).
Economy: Employment by occupation: 6.8% management, 18.5% professional, 26.6% services, 22.1% sales, 1.9% farming, 10.8% construction, 13.2% production (2000).
Income: Per capita income: $14,538 (2000); Median household income: $26,637 (2000); Poverty rate: 10.4% (2000).
Taxes: Total city taxes per capita: $110 (1997); City property taxes per capita: $109 (1997).
Education: High school graduation rate: 80.4% (2000); College graduation rate: 13.4% (2000).

School District(s)

Forest Park School District (PK-12)
2000 Enrollment: 722 906-875-6761
Housing: Homeownership rate: 78.6% (2000); Median home value: $46,500 (2000); Median rent: $241 per month (2000); Median age of housing: 60+ years (2000).
Hospitals: Crystal Falls Community Hospital (35 beds)

Safety: Violent crime rate: 0.0 per 10,000 population; Property crime rate: 33.3 per 10,000 population (2001).
Transportation: Commute to work: 86.6% car, 0.3% public transportation, 7.6% walk, 5.2% work from home (2000); Travel time to work: 58.7% less than 15 minutes, 20.3% 15 to 30 minutes, 10.6% 30 to 45 minutes, 4.9% 45 to 60 minutes, 5.5% 60 minutes or more (2000)

CRYSTAL FALLS (township). Covers a land area of 228.724 square miles and a water area of 6.442 square miles. Located at 46.20° N. Lat.; 88.33° W. Long. Elevation is 1,517 feet.
History: Incorporated as village 1889, as city 1899.
Population: 1,722 (2000); Race: 97.2% White, 0.1% Black, 0.3% Asian, 0.3% American Indian and Alaska Native, 0.1% Hispanic of any race, 2.0% two or more races (2000); Density: 7.5 persons per square mile (2000); Age: 18.2% under 18, 25.1% over 64 (2000); Marriage status: 17.0% never married, 56.9% now married, 13.3% widowed, 12.8% divorced (2000); Foreign born: 0.9% (2000); Ancestry (includes multiple ancestries): 22.2% Finnish, 18.6% German, 13.5% Swedish, 12.3% Italian, 12.0% Polish (2000).
Economy: Lumbering; dairy farming. Manufacturing: wood products. Its many lakes attract tourists. Crystella Ski Area to Southwest. Employment by occupation: 9.9% management, 22.9% professional, 18.0% services, 22.8% sales, 1.9% farming, 11.8% construction, 12.6% production (2000).
Income: Per capita income: $18,213 (2000); Median household income: $34,688 (2000); Poverty rate: 6.9% (2000).
Taxes: Total city taxes per capita: $234 (1997); City property taxes per capita: $232 (1997).
Education: High school graduation rate: 85.4% (2000); College graduation rate: 15.3% (2000).
Housing: Homeownership rate: 91.0% (2000); Median home value: $68,300 (2000); Median rent: $271 per month (2000); Median age of housing: 37 years (2000).
Transportation: Commute to work: 95.4% car, 0.0% public transportation, 1.5% walk, 2.8% work from home (2000); Travel time to work: 47.7% less than 15 minutes, 26.5% 15 to 30 minutes, 11.7% 30 to 45 minutes, 8.5% 45 to 60 minutes, 5.7% 60 minutes or more (2000)

GAASTRA (city). Covers a land area of 1.647 square miles and a water area of 0 square miles. Located at 46.06° N. Lat.; 88.60° W. Long.
History: Gaastra was laid out in 1908 and named for Douwe Gaastra, a real estate speculator who owned the land. Gaastra was incorporated as a village in 1919 and as a city in 1949.
Population: 339 (2000); Race: 96.1% White, 0.9% Black, 0.0% Asian, 0.9% American Indian and Alaska Native, 0.0% Hispanic of any race, 2.1% two or more races (2000); Density: 205.9 persons per square mile (2000); Age: 24.3% under 18, 30.3% over 64 (2000); Marriage status: 19.5% never married, 67.8% now married, 10.1% widowed, 2.6% divorced (2000); Foreign born: 0.3% (2000); Ancestry (includes multiple ancestries): 29.1% Polish, 19.5% Italian, 17.1% Finnish, 11.4% French (except Basque), 6.6% United States or American (2000).
Economy: Employment by occupation: 11.7% management, 15.3% professional, 22.5% services, 24.3% sales, 1.8% farming, 4.5% construction, 19.8% production (2000).
Income: Per capita income: $15,797 (2000); Median household income: $23,125 (2000); Poverty rate: 22.2% (2000).
Taxes: Total city taxes per capita: $106 (1997); City property taxes per capita: $106 (1997).
Education: High school graduation rate: 85.8% (2000); College graduation rate: 13.7% (2000).
Housing: Homeownership rate: 84.5% (2000); Median home value: $34,500 (2000); Median rent: $282 per month (2000); Median age of housing: 56 years (2000).
Transportation: Commute to work: 97.3% car, 0.0% public transportation, 2.7% walk, 0.0% work from home (2000); Travel time to work: 48.6% less than 15 minutes, 25.2% 15 to 30 minutes, 6.3% 30 to 45 minutes, 19.8% 45 to 60 minutes, 0.0% 60 minutes or more (2000)

HEMATITE (township). Covers a land area of 153.451 square miles and a water area of 2.312 square miles. Located at 46.31° N. Lat.; 88.50° W. Long.
Population: 352 (2000); Race: 96.5% White, 0.0% Black, 0.0% Asian, 0.6% American Indian and Alaska Native, 0.9% Hispanic of any race, 2.9% two or more races (2000); Density: 2.3 persons per square mile (2000); Age: 20.6% under 18, 22.1% over 64 (2000); Marriage status: 27.5% never married, 52.6% now married, 10.1% widowed, 9.8% divorced (2000); Foreign born: 0.6% (2000); Ancestry (includes multiple ancestries): 32.6% Finnish, 16.3% German, 11.3% Italian, 10.2% Swedish, 7.3% Other groups (2000).
Economy: Employment by occupation: 5.6% management, 6.3% professional, 34.5% services, 16.2% sales, 6.3% farming, 9.2% construction, 21.8% production (2000).
Income: Per capita income: $13,931 (2000); Median household income: $26,964 (2000); Poverty rate: 17.9% (2000).
Taxes: Total city taxes per capita: $206 (1997); City property taxes per capita: $206 (1997).
Education: High school graduation rate: 85.7% (2000); College graduation rate: 8.4% (2000).
Housing: Homeownership rate: 83.1% (2000); Median home value: $34,800 (2000); Median rent: $175 per month (2000); Median age of housing: 33 years (2000).
Transportation: Commute to work: 89.3% car, 0.0% public transportation, 3.6% walk, 1.4% work from home (2000); Travel time to work: 42.0% less than 15 minutes, 34.8% 15 to 30 minutes, 9.4% 30 to 45 minutes, 6.5% 45 to 60 minutes, 7.2% 60 minutes or more (2000)

IRON RIVER (city). Covers a land area of 3.471 square miles and a water area of 0.020 square miles. Located at 46.09° N. Lat.; 88.64° W. Long. Elevation is 1,510 feet.
History: Iron River was settled in 1881 when the Nanaina Mine was producing, and was known for a time as Nanaina. Iron River was incorporated as a village in 1885 and as a city in 1926.
Population: 1,929 (2000); Race: 95.4% White, 0.0% Black, 0.2% Asian, 2.0% American Indian and Alaska Native, 0.9% Hispanic of any race, 2.2% two or more races (2000); Density: 555.7 persons per square mile (2000); Age: 19.2% under 18, 31.6% over 64 (2000); Marriage status: 18.9% never married, 55.5% now married, 14.2% widowed, 11.5% divorced (2000); Foreign born: 0.5% (2000); Ancestry (includes multiple ancestries): 19.4% German, 15.8% Swedish, 12.1% Polish, 12.1% Italian, 10.9% English (2000).
Economy: Employment by occupation: 9.1% management, 15.5% professional, 25.7% services, 27.2% sales, 1.3% farming, 7.9% construction, 13.4% production (2000).
Income: Per capita income: $15,728 (2000); Median household income: $23,438 (2000); Poverty rate: 11.9% (2000).
Taxes: Total city taxes per capita: $265 (1997); City property taxes per capita: $265 (1997).
Education: High school graduation rate: 83.5% (2000); College graduation rate: 13.7% (2000).
Housing: Homeownership rate: 71.8% (2000); Median home value: $43,100 (2000); Median rent: $274 per month (2000); Median age of housing: 60+ years (2000).
Hospitals: Iron County Community Hospitals (67 beds)
Safety: Violent crime rate: 67.0 per 10,000 population; Property crime rate: 618.9 per 10,000 population (2001).
Newspapers: Iron County Reporter (1 x week)
Transportation: Commute to work: 84.9% car, 0.0% public transportation, 10.3% walk, 4.7% work from home (2000); Travel time to work: 65.0% less than 15 minutes, 18.3% 15 to 30 minutes, 10.1% 30 to 45 minutes, 2.2% 45 to 60 minutes, 4.5% 60 minutes or more (2000)
Additional Information Contacts
Iron County Chamber of Commerce 906-265-3822

IRON RIVER (township). Covers a land area of 239.554 square miles and a water area of 4.378 square miles. Located at 46.26° N. Lat.; 88.79° W. Long. Elevation is 1,510 feet.
History: Settled by iron-ore prospectors c.1881; incorporated as village 1885, as city 1926.
Population: 1,585 (2000); Race: 89.6% White, 6.6% Black, 0.4% Asian, 0.4% American Indian and Alaska Native, 1.3% Hispanic of any race, 1.7% two or more races (2000); Density: 6.6 persons per square mile (2000); Age: 20.0% under 18, 16.3% over 64 (2000); Marriage status: 28.3% never married, 52.1% now married, 7.4% widowed, 12.3% divorced (2000); Foreign born: 0.9% (2000); Ancestry (includes multiple ancestries): 17.5% German, 11.9% Swedish, 10.4% Finnish, 10.3% Polish, 9.7% Italian (2000).
Economy: In lumbering region. Livestock; potatoes; dairy products. Manufacturing: machining, naval equipment and cranes. Lake resort. Ottawa National Forest to Northwest; Brule Mt. Ski Area to Southwest. Employment by occupation: 8.7% management, 14.6% professional, 24.8% services, 19.9% sales, 2.7% farming, 15.2% construction, 14.1% production (2000).
Income: Per capita income: $14,679 (2000); Median household income: $32,024 (2000); Poverty rate: 12.8% (2000).
Taxes: Total city taxes per capita: $88 (1997); City property taxes per capita: $88 (1997).
Education: High school graduation rate: 84.1% (2000); College graduation rate: 7.8% (2000).

Housing: Homeownership rate: 86.7% (2000); Median home value: $46,000 (2000); Median rent: $210 per month (2000); Median age of housing: 40 years (2000).
Transportation: Commute to work: 93.1% car, 0.3% public transportation, 1.4% walk, 5.0% work from home (2000); Travel time to work: 46.3% less than 15 minutes, 27.3% 15 to 30 minutes, 13.9% 30 to 45 minutes, 4.2% 45 to 60 minutes, 8.3% 60 minutes or more (2000)

MANSFIELD (township). Covers a land area of 99.314 square miles and a water area of 8.382 square miles. Located at 46.18° N. Lat.; 88.19° W. Long. Elevation is 1,377 feet.
Population: 243 (2000); Race: 96.3% White, 0.0% Black, 0.0% Asian, 3.7% American Indian and Alaska Native, 0.0% Hispanic of any race, 0.0% two or more races (2000); Density: 2.4 persons per square mile (2000); Age: 18.4% under 18, 15.2% over 64 (2000); Marriage status: 16.7% never married, 62.9% now married, 8.6% widowed, 11.9% divorced (2000); Foreign born: 1.2% (2000); Ancestry (includes multiple ancestries): 23.4% Polish, 18.4% English, 13.9% Swedish, 12.7% Finnish, 12.7% German (2000).
Economy: Employment by occupation: 11.4% management, 18.1% professional, 12.4% services, 26.7% sales, 1.9% farming, 13.3% construction, 16.2% production (2000).
Income: Per capita income: $17,154 (2000); Median household income: $36,458 (2000); Poverty rate: 5.3% (2000).
Taxes: Total city taxes per capita: $133 (1997); City property taxes per capita: $125 (1997).
Education: High school graduation rate: 87.4% (2000); College graduation rate: 17.5% (2000).
Housing: Homeownership rate: 95.9% (2000); Median home value: $60,000 (2000); Median rent: $325 per month (2000); Median age of housing: 29 years (2000).
Transportation: Commute to work: 89.2% car, 0.0% public transportation, 6.9% walk, 3.9% work from home (2000); Travel time to work: 23.5% less than 15 minutes, 24.5% 15 to 30 minutes, 40.8% 30 to 45 minutes, 9.2% 45 to 60 minutes, 2.0% 60 minutes or more (2000)

MASTODON (township). Covers a land area of 126.591 square miles and a water area of 8.749 square miles. Located at 46.03° N. Lat.; 88.31° W. Long.
Population: 668 (2000); Race: 100.0% White, 0.0% Black, 0.0% Asian, 0.0% American Indian and Alaska Native, 0.8% Hispanic of any race, 0.0% two or more races (2000); Density: 5.3 persons per square mile (2000); Age: 16.4% under 18, 26.8% over 64 (2000); Marriage status: 17.9% never married, 60.6% now married, 12.8% widowed, 8.6% divorced (2000); Foreign born: 1.1% (2000); Ancestry (includes multiple ancestries): 26.2% German, 22.2% Polish, 16.4% Finnish, 10.3% Swedish, 9.8% English (2000).
Economy: Employment by occupation: 14.6% management, 19.6% professional, 15.0% services, 23.3% sales, 0.4% farming, 7.5% construction, 19.6% production (2000).
Income: Per capita income: $16,823 (2000); Median household income: $27,917 (2000); Poverty rate: 13.2% (2000).
Taxes: Total city taxes per capita: $254 (1997); City property taxes per capita: $254 (1997).
Education: High school graduation rate: 90.9% (2000); College graduation rate: 20.0% (2000).
Housing: Homeownership rate: 96.1% (2000); Median home value: $62,100 (2000); Median rent: $250 per month (2000); Median age of housing: 40 years (2000).
Transportation: Commute to work: 92.5% car, 0.0% public transportation, 5.4% walk, 1.3% work from home (2000); Travel time to work: 28.7% less than 15 minutes, 24.9% 15 to 30 minutes, 21.5% 30 to 45 minutes, 12.7% 45 to 60 minutes, 12.2% 60 minutes or more (2000)

MINERAL HILLS (village). Covers a land area of 1.450 square miles and a water area of 0 square miles. Located at 46.11° N. Lat.; 88.64° W. Long.
Population: 214 (2000); Race: 98.2% White, 0.0% Black, 0.0% Asian, 0.0% American Indian and Alaska Native, 0.9% Hispanic of any race, 0.9% two or more races (2000); Density: 147.6 persons per square mile (2000); Age: 30.2% under 18, 9.5% over 64 (2000); Marriage status: 35.1% never married, 43.1% now married, 5.7% widowed, 16.1% divorced (2000); Foreign born: 0.0% (2000); Ancestry (includes multiple ancestries): 12.6% English, 10.8% Italian, 9.9% German, 8.1% Irish, 7.7% French (except Basque) (2000).
Economy: Employment by occupation: 3.7% management, 5.6% professional, 38.3% services, 16.8% sales, 3.7% farming, 15.9% construction, 15.9% production (2000).
Income: Per capita income: $12,486 (2000); Median household income: $30,750 (2000); Poverty rate: 13.6% (2000).
Taxes: Total city taxes per capita: $118 (1997); City property taxes per capita: $118 (1997).
Education: High school graduation rate: 91.0% (2000); College graduation rate: 7.5% (2000).
Housing: Homeownership rate: 73.0% (2000); Median home value: $35,800 (2000); Median rent: $175 per month (2000); Median age of housing: 56 years (2000).
Transportation: Commute to work: 95.2% car, 0.0% public transportation, 0.0% walk, 4.8% work from home (2000); Travel time to work: 51.0% less than 15 minutes, 21.0% 15 to 30 minutes, 13.0% 30 to 45 minutes, 8.0% 45 to 60 minutes, 7.0% 60 minutes or more (2000)

STAMBAUGH (city). Covers a land area of 1.643 square miles and a water area of 0 square miles. Located at 46.08° N. Lat.; 88.63° W. Long. Elevation is 1,539 feet.
History: Stambaugh began in 1878 when prospectors from Quinnesec came looking for iron ore. The village was platted in 1882, and named for John Stambaugh, president of the company that owned the Iron River Mine. Stambaugh was incorporated as a village in 1890 and as a city in 1923.
Population: 1,243 (2000); Race: 96.4% White, 0.0% Black, 0.2% Asian, 2.3% American Indian and Alaska Native, 1.3% Hispanic of any race, 0.6% two or more races (2000); Density: 756.5 persons per square mile (2000); Age: 22.3% under 18, 26.6% over 64 (2000); Marriage status: 22.0% never married, 51.0% now married, 14.4% widowed, 12.6% divorced (2000); Foreign born: 0.9% (2000); Ancestry (includes multiple ancestries): 21.8% German, 14.1% Swedish, 13.2% Finnish, 13.1% English, 11.3% Polish (2000).
Economy: Employment by occupation: 6.2% management, 17.0% professional, 29.5% services, 19.7% sales, 3.3% farming, 9.3% construction, 14.9% production (2000).
Income: Per capita income: $15,890 (2000); Median household income: $23,643 (2000); Poverty rate: 13.5% (2000).
Taxes: Total city taxes per capita: $138 (1997); City property taxes per capita: $138 (1997).
Education: High school graduation rate: 84.3% (2000); College graduation rate: 13.4% (2000).

School District(s)

West Iron County Public Schools (KG-12)
2000 Enrollment: 1,313 906-265-9218

Housing: Homeownership rate: 68.4% (2000); Median home value: $37,700 (2000); Median rent: $268 per month (2000); Median age of housing: 58 years (2000).
Transportation: Commute to work: 92.0% car, 0.0% public transportation, 6.1% walk, 1.5% work from home (2000); Travel time to work: 63.7% less than 15 minutes, 16.0% 15 to 30 minutes, 7.7% 30 to 45 minutes, 3.4% 45 to 60 minutes, 9.2% 60 minutes or more (2000)

STAMBAUGH (township). Covers a land area of 181.781 square miles and a water area of 8.290 square miles. Located at 46.16° N. Lat.; 88.87° W. Long. Elevation is 1,539 feet.
History: Settled c.1878; incorporated as village 1895, as city 1923.
Population: 1,248 (2000); Race: 98.3% White, 0.0% Black, 0.0% Asian, 1.1% American Indian and Alaska Native, 0.2% Hispanic of any race, 0.6% two or more races (2000); Density: 6.9 persons per square mile (2000); Age: 18.0% under 18, 23.2% over 64 (2000); Marriage status: 17.2% never married, 67.3% now married, 5.4% widowed, 10.1% divorced (2000); Foreign born: 1.1% (2000); Ancestry (includes multiple ancestries): 24.6% German, 12.9% Italian, 12.8% Polish, 12.6% Swedish, 11.0% Finnish (2000).
Economy: Employment by occupation: 8.6% management, 18.2% professional, 23.1% services, 22.9% sales, 3.1% farming, 12.8% construction, 11.3% production (2000).
Income: Per capita income: $20,997 (2000); Median household income: $37,656 (2000); Poverty rate: 6.7% (2000).
Taxes: Total city taxes per capita: $125 (1997); City property taxes per capita: $123 (1997).
Education: High school graduation rate: 85.6% (2000); College graduation rate: 20.0% (2000).
Housing: Homeownership rate: 90.7% (2000); Median home value: $84,100 (2000); Median rent: $319 per month (2000); Median age of housing: 30 years (2000).
Transportation: Commute to work: 91.2% car, 0.8% public transportation, 3.5% walk, 3.9% work from home (2000); Travel time to work: 44.1% less than 15 minutes, 39.0% 15 to 30 minutes, 8.4% 30 to 45 minutes, 1.6% 45 to 60 minutes, 6.9% 60 minutes or more (2000)

Isabella County

Located in central Michigan; drained by the Chippewa and Pine Rivers. Covers a land area of 574.30 square miles, a water area of 3.50 square miles, and is located in the Eastern Time Zone. The county government was organized in 1831. County seat is Mount Pleasant.

Weather Station: Mount Pleasant University Elevation: 793 feet

	Jan	Feb	Mar	Apr	May	Jun	Jul	Aug	Sep	Oct	Nov	Dec
High	28	31	41	55	69	78	83	80	71	59	45	33
Low	13	14	22	34	45	54	59	57	49	39	29	20
Precip	1.5	1.1	2.2	3.1	2.7	3.5	2.8	3.7	3.7	3.0	2.8	1.9
Snow	na	4.7	na	1.7	tr	0.0	0.0	0.0	0.0	tr	na	na

High and Low temperatures in degrees Fahrenheit; Precipitation and Snow in inches

Population: 63,351 (2000); Race: 91.6% White, 2.0% Black, 1.3% Asian, 2.8% American Indian and Alaska Native, 2.4% Hispanic of any race, 1.6% two or more races (2000); Density: 110.3 persons per square mile (2000); Age: 20.4% under 18, 9.0% over 64 (2000).
Religion: Five largest groups: 15.2% Catholic Church, 2.9% The United Methodist Church, 1.0% Presbyterian Church (U.S.A.), 0.9% Evangelical Lutheran Church in America, 0.7% Christian Churches and Churches of Christ (2000).
Economy: Unemployment rate: 2.9% (11/2002); Total civilian labor force: 34,407 (11/2002); Leading industries: 17.1% retail trade; 14.5% accommodation & food services; 14.2% health care and social assistance (2000); Companies that employ more than 1,000 persons: 0 (2000); Companies that employ more than 100 persons: 28 (2000); Farms: 911 totaling 216,651 acres (1997); Minority business ownership rate: 4.4% (1997); Women business ownership rate: 24.0% (1997); Retail sales per capita: $7,946 (1997). Single-family building permits issued: 278 (2001) / 299 (2000); Multi-family building permits issued: 234 (2001) / 911 (2000).
Income: Per capita income: $16,242 (2000); Median household income: $34,262 (2000); Poverty rate: 20.4% (2000); Bankruptcy rate: 3.49% (2001).
Taxes: Total county taxes per capita: $99 (2000); County property taxes per capita: $89 (2000).
Education: High school graduation rate: 86.1% (2000); College graduation rate: 23.9% (2000).
Housing: Homeownership rate: 63.3% (2000); Median home value: $91,800 (2000); Median rent: $407 per month (2000); Median age of housing: 26 years (2000).
Health: Birth rate: 102.8 per 10,000 population (1998); Age adjusted death rate: 85.4 per 10,000 population (1999); Age adjusted cancer mortality rate: 198.1 deaths per 100,000 population (1999). Number of physicians: 9.2 per 10,000 population (1999); Number of hospital beds: 11.0 per 10,000 population (1999).
Elections: 2000 Presidential election results: 48.6% Gore, 47.7% Bush, 3.2% Nader, 0.0% Buchanan
Additional Information Contacts
Isabella County Government Offices 989-772-0911
Central Michigan Association of Realtors 989-773-2564
Mt Pleasant Chamber of Commerce 989-772-2396

Isabella County Communities

BEAL CITY (CDP). Covers a land area of 4.009 square miles and a water area of 0 square miles. Located at 43.67° N. Lat.; 84.91° W. Long. Elevation is 865 feet.
History: Beal City was founded by a Mr. Beal who operated a grocery store here in the 1880's.
Population: 345 (2000); Race: 99.5% White, 0.0% Black, 0.0% Asian, 0.5% American Indian and Alaska Native, 0.5% Hispanic of any race, 0.0% two or more races (2000); Density: 86.1 persons per square mile (2000); Age: 33.2% under 18, 16.0% over 64 (2000); Marriage status: 17.4% never married, 68.3% now married, 8.7% widowed, 5.7% divorced (2000); Foreign born: 0.0% (2000); Ancestry (includes multiple ancestries): 60.1% German, 12.2% Irish, 6.3% United States or American, 6.0% French Canadian, 5.4% French (except Basque) (2000).
Economy: Employment by occupation: 10.7% management, 12.1% professional, 15.7% services, 22.1% sales, 2.1% farming, 14.3% construction, 22.9% production (2000).
Income: Per capita income: $16,185 (2000); Median household income: $37,500 (2000); Poverty rate: 10.3% (2000).
Education: High school graduation rate: 91.9% (2000); College graduation rate: 10.3% (2000).
Housing: Homeownership rate: 83.7% (2000); Median home value: $105,900 (2000); Median rent: $429 per month (2000); Median age of housing: 48 years (2000).
Transportation: Commute to work: 93.4% car, 0.0% public transportation, 1.5% walk, 2.9% work from home (2000); Travel time to work: 23.5% less than 15 minutes, 70.5% 15 to 30 minutes, 4.5% 30 to 45 minutes, 1.5% 45 to 60 minutes, 0.0% 60 minutes or more (2000)

BLANCHARD (unincorporated postal area, zip code 49310). Covers a land area of 86.689 square miles and a water area of 0.134 square miles. Located at 43.52° N. Lat.; 85.04° W. Long.
History: Blanchard was founded by Peter G. Blanchard, a lumberman, and named for Herbert P. Blanchard, the first postmaster. It was incorporated as a village in 1879.
Population: 2,757 (2000); Race: 95.0% White, 1.0% Black, 0.2% Asian, 0.1% American Indian and Alaska Native, 1.7% Hispanic of any race, 2.8% two or more races (2000); Density: 31.8 persons per square mile (2000); Age: 26.9% under 18, 11.8% over 64 (2000); Marriage status: 20.5% never married, 64.6% now married, 5.1% widowed, 9.9% divorced (2000); Foreign born: 1.5% (2000); Ancestry (includes multiple ancestries): 27.4% German, 14.5% English, 10.3% Irish, 8.7% Other groups, 7.7% United States or American (2000).
Economy: Employment by occupation: 12.5% management, 13.6% professional, 15.9% services, 21.3% sales, 1.7% farming, 10.4% construction, 24.6% production (2000).
Income: Per capita income: $17,563 (2000); Median household income: $36,636 (2000); Poverty rate: 10.7% (2000).
Education: High school graduation rate: 85.5% (2000); College graduation rate: 11.4% (2000).
Housing: Homeownership rate: 90.8% (2000); Median home value: $72,300 (2000); Median rent: $319 per month (2000); Median age of housing: 30 years (2000).
Transportation: Commute to work: 90.4% car, 0.0% public transportation, 2.1% walk, 6.8% work from home (2000); Travel time to work: 24.6% less than 15 minutes, 35.1% 15 to 30 minutes, 21.7% 30 to 45 minutes, 9.3% 45 to 60 minutes, 9.3% 60 minutes or more (2000)

BROOMFIELD (township). Covers a land area of 34.893 square miles and a water area of 0.812 square miles. Located at 43.61° N. Lat.; 85.01° W. Long.
History: Broomfield Township was organized in 1866 and named for William Broomfield, an early settler.
Population: 1,620 (2000); Race: 95.9% White, 0.3% Black, 0.2% Asian, 0.4% American Indian and Alaska Native, 2.3% Hispanic of any race, 1.1% two or more races (2000); Density: 46.4 persons per square mile (2000); Age: 25.1% under 18, 15.3% over 64 (2000); Marriage status: 23.4% never married, 62.5% now married, 4.5% widowed, 9.6% divorced (2000); Foreign born: 1.3% (2000); Ancestry (includes multiple ancestries): 27.8% German, 12.1% Irish, 11.8% English, 9.6% United States or American, 6.6% Other groups (2000).
Economy: Employment by occupation: 11.9% management, 14.7% professional, 23.0% services, 19.5% sales, 0.6% farming, 9.4% construction, 20.9% production (2000).
Income: Per capita income: $17,227 (2000); Median household income: $36,711 (2000); Poverty rate: 15.1% (2000).
Taxes: Total city taxes per capita: $15 (1997); City property taxes per capita: $14 (1997).
Education: High school graduation rate: 87.5% (2000); College graduation rate: 16.1% (2000).
Housing: Homeownership rate: 86.2% (2000); Median home value: $98,600 (2000); Median rent: $318 per month (2000); Median age of housing: 24 years (2000).
Transportation: Commute to work: 93.0% car, 0.3% public transportation, 0.6% walk, 5.7% work from home (2000); Travel time to work: 17.4% less than 15 minutes, 58.7% 15 to 30 minutes, 14.0% 30 to 45 minutes, 5.3% 45 to 60 minutes, 4.7% 60 minutes or more (2000)

CHIPPEWA (township). Covers a land area of 36.169 square miles and a water area of 0.127 square miles. Located at 43.60° N. Lat.; 84.67° W. Long.
Population: 4,617 (2000); Race: 80.7% White, 0.5% Black, 0.3% Asian, 14.1% American Indian and Alaska Native, 3.5% Hispanic of any race, 3.7% two or more races (2000); Density: 127.6 persons per square mile (2000); Age: 28.8% under 18, 8.7% over 64 (2000); Marriage status: 29.2% never married, 52.5% now married, 4.4% widowed, 13.8% divorced (2000); Foreign born: 1.5% (2000); Ancestry (includes multiple ancestries): 22.1%

Other groups, 20.3% German, 10.9% Irish, 10.3% United States or American, 8.7% English (2000).
Economy: Single-family building permits issued: 0 (2001) / 0 (2000); Multi-family building permits issued: 0 (2001) / 0 (2000); Employment by occupation: 7.8% management, 13.1% professional, 27.6% services, 21.9% sales, 0.1% farming, 12.6% construction, 16.8% production (2000).
Income: Per capita income: $16,312 (2000); Median household income: $35,676 (2000); Poverty rate: 13.9% (2000).
Taxes: Total city taxes per capita: $15 (1997); City property taxes per capita: $11 (1997).
Education: High school graduation rate: 81.3% (2000); College graduation rate: 11.8% (2000).
Housing: Homeownership rate: 74.1% (2000); Median home value: $81,600 (2000); Median rent: $365 per month (2000); Median age of housing: 25 years (2000).
Transportation: Commute to work: 95.9% car, 0.4% public transportation, 0.4% walk, 1.6% work from home (2000); Travel time to work: 43.1% less than 15 minutes, 38.5% 15 to 30 minutes, 11.2% 30 to 45 minutes, 2.0% 45 to 60 minutes, 5.1% 60 minutes or more (2000)

COE (township). Covers a land area of 36.229 square miles and a water area of 0 square miles. Located at 43.51° N. Lat.; 84.67° W. Long.
History: Coe Township was organized in 1855 and named for Lt. Governor George A. Coe.
Population: 2,993 (2000); Race: 96.3% White, 0.3% Black, 0.6% Asian, 0.3% American Indian and Alaska Native, 2.4% Hispanic of any race, 2.0% two or more races (2000); Density: 82.6 persons per square mile (2000); Age: 29.0% under 18, 10.1% over 64 (2000); Marriage status: 25.3% never married, 58.8% now married, 4.9% widowed, 11.0% divorced (2000); Foreign born: 0.8% (2000); Ancestry (includes multiple ancestries): 37.5% German, 15.9% Irish, 13.8% English, 7.7% Other groups, 6.6% United States or American (2000).
Economy: Employment by occupation: 8.9% management, 22.0% professional, 16.2% services, 26.4% sales, 0.3% farming, 9.1% construction, 17.2% production (2000).
Income: Per capita income: $19,435 (2000); Median household income: $45,182 (2000); Poverty rate: 6.4% (2000).
Education: High school graduation rate: 89.8% (2000); College graduation rate: 20.4% (2000).
Housing: Homeownership rate: 81.4% (2000); Median home value: $86,600 (2000); Median rent: $372 per month (2000); Median age of housing: 36 years (2000).
Transportation: Commute to work: 93.8% car, 0.0% public transportation, 2.8% walk, 3.1% work from home (2000); Travel time to work: 36.7% less than 15 minutes, 44.0% 15 to 30 minutes, 7.9% 30 to 45 minutes, 5.5% 45 to 60 minutes, 5.9% 60 minutes or more (2000)

COLDWATER (township). Covers a land area of 35.885 square miles and a water area of 0.078 square miles. Located at 43.75° N. Lat.; 85.02° W. Long.
Population: 737 (2000); Race: 96.6% White, 0.0% Black, 0.0% Asian, 1.3% American Indian and Alaska Native, 0.1% Hispanic of any race, 2.1% two or more races (2000); Density: 20.5 persons per square mile (2000); Age: 25.1% under 18, 15.8% over 64 (2000); Marriage status: 18.4% never married, 64.1% now married, 8.2% widowed, 9.3% divorced (2000); Foreign born: 0.9% (2000); Ancestry (includes multiple ancestries): 25.5% German, 14.5% Irish, 12.8% English, 9.4% United States or American, 8.5% Other groups (2000).
Economy: Employment by occupation: 9.9% management, 10.8% professional, 16.0% services, 22.9% sales, 1.8% farming, 14.8% construction, 23.8% production (2000).
Income: Per capita income: $16,477 (2000); Median household income: $34,853 (2000); Poverty rate: 6.9% (2000).
Taxes: Total city taxes per capita: $21 (1997); City property taxes per capita: $21 (1997).
Education: High school graduation rate: 74.8% (2000); College graduation rate: 10.5% (2000).
Housing: Homeownership rate: 90.8% (2000); Median home value: $70,000 (2000); Median rent: $316 per month (2000); Median age of housing: 25 years (2000).
Transportation: Commute to work: 87.6% car, 0.0% public transportation, 3.3% walk, 9.1% work from home (2000); Travel time to work: 17.7% less than 15 minutes, 29.7% 15 to 30 minutes, 35.0% 30 to 45 minutes, 8.3% 45 to 60 minutes, 9.3% 60 minutes or more (2000)

DEERFIELD (township). Covers a land area of 35.761 square miles and a water area of 0.115 square miles. Located at 43.58° N. Lat.; 84.90° W. Long.
Population: 3,081 (2000); Race: 97.7% White, 0.4% Black, 0.4% Asian, 0.7% American Indian and Alaska Native, 0.8% Hispanic of any race, 0.7% two or more races (2000); Density: 86.2 persons per square mile (2000); Age: 29.5% under 18, 9.3% over 64 (2000); Marriage status: 22.8% never married, 67.4% now married, 3.8% widowed, 6.0% divorced (2000); Foreign born: 1.4% (2000); Ancestry (includes multiple ancestries): 34.7% German, 15.5% English, 14.3% Irish, 6.8% United States or American, 5.5% French (except Basque) (2000).
Economy: Single-family building permits issued: 23 (2001) / 25 (2000); Multi-family building permits issued: 4 (2001) / 0 (2000); Employment by occupation: 15.6% management, 24.7% professional, 15.5% services, 22.0% sales, 0.8% farming, 9.9% construction, 11.5% production (2000).
Income: Per capita income: $25,618 (2000); Median household income: $56,250 (2000); Poverty rate: 4.6% (2000).
Taxes: Total city taxes per capita: $35 (1997); City property taxes per capita: $35 (1997).
Education: High school graduation rate: 90.3% (2000); College graduation rate: 35.3% (2000).
Housing: Homeownership rate: 92.3% (2000); Median home value: $125,900 (2000); Median rent: $394 per month (2000); Median age of housing: 21 years (2000).
Transportation: Commute to work: 97.1% car, 0.1% public transportation, 0.3% walk, 1.9% work from home (2000); Travel time to work: 33.0% less than 15 minutes, 49.3% 15 to 30 minutes, 7.3% 30 to 45 minutes, 5.3% 45 to 60 minutes, 5.1% 60 minutes or more (2000)

DENVER (township). Covers a land area of 36.517 square miles and a water area of 0.016 square miles. Located at 43.68° N. Lat.; 84.67° W. Long.
Population: 1,147 (2000); Race: 92.7% White, 0.1% Black, 0.0% Asian, 4.2% American Indian and Alaska Native, 2.9% Hispanic of any race, 3.0% two or more races (2000); Density: 31.4 persons per square mile (2000); Age: 28.4% under 18, 8.1% over 64 (2000); Marriage status: 25.1% never married, 57.6% now married, 4.9% widowed, 12.4% divorced (2000); Foreign born: 0.3% (2000); Ancestry (includes multiple ancestries): 32.6% German, 11.0% Other groups, 10.6% United States or American, 9.4% English, 8.9% Irish (2000).
Economy: Employment by occupation: 8.8% management, 14.1% professional, 23.8% services, 24.2% sales, 1.2% farming, 13.2% construction, 14.6% production (2000).
Income: Per capita income: $17,480 (2000); Median household income: $41,181 (2000); Poverty rate: 9.6% (2000).
Taxes: Total city taxes per capita: $12 (1997); City property taxes per capita: $12 (1997).
Education: High school graduation rate: 83.0% (2000); College graduation rate: 10.1% (2000).
Housing: Homeownership rate: 88.0% (2000); Median home value: $76,800 (2000); Median rent: $400 per month (2000); Median age of housing: 25 years (2000).
Transportation: Commute to work: 95.1% car, 0.0% public transportation, 1.1% walk, 3.4% work from home (2000); Travel time to work: 24.2% less than 15 minutes, 50.9% 15 to 30 minutes, 16.7% 30 to 45 minutes, 2.2% 45 to 60 minutes, 6.0% 60 minutes or more (2000)

FREMONT (township). Covers a land area of 35.833 square miles and a water area of 0.036 square miles. Located at 43.51° N. Lat.; 84.90° W. Long.
Population: 1,358 (2000); Race: 98.2% White, 0.0% Black, 0.0% Asian, 0.0% American Indian and Alaska Native, 2.5% Hispanic of any race, 0.7% two or more races (2000); Density: 37.9 persons per square mile (2000); Age: 30.2% under 18, 8.9% over 64 (2000); Marriage status: 23.3% never married, 64.3% now married, 4.5% widowed, 7.9% divorced (2000); Foreign born: 0.1% (2000); Ancestry (includes multiple ancestries): 31.2% German, 12.5% Irish, 11.9% English, 7.9% Other groups, 7.0% Dutch (2000).
Economy: Single-family building permits issued: 16 (2001) / 12 (2000); Multi-family building permits issued: 0 (2001) / 0 (2000); Employment by occupation: 10.2% management, 12.5% professional, 19.2% services, 25.6% sales, 2.0% farming, 10.1% construction, 20.3% production (2000).
Income: Per capita income: $16,644 (2000); Median household income: $40,577 (2000); Poverty rate: 7.0% (2000).
Taxes: Total city taxes per capita: $30 (1997); City property taxes per capita: $30 (1997).
Education: High school graduation rate: 87.1% (2000); College graduation rate: 12.0% (2000).

Housing: Homeownership rate: 90.8% (2000); Median home value: $76,700 (2000); Median rent: $367 per month (2000); Median age of housing: 28 years (2000).
Transportation: Commute to work: 93.2% car, 0.3% public transportation, 0.9% walk, 5.0% work from home (2000); Travel time to work: 18.9% less than 15 minutes, 54.2% 15 to 30 minutes, 18.8% 30 to 45 minutes, 2.3% 45 to 60 minutes, 5.9% 60 minutes or more (2000)

GILMORE (township). Covers a land area of 35.738 square miles and a water area of 0.339 square miles. Located at 43.76° N. Lat.; 84.91° W. Long.
History: Gilmore Township was organized in 1870 and named for General Gilmore.
Population: 1,376 (2000); Race: 96.5% White, 0.0% Black, 0.4% Asian, 2.1% American Indian and Alaska Native, 3.6% Hispanic of any race, 0.5% two or more races (2000); Density: 38.5 persons per square mile (2000); Age: 23.1% under 18, 14.0% over 64 (2000); Marriage status: 18.8% never married, 68.0% now married, 4.2% widowed, 8.9% divorced (2000); Foreign born: 0.8% (2000); Ancestry (includes multiple ancestries): 24.6% German, 15.5% English, 12.5% Irish, 9.1% Other groups, 7.3% United States or American (2000).
Economy: Employment by occupation: 8.7% management, 15.2% professional, 17.3% services, 25.3% sales, 1.0% farming, 13.9% construction, 18.6% production (2000).
Income: Per capita income: $16,277 (2000); Median household income: $37,000 (2000); Poverty rate: 9.9% (2000).
Taxes: Total city taxes per capita: $24 (1997); City property taxes per capita: $24 (1997).
Education: High school graduation rate: 81.4% (2000); College graduation rate: 8.9% (2000).
Housing: Homeownership rate: 92.0% (2000); Median home value: $82,300 (2000); Median rent: $288 per month (2000); Median age of housing: 25 years (2000).
Transportation: Commute to work: 93.2% car, 0.0% public transportation, 1.7% walk, 4.8% work from home (2000); Travel time to work: 26.7% less than 15 minutes, 37.2% 15 to 30 minutes, 22.1% 30 to 45 minutes, 7.9% 45 to 60 minutes, 6.1% 60 minutes or more (2000)

ISABELLA (township). Covers a land area of 36.355 square miles and a water area of 0.021 square miles. Located at 43.68° N. Lat.; 84.77° W. Long.
Population: 2,145 (2000); Race: 95.3% White, 0.1% Black, 0.3% Asian, 3.2% American Indian and Alaska Native, 1.3% Hispanic of any race, 0.8% two or more races (2000); Density: 59.0 persons per square mile (2000); Age: 28.4% under 18, 10.8% over 64 (2000); Marriage status: 25.1% never married, 60.8% now married, 5.0% widowed, 9.1% divorced (2000); Foreign born: 0.9% (2000); Ancestry (includes multiple ancestries): 30.1% German, 15.9% Irish, 10.9% English, 9.4% United States or American, 7.7% Other groups (2000).
Economy: Employment by occupation: 10.6% management, 15.7% professional, 16.2% services, 27.0% sales, 1.9% farming, 13.4% construction, 15.2% production (2000).
Income: Per capita income: $16,995 (2000); Median household income: $36,573 (2000); Poverty rate: 9.6% (2000).
Taxes: Total city taxes per capita: $13 (1997); City property taxes per capita: $12 (1997).
Education: High school graduation rate: 85.5% (2000); College graduation rate: 11.5% (2000).
Housing: Homeownership rate: 87.9% (2000); Median home value: $85,300 (2000); Median rent: $338 per month (2000); Median age of housing: 29 years (2000).
Transportation: Commute to work: 90.3% car, 0.3% public transportation, 2.2% walk, 6.4% work from home (2000); Travel time to work: 44.6% less than 15 minutes, 40.4% 15 to 30 minutes, 6.4% 30 to 45 minutes, 3.7% 45 to 60 minutes, 4.9% 60 minutes or more (2000)

LINCOLN (township). Covers a land area of 36.126 square miles and a water area of 0.067 square miles. Located at 43.51° N. Lat.; 84.78° W. Long.
Population: 1,936 (2000); Race: 96.3% White, 0.5% Black, 0.1% Asian, 0.5% American Indian and Alaska Native, 3.0% Hispanic of any race, 1.3% two or more races (2000); Density: 53.6 persons per square mile (2000); Age: 27.1% under 18, 10.5% over 64 (2000); Marriage status: 25.0% never married, 61.6% now married, 5.0% widowed, 8.5% divorced (2000); Foreign born: 0.7% (2000); Ancestry (includes multiple ancestries): 31.9% German, 15.4% English, 11.6% Irish, 8.4% Other groups, 5.8% United States or American (2000).
Economy: Employment by occupation: 12.0% management, 14.0% professional, 18.5% services, 25.1% sales, 1.7% farming, 9.8% construction, 19.0% production (2000).
Income: Per capita income: $18,734 (2000); Median household income: $44,871 (2000); Poverty rate: 7.0% (2000).
Taxes: Total city taxes per capita: $19 (1997); City property taxes per capita: $19 (1997).
Education: High school graduation rate: 87.3% (2000); College graduation rate: 16.9% (2000).
Housing: Homeownership rate: 85.0% (2000); Median home value: $96,300 (2000); Median rent: $386 per month (2000); Median age of housing: 25 years (2000).
Transportation: Commute to work: 93.5% car, 0.0% public transportation, 1.1% walk, 5.1% work from home (2000); Travel time to work: 35.1% less than 15 minutes, 49.8% 15 to 30 minutes, 7.0% 30 to 45 minutes, 3.8% 45 to 60 minutes, 4.3% 60 minutes or more (2000)

MOUNT PLEASANT (city). Covers a land area of 7.798 square miles and a water area of 0 square miles. Located at 43.60° N. Lat.; 84.77° W. Long. Elevation is 761 feet.
History: Mount Pleasant, which began as a trading post, developed as a residential and college city. The Central State Teachers College was founded here in 1895.
Population: 25,946 (2000); Race: 89.2% White, 3.7% Black, 2.5% Asian, 1.9% American Indian and Alaska Native, 2.6% Hispanic of any race, 1.7% two or more races (2000); Density: 3,327.2 persons per square mile (2000); Age: 11.6% under 18, 7.3% over 64 (2000); Marriage status: 62.7% never married, 28.8% now married, 3.4% widowed, 5.1% divorced (2000); Foreign born: 4.0% (2000); Ancestry (includes multiple ancestries): 25.9% German, 12.7% Other groups, 12.3% Irish, 10.5% English, 8.8% Polish (2000).
Vital Statistics: Birth rate: 82.9 per 10,000 population (1998)
Economy: Single-family building permits issued: 28 (2001) / 35 (2000); Multi-family building permits issued: 206 (2001) / 289 (2000); Employment by occupation: 8.0% management, 21.2% professional, 28.5% services, 32.2% sales, 0.3% farming, 3.6% construction, 6.1% production (2000).
Income: Per capita income: $13,177 (2000); Median household income: $24,572 (2000); Poverty rate: 37.2% (2000).
Taxes: Total city taxes per capita: $180 (1997); City property taxes per capita: $170 (1997).
Education: High school graduation rate: 88.2% (2000); College graduation rate: 40.3% (2000).

School District(s)

Beal City Public Schools (PK-12)
2000 Enrollment: 624 517-644-3901
Mount Pleasant City School District (PK-12)
2000 Enrollment: 4,350 517-775-2301
Renaissance Public School Academ (PK-06)
2000 Enrollment: 92 517-774-2100

Four-year College(s)

Central Michigan University (Public)
2001 Enrollment: 27,797 517-774-4000
2001 Tuition: In-state $3,567; Out-of-state $9,258

Housing: Homeownership rate: 34.5% (2000); Median home value: $95,500 (2000); Median rent: $409 per month (2000); Median age of housing: 29 years (2000).
Hospitals: Central Michigan Community Hospital (151 beds)
Safety: Violent crime rate: 13.8 per 10,000 population; Property crime rate: 162.2 per 10,000 population (2001).
Newspapers: Morning Sun (6 x week)
Transportation: Commute to work: 79.1% car, 0.7% public transportation, 15.5% walk, 2.7% work from home (2000); Travel time to work: 75.7% less than 15 minutes, 13.8% 15 to 30 minutes, 4.9% 30 to 45 minutes, 1.6% 45 to 60 minutes, 4.0% 60 minutes or more (2000)
Airports: Mount Pleasant Municipal
Additional Information Contacts
Central Michigan Association of Realtors 989-773-2564
Mt Pleasant Chamber of Commerce 989-772-2396

NOTTAWA (township). Covers a land area of 35.348 square miles and a water area of 0.605 square miles. Located at 43.67° N. Lat.; 84.93° W. Long.
Population: 2,278 (2000); Race: 97.3% White, 0.0% Black, 0.7% Asian, 2.0% American Indian and Alaska Native, 0.8% Hispanic of any race, 0.1% two or more races (2000); Density: 64.4 persons per square mile (2000); Age: 28.6% under 18, 11.3% over 64 (2000); Marriage status: 22.2% never married, 64.7% now married, 5.2% widowed, 7.9% divorced (2000); Foreign born: 1.2% (2000); Ancestry (includes multiple ancestries): 47.3% German,

12.5% Irish, 8.0% United States or American, 7.9% English, 7.0% Other groups (2000).
Economy: Single-family building permits issued: 17 (2001) / 15 (2000); Multi-family building permits issued: 0 (2001) / 0 (2000); Employment by occupation: 12.1% management, 12.2% professional, 15.9% services, 26.4% sales, 1.3% farming, 11.5% construction, 20.7% production (2000).
Income: Per capita income: $18,340 (2000); Median household income: $40,766 (2000); Poverty rate: 6.5% (2000).
Taxes: Total city taxes per capita: $15 (1997); City property taxes per capita: $15 (1997).
Education: High school graduation rate: 85.5% (2000); College graduation rate: 11.9% (2000).
Housing: Homeownership rate: 89.3% (2000); Median home value: $95,000 (2000); Median rent: $432 per month (2000); Median age of housing: 28 years (2000).
Transportation: Commute to work: 90.7% car, 0.3% public transportation, 1.7% walk, 5.9% work from home (2000); Travel time to work: 19.7% less than 15 minutes, 55.0% 15 to 30 minutes, 12.9% 30 to 45 minutes, 4.6% 45 to 60 minutes, 7.9% 60 minutes or more (2000)

ROLLAND (township). Covers a land area of 35.711 square miles and a water area of 0.071 square miles. Located at 43.51° N. Lat.; 85.04° W. Long.
Population: 1,210 (2000); Race: 94.0% White, 2.2% Black, 0.2% Asian, 0.0% American Indian and Alaska Native, 1.5% Hispanic of any race, 3.1% two or more races (2000); Density: 33.9 persons per square mile (2000); Age: 25.4% under 18, 11.0% over 64 (2000); Marriage status: 21.0% never married, 64.3% now married, 3.5% widowed, 11.3% divorced (2000); Foreign born: 0.9% (2000); Ancestry (includes multiple ancestries): 27.1% German, 14.3% English, 11.1% Irish, 9.4% Other groups, 5.4% United States or American (2000).
Economy: Single-family building permits issued: 17 (2001) / 8 (2000); Multi-family building permits issued: 0 (2001) / 0 (2000); Employment by occupation: 13.9% management, 15.0% professional, 13.6% services, 19.9% sales, 1.9% farming, 10.0% construction, 25.7% production (2000).
Income: Per capita income: $18,145 (2000); Median household income: $36,643 (2000); Poverty rate: 11.6% (2000).
Taxes: Total city taxes per capita: $27 (1997); City property taxes per capita: $27 (1997).
Education: High school graduation rate: 86.3% (2000); College graduation rate: 14.6% (2000).
Housing: Homeownership rate: 89.0% (2000); Median home value: $65,900 (2000); Median rent: $321 per month (2000); Median age of housing: 32 years (2000).
Transportation: Commute to work: 93.1% car, 0.0% public transportation, 2.3% walk, 4.3% work from home (2000); Travel time to work: 26.9% less than 15 minutes, 33.5% 15 to 30 minutes, 19.3% 30 to 45 minutes, 9.4% 45 to 60 minutes, 10.9% 60 minutes or more (2000)

ROSEBUSH (village). Covers a land area of 0.866 square miles and a water area of 0 square miles. Located at 43.69° N. Lat.; 84.76° W. Long. Elevation is 775 feet.
History: Rosebush was settled in the 1840's. In 1868, James L. Bush platted the village, donating land to the Ann Arbor Railroad for a station. He named the village for his wife, Rose Bush.
Population: 379 (2000); Race: 95.9% White, 0.0% Black, 0.0% Asian, 3.0% American Indian and Alaska Native, 6.1% Hispanic of any race, 0.0% two or more races (2000); Density: 437.6 persons per square mile (2000); Age: 29.2% under 18, 10.2% over 64 (2000); Marriage status: 30.3% never married, 52.0% now married, 4.4% widowed, 13.3% divorced (2000); Foreign born: 0.6% (2000); Ancestry (includes multiple ancestries): 26.7% German, 15.7% United States or American, 14.0% English, 10.5% Irish, 9.4% Other groups (2000).
Economy: Employment by occupation: 10.9% management, 12.1% professional, 17.0% services, 27.9% sales, 0.0% farming, 11.5% construction, 20.6% production (2000).
Income: Per capita income: $14,041 (2000); Median household income: $31,111 (2000); Poverty rate: 20.4% (2000).
Taxes: Total city taxes per capita: $123 (1997); City property taxes per capita: $123 (1997).
Education: High school graduation rate: 87.7% (2000); College graduation rate: 13.3% (2000).
Housing: Homeownership rate: 68.1% (2000); Median home value: $64,200 (2000); Median rent: $275 per month (2000); Median age of housing: 48 years (2000).
Transportation: Commute to work: 88.1% car, 0.0% public transportation, 5.0% walk, 6.9% work from home (2000); Travel time to work: 57.7% less than 15 minutes, 27.5% 15 to 30 minutes, 8.1% 30 to 45 minutes, 3.4% 45 to 60 minutes, 3.4% 60 minutes or more (2000)

SHEPHERD (village). Covers a land area of 0.968 square miles and a water area of 0 square miles. Located at 43.52° N. Lat.; 84.69° W. Long. Elevation is 771 feet.
History: Shepherd was founded by lumberman Isaac N. Shepherd.
Population: 1,536 (2000); Race: 95.9% White, 0.0% Black, 0.5% Asian, 0.7% American Indian and Alaska Native, 4.1% Hispanic of any race, 2.3% two or more races (2000); Density: 1,586.7 persons per square mile (2000); Age: 28.0% under 18, 11.1% over 64 (2000); Marriage status: 26.7% never married, 54.9% now married, 5.5% widowed, 12.9% divorced (2000); Foreign born: 0.9% (2000); Ancestry (includes multiple ancestries): 33.9% German, 18.3% Irish, 12.8% English, 9.2% Other groups, 5.6% Polish (2000).
Economy: Employment by occupation: 7.7% management, 23.4% professional, 16.0% services, 30.1% sales, 0.2% farming, 8.0% construction, 14.7% production (2000).
Income: Per capita income: $17,689 (2000); Median household income: $40,804 (2000); Poverty rate: 10.5% (2000).
Taxes: Total city taxes per capita: $136 (1997); City property taxes per capita: $136 (1997).
Education: High school graduation rate: 90.1% (2000); College graduation rate: 26.0% (2000).

School District(s)

Morey Charter School (KG-10)
2000 Enrollment: 388 517-774-2100
Shepherd Public School District (KG-12)
2000 Enrollment: 1,742 517-828-5520

Housing: Homeownership rate: 71.5% (2000); Median home value: $81,000 (2000); Median rent: $371 per month (2000); Median age of housing: 43 years (2000).
Safety: Violent crime rate: 6.5 per 10,000 population; Property crime rate: 226.7 per 10,000 population (2001).
Newspapers: The Shepherd Argus (1 x week); Sanford Express (1 x week); Freeland Globe (1 x week); Auburn Record (1 x month)
Transportation: Commute to work: 93.3% car, 0.0% public transportation, 4.2% walk, 2.3% work from home (2000); Travel time to work: 41.1% less than 15 minutes, 44.3% 15 to 30 minutes, 5.0% 30 to 45 minutes, 4.1% 45 to 60 minutes, 5.4% 60 minutes or more (2000)

SHERMAN (township). Covers a land area of 34.805 square miles and a water area of 0.790 square miles. Located at 43.67° N. Lat.; 85.02° W. Long.
Population: 2,616 (2000); Race: 95.7% White, 0.3% Black, 0.0% Asian, 1.2% American Indian and Alaska Native, 1.6% Hispanic of any race, 1.8% two or more races (2000); Density: 75.2 persons per square mile (2000); Age: 24.8% under 18, 13.2% over 64 (2000); Marriage status: 20.9% never married, 65.1% now married, 5.4% widowed, 8.6% divorced (2000); Foreign born: 0.8% (2000); Ancestry (includes multiple ancestries): 28.8% German, 14.2% English, 12.2% Irish, 9.4% United States or American, 7.7% Polish (2000).
Economy: Single-family building permits issued: 6 (2001) / 12 (2000); Multi-family building permits issued: 2 (2001) / 4 (2000); Employment by occupation: 10.3% management, 11.6% professional, 23.1% services, 21.9% sales, 1.4% farming, 11.7% construction, 20.0% production (2000).
Income: Per capita income: $18,296 (2000); Median household income: $36,371 (2000); Poverty rate: 10.7% (2000).
Taxes: Total city taxes per capita: $34 (1997); City property taxes per capita: $33 (1997).
Education: High school graduation rate: 78.3% (2000); College graduation rate: 12.1% (2000).
Housing: Homeownership rate: 90.6% (2000); Median home value: $94,000 (2000); Median rent: $323 per month (2000); Median age of housing: 22 years (2000).
Transportation: Commute to work: 92.1% car, 0.7% public transportation, 1.5% walk, 5.0% work from home (2000); Travel time to work: 18.9% less than 15 minutes, 38.8% 15 to 30 minutes, 28.6% 30 to 45 minutes, 8.1% 45 to 60 minutes, 5.7% 60 minutes or more (2000)

UNION CHARTER (township). Covers a land area of 28.479 square miles and a water area of 0.116 square miles. Located at 43.59° N. Lat.; 84.76° W. Long.
Population: 7,615 (2000); Race: 91.3% White, 2.7% Black, 0.8% Asian, 3.4% American Indian and Alaska Native, 2.4% Hispanic of any race, 1.0% two or more races (2000); Density: 267.4 persons per square mile (2000); Age: 21.9% under 18, 7.4% over 64 (2000); Marriage status: 45.4% never

married, 42.9% now married, 3.1% widowed, 8.5% divorced (2000); Foreign born: 1.4% (2000); Ancestry (includes multiple ancestries): 26.8% German, 13.1% Irish, 12.0% English, 11.1% Other groups, 5.3% Polish (2000).
Economy: Employment by occupation: 11.0% management, 20.7% professional, 24.5% services, 26.8% sales, 0.4% farming, 7.8% construction, 8.7% production (2000).
Income: Per capita income: $18,248 (2000); Median household income: $35,448 (2000); Poverty rate: 19.2% (2000).
Taxes: Total city taxes per capita: $176 (2000); City property taxes per capita: $162 (2000).
Education: High school graduation rate: 88.3% (2000); College graduation rate: 27.1% (2000).
Housing: Homeownership rate: 61.0% (2000); Median home value: $101,800 (2000); Median rent: $572 per month (2000); Median age of housing: 17 years (2000).
Transportation: Commute to work: 95.1% car, 0.6% public transportation, 1.3% walk, 1.9% work from home (2000); Travel time to work: 66.0% less than 15 minutes, 21.3% 15 to 30 minutes, 7.3% 30 to 45 minutes, 2.4% 45 to 60 minutes, 3.1% 60 minutes or more (2000)

VERNON (township). Covers a land area of 35.439 square miles and a water area of 0.249 square miles. Located at 43.76° N. Lat.; 84.78° W. Long.
Population: 1,342 (2000); Race: 95.4% White, 0.7% Black, 0.4% Asian, 1.3% American Indian and Alaska Native, 2.9% Hispanic of any race, 1.7% two or more races (2000); Density: 37.9 persons per square mile (2000); Age: 26.3% under 18, 11.7% over 64 (2000); Marriage status: 19.5% never married, 67.4% now married, 5.4% widowed, 7.7% divorced (2000); Foreign born: 2.5% (2000); Ancestry (includes multiple ancestries): 26.5% German, 17.5% English, 13.0% Irish, 10.6% United States or American, 7.0% Other groups (2000).
Economy: Employment by occupation: 11.2% management, 18.4% professional, 15.4% services, 24.6% sales, 2.1% farming, 10.7% construction, 17.6% production (2000).
Income: Per capita income: $18,291 (2000); Median household income: $43,594 (2000); Poverty rate: 8.0% (2000).
Taxes: Total city taxes per capita: $49 (1997); City property taxes per capita: $49 (1997).
Education: High school graduation rate: 85.0% (2000); College graduation rate: 17.5% (2000).
Housing: Homeownership rate: 90.5% (2000); Median home value: $78,800 (2000); Median rent: $353 per month (2000); Median age of housing: 30 years (2000).
Transportation: Commute to work: 93.3% car, 0.3% public transportation, 1.9% walk, 4.6% work from home (2000); Travel time to work: 30.3% less than 15 minutes, 43.2% 15 to 30 minutes, 13.8% 30 to 45 minutes, 6.8% 45 to 60 minutes, 5.9% 60 minutes or more (2000)

VILLAGE OF LAKE ISABELLA (village). Covers a land area of 3.492 square miles and a water area of 1.107 square miles. Located at 43.64° N. Lat.; 85.00° W. Long.
Population: 1,243 (2000); Race: 94.5% White, 0.0% Black, 0.0% Asian, 2.4% American Indian and Alaska Native, 1.5% Hispanic of any race, 2.2% two or more races (2000); Density: 356.0 persons per square mile (2000); Age: 20.1% under 18, 14.5% over 64 (2000); Marriage status: 18.9% never married, 66.6% now married, 5.9% widowed, 8.5% divorced (2000); Foreign born: 0.4% (2000); Ancestry (includes multiple ancestries): 34.1% German, 16.4% English, 14.9% Irish, 9.8% United States or American, 6.6% Other groups (2000).
Economy: Employment by occupation: 13.1% management, 13.6% professional, 22.1% services, 26.7% sales, 0.9% farming, 10.8% construction, 12.7% production (2000).
Income: Per capita income: $23,324 (2000); Median household income: $40,833 (2000); Poverty rate: 11.3% (2000).
Education: High school graduation rate: 87.0% (2000); College graduation rate: 18.7% (2000).
Housing: Homeownership rate: 92.5% (2000); Median home value: $114,400 (2000); Median rent: $335 per month (2000); Median age of housing: 19 years (2000).
Transportation: Commute to work: 95.3% car, 0.0% public transportation, 0.4% walk, 3.8% work from home (2000); Travel time to work: 15.6% less than 15 minutes, 53.6% 15 to 30 minutes, 19.5% 30 to 45 minutes, 6.2% 45 to 60 minutes, 5.1% 60 minutes or more (2000)

WEIDMAN (CDP). Covers a land area of 5.515 square miles and a water area of 0.284 square miles. Located at 43.69° N. Lat.; 84.96° W. Long. Elevation is 892 feet.
Population: 879 (2000); Race: 95.3% White, 0.5% Black, 0.9% Asian, 2.4% American Indian and Alaska Native, 2.5% Hispanic of any race, 0.2% two or more races (2000); Density: 159.4 persons per square mile (2000); Age: 25.5% under 18, 14.4% over 64 (2000); Marriage status: 24.8% never married, 58.8% now married, 6.8% widowed, 9.6% divorced (2000); Foreign born: 2.6% (2000); Ancestry (includes multiple ancestries): 25.6% German, 15.0% United States or American, 12.4% English, 12.3% Irish, 9.1% Other groups (2000).
Economy: In agricultural area; manufacturing of refrigerators and freezers; sawmill. Employment by occupation: 11.8% management, 14.5% professional, 18.9% services, 24.3% sales, 1.5% farming, 8.6% construction, 20.6% production (2000).
Income: Per capita income: $15,968 (2000); Median household income: $36,042 (2000); Poverty rate: 9.9% (2000).
Education: High school graduation rate: 73.9% (2000); College graduation rate: 10.5% (2000).
Housing: Homeownership rate: 88.7% (2000); Median home value: $80,000 (2000); Median rent: $334 per month (2000); Median age of housing: 26 years (2000).
Transportation: Commute to work: 90.7% car, 2.2% public transportation, 0.5% walk, 4.9% work from home (2000); Travel time to work: 24.6% less than 15 minutes, 38.4% 15 to 30 minutes, 22.3% 30 to 45 minutes, 9.7% 45 to 60 minutes, 4.9% 60 minutes or more (2000)

WISE (township). Covers a land area of 36.628 square miles and a water area of 0.037 square miles. Located at 43.76° N. Lat.; 84.67° W. Long. Elevation is 751 feet.
Population: 1,301 (2000); Race: 95.1% White, 0.0% Black, 0.2% Asian, 4.1% American Indian and Alaska Native, 1.2% Hispanic of any race, 0.0% two or more races (2000); Density: 35.5 persons per square mile (2000); Age: 29.7% under 18, 11.7% over 64 (2000); Marriage status: 22.6% never married, 62.5% now married, 5.1% widowed, 9.8% divorced (2000); Foreign born: 0.8% (2000); Ancestry (includes multiple ancestries): 28.3% German, 12.1% Irish, 10.2% English, 9.9% Other groups, 9.4% French (except Basque) (2000).
Economy: Single-family building permits issued: 14 (2001) / 14 (2000); Multi-family building permits issued: 0 (2001) / 0 (2000); Employment by occupation: 11.1% management, 10.5% professional, 12.0% services, 29.1% sales, 1.2% farming, 17.1% construction, 19.1% production (2000).
Income: Per capita income: $16,346 (2000); Median household income: $41,333 (2000); Poverty rate: 7.8% (2000).
Taxes: Total city taxes per capita: $39 (1997); City property taxes per capita: $39 (1997).
Education: High school graduation rate: 81.3% (2000); College graduation rate: 7.2% (2000).
Housing: Homeownership rate: 86.9% (2000); Median home value: $73,800 (2000); Median rent: $378 per month (2000); Median age of housing: 30 years (2000).
Transportation: Commute to work: 92.4% car, 0.0% public transportation, 2.5% walk, 4.6% work from home (2000); Travel time to work: 30.6% less than 15 minutes, 37.2% 15 to 30 minutes, 20.6% 30 to 45 minutes, 3.7% 45 to 60 minutes, 7.8% 60 minutes or more (2000)

Jackson County

Located in southern Michigan; drained by the Grand and Raisin Rivers; includes many small lakes. Covers a land area of 706.60 square miles, a water area of 17.20 square miles, and is located in the Eastern Time Zone. The county government was organized in 1832. County seat is Jackson.

Jackson County is part of the Jackson, MI MSA. The entire metro area includes: Jackson County

Weather Station: Jackson Reynolds Field — Elevation: 997 feet

	Jan	Feb	Mar	Apr	May	Jun	Jul	Aug	Sep	Oct	Nov	Dec
High	29	33	44	57	70	79	83	80	73	60	47	35
Low	15	17	26	37	47	56	61	59	52	40	32	22
Precip	1.4	1.2	2.1	2.7	2.8	3.2	3.4	3.4	3.5	2.3	2.6	2.1
Snow	12.5	7.2	6.3	1.5	tr	tr	0.0	0.0	0.0	0.2	2.1	9.3

High and Low temperatures in degrees Fahrenheit; Precipitation and Snow in inches

Population: 158,422 (2000); Race: 88.5% White, 7.6% Black, 0.5% Asian, 0.4% American Indian and Alaska Native, 2.4% Hispanic of any race, 1.9% two or more races (2000); Density: 224.2 persons per square mile (2000); Age: 25.6% under 18, 12.9% over 64 (2000).

Religion: Five largest groups: 16.0% Catholic Church, 2.5% The Wesleyan Church, 2.3% The United Methodist Church, 1.5% Lutheran Church—Missouri Synod, 1.3% Southern Baptist Convention (2000).
Economy: Unemployment rate: 5.7% (11/2002); Total civilian labor force: 81,650 (11/2002); Leading industries: 22.6% manufacturing; 15.5% retail trade; 14.3% health care and social assistance (2000); Companies that employ more than 1,000 persons: 1 (2000); Companies that employ more than 100 persons: 90 (2000); Farms: 987 totaling 181,287 acres (1997); Minority business ownership rate: 4.3% (1997); Women business ownership rate: 25.6% (1997); Retail sales per capita: $8,292 (1997). Single-family building permits issued: 727 (2001) / 688 (2000); Multi-family building permits issued: 218 (2001) / 231 (2000).
Income: Per capita income: $20,171 (2000); Median household income: $43,171 (2000); Poverty rate: 9.0% (2000); Bankruptcy rate: 5.58% (2001).
Taxes: Total county taxes per capita: $97 (2000); County property taxes per capita: $91 (2000).
Education: High school graduation rate: 84.2% (2000); College graduation rate: 16.3% (2000).
Housing: Homeownership rate: 76.5% (2000); Median home value: $96,900 (2000); Median rent: $441 per month (2000); Median age of housing: 39 years (2000).
Health: Birth rate: 129.7 per 10,000 population (1998); Age adjusted death rate: 89.4 per 10,000 population (1999); Age adjusted cancer mortality rate: 207.4 deaths per 100,000 population (1999). Number of physicians: 11.2 per 10,000 population (1999); Number of hospital beds: 35.7 per 10,000 population (1999).
Elections: 2000 Presidential election results: 45.5% Gore, 51.8% Bush, 2.2% Nader, 0.1% Buchanan
National and State Parks: Onsted State Wildlife Management; Waterloo State Recreation Area
Additional Information Contacts
Jackson County Government Offices 517-788-4336
Brooklyn Chamber of Commerce 517-592-8907
Concord Economic Development 517-563-3337
Jackson Area Association of Realtors 517-787-6175
Jackson Chamber of Commerce 517-782-8221
Jackson Convention & Tourist Bureau 517-764-4440
Napoleon Chamber of Commerce 517-536-0547
Napoleon Chamber of Commerce 517-536-0547

Jackson County Communities

BLACKMAN (township). Covers a land area of 31.819 square miles and a water area of 0 square miles. Located at 42.27° N. Lat.; 84.42° W. Long.
History: Blackman Township was organized in 1857 and named for Horace Blackman who had settled here in 1829.
Population: 22,800 (2000); Race: 79.2% White, 17.1% Black, 0.6% Asian, 0.7% American Indian and Alaska Native, 2.1% Hispanic of any race, 1.1% two or more races (2000); Density: 716.6 persons per square mile (2000); Age: 16.8% under 18, 13.3% over 64 (2000); Marriage status: 15.7% never married, 67.0% now married, 8.7% widowed, 8.7% divorced (2000); Foreign born: 1.9% (2000); Ancestry (includes multiple ancestries): 17.0% German, 10.8% English, 9.1% Irish, 6.7% Other groups, 6.1% United States or American (2000).
Economy: Single-family building permits issued: 67 (2001) / 130 (2000); Multi-family building permits issued: 171 (2001) / 149 (2000); Employment by occupation: 8.6% management, 17.7% professional, 18.6% services, 25.4% sales, 0.2% farming, 10.4% construction, 19.1% production (2000).
Income: Per capita income: $18,708 (2000); Median household income: $40,286 (2000); Poverty rate: 6.6% (2000).
Taxes: Total city taxes per capita: $59 (1997); City property taxes per capita: $52 (1997).
Education: High school graduation rate: 84.1% (2000); College graduation rate: 12.9% (2000).
Housing: Homeownership rate: 67.3% (2000); Median home value: $93,900 (2000); Median rent: $474 per month (2000); Median age of housing: 29 years (2000).
Safety: Violent crime rate: 25.7 per 10,000 population; Property crime rate: 259.2 per 10,000 population (2001).
Transportation: Commute to work: 94.7% car, 0.4% public transportation, 1.3% walk, 3.0% work from home (2000); Travel time to work: 47.7% less than 15 minutes, 33.5% 15 to 30 minutes, 9.1% 30 to 45 minutes, 5.4% 45 to 60 minutes, 4.3% 60 minutes or more (2000)

BROOKLYN (village). Covers a land area of 1.004 square miles and a water area of 0.012 square miles. Located at 42.10° N. Lat.; 84.24° W. Long. Elevation is 992 feet.
History: Brooklyn was first called Swainesville for early settler Calvin H. Swaine, who built a sawmill in 1833. The name was changed in 1836 after Brooklyn, New York.
Population: 1,176 (2000); Race: 96.2% White, 0.0% Black, 0.2% Asian, 0.4% American Indian and Alaska Native, 1.8% Hispanic of any race, 1.5% two or more races (2000); Density: 1,171.1 persons per square mile (2000); Age: 21.6% under 18, 21.0% over 64 (2000); Marriage status: 22.2% never married, 48.2% now married, 13.2% widowed, 16.4% divorced (2000); Foreign born: 3.1% (2000); Ancestry (includes multiple ancestries): 27.3% German, 13.0% Irish, 12.6% English, 7.8% United States or American, 6.6% Other groups (2000).
Economy: Single-family building permits issued: 11 (2001) / 9 (2000); Multi-family building permits issued: 0 (2001) / 0 (2000); Employment by occupation: 11.0% management, 13.0% professional, 22.1% services, 20.1% sales, 0.8% farming, 5.8% construction, 27.3% production (2000).
Income: Per capita income: $18,933 (2000); Median household income: $31,964 (2000); Poverty rate: 12.1% (2000).
Taxes: Total city taxes per capita: $311 (1997); City property taxes per capita: $300 (1997).
Education: High school graduation rate: 83.0% (2000); College graduation rate: 15.0% (2000).

School District(s)
Columbia School District (KG-12)
2000 Enrollment: 1,886 517-592-6641
Housing: Homeownership rate: 58.3% (2000); Median home value: $93,800 (2000); Median rent: $415 per month (2000); Median age of housing: 46 years (2000).
Safety: Violent crime rate: 17.9 per 10,000 population; Property crime rate: 305.3 per 10,000 population (2001).
Newspapers: The Exponent (1 x week)
Transportation: Commute to work: 92.5% car, 0.0% public transportation, 4.2% walk, 2.4% work from home (2000); Travel time to work: 35.0% less than 15 minutes, 28.5% 15 to 30 minutes, 17.4% 30 to 45 minutes, 10.5% 45 to 60 minutes, 8.5% 60 minutes or more (2000)
Additional Information Contacts
Brooklyn Chamber of Commerce 517-592-8907

CLARKLAKE (unincorporated postal area, zip code 49234). Covers a land area of 21.324 square miles and a water area of 1.236 square miles. Located at 42.12° N. Lat.; 84.36° W. Long. Elevation is 974 feet.
History: The lake on which Clarklake was settled was named in 1824 by Robert Clark, a government surveyor. The first settler was George Stranahan, who came in 1833.
Population: 2,704 (2000); Race: 98.4% White, 0.0% Black, 0.0% Asian, 0.4% American Indian and Alaska Native, 1.8% Hispanic of any race, 1.1% two or more races (2000); Density: 126.8 persons per square mile (2000); Age: 24.6% under 18, 15.1% over 64 (2000); Marriage status: 15.8% never married, 63.9% now married, 10.3% widowed, 10.0% divorced (2000); Foreign born: 1.0% (2000); Ancestry (includes multiple ancestries): 27.5% German, 20.4% English, 14.5% United States or American, 14.1% Irish, 7.8% Other groups (2000).
Economy: Employment by occupation: 18.2% management, 20.8% professional, 9.6% services, 25.4% sales, 0.0% farming, 10.6% construction, 15.4% production (2000).
Income: Per capita income: $29,999 (2000); Median household income: $57,963 (2000); Poverty rate: 2.9% (2000).
Education: High school graduation rate: 89.5% (2000); College graduation rate: 28.1% (2000).
Housing: Homeownership rate: 88.7% (2000); Median home value: $145,800 (2000); Median rent: $533 per month (2000); Median age of housing: 41 years (2000).
Transportation: Commute to work: 97.7% car, 0.0% public transportation, 0.0% walk, 2.3% work from home (2000); Travel time to work: 16.0% less than 15 minutes, 53.3% 15 to 30 minutes, 13.8% 30 to 45 minutes, 7.7% 45 to 60 minutes, 9.1% 60 minutes or more (2000)

COLUMBIA (township). Covers a land area of 36.574 square miles and a water area of 2.709 square miles. Located at 42.10° N. Lat.; 84.28° W. Long.
Population: 7,234 (2000); Race: 98.0% White, 0.1% Black, 0.0% Asian, 0.3% American Indian and Alaska Native, 0.9% Hispanic of any race, 1.3% two or more races (2000); Density: 197.8 persons per square mile (2000); Age: 23.2% under 18, 15.5% over 64 (2000); Marriage status: 16.5% never

married, 64.5% now married, 9.2% widowed, 9.8% divorced (2000); Foreign born: 1.9% (2000); Ancestry (includes multiple ancestries): 25.3% German, 17.4% English, 11.2% Irish, 9.2% Polish, 7.5% United States or American (2000).
Economy: Single-family building permits issued: 58 (2001) / 34 (2000); Multi-family building permits issued: 0 (2001) / 0 (2000); Employment by occupation: 14.1% management, 17.7% professional, 13.1% services, 23.0% sales, 0.8% farming, 9.8% construction, 21.5% production (2000).
Income: Per capita income: $25,763 (2000); Median household income: $51,632 (2000); Poverty rate: 4.9% (2000).
Taxes: Total city taxes per capita: $78 (1997); City property taxes per capita: $65 (1997).
Education: High school graduation rate: 87.4% (2000); College graduation rate: 22.0% (2000).
Housing: Homeownership rate: 85.4% (2000); Median home value: $141,700 (2000); Median rent: $450 per month (2000); Median age of housing: 33 years (2000).
Transportation: Commute to work: 95.8% car, 0.1% public transportation, 0.8% walk, 2.7% work from home (2000); Travel time to work: 22.9% less than 15 minutes, 36.8% 15 to 30 minutes, 15.5% 30 to 45 minutes, 8.4% 45 to 60 minutes, 16.5% 60 minutes or more (2000)

CONCORD (village). Covers a land area of 1.471 square miles and a water area of 0.100 square miles. Located at 42.17° N. Lat.; 84.64° W. Long. Elevation is 999 feet.
History: The name of Concord reflects the good relationship among the residents when they applied for a post office. The community was first called Van Fossenville for William Van Fossen, the first settler here in 1832.
Population: 1,101 (2000); Race: 98.9% White, 0.0% Black, 0.0% Asian, 0.2% American Indian and Alaska Native, 1.5% Hispanic of any race, 0.5% two or more races (2000); Density: 748.4 persons per square mile (2000); Age: 26.5% under 18, 15.4% over 64 (2000); Marriage status: 19.7% never married, 63.4% now married, 7.2% widowed, 9.7% divorced (2000); Foreign born: 0.5% (2000); Ancestry (includes multiple ancestries): 22.1% English, 20.9% German, 10.1% United States or American, 8.7% Irish, 8.6% Other groups (2000).
Economy: Single-family building permits issued: 4 (2001) / 3 (2000); Multi-family building permits issued: 0 (2001) / 0 (2000); Employment by occupation: 10.1% management, 15.5% professional, 16.4% services, 26.7% sales, 0.0% farming, 11.2% construction, 20.1% production (2000).
Income: Per capita income: $19,348 (2000); Median household income: $46,500 (2000); Poverty rate: 5.2% (2000).
Taxes: Total city taxes per capita: $193 (1997); City property taxes per capita: $188 (1997).
Education: High school graduation rate: 87.5% (2000); College graduation rate: 16.7% (2000).

School District(s)

Concord Community Schools (KG-12)
2000 Enrollment: 977 517-524-8850
Housing: Homeownership rate: 73.6% (2000); Median home value: $91,000 (2000); Median rent: $409 per month (2000); Median age of housing: 47 years (2000).
Transportation: Commute to work: 91.2% car, 0.0% public transportation, 4.1% walk, 4.7% work from home (2000); Travel time to work: 31.3% less than 15 minutes, 40.2% 15 to 30 minutes, 16.6% 30 to 45 minutes, 2.1% 45 to 60 minutes, 9.8% 60 minutes or more (2000)
Additional Information Contacts
Concord Economic Development 517-563-3337

CONCORD (township). Covers a land area of 35.851 square miles and a water area of 0.374 square miles. Located at 42.19° N. Lat.; 84.65° W. Long. Elevation is 999 feet.
Population: 2,692 (2000); Race: 98.2% White, 0.0% Black, 0.1% Asian, 0.2% American Indian and Alaska Native, 1.3% Hispanic of any race, 0.9% two or more races (2000); Density: 75.1 persons per square mile (2000); Age: 27.2% under 18, 12.0% over 64 (2000); Marriage status: 19.8% never married, 65.3% now married, 5.3% widowed, 9.5% divorced (2000); Foreign born: 0.7% (2000); Ancestry (includes multiple ancestries): 23.6% German, 19.2% English, 10.9% Irish, 10.7% United States or American, 8.4% Other groups (2000).
Economy: In livestock, poultry, and grain area; grain milling; manufacturing. Single-family building permits issued: 17 (2001) / 6 (2000); Multi-family building permits issued: 0 (2001) / 0 (2000); Employment by occupation: 9.8% management, 17.0% professional, 15.4% services, 22.3% sales, 0.0% farming, 12.2% construction, 23.3% production (2000).
Income: Per capita income: $19,417 (2000); Median household income: $50,000 (2000); Poverty rate: 5.2% (2000).
Taxes: Total city taxes per capita: $35 (1997); City property taxes per capita: $30 (1997).
Education: High school graduation rate: 88.7% (2000); College graduation rate: 14.7% (2000).
Housing: Homeownership rate: 78.8% (2000); Median home value: $104,900 (2000); Median rent: $436 per month (2000); Median age of housing: 42 years (2000).
Transportation: Commute to work: 93.7% car, 0.0% public transportation, 1.9% walk, 4.3% work from home (2000); Travel time to work: 28.3% less than 15 minutes, 41.9% 15 to 30 minutes, 18.0% 30 to 45 minutes, 3.3% 45 to 60 minutes, 8.5% 60 minutes or more (2000)

GRASS LAKE (village). Covers a land area of 0.962 square miles and a water area of 0 square miles. Located at 42.25° N. Lat.; 84.20° W. Long. Elevation is 996 feet.
History: The village of Grass Lake was established in the 1840's on the south shore of the lake for which it was named. For a time, Grass Lake's economy was supported by a furniture factory. Later it depended on dairying and agriculture.
Population: 1,082 (2000); Race: 98.9% White, 0.0% Black, 0.1% Asian, 0.7% American Indian and Alaska Native, 0.0% Hispanic of any race, 0.3% two or more races (2000); Density: 1,124.2 persons per square mile (2000); Age: 24.8% under 18, 14.7% over 64 (2000); Marriage status: 23.1% never married, 55.0% now married, 7.8% widowed, 14.1% divorced (2000); Foreign born: 1.8% (2000); Ancestry (includes multiple ancestries): 34.9% German, 18.6% English, 13.9% Irish, 10.3% United States or American, 6.2% Other groups (2000).
Economy: In agricultural and dairy area. Manufacturing: transportation equipment. Single-family building permits issued: 46 (2001) / 5 (2000); Multi-family building permits issued: 0 (2001) / 2 (2000); Employment by occupation: 11.7% management, 17.7% professional, 15.9% services, 21.8% sales, 0.0% farming, 9.1% construction, 23.8% production (2000).
Income: Per capita income: $20,210 (2000); Median household income: $45,078 (2000); Poverty rate: 4.3% (2000).
Taxes: Total city taxes per capita: $155 (1997); City property taxes per capita: $152 (1997).
Education: High school graduation rate: 83.0% (2000); College graduation rate: 18.7% (2000).

School District(s)

Grass Lake Community Schools (KG-12)
2000 Enrollment: 962 517-522-8491
Housing: Homeownership rate: 68.8% (2000); Median home value: $116,100 (2000); Median rent: $518 per month (2000); Median age of housing: 59 years (2000).
Transportation: Commute to work: 95.2% car, 0.0% public transportation, 2.4% walk, 1.6% work from home (2000); Travel time to work: 14.2% less than 15 minutes, 43.5% 15 to 30 minutes, 27.4% 30 to 45 minutes, 10.2% 45 to 60 minutes, 4.7% 60 minutes or more (2000)

GRASS LAKE CHARTER (township). Covers a land area of 47.187 square miles and a water area of 1.300 square miles. Located at 42.25° N. Lat.; 84.20° W. Long. Elevation is 996 feet.
Population: 4,586 (2000); Race: 98.4% White, 0.2% Black, 0.1% Asian, 0.3% American Indian and Alaska Native, 1.0% Hispanic of any race, 0.8% two or more races (2000); Density: 97.2 persons per square mile (2000); Age: 25.6% under 18, 12.1% over 64 (2000); Marriage status: 17.9% never married, 64.6% now married, 6.7% widowed, 10.7% divorced (2000); Foreign born: 1.3% (2000); Ancestry (includes multiple ancestries): 29.7% German, 12.8% Irish, 12.5% English, 11.7% United States or American, 7.1% Polish (2000).
Economy: Employment by occupation: 14.4% management, 17.1% professional, 12.9% services, 24.1% sales, 1.7% farming, 11.5% construction, 18.2% production (2000).
Income: Per capita income: $23,976 (2000); Median household income: $55,280 (2000); Poverty rate: 2.3% (2000).
Taxes: Total city taxes per capita: $64 (1997); City property taxes per capita: $48 (1997).
Education: High school graduation rate: 87.2% (2000); College graduation rate: 20.3% (2000).
Housing: Homeownership rate: 85.2% (2000); Median home value: $136,100 (2000); Median rent: $489 per month (2000); Median age of housing: 31 years (2000).
Transportation: Commute to work: 94.3% car, 0.0% public transportation, 1.6% walk, 3.0% work from home (2000); Travel time to work: 15.0% less

than 15 minutes, 39.6% 15 to 30 minutes, 25.9% 30 to 45 minutes, 13.7% 45 to 60 minutes, 5.8% 60 minutes or more (2000)

HANOVER (village). Covers a land area of 0.411 square miles and a water area of 0.008 square miles. Located at 42.10° N. Lat.; 84.55° W. Long. Elevation is 1,117 feet.
History: Hanover was named for Hanover, Germany, the former home of Henry Wickman who came here in 1836. The village was platted when the railroad came in 1870.
Population: 424 (2000); Race: 99.0% White, 0.5% Black, 0.0% Asian, 0.0% American Indian and Alaska Native, 0.0% Hispanic of any race, 0.5% two or more races (2000); Density: 1,031.2 persons per square mile (2000); Age: 31.2% under 18, 14.7% over 64 (2000); Marriage status: 25.2% never married, 54.6% now married, 7.6% widowed, 12.6% divorced (2000); Foreign born: 1.5% (2000); Ancestry (includes multiple ancestries): 24.3% German, 11.1% English, 8.4% United States or American, 7.9% Irish, 4.2% Other groups (2000).
Economy: Single-family building permits issued: 1 (2001) / 3 (2000); Multi-family building permits issued: 0 (2001) / 0 (2000); Employment by occupation: 2.6% management, 16.9% professional, 12.3% services, 31.2% sales, 1.3% farming, 16.2% construction, 19.5% production (2000).
Income: Per capita income: $13,254 (2000); Median household income: $38,750 (2000); Poverty rate: 18.7% (2000).
Taxes: Total city taxes per capita: $67 (1997); City property taxes per capita: $67 (1997).
Education: High school graduation rate: 86.5% (2000); College graduation rate: 6.3% (2000).
Housing: Homeownership rate: 73.4% (2000); Median home value: $73,800 (2000); Median rent: $297 per month (2000); Median age of housing: 60+ years (2000).
Transportation: Commute to work: 91.6% car, 0.0% public transportation, 2.6% walk, 4.5% work from home (2000); Travel time to work: 29.9% less than 15 minutes, 28.6% 15 to 30 minutes, 34.0% 30 to 45 minutes, 6.8% 45 to 60 minutes, 0.7% 60 minutes or more (2000)

HANOVER (township). Covers a land area of 34.981 square miles and a water area of 0.756 square miles. Located at 42.10° N. Lat.; 84.52° W. Long. Elevation is 1,117 feet.
Population: 3,792 (2000); Race: 97.5% White, 1.1% Black, 0.6% Asian, 0.2% American Indian and Alaska Native, 0.2% Hispanic of any race, 0.3% two or more races (2000); Density: 108.4 persons per square mile (2000); Age: 27.5% under 18, 10.3% over 64 (2000); Marriage status: 20.4% never married, 67.2% now married, 4.1% widowed, 8.3% divorced (2000); Foreign born: 0.4% (2000); Ancestry (includes multiple ancestries): 28.6% German, 18.6% English, 12.2% Irish, 8.0% United States or American, 6.4% Polish (2000).
Economy: In diversified farming area. Machining. Single-family building permits issued: 10 (2001) / 13 (2000); Multi-family building permits issued: 0 (2001) / 0 (2000); Employment by occupation: 10.5% management, 21.1% professional, 15.5% services, 27.3% sales, 0.6% farming, 9.8% construction, 15.2% production (2000).
Income: Per capita income: $22,648 (2000); Median household income: $49,966 (2000); Poverty rate: 4.0% (2000).
Taxes: Total city taxes per capita: $36 (1997); City property taxes per capita: $30 (1997).
Education: High school graduation rate: 89.7% (2000); College graduation rate: 21.1% (2000).
Housing: Homeownership rate: 90.3% (2000); Median home value: $113,800 (2000); Median rent: $404 per month (2000); Median age of housing: 29 years (2000).
Transportation: Commute to work: 95.8% car, 0.4% public transportation, 1.2% walk, 2.5% work from home (2000); Travel time to work: 12.0% less than 15 minutes, 44.8% 15 to 30 minutes, 30.3% 30 to 45 minutes, 7.6% 45 to 60 minutes, 5.2% 60 minutes or more (2000)

HENRIETTA (township). Covers a land area of 36.241 square miles and a water area of 0.899 square miles. Located at 42.38° N. Lat.; 84.31° W. Long.
History: Henrietta Township was organized in 1837 and named West Portage until 1839, when it was renamed for Henrietta, New York, former home of settler Henry Hurd.
Population: 4,483 (2000); Race: 96.4% White, 0.3% Black, 0.0% Asian, 0.0% American Indian and Alaska Native, 1.9% Hispanic of any race, 1.7% two or more races (2000); Density: 123.7 persons per square mile (2000); Age: 29.2% under 18, 10.1% over 64 (2000); Marriage status: 24.2% never married, 62.3% now married, 5.3% widowed, 8.2% divorced (2000); Foreign born: 0.9% (2000); Ancestry (includes multiple ancestries): 28.0% German, 12.6% United States or American, 11.2% Other groups, 10.8% Irish, 10.5% English (2000).
Economy: Single-family building permits issued: 36 (2001) / 31 (2000); Multi-family building permits issued: 0 (2001) / 0 (2000); Employment by occupation: 9.2% management, 11.4% professional, 14.0% services, 28.7% sales, 0.4% farming, 13.3% construction, 23.1% production (2000).
Income: Per capita income: $19,904 (2000); Median household income: $48,517 (2000); Poverty rate: 3.3% (2000).
Taxes: Total city taxes per capita: $33 (1997); City property taxes per capita: $28 (1997).
Education: High school graduation rate: 79.6% (2000); College graduation rate: 11.1% (2000).
Housing: Homeownership rate: 89.6% (2000); Median home value: $117,000 (2000); Median rent: $517 per month (2000); Median age of housing: 28 years (2000).
Transportation: Commute to work: 94.0% car, 0.0% public transportation, 2.5% walk, 3.1% work from home (2000); Travel time to work: 13.3% less than 15 minutes, 47.9% 15 to 30 minutes, 21.8% 30 to 45 minutes, 8.6% 45 to 60 minutes, 8.4% 60 minutes or more (2000)

HORTON (unincorporated postal area, zip code 49246). Covers a land area of 35.885 square miles and a water area of 0.969 square miles. Located at 42.11° N. Lat.; 84.49° W. Long. Elevation is 1,042 feet.
History: Horton grew up around a flour mill built in 1842 by George A. Baldwin, who gave the land for the village. First called Baldwin, the name was changed to Horton in 1874 because there was another Baldwin in the state.
Population: 3,309 (2000); Race: 97.4% White, 1.0% Black, 1.1% Asian, 0.2% American Indian and Alaska Native, 0.7% Hispanic of any race, 0.1% two or more races (2000); Density: 92.2 persons per square mile (2000); Age: 25.7% under 18, 9.3% over 64 (2000); Marriage status: 18.7% never married, 69.0% now married, 4.0% widowed, 8.3% divorced (2000); Foreign born: 0.8% (2000); Ancestry (includes multiple ancestries): 30.4% German, 19.3% English, 14.0% Irish, 9.1% Polish, 7.7% United States or American (2000).
Economy: Employment by occupation: 12.4% management, 22.6% professional, 13.7% services, 26.9% sales, 0.3% farming, 9.9% construction, 14.2% production (2000).
Income: Per capita income: $25,391 (2000); Median household income: $57,008 (2000); Poverty rate: 2.1% (2000).
Education: High school graduation rate: 92.3% (2000); College graduation rate: 25.3% (2000).

School District(s)

Hanover-Horton Schools (KG-12)
2000 Enrollment: 1,330 517-563-0100

Housing: Homeownership rate: 91.8% (2000); Median home value: $127,400 (2000); Median rent: $434 per month (2000); Median age of housing: 30 years (2000).
Transportation: Commute to work: 97.6% car, 0.0% public transportation, 0.0% walk, 2.4% work from home (2000); Travel time to work: 9.7% less than 15 minutes, 51.6% 15 to 30 minutes, 23.8% 30 to 45 minutes, 7.9% 45 to 60 minutes, 7.1% 60 minutes or more (2000)

JACKSON (city). Covers a land area of 11.089 square miles and a water area of 0 square miles. Located at 42.24° N. Lat.; 84.40° W. Long. Elevation is 940 feet.
History: The site chosen for Jackson was at the intersection of the Grand River and an old trail. Lumbering was the first industry, followed by a gristmill. Jackson achieved fame in 1854 when the Republican Pary was formed and named at a convention held here. The convention meetings were held outdoors under the oak trees. The party's first platform included repeal of the fugitive slave law. Jackson's industrial importance grew when the Michigan Central Railroad established its shops here in 1871. The manufacture of carriages was an early industry, replaced in the early 1900's by industries related to auto manufacturing.
Population: 36,316 (2000); Race: 74.2% White, 19.0% Black, 0.4% Asian, 0.7% American Indian and Alaska Native, 4.5% Hispanic of any race, 3.8% two or more races (2000); Density: 3,274.9 persons per square mile (2000); Age: 29.7% under 18, 12.0% over 64 (2000); Marriage status: 31.6% never married, 44.2% now married, 8.0% widowed, 16.3% divorced (2000); Foreign born: 1.8% (2000); Ancestry (includes multiple ancestries): 26.8% Other groups, 16.4% German, 11.2% Irish, 9.9% English, 7.1% Polish (2000).
Vital Statistics: Birth rate: 263.0 per 10,000 population (1998)
Economy: Unemployment rate: 8.3% (11/2002); Total civilian labor force: 19,370 (11/2002); Single-family building permits issued: 20 (2001) / 12

(2000); Multi-family building permits issued: 0 (2001) / 0 (2000); Employment by occupation: 9.3% management, 13.7% professional, 22.3% services, 22.3% sales, 0.0% farming, 7.4% construction, 25.0% production (2000).
Income: Per capita income: $15,230 (2000); Median household income: $31,294 (2000); Poverty rate: 19.6% (2000).
Taxes: Total city taxes per capita: $424 (2000); City property taxes per capita: $217 (2000).
Education: High school graduation rate: 77.3% (2000); College graduation rate: 13.1% (2000).

School District(s)

Da Vinci Institute (KG-12)
2000 Enrollment: 205 517-774-2100
East Jackson Community Schools (KG-12)
2000 Enrollment: 1,613 517-764-2090
Jackson Public Schools (PK-12)
2000 Enrollment: 7,345 517-789-8144
Northwest Community Schools (PK-12)
2000 Enrollment: 3,590 517-569-2247
Paragon Charter Academy (KG-08)
2000 Enrollment: 486 616-895-3029
Vandercook Lake Public Schools (PK-12)
2000 Enrollment: 1,225 517-782-9044

Four-year College(s)

Baker College of Jackson (Private, Not-for-profit)
2001 Enrollment: 1,236 517-789-6123
2001 Tuition: In-state $7,440; Out-of-state $7,440

Two-year College(s)

Jackson Community College (Public)
2001 Enrollment: 5,285 517-796-8400
2001 Tuition: In-state $2,263; Out-of-state $2,511
New Tribes Mission Inc-New Tribes Bible Institute (Private, Not-for-profit)
2001 Enrollment: n/a 517-782-9309

Housing: Homeownership rate: 57.6% (2000); Median home value: $64,300 (2000); Median rent: $412 per month (2000); Median age of housing: 60+ years (2000).
Hospitals: Doctors Hospital (65 beds); Foote Memorial Hospital (325 beds)
Safety: Violent crime rate: 139.6 per 10,000 population; Property crime rate: 752.5 per 10,000 population (2001).
Newspapers: Jackson Citizen Patriot (7 x week); The Blazer News (1 x week)
Transportation: Commute to work: 92.5% car, 1.5% public transportation, 3.0% walk, 2.0% work from home (2000); Travel time to work: 50.4% less than 15 minutes, 30.2% 15 to 30 minutes, 9.4% 30 to 45 minutes, 5.8% 45 to 60 minutes, 4.3% 60 minutes or more (2000); Amtrak: Service available.
Airports: Jackson County-Reynolds Field

Additional Information Contacts

Jackson Area Association of Realtors 517-787-6175
Jackson Chamber of Commerce 517-782-8221
Jackson Convention & Tourist Bureau 517-764-4440
Napoleon Chamber of Commerce 517-536-0547

LEONI (township). Covers a land area of 49.097 square miles and a water area of 2.115 square miles. Located at 42.25° N. Lat.; 84.31° W. Long.
Population: 13,459 (2000); Race: 96.2% White, 0.8% Black, 0.2% Asian, 0.4% American Indian and Alaska Native, 1.0% Hispanic of any race, 2.0% two or more races (2000); Density: 274.1 persons per square mile (2000); Age: 26.0% under 18, 12.4% over 64 (2000); Marriage status: 21.8% never married, 62.1% now married, 5.7% widowed, 10.4% divorced (2000); Foreign born: 0.8% (2000); Ancestry (includes multiple ancestries): 24.1% German, 15.1% English, 11.9% Irish, 10.6% Polish, 10.3% United States or American (2000).
Economy: Single-family building permits issued: 59 (2001) / 44 (2000); Multi-family building permits issued: 0 (2001) / 0 (2000); Employment by occupation: 10.6% management, 14.9% professional, 14.4% services, 22.9% sales, 0.5% farming, 10.1% construction, 26.6% production (2000).
Income: Per capita income: $19,329 (2000); Median household income: $43,551 (2000); Poverty rate: 7.9% (2000).
Taxes: Total city taxes per capita: $68 (2000); City property taxes per capita: $62 (2000).
Education: High school graduation rate: 82.5% (2000); College graduation rate: 10.0% (2000).
Housing: Homeownership rate: 86.0% (2000); Median home value: $95,900 (2000); Median rent: $391 per month (2000); Median age of housing: 41 years (2000).
Safety: Violent crime rate: 21.4 per 10,000 population; Property crime rate: 362.9 per 10,000 population (2001).
Transportation: Commute to work: 96.3% car, 0.3% public transportation, 1.0% walk, 1.8% work from home (2000); Travel time to work: 30.2% less than 15 minutes, 42.9% 15 to 30 minutes, 11.8% 30 to 45 minutes, 7.5% 45 to 60 minutes, 7.6% 60 minutes or more (2000)

LIBERTY (township). Covers a land area of 34.757 square miles and a water area of 1.011 square miles. Located at 42.10° N. Lat.; 84.41° W. Long.
History: Liberty Township was organized in 1837. The patriotic name was inspired by Patrick Henry's words, "Give me liberty or give me death."
Population: 2,903 (2000); Race: 98.3% White, 0.0% Black, 0.5% Asian, 0.3% American Indian and Alaska Native, 2.4% Hispanic of any race, 0.9% two or more races (2000); Density: 83.5 persons per square mile (2000); Age: 25.4% under 18, 13.3% over 64 (2000); Marriage status: 16.0% never married, 69.6% now married, 4.4% widowed, 10.1% divorced (2000); Foreign born: 1.1% (2000); Ancestry (includes multiple ancestries): 29.0% German, 19.8% English, 13.5% Irish, 11.6% United States or American, 8.2% Polish (2000).
Economy: Single-family building permits issued: 26 (2001) / 29 (2000); Multi-family building permits issued: 0 (2001) / 0 (2000); Employment by occupation: 13.9% management, 18.9% professional, 13.0% services, 25.7% sales, 0.7% farming, 12.8% construction, 15.0% production (2000).
Income: Per capita income: $27,433 (2000); Median household income: $55,046 (2000); Poverty rate: 2.9% (2000).
Taxes: Total city taxes per capita: $35 (1997); City property taxes per capita: $24 (1997).
Education: High school graduation rate: 91.1% (2000); College graduation rate: 22.0% (2000).
Housing: Homeownership rate: 92.8% (2000); Median home value: $137,500 (2000); Median rent: $513 per month (2000); Median age of housing: 28 years (2000).
Transportation: Commute to work: 95.9% car, 0.0% public transportation, 0.0% walk, 3.8% work from home (2000); Travel time to work: 17.3% less than 15 minutes, 53.4% 15 to 30 minutes, 18.2% 30 to 45 minutes, 3.1% 45 to 60 minutes, 7.9% 60 minutes or more (2000)

MICHIGAN CENTER (CDP). Covers a land area of 5.182 square miles and a water area of 0.481 square miles. Located at 42.22° N. Lat.; 84.32° W. Long. Elevation is 945 feet.
Population: 4,641 (2000); Race: 98.3% White, 0.1% Black, 0.4% Asian, 0.4% American Indian and Alaska Native, 0.8% Hispanic of any race, 0.6% two or more races (2000); Density: 895.6 persons per square mile (2000); Age: 26.2% under 18, 13.6% over 64 (2000); Marriage status: 22.7% never married, 59.8% now married, 6.6% widowed, 10.8% divorced (2000); Foreign born: 1.2% (2000); Ancestry (includes multiple ancestries): 26.5% German, 15.0% Irish, 13.8% English, 12.3% Polish, 7.8% Other groups (2000).
Economy: Employment by occupation: 8.8% management, 11.9% professional, 15.9% services, 23.0% sales, 0.4% farming, 11.1% construction, 29.0% production (2000).
Income: Per capita income: $18,701 (2000); Median household income: $43,056 (2000); Poverty rate: 4.9% (2000).
Education: High school graduation rate: 82.9% (2000); College graduation rate: 7.8% (2000).

School District(s)

Michigan Center School District (PK-12)
2000 Enrollment: 1,417 517-764-5778

Housing: Homeownership rate: 87.9% (2000); Median home value: $94,000 (2000); Median rent: $428 per month (2000); Median age of housing: 48 years (2000).
Transportation: Commute to work: 96.0% car, 0.0% public transportation, 0.5% walk, 2.4% work from home (2000); Travel time to work: 28.2% less than 15 minutes, 47.7% 15 to 30 minutes, 7.5% 30 to 45 minutes, 7.0% 45 to 60 minutes, 9.6% 60 minutes or more (2000)

MUNITH (unincorporated postal area, zip code 49259). Covers a land area of 30.791 square miles and a water area of 0.110 square miles. Located at 42.37° N. Lat.; 84.25° W. Long.
Population: 2,789 (2000); Race: 97.2% White, 0.0% Black, 0.0% Asian, 0.0% American Indian and Alaska Native, 0.7% Hispanic of any race, 1.8% two or more races (2000); Density: 90.6 persons per square mile (2000); Age: 34.2% under 18, 8.1% over 64 (2000); Marriage status: 23.7% never married, 63.6% now married, 3.7% widowed, 8.9% divorced (2000); Foreign born: 0.7% (2000); Ancestry (includes multiple ancestries): 33.6% German, 13.7%

Irish, 10.3% English, 8.2% United States or American, 7.3% French (except Basque) (2000).
Economy: Employment by occupation: 8.1% management, 10.3% professional, 13.0% services, 24.7% sales, 2.5% farming, 16.2% construction, 25.2% production (2000).
Income: Per capita income: $21,012 (2000); Median household income: $50,125 (2000); Poverty rate: 4.3% (2000).
Education: High school graduation rate: 80.7% (2000); College graduation rate: 8.1% (2000).
Housing: Homeownership rate: 91.5% (2000); Median home value: $110,700 (2000); Median rent: $431 per month (2000); Median age of housing: 25 years (2000).
Transportation: Commute to work: 95.8% car, 0.0% public transportation, 1.6% walk, 1.9% work from home (2000); Travel time to work: 9.6% less than 15 minutes, 34.6% 15 to 30 minutes, 30.1% 30 to 45 minutes, 14.4% 45 to 60 minutes, 11.3% 60 minutes or more (2000)

NAPOLEON (township). Covers a land area of 29.447 square miles and a water area of 1.990 square miles. Located at 42.17° N. Lat.; 84.28° W. Long. Elevation is 962 feet.
Population: 6,962 (2000); Race: 96.7% White, 0.2% Black, 0.3% Asian, 0.5% American Indian and Alaska Native, 1.8% Hispanic of any race, 1.1% two or more races (2000); Density: 236.4 persons per square mile (2000); Age: 27.0% under 18, 11.0% over 64 (2000); Marriage status: 21.8% never married, 61.4% now married, 5.7% widowed, 11.0% divorced (2000); Foreign born: 2.4% (2000); Ancestry (includes multiple ancestries): 23.9% German, 16.2% English, 13.0% Irish, 8.3% Polish, 8.0% United States or American (2000).
Economy: Single-family building permits issued: 39 (2001) / 39 (2000); Multi-family building permits issued: 0 (2001) / 0 (2000); Employment by occupation: 7.8% management, 14.1% professional, 14.0% services, 28.2% sales, 0.1% farming, 12.5% construction, 23.2% production (2000).
Income: Per capita income: $22,436 (2000); Median household income: $48,065 (2000); Poverty rate: 4.0% (2000).
Taxes: Total city taxes per capita: $36 (2000); City property taxes per capita: $26 (2000).
Education: High school graduation rate: 88.6% (2000); College graduation rate: 14.2% (2000).

School District(s)

Napoleon Community Schools (KG-12)
2000 Enrollment: 1,673 517-536-8667
Housing: Homeownership rate: 84.1% (2000); Median home value: $120,800 (2000); Median rent: $502 per month (2000); Median age of housing: 30 years (2000).
Transportation: Commute to work: 93.0% car, 0.1% public transportation, 0.9% walk, 5.4% work from home (2000); Travel time to work: 23.5% less than 15 minutes, 39.9% 15 to 30 minutes, 20.6% 30 to 45 minutes, 8.7% 45 to 60 minutes, 7.3% 60 minutes or more (2000)
Additional Information Contacts
Napoleon Chamber of Commerce 517-536-0547

NORVELL (township). Covers a land area of 30.012 square miles and a water area of 2.041 square miles. Located at 42.12° N. Lat.; 84.18° W. Long.
Population: 2,922 (2000); Race: 97.8% White, 0.0% Black, 0.0% Asian, 0.1% American Indian and Alaska Native, 0.7% Hispanic of any race, 2.0% two or more races (2000); Density: 97.4 persons per square mile (2000); Age: 25.2% under 18, 13.2% over 64 (2000); Marriage status: 17.0% never married, 65.0% now married, 7.0% widowed, 11.0% divorced (2000); Foreign born: 1.6% (2000); Ancestry (includes multiple ancestries): 29.5% German, 14.4% English, 12.7% Irish, 8.4% Polish, 7.7% United States or American (2000).
Economy: Single-family building permits issued: 24 (2001) / 36 (2000); Multi-family building permits issued: 0 (2001) / 0 (2000); Employment by occupation: 9.4% management, 11.9% professional, 14.2% services, 21.8% sales, 0.3% farming, 15.9% construction, 26.6% production (2000).
Income: Per capita income: $20,488 (2000); Median household income: $49,167 (2000); Poverty rate: 6.6% (2000).
Taxes: Total city taxes per capita: $68 (1997); City property taxes per capita: $55 (1997).
Education: High school graduation rate: 85.0% (2000); College graduation rate: 11.9% (2000).
Housing: Homeownership rate: 92.7% (2000); Median home value: $124,600 (2000); Median rent: $509 per month (2000); Median age of housing: 36 years (2000).
Safety: Violent crime rate: 20.4 per 10,000 population; Property crime rate: 126.0 per 10,000 population (2001).
Transportation: Commute to work: 95.3% car, 0.0% public transportation, 0.4% walk, 4.3% work from home (2000); Travel time to work: 13.9% less than 15 minutes, 21.1% 15 to 30 minutes, 31.4% 30 to 45 minutes, 15.1% 45 to 60 minutes, 18.5% 60 minutes or more (2000)

PARMA (village). Covers a land area of 0.589 square miles and a water area of 0 square miles. Located at 42.25° N. Lat.; 84.59° W. Long. Elevation is 992 feet.
History: Parma was settled in the 1830's, at a place known as Cracker Hill. Many of the early residents were Quakers, and for a time there was a Quaker meeting house in Parma.
Population: 907 (2000); Race: 97.4% White, 0.0% Black, 0.0% Asian, 1.1% American Indian and Alaska Native, 1.3% Hispanic of any race, 0.5% two or more races (2000); Density: 1,541.2 persons per square mile (2000); Age: 35.0% under 18, 7.5% over 64 (2000); Marriage status: 25.5% never married, 60.5% now married, 4.5% widowed, 9.5% divorced (2000); Foreign born: 0.0% (2000); Ancestry (includes multiple ancestries): 22.5% German, 15.0% English, 12.3% Other groups, 11.3% United States or American, 7.5% Irish (2000).
Economy: Single-family building permits issued: 0 (2001) / 1 (2000); Multi-family building permits issued: 0 (2001) / 0 (2000); Employment by occupation: 8.6% management, 15.4% professional, 14.2% services, 27.5% sales, 1.2% farming, 8.9% construction, 24.2% production (2000).
Income: Per capita income: $16,483 (2000); Median household income: $39,531 (2000); Poverty rate: 3.3% (2000).
Taxes: Total city taxes per capita: $272 (1997); City property taxes per capita: $263 (1997).
Education: High school graduation rate: 86.8% (2000); College graduation rate: 14.5% (2000).

School District(s)

Western School District (PK-12)
2000 Enrollment: 2,692 517-841-8100
Housing: Homeownership rate: 75.9% (2000); Median home value: $85,500 (2000); Median rent: $434 per month (2000); Median age of housing: 57 years (2000).
Newspapers: County Press (1 x week)
Transportation: Commute to work: 94.9% car, 0.5% public transportation, 3.4% walk, 0.7% work from home (2000); Travel time to work: 29.9% less than 15 minutes, 49.5% 15 to 30 minutes, 12.1% 30 to 45 minutes, 3.4% 45 to 60 minutes, 5.1% 60 minutes or more (2000)

PARMA (township). Covers a land area of 36.316 square miles and a water area of 0.054 square miles. Located at 42.27° N. Lat.; 84.66° W. Long. Elevation is 992 feet.
Population: 2,696 (2000); Race: 93.3% White, 2.4% Black, 0.6% Asian, 0.6% American Indian and Alaska Native, 3.7% Hispanic of any race, 1.8% two or more races (2000); Density: 74.2 persons per square mile (2000); Age: 27.4% under 18, 10.5% over 64 (2000); Marriage status: 22.4% never married, 64.7% now married, 4.7% widowed, 8.2% divorced (2000); Foreign born: 1.8% (2000); Ancestry (includes multiple ancestries): 23.1% German, 16.1% English, 11.0% Other groups, 10.3% Irish, 9.5% United States or American (2000).
Economy: In farm area: fruit; dairy products. Manufacturing of motor vehicle parts, appliances. Single-family building permits issued: 21 (2001) / 21 (2000); Multi-family building permits issued: 0 (2001) / 0 (2000); Employment by occupation: 8.3% management, 16.3% professional, 15.1% services, 23.7% sales, 1.3% farming, 12.4% construction, 22.8% production (2000).
Income: Per capita income: $19,026 (2000); Median household income: $48,510 (2000); Poverty rate: 7.1% (2000).
Taxes: Total city taxes per capita: $20 (1997); City property taxes per capita: $16 (1997).
Education: High school graduation rate: 84.0% (2000); College graduation rate: 15.9% (2000).
Housing: Homeownership rate: 88.0% (2000); Median home value: $92,000 (2000); Median rent: $396 per month (2000); Median age of housing: 32 years (2000).
Transportation: Commute to work: 94.9% car, 0.0% public transportation, 1.9% walk, 1.9% work from home (2000); Travel time to work: 28.9% less than 15 minutes, 43.9% 15 to 30 minutes, 14.5% 30 to 45 minutes, 4.3% 45 to 60 minutes, 8.3% 60 minutes or more (2000)

PLEASANT LAKE (unincorporated postal area, zip code 49272). Covers a land area of 13.932 square miles and a water area of 0.771 square miles. Located at 42.39° N. Lat.; 84.34° W. Long.

History: Pleasant Lake was first called Spring Lake. John Wenstren acquired land here and renamed the settlement in 1836. The village of Pleasant Lake was laid out in 1868.
Population: 2,411 (2000); Race: 98.0% White, 0.5% Black, 0.0% Asian, 0.0% American Indian and Alaska Native, 1.2% Hispanic of any race, 0.9% two or more races (2000); Density: 173.1 persons per square mile (2000); Age: 25.4% under 18, 11.3% over 64 (2000); Marriage status: 21.4% never married, 62.0% now married, 7.1% widowed, 9.5% divorced (2000); Foreign born: 1.0% (2000); Ancestry (includes multiple ancestries): 32.8% German, 12.6% Polish, 12.3% English, 11.6% Irish, 11.4% United States or American (2000).
Economy: Employment by occupation: 10.4% management, 12.3% professional, 12.5% services, 32.8% sales, 0.8% farming, 8.7% construction, 22.5% production (2000).
Income: Per capita income: $20,127 (2000); Median household income: $50,938 (2000); Poverty rate: 2.0% (2000).
Education: High school graduation rate: 82.5% (2000); College graduation rate: 14.0% (2000).
Housing: Homeownership rate: 92.1% (2000); Median home value: $118,500 (2000); Median rent: $676 per month (2000); Median age of housing: 33 years (2000).
Transportation: Commute to work: 93.6% car, 0.0% public transportation, 3.9% walk, 1.8% work from home (2000); Travel time to work: 13.7% less than 15 minutes, 51.2% 15 to 30 minutes, 17.5% 30 to 45 minutes, 11.1% 45 to 60 minutes, 6.4% 60 minutes or more (2000)

PULASKI (township). Covers a land area of 36.225 square miles and a water area of 0.426 square miles. Located at 42.10° N. Lat.; 84.65° W. Long. Elevation is 1,088 feet.
History: Pulaski Township was organized in 1838 and named for Count Casimir Pulaski, Polish hero in the American Revolution.
Population: 1,931 (2000); Race: 98.2% White, 0.1% Black, 0.3% Asian, 0.3% American Indian and Alaska Native, 0.8% Hispanic of any race, 0.9% two or more races (2000); Density: 53.3 persons per square mile (2000); Age: 29.9% under 18, 9.8% over 64 (2000); Marriage status: 22.0% never married, 63.5% now married, 4.5% widowed, 10.0% divorced (2000); Foreign born: 0.7% (2000); Ancestry (includes multiple ancestries): 23.3% German, 16.6% English, 13.7% Irish, 12.4% United States or American, 5.8% Polish (2000).
Economy: Single-family building permits issued: 20 (2001) / 13 (2000); Multi-family building permits issued: 0 (2001) / 0 (2000); Employment by occupation: 9.1% management, 16.8% professional, 15.9% services, 17.8% sales, 0.5% farming, 9.8% construction, 30.1% production (2000).
Income: Per capita income: $18,126 (2000); Median household income: $44,306 (2000); Poverty rate: 6.2% (2000).
Taxes: Total city taxes per capita: $25 (1997); City property taxes per capita: $22 (1997).
Education: High school graduation rate: 84.8% (2000); College graduation rate: 12.6% (2000).
Housing: Homeownership rate: 87.0% (2000); Median home value: $103,100 (2000); Median rent: $394 per month (2000); Median age of housing: 28 years (2000).
Transportation: Commute to work: 93.7% car, 0.0% public transportation, 0.8% walk, 3.5% work from home (2000); Travel time to work: 22.4% less than 15 minutes, 39.4% 15 to 30 minutes, 27.7% 30 to 45 minutes, 4.9% 45 to 60 minutes, 5.5% 60 minutes or more (2000)

RIVES (township). Covers a land area of 35.899 square miles and a water area of 0.344 square miles. Located at 42.38° N. Lat.; 84.42° W. Long.
Population: 4,725 (2000); Race: 97.4% White, 0.0% Black, 0.2% Asian, 0.0% American Indian and Alaska Native, 2.1% Hispanic of any race, 1.6% two or more races (2000); Density: 131.6 persons per square mile (2000); Age: 28.1% under 18, 9.4% over 64 (2000); Marriage status: 19.5% never married, 68.0% now married, 4.7% widowed, 7.7% divorced (2000); Foreign born: 0.7% (2000); Ancestry (includes multiple ancestries): 22.0% German, 15.1% English, 12.6% Irish, 12.4% United States or American, 7.6% Other groups (2000).
Economy: Single-family building permits issued: 42 (2001) / 42 (2000); Multi-family building permits issued: 0 (2001) / 0 (2000); Employment by occupation: 11.5% management, 18.1% professional, 15.5% services, 27.8% sales, 0.0% farming, 7.6% construction, 19.5% production (2000).
Income: Per capita income: $22,942 (2000); Median household income: $53,819 (2000); Poverty rate: 8.6% (2000).
Taxes: Total city taxes per capita: $16 (1997); City property taxes per capita: $10 (1997).
Education: High school graduation rate: 88.0% (2000); College graduation rate: 11.9% (2000).
Housing: Homeownership rate: 93.8% (2000); Median home value: $117,700 (2000); Median rent: $470 per month (2000); Median age of housing: 25 years (2000).
Transportation: Commute to work: 96.0% car, 0.0% public transportation, 0.0% walk, 2.3% work from home (2000); Travel time to work: 21.0% less than 15 minutes, 51.3% 15 to 30 minutes, 16.0% 30 to 45 minutes, 7.5% 45 to 60 minutes, 4.3% 60 minutes or more (2000)

RIVES JUNCTION (unincorporated postal area, zip code 49277). Covers a land area of 37.493 square miles and a water area of 0.113 square miles. Located at 42.39° N. Lat.; 84.46° W. Long. Elevation is 917 feet.
History: Rives Junction was founded in 1834 by Samuel Prescott and Henry Fifield, and grew up around the Michigan Central Railroad junction.
Population: 3,740 (2000); Race: 98.5% White, 0.1% Black, 0.1% Asian, 0.0% American Indian and Alaska Native, 1.5% Hispanic of any race, 0.9% two or more races (2000); Density: 99.8 persons per square mile (2000); Age: 27.8% under 18, 7.8% over 64 (2000); Marriage status: 20.6% never married, 68.8% now married, 4.3% widowed, 6.3% divorced (2000); Foreign born: 0.6% (2000); Ancestry (includes multiple ancestries): 18.9% English, 18.3% German, 13.8% United States or American, 13.5% Irish, 7.1% Polish (2000).
Economy: Employment by occupation: 10.5% management, 17.5% professional, 15.1% services, 27.7% sales, 0.0% farming, 10.3% construction, 18.9% production (2000).
Income: Per capita income: $19,253 (2000); Median household income: $50,486 (2000); Poverty rate: 8.2% (2000).
Education: High school graduation rate: 87.7% (2000); College graduation rate: 12.0% (2000).
Housing: Homeownership rate: 92.9% (2000); Median home value: $114,000 (2000); Median rent: $454 per month (2000); Median age of housing: 28 years (2000).
Transportation: Commute to work: 94.2% car, 0.0% public transportation, 0.3% walk, 3.8% work from home (2000); Travel time to work: 16.2% less than 15 minutes, 55.7% 15 to 30 minutes, 18.3% 30 to 45 minutes, 4.5% 45 to 60 minutes, 5.3% 60 minutes or more (2000)

SANDSTONE (township). Covers a land area of 36.277 square miles and a water area of 0.039 square miles. Located at 42.28° N. Lat.; 84.54° W. Long.
History: Sandstone was settled in the 1830's and named for the large deposit of sandstone along Sandstone Creek.
Population: 3,801 (2000); Race: 98.1% White, 0.3% Black, 0.0% Asian, 0.3% American Indian and Alaska Native, 1.3% Hispanic of any race, 0.7% two or more races (2000); Density: 104.8 persons per square mile (2000); Age: 28.9% under 18, 11.4% over 64 (2000); Marriage status: 18.1% never married, 64.9% now married, 7.0% widowed, 10.0% divorced (2000); Foreign born: 0.9% (2000); Ancestry (includes multiple ancestries): 27.5% German, 18.5% English, 12.4% Other groups, 9.4% Irish, 8.7% United States or American (2000).
Economy: Single-family building permits issued: 31 (2001) / 26 (2000); Multi-family building permits issued: 0 (2001) / 0 (2000); Employment by occupation: 13.8% management, 21.2% professional, 12.2% services, 23.7% sales, 0.6% farming, 8.5% construction, 20.1% production (2000).
Income: Per capita income: $22,622 (2000); Median household income: $50,396 (2000); Poverty rate: 4.7% (2000).
Taxes: Total city taxes per capita: $29 (1997); City property taxes per capita: $22 (1997).
Education: High school graduation rate: 88.2% (2000); College graduation rate: 20.4% (2000).
Housing: Homeownership rate: 87.3% (2000); Median home value: $116,400 (2000); Median rent: $428 per month (2000); Median age of housing: 30 years (2000).
Transportation: Commute to work: 93.2% car, 0.4% public transportation, 1.9% walk, 3.8% work from home (2000); Travel time to work: 29.9% less than 15 minutes, 52.5% 15 to 30 minutes, 8.0% 30 to 45 minutes, 6.7% 45 to 60 minutes, 3.0% 60 minutes or more (2000)

SPRING ARBOR (township). Covers a land area of 35.389 square miles and a water area of 0.394 square miles. Located at 42.21° N. Lat.; 84.53° W. Long.
History: Spring Arbor was settled in the 1830's, and named for a spring in the area. Isaac N. Swain founded the village of Spring Arbor in 1839.
Population: 7,577 (2000); Race: 97.6% White, 0.4% Black, 0.3% Asian, 0.1% American Indian and Alaska Native, 2.4% Hispanic of any race, 0.6% two or more races (2000); Density: 214.1 persons per square mile (2000); Age: 24.8% under 18, 13.5% over 64 (2000); Marriage status: 23.9% never married, 62.3% now married, 6.2% widowed, 7.6% divorced (2000); Foreign

born: 0.8% (2000); Ancestry (includes multiple ancestries): 22.1% German, 14.4% English, 11.3% Irish, 10.5% United States or American, 6.2% Polish (2000).
Economy: Single-family building permits issued: 36 (2001) / 36 (2000); Multi-family building permits issued: 12 (2001) / 12 (2000); Employment by occupation: 11.6% management, 21.6% professional, 18.5% services, 22.8% sales, 0.5% farming, 8.9% construction, 16.1% production (2000).
Income: Per capita income: $19,622 (2000); Median household income: $51,770 (2000); Poverty rate: 7.9% (2000).
Taxes: Total city taxes per capita: $18 (1997); City property taxes per capita: $12 (1997).
Education: High school graduation rate: 87.5% (2000); College graduation rate: 27.9% (2000).

Four-year College(s)

Spring Arbor University (Private, Not-for-profit, Free Methodist)
2001 Enrollment: 2,616 517-750-1200
2001 Tuition: In-state $12,920; Out-of-state $12,920
Housing: Homeownership rate: 81.1% (2000); Median home value: $128,500 (2000); Median rent: $438 per month (2000); Median age of housing: 27 years (2000).
Safety: Violent crime rate: 7.9 per 10,000 population; Property crime rate: 93.2 per 10,000 population (2001).
Transportation: Commute to work: 87.5% car, 0.8% public transportation, 8.1% walk, 3.0% work from home (2000); Travel time to work: 40.6% less than 15 minutes, 39.9% 15 to 30 minutes, 7.2% 30 to 45 minutes, 6.6% 45 to 60 minutes, 5.7% 60 minutes or more (2000)

SPRINGPORT (village). Covers a land area of 1.276 square miles and a water area of 0 square miles. Located at 42.37° N. Lat.; 84.69° W. Long. Elevation is 996 feet.
History: Springport was founded in 1836 by John Oyer, when it was called Oyer's Corners. It developed around a station of the Lake Shore & Michigan Southern Railroad which arrived here in 1876.
Population: 704 (2000); Race: 92.8% White, 0.9% Black, 0.0% Asian, 0.0% American Indian and Alaska Native, 3.8% Hispanic of any race, 4.7% two or more races (2000); Density: 551.7 persons per square mile (2000); Age: 29.6% under 18, 11.3% over 64 (2000); Marriage status: 28.0% never married, 52.1% now married, 7.7% widowed, 12.1% divorced (2000); Foreign born: 1.3% (2000); Ancestry (includes multiple ancestries): 17.7% German, 12.8% United States or American, 10.9% English, 10.8% Other groups, 8.9% Irish (2000).
Economy: Employment by occupation: 3.4% management, 10.7% professional, 15.6% services, 18.1% sales, 0.9% farming, 15.6% construction, 35.6% production (2000).
Income: Per capita income: $13,887 (2000); Median household income: $40,052 (2000); Poverty rate: 8.9% (2000).
Taxes: Total city taxes per capita: $140 (1997); City property taxes per capita: $138 (1997).
Education: High school graduation rate: 76.0% (2000); College graduation rate: 11.4% (2000).

School District(s)

Springport Public Schools (KG-12)
2000 Enrollment: 1,079 517-857-3495
Housing: Homeownership rate: 68.5% (2000); Median home value: $67,600 (2000); Median rent: $350 per month (2000); Median age of housing: 60+ years (2000).
Newspapers: Springport Signal (1 x week)
Transportation: Commute to work: 90.3% car, 0.0% public transportation, 6.2% walk, 3.4% work from home (2000); Travel time to work: 29.0% less than 15 minutes, 41.9% 15 to 30 minutes, 17.7% 30 to 45 minutes, 6.5% 45 to 60 minutes, 4.8% 60 minutes or more (2000)

SPRINGPORT (township). Covers a land area of 36.137 square miles and a water area of 0.204 square miles. Located at 42.37° N. Lat.; 84.67° W. Long. Elevation is 996 feet.
Population: 2,182 (2000); Race: 96.5% White, 0.3% Black, 0.0% Asian, 0.2% American Indian and Alaska Native, 1.7% Hispanic of any race, 2.3% two or more races (2000); Density: 60.4 persons per square mile (2000); Age: 28.1% under 18, 11.0% over 64 (2000); Marriage status: 24.4% never married, 59.3% now married, 4.3% widowed, 12.0% divorced (2000); Foreign born: 0.6% (2000); Ancestry (includes multiple ancestries): 21.7% German, 10.2% English, 10.0% Other groups, 8.8% Irish, 8.8% United States or American (2000).
Economy: In agricultural area; manufacturing of metal stampings. Single-family building permits issued: 10 (2001) / 10 (2000); Multi-family building permits issued: 0 (2001) / 0 (2000); Employment by occupation: 6.3% management, 10.9% professional, 12.7% services, 22.5% sales, 0.3% farming, 15.9% construction, 31.4% production (2000).
Income: Per capita income: $16,417 (2000); Median household income: $42,344 (2000); Poverty rate: 7.8% (2000).
Taxes: Total city taxes per capita: $37 (1997); City property taxes per capita: $34 (1997).
Education: High school graduation rate: 81.0% (2000); College graduation rate: 9.1% (2000).
Housing: Homeownership rate: 78.6% (2000); Median home value: $79,200 (2000); Median rent: $382 per month (2000); Median age of housing: 45 years (2000).
Transportation: Commute to work: 94.9% car, 0.7% public transportation, 2.3% walk, 1.9% work from home (2000); Travel time to work: 19.2% less than 15 minutes, 39.2% 15 to 30 minutes, 27.4% 30 to 45 minutes, 7.4% 45 to 60 minutes, 6.8% 60 minutes or more (2000)

SUMMIT (township). Covers a land area of 29.284 square miles and a water area of 0.601 square miles. Located at 42.20° N. Lat.; 84.41° W. Long.
History: Summit Township was set off in 1857 from the old township of Jackson, and named for having the highest elevation in the county.
Population: 21,534 (2000); Race: 91.7% White, 3.8% Black, 1.4% Asian, 0.4% American Indian and Alaska Native, 2.5% Hispanic of any race, 1.5% two or more races (2000); Density: 735.4 persons per square mile (2000); Age: 25.0% under 18, 17.8% over 64 (2000); Marriage status: 19.2% never married, 63.1% now married, 8.4% widowed, 9.3% divorced (2000); Foreign born: 3.1% (2000); Ancestry (includes multiple ancestries): 24.0% German, 15.6% Irish, 15.0% English, 11.1% Other groups, 7.8% Polish (2000).
Economy: Single-family building permits issued: 96 (2001) / 63 (2000); Multi-family building permits issued: 33 (2001) / 68 (2000); Employment by occupation: 14.0% management, 20.0% professional, 14.2% services, 27.7% sales, 0.2% farming, 5.9% construction, 18.0% production (2000).
Income: Per capita income: $25,738 (2000); Median household income: $50,492 (2000); Poverty rate: 5.1% (2000).
Taxes: Total city taxes per capita: $31 (1997); City property taxes per capita: $24 (1997).
Education: High school graduation rate: 87.8% (2000); College graduation rate: 25.1% (2000).
Housing: Homeownership rate: 80.7% (2000); Median home value: $102,700 (2000); Median rent: $513 per month (2000); Median age of housing: 39 years (2000).
Safety: Violent crime rate: 18.9 per 10,000 population; Property crime rate: 186.2 per 10,000 population (2001).
Transportation: Commute to work: 96.3% car, 0.2% public transportation, 0.8% walk, 2.2% work from home (2000); Travel time to work: 42.2% less than 15 minutes, 41.0% 15 to 30 minutes, 7.8% 30 to 45 minutes, 5.3% 45 to 60 minutes, 3.7% 60 minutes or more (2000)

TOMPKINS (township). Aka Tompkins Center. Covers a land area of 36.093 square miles and a water area of 0.284 square miles. Located at 42.37° N. Lat.; 84.54° W. Long.
Population: 2,758 (2000); Race: 97.6% White, 0.1% Black, 0.1% Asian, 0.3% American Indian and Alaska Native, 0.8% Hispanic of any race, 1.1% two or more races (2000); Density: 76.4 persons per square mile (2000); Age: 30.1% under 18, 10.3% over 64 (2000); Marriage status: 18.5% never married, 67.2% now married, 5.9% widowed, 8.3% divorced (2000); Foreign born: 0.5% (2000); Ancestry (includes multiple ancestries): 22.3% German, 17.6% English, 12.4% Irish, 9.4% United States or American, 7.9% Other groups (2000).
Economy: Single-family building permits issued: 20 (2001) / 15 (2000); Multi-family building permits issued: 0 (2001) / 0 (2000); Employment by occupation: 8.2% management, 16.9% professional, 13.6% services, 24.4% sales, 1.1% farming, 12.9% construction, 22.9% production (2000).
Income: Per capita income: $17,094 (2000); Median household income: $43,203 (2000); Poverty rate: 6.8% (2000).
Taxes: Total city taxes per capita: $19 (1997); City property taxes per capita: $16 (1997).
Education: High school graduation rate: 86.0% (2000); College graduation rate: 11.4% (2000).
Housing: Homeownership rate: 90.8% (2000); Median home value: $110,900 (2000); Median rent: $423 per month (2000); Median age of housing: 28 years (2000).
Transportation: Commute to work: 91.6% car, 0.0% public transportation, 1.4% walk, 5.5% work from home (2000); Travel time to work: 13.9% less than 15 minutes, 52.3% 15 to 30 minutes, 21.8% 30 to 45 minutes, 6.1% 45 to 60 minutes, 5.8% 60 minutes or more (2000)

VANDERCOOK LAKE (CDP). Aka Vandercook. Covers a land area of 4.562 square miles and a water area of 0.186 square miles. Located at 42.19° N. Lat.; 84.39° W. Long.
Population: 4,809 (2000); Race: 96.7% White, 1.1% Black, 0.0% Asian, 0.5% American Indian and Alaska Native, 3.3% Hispanic of any race, 0.7% two or more races (2000); Density: 1,054.1 persons per square mile (2000); Age: 28.2% under 18, 14.3% over 64 (2000); Marriage status: 24.2% never married, 54.8% now married, 7.3% widowed, 13.7% divorced (2000); Foreign born: 0.9% (2000); Ancestry (includes multiple ancestries): 23.2% German, 12.9% United States or American, 12.2% Irish, 11.8% English, 8.5% Other groups (2000).
Economy: Michigan Space Center to South. Employment by occupation: 5.6% management, 14.6% professional, 16.6% services, 27.1% sales, 0.0% farming, 8.4% construction, 27.8% production (2000).
Income: Per capita income: $17,359 (2000); Median household income: $40,238 (2000); Poverty rate: 5.7% (2000).
Education: High school graduation rate: 81.5% (2000); College graduation rate: 9.9% (2000).
Housing: Homeownership rate: 88.8% (2000); Median home value: $83,000 (2000); Median rent: $434 per month (2000); Median age of housing: 45 years (2000).
Transportation: Commute to work: 97.8% car, 0.0% public transportation, 1.1% walk, 1.1% work from home (2000); Travel time to work: 38.6% less than 15 minutes, 44.2% 15 to 30 minutes, 8.6% 30 to 45 minutes, 6.0% 45 to 60 minutes, 2.6% 60 minutes or more (2000)

WATERLOO (township). Covers a land area of 47.925 square miles and a water area of 1.625 square miles. Located at 42.34° N. Lat.; 84.20° W. Long.
Population: 3,069 (2000); Race: 95.7% White, 2.8% Black, 0.0% Asian, 0.0% American Indian and Alaska Native, 0.0% Hispanic of any race, 1.2% two or more races (2000); Density: 64.0 persons per square mile (2000); Age: 24.3% under 18, 9.4% over 64 (2000); Marriage status: 16.7% never married, 70.8% now married, 4.2% widowed, 8.3% divorced (2000); Foreign born: 0.6% (2000); Ancestry (includes multiple ancestries): 34.1% German, 12.4% Irish, 9.9% United States or American, 9.2% English, 5.7% French (except Basque) (2000).
Economy: Single-family building permits issued: 28 (2001) / 21 (2000); Multi-family building permits issued: 0 (2001) / 0 (2000); Employment by occupation: 15.0% management, 16.7% professional, 10.7% services, 26.8% sales, 2.3% farming, 11.2% construction, 17.5% production (2000).
Income: Per capita income: $22,609 (2000); Median household income: $55,119 (2000); Poverty rate: 3.2% (2000).
Taxes: Total city taxes per capita: $51 (1997); City property taxes per capita: $36 (1997).
Education: High school graduation rate: 89.8% (2000); College graduation rate: 15.8% (2000).
Housing: Homeownership rate: 92.5% (2000); Median home value: $151,200 (2000); Median rent: $716 per month (2000); Median age of housing: 26 years (2000).
Safety: Violent crime rate: 6.5 per 10,000 population; Property crime rate: 81.0 per 10,000 population (2001).
Transportation: Commute to work: 91.6% car, 0.0% public transportation, 1.7% walk, 6.0% work from home (2000); Travel time to work: 10.9% less than 15 minutes, 30.8% 15 to 30 minutes, 26.1% 30 to 45 minutes, 19.2% 45 to 60 minutes, 13.0% 60 minutes or more (2000)

Kalamazoo County

Located in southwestern Michigan; drained by the Kalamazoo and Portage Rivers; includes many small lakes. Covers a land area of 561.90 square miles, a water area of 18.30 square miles, and is located in the Eastern Time Zone. The county government was organized in 1829. County seat is Kalamazoo.

Kalamazoo County is part of the Kalamazoo-Battle Creek, MI MSA. The entire metro area includes: Calhoun County; Kalamazoo County; Van Buren County

Weather Station: Gull Lake Biological Station — Elevation: 908 feet

	Jan	Feb	Mar	Apr	May	Jun	Jul	Aug	Sep	Oct	Nov	Dec
High	31	35	46	59	72	81	84	82	75	63	48	36
Low	16	17	26	36	47	57	62	60	53	42	33	22
Precip	2.0	1.7	2.7	3.8	3.3	3.8	3.7	3.8	4.2	3.2	3.3	2.9
Snow	18.3	10.7	5.4	1.4	tr	0.0	0.0	0.0	0.0	0.4	4.0	15.2

High and Low temperatures in degrees Fahrenheit; Precipitation and Snow in inches

Population: 238,603 (2000); Race: 84.6% White, 9.1% Black, 1.8% Asian, 0.5% American Indian and Alaska Native, 2.7% Hispanic of any race, 2.6% two or more races (2000); Density: 424.7 persons per square mile (2000); Age: 24.0% under 18, 11.3% over 64 (2000).
Religion: Five largest groups: 8.8% Catholic Church, 3.9% Reformed Church in America, 3.0% The United Methodist Church, 2.6% Independent, Non-Charismatic Churches, 2.3% Christian Reformed Church in North America (2000).
Economy: Unemployment rate: 3.7% (11/2002); Total civilian labor force: 130,758 (11/2002); Leading industries: 18.1% manufacturing; 13.9% retail trade; 13.4% health care and social assistance (2000); Companies that employ more than 1,000 persons: 5 (2000); Companies that employ more than 100 persons: 184 (2000); Farms: 696 totaling 146,927 acres (1997); Minority business ownership rate: 3.8% (1997); Women business ownership rate: 26.9% (1997); Retail sales per capita: $10,407 (1997). Single-family building permits issued: 954 (2001) / 907 (2000); Multi-family building permits issued: 272 (2001) / 580 (2000).
Income: Per capita income: $21,739 (2000); Median household income: $42,022 (2000); Poverty rate: 12.0% (2000); Bankruptcy rate: 5.01% (2001).
Taxes: Total county taxes per capita: $135 (2000); County property taxes per capita: $129 (2000).
Education: High school graduation rate: 88.8% (2000); College graduation rate: 31.2% (2000).
Housing: Homeownership rate: 65.8% (2000); Median home value: $108,000 (2000); Median rent: $484 per month (2000); Median age of housing: 32 years (2000).
Health: Birth rate: 133.4 per 10,000 population (1998); Age adjusted death rate: 86.6 per 10,000 population (1999); Age adjusted cancer mortality rate: 205.7 deaths per 100,000 population (1999). Air Quality Index: 69% good, 31% moderate, 0% unhealthy (percent of days in 2000). Number of physicians: 33.7 per 10,000 population (1999); Number of hospital beds: 37.3 per 10,000 population (1999).
Elections: 2000 Presidential election results: 48.5% Gore, 47.9% Bush, 3.1% Nader, 0.0% Buchanan
National and State Parks: Fort Custer State Park; Gourdneck State Game Area
Additional Information Contacts
Kalamazoo County Government Offices 616-384-8111
Greater Kalamazoo Association of Realtors 616-382-1597
Kalamazoo County Chamber of Commerce 616-381-4000

Kalamazoo County Communities

ALAMO (township). Covers a land area of 36.285 square miles and a water area of 0.151 square miles. Located at 42.38° N. Lat.; 85.69° W. Long. Elevation is 783 feet.
History: Alamo Township was formed in 1838 and named for the Alamo in Texas.
Population: 3,820 (2000); Race: 97.4% White, 0.4% Black, 0.8% Asian, 0.0% American Indian and Alaska Native, 0.9% Hispanic of any race, 1.0% two or more races (2000); Density: 105.3 persons per square mile (2000); Age: 26.1% under 18, 15.5% over 64 (2000); Marriage status: 18.5% never married, 67.6% now married, 6.6% widowed, 7.4% divorced (2000); Foreign born: 2.4% (2000); Ancestry (includes multiple ancestries): 24.8% Dutch, 21.7% German, 15.1% English, 10.2% United States or American, 9.6% Irish (2000).
Economy: Single-family building permits issued: 13 (2001) / 15 (2000); Multi-family building permits issued: 0 (2001) / 0 (2000); Employment by occupation: 13.9% management, 16.2% professional, 13.7% services, 25.9% sales, 1.3% farming, 12.7% construction, 16.2% production (2000).
Income: Per capita income: $22,116 (2000); Median household income: $50,409 (2000); Poverty rate: 5.2% (2000).
Taxes: Total city taxes per capita: $41 (1997); City property taxes per capita: $37 (1997).
Education: High school graduation rate: 90.8% (2000); College graduation rate: 22.1% (2000).
Housing: Homeownership rate: 92.7% (2000); Median home value: $120,900 (2000); Median rent: $482 per month (2000); Median age of housing: 23 years (2000).
Transportation: Commute to work: 92.6% car, 0.5% public transportation, 1.6% walk, 5.3% work from home (2000); Travel time to work: 26.3% less than 15 minutes, 52.4% 15 to 30 minutes, 13.5% 30 to 45 minutes, 4.1% 45 to 60 minutes, 3.6% 60 minutes or more (2000)

AUGUSTA (village). Covers a land area of 0.934 square miles and a water area of 0.013 square miles. Located at 42.33° N. Lat.; 85.35° W. Long.
History: Augusta was the home of scientist Dr. William T. Bovie. The village was platted in 1836, and incorporated in 1869.
Population: 899 (2000); Race: 97.2% White, 0.0% Black, 0.0% Asian, 0.9% American Indian and Alaska Native, 0.4% Hispanic of any race, 1.7% two or more races (2000); Density: 962.7 persons per square mile (2000); Age: 29.4% under 18, 10.2% over 64 (2000); Marriage status: 21.1% never married, 59.9% now married, 6.5% widowed, 12.4% divorced (2000); Foreign born: 1.6% (2000); Ancestry (includes multiple ancestries): 21.1% German, 19.9% Irish, 19.2% English, 15.1% Other groups, 10.2% French (except Basque) (2000).
Economy: Single-family building permits issued: 2 (2001) / 1 (2000); Multi-family building permits issued: 0 (2001) / 0 (2000); Employment by occupation: 9.7% management, 17.5% professional, 10.6% services, 25.6% sales, 0.0% farming, 9.4% construction, 27.2% production (2000).
Income: Per capita income: $19,207 (2000); Median household income: $44,375 (2000); Poverty rate: 4.8% (2000).
Taxes: Total city taxes per capita: $115 (1997); City property taxes per capita: $105 (1997).
Education: High school graduation rate: 90.5% (2000); College graduation rate: 15.2% (2000).
Housing: Homeownership rate: 75.1% (2000); Median home value: $84,800 (2000); Median rent: $431 per month (2000); Median age of housing: 52 years (2000).
Safety: Violent crime rate: 0.0 per 10,000 population; Property crime rate: 199.1 per 10,000 population (2001).
Transportation: Commute to work: 95.5% car, 0.0% public transportation, 0.9% walk, 2.5% work from home (2000); Travel time to work: 29.8% less than 15 minutes, 46.5% 15 to 30 minutes, 17.9% 30 to 45 minutes, 2.6% 45 to 60 minutes, 3.3% 60 minutes or more (2000)

BRADY (township). Covers a land area of 34.903 square miles and a water area of 1.240 square miles. Located at 42.12° N. Lat.; 85.48° W. Long.
Population: 4,263 (2000); Race: 97.0% White, 0.3% Black, 0.1% Asian, 0.3% American Indian and Alaska Native, 0.7% Hispanic of any race, 2.0% two or more races (2000); Density: 122.1 persons per square mile (2000); Age: 28.5% under 18, 11.5% over 64 (2000); Marriage status: 18.5% never married, 68.0% now married, 4.3% widowed, 9.2% divorced (2000); Foreign born: 1.0% (2000); Ancestry (includes multiple ancestries): 23.5% German, 17.6% English, 11.3% Irish, 11.2% Dutch, 9.4% United States or American (2000).
Economy: Employment by occupation: 11.8% management, 15.9% professional, 13.1% services, 24.2% sales, 0.4% farming, 12.2% construction, 22.5% production (2000).
Income: Per capita income: $22,229 (2000); Median household income: $52,202 (2000); Poverty rate: 3.4% (2000).
Taxes: Total city taxes per capita: $30 (1997); City property taxes per capita: $21 (1997).
Education: High school graduation rate: 88.9% (2000); College graduation rate: 18.6% (2000).
Housing: Homeownership rate: 92.1% (2000); Median home value: $111,000 (2000); Median rent: $404 per month (2000); Median age of housing: 33 years (2000).
Transportation: Commute to work: 94.9% car, 0.0% public transportation, 0.8% walk, 4.0% work from home (2000); Travel time to work: 23.7% less than 15 minutes, 43.2% 15 to 30 minutes, 22.6% 30 to 45 minutes, 6.1% 45 to 60 minutes, 4.4% 60 minutes or more (2000)

CHARLESTON (township). Covers a land area of 34.893 square miles and a water area of 0.729 square miles. Located at 42.28° N. Lat.; 85.36° W. Long.
Population: 1,813 (2000); Race: 96.8% White, 0.6% Black, 0.6% Asian, 1.3% American Indian and Alaska Native, 1.9% Hispanic of any race, 0.3% two or more races (2000); Density: 52.0 persons per square mile (2000); Age: 24.1% under 18, 13.2% over 64 (2000); Marriage status: 18.6% never married, 67.2% now married, 6.1% widowed, 8.1% divorced (2000); Foreign born: 1.8% (2000); Ancestry (includes multiple ancestries): 20.5% German, 14.0% English, 11.6% Irish, 10.7% United States or American, 9.6% Dutch (2000).
Economy: Single-family building permits issued: 9 (2001) / 3 (2000); Multi-family building permits issued: 0 (2001) / 0 (2000); Employment by occupation: 12.4% management, 15.8% professional, 13.8% services, 23.8% sales, 2.0% farming, 11.3% construction, 20.9% production (2000).
Income: Per capita income: $20,921 (2000); Median household income: $50,707 (2000); Poverty rate: 7.0% (2000).
Taxes: Total city taxes per capita: $50 (1997); City property taxes per capita: $46 (1997).
Education: High school graduation rate: 86.9% (2000); College graduation rate: 17.4% (2000).
Housing: Homeownership rate: 92.6% (2000); Median home value: $108,600 (2000); Median rent: $475 per month (2000); Median age of housing: 36 years (2000).
Transportation: Commute to work: 94.3% car, 0.0% public transportation, 0.6% walk, 4.5% work from home (2000); Travel time to work: 28.5% less than 15 minutes, 54.3% 15 to 30 minutes, 12.3% 30 to 45 minutes, 1.8% 45 to 60 minutes, 3.0% 60 minutes or more (2000)

CLIMAX (village). Covers a land area of 1.027 square miles and a water area of 0 square miles. Located at 42.23° N. Lat.; 85.33° W. Long. Elevation is 972 feet.
History: The village of Climax was settled in 1838 and took the name of the township, referring to the settlers end of a search for a place to live.
Population: 791 (2000); Race: 94.9% White, 1.2% Black, 0.0% Asian, 0.4% American Indian and Alaska Native, 2.2% Hispanic of any race, 2.3% two or more races (2000); Density: 769.9 persons per square mile (2000); Age: 33.9% under 18, 5.4% over 64 (2000); Marriage status: 22.2% never married, 61.7% now married, 5.0% widowed, 11.1% divorced (2000); Foreign born: 1.4% (2000); Ancestry (includes multiple ancestries): 28.7% German, 17.6% English, 12.2% Irish, 11.8% United States or American, 6.5% Other groups (2000).
Economy: Employment by occupation: 9.0% management, 17.0% professional, 12.5% services, 23.9% sales, 0.5% farming, 14.4% construction, 22.6% production (2000).
Income: Per capita income: $18,658 (2000); Median household income: $44,464 (2000); Poverty rate: 4.7% (2000).
Taxes: Total city taxes per capita: $123 (1997); City property taxes per capita: $120 (1997).
Education: High school graduation rate: 87.1% (2000); College graduation rate: 18.7% (2000).

School District(s)

Climax-Scotts Community Schools (KG-12)
2000 Enrollment: 723 616-746-2400

Housing: Homeownership rate: 78.0% (2000); Median home value: $94,100 (2000); Median rent: $441 per month (2000); Median age of housing: 48 years (2000).
Newspapers: The Climax Crescent (1 x week)
Transportation: Commute to work: 95.4% car, 0.0% public transportation, 2.4% walk, 1.1% work from home (2000); Travel time to work: 17.9% less than 15 minutes, 60.3% 15 to 30 minutes, 14.7% 30 to 45 minutes, 3.8% 45 to 60 minutes, 3.3% 60 minutes or more (2000)

CLIMAX (township). Covers a land area of 36.213 square miles and a water area of 0.167 square miles. Located at 42.20° N. Lat.; 85.36° W. Long. Elevation is 972 feet.
History: Climax was named Climax Prairie by its early settlers because it climaxed the end of their search for a place to live.
Population: 2,412 (2000); Race: 96.1% White, 0.5% Black, 0.0% Asian, 0.7% American Indian and Alaska Native, 1.5% Hispanic of any race, 2.2% two or more races (2000); Density: 66.6 persons per square mile (2000); Age: 27.9% under 18, 10.4% over 64 (2000); Marriage status: 19.6% never married, 69.1% now married, 4.3% widowed, 7.0% divorced (2000); Foreign born: 0.9% (2000); Ancestry (includes multiple ancestries): 25.9% German, 16.6% English, 15.2% Irish, 11.0% Dutch, 8.8% United States or American (2000).
Economy: Employment by occupation: 10.9% management, 13.2% professional, 12.2% services, 24.5% sales, 2.1% farming, 12.7% construction, 24.5% production (2000).
Income: Per capita income: $19,381 (2000); Median household income: $47,620 (2000); Poverty rate: 3.7% (2000).
Taxes: Total city taxes per capita: $53 (1997); City property taxes per capita: $48 (1997).
Education: High school graduation rate: 88.1% (2000); College graduation rate: 13.1% (2000).
Housing: Homeownership rate: 87.4% (2000); Median home value: $98,000 (2000); Median rent: $443 per month (2000); Median age of housing: 41 years (2000).
Transportation: Commute to work: 94.8% car, 0.0% public transportation, 1.3% walk, 2.9% work from home (2000); Travel time to work: 14.8% less

than 15 minutes, 52.9% 15 to 30 minutes, 24.4% 30 to 45 minutes, 2.3% 45 to 60 minutes, 5.6% 60 minutes or more (2000)

COMSTOCK (township). Covers a land area of 32.961 square miles and a water area of 1.983 square miles. Located at 42.29° N. Lat.; 85.49° W. Long.
History: Comstock was named for General Horace Comstock, who supported the development of the settlement in 1831 and became the first postmaster. His efforts to have Comstock named as the seat of Kalamazoo County were unsuccessful, and he returned to New York.
Population: 13,851 (2000); Race: 91.8% White, 3.8% Black, 1.0% Asian, 0.4% American Indian and Alaska Native, 1.2% Hispanic of any race, 2.6% two or more races (2000); Density: 420.2 persons per square mile (2000); Age: 26.2% under 18, 11.7% over 64 (2000); Marriage status: 23.3% never married, 59.0% now married, 6.4% widowed, 11.3% divorced (2000); Foreign born: 2.6% (2000); Ancestry (includes multiple ancestries): 20.4% German, 14.2% Dutch, 13.7% English, 12.7% Irish, 11.1% United States or American (2000).
Economy: Single-family building permits issued: 80 (2001) / 75 (2000); Multi-family building permits issued: 98 (2001) / 180 (2000); Employment by occupation: 10.6% management, 20.2% professional, 12.8% services, 25.8% sales, 1.2% farming, 9.7% construction, 19.6% production (2000).
Income: Per capita income: $22,857 (2000); Median household income: $46,140 (2000); Poverty rate: 7.1% (2000).
Taxes: Total city taxes per capita: $85 (1997); City property taxes per capita: $71 (1997).
Education: High school graduation rate: 86.3% (2000); College graduation rate: 22.0% (2000).
Housing: Homeownership rate: 73.8% (2000); Median home value: $109,400 (2000); Median rent: $517 per month (2000); Median age of housing: 29 years (2000).
Transportation: Commute to work: 95.5% car, 0.2% public transportation, 1.1% walk, 2.8% work from home (2000); Travel time to work: 34.8% less than 15 minutes, 49.5% 15 to 30 minutes, 9.3% 30 to 45 minutes, 2.2% 45 to 60 minutes, 4.2% 60 minutes or more (2000)

COMSTOCK NORTHWEST (CDP). Covers a land area of 3.184 square miles and a water area of 0.008 square miles. Located at 42.32° N. Lat.; 85.51° W. Long.
Population: 4,472 (2000); Race: 86.4% White, 7.0% Black, 1.5% Asian, 0.0% American Indian and Alaska Native, 1.4% Hispanic of any race, 4.2% two or more races (2000); Density: 1,404.3 persons per square mile (2000); Age: 24.6% under 18, 14.5% over 64 (2000); Marriage status: 25.8% never married, 56.0% now married, 7.0% widowed, 11.3% divorced (2000); Foreign born: 4.4% (2000); Ancestry (includes multiple ancestries): 20.1% German, 14.9% Dutch, 13.9% English, 12.7% Irish, 12.0% Other groups (2000).
Economy: Employment by occupation: 9.9% management, 23.3% professional, 12.9% services, 27.8% sales, 0.8% farming, 7.4% construction, 17.9% production (2000).
Income: Per capita income: $23,961 (2000); Median household income: $43,590 (2000); Poverty rate: 6.1% (2000).
Education: High school graduation rate: 89.7% (2000); College graduation rate: 23.7% (2000).
Housing: Homeownership rate: 55.3% (2000); Median home value: $115,800 (2000); Median rent: $534 per month (2000); Median age of housing: 21 years (2000).
Transportation: Commute to work: 96.6% car, 0.4% public transportation, 0.7% walk, 2.3% work from home (2000); Travel time to work: 33.8% less than 15 minutes, 48.2% 15 to 30 minutes, 11.4% 30 to 45 minutes, 2.2% 45 to 60 minutes, 4.5% 60 minutes or more (2000)

COOPER (township). Covers a land area of 36.293 square miles and a water area of 0.388 square miles. Located at 42.36° N. Lat.; 85.57° W. Long. Elevation is 875 feet.
History: Cooper Township was organized in 1836 by General Horace Comstock, who named it for his wife, a niece of James Fenimore Cooper.
Population: 8,754 (2000); Race: 96.1% White, 0.5% Black, 0.3% Asian, 0.8% American Indian and Alaska Native, 0.9% Hispanic of any race, 1.9% two or more races (2000); Density: 241.2 persons per square mile (2000); Age: 26.3% under 18, 12.6% over 64 (2000); Marriage status: 18.1% never married, 70.0% now married, 5.4% widowed, 6.5% divorced (2000); Foreign born: 1.7% (2000); Ancestry (includes multiple ancestries): 22.5% German, 18.3% Dutch, 13.2% Irish, 12.6% English, 9.3% United States or American (2000).
Economy: Single-family building permits issued: 60 (2001) / 68 (2000); Multi-family building permits issued: 132 (2001) / 0 (2000); Employment by occupation: 11.0% management, 20.4% professional, 14.2% services, 23.8% sales, 0.6% farming, 12.4% construction, 17.6% production (2000).
Income: Per capita income: $21,566 (2000); Median household income: $47,004 (2000); Poverty rate: 3.5% (2000).
Taxes: Total city taxes per capita: $28 (1997); City property taxes per capita: $21 (1997).
Education: High school graduation rate: 86.9% (2000); College graduation rate: 23.6% (2000).
Housing: Homeownership rate: 90.9% (2000); Median home value: $107,200 (2000); Median rent: $499 per month (2000); Median age of housing: 35 years (2000).
Transportation: Commute to work: 95.0% car, 0.7% public transportation, 0.2% walk, 3.2% work from home (2000); Travel time to work: 28.7% less than 15 minutes, 47.7% 15 to 30 minutes, 16.5% 30 to 45 minutes, 3.9% 45 to 60 minutes, 3.2% 60 minutes or more (2000)

EASTWOOD (CDP). Covers a land area of 1.996 square miles and a water area of 0.004 square miles. Located at 42.30° N. Lat.; 85.54° W. Long.
Population: 6,265 (2000); Race: 74.6% White, 20.3% Black, 1.7% Asian, 0.6% American Indian and Alaska Native, 2.5% Hispanic of any race, 1.4% two or more races (2000); Density: 3,139.3 persons per square mile (2000); Age: 24.7% under 18, 13.2% over 64 (2000); Marriage status: 31.0% never married, 50.3% now married, 6.0% widowed, 12.7% divorced (2000); Foreign born: 4.0% (2000); Ancestry (includes multiple ancestries): 25.3% Other groups, 12.0% German, 8.7% English, 7.8% Dutch, 7.8% Irish (2000).
Economy: Employment by occupation: 6.2% management, 16.3% professional, 17.8% services, 24.2% sales, 0.2% farming, 11.7% construction, 23.6% production (2000).
Income: Per capita income: $17,313 (2000); Median household income: $35,763 (2000); Poverty rate: 12.1% (2000).
Education: High school graduation rate: 86.7% (2000); College graduation rate: 14.3% (2000).
Housing: Homeownership rate: 66.2% (2000); Median home value: $67,000 (2000); Median rent: $459 per month (2000); Median age of housing: 46 years (2000).
Transportation: Commute to work: 93.9% car, 2.1% public transportation, 1.8% walk, 1.8% work from home (2000); Travel time to work: 36.3% less than 15 minutes, 46.9% 15 to 30 minutes, 10.0% 30 to 45 minutes, 3.9% 45 to 60 minutes, 2.8% 60 minutes or more (2000)

FULTON (unincorporated postal area, zip code 49052). Covers a land area of 29.406 square miles and a water area of 0 square miles. Located at 42.11° N. Lat.; 85.31° W. Long.
Population: 850 (2000); Race: 95.2% White, 0.0% Black, 0.5% Asian, 3.4% American Indian and Alaska Native, 1.0% Hispanic of any race, 0.0% two or more races (2000); Density: 28.9 persons per square mile (2000); Age: 25.5% under 18, 10.4% over 64 (2000); Marriage status: 19.6% never married, 66.2% now married, 5.7% widowed, 8.5% divorced (2000); Foreign born: 2.3% (2000); Ancestry (includes multiple ancestries): 31.2% German, 13.6% English, 12.2% Irish, 10.9% Other groups, 10.6% United States or American (2000).
Economy: Employment by occupation: 12.3% management, 12.6% professional, 13.1% services, 21.7% sales, 2.7% farming, 10.9% construction, 26.7% production (2000).
Income: Per capita income: $17,761 (2000); Median household income: $44,479 (2000); Poverty rate: 8.8% (2000).
Education: High school graduation rate: 85.9% (2000); College graduation rate: 9.6% (2000).
Housing: Homeownership rate: 93.5% (2000); Median home value: $78,100 (2000); Median rent: $375 per month (2000); Median age of housing: 55 years (2000).
Transportation: Commute to work: 95.9% car, 0.0% public transportation, 0.3% walk, 3.8% work from home (2000); Travel time to work: 7.9% less than 15 minutes, 35.2% 15 to 30 minutes, 46.3% 30 to 45 minutes, 7.9% 45 to 60 minutes, 2.6% 60 minutes or more (2000)

GALESBURG (city). Covers a land area of 1.390 square miles and a water area of 0.053 square miles. Located at 42.28° N. Lat.; 85.41° W. Long. Elevation is 789 feet.
History: Galesburg, established at the intersection of several trails, was a stopping place for travelers going between St. Joseph and Fort Dearborn. The town was first called Morton when it was founded in 1835 by George L. Gale, but in 1838 the residents changed the name to Galesburg, in honor of the founder.

Population: 1,988 (2000); Race: 95.7% White, 0.9% Black, 0.0% Asian, 0.7% American Indian and Alaska Native, 0.4% Hispanic of any race, 2.5% two or more races (2000); Density: 1,429.8 persons per square mile (2000); Age: 27.2% under 18, 12.5% over 64 (2000); Marriage status: 30.7% never married, 49.3% now married, 6.5% widowed, 13.5% divorced (2000); Foreign born: 0.6% (2000); Ancestry (includes multiple ancestries): 21.4% German, 14.1% English, 12.8% Irish, 12.5% Dutch, 7.8% United States or American (2000).
Economy: Single-family building permits issued: 3 (2001) / 3 (2000); Multi-family building permits issued: 0 (2001) / 0 (2000); Employment by occupation: 10.3% management, 8.6% professional, 19.7% services, 21.5% sales, 1.3% farming, 16.4% construction, 22.3% production (2000).
Income: Per capita income: $16,785 (2000); Median household income: $34,663 (2000); Poverty rate: 12.9% (2000).
Taxes: Total city taxes per capita: $99 (1997); City property taxes per capita: $89 (1997).
Education: High school graduation rate: 81.3% (2000); College graduation rate: 11.9% (2000).

School District(s)

Galesburg-Augusta Community Scho (KG-12)
2000 Enrollment: 1,198 616-665-7088

Housing: Homeownership rate: 67.7% (2000); Median home value: $83,200 (2000); Median rent: $365 per month (2000); Median age of housing: 30 years (2000).
Safety: Violent crime rate: 0.0 per 10,000 population; Property crime rate: 220.2 per 10,000 population (2001).
Transportation: Commute to work: 96.9% car, 0.0% public transportation, 1.0% walk, 1.7% work from home (2000); Travel time to work: 24.5% less than 15 minutes, 60.5% 15 to 30 minutes, 10.7% 30 to 45 minutes, 1.0% 45 to 60 minutes, 3.3% 60 minutes or more (2000)

GREATER GALESBURG (CDP). Covers a land area of 6.651 square miles and a water area of 0.998 square miles. Located at 42.28° N. Lat.; 85.42° W. Long.
Population: 1,631 (2000); Race: 96.7% White, 0.7% Black, 0.4% Asian, 0.1% American Indian and Alaska Native, 2.2% Hispanic of any race, 0.7% two or more races (2000); Density: 245.2 persons per square mile (2000); Age: 28.2% under 18, 9.3% over 64 (2000); Marriage status: 23.6% never married, 57.5% now married, 7.3% widowed, 11.7% divorced (2000); Foreign born: 0.5% (2000); Ancestry (includes multiple ancestries): 23.6% German, 15.8% Irish, 11.1% Dutch, 10.5% English, 7.9% United States or American (2000).
Economy: Employment by occupation: 10.1% management, 17.6% professional, 16.1% services, 25.3% sales, 1.6% farming, 10.1% construction, 19.2% production (2000).
Income: Per capita income: $19,368 (2000); Median household income: $47,125 (2000); Poverty rate: 9.6% (2000).
Education: High school graduation rate: 86.5% (2000); College graduation rate: 20.7% (2000).
Housing: Homeownership rate: 87.5% (2000); Median home value: $106,200 (2000); Median rent: $428 per month (2000); Median age of housing: 29 years (2000).
Transportation: Commute to work: 93.8% car, 0.0% public transportation, 3.2% walk, 2.7% work from home (2000); Travel time to work: 30.7% less than 15 minutes, 57.5% 15 to 30 minutes, 8.0% 30 to 45 minutes, 0.4% 45 to 60 minutes, 3.4% 60 minutes or more (2000)

KALAMAZOO (city). Covers a land area of 24.683 square miles and a water area of 0.499 square miles. Located at 42.27° N. Lat.; 85.58° W. Long. Elevation is 753 feet.
History: The name first applied to the river was Kee-Kalamazoo, meaning "where the water boils in the pot," in reference to the bubbling springs in the river. A trading post was established here in 1823, followed in 1847 by a group of Hollanders seeking religious freedom. Kalamazoo was the birthplace of celery, whose seeds were introduced about 1850 by Scotsman James Taylor. Cultivation was begun by Marinus DeBruin, and by 1870 much swampland had been converted into celery farms. Other industries that began before the turn of the century were the Kalamazoo Paper Company, forerunner of a group that made the city a paper-mill center, and Dr. William E. Upjohn's pill company, which developed into the pharmaceutical industry.
Population: 77,145 (2000); Race: 70.6% White, 19.7% Black, 2.1% Asian, 0.6% American Indian and Alaska Native, 4.4% Hispanic of any race, 4.1% two or more races (2000); Density: 3,125.4 persons per square mile (2000); Age: 20.3% under 18, 10.0% over 64 (2000); Marriage status: 46.2% never married, 38.5% now married, 5.0% widowed, 10.4% divorced (2000); Foreign born: 5.2% (2000); Ancestry (includes multiple ancestries): 26.0% Other groups, 17.3% German, 10.0% Irish, 9.8% English, 7.7% Dutch (2000).
Vital Statistics: Birth rate: 188.2 per 10,000 population (1998)
Economy: Unemployment rate: 5.5% (11/2002); Total civilian labor force: 43,520 (11/2002); Single-family building permits issued: 37 (2001) / 22 (2000); Multi-family building permits issued: 8 (2001) / 24 (2000); Employment by occupation: 9.6% management, 22.6% professional, 20.9% services, 25.4% sales, 0.8% farming, 5.9% construction, 14.7% production (2000).
Income: Per capita income: $16,897 (2000); Median household income: $31,189 (2000); Poverty rate: 24.3% (2000).
Taxes: Total city taxes per capita: $377 (2000); City property taxes per capita: $365 (2000).
Education: High school graduation rate: 84.2% (2000); College graduation rate: 32.7% (2000).

School District(s)

Comstock Public Schools (KG-12)
2000 Enrollment: 2,985 616-388-9461
Family Institute Early Childhood (KG-03)
2000 Enrollment: 10 616-895-3029
Kalamazoo Advantage Academy (KG-07)
2000 Enrollment: 535 616-895-3029
Kalamazoo Public School District (PK-12)
2000 Enrollment: 11,105 616-337-0123
Navigator Academy (KG-06)
2000 Enrollment: 52 616-895-3029
Paramount Charter Academy (KG-07)
2000 Enrollment: 516 616-895-3029

Four-year College(s)

Davenport University-Western Region-Kalamazoo (Private, Not-for-profit)
2001 Enrollment: 1,063 616-382-2835
2001 Tuition: In-state $9,570; Out-of-state $9,570
Kalamazoo College (Private, Not-for-profit)
2001 Enrollment: 1,384 616-337-7000
2001 Tuition: In-state $20,652; Out-of-state $20,652
Western Michigan University (Public)
2001 Enrollment: 28,931 616-387-3530
2001 Tuition: In-state $3,897; Out-of-state $9,653

Two-year College(s)

Kalamazoo Valley Community College (Public)
2001 Enrollment: 9,911 616-372-5000
2001 Tuition: In-state $2,478; Out-of-state $3,542

Housing: Homeownership rate: 47.8% (2000); Median home value: $83,000 (2000); Median rent: $476 per month (2000); Median age of housing: 44 years (2000).
Hospitals: Borgess Medical Center (424 beds); Bronson Total Health Care (439 beds); Kalamazoo Psychiatric Hospital (163 beds)
Safety: Violent crime rate: 117.0 per 10,000 population; Property crime rate: 694.8 per 10,000 population (2001).
Newspapers: Kalamazoo Gazette (7 x week); The Hometown Gazette (1 x week)
Transportation: Commute to work: 85.6% car, 3.2% public transportation, 7.0% walk, 3.2% work from home (2000); Travel time to work: 48.8% less than 15 minutes, 36.2% 15 to 30 minutes, 8.6% 30 to 45 minutes, 2.7% 45 to 60 minutes, 3.7% 60 minutes or more (2000); Amtrak: Service available.
Airports: Kalamazoo/Battle Creek International (primary service)
Additional Information Contacts
Greater Kalamazoo Association of Realtors 616-382-1597
Kalamazoo County Chamber of Commerce 616-381-4000

KALAMAZOO (township). Covers a land area of 11.676 square miles and a water area of 0.125 square miles. Located at 42.31° N. Lat.; 85.58° W. Long. Elevation is 753 feet.
History: The seat of Western Michigan University, Kalamazoo College and Nazareth College. Incorporated 1883.
Population: 21,675 (2000); Race: 83.0% White, 11.5% Black, 1.4% Asian, 0.4% American Indian and Alaska Native, 2.5% Hispanic of any race, 2.2% two or more races (2000); Density: 1,856.4 persons per square mile (2000); Age: 22.4% under 18, 15.0% over 64 (2000); Marriage status: 32.4% never married, 49.4% now married, 7.0% widowed, 11.2% divorced (2000); Foreign born: 3.1% (2000); Ancestry (includes multiple ancestries): 18.3% Other groups, 17.5% German, 14.1% Dutch, 12.2% English, 10.6% Irish (2000).
Vital Statistics: Birth rate: 144.4 per 10,000 population (1998)
Economy: Industrial and commercial center in a fertile farm area. Agriculture includes celery, peppermint and fruit. Important paper industry.

Manufacturing includes paper products, hydraulic equipment, handling devices, meat products, furniture, concrete, motor vehicle parts, printing plates, sheet metal products and pharmaceuticals. Winery. Railroad junction. Single-family building permits issued: 40 (2001) / 64 (2000); Multi-family building permits issued: 2 (2001) / 50 (2000); Employment by occupation: 10.1% management, 22.6% professional, 17.0% services, 25.5% sales, 0.3% farming, 7.2% construction, 17.4% production (2000).
Income: Per capita income: $19,844 (2000); Median household income: $37,463 (2000); Poverty rate: 11.0% (2000).
Taxes: Total city taxes per capita: $150 (2000); City property taxes per capita: $140 (2000).
Education: High school graduation rate: 87.7% (2000); College graduation rate: 26.8% (2000).
Housing: Homeownership rate: 68.1% (2000); Median home value: $84,700 (2000); Median rent: $506 per month (2000); Median age of housing: 39 years (2000).
Safety: Violent crime rate: 38.1 per 10,000 population; Property crime rate: 439.7 per 10,000 population (2001).
Transportation: Commute to work: 93.7% car, 1.4% public transportation, 2.0% walk, 2.2% work from home (2000); Travel time to work: 37.2% less than 15 minutes, 44.5% 15 to 30 minutes, 11.7% 30 to 45 minutes, 3.4% 45 to 60 minutes, 3.2% 60 minutes or more (2000); Amtrak: Service available.

OSHTEMO (township). Covers a land area of 35.959 square miles and a water area of 0.146 square miles. Located at 42.28° N. Lat.; 85.68° W. Long.
History: Oshtemo developed as a trading center for grape and apple growers. The township was established in 1838, and the post office was founded in 1857.
Population: 17,003 (2000); Race: 85.6% White, 7.8% Black, 2.5% Asian, 0.3% American Indian and Alaska Native, 3.2% Hispanic of any race, 2.4% two or more races (2000); Density: 472.8 persons per square mile (2000); Age: 21.1% under 18, 13.2% over 64 (2000); Marriage status: 33.8% never married, 51.4% now married, 6.3% widowed, 8.5% divorced (2000); Foreign born: 5.4% (2000); Ancestry (includes multiple ancestries): 22.4% German, 16.2% Other groups, 14.2% English, 13.0% Dutch, 11.4% Irish (2000).
Economy: Single-family building permits issued: 98 (2001) / 94 (2000); Multi-family building permits issued: 26 (2001) / 326 (2000); Employment by occupation: 16.9% management, 23.1% professional, 15.4% services, 24.7% sales, 0.7% farming, 7.2% construction, 12.0% production (2000).
Income: Per capita income: $24,249 (2000); Median household income: $38,433 (2000); Poverty rate: 13.8% (2000).
Taxes: Total city taxes per capita: $96 (1997); City property taxes per capita: $81 (1997).
Education: High school graduation rate: 92.1% (2000); College graduation rate: 38.1% (2000).
Housing: Homeownership rate: 54.4% (2000); Median home value: $150,300 (2000); Median rent: $452 per month (2000); Median age of housing: 21 years (2000).
Transportation: Commute to work: 94.5% car, 1.1% public transportation, 2.0% walk, 2.3% work from home (2000); Travel time to work: 32.5% less than 15 minutes, 50.2% 15 to 30 minutes, 10.4% 30 to 45 minutes, 3.3% 45 to 60 minutes, 3.7% 60 minutes or more (2000)

PARCHMENT (city). Covers a land area of 0.855 square miles and a water area of 0.034 square miles. Located at 42.32° N. Lat.; 85.56° W. Long. Elevation is 846 feet.
History: Parchment was established as a model village around the Kalamazoo Vegetable Parchment Paper factory. Jacob Kindleberger built the town for the factory workers in 1909, when he opened the paper mill.
Population: 1,936 (2000); Race: 92.5% White, 4.0% Black, 0.4% Asian, 0.7% American Indian and Alaska Native, 1.1% Hispanic of any race, 1.5% two or more races (2000); Density: 2,263.6 persons per square mile (2000); Age: 27.0% under 18, 12.8% over 64 (2000); Marriage status: 26.9% never married, 54.4% now married, 7.0% widowed, 11.7% divorced (2000); Foreign born: 2.0% (2000); Ancestry (includes multiple ancestries): 20.0% German, 17.7% Irish, 15.5% English, 14.0% Dutch, 9.3% Other groups (2000).
Economy: Single-family building permits issued: 0 (2001) / 0 (2000); Multi-family building permits issued: 0 (2001) / 0 (2000); Employment by occupation: 12.5% management, 19.3% professional, 20.7% services, 26.0% sales, 0.4% farming, 5.3% construction, 15.8% production (2000).
Income: Per capita income: $18,911 (2000); Median household income: $40,074 (2000); Poverty rate: 4.4% (2000).
Taxes: Total city taxes per capita: $327 (1997); City property taxes per capita: $295 (1997).
Education: High school graduation rate: 90.6% (2000); College graduation rate: 27.7% (2000).

School District(s)

Parchment School District (KG-12)
2000 Enrollment: 1,858 616-342-7405
Housing: Homeownership rate: 66.3% (2000); Median home value: $90,800 (2000); Median rent: $488 per month (2000); Median age of housing: 46 years (2000).
Safety: Violent crime rate: 25.7 per 10,000 population; Property crime rate: 231.2 per 10,000 population (2001).
Transportation: Commute to work: 93.0% car, 1.0% public transportation, 3.4% walk, 2.6% work from home (2000); Travel time to work: 44.7% less than 15 minutes, 40.0% 15 to 30 minutes, 8.8% 30 to 45 minutes, 3.0% 45 to 60 minutes, 3.5% 60 minutes or more (2000)

PAVILION (township). Covers a land area of 34.884 square miles and a water area of 1.366 square miles. Located at 42.19° N. Lat.; 85.47° W. Long.
Population: 5,829 (2000); Race: 95.1% White, 1.5% Black, 0.2% Asian, 0.0% American Indian and Alaska Native, 1.0% Hispanic of any race, 2.5% two or more races (2000); Density: 167.1 persons per square mile (2000); Age: 28.3% under 18, 9.2% over 64 (2000); Marriage status: 23.2% never married, 62.9% now married, 5.4% widowed, 8.5% divorced (2000); Foreign born: 0.4% (2000); Ancestry (includes multiple ancestries): 22.0% German, 16.7% Dutch, 14.7% English, 14.4% Irish, 6.7% United States or American (2000).
Economy: Employment by occupation: 10.7% management, 16.3% professional, 11.9% services, 29.1% sales, 0.8% farming, 12.9% construction, 18.3% production (2000).
Income: Per capita income: $20,351 (2000); Median household income: $46,675 (2000); Poverty rate: 7.5% (2000).
Taxes: Total city taxes per capita: $29 (1997); City property taxes per capita: $22 (1997).
Education: High school graduation rate: 86.9% (2000); College graduation rate: 20.5% (2000).
Housing: Homeownership rate: 93.0% (2000); Median home value: $119,400 (2000); Median rent: $434 per month (2000); Median age of housing: 26 years (2000).
Transportation: Commute to work: 96.3% car, 0.0% public transportation, 0.0% walk, 3.7% work from home (2000); Travel time to work: 21.3% less than 15 minutes, 55.0% 15 to 30 minutes, 12.8% 30 to 45 minutes, 2.7% 45 to 60 minutes, 8.1% 60 minutes or more (2000)

PORTAGE (city). Covers a land area of 32.203 square miles and a water area of 2.823 square miles. Located at 42.21° N. Lat.; 85.58° W. Long. Elevation is 877 feet.
History: Portage was settled in 1830, and given a post office in 1836, when it was called Sweetland. In 1839 it was renamed Portage, like the township.
Population: 44,897 (2000); Race: 91.3% White, 3.1% Black, 2.6% Asian, 0.4% American Indian and Alaska Native, 2.1% Hispanic of any race, 1.8% two or more races (2000); Density: 1,394.2 persons per square mile (2000); Age: 26.5% under 18, 11.8% over 64 (2000); Marriage status: 24.3% never married, 59.7% now married, 6.1% widowed, 9.9% divorced (2000); Foreign born: 4.8% (2000); Ancestry (includes multiple ancestries): 25.7% German, 14.3% English, 12.9% Irish, 12.0% Dutch, 11.4% Other groups (2000).
Vital Statistics: Birth rate: 120.3 per 10,000 population (1998)
Economy: Unemployment rate: 2.4% (11/2002); Total civilian labor force: 25,804 (11/2002); Single-family building permits issued: 204 (2001) / 203 (2000); Multi-family building permits issued: 4 (2001) / 0 (2000); Employment by occupation: 15.2% management, 23.8% professional, 11.9% services, 28.4% sales, 0.3% farming, 7.1% construction, 13.3% production (2000).
Income: Per capita income: $25,414 (2000); Median household income: $49,410 (2000); Poverty rate: 4.8% (2000).
Taxes: Total city taxes per capita: $472 (2000); City property taxes per capita: $455 (2000).
Education: High school graduation rate: 92.6% (2000); College graduation rate: 36.8% (2000).

School District(s)

Oakland Academy (KG-05)
2000 Enrollment: 42 616-895-3029
Portage Public Schools (KG-12)
2000 Enrollment: 8,886 616-323-5182
Housing: Homeownership rate: 69.0% (2000); Median home value: $120,800 (2000); Median rent: $500 per month (2000); Median age of housing: 28 years (2000).

Safety: Violent crime rate: 20.6 per 10,000 population; Property crime rate: 475.9 per 10,000 population (2001).
Newspapers: Kalamazoo Flashes Shopping Guide (1 x week); Portage Gazette (1 x week); West Michigan Senior Times (1 x month); Zeeland Flashes Community Shopper (1 x week)
Transportation: Commute to work: 95.3% car, 0.3% public transportation, 0.8% walk, 3.2% work from home (2000); Travel time to work: 37.9% less than 15 minutes, 44.3% 15 to 30 minutes, 11.2% 30 to 45 minutes, 2.7% 45 to 60 minutes, 3.9% 60 minutes or more (2000)

PRAIRIE RONDE (township). Covers a land area of 35.777 square miles and a water area of 0.633 square miles. Located at 42.10° N. Lat.; 85.70° W. Long.
Population: 2,086 (2000); Race: 97.3% White, 0.1% Black, 1.3% Asian, 0.0% American Indian and Alaska Native, 0.9% Hispanic of any race, 1.3% two or more races (2000); Density: 58.3 persons per square mile (2000); Age: 32.1% under 18, 6.2% over 64 (2000); Marriage status: 17.8% never married, 72.7% now married, 3.3% widowed, 6.2% divorced (2000); Foreign born: 1.4% (2000); Ancestry (includes multiple ancestries): 26.8% German, 12.8% Dutch, 11.8% Irish, 9.2% English, 7.0% Polish (2000).
Economy: Employment by occupation: 16.4% management, 19.6% professional, 8.7% services, 25.1% sales, 0.0% farming, 11.0% construction, 19.3% production (2000).
Income: Per capita income: $23,431 (2000); Median household income: $65,385 (2000); Poverty rate: 4.2% (2000).
Taxes: Total city taxes per capita: $44 (1997); City property taxes per capita: $43 (1997).
Education: High school graduation rate: 96.9% (2000); College graduation rate: 24.9% (2000).
Housing: Homeownership rate: 96.5% (2000); Median home value: $146,500 (2000); Median rent: $488 per month (2000); Median age of housing: 17 years (2000).
Transportation: Commute to work: 94.8% car, 0.0% public transportation, 0.0% walk, 5.2% work from home (2000); Travel time to work: 11.1% less than 15 minutes, 56.7% 15 to 30 minutes, 24.1% 30 to 45 minutes, 1.5% 45 to 60 minutes, 6.6% 60 minutes or more (2000)

RICHLAND (village). Covers a land area of 1.199 square miles and a water area of <.001 square miles. Located at 42.37° N. Lat.; 85.45° W. Long. Elevation is 928 feet.
History: The village of Richland was platted in 1833 and called Gull Corners, for nearby Gull Lake. It was renamed for the township in 1840, and incorporated as a village in 1871.
Population: 593 (2000); Race: 93.6% White, 1.2% Black, 2.5% Asian, 0.0% American Indian and Alaska Native, 0.9% Hispanic of any race, 2.7% two or more races (2000); Density: 494.4 persons per square mile (2000); Age: 21.9% under 18, 16.5% over 64 (2000); Marriage status: 19.0% never married, 63.2% now married, 7.6% widowed, 10.1% divorced (2000); Foreign born: 3.7% (2000); Ancestry (includes multiple ancestries): 22.6% German, 17.8% Irish, 15.7% English, 13.5% Dutch, 8.2% Other groups (2000).
Economy: Single-family building permits issued: 18 (2001) / 14 (2000); Multi-family building permits issued: 0 (2001) / 0 (2000); Employment by occupation: 13.1% management, 29.0% professional, 15.0% services, 27.1% sales, 0.9% farming, 6.9% construction, 8.1% production (2000).
Income: Per capita income: $23,777 (2000); Median household income: $50,938 (2000); Poverty rate: 1.4% (2000).
Taxes: Total city taxes per capita: $243 (1997); City property taxes per capita: $233 (1997).
Education: High school graduation rate: 92.6% (2000); College graduation rate: 32.9% (2000).

School District(s)

Gull Lake Community Schools (KG-12)
2000 Enrollment: 3,051 616-629-5880
Housing: Homeownership rate: 79.4% (2000); Median home value: $111,200 (2000); Median rent: $622 per month (2000); Median age of housing: 33 years (2000).
Transportation: Commute to work: 95.0% car, 0.0% public transportation, 2.2% walk, 0.6% work from home (2000); Travel time to work: 28.2% less than 15 minutes, 44.6% 15 to 30 minutes, 17.4% 30 to 45 minutes, 4.4% 45 to 60 minutes, 5.4% 60 minutes or more (2000)

RICHLAND (township). Covers a land area of 34.749 square miles and a water area of 1.729 square miles. Located at 42.37° N. Lat.; 85.47° W. Long. Elevation is 928 feet.
History: Richland Township was organized in 1832 and named by Simeon Mills.
Population: 6,491 (2000); Race: 93.1% White, 3.4% Black, 0.9% Asian, 0.3% American Indian and Alaska Native, 3.2% Hispanic of any race, 2.0% two or more races (2000); Density: 186.8 persons per square mile (2000); Age: 28.7% under 18, 9.8% over 64 (2000); Marriage status: 18.0% never married, 69.0% now married, 4.1% widowed, 9.0% divorced (2000); Foreign born: 1.9% (2000); Ancestry (includes multiple ancestries): 23.0% German, 17.2% English, 15.6% Dutch, 11.4% Irish, 9.9% Other groups (2000).
Economy: Employment by occupation: 16.9% management, 25.5% professional, 9.8% services, 26.1% sales, 0.6% farming, 7.9% construction, 13.3% production (2000).
Income: Per capita income: $29,613 (2000); Median household income: $59,432 (2000); Poverty rate: 4.8% (2000).
Taxes: Total city taxes per capita: $72 (1997); City property taxes per capita: $57 (1997).
Education: High school graduation rate: 93.1% (2000); College graduation rate: 37.5% (2000).
Housing: Homeownership rate: 81.2% (2000); Median home value: $137,500 (2000); Median rent: $491 per month (2000); Median age of housing: 25 years (2000).
Transportation: Commute to work: 94.1% car, 0.5% public transportation, 1.4% walk, 3.7% work from home (2000); Travel time to work: 23.0% less than 15 minutes, 50.7% 15 to 30 minutes, 18.1% 30 to 45 minutes, 3.6% 45 to 60 minutes, 4.6% 60 minutes or more (2000)

ROSS (township). Covers a land area of 33.316 square miles and a water area of 2.672 square miles. Located at 42.36° N. Lat.; 85.36° W. Long.
History: Ross Township was organized in 1839 and named by the legislature. John Van Vleck built a tavern here in 1843.
Population: 5,047 (2000); Race: 96.3% White, 0.6% Black, 0.3% Asian, 0.2% American Indian and Alaska Native, 0.8% Hispanic of any race, 1.6% two or more races (2000); Density: 151.5 persons per square mile (2000); Age: 24.7% under 18, 13.0% over 64 (2000); Marriage status: 17.0% never married, 67.3% now married, 5.2% widowed, 10.6% divorced (2000); Foreign born: 1.8% (2000); Ancestry (includes multiple ancestries): 26.0% German, 20.5% English, 14.9% Irish, 10.5% Dutch, 6.8% Other groups (2000).
Economy: Single-family building permits issued: 23 (2001) / 29 (2000); Multi-family building permits issued: 0 (2001) / 0 (2000); Employment by occupation: 15.2% management, 22.3% professional, 10.0% services, 25.5% sales, 0.3% farming, 9.6% construction, 17.1% production (2000).
Income: Per capita income: $32,715 (2000); Median household income: $58,446 (2000); Poverty rate: 3.2% (2000).
Taxes: Total city taxes per capita: $67 (1997); City property taxes per capita: $60 (1997).
Education: High school graduation rate: 93.3% (2000); College graduation rate: 31.8% (2000).
Housing: Homeownership rate: 84.9% (2000); Median home value: $143,200 (2000); Median rent: $420 per month (2000); Median age of housing: 42 years (2000).
Transportation: Commute to work: 94.4% car, 0.0% public transportation, 0.7% walk, 4.5% work from home (2000); Travel time to work: 24.6% less than 15 minutes, 45.8% 15 to 30 minutes, 20.8% 30 to 45 minutes, 3.8% 45 to 60 minutes, 5.0% 60 minutes or more (2000)

SCHOOLCRAFT (village). Covers a land area of 0.932 square miles and a water area of 0 square miles. Located at 42.11° N. Lat.; 85.63° W. Long. Elevation is 893 feet.
History: It was in Schoolcraft that James Fenimore Cooper stayed while collecting material for his book "Oak Openings." Schoolcraft was a station on the Underground Railroad to freedom for slaves from the south. The town was named for Henry Rowe Schoolcraft when it was founded in 1831 by Lucius Lyon, a surveyor.
Population: 1,587 (2000); Race: 96.1% White, 0.6% Black, 0.8% Asian, 0.0% American Indian and Alaska Native, 1.6% Hispanic of any race, 2.3% two or more races (2000); Density: 1,703.2 persons per square mile (2000); Age: 29.0% under 18, 12.3% over 64 (2000); Marriage status: 22.2% never married, 59.4% now married, 8.0% widowed, 10.3% divorced (2000); Foreign born: 1.3% (2000); Ancestry (includes multiple ancestries): 26.5% German, 16.6% English, 16.5% Dutch, 14.8% Irish, 7.2% Other groups (2000).
Economy: Single-family building permits issued: 1 (2001) / 2 (2000); Multi-family building permits issued: 2 (2001) / 0 (2000); Employment by occupation: 12.4% management, 16.9% professional, 14.7% services, 27.7% sales, 0.2% farming, 9.1% construction, 18.9% production (2000).

Income: Per capita income: $20,223 (2000); Median household income: $45,380 (2000); Poverty rate: 6.9% (2000).
Taxes: Total city taxes per capita: $275 (1997); City property taxes per capita: $264 (1997).
Education: High school graduation rate: 91.9% (2000); College graduation rate: 22.5% (2000).

School District(s)

Schoolcraft Community Schools (KG-12)
2000 Enrollment: 1,155 616-679-4331

Housing: Homeownership rate: 71.5% (2000); Median home value: $102,500 (2000); Median rent: $442 per month (2000); Median age of housing: 44 years (2000).
Safety: Violent crime rate: 6.3 per 10,000 population; Property crime rate: 144.2 per 10,000 population (2001).
Transportation: Commute to work: 93.8% car, 0.0% public transportation, 2.8% walk, 2.3% work from home (2000); Travel time to work: 35.8% less than 15 minutes, 46.5% 15 to 30 minutes, 12.7% 30 to 45 minutes, 2.0% 45 to 60 minutes, 2.9% 60 minutes or more (2000)

SCHOOLCRAFT (township). Covers a land area of 34.359 square miles and a water area of 1.687 square miles. Located at 42.11° N. Lat.; 85.58° W. Long. Elevation is 893 feet.
Population: 7,260 (2000); Race: 96.8% White, 0.7% Black, 1.1% Asian, 0.0% American Indian and Alaska Native, 2.8% Hispanic of any race, 1.4% two or more races (2000); Density: 211.3 persons per square mile (2000); Age: 26.9% under 18, 11.3% over 64 (2000); Marriage status: 21.4% never married, 61.9% now married, 5.7% widowed, 11.0% divorced (2000); Foreign born: 3.0% (2000); Ancestry (includes multiple ancestries): 24.1% German, 16.2% Dutch, 16.0% English, 11.6% Irish, 9.1% United States or American (2000).
Economy: Railroad junction. Manufacturing: plastic molds, aircraft parts, marble bath products. Cattle; forage crops. Employment by occupation: 13.4% management, 17.0% professional, 12.0% services, 29.6% sales, 0.2% farming, 9.4% construction, 18.3% production (2000).
Income: Per capita income: $21,512 (2000); Median household income: $48,737 (2000); Poverty rate: 5.3% (2000).
Taxes: Total city taxes per capita: $33 (1997); City property taxes per capita: $27 (1997).
Education: High school graduation rate: 90.8% (2000); College graduation rate: 22.5% (2000).
Housing: Homeownership rate: 76.9% (2000); Median home value: $119,100 (2000); Median rent: $446 per month (2000); Median age of housing: 30 years (2000).
Transportation: Commute to work: 94.7% car, 0.1% public transportation, 1.9% walk, 2.5% work from home (2000); Travel time to work: 29.3% less than 15 minutes, 48.3% 15 to 30 minutes, 15.3% 30 to 45 minutes, 4.0% 45 to 60 minutes, 3.1% 60 minutes or more (2000)

SCOTTS (unincorporated postal area, zip code 49088). Covers a land area of 35.441 square miles and a water area of 0.492 square miles. Located at 42.18° N. Lat.; 85.42° W. Long.
History: Scotts, first called Scotts Crossing, was settled in 1847 by Samuel Scott.
Population: 3,019 (2000); Race: 98.1% White, 0.0% Black, 0.0% Asian, 0.0% American Indian and Alaska Native, 0.4% Hispanic of any race, 1.9% two or more races (2000); Density: 85.2 persons per square mile (2000); Age: 26.0% under 18, 9.0% over 64 (2000); Marriage status: 19.1% never married, 71.3% now married, 3.6% widowed, 6.0% divorced (2000); Foreign born: 0.2% (2000); Ancestry (includes multiple ancestries): 24.3% German, 17.6% Irish, 15.4% Dutch, 15.3% English, 7.0% United States or American (2000).
Economy: Employment by occupation: 12.6% management, 16.4% professional, 9.3% services, 28.0% sales, 1.6% farming, 13.0% construction, 19.1% production (2000).
Income: Per capita income: $23,275 (2000); Median household income: $60,385 (2000); Poverty rate: 4.3% (2000).
Education: High school graduation rate: 88.7% (2000); College graduation rate: 20.9% (2000).
Housing: Homeownership rate: 92.5% (2000); Median home value: $118,000 (2000); Median rent: $457 per month (2000); Median age of housing: 28 years (2000).
Transportation: Commute to work: 95.1% car, 0.0% public transportation, 0.0% walk, 4.3% work from home (2000); Travel time to work: 16.0% less than 15 minutes, 53.7% 15 to 30 minutes, 19.9% 30 to 45 minutes, 1.7% 45 to 60 minutes, 8.8% 60 minutes or more (2000)

SOUTH GULL LAKE (CDP). Covers a land area of 1.314 square miles and a water area of 1.814 square miles. Located at 42.38° N. Lat.; 85.39° W. Long.
Population: 1,526 (2000); Race: 96.3% White, 0.9% Black, 0.0% Asian, 0.3% American Indian and Alaska Native, 0.4% Hispanic of any race, 1.3% two or more races (2000); Density: 1,161.2 persons per square mile (2000); Age: 28.2% under 18, 13.4% over 64 (2000); Marriage status: 16.4% never married, 64.6% now married, 5.5% widowed, 13.5% divorced (2000); Foreign born: 1.8% (2000); Ancestry (includes multiple ancestries): 23.6% German, 20.6% English, 12.0% Dutch, 9.3% Irish, 5.5% United States or American (2000).
Economy: Employment by occupation: 24.3% management, 24.2% professional, 13.2% services, 21.6% sales, 0.0% farming, 3.8% construction, 13.0% production (2000).
Income: Per capita income: $45,175 (2000); Median household income: $65,833 (2000); Poverty rate: 1.6% (2000).
Education: High school graduation rate: 97.9% (2000); College graduation rate: 48.9% (2000).
Housing: Homeownership rate: 85.1% (2000); Median home value: $311,300 (2000); Median rent: $583 per month (2000); Median age of housing: 46 years (2000).
Transportation: Commute to work: 91.3% car, 0.0% public transportation, 0.9% walk, 7.8% work from home (2000); Travel time to work: 26.5% less than 15 minutes, 35.4% 15 to 30 minutes, 25.8% 30 to 45 minutes, 3.9% 45 to 60 minutes, 8.4% 60 minutes or more (2000)

TEXAS (township). Covers a land area of 34.451 square miles and a water area of 1.890 square miles. Located at 42.21° N. Lat.; 85.69° W. Long.
Population: 10,919 (2000); Race: 93.1% White, 1.8% Black, 3.3% Asian, 0.4% American Indian and Alaska Native, 1.0% Hispanic of any race, 1.1% two or more races (2000); Density: 316.9 persons per square mile (2000); Age: 29.2% under 18, 7.6% over 64 (2000); Marriage status: 20.9% never married, 68.2% now married, 3.1% widowed, 7.8% divorced (2000); Foreign born: 5.4% (2000); Ancestry (includes multiple ancestries): 29.2% German, 15.7% English, 14.4% Irish, 13.4% Dutch, 8.5% Other groups (2000).
Economy: Single-family building permits issued: 141 (2001) / 98 (2000); Multi-family building permits issued: 0 (2001) / 0 (2000); Employment by occupation: 19.0% management, 29.6% professional, 9.4% services, 23.6% sales, 0.7% farming, 6.3% construction, 11.4% production (2000).
Income: Per capita income: $32,151 (2000); Median household income: $69,854 (2000); Poverty rate: 3.3% (2000).
Taxes: Total city taxes per capita: $46 (1997); City property taxes per capita: $31 (1997).
Education: High school graduation rate: 95.8% (2000); College graduation rate: 45.8% (2000).
Housing: Homeownership rate: 90.1% (2000); Median home value: $193,000 (2000); Median rent: $555 per month (2000); Median age of housing: 15 years (2000).
Transportation: Commute to work: 94.9% car, 0.4% public transportation, 0.7% walk, 3.4% work from home (2000); Travel time to work: 27.0% less than 15 minutes, 55.7% 15 to 30 minutes, 11.4% 30 to 45 minutes, 3.2% 45 to 60 minutes, 2.8% 60 minutes or more (2000)

VICKSBURG (village). Covers a land area of 1.833 square miles and a water area of 0.056 square miles. Located at 42.12° N. Lat.; 85.53° W. Long. Elevation is 860 feet.
History: Known for Egyptian lotuses grown nearby. Annual Vicksburg Old Car Festival. Incorporated 1871.
Population: 2,320 (2000); Race: 96.3% White, 1.4% Black, 0.8% Asian, 0.0% American Indian and Alaska Native, 2.0% Hispanic of any race, 1.2% two or more races (2000); Density: 1,265.9 persons per square mile (2000); Age: 28.8% under 18, 12.3% over 64 (2000); Marriage status: 23.6% never married, 55.3% now married, 6.2% widowed, 14.9% divorced (2000); Foreign born: 2.6% (2000); Ancestry (includes multiple ancestries): 18.6% German, 15.3% English, 13.7% Irish, 13.0% Dutch, 11.6% United States or American (2000).
Economy: In farm area: livestock; soybeans, fruit, grain, peppermint; dairy products. Manufacturing of paper products and plastic molding. Employment by occupation: 9.5% management, 12.2% professional, 12.0% services, 24.3% sales, 0.0% farming, 14.9% construction, 27.1% production (2000).
Income: Per capita income: $18,178 (2000); Median household income: $41,780 (2000); Poverty rate: 6.8% (2000).
Taxes: Total city taxes per capita: $355 (1997); City property taxes per capita: $351 (1997).

Education: High school graduation rate: 85.2% (2000); College graduation rate: 17.9% (2000).

School District(s)

Vicksburg Community Schools (PK-12)
2000 Enrollment: 2,774 616-321-1000

Housing: Homeownership rate: 66.9% (2000); Median home value: $88,300 (2000); Median rent: $434 per month (2000); Median age of housing: 51 years (2000).

Hospitals: Bronson Vicksburg Hospital (41 beds)

Safety: Violent crime rate: 4.3 per 10,000 population; Property crime rate: 85.8 per 10,000 population (2001).

Newspapers: The Vicksburg Commercial Express (1 x week); The Broadcast (1 x week)

Transportation: Commute to work: 92.9% car, 0.0% public transportation, 2.9% walk, 2.0% work from home (2000); Travel time to work: 26.7% less than 15 minutes, 46.0% 15 to 30 minutes, 16.0% 30 to 45 minutes, 6.9% 45 to 60 minutes, 4.4% 60 minutes or more (2000)

WAKESHMA (township). Covers a land area of 36.012 square miles and a water area of 0 square miles. Located at 42.11° N. Lat.; 85.35° W. Long.

Population: 1,414 (2000); Race: 96.7% White, 0.3% Black, 0.3% Asian, 0.1% American Indian and Alaska Native, 1.0% Hispanic of any race, 1.2% two or more races (2000); Density: 39.3 persons per square mile (2000); Age: 28.4% under 18, 10.2% over 64 (2000); Marriage status: 21.2% never married, 64.5% now married, 4.5% widowed, 9.9% divorced (2000); Foreign born: 1.3% (2000); Ancestry (includes multiple ancestries): 26.0% German, 14.4% Irish, 12.4% English, 12.3% Dutch, 10.4% Other groups (2000).

Economy: Employment by occupation: 12.5% management, 9.9% professional, 14.1% services, 23.1% sales, 2.1% farming, 12.5% construction, 25.8% production (2000).

Income: Per capita income: $20,051 (2000); Median household income: $52,328 (2000); Poverty rate: 8.7% (2000).

Taxes: Total city taxes per capita: $14 (1997); City property taxes per capita: $14 (1997).

Education: High school graduation rate: 83.6% (2000); College graduation rate: 8.5% (2000).

Housing: Homeownership rate: 91.6% (2000); Median home value: $82,500 (2000); Median rent: $394 per month (2000); Median age of housing: 49 years (2000).

Transportation: Commute to work: 92.7% car, 0.0% public transportation, 0.4% walk, 5.7% work from home (2000); Travel time to work: 8.7% less than 15 minutes, 40.6% 15 to 30 minutes, 38.9% 30 to 45 minutes, 6.7% 45 to 60 minutes, 5.2% 60 minutes or more (2000)

WESTWOOD (CDP). Covers a land area of 2.800 square miles and a water area of 0 square miles. Located at 42.30° N. Lat.; 85.62° W. Long.

Population: 9,122 (2000); Race: 86.1% White, 9.2% Black, 1.8% Asian, 0.2% American Indian and Alaska Native, 1.9% Hispanic of any race, 2.0% two or more races (2000); Density: 3,258.0 persons per square mile (2000); Age: 17.2% under 18, 16.7% over 64 (2000); Marriage status: 40.0% never married, 42.8% now married, 8.0% widowed, 9.2% divorced (2000); Foreign born: 3.7% (2000); Ancestry (includes multiple ancestries): 20.8% German, 15.7% English, 15.3% Dutch, 15.0% Other groups, 11.6% Irish (2000).

Economy: Employment by occupation: 12.9% management, 28.8% professional, 15.6% services, 26.0% sales, 0.2% farming, 5.1% construction, 11.4% production (2000).

Income: Per capita income: $22,686 (2000); Median household income: $37,407 (2000); Poverty rate: 12.7% (2000).

Education: High school graduation rate: 93.8% (2000); College graduation rate: 41.9% (2000).

Housing: Homeownership rate: 59.1% (2000); Median home value: $94,500 (2000); Median rent: $542 per month (2000); Median age of housing: 36 years (2000).

Transportation: Commute to work: 92.4% car, 1.6% public transportation, 2.2% walk, 3.0% work from home (2000); Travel time to work: 41.2% less than 15 minutes, 43.0% 15 to 30 minutes, 10.1% 30 to 45 minutes, 3.2% 45 to 60 minutes, 2.6% 60 minutes or more (2000)

Kalkaska County

Located in northwest central Michigan; drained by the Manistee and Boardman Rivers; includes many lakes. Covers a land area of 561.00 square miles, a water area of 9.70 square miles, and is located in the Eastern Time Zone. The county government was organized in 1870. County seat is Kalkaska.

Population: 16,571 (2000); Race: 97.4% White, 0.2% Black, 0.2% Asian, 1.1% American Indian and Alaska Native, 0.8% Hispanic of any race, 1.0% two or more races (2000); Density: 29.5 persons per square mile (2000); Age: 25.6% under 18, 13.8% over 64 (2000).

Religion: Five largest groups: 6.4% Catholic Church, 2.7% Christian Churches and Churches of Christ, 2.1% The United Methodist Church, 2.0% Lutheran Church—Missouri Synod, 1.2% Assemblies of God (2000).

Economy: Unemployment rate: 7.9% (11/2002); Total civilian labor force: 7,925 (11/2002); Leading industries: 29.1% manufacturing; 15.5% retail trade; 10.6% health care and social assistance (2000); Companies that employ more than 1,000 persons: 0 (2000); Companies that employ more than 100 persons: 8 (2000); Farms: 139 totaling 21,375 acres (1997); Minority business ownership rate: 0.0% (1997); Women business ownership rate: 23.3% (1997); Retail sales per capita: $9,353 (1997). Single-family building permits issued: 147 (2001) / 130 (2000); Multi-family building permits issued: 0 (2001) / 2 (2000).

Income: Per capita income: $16,309 (2000); Median household income: $36,072 (2000); Poverty rate: 10.5% (2000); Bankruptcy rate: 4.99% (2001).

Taxes: Total county taxes per capita: $182 (1997); County property taxes per capita: $165 (1997).

Education: High school graduation rate: 80.0% (2000); College graduation rate: 9.7% (2000).

Housing: Homeownership rate: 85.4% (2000); Median home value: $85,100 (2000); Median rent: $376 per month (2000); Median age of housing: 25 years (2000).

Health: Birth rate: 106.8 per 10,000 population (1998); Age adjusted death rate: 95.9 per 10,000 population (1999); Age adjusted cancer mortality rate: 218.2 deaths per 100,000 population (1999). Number of physicians: 1.8 per 10,000 population (1999); Number of hospital beds: 57.9 per 10,000 population (1999).

Elections: 2000 Presidential election results: 40.5% Gore, 56.1% Bush, 2.5% Nader, 0.1% Buchanan

National and State Parks: Kalkaska State Forest

Additional Information Contacts

Kalkaska County Government Offices. 231-258-3300
Kalkaska Chamber of Commerce. 231-258-9103

Kalkaska County Communities

BEAR LAKE (township). Covers a land area of 71.540 square miles and a water area of 0.857 square miles. Located at 44.68° N. Lat.; 84.90° W. Long.

Population: 746 (2000); Race: 97.0% White, 0.4% Black, 0.0% Asian, 0.4% American Indian and Alaska Native, 0.3% Hispanic of any race, 2.2% two or more races (2000); Density: 10.4 persons per square mile (2000); Age: 16.7% under 18, 18.8% over 64 (2000); Marriage status: 15.3% never married, 65.4% now married, 8.2% widowed, 11.0% divorced (2000); Foreign born: 1.9% (2000); Ancestry (includes multiple ancestries): 20.4% German, 15.2% English, 13.8% Irish, 11.4% United States or American, 8.3% Polish (2000).

Economy: Employment by occupation: 14.8% management, 11.4% professional, 17.1% services, 21.1% sales, 1.0% farming, 13.8% construction, 20.8% production (2000).

Income: Per capita income: $17,570 (2000); Median household income: $36,875 (2000); Poverty rate: 8.9% (2000).

Taxes: Total city taxes per capita: $155 (1997); City property taxes per capita: $155 (1997).

Education: High school graduation rate: 77.1% (2000); College graduation rate: 6.6% (2000).

Housing: Homeownership rate: 91.3% (2000); Median home value: $85,600 (2000); Median rent: $406 per month (2000); Median age of housing: 26 years (2000).

Transportation: Commute to work: 97.9% car, 0.0% public transportation, 1.0% walk, 1.0% work from home (2000); Travel time to work: 12.2% less than 15 minutes, 50.0% 15 to 30 minutes, 19.4% 30 to 45 minutes, 7.3% 45 to 60 minutes, 11.1% 60 minutes or more (2000)

BLUE LAKE (township). Covers a land area of 34.653 square miles and a water area of 1.579 square miles. Located at 44.81° N. Lat.; 84.90° W. Long.

Population: 428 (2000); Race: 99.5% White, 0.0% Black, 0.0% Asian, 0.0% American Indian and Alaska Native, 0.5% Hispanic of any race, 0.5% two or more races (2000); Density: 12.4 persons per square mile (2000); Age: 9.4% under 18, 36.4% over 64 (2000); Marriage status: 8.9% never married, 78.9% now married, 9.1% widowed, 3.0% divorced (2000); Foreign born: 1.9%

(2000); Ancestry (includes multiple ancestries): 27.2% German, 18.8% English, 9.6% Irish, 8.7% French (except Basque), 6.8% Scottish (2000).
Economy: Employment by occupation: 9.9% management, 13.7% professional, 18.3% services, 31.3% sales, 0.0% farming, 13.7% construction, 13.0% production (2000).
Income: Per capita income: $20,543 (2000); Median household income: $37,045 (2000); Poverty rate: 4.0% (2000).
Taxes: Total city taxes per capita: $298 (1997); City property taxes per capita: $293 (1997).
Education: High school graduation rate: 80.5% (2000); College graduation rate: 13.9% (2000).
Housing: Homeownership rate: 92.5% (2000); Median home value: $110,400 (2000); Median rent: $625 per month (2000); Median age of housing: 28 years (2000).
Transportation: Commute to work: 88.4% car, 0.0% public transportation, 3.1% walk, 8.5% work from home (2000); Travel time to work: 12.7% less than 15 minutes, 26.3% 15 to 30 minutes, 40.7% 30 to 45 minutes, 9.3% 45 to 60 minutes, 11.0% 60 minutes or more (2000)

BOARDMAN (township). Covers a land area of 35.927 square miles and a water area of 0.221 square miles. Located at 44.64° N. Lat.; 85.27° W. Long.
Population: 1,373 (2000); Race: 97.4% White, 0.4% Black, 0.4% Asian, 1.0% American Indian and Alaska Native, 0.9% Hispanic of any race, 0.8% two or more races (2000); Density: 38.2 persons per square mile (2000); Age: 32.4% under 18, 9.1% over 64 (2000); Marriage status: 23.7% never married, 61.9% now married, 4.0% widowed, 10.4% divorced (2000); Foreign born: 1.1% (2000); Ancestry (includes multiple ancestries): 23.1% German, 14.9% English, 10.9% Irish, 10.8% United States or American, 7.1% Other groups (2000).
Economy: Employment by occupation: 8.2% management, 11.0% professional, 15.2% services, 24.1% sales, 1.1% farming, 18.3% construction, 22.1% production (2000).
Income: Per capita income: $14,123 (2000); Median household income: $35,850 (2000); Poverty rate: 13.7% (2000).
Taxes: Total city taxes per capita: $44 (1997); City property taxes per capita: $44 (1997).
Education: High school graduation rate: 77.3% (2000); College graduation rate: 7.4% (2000).
Housing: Homeownership rate: 86.7% (2000); Median home value: $76,600 (2000); Median rent: $366 per month (2000); Median age of housing: 25 years (2000).
Transportation: Commute to work: 91.4% car, 0.8% public transportation, 2.3% walk, 5.1% work from home (2000); Travel time to work: 22.1% less than 15 minutes, 25.6% 15 to 30 minutes, 30.1% 30 to 45 minutes, 12.0% 45 to 60 minutes, 10.3% 60 minutes or more (2000)

CLEARWATER (township). Covers a land area of 31.147 square miles and a water area of 2.619 square miles. Located at 44.82° N. Lat.; 85.28° W. Long.
Population: 2,382 (2000); Race: 97.7% White, 0.0% Black, 0.2% Asian, 0.7% American Indian and Alaska Native, 0.7% Hispanic of any race, 1.3% two or more races (2000); Density: 76.5 persons per square mile (2000); Age: 24.9% under 18, 12.8% over 64 (2000); Marriage status: 21.9% never married, 63.1% now married, 6.1% widowed, 9.0% divorced (2000); Foreign born: 1.1% (2000); Ancestry (includes multiple ancestries): 27.5% German, 16.3% English, 13.6% Irish, 9.6% French (except Basque), 7.7% Other groups (2000).
Economy: Employment by occupation: 8.4% management, 12.6% professional, 18.3% services, 24.3% sales, 0.4% farming, 16.1% construction, 20.0% production (2000).
Income: Per capita income: $16,961 (2000); Median household income: $37,008 (2000); Poverty rate: 7.9% (2000).
Taxes: Total city taxes per capita: $44 (1997); City property taxes per capita: $43 (1997).
Education: High school graduation rate: 83.9% (2000); College graduation rate: 14.8% (2000).
Housing: Homeownership rate: 86.0% (2000); Median home value: $95,000 (2000); Median rent: $378 per month (2000); Median age of housing: 25 years (2000).
Transportation: Commute to work: 95.1% car, 0.7% public transportation, 1.3% walk, 2.1% work from home (2000); Travel time to work: 17.9% less than 15 minutes, 43.4% 15 to 30 minutes, 19.9% 30 to 45 minutes, 9.5% 45 to 60 minutes, 9.4% 60 minutes or more (2000)

COLDSPRINGS (township). Covers a land area of 34.424 square miles and a water area of 1.845 square miles. Located at 44.80° N. Lat.; 85.02° W. Long.
Population: 1,449 (2000); Race: 97.9% White, 0.0% Black, 0.1% Asian, 1.2% American Indian and Alaska Native, 0.0% Hispanic of any race, 0.8% two or more races (2000); Density: 42.1 persons per square mile (2000); Age: 20.4% under 18, 16.6% over 64 (2000); Marriage status: 16.2% never married, 70.4% now married, 5.0% widowed, 8.4% divorced (2000); Foreign born: 0.6% (2000); Ancestry (includes multiple ancestries): 24.6% German, 15.9% English, 11.4% Irish, 7.2% Polish, 7.0% United States or American (2000).
Economy: Employment by occupation: 7.6% management, 7.6% professional, 16.2% services, 23.9% sales, 2.1% farming, 17.3% construction, 25.4% production (2000).
Income: Per capita income: $17,396 (2000); Median household income: $33,839 (2000); Poverty rate: 8.8% (2000).
Education: High school graduation rate: 78.6% (2000); College graduation rate: 9.4% (2000).
Housing: Homeownership rate: 92.7% (2000); Median home value: $97,300 (2000); Median rent: $333 per month (2000); Median age of housing: 21 years (2000).
Transportation: Commute to work: 95.2% car, 0.0% public transportation, 0.0% walk, 2.0% work from home (2000); Travel time to work: 14.9% less than 15 minutes, 43.8% 15 to 30 minutes, 14.6% 30 to 45 minutes, 13.0% 45 to 60 minutes, 13.7% 60 minutes or more (2000)

EXCELSIOR (township). Covers a land area of 35.620 square miles and a water area of 0.620 square miles. Located at 44.73° N. Lat.; 85.02° W. Long.
Population: 855 (2000); Race: 98.9% White, 0.0% Black, 0.2% Asian, 0.2% American Indian and Alaska Native, 0.0% Hispanic of any race, 0.6% two or more races (2000); Density: 24.0 persons per square mile (2000); Age: 26.9% under 18, 15.8% over 64 (2000); Marriage status: 18.4% never married, 66.7% now married, 6.3% widowed, 8.6% divorced (2000); Foreign born: 1.8% (2000); Ancestry (includes multiple ancestries): 23.1% German, 12.0% Irish, 9.1% English, 7.3% Other groups, 6.7% United States or American (2000).
Economy: Employment by occupation: 14.3% management, 11.5% professional, 12.9% services, 26.9% sales, 1.4% farming, 10.9% construction, 22.1% production (2000).
Income: Per capita income: $16,476 (2000); Median household income: $36,932 (2000); Poverty rate: 9.0% (2000).
Taxes: Total city taxes per capita: $99 (1997); City property taxes per capita: $99 (1997).
Education: High school graduation rate: 79.4% (2000); College graduation rate: 7.0% (2000).
Housing: Homeownership rate: 87.8% (2000); Median home value: $85,500 (2000); Median rent: $403 per month (2000); Median age of housing: 24 years (2000).
Transportation: Commute to work: 88.7% car, 0.6% public transportation, 3.5% walk, 7.3% work from home (2000); Travel time to work: 27.0% less than 15 minutes, 36.4% 15 to 30 minutes, 16.6% 30 to 45 minutes, 13.8% 45 to 60 minutes, 6.3% 60 minutes or more (2000)

GARFIELD (township). Covers a land area of 106.737 square miles and a water area of 0.043 square miles. Located at 44.55° N. Lat.; 85.07° W. Long.
Population: 794 (2000); Race: 98.5% White, 0.0% Black, 0.0% Asian, 0.0% American Indian and Alaska Native, 1.3% Hispanic of any race, 0.3% two or more races (2000); Density: 7.4 persons per square mile (2000); Age: 23.5% under 18, 15.0% over 64 (2000); Marriage status: 15.8% never married, 68.8% now married, 5.1% widowed, 10.2% divorced (2000); Foreign born: 0.3% (2000); Ancestry (includes multiple ancestries): 25.2% German, 13.7% English, 13.1% Irish, 9.9% United States or American, 5.6% Dutch (2000).
Economy: Employment by occupation: 7.4% management, 5.8% professional, 21.0% services, 25.2% sales, 1.3% farming, 15.9% construction, 23.3% production (2000).
Income: Per capita income: $15,552 (2000); Median household income: $34,444 (2000); Poverty rate: 11.9% (2000).
Taxes: Total city taxes per capita: $77 (1997); City property taxes per capita: $76 (1997).
Education: High school graduation rate: 72.5% (2000); College graduation rate: 9.0% (2000).

Housing: Homeownership rate: 93.5% (2000); Median home value: $81,100 (2000); Median rent: $225 per month (2000); Median age of housing: 29 years (2000).
Transportation: Commute to work: 93.4% car, 0.0% public transportation, 0.0% walk, 4.3% work from home (2000); Travel time to work: 9.3% less than 15 minutes, 40.1% 15 to 30 minutes, 28.0% 30 to 45 minutes, 14.2% 45 to 60 minutes, 8.3% 60 minutes or more (2000)

KALKASKA (village). Covers a land area of 2.499 square miles and a water area of 0.020 square miles. Located at 44.73° N. Lat.; 85.18° W. Long. Elevation is 1,035 feet.
History: Kalkaska was first settled as a logging and railroad grading camp. In 1873, a tannery and sawmill were established, and the village became a supply center for the nearby farms. Later, Kalkaska developed as a resort area for fishermen and vacationers.
Population: 2,226 (2000); Race: 97.1% White, 0.3% Black, 0.0% Asian, 2.6% American Indian and Alaska Native, 1.9% Hispanic of any race, 0.0% two or more races (2000); Density: 890.7 persons per square mile (2000); Age: 26.9% under 18, 16.6% over 64 (2000); Marriage status: 26.0% never married, 49.8% now married, 10.0% widowed, 14.2% divorced (2000); Foreign born: 0.5% (2000); Ancestry (includes multiple ancestries): 24.2% German, 15.5% Irish, 11.6% English, 10.3% Other groups, 6.9% French (except Basque) (2000).
Economy: Employment by occupation: 5.8% management, 10.3% professional, 20.8% services, 19.3% sales, 0.0% farming, 13.7% construction, 30.2% production (2000).
Income: Per capita income: $13,028 (2000); Median household income: $27,891 (2000); Poverty rate: 16.4% (2000).
Taxes: Total city taxes per capita: $201 (1997); City property taxes per capita: $201 (1997).
Education: High school graduation rate: 76.0% (2000); College graduation rate: 9.9% (2000).

School District(s)

Excelsior Township School District #1 (KG-08)
2000 Enrollment: 33 231-258-8438
Kalkaska Public Schools (KG-12)
2000 Enrollment: 1,916 231-258-9109

Housing: Homeownership rate: 57.5% (2000); Median home value: $72,700 (2000); Median rent: $386 per month (2000); Median age of housing: 31 years (2000).
Hospitals: Kalkaska Memorial Hospital (96 beds)
Safety: Violent crime rate: 26.8 per 10,000 population; Property crime rate: 960.7 per 10,000 population (2001).
Newspapers: The Leader and Kalkaskian (1 x week); The Star Advertiser (1 x week)
Transportation: Commute to work: 90.4% car, 0.5% public transportation, 6.0% walk, 2.7% work from home (2000); Travel time to work: 56.9% less than 15 minutes, 19.4% 15 to 30 minutes, 11.8% 30 to 45 minutes, 8.1% 45 to 60 minutes, 3.7% 60 minutes or more (2000); Amtrak: Service available.

Additional Information Contacts

Kalkaska Chamber of Commerce. 231-258-9103

KALKASKA (township). Covers a land area of 70.351 square miles and a water area of 0.817 square miles. Located at 44.73° N. Lat.; 85.19° W. Long. Elevation is 1,035 feet.
History: Incorporated 1887.
Population: 4,830 (2000); Race: 96.8% White, 0.4% Black, 0.1% Asian, 1.7% American Indian and Alaska Native, 1.2% Hispanic of any race, 1.0% two or more races (2000); Density: 68.7 persons per square mile (2000); Age: 27.1% under 18, 13.9% over 64 (2000); Marriage status: 23.9% never married, 56.1% now married, 6.6% widowed, 13.4% divorced (2000); Foreign born: 0.6% (2000); Ancestry (includes multiple ancestries): 26.5% German, 14.2% Irish, 12.3% English, 8.4% Other groups, 6.7% Polish (2000).
Economy: Supply center for farm and lake area. Manufacturing: steel parts, crafts, wire products. Employment by occupation: 6.8% management, 15.1% professional, 17.5% services, 23.1% sales, 0.2% farming, 13.5% construction, 23.8% production (2000).
Income: Per capita income: $16,595 (2000); Median household income: $36,278 (2000); Poverty rate: 12.5% (2000).
Taxes: Total city taxes per capita: $30 (1997); City property taxes per capita: $30 (1997).
Education: High school graduation rate: 83.2% (2000); College graduation rate: 11.8% (2000).
Housing: Homeownership rate: 74.9% (2000); Median home value: $83,700 (2000); Median rent: $384 per month (2000); Median age of housing: 25 years (2000).
Transportation: Commute to work: 91.0% car, 0.9% public transportation, 4.1% walk, 3.4% work from home (2000); Travel time to work: 52.3% less than 15 minutes, 17.3% 15 to 30 minutes, 15.2% 30 to 45 minutes, 8.4% 45 to 60 minutes, 6.8% 60 minutes or more (2000); Amtrak: Service available.

OLIVER (township). Covers a land area of 36.054 square miles and a water area of 0.051 square miles. Located at 44.63° N. Lat.; 85.02° W. Long.
Population: 263 (2000); Race: 96.3% White, 0.0% Black, 0.0% Asian, 3.0% American Indian and Alaska Native, 0.0% Hispanic of any race, 0.7% two or more races (2000); Density: 7.3 persons per square mile (2000); Age: 18.2% under 18, 19.9% over 64 (2000); Marriage status: 19.6% never married, 63.7% now married, 8.6% widowed, 8.2% divorced (2000); Foreign born: 2.0% (2000); Ancestry (includes multiple ancestries): 14.9% German, 13.9% English, 12.2% Irish, 9.5% Other groups, 9.5% United States or American (2000).
Economy: Employment by occupation: 6.2% management, 11.6% professional, 19.4% services, 23.3% sales, 2.3% farming, 12.4% construction, 24.8% production (2000).
Income: Per capita income: $15,153 (2000); Median household income: $30,104 (2000); Poverty rate: 8.4% (2000).
Taxes: Total city taxes per capita: $21 (1997); City property taxes per capita: $21 (1997).
Education: High school graduation rate: 81.9% (2000); College graduation rate: 7.9% (2000).
Housing: Homeownership rate: 93.0% (2000); Median home value: $74,300 (2000); Median rent: $325 per month (2000); Median age of housing: 23 years (2000).
Transportation: Commute to work: 89.3% car, 0.0% public transportation, 0.0% walk, 9.0% work from home (2000); Travel time to work: 9.0% less than 15 minutes, 52.3% 15 to 30 minutes, 15.3% 30 to 45 minutes, 12.6% 45 to 60 minutes, 10.8% 60 minutes or more (2000)

ORANGE (township). Covers a land area of 34.170 square miles and a water area of 0.663 square miles. Located at 44.64° N. Lat.; 85.15° W. Long.
Population: 1,176 (2000); Race: 97.9% White, 0.2% Black, 0.0% Asian, 0.9% American Indian and Alaska Native, 0.2% Hispanic of any race, 0.9% two or more races (2000); Density: 34.4 persons per square mile (2000); Age: 28.4% under 18, 10.7% over 64 (2000); Marriage status: 21.5% never married, 62.3% now married, 4.7% widowed, 11.4% divorced (2000); Foreign born: 0.1% (2000); Ancestry (includes multiple ancestries): 22.3% German, 12.9% English, 12.0% Irish, 7.8% Other groups, 7.0% Dutch (2000).
Economy: Employment by occupation: 6.8% management, 11.0% professional, 18.5% services, 20.1% sales, 1.5% farming, 18.0% construction, 24.1% production (2000).
Income: Per capita income: $15,448 (2000); Median household income: $35,380 (2000); Poverty rate: 10.0% (2000).
Taxes: Total city taxes per capita: $27 (1997); City property taxes per capita: $27 (1997).
Education: High school graduation rate: 75.5% (2000); College graduation rate: 5.9% (2000).
Housing: Homeownership rate: 87.7% (2000); Median home value: $74,500 (2000); Median rent: $332 per month (2000); Median age of housing: 23 years (2000).
Transportation: Commute to work: 92.2% car, 0.6% public transportation, 0.2% walk, 6.0% work from home (2000); Travel time to work: 24.3% less than 15 minutes, 38.8% 15 to 30 minutes, 17.7% 30 to 45 minutes, 11.5% 45 to 60 minutes, 7.6% 60 minutes or more (2000)

RAPID CITY (unincorporated postal area, zip code 49676). Covers a land area of 38.102 square miles and a water area of 0.047 square miles. Located at 44.82° N. Lat.; 85.28° W. Long. Elevation is 626 feet.
History: Rapid City began in 1891 as a station on the Chicago & Western Michigan Railroad, named Van Buren for Charles and Carrie Van Buren who platted the village. The name was changed in 1898 to reflect the village location on the Rapid River.
Population: 3,104 (2000); Race: 97.4% White, 0.0% Black, 0.2% Asian, 0.9% American Indian and Alaska Native, 0.9% Hispanic of any race, 1.1% two or more races (2000); Density: 81.5 persons per square mile (2000); Age: 24.4% under 18, 15.1% over 64 (2000); Marriage status: 19.3% never married, 65.4% now married, 5.9% widowed, 9.4% divorced (2000); Foreign born: 1.2% (2000); Ancestry (includes multiple ancestries): 29.1% German,

17.0% English, 13.5% Irish, 9.5% French (except Basque), 7.7% Other groups (2000).
Economy: Employment by occupation: 8.8% management, 15.0% professional, 15.9% services, 23.9% sales, 0.3% farming, 16.9% construction, 19.3% production (2000).
Income: Per capita income: $20,934 (2000); Median household income: $40,574 (2000); Poverty rate: 6.9% (2000).
Education: High school graduation rate: 87.2% (2000); College graduation rate: 18.7% (2000).
Housing: Homeownership rate: 88.0% (2000); Median home value: $115,600 (2000); Median rent: $382 per month (2000); Median age of housing: 26 years (2000).
Transportation: Commute to work: 94.5% car, 0.2% public transportation, 1.4% walk, 3.0% work from home (2000); Travel time to work: 19.6% less than 15 minutes, 41.3% 15 to 30 minutes, 19.2% 30 to 45 minutes, 10.8% 45 to 60 minutes, 9.1% 60 minutes or more (2000)

RAPID RIVER (township). Covers a land area of 35.167 square miles and a water area of 0.143 square miles. Located at 44.81° N. Lat.; 85.15° W. Long.
Population: 1,005 (2000); Race: 97.6% White, 0.0% Black, 0.0% Asian, 1.4% American Indian and Alaska Native, 2.1% Hispanic of any race, 0.8% two or more races (2000); Density: 28.6 persons per square mile (2000); Age: 28.4% under 18, 7.4% over 64 (2000); Marriage status: 26.6% never married, 62.6% now married, 2.9% widowed, 7.8% divorced (2000); Foreign born: 0.4% (2000); Ancestry (includes multiple ancestries): 19.8% German, 10.4% English, 10.0% United States or American, 9.7% Other groups, 7.0% French (except Basque) (2000).
Economy: Employment by occupation: 7.9% management, 6.3% professional, 16.8% services, 28.1% sales, 0.5% farming, 13.6% construction, 26.8% production (2000).
Income: Per capita income: $14,670 (2000); Median household income: $37,857 (2000); Poverty rate: 10.7% (2000).
Taxes: Total city taxes per capita: $92 (1997); City property taxes per capita: $92 (1997).
Education: High school graduation rate: 77.5% (2000); College graduation rate: 3.4% (2000).
Housing: Homeownership rate: 89.2% (2000); Median home value: $77,500 (2000); Median rent: $327 per month (2000); Median age of housing: 23 years (2000).
Transportation: Commute to work: 96.0% car, 0.0% public transportation, 0.9% walk, 2.1% work from home (2000); Travel time to work: 30.5% less than 15 minutes, 36.4% 15 to 30 minutes, 17.1% 30 to 45 minutes, 10.5% 45 to 60 minutes, 5.5% 60 minutes or more (2000)

SOUTH BOARDMAN (unincorporated postal area, zip code 49680). Covers a land area of 53.772 square miles and a water area of 0.401 square miles. Located at 44.65° N. Lat.; 85.26° W. Long. Elevation is 1,010 feet.
History: South Boardman grew up around a railroad station where the line crossed the south branch of the Boardman River. The depot and a hotel were built by Hamilton Stone in 1874.
Population: 1,811 (2000); Race: 97.9% White, 0.3% Black, 0.3% Asian, 1.0% American Indian and Alaska Native, 0.7% Hispanic of any race, 0.5% two or more races (2000); Density: 33.7 persons per square mile (2000); Age: 30.5% under 18, 9.6% over 64 (2000); Marriage status: 24.3% never married, 61.7% now married, 4.2% widowed, 9.8% divorced (2000); Foreign born: 1.1% (2000); Ancestry (includes multiple ancestries): 23.3% German, 14.6% English, 10.0% Irish, 9.1% United States or American, 7.2% Other groups (2000).
Economy: Employment by occupation: 7.5% management, 11.5% professional, 14.7% services, 23.6% sales, 0.6% farming, 18.7% construction, 23.4% production (2000).
Income: Per capita income: $15,281 (2000); Median household income: $37,904 (2000); Poverty rate: 11.3% (2000).
Education: High school graduation rate: 77.1% (2000); College graduation rate: 6.4% (2000).
Housing: Homeownership rate: 88.0% (2000); Median home value: $76,800 (2000); Median rent: $356 per month (2000); Median age of housing: 25 years (2000).
Transportation: Commute to work: 92.1% car, 1.1% public transportation, 1.7% walk, 4.7% work from home (2000); Travel time to work: 20.7% less than 15 minutes, 29.4% 15 to 30 minutes, 26.3% 30 to 45 minutes, 13.1% 45 to 60 minutes, 10.5% 60 minutes or more (2000)

SPRINGFIELD (township). Covers a land area of 35.226 square miles and a water area of 0.288 square miles. Located at 44.55° N. Lat.; 85.27° W. Long.
Population: 1,270 (2000); Race: 95.5% White, 0.9% Black, 0.6% Asian, 1.0% American Indian and Alaska Native, 0.3% Hispanic of any race, 1.6% two or more races (2000); Density: 36.1 persons per square mile (2000); Age: 28.3% under 18, 10.3% over 64 (2000); Marriage status: 20.3% never married, 61.0% now married, 6.5% widowed, 12.2% divorced (2000); Foreign born: 0.5% (2000); Ancestry (includes multiple ancestries): 24.7% German, 11.1% Irish, 8.5% English, 8.1% Other groups, 6.1% United States or American (2000).
Economy: Employment by occupation: 7.5% management, 8.2% professional, 16.3% services, 26.3% sales, 0.7% farming, 11.8% construction, 29.2% production (2000).
Income: Per capita income: $15,666 (2000); Median household income: $38,667 (2000); Poverty rate: 10.2% (2000).
Taxes: Total city taxes per capita: $39 (1997); City property taxes per capita: $39 (1997).
Education: High school graduation rate: 77.1% (2000); College graduation rate: 6.1% (2000).
Housing: Homeownership rate: 92.8% (2000); Median home value: $87,100 (2000); Median rent: $354 per month (2000); Median age of housing: 24 years (2000).
Transportation: Commute to work: 95.6% car, 0.0% public transportation, 0.0% walk, 3.1% work from home (2000); Travel time to work: 14.3% less than 15 minutes, 25.1% 15 to 30 minutes, 34.8% 30 to 45 minutes, 16.6% 45 to 60 minutes, 9.2% 60 minutes or more (2000)

Kent County

Located in southwestern Michigan; crossed by the Grand River; drained by the Flat, Rogue, and Thornapple Rivers. Covers a land area of 856.20 square miles, a water area of 16.00 square miles, and is located in the Eastern Time Zone. The county government was organized in 1836. County seat is Grand Rapids.

Kent County is part of the Grand Rapids-Muskegon-Holland, MI MSA. The entire metro area includes: Allegan County; Kent County; Muskegon County; Ottawa County

Weather Station: Grand Rapids Int'l Airport Elevation: 784 feet

	Jan	Feb	Mar	Apr	May	Jun	Jul	Aug	Sep	Oct	Nov	Dec
High	29	32	43	57	70	79	83	80	72	60	46	34
Low	15	17	25	36	46	56	61	59	51	40	31	22
Precip	2.0	1.5	2.6	3.5	3.2	3.7	3.6	3.8	4.3	2.9	3.4	2.7
Snow	21.3	11.8	9.3	2.8	tr	0.0	tr	tr	0.0	0.6	7.2	18.0

High and Low temperatures in degrees Fahrenheit; Precipitation and Snow in inches

Population: 574,335 (2000); Race: 83.1% White, 9.0% Black, 1.8% Asian, 0.6% American Indian and Alaska Native, 7.0% Hispanic of any race, 2.2% two or more races (2000); Density: 670.8 persons per square mile (2000); Age: 28.3% under 18, 10.4% over 64 (2000).
Religion: Five largest groups: 19.9% Catholic Church, 8.5% Christian Reformed Church in North America, 3.0% Reformed Church in America, 2.0% General Association of Regular Baptist Churches, 1.8% The United Methodist Church (2000).
Economy: Unemployment rate: 5.5% (11/2002); Total civilian labor force: 337,665 (11/2002); Leading industries: 23.9% manufacturing; 12.5% retail trade; 10.1% health care and social assistance (2000); Companies that employ more than 1,000 persons: 18 (2000); Companies that employ more than 100 persons: 588 (2000); Farms: 1,136 totaling 186,453 acres (1997); Minority business ownership rate: 6.2% (1997); Women business ownership rate: 26.5% (1997); Retail sales per capita: $11,996 (1997). Single-family building permits issued: 2,938 (2001) / 2,697 (2000); Multi-family building permits issued: 301 (2001) / 353 (2000).
Income: Per capita income: $21,629 (2000); Median household income: $45,980 (2000); Poverty rate: 8.9% (2000); Bankruptcy rate: 4.29% (2001).
Taxes: Total county taxes per capita: $127 (2000); County property taxes per capita: $122 (2000).
Education: High school graduation rate: 84.6% (2000); College graduation rate: 25.8% (2000).
Housing: Homeownership rate: 70.3% (2000); Median home value: $115,100 (2000); Median rent: $503 per month (2000); Median age of housing: 32 years (2000).

Health: Birth rate: 159.5 per 10,000 population (1998); Age adjusted death rate: 83.0 per 10,000 population (1999); Infant mortality rate: 7.0 per 1,000 live births (1998); Age adjusted cancer mortality rate: 190.8 deaths per 100,000 population (1999). Air Quality Index: 79% good, 21% moderate, 0% unhealthy (percent of days in 2000). Number of physicians: 24.9 per 10,000 population (1999); Number of hospital beds: 33.3 per 10,000 population (1999).
Elections: 2000 Presidential election results: 38.1% Gore, 59.4% Bush, 2.0% Nader, 0.1% Buchanan
National and State Parks: Cannonsburg State Game Area; Rogue River State Game Area
Additional Information Contacts
Kent County Government Offices 616-336-3512
Byron Center Chamber of Commerce 616-878-0108
Cedar Springs Chamber of Commerce. 616-696-3260
Grand Rapids Association of Realtors 616-940-8200
Grand Rapids Chamber of Commerce 616-771-0300
Grandville Chamber of Commerce 616-531-8890
Lowell Area Chamber of Commerce 616-897-9161
Rockford Chamber of Commerce 616-866-2000
Sparta Chamber of Commerce 616-887-2454
Wyoming Chamber of Commerce 616-531-5990

Kent County Communities

ADA (township). Covers a land area of 36.077 square miles and a water area of 0.958 square miles. Located at 42.97° N. Lat.; 85.49° W. Long.
History: Ada was founded in 1821 as a trading post and sawmill site. It later became a trading center for a farming area. Both the township and the town of Ada were named for Ada Smith, the daughter of the first postmaster in 1837.
Population: 9,882 (2000); Race: 95.2% White, 0.7% Black, 1.7% Asian, 0.3% American Indian and Alaska Native, 1.1% Hispanic of any race, 1.4% two or more races (2000); Density: 273.9 persons per square mile (2000); Age: 32.4% under 18, 7.3% over 64 (2000); Marriage status: 17.2% never married, 75.2% now married, 3.1% widowed, 4.5% divorced (2000); Foreign born: 4.7% (2000); Ancestry (includes multiple ancestries): 26.8% German, 21.9% Dutch, 16.1% English, 15.4% Irish, 8.5% Polish (2000).
Economy: Single-family building permits issued: 166 (2001) / 191 (2000); Multi-family building permits issued: 0 (2001) / 0 (2000); Employment by occupation: 23.0% management, 28.7% professional, 7.3% services, 27.2% sales, 0.3% farming, 4.6% construction, 8.8% production (2000).
Income: Per capita income: $37,840 (2000); Median household income: $83,357 (2000); Poverty rate: 1.9% (2000).
Taxes: Total city taxes per capita: $145 (2000); City property taxes per capita: $126 (2000).
Education: High school graduation rate: 96.5% (2000); College graduation rate: 50.6% (2000).
Housing: Homeownership rate: 94.7% (2000); Median home value: $189,200 (2000); Median rent: $906 per month (2000); Median age of housing: 20 years (2000).
Transportation: Commute to work: 95.2% car, 0.0% public transportation, 0.3% walk, 4.0% work from home (2000); Travel time to work: 26.6% less than 15 minutes, 57.2% 15 to 30 minutes, 11.0% 30 to 45 minutes, 2.7% 45 to 60 minutes, 2.5% 60 minutes or more (2000)

ALGOMA (township). Covers a land area of 34.861 square miles and a water area of 0.403 square miles. Located at 43.16° N. Lat.; 85.60° W. Long.
History: Algoma Township was organized in 1849 and named for a steamer, the "Algoma," which operated on the Grand River between Grand Rapids and Grand Haven.
Population: 7,596 (2000); Race: 97.3% White, 0.0% Black, 1.1% Asian, 0.0% American Indian and Alaska Native, 0.9% Hispanic of any race, 1.3% two or more races (2000); Density: 217.9 persons per square mile (2000); Age: 30.1% under 18, 7.7% over 64 (2000); Marriage status: 19.9% never married, 69.1% now married, 3.5% widowed, 7.5% divorced (2000); Foreign born: 1.9% (2000); Ancestry (includes multiple ancestries): 24.2% German, 20.7% Dutch, 16.7% English, 14.2% Irish, 10.0% Polish (2000).
Economy: Single-family building permits issued: 162 (2001) / 120 (2000); Multi-family building permits issued: 0 (2001) / 2 (2000); Employment by occupation: 10.8% management, 15.6% professional, 10.3% services, 29.4% sales, 0.0% farming, 11.5% construction, 22.4% production (2000).
Income: Per capita income: $23,150 (2000); Median household income: $58,285 (2000); Poverty rate: 3.7% (2000).
Taxes: Total city taxes per capita: $74 (1997); City property taxes per capita: $66 (1997).
Education: High school graduation rate: 89.0% (2000); College graduation rate: 18.1% (2000).
Housing: Homeownership rate: 95.9% (2000); Median home value: $148,600 (2000); Median rent: $436 per month (2000); Median age of housing: 19 years (2000).
Transportation: Commute to work: 95.1% car, 0.0% public transportation, 0.9% walk, 3.8% work from home (2000); Travel time to work: 16.0% less than 15 minutes, 47.9% 15 to 30 minutes, 25.0% 30 to 45 minutes, 6.7% 45 to 60 minutes, 4.5% 60 minutes or more (2000)

ALPINE (township). Covers a land area of 35.848 square miles and a water area of 0.138 square miles. Located at 43.06° N. Lat.; 85.71° W. Long. Elevation is 751 feet.
History: Alpine Township was organized in 1847 and named for the pine trees that grew in the area.
Population: 13,976 (2000); Race: 89.8% White, 3.5% Black, 1.6% Asian, 1.2% American Indian and Alaska Native, 6.4% Hispanic of any race, 1.0% two or more races (2000); Density: 389.9 persons per square mile (2000); Age: 24.7% under 18, 8.9% over 64 (2000); Marriage status: 35.1% never married, 49.4% now married, 4.1% widowed, 11.4% divorced (2000); Foreign born: 5.0% (2000); Ancestry (includes multiple ancestries): 24.3% German, 15.3% Dutch, 14.8% Other groups, 11.2% English, 10.5% Irish (2000).
Economy: Single-family building permits issued: 45 (2001) / 38 (2000); Multi-family building permits issued: 0 (2001) / 5 (2000); Employment by occupation: 11.3% management, 14.0% professional, 13.5% services, 29.3% sales, 0.9% farming, 8.2% construction, 22.9% production (2000).
Income: Per capita income: $20,412 (2000); Median household income: $42,484 (2000); Poverty rate: 8.9% (2000).
Taxes: Total city taxes per capita: $56 (2000); City property taxes per capita: $41 (2000).
Education: High school graduation rate: 87.2% (2000); College graduation rate: 17.5% (2000).
Housing: Homeownership rate: 56.2% (2000); Median home value: $120,500 (2000); Median rent: $586 per month (2000); Median age of housing: 17 years (2000).
Transportation: Commute to work: 96.3% car, 0.5% public transportation, 0.6% walk, 2.4% work from home (2000); Travel time to work: 33.5% less than 15 minutes, 43.6% 15 to 30 minutes, 15.9% 30 to 45 minutes, 3.3% 45 to 60 minutes, 3.7% 60 minutes or more (2000)

ALTO (unincorporated postal area, zip code 49302). Covers a land area of 48.362 square miles and a water area of 0.425 square miles. Located at 42.83° N. Lat.; 85.41° W. Long. Elevation is 817 feet.
History: Alto was founded by David N. Skidmore in 1845, and grew around a station on the Detroit, Grand Rapids & Western Railroad. The name refers to its elevation, being at the highest point between Grand Rapids and Detroit.
Population: 6,467 (2000); Race: 97.8% White, 0.1% Black, 1.0% Asian, 0.0% American Indian and Alaska Native, 0.9% Hispanic of any race, 0.4% two or more races (2000); Density: 133.7 persons per square mile (2000); Age: 31.0% under 18, 7.1% over 64 (2000); Marriage status: 20.5% never married, 70.6% now married, 2.8% widowed, 6.0% divorced (2000); Foreign born: 1.7% (2000); Ancestry (includes multiple ancestries): 25.2% German, 21.9% Dutch, 11.7% English, 10.0% Irish, 8.2% United States or American (2000).
Economy: Employment by occupation: 16.6% management, 18.4% professional, 9.8% services, 27.8% sales, 0.2% farming, 10.7% construction, 16.5% production (2000).
Income: Per capita income: $25,266 (2000); Median household income: $62,520 (2000); Poverty rate: 2.7% (2000).
Education: High school graduation rate: 92.9% (2000); College graduation rate: 30.0% (2000).
Housing: Homeownership rate: 93.2% (2000); Median home value: $169,900 (2000); Median rent: $383 per month (2000); Median age of housing: 24 years (2000).
Transportation: Commute to work: 93.3% car, 0.2% public transportation, 1.0% walk, 5.5% work from home (2000); Travel time to work: 15.6% less than 15 minutes, 51.1% 15 to 30 minutes, 26.0% 30 to 45 minutes, 2.4% 45 to 60 minutes, 4.9% 60 minutes or more (2000)

BELMONT (unincorporated postal area, zip code 49306). Covers a land area of 17.697 square miles and a water area of 0.187 square miles. Located at 43.07° N. Lat.; 85.59° W. Long. Elevation is 667 feet.

Population: 8,008 (2000); Race: 96.4% White, 1.1% Black, 0.9% Asian, 0.4% American Indian and Alaska Native, 1.4% Hispanic of any race, 1.1% two or more races (2000); Density: 452.5 persons per square mile (2000); Age: 29.1% under 18, 10.5% over 64 (2000); Marriage status: 20.8% never married, 65.0% now married, 6.5% widowed, 7.7% divorced (2000); Foreign born: 1.5% (2000); Ancestry (includes multiple ancestries): 24.8% German, 19.5% Dutch, 15.7% Irish, 15.1% English, 10.4% Polish (2000).
Economy: Employment by occupation: 12.5% management, 22.0% professional, 10.0% services, 27.9% sales, 0.2% farming, 10.9% construction, 16.5% production (2000).
Income: Per capita income: $27,043 (2000); Median household income: $61,601 (2000); Poverty rate: 1.9% (2000).
Education: High school graduation rate: 92.8% (2000); College graduation rate: 29.4% (2000).

School District(s)

Chandler Woods Charter Academy (KG-06)
2000 Enrollment: 364 616-895-3029
Housing: Homeownership rate: 97.9% (2000); Median home value: $154,700 (2000); Median rent: $558 per month (2000); Median age of housing: 17 years (2000).
Transportation: Commute to work: 95.2% car, 0.2% public transportation, 0.4% walk, 3.7% work from home (2000); Travel time to work: 22.1% less than 15 minutes, 49.7% 15 to 30 minutes, 19.2% 30 to 45 minutes, 5.7% 45 to 60 minutes, 3.3% 60 minutes or more (2000)

BOWNE (township). Covers a land area of 35.853 square miles and a water area of 0.176 square miles. Located at 42.82° N. Lat.; 85.36° W. Long.
Population: 2,743 (2000); Race: 95.8% White, 0.0% Black, 1.8% Asian, 0.0% American Indian and Alaska Native, 3.6% Hispanic of any race, 0.9% two or more races (2000); Density: 76.5 persons per square mile (2000); Age: 31.1% under 18, 6.6% over 64 (2000); Marriage status: 21.7% never married, 71.6% now married, 2.1% widowed, 4.7% divorced (2000); Foreign born: 1.9% (2000); Ancestry (includes multiple ancestries): 23.1% German, 22.5% Dutch, 10.0% English, 9.6% Irish, 8.5% Other groups (2000).
Economy: Single-family building permits issued: 22 (2001) / 11 (2000); Multi-family building permits issued: 0 (2001) / 0 (2000); Employment by occupation: 13.4% management, 17.6% professional, 12.6% services, 25.3% sales, 0.5% farming, 9.6% construction, 21.0% production (2000).
Income: Per capita income: $22,675 (2000); Median household income: $60,909 (2000); Poverty rate: 5.6% (2000).
Taxes: Total city taxes per capita: $130 (1997); City property taxes per capita: $120 (1997).
Education: High school graduation rate: 91.1% (2000); College graduation rate: 28.2% (2000).
Housing: Homeownership rate: 91.3% (2000); Median home value: $164,900 (2000); Median rent: $392 per month (2000); Median age of housing: 27 years (2000).
Transportation: Commute to work: 92.4% car, 0.0% public transportation, 1.7% walk, 5.9% work from home (2000); Travel time to work: 15.4% less than 15 minutes, 47.9% 15 to 30 minutes, 29.0% 30 to 45 minutes, 2.9% 45 to 60 minutes, 4.8% 60 minutes or more (2000)

BYRON (township). Covers a land area of 36.558 square miles and a water area of 0.020 square miles. Located at 42.82° N. Lat.; 85.70° W. Long.
History: Byron Township was organized in 1836.
Population: 17,553 (2000); Race: 94.2% White, 1.6% Black, 0.6% Asian, 0.5% American Indian and Alaska Native, 2.3% Hispanic of any race, 2.2% two or more races (2000); Density: 480.1 persons per square mile (2000); Age: 28.9% under 18, 10.6% over 64 (2000); Marriage status: 25.8% never married, 61.0% now married, 4.4% widowed, 8.8% divorced (2000); Foreign born: 3.0% (2000); Ancestry (includes multiple ancestries): 36.7% Dutch, 18.9% German, 8.9% Irish, 8.3% English, 7.5% Other groups (2000).
Economy: Single-family building permits issued: 142 (2001) / 118 (2000); Multi-family building permits issued: 47 (2001) / 31 (2000); Employment by occupation: 13.2% management, 15.1% professional, 10.6% services, 26.6% sales, 0.5% farming, 10.3% construction, 23.8% production (2000).
Income: Per capita income: $24,206 (2000); Median household income: $49,672 (2000); Poverty rate: 4.1% (2000).
Taxes: Total city taxes per capita: $72 (2000); City property taxes per capita: $54 (2000).
Education: High school graduation rate: 83.1% (2000); College graduation rate: 19.6% (2000).
Housing: Homeownership rate: 82.1% (2000); Median home value: $141,000 (2000); Median rent: $562 per month (2000); Median age of housing: 15 years (2000).
Transportation: Commute to work: 94.8% car, 0.7% public transportation, 1.2% walk, 2.7% work from home (2000); Travel time to work: 32.5% less than 15 minutes, 46.9% 15 to 30 minutes, 14.2% 30 to 45 minutes, 3.0% 45 to 60 minutes, 3.4% 60 minutes or more (2000)

BYRON CENTER (CDP). Covers a land area of 5.024 square miles and a water area of 0 square miles. Located at 42.81° N. Lat.; 85.72° W. Long. Elevation is 757 feet.
Population: 3,777 (2000); Race: 98.0% White, 0.9% Black, 0.4% Asian, 0.4% American Indian and Alaska Native, 1.9% Hispanic of any race, 0.2% two or more races (2000); Density: 751.8 persons per square mile (2000); Age: 32.7% under 18, 10.9% over 64 (2000); Marriage status: 19.8% never married, 70.7% now married, 3.9% widowed, 5.5% divorced (2000); Foreign born: 1.4% (2000); Ancestry (includes multiple ancestries): 43.4% Dutch, 21.5% German, 8.7% English, 6.8% Irish, 5.1% Polish (2000).
Economy: Employment by occupation: 15.2% management, 18.4% professional, 10.7% services, 27.4% sales, 0.6% farming, 8.6% construction, 19.0% production (2000).
Income: Per capita income: $29,028 (2000); Median household income: $58,508 (2000); Poverty rate: 3.2% (2000).
Education: High school graduation rate: 86.0% (2000); College graduation rate: 35.2% (2000).

School District(s)

Byron Center Public Schools (KG-12)
2000 Enrollment: 2,519 616-878-6100
Cross Creek Charter Academy (KG-08)
2000 Enrollment: 457 517-774-2400
The Learning Center Academy (KG-12)
2000 Enrollment: 163 616-895-3029
Housing: Homeownership rate: 90.3% (2000); Median home value: $158,500 (2000); Median rent: $648 per month (2000); Median age of housing: 13 years (2000).
Transportation: Commute to work: 92.6% car, 0.0% public transportation, 2.7% walk, 3.4% work from home (2000); Travel time to work: 38.6% less than 15 minutes, 42.5% 15 to 30 minutes, 14.3% 30 to 45 minutes, 1.8% 45 to 60 minutes, 2.9% 60 minutes or more (2000)
Additional Information Contacts
Byron Center Chamber of Commerce 616-878-0108

CALEDONIA (village). Covers a land area of 1.350 square miles and a water area of 0.038 square miles. Located at 42.79° N. Lat.; 85.51° W. Long. Elevation is 814 feet.
History: Caledonia was settled in 1838 and named for Caledonia, New York. The village was incorporated in 1888.
Population: 1,102 (2000); Race: 98.6% White, 0.1% Black, 0.1% Asian, 0.5% American Indian and Alaska Native, 1.2% Hispanic of any race, 0.5% two or more races (2000); Density: 816.3 persons per square mile (2000); Age: 32.1% under 18, 13.0% over 64 (2000); Marriage status: 19.9% never married, 63.3% now married, 5.6% widowed, 11.2% divorced (2000); Foreign born: 0.6% (2000); Ancestry (includes multiple ancestries): 22.4% German, 20.0% Dutch, 11.3% English, 11.1% Irish, 8.2% United States or American (2000).
Economy: Employment by occupation: 16.0% management, 16.2% professional, 16.9% services, 25.6% sales, 0.9% farming, 5.6% construction, 19.0% production (2000).
Income: Per capita income: $22,386 (2000); Median household income: $50,724 (2000); Poverty rate: 3.7% (2000).
Taxes: Total city taxes per capita: $210 (1997); City property taxes per capita: $204 (1997).
Education: High school graduation rate: 94.9% (2000); College graduation rate: 29.9% (2000).

School District(s)

Caledonia Community Schools (KG-12)
2000 Enrollment: 3,185 616-891-8185
Housing: Homeownership rate: 61.8% (2000); Median home value: $119,200 (2000); Median rent: $472 per month (2000); Median age of housing: 28 years (2000).
Transportation: Commute to work: 91.3% car, 0.0% public transportation, 4.1% walk, 4.2% work from home (2000); Travel time to work: 27.5% less than 15 minutes, 47.8% 15 to 30 minutes, 19.0% 30 to 45 minutes, 2.4% 45 to 60 minutes, 3.3% 60 minutes or more (2000)

CALEDONIA (township). Covers a land area of 35.150 square miles and a water area of 0.621 square miles. Located at 42.81° N. Lat.; 85.48° W. Long. Elevation is 814 feet.

Population: 8,964 (2000); Race: 98.3% White, 0.2% Black, 1.1% Asian, 0.1% American Indian and Alaska Native, 0.5% Hispanic of any race, 0.2% two or more races (2000); Density: 255.0 persons per square mile (2000); Age: 31.3% under 18, 7.3% over 64 (2000); Marriage status: 21.4% never married, 67.9% now married, 3.5% widowed, 7.1% divorced (2000); Foreign born: 2.2% (2000); Ancestry (includes multiple ancestries): 24.8% German, 23.1% Dutch, 13.6% English, 10.0% Irish, 6.8% Polish (2000).
Economy: Agriculture: dairying. Manufacturing: paint, motor vehicle parts, thermoplastic materials. Middleville Ski Area to Southeast. Single-family building permits issued: 108 (2001) / 99 (2000); Multi-family building permits issued: 28 (2001) / 76 (2000); Employment by occupation: 16.9% management, 19.1% professional, 10.7% services, 28.3% sales, 0.1% farming, 10.0% construction, 15.0% production (2000).
Income: Per capita income: $25,710 (2000); Median household income: $63,032 (2000); Poverty rate: 2.3% (2000).
Taxes: Total city taxes per capita: $102 (1997); City property taxes per capita: $82 (1997).
Education: High school graduation rate: 93.6% (2000); College graduation rate: 33.4% (2000).
Housing: Homeownership rate: 89.8% (2000); Median home value: $170,000 (2000); Median rent: $470 per month (2000); Median age of housing: 20 years (2000).
Transportation: Commute to work: 94.8% car, 0.3% public transportation, 0.7% walk, 4.1% work from home (2000); Travel time to work: 24.7% less than 15 minutes, 48.0% 15 to 30 minutes, 20.0% 30 to 45 minutes, 3.2% 45 to 60 minutes, 4.1% 60 minutes or more (2000)

CANNON (township). Covers a land area of 35.887 square miles and a water area of 1.220 square miles. Located at 43.07° N. Lat.; 85.48° W. Long.
Population: 12,075 (2000); Race: 98.0% White, 0.5% Black, 0.7% Asian, 0.0% American Indian and Alaska Native, 0.2% Hispanic of any race, 0.5% two or more races (2000); Density: 336.5 persons per square mile (2000); Age: 34.1% under 18, 6.1% over 64 (2000); Marriage status: 18.4% never married, 72.7% now married, 3.7% widowed, 5.1% divorced (2000); Foreign born: 1.9% (2000); Ancestry (includes multiple ancestries): 31.4% German, 18.9% Dutch, 16.7% Irish, 14.3% English, 9.2% Polish (2000).
Economy: Single-family building permits issued: 121 (2001) / 117 (2000); Multi-family building permits issued: 0 (2001) / 0 (2000); Employment by occupation: 18.7% management, 25.7% professional, 9.4% services, 26.5% sales, 0.0% farming, 8.7% construction, 10.9% production (2000).
Income: Per capita income: $27,383 (2000); Median household income: $70,925 (2000); Poverty rate: 2.5% (2000).
Taxes: Total city taxes per capita: $89 (1997); City property taxes per capita: $62 (1997).
Education: High school graduation rate: 95.8% (2000); College graduation rate: 37.9% (2000).
Housing: Homeownership rate: 93.0% (2000); Median home value: $185,000 (2000); Median rent: $655 per month (2000); Median age of housing: 16 years (2000).
Transportation: Commute to work: 94.7% car, 0.2% public transportation, 0.8% walk, 3.9% work from home (2000); Travel time to work: 17.3% less than 15 minutes, 42.9% 15 to 30 minutes, 29.3% 30 to 45 minutes, 5.2% 45 to 60 minutes, 5.3% 60 minutes or more (2000)

CASCADE (township). Covers a land area of 33.898 square miles and a water area of 0.879 square miles. Located at 42.90° N. Lat.; 85.49° W. Long.
History: Mineral springs in the Cascade area attracted health seekers when they were first discovered, but soon the springs undermined the hotel and it collapsed. The area developed as a residential suburb of Grand Rapids.
Population: 15,107 (2000); Race: 95.5% White, 1.3% Black, 2.3% Asian, 0.2% American Indian and Alaska Native, 1.1% Hispanic of any race, 0.6% two or more races (2000); Density: 445.7 persons per square mile (2000); Age: 29.3% under 18, 11.4% over 64 (2000); Marriage status: 17.7% never married, 72.9% now married, 3.9% widowed, 5.5% divorced (2000); Foreign born: 5.3% (2000); Ancestry (includes multiple ancestries): 23.4% German, 18.3% Dutch, 16.5% English, 13.7% Irish, 7.1% Polish (2000).
Economy: Single-family building permits issued: 33 (2001) / 121 (2000); Multi-family building permits issued: 48 (2001) / 0 (2000); Employment by occupation: 23.5% management, 29.8% professional, 9.3% services, 27.2% sales, 0.2% farming, 3.6% construction, 6.5% production (2000).
Income: Per capita income: $39,470 (2000); Median household income: $87,290 (2000); Poverty rate: 2.3% (2000).
Taxes: Total city taxes per capita: $294 (2000); City property taxes per capita: $226 (2000).
Education: High school graduation rate: 96.0% (2000); College graduation rate: 54.6% (2000).
Housing: Homeownership rate: 92.8% (2000); Median home value: $220,100 (2000); Median rent: $817 per month (2000); Median age of housing: 22 years (2000).
Transportation: Commute to work: 91.2% car, 0.2% public transportation, 0.8% walk, 6.7% work from home (2000); Travel time to work: 35.1% less than 15 minutes, 49.1% 15 to 30 minutes, 8.5% 30 to 45 minutes, 2.8% 45 to 60 minutes, 4.5% 60 minutes or more (2000)

CASNOVIA (village). Covers a land area of 1.095 square miles and a water area of 0 square miles. Located at 43.23° N. Lat.; 85.78° W. Long.
Population: 315 (2000); Race: 100.0% White, 0.0% Black, 0.0% Asian, 0.0% American Indian and Alaska Native, 0.0% Hispanic of any race, 0.0% two or more races (2000); Density: 287.6 persons per square mile (2000); Age: 23.7% under 18, 13.0% over 64 (2000); Marriage status: 25.5% never married, 60.3% now married, 8.5% widowed, 5.7% divorced (2000); Foreign born: 2.0% (2000); Ancestry (includes multiple ancestries): 19.4% German, 18.7% Dutch, 13.4% English, 12.0% Irish, 10.7% United States or American (2000).
Economy: Single-family building permits issued: 0 (2001) / 3 (2000); Multi-family building permits issued: 0 (2001) / 0 (2000); Employment by occupation: 5.0% management, 10.7% professional, 10.0% services, 17.1% sales, 0.0% farming, 13.6% construction, 43.6% production (2000).
Income: Per capita income: $18,962 (2000); Median household income: $42,019 (2000); Poverty rate: 4.7% (2000).
Education: High school graduation rate: 75.4% (2000); College graduation rate: 7.5% (2000).
Housing: Homeownership rate: 88.5% (2000); Median home value: $84,000 (2000); Median rent: $404 per month (2000); Median age of housing: 60+ years (2000).
Transportation: Commute to work: 87.1% car, 0.0% public transportation, 10.0% walk, 0.7% work from home (2000); Travel time to work: 35.3% less than 15 minutes, 15.1% 15 to 30 minutes, 34.5% 30 to 45 minutes, 10.1% 45 to 60 minutes, 5.0% 60 minutes or more (2000)

CEDAR SPRINGS (city). Covers a land area of 1.829 square miles and a water area of 0.018 square miles. Located at 43.22° N. Lat.; 85.55° W. Long. Elevation is 844 feet.
History: Cedar Springs was settled in 1855 and platted in 1859. On the Grand Rapids & Indiana Railroad after 1868, Cedar Springs developed as a summer resort.
Population: 3,112 (2000); Race: 97.2% White, 0.6% Black, 0.1% Asian, 0.5% American Indian and Alaska Native, 4.2% Hispanic of any race, 0.9% two or more races (2000); Density: 1,701.9 persons per square mile (2000); Age: 31.4% under 18, 9.6% over 64 (2000); Marriage status: 29.8% never married, 49.2% now married, 6.1% widowed, 14.9% divorced (2000); Foreign born: 2.4% (2000); Ancestry (includes multiple ancestries): 23.6% German, 13.9% United States or American, 13.5% Dutch, 9.7% Irish, 9.6% Other groups (2000).
Economy: Single-family building permits issued: 7 (2001) / 8 (2000); Multi-family building permits issued: 6 (2001) / 2 (2000); Employment by occupation: 6.8% management, 12.2% professional, 20.7% services, 20.5% sales, 1.7% farming, 11.4% construction, 26.7% production (2000).
Income: Per capita income: $16,040 (2000); Median household income: $39,542 (2000); Poverty rate: 13.8% (2000).
Taxes: Total city taxes per capita: $192 (1997); City property taxes per capita: $189 (1997).
Education: High school graduation rate: 79.4% (2000); College graduation rate: 11.7% (2000).

School District(s)

Cedar Springs Public Schools (PK-12)
2000 Enrollment: 3,221 616-696-1204
Creative Technologies Academy (07-12)
2000 Enrollment: 147 616-592-5819

Housing: Homeownership rate: 65.8% (2000); Median home value: $88,900 (2000); Median rent: $440 per month (2000); Median age of housing: 33 years (2000).
Safety: Violent crime rate: 44.8 per 10,000 population; Property crime rate: 636.2 per 10,000 population (2001).
Newspapers: Cedar Springs Post (1 x week)
Transportation: Commute to work: 94.8% car, 0.0% public transportation, 3.2% walk, 1.8% work from home (2000); Travel time to work: 28.8% less than 15 minutes, 27.4% 15 to 30 minutes, 30.0% 30 to 45 minutes, 7.6% 45 to 60 minutes, 6.2% 60 minutes or more (2000)
Additional Information Contacts
Cedar Springs Chamber of Commerce. 616-696-3260

COMSTOCK PARK (CDP). Covers a land area of 3.903 square miles and a water area of 0 square miles. Located at 43.04° N. Lat.; 85.67° W. Long. Elevation is 705 feet.
History: Previously known as North Park and Mill Creek, Comstock Park was renamed in 1906 for Charles C. Comstock, a congressional representative from the district.
Population: 10,674 (2000); Race: 87.9% White, 4.4% Black, 2.2% Asian, 1.0% American Indian and Alaska Native, 7.6% Hispanic of any race, 0.8% two or more races (2000); Density: 2,735.0 persons per square mile (2000); Age: 23.7% under 18, 8.0% over 64 (2000); Marriage status: 38.5% never married, 43.6% now married, 4.2% widowed, 13.8% divorced (2000); Foreign born: 6.1% (2000); Ancestry (includes multiple ancestries): 21.3% German, 17.8% Other groups, 14.3% Dutch, 12.8% English, 10.5% Irish (2000).
Economy: Employment by occupation: 10.6% management, 15.6% professional, 14.6% services, 28.6% sales, 0.7% farming, 8.6% construction, 21.4% production (2000).
Income: Per capita income: $19,911 (2000); Median household income: $40,202 (2000); Poverty rate: 9.7% (2000).
Education: High school graduation rate: 86.1% (2000); College graduation rate: 19.5% (2000).

School District(s)

Comstock Park Public Schools (KG-12)
2000 Enrollment: 2,215 616-254-5001

Housing: Homeownership rate: 42.1% (2000); Median home value: $114,100 (2000); Median rent: $582 per month (2000); Median age of housing: 13 years (2000).
Transportation: Commute to work: 96.6% car, 0.2% public transportation, 0.6% walk, 2.3% work from home (2000); Travel time to work: 30.5% less than 15 minutes, 47.3% 15 to 30 minutes, 15.3% 30 to 45 minutes, 3.0% 45 to 60 minutes, 3.8% 60 minutes or more (2000)

COURTLAND (township). Covers a land area of 35.460 square miles and a water area of 0.524 square miles. Located at 43.15° N. Lat.; 85.49° W. Long.
Population: 5,817 (2000); Race: 98.2% White, 0.5% Black, 0.3% Asian, 0.0% American Indian and Alaska Native, 1.1% Hispanic of any race, 0.9% two or more races (2000); Density: 164.0 persons per square mile (2000); Age: 30.5% under 18, 7.0% over 64 (2000); Marriage status: 18.5% never married, 71.3% now married, 2.7% widowed, 7.5% divorced (2000); Foreign born: 0.7% (2000); Ancestry (includes multiple ancestries): 28.7% German, 16.7% English, 15.9% Dutch, 12.7% Polish, 12.6% Irish (2000).
Economy: Single-family building permits issued: 92 (2001) / 79 (2000); Multi-family building permits issued: 0 (2001) / 0 (2000); Employment by occupation: 15.0% management, 19.0% professional, 9.8% services, 24.3% sales, 0.4% farming, 13.2% construction, 18.3% production (2000).
Income: Per capita income: $26,254 (2000); Median household income: $64,430 (2000); Poverty rate: 2.4% (2000).
Taxes: Total city taxes per capita: $76 (1997); City property taxes per capita: $54 (1997).
Education: High school graduation rate: 91.2% (2000); College graduation rate: 25.0% (2000).
Housing: Homeownership rate: 95.5% (2000); Median home value: $151,300 (2000); Median rent: $664 per month (2000); Median age of housing: 21 years (2000).
Transportation: Commute to work: 95.2% car, 0.4% public transportation, 0.0% walk, 4.2% work from home (2000); Travel time to work: 19.4% less than 15 minutes, 34.6% 15 to 30 minutes, 32.2% 30 to 45 minutes, 8.4% 45 to 60 minutes, 5.4% 60 minutes or more (2000)

CUTLERVILLE (CDP). Covers a land area of 5.981 square miles and a water area of 0 square miles. Located at 42.83° N. Lat.; 85.66° W. Long. Elevation is 678 feet.
History: Cutlerville was settled in 1853 by John Cutler and his family of ten children. One of his sons, John, built the Cutler mansion in 1891, which became the Pine Rest Christian Hospital in 1910.
Population: 15,114 (2000); Race: 88.8% White, 4.8% Black, 1.3% Asian, 0.6% American Indian and Alaska Native, 4.3% Hispanic of any race, 2.9% two or more races (2000); Density: 2,527.2 persons per square mile (2000); Age: 27.2% under 18, 10.2% over 64 (2000); Marriage status: 31.6% never married, 52.1% now married, 4.5% widowed, 11.8% divorced (2000); Foreign born: 5.2% (2000); Ancestry (includes multiple ancestries): 27.9% Dutch, 18.5% German, 12.9% Other groups, 10.2% English, 9.5% Irish (2000).
Economy: Employment by occupation: 11.1% management, 12.4% professional, 12.6% services, 25.8% sales, 0.2% farming, 9.6% construction, 28.3% production (2000).
Income: Per capita income: $19,648 (2000); Median household income: $40,809 (2000); Poverty rate: 7.2% (2000).
Education: High school graduation rate: 79.9% (2000); College graduation rate: 13.5% (2000).
Housing: Homeownership rate: 70.8% (2000); Median home value: $117,500 (2000); Median rent: $552 per month (2000); Median age of housing: 15 years (2000).
Transportation: Commute to work: 95.5% car, 1.8% public transportation, 0.5% walk, 1.8% work from home (2000); Travel time to work: 30.7% less than 15 minutes, 49.6% 15 to 30 minutes, 13.9% 30 to 45 minutes, 3.4% 45 to 60 minutes, 2.4% 60 minutes or more (2000)

EAST GRAND RAPIDS (city). Covers a land area of 2.927 square miles and a water area of 0.474 square miles. Located at 42.94° N. Lat.; 85.61° W. Long. Elevation is 756 feet.
Population: 10,764 (2000); Race: 97.9% White, 0.9% Black, 0.7% Asian, 0.1% American Indian and Alaska Native, 1.8% Hispanic of any race, 0.2% two or more races (2000); Density: 3,678.0 persons per square mile (2000); Age: 32.4% under 18, 10.2% over 64 (2000); Marriage status: 18.9% never married, 68.9% now married, 4.2% widowed, 7.9% divorced (2000); Foreign born: 3.1% (2000); Ancestry (includes multiple ancestries): 26.2% German, 20.0% Irish, 19.0% English, 16.6% Dutch, 6.7% Polish (2000).
Vital Statistics: Birth rate: 109.6 per 10,000 population (1998)
Economy: Single-family building permits issued: 5 (2001) / 6 (2000); Multi-family building permits issued: 0 (2001) / 0 (2000); Employment by occupation: 24.3% management, 37.5% professional, 6.6% services, 26.1% sales, 0.3% farming, 1.9% construction, 3.3% production (2000).
Income: Per capita income: $41,388 (2000); Median household income: $84,772 (2000); Poverty rate: 2.8% (2000).
Taxes: Total city taxes per capita: $443 (1997); City property taxes per capita: $432 (1997).
Education: High school graduation rate: 99.0% (2000); College graduation rate: 71.1% (2000).

School District(s)

East Grand Rapids Public Schools (PK-12)
2000 Enrollment: 2,708 616-235-3535

Housing: Homeownership rate: 93.8% (2000); Median home value: $205,600 (2000); Median rent: $711 per month (2000); Median age of housing: 48 years (2000).
Safety: Violent crime rate: 1.8 per 10,000 population; Property crime rate: 132.2 per 10,000 population (2001).
Transportation: Commute to work: 92.2% car, 0.2% public transportation, 1.7% walk, 5.5% work from home (2000); Travel time to work: 42.8% less than 15 minutes, 46.7% 15 to 30 minutes, 5.4% 30 to 45 minutes, 2.3% 45 to 60 minutes, 2.7% 60 minutes or more (2000)

FOREST HILLS (CDP). Covers a land area of 49.386 square miles and a water area of 1.371 square miles. Located at 42.94° N. Lat.; 85.49° W. Long.
Population: 20,942 (2000); Race: 95.5% White, 0.9% Black, 2.0% Asian, 0.2% American Indian and Alaska Native, 1.1% Hispanic of any race, 1.0% two or more races (2000); Density: 424.0 persons per square mile (2000); Age: 31.2% under 18, 9.0% over 64 (2000); Marriage status: 17.1% never married, 75.0% now married, 2.9% widowed, 5.0% divorced (2000); Foreign born: 5.2% (2000); Ancestry (includes multiple ancestries): 25.0% German, 20.3% Dutch, 16.3% English, 14.3% Irish, 7.9% Polish (2000).
Economy: Employment by occupation: 23.4% management, 29.4% professional, 8.3% services, 27.3% sales, 0.2% farming, 4.1% construction, 7.2% production (2000).
Income: Per capita income: $39,517 (2000); Median household income: $87,266 (2000); Poverty rate: 2.0% (2000).
Education: High school graduation rate: 95.9% (2000); College graduation rate: 54.1% (2000).
Housing: Homeownership rate: 95.2% (2000); Median home value: $212,600 (2000); Median rent: $722 per month (2000); Median age of housing: 21 years (2000).
Transportation: Commute to work: 93.7% car, 0.1% public transportation, 0.6% walk, 4.8% work from home (2000); Travel time to work: 31.3% less than 15 minutes, 52.0% 15 to 30 minutes, 9.8% 30 to 45 minutes, 3.0% 45 to 60 minutes, 4.0% 60 minutes or more (2000)

GAINES (township). Covers a land area of 35.926 square miles and a water area of 0.021 square miles. Located at 42.83° N. Lat.; 85.63° W. Long.

Population: 20,112 (2000); Race: 89.4% White, 5.3% Black, 1.4% Asian, 0.7% American Indian and Alaska Native, 3.4% Hispanic of any race, 2.3% two or more races (2000); Density: 559.8 persons per square mile (2000); Age: 28.9% under 18, 9.7% over 64 (2000); Marriage status: 28.4% never married, 59.0% now married, 4.4% widowed, 8.2% divorced (2000); Foreign born: 4.2% (2000); Ancestry (includes multiple ancestries): 32.0% Dutch, 17.6% German, 12.4% Other groups, 10.2% English, 8.9% Irish (2000).
Economy: Single-family building permits issued: 263 (2001) / 300 (2000); Multi-family building permits issued: 0 (2001) / 0 (2000); Employment by occupation: 15.0% management, 14.3% professional, 12.3% services, 28.9% sales, 0.4% farming, 8.2% construction, 20.9% production (2000).
Income: Per capita income: $23,459 (2000); Median household income: $48,482 (2000); Poverty rate: 5.4% (2000).
Taxes: Total city taxes per capita: $36 (2000); City property taxes per capita: $18 (2000).
Education: High school graduation rate: 85.6% (2000); College graduation rate: 21.0% (2000).
Housing: Homeownership rate: 71.2% (2000); Median home value: $145,400 (2000); Median rent: $556 per month (2000); Median age of housing: 15 years (2000).
Transportation: Commute to work: 94.4% car, 1.2% public transportation, 0.4% walk, 3.6% work from home (2000); Travel time to work: 31.8% less than 15 minutes, 49.8% 15 to 30 minutes, 13.1% 30 to 45 minutes, 2.9% 45 to 60 minutes, 2.4% 60 minutes or more (2000)

GRAND RAPIDS (city). Covers a land area of 44.638 square miles and a water area of 0.682 square miles. Located at 42.96° N. Lat.; 85.65° W. Long. Elevation is 610 feet.
History: A Baptist mission in 1826 and a fur trading post in 1827 were the beginnings of Grand Rapids, named for the rapids on the Grand River. Louis Campau, who had built the trading post, laid out the town in 1831, besting Lucius Lyon's attempts in a similar endeavor. For a time Lyon's town name of Kent was the official post office name, but in 1842 the town again became Grand Rapids. Logging, the first industry of importance, led to furniture making as early as 1838. By 1876 the Grand Rapids furniture trade was established.
Population: 197,800 (2000); Race: 67.0% White, 20.4% Black, 1.6% Asian, 0.8% American Indian and Alaska Native, 13.0% Hispanic of any race, 3.4% two or more races (2000); Density: 4,431.2 persons per square mile (2000); Age: 27.0% under 18, 11.6% over 64 (2000); Marriage status: 36.7% never married, 46.0% now married, 6.6% widowed, 10.6% divorced (2000); Foreign born: 10.5% (2000); Ancestry (includes multiple ancestries): 32.2% Other groups, 15.7% Dutch, 13.8% German, 8.6% Irish, 7.8% Polish (2000).
Vital Statistics: Birth rate: 198.6 per 10,000 population (1998)
Economy: Unemployment rate: 7.6% (11/2002); Total civilian labor force: 119,799 (11/2002); Single-family building permits issued: 225 (2001) / 237 (2000); Multi-family building permits issued: 16 (2001) / 0 (2000); Employment by occupation: 10.1% management, 19.1% professional, 16.7% services, 24.9% sales, 0.7% farming, 6.7% construction, 21.7% production (2000).
Income: Per capita income: $17,661 (2000); Median household income: $37,224 (2000); Poverty rate: 15.7% (2000).
Taxes: Total city taxes per capita: $469 (2000); City property taxes per capita: $178 (2000).
Education: High school graduation rate: 78.0% (2000); College graduation rate: 23.8% (2000).

School District(s)

Forest Hills Public Schools (KG-12)
2000 Enrollment: 8,287 616-493-8800
Gateway Middle/High School (07-12)
2000 Enrollment: 199 616-895-3029
Grand Rapids Child Discovery Cen (KG-02)
2000 Enrollment: 83 616-459-0330
Grand Rapids Public Schools (PK-12)
2000 Enrollment: 25,625 616-771-2000
Kelloggsville Public Schools (KG-12)
2000 Enrollment: 2,095 616-538-7460
Kenowa Hills Public Schools (KG-12)
2000 Enrollment: 3,445 616-784-2511
Northview Public School District (KG-12)
2000 Enrollment: 3,181 616-363-6861

Four-year College(s)

Aquinas College (Private, Not-for-profit, Roman Catholic)
2001 Enrollment: 2,571 616-459-8281
2001 Tuition: In-state $14,876; Out-of-state $14,876
Calvin College (Private, Not-for-profit, Christian Reformed Church)
2001 Enrollment: 4,258 616-957-6000
2001 Tuition: In-state $14,870; Out-of-state $14,870
Calvin Theological Seminary (Private, Not-for-profit, Christian Reformed Church)
2001 Enrollment: 274 616-957-6036
Davenport University-Western Region-Grand Rapids (Private, Not-for-profit)
2001 Enrollment: 2,127 616-451-3511
2001 Tuition: In-state $8,586; Out-of-state $8,586
Cornerstone University (Private, Not-for-profit, Baptist)
2001 Enrollment: 1,941 616-949-5300
2001 Tuition: In-state $12,215; Out-of-state $12,215
David Wolcott Kendall Memorial School (Private, Not-for-profit)
2001 Enrollment: n/a 616-451-2787
Reformed Bible College (Private, Not-for-profit, Other Protestant)
2001 Enrollment: 294 616-222-3000
2001 Tuition: In-state $8,400; Out-of-state $8,400
University of Phoenix-Grand Rapids Campus (Private, For-profit)
2001 Enrollment: 586 616-956-5100

Two-year College(s)

Grand Rapids Community College (Public)
2001 Enrollment: 13,483 616-234-4000
2001 Tuition: In-state $2,640; Out-of-state $3,060
ITT Technical Institute (Private, For-profit)
2001 Enrollment: 519 616-956-1060
2001 Tuition: In-state $10,548; Out-of-state $10,548

Housing: Homeownership rate: 59.8% (2000); Median home value: $91,400 (2000); Median rent: $465 per month (2000); Median age of housing: 49 years (2000).
Hospitals: Forest View Psychiatric Hospital (62 beds); Mary Free Bed Hospital & Rehabilitation Center (80 beds); Metropolitan Hospital (238 beds); Pine Rest Christian Mental Health Services (162 beds); Saint Mary's Mercy Medical Center (324 beds); Spectrum Health (529 beds); Spectrum Health - East Campus (410 beds); Spectrum Health - Kent Community Campus (484 beds)
Safety: Violent crime rate: 103.0 per 10,000 population; Property crime rate: 501.8 per 10,000 population (2001).
Newspapers: The Paper (1 x week); The Grand Rapids Press (7 x week); Grand Rapids Times (1 x week)
Transportation: Commute to work: 89.4% car, 2.4% public transportation, 4.0% walk, 2.7% work from home (2000); Travel time to work: 36.1% less than 15 minutes, 47.1% 15 to 30 minutes, 10.7% 30 to 45 minutes, 2.7% 45 to 60 minutes, 3.3% 60 minutes or more (2000); Amtrak: Service available.
Airports: Gerald R. Ford International (primary service/small hub)
Additional Information Contacts
Grand Rapids Association of Realtors 616-940-8200
Grand Rapids Chamber of Commerce 616-771-0300

GRAND RAPIDS CHARTER (township). Covers a land area of 15.420 square miles and a water area of 0.149 square miles. Located at 42.98° N. Lat.; 85.58° W. Long.
Population: 14,056 (2000); Race: 96.5% White, 1.3% Black, 0.9% Asian, 0.2% American Indian and Alaska Native, 1.0% Hispanic of any race, 0.7% two or more races (2000); Density: 911.6 persons per square mile (2000); Age: 29.1% under 18, 15.8% over 64 (2000); Marriage status: 20.3% never married, 67.2% now married, 7.6% widowed, 4.9% divorced (2000); Foreign born: 3.4% (2000); Ancestry (includes multiple ancestries): 25.3% German, 21.2% Dutch, 16.6% English, 12.5% Irish, 8.1% Polish (2000).
Economy: Employment by occupation: 19.6% management, 27.0% professional, 12.2% services, 26.4% sales, 0.0% farming, 4.5% construction, 10.3% production (2000).
Income: Per capita income: $30,531 (2000); Median household income: $66,250 (2000); Poverty rate: 3.2% (2000).
Taxes: Total city taxes per capita: $82 (2000); City property taxes per capita: $57 (2000).
Education: High school graduation rate: 91.6% (2000); College graduation rate: 46.0% (2000).
Housing: Homeownership rate: 88.6% (2000); Median home value: $166,300 (2000); Median rent: $1,063 per month (2000); Median age of housing: 24 years (2000).
Transportation: Commute to work: 93.3% car, 0.1% public transportation, 0.9% walk, 4.5% work from home (2000); Travel time to work: 42.5% less than 15 minutes, 45.1% 15 to 30 minutes, 7.6% 30 to 45 minutes, 1.9% 45 to 60 minutes, 3.0% 60 minutes or more (2000)

GRANDVILLE (city). Covers a land area of 7.407 square miles and a water area of 0.200 square miles. Located at 42.90° N. Lat.; 85.75° W. Long. Elevation is 604 feet.
History: Grandville was established in the 1830's by a company of land operators from an eastern state. Grandville was incorporated as a village in 1887 and as a city in 1933.
Population: 16,263 (2000); Race: 94.5% White, 2.0% Black, 0.7% Asian, 0.5% American Indian and Alaska Native, 2.9% Hispanic of any race, 1.4% two or more races (2000); Density: 2,195.6 persons per square mile (2000); Age: 28.2% under 18, 12.7% over 64 (2000); Marriage status: 26.6% never married, 60.4% now married, 5.6% widowed, 7.4% divorced (2000); Foreign born: 2.6% (2000); Ancestry (includes multiple ancestries): 37.3% Dutch, 18.6% German, 10.7% English, 7.7% Other groups, 7.4% Irish (2000).
Vital Statistics: Birth rate: 158.0 per 10,000 population (1998)
Economy: Single-family building permits issued: 80 (2001) / 76 (2000); Multi-family building permits issued: 0 (2001) / 0 (2000); Employment by occupation: 12.1% management, 18.6% professional, 14.1% services, 30.4% sales, 0.1% farming, 6.3% construction, 18.4% production (2000).
Income: Per capita income: $21,306 (2000); Median household income: $47,570 (2000); Poverty rate: 4.5% (2000).
Taxes: Total city taxes per capita: $206 (1997); City property taxes per capita: $197 (1997).
Education: High school graduation rate: 88.2% (2000); College graduation rate: 22.2% (2000).

School District(s)

Grandville Public Schools (PK-12)
2000 Enrollment: 5,907 616-254-6550

Four-year College(s)

Theological School of the Protestant Reform Church (Private, Not-for-profit, Other Protestant)
2001 Enrollment: n/a 616-531-1490
Housing: Homeownership rate: 73.6% (2000); Median home value: $122,200 (2000); Median rent: $515 per month (2000); Median age of housing: 28 years (2000).
Safety: Violent crime rate: 19.6 per 10,000 population; Property crime rate: 567.0 per 10,000 population (2001).
Transportation: Commute to work: 93.8% car, 1.0% public transportation, 2.0% walk, 2.4% work from home (2000); Travel time to work: 34.6% less than 15 minutes, 45.1% 15 to 30 minutes, 15.1% 30 to 45 minutes, 2.3% 45 to 60 minutes, 2.8% 60 minutes or more (2000)
Additional Information Contacts
Grandville Chamber of Commerce 616-531-8890

GRATTAN (township). Aka Grattan Center. Covers a land area of 34.991 square miles and a water area of 1.948 square miles. Located at 43.08° N. Lat.; 85.37° W. Long.
History: Grattan Township was named for Henry Grattan, an Irish statesman and orator. The first settlers here in the mid-1840's were Irish. Edward S. Bellamy and Nathan Holmes built a grist mill in 1850.
Population: 3,551 (2000); Race: 96.9% White, 0.2% Black, 0.1% Asian, 0.2% American Indian and Alaska Native, 2.9% Hispanic of any race, 1.8% two or more races (2000); Density: 101.5 persons per square mile (2000); Age: 27.8% under 18, 9.0% over 64 (2000); Marriage status: 22.7% never married, 64.2% now married, 4.1% widowed, 9.0% divorced (2000); Foreign born: 1.7% (2000); Ancestry (includes multiple ancestries): 26.4% German, 18.8% Irish, 15.0% English, 12.7% Dutch, 8.2% Polish (2000).
Economy: Single-family building permits issued: 24 (2001) / 22 (2000); Multi-family building permits issued: 0 (2001) / 0 (2000); Employment by occupation: 15.0% management, 14.9% professional, 9.9% services, 29.2% sales, 1.2% farming, 7.6% construction, 22.1% production (2000).
Income: Per capita income: $23,213 (2000); Median household income: $56,467 (2000); Poverty rate: 2.3% (2000).
Taxes: Total city taxes per capita: $75 (1997); City property taxes per capita: $61 (1997).
Education: High school graduation rate: 88.9% (2000); College graduation rate: 22.0% (2000).
Housing: Homeownership rate: 92.3% (2000); Median home value: $149,900 (2000); Median rent: $591 per month (2000); Median age of housing: 30 years (2000).
Transportation: Commute to work: 96.2% car, 0.0% public transportation, 0.2% walk, 3.2% work from home (2000); Travel time to work: 11.2% less than 15 minutes, 33.0% 15 to 30 minutes, 37.1% 30 to 45 minutes, 11.8% 45 to 60 minutes, 7.0% 60 minutes or more (2000)

KENT CITY (village). Covers a land area of 1.095 square miles and a water area of 0.011 square miles. Located at 43.21° N. Lat.; 85.75° W. Long. Elevation is 800 feet.
History: Kent City was platted in 1870 for John W. Thompson. It was named after its township, which had been named for New York jurist James Kent (1763-1847).
Population: 1,061 (2000); Race: 95.6% White, 0.0% Black, 0.0% Asian, 0.0% American Indian and Alaska Native, 15.3% Hispanic of any race, 1.0% two or more races (2000); Density: 969.2 persons per square mile (2000); Age: 37.6% under 18, 7.5% over 64 (2000); Marriage status: 24.4% never married, 56.4% now married, 6.1% widowed, 13.1% divorced (2000); Foreign born: 10.5% (2000); Ancestry (includes multiple ancestries): 20.3% United States or American, 17.0% Other groups, 15.7% German, 10.8% Dutch, 9.2% English (2000).
Economy: Single-family building permits issued: 0 (2001) / 0 (2000); Multi-family building permits issued: 0 (2001) / 0 (2000); Employment by occupation: 8.5% management, 8.1% professional, 16.1% services, 25.6% sales, 0.0% farming, 7.2% construction, 34.5% production (2000).
Income: Per capita income: $13,084 (2000); Median household income: $35,341 (2000); Poverty rate: 12.0% (2000).
Taxes: Total city taxes per capita: $115 (1997); City property taxes per capita: $115 (1997).
Education: High school graduation rate: 79.7% (2000); College graduation rate: 7.4% (2000).

School District(s)

Kent City Community Schools (PK-12)
2000 Enrollment: 1,491 616-678-7714
Housing: Homeownership rate: 74.9% (2000); Median home value: $81,700 (2000); Median rent: $345 per month (2000); Median age of housing: 32 years (2000).
Transportation: Commute to work: 96.0% car, 0.0% public transportation, 1.3% walk, 1.1% work from home (2000); Travel time to work: 21.2% less than 15 minutes, 43.9% 15 to 30 minutes, 29.6% 30 to 45 minutes, 3.8% 45 to 60 minutes, 1.6% 60 minutes or more (2000)

KENTWOOD (city). Covers a land area of 21.043 square miles and a water area of 0 square miles. Located at 42.88° N. Lat.; 85.60° W. Long. Elevation is 689 feet.
Population: 45,255 (2000); Race: 80.8% White, 9.1% Black, 5.5% Asian, 0.6% American Indian and Alaska Native, 3.8% Hispanic of any race, 2.2% two or more races (2000); Density: 2,150.6 persons per square mile (2000); Age: 26.7% under 18, 10.1% over 64 (2000); Marriage status: 27.9% never married, 55.5% now married, 5.2% widowed, 11.4% divorced (2000); Foreign born: 9.3% (2000); Ancestry (includes multiple ancestries): 19.4% Other groups, 18.3% German, 17.9% Dutch, 9.9% English, 9.7% Irish (2000).
Vital Statistics: Birth rate: 162.2 per 10,000 population (1998)
Economy: Manufacturing: plastics, transportation equipment, furniture. International Airport to Southeast. Unemployment rate: 3.6% (11/2002); Total civilian labor force: 28,150 (11/2002); Single-family building permits issued: 234 (2001) / 246 (2000); Multi-family building permits issued: 4 (2001) / 4 (2000); Employment by occupation: 14.6% management, 20.5% professional, 11.0% services, 28.9% sales, 0.1% farming, 5.5% construction, 19.4% production (2000).
Income: Per capita income: $22,463 (2000); Median household income: $45,812 (2000); Poverty rate: 6.3% (2000).
Taxes: Total city taxes per capita: $288 (2000); City property taxes per capita: $264 (2000).
Education: High school graduation rate: 89.2% (2000); College graduation rate: 31.5% (2000).

School District(s)

Kentwood Public Schools (PK-12)
2000 Enrollment: 8,644 616-455-4400
Housing: Homeownership rate: 61.0% (2000); Median home value: $120,600 (2000); Median rent: $536 per month (2000); Median age of housing: 21 years (2000).
Safety: Violent crime rate: 27.3 per 10,000 population; Property crime rate: 366.4 per 10,000 population (2001).
Transportation: Commute to work: 95.5% car, 0.6% public transportation, 0.7% walk, 2.7% work from home (2000); Travel time to work: 36.6% less than 15 minutes, 46.6% 15 to 30 minutes, 10.6% 30 to 45 minutes, 3.5% 45 to 60 minutes, 2.7% 60 minutes or more (2000)

LOWELL (city). Covers a land area of 2.884 square miles and a water area of 0.204 square miles. Located at 42.93° N. Lat.; 85.34° W. Long. Elevation is 639 feet.
History: Lowell was settled in 1821 at the mouth of the Flat River, and incorporated as a village in 1861. Industries in the early 1900's included a milling plant, chick hatchery, and a button factory that used mussel shells gathered by clam-diggers on the Grand, Flat, and Thornapple Rivers.
Population: 4,013 (2000); Race: 97.2% White, 0.0% Black, 1.0% Asian, 1.1% American Indian and Alaska Native, 1.8% Hispanic of any race, 0.6% two or more races (2000); Density: 1,391.2 persons per square mile (2000); Age: 28.1% under 18, 15.1% over 64 (2000); Marriage status: 24.7% never married, 54.0% now married, 8.0% widowed, 13.3% divorced (2000); Foreign born: 2.7% (2000); Ancestry (includes multiple ancestries): 22.5% German, 15.3% Irish, 14.7% English, 11.3% Dutch, 9.2% United States or American (2000).
Economy: Single-family building permits issued: 29 (2001) / 20 (2000); Multi-family building permits issued: 2 (2001) / 8 (2000); Employment by occupation: 11.6% management, 11.5% professional, 20.1% services, 24.4% sales, 0.0% farming, 8.8% construction, 23.7% production (2000).
Income: Per capita income: $17,843 (2000); Median household income: $42,326 (2000); Poverty rate: 6.0% (2000).
Taxes: Total city taxes per capita: $296 (1997); City property taxes per capita: $292 (1997).
Education: High school graduation rate: 85.9% (2000); College graduation rate: 15.5% (2000).

School District(s)

Lowell Area Schools (KG-12)
2000 Enrollment: 3,797 616-897-8415
Housing: Homeownership rate: 68.5% (2000); Median home value: $98,500 (2000); Median rent: $434 per month (2000); Median age of housing: 37 years (2000).
Safety: Violent crime rate: 32.2 per 10,000 population; Property crime rate: 158.7 per 10,000 population (2001).
Newspapers: The Lowell Ledger (1 x week)
Transportation: Commute to work: 90.1% car, 0.0% public transportation, 6.3% walk, 2.5% work from home (2000); Travel time to work: 35.0% less than 15 minutes, 34.5% 15 to 30 minutes, 25.1% 30 to 45 minutes, 2.5% 45 to 60 minutes, 2.9% 60 minutes or more (2000)
Additional Information Contacts
Lowell Area Chamber of Commerce 616-897-9161

LOWELL (township). Covers a land area of 32.632 square miles and a water area of 0.696 square miles. Located at 42.90° N. Lat.; 85.36° W. Long. Elevation is 639 feet.
History: Resort. Settled 1821, incorporated 1859.
Population: 5,219 (2000); Race: 98.1% White, 0.2% Black, 0.2% Asian, 0.3% American Indian and Alaska Native, 1.1% Hispanic of any race, 0.8% two or more races (2000); Density: 159.9 persons per square mile (2000); Age: 31.2% under 18, 7.9% over 64 (2000); Marriage status: 21.5% never married, 65.6% now married, 5.2% widowed, 7.7% divorced (2000); Foreign born: 1.5% (2000); Ancestry (includes multiple ancestries): 22.2% German, 22.2% Dutch, 14.2% English, 11.3% Irish, 6.7% United States or American (2000).
Economy: Railroad junction. In agricultural area: apples, cherries. Manufacturing: motor vehicle parts, wire products, chemical sprayers. Resort. Single-family building permits issued: 285 (2001) / 26 (2000); Multi-family building permits issued: 99 (2001) / 0 (2000); Employment by occupation: 13.5% management, 14.9% professional, 14.8% services, 25.3% sales, 0.0% farming, 6.7% construction, 24.8% production (2000).
Income: Per capita income: $22,560 (2000); Median household income: $58,639 (2000); Poverty rate: 3.0% (2000).
Taxes: Total city taxes per capita: $18 (1997); City property taxes per capita: $14 (1997).
Education: High school graduation rate: 86.8% (2000); College graduation rate: 21.5% (2000).
Housing: Homeownership rate: 93.2% (2000); Median home value: $119,600 (2000); Median rent: $598 per month (2000); Median age of housing: 23 years (2000).
Transportation: Commute to work: 95.5% car, 0.0% public transportation, 0.4% walk, 3.8% work from home (2000); Travel time to work: 21.9% less than 15 minutes, 46.7% 15 to 30 minutes, 23.6% 30 to 45 minutes, 3.2% 45 to 60 minutes, 4.7% 60 minutes or more (2000)

NELSON (township). Covers a land area of 36.020 square miles and a water area of 0.199 square miles. Located at 43.27° N. Lat.; 85.50° W. Long.
Population: 4,192 (2000); Race: 96.7% White, 0.4% Black, 0.7% Asian, 0.6% American Indian and Alaska Native, 1.8% Hispanic of any race, 1.0% two or more races (2000); Density: 116.4 persons per square mile (2000); Age: 32.3% under 18, 8.2% over 64 (2000); Marriage status: 21.9% never married, 65.7% now married, 4.0% widowed, 8.4% divorced (2000); Foreign born: 2.3% (2000); Ancestry (includes multiple ancestries): 29.5% German, 13.0% Dutch, 12.9% Irish, 11.2% English, 7.7% United States or American (2000).
Economy: Single-family building permits issued: 33 (2001) / 36 (2000); Multi-family building permits issued: 0 (2001) / 0 (2000); Employment by occupation: 14.7% management, 13.0% professional, 11.0% services, 18.0% sales, 0.6% farming, 15.3% construction, 27.4% production (2000).
Income: Per capita income: $18,861 (2000); Median household income: $50,521 (2000); Poverty rate: 11.7% (2000).
Taxes: Total city taxes per capita: $31 (1997); City property taxes per capita: $21 (1997).
Education: High school graduation rate: 77.8% (2000); College graduation rate: 10.3% (2000).
Housing: Homeownership rate: 88.1% (2000); Median home value: $105,700 (2000); Median rent: $300 per month (2000); Median age of housing: 20 years (2000).
Transportation: Commute to work: 94.6% car, 0.0% public transportation, 2.3% walk, 2.6% work from home (2000); Travel time to work: 15.9% less than 15 minutes, 28.3% 15 to 30 minutes, 31.9% 30 to 45 minutes, 17.1% 45 to 60 minutes, 6.8% 60 minutes or more (2000)

NORTHVIEW (CDP). Covers a land area of 10.413 square miles and a water area of 0.648 square miles. Located at 43.03° N. Lat.; 85.61° W. Long.
Population: 14,730 (2000); Race: 94.1% White, 2.2% Black, 1.0% Asian, 0.5% American Indian and Alaska Native, 2.0% Hispanic of any race, 1.3% two or more races (2000); Density: 1,414.6 persons per square mile (2000); Age: 28.6% under 18, 10.2% over 64 (2000); Marriage status: 27.1% never married, 57.0% now married, 4.9% widowed, 11.0% divorced (2000); Foreign born: 2.8% (2000); Ancestry (includes multiple ancestries): 23.8% German, 20.3% Dutch, 13.1% English, 12.9% Irish, 10.9% Polish (2000).
Economy: Employment by occupation: 12.7% management, 18.3% professional, 13.4% services, 30.2% sales, 0.2% farming, 8.3% construction, 16.9% production (2000).
Income: Per capita income: $21,215 (2000); Median household income: $46,888 (2000); Poverty rate: 6.0% (2000).
Education: High school graduation rate: 90.4% (2000); College graduation rate: 25.8% (2000).
Housing: Homeownership rate: 72.1% (2000); Median home value: $118,200 (2000); Median rent: $549 per month (2000); Median age of housing: 27 years (2000).
Transportation: Commute to work: 94.6% car, 0.7% public transportation, 1.2% walk, 3.4% work from home (2000); Travel time to work: 31.3% less than 15 minutes, 50.1% 15 to 30 minutes, 12.7% 30 to 45 minutes, 3.0% 45 to 60 minutes, 2.9% 60 minutes or more (2000)

OAKFIELD (township). Covers a land area of 34.616 square miles and a water area of 1.800 square miles. Located at 43.16° N. Lat.; 85.36° W. Long.
Population: 5,058 (2000); Race: 97.3% White, 0.6% Black, 0.0% Asian, 0.4% American Indian and Alaska Native, 1.0% Hispanic of any race, 1.1% two or more races (2000); Density: 146.1 persons per square mile (2000); Age: 28.2% under 18, 8.3% over 64 (2000); Marriage status: 21.3% never married, 65.6% now married, 3.2% widowed, 9.8% divorced (2000); Foreign born: 0.7% (2000); Ancestry (includes multiple ancestries): 26.6% German, 16.9% Irish, 14.6% Dutch, 14.2% English, 8.0% Other groups (2000).
Economy: Single-family building permits issued: 50 (2001) / 49 (2000); Multi-family building permits issued: 0 (2001) / 0 (2000); Employment by occupation: 12.2% management, 15.5% professional, 10.7% services, 22.6% sales, 0.0% farming, 10.3% construction, 28.6% production (2000).
Income: Per capita income: $20,463 (2000); Median household income: $49,429 (2000); Poverty rate: 7.2% (2000).
Taxes: Total city taxes per capita: $34 (1997); City property taxes per capita: $20 (1997).
Education: High school graduation rate: 85.4% (2000); College graduation rate: 14.9% (2000).
Housing: Homeownership rate: 92.3% (2000); Median home value: $128,100 (2000); Median rent: $425 per month (2000); Median age of housing: 23 years (2000).
Transportation: Commute to work: 93.1% car, 0.0% public transportation, 1.4% walk, 5.1% work from home (2000); Travel time to work: 20.1% less than 15 minutes, 29.0% 15 to 30 minutes, 33.5% 30 to 45 minutes, 13.6% 45 to 60 minutes, 3.8% 60 minutes or more (2000)

PLAINFIELD (township). Covers a land area of 35.141 square miles and a water area of 1.383 square miles. Located at 43.05° N. Lat.; 85.61° W. Long.
History: Plainfield Township was organized in 1838 and named for the level of much of the land within its boundaries.
Population: 30,195 (2000); Race: 95.4% White, 1.4% Black, 1.2% Asian, 0.4% American Indian and Alaska Native, 1.7% Hispanic of any race, 1.0% two or more races (2000); Density: 859.2 persons per square mile (2000); Age: 30.3% under 18, 9.3% over 64 (2000); Marriage status: 24.0% never married, 61.3% now married, 4.7% widowed, 10.0% divorced (2000); Foreign born: 2.4% (2000); Ancestry (includes multiple ancestries): 23.8% German, 19.3% Dutch, 15.6% Irish, 13.5% English, 11.2% Polish (2000).
Economy: Unemployment rate: 3.6% (11/2002); Total civilian labor force: 17,772 (11/2002); Single-family building permits issued: 152 (2001) / 178 (2000); Multi-family building permits issued: 6 (2001) / 0 (2000); Employment by occupation: 13.1% management, 18.4% professional, 12.3% services, 29.5% sales, 0.2% farming, 9.4% construction, 17.1% production (2000).
Income: Per capita income: $23,753 (2000); Median household income: $55,181 (2000); Poverty rate: 4.2% (2000).
Taxes: Total city taxes per capita: $20 (2000); City property taxes per capita: $2 (2000).
Education: High school graduation rate: 91.0% (2000); College graduation rate: 27.9% (2000).
Housing: Homeownership rate: 82.1% (2000); Median home value: $135,300 (2000); Median rent: $546 per month (2000); Median age of housing: 23 years (2000).
Transportation: Commute to work: 94.8% car, 0.4% public transportation, 1.3% walk, 3.3% work from home (2000); Travel time to work: 28.1% less than 15 minutes, 50.0% 15 to 30 minutes, 15.2% 30 to 45 minutes, 3.7% 45 to 60 minutes, 3.0% 60 minutes or more (2000)

ROCKFORD (city). Covers a land area of 2.996 square miles and a water area of 0.030 square miles. Located at 43.12° N. Lat.; 85.55° W. Long. Elevation is 693 feet.
History: Rockford was settled in the 1840's, and was known for a time as Laphamsville for its first settler, Smith Lapham. Renamed Rockford in 1866, the town grew up around a tanning, shoe, and glove factory. Its location on the Rogue River and Rum Creek also made it a resort area.
Population: 4,626 (2000); Race: 95.7% White, 0.3% Black, 1.4% Asian, 0.2% American Indian and Alaska Native, 1.9% Hispanic of any race, 1.5% two or more races (2000); Density: 1,544.2 persons per square mile (2000); Age: 33.8% under 18, 8.9% over 64 (2000); Marriage status: 23.3% never married, 60.0% now married, 6.1% widowed, 10.7% divorced (2000); Foreign born: 2.2% (2000); Ancestry (includes multiple ancestries): 23.9% German, 18.2% Dutch, 13.4% English, 12.8% Irish, 12.3% Polish (2000).
Economy: Single-family building permits issued: 33 (2001) / 30 (2000); Multi-family building permits issued: 3 (2001) / 4 (2000); Employment by occupation: 15.6% management, 19.7% professional, 13.2% services, 26.7% sales, 0.0% farming, 7.0% construction, 17.9% production (2000).
Income: Per capita income: $19,906 (2000); Median household income: $50,562 (2000); Poverty rate: 8.1% (2000).
Taxes: Total city taxes per capita: $280 (1997); City property taxes per capita: $279 (1997).
Education: High school graduation rate: 89.5% (2000); College graduation rate: 27.9% (2000).

School District(s)

Rockford Public Schools (PK-12)
2000 Enrollment: 7,543 616-866-1597
Housing: Homeownership rate: 66.3% (2000); Median home value: $116,400 (2000); Median rent: $433 per month (2000); Median age of housing: 27 years (2000).
Safety: Violent crime rate: 10.8 per 10,000 population; Property crime rate: 273.1 per 10,000 population (2001).
Newspapers: Rockford Squire (1 x week)
Transportation: Commute to work: 92.9% car, 0.0% public transportation, 2.5% walk, 4.2% work from home (2000); Travel time to work: 34.5% less than 15 minutes, 29.9% 15 to 30 minutes, 27.9% 30 to 45 minutes, 5.2% 45 to 60 minutes, 2.5% 60 minutes or more (2000); Amtrak: Service available.
Additional Information Contacts
Rockford Chamber of Commerce 616-866-2000

SAND LAKE (village). Covers a land area of 0.734 square miles and a water area of 0.027 square miles. Located at 43.29° N. Lat.; 85.51° W. Long. Elevation is 912 feet.
History: Lumber operations began in the Sand Lake area in the late 1860's. The village was platted and named in 1871. Sand Lake grew as a resort area.
Population: 492 (2000); Race: 95.9% White, 1.6% Black, 1.4% Asian, 0.0% American Indian and Alaska Native, 0.4% Hispanic of any race, 1.0% two or more races (2000); Density: 670.5 persons per square mile (2000); Age: 29.9% under 18, 10.2% over 64 (2000); Marriage status: 23.4% never married, 58.7% now married, 7.9% widowed, 10.1% divorced (2000); Foreign born: 2.9% (2000); Ancestry (includes multiple ancestries): 30.1% German, 12.0% Irish, 11.4% English, 10.6% Dutch, 9.0% United States or American (2000).
Economy: Employment by occupation: 8.7% management, 18.4% professional, 11.6% services, 21.7% sales, 0.0% farming, 13.0% construction, 26.6% production (2000).
Income: Per capita income: $14,184 (2000); Median household income: $31,875 (2000); Poverty rate: 14.5% (2000).
Taxes: Total city taxes per capita: $266 (1997); City property taxes per capita: $264 (1997).
Education: High school graduation rate: 74.7% (2000); College graduation rate: 9.7% (2000).
Housing: Homeownership rate: 62.1% (2000); Median home value: $72,700 (2000); Median rent: $268 per month (2000); Median age of housing: 30 years (2000).
Transportation: Commute to work: 90.7% car, 0.0% public transportation, 3.9% walk, 4.4% work from home (2000); Travel time to work: 17.4% less than 15 minutes, 31.8% 15 to 30 minutes, 30.3% 30 to 45 minutes, 13.3% 45 to 60 minutes, 7.2% 60 minutes or more (2000)

SOLON (township). Covers a land area of 35.834 square miles and a water area of 0.500 square miles. Located at 43.24° N. Lat.; 85.61° W. Long.
History: Solon Township was organized in 1857, a few years after the area was settled by J.M. Rounds and a Mr. Beals.
Population: 4,662 (2000); Race: 97.5% White, 0.5% Black, 0.2% Asian, 0.5% American Indian and Alaska Native, 1.2% Hispanic of any race, 1.2% two or more races (2000); Density: 130.1 persons per square mile (2000); Age: 29.1% under 18, 9.9% over 64 (2000); Marriage status: 22.5% never married, 61.7% now married, 4.5% widowed, 11.2% divorced (2000); Foreign born: 0.8% (2000); Ancestry (includes multiple ancestries): 22.9% German, 17.2% Dutch, 12.9% English, 12.5% Irish, 9.1% United States or American (2000).
Economy: Single-family building permits issued: 87 (2001) / 87 (2000); Multi-family building permits issued: 0 (2001) / 0 (2000); Employment by occupation: 6.1% management, 13.7% professional, 11.3% services, 19.5% sales, 1.5% farming, 15.0% construction, 32.9% production (2000).
Income: Per capita income: $17,540 (2000); Median household income: $44,814 (2000); Poverty rate: 5.1% (2000).
Taxes: Total city taxes per capita: $41 (1997); City property taxes per capita: $31 (1997).
Education: High school graduation rate: 85.6% (2000); College graduation rate: 13.6% (2000).
Housing: Homeownership rate: 93.8% (2000); Median home value: $119,300 (2000); Median rent: $496 per month (2000); Median age of housing: 17 years (2000).
Transportation: Commute to work: 94.2% car, 0.0% public transportation, 0.6% walk, 4.2% work from home (2000); Travel time to work: 16.3% less than 15 minutes, 34.1% 15 to 30 minutes, 33.3% 30 to 45 minutes, 10.4% 45 to 60 minutes, 5.9% 60 minutes or more (2000)

SPARTA (village). Covers a land area of 2.441 square miles and a water area of 0 square miles. Located at 43.15° N. Lat.; 85.70° W. Long. Elevation is 753 feet.
History: Sparta was founded by Jonathan P. Nash, and first called Nashville. In 1850, Sparta took the name of its township.
Population: 4,159 (2000); Race: 97.0% White, 0.7% Black, 0.2% Asian, 0.5% American Indian and Alaska Native, 1.3% Hispanic of any race, 0.7% two or more races (2000); Density: 1,703.9 persons per square mile (2000); Age: 28.6% under 18, 13.5% over 64 (2000); Marriage status: 26.2% never married, 57.2% now married, 6.9% widowed, 9.7% divorced (2000); Foreign born: 0.4% (2000); Ancestry (includes multiple ancestries): 28.4% German, 17.4% Dutch, 15.4% Irish, 10.7% English, 8.2% United States or American (2000).
Economy: Single-family building permits issued: 9 (2001) / 0 (2000); Multi-family building permits issued: 0 (2001) / 0 (2000); Employment by occupation: 8.8% management, 11.4% professional, 13.5% services, 29.8% sales, 0.8% farming, 12.4% construction, 23.4% production (2000).
Income: Per capita income: $17,920 (2000); Median household income: $39,047 (2000); Poverty rate: 7.2% (2000).

Taxes: Total city taxes per capita: $361 (1997); City property taxes per capita: $355 (1997).
Education: High school graduation rate: 81.7% (2000); College graduation rate: 15.3% (2000).

School District(s)

Sparta Area Schools (KG-12)
2000 Enrollment: 3,009 616-887-8253
Housing: Homeownership rate: 65.3% (2000); Median home value: $88,400 (2000); Median rent: $427 per month (2000); Median age of housing: 41 years (2000).
Safety: Violent crime rate: 12.0 per 10,000 population; Property crime rate: 354.0 per 10,000 population (2001).
Transportation: Commute to work: 95.1% car, 0.0% public transportation, 2.7% walk, 1.6% work from home (2000); Travel time to work: 32.5% less than 15 minutes, 37.9% 15 to 30 minutes, 21.1% 30 to 45 minutes, 5.2% 45 to 60 minutes, 3.3% 60 minutes or more (2000)
Additional Information Contacts
Sparta Chamber of Commerce 616-887-2454

SPARTA (township). Covers a land area of 36.521 square miles and a water area of 0.031 square miles. Located at 43.16° N. Lat.; 85.71° W. Long. Elevation is 753 feet.
History: Plotted 1869, incorporated 1883.
Population: 8,938 (2000); Race: 97.1% White, 0.6% Black, 0.3% Asian, 0.4% American Indian and Alaska Native, 3.2% Hispanic of any race, 1.0% two or more races (2000); Density: 244.7 persons per square mile (2000); Age: 29.5% under 18, 12.0% over 64 (2000); Marriage status: 24.5% never married, 60.8% now married, 5.6% widowed, 9.1% divorced (2000); Foreign born: 1.0% (2000); Ancestry (includes multiple ancestries): 27.0% German, 14.6% Dutch, 14.4% Irish, 12.5% English, 9.2% Polish (2000).
Economy: In dairy and fruit-farming area. Manufacturing: transportation equipment, paper products, structural wood, plastic products. Airport here. Single-family building permits issued: 23 (2001) / 46 (2000); Multi-family building permits issued: 0 (2001) / 0 (2000); Employment by occupation: 10.1% management, 11.0% professional, 13.8% services, 24.9% sales, 1.4% farming, 11.6% construction, 27.2% production (2000).
Income: Per capita income: $18,345 (2000); Median household income: $42,992 (2000); Poverty rate: 5.5% (2000).
Taxes: Total city taxes per capita: $22 (1997); City property taxes per capita: $19 (1997).
Education: High school graduation rate: 81.9% (2000); College graduation rate: 14.0% (2000).
Housing: Homeownership rate: 79.0% (2000); Median home value: $95,100 (2000); Median rent: $421 per month (2000); Median age of housing: 32 years (2000).
Transportation: Commute to work: 95.2% car, 0.1% public transportation, 1.6% walk, 2.3% work from home (2000); Travel time to work: 30.8% less than 15 minutes, 36.6% 15 to 30 minutes, 23.8% 30 to 45 minutes, 5.2% 45 to 60 minutes, 3.7% 60 minutes or more (2000)

SPENCER (township). Covers a land area of 35.094 square miles and a water area of 1.563 square miles. Located at 43.25° N. Lat.; 85.35° W. Long.
Population: 3,681 (2000); Race: 95.6% White, 1.2% Black, 0.4% Asian, 0.4% American Indian and Alaska Native, 1.9% Hispanic of any race, 2.2% two or more races (2000); Density: 104.9 persons per square mile (2000); Age: 26.1% under 18, 9.8% over 64 (2000); Marriage status: 20.0% never married, 65.8% now married, 5.9% widowed, 8.3% divorced (2000); Foreign born: 0.9% (2000); Ancestry (includes multiple ancestries): 27.8% German, 14.3% English, 14.1% Dutch, 11.8% Irish, 8.9% Other groups (2000).
Economy: Single-family building permits issued: 21 (2001) / 26 (2000); Multi-family building permits issued: 0 (2001) / 0 (2000); Employment by occupation: 8.9% management, 9.1% professional, 8.4% services, 26.8% sales, 0.0% farming, 16.8% construction, 30.0% production (2000).
Income: Per capita income: $18,692 (2000); Median household income: $51,765 (2000); Poverty rate: 5.2% (2000).
Taxes: Total city taxes per capita: $48 (1997); City property taxes per capita: $36 (1997).
Education: High school graduation rate: 82.5% (2000); College graduation rate: 7.7% (2000).
Housing: Homeownership rate: 93.9% (2000); Median home value: $114,000 (2000); Median rent: $429 per month (2000); Median age of housing: 21 years (2000).
Transportation: Commute to work: 95.7% car, 0.0% public transportation, 0.5% walk, 2.8% work from home (2000); Travel time to work: 10.6% less than 15 minutes, 36.5% 15 to 30 minutes, 18.5% 30 to 45 minutes, 22.6% 45 to 60 minutes, 11.9% 60 minutes or more (2000)

TYRONE (township). Covers a land area of 36.373 square miles and a water area of 0.105 square miles. Located at 43.24° N. Lat.; 85.73° W. Long.
Population: 4,304 (2000); Race: 96.5% White, 0.1% Black, 0.0% Asian, 0.4% American Indian and Alaska Native, 5.2% Hispanic of any race, 1.4% two or more races (2000); Density: 118.3 persons per square mile (2000); Age: 31.2% under 18, 8.0% over 64 (2000); Marriage status: 22.5% never married, 62.8% now married, 4.5% widowed, 10.2% divorced (2000); Foreign born: 3.6% (2000); Ancestry (includes multiple ancestries): 25.1% German, 16.8% Dutch, 13.1% English, 10.8% Irish, 10.0% United States or American (2000).
Economy: Single-family building permits issued: 18 (2001) / 18 (2000); Multi-family building permits issued: 0 (2001) / 0 (2000); Employment by occupation: 10.4% management, 11.1% professional, 12.1% services, 22.9% sales, 0.2% farming, 16.0% construction, 27.3% production (2000).
Income: Per capita income: $18,879 (2000); Median household income: $48,006 (2000); Poverty rate: 9.4% (2000).
Taxes: Total city taxes per capita: $33 (1997); City property taxes per capita: $28 (1997).
Education: High school graduation rate: 84.6% (2000); College graduation rate: 7.8% (2000).
Housing: Homeownership rate: 88.2% (2000); Median home value: $99,800 (2000); Median rent: $348 per month (2000); Median age of housing: 28 years (2000).
Transportation: Commute to work: 95.1% car, 0.0% public transportation, 1.5% walk, 3.1% work from home (2000); Travel time to work: 20.3% less than 15 minutes, 24.0% 15 to 30 minutes, 35.1% 30 to 45 minutes, 13.1% 45 to 60 minutes, 7.5% 60 minutes or more (2000)

VERGENNES (township). Covers a land area of 34.712 square miles and a water area of 0.700 square miles. Located at 42.98° N. Lat.; 85.36° W. Long.
Population: 3,611 (2000); Race: 97.0% White, 0.4% Black, 1.3% Asian, 0.0% American Indian and Alaska Native, 2.2% Hispanic of any race, 0.1% two or more races (2000); Density: 104.0 persons per square mile (2000); Age: 34.0% under 18, 6.3% over 64 (2000); Marriage status: 22.4% never married, 71.3% now married, 2.8% widowed, 3.5% divorced (2000); Foreign born: 3.5% (2000); Ancestry (includes multiple ancestries): 24.5% German, 21.0% Dutch, 16.6% Irish, 11.5% English, 9.2% United States or American (2000).
Economy: Single-family building permits issued: 36 (2001) / 46 (2000); Multi-family building permits issued: 0 (2001) / 0 (2000); Employment by occupation: 17.6% management, 17.0% professional, 8.8% services, 28.5% sales, 0.7% farming, 8.7% construction, 18.7% production (2000).
Income: Per capita income: $21,339 (2000); Median household income: $61,500 (2000); Poverty rate: 6.2% (2000).
Taxes: Total city taxes per capita: $44 (1997); City property taxes per capita: $23 (1997).
Education: High school graduation rate: 94.1% (2000); College graduation rate: 27.4% (2000).
Housing: Homeownership rate: 93.2% (2000); Median home value: $158,700 (2000); Median rent: $410 per month (2000); Median age of housing: 15 years (2000).
Transportation: Commute to work: 93.7% car, 0.0% public transportation, 0.0% walk, 5.5% work from home (2000); Travel time to work: 19.4% less than 15 minutes, 35.2% 15 to 30 minutes, 34.5% 30 to 45 minutes, 6.0% 45 to 60 minutes, 4.8% 60 minutes or more (2000)

WALKER (city). Covers a land area of 25.155 square miles and a water area of 0.277 square miles. Located at 43.00° N. Lat.; 85.74° W. Long. Elevation is 742 feet.
Population: 21,842 (2000); Race: 94.2% White, 1.6% Black, 1.5% Asian, 0.3% American Indian and Alaska Native, 2.7% Hispanic of any race, 1.5% two or more races (2000); Density: 868.3 persons per square mile (2000); Age: 25.7% under 18, 10.4% over 64 (2000); Marriage status: 30.7% never married, 54.8% now married, 5.9% widowed, 8.7% divorced (2000); Foreign born: 3.2% (2000); Ancestry (includes multiple ancestries): 25.1% Dutch, 22.6% German, 15.4% Polish, 12.1% Irish, 8.4% Other groups (2000).
Vital Statistics: Birth rate: 114.0 per 10,000 population (1998)
Economy: Manufacturing: metal stampings, iron castings, theater and auditorium seating, assembly tracks. Single-family building permits issued: 139 (2001) / 129 (2000); Multi-family building permits issued: 40 (2001) / 189 (2000); Employment by occupation: 11.0% management, 17.5% professional, 12.5% services, 29.2% sales, 0.2% farming, 8.3% construction, 21.2% production (2000).

Income: Per capita income: $21,198 (2000); Median household income: $44,818 (2000); Poverty rate: 6.1% (2000).
Taxes: Total city taxes per capita: $329 (1997); City property taxes per capita: $79 (1997).
Education: High school graduation rate: 88.3% (2000); College graduation rate: 22.0% (2000).

School District(s)

Walker Charter Academy (KG-08)
2000 Enrollment: 585 616-895-3029
West Mi Academy of Environmental (KG-09)
2000 Enrollment: 439 517-774-2100

Housing: Homeownership rate: 62.4% (2000); Median home value: $120,400 (2000); Median rent: $500 per month (2000); Median age of housing: 22 years (2000).
Safety: Violent crime rate: 21.0 per 10,000 population; Property crime rate: 455.9 per 10,000 population (2001).
Transportation: Commute to work: 95.8% car, 0.9% public transportation, 1.4% walk, 1.5% work from home (2000); Travel time to work: 34.8% less than 15 minutes, 47.9% 15 to 30 minutes, 13.7% 30 to 45 minutes, 2.0% 45 to 60 minutes, 1.5% 60 minutes or more (2000)

WYOMING (city). Covers a land area of 24.424 square miles and a water area of 0.087 square miles. Located at 42.90° N. Lat.; 85.69° W. Long. Elevation is 646 feet.
History: Native American mounds in adjacent Grandville. Settled 1832, incorporated 1959.
Population: 69,368 (2000); Race: 84.3% White, 4.7% Black, 2.9% Asian, 0.5% American Indian and Alaska Native, 9.7% Hispanic of any race, 3.0% two or more races (2000); Density: 2,840.1 persons per square mile (2000); Age: 28.1% under 18, 9.3% over 64 (2000); Marriage status: 29.8% never married, 53.9% now married, 4.7% widowed, 11.6% divorced (2000); Foreign born: 7.9% (2000); Ancestry (includes multiple ancestries): 22.6% Dutch, 19.0% Other groups, 18.8% German, 10.2% Irish, 9.1% English (2000).
Economy: Manufacturing: fabricated metal products, transportation equipment, food processing. Unemployment rate: 5.3% (11/2002); Total civilian labor force: 45,712 (11/2002); Single-family building permits issued: 287 (2001) / 207 (2000); Multi-family building permits issued: 2 (2001) / 32 (2000); Employment by occupation: 9.8% management, 13.6% professional, 12.3% services, 27.8% sales, 0.5% farming, 9.0% construction, 26.9% production (2000).
Income: Per capita income: $19,287 (2000); Median household income: $43,164 (2000); Poverty rate: 7.3% (2000).
Taxes: Total city taxes per capita: $296 (2000); City property taxes per capita: $270 (2000).
Education: High school graduation rate: 81.9% (2000); College graduation rate: 17.0% (2000).

School District(s)

Godfrey-Lee Public Schools (KG-12)
2000 Enrollment: 1,368 616-241-4722
Godwin Heights Public Schools (PK-12)
2000 Enrollment: 2,283 616-245-0091
Horizons Community High School (09-12)
2000 Enrollment: 211 616-530-7550
Vanguard Charter Academy (KG-08)
2000 Enrollment: 590 616-895-3029
Wyoming Public Schools (PK-12)
2000 Enrollment: 5,669 616-530-7550

Four-year College(s)

Grace Bible College (Private, Not-for-profit, Other Protestant)
2001 Enrollment: 149 616-538-2330
2001 Tuition: In-state $7,600; Out-of-state $7,600

Housing: Homeownership rate: 67.7% (2000); Median home value: $93,000 (2000); Median rent: $516 per month (2000); Median age of housing: 35 years (2000).
Safety: Violent crime rate: 47.6 per 10,000 population; Property crime rate: 333.4 per 10,000 population (2001).
Transportation: Commute to work: 94.2% car, 1.1% public transportation, 1.8% walk, 2.0% work from home (2000); Travel time to work: 34.8% less than 15 minutes, 46.0% 15 to 30 minutes, 14.6% 30 to 45 minutes, 2.1% 45 to 60 minutes, 2.5% 60 minutes or more (2000)
Additional Information Contacts
Wyoming Chamber of Commerce 616-531-5990

Keweenaw County

Located in northwestern Michigan, on the Upper Peninsula; on the Keweenaw Peninsula in Lake Superior; includes Isle Royale. Covers a land area of 541.00 square miles, a water area of 5,425.00 square miles, and is located in the Eastern Time Zone. The county government was organized in 1861. County seat is Eagle River.
Population: 2,301 (2000); Race: 95.8% White, 2.6% Black, 0.0% Asian, 0.4% American Indian and Alaska Native, 1.2% Hispanic of any race, 1.1% two or more races (2000); Density: 4.3 persons per square mile (2000); Age: 22.5% under 18, 20.2% over 64 (2000).
Religion: Five largest groups: 21.9% Evangelical Lutheran Church in America, 16.7% Catholic Church, 1.8% Episcopal Church, 1.4% The United Methodist Church, 0.0% Bahá'í (2000).
Economy: Unemployment rate: 13.8% (11/2002); Total civilian labor force: 914 (11/2002); Leading industries: Companies that employ more than 1,000 persons: 0 (2000); Companies that employ more than 100 persons: 1 (2000); Farms: 5 (1997); Minority business ownership rate: 0.0% (1997); Women business ownership rate: 0.0% (1997); Retail sales per capita: $1,293 (1997). Single-family building permits issued: 25 (2001) / 25 (2000); Multi-family building permits issued: 0 (2001) / 0 (2000).
Income: Per capita income: $16,769 (2000); Median household income: $28,140 (2000); Poverty rate: 12.7% (2000); Bankruptcy rate: 1.85% (2001).
Taxes: Total county taxes per capita: $238 (1997); County property taxes per capita: $223 (1997).
Education: High school graduation rate: 83.7% (2000); College graduation rate: 19.1% (2000).
Housing: Homeownership rate: 89.3% (2000); Median home value: $44,100 (2000); Median rent: $225 per month (2000); Median age of housing: 55 years (2000).
Health: Birth rate: 130.4 per 10,000 population (1998); Age adjusted death rate: 94.8 per 10,000 population (1999); Age adjusted cancer mortality rate: n/a (1999). Number of physicians: 13.0 per 10,000 population (1999); Number of hospital beds: n/a (1999).
Elections: 2000 Presidential election results: 40.2% Gore, 55.1% Bush, 4.0% Nader, 0.2% Buchanan
National and State Parks: Fort Wilkins State Park; Hobard State Park; Isle Royale National Park
Additional Information Contacts
Keweenaw County Government Offices 906-337-2229

Keweenaw County Communities

AHMEEK (village). Covers a land area of 0.070 square miles and a water area of 0 square miles. Located at 47.29° N. Lat.; 88.39° W. Long.
History: Ahmeek grew up around the Ahmeek Copper Mine. The village was founded in 1904 by John Bosch, and incorporated as a village in 1909. The name is Chippewa for "beaver."
Population: 157 (2000); Race: 100.0% White, 0.0% Black, 0.0% Asian, 0.0% American Indian and Alaska Native, 0.0% Hispanic of any race, 0.0% two or more races (2000); Density: 2,237.9 persons per square mile (2000); Age: 21.2% under 18, 20.6% over 64 (2000); Marriage status: 18.0% never married, 49.6% now married, 11.3% widowed, 21.1% divorced (2000); Foreign born: 0.0% (2000); Ancestry (includes multiple ancestries): 35.8% Finnish, 22.4% Italian, 14.5% German, 12.1% English, 11.5% French (except Basque) (2000).
Economy: Single-family building permits issued: 0 (2001) / 0 (2000); Multi-family building permits issued: 0 (2001) / 0 (2000); Employment by occupation: 2.4% management, 9.4% professional, 24.7% services, 23.5% sales, 8.2% farming, 11.8% construction, 20.0% production (2000).
Income: Per capita income: $16,188 (2000); Median household income: $24,231 (2000); Poverty rate: 11.5% (2000).
Taxes: Total city taxes per capita: $64 (1997); City property taxes per capita: $64 (1997).
Education: High school graduation rate: 76.0% (2000); College graduation rate: 12.0% (2000).
Housing: Homeownership rate: 86.6% (2000); Median home value: $27,100 (2000); Median rent: $288 per month (2000); Median age of housing: 60+ years (2000).
Transportation: Commute to work: 88.9% car, 0.0% public transportation, 1.2% walk, 9.9% work from home (2000); Travel time to work: 39.7% less than 15 minutes, 42.5% 15 to 30 minutes, 15.1% 30 to 45 minutes, 2.7% 45 to 60 minutes, 0.0% 60 minutes or more (2000)

ALLOUEZ (township). Covers a land area of 54.692 square miles and a water area of 0.042 square miles. Located at 47.31° N. Lat.; 88.38° W. Long.
History: Allouez took its name from the Allouez Mining Company, which had been named for Claude Jean Allouez, a French Jesuit missionary. The Allouez Mining Company opened a copper mine here in 1859.
Population: 1,584 (2000); Race: 98.8% White, 0.0% Black, 0.0% Asian, 0.1% American Indian and Alaska Native, 0.0% Hispanic of any race, 1.0% two or more races (2000); Density: 29.0 persons per square mile (2000); Age: 22.9% under 18, 18.4% over 64 (2000); Marriage status: 20.2% never married, 57.7% now married, 9.0% widowed, 13.1% divorced (2000); Foreign born: 1.2% (2000); Ancestry (includes multiple ancestries): 46.9% Finnish, 13.8% German, 10.0% English, 9.5% French (except Basque), 9.3% Italian (2000).
Economy: Employment by occupation: 8.2% management, 17.8% professional, 25.3% services, 21.5% sales, 2.2% farming, 9.4% construction, 15.5% production (2000).
Income: Per capita income: $14,974 (2000); Median household income: $26,500 (2000); Poverty rate: 14.7% (2000).
Taxes: Total city taxes per capita: $23 (1997); City property taxes per capita: $23 (1997).
Education: High school graduation rate: 81.4% (2000); College graduation rate: 12.0% (2000).
Housing: Homeownership rate: 87.9% (2000); Median home value: $36,600 (2000); Median rent: $223 per month (2000); Median age of housing: 60+ years (2000).
Transportation: Commute to work: 89.2% car, 0.0% public transportation, 4.3% walk, 6.1% work from home (2000); Travel time to work: 37.2% less than 15 minutes, 39.3% 15 to 30 minutes, 17.1% 30 to 45 minutes, 4.0% 45 to 60 minutes, 2.4% 60 minutes or more (2000)

EAGLE HARBOR (township). Covers a land area of 180.514 square miles and a water area of 362.538 square miles. Located at 47.43° N. Lat.; 88.22° W. Long.
History: The Eagle Harbor area developed as a resort center, after the days when copper was shipped from here to the markets of the world. It was in Eagle Harbor that Justus H. Rathbone, a school teacher, wrote the rituals for the Order of Knights of Pythias, later founded in Washington, D.C.
Population: 281 (2000); Race: 99.3% White, 0.0% Black, 0.0% Asian, 0.0% American Indian and Alaska Native, 4.2% Hispanic of any race, 0.0% two or more races (2000); Density: 1.6 persons per square mile (2000); Age: 4.2% under 18, 30.4% over 64 (2000); Marriage status: 13.7% never married, 76.6% now married, 5.0% widowed, 4.7% divorced (2000); Foreign born: 0.0% (2000); Ancestry (includes multiple ancestries): 30.4% German, 27.2% English, 13.1% Polish, 12.7% Irish, 9.5% French (except Basque) (2000).
Economy: Employment by occupation: 33.0% management, 32.1% professional, 2.8% services, 15.6% sales, 0.9% farming, 9.2% construction, 6.4% production (2000).
Income: Per capita income: $29,091 (2000); Median household income: $38,000 (2000); Poverty rate: 3.6% (2000).
Taxes: Total city taxes per capita: $711 (1997); City property taxes per capita: $711 (1997).
Education: High school graduation rate: 96.6% (2000); College graduation rate: 45.3% (2000).
Housing: Homeownership rate: 98.4% (2000); Median home value: $123,000 (2000); Median age of housing: 37 years (2000).
Transportation: Commute to work: 86.5% car, 0.0% public transportation, 7.7% walk, 5.8% work from home (2000); Travel time to work: 61.2% less than 15 minutes, 6.1% 15 to 30 minutes, 10.2% 30 to 45 minutes, 12.2% 45 to 60 minutes, 10.2% 60 minutes or more (2000)

GRANT (township). Covers a land area of 119.281 square miles and a water area of 83.410 square miles. Located at 47.40° N. Lat.; 87.96° W. Long.
Population: 172 (2000); Race: 98.6% White, 0.0% Black, 0.0% Asian, 0.0% American Indian and Alaska Native, 1.4% Hispanic of any race, 1.4% two or more races (2000); Density: 1.4 persons per square mile (2000); Age: 8.1% under 18, 29.1% over 64 (2000); Marriage status: 23.0% never married, 61.9% now married, 7.2% widowed, 7.9% divorced (2000); Foreign born: 2.0% (2000); Ancestry (includes multiple ancestries): 33.8% Finnish, 14.2% French (except Basque), 12.2% English, 11.5% German, 9.5% Irish (2000).
Economy: Employment by occupation: 22.4% management, 14.9% professional, 23.9% services, 14.9% sales, 0.0% farming, 10.4% construction, 13.4% production (2000).
Income: Per capita income: $24,336 (2000); Median household income: $34,464 (2000); Poverty rate: 10.8% (2000).
Taxes: Total city taxes per capita: $1,107 (1997); City property taxes per capita: $1,107 (1997).
Education: High school graduation rate: 81.8% (2000); College graduation rate: 23.1% (2000).
Housing: Homeownership rate: 86.1% (2000); Median home value: $95,000 (2000); Median rent: $188 per month (2000); Median age of housing: 49 years (2000).
Transportation: Commute to work: 75.8% car, 0.0% public transportation, 19.4% walk, 4.8% work from home (2000); Travel time to work: 45.8% less than 15 minutes, 10.2% 15 to 30 minutes, 16.9% 30 to 45 minutes, 15.3% 45 to 60 minutes, 11.9% 60 minutes or more (2000)

HOUGHTON (township). Covers a land area of 121.399 square miles and a water area of 396.185 square miles. Located at 47.41° N. Lat.; 88.29° W. Long.
Population: 204 (2000); Race: 66.2% White, 27.4% Black, 0.0% Asian, 3.2% American Indian and Alaska Native, 5.9% Hispanic of any race, 3.2% two or more races (2000); Density: 1.7 persons per square mile (2000); Age: 55.3% under 18, 10.0% over 64 (2000); Marriage status: 63.2% never married, 28.5% now married, 5.7% widowed, 2.6% divorced (2000); Foreign born: 0.9% (2000); Ancestry (includes multiple ancestries): 21.9% Other groups, 15.5% Finnish, 10.0% English, 8.7% Irish, 7.8% Italian (2000).
Economy: Employment by occupation: 16.2% management, 29.7% professional, 18.9% services, 13.5% sales, 0.0% farming, 5.4% construction, 16.2% production (2000).
Income: Per capita income: $8,505 (2000); Median household income: $28,750 (2000); Poverty rate: 7.0% (2000).
Taxes: Total city taxes per capita: $286 (1997); City property taxes per capita: $286 (1997).
Education: High school graduation rate: 80.8% (2000); College graduation rate: 28.8% (2000).
Housing: Homeownership rate: 81.8% (2000); Median home value: $106,300 (2000); Median rent: $325 per month (2000); Median age of housing: 43 years (2000).
Transportation: Commute to work: 56.8% car, 0.0% public transportation, 27.0% walk, 16.2% work from home (2000); Travel time to work: 38.7% less than 15 minutes, 51.6% 15 to 30 minutes, 9.7% 30 to 45 minutes, 0.0% 45 to 60 minutes, 0.0% 60 minutes or more (2000)

MOHAWK (unincorporated postal area, zip code 49950). Covers a land area of 204.090 square miles and a water area of 3.496 square miles. Located at 47.40° N. Lat.; 88.14° W. Long. Elevation is 1,062 feet.
History: Mohawk was settled in 1898 and became a mining center of a substance called mohawkite, a compound of copper and arsenic. The mine was active until 1934.
Population: 1,419 (2000); Race: 93.7% White, 4.3% Black, 0.0% Asian, 0.5% American Indian and Alaska Native, 1.8% Hispanic of any race, 1.3% two or more races (2000); Density: 7.0 persons per square mile (2000); Age: 25.7% under 18, 18.9% over 64 (2000); Marriage status: 26.6% never married, 56.3% now married, 7.8% widowed, 9.3% divorced (2000); Foreign born: 1.0% (2000); Ancestry (includes multiple ancestries): 35.4% Finnish, 15.2% German, 12.8% English, 8.9% French (except Basque), 8.0% Italian (2000).
Economy: Employment by occupation: 14.4% management, 23.1% professional, 21.2% services, 18.6% sales, 0.8% farming, 8.9% construction, 13.0% production (2000).
Income: Per capita income: $17,391 (2000); Median household income: $30,648 (2000); Poverty rate: 12.7% (2000).
Education: High school graduation rate: 87.4% (2000); College graduation rate: 22.5% (2000).
Housing: Homeownership rate: 88.0% (2000); Median home value: $49,400 (2000); Median rent: $242 per month (2000); Median age of housing: 53 years (2000).
Transportation: Commute to work: 83.2% car, 0.0% public transportation, 9.3% walk, 7.1% work from home (2000); Travel time to work: 40.4% less than 15 minutes, 33.4% 15 to 30 minutes, 16.0% 30 to 45 minutes, 5.7% 45 to 60 minutes, 4.5% 60 minutes or more (2000)

SHERMAN (township). Covers a land area of 65.089 square miles and a water area of 4.179 square miles. Located at 47.24° N. Lat.; 88.23° W. Long.
Population: 60 (2000); Race: 100.0% White, 0.0% Black, 0.0% Asian, 0.0% American Indian and Alaska Native, 0.0% Hispanic of any race, 0.0% two or more races (2000); Density: 0.9 persons per square mile (2000); Age: 14.5% under 18, 38.2% over 64 (2000); Marriage status: 29.2% never married, 35.4% now married, 22.9% widowed, 12.5% divorced (2000); Foreign born:

0.0% (2000); Ancestry (includes multiple ancestries): 43.6% Finnish, 20.0% Polish, 14.5% Irish, 12.7% French (except Basque), 10.9% German (2000).
Economy: Employment by occupation: 12.5% management, 25.0% professional, 8.3% services, 29.2% sales, 0.0% farming, 0.0% construction, 25.0% production (2000).
Income: Per capita income: $17,989 (2000); Median household income: $27,000 (2000); Poverty rate: 12.7% (2000).
Taxes: Total city taxes per capita: $244 (1997); City property taxes per capita: $244 (1997).
Education: High school graduation rate: 75.0% (2000); College graduation rate: 15.9% (2000).
Housing: Homeownership rate: 100.0% (2000); Median home value: $43,000 (2000); Median age of housing: 60+ years (2000).
Transportation: Commute to work: 79.2% car, 0.0% public transportation, 8.3% walk, 12.5% work from home (2000); Travel time to work: 9.5% less than 15 minutes, 33.3% 15 to 30 minutes, 47.6% 30 to 45 minutes, 0.0% 45 to 60 minutes, 9.5% 60 minutes or more (2000)

Lake County

Located in west central Michigan; drained by Pere Marquette and Little Manistee Rivers; includes part of Manistee National Forest. Covers a land area of 567.40 square miles, a water area of 7.20 square miles, and is located in the Eastern Time Zone. The county government was organized in 1870. County seat is Baldwin.

Weather Station: Baldwin — Elevation: 833 feet

	Jan	Feb	Mar	Apr	May	Jun	Jul	Aug	Sep	Oct	Nov	Dec
High	29	32	42	56	69	78	82	80	71	59	45	33
Low	10	10	19	31	42	51	55	53	45	35	26	17
Precip	2.4	1.6	2.3	2.9	2.8	3.5	2.7	4.0	3.7	3.2	3.1	2.3
Snow	25.7	17.4	10.0	2.0	tr	0.0	0.0	0.0	0.0	0.2	8.3	18.6

High and Low temperatures in degrees Fahrenheit; Precipitation and Snow in inches

Population: 11,333 (2000); Race: 84.7% White, 10.7% Black, 0.1% Asian, 1.2% American Indian and Alaska Native, 1.6% Hispanic of any race, 3.0% two or more races (2000); Density: 20.0 persons per square mile (2000); Age: 22.0% under 18, 19.6% over 64 (2000).
Religion: Five largest groups: 17.2% Catholic Church, 1.6% United Church of Christ, 1.4% The Christian and Missionary Alliance, 1.2% International Council of Community Churches, 1.2% The United Methodist Church (2000).
Economy: Unemployment rate: 8.6% (11/2002); Total civilian labor force: 3,816 (11/2002); Leading industries: 21.2% retail trade; 19.9% accommodation & food services; 19.3% health care and social assistance (2000); Companies that employ more than 1,000 persons: 0 (2000); Companies that employ more than 100 persons: 0 (2000); Farms: 126 totaling 22,971 acres (1997); Minority business ownership rate: 0.0% (1997); Women business ownership rate: 34.0% (1997); Retail sales per capita: $3,626 (1997). Single-family building permits issued: 113 (2001) / 113 (2000); Multi-family building permits issued: 0 (2001) / 0 (2000).
Income: Per capita income: $14,457 (2000); Median household income: $26,622 (2000); Poverty rate: 19.4% (2000); Bankruptcy rate: 4.18% (2001).
Taxes: Total county taxes per capita: $263 (1997); County property taxes per capita: $240 (1997).
Education: High school graduation rate: 72.2% (2000); College graduation rate: 7.8% (2000).
Housing: Homeownership rate: 82.9% (2000); Median home value: $61,300 (2000); Median rent: $301 per month (2000); Median age of housing: 25 years (2000).
Health: Birth rate: 118.2 per 10,000 population (1998); Age adjusted death rate: 102.7 per 10,000 population (1999); Age adjusted cancer mortality rate: 251.3 deaths per 100,000 population (1999). Number of physicians: 0.9 per 10,000 population (1999); Number of hospital beds: n/a (1999).
Elections: 2000 Presidential election results: 55.1% Gore, 41.8% Bush, 2.3% Nader, 0.1% Buchanan
National and State Parks: North Country National Scenic Trail; Pere Marquette State Forest
Additional Information Contacts
Lake County Government Offices 231-745-4641

Lake County Communities

BALDWIN (village). Covers a land area of 1.268 square miles and a water area of <.001 square miles. Located at 43.89° N. Lat.; 85.85° W. Long. Elevation is 838 feet.
History: Baldwin grew up at the junction of two rail lines, in an area of many lakes and streams that attracted vacationers. After being called Hannibal for an early settler, the name was changed to Baldwin in 1872 to honor Henry P. Baldwin, a governor of Michigan.
Population: 1,107 (2000); Race: 65.8% White, 27.7% Black, 0.0% Asian, 0.3% American Indian and Alaska Native, 2.4% Hispanic of any race, 6.3% two or more races (2000); Density: 873.2 persons per square mile (2000); Age: 21.7% under 18, 28.4% over 64 (2000); Marriage status: 24.8% never married, 46.6% now married, 18.2% widowed, 10.4% divorced (2000); Foreign born: 0.7% (2000); Ancestry (includes multiple ancestries): 29.5% Other groups, 12.7% German, 6.9% Dutch, 6.0% Irish, 4.6% English (2000).
Economy: Single-family building permits issued: 4 (2001) / 2 (2000); Multi-family building permits issued: 0 (2001) / 0 (2000); Employment by occupation: 4.5% management, 15.6% professional, 25.6% services, 25.6% sales, 0.7% farming, 9.0% construction, 19.0% production (2000).
Income: Per capita income: $9,619 (2000); Median household income: $15,550 (2000); Poverty rate: 35.9% (2000).
Taxes: Total city taxes per capita: $126 (1997); City property taxes per capita: $126 (1997).
Education: High school graduation rate: 64.8% (2000); College graduation rate: 9.5% (2000).

School District(s)

Baldwin Community Schools (PK-12)
2000 Enrollment: 774 231-745-4791
Housing: Homeownership rate: 36.7% (2000); Median home value: $39,700 (2000); Median rent: $185 per month (2000); Median age of housing: 31 years (2000).
Newspapers: Lake County Star (1 x week)
Transportation: Commute to work: 86.4% car, 1.4% public transportation, 6.5% walk, 2.2% work from home (2000); Travel time to work: 68.9% less than 15 minutes, 11.0% 15 to 30 minutes, 8.4% 30 to 45 minutes, 6.2% 45 to 60 minutes, 5.5% 60 minutes or more (2000)

CHASE (township). Covers a land area of 35.390 square miles and a water area of 0.174 square miles. Located at 43.87° N. Lat.; 85.62° W. Long. Elevation is 1,077 feet.
History: Chase Township was named for Salmon Portland Chase, a governor of Ohio.
Population: 1,194 (2000); Race: 97.3% White, 0.8% Black, 0.0% Asian, 0.2% American Indian and Alaska Native, 1.2% Hispanic of any race, 0.9% two or more races (2000); Density: 33.7 persons per square mile (2000); Age: 29.8% under 18, 9.3% over 64 (2000); Marriage status: 24.8% never married, 63.2% now married, 3.2% widowed, 8.8% divorced (2000); Foreign born: 0.3% (2000); Ancestry (includes multiple ancestries): 28.4% German, 13.4% United States or American, 11.5% English, 6.9% Irish, 5.8% Other groups (2000).
Economy: Employment by occupation: 11.8% management, 11.6% professional, 12.6% services, 21.1% sales, 2.6% farming, 14.8% construction, 25.5% production (2000).
Income: Per capita income: $14,882 (2000); Median household income: $36,776 (2000); Poverty rate: 12.9% (2000).
Taxes: Total city taxes per capita: $13 (1997); City property taxes per capita: $13 (1997).
Education: High school graduation rate: 80.9% (2000); College graduation rate: 9.2% (2000).
Housing: Homeownership rate: 89.3% (2000); Median home value: $65,500 (2000); Median rent: $353 per month (2000); Median age of housing: 24 years (2000).
Transportation: Commute to work: 92.4% car, 0.0% public transportation, 1.3% walk, 5.6% work from home (2000); Travel time to work: 26.0% less than 15 minutes, 47.7% 15 to 30 minutes, 14.0% 30 to 45 minutes, 4.1% 45 to 60 minutes, 8.1% 60 minutes or more (2000)

CHERRY VALLEY (township). Covers a land area of 35.599 square miles and a water area of 0 square miles. Located at 43.91° N. Lat.; 85.75° W. Long.
Population: 368 (2000); Race: 89.2% White, 2.2% Black, 0.0% Asian, 4.1% American Indian and Alaska Native, 2.6% Hispanic of any race, 4.6% two or more races (2000); Density: 10.3 persons per square mile (2000); Age: 20.4% under 18, 21.6% over 64 (2000); Marriage status: 18.4% never married, 64.8% now married, 8.7% widowed, 8.1% divorced (2000); Foreign born: 0.0% (2000); Ancestry (includes multiple ancestries): 21.6% Other groups, 19.2% German, 11.8% English, 10.3% Irish, 6.7% French (except Basque) (2000).

Economy: Employment by occupation: 4.3% management, 8.6% professional, 22.1% services, 17.8% sales, 1.2% farming, 15.3% construction, 30.7% production (2000).
Income: Per capita income: $15,030 (2000); Median household income: $31,250 (2000); Poverty rate: 19.9% (2000).
Taxes: Total city taxes per capita: $141 (1997); City property taxes per capita: $141 (1997).
Education: High school graduation rate: 63.0% (2000); College graduation rate: 2.0% (2000).
Housing: Homeownership rate: 82.9% (2000); Median home value: $39,800 (2000); Median rent: $325 per month (2000); Median age of housing: 23 years (2000).
Transportation: Commute to work: 94.2% car, 1.9% public transportation, 0.0% walk, 3.9% work from home (2000); Travel time to work: 19.5% less than 15 minutes, 38.9% 15 to 30 minutes, 20.8% 30 to 45 minutes, 5.4% 45 to 60 minutes, 15.4% 60 minutes or more (2000)

DOVER (township). Covers a land area of 36.800 square miles and a water area of 0.182 square miles. Located at 44.12° N. Lat.; 85.60° W. Long.
Population: 332 (2000); Race: 97.1% White, 0.0% Black, 0.0% Asian, 0.0% American Indian and Alaska Native, 1.8% Hispanic of any race, 2.9% two or more races (2000); Density: 9.0 persons per square mile (2000); Age: 16.2% under 18, 22.8% over 64 (2000); Marriage status: 20.3% never married, 54.4% now married, 15.4% widowed, 10.0% divorced (2000); Foreign born: 0.0% (2000); Ancestry (includes multiple ancestries): 22.1% German, 21.7% English, 11.0% United States or American, 8.8% Swedish, 7.7% Irish (2000).
Economy: Employment by occupation: 2.0% management, 16.7% professional, 7.8% services, 14.7% sales, 2.9% farming, 19.6% construction, 36.3% production (2000).
Income: Per capita income: $15,836 (2000); Median household income: $27,344 (2000); Poverty rate: 10.7% (2000).
Taxes: Total city taxes per capita: $76 (1997); City property taxes per capita: $76 (1997).
Education: High school graduation rate: 78.6% (2000); College graduation rate: 14.4% (2000).
Housing: Homeownership rate: 87.1% (2000); Median home value: $77,500 (2000); Median rent: $350 per month (2000); Median age of housing: 32 years (2000).
Transportation: Commute to work: 86.3% car, 0.0% public transportation, 4.9% walk, 5.9% work from home (2000); Travel time to work: 15.6% less than 15 minutes, 34.4% 15 to 30 minutes, 39.6% 30 to 45 minutes, 6.3% 45 to 60 minutes, 4.2% 60 minutes or more (2000)

EDEN (township). Covers a land area of 36.379 square miles and a water area of 0.149 square miles. Located at 44.12° N. Lat.; 85.85° W. Long.
Population: 377 (2000); Race: 96.5% White, 0.0% Black, 0.0% Asian, 0.0% American Indian and Alaska Native, 1.1% Hispanic of any race, 2.7% two or more races (2000); Density: 10.4 persons per square mile (2000); Age: 15.2% under 18, 19.8% over 64 (2000); Marriage status: 14.8% never married, 58.0% now married, 6.8% widowed, 20.4% divorced (2000); Foreign born: 1.4% (2000); Ancestry (includes multiple ancestries): 19.0% German, 13.9% Irish, 9.8% English, 9.5% United States or American, 7.9% Other groups (2000).
Economy: Employment by occupation: 7.5% management, 10.4% professional, 19.8% services, 24.5% sales, 0.0% farming, 19.8% construction, 17.9% production (2000).
Income: Per capita income: $12,895 (2000); Median household income: $23,646 (2000); Poverty rate: 25.9% (2000).
Taxes: Total city taxes per capita: $106 (1997); City property taxes per capita: $106 (1997).
Education: High school graduation rate: 56.2% (2000); College graduation rate: 5.1% (2000).
Housing: Homeownership rate: 74.9% (2000); Median home value: $60,000 (2000); Median rent: $289 per month (2000); Median age of housing: 23 years (2000).
Transportation: Commute to work: 95.1% car, 0.0% public transportation, 0.0% walk, 2.0% work from home (2000); Travel time to work: 9.0% less than 15 minutes, 31.0% 15 to 30 minutes, 29.0% 30 to 45 minutes, 20.0% 45 to 60 minutes, 11.0% 60 minutes or more (2000)

ELK (township). Covers a land area of 35.580 square miles and a water area of 1.227 square miles. Located at 44.12° N. Lat.; 85.97° W. Long.
Population: 900 (2000); Race: 98.3% White, 0.0% Black, 0.4% Asian, 1.0% American Indian and Alaska Native, 0.0% Hispanic of any race, 0.2% two or more races (2000); Density: 25.3 persons per square mile (2000); Age: 17.0% under 18, 23.9% over 64 (2000); Marriage status: 12.6% never married, 69.0% now married, 8.8% widowed, 9.6% divorced (2000); Foreign born: 1.2% (2000); Ancestry (includes multiple ancestries): 23.0% German, 14.5% Irish, 12.4% English, 9.7% Dutch, 9.2% United States or American (2000).
Economy: Employment by occupation: 8.9% management, 14.4% professional, 15.3% services, 26.5% sales, 3.5% farming, 13.7% construction, 17.6% production (2000).
Income: Per capita income: $16,293 (2000); Median household income: $31,917 (2000); Poverty rate: 12.1% (2000).
Taxes: Total city taxes per capita: $84 (2000); City property taxes per capita: $84 (2000).
Education: High school graduation rate: 80.0% (2000); College graduation rate: 7.2% (2000).
Housing: Homeownership rate: 92.4% (2000); Median home value: $99,400 (2000); Median rent: $350 per month (2000); Median age of housing: 19 years (2000).
Transportation: Commute to work: 96.0% car, 0.0% public transportation, 0.0% walk, 3.7% work from home (2000); Travel time to work: 17.7% less than 15 minutes, 19.8% 15 to 30 minutes, 38.5% 30 to 45 minutes, 11.1% 45 to 60 minutes, 12.8% 60 minutes or more (2000)

ELLSWORTH (township). Covers a land area of 35.167 square miles and a water area of 0.197 square miles. Located at 44.02° N. Lat.; 85.65° W. Long.
Population: 821 (2000); Race: 98.2% White, 0.5% Black, 0.0% Asian, 1.0% American Indian and Alaska Native, 0.0% Hispanic of any race, 0.1% two or more races (2000); Density: 23.3 persons per square mile (2000); Age: 29.2% under 18, 12.3% over 64 (2000); Marriage status: 19.2% never married, 65.0% now married, 6.0% widowed, 9.8% divorced (2000); Foreign born: 0.6% (2000); Ancestry (includes multiple ancestries): 24.2% German, 14.0% United States or American, 11.4% Irish, 6.5% Polish, 6.3% Other groups (2000).
Economy: Employment by occupation: 6.5% management, 11.5% professional, 10.9% services, 23.7% sales, 5.0% farming, 17.2% construction, 25.1% production (2000).
Income: Per capita income: $15,927 (2000); Median household income: $35,489 (2000); Poverty rate: 10.7% (2000).
Taxes: Total city taxes per capita: $47 (1997); City property taxes per capita: $47 (1997).
Education: High school graduation rate: 78.3% (2000); College graduation rate: 6.0% (2000).
Housing: Homeownership rate: 87.3% (2000); Median home value: $56,000 (2000); Median rent: $263 per month (2000); Median age of housing: 24 years (2000).
Transportation: Commute to work: 94.4% car, 0.6% public transportation, 1.5% walk, 2.5% work from home (2000); Travel time to work: 13.6% less than 15 minutes, 34.2% 15 to 30 minutes, 31.6% 30 to 45 minutes, 8.2% 45 to 60 minutes, 12.3% 60 minutes or more (2000)

IDLEWILD (unincorporated postal area, zip code 49642). Covers a land area of 19.646 square miles and a water area of 0.270 square miles. Located at 43.88° N. Lat.; 85.79° W. Long. Elevation is 856 feet.
History: Idlewild was platted in 1915 and developed as a summer resort and recreation area on Idlewild Lake, one of several lakes in the vicinity.
Population: 685 (2000); Race: 45.1% White, 48.9% Black, 0.0% Asian, 1.3% American Indian and Alaska Native, 2.8% Hispanic of any race, 4.3% two or more races (2000); Density: 34.9 persons per square mile (2000); Age: 24.7% under 18, 23.5% over 64 (2000); Marriage status: 24.8% never married, 53.1% now married, 11.1% widowed, 10.9% divorced (2000); Foreign born: 0.6% (2000); Ancestry (includes multiple ancestries): 59.0% Other groups, 9.6% German, 5.8% United States or American, 4.6% Irish, 2.8% African (2000).
Economy: Employment by occupation: 8.7% management, 6.7% professional, 23.6% services, 16.9% sales, 1.0% farming, 16.9% construction, 26.2% production (2000).
Income: Per capita income: $13,336 (2000); Median household income: $19,716 (2000); Poverty rate: 28.5% (2000).
Education: High school graduation rate: 66.7% (2000); College graduation rate: 6.2% (2000).
Housing: Homeownership rate: 71.4% (2000); Median home value: $44,800 (2000); Median rent: $311 per month (2000); Median age of housing: 34 years (2000).
Transportation: Commute to work: 83.9% car, 1.6% public transportation, 6.3% walk, 7.3% work from home (2000); Travel time to work: 36.5% less than 15 minutes, 22.5% 15 to 30 minutes, 13.5% 30 to 45 minutes, 8.4% 45 to 60 minutes, 19.1% 60 minutes or more (2000)

IRONS (unincorporated postal area, zip code 49644). Covers a land area of 120.061 square miles and a water area of 2.029 square miles. Located at 44.10° N. Lat.; 85.92° W. Long.
History: Irons grew up around a station on the Chicago & Western Michigan Railroad established in 1894. The village was platted in the early 1900's and named for the Irons family, early residents.
Population: 1,766 (2000); Race: 98.0% White, 0.2% Black, 0.2% Asian, 0.5% American Indian and Alaska Native, 0.3% Hispanic of any race, 0.9% two or more races (2000); Density: 14.7 persons per square mile (2000); Age: 15.7% under 18, 24.6% over 64 (2000); Marriage status: 12.5% never married, 65.4% now married, 8.2% widowed, 13.9% divorced (2000); Foreign born: 1.2% (2000); Ancestry (includes multiple ancestries): 22.2% German, 14.4% Irish, 12.9% English, 9.5% United States or American, 8.5% Dutch (2000).
Economy: Employment by occupation: 6.9% management, 10.8% professional, 19.0% services, 26.9% sales, 2.0% farming, 15.0% construction, 19.3% production (2000).
Income: Per capita income: $15,644 (2000); Median household income: $28,375 (2000); Poverty rate: 15.5% (2000).
Education: High school graduation rate: 75.1% (2000); College graduation rate: 6.4% (2000).
Housing: Homeownership rate: 87.3% (2000); Median home value: $89,500 (2000); Median rent: $336 per month (2000); Median age of housing: 21 years (2000).
Transportation: Commute to work: 96.4% car, 0.0% public transportation, 0.4% walk, 2.5% work from home (2000); Travel time to work: 17.0% less than 15 minutes, 21.1% 15 to 30 minutes, 35.2% 30 to 45 minutes, 12.4% 45 to 60 minutes, 14.3% 60 minutes or more (2000)

LAKE (township). Covers a land area of 34.066 square miles and a water area of 1.910 square miles. Located at 43.84° N. Lat.; 85.96° W. Long.
Population: 849 (2000); Race: 95.3% White, 1.1% Black, 0.1% Asian, 1.1% American Indian and Alaska Native, 1.5% Hispanic of any race, 1.9% two or more races (2000); Density: 24.9 persons per square mile (2000); Age: 12.1% under 18, 26.2% over 64 (2000); Marriage status: 11.7% never married, 69.6% now married, 7.0% widowed, 11.7% divorced (2000); Foreign born: 2.7% (2000); Ancestry (includes multiple ancestries): 19.3% German, 12.3% Dutch, 10.0% United States or American, 10.0% English, 9.7% Irish (2000).
Economy: Employment by occupation: 12.6% management, 8.3% professional, 14.6% services, 28.6% sales, 1.3% farming, 8.3% construction, 26.2% production (2000).
Income: Per capita income: $19,053 (2000); Median household income: $26,806 (2000); Poverty rate: 16.0% (2000).
Taxes: Total city taxes per capita: $202 (1997); City property taxes per capita: $168 (1997).
Education: High school graduation rate: 73.8% (2000); College graduation rate: 9.4% (2000).
Housing: Homeownership rate: 94.0% (2000); Median home value: $69,100 (2000); Median rent: $338 per month (2000); Median age of housing: 27 years (2000).
Transportation: Commute to work: 90.7% car, 0.0% public transportation, 0.7% walk, 6.9% work from home (2000); Travel time to work: 25.9% less than 15 minutes, 38.5% 15 to 30 minutes, 11.1% 30 to 45 minutes, 11.9% 45 to 60 minutes, 12.6% 60 minutes or more (2000)

LUTHER (village). Covers a land area of 0.929 square miles and a water area of 0.019 square miles. Located at 44.04° N. Lat.; 85.68° W. Long. Elevation is 1,023 feet.
History: When Luther was settled in 1880, it was called Wilson, for the owner of the sawmill. The next year it was platted and renamed for B.T. Luther, the other owner of the sawmill. Luther was incorporated as a village in 1893.
Population: 339 (2000); Race: 91.6% White, 1.1% Black, 0.5% Asian, 4.1% American Indian and Alaska Native, 0.5% Hispanic of any race, 2.7% two or more races (2000); Density: 364.8 persons per square mile (2000); Age: 28.3% under 18, 20.2% over 64 (2000); Marriage status: 22.8% never married, 47.8% now married, 11.6% widowed, 17.8% divorced (2000); Foreign born: 1.1% (2000); Ancestry (includes multiple ancestries): 14.4% Irish, 13.6% German, 8.2% United States or American, 6.8% French (except Basque), 6.0% Polish (2000).
Economy: Employment by occupation: 4.0% management, 5.6% professional, 12.1% services, 20.2% sales, 0.8% farming, 15.3% construction, 41.9% production (2000).
Income: Per capita income: $10,715 (2000); Median household income: $24,583 (2000); Poverty rate: 22.2% (2000).
Taxes: Total city taxes per capita: $62 (1997); City property taxes per capita: $62 (1997).
Education: High school graduation rate: 64.7% (2000); College graduation rate: 2.9% (2000).
Housing: Homeownership rate: 78.7% (2000); Median home value: $35,000 (2000); Median rent: $313 per month (2000); Median age of housing: 44 years (2000).
Transportation: Commute to work: 83.5% car, 0.9% public transportation, 7.0% walk, 6.1% work from home (2000); Travel time to work: 24.1% less than 15 minutes, 13.9% 15 to 30 minutes, 42.6% 30 to 45 minutes, 15.7% 45 to 60 minutes, 3.7% 60 minutes or more (2000)

NEWKIRK (township). Covers a land area of 72.758 square miles and a water area of 0.076 square miles. Located at 44.06° N. Lat.; 85.72° W. Long.
Population: 719 (2000); Race: 94.1% White, 0.0% Black, 0.6% Asian, 2.4% American Indian and Alaska Native, 0.8% Hispanic of any race, 2.6% two or more races (2000); Density: 9.9 persons per square mile (2000); Age: 30.5% under 18, 16.5% over 64 (2000); Marriage status: 17.7% never married, 57.6% now married, 10.3% widowed, 14.4% divorced (2000); Foreign born: 0.9% (2000); Ancestry (includes multiple ancestries): 19.2% German, 16.3% Irish, 9.4% United States or American, 9.0% English, 6.9% Other groups (2000).
Economy: Employment by occupation: 7.7% management, 5.0% professional, 17.3% services, 18.1% sales, 1.9% farming, 12.7% construction, 37.3% production (2000).
Income: Per capita income: $11,432 (2000); Median household income: $23,636 (2000); Poverty rate: 25.1% (2000).
Taxes: Total city taxes per capita: $46 (1997); City property taxes per capita: $46 (1997).
Education: High school graduation rate: 65.9% (2000); College graduation rate: 4.7% (2000).
Housing: Homeownership rate: 89.5% (2000); Median home value: $39,300 (2000); Median rent: $327 per month (2000); Median age of housing: 26 years (2000).
Transportation: Commute to work: 91.6% car, 0.4% public transportation, 2.0% walk, 3.6% work from home (2000); Travel time to work: 18.3% less than 15 minutes, 20.8% 15 to 30 minutes, 35.4% 30 to 45 minutes, 14.6% 45 to 60 minutes, 10.8% 60 minutes or more (2000)

PEACOCK (township). Covers a land area of 34.834 square miles and a water area of 0.942 square miles. Located at 44.02° N. Lat.; 85.86° W. Long. Elevation is 869 feet.
Population: 445 (2000); Race: 97.8% White, 0.0% Black, 0.0% Asian, 0.0% American Indian and Alaska Native, 1.5% Hispanic of any race, 1.7% two or more races (2000); Density: 12.8 persons per square mile (2000); Age: 7.4% under 18, 27.2% over 64 (2000); Marriage status: 9.1% never married, 65.4% now married, 8.6% widowed, 16.9% divorced (2000); Foreign born: 0.0% (2000); Ancestry (includes multiple ancestries): 20.8% German, 13.4% English, 9.7% Dutch, 9.2% United States or American, 9.2% French (except Basque) (2000).
Economy: Employment by occupation: 20.3% management, 7.6% professional, 15.8% services, 19.6% sales, 0.0% farming, 11.4% construction, 25.3% production (2000).
Income: Per capita income: $17,638 (2000); Median household income: $24,167 (2000); Poverty rate: 16.8% (2000).
Taxes: Total city taxes per capita: $137 (1997); City property taxes per capita: $137 (1997).
Education: High school graduation rate: 78.4% (2000); College graduation rate: 8.6% (2000).
Housing: Homeownership rate: 95.9% (2000); Median home value: $80,000 (2000); Median rent: $338 per month (2000); Median age of housing: 24 years (2000).
Transportation: Commute to work: 89.7% car, 0.0% public transportation, 4.5% walk, 3.9% work from home (2000); Travel time to work: 28.9% less than 15 minutes, 35.6% 15 to 30 minutes, 13.4% 30 to 45 minutes, 2.7% 45 to 60 minutes, 19.5% 60 minutes or more (2000)

PINORA (township). Covers a land area of 35.526 square miles and a water area of 0.047 square miles. Located at 43.95° N. Lat.; 85.64° W. Long.
Population: 643 (2000); Race: 94.7% White, 0.0% Black, 0.3% Asian, 0.7% American Indian and Alaska Native, 0.8% Hispanic of any race, 4.1% two or more races (2000); Density: 18.1 persons per square mile (2000); Age: 21.4% under 18, 14.8% over 64 (2000); Marriage status: 20.4% never married, 59.3% now married, 6.4% widowed, 13.8% divorced (2000); Foreign born: 2.6% (2000); Ancestry (includes multiple ancestries): 23.9% German, 18.5%

United States or American, 11.7% Irish, 6.3% English, 5.9% Other groups (2000).
Economy: Employment by occupation: 3.9% management, 13.3% professional, 10.2% services, 18.4% sales, 2.0% farming, 19.1% construction, 33.2% production (2000).
Income: Per capita income: $17,285 (2000); Median household income: $37,222 (2000); Poverty rate: 9.8% (2000).
Taxes: Total city taxes per capita: $41 (1997); City property taxes per capita: $41 (1997).
Education: High school graduation rate: 72.4% (2000); College graduation rate: 9.1% (2000).
Housing: Homeownership rate: 91.6% (2000); Median home value: $68,800 (2000); Median rent: $270 per month (2000); Median age of housing: 17 years (2000).
Transportation: Commute to work: 94.9% car, 1.2% public transportation, 0.8% walk, 3.2% work from home (2000); Travel time to work: 15.5% less than 15 minutes, 46.9% 15 to 30 minutes, 24.1% 30 to 45 minutes, 4.9% 45 to 60 minutes, 8.6% 60 minutes or more (2000)

PLEASANT PLAINS (township). Covers a land area of 34.718 square miles and a water area of 0.572 square miles. Located at 43.86° N. Lat.; 85.84° W. Long.
Population: 1,535 (2000); Race: 74.3% White, 19.7% Black, 0.0% Asian, 0.8% American Indian and Alaska Native, 3.8% Hispanic of any race, 4.6% two or more races (2000); Density: 44.2 persons per square mile (2000); Age: 23.3% under 18, 18.1% over 64 (2000); Marriage status: 22.2% never married, 53.0% now married, 11.0% widowed, 13.8% divorced (2000); Foreign born: 1.3% (2000); Ancestry (includes multiple ancestries): 27.5% Other groups, 18.5% German, 8.3% English, 7.4% Irish, 6.6% United States or American (2000).
Economy: Employment by occupation: 8.0% management, 17.7% professional, 20.1% services, 23.7% sales, 0.7% farming, 8.0% construction, 21.6% production (2000).
Income: Per capita income: $15,571 (2000); Median household income: $22,353 (2000); Poverty rate: 25.6% (2000).
Taxes: Total city taxes per capita: $170 (1997); City property taxes per capita: $169 (1997).
Education: High school graduation rate: 71.7% (2000); College graduation rate: 11.7% (2000).
Housing: Homeownership rate: 71.4% (2000); Median home value: $47,900 (2000); Median rent: $334 per month (2000); Median age of housing: 33 years (2000).
Transportation: Commute to work: 90.8% car, 0.8% public transportation, 5.7% walk, 1.2% work from home (2000); Travel time to work: 58.2% less than 15 minutes, 14.2% 15 to 30 minutes, 11.2% 30 to 45 minutes, 5.9% 45 to 60 minutes, 10.5% 60 minutes or more (2000)

SAUBLE (township). Covers a land area of 34.618 square miles and a water area of 0.746 square miles. Located at 44.03° N. Lat.; 85.97° W. Long. Elevation is 737 feet.
Population: 323 (2000); Race: 97.7% White, 1.0% Black, 0.0% Asian, 0.0% American Indian and Alaska Native, 0.7% Hispanic of any race, 1.3% two or more races (2000); Density: 9.3 persons per square mile (2000); Age: 12.4% under 18, 38.1% over 64 (2000); Marriage status: 6.2% never married, 68.9% now married, 9.9% widowed, 15.0% divorced (2000); Foreign born: 0.7% (2000); Ancestry (includes multiple ancestries): 23.1% German, 18.2% English, 17.9% Irish, 7.5% French (except Basque), 7.5% Dutch (2000).
Economy: Employment by occupation: 4.7% management, 2.4% professional, 23.5% services, 34.1% sales, 0.0% farming, 7.1% construction, 28.2% production (2000).
Income: Per capita income: $18,528 (2000); Median household income: $28,636 (2000); Poverty rate: 12.1% (2000).
Taxes: Total city taxes per capita: $61 (1997); City property taxes per capita: $61 (1997).
Education: High school graduation rate: 83.1% (2000); College graduation rate: 6.9% (2000).
Housing: Homeownership rate: 85.3% (2000); Median home value: $83,900 (2000); Median rent: $425 per month (2000); Median age of housing: 22 years (2000).
Transportation: Commute to work: 97.5% car, 0.0% public transportation, 2.5% walk, 0.0% work from home (2000); Travel time to work: 21.0% less than 15 minutes, 14.8% 15 to 30 minutes, 34.6% 30 to 45 minutes, 17.3% 45 to 60 minutes, 12.3% 60 minutes or more (2000)

SWEETWATER (township). Covers a land area of 35.726 square miles and a water area of 0.068 square miles. Located at 43.92° N. Lat.; 85.98° W. Long.
Population: 238 (2000); Race: 87.5% White, 11.3% Black, 0.0% Asian, 0.8% American Indian and Alaska Native, 3.5% Hispanic of any race, 0.4% two or more races (2000); Density: 6.7 persons per square mile (2000); Age: 20.6% under 18, 19.1% over 64 (2000); Marriage status: 14.1% never married, 68.5% now married, 11.7% widowed, 5.6% divorced (2000); Foreign born: 1.2% (2000); Ancestry (includes multiple ancestries): 18.7% United States or American, 16.7% Other groups, 13.6% German, 8.6% English, 8.6% French (except Basque) (2000).
Economy: Employment by occupation: 9.3% management, 17.3% professional, 10.7% services, 33.3% sales, 1.3% farming, 8.0% construction, 20.0% production (2000).
Income: Per capita income: $12,037 (2000); Median household income: $24,107 (2000); Poverty rate: 18.5% (2000).
Taxes: Total city taxes per capita: $96 (1997); City property taxes per capita: $96 (1997).
Education: High school graduation rate: 69.7% (2000); College graduation rate: 10.1% (2000).
Housing: Homeownership rate: 94.1% (2000); Median home value: $55,500 (2000); Median rent: $275 per month (2000); Median age of housing: 22 years (2000).
Transportation: Commute to work: 100.0% car, 0.0% public transportation, 0.0% walk, 0.0% work from home (2000); Travel time to work: 12.5% less than 15 minutes, 48.6% 15 to 30 minutes, 11.1% 30 to 45 minutes, 5.6% 45 to 60 minutes, 22.2% 60 minutes or more (2000)

WEBBER (township). Covers a land area of 34.883 square miles and a water area of 0.564 square miles. Located at 43.92° N. Lat.; 85.85° W. Long.
Population: 1,875 (2000); Race: 63.5% White, 27.2% Black, 0.1% Asian, 2.3% American Indian and Alaska Native, 1.9% Hispanic of any race, 6.8% two or more races (2000); Density: 53.8 persons per square mile (2000); Age: 21.0% under 18, 21.6% over 64 (2000); Marriage status: 34.8% never married, 42.1% now married, 11.5% widowed, 11.5% divorced (2000); Foreign born: 0.5% (2000); Ancestry (includes multiple ancestries): 28.4% Other groups, 13.0% German, 6.7% Irish, 6.6% Dutch, 5.8% English (2000).
Economy: Employment by occupation: 4.6% management, 10.2% professional, 25.0% services, 24.0% sales, 0.4% farming, 10.2% construction, 25.6% production (2000).
Income: Per capita income: $9,512 (2000); Median household income: $20,822 (2000); Poverty rate: 28.1% (2000).
Education: High school graduation rate: 62.2% (2000); College graduation rate: 5.4% (2000).
Housing: Homeownership rate: 66.1% (2000); Median home value: $54,300 (2000); Median rent: $191 per month (2000); Median age of housing: 24 years (2000).
Transportation: Commute to work: 85.3% car, 2.8% public transportation, 5.0% walk, 3.0% work from home (2000); Travel time to work: 48.2% less than 15 minutes, 20.8% 15 to 30 minutes, 12.1% 30 to 45 minutes, 11.4% 45 to 60 minutes, 7.6% 60 minutes or more (2000)

YATES (township). Covers a land area of 35.391 square miles and a water area of 0.315 square miles. Located at 43.88° N. Lat.; 85.78° W. Long.
Population: 714 (2000); Race: 51.4% White, 45.5% Black, 0.0% Asian, 0.9% American Indian and Alaska Native, 1.3% Hispanic of any race, 2.3% two or more races (2000); Density: 20.2 persons per square mile (2000); Age: 27.5% under 18, 24.0% over 64 (2000); Marriage status: 23.7% never married, 54.2% now married, 9.8% widowed, 12.2% divorced (2000); Foreign born: 1.3% (2000); Ancestry (includes multiple ancestries): 54.6% Other groups, 11.4% German, 9.4% Irish, 4.7% United States or American, 3.9% Polish (2000).
Economy: Employment by occupation: 7.8% management, 10.8% professional, 25.5% services, 17.6% sales, 1.0% farming, 15.2% construction, 22.1% production (2000).
Income: Per capita income: $13,570 (2000); Median household income: $20,417 (2000); Poverty rate: 30.6% (2000).
Taxes: Total city taxes per capita: $336 (1997); City property taxes per capita: $327 (1997).
Education: High school graduation rate: 74.1% (2000); College graduation rate: 8.0% (2000).
Housing: Homeownership rate: 76.7% (2000); Median home value: $53,900 (2000); Median rent: $311 per month (2000); Median age of housing: 32 years (2000).

Transportation: Commute to work: 84.6% car, 0.0% public transportation, 6.0% walk, 8.5% work from home (2000); Travel time to work: 34.8% less than 15 minutes, 25.0% 15 to 30 minutes, 14.7% 30 to 45 minutes, 10.3% 45 to 60 minutes, 15.2% 60 minutes or more (2000)

Lapeer County

Located in eastern Michigan; drained by the Flint and Belle Rivers; includes many small lakes. Covers a land area of 654.20 square miles, a water area of 8.90 square miles, and is located in the Eastern Time Zone. The county government was organized in 1837. County seat is Lapeer.

Lapeer County is part of the Detroit, MI PMSA. The entire metro area includes: Lapeer County; Macomb County; Monroe County; Oakland County; St. Clair County; Wayne County

Weather Station: Lapeer WWTP Elevation: 816 feet

	Jan	Feb	Mar	Apr	May	Jun	Jul	Aug	Sep	Oct	Nov	Dec
High	29	33	44	57	70	79	83	80	73	61	47	35
Low	14	16	24	35	45	54	59	56	50	39	30	20
Precip	1.5	1.1	2.0	2.8	2.8	3.1	3.0	3.4	3.7	2.7	2.7	1.9
Snow	9.5	7.8	6.7	1.1	tr	0.0	0.0	0.0	0.0	tr	1.9	9.3

High and Low temperatures in degrees Fahrenheit; Precipitation and Snow in inches

Population: 87,904 (2000); Race: 96.4% White, 0.7% Black, 0.2% Asian, 0.5% American Indian and Alaska Native, 2.9% Hispanic of any race, 1.2% two or more races (2000); Density: 134.4 persons per square mile (2000); Age: 28.2% under 18, 9.5% over 64 (2000).
Religion: Five largest groups: 17.9% Catholic Church, 3.2% Lutheran Church—Missouri Synod, 2.2% The United Methodist Church, 0.8% Christian Churches and Churches of Christ, 0.8% The Wesleyan Church (2000).
Economy: Unemployment rate: 6.5% (11/2002); Total civilian labor force: 45,237 (11/2002); Leading industries: 28.4% manufacturing; 18.7% retail trade; 9.6% health care and social assistance (2000); Companies that employ more than 1,000 persons: 0 (2000); Companies that employ more than 100 persons: 34 (2000); Farms: 1,020 totaling 178,249 acres (1997); Minority business ownership rate: 1.9% (1997); Women business ownership rate: 28.2% (1997); Retail sales per capita: $8,124 (1997). Single-family building permits issued: 461 (2001) / 566 (2000); Multi-family building permits issued: 0 (2001) / 0 (2000).
Income: Per capita income: $21,462 (2000); Median household income: $51,717 (2000); Poverty rate: 5.4% (2000); Bankruptcy rate: 4.76% (2001).
Taxes: Total county taxes per capita: $93 (2000); County property taxes per capita: $83 (2000).
Education: High school graduation rate: 84.5% (2000); College graduation rate: 12.7% (2000).
Housing: Homeownership rate: 85.0% (2000); Median home value: $134,600 (2000); Median rent: $461 per month (2000); Median age of housing: 26 years (2000).
Health: Birth rate: 124.2 per 10,000 population (1998); Age adjusted death rate: 86.0 per 10,000 population (1999); Age adjusted cancer mortality rate: 186.6 deaths per 100,000 population (1999). Number of physicians: 4.1 per 10,000 population (1999); Number of hospital beds: 18.1 per 10,000 population (1999).
Elections: 2000 Presidential election results: 42.3% Gore, 54.7% Bush, 2.1% Nader, 0.2% Buchanan
National and State Parks: Lapeer State Game Area; Metamora-Hadley State Recreation Area; Ortonville State Recreation Area
Additional Information Contacts
Lapeer County Government Offices 810-667-0340
Almont Area Chamber of Commerce 810-798-2410
Dryden Chamber of Commerce 810-796-3700
Imlay City Chamber of Commerce 810-724-1361
Lapeer & Upper Thumb Association of Realtors 810-664-0271
Lapeer Area Chamber of Commerce 810-664-6641
Metamore Chamber of Commerce 810-678-6222

Lapeer County Communities

ALMONT (village). Covers a land area of 1.509 square miles and a water area of <.001 square miles. Located at 42.92° N. Lat.; 83.04° W. Long. Elevation is 839 feet.
History: Almont was first settled by James Deneen in 1828. First called Newburg, the name was changed in 1846 to honor the Mexican general Juan N. Almonte.
Population: 2,803 (2000); Race: 97.2% White, 0.0% Black, 0.3% Asian, 0.2% American Indian and Alaska Native, 3.7% Hispanic of any race, 1.0% two or more races (2000); Density: 1,857.2 persons per square mile (2000); Age: 30.1% under 18, 9.1% over 64 (2000); Marriage status: 21.8% never married, 60.0% now married, 6.3% widowed, 11.8% divorced (2000); Foreign born: 2.9% (2000); Ancestry (includes multiple ancestries): 26.5% German, 15.6% Polish, 12.9% Irish, 12.2% English, 8.4% Italian (2000).
Economy: Single-family building permits issued: 5 (2001) / 11 (2000); Multi-family building permits issued: 0 (2001) / 0 (2000); Employment by occupation: 9.4% management, 18.5% professional, 12.1% services, 21.2% sales, 0.4% farming, 13.3% construction, 25.0% production (2000).
Income: Per capita income: $21,252 (2000); Median household income: $53,984 (2000); Poverty rate: 5.6% (2000).
Taxes: Total city taxes per capita: $306 (1997); City property taxes per capita: $294 (1997).
Education: High school graduation rate: 86.9% (2000); College graduation rate: 14.8% (2000).

School District(s)

Almont Community Schools (KG-12)
2000 Enrollment: 1,629 810-798-8561
Housing: Homeownership rate: 88.1% (2000); Median home value: $135,400 (2000); Median rent: $449 per month (2000); Median age of housing: 24 years (2000).
Transportation: Commute to work: 94.3% car, 0.1% public transportation, 2.2% walk, 3.0% work from home (2000); Travel time to work: 24.2% less than 15 minutes, 21.9% 15 to 30 minutes, 23.6% 30 to 45 minutes, 18.6% 45 to 60 minutes, 11.7% 60 minutes or more (2000)
Additional Information Contacts
Almont Area Chamber of Commerce 810-798-2410

ALMONT (township). Covers a land area of 36.988 square miles and a water area of 0.097 square miles. Located at 42.93° N. Lat.; 83.05° W. Long. Elevation is 839 feet.
History: Incorporated 1885.
Population: 6,041 (2000); Race: 97.6% White, 0.1% Black, 0.2% Asian, 0.3% American Indian and Alaska Native, 2.5% Hispanic of any race, 1.2% two or more races (2000); Density: 163.3 persons per square mile (2000); Age: 29.1% under 18, 8.6% over 64 (2000); Marriage status: 20.9% never married, 67.4% now married, 4.3% widowed, 7.4% divorced (2000); Foreign born: 2.7% (2000); Ancestry (includes multiple ancestries): 28.2% German, 16.6% Polish, 13.1% English, 11.7% Irish, 6.3% United States or American (2000).
Economy: In farm area: fruit, grain, dairy products. Manufactures auto parts and metal tubing. Single-family building permits issued: 50 (2001) / 70 (2000); Multi-family building permits issued: 0 (2001) / 0 (2000); Employment by occupation: 9.9% management, 19.0% professional, 10.4% services, 22.5% sales, 0.2% farming, 14.1% construction, 23.9% production (2000).
Income: Per capita income: $23,608 (2000); Median household income: $65,000 (2000); Poverty rate: 3.0% (2000).
Taxes: Total city taxes per capita: $64 (1997); City property taxes per capita: $54 (1997).
Education: High school graduation rate: 86.5% (2000); College graduation rate: 15.4% (2000).
Housing: Homeownership rate: 92.7% (2000); Median home value: $157,100 (2000); Median rent: $457 per month (2000); Median age of housing: 21 years (2000).
Transportation: Commute to work: 94.2% car, 0.4% public transportation, 1.6% walk, 3.6% work from home (2000); Travel time to work: 23.7% less than 15 minutes, 19.8% 15 to 30 minutes, 24.4% 30 to 45 minutes, 19.5% 45 to 60 minutes, 12.6% 60 minutes or more (2000)

ARCADIA (township). Covers a land area of 35.330 square miles and a water area of 0.861 square miles. Located at 43.11° N. Lat.; 83.16° W. Long.
Population: 3,197 (2000); Race: 97.8% White, 1.0% Black, 0.0% Asian, 0.1% American Indian and Alaska Native, 1.8% Hispanic of any race, 0.4% two or more races (2000); Density: 90.5 persons per square mile (2000); Age: 27.7% under 18, 9.6% over 64 (2000); Marriage status: 20.3% never married, 68.1% now married, 3.4% widowed, 8.1% divorced (2000); Foreign born: 1.5% (2000); Ancestry (includes multiple ancestries): 30.2% German, 16.4% English, 12.2% Irish, 8.9% United States or American, 8.1% Polish (2000).
Economy: Employment by occupation: 10.1% management, 17.9% professional, 13.0% services, 21.3% sales, 0.5% farming, 12.8% construction, 24.5% production (2000).
Income: Per capita income: $22,080 (2000); Median household income: $56,458 (2000); Poverty rate: 4.9% (2000).

Taxes: Total city taxes per capita: $34 (1997); City property taxes per capita: $33 (1997).
Education: High school graduation rate: 82.6% (2000); College graduation rate: 12.3% (2000).
Housing: Homeownership rate: 94.4% (2000); Median home value: $142,800 (2000); Median rent: $468 per month (2000); Median age of housing: 23 years (2000).
Transportation: Commute to work: 95.2% car, 0.0% public transportation, 0.5% walk, 3.6% work from home (2000); Travel time to work: 12.0% less than 15 minutes, 36.1% 15 to 30 minutes, 14.4% 30 to 45 minutes, 14.2% 45 to 60 minutes, 23.3% 60 minutes or more (2000)

ATTICA (township). Covers a land area of 35.767 square miles and a water area of 0.479 square miles. Located at 43.01° N. Lat.; 83.16° W. Long.
Population: 4,678 (2000); Race: 97.1% White, 0.2% Black, 0.6% Asian, 0.0% American Indian and Alaska Native, 1.9% Hispanic of any race, 0.9% two or more races (2000); Density: 130.8 persons per square mile (2000); Age: 29.6% under 18, 8.9% over 64 (2000); Marriage status: 19.6% never married, 65.7% now married, 5.9% widowed, 8.9% divorced (2000); Foreign born: 1.3% (2000); Ancestry (includes multiple ancestries): 22.0% German, 11.6% English, 10.7% Irish, 7.8% Polish, 7.7% Other groups (2000).
Economy: Employment by occupation: 8.3% management, 15.5% professional, 16.7% services, 15.3% sales, 0.0% farming, 14.9% construction, 29.3% production (2000).
Income: Per capita income: $22,226 (2000); Median household income: $50,392 (2000); Poverty rate: 3.6% (2000).
Taxes: Total city taxes per capita: $53 (1997); City property taxes per capita: $48 (1997).
Education: High school graduation rate: 81.8% (2000); College graduation rate: 8.3% (2000).
Housing: Homeownership rate: 90.8% (2000); Median home value: $146,700 (2000); Median rent: $481 per month (2000); Median age of housing: 29 years (2000).
Transportation: Commute to work: 96.1% car, 0.0% public transportation, 1.8% walk, 2.2% work from home (2000); Travel time to work: 19.3% less than 15 minutes, 21.2% 15 to 30 minutes, 15.1% 30 to 45 minutes, 16.9% 45 to 60 minutes, 27.4% 60 minutes or more (2000)

BARNES LAKE-MILLERS LAKE (CDP). Covers a land area of 3.064 square miles and a water area of 0.378 square miles. Located at 43.18° N. Lat.; 83.30° W. Long.
Population: 1,187 (2000); Race: 99.5% White, 0.0% Black, 0.0% Asian, 0.0% American Indian and Alaska Native, 2.7% Hispanic of any race, 0.0% two or more races (2000); Density: 387.4 persons per square mile (2000); Age: 26.2% under 18, 8.8% over 64 (2000); Marriage status: 16.7% never married, 68.5% now married, 3.9% widowed, 10.9% divorced (2000); Foreign born: 0.0% (2000); Ancestry (includes multiple ancestries): 20.2% German, 10.9% United States or American, 10.6% Irish, 10.2% Polish, 7.8% English (2000).
Economy: Employment by occupation: 17.6% management, 17.6% professional, 5.6% services, 21.2% sales, 0.0% farming, 8.3% construction, 29.8% production (2000).
Income: Per capita income: $22,103 (2000); Median household income: $48,889 (2000); Poverty rate: 2.5% (2000).
Education: High school graduation rate: 89.0% (2000); College graduation rate: 10.8% (2000).
Housing: Homeownership rate: 83.9% (2000); Median home value: $124,500 (2000); Median rent: $476 per month (2000); Median age of housing: 29 years (2000).
Transportation: Commute to work: 94.3% car, 0.0% public transportation, 0.0% walk, 5.7% work from home (2000); Travel time to work: 9.7% less than 15 minutes, 37.9% 15 to 30 minutes, 5.0% 30 to 45 minutes, 18.8% 45 to 60 minutes, 28.6% 60 minutes or more (2000)

BURLINGTON (township). Covers a land area of 35.595 square miles and a water area of 0.018 square miles. Located at 43.30° N. Lat.; 83.19° W. Long.
Population: 1,402 (2000); Race: 97.0% White, 0.3% Black, 0.4% Asian, 0.0% American Indian and Alaska Native, 2.0% Hispanic of any race, 1.5% two or more races (2000); Density: 39.4 persons per square mile (2000); Age: 27.5% under 18, 10.2% over 64 (2000); Marriage status: 19.9% never married, 61.7% now married, 7.9% widowed, 10.5% divorced (2000); Foreign born: 1.3% (2000); Ancestry (includes multiple ancestries): 23.3% German, 14.9% English, 13.6% United States or American, 9.8% Irish, 7.9% Other groups (2000).
Economy: Employment by occupation: 10.5% management, 8.0% professional, 14.2% services, 19.6% sales, 1.9% farming, 14.4% construction, 31.3% production (2000).
Income: Per capita income: $17,108 (2000); Median household income: $42,794 (2000); Poverty rate: 8.8% (2000).
Taxes: Total city taxes per capita: $19 (1997); City property taxes per capita: $19 (1997).
Education: High school graduation rate: 74.3% (2000); College graduation rate: 6.3% (2000).
Housing: Homeownership rate: 88.0% (2000); Median home value: $91,400 (2000); Median rent: $421 per month (2000); Median age of housing: 36 years (2000).
Transportation: Commute to work: 88.5% car, 0.0% public transportation, 2.8% walk, 7.4% work from home (2000); Travel time to work: 29.8% less than 15 minutes, 15.5% 15 to 30 minutes, 20.1% 30 to 45 minutes, 11.7% 45 to 60 minutes, 22.9% 60 minutes or more (2000)

BURNSIDE (township). Covers a land area of 54.100 square miles and a water area of 0.008 square miles. Located at 43.22° N. Lat.; 83.06° W. Long.
History: Burnside Township began as Allison Township, organized in 1855. The name was changed in 1866 to honor Union General Ambrose E. Burnside.
Population: 1,920 (2000); Race: 97.1% White, 0.4% Black, 0.3% Asian, 0.2% American Indian and Alaska Native, 2.1% Hispanic of any race, 1.0% two or more races (2000); Density: 35.5 persons per square mile (2000); Age: 30.8% under 18, 9.0% over 64 (2000); Marriage status: 21.4% never married, 67.6% now married, 3.7% widowed, 7.3% divorced (2000); Foreign born: 1.4% (2000); Ancestry (includes multiple ancestries): 28.2% German, 13.6% English, 12.3% Irish, 8.3% Other groups, 7.3% Polish (2000).
Economy: Single-family building permits issued: 9 (2001) / 10 (2000); Multi-family building permits issued: 0 (2001) / 0 (2000); Employment by occupation: 10.2% management, 8.9% professional, 10.3% services, 18.2% sales, 2.0% farming, 19.5% construction, 30.9% production (2000).
Income: Per capita income: $18,212 (2000); Median household income: $43,913 (2000); Poverty rate: 10.6% (2000).
Taxes: Total city taxes per capita: $32 (1997); City property taxes per capita: $28 (1997).
Education: High school graduation rate: 76.6% (2000); College graduation rate: 5.5% (2000).
Housing: Homeownership rate: 83.9% (2000); Median home value: $124,100 (2000); Median rent: $411 per month (2000); Median age of housing: 27 years (2000).
Transportation: Commute to work: 91.2% car, 0.0% public transportation, 2.2% walk, 5.9% work from home (2000); Travel time to work: 26.4% less than 15 minutes, 22.4% 15 to 30 minutes, 15.8% 30 to 45 minutes, 8.1% 45 to 60 minutes, 27.4% 60 minutes or more (2000)

CLIFFORD (village). Covers a land area of 1.509 square miles and a water area of 0 square miles. Located at 43.31° N. Lat.; 83.18° W. Long. Elevation is 828 feet.
History: Clifford was founded in the early 1860's by Arden W. Lyman, who operated a store and post office from his home. Lyman named the village for his son, Clifford Lyman.
Population: 324 (2000); Race: 91.6% White, 1.1% Black, 0.5% Asian, 0.0% American Indian and Alaska Native, 5.5% Hispanic of any race, 3.7% two or more races (2000); Density: 214.7 persons per square mile (2000); Age: 28.9% under 18, 12.1% over 64 (2000); Marriage status: 22.0% never married, 54.9% now married, 9.1% widowed, 14.0% divorced (2000); Foreign born: 1.8% (2000); Ancestry (includes multiple ancestries): 23.2% United States or American, 15.3% German, 15.0% Other groups, 10.0% Irish, 7.6% English (2000).
Economy: Employment by occupation: 14.9% management, 9.1% professional, 18.8% services, 13.0% sales, 0.0% farming, 13.0% construction, 31.2% production (2000).
Income: Per capita income: $16,426 (2000); Median household income: $36,875 (2000); Poverty rate: 13.7% (2000).
Taxes: Total city taxes per capita: $318 (1997); City property taxes per capita: $318 (1997).
Education: High school graduation rate: 63.8% (2000); College graduation rate: 4.5% (2000).
Housing: Homeownership rate: 84.0% (2000); Median home value: $73,600 (2000); Median rent: $431 per month (2000); Median age of housing: 45 years (2000).
Transportation: Commute to work: 84.0% car, 0.0% public transportation, 8.7% walk, 7.3% work from home (2000); Travel time to work: 32.4% less

than 15 minutes, 11.5% 15 to 30 minutes, 28.8% 30 to 45 minutes, 4.3% 45 to 60 minutes, 23.0% 60 minutes or more (2000)

COLUMBIAVILLE (village). Covers a land area of 0.866 square miles and a water area of 0.267 square miles. Located at 43.15° N. Lat.; 83.40° W. Long. Elevation is 780 feet.
History: Columbiaville was settled in 1847 and developed around a sawmill. It was first known as Niverville, and later renamed for Columbia County, New York.
Population: 815 (2000); Race: 95.2% White, 0.0% Black, 1.0% Asian, 0.8% American Indian and Alaska Native, 2.2% Hispanic of any race, 1.3% two or more races (2000); Density: 940.8 persons per square mile (2000); Age: 27.4% under 18, 11.5% over 64 (2000); Marriage status: 22.3% never married, 58.9% now married, 8.3% widowed, 10.5% divorced (2000); Foreign born: 1.4% (2000); Ancestry (includes multiple ancestries): 25.1% German, 13.4% English, 12.5% Irish, 8.8% Other groups, 8.4% French (except Basque) (2000).
Economy: Employment by occupation: 8.2% management, 6.8% professional, 15.5% services, 25.1% sales, 0.6% farming, 17.5% construction, 26.3% production (2000).
Income: Per capita income: $16,216 (2000); Median household income: $39,844 (2000); Poverty rate: 4.3% (2000).
Taxes: Total city taxes per capita: $172 (1997); City property taxes per capita: $170 (1997).
Education: High school graduation rate: 79.0% (2000); College graduation rate: 5.5% (2000).
Housing: Homeownership rate: 68.8% (2000); Median home value: $93,400 (2000); Median rent: $386 per month (2000); Median age of housing: 55 years (2000).
Transportation: Commute to work: 92.7% car, 0.0% public transportation, 5.2% walk, 2.0% work from home (2000); Travel time to work: 21.1% less than 15 minutes, 26.8% 15 to 30 minutes, 22.6% 30 to 45 minutes, 11.6% 45 to 60 minutes, 17.9% 60 minutes or more (2000)

DEERFIELD (township). Covers a land area of 35.874 square miles and a water area of 0.494 square miles. Located at 43.18° N. Lat.; 83.29° W. Long.
Population: 5,736 (2000); Race: 97.0% White, 0.1% Black, 0.0% Asian, 0.0% American Indian and Alaska Native, 3.6% Hispanic of any race, 2.4% two or more races (2000); Density: 159.9 persons per square mile (2000); Age: 31.2% under 18, 6.6% over 64 (2000); Marriage status: 20.8% never married, 67.7% now married, 3.4% widowed, 8.1% divorced (2000); Foreign born: 1.2% (2000); Ancestry (includes multiple ancestries): 20.3% German, 12.5% English, 9.2% Other groups, 9.2% United States or American, 8.9% Irish (2000).
Economy: Employment by occupation: 11.2% management, 20.5% professional, 12.2% services, 17.5% sales, 0.2% farming, 13.4% construction, 25.1% production (2000).
Income: Per capita income: $19,609 (2000); Median household income: $47,804 (2000); Poverty rate: 3.9% (2000).
Taxes: Total city taxes per capita: $36 (1997); City property taxes per capita: $34 (1997).
Education: High school graduation rate: 87.9% (2000); College graduation rate: 11.2% (2000).
Housing: Homeownership rate: 92.1% (2000); Median home value: $118,000 (2000); Median rent: $476 per month (2000); Median age of housing: 25 years (2000).
Transportation: Commute to work: 95.5% car, 0.0% public transportation, 1.3% walk, 2.6% work from home (2000); Travel time to work: 16.2% less than 15 minutes, 37.6% 15 to 30 minutes, 13.5% 30 to 45 minutes, 10.2% 45 to 60 minutes, 22.6% 60 minutes or more (2000)

DRYDEN (village). Covers a land area of 1.120 square miles and a water area of 0 square miles. Located at 42.94° N. Lat.; 83.12° W. Long. Elevation is 919 feet.
History: Dryden was first called Lamb's Corners, but was renamed for the English poet, John Dryden. The village developed as the center of a farming and horse-breeding region.
Population: 815 (2000); Race: 96.6% White, 0.4% Black, 0.0% Asian, 0.4% American Indian and Alaska Native, 0.0% Hispanic of any race, 2.7% two or more races (2000); Density: 727.8 persons per square mile (2000); Age: 28.4% under 18, 8.3% over 64 (2000); Marriage status: 20.1% never married, 67.6% now married, 3.0% widowed, 9.3% divorced (2000); Foreign born: 1.3% (2000); Ancestry (includes multiple ancestries): 24.3% German, 12.4% Irish, 11.0% English, 9.4% Polish, 7.3% United States or American (2000).
Economy: Employment by occupation: 6.5% management, 14.7% professional, 15.7% services, 15.9% sales, 0.0% farming, 17.9% construction, 29.2% production (2000).
Income: Per capita income: $21,180 (2000); Median household income: $54,375 (2000); Poverty rate: 5.7% (2000).
Taxes: Total city taxes per capita: $159 (1997); City property taxes per capita: $154 (1997).
Education: High school graduation rate: 85.0% (2000); College graduation rate: 10.9% (2000).

School District(s)

Dryden Community Schools (KG-12)
2000 Enrollment: 846 810-796-9534

Housing: Homeownership rate: 83.6% (2000); Median home value: $113,400 (2000); Median rent: $506 per month (2000); Median age of housing: 37 years (2000).
Transportation: Commute to work: 93.8% car, 0.0% public transportation, 4.0% walk, 0.5% work from home (2000); Travel time to work: 12.4% less than 15 minutes, 31.3% 15 to 30 minutes, 21.6% 30 to 45 minutes, 21.4% 45 to 60 minutes, 13.2% 60 minutes or more (2000)

Additional Information Contacts

Dryden Chamber of Commerce 810-796-3700

DRYDEN (township). Covers a land area of 35.873 square miles and a water area of 0.328 square miles. Located at 42.92° N. Lat.; 83.15° W. Long. Elevation is 919 feet.
Population: 4,624 (2000); Race: 98.2% White, 0.1% Black, 0.3% Asian, 0.1% American Indian and Alaska Native, 0.9% Hispanic of any race, 1.1% two or more races (2000); Density: 128.9 persons per square mile (2000); Age: 28.4% under 18, 8.0% over 64 (2000); Marriage status: 19.3% never married, 70.4% now married, 4.2% widowed, 6.1% divorced (2000); Foreign born: 1.9% (2000); Ancestry (includes multiple ancestries): 26.3% German, 13.1% English, 12.5% Polish, 11.1% Irish, 8.4% Italian (2000).
Economy: Trade center for agricultural and horse-breeding area. Manufacturing: automotive accessories. Employment by occupation: 10.8% management, 21.0% professional, 11.5% services, 22.2% sales, 0.3% farming, 11.7% construction, 22.5% production (2000).
Income: Per capita income: $26,902 (2000); Median household income: $69,659 (2000); Poverty rate: 2.5% (2000).
Taxes: Total city taxes per capita: $335 (2000); City property taxes per capita: $335 (2000).
Education: High school graduation rate: 90.7% (2000); College graduation rate: 18.2% (2000).
Housing: Homeownership rate: 92.8% (2000); Median home value: $151,100 (2000); Median rent: $546 per month (2000); Median age of housing: 21 years (2000).
Safety: Violent crime rate: 2.2 per 10,000 population; Property crime rate: 68.8 per 10,000 population (2001).
Transportation: Commute to work: 94.0% car, 1.0% public transportation, 1.1% walk, 3.4% work from home (2000); Travel time to work: 11.3% less than 15 minutes, 18.3% 15 to 30 minutes, 26.0% 30 to 45 minutes, 22.3% 45 to 60 minutes, 22.1% 60 minutes or more (2000)

ELBA (township). Covers a land area of 32.790 square miles and a water area of 1.209 square miles. Located at 43.02° N. Lat.; 83.41° W. Long. Elevation is 854 feet.
Population: 5,462 (2000); Race: 96.7% White, 0.0% Black, 0.0% Asian, 2.0% American Indian and Alaska Native, 0.4% Hispanic of any race, 1.3% two or more races (2000); Density: 166.6 persons per square mile (2000); Age: 25.2% under 18, 9.3% over 64 (2000); Marriage status: 21.7% never married, 63.2% now married, 4.6% widowed, 10.5% divorced (2000); Foreign born: 1.1% (2000); Ancestry (includes multiple ancestries): 26.2% German, 15.2% English, 13.5% Irish, 8.9% Polish, 7.2% Other groups (2000).
Economy: Employment by occupation: 9.4% management, 19.2% professional, 14.5% services, 21.7% sales, 0.3% farming, 18.2% construction, 16.7% production (2000).
Income: Per capita income: $22,863 (2000); Median household income: $53,614 (2000); Poverty rate: 5.5% (2000).
Taxes: Total city taxes per capita: $55 (1997); City property taxes per capita: $51 (1997).
Education: High school graduation rate: 87.6% (2000); College graduation rate: 16.3% (2000).
Housing: Homeownership rate: 90.8% (2000); Median home value: $139,100 (2000); Median rent: $498 per month (2000); Median age of housing: 26 years (2000).

Transportation: Commute to work: 93.8% car, 0.7% public transportation, 0.4% walk, 5.1% work from home (2000); Travel time to work: 18.3% less than 15 minutes, 34.9% 15 to 30 minutes, 17.1% 30 to 45 minutes, 10.7% 45 to 60 minutes, 19.1% 60 minutes or more (2000)

GOODLAND (township). Covers a land area of 35.646 square miles and a water area of 0.018 square miles. Located at 43.12° N. Lat.; 83.05° W. Long.
History: Goodland Township was organized in 1855. The name was suggested by James Hill, who had settled here in 1851.
Population: 1,734 (2000); Race: 99.0% White, 0.0% Black, 0.2% Asian, 0.0% American Indian and Alaska Native, 2.3% Hispanic of any race, 0.8% two or more races (2000); Density: 48.6 persons per square mile (2000); Age: 29.1% under 18, 9.3% over 64 (2000); Marriage status: 20.9% never married, 66.7% now married, 5.6% widowed, 6.8% divorced (2000); Foreign born: 4.2% (2000); Ancestry (includes multiple ancestries): 37.8% German, 14.1% Polish, 12.6% English, 11.0% Irish, 5.9% United States or American (2000).
Economy: Employment by occupation: 8.4% management, 15.8% professional, 11.1% services, 18.8% sales, 0.9% farming, 18.2% construction, 26.9% production (2000).
Income: Per capita income: $19,999 (2000); Median household income: $51,313 (2000); Poverty rate: 7.0% (2000).
Taxes: Total city taxes per capita: $78 (1997); City property taxes per capita: $76 (1997).
Education: High school graduation rate: 86.3% (2000); College graduation rate: 10.0% (2000).
Housing: Homeownership rate: 88.5% (2000); Median home value: $135,100 (2000); Median rent: $427 per month (2000); Median age of housing: 25 years (2000).
Transportation: Commute to work: 95.5% car, 0.0% public transportation, 0.8% walk, 3.7% work from home (2000); Travel time to work: 18.2% less than 15 minutes, 29.2% 15 to 30 minutes, 13.4% 30 to 45 minutes, 13.5% 45 to 60 minutes, 25.8% 60 minutes or more (2000)

HADLEY (township). Covers a land area of 35.279 square miles and a water area of 0.771 square miles. Located at 42.92° N. Lat.; 83.39° W. Long.
Population: 4,655 (2000); Race: 99.1% White, 0.0% Black, 0.2% Asian, 0.0% American Indian and Alaska Native, 1.4% Hispanic of any race, 0.5% two or more races (2000); Density: 131.9 persons per square mile (2000); Age: 28.0% under 18, 7.2% over 64 (2000); Marriage status: 20.0% never married, 70.2% now married, 4.5% widowed, 5.3% divorced (2000); Foreign born: 3.0% (2000); Ancestry (includes multiple ancestries): 19.1% German, 18.8% English, 15.4% Irish, 13.9% Polish, 5.9% United States or American (2000).
Economy: Employment by occupation: 11.2% management, 15.5% professional, 13.1% services, 19.5% sales, 0.9% farming, 16.6% construction, 23.1% production (2000).
Income: Per capita income: $26,859 (2000); Median household income: $72,381 (2000); Poverty rate: 1.4% (2000).
Taxes: Total city taxes per capita: $57 (1997); City property taxes per capita: $57 (1997).
Education: High school graduation rate: 89.9% (2000); College graduation rate: 16.8% (2000).
Housing: Homeownership rate: 97.6% (2000); Median home value: $168,400 (2000); Median rent: $416 per month (2000); Median age of housing: 23 years (2000).
Transportation: Commute to work: 95.6% car, 0.0% public transportation, 0.6% walk, 3.8% work from home (2000); Travel time to work: 9.1% less than 15 minutes, 23.8% 15 to 30 minutes, 21.5% 30 to 45 minutes, 26.5% 45 to 60 minutes, 19.1% 60 minutes or more (2000)

IMLAY (township). Covers a land area of 33.587 square miles and a water area of 0.136 square miles. Located at 43.01° N. Lat.; 83.04° W. Long.
History: Imlay Township was organized in 1850 and named for William H. Imlay, a Connecticut capitalist who owned land here.
Population: 2,713 (2000); Race: 97.2% White, 0.0% Black, 0.0% Asian, 0.3% American Indian and Alaska Native, 7.7% Hispanic of any race, 0.7% two or more races (2000); Density: 80.8 persons per square mile (2000); Age: 28.6% under 18, 9.8% over 64 (2000); Marriage status: 20.2% never married, 68.8% now married, 4.8% widowed, 6.3% divorced (2000); Foreign born: 4.3% (2000); Ancestry (includes multiple ancestries): 32.2% German, 12.5% English, 10.2% Irish, 9.6% Other groups, 8.4% United States or American (2000).
Economy: Single-family building permits issued: 26 (2001) / 30 (2000); Multi-family building permits issued: 0 (2001) / 0 (2000); Employment by occupation: 10.7% management, 12.6% professional, 12.0% services, 22.6% sales, 0.8% farming, 13.4% construction, 28.0% production (2000).
Income: Per capita income: $21,222 (2000); Median household income: $60,362 (2000); Poverty rate: 4.4% (2000).
Taxes: Total city taxes per capita: $47 (1997); City property taxes per capita: $34 (1997).
Education: High school graduation rate: 83.6% (2000); College graduation rate: 7.6% (2000).
Housing: Homeownership rate: 91.0% (2000); Median home value: $145,300 (2000); Median rent: $452 per month (2000); Median age of housing: 31 years (2000).
Transportation: Commute to work: 95.1% car, 0.0% public transportation, 0.0% walk, 4.5% work from home (2000); Travel time to work: 28.7% less than 15 minutes, 18.6% 15 to 30 minutes, 11.1% 30 to 45 minutes, 20.5% 45 to 60 minutes, 21.0% 60 minutes or more (2000)

IMLAY CITY (city). Covers a land area of 2.289 square miles and a water area of 0 square miles. Located at 43.02° N. Lat.; 83.07° W. Long. Elevation is 830 feet.
History: Imlay City, named for landowner William H. Imlay, began in 1870 when the Port Huron & Lake Michigan Railroad arrived. The town grew as a market center for an agricultural area. Celery was a leading crop in the early 1900's.
Population: 3,869 (2000); Race: 90.1% White, 0.6% Black, 0.7% Asian, 0.0% American Indian and Alaska Native, 18.6% Hispanic of any race, 0.4% two or more races (2000); Density: 1,690.4 persons per square mile (2000); Age: 28.3% under 18, 15.8% over 64 (2000); Marriage status: 25.6% never married, 54.0% now married, 10.2% widowed, 10.2% divorced (2000); Foreign born: 11.3% (2000); Ancestry (includes multiple ancestries): 20.2% Other groups, 18.8% German, 11.1% Irish, 10.6% English, 9.2% Polish (2000).
Economy: Employment by occupation: 8.8% management, 11.0% professional, 16.9% services, 18.1% sales, 0.0% farming, 10.4% construction, 34.9% production (2000).
Income: Per capita income: $16,021 (2000); Median household income: $32,436 (2000); Poverty rate: 8.1% (2000).
Taxes: Total city taxes per capita: $425 (1997); City property taxes per capita: $420 (1997).
Education: High school graduation rate: 72.1% (2000); College graduation rate: 9.9% (2000).

School District(s)

Imlay City Community Schools (PK-12)
2000 Enrollment: 2,211 810-724-9861

Housing: Homeownership rate: 57.0% (2000); Median home value: $112,400 (2000); Median rent: $481 per month (2000); Median age of housing: 27 years (2000).
Safety: Violent crime rate: 38.6 per 10,000 population; Property crime rate: 411.4 per 10,000 population (2001).
Newspapers: Tri-City Times (1 x week)
Transportation: Commute to work: 94.4% car, 0.0% public transportation, 2.5% walk, 2.5% work from home (2000); Travel time to work: 35.8% less than 15 minutes, 16.6% 15 to 30 minutes, 15.5% 30 to 45 minutes, 15.0% 45 to 60 minutes, 17.0% 60 minutes or more (2000)

Additional Information Contacts

Imlay City Chamber of Commerce 810-724-1361

LAPEER (city). Covers a land area of 5.547 square miles and a water area of 0 square miles. Located at 43.05° N. Lat.; 83.31° W. Long. Elevation is 827 feet.
History: Lapeer was founded in 1831, when the Pontiac Mill Company built a sawmill here. Its name comes from the French word for stone, perhaps referring to the flints found along the Flint River. First a lumber town, Lapeer became a furniture manufacturing center.
Population: 9,072 (2000); Race: 91.7% White, 5.6% Black, 0.5% Asian, 0.2% American Indian and Alaska Native, 3.2% Hispanic of any race, 1.3% two or more races (2000); Density: 1,635.5 persons per square mile (2000); Age: 25.0% under 18, 12.0% over 64 (2000); Marriage status: 24.9% never married, 54.1% now married, 7.2% widowed, 13.8% divorced (2000); Foreign born: 1.8% (2000); Ancestry (includes multiple ancestries): 27.2% German, 13.9% English, 13.6% Irish, 8.6% Polish, 8.4% Other groups (2000).
Economy: Single-family building permits issued: 14 (2001) / 26 (2000); Multi-family building permits issued: 0 (2001) / 0 (2000); Employment by occupation: 9.0% management, 15.5% professional, 16.4% services, 23.7% sales, 0.0% farming, 10.6% construction, 24.7% production (2000).

Income: Per capita income: $16,608 (2000); Median household income: $35,526 (2000); Poverty rate: 10.2% (2000).
Taxes: Total city taxes per capita: $558 (2000); City property taxes per capita: $318 (2000).
Education: High school graduation rate: 77.7% (2000); College graduation rate: 8.8% (2000).

School District(s)

Chatfield School (KG-06)
2000 Enrollment: 266 517-790-4000
Lapeer Community Schools (PK-12)
2000 Enrollment: 7,481 810-667-2401

Housing: Homeownership rate: 52.1% (2000); Median home value: $107,900 (2000); Median rent: $468 per month (2000); Median age of housing: 27 years (2000).
Hospitals: Lapeer Regional Hospital (185 beds)
Safety: Violent crime rate: 30.7 per 10,000 population; Property crime rate: 723.7 per 10,000 population (2001).
Transportation: Commute to work: 93.9% car, 1.2% public transportation, 3.1% walk, 0.6% work from home (2000); Travel time to work: 45.2% less than 15 minutes, 15.3% 15 to 30 minutes, 14.2% 30 to 45 minutes, 13.8% 45 to 60 minutes, 11.5% 60 minutes or more (2000); Amtrak: Service available.

Additional Information Contacts

Lapeer & Upper Thumb Association of Realtors...........810-664-0271
Lapeer Area Chamber of Commerce 810-664-6641

LAPEER (township). Covers a land area of 31.990 square miles and a water area of 0.319 square miles. Located at 43.02° N. Lat.; 83.29° W. Long. Elevation is 827 feet.
History: Settled 1831, incorporated as city 1869.
Population: 5,078 (2000); Race: 96.6% White, 0.1% Black, 0.0% Asian, 0.8% American Indian and Alaska Native, 3.1% Hispanic of any race, 2.2% two or more races (2000); Density: 158.7 persons per square mile (2000); Age: 27.4% under 18, 9.6% over 64 (2000); Marriage status: 22.1% never married, 65.4% now married, 4.5% widowed, 8.0% divorced (2000); Foreign born: 1.4% (2000); Ancestry (includes multiple ancestries): 25.5% German, 18.7% English, 16.4% Irish, 8.0% Other groups, 6.8% Polish (2000).
Economy: In dairying and grain-growing area. Manufacturing: metal products, transportation equipment, plastics products, furniture. Has state home and school for mentally ill. Airport to East. Employment by occupation: 13.4% management, 22.4% professional, 14.1% services, 16.2% sales, 0.0% farming, 15.0% construction, 18.9% production (2000).
Income: Per capita income: $23,383 (2000); Median household income: $63,411 (2000); Poverty rate: 4.1% (2000).
Taxes: Total city taxes per capita: $38 (1997); City property taxes per capita: $36 (1997).
Education: High school graduation rate: 88.7% (2000); College graduation rate: 16.5% (2000).
Housing: Homeownership rate: 91.1% (2000); Median home value: $140,300 (2000); Median rent: $445 per month (2000); Median age of housing: 27 years (2000).
Transportation: Commute to work: 95.7% car, 0.0% public transportation, 0.5% walk, 2.5% work from home (2000); Travel time to work: 32.7% less than 15 minutes, 17.5% 15 to 30 minutes, 15.0% 30 to 45 minutes, 15.2% 45 to 60 minutes, 19.6% 60 minutes or more (2000); Amtrak: Service available.

MARATHON (township). Covers a land area of 33.427 square miles and a water area of 0.960 square miles. Located at 43.19° N. Lat.; 83.41° W. Long.
Population: 4,701 (2000); Race: 95.7% White, 0.6% Black, 0.2% Asian, 0.6% American Indian and Alaska Native, 2.3% Hispanic of any race, 1.3% two or more races (2000); Density: 140.6 persons per square mile (2000); Age: 28.7% under 18, 8.9% over 64 (2000); Marriage status: 23.3% never married, 63.8% now married, 5.0% widowed, 8.0% divorced (2000); Foreign born: 0.8% (2000); Ancestry (includes multiple ancestries): 23.6% German, 14.4% English, 13.7% Irish, 10.3% United States or American, 9.7% Other groups (2000).
Economy: Single-family building permits issued: 22 (2001) / 25 (2000); Multi-family building permits issued: 0 (2001) / 0 (2000); Employment by occupation: 7.2% management, 12.8% professional, 11.6% services, 24.3% sales, 0.4% farming, 15.5% construction, 28.2% production (2000).
Income: Per capita income: $19,469 (2000); Median household income: $49,255 (2000); Poverty rate: 7.8% (2000).
Taxes: Total city taxes per capita: $28 (1997); City property taxes per capita: $19 (1997).
Education: High school graduation rate: 79.9% (2000); College graduation rate: 8.0% (2000).
Housing: Homeownership rate: 87.8% (2000); Median home value: $108,300 (2000); Median rent: $415 per month (2000); Median age of housing: 33 years (2000).
Transportation: Commute to work: 94.5% car, 0.6% public transportation, 1.3% walk, 2.9% work from home (2000); Travel time to work: 9.1% less than 15 minutes, 25.8% 15 to 30 minutes, 25.2% 30 to 45 minutes, 14.4% 45 to 60 minutes, 25.5% 60 minutes or more (2000)

MAYFIELD (township). Covers a land area of 34.782 square miles and a water area of 0.277 square miles. Located at 43.09° N. Lat.; 83.28° W. Long.
Population: 7,659 (2000); Race: 97.1% White, 0.0% Black, 0.0% Asian, 1.2% American Indian and Alaska Native, 1.5% Hispanic of any race, 1.5% two or more races (2000); Density: 220.2 persons per square mile (2000); Age: 28.5% under 18, 11.5% over 64 (2000); Marriage status: 19.8% never married, 66.5% now married, 4.5% widowed, 9.2% divorced (2000); Foreign born: 1.6% (2000); Ancestry (includes multiple ancestries): 26.4% German, 15.3% English, 12.0% Irish, 9.5% Other groups, 8.4% Polish (2000).
Economy: Employment by occupation: 9.5% management, 14.2% professional, 13.8% services, 23.2% sales, 0.3% farming, 14.6% construction, 24.4% production (2000).
Income: Per capita income: $20,399 (2000); Median household income: $50,822 (2000); Poverty rate: 4.7% (2000).
Taxes: Total city taxes per capita: $33 (1997); City property taxes per capita: $30 (1997).
Education: High school graduation rate: 84.4% (2000); College graduation rate: 11.9% (2000).
Housing: Homeownership rate: 90.8% (2000); Median home value: $137,800 (2000); Median rent: $383 per month (2000); Median age of housing: 24 years (2000).
Transportation: Commute to work: 96.8% car, 0.2% public transportation, 0.4% walk, 2.1% work from home (2000); Travel time to work: 31.0% less than 15 minutes, 20.7% 15 to 30 minutes, 14.8% 30 to 45 minutes, 11.8% 45 to 60 minutes, 21.6% 60 minutes or more (2000)

METAMORA (village). Covers a land area of 0.662 square miles and a water area of 0 square miles. Located at 42.94° N. Lat.; 83.28° W. Long. Elevation is 1,053 feet.
Population: 507 (2000); Race: 97.3% White, 0.0% Black, 0.2% Asian, 0.5% American Indian and Alaska Native, 1.4% Hispanic of any race, 2.0% two or more races (2000); Density: 765.4 persons per square mile (2000); Age: 26.0% under 18, 9.6% over 64 (2000); Marriage status: 23.2% never married, 60.6% now married, 3.9% widowed, 12.4% divorced (2000); Foreign born: 1.4% (2000); Ancestry (includes multiple ancestries): 28.7% German, 14.4% English, 10.3% Polish, 9.3% Italian, 8.9% Other groups (2000).
Economy: Employment by occupation: 7.5% management, 20.4% professional, 8.6% services, 31.8% sales, 0.0% farming, 12.1% construction, 19.6% production (2000).
Income: Per capita income: $19,548 (2000); Median household income: $58,088 (2000); Poverty rate: 3.6% (2000).
Taxes: Total city taxes per capita: $209 (1997); City property taxes per capita: $206 (1997).
Education: High school graduation rate: 88.2% (2000); College graduation rate: 20.4% (2000).
Housing: Homeownership rate: 83.9% (2000); Median home value: $144,900 (2000); Median rent: $675 per month (2000); Median age of housing: 42 years (2000).
Safety: Violent crime rate: 78.4 per 10,000 population; Property crime rate: 1,568.6 per 10,000 population (2001).
Transportation: Commute to work: 92.3% car, 0.0% public transportation, 4.7% walk, 2.6% work from home (2000); Travel time to work: 26.2% less than 15 minutes, 18.7% 15 to 30 minutes, 22.5% 30 to 45 minutes, 15.4% 45 to 60 minutes, 17.2% 60 minutes or more (2000)

Additional Information Contacts

Metamore Chamber of Commerce 810-678-6222

METAMORA (township). Covers a land area of 34.759 square miles and a water area of 0.560 square miles. Located at 42.92° N. Lat.; 83.29° W. Long. Elevation is 1,053 feet.
Population: 4,184 (2000); Race: 97.4% White, 0.0% Black, 0.1% Asian, 0.3% American Indian and Alaska Native, 0.8% Hispanic of any race, 1.7% two or more races (2000); Density: 120.4 persons per square mile (2000); Age: 26.1% under 18, 9.6% over 64 (2000); Marriage status: 19.6% never married, 67.8% now married, 4.4% widowed, 8.2% divorced (2000); Foreign born: 1.3% (2000); Ancestry (includes multiple ancestries): 27.6% German, 14.8% English, 11.8% Irish, 11.0% Polish, 8.7% United States or American (2000).

Economy: In farm area. Manufacturing: plastic molding, machining. Metamura-Hadley State Recreation Area to West. Single-family building permits issued: 21 (2001) / 24 (2000); Multi-family building permits issued: 0 (2001) / 0 (2000); Employment by occupation: 14.5% management, 22.5% professional, 12.1% services, 22.6% sales, 0.1% farming, 11.9% construction, 16.3% production (2000).
Income: Per capita income: $29,255 (2000); Median household income: $61,250 (2000); Poverty rate: 5.4% (2000).
Taxes: Total city taxes per capita: $146 (1997); City property taxes per capita: $125 (1997).
Education: High school graduation rate: 89.1% (2000); College graduation rate: 23.5% (2000).
Housing: Homeownership rate: 90.5% (2000); Median home value: $176,400 (2000); Median rent: $519 per month (2000); Median age of housing: 23 years (2000).
Transportation: Commute to work: 94.1% car, 0.0% public transportation, 3.8% walk, 1.5% work from home (2000); Travel time to work: 19.0% less than 15 minutes, 23.0% 15 to 30 minutes, 22.6% 30 to 45 minutes, 19.0% 45 to 60 minutes, 16.4% 60 minutes or more (2000)

NORTH BRANCH (village). Covers a land area of 1.276 square miles and a water area of 0 square miles. Located at 43.23° N. Lat.; 83.19° W. Long. Elevation is 816 feet.
Population: 1,027 (2000); Race: 96.6% White, 0.6% Black, 0.0% Asian, 1.0% American Indian and Alaska Native, 3.0% Hispanic of any race, 1.1% two or more races (2000); Density: 804.6 persons per square mile (2000); Age: 29.1% under 18, 16.8% over 64 (2000); Marriage status: 23.6% never married, 51.1% now married, 13.0% widowed, 12.3% divorced (2000); Foreign born: 0.6% (2000); Ancestry (includes multiple ancestries): 23.5% German, 14.5% English, 12.6% Irish, 9.4% Other groups, 6.7% French (except Basque) (2000).
Economy: Employment by occupation: 5.5% management, 13.2% professional, 14.1% services, 29.3% sales, 0.9% farming, 7.3% construction, 29.8% production (2000).
Income: Per capita income: $15,782 (2000); Median household income: $31,071 (2000); Poverty rate: 13.8% (2000).
Taxes: Total city taxes per capita: $197 (1997); City property taxes per capita: $195 (1997).
Education: High school graduation rate: 77.9% (2000); College graduation rate: 6.1% (2000).

School District(s)

North Branch Area Schools (KG-12)
2000 Enrollment: 2,575 810-688-3570
Housing: Homeownership rate: 56.4% (2000); Median home value: $92,400 (2000); Median rent: $382 per month (2000); Median age of housing: 49 years (2000).
Safety: Violent crime rate: 9.7 per 10,000 population; Property crime rate: 271.3 per 10,000 population (2001).
Transportation: Commute to work: 94.0% car, 0.0% public transportation, 4.3% walk, 1.7% work from home (2000); Travel time to work: 29.2% less than 15 minutes, 21.7% 15 to 30 minutes, 24.8% 30 to 45 minutes, 7.8% 45 to 60 minutes, 16.5% 60 minutes or more (2000)

NORTH BRANCH (township). Covers a land area of 36.146 square miles and a water area of 0.173 square miles. Located at 43.20° N. Lat.; 83.18° W. Long. Elevation is 816 feet.
Population: 3,595 (2000); Race: 97.4% White, 0.2% Black, 0.4% Asian, 1.1% American Indian and Alaska Native, 2.4% Hispanic of any race, 0.6% two or more races (2000); Density: 99.5 persons per square mile (2000); Age: 31.9% under 18, 9.8% over 64 (2000); Marriage status: 23.0% never married, 63.3% now married, 6.4% widowed, 7.4% divorced (2000); Foreign born: 0.9% (2000); Ancestry (includes multiple ancestries): 31.1% German, 11.1% Irish, 10.8% English, 8.9% United States or American, 8.6% Polish (2000).
Economy: In area producing livestock; grain, apples, soybeans; dairying. Manufacturing: screw machine products, rolled thread and nuts. Employment by occupation: 6.4% management, 14.8% professional, 13.4% services, 23.5% sales, 1.7% farming, 12.2% construction, 28.1% production (2000).
Income: Per capita income: $16,972 (2000); Median household income: $46,020 (2000); Poverty rate: 5.8% (2000).
Taxes: Total city taxes per capita: $92 (2000); City property taxes per capita: $92 (2000).
Education: High school graduation rate: 84.8% (2000); College graduation rate: 7.4% (2000).
Housing: Homeownership rate: 81.1% (2000); Median home value: $116,700 (2000); Median rent: $383 per month (2000); Median age of housing: 27 years (2000).
Transportation: Commute to work: 94.9% car, 0.0% public transportation, 2.1% walk, 3.0% work from home (2000); Travel time to work: 22.6% less than 15 minutes, 26.5% 15 to 30 minutes, 18.9% 30 to 45 minutes, 9.4% 45 to 60 minutes, 22.6% 60 minutes or more (2000)

OREGON (township). Covers a land area of 33.181 square miles and a water area of 2.073 square miles. Located at 43.10° N. Lat.; 83.40° W. Long.
Population: 6,166 (2000); Race: 97.9% White, 0.1% Black, 0.0% Asian, 0.7% American Indian and Alaska Native, 1.1% Hispanic of any race, 0.8% two or more races (2000); Density: 185.8 persons per square mile (2000); Age: 28.3% under 18, 6.8% over 64 (2000); Marriage status: 22.0% never married, 67.9% now married, 3.3% widowed, 6.9% divorced (2000); Foreign born: 1.6% (2000); Ancestry (includes multiple ancestries): 26.8% German, 14.3% Irish, 12.0% English, 8.6% Other groups, 8.3% United States or American (2000).
Economy: Single-family building permits issued: 20 (2001) / 31 (2000); Multi-family building permits issued: 0 (2001) / 0 (2000); Employment by occupation: 10.3% management, 17.1% professional, 17.4% services, 21.4% sales, 0.2% farming, 11.8% construction, 21.8% production (2000).
Income: Per capita income: $22,788 (2000); Median household income: $60,137 (2000); Poverty rate: 5.7% (2000).
Taxes: Total city taxes per capita: $25 (1997); City property taxes per capita: $23 (1997).
Education: High school graduation rate: 90.3% (2000); College graduation rate: 16.1% (2000).
Housing: Homeownership rate: 94.6% (2000); Median home value: $130,900 (2000); Median rent: $637 per month (2000); Median age of housing: 26 years (2000).
Transportation: Commute to work: 97.5% car, 0.2% public transportation, 0.2% walk, 2.1% work from home (2000); Travel time to work: 16.2% less than 15 minutes, 33.0% 15 to 30 minutes, 22.1% 30 to 45 minutes, 10.8% 45 to 60 minutes, 17.9% 60 minutes or more (2000)

OTTER LAKE (village). Covers a land area of 0.679 square miles and a water area of 0.084 square miles. Located at 43.21° N. Lat.; 83.45° W. Long.
Population: 437 (2000); Race: 92.9% White, 0.0% Black, 0.0% Asian, 2.9% American Indian and Alaska Native, 4.9% Hispanic of any race, 2.7% two or more races (2000); Density: 643.3 persons per square mile (2000); Age: 31.0% under 18, 7.3% over 64 (2000); Marriage status: 27.3% never married, 57.7% now married, 3.6% widowed, 11.4% divorced (2000); Foreign born: 0.7% (2000); Ancestry (includes multiple ancestries): 24.3% German, 18.9% English, 17.4% Other groups, 11.8% United States or American, 9.6% Irish (2000).
Economy: Employment by occupation: 6.2% management, 13.8% professional, 15.2% services, 23.3% sales, 0.0% farming, 17.1% construction, 24.3% production (2000).
Income: Per capita income: $17,927 (2000); Median household income: $49,000 (2000); Poverty rate: 7.8% (2000).
Taxes: Total city taxes per capita: $134 (1997); City property taxes per capita: $134 (1997).
Education: High school graduation rate: 80.4% (2000); College graduation rate: 10.9% (2000).
Housing: Homeownership rate: 71.3% (2000); Median home value: $79,300 (2000); Median rent: $423 per month (2000); Median age of housing: 51 years (2000).
Transportation: Commute to work: 92.7% car, 0.0% public transportation, 4.4% walk, 2.9% work from home (2000); Travel time to work: 13.6% less than 15 minutes, 15.1% 15 to 30 minutes, 36.2% 30 to 45 minutes, 14.1% 45 to 60 minutes, 21.1% 60 minutes or more (2000)

RICH (township). Covers a land area of 35.239 square miles and a water area of 0.098 square miles. Located at 43.28° N. Lat.; 83.29° W. Long.
History: Rich was settled in the mid-1850's and grew around a grist mill. Rich Township, organized in 1858, was named for Charles Rich.
Population: 1,412 (2000); Race: 97.5% White, 1.0% Black, 0.0% Asian, 0.8% American Indian and Alaska Native, 1.0% Hispanic of any race, 0.8% two or more races (2000); Density: 40.1 persons per square mile (2000); Age: 29.3% under 18, 10.3% over 64 (2000); Marriage status: 21.8% never married, 66.3% now married, 5.5% widowed, 6.4% divorced (2000); Foreign born: 1.4% (2000); Ancestry (includes multiple ancestries): 26.1% German, 12.5% English, 9.6% Irish, 9.4% United States or American, 8.7% Other groups (2000).
Economy: Employment by occupation: 11.4% management, 16.3% professional, 13.1% services, 20.2% sales, 1.5% farming, 14.1% construction, 23.4% production (2000).

Income: Per capita income: $19,968 (2000); Median household income: $47,212 (2000); Poverty rate: 5.5% (2000).
Taxes: Total city taxes per capita: $34 (1997); City property taxes per capita: $33 (1997).
Education: High school graduation rate: 83.0% (2000); College graduation rate: 9.1% (2000).
Housing: Homeownership rate: 86.7% (2000); Median home value: $105,600 (2000); Median rent: $425 per month (2000); Median age of housing: 30 years (2000).
Transportation: Commute to work: 93.2% car, 0.0% public transportation, 2.4% walk, 3.3% work from home (2000); Travel time to work: 15.0% less than 15 minutes, 34.3% 15 to 30 minutes, 13.6% 30 to 45 minutes, 13.1% 45 to 60 minutes, 23.9% 60 minutes or more (2000)

SILVERWOOD (unincorporated postal area, zip code 48760). Covers a land area of 26.310 square miles and a water area of 0.177 square miles. Located at 43.33° N. Lat.; 83.25° W. Long.
Population: 1,133 (2000); Race: 92.9% White, 4.5% Black, 0.4% Asian, 0.0% American Indian and Alaska Native, 0.9% Hispanic of any race, 1.5% two or more races (2000); Density: 43.1 persons per square mile (2000); Age: 26.4% under 18, 14.1% over 64 (2000); Marriage status: 21.4% never married, 59.8% now married, 6.8% widowed, 11.9% divorced (2000); Foreign born: 1.9% (2000); Ancestry (includes multiple ancestries): 21.3% German, 13.7% English, 10.4% Irish, 9.3% Polish, 7.7% Other groups (2000).
Economy: Employment by occupation: 10.4% management, 13.6% professional, 11.7% services, 17.1% sales, 4.5% farming, 16.6% construction, 26.1% production (2000).
Income: Per capita income: $16,909 (2000); Median household income: $36,136 (2000); Poverty rate: 9.2% (2000).
Education: High school graduation rate: 82.8% (2000); College graduation rate: 6.5% (2000).
Housing: Homeownership rate: 87.2% (2000); Median home value: $91,900 (2000); Median rent: $402 per month (2000); Median age of housing: 33 years (2000).
Transportation: Commute to work: 89.8% car, 0.0% public transportation, 2.4% walk, 6.0% work from home (2000); Travel time to work: 17.0% less than 15 minutes, 27.7% 15 to 30 minutes, 17.5% 30 to 45 minutes, 11.1% 45 to 60 minutes, 26.7% 60 minutes or more (2000)

Leelanau County

Located in northwestern Michigan; a peninsula, bounded on the west by Lake Michigan, and on the east by Grand Traverse Bay; includes Leelanau and Glen Lakes. Covers a land area of 348.50 square miles, a water area of 2,183.90 square miles, and is located in the Eastern Time Zone. The county government was organized in 1863. County seat is Leland.

Weather Station: Maple City — Elevation: 728 feet

	Jan	Feb	Mar	Apr	May	Jun	Jul	Aug	Sep	Oct	Nov	Dec
High	28	32	41	54	68	77	81	79	71	59	45	33
Low	15	15	22	32	42	51	57	56	50	40	30	21
Precip	2.9	1.8	2.2	2.6	2.7	2.9	3.0	3.3	4.1	3.3	3.2	2.8
Snow	51.0	29.2	16.2	3.8	tr	0.0	0.0	0.0	tr	0.3	12.9	38.0

High and Low temperatures in degrees Fahrenheit; Precipitation and Snow in inches

Population: 21,119 (2000); Race: 93.7% White, 0.1% Black, 0.3% Asian, 3.8% American Indian and Alaska Native, 2.7% Hispanic of any race, 1.1% two or more races (2000); Density: 60.6 persons per square mile (2000); Age: 24.4% under 18, 17.4% over 64 (2000).
Religion: Five largest groups: 24.3% Catholic Church, 2.4% The United Methodist Church, 2.3% Lutheran Church—Missouri Synod, 2.3% Evangelical Lutheran Church in America, 1.8% Reformed Church in America (2000).
Economy: Unemployment rate: 3.8% (11/2002); Total civilian labor force: 11,268 (11/2002); Leading industries: 18.6% construction; 16.5% accommodation & food services; 14.7% retail trade (2000); Companies that employ more than 1,000 persons: 0 (2000); Companies that employ more than 100 persons: 3 (2000); Farms: 369 totaling 62,129 acres (1997); Minority business ownership rate: 0.0% (1997); Women business ownership rate: 18.3% (1997); Retail sales per capita: $4,887 (1997). Single-family building permits issued: 252 (2001) / 276 (2000); Multi-family building permits issued: 0 (2001) / 53 (2000).
Income: Per capita income: $24,686 (2000); Median household income: $47,062 (2000); Poverty rate: 5.4% (2000); Bankruptcy rate: 1.73% (2001).
Taxes: Total county taxes per capita: $303 (2000); County property taxes per capita: $269 (2000).
Education: High school graduation rate: 90.7% (2000); College graduation rate: 31.4% (2000).
Housing: Homeownership rate: 84.7% (2000); Median home value: $165,400 (2000); Median rent: $466 per month (2000); Median age of housing: 24 years (2000).
Health: Birth rate: 88.6 per 10,000 population (1998); Age adjusted death rate: 73.2 per 10,000 population (1999); Age adjusted cancer mortality rate: 188.5 deaths per 100,000 population (1999). Number of physicians: 7.1 per 10,000 population (1999); Number of hospital beds: 45.0 per 10,000 population (1999).
Elections: 2000 Presidential election results: 38.6% Gore, 57.0% Bush, 3.8% Nader, 0.1% Buchanan
National and State Parks: D H Day State Park; Fife Lake State Forest; Sleeping Bear Dunes National Lakeshore
Additional Information Contacts
Leelanau County Government Offices.................... 231-256-9711
Glen Lake Chamber of Commerce.......................... 231-334-3238
Leelanau Chamber of Commerce............................ 231-256-9895
Sutton Bay Chamber of Commerce......................... 231-271-5077

Leelanau County Communities

BINGHAM (township). Covers a land area of 23.579 square miles and a water area of 15.745 square miles. Located at 44.92° N. Lat.; 85.66° W. Long.
History: Bingham Township was named for former Michigan Governor Kingsley Bingham in 1861.
Population: 2,425 (2000); Race: 97.1% White, 0.0% Black, 0.2% Asian, 1.6% American Indian and Alaska Native, 1.8% Hispanic of any race, 0.9% two or more races (2000); Density: 102.8 persons per square mile (2000); Age: 24.3% under 18, 16.1% over 64 (2000); Marriage status: 19.7% never married, 69.7% now married, 4.0% widowed, 6.5% divorced (2000); Foreign born: 2.2% (2000); Ancestry (includes multiple ancestries): 30.2% German, 14.7% English, 11.3% Irish, 11.3% Polish, 11.1% French (except Basque) (2000).
Economy: Employment by occupation: 14.6% management, 22.1% professional, 14.7% services, 27.6% sales, 1.3% farming, 11.4% construction, 8.3% production (2000).
Income: Per capita income: $25,936 (2000); Median household income: $52,813 (2000); Poverty rate: 5.1% (2000).
Taxes: Total city taxes per capita: $36 (1997); City property taxes per capita: $33 (1997).
Education: High school graduation rate: 92.3% (2000); College graduation rate: 32.8% (2000).
Housing: Homeownership rate: 89.5% (2000); Median home value: $164,100 (2000); Median rent: $575 per month (2000); Median age of housing: 22 years (2000).
Transportation: Commute to work: 89.2% car, 0.9% public transportation, 2.3% walk, 7.5% work from home (2000); Travel time to work: 27.2% less than 15 minutes, 44.8% 15 to 30 minutes, 23.2% 30 to 45 minutes, 2.6% 45 to 60 minutes, 2.3% 60 minutes or more (2000)

CEDAR (unincorporated postal area, zip code 49621). Covers a land area of 54.758 square miles and a water area of 0.068 square miles. Located at 44.87° N. Lat.; 85.78° W. Long. Elevation is 596 feet.
History: Benjamin Boughey founded the community of Cedar in 1885 as a lumber town, named for the cedar forests that surrounded it.
Population: 2,711 (2000); Race: 97.7% White, 0.2% Black, 0.2% Asian, 0.6% American Indian and Alaska Native, 2.1% Hispanic of any race, 0.8% two or more races (2000); Density: 49.5 persons per square mile (2000); Age: 27.7% under 18, 14.8% over 64 (2000); Marriage status: 21.5% never married, 66.5% now married, 5.3% widowed, 6.7% divorced (2000); Foreign born: 1.5% (2000); Ancestry (includes multiple ancestries): 27.9% German, 21.4% Polish, 13.5% English, 12.1% Irish, 10.9% French (except Basque) (2000).
Economy: Employment by occupation: 13.2% management, 18.8% professional, 15.9% services, 22.3% sales, 3.1% farming, 15.7% construction, 11.0% production (2000).
Income: Per capita income: $19,067 (2000); Median household income: $44,261 (2000); Poverty rate: 6.2% (2000).
Education: High school graduation rate: 86.1% (2000); College graduation rate: 23.3% (2000).

Housing: Homeownership rate: 88.0% (2000); Median home value: $136,000 (2000); Median rent: $458 per month (2000); Median age of housing: 22 years (2000).
Transportation: Commute to work: 90.1% car, 0.4% public transportation, 1.9% walk, 7.6% work from home (2000); Travel time to work: 21.0% less than 15 minutes, 42.6% 15 to 30 minutes, 27.6% 30 to 45 minutes, 2.9% 45 to 60 minutes, 6.0% 60 minutes or more (2000)

CENTERVILLE (township). Covers a land area of 27.735 square miles and a water area of 2.695 square miles. Located at 44.91° N. Lat.; 85.76° W. Long.
Population: 1,095 (2000); Race: 98.5% White, 0.0% Black, 0.0% Asian, 0.9% American Indian and Alaska Native, 3.5% Hispanic of any race, 0.0% two or more races (2000); Density: 39.5 persons per square mile (2000); Age: 24.3% under 18, 18.1% over 64 (2000); Marriage status: 16.3% never married, 72.2% now married, 4.7% widowed, 6.7% divorced (2000); Foreign born: 2.0% (2000); Ancestry (includes multiple ancestries): 32.2% German, 24.5% Polish, 13.2% Irish, 11.3% French (except Basque), 11.3% English (2000).
Economy: Employment by occupation: 13.1% management, 17.3% professional, 14.2% services, 20.6% sales, 5.0% farming, 19.0% construction, 10.9% production (2000).
Income: Per capita income: $18,707 (2000); Median household income: $43,214 (2000); Poverty rate: 7.0% (2000).
Taxes: Total city taxes per capita: $30 (1997); City property taxes per capita: $29 (1997).
Education: High school graduation rate: 85.8% (2000); College graduation rate: 22.0% (2000).
Housing: Homeownership rate: 87.4% (2000); Median home value: $150,000 (2000); Median rent: $465 per month (2000); Median age of housing: 22 years (2000).
Transportation: Commute to work: 91.9% car, 0.0% public transportation, 2.3% walk, 5.8% work from home (2000); Travel time to work: 21.9% less than 15 minutes, 34.1% 15 to 30 minutes, 29.7% 30 to 45 minutes, 4.2% 45 to 60 minutes, 10.2% 60 minutes or more (2000)

CLEVELAND (township). Covers a land area of 30.948 square miles and a water area of 39.707 square miles. Located at 44.90° N. Lat.; 85.86° W. Long.
Population: 1,040 (2000); Race: 98.3% White, 0.0% Black, 0.0% Asian, 0.0% American Indian and Alaska Native, 0.8% Hispanic of any race, 1.1% two or more races (2000); Density: 33.6 persons per square mile (2000); Age: 23.3% under 18, 18.8% over 64 (2000); Marriage status: 19.5% never married, 65.9% now married, 8.1% widowed, 6.5% divorced (2000); Foreign born: 1.9% (2000); Ancestry (includes multiple ancestries): 29.3% German, 18.0% Polish, 12.3% Irish, 11.5% English, 7.7% United States or American (2000).
Economy: Employment by occupation: 18.0% management, 21.3% professional, 11.1% services, 22.3% sales, 1.0% farming, 12.3% construction, 14.0% production (2000).
Income: Per capita income: $25,796 (2000); Median household income: $45,625 (2000); Poverty rate: 6.2% (2000).
Taxes: Total city taxes per capita: $37 (1997); City property taxes per capita: $36 (1997).
Education: High school graduation rate: 88.5% (2000); College graduation rate: 28.9% (2000).
Housing: Homeownership rate: 89.0% (2000); Median home value: $172,700 (2000); Median rent: $450 per month (2000); Median age of housing: 23 years (2000).
Transportation: Commute to work: 91.6% car, 1.8% public transportation, 1.1% walk, 5.1% work from home (2000); Travel time to work: 24.5% less than 15 minutes, 29.4% 15 to 30 minutes, 34.3% 30 to 45 minutes, 6.7% 45 to 60 minutes, 5.1% 60 minutes or more (2000)

ELMWOOD CHARTER (township). Covers a land area of 20.056 square miles and a water area of 10.842 square miles. Located at 44.80° N. Lat.; 85.67° W. Long.
Population: 4,264 (2000); Race: 97.1% White, 0.0% Black, 0.2% Asian, 1.5% American Indian and Alaska Native, 0.9% Hispanic of any race, 0.9% two or more races (2000); Density: 212.6 persons per square mile (2000); Age: 24.2% under 18, 14.8% over 64 (2000); Marriage status: 20.6% never married, 66.3% now married, 6.0% widowed, 7.2% divorced (2000); Foreign born: 1.9% (2000); Ancestry (includes multiple ancestries): 32.1% German, 16.9% Irish, 15.1% English, 9.8% Polish, 8.6% French (except Basque) (2000).
Economy: Employment by occupation: 11.8% management, 23.3% professional, 15.1% services, 27.7% sales, 0.7% farming, 10.0% construction, 11.5% production (2000).
Income: Per capita income: $27,574 (2000); Median household income: $51,063 (2000); Poverty rate: 3.3% (2000).
Taxes: Total city taxes per capita: $55 (1997); City property taxes per capita: $53 (1997).
Education: High school graduation rate: 92.1% (2000); College graduation rate: 30.0% (2000).
Housing: Homeownership rate: 87.2% (2000); Median home value: $145,900 (2000); Median rent: $525 per month (2000); Median age of housing: 23 years (2000).
Transportation: Commute to work: 93.9% car, 0.3% public transportation, 0.9% walk, 4.6% work from home (2000); Travel time to work: 26.1% less than 15 minutes, 56.7% 15 to 30 minutes, 11.4% 30 to 45 minutes, 2.2% 45 to 60 minutes, 3.6% 60 minutes or more (2000)

EMPIRE (village). Covers a land area of 1.151 square miles and a water area of 0.086 square miles. Located at 44.81° N. Lat.; 86.05° W. Long. Elevation is 619 feet.
History: Empire began as a lumber town, boasting the largest sawmill in Leelanau County at one time. Later, cherry orchards became the source of revenue.
Population: 378 (2000); Race: 97.1% White, 0.5% Black, 1.9% Asian, 0.5% American Indian and Alaska Native, 0.0% Hispanic of any race, 0.0% two or more races (2000); Density: 328.5 persons per square mile (2000); Age: 13.5% under 18, 22.2% over 64 (2000); Marriage status: 20.8% never married, 58.5% now married, 8.6% widowed, 12.2% divorced (2000); Foreign born: 2.4% (2000); Ancestry (includes multiple ancestries): 25.7% German, 22.2% English, 21.7% Irish, 7.1% French (except Basque), 6.6% Polish (2000).
Economy: Employment by occupation: 13.9% management, 17.5% professional, 16.5% services, 24.7% sales, 1.0% farming, 17.0% construction, 9.3% production (2000).
Income: Per capita income: $27,850 (2000); Median household income: $39,722 (2000); Poverty rate: 7.4% (2000).
Taxes: Total city taxes per capita: $362 (1997); City property taxes per capita: $362 (1997).
Education: High school graduation rate: 92.8% (2000); College graduation rate: 30.3% (2000).
Housing: Homeownership rate: 74.3% (2000); Median home value: $129,700 (2000); Median rent: $432 per month (2000); Median age of housing: 49 years (2000).
Transportation: Commute to work: 81.7% car, 0.0% public transportation, 5.4% walk, 10.8% work from home (2000); Travel time to work: 39.2% less than 15 minutes, 18.1% 15 to 30 minutes, 19.3% 30 to 45 minutes, 20.5% 45 to 60 minutes, 3.0% 60 minutes or more (2000)

EMPIRE (township). Covers a land area of 35.266 square miles and a water area of 7.556 square miles. Located at 44.83° N. Lat.; 86.01° W. Long. Elevation is 619 feet.
Population: 1,085 (2000); Race: 98.2% White, 0.2% Black, 0.6% Asian, 1.0% American Indian and Alaska Native, 0.0% Hispanic of any race, 0.0% two or more races (2000); Density: 30.8 persons per square mile (2000); Age: 19.3% under 18, 20.9% over 64 (2000); Marriage status: 18.4% never married, 63.7% now married, 7.1% widowed, 10.9% divorced (2000); Foreign born: 1.5% (2000); Ancestry (includes multiple ancestries): 27.6% German, 19.2% English, 17.6% Irish, 7.6% French (except Basque), 7.5% Dutch (2000).
Economy: In cherry and grape-growing region; winery; apple juice and fruit processing. Resort area. Sleeping Bear Dunes National Lakeshore to North and South; Timber Lake ski area to East. Employment by occupation: 15.1% management, 21.3% professional, 17.5% services, 20.9% sales, 0.4% farming, 16.1% construction, 8.6% production (2000).
Income: Per capita income: $24,975 (2000); Median household income: $40,263 (2000); Poverty rate: 6.3% (2000).
Taxes: Total city taxes per capita: $101 (1997); City property taxes per capita: $99 (1997).
Education: High school graduation rate: 93.0% (2000); College graduation rate: 33.9% (2000).
Housing: Homeownership rate: 83.1% (2000); Median home value: $148,300 (2000); Median rent: $446 per month (2000); Median age of housing: 34 years (2000).
Transportation: Commute to work: 85.8% car, 0.4% public transportation, 2.7% walk, 9.8% work from home (2000); Travel time to work: 33.3% less

than 15 minutes, 24.5% 15 to 30 minutes, 27.5% 30 to 45 minutes, 12.5% 45 to 60 minutes, 2.1% 60 minutes or more (2000)

GLEN ARBOR (township). Covers a land area of 28.590 square miles and a water area of 58.985 square miles. Located at 44.89° N. Lat.; 85.99° W. Long. Elevation is 591 feet.
Population: 788 (2000); Race: 99.4% White, 0.0% Black, 0.0% Asian, 0.0% American Indian and Alaska Native, 0.6% Hispanic of any race, 0.6% two or more races (2000); Density: 27.6 persons per square mile (2000); Age: 16.7% under 18, 31.0% over 64 (2000); Marriage status: 15.2% never married, 70.6% now married, 7.6% widowed, 6.6% divorced (2000); Foreign born: 1.6% (2000); Ancestry (includes multiple ancestries): 31.4% German, 23.8% English, 12.6% Irish, 7.4% Scottish, 6.7% United States or American (2000).
Economy: Employment by occupation: 24.9% management, 27.7% professional, 10.8% services, 21.8% sales, 0.0% farming, 8.3% construction, 6.5% production (2000).
Income: Per capita income: $29,070 (2000); Median household income: $46,719 (2000); Poverty rate: 5.1% (2000).
Taxes: Total city taxes per capita: $512 (1997); City property taxes per capita: $511 (1997).
Education: High school graduation rate: 96.1% (2000); College graduation rate: 53.8% (2000).
Housing: Homeownership rate: 89.6% (2000); Median home value: $298,000 (2000); Median rent: $575 per month (2000); Median age of housing: 22 years (2000).
Transportation: Commute to work: 79.6% car, 0.6% public transportation, 6.3% walk, 12.6% work from home (2000); Travel time to work: 57.9% less than 15 minutes, 12.9% 15 to 30 minutes, 17.6% 30 to 45 minutes, 8.3% 45 to 60 minutes, 3.2% 60 minutes or more (2000)
Additional Information Contacts
Glen Lake Chamber of Commerce........................231-334-3238

GREILICKVILLE (CDP). Covers a land area of 4.501 square miles and a water area of 2.384 square miles. Located at 44.79° N. Lat.; 85.64° W. Long.
History: Greilickville was first called Norristown in honor of two brothers who founded the village and built a gristmill, tannery and brickyard. The name of Greilickville came from Godfrey Greilick and his sons (John, Anthony, and Edward) who came from Austria in 1848. One of the seven sawmills operated by the Greilicks was at Morristown. The Greilickville name came into use when the Manistee & Northwestern Railroad called its station that in 1893.
Population: 1,415 (2000); Race: 97.6% White, 0.0% Black, 0.0% Asian, 0.3% American Indian and Alaska Native, 1.5% Hispanic of any race, 1.5% two or more races (2000); Density: 314.4 persons per square mile (2000); Age: 20.3% under 18, 23.6% over 64 (2000); Marriage status: 18.4% never married, 64.2% now married, 10.0% widowed, 7.5% divorced (2000); Foreign born: 1.6% (2000); Ancestry (includes multiple ancestries): 36.9% German, 21.0% Irish, 18.9% English, 9.6% Polish, 8.2% French (except Basque) (2000).
Economy: Employment by occupation: 9.9% management, 24.4% professional, 24.7% services, 26.6% sales, 0.0% farming, 7.7% construction, 6.7% production (2000).
Income: Per capita income: $30,822 (2000); Median household income: $48,269 (2000); Poverty rate: 1.2% (2000).
Education: High school graduation rate: 89.8% (2000); College graduation rate: 27.5% (2000).
Housing: Homeownership rate: 87.2% (2000); Median home value: $136,100 (2000); Median rent: $603 per month (2000); Median age of housing: 25 years (2000).
Transportation: Commute to work: 95.4% car, 1.0% public transportation, 0.9% walk, 2.7% work from home (2000); Travel time to work: 31.7% less than 15 minutes, 47.6% 15 to 30 minutes, 12.7% 30 to 45 minutes, 3.5% 45 to 60 minutes, 4.5% 60 minutes or more (2000)

KASSON (township). Covers a land area of 35.922 square miles and a water area of 0.303 square miles. Located at 44.82° N. Lat.; 85.87° W. Long.
History: Kasson Township was organized in 1865 and named for Kasson Freeman, county surveyor.
Population: 1,577 (2000); Race: 97.7% White, 0.3% Black, 0.0% Asian, 1.1% American Indian and Alaska Native, 2.0% Hispanic of any race, 0.7% two or more races (2000); Density: 43.9 persons per square mile (2000); Age: 30.9% under 18, 9.5% over 64 (2000); Marriage status: 20.6% never married, 63.5% now married, 5.6% widowed, 10.2% divorced (2000); Foreign born: 1.0% (2000); Ancestry (includes multiple ancestries): 32.2% German, 16.8% English, 16.3% Polish, 12.8% Irish, 7.1% French (except Basque) (2000).
Economy: Employment by occupation: 9.5% management, 16.9% professional, 17.2% services, 23.1% sales, 0.4% farming, 18.5% construction, 14.3% production (2000).
Income: Per capita income: $19,319 (2000); Median household income: $41,726 (2000); Poverty rate: 5.1% (2000).
Taxes: Total city taxes per capita: $23 (1997); City property taxes per capita: $22 (1997).
Education: High school graduation rate: 89.6% (2000); College graduation rate: 20.2% (2000).
Housing: Homeownership rate: 80.2% (2000); Median home value: $116,700 (2000); Median rent: $428 per month (2000); Median age of housing: 23 years (2000).
Transportation: Commute to work: 91.1% car, 0.7% public transportation, 0.6% walk, 7.0% work from home (2000); Travel time to work: 20.3% less than 15 minutes, 41.6% 15 to 30 minutes, 27.5% 30 to 45 minutes, 5.4% 45 to 60 minutes, 5.1% 60 minutes or more (2000)

LAKE LEELANAU (unincorporated postal area, zip code 49653). Covers a land area of 30.697 square miles and a water area of 0.055 square miles. Located at 44.97° N. Lat.; 85.72° W. Long. Elevation is 607 feet.
History: The town of Lake Leelanau was located at the narrows of Carp Lake and first called Le Naro. The name of Leelanau is of Indian origin meaning "delight of life."
Population: 2,086 (2000); Race: 96.1% White, 0.0% Black, 0.4% Asian, 1.7% American Indian and Alaska Native, 3.6% Hispanic of any race, 0.6% two or more races (2000); Density: 68.0 persons per square mile (2000); Age: 24.7% under 18, 17.4% over 64 (2000); Marriage status: 19.2% never married, 69.0% now married, 5.0% widowed, 6.9% divorced (2000); Foreign born: 2.6% (2000); Ancestry (includes multiple ancestries): 31.2% German, 16.5% French (except Basque), 14.0% Polish, 11.3% English, 10.7% Irish (2000).
Economy: Employment by occupation: 14.8% management, 17.7% professional, 15.4% services, 25.7% sales, 1.4% farming, 15.8% construction, 9.3% production (2000).
Income: Per capita income: $25,453 (2000); Median household income: $45,183 (2000); Poverty rate: 3.2% (2000).
Education: High school graduation rate: 90.7% (2000); College graduation rate: 31.0% (2000).
Housing: Homeownership rate: 84.7% (2000); Median home value: $175,400 (2000); Median rent: $437 per month (2000); Median age of housing: 30 years (2000).
Transportation: Commute to work: 89.6% car, 1.1% public transportation, 2.6% walk, 6.4% work from home (2000); Travel time to work: 39.7% less than 15 minutes, 25.6% 15 to 30 minutes, 24.8% 30 to 45 minutes, 6.3% 45 to 60 minutes, 3.6% 60 minutes or more (2000)
Additional Information Contacts
Leelanau Chamber of Commerce............................231-256-9895

LEELANAU (township). Covers a land area of 49.210 square miles and a water area of 178.349 square miles. Located at 45.10° N. Lat.; 85.62° W. Long.
History: The name of Leelanau is of Indian origin and means "delight of life."
Population: 2,139 (2000); Race: 93.0% White, 0.0% Black, 0.0% Asian, 3.6% American Indian and Alaska Native, 6.8% Hispanic of any race, 2.1% two or more races (2000); Density: 43.5 persons per square mile (2000); Age: 19.9% under 18, 26.0% over 64 (2000); Marriage status: 14.6% never married, 66.4% now married, 8.8% widowed, 10.2% divorced (2000); Foreign born: 3.6% (2000); Ancestry (includes multiple ancestries): 22.1% German, 20.0% English, 13.0% Irish, 11.0% Other groups, 8.2% Norwegian (2000).
Economy: Employment by occupation: 13.3% management, 21.0% professional, 15.6% services, 21.5% sales, 2.9% farming, 12.2% construction, 13.5% production (2000).
Income: Per capita income: $23,799 (2000); Median household income: $42,112 (2000); Poverty rate: 8.6% (2000).
Taxes: Total city taxes per capita: $216 (1997); City property taxes per capita: $214 (1997).
Education: High school graduation rate: 89.4% (2000); College graduation rate: 34.9% (2000).
Housing: Homeownership rate: 82.5% (2000); Median home value: $178,100 (2000); Median rent: $461 per month (2000); Median age of housing: 26 years (2000).
Transportation: Commute to work: 85.8% car, 0.2% public transportation, 5.2% walk, 8.3% work from home (2000); Travel time to work: 54.3% less

than 15 minutes, 21.3% 15 to 30 minutes, 12.5% 30 to 45 minutes, 5.6% 45 to 60 minutes, 6.3% 60 minutes or more (2000)

LELAND (township). Covers a land area of 45.607 square miles and a water area of 100.878 square miles. Located at 45.01° N. Lat.; 85.73° W. Long. Elevation is 602 feet.
History: Leland developed as a summer resort and a community of commercial fishermen. A sawmill was erected here in 1853, and docks supplied cordwood to steamers.
Population: 2,033 (2000); Race: 96.4% White, 0.0% Black, 0.4% Asian, 0.8% American Indian and Alaska Native, 3.7% Hispanic of any race, 1.2% two or more races (2000); Density: 44.6 persons per square mile (2000); Age: 22.2% under 18, 21.6% over 64 (2000); Marriage status: 18.0% never married, 66.9% now married, 6.7% widowed, 8.3% divorced (2000); Foreign born: 2.1% (2000); Ancestry (includes multiple ancestries): 31.0% German, 17.0% English, 12.8% Irish, 12.2% French (except Basque), 10.6% Polish (2000).
Economy: Employment by occupation: 17.7% management, 16.8% professional, 15.0% services, 28.7% sales, 1.0% farming, 11.6% construction, 9.1% production (2000).
Income: Per capita income: $27,556 (2000); Median household income: $46,629 (2000); Poverty rate: 3.2% (2000).
Taxes: Total city taxes per capita: $120 (1997); City property taxes per capita: $119 (1997).
Education: High school graduation rate: 92.4% (2000); College graduation rate: 38.9% (2000).

School District(s)

Leland Public School District (KG-12)
2000 Enrollment: 423 231-256-9857

Housing: Homeownership rate: 84.5% (2000); Median home value: $223,200 (2000); Median rent: $442 per month (2000); Median age of housing: 37 years (2000).
Newspapers: The Leelanau Enterprise and Tribune (1 x week)
Transportation: Commute to work: 85.0% car, 1.7% public transportation, 3.8% walk, 8.5% work from home (2000); Travel time to work: 44.6% less than 15 minutes, 21.4% 15 to 30 minutes, 23.0% 30 to 45 minutes, 8.8% 45 to 60 minutes, 2.1% 60 minutes or more (2000)

MAPLE CITY (unincorporated postal area, zip code 49664). Covers a land area of 83.521 square miles and a water area of 1.268 square miles. Located at 44.88° N. Lat.; 85.89° W. Long. Elevation is 716 feet.
Population: 2,047 (2000); Race: 98.1% White, 0.1% Black, 0.0% Asian, 0.6% American Indian and Alaska Native, 1.0% Hispanic of any race, 0.9% two or more races (2000); Density: 24.5 persons per square mile (2000); Age: 26.2% under 18, 13.7% over 64 (2000); Marriage status: 19.7% never married, 65.3% now married, 6.7% widowed, 8.3% divorced (2000); Foreign born: 0.8% (2000); Ancestry (includes multiple ancestries): 34.1% German, 16.4% Polish, 15.2% English, 12.6% Irish, 6.8% French (except Basque) (2000).
Economy: Employment by occupation: 13.3% management, 17.9% professional, 16.0% services, 23.6% sales, 0.4% farming, 15.5% construction, 13.2% production (2000).
Income: Per capita income: $23,906 (2000); Median household income: $44,837 (2000); Poverty rate: 5.5% (2000).
Education: High school graduation rate: 90.6% (2000); College graduation rate: 26.3% (2000).

School District(s)

Glen Lake Community Schools (KG-12)
2000 Enrollment: 949 231-334-3061

Housing: Homeownership rate: 82.2% (2000); Median home value: $152,800 (2000); Median rent: $447 per month (2000); Median age of housing: 26 years (2000).
Transportation: Commute to work: 90.9% car, 1.2% public transportation, 0.6% walk, 6.5% work from home (2000); Travel time to work: 26.1% less than 15 minutes, 34.5% 15 to 30 minutes, 28.9% 30 to 45 minutes, 6.9% 45 to 60 minutes, 3.6% 60 minutes or more (2000)

NORTHPORT (village). Covers a land area of 1.663 square miles and a water area of 0 square miles. Located at 45.13° N. Lat.; 85.61° W. Long. Elevation is 624 feet.
History: Northport was an important shipping center during the last half of the 19th century.
Population: 648 (2000); Race: 93.9% White, 0.0% Black, 0.0% Asian, 3.2% American Indian and Alaska Native, 5.1% Hispanic of any race, 1.5% two or more races (2000); Density: 389.7 persons per square mile (2000); Age: 15.6% under 18, 36.0% over 64 (2000); Marriage status: 14.9% never married, 55.7% now married, 13.8% widowed, 15.6% divorced (2000); Foreign born: 2.0% (2000); Ancestry (includes multiple ancestries): 22.8% German, 18.2% English, 15.0% Irish, 10.3% Other groups, 9.5% Norwegian (2000).
Economy: Employment by occupation: 11.9% management, 24.6% professional, 17.3% services, 20.8% sales, 1.5% farming, 8.8% construction, 15.0% production (2000).
Income: Per capita income: $23,786 (2000); Median household income: $40,368 (2000); Poverty rate: 9.1% (2000).
Taxes: Total city taxes per capita: $282 (1997); City property taxes per capita: $280 (1997).
Education: High school graduation rate: 87.5% (2000); College graduation rate: 32.2% (2000).

School District(s)

Northport Public School District (KG-12)
2000 Enrollment: 290 231-386-5153

Housing: Homeownership rate: 79.2% (2000); Median home value: $136,200 (2000); Median rent: $498 per month (2000); Median age of housing: 42 years (2000).
Hospitals: Leelanau Memorial Health Center (95 beds)
Transportation: Commute to work: 82.6% car, 0.8% public transportation, 11.2% walk, 5.4% work from home (2000); Travel time to work: 66.1% less than 15 minutes, 14.3% 15 to 30 minutes, 9.0% 30 to 45 minutes, 5.7% 45 to 60 minutes, 4.9% 60 minutes or more (2000)

SOLON (township). Covers a land area of 26.613 square miles and a water area of 3.087 square miles. Located at 44.81° N. Lat.; 85.77° W. Long.
History: Solon Township was settled in the 1860's and named for Solon, Ohio, the former home of some of the early residents.
Population: 1,542 (2000); Race: 97.3% White, 0.3% Black, 0.3% Asian, 0.7% American Indian and Alaska Native, 0.5% Hispanic of any race, 1.2% two or more races (2000); Density: 57.9 persons per square mile (2000); Age: 26.1% under 18, 11.8% over 64 (2000); Marriage status: 22.1% never married, 68.1% now married, 3.4% widowed, 6.4% divorced (2000); Foreign born: 0.5% (2000); Ancestry (includes multiple ancestries): 27.4% German, 20.0% Polish, 13.3% English, 12.4% French (except Basque), 12.1% Irish (2000).
Economy: Employment by occupation: 13.3% management, 22.9% professional, 17.4% services, 19.3% sales, 1.7% farming, 13.8% construction, 11.6% production (2000).
Income: Per capita income: $22,987 (2000); Median household income: $47,448 (2000); Poverty rate: 3.6% (2000).
Taxes: Total city taxes per capita: $20 (1997); City property taxes per capita: $19 (1997).
Education: High school graduation rate: 87.5% (2000); College graduation rate: 22.7% (2000).
Housing: Homeownership rate: 88.7% (2000); Median home value: $126,600 (2000); Median rent: $471 per month (2000); Median age of housing: 22 years (2000).
Transportation: Commute to work: 88.9% car, 0.4% public transportation, 1.1% walk, 9.0% work from home (2000); Travel time to work: 18.1% less than 15 minutes, 53.3% 15 to 30 minutes, 25.1% 30 to 45 minutes, 2.0% 45 to 60 minutes, 1.5% 60 minutes or more (2000)

SUTTONS BAY (village). Covers a land area of 1.093 square miles and a water area of 0 square miles. Located at 44.97° N. Lat.; 85.65° W. Long.
History: Suttons Bay was founded in 1854 on land owned by Harry C. Sutton. The town developed around sawmills and docks, where lumber was shipped. The location on Suttons Bay later became a resort area.
Population: 589 (2000); Race: 96.4% White, 0.0% Black, 0.4% Asian, 2.9% American Indian and Alaska Native, 1.8% Hispanic of any race, 0.4% two or more races (2000); Density: 538.7 persons per square mile (2000); Age: 19.4% under 18, 23.8% over 64 (2000); Marriage status: 21.7% never married, 59.9% now married, 7.9% widowed, 10.5% divorced (2000); Foreign born: 1.1% (2000); Ancestry (includes multiple ancestries): 26.1% German, 15.8% English, 11.4% Irish, 9.8% Norwegian, 7.8% Polish (2000).
Economy: Employment by occupation: 21.7% management, 23.5% professional, 15.7% services, 24.2% sales, 1.1% farming, 6.0% construction, 7.8% production (2000).
Income: Per capita income: $24,097 (2000); Median household income: $44,063 (2000); Poverty rate: 6.0% (2000).
Taxes: Total city taxes per capita: $318 (1997); City property taxes per capita: $316 (1997).
Education: High school graduation rate: 93.3% (2000); College graduation rate: 34.5% (2000).

School District(s)

Suttons Bay Public Schools (KG-12)
2000 Enrollment: 1,085 231-271-3846

Housing: Homeownership rate: 74.0% (2000); Median home value: $144,200 (2000); Median rent: $553 per month (2000); Median age of housing: 34 years (2000).
Transportation: Commute to work: 81.3% car, 0.0% public transportation, 11.5% walk, 6.5% work from home (2000); Travel time to work: 55.8% less than 15 minutes, 17.7% 15 to 30 minutes, 20.8% 30 to 45 minutes, 3.1% 45 to 60 minutes, 2.7% 60 minutes or more (2000)
Additional Information Contacts
Sutton Bay Chamber of Commerce 231-271-5077

SUTTONS BAY (township). Covers a land area of 24.597 square miles and a water area of 17.325 square miles. Located at 44.99° N. Lat.; 85.63° W. Long.
Population: 2,982 (2000); Race: 74.5% White, 0.4% Black, 1.2% Asian, 18.6% American Indian and Alaska Native, 5.9% Hispanic of any race, 1.7% two or more races (2000); Density: 121.2 persons per square mile (2000); Age: 29.5% under 18, 14.3% over 64 (2000); Marriage status: 24.1% never married, 61.3% now married, 5.4% widowed, 9.2% divorced (2000); Foreign born: 3.9% (2000); Ancestry (includes multiple ancestries): 24.4% German, 22.6% Other groups, 11.7% English, 10.4% Irish, 6.3% French (except Basque) (2000).
Economy: In fruit growing and resort area; winery; fruit processing. Manufacturing of hoses. Employment by occupation: 13.6% management, 20.1% professional, 18.4% services, 25.2% sales, 2.0% farming, 9.5% construction, 11.1% production (2000).
Income: Per capita income: $22,640 (2000); Median household income: $48,068 (2000); Poverty rate: 7.1% (2000).
Taxes: Total city taxes per capita: $40 (1997); City property taxes per capita: $38 (1997).
Education: High school graduation rate: 89.6% (2000); College graduation rate: 30.2% (2000).
Housing: Homeownership rate: 76.5% (2000); Median home value: $193,300 (2000); Median rent: $417 per month (2000); Median age of housing: 22 years (2000).
Transportation: Commute to work: 85.7% car, 0.5% public transportation, 6.6% walk, 6.5% work from home (2000); Travel time to work: 51.1% less than 15 minutes, 22.3% 15 to 30 minutes, 20.2% 30 to 45 minutes, 3.5% 45 to 60 minutes, 2.8% 60 minutes or more (2000)

Lenawee County

Located in southeastern Michigan; bounded on the south by Ohio; drained by the Raisin and Tiffin Rivers. Covers a land area of 750.50 square miles, a water area of 10.80 square miles, and is located in the Eastern Time Zone. The county government was organized in 1822. County seat is Adrian.

Lenawee County is part of the Ann Arbor, MI PMSA. The entire metro area includes: Lenawee County; Livingston County; Washtenaw County

Weather Station: Adrian 2 NNE Elevation: 757 feet

	Jan	Feb	Mar	Apr	May	Jun	Jul	Aug	Sep	Oct	Nov	Dec
High	32	35	45	58	71	80	83	81	74	62	48	36
Low	15	17	25	35	46	55	59	57	49	38	30	21
Precip	2.0	1.8	2.7	3.3	3.3	3.8	3.2	3.5	3.5	2.6	3.0	2.6
Snow	8.5	6.4	4.7	0.8	0.0	0.0	0.0	0.0	0.0	0.1	2.7	6.9

High and Low temperatures in degrees Fahrenheit; Precipitation and Snow in inches

Population: 98,890 (2000); Race: 92.5% White, 2.1% Black, 0.5% Asian, 0.4% American Indian and Alaska Native, 6.9% Hispanic of any race, 1.5% two or more races (2000); Density: 131.8 persons per square mile (2000); Age: 25.9% under 18, 12.7% over 64 (2000).
Religion: Five largest groups: 13.6% Catholic Church, 6.0% Assemblies of God, 3.5% The United Methodist Church, 2.4% Lutheran Church—Missouri Synod, 1.8% Evangelical Lutheran Church in America (2000).
Economy: Unemployment rate: 4.9% (11/2002); Total civilian labor force: 50,330 (11/2002); Leading industries: 31.1% manufacturing; 16.6% retail trade; 11.6% health care and social assistance (2000); Companies that employ more than 1,000 persons: 1 (2000); Companies that employ more than 100 persons: 46 (2000); Farms: 1,317 totaling 336,468 acres (1997); Minority business ownership rate: 6.8% (1997); Women business ownership rate: 22.6% (1997); Retail sales per capita: $8,441 (1997). Single-family building permits issued: 538 (2001) / 475 (2000); Multi-family building permits issued: 12 (2001) / 23 (2000).
Income: Per capita income: $20,186 (2000); Median household income: $45,739 (2000); Poverty rate: 6.7% (2000); Bankruptcy rate: 4.49% (2001).
Taxes: Total county taxes per capita: $117 (2000); County property taxes per capita: $104 (2000).
Education: High school graduation rate: 83.4% (2000); College graduation rate: 16.3% (2000).
Housing: Homeownership rate: 78.2% (2000); Median home value: $109,500 (2000); Median rent: $446 per month (2000); Median age of housing: 41 years (2000).
Health: Birth rate: 122.5 per 10,000 population (1998); Age adjusted death rate: 90.3 per 10,000 population (1999); Age adjusted cancer mortality rate: 197.1 deaths per 100,000 population (1999). Air Quality Index: 64% good, 36% moderate, 0% unhealthy (percent of days in 2000). Number of physicians: 8.8 per 10,000 population (1999); Number of hospital beds: 18.0 per 10,000 population (1999).
Elections: 2000 Presidential election results: 45.8% Gore, 51.6% Bush, 1.9% Nader, 0.1% Buchanan
National and State Parks: Hayes State Park
Additional Information Contacts
Lenawee County Government Offices 517-264-4508
Clinton Chamber of Commerce 517-456-4848
Lenawee County Association of Realtors 517-263-0325
Lenawee County Chamber of Commerce 517-265-5141
Tecumseh Area Chamber of Commerce 517-423-3740

Lenawee County Communities

ADDISON (village). Covers a land area of 0.976 square miles and a water area of 0.033 square miles. Located at 41.98° N. Lat.; 84.34° W. Long.
History: Addison was named for Addison J. Comstock, a banker who owned land here and had the town platted in 1851. Before that, the settlement had been called Manetau, Peru, Brownell's Mills, Jackson's Mills, and Harrison. Addison was incorporated in 1893.
Population: 627 (2000); Race: 99.7% White, 0.0% Black, 0.3% Asian, 0.0% American Indian and Alaska Native, 0.8% Hispanic of any race, 0.0% two or more races (2000); Density: 642.6 persons per square mile (2000); Age: 31.9% under 18, 10.1% over 64 (2000); Marriage status: 32.8% never married, 48.3% now married, 6.5% widowed, 12.4% divorced (2000); Foreign born: 0.8% (2000); Ancestry (includes multiple ancestries): 28.7% German, 15.8% United States or American, 13.6% Irish, 12.5% English, 7.0% Other groups (2000).
Economy: Single-family building permits issued: 0 (2001) / 2 (2000); Multi-family building permits issued: 0 (2001) / 0 (2000); Employment by occupation: 12.1% management, 5.4% professional, 21.5% services, 25.8% sales, 0.0% farming, 9.1% construction, 26.2% production (2000).
Income: Per capita income: $15,883 (2000); Median household income: $35,781 (2000); Poverty rate: 8.1% (2000).
Taxes: Total city taxes per capita: $138 (1997); City property taxes per capita: $133 (1997).
Education: High school graduation rate: 87.9% (2000); College graduation rate: 9.2% (2000).

School District(s)

Addison Community Schools (KG-12)
2000 Enrollment: 1,340 517-547-6123

Housing: Homeownership rate: 59.3% (2000); Median home value: $80,700 (2000); Median rent: $402 per month (2000); Median age of housing: 44 years (2000).
Transportation: Commute to work: 90.1% car, 0.0% public transportation, 8.5% walk, 1.0% work from home (2000); Travel time to work: 36.2% less than 15 minutes, 19.7% 15 to 30 minutes, 31.4% 30 to 45 minutes, 3.4% 45 to 60 minutes, 9.3% 60 minutes or more (2000)

ADRIAN (city). Covers a land area of 7.135 square miles and a water area of 0.127 square miles. Located at 41.89° N. Lat.; 84.03° W. Long. Elevation is 813 feet.
History: Adrian was founded as Logan in 1828 by Addison J. Comstock. His wife wanted the town named for her hero, the Roman emperor Hadrian, and it became Adrian. Adrian was incorporated as a village in 1836 and as a city in 1853. This was the home of Elmer D. Smith, who originated 586 varieties of chrysanthemums.
Population: 21,574 (2000); Race: 85.0% White, 3.3% Black, 1.0% Asian, 0.6% American Indian and Alaska Native, 16.6% Hispanic of any race, 2.2% two or more races (2000); Density: 3,023.5 persons per square mile (2000); Age: 25.1% under 18, 14.6% over 64 (2000); Marriage status: 33.6% never married, 46.5% now married, 8.6% widowed, 11.3% divorced (2000);

Foreign born: 3.1% (2000); Ancestry (includes multiple ancestries): 25.3% Other groups, 24.6% German, 11.6% English, 9.4% Irish, 7.0% United States or American (2000).
Vital Statistics: Birth rate: 194.2 per 10,000 population (1998)
Economy: Single-family building permits issued: 10 (2001) / 9 (2000); Multi-family building permits issued: 3 (2001) / 9 (2000); Employment by occupation: 6.6% management, 17.1% professional, 18.7% services, 27.5% sales, 0.3% farming, 7.5% construction, 22.3% production (2000).
Income: Per capita income: $16,528 (2000); Median household income: $34,203 (2000); Poverty rate: 13.8% (2000).
Taxes: Total city taxes per capita: $237 (1997); City property taxes per capita: $223 (1997).
Education: High school graduation rate: 79.1% (2000); College graduation rate: 20.1% (2000).

School District(s)

Adrian City School District (KG-12)
2000 Enrollment: 4,198 517-263-2115
Madison School District (Lenawee (PK-12)
2000 Enrollment: 1,154 517-263-0741

Four-year College(s)

Adrian College (Private, Not-for-profit, United Methodist)
2001 Enrollment: 1,054 517-265-5161
2001 Tuition: In-state $14,750; Out-of-state $14,750
Siena Heights University (Private, Not-for-profit, Roman Catholic)
2001 Enrollment: 2,024 517-263-0731
2001 Tuition: In-state $12,700; Out-of-state $12,700

Housing: Homeownership rate: 56.0% (2000); Median home value: $86,100 (2000); Median rent: $447 per month (2000); Median age of housing: 49 years (2000).
Hospitals: Lenawee Health Alliance (126 beds)
Safety: Violent crime rate: 50.3 per 10,000 population; Property crime rate: 452.3 per 10,000 population (2001).
Newspapers: The Daily Telegram (7 x week)
Transportation: Commute to work: 91.3% car, 0.6% public transportation, 5.4% walk, 1.5% work from home (2000); Travel time to work: 58.6% less than 15 minutes, 20.7% 15 to 30 minutes, 8.9% 30 to 45 minutes, 6.9% 45 to 60 minutes, 5.0% 60 minutes or more (2000)
Additional Information Contacts
Lenawee County Association of Realtors 517-263-0325
Lenawee County Chamber of Commerce 517-265-5141

ADRIAN (township). Covers a land area of 34.557 square miles and a water area of 0.005 square miles. Located at 41.93° N. Lat.; 84.05° W. Long. Elevation is 813 feet.
History: The township was named Logan until 1838, when the name was changed to Adrian by the legislature.
Population: 5,749 (2000); Race: 93.5% White, 0.8% Black, 1.2% Asian, 0.5% American Indian and Alaska Native, 5.6% Hispanic of any race, 1.6% two or more races (2000); Density: 166.4 persons per square mile (2000); Age: 23.9% under 18, 13.5% over 64 (2000); Marriage status: 20.8% never married, 67.5% now married, 4.4% widowed, 7.3% divorced (2000); Foreign born: 1.1% (2000); Ancestry (includes multiple ancestries): 29.0% German, 15.5% English, 12.3% Other groups, 11.3% Irish, 7.8% United States or American (2000).
Economy: Single-family building permits issued: 97 (2001) / 93 (2000); Multi-family building permits issued: 0 (2001) / 0 (2000); Employment by occupation: 11.3% management, 18.8% professional, 16.5% services, 23.4% sales, 0.2% farming, 11.5% construction, 18.3% production (2000).
Income: Per capita income: $24,881 (2000); Median household income: $60,640 (2000); Poverty rate: 3.2% (2000).
Taxes: Total city taxes per capita: $46 (2000); City property taxes per capita: $38 (2000).
Education: High school graduation rate: 86.9% (2000); College graduation rate: 23.9% (2000).
Housing: Homeownership rate: 87.9% (2000); Median home value: $135,500 (2000); Median rent: $503 per month (2000); Median age of housing: 25 years (2000).
Transportation: Commute to work: 92.4% car, 0.0% public transportation, 1.3% walk, 5.9% work from home (2000); Travel time to work: 52.2% less than 15 minutes, 27.0% 15 to 30 minutes, 8.5% 30 to 45 minutes, 7.0% 45 to 60 minutes, 5.3% 60 minutes or more (2000)

BLISSFIELD (village). Covers a land area of 2.119 square miles and a water area of 0.011 square miles. Located at 41.83° N. Lat.; 83.86° W. Long. Elevation is 694 feet.
History: Blissfield was incorporated as a village in 1875.
Population: 3,223 (2000); Race: 95.9% White, 0.0% Black, 0.2% Asian, 0.0% American Indian and Alaska Native, 5.3% Hispanic of any race, 0.8% two or more races (2000); Density: 1,520.7 persons per square mile (2000); Age: 25.7% under 18, 16.1% over 64 (2000); Marriage status: 19.6% never married, 61.0% now married, 8.9% widowed, 10.6% divorced (2000); Foreign born: 1.0% (2000); Ancestry (includes multiple ancestries): 41.9% German, 14.3% English, 12.4% Irish, 8.3% Other groups, 8.2% French (except Basque) (2000).
Economy: Single-family building permits issued: 8 (2001) / 4 (2000); Multi-family building permits issued: 0 (2001) / 10 (2000); Employment by occupation: 11.6% management, 15.4% professional, 18.3% services, 24.6% sales, 0.5% farming, 9.9% construction, 19.8% production (2000).
Income: Per capita income: $19,255 (2000); Median household income: $39,438 (2000); Poverty rate: 8.4% (2000).
Taxes: Total city taxes per capita: $250 (1997); City property taxes per capita: $243 (1997).
Education: High school graduation rate: 88.3% (2000); College graduation rate: 19.0% (2000).

School District(s)

Blissfield Community Schools (KG-12)
2000 Enrollment: 1,409 517-486-2205

Housing: Homeownership rate: 79.5% (2000); Median home value: $105,100 (2000); Median rent: $430 per month (2000); Median age of housing: 49 years (2000).
Safety: Violent crime rate: 18.5 per 10,000 population; Property crime rate: 308.6 per 10,000 population (2001).
Newspapers: Blissfield Advance (1 x week)
Transportation: Commute to work: 93.1% car, 0.0% public transportation, 3.2% walk, 2.7% work from home (2000); Travel time to work: 31.1% less than 15 minutes, 38.7% 15 to 30 minutes, 18.9% 30 to 45 minutes, 5.2% 45 to 60 minutes, 6.1% 60 minutes or more (2000)

BLISSFIELD (township). Covers a land area of 21.059 square miles and a water area of 0.023 square miles. Located at 41.84° N. Lat.; 83.86° W. Long. Elevation is 694 feet.
History: Blissfield Township was organized in 1827 and named for Hervey Bliss, who settled here in 1824.
Population: 3,915 (2000); Race: 96.1% White, 0.0% Black, 0.2% Asian, 0.0% American Indian and Alaska Native, 5.5% Hispanic of any race, 0.6% two or more races (2000); Density: 185.9 persons per square mile (2000); Age: 26.2% under 18, 15.8% over 64 (2000); Marriage status: 19.1% never married, 62.2% now married, 8.8% widowed, 10.0% divorced (2000); Foreign born: 0.8% (2000); Ancestry (includes multiple ancestries): 41.5% German, 13.9% English, 11.7% Irish, 8.6% Other groups, 7.1% French (except Basque) (2000).
Economy: Single-family building permits issued: 3 (2001) / 2 (2000); Multi-family building permits issued: 0 (2001) / 0 (2000); Employment by occupation: 11.9% management, 16.9% professional, 16.2% services, 23.1% sales, 0.7% farming, 10.9% construction, 20.4% production (2000).
Income: Per capita income: $19,406 (2000); Median household income: $40,306 (2000); Poverty rate: 7.7% (2000).
Taxes: Total city taxes per capita: $45 (1997); City property taxes per capita: $45 (1997).
Education: High school graduation rate: 88.5% (2000); College graduation rate: 18.6% (2000).
Housing: Homeownership rate: 78.9% (2000); Median home value: $106,200 (2000); Median rent: $436 per month (2000); Median age of housing: 51 years (2000).
Transportation: Commute to work: 90.5% car, 0.0% public transportation, 4.0% walk, 4.6% work from home (2000); Travel time to work: 31.3% less than 15 minutes, 38.6% 15 to 30 minutes, 17.9% 30 to 45 minutes, 5.9% 45 to 60 minutes, 6.3% 60 minutes or more (2000)

BRITTON (village). Covers a land area of 0.874 square miles and a water area of 0 square miles. Located at 41.98° N. Lat.; 83.83° W. Long.
History: Britton was named for John Britton, who operated a store here and became the first postmaster in 1881.
Population: 699 (2000); Race: 99.6% White, 0.0% Black, 0.0% Asian, 0.0% American Indian and Alaska Native, 2.7% Hispanic of any race, 0.4% two or more races (2000); Density: 799.6 persons per square mile (2000); Age: 29.7% under 18, 10.8% over 64 (2000); Marriage status: 23.0% never married, 65.1% now married, 5.8% widowed, 6.0% divorced (2000); Foreign born: 1.1% (2000); Ancestry (includes multiple ancestries): 36.1% German, 16.9% English, 15.3% Irish, 8.0% United States or American, 7.6% French (except Basque) (2000).

Economy: Single-family building permits issued: 1 (2001) / 1 (2000); Multi-family building permits issued: 0 (2001) / 0 (2000); Employment by occupation: 7.1% management, 12.3% professional, 18.5% services, 24.1% sales, 0.0% farming, 20.1% construction, 17.9% production (2000).
Income: Per capita income: $18,087 (2000); Median household income: $49,091 (2000); Poverty rate: 7.3% (2000).
Taxes: Total city taxes per capita: $129 (1997); City property taxes per capita: $126 (1997).
Education: High school graduation rate: 84.3% (2000); College graduation rate: 11.8% (2000).

School District(s)

Britton-Macon Area School District (KG-12)
2000 Enrollment: 530 517-451-4581

Housing: Homeownership rate: 77.0% (2000); Median home value: $94,800 (2000); Median rent: $410 per month (2000); Median age of housing: 60 years (2000).
Transportation: Commute to work: 95.8% car, 0.6% public transportation, 2.9% walk, 0.6% work from home (2000); Travel time to work: 18.7% less than 15 minutes, 32.3% 15 to 30 minutes, 28.1% 30 to 45 minutes, 12.9% 45 to 60 minutes, 8.1% 60 minutes or more (2000)

CAMBRIDGE (township). Covers a land area of 32.017 square miles and a water area of 3.479 square miles. Located at 42.04° N. Lat.; 84.18° W. Long.
History: Cambridge Junction was originally the intersection of the Chicago Turnpike and the Monroe Turnpike from Lake Erie. The Walker Tavern was a stopover spot on the stagecoach journey between Chicago and Detroit. As such, it entertained such guests as Daniel Webster and James Fenimore Cooper.
Population: 5,299 (2000); Race: 96.0% White, 0.7% Black, 0.6% Asian, 0.3% American Indian and Alaska Native, 2.1% Hispanic of any race, 1.7% two or more races (2000); Density: 165.5 persons per square mile (2000); Age: 26.1% under 18, 12.0% over 64 (2000); Marriage status: 15.0% never married, 69.9% now married, 4.6% widowed, 10.5% divorced (2000); Foreign born: 1.7% (2000); Ancestry (includes multiple ancestries): 27.3% German, 17.8% Irish, 15.7% English, 9.0% Other groups, 7.0% French (except Basque) (2000).
Economy: Single-family building permits issued: 62 (2001) / 49 (2000); Multi-family building permits issued: 0 (2001) / 0 (2000); Employment by occupation: 13.2% management, 17.9% professional, 11.7% services, 25.9% sales, 0.1% farming, 10.1% construction, 21.2% production (2000).
Income: Per capita income: $26,705 (2000); Median household income: $59,450 (2000); Poverty rate: 3.4% (2000).
Taxes: Total city taxes per capita: $92 (1997); City property taxes per capita: $76 (1997).
Education: High school graduation rate: 88.2% (2000); College graduation rate: 16.7% (2000).
Housing: Homeownership rate: 89.0% (2000); Median home value: $159,000 (2000); Median rent: $461 per month (2000); Median age of housing: 26 years (2000).
Safety: Violent crime rate: 3.8 per 10,000 population; Property crime rate: 58.2 per 10,000 population (2001).
Transportation: Commute to work: 93.4% car, 0.0% public transportation, 0.9% walk, 5.6% work from home (2000); Travel time to work: 17.3% less than 15 minutes, 31.2% 15 to 30 minutes, 20.1% 30 to 45 minutes, 11.3% 45 to 60 minutes, 20.1% 60 minutes or more (2000)

CEMENT CITY (village). Covers a land area of 0.878 square miles and a water area of 0.036 square miles. Located at 42.06° N. Lat.; 84.33° W. Long. Elevation is 1,061 feet.
History: Cement City began as Woodstock. It was renamed in 1900 when a cement company built a plant here. The village was incorporated in 1953.
Population: 452 (2000); Race: 99.1% White, 0.0% Black, 0.5% Asian, 0.0% American Indian and Alaska Native, 1.1% Hispanic of any race, 0.5% two or more races (2000); Density: 514.6 persons per square mile (2000); Age: 28.2% under 18, 11.1% over 64 (2000); Marriage status: 22.1% never married, 60.5% now married, 3.8% widowed, 13.7% divorced (2000); Foreign born: 0.5% (2000); Ancestry (includes multiple ancestries): 24.1% German, 18.9% English, 14.5% Irish, 7.5% Other groups, 4.8% French (except Basque) (2000).
Economy: Single-family building permits issued: 0 (2001) / 0 (2000); Multi-family building permits issued: 0 (2001) / 0 (2000); Employment by occupation: 9.3% management, 9.8% professional, 16.1% services, 22.4% sales, 0.0% farming, 7.8% construction, 34.6% production (2000).
Income: Per capita income: $17,015 (2000); Median household income: $40,500 (2000); Poverty rate: 5.9% (2000).
Taxes: Total city taxes per capita: $61 (1997); City property taxes per capita: $61 (1997).
Education: High school graduation rate: 74.0% (2000); College graduation rate: 6.1% (2000).
Housing: Homeownership rate: 89.4% (2000); Median home value: $80,600 (2000); Median rent: $400 per month (2000); Median age of housing: 56 years (2000).
Transportation: Commute to work: 94.8% car, 0.0% public transportation, 3.1% walk, 1.0% work from home (2000); Travel time to work: 21.4% less than 15 minutes, 50.5% 15 to 30 minutes, 15.6% 30 to 45 minutes, 6.3% 45 to 60 minutes, 6.3% 60 minutes or more (2000)

CLAYTON (village). Covers a land area of 0.761 square miles and a water area of 0 square miles. Located at 41.86° N. Lat.; 84.23° W. Long. Elevation is 891 feet.
History: Clayton was settled in 1836 and platted in 1843. It was named for a Presbyterian minister in New York, a friend of Reuben E. Bird who platted the village.
Population: 326 (2000); Race: 96.9% White, 0.0% Black, 0.0% Asian, 0.6% American Indian and Alaska Native, 2.3% Hispanic of any race, 2.0% two or more races (2000); Density: 428.2 persons per square mile (2000); Age: 29.9% under 18, 8.5% over 64 (2000); Marriage status: 28.2% never married, 56.4% now married, 3.8% widowed, 11.7% divorced (2000); Foreign born: 0.0% (2000); Ancestry (includes multiple ancestries): 26.3% German, 16.7% English, 9.0% Irish, 8.8% Polish, 7.3% Other groups (2000).
Economy: Employment by occupation: 6.8% management, 11.6% professional, 13.2% services, 18.9% sales, 0.0% farming, 13.2% construction, 36.3% production (2000).
Income: Per capita income: $17,941 (2000); Median household income: $41,875 (2000); Poverty rate: 6.5% (2000).
Taxes: Total city taxes per capita: $59 (1997); City property taxes per capita: $59 (1997).
Education: High school graduation rate: 75.4% (2000); College graduation rate: 10.3% (2000).
Housing: Homeownership rate: 84.0% (2000); Median home value: $71,000 (2000); Median rent: $363 per month (2000); Median age of housing: 60+ years (2000).
Transportation: Commute to work: 97.3% car, 0.0% public transportation, 1.6% walk, 1.1% work from home (2000); Travel time to work: 13.2% less than 15 minutes, 44.5% 15 to 30 minutes, 28.6% 30 to 45 minutes, 4.4% 45 to 60 minutes, 9.3% 60 minutes or more (2000)

CLINTON (village). Covers a land area of 1.495 square miles and a water area of 0.030 square miles. Located at 42.07° N. Lat.; 83.97° W. Long. Elevation is 833 feet.
History: Clinton was called Oak Plains when it was incorporated in 1838. An early industry in Clinton was the woolen mill. The town was named for DeWitt Clinton of New York.
Population: 2,293 (2000); Race: 100.0% White, 0.0% Black, 0.0% Asian, 0.0% American Indian and Alaska Native, 0.4% Hispanic of any race, 0.0% two or more races (2000); Density: 1,533.8 persons per square mile (2000); Age: 27.1% under 18, 14.9% over 64 (2000); Marriage status: 22.6% never married, 54.4% now married, 9.1% widowed, 13.9% divorced (2000); Foreign born: 0.6% (2000); Ancestry (includes multiple ancestries): 32.2% German, 14.5% Irish, 13.2% English, 7.5% United States or American, 6.3% Polish (2000).
Economy: Single-family building permits issued: 16 (2001) / 4 (2000); Multi-family building permits issued: 0 (2001) / 0 (2000); Employment by occupation: 9.1% management, 15.9% professional, 17.2% services, 24.0% sales, 0.3% farming, 10.2% construction, 23.3% production (2000).
Income: Per capita income: $20,513 (2000); Median household income: $47,961 (2000); Poverty rate: 6.5% (2000).
Taxes: Total city taxes per capita: $162 (1997); City property taxes per capita: $153 (1997).
Education: High school graduation rate: 90.2% (2000); College graduation rate: 16.2% (2000).

School District(s)

Clinton Community Schools (KG-12)
2000 Enrollment: 1,231 517-456-6501

Housing: Homeownership rate: 82.0% (2000); Median home value: $117,300 (2000); Median rent: $490 per month (2000); Median age of housing: 42 years (2000).
Safety: Violent crime rate: 21.7 per 10,000 population; Property crime rate: 251.6 per 10,000 population (2001).
Newspapers: The Clinton Local (1 x week)

Transportation: Commute to work: 93.2% car, 0.3% public transportation, 3.9% walk, 1.7% work from home (2000); Travel time to work: 23.8% less than 15 minutes, 33.6% 15 to 30 minutes, 25.2% 30 to 45 minutes, 11.1% 45 to 60 minutes, 6.3% 60 minutes or more (2000)
Additional Information Contacts
Clinton Chamber of Commerce 517-456-4848

CLINTON (township). Covers a land area of 18.078 square miles and a water area of 0.068 square miles. Located at 42.06° N. Lat.; 83.96° W. Long. Elevation is 833 feet.
Population: 3,624 (2000); Race: 99.3% White, 0.0% Black, 0.0% Asian, 0.0% American Indian and Alaska Native, 1.3% Hispanic of any race, 0.4% two or more races (2000); Density: 200.5 persons per square mile (2000); Age: 27.4% under 18, 10.8% over 64 (2000); Marriage status: 22.7% never married, 59.1% now married, 6.9% widowed, 11.4% divorced (2000); Foreign born: 0.5% (2000); Ancestry (includes multiple ancestries): 33.2% German, 15.3% Irish, 11.2% English, 7.5% Polish, 6.3% United States or American (2000).
Economy: Single-family building permits issued: 10 (2001) / 7 (2000); Multi-family building permits issued: 0 (2001) / 0 (2000); Employment by occupation: 9.5% management, 18.0% professional, 15.6% services, 22.3% sales, 0.3% farming, 9.8% construction, 24.5% production (2000).
Income: Per capita income: $21,554 (2000); Median household income: $51,661 (2000); Poverty rate: 6.1% (2000).
Taxes: Total city taxes per capita: $26 (1997); City property taxes per capita: $23 (1997).
Education: High school graduation rate: 90.5% (2000); College graduation rate: 17.3% (2000).
Housing: Homeownership rate: 82.8% (2000); Median home value: $123,100 (2000); Median rent: $485 per month (2000); Median age of housing: 36 years (2000).
Transportation: Commute to work: 94.6% car, 0.3% public transportation, 2.3% walk, 2.3% work from home (2000); Travel time to work: 20.0% less than 15 minutes, 33.1% 15 to 30 minutes, 27.3% 30 to 45 minutes, 14.1% 45 to 60 minutes, 5.5% 60 minutes or more (2000)

DEERFIELD (village). Covers a land area of 0.936 square miles and a water area of 0 square miles. Located at 41.88° N. Lat.; 83.77° W. Long. Elevation is 673 feet.
Population: 1,005 (2000); Race: 99.1% White, 0.0% Black, 0.5% Asian, 0.0% American Indian and Alaska Native, 2.3% Hispanic of any race, 0.4% two or more races (2000); Density: 1,073.2 persons per square mile (2000); Age: 31.5% under 18, 10.4% over 64 (2000); Marriage status: 26.9% never married, 60.1% now married, 6.4% widowed, 6.6% divorced (2000); Foreign born: 0.8% (2000); Ancestry (includes multiple ancestries): 35.8% German, 11.7% United States or American, 11.2% Irish, 9.7% English, 7.4% French (except Basque) (2000).
Economy: Single-family building permits issued: 0 (2001) / 0 (2000); Multi-family building permits issued: 0 (2001) / 0 (2000); Employment by occupation: 11.3% management, 12.1% professional, 15.0% services, 23.5% sales, 0.8% farming, 8.8% construction, 28.4% production (2000).
Income: Per capita income: $19,569 (2000); Median household income: $49,276 (2000); Poverty rate: 5.3% (2000).
Taxes: Total city taxes per capita: $121 (1997); City property taxes per capita: $120 (1997).
Education: High school graduation rate: 87.9% (2000); College graduation rate: 12.7% (2000).
School District(s)
Deerfield Public Schools (PK-12)
2000 Enrollment: 422 517-447-3215
Housing: Homeownership rate: 81.0% (2000); Median home value: $107,300 (2000); Median rent: $368 per month (2000); Median age of housing: 50 years (2000).
Transportation: Commute to work: 95.2% car, 0.0% public transportation, 2.1% walk, 1.5% work from home (2000); Travel time to work: 14.3% less than 15 minutes, 39.1% 15 to 30 minutes, 30.2% 30 to 45 minutes, 12.3% 45 to 60 minutes, 4.0% 60 minutes or more (2000)

DEERFIELD (township). Covers a land area of 25.126 square miles and a water area of 0.003 square miles. Located at 41.88° N. Lat.; 83.80° W. Long. Elevation is 673 feet.
Population: 1,770 (2000); Race: 96.7% White, 0.0% Black, 0.3% Asian, 0.0% American Indian and Alaska Native, 5.4% Hispanic of any race, 0.3% two or more races (2000); Density: 70.4 persons per square mile (2000); Age: 29.3% under 18, 10.4% over 64 (2000); Marriage status: 26.2% never married, 62.7% now married, 4.7% widowed, 6.4% divorced (2000); Foreign born: 1.4% (2000); Ancestry (includes multiple ancestries): 38.5% German, 9.8% Irish, 9.0% French (except Basque), 9.0% United States or American, 8.1% Other groups (2000).
Economy: In farm area. Employment by occupation: 12.5% management, 12.8% professional, 13.0% services, 23.5% sales, 1.8% farming, 9.0% construction, 27.4% production (2000).
Income: Per capita income: $19,878 (2000); Median household income: $50,000 (2000); Poverty rate: 6.3% (2000).
Taxes: Total city taxes per capita: $89 (1997); City property taxes per capita: $89 (1997).
Education: High school graduation rate: 86.9% (2000); College graduation rate: 12.7% (2000).
Housing: Homeownership rate: 82.0% (2000); Median home value: $112,100 (2000); Median rent: $398 per month (2000); Median age of housing: 53 years (2000).
Transportation: Commute to work: 96.0% car, 0.0% public transportation, 1.3% walk, 2.0% work from home (2000); Travel time to work: 19.5% less than 15 minutes, 34.5% 15 to 30 minutes, 27.6% 30 to 45 minutes, 12.5% 45 to 60 minutes, 5.8% 60 minutes or more (2000)

DOVER (township). Covers a land area of 35.088 square miles and a water area of 0.104 square miles. Located at 41.85° N. Lat.; 84.16° W. Long.
Population: 1,787 (2000); Race: 96.8% White, 0.0% Black, 0.4% Asian, 0.3% American Indian and Alaska Native, 4.2% Hispanic of any race, 0.9% two or more races (2000); Density: 50.9 persons per square mile (2000); Age: 28.9% under 18, 10.1% over 64 (2000); Marriage status: 19.7% never married, 66.6% now married, 5.7% widowed, 8.1% divorced (2000); Foreign born: 1.2% (2000); Ancestry (includes multiple ancestries): 27.0% German, 11.9% English, 11.2% Irish, 10.5% United States or American, 8.8% Other groups (2000).
Economy: Employment by occupation: 10.6% management, 10.0% professional, 15.2% services, 21.2% sales, 0.4% farming, 11.5% construction, 31.2% production (2000).
Income: Per capita income: $18,299 (2000); Median household income: $45,329 (2000); Poverty rate: 10.7% (2000).
Taxes: Total city taxes per capita: $12 (1997); City property taxes per capita: $11 (1997).
Education: High school graduation rate: 83.0% (2000); College graduation rate: 10.1% (2000).
Housing: Homeownership rate: 84.2% (2000); Median home value: $92,700 (2000); Median rent: $408 per month (2000); Median age of housing: 45 years (2000).
Transportation: Commute to work: 91.4% car, 0.0% public transportation, 1.3% walk, 6.4% work from home (2000); Travel time to work: 17.4% less than 15 minutes, 51.2% 15 to 30 minutes, 13.8% 30 to 45 minutes, 5.7% 45 to 60 minutes, 11.9% 60 minutes or more (2000)

FAIRFIELD (township). Covers a land area of 41.961 square miles and a water area of 0 square miles. Located at 41.77° N. Lat.; 84.06° W. Long.
Population: 1,756 (2000); Race: 96.7% White, 0.3% Black, 0.0% Asian, 0.4% American Indian and Alaska Native, 3.8% Hispanic of any race, 1.4% two or more races (2000); Density: 41.8 persons per square mile (2000); Age: 30.1% under 18, 10.9% over 64 (2000); Marriage status: 19.4% never married, 67.8% now married, 5.7% widowed, 7.2% divorced (2000); Foreign born: 0.3% (2000); Ancestry (includes multiple ancestries): 29.8% German, 12.6% English, 10.0% Irish, 9.6% United States or American, 8.1% Other groups (2000).
Economy: Single-family building permits issued: 4 (2001) / 5 (2000); Multi-family building permits issued: 0 (2001) / 0 (2000); Employment by occupation: 7.2% management, 10.9% professional, 15.7% services, 20.7% sales, 0.5% farming, 9.3% construction, 35.7% production (2000).
Income: Per capita income: $17,496 (2000); Median household income: $42,900 (2000); Poverty rate: 4.8% (2000).
Taxes: Total city taxes per capita: $68 (1997); City property taxes per capita: $65 (1997).
Education: High school graduation rate: 80.0% (2000); College graduation rate: 9.2% (2000).
Housing: Homeownership rate: 86.6% (2000); Median home value: $84,300 (2000); Median rent: $445 per month (2000); Median age of housing: 59 years (2000).
Transportation: Commute to work: 97.3% car, 0.0% public transportation, 0.4% walk, 2.1% work from home (2000); Travel time to work: 25.2% less than 15 minutes, 46.3% 15 to 30 minutes, 15.9% 30 to 45 minutes, 5.4% 45 to 60 minutes, 7.2% 60 minutes or more (2000)

FRANKLIN (township). Covers a land area of 38.484 square miles and a water area of 0.835 square miles. Located at 42.03° N. Lat.; 84.07° W. Long.
Population: 2,939 (2000); Race: 96.8% White, 0.3% Black, 0.2% Asian, 0.3% American Indian and Alaska Native, 1.1% Hispanic of any race, 1.9% two or more races (2000); Density: 76.4 persons per square mile (2000); Age: 26.7% under 18, 7.8% over 64 (2000); Marriage status: 19.3% never married, 68.3% now married, 4.5% widowed, 7.9% divorced (2000); Foreign born: 1.1% (2000); Ancestry (includes multiple ancestries): 31.1% German, 18.5% Irish, 12.9% English, 8.5% United States or American, 8.2% Other groups (2000).
Economy: Single-family building permits issued: 22 (2001) / 23 (2000); Multi-family building permits issued: 0 (2001) / 0 (2000); Employment by occupation: 10.0% management, 15.2% professional, 12.5% services, 23.6% sales, 0.0% farming, 15.4% construction, 23.3% production (2000).
Income: Per capita income: $24,300 (2000); Median household income: $56,296 (2000); Poverty rate: 2.7% (2000).
Taxes: Total city taxes per capita: $29 (1997); City property taxes per capita: $19 (1997).
Education: High school graduation rate: 88.8% (2000); College graduation rate: 15.3% (2000).
Housing: Homeownership rate: 90.9% (2000); Median home value: $139,600 (2000); Median rent: $463 per month (2000); Median age of housing: 31 years (2000).
Transportation: Commute to work: 96.5% car, 0.0% public transportation, 0.5% walk, 1.9% work from home (2000); Travel time to work: 17.3% less than 15 minutes, 36.9% 15 to 30 minutes, 19.5% 30 to 45 minutes, 11.9% 45 to 60 minutes, 14.5% 60 minutes or more (2000)

HUDSON (city). Covers a land area of 2.163 square miles and a water area of 0.007 square miles. Located at 41.85° N. Lat.; 84.35° W. Long. Elevation is 918 feet.
History: Hudson was settled in the 1830's and first known as Bean Creek, then Lanesville. Renamed Hudson in 1840, it developed as a shipping point for a farming area, and the home of industries producing harnesses and pumps. Hudson was incorporated as a city in 1893.
Population: 2,499 (2000); Race: 97.1% White, 0.4% Black, 0.5% Asian, 0.3% American Indian and Alaska Native, 0.9% Hispanic of any race, 1.7% two or more races (2000); Density: 1,155.4 persons per square mile (2000); Age: 28.9% under 18, 11.9% over 64 (2000); Marriage status: 26.2% never married, 55.2% now married, 6.5% widowed, 12.1% divorced (2000); Foreign born: 1.2% (2000); Ancestry (includes multiple ancestries): 28.5% German, 15.9% English, 13.9% Irish, 11.7% United States or American, 11.0% Other groups (2000).
Economy: Single-family building permits issued: 0 (2001) / 1 (2000); Multi-family building permits issued: 0 (2001) / 0 (2000); Employment by occupation: 4.2% management, 17.0% professional, 14.5% services, 22.5% sales, 0.5% farming, 8.7% construction, 32.6% production (2000).
Income: Per capita income: $16,340 (2000); Median household income: $41,122 (2000); Poverty rate: 8.0% (2000).
Taxes: Total city taxes per capita: $261 (2000); City property taxes per capita: $259 (2000).
Education: High school graduation rate: 81.6% (2000); College graduation rate: 12.1% (2000).

School District(s)

Hudson Area Schools (KG-12)
2000 Enrollment: 1,096 517-448-8912

Housing: Homeownership rate: 72.3% (2000); Median home value: $78,100 (2000); Median rent: $400 per month (2000); Median age of housing: 60+ years (2000).
Safety: Violent crime rate: 31.8 per 10,000 population; Property crime rate: 326.4 per 10,000 population (2001).
Newspapers: Post-Gazette (1 x week)
Transportation: Commute to work: 91.8% car, 0.8% public transportation, 3.1% walk, 2.7% work from home (2000); Travel time to work: 35.0% less than 15 minutes, 29.1% 15 to 30 minutes, 23.4% 30 to 45 minutes, 6.4% 45 to 60 minutes, 6.1% 60 minutes or more (2000)

HUDSON (township). Covers a land area of 35.433 square miles and a water area of 1.098 square miles. Located at 41.85° N. Lat.; 84.30° W. Long. Elevation is 918 feet.
History: Hudson Township was named for Dr. Daniel Hudson, one of the first landowners, who had come from New York.
Population: 1,576 (2000); Race: 98.6% White, 0.0% Black, 0.0% Asian, 0.0% American Indian and Alaska Native, 1.0% Hispanic of any race, 1.1% two or more races (2000); Density: 44.5 persons per square mile (2000); Age: 24.1% under 18, 15.8% over 64 (2000); Marriage status: 22.2% never married, 62.7% now married, 7.2% widowed, 7.9% divorced (2000); Foreign born: 0.3% (2000); Ancestry (includes multiple ancestries): 33.2% German, 14.0% English, 13.4% Irish, 7.4% United States or American, 6.5% French (except Basque) (2000).
Economy: Single-family building permits issued: 10 (2001) / 8 (2000); Multi-family building permits issued: 0 (2001) / 0 (2000); Employment by occupation: 10.2% management, 9.9% professional, 12.0% services, 23.0% sales, 2.1% farming, 13.0% construction, 29.8% production (2000).
Income: Per capita income: $19,771 (2000); Median household income: $41,354 (2000); Poverty rate: 4.3% (2000).
Taxes: Total city taxes per capita: $52 (1997); City property taxes per capita: $50 (1997).
Education: High school graduation rate: 81.8% (2000); College graduation rate: 8.3% (2000).
Housing: Homeownership rate: 91.3% (2000); Median home value: $94,800 (2000); Median rent: $388 per month (2000); Median age of housing: 36 years (2000).
Transportation: Commute to work: 94.0% car, 1.1% public transportation, 1.6% walk, 2.9% work from home (2000); Travel time to work: 28.5% less than 15 minutes, 36.2% 15 to 30 minutes, 16.0% 30 to 45 minutes, 9.9% 45 to 60 minutes, 9.4% 60 minutes or more (2000)

JASPER (unincorporated postal area, zip code 49248). Covers a land area of 34.130 square miles and a water area of 0 square miles. Located at 41.76° N. Lat.; 84.01° W. Long. Elevation is 734 feet.
Population: 912 (2000); Race: 97.8% White, 0.0% Black, 0.0% Asian, 0.4% American Indian and Alaska Native, 3.8% Hispanic of any race, 0.8% two or more races (2000); Density: 26.7 persons per square mile (2000); Age: 29.5% under 18, 12.5% over 64 (2000); Marriage status: 18.0% never married, 68.2% now married, 5.3% widowed, 8.5% divorced (2000); Foreign born: 0.7% (2000); Ancestry (includes multiple ancestries): 40.0% German, 12.8% English, 12.6% Irish, 7.7% United States or American, 7.7% Other groups (2000).
Economy: Employment by occupation: 9.3% management, 12.1% professional, 15.8% services, 20.6% sales, 1.2% farming, 10.3% construction, 30.6% production (2000).
Income: Per capita income: $20,608 (2000); Median household income: $46,827 (2000); Poverty rate: 3.7% (2000).
Education: High school graduation rate: 84.8% (2000); College graduation rate: 12.6% (2000).
Housing: Homeownership rate: 88.1% (2000); Median home value: $86,100 (2000); Median rent: $519 per month (2000); Median age of housing: 60+ years (2000).
Transportation: Commute to work: 96.4% car, 0.0% public transportation, 1.5% walk, 2.1% work from home (2000); Travel time to work: 19.7% less than 15 minutes, 54.3% 15 to 30 minutes, 15.2% 30 to 45 minutes, 6.5% 45 to 60 minutes, 4.3% 60 minutes or more (2000)

MACON (township). Covers a land area of 32.626 square miles and a water area of 0 square miles. Located at 42.04° N. Lat.; 83.83° W. Long. Elevation is 835 feet.
History: The Macon area was owned by Henry Ford, and devoted largely to soy-bean production.
Population: 1,448 (2000); Race: 97.2% White, 0.0% Black, 0.4% Asian, 1.1% American Indian and Alaska Native, 0.6% Hispanic of any race, 0.7% two or more races (2000); Density: 44.4 persons per square mile (2000); Age: 26.1% under 18, 10.8% over 64 (2000); Marriage status: 19.0% never married, 68.9% now married, 3.9% widowed, 8.1% divorced (2000); Foreign born: 1.7% (2000); Ancestry (includes multiple ancestries): 32.7% German, 17.6% English, 13.6% Irish, 6.7% Polish, 6.3% Other groups (2000).
Economy: Single-family building permits issued: 10 (2001) / 5 (2000); Multi-family building permits issued: 0 (2001) / 0 (2000); Employment by occupation: 13.8% management, 11.8% professional, 14.7% services, 22.9% sales, 0.0% farming, 12.0% construction, 24.8% production (2000).
Income: Per capita income: $24,059 (2000); Median household income: $61,818 (2000); Poverty rate: 1.6% (2000).
Taxes: Total city taxes per capita: $60 (1997); City property taxes per capita: $57 (1997).
Education: High school graduation rate: 90.9% (2000); College graduation rate: 15.5% (2000).
Housing: Homeownership rate: 92.6% (2000); Median home value: $132,100 (2000); Median rent: $535 per month (2000); Median age of housing: 44 years (2000).
Transportation: Commute to work: 94.9% car, 0.0% public transportation, 1.5% walk, 2.5% work from home (2000); Travel time to work: 12.4% less

than 15 minutes, 42.8% 15 to 30 minutes, 30.6% 30 to 45 minutes, 8.7% 45 to 60 minutes, 5.5% 60 minutes or more (2000)

MADISON CHARTER (township). Covers a land area of 30.666 square miles and a water area of 0.245 square miles. Located at 41.86° N. Lat.; 84.05° W. Long.
Population: 8,200 (2000); Race: 80.8% White, 13.4% Black, 0.5% Asian, 0.2% American Indian and Alaska Native, 8.5% Hispanic of any race, 1.3% two or more races (2000); Density: 267.4 persons per square mile (2000); Age: 20.5% under 18, 11.1% over 64 (2000); Marriage status: 15.0% never married, 74.4% now married, 4.0% widowed, 6.7% divorced (2000); Foreign born: 1.4% (2000); Ancestry (includes multiple ancestries): 20.3% German, 12.8% Other groups, 8.2% Irish, 8.1% United States or American, 7.6% English (2000).
Economy: Single-family building permits issued: 66 (2001) / 48 (2000); Multi-family building permits issued: 9 (2001) / 4 (2000); Employment by occupation: 6.0% management, 17.7% professional, 13.3% services, 26.4% sales, 0.0% farming, 10.9% construction, 25.7% production (2000).
Income: Per capita income: $17,749 (2000); Median household income: $47,114 (2000); Poverty rate: 2.1% (2000).
Taxes: Total city taxes per capita: $95 (2000); City property taxes per capita: $89 (2000).
Education: High school graduation rate: 75.1% (2000); College graduation rate: 10.8% (2000).
Housing: Homeownership rate: 90.0% (2000); Median home value: $98,900 (2000); Median rent: $610 per month (2000); Median age of housing: 36 years (2000).
Transportation: Commute to work: 94.2% car, 0.0% public transportation, 2.0% walk, 2.8% work from home (2000); Travel time to work: 51.5% less than 15 minutes, 29.5% 15 to 30 minutes, 5.1% 30 to 45 minutes, 5.7% 45 to 60 minutes, 8.2% 60 minutes or more (2000)

MANITOU BEACH-DEVILS LAKE (CDP). Covers a land area of 6.997 square miles and a water area of 2.744 square miles. Located at 41.98° N. Lat.; 84.28° W. Long.
Population: 2,080 (2000); Race: 99.1% White, 0.0% Black, 0.3% Asian, 0.0% American Indian and Alaska Native, 1.4% Hispanic of any race, 0.3% two or more races (2000); Density: 297.3 persons per square mile (2000); Age: 18.6% under 18, 17.0% over 64 (2000); Marriage status: 17.5% never married, 60.8% now married, 8.6% widowed, 13.1% divorced (2000); Foreign born: 1.6% (2000); Ancestry (includes multiple ancestries): 33.7% German, 13.6% Irish, 12.8% English, 11.8% United States or American, 6.6% French (except Basque) (2000).
Economy: Employment by occupation: 9.3% management, 14.4% professional, 9.6% services, 25.6% sales, 0.0% farming, 10.9% construction, 30.2% production (2000).
Income: Per capita income: $24,561 (2000); Median household income: $37,938 (2000); Poverty rate: 6.8% (2000).
Education: High school graduation rate: 81.0% (2000); College graduation rate: 18.9% (2000).
Housing: Homeownership rate: 88.7% (2000); Median home value: $145,000 (2000); Median rent: $411 per month (2000); Median age of housing: 45 years (2000).
Transportation: Commute to work: 94.9% car, 0.0% public transportation, 1.3% walk, 3.8% work from home (2000); Travel time to work: 16.2% less than 15 minutes, 31.3% 15 to 30 minutes, 27.7% 30 to 45 minutes, 7.2% 45 to 60 minutes, 17.6% 60 minutes or more (2000)

MEDINA (township). Covers a land area of 47.562 square miles and a water area of 0.069 square miles. Located at 41.75° N. Lat.; 84.29° W. Long.
Population: 1,227 (2000); Race: 98.1% White, 0.0% Black, 0.2% Asian, 0.0% American Indian and Alaska Native, 3.3% Hispanic of any race, 1.0% two or more races (2000); Density: 25.8 persons per square mile (2000); Age: 25.3% under 18, 15.1% over 64 (2000); Marriage status: 21.3% never married, 64.6% now married, 7.4% widowed, 6.7% divorced (2000); Foreign born: 0.0% (2000); Ancestry (includes multiple ancestries): 35.9% German, 12.6% English, 10.2% Irish, 9.3% Other groups, 7.4% United States or American (2000).
Economy: Single-family building permits issued: 10 (2001) / 10 (2000); Multi-family building permits issued: 0 (2001) / 0 (2000); Employment by occupation: 9.7% management, 8.5% professional, 14.3% services, 16.3% sales, 2.4% farming, 9.2% construction, 39.7% production (2000).
Income: Per capita income: $18,008 (2000); Median household income: $40,347 (2000); Poverty rate: 6.2% (2000).
Taxes: Total city taxes per capita: $52 (1997); City property taxes per capita: $48 (1997).
Education: High school graduation rate: 75.2% (2000); College graduation rate: 6.6% (2000).
Housing: Homeownership rate: 85.1% (2000); Median home value: $82,600 (2000); Median rent: $400 per month (2000); Median age of housing: 60+ years (2000).
Transportation: Commute to work: 91.2% car, 0.0% public transportation, 1.7% walk, 6.9% work from home (2000); Travel time to work: 23.0% less than 15 minutes, 31.9% 15 to 30 minutes, 29.1% 30 to 45 minutes, 6.9% 45 to 60 minutes, 9.3% 60 minutes or more (2000)

MORENCI (city). Covers a land area of 2.114 square miles and a water area of 0 square miles. Located at 41.72° N. Lat.; 84.21° W. Long. Elevation is 770 feet.
History: Incorporated as city 1934.
Population: 2,398 (2000); Race: 94.5% White, 1.2% Black, 0.9% Asian, 0.5% American Indian and Alaska Native, 1.7% Hispanic of any race, 2.8% two or more races (2000); Density: 1,134.1 persons per square mile (2000); Age: 28.8% under 18, 14.6% over 64 (2000); Marriage status: 22.4% never married, 59.5% now married, 7.2% widowed, 10.9% divorced (2000); Foreign born: 1.5% (2000); Ancestry (includes multiple ancestries): 26.6% German, 14.8% English, 10.0% Irish, 9.1% Other groups, 7.9% United States or American (2000).
Economy: In diversified farm area: corn, grain, apples, sugar beets; livestock; dairy. Manufacturing: broaching tools, metal fabrication. Single-family building permits issued: 4 (2001) / 1 (2000); Multi-family building permits issued: 0 (2001) / 0 (2000); Employment by occupation: 6.2% management, 17.9% professional, 15.4% services, 18.0% sales, 0.3% farming, 8.7% construction, 33.4% production (2000).
Income: Per capita income: $16,557 (2000); Median household income: $40,050 (2000); Poverty rate: 9.7% (2000).
Taxes: Total city taxes per capita: $194 (1997); City property taxes per capita: $191 (1997).
Education: High school graduation rate: 82.6% (2000); College graduation rate: 13.4% (2000).

School District(s)

Morenci Area Schools (PK-12)
2000 Enrollment: 927 517-458-7501
Housing: Homeownership rate: 71.9% (2000); Median home value: $77,800 (2000); Median rent: $405 per month (2000); Median age of housing: 58 years (2000).
Safety: Violent crime rate: 8.3 per 10,000 population; Property crime rate: 83.0 per 10,000 population (2001).
Newspapers: Morenci Observer (1 x week)
Transportation: Commute to work: 93.4% car, 0.4% public transportation, 4.3% walk, 1.4% work from home (2000); Travel time to work: 26.5% less than 15 minutes, 28.0% 15 to 30 minutes, 29.1% 30 to 45 minutes, 8.2% 45 to 60 minutes, 8.1% 60 minutes or more (2000)

OGDEN (township). Covers a land area of 41.983 square miles and a water area of 0 square miles. Located at 41.76° N. Lat.; 83.94° W. Long. Elevation is 710 feet.
Population: 1,063 (2000); Race: 97.6% White, 0.0% Black, 0.0% Asian, 0.6% American Indian and Alaska Native, 3.1% Hispanic of any race, 0.8% two or more races (2000); Density: 25.3 persons per square mile (2000); Age: 26.5% under 18, 12.8% over 64 (2000); Marriage status: 21.3% never married, 66.6% now married, 5.0% widowed, 7.2% divorced (2000); Foreign born: 0.2% (2000); Ancestry (includes multiple ancestries): 39.8% German, 16.6% English, 13.2% Irish, 8.4% French (except Basque), 8.2% United States or American (2000).
Economy: Employment by occupation: 10.8% management, 13.5% professional, 12.6% services, 25.0% sales, 1.7% farming, 11.4% construction, 25.0% production (2000).
Income: Per capita income: $22,545 (2000); Median household income: $51,250 (2000); Poverty rate: 4.0% (2000).
Taxes: Total city taxes per capita: $113 (1997); City property taxes per capita: $113 (1997).
Education: High school graduation rate: 88.4% (2000); College graduation rate: 13.2% (2000).
Housing: Homeownership rate: 84.3% (2000); Median home value: $101,500 (2000); Median rent: $415 per month (2000); Median age of housing: 60+ years (2000).
Transportation: Commute to work: 95.7% car, 0.0% public transportation, 1.1% walk, 3.2% work from home (2000); Travel time to work: 22.0% less than 15 minutes, 48.8% 15 to 30 minutes, 19.6% 30 to 45 minutes, 6.1% 45 to 60 minutes, 3.5% 60 minutes or more (2000)

ONSTED (village). Covers a land area of 0.957 square miles and a water area of 0 square miles. Located at 42.00° N. Lat.; 84.18° W. Long. Elevation is 989 feet.
Population: 813 (2000); Race: 95.9% White, 0.0% Black, 0.5% Asian, 1.1% American Indian and Alaska Native, 1.9% Hispanic of any race, 2.1% two or more races (2000); Density: 849.7 persons per square mile (2000); Age: 26.9% under 18, 15.9% over 64 (2000); Marriage status: 23.0% never married, 54.8% now married, 8.4% widowed, 13.8% divorced (2000); Foreign born: 1.7% (2000); Ancestry (includes multiple ancestries): 38.3% German, 26.3% Irish, 17.2% English, 7.9% Other groups, 6.3% French (except Basque) (2000).
Economy: In farm area. Manufacturing: hardware. Single-family building permits issued: 13 (2001) / 20 (2000); Multi-family building permits issued: 0 (2001) / 0 (2000); Employment by occupation: 7.1% management, 18.4% professional, 12.1% services, 26.2% sales, 0.5% farming, 11.6% construction, 24.2% production (2000).
Income: Per capita income: $19,862 (2000); Median household income: $34,539 (2000); Poverty rate: 8.0% (2000).
Taxes: Total city taxes per capita: $95 (1997); City property taxes per capita: $91 (1997).
Education: High school graduation rate: 85.7% (2000); College graduation rate: 10.3% (2000).

School District(s)

Onsted Community Schools (KG-12)
2000 Enrollment: 1,835 517-467-2174

Housing: Homeownership rate: 59.7% (2000); Median home value: $115,000 (2000); Median rent: $369 per month (2000); Median age of housing: 43 years (2000).
Transportation: Commute to work: 91.2% car, 0.0% public transportation, 4.9% walk, 3.9% work from home (2000); Travel time to work: 19.3% less than 15 minutes, 45.3% 15 to 30 minutes, 15.3% 30 to 45 minutes, 7.0% 45 to 60 minutes, 13.1% 60 minutes or more (2000)

PALMYRA (township). Covers a land area of 36.679 square miles and a water area of 0.009 square miles. Located at 41.86° N. Lat.; 83.94° W. Long.
History: Palmyra was settled in 1827 and named for Palmyra, New York, the former home of an early settler.
Population: 2,366 (2000); Race: 85.4% White, 1.2% Black, 0.0% Asian, 0.3% American Indian and Alaska Native, 13.7% Hispanic of any race, 4.8% two or more races (2000); Density: 64.5 persons per square mile (2000); Age: 27.8% under 18, 10.5% over 64 (2000); Marriage status: 24.7% never married, 60.6% now married, 5.7% widowed, 9.0% divorced (2000); Foreign born: 1.5% (2000); Ancestry (includes multiple ancestries): 28.4% German, 11.7% Other groups, 9.0% English, 7.8% Irish, 7.7% United States or American (2000).
Economy: Single-family building permits issued: 5 (2001) / 5 (2000); Multi-family building permits issued: 0 (2001) / 0 (2000); Employment by occupation: 8.4% management, 14.7% professional, 13.6% services, 19.3% sales, 1.5% farming, 12.4% construction, 30.2% production (2000).
Income: Per capita income: $18,843 (2000); Median household income: $49,598 (2000); Poverty rate: 6.1% (2000).
Taxes: Total city taxes per capita: $25 (1997); City property taxes per capita: $20 (1997).
Education: High school graduation rate: 79.7% (2000); College graduation rate: 10.7% (2000).
Housing: Homeownership rate: 84.7% (2000); Median home value: $106,600 (2000); Median rent: $398 per month (2000); Median age of housing: 51 years (2000).
Transportation: Commute to work: 91.8% car, 0.3% public transportation, 3.9% walk, 3.3% work from home (2000); Travel time to work: 40.9% less than 15 minutes, 35.9% 15 to 30 minutes, 11.2% 30 to 45 minutes, 6.0% 45 to 60 minutes, 6.0% 60 minutes or more (2000)

RAISIN (township). Covers a land area of 36.253 square miles and a water area of 0.204 square miles. Located at 41.94° N. Lat.; 83.94° W. Long.
Population: 6,507 (2000); Race: 96.4% White, 0.7% Black, 0.2% Asian, 0.2% American Indian and Alaska Native, 4.9% Hispanic of any race, 0.9% two or more races (2000); Density: 179.5 persons per square mile (2000); Age: 28.9% under 18, 8.9% over 64 (2000); Marriage status: 20.1% never married, 69.6% now married, 4.7% widowed, 5.5% divorced (2000); Foreign born: 1.4% (2000); Ancestry (includes multiple ancestries): 34.0% German, 15.1% English, 14.9% Irish, 9.5% Other groups, 7.7% French (except Basque) (2000).
Economy: Single-family building permits issued: 58 (2001) / 56 (2000); Multi-family building permits issued: 0 (2001) / 0 (2000); Employment by occupation: 10.0% management, 16.6% professional, 12.9% services, 24.2% sales, 0.4% farming, 9.5% construction, 26.3% production (2000).
Income: Per capita income: $21,703 (2000); Median household income: $57,088 (2000); Poverty rate: 2.9% (2000).
Taxes: Total city taxes per capita: $38 (2000); City property taxes per capita: $29 (2000).
Education: High school graduation rate: 86.6% (2000); College graduation rate: 16.1% (2000).
Housing: Homeownership rate: 93.8% (2000); Median home value: $127,000 (2000); Median rent: $511 per month (2000); Median age of housing: 26 years (2000).
Transportation: Commute to work: 97.1% car, 0.0% public transportation, 0.3% walk, 2.4% work from home (2000); Travel time to work: 34.8% less than 15 minutes, 30.8% 15 to 30 minutes, 16.8% 30 to 45 minutes, 12.1% 45 to 60 minutes, 5.4% 60 minutes or more (2000)

RIDGEWAY (township). Covers a land area of 28.658 square miles and a water area of 0.032 square miles. Located at 41.97° N. Lat.; 83.83° W. Long.
History: Ridgeway was settled in the late 1820's. It was named for an old path over a ridge, called the ridge way.
Population: 1,580 (2000); Race: 98.7% White, 0.0% Black, 0.1% Asian, 0.1% American Indian and Alaska Native, 3.0% Hispanic of any race, 0.3% two or more races (2000); Density: 55.1 persons per square mile (2000); Age: 28.8% under 18, 12.2% over 64 (2000); Marriage status: 21.7% never married, 65.3% now married, 6.4% widowed, 6.6% divorced (2000); Foreign born: 1.5% (2000); Ancestry (includes multiple ancestries): 35.2% German, 15.5% English, 13.8% Irish, 8.6% United States or American, 7.2% Other groups (2000).
Economy: Single-family building permits issued: 15 (2001) / 5 (2000); Multi-family building permits issued: 0 (2001) / 0 (2000); Employment by occupation: 6.1% management, 12.6% professional, 14.2% services, 25.4% sales, 1.6% farming, 16.8% construction, 23.3% production (2000).
Income: Per capita income: $19,111 (2000); Median household income: $50,642 (2000); Poverty rate: 4.5% (2000).
Taxes: Total city taxes per capita: $93 (1997); City property taxes per capita: $92 (1997).
Education: High school graduation rate: 84.8% (2000); College graduation rate: 9.1% (2000).
Housing: Homeownership rate: 81.5% (2000); Median home value: $102,300 (2000); Median rent: $431 per month (2000); Median age of housing: 60+ years (2000).
Transportation: Commute to work: 95.6% car, 0.3% public transportation, 1.8% walk, 1.9% work from home (2000); Travel time to work: 22.9% less than 15 minutes, 30.1% 15 to 30 minutes, 28.4% 30 to 45 minutes, 11.7% 45 to 60 minutes, 6.9% 60 minutes or more (2000)

RIGA (township). Covers a land area of 40.879 square miles and a water area of 0 square miles. Located at 41.78° N. Lat.; 83.81° W. Long. Elevation is 696 feet.
Population: 1,439 (2000); Race: 98.2% White, 0.2% Black, 0.1% Asian, 0.0% American Indian and Alaska Native, 2.4% Hispanic of any race, 0.9% two or more races (2000); Density: 35.2 persons per square mile (2000); Age: 28.1% under 18, 13.5% over 64 (2000); Marriage status: 21.2% never married, 64.5% now married, 9.0% widowed, 5.3% divorced (2000); Foreign born: 1.1% (2000); Ancestry (includes multiple ancestries): 46.4% German, 12.0% English, 9.2% Irish, 6.6% United States or American, 4.6% Polish (2000).
Economy: Single-family building permits issued: 1 (2001) / 1 (2000); Multi-family building permits issued: 0 (2001) / 0 (2000); Employment by occupation: 10.5% management, 13.0% professional, 12.9% services, 25.1% sales, 0.8% farming, 14.0% construction, 23.7% production (2000).
Income: Per capita income: $20,968 (2000); Median household income: $50,368 (2000); Poverty rate: 5.2% (2000).
Taxes: Total city taxes per capita: $127 (2000); City property taxes per capita: $118 (2000).
Education: High school graduation rate: 84.9% (2000); College graduation rate: 10.0% (2000).
Housing: Homeownership rate: 93.0% (2000); Median home value: $113,900 (2000); Median rent: $467 per month (2000); Median age of housing: 60+ years (2000).
Transportation: Commute to work: 93.9% car, 0.0% public transportation, 0.3% walk, 5.6% work from home (2000); Travel time to work: 21.8% less than 15 minutes, 36.2% 15 to 30 minutes, 29.0% 30 to 45 minutes, 8.3% 45 to 60 minutes, 4.8% 60 minutes or more (2000)

ROLLIN (township). Covers a land area of 33.901 square miles and a water area of 2.292 square miles. Located at 41.95° N. Lat.; 84.31° W. Long. Elevation is 983 feet.
History: Rollin Township was named for Reverend David Rollin. It was settled in the mid-1830's and grew up around a sawmill.
Population: 3,176 (2000); Race: 99.2% White, 0.0% Black, 0.5% Asian, 0.2% American Indian and Alaska Native, 0.9% Hispanic of any race, 0.1% two or more races (2000); Density: 93.7 persons per square mile (2000); Age: 23.7% under 18, 13.8% over 64 (2000); Marriage status: 19.4% never married, 61.5% now married, 6.8% widowed, 12.3% divorced (2000); Foreign born: 1.4% (2000); Ancestry (includes multiple ancestries): 34.7% German, 14.3% English, 12.5% Irish, 10.3% United States or American, 6.2% French (except Basque) (2000).
Economy: Single-family building permits issued: 8 (2001) / 17 (2000); Multi-family building permits issued: 0 (2001) / 0 (2000); Employment by occupation: 9.7% management, 11.4% professional, 12.6% services, 20.7% sales, 1.2% farming, 11.8% construction, 32.7% production (2000).
Income: Per capita income: $21,103 (2000); Median household income: $39,638 (2000); Poverty rate: 6.5% (2000).
Taxes: Total city taxes per capita: $33 (1997); City property taxes per capita: $26 (1997).
Education: High school graduation rate: 81.3% (2000); College graduation rate: 17.5% (2000).
Housing: Homeownership rate: 82.1% (2000); Median home value: $111,000 (2000); Median rent: $416 per month (2000); Median age of housing: 44 years (2000).
Transportation: Commute to work: 91.9% car, 0.3% public transportation, 1.7% walk, 5.4% work from home (2000); Travel time to work: 17.7% less than 15 minutes, 26.4% 15 to 30 minutes, 31.8% 30 to 45 minutes, 6.9% 45 to 60 minutes, 17.2% 60 minutes or more (2000)

ROME (township). Covers a land area of 35.881 square miles and a water area of 0.026 square miles. Located at 41.94° N. Lat.; 84.18° W. Long.
Population: 1,772 (2000); Race: 97.9% White, 0.0% Black, 0.0% Asian, 0.6% American Indian and Alaska Native, 3.1% Hispanic of any race, 1.1% two or more races (2000); Density: 49.4 persons per square mile (2000); Age: 26.9% under 18, 9.1% over 64 (2000); Marriage status: 21.1% never married, 68.8% now married, 4.2% widowed, 5.9% divorced (2000); Foreign born: 0.4% (2000); Ancestry (includes multiple ancestries): 31.5% German, 13.6% English, 12.7% Irish, 9.7% United States or American, 7.0% Other groups (2000).
Economy: Single-family building permits issued: 5 (2001) / 6 (2000); Multi-family building permits issued: 0 (2001) / 0 (2000); Employment by occupation: 9.7% management, 12.8% professional, 13.1% services, 23.8% sales, 1.4% farming, 13.2% construction, 26.0% production (2000).
Income: Per capita income: $20,715 (2000); Median household income: $54,145 (2000); Poverty rate: 3.9% (2000).
Taxes: Total city taxes per capita: $45 (1997); City property taxes per capita: $40 (1997).
Education: High school graduation rate: 84.3% (2000); College graduation rate: 9.5% (2000).
Housing: Homeownership rate: 92.0% (2000); Median home value: $96,900 (2000); Median rent: $520 per month (2000); Median age of housing: 32 years (2000).
Transportation: Commute to work: 94.4% car, 0.1% public transportation, 0.6% walk, 4.7% work from home (2000); Travel time to work: 18.9% less than 15 minutes, 49.9% 15 to 30 minutes, 11.0% 30 to 45 minutes, 7.7% 45 to 60 minutes, 12.6% 60 minutes or more (2000)

SAND CREEK (unincorporated postal area, zip code 49279). Aka Sandcreek. Covers a land area of 26.203 square miles and a water area of 0 square miles. Located at 41.79° N. Lat.; 84.10° W. Long. Elevation is 779 feet.
History: Sand Creek was first called Thurber for its first settlers, Joshua and Rebecca Thurber, who came in 1820.
Population: 930 (2000); Race: 95.0% White, 0.4% Black, 0.3% Asian, 1.0% American Indian and Alaska Native, 1.8% Hispanic of any race, 2.0% two or more races (2000); Density: 35.5 persons per square mile (2000); Age: 31.8% under 18, 12.9% over 64 (2000); Marriage status: 18.7% never married, 71.7% now married, 5.6% widowed, 4.0% divorced (2000); Foreign born: 0.3% (2000); Ancestry (includes multiple ancestries): 26.1% German, 11.8% English, 10.2% Irish, 8.4% Other groups, 5.2% United States or American (2000).
Economy: Employment by occupation: 10.4% management, 8.9% professional, 12.9% services, 23.1% sales, 0.0% farming, 13.2% construction, 31.5% production (2000).
Income: Per capita income: $16,331 (2000); Median household income: $42,065 (2000); Poverty rate: 3.0% (2000).
Education: High school graduation rate: 87.7% (2000); College graduation rate: 7.3% (2000).

School District(s)

Sand Creek Community Schools (KG-12)
2000 Enrollment: 983 517-436-3121
Housing: Homeownership rate: 86.2% (2000); Median home value: $90,000 (2000); Median rent: $425 per month (2000); Median age of housing: 60+ years (2000).
Transportation: Commute to work: 92.8% car, 0.5% public transportation, 3.2% walk, 3.2% work from home (2000); Travel time to work: 18.3% less than 15 minutes, 47.7% 15 to 30 minutes, 16.5% 30 to 45 minutes, 8.5% 45 to 60 minutes, 9.0% 60 minutes or more (2000)

SENECA (township). Covers a land area of 40.005 square miles and a water area of 0.058 square miles. Located at 41.76° N. Lat.; 84.16° W. Long. Elevation is 798 feet.
History: Seneca Township was organized in 1836 and named for Seneca County, New York, the former home of many of its first residents.
Population: 1,303 (2000); Race: 96.6% White, 0.3% Black, 0.2% Asian, 0.9% American Indian and Alaska Native, 1.5% Hispanic of any race, 1.2% two or more races (2000); Density: 32.6 persons per square mile (2000); Age: 27.4% under 18, 9.8% over 64 (2000); Marriage status: 21.6% never married, 65.5% now married, 5.1% widowed, 7.9% divorced (2000); Foreign born: 0.9% (2000); Ancestry (includes multiple ancestries): 25.3% German, 13.3% English, 11.9% Other groups, 11.5% Irish, 8.9% United States or American (2000).
Economy: Single-family building permits issued: 4 (2001) / 2 (2000); Multi-family building permits issued: 0 (2001) / 0 (2000); Employment by occupation: 8.3% management, 12.6% professional, 15.3% services, 18.8% sales, 2.2% farming, 13.1% construction, 29.8% production (2000).
Income: Per capita income: $17,758 (2000); Median household income: $44,107 (2000); Poverty rate: 5.7% (2000).
Taxes: Total city taxes per capita: $23 (1997); City property taxes per capita: $20 (1997).
Education: High school graduation rate: 79.3% (2000); College graduation rate: 10.5% (2000).
Housing: Homeownership rate: 83.7% (2000); Median home value: $89,800 (2000); Median rent: $356 per month (2000); Median age of housing: 51 years (2000).
Transportation: Commute to work: 95.9% car, 0.3% public transportation, 0.6% walk, 3.1% work from home (2000); Travel time to work: 28.2% less than 15 minutes, 31.4% 15 to 30 minutes, 25.9% 30 to 45 minutes, 8.3% 45 to 60 minutes, 6.2% 60 minutes or more (2000)

TECUMSEH (city). Covers a land area of 5.167 square miles and a water area of 0.233 square miles. Located at 42.00° N. Lat.; 83.94° W. Long. Elevation is 795 feet.
History: Tecumseh was incorporated as a village in 1837, and was named for the great Shawnee chief Tecumseh. The first house built in Lenawee County was erected by Musgrove and Abi Evans in 1824 in Tecumseh. The village grew as a trading center for a farm area that raised celery.
Population: 8,574 (2000); Race: 95.1% White, 0.0% Black, 0.8% Asian, 0.9% American Indian and Alaska Native, 5.4% Hispanic of any race, 1.7% two or more races (2000); Density: 1,659.4 persons per square mile (2000); Age: 26.5% under 18, 15.3% over 64 (2000); Marriage status: 23.3% never married, 58.5% now married, 6.8% widowed, 11.3% divorced (2000); Foreign born: 1.5% (2000); Ancestry (includes multiple ancestries): 30.4% German, 16.0% Irish, 12.7% English, 11.4% Other groups, 6.4% United States or American (2000).
Economy: Single-family building permits issued: 56 (2001) / 45 (2000); Multi-family building permits issued: 0 (2001) / 0 (2000); Employment by occupation: 11.0% management, 19.5% professional, 13.9% services, 24.7% sales, 0.1% farming, 8.2% construction, 22.6% production (2000).
Income: Per capita income: $22,797 (2000); Median household income: $46,106 (2000); Poverty rate: 4.9% (2000).
Taxes: Total city taxes per capita: $470 (1997); City property taxes per capita: $428 (1997).
Education: High school graduation rate: 88.0% (2000); College graduation rate: 21.2% (2000).

School District(s)

Tecumseh Public Schools (KG-12)
 2000 Enrollment: 3,266 517-423-2167

Housing: Homeownership rate: 71.6% (2000); Median home value: $119,300 (2000); Median rent: $510 per month (2000); Median age of housing: 40 years (2000).

Hospitals: Herrick Memorial Hospital (94 beds)

Safety: Violent crime rate: 11.6 per 10,000 population; Property crime rate: 276.1 per 10,000 population (2001).

Newspapers: The Tecumseh Herald (1 x week)

Transportation: Commute to work: 93.2% car, 0.3% public transportation, 3.2% walk, 2.6% work from home (2000); Travel time to work: 36.7% less than 15 minutes, 17.5% 15 to 30 minutes, 24.3% 30 to 45 minutes, 14.4% 45 to 60 minutes, 7.1% 60 minutes or more (2000)

Additional Information Contacts

Tecumseh Area Chamber of Commerce 517-423-3740

TECUMSEH (township). Covers a land area of 13.124 square miles and a water area of 0.066 square miles. Located at 42.02° N. Lat.; 83.93° W. Long. Elevation is 795 feet.

History: Has Native-American village sites and earthworks. Settled 1824, incorporated 1837.

Population: 1,881 (2000); Race: 98.2% White, 0.1% Black, 0.3% Asian, 1.0% American Indian and Alaska Native, 2.7% Hispanic of any race, 0.4% two or more races (2000); Density: 143.3 persons per square mile (2000); Age: 25.1% under 18, 13.8% over 64 (2000); Marriage status: 16.6% never married, 75.1% now married, 4.4% widowed, 3.9% divorced (2000); Foreign born: 2.2% (2000); Ancestry (includes multiple ancestries): 32.0% German, 14.9% Irish, 14.5% English, 7.6% United States or American, 6.7% Other groups (2000).

Economy: Ships sand, gravel. Manufacturing includes machinery, motor vehicle parts, paper products, metal products. Single-family building permits issued: 9 (2001) / 16 (2000); Multi-family building permits issued: 0 (2001) / 0 (2000); Employment by occupation: 13.1% management, 22.3% professional, 10.4% services, 24.1% sales, 0.6% farming, 10.1% construction, 19.3% production (2000).

Income: Per capita income: $28,398 (2000); Median household income: $69,276 (2000); Poverty rate: 2.7% (2000).

Taxes: Total city taxes per capita: $41 (1997); City property taxes per capita: $34 (1997).

Education: High school graduation rate: 91.2% (2000); College graduation rate: 23.4% (2000).

Housing: Homeownership rate: 94.7% (2000); Median home value: $157,800 (2000); Median rent: $538 per month (2000); Median age of housing: 27 years (2000).

Transportation: Commute to work: 95.3% car, 0.0% public transportation, 0.8% walk, 3.9% work from home (2000); Travel time to work: 33.8% less than 15 minutes, 23.7% 15 to 30 minutes, 23.0% 30 to 45 minutes, 15.7% 45 to 60 minutes, 3.8% 60 minutes or more (2000)

TIPTON (unincorporated postal area, zip code 49287). Covers a land area of 27.388 square miles and a water area of 0.604 square miles. Located at 42.03° N. Lat.; 84.09° W. Long. Elevation is 904 feet.

Population: 1,925 (2000); Race: 97.9% White, 0.2% Black, 0.3% Asian, 0.2% American Indian and Alaska Native, 1.0% Hispanic of any race, 0.2% two or more races (2000); Density: 70.3 persons per square mile (2000); Age: 23.2% under 18, 7.6% over 64 (2000); Marriage status: 20.9% never married, 66.9% now married, 4.2% widowed, 8.0% divorced (2000); Foreign born: 1.6% (2000); Ancestry (includes multiple ancestries): 30.2% German, 19.5% Irish, 13.1% English, 8.7% Polish, 7.9% United States or American (2000).

Economy: Employment by occupation: 9.7% management, 18.8% professional, 11.4% services, 24.2% sales, 0.0% farming, 15.6% construction, 20.2% production (2000).

Income: Per capita income: $24,901 (2000); Median household income: $55,500 (2000); Poverty rate: 3.2% (2000).

Education: High school graduation rate: 88.2% (2000); College graduation rate: 15.0% (2000).

Housing: Homeownership rate: 90.6% (2000); Median home value: $134,800 (2000); Median rent: $435 per month (2000); Median age of housing: 35 years (2000).

Transportation: Commute to work: 96.7% car, 0.0% public transportation, 0.5% walk, 2.0% work from home (2000); Travel time to work: 15.8% less than 15 minutes, 38.2% 15 to 30 minutes, 22.1% 30 to 45 minutes, 11.7% 45 to 60 minutes, 12.1% 60 minutes or more (2000)

WOODSTOCK (township). Covers a land area of 33.902 square miles and a water area of 1.829 square miles. Located at 42.02° N. Lat.; 84.30° W. Long.

Population: 3,468 (2000); Race: 98.1% White, 0.3% Black, 0.2% Asian, 0.0% American Indian and Alaska Native, 1.6% Hispanic of any race, 1.0% two or more races (2000); Density: 102.3 persons per square mile (2000); Age: 26.8% under 18, 12.4% over 64 (2000); Marriage status: 21.7% never married, 63.1% now married, 5.2% widowed, 10.1% divorced (2000); Foreign born: 1.8% (2000); Ancestry (includes multiple ancestries): 24.7% German, 19.3% Irish, 12.6% English, 7.9% Other groups, 6.7% United States or American (2000).

Economy: Single-family building permits issued: 31 (2001) / 30 (2000); Multi-family building permits issued: 0 (2001) / 0 (2000); Employment by occupation: 8.4% management, 10.3% professional, 12.5% services, 29.4% sales, 0.0% farming, 11.7% construction, 27.7% production (2000).

Income: Per capita income: $20,551 (2000); Median household income: $42,882 (2000); Poverty rate: 6.6% (2000).

Taxes: Total city taxes per capita: $67 (1997); City property taxes per capita: $64 (1997).

Education: High school graduation rate: 81.1% (2000); College graduation rate: 11.3% (2000).

Housing: Homeownership rate: 87.0% (2000); Median home value: $139,100 (2000); Median rent: $384 per month (2000); Median age of housing: 35 years (2000).

Transportation: Commute to work: 94.7% car, 0.6% public transportation, 3.0% walk, 1.2% work from home (2000); Travel time to work: 24.9% less than 15 minutes, 34.5% 15 to 30 minutes, 19.1% 30 to 45 minutes, 8.5% 45 to 60 minutes, 13.0% 60 minutes or more (2000)

Livingston County

Located in southeastern Michigan; drained by the Red Cedar, Huron, and Shiawassee Rivers; includes many lakes. Covers a land area of 568.40 square miles, a water area of 17.00 square miles, and is located in the Eastern Time Zone. The county government was organized in 1836. County seat is Howell.

Livingston County is part of the Ann Arbor, MI PMSA. The entire metro area includes: Lenawee County; Livingston County; Washtenaw County

Population: 156,951 (2000); Race: 96.9% White, 0.5% Black, 0.7% Asian, 0.5% American Indian and Alaska Native, 1.1% Hispanic of any race, 1.1% two or more races (2000); Density: 276.1 persons per square mile (2000); Age: 28.7% under 18, 8.2% over 64 (2000).

Religion: Five largest groups: 22.1% Catholic Church, 2.6% Lutheran Church—Missouri Synod, 1.9% Evangelical Lutheran Church in America, 1.8% The United Methodist Church, 1.2% Evangelical Presbyterian Church (2000).

Economy: Unemployment rate: 3.1% (11/2002); Total civilian labor force: 85,408 (11/2002); Leading industries: 23.7% manufacturing; 18.0% retail trade; 10.1% construction (2000); Companies that employ more than 1,000 persons: 0 (2000); Companies that employ more than 100 persons: 64 (2000); Farms: 637 totaling 98,297 acres (1997); Minority business ownership rate: 2.4% (1997); Women business ownership rate: 26.9% (1997); Retail sales per capita: $9,223 (1997). Single-family building permits issued: 1,741 (2001) / 1,877 (2000); Multi-family building permits issued: 428 (2001) / 290 (2000).

Income: Per capita income: $28,069 (2000); Median household income: $67,400 (2000); Poverty rate: 3.4% (2000); Bankruptcy rate: 2.44% (2001).

Taxes: Total county taxes per capita: $137 (2000); County property taxes per capita: $124 (2000).

Education: High school graduation rate: 91.4% (2000); College graduation rate: 28.2% (2000).

Housing: Homeownership rate: 88.1% (2000); Median home value: $187,500 (2000); Median rent: $616 per month (2000); Median age of housing: 21 years (2000).

Health: Birth rate: 124.5 per 10,000 population (1998); Age adjusted death rate: 88.5 per 10,000 population (1999); Age adjusted cancer mortality rate: 225.7 deaths per 100,000 population (1999). Number of physicians: 8.7 per 10,000 population (1999); Number of hospital beds: 8.4 per 10,000 population (1999).

Elections: 2000 Presidential election results: 38.1% Gore, 59.1% Bush, 2.0% Nader, 0.0% Buchanan

National and State Parks: Brighton State Recreation Area; Gregory State Game Area; Island Lake State Recreation Area; Oak Grove State Game Area; Southern Michigan State Forest Nursery; Unadilla State Wildlife Area

Additional Information Contacts

Livingston County Government Offices 517-546-0500
Hartland Chamber of Commerce 810-632-9130
Hell Michigan Chamber of Commerce 734-878-1099
Livingston County Association of Realtors 517-546-8300

Livingston County Communities

BRIGHTON (city). Covers a land area of 3.608 square miles and a water area of 0.117 square miles. Located at 42.52° N. Lat.; 83.78° W. Long. Elevation is 927 feet.
History: Brighton was first settled in 1832 by Maynard Maltby, who called it Ore Creek. The community, renamed by residents from New York for the town of Brighton there, developed around a grist mill.
Population: 6,701 (2000); Race: 97.5% White, 0.2% Black, 0.6% Asian, 0.2% American Indian and Alaska Native, 1.2% Hispanic of any race, 1.0% two or more races (2000); Density: 1,857.0 persons per square mile (2000); Age: 22.0% under 18, 15.4% over 64 (2000); Marriage status: 26.4% never married, 51.8% now married, 9.0% widowed, 12.8% divorced (2000); Foreign born: 3.5% (2000); Ancestry (includes multiple ancestries): 22.8% German, 17.1% English, 13.7% Irish, 11.7% Polish, 7.6% Italian (2000).
Economy: Single-family building permits issued: 74 (2001) / 58 (2000); Multi-family building permits issued: 0 (2001) / 0 (2000); Employment by occupation: 14.9% management, 21.9% professional, 15.3% services, 26.5% sales, 0.0% farming, 9.3% construction, 12.1% production (2000).
Income: Per capita income: $28,393 (2000); Median household income: $47,897 (2000); Poverty rate: 5.1% (2000).
Taxes: Total city taxes per capita: $569 (1997); City property taxes per capita: $550 (1997).
Education: High school graduation rate: 91.2% (2000); College graduation rate: 31.0% (2000).

School District(s)

Brighton Area Schools (KG-12)
2000 Enrollment: 7,025 810-229-1450
Housing: Homeownership rate: 62.4% (2000); Median home value: $156,400 (2000); Median rent: $605 per month (2000); Median age of housing: 21 years (2000).
Hospitals: Brighton Hospital (63 beds)
Safety: Violent crime rate: 32.7 per 10,000 population; Property crime rate: 433.5 per 10,000 population (2001).
Transportation: Commute to work: 91.0% car, 0.2% public transportation, 4.2% walk, 2.9% work from home (2000); Travel time to work: 34.2% less than 15 minutes, 23.1% 15 to 30 minutes, 25.4% 30 to 45 minutes, 12.1% 45 to 60 minutes, 5.3% 60 minutes or more (2000)

BRIGHTON (township). Covers a land area of 33.115 square miles and a water area of 1.447 square miles. Located at 42.55° N. Lat.; 83.75° W. Long. Elevation is 927 feet.
History: Settled 1832; incorporated 1867 as village and 1928 as city.
Population: 17,673 (2000); Race: 97.0% White, 0.7% Black, 1.1% Asian, 0.3% American Indian and Alaska Native, 0.9% Hispanic of any race, 0.8% two or more races (2000); Density: 533.7 persons per square mile (2000); Age: 29.7% under 18, 7.2% over 64 (2000); Marriage status: 19.5% never married, 69.9% now married, 3.3% widowed, 7.4% divorced (2000); Foreign born: 4.8% (2000); Ancestry (includes multiple ancestries): 25.8% German, 15.1% Irish, 13.8% Polish, 12.9% English, 8.6% Italian (2000).
Economy: In rich agricultural area; timber. Manufacturing: transportation equipment, fences, chemicals, wood products, thermoplastics. Summer resort. Single-family building permits issued: 109 (2001) / 111 (2000); Multi-family building permits issued: 0 (2001) / 0 (2000); Employment by occupation: 20.2% management, 25.1% professional, 9.2% services, 26.4% sales, 0.1% farming, 8.5% construction, 10.5% production (2000).
Income: Per capita income: $33,070 (2000); Median household income: $83,940 (2000); Poverty rate: 2.5% (2000).
Taxes: Total city taxes per capita: $56 (1997); City property taxes per capita: $30 (1997).
Education: High school graduation rate: 93.1% (2000); College graduation rate: 37.9% (2000).
Housing: Homeownership rate: 94.0% (2000); Median home value: $222,900 (2000); Median rent: $589 per month (2000); Median age of housing: 21 years (2000).
Transportation: Commute to work: 94.6% car, 0.2% public transportation, 0.9% walk, 4.1% work from home (2000); Travel time to work: 23.7% less than 15 minutes, 21.8% 15 to 30 minutes, 29.6% 30 to 45 minutes, 15.6% 45 to 60 minutes, 9.3% 60 minutes or more (2000)

COHOCTAH (township). Aka East Cohoctah. Covers a land area of 38.096 square miles and a water area of 0.232 square miles. Located at 42.73° N. Lat.; 83.97° W. Long. Elevation is 887 feet.
Population: 3,394 (2000); Race: 98.3% White, 0.0% Black, 1.0% Asian, 0.0% American Indian and Alaska Native, 1.0% Hispanic of any race, 0.7% two or more races (2000); Density: 89.1 persons per square mile (2000); Age: 29.6% under 18, 6.1% over 64 (2000); Marriage status: 21.7% never married, 65.2% now married, 5.8% widowed, 7.3% divorced (2000); Foreign born: 1.7% (2000); Ancestry (includes multiple ancestries): 18.6% German, 17.4% Irish, 12.7% Other groups, 9.0% English, 7.7% United States or American (2000).
Economy: Employment by occupation: 9.1% management, 17.3% professional, 9.1% services, 33.8% sales, 0.0% farming, 14.2% construction, 16.5% production (2000).
Income: Per capita income: $21,582 (2000); Median household income: $57,500 (2000); Poverty rate: 2.6% (2000).
Taxes: Total city taxes per capita: $35 (1997); City property taxes per capita: $33 (1997).
Education: High school graduation rate: 88.2% (2000); College graduation rate: 12.8% (2000).
Housing: Homeownership rate: 95.9% (2000); Median home value: $150,400 (2000); Median rent: $671 per month (2000); Median age of housing: 25 years (2000).
Transportation: Commute to work: 94.3% car, 0.0% public transportation, 1.6% walk, 4.1% work from home (2000); Travel time to work: 14.9% less than 15 minutes, 28.3% 15 to 30 minutes, 21.4% 30 to 45 minutes, 18.2% 45 to 60 minutes, 17.1% 60 minutes or more (2000)

CONWAY (township). Covers a land area of 37.765 square miles and a water area of 0.026 square miles. Located at 42.72° N. Lat.; 84.10° W. Long.
Population: 2,732 (2000); Race: 95.3% White, 0.1% Black, 0.0% Asian, 2.3% American Indian and Alaska Native, 0.5% Hispanic of any race, 2.3% two or more races (2000); Density: 72.3 persons per square mile (2000); Age: 31.1% under 18, 7.2% over 64 (2000); Marriage status: 21.9% never married, 65.3% now married, 4.4% widowed, 8.3% divorced (2000); Foreign born: 1.5% (2000); Ancestry (includes multiple ancestries): 27.9% German, 14.6% English, 12.3% Irish, 9.3% Polish, 8.6% Other groups (2000).
Economy: Employment by occupation: 13.9% management, 10.5% professional, 13.5% services, 26.4% sales, 0.8% farming, 18.1% construction, 16.8% production (2000).
Income: Per capita income: $23,796 (2000); Median household income: $64,306 (2000); Poverty rate: 4.1% (2000).
Taxes: Total city taxes per capita: $35 (1997); City property taxes per capita: $34 (1997).
Education: High school graduation rate: 87.4% (2000); College graduation rate: 10.8% (2000).
Housing: Homeownership rate: 97.1% (2000); Median home value: $154,200 (2000); Median rent: $625 per month (2000); Median age of housing: 21 years (2000).
Transportation: Commute to work: 96.3% car, 0.0% public transportation, 0.5% walk, 2.3% work from home (2000); Travel time to work: 14.3% less than 15 minutes, 31.9% 15 to 30 minutes, 24.2% 30 to 45 minutes, 13.6% 45 to 60 minutes, 16.1% 60 minutes or more (2000)

DEERFIELD (township). Covers a land area of 36.412 square miles and a water area of 1.302 square miles. Located at 42.75° N. Lat.; 83.85° W. Long.
Population: 4,087 (2000); Race: 97.4% White, 0.0% Black, 0.0% Asian, 0.9% American Indian and Alaska Native, 1.2% Hispanic of any race, 1.7% two or more races (2000); Density: 112.2 persons per square mile (2000); Age: 30.0% under 18, 6.6% over 64 (2000); Marriage status: 19.0% never married, 69.0% now married, 3.6% widowed, 8.4% divorced (2000); Foreign born: 0.9% (2000); Ancestry (includes multiple ancestries): 32.9% German, 15.4% Irish, 13.4% English, 11.2% Polish, 7.6% French (except Basque) (2000).
Economy: Single-family building permits issued: 6 (2001) / 27 (2000); Multi-family building permits issued: 0 (2001) / 0 (2000); Employment by occupation: 13.2% management, 16.7% professional, 9.7% services, 29.3% sales, 0.2% farming, 13.4% construction, 17.5% production (2000).
Income: Per capita income: $28,140 (2000); Median household income: $65,756 (2000); Poverty rate: 2.4% (2000).
Taxes: Total city taxes per capita: $63 (1997); City property taxes per capita: $46 (1997).
Education: High school graduation rate: 91.0% (2000); College graduation rate: 18.6% (2000).

Housing: Homeownership rate: 94.1% (2000); Median home value: $172,300 (2000); Median rent: $475 per month (2000); Median age of housing: 23 years (2000).
Transportation: Commute to work: 94.7% car, 0.0% public transportation, 0.8% walk, 4.5% work from home (2000); Travel time to work: 10.7% less than 15 minutes, 32.2% 15 to 30 minutes, 26.1% 30 to 45 minutes, 16.3% 45 to 60 minutes, 14.6% 60 minutes or more (2000)

FOWLERVILLE (village). Covers a land area of 2.312 square miles and a water area of 0.035 square miles. Located at 42.65° N. Lat.; 84.07° W. Long. Elevation is 893 feet.
History: Fowlerville was established in 1835.
Population: 2,972 (2000); Race: 96.7% White, 0.0% Black, 0.3% Asian, 1.6% American Indian and Alaska Native, 0.6% Hispanic of any race, 0.8% two or more races (2000); Density: 1,285.2 persons per square mile (2000); Age: 29.8% under 18, 12.7% over 64 (2000); Marriage status: 26.9% never married, 45.8% now married, 8.4% widowed, 18.9% divorced (2000); Foreign born: 2.2% (2000); Ancestry (includes multiple ancestries): 20.9% German, 13.7% English, 11.0% Irish, 10.8% United States or American, 7.9% Other groups (2000).
Economy: Employment by occupation: 8.5% management, 10.7% professional, 19.3% services, 23.1% sales, 0.3% farming, 13.6% construction, 24.5% production (2000).
Income: Per capita income: $18,074 (2000); Median household income: $41,628 (2000); Poverty rate: 9.0% (2000).
Taxes: Total city taxes per capita: $448 (1997); City property taxes per capita: $443 (1997).
Education: High school graduation rate: 82.3% (2000); College graduation rate: 11.0% (2000).

School District(s)

Fowlerville Community Schools (KG-12)
2000 Enrollment: 3,164 517-223-8459

Housing: Homeownership rate: 66.7% (2000); Median home value: $123,900 (2000); Median rent: $533 per month (2000); Median age of housing: 30 years (2000).
Safety: Violent crime rate: 6.7 per 10,000 population; Property crime rate: 237.6 per 10,000 population (2001).
Transportation: Commute to work: 93.3% car, 0.0% public transportation, 3.5% walk, 2.7% work from home (2000); Travel time to work: 29.5% less than 15 minutes, 36.2% 15 to 30 minutes, 18.6% 30 to 45 minutes, 9.2% 45 to 60 minutes, 6.5% 60 minutes or more (2000)

GENOA (township). Covers a land area of 34.255 square miles and a water area of 2.095 square miles. Located at 42.56° N. Lat.; 83.84° W. Long.
Population: 15,901 (2000); Race: 97.4% White, 0.3% Black, 0.5% Asian, 0.6% American Indian and Alaska Native, 1.0% Hispanic of any race, 1.1% two or more races (2000); Density: 464.2 persons per square mile (2000); Age: 27.4% under 18, 8.9% over 64 (2000); Marriage status: 19.7% never married, 67.2% now married, 4.0% widowed, 9.1% divorced (2000); Foreign born: 3.6% (2000); Ancestry (includes multiple ancestries): 22.6% German, 14.7% Irish, 13.4% English, 12.0% Polish, 8.7% Italian (2000).
Economy: Employment by occupation: 17.4% management, 20.6% professional, 12.0% services, 26.4% sales, 0.2% farming, 10.1% construction, 13.2% production (2000).
Income: Per capita income: $32,601 (2000); Median household income: $71,398 (2000); Poverty rate: 2.7% (2000).
Taxes: Total city taxes per capita: $61 (2000); City property taxes per capita: $43 (2000).
Education: High school graduation rate: 91.3% (2000); College graduation rate: 32.8% (2000).
Housing: Homeownership rate: 88.8% (2000); Median home value: $224,900 (2000); Median rent: $695 per month (2000); Median age of housing: 17 years (2000).
Transportation: Commute to work: 94.9% car, 0.0% public transportation, 0.6% walk, 4.2% work from home (2000); Travel time to work: 22.9% less than 15 minutes, 25.9% 15 to 30 minutes, 24.7% 30 to 45 minutes, 17.2% 45 to 60 minutes, 9.4% 60 minutes or more (2000)

GREEN OAK (township). Covers a land area of 34.727 square miles and a water area of 2.016 square miles. Located at 42.47° N. Lat.; 83.72° W. Long.
Population: 15,618 (2000); Race: 96.3% White, 1.4% Black, 0.7% Asian, 0.5% American Indian and Alaska Native, 0.7% Hispanic of any race, 1.0% two or more races (2000); Density: 449.7 persons per square mile (2000); Age: 29.5% under 18, 8.9% over 64 (2000); Marriage status: 22.0% never married, 66.8% now married, 4.4% widowed, 6.8% divorced (2000); Foreign born: 1.8% (2000); Ancestry (includes multiple ancestries): 27.3% German, 15.5% Irish, 14.3% Polish, 13.5% English, 6.7% Italian (2000).
Economy: Single-family building permits issued: 127 (2001) / 162 (2000); Multi-family building permits issued: 104 (2001) / 0 (2000); Employment by occupation: 17.1% management, 22.5% professional, 12.1% services, 24.9% sales, 0.0% farming, 11.7% construction, 11.7% production (2000).
Income: Per capita income: $29,923 (2000); Median household income: $75,173 (2000); Poverty rate: 2.6% (2000).
Taxes: Total city taxes per capita: $121 (1997); City property taxes per capita: $86 (1997).
Education: High school graduation rate: 93.2% (2000); College graduation rate: 33.0% (2000).
Housing: Homeownership rate: 91.0% (2000); Median home value: $201,300 (2000); Median rent: $582 per month (2000); Median age of housing: 23 years (2000).
Safety: Violent crime rate: 11.5 per 10,000 population; Property crime rate: 138.2 per 10,000 population (2001).
Transportation: Commute to work: 94.5% car, 0.1% public transportation, 1.0% walk, 3.7% work from home (2000); Travel time to work: 15.9% less than 15 minutes, 30.5% 15 to 30 minutes, 31.6% 30 to 45 minutes, 14.4% 45 to 60 minutes, 7.6% 60 minutes or more (2000)

GREGORY (unincorporated postal area, zip code 48137). Covers a land area of 42.575 square miles and a water area of 1.730 square miles. Located at 42.44° N. Lat.; 84.06° W. Long. Elevation is 950 feet.
History: Halstead Gregory owned the farm through which the Grand Trunk Railroad ran its line in 1884. Gregory built a store, which also served as the post office, near the depot. The community that grew up around Gregory's store was named for him.
Population: 4,511 (2000); Race: 95.8% White, 0.8% Black, 0.5% Asian, 0.4% American Indian and Alaska Native, 2.3% Hispanic of any race, 0.7% two or more races (2000); Density: 106.0 persons per square mile (2000); Age: 26.8% under 18, 10.4% over 64 (2000); Marriage status: 20.3% never married, 66.1% now married, 5.0% widowed, 8.6% divorced (2000); Foreign born: 2.9% (2000); Ancestry (includes multiple ancestries): 29.9% German, 13.7% Irish, 12.9% English, 9.5% Other groups, 7.7% French (except Basque) (2000).
Economy: Employment by occupation: 13.5% management, 17.7% professional, 14.2% services, 22.3% sales, 2.1% farming, 14.6% construction, 15.6% production (2000).
Income: Per capita income: $23,619 (2000); Median household income: $58,429 (2000); Poverty rate: 3.1% (2000).
Education: High school graduation rate: 86.1% (2000); College graduation rate: 20.8% (2000).
Housing: Homeownership rate: 92.0% (2000); Median home value: $161,900 (2000); Median rent: $697 per month (2000); Median age of housing: 28 years (2000).
Transportation: Commute to work: 93.3% car, 1.2% public transportation, 2.1% walk, 3.3% work from home (2000); Travel time to work: 8.9% less than 15 minutes, 28.5% 15 to 30 minutes, 29.6% 30 to 45 minutes, 20.8% 45 to 60 minutes, 12.1% 60 minutes or more (2000)

HAMBURG (township). Covers a land area of 32.389 square miles and a water area of 3.628 square miles. Located at 42.46° N. Lat.; 83.84° W. Long.
Population: 20,627 (2000); Race: 96.6% White, 1.0% Black, 0.8% Asian, 0.4% American Indian and Alaska Native, 1.1% Hispanic of any race, 1.2% two or more races (2000); Density: 636.9 persons per square mile (2000); Age: 29.3% under 18, 6.2% over 64 (2000); Marriage status: 19.6% never married, 69.3% now married, 3.1% widowed, 8.0% divorced (2000); Foreign born: 2.9% (2000); Ancestry (includes multiple ancestries): 27.6% German, 17.6% Irish, 13.8% English, 13.3% Polish, 7.2% United States or American (2000).
Economy: Manufacturing: electrical equipment, fabricated metal products. Employment by occupation: 17.5% management, 23.7% professional, 10.8% services, 25.8% sales, 0.0% farming, 10.6% construction, 11.6% production (2000).
Income: Per capita income: $30,283 (2000); Median household income: $75,960 (2000); Poverty rate: 2.4% (2000).
Taxes: Total city taxes per capita: $112 (2000); City property taxes per capita: $102 (2000).
Education: High school graduation rate: 93.1% (2000); College graduation rate: 32.8% (2000).
Housing: Homeownership rate: 93.7% (2000); Median home value: $204,200 (2000); Median rent: $726 per month (2000); Median age of housing: 19 years (2000).

Safety: Violent crime rate: 2.9 per 10,000 population; Property crime rate: 89.7 per 10,000 population (2001).
Transportation: Commute to work: 97.1% car, 0.1% public transportation, 0.2% walk, 2.3% work from home (2000); Travel time to work: 13.7% less than 15 minutes, 25.1% 15 to 30 minutes, 35.3% 30 to 45 minutes, 15.9% 45 to 60 minutes, 10.0% 60 minutes or more (2000)

HANDY (township). Covers a land area of 34.495 square miles and a water area of 0.109 square miles. Located at 42.65° N. Lat.; 84.08° W. Long.
Population: 7,004 (2000); Race: 97.1% White, 0.4% Black, 0.1% Asian, 0.9% American Indian and Alaska Native, 0.4% Hispanic of any race, 1.3% two or more races (2000); Density: 203.0 persons per square mile (2000); Age: 31.4% under 18, 9.4% over 64 (2000); Marriage status: 24.3% never married, 55.6% now married, 6.4% widowed, 13.7% divorced (2000); Foreign born: 2.2% (2000); Ancestry (includes multiple ancestries): 22.3% German, 14.8% English, 14.0% Irish, 10.3% United States or American, 6.9% Polish (2000).
Economy: Employment by occupation: 10.4% management, 13.3% professional, 17.1% services, 24.1% sales, 0.2% farming, 13.7% construction, 21.2% production (2000).
Income: Per capita income: $20,159 (2000); Median household income: $49,447 (2000); Poverty rate: 6.2% (2000).
Taxes: Total city taxes per capita: $32 (1997); City property taxes per capita: $29 (1997).
Education: High school graduation rate: 85.3% (2000); College graduation rate: 14.9% (2000).
Housing: Homeownership rate: 78.2% (2000); Median home value: $141,700 (2000); Median rent: $482 per month (2000); Median age of housing: 26 years (2000).
Transportation: Commute to work: 94.2% car, 0.0% public transportation, 2.3% walk, 3.3% work from home (2000); Travel time to work: 25.3% less than 15 minutes, 34.0% 15 to 30 minutes, 16.8% 30 to 45 minutes, 14.9% 45 to 60 minutes, 8.9% 60 minutes or more (2000)

HARTLAND (township). Covers a land area of 36.349 square miles and a water area of 1.306 square miles. Located at 42.63° N. Lat.; 83.73° W. Long.
Population: 10,996 (2000); Race: 96.8% White, 0.4% Black, 0.9% Asian, 0.2% American Indian and Alaska Native, 2.1% Hispanic of any race, 0.6% two or more races (2000); Density: 302.5 persons per square mile (2000); Age: 30.2% under 18, 6.8% over 64 (2000); Marriage status: 18.1% never married, 72.6% now married, 3.3% widowed, 6.0% divorced (2000); Foreign born: 2.4% (2000); Ancestry (includes multiple ancestries): 28.5% German, 18.6% Irish, 17.7% English, 10.4% Polish, 5.9% French (except Basque) (2000).
Economy: In farm area. Employment by occupation: 17.5% management, 24.4% professional, 8.9% services, 26.0% sales, 0.2% farming, 11.2% construction, 11.9% production (2000).
Income: Per capita income: $28,971 (2000); Median household income: $75,908 (2000); Poverty rate: 1.7% (2000).
Taxes: Total city taxes per capita: $80 (1997); City property taxes per capita: $73 (1997).
Education: High school graduation rate: 95.1% (2000); College graduation rate: 33.3% (2000).

School District(s)

Hartland Consolidated Schools (KG-12)
2000 Enrollment: 4,582 810-632-7481

Housing: Homeownership rate: 95.8% (2000); Median home value: $198,300 (2000); Median rent: $637 per month (2000); Median age of housing: 17 years (2000).
Transportation: Commute to work: 95.7% car, 0.3% public transportation, 0.4% walk, 3.5% work from home (2000); Travel time to work: 13.4% less than 15 minutes, 28.9% 15 to 30 minutes, 28.4% 30 to 45 minutes, 17.9% 45 to 60 minutes, 11.4% 60 minutes or more (2000)
Additional Information Contacts
Hartland Chamber of Commerce 810-632-9130

HOWELL (city). Covers a land area of 4.111 square miles and a water area of 0.195 square miles. Located at 42.61° N. Lat.; 83.93° W. Long. Elevation is 922 feet.
History: Howell began as a lumber town, but later turned to dairying, becoming a center for Holstein cattle. The Know-Nothing movement, organized to influence changes in the immigration laws, was strong in Howell in the 1850's.
Population: 9,232 (2000); Race: 96.5% White, 0.3% Black, 1.1% Asian, 0.4% American Indian and Alaska Native, 2.3% Hispanic of any race, 0.9% two or more races (2000); Density: 2,245.8 persons per square mile (2000); Age: 24.1% under 18, 12.5% over 64 (2000); Marriage status: 27.5% never married, 48.5% now married, 8.1% widowed, 15.9% divorced (2000); Foreign born: 3.9% (2000); Ancestry (includes multiple ancestries): 28.4% German, 16.5% Irish, 14.0% English, 8.8% Polish, 7.6% United States or American (2000).
Economy: Single-family building permits issued: 31 (2001) / 18 (2000); Multi-family building permits issued: 42 (2001) / 0 (2000); Employment by occupation: 11.1% management, 19.3% professional, 13.9% services, 29.4% sales, 0.0% farming, 10.1% construction, 16.2% production (2000).
Income: Per capita income: $22,254 (2000); Median household income: $43,958 (2000); Poverty rate: 6.6% (2000).
Taxes: Total city taxes per capita: $394 (1997); City property taxes per capita: $383 (1997).
Education: High school graduation rate: 88.0% (2000); College graduation rate: 23.6% (2000).

School District(s)

Howell Public Schools (KG-12)
2000 Enrollment: 7,552 517-548-6234
Livingston Developmental Academy (KG-08)
2000 Enrollment: 398 517-774-2100
Livingston Technical Academy (09-12)
2000 Enrollment: 130 517-774-2100

Four-year College(s)

Cleary College (Private, Not-for-profit)
2001 Enrollment: n/a 517-548-3670
2001 Tuition: In-state $13,800; Out-of-state $13,800

Housing: Homeownership rate: 56.9% (2000); Median home value: $145,200 (2000); Median rent: $625 per month (2000); Median age of housing: 26 years (2000).
Hospitals: McPherson Hospital (136 beds)
Safety: Violent crime rate: 16.2 per 10,000 population; Property crime rate: 296.3 per 10,000 population (2001).
Newspapers: The Livingston County Daily Press & Argus (7 x week)
Transportation: Commute to work: 93.1% car, 0.6% public transportation, 3.0% walk, 2.7% work from home (2000); Travel time to work: 37.9% less than 15 minutes, 22.7% 15 to 30 minutes, 16.7% 30 to 45 minutes, 13.2% 45 to 60 minutes, 9.5% 60 minutes or more (2000)
Additional Information Contacts
Livingston County Association of Realtors 517-546-8300

HOWELL (township). Covers a land area of 31.734 square miles and a water area of 0.161 square miles. Located at 42.63° N. Lat.; 83.97° W. Long. Elevation is 922 feet.
History: Settled 1834; Incorporated as village 1863, as city 1915.
Population: 5,679 (2000); Race: 98.8% White, 0.3% Black, 0.0% Asian, 0.0% American Indian and Alaska Native, 1.6% Hispanic of any race, 0.9% two or more races (2000); Density: 179.0 persons per square mile (2000); Age: 27.9% under 18, 10.8% over 64 (2000); Marriage status: 20.5% never married, 66.5% now married, 5.9% widowed, 7.2% divorced (2000); Foreign born: 1.3% (2000); Ancestry (includes multiple ancestries): 26.4% German, 15.5% English, 14.0% Irish, 10.4% United States or American, 10.1% Polish (2000).
Economy: Railroad junction. In agricultural and dairying area. Manufacturing of electronic equipment, chemicals, metal products, lubricants and hydraulic fluids, metal plating, plastic molding, transformers, soft drinks, baking containers, electric breakers,hospital supplies and aluminum wheels. Summer resort. Airport. Employment by occupation: 12.9% management, 17.4% professional, 12.3% services, 26.5% sales, 0.0% farming, 15.0% construction, 15.9% production (2000).
Income: Per capita income: $23,840 (2000); Median household income: $63,114 (2000); Poverty rate: 2.8% (2000).
Taxes: Total city taxes per capita: $58 (1997); City property taxes per capita: $52 (1997).
Education: High school graduation rate: 87.3% (2000); College graduation rate: 18.6% (2000).
Housing: Homeownership rate: 93.6% (2000); Median home value: $161,200 (2000); Median rent: $697 per month (2000); Median age of housing: 23 years (2000).
Transportation: Commute to work: 95.0% car, 0.5% public transportation, 0.3% walk, 3.3% work from home (2000); Travel time to work: 27.9% less than 15 minutes, 24.1% 15 to 30 minutes, 15.5% 30 to 45 minutes, 19.3% 45 to 60 minutes, 13.2% 60 minutes or more (2000)

IOSCO (township). Covers a land area of 35.485 square miles and a water area of 0.054 square miles. Located at 42.55° N. Lat.; 84.07° W. Long.

Population: 3,039 (2000); Race: 95.2% White, 0.0% Black, 1.7% Asian, 0.0% American Indian and Alaska Native, 2.8% Hispanic of any race, 0.7% two or more races (2000); Density: 85.6 persons per square mile (2000); Age: 32.6% under 18, 4.9% over 64 (2000); Marriage status: 20.3% never married, 69.7% now married, 3.1% widowed, 6.9% divorced (2000); Foreign born: 2.6% (2000); Ancestry (includes multiple ancestries): 26.7% German, 13.4% Irish, 12.4% English, 12.0% Polish, 9.5% Other groups (2000).
Economy: Employment by occupation: 15.0% management, 16.3% professional, 12.6% services, 21.7% sales, 3.6% farming, 13.4% construction, 17.5% production (2000).
Income: Per capita income: $20,675 (2000); Median household income: $63,808 (2000); Poverty rate: 6.6% (2000).
Taxes: Total city taxes per capita: $60 (1997); City property taxes per capita: $59 (1997).
Education: High school graduation rate: 84.7% (2000); College graduation rate: 15.3% (2000).
Housing: Homeownership rate: 96.4% (2000); Median home value: $170,900 (2000); Median rent: $675 per month (2000); Median age of housing: 12 years (2000).
Transportation: Commute to work: 92.6% car, 1.7% public transportation, 1.3% walk, 4.2% work from home (2000); Travel time to work: 11.3% less than 15 minutes, 44.4% 15 to 30 minutes, 18.0% 30 to 45 minutes, 12.9% 45 to 60 minutes, 13.5% 60 minutes or more (2000)

MARION (township). Covers a land area of 35.572 square miles and a water area of 0.760 square miles. Located at 42.56° N. Lat.; 83.96° W. Long.
Population: 6,757 (2000); Race: 97.1% White, 0.0% Black, 0.3% Asian, 0.5% American Indian and Alaska Native, 0.7% Hispanic of any race, 2.0% two or more races (2000); Density: 190.0 persons per square mile (2000); Age: 29.7% under 18, 7.3% over 64 (2000); Marriage status: 19.4% never married, 70.3% now married, 3.8% widowed, 6.5% divorced (2000); Foreign born: 3.8% (2000); Ancestry (includes multiple ancestries): 31.0% German, 15.5% Polish, 14.9% English, 13.6% Irish, 6.2% Other groups (2000).
Economy: Employment by occupation: 12.0% management, 19.2% professional, 10.2% services, 26.7% sales, 0.2% farming, 12.5% construction, 19.3% production (2000).
Income: Per capita income: $26,862 (2000); Median household income: $72,378 (2000); Poverty rate: 2.0% (2000).
Taxes: Total city taxes per capita: $30 (1997); City property taxes per capita: $24 (1997).
Education: High school graduation rate: 94.1% (2000); College graduation rate: 23.2% (2000).
Housing: Homeownership rate: 95.6% (2000); Median home value: $186,600 (2000); Median rent: $842 per month (2000); Median age of housing: 21 years (2000).
Transportation: Commute to work: 95.7% car, 0.3% public transportation, 0.8% walk, 2.5% work from home (2000); Travel time to work: 15.6% less than 15 minutes, 35.1% 15 to 30 minutes, 22.6% 30 to 45 minutes, 14.0% 45 to 60 minutes, 12.7% 60 minutes or more (2000)

OCEOLA (township). Covers a land area of 36.290 square miles and a water area of 0.501 square miles. Located at 42.63° N. Lat.; 83.86° W. Long.
Population: 8,362 (2000); Race: 96.6% White, 0.0% Black, 0.6% Asian, 1.0% American Indian and Alaska Native, 0.9% Hispanic of any race, 1.0% two or more races (2000); Density: 230.4 persons per square mile (2000); Age: 32.0% under 18, 5.8% over 64 (2000); Marriage status: 17.3% never married, 74.3% now married, 2.4% widowed, 6.0% divorced (2000); Foreign born: 4.2% (2000); Ancestry (includes multiple ancestries): 22.6% German, 16.2% Irish, 12.5% English, 12.1% Polish, 7.0% French (except Basque) (2000).
Economy: Employment by occupation: 14.5% management, 22.3% professional, 11.7% services, 27.2% sales, 0.0% farming, 11.0% construction, 13.3% production (2000).
Income: Per capita income: $27,052 (2000); Median household income: $76,139 (2000); Poverty rate: 4.6% (2000).
Taxes: Total city taxes per capita: $61 (2000); City property taxes per capita: $59 (2000).
Education: High school graduation rate: 93.4% (2000); College graduation rate: 25.3% (2000).
Housing: Homeownership rate: 95.0% (2000); Median home value: $189,200 (2000); Median rent: $572 per month (2000); Median age of housing: 12 years (2000).
Transportation: Commute to work: 95.8% car, 0.2% public transportation, 0.7% walk, 3.2% work from home (2000); Travel time to work: 18.8% less than 15 minutes, 28.1% 15 to 30 minutes, 21.1% 30 to 45 minutes, 19.2% 45 to 60 minutes, 12.8% 60 minutes or more (2000)

PINCKNEY (village). Covers a land area of 1.490 square miles and a water area of 0.050 square miles. Located at 42.45° N. Lat.; 83.94° W. Long.
History: Pinckney was founded by William Kirkland, who named the village for his brother, Charles Pinckney Kirkland, a New York lawyer. The village was first settled in 1836.
Population: 2,141 (2000); Race: 97.5% White, 0.2% Black, 0.4% Asian, 0.0% American Indian and Alaska Native, 0.9% Hispanic of any race, 1.7% two or more races (2000); Density: 1,436.8 persons per square mile (2000); Age: 34.5% under 18, 5.2% over 64 (2000); Marriage status: 25.1% never married, 61.3% now married, 2.7% widowed, 10.9% divorced (2000); Foreign born: 2.3% (2000); Ancestry (includes multiple ancestries): 25.1% German, 15.7% Irish, 12.9% Polish, 10.9% English, 9.3% United States or American (2000).
Economy: Employment by occupation: 10.6% management, 18.4% professional, 15.5% services, 24.4% sales, 0.0% farming, 15.5% construction, 15.5% production (2000).
Income: Per capita income: $20,429 (2000); Median household income: $58,077 (2000); Poverty rate: 5.7% (2000).
Taxes: Total city taxes per capita: $162 (1997); City property taxes per capita: $153 (1997).
Education: High school graduation rate: 92.0% (2000); College graduation rate: 22.8% (2000).

School District(s)

Pinckney Community Schools (KG-12)
2000 Enrollment: 4,903 810-225-3900

Housing: Homeownership rate: 82.6% (2000); Median home value: $150,100 (2000); Median rent: $607 per month (2000); Median age of housing: 21 years (2000).
Safety: Violent crime rate: 9.3 per 10,000 population; Property crime rate: 520.4 per 10,000 population (2001).
Newspapers: The Express (1 x week)
Transportation: Commute to work: 93.7% car, 0.0% public transportation, 3.4% walk, 2.7% work from home (2000); Travel time to work: 19.8% less than 15 minutes, 23.9% 15 to 30 minutes, 29.5% 30 to 45 minutes, 13.6% 45 to 60 minutes, 13.2% 60 minutes or more (2000)

Additional Information Contacts

Hell Michigan Chamber of Commerce 734-878-1099

PUTNAM (township). Covers a land area of 34.357 square miles and a water area of 1.176 square miles. Located at 42.45° N. Lat.; 83.95° W. Long.
Population: 7,500 (2000); Race: 98.1% White, 0.2% Black, 0.2% Asian, 0.6% American Indian and Alaska Native, 0.3% Hispanic of any race, 0.9% two or more races (2000); Density: 218.3 persons per square mile (2000); Age: 27.6% under 18, 7.1% over 64 (2000); Marriage status: 22.5% never married, 64.0% now married, 3.6% widowed, 10.0% divorced (2000); Foreign born: 2.0% (2000); Ancestry (includes multiple ancestries): 26.9% German, 15.2% Irish, 12.0% English, 11.3% Polish, 11.1% United States or American (2000).
Economy: Employment by occupation: 12.3% management, 16.6% professional, 15.0% services, 26.6% sales, 0.0% farming, 13.2% construction, 16.2% production (2000).
Income: Per capita income: $23,974 (2000); Median household income: $61,388 (2000); Poverty rate: 3.9% (2000).
Taxes: Total city taxes per capita: $57 (2000); City property taxes per capita: $54 (2000).
Education: High school graduation rate: 89.3% (2000); College graduation rate: 19.1% (2000).
Housing: Homeownership rate: 87.2% (2000); Median home value: $164,900 (2000); Median rent: $542 per month (2000); Median age of housing: 27 years (2000).
Transportation: Commute to work: 94.1% car, 0.0% public transportation, 2.3% walk, 2.7% work from home (2000); Travel time to work: 18.3% less than 15 minutes, 24.7% 15 to 30 minutes, 30.1% 30 to 45 minutes, 16.5% 45 to 60 minutes, 10.4% 60 minutes or more (2000)

TYRONE (township). Covers a land area of 35.645 square miles and a water area of 1.099 square miles. Located at 42.74° N. Lat.; 83.75° W. Long.
Population: 8,459 (2000); Race: 96.2% White, 0.6% Black, 1.2% Asian, 0.5% American Indian and Alaska Native, 1.9% Hispanic of any race, 1.1% two or more races (2000); Density: 237.3 persons per square mile (2000); Age: 28.3% under 18, 8.1% over 64 (2000); Marriage status: 19.9% never married, 69.8% now married, 4.2% widowed, 6.1% divorced (2000); Foreign born: 3.6% (2000); Ancestry (includes multiple ancestries): 24.1% German, 17.8% English, 17.5% Irish, 13.1% Polish, 7.8% Other groups (2000).

Economy: Employment by occupation: 17.1% management, 25.6% professional, 11.5% services, 21.0% sales, 0.2% farming, 11.0% construction, 13.5% production (2000).
Income: Per capita income: $29,292 (2000); Median household income: $75,994 (2000); Poverty rate: 4.2% (2000).
Taxes: Total city taxes per capita: $46 (2000); City property taxes per capita: $41 (2000).
Education: High school graduation rate: 92.4% (2000); College graduation rate: 31.6% (2000).
Housing: Homeownership rate: 94.5% (2000); Median home value: $193,200 (2000); Median rent: $613 per month (2000); Median age of housing: 24 years (2000).
Transportation: Commute to work: 93.5% car, 0.0% public transportation, 0.3% walk, 5.1% work from home (2000); Travel time to work: 20.2% less than 15 minutes, 31.3% 15 to 30 minutes, 23.9% 30 to 45 minutes, 9.9% 45 to 60 minutes, 14.7% 60 minutes or more (2000)

UNADILLA (township). Covers a land area of 33.994 square miles and a water area of 0.810 square miles. Located at 42.46° N. Lat.; 84.07° W. Long.
Population: 3,190 (2000); Race: 97.5% White, 0.3% Black, 0.2% Asian, 0.3% American Indian and Alaska Native, 0.4% Hispanic of any race, 1.8% two or more races (2000); Density: 93.8 persons per square mile (2000); Age: 26.1% under 18, 10.6% over 64 (2000); Marriage status: 22.0% never married, 61.9% now married, 6.2% widowed, 9.9% divorced (2000); Foreign born: 1.3% (2000); Ancestry (includes multiple ancestries): 28.9% German, 15.1% Irish, 14.5% English, 7.7% United States or American, 7.4% Polish (2000).
Economy: Employment by occupation: 10.2% management, 16.9% professional, 16.4% services, 19.3% sales, 0.7% farming, 16.9% construction, 19.5% production (2000).
Income: Per capita income: $21,689 (2000); Median household income: $52,433 (2000); Poverty rate: 3.2% (2000).
Taxes: Total city taxes per capita: $35 (1997); City property taxes per capita: $32 (1997).
Education: High school graduation rate: 84.6% (2000); College graduation rate: 14.7% (2000).
Housing: Homeownership rate: 91.1% (2000); Median home value: $137,200 (2000); Median rent: $621 per month (2000); Median age of housing: 27 years (2000).
Safety: Violent crime rate: 9.4 per 10,000 population; Property crime rate: 40.5 per 10,000 population (2001).
Transportation: Commute to work: 92.7% car, 0.3% public transportation, 2.3% walk, 3.8% work from home (2000); Travel time to work: 8.8% less than 15 minutes, 27.7% 15 to 30 minutes, 27.3% 30 to 45 minutes, 21.6% 45 to 60 minutes, 14.6% 60 minutes or more (2000)

WHITMORE LAKE (CDP). Covers a land area of 4.358 square miles and a water area of 1.052 square miles. Located at 42.41° N. Lat.; 83.75° W. Long.
History: The community of Whitmore Lake, on the lake of the same name, grew as a resort center, popular with local residents for its fishing and swimming.
Population: 6,574 (2000); Race: 96.5% White, 0.6% Black, 1.4% Asian, 0.0% American Indian and Alaska Native, 1.2% Hispanic of any race, 1.4% two or more races (2000); Density: 1,508.5 persons per square mile (2000); Age: 23.1% under 18, 8.1% over 64 (2000); Marriage status: 23.7% never married, 59.1% now married, 4.2% widowed, 13.0% divorced (2000); Foreign born: 3.2% (2000); Ancestry (includes multiple ancestries): 21.9% German, 11.9% Irish, 11.3% Polish, 9.1% English, 8.3% Other groups (2000).
Economy: Employment by occupation: 12.8% management, 18.0% professional, 14.4% services, 26.5% sales, 0.2% farming, 11.7% construction, 16.4% production (2000).
Income: Per capita income: $26,066 (2000); Median household income: $51,504 (2000); Poverty rate: 5.2% (2000).
Education: High school graduation rate: 89.6% (2000); College graduation rate: 25.5% (2000).

School District(s)

Whitmore Lake Public Schools (KG-12)
2000 Enrollment: 1,262 734-449-4464

Housing: Homeownership rate: 81.0% (2000); Median home value: $161,200 (2000); Median rent: $652 per month (2000); Median age of housing: 18 years (2000).
Transportation: Commute to work: 98.1% car, 0.2% public transportation, 0.0% walk, 1.7% work from home (2000); Travel time to work: 15.9% less than 15 minutes, 44.7% 15 to 30 minutes, 25.3% 30 to 45 minutes, 8.6% 45 to 60 minutes, 5.5% 60 minutes or more (2000)

Luce County

Located in northwestern Michigan, on the Upper Peninsula; bounded on the north by Lake Superior; drained by the Tahquamenon and Two Hearted Rivers; includes part of Manistique and North Manistique Lakes, and Tahquamenon Falls. Covers a land area of 903.10 square miles, a water area of 1,008.80 square miles, and is located in the Eastern Time Zone. The county government was organized in 1887. County seat is Newberry.

Weather Station: Newberry 3 S — Elevation: 849 feet

	Jan	Feb	Mar	Apr	May	Jun	Jul	Aug	Sep	Oct	Nov	Dec
High	23	26	35	49	63	72	77	74	65	53	39	28
Low	7	8	17	29	39	48	53	53	45	36	26	14
Precip	2.1	1.2	2.0	1.9	2.7	3.0	3.3	3.5	3.7	3.2	2.5	2.1
Snow	33.1	19.7	15.4	6.3	0.1	0.0	0.0	0.0	tr	0.8	12.4	26.9

High and Low temperatures in degrees Fahrenheit; Precipitation and Snow in inches

Population: 7,024 (2000); Race: 82.6% White, 8.0% Black, 0.1% Asian, 5.7% American Indian and Alaska Native, 1.3% Hispanic of any race, 3.3% two or more races (2000); Density: 7.8 persons per square mile (2000); Age: 21.4% under 18, 15.4% over 64 (2000).
Religion: Five largest groups: 9.6% Catholic Church, 5.1% Evangelical Lutheran Church in America, 3.1% Lutheran Church—Missouri Synod, 3.0% The United Methodist Church, 1.8% Presbyterian Church (U.S.A.) (2000).
Economy: Unemployment rate: 5.9% (11/2002); Total civilian labor force: 2,647 (11/2002); Leading industries: 22.0% retail trade; 18.8% health care and social assistance; 13.8% accommodation & food services (2000); Companies that employ more than 1,000 persons: 0 (2000); Companies that employ more than 100 persons: 3 (2000); Farms: 31 (1997); Minority business ownership rate: 0.0% (1997); Women business ownership rate: 21.9% (1997); Retail sales per capita: $9,792 (1997). Single-family building permits issued: 54 (2001) / 30 (2000); Multi-family building permits issued: 0 (2001) / 0 (2000).
Income: Per capita income: $16,828 (2000); Median household income: $32,031 (2000); Poverty rate: 14.9% (2000); Bankruptcy rate: 3.54% (2001).
Taxes: Total county taxes per capita: $146 (2000); County property taxes per capita: $139 (2000).
Education: High school graduation rate: 75.5% (2000); College graduation rate: 11.8% (2000).
Housing: Homeownership rate: 79.6% (2000); Median home value: $67,800 (2000); Median rent: $374 per month (2000); Median age of housing: 33 years (2000).
Health: Birth rate: 69.8 per 10,000 population (1998); Age adjusted death rate: 94.1 per 10,000 population (1999); Age adjusted cancer mortality rate: 242.1 (Unreliable figure as per CDC) deaths per 100,000 population (1999). Number of physicians: 10.0 per 10,000 population (1999); Number of hospital beds: 103.9 per 10,000 population (1999).
Elections: 2000 Presidential election results: 37.7% Gore, 58.4% Bush, 2.9% Nader, 0.0% Buchanan
National and State Parks: Lake Superior State Forest; Muskallonge Lake State Park; Tahquamenon River State Forest
Additional Information Contacts
Luce County Government Offices 906-293-5521
Newberry Area Chamber of Commerce. 906-293-5562

Luce County Communities

COLUMBUS (township). Covers a land area of 140.776 square miles and a water area of 2.491 square miles. Located at 46.41° N. Lat.; 85.74° W. Long.
Population: 215 (2000); Race: 99.0% White, 0.0% Black, 0.0% Asian, 0.5% American Indian and Alaska Native, 1.0% Hispanic of any race, 0.5% two or more races (2000); Density: 1.5 persons per square mile (2000); Age: 19.4% under 18, 15.9% over 64 (2000); Marriage status: 17.3% never married, 59.0% now married, 12.7% widowed, 11.0% divorced (2000); Foreign born: 0.0% (2000); Ancestry (includes multiple ancestries): 22.4% German, 12.4% English, 10.4% French (except Basque), 10.0% Other groups, 8.5% United States or American (2000).
Economy: Employment by occupation: 2.5% management, 14.8% professional, 29.6% services, 27.2% sales, 0.0% farming, 7.4% construction, 18.5% production (2000).
Income: Per capita income: $18,289 (2000); Median household income: $30,469 (2000); Poverty rate: 12.9% (2000).

Taxes: Total city taxes per capita: $45 (1997); City property taxes per capita: $45 (1997).
Education: High school graduation rate: 83.1% (2000); College graduation rate: 5.2% (2000).
Housing: Homeownership rate: 84.5% (2000); Median home value: $55,000 (2000); Median rent: $175 per month (2000); Median age of housing: 37 years (2000).
Transportation: Commute to work: 82.7% car, 0.0% public transportation, 6.2% walk, 11.1% work from home (2000); Travel time to work: 20.8% less than 15 minutes, 41.7% 15 to 30 minutes, 12.5% 30 to 45 minutes, 8.3% 45 to 60 minutes, 16.7% 60 minutes or more (2000)

LAKEFIELD (township). Covers a land area of 63.365 square miles and a water area of 8.698 square miles. Located at 46.27° N. Lat.; 85.71° W. Long.
Population: 1,074 (2000); Race: 92.2% White, 0.1% Black, 0.0% Asian, 4.1% American Indian and Alaska Native, 0.2% Hispanic of any race, 3.2% two or more races (2000); Density: 16.9 persons per square mile (2000); Age: 20.3% under 18, 19.4% over 64 (2000); Marriage status: 17.0% never married, 73.6% now married, 3.6% widowed, 5.9% divorced (2000); Foreign born: 1.1% (2000); Ancestry (includes multiple ancestries): 22.1% German, 15.6% English, 10.7% Irish, 9.4% United States or American, 9.0% French (except Basque) (2000).
Economy: Employment by occupation: 13.2% management, 13.9% professional, 23.9% services, 24.9% sales, 1.7% farming, 12.2% construction, 10.3% production (2000).
Income: Per capita income: $16,671 (2000); Median household income: $34,773 (2000); Poverty rate: 11.2% (2000).
Taxes: Total city taxes per capita: $26 (1997); City property taxes per capita: $26 (1997).
Education: High school graduation rate: 82.3% (2000); College graduation rate: 15.6% (2000).
Housing: Homeownership rate: 92.5% (2000); Median home value: $98,000 (2000); Median rent: $416 per month (2000); Median age of housing: 27 years (2000).
Transportation: Commute to work: 91.0% car, 0.0% public transportation, 0.5% walk, 7.7% work from home (2000); Travel time to work: 20.5% less than 15 minutes, 62.5% 15 to 30 minutes, 10.5% 30 to 45 minutes, 1.8% 45 to 60 minutes, 4.7% 60 minutes or more (2000)

MCMILLAN (township). Covers a land area of 592.031 square miles and a water area of 12.600 square miles. Located at 46.53° N. Lat.; 85.50° W. Long. Elevation is 750 feet.
History: McMillan developed as a supply base for lumber and charcoal camps. It was named in 1881 for James Stoughton McMillan, a railroad executive and U.S. senator.
Population: 3,947 (2000); Race: 76.1% White, 14.0% Black, 0.1% Asian, 5.7% American Indian and Alaska Native, 2.1% Hispanic of any race, 3.5% two or more races (2000); Density: 6.7 persons per square mile (2000); Age: 19.3% under 18, 14.3% over 64 (2000); Marriage status: 23.6% never married, 59.2% now married, 7.5% widowed, 9.7% divorced (2000); Foreign born: 1.2% (2000); Ancestry (includes multiple ancestries): 16.7% German, 11.5% Other groups, 9.5% Irish, 9.3% English, 7.3% French (except Basque) (2000).
Economy: Employment by occupation: 9.4% management, 13.8% professional, 32.5% services, 22.7% sales, 2.8% farming, 7.8% construction, 11.1% production (2000).
Income: Per capita income: $17,007 (2000); Median household income: $30,514 (2000); Poverty rate: 16.9% (2000).
Taxes: Total city taxes per capita: $18 (1997); City property taxes per capita: $18 (1997).
Education: High school graduation rate: 70.0% (2000); College graduation rate: 9.3% (2000).
Housing: Homeownership rate: 73.5% (2000); Median home value: $53,300 (2000); Median rent: $365 per month (2000); Median age of housing: 42 years (2000).
Transportation: Commute to work: 86.4% car, 0.2% public transportation, 6.0% walk, 6.1% work from home (2000); Travel time to work: 71.8% less than 15 minutes, 11.8% 15 to 30 minutes, 4.1% 30 to 45 minutes, 3.3% 45 to 60 minutes, 9.1% 60 minutes or more (2000)

NEWBERRY (village). Covers a land area of 0.981 square miles and a water area of 0 square miles. Located at 46.35° N. Lat.; 85.51° W. Long. Elevation is 788 feet.
History: Newberry developed as a lumber town, changing gradually to woodworking and trading for the Tahquamenon Valley. The Newberry Lumber and Chemical Company was founded here in 1882 as a charcoal kiln and iron-furnace operation, converting hardwood into charcoal for use in smelting iron ore.
Population: 2,686 (2000); Race: 69.9% White, 20.5% Black, 0.0% Asian, 4.9% American Indian and Alaska Native, 2.5% Hispanic of any race, 4.0% two or more races (2000); Density: 2,737.1 persons per square mile (2000); Age: 17.8% under 18, 13.6% over 64 (2000); Marriage status: 25.6% never married, 57.1% now married, 7.1% widowed, 10.2% divorced (2000); Foreign born: 1.5% (2000); Ancestry (includes multiple ancestries): 13.8% Other groups, 13.3% German, 8.8% Irish, 8.5% English, 7.2% French (except Basque) (2000).
Economy: Employment by occupation: 5.7% management, 14.7% professional, 33.2% services, 25.2% sales, 3.0% farming, 8.8% construction, 9.4% production (2000).
Income: Per capita income: $17,224 (2000); Median household income: $29,052 (2000); Poverty rate: 18.1% (2000).
Taxes: Total city taxes per capita: $103 (1997); City property taxes per capita: $102 (1997).
Education: High school graduation rate: 68.0% (2000); College graduation rate: 9.3% (2000).

School District(s)

Tahquamenon Area Schools (PK-12)
2000 Enrollment: 1,238 906-293-3226
Housing: Homeownership rate: 68.0% (2000); Median home value: $53,900 (2000); Median rent: $360 per month (2000); Median age of housing: 57 years (2000).
Hospitals: Helen Newberry Joy Hospital (73 beds)
Newspapers: The Newberry News (1 x week)
Transportation: Commute to work: 84.9% car, 0.3% public transportation, 9.5% walk, 4.1% work from home (2000); Travel time to work: 82.7% less than 15 minutes, 5.6% 15 to 30 minutes, 3.8% 30 to 45 minutes, 1.4% 45 to 60 minutes, 6.4% 60 minutes or more (2000)
Airports: Luce County
Additional Information Contacts
Newberry Area Chamber of Commerce. 906-293-5562

PENTLAND (township). Covers a land area of 106.912 square miles and a water area of 0.428 square miles. Located at 46.30° N. Lat.; 85.48° W. Long.
Population: 1,788 (2000); Race: 89.4% White, 0.2% Black, 0.0% Asian, 7.2% American Indian and Alaska Native, 0.0% Hispanic of any race, 3.2% two or more races (2000); Density: 16.7 persons per square mile (2000); Age: 27.1% under 18, 15.3% over 64 (2000); Marriage status: 19.5% never married, 64.0% now married, 6.5% widowed, 10.1% divorced (2000); Foreign born: 1.0% (2000); Ancestry (includes multiple ancestries): 23.8% German, 14.2% English, 11.3% Other groups, 9.0% Irish, 8.9% United States or American (2000).
Economy: Employment by occupation: 8.9% management, 17.4% professional, 26.9% services, 20.7% sales, 2.3% farming, 12.1% construction, 11.7% production (2000).
Income: Per capita income: $16,352 (2000); Median household income: $35,990 (2000); Poverty rate: 14.0% (2000).
Taxes: Total city taxes per capita: $10 (1997); City property taxes per capita: $10 (1997).
Education: High school graduation rate: 83.0% (2000); College graduation rate: 15.9% (2000).
Housing: Homeownership rate: 81.4% (2000); Median home value: $75,000 (2000); Median rent: $400 per month (2000); Median age of housing: 27 years (2000).
Transportation: Commute to work: 92.3% car, 0.4% public transportation, 1.6% walk, 5.2% work from home (2000); Travel time to work: 72.8% less than 15 minutes, 17.4% 15 to 30 minutes, 2.8% 30 to 45 minutes, 0.8% 45 to 60 minutes, 6.3% 60 minutes or more (2000)

Mackinac County

Located in northwestern Michigan on the Upper Peninsula; bounded on the south by Lakes Michigan and Huron and the Straits of Mackinac; drained by the Carp and Pine Rivers; includes Mackinac and Bois Blanc Islands, several lakes, and part of Marquette National Forest. Covers a land area of 1,021.60 square miles, a water area of 1,079.00 square miles, and is located in the Eastern Time Zone. The county government was organized in 1818. County seat is St. Ignace.
Population: 11,943 (2000); Race: 79.5% White, 0.1% Black, 0.2% Asian, 14.7% American Indian and Alaska Native, 0.6% Hispanic of any race, 5.0%

two or more races (2000); Density: 11.7 persons per square mile (2000); Age: 22.3% under 18, 18.3% over 64 (2000).
Religion: Five largest groups: 21.5% Catholic Church, 3.9% Evangelical Lutheran Church in America, 3.1% The United Methodist Church, 2.2% General Association of Regular Baptist Churches, 1.9% Lutheran Church—Missouri Synod (2000).
Economy: Unemployment rate: 10.5% (11/2002); Total civilian labor force: 6,184 (11/2002); Leading industries: 28.0% accommodation & food services; 18.4% retail trade; 11.4% construction (2000); Companies that employ more than 1,000 persons: 0 (2000); Companies that employ more than 100 persons: 1 (2000); Farms: 72 totaling 21,513 acres (1997); Minority business ownership rate: 0.0% (1997); Women business ownership rate: 21.4% (1997); Retail sales per capita: $7,549 (1997). Single-family building permits issued: 109 (2001) / 112 (2000); Multi-family building permits issued: 0 (2001) / 2 (2000).
Income: Per capita income: $17,777 (2000); Median household income: $33,356 (2000); Poverty rate: 10.5% (2000); Bankruptcy rate: 1.70% (2001).
Taxes: Total county taxes per capita: $222 (1997); County property taxes per capita: $218 (1997).
Education: High school graduation rate: 82.5% (2000); College graduation rate: 14.9% (2000).
Housing: Homeownership rate: 79.1% (2000); Median home value: $91,800 (2000); Median rent: $351 per month (2000); Median age of housing: 34 years (2000).
Health: Birth rate: 87.9 per 10,000 population (1998); Age adjusted death rate: 102.7 per 10,000 population (1999); Age adjusted cancer mortality rate: 298.9 deaths per 100,000 population (1999). Number of physicians: 8.4 per 10,000 population (1999); Number of hospital beds: 89.6 per 10,000 population (1999).
Elections: 2000 Presidential election results: 42.4% Gore, 54.8% Bush, 2.3% Nader, 0.1% Buchanan
National and State Parks: Mackinac Island State Park; Mackinac State Forest; Straits State Park
Additional Information Contacts
Mackinac County Government Offices 906-643-7300
Mackinac Island Chamber of Commerce. 906-847-6418
St. Ignace Chamber of Commerce 906-643-8717

Mackinac County Communities

BOIS BLANC (township). Covers a land area of 35.270 square miles and a water area of 13.739 square miles. Located at 45.75° N. Lat.; 84.46° W. Long.
History: The name of Bois Blanc is French for "white wood," referring to the many birch trees here.
Population: 71 (2000); Race: 100.0% White, 0.0% Black, 0.0% Asian, 0.0% American Indian and Alaska Native, 0.0% Hispanic of any race, 0.0% two or more races (2000); Density: 2.0 persons per square mile (2000); Age: 20.0% under 18, 17.5% over 64 (2000); Marriage status: 13.8% never married, 56.9% now married, 6.2% widowed, 23.1% divorced (2000); Foreign born: 0.0% (2000); Ancestry (includes multiple ancestries): 32.5% German, 17.5% English, 8.8% Irish, 5.0% United States or American, 5.0% French (except Basque) (2000).
Economy: Employment by occupation: 36.0% management, 8.0% professional, 0.0% services, 16.0% sales, 0.0% farming, 24.0% construction, 16.0% production (2000).
Income: Per capita income: $27,131 (2000); Median household income: $40,833 (2000); Poverty rate: 3.8% (2000).
Taxes: Total city taxes per capita: $2,468 (1997); City property taxes per capita: $2,355 (1997).
Education: High school graduation rate: 86.2% (2000); College graduation rate: 27.6% (2000).
Housing: Homeownership rate: 100.0% (2000); Median home value: $62,500 (2000); Median age of housing: 29 years (2000).
Transportation: Commute to work: 62.5% car, 8.3% public transportation, 12.5% walk, 16.7% work from home (2000); Travel time to work: 60.0% less than 15 minutes, 30.0% 15 to 30 minutes, 0.0% 30 to 45 minutes, 5.0% 45 to 60 minutes, 5.0% 60 minutes or more (2000)

BREVORT (township). Covers a land area of 92.469 square miles and a water area of 6.374 square miles. Located at 46.04° N. Lat.; 84.84° W. Long. Elevation is 685 feet.
History: The township, lake, river, and village were named for Henry Brevort, a surveyor who subdivided the area in 1845. Many people of Swedish ancestry settled in Brevort in the 1860's. The post office was established in 1890.
Population: 649 (2000); Race: 80.0% White, 0.3% Black, 0.0% Asian, 11.1% American Indian and Alaska Native, 0.0% Hispanic of any race, 8.6% two or more races (2000); Density: 7.0 persons per square mile (2000); Age: 22.1% under 18, 14.6% over 64 (2000); Marriage status: 24.0% never married, 52.1% now married, 7.7% widowed, 16.3% divorced (2000); Foreign born: 0.2% (2000); Ancestry (includes multiple ancestries): 26.4% German, 14.9% Other groups, 9.8% French (except Basque), 9.2% Irish, 9.2% Polish (2000).
Economy: Single-family building permits issued: 4 (2001) / 1 (2000); Multi-family building permits issued: 0 (2001) / 0 (2000); Employment by occupation: 5.9% management, 12.6% professional, 23.8% services, 20.1% sales, 2.5% farming, 21.8% construction, 13.4% production (2000).
Income: Per capita income: $19,878 (2000); Median household income: $33,611 (2000); Poverty rate: 9.5% (2000).
Taxes: Total city taxes per capita: $197 (1997); City property taxes per capita: $193 (1997).
Education: High school graduation rate: 74.7% (2000); College graduation rate: 9.0% (2000).
Housing: Homeownership rate: 93.8% (2000); Median home value: $87,000 (2000); Median rent: $433 per month (2000); Median age of housing: 35 years (2000).
Transportation: Commute to work: 94.4% car, 0.0% public transportation, 0.0% walk, 1.7% work from home (2000); Travel time to work: 21.8% less than 15 minutes, 54.1% 15 to 30 minutes, 6.6% 30 to 45 minutes, 3.1% 45 to 60 minutes, 14.4% 60 minutes or more (2000)

CEDARVILLE (unincorporated postal area, zip code 49719). Covers a land area of 64.675 square miles and a water area of 0.207 square miles. Located at 45.99° N. Lat.; 84.32° W. Long.
History: Cedarville grew up around the lumber camps on the shores of Lake Huron in 1884.
Population: 1,662 (2000); Race: 91.9% White, 0.0% Black, 0.2% Asian, 5.2% American Indian and Alaska Native, 0.1% Hispanic of any race, 2.6% two or more races (2000); Density: 25.7 persons per square mile (2000); Age: 21.0% under 18, 21.3% over 64 (2000); Marriage status: 15.4% never married, 64.1% now married, 9.0% widowed, 11.5% divorced (2000); Foreign born: 1.3% (2000); Ancestry (includes multiple ancestries): 23.4% German, 16.3% English, 12.1% Irish, 9.1% Polish, 9.0% Swedish (2000).
Economy: Employment by occupation: 12.3% management, 15.7% professional, 19.0% services, 23.4% sales, 1.1% farming, 17.5% construction, 10.9% production (2000).
Income: Per capita income: $19,781 (2000); Median household income: $35,375 (2000); Poverty rate: 6.5% (2000).
Education: High school graduation rate: 89.8% (2000); College graduation rate: 20.6% (2000).

School District(s)
Les Cheneaux Community Schools (KG-12)
2000 Enrollment: 440 906-484-2256
Housing: Homeownership rate: 84.9% (2000); Median home value: $127,000 (2000); Median rent: $339 per month (2000); Median age of housing: 31 years (2000).
Transportation: Commute to work: 90.6% car, 0.0% public transportation, 2.5% walk, 4.7% work from home (2000); Travel time to work: 53.1% less than 15 minutes, 18.7% 15 to 30 minutes, 13.6% 30 to 45 minutes, 10.0% 45 to 60 minutes, 4.6% 60 minutes or more (2000)

CLARK (township). Covers a land area of 79.095 square miles and a water area of 22.454 square miles. Located at 45.99° N. Lat.; 84.34° W. Long.
Population: 2,200 (2000); Race: 84.8% White, 0.0% Black, 0.3% Asian, 12.2% American Indian and Alaska Native, 0.2% Hispanic of any race, 2.7% two or more races (2000); Density: 27.8 persons per square mile (2000); Age: 22.8% under 18, 19.1% over 64 (2000); Marriage status: 17.4% never married, 62.7% now married, 8.7% widowed, 11.3% divorced (2000); Foreign born: 1.4% (2000); Ancestry (includes multiple ancestries): 20.3% German, 14.9% English, 10.9% Other groups, 10.8% Irish, 8.9% Swedish (2000).
Economy: Single-family building permits issued: 24 (2001) / 12 (2000); Multi-family building permits issued: 0 (2001) / 2 (2000); Employment by occupation: 12.2% management, 15.1% professional, 19.1% services, 24.1% sales, 0.8% farming, 18.9% construction, 9.8% production (2000).
Income: Per capita income: $18,357 (2000); Median household income: $33,975 (2000); Poverty rate: 9.9% (2000).
Taxes: Total city taxes per capita: $171 (2000); City property taxes per capita: $161 (2000).

Education: High school graduation rate: 88.4% (2000); College graduation rate: 19.7% (2000).
Housing: Homeownership rate: 82.8% (2000); Median home value: $111,900 (2000); Median rent: $329 per month (2000); Median age of housing: 32 years (2000).
Transportation: Commute to work: 89.9% car, 0.2% public transportation, 2.8% walk, 5.2% work from home (2000); Travel time to work: 54.5% less than 15 minutes, 16.3% 15 to 30 minutes, 14.1% 30 to 45 minutes, 9.5% 45 to 60 minutes, 5.6% 60 minutes or more (2000)

CURTIS (unincorporated postal area, zip code 49820). Covers a land area of 43.499 square miles and a water area of 0.292 square miles. Located at 46.19° N. Lat.; 85.72° W. Long.
History: First called Portage, the settlement was renamed Curtis in 1905 for William L. Curtis, a state senator.
Population: 844 (2000); Race: 95.9% White, 0.0% Black, 0.0% Asian, 3.9% American Indian and Alaska Native, 0.2% Hispanic of any race, 0.2% two or more races (2000); Density: 19.4 persons per square mile (2000); Age: 19.4% under 18, 18.7% over 64 (2000); Marriage status: 18.8% never married, 65.3% now married, 9.7% widowed, 6.3% divorced (2000); Foreign born: 1.2% (2000); Ancestry (includes multiple ancestries): 27.6% German, 12.4% English, 12.2% Irish, 8.2% French (except Basque), 6.9% Polish (2000).
Economy: Employment by occupation: 5.6% management, 16.9% professional, 22.5% services, 18.4% sales, 1.9% farming, 17.2% construction, 17.6% production (2000).
Income: Per capita income: $15,107 (2000); Median household income: $27,125 (2000); Poverty rate: 14.6% (2000).
Education: High school graduation rate: 74.3% (2000); College graduation rate: 10.7% (2000).
Housing: Homeownership rate: 84.8% (2000); Median home value: $88,100 (2000); Median rent: $188 per month (2000); Median age of housing: 35 years (2000).
Transportation: Commute to work: 81.3% car, 0.0% public transportation, 9.9% walk, 4.8% work from home (2000); Travel time to work: 39.6% less than 15 minutes, 11.3% 15 to 30 minutes, 26.7% 30 to 45 minutes, 3.3% 45 to 60 minutes, 19.2% 60 minutes or more (2000)

ENGADINE (unincorporated postal area, zip code 49827). Covers a land area of 110.496 square miles and a water area of 2.438 square miles. Located at 46.15° N. Lat.; 85.57° W. Long. Elevation is 712 feet.
History: Engadine developed around a railway station, as a supply center for a resort area.
Population: 945 (2000); Race: 88.6% White, 0.0% Black, 0.2% Asian, 8.1% American Indian and Alaska Native, 1.4% Hispanic of any race, 1.9% two or more races (2000); Density: 8.6 persons per square mile (2000); Age: 19.3% under 18, 22.1% over 64 (2000); Marriage status: 20.5% never married, 61.5% now married, 11.3% widowed, 6.7% divorced (2000); Foreign born: 0.7% (2000); Ancestry (includes multiple ancestries): 23.2% German, 9.3% Other groups, 8.9% United States or American, 8.8% English, 7.3% Irish (2000).
Economy: Employment by occupation: 8.9% management, 17.3% professional, 19.6% services, 21.5% sales, 6.5% farming, 13.1% construction, 13.1% production (2000).
Income: Per capita income: $15,725 (2000); Median household income: $31,250 (2000); Poverty rate: 13.7% (2000).
Education: High school graduation rate: 77.9% (2000); College graduation rate: 12.9% (2000).

School District(s)

Engadine Consolidated Schools (KG-12)
2000 Enrollment: 303 906-477-6313
Housing: Homeownership rate: 81.0% (2000); Median home value: $77,400 (2000); Median rent: $232 per month (2000); Median age of housing: 39 years (2000).
Transportation: Commute to work: 83.1% car, 0.5% public transportation, 5.6% walk, 10.8% work from home (2000); Travel time to work: 38.9% less than 15 minutes, 35.9% 15 to 30 minutes, 14.8% 30 to 45 minutes, 1.8% 45 to 60 minutes, 8.6% 60 minutes or more (2000)

GARFIELD (township). Covers a land area of 134.142 square miles and a water area of 3.240 square miles. Located at 46.14° N. Lat.; 85.50° W. Long.
Population: 1,251 (2000); Race: 83.6% White, 0.0% Black, 0.2% Asian, 13.3% American Indian and Alaska Native, 1.0% Hispanic of any race, 2.1% two or more races (2000); Density: 9.3 persons per square mile (2000); Age: 17.8% under 18, 23.2% over 64 (2000); Marriage status: 17.1% never married, 67.0% now married, 9.9% widowed, 6.0% divorced (2000); Foreign born: 0.7% (2000); Ancestry (includes multiple ancestries): 22.1% German, 12.3% Other groups, 9.9% English, 7.0% French (except Basque), 7.0% United States or American (2000).
Economy: Single-family building permits issued: 11 (2001) / 12 (2000); Multi-family building permits issued: 0 (2001) / 0 (2000); Employment by occupation: 10.8% management, 17.7% professional, 17.5% services, 23.8% sales, 6.1% farming, 11.0% construction, 13.2% production (2000).
Income: Per capita income: $17,315 (2000); Median household income: $34,712 (2000); Poverty rate: 10.0% (2000).
Taxes: Total city taxes per capita: $15 (1997); City property taxes per capita: $15 (1997).
Education: High school graduation rate: 80.8% (2000); College graduation rate: 16.4% (2000).
Housing: Homeownership rate: 84.0% (2000); Median home value: $81,400 (2000); Median rent: $252 per month (2000); Median age of housing: 37 years (2000).
Transportation: Commute to work: 80.2% car, 0.4% public transportation, 9.0% walk, 9.8% work from home (2000); Travel time to work: 44.7% less than 15 minutes, 30.5% 15 to 30 minutes, 14.2% 30 to 45 minutes, 1.8% 45 to 60 minutes, 8.8% 60 minutes or more (2000)

GOULD CITY (unincorporated postal area, zip code 49838). Covers a land area of 138.368 square miles and a water area of 5.402 square miles. Located at 46.09° N. Lat.; 85.71° W. Long. Elevation is 743 feet.
History: Gould City was founded in 1886 by Sam Stiles, who operated a grocery store. The town, named for a lumberman, began as a lumber center for hemlock and hardwood timber.
Population: 341 (2000); Race: 86.3% White, 0.0% Black, 0.0% Asian, 11.4% American Indian and Alaska Native, 0.0% Hispanic of any race, 2.3% two or more races (2000); Density: 2.5 persons per square mile (2000); Age: 14.3% under 18, 30.9% over 64 (2000); Marriage status: 15.8% never married, 60.9% now married, 12.9% widowed, 10.4% divorced (2000); Foreign born: 0.7% (2000); Ancestry (includes multiple ancestries): 17.9% German, 13.7% Other groups, 10.7% English, 9.8% Irish, 6.2% United States or American (2000).
Economy: Employment by occupation: 18.4% management, 3.5% professional, 29.8% services, 17.5% sales, 1.8% farming, 21.1% construction, 7.9% production (2000).
Income: Per capita income: $23,310 (2000); Median household income: $26,429 (2000); Poverty rate: 11.7% (2000).
Education: High school graduation rate: 80.2% (2000); College graduation rate: 6.7% (2000).
Housing: Homeownership rate: 89.9% (2000); Median home value: $57,700 (2000); Median rent: $338 per month (2000); Median age of housing: 34 years (2000).
Transportation: Commute to work: 96.3% car, 0.0% public transportation, 1.8% walk, 1.8% work from home (2000); Travel time to work: 22.4% less than 15 minutes, 29.0% 15 to 30 minutes, 32.7% 30 to 45 minutes, 2.8% 45 to 60 minutes, 13.1% 60 minutes or more (2000)

HENDRICKS (township). Covers a land area of 78.908 square miles and a water area of 2.209 square miles. Located at 46.14° N. Lat.; 85.18° W. Long.
Population: 183 (2000); Race: 84.5% White, 0.0% Black, 0.0% Asian, 10.7% American Indian and Alaska Native, 0.0% Hispanic of any race, 4.8% two or more races (2000); Density: 2.3 persons per square mile (2000); Age: 23.5% under 18, 23.0% over 64 (2000); Marriage status: 11.2% never married, 71.3% now married, 3.5% widowed, 14.0% divorced (2000); Foreign born: 1.1% (2000); Ancestry (includes multiple ancestries): 26.7% Other groups, 12.8% French (except Basque), 12.3% German, 11.8% English, 8.6% Irish (2000).
Economy: Employment by occupation: 8.7% management, 10.9% professional, 23.9% services, 21.7% sales, 10.9% farming, 17.4% construction, 6.5% production (2000).
Income: Per capita income: $13,772 (2000); Median household income: $32,500 (2000); Poverty rate: 23.5% (2000).
Taxes: Total city taxes per capita: $147 (1997); City property taxes per capita: $147 (1997).
Education: High school graduation rate: 71.2% (2000); College graduation rate: 3.0% (2000).
Housing: Homeownership rate: 86.8% (2000); Median home value: $85,700 (2000); Median rent: $450 per month (2000); Median age of housing: 34 years (2000).
Transportation: Commute to work: 88.6% car, 0.0% public transportation, 6.8% walk, 4.5% work from home (2000); Travel time to work: 26.2% less

than 15 minutes, 0.0% 15 to 30 minutes, 40.5% 30 to 45 minutes, 28.6% 45 to 60 minutes, 4.8% 60 minutes or more (2000)

HESSEL (unincorporated postal area, zip code 49745). Covers a land area of 5.351 square miles and a water area of 0.014 square miles. Located at 46.02° N. Lat.; 84.42° W. Long.
Population: 204 (2000); Race: 73.6% White, 0.0% Black, 0.0% Asian, 23.4% American Indian and Alaska Native, 0.0% Hispanic of any race, 3.0% two or more races (2000); Density: 38.1 persons per square mile (2000); Age: 20.4% under 18, 17.0% over 64 (2000); Marriage status: 19.8% never married, 64.4% now married, 6.9% widowed, 8.9% divorced (2000); Foreign born: 2.1% (2000); Ancestry (includes multiple ancestries): 21.3% Other groups, 14.5% Swedish, 13.2% English, 12.3% German, 6.8% Irish (2000).
Economy: Employment by occupation: 14.4% management, 17.3% professional, 16.3% services, 23.1% sales, 1.9% farming, 25.0% construction, 1.9% production (2000).
Income: Per capita income: $17,507 (2000); Median household income: $29,375 (2000); Poverty rate: 10.6% (2000).
Education: High school graduation rate: 92.9% (2000); College graduation rate: 23.6% (2000).
Housing: Homeownership rate: 80.8% (2000); Median home value: $81,300 (2000); Median rent: $370 per month (2000); Median age of housing: 50 years (2000).
Transportation: Commute to work: 92.1% car, 0.0% public transportation, 2.0% walk, 5.9% work from home (2000); Travel time to work: 62.1% less than 15 minutes, 8.4% 15 to 30 minutes, 11.6% 30 to 45 minutes, 10.5% 45 to 60 minutes, 7.4% 60 minutes or more (2000)

HUDSON (township). Covers a land area of 68.742 square miles and a water area of 0.741 square miles. Located at 46.14° N. Lat.; 85.29° W. Long.
Population: 214 (2000); Race: 61.8% White, 0.0% Black, 0.0% Asian, 20.3% American Indian and Alaska Native, 8.8% Hispanic of any race, 10.1% two or more races (2000); Density: 3.1 persons per square mile (2000); Age: 26.7% under 18, 17.5% over 64 (2000); Marriage status: 17.9% never married, 61.8% now married, 5.8% widowed, 14.5% divorced (2000); Foreign born: 2.3% (2000); Ancestry (includes multiple ancestries): 29.5% Other groups, 18.9% United States or American, 18.4% German, 11.5% Irish, 9.2% English (2000).
Economy: Employment by occupation: 0.0% management, 0.0% professional, 40.3% services, 16.4% sales, 9.0% farming, 16.4% construction, 17.9% production (2000).
Income: Per capita income: $13,025 (2000); Median household income: $26,250 (2000); Poverty rate: 27.2% (2000).
Taxes: Total city taxes per capita: $163 (1997); City property taxes per capita: $163 (1997).
Education: High school graduation rate: 59.5% (2000); College graduation rate: 4.1% (2000).
Housing: Homeownership rate: 87.4% (2000); Median home value: $69,400 (2000); Median rent: $275 per month (2000); Median age of housing: 25 years (2000).
Transportation: Commute to work: 88.1% car, 0.0% public transportation, 9.0% walk, 0.0% work from home (2000); Travel time to work: 19.4% less than 15 minutes, 22.4% 15 to 30 minutes, 11.9% 30 to 45 minutes, 14.9% 45 to 60 minutes, 31.3% 60 minutes or more (2000)

MACKINAC ISLAND (city). Covers a land area of 4.365 square miles and a water area of 1.217 square miles. Located at 45.85° N. Lat.; 84.62° W. Long. Elevation is 744 feet.
History: The island, first called Michilimackinac ("the great turtle"), stands in the Straits of Mackinac between Lake Huron and Lake Michigan, and attracts many tourists. The British transferred their garrison from the mainland to Mackinac Island in 1781, and refused to evacuate the post when the island was ceded to America by the Treaty of Paris in 1783. The island changed hands several times until coming under permanent American rule in 1814, and John Jacob Astor soon centered the activities of the American Fur Company at Mackinac Island. When fur trading declined after 1830, Mackinac Island was promoted as a resort center and a place for summer estates, especially after ferry service was begun in 1881.
Population: 523 (2000); Race: 74.5% White, 0.0% Black, 0.6% Asian, 16.7% American Indian and Alaska Native, 1.0% Hispanic of any race, 7.6% two or more races (2000); Density: 119.8 persons per square mile (2000); Age: 19.2% under 18, 13.7% over 64 (2000); Marriage status: 29.8% never married, 54.0% now married, 4.2% widowed, 12.1% divorced (2000); Foreign born: 2.2% (2000); Ancestry (includes multiple ancestries): 24.5% German, 19.0% Other groups, 17.1% Irish, 12.2% English, 9.0% French (except Basque) (2000).
Economy: Single-family building permits issued: 5 (2001) / 17 (2000); Multi-family building permits issued: 0 (2001) / 0 (2000); Employment by occupation: 16.1% management, 22.5% professional, 19.1% services, 24.6% sales, 0.0% farming, 11.0% construction, 6.8% production (2000).
Income: Per capita income: $27,965 (2000); Median household income: $36,964 (2000); Poverty rate: 3.5% (2000).
Taxes: Total city taxes per capita: $3,444 (1997); City property taxes per capita: $2,848 (1997).
Education: High school graduation rate: 84.1% (2000); College graduation rate: 31.1% (2000).

School District(s)

Mackinac Island Public Schools (KG-12)
2000 Enrollment: 81 906-847-3377
Housing: Homeownership rate: 56.0% (2000); Median home value: $170,000 (2000); Median rent: $389 per month (2000); Median age of housing: 57 years (2000).
Newspapers: Mackinac Island Town Crier
Transportation: Commute to work: 14.7% car, 0.0% public transportation, 16.6% walk, 6.5% work from home (2000); Travel time to work: 78.3% less than 15 minutes, 19.2% 15 to 30 minutes, 0.0% 30 to 45 minutes, 1.0% 45 to 60 minutes, 1.5% 60 minutes or more (2000)
Airports: Mackinac Island
Additional Information Contacts
Mackinac Island Chamber of Commerce 906-847-6418

MARQUETTE (township). Covers a land area of 97.191 square miles and a water area of 39.027 square miles. Located at 46.09° N. Lat.; 84.52° W. Long.
Population: 659 (2000); Race: 91.8% White, 0.0% Black, 0.0% Asian, 7.1% American Indian and Alaska Native, 0.3% Hispanic of any race, 1.2% two or more races (2000); Density: 6.8 persons per square mile (2000); Age: 27.2% under 18, 15.4% over 64 (2000); Marriage status: 15.3% never married, 73.3% now married, 5.0% widowed, 6.4% divorced (2000); Foreign born: 1.2% (2000); Ancestry (includes multiple ancestries): 23.1% German, 15.1% English, 10.7% Irish, 9.0% Other groups, 7.8% Polish (2000).
Economy: Single-family building permits issued: 5 (2001) / 7 (2000); Multi-family building permits issued: 0 (2001) / 0 (2000); Employment by occupation: 7.6% management, 11.0% professional, 21.6% services, 20.8% sales, 3.0% farming, 20.5% construction, 15.5% production (2000).
Income: Per capita income: $14,538 (2000); Median household income: $30,069 (2000); Poverty rate: 11.8% (2000).
Taxes: Total city taxes per capita: $85 (1997); City property taxes per capita: $83 (1997).
Education: High school graduation rate: 86.2% (2000); College graduation rate: 4.5% (2000).
Housing: Homeownership rate: 93.1% (2000); Median home value: $69,600 (2000); Median rent: $325 per month (2000); Median age of housing: 24 years (2000).
Transportation: Commute to work: 87.9% car, 0.8% public transportation, 1.9% walk, 7.8% work from home (2000); Travel time to work: 27.0% less than 15 minutes, 38.0% 15 to 30 minutes, 22.4% 30 to 45 minutes, 5.1% 45 to 60 minutes, 7.6% 60 minutes or more (2000)

MORAN (township). Covers a land area of 127.509 square miles and a water area of 6.927 square miles. Located at 45.97° N. Lat.; 84.92° W. Long. Elevation is 701 feet.
Population: 1,080 (2000); Race: 73.3% White, 0.4% Black, 0.0% Asian, 16.5% American Indian and Alaska Native, 0.8% Hispanic of any race, 8.6% two or more races (2000); Density: 8.5 persons per square mile (2000); Age: 23.2% under 18, 14.7% over 64 (2000); Marriage status: 23.0% never married, 61.4% now married, 7.6% widowed, 8.1% divorced (2000); Foreign born: 1.3% (2000); Ancestry (includes multiple ancestries): 22.3% German, 20.4% Other groups, 13.7% Irish, 12.2% English, 10.7% French (except Basque) (2000).
Economy: Single-family building permits issued: 18 (2001) / 17 (2000); Multi-family building permits issued: 0 (2001) / 0 (2000); Employment by occupation: 13.6% management, 15.1% professional, 23.2% services, 22.3% sales, 0.0% farming, 15.1% construction, 10.7% production (2000).
Income: Per capita income: $19,209 (2000); Median household income: $40,208 (2000); Poverty rate: 6.9% (2000).
Taxes: Total city taxes per capita: $207 (1997); City property taxes per capita: $199 (1997).
Education: High school graduation rate: 89.0% (2000); College graduation rate: 16.6% (2000).

Housing: Homeownership rate: 86.7% (2000); Median home value: $112,800 (2000); Median rent: $382 per month (2000); Median age of housing: 32 years (2000).
Transportation: Commute to work: 91.9% car, 2.5% public transportation, 1.8% walk, 3.8% work from home (2000); Travel time to work: 57.6% less than 15 minutes, 16.2% 15 to 30 minutes, 9.4% 30 to 45 minutes, 7.8% 45 to 60 minutes, 8.9% 60 minutes or more (2000)

NAUBINWAY (unincorporated postal area, zip code 49762). Covers a land area of 183.037 square miles and a water area of 2.594 square miles. Located at 46.14° N. Lat.; 85.29° W. Long. Elevation is 595 feet.
History: Naubinway was settled in 1880 by French fishermen. For a time it had a sawmill, but commercial fishing emerged as the main source of revenue.
Population: 731 (2000); Race: 72.0% White, 0.0% Black, 0.0% Asian, 20.2% American Indian and Alaska Native, 2.5% Hispanic of any race, 5.5% two or more races (2000); Density: 4.0 persons per square mile (2000); Age: 20.9% under 18, 22.0% over 64 (2000); Marriage status: 11.5% never married, 73.2% now married, 5.3% widowed, 10.0% divorced (2000); Foreign born: 1.2% (2000); Ancestry (includes multiple ancestries): 24.1% Other groups, 16.1% German, 12.2% English, 8.7% United States or American, 8.0% Irish (2000).
Economy: Employment by occupation: 9.7% management, 11.7% professional, 21.1% services, 25.1% sales, 7.7% farming, 10.5% construction, 14.2% production (2000).
Income: Per capita income: $17,050 (2000); Median household income: $33,167 (2000); Poverty rate: 14.4% (2000).
Education: High school graduation rate: 76.8% (2000); College graduation rate: 14.2% (2000).
Housing: Homeownership rate: 88.9% (2000); Median home value: $87,300 (2000); Median rent: $339 per month (2000); Median age of housing: 29 years (2000).
Transportation: Commute to work: 79.3% car, 0.0% public transportation, 13.7% walk, 5.0% work from home (2000); Travel time to work: 41.0% less than 15 minutes, 13.5% 15 to 30 minutes, 19.2% 30 to 45 minutes, 9.6% 45 to 60 minutes, 16.6% 60 minutes or more (2000)

NEWTON (township). Covers a land area of 148.625 square miles and a water area of 6.293 square miles. Located at 46.07° N. Lat.; 85.70° W. Long.
Population: 356 (2000); Race: 89.0% White, 0.0% Black, 0.0% Asian, 9.0% American Indian and Alaska Native, 0.0% Hispanic of any race, 2.0% two or more races (2000); Density: 2.4 persons per square mile (2000); Age: 17.4% under 18, 24.9% over 64 (2000); Marriage status: 19.2% never married, 59.0% now married, 10.1% widowed, 11.7% divorced (2000); Foreign born: 0.6% (2000); Ancestry (includes multiple ancestries): 17.4% German, 13.6% English, 12.8% Irish, 11.6% Other groups, 8.1% United States or American (2000).
Economy: Single-family building permits issued: 5 (2001) / 5 (2000); Multi-family building permits issued: 0 (2001) / 0 (2000); Employment by occupation: 18.9% management, 8.2% professional, 26.2% services, 14.8% sales, 3.3% farming, 17.2% construction, 11.5% production (2000).
Income: Per capita income: $22,053 (2000); Median household income: $26,477 (2000); Poverty rate: 12.6% (2000).
Taxes: Total city taxes per capita: $93 (1997); City property taxes per capita: $88 (1997).
Education: High school graduation rate: 82.5% (2000); College graduation rate: 7.4% (2000).
Housing: Homeownership rate: 89.3% (2000); Median home value: $56,700 (2000); Median rent: $313 per month (2000); Median age of housing: 34 years (2000).
Transportation: Commute to work: 93.4% car, 0.0% public transportation, 0.0% walk, 4.9% work from home (2000); Travel time to work: 24.1% less than 15 minutes, 24.1% 15 to 30 minutes, 36.2% 30 to 45 minutes, 2.6% 45 to 60 minutes, 12.9% 60 minutes or more (2000)

POINTE AUX PINS (unincorporated postal area, zip code 49775). Covers a land area of 35.860 square miles and a water area of 1.784 square miles. Located at 45.75° N. Lat.; 84.46° W. Long. Elevation is 608 feet.
History: Pointe aux Pins was laid out in 1888 as a resort village on Bois Blanc Island. The name is French for "point of pines."
Population: 71 (2000); Race: 100.0% White, 0.0% Black, 0.0% Asian, 0.0% American Indian and Alaska Native, 0.0% Hispanic of any race, 0.0% two or more races (2000); Density: 2.0 persons per square mile (2000); Age: 20.0% under 18, 17.5% over 64 (2000); Marriage status: 13.8% never married, 56.9% now married, 6.2% widowed, 23.1% divorced (2000); Foreign born: 0.0% (2000); Ancestry (includes multiple ancestries): 32.5% German, 17.5% English, 8.8% Irish, 5.0% French (except Basque), 5.0% United States or American (2000).
Economy: Employment by occupation: 36.0% management, 8.0% professional, 0.0% services, 16.0% sales, 0.0% farming, 24.0% construction, 16.0% production (2000).
Income: Per capita income: $27,131 (2000); Median household income: $40,833 (2000); Poverty rate: 3.8% (2000).
Education: High school graduation rate: 86.2% (2000); College graduation rate: 27.6% (2000).

School District(s)

Bois Blanc Pines School District (KG-08)
2000 Enrollment: 3 906-632-3373
Housing: Homeownership rate: 100.0% (2000); Median home value: $62,500 (2000); Median age of housing: 29 years (2000).
Transportation: Commute to work: 62.5% car, 8.3% public transportation, 12.5% walk, 16.7% work from home (2000); Travel time to work: 60.0% less than 15 minutes, 30.0% 15 to 30 minutes, 0.0% 30 to 45 minutes, 5.0% 45 to 60 minutes, 5.0% 60 minutes or more (2000)
Airports: Bois Blanc

PORTAGE (township). Covers a land area of 55.423 square miles and a water area of 16.775 square miles. Located at 46.20° N. Lat.; 85.73° W. Long.
Population: 1,055 (2000); Race: 95.3% White, 0.0% Black, 0.0% Asian, 4.5% American Indian and Alaska Native, 0.2% Hispanic of any race, 0.2% two or more races (2000); Density: 19.0 persons per square mile (2000); Age: 17.9% under 18, 21.5% over 64 (2000); Marriage status: 16.5% never married, 66.5% now married, 10.2% widowed, 6.7% divorced (2000); Foreign born: 1.0% (2000); Ancestry (includes multiple ancestries): 28.8% German, 12.3% English, 11.9% Irish, 7.9% French (except Basque), 7.1% Polish (2000).
Economy: Single-family building permits issued: 15 (2001) / 25 (2000); Multi-family building permits issued: 0 (2001) / 0 (2000); Employment by occupation: 6.8% management, 14.8% professional, 22.2% services, 20.9% sales, 1.5% farming, 16.9% construction, 16.9% production (2000).
Income: Per capita income: $15,435 (2000); Median household income: $27,037 (2000); Poverty rate: 16.3% (2000).
Taxes: Total city taxes per capita: $234 (1997); City property taxes per capita: $218 (1997).
Education: High school graduation rate: 75.0% (2000); College graduation rate: 9.0% (2000).
Housing: Homeownership rate: 86.8% (2000); Median home value: $94,600 (2000); Median rent: $225 per month (2000); Median age of housing: 35 years (2000).
Transportation: Commute to work: 83.3% car, 0.0% public transportation, 8.9% walk, 5.2% work from home (2000); Travel time to work: 36.7% less than 15 minutes, 15.2% 15 to 30 minutes, 28.0% 30 to 45 minutes, 2.8% 45 to 60 minutes, 17.3% 60 minutes or more (2000)

SAINT IGNACE (city). Covers a land area of 2.703 square miles and a water area of 0.009 square miles. Located at 45.86° N. Lat.; 84.72° W. Long. Elevation is 595 feet.
History: The town of St. Ignace had its beginning when Father Jacques Marquette built a mission here in 1671. In 1706, seeing that he had few parishioners, the last priest burned the chapel as he left. When the Jesuits came again in 1834, they found that fishermen had settled here. It was the establishment of railroad ferry service across the Mackinac Straits that brought about the founding of an iron smelting furnace, the rise of the lumber industry, and the settlement of a town. St. Ignace was incorporated as a village in 1882, and as a city in 1883. The iron smelter and the lumber industry soon declined, but St. Ignace developed as an entry to the Upper Peninsula and as a commercial fishing center.
Population: 2,678 (2000); Race: 71.3% White, 0.0% Black, 0.3% Asian, 19.8% American Indian and Alaska Native, 0.5% Hispanic of any race, 8.3% two or more races (2000); Density: 990.7 persons per square mile (2000); Age: 23.1% under 18, 19.5% over 64 (2000); Marriage status: 26.0% never married, 52.9% now married, 11.7% widowed, 9.5% divorced (2000); Foreign born: 1.7% (2000); Ancestry (includes multiple ancestries): 21.8% Other groups, 20.1% German, 12.8% Irish, 11.0% French (except Basque), 9.1% English (2000).
Economy: Single-family building permits issued: 7 (2001) / 4 (2000); Multi-family building permits issued: 0 (2001) / 0 (2000); Employment by occupation: 11.0% management, 16.4% professional, 24.1% services, 28.1% sales, 1.0% farming, 11.5% construction, 7.9% production (2000).
Income: Per capita income: $17,340 (2000); Median household income: $34,447 (2000); Poverty rate: 9.0% (2000).

Education: High school graduation rate: 83.5% (2000); College graduation rate: 17.7% (2000).

School District(s)

Moran Township School District (KG-08)
2000 Enrollment: 116 906-643-7970

Saint Ignace Area Schools (KG-12)
2000 Enrollment: 830 906-643-8145

Housing: Homeownership rate: 63.2% (2000); Median home value: $86,400 (2000); Median rent: $384 per month (2000); Median age of housing: 44 years (2000).

Hospitals: Mackinac Straits Hospital & Health Center (114 beds)

Safety: Violent crime rate: 18.6 per 10,000 population; Property crime rate: 334.3 per 10,000 population (2001).

Newspapers: The Saint Ignace News (1 x week)

Transportation: Commute to work: 85.4% car, 5.9% public transportation, 2.5% walk, 4.6% work from home (2000); Travel time to work: 71.7% less than 15 minutes, 10.5% 15 to 30 minutes, 7.7% 30 to 45 minutes, 4.7% 45 to 60 minutes, 5.4% 60 minutes or more (2000); Amtrak: Service available.

Additional Information Contacts

St. Ignace Chamber of Commerce 906-643-8717

SAINT IGNACE (township). Covers a land area of 97.140 square miles and a water area of 45.089 square miles. Located at 45.99° N. Lat.; 84.70° W. Long. Elevation is 595 feet.

Population: 1,024 (2000); Race: 68.1% White, 0.0% Black, 0.6% Asian, 25.4% American Indian and Alaska Native, 0.5% Hispanic of any race, 5.6% two or more races (2000); Density: 10.5 persons per square mile (2000); Age: 26.6% under 18, 12.5% over 64 (2000); Marriage status: 21.6% never married, 60.3% now married, 6.6% widowed, 11.4% divorced (2000); Foreign born: 0.2% (2000); Ancestry (includes multiple ancestries): 21.4% Other groups, 14.5% German, 11.1% French (except Basque), 7.6% English, 6.7% Irish (2000).

Economy: Single-family building permits issued: 15 (2001) / 12 (2000); Multi-family building permits issued: 0 (2001) / 0 (2000); Employment by occupation: 8.6% management, 13.4% professional, 31.3% services, 21.5% sales, 0.0% farming, 17.9% construction, 7.2% production (2000).

Income: Per capita income: $14,768 (2000); Median household income: $35,461 (2000); Poverty rate: 11.0% (2000).

Education: High school graduation rate: 78.5% (2000); College graduation rate: 7.5% (2000).

Housing: Homeownership rate: 75.6% (2000); Median home value: $82,900 (2000); Median rent: $280 per month (2000); Median age of housing: 27 years (2000).

Transportation: Commute to work: 93.9% car, 0.0% public transportation, 4.4% walk, 1.7% work from home (2000); Travel time to work: 39.1% less than 15 minutes, 34.8% 15 to 30 minutes, 16.2% 30 to 45 minutes, 3.5% 45 to 60 minutes, 6.5% 60 minutes or more (2000); Amtrak: Service available.

Macomb County

Located in southeastern Michigan; bounded on the southeast by Lake St. Clair and Anchor Bay; drained by the Clinton River. Covers a land area of 480.40 square miles, a water area of 89.30 square miles, and is located in the Eastern Time Zone. The county government was organized in 1818. County seat is Mount Clemens.

Macomb County is part of the Detroit, MI PMSA. The entire metro area includes: Lapeer County; Macomb County; Monroe County; Oakland County; St. Clair County; Wayne County

Population: 788,149 (2000); Race: 92.4% White, 2.6% Black, 2.2% Asian, 0.4% American Indian and Alaska Native, 1.6% Hispanic of any race, 2.0% two or more races (2000); Density: 1,640.5 persons per square mile (2000); Age: 24.1% under 18, 13.6% over 64 (2000).

Religion: Five largest groups: 30.9% Catholic Church, 3.5% Lutheran Church—Missouri Synod, 1.7% Evangelical Lutheran Church in America, 0.7% Greek Orthodox Archdiocese of America, 0.7% The United Methodist Church (2000).

Economy: Unemployment rate: 4.7% (11/2002); Total civilian labor force: 442,548 (11/2002); Leading industries: 27.5% manufacturing; 14.5% retail trade; 9.0% health care and social assistance (2000); Companies that employ more than 1,000 persons: 24 (2000); Companies that employ more than 100 persons: 525 (2000); Farms: 523 totaling 68,829 acres (1997); Minority business ownership rate: 4.6% (1997); Women business ownership rate: 25.5% (1997); Retail sales per capita: $11,508 (1997). Single-family building permits issued: 3,793 (2001) / 5,093 (2000); Multi-family building permits issued: 821 (2001) / 870 (2000).

Income: Per capita income: $24,446 (2000); Median household income: $52,102 (2000); Poverty rate: 5.6% (2000); Bankruptcy rate: 4.56% (2001).

Taxes: Total county taxes per capita: $108 (2000); County property taxes per capita: $101 (2000).

Education: High school graduation rate: 82.9% (2000); College graduation rate: 17.6% (2000).

Housing: Homeownership rate: 78.9% (2000); Median home value: $139,200 (2000); Median rent: $543 per month (2000); Median age of housing: 30 years (2000).

Health: Birth rate: 125.7 per 10,000 population (1998); Age adjusted death rate: 88.2 per 10,000 population (1999); Infant mortality rate: 6.9 per 1,000 live births (1998); Age adjusted cancer mortality rate: 207.6 deaths per 100,000 population (1999). Air Quality Index: 77% good, 23% moderate, <1% unhealthy (percent of days in 2000). Number of physicians: 12.4 per 10,000 population (1999); Number of hospital beds: 16.0 per 10,000 population (1999).

Elections: 2000 Presidential election results: 50.0% Gore, 47.5% Bush, 1.8% Nader, 0.1% Buchanan

National and State Parks: Dodge Brothers State Park Number 8; Rochester-Utica State Recreation Area

Additional Information Contacts

Macomb County Government Offices 586-469-5100
Eastpointe Chamber of Commerce. 810-776-5520
Mt Clemens Chamber of Commerce 810-463-1528
New Baltimore Chamber of Commerce. 810-725-5148
St. Clair Shores Chamber of Commerce 810-777-2741
Sterling Heights Chamber of Commerce 810-731-5400

Macomb County Communities

ARMADA (village). Covers a land area of 0.708 square miles and a water area of 0 square miles. Located at 42.84° N. Lat.; 82.88° W. Long. Elevation is 737 feet.

History: Armada was established in 1834 when Henry B. Ten Eyck hosted the first town meeting in his home. Armada was incorporated as a village in 1867.

Population: 1,573 (2000); Race: 98.5% White, 0.0% Black, 0.3% Asian, 0.4% American Indian and Alaska Native, 2.0% Hispanic of any race, 0.5% two or more races (2000); Density: 2,221.8 persons per square mile (2000); Age: 30.8% under 18, 8.3% over 64 (2000); Marriage status: 23.3% never married, 62.4% now married, 6.7% widowed, 7.5% divorced (2000); Foreign born: 1.7% (2000); Ancestry (includes multiple ancestries): 30.2% German, 15.2% Polish, 13.4% Irish, 10.3% English, 9.0% United States or American (2000).

Economy: Single-family building permits issued: 9 (2001) / 16 (2000); Multi-family building permits issued: 0 (2001) / 0 (2000); Employment by occupation: 12.7% management, 16.3% professional, 14.6% services, 25.4% sales, 0.3% farming, 13.1% construction, 17.6% production (2000).

Income: Per capita income: $22,446 (2000); Median household income: $61,700 (2000); Poverty rate: 3.6% (2000).

Taxes: Total city taxes per capita: $334 (1997); City property taxes per capita: $329 (1997).

Education: High school graduation rate: 90.7% (2000); College graduation rate: 17.1% (2000).

School District(s)

Armada Area Schools (PK-12)
2000 Enrollment: 1,912 810-784-4511

Housing: Homeownership rate: 80.9% (2000); Median home value: $142,900 (2000); Median rent: $489 per month (2000); Median age of housing: 48 years (2000).

Safety: Violent crime rate: 0.0 per 10,000 population; Property crime rate: 170.8 per 10,000 population (2001).

Newspapers: Armada Times (1 x week)

Transportation: Commute to work: 92.6% car, 0.3% public transportation, 4.2% walk, 2.7% work from home (2000); Travel time to work: 20.5% less than 15 minutes, 24.4% 15 to 30 minutes, 28.9% 30 to 45 minutes, 13.0% 45 to 60 minutes, 13.2% 60 minutes or more (2000)

ARMADA (township). Covers a land area of 36.495 square miles and a water area of 0 square miles. Located at 42.84° N. Lat.; 82.91° W. Long. Elevation is 737 feet.

Population: 5,246 (2000); Race: 97.0% White, 1.4% Black, 0.2% Asian, 0.2% American Indian and Alaska Native, 1.0% Hispanic of any race, 0.9%

two or more races (2000); Density: 143.7 persons per square mile (2000); Age: 28.9% under 18, 8.8% over 64 (2000); Marriage status: 23.0% never married, 65.7% now married, 5.6% widowed, 5.7% divorced (2000); Foreign born: 2.0% (2000); Ancestry (includes multiple ancestries): 31.3% German, 15.8% Polish, 11.2% Irish, 9.5% English, 8.9% Italian (2000).
Economy: In grain and fruit-growing area. Manufacturing: rubber products, ball-bearing lead screws. Satellite community of Detroit. Single-family building permits issued: 22 (2001) / 23 (2000); Multi-family building permits issued: 0 (2001) / 0 (2000); Employment by occupation: 9.8% management, 16.5% professional, 9.9% services, 27.5% sales, 1.4% farming, 15.0% construction, 19.8% production (2000).
Income: Per capita income: $24,766 (2000); Median household income: $68,421 (2000); Poverty rate: 2.0% (2000).
Taxes: Total city taxes per capita: $65 (1997); City property taxes per capita: $55 (1997).
Education: High school graduation rate: 86.2% (2000); College graduation rate: 14.8% (2000).
Housing: Homeownership rate: 91.4% (2000); Median home value: $165,900 (2000); Median rent: $491 per month (2000); Median age of housing: 28 years (2000).
Transportation: Commute to work: 94.4% car, 0.3% public transportation, 2.2% walk, 3.1% work from home (2000); Travel time to work: 16.6% less than 15 minutes, 23.9% 15 to 30 minutes, 30.3% 30 to 45 minutes, 15.5% 45 to 60 minutes, 13.6% 60 minutes or more (2000)

BRUCE (township). Covers a land area of 36.400 square miles and a water area of 0.204 square miles. Located at 42.82° N. Lat.; 83.03° W. Long.
Population: 8,158 (2000); Race: 96.2% White, 1.2% Black, 0.3% Asian, 0.4% American Indian and Alaska Native, 2.6% Hispanic of any race, 1.5% two or more races (2000); Density: 224.1 persons per square mile (2000); Age: 29.1% under 18, 8.2% over 64 (2000); Marriage status: 23.0% never married, 67.7% now married, 2.7% widowed, 6.6% divorced (2000); Foreign born: 3.8% (2000); Ancestry (includes multiple ancestries): 31.2% German, 18.2% Polish, 16.6% Irish, 10.2% English, 9.7% Italian (2000).
Economy: Single-family building permits issued: 55 (2001) / 50 (2000); Multi-family building permits issued: 0 (2001) / 0 (2000); Employment by occupation: 14.5% management, 23.2% professional, 10.0% services, 23.6% sales, 0.7% farming, 9.6% construction, 18.5% production (2000).
Income: Per capita income: $27,561 (2000); Median household income: $65,469 (2000); Poverty rate: 4.1% (2000).
Taxes: Total city taxes per capita: $146 (2000); City property taxes per capita: $132 (2000).
Education: High school graduation rate: 88.3% (2000); College graduation rate: 24.2% (2000).
Housing: Homeownership rate: 93.1% (2000); Median home value: $204,500 (2000); Median rent: $421 per month (2000); Median age of housing: 24 years (2000).
Transportation: Commute to work: 94.4% car, 0.8% public transportation, 1.6% walk, 3.2% work from home (2000); Travel time to work: 26.4% less than 15 minutes, 23.6% 15 to 30 minutes, 24.0% 30 to 45 minutes, 14.9% 45 to 60 minutes, 11.1% 60 minutes or more (2000)

CENTER LINE (city). Covers a land area of 1.737 square miles and a water area of 0 square miles. Located at 42.47° N. Lat.; 83.02° W. Long. Elevation is 632 feet.
History: Center Line was named by the French because it was on the middle of three trails from Detroit to the northern trading posts. The first general store was opened here in 1863.
Population: 8,531 (2000); Race: 93.3% White, 2.5% Black, 1.1% Asian, 0.1% American Indian and Alaska Native, 1.1% Hispanic of any race, 2.9% two or more races (2000); Density: 4,912.6 persons per square mile (2000); Age: 21.5% under 18, 22.7% over 64 (2000); Marriage status: 25.6% never married, 46.1% now married, 15.1% widowed, 13.2% divorced (2000); Foreign born: 7.2% (2000); Ancestry (includes multiple ancestries): 22.4% Polish, 17.2% German, 12.9% Irish, 8.6% Other groups, 8.2% Italian (2000).
Economy: Single-family building permits issued: 0 (2001) / 3 (2000); Multi-family building permits issued: 0 (2001) / 0 (2000); Employment by occupation: 8.3% management, 10.8% professional, 18.3% services, 29.6% sales, 0.0% farming, 13.1% construction, 20.0% production (2000).
Income: Per capita income: $19,066 (2000); Median household income: $31,677 (2000); Poverty rate: 13.3% (2000).
Taxes: Total city taxes per capita: $431 (1997); City property taxes per capita: $406 (1997).
Education: High school graduation rate: 73.7% (2000); College graduation rate: 6.1% (2000).

School District(s)

Center Line Public Schools (KG-12)
2000 Enrollment: 2,810 810-757-7000

Housing: Homeownership rate: 58.7% (2000); Median home value: $104,400 (2000); Median rent: $211 per month (2000); Median age of housing: 44 years (2000).
Safety: Violent crime rate: 31.5 per 10,000 population; Property crime rate: 346.3 per 10,000 population (2001).
Transportation: Commute to work: 95.0% car, 1.0% public transportation, 2.1% walk, 1.0% work from home (2000); Travel time to work: 27.9% less than 15 minutes, 42.0% 15 to 30 minutes, 18.6% 30 to 45 minutes, 5.3% 45 to 60 minutes, 6.3% 60 minutes or more (2000)

CHESTERFIELD (township). Covers a land area of 27.880 square miles and a water area of 2.784 square miles. Located at 42.67° N. Lat.; 82.80° W. Long.
Population: 37,405 (2000); Race: 92.7% White, 3.0% Black, 0.9% Asian, 0.7% American Indian and Alaska Native, 2.6% Hispanic of any race, 1.6% two or more races (2000); Density: 1,341.7 persons per square mile (2000); Age: 29.5% under 18, 6.5% over 64 (2000); Marriage status: 23.8% never married, 63.4% now married, 4.0% widowed, 8.7% divorced (2000); Foreign born: 4.0% (2000); Ancestry (includes multiple ancestries): 27.6% German, 18.3% Polish, 13.2% Italian, 12.2% Irish, 10.1% Other groups (2000).
Vital Statistics: Birth rate: 120.0 per 10,000 population (1998)
Economy: Unemployment rate: 4.2% (11/2002); Total civilian labor force: 16,095 (11/2002); Single-family building permits issued: 499 (2001) / 639 (2000); Multi-family building permits issued: 0 (2001) / 0 (2000); Employment by occupation: 13.2% management, 18.0% professional, 12.8% services, 25.4% sales, 0.2% farming, 11.0% construction, 19.5% production (2000).
Income: Per capita income: $24,410 (2000); Median household income: $61,630 (2000); Poverty rate: 4.7% (2000).
Taxes: Total city taxes per capita: $223 (2000); City property taxes per capita: $182 (2000).
Education: High school graduation rate: 88.7% (2000); College graduation rate: 16.4% (2000).
Housing: Homeownership rate: 81.4% (2000); Median home value: $167,900 (2000); Median rent: $561 per month (2000); Median age of housing: 16 years (2000).
Safety: Violent crime rate: 6.4 per 10,000 population; Property crime rate: 195.7 per 10,000 population (2001).
Transportation: Commute to work: 97.3% car, 0.2% public transportation, 0.4% walk, 1.9% work from home (2000); Travel time to work: 21.7% less than 15 minutes, 31.3% 15 to 30 minutes, 25.9% 30 to 45 minutes, 12.3% 45 to 60 minutes, 8.8% 60 minutes or more (2000)

CLINTON (CDP). Aka Clinton Township. Covers a land area of 28.194 square miles and a water area of 0.026 square miles. Located at 42.58° N. Lat.; 82.91° W. Long.
Population: 95,648 (2000); Race: 90.9% White, 4.3% Black, 1.9% Asian, 0.4% American Indian and Alaska Native, 1.8% Hispanic of any race, 2.0% two or more races (2000); Density: 3,392.5 persons per square mile (2000); Age: 22.4% under 18, 14.3% over 64 (2000); Marriage status: 27.0% never married, 54.4% now married, 7.3% widowed, 11.3% divorced (2000); Foreign born: 8.2% (2000); Ancestry (includes multiple ancestries): 24.0% German, 18.3% Polish, 16.0% Italian, 11.7% Irish, 10.3% Other groups (2000).
Vital Statistics: Birth rate: 129.3 per 10,000 population (1998)
Economy: Unemployment rate: 4.6% (11/2002); Total civilian labor force: 54,442 (11/2002); Employment by occupation: 13.0% management, 18.9% professional, 12.9% services, 29.2% sales, 0.0% farming, 9.0% construction, 16.9% production (2000).
Income: Per capita income: $25,758 (2000); Median household income: $50,067 (2000); Poverty rate: 5.8% (2000).
Education: High school graduation rate: 84.9% (2000); College graduation rate: 18.0% (2000).
Housing: Homeownership rate: 69.5% (2000); Median home value: $145,400 (2000); Median rent: $543 per month (2000); Median age of housing: 23 years (2000).
Transportation: Commute to work: 97.0% car, 0.5% public transportation, 0.9% walk, 1.1% work from home (2000); Travel time to work: 20.9% less than 15 minutes, 37.2% 15 to 30 minutes, 24.7% 30 to 45 minutes, 10.6% 45 to 60 minutes, 6.6% 60 minutes or more (2000)

EASTPOINTE (city). Aka East Detroit. Covers a land area of 5.102 square miles and a water area of 0 square miles. Located at 42.46° N. Lat.; 82.94° W. Long.
Population: 34,077 (2000); Race: 91.8% White, 4.6% Black, 0.5% Asian, 0.5% American Indian and Alaska Native, 1.1% Hispanic of any race, 2.3% two or more races (2000); Density: 6,678.8 persons per square mile (2000); Age: 24.3% under 18, 16.6% over 64 (2000); Marriage status: 26.4% never married, 53.1% now married, 9.9% widowed, 10.6% divorced (2000); Foreign born: 4.9% (2000); Ancestry (includes multiple ancestries): 27.1% German, 18.4% Polish, 16.7% Italian, 13.9% Irish, 9.3% Other groups (2000).
Vital Statistics: Birth rate: 124.4 per 10,000 population (1998)
Economy: Unemployment rate: 4.1% (11/2002); Total civilian labor force: 19,791 (11/2002); Single-family building permits issued: 8 (2001) / 5 (2000); Multi-family building permits issued: 0 (2001) / 0 (2000); Employment by occupation: 8.3% management, 14.8% professional, 16.3% services, 28.3% sales, 0.0% farming, 11.1% construction, 21.2% production (2000).
Income: Per capita income: $20,665 (2000); Median household income: $46,261 (2000); Poverty rate: 6.4% (2000).
Taxes: Total city taxes per capita: $309 (1997); City property taxes per capita: $295 (1997).
Education: High school graduation rate: 79.3% (2000); College graduation rate: 11.3% (2000).

School District(s)

East Detroit Public Schools (KG-12)
2000 Enrollment: 6,603 810-445-4400
Housing: Homeownership rate: 87.9% (2000); Median home value: $98,100 (2000); Median rent: $485 per month (2000); Median age of housing: 46 years (2000).
Safety: Violent crime rate: 42.9 per 10,000 population; Property crime rate: 348.2 per 10,000 population (2001).
Transportation: Commute to work: 95.7% car, 1.0% public transportation, 1.3% walk, 1.5% work from home (2000); Travel time to work: 25.7% less than 15 minutes, 39.5% 15 to 30 minutes, 22.2% 30 to 45 minutes, 8.4% 45 to 60 minutes, 4.1% 60 minutes or more (2000)
Additional Information Contacts
Eastpointe Chamber of Commerce. 810-776-5520

FRASER (city). Covers a land area of 4.188 square miles and a water area of 0 square miles. Located at 42.53° N. Lat.; 82.95° W. Long. Elevation is 604 feet.
History: Incorporated as a village 1894, as a city 1957.
Population: 15,297 (2000); Race: 96.7% White, 0.4% Black, 0.8% Asian, 0.4% American Indian and Alaska Native, 2.0% Hispanic of any race, 1.0% two or more races (2000); Density: 3,652.5 persons per square mile (2000); Age: 24.4% under 18, 15.4% over 64 (2000); Marriage status: 23.3% never married, 55.1% now married, 9.8% widowed, 11.9% divorced (2000); Foreign born: 6.0% (2000); Ancestry (includes multiple ancestries): 25.7% German, 20.9% Polish, 15.9% Italian, 14.0% Irish, 8.4% English (2000).
Vital Statistics: Birth rate: 105.9 per 10,000 population (1998)
Economy: Tools, dies, and jigs, plastic and plaster products, heating equipment, and steel products are manufactured here. Single-family building permits issued: 11 (2001) / 39 (2000); Multi-family building permits issued: 0 (2001) / 0 (2000); Employment by occupation: 11.6% management, 19.5% professional, 13.2% services, 32.2% sales, 0.0% farming, 7.9% construction, 15.6% production (2000).
Income: Per capita income: $22,864 (2000); Median household income: $50,339 (2000); Poverty rate: 4.2% (2000).
Taxes: Total city taxes per capita: $571 (2000); City property taxes per capita: $557 (2000).
Education: High school graduation rate: 82.4% (2000); College graduation rate: 14.6% (2000).

School District(s)

Fraser Public Schools (KG-12)
2000 Enrollment: 4,598 810-293-5100
Housing: Homeownership rate: 73.6% (2000); Median home value: $139,000 (2000); Median rent: $489 per month (2000); Median age of housing: 29 years (2000).
Newspapers: The Detroit Monitor (1 x week)
Transportation: Commute to work: 96.9% car, 0.4% public transportation, 0.8% walk, 1.6% work from home (2000); Travel time to work: 24.4% less than 15 minutes, 41.1% 15 to 30 minutes, 21.4% 30 to 45 minutes, 8.5% 45 to 60 minutes, 4.7% 60 minutes or more (2000)

HARRISON (CDP). Aka Harrison Township. Covers a land area of 14.303 square miles and a water area of 9.449 square miles. Located at 42.58° N. Lat.; 82.82° W. Long.
Population: 24,461 (2000); Race: 95.0% White, 2.3% Black, 0.1% Asian, 0.4% American Indian and Alaska Native, 1.3% Hispanic of any race, 1.6% two or more races (2000); Density: 1,710.2 persons per square mile (2000); Age: 21.8% under 18, 10.9% over 64 (2000); Marriage status: 27.7% never married, 53.7% now married, 6.0% widowed, 12.7% divorced (2000); Foreign born: 4.1% (2000); Ancestry (includes multiple ancestries): 28.0% German, 16.7% Polish, 12.9% Italian, 12.3% Irish, 10.3% English (2000).
Vital Statistics: Birth rate: 123.9 per 10,000 population (1998)
Economy: Unemployment rate: 4.7% (11/2002); Total civilian labor force: 15,893 (11/2002); Single-family building permits issued: 81 (2001) / 110 (2000); Multi-family building permits issued: 196 (2001) / 156 (2000); Employment by occupation: 14.1% management, 18.2% professional, 11.4% services, 29.2% sales, 0.0% farming, 9.9% construction, 17.1% production (2000).
Income: Per capita income: $29,491 (2000); Median household income: $51,892 (2000); Poverty rate: 5.7% (2000).
Education: High school graduation rate: 88.2% (2000); College graduation rate: 19.8% (2000).
Housing: Homeownership rate: 69.8% (2000); Median home value: $166,600 (2000); Median rent: $572 per month (2000); Median age of housing: 26 years (2000).
Transportation: Commute to work: 97.1% car, 0.2% public transportation, 0.5% walk, 1.5% work from home (2000); Travel time to work: 20.3% less than 15 minutes, 36.7% 15 to 30 minutes, 26.3% 30 to 45 minutes, 10.0% 45 to 60 minutes, 6.6% 60 minutes or more (2000)

LAKE (township). Covers a land area of 0.156 square miles and a water area of 0.486 square miles. Located at 42.45° N. Lat.; 82.87° W. Long.
Population: 80 (2000); Race: 100.0% White, 0.0% Black, 0.0% Asian, 0.0% American Indian and Alaska Native, 0.0% Hispanic of any race, 0.0% two or more races (2000); Density: 511.5 persons per square mile (2000); Age: 9.6% under 18, 44.2% over 64 (2000); Marriage status: 4.2% never married, 66.7% now married, 27.1% widowed, 2.1% divorced (2000); Foreign born: 15.4% (2000); Ancestry (includes multiple ancestries): 19.2% Polish, 19.2% German, 13.5% English, 11.5% French (except Basque), 9.6% Irish (2000).
Economy: Employment by occupation: 14.3% management, 42.9% professional, 0.0% services, 42.9% sales, 0.0% farming, 0.0% construction, 0.0% production (2000).
Income: Per capita income: $64,812 (2000); Median household income: $97,278 (2000); Poverty rate: 3.8% (2000).
Taxes: Total city taxes per capita: $102 (1997); City property taxes per capita: $102 (1997).
Education: High school graduation rate: 89.4% (2000); College graduation rate: 42.6% (2000).
Housing: Homeownership rate: 94.4% (2000); Median home value: $487,500 (2000); Median rent: $1,125 per month (2000); Median age of housing: 45 years (2000).
Transportation: Commute to work: 100.0% car, 0.0% public transportation, 0.0% walk, 0.0% work from home (2000); Travel time to work: 19.0% less than 15 minutes, 52.4% 15 to 30 minutes, 23.8% 30 to 45 minutes, 4.8% 45 to 60 minutes, 0.0% 60 minutes or more (2000)

LENOX (township). Covers a land area of 38.828 square miles and a water area of 0 square miles. Located at 42.74° N. Lat.; 82.80° W. Long.
Population: 8,433 (2000); Race: 78.6% White, 16.2% Black, 0.7% Asian, 0.7% American Indian and Alaska Native, 3.4% Hispanic of any race, 3.2% two or more races (2000); Density: 217.2 persons per square mile (2000); Age: 24.8% under 18, 7.1% over 64 (2000); Marriage status: 30.2% never married, 51.7% now married, 5.0% widowed, 13.1% divorced (2000); Foreign born: 3.2% (2000); Ancestry (includes multiple ancestries): 25.5% German, 18.8% Other groups, 14.4% Polish, 10.0% Irish, 7.5% Italian (2000).
Economy: Single-family building permits issued: 21 (2001) / 20 (2000); Multi-family building permits issued: 0 (2001) / 0 (2000); Employment by occupation: 8.0% management, 10.2% professional, 12.0% services, 26.0% sales, 0.1% farming, 17.6% construction, 26.1% production (2000).
Income: Per capita income: $18,800 (2000); Median household income: $50,659 (2000); Poverty rate: 10.1% (2000).
Taxes: Total city taxes per capita: $91 (1997); City property taxes per capita: $83 (1997).
Education: High school graduation rate: 80.4% (2000); College graduation rate: 8.2% (2000).

Housing: Homeownership rate: 87.3% (2000); Median home value: $126,100 (2000); Median rent: $403 per month (2000); Median age of housing: 20 years (2000).
Transportation: Commute to work: 96.4% car, 0.0% public transportation, 1.3% walk, 1.6% work from home (2000); Travel time to work: 21.6% less than 15 minutes, 30.0% 15 to 30 minutes, 24.2% 30 to 45 minutes, 13.0% 45 to 60 minutes, 11.2% 60 minutes or more (2000)

MACOMB (township). Covers a land area of 36.271 square miles and a water area of 0.022 square miles. Located at 42.65° N. Lat.; 82.93° W. Long. Elevation is 628 feet.
Population: 50,478 (2000); Race: 96.2% White, 0.6% Black, 1.4% Asian, 0.1% American Indian and Alaska Native, 1.3% Hispanic of any race, 1.4% two or more races (2000); Density: 1,391.7 persons per square mile (2000); Age: 30.3% under 18, 7.4% over 64 (2000); Marriage status: 20.2% never married, 70.5% now married, 3.3% widowed, 6.0% divorced (2000); Foreign born: 7.5% (2000); Ancestry (includes multiple ancestries): 27.2% German, 21.2% Italian, 19.6% Polish, 11.6% Irish, 8.1% English (2000).
Economy: Unemployment rate: 4.7% (11/2002); Total civilian labor force: 14,021 (11/2002); Single-family building permits issued: 1,078 (2001) / 1,856 (2000); Multi-family building permits issued: 191 (2001) / 133 (2000); Employment by occupation: 15.0% management, 21.9% professional, 10.7% services, 27.4% sales, 0.2% farming, 9.1% construction, 15.7% production (2000).
Income: Per capita income: $25,907 (2000); Median household income: $72,319 (2000); Poverty rate: 2.1% (2000).
Taxes: Total city taxes per capita: $149 (2000); City property taxes per capita: $93 (2000).
Education: High school graduation rate: 88.9% (2000); College graduation rate: 22.0% (2000).
Housing: Homeownership rate: 96.6% (2000); Median home value: $205,900 (2000); Median rent: $607 per month (2000); Median age of housing: 7 years (2000).
Transportation: Commute to work: 97.5% car, 0.2% public transportation, 0.3% walk, 1.7% work from home (2000); Travel time to work: 19.6% less than 15 minutes, 32.2% 15 to 30 minutes, 27.4% 30 to 45 minutes, 12.5% 45 to 60 minutes, 8.2% 60 minutes or more (2000)

MEMPHIS (city). Covers a land area of 1.123 square miles and a water area of 0.028 square miles. Located at 42.89° N. Lat.; 82.77° W. Long. Elevation is 718 feet.
Population: 1,129 (2000); Race: 97.0% White, 1.2% Black, 0.0% Asian, 1.0% American Indian and Alaska Native, 0.9% Hispanic of any race, 0.8% two or more races (2000); Density: 1,005.6 persons per square mile (2000); Age: 26.4% under 18, 16.0% over 64 (2000); Marriage status: 23.7% never married, 54.7% now married, 10.0% widowed, 11.7% divorced (2000); Foreign born: 1.5% (2000); Ancestry (includes multiple ancestries): 24.4% German, 16.3% Polish, 13.9% Irish, 10.0% French (except Basque), 9.0% English (2000).
Economy: Single-family building permits issued: 10 (2001) / 0 (2000); Multi-family building permits issued: 0 (2001) / 0 (2000); Employment by occupation: 7.0% management, 14.2% professional, 15.3% services, 14.3% sales, 0.0% farming, 17.7% construction, 31.5% production (2000).
Income: Per capita income: $19,983 (2000); Median household income: $41,705 (2000); Poverty rate: 10.0% (2000).
Taxes: Total city taxes per capita: $246 (1997); City property taxes per capita: $240 (1997).
Education: High school graduation rate: 80.2% (2000); College graduation rate: 12.7% (2000).

School District(s)

Memphis Community Schools (KG-12)
2000 Enrollment: 1,015 810-392-2151
Housing: Homeownership rate: 63.9% (2000); Median home value: $119,200 (2000); Median rent: $376 per month (2000); Median age of housing: 43 years (2000).
Safety: Violent crime rate: 44.1 per 10,000 population; Property crime rate: 449.3 per 10,000 population (2001).
Transportation: Commute to work: 90.2% car, 0.0% public transportation, 6.9% walk, 1.7% work from home (2000); Travel time to work: 21.6% less than 15 minutes, 22.4% 15 to 30 minutes, 25.7% 30 to 45 minutes, 16.9% 45 to 60 minutes, 13.4% 60 minutes or more (2000)

MOUNT CLEMENS (city). Covers a land area of 4.215 square miles and a water area of 0 square miles. Located at 42.59° N. Lat.; 82.88° W. Long. Elevation is 614 feet.
History: Mount Clemens developed around sulphur springs as a spa with bathhouses and hotels. The water, which contained about 30 different chemical elements, was also marketed in containers for medicinal purposes. In Mount Clemens, at the Grand Trunk Station, Thomas Edison learned telegraphy.
Population: 17,312 (2000); Race: 75.8% White, 20.1% Black, 1.5% Asian, 0.5% American Indian and Alaska Native, 2.2% Hispanic of any race, 1.8% two or more races (2000); Density: 4,107.0 persons per square mile (2000); Age: 21.8% under 18, 13.4% over 64 (2000); Marriage status: 32.4% never married, 44.6% now married, 8.8% widowed, 14.2% divorced (2000); Foreign born: 3.9% (2000); Ancestry (includes multiple ancestries): 22.8% Other groups, 22.6% German, 10.9% Irish, 9.7% Polish, 7.7% English (2000).
Vital Statistics: Birth rate: 156.5 per 10,000 population (1998)
Economy: Single-family building permits issued: 14 (2001) / 20 (2000); Multi-family building permits issued: 2 (2001) / 30 (2000); Employment by occupation: 9.3% management, 16.6% professional, 15.7% services, 26.3% sales, 0.0% farming, 10.9% construction, 21.1% production (2000).
Income: Per capita income: $21,741 (2000); Median household income: $37,856 (2000); Poverty rate: 14.1% (2000).
Taxes: Total city taxes per capita: $351 (1997); City property taxes per capita: $330 (1997).
Education: High school graduation rate: 78.5% (2000); College graduation rate: 13.5% (2000).

School District(s)

Mount Clemens Community School District (KG-12)
2000 Enrollment: 3,354 810-469-6100
Housing: Homeownership rate: 60.6% (2000); Median home value: $99,900 (2000); Median rent: $439 per month (2000); Median age of housing: 46 years (2000).
Hospitals: Mount Clemens General Hospital (288 beds)
Safety: Violent crime rate: 81.0 per 10,000 population; Property crime rate: 412.0 per 10,000 population (2001).
Newspapers: The Macomb Daily (7 x week)
Transportation: Commute to work: 93.3% car, 1.4% public transportation, 2.8% walk, 1.0% work from home (2000); Travel time to work: 33.2% less than 15 minutes, 32.2% 15 to 30 minutes, 20.2% 30 to 45 minutes, 9.1% 45 to 60 minutes, 5.2% 60 minutes or more (2000)
Additional Information Contacts
Mt Clemens Chamber of Commerce 810-463-1528

NEW BALTIMORE (city). Covers a land area of 4.615 square miles and a water area of 2.120 square miles. Located at 42.68° N. Lat.; 82.73° W. Long. Elevation is 588 feet.
History: First a lumbering center with a sawmill and dock, New Baltimore became a year-round resort with fishing, duck hunting, and ice fishing on Lake St. Clair.
Population: 7,405 (2000); Race: 96.2% White, 0.5% Black, 0.6% Asian, 0.1% American Indian and Alaska Native, 3.1% Hispanic of any race, 1.4% two or more races (2000); Density: 1,604.5 persons per square mile (2000); Age: 25.3% under 18, 9.6% over 64 (2000); Marriage status: 21.2% never married, 63.2% now married, 6.3% widowed, 9.3% divorced (2000); Foreign born: 4.5% (2000); Ancestry (includes multiple ancestries): 30.1% German, 21.2% Polish, 11.1% Italian, 10.9% Irish, 9.9% French (except Basque) (2000).
Economy: Single-family building permits issued: 269 (2001) / 317 (2000); Multi-family building permits issued: 0 (2001) / 116 (2000); Employment by occupation: 14.9% management, 21.8% professional, 10.9% services, 24.8% sales, 0.4% farming, 11.1% construction, 16.1% production (2000).
Income: Per capita income: $26,921 (2000); Median household income: $60,699 (2000); Poverty rate: 3.5% (2000).
Taxes: Total city taxes per capita: $280 (1997); City property taxes per capita: $257 (1997).
Education: High school graduation rate: 86.9% (2000); College graduation rate: 22.7% (2000).

School District(s)

Anchor Bay School District (KG-12)
2000 Enrollment: 5,597 810-725-2861
Housing: Homeownership rate: 71.5% (2000); Median home value: $165,800 (2000); Median rent: $509 per month (2000); Median age of housing: 24 years (2000).
Hospitals: Harbor Oaks Hospital (64 beds)
Safety: Violent crime rate: 9.4 per 10,000 population; Property crime rate: 300.9 per 10,000 population (2001).

Newspapers: The Bay Voice (1 x week); The North Macomb Voice (1 x week); The Macomb Township Voice (1 x week); The Downriver Voice (1 x week); The Blue Water Voice (1 x week)
Transportation: Commute to work: 97.3% car, 0.1% public transportation, 0.5% walk, 1.1% work from home (2000); Travel time to work: 20.3% less than 15 minutes, 30.2% 15 to 30 minutes, 27.1% 30 to 45 minutes, 13.8% 45 to 60 minutes, 8.6% 60 minutes or more (2000)
Additional Information Contacts
New Baltimore Chamber of Commerce. 810-725-5148

NEW HAVEN (village). Covers a land area of 2.419 square miles and a water area of 0 square miles. Located at 42.73° N. Lat.; 82.79° W. Long. Elevation is 627 feet.
History: Incorporated 1869.
Population: 3,071 (2000); Race: 73.5% White, 18.9% Black, 0.8% Asian, 1.2% American Indian and Alaska Native, 4.1% Hispanic of any race, 4.4% two or more races (2000); Density: 1,269.6 persons per square mile (2000); Age: 32.3% under 18, 5.8% over 64 (2000); Marriage status: 30.2% never married, 48.2% now married, 6.0% widowed, 15.6% divorced (2000); Foreign born: 3.5% (2000); Ancestry (includes multiple ancestries): 26.8% Other groups, 22.4% German, 12.5% Polish, 9.9% Irish, 7.1% Italian (2000).
Economy: In farm area. Manufacturing: motor vehicle parts, iron foundry. Single-family building permits issued: 96 (2001) / 4 (2000); Multi-family building permits issued: 0 (2001) / 0 (2000); Employment by occupation: 5.0% management, 8.5% professional, 12.1% services, 27.3% sales, 0.0% farming, 16.8% construction, 30.3% production (2000).
Income: Per capita income: $16,739 (2000); Median household income: $40,699 (2000); Poverty rate: 14.5% (2000).
Taxes: Total city taxes per capita: $144 (1997); City property taxes per capita: $124 (1997).
Education: High school graduation rate: 77.8% (2000); College graduation rate: 6.1% (2000).

School District(s)
New Haven Community Schools (PK-12)
2000 Enrollment: 1,149 810-749-5123
Housing: Homeownership rate: 81.2% (2000); Median home value: $90,500 (2000); Median rent: $314 per month (2000); Median age of housing: 17 years (2000).
Safety: Violent crime rate: 32.4 per 10,000 population; Property crime rate: 35.6 per 10,000 population (2001).
Transportation: Commute to work: 95.0% car, 0.0% public transportation, 2.7% walk, 1.3% work from home (2000); Travel time to work: 26.4% less than 15 minutes, 33.8% 15 to 30 minutes, 24.2% 30 to 45 minutes, 9.1% 45 to 60 minutes, 6.5% 60 minutes or more (2000)

RAY (township). Covers a land area of 36.830 square miles and a water area of 0 square miles. Located at 42.75° N. Lat.; 82.92° W. Long.
Population: 3,740 (2000); Race: 97.4% White, 0.6% Black, 0.0% Asian, 1.5% American Indian and Alaska Native, 1.0% Hispanic of any race, 0.5% two or more races (2000); Density: 101.5 persons per square mile (2000); Age: 25.7% under 18, 9.5% over 64 (2000); Marriage status: 20.9% never married, 69.8% now married, 4.0% widowed, 5.3% divorced (2000); Foreign born: 1.8% (2000); Ancestry (includes multiple ancestries): 39.0% German, 14.3% English, 12.9% Polish, 11.0% Irish, 9.2% French (except Basque) (2000).
Economy: Single-family building permits issued: 19 (2001) / 33 (2000); Multi-family building permits issued: 0 (2001) / 0 (2000); Employment by occupation: 11.7% management, 17.4% professional, 12.9% services, 25.3% sales, 0.2% farming, 13.4% construction, 19.1% production (2000).
Income: Per capita income: $26,604 (2000); Median household income: $70,081 (2000); Poverty rate: 1.8% (2000).
Education: High school graduation rate: 88.0% (2000); College graduation rate: 18.3% (2000).
Housing: Homeownership rate: 91.1% (2000); Median home value: $187,000 (2000); Median rent: $633 per month (2000); Median age of housing: 27 years (2000).
Transportation: Commute to work: 97.3% car, 0.0% public transportation, 1.0% walk, 1.7% work from home (2000); Travel time to work: 13.9% less than 15 minutes, 32.0% 15 to 30 minutes, 29.1% 30 to 45 minutes, 18.2% 45 to 60 minutes, 6.8% 60 minutes or more (2000)

RICHMOND (city). Covers a land area of 2.895 square miles and a water area of 0.055 square miles. Located at 42.81° N. Lat.; 82.75° W. Long. Elevation is 735 feet.
History: Richmond was first known as Beebe's Corners. A settlement about a mile east was called Ridgeway, and later Lenox. A business district developed between the two settlements, and in 1879 the whole was merged and incorporated as Richmond. Harness racing was popular at the Sportsman's Park in Richmond beginning in the 1880's.
Population: 4,897 (2000); Race: 96.0% White, 1.4% Black, 0.2% Asian, 0.3% American Indian and Alaska Native, 4.0% Hispanic of any race, 0.5% two or more races (2000); Density: 1,691.6 persons per square mile (2000); Age: 24.3% under 18, 13.3% over 64 (2000); Marriage status: 26.6% never married, 57.8% now married, 7.4% widowed, 8.1% divorced (2000); Foreign born: 6.4% (2000); Ancestry (includes multiple ancestries): 28.7% German, 14.4% Polish, 10.1% Irish, 9.6% English, 9.0% Other groups (2000).
Economy: Single-family building permits issued: 72 (2001) / 76 (2000); Multi-family building permits issued: 0 (2001) / 0 (2000); Employment by occupation: 10.5% management, 14.8% professional, 11.4% services, 24.3% sales, 0.7% farming, 12.5% construction, 25.8% production (2000).
Income: Per capita income: $21,384 (2000); Median household income: $43,378 (2000); Poverty rate: 6.2% (2000).
Taxes: Total city taxes per capita: $460 (2000); City property taxes per capita: $429 (2000).
Education: High school graduation rate: 83.7% (2000); College graduation rate: 13.7% (2000).

School District(s)
Richmond Community Schools (KG-12)
2000 Enrollment: 1,948 810-727-3565
Housing: Homeownership rate: 71.7% (2000); Median home value: $135,300 (2000); Median rent: $445 per month (2000); Median age of housing: 28 years (2000).
Safety: Violent crime rate: 73.1 per 10,000 population; Property crime rate: 288.4 per 10,000 population (2001).
Transportation: Commute to work: 95.5% car, 0.0% public transportation, 2.4% walk, 1.7% work from home (2000); Travel time to work: 25.2% less than 15 minutes, 24.5% 15 to 30 minutes, 22.3% 30 to 45 minutes, 16.9% 45 to 60 minutes, 11.1% 60 minutes or more (2000)

RICHMOND (township). Covers a land area of 37.267 square miles and a water area of 0 square miles. Located at 42.85° N. Lat.; 82.79° W. Long. Elevation is 735 feet.
History: Richmond Township was named in 1840 for Richmond, New York, by its first postmaster, who had formerly lived in New York.
Population: 3,416 (2000); Race: 97.9% White, 0.6% Black, 0.0% Asian, 0.0% American Indian and Alaska Native, 0.5% Hispanic of any race, 1.5% two or more races (2000); Density: 91.7 persons per square mile (2000); Age: 27.8% under 18, 11.5% over 64 (2000); Marriage status: 24.5% never married, 62.7% now married, 9.2% widowed, 3.6% divorced (2000); Foreign born: 0.9% (2000); Ancestry (includes multiple ancestries): 36.3% German, 16.9% Polish, 14.3% Irish, 8.0% Italian, 7.0% English (2000).
Economy: Single-family building permits issued: 30 (2001) / 32 (2000); Multi-family building permits issued: 0 (2001) / 0 (2000); Employment by occupation: 12.1% management, 18.8% professional, 15.2% services, 19.8% sales, 0.9% farming, 16.6% construction, 16.4% production (2000).
Income: Per capita income: $24,937 (2000); Median household income: $69,449 (2000); Poverty rate: 5.9% (2000).
Taxes: Total city taxes per capita: $51 (1997); City property taxes per capita: $38 (1997).
Education: High school graduation rate: 84.6% (2000); College graduation rate: 14.0% (2000).
Housing: Homeownership rate: 93.3% (2000); Median home value: $184,400 (2000); Median rent: $506 per month (2000); Median age of housing: 27 years (2000).
Transportation: Commute to work: 93.1% car, 0.0% public transportation, 2.1% walk, 4.8% work from home (2000); Travel time to work: 25.1% less than 15 minutes, 21.7% 15 to 30 minutes, 24.4% 30 to 45 minutes, 15.5% 45 to 60 minutes, 13.3% 60 minutes or more (2000)

ROMEO (village). Covers a land area of 2.019 square miles and a water area of 0 square miles. Located at 42.80° N. Lat.; 83.01° W. Long. Elevation is 804 feet.
History: Romeo was settled by a group of New Englanders in the 1820's. Their interest in culture and education led to the literary name for the town, as well as to a number of academies that flourished in the 1800's.
Population: 3,721 (2000); Race: 92.6% White, 3.8% Black, 0.9% Asian, 0.1% American Indian and Alaska Native, 4.0% Hispanic of any race, 1.6% two or more races (2000); Density: 1,842.8 persons per square mile (2000); Age: 25.9% under 18, 14.1% over 64 (2000); Marriage status: 27.5% never married, 52.2% now married, 7.3% widowed, 12.9% divorced (2000); Foreign born: 3.4% (2000); Ancestry (includes multiple ancestries): 31.7%

German, 15.8% Irish, 13.6% English, 12.7% Polish, 8.3% Other groups (2000).
Economy: Single-family building permits issued: 0 (2001) / 1 (2000); Multi-family building permits issued: 16 (2001) / 8 (2000); Employment by occupation: 12.7% management, 17.3% professional, 17.5% services, 22.6% sales, 0.0% farming, 11.6% construction, 18.3% production (2000).
Income: Per capita income: $22,588 (2000); Median household income: $48,015 (2000); Poverty rate: 3.9% (2000).
Taxes: Total city taxes per capita: $593 (1997); City property taxes per capita: $584 (1997).
Education: High school graduation rate: 84.4% (2000); College graduation rate: 23.3% (2000).

School District(s)

Romeo Community Schools (KG-12)
2000 Enrollment: 5,332 810-752-0200

Housing: Homeownership rate: 69.6% (2000); Median home value: $151,600 (2000); Median rent: $420 per month (2000); Median age of housing: 43 years (2000).
Safety: Violent crime rate: 26.7 per 10,000 population; Property crime rate: 216.5 per 10,000 population (2001).
Newspapers: The Romeo Observer (1 x week); Countryman (1 x week)
Transportation: Commute to work: 92.7% car, 0.0% public transportation, 4.0% walk, 2.5% work from home (2000); Travel time to work: 32.3% less than 15 minutes, 25.6% 15 to 30 minutes, 25.7% 30 to 45 minutes, 8.4% 45 to 60 minutes, 8.0% 60 minutes or more (2000)

ROSEVILLE (city). Covers a land area of 9.811 square miles and a water area of 0.016 square miles. Located at 42.50° N. Lat.; 82.93° W. Long. Elevation is 615 feet.
History: Roseville began in the 1840's, but grew with the industrial expansion of Detroit in the 1900's, when many residences were built here for people employed in the larger city.
Population: 48,129 (2000); Race: 93.3% White, 2.5% Black, 1.8% Asian, 0.3% American Indian and Alaska Native, 1.5% Hispanic of any race, 1.7% two or more races (2000); Density: 4,905.6 persons per square mile (2000); Age: 23.2% under 18, 15.4% over 64 (2000); Marriage status: 28.1% never married, 50.2% now married, 9.1% widowed, 12.5% divorced (2000); Foreign born: 5.4% (2000); Ancestry (includes multiple ancestries): 24.5% German, 19.8% Polish, 14.4% Italian, 13.4% Irish, 9.1% Other groups (2000).
Vital Statistics: Birth rate: 133.8 per 10,000 population (1998)
Economy: Unemployment rate: 5.8% (11/2002); Total civilian labor force: 31,130 (11/2002); Single-family building permits issued: 71 (2001) / 148 (2000); Multi-family building permits issued: 0 (2001) / 24 (2000); Employment by occupation: 7.1% management, 12.4% professional, 16.1% services, 29.0% sales, 0.1% farming, 13.6% construction, 21.6% production (2000).
Income: Per capita income: $19,823 (2000); Median household income: $41,220 (2000); Poverty rate: 7.9% (2000).
Taxes: Total city taxes per capita: $370 (2000); City property taxes per capita: $354 (2000).
Education: High school graduation rate: 76.2% (2000); College graduation rate: 7.2% (2000).

School District(s)

Conner Creek Academy East (KG-08)
2000 Enrollment: 397 231-591-5802
Roseville Community Schools (KG-12)
2000 Enrollment: 6,162 810-445-5505

Housing: Homeownership rate: 75.2% (2000); Median home value: $97,800 (2000); Median rent: $504 per month (2000); Median age of housing: 41 years (2000).
Safety: Violent crime rate: 31.4 per 10,000 population; Property crime rate: 477.9 per 10,000 population (2001).
Transportation: Commute to work: 95.9% car, 1.0% public transportation, 1.1% walk, 1.2% work from home (2000); Travel time to work: 26.6% less than 15 minutes, 40.3% 15 to 30 minutes, 21.2% 30 to 45 minutes, 7.1% 45 to 60 minutes, 4.8% 60 minutes or more (2000)

SAINT CLAIR SHORES (city). Covers a land area of 11.530 square miles and a water area of 2.721 square miles. Located at 42.48° N. Lat.; 82.89° W. Long. Elevation is 585 feet.
History: The area of St. Clair Shores was settled in the 1770's by French familes from Detroit. The village was named and incorporated in 1925, after having been called L'Anse Cruise (deep bay) by the residents. St. Clair Shores was incorporated as a city in 1950.
Population: 63,096 (2000); Race: 96.5% White, 0.7% Black, 0.8% Asian, 0.4% American Indian and Alaska Native, 1.2% Hispanic of any race, 1.3% two or more races (2000); Density: 5,472.3 persons per square mile (2000); Age: 20.1% under 18, 21.8% over 64 (2000); Marriage status: 24.1% never married, 55.1% now married, 10.7% widowed, 10.1% divorced (2000); Foreign born: 5.7% (2000); Ancestry (includes multiple ancestries): 25.9% German, 17.1% Polish, 16.6% Italian, 15.8% Irish, 9.3% English (2000).
Vital Statistics: Birth rate: 102.4 per 10,000 population (1998)
Economy: Unemployment rate: 4.3% (11/2002); Total civilian labor force: 40,907 (11/2002); Single-family building permits issued: 35 (2001) / 39 (2000); Multi-family building permits issued: 0 (2001) / 0 (2000); Employment by occupation: 12.1% management, 19.3% professional, 12.8% services, 30.3% sales, 0.0% farming, 9.9% construction, 15.6% production (2000).
Income: Per capita income: $25,009 (2000); Median household income: $49,047 (2000); Poverty rate: 3.7% (2000).
Education: High school graduation rate: 84.4% (2000); College graduation rate: 18.1% (2000).

School District(s)

Lake Shore Public Schools (Macom (KG-12)
2000 Enrollment: 3,245 810-285-8480
Lakeview Public Schools (Macomb) (KG-12)
2000 Enrollment: 2,714 810-445-4015
South Lake Schools (KG-12)
2000 Enrollment: 2,220 810-445-4209

Housing: Homeownership rate: 85.8% (2000); Median home value: $123,700 (2000); Median rent: $552 per month (2000); Median age of housing: 43 years (2000).
Safety: Violent crime rate: 27.1 per 10,000 population; Property crime rate: 222.3 per 10,000 population (2001).
Transportation: Commute to work: 95.8% car, 0.6% public transportation, 1.0% walk, 2.3% work from home (2000); Travel time to work: 25.5% less than 15 minutes, 38.1% 15 to 30 minutes, 23.0% 30 to 45 minutes, 9.2% 45 to 60 minutes, 4.2% 60 minutes or more (2000)

Additional Information Contacts

St. Clair Shores Chamber of Commerce 810-777-2741

SHELBY (CDP). Covers a land area of 34.682 square miles and a water area of 0.541 square miles. Located at 42.67° N. Lat.; 83.03° W. Long.
History: Shelby Township was settled in the 1820's and named for General Isaac Shelby, leader of the Kentucky Rangers in the War of 1812.
Population: 65,159 (2000); Race: 94.7% White, 0.9% Black, 1.9% Asian, 0.3% American Indian and Alaska Native, 1.5% Hispanic of any race, 1.9% two or more races (2000); Density: 1,878.7 persons per square mile (2000); Age: 24.9% under 18, 10.5% over 64 (2000); Marriage status: 24.4% never married, 62.6% now married, 5.2% widowed, 7.9% divorced (2000); Foreign born: 9.7% (2000); Ancestry (includes multiple ancestries): 24.8% German, 19.2% Polish, 14.5% Italian, 11.0% Irish, 9.4% English (2000).
Vital Statistics: Birth rate: 93.9 per 10,000 population (1998)
Economy: Unemployment rate: 3.9% (11/2002); Total civilian labor force: 32,685 (11/2002); Employment by occupation: 15.5% management, 23.5% professional, 11.2% services, 26.5% sales, 0.1% farming, 8.8% construction, 14.4% production (2000).
Income: Per capita income: $30,131 (2000); Median household income: $65,291 (2000); Poverty rate: 3.7% (2000).
Education: High school graduation rate: 87.4% (2000); College graduation rate: 26.3% (2000).
Housing: Homeownership rate: 78.3% (2000); Median home value: $195,900 (2000); Median rent: $639 per month (2000); Median age of housing: 18 years (2000).
Newspapers: Great Lakes Senior Living News (1 x month); The Advisor - Warren (1 x week); The Source - Sterling Heights, Utica & Shelby (1 x week); The Source - Romeo, Washington & Bruce Edition (1 x week); The Advisor - Eastpointe, Roseville & Saint Clair Shores (1 x week); The Advisor - Mt. Clemens, Macomb, Clinton, Harrison & Fraser (1 x week)
Transportation: Commute to work: 96.1% car, 0.4% public transportation, 0.5% walk, 2.5% work from home (2000); Travel time to work: 20.9% less than 15 minutes, 36.3% 15 to 30 minutes, 25.4% 30 to 45 minutes, 10.3% 45 to 60 minutes, 7.1% 60 minutes or more (2000)

STERLING HEIGHTS (city). Covers a land area of 36.641 square miles and a water area of 0.052 square miles. Located at 42.58° N. Lat.; 83.02° W. Long. Elevation is 625 feet.
History: Sterling Heights began as the township of Jefferson, but was renamed to honor early settler Azariah W. Sterling. In 1966 the township was incorporated as a city.

Population: 124,471 (2000); Race: 90.2% White, 1.1% Black, 5.2% Asian, 0.4% American Indian and Alaska Native, 1.3% Hispanic of any race, 2.7% two or more races (2000); Density: 3,397.0 persons per square mile (2000); Age: 24.1% under 18, 11.7% over 64 (2000); Marriage status: 25.6% never married, 60.5% now married, 6.2% widowed, 7.6% divorced (2000); Foreign born: 17.0% (2000); Ancestry (includes multiple ancestries): 21.0% Polish, 19.9% German, 13.3% Italian, 9.6% Irish, 9.2% Other groups (2000).
Vital Statistics: Birth rate: 123.2 per 10,000 population (1998)
Economy: Unemployment rate: 3.8% (11/2002); Total civilian labor force: 77,106 (11/2002); Single-family building permits issued: 503 (2001) / 529 (2000); Multi-family building permits issued: 15 (2001) / 222 (2000); Employment by occupation: 14.1% management, 21.5% professional, 12.3% services, 29.9% sales, 0.1% farming, 7.7% construction, 14.6% production (2000).
Income: Per capita income: $24,958 (2000); Median household income: $60,494 (2000); Poverty rate: 5.2% (2000).
Taxes: Total city taxes per capita: $357 (2000); City property taxes per capita: $334 (2000).
Education: High school graduation rate: 84.0% (2000); College graduation rate: 23.0% (2000).

School District(s)

Huron Academy (KG-08)
2000 Enrollment: 269 231-591-5802
Utica Community Schools (KG-12)
2000 Enrollment: 27,786 810-795-2300

Housing: Homeownership rate: 79.0% (2000); Median home value: $160,700 (2000); Median rent: $585 per month (2000); Median age of housing: 25 years (2000).
Safety: Violent crime rate: 20.8 per 10,000 population; Property crime rate: 263.1 per 10,000 population (2001).
Transportation: Commute to work: 97.1% car, 0.3% public transportation, 0.7% walk, 1.6% work from home (2000); Travel time to work: 21.8% less than 15 minutes, 41.6% 15 to 30 minutes, 23.4% 30 to 45 minutes, 8.1% 45 to 60 minutes, 5.2% 60 minutes or more (2000)
Additional Information Contacts
Sterling Heights Chamber of Commerce 810-731-5400

UTICA (city). Covers a land area of 1.775 square miles and a water area of 0 square miles. Located at 42.62° N. Lat.; 83.02° W. Long. Elevation is 645 feet.
History: Utica was first called Hog's Hollow. It was settled by a group of German immigrants in 1817.
Population: 4,577 (2000); Race: 95.1% White, 0.3% Black, 3.3% Asian, 0.6% American Indian and Alaska Native, 2.7% Hispanic of any race, 0.3% two or more races (2000); Density: 2,578.2 persons per square mile (2000); Age: 21.1% under 18, 14.6% over 64 (2000); Marriage status: 27.1% never married, 50.6% now married, 8.9% widowed, 13.3% divorced (2000); Foreign born: 13.0% (2000); Ancestry (includes multiple ancestries): 27.3% German, 14.8% Polish, 9.9% English, 9.4% Irish, 8.3% Other groups (2000).
Economy: Single-family building permits issued: 24 (2001) / 33 (2000); Multi-family building permits issued: 0 (2001) / 0 (2000); Employment by occupation: 9.7% management, 19.5% professional, 15.2% services, 28.1% sales, 0.0% farming, 11.6% construction, 15.9% production (2000).
Income: Per capita income: $21,615 (2000); Median household income: $38,683 (2000); Poverty rate: 7.0% (2000).
Taxes: Total city taxes per capita: $713 (2000); City property taxes per capita: $666 (2000).
Education: High school graduation rate: 80.8% (2000); College graduation rate: 18.3% (2000).
Housing: Homeownership rate: 54.0% (2000); Median home value: $145,800 (2000); Median rent: $474 per month (2000); Median age of housing: 34 years (2000).
Transportation: Commute to work: 95.8% car, 0.3% public transportation, 1.8% walk, 1.0% work from home (2000); Travel time to work: 25.8% less than 15 minutes, 40.2% 15 to 30 minutes, 19.5% 30 to 45 minutes, 7.7% 45 to 60 minutes, 6.7% 60 minutes or more (2000)

WARREN (city). Covers a land area of 34.289 square miles and a water area of 0.025 square miles. Located at 42.49° N. Lat.; 83.02° W. Long. Elevation is 619 feet.
History: Established 1837; Incorporated as a city 1957.
Population: 138,247 (2000); Race: 91.0% White, 2.5% Black, 3.1% Asian, 0.3% American Indian and Alaska Native, 1.4% Hispanic of any race, 2.7% two or more races (2000); Density: 4,031.8 persons per square mile (2000); Age: 22.9% under 18, 17.2% over 64 (2000); Marriage status: 27.0% never married, 53.2% now married, 8.9% widowed, 10.9% divorced (2000); Foreign born: 10.3% (2000); Ancestry (includes multiple ancestries): 21.0% Polish, 20.4% German, 11.4% Irish, 10.6% Italian, 10.4% Other groups (2000).
Vital Statistics: Birth rate: 127.8 per 10,000 population (1998)
Economy: Important metalworking center where steel is processed. Manufacturing includes tool and die and transportation equipment. A large General Motors technical center is in Warren. U.S. Army Mobility Command Arsenal here. Unemployment rate: 5.5% (11/2002); Total civilian labor force: 86,812 (11/2002); Single-family building permits issued: 85 (2001) / 68 (2000); Multi-family building permits issued: 2 (2001) / 51 (2000); Employment by occupation: 10.0% management, 15.4% professional, 14.9% services, 27.8% sales, 0.1% farming, 10.2% construction, 21.7% production (2000).
Income: Per capita income: $21,407 (2000); Median household income: $44,626 (2000); Poverty rate: 7.4% (2000).
Taxes: Total city taxes per capita: $474 (2000); City property taxes per capita: $458 (2000).
Education: High school graduation rate: 76.9% (2000); College graduation rate: 13.0% (2000).

School District(s)

Conner Creek Academy (KG-08)
2000 Enrollment: 525 517-774-2100
Fitzgerald Public Schools (KG-12)
2000 Enrollment: 3,152 810-757-1750
Van Dyke Public Schools (KG-12)
2000 Enrollment: 4,205 810-758-8333
Warren Consolidated Schools (KG-12)
2000 Enrollment: 14,602 810-825-2400
Warren Woods Public Schools (KG-12)
2000 Enrollment: 3,069 810-439-4401

Four-year College(s)

Davenport University-Eastern Region-Warren (Private, Not-for-profit)
2001 Enrollment: 2,486 810-558-8700
2001 Tuition: In-state $7,344; Out-of-state $7,344

Two-year College(s)

Macomb Community College (Public)
2001 Enrollment: 21,818 810-445-7999
2001 Tuition: In-state $2,604; Out-of-state $3,069

Housing: Homeownership rate: 80.3% (2000); Median home value: $117,800 (2000); Median rent: $539 per month (2000); Median age of housing: 37 years (2000).
Hospitals: Bi-County Community Hospital (231 beds); Kern Hospital & Medical Center (20 beds); Saint John Macomb Hospital (376 beds)
Safety: Violent crime rate: 58.9 per 10,000 population; Property crime rate: 346.5 per 10,000 population (2001).
Newspapers: Warren Weekly (1 x week); Eastside Advertiser Times; Grosse Pointe Times (2 x month); Eastsider; Troy Times (1 x week); Saint Clair Shores Sentinel (1 x week); Shelby-Utica News (1 x week); Madison Park News (2 x month); Sterling Heights Sentry (1 x week); Chronicle; The Journal
Transportation: Commute to work: 96.1% car, 0.7% public transportation, 1.2% walk, 1.3% work from home (2000); Travel time to work: 25.8% less than 15 minutes, 41.0% 15 to 30 minutes, 22.1% 30 to 45 minutes, 7.3% 45 to 60 minutes, 3.9% 60 minutes or more (2000)

WASHINGTON (township). Covers a land area of 35.949 square miles and a water area of 0.860 square miles. Located at 42.75° N. Lat.; 83.03° W. Long. Elevation is 700 feet.
Population: 19,080 (2000); Race: 97.2% White, 0.5% Black, 0.5% Asian, 0.5% American Indian and Alaska Native, 2.7% Hispanic of any race, 0.6% two or more races (2000); Density: 530.7 persons per square mile (2000); Age: 26.7% under 18, 8.9% over 64 (2000); Marriage status: 22.9% never married, 65.4% now married, 4.8% widowed, 6.9% divorced (2000); Foreign born: 6.1% (2000); Ancestry (includes multiple ancestries): 29.0% German, 19.8% Polish, 12.9% Irish, 12.8% Italian, 10.4% English (2000).
Economy: Manufacturing: iron grinding, transportation equipment. Stony Creek Metropark to West. Single-family building permits issued: 268 (2001) / 302 (2000); Multi-family building permits issued: 2 (2001) / 58 (2000); Employment by occupation: 15.9% management, 19.6% professional, 11.2% services, 26.7% sales, 0.1% farming, 11.9% construction, 14.5% production (2000).
Income: Per capita income: $30,740 (2000); Median household income: $68,841 (2000); Poverty rate: 3.7% (2000).
Taxes: Total city taxes per capita: $129 (2000); City property taxes per capita: $90 (2000).

Education: High school graduation rate: 87.9% (2000); College graduation rate: 22.6% (2000).
Housing: Homeownership rate: 85.2% (2000); Median home value: $221,000 (2000); Median rent: $519 per month (2000); Median age of housing: 16 years (2000).
Transportation: Commute to work: 96.4% car, 0.1% public transportation, 0.8% walk, 2.1% work from home (2000); Travel time to work: 18.9% less than 15 minutes, 31.4% 15 to 30 minutes, 29.4% 30 to 45 minutes, 12.4% 45 to 60 minutes, 7.9% 60 minutes or more (2000)

Manistee County

Located in northwestern Michigan; bounded on the west by Lake Michigan; drained by the Manistee and Little Manistee Rivers; includes part of Manistee National Forest, and several lakes. Covers a land area of 543.60 square miles, a water area of 737.20 square miles, and is located in the Eastern Time Zone. The county government was organized in 1855. County seat is Manistee.
Population: 24,527 (2000); Race: 94.1% White, 1.4% Black, 0.3% Asian, 1.3% American Indian and Alaska Native, 2.8% Hispanic of any race, 2.0% two or more races (2000); Density: 45.1 persons per square mile (2000); Age: 22.8% under 18, 18.1% over 64 (2000).
Religion: Five largest groups: 26.3% Catholic Church, 7.2% Lutheran Church—Missouri Synod, 4.7% Evangelical Lutheran Church in America, 2.8% The United Methodist Church, 1.9% General Association of Regular Baptist Churches (2000).
Economy: Unemployment rate: 7.1% (11/2002); Total civilian labor force: 11,652 (11/2002); Leading industries: 22.3% manufacturing; 18.0% health care and social assistance; 17.0% retail trade (2000); Companies that employ more than 1,000 persons: 0 (2000); Companies that employ more than 100 persons: 9 (2000); Farms: 284 totaling 47,521 acres (1997); Minority business ownership rate: 0.0% (1997); Women business ownership rate: 20.5% (1997); Retail sales per capita: $8,156 (1997). Single-family building permits issued: 52 (2001) / 34 (2000); Multi-family building permits issued: 48 (2001) / 18 (2000).
Income: Per capita income: $17,204 (2000); Median household income: $34,208 (2000); Poverty rate: 10.3% (2000); Bankruptcy rate: 3.71% (2001).
Taxes: Total county taxes per capita: $174 (1997); County property taxes per capita: $164 (1997).
Education: High school graduation rate: 81.4% (2000); College graduation rate: 14.2% (2000).
Housing: Homeownership rate: 81.0% (2000); Median home value: $77,400 (2000); Median rent: $339 per month (2000); Median age of housing: 36 years (2000).
Health: Birth rate: 97.9 per 10,000 population (1998); Age adjusted death rate: 86.9 per 10,000 population (1999); Age adjusted cancer mortality rate: 209.4 deaths per 100,000 population (1999). Number of physicians: 10.6 per 10,000 population (1999); Number of hospital beds: 22.0 per 10,000 population (1999).
Elections: 2000 Presidential election results: 49.3% Gore, 47.3% Bush, 2.8% Nader, 0.1% Buchanan
National and State Parks: Manistee National Forest; Manistee River State Game Area; Orchard Beach State Park
Additional Information Contacts
Manistee County Government Offices.................... 231-723-4575
Manistee Area Chamber of Commerce.................... 231-723-2575

Manistee County Communities

ARCADIA (township). Covers a land area of 18.626 square miles and a water area of 0.322 square miles. Located at 44.48° N. Lat.; 86.22° W. Long. Elevation is 587 feet.
History: Arcadia Township was organized in 1870. The village of Arcadia was settled by a German immigrant.
Population: 621 (2000); Race: 98.7% White, 0.0% Black, 0.0% Asian, 0.6% American Indian and Alaska Native, 1.1% Hispanic of any race, 0.3% two or more races (2000); Density: 33.3 persons per square mile (2000); Age: 19.7% under 18, 23.5% over 64 (2000); Marriage status: 16.9% never married, 66.2% now married, 6.3% widowed, 10.6% divorced (2000); Foreign born: 1.1% (2000); Ancestry (includes multiple ancestries): 31.6% German, 14.3% English, 9.9% Irish, 8.7% United States or American, 6.7% French (except Basque) (2000).
Economy: Employment by occupation: 14.3% management, 24.9% professional, 9.7% services, 19.4% sales, 1.3% farming, 17.3% construction, 13.1% production (2000).
Income: Per capita income: $23,089 (2000); Median household income: $34,844 (2000); Poverty rate: 13.3% (2000).
Taxes: Total city taxes per capita: $141 (1997); City property taxes per capita: $140 (1997).
Education: High school graduation rate: 83.0% (2000); College graduation rate: 27.9% (2000).
Housing: Homeownership rate: 83.7% (2000); Median home value: $99,200 (2000); Median rent: $344 per month (2000); Median age of housing: 39 years (2000).
Transportation: Commute to work: 86.8% car, 1.3% public transportation, 5.7% walk, 6.1% work from home (2000); Travel time to work: 25.2% less than 15 minutes, 42.5% 15 to 30 minutes, 14.0% 30 to 45 minutes, 7.9% 45 to 60 minutes, 10.3% 60 minutes or more (2000)

BEAR LAKE (village). Covers a land area of 0.315 square miles and a water area of 0.017 square miles. Located at 44.42° N. Lat.; 86.14° W. Long. Elevation is 878 feet.
History: Bear Lake Village, on the shores of Bear Lake, was first a lumber center, but became a tourist trading center and a shipping point for fruit from the surrounding farms and orchards. The village was settled in 1863 by Russell F. Smith, and incorporated in 1893.
Population: 318 (2000); Race: 93.6% White, 0.0% Black, 0.0% Asian, 2.4% American Indian and Alaska Native, 6.1% Hispanic of any race, 2.4% two or more races (2000); Density: 1,011.1 persons per square mile (2000); Age: 25.6% under 18, 18.3% over 64 (2000); Marriage status: 28.1% never married, 51.0% now married, 8.7% widowed, 12.2% divorced (2000); Foreign born: 0.9% (2000); Ancestry (includes multiple ancestries): 24.1% German, 22.0% English, 9.8% Other groups, 7.3% Irish, 6.4% French (except Basque) (2000).
Economy: Employment by occupation: 6.6% management, 14.0% professional, 23.5% services, 19.9% sales, 0.0% farming, 9.6% construction, 26.5% production (2000).
Income: Per capita income: $15,170 (2000); Median household income: $31,389 (2000); Poverty rate: 12.7% (2000).
Taxes: Total city taxes per capita: $73 (1997); City property taxes per capita: $73 (1997).
Education: High school graduation rate: 82.2% (2000); College graduation rate: 15.5% (2000).

School District(s)

Bear Lake School District (KG-12)
2000 Enrollment: 358 231-864-3133
Housing: Homeownership rate: 78.3% (2000); Median home value: $71,300 (2000); Median rent: $400 per month (2000); Median age of housing: 53 years (2000).
Transportation: Commute to work: 82.1% car, 0.0% public transportation, 10.4% walk, 7.5% work from home (2000); Travel time to work: 43.5% less than 15 minutes, 33.9% 15 to 30 minutes, 15.3% 30 to 45 minutes, 3.2% 45 to 60 minutes, 4.0% 60 minutes or more (2000)

BEAR LAKE (township). Covers a land area of 34.735 square miles and a water area of 1.336 square miles. Located at 44.39° N. Lat.; 86.13° W. Long. Elevation is 878 feet.
Population: 1,587 (2000); Race: 96.7% White, 0.0% Black, 0.4% Asian, 1.3% American Indian and Alaska Native, 2.5% Hispanic of any race, 0.7% two or more races (2000); Density: 45.7 persons per square mile (2000); Age: 25.4% under 18, 16.6% over 64 (2000); Marriage status: 19.6% never married, 63.8% now married, 8.0% widowed, 8.5% divorced (2000); Foreign born: 1.5% (2000); Ancestry (includes multiple ancestries): 25.4% German, 14.0% English, 10.1% United States or American, 7.5% Irish, 5.7% French (except Basque) (2000).
Economy: Trade and shipping center for resort and farm area: apples, cherries, berries. Manufacturing: food and beverages. Employment by occupation: 10.9% management, 13.5% professional, 23.7% services, 21.3% sales, 1.3% farming, 13.2% construction, 16.1% production (2000).
Income: Per capita income: $18,186 (2000); Median household income: $37,898 (2000); Poverty rate: 8.2% (2000).
Taxes: Total city taxes per capita: $41 (1997); City property taxes per capita: $39 (1997).
Education: High school graduation rate: 86.9% (2000); College graduation rate: 15.2% (2000).
Housing: Homeownership rate: 87.3% (2000); Median home value: $91,800 (2000); Median rent: $401 per month (2000); Median age of housing: 38 years (2000).
Transportation: Commute to work: 89.0% car, 0.0% public transportation, 3.4% walk, 7.6% work from home (2000); Travel time to work: 32.3% less

than 15 minutes, 45.5% 15 to 30 minutes, 12.9% 30 to 45 minutes, 3.6% 45 to 60 minutes, 5.6% 60 minutes or more (2000)

BRETHREN (unincorporated postal area, zip code 49619). Covers a land area of 61.153 square miles and a water area of 0.162 square miles. Located at 44.30° N. Lat.; 86.01° W. Long. Elevation is 729 feet.
History: Brethren was founded in 1900 by Samuel S. Thorpe of the German Baptist Brethren Church.
Population: 1,060 (2000); Race: 97.2% White, 0.0% Black, 0.2% Asian, 0.9% American Indian and Alaska Native, 0.6% Hispanic of any race, 1.8% two or more races (2000); Density: 17.3 persons per square mile (2000); Age: 21.7% under 18, 20.5% over 64 (2000); Marriage status: 17.9% never married, 62.7% now married, 6.3% widowed, 13.0% divorced (2000); Foreign born: 0.4% (2000); Ancestry (includes multiple ancestries): 30.8% German, 14.5% English, 9.3% Dutch, 8.4% United States or American, 7.9% Irish (2000).
Economy: Employment by occupation: 8.8% management, 8.8% professional, 20.9% services, 16.3% sales, 0.7% farming, 20.7% construction, 23.7% production (2000).
Income: Per capita income: $15,896 (2000); Median household income: $34,444 (2000); Poverty rate: 8.5% (2000).
Education: High school graduation rate: 80.8% (2000); College graduation rate: 6.5% (2000).

School District(s)

Kaleva Norman Dickson School District (KG-12)
2000 Enrollment: 897 231-477-5353

Housing: Homeownership rate: 88.7% (2000); Median home value: $68,900 (2000); Median rent: $352 per month (2000); Median age of housing: 29 years (2000).
Transportation: Commute to work: 91.2% car, 0.0% public transportation, 3.3% walk, 5.0% work from home (2000); Travel time to work: 22.8% less than 15 minutes, 42.3% 15 to 30 minutes, 18.5% 30 to 45 minutes, 9.3% 45 to 60 minutes, 7.2% 60 minutes or more (2000)

BROWN (township). Covers a land area of 35.671 square miles and a water area of 0.492 square miles. Located at 44.30° N. Lat.; 86.12° W. Long.
History: Brown Township was organized in 1855 and named for Henry L. Brown, who settled here in 1853.
Population: 712 (2000); Race: 96.4% White, 0.0% Black, 0.3% Asian, 1.6% American Indian and Alaska Native, 0.9% Hispanic of any race, 1.5% two or more races (2000); Density: 20.0 persons per square mile (2000); Age: 25.8% under 18, 17.2% over 64 (2000); Marriage status: 17.0% never married, 63.8% now married, 7.8% widowed, 11.4% divorced (2000); Foreign born: 0.7% (2000); Ancestry (includes multiple ancestries): 34.3% German, 12.1% English, 9.7% Polish, 8.9% United States or American, 8.0% Dutch (2000).
Economy: Employment by occupation: 15.0% management, 12.8% professional, 20.4% services, 17.9% sales, 1.1% farming, 10.2% construction, 22.6% production (2000).
Income: Per capita income: $17,286 (2000); Median household income: $40,380 (2000); Poverty rate: 8.0% (2000).
Taxes: Total city taxes per capita: $41 (1997); City property taxes per capita: $41 (1997).
Education: High school graduation rate: 81.6% (2000); College graduation rate: 10.7% (2000).
Housing: Homeownership rate: 91.7% (2000); Median home value: $86,500 (2000); Median rent: $455 per month (2000); Median age of housing: 29 years (2000).
Transportation: Commute to work: 86.2% car, 0.7% public transportation, 1.5% walk, 10.4% work from home (2000); Travel time to work: 24.2% less than 15 minutes, 59.6% 15 to 30 minutes, 6.3% 30 to 45 minutes, 3.3% 45 to 60 minutes, 6.7% 60 minutes or more (2000)

CLEON (township). Covers a land area of 35.986 square miles and a water area of 0.076 square miles. Located at 44.47° N. Lat.; 85.88° W. Long.
Population: 932 (2000); Race: 96.1% White, 0.0% Black, 0.5% Asian, 2.2% American Indian and Alaska Native, 1.9% Hispanic of any race, 0.2% two or more races (2000); Density: 25.9 persons per square mile (2000); Age: 27.5% under 18, 11.1% over 64 (2000); Marriage status: 27.5% never married, 55.0% now married, 6.2% widowed, 11.2% divorced (2000); Foreign born: 2.2% (2000); Ancestry (includes multiple ancestries): 20.6% German, 19.0% United States or American, 11.3% English, 9.4% Other groups, 9.2% Irish (2000).
Economy: Employment by occupation: 4.8% management, 9.1% professional, 18.6% services, 20.8% sales, 1.4% farming, 22.0% construction, 23.4% production (2000).
Income: Per capita income: $13,523 (2000); Median household income: $30,547 (2000); Poverty rate: 13.2% (2000).
Taxes: Total city taxes per capita: $62 (1997); City property taxes per capita: $53 (1997).
Education: High school graduation rate: 72.9% (2000); College graduation rate: 6.0% (2000).
Housing: Homeownership rate: 85.3% (2000); Median home value: $61,300 (2000); Median rent: $375 per month (2000); Median age of housing: 30 years (2000).
Transportation: Commute to work: 91.8% car, 0.0% public transportation, 1.2% walk, 5.1% work from home (2000); Travel time to work: 14.7% less than 15 minutes, 25.4% 15 to 30 minutes, 35.0% 30 to 45 minutes, 16.8% 45 to 60 minutes, 8.1% 60 minutes or more (2000)

COPEMISH (village). Covers a land area of 0.869 square miles and a water area of 0.061 square miles. Located at 44.48° N. Lat.; 85.92° W. Long. Elevation is 808 feet.
History: The Buckley Douglass Lumber Company began operations here about 1883. The town of Copemish was established when the railroad came in 1889. The name means "big beech" referring to a legendary beech tree in the community.
Population: 232 (2000); Race: 90.2% White, 0.0% Black, 0.0% Asian, 5.7% American Indian and Alaska Native, 6.4% Hispanic of any race, 0.8% two or more races (2000); Density: 267.0 persons per square mile (2000); Age: 32.5% under 18, 12.1% over 64 (2000); Marriage status: 35.8% never married, 38.4% now married, 12.6% widowed, 13.2% divorced (2000); Foreign born: 1.1% (2000); Ancestry (includes multiple ancestries): 23.0% United States or American, 18.9% Other groups, 18.5% German, 8.3% Irish, 7.9% Polish (2000).
Economy: Employment by occupation: 0.0% management, 4.2% professional, 21.2% services, 23.7% sales, 1.7% farming, 18.6% construction, 30.5% production (2000).
Income: Per capita income: $10,884 (2000); Median household income: $25,357 (2000); Poverty rate: 13.2% (2000).
Taxes: Total city taxes per capita: $85 (1997); City property taxes per capita: $85 (1997).
Education: High school graduation rate: 68.6% (2000); College graduation rate: 3.8% (2000).
Housing: Homeownership rate: 79.5% (2000); Median home value: $36,700 (2000); Median rent: $340 per month (2000); Median age of housing: 52 years (2000).
Transportation: Commute to work: 88.8% car, 0.0% public transportation, 0.9% walk, 7.8% work from home (2000); Travel time to work: 24.3% less than 15 minutes, 29.9% 15 to 30 minutes, 28.0% 30 to 45 minutes, 17.8% 45 to 60 minutes, 0.0% 60 minutes or more (2000)

DICKSON (township). Covers a land area of 70.059 square miles and a water area of 1.641 square miles. Located at 44.29° N. Lat.; 85.94° W. Long.
Population: 929 (2000); Race: 96.2% White, 0.0% Black, 0.0% Asian, 1.1% American Indian and Alaska Native, 0.7% Hispanic of any race, 2.7% two or more races (2000); Density: 13.3 persons per square mile (2000); Age: 21.9% under 18, 18.4% over 64 (2000); Marriage status: 20.1% never married, 58.5% now married, 6.8% widowed, 14.5% divorced (2000); Foreign born: 0.8% (2000); Ancestry (includes multiple ancestries): 28.4% German, 13.4% English, 9.3% Irish, 9.1% United States or American, 8.0% Dutch (2000).
Economy: Single-family building permits issued: 8 (2001) / 8 (2000); Multi-family building permits issued: 0 (2001) / 0 (2000); Employment by occupation: 4.6% management, 10.2% professional, 22.3% services, 18.8% sales, 0.0% farming, 20.7% construction, 23.4% production (2000).
Income: Per capita income: $15,479 (2000); Median household income: $33,309 (2000); Poverty rate: 10.2% (2000).
Taxes: Total city taxes per capita: $97 (1997); City property taxes per capita: $96 (1997).
Education: High school graduation rate: 79.6% (2000); College graduation rate: 5.0% (2000).
Housing: Homeownership rate: 87.5% (2000); Median home value: $68,500 (2000); Median rent: $353 per month (2000); Median age of housing: 27 years (2000).
Transportation: Commute to work: 92.2% car, 0.0% public transportation, 3.6% walk, 3.6% work from home (2000); Travel time to work: 21.3% less than 15 minutes, 36.0% 15 to 30 minutes, 23.3% 30 to 45 minutes, 10.1% 45 to 60 minutes, 9.2% 60 minutes or more (2000)

EASTLAKE (village). Aka East Lake. Covers a land area of 1.183 square miles and a water area of 0.334 square miles. Located at 44.24° N. Lat.; 86.29° W. Long.

Population: 441 (2000); Race: 94.1% White, 0.7% Black, 1.1% Asian, 2.3% American Indian and Alaska Native, 1.6% Hispanic of any race, 1.1% two or more races (2000); Density: 372.6 persons per square mile (2000); Age: 23.0% under 18, 14.5% over 64 (2000); Marriage status: 24.6% never married, 60.6% now married, 8.1% widowed, 6.7% divorced (2000); Foreign born: 1.8% (2000); Ancestry (includes multiple ancestries): 24.3% Polish, 19.1% German, 9.8% Irish, 7.7% French (except Basque), 6.8% English (2000).
Economy: Employment by occupation: 2.7% management, 8.6% professional, 28.2% services, 21.4% sales, 0.9% farming, 9.1% construction, 29.1% production (2000).
Income: Per capita income: $15,034 (2000); Median household income: $31,750 (2000); Poverty rate: 3.4% (2000).
Taxes: Total city taxes per capita: $53 (1997); City property taxes per capita: $51 (1997).
Education: High school graduation rate: 82.0% (2000); College graduation rate: 7.7% (2000).
Housing: Homeownership rate: 89.2% (2000); Median home value: $59,800 (2000); Median rent: $275 per month (2000); Median age of housing: 52 years (2000).
Transportation: Commute to work: 93.1% car, 0.9% public transportation, 4.2% walk, 1.9% work from home (2000); Travel time to work: 64.6% less than 15 minutes, 23.6% 15 to 30 minutes, 6.6% 30 to 45 minutes, 5.2% 45 to 60 minutes, 0.0% 60 minutes or more (2000)

FILER CHARTER (township). Covers a land area of 15.832 square miles and a water area of 0.355 square miles. Located at 44.21° N. Lat.; 86.30° W. Long.
Population: 2,208 (2000); Race: 96.1% White, 0.2% Black, 0.2% Asian, 0.2% American Indian and Alaska Native, 1.7% Hispanic of any race, 2.0% two or more races (2000); Density: 139.5 persons per square mile (2000); Age: 23.1% under 18, 19.2% over 64 (2000); Marriage status: 21.1% never married, 66.7% now married, 6.6% widowed, 5.6% divorced (2000); Foreign born: 0.8% (2000); Ancestry (includes multiple ancestries): 36.9% Polish, 29.6% German, 7.6% Swedish, 7.2% Irish, 5.7% English (2000).
Economy: Employment by occupation: 8.6% management, 18.0% professional, 15.8% services, 21.6% sales, 0.1% farming, 10.0% construction, 25.9% production (2000).
Income: Per capita income: $19,811 (2000); Median household income: $40,972 (2000); Poverty rate: 7.2% (2000).
Taxes: Total city taxes per capita: $124 (1997); City property taxes per capita: $117 (1997).
Education: High school graduation rate: 83.3% (2000); College graduation rate: 15.1% (2000).
Housing: Homeownership rate: 89.8% (2000); Median home value: $87,700 (2000); Median rent: $392 per month (2000); Median age of housing: 35 years (2000).
Transportation: Commute to work: 92.4% car, 0.9% public transportation, 1.9% walk, 3.9% work from home (2000); Travel time to work: 63.6% less than 15 minutes, 27.7% 15 to 30 minutes, 4.9% 30 to 45 minutes, 0.5% 45 to 60 minutes, 3.3% 60 minutes or more (2000)

KALEVA (village). Covers a land area of 1.107 square miles and a water area of 0 square miles. Located at 44.37° N. Lat.; 86.01° W. Long. Elevation is 738 feet.
History: The name of Kaleva came from the Finnish national epic, the Kalevala. Kaleva was founded as a Finnish settlement by the Michigan Land Society in the 1890's, at a railroad junction. The village was platted in 1894.
Population: 509 (2000); Race: 91.2% White, 0.0% Black, 0.0% Asian, 3.6% American Indian and Alaska Native, 7.4% Hispanic of any race, 1.7% two or more races (2000); Density: 459.6 persons per square mile (2000); Age: 29.1% under 18, 14.3% over 64 (2000); Marriage status: 19.5% never married, 51.6% now married, 12.8% widowed, 16.0% divorced (2000); Foreign born: 2.1% (2000); Ancestry (includes multiple ancestries): 22.3% German, 12.6% Other groups, 11.6% Irish, 8.4% English, 7.4% Finnish (2000).
Economy: Single-family building permits issued: 1 (2001) / 1 (2000); Multi-family building permits issued: 0 (2001) / 0 (2000); Employment by occupation: 3.4% management, 12.6% professional, 24.6% services, 21.7% sales, 2.4% farming, 15.9% construction, 19.3% production (2000).
Income: Per capita income: $13,400 (2000); Median household income: $30,714 (2000); Poverty rate: 17.4% (2000).
Taxes: Total city taxes per capita: $52 (1997); City property taxes per capita: $50 (1997).
Education: High school graduation rate: 69.3% (2000); College graduation rate: 7.3% (2000).
Housing: Homeownership rate: 75.8% (2000); Median home value: $52,900 (2000); Median rent: $286 per month (2000); Median age of housing: 48 years (2000).
Transportation: Commute to work: 87.7% car, 0.0% public transportation, 7.4% walk, 3.9% work from home (2000); Travel time to work: 32.7% less than 15 minutes, 23.5% 15 to 30 minutes, 23.5% 30 to 45 minutes, 9.2% 45 to 60 minutes, 11.2% 60 minutes or more (2000)

MANISTEE (city). Covers a land area of 3.254 square miles and a water area of 1.096 square miles. Located at 44.24° N. Lat.; 86.32° W. Long. Elevation is 598 feet.
History: Many of the early residents of Manistee were of Swedish and Norwegian descent. The name is of Chippewa origin meaning "spirit of the woods."
Population: 6,586 (2000); Race: 94.0% White, 0.1% Black, 0.4% Asian, 1.2% American Indian and Alaska Native, 3.2% Hispanic of any race, 3.2% two or more races (2000); Density: 2,023.7 persons per square mile (2000); Age: 23.8% under 18, 19.5% over 64 (2000); Marriage status: 23.7% never married, 51.1% now married, 12.1% widowed, 13.2% divorced (2000); Foreign born: 1.2% (2000); Ancestry (includes multiple ancestries): 26.9% German, 22.8% Polish, 11.2% Irish, 9.4% English, 8.8% Other groups (2000).
Economy: Single-family building permits issued: 23 (2001) / 6 (2000); Multi-family building permits issued: 48 (2001) / 14 (2000); Employment by occupation: 7.7% management, 16.3% professional, 27.5% services, 23.0% sales, 0.6% farming, 8.7% construction, 16.3% production (2000).
Income: Per capita income: $16,810 (2000); Median household income: $30,351 (2000); Poverty rate: 11.1% (2000).
Taxes: Total city taxes per capita: $346 (1997); City property taxes per capita: $335 (1997).
Education: High school graduation rate: 84.5% (2000); College graduation rate: 17.4% (2000).

School District(s)

Casman Alternative Academy (07-12)
2000 Enrollment: 67 231-723-3521
Manistee Area Schools (KG-12)
2000 Enrollment: 1,776 231-723-3521
Shoreline Academy of Business & (11-12)
2000 Enrollment: 0 231-723-4264

Housing: Homeownership rate: 64.7% (2000); Median home value: $66,500 (2000); Median rent: $311 per month (2000); Median age of housing: 60+ years (2000).
Hospitals: West Shore Medical Center (54 beds)
Newspapers: Manistee News-Advocate (6 x week); Westshore Shopper & Manistee Observer (1 x week)
Transportation: Commute to work: 89.6% car, 0.5% public transportation, 4.3% walk, 4.4% work from home (2000); Travel time to work: 67.4% less than 15 minutes, 15.6% 15 to 30 minutes, 8.2% 30 to 45 minutes, 3.8% 45 to 60 minutes, 5.0% 60 minutes or more (2000)
Additional Information Contacts
Manistee Area Chamber of Commerce 231-723-2575

MANISTEE (township). Covers a land area of 44.478 square miles and a water area of 3.742 square miles. Located at 44.27° N. Lat.; 86.26° W. Long. Elevation is 598 feet.
History: Incorporated as city 1869.
Population: 3,764 (2000); Race: 84.9% White, 8.7% Black, 0.5% Asian, 2.2% American Indian and Alaska Native, 2.9% Hispanic of any race, 3.0% two or more races (2000); Density: 84.6 persons per square mile (2000); Age: 17.4% under 18, 16.1% over 64 (2000); Marriage status: 26.9% never married, 60.5% now married, 5.8% widowed, 6.7% divorced (2000); Foreign born: 1.7% (2000); Ancestry (includes multiple ancestries): 26.1% German, 18.9% Polish, 10.8% Other groups, 10.3% English, 9.7% Irish (2000).
Economy: Resort, shipping and industrial center; salt mining and processing. Manufacturing includes salt, salt products, bulk bags, chemicals, paper, furniture, wood products, boats, textiles and fisheries. Agricultural products are fruit, potatoes, cattle, hogs and poultry. Employment by occupation: 8.6% management, 16.6% professional, 22.6% services, 23.8% sales, 0.4% farming, 10.5% construction, 17.5% production (2000).
Income: Per capita income: $16,442 (2000); Median household income: $39,946 (2000); Poverty rate: 4.8% (2000).
Taxes: Total city taxes per capita: $56 (1997); City property taxes per capita: $52 (1997).
Education: High school graduation rate: 78.7% (2000); College graduation rate: 12.9% (2000).

Housing: Homeownership rate: 91.4% (2000); Median home value: $86,500 (2000); Median rent: $414 per month (2000); Median age of housing: 35 years (2000).
Transportation: Commute to work: 94.9% car, 0.5% public transportation, 1.5% walk, 2.8% work from home (2000); Travel time to work: 61.1% less than 15 minutes, 25.9% 15 to 30 minutes, 5.5% 30 to 45 minutes, 4.4% 45 to 60 minutes, 3.1% 60 minutes or more (2000)

MAPLE GROVE (township). Covers a land area of 35.654 square miles and a water area of 0.097 square miles. Located at 44.37° N. Lat.; 86.00° W. Long.
Population: 1,285 (2000); Race: 94.0% White, 0.2% Black, 0.0% Asian, 2.2% American Indian and Alaska Native, 5.5% Hispanic of any race, 1.8% two or more races (2000); Density: 36.0 persons per square mile (2000); Age: 25.6% under 18, 14.9% over 64 (2000); Marriage status: 19.1% never married, 59.1% now married, 9.7% widowed, 12.1% divorced (2000); Foreign born: 0.9% (2000); Ancestry (includes multiple ancestries): 23.8% German, 11.4% English, 11.1% Other groups, 11.1% Irish, 8.2% Polish (2000).
Economy: Employment by occupation: 6.9% management, 10.5% professional, 18.2% services, 24.5% sales, 2.1% farming, 17.4% construction, 20.3% production (2000).
Income: Per capita income: $14,652 (2000); Median household income: $32,011 (2000); Poverty rate: 14.8% (2000).
Taxes: Total city taxes per capita: $86 (1997); City property taxes per capita: $85 (1997).
Education: High school graduation rate: 75.6% (2000); College graduation rate: 6.5% (2000).
Housing: Homeownership rate: 85.2% (2000); Median home value: $59,700 (2000); Median rent: $321 per month (2000); Median age of housing: 30 years (2000).
Transportation: Commute to work: 92.6% car, 0.0% public transportation, 3.5% walk, 2.9% work from home (2000); Travel time to work: 32.1% less than 15 minutes, 27.4% 15 to 30 minutes, 21.4% 30 to 45 minutes, 7.9% 45 to 60 minutes, 11.3% 60 minutes or more (2000)

MARILLA (township). Covers a land area of 35.383 square miles and a water area of 0.015 square miles. Located at 44.37° N. Lat.; 85.89° W. Long. Elevation is 934 feet.
Population: 362 (2000); Race: 99.4% White, 0.0% Black, 0.0% Asian, 0.0% American Indian and Alaska Native, 0.0% Hispanic of any race, 0.6% two or more races (2000); Density: 10.2 persons per square mile (2000); Age: 17.7% under 18, 16.9% over 64 (2000); Marriage status: 18.0% never married, 64.0% now married, 7.1% widowed, 10.9% divorced (2000); Foreign born: 0.0% (2000); Ancestry (includes multiple ancestries): 26.6% German, 16.3% English, 11.1% United States or American, 8.3% Irish, 8.0% French (except Basque) (2000).
Economy: Employment by occupation: 13.3% management, 11.0% professional, 13.3% services, 26.0% sales, 1.7% farming, 22.0% construction, 12.7% production (2000).
Income: Per capita income: $17,643 (2000); Median household income: $40,000 (2000); Poverty rate: 5.8% (2000).
Taxes: Total city taxes per capita: $58 (1997); City property taxes per capita: $58 (1997).
Education: High school graduation rate: 83.5% (2000); College graduation rate: 8.4% (2000).
Housing: Homeownership rate: 95.5% (2000); Median home value: $72,100 (2000); Median rent: $325 per month (2000); Median age of housing: 26 years (2000).
Transportation: Commute to work: 85.9% car, 0.0% public transportation, 2.4% walk, 8.8% work from home (2000); Travel time to work: 24.5% less than 15 minutes, 25.2% 15 to 30 minutes, 18.7% 30 to 45 minutes, 20.6% 45 to 60 minutes, 11.0% 60 minutes or more (2000)

NORMAN (township). Covers a land area of 70.812 square miles and a water area of 1.341 square miles. Located at 44.21° N. Lat.; 85.95° W. Long.
Population: 1,676 (2000); Race: 97.2% White, 0.0% Black, 0.0% Asian, 1.2% American Indian and Alaska Native, 0.2% Hispanic of any race, 1.6% two or more races (2000); Density: 23.7 persons per square mile (2000); Age: 24.1% under 18, 16.7% over 64 (2000); Marriage status: 18.7% never married, 61.5% now married, 6.1% widowed, 13.7% divorced (2000); Foreign born: 1.0% (2000); Ancestry (includes multiple ancestries): 22.8% German, 12.2% English, 10.7% United States or American, 8.6% Irish, 7.5% Polish (2000).
Economy: Employment by occupation: 6.7% management, 9.0% professional, 30.7% services, 18.7% sales, 1.1% farming, 14.1% construction, 19.7% production (2000).
Income: Per capita income: $16,081 (2000); Median household income: $31,010 (2000); Poverty rate: 15.2% (2000).
Taxes: Total city taxes per capita: $122 (1997); City property taxes per capita: $122 (1997).
Education: High school graduation rate: 72.7% (2000); College graduation rate: 6.4% (2000).
Housing: Homeownership rate: 84.7% (2000); Median home value: $64,100 (2000); Median rent: $360 per month (2000); Median age of housing: 28 years (2000).
Transportation: Commute to work: 89.3% car, 0.0% public transportation, 1.9% walk, 8.5% work from home (2000); Travel time to work: 17.5% less than 15 minutes, 34.4% 15 to 30 minutes, 27.6% 30 to 45 minutes, 7.0% 45 to 60 minutes, 13.6% 60 minutes or more (2000)

ONEKAMA (village). Aka Brookfields. Covers a land area of 0.597 square miles and a water area of 0 square miles. Located at 44.36° N. Lat.; 86.20° W. Long. Elevation is 868 feet.
History: Onekama developed around the cucumber fields of the nearby farms, and as a supply center for the resorts in Manistee County. A channel dredged between Portage Lake and Lake Michigan made Onekama a harbor town.
Population: 647 (2000); Race: 94.1% White, 0.3% Black, 0.0% Asian, 0.8% American Indian and Alaska Native, 23.6% Hispanic of any race, 0.5% two or more races (2000); Density: 1,083.9 persons per square mile (2000); Age: 30.4% under 18, 19.9% over 64 (2000); Marriage status: 31.7% never married, 52.5% now married, 6.1% widowed, 9.7% divorced (2000); Foreign born: 0.8% (2000); Ancestry (includes multiple ancestries): 16.6% German, 10.8% Irish, 10.3% English, 5.9% French (except Basque), 5.8% Swedish (2000).
Economy: Employment by occupation: 9.4% management, 22.8% professional, 18.3% services, 15.2% sales, 12.5% farming, 11.2% construction, 10.7% production (2000).
Income: Per capita income: $16,718 (2000); Median household income: $29,091 (2000); Poverty rate: 16.0% (2000).
Taxes: Total city taxes per capita: $114 (1997); City property taxes per capita: $114 (1997).
Education: High school graduation rate: 81.2% (2000); College graduation rate: 20.3% (2000).

School District(s)

Onekama Consolidated Schools (KG-12)
2000 Enrollment: 537 231-889-4251
Housing: Homeownership rate: 72.3% (2000); Median home value: $82,700 (2000); Median rent: $358 per month (2000); Median age of housing: 43 years (2000).
Transportation: Commute to work: 89.7% car, 0.0% public transportation, 5.4% walk, 3.1% work from home (2000); Travel time to work: 44.7% less than 15 minutes, 37.8% 15 to 30 minutes, 7.4% 30 to 45 minutes, 2.3% 45 to 60 minutes, 7.8% 60 minutes or more (2000)

ONEKAMA (township). Aka Brookfields. Covers a land area of 18.441 square miles and a water area of 4.956 square miles. Located at 44.36° N. Lat.; 86.21° W. Long. Elevation is 868 feet.
Population: 1,514 (2000); Race: 97.1% White, 0.1% Black, 0.0% Asian, 0.7% American Indian and Alaska Native, 9.7% Hispanic of any race, 0.3% two or more races (2000); Density: 82.1 persons per square mile (2000); Age: 23.9% under 18, 22.2% over 64 (2000); Marriage status: 22.9% never married, 61.3% now married, 6.9% widowed, 9.0% divorced (2000); Foreign born: 1.3% (2000); Ancestry (includes multiple ancestries): 23.7% German, 16.0% English, 9.5% Irish, 9.0% Polish, 6.7% United States or American (2000).
Economy: Manufacturing: electrical wire harnesses. Resort. Employment by occupation: 12.2% management, 24.0% professional, 15.6% services, 21.7% sales, 5.3% farming, 10.4% construction, 10.9% production (2000).
Income: Per capita income: $20,919 (2000); Median household income: $39,792 (2000); Poverty rate: 9.6% (2000).
Taxes: Total city taxes per capita: $89 (1997); City property taxes per capita: $87 (1997).
Education: High school graduation rate: 86.8% (2000); College graduation rate: 27.9% (2000).
Housing: Homeownership rate: 82.9% (2000); Median home value: $107,000 (2000); Median rent: $391 per month (2000); Median age of housing: 34 years (2000).

Transportation: Commute to work: 84.7% car, 0.2% public transportation, 5.4% walk, 8.6% work from home (2000); Travel time to work: 41.7% less than 15 minutes, 40.4% 15 to 30 minutes, 9.9% 30 to 45 minutes, 2.8% 45 to 60 minutes, 5.3% 60 minutes or more (2000)

PLEASANTON (township). Covers a land area of 33.571 square miles and a water area of 1.875 square miles. Located at 44.46° N. Lat.; 86.13° W. Long. Elevation is 894 feet.
Population: 817 (2000); Race: 97.9% White, 0.4% Black, 0.4% Asian, 0.2% American Indian and Alaska Native, 2.0% Hispanic of any race, 1.2% two or more races (2000); Density: 24.3 persons per square mile (2000); Age: 23.1% under 18, 24.4% over 64 (2000); Marriage status: 16.8% never married, 66.2% now married, 8.2% widowed, 8.8% divorced (2000); Foreign born: 1.7% (2000); Ancestry (includes multiple ancestries): 31.8% German, 11.7% English, 11.0% Irish, 10.5% Polish, 6.6% Other groups (2000).
Economy: Employment by occupation: 9.3% management, 9.0% professional, 16.8% services, 23.7% sales, 1.6% farming, 14.3% construction, 25.2% production (2000).
Income: Per capita income: $15,450 (2000); Median household income: $33,977 (2000); Poverty rate: 12.4% (2000).
Taxes: Total city taxes per capita: $65 (2000); City property taxes per capita: $62 (2000).
Education: High school graduation rate: 84.8% (2000); College graduation rate: 10.7% (2000).
Housing: Homeownership rate: 91.0% (2000); Median home value: $105,700 (2000); Median rent: $275 per month (2000); Median age of housing: 30 years (2000).
Transportation: Commute to work: 91.7% car, 0.0% public transportation, 2.9% walk, 3.8% work from home (2000); Travel time to work: 29.5% less than 15 minutes, 33.8% 15 to 30 minutes, 18.9% 30 to 45 minutes, 10.9% 45 to 60 minutes, 7.0% 60 minutes or more (2000)

SPRINGDALE (township). Covers a land area of 35.648 square miles and a water area of 0.069 square miles. Located at 44.46° N. Lat.; 85.99° W. Long.
History: Springdale Township was organized in 1870 and named for the many perennial springs in the area.
Population: 730 (2000); Race: 96.1% White, 0.4% Black, 0.0% Asian, 2.2% American Indian and Alaska Native, 2.1% Hispanic of any race, 1.0% two or more races (2000); Density: 20.5 persons per square mile (2000); Age: 22.1% under 18, 17.1% over 64 (2000); Marriage status: 19.0% never married, 57.8% now married, 5.8% widowed, 17.5% divorced (2000); Foreign born: 2.4% (2000); Ancestry (includes multiple ancestries): 20.6% German, 11.6% Irish, 10.4% Polish, 10.1% English, 7.6% Other groups (2000).
Economy: Single-family building permits issued: 9 (2001) / 8 (2000); Multi-family building permits issued: 0 (2001) / 4 (2000); Employment by occupation: 11.4% management, 8.1% professional, 18.5% services, 22.1% sales, 1.6% farming, 12.0% construction, 26.3% production (2000).
Income: Per capita income: $16,612 (2000); Median household income: $29,417 (2000); Poverty rate: 22.2% (2000).
Taxes: Total city taxes per capita: $75 (1997); City property taxes per capita: $59 (1997).
Education: High school graduation rate: 78.5% (2000); College graduation rate: 11.6% (2000).
Housing: Homeownership rate: 83.4% (2000); Median home value: $100,000 (2000); Median rent: $348 per month (2000); Median age of housing: 20 years (2000).
Transportation: Commute to work: 93.3% car, 0.0% public transportation, 0.7% walk, 6.0% work from home (2000); Travel time to work: 33.3% less than 15 minutes, 34.0% 15 to 30 minutes, 16.0% 30 to 45 minutes, 10.3% 45 to 60 minutes, 6.4% 60 minutes or more (2000)

STRONACH (township). Covers a land area of 55.458 square miles and a water area of 0.250 square miles. Located at 44.20° N. Lat.; 86.17° W. Long. Elevation is 607 feet.
Population: 804 (2000); Race: 96.7% White, 0.0% Black, 0.0% Asian, 2.8% American Indian and Alaska Native, 0.3% Hispanic of any race, 0.1% two or more races (2000); Density: 14.5 persons per square mile (2000); Age: 21.9% under 18, 16.0% over 64 (2000); Marriage status: 18.3% never married, 63.7% now married, 6.8% widowed, 11.3% divorced (2000); Foreign born: 0.9% (2000); Ancestry (includes multiple ancestries): 27.3% German, 25.8% Polish, 10.7% United States or American, 9.2% Irish, 8.2% English (2000).
Economy: Single-family building permits issued: 11 (2001) / 11 (2000); Multi-family building permits issued: 0 (2001) / 0 (2000); Employment by occupation: 7.8% management, 11.7% professional, 18.3% services, 22.2% sales, 1.1% farming, 18.9% construction, 20.0% production (2000).
Income: Per capita income: $17,683 (2000); Median household income: $36,181 (2000); Poverty rate: 5.4% (2000).
Taxes: Total city taxes per capita: $144 (1997); City property taxes per capita: $140 (1997).
Education: High school graduation rate: 79.5% (2000); College graduation rate: 10.5% (2000).
Housing: Homeownership rate: 89.7% (2000); Median home value: $72,000 (2000); Median rent: $333 per month (2000); Median age of housing: 28 years (2000).
Transportation: Commute to work: 90.6% car, 1.1% public transportation, 0.9% walk, 7.4% work from home (2000); Travel time to work: 33.2% less than 15 minutes, 49.5% 15 to 30 minutes, 8.6% 30 to 45 minutes, 2.8% 45 to 60 minutes, 5.8% 60 minutes or more (2000)

WELLSTON (unincorporated postal area, zip code 49689). Covers a land area of 76.065 square miles and a water area of 0.173 square miles. Located at 44.21° N. Lat.; 85.91° W. Long. Elevation is 773 feet.
Population: 1,630 (2000); Race: 96.6% White, 0.0% Black, 0.0% Asian, 1.2% American Indian and Alaska Native, 0.2% Hispanic of any race, 2.2% two or more races (2000); Density: 21.4 persons per square mile (2000); Age: 24.0% under 18, 17.9% over 64 (2000); Marriage status: 18.3% never married, 59.5% now married, 7.7% widowed, 14.5% divorced (2000); Foreign born: 1.0% (2000); Ancestry (includes multiple ancestries): 23.0% German, 11.4% English, 9.0% United States or American, 7.3% Irish, 7.1% Polish (2000).
Economy: Employment by occupation: 7.4% management, 9.8% professional, 29.3% services, 16.8% sales, 1.4% farming, 13.6% construction, 21.7% production (2000).
Income: Per capita income: $16,022 (2000); Median household income: $29,778 (2000); Poverty rate: 16.7% (2000).
Education: High school graduation rate: 73.0% (2000); College graduation rate: 6.3% (2000).
Housing: Homeownership rate: 85.0% (2000); Median home value: $62,300 (2000); Median rent: $348 per month (2000); Median age of housing: 29 years (2000).
Transportation: Commute to work: 87.9% car, 0.0% public transportation, 2.2% walk, 9.7% work from home (2000); Travel time to work: 16.6% less than 15 minutes, 32.4% 15 to 30 minutes, 29.1% 30 to 45 minutes, 7.2% 45 to 60 minutes, 14.7% 60 minutes or more (2000)

Marquette County

Located in northwestern Michigan on the Upper Peninsula; bounded on the north by Lake Superior; drained by the Dead and Michigamme Rivers; includes the Marquette Iron Range and Huron Mountains, and several lakes. Covers a land area of 1,821.10 square miles, a water area of 1,604.10 square miles, and is located in the Eastern Time Zone. The county government was organized in 1843. County seat is Marquette.

Weather Station: Champion Van Riper Park — Elevation: 1,564 feet

	Jan	Feb	Mar	Apr	May	Jun	Jul	Aug	Sep	Oct	Nov	Dec
High	22	27	37	51	66	74	79	76	67	55	38	26
Low	0	2	11	24	35	44	50	49	41	32	20	8
Precip	1.8	1.3	2.2	2.4	3.2	3.3	3.8	3.8	4.0	3.4	2.6	1.9
Snow	29.8	18.2	21.9	8.8	1.1	0.0	0.0	0.0	tr	4.8	19.9	27.2

High and Low temperatures in degrees Fahrenheit; Precipitation and Snow in inches

Weather Station: Marquette County Airport — Elevation: 1,414 feet

	Jan	Feb	Mar	Apr	May	Jun	Jul	Aug	Sep	Oct	Nov	Dec
High	21	25	34	47	62	72	76	74	64	52	37	25
Low	4	6	14	27	39	49	54	52	44	34	23	11
Precip	2.6	1.8	3.1	2.8	3.2	3.1	3.1	3.5	3.9	3.7	3.2	2.4
Snow	41.7	29.0	31.0	12.3	1.6	tr	0.0	tr	0.1	5.5	21.8	36.8

High and Low temperatures in degrees Fahrenheit; Precipitation and Snow in inches

Weather Station: Marquette WBO — Elevation: 675 feet

	Jan	Feb	Mar	Apr	May	Jun	Jul	Aug	Sep	Oct	Nov	Dec
High	25	29	36	48	60	70	76	75	66	55	40	30
Low	11	13	21	32	41	50	57	57	49	39	28	17
Precip	2.0	1.3	2.2	2.4	2.8	2.7	2.8	3.0	3.6	3.0	2.6	2.0
Snow	31.0	19.3	20.0	7.7	1.1	0.0	0.0	0.0	0.2	1.7	12.0	25.2

High and Low temperatures in degrees Fahrenheit; Precipitation and Snow in inches

Population: 64,634 (2000); Race: 95.2% White, 1.2% Black, 0.5% Asian, 1.4% American Indian and Alaska Native, 0.7% Hispanic of any race, 1.6% two or more races (2000); Density: 35.5 persons per square mile (2000); Age: 21.4% under 18, 13.5% over 64 (2000).

Religion: Five largest groups: 29.7% Catholic Church, 13.1% Evangelical Lutheran Church in America, 3.5% The United Methodist Church, 2.5% Lutheran Church—Missouri Synod, 1.0% Presbyterian Church (U.S.A.) (2000).
Economy: Unemployment rate: 5.2% (11/2002); Total civilian labor force: 33,911 (11/2002); Leading industries: 24.8% health care and social assistance; 17.6% retail trade; 12.0% accommodation & food services (2000); Companies that employ more than 1,000 persons: 1 (2000); Companies that employ more than 100 persons: 25 (2000); Farms: 108 totaling 26,624 acres (1997); Minority business ownership rate: 5.0% (1997); Women business ownership rate: 28.6% (1997); Retail sales per capita: $8,400 (1997). Single-family building permits issued: 187 (2001) / 239 (2000); Multi-family building permits issued: 2 (2001) / 28 (2000).
Income: Per capita income: $18,070 (2000); Median household income: $35,548 (2000); Poverty rate: 10.9% (2000); Bankruptcy rate: 2.81% (2001).
Taxes: Total county taxes per capita: $188 (2000); County property taxes per capita: $180 (2000).
Education: High school graduation rate: 88.5% (2000); College graduation rate: 23.7% (2000).
Housing: Homeownership rate: 69.8% (2000); Median home value: $77,200 (2000); Median rent: $358 per month (2000); Median age of housing: 36 years (2000).
Health: Birth rate: 91.1 per 10,000 population (1998); Age adjusted death rate: 99.4 per 10,000 population (1999); Age adjusted cancer mortality rate: 194.3 deaths per 100,000 population (1999). Number of physicians: 30.6 per 10,000 population (1999); Number of hospital beds: 48.3 per 10,000 population (1999).
Elections: 2000 Presidential election results: 53.1% Gore, 43.1% Bush, 3.2% Nader, 0.1% Buchanan
National and State Parks: Escanaba River State Forest; Huron National Wildlife Refuge; Michigamme State Forest; Michigamme State Forest
Additional Information Contacts
Marquette County Government Offices 906-228-1559
Gwinn Chamber of Commerce 906-346-9666
Ishpeming Chamber of Commerce 906-486-4841
Marquette Chamber of Commerce 906-226-6591
Upper Peninsula Association of Realtors 906-228-4870

Marquette County Communities

BIG BAY (CDP). Covers a land area of 3.831 square miles and a water area of 2.124 square miles. Located at 46.81° N. Lat.; 87.72° W. Long. Elevation is 685 feet.
Population: 265 (2000); Race: 93.0% White, 0.0% Black, 0.0% Asian, 2.1% American Indian and Alaska Native, 0.4% Hispanic of any race, 4.6% two or more races (2000); Density: 69.2 persons per square mile (2000); Age: 17.3% under 18, 22.9% over 64 (2000); Marriage status: 19.5% never married, 65.9% now married, 2.8% widowed, 11.8% divorced (2000); Foreign born: 0.0% (2000); Ancestry (includes multiple ancestries): 22.5% German, 17.6% French (except Basque), 13.7% English, 13.0% Irish, 8.8% Swedish (2000).
Economy: Employment by occupation: 4.0% management, 14.1% professional, 33.3% services, 17.2% sales, 0.0% farming, 8.1% construction, 23.2% production (2000).
Income: Per capita income: $18,620 (2000); Median household income: $34,750 (2000); Poverty rate: 11.4% (2000).
Education: High school graduation rate: 86.5% (2000); College graduation rate: 22.6% (2000).

School District(s)

Powell Township Schools (PK-08)
2000 Enrollment: 57 906-345-9355
Housing: Homeownership rate: 92.5% (2000); Median home value: $81,700 (2000); Median rent: $250 per month (2000); Median age of housing: 30 years (2000).
Transportation: Commute to work: 73.6% car, 0.0% public transportation, 18.7% walk, 7.7% work from home (2000); Travel time to work: 51.2% less than 15 minutes, 8.3% 15 to 30 minutes, 35.7% 30 to 45 minutes, 4.8% 45 to 60 minutes, 0.0% 60 minutes or more (2000)

CHAMPION (township). Covers a land area of 120.920 square miles and a water area of 4.043 square miles. Located at 46.60° N. Lat.; 87.89° W. Long. Elevation is 1,598 feet.
Population: 297 (2000); Race: 100.0% White, 0.0% Black, 0.0% Asian, 0.0% American Indian and Alaska Native, 0.0% Hispanic of any race, 0.0% two or more races (2000); Density: 2.5 persons per square mile (2000); Age: 17.0% under 18, 14.8% over 64 (2000); Marriage status: 23.0% never married, 56.4% now married, 8.2% widowed, 12.3% divorced (2000); Foreign born: 0.0% (2000); Ancestry (includes multiple ancestries): 30.6% Finnish, 25.5% French (except Basque), 25.5% German, 10.7% French Canadian, 9.2% English (2000).
Economy: Employment by occupation: 3.3% management, 8.2% professional, 30.3% services, 14.8% sales, 3.3% farming, 15.6% construction, 24.6% production (2000).
Income: Per capita income: $17,396 (2000); Median household income: $33,571 (2000); Poverty rate: 12.3% (2000).
Taxes: Total city taxes per capita: $158 (1997); City property taxes per capita: $158 (1997).
Education: High school graduation rate: 90.4% (2000); College graduation rate: 7.2% (2000).
Housing: Homeownership rate: 98.3% (2000); Median home value: $36,900 (2000); Median rent: $275 per month (2000); Median age of housing: 44 years (2000).
Transportation: Commute to work: 93.2% car, 0.8% public transportation, 3.4% walk, 2.5% work from home (2000); Travel time to work: 16.5% less than 15 minutes, 29.6% 15 to 30 minutes, 33.0% 30 to 45 minutes, 15.7% 45 to 60 minutes, 5.2% 60 minutes or more (2000)

CHOCOLAY (township). Covers a land area of 59.659 square miles and a water area of 1.154 square miles. Located at 46.47° N. Lat.; 87.31° W. Long.
History: The name of Chocolay Township came from that of a French fur trader, M. Choquette.
Population: 7,148 (2000); Race: 87.6% White, 7.6% Black, 1.0% Asian, 1.1% American Indian and Alaska Native, 1.6% Hispanic of any race, 2.4% two or more races (2000); Density: 119.8 persons per square mile (2000); Age: 22.7% under 18, 7.8% over 64 (2000); Marriage status: 31.1% never married, 57.5% now married, 3.5% widowed, 8.0% divorced (2000); Foreign born: 2.2% (2000); Ancestry (includes multiple ancestries): 15.3% German, 14.0% French (except Basque), 13.0% Finnish, 12.2% English, 9.3% Irish (2000).
Economy: Employment by occupation: 12.3% management, 25.6% professional, 15.0% services, 26.4% sales, 0.0% farming, 11.3% construction, 9.5% production (2000).
Income: Per capita income: $19,569 (2000); Median household income: $49,438 (2000); Poverty rate: 4.9% (2000).
Taxes: Total city taxes per capita: $100 (1997); City property taxes per capita: $99 (1997).
Education: High school graduation rate: 85.2% (2000); College graduation rate: 25.7% (2000).
Housing: Homeownership rate: 84.5% (2000); Median home value: $97,000 (2000); Median rent: $357 per month (2000); Median age of housing: 26 years (2000).
Safety: Violent crime rate: 0.0 per 10,000 population; Property crime rate: 61.2 per 10,000 population (2001).
Transportation: Commute to work: 91.9% car, 0.6% public transportation, 2.7% walk, 3.1% work from home (2000); Travel time to work: 35.1% less than 15 minutes, 53.5% 15 to 30 minutes, 7.1% 30 to 45 minutes, 2.3% 45 to 60 minutes, 2.0% 60 minutes or more (2000)

ELY (township). Covers a land area of 137.650 square miles and a water area of 2.912 square miles. Located at 46.43° N. Lat.; 87.80° W. Long.
Population: 2,010 (2000); Race: 98.7% White, 0.1% Black, 0.1% Asian, 0.7% American Indian and Alaska Native, 0.3% Hispanic of any race, 0.4% two or more races (2000); Density: 14.6 persons per square mile (2000); Age: 28.1% under 18, 7.9% over 64 (2000); Marriage status: 22.4% never married, 67.4% now married, 3.7% widowed, 6.5% divorced (2000); Foreign born: 0.8% (2000); Ancestry (includes multiple ancestries): 36.0% Finnish, 15.7% English, 15.2% French (except Basque), 14.7% German, 10.4% Swedish (2000).
Economy: Employment by occupation: 5.8% management, 13.4% professional, 19.9% services, 23.6% sales, 0.4% farming, 20.8% construction, 16.0% production (2000).
Income: Per capita income: $16,901 (2000); Median household income: $42,326 (2000); Poverty rate: 5.1% (2000).
Education: High school graduation rate: 89.9% (2000); College graduation rate: 11.7% (2000).
Housing: Homeownership rate: 92.2% (2000); Median home value: $68,200 (2000); Median rent: $305 per month (2000); Median age of housing: 28 years (2000).
Transportation: Commute to work: 94.8% car, 0.0% public transportation, 1.6% walk, 3.6% work from home (2000); Travel time to work: 26.6% less

than 15 minutes, 40.4% 15 to 30 minutes, 23.4% 30 to 45 minutes, 4.6% 45 to 60 minutes, 5.0% 60 minutes or more (2000)

EWING (township). Covers a land area of 48.423 square miles and a water area of 0.393 square miles. Located at 46.05° N. Lat.; 87.30° W. Long.
Population: 159 (2000); Race: 98.7% White, 1.3% Black, 0.0% Asian, 0.0% American Indian and Alaska Native, 0.0% Hispanic of any race, 0.0% two or more races (2000); Density: 3.3 persons per square mile (2000); Age: 27.0% under 18, 12.5% over 64 (2000); Marriage status: 26.0% never married, 57.5% now married, 10.2% widowed, 6.3% divorced (2000); Foreign born: 0.0% (2000); Ancestry (includes multiple ancestries): 35.5% Finnish, 15.1% Polish, 7.9% German, 7.2% Swedish, 7.2% French Canadian (2000).
Economy: Employment by occupation: 15.0% management, 17.5% professional, 30.0% services, 5.0% sales, 5.0% farming, 0.0% construction, 27.5% production (2000).
Income: Per capita income: $13,183 (2000); Median household income: $17,813 (2000); Poverty rate: 9.3% (2000).
Taxes: Total city taxes per capita: $35 (1997); City property taxes per capita: $35 (1997).
Education: High school graduation rate: 86.9% (2000); College graduation rate: 6.5% (2000).
Housing: Homeownership rate: 94.1% (2000); Median home value: $32,500 (2000); Median age of housing: 36 years (2000).
Transportation: Commute to work: 100.0% car, 0.0% public transportation, 0.0% walk, 0.0% work from home (2000); Travel time to work: 15.8% less than 15 minutes, 0.0% 15 to 30 minutes, 26.3% 30 to 45 minutes, 36.8% 45 to 60 minutes, 21.1% 60 minutes or more (2000)

FORSYTH (township). Covers a land area of 175.208 square miles and a water area of 3.925 square miles. Located at 46.28° N. Lat.; 87.42° W. Long.
Population: 4,824 (2000); Race: 96.0% White, 0.5% Black, 0.2% Asian, 0.8% American Indian and Alaska Native, 0.7% Hispanic of any race, 2.2% two or more races (2000); Density: 27.5 persons per square mile (2000); Age: 23.1% under 18, 12.9% over 64 (2000); Marriage status: 21.4% never married, 62.1% now married, 5.2% widowed, 11.4% divorced (2000); Foreign born: 2.4% (2000); Ancestry (includes multiple ancestries): 21.0% Finnish, 17.7% German, 16.4% English, 13.5% Irish, 11.1% Italian (2000).
Economy: Employment by occupation: 6.5% management, 14.2% professional, 21.3% services, 25.2% sales, 0.0% farming, 17.9% construction, 14.8% production (2000).
Income: Per capita income: $16,550 (2000); Median household income: $34,944 (2000); Poverty rate: 14.4% (2000).
Taxes: Total city taxes per capita: $122 (1997); City property taxes per capita: $122 (1997).
Education: High school graduation rate: 90.7% (2000); College graduation rate: 15.9% (2000).
Housing: Homeownership rate: 72.7% (2000); Median home value: $71,500 (2000); Median rent: $361 per month (2000); Median age of housing: 33 years (2000).
Safety: Violent crime rate: 6.2 per 10,000 population; Property crime rate: 115.5 per 10,000 population (2001).
Transportation: Commute to work: 96.0% car, 0.2% public transportation, 0.9% walk, 2.8% work from home (2000); Travel time to work: 26.8% less than 15 minutes, 25.3% 15 to 30 minutes, 35.0% 30 to 45 minutes, 7.9% 45 to 60 minutes, 4.9% 60 minutes or more (2000)

GWINN (CDP). Covers a land area of 5.084 square miles and a water area of 0 square miles. Located at 46.28° N. Lat.; 87.43° W. Long. Elevation is 1,090 feet.
History: Gwinn was built in 1907 by the Cleveland Cliffs Iron Company as a model community for its employees. It was named by William Gwinn Mather, the company president, for his mother whose maiden name was Gwinn.
Population: 1,965 (2000); Race: 95.9% White, 1.2% Black, 0.3% Asian, 0.0% American Indian and Alaska Native, 0.3% Hispanic of any race, 2.6% two or more races (2000); Density: 386.5 persons per square mile (2000); Age: 22.2% under 18, 16.4% over 64 (2000); Marriage status: 21.6% never married, 58.3% now married, 6.4% widowed, 13.7% divorced (2000); Foreign born: 1.4% (2000); Ancestry (includes multiple ancestries): 24.0% Finnish, 17.0% Italian, 14.2% English, 13.1% French (except Basque), 12.7% German (2000).
Economy: Employment by occupation: 6.0% management, 15.9% professional, 18.8% services, 26.3% sales, 0.0% farming, 18.0% construction, 15.0% production (2000).
Income: Per capita income: $16,511 (2000); Median household income: $30,772 (2000); Poverty rate: 17.3% (2000).
Education: High school graduation rate: 91.8% (2000); College graduation rate: 14.0% (2000).

School District(s)

Gwinn Area Community Schools (PK-12)
2000 Enrollment: 1,420 906-346-9283
Housing: Homeownership rate: 80.7% (2000); Median home value: $62,800 (2000); Median rent: $284 per month (2000); Median age of housing: 30 years (2000).
Transportation: Commute to work: 96.1% car, 0.6% public transportation, 0.7% walk, 2.6% work from home (2000); Travel time to work: 33.4% less than 15 minutes, 25.3% 15 to 30 minutes, 31.2% 30 to 45 minutes, 5.3% 45 to 60 minutes, 4.9% 60 minutes or more (2000)
Airports: Sawyer International (primary service)
Additional Information Contacts
Gwinn Chamber of Commerce. 906-346-9666

HARVEY (CDP). Covers a land area of 2.042 square miles and a water area of 0.539 square miles. Located at 46.49° N. Lat.; 87.35° W. Long. Elevation is 650 feet.
History: Harvey grew up in 1860 around the blast furnace of the Northern Iron Company. Established on the Chocolay River near the shore of Lake Superior, Harvey was named for Charles T. Harvey. The town developed as an agricultural center, and later as a summer resort.
Population: 1,321 (2000); Race: 94.0% White, 0.0% Black, 0.0% Asian, 2.9% American Indian and Alaska Native, 0.0% Hispanic of any race, 3.2% two or more races (2000); Density: 646.9 persons per square mile (2000); Age: 26.2% under 18, 9.8% over 64 (2000); Marriage status: 30.4% never married, 51.1% now married, 7.2% widowed, 11.2% divorced (2000); Foreign born: 0.3% (2000); Ancestry (includes multiple ancestries): 19.2% French (except Basque), 15.8% German, 13.4% English, 13.0% Finnish, 10.7% Irish (2000).
Economy: Employment by occupation: 12.6% management, 20.3% professional, 18.8% services, 24.9% sales, 0.0% farming, 8.6% construction, 14.8% production (2000).
Income: Per capita income: $18,733 (2000); Median household income: $37,321 (2000); Poverty rate: 7.0% (2000).
Education: High school graduation rate: 88.6% (2000); College graduation rate: 30.0% (2000).
Housing: Homeownership rate: 68.8% (2000); Median home value: $97,000 (2000); Median rent: $275 per month (2000); Median age of housing: 28 years (2000).
Transportation: Commute to work: 94.1% car, 0.0% public transportation, 2.2% walk, 1.2% work from home (2000); Travel time to work: 51.0% less than 15 minutes, 44.3% 15 to 30 minutes, 4.7% 30 to 45 minutes, 0.0% 45 to 60 minutes, 0.0% 60 minutes or more (2000)

HUMBOLDT (township). Covers a land area of 93.759 square miles and a water area of 1.913 square miles. Located at 46.42° N. Lat.; 87.92° W. Long. Elevation is 1,537 feet.
Population: 469 (2000); Race: 99.1% White, 0.0% Black, 0.4% Asian, 0.0% American Indian and Alaska Native, 0.0% Hispanic of any race, 0.4% two or more races (2000); Density: 5.0 persons per square mile (2000); Age: 18.6% under 18, 14.9% over 64 (2000); Marriage status: 25.6% never married, 61.8% now married, 6.3% widowed, 6.3% divorced (2000); Foreign born: 1.1% (2000); Ancestry (includes multiple ancestries): 55.4% Finnish, 14.9% German, 11.1% English, 6.9% Swedish, 6.2% French (except Basque) (2000).
Economy: Employment by occupation: 6.1% management, 14.2% professional, 19.3% services, 25.9% sales, 0.0% farming, 23.1% construction, 11.3% production (2000).
Income: Per capita income: $16,872 (2000); Median household income: $35,625 (2000); Poverty rate: 8.7% (2000).
Taxes: Total city taxes per capita: $100 (1997); City property taxes per capita: $100 (1997).
Education: High school graduation rate: 84.7% (2000); College graduation rate: 10.0% (2000).
Housing: Homeownership rate: 88.0% (2000); Median home value: $55,300 (2000); Median rent: $356 per month (2000); Median age of housing: 32 years (2000).
Transportation: Commute to work: 94.2% car, 0.0% public transportation, 2.9% walk, 2.9% work from home (2000); Travel time to work: 22.3% less than 15 minutes, 39.6% 15 to 30 minutes, 23.3% 30 to 45 minutes, 6.4% 45 to 60 minutes, 8.4% 60 minutes or more (2000)

ISHPEMING (city). Covers a land area of 8.686 square miles and a water area of 0.569 square miles. Located at 46.49° N. Lat.; 87.66° W. Long. Elevation is 1,411 feet.

History: The name of Ishpeming is of Indian origin meaning "high grounds" or "heaven." The city developed around the mining of ore from the Marquette Range, with the Cleveland Cliffs Iron Company, the Oliver Mining Company, and a mine opened by Henry Ford. The Norden Ski Club was formed in 1888 in Ishpeming and instituted jumping contests, which became the Ishpeming Ski Tournament.

Population: 6,686 (2000); Race: 96.4% White, 0.1% Black, 0.2% Asian, 2.2% American Indian and Alaska Native, 0.2% Hispanic of any race, 1.0% two or more races (2000); Density: 769.8 persons per square mile (2000); Age: 23.6% under 18, 19.3% over 64 (2000); Marriage status: 25.2% never married, 54.4% now married, 9.8% widowed, 10.5% divorced (2000); Foreign born: 1.2% (2000); Ancestry (includes multiple ancestries): 29.5% Finnish, 19.6% English, 18.9% French (except Basque), 15.9% Italian, 11.2% German (2000).

Economy: Employment by occupation: 8.3% management, 13.7% professional, 25.1% services, 24.6% sales, 0.1% farming, 14.6% construction, 13.7% production (2000).

Income: Per capita income: $16,946 (2000); Median household income: $31,347 (2000); Poverty rate: 11.1% (2000).

Taxes: Total city taxes per capita: $291 (1997); City property taxes per capita: $283 (1997).

Education: High school graduation rate: 87.0% (2000); College graduation rate: 16.7% (2000).

School District(s)

Ishpeming Public School District (PK-12)
2000 Enrollment: 1,053 906-485-5501
N.I.C.E. Community Schools (PK-12)
2000 Enrollment: 1,355 906-485-1021
Northstar Academy (07-12)
2000 Enrollment: 67 906-227-2920

Housing: Homeownership rate: 65.9% (2000); Median home value: $52,100 (2000); Median rent: $298 per month (2000); Median age of housing: 60+ years (2000).

Hospitals: Bell Memorial (69 beds)

Safety: Violent crime rate: 16.4 per 10,000 population; Property crime rate: 202.4 per 10,000 population (2001).

Transportation: Commute to work: 92.8% car, 1.1% public transportation, 3.4% walk, 2.1% work from home (2000); Travel time to work: 42.7% less than 15 minutes, 41.2% 15 to 30 minutes, 10.6% 30 to 45 minutes, 1.2% 45 to 60 minutes, 4.3% 60 minutes or more (2000)

Additional Information Contacts

Ishpeming Chamber of Commerce. 906-486-4841

ISHPEMING (township). Covers a land area of 86.465 square miles and a water area of 4.982 square miles. Located at 46.56° N. Lat.; 87.69° W. Long. Elevation is 1,411 feet.

History: U.S. National Ski Hall of Fame; birthplace of skiing in America; ski tournaments held here since 1888. Incorporated as village 1871, as city 1873.

Population: 3,522 (2000); Race: 96.4% White, 0.0% Black, 0.4% Asian, 0.9% American Indian and Alaska Native, 1.1% Hispanic of any race, 2.1% two or more races (2000); Density: 40.7 persons per square mile (2000); Age: 23.9% under 18, 15.8% over 64 (2000); Marriage status: 21.8% never married, 64.6% now married, 5.3% widowed, 8.3% divorced (2000); Foreign born: 1.1% (2000); Ancestry (includes multiple ancestries): 34.2% Finnish, 22.9% English, 13.6% French (except Basque), 12.2% Italian, 10.7% Swedish (2000).

Economy: Railroad junction. Lumbering; cattle. Manufacturing: logging, construction, sand and gravel, hardwood parquet; iron mining. Single-family building permits issued: 16 (2001) / 17 (2000); Multi-family building permits issued: 0 (2001) / 0 (2000); Employment by occupation: 7.6% management, 20.3% professional, 19.3% services, 31.0% sales, 0.1% farming, 13.0% construction, 8.6% production (2000).

Income: Per capita income: $17,736 (2000); Median household income: $43,139 (2000); Poverty rate: 6.8% (2000).

Taxes: Total city taxes per capita: $34 (1997); City property taxes per capita: $33 (1997).

Education: High school graduation rate: 88.8% (2000); College graduation rate: 20.8% (2000).

Housing: Homeownership rate: 91.7% (2000); Median home value: $76,300 (2000); Median rent: $315 per month (2000); Median age of housing: 31 years (2000).

Transportation: Commute to work: 97.6% car, 0.0% public transportation, 0.3% walk, 2.1% work from home (2000); Travel time to work: 45.3% less than 15 minutes, 32.2% 15 to 30 minutes, 14.8% 30 to 45 minutes, 1.3% 45 to 60 minutes, 6.4% 60 minutes or more (2000)

K. I. SAWYER AFB (CDP). Covers a land area of 8.440 square miles and a water area of 0.020 square miles. Located at 46.33° N. Lat.; 87.37° W. Long.

Population: 1,443 (2000); Race: 93.3% White, 0.0% Black, 0.0% Asian, 3.9% American Indian and Alaska Native, 1.0% Hispanic of any race, 2.8% two or more races (2000); Density: 171.0 persons per square mile (2000); Age: 40.5% under 18, 1.1% over 64 (2000); Marriage status: 28.0% never married, 49.9% now married, 1.8% widowed, 20.3% divorced (2000); Foreign born: 1.4% (2000); Ancestry (includes multiple ancestries): 21.8% German, 17.0% Irish, 10.7% English, 10.4% Finnish, 10.1% Other groups (2000).

Economy: Employment by occupation: 4.3% management, 9.8% professional, 24.6% services, 25.9% sales, 0.0% farming, 17.3% construction, 18.1% production (2000).

Income: Per capita income: $10,029 (2000); Median household income: $26,550 (2000); Poverty rate: 26.6% (2000).

Education: High school graduation rate: 93.6% (2000); College graduation rate: 14.1% (2000).

Housing: Homeownership rate: 0.0% (2000); Median rent: $421 per month (2000); Median age of housing: 36 years (2000).

Transportation: Commute to work: 96.6% car, 0.0% public transportation, 2.5% walk, 1.0% work from home (2000); Travel time to work: 28.4% less than 15 minutes, 19.6% 15 to 30 minutes, 41.4% 30 to 45 minutes, 6.9% 45 to 60 minutes, 3.6% 60 minutes or more (2000)

LITTLE LAKE (unincorporated postal area, zip code 49833). Covers a land area of 6.653 square miles and a water area of 0.123 square miles. Located at 46.29° N. Lat.; 87.33° W. Long. Elevation is 1,128 feet.

History: Little Lake grew up around a mill and general store of the Cheshire Iron Manufacturing Company in 1863.

Population: 249 (2000); Race: 95.9% White, 0.0% Black, 0.0% Asian, 4.1% American Indian and Alaska Native, 0.0% Hispanic of any race, 0.0% two or more races (2000); Density: 37.4 persons per square mile (2000); Age: 5.8% under 18, 17.0% over 64 (2000); Marriage status: 8.1% never married, 81.4% now married, 0.0% widowed, 10.6% divorced (2000); Foreign born: 0.0% (2000); Ancestry (includes multiple ancestries): 33.3% Irish, 17.5% German, 16.4% Finnish, 10.5% French Canadian, 5.3% Dutch (2000).

Economy: Employment by occupation: 13.0% management, 0.0% professional, 52.2% services, 8.7% sales, 0.0% farming, 14.5% construction, 11.6% production (2000).

Income: Per capita income: $19,768 (2000); Median household income: $27,232 (2000); Poverty rate: 8.2% (2000).

Education: High school graduation rate: 81.1% (2000); College graduation rate: 14.9% (2000).

Housing: Homeownership rate: 90.2% (2000); Median home value: $83,600 (2000); Median rent: $475 per month (2000); Median age of housing: 34 years (2000).

Transportation: Commute to work: 100.0% car, 0.0% public transportation, 0.0% walk, 0.0% work from home (2000); Travel time to work: 44.9% less than 15 minutes, 40.6% 15 to 30 minutes, 0.0% 30 to 45 minutes, 5.8% 45 to 60 minutes, 8.7% 60 minutes or more (2000)

MARQUETTE (city). Covers a land area of 11.405 square miles and a water area of 7.961 square miles. Located at 46.54° N. Lat.; 87.40° W. Long. Elevation is 628 feet.

History: In 1830 iron ore was discovered on the south shore of Lake Superior, and in 1846 the Jackson mine was opened about 14 miles inland from the site of Marquette. A shipping point was needed for the ore, and the site selected was the natural harbor at the mouth of the Carp River. The community that grew up here was first called Worcester, for the Massachusetts home of an early resident. In 1850 the town was renamed for the Jesuit missionary Marquette, whose explorations had helped to open the Northwest Territory. Marquette was incorporated as a village in 1859, and as a city in 1871.

Population: 19,661 (2000); Race: 94.7% White, 1.0% Black, 0.6% Asian, 1.8% American Indian and Alaska Native, 1.0% Hispanic of any race, 1.6% two or more races (2000); Density: 1,723.9 persons per square mile (2000); Age: 16.3% under 18, 14.1% over 64 (2000); Marriage status: 44.5% never married, 39.8% now married, 6.3% widowed, 9.4% divorced (2000); Foreign born: 1.9% (2000); Ancestry (includes multiple ancestries): 20.4% German,

13.5% Finnish, 13.0% French (except Basque), 12.6% English, 11.7% Irish (2000).
Vital Statistics: Birth rate: 92.1 per 10,000 population (1998)
Economy: Employment by occupation: 10.4% management, 23.4% professional, 23.4% services, 28.4% sales, 0.0% farming, 6.8% construction, 7.6% production (2000).
Income: Per capita income: $17,787 (2000); Median household income: $29,918 (2000); Poverty rate: 17.0% (2000).
Taxes: Total city taxes per capita: $343 (2000); City property taxes per capita: $334 (2000).
Education: High school graduation rate: 91.5% (2000); College graduation rate: 34.2% (2000).

School District(s)

Marquette Area Public Schools (KG-12)
2000 Enrollment: 4,120 906-225-4200

Four-year College(s)

Northern Michigan University (Public)
2001 Enrollment: 8,577 906-227-1000
2001 Tuition: In-state $3,192; Out-of-state $5,976

Two-year College(s)

Marquette General Hospital (Private, Not-for-profit)
2001 Enrollment: 13 906-225-4916
2001 Tuition: In-state $1,500; Out-of-state $1,500

Housing: Homeownership rate: 49.7% (2000); Median home value: $86,400 (2000); Median rent: $387 per month (2000); Median age of housing: 41 years (2000).
Hospitals: Marquette General Health System
Safety: Violent crime rate: 15.7 per 10,000 population; Property crime rate: 212.5 per 10,000 population (2001).
Newspapers: The Mining Journal (7 x week); Upper Peninsula Catholic (2 x month)
Transportation: Commute to work: 85.2% car, 0.9% public transportation, 10.7% walk, 1.6% work from home (2000); Travel time to work: 76.1% less than 15 minutes, 17.2% 15 to 30 minutes, 3.8% 30 to 45 minutes, 0.7% 45 to 60 minutes, 2.2% 60 minutes or more (2000); Amtrak: Service available.

Additional Information Contacts

Marquette Chamber of Commerce.......................... 906-226-6591
Upper Peninsula Association of Realtors.......................... 906-228-4870

MARQUETTE (township). Covers a land area of 54.734 square miles and a water area of 5.420 square miles. Located at 46.57° N. Lat.; 87.46° W. Long. Elevation is 628 feet.
History: Once an iron ore shipping port. Seat of Northern Michigan University (has Olympic Training Center). Maritime Museum. Settled 1849, Incorporated as a city 1871.
Population: 3,286 (2000); Race: 98.4% White, 0.0% Black, 0.0% Asian, 0.5% American Indian and Alaska Native, 0.1% Hispanic of any race, 1.1% two or more races (2000); Density: 60.0 persons per square mile (2000); Age: 23.0% under 18, 12.6% over 64 (2000); Marriage status: 24.9% never married, 59.7% now married, 6.6% widowed, 8.9% divorced (2000); Foreign born: 1.1% (2000); Ancestry (includes multiple ancestries): 18.7% German, 18.0% Finnish, 16.5% English, 12.8% Irish, 12.5% French (except Basque) (2000).
Economy: A shipping center for a lumber, cattle and resort region. Railroad spur terminus (ship railroad transfer). Manufacturing includes chemicals, wood products and mining machinery, dairy and bakery products and publishing. Ore Docks handle 7 million tons of iron ore annually. Cliffs Ridge Ski Area to south. Employment by occupation: 8.8% management, 25.3% professional, 13.8% services, 29.4% sales, 0.0% farming, 9.8% construction, 12.9% production (2000).
Income: Per capita income: $23,056 (2000); Median household income: $42,385 (2000); Poverty rate: 5.2% (2000).
Taxes: Total city taxes per capita: $435 (1997); City property taxes per capita: $430 (1997).
Education: High school graduation rate: 89.1% (2000); College graduation rate: 30.0% (2000).
Housing: Homeownership rate: 75.3% (2000); Median home value: $97,400 (2000); Median rent: $421 per month (2000); Median age of housing: 24 years (2000).
Transportation: Commute to work: 95.3% car, 0.0% public transportation, 1.1% walk, 3.6% work from home (2000); Travel time to work: 69.0% less than 15 minutes, 22.9% 15 to 30 minutes, 2.4% 30 to 45 minutes, 0.9% 45 to 60 minutes, 4.8% 60 minutes or more (2000); Amtrak: Service available.

MICHIGAMME (township). Covers a land area of 133.665 square miles and a water area of 8.131 square miles. Located at 46.61° N. Lat.; 88.02° W. Long.
Population: 377 (2000); Race: 99.5% White, 0.0% Black, 0.5% Asian, 0.0% American Indian and Alaska Native, 0.0% Hispanic of any race, 0.0% two or more races (2000); Density: 2.8 persons per square mile (2000); Age: 14.4% under 18, 27.3% over 64 (2000); Marriage status: 12.9% never married, 68.7% now married, 10.1% widowed, 8.3% divorced (2000); Foreign born: 1.3% (2000); Ancestry (includes multiple ancestries): 22.4% Finnish, 17.8% German, 11.3% French (except Basque), 9.8% Irish, 8.8% English (2000).
Economy: Employment by occupation: 13.2% management, 16.9% professional, 13.2% services, 25.0% sales, 2.9% farming, 12.5% construction, 16.2% production (2000).
Income: Per capita income: $24,549 (2000); Median household income: $29,750 (2000); Poverty rate: 8.8% (2000).
Taxes: Total city taxes per capita: $34 (1997); City property taxes per capita: $34 (1997).
Education: High school graduation rate: 84.7% (2000); College graduation rate: 20.2% (2000).
Housing: Homeownership rate: 95.0% (2000); Median home value: $49,600 (2000); Median rent: $288 per month (2000); Median age of housing: 40 years (2000).
Transportation: Commute to work: 83.8% car, 0.0% public transportation, 1.5% walk, 10.3% work from home (2000); Travel time to work: 16.4% less than 15 minutes, 15.6% 15 to 30 minutes, 28.7% 30 to 45 minutes, 27.0% 45 to 60 minutes, 12.3% 60 minutes or more (2000)

NEGAUNEE (city). Covers a land area of 13.778 square miles and a water area of 0.887 square miles. Located at 46.50° N. Lat.; 87.60° W. Long. Elevation is 1,375 feet.
History: Iron ore was discovered in 1844 in the Marquette Range by a surveying party. Development of the community of Negaunee was slow, because of the difficulty of transporting the ore via forest trails to the dock at Marquette, and then unloading it to be carried around the rapids at Sault Ste. Marie. By 1855 a plank road had been completed, and the first locks at Sault Ste. Marie made shipping easier. The railroad connection between Negaunee and Marquette in 1857 brought more growth, and Negaunee was platted in 1865.
Population: 4,576 (2000); Race: 97.6% White, 0.0% Black, 0.3% Asian, 0.8% American Indian and Alaska Native, 0.1% Hispanic of any race, 1.3% two or more races (2000); Density: 332.1 persons per square mile (2000); Age: 22.0% under 18, 20.1% over 64 (2000); Marriage status: 24.3% never married, 57.4% now married, 8.7% widowed, 9.7% divorced (2000); Foreign born: 1.0% (2000); Ancestry (includes multiple ancestries): 29.5% Finnish, 19.0% English, 14.8% Italian, 14.8% Swedish, 13.5% German (2000).
Economy: Employment by occupation: 7.2% management, 15.5% professional, 22.1% services, 25.7% sales, 0.0% farming, 12.7% construction, 16.8% production (2000).
Income: Per capita income: $16,889 (2000); Median household income: $33,117 (2000); Poverty rate: 9.4% (2000).
Taxes: Total city taxes per capita: $268 (1997); City property taxes per capita: $258 (1997).
Education: High school graduation rate: 84.9% (2000); College graduation rate: 19.4% (2000).

School District(s)

Negaunee Public Schools (PK-12)
2000 Enrollment: 1,524 906-475-4157

Housing: Homeownership rate: 69.6% (2000); Median home value: $61,300 (2000); Median rent: $310 per month (2000); Median age of housing: 59 years (2000).
Safety: Violent crime rate: 8.7 per 10,000 population; Property crime rate: 121.7 per 10,000 population (2001).
Transportation: Commute to work: 93.9% car, 1.4% public transportation, 3.4% walk, 1.3% work from home (2000); Travel time to work: 36.3% less than 15 minutes, 53.6% 15 to 30 minutes, 7.3% 30 to 45 minutes, 0.9% 45 to 60 minutes, 1.9% 60 minutes or more (2000)

NEGAUNEE (township). Covers a land area of 42.052 square miles and a water area of 1.601 square miles. Located at 46.53° N. Lat.; 87.54° W. Long. Elevation is 1,375 feet.
History: Iron was discovered here in 1844. Michigan Iron Industry Museum. Settled 1846; incorporated as village 1862, as city 1873.
Population: 2,707 (2000); Race: 96.7% White, 0.0% Black, 1.0% Asian, 0.6% American Indian and Alaska Native, 0.6% Hispanic of any race, 1.6% two or more races (2000); Density: 64.4 persons per square mile (2000); Age:

24.4% under 18, 6.7% over 64 (2000); Marriage status: 22.0% never married, 66.1% now married, 4.1% widowed, 7.7% divorced (2000); Foreign born: 1.0% (2000); Ancestry (includes multiple ancestries): 40.2% Finnish, 15.0% English, 14.0% German, 12.5% Swedish, 12.1% French (except Basque) (2000).
Economy: Railroad junction for mining spurs and railroad spur to Marquette. Iron mining; wood products; cattle farming. Resort. Employment by occupation: 10.1% management, 20.6% professional, 17.2% services, 27.4% sales, 0.0% farming, 14.2% construction, 10.6% production (2000).
Income: Per capita income: $18,894 (2000); Median household income: $47,348 (2000); Poverty rate: 3.7% (2000).
Taxes: Total city taxes per capita: $121 (1997); City property taxes per capita: $120 (1997).
Education: High school graduation rate: 89.5% (2000); College graduation rate: 26.0% (2000).
Housing: Homeownership rate: 90.9% (2000); Median home value: $91,000 (2000); Median rent: $363 per month (2000); Median age of housing: 28 years (2000).
Transportation: Commute to work: 95.5% car, 0.0% public transportation, 2.0% walk, 2.0% work from home (2000); Travel time to work: 35.6% less than 15 minutes, 52.0% 15 to 30 minutes, 10.3% 30 to 45 minutes, 0.5% 45 to 60 minutes, 1.7% 60 minutes or more (2000)

PALMER (CDP). Covers a land area of 0.590 square miles and a water area of 0 square miles. Located at 46.44° N. Lat.; 87.59° W. Long. Elevation is 1,298 feet.
Population: 449 (2000); Race: 97.8% White, 0.0% Black, 0.0% Asian, 0.7% American Indian and Alaska Native, 0.2% Hispanic of any race, 1.3% two or more races (2000); Density: 760.8 persons per square mile (2000); Age: 17.0% under 18, 25.3% over 64 (2000); Marriage status: 27.5% never married, 49.0% now married, 10.9% widowed, 12.7% divorced (2000); Foreign born: 1.1% (2000); Ancestry (includes multiple ancestries): 41.5% Finnish, 13.2% French (except Basque), 10.5% English, 9.9% German, 9.6% Swedish (2000).
Economy: Employment by occupation: 7.2% management, 10.8% professional, 21.1% services, 19.9% sales, 0.0% farming, 15.7% construction, 25.3% production (2000).
Income: Per capita income: $21,309 (2000); Median household income: $29,063 (2000); Poverty rate: 13.5% (2000).
Education: High school graduation rate: 80.1% (2000); College graduation rate: 8.3% (2000).
Housing: Homeownership rate: 84.9% (2000); Median home value: $38,200 (2000); Median rent: $213 per month (2000); Median age of housing: 55 years (2000).
Transportation: Commute to work: 86.9% car, 0.0% public transportation, 6.9% walk, 1.9% work from home (2000); Travel time to work: 30.6% less than 15 minutes, 49.0% 15 to 30 minutes, 14.6% 30 to 45 minutes, 0.0% 45 to 60 minutes, 5.7% 60 minutes or more (2000)

POWELL (township). Covers a land area of 154.170 square miles and a water area of 8.145 square miles. Located at 46.79° N. Lat.; 87.73° W. Long.
Population: 724 (2000); Race: 94.5% White, 0.0% Black, 0.4% Asian, 1.8% American Indian and Alaska Native, 0.1% Hispanic of any race, 3.2% two or more races (2000); Density: 4.7 persons per square mile (2000); Age: 18.7% under 18, 17.3% over 64 (2000); Marriage status: 19.2% never married, 65.3% now married, 4.4% widowed, 11.1% divorced (2000); Foreign born: 0.4% (2000); Ancestry (includes multiple ancestries): 22.0% German, 15.5% Irish, 12.3% French (except Basque), 11.3% English, 8.4% French Canadian (2000).
Economy: Employment by occupation: 8.7% management, 18.1% professional, 23.2% services, 17.7% sales, 3.2% farming, 13.5% construction, 15.5% production (2000).
Income: Per capita income: $19,391 (2000); Median household income: $34,659 (2000); Poverty rate: 8.1% (2000).
Taxes: Total city taxes per capita: $189 (1997); City property taxes per capita: $189 (1997).
Education: High school graduation rate: 86.4% (2000); College graduation rate: 18.4% (2000).
Housing: Homeownership rate: 89.1% (2000); Median home value: $69,700 (2000); Median rent: $271 per month (2000); Median age of housing: 33 years (2000).
Transportation: Commute to work: 82.6% car, 0.0% public transportation, 11.4% walk, 5.4% work from home (2000); Travel time to work: 29.3% less than 15 minutes, 16.3% 15 to 30 minutes, 39.2% 30 to 45 minutes, 11.3% 45 to 60 minutes, 3.9% 60 minutes or more (2000)

REPUBLIC (township). Covers a land area of 113.222 square miles and a water area of 6.348 square miles. Located at 46.35° N. Lat.; 88.02° W. Long. Elevation is 1,520 feet.
History: Republic was named for the Republic Mine, which began operation in 1871.
Population: 1,106 (2000); Race: 97.9% White, 0.0% Black, 0.0% Asian, 1.4% American Indian and Alaska Native, 0.2% Hispanic of any race, 0.7% two or more races (2000); Density: 9.8 persons per square mile (2000); Age: 19.2% under 18, 23.1% over 64 (2000); Marriage status: 19.7% never married, 63.5% now married, 7.7% widowed, 9.1% divorced (2000); Foreign born: 0.4% (2000); Ancestry (includes multiple ancestries): 42.0% Finnish, 16.0% German, 10.8% French (except Basque), 10.5% Swedish, 8.5% English (2000).
Economy: Employment by occupation: 8.0% management, 15.2% professional, 19.5% services, 21.4% sales, 2.7% farming, 16.8% construction, 16.3% production (2000).
Income: Per capita income: $15,524 (2000); Median household income: $27,500 (2000); Poverty rate: 11.2% (2000).
Taxes: Total city taxes per capita: $129 (1997); City property taxes per capita: $129 (1997).
Education: High school graduation rate: 82.3% (2000); College graduation rate: 8.9% (2000).

School District(s)

Republic-Michigamme Schools (KG-12)
2000 Enrollment: 191 906-376-2277

Housing: Homeownership rate: 87.5% (2000); Median home value: $39,500 (2000); Median rent: $195 per month (2000); Median age of housing: 39 years (2000).
Transportation: Commute to work: 94.1% car, 0.8% public transportation, 4.5% walk, 0.6% work from home (2000); Travel time to work: 21.9% less than 15 minutes, 12.9% 15 to 30 minutes, 23.0% 30 to 45 minutes, 23.9% 45 to 60 minutes, 18.3% 60 minutes or more (2000)

RICHMOND (township). Covers a land area of 55.596 square miles and a water area of 1.864 square miles. Located at 46.41° N. Lat.; 87.58° W. Long.
Population: 974 (2000); Race: 98.7% White, 0.0% Black, 0.0% Asian, 0.3% American Indian and Alaska Native, 0.1% Hispanic of any race, 0.9% two or more races (2000); Density: 17.5 persons per square mile (2000); Age: 20.4% under 18, 19.8% over 64 (2000); Marriage status: 24.5% never married, 54.4% now married, 9.4% widowed, 11.7% divorced (2000); Foreign born: 0.9% (2000); Ancestry (includes multiple ancestries): 43.1% Finnish, 12.1% French (except Basque), 10.8% German, 9.0% English, 8.2% Irish (2000).
Economy: Employment by occupation: 8.2% management, 10.6% professional, 18.8% services, 20.9% sales, 0.5% farming, 19.8% construction, 21.1% production (2000).
Income: Per capita income: $19,084 (2000); Median household income: $31,917 (2000); Poverty rate: 10.8% (2000).
Taxes: Total city taxes per capita: $250 (1997); City property taxes per capita: $250 (1997).
Education: High school graduation rate: 81.2% (2000); College graduation rate: 7.9% (2000).
Housing: Homeownership rate: 85.0% (2000); Median home value: $43,200 (2000); Median rent: $242 per month (2000); Median age of housing: 48 years (2000).
Transportation: Commute to work: 89.7% car, 0.0% public transportation, 4.5% walk, 3.9% work from home (2000); Travel time to work: 23.0% less than 15 minutes, 45.5% 15 to 30 minutes, 27.7% 30 to 45 minutes, 1.4% 45 to 60 minutes, 2.5% 60 minutes or more (2000)

SANDS (township). Covers a land area of 70.842 square miles and a water area of 0.280 square miles. Located at 46.41° N. Lat.; 87.40° W. Long. Elevation is 1,200 feet.
Population: 2,127 (2000); Race: 95.5% White, 0.5% Black, 1.2% Asian, 1.5% American Indian and Alaska Native, 0.5% Hispanic of any race, 1.3% two or more races (2000); Density: 30.0 persons per square mile (2000); Age: 26.3% under 18, 3.8% over 64 (2000); Marriage status: 22.6% never married, 64.5% now married, 2.3% widowed, 10.5% divorced (2000); Foreign born: 1.2% (2000); Ancestry (includes multiple ancestries): 23.7% German, 18.7% Finnish, 13.5% French (except Basque), 11.3% English, 10.6% Irish (2000).
Economy: Employment by occupation: 10.5% management, 22.0% professional, 15.9% services, 27.9% sales, 1.0% farming, 12.5% construction, 10.2% production (2000).
Income: Per capita income: $21,943 (2000); Median household income: $51,948 (2000); Poverty rate: 4.2% (2000).

Taxes: Total city taxes per capita: $84 (1997); City property taxes per capita: $83 (1997).
Education: High school graduation rate: 93.6% (2000); College graduation rate: 28.4% (2000).
Housing: Homeownership rate: 93.2% (2000); Median home value: $99,400 (2000); Median rent: $269 per month (2000); Median age of housing: 20 years (2000).
Transportation: Commute to work: 96.6% car, 0.0% public transportation, 1.2% walk, 2.1% work from home (2000); Travel time to work: 27.5% less than 15 minutes, 61.1% 15 to 30 minutes, 6.4% 30 to 45 minutes, 1.8% 45 to 60 minutes, 3.2% 60 minutes or more (2000)

SKANDIA (township). Covers a land area of 72.031 square miles and a water area of 0.058 square miles. Located at 46.35° N. Lat.; 87.20° W. Long.
Population: 907 (2000); Race: 95.9% White, 0.0% Black, 0.0% Asian, 1.6% American Indian and Alaska Native, 0.0% Hispanic of any race, 2.5% two or more races (2000); Density: 12.6 persons per square mile (2000); Age: 26.1% under 18, 9.6% over 64 (2000); Marriage status: 25.2% never married, 61.3% now married, 5.9% widowed, 7.7% divorced (2000); Foreign born: 0.1% (2000); Ancestry (includes multiple ancestries): 24.8% German, 15.0% Irish, 14.7% Swedish, 14.0% Finnish, 11.3% French (except Basque) (2000).
Economy: Employment by occupation: 8.1% management, 17.8% professional, 20.2% services, 24.0% sales, 2.6% farming, 14.5% construction, 12.7% production (2000).
Income: Per capita income: $16,941 (2000); Median household income: $38,125 (2000); Poverty rate: 6.7% (2000).
Taxes: Total city taxes per capita: $36 (1997); City property taxes per capita: $36 (1997).
Education: High school graduation rate: 84.2% (2000); College graduation rate: 17.0% (2000).
Housing: Homeownership rate: 88.3% (2000); Median home value: $64,300 (2000); Median rent: $338 per month (2000); Median age of housing: 29 years (2000).
Transportation: Commute to work: 94.3% car, 0.0% public transportation, 2.7% walk, 2.5% work from home (2000); Travel time to work: 13.1% less than 15 minutes, 41.3% 15 to 30 minutes, 35.9% 30 to 45 minutes, 6.8% 45 to 60 minutes, 3.0% 60 minutes or more (2000)

TILDEN (township). Covers a land area of 94.254 square miles and a water area of 1.752 square miles. Located at 46.40° N. Lat.; 87.69° W. Long.
Population: 1,003 (2000); Race: 99.8% White, 0.0% Black, 0.0% Asian, 0.0% American Indian and Alaska Native, 0.0% Hispanic of any race, 0.2% two or more races (2000); Density: 10.6 persons per square mile (2000); Age: 22.7% under 18, 11.1% over 64 (2000); Marriage status: 24.1% never married, 62.0% now married, 4.0% widowed, 9.8% divorced (2000); Foreign born: 0.4% (2000); Ancestry (includes multiple ancestries): 41.1% Finnish, 19.4% English, 13.7% French (except Basque), 13.1% Swedish, 11.9% Italian (2000).
Economy: Employment by occupation: 9.7% management, 14.3% professional, 17.4% services, 21.6% sales, 1.0% farming, 19.1% construction, 17.0% production (2000).
Income: Per capita income: $17,199 (2000); Median household income: $43,450 (2000); Poverty rate: 4.6% (2000).
Taxes: Total city taxes per capita: $135 (1997); City property taxes per capita: $135 (1997).
Education: High school graduation rate: 85.4% (2000); College graduation rate: 13.3% (2000).
Housing: Homeownership rate: 92.5% (2000); Median home value: $57,700 (2000); Median rent: $306 per month (2000); Median age of housing: 34 years (2000).
Transportation: Commute to work: 97.6% car, 0.0% public transportation, 1.2% walk, 1.2% work from home (2000); Travel time to work: 46.6% less than 15 minutes, 28.2% 15 to 30 minutes, 17.8% 30 to 45 minutes, 6.0% 45 to 60 minutes, 1.4% 60 minutes or more (2000)

TROWBRIDGE PARK (CDP). Covers a land area of 1.376 square miles and a water area of 0.014 square miles. Located at 46.55° N. Lat.; 87.43° W. Long.
Population: 2,012 (2000); Race: 97.7% White, 0.0% Black, 0.0% Asian, 0.8% American Indian and Alaska Native, 0.0% Hispanic of any race, 1.5% two or more races (2000); Density: 1,462.1 persons per square mile (2000); Age: 22.7% under 18, 10.4% over 64 (2000); Marriage status: 26.4% never married, 60.0% now married, 4.0% widowed, 9.5% divorced (2000); Foreign born: 1.3% (2000); Ancestry (includes multiple ancestries): 20.3% German, 18.3% English, 15.2% Finnish, 15.2% Irish, 14.2% French (except Basque) (2000).
Economy: Employment by occupation: 8.1% management, 20.1% professional, 17.1% services, 31.1% sales, 0.0% farming, 12.6% construction, 11.0% production (2000).
Income: Per capita income: $20,346 (2000); Median household income: $42,422 (2000); Poverty rate: 6.1% (2000).
Education: High school graduation rate: 87.2% (2000); College graduation rate: 23.3% (2000).
Housing: Homeownership rate: 81.8% (2000); Median home value: $85,400 (2000); Median rent: $443 per month (2000); Median age of housing: 28 years (2000).
Transportation: Commute to work: 95.7% car, 0.0% public transportation, 1.7% walk, 2.6% work from home (2000); Travel time to work: 72.6% less than 15 minutes, 17.8% 15 to 30 minutes, 2.4% 30 to 45 minutes, 0.8% 45 to 60 minutes, 6.3% 60 minutes or more (2000)

TURIN (township). Covers a land area of 84.183 square miles and a water area of 0.050 square miles. Located at 46.19° N. Lat.; 87.25° W. Long.
Population: 131 (2000); Race: 97.3% White, 0.0% Black, 0.0% Asian, 2.7% American Indian and Alaska Native, 0.0% Hispanic of any race, 0.0% two or more races (2000); Density: 1.6 persons per square mile (2000); Age: 21.9% under 18, 9.6% over 64 (2000); Marriage status: 23.3% never married, 60.0% now married, 5.8% widowed, 10.8% divorced (2000); Foreign born: 1.4% (2000); Ancestry (includes multiple ancestries): 31.5% Finnish, 24.0% Swedish, 20.5% French (except Basque), 19.9% German, 10.3% Italian (2000).
Economy: Employment by occupation: 14.3% management, 11.1% professional, 15.9% services, 15.9% sales, 0.0% farming, 17.5% construction, 25.4% production (2000).
Income: Per capita income: $12,832 (2000); Median household income: $30,625 (2000); Poverty rate: 19.2% (2000).
Taxes: Total city taxes per capita: $23 (2000); City property taxes per capita: $23 (2000).
Education: High school graduation rate: 83.7% (2000); College graduation rate: 2.0% (2000).
Housing: Homeownership rate: 84.6% (2000); Median home value: $55,000 (2000); Median rent: $225 per month (2000); Median age of housing: 25 years (2000).
Transportation: Commute to work: 87.3% car, 0.0% public transportation, 0.0% walk, 12.7% work from home (2000); Travel time to work: 14.5% less than 15 minutes, 43.6% 15 to 30 minutes, 21.8% 30 to 45 minutes, 12.7% 45 to 60 minutes, 7.3% 60 minutes or more (2000)

WELLS (township). Covers a land area of 154.867 square miles and a water area of 0.343 square miles. Located at 46.04° N. Lat.; 87.46° W. Long.
Population: 292 (2000); Race: 99.3% White, 0.0% Black, 0.0% Asian, 0.7% American Indian and Alaska Native, 0.0% Hispanic of any race, 0.0% two or more races (2000); Density: 1.9 persons per square mile (2000); Age: 20.6% under 18, 15.1% over 64 (2000); Marriage status: 28.7% never married, 55.7% now married, 6.1% widowed, 9.6% divorced (2000); Foreign born: 0.0% (2000); Ancestry (includes multiple ancestries): 22.8% French (except Basque), 19.5% Finnish, 15.8% Irish, 13.6% German, 10.3% Dutch (2000).
Economy: Employment by occupation: 14.8% management, 9.8% professional, 23.8% services, 16.4% sales, 9.0% farming, 10.7% construction, 15.6% production (2000).
Income: Per capita income: $15,333 (2000); Median household income: $28,906 (2000); Poverty rate: 9.3% (2000).
Taxes: Total city taxes per capita: $322 (2000); City property taxes per capita: $322 (2000).
Education: High school graduation rate: 76.7% (2000); College graduation rate: 6.7% (2000).
Housing: Homeownership rate: 83.9% (2000); Median home value: $56,300 (2000); Median rent: $213 per month (2000); Median age of housing: 30 years (2000).
Transportation: Commute to work: 80.0% car, 1.7% public transportation, 8.3% walk, 10.0% work from home (2000); Travel time to work: 25.9% less than 15 minutes, 12.0% 15 to 30 minutes, 31.5% 30 to 45 minutes, 18.5% 45 to 60 minutes, 12.0% 60 minutes or more (2000)

WEST BRANCH (township). Covers a land area of 35.481 square miles and a water area of 0.207 square miles. Located at 46.35° N. Lat.; 87.32° W. Long.
Population: 1,648 (2000); Race: 93.0% White, 0.0% Black, 0.0% Asian, 3.8% American Indian and Alaska Native, 0.8% Hispanic of any race, 2.8% two or more races (2000); Density: 46.4 persons per square mile (2000); Age: 34.0% under 18, 5.8% over 64 (2000); Marriage status: 19.1% never married, 60.2% now married, 3.7% widowed, 17.0% divorced (2000); Foreign born:

0.0% (2000); Ancestry (includes multiple ancestries): 21.0% German, 12.2% English, 10.5% Other groups, 9.8% Finnish, 9.5% Irish (2000).
Economy: Employment by occupation: 11.3% management, 16.5% professional, 16.9% services, 24.1% sales, 0.0% farming, 17.6% construction, 13.8% production (2000).
Income: Per capita income: $14,685 (2000); Median household income: $30,183 (2000); Poverty rate: 17.1% (2000).
Taxes: Total city taxes per capita: $16 (1997); City property taxes per capita: $16 (1997).
Education: High school graduation rate: 88.7% (2000); College graduation rate: 16.6% (2000).
Housing: Homeownership rate: 49.3% (2000); Median home value: $84,200 (2000); Median rent: $417 per month (2000); Median age of housing: 35 years (2000).
Transportation: Commute to work: 94.0% car, 0.0% public transportation, 1.6% walk, 4.4% work from home (2000); Travel time to work: 21.6% less than 15 minutes, 33.3% 15 to 30 minutes, 37.4% 30 to 45 minutes, 5.2% 45 to 60 minutes, 2.4% 60 minutes or more (2000)

WEST ISHPEMING (CDP). Covers a land area of 3.004 square miles and a water area of 0.045 square miles. Located at 46.48° N. Lat.; 87.71° W. Long.
Population: 2,792 (2000); Race: 96.5% White, 0.0% Black, 0.5% Asian, 0.0% American Indian and Alaska Native, 1.4% Hispanic of any race, 2.7% two or more races (2000); Density: 929.4 persons per square mile (2000); Age: 23.5% under 18, 17.8% over 64 (2000); Marriage status: 21.9% never married, 63.9% now married, 5.0% widowed, 9.2% divorced (2000); Foreign born: 1.0% (2000); Ancestry (includes multiple ancestries): 34.0% Finnish, 22.2% English, 13.7% Italian, 13.5% French (except Basque), 11.2% Swedish (2000).
Economy: Employment by occupation: 6.2% management, 20.4% professional, 20.1% services, 30.8% sales, 0.0% farming, 12.7% construction, 9.8% production (2000).
Income: Per capita income: $16,928 (2000); Median household income: $41,758 (2000); Poverty rate: 7.5% (2000).
Education: High school graduation rate: 88.9% (2000); College graduation rate: 17.6% (2000).
Housing: Homeownership rate: 91.4% (2000); Median home value: $73,200 (2000); Median rent: $312 per month (2000); Median age of housing: 29 years (2000).
Transportation: Commute to work: 97.2% car, 0.0% public transportation, 0.7% walk, 2.1% work from home (2000); Travel time to work: 51.8% less than 15 minutes, 31.3% 15 to 30 minutes, 10.9% 30 to 45 minutes, 1.1% 45 to 60 minutes, 4.8% 60 minutes or more (2000)

Mason County

Located in western Michigan; bounded on the west by Lake Michigan; drained by the Pere Marquette, Big Sable, and Little Manistee Rivers; includes Hamlin Lake, and Manistee National Forest. Covers a land area of 495.20 square miles, a water area of 746.70 square miles, and is located in the Eastern Time Zone. The county government was organized in 1855. County seat is Ludington.
Population: 28,274 (2000); Race: 95.2% White, 0.9% Black, 0.2% Asian, 0.8% American Indian and Alaska Native, 3.1% Hispanic of any race, 2.0% two or more races (2000); Density: 57.1 persons per square mile (2000); Age: 24.2% under 18, 16.9% over 64 (2000).
Religion: Five largest groups: 14.6% Catholic Church, 4.0% Lutheran Church—Missouri Synod, 3.8% Evangelical Lutheran Church in America, 3.7% The United Methodist Church, 2.6% Congregational Christian Churches, Additional (not part of any national
Economy: Unemployment rate: 11.9% (11/2002); Total civilian labor force: 15,839 (11/2002); Leading industries: 29.7% manufacturing; 16.6% retail trade; 11.4% health care and social assistance (2000); Companies that employ more than 1,000 persons: 0 (2000); Companies that employ more than 100 persons: 13 (2000); Farms: 413 totaling 77,103 acres (1997); Minority business ownership rate: 0.0% (1997); Women business ownership rate: 29.0% (1997); Retail sales per capita: $8,027 (1997). Single-family building permits issued: 144 (2001) / 145 (2000); Multi-family building permits issued: 4 (2001) / 46 (2000).
Income: Per capita income: $17,713 (2000); Median household income: $34,704 (2000); Poverty rate: 11.0% (2000); Bankruptcy rate: 2.59% (2001).
Taxes: Total county taxes per capita: $199 (1997); County property taxes per capita: $192 (1997).
Education: High school graduation rate: 82.7% (2000); College graduation rate: 15.9% (2000).
Housing: Homeownership rate: 78.3% (2000); Median home value: $81,500 (2000); Median rent: $349 per month (2000); Median age of housing: 33 years (2000).
Health: Birth rate: 108.9 per 10,000 population (1998); Age adjusted death rate: 92.7 per 10,000 population (1999); Age adjusted cancer mortality rate: 229.2 deaths per 100,000 population (1999). Air Quality Index: 69% good, 30% moderate, 1% unhealthy (percent of days in 2000). Number of physicians: 10.3 per 10,000 population (1999); Number of hospital beds: 30.1 per 10,000 population (1999).
Elections: 2000 Presidential election results: 42.9% Gore, 54.3% Bush, 2.3% Nader, 0.0% Buchanan
National and State Parks: Ludington State Park
Additional Information Contacts
Mason County Government Offices. 231-843-8202
Ludington Chamber of Commerce. 231-845-0324
Mason Oceana Manistee Board of Realtors 231-845-1896

Mason County Communities

AMBER (township). Covers a land area of 27.611 square miles and a water area of 0.179 square miles. Located at 43.95° N. Lat.; 86.34° W. Long. Elevation is 681 feet.
History: Amber Township was formed in 1867, and probably named by Charles W. Jones for his hometown of Amber, Indiana.
Population: 2,054 (2000); Race: 95.7% White, 0.4% Black, 0.4% Asian, 0.1% American Indian and Alaska Native, 4.0% Hispanic of any race, 2.1% two or more races (2000); Density: 74.4 persons per square mile (2000); Age: 25.7% under 18, 15.6% over 64 (2000); Marriage status: 18.7% never married, 64.8% now married, 5.8% widowed, 10.7% divorced (2000); Foreign born: 1.8% (2000); Ancestry (includes multiple ancestries): 24.0% German, 12.7% Irish, 12.2% Polish, 11.8% English, 8.5% Other groups (2000).
Economy: Employment by occupation: 10.1% management, 14.4% professional, 14.4% services, 25.9% sales, 1.5% farming, 11.4% construction, 22.3% production (2000).
Income: Per capita income: $17,833 (2000); Median household income: $43,458 (2000); Poverty rate: 4.9% (2000).
Taxes: Total city taxes per capita: $44 (2000); City property taxes per capita: $44 (2000).
Education: High school graduation rate: 87.1% (2000); College graduation rate: 14.9% (2000).
Housing: Homeownership rate: 88.2% (2000); Median home value: $95,200 (2000); Median rent: $356 per month (2000); Median age of housing: 25 years (2000).
Transportation: Commute to work: 94.0% car, 0.2% public transportation, 2.0% walk, 3.0% work from home (2000); Travel time to work: 60.2% less than 15 minutes, 28.6% 15 to 30 minutes, 4.9% 30 to 45 minutes, 1.9% 45 to 60 minutes, 4.5% 60 minutes or more (2000)

BRANCH (township). Covers a land area of 35.446 square miles and a water area of 0.525 square miles. Located at 43.95° N. Lat.; 86.10° W. Long.
History: Branch was founded in 1875 as a lumber center, established around a station of the Pere Marquette Railway. Besides the sawmills, an early industry was pickle-making.
Population: 1,181 (2000); Race: 97.4% White, 0.6% Black, 0.0% Asian, 0.3% American Indian and Alaska Native, 1.9% Hispanic of any race, 0.6% two or more races (2000); Density: 33.3 persons per square mile (2000); Age: 20.3% under 18, 16.7% over 64 (2000); Marriage status: 17.5% never married, 59.6% now married, 9.5% widowed, 13.4% divorced (2000); Foreign born: 0.9% (2000); Ancestry (includes multiple ancestries): 25.9% German, 13.0% Irish, 10.5% English, 7.4% Dutch, 6.6% United States or American (2000).
Economy: Employment by occupation: 7.1% management, 17.1% professional, 18.8% services, 18.6% sales, 3.7% farming, 15.6% construction, 19.2% production (2000).
Income: Per capita income: $15,659 (2000); Median household income: $27,593 (2000); Poverty rate: 9.9% (2000).
Taxes: Total city taxes per capita: $27 (1997); City property taxes per capita: $27 (1997).
Education: High school graduation rate: 74.1% (2000); College graduation rate: 12.2% (2000).

Housing: Homeownership rate: 88.1% (2000); Median home value: $68,000 (2000); Median rent: $350 per month (2000); Median age of housing: 26 years (2000).
Transportation: Commute to work: 94.5% car, 0.0% public transportation, 0.7% walk, 4.9% work from home (2000); Travel time to work: 13.2% less than 15 minutes, 46.4% 15 to 30 minutes, 25.3% 30 to 45 minutes, 4.9% 45 to 60 minutes, 10.2% 60 minutes or more (2000)

CUSTER (village). Covers a land area of 0.992 square miles and a water area of 0 square miles. Located at 43.95° N. Lat.; 86.22° W. Long. Elevation is 698 feet.
History: Custer was founded in 1876 as a station on the Pere Marquette Railroad. The village and township were named for General George A. Custer (1839-1876).
Population: 318 (2000); Race: 92.8% White, 0.0% Black, 0.0% Asian, 1.0% American Indian and Alaska Native, 0.7% Hispanic of any race, 5.5% two or more races (2000); Density: 320.7 persons per square mile (2000); Age: 24.7% under 18, 17.1% over 64 (2000); Marriage status: 20.7% never married, 54.4% now married, 9.7% widowed, 15.2% divorced (2000); Foreign born: 0.0% (2000); Ancestry (includes multiple ancestries): 27.7% German, 15.4% Irish, 8.2% English, 7.9% Other groups, 6.5% Italian (2000).
Economy: Employment by occupation: 4.6% management, 7.6% professional, 22.1% services, 29.8% sales, 1.5% farming, 13.7% construction, 20.6% production (2000).
Income: Per capita income: $15,436 (2000); Median household income: $29,444 (2000); Poverty rate: 10.1% (2000).
Taxes: Total city taxes per capita: $33 (1997); City property taxes per capita: $33 (1997).
Education: High school graduation rate: 84.8% (2000); College graduation rate: 7.1% (2000).

School District(s)

Mason County Eastern Schools (KG-12)
2000 Enrollment: 628 231-757-3733

Housing: Homeownership rate: 71.1% (2000); Median home value: $65,600 (2000); Median rent: $369 per month (2000); Median age of housing: 46 years (2000).
Transportation: Commute to work: 88.7% car, 0.8% public transportation, 6.5% walk, 4.0% work from home (2000); Travel time to work: 36.1% less than 15 minutes, 36.1% 15 to 30 minutes, 11.8% 30 to 45 minutes, 4.2% 45 to 60 minutes, 11.8% 60 minutes or more (2000)

CUSTER (township). Covers a land area of 34.925 square miles and a water area of 0.061 square miles. Located at 43.94° N. Lat.; 86.22° W. Long. Elevation is 698 feet.
Population: 1,307 (2000); Race: 96.3% White, 0.2% Black, 0.0% Asian, 2.0% American Indian and Alaska Native, 0.6% Hispanic of any race, 1.4% two or more races (2000); Density: 37.4 persons per square mile (2000); Age: 23.9% under 18, 15.4% over 64 (2000); Marriage status: 21.4% never married, 62.3% now married, 8.0% widowed, 8.4% divorced (2000); Foreign born: 2.0% (2000); Ancestry (includes multiple ancestries): 31.2% German, 10.3% Irish, 8.6% English, 7.8% Polish, 6.4% Other groups (2000).
Economy: In farm and resort area; meat processing. Railroad junction to East at Walhalla. Employment by occupation: 10.1% management, 17.6% professional, 17.7% services, 21.6% sales, 1.4% farming, 11.1% construction, 20.4% production (2000).
Income: Per capita income: $17,407 (2000); Median household income: $36,597 (2000); Poverty rate: 9.8% (2000).
Taxes: Total city taxes per capita: $18 (1997); City property taxes per capita: $18 (1997).
Education: High school graduation rate: 83.4% (2000); College graduation rate: 15.6% (2000).
Housing: Homeownership rate: 85.0% (2000); Median home value: $68,000 (2000); Median rent: $378 per month (2000); Median age of housing: 44 years (2000).
Transportation: Commute to work: 89.5% car, 0.2% public transportation, 3.7% walk, 6.3% work from home (2000); Travel time to work: 31.1% less than 15 minutes, 49.6% 15 to 30 minutes, 10.1% 30 to 45 minutes, 2.8% 45 to 60 minutes, 6.4% 60 minutes or more (2000)

EDEN (township). Covers a land area of 35.419 square miles and a water area of 0.440 square miles. Located at 43.86° N. Lat.; 86.23° W. Long.
Population: 555 (2000); Race: 98.6% White, 0.0% Black, 0.0% Asian, 0.5% American Indian and Alaska Native, 0.0% Hispanic of any race, 0.6% two or more races (2000); Density: 15.7 persons per square mile (2000); Age: 30.3% under 18, 12.1% over 64 (2000); Marriage status: 23.3% never married, 64.9% now married, 5.3% widowed, 6.5% divorced (2000); Foreign born: 0.3% (2000); Ancestry (includes multiple ancestries): 33.1% German, 13.0% Irish, 10.9% English, 8.8% Dutch, 5.3% United States or American (2000).
Economy: Employment by occupation: 6.3% management, 11.1% professional, 9.4% services, 22.6% sales, 5.6% farming, 14.6% construction, 30.6% production (2000).
Income: Per capita income: $13,488 (2000); Median household income: $36,985 (2000); Poverty rate: 10.5% (2000).
Taxes: Total city taxes per capita: $24 (1997); City property taxes per capita: $24 (1997).
Education: High school graduation rate: 74.6% (2000); College graduation rate: 8.4% (2000).
Housing: Homeownership rate: 89.5% (2000); Median home value: $79,000 (2000); Median rent: $213 per month (2000); Median age of housing: 33 years (2000).
Transportation: Commute to work: 79.8% car, 7.8% public transportation, 2.1% walk, 9.6% work from home (2000); Travel time to work: 14.1% less than 15 minutes, 49.4% 15 to 30 minutes, 22.7% 30 to 45 minutes, 0.0% 45 to 60 minutes, 13.7% 60 minutes or more (2000)

FOUNTAIN (village). Covers a land area of 1.008 square miles and a water area of 0 square miles. Located at 44.04° N. Lat.; 86.17° W. Long. Elevation is 696 feet.
Population: 175 (2000); Race: 93.0% White, 0.0% Black, 0.0% Asian, 3.7% American Indian and Alaska Native, 1.1% Hispanic of any race, 1.6% two or more races (2000); Density: 173.7 persons per square mile (2000); Age: 20.3% under 18, 17.1% over 64 (2000); Marriage status: 16.8% never married, 59.1% now married, 14.1% widowed, 10.1% divorced (2000); Foreign born: 3.7% (2000); Ancestry (includes multiple ancestries): 30.5% German, 8.6% Dutch, 7.5% Irish, 7.0% Welsh, 4.8% English (2000).
Economy: In farm and resort area; lumber; cheese; pallets and boxes. Manistee National Forest to North and East. Employment by occupation: 8.4% management, 4.2% professional, 21.1% services, 26.3% sales, 0.0% farming, 12.6% construction, 27.4% production (2000).
Income: Per capita income: $19,396 (2000); Median household income: $30,000 (2000); Poverty rate: 5.5% (2000).
Taxes: Total city taxes per capita: $48 (1997); City property taxes per capita: $48 (1997).
Education: High school graduation rate: 81.7% (2000); College graduation rate: 4.0% (2000).
Housing: Homeownership rate: 85.9% (2000); Median home value: $62,700 (2000); Median rent: $313 per month (2000); Median age of housing: 50 years (2000).
Transportation: Commute to work: 100.0% car, 0.0% public transportation, 0.0% walk, 0.0% work from home (2000); Travel time to work: 24.1% less than 15 minutes, 35.6% 15 to 30 minutes, 40.2% 30 to 45 minutes, 0.0% 45 to 60 minutes, 0.0% 60 minutes or more (2000)

FREE SOIL (village). Aka Freesoil. Covers a land area of 1.034 square miles and a water area of 0 square miles. Located at 44.10° N. Lat.; 86.21° W. Long. Elevation is 677 feet.
Population: 177 (2000); Race: 94.4% White, 0.0% Black, 0.0% Asian, 1.0% American Indian and Alaska Native, 0.0% Hispanic of any race, 4.6% two or more races (2000); Density: 171.2 persons per square mile (2000); Age: 27.0% under 18, 22.4% over 64 (2000); Marriage status: 18.3% never married, 61.4% now married, 11.1% widowed, 9.2% divorced (2000); Foreign born: 0.0% (2000); Ancestry (includes multiple ancestries): 21.4% Polish, 17.9% German, 14.3% English, 11.2% United States or American, 10.2% Irish (2000).
Economy: Employment by occupation: 11.1% management, 3.2% professional, 39.7% services, 11.1% sales, 0.0% farming, 12.7% construction, 22.2% production (2000).
Income: Per capita income: $13,329 (2000); Median household income: $27,083 (2000); Poverty rate: 9.8% (2000).
Taxes: Total city taxes per capita: $25 (1997); City property taxes per capita: $25 (1997).
Education: High school graduation rate: 77.1% (2000); College graduation rate: 6.1% (2000).

School District(s)

Free Soil Community Schools (KG-12)
2000 Enrollment: 172 231-464-5651

Housing: Homeownership rate: 85.0% (2000); Median home value: $45,000 (2000); Median rent: $368 per month (2000); Median age of housing: 52 years (2000).
Transportation: Commute to work: 85.7% car, 0.0% public transportation, 3.2% walk, 11.1% work from home (2000); Travel time to work: 14.3% less

than 15 minutes, 67.9% 15 to 30 minutes, 5.4% 30 to 45 minutes, 0.0% 45 to 60 minutes, 12.5% 60 minutes or more (2000)

FREE SOIL (township). Aka Freesoil. Covers a land area of 38.703 square miles and a water area of 0.372 square miles. Located at 44.12° N. Lat.; 86.22° W. Long. Elevation is 677 feet.
Population: 809 (2000); Race: 93.2% White, 0.8% Black, 0.7% Asian, 1.0% American Indian and Alaska Native, 1.3% Hispanic of any race, 4.2% two or more races (2000); Density: 20.9 persons per square mile (2000); Age: 25.4% under 18, 18.8% over 64 (2000); Marriage status: 18.6% never married, 67.9% now married, 8.5% widowed, 4.9% divorced (2000); Foreign born: 1.5% (2000); Ancestry (includes multiple ancestries): 28.3% Polish, 19.6% German, 12.3% English, 7.3% Irish, 6.7% Other groups (2000).
Economy: Employment by occupation: 4.8% management, 12.3% professional, 23.4% services, 20.7% sales, 1.2% farming, 17.4% construction, 20.1% production (2000).
Income: Per capita income: $15,318 (2000); Median household income: $34,375 (2000); Poverty rate: 8.0% (2000).
Taxes: Total city taxes per capita: $15 (1997); City property taxes per capita: $15 (1997).
Education: High school graduation rate: 82.5% (2000); College graduation rate: 10.2% (2000).
Housing: Homeownership rate: 90.3% (2000); Median home value: $64,100 (2000); Median rent: $319 per month (2000); Median age of housing: 36 years (2000).
Transportation: Commute to work: 94.8% car, 0.6% public transportation, 0.6% walk, 4.0% work from home (2000); Travel time to work: 20.4% less than 15 minutes, 55.1% 15 to 30 minutes, 16.2% 30 to 45 minutes, 0.0% 45 to 60 minutes, 8.3% 60 minutes or more (2000)

GRANT (township). Covers a land area of 48.673 square miles and a water area of 0.190 square miles. Located at 44.13° N. Lat.; 86.36° W. Long.
History: Grant Township was organized in 1867 and named for Civil War General U.S. Grant.
Population: 850 (2000); Race: 94.6% White, 0.2% Black, 0.2% Asian, 1.9% American Indian and Alaska Native, 0.7% Hispanic of any race, 3.1% two or more races (2000); Density: 17.5 persons per square mile (2000); Age: 24.3% under 18, 10.4% over 64 (2000); Marriage status: 19.9% never married, 68.4% now married, 2.2% widowed, 9.4% divorced (2000); Foreign born: 1.0% (2000); Ancestry (includes multiple ancestries): 26.7% German, 23.1% Polish, 10.5% Irish, 9.8% United States or American, 7.9% English (2000).
Economy: Employment by occupation: 10.4% management, 9.9% professional, 19.1% services, 19.6% sales, 0.5% farming, 13.7% construction, 26.9% production (2000).
Income: Per capita income: $16,611 (2000); Median household income: $39,018 (2000); Poverty rate: 11.4% (2000).
Taxes: Total city taxes per capita: $100 (1997); City property taxes per capita: $99 (1997).
Education: High school graduation rate: 85.8% (2000); College graduation rate: 10.1% (2000).
Housing: Homeownership rate: 86.3% (2000); Median home value: $91,300 (2000); Median rent: $319 per month (2000); Median age of housing: 23 years (2000).
Transportation: Commute to work: 93.7% car, 0.0% public transportation, 1.9% walk, 2.9% work from home (2000); Travel time to work: 27.4% less than 15 minutes, 54.0% 15 to 30 minutes, 9.5% 30 to 45 minutes, 2.7% 45 to 60 minutes, 6.5% 60 minutes or more (2000)

HAMLIN (township). Covers a land area of 27.487 square miles and a water area of 6.887 square miles. Located at 44.03° N. Lat.; 86.44° W. Long.
Population: 3,192 (2000); Race: 94.7% White, 1.1% Black, 0.4% Asian, 0.5% American Indian and Alaska Native, 1.9% Hispanic of any race, 2.6% two or more races (2000); Density: 116.1 persons per square mile (2000); Age: 21.4% under 18, 17.4% over 64 (2000); Marriage status: 17.3% never married, 69.2% now married, 4.7% widowed, 8.8% divorced (2000); Foreign born: 1.7% (2000); Ancestry (includes multiple ancestries): 27.2% German, 13.4% English, 11.0% Irish, 10.1% United States or American, 9.6% Other groups (2000).
Economy: Employment by occupation: 10.7% management, 24.9% professional, 12.4% services, 24.6% sales, 0.5% farming, 8.2% construction, 18.7% production (2000).
Income: Per capita income: $21,658 (2000); Median household income: $41,594 (2000); Poverty rate: 7.0% (2000).
Taxes: Total city taxes per capita: $56 (1997); City property taxes per capita: $54 (1997).
Education: High school graduation rate: 85.1% (2000); College graduation rate: 19.9% (2000).
Housing: Homeownership rate: 93.3% (2000); Median home value: $115,300 (2000); Median rent: $393 per month (2000); Median age of housing: 25 years (2000).
Transportation: Commute to work: 93.6% car, 0.9% public transportation, 0.1% walk, 4.0% work from home (2000); Travel time to work: 51.0% less than 15 minutes, 37.5% 15 to 30 minutes, 6.2% 30 to 45 minutes, 0.4% 45 to 60 minutes, 5.0% 60 minutes or more (2000)

LOGAN (township). Covers a land area of 35.912 square miles and a water area of 0.129 square miles. Located at 43.85° N. Lat.; 86.11° W. Long.
Population: 329 (2000); Race: 98.8% White, 0.0% Black, 0.0% Asian, 0.0% American Indian and Alaska Native, 1.2% Hispanic of any race, 1.2% two or more races (2000); Density: 9.2 persons per square mile (2000); Age: 16.4% under 18, 21.9% over 64 (2000); Marriage status: 14.1% never married, 71.8% now married, 4.6% widowed, 9.5% divorced (2000); Foreign born: 0.6% (2000); Ancestry (includes multiple ancestries): 28.4% German, 11.1% United States or American, 11.1% English, 10.2% Dutch, 9.6% Polish (2000).
Economy: Employment by occupation: 10.7% management, 8.3% professional, 21.5% services, 24.0% sales, 2.5% farming, 5.8% construction, 27.3% production (2000).
Income: Per capita income: $16,762 (2000); Median household income: $30,341 (2000); Poverty rate: 14.2% (2000).
Taxes: Total city taxes per capita: $145 (1997); City property taxes per capita: $145 (1997).
Education: High school graduation rate: 80.6% (2000); College graduation rate: 8.7% (2000).
Housing: Homeownership rate: 88.7% (2000); Median home value: $86,500 (2000); Median rent: $345 per month (2000); Median age of housing: 20 years (2000).
Transportation: Commute to work: 93.0% car, 0.0% public transportation, 0.0% walk, 7.0% work from home (2000); Travel time to work: 15.1% less than 15 minutes, 43.4% 15 to 30 minutes, 27.4% 30 to 45 minutes, 6.6% 45 to 60 minutes, 7.5% 60 minutes or more (2000)

LUDINGTON (city). Covers a land area of 3.367 square miles and a water area of 0.327 square miles. Located at 43.95° N. Lat.; 86.44° W. Long. Elevation is 584 feet.
History: Ludington was first called Marquette, in honor of Father Jacques Marquette, the missionary and explorer, who died here in 1675. It was later renamed Ludington for James Ludington, a lumberman who lived here in the 1880's. Ludington became an important shipping center, bordering both Lake Michigan and Pere Marquette Lake, which provided a safe harbor for boats, ferries, and lake freighters.
Population: 8,357 (2000); Race: 94.0% White, 1.2% Black, 0.0% Asian, 1.0% American Indian and Alaska Native, 3.7% Hispanic of any race, 2.4% two or more races (2000); Density: 2,482.2 persons per square mile (2000); Age: 23.8% under 18, 19.6% over 64 (2000); Marriage status: 22.8% never married, 52.5% now married, 11.7% widowed, 12.9% divorced (2000); Foreign born: 1.7% (2000); Ancestry (includes multiple ancestries): 27.5% German, 13.1% Irish, 11.3% Other groups, 11.2% English, 10.0% Polish (2000).
Economy: Single-family building permits issued: 5 (2001) / 8 (2000); Multi-family building permits issued: 4 (2001) / 46 (2000); Employment by occupation: 8.8% management, 21.3% professional, 18.6% services, 22.9% sales, 0.9% farming, 9.8% construction, 17.7% production (2000).
Income: Per capita income: $17,215 (2000); Median household income: $28,089 (2000); Poverty rate: 16.3% (2000).
Taxes: Total city taxes per capita: $313 (1997); City property taxes per capita: $307 (1997).
Education: High school graduation rate: 82.1% (2000); College graduation rate: 18.1% (2000).

School District(s)

Ludington Area School District (KG-12)
2000 Enrollment: 2,715 231-845-7303
Housing: Homeownership rate: 58.6% (2000); Median home value: $73,000 (2000); Median rent: $355 per month (2000); Median age of housing: 53 years (2000).
Hospitals: Memorial Medical Center West Michigan (95 beds)
Safety: Violent crime rate: 34.5 per 10,000 population; Property crime rate: 465.4 per 10,000 population (2001).
Newspapers: Ludington Daily News (6 x week)
Transportation: Commute to work: 89.4% car, 1.8% public transportation, 4.9% walk, 3.0% work from home (2000); Travel time to work: 78.7% less

than 15 minutes, 13.8% 15 to 30 minutes, 4.6% 30 to 45 minutes, 0.7% 45 to 60 minutes, 2.2% 60 minutes or more (2000)
Airports: Mason County
Additional Information Contacts
Ludington Chamber of Commerce........................231-845-0324
Mason Oceana Manistee Board of Realtors................231-845-1896

MEADE (township). Covers a land area of 37.559 square miles and a water area of 0.086 square miles. Located at 44.14° N. Lat.; 86.09° W. Long.
Population: 287 (2000); Race: 80.2% White, 13.9% Black, 2.4% Asian, 1.4% American Indian and Alaska Native, 4.2% Hispanic of any race, 0.3% two or more races (2000); Density: 7.6 persons per square mile (2000); Age: 7.6% under 18, 6.9% over 64 (2000); Marriage status: 21.5% never married, 58.2% now married, 3.3% widowed, 17.1% divorced (2000); Foreign born: 0.0% (2000); Ancestry (includes multiple ancestries): 25.3% German, 15.6% Irish, 10.4% Other groups, 7.6% Polish, 7.3% English (2000).
Economy: Employment by occupation: 16.2% management, 13.2% professional, 4.4% services, 20.6% sales, 0.0% farming, 19.1% construction, 26.5% production (2000).
Income: Per capita income: $14,334 (2000); Median household income: $50,536 (2000); Poverty rate: 8.4% (2000).
Taxes: Total city taxes per capita: $113 (1997); City property taxes per capita: $113 (1997).
Education: High school graduation rate: 82.8% (2000); College graduation rate: 6.7% (2000).
Housing: Homeownership rate: 83.1% (2000); Median home value: $82,800 (2000); Median rent: $313 per month (2000); Median age of housing: 27 years (2000).
Transportation: Commute to work: 96.9% car, 0.0% public transportation, 0.0% walk, 3.1% work from home (2000); Travel time to work: 0.0% less than 15 minutes, 29.0% 15 to 30 minutes, 40.3% 30 to 45 minutes, 16.1% 45 to 60 minutes, 14.5% 60 minutes or more (2000)

PERE MARQUETTE CHARTER (township). Covers a land area of 14.097 square miles and a water area of 1.647 square miles. Located at 43.94° N. Lat.; 86.42° W. Long.
Population: 2,228 (2000); Race: 98.8% White, 0.3% Black, 0.0% Asian, 0.1% American Indian and Alaska Native, 1.9% Hispanic of any race, 0.2% two or more races (2000); Density: 158.0 persons per square mile (2000); Age: 25.6% under 18, 17.7% over 64 (2000); Marriage status: 17.2% never married, 66.3% now married, 7.9% widowed, 8.6% divorced (2000); Foreign born: 2.7% (2000); Ancestry (includes multiple ancestries): 29.4% German, 15.5% English, 12.2% Irish, 10.2% Polish, 7.7% Swedish (2000).
Economy: Single-family building permits issued: 28 (2001) / 21 (2000); Multi-family building permits issued: 0 (2001) / 0 (2000); Employment by occupation: 12.0% management, 23.1% professional, 18.0% services, 22.3% sales, 1.1% farming, 7.1% construction, 16.3% production (2000).
Income: Per capita income: $21,160 (2000); Median household income: $44,432 (2000); Poverty rate: 4.5% (2000).
Taxes: Total city taxes per capita: $300 (1997); City property taxes per capita: $291 (1997).
Education: High school graduation rate: 90.1% (2000); College graduation rate: 23.6% (2000).
Housing: Homeownership rate: 88.3% (2000); Median home value: $123,300 (2000); Median rent: $413 per month (2000); Median age of housing: 30 years (2000).
Transportation: Commute to work: 94.1% car, 0.0% public transportation, 0.6% walk, 4.8% work from home (2000); Travel time to work: 66.4% less than 15 minutes, 19.5% 15 to 30 minutes, 8.8% 30 to 45 minutes, 1.5% 45 to 60 minutes, 3.9% 60 minutes or more (2000)

RIVERTON (township). Covers a land area of 35.224 square miles and a water area of 0.419 square miles. Located at 43.86° N. Lat.; 86.32° W. Long.
Population: 1,335 (2000); Race: 94.8% White, 0.8% Black, 0.0% Asian, 0.2% American Indian and Alaska Native, 6.8% Hispanic of any race, 1.3% two or more races (2000); Density: 37.9 persons per square mile (2000); Age: 31.7% under 18, 11.5% over 64 (2000); Marriage status: 24.0% never married, 64.9% now married, 4.3% widowed, 6.8% divorced (2000); Foreign born: 1.5% (2000); Ancestry (includes multiple ancestries): 38.7% German, 11.3% Irish, 9.1% English, 9.1% Other groups, 8.4% Polish (2000).
Economy: Employment by occupation: 13.7% management, 17.0% professional, 14.2% services, 20.5% sales, 1.9% farming, 10.4% construction, 22.3% production (2000).
Income: Per capita income: $14,566 (2000); Median household income: $38,482 (2000); Poverty rate: 16.8% (2000).
Taxes: Total city taxes per capita: $20 (1997); City property taxes per capita: $20 (1997).
Education: High school graduation rate: 78.6% (2000); College graduation rate: 16.0% (2000).
Housing: Homeownership rate: 88.3% (2000); Median home value: $73,400 (2000); Median rent: $350 per month (2000); Median age of housing: 47 years (2000).
Transportation: Commute to work: 82.5% car, 0.0% public transportation, 1.8% walk, 14.8% work from home (2000); Travel time to work: 26.4% less than 15 minutes, 55.0% 15 to 30 minutes, 10.0% 30 to 45 minutes, 2.9% 45 to 60 minutes, 5.6% 60 minutes or more (2000)

SCOTTVILLE (city). Covers a land area of 1.461 square miles and a water area of 0 square miles. Located at 43.95° N. Lat.; 86.28° W. Long. Elevation is 678 feet.
History: Scottville was settled in 1876 and first called Mason Center. In 1881 it was renamed Sweetland in honor of James Sweetland, who platted the community. When it was incorporated as a village in 1889, the name was changed to Scottville to honor Hiram Scott, an early resident. All three names continued to be used until 1907, when incorporation as a city settled the name of Scottville.
Population: 1,266 (2000); Race: 92.2% White, 1.0% Black, 0.1% Asian, 1.0% American Indian and Alaska Native, 9.8% Hispanic of any race, 4.9% two or more races (2000); Density: 866.5 persons per square mile (2000); Age: 27.9% under 18, 16.4% over 64 (2000); Marriage status: 25.4% never married, 47.8% now married, 8.5% widowed, 18.3% divorced (2000); Foreign born: 2.5% (2000); Ancestry (includes multiple ancestries): 27.2% German, 13.9% Other groups, 12.0% Irish, 11.6% English, 6.0% Swedish (2000).
Economy: Employment by occupation: 6.9% management, 16.4% professional, 23.3% services, 21.0% sales, 4.6% farming, 8.1% construction, 19.7% production (2000).
Income: Per capita income: $15,703 (2000); Median household income: $27,750 (2000); Poverty rate: 18.4% (2000).
Taxes: Total city taxes per capita: $252 (1997); City property taxes per capita: $250 (1997).
Education: High school graduation rate: 80.9% (2000); College graduation rate: 11.6% (2000).

School District(s)

Mason County Central Schools (KG-12)
2000 Enrollment: 1,640..........................231-757-3713

Two-year College(s)

West Shore Community College (Public)
2001 Enrollment: 1,280..........................231-845-6211
2001 Tuition: In-state $2,034; Out-of-state $2,544
Housing: Homeownership rate: 67.9% (2000); Median home value: $53,500 (2000); Median rent: $314 per month (2000); Median age of housing: 50 years (2000).
Safety: Violent crime rate: 23.6 per 10,000 population; Property crime rate: 243.5 per 10,000 population (2001).
Transportation: Commute to work: 89.4% car, 1.0% public transportation, 5.7% walk, 3.1% work from home (2000); Travel time to work: 51.6% less than 15 minutes, 33.8% 15 to 30 minutes, 8.9% 30 to 45 minutes, 1.0% 45 to 60 minutes, 4.7% 60 minutes or more (2000)

SHERIDAN (township). Covers a land area of 34.352 square miles and a water area of 1.579 square miles. Located at 44.02° N. Lat.; 86.11° W. Long.
Population: 969 (2000); Race: 98.2% White, 0.0% Black, 0.0% Asian, 1.2% American Indian and Alaska Native, 1.7% Hispanic of any race, 0.6% two or more races (2000); Density: 28.2 persons per square mile (2000); Age: 22.1% under 18, 15.3% over 64 (2000); Marriage status: 19.2% never married, 64.0% now married, 6.9% widowed, 9.9% divorced (2000); Foreign born: 0.4% (2000); Ancestry (includes multiple ancestries): 18.4% German, 14.2% English, 9.9% Irish, 9.1% Other groups, 8.1% Polish (2000).
Economy: Employment by occupation: 15.4% management, 13.2% professional, 13.9% services, 23.2% sales, 0.2% farming, 10.2% construction, 23.9% production (2000).
Income: Per capita income: $17,679 (2000); Median household income: $30,357 (2000); Poverty rate: 15.3% (2000).
Taxes: Total city taxes per capita: $34 (1997); City property taxes per capita: $28 (1997).
Education: High school graduation rate: 74.9% (2000); College graduation rate: 9.2% (2000).
Housing: Homeownership rate: 90.1% (2000); Median home value: $66,300 (2000); Median rent: $358 per month (2000); Median age of housing: 26 years (2000).

Transportation: Commute to work: 93.7% car, 0.0% public transportation, 1.2% walk, 3.6% work from home (2000); Travel time to work: 8.3% less than 15 minutes, 34.7% 15 to 30 minutes, 44.5% 30 to 45 minutes, 3.0% 45 to 60 minutes, 9.5% 60 minutes or more (2000)

SHERMAN (township). Covers a land area of 36.163 square miles and a water area of 0.058 square miles. Located at 44.04° N. Lat.; 86.20° W. Long.
History: Sherman Township was organized in 1867 and named for General William T. Sherman.
Population: 1,090 (2000); Race: 95.6% White, 0.6% Black, 0.1% Asian, 1.9% American Indian and Alaska Native, 0.6% Hispanic of any race, 1.5% two or more races (2000); Density: 30.1 persons per square mile (2000); Age: 25.9% under 18, 11.4% over 64 (2000); Marriage status: 18.0% never married, 66.6% now married, 6.0% widowed, 9.4% divorced (2000); Foreign born: 1.8% (2000); Ancestry (includes multiple ancestries): 23.6% German, 12.3% Polish, 9.6% Irish, 8.7% English, 6.8% Swedish (2000).
Economy: Employment by occupation: 8.2% management, 11.7% professional, 13.9% services, 22.8% sales, 1.8% farming, 12.6% construction, 29.0% production (2000).
Income: Per capita income: $16,251 (2000); Median household income: $34,083 (2000); Poverty rate: 4.8% (2000).
Taxes: Total city taxes per capita: $18 (1997); City property taxes per capita: $18 (1997).
Education: High school graduation rate: 81.6% (2000); College graduation rate: 9.5% (2000).
Housing: Homeownership rate: 89.0% (2000); Median home value: $65,200 (2000); Median rent: $320 per month (2000); Median age of housing: 37 years (2000).
Transportation: Commute to work: 93.8% car, 0.0% public transportation, 1.9% walk, 3.8% work from home (2000); Travel time to work: 26.6% less than 15 minutes, 45.3% 15 to 30 minutes, 20.9% 30 to 45 minutes, 2.2% 45 to 60 minutes, 5.1% 60 minutes or more (2000)

SUMMIT (township). Covers a land area of 12.859 square miles and a water area of 1.447 square miles. Located at 43.84° N. Lat.; 86.41° W. Long.
Population: 1,021 (2000); Race: 95.4% White, 0.0% Black, 0.5% Asian, 1.1% American Indian and Alaska Native, 3.0% Hispanic of any race, 1.1% two or more races (2000); Density: 79.4 persons per square mile (2000); Age: 23.6% under 18, 20.6% over 64 (2000); Marriage status: 14.9% never married, 70.4% now married, 6.8% widowed, 7.9% divorced (2000); Foreign born: 1.8% (2000); Ancestry (includes multiple ancestries): 31.5% German, 14.9% English, 9.9% Polish, 8.9% Irish, 5.8% Other groups (2000).
Economy: Employment by occupation: 14.6% management, 20.2% professional, 10.1% services, 25.2% sales, 1.6% farming, 16.9% construction, 11.5% production (2000).
Income: Per capita income: $20,335 (2000); Median household income: $44,432 (2000); Poverty rate: 3.1% (2000).
Taxes: Total city taxes per capita: $103 (1997); City property taxes per capita: $103 (1997).
Education: High school graduation rate: 86.2% (2000); College graduation rate: 17.9% (2000).
Housing: Homeownership rate: 92.3% (2000); Median home value: $95,000 (2000); Median rent: $390 per month (2000); Median age of housing: 32 years (2000).
Transportation: Commute to work: 92.4% car, 0.0% public transportation, 1.2% walk, 6.5% work from home (2000); Travel time to work: 23.9% less than 15 minutes, 62.3% 15 to 30 minutes, 6.9% 30 to 45 minutes, 3.0% 45 to 60 minutes, 3.9% 60 minutes or more (2000)

VICTORY (township). Covers a land area of 35.909 square miles and a water area of 0.557 square miles. Located at 44.03° N. Lat.; 86.34° W. Long.
Population: 1,444 (2000); Race: 96.5% White, 0.3% Black, 0.4% Asian, 1.4% American Indian and Alaska Native, 2.7% Hispanic of any race, 0.8% two or more races (2000); Density: 40.2 persons per square mile (2000); Age: 23.6% under 18, 15.7% over 64 (2000); Marriage status: 20.6% never married, 63.4% now married, 7.0% widowed, 9.0% divorced (2000); Foreign born: 0.9% (2000); Ancestry (includes multiple ancestries): 27.4% German, 9.9% English, 9.4% Irish, 9.3% Polish, 8.8% Other groups (2000).
Economy: Employment by occupation: 12.3% management, 14.0% professional, 15.5% services, 15.5% sales, 3.0% farming, 14.6% construction, 25.0% production (2000).
Income: Per capita income: $17,140 (2000); Median household income: $41,667 (2000); Poverty rate: 7.8% (2000).
Taxes: Total city taxes per capita: $21 (1997); City property taxes per capita: $21 (1997).
Education: High school graduation rate: 79.4% (2000); College graduation rate: 11.6% (2000).
Housing: Homeownership rate: 86.1% (2000); Median home value: $85,600 (2000); Median rent: $343 per month (2000); Median age of housing: 26 years (2000).
Transportation: Commute to work: 90.3% car, 0.0% public transportation, 2.7% walk, 6.3% work from home (2000); Travel time to work: 28.5% less than 15 minutes, 52.8% 15 to 30 minutes, 11.6% 30 to 45 minutes, 1.0% 45 to 60 minutes, 6.2% 60 minutes or more (2000)

Mecosta County

Located in central Michigan; drained by the Muskegon, Little Muskegon, Chippewa, and Pine Rivers; includes part of Manistee National Forest. Covers a land area of 555.70 square miles, a water area of 15.40 square miles, and is located in the Eastern Time Zone. The county government was organized in 1859. County seat is Big Rapids.

Weather Station: Big Rapids Waterworks Elevation: 928 feet

	Jan	Feb	Mar	Apr	May	Jun	Jul	Aug	Sep	Oct	Nov	Dec
High	28	32	42	56	69	78	82	79	71	58	44	33
Low	11	13	21	32	43	52	57	55	47	36	28	18
Precip	2.2	1.5	2.4	2.9	3.1	3.2	2.6	4.2	4.0	3.0	3.0	2.3
Snow	20.6	13.1	9.9	2.3	tr	0.0	0.0	0.0	tr	0.4	6.6	16.4

High and Low temperatures in degrees Fahrenheit; Precipitation and Snow in inches

Population: 40,553 (2000); Race: 92.8% White, 3.5% Black, 0.6% Asian, 0.6% American Indian and Alaska Native, 1.2% Hispanic of any race, 2.0% two or more races (2000); Density: 73.0 persons per square mile (2000); Age: 22.5% under 18, 13.1% over 64 (2000).
Religion: Five largest groups: 7.5% Catholic Church, 3.7% The United Methodist Church, 2.8% Lutheran Church—Missouri Synod, 1.4% United Church of Christ, 1.4% The Wesleyan Church (2000).
Economy: Unemployment rate: 4.3% (11/2002); Total civilian labor force: 19,409 (11/2002); Leading industries: 21.2% manufacturing; 20.5% retail trade; 16.4% accommodation & food services (2000); Companies that employ more than 1,000 persons: 0 (2000); Companies that employ more than 100 persons: 15 (2000); Farms: 597 totaling 111,974 acres (1997); Minority business ownership rate: 0.0% (1997); Women business ownership rate: 19.0% (1997); Retail sales per capita: $7,643 (1997). Single-family building permits issued: 247 (2001) / 263 (2000); Multi-family building permits issued: 34 (2001) / 0 (2000).
Income: Per capita income: $16,372 (2000); Median household income: $33,849 (2000); Poverty rate: 16.1% (2000); Bankruptcy rate: 3.38% (2001).
Taxes: Total county taxes per capita: $122 (1997); County property taxes per capita: $112 (1997).
Education: High school graduation rate: 83.8% (2000); College graduation rate: 19.1% (2000).
Housing: Homeownership rate: 73.6% (2000); Median home value: $90,100 (2000); Median rent: $399 per month (2000); Median age of housing: 27 years (2000).
Health: Birth rate: 120.8 per 10,000 population (1998); Age adjusted death rate: 83.0 per 10,000 population (1999); Age adjusted cancer mortality rate: 195.4 deaths per 100,000 population (1999). Number of physicians: 9.1 per 10,000 population (1999); Number of hospital beds: 12.3 per 10,000 population (1999).
Elections: 2000 Presidential election results: 42.7% Gore, 54.7% Bush, 2.2% Nader, 0.0% Buchanan
National and State Parks: Haymarsh Lake State Game Area
Additional Information Contacts
Mecosta County Government Offices 231-592-0184
Big Rapids Chamber of Commerce 231-796-7649

Mecosta County Communities

AETNA (township). Covers a land area of 35.615 square miles and a water area of 0.307 square miles. Located at 43.49° N. Lat.; 85.47° W. Long.
Population: 2,044 (2000); Race: 95.4% White, 0.6% Black, 0.1% Asian, 1.2% American Indian and Alaska Native, 0.7% Hispanic of any race, 2.4% two or more races (2000); Density: 57.4 persons per square mile (2000); Age: 30.3% under 18, 9.0% over 64 (2000); Marriage status: 24.8% never married, 56.0% now married, 5.6% widowed, 13.6% divorced (2000); Foreign born: 0.8% (2000); Ancestry (includes multiple ancestries): 18.4% German, 12.4% Irish, 11.6% United States or American, 11.1% English, 9.2% Other groups (2000).

Economy: Employment by occupation: 9.6% management, 6.7% professional, 18.5% services, 16.2% sales, 0.9% farming, 20.7% construction, 27.4% production (2000).
Income: Per capita income: $14,141 (2000); Median household income: $34,571 (2000); Poverty rate: 18.3% (2000).
Taxes: Total city taxes per capita: $16 (1997); City property taxes per capita: $16 (1997).
Education: High school graduation rate: 78.2% (2000); College graduation rate: 4.7% (2000).
Housing: Homeownership rate: 82.2% (2000); Median home value: $75,500 (2000); Median rent: $365 per month (2000); Median age of housing: 25 years (2000).
Transportation: Commute to work: 90.7% car, 0.5% public transportation, 2.4% walk, 5.0% work from home (2000); Travel time to work: 16.9% less than 15 minutes, 21.6% 15 to 30 minutes, 18.1% 30 to 45 minutes, 23.8% 45 to 60 minutes, 19.6% 60 minutes or more (2000)

AUSTIN (township). Covers a land area of 35.659 square miles and a water area of 0.049 square miles. Located at 43.59° N. Lat.; 85.37° W. Long.
History: Austin Township was organized in 1869.
Population: 1,415 (2000); Race: 98.1% White, 0.9% Black, 0.0% Asian, 0.1% American Indian and Alaska Native, 0.7% Hispanic of any race, 0.6% two or more races (2000); Density: 39.7 persons per square mile (2000); Age: 31.2% under 18, 14.7% over 64 (2000); Marriage status: 18.4% never married, 67.9% now married, 5.7% widowed, 8.0% divorced (2000); Foreign born: 0.9% (2000); Ancestry (includes multiple ancestries): 24.9% German, 15.8% English, 10.0% Irish, 8.9% United States or American, 6.6% Dutch (2000).
Economy: Employment by occupation: 14.0% management, 12.4% professional, 12.0% services, 22.2% sales, 1.6% farming, 11.7% construction, 26.0% production (2000).
Income: Per capita income: $15,986 (2000); Median household income: $34,674 (2000); Poverty rate: 11.6% (2000).
Taxes: Total city taxes per capita: $42 (1997); City property taxes per capita: $41 (1997).
Education: High school graduation rate: 82.7% (2000); College graduation rate: 14.5% (2000).
Housing: Homeownership rate: 90.3% (2000); Median home value: $94,700 (2000); Median rent: $419 per month (2000); Median age of housing: 23 years (2000).
Transportation: Commute to work: 86.2% car, 1.7% public transportation, 0.9% walk, 10.8% work from home (2000); Travel time to work: 18.3% less than 15 minutes, 48.8% 15 to 30 minutes, 9.1% 30 to 45 minutes, 9.3% 45 to 60 minutes, 14.4% 60 minutes or more (2000)

BARRYTON (village). Covers a land area of 0.946 square miles and a water area of 0.080 square miles. Located at 43.75° N. Lat.; 85.14° W. Long. Elevation is 976 feet.
History: Barryton was founded in 1894 by Frank Barry, who opened a grocery and drug store.
Population: 381 (2000); Race: 96.8% White, 0.0% Black, 0.0% Asian, 1.0% American Indian and Alaska Native, 1.0% Hispanic of any race, 2.2% two or more races (2000); Density: 402.6 persons per square mile (2000); Age: 32.3% under 18, 15.6% over 64 (2000); Marriage status: 20.2% never married, 57.5% now married, 9.9% widowed, 12.3% divorced (2000); Foreign born: 0.5% (2000); Ancestry (includes multiple ancestries): 30.3% German, 10.7% Dutch, 9.4% Irish, 8.2% Scottish, 7.9% English (2000).
Economy: Employment by occupation: 1.3% management, 12.5% professional, 25.7% services, 21.1% sales, 1.3% farming, 8.6% construction, 29.6% production (2000).
Income: Per capita income: $12,166 (2000); Median household income: $23,333 (2000); Poverty rate: 18.0% (2000).
Taxes: Total city taxes per capita: $69 (1997); City property taxes per capita: $69 (1997).
Education: High school graduation rate: 78.9% (2000); College graduation rate: 12.4% (2000).
Housing: Homeownership rate: 69.5% (2000); Median home value: $43,100 (2000); Median rent: $233 per month (2000); Median age of housing: 52 years (2000).
Transportation: Commute to work: 88.5% car, 1.4% public transportation, 8.8% walk, 1.4% work from home (2000); Travel time to work: 32.2% less than 15 minutes, 19.9% 15 to 30 minutes, 28.1% 30 to 45 minutes, 14.4% 45 to 60 minutes, 5.5% 60 minutes or more (2000)

BIG RAPIDS (city). Covers a land area of 4.245 square miles and a water area of 0.148 square miles. Located at 43.69° N. Lat.; 85.48° W. Long. Elevation is 928 feet.
History: Big Rapids was first known as Leonard, for an early settler, but the rapids on the Muskegon River became the feature by which the community was known. The first house was built here in 1854. A lumber boom brought early growth to the settlement. When the timber was depleted, Big Rapids became a year-round vacation resort. Natural gas was discovered here in the early 1930's, giving a boost to the economy.
Population: 10,849 (2000); Race: 83.6% White, 11.1% Black, 1.7% Asian, 0.5% American Indian and Alaska Native, 1.7% Hispanic of any race, 2.5% two or more races (2000); Density: 2,555.5 persons per square mile (2000); Age: 14.3% under 18, 7.5% over 64 (2000); Marriage status: 47.4% never married, 40.8% now married, 4.3% widowed, 7.5% divorced (2000); Foreign born: 3.6% (2000); Ancestry (includes multiple ancestries): 24.2% German, 13.8% Other groups, 11.5% Irish, 8.3% English, 6.5% Polish (2000).
Vital Statistics: Birth rate: 99.6 per 10,000 population (1998)
Economy: Single-family building permits issued: 14 (2001) / 6 (2000); Multi-family building permits issued: 4 (2001) / 0 (2000); Employment by occupation: 6.2% management, 22.4% professional, 25.0% services, 29.3% sales, 0.1% farming, 5.8% construction, 11.3% production (2000).
Income: Per capita income: $10,719 (2000); Median household income: $20,192 (2000); Poverty rate: 35.0% (2000).
Taxes: Total city taxes per capita: $262 (1997); City property taxes per capita: $136 (1997).
Education: High school graduation rate: 87.3% (2000); College graduation rate: 31.7% (2000).

School District(s)

Big Rapids Public Schools (KG-12)
2000 Enrollment: 2,257 231-796-2627
Crossroads Charter Academy (KG-10)
2000 Enrollment: 449 616-895-3029

Four-year College(s)

Ferris State University (Public)
2001 Enrollment: 10,930 231-591-2000
2001 Tuition: In-state $4,670; Out-of-state $9,890

Housing: Homeownership rate: 35.1% (2000); Median home value: $75,400 (2000); Median rent: $419 per month (2000); Median age of housing: 36 years (2000).
Hospitals: Mecosta County General Hospital (74 beds)
Newspapers: The Pioneer (6 x week)
Transportation: Commute to work: 73.8% car, 1.8% public transportation, 19.0% walk, 2.8% work from home (2000); Travel time to work: 74.3% less than 15 minutes, 13.1% 15 to 30 minutes, 3.4% 30 to 45 minutes, 3.0% 45 to 60 minutes, 6.1% 60 minutes or more (2000); Amtrak: Service available.
Additional Information Contacts
Big Rapids Chamber of Commerce 231-796-7649

BIG RAPIDS (township). Covers a land area of 30.671 square miles and a water area of 0.370 square miles. Located at 43.68° N. Lat.; 85.49° W. Long. Elevation is 928 feet.
History: Incorporated 1869.
Population: 3,249 (2000); Race: 95.3% White, 1.1% Black, 1.5% Asian, 0.2% American Indian and Alaska Native, 0.4% Hispanic of any race, 2.0% two or more races (2000); Density: 105.9 persons per square mile (2000); Age: 24.7% under 18, 13.0% over 64 (2000); Marriage status: 26.6% never married, 62.9% now married, 4.1% widowed, 6.3% divorced (2000); Foreign born: 2.9% (2000); Ancestry (includes multiple ancestries): 26.9% German, 16.8% English, 12.7% Irish, 8.6% United States or American, 7.4% Other groups (2000).
Economy: Agriculture and light manufacturing include fabricated metal products, transportation equipment, tools, footwear, building materials; publishing. Big Rapids serves as a shipping point for the region's grains. Extensive natural gas wells are nearby. Airport here. Employment by occupation: 10.6% management, 30.2% professional, 12.9% services, 24.3% sales, 0.0% farming, 9.0% construction, 13.0% production (2000).
Income: Per capita income: $22,761 (2000); Median household income: $47,933 (2000); Poverty rate: 10.6% (2000).
Taxes: Total city taxes per capita: $37 (1997); City property taxes per capita: $36 (1997).
Education: High school graduation rate: 89.7% (2000); College graduation rate: 35.7% (2000).
Housing: Homeownership rate: 79.0% (2000); Median home value: $112,300 (2000); Median rent: $552 per month (2000); Median age of housing: 24 years (2000).

Transportation: Commute to work: 92.8% car, 0.0% public transportation, 1.4% walk, 5.4% work from home (2000); Travel time to work: 61.5% less than 15 minutes, 23.0% 15 to 30 minutes, 4.8% 30 to 45 minutes, 5.1% 45 to 60 minutes, 5.6% 60 minutes or more (2000); Amtrak: Service available.

CANADIAN LAKES (CDP). Covers a land area of 9.499 square miles and a water area of 1.161 square miles. Located at 43.58° N. Lat.; 85.30° W. Long.
Population: 1,922 (2000); Race: 98.2% White, 0.9% Black, 0.1% Asian, 0.0% American Indian and Alaska Native, 0.4% Hispanic of any race, 0.7% two or more races (2000); Density: 202.3 persons per square mile (2000); Age: 11.0% under 18, 36.4% over 64 (2000); Marriage status: 7.8% never married, 80.9% now married, 6.5% widowed, 4.9% divorced (2000); Foreign born: 2.9% (2000); Ancestry (includes multiple ancestries): 30.6% German, 20.2% English, 12.7% Irish, 10.7% Polish, 5.9% French (except Basque) (2000).
Economy: Employment by occupation: 22.7% management, 23.2% professional, 10.6% services, 26.3% sales, 0.0% farming, 9.5% construction, 7.8% production (2000).
Income: Per capita income: $30,770 (2000); Median household income: $51,595 (2000); Poverty rate: 5.1% (2000).
Education: High school graduation rate: 93.8% (2000); College graduation rate: 31.9% (2000).
Housing: Homeownership rate: 95.0% (2000); Median home value: $148,500 (2000); Median rent: $566 per month (2000); Median age of housing: 14 years (2000).
Transportation: Commute to work: 91.0% car, 0.0% public transportation, 0.9% walk, 7.7% work from home (2000); Travel time to work: 25.7% less than 15 minutes, 30.7% 15 to 30 minutes, 16.8% 30 to 45 minutes, 7.8% 45 to 60 minutes, 19.0% 60 minutes or more (2000)

CHIPPEWA (township). Covers a land area of 33.072 square miles and a water area of 2.357 square miles. Located at 43.76° N. Lat.; 85.27° W. Long.
Population: 1,239 (2000); Race: 99.3% White, 0.0% Black, 0.0% Asian, 0.0% American Indian and Alaska Native, 0.3% Hispanic of any race, 0.7% two or more races (2000); Density: 37.5 persons per square mile (2000); Age: 19.7% under 18, 19.3% over 64 (2000); Marriage status: 20.7% never married, 58.2% now married, 7.1% widowed, 14.0% divorced (2000); Foreign born: 0.9% (2000); Ancestry (includes multiple ancestries): 26.3% German, 14.1% Irish, 14.0% English, 8.3% United States or American, 7.4% Other groups (2000).
Economy: Employment by occupation: 9.3% management, 10.2% professional, 13.3% services, 21.8% sales, 1.9% farming, 10.0% construction, 33.5% production (2000).
Income: Per capita income: $17,336 (2000); Median household income: $33,859 (2000); Poverty rate: 10.0% (2000).
Taxes: Total city taxes per capita: $67 (1997); City property taxes per capita: $67 (1997).
Education: High school graduation rate: 78.1% (2000); College graduation rate: 9.7% (2000).
Housing: Homeownership rate: 85.8% (2000); Median home value: $75,900 (2000); Median rent: $392 per month (2000); Median age of housing: 32 years (2000).
Transportation: Commute to work: 93.3% car, 0.0% public transportation, 1.3% walk, 5.2% work from home (2000); Travel time to work: 11.8% less than 15 minutes, 58.1% 15 to 30 minutes, 16.2% 30 to 45 minutes, 5.0% 45 to 60 minutes, 8.9% 60 minutes or more (2000)

COLFAX (township). Covers a land area of 35.131 square miles and a water area of 0.672 square miles. Located at 43.68° N. Lat.; 85.38° W. Long.
History: Colfax Township was organized in 1869 and named for Vice President Schuyler Colfax.
Population: 1,975 (2000); Race: 97.0% White, 0.9% Black, 0.0% Asian, 0.7% American Indian and Alaska Native, 0.0% Hispanic of any race, 1.4% two or more races (2000); Density: 56.2 persons per square mile (2000); Age: 27.7% under 18, 11.1% over 64 (2000); Marriage status: 24.4% never married, 60.7% now married, 5.2% widowed, 9.7% divorced (2000); Foreign born: 1.7% (2000); Ancestry (includes multiple ancestries): 26.5% German, 12.9% Irish, 12.6% English, 8.5% Dutch, 5.8% Polish (2000).
Economy: Employment by occupation: 9.7% management, 23.4% professional, 11.0% services, 26.9% sales, 0.8% farming, 8.5% construction, 19.6% production (2000).
Income: Per capita income: $19,418 (2000); Median household income: $46,071 (2000); Poverty rate: 8.9% (2000).
Taxes: Total city taxes per capita: $17 (1997); City property taxes per capita: $17 (1997).
Education: High school graduation rate: 84.7% (2000); College graduation rate: 26.2% (2000).
Housing: Homeownership rate: 88.7% (2000); Median home value: $112,200 (2000); Median rent: $435 per month (2000); Median age of housing: 26 years (2000).
Transportation: Commute to work: 93.7% car, 0.0% public transportation, 1.0% walk, 4.6% work from home (2000); Travel time to work: 48.1% less than 15 minutes, 31.6% 15 to 30 minutes, 8.0% 30 to 45 minutes, 3.4% 45 to 60 minutes, 8.9% 60 minutes or more (2000)

DEERFIELD (township). Covers a land area of 35.751 square miles and a water area of 0.133 square miles. Located at 43.50° N. Lat.; 85.40° W. Long.
Population: 1,630 (2000); Race: 95.8% White, 0.9% Black, 0.2% Asian, 1.1% American Indian and Alaska Native, 2.7% Hispanic of any race, 1.4% two or more races (2000); Density: 45.6 persons per square mile (2000); Age: 33.2% under 18, 10.0% over 64 (2000); Marriage status: 23.8% never married, 64.3% now married, 4.8% widowed, 7.1% divorced (2000); Foreign born: 0.7% (2000); Ancestry (includes multiple ancestries): 24.9% German, 11.7% English, 8.9% Other groups, 8.0% United States or American, 7.9% Irish (2000).
Economy: Employment by occupation: 9.8% management, 12.1% professional, 14.5% services, 21.0% sales, 2.1% farming, 9.9% construction, 30.6% production (2000).
Income: Per capita income: $13,693 (2000); Median household income: $36,293 (2000); Poverty rate: 13.4% (2000).
Taxes: Total city taxes per capita: $11 (1997); City property taxes per capita: $11 (1997).
Education: High school graduation rate: 77.3% (2000); College graduation rate: 11.1% (2000).
Housing: Homeownership rate: 84.5% (2000); Median home value: $75,900 (2000); Median rent: $395 per month (2000); Median age of housing: 28 years (2000).
Transportation: Commute to work: 90.0% car, 0.9% public transportation, 3.0% walk, 5.3% work from home (2000); Travel time to work: 20.2% less than 15 minutes, 22.3% 15 to 30 minutes, 13.2% 30 to 45 minutes, 22.5% 45 to 60 minutes, 21.8% 60 minutes or more (2000)

FORK (township). Covers a land area of 34.953 square miles and a water area of 0.317 square miles. Located at 43.76° N. Lat.; 85.14° W. Long.
Population: 1,678 (2000); Race: 97.5% White, 0.5% Black, 0.0% Asian, 0.8% American Indian and Alaska Native, 1.6% Hispanic of any race, 0.9% two or more races (2000); Density: 48.0 persons per square mile (2000); Age: 25.0% under 18, 17.4% over 64 (2000); Marriage status: 18.3% never married, 63.9% now married, 8.6% widowed, 9.1% divorced (2000); Foreign born: 0.7% (2000); Ancestry (includes multiple ancestries): 20.5% German, 12.8% United States or American, 11.3% English, 9.4% Irish, 8.9% Other groups (2000).
Economy: Employment by occupation: 9.3% management, 12.3% professional, 16.7% services, 20.3% sales, 3.0% farming, 12.1% construction, 26.4% production (2000).
Income: Per capita income: $14,124 (2000); Median household income: $28,750 (2000); Poverty rate: 14.8% (2000).
Taxes: Total city taxes per capita: $22 (1997); City property taxes per capita: $22 (1997).
Education: High school graduation rate: 78.0% (2000); College graduation rate: 10.7% (2000).
Housing: Homeownership rate: 85.0% (2000); Median home value: $50,800 (2000); Median rent: $309 per month (2000); Median age of housing: 33 years (2000).
Transportation: Commute to work: 91.8% car, 0.6% public transportation, 2.4% walk, 4.5% work from home (2000); Travel time to work: 27.8% less than 15 minutes, 21.0% 15 to 30 minutes, 31.8% 30 to 45 minutes, 6.9% 45 to 60 minutes, 12.5% 60 minutes or more (2000)

GRANT (township). Covers a land area of 32.595 square miles and a water area of 1.459 square miles. Located at 43.77° N. Lat.; 85.39° W. Long.
Population: 680 (2000); Race: 96.9% White, 0.0% Black, 0.3% Asian, 1.6% American Indian and Alaska Native, 0.8% Hispanic of any race, 1.0% two or more races (2000); Density: 20.9 persons per square mile (2000); Age: 25.6% under 18, 15.0% over 64 (2000); Marriage status: 15.7% never married, 70.9% now married, 5.4% widowed, 8.0% divorced (2000); Foreign born: 1.6% (2000); Ancestry (includes multiple ancestries): 31.2% German, 15.5% Irish, 11.4% English, 7.9% Other groups, 7.3% Dutch (2000).

Economy: Employment by occupation: 9.6% management, 20.2% professional, 14.6% services, 20.2% sales, 0.9% farming, 12.9% construction, 21.6% production (2000).
Income: Per capita income: $17,886 (2000); Median household income: $36,071 (2000); Poverty rate: 7.2% (2000).
Taxes: Total city taxes per capita: $37 (1997); City property taxes per capita: $37 (1997).
Education: High school graduation rate: 82.2% (2000); College graduation rate: 14.2% (2000).
Housing: Homeownership rate: 90.0% (2000); Median home value: $85,800 (2000); Median rent: $325 per month (2000); Median age of housing: 29 years (2000).
Transportation: Commute to work: 90.2% car, 0.9% public transportation, 1.5% walk, 7.3% work from home (2000); Travel time to work: 13.9% less than 15 minutes, 65.0% 15 to 30 minutes, 9.9% 30 to 45 minutes, 1.3% 45 to 60 minutes, 9.9% 60 minutes or more (2000)

GREEN CHARTER (township). Covers a land area of 36.928 square miles and a water area of 0.657 square miles. Located at 43.76° N. Lat.; 85.51° W. Long.
History: Green Township was organized in 1858 and named for Andrew and Lewis H. Green, who had settled here the year before.
Population: 3,209 (2000); Race: 96.8% White, 0.8% Black, 0.0% Asian, 1.2% American Indian and Alaska Native, 0.7% Hispanic of any race, 1.2% two or more races (2000); Density: 86.9 persons per square mile (2000); Age: 26.3% under 18, 10.6% over 64 (2000); Marriage status: 22.1% never married, 63.4% now married, 5.3% widowed, 9.3% divorced (2000); Foreign born: 0.2% (2000); Ancestry (includes multiple ancestries): 26.7% German, 13.1% English, 11.8% Irish, 8.3% Other groups, 8.2% United States or American (2000).
Economy: Employment by occupation: 8.9% management, 20.8% professional, 17.5% services, 22.8% sales, 0.0% farming, 7.0% construction, 23.0% production (2000).
Income: Per capita income: $18,212 (2000); Median household income: $39,036 (2000); Poverty rate: 10.6% (2000).
Taxes: Total city taxes per capita: $15 (1997); City property taxes per capita: $15 (1997).
Education: High school graduation rate: 88.8% (2000); College graduation rate: 21.0% (2000).
Housing: Homeownership rate: 81.9% (2000); Median home value: $90,400 (2000); Median rent: $341 per month (2000); Median age of housing: 23 years (2000).
Transportation: Commute to work: 90.5% car, 1.6% public transportation, 0.4% walk, 6.3% work from home (2000); Travel time to work: 51.0% less than 15 minutes, 33.9% 15 to 30 minutes, 5.9% 30 to 45 minutes, 4.2% 45 to 60 minutes, 5.0% 60 minutes or more (2000)

HINTON (township). Covers a land area of 35.726 square miles and a water area of 0.019 square miles. Located at 43.51° N. Lat.; 85.27° W. Long.
History: Hinton Township was organized in 1860 and named for John Hinton, who had settled here in 1855.
Population: 1,035 (2000); Race: 96.1% White, 0.2% Black, 0.0% Asian, 1.1% American Indian and Alaska Native, 3.1% Hispanic of any race, 1.0% two or more races (2000); Density: 29.0 persons per square mile (2000); Age: 25.0% under 18, 12.8% over 64 (2000); Marriage status: 21.2% never married, 65.8% now married, 5.3% widowed, 7.6% divorced (2000); Foreign born: 0.6% (2000); Ancestry (includes multiple ancestries): 27.5% German, 13.4% English, 9.5% Irish, 9.5% United States or American, 6.6% Other groups (2000).
Economy: Employment by occupation: 9.6% management, 9.8% professional, 11.6% services, 23.0% sales, 1.8% farming, 16.9% construction, 27.3% production (2000).
Income: Per capita income: $16,964 (2000); Median household income: $37,976 (2000); Poverty rate: 9.9% (2000).
Taxes: Total city taxes per capita: $21 (1997); City property taxes per capita: $21 (1997).
Education: High school graduation rate: 80.3% (2000); College graduation rate: 10.0% (2000).
Housing: Homeownership rate: 83.4% (2000); Median home value: $74,100 (2000); Median rent: $392 per month (2000); Median age of housing: 32 years (2000).
Transportation: Commute to work: 91.2% car, 0.0% public transportation, 3.5% walk, 4.9% work from home (2000); Travel time to work: 21.4% less than 15 minutes, 25.1% 15 to 30 minutes, 21.2% 30 to 45 minutes, 17.0% 45 to 60 minutes, 15.3% 60 minutes or more (2000)

MARTINY (township). Covers a land area of 32.218 square miles and a water area of 3.215 square miles. Located at 43.69° N. Lat.; 85.25° W. Long.
Population: 1,606 (2000); Race: 98.4% White, 0.3% Black, 0.0% Asian, 0.3% American Indian and Alaska Native, 0.0% Hispanic of any race, 1.0% two or more races (2000); Density: 49.8 persons per square mile (2000); Age: 19.9% under 18, 21.5% over 64 (2000); Marriage status: 16.1% never married, 67.0% now married, 7.4% widowed, 9.5% divorced (2000); Foreign born: 0.4% (2000); Ancestry (includes multiple ancestries): 27.5% German, 15.2% English, 11.8% Irish, 11.7% United States or American, 7.6% Other groups (2000).
Economy: Employment by occupation: 8.0% management, 11.0% professional, 15.2% services, 26.2% sales, 1.4% farming, 13.7% construction, 24.5% production (2000).
Income: Per capita income: $18,825 (2000); Median household income: $31,681 (2000); Poverty rate: 7.7% (2000).
Taxes: Total city taxes per capita: $23 (1997); City property taxes per capita: $23 (1997).
Education: High school graduation rate: 75.2% (2000); College graduation rate: 6.8% (2000).
Housing: Homeownership rate: 88.3% (2000); Median home value: $92,800 (2000); Median rent: $313 per month (2000); Median age of housing: 29 years (2000).
Transportation: Commute to work: 93.0% car, 1.4% public transportation, 0.3% walk, 4.9% work from home (2000); Travel time to work: 16.0% less than 15 minutes, 40.9% 15 to 30 minutes, 18.0% 30 to 45 minutes, 7.5% 45 to 60 minutes, 17.6% 60 minutes or more (2000)

MECOSTA (village). Covers a land area of 1.144 square miles and a water area of 0 square miles. Located at 43.62° N. Lat.; 85.23° W. Long.
Population: 440 (2000); Race: 84.3% White, 3.9% Black, 0.7% Asian, 0.0% American Indian and Alaska Native, 3.9% Hispanic of any race, 9.4% two or more races (2000); Density: 384.7 persons per square mile (2000); Age: 31.2% under 18, 14.4% over 64 (2000); Marriage status: 26.0% never married, 52.4% now married, 11.2% widowed, 10.4% divorced (2000); Foreign born: 1.5% (2000); Ancestry (includes multiple ancestries): 20.3% German, 17.9% Other groups, 17.2% United States or American, 11.5% English, 8.7% Irish (2000).
Economy: Employment by occupation: 12.0% management, 2.1% professional, 28.1% services, 18.2% sales, 5.2% farming, 9.9% construction, 24.5% production (2000).
Income: Per capita income: $14,620 (2000); Median household income: $32,857 (2000); Poverty rate: 17.9% (2000).
Taxes: Total city taxes per capita: $27 (1997); City property taxes per capita: $27 (1997).
Education: High school graduation rate: 73.4% (2000); College graduation rate: 7.7% (2000).
Housing: Homeownership rate: 83.6% (2000); Median home value: $59,600 (2000); Median rent: $338 per month (2000); Median age of housing: 37 years (2000).
Transportation: Commute to work: 86.7% car, 0.0% public transportation, 3.2% walk, 6.9% work from home (2000); Travel time to work: 21.7% less than 15 minutes, 21.1% 15 to 30 minutes, 32.6% 30 to 45 minutes, 12.6% 45 to 60 minutes, 12.0% 60 minutes or more (2000)

MECOSTA (township). Covers a land area of 33.927 square miles and a water area of 2.001 square miles. Located at 43.60° N. Lat.; 85.48° W. Long.
Population: 2,435 (2000); Race: 96.8% White, 0.5% Black, 0.2% Asian, 0.5% American Indian and Alaska Native, 0.7% Hispanic of any race, 1.7% two or more races (2000); Density: 71.8 persons per square mile (2000); Age: 27.0% under 18, 11.5% over 64 (2000); Marriage status: 21.1% never married, 61.4% now married, 5.4% widowed, 12.1% divorced (2000); Foreign born: 1.5% (2000); Ancestry (includes multiple ancestries): 24.2% German, 13.2% English, 10.9% Irish, 7.0% United States or American, 6.8% Dutch (2000).
Economy: In lake-resort and farm area. Employment by occupation: 8.3% management, 13.3% professional, 17.0% services, 23.7% sales, 0.2% farming, 11.8% construction, 25.7% production (2000).
Income: Per capita income: $18,494 (2000); Median household income: $37,287 (2000); Poverty rate: 11.5% (2000).
Taxes: Total city taxes per capita: $45 (1997); City property taxes per capita: $44 (1997).
Education: High school graduation rate: 83.6% (2000); College graduation rate: 12.5% (2000).

Housing: Homeownership rate: 75.2% (2000); Median home value: $84,200 (2000); Median rent: $384 per month (2000); Median age of housing: 28 years (2000).
Transportation: Commute to work: 93.8% car, 0.7% public transportation, 0.5% walk, 4.8% work from home (2000); Travel time to work: 27.5% less than 15 minutes, 38.9% 15 to 30 minutes, 10.3% 30 to 45 minutes, 8.7% 45 to 60 minutes, 14.6% 60 minutes or more (2000)

MILLBROOK (township). Covers a land area of 35.735 square miles and a water area of 0.052 square miles. Located at 43.50° N. Lat.; 85.14° W. Long.
Population: 1,081 (2000); Race: 95.5% White, 0.2% Black, 0.0% Asian, 0.3% American Indian and Alaska Native, 1.9% Hispanic of any race, 2.4% two or more races (2000); Density: 30.3 persons per square mile (2000); Age: 26.3% under 18, 13.5% over 64 (2000); Marriage status: 19.5% never married, 62.6% now married, 7.9% widowed, 10.0% divorced (2000); Foreign born: 2.4% (2000); Ancestry (includes multiple ancestries): 25.5% German, 15.0% English, 10.1% United States or American, 8.4% Irish, 5.5% Other groups (2000).
Economy: Employment by occupation: 9.5% management, 13.4% professional, 16.3% services, 18.2% sales, 3.1% farming, 11.8% construction, 27.7% production (2000).
Income: Per capita income: $16,064 (2000); Median household income: $35,238 (2000); Poverty rate: 11.9% (2000).
Taxes: Total city taxes per capita: $30 (1997); City property taxes per capita: $30 (1997).
Education: High school graduation rate: 82.5% (2000); College graduation rate: 8.7% (2000).
Housing: Homeownership rate: 86.8% (2000); Median home value: $74,800 (2000); Median rent: $279 per month (2000); Median age of housing: 27 years (2000).
Transportation: Commute to work: 88.0% car, 0.0% public transportation, 2.5% walk, 8.5% work from home (2000); Travel time to work: 19.7% less than 15 minutes, 31.3% 15 to 30 minutes, 26.1% 30 to 45 minutes, 12.9% 45 to 60 minutes, 10.0% 60 minutes or more (2000)

MORLEY (village). Covers a land area of 0.922 square miles and a water area of 0.079 square miles. Located at 43.49° N. Lat.; 85.44° W. Long. Elevation is 880 feet.
History: Morley was settled in 1869 as a trading and supply center for the surrounding area.
Population: 495 (2000); Race: 97.1% White, 0.0% Black, 0.4% Asian, 0.2% American Indian and Alaska Native, 1.0% Hispanic of any race, 1.8% two or more races (2000); Density: 536.9 persons per square mile (2000); Age: 31.3% under 18, 13.9% over 64 (2000); Marriage status: 25.5% never married, 49.3% now married, 11.9% widowed, 13.3% divorced (2000); Foreign born: 1.4% (2000); Ancestry (includes multiple ancestries): 21.3% German, 18.6% Irish, 15.6% United States or American, 9.8% Other groups, 8.2% English (2000).
Economy: Employment by occupation: 5.5% management, 11.5% professional, 20.3% services, 16.5% sales, 1.6% farming, 13.2% construction, 31.3% production (2000).
Income: Per capita income: $11,634 (2000); Median household income: $31,442 (2000); Poverty rate: 17.7% (2000).
Taxes: Total city taxes per capita: $71 (1997); City property taxes per capita: $71 (1997).
Education: High school graduation rate: 68.3% (2000); College graduation rate: 7.1% (2000).

School District(s)

Morley Stanwood Community School (KG-12)
2000 Enrollment: 1,600 231-856-4392
Housing: Homeownership rate: 75.5% (2000); Median home value: $55,000 (2000); Median rent: $336 per month (2000); Median age of housing: 50 years (2000).
Transportation: Commute to work: 89.6% car, 0.0% public transportation, 4.4% walk, 3.8% work from home (2000); Travel time to work: 26.9% less than 15 minutes, 20.6% 15 to 30 minutes, 10.3% 30 to 45 minutes, 24.6% 45 to 60 minutes, 17.7% 60 minutes or more (2000)

MORTON (township). Covers a land area of 33.141 square miles and a water area of 2.511 square miles. Located at 43.59° N. Lat.; 85.28° W. Long.
Population: 3,597 (2000); Race: 94.6% White, 1.3% Black, 0.3% Asian, 0.1% American Indian and Alaska Native, 2.0% Hispanic of any race, 3.0% two or more races (2000); Density: 108.5 persons per square mile (2000); Age: 16.9% under 18, 28.8% over 64 (2000); Marriage status: 11.9% never married, 72.9% now married, 7.1% widowed, 8.1% divorced (2000); Foreign born: 2.6% (2000); Ancestry (includes multiple ancestries): 28.6% German, 16.1% English, 11.6% Irish, 8.0% Other groups, 8.0% Polish (2000).
Economy: Single-family building permits issued: 67 (2001) / 63 (2000); Multi-family building permits issued: 30 (2001) / 0 (2000); Employment by occupation: 16.3% management, 15.9% professional, 17.2% services, 22.0% sales, 1.9% farming, 10.0% construction, 16.7% production (2000).
Income: Per capita income: $24,729 (2000); Median household income: $41,422 (2000); Poverty rate: 9.1% (2000).
Taxes: Total city taxes per capita: $147 (1997); City property taxes per capita: $131 (1997).
Education: High school graduation rate: 88.0% (2000); College graduation rate: 23.5% (2000).
Housing: Homeownership rate: 91.7% (2000); Median home value: $136,900 (2000); Median rent: $348 per month (2000); Median age of housing: 21 years (2000).
Transportation: Commute to work: 91.0% car, 0.8% public transportation, 1.2% walk, 6.1% work from home (2000); Travel time to work: 26.0% less than 15 minutes, 28.5% 15 to 30 minutes, 22.2% 30 to 45 minutes, 7.0% 45 to 60 minutes, 16.3% 60 minutes or more (2000)

PARIS (unincorporated postal area, zip code 49338). Covers a land area of 57.086 square miles and a water area of 0.081 square miles. Located at 43.76° N. Lat.; 85.57° W. Long.
History: A trapper named John Parish came to this area in the 1850's, and the settlement that grew up around his cabin was named for him. The "h" was dropped through usage.
Population: 1,912 (2000); Race: 98.5% White, 0.0% Black, 0.1% Asian, 0.7% American Indian and Alaska Native, 0.9% Hispanic of any race, 0.4% two or more races (2000); Density: 33.5 persons per square mile (2000); Age: 32.9% under 18, 7.4% over 64 (2000); Marriage status: 21.6% never married, 61.2% now married, 5.5% widowed, 11.6% divorced (2000); Foreign born: 0.5% (2000); Ancestry (includes multiple ancestries): 28.8% German, 16.4% Irish, 10.1% United States or American, 9.8% English, 8.3% Dutch (2000).
Economy: Employment by occupation: 11.9% management, 17.4% professional, 16.1% services, 18.3% sales, 0.6% farming, 10.0% construction, 25.7% production (2000).
Income: Per capita income: $16,148 (2000); Median household income: $40,020 (2000); Poverty rate: 10.2% (2000).
Education: High school graduation rate: 85.5% (2000); College graduation rate: 18.1% (2000).
Housing: Homeownership rate: 77.9% (2000); Median home value: $79,700 (2000); Median rent: $362 per month (2000); Median age of housing: 22 years (2000).
Transportation: Commute to work: 91.1% car, 0.5% public transportation, 0.1% walk, 7.8% work from home (2000); Travel time to work: 39.8% less than 15 minutes, 40.1% 15 to 30 minutes, 4.7% 30 to 45 minutes, 3.5% 45 to 60 minutes, 11.9% 60 minutes or more (2000)

REMUS (unincorporated postal area, zip code 49340). Covers a land area of 84.808 square miles and a water area of 0.728 square miles. Located at 43.61° N. Lat.; 85.09° W. Long.
History: Remus began as Bingen, at a sawmill site just west of the present site. The town was moved in 1869 to take advantage of the Detroit, Lansing & Northern Railroad line, and was renamed for surveyor William John Remus, who owned land here.
Population: 2,935 (2000); Race: 93.3% White, 1.3% Black, 0.1% Asian, 0.8% American Indian and Alaska Native, 1.0% Hispanic of any race, 3.2% two or more races (2000); Density: 34.6 persons per square mile (2000); Age: 29.3% under 18, 13.4% over 64 (2000); Marriage status: 21.6% never married, 63.4% now married, 5.8% widowed, 9.2% divorced (2000); Foreign born: 0.8% (2000); Ancestry (includes multiple ancestries): 33.2% German, 12.3% English, 11.3% Irish, 9.3% Other groups, 8.3% United States or American (2000).
Economy: Employment by occupation: 9.0% management, 14.8% professional, 20.0% services, 19.3% sales, 1.9% farming, 11.0% construction, 24.1% production (2000).
Income: Per capita income: $15,779 (2000); Median household income: $34,833 (2000); Poverty rate: 13.7% (2000).
Education: High school graduation rate: 82.1% (2000); College graduation rate: 11.8% (2000).

School District(s)

Chippewa Hills School District (KG-12)
2000 Enrollment: 2,612 517-967-8356
Housing: Homeownership rate: 83.1% (2000); Median home value: $68,600 (2000); Median rent: $308 per month (2000); Median age of housing: 28 years (2000).

Transportation: Commute to work: 91.7% car, 0.2% public transportation, 2.9% walk, 4.7% work from home (2000); Travel time to work: 25.1% less than 15 minutes, 32.6% 15 to 30 minutes, 25.0% 30 to 45 minutes, 8.0% 45 to 60 minutes, 9.3% 60 minutes or more (2000)

RODNEY (unincorporated postal area, zip code 49342). Covers a land area of 37.069 square miles and a water area of 0.871 square miles. Located at 43.69° N. Lat.; 85.31° W. Long. Elevation is 1,081 feet.
History: Rodney grew up around a station on the Detroit, Grand Rapids & Western Railroad. The village was founded in 1879 and named for Rodney Hood of the Hood & Gale lumber company.
Population: 1,812 (2000); Race: 96.8% White, 0.8% Black, 0.3% Asian, 0.0% American Indian and Alaska Native, 0.5% Hispanic of any race, 1.9% two or more races (2000); Density: 48.9 persons per square mile (2000); Age: 24.5% under 18, 16.9% over 64 (2000); Marriage status: 20.8% never married, 61.5% now married, 5.9% widowed, 11.8% divorced (2000); Foreign born: 0.8% (2000); Ancestry (includes multiple ancestries): 24.2% German, 13.3% English, 12.8% Irish, 10.2% Other groups, 9.8% United States or American (2000).
Economy: Employment by occupation: 8.8% management, 12.7% professional, 14.7% services, 25.2% sales, 1.6% farming, 11.7% construction, 25.2% production (2000).
Income: Per capita income: $16,146 (2000); Median household income: $32,500 (2000); Poverty rate: 10.0% (2000).
Education: High school graduation rate: 78.5% (2000); College graduation rate: 11.7% (2000).
Housing: Homeownership rate: 87.4% (2000); Median home value: $87,500 (2000); Median rent: $327 per month (2000); Median age of housing: 29 years (2000).
Transportation: Commute to work: 92.0% car, 0.8% public transportation, 1.3% walk, 5.6% work from home (2000); Travel time to work: 19.5% less than 15 minutes, 54.4% 15 to 30 minutes, 10.6% 30 to 45 minutes, 4.4% 45 to 60 minutes, 11.0% 60 minutes or more (2000)

SHERIDAN (township). Covers a land area of 34.795 square miles and a water area of 0.970 square miles. Located at 43.70° N. Lat.; 85.16° W. Long.
History: Sheridan Township was organized in 1867 and named for General Philip H. Sheridan.
Population: 1,357 (2000); Race: 91.8% White, 1.7% Black, 0.1% Asian, 0.8% American Indian and Alaska Native, 0.6% Hispanic of any race, 5.6% two or more races (2000); Density: 39.0 persons per square mile (2000); Age: 27.8% under 18, 13.0% over 64 (2000); Marriage status: 21.8% never married, 60.6% now married, 5.7% widowed, 11.9% divorced (2000); Foreign born: 0.4% (2000); Ancestry (includes multiple ancestries): 28.0% German, 16.6% Other groups, 14.0% Irish, 12.8% English, 9.2% United States or American (2000).
Economy: Employment by occupation: 7.6% management, 12.3% professional, 16.0% services, 18.2% sales, 3.9% farming, 11.9% construction, 29.9% production (2000).
Income: Per capita income: $15,076 (2000); Median household income: $31,050 (2000); Poverty rate: 14.9% (2000).
Taxes: Total city taxes per capita: $18 (1997); City property taxes per capita: $18 (1997).
Education: High school graduation rate: 76.4% (2000); College graduation rate: 6.7% (2000).
Housing: Homeownership rate: 89.5% (2000); Median home value: $67,700 (2000); Median rent: $334 per month (2000); Median age of housing: 31 years (2000).
Transportation: Commute to work: 94.3% car, 0.6% public transportation, 0.4% walk, 4.3% work from home (2000); Travel time to work: 20.1% less than 15 minutes, 27.6% 15 to 30 minutes, 29.5% 30 to 45 minutes, 14.3% 45 to 60 minutes, 8.5% 60 minutes or more (2000)

STANWOOD (village). Covers a land area of 0.244 square miles and a water area of 0 square miles. Located at 43.58° N. Lat.; 85.44° W. Long.
History: Stanwood was settled in 1870 and named for the plentiful timber in the area. It was incorporated as a village in 1907.
Population: 204 (2000); Race: 100.0% White, 0.0% Black, 0.0% Asian, 0.0% American Indian and Alaska Native, 0.0% Hispanic of any race, 0.0% two or more races (2000); Density: 836.0 persons per square mile (2000); Age: 28.3% under 18, 9.9% over 64 (2000); Marriage status: 22.2% never married, 61.1% now married, 4.9% widowed, 11.7% divorced (2000); Foreign born: 0.9% (2000); Ancestry (includes multiple ancestries): 37.7% German, 13.2% Irish, 10.8% English, 7.5% Dutch, 5.2% United States or American (2000).
Economy: Employment by occupation: 2.2% management, 16.9% professional, 23.6% services, 21.3% sales, 0.0% farming, 3.4% construction, 32.6% production (2000).
Income: Per capita income: $17,121 (2000); Median household income: $39,000 (2000); Poverty rate: 3.8% (2000).
Taxes: Total city taxes per capita: $67 (1997); City property taxes per capita: $62 (1997).
Education: High school graduation rate: 88.1% (2000); College graduation rate: 19.4% (2000).
Housing: Homeownership rate: 68.4% (2000); Median home value: $60,000 (2000); Median rent: $371 per month (2000); Median age of housing: 57 years (2000).
Transportation: Commute to work: 94.4% car, 3.4% public transportation, 0.0% walk, 2.2% work from home (2000); Travel time to work: 16.1% less than 15 minutes, 42.5% 15 to 30 minutes, 11.5% 30 to 45 minutes, 18.4% 45 to 60 minutes, 11.5% 60 minutes or more (2000)

WHEATLAND (township). Covers a land area of 35.530 square miles and a water area of 0.175 square miles. Located at 43.59° N. Lat.; 85.14° W. Long.
Population: 1,474 (2000); Race: 94.4% White, 1.0% Black, 0.0% Asian, 1.5% American Indian and Alaska Native, 0.4% Hispanic of any race, 2.6% two or more races (2000); Density: 41.5 persons per square mile (2000); Age: 28.3% under 18, 14.7% over 64 (2000); Marriage status: 21.6% never married, 62.6% now married, 6.9% widowed, 9.0% divorced (2000); Foreign born: 0.5% (2000); Ancestry (includes multiple ancestries): 38.2% German, 12.1% English, 9.6% United States or American, 9.4% Irish, 7.0% Other groups (2000).
Economy: Employment by occupation: 8.5% management, 15.2% professional, 19.9% services, 21.4% sales, 1.7% farming, 10.5% construction, 22.8% production (2000).
Income: Per capita income: $16,405 (2000); Median household income: $33,654 (2000); Poverty rate: 11.7% (2000).
Taxes: Total city taxes per capita: $35 (1997); City property taxes per capita: $35 (1997).
Education: High school graduation rate: 82.4% (2000); College graduation rate: 12.0% (2000).
Housing: Homeownership rate: 78.9% (2000); Median home value: $66,100 (2000); Median rent: $277 per month (2000); Median age of housing: 30 years (2000).
Transportation: Commute to work: 90.7% car, 0.1% public transportation, 5.1% walk, 3.6% work from home (2000); Travel time to work: 32.3% less than 15 minutes, 25.6% 15 to 30 minutes, 26.2% 30 to 45 minutes, 6.0% 45 to 60 minutes, 9.9% 60 minutes or more (2000)

Menominee County

Located in northwestern Michigan on the Upper Peninsula; bounded on the southeast by Green Bay, and on the southwest by Wisconsin; drained by the Menominee, Cedar, and Little Cedar Rivers. Covers a land area of 1,043.50 square miles, a water area of 294.50 square miles, and is located in the Central Time Zone. The county government was organized in 1863. County seat is Menominee.

Weather Station: Stephenson 8 WNW — Elevation: 708 feet

	Jan	Feb	Mar	Apr	May	Jun	Jul	Aug	Sep	Oct	Nov	Dec
High	25	29	39	54	68	76	80	78	69	57	41	29
Low	3	6	18	30	40	50	55	53	45	34	24	11
Precip	1.5	0.9	1.9	2.3	3.3	3.3	3.7	3.7	3.6	2.7	2.5	1.8
Snow	18.0	8.8	11.6	3.7	0.6	0.0	0.0	0.0	tr	0.5	5.7	15.7

High and Low temperatures in degrees Fahrenheit; Precipitation and Snow in inches

Population: 25,326 (2000); Race: 96.2% White, 0.2% Black, 0.1% Asian, 2.3% American Indian and Alaska Native, 0.5% Hispanic of any race, 1.0% two or more races (2000); Density: 24.3 persons per square mile (2000); Age: 24.1% under 18, 17.3% over 64 (2000).
Religion: Five largest groups: 43.7% Catholic Church, 12.1% Evangelical Lutheran Church in America, 3.3% Wisconsin Evangelical Lutheran Synod, 2.1% The United Methodist Church, 1.5% Presbyterian Church (U.S.A.) (2000).
Economy: Unemployment rate: 5.9% (11/2002); Total civilian labor force: 12,054 (11/2002); Leading industries: 42.7% manufacturing; 10.6% retail trade; 7.4% health care and social assistance (2000); Companies that employ more than 1,000 persons: 0 (2000); Companies that employ more than 100 persons: 13 (2000); Farms: 348 totaling 109,661 acres (1997); Minority business ownership rate: 0.0% (1997); Women business ownership rate:

19.7% (1997); Retail sales per capita: $6,626 (1997). Single-family building permits issued: 124 (2001) / 138 (2000); Multi-family building permits issued: 0 (2001) / 0 (2000).
Income: Per capita income: $16,909 (2000); Median household income: $32,888 (2000); Poverty rate: 11.5% (2000); Bankruptcy rate: 2.65% (2001).
Taxes: Total county taxes per capita: $124 (1997); County property taxes per capita: $120 (1997).
Education: High school graduation rate: 83.5% (2000); College graduation rate: 11.0% (2000).
Housing: Homeownership rate: 79.5% (2000); Median home value: $63,400 (2000); Median rent: $294 per month (2000); Median age of housing: 41 years (2000).
Health: Birth rate: 121.2 per 10,000 population (1998); Age adjusted death rate: 96.2 per 10,000 population (1999); Age adjusted cancer mortality rate: 199.4 deaths per 100,000 population (1999). Number of physicians: 2.4 per 10,000 population (1999); Number of hospital beds: n/a (1999).
Elections: 2000 Presidential election results: 44.1% Gore, 53.0% Bush, 2.6% Nader, 0.1% Buchanan
National and State Parks: Escanaba River State Forest; J W Wells State Park
Additional Information Contacts
Menominee County Government Offices 906-863-9648
Cedarville Chamber of Commerce. 906-484-3935
Menominee Chamber of Commerce 906-863-2679

Menominee County Communities

CARNEY (village). Covers a land area of 0.995 square miles and a water area of 0 square miles. Located at 45.58° N. Lat.; 87.55° W. Long.
History: Carney grew up around a station on the Chicago & Northwestern Railroad in 1879. It was named for Fred Carney, who owned land in the area.
Population: 225 (2000); Race: 96.9% White, 0.0% Black, 0.9% Asian, 0.0% American Indian and Alaska Native, 1.3% Hispanic of any race, 2.2% two or more races (2000); Density: 226.1 persons per square mile (2000); Age: 22.5% under 18, 11.9% over 64 (2000); Marriage status: 25.0% never married, 51.0% now married, 8.3% widowed, 15.6% divorced (2000); Foreign born: 0.9% (2000); Ancestry (includes multiple ancestries): 30.0% German, 13.7% French (except Basque), 8.4% Irish, 8.4% Polish, 8.4% Italian (2000).
Economy: Employment by occupation: 6.7% management, 17.1% professional, 14.3% services, 24.8% sales, 3.8% farming, 9.5% construction, 23.8% production (2000).
Income: Per capita income: $15,481 (2000); Median household income: $31,111 (2000); Poverty rate: 11.1% (2000).
Taxes: Total city taxes per capita: $24 (1997); City property taxes per capita: $24 (1997).
Education: High school graduation rate: 77.5% (2000); College graduation rate: 12.6% (2000).

School District(s)

Carney-Nadeau Public Schools (KG-12)
2000 Enrollment: 233 906-639-2000
Housing: Homeownership rate: 85.7% (2000); Median home value: $45,000 (2000); Median rent: $275 per month (2000); Median age of housing: 43 years (2000).
Transportation: Commute to work: 96.1% car, 0.0% public transportation, 3.9% walk, 0.0% work from home (2000); Travel time to work: 40.8% less than 15 minutes, 21.4% 15 to 30 minutes, 16.5% 30 to 45 minutes, 18.4% 45 to 60 minutes, 2.9% 60 minutes or more (2000)

CEDAR RIVER (unincorporated postal area, zip code 49813). Covers a land area of 68.660 square miles and a water area of 0.103 square miles. Located at 45.43° N. Lat.; 87.37° W. Long. Elevation is 592 feet.
History: The community of Cedar River was settled in 1854 at the mouth of the Big Cedar River, and grew up around a sawmill. It became a popular lake trout fishing center, with other varieties of fish plentiful further upstream.
Population: 230 (2000); Race: 96.3% White, 0.0% Black, 0.0% Asian, 2.9% American Indian and Alaska Native, 0.0% Hispanic of any race, 0.8% two or more races (2000); Density: 3.3 persons per square mile (2000); Age: 9.1% under 18, 21.9% over 64 (2000); Marriage status: 16.5% never married, 69.6% now married, 9.8% widowed, 4.0% divorced (2000); Foreign born: 2.9% (2000); Ancestry (includes multiple ancestries): 29.8% German, 15.7% English, 13.6% French (except Basque), 12.8% Irish, 12.0% Swedish (2000).
Economy: Employment by occupation: 4.7% management, 21.2% professional, 10.6% services, 24.7% sales, 7.1% farming, 12.9% construction, 18.8% production (2000).
Income: Per capita income: $18,857 (2000); Median household income: $31,364 (2000); Poverty rate: 12.0% (2000).
Education: High school graduation rate: 86.8% (2000); College graduation rate: 21.6% (2000).
Housing: Homeownership rate: 96.6% (2000); Median home value: $112,500 (2000); Median rent: $275 per month (2000); Median age of housing: 31 years (2000).
Transportation: Commute to work: 91.5% car, 0.0% public transportation, 0.0% walk, 8.5% work from home (2000); Travel time to work: 8.0% less than 15 minutes, 21.3% 15 to 30 minutes, 49.3% 30 to 45 minutes, 13.3% 45 to 60 minutes, 8.0% 60 minutes or more (2000)

CEDARVILLE (township). Covers a land area of 78.949 square miles and a water area of 0.096 square miles. Located at 45.48° N. Lat.; 87.38° W. Long.
Population: 276 (2000); Race: 94.1% White, 0.7% Black, 0.0% Asian, 2.4% American Indian and Alaska Native, 0.0% Hispanic of any race, 2.8% two or more races (2000); Density: 3.5 persons per square mile (2000); Age: 12.2% under 18, 21.3% over 64 (2000); Marriage status: 14.1% never married, 68.4% now married, 11.3% widowed, 6.3% divorced (2000); Foreign born: 1.4% (2000); Ancestry (includes multiple ancestries): 24.0% German, 15.0% Swedish, 13.6% French (except Basque), 12.9% English, 11.5% French Canadian (2000).
Economy: Employment by occupation: 7.1% management, 19.2% professional, 16.2% services, 20.2% sales, 10.1% farming, 8.1% construction, 19.2% production (2000).
Income: Per capita income: $18,279 (2000); Median household income: $29,107 (2000); Poverty rate: 12.9% (2000).
Taxes: Total city taxes per capita: $48 (1997); City property taxes per capita: $48 (1997).
Education: High school graduation rate: 87.7% (2000); College graduation rate: 19.8% (2000).
Housing: Homeownership rate: 95.8% (2000); Median home value: $120,000 (2000); Median rent: $250 per month (2000); Median age of housing: 29 years (2000).
Transportation: Commute to work: 92.7% car, 0.0% public transportation, 0.0% walk, 7.3% work from home (2000); Travel time to work: 9.0% less than 15 minutes, 23.6% 15 to 30 minutes, 42.7% 30 to 45 minutes, 15.7% 45 to 60 minutes, 9.0% 60 minutes or more (2000)
Additional Information Contacts
Cedarville Chamber of Commerce. 906-484-3935

DAGGETT (village). Covers a land area of 1.105 square miles and a water area of 0 square miles. Located at 45.46° N. Lat.; 87.60° W. Long. Elevation is 772 feet.
Population: 270 (2000); Race: 93.1% White, 0.0% Black, 0.0% Asian, 0.8% American Indian and Alaska Native, 2.4% Hispanic of any race, 4.5% two or more races (2000); Density: 244.3 persons per square mile (2000); Age: 38.0% under 18, 16.7% over 64 (2000); Marriage status: 20.7% never married, 62.6% now married, 9.8% widowed, 6.9% divorced (2000); Foreign born: 0.0% (2000); Ancestry (includes multiple ancestries): 39.6% German, 15.1% French (except Basque), 13.1% Swedish, 7.8% Other groups, 7.3% Irish (2000).
Economy: Employment by occupation: 9.6% management, 12.3% professional, 11.0% services, 21.9% sales, 0.0% farming, 11.0% construction, 34.2% production (2000).
Income: Per capita income: $9,910 (2000); Median household income: $24,583 (2000); Poverty rate: 24.1% (2000).
Education: High school graduation rate: 79.1% (2000); College graduation rate: 11.5% (2000).
Housing: Homeownership rate: 84.4% (2000); Median home value: $44,700 (2000); Median rent: $250 per month (2000); Median age of housing: 54 years (2000).
Transportation: Commute to work: 98.6% car, 0.0% public transportation, 0.0% walk, 1.4% work from home (2000); Travel time to work: 52.8% less than 15 minutes, 2.8% 15 to 30 minutes, 20.8% 30 to 45 minutes, 23.6% 45 to 60 minutes, 0.0% 60 minutes or more (2000)

DAGGETT (township). Covers a land area of 35.913 square miles and a water area of 0.157 square miles. Located at 45.47° N. Lat.; 87.57° W. Long. Elevation is 772 feet.
Population: 740 (2000); Race: 95.6% White, 0.3% Black, 0.0% Asian, 0.7% American Indian and Alaska Native, 2.8% Hispanic of any race, 1.5% two or more races (2000); Density: 20.6 persons per square mile (2000); Age: 28.4% under 18, 14.9% over 64 (2000); Marriage status: 21.2% never married, 64.0% now married, 8.0% widowed, 6.8% divorced (2000); Foreign born:

0.3% (2000); Ancestry (includes multiple ancestries): 33.1% German, 17.3% Swedish, 12.3% French (except Basque), 7.8% English, 6.9% Polish (2000).
Economy: Employment by occupation: 13.6% management, 10.8% professional, 15.7% services, 14.8% sales, 5.4% farming, 10.2% construction, 29.5% production (2000).
Income: Per capita income: $13,767 (2000); Median household income: $32,727 (2000); Poverty rate: 13.0% (2000).
Taxes: Total city taxes per capita: $39 (1997); City property taxes per capita: $39 (1997).
Education: High school graduation rate: 83.8% (2000); College graduation rate: 12.1% (2000).
Housing: Homeownership rate: 92.4% (2000); Median home value: $49,300 (2000); Median rent: $238 per month (2000); Median age of housing: 38 years (2000).
Transportation: Commute to work: 90.1% car, 0.0% public transportation, 3.1% walk, 6.8% work from home (2000); Travel time to work: 50.0% less than 15 minutes, 11.3% 15 to 30 minutes, 19.5% 30 to 45 minutes, 15.2% 45 to 60 minutes, 4.0% 60 minutes or more (2000)

FAITHORN (township). Covers a land area of 53.556 square miles and a water area of 0.711 square miles. Located at 45.66° N. Lat.; 87.75° W. Long. Elevation is 849 feet.
Population: 214 (2000); Race: 100.0% White, 0.0% Black, 0.0% Asian, 0.0% American Indian and Alaska Native, 0.0% Hispanic of any race, 0.0% two or more races (2000); Density: 4.0 persons per square mile (2000); Age: 19.3% under 18, 18.4% over 64 (2000); Marriage status: 12.2% never married, 79.7% now married, 7.0% widowed, 1.2% divorced (2000); Foreign born: 0.0% (2000); Ancestry (includes multiple ancestries): 33.3% German, 16.4% English, 12.6% French (except Basque), 12.1% Swedish, 10.1% Italian (2000).
Economy: Employment by occupation: 2.4% management, 8.2% professional, 28.2% services, 18.8% sales, 2.4% farming, 4.7% construction, 35.3% production (2000).
Income: Per capita income: $20,422 (2000); Median household income: $41,250 (2000); Poverty rate: 4.3% (2000).
Taxes: Total city taxes per capita: $65 (1997); City property taxes per capita: $65 (1997).
Education: High school graduation rate: 78.5% (2000); College graduation rate: 13.3% (2000).
Housing: Homeownership rate: 100.0% (2000); Median home value: $53,300 (2000); Median age of housing: 27 years (2000).
Transportation: Commute to work: 100.0% car, 0.0% public transportation, 0.0% walk, 0.0% work from home (2000); Travel time to work: 4.7% less than 15 minutes, 54.1% 15 to 30 minutes, 21.2% 30 to 45 minutes, 4.7% 45 to 60 minutes, 15.3% 60 minutes or more (2000)

GOURLEY (township). Covers a land area of 35.744 square miles and a water area of 0.035 square miles. Located at 45.60° N. Lat.; 87.37° W. Long.
History: Gourley developed around a mill which was purchased by Arthur Gourley and his partner, Samuel L. Hall. Gourley and Hall founded the village of Gourley. When the township was divided out from Cedarville Township in 1920, the new township was also called Gourley.
Population: 409 (2000); Race: 88.1% White, 0.0% Black, 0.0% Asian, 11.0% American Indian and Alaska Native, 0.2% Hispanic of any race, 0.9% two or more races (2000); Density: 11.4 persons per square mile (2000); Age: 25.6% under 18, 14.5% over 64 (2000); Marriage status: 22.1% never married, 69.3% now married, 6.1% widowed, 2.5% divorced (2000); Foreign born: 0.0% (2000); Ancestry (includes multiple ancestries): 28.9% German, 17.2% French (except Basque), 13.8% Other groups, 12.8% Irish, 11.0% Belgian (2000).
Economy: Employment by occupation: 6.6% management, 12.2% professional, 19.3% services, 22.3% sales, 2.0% farming, 14.2% construction, 23.4% production (2000).
Income: Per capita income: $14,215 (2000); Median household income: $27,063 (2000); Poverty rate: 14.5% (2000).
Taxes: Total city taxes per capita: $71 (1997); City property taxes per capita: $71 (1997).
Education: High school graduation rate: 78.2% (2000); College graduation rate: 9.3% (2000).
Housing: Homeownership rate: 82.0% (2000); Median home value: $73,200 (2000); Median rent: $238 per month (2000); Median age of housing: 23 years (2000).
Transportation: Commute to work: 91.6% car, 0.0% public transportation, 0.5% walk, 6.8% work from home (2000); Travel time to work: 12.9% less than 15 minutes, 33.1% 15 to 30 minutes, 32.6% 30 to 45 minutes, 8.4% 45 to 60 minutes, 12.9% 60 minutes or more (2000)

HARRIS (township). Covers a land area of 143.095 square miles and a water area of 0.141 square miles. Located at 45.74° N. Lat.; 87.39° W. Long. Elevation is 795 feet.
History: Harris was named for early settler Michael B. Harris, who came here in 1875 to work in the lumber industry. Harris is credited with saving a group of Potawatomi from starvation by taking food and milk to them when they were quarantined by a smallpox epidemic.
Population: 1,895 (2000); Race: 75.8% White, 0.2% Black, 0.4% Asian, 21.3% American Indian and Alaska Native, 1.3% Hispanic of any race, 1.1% two or more races (2000); Density: 13.2 persons per square mile (2000); Age: 30.3% under 18, 10.7% over 64 (2000); Marriage status: 26.1% never married, 59.3% now married, 4.9% widowed, 9.7% divorced (2000); Foreign born: 0.9% (2000); Ancestry (includes multiple ancestries): 21.6% Other groups, 16.0% French (except Basque), 14.9% German, 13.9% Polish, 9.2% Swedish (2000).
Economy: Employment by occupation: 10.8% management, 10.0% professional, 23.1% services, 17.7% sales, 4.7% farming, 9.4% construction, 24.3% production (2000).
Income: Per capita income: $14,764 (2000); Median household income: $32,950 (2000); Poverty rate: 14.5% (2000).
Taxes: Total city taxes per capita: $33 (1997); City property taxes per capita: $32 (1997).
Education: High school graduation rate: 82.8% (2000); College graduation rate: 6.1% (2000).
Housing: Homeownership rate: 75.3% (2000); Median home value: $69,800 (2000); Median rent: $182 per month (2000); Median age of housing: 25 years (2000).
Transportation: Commute to work: 88.6% car, 0.0% public transportation, 2.0% walk, 8.2% work from home (2000); Travel time to work: 38.4% less than 15 minutes, 32.0% 15 to 30 minutes, 17.8% 30 to 45 minutes, 4.7% 45 to 60 minutes, 7.1% 60 minutes or more (2000)

HERMANSVILLE (unincorporated postal area, zip code 49847). Covers a land area of 55.936 square miles and a water area of 0.427 square miles. Located at 45.71° N. Lat.; 87.61° W. Long. Elevation is 887 feet.
History: Hermansville grew up around the Wisconsin Land and Lumber Company's hardwood flooring mill. Charles J.L. Meyer, who founded the company in 1883, named the town for his younger son, Herman.
Population: 1,041 (2000); Race: 99.2% White, 0.2% Black, 0.0% Asian, 0.2% American Indian and Alaska Native, 1.0% Hispanic of any race, 0.5% two or more races (2000); Density: 18.6 persons per square mile (2000); Age: 24.4% under 18, 19.0% over 64 (2000); Marriage status: 20.8% never married, 61.3% now married, 7.4% widowed, 10.4% divorced (2000); Foreign born: 1.0% (2000); Ancestry (includes multiple ancestries): 20.8% French (except Basque), 20.6% German, 10.4% French Canadian, 9.5% Italian, 8.3% Polish (2000).
Economy: Employment by occupation: 5.4% management, 10.4% professional, 20.5% services, 18.8% sales, 2.3% farming, 7.5% construction, 35.2% production (2000).
Income: Per capita income: $16,275 (2000); Median household income: $33,409 (2000); Poverty rate: 8.7% (2000).
Education: High school graduation rate: 78.6% (2000); College graduation rate: 7.2% (2000).
Housing: Homeownership rate: 80.8% (2000); Median home value: $47,400 (2000); Median rent: $276 per month (2000); Median age of housing: 43 years (2000).
Transportation: Commute to work: 93.7% car, 0.2% public transportation, 2.5% walk, 2.9% work from home (2000); Travel time to work: 43.6% less than 15 minutes, 21.9% 15 to 30 minutes, 21.3% 30 to 45 minutes, 5.4% 45 to 60 minutes, 7.8% 60 minutes or more (2000)

HOLMES (township). Covers a land area of 71.251 square miles and a water area of 1.158 square miles. Located at 45.51° N. Lat.; 87.73° W. Long.
Population: 296 (2000); Race: 98.4% White, 0.6% Black, 0.0% Asian, 0.0% American Indian and Alaska Native, 0.0% Hispanic of any race, 1.0% two or more races (2000); Density: 4.2 persons per square mile (2000); Age: 22.3% under 18, 22.9% over 64 (2000); Marriage status: 15.7% never married, 68.5% now married, 7.1% widowed, 8.7% divorced (2000); Foreign born: 1.0% (2000); Ancestry (includes multiple ancestries): 46.5% German, 14.5% Swedish, 14.5% Polish, 8.4% French (except Basque), 7.7% English (2000).
Economy: Employment by occupation: 11.5% management, 11.5% professional, 13.8% services, 5.4% sales, 13.8% farming, 7.7% construction, 36.2% production (2000).
Income: Per capita income: $15,196 (2000); Median household income: $35,547 (2000); Poverty rate: 14.8% (2000).

Taxes: Total city taxes per capita: $84 (1997); City property taxes per capita: $84 (1997).
Education: High school graduation rate: 86.1% (2000); College graduation rate: 7.6% (2000).
Housing: Homeownership rate: 85.3% (2000); Median home value: $75,700 (2000); Median rent: $367 per month (2000); Median age of housing: 26 years (2000).
Transportation: Commute to work: 98.5% car, 0.0% public transportation, 0.0% walk, 1.5% work from home (2000); Travel time to work: 17.2% less than 15 minutes, 25.8% 15 to 30 minutes, 18.8% 30 to 45 minutes, 24.2% 45 to 60 minutes, 14.1% 60 minutes or more (2000)

INGALLS (unincorporated postal area, zip code 49848). Covers a land area of 5.751 square miles and a water area of 0 square miles. Located at 45.37° N. Lat.; 87.63° W. Long. Elevation is 696 feet.
History: The first settler came to Ingalls in 1858. It was named for Judge Eleazer S. Ingalls, a community leader.
Population: 189 (2000); Race: 98.1% White, 0.0% Black, 1.0% Asian, 1.0% American Indian and Alaska Native, 1.0% Hispanic of any race, 0.0% two or more races (2000); Density: 32.9 persons per square mile (2000); Age: 35.3% under 18, 5.8% over 64 (2000); Marriage status: 28.3% never married, 55.9% now married, 10.5% widowed, 5.3% divorced (2000); Foreign born: 1.0% (2000); Ancestry (includes multiple ancestries): 32.9% German, 17.4% Polish, 11.6% French (except Basque), 10.6% French Canadian, 7.7% Other groups (2000).
Economy: Employment by occupation: 15.4% management, 12.8% professional, 6.4% services, 10.3% sales, 0.0% farming, 14.1% construction, 41.0% production (2000).
Income: Per capita income: $12,199 (2000); Median household income: $32,917 (2000); Poverty rate: 10.1% (2000).
Education: High school graduation rate: 72.1% (2000); College graduation rate: 6.6% (2000).
Housing: Homeownership rate: 75.3% (2000); Median home value: $77,500 (2000); Median rent: $275 per month (2000); Median age of housing: 36 years (2000).
Transportation: Commute to work: 94.7% car, 0.0% public transportation, 0.0% walk, 5.3% work from home (2000); Travel time to work: 29.2% less than 15 minutes, 18.1% 15 to 30 minutes, 38.9% 30 to 45 minutes, 4.2% 45 to 60 minutes, 9.7% 60 minutes or more (2000)

INGALLSTON (township). Covers a land area of 70.824 square miles and a water area of 0.817 square miles. Located at 45.29° N. Lat.; 87.46° W. Long.
History: Ingallston Township was organized in 1863 and named for Eleazer S. and Charles B. Ingalls, brothers who built a sawmill here in 1866.
Population: 1,042 (2000); Race: 97.0% White, 0.0% Black, 0.5% Asian, 0.9% American Indian and Alaska Native, 0.0% Hispanic of any race, 1.6% two or more races (2000); Density: 14.7 persons per square mile (2000); Age: 21.2% under 18, 18.0% over 64 (2000); Marriage status: 19.8% never married, 63.9% now married, 7.3% widowed, 9.1% divorced (2000); Foreign born: 2.7% (2000); Ancestry (includes multiple ancestries): 36.7% German, 17.7% Polish, 15.0% French (except Basque), 14.6% Swedish, 9.3% Irish (2000).
Economy: Employment by occupation: 9.5% management, 15.6% professional, 14.3% services, 19.4% sales, 1.3% farming, 11.6% construction, 28.4% production (2000).
Income: Per capita income: $18,232 (2000); Median household income: $37,361 (2000); Poverty rate: 8.3% (2000).
Taxes: Total city taxes per capita: $31 (1997); City property taxes per capita: $30 (1997).
Education: High school graduation rate: 85.4% (2000); College graduation rate: 13.9% (2000).
Housing: Homeownership rate: 90.6% (2000); Median home value: $98,200 (2000); Median rent: $505 per month (2000); Median age of housing: 31 years (2000).
Transportation: Commute to work: 92.2% car, 0.4% public transportation, 0.9% walk, 5.4% work from home (2000); Travel time to work: 12.4% less than 15 minutes, 59.3% 15 to 30 minutes, 20.9% 30 to 45 minutes, 4.1% 45 to 60 minutes, 3.2% 60 minutes or more (2000)

LAKE (township). Covers a land area of 70.781 square miles and a water area of 1.954 square miles. Located at 45.42° N. Lat.; 87.76° W. Long.
Population: 576 (2000); Race: 97.8% White, 0.0% Black, 0.4% Asian, 0.9% American Indian and Alaska Native, 0.0% Hispanic of any race, 0.9% two or more races (2000); Density: 8.1 persons per square mile (2000); Age: 18.0% under 18, 17.3% over 64 (2000); Marriage status: 19.8% never married, 67.3% now married, 5.8% widowed, 7.2% divorced (2000); Foreign born: 2.3% (2000); Ancestry (includes multiple ancestries): 34.1% German, 14.6% French (except Basque), 13.3% Polish, 13.2% Swedish, 9.0% French Canadian (2000).
Economy: Employment by occupation: 8.6% management, 10.4% professional, 14.3% services, 16.8% sales, 7.9% farming, 6.8% construction, 35.4% production (2000).
Income: Per capita income: $17,244 (2000); Median household income: $35,446 (2000); Poverty rate: 9.8% (2000).
Taxes: Total city taxes per capita: $127 (1997); City property taxes per capita: $127 (1997).
Education: High school graduation rate: 81.8% (2000); College graduation rate: 9.7% (2000).
Housing: Homeownership rate: 84.2% (2000); Median home value: $71,200 (2000); Median rent: $234 per month (2000); Median age of housing: 34 years (2000).
Transportation: Commute to work: 91.9% car, 0.0% public transportation, 3.3% walk, 4.0% work from home (2000); Travel time to work: 25.6% less than 15 minutes, 18.3% 15 to 30 minutes, 27.9% 30 to 45 minutes, 16.0% 45 to 60 minutes, 12.2% 60 minutes or more (2000)

MELLEN (township). Covers a land area of 30.804 square miles and a water area of 0.586 square miles. Located at 45.34° N. Lat.; 87.62° W. Long.
Population: 1,260 (2000); Race: 97.6% White, 0.2% Black, 1.1% Asian, 1.0% American Indian and Alaska Native, 0.5% Hispanic of any race, 0.1% two or more races (2000); Density: 40.9 persons per square mile (2000); Age: 26.8% under 18, 12.0% over 64 (2000); Marriage status: 22.7% never married, 63.8% now married, 5.1% widowed, 8.5% divorced (2000); Foreign born: 1.1% (2000); Ancestry (includes multiple ancestries): 36.3% German, 16.1% French (except Basque), 12.4% Polish, 12.4% Swedish, 7.3% Irish (2000).
Economy: Employment by occupation: 4.1% management, 8.6% professional, 11.2% services, 17.5% sales, 1.7% farming, 15.1% construction, 41.9% production (2000).
Income: Per capita income: $16,096 (2000); Median household income: $35,435 (2000); Poverty rate: 10.3% (2000).
Education: High school graduation rate: 83.7% (2000); College graduation rate: 6.5% (2000).
Housing: Homeownership rate: 83.7% (2000); Median home value: $82,100 (2000); Median rent: $298 per month (2000); Median age of housing: 29 years (2000).
Transportation: Commute to work: 93.3% car, 0.0% public transportation, 3.1% walk, 3.3% work from home (2000); Travel time to work: 21.5% less than 15 minutes, 41.4% 15 to 30 minutes, 29.1% 30 to 45 minutes, 1.8% 45 to 60 minutes, 6.2% 60 minutes or more (2000)

MENOMINEE (city). Covers a land area of 5.179 square miles and a water area of 0.315 square miles. Located at 45.12° N. Lat.; 87.61° W. Long. Elevation is 594 feet.
History: A trading post was established at this spot on the Menominee River in 1796. By the 1830's, a sawmill and dam had been constructed, and soon fish joined lumber as a marketable product. When lumbering declined after 1910, a dairying industry developed. Water power provided by plants on the Menominee River later made this a manufacturing city, as well as a destination for vacationers.
Population: 9,131 (2000); Race: 97.7% White, 0.3% Black, 0.0% Asian, 0.6% American Indian and Alaska Native, 0.3% Hispanic of any race, 1.4% two or more races (2000); Density: 1,763.2 persons per square mile (2000); Age: 24.0% under 18, 17.9% over 64 (2000); Marriage status: 26.2% never married, 51.8% now married, 9.3% widowed, 12.7% divorced (2000); Foreign born: 0.8% (2000); Ancestry (includes multiple ancestries): 34.2% German, 14.0% French (except Basque), 10.5% Polish, 10.0% Swedish, 9.2% Irish (2000).
Economy: Single-family building permits issued: 15 (2001) / 15 (2000); Multi-family building permits issued: 0 (2001) / 0 (2000); Employment by occupation: 9.6% management, 12.7% professional, 17.2% services, 21.7% sales, 0.3% farming, 8.4% construction, 30.1% production (2000).
Income: Per capita income: $17,500 (2000); Median household income: $30,523 (2000); Poverty rate: 13.3% (2000).
Taxes: Total city taxes per capita: $354 (1997); City property taxes per capita: $343 (1997).
Education: High school graduation rate: 85.4% (2000); College graduation rate: 13.1% (2000).

School District(s)

Menominee Area Public Schools (KG-12)
2000 Enrollment: 2,111 906-863-9951

Housing: Homeownership rate: 69.7% (2000); Median home value: $56,300 (2000); Median rent: $307 per month (2000); Median age of housing: 54 years (2000).
Safety: Violent crime rate: 21.8 per 10,000 population; Property crime rate: 378.0 per 10,000 population (2001).
Transportation: Commute to work: 92.3% car, 0.5% public transportation, 3.5% walk, 1.5% work from home (2000); Travel time to work: 75.3% less than 15 minutes, 18.4% 15 to 30 minutes, 3.4% 30 to 45 minutes, 1.1% 45 to 60 minutes, 1.9% 60 minutes or more (2000)
Additional Information Contacts
Menominee Chamber of Commerce 906-863-2679

MENOMINEE (township). Covers a land area of 72.665 square miles and a water area of 0.812 square miles. Located at 45.19° N. Lat.; 87.63° W. Long. Elevation is 594 feet.
History: Of interest is the mystery ship, raised (1969) from the bottom of Green Bay, where it sank in 1864. Incorporated 1883.
Population: 3,939 (2000); Race: 99.4% White, 0.0% Black, 0.1% Asian, 0.3% American Indian and Alaska Native, 0.6% Hispanic of any race, 0.3% two or more races (2000); Density: 54.2 persons per square mile (2000); Age: 23.2% under 18, 15.1% over 64 (2000); Marriage status: 17.4% never married, 68.5% now married, 6.5% widowed, 7.6% divorced (2000); Foreign born: 0.6% (2000); Ancestry (includes multiple ancestries): 32.5% German, 15.4% Polish, 15.0% French (except Basque), 8.1% Irish, 7.7% French Canadian (2000).
Economy: A distribution center for upper Michigan and Northern Wisconsin. Manufacturing includes fabricated metal products, machinery, consumer goods, paper products, lumber and wood products. Employment by occupation: 6.7% management, 14.0% professional, 10.7% services, 21.7% sales, 0.5% farming, 9.8% construction, 36.5% production (2000).
Income: Per capita income: $18,815 (2000); Median household income: $41,435 (2000); Poverty rate: 7.2% (2000).
Taxes: Total city taxes per capita: $20 (1997); City property taxes per capita: $19 (1997).
Education: High school graduation rate: 85.2% (2000); College graduation rate: 11.8% (2000).
Housing: Homeownership rate: 90.3% (2000); Median home value: $87,600 (2000); Median rent: $363 per month (2000); Median age of housing: 30 years (2000).
Transportation: Commute to work: 95.8% car, 0.7% public transportation, 0.5% walk, 2.2% work from home (2000); Travel time to work: 39.8% less than 15 minutes, 49.1% 15 to 30 minutes, 6.0% 30 to 45 minutes, 1.3% 45 to 60 minutes, 3.9% 60 minutes or more (2000)

MEYER (township). Covers a land area of 89.768 square miles and a water area of 0.426 square miles. Located at 45.72° N. Lat.; 87.62° W. Long.
Population: 1,036 (2000); Race: 98.8% White, 0.2% Black, 0.0% Asian, 0.4% American Indian and Alaska Native, 1.0% Hispanic of any race, 0.7% two or more races (2000); Density: 11.5 persons per square mile (2000); Age: 25.1% under 18, 19.0% over 64 (2000); Marriage status: 20.4% never married, 60.8% now married, 8.2% widowed, 10.6% divorced (2000); Foreign born: 1.0% (2000); Ancestry (includes multiple ancestries): 20.7% German, 20.0% French (except Basque), 11.1% French Canadian, 9.5% Italian, 8.4% Polish (2000).
Economy: Employment by occupation: 5.0% management, 10.6% professional, 20.7% services, 19.5% sales, 2.7% farming, 7.0% construction, 34.6% production (2000).
Income: Per capita income: $15,256 (2000); Median household income: $33,466 (2000); Poverty rate: 8.3% (2000).
Taxes: Total city taxes per capita: $40 (1997); City property taxes per capita: $40 (1997).
Education: High school graduation rate: 78.5% (2000); College graduation rate: 6.9% (2000).
Housing: Homeownership rate: 81.2% (2000); Median home value: $46,200 (2000); Median rent: $269 per month (2000); Median age of housing: 45 years (2000).
Transportation: Commute to work: 94.9% car, 0.2% public transportation, 2.1% walk, 2.1% work from home (2000); Travel time to work: 42.8% less than 15 minutes, 23.2% 15 to 30 minutes, 22.6% 30 to 45 minutes, 4.7% 45 to 60 minutes, 6.7% 60 minutes or more (2000)

NADEAU (township). Covers a land area of 80.689 square miles and a water area of 0.139 square miles. Located at 45.58° N. Lat.; 87.56° W. Long. Elevation is 810 feet.
Population: 1,160 (2000); Race: 97.7% White, 0.0% Black, 0.2% Asian, 0.9% American Indian and Alaska Native, 0.3% Hispanic of any race, 1.2% two or more races (2000); Density: 14.4 persons per square mile (2000); Age: 25.9% under 18, 13.4% over 64 (2000); Marriage status: 22.8% never married, 57.7% now married, 6.1% widowed, 13.4% divorced (2000); Foreign born: 0.4% (2000); Ancestry (includes multiple ancestries): 34.1% German, 10.3% Swedish, 10.1% French (except Basque), 9.3% Polish, 8.4% English (2000).
Economy: Employment by occupation: 8.4% management, 15.8% professional, 16.1% services, 17.3% sales, 2.3% farming, 11.7% construction, 28.4% production (2000).
Income: Per capita income: $15,983 (2000); Median household income: $29,375 (2000); Poverty rate: 11.6% (2000).
Taxes: Total city taxes per capita: $41 (1997); City property taxes per capita: $41 (1997).
Education: High school graduation rate: 82.0% (2000); College graduation rate: 7.7% (2000).
Housing: Homeownership rate: 89.8% (2000); Median home value: $48,600 (2000); Median rent: $261 per month (2000); Median age of housing: 36 years (2000).
Transportation: Commute to work: 88.6% car, 0.0% public transportation, 3.6% walk, 6.0% work from home (2000); Travel time to work: 34.3% less than 15 minutes, 29.4% 15 to 30 minutes, 10.6% 30 to 45 minutes, 14.9% 45 to 60 minutes, 10.9% 60 minutes or more (2000)

PERRONVILLE (unincorporated postal area, zip code 49873). Covers a land area of 82.367 square miles and a water area of 0.228 square miles. Located at 45.89° N. Lat.; 87.50° W. Long.
History: Perronville began when the railroad was built here in 1873 to haul ore and logs. A dam and sawmill were built in 1883 by Manazipe Perron, who became the first postmaster in 1897. Many farmers of Polish descent settled here after the lumbering declined.
Population: 100 (2000); Race: 94.8% White, 0.0% Black, 0.0% Asian, 0.0% American Indian and Alaska Native, 6.2% Hispanic of any race, 2.1% two or more races (2000); Density: 1.2 persons per square mile (2000); Age: 22.7% under 18, 24.7% over 64 (2000); Marriage status: 0.0% never married, 80.0% now married, 8.0% widowed, 12.0% divorced (2000); Foreign born: 0.0% (2000); Ancestry (includes multiple ancestries): 23.7% French (except Basque), 13.4% German, 12.4% Polish, 9.3% Irish, 9.3% Finnish (2000).
Economy: Employment by occupation: 11.8% management, 11.8% professional, 11.8% services, 14.7% sales, 0.0% farming, 17.6% construction, 32.4% production (2000).
Income: Per capita income: $19,048 (2000); Median household income: $40,938 (2000); Poverty rate: 11.3% (2000).
Education: High school graduation rate: 71.6% (2000); College graduation rate: 4.1% (2000).
Housing: Homeownership rate: 87.0% (2000); Median home value: $37,500 (2000); Median age of housing: 37 years (2000).
Transportation: Commute to work: 94.1% car, 0.0% public transportation, 5.9% walk, 0.0% work from home (2000); Travel time to work: 0.0% less than 15 minutes, 44.1% 15 to 30 minutes, 29.4% 30 to 45 minutes, 11.8% 45 to 60 minutes, 14.7% 60 minutes or more (2000)

POWERS (village). Covers a land area of 0.991 square miles and a water area of 0 square miles. Located at 45.69° N. Lat.; 87.52° W. Long. Elevation is 869 feet.
History: The village of Powers was platted and named by Edward Powers, a civil engineer with the Chicago & Northwestern Railroad.
Population: 430 (2000); Race: 100.0% White, 0.0% Black, 0.0% Asian, 0.0% American Indian and Alaska Native, 0.0% Hispanic of any race, 0.0% two or more races (2000); Density: 433.8 persons per square mile (2000); Age: 5.6% under 18, 56.8% over 64 (2000); Marriage status: 14.1% never married, 32.1% now married, 40.0% widowed, 13.8% divorced (2000); Foreign born: 0.0% (2000); Ancestry (includes multiple ancestries): 26.4% French (except Basque), 24.5% German, 14.4% Irish, 10.7% English, 9.9% Swedish (2000).
Economy: Employment by occupation: 7.4% management, 10.6% professional, 25.5% services, 13.8% sales, 2.1% farming, 8.5% construction, 31.9% production (2000).
Income: Per capita income: $14,207 (2000); Median household income: $20,250 (2000); Poverty rate: 17.9% (2000).
Taxes: Total city taxes per capita: $19 (1997); City property taxes per capita: $19 (1997).
Education: High school graduation rate: 60.5% (2000); College graduation rate: 4.7% (2000).

School District(s)

North Central Area Schools (PK-12)
2000 Enrollment: 571 906-497-5821

Housing: Homeownership rate: 52.9% (2000); Median home value: $55,900 (2000); Median rent: $230 per month (2000); Median age of housing: 43 years (2000).
Transportation: Commute to work: 73.3% car, 0.0% public transportation, 21.1% walk, 2.2% work from home (2000); Travel time to work: 58.0% less than 15 minutes, 14.8% 15 to 30 minutes, 17.0% 30 to 45 minutes, 2.3% 45 to 60 minutes, 8.0% 60 minutes or more (2000)

SPALDING (township). Covers a land area of 162.465 square miles and a water area of 0.412 square miles. Located at 45.76° N. Lat.; 87.52° W. Long. Elevation is 853 feet.
History: Spalding Township was named for Jesse Spalding, who owned land in the area.
Population: 1,761 (2000); Race: 98.4% White, 0.1% Black, 0.0% Asian, 0.7% American Indian and Alaska Native, 0.3% Hispanic of any race, 0.8% two or more races (2000); Density: 10.8 persons per square mile (2000); Age: 22.3% under 18, 22.3% over 64 (2000); Marriage status: 20.9% never married, 54.5% now married, 14.4% widowed, 10.3% divorced (2000); Foreign born: 0.5% (2000); Ancestry (includes multiple ancestries): 27.6% German, 26.5% French (except Basque), 11.6% Polish, 10.8% French Canadian, 10.2% Irish (2000).
Economy: Employment by occupation: 9.4% management, 9.5% professional, 19.2% services, 17.7% sales, 4.5% farming, 10.6% construction, 28.9% production (2000).
Income: Per capita income: $15,423 (2000); Median household income: $31,625 (2000); Poverty rate: 12.8% (2000).
Taxes: Total city taxes per capita: $38 (1997); City property taxes per capita: $38 (1997).
Education: High school graduation rate: 76.5% (2000); College graduation rate: 6.2% (2000).
Housing: Homeownership rate: 81.0% (2000); Median home value: $65,000 (2000); Median rent: $289 per month (2000); Median age of housing: 34 years (2000).
Transportation: Commute to work: 86.2% car, 0.0% public transportation, 7.7% walk, 4.5% work from home (2000); Travel time to work: 50.1% less than 15 minutes, 21.6% 15 to 30 minutes, 14.9% 30 to 45 minutes, 4.8% 45 to 60 minutes, 8.5% 60 minutes or more (2000)

STEPHENSON (city). Covers a land area of 1.094 square miles and a water area of 0 square miles. Located at 45.41° N. Lat.; 87.60° W. Long.
History: Stephenson began as a producer of charcoal and tan bark. The Chicago & Northwestern Railroad established a station here in 1872. The town was named for Samuel Stephenson, a member of congress from this district.
Population: 875 (2000); Race: 98.9% White, 0.0% Black, 0.0% Asian, 0.0% American Indian and Alaska Native, 0.0% Hispanic of any race, 1.1% two or more races (2000); Density: 800.1 persons per square mile (2000); Age: 19.4% under 18, 34.8% over 64 (2000); Marriage status: 16.5% never married, 48.9% now married, 24.8% widowed, 9.8% divorced (2000); Foreign born: 0.4% (2000); Ancestry (includes multiple ancestries): 33.6% German, 15.2% French (except Basque), 15.2% Swedish, 9.9% Polish, 8.9% French Canadian (2000).
Economy: Single-family building permits issued: 2 (2001) / 0 (2000); Multi-family building permits issued: 0 (2001) / 0 (2000); Employment by occupation: 10.1% management, 16.9% professional, 18.2% services, 16.9% sales, 0.0% farming, 9.4% construction, 28.6% production (2000).
Income: Per capita income: $16,615 (2000); Median household income: $25,357 (2000); Poverty rate: 11.8% (2000).
Taxes: Total city taxes per capita: $52 (1997); City property taxes per capita: $52 (1997).
Education: High school graduation rate: 77.0% (2000); College graduation rate: 14.2% (2000).

School District(s)

Stephenson Area Public Schools (KG-12)
2000 Enrollment: 925 906-753-2221

Housing: Homeownership rate: 76.5% (2000); Median home value: $60,200 (2000); Median rent: $282 per month (2000); Median age of housing: 48 years (2000).
Newspapers: The Menominee County Journal (1 x week)
Transportation: Commute to work: 91.0% car, 0.0% public transportation, 6.3% walk, 1.3% work from home (2000); Travel time to work: 47.5% less than 15 minutes, 15.2% 15 to 30 minutes, 29.0% 30 to 45 minutes, 3.4% 45 to 60 minutes, 5.1% 60 minutes or more (2000)

STEPHENSON (township). Covers a land area of 40.745 square miles and a water area of 0.472 square miles. Located at 45.41° N. Lat.; 87.54° W. Long.
Population: 716 (2000); Race: 99.0% White, 0.0% Black, 0.4% Asian, 0.0% American Indian and Alaska Native, 0.3% Hispanic of any race, 0.6% two or more races (2000); Density: 17.6 persons per square mile (2000); Age: 23.7% under 18, 17.9% over 64 (2000); Marriage status: 20.5% never married, 67.3% now married, 6.4% widowed, 5.7% divorced (2000); Foreign born: 1.3% (2000); Ancestry (includes multiple ancestries): 35.4% German, 17.6% Swedish, 14.1% French (except Basque), 13.2% Polish, 4.7% Belgian (2000).
Economy: In dairying and agricultural area. Employment by occupation: 15.0% management, 12.2% professional, 9.7% services, 15.0% sales, 3.1% farming, 16.6% construction, 28.4% production (2000).
Income: Per capita income: $15,727 (2000); Median household income: $33,000 (2000); Poverty rate: 9.8% (2000).
Taxes: Total city taxes per capita: $23 (1997); City property taxes per capita: $23 (1997).
Education: High school graduation rate: 85.8% (2000); College graduation rate: 10.1% (2000).
Housing: Homeownership rate: 90.1% (2000); Median home value: $61,800 (2000); Median rent: $263 per month (2000); Median age of housing: 51 years (2000).
Transportation: Commute to work: 80.9% car, 0.0% public transportation, 5.9% walk, 11.9% work from home (2000); Travel time to work: 42.6% less than 15 minutes, 12.8% 15 to 30 minutes, 27.3% 30 to 45 minutes, 8.9% 45 to 60 minutes, 8.5% 60 minutes or more (2000)

WALLACE (unincorporated postal area, zip code 49893). Covers a land area of 52.710 square miles and a water area of 0.409 square miles. Located at 45.31° N. Lat.; 87.63° W. Long.
Population: 1,679 (2000); Race: 97.7% White, 0.1% Black, 1.0% Asian, 0.6% American Indian and Alaska Native, 1.2% Hispanic of any race, 0.3% two or more races (2000); Density: 31.9 persons per square mile (2000); Age: 27.5% under 18, 12.4% over 64 (2000); Marriage status: 22.2% never married, 64.0% now married, 5.4% widowed, 8.4% divorced (2000); Foreign born: 1.0% (2000); Ancestry (includes multiple ancestries): 36.5% German, 16.3% Polish, 14.5% Swedish, 13.9% French (except Basque), 5.6% Norwegian (2000).
Economy: Employment by occupation: 6.0% management, 10.6% professional, 9.8% services, 18.7% sales, 1.0% farming, 15.5% construction, 38.6% production (2000).
Income: Per capita income: $15,883 (2000); Median household income: $34,750 (2000); Poverty rate: 8.0% (2000).
Education: High school graduation rate: 85.5% (2000); College graduation rate: 7.7% (2000).
Housing: Homeownership rate: 86.7% (2000); Median home value: $83,400 (2000); Median rent: $356 per month (2000); Median age of housing: 29 years (2000).
Transportation: Commute to work: 93.2% car, 0.0% public transportation, 2.1% walk, 3.6% work from home (2000); Travel time to work: 16.2% less than 15 minutes, 52.4% 15 to 30 minutes, 25.6% 30 to 45 minutes, 0.9% 45 to 60 minutes, 5.0% 60 minutes or more (2000)

WILSON (unincorporated postal area, zip code 49896). Covers a land area of 59.016 square miles and a water area of 0.087 square miles. Located at 45.68° N. Lat.; 87.37° W. Long.
Population: 1,652 (2000); Race: 72.9% White, 0.2% Black, 0.3% Asian, 24.8% American Indian and Alaska Native, 1.2% Hispanic of any race, 0.9% two or more races (2000); Density: 28.0 persons per square mile (2000); Age: 31.6% under 18, 10.3% over 64 (2000); Marriage status: 28.0% never married, 58.2% now married, 5.3% widowed, 8.5% divorced (2000); Foreign born: 0.6% (2000); Ancestry (includes multiple ancestries): 24.5% Other groups, 18.7% German, 15.9% French (except Basque), 8.7% Polish, 8.2% French Canadian (2000).
Economy: Employment by occupation: 9.9% management, 9.2% professional, 23.5% services, 18.0% sales, 5.5% farming, 10.5% construction, 23.5% production (2000).
Income: Per capita income: $13,029 (2000); Median household income: $30,938 (2000); Poverty rate: 17.0% (2000).
Education: High school graduation rate: 81.5% (2000); College graduation rate: 6.1% (2000).

School District(s)

Nah Tah Wahsh Public School Acad (KG-12)
2000 Enrollment: 156 906-227-2400

Housing: Homeownership rate: 72.7% (2000); Median home value: $69,300 (2000); Median rent: $182 per month (2000); Median age of housing: 24 years (2000).
Transportation: Commute to work: 89.3% car, 0.0% public transportation, 1.9% walk, 7.1% work from home (2000); Travel time to work: 39.4% less than 15 minutes, 29.8% 15 to 30 minutes, 18.4% 30 to 45 minutes, 4.8% 45 to 60 minutes, 7.5% 60 minutes or more (2000)

Midland County

Located in east central Michigan; drained by the Tittabawassee, Pine, and Chippewa Rivers. Covers a land area of 521.20 square miles, a water area of 6.70 square miles, and is located in the Eastern Time Zone. The county government was organized in 1850. County seat is Midland.

Midland County is part of the Saginaw-Bay City-Midland, MI MSA. The entire metro area includes: Bay County; Midland County; Saginaw County

Weather Station: Midland Elevation: 639 feet

	Jan	Feb	Mar	Apr	May	Jun	Jul	Aug	Sep	Oct	Nov	Dec
High	29	33	43	58	71	80	84	81	73	61	46	35
Low	15	17	25	35	46	56	60	59	51	41	32	22
Precip	1.6	1.2	2.3	2.8	2.7	3.0	2.5	3.6	3.9	2.6	2.5	1.9
Snow	na	na	na	0.4	0.0	0.0	0.0	0.0	0.0	tr	na	na

High and Low temperatures in degrees Fahrenheit; Precipitation and Snow in inches

Population: 82,874 (2000); Race: 95.3% White, 1.1% Black, 1.4% Asian, 0.5% American Indian and Alaska Native, 1.5% Hispanic of any race, 1.2% two or more races (2000); Density: 159.0 persons per square mile (2000); Age: 26.9% under 18, 12.0% over 64 (2000).
Religion: Five largest groups: 14.2% Catholic Church, 6.0% The United Methodist Church, 4.5% Lutheran Church—Missouri Synod, 2.6% Presbyterian Church (U.S.A.), 2.1% Evangelical Lutheran Church in America (2000).
Economy: Unemployment rate: 4.2% (11/2002); Total civilian labor force: 42,632 (11/2002); Leading industries: 16.3% manufacturing; 14.9% health care and social assistance; 14.1% retail trade (2000); Companies that employ more than 1,000 persons: 3 (2000); Companies that employ more than 100 persons: 49 (2000); Farms: 418 totaling 79,667 acres (1997); Minority business ownership rate: 3.0% (1997); Women business ownership rate: 25.9% (1997); Retail sales per capita: $8,893 (1997). Single-family building permits issued: 251 (2001) / 234 (2000); Multi-family building permits issued: 96 (2001) / 65 (2000).
Income: Per capita income: $23,383 (2000); Median household income: $45,674 (2000); Poverty rate: 8.4% (2000); Bankruptcy rate: 3.56% (2001).
Taxes: Total county taxes per capita: $284 (2000); County property taxes per capita: $276 (2000).
Education: High school graduation rate: 89.0% (2000); College graduation rate: 29.3% (2000).
Housing: Homeownership rate: 78.4% (2000); Median home value: $101,800 (2000); Median rent: $438 per month (2000); Median age of housing: 29 years (2000).
Health: Birth rate: 123.8 per 10,000 population (1998); Age adjusted death rate: 80.0 per 10,000 population (1999); Age adjusted cancer mortality rate: 197.1 deaths per 100,000 population (1999). Number of physicians: 22.8 per 10,000 population (1999); Number of hospital beds: 30.2 per 10,000 population (1999).
Elections: 2000 Presidential election results: 41.0% Gore, 56.3% Bush, 2.0% Nader, 0.0% Buchanan
National and State Parks: Tittabawassee River State Forest
Additional Information Contacts
Midland County Government Offices 989-832-6775
Midland Board of Realtors 989-631-6350
Midland Chamber of Commerce 989-839-9901
Sanford Chamber of Commerce 989-687-2800

Midland County Communities

COLEMAN (city). Covers a land area of 1.125 square miles and a water area of 0 square miles. Located at 43.75° N. Lat.; 84.58° W. Long. Elevation is 757 feet.
History: Coleman was surveyed in the 1860's by Seymour Coleman, who donated land for the Pere Marquette Railroad depot in 1871.
Population: 1,296 (2000); Race: 95.6% White, 0.0% Black, 0.0% Asian, 1.2% American Indian and Alaska Native, 2.3% Hispanic of any race, 1.6% two or more races (2000); Density: 1,151.7 persons per square mile (2000); Age: 26.7% under 18, 15.5% over 64 (2000); Marriage status: 23.3% never married, 56.4% now married, 7.2% widowed, 13.1% divorced (2000); Foreign born: 0.2% (2000); Ancestry (includes multiple ancestries): 25.7% German, 11.9% Irish, 10.9% English, 8.6% Other groups, 8.0% United States or American (2000).
Economy: Single-family building permits issued: 1 (2001) / 0 (2000); Multi-family building permits issued: 0 (2001) / 0 (2000); Employment by occupation: 4.8% management, 12.0% professional, 25.5% services, 19.2% sales, 0.0% farming, 16.4% construction, 22.0% production (2000).
Income: Per capita income: $15,921 (2000); Median household income: $28,750 (2000); Poverty rate: 17.0% (2000).
Taxes: Total city taxes per capita: $148 (1997); City property taxes per capita: $148 (1997).
Education: High school graduation rate: 79.2% (2000); College graduation rate: 5.7% (2000).

School District(s)
Coleman Community School District (KG-12)
2000 Enrollment: 1,054 517-465-6060
Housing: Homeownership rate: 70.9% (2000); Median home value: $63,500 (2000); Median rent: $361 per month (2000); Median age of housing: 42 years (2000).
Safety: Violent crime rate: 0.0 per 10,000 population; Property crime rate: 291.6 per 10,000 population (2001).
Transportation: Commute to work: 93.4% car, 0.2% public transportation, 2.5% walk, 2.9% work from home (2000); Travel time to work: 28.0% less than 15 minutes, 25.1% 15 to 30 minutes, 34.0% 30 to 45 minutes, 4.5% 45 to 60 minutes, 8.5% 60 minutes or more (2000)

EDENVILLE (township). Covers a land area of 34.836 square miles and a water area of 1.043 square miles. Located at 43.77° N. Lat.; 84.40° W. Long.
Population: 2,528 (2000); Race: 95.5% White, 0.0% Black, 0.2% Asian, 3.2% American Indian and Alaska Native, 0.2% Hispanic of any race, 1.1% two or more races (2000); Density: 72.6 persons per square mile (2000); Age: 24.2% under 18, 10.7% over 64 (2000); Marriage status: 18.2% never married, 66.9% now married, 3.3% widowed, 11.5% divorced (2000); Foreign born: 1.9% (2000); Ancestry (includes multiple ancestries): 25.2% German, 14.6% English, 13.6% Irish, 8.5% Other groups, 7.6% French (except Basque) (2000).
Economy: Single-family building permits issued: 18 (2001) / 12 (2000); Multi-family building permits issued: 0 (2001) / 0 (2000); Employment by occupation: 7.5% management, 19.2% professional, 13.0% services, 29.0% sales, 0.0% farming, 14.9% construction, 16.4% production (2000).
Income: Per capita income: $20,470 (2000); Median household income: $42,847 (2000); Poverty rate: 8.1% (2000).
Taxes: Total city taxes per capita: $34 (1997); City property taxes per capita: $28 (1997).
Education: High school graduation rate: 82.8% (2000); College graduation rate: 15.7% (2000).
Housing: Homeownership rate: 90.1% (2000); Median home value: $97,200 (2000); Median rent: $398 per month (2000); Median age of housing: 25 years (2000).
Transportation: Commute to work: 98.2% car, 0.0% public transportation, 0.6% walk, 0.4% work from home (2000); Travel time to work: 12.4% less than 15 minutes, 41.5% 15 to 30 minutes, 27.7% 30 to 45 minutes, 11.6% 45 to 60 minutes, 6.8% 60 minutes or more (2000)

GENEVA (township). Covers a land area of 36.021 square miles and a water area of 0 square miles. Located at 43.69° N. Lat.; 84.53° W. Long.
Population: 1,137 (2000); Race: 98.0% White, 0.0% Black, 0.0% Asian, 1.7% American Indian and Alaska Native, 2.5% Hispanic of any race, 0.4% two or more races (2000); Density: 31.6 persons per square mile (2000); Age: 24.6% under 18, 12.6% over 64 (2000); Marriage status: 18.3% never married, 67.0% now married, 5.0% widowed, 9.8% divorced (2000); Foreign born: 0.1% (2000); Ancestry (includes multiple ancestries): 29.4% German, 13.9% Irish, 12.8% English, 12.5% United States or American, 6.6% Other groups (2000).
Economy: Employment by occupation: 6.6% management, 15.4% professional, 17.2% services, 22.6% sales, 0.0% farming, 14.4% construction, 23.8% production (2000).
Income: Per capita income: $17,479 (2000); Median household income: $41,908 (2000); Poverty rate: 8.5% (2000).
Taxes: Total city taxes per capita: $28 (1997); City property taxes per capita: $28 (1997).
Education: High school graduation rate: 84.9% (2000); College graduation rate: 8.8% (2000).

Housing: Homeownership rate: 89.7% (2000); Median home value: $72,800 (2000); Median rent: $385 per month (2000); Median age of housing: 27 years (2000).
Transportation: Commute to work: 95.0% car, 0.0% public transportation, 0.4% walk, 3.2% work from home (2000); Travel time to work: 13.3% less than 15 minutes, 43.8% 15 to 30 minutes, 31.3% 30 to 45 minutes, 5.6% 45 to 60 minutes, 6.0% 60 minutes or more (2000)

GREENDALE (township). Covers a land area of 36.096 square miles and a water area of 0 square miles. Located at 43.59° N. Lat.; 84.56° W. Long.
Population: 1,788 (2000); Race: 94.5% White, 0.4% Black, 0.5% Asian, 1.4% American Indian and Alaska Native, 0.8% Hispanic of any race, 3.0% two or more races (2000); Density: 49.5 persons per square mile (2000); Age: 32.1% under 18, 7.2% over 64 (2000); Marriage status: 20.5% never married, 62.9% now married, 5.8% widowed, 10.8% divorced (2000); Foreign born: 0.8% (2000); Ancestry (includes multiple ancestries): 22.7% German, 15.7% United States or American, 8.9% Other groups, 8.8% English, 8.5% Irish (2000).
Economy: Single-family building permits issued: 15 (2001) / 15 (2000); Multi-family building permits issued: 0 (2001) / 0 (2000); Employment by occupation: 4.9% management, 12.5% professional, 21.2% services, 21.4% sales, 0.7% farming, 18.9% construction, 20.5% production (2000).
Income: Per capita income: $14,522 (2000); Median household income: $33,587 (2000); Poverty rate: 13.7% (2000).
Taxes: Total city taxes per capita: $17 (1997); City property taxes per capita: $13 (1997).
Education: High school graduation rate: 77.9% (2000); College graduation rate: 5.8% (2000).
Housing: Homeownership rate: 85.6% (2000); Median home value: $67,100 (2000); Median rent: $348 per month (2000); Median age of housing: 23 years (2000).
Transportation: Commute to work: 93.9% car, 1.3% public transportation, 0.3% walk, 2.8% work from home (2000); Travel time to work: 10.2% less than 15 minutes, 52.3% 15 to 30 minutes, 23.1% 30 to 45 minutes, 3.0% 45 to 60 minutes, 11.4% 60 minutes or more (2000)

HOMER (township). Covers a land area of 21.410 square miles and a water area of 0.146 square miles. Located at 43.60° N. Lat.; 84.32° W. Long.
Population: 3,924 (2000); Race: 99.4% White, 0.2% Black, 0.0% Asian, 0.2% American Indian and Alaska Native, 1.4% Hispanic of any race, 0.2% two or more races (2000); Density: 183.3 persons per square mile (2000); Age: 26.6% under 18, 12.2% over 64 (2000); Marriage status: 18.4% never married, 67.8% now married, 4.9% widowed, 8.8% divorced (2000); Foreign born: 1.1% (2000); Ancestry (includes multiple ancestries): 26.7% German, 15.2% English, 12.0% United States or American, 10.3% Irish, 7.2% French (except Basque) (2000).
Economy: Single-family building permits issued: 28 (2001) / 28 (2000); Multi-family building permits issued: 0 (2001) / 0 (2000); Employment by occupation: 8.5% management, 23.1% professional, 15.4% services, 24.9% sales, 0.4% farming, 11.6% construction, 15.9% production (2000).
Income: Per capita income: $20,574 (2000); Median household income: $44,924 (2000); Poverty rate: 5.7% (2000).
Taxes: Total city taxes per capita: $69 (1997); City property taxes per capita: $64 (1997).
Education: High school graduation rate: 86.9% (2000); College graduation rate: 21.2% (2000).
Housing: Homeownership rate: 88.7% (2000); Median home value: $89,100 (2000); Median rent: $459 per month (2000); Median age of housing: 31 years (2000).
Transportation: Commute to work: 96.1% car, 0.5% public transportation, 0.0% walk, 3.2% work from home (2000); Travel time to work: 29.5% less than 15 minutes, 47.7% 15 to 30 minutes, 10.6% 30 to 45 minutes, 3.0% 45 to 60 minutes, 9.1% 60 minutes or more (2000)

HOPE (township). Covers a land area of 23.040 square miles and a water area of 0.352 square miles. Located at 43.79° N. Lat.; 84.33° W. Long. Elevation is 678 feet.
History: There were settlers in Hope in the 1850's. The township was organized in 1871, and named by the residents.
Population: 1,286 (2000); Race: 97.7% White, 1.3% Black, 0.0% Asian, 0.0% American Indian and Alaska Native, 0.3% Hispanic of any race, 1.0% two or more races (2000); Density: 55.8 persons per square mile (2000); Age: 22.4% under 18, 14.4% over 64 (2000); Marriage status: 16.9% never married, 69.9% now married, 4.4% widowed, 8.9% divorced (2000); Foreign born: 1.1% (2000); Ancestry (includes multiple ancestries): 31.8% German, 16.0% English, 12.0% Irish, 6.9% French (except Basque), 5.2% Polish (2000).
Economy: Single-family building permits issued: 4 (2001) / 4 (2000); Multi-family building permits issued: 0 (2001) / 0 (2000); Employment by occupation: 12.2% management, 16.9% professional, 13.4% services, 25.6% sales, 0.0% farming, 16.7% construction, 15.2% production (2000).
Income: Per capita income: $23,660 (2000); Median household income: $45,313 (2000); Poverty rate: 3.3% (2000).
Taxes: Total city taxes per capita: $25 (1997); City property taxes per capita: $24 (1997).
Education: High school graduation rate: 84.3% (2000); College graduation rate: 14.7% (2000).
Housing: Homeownership rate: 91.6% (2000); Median home value: $86,800 (2000); Median rent: $280 per month (2000); Median age of housing: 30 years (2000).
Transportation: Commute to work: 96.2% car, 0.0% public transportation, 0.3% walk, 3.2% work from home (2000); Travel time to work: 11.2% less than 15 minutes, 43.7% 15 to 30 minutes, 26.3% 30 to 45 minutes, 11.9% 45 to 60 minutes, 6.9% 60 minutes or more (2000)

INGERSOLL (township). Covers a land area of 36.388 square miles and a water area of 0.126 square miles. Located at 43.53° N. Lat.; 84.22° W. Long.
Population: 3,018 (2000); Race: 98.5% White, 0.8% Black, 0.0% Asian, 0.0% American Indian and Alaska Native, 0.7% Hispanic of any race, 0.5% two or more races (2000); Density: 82.9 persons per square mile (2000); Age: 25.4% under 18, 16.2% over 64 (2000); Marriage status: 20.9% never married, 64.9% now married, 8.2% widowed, 6.0% divorced (2000); Foreign born: 0.9% (2000); Ancestry (includes multiple ancestries): 34.0% German, 14.1% English, 11.8% United States or American, 11.6% Irish, 6.1% French (except Basque) (2000).
Economy: Single-family building permits issued: 6 (2001) / 6 (2000); Multi-family building permits issued: 0 (2001) / 0 (2000); Employment by occupation: 12.0% management, 18.8% professional, 17.7% services, 20.5% sales, 0.3% farming, 13.4% construction, 17.2% production (2000).
Income: Per capita income: $22,249 (2000); Median household income: $49,673 (2000); Poverty rate: 6.1% (2000).
Taxes: Total city taxes per capita: $72 (1997); City property taxes per capita: $66 (1997).
Education: High school graduation rate: 88.0% (2000); College graduation rate: 18.1% (2000).
Housing: Homeownership rate: 84.0% (2000); Median home value: $92,100 (2000); Median rent: $631 per month (2000); Median age of housing: 32 years (2000).
Transportation: Commute to work: 95.1% car, 0.0% public transportation, 0.1% walk, 4.4% work from home (2000); Travel time to work: 20.2% less than 15 minutes, 52.0% 15 to 30 minutes, 18.2% 30 to 45 minutes, 4.9% 45 to 60 minutes, 4.6% 60 minutes or more (2000)

JASPER (township). Covers a land area of 36.101 square miles and a water area of 0 square miles. Located at 43.51° N. Lat.; 84.54° W. Long.
Population: 1,145 (2000); Race: 98.8% White, 0.0% Black, 0.0% Asian, 0.3% American Indian and Alaska Native, 1.0% Hispanic of any race, 0.9% two or more races (2000); Density: 31.7 persons per square mile (2000); Age: 27.6% under 18, 9.9% over 64 (2000); Marriage status: 22.2% never married, 64.7% now married, 5.7% widowed, 7.4% divorced (2000); Foreign born: 0.0% (2000); Ancestry (includes multiple ancestries): 22.1% German, 11.6% English, 11.1% United States or American, 8.5% Irish, 7.6% Other groups (2000).
Economy: Single-family building permits issued: 2 (2001) / 2 (2000); Multi-family building permits issued: 0 (2001) / 0 (2000); Employment by occupation: 6.4% management, 12.7% professional, 13.3% services, 20.6% sales, 1.1% farming, 16.8% construction, 29.2% production (2000).
Income: Per capita income: $16,741 (2000); Median household income: $39,432 (2000); Poverty rate: 7.1% (2000).
Taxes: Total city taxes per capita: $55 (1997); City property taxes per capita: $53 (1997).
Education: High school graduation rate: 84.2% (2000); College graduation rate: 8.1% (2000).
Housing: Homeownership rate: 92.1% (2000); Median home value: $70,600 (2000); Median rent: $338 per month (2000); Median age of housing: 26 years (2000).
Transportation: Commute to work: 93.3% car, 0.0% public transportation, 0.8% walk, 5.4% work from home (2000); Travel time to work: 14.3% less than 15 minutes, 48.7% 15 to 30 minutes, 21.8% 30 to 45 minutes, 3.3% 45 to 60 minutes, 12.0% 60 minutes or more (2000)

JEROME (township). Covers a land area of 33.968 square miles and a water area of 1.668 square miles. Located at 43.68° N. Lat.; 84.40° W. Long.
Population: 4,888 (2000); Race: 96.5% White, 0.0% Black, 0.1% Asian, 1.7% American Indian and Alaska Native, 0.4% Hispanic of any race, 1.7% two or more races (2000); Density: 143.9 persons per square mile (2000); Age: 24.5% under 18, 11.8% over 64 (2000); Marriage status: 17.3% never married, 69.1% now married, 5.5% widowed, 8.1% divorced (2000); Foreign born: 1.0% (2000); Ancestry (includes multiple ancestries): 26.4% German, 12.9% English, 12.2% Irish, 10.7% United States or American, 9.1% French (except Basque) (2000).
Economy: Single-family building permits issued: 0 (2001) / 0 (2000); Multi-family building permits issued: 0 (2001) / 0 (2000); Employment by occupation: 11.5% management, 17.2% professional, 20.2% services, 21.6% sales, 0.1% farming, 14.4% construction, 15.0% production (2000).
Income: Per capita income: $19,328 (2000); Median household income: $39,854 (2000); Poverty rate: 6.7% (2000).
Taxes: Total city taxes per capita: $47 (1997); City property taxes per capita: $42 (1997).
Education: High school graduation rate: 86.0% (2000); College graduation rate: 14.0% (2000).
Housing: Homeownership rate: 88.3% (2000); Median home value: $92,700 (2000); Median rent: $341 per month (2000); Median age of housing: 28 years (2000).
Transportation: Commute to work: 93.5% car, 0.5% public transportation, 1.5% walk, 4.3% work from home (2000); Travel time to work: 22.1% less than 15 minutes, 53.1% 15 to 30 minutes, 14.3% 30 to 45 minutes, 6.1% 45 to 60 minutes, 4.5% 60 minutes or more (2000)

LARKIN CHARTER (township). Covers a land area of 32.756 square miles and a water area of 0.011 square miles. Located at 43.69° N. Lat.; 84.23° W. Long.
History: Larkin Township was organized in 1879 and named for John Larkin, early landowner and lumber camp operator who had petitioned for the township.
Population: 4,514 (2000); Race: 97.3% White, 0.0% Black, 0.7% Asian, 0.8% American Indian and Alaska Native, 1.2% Hispanic of any race, 1.0% two or more races (2000); Density: 137.8 persons per square mile (2000); Age: 32.5% under 18, 7.2% over 64 (2000); Marriage status: 20.8% never married, 71.3% now married, 2.5% widowed, 5.3% divorced (2000); Foreign born: 4.9% (2000); Ancestry (includes multiple ancestries): 33.3% German, 16.6% English, 12.5% Polish, 10.6% Irish, 6.1% French (except Basque) (2000).
Economy: Employment by occupation: 18.8% management, 29.7% professional, 15.4% services, 20.4% sales, 0.2% farming, 6.0% construction, 9.5% production (2000).
Income: Per capita income: $29,996 (2000); Median household income: $80,177 (2000); Poverty rate: 2.5% (2000).
Taxes: Total city taxes per capita: $30 (1997); City property taxes per capita: $24 (1997).
Education: High school graduation rate: 93.8% (2000); College graduation rate: 39.7% (2000).
Housing: Homeownership rate: 95.3% (2000); Median home value: $173,000 (2000); Median rent: $509 per month (2000); Median age of housing: 21 years (2000).
Transportation: Commute to work: 94.8% car, 0.6% public transportation, 0.8% walk, 3.6% work from home (2000); Travel time to work: 25.6% less than 15 minutes, 60.7% 15 to 30 minutes, 8.7% 30 to 45 minutes, 3.0% 45 to 60 minutes, 1.9% 60 minutes or more (2000)

LEE (township). Covers a land area of 35.975 square miles and a water area of 0.012 square miles. Located at 43.59° N. Lat.; 84.41° W. Long.
Population: 4,411 (2000); Race: 96.8% White, 0.0% Black, 0.2% Asian, 1.5% American Indian and Alaska Native, 1.0% Hispanic of any race, 1.5% two or more races (2000); Density: 122.6 persons per square mile (2000); Age: 31.7% under 18, 6.6% over 64 (2000); Marriage status: 24.3% never married, 62.6% now married, 2.8% widowed, 10.2% divorced (2000); Foreign born: 0.4% (2000); Ancestry (includes multiple ancestries): 23.5% German, 10.6% English, 10.6% Other groups, 10.1% United States or American, 8.2% Irish (2000).
Economy: Employment by occupation: 8.1% management, 12.4% professional, 21.5% services, 22.5% sales, 0.0% farming, 19.1% construction, 16.4% production (2000).
Income: Per capita income: $15,289 (2000); Median household income: $36,518 (2000); Poverty rate: 14.9% (2000).
Education: High school graduation rate: 80.4% (2000); College graduation rate: 12.3% (2000).
Housing: Homeownership rate: 81.6% (2000); Median home value: $82,300 (2000); Median rent: $344 per month (2000); Median age of housing: 24 years (2000).
Transportation: Commute to work: 95.3% car, 0.6% public transportation, 1.1% walk, 1.8% work from home (2000); Travel time to work: 8.8% less than 15 minutes, 58.9% 15 to 30 minutes, 19.0% 30 to 45 minutes, 7.0% 45 to 60 minutes, 6.3% 60 minutes or more (2000)

LINCOLN (township). Covers a land area of 23.408 square miles and a water area of 0.079 square miles. Located at 43.68° N. Lat.; 84.33° W. Long.
Population: 2,277 (2000); Race: 97.3% White, 0.0% Black, 0.4% Asian, 0.0% American Indian and Alaska Native, 1.8% Hispanic of any race, 1.8% two or more races (2000); Density: 97.3 persons per square mile (2000); Age: 28.2% under 18, 8.7% over 64 (2000); Marriage status: 21.7% never married, 67.8% now married, 3.2% widowed, 7.3% divorced (2000); Foreign born: 0.8% (2000); Ancestry (includes multiple ancestries): 30.7% German, 13.8% English, 11.3% Irish, 10.5% United States or American, 8.2% Polish (2000).
Economy: Single-family building permits issued: 13 (2001) / 17 (2000); Multi-family building permits issued: 0 (2001) / 0 (2000); Employment by occupation: 9.0% management, 19.6% professional, 17.0% services, 26.7% sales, 0.5% farming, 12.5% construction, 14.7% production (2000).
Income: Per capita income: $19,168 (2000); Median household income: $42,167 (2000); Poverty rate: 7.6% (2000).
Taxes: Total city taxes per capita: $35 (1997); City property taxes per capita: $32 (1997).
Education: High school graduation rate: 91.5% (2000); College graduation rate: 17.1% (2000).
Housing: Homeownership rate: 84.7% (2000); Median home value: $97,300 (2000); Median rent: $385 per month (2000); Median age of housing: 22 years (2000).
Transportation: Commute to work: 95.7% car, 0.6% public transportation, 1.0% walk, 1.9% work from home (2000); Travel time to work: 32.6% less than 15 minutes, 52.2% 15 to 30 minutes, 10.0% 30 to 45 minutes, 1.6% 45 to 60 minutes, 3.5% 60 minutes or more (2000)

MIDLAND (city). Covers a land area of 33.218 square miles and a water area of 1.733 square miles. Located at 43.62° N. Lat.; 84.23° W. Long. Elevation is 629 feet.
History: Midland developed first as a lumber town, but later became the home of the Dow Chemical Company, organized by Dr. Herbert H. Dow in 1890 as the Midland Chemical Company. Dr. Dow began his experiments in the extraction of bromine and other chemicals from the salt brine underlying the Midland region.
Population: 41,685 (2000); Race: 93.2% White, 2.0% Black, 2.6% Asian, 0.2% American Indian and Alaska Native, 1.9% Hispanic of any race, 1.2% two or more races (2000); Density: 1,254.9 persons per square mile (2000); Age: 25.6% under 18, 13.9% over 64 (2000); Marriage status: 24.7% never married, 59.8% now married, 6.1% widowed, 9.5% divorced (2000); Foreign born: 5.0% (2000); Ancestry (includes multiple ancestries): 31.1% German, 13.7% English, 13.4% Irish, 9.0% Other groups, 7.4% Polish (2000).
Vital Statistics: Birth rate: 120.2 per 10,000 population (1998)
Economy: Unemployment rate: 3.1% (11/2002); Total civilian labor force: 22,113 (11/2002); Single-family building permits issued: 76 (2001) / 72 (2000); Multi-family building permits issued: 96 (2001) / 65 (2000); Employment by occupation: 15.1% management, 31.1% professional, 14.7% services, 23.7% sales, 0.1% farming, 5.8% construction, 9.5% production (2000).
Income: Per capita income: $26,818 (2000); Median household income: $48,444 (2000); Poverty rate: 8.8% (2000).
Taxes: Total city taxes per capita: $691 (2000); City property taxes per capita: $680 (2000).
Education: High school graduation rate: 92.2% (2000); College graduation rate: 41.9% (2000).

School District(s)

Bullock Creek School District (KG-12)
2000 Enrollment: 2,082 517-631-9022
Midland Acad. Advanced/Creative (KG-09)
2000 Enrollment: 212 517-774-2100
Midland Public Schools (KG-12)
2000 Enrollment: 9,485 517-839-2401
Windover High School (09-12)
2000 Enrollment: 90 517-631-5890

Four-year College(s)

Northwood University (Private, Not-for-profit)
2001 Enrollment: 3,654 989-837-4200
2001 Tuition: In-state $12,231; Out-of-state $12,231

Davenport University-Central Region (Private, Not-for-profit)
2001 Enrollment: 1,875 517-835-5588
2001 Tuition: In-state $5,424; Out-of-state $5,424

Two-year College(s)

Delta College (Public)
2001 Enrollment: 9,764 989-686-9000
2001 Tuition: In-state $2,520; Out-of-state $3,600

Housing: Homeownership rate: 69.6% (2000); Median home value: $114,400 (2000); Median rent: $456 per month (2000); Median age of housing: 32 years (2000).

Hospitals: MidMichigan Medical Center (259 beds)

Safety: Violent crime rate: 17.7 per 10,000 population; Property crime rate: 214.5 per 10,000 population (2001).

Newspapers: Midland Daily News (7 x week)

Transportation: Commute to work: 93.7% car, 0.6% public transportation, 1.8% walk, 3.1% work from home (2000); Travel time to work: 57.8% less than 15 minutes, 26.1% 15 to 30 minutes, 10.9% 30 to 45 minutes, 2.6% 45 to 60 minutes, 2.6% 60 minutes or more (2000)

Additional Information Contacts

Midland Board of Realtors 989-631-6350
Midland Chamber of Commerce 989-839-9901

MIDLAND (township). Covers a land area of 7.777 square miles and a water area of 0.480 square miles. Located at 43.59° N. Lat.; 84.23° W. Long. Elevation is 629 feet.

History: Midland owes its development after 1890 to the Dow Chemical Company. Dow Gardens, original gardens at home of Dr. Herbert H. Dow, founder of Dow Chemical Corporation, and Dow Gardens Library and Center for Arts are in Midland; Saginaw Valley State University at University Center, 12 miles east. Incorporated 1887.

Population: 2,297 (2000); Race: 97.4% White, 1.0% Black, 0.2% Asian, 0.0% American Indian and Alaska Native, 1.1% Hispanic of any race, 1.4% two or more races (2000); Density: 295.3 persons per square mile (2000); Age: 33.8% under 18, 5.6% over 64 (2000); Marriage status: 17.8% never married, 70.6% now married, 2.7% widowed, 8.9% divorced (2000); Foreign born: 0.9% (2000); Ancestry (includes multiple ancestries): 29.9% German, 10.6% French (except Basque), 9.3% English, 9.0% Polish, 8.5% United States or American (2000).

Economy: Owes its development to the Dow Chemical Company; corporate headquarters here. Manufacturing includes silicone products, chemicals, magnesium, and plastics. Other manufacturing includes exhibits, metal cutting machinery and printing. Oil, coal and salt are found in the area. Single-family building permits issued: 7 (2001) / 6 (2000); Multi-family building permits issued: 0 (2001) / 0 (2000); Employment by occupation: 10.6% management, 20.2% professional, 14.2% services, 21.1% sales, 0.3% farming, 14.6% construction, 19.1% production (2000).

Income: Per capita income: $21,538 (2000); Median household income: $50,327 (2000); Poverty rate: 3.0% (2000).

Taxes: Total city taxes per capita: $237 (1997); City property taxes per capita: $228 (1997).

Education: High school graduation rate: 91.9% (2000); College graduation rate: 18.1% (2000).

Housing: Homeownership rate: 91.4% (2000); Median home value: $93,900 (2000); Median rent: $382 per month (2000); Median age of housing: 39 years (2000).

Transportation: Commute to work: 92.5% car, 0.9% public transportation, 0.9% walk, 4.6% work from home (2000); Travel time to work: 47.0% less than 15 minutes, 31.1% 15 to 30 minutes, 11.7% 30 to 45 minutes, 3.8% 45 to 60 minutes, 6.4% 60 minutes or more (2000)

MILLS (township). Covers a land area of 34.979 square miles and a water area of 1.023 square miles. Located at 43.78° N. Lat.; 84.24° W. Long.

Population: 1,871 (2000); Race: 98.3% White, 0.0% Black, 0.0% Asian, 0.8% American Indian and Alaska Native, 1.2% Hispanic of any race, 0.4% two or more races (2000); Density: 53.5 persons per square mile (2000); Age: 29.5% under 18, 7.0% over 64 (2000); Marriage status: 19.9% never married, 64.4% now married, 4.9% widowed, 10.9% divorced (2000); Foreign born: 0.5% (2000); Ancestry (includes multiple ancestries): 27.9% German, 13.6% English, 10.3% Irish, 7.8% United States or American, 7.3% Other groups (2000).

Economy: Single-family building permits issued: 19 (2001) / 14 (2000); Multi-family building permits issued: 0 (2001) / 0 (2000); Employment by occupation: 6.7% management, 13.0% professional, 16.5% services, 22.6% sales, 0.5% farming, 24.0% construction, 16.7% production (2000).

Income: Per capita income: $16,718 (2000); Median household income: $40,530 (2000); Poverty rate: 10.1% (2000).

Taxes: Total city taxes per capita: $44 (1997); City property taxes per capita: $40 (1997).

Education: High school graduation rate: 82.4% (2000); College graduation rate: 11.7% (2000).

Housing: Homeownership rate: 90.0% (2000); Median home value: $85,400 (2000); Median rent: $297 per month (2000); Median age of housing: 23 years (2000).

Transportation: Commute to work: 95.6% car, 0.0% public transportation, 1.8% walk, 2.4% work from home (2000); Travel time to work: 9.8% less than 15 minutes, 52.6% 15 to 30 minutes, 20.6% 30 to 45 minutes, 8.5% 45 to 60 minutes, 8.5% 60 minutes or more (2000)

MOUNT HALEY (township). Covers a land area of 23.783 square miles and a water area of 0 square miles. Located at 43.53° N. Lat.; 84.34° W. Long.

Population: 1,654 (2000); Race: 98.1% White, 0.0% Black, 0.8% Asian, 0.1% American Indian and Alaska Native, 1.0% Hispanic of any race, 0.7% two or more races (2000); Density: 69.5 persons per square mile (2000); Age: 26.3% under 18, 9.1% over 64 (2000); Marriage status: 21.2% never married, 66.4% now married, 3.2% widowed, 9.1% divorced (2000); Foreign born: 1.1% (2000); Ancestry (includes multiple ancestries): 29.4% German, 13.4% Irish, 12.6% English, 9.5% French (except Basque), 6.6% United States or American (2000).

Economy: Single-family building permits issued: 0 (2001) / 0 (2000); Multi-family building permits issued: 0 (2001) / 0 (2000); Employment by occupation: 10.6% management, 14.3% professional, 14.1% services, 25.0% sales, 0.0% farming, 14.9% construction, 21.0% production (2000).

Income: Per capita income: $18,553 (2000); Median household income: $42,321 (2000); Poverty rate: 8.3% (2000).

Taxes: Total city taxes per capita: $60 (1997); City property taxes per capita: $58 (1997).

Education: High school graduation rate: 87.4% (2000); College graduation rate: 11.9% (2000).

Housing: Homeownership rate: 91.8% (2000); Median home value: $86,300 (2000); Median rent: $425 per month (2000); Median age of housing: 29 years (2000).

Transportation: Commute to work: 94.9% car, 0.0% public transportation, 0.5% walk, 3.9% work from home (2000); Travel time to work: 12.2% less than 15 minutes, 48.0% 15 to 30 minutes, 23.2% 30 to 45 minutes, 8.6% 45 to 60 minutes, 8.0% 60 minutes or more (2000)

PORTER (township). Covers a land area of 35.741 square miles and a water area of 0 square miles. Located at 43.51° N. Lat.; 84.42° W. Long.

Population: 1,270 (2000); Race: 98.8% White, 0.0% Black, 0.2% Asian, 0.0% American Indian and Alaska Native, 1.3% Hispanic of any race, 0.6% two or more races (2000); Density: 35.5 persons per square mile (2000); Age: 27.9% under 18, 10.6% over 64 (2000); Marriage status: 17.0% never married, 67.7% now married, 4.9% widowed, 10.3% divorced (2000); Foreign born: 0.6% (2000); Ancestry (includes multiple ancestries): 28.3% German, 11.5% English, 11.1% Irish, 10.3% United States or American, 8.4% Other groups (2000).

Economy: Single-family building permits issued: 3 (2001) / 3 (2000); Multi-family building permits issued: 0 (2001) / 0 (2000); Employment by occupation: 7.7% management, 14.6% professional, 16.7% services, 23.9% sales, 1.3% farming, 12.8% construction, 23.0% production (2000).

Income: Per capita income: $16,681 (2000); Median household income: $37,315 (2000); Poverty rate: 10.9% (2000).

Taxes: Total city taxes per capita: $29 (1997); City property taxes per capita: $25 (1997).

Education: High school graduation rate: 80.4% (2000); College graduation rate: 6.6% (2000).

Housing: Homeownership rate: 90.9% (2000); Median home value: $76,000 (2000); Median rent: $331 per month (2000); Median age of housing: 24 years (2000).

Transportation: Commute to work: 93.3% car, 0.0% public transportation, 0.0% walk, 5.4% work from home (2000); Travel time to work: 17.6% less than 15 minutes, 36.9% 15 to 30 minutes, 29.8% 30 to 45 minutes, 11.8% 45 to 60 minutes, 3.9% 60 minutes or more (2000)

SANFORD (village). Covers a land area of 1.271 square miles and a water area of 0.283 square miles. Located at 43.67° N. Lat.; 84.37° W. Long. Elevation is 620 feet.

History: The village of Sanford was laid out in 1870 by Charles S. Sanford, who had come here from New York.
Population: 943 (2000); Race: 98.3% White, 0.0% Black, 0.3% Asian, 0.0% American Indian and Alaska Native, 2.1% Hispanic of any race, 1.3% two or more races (2000); Density: 742.1 persons per square mile (2000); Age: 22.7% under 18, 10.8% over 64 (2000); Marriage status: 20.6% never married, 58.4% now married, 6.5% widowed, 14.5% divorced (2000); Foreign born: 1.1% (2000); Ancestry (includes multiple ancestries): 28.2% German, 14.0% English, 13.0% Irish, 9.4% United States or American, 9.0% Polish (2000).
Economy: Single-family building permits issued: 2 (2001) / 3 (2000); Multi-family building permits issued: 0 (2001) / 0 (2000); Employment by occupation: 10.2% management, 24.8% professional, 19.4% services, 24.4% sales, 0.0% farming, 9.0% construction, 12.2% production (2000).
Income: Per capita income: $20,599 (2000); Median household income: $39,063 (2000); Poverty rate: 8.7% (2000).
Taxes: Total city taxes per capita: $38 (1997); City property taxes per capita: $33 (1997).
Education: High school graduation rate: 89.5% (2000); College graduation rate: 23.9% (2000).

School District(s)

Meridian Public Schools (KG-12)
2000 Enrollment: 1,638 517-687-3200

Housing: Homeownership rate: 80.3% (2000); Median home value: $97,400 (2000); Median rent: $394 per month (2000); Median age of housing: 36 years (2000).
Transportation: Commute to work: 91.0% car, 0.0% public transportation, 3.6% walk, 5.0% work from home (2000); Travel time to work: 26.9% less than 15 minutes, 51.2% 15 to 30 minutes, 13.5% 30 to 45 minutes, 1.7% 45 to 60 minutes, 6.7% 60 minutes or more (2000)

Additional Information Contacts

Sanford Chamber of Commerce. 989-687-2800

WARREN (township). Covers a land area of 35.012 square miles and a water area of 0.024 square miles. Located at 43.76° N. Lat.; 84.54° W. Long.
Population: 2,107 (2000); Race: 99.3% White, 0.0% Black, 0.0% Asian, 0.1% American Indian and Alaska Native, 1.2% Hispanic of any race, 0.3% two or more races (2000); Density: 60.2 persons per square mile (2000); Age: 28.4% under 18, 12.1% over 64 (2000); Marriage status: 19.4% never married, 68.7% now married, 5.7% widowed, 6.1% divorced (2000); Foreign born: 0.8% (2000); Ancestry (includes multiple ancestries): 28.9% German, 12.4% United States or American, 10.1% Irish, 10.0% English, 5.8% Other groups (2000).
Economy: Employment by occupation: 11.5% management, 10.8% professional, 17.6% services, 21.1% sales, 0.3% farming, 12.3% construction, 26.3% production (2000).
Income: Per capita income: $16,928 (2000); Median household income: $40,063 (2000); Poverty rate: 9.0% (2000).
Taxes: Total city taxes per capita: $20 (1997); City property taxes per capita: $20 (1997).
Education: High school graduation rate: 82.2% (2000); College graduation rate: 11.3% (2000).
Housing: Homeownership rate: 92.4% (2000); Median home value: $82,400 (2000); Median rent: $381 per month (2000); Median age of housing: 25 years (2000).
Transportation: Commute to work: 97.2% car, 0.0% public transportation, 0.0% walk, 2.5% work from home (2000); Travel time to work: 27.3% less than 15 minutes, 30.0% 15 to 30 minutes, 29.9% 30 to 45 minutes, 8.5% 45 to 60 minutes, 4.2% 60 minutes or more (2000)

Missaukee County

Located in north central Michigan; drained by the Muskegon River; includes part of Manistee National Forest. Covers a land area of 566.70 square miles, a water area of 7.10 square miles, and is located in the Eastern Time Zone. The county government was organized in 1840. County seat is Lake City.

Weather Station: Houghton Lake 6 WSW — Elevation: 1,131 feet

	Jan	Feb	Mar	Apr	May	Jun	Jul	Aug	Sep	Oct	Nov	Dec
High	26	29	39	53	67	76	81	78	69	56	43	31
Low	8	8	17	30	40	48	53	50	43	34	25	15
Precip	1.6	1.2	1.6	2.3	2.6	3.2	2.9	3.8	3.6	2.8	2.3	1.8
Snow	na	9.7	na	1.5	tr	0.0	0.0	0.0	0.0	0.3	5.9	na

High and Low temperatures in degrees Fahrenheit; Precipitation and Snow in inches

Weather Station: Lake City Exp. Farm — Elevation: 1,240 feet

	Jan	Feb	Mar	Apr	May	Jun	Jul	Aug	Sep	Oct	Nov	Dec
High	26	29	39	53	67	76	80	77	69	56	42	31
Low	8	9	17	30	41	50	54	53	45	35	26	16
Precip	1.6	1.2	2.0	2.8	2.7	3.0	2.9	3.6	3.8	3.0	2.5	1.8
Snow	20.0	14.8	11.9	4.2	0.5	0.0	0.0	0.0	tr	1.3	9.1	15.6

High and Low temperatures in degrees Fahrenheit; Precipitation and Snow in inches

Population: 14,478 (2000); Race: 98.1% White, 0.1% Black, 0.3% Asian, 0.4% American Indian and Alaska Native, 0.9% Hispanic of any race, 0.9% two or more races (2000); Density: 25.5 persons per square mile (2000); Age: 27.1% under 18, 14.9% over 64 (2000).
Religion: Five largest groups: 16.4% Christian Reformed Church in North America, 4.4% Reformed Church in America, 3.3% Catholic Church, 2.4% The United Methodist Church, 1.9% Evangelical Lutheran Church in America (2000).
Economy: Unemployment rate: 6.0% (11/2002); Total civilian labor force: 6,708 (11/2002); Leading industries: 20.9% retail trade; 17.7% manufacturing; 12.4% accommodation & food services (2000); Companies that employ more than 1,000 persons: 0 (2000); Companies that employ more than 100 persons: 0 (2000); Farms: 335 totaling 90,027 acres (1997); Minority business ownership rate: 0.0% (1997); Women business ownership rate: 27.2% (1997); Retail sales per capita: $7,566 (1997). Single-family building permits issued: 79 (2001) / 87 (2000); Multi-family building permits issued: 0 (2001) / 6 (2000).
Income: Per capita income: $16,072 (2000); Median household income: $35,224 (2000); Poverty rate: 10.7% (2000); Bankruptcy rate: 3.76% (2001).
Taxes: Total county taxes per capita: $133 (1997); County property taxes per capita: $112 (1997).
Education: High school graduation rate: 78.6% (2000); College graduation rate: 10.2% (2000).
Housing: Homeownership rate: 83.5% (2000); Median home value: $78,700 (2000); Median rent: $349 per month (2000); Median age of housing: 26 years (2000).
Health: Birth rate: 102.2 per 10,000 population (1998); Age adjusted death rate: 84.5 per 10,000 population (1999); Age adjusted cancer mortality rate: 163.7 deaths per 100,000 population (1999). Air Quality Index: 72% good, 28% moderate, 0% unhealthy (percent of days in 2000). Number of physicians: 2.8 per 10,000 population (1999); Number of hospital beds: n/a (1999).
Elections: 2000 Presidential election results: 31.7% Gore, 65.8% Bush, 1.9% Nader, 0.0% Buchanan

Additional Information Contacts

Missaukee County Government Offices 231-839-4967
Lake City Chamber of Commerce. 231-839-4969
McBain Chamber of Commerce. 231-825-2893

Missaukee County Communities

AETNA (township). Covers a land area of 35.871 square miles and a water area of 0 square miles. Located at 44.28° N. Lat.; 85.02° W. Long.
Population: 491 (2000); Race: 98.0% White, 0.7% Black, 0.0% Asian, 0.9% American Indian and Alaska Native, 0.0% Hispanic of any race, 0.4% two or more races (2000); Density: 13.7 persons per square mile (2000); Age: 26.6% under 18, 15.7% over 64 (2000); Marriage status: 28.1% never married, 62.3% now married, 6.6% widowed, 2.9% divorced (2000); Foreign born: 0.0% (2000); Ancestry (includes multiple ancestries): 34.7% Dutch, 22.7% German, 17.2% English, 11.8% United States or American, 10.0% Irish (2000).
Economy: Employment by occupation: 14.6% management, 10.2% professional, 14.2% services, 14.6% sales, 12.4% farming, 6.6% construction, 27.4% production (2000).
Income: Per capita income: $15,530 (2000); Median household income: $36,964 (2000); Poverty rate: 5.4% (2000).
Taxes: Total city taxes per capita: $66 (1997); City property taxes per capita: $66 (1997).
Education: High school graduation rate: 80.8% (2000); College graduation rate: 6.2% (2000).
Housing: Homeownership rate: 85.6% (2000); Median home value: $63,200 (2000); Median rent: $275 per month (2000); Median age of housing: 28 years (2000).
Transportation: Commute to work: 84.7% car, 0.9% public transportation, 4.6% walk, 8.8% work from home (2000); Travel time to work: 26.9% less than 15 minutes, 32.0% 15 to 30 minutes, 28.9% 30 to 45 minutes, 1.5% 45 to 60 minutes, 10.7% 60 minutes or more (2000)

BLOOMFIELD (township). Covers a land area of 35.664 square miles and a water area of 0 square miles. Located at 44.47° N. Lat.; 85.27° W. Long.
Population: 475 (2000); Race: 98.6% White, 0.0% Black, 0.0% Asian, 0.0% American Indian and Alaska Native, 0.0% Hispanic of any race, 1.4% two or more races (2000); Density: 13.3 persons per square mile (2000); Age: 24.6% under 18, 12.5% over 64 (2000); Marriage status: 16.0% never married, 71.9% now married, 2.8% widowed, 9.3% divorced (2000); Foreign born: 0.0% (2000); Ancestry (includes multiple ancestries): 25.6% German, 13.1% Irish, 10.7% United States or American, 10.5% English, 7.3% Dutch (2000).
Economy: Employment by occupation: 4.4% management, 12.7% professional, 10.3% services, 21.1% sales, 2.5% farming, 24.0% construction, 25.0% production (2000).
Income: Per capita income: $15,658 (2000); Median household income: $37,500 (2000); Poverty rate: 12.9% (2000).
Taxes: Total city taxes per capita: $34 (1997); City property taxes per capita: $34 (1997).
Education: High school graduation rate: 73.1% (2000); College graduation rate: 4.6% (2000).
Housing: Homeownership rate: 93.4% (2000); Median home value: $87,500 (2000); Median rent: $275 per month (2000); Median age of housing: 24 years (2000).
Transportation: Commute to work: 93.5% car, 0.0% public transportation, 4.0% walk, 1.0% work from home (2000); Travel time to work: 16.2% less than 15 minutes, 31.5% 15 to 30 minutes, 32.5% 30 to 45 minutes, 9.1% 45 to 60 minutes, 10.7% 60 minutes or more (2000)

BUTTERFIELD (township). Covers a land area of 35.811 square miles and a water area of 0.163 square miles. Located at 44.29° N. Lat.; 84.92° W. Long. Elevation is 1,166 feet.
Population: 548 (2000); Race: 97.6% White, 1.1% Black, 0.0% Asian, 0.5% American Indian and Alaska Native, 0.5% Hispanic of any race, 0.7% two or more races (2000); Density: 15.3 persons per square mile (2000); Age: 28.7% under 18, 10.3% over 64 (2000); Marriage status: 21.7% never married, 62.4% now married, 4.2% widowed, 11.8% divorced (2000); Foreign born: 0.4% (2000); Ancestry (includes multiple ancestries): 15.2% German, 15.2% Dutch, 12.3% English, 12.2% Irish, 6.9% United States or American (2000).
Economy: Employment by occupation: 8.6% management, 8.2% professional, 23.0% services, 18.4% sales, 2.3% farming, 15.2% construction, 24.2% production (2000).
Income: Per capita income: $16,993 (2000); Median household income: $37,188 (2000); Poverty rate: 8.8% (2000).
Taxes: Total city taxes per capita: $49 (1997); City property taxes per capita: $49 (1997).
Education: High school graduation rate: 77.8% (2000); College graduation rate: 6.5% (2000).
Housing: Homeownership rate: 83.0% (2000); Median home value: $51,400 (2000); Median rent: $292 per month (2000); Median age of housing: 20 years (2000).
Transportation: Commute to work: 89.4% car, 1.6% public transportation, 2.8% walk, 3.7% work from home (2000); Travel time to work: 19.4% less than 15 minutes, 32.9% 15 to 30 minutes, 28.3% 30 to 45 minutes, 10.5% 45 to 60 minutes, 8.9% 60 minutes or more (2000)

CALDWELL (township). Covers a land area of 34.429 square miles and a water area of 1.177 square miles. Located at 44.37° N. Lat.; 85.25° W. Long.
History: Caldwell Township was first called Quilna Township, renamed in 1873 for Thomas T. Caldwell. James C. Caldwell was the first postmaster here.
Population: 1,363 (2000); Race: 97.0% White, 0.0% Black, 1.6% Asian, 0.0% American Indian and Alaska Native, 0.7% Hispanic of any race, 1.4% two or more races (2000); Density: 39.6 persons per square mile (2000); Age: 27.7% under 18, 14.0% over 64 (2000); Marriage status: 22.5% never married, 59.0% now married, 7.2% widowed, 11.3% divorced (2000); Foreign born: 1.8% (2000); Ancestry (includes multiple ancestries): 25.5% German, 14.5% English, 13.3% Irish, 10.1% United States or American, 8.6% Dutch (2000).
Economy: Employment by occupation: 5.0% management, 8.6% professional, 18.2% services, 20.2% sales, 2.8% farming, 15.8% construction, 29.5% production (2000).
Income: Per capita income: $14,674 (2000); Median household income: $31,719 (2000); Poverty rate: 19.4% (2000).
Taxes: Total city taxes per capita: $17 (1997); City property taxes per capita: $13 (1997).
Education: High school graduation rate: 76.0% (2000); College graduation rate: 8.0% (2000).
Housing: Homeownership rate: 82.4% (2000); Median home value: $72,900 (2000); Median rent: $372 per month (2000); Median age of housing: 26 years (2000).
Transportation: Commute to work: 89.9% car, 2.8% public transportation, 2.2% walk, 2.8% work from home (2000); Travel time to work: 25.0% less than 15 minutes, 41.0% 15 to 30 minutes, 16.5% 30 to 45 minutes, 3.8% 45 to 60 minutes, 13.7% 60 minutes or more (2000)

CLAM UNION (township). Covers a land area of 35.805 square miles and a water area of 0.203 square miles. Located at 44.20° N. Lat.; 85.03° W. Long.
Population: 882 (2000); Race: 98.4% White, 0.0% Black, 0.2% Asian, 0.3% American Indian and Alaska Native, 0.5% Hispanic of any race, 1.0% two or more races (2000); Density: 24.6 persons per square mile (2000); Age: 32.0% under 18, 12.0% over 64 (2000); Marriage status: 22.1% never married, 67.4% now married, 5.7% widowed, 4.8% divorced (2000); Foreign born: 0.9% (2000); Ancestry (includes multiple ancestries): 47.2% Dutch, 7.9% German, 7.0% Irish, 5.5% English, 3.9% United States or American (2000).
Economy: Employment by occupation: 13.5% management, 9.6% professional, 14.4% services, 23.6% sales, 5.7% farming, 13.5% construction, 19.5% production (2000).
Income: Per capita income: $13,542 (2000); Median household income: $35,542 (2000); Poverty rate: 10.4% (2000).
Taxes: Total city taxes per capita: $46 (1997); City property taxes per capita: $46 (1997).
Education: High school graduation rate: 81.9% (2000); College graduation rate: 5.0% (2000).
Housing: Homeownership rate: 87.9% (2000); Median home value: $67,800 (2000); Median rent: $325 per month (2000); Median age of housing: 33 years (2000).
Transportation: Commute to work: 82.5% car, 0.0% public transportation, 7.7% walk, 9.8% work from home (2000); Travel time to work: 34.9% less than 15 minutes, 28.2% 15 to 30 minutes, 23.3% 30 to 45 minutes, 4.4% 45 to 60 minutes, 9.3% 60 minutes or more (2000)

ENTERPRISE (township). Covers a land area of 34.666 square miles and a water area of 0.338 square miles. Located at 44.36° N. Lat.; 84.91° W. Long.
Population: 194 (2000); Race: 98.9% White, 0.0% Black, 0.0% Asian, 0.0% American Indian and Alaska Native, 1.1% Hispanic of any race, 1.1% two or more races (2000); Density: 5.6 persons per square mile (2000); Age: 33.7% under 18, 12.7% over 64 (2000); Marriage status: 10.8% never married, 79.2% now married, 6.7% widowed, 3.3% divorced (2000); Foreign born: 0.0% (2000); Ancestry (includes multiple ancestries): 19.3% German, 10.5% United States or American, 8.3% Polish, 7.2% Irish, 7.2% Dutch (2000).
Economy: Employment by occupation: 3.4% management, 8.6% professional, 17.2% services, 27.6% sales, 0.0% farming, 20.7% construction, 22.4% production (2000).
Income: Per capita income: $14,061 (2000); Median household income: $33,889 (2000); Poverty rate: 3.9% (2000).
Taxes: Total city taxes per capita: $378 (1997); City property taxes per capita: $378 (1997).
Education: High school graduation rate: 85.1% (2000); College graduation rate: 14.9% (2000).
Housing: Homeownership rate: 70.0% (2000); Median home value: $62,500 (2000); Median rent: $306 per month (2000); Median age of housing: 20 years (2000).
Transportation: Commute to work: 90.9% car, 0.0% public transportation, 0.0% walk, 9.1% work from home (2000); Travel time to work: 4.0% less than 15 minutes, 46.0% 15 to 30 minutes, 38.0% 30 to 45 minutes, 12.0% 45 to 60 minutes, 0.0% 60 minutes or more (2000)

FALMOUTH (unincorporated postal area, zip code 49632). Covers a land area of 84.463 square miles and a water area of 0.254 square miles. Located at 44.23° N. Lat.; 84.97° W. Long. Elevation is 1,180 feet.
Population: 1,148 (2000); Race: 98.5% White, 0.3% Black, 0.0% Asian, 0.3% American Indian and Alaska Native, 0.9% Hispanic of any race, 0.9% two or more races (2000); Density: 13.6 persons per square mile (2000); Age: 27.6% under 18, 14.5% over 64 (2000); Marriage status: 21.7% never married, 65.5% now married, 6.9% widowed, 5.9% divorced (2000); Foreign born: 0.4% (2000); Ancestry (includes multiple ancestries): 38.8% Dutch, 17.7% German, 8.3% United States or American, 8.1% Irish, 7.9% English (2000).

Economy: Employment by occupation: 10.5% management, 9.0% professional, 18.1% services, 19.7% sales, 6.5% farming, 14.0% construction, 22.1% production (2000).
Income: Per capita income: $15,285 (2000); Median household income: $36,211 (2000); Poverty rate: 8.1% (2000).
Education: High school graduation rate: 79.2% (2000); College graduation rate: 7.4% (2000).
Housing: Homeownership rate: 86.7% (2000); Median home value: $65,500 (2000); Median rent: $271 per month (2000); Median age of housing: 29 years (2000).
Transportation: Commute to work: 84.4% car, 0.4% public transportation, 7.8% walk, 7.0% work from home (2000); Travel time to work: 28.2% less than 15 minutes, 30.8% 15 to 30 minutes, 28.4% 30 to 45 minutes, 4.7% 45 to 60 minutes, 8.0% 60 minutes or more (2000)

FOREST (township). Covers a land area of 35.168 square miles and a water area of 0 square miles. Located at 44.36° N. Lat.; 85.15° W. Long.
Population: 1,082 (2000); Race: 97.8% White, 0.0% Black, 0.4% Asian, 0.4% American Indian and Alaska Native, 1.0% Hispanic of any race, 1.0% two or more races (2000); Density: 30.8 persons per square mile (2000); Age: 25.4% under 18, 14.1% over 64 (2000); Marriage status: 19.0% never married, 62.8% now married, 6.1% widowed, 12.0% divorced (2000); Foreign born: 1.2% (2000); Ancestry (includes multiple ancestries): 25.6% German, 13.5% English, 7.8% United States or American, 7.4% Irish, 7.4% Dutch (2000).
Economy: Employment by occupation: 7.4% management, 12.4% professional, 18.5% services, 18.5% sales, 1.4% farming, 10.6% construction, 31.3% production (2000).
Income: Per capita income: $15,417 (2000); Median household income: $33,359 (2000); Poverty rate: 11.3% (2000).
Taxes: Total city taxes per capita: $19 (1997); City property taxes per capita: $19 (1997).
Education: High school graduation rate: 74.8% (2000); College graduation rate: 9.3% (2000).
Housing: Homeownership rate: 73.6% (2000); Median home value: $62,900 (2000); Median rent: $358 per month (2000); Median age of housing: 24 years (2000).
Transportation: Commute to work: 90.7% car, 1.4% public transportation, 2.0% walk, 5.1% work from home (2000); Travel time to work: 27.0% less than 15 minutes, 34.7% 15 to 30 minutes, 22.7% 30 to 45 minutes, 7.7% 45 to 60 minutes, 7.9% 60 minutes or more (2000)

HOLLAND (township). Covers a land area of 35.839 square miles and a water area of 0.050 square miles. Located at 44.20° N. Lat.; 84.91° W. Long.
Population: 223 (2000); Race: 100.0% White, 0.0% Black, 0.0% Asian, 0.0% American Indian and Alaska Native, 0.0% Hispanic of any race, 0.0% two or more races (2000); Density: 6.2 persons per square mile (2000); Age: 18.6% under 18, 24.3% over 64 (2000); Marriage status: 15.6% never married, 59.2% now married, 12.2% widowed, 12.9% divorced (2000); Foreign born: 0.0% (2000); Ancestry (includes multiple ancestries): 23.2% Dutch, 23.2% German, 18.1% English, 11.9% Other groups, 8.5% Irish (2000).
Economy: Unemployment rate: 4.6% (11/2002); Total civilian labor force: 14,772 (11/2002); Employment by occupation: 6.0% management, 10.4% professional, 14.9% services, 22.4% sales, 7.5% farming, 20.9% construction, 17.9% production (2000).
Income: Per capita income: $16,200 (2000); Median household income: $31,000 (2000); Poverty rate: 11.9% (2000).
Taxes: Total city taxes per capita: $73 (1997); City property taxes per capita: $73 (1997).
Education: High school graduation rate: 73.3% (2000); College graduation rate: 16.3% (2000).
Housing: Homeownership rate: 83.5% (2000); Median home value: $57,500 (2000); Median rent: $288 per month (2000); Median age of housing: 30 years (2000).
Transportation: Commute to work: 85.1% car, 0.0% public transportation, 10.4% walk, 4.5% work from home (2000); Travel time to work: 23.4% less than 15 minutes, 23.4% 15 to 30 minutes, 37.5% 30 to 45 minutes, 9.4% 45 to 60 minutes, 6.3% 60 minutes or more (2000)

LAKE (township). Covers a land area of 31.663 square miles and a water area of 4.351 square miles. Located at 44.30° N. Lat.; 85.26° W. Long.
Population: 2,468 (2000); Race: 98.7% White, 0.0% Black, 0.6% Asian, 0.5% American Indian and Alaska Native, 0.7% Hispanic of any race, 0.1% two or more races (2000); Density: 77.9 persons per square mile (2000); Age: 23.4% under 18, 16.6% over 64 (2000); Marriage status: 17.6% never married, 64.2% now married, 7.0% widowed, 11.2% divorced (2000); Foreign born: 0.7% (2000); Ancestry (includes multiple ancestries): 21.7% German, 13.8% English, 10.9% Irish, 10.7% Dutch, 8.4% United States or American (2000).
Economy: Employment by occupation: 7.9% management, 15.7% professional, 12.7% services, 27.8% sales, 0.4% farming, 11.0% construction, 24.5% production (2000).
Income: Per capita income: $18,332 (2000); Median household income: $36,934 (2000); Poverty rate: 9.4% (2000).
Taxes: Total city taxes per capita: $49 (1997); City property taxes per capita: $49 (1997).
Education: High school graduation rate: 84.2% (2000); College graduation rate: 13.8% (2000).
Housing: Homeownership rate: 86.2% (2000); Median home value: $93,900 (2000); Median rent: $360 per month (2000); Median age of housing: 23 years (2000).
Transportation: Commute to work: 92.9% car, 0.2% public transportation, 1.7% walk, 4.7% work from home (2000); Travel time to work: 32.4% less than 15 minutes, 52.4% 15 to 30 minutes, 5.5% 30 to 45 minutes, 4.8% 45 to 60 minutes, 4.9% 60 minutes or more (2000)

LAKE CITY (city). Covers a land area of 1.080 square miles and a water area of 0 square miles. Located at 44.33° N. Lat.; 85.21° W. Long. Elevation is 1,260 feet.
History: Daniel Reeder settled here in 1868. The community was first called Reeder, but was renamed Lake City in 1877, incorporated as a village in 1889 and as a city in 1932.
Population: 923 (2000); Race: 98.5% White, 0.0% Black, 0.0% Asian, 0.4% American Indian and Alaska Native, 1.2% Hispanic of any race, 1.1% two or more races (2000); Density: 854.9 persons per square mile (2000); Age: 24.3% under 18, 21.8% over 64 (2000); Marriage status: 22.8% never married, 54.8% now married, 10.9% widowed, 11.5% divorced (2000); Foreign born: 1.7% (2000); Ancestry (includes multiple ancestries): 26.3% German, 16.4% English, 12.5% Irish, 9.2% Dutch, 7.0% Other groups (2000).
Economy: Employment by occupation: 10.9% management, 17.9% professional, 14.0% services, 29.1% sales, 2.0% farming, 9.5% construction, 16.8% production (2000).
Income: Per capita income: $17,067 (2000); Median household income: $28,864 (2000); Poverty rate: 13.1% (2000).
Taxes: Total city taxes per capita: $240 (1997); City property taxes per capita: $233 (1997).
Education: High school graduation rate: 83.9% (2000); College graduation rate: 18.0% (2000).

School District(s)

Lake City Area School District (KG-12)
2000 Enrollment: 1,328 231-839-4333
Housing: Homeownership rate: 73.3% (2000); Median home value: $72,100 (2000); Median rent: $358 per month (2000); Median age of housing: 42 years (2000).
Transportation: Commute to work: 87.6% car, 0.0% public transportation, 3.9% walk, 8.2% work from home (2000); Travel time to work: 43.6% less than 15 minutes, 38.7% 15 to 30 minutes, 7.7% 30 to 45 minutes, 4.0% 45 to 60 minutes, 6.1% 60 minutes or more (2000)
Additional Information Contacts
Lake City Chamber of Commerce 231-839-4969

MCBAIN (city). Covers a land area of 1.220 square miles and a water area of 0 square miles. Located at 44.19° N. Lat.; 85.21° W. Long. Elevation is 1,236 feet.
Population: 584 (2000); Race: 98.3% White, 0.0% Black, 0.3% Asian, 0.0% American Indian and Alaska Native, 0.0% Hispanic of any race, 1.4% two or more races (2000); Density: 478.6 persons per square mile (2000); Age: 20.9% under 18, 23.8% over 64 (2000); Marriage status: 21.0% never married, 60.1% now married, 12.3% widowed, 6.7% divorced (2000); Foreign born: 0.9% (2000); Ancestry (includes multiple ancestries): 50.3% Dutch, 13.7% German, 7.1% United States or American, 6.8% Irish, 6.4% English (2000).
Economy: Manufacturing: sawmill; feeds. Employment by occupation: 8.6% management, 23.3% professional, 12.0% services, 20.5% sales, 3.1% farming, 5.8% construction, 26.7% production (2000).
Income: Per capita income: $19,356 (2000); Median household income: $35,156 (2000); Poverty rate: 5.2% (2000).
Taxes: Total city taxes per capita: $772 (1997); City property taxes per capita: $772 (1997).

Education: High school graduation rate: 76.0% (2000); College graduation rate: 18.4% (2000).

School District(s)

Mcbain Rural Agricultural School (PK-12)
2000 Enrollment: 1,052 616-825-2165

Housing: Homeownership rate: 64.0% (2000); Median home value: $69,500 (2000); Median rent: $328 per month (2000); Median age of housing: 43 years (2000).

Transportation: Commute to work: 82.6% car, 2.4% public transportation, 13.5% walk, 1.4% work from home (2000); Travel time to work: 45.1% less than 15 minutes, 38.4% 15 to 30 minutes, 9.5% 30 to 45 minutes, 1.8% 45 to 60 minutes, 5.3% 60 minutes or more (2000)

Additional Information Contacts

McBain Chamber of Commerce. 231-825-2893

MERRITT (unincorporated postal area, zip code 49667). Covers a land area of 56.660 square miles and a water area of 0.501 square miles. Located at 44.33° N. Lat.; 84.91° W. Long. Elevation is 1,153 feet.

Population: 550 (2000); Race: 98.2% White, 1.1% Black, 0.0% Asian, 0.0% American Indian and Alaska Native, 0.4% Hispanic of any race, 0.7% two or more races (2000); Density: 9.7 persons per square mile (2000); Age: 29.6% under 18, 12.0% over 64 (2000); Marriage status: 19.0% never married, 62.9% now married, 6.1% widowed, 12.0% divorced (2000); Foreign born: 0.4% (2000); Ancestry (includes multiple ancestries): 16.0% German, 12.5% English, 11.6% Irish, 7.8% Dutch, 6.4% United States or American (2000).

Economy: Employment by occupation: 11.4% management, 11.0% professional, 13.1% services, 21.6% sales, 2.5% farming, 15.7% construction, 24.6% production (2000).

Income: Per capita income: $16,818 (2000); Median household income: $35,729 (2000); Poverty rate: 6.4% (2000).

Education: High school graduation rate: 78.0% (2000); College graduation rate: 9.6% (2000).

Housing: Homeownership rate: 79.1% (2000); Median home value: $51,000 (2000); Median rent: $331 per month (2000); Median age of housing: 24 years (2000).

Transportation: Commute to work: 86.7% car, 0.9% public transportation, 3.5% walk, 6.2% work from home (2000); Travel time to work: 19.3% less than 15 minutes, 34.0% 15 to 30 minutes, 26.9% 30 to 45 minutes, 13.2% 45 to 60 minutes, 6.6% 60 minutes or more (2000)

NORWICH (township). Covers a land area of 71.865 square miles and a water area of 0.631 square miles. Located at 44.48° N. Lat.; 84.95° W. Long.

Population: 646 (2000); Race: 98.6% White, 0.0% Black, 0.3% Asian, 0.9% American Indian and Alaska Native, 1.1% Hispanic of any race, 0.2% two or more races (2000); Density: 9.0 persons per square mile (2000); Age: 25.1% under 18, 15.4% over 64 (2000); Marriage status: 20.4% never married, 66.9% now married, 6.9% widowed, 5.9% divorced (2000); Foreign born: 1.1% (2000); Ancestry (includes multiple ancestries): 23.4% German, 14.2% Irish, 10.9% United States or American, 9.1% Polish, 7.1% Other groups (2000).

Economy: Employment by occupation: 7.2% management, 10.0% professional, 27.7% services, 14.9% sales, 6.8% farming, 10.8% construction, 22.5% production (2000).

Income: Per capita income: $16,460 (2000); Median household income: $27,788 (2000); Poverty rate: 18.2% (2000).

Taxes: Total city taxes per capita: $90 (1997); City property taxes per capita: $90 (1997).

Education: High school graduation rate: 71.5% (2000); College graduation rate: 6.1% (2000).

Housing: Homeownership rate: 87.0% (2000); Median home value: $77,000 (2000); Median rent: $311 per month (2000); Median age of housing: 24 years (2000).

Transportation: Commute to work: 90.2% car, 0.0% public transportation, 5.3% walk, 4.5% work from home (2000); Travel time to work: 19.7% less than 15 minutes, 27.9% 15 to 30 minutes, 28.8% 30 to 45 minutes, 11.6% 45 to 60 minutes, 12.0% 60 minutes or more (2000)

PIONEER (township). Covers a land area of 35.894 square miles and a water area of 0.032 square miles. Located at 44.47° N. Lat.; 85.16° W. Long. Elevation is 1,331 feet.

Population: 460 (2000); Race: 98.1% White, 0.0% Black, 0.0% Asian, 1.2% American Indian and Alaska Native, 0.9% Hispanic of any race, 0.7% two or more races (2000); Density: 12.8 persons per square mile (2000); Age: 19.3% under 18, 11.8% over 64 (2000); Marriage status: 18.2% never married, 66.3% now married, 5.8% widowed, 9.7% divorced (2000); Foreign born: 0.0% (2000); Ancestry (includes multiple ancestries): 34.1% German, 12.2% English, 11.3% Irish, 7.5% United States or American, 5.4% Polish (2000).

Economy: Employment by occupation: 8.0% management, 10.9% professional, 9.2% services, 19.0% sales, 8.6% farming, 17.2% construction, 27.0% production (2000).

Income: Per capita income: $16,837 (2000); Median household income: $32,000 (2000); Poverty rate: 8.9% (2000).

Taxes: Total city taxes per capita: $34 (1997); City property taxes per capita: $34 (1997).

Education: High school graduation rate: 77.0% (2000); College graduation rate: 5.7% (2000).

Housing: Homeownership rate: 88.8% (2000); Median home value: $62,500 (2000); Median rent: $331 per month (2000); Median age of housing: 29 years (2000).

Transportation: Commute to work: 91.2% car, 0.0% public transportation, 3.5% walk, 2.4% work from home (2000); Travel time to work: 13.9% less than 15 minutes, 28.9% 15 to 30 minutes, 33.7% 30 to 45 minutes, 16.3% 45 to 60 minutes, 7.2% 60 minutes or more (2000)

REEDER (township). Covers a land area of 34.888 square miles and a water area of 0.046 square miles. Located at 44.28° N. Lat.; 85.15° W. Long.

Population: 1,112 (2000); Race: 95.9% White, 0.2% Black, 0.0% Asian, 1.6% American Indian and Alaska Native, 2.7% Hispanic of any race, 2.4% two or more races (2000); Density: 31.9 persons per square mile (2000); Age: 32.2% under 18, 10.8% over 64 (2000); Marriage status: 19.8% never married, 68.2% now married, 3.1% widowed, 8.8% divorced (2000); Foreign born: 0.3% (2000); Ancestry (includes multiple ancestries): 18.5% German, 16.9% Dutch, 10.7% Other groups, 10.4% Irish, 9.4% English (2000).

Economy: Employment by occupation: 9.4% management, 11.0% professional, 11.7% services, 23.1% sales, 2.9% farming, 12.6% construction, 29.2% production (2000).

Income: Per capita income: $13,962 (2000); Median household income: $33,424 (2000); Poverty rate: 10.6% (2000).

Taxes: Total city taxes per capita: $24 (1997); City property taxes per capita: $24 (1997).

Education: High school graduation rate: 78.4% (2000); College graduation rate: 6.3% (2000).

Housing: Homeownership rate: 83.6% (2000); Median home value: $76,300 (2000); Median rent: $373 per month (2000); Median age of housing: 23 years (2000).

Transportation: Commute to work: 92.7% car, 0.5% public transportation, 0.9% walk, 5.5% work from home (2000); Travel time to work: 27.1% less than 15 minutes, 41.1% 15 to 30 minutes, 19.1% 30 to 45 minutes, 4.8% 45 to 60 minutes, 8.0% 60 minutes or more (2000)

RICHLAND (township). Covers a land area of 35.614 square miles and a water area of 0.022 square miles. Located at 44.21° N. Lat.; 85.27° W. Long.

Population: 1,445 (2000); Race: 98.2% White, 0.0% Black, 0.3% Asian, 0.3% American Indian and Alaska Native, 0.1% Hispanic of any race, 1.0% two or more races (2000); Density: 40.6 persons per square mile (2000); Age: 33.8% under 18, 9.6% over 64 (2000); Marriage status: 24.1% never married, 68.7% now married, 3.6% widowed, 3.6% divorced (2000); Foreign born: 1.1% (2000); Ancestry (includes multiple ancestries): 48.0% Dutch, 15.5% German, 9.2% United States or American, 7.2% English, 5.1% Irish (2000).

Economy: Employment by occupation: 10.5% management, 17.7% professional, 13.7% services, 20.7% sales, 5.7% farming, 12.0% construction, 19.6% production (2000).

Income: Per capita income: $15,834 (2000); Median household income: $45,833 (2000); Poverty rate: 4.6% (2000).

Taxes: Total city taxes per capita: $22 (1997); City property taxes per capita: $22 (1997).

Education: High school graduation rate: 86.4% (2000); College graduation rate: 14.2% (2000).

Housing: Homeownership rate: 89.8% (2000); Median home value: $87,600 (2000); Median rent: $442 per month (2000); Median age of housing: 27 years (2000).

Transportation: Commute to work: 88.2% car, 0.6% public transportation, 3.4% walk, 7.9% work from home (2000); Travel time to work: 39.2% less than 15 minutes, 48.3% 15 to 30 minutes, 6.4% 30 to 45 minutes, 4.1% 45 to 60 minutes, 2.0% 60 minutes or more (2000)

RIVERSIDE (township). Covers a land area of 35.592 square miles and a water area of 0.032 square miles. Located at 44.21° N. Lat.; 85.15° W. Long.

Population: 1,050 (2000); Race: 97.6% White, 0.2% Black, 0.0% Asian, 0.0% American Indian and Alaska Native, 1.8% Hispanic of any race, 1.3% two or more races (2000); Density: 29.5 persons per square mile (2000); Age:

28.3% under 18, 20.4% over 64 (2000); Marriage status: 21.6% never married, 68.7% now married, 4.5% widowed, 5.2% divorced (2000); Foreign born: 2.4% (2000); Ancestry (includes multiple ancestries): 39.9% Dutch, 12.7% German, 11.4% Irish, 5.4% French (except Basque), 4.2% English (2000).
Economy: Employment by occupation: 13.7% management, 14.5% professional, 14.2% services, 22.0% sales, 4.3% farming, 12.6% construction, 18.7% production (2000).
Income: Per capita income: $16,167 (2000); Median household income: $37,857 (2000); Poverty rate: 10.3% (2000).
Taxes: Total city taxes per capita: $37 (1997); City property taxes per capita: $37 (1997).
Education: High school graduation rate: 70.0% (2000); College graduation rate: 7.9% (2000).

School District(s)

Hagar Township School District #6 (KG-08)
2000 Enrollment: 69 616-849-1343

Housing: Homeownership rate: 92.9% (2000); Median home value: $88,200 (2000); Median rent: $294 per month (2000); Median age of housing: 28 years (2000).
Transportation: Commute to work: 88.5% car, 0.5% public transportation, 3.1% walk, 8.0% work from home (2000); Travel time to work: 35.5% less than 15 minutes, 41.8% 15 to 30 minutes, 13.8% 30 to 45 minutes, 4.3% 45 to 60 minutes, 4.6% 60 minutes or more (2000)

WEST BRANCH (township). Covers a land area of 35.678 square miles and a water area of 0.031 square miles. Located at 44.36° N. Lat.; 85.02° W. Long.
Population: 532 (2000); Race: 99.6% White, 0.0% Black, 0.0% Asian, 0.0% American Indian and Alaska Native, 1.0% Hispanic of any race, 0.4% two or more races (2000); Density: 14.9 persons per square mile (2000); Age: 28.1% under 18, 12.4% over 64 (2000); Marriage status: 20.8% never married, 64.3% now married, 7.1% widowed, 7.8% divorced (2000); Foreign born: 0.8% (2000); Ancestry (includes multiple ancestries): 22.1% German, 14.4% English, 10.6% United States or American, 9.5% Dutch, 8.6% Other groups (2000).
Economy: Employment by occupation: 12.7% management, 6.8% professional, 11.8% services, 24.0% sales, 4.5% farming, 16.3% construction, 24.0% production (2000).
Income: Per capita income: $14,057 (2000); Median household income: $36,161 (2000); Poverty rate: 12.0% (2000).
Taxes: Total city taxes per capita: $26 (1997); City property taxes per capita: $26 (1997).
Education: High school graduation rate: 67.1% (2000); College graduation rate: 4.1% (2000).
Housing: Homeownership rate: 87.9% (2000); Median home value: $66,500 (2000); Median rent: $241 per month (2000); Median age of housing: 25 years (2000).
Transportation: Commute to work: 83.3% car, 5.2% public transportation, 2.9% walk, 5.7% work from home (2000); Travel time to work: 21.7% less than 15 minutes, 28.3% 15 to 30 minutes, 25.3% 30 to 45 minutes, 10.6% 45 to 60 minutes, 14.1% 60 minutes or more (2000)

Monroe County

Located in southeastern Michigan; bounded on the south by Ohio, on the east by Lake Erie, and on the northeast by the Huron River; drained by the Raisin River. Covers a land area of 551.10 square miles, a water area of 128.90 square miles, and is located in the Eastern Time Zone. The county government was organized in 1817. County seat is Monroe.

Monroe County is part of the Detroit, MI PMSA. The entire metro area includes: Lapeer County; Macomb County; Monroe County; Oakland County; St. Clair County; Wayne County

Weather Station: Monroe — Elevation: 587 feet

	Jan	Feb	Mar	Apr	May	Jun	Jul	Aug	Sep	Oct	Nov	Dec
High	31	35	45	58	71	81	85	83	75	62	48	37
Low	17	19	28	38	49	59	64	62	54	42	33	23
Precip	1.8	1.7	2.7	3.2	3.1	3.6	3.0	3.4	3.0	2.3	2.9	2.5
Snow	na	5.7	5.4	1.0	0.0	0.0	0.0	0.0	0.0	tr	na	na

High and Low temperatures in degrees Fahrenheit; Precipitation and Snow in inches

Population: 145,945 (2000); Race: 95.3% White, 1.8% Black, 0.6% Asian, 0.2% American Indian and Alaska Native, 1.8% Hispanic of any race, 1.5% two or more races (2000); Density: 264.8 persons per square mile (2000); Age: 27.3% under 18, 11.1% over 64 (2000).
Religion: Five largest groups: 27.2% Catholic Church, 4.2% Evangelical Lutheran Church in America, 3.8% Southern Baptist Convention, 3.7% Lutheran Church—Missouri Synod, 2.8% Jewish estimate (2000).
Economy: Unemployment rate: 4.1% (11/2002); Total civilian labor force: 73,961 (11/2002); Leading industries: 26.4% manufacturing; 15.0% retail trade; 10.8% health care and social assistance (2000); Companies that employ more than 1,000 persons: 3 (2000); Companies that employ more than 100 persons: 64 (2000); Farms: 1,058 totaling 209,715 acres (1997); Minority business ownership rate: 5.2% (1997); Women business ownership rate: 34.4% (1997); Retail sales per capita: $7,283 (1997). Single-family building permits issued: 678 (2001) / 720 (2000); Multi-family building permits issued: 143 (2001) / 482 (2000).
Income: Per capita income: $22,458 (2000); Median household income: $51,743 (2000); Poverty rate: 7.0% (2000); Bankruptcy rate: 4.76% (2001).
Taxes: Total county taxes per capita: $181 (2000); County property taxes per capita: $173 (2000).
Education: High school graduation rate: 83.1% (2000); College graduation rate: 14.3% (2000).
Housing: Homeownership rate: 80.9% (2000); Median home value: $132,000 (2000); Median rent: $471 per month (2000); Median age of housing: 34 years (2000).
Health: Birth rate: 127.8 per 10,000 population (1998); Age adjusted death rate: 87.7 per 10,000 population (1999); Age adjusted cancer mortality rate: 210.9 deaths per 100,000 population (1999). Number of physicians: 7.9 per 10,000 population (1999); Number of hospital beds: 17.1 per 10,000 population (1999).
Elections: 2000 Presidential election results: 51.1% Gore, 46.8% Bush, 1.6% Nader, 0.1% Buchanan
National and State Parks: Erie State Game Area; Petersburg State Game Management Area; Pointe Mouillee State Game Area; Sterling State Park
Additional Information Contacts
Monroe County Government Offices 734-243-7081
Monroe County Association of Realtors 734-242-6866
Monroe County Chamber of Commerce 734-242-3366
Monroe County Convention Bureau 734-457-1030

Monroe County Communities

ASH (township). Covers a land area of 34.596 square miles and a water area of 0.197 square miles. Located at 42.05° N. Lat.; 83.37° W. Long.
Population: 7,610 (2000); Race: 96.3% White, 0.2% Black, 0.1% Asian, 0.3% American Indian and Alaska Native, 1.5% Hispanic of any race, 2.8% two or more races (2000); Density: 220.0 persons per square mile (2000); Age: 27.6% under 18, 10.0% over 64 (2000); Marriage status: 21.1% never married, 63.5% now married, 6.5% widowed, 8.9% divorced (2000); Foreign born: 1.6% (2000); Ancestry (includes multiple ancestries): 27.2% German, 14.2% Irish, 13.7% Polish, 10.2% French (except Basque), 9.6% United States or American (2000).
Economy: Single-family building permits issued: 25 (2001) / 33 (2000); Multi-family building permits issued: 0 (2001) / 0 (2000); Employment by occupation: 7.2% management, 13.9% professional, 13.5% services, 23.4% sales, 0.6% farming, 15.7% construction, 25.9% production (2000).
Income: Per capita income: $24,271 (2000); Median household income: $54,439 (2000); Poverty rate: 6.3% (2000).
Education: High school graduation rate: 83.9% (2000); College graduation rate: 8.4% (2000).
Housing: Homeownership rate: 90.1% (2000); Median home value: $147,500 (2000); Median rent: $415 per month (2000); Median age of housing: 26 years (2000).
Transportation: Commute to work: 96.6% car, 0.2% public transportation, 1.0% walk, 2.2% work from home (2000); Travel time to work: 21.6% less than 15 minutes, 41.4% 15 to 30 minutes, 23.1% 30 to 45 minutes, 9.6% 45 to 60 minutes, 4.2% 60 minutes or more (2000)

BEDFORD (township). Covers a land area of 39.107 square miles and a water area of 0.160 square miles. Located at 41.76° N. Lat.; 83.58° W. Long.
Population: 28,606 (2000); Race: 97.1% White, 0.4% Black, 0.7% Asian, 0.2% American Indian and Alaska Native, 1.5% Hispanic of any race, 1.2% two or more races (2000); Density: 731.5 persons per square mile (2000); Age: 27.7% under 18, 10.8% over 64 (2000); Marriage status: 20.1% never married, 65.1% now married, 6.2% widowed, 8.7% divorced (2000); Foreign born: 2.0% (2000); Ancestry (includes multiple ancestries): 35.2% German,

13.4% Polish, 13.1% Irish, 12.1% English, 8.3% French (except Basque) (2000).
Economy: Unemployment rate: 3.5% (11/2002); Total civilian labor force: 13,779 (11/2002); Single-family building permits issued: 202 (2001) / 228 (2000); Multi-family building permits issued: 4 (2001) / 88 (2000); Employment by occupation: 11.4% management, 19.4% professional, 11.1% services, 25.0% sales, 0.2% farming, 12.6% construction, 20.4% production (2000).
Income: Per capita income: $24,131 (2000); Median household income: $59,835 (2000); Poverty rate: 4.5% (2000).
Taxes: Total city taxes per capita: $55 (1997); City property taxes per capita: $39 (1997).
Education: High school graduation rate: 90.3% (2000); College graduation rate: 20.7% (2000).
Housing: Homeownership rate: 88.9% (2000); Median home value: $142,000 (2000); Median rent: $499 per month (2000); Median age of housing: 29 years (2000).
Transportation: Commute to work: 96.4% car, 0.1% public transportation, 0.6% walk, 2.7% work from home (2000); Travel time to work: 27.1% less than 15 minutes, 44.5% 15 to 30 minutes, 17.4% 30 to 45 minutes, 5.9% 45 to 60 minutes, 5.2% 60 minutes or more (2000)

BERLIN CHARTER (township). Covers a land area of 32.078 square miles and a water area of 5.052 square miles. Located at 42.03° N. Lat.; 83.26° W. Long.
Population: 6,924 (2000); Race: 96.8% White, 0.1% Black, 0.4% Asian, 0.3% American Indian and Alaska Native, 1.4% Hispanic of any race, 1.7% two or more races (2000); Density: 215.8 persons per square mile (2000); Age: 26.3% under 18, 8.5% over 64 (2000); Marriage status: 23.1% never married, 64.9% now married, 4.6% widowed, 7.4% divorced (2000); Foreign born: 1.1% (2000); Ancestry (includes multiple ancestries): 25.7% German, 14.8% French (except Basque), 10.9% Irish, 9.6% Other groups, 9.3% Polish (2000).
Economy: Single-family building permits issued: 23 (2001) / 22 (2000); Multi-family building permits issued: 0 (2001) / 0 (2000); Employment by occupation: 9.3% management, 14.0% professional, 11.9% services, 21.5% sales, 0.3% farming, 17.3% construction, 25.7% production (2000).
Income: Per capita income: $23,898 (2000); Median household income: $57,403 (2000); Poverty rate: 5.6% (2000).
Taxes: Total city taxes per capita: $48 (2000); City property taxes per capita: $18 (2000).
Education: High school graduation rate: 83.1% (2000); College graduation rate: 10.9% (2000).
Housing: Homeownership rate: 84.9% (2000); Median home value: $145,000 (2000); Median rent: $526 per month (2000); Median age of housing: 34 years (2000).
Transportation: Commute to work: 98.1% car, 0.2% public transportation, 0.0% walk, 1.1% work from home (2000); Travel time to work: 23.6% less than 15 minutes, 38.2% 15 to 30 minutes, 24.3% 30 to 45 minutes, 8.3% 45 to 60 minutes, 5.7% 60 minutes or more (2000)

CARLETON (village). Covers a land area of 0.994 square miles and a water area of 0 square miles. Located at 42.05° N. Lat.; 83.39° W. Long. Elevation is 615 feet.
History: Carleton was laid out in 1872 by Daniel A. Matthews, who operated an inn here and became the first postmaster. The village was named for Michigan poet Will Carleton (1845-1912).
Population: 2,562 (2000); Race: 95.6% White, 0.5% Black, 0.2% Asian, 0.7% American Indian and Alaska Native, 1.2% Hispanic of any race, 2.5% two or more races (2000); Density: 2,577.3 persons per square mile (2000); Age: 30.5% under 18, 9.6% over 64 (2000); Marriage status: 27.3% never married, 51.1% now married, 8.6% widowed, 13.0% divorced (2000); Foreign born: 0.9% (2000); Ancestry (includes multiple ancestries): 24.4% German, 12.8% Irish, 11.4% English, 9.6% United States or American, 8.9% Other groups (2000).
Economy: Single-family building permits issued: 4 (2001) / 6 (2000); Multi-family building permits issued: 81 (2001) / 77 (2000); Employment by occupation: 3.6% management, 13.5% professional, 12.6% services, 25.9% sales, 0.6% farming, 13.3% construction, 30.6% production (2000).
Income: Per capita income: $20,394 (2000); Median household income: $44,205 (2000); Poverty rate: 10.6% (2000).
Taxes: Total city taxes per capita: $89 (1997); City property taxes per capita: $82 (1997).
Education: High school graduation rate: 81.1% (2000); College graduation rate: 5.8% (2000).

School District(s)

Airport Community School District (KG-12)
2000 Enrollment: 3,288 734-654-2414
Housing: Homeownership rate: 82.7% (2000); Median home value: $117,600 (2000); Median rent: $396 per month (2000); Median age of housing: 24 years (2000).
Safety: Violent crime rate: 19.4 per 10,000 population; Property crime rate: 205.7 per 10,000 population (2001).
Transportation: Commute to work: 97.0% car, 0.0% public transportation, 0.5% walk, 2.5% work from home (2000); Travel time to work: 22.0% less than 15 minutes, 41.7% 15 to 30 minutes, 22.6% 30 to 45 minutes, 9.2% 45 to 60 minutes, 4.5% 60 minutes or more (2000)

DETROIT BEACH (CDP). Covers a land area of 0.628 square miles and a water area of 0.042 square miles. Located at 41.93° N. Lat.; 83.32° W. Long. Elevation is 575 feet.
Population: 2,289 (2000); Race: 97.9% White, 0.0% Black, 0.5% Asian, 0.3% American Indian and Alaska Native, 0.0% Hispanic of any race, 1.3% two or more races (2000); Density: 3,643.1 persons per square mile (2000); Age: 26.3% under 18, 9.7% over 64 (2000); Marriage status: 25.7% never married, 58.9% now married, 6.5% widowed, 8.8% divorced (2000); Foreign born: 0.8% (2000); Ancestry (includes multiple ancestries): 20.1% German, 14.2% Irish, 11.8% French (except Basque), 10.0% United States or American, 9.6% Other groups (2000).
Economy: Employment by occupation: 7.1% management, 10.5% professional, 11.8% services, 24.9% sales, 0.6% farming, 14.6% construction, 30.5% production (2000).
Income: Per capita income: $21,025 (2000); Median household income: $56,528 (2000); Poverty rate: 3.9% (2000).
Education: High school graduation rate: 74.3% (2000); College graduation rate: 5.6% (2000).
Housing: Homeownership rate: 87.8% (2000); Median home value: $105,900 (2000); Median rent: $605 per month (2000); Median age of housing: 43 years (2000).
Transportation: Commute to work: 98.3% car, 0.0% public transportation, 1.7% walk, 0.0% work from home (2000); Travel time to work: 40.3% less than 15 minutes, 30.5% 15 to 30 minutes, 16.7% 30 to 45 minutes, 8.6% 45 to 60 minutes, 3.9% 60 minutes or more (2000)

DUNDEE (village). Covers a land area of 3.227 square miles and a water area of 0.001 square miles. Located at 41.95° N. Lat.; 83.65° W. Long. Elevation is 665 feet.
History: The village of Dundee was laid out in the early 1830's by S. Van Ness, when it became known as Van Ness's Mills. The village was incorporated in 1855 under the name of the township.
Population: 3,522 (2000); Race: 97.2% White, 1.1% Black, 0.1% Asian, 0.0% American Indian and Alaska Native, 0.6% Hispanic of any race, 1.4% two or more races (2000); Density: 1,091.5 persons per square mile (2000); Age: 28.1% under 18, 9.8% over 64 (2000); Marriage status: 26.3% never married, 50.8% now married, 8.9% widowed, 13.9% divorced (2000); Foreign born: 0.3% (2000); Ancestry (includes multiple ancestries): 39.7% German, 12.5% Irish, 10.6% English, 10.6% French (except Basque), 6.4% Polish (2000).
Economy: Single-family building permits issued: 9 (2001) / 9 (2000); Multi-family building permits issued: 0 (2001) / 0 (2000); Employment by occupation: 4.8% management, 22.7% professional, 18.1% services, 21.0% sales, 0.4% farming, 11.6% construction, 21.4% production (2000).
Income: Per capita income: $18,389 (2000); Median household income: $41,563 (2000); Poverty rate: 9.0% (2000).
Taxes: Total city taxes per capita: $277 (1997); City property taxes per capita: $259 (1997).
Education: High school graduation rate: 84.4% (2000); College graduation rate: 17.5% (2000).

School District(s)

Dundee Community Schools (KG-12)
2000 Enrollment: 1,559 734-529-2350
Housing: Homeownership rate: 63.0% (2000); Median home value: $113,600 (2000); Median rent: $446 per month (2000); Median age of housing: 39 years (2000).
Newspapers: The Independent (1 x week)
Transportation: Commute to work: 95.5% car, 0.0% public transportation, 2.5% walk, 0.9% work from home (2000); Travel time to work: 30.6% less than 15 minutes, 27.5% 15 to 30 minutes, 27.1% 30 to 45 minutes, 7.8% 45 to 60 minutes, 7.0% 60 minutes or more (2000)

DUNDEE (township). Covers a land area of 48.424 square miles and a water area of 0.206 square miles. Located at 41.96° N. Lat.; 83.67° W. Long. Elevation is 665 feet.
History: Dundee Township was named by Alonzo Curtis, the postmaster, for the city in Scotland where his forebears had lived.
Population: 6,341 (2000); Race: 97.9% White, 0.6% Black, 0.2% Asian, 0.0% American Indian and Alaska Native, 0.5% Hispanic of any race, 1.2% two or more races (2000); Density: 130.9 persons per square mile (2000); Age: 28.1% under 18, 9.6% over 64 (2000); Marriage status: 23.0% never married, 59.7% now married, 6.9% widowed, 10.4% divorced (2000); Foreign born: 0.7% (2000); Ancestry (includes multiple ancestries): 39.7% German, 13.9% Irish, 10.9% French (except Basque), 10.7% English, 7.3% Polish (2000).
Economy: Single-family building permits issued: 6 (2001) / 13 (2000); Multi-family building permits issued: 0 (2001) / 0 (2000); Employment by occupation: 6.5% management, 19.2% professional, 16.2% services, 19.1% sales, 0.2% farming, 13.0% construction, 25.8% production (2000).
Income: Per capita income: $20,361 (2000); Median household income: $47,279 (2000); Poverty rate: 7.7% (2000).
Taxes: Total city taxes per capita: $55 (1997); City property taxes per capita: $50 (1997).
Education: High school graduation rate: 83.5% (2000); College graduation rate: 14.6% (2000).
Housing: Homeownership rate: 75.4% (2000); Median home value: $123,100 (2000); Median rent: $441 per month (2000); Median age of housing: 38 years (2000).
Transportation: Commute to work: 96.2% car, 0.0% public transportation, 1.3% walk, 1.6% work from home (2000); Travel time to work: 25.2% less than 15 minutes, 26.8% 15 to 30 minutes, 29.7% 30 to 45 minutes, 10.8% 45 to 60 minutes, 7.5% 60 minutes or more (2000)

ERIE (township). Covers a land area of 24.113 square miles and a water area of 5.560 square miles. Located at 41.77° N. Lat.; 83.48° W. Long.
Population: 4,850 (2000); Race: 96.6% White, 0.8% Black, 0.0% Asian, 0.1% American Indian and Alaska Native, 4.3% Hispanic of any race, 2.0% two or more races (2000); Density: 201.1 persons per square mile (2000); Age: 26.6% under 18, 10.2% over 64 (2000); Marriage status: 21.8% never married, 61.4% now married, 5.7% widowed, 11.1% divorced (2000); Foreign born: 0.5% (2000); Ancestry (includes multiple ancestries): 33.8% German, 17.4% French (except Basque), 15.8% Irish, 12.7% Other groups, 11.0% Polish (2000).
Economy: Single-family building permits issued: 18 (2001) / 9 (2000); Multi-family building permits issued: 0 (2001) / 0 (2000); Employment by occupation: 6.1% management, 16.9% professional, 10.7% services, 25.3% sales, 0.4% farming, 15.3% construction, 25.3% production (2000).
Income: Per capita income: $21,494 (2000); Median household income: $52,442 (2000); Poverty rate: 5.1% (2000).
Taxes: Total city taxes per capita: $97 (2000); City property taxes per capita: $63 (2000).
Education: High school graduation rate: 86.1% (2000); College graduation rate: 13.2% (2000).

School District(s)

Mason Consolidated Schools (Monr (PK-12)
2000 Enrollment: 1,554 734-848-4849

Housing: Homeownership rate: 89.7% (2000); Median home value: $118,000 (2000); Median rent: $448 per month (2000); Median age of housing: 36 years (2000).
Safety: Violent crime rate: 6.2 per 10,000 population; Property crime rate: 71.8 per 10,000 population (2001).
Transportation: Commute to work: 98.2% car, 0.0% public transportation, 0.7% walk, 1.0% work from home (2000); Travel time to work: 27.2% less than 15 minutes, 44.8% 15 to 30 minutes, 17.5% 30 to 45 minutes, 5.1% 45 to 60 minutes, 5.4% 60 minutes or more (2000)

ESTRAL BEACH (village). Covers a land area of 0.494 square miles and a water area of 0.003 square miles. Located at 41.98° N. Lat.; 83.23° W. Long.
Population: 486 (2000); Race: 93.4% White, 0.0% Black, 0.0% Asian, 0.0% American Indian and Alaska Native, 0.0% Hispanic of any race, 6.6% two or more races (2000); Density: 983.7 persons per square mile (2000); Age: 28.3% under 18, 11.6% over 64 (2000); Marriage status: 23.5% never married, 59.9% now married, 3.3% widowed, 13.3% divorced (2000); Foreign born: 1.1% (2000); Ancestry (includes multiple ancestries): 19.2% German, 16.5% Irish, 14.4% Polish, 10.1% French (except Basque), 7.0% English (2000).
Economy: Single-family building permits issued: 1 (2001) / 3 (2000); Multi-family building permits issued: 0 (2001) / 0 (2000); Employment by occupation: 10.3% management, 9.8% professional, 21.6% services, 15.2% sales, 1.5% farming, 20.6% construction, 21.1% production (2000).
Income: Per capita income: $21,873 (2000); Median household income: $48,194 (2000); Poverty rate: 7.2% (2000).
Taxes: Total city taxes per capita: $110 (1997); City property taxes per capita: $101 (1997).
Education: High school graduation rate: 76.6% (2000); College graduation rate: 7.7% (2000).
Housing: Homeownership rate: 85.4% (2000); Median home value: $108,300 (2000); Median rent: $442 per month (2000); Median age of housing: 48 years (2000).
Transportation: Commute to work: 96.5% car, 1.0% public transportation, 0.0% walk, 2.5% work from home (2000); Travel time to work: 14.9% less than 15 minutes, 34.4% 15 to 30 minutes, 29.7% 30 to 45 minutes, 13.3% 45 to 60 minutes, 7.7% 60 minutes or more (2000)

EXETER (township). Covers a land area of 36.553 square miles and a water area of 0.086 square miles. Located at 42.03° N. Lat.; 83.47° W. Long.
Population: 3,727 (2000); Race: 91.9% White, 5.6% Black, 0.0% Asian, 0.9% American Indian and Alaska Native, 1.1% Hispanic of any race, 0.5% two or more races (2000); Density: 102.0 persons per square mile (2000); Age: 27.9% under 18, 9.1% over 64 (2000); Marriage status: 23.3% never married, 62.7% now married, 7.9% widowed, 6.1% divorced (2000); Foreign born: 1.0% (2000); Ancestry (includes multiple ancestries): 33.4% German, 9.8% Irish, 9.6% French (except Basque), 9.5% Other groups, 8.5% Polish (2000).
Economy: Single-family building permits issued: 27 (2001) / 29 (2000); Multi-family building permits issued: 0 (2001) / 0 (2000); Employment by occupation: 6.6% management, 14.8% professional, 12.7% services, 22.4% sales, 1.6% farming, 15.5% construction, 26.3% production (2000).
Income: Per capita income: $24,308 (2000); Median household income: $63,806 (2000); Poverty rate: 4.8% (2000).
Taxes: Total city taxes per capita: $49 (1997); City property taxes per capita: $22 (1997).
Education: High school graduation rate: 81.1% (2000); College graduation rate: 9.9% (2000).
Housing: Homeownership rate: 90.6% (2000); Median home value: $144,800 (2000); Median rent: $453 per month (2000); Median age of housing: 41 years (2000).
Transportation: Commute to work: 97.9% car, 0.0% public transportation, 0.4% walk, 1.5% work from home (2000); Travel time to work: 14.1% less than 15 minutes, 44.3% 15 to 30 minutes, 28.2% 30 to 45 minutes, 7.6% 45 to 60 minutes, 5.8% 60 minutes or more (2000)

FRENCHTOWN (township). Covers a land area of 42.109 square miles and a water area of 1.145 square miles. Located at 41.95° N. Lat.; 83.33° W. Long.
Population: 20,777 (2000); Race: 95.6% White, 1.1% Black, 0.9% Asian, 0.4% American Indian and Alaska Native, 2.2% Hispanic of any race, 1.3% two or more races (2000); Density: 493.4 persons per square mile (2000); Age: 27.5% under 18, 10.1% over 64 (2000); Marriage status: 24.1% never married, 60.4% now married, 6.1% widowed, 9.4% divorced (2000); Foreign born: 2.5% (2000); Ancestry (includes multiple ancestries): 24.1% German, 11.8% French (except Basque), 11.7% Irish, 11.2% Other groups, 8.2% English (2000).
Economy: Single-family building permits issued: 69 (2001) / 100 (2000); Multi-family building permits issued: 0 (2001) / 150 (2000); Employment by occupation: 7.8% management, 9.8% professional, 15.0% services, 23.7% sales, 1.2% farming, 14.0% construction, 28.5% production (2000).
Income: Per capita income: $21,335 (2000); Median household income: $47,699 (2000); Poverty rate: 7.0% (2000).
Taxes: Total city taxes per capita: $252 (2000); City property taxes per capita: $226 (2000).
Education: High school graduation rate: 77.3% (2000); College graduation rate: 9.2% (2000).
Housing: Homeownership rate: 77.0% (2000); Median home value: $125,000 (2000); Median rent: $524 per month (2000); Median age of housing: 28 years (2000).
Transportation: Commute to work: 96.6% car, 0.5% public transportation, 1.2% walk, 1.3% work from home (2000); Travel time to work: 31.9% less than 15 minutes, 35.3% 15 to 30 minutes, 19.0% 30 to 45 minutes, 9.4% 45 to 60 minutes, 4.5% 60 minutes or more (2000)

IDA (township). Covers a land area of 36.748 square miles and a water area of 0.104 square miles. Located at 41.86° N. Lat.; 83.58° W. Long. Elevation is 639 feet.
History: Ida Township was organized in 1837 and named for Ida M. Taylor, a community leader.
Population: 4,949 (2000); Race: 99.1% White, 0.0% Black, 0.0% Asian, 0.0% American Indian and Alaska Native, 0.3% Hispanic of any race, 0.6% two or more races (2000); Density: 134.7 persons per square mile (2000); Age: 29.5% under 18, 8.2% over 64 (2000); Marriage status: 21.9% never married, 70.1% now married, 3.1% widowed, 4.9% divorced (2000); Foreign born: 1.3% (2000); Ancestry (includes multiple ancestries): 42.6% German, 9.4% Polish, 9.3% Irish, 9.3% English, 9.0% French (except Basque) (2000).
Economy: Single-family building permits issued: 48 (2001) / 21 (2000); Multi-family building permits issued: 0 (2001) / 0 (2000); Employment by occupation: 10.7% management, 16.3% professional, 12.0% services, 23.7% sales, 0.4% farming, 16.5% construction, 20.4% production (2000).
Income: Per capita income: $21,074 (2000); Median household income: $57,106 (2000); Poverty rate: 2.6% (2000).
Education: High school graduation rate: 88.1% (2000); College graduation rate: 13.6% (2000).

School District(s)

Ida Public School District (KG-12)
2000 Enrollment: 1,622 734-269-3110
Housing: Homeownership rate: 91.1% (2000); Median home value: $149,200 (2000); Median rent: $525 per month (2000); Median age of housing: 32 years (2000).
Transportation: Commute to work: 95.6% car, 0.0% public transportation, 0.4% walk, 3.7% work from home (2000); Travel time to work: 16.0% less than 15 minutes, 39.8% 15 to 30 minutes, 27.2% 30 to 45 minutes, 10.6% 45 to 60 minutes, 6.5% 60 minutes or more (2000)

LA SALLE (township). Covers a land area of 26.647 square miles and a water area of 0.165 square miles. Located at 41.84° N. Lat.; 83.45° W. Long.
Population: 5,001 (2000); Race: 96.9% White, 0.2% Black, 0.5% Asian, 0.5% American Indian and Alaska Native, 1.0% Hispanic of any race, 1.7% two or more races (2000); Density: 187.7 persons per square mile (2000); Age: 25.5% under 18, 10.3% over 64 (2000); Marriage status: 21.1% never married, 68.2% now married, 4.0% widowed, 6.6% divorced (2000); Foreign born: 1.7% (2000); Ancestry (includes multiple ancestries): 31.8% German, 13.9% French (except Basque), 11.4% English, 10.1% United States or American, 10.1% Irish (2000).
Economy: Single-family building permits issued: 16 (2001) / 16 (2000); Multi-family building permits issued: 0 (2001) / 0 (2000); Employment by occupation: 9.9% management, 17.6% professional, 16.2% services, 17.6% sales, 0.3% farming, 13.8% construction, 24.7% production (2000).
Income: Per capita income: $24,237 (2000); Median household income: $63,693 (2000); Poverty rate: 3.6% (2000).
Taxes: Total city taxes per capita: $74 (1997); City property taxes per capita: $63 (1997).
Education: High school graduation rate: 80.9% (2000); College graduation rate: 11.1% (2000).
Housing: Homeownership rate: 91.8% (2000); Median home value: $141,800 (2000); Median rent: $396 per month (2000); Median age of housing: 36 years (2000).
Transportation: Commute to work: 97.6% car, 0.2% public transportation, 0.2% walk, 1.7% work from home (2000); Travel time to work: 20.7% less than 15 minutes, 50.1% 15 to 30 minutes, 15.0% 30 to 45 minutes, 8.2% 45 to 60 minutes, 5.9% 60 minutes or more (2000)

LAMBERTVILLE (CDP). Covers a land area of 6.077 square miles and a water area of 0.019 square miles. Located at 41.75° N. Lat.; 83.62° W. Long.
History: Lambertville was founded in 1832 by John Lambert, and named for him.
Population: 9,299 (2000); Race: 97.6% White, 0.1% Black, 1.1% Asian, 0.0% American Indian and Alaska Native, 2.0% Hispanic of any race, 0.6% two or more races (2000); Density: 1,530.1 persons per square mile (2000); Age: 28.1% under 18, 9.8% over 64 (2000); Marriage status: 19.1% never married, 67.5% now married, 4.9% widowed, 8.5% divorced (2000); Foreign born: 2.3% (2000); Ancestry (includes multiple ancestries): 36.9% German, 14.9% English, 14.9% Irish, 12.7% Polish, 8.1% French (except Basque) (2000).
Economy: Employment by occupation: 13.8% management, 20.0% professional, 10.8% services, 27.1% sales, 0.0% farming, 11.3% construction, 17.1% production (2000).
Income: Per capita income: $26,475 (2000); Median household income: $62,221 (2000); Poverty rate: 4.8% (2000).
Education: High school graduation rate: 92.4% (2000); College graduation rate: 23.9% (2000).

School District(s)

New Bedford Academy (KG-08)
2000 Enrollment: 191 231-591-5803
Housing: Homeownership rate: 91.1% (2000); Median home value: $142,900 (2000); Median rent: $633 per month (2000); Median age of housing: 31 years (2000).
Transportation: Commute to work: 96.1% car, 0.2% public transportation, 0.5% walk, 2.5% work from home (2000); Travel time to work: 28.2% less than 15 minutes, 43.5% 15 to 30 minutes, 17.8% 30 to 45 minutes, 5.6% 45 to 60 minutes, 4.8% 60 minutes or more (2000)
Airports: Toledo Suburban

LONDON (township). Covers a land area of 35.710 square miles and a water area of 0.147 square miles. Located at 42.03° N. Lat.; 83.59° W. Long.
History: London Township was organized in 1833.
Population: 3,024 (2000); Race: 85.5% White, 12.1% Black, 0.3% Asian, 0.0% American Indian and Alaska Native, 1.4% Hispanic of any race, 1.4% two or more races (2000); Density: 84.7 persons per square mile (2000); Age: 29.4% under 18, 8.3% over 64 (2000); Marriage status: 23.2% never married, 62.9% now married, 4.7% widowed, 9.2% divorced (2000); Foreign born: 1.3% (2000); Ancestry (includes multiple ancestries): 27.3% German, 16.9% Other groups, 11.4% Irish, 9.8% United States or American, 8.5% English (2000).
Economy: Single-family building permits issued: 20 (2001) / 14 (2000); Multi-family building permits issued: 0 (2001) / 0 (2000); Employment by occupation: 5.8% management, 8.5% professional, 16.9% services, 20.9% sales, 0.8% farming, 14.8% construction, 32.2% production (2000).
Income: Per capita income: $20,285 (2000); Median household income: $56,250 (2000); Poverty rate: 8.4% (2000).
Taxes: Total city taxes per capita: $71 (1997); City property taxes per capita: $35 (1997).
Education: High school graduation rate: 78.0% (2000); College graduation rate: 9.6% (2000).
Housing: Homeownership rate: 91.1% (2000); Median home value: $124,600 (2000); Median rent: $511 per month (2000); Median age of housing: 34 years (2000).
Transportation: Commute to work: 94.7% car, 0.0% public transportation, 1.1% walk, 4.1% work from home (2000); Travel time to work: 11.5% less than 15 minutes, 39.9% 15 to 30 minutes, 34.7% 30 to 45 minutes, 9.0% 45 to 60 minutes, 4.9% 60 minutes or more (2000)

LUNA PIER (city). Covers a land area of 1.550 square miles and a water area of 0.156 square miles. Located at 41.80° N. Lat.; 83.44° W. Long. Elevation is 589 feet.
History: The Luna Pier post office was established in 1929. Luna Pier was incorporated as a city in 1963.
Population: 1,483 (2000); Race: 94.7% White, 0.1% Black, 0.0% Asian, 0.7% American Indian and Alaska Native, 3.0% Hispanic of any race, 2.8% two or more races (2000); Density: 956.9 persons per square mile (2000); Age: 30.6% under 18, 9.9% over 64 (2000); Marriage status: 23.1% never married, 57.1% now married, 7.4% widowed, 12.4% divorced (2000); Foreign born: 1.6% (2000); Ancestry (includes multiple ancestries): 33.6% German, 13.6% French (except Basque), 13.6% Irish, 12.0% Other groups, 9.4% Polish (2000).
Economy: Single-family building permits issued: 2 (2001) / 4 (2000); Multi-family building permits issued: 0 (2001) / 0 (2000); Employment by occupation: 6.2% management, 12.8% professional, 17.2% services, 22.2% sales, 0.0% farming, 11.8% construction, 29.8% production (2000).
Income: Per capita income: $19,325 (2000); Median household income: $40,909 (2000); Poverty rate: 14.0% (2000).
Taxes: Total city taxes per capita: $521 (1997); City property taxes per capita: $507 (1997).
Education: High school graduation rate: 75.5% (2000); College graduation rate: 8.1% (2000).
Housing: Homeownership rate: 69.6% (2000); Median home value: $99,300 (2000); Median rent: $357 per month (2000); Median age of housing: 47 years (2000).
Safety: Violent crime rate: 80.5 per 10,000 population; Property crime rate: 355.5 per 10,000 population (2001).
Transportation: Commute to work: 94.9% car, 0.0% public transportation, 3.7% walk, 0.5% work from home (2000); Travel time to work: 29.9% less

than 15 minutes, 38.2% 15 to 30 minutes, 15.6% 30 to 45 minutes, 8.2% 45 to 60 minutes, 8.0% 60 minutes or more (2000)

MAYBEE (village). Covers a land area of 1.168 square miles and a water area of 0 square miles. Located at 42.00° N. Lat.; 83.51° W. Long.
Population: 505 (2000); Race: 100.0% White, 0.0% Black, 0.0% Asian, 0.0% American Indian and Alaska Native, 1.1% Hispanic of any race, 0.0% two or more races (2000); Density: 432.3 persons per square mile (2000); Age: 29.7% under 18, 5.9% over 64 (2000); Marriage status: 27.3% never married, 53.1% now married, 10.9% widowed, 8.7% divorced (2000); Foreign born: 0.6% (2000); Ancestry (includes multiple ancestries): 43.5% German, 14.9% French (except Basque), 12.9% Polish, 11.5% Irish, 6.4% Italian (2000).
Economy: In farm area. Limestone. Single-family building permits issued: 3 (2001) / 4 (2000); Multi-family building permits issued: 0 (2001) / 0 (2000); Employment by occupation: 7.4% management, 12.5% professional, 11.0% services, 26.1% sales, 0.7% farming, 20.2% construction, 22.1% production (2000).
Income: Per capita income: $18,716 (2000); Median household income: $50,962 (2000); Poverty rate: 4.4% (2000).
Taxes: Total city taxes per capita: $103 (1997); City property taxes per capita: $101 (1997).
Education: High school graduation rate: 87.8% (2000); College graduation rate: 6.4% (2000).
Housing: Homeownership rate: 76.3% (2000); Median home value: $115,700 (2000); Median rent: $533 per month (2000); Median age of housing: 60+ years (2000).
Transportation: Commute to work: 95.9% car, 0.0% public transportation, 1.5% walk, 1.5% work from home (2000); Travel time to work: 19.0% less than 15 minutes, 50.2% 15 to 30 minutes, 19.4% 30 to 45 minutes, 8.0% 45 to 60 minutes, 3.4% 60 minutes or more (2000)

MILAN (township). Covers a land area of 35.052 square miles and a water area of 0.014 square miles. Located at 42.03° N. Lat.; 83.70° W. Long.
Population: 1,670 (2000); Race: 98.5% White, 0.4% Black, 0.0% Asian, 0.0% American Indian and Alaska Native, 1.7% Hispanic of any race, 0.4% two or more races (2000); Density: 47.6 persons per square mile (2000); Age: 25.2% under 18, 11.0% over 64 (2000); Marriage status: 17.1% never married, 72.0% now married, 4.5% widowed, 6.4% divorced (2000); Foreign born: 0.4% (2000); Ancestry (includes multiple ancestries): 34.3% German, 12.2% Irish, 12.2% English, 9.3% Other groups, 7.7% United States or American (2000).
Economy: Single-family building permits issued: 4 (2001) / 6 (2000); Multi-family building permits issued: 0 (2001) / 0 (2000); Employment by occupation: 14.5% management, 16.9% professional, 13.5% services, 18.4% sales, 0.2% farming, 11.7% construction, 24.8% production (2000).
Income: Per capita income: $23,269 (2000); Median household income: $57,361 (2000); Poverty rate: 4.5% (2000).
Taxes: Total city taxes per capita: $80 (1997); City property taxes per capita: $72 (1997).
Education: High school graduation rate: 87.7% (2000); College graduation rate: 16.5% (2000).
Housing: Homeownership rate: 88.7% (2000); Median home value: $137,100 (2000); Median rent: $406 per month (2000); Median age of housing: 47 years (2000).
Transportation: Commute to work: 94.9% car, 0.5% public transportation, 1.5% walk, 2.9% work from home (2000); Travel time to work: 21.9% less than 15 minutes, 37.9% 15 to 30 minutes, 25.3% 30 to 45 minutes, 8.5% 45 to 60 minutes, 6.4% 60 minutes or more (2000)

MONROE (city). Covers a land area of 9.044 square miles and a water area of 1.019 square miles. Located at 41.91° N. Lat.; 83.39° W. Long. Elevation is 593 feet.
History: First called Frenchtown because of its French settlers, the city was renamed Monroe when a visit from President Monroe was expected. Its location on the River Raisin, a few miles from Lake Erie, placed Monroe in an area where the border was in question. The so-called "Toledo War" dispute between Michigan and Ohio centered in Monroe in 1835, ending with Michigan giving up to Ohio the area to the south that included Toledo, and getting in exchange the Upper Peninsula. An early industry in Monroe was glass making, using local siliceous sand and sandstone. Nurseries and paper plants added to the early economic base. A prominent resident of Monroe was General George A. Custer.
Population: 22,076 (2000); Race: 90.4% White, 5.2% Black, 1.4% Asian, 0.1% American Indian and Alaska Native, 2.4% Hispanic of any race, 2.2% two or more races (2000); Density: 2,440.9 persons per square mile (2000); Age: 27.0% under 18, 14.6% over 64 (2000); Marriage status: 27.8% never married, 52.5% now married, 7.7% widowed, 12.0% divorced (2000); Foreign born: 2.9% (2000); Ancestry (includes multiple ancestries): 25.9% German, 12.8% Other groups, 12.6% Irish, 10.3% French (except Basque), 8.1% English (2000).
Vital Statistics: Birth rate: 341.6 per 10,000 population (1998)
Economy: Single-family building permits issued: 95 (2001) / 34 (2000); Multi-family building permits issued: 0 (2001) / 55 (2000); Employment by occupation: 8.9% management, 17.5% professional, 18.3% services, 23.6% sales, 0.3% farming, 9.0% construction, 22.5% production (2000).
Income: Per capita income: $19,948 (2000); Median household income: $41,810 (2000); Poverty rate: 12.6% (2000).
Taxes: Total city taxes per capita: $530 (1997); City property taxes per capita: $510 (1997).
Education: High school graduation rate: 79.3% (2000); College graduation rate: 16.7% (2000).

School District(s)

Jefferson Schools (Monroe) (PK-12)
2000 Enrollment: 2,736 734-289-5599
Monroe Public Schools (KG-12)
2000 Enrollment: 6,981 734-241-0330

Two-year College(s)

Monroe County Community College (Public)
2001 Enrollment: 3,649 734-242-7300
2001 Tuition: In-state $2,550; Out-of-state $2,790

Housing: Homeownership rate: 61.6% (2000); Median home value: $115,500 (2000); Median rent: $449 per month (2000); Median age of housing: 50 years (2000).
Hospitals: Mercy-Memorial Hospital (239 beds)
Safety: Violent crime rate: 33.3 per 10,000 population; Property crime rate: 303.7 per 10,000 population (2001).
Newspapers: The Monroe Evening News (7 x week); The Guardian (1 x week)
Transportation: Commute to work: 94.4% car, 1.1% public transportation, 2.6% walk, 1.2% work from home (2000); Travel time to work: 51.2% less than 15 minutes, 20.9% 15 to 30 minutes, 14.1% 30 to 45 minutes, 7.6% 45 to 60 minutes, 6.2% 60 minutes or more (2000)
Additional Information Contacts
Monroe County Association of Realtors 734-242-6866
Monroe County Chamber of Commerce 734-242-3366
Monroe County Convention Bureau 734-457-1030

MONROE CHARTER (township). Covers a land area of 17.363 square miles and a water area of 1.074 square miles. Located at 41.89° N. Lat.; 83.41° W. Long. Elevation is 593 feet.
History: Monroe was the scene of the River Raisin massacre during the War of 1812 and the center of the Toledo War. George A. Custer lived here, and the local Museum has a large collection of Custer memorabilia. General Custer Historic Site to northeast. Settled 1778, Incorporated 1837.
Population: 13,491 (2000); Race: 94.5% White, 1.6% Black, 0.9% Asian, 0.5% American Indian and Alaska Native, 1.8% Hispanic of any race, 2.0% two or more races (2000); Density: 777.0 persons per square mile (2000); Age: 26.2% under 18, 14.4% over 64 (2000); Marriage status: 21.9% never married, 57.7% now married, 8.9% widowed, 11.5% divorced (2000); Foreign born: 1.9% (2000); Ancestry (includes multiple ancestries): 25.4% German, 12.4% French (except Basque), 10.1% English, 9.8% Other groups, 9.3% Irish (2000).
Economy: Paper products, heating equipment, plastic tubing, flour and auto parts are made. The cityhas large nurseries and is the shipping point for a farm region. Employment by occupation: 9.3% management, 14.2% professional, 14.6% services, 26.0% sales, 0.2% farming, 10.7% construction, 25.0% production (2000).
Income: Per capita income: $23,276 (2000); Median household income: $45,694 (2000); Poverty rate: 10.7% (2000).
Taxes: Total city taxes per capita: $144 (1997); City property taxes per capita: $126 (1997).
Education: High school graduation rate: 78.1% (2000); College graduation rate: 13.8% (2000).
Housing: Homeownership rate: 80.5% (2000); Median home value: $129,000 (2000); Median rent: $414 per month (2000); Median age of housing: 26 years (2000).
Transportation: Commute to work: 97.6% car, 0.9% public transportation, 0.5% walk, 0.4% work from home (2000); Travel time to work: 40.3% less than 15 minutes, 32.9% 15 to 30 minutes, 14.4% 30 to 45 minutes, 6.8% 45 to 60 minutes, 5.5% 60 minutes or more (2000)

NEWPORT (unincorporated postal area, zip code 48166). Covers a land area of 28.984 square miles and a water area of 0.673 square miles. Located at 41.98° N. Lat.; 83.29° W. Long.
Population: 10,420 (2000); Race: 96.3% White, 0.3% Black, 0.8% Asian, 0.1% American Indian and Alaska Native, 2.5% Hispanic of any race, 1.7% two or more races (2000); Density: 359.5 persons per square mile (2000); Age: 30.9% under 18, 6.2% over 64 (2000); Marriage status: 23.0% never married, 63.2% now married, 3.6% widowed, 10.2% divorced (2000); Foreign born: 1.6% (2000); Ancestry (includes multiple ancestries): 22.8% German, 12.6% French (except Basque), 12.6% Irish, 11.8% Other groups, 7.1% Polish (2000).
Economy: Employment by occupation: 6.8% management, 10.7% professional, 13.2% services, 22.8% sales, 0.8% farming, 15.5% construction, 30.2% production (2000).
Income: Per capita income: $21,241 (2000); Median household income: $52,300 (2000); Poverty rate: 6.8% (2000).
Education: High school graduation rate: 81.2% (2000); College graduation rate: 7.5% (2000).
Housing: Homeownership rate: 89.6% (2000); Median home value: $141,400 (2000); Median rent: $538 per month (2000); Median age of housing: 20 years (2000).
Transportation: Commute to work: 97.4% car, 0.4% public transportation, 0.3% walk, 1.3% work from home (2000); Travel time to work: 17.8% less than 15 minutes, 40.4% 15 to 30 minutes, 23.8% 30 to 45 minutes, 10.6% 45 to 60 minutes, 7.4% 60 minutes or more (2000)

OTTAWA LAKE (unincorporated postal area, zip code 49267). Covers a land area of 38.889 square miles and a water area of 0.357 square miles. Located at 41.75° N. Lat.; 83.71° W. Long.
Population: 4,038 (2000); Race: 97.2% White, 2.0% Black, 0.0% Asian, 0.0% American Indian and Alaska Native, 1.8% Hispanic of any race, 0.1% two or more races (2000); Density: 103.8 persons per square mile (2000); Age: 25.6% under 18, 10.7% over 64 (2000); Marriage status: 23.0% never married, 64.6% now married, 5.6% widowed, 6.8% divorced (2000); Foreign born: 1.3% (2000); Ancestry (includes multiple ancestries): 37.4% German, 12.6% English, 12.5% Polish, 10.1% Irish, 6.1% French (except Basque) (2000).
Economy: Employment by occupation: 11.4% management, 17.0% professional, 8.7% services, 25.7% sales, 0.6% farming, 15.1% construction, 21.5% production (2000).
Income: Per capita income: $22,555 (2000); Median household income: $55,085 (2000); Poverty rate: 5.1% (2000).
Education: High school graduation rate: 87.6% (2000); College graduation rate: 14.4% (2000).

School District(s)

Whiteford Agricultural Schools (KG-12)
2000 Enrollment: 784 734-856-2656

Housing: Homeownership rate: 88.1% (2000); Median home value: $127,100 (2000); Median rent: $385 per month (2000); Median age of housing: 41 years (2000).
Transportation: Commute to work: 94.5% car, 1.0% public transportation, 0.1% walk, 3.6% work from home (2000); Travel time to work: 23.0% less than 15 minutes, 47.7% 15 to 30 minutes, 20.4% 30 to 45 minutes, 2.7% 45 to 60 minutes, 6.1% 60 minutes or more (2000)

PETERSBURG (city). Covers a land area of 0.463 square miles and a water area of 0 square miles. Located at 41.89° N. Lat.; 83.71° W. Long. Elevation is 686 feet.
History: Petersburg was established on the farm of Richard Peters, who settled here in 1824. Petersburg was incorporated as a village in 1869 and as a city in 1967.
Population: 1,157 (2000); Race: 98.4% White, 0.0% Black, 0.0% Asian, 0.2% American Indian and Alaska Native, 0.9% Hispanic of any race, 1.0% two or more races (2000); Density: 2,497.8 persons per square mile (2000); Age: 30.3% under 18, 10.0% over 64 (2000); Marriage status: 21.4% never married, 62.6% now married, 7.0% widowed, 9.0% divorced (2000); Foreign born: 0.6% (2000); Ancestry (includes multiple ancestries): 34.3% German, 10.0% Irish, 9.6% English, 8.1% United States or American, 7.4% Other groups (2000).
Economy: Single-family building permits issued: 3 (2001) / 3 (2000); Multi-family building permits issued: 0 (2001) / 0 (2000); Employment by occupation: 10.2% management, 14.5% professional, 15.1% services, 20.9% sales, 0.5% farming, 11.3% construction, 27.6% production (2000).
Income: Per capita income: $21,657 (2000); Median household income: $44,861 (2000); Poverty rate: 9.3% (2000).
Taxes: Total city taxes per capita: $252 (1997); City property taxes per capita: $250 (1997).
Education: High school graduation rate: 88.3% (2000); College graduation rate: 12.5% (2000).

School District(s)

Summerfield School District (KG-12)
2000 Enrollment: 883 734-279-1035

Housing: Homeownership rate: 74.3% (2000); Median home value: $105,000 (2000); Median rent: $435 per month (2000); Median age of housing: 53 years (2000).
Transportation: Commute to work: 93.2% car, 0.7% public transportation, 2.4% walk, 3.0% work from home (2000); Travel time to work: 28.5% less than 15 minutes, 21.9% 15 to 30 minutes, 34.4% 30 to 45 minutes, 8.6% 45 to 60 minutes, 6.7% 60 minutes or more (2000)

RAISINVILLE (township). Covers a land area of 48.191 square miles and a water area of 0.437 square miles. Located at 41.94° N. Lat.; 83.53° W. Long.
History: Raisinville Township was organized in 1823, and named for the River Raisin, where wild grapes ("raisin" in French) grew.
Population: 4,896 (2000); Race: 98.2% White, 0.4% Black, 0.3% Asian, 0.0% American Indian and Alaska Native, 0.7% Hispanic of any race, 1.0% two or more races (2000); Density: 101.6 persons per square mile (2000); Age: 25.7% under 18, 10.7% over 64 (2000); Marriage status: 20.3% never married, 66.7% now married, 5.1% widowed, 7.9% divorced (2000); Foreign born: 1.3% (2000); Ancestry (includes multiple ancestries): 41.4% German, 12.8% Irish, 12.3% French (except Basque), 10.1% English, 7.1% Polish (2000).
Economy: Single-family building permits issued: 21 (2001) / 22 (2000); Multi-family building permits issued: 0 (2001) / 0 (2000); Employment by occupation: 10.0% management, 14.8% professional, 12.4% services, 25.9% sales, 1.2% farming, 13.0% construction, 22.7% production (2000).
Income: Per capita income: $26,520 (2000); Median household income: $62,734 (2000); Poverty rate: 2.9% (2000).
Taxes: Total city taxes per capita: $27 (1997); City property taxes per capita: $18 (1997).
Education: High school graduation rate: 87.7% (2000); College graduation rate: 14.7% (2000).
Housing: Homeownership rate: 93.5% (2000); Median home value: $142,700 (2000); Median rent: $445 per month (2000); Median age of housing: 32 years (2000).
Transportation: Commute to work: 97.6% car, 0.2% public transportation, 0.3% walk, 1.9% work from home (2000); Travel time to work: 24.8% less than 15 minutes, 40.0% 15 to 30 minutes, 19.4% 30 to 45 minutes, 11.2% 45 to 60 minutes, 4.7% 60 minutes or more (2000)

SOUTH MONROE (CDP). Covers a land area of 2.380 square miles and a water area of 0 square miles. Located at 41.89° N. Lat.; 83.41° W. Long.
Population: 6,370 (2000); Race: 90.5% White, 3.2% Black, 2.0% Asian, 0.8% American Indian and Alaska Native, 2.7% Hispanic of any race, 2.5% two or more races (2000); Density: 2,675.9 persons per square mile (2000); Age: 26.1% under 18, 17.3% over 64 (2000); Marriage status: 20.0% never married, 58.7% now married, 11.2% widowed, 10.1% divorced (2000); Foreign born: 2.7% (2000); Ancestry (includes multiple ancestries): 24.8% German, 12.9% French (except Basque), 12.1% Other groups, 12.0% English, 9.1% Irish (2000).
Economy: Employment by occupation: 9.5% management, 15.1% professional, 13.9% services, 26.4% sales, 0.0% farming, 10.5% construction, 24.7% production (2000).
Income: Per capita income: $23,490 (2000); Median household income: $43,665 (2000); Poverty rate: 10.6% (2000).
Education: High school graduation rate: 77.2% (2000); College graduation rate: 13.5% (2000).
Housing: Homeownership rate: 71.4% (2000); Median home value: $121,500 (2000); Median rent: $409 per month (2000); Median age of housing: 26 years (2000).
Transportation: Commute to work: 98.8% car, 0.6% public transportation, 0.4% walk, 0.2% work from home (2000); Travel time to work: 44.7% less than 15 minutes, 26.7% 15 to 30 minutes, 14.8% 30 to 45 minutes, 8.0% 45 to 60 minutes, 5.7% 60 minutes or more (2000)

SOUTH ROCKWOOD (village). Covers a land area of 2.440 square miles and a water area of 0 square miles. Located at 42.06° N. Lat.; 83.25° W. Long. Elevation is 586 feet.

History: South Rockwood was founded in 1863 by John Strong, who operated a store here. He named the village for Rockwood, Ontario.
Population: 1,284 (2000); Race: 96.6% White, 0.0% Black, 0.6% Asian, 0.2% American Indian and Alaska Native, 0.7% Hispanic of any race, 2.6% two or more races (2000); Density: 526.1 persons per square mile (2000); Age: 27.8% under 18, 8.4% over 64 (2000); Marriage status: 22.9% never married, 64.9% now married, 5.2% widowed, 7.0% divorced (2000); Foreign born: 1.0% (2000); Ancestry (includes multiple ancestries): 27.1% German, 17.2% French (except Basque), 13.6% Irish, 9.6% Other groups, 7.9% United States or American (2000).
Economy: Single-family building permits issued: 4 (2001) / 7 (2000); Multi-family building permits issued: 0 (2001) / 112 (2000); Employment by occupation: 8.8% management, 14.1% professional, 12.1% services, 23.8% sales, 0.0% farming, 16.5% construction, 24.6% production (2000).
Income: Per capita income: $22,245 (2000); Median household income: $62,500 (2000); Poverty rate: 4.1% (2000).
Taxes: Total city taxes per capita: $240 (1997); City property taxes per capita: $223 (1997).
Education: High school graduation rate: 84.7% (2000); College graduation rate: 10.7% (2000).
Housing: Homeownership rate: 88.4% (2000); Median home value: $121,700 (2000); Median rent: $425 per month (2000); Median age of housing: 45 years (2000).
Transportation: Commute to work: 99.0% car, 0.0% public transportation, 0.0% walk, 0.7% work from home (2000); Travel time to work: 26.3% less than 15 minutes, 42.1% 15 to 30 minutes, 21.9% 30 to 45 minutes, 7.3% 45 to 60 minutes, 2.4% 60 minutes or more (2000)

STONY POINT (CDP). Covers a land area of 1.142 square miles and a water area of 0.013 square miles. Located at 41.94° N. Lat.; 83.26° W. Long. Elevation is 575 feet.
Population: 1,775 (2000); Race: 90.8% White, 0.0% Black, 2.9% Asian, 0.0% American Indian and Alaska Native, 4.7% Hispanic of any race, 4.5% two or more races (2000); Density: 1,553.6 persons per square mile (2000); Age: 27.3% under 18, 9.7% over 64 (2000); Marriage status: 21.4% never married, 61.3% now married, 5.0% widowed, 12.3% divorced (2000); Foreign born: 3.2% (2000); Ancestry (includes multiple ancestries): 18.7% German, 15.7% Other groups, 13.1% Irish, 10.5% French (except Basque), 7.9% United States or American (2000).
Economy: Employment by occupation: 4.6% management, 9.6% professional, 14.7% services, 24.8% sales, 1.2% farming, 15.0% construction, 30.2% production (2000).
Income: Per capita income: $22,667 (2000); Median household income: $49,167 (2000); Poverty rate: 4.2% (2000).
Education: High school graduation rate: 78.4% (2000); College graduation rate: 8.7% (2000).
Housing: Homeownership rate: 86.7% (2000); Median home value: $104,700 (2000); Median rent: $448 per month (2000); Median age of housing: 47 years (2000).
Transportation: Commute to work: 96.6% car, 1.1% public transportation, 0.0% walk, 1.1% work from home (2000); Travel time to work: 10.4% less than 15 minutes, 48.2% 15 to 30 minutes, 16.4% 30 to 45 minutes, 18.5% 45 to 60 minutes, 6.4% 60 minutes or more (2000)

SUMMERFIELD (township). Covers a land area of 42.213 square miles and a water area of 0.155 square miles. Located at 41.87° N. Lat.; 83.71° W. Long.
Population: 3,233 (2000); Race: 97.9% White, 0.1% Black, 0.0% Asian, 0.0% American Indian and Alaska Native, 2.2% Hispanic of any race, 0.6% two or more races (2000); Density: 76.6 persons per square mile (2000); Age: 27.0% under 18, 9.3% over 64 (2000); Marriage status: 20.8% never married, 70.1% now married, 4.0% widowed, 5.1% divorced (2000); Foreign born: 1.8% (2000); Ancestry (includes multiple ancestries): 35.2% German, 12.6% Irish, 10.5% English, 10.2% French (except Basque), 8.4% Polish (2000).
Economy: Single-family building permits issued: 11 (2001) / 16 (2000); Multi-family building permits issued: 0 (2001) / 0 (2000); Employment by occupation: 10.2% management, 16.4% professional, 9.5% services, 21.8% sales, 3.4% farming, 13.0% construction, 25.8% production (2000).
Income: Per capita income: $24,057 (2000); Median household income: $62,105 (2000); Poverty rate: 3.8% (2000).
Taxes: Total city taxes per capita: $88 (1997); City property taxes per capita: $76 (1997).
Education: High school graduation rate: 84.3% (2000); College graduation rate: 14.3% (2000).
Housing: Homeownership rate: 88.5% (2000); Median home value: $135,600 (2000); Median rent: $473 per month (2000); Median age of housing: 30 years (2000).
Transportation: Commute to work: 95.3% car, 0.1% public transportation, 0.6% walk, 3.4% work from home (2000); Travel time to work: 20.3% less than 15 minutes, 38.5% 15 to 30 minutes, 26.5% 30 to 45 minutes, 8.9% 45 to 60 minutes, 5.7% 60 minutes or more (2000)

TEMPERANCE (CDP). Covers a land area of 4.595 square miles and a water area of 0.053 square miles. Located at 41.76° N. Lat.; 83.57° W. Long. Elevation is 620 feet.
Population: 7,757 (2000); Race: 97.1% White, 0.1% Black, 0.7% Asian, 0.1% American Indian and Alaska Native, 1.6% Hispanic of any race, 1.3% two or more races (2000); Density: 1,688.0 persons per square mile (2000); Age: 25.9% under 18, 13.0% over 64 (2000); Marriage status: 19.7% never married, 65.3% now married, 8.1% widowed, 6.9% divorced (2000); Foreign born: 1.9% (2000); Ancestry (includes multiple ancestries): 34.4% German, 14.6% Polish, 11.8% Irish, 10.5% English, 8.1% French (except Basque) (2000).
Economy: Manufacturing: furniture, metal fabrication. Employment by occupation: 11.5% management, 20.0% professional, 10.5% services, 25.5% sales, 0.1% farming, 9.9% construction, 22.4% production (2000).
Income: Per capita income: $24,237 (2000); Median household income: $61,090 (2000); Poverty rate: 3.6% (2000).
Education: High school graduation rate: 90.5% (2000); College graduation rate: 21.3% (2000).

School District(s)

Bedford Public Schools (KG-12)
2000 Enrollment: 5,329 734-850-6000
Housing: Homeownership rate: 84.8% (2000); Median home value: $138,300 (2000); Median rent: $527 per month (2000); Median age of housing: 30 years (2000).
Transportation: Commute to work: 97.0% car, 0.1% public transportation, 0.6% walk, 2.3% work from home (2000); Travel time to work: 28.7% less than 15 minutes, 44.0% 15 to 30 minutes, 16.0% 30 to 45 minutes, 6.3% 45 to 60 minutes, 5.0% 60 minutes or more (2000)

WEST MONROE (CDP). Covers a land area of 1.256 square miles and a water area of 0.030 square miles. Located at 41.91° N. Lat.; 83.42° W. Long.
Population: 3,893 (2000); Race: 98.8% White, 0.5% Black, 0.0% Asian, 0.3% American Indian and Alaska Native, 1.9% Hispanic of any race, 0.2% two or more races (2000); Density: 3,100.4 persons per square mile (2000); Age: 27.6% under 18, 10.6% over 64 (2000); Marriage status: 25.9% never married, 53.7% now married, 6.9% widowed, 13.5% divorced (2000); Foreign born: 0.6% (2000); Ancestry (includes multiple ancestries): 21.1% German, 11.5% French (except Basque), 10.3% Irish, 9.3% United States or American, 8.9% Other groups (2000).
Economy: Employment by occupation: 4.6% management, 13.2% professional, 19.2% services, 20.5% sales, 0.4% farming, 13.4% construction, 28.7% production (2000).
Income: Per capita income: $20,067 (2000); Median household income: $42,986 (2000); Poverty rate: 12.0% (2000).
Education: High school graduation rate: 74.2% (2000); College graduation rate: 7.9% (2000).
Housing: Homeownership rate: 91.6% (2000); Median home value: $99,300 (2000); Median rent: $333 per month (2000); Median age of housing: 24 years (2000).
Transportation: Commute to work: 98.2% car, 0.5% public transportation, 0.9% walk, 0.0% work from home (2000); Travel time to work: 35.5% less than 15 minutes, 41.9% 15 to 30 minutes, 12.3% 30 to 45 minutes, 3.5% 45 to 60 minutes, 6.8% 60 minutes or more (2000)

WHITEFORD (township). Covers a land area of 39.832 square miles and a water area of 0.439 square miles. Located at 41.77° N. Lat.; 83.69° W. Long.
Population: 4,420 (2000); Race: 95.7% White, 1.9% Black, 0.0% Asian, 0.0% American Indian and Alaska Native, 3.3% Hispanic of any race, 0.0% two or more races (2000); Density: 111.0 persons per square mile (2000); Age: 25.1% under 18, 10.8% over 64 (2000); Marriage status: 23.3% never married, 64.7% now married, 5.3% widowed, 6.8% divorced (2000); Foreign born: 2.6% (2000); Ancestry (includes multiple ancestries): 33.7% German, 12.1% Polish, 10.3% English, 9.9% Irish, 7.1% French (except Basque) (2000).
Economy: Single-family building permits issued: 30 (2001) / 29 (2000); Multi-family building permits issued: 0 (2001) / 0 (2000); Employment by

occupation: 11.0% management, 15.2% professional, 8.8% services, 26.7% sales, 2.0% farming, 12.8% construction, 23.5% production (2000).
Income: Per capita income: $21,899 (2000); Median household income: $56,280 (2000); Poverty rate: 5.1% (2000).
Taxes: Total city taxes per capita: $88 (1997); City property taxes per capita: $87 (1997).
Education: High school graduation rate: 85.3% (2000); College graduation rate: 13.9% (2000).
Housing: Homeownership rate: 87.3% (2000); Median home value: $129,800 (2000); Median rent: $388 per month (2000); Median age of housing: 39 years (2000).
Transportation: Commute to work: 95.3% car, 0.9% public transportation, 0.0% walk, 3.1% work from home (2000); Travel time to work: 25.2% less than 15 minutes, 47.6% 15 to 30 minutes, 19.6% 30 to 45 minutes, 2.4% 45 to 60 minutes, 5.1% 60 minutes or more (2000)

WOODLAND BEACH (CDP). Covers a land area of 0.524 square miles and a water area of 0.004 square miles. Located at 41.94° N. Lat.; 83.31° W. Long.
Population: 2,179 (2000); Race: 98.1% White, 0.0% Black, 0.0% Asian, 0.0% American Indian and Alaska Native, 1.4% Hispanic of any race, 1.2% two or more races (2000); Density: 4,155.0 persons per square mile (2000); Age: 30.3% under 18, 3.7% over 64 (2000); Marriage status: 21.9% never married, 67.4% now married, 6.2% widowed, 4.5% divorced (2000); Foreign born: 0.0% (2000); Ancestry (includes multiple ancestries): 26.1% German, 18.0% French (except Basque), 11.0% Other groups, 10.5% United States or American, 8.9% Polish (2000).
Economy: Employment by occupation: 8.9% management, 6.7% professional, 19.5% services, 28.6% sales, 0.0% farming, 12.9% construction, 23.6% production (2000).
Income: Per capita income: $17,824 (2000); Median household income: $45,417 (2000); Poverty rate: 7.1% (2000).
Education: High school graduation rate: 82.6% (2000); College graduation rate: 9.2% (2000).
Housing: Homeownership rate: 86.0% (2000); Median home value: $108,900 (2000); Median rent: $507 per month (2000); Median age of housing: 46 years (2000).
Transportation: Commute to work: 97.0% car, 0.9% public transportation, 0.0% walk, 0.7% work from home (2000); Travel time to work: 30.8% less than 15 minutes, 33.2% 15 to 30 minutes, 19.9% 30 to 45 minutes, 11.1% 45 to 60 minutes, 5.0% 60 minutes or more (2000)

Montcalm County

Located in central Michigan; drained by the Flat, Pine, and Tamarack Rivers; includes several lakes. Covers a land area of 708.00 square miles, a water area of 12.90 square miles, and is located in the Eastern Time Zone. The county government was organized in 1831. County seat is Stanton.

Weather Station: Greenville 2 NNE Elevation: 879 feet

	Jan	Feb	Mar	Apr	May	Jun	Jul	Aug	Sep	Oct	Nov	Dec
High	29	33	43	58	71	79	83	81	73	61	46	34
Low	13	15	23	34	45	54	58	56	49	39	29	19
Precip	1.8	1.4	2.4	3.0	3.3	3.4	2.8	4.2	3.8	3.0	3.2	2.5
Snow	20.5	12.7	10.4	2.6	tr	0.0	0.0	0.0	0.0	0.4	5.8	16.3

High and Low temperatures in degrees Fahrenheit; Precipitation and Snow in inches

Population: 61,266 (2000); Race: 94.4% White, 2.1% Black, 0.3% Asian, 0.6% American Indian and Alaska Native, 2.1% Hispanic of any race, 1.8% two or more races (2000); Density: 86.5 persons per square mile (2000); Age: 27.2% under 18, 12.1% over 64 (2000).
Religion: Five largest groups: 9.7% Catholic Church, 3.2% The United Methodist Church, 2.3% Evangelical Lutheran Church in America, 2.1% Lutheran Church—Missouri Synod, 2.1% The Wesleyan Church (2000).
Economy: Unemployment rate: 7.2% (11/2002); Total civilian labor force: 26,674 (11/2002); Leading industries: 38.3% manufacturing; 18.1% retail trade; 10.4% health care and social assistance (2000); Companies that employ more than 1,000 persons: 1 (2000); Companies that employ more than 100 persons: 22 (2000); Farms: 954 totaling 237,771 acres (1997); Minority business ownership rate: 0.0% (1997); Women business ownership rate: 21.8% (1997); Retail sales per capita: $6,763 (1997). Single-family building permits issued: 206 (2001) / 240 (2000); Multi-family building permits issued: 42 (2001) / 32 (2000).
Income: Per capita income: $16,183 (2000); Median household income: $37,218 (2000); Poverty rate: 10.9% (2000); Bankruptcy rate: 5.15% (2001).
Taxes: Total county taxes per capita: $91 (2000); County property taxes per capita: $87 (2000).
Education: High school graduation rate: 81.2% (2000); College graduation rate: 10.8% (2000).
Housing: Homeownership rate: 81.6% (2000); Median home value: $84,900 (2000); Median rent: $375 per month (2000); Median age of housing: 31 years (2000).
Health: Birth rate: 135.6 per 10,000 population (1998); Age adjusted death rate: 98.2 per 10,000 population (1999); Age adjusted cancer mortality rate: 262.7 deaths per 100,000 population (1999). Number of physicians: 5.2 per 10,000 population (1999); Number of hospital beds: 41.1 per 10,000 population (1999).
Elections: 2000 Presidential election results: 42.0% Gore, 55.4% Bush, 2.1% Nader, 0.0% Buchanan
National and State Parks: Edmore State Game Area; Flat River State Game Area; Stanton State Game Area
Additional Information Contacts
Montcalm County Government Offices 989-831-7300
Greenville Chamber of Commerce. 616-754-5697
Lakeview Area Chamber of Commerce 989-352-1200
Montcalm County Association of Realtors 616-754-8896

Montcalm County Communities

BELVIDERE (township). Covers a land area of 34.843 square miles and a water area of 1.217 square miles. Located at 43.43° N. Lat.; 85.14° W. Long.
History: Belvidere Township was established in 1866.
Population: 2,438 (2000); Race: 96.3% White, 0.0% Black, 0.3% Asian, 2.0% American Indian and Alaska Native, 1.0% Hispanic of any race, 1.1% two or more races (2000); Density: 70.0 persons per square mile (2000); Age: 25.4% under 18, 16.6% over 64 (2000); Marriage status: 20.4% never married, 62.3% now married, 8.1% widowed, 9.2% divorced (2000); Foreign born: 1.5% (2000); Ancestry (includes multiple ancestries): 27.4% German, 15.1% English, 9.4% Irish, 7.3% Dutch, 7.1% Other groups (2000).
Economy: Employment by occupation: 7.8% management, 9.5% professional, 16.3% services, 21.1% sales, 1.5% farming, 12.9% construction, 30.9% production (2000).
Income: Per capita income: $15,920 (2000); Median household income: $33,477 (2000); Poverty rate: 10.6% (2000).
Taxes: Total city taxes per capita: $97 (2000); City property taxes per capita: $95 (2000).
Education: High school graduation rate: 82.4% (2000); College graduation rate: 10.0% (2000).
Housing: Homeownership rate: 87.5% (2000); Median home value: $71,800 (2000); Median rent: $347 per month (2000); Median age of housing: 34 years (2000).
Transportation: Commute to work: 93.2% car, 0.0% public transportation, 3.2% walk, 3.2% work from home (2000); Travel time to work: 34.1% less than 15 minutes, 26.3% 15 to 30 minutes, 19.0% 30 to 45 minutes, 8.8% 45 to 60 minutes, 11.8% 60 minutes or more (2000)

BLOOMER (township). Covers a land area of 35.208 square miles and a water area of 0.031 square miles. Located at 43.16° N. Lat.; 84.87° W. Long.
History: Bloomer Township was organized in 1852, and reportedly named for the shocking new item of ladies' clothing that was coming into vogue at that time.
Population: 3,039 (2000); Race: 64.3% White, 27.5% Black, 0.2% Asian, 2.4% American Indian and Alaska Native, 3.7% Hispanic of any race, 4.8% two or more races (2000); Density: 86.3 persons per square mile (2000); Age: 15.6% under 18, 5.6% over 64 (2000); Marriage status: 45.5% never married, 38.3% now married, 2.8% widowed, 13.4% divorced (2000); Foreign born: 1.2% (2000); Ancestry (includes multiple ancestries): 22.3% Other groups, 18.4% German, 10.0% Irish, 7.6% English, 6.6% United States or American (2000).
Economy: Employment by occupation: 11.3% management, 15.4% professional, 17.8% services, 21.9% sales, 0.7% farming, 12.1% construction, 20.8% production (2000).
Income: Per capita income: $11,351 (2000); Median household income: $36,488 (2000); Poverty rate: 15.8% (2000).
Taxes: Total city taxes per capita: $9 (1997); City property taxes per capita: $9 (1997).
Education: High school graduation rate: 82.9% (2000); College graduation rate: 8.6% (2000).

Housing: Homeownership rate: 87.5% (2000); Median home value: $76,400 (2000); Median rent: $363 per month (2000); Median age of housing: 37 years (2000).
Transportation: Commute to work: 89.3% car, 0.0% public transportation, 5.1% walk, 5.6% work from home (2000); Travel time to work: 42.4% less than 15 minutes, 19.1% 15 to 30 minutes, 15.2% 30 to 45 minutes, 8.1% 45 to 60 minutes, 15.2% 60 minutes or more (2000)

BUSHNELL (township). Covers a land area of 35.597 square miles and a water area of 0.138 square miles. Located at 43.15° N. Lat.; 85.01° W. Long.
History: Bushnell Township was organized in 1850 and named for Daniel P. Bushnell, a clerk of the state legislature.
Population: 2,111 (2000); Race: 80.8% White, 14.6% Black, 0.3% Asian, 0.4% American Indian and Alaska Native, 4.3% Hispanic of any race, 1.7% two or more races (2000); Density: 59.3 persons per square mile (2000); Age: 19.9% under 18, 7.1% over 64 (2000); Marriage status: 32.3% never married, 49.6% now married, 4.1% widowed, 13.9% divorced (2000); Foreign born: 3.0% (2000); Ancestry (includes multiple ancestries): 20.3% Other groups, 17.2% German, 11.0% English, 7.9% United States or American, 7.0% Dutch (2000).
Economy: Employment by occupation: 11.1% management, 8.5% professional, 16.3% services, 18.3% sales, 3.7% farming, 11.3% construction, 30.9% production (2000).
Income: Per capita income: $13,376 (2000); Median household income: $35,573 (2000); Poverty rate: 14.6% (2000).
Taxes: Total city taxes per capita: $13 (1997); City property taxes per capita: $13 (1997).
Education: High school graduation rate: 78.3% (2000); College graduation rate: 4.7% (2000).
Housing: Homeownership rate: 89.3% (2000); Median home value: $73,800 (2000); Median rent: $336 per month (2000); Median age of housing: 32 years (2000).
Transportation: Commute to work: 88.2% car, 0.0% public transportation, 3.1% walk, 7.9% work from home (2000); Travel time to work: 14.9% less than 15 minutes, 50.2% 15 to 30 minutes, 17.1% 30 to 45 minutes, 6.9% 45 to 60 minutes, 11.0% 60 minutes or more (2000)

CARSON CITY (city). Covers a land area of 0.712 square miles and a water area of 0.013 square miles. Located at 43.17° N. Lat.; 84.84° W. Long. Elevation is 779 feet.
History: Carson City developed around a sawmill and a grist mill built in 1868 and 1870. The settlement was named for Carson City, Nevada.
Population: 1,190 (2000); Race: 96.4% White, 0.7% Black, 0.0% Asian, 0.0% American Indian and Alaska Native, 3.5% Hispanic of any race, 2.2% two or more races (2000); Density: 1,670.8 persons per square mile (2000); Age: 27.9% under 18, 17.1% over 64 (2000); Marriage status: 20.9% never married, 55.0% now married, 13.7% widowed, 10.4% divorced (2000); Foreign born: 0.2% (2000); Ancestry (includes multiple ancestries): 22.1% German, 19.2% Irish, 16.3% English, 10.4% Other groups, 8.0% United States or American (2000).
Economy: Employment by occupation: 8.8% management, 20.6% professional, 18.3% services, 21.4% sales, 0.2% farming, 5.4% construction, 25.3% production (2000).
Income: Per capita income: $19,178 (2000); Median household income: $32,500 (2000); Poverty rate: 15.2% (2000).
Taxes: Total city taxes per capita: $238 (1997); City property taxes per capita: $238 (1997).
Education: High school graduation rate: 83.9% (2000); College graduation rate: 12.4% (2000).

School District(s)

Carson City-Crystal Area Schools (PK-12)
2000 Enrollment: 1,355 517-584-3138

Housing: Homeownership rate: 63.6% (2000); Median home value: $73,600 (2000); Median rent: $317 per month (2000); Median age of housing: 54 years (2000).
Hospitals: Carson City Hospital (99 beds)
Newspapers: Carson City Gazette (1 x week)
Transportation: Commute to work: 86.6% car, 0.0% public transportation, 10.5% walk, 2.0% work from home (2000); Travel time to work: 51.4% less than 15 minutes, 11.7% 15 to 30 minutes, 18.5% 30 to 45 minutes, 8.5% 45 to 60 minutes, 9.9% 60 minutes or more (2000)

CATO (township). Covers a land area of 35.270 square miles and a water area of 0.781 square miles. Located at 43.44° N. Lat.; 85.26° W. Long.
History: Cato Township was organized in 1857 and named for Cato, New York.
Population: 2,920 (2000); Race: 98.1% White, 0.0% Black, 0.0% Asian, 0.0% American Indian and Alaska Native, 1.6% Hispanic of any race, 1.4% two or more races (2000); Density: 82.8 persons per square mile (2000); Age: 28.3% under 18, 14.6% over 64 (2000); Marriage status: 21.6% never married, 60.6% now married, 8.8% widowed, 9.0% divorced (2000); Foreign born: 0.3% (2000); Ancestry (includes multiple ancestries): 22.9% German, 12.5% English, 10.8% United States or American, 10.0% Irish, 6.1% Danish (2000).
Economy: Employment by occupation: 8.2% management, 11.7% professional, 15.7% services, 21.5% sales, 0.8% farming, 12.0% construction, 30.1% production (2000).
Income: Per capita income: $15,495 (2000); Median household income: $35,919 (2000); Poverty rate: 11.4% (2000).
Taxes: Total city taxes per capita: $32 (1997); City property taxes per capita: $31 (1997).
Education: High school graduation rate: 82.3% (2000); College graduation rate: 11.8% (2000).
Housing: Homeownership rate: 78.1% (2000); Median home value: $77,200 (2000); Median rent: $363 per month (2000); Median age of housing: 33 years (2000).
Transportation: Commute to work: 91.3% car, 0.0% public transportation, 3.8% walk, 3.9% work from home (2000); Travel time to work: 38.7% less than 15 minutes, 24.9% 15 to 30 minutes, 16.1% 30 to 45 minutes, 11.7% 45 to 60 minutes, 8.5% 60 minutes or more (2000)

CORAL (unincorporated postal area, zip code 49322). Covers a land area of 26.394 square miles and a water area of 0.827 square miles. Located at 43.36° N. Lat.; 85.37° W. Long.
History: Coral was first called Stumptown, for one of the owners of a sawmill, a Mr. Stump. The name was changed when the town was platted.
Population: 1,261 (2000); Race: 95.7% White, 0.2% Black, 1.1% Asian, 0.2% American Indian and Alaska Native, 0.3% Hispanic of any race, 2.4% two or more races (2000); Density: 47.8 persons per square mile (2000); Age: 28.4% under 18, 12.9% over 64 (2000); Marriage status: 21.1% never married, 65.0% now married, 5.7% widowed, 8.3% divorced (2000); Foreign born: 1.4% (2000); Ancestry (includes multiple ancestries): 22.5% German, 14.8% Irish, 11.4% English, 10.1% United States or American, 9.5% Dutch (2000).
Economy: Employment by occupation: 8.0% management, 11.8% professional, 15.7% services, 21.9% sales, 2.6% farming, 17.5% construction, 22.5% production (2000).
Income: Per capita income: $15,075 (2000); Median household income: $37,269 (2000); Poverty rate: 6.7% (2000).
Education: High school graduation rate: 79.0% (2000); College graduation rate: 8.6% (2000).
Housing: Homeownership rate: 86.3% (2000); Median home value: $76,400 (2000); Median rent: $394 per month (2000); Median age of housing: 42 years (2000).
Transportation: Commute to work: 89.4% car, 0.0% public transportation, 3.9% walk, 5.5% work from home (2000); Travel time to work: 19.5% less than 15 minutes, 22.5% 15 to 30 minutes, 21.2% 30 to 45 minutes, 21.9% 45 to 60 minutes, 14.9% 60 minutes or more (2000)

CRYSTAL (township). Covers a land area of 34.134 square miles and a water area of 1.703 square miles. Located at 43.26° N. Lat.; 84.90° W. Long.
Population: 2,824 (2000); Race: 95.6% White, 1.0% Black, 0.2% Asian, 1.1% American Indian and Alaska Native, 0.6% Hispanic of any race, 1.8% two or more races (2000); Density: 82.7 persons per square mile (2000); Age: 26.8% under 18, 13.1% over 64 (2000); Marriage status: 22.4% never married, 57.2% now married, 8.8% widowed, 11.6% divorced (2000); Foreign born: 1.4% (2000); Ancestry (includes multiple ancestries): 24.5% German, 12.3% English, 11.0% Irish, 10.1% Other groups, 9.3% United States or American (2000).
Economy: Employment by occupation: 8.5% management, 10.9% professional, 20.2% services, 19.3% sales, 0.3% farming, 12.8% construction, 28.0% production (2000).
Income: Per capita income: $17,231 (2000); Median household income: $34,421 (2000); Poverty rate: 10.0% (2000).
Taxes: Total city taxes per capita: $73 (1997); City property taxes per capita: $66 (1997).
Education: High school graduation rate: 82.6% (2000); College graduation rate: 10.7% (2000).
Housing: Homeownership rate: 86.0% (2000); Median home value: $74,400 (2000); Median rent: $341 per month (2000); Median age of housing: 36 years (2000).

Safety: Violent crime rate: 3.5 per 10,000 population; Property crime rate: 183.2 per 10,000 population (2001).
Transportation: Commute to work: 92.8% car, 0.2% public transportation, 1.1% walk, 4.5% work from home (2000); Travel time to work: 19.7% less than 15 minutes, 23.3% 15 to 30 minutes, 25.2% 30 to 45 minutes, 9.7% 45 to 60 minutes, 22.1% 60 minutes or more (2000)

DAY (township). Covers a land area of 35.214 square miles and a water area of 0.075 square miles. Located at 43.34° N. Lat.; 85.03° W. Long.
Population: 1,282 (2000); Race: 96.0% White, 0.1% Black, 0.0% Asian, 0.0% American Indian and Alaska Native, 2.5% Hispanic of any race, 2.7% two or more races (2000); Density: 36.4 persons per square mile (2000); Age: 27.7% under 18, 14.0% over 64 (2000); Marriage status: 22.1% never married, 66.7% now married, 5.7% widowed, 5.6% divorced (2000); Foreign born: 0.8% (2000); Ancestry (includes multiple ancestries): 30.6% German, 11.8% English, 9.5% Irish, 9.0% Other groups, 8.8% Danish (2000).
Economy: Employment by occupation: 14.1% management, 9.5% professional, 14.3% services, 18.4% sales, 7.7% farming, 11.2% construction, 24.9% production (2000).
Income: Per capita income: $16,724 (2000); Median household income: $35,500 (2000); Poverty rate: 13.3% (2000).
Taxes: Total city taxes per capita: $69 (2000); City property taxes per capita: $69 (2000).
Education: High school graduation rate: 81.9% (2000); College graduation rate: 10.3% (2000).
Housing: Homeownership rate: 90.6% (2000); Median home value: $69,700 (2000); Median rent: $292 per month (2000); Median age of housing: 48 years (2000).
Transportation: Commute to work: 84.3% car, 0.0% public transportation, 3.8% walk, 9.0% work from home (2000); Travel time to work: 41.4% less than 15 minutes, 25.6% 15 to 30 minutes, 21.1% 30 to 45 minutes, 3.2% 45 to 60 minutes, 8.7% 60 minutes or more (2000)

DOUGLASS (township). Covers a land area of 34.950 square miles and a water area of 0.756 square miles. Located at 43.34° N. Lat.; 85.15° W. Long.
Population: 2,377 (2000); Race: 96.2% White, 0.0% Black, 0.4% Asian, 0.8% American Indian and Alaska Native, 2.0% Hispanic of any race, 1.5% two or more races (2000); Density: 68.0 persons per square mile (2000); Age: 28.1% under 18, 12.6% over 64 (2000); Marriage status: 19.5% never married, 62.6% now married, 5.4% widowed, 12.5% divorced (2000); Foreign born: 1.2% (2000); Ancestry (includes multiple ancestries): 24.6% German, 16.4% English, 15.7% Irish, 8.9% Other groups, 7.6% United States or American (2000).
Economy: Employment by occupation: 8.3% management, 15.3% professional, 13.5% services, 22.7% sales, 1.7% farming, 12.2% construction, 26.2% production (2000).
Income: Per capita income: $17,892 (2000); Median household income: $44,309 (2000); Poverty rate: 4.6% (2000).
Taxes: Total city taxes per capita: $20 (1997); City property taxes per capita: $19 (1997).
Education: High school graduation rate: 83.5% (2000); College graduation rate: 11.2% (2000).
Housing: Homeownership rate: 89.1% (2000); Median home value: $93,200 (2000); Median rent: $390 per month (2000); Median age of housing: 27 years (2000).
Transportation: Commute to work: 90.9% car, 0.0% public transportation, 2.4% walk, 5.7% work from home (2000); Travel time to work: 22.1% less than 15 minutes, 31.1% 15 to 30 minutes, 16.0% 30 to 45 minutes, 11.9% 45 to 60 minutes, 18.8% 60 minutes or more (2000)

EDMORE (village). Covers a land area of 1.421 square miles and a water area of 0 square miles. Located at 43.40° N. Lat.; 85.04° W. Long. Elevation is 965 feet.
History: The village of Edmore was platted in 1878 by Edwin Moore, and named for him. After its heyday as a lumber town, Edmore turned to dairying and milling, and later to gas and oil as its economic base.
Population: 1,244 (2000); Race: 95.5% White, 0.8% Black, 0.0% Asian, 0.6% American Indian and Alaska Native, 3.0% Hispanic of any race, 2.5% two or more races (2000); Density: 875.7 persons per square mile (2000); Age: 31.0% under 18, 16.2% over 64 (2000); Marriage status: 20.6% never married, 55.2% now married, 11.0% widowed, 13.2% divorced (2000); Foreign born: 1.1% (2000); Ancestry (includes multiple ancestries): 22.6% German, 16.3% English, 13.0% Irish, 10.6% Other groups, 8.4% United States or American (2000).
Economy: Employment by occupation: 6.9% management, 18.7% professional, 22.2% services, 18.7% sales, 1.2% farming, 6.3% construction, 25.9% production (2000).
Income: Per capita income: $12,853 (2000); Median household income: $24,926 (2000); Poverty rate: 20.7% (2000).
Taxes: Total city taxes per capita: $139 (1997); City property taxes per capita: $138 (1997).
Education: High school graduation rate: 79.1% (2000); College graduation rate: 15.0% (2000).

School District(s)

Montabella Community Schools (KG-12)
2000 Enrollment: 1,092 517-427-5148

Housing: Homeownership rate: 70.4% (2000); Median home value: $67,300 (2000); Median rent: $267 per month (2000); Median age of housing: 43 years (2000).
Transportation: Commute to work: 93.4% car, 0.0% public transportation, 4.1% walk, 1.6% work from home (2000); Travel time to work: 50.7% less than 15 minutes, 19.7% 15 to 30 minutes, 15.9% 30 to 45 minutes, 7.1% 45 to 60 minutes, 6.5% 60 minutes or more (2000)

EUREKA (township). Covers a land area of 29.561 square miles and a water area of 0.714 square miles. Located at 43.15° N. Lat.; 85.25° W. Long.
Population: 3,271 (2000); Race: 96.9% White, 0.1% Black, 0.4% Asian, 0.4% American Indian and Alaska Native, 2.9% Hispanic of any race, 1.0% two or more races (2000); Density: 110.7 persons per square mile (2000); Age: 28.1% under 18, 10.4% over 64 (2000); Marriage status: 20.3% never married, 69.6% now married, 3.7% widowed, 6.5% divorced (2000); Foreign born: 2.0% (2000); Ancestry (includes multiple ancestries): 28.2% German, 14.6% English, 13.9% Irish, 9.2% Dutch, 7.5% Other groups (2000).
Economy: Single-family building permits issued: 39 (2001) / 38 (2000); Multi-family building permits issued: 0 (2001) / 0 (2000); Employment by occupation: 15.7% management, 16.8% professional, 10.5% services, 23.3% sales, 1.2% farming, 11.3% construction, 21.1% production (2000).
Income: Per capita income: $20,223 (2000); Median household income: $50,566 (2000); Poverty rate: 5.4% (2000).
Taxes: Total city taxes per capita: $55 (1997); City property taxes per capita: $38 (1997).
Education: High school graduation rate: 85.7% (2000); College graduation rate: 20.0% (2000).
Housing: Homeownership rate: 91.7% (2000); Median home value: $119,600 (2000); Median rent: $421 per month (2000); Median age of housing: 26 years (2000).
Transportation: Commute to work: 93.3% car, 0.6% public transportation, 1.4% walk, 4.7% work from home (2000); Travel time to work: 41.7% less than 15 minutes, 21.5% 15 to 30 minutes, 17.6% 30 to 45 minutes, 11.1% 45 to 60 minutes, 8.2% 60 minutes or more (2000)

EVERGREEN (township). Covers a land area of 34.657 square miles and a water area of 0.636 square miles. Located at 43.24° N. Lat.; 85.02° W. Long.
Population: 2,922 (2000); Race: 97.8% White, 0.1% Black, 0.2% Asian, 0.3% American Indian and Alaska Native, 1.1% Hispanic of any race, 0.8% two or more races (2000); Density: 84.3 persons per square mile (2000); Age: 27.0% under 18, 12.3% over 64 (2000); Marriage status: 20.4% never married, 62.9% now married, 6.3% widowed, 10.4% divorced (2000); Foreign born: 0.3% (2000); Ancestry (includes multiple ancestries): 23.8% German, 14.8% English, 11.9% Irish, 10.0% United States or American, 6.3% Other groups (2000).
Economy: Employment by occupation: 6.4% management, 11.2% professional, 14.0% services, 20.8% sales, 0.0% farming, 15.8% construction, 31.7% production (2000).
Income: Per capita income: $15,563 (2000); Median household income: $33,604 (2000); Poverty rate: 13.5% (2000).
Taxes: Total city taxes per capita: $13 (1997); City property taxes per capita: $13 (1997).
Education: High school graduation rate: 79.2% (2000); College graduation rate: 9.1% (2000).
Housing: Homeownership rate: 83.8% (2000); Median home value: $82,400 (2000); Median rent: $367 per month (2000); Median age of housing: 29 years (2000).
Transportation: Commute to work: 96.0% car, 0.0% public transportation, 1.4% walk, 2.6% work from home (2000); Travel time to work: 21.9% less than 15 minutes, 38.9% 15 to 30 minutes, 15.3% 30 to 45 minutes, 10.3% 45 to 60 minutes, 13.5% 60 minutes or more (2000)

FAIRPLAIN (township). Covers a land area of 35.466 square miles and a water area of 0.472 square miles. Located at 43.16° N. Lat.; 85.12° W. Long.
Population: 1,826 (2000); Race: 96.1% White, 1.0% Black, 0.0% Asian, 0.7% American Indian and Alaska Native, 1.7% Hispanic of any race, 1.2% two or more races (2000); Density: 51.5 persons per square mile (2000); Age: 28.4% under 18, 10.2% over 64 (2000); Marriage status: 23.2% never married, 59.3% now married, 6.0% widowed, 11.5% divorced (2000); Foreign born: 0.7% (2000); Ancestry (includes multiple ancestries): 21.2% German, 15.9% English, 10.8% Irish, 9.3% United States or American, 8.7% Other groups (2000).
Economy: Employment by occupation: 6.9% management, 10.7% professional, 12.7% services, 20.8% sales, 0.2% farming, 15.2% construction, 33.5% production (2000).
Income: Per capita income: $15,833 (2000); Median household income: $42,955 (2000); Poverty rate: 8.3% (2000).
Taxes: Total city taxes per capita: $15 (1997); City property taxes per capita: $15 (1997).
Education: High school graduation rate: 78.4% (2000); College graduation rate: 7.0% (2000).
Housing: Homeownership rate: 86.9% (2000); Median home value: $90,100 (2000); Median rent: $353 per month (2000); Median age of housing: 27 years (2000).
Transportation: Commute to work: 94.6% car, 0.0% public transportation, 1.1% walk, 4.1% work from home (2000); Travel time to work: 26.0% less than 15 minutes, 43.8% 15 to 30 minutes, 7.7% 30 to 45 minutes, 10.6% 45 to 60 minutes, 12.0% 60 minutes or more (2000)

FENWICK (unincorporated postal area, zip code 48834). Covers a land area of 50.562 square miles and a water area of 0.299 square miles. Located at 43.14° N. Lat.; 85.04° W. Long.
Population: 2,412 (2000); Race: 96.7% White, 0.6% Black, 0.0% Asian, 0.3% American Indian and Alaska Native, 2.5% Hispanic of any race, 1.6% two or more races (2000); Density: 47.7 persons per square mile (2000); Age: 28.2% under 18, 8.1% over 64 (2000); Marriage status: 23.5% never married, 60.9% now married, 4.9% widowed, 10.7% divorced (2000); Foreign born: 0.7% (2000); Ancestry (includes multiple ancestries): 18.8% German, 15.4% English, 13.6% United States or American, 9.1% Other groups, 8.1% Irish (2000).
Economy: Employment by occupation: 8.7% management, 11.5% professional, 15.8% services, 19.4% sales, 1.1% farming, 12.5% construction, 31.1% production (2000).
Income: Per capita income: $17,074 (2000); Median household income: $40,938 (2000); Poverty rate: 8.8% (2000).
Education: High school graduation rate: 77.6% (2000); College graduation rate: 6.3% (2000).
Housing: Homeownership rate: 88.5% (2000); Median home value: $77,100 (2000); Median rent: $372 per month (2000); Median age of housing: 30 years (2000).
Transportation: Commute to work: 93.4% car, 0.0% public transportation, 1.1% walk, 5.1% work from home (2000); Travel time to work: 12.9% less than 15 minutes, 47.6% 15 to 30 minutes, 15.4% 30 to 45 minutes, 9.8% 45 to 60 minutes, 14.3% 60 minutes or more (2000)

FERRIS (township). Covers a land area of 36.110 square miles and a water area of 0.033 square miles. Located at 43.33° N. Lat.; 84.91° W. Long.
Population: 1,379 (2000); Race: 99.1% White, 0.0% Black, 0.0% Asian, 0.1% American Indian and Alaska Native, 1.6% Hispanic of any race, 0.5% two or more races (2000); Density: 38.2 persons per square mile (2000); Age: 30.4% under 18, 10.4% over 64 (2000); Marriage status: 18.5% never married, 68.3% now married, 4.1% widowed, 9.1% divorced (2000); Foreign born: 0.4% (2000); Ancestry (includes multiple ancestries): 15.8% German, 10.8% English, 9.1% United States or American, 7.9% Irish, 7.2% Other groups (2000).
Economy: Employment by occupation: 5.9% management, 11.4% professional, 16.7% services, 18.4% sales, 2.8% farming, 13.9% construction, 30.9% production (2000).
Income: Per capita income: $15,184 (2000); Median household income: $35,820 (2000); Poverty rate: 9.7% (2000).
Taxes: Total city taxes per capita: $26 (1997); City property taxes per capita: $26 (1997).
Education: High school graduation rate: 77.8% (2000); College graduation rate: 8.3% (2000).
Housing: Homeownership rate: 91.5% (2000); Median home value: $81,200 (2000); Median rent: $358 per month (2000); Median age of housing: 23 years (2000).
Transportation: Commute to work: 92.6% car, 0.3% public transportation, 1.0% walk, 5.8% work from home (2000); Travel time to work: 18.2% less than 15 minutes, 33.3% 15 to 30 minutes, 24.7% 30 to 45 minutes, 14.2% 45 to 60 minutes, 9.6% 60 minutes or more (2000)

GOWEN (unincorporated postal area, zip code 49326). Covers a land area of 25.271 square miles and a water area of 1.173 square miles. Located at 43.24° N. Lat.; 85.34° W. Long. Elevation is 860 feet.
History: Gowen began in the 1840's as a lumbering center. It was first called Gregor's Mills, and then Kaywood. When Colonel James Gowen of Pennsylvania platted a village here in 1871, it was named for him.
Population: 3,445 (2000); Race: 95.3% White, 1.3% Black, 0.4% Asian, 0.7% American Indian and Alaska Native, 3.0% Hispanic of any race, 1.7% two or more races (2000); Density: 136.3 persons per square mile (2000); Age: 24.2% under 18, 11.2% over 64 (2000); Marriage status: 17.0% never married, 66.1% now married, 6.7% widowed, 10.3% divorced (2000); Foreign born: 0.8% (2000); Ancestry (includes multiple ancestries): 24.9% German, 12.4% English, 12.3% Dutch, 11.6% Other groups, 10.6% Irish (2000).
Economy: Employment by occupation: 13.0% management, 9.6% professional, 8.3% services, 27.2% sales, 0.3% farming, 11.3% construction, 30.3% production (2000).
Income: Per capita income: $19,442 (2000); Median household income: $48,517 (2000); Poverty rate: 5.5% (2000).
Education: High school graduation rate: 82.1% (2000); College graduation rate: 8.0% (2000).
Housing: Homeownership rate: 94.2% (2000); Median home value: $103,800 (2000); Median rent: $460 per month (2000); Median age of housing: 21 years (2000).
Transportation: Commute to work: 94.3% car, 0.0% public transportation, 0.8% walk, 4.2% work from home (2000); Travel time to work: 20.8% less than 15 minutes, 31.6% 15 to 30 minutes, 18.4% 30 to 45 minutes, 22.4% 45 to 60 minutes, 6.8% 60 minutes or more (2000)

GREENVILLE (city). Covers a land area of 5.712 square miles and a water area of 0.243 square miles. Located at 43.18° N. Lat.; 85.25° W. Long. Elevation is 813 feet.
History: Greenville began as a lumber center, founded by John Green in 1844 and platted in 1853. It later became an important potato market on the Flat River.
Population: 7,935 (2000); Race: 95.2% White, 0.3% Black, 0.5% Asian, 0.1% American Indian and Alaska Native, 3.5% Hispanic of any race, 2.1% two or more races (2000); Density: 1,389.2 persons per square mile (2000); Age: 25.9% under 18, 17.1% over 64 (2000); Marriage status: 22.2% never married, 52.5% now married, 10.9% widowed, 14.3% divorced (2000); Foreign born: 1.6% (2000); Ancestry (includes multiple ancestries): 20.2% German, 19.4% English, 10.7% Irish, 9.6% Other groups, 8.9% United States or American (2000).
Economy: Single-family building permits issued: 1 (2001) / 5 (2000); Multi-family building permits issued: 40 (2001) / 19 (2000); Employment by occupation: 7.4% management, 17.9% professional, 16.8% services, 23.4% sales, 0.7% farming, 6.7% construction, 27.1% production (2000).
Income: Per capita income: $15,933 (2000); Median household income: $30,453 (2000); Poverty rate: 15.2% (2000).
Taxes: Total city taxes per capita: $290 (1997); City property taxes per capita: $283 (1997).
Education: High school graduation rate: 78.4% (2000); College graduation rate: 12.8% (2000).

School District(s)

Greenville Public Schools (KG-12)
2000 Enrollment: 3,883 616-754-3686
Threshold Academy (KG-06)
2000 Enrollment: 184 517-774-2100

Housing: Homeownership rate: 61.2% (2000); Median home value: $80,900 (2000); Median rent: $406 per month (2000); Median age of housing: 38 years (2000).
Hospitals: United Memorial Health Center (105 beds)
Newspapers: Spartan (2 x month); The Daily News (6 x week); Buyline South (1 x week); Buyline Central (1 x week); Buyline North (1 x week)
Transportation: Commute to work: 91.0% car, 0.2% public transportation, 4.3% walk, 3.5% work from home (2000); Travel time to work: 47.2% less than 15 minutes, 20.2% 15 to 30 minutes, 12.5% 30 to 45 minutes, 13.2% 45 to 60 minutes, 6.9% 60 minutes or more (2000)
Airports: Greenville Municipal
Additional Information Contacts
Greenville Chamber of Commerce 616-754-5697

Montcalm County Association of Realtors 616-754-8896

HOME (township). Covers a land area of 35.999 square miles and a water area of 0.108 square miles. Located at 43.41° N. Lat.; 85.03° W. Long.
Population: 2,708 (2000); Race: 97.2% White, 0.4% Black, 0.3% Asian, 0.3% American Indian and Alaska Native, 3.1% Hispanic of any race, 1.5% two or more races (2000); Density: 75.2 persons per square mile (2000); Age: 27.9% under 18, 15.3% over 64 (2000); Marriage status: 18.6% never married, 62.5% now married, 8.2% widowed, 10.7% divorced (2000); Foreign born: 1.8% (2000); Ancestry (includes multiple ancestries): 22.0% German, 15.6% English, 13.3% Irish, 9.8% United States or American, 8.7% Other groups (2000).
Economy: Employment by occupation: 10.6% management, 17.1% professional, 17.1% services, 20.3% sales, 0.8% farming, 8.1% construction, 26.0% production (2000).
Income: Per capita income: $14,522 (2000); Median household income: $30,590 (2000); Poverty rate: 16.3% (2000).
Taxes: Total city taxes per capita: $59 (1997); City property taxes per capita: $59 (1997).
Education: High school graduation rate: 82.5% (2000); College graduation rate: 13.3% (2000).
Housing: Homeownership rate: 76.0% (2000); Median home value: $74,400 (2000); Median rent: $325 per month (2000); Median age of housing: 37 years (2000).
Transportation: Commute to work: 90.1% car, 0.0% public transportation, 4.6% walk, 4.8% work from home (2000); Travel time to work: 49.8% less than 15 minutes, 21.3% 15 to 30 minutes, 16.3% 30 to 45 minutes, 6.2% 45 to 60 minutes, 6.5% 60 minutes or more (2000)

HOWARD CITY (village). Covers a land area of 2.510 square miles and a water area of 0 square miles. Located at 43.39° N. Lat.; 85.46° W. Long. Elevation is 870 feet.
History: The land on which Howard City was platted in 1868 belonged to Benjamin Ensley. Howard City, formed as a lumber center, turned to farming. Discovery of oil and gas in the 1930's supported the economy.
Population: 1,585 (2000); Race: 93.7% White, 0.2% Black, 0.4% Asian, 1.7% American Indian and Alaska Native, 3.0% Hispanic of any race, 3.0% two or more races (2000); Density: 631.5 persons per square mile (2000); Age: 30.8% under 18, 14.6% over 64 (2000); Marriage status: 21.8% never married, 58.7% now married, 8.6% widowed, 11.0% divorced (2000); Foreign born: 1.1% (2000); Ancestry (includes multiple ancestries): 24.3% German, 14.1% Irish, 11.5% English, 11.3% Dutch, 9.5% United States or American (2000).
Economy: Employment by occupation: 7.3% management, 8.6% professional, 15.5% services, 24.1% sales, 0.3% farming, 14.8% construction, 29.5% production (2000).
Income: Per capita income: $14,076 (2000); Median household income: $34,556 (2000); Poverty rate: 10.4% (2000).
Taxes: Total city taxes per capita: $105 (1997); City property taxes per capita: $104 (1997).
Education: High school graduation rate: 74.3% (2000); College graduation rate: 7.8% (2000).

School District(s)

Tri County Area Schools (KG-12)
2000 Enrollment: 2,358 231-937-5611
Housing: Homeownership rate: 70.5% (2000); Median home value: $76,100 (2000); Median rent: $383 per month (2000); Median age of housing: 35 years (2000).
Safety: Violent crime rate: 69.1 per 10,000 population; Property crime rate: 514.8 per 10,000 population (2001).
Newspapers: River Valley News Shopper (1 x week); Lakeview Enterprise (1 x week)
Transportation: Commute to work: 92.5% car, 0.0% public transportation, 2.8% walk, 4.1% work from home (2000); Travel time to work: 30.1% less than 15 minutes, 9.3% 15 to 30 minutes, 25.8% 30 to 45 minutes, 24.3% 45 to 60 minutes, 10.4% 60 minutes or more (2000); Amtrak: Service available.

LAKEVIEW (village). Covers a land area of 1.572 square miles and a water area of 0.332 square miles. Located at 43.44° N. Lat.; 85.27° W. Long. Elevation is 953 feet.
History: Lakeview was first settled in 1858 on the shore of Tamarck Lake by Albert S. French from New York. It was incorporated as a village in 1881.
Population: 1,112 (2000); Race: 97.5% White, 0.0% Black, 0.0% Asian, 0.0% American Indian and Alaska Native, 0.9% Hispanic of any race, 1.9% two or more races (2000); Density: 707.2 persons per square mile (2000); Age: 30.1% under 18, 19.0% over 64 (2000); Marriage status: 22.4% never married, 55.3% now married, 13.5% widowed, 8.8% divorced (2000); Foreign born: 0.3% (2000); Ancestry (includes multiple ancestries): 19.0% German, 15.3% English, 12.2% United States or American, 11.6% Irish, 6.5% Danish (2000).
Economy: Employment by occupation: 6.9% management, 14.2% professional, 20.8% services, 19.5% sales, 1.3% farming, 7.3% construction, 30.1% production (2000).
Income: Per capita income: $14,154 (2000); Median household income: $33,611 (2000); Poverty rate: 9.9% (2000).
Taxes: Total city taxes per capita: $204 (1997); City property taxes per capita: $200 (1997).
Education: High school graduation rate: 78.7% (2000); College graduation rate: 9.9% (2000).

School District(s)

Lakeview Community Schools (KG-12)
2000 Enrollment: 1,886 517-352-6226
Housing: Homeownership rate: 70.4% (2000); Median home value: $68,800 (2000); Median rent: $371 per month (2000); Median age of housing: 53 years (2000).
Hospitals: Kelsey Memorial Hospital (94 beds)
Safety: Violent crime rate: 8.9 per 10,000 population; Property crime rate: 98.4 per 10,000 population (2001).
Transportation: Commute to work: 90.8% car, 0.0% public transportation, 6.6% walk, 2.3% work from home (2000); Travel time to work: 39.1% less than 15 minutes, 19.7% 15 to 30 minutes, 19.9% 30 to 45 minutes, 14.5% 45 to 60 minutes, 6.8% 60 minutes or more (2000)

Additional Information Contacts

Lakeview Area Chamber of Commerce 989-352-1200

MAPLE VALLEY (township). Covers a land area of 35.409 square miles and a water area of 0.723 square miles. Located at 43.33° N. Lat.; 85.39° W. Long.
Population: 2,083 (2000); Race: 96.0% White, 0.3% Black, 0.7% Asian, 0.2% American Indian and Alaska Native, 0.5% Hispanic of any race, 2.5% two or more races (2000); Density: 58.8 persons per square mile (2000); Age: 28.4% under 18, 12.4% over 64 (2000); Marriage status: 21.8% never married, 63.2% now married, 5.9% widowed, 9.1% divorced (2000); Foreign born: 1.2% (2000); Ancestry (includes multiple ancestries): 25.4% German, 13.0% Irish, 13.0% English, 9.3% Dutch, 8.8% Danish (2000).
Economy: Employment by occupation: 9.3% management, 13.2% professional, 12.1% services, 20.7% sales, 4.0% farming, 14.4% construction, 26.2% production (2000).
Income: Per capita income: $15,163 (2000); Median household income: $36,583 (2000); Poverty rate: 7.8% (2000).
Taxes: Total city taxes per capita: $27 (1997); City property taxes per capita: $27 (1997).
Education: High school graduation rate: 78.5% (2000); College graduation rate: 11.5% (2000).
Housing: Homeownership rate: 87.6% (2000); Median home value: $79,800 (2000); Median rent: $425 per month (2000); Median age of housing: 41 years (2000).
Transportation: Commute to work: 90.3% car, 0.0% public transportation, 3.1% walk, 5.2% work from home (2000); Travel time to work: 16.7% less than 15 minutes, 26.3% 15 to 30 minutes, 20.9% 30 to 45 minutes, 22.9% 45 to 60 minutes, 13.1% 60 minutes or more (2000)

MCBRIDE (village). Covers a land area of 0.361 square miles and a water area of 0 square miles. Located at 43.35° N. Lat.; 85.04° W. Long.
Population: 232 (2000); Race: 91.7% White, 0.0% Black, 0.0% Asian, 0.0% American Indian and Alaska Native, 1.4% Hispanic of any race, 8.3% two or more races (2000); Density: 642.3 persons per square mile (2000); Age: 27.5% under 18, 11.5% over 64 (2000); Marriage status: 22.9% never married, 66.3% now married, 6.0% widowed, 4.8% divorced (2000); Foreign born: 0.0% (2000); Ancestry (includes multiple ancestries): 25.7% German, 7.8% Danish, 7.8% United States or American, 7.8% English, 4.1% French Canadian (2000).
Economy: In agricultural area. Employment by occupation: 6.8% management, 16.5% professional, 10.7% services, 14.6% sales, 1.9% farming, 15.5% construction, 34.0% production (2000).
Income: Per capita income: $13,376 (2000); Median household income: $30,568 (2000); Poverty rate: 18.8% (2000).
Taxes: Total city taxes per capita: $24 (1997); City property taxes per capita: $24 (1997).
Education: High school graduation rate: 85.0% (2000); College graduation rate: 5.0% (2000).

Housing: Homeownership rate: 92.4% (2000); Median home value: $49,500 (2000); Median rent: $375 per month (2000); Median age of housing: 60+ years (2000).
Transportation: Commute to work: 84.5% car, 0.0% public transportation, 3.9% walk, 3.9% work from home (2000); Travel time to work: 42.4% less than 15 minutes, 27.3% 15 to 30 minutes, 22.2% 30 to 45 minutes, 2.0% 45 to 60 minutes, 6.1% 60 minutes or more (2000)

MONTCALM (township). Covers a land area of 35.710 square miles and a water area of 0.711 square miles. Located at 43.24° N. Lat.; 85.26° W. Long.
Population: 3,178 (2000); Race: 97.5% White, 0.0% Black, 0.3% Asian, 1.1% American Indian and Alaska Native, 1.5% Hispanic of any race, 0.9% two or more races (2000); Density: 89.0 persons per square mile (2000); Age: 28.4% under 18, 9.7% over 64 (2000); Marriage status: 21.3% never married, 62.6% now married, 4.8% widowed, 11.4% divorced (2000); Foreign born: 0.7% (2000); Ancestry (includes multiple ancestries): 27.5% German, 15.5% English, 9.7% Irish, 9.4% Other groups, 8.7% Danish (2000).
Economy: Single-family building permits issued: 17 (2001) / 34 (2000); Multi-family building permits issued: 0 (2001) / 0 (2000); Employment by occupation: 10.6% management, 9.7% professional, 10.1% services, 23.5% sales, 0.8% farming, 11.4% construction, 33.9% production (2000).
Income: Per capita income: $17,591 (2000); Median household income: $43,485 (2000); Poverty rate: 7.4% (2000).
Taxes: Total city taxes per capita: $375 (1997); City property taxes per capita: $368 (1997).
Education: High school graduation rate: 80.5% (2000); College graduation rate: 7.8% (2000).
Housing: Homeownership rate: 87.6% (2000); Median home value: $92,600 (2000); Median rent: $429 per month (2000); Median age of housing: 27 years (2000).
Transportation: Commute to work: 95.9% car, 0.0% public transportation, 1.8% walk, 2.0% work from home (2000); Travel time to work: 38.4% less than 15 minutes, 24.9% 15 to 30 minutes, 10.2% 30 to 45 minutes, 16.4% 45 to 60 minutes, 10.2% 60 minutes or more (2000)

PIERSON (village). Covers a land area of 0.253 square miles and a water area of 0 square miles. Located at 43.31° N. Lat.; 85.49° W. Long. Elevation is 900 feet.
History: Pierson was founded in 1856 on land acquired by David S. Pierson. It became a trading center for nearby resorts.
Population: 185 (2000); Race: 97.6% White, 0.0% Black, 0.0% Asian, 0.9% American Indian and Alaska Native, 3.3% Hispanic of any race, 1.4% two or more races (2000); Density: 730.2 persons per square mile (2000); Age: 36.0% under 18, 7.6% over 64 (2000); Marriage status: 28.5% never married, 61.1% now married, 4.2% widowed, 6.3% divorced (2000); Foreign born: 0.0% (2000); Ancestry (includes multiple ancestries): 23.2% Irish, 22.7% German, 21.3% English, 12.8% Other groups, 7.6% United States or American (2000).
Economy: Employment by occupation: 2.6% management, 0.0% professional, 9.0% services, 24.4% sales, 0.0% farming, 23.1% construction, 41.0% production (2000).
Income: Per capita income: $10,456 (2000); Median household income: $37,500 (2000); Poverty rate: 11.8% (2000).
Taxes: Total city taxes per capita: $57 (1997); City property taxes per capita: $57 (1997).
Education: High school graduation rate: 67.0% (2000); College graduation rate: 1.8% (2000).
Housing: Homeownership rate: 76.6% (2000); Median home value: $51,400 (2000); Median rent: $345 per month (2000); Median age of housing: 60+ years (2000).
Transportation: Commute to work: 87.2% car, 0.0% public transportation, 5.1% walk, 0.0% work from home (2000); Travel time to work: 25.6% less than 15 minutes, 26.9% 15 to 30 minutes, 24.4% 30 to 45 minutes, 10.3% 45 to 60 minutes, 12.8% 60 minutes or more (2000)

PIERSON (township). Covers a land area of 34.677 square miles and a water area of 1.540 square miles. Located at 43.32° N. Lat.; 85.50° W. Long. Elevation is 900 feet.
Population: 2,866 (2000); Race: 95.8% White, 0.2% Black, 0.3% Asian, 0.5% American Indian and Alaska Native, 1.8% Hispanic of any race, 2.1% two or more races (2000); Density: 82.6 persons per square mile (2000); Age: 30.7% under 18, 8.6% over 64 (2000); Marriage status: 20.4% never married, 66.4% now married, 4.8% widowed, 8.4% divorced (2000); Foreign born: 0.8% (2000); Ancestry (includes multiple ancestries): 23.6% German, 14.4% English, 13.3% Dutch, 13.1% Irish, 9.6% United States or American (2000).
Economy: In lake and farm area. Employment by occupation: 10.9% management, 12.6% professional, 10.0% services, 24.5% sales, 0.3% farming, 13.1% construction, 28.7% production (2000).
Income: Per capita income: $19,216 (2000); Median household income: $48,519 (2000); Poverty rate: 5.0% (2000).
Taxes: Total city taxes per capita: $17 (1997); City property taxes per capita: $16 (1997).
Education: High school graduation rate: 83.3% (2000); College graduation rate: 13.8% (2000).
Housing: Homeownership rate: 91.3% (2000); Median home value: $109,700 (2000); Median rent: $383 per month (2000); Median age of housing: 26 years (2000).
Transportation: Commute to work: 94.4% car, 0.1% public transportation, 1.6% walk, 3.2% work from home (2000); Travel time to work: 16.0% less than 15 minutes, 18.3% 15 to 30 minutes, 38.0% 30 to 45 minutes, 19.9% 45 to 60 minutes, 7.8% 60 minutes or more (2000)

PINE (township). Covers a land area of 35.168 square miles and a water area of 0.950 square miles. Located at 43.33° N. Lat.; 85.25° W. Long.
Population: 1,654 (2000); Race: 96.4% White, 0.1% Black, 0.2% Asian, 1.7% American Indian and Alaska Native, 0.2% Hispanic of any race, 1.1% two or more races (2000); Density: 47.0 persons per square mile (2000); Age: 28.2% under 18, 11.8% over 64 (2000); Marriage status: 17.4% never married, 67.7% now married, 5.3% widowed, 9.6% divorced (2000); Foreign born: 0.7% (2000); Ancestry (includes multiple ancestries): 22.7% German, 13.6% English, 9.6% Irish, 9.2% Danish, 7.2% Dutch (2000).
Economy: Employment by occupation: 8.1% management, 10.6% professional, 12.7% services, 24.9% sales, 1.6% farming, 14.2% construction, 28.0% production (2000).
Income: Per capita income: $17,381 (2000); Median household income: $41,583 (2000); Poverty rate: 8.5% (2000).
Taxes: Total city taxes per capita: $21 (1997); City property taxes per capita: $19 (1997).
Education: High school graduation rate: 83.5% (2000); College graduation rate: 7.5% (2000).
Housing: Homeownership rate: 87.3% (2000); Median home value: $97,100 (2000); Median rent: $392 per month (2000); Median age of housing: 27 years (2000).
Transportation: Commute to work: 88.5% car, 0.0% public transportation, 2.0% walk, 7.1% work from home (2000); Travel time to work: 13.7% less than 15 minutes, 45.6% 15 to 30 minutes, 14.1% 30 to 45 minutes, 9.5% 45 to 60 minutes, 17.1% 60 minutes or more (2000)

REYNOLDS (township). Covers a land area of 36.039 square miles and a water area of 0.061 square miles. Located at 43.40° N. Lat.; 85.47° W. Long.
Population: 4,279 (2000); Race: 94.5% White, 0.1% Black, 0.3% Asian, 1.1% American Indian and Alaska Native, 2.2% Hispanic of any race, 3.4% two or more races (2000); Density: 118.7 persons per square mile (2000); Age: 30.9% under 18, 8.6% over 64 (2000); Marriage status: 19.2% never married, 63.1% now married, 5.5% widowed, 12.2% divorced (2000); Foreign born: 1.4% (2000); Ancestry (includes multiple ancestries): 21.1% German, 13.5% Irish, 12.9% English, 11.5% Dutch, 10.6% United States or American (2000).
Economy: Employment by occupation: 6.8% management, 8.9% professional, 11.8% services, 26.2% sales, 0.4% farming, 15.7% construction, 30.3% production (2000).
Income: Per capita income: $15,589 (2000); Median household income: $40,799 (2000); Poverty rate: 11.6% (2000).
Taxes: Total city taxes per capita: $48 (1997); City property taxes per capita: $48 (1997).
Education: High school graduation rate: 80.3% (2000); College graduation rate: 10.1% (2000).
Housing: Homeownership rate: 82.7% (2000); Median home value: $92,200 (2000); Median rent: $401 per month (2000); Median age of housing: 18 years (2000).
Transportation: Commute to work: 94.5% car, 0.0% public transportation, 1.0% walk, 3.9% work from home (2000); Travel time to work: 19.7% less than 15 minutes, 21.4% 15 to 30 minutes, 24.5% 30 to 45 minutes, 23.4% 45 to 60 minutes, 11.1% 60 minutes or more (2000)

RICHLAND (township). Covers a land area of 35.884 square miles and a water area of 0.380 square miles. Located at 43.40° N. Lat.; 84.92° W. Long.
Population: 2,868 (2000); Race: 97.3% White, 0.4% Black, 0.0% Asian, 0.1% American Indian and Alaska Native, 2.0% Hispanic of any race, 2.0% two or more races (2000); Density: 79.9 persons per square mile (2000); Age: 28.8% under 18, 11.5% over 64 (2000); Marriage status: 21.9% never

married, 63.4% now married, 5.6% widowed, 9.1% divorced (2000); Foreign born: 0.9% (2000); Ancestry (includes multiple ancestries): 18.6% German, 12.7% English, 11.3% Irish, 8.9% United States or American, 8.3% Other groups (2000).
Economy: Employment by occupation: 7.1% management, 10.9% professional, 16.0% services, 22.4% sales, 2.2% farming, 12.7% construction, 28.7% production (2000).
Income: Per capita income: $14,889 (2000); Median household income: $34,847 (2000); Poverty rate: 10.5% (2000).
Taxes: Total city taxes per capita: $34 (1997); City property taxes per capita: $33 (1997).
Education: High school graduation rate: 80.9% (2000); College graduation rate: 8.3% (2000).
Housing: Homeownership rate: 86.2% (2000); Median home value: $73,400 (2000); Median rent: $307 per month (2000); Median age of housing: 32 years (2000).
Transportation: Commute to work: 91.5% car, 0.0% public transportation, 3.5% walk, 4.1% work from home (2000); Travel time to work: 25.6% less than 15 minutes, 45.0% 15 to 30 minutes, 16.4% 30 to 45 minutes, 6.0% 45 to 60 minutes, 7.0% 60 minutes or more (2000)

SHERIDAN (village). Covers a land area of 0.919 square miles and a water area of 0.051 square miles. Located at 43.21° N. Lat.; 85.07° W. Long.
History: Sheridan grew around a sawmill founded by John W. Winsor in the 1850's. The village was named for General Philip H. Sheridan.
Population: 705 (2000); Race: 96.4% White, 0.0% Black, 0.0% Asian, 1.0% American Indian and Alaska Native, 1.1% Hispanic of any race, 2.2% two or more races (2000); Density: 767.1 persons per square mile (2000); Age: 28.3% under 18, 18.1% over 64 (2000); Marriage status: 22.2% never married, 57.3% now married, 8.7% widowed, 11.7% divorced (2000); Foreign born: 0.7% (2000); Ancestry (includes multiple ancestries): 17.4% German, 17.4% English, 11.8% Irish, 8.8% United States or American, 7.9% Danish (2000).
Economy: Employment by occupation: 7.6% management, 13.3% professional, 14.2% services, 32.0% sales, 0.0% farming, 10.8% construction, 22.2% production (2000).
Income: Per capita income: $16,781 (2000); Median household income: $30,556 (2000); Poverty rate: 9.6% (2000).
Taxes: Total city taxes per capita: $147 (1997); City property taxes per capita: $147 (1997).
Education: High school graduation rate: 85.1% (2000); College graduation rate: 10.7% (2000).
Housing: Homeownership rate: 72.4% (2000); Median home value: $74,400 (2000); Median rent: $348 per month (2000); Median age of housing: 38 years (2000).
Hospitals: Sheridan Community Hospital (31 beds)
Transportation: Commute to work: 93.4% car, 0.0% public transportation, 2.0% walk, 4.0% work from home (2000); Travel time to work: 37.7% less than 15 minutes, 39.4% 15 to 30 minutes, 5.9% 30 to 45 minutes, 6.2% 45 to 60 minutes, 10.7% 60 minutes or more (2000)

SIDNEY (township). Covers a land area of 34.061 square miles and a water area of 1.010 square miles. Located at 43.24° N. Lat.; 85.14° W. Long. Elevation is 898 feet.
History: Sidney Township was organized in 1857 and named for Sidney, Ohio, the former home of some of the early residents.
Population: 2,563 (2000); Race: 97.9% White, 0.0% Black, 0.3% Asian, 0.6% American Indian and Alaska Native, 0.6% Hispanic of any race, 0.8% two or more races (2000); Density: 75.2 persons per square mile (2000); Age: 26.1% under 18, 12.3% over 64 (2000); Marriage status: 22.0% never married, 62.1% now married, 6.2% widowed, 9.7% divorced (2000); Foreign born: 0.4% (2000); Ancestry (includes multiple ancestries): 25.3% German, 15.2% English, 10.8% United States or American, 10.8% Irish, 8.4% Danish (2000).
Economy: Employment by occupation: 5.8% management, 14.8% professional, 15.2% services, 17.7% sales, 1.9% farming, 11.2% construction, 33.3% production (2000).
Income: Per capita income: $17,045 (2000); Median household income: $40,682 (2000); Poverty rate: 8.6% (2000).
Taxes: Total city taxes per capita: $16 (1997); City property taxes per capita: $15 (1997).
Education: High school graduation rate: 81.7% (2000); College graduation rate: 10.3% (2000).

Two-year College(s)

Montcalm Community College (Public)
2001 Enrollment: 1,520 517-328-2111
2001 Tuition: In-state $2,519; Out-of-state $3,214
Housing: Homeownership rate: 89.4% (2000); Median home value: $83,500 (2000); Median rent: $412 per month (2000); Median age of housing: 28 years (2000).
Transportation: Commute to work: 95.7% car, 0.3% public transportation, 0.2% walk, 2.9% work from home (2000); Travel time to work: 23.2% less than 15 minutes, 52.6% 15 to 30 minutes, 9.8% 30 to 45 minutes, 5.7% 45 to 60 minutes, 8.7% 60 minutes or more (2000)

SIX LAKES (unincorporated postal area, zip code 48886). Covers a land area of 29.198 square miles and a water area of 0.760 square miles. Located at 43.42° N. Lat.; 85.15° W. Long.
History: The railway established a station here in 1875, drawing the residents of nearby Summerville to abandon their village and move to Six Lakes. The many small lakes offered fishing to summer vacationers.
Population: 2,215 (2000); Race: 95.4% White, 0.0% Black, 0.4% Asian, 1.7% American Indian and Alaska Native, 2.0% Hispanic of any race, 1.5% two or more races (2000); Density: 75.9 persons per square mile (2000); Age: 27.7% under 18, 14.2% over 64 (2000); Marriage status: 21.5% never married, 60.8% now married, 7.2% widowed, 10.5% divorced (2000); Foreign born: 1.6% (2000); Ancestry (includes multiple ancestries): 26.2% German, 12.7% English, 10.4% Irish, 7.9% Other groups, 7.0% Dutch (2000).
Economy: Employment by occupation: 7.2% management, 7.2% professional, 16.4% services, 22.4% sales, 2.0% farming, 13.9% construction, 31.0% production (2000).
Income: Per capita income: $15,151 (2000); Median household income: $32,672 (2000); Poverty rate: 10.8% (2000).
Education: High school graduation rate: 82.0% (2000); College graduation rate: 8.8% (2000).
Housing: Homeownership rate: 84.6% (2000); Median home value: $72,800 (2000); Median rent: $341 per month (2000); Median age of housing: 35 years (2000).
Transportation: Commute to work: 92.2% car, 0.0% public transportation, 4.4% walk, 2.9% work from home (2000); Travel time to work: 34.2% less than 15 minutes, 28.8% 15 to 30 minutes, 18.4% 30 to 45 minutes, 6.6% 45 to 60 minutes, 12.0% 60 minutes or more (2000)

STANTON (city). Covers a land area of 2.144 square miles and a water area of 0 square miles. Located at 43.29° N. Lat.; 85.08° W. Long. Elevation is 919 feet.
History: Stanton was founded as the seat of Montcalm County in 1860. It was first named Fred, for Fred Hall who had previously owned the land, but was renamed in 1863 for Edwin M. Stanton, secretary of war.
Population: 1,504 (2000); Race: 96.6% White, 0.5% Black, 0.0% Asian, 0.2% American Indian and Alaska Native, 3.6% Hispanic of any race, 1.2% two or more races (2000); Density: 701.6 persons per square mile (2000); Age: 30.2% under 18, 13.0% over 64 (2000); Marriage status: 26.1% never married, 51.0% now married, 8.6% widowed, 14.3% divorced (2000); Foreign born: 1.1% (2000); Ancestry (includes multiple ancestries): 28.9% German, 10.4% Other groups, 9.8% Irish, 9.7% English, 6.7% Danish (2000).
Economy: Employment by occupation: 5.0% management, 13.6% professional, 21.7% services, 19.6% sales, 0.4% farming, 12.6% construction, 27.1% production (2000).
Income: Per capita income: $13,901 (2000); Median household income: $29,286 (2000); Poverty rate: 21.7% (2000).
Taxes: Total city taxes per capita: $152 (1997); City property taxes per capita: $149 (1997).
Education: High school graduation rate: 77.4% (2000); College graduation rate: 9.7% (2000).

School District(s)

Central Montcalm Public Schools (KG-12)
2000 Enrollment: 2,196 517-831-5243
Housing: Homeownership rate: 62.1% (2000); Median home value: $64,000 (2000); Median rent: $351 per month (2000); Median age of housing: 40 years (2000).
Transportation: Commute to work: 90.7% car, 0.2% public transportation, 4.6% walk, 3.0% work from home (2000); Travel time to work: 35.6% less than 15 minutes, 30.5% 15 to 30 minutes, 16.6% 30 to 45 minutes, 7.4% 45 to 60 minutes, 10.0% 60 minutes or more (2000)

TRUFANT (unincorporated postal area, zip code 49347). Covers a land area of 18.300 square miles and a water area of 0.461 square miles. Located at 43.31° N. Lat.; 85.35° W. Long. Elevation is 891 feet.
Population: 1,292 (2000); Race: 98.4% White, 0.0% Black, 0.2% Asian, 0.4% American Indian and Alaska Native, 0.2% Hispanic of any race, 1.0% two or more races (2000); Density: 70.6 persons per square mile (2000); Age: 25.5% under 18, 12.2% over 64 (2000); Marriage status: 20.7% never married, 61.9% now married, 6.1% widowed, 11.3% divorced (2000); Foreign born: 0.4% (2000); Ancestry (includes multiple ancestries): 27.3% German, 16.1% English, 13.4% Irish, 12.7% Danish, 8.9% Dutch (2000).
Economy: Employment by occupation: 9.5% management, 12.3% professional, 10.1% services, 23.9% sales, 2.6% farming, 11.9% construction, 29.7% production (2000).
Income: Per capita income: $17,686 (2000); Median household income: $39,167 (2000); Poverty rate: 7.2% (2000).
Education: High school graduation rate: 83.8% (2000); College graduation rate: 12.8% (2000).
Housing: Homeownership rate: 88.7% (2000); Median home value: $91,100 (2000); Median rent: $461 per month (2000); Median age of housing: 34 years (2000).
Transportation: Commute to work: 93.5% car, 0.0% public transportation, 1.9% walk, 3.0% work from home (2000); Travel time to work: 10.6% less than 15 minutes, 38.6% 15 to 30 minutes, 16.2% 30 to 45 minutes, 18.9% 45 to 60 minutes, 15.7% 60 minutes or more (2000)

VESTABURG (unincorporated postal area, zip code 48891). Covers a land area of 40.748 square miles and a water area of 0.305 square miles. Located at 43.40° N. Lat.; 84.92° W. Long. Elevation is 918 feet.
Population: 3,029 (2000); Race: 98.3% White, 0.4% Black, 0.0% Asian, 0.1% American Indian and Alaska Native, 3.0% Hispanic of any race, 1.1% two or more races (2000); Density: 74.3 persons per square mile (2000); Age: 27.9% under 18, 11.9% over 64 (2000); Marriage status: 20.7% never married, 64.0% now married, 5.9% widowed, 9.4% divorced (2000); Foreign born: 1.2% (2000); Ancestry (includes multiple ancestries): 16.9% German, 12.3% English, 10.0% United States or American, 9.8% Irish, 7.5% Other groups (2000).
Economy: Employment by occupation: 8.4% management, 12.0% professional, 13.7% services, 20.5% sales, 2.0% farming, 14.4% construction, 29.1% production (2000).
Income: Per capita income: $14,663 (2000); Median household income: $33,641 (2000); Poverty rate: 9.3% (2000).
Education: High school graduation rate: 79.6% (2000); College graduation rate: 9.2% (2000).

School District(s)

Vestaburg Community Schools (KG-12)
2000 Enrollment: 755 517-268-5353

Housing: Homeownership rate: 85.0% (2000); Median home value: $75,400 (2000); Median rent: $348 per month (2000); Median age of housing: 32 years (2000).
Transportation: Commute to work: 91.2% car, 0.2% public transportation, 4.0% walk, 4.0% work from home (2000); Travel time to work: 28.5% less than 15 minutes, 37.5% 15 to 30 minutes, 18.2% 30 to 45 minutes, 9.0% 45 to 60 minutes, 6.8% 60 minutes or more (2000)

WINFIELD (township). Covers a land area of 35.515 square miles and a water area of 0.650 square miles. Located at 43.42° N. Lat.; 85.39° W. Long.
Population: 2,049 (2000); Race: 98.1% White, 0.1% Black, 0.1% Asian, 0.3% American Indian and Alaska Native, 0.2% Hispanic of any race, 1.3% two or more races (2000); Density: 57.7 persons per square mile (2000); Age: 30.1% under 18, 10.8% over 64 (2000); Marriage status: 17.5% never married, 70.5% now married, 4.1% widowed, 7.9% divorced (2000); Foreign born: 0.4% (2000); Ancestry (includes multiple ancestries): 24.1% German, 18.1% Dutch, 14.4% English, 11.4% Irish, 8.1% United States or American (2000).
Economy: Employment by occupation: 13.1% management, 10.9% professional, 13.5% services, 24.4% sales, 2.3% farming, 13.1% construction, 22.7% production (2000).
Income: Per capita income: $17,779 (2000); Median household income: $44,524 (2000); Poverty rate: 8.6% (2000).
Taxes: Total city taxes per capita: $38 (1997); City property taxes per capita: $36 (1997).
Education: High school graduation rate: 83.0% (2000); College graduation rate: 9.9% (2000).
Housing: Homeownership rate: 91.4% (2000); Median home value: $108,300 (2000); Median rent: $380 per month (2000); Median age of housing: 20 years (2000).
Transportation: Commute to work: 94.8% car, 0.0% public transportation, 1.0% walk, 3.6% work from home (2000); Travel time to work: 22.4% less than 15 minutes, 17.0% 15 to 30 minutes, 22.6% 30 to 45 minutes, 24.6% 45 to 60 minutes, 13.3% 60 minutes or more (2000)

Montmorency County

Located in northern Michigan; drained by the Thunder Bay, Rainy, and Black Rivers; includes Rush, Long, Grass, Avalon, and East Twin Lakes. Covers a land area of 547.60 square miles, a water area of 14.80 square miles, and is located in the Eastern Time Zone. The county government was organized in 1881. County seat is Atlanta.
Population: 10,315 (2000); Race: 98.0% White, 0.2% Black, 0.1% Asian, 0.3% American Indian and Alaska Native, 0.5% Hispanic of any race, 1.3% two or more races (2000); Density: 18.8 persons per square mile (2000); Age: 20.4% under 18, 23.8% over 64 (2000).
Religion: Five largest groups: 22.6% Catholic Church, 7.2% Lutheran Church—Missouri Synod, 3.0% United Church of Christ, 1.6% Assemblies of God, 1.5% The United Methodist Church (2000).
Economy: Unemployment rate: 11.9% (11/2002); Total civilian labor force: 3,656 (11/2002); Leading industries: 22.2% manufacturing; 16.7% retail trade; 14.3% accommodation & food services (2000); Companies that employ more than 1,000 persons: 0 (2000); Companies that employ more than 100 persons: 1 (2000); Farms: 103 totaling 21,025 acres (1997); Minority business ownership rate: 0.0% (1997); Women business ownership rate: 22.5% (1997); Retail sales per capita: $5,000 (1997). Single-family building permits issued: 97 (2001) / 99 (2000); Multi-family building permits issued: 0 (2001) / 0 (2000).
Income: Per capita income: $16,493 (2000); Median household income: $30,005 (2000); Poverty rate: 12.8% (2000); Bankruptcy rate: 5.11% (2001).
Taxes: Total county taxes per capita: $173 (1997); County property taxes per capita: $165 (1997).
Education: High school graduation rate: 74.8% (2000); College graduation rate: 8.2% (2000).
Housing: Homeownership rate: 86.1% (2000); Median home value: $76,900 (2000); Median rent: $338 per month (2000); Median age of housing: 29 years (2000).
Health: Birth rate: 104.7 per 10,000 population (1998); Age adjusted death rate: 95.6 per 10,000 population (1999); Age adjusted cancer mortality rate: 265.9 deaths per 100,000 population (1999). Number of physicians: 2.9 per 10,000 population (1999); Number of hospital beds: n/a (1999).
Elections: 2000 Presidential election results: 42.7% Gore, 54.9% Bush, 1.8% Nader, 0.1% Buchanan
National and State Parks: Presque Isle State Forest
Additional Information Contacts
Montmorency County Government Offices. 989-785-4794
Atlanta Chamber of Commerce 989-785-3400
Hillman Chamber of Commerce 989-742-3739
Lewiston Chamber of Commerce. 989-786-2293

Montmorency County Communities

ALBERT (township). Covers a land area of 65.813 square miles and a water area of 4.651 square miles. Located at 44.88° N. Lat.; 84.27° W. Long.
Population: 2,695 (2000); Race: 97.2% White, 0.1% Black, 0.0% Asian, 0.3% American Indian and Alaska Native, 0.8% Hispanic of any race, 2.4% two or more races (2000); Density: 40.9 persons per square mile (2000); Age: 18.6% under 18, 27.1% over 64 (2000); Marriage status: 14.6% never married, 66.4% now married, 10.9% widowed, 8.2% divorced (2000); Foreign born: 1.6% (2000); Ancestry (includes multiple ancestries): 27.7% German, 12.6% English, 12.1% Irish, 8.8% French (except Basque), 6.1% United States or American (2000).
Economy: Employment by occupation: 7.1% management, 11.9% professional, 20.7% services, 25.9% sales, 0.7% farming, 12.9% construction, 20.8% production (2000).
Income: Per capita income: $18,206 (2000); Median household income: $30,445 (2000); Poverty rate: 10.7% (2000).
Taxes: Total city taxes per capita: $135 (1997); City property taxes per capita: $133 (1997).
Education: High school graduation rate: 78.6% (2000); College graduation rate: 8.8% (2000).

Housing: Homeownership rate: 84.8% (2000); Median home value: $81,000 (2000); Median rent: $455 per month (2000); Median age of housing: 26 years (2000).
Transportation: Commute to work: 94.2% car, 0.0% public transportation, 1.5% walk, 3.5% work from home (2000); Travel time to work: 47.0% less than 15 minutes, 15.8% 15 to 30 minutes, 19.2% 30 to 45 minutes, 12.7% 45 to 60 minutes, 5.3% 60 minutes or more (2000)

ATLANTA (CDP). Covers a land area of 2.714 square miles and a water area of 0.167 square miles. Located at 45.00° N. Lat.; 84.15° W. Long. Elevation is 995 feet.
History: Atlanta was founded by Alfred J. West in 1881. West, a Civil War veteran, named the village after Atlanta, Georgia.
Population: 757 (2000); Race: 96.9% White, 0.5% Black, 0.3% Asian, 0.9% American Indian and Alaska Native, 0.4% Hispanic of any race, 1.3% two or more races (2000); Density: 278.9 persons per square mile (2000); Age: 21.7% under 18, 18.3% over 64 (2000); Marriage status: 21.1% never married, 54.2% now married, 12.0% widowed, 12.7% divorced (2000); Foreign born: 0.4% (2000); Ancestry (includes multiple ancestries): 26.3% German, 15.2% English, 10.2% French (except Basque), 8.5% Other groups, 8.2% Irish (2000).
Economy: Employment by occupation: 6.7% management, 7.1% professional, 27.3% services, 25.7% sales, 2.4% farming, 15.4% construction, 15.4% production (2000).
Income: Per capita income: $15,178 (2000); Median household income: $23,529 (2000); Poverty rate: 23.8% (2000).
Education: High school graduation rate: 69.7% (2000); College graduation rate: 6.9% (2000).

School District(s)

Atlanta Community Schools (KG-12)
2000 Enrollment: 517 517-785-4877
Housing: Homeownership rate: 76.8% (2000); Median home value: $66,200 (2000); Median rent: $296 per month (2000); Median age of housing: 35 years (2000).
Newspapers: The Montmorency County Tribune (1 x week)
Transportation: Commute to work: 85.2% car, 0.0% public transportation, 4.6% walk, 7.2% work from home (2000); Travel time to work: 50.0% less than 15 minutes, 11.4% 15 to 30 minutes, 15.5% 30 to 45 minutes, 11.8% 45 to 60 minutes, 11.4% 60 minutes or more (2000)
Additional Information Contacts
Atlanta Chamber of Commerce 989-785-3400

AVERY (township). Covers a land area of 35.032 square miles and a water area of 0.257 square miles. Located at 44.97° N. Lat.; 84.07° W. Long. Elevation is 799 feet.
Population: 717 (2000); Race: 98.4% White, 0.3% Black, 0.0% Asian, 0.6% American Indian and Alaska Native, 0.0% Hispanic of any race, 0.7% two or more races (2000); Density: 20.5 persons per square mile (2000); Age: 20.8% under 18, 18.7% over 64 (2000); Marriage status: 14.1% never married, 65.3% now married, 9.1% widowed, 11.5% divorced (2000); Foreign born: 2.0% (2000); Ancestry (includes multiple ancestries): 29.3% German, 13.5% Irish, 11.9% English, 11.6% French (except Basque), 8.9% United States or American (2000).
Economy: Employment by occupation: 7.6% management, 11.2% professional, 25.9% services, 23.4% sales, 0.0% farming, 11.7% construction, 20.3% production (2000).
Income: Per capita income: $14,677 (2000); Median household income: $27,723 (2000); Poverty rate: 17.4% (2000).
Taxes: Total city taxes per capita: $77 (1997); City property taxes per capita: $75 (1997).
Education: High school graduation rate: 72.8% (2000); College graduation rate: 5.6% (2000).
Housing: Homeownership rate: 90.2% (2000); Median home value: $62,400 (2000); Median rent: $316 per month (2000); Median age of housing: 29 years (2000).
Transportation: Commute to work: 89.5% car, 0.0% public transportation, 1.7% walk, 7.2% work from home (2000); Travel time to work: 45.2% less than 15 minutes, 26.8% 15 to 30 minutes, 8.9% 30 to 45 minutes, 13.7% 45 to 60 minutes, 5.4% 60 minutes or more (2000)

BRILEY (township). Covers a land area of 68.372 square miles and a water area of 1.953 square miles. Located at 45.01° N. Lat.; 84.17° W. Long.
Population: 2,029 (2000); Race: 97.6% White, 0.2% Black, 0.6% Asian, 0.2% American Indian and Alaska Native, 0.6% Hispanic of any race, 1.3% two or more races (2000); Density: 29.7 persons per square mile (2000); Age: 21.0% under 18, 20.8% over 64 (2000); Marriage status: 18.2% never married, 58.9% now married, 11.8% widowed, 11.0% divorced (2000); Foreign born: 0.7% (2000); Ancestry (includes multiple ancestries): 23.8% German, 16.4% English, 10.1% Irish, 9.1% French (except Basque), 7.8% United States or American (2000).
Economy: Employment by occupation: 8.9% management, 12.0% professional, 21.2% services, 26.4% sales, 1.3% farming, 13.1% construction, 16.9% production (2000).
Income: Per capita income: $15,906 (2000); Median household income: $27,264 (2000); Poverty rate: 18.5% (2000).
Taxes: Total city taxes per capita: $48 (1997); City property taxes per capita: $47 (1997).
Education: High school graduation rate: 71.2% (2000); College graduation rate: 7.5% (2000).
Housing: Homeownership rate: 85.7% (2000); Median home value: $67,600 (2000); Median rent: $322 per month (2000); Median age of housing: 31 years (2000).
Transportation: Commute to work: 91.8% car, 0.0% public transportation, 2.0% walk, 4.3% work from home (2000); Travel time to work: 45.5% less than 15 minutes, 20.2% 15 to 30 minutes, 16.2% 30 to 45 minutes, 11.7% 45 to 60 minutes, 6.5% 60 minutes or more (2000)

CANADA CREEK RANCH (CDP). Covers a land area of 7.780 square miles and a water area of 0.483 square miles. Located at 45.16° N. Lat.; 84.20° W. Long.
Population: 405 (2000); Race: 96.9% White, 2.6% Black, 0.0% Asian, 0.0% American Indian and Alaska Native, 0.5% Hispanic of any race, 0.5% two or more races (2000); Density: 52.1 persons per square mile (2000); Age: 11.5% under 18, 45.2% over 64 (2000); Marriage status: 6.9% never married, 74.8% now married, 12.7% widowed, 5.5% divorced (2000); Foreign born: 2.8% (2000); Ancestry (includes multiple ancestries): 30.1% German, 26.3% English, 12.0% Irish, 7.1% French (except Basque), 6.1% Other groups (2000).
Economy: Employment by occupation: 5.6% management, 19.7% professional, 29.6% services, 31.0% sales, 0.0% farming, 7.0% construction, 7.0% production (2000).
Income: Per capita income: $20,227 (2000); Median household income: $32,857 (2000); Poverty rate: 2.6% (2000).
Education: High school graduation rate: 89.5% (2000); College graduation rate: 22.1% (2000).
Housing: Homeownership rate: 97.6% (2000); Median home value: $103,500 (2000); Median rent: $125 per month (2000); Median age of housing: 35 years (2000).
Transportation: Commute to work: 100.0% car, 0.0% public transportation, 0.0% walk, 0.0% work from home (2000); Travel time to work: 39.4% less than 15 minutes, 32.4% 15 to 30 minutes, 11.3% 30 to 45 minutes, 16.9% 45 to 60 minutes, 0.0% 60 minutes or more (2000)

HILLMAN (village). Covers a land area of 1.685 square miles and a water area of 0.012 square miles. Located at 45.06° N. Lat.; 83.90° W. Long. Elevation is 813 feet.
History: Hillman was founded in 1880 by John Hillman Stevens, who owned the land. Hillman developed as a popular destination for fishermen in the summer, and for deer hunters in the fall. A number of private hunting clubs were established in this area.
Population: 685 (2000); Race: 99.4% White, 0.0% Black, 0.0% Asian, 0.3% American Indian and Alaska Native, 0.3% Hispanic of any race, 0.0% two or more races (2000); Density: 406.6 persons per square mile (2000); Age: 15.0% under 18, 39.1% over 64 (2000); Marriage status: 22.5% never married, 51.5% now married, 13.3% widowed, 12.7% divorced (2000); Foreign born: 2.7% (2000); Ancestry (includes multiple ancestries): 28.7% German, 11.8% English, 10.4% French (except Basque), 7.8% Polish, 7.8% Irish (2000).
Economy: Employment by occupation: 7.9% management, 8.9% professional, 25.7% services, 18.8% sales, 2.6% farming, 5.8% construction, 30.4% production (2000).
Income: Per capita income: $13,818 (2000); Median household income: $21,250 (2000); Poverty rate: 14.7% (2000).
Taxes: Total city taxes per capita: $187 (1997); City property taxes per capita: $187 (1997).
Education: High school graduation rate: 69.8% (2000); College graduation rate: 6.3% (2000).

School District(s)

Hillman Community Schools (KG-12)
2000 Enrollment: 602 517-742-2908

Housing: Homeownership rate: 64.7% (2000); Median home value: $59,700 (2000); Median rent: $301 per month (2000); Median age of housing: 28 years (2000).
Transportation: Commute to work: 92.1% car, 0.0% public transportation, 5.8% walk, 2.1% work from home (2000); Travel time to work: 63.8% less than 15 minutes, 11.9% 15 to 30 minutes, 15.1% 30 to 45 minutes, 3.8% 45 to 60 minutes, 5.4% 60 minutes or more (2000)
Additional Information Contacts
Hillman Chamber of Commerce 989-742-3739

HILLMAN (township). Covers a land area of 67.622 square miles and a water area of 1.259 square miles. Located at 45.06° N. Lat.; 83.98° W. Long. Elevation is 813 feet.
Population: 2,267 (2000); Race: 98.7% White, 0.0% Black, 0.0% Asian, 0.3% American Indian and Alaska Native, 0.2% Hispanic of any race, 0.9% two or more races (2000); Density: 33.5 persons per square mile (2000); Age: 20.9% under 18, 24.0% over 64 (2000); Marriage status: 19.6% never married, 59.6% now married, 10.5% widowed, 10.4% divorced (2000); Foreign born: 1.3% (2000); Ancestry (includes multiple ancestries): 28.9% German, 13.2% English, 10.8% Polish, 10.0% French (except Basque), 8.8% Irish (2000).
Economy: Manufacturing: wire cloth and filters. Employment by occupation: 10.1% management, 8.4% professional, 22.2% services, 18.4% sales, 3.0% farming, 13.0% construction, 24.8% production (2000).
Income: Per capita income: $14,660 (2000); Median household income: $27,011 (2000); Poverty rate: 11.8% (2000).
Taxes: Total city taxes per capita: $43 (1997); City property taxes per capita: $42 (1997).
Education: High school graduation rate: 72.5% (2000); College graduation rate: 6.3% (2000).
Housing: Homeownership rate: 82.0% (2000); Median home value: $73,000 (2000); Median rent: $309 per month (2000); Median age of housing: 29 years (2000).
Transportation: Commute to work: 92.7% car, 0.3% public transportation, 1.8% walk, 4.9% work from home (2000); Travel time to work: 49.3% less than 15 minutes, 16.6% 15 to 30 minutes, 20.7% 30 to 45 minutes, 6.2% 45 to 60 minutes, 7.2% 60 minutes or more (2000)

LEWISTON (CDP). Covers a land area of 5.288 square miles and a water area of 3.285 square miles. Located at 44.87° N. Lat.; 84.32° W. Long. Elevation is 1,240 feet.
History: Lewiston grew up around the mill and general store of the Michelson & Hanson Lumber Company. It was named for Lewiston, New York.
Population: 990 (2000); Race: 98.5% White, 0.0% Black, 0.0% Asian, 0.5% American Indian and Alaska Native, 2.0% Hispanic of any race, 0.9% two or more races (2000); Density: 187.2 persons per square mile (2000); Age: 13.4% under 18, 31.3% over 64 (2000); Marriage status: 11.4% never married, 68.2% now married, 11.5% widowed, 8.8% divorced (2000); Foreign born: 3.0% (2000); Ancestry (includes multiple ancestries): 30.5% German, 13.0% English, 12.7% Irish, 11.9% French (except Basque), 7.3% Polish (2000).
Economy: Employment by occupation: 9.0% management, 6.1% professional, 24.8% services, 34.1% sales, 0.0% farming, 12.2% construction, 13.8% production (2000).
Income: Per capita income: $20,393 (2000); Median household income: $31,429 (2000); Poverty rate: 6.5% (2000).
Education: High school graduation rate: 81.9% (2000); College graduation rate: 6.3% (2000).
Housing: Homeownership rate: 88.7% (2000); Median home value: $80,100 (2000); Median rent: $380 per month (2000); Median age of housing: 29 years (2000).
Transportation: Commute to work: 88.7% car, 0.0% public transportation, 4.2% walk, 4.8% work from home (2000); Travel time to work: 54.1% less than 15 minutes, 14.5% 15 to 30 minutes, 11.5% 30 to 45 minutes, 15.2% 45 to 60 minutes, 4.7% 60 minutes or more (2000)
Additional Information Contacts
Lewiston Chamber of Commerce. 989-786-2293

LOUD (township). Covers a land area of 35.788 square miles and a water area of 0.020 square miles. Located at 44.89° N. Lat.; 84.06° W. Long.
Population: 284 (2000); Race: 96.7% White, 0.0% Black, 0.0% Asian, 1.2% American Indian and Alaska Native, 0.0% Hispanic of any race, 2.1% two or more races (2000); Density: 7.9 persons per square mile (2000); Age: 13.2% under 18, 36.6% over 64 (2000); Marriage status: 10.1% never married, 62.2% now married, 17.1% widowed, 10.6% divorced (2000); Foreign born: 0.8% (2000); Ancestry (includes multiple ancestries): 18.9% Irish, 18.9% German, 9.5% English, 8.2% United States or American, 8.2% Other groups (2000).
Economy: Employment by occupation: 19.7% management, 12.1% professional, 12.1% services, 31.8% sales, 0.0% farming, 7.6% construction, 16.7% production (2000).
Income: Per capita income: $16,031 (2000); Median household income: $26,750 (2000); Poverty rate: 10.7% (2000).
Taxes: Total city taxes per capita: $227 (1997); City property taxes per capita: $227 (1997).
Education: High school graduation rate: 69.9% (2000); College graduation rate: 2.0% (2000).
Housing: Homeownership rate: 89.4% (2000); Median home value: $72,200 (2000); Median rent: $325 per month (2000); Median age of housing: 34 years (2000).
Transportation: Commute to work: 85.7% car, 0.0% public transportation, 6.3% walk, 7.9% work from home (2000); Travel time to work: 24.1% less than 15 minutes, 56.9% 15 to 30 minutes, 12.1% 30 to 45 minutes, 3.4% 45 to 60 minutes, 3.4% 60 minutes or more (2000)

MONTMORENCY (township). Covers a land area of 137.386 square miles and a water area of 3.134 square miles. Located at 45.15° N. Lat.; 84.16° W. Long.
Population: 1,202 (2000); Race: 98.4% White, 0.8% Black, 0.0% Asian, 0.0% American Indian and Alaska Native, 0.4% Hispanic of any race, 0.7% two or more races (2000); Density: 8.7 persons per square mile (2000); Age: 19.6% under 18, 28.0% over 64 (2000); Marriage status: 16.5% never married, 68.6% now married, 7.8% widowed, 7.1% divorced (2000); Foreign born: 1.2% (2000); Ancestry (includes multiple ancestries): 33.6% German, 17.2% English, 10.9% Irish, 9.0% French (except Basque), 6.0% Polish (2000).
Economy: Employment by occupation: 11.4% management, 19.1% professional, 12.8% services, 22.2% sales, 2.3% farming, 11.1% construction, 21.1% production (2000).
Income: Per capita income: $17,701 (2000); Median household income: $34,500 (2000); Poverty rate: 8.6% (2000).
Taxes: Total city taxes per capita: $59 (1997); City property taxes per capita: $57 (1997).
Education: High school graduation rate: 79.3% (2000); College graduation rate: 13.3% (2000).
Housing: Homeownership rate: 92.2% (2000); Median home value: $101,400 (2000); Median rent: $279 per month (2000); Median age of housing: 29 years (2000).
Transportation: Commute to work: 89.9% car, 0.0% public transportation, 1.4% walk, 8.7% work from home (2000); Travel time to work: 29.5% less than 15 minutes, 37.8% 15 to 30 minutes, 17.1% 30 to 45 minutes, 13.3% 45 to 60 minutes, 2.2% 60 minutes or more (2000)

RUST (township). Covers a land area of 68.586 square miles and a water area of 3.275 square miles. Located at 44.91° N. Lat.; 83.95° W. Long.
Population: 549 (2000); Race: 99.0% White, 0.0% Black, 0.0% Asian, 0.3% American Indian and Alaska Native, 0.6% Hispanic of any race, 0.0% two or more races (2000); Density: 8.0 persons per square mile (2000); Age: 24.5% under 18, 20.3% over 64 (2000); Marriage status: 18.3% never married, 65.7% now married, 7.9% widowed, 8.1% divorced (2000); Foreign born: 1.0% (2000); Ancestry (includes multiple ancestries): 30.3% German, 12.7% Irish, 8.7% English, 8.5% French (except Basque), 7.4% Scottish (2000).
Economy: Employment by occupation: 15.5% management, 11.9% professional, 20.4% services, 11.1% sales, 1.8% farming, 18.1% construction, 21.2% production (2000).
Income: Per capita income: $15,129 (2000); Median household income: $30,870 (2000); Poverty rate: 12.2% (2000).
Taxes: Total city taxes per capita: $67 (1997); City property taxes per capita: $67 (1997).
Education: High school graduation rate: 73.6% (2000); College graduation rate: 9.3% (2000).
Housing: Homeownership rate: 86.5% (2000); Median home value: $66,800 (2000); Median rent: $275 per month (2000); Median age of housing: 29 years (2000).
Transportation: Commute to work: 93.6% car, 0.9% public transportation, 0.5% walk, 5.0% work from home (2000); Travel time to work: 21.3% less than 15 minutes, 42.0% 15 to 30 minutes, 19.3% 30 to 45 minutes, 8.2% 45 to 60 minutes, 9.2% 60 minutes or more (2000)

VIENNA (township). Covers a land area of 69.028 square miles and a water area of 0.264 square miles. Located at 45.02° N. Lat.; 84.31° W. Long.

Population: 572 (2000); Race: 98.7% White, 0.0% Black, 0.0% Asian, 0.0% American Indian and Alaska Native, 1.3% Hispanic of any race, 0.5% two or more races (2000); Density: 8.3 persons per square mile (2000); Age: 24.3% under 18, 15.5% over 64 (2000); Marriage status: 15.0% never married, 72.2% now married, 6.6% widowed, 6.2% divorced (2000); Foreign born: 2.5% (2000); Ancestry (includes multiple ancestries): 24.0% German, 16.0% English, 13.2% Irish, 8.9% Polish, 7.8% French (except Basque) (2000).
Economy: Employment by occupation: 8.9% management, 13.2% professional, 12.8% services, 28.9% sales, 3.0% farming, 16.2% construction, 17.0% production (2000).
Income: Per capita income: $18,923 (2000); Median household income: $35,909 (2000); Poverty rate: 11.6% (2000).
Taxes: Total city taxes per capita: $138 (1997); City property taxes per capita: $138 (1997).
Education: High school graduation rate: 74.7% (2000); College graduation rate: 9.5% (2000).
Housing: Homeownership rate: 89.2% (2000); Median home value: $72,900 (2000); Median rent: $319 per month (2000); Median age of housing: 27 years (2000).
Transportation: Commute to work: 93.1% car, 0.0% public transportation, 0.0% walk, 6.9% work from home (2000); Travel time to work: 24.4% less than 15 minutes, 30.4% 15 to 30 minutes, 27.2% 30 to 45 minutes, 8.3% 45 to 60 minutes, 9.7% 60 minutes or more (2000)

Muskegon County

Located in southwestern Michigan; bounded on the west by Lake Michigan; drained by the Muskegon and White Rivers; includes part of Manistee National Forest. Covers a land area of 509.10 square miles, a water area of 950.20 square miles, and is located in the Eastern Time Zone. The county government was organized in 1859. County seat is Muskegon.

Muskegon County is part of the Grand Rapids-Muskegon-Holland, MI MSA. The entire metro area includes: Allegan County; Kent County; Muskegon County; Ottawa County

Weather Station: Montague 4 NW Elevation: 649 feet

	Jan	Feb	Mar	Apr	May	Jun	Jul	Aug	Sep	Oct	Nov	Dec
High	30	33	42	55	67	75	79	78	70	59	46	35
Low	16	17	24	33	43	52	57	56	50	40	31	22
Precip	1.7	1.1	2.4	3.1	2.6	2.8	2.8	4.2	3.5	3.3	3.1	1.8
Snow	25.8	14.5	5.6	1.6	tr	0.0	0.0	0.0	0.0	0.1	4.1	19.0

High and Low temperatures in degrees Fahrenheit; Precipitation and Snow in inches

Weather Station: Muskegon County Airport Elevation: 623 feet

	Jan	Feb	Mar	Apr	May	Jun	Jul	Aug	Sep	Oct	Nov	Dec
High	29	32	42	55	67	76	80	78	70	59	45	34
Low	17	18	25	36	46	55	60	59	51	41	32	23
Precip	2.3	1.6	2.4	2.9	2.8	2.6	2.3	3.8	3.6	2.8	3.2	2.7
Snow	35.5	18.7	10.9	3.2	tr	0.0	tr	0.0	tr	0.6	8.7	28.3

High and Low temperatures in degrees Fahrenheit; Precipitation and Snow in inches

Population: 170,200 (2000); Race: 81.3% White, 14.1% Black, 0.4% Asian, 0.7% American Indian and Alaska Native, 3.4% Hispanic of any race, 2.2% two or more races (2000); Density: 334.3 persons per square mile (2000); Age: 27.4% under 18, 12.9% over 64 (2000).
Religion: Five largest groups: 11.7% Catholic Church, 3.1% Reformed Church in America, 2.4% The United Methodist Church, 2.3% Evangelical Lutheran Church in America, 1.8% Lutheran Church—Missouri Synod (2000).
Economy: Unemployment rate: 8.5% (11/2002); Total civilian labor force: 88,599 (11/2002); Leading industries: 28.1% manufacturing; 15.4% retail trade; 13.1% health care and social assistance (2000); Companies that employ more than 1,000 persons: 3 (2000); Companies that employ more than 100 persons: 97 (2000); Farms: 410 totaling 73,113 acres (1997); Minority business ownership rate: 3.6% (1997); Women business ownership rate: 28.7% (1997); Retail sales per capita: $8,230 (1997). Single-family building permits issued: 816 (2001) / 803 (2000); Multi-family building permits issued: 82 (2001) / 33 (2000).
Income: Per capita income: $17,967 (2000); Median household income: $38,008 (2000); Poverty rate: 11.4% (2000); Bankruptcy rate: 5.47% (2001).
Taxes: Total county taxes per capita: $105 (2000); County property taxes per capita: $98 (2000).
Education: High school graduation rate: 83.1% (2000); College graduation rate: 13.9% (2000).
Housing: Homeownership rate: 77.7% (2000); Median home value: $85,900 (2000); Median rent: $381 per month (2000); Median age of housing: 38 years (2000).
Health: Birth rate: 139.3 per 10,000 population (1998); Age adjusted death rate: 95.3 per 10,000 population (1999); Age adjusted cancer mortality rate: 213.7 deaths per 100,000 population (1999). Air Quality Index: 67% good, 32% moderate, 1% unhealthy (percent of days in 2000). Number of physicians: 12.9 per 10,000 population (1999); Number of hospital beds: 21.9 per 10,000 population (1999).
Elections: 2000 Presidential election results: 54.7% Gore, 43.4% Bush, 1.6% Nader, 0.0% Buchanan
National and State Parks: Muskegon State Game Area; Muskegon State Park; P J Hoffmaster State Park
Additional Information Contacts
Muskegon County Government Offices. 231-724-6211
Muskegon Area Chamber of Commerce 231-722-3751
Muskegon Chamber of Commerce. 231-737-2259
White Lake Chamber of Commerce. 231-893-4585

Muskegon County Communities

BAILEY (unincorporated postal area, zip code 49303). Covers a land area of 14.074 square miles and a water area of 0.028 square miles. Located at 43.27° N. Lat.; 85.84° W. Long. Elevation is 832 feet.
History: A post office was established at Bailey in 1872, and named for a settler who had come in 1865.
Population: 1,024 (2000); Race: 89.1% White, 0.0% Black, 0.7% Asian, 0.0% American Indian and Alaska Native, 8.8% Hispanic of any race, 2.3% two or more races (2000); Density: 72.8 persons per square mile (2000); Age: 30.7% under 18, 7.4% over 64 (2000); Marriage status: 22.4% never married, 67.0% now married, 2.8% widowed, 7.9% divorced (2000); Foreign born: 4.9% (2000); Ancestry (includes multiple ancestries): 21.7% German, 16.3% Other groups, 11.7% Dutch, 10.2% Irish, 7.9% French (except Basque) (2000).
Economy: Employment by occupation: 7.7% management, 12.8% professional, 12.6% services, 19.8% sales, 6.1% farming, 11.5% construction, 29.5% production (2000).
Income: Per capita income: $15,991 (2000); Median household income: $37,778 (2000); Poverty rate: 9.2% (2000).
Education: High school graduation rate: 81.7% (2000); College graduation rate: 12.4% (2000).
Housing: Homeownership rate: 88.4% (2000); Median home value: $84,100 (2000); Median rent: $433 per month (2000); Median age of housing: 34 years (2000).
Transportation: Commute to work: 95.6% car, 0.0% public transportation, 2.1% walk, 2.3% work from home (2000); Travel time to work: 32.2% less than 15 minutes, 20.8% 15 to 30 minutes, 18.9% 30 to 45 minutes, 24.6% 45 to 60 minutes, 3.6% 60 minutes or more (2000)

BLUE LAKE (township). Covers a land area of 34.419 square miles and a water area of 1.290 square miles. Located at 43.43° N. Lat.; 86.22° W. Long.
Population: 1,990 (2000); Race: 86.2% White, 6.3% Black, 0.5% Asian, 2.0% American Indian and Alaska Native, 1.7% Hispanic of any race, 4.2% two or more races (2000); Density: 57.8 persons per square mile (2000); Age: 31.2% under 18, 6.8% over 64 (2000); Marriage status: 22.2% never married, 64.7% now married, 3.7% widowed, 9.4% divorced (2000); Foreign born: 1.9% (2000); Ancestry (includes multiple ancestries): 22.9% German, 13.1% Other groups, 11.1% Irish, 10.6% English, 10.4% Dutch (2000).
Economy: Single-family building permits issued: 37 (2001) / 45 (2000); Multi-family building permits issued: 0 (2001) / 0 (2000); Employment by occupation: 9.5% management, 17.4% professional, 13.3% services, 24.9% sales, 0.2% farming, 9.9% construction, 24.7% production (2000).
Income: Per capita income: $18,866 (2000); Median household income: $50,000 (2000); Poverty rate: 11.5% (2000).
Taxes: Total city taxes per capita: $107 (2000); City property taxes per capita: $83 (2000).
Education: High school graduation rate: 87.1% (2000); College graduation rate: 14.6% (2000).
Housing: Homeownership rate: 86.0% (2000); Median home value: $101,400 (2000); Median rent: $206 per month (2000); Median age of housing: 19 years (2000).
Transportation: Commute to work: 95.0% car, 0.0% public transportation, 0.7% walk, 3.9% work from home (2000); Travel time to work: 13.5% less

than 15 minutes, 49.4% 15 to 30 minutes, 26.3% 30 to 45 minutes, 4.7% 45 to 60 minutes, 5.9% 60 minutes or more (2000)

CASNOVIA (township). Covers a land area of 35.691 square miles and a water area of 0.119 square miles. Located at 43.25° N. Lat.; 85.84° W. Long. Elevation is 881 feet.
Population: 2,652 (2000); Race: 93.5% White, 0.0% Black, 0.5% Asian, 0.0% American Indian and Alaska Native, 5.9% Hispanic of any race, 2.3% two or more races (2000); Density: 74.3 persons per square mile (2000); Age: 29.6% under 18, 6.8% over 64 (2000); Marriage status: 24.4% never married, 64.2% now married, 3.7% widowed, 7.7% divorced (2000); Foreign born: 3.0% (2000); Ancestry (includes multiple ancestries): 25.5% German, 14.8% Dutch, 11.3% Irish, 11.2% Other groups, 7.4% Swedish (2000).
Economy: Single-family building permits issued: 14 (2001) / 12 (2000); Multi-family building permits issued: 0 (2001) / 0 (2000); Employment by occupation: 9.8% management, 10.9% professional, 11.2% services, 22.7% sales, 3.7% farming, 12.4% construction, 29.4% production (2000).
Income: Per capita income: $16,880 (2000); Median household income: $41,711 (2000); Poverty rate: 7.9% (2000).
Taxes: Total city taxes per capita: $33 (1997); City property taxes per capita: $30 (1997).
Education: High school graduation rate: 81.6% (2000); College graduation rate: 10.4% (2000).
Housing: Homeownership rate: 88.7% (2000); Median home value: $91,100 (2000); Median rent: $418 per month (2000); Median age of housing: 31 years (2000).
Transportation: Commute to work: 93.8% car, 0.2% public transportation, 3.1% walk, 2.7% work from home (2000); Travel time to work: 28.5% less than 15 minutes, 22.4% 15 to 30 minutes, 27.9% 30 to 45 minutes, 15.9% 45 to 60 minutes, 5.3% 60 minutes or more (2000)

CEDAR CREEK (township). Covers a land area of 35.207 square miles and a water area of 1.025 square miles. Located at 43.34° N. Lat.; 86.09° W. Long.
Population: 3,109 (2000); Race: 95.1% White, 0.9% Black, 0.0% Asian, 0.3% American Indian and Alaska Native, 4.2% Hispanic of any race, 2.4% two or more races (2000); Density: 88.3 persons per square mile (2000); Age: 28.5% under 18, 6.8% over 64 (2000); Marriage status: 27.2% never married, 53.8% now married, 3.7% widowed, 15.3% divorced (2000); Foreign born: 0.0% (2000); Ancestry (includes multiple ancestries): 26.9% German, 10.7% English, 10.2% Dutch, 9.9% Irish, 9.4% Other groups (2000).
Economy: Single-family building permits issued: 31 (2001) / 30 (2000); Multi-family building permits issued: 0 (2001) / 0 (2000); Employment by occupation: 8.1% management, 10.1% professional, 12.4% services, 22.5% sales, 0.7% farming, 15.0% construction, 31.1% production (2000).
Income: Per capita income: $16,775 (2000); Median household income: $36,179 (2000); Poverty rate: 10.6% (2000).
Taxes: Total city taxes per capita: $16 (1997); City property taxes per capita: $11 (1997).
Education: High school graduation rate: 89.1% (2000); College graduation rate: 4.8% (2000).
Housing: Homeownership rate: 91.4% (2000); Median home value: $84,400 (2000); Median rent: $323 per month (2000); Median age of housing: 25 years (2000).
Transportation: Commute to work: 96.6% car, 0.0% public transportation, 0.6% walk, 2.3% work from home (2000); Travel time to work: 9.8% less than 15 minutes, 55.4% 15 to 30 minutes, 23.3% 30 to 45 minutes, 6.4% 45 to 60 minutes, 5.2% 60 minutes or more (2000)

DALTON (township). Covers a land area of 35.681 square miles and a water area of 0.815 square miles. Located at 43.34° N. Lat.; 86.22° W. Long. Elevation is 659 feet.
Population: 8,047 (2000); Race: 93.2% White, 3.0% Black, 0.2% Asian, 1.7% American Indian and Alaska Native, 1.6% Hispanic of any race, 1.5% two or more races (2000); Density: 225.5 persons per square mile (2000); Age: 29.1% under 18, 8.5% over 64 (2000); Marriage status: 20.1% never married, 64.6% now married, 4.8% widowed, 10.5% divorced (2000); Foreign born: 0.4% (2000); Ancestry (includes multiple ancestries): 21.5% German, 12.6% Dutch, 11.6% Irish, 11.1% Other groups, 11.0% English (2000).
Economy: Single-family building permits issued: 73 (2001) / 59 (2000); Multi-family building permits issued: 0 (2001) / 0 (2000); Employment by occupation: 6.5% management, 12.4% professional, 13.6% services, 25.3% sales, 0.5% farming, 11.4% construction, 30.3% production (2000).
Income: Per capita income: $18,036 (2000); Median household income: $47,127 (2000); Poverty rate: 5.9% (2000).
Taxes: Total city taxes per capita: $64 (1997); City property taxes per capita: $54 (1997).
Education: High school graduation rate: 85.7% (2000); College graduation rate: 9.8% (2000).
Housing: Homeownership rate: 91.9% (2000); Median home value: $89,900 (2000); Median rent: $417 per month (2000); Median age of housing: 26 years (2000).
Transportation: Commute to work: 97.0% car, 0.0% public transportation, 0.5% walk, 1.7% work from home (2000); Travel time to work: 19.5% less than 15 minutes, 58.7% 15 to 30 minutes, 13.6% 30 to 45 minutes, 4.1% 45 to 60 minutes, 4.2% 60 minutes or more (2000)

EGELSTON (township). Covers a land area of 34.954 square miles and a water area of 0.630 square miles. Located at 43.24° N. Lat.; 86.10° W. Long.
Population: 9,537 (2000); Race: 95.0% White, 0.7% Black, 0.5% Asian, 0.7% American Indian and Alaska Native, 4.4% Hispanic of any race, 1.7% two or more races (2000); Density: 272.8 persons per square mile (2000); Age: 28.9% under 18, 9.8% over 64 (2000); Marriage status: 22.1% never married, 61.2% now married, 5.3% widowed, 11.4% divorced (2000); Foreign born: 1.1% (2000); Ancestry (includes multiple ancestries): 21.7% German, 11.9% Irish, 11.4% Dutch, 11.2% Other groups, 10.6% United States or American (2000).
Economy: Single-family building permits issued: 42 (2001) / 38 (2000); Multi-family building permits issued: 0 (2001) / 0 (2000); Employment by occupation: 4.7% management, 8.2% professional, 17.6% services, 23.7% sales, 0.6% farming, 12.0% construction, 33.2% production (2000).
Income: Per capita income: $16,489 (2000); Median household income: $37,557 (2000); Poverty rate: 8.7% (2000).
Taxes: Total city taxes per capita: $94 (1997); City property taxes per capita: $81 (1997).
Education: High school graduation rate: 79.4% (2000); College graduation rate: 6.5% (2000).
Housing: Homeownership rate: 90.9% (2000); Median home value: $81,900 (2000); Median rent: $411 per month (2000); Median age of housing: 23 years (2000).
Transportation: Commute to work: 96.0% car, 0.1% public transportation, 0.8% walk, 2.4% work from home (2000); Travel time to work: 25.2% less than 15 minutes, 47.1% 15 to 30 minutes, 17.4% 30 to 45 minutes, 5.8% 45 to 60 minutes, 4.5% 60 minutes or more (2000)

FRUITLAND (township). Covers a land area of 36.514 square miles and a water area of 3.161 square miles. Located at 43.35° N. Lat.; 86.34° W. Long.
Population: 5,235 (2000); Race: 96.2% White, 0.5% Black, 0.4% Asian, 1.4% American Indian and Alaska Native, 1.2% Hispanic of any race, 0.7% two or more races (2000); Density: 143.4 persons per square mile (2000); Age: 28.4% under 18, 9.0% over 64 (2000); Marriage status: 20.6% never married, 67.7% now married, 5.2% widowed, 6.5% divorced (2000); Foreign born: 2.2% (2000); Ancestry (includes multiple ancestries): 24.1% German, 10.9% Dutch, 10.4% Irish, 10.3% Other groups, 9.7% English (2000).
Economy: Single-family building permits issued: 44 (2001) / 33 (2000); Multi-family building permits issued: 0 (2001) / 0 (2000); Employment by occupation: 11.2% management, 23.5% professional, 8.2% services, 24.5% sales, 0.3% farming, 9.8% construction, 22.5% production (2000).
Income: Per capita income: $23,216 (2000); Median household income: $53,977 (2000); Poverty rate: 3.3% (2000).
Taxes: Total city taxes per capita: $46 (1997); City property taxes per capita: $24 (1997).
Education: High school graduation rate: 90.9% (2000); College graduation rate: 24.5% (2000).
Housing: Homeownership rate: 90.7% (2000); Median home value: $116,600 (2000); Median rent: $486 per month (2000); Median age of housing: 28 years (2000).
Transportation: Commute to work: 96.9% car, 0.0% public transportation, 0.9% walk, 1.7% work from home (2000); Travel time to work: 23.9% less than 15 minutes, 48.9% 15 to 30 minutes, 18.4% 30 to 45 minutes, 2.3% 45 to 60 minutes, 6.5% 60 minutes or more (2000)

FRUITPORT (village). Covers a land area of 0.938 square miles and a water area of 0.071 square miles. Located at 43.12° N. Lat.; 86.15° W. Long. Elevation is 625 feet.
Population: 1,124 (2000); Race: 97.6% White, 0.0% Black, 0.3% Asian, 0.6% American Indian and Alaska Native, 1.2% Hispanic of any race, 0.9% two or more races (2000); Density: 1,197.8 persons per square mile (2000); Age: 23.9% under 18, 13.2% over 64 (2000); Marriage status: 20.7% never married, 61.1% now married, 5.4% widowed, 12.8% divorced (2000);

Foreign born: 1.1% (2000); Ancestry (includes multiple ancestries): 23.3% German, 18.2% Dutch, 13.4% English, 12.2% Irish, 7.5% French (except Basque) (2000).
Economy: Employment by occupation: 11.1% management, 17.2% professional, 13.4% services, 24.0% sales, 0.0% farming, 9.5% construction, 24.8% production (2000).
Income: Per capita income: $22,364 (2000); Median household income: $48,125 (2000); Poverty rate: 5.8% (2000).
Taxes: Total city taxes per capita: $166 (1997); City property taxes per capita: $161 (1997).
Education: High school graduation rate: 91.0% (2000); College graduation rate: 17.5% (2000).

School District(s)

Fruitport Community Schools (PK-12)
2000 Enrollment: 3,283 231-865-3154
Housing: Homeownership rate: 84.2% (2000); Median home value: $96,900 (2000); Median rent: $525 per month (2000); Median age of housing: 43 years (2000).
Transportation: Commute to work: 94.4% car, 0.0% public transportation, 2.0% walk, 3.1% work from home (2000); Travel time to work: 37.5% less than 15 minutes, 40.5% 15 to 30 minutes, 14.6% 30 to 45 minutes, 5.1% 45 to 60 minutes, 2.4% 60 minutes or more (2000)

FRUITPORT CHARTER (township). Covers a land area of 30.012 square miles and a water area of 0.132 square miles. Located at 43.15° N. Lat.; 86.17° W. Long. Elevation is 625 feet.
Population: 12,533 (2000); Race: 96.4% White, 1.1% Black, 0.2% Asian, 0.5% American Indian and Alaska Native, 1.0% Hispanic of any race, 1.5% two or more races (2000); Density: 417.6 persons per square mile (2000); Age: 27.5% under 18, 11.0% over 64 (2000); Marriage status: 21.1% never married, 64.5% now married, 4.7% widowed, 9.6% divorced (2000); Foreign born: 0.9% (2000); Ancestry (includes multiple ancestries): 21.9% German, 17.6% Dutch, 12.3% English, 11.5% Irish, 8.7% Polish (2000).
Economy: Single-family building permits issued: 70 (2001) / 75 (2000); Multi-family building permits issued: 0 (2001) / 0 (2000); Employment by occupation: 10.2% management, 15.1% professional, 12.9% services, 28.7% sales, 0.1% farming, 10.4% construction, 22.7% production (2000).
Income: Per capita income: $20,582 (2000); Median household income: $49,065 (2000); Poverty rate: 6.6% (2000).
Taxes: Total city taxes per capita: $66 (2000); City property taxes per capita: $60 (2000).
Education: High school graduation rate: 86.1% (2000); College graduation rate: 15.2% (2000).
Housing: Homeownership rate: 91.3% (2000); Median home value: $98,400 (2000); Median rent: $453 per month (2000); Median age of housing: 33 years (2000).
Transportation: Commute to work: 94.8% car, 0.3% public transportation, 1.2% walk, 3.5% work from home (2000); Travel time to work: 40.3% less than 15 minutes, 40.5% 15 to 30 minutes, 10.8% 30 to 45 minutes, 5.3% 45 to 60 minutes, 3.0% 60 minutes or more (2000)

HOLTON (township). Covers a land area of 35.208 square miles and a water area of 0.507 square miles. Located at 43.41° N. Lat.; 86.08° W. Long. Elevation is 990 feet.
Population: 2,532 (2000); Race: 95.7% White, 0.0% Black, 0.4% Asian, 1.1% American Indian and Alaska Native, 2.4% Hispanic of any race, 1.5% two or more races (2000); Density: 71.9 persons per square mile (2000); Age: 26.8% under 18, 11.6% over 64 (2000); Marriage status: 20.7% never married, 63.4% now married, 4.6% widowed, 11.3% divorced (2000); Foreign born: 0.5% (2000); Ancestry (includes multiple ancestries): 22.7% German, 12.0% Irish, 10.4% English, 8.9% Other groups, 7.6% Dutch (2000).
Economy: Single-family building permits issued: 13 (2001) / 6 (2000); Multi-family building permits issued: 0 (2001) / 0 (2000); Employment by occupation: 9.7% management, 8.8% professional, 12.6% services, 23.8% sales, 2.8% farming, 12.3% construction, 30.0% production (2000).
Income: Per capita income: $16,210 (2000); Median household income: $37,813 (2000); Poverty rate: 9.5% (2000).
Taxes: Total city taxes per capita: $43 (1997); City property taxes per capita: $39 (1997).
Education: High school graduation rate: 75.9% (2000); College graduation rate: 5.8% (2000).

School District(s)

Holton Public Schools (PK-12)
2000 Enrollment: 1,167 231-821-2178

Housing: Homeownership rate: 85.5% (2000); Median home value: $80,400 (2000); Median rent: $333 per month (2000); Median age of housing: 28 years (2000).
Transportation: Commute to work: 93.7% car, 0.9% public transportation, 1.5% walk, 2.5% work from home (2000); Travel time to work: 19.7% less than 15 minutes, 34.2% 15 to 30 minutes, 28.8% 30 to 45 minutes, 8.9% 45 to 60 minutes, 8.3% 60 minutes or more (2000)

LAKETON (township). Covers a land area of 17.309 square miles and a water area of 1.365 square miles. Located at 43.26° N. Lat.; 86.30° W. Long.
History: Laketon Township was created by a division in Muskegon Township in 1865. Its name came from its setting, surrounded on three sides by lakes.
Population: 7,363 (2000); Race: 96.6% White, 0.1% Black, 0.3% Asian, 0.7% American Indian and Alaska Native, 2.9% Hispanic of any race, 1.2% two or more races (2000); Density: 425.4 persons per square mile (2000); Age: 27.3% under 18, 12.0% over 64 (2000); Marriage status: 19.3% never married, 67.3% now married, 5.1% widowed, 8.2% divorced (2000); Foreign born: 2.1% (2000); Ancestry (includes multiple ancestries): 25.4% German, 13.5% Irish, 13.2% Dutch, 11.5% English, 10.2% Polish (2000).
Economy: Single-family building permits issued: 68 (2001) / 48 (2000); Multi-family building permits issued: 4 (2001) / 0 (2000); Employment by occupation: 14.1% management, 25.2% professional, 12.6% services, 24.0% sales, 0.3% farming, 8.3% construction, 15.5% production (2000).
Income: Per capita income: $21,411 (2000); Median household income: $50,913 (2000); Poverty rate: 5.6% (2000).
Taxes: Total city taxes per capita: $44 (1997); City property taxes per capita: $26 (1997).
Education: High school graduation rate: 93.2% (2000); College graduation rate: 22.0% (2000).
Housing: Homeownership rate: 92.5% (2000); Median home value: $105,500 (2000); Median rent: $485 per month (2000); Median age of housing: 30 years (2000).
Transportation: Commute to work: 95.2% car, 0.0% public transportation, 1.3% walk, 3.0% work from home (2000); Travel time to work: 29.4% less than 15 minutes, 54.5% 15 to 30 minutes, 8.4% 30 to 45 minutes, 3.3% 45 to 60 minutes, 4.5% 60 minutes or more (2000)

LAKEWOOD CLUB (village). Covers a land area of 1.893 square miles and a water area of 0.140 square miles. Located at 43.37° N. Lat.; 86.25° W. Long. Elevation is 680 feet.
Population: 1,006 (2000); Race: 91.1% White, 1.7% Black, 0.0% Asian, 1.9% American Indian and Alaska Native, 5.9% Hispanic of any race, 2.3% two or more races (2000); Density: 531.4 persons per square mile (2000); Age: 36.8% under 18, 5.6% over 64 (2000); Marriage status: 17.3% never married, 68.0% now married, 5.5% widowed, 9.2% divorced (2000); Foreign born: 0.5% (2000); Ancestry (includes multiple ancestries): 18.6% Other groups, 17.0% German, 14.4% Irish, 10.9% United States or American, 9.9% Dutch (2000).
Economy: Single-family building permits issued: 22 (2001) / 26 (2000); Multi-family building permits issued: 0 (2001) / 0 (2000); Employment by occupation: 5.9% management, 6.6% professional, 13.9% services, 23.4% sales, 1.0% farming, 10.5% construction, 38.8% production (2000).
Income: Per capita income: $13,451 (2000); Median household income: $40,313 (2000); Poverty rate: 15.5% (2000).
Taxes: Total city taxes per capita: $134 (1997); City property taxes per capita: $119 (1997).
Education: High school graduation rate: 77.8% (2000); College graduation rate: 2.2% (2000).
Housing: Homeownership rate: 95.9% (2000); Median home value: $70,500 (2000); Median rent: $375 per month (2000); Median age of housing: 25 years (2000).
Transportation: Commute to work: 96.0% car, 0.0% public transportation, 0.0% walk, 2.8% work from home (2000); Travel time to work: 14.9% less than 15 minutes, 60.4% 15 to 30 minutes, 16.5% 30 to 45 minutes, 2.8% 45 to 60 minutes, 5.4% 60 minutes or more (2000)

MONTAGUE (city). Covers a land area of 2.659 square miles and a water area of 0.543 square miles. Located at 43.41° N. Lat.; 86.36° W. Long. Elevation is 589 feet.
History: Montague was established at the head of White Lake. Industries in the early 1900's included a foundry and canning factory. Navy beans, grown in the area, were shipped from Montague.
Population: 2,407 (2000); Race: 97.2% White, 0.5% Black, 1.0% Asian, 0.0% American Indian and Alaska Native, 0.6% Hispanic of any race, 1.3% two or more races (2000); Density: 905.1 persons per square mile (2000);

Age: 26.3% under 18, 15.1% over 64 (2000); Marriage status: 24.5% never married, 56.3% now married, 8.0% widowed, 11.2% divorced (2000); Foreign born: 1.2% (2000); Ancestry (includes multiple ancestries): 31.0% German, 15.7% English, 12.6% Irish, 8.3% Polish, 7.6% Swedish (2000).
Economy: Employment by occupation: 11.8% management, 17.8% professional, 15.6% services, 23.2% sales, 0.4% farming, 8.5% construction, 22.7% production (2000).
Income: Per capita income: $21,238 (2000); Median household income: $40,677 (2000); Poverty rate: 9.5% (2000).
Taxes: Total city taxes per capita: $325 (1997); City property taxes per capita: $322 (1997).
Education: High school graduation rate: 88.8% (2000); College graduation rate: 18.3% (2000).

School District(s)

Montague Area Public Schools (KG-12)
2000 Enrollment: 1,518 231-893-1515

Housing: Homeownership rate: 73.3% (2000); Median home value: $89,100 (2000); Median rent: $394 per month (2000); Median age of housing: 41 years (2000).
Safety: Violent crime rate: 20.7 per 10,000 population; Property crime rate: 202.5 per 10,000 population (2001).
Transportation: Commute to work: 92.6% car, 0.4% public transportation, 3.8% walk, 2.5% work from home (2000); Travel time to work: 47.4% less than 15 minutes, 28.2% 15 to 30 minutes, 12.5% 30 to 45 minutes, 5.9% 45 to 60 minutes, 6.0% 60 minutes or more (2000)

MONTAGUE (township). Covers a land area of 18.900 square miles and a water area of 0.374 square miles. Located at 43.43° N. Lat.; 86.34° W. Long. Elevation is 589 feet.
History: Incorporated as village 1883, as city 1935.
Population: 1,637 (2000); Race: 96.9% White, 0.2% Black, 0.1% Asian, 1.9% American Indian and Alaska Native, 1.6% Hispanic of any race, 0.6% two or more races (2000); Density: 86.6 persons per square mile (2000); Age: 25.5% under 18, 11.5% over 64 (2000); Marriage status: 21.8% never married, 61.9% now married, 6.3% widowed, 10.0% divorced (2000); Foreign born: 0.9% (2000); Ancestry (includes multiple ancestries): 28.8% German, 14.6% English, 12.9% Dutch, 10.1% Irish, 7.2% Other groups (2000).
Economy: Shipping point for agriculture: fruits and vegetables; poultry. Dairying area. Manufacturing: food products, horticultural labels, pharmaceuticals, cast aluminum products, machining. Resort; winter ice fishing. Employment by occupation: 9.8% management, 15.4% professional, 10.7% services, 21.8% sales, 1.7% farming, 14.7% construction, 25.9% production (2000).
Income: Per capita income: $17,695 (2000); Median household income: $41,534 (2000); Poverty rate: 7.1% (2000).
Taxes: Total city taxes per capita: $31 (1997); City property taxes per capita: $31 (1997).
Education: High school graduation rate: 85.7% (2000); College graduation rate: 14.7% (2000).
Housing: Homeownership rate: 93.1% (2000); Median home value: $93,300 (2000); Median rent: $446 per month (2000); Median age of housing: 29 years (2000).
Transportation: Commute to work: 95.0% car, 0.3% public transportation, 0.9% walk, 3.7% work from home (2000); Travel time to work: 40.3% less than 15 minutes, 36.8% 15 to 30 minutes, 14.5% 30 to 45 minutes, 3.7% 45 to 60 minutes, 4.8% 60 minutes or more (2000)

MOORLAND (township). Covers a land area of 36.430 square miles and a water area of 0 square miles. Located at 43.26° N. Lat.; 85.95° W. Long. Elevation is 689 feet.
Population: 1,616 (2000); Race: 97.6% White, 0.0% Black, 0.1% Asian, 0.1% American Indian and Alaska Native, 2.8% Hispanic of any race, 1.5% two or more races (2000); Density: 44.4 persons per square mile (2000); Age: 30.8% under 18, 12.3% over 64 (2000); Marriage status: 21.1% never married, 65.2% now married, 5.4% widowed, 8.3% divorced (2000); Foreign born: 1.3% (2000); Ancestry (includes multiple ancestries): 26.2% German, 14.3% Irish, 11.8% Other groups, 9.7% Dutch, 9.6% United States or American (2000).
Economy: Single-family building permits issued: 19 (2001) / 21 (2000); Multi-family building permits issued: 0 (2001) / 0 (2000); Employment by occupation: 7.2% management, 8.8% professional, 14.3% services, 22.0% sales, 2.4% farming, 15.3% construction, 29.9% production (2000).
Income: Per capita income: $16,347 (2000); Median household income: $40,669 (2000); Poverty rate: 7.8% (2000).
Taxes: Total city taxes per capita: $44 (1997); City property taxes per capita: $40 (1997).
Education: High school graduation rate: 78.1% (2000); College graduation rate: 5.5% (2000).
Housing: Homeownership rate: 93.5% (2000); Median home value: $91,800 (2000); Median rent: $367 per month (2000); Median age of housing: 26 years (2000).
Transportation: Commute to work: 92.6% car, 1.0% public transportation, 0.9% walk, 5.2% work from home (2000); Travel time to work: 14.9% less than 15 minutes, 29.1% 15 to 30 minutes, 37.1% 30 to 45 minutes, 13.6% 45 to 60 minutes, 5.3% 60 minutes or more (2000)

MUSKEGON (city). Covers a land area of 14.351 square miles and a water area of 3.671 square miles. Located at 43.22° N. Lat.; 86.24° W. Long. Elevation is 613 feet.
History: Muskegon's location along the south shore of Muskegon Lake, an arm of Lake Michigan, shaped its development as a lumber center for the Muskegon River valley. In the 1880's, the town had 47 sawmills, earning for it the reputation of Lumber Queen as well as Saloon Queen and Gambling Queen. With the decline of lumbering in the 1890's, Muskegon began to utilize its port for other shipping and more diversified industry. The parent factory of the Continental Motors Corporation was established in Muskegon. In 1927, discovery of oil under the city attracted additional industry.
Population: 40,105 (2000); Race: 60.9% White, 31.0% Black, 0.6% Asian, 1.1% American Indian and Alaska Native, 6.0% Hispanic of any race, 4.2% two or more races (2000); Density: 2,794.5 persons per square mile (2000); Age: 25.7% under 18, 12.4% over 64 (2000); Marriage status: 33.0% never married, 44.2% now married, 7.8% widowed, 15.0% divorced (2000); Foreign born: 2.9% (2000); Ancestry (includes multiple ancestries): 34.3% Other groups, 14.1% German, 7.2% Irish, 6.6% Dutch, 6.5% English (2000).
Vital Statistics: Birth rate: 203.2 per 10,000 population (1998)
Economy: Unemployment rate: 11.2% (11/2002); Total civilian labor force: 19,493 (11/2002); Single-family building permits issued: 56 (2001) / 69 (2000); Multi-family building permits issued: 0 (2001) / 0 (2000); Employment by occupation: 6.4% management, 12.8% professional, 21.9% services, 23.4% sales, 0.2% farming, 6.6% construction, 28.7% production (2000).
Income: Per capita income: $14,283 (2000); Median household income: $27,929 (2000); Poverty rate: 20.5% (2000).
Taxes: Total city taxes per capita: $359 (2000); City property taxes per capita: $173 (2000).
Education: High school graduation rate: 77.7% (2000); College graduation rate: 8.7% (2000).

School District(s)

Muskegon City School District (PK-12)
2000 Enrollment: 6,649 231-720-2000
Muskegon Technical Academy (07-09)
2000 Enrollment: 0 231-767-8457
Oakridge Public Schools (PK-12)
2000 Enrollment: 1,982 231-788-2361
Orchard View Schools (KG-12)
2000 Enrollment: 2,714 231-760-1309
Reeths-Puffer Schools (PK-12)
2000 Enrollment: 4,582 231-744-4736
Timberland Academy (KG-05)
2000 Enrollment: 312 616-895-3029

Four-year College(s)

Baker College of Muskegon (Private, Not-for-profit)
2001 Enrollment: 2,929 231-777-8800
2001 Tuition: In-state $7,440; Out-of-state $7,440

Two-year College(s)

Muskegon Community College (Public)
2001 Enrollment: 4,407 616-777-0311
2001 Tuition: In-state $2,130; Out-of-state $2,610

Housing: Homeownership rate: 57.0% (2000); Median home value: $59,800 (2000); Median rent: $361 per month (2000); Median age of housing: 50 years (2000).
Hospitals: Hackley Hospital (181 beds); Mercy General Health Partners (302 beds); Muskegon General Hospital (127 beds)
Safety: Violent crime rate: 106.9 per 10,000 population; Property crime rate: 738.2 per 10,000 population (2001).
Newspapers: The Muskegon Chronicle (7 x week); Norton Lake Shore Examiner (1 x week)
Transportation: Commute to work: 91.4% car, 1.2% public transportation, 2.9% walk, 2.5% work from home (2000); Travel time to work: 43.8% less

than 15 minutes, 37.6% 15 to 30 minutes, 9.4% 30 to 45 minutes, 4.9% 45 to 60 minutes, 4.3% 60 minutes or more (2000)
Airports: Muskegon County (primary service)
Additional Information Contacts
Muskegon Area Chamber of Commerce 231-722-3751
Muskegon Chamber of Commerce. 231-737-2259

MUSKEGON (township). Covers a land area of 23.842 square miles and a water area of 0.064 square miles. Located at 43.24° N. Lat.; 86.19° W. Long. Elevation is 613 feet.
History: A fur-trading post was established here c.1810. The first sawmill was built in 1837, and the lumber industry thrived until 1890, when the city was swept by fire. Incorporated as a city 1869.
Population: 17,737 (2000); Race: 91.3% White, 4.8% Black, 0.3% Asian, 0.6% American Indian and Alaska Native, 3.0% Hispanic of any race, 2.2% two or more races (2000); Density: 743.9 persons per square mile (2000); Age: 29.2% under 18, 13.8% over 64 (2000); Marriage status: 21.7% never married, 58.4% now married, 8.3% widowed, 11.6% divorced (2000); Foreign born: 1.0% (2000); Ancestry (includes multiple ancestries): 21.5% German, 13.6% Dutch, 13.5% Irish, 11.8% Other groups, 11.1% English (2000).
Economy: A port of entry, the city is a car-ferry terminus and a ship railroad transfer point for a farm, fruit and industrial region. Manufacturing includes motor vehicle equipment and parts, foundry products, chemicals, paper products, sporting goods equipment, ink pigments, gasoline pumps and heavy machinery. Single-family building permits issued: 94 (2001) / 82 (2000); Multi-family building permits issued: 7 (2001) / 18 (2000); Employment by occupation: 8.3% management, 12.2% professional, 14.1% services, 29.2% sales, 0.2% farming, 8.1% construction, 27.9% production (2000).
Income: Per capita income: $16,623 (2000); Median household income: $38,634 (2000); Poverty rate: 9.1% (2000).
Taxes: Total city taxes per capita: $136 (2000); City property taxes per capita: $117 (2000).
Education: High school graduation rate: 82.3% (2000); College graduation rate: 9.3% (2000).
Housing: Homeownership rate: 81.9% (2000); Median home value: $81,700 (2000); Median rent: $350 per month (2000); Median age of housing: 30 years (2000).
Safety: Violent crime rate: 24.1 per 10,000 population; Property crime rate: 591.1 per 10,000 population (2001).
Transportation: Commute to work: 96.0% car, 0.3% public transportation, 0.6% walk, 2.1% work from home (2000); Travel time to work: 39.8% less than 15 minutes, 42.8% 15 to 30 minutes, 9.4% 30 to 45 minutes, 4.8% 45 to 60 minutes, 3.1% 60 minutes or more (2000)
Airports: Muskegon County (primary service)

MUSKEGON HEIGHTS (city). Covers a land area of 3.167 square miles and a water area of 0 square miles. Located at 43.20° N. Lat.; 86.24° W. Long. Elevation is 629 feet.
Population: 12,049 (2000); Race: 17.9% White, 78.6% Black, 0.2% Asian, 0.2% American Indian and Alaska Native, 3.4% Hispanic of any race, 1.3% two or more races (2000); Density: 3,804.2 persons per square mile (2000); Age: 34.8% under 18, 11.3% over 64 (2000); Marriage status: 43.2% never married, 31.8% now married, 9.0% widowed, 16.0% divorced (2000); Foreign born: 1.4% (2000); Ancestry (includes multiple ancestries): 69.8% Other groups, 3.6% German, 3.5% United States or American, 3.1% African, 1.9% Irish (2000).
Vital Statistics: Birth rate: 209.2 per 10,000 population (1998)
Economy: Single-family building permits issued: 3 (2001) / 3 (2000); Multi-family building permits issued: 15 (2001) / 15 (2000); Employment by occupation: 3.3% management, 8.8% professional, 24.7% services, 20.7% sales, 0.0% farming, 5.1% construction, 37.4% production (2000).
Income: Per capita income: $12,456 (2000); Median household income: $21,778 (2000); Poverty rate: 29.6% (2000).
Taxes: Total city taxes per capita: $250 (1997); City property taxes per capita: $152 (1997).
Education: High school graduation rate: 68.0% (2000); College graduation rate: 4.5% (2000).

School District(s)
Muskegon Heights School District (KG-12)
2000 Enrollment: 2,278 231-739-9302
Housing: Homeownership rate: 57.2% (2000); Median home value: $42,400 (2000); Median rent: $360 per month (2000); Median age of housing: 53 years (2000).
Safety: Violent crime rate: 227.0 per 10,000 population; Property crime rate: 935.4 per 10,000 population (2001).
Transportation: Commute to work: 92.3% car, 3.1% public transportation, 1.9% walk, 1.7% work from home (2000); Travel time to work: 47.2% less than 15 minutes, 36.1% 15 to 30 minutes, 8.7% 30 to 45 minutes, 5.4% 45 to 60 minutes, 2.6% 60 minutes or more (2000)

NORTH MUSKEGON (city). Covers a land area of 1.784 square miles and a water area of 2.305 square miles. Located at 43.25° N. Lat.; 86.27° W. Long. Elevation is 621 feet.
History: Incorporated as village 1881, as city 1891.
Population: 4,031 (2000); Race: 98.0% White, 0.8% Black, 0.0% Asian, 0.3% American Indian and Alaska Native, 1.8% Hispanic of any race, 0.9% two or more races (2000); Density: 2,259.2 persons per square mile (2000); Age: 25.2% under 18, 19.1% over 64 (2000); Marriage status: 19.1% never married, 63.3% now married, 6.5% widowed, 11.1% divorced (2000); Foreign born: 1.2% (2000); Ancestry (includes multiple ancestries): 24.4% German, 16.3% Dutch, 12.2% Irish, 12.1% English, 7.6% Swedish (2000).
Economy: Railroad junction. Manufacturing of agricultural chemicals. Fruit and vegetable farming. Manistee National Forest to Northeast. Single-family building permits issued: 11 (2001) / 22 (2000); Multi-family building permits issued: 0 (2001) / 0 (2000); Employment by occupation: 17.5% management, 31.7% professional, 7.0% services, 26.7% sales, 0.5% farming, 4.7% construction, 12.0% production (2000).
Income: Per capita income: $27,140 (2000); Median household income: $55,063 (2000); Poverty rate: 3.4% (2000).
Taxes: Total city taxes per capita: $275 (1997); City property taxes per capita: $260 (1997).
Education: High school graduation rate: 92.7% (2000); College graduation rate: 35.9% (2000).

School District(s)
North Muskegon Public Schools (KG-12)
2000 Enrollment: 929 231-719-4100
Housing: Homeownership rate: 79.2% (2000); Median home value: $123,300 (2000); Median rent: $484 per month (2000); Median age of housing: 45 years (2000).
Safety: Violent crime rate: 4.9 per 10,000 population; Property crime rate: 281.3 per 10,000 population (2001).
Transportation: Commute to work: 95.5% car, 0.0% public transportation, 1.2% walk, 3.3% work from home (2000); Travel time to work: 32.0% less than 15 minutes, 49.3% 15 to 30 minutes, 8.7% 30 to 45 minutes, 4.9% 45 to 60 minutes, 5.2% 60 minutes or more (2000)

NORTON SHORES (city). Covers a land area of 23.244 square miles and a water area of 1.218 square miles. Located at 43.17° N. Lat.; 86.25° W. Long. Elevation is 612 feet.
Population: 22,527 (2000); Race: 95.0% White, 2.0% Black, 0.8% Asian, 0.2% American Indian and Alaska Native, 2.3% Hispanic of any race, 1.5% two or more races (2000); Density: 969.2 persons per square mile (2000); Age: 24.8% under 18, 17.3% over 64 (2000); Marriage status: 20.9% never married, 61.5% now married, 7.6% widowed, 10.0% divorced (2000); Foreign born: 2.6% (2000); Ancestry (includes multiple ancestries): 23.7% German, 14.4% Dutch, 13.6% Irish, 11.5% English, 8.7% Swedish (2000).
Vital Statistics: Birth rate: 87.9 per 10,000 population (1998)
Economy: Airport is here. Single-family building permits issued: 166 (2001) / 137 (2000); Multi-family building permits issued: 56 (2001) / 0 (2000); Employment by occupation: 13.8% management, 18.6% professional, 13.4% services, 26.2% sales, 0.4% farming, 8.3% construction, 19.4% production (2000).
Income: Per capita income: $22,713 (2000); Median household income: $45,457 (2000); Poverty rate: 5.3% (2000).
Taxes: Total city taxes per capita: $200 (1997); City property taxes per capita: $178 (1997).
Education: High school graduation rate: 87.8% (2000); College graduation rate: 24.0% (2000).

School District(s)
Mona Shores Public School District (PK-12)
2000 Enrollment: 4,190 231-780-4751
Housing: Homeownership rate: 89.5% (2000); Median home value: $106,100 (2000); Median rent: $478 per month (2000); Median age of housing: 33 years (2000).
Safety: Violent crime rate: 21.6 per 10,000 population; Property crime rate: 463.2 per 10,000 population (2001).
Transportation: Commute to work: 95.4% car, 0.0% public transportation, 0.6% walk, 3.3% work from home (2000); Travel time to work: 43.5% less than 15 minutes, 40.4% 15 to 30 minutes, 9.1% 30 to 45 minutes, 4.8% 45 to 60 minutes, 2.2% 60 minutes or more (2000)

RAVENNA (village). Covers a land area of 1.259 square miles and a water area of 0 square miles. Located at 43.18° N. Lat.; 85.94° W. Long. Elevation is 695 feet.

History: The village of Ravenna was first settled in 1847 by Benjamin Smith, and was incorporated in 1922. Ravenna took its name from the township, which was named for Ravenna, Ohio.

Population: 1,206 (2000); Race: 97.3% White, 0.0% Black, 0.0% Asian, 0.6% American Indian and Alaska Native, 1.8% Hispanic of any race, 0.4% two or more races (2000); Density: 958.1 persons per square mile (2000); Age: 29.4% under 18, 10.9% over 64 (2000); Marriage status: 17.6% never married, 69.7% now married, 6.0% widowed, 6.7% divorced (2000); Foreign born: 1.4% (2000); Ancestry (includes multiple ancestries): 22.4% German, 16.1% United States or American, 15.2% English, 13.9% Dutch, 13.1% Irish (2000).

Economy: Single-family building permits issued: 8 (2001) / 13 (2000); Multi-family building permits issued: 0 (2001) / 0 (2000); Employment by occupation: 11.5% management, 19.5% professional, 10.5% services, 23.0% sales, 1.5% farming, 8.4% construction, 25.6% production (2000).

Income: Per capita income: $19,197 (2000); Median household income: $47,167 (2000); Poverty rate: 3.7% (2000).

Taxes: Total city taxes per capita: $108 (1997); City property taxes per capita: $103 (1997).

Education: High school graduation rate: 90.2% (2000); College graduation rate: 16.0% (2000).

School District(s)

Ravenna Public Schools (KG-12)
2000 Enrollment: 1,241 231-853-2231

Housing: Homeownership rate: 86.2% (2000); Median home value: $97,400 (2000); Median rent: $435 per month (2000); Median age of housing: 35 years (2000).

Transportation: Commute to work: 94.9% car, 0.0% public transportation, 2.2% walk, 2.5% work from home (2000); Travel time to work: 23.1% less than 15 minutes, 30.6% 15 to 30 minutes, 29.9% 30 to 45 minutes, 11.5% 45 to 60 minutes, 4.9% 60 minutes or more (2000)

RAVENNA (township). Covers a land area of 36.339 square miles and a water area of 0 square miles. Located at 43.17° N. Lat.; 85.95° W. Long. Elevation is 695 feet.

History: Ravenna grew around a sawmill built in 1844 by E.B. Bostwick. The township was organized in 1848, and named for Ravenna, Ohio, the former home of the surveyor.

Population: 2,856 (2000); Race: 96.4% White, 0.1% Black, 0.1% Asian, 0.6% American Indian and Alaska Native, 2.8% Hispanic of any race, 1.2% two or more races (2000); Density: 78.6 persons per square mile (2000); Age: 28.7% under 18, 11.6% over 64 (2000); Marriage status: 20.7% never married, 66.0% now married, 5.4% widowed, 7.9% divorced (2000); Foreign born: 1.8% (2000); Ancestry (includes multiple ancestries): 23.0% German, 17.2% Dutch, 15.5% United States or American, 10.2% Irish, 9.5% English (2000).

Economy: Single-family building permits issued: 6 (2001) / 7 (2000); Multi-family building permits issued: 0 (2001) / 0 (2000); Employment by occupation: 10.2% management, 12.8% professional, 10.7% services, 22.8% sales, 2.0% farming, 11.4% construction, 30.2% production (2000).

Income: Per capita income: $18,440 (2000); Median household income: $44,315 (2000); Poverty rate: 8.1% (2000).

Taxes: Total city taxes per capita: $46 (1997); City property taxes per capita: $42 (1997).

Education: High school graduation rate: 85.7% (2000); College graduation rate: 12.3% (2000).

Housing: Homeownership rate: 84.4% (2000); Median home value: $95,100 (2000); Median rent: $384 per month (2000); Median age of housing: 34 years (2000).

Transportation: Commute to work: 92.9% car, 0.5% public transportation, 2.0% walk, 4.5% work from home (2000); Travel time to work: 23.0% less than 15 minutes, 30.1% 15 to 30 minutes, 30.2% 30 to 45 minutes, 10.6% 45 to 60 minutes, 6.1% 60 minutes or more (2000)

ROOSEVELT PARK (city). Covers a land area of 1.006 square miles and a water area of 0 square miles. Located at 43.19° N. Lat.; 86.27° W. Long. Elevation is 622 feet.

History: Incorporated 1946.

Population: 3,890 (2000); Race: 93.2% White, 2.4% Black, 1.2% Asian, 0.6% American Indian and Alaska Native, 2.7% Hispanic of any race, 1.6% two or more races (2000); Density: 3,865.3 persons per square mile (2000); Age: 22.1% under 18, 23.3% over 64 (2000); Marriage status: 19.7% never married, 57.5% now married, 11.3% widowed, 11.5% divorced (2000); Foreign born: 3.3% (2000); Ancestry (includes multiple ancestries): 27.0% German, 14.1% Dutch, 11.6% Polish, 9.8% English, 9.6% Irish (2000).

Economy: Single-family building permits issued: 5 (2001) / 3 (2000); Multi-family building permits issued: 0 (2001) / 0 (2000); Employment by occupation: 11.6% management, 23.2% professional, 13.3% services, 29.1% sales, 0.0% farming, 6.1% construction, 16.7% production (2000).

Income: Per capita income: $19,825 (2000); Median household income: $37,035 (2000); Poverty rate: 4.8% (2000).

Taxes: Total city taxes per capita: $211 (1997); City property taxes per capita: $198 (1997).

Education: High school graduation rate: 88.1% (2000); College graduation rate: 25.8% (2000).

Housing: Homeownership rate: 62.7% (2000); Median home value: $95,500 (2000); Median rent: $578 per month (2000); Median age of housing: 35 years (2000).

Safety: Violent crime rate: 25.6 per 10,000 population; Property crime rate: 542.2 per 10,000 population (2001).

Transportation: Commute to work: 96.2% car, 0.0% public transportation, 0.7% walk, 3.1% work from home (2000); Travel time to work: 48.3% less than 15 minutes, 33.5% 15 to 30 minutes, 7.6% 30 to 45 minutes, 5.8% 45 to 60 minutes, 4.9% 60 minutes or more (2000)

SULLIVAN (township). Covers a land area of 24.089 square miles and a water area of 0 square miles. Located at 43.16° N. Lat.; 86.07° W. Long.

Population: 2,477 (2000); Race: 96.4% White, 0.3% Black, 0.3% Asian, 1.2% American Indian and Alaska Native, 3.5% Hispanic of any race, 0.9% two or more races (2000); Density: 102.8 persons per square mile (2000); Age: 28.4% under 18, 10.7% over 64 (2000); Marriage status: 23.2% never married, 62.6% now married, 4.6% widowed, 9.6% divorced (2000); Foreign born: 1.6% (2000); Ancestry (includes multiple ancestries): 23.0% German, 14.9% Dutch, 12.2% Irish, 10.7% Polish, 10.6% English (2000).

Economy: Employment by occupation: 8.2% management, 8.0% professional, 15.5% services, 25.5% sales, 0.9% farming, 12.6% construction, 29.2% production (2000).

Income: Per capita income: $19,360 (2000); Median household income: $46,447 (2000); Poverty rate: 5.3% (2000).

Taxes: Total city taxes per capita: $20 (1997); City property taxes per capita: $18 (1997).

Education: High school graduation rate: 83.7% (2000); College graduation rate: 8.2% (2000).

Housing: Homeownership rate: 96.2% (2000); Median home value: $89,300 (2000); Median rent: $505 per month (2000); Median age of housing: 30 years (2000).

Transportation: Commute to work: 94.1% car, 0.5% public transportation, 1.3% walk, 2.5% work from home (2000); Travel time to work: 23.6% less than 15 minutes, 47.9% 15 to 30 minutes, 16.6% 30 to 45 minutes, 8.1% 45 to 60 minutes, 3.7% 60 minutes or more (2000)

TWIN LAKE (CDP). Covers a land area of 2.381 square miles and a water area of 0.521 square miles. Located at 43.36° N. Lat.; 86.17° W. Long. Elevation is 688 feet.

Population: 1,613 (2000); Race: 97.0% White, 0.0% Black, 0.0% Asian, 0.0% American Indian and Alaska Native, 1.5% Hispanic of any race, 3.0% two or more races (2000); Density: 677.4 persons per square mile (2000); Age: 28.5% under 18, 10.7% over 64 (2000); Marriage status: 17.4% never married, 67.1% now married, 4.4% widowed, 11.1% divorced (2000); Foreign born: 0.5% (2000); Ancestry (includes multiple ancestries): 26.3% German, 13.7% English, 12.1% Polish, 11.9% Dutch, 11.4% Irish (2000).

Economy: Employment by occupation: 4.7% management, 15.0% professional, 13.4% services, 27.6% sales, 0.0% farming, 14.5% construction, 24.7% production (2000).

Income: Per capita income: $18,501 (2000); Median household income: $49,141 (2000); Poverty rate: 10.2% (2000).

Education: High school graduation rate: 92.0% (2000); College graduation rate: 14.0% (2000).

Housing: Homeownership rate: 88.0% (2000); Median home value: $119,100 (2000); Median rent: $418 per month (2000); Median age of housing: 29 years (2000).

Transportation: Commute to work: 97.2% car, 0.0% public transportation, 0.5% walk, 1.5% work from home (2000); Travel time to work: 8.2% less than 15 minutes, 65.6% 15 to 30 minutes, 17.3% 30 to 45 minutes, 3.8% 45 to 60 minutes, 5.1% 60 minutes or more (2000)

WHITE RIVER (township). Covers a land area of 15.872 square miles and a water area of 0.040 square miles. Located at 43.42° N. Lat.; 86.42° W. Long.
Population: 1,338 (2000); Race: 96.0% White, 0.0% Black, 0.0% Asian, 0.4% American Indian and Alaska Native, 3.7% Hispanic of any race, 3.1% two or more races (2000); Density: 84.3 persons per square mile (2000); Age: 24.2% under 18, 16.7% over 64 (2000); Marriage status: 17.7% never married, 66.5% now married, 8.1% widowed, 7.7% divorced (2000); Foreign born: 1.5% (2000); Ancestry (includes multiple ancestries): 29.4% German, 12.3% Irish, 11.9% Polish, 10.7% English, 9.6% Dutch (2000).
Economy: Single-family building permits issued: 9 (2001) / 17 (2000); Multi-family building permits issued: 0 (2001) / 0 (2000); Employment by occupation: 12.4% management, 22.6% professional, 12.7% services, 19.4% sales, 1.1% farming, 11.9% construction, 19.9% production (2000).
Income: Per capita income: $21,797 (2000); Median household income: $48,077 (2000); Poverty rate: 6.3% (2000).
Taxes: Total city taxes per capita: $54 (1997); City property taxes per capita: $41 (1997).
Education: High school graduation rate: 91.2% (2000); College graduation rate: 26.4% (2000).
Housing: Homeownership rate: 97.3% (2000); Median home value: $116,300 (2000); Median rent: $470 per month (2000); Median age of housing: 27 years (2000).
Transportation: Commute to work: 92.5% car, 0.5% public transportation, 1.8% walk, 5.2% work from home (2000); Travel time to work: 31.5% less than 15 minutes, 36.7% 15 to 30 minutes, 22.0% 30 to 45 minutes, 5.7% 45 to 60 minutes, 4.2% 60 minutes or more (2000)

WHITEHALL (city). Covers a land area of 3.004 square miles and a water area of 0.663 square miles. Located at 43.40° N. Lat.; 86.34° W. Long. Elevation is 593 feet.
History: Whitehall, rival of Montague at the head of White Lake, depended on fruit raising for its source of revenue.
Population: 2,884 (2000); Race: 95.9% White, 1.7% Black, 0.0% Asian, 0.9% American Indian and Alaska Native, 1.9% Hispanic of any race, 1.5% two or more races (2000); Density: 960.0 persons per square mile (2000); Age: 25.3% under 18, 21.1% over 64 (2000); Marriage status: 22.4% never married, 55.0% now married, 13.8% widowed, 8.7% divorced (2000); Foreign born: 2.5% (2000); Ancestry (includes multiple ancestries): 21.7% German, 17.3% Irish, 11.1% Other groups, 10.2% English, 8.3% Dutch (2000).
Economy: Employment by occupation: 9.6% management, 21.2% professional, 22.6% services, 17.2% sales, 0.0% farming, 5.9% construction, 23.6% production (2000).
Income: Per capita income: $18,544 (2000); Median household income: $37,641 (2000); Poverty rate: 7.3% (2000).
Taxes: Total city taxes per capita: $446 (1997); City property taxes per capita: $443 (1997).
Education: High school graduation rate: 86.1% (2000); College graduation rate: 14.7% (2000).

School District(s)

Whitehall School District (PK-12)
2000 Enrollment: 2,183 231-893-7335

Housing: Homeownership rate: 63.7% (2000); Median home value: $88,700 (2000); Median rent: $366 per month (2000); Median age of housing: 41 years (2000).
Safety: Violent crime rate: 34.5 per 10,000 population; Property crime rate: 651.9 per 10,000 population (2001).
Newspapers: White Lake Beacon (1 x week)
Transportation: Commute to work: 90.9% car, 0.3% public transportation, 2.8% walk, 4.9% work from home (2000); Travel time to work: 60.3% less than 15 minutes, 21.0% 15 to 30 minutes, 5.6% 30 to 45 minutes, 3.9% 45 to 60 minutes, 9.2% 60 minutes or more (2000)

Additional Information Contacts

White Lake Chamber of Commerce 231-893-4585

WHITEHALL (township). Covers a land area of 9.433 square miles and a water area of 0.163 square miles. Located at 43.41° N. Lat.; 86.30° W. Long. Elevation is 593 feet.
History: White River Station Museum. Incorporated 1867 as village, as city 1943.
Population: 1,648 (2000); Race: 97.9% White, 1.0% Black, 0.0% Asian, 0.4% American Indian and Alaska Native, 1.0% Hispanic of any race, 0.7% two or more races (2000); Density: 174.7 persons per square mile (2000); Age: 25.8% under 18, 10.7% over 64 (2000); Marriage status: 22.6% never married, 64.2% now married, 3.7% widowed, 9.5% divorced (2000); Foreign born: 0.4% (2000); Ancestry (includes multiple ancestries): 35.0% German, 13.9% English, 13.9% Irish, 12.2% Dutch, 6.4% Other groups (2000).
Economy: In fruit-growing area near Lake Michigan. Manufacturing: fabricated metal products, electronic equipment, machinery. Resort. Swedish midsummer festival held here. Manistee National Forest to Northeast. Employment by occupation: 10.7% management, 22.0% professional, 11.2% services, 25.0% sales, 0.2% farming, 6.6% construction, 24.3% production (2000).
Income: Per capita income: $21,989 (2000); Median household income: $50,375 (2000); Poverty rate: 4.1% (2000).
Taxes: Total city taxes per capita: $33 (1997); City property taxes per capita: $31 (1997).
Education: High school graduation rate: 91.4% (2000); College graduation rate: 19.2% (2000).
Housing: Homeownership rate: 92.2% (2000); Median home value: $104,900 (2000); Median rent: $445 per month (2000); Median age of housing: 22 years (2000).
Transportation: Commute to work: 94.8% car, 1.4% public transportation, 0.8% walk, 2.5% work from home (2000); Travel time to work: 44.0% less than 15 minutes, 31.9% 15 to 30 minutes, 13.7% 30 to 45 minutes, 5.6% 45 to 60 minutes, 4.8% 60 minutes or more (2000)

WOLF LAKE (CDP). Covers a land area of 3.483 square miles and a water area of 0.362 square miles. Located at 43.24° N. Lat.; 86.11° W. Long. Elevation is 634 feet.
Population: 4,455 (2000); Race: 96.3% White, 0.5% Black, 0.0% Asian, 1.0% American Indian and Alaska Native, 3.2% Hispanic of any race, 1.8% two or more races (2000); Density: 1,279.0 persons per square mile (2000); Age: 27.8% under 18, 10.6% over 64 (2000); Marriage status: 20.5% never married, 58.5% now married, 7.2% widowed, 13.8% divorced (2000); Foreign born: 1.3% (2000); Ancestry (includes multiple ancestries): 20.7% German, 15.9% Irish, 13.7% Dutch, 10.1% English, 9.5% Other groups (2000).
Economy: Employment by occupation: 5.0% management, 9.7% professional, 18.7% services, 22.4% sales, 1.3% farming, 13.0% construction, 30.0% production (2000).
Income: Per capita income: $16,214 (2000); Median household income: $34,799 (2000); Poverty rate: 8.1% (2000).
Education: High school graduation rate: 79.4% (2000); College graduation rate: 8.4% (2000).
Housing: Homeownership rate: 91.6% (2000); Median home value: $74,500 (2000); Median rent: $412 per month (2000); Median age of housing: 27 years (2000).
Transportation: Commute to work: 96.1% car, 0.3% public transportation, 0.0% walk, 3.1% work from home (2000); Travel time to work: 25.2% less than 15 minutes, 46.7% 15 to 30 minutes, 16.1% 30 to 45 minutes, 6.7% 45 to 60 minutes, 5.2% 60 minutes or more (2000)

Newaygo County

Located in west central Michigan; drained by the Muskegon, Pere Marquette, and White Rivers; includes part of Manistee National Forest. Covers a land area of 842.40 square miles, a water area of 19.00 square miles, and is located in the Eastern Time Zone. The county government was organized in 1840. County seat is White Cloud.
Population: 47,874 (2000); Race: 94.9% White, 1.0% Black, 0.3% Asian, 0.6% American Indian and Alaska Native, 4.0% Hispanic of any race, 1.6% two or more races (2000); Density: 56.8 persons per square mile (2000); Age: 29.1% under 18, 12.8% over 64 (2000).
Religion: Five largest groups: 9.9% Catholic Church, 5.0% Christian Reformed Church in North America, 3.1% Reformed Church in America, 2.9% The United Methodist Church, 2.2% The Wesleyan Church (2000).
Economy: Unemployment rate: 7.9% (11/2002); Total civilian labor force: 22,291 (11/2002); Leading industries: 21.2% manufacturing; 17.4% retail trade; 11.9% health care and social assistance (2000); Companies that employ more than 1,000 persons: 0 (2000); Companies that employ more than 100 persons: 10 (2000); Farms: 670 totaling 122,294 acres (1997); Minority business ownership rate: 4.2% (1997); Women business ownership rate: 21.6% (1997); Retail sales per capita: $5,423 (1997). Single-family building permits issued: 249 (2001) / 210 (2000); Multi-family building permits issued: 20 (2001) / 0 (2000).
Income: Per capita income: $16,976 (2000); Median household income: $37,130 (2000); Poverty rate: 11.6% (2000); Bankruptcy rate: 4.82% (2001).

Taxes: Total county taxes per capita: $118 (2000); County property taxes per capita: $115 (2000).
Education: High school graduation rate: 78.7% (2000); College graduation rate: 11.4% (2000).
Housing: Homeownership rate: 84.5% (2000); Median home value: $88,700 (2000); Median rent: $362 per month (2000); Median age of housing: 29 years (2000).
Health: Birth rate: 132.6 per 10,000 population (1998); Age adjusted death rate: 90.5 per 10,000 population (1999); Age adjusted cancer mortality rate: 158.7 deaths per 100,000 population (1999). Number of physicians: 6.7 per 10,000 population (1999); Number of hospital beds: 17.3 per 10,000 population (1999).
Elections: 2000 Presidential election results: 39.3% Gore, 58.3% Bush, 1.9% Nader, 0.1% Buchanan
National and State Parks: Newaygo State Park; White Cloud State Park
Additional Information Contacts
Newaygo County Government Offices 231-689-7200
Fremont Chamber of Commerce 231-924-0770
Newaygo Chamber of Commerce 231-652-3068
Newaygo County Tourist Council 231-652-9298
West Central Board of Realtors 231-924-6555
White Cloud Chamber of Commerce. 231-689-6607

Newaygo County Communities

ASHLAND (township). Covers a land area of 34.901 square miles and a water area of 0.389 square miles. Located at 43.34° N. Lat.; 85.86° W. Long. Elevation is 784 feet.
History: Ashland Township was organized in 1854 and named for the quantity of white ash timber in the area.
Population: 2,570 (2000); Race: 95.7% White, 0.1% Black, 0.0% Asian, 0.5% American Indian and Alaska Native, 9.7% Hispanic of any race, 2.1% two or more races (2000); Density: 73.6 persons per square mile (2000); Age: 32.3% under 18, 8.5% over 64 (2000); Marriage status: 21.4% never married, 64.0% now married, 4.5% widowed, 10.1% divorced (2000); Foreign born: 3.3% (2000); Ancestry (includes multiple ancestries): 21.1% German, 11.9% Dutch, 11.7% United States or American, 11.6% Other groups, 9.7% Irish (2000).
Economy: Employment by occupation: 7.5% management, 12.0% professional, 13.2% services, 19.5% sales, 1.8% farming, 14.9% construction, 31.0% production (2000).
Income: Per capita income: $18,232 (2000); Median household income: $42,151 (2000); Poverty rate: 12.5% (2000).
Taxes: Total city taxes per capita: $83 (1997); City property taxes per capita: $83 (1997).
Education: High school graduation rate: 78.6% (2000); College graduation rate: 7.9% (2000).
Housing: Homeownership rate: 89.6% (2000); Median home value: $94,100 (2000); Median rent: $405 per month (2000); Median age of housing: 26 years (2000).
Transportation: Commute to work: 94.7% car, 0.0% public transportation, 0.8% walk, 4.0% work from home (2000); Travel time to work: 18.0% less than 15 minutes, 22.7% 15 to 30 minutes, 23.9% 30 to 45 minutes, 20.9% 45 to 60 minutes, 14.5% 60 minutes or more (2000)

BARTON (township). Covers a land area of 35.862 square miles and a water area of 0.043 square miles. Located at 43.77° N. Lat.; 85.62° W. Long.
Population: 820 (2000); Race: 97.9% White, 0.0% Black, 0.3% Asian, 0.3% American Indian and Alaska Native, 0.8% Hispanic of any race, 0.9% two or more races (2000); Density: 22.9 persons per square mile (2000); Age: 26.2% under 18, 10.0% over 64 (2000); Marriage status: 18.7% never married, 63.4% now married, 5.2% widowed, 12.7% divorced (2000); Foreign born: 1.3% (2000); Ancestry (includes multiple ancestries): 25.2% German, 24.9% Irish, 11.0% United States or American, 6.8% Other groups, 6.7% Dutch (2000).
Economy: Single-family building permits issued: 5 (2001) / 3 (2000); Multi-family building permits issued: 0 (2001) / 0 (2000); Employment by occupation: 11.0% management, 11.0% professional, 20.4% services, 17.9% sales, 1.9% farming, 17.6% construction, 20.1% production (2000).
Income: Per capita income: $16,243 (2000); Median household income: $35,000 (2000); Poverty rate: 9.4% (2000).
Taxes: Total city taxes per capita: $53 (1997); City property taxes per capita: $48 (1997).
Education: High school graduation rate: 83.0% (2000); College graduation rate: 11.6% (2000).
Housing: Homeownership rate: 89.1% (2000); Median home value: $77,500 (2000); Median rent: $379 per month (2000); Median age of housing: 21 years (2000).
Transportation: Commute to work: 92.8% car, 0.9% public transportation, 0.3% walk, 5.4% work from home (2000); Travel time to work: 24.2% less than 15 minutes, 53.0% 15 to 30 minutes, 6.4% 30 to 45 minutes, 2.7% 45 to 60 minutes, 13.6% 60 minutes or more (2000)

BEAVER (township). Covers a land area of 35.627 square miles and a water area of 0.208 square miles. Located at 43.68° N. Lat.; 85.99° W. Long.
Population: 608 (2000); Race: 90.3% White, 3.3% Black, 0.0% Asian, 1.3% American Indian and Alaska Native, 4.5% Hispanic of any race, 1.8% two or more races (2000); Density: 17.1 persons per square mile (2000); Age: 32.6% under 18, 9.2% over 64 (2000); Marriage status: 25.7% never married, 60.8% now married, 3.4% widowed, 10.1% divorced (2000); Foreign born: 2.4% (2000); Ancestry (includes multiple ancestries): 18.9% German, 13.2% Other groups, 11.9% English, 10.5% Dutch, 8.8% Irish (2000).
Economy: Employment by occupation: 8.2% management, 11.1% professional, 19.8% services, 14.0% sales, 5.8% farming, 13.0% construction, 28.0% production (2000).
Income: Per capita income: $11,098 (2000); Median household income: $29,500 (2000); Poverty rate: 20.4% (2000).
Taxes: Total city taxes per capita: $22 (1997); City property taxes per capita: $22 (1997).
Education: High school graduation rate: 64.1% (2000); College graduation rate: 4.7% (2000).
Housing: Homeownership rate: 85.6% (2000); Median home value: $74,200 (2000); Median rent: $308 per month (2000); Median age of housing: 30 years (2000).
Transportation: Commute to work: 96.1% car, 0.0% public transportation, 1.5% walk, 2.4% work from home (2000); Travel time to work: 14.4% less than 15 minutes, 23.9% 15 to 30 minutes, 21.9% 30 to 45 minutes, 16.9% 45 to 60 minutes, 22.9% 60 minutes or more (2000)

BIG PRAIRIE (township). Covers a land area of 31.508 square miles and a water area of 4.721 square miles. Located at 43.51° N. Lat.; 85.62° W. Long. Elevation is 946 feet.
History: Big Prairie Township was organized in 1852 and named because it was then on prairie land. Later, pine trees were planted here.
Population: 2,465 (2000); Race: 96.9% White, 0.4% Black, 0.0% Asian, 0.5% American Indian and Alaska Native, 1.5% Hispanic of any race, 1.6% two or more races (2000); Density: 78.2 persons per square mile (2000); Age: 27.3% under 18, 13.3% over 64 (2000); Marriage status: 17.6% never married, 62.4% now married, 6.5% widowed, 13.5% divorced (2000); Foreign born: 0.5% (2000); Ancestry (includes multiple ancestries): 21.4% German, 11.5% Dutch, 11.0% English, 10.8% Irish, 8.2% Other groups (2000).
Economy: Employment by occupation: 6.5% management, 7.3% professional, 15.4% services, 19.3% sales, 0.9% farming, 16.9% construction, 33.6% production (2000).
Income: Per capita income: $14,900 (2000); Median household income: $32,879 (2000); Poverty rate: 12.2% (2000).
Taxes: Total city taxes per capita: $29 (1997); City property taxes per capita: $23 (1997).
Education: High school graduation rate: 72.1% (2000); College graduation rate: 4.1% (2000).
Housing: Homeownership rate: 87.0% (2000); Median home value: $76,100 (2000); Median rent: $356 per month (2000); Median age of housing: 26 years (2000).
Transportation: Commute to work: 95.0% car, 0.1% public transportation, 1.1% walk, 3.1% work from home (2000); Travel time to work: 12.8% less than 15 minutes, 21.7% 15 to 30 minutes, 16.2% 30 to 45 minutes, 22.5% 45 to 60 minutes, 26.8% 60 minutes or more (2000)

BITELY (unincorporated postal area, zip code 49309). Covers a land area of 139.977 square miles and a water area of 1.955 square miles. Located at 43.74° N. Lat.; 85.86° W. Long. Elevation is 861 feet.
History: Bitely was founded in 1889 by Steven and Jerome Bitely, who built a sawmill near the railroad station that had been placed here in 1884.
Population: 1,869 (2000); Race: 86.6% White, 8.5% Black, 0.0% Asian, 0.8% American Indian and Alaska Native, 3.5% Hispanic of any race, 2.7% two or more races (2000); Density: 13.4 persons per square mile (2000); Age: 25.1% under 18, 17.9% over 64 (2000); Marriage status: 18.7% never married, 62.9% now married, 7.4% widowed, 11.0% divorced (2000); Foreign born: 0.9% (2000); Ancestry (includes multiple ancestries): 19.3%

German, 16.1% Other groups, 10.8% Irish, 9.5% English, 6.8% Dutch (2000).
Economy: Employment by occupation: 8.1% management, 8.8% professional, 20.2% services, 21.7% sales, 3.9% farming, 13.5% construction, 23.9% production (2000).
Income: Per capita income: $13,251 (2000); Median household income: $25,711 (2000); Poverty rate: 15.9% (2000).
Education: High school graduation rate: 69.8% (2000); College graduation rate: 7.4% (2000).
Housing: Homeownership rate: 89.7% (2000); Median home value: $71,300 (2000); Median rent: $340 per month (2000); Median age of housing: 30 years (2000).
Transportation: Commute to work: 94.1% car, 0.3% public transportation, 2.3% walk, 3.0% work from home (2000); Travel time to work: 21.0% less than 15 minutes, 29.9% 15 to 30 minutes, 20.3% 30 to 45 minutes, 9.9% 45 to 60 minutes, 18.9% 60 minutes or more (2000)

BRIDGETON (township). Covers a land area of 35.472 square miles and a water area of 0.480 square miles. Located at 43.33° N. Lat.; 85.97° W. Long.
History: Bridgeton Township was organized in 1852 and named because of the bridge across the Muskegon River.
Population: 2,098 (2000); Race: 94.4% White, 0.1% Black, 0.1% Asian, 0.5% American Indian and Alaska Native, 3.1% Hispanic of any race, 3.4% two or more races (2000); Density: 59.1 persons per square mile (2000); Age: 31.7% under 18, 7.8% over 64 (2000); Marriage status: 20.5% never married, 63.9% now married, 4.9% widowed, 10.7% divorced (2000); Foreign born: 1.0% (2000); Ancestry (includes multiple ancestries): 19.0% German, 12.6% United States or American, 12.5% Irish, 10.8% Dutch, 10.8% Other groups (2000).
Economy: Single-family building permits issued: 18 (2001) / 27 (2000); Multi-family building permits issued: 0 (2001) / 0 (2000); Employment by occupation: 5.4% management, 11.0% professional, 11.7% services, 18.5% sales, 1.3% farming, 17.5% construction, 34.4% production (2000).
Income: Per capita income: $17,173 (2000); Median household income: $38,750 (2000); Poverty rate: 11.8% (2000).
Taxes: Total city taxes per capita: $39 (1997); City property taxes per capita: $35 (1997).
Education: High school graduation rate: 72.9% (2000); College graduation rate: 6.7% (2000).
Housing: Homeownership rate: 87.1% (2000); Median home value: $88,100 (2000); Median rent: $378 per month (2000); Median age of housing: 22 years (2000).
Transportation: Commute to work: 95.3% car, 0.0% public transportation, 0.8% walk, 2.9% work from home (2000); Travel time to work: 10.0% less than 15 minutes, 31.9% 15 to 30 minutes, 24.8% 30 to 45 minutes, 19.8% 45 to 60 minutes, 13.4% 60 minutes or more (2000)

BROOKS (township). Covers a land area of 31.750 square miles and a water area of 2.303 square miles. Located at 43.42° N. Lat.; 85.75° W. Long.
History: Brooks Township was named for John A. Brooks, a lumberman.
Population: 3,671 (2000); Race: 95.9% White, 0.4% Black, 0.2% Asian, 0.6% American Indian and Alaska Native, 2.7% Hispanic of any race, 1.2% two or more races (2000); Density: 115.6 persons per square mile (2000); Age: 27.2% under 18, 13.9% over 64 (2000); Marriage status: 17.8% never married, 64.0% now married, 5.2% widowed, 13.0% divorced (2000); Foreign born: 1.3% (2000); Ancestry (includes multiple ancestries): 21.9% German, 13.9% Dutch, 12.8% English, 12.0% Irish, 9.9% Other groups (2000).
Economy: Employment by occupation: 9.2% management, 16.6% professional, 12.8% services, 24.1% sales, 1.0% farming, 11.5% construction, 24.8% production (2000).
Income: Per capita income: $19,088 (2000); Median household income: $42,434 (2000); Poverty rate: 11.1% (2000).
Taxes: Total city taxes per capita: $34 (1997); City property taxes per capita: $34 (1997).
Education: High school graduation rate: 82.2% (2000); College graduation rate: 16.1% (2000).
Housing: Homeownership rate: 89.6% (2000); Median home value: $111,600 (2000); Median rent: $406 per month (2000); Median age of housing: 29 years (2000).
Transportation: Commute to work: 95.1% car, 0.0% public transportation, 0.4% walk, 3.9% work from home (2000); Travel time to work: 27.7% less than 15 minutes, 21.5% 15 to 30 minutes, 15.6% 30 to 45 minutes, 17.4% 45 to 60 minutes, 17.9% 60 minutes or more (2000)

CROTON (township). Covers a land area of 34.040 square miles and a water area of 2.322 square miles. Located at 43.42° N. Lat.; 85.63° W. Long. Elevation is 752 feet.
History: Croton was settled in 1840. First called Stearns Mills after a settler who built a sawmill here, the name was changed in 1850 to Croton, after the Croton Water Works in New York.
Population: 3,042 (2000); Race: 97.4% White, 0.0% Black, 0.3% Asian, 0.3% American Indian and Alaska Native, 1.4% Hispanic of any race, 1.2% two or more races (2000); Density: 89.4 persons per square mile (2000); Age: 25.4% under 18, 13.4% over 64 (2000); Marriage status: 19.0% never married, 64.9% now married, 6.8% widowed, 9.3% divorced (2000); Foreign born: 0.8% (2000); Ancestry (includes multiple ancestries): 21.0% German, 14.9% Dutch, 13.1% English, 12.1% Irish, 9.5% United States or American (2000).
Economy: Single-family building permits issued: 29 (2001) / 40 (2000); Multi-family building permits issued: 0 (2001) / 0 (2000); Employment by occupation: 11.4% management, 10.6% professional, 11.3% services, 20.4% sales, 1.0% farming, 16.8% construction, 28.4% production (2000).
Income: Per capita income: $21,036 (2000); Median household income: $41,596 (2000); Poverty rate: 7.4% (2000).
Taxes: Total city taxes per capita: $61 (1997); City property taxes per capita: $53 (1997).
Education: High school graduation rate: 78.8% (2000); College graduation rate: 8.1% (2000).
Housing: Homeownership rate: 88.5% (2000); Median home value: $115,600 (2000); Median rent: $401 per month (2000); Median age of housing: 24 years (2000).
Transportation: Commute to work: 92.9% car, 0.8% public transportation, 1.3% walk, 3.9% work from home (2000); Travel time to work: 17.5% less than 15 minutes, 23.0% 15 to 30 minutes, 18.8% 30 to 45 minutes, 24.4% 45 to 60 minutes, 16.4% 60 minutes or more (2000)

DAYTON (township). Covers a land area of 33.812 square miles and a water area of 0.367 square miles. Located at 43.50° N. Lat.; 85.98° W. Long.
Population: 2,002 (2000); Race: 97.2% White, 0.0% Black, 0.9% Asian, 0.2% American Indian and Alaska Native, 3.0% Hispanic of any race, 1.2% two or more races (2000); Density: 59.2 persons per square mile (2000); Age: 31.5% under 18, 11.1% over 64 (2000); Marriage status: 23.3% never married, 69.2% now married, 3.2% widowed, 4.3% divorced (2000); Foreign born: 1.2% (2000); Ancestry (includes multiple ancestries): 25.9% Dutch, 25.6% German, 13.5% English, 11.6% Irish, 11.1% Other groups (2000).
Economy: Employment by occupation: 13.1% management, 14.7% professional, 13.4% services, 25.6% sales, 3.6% farming, 11.3% construction, 18.4% production (2000).
Income: Per capita income: $19,433 (2000); Median household income: $44,770 (2000); Poverty rate: 8.5% (2000).
Taxes: Total city taxes per capita: $18 (1997); City property taxes per capita: $18 (1997).
Education: High school graduation rate: 87.0% (2000); College graduation rate: 14.6% (2000).
Housing: Homeownership rate: 90.2% (2000); Median home value: $94,900 (2000); Median rent: $375 per month (2000); Median age of housing: 41 years (2000).
Transportation: Commute to work: 90.4% car, 0.0% public transportation, 2.4% walk, 7.2% work from home (2000); Travel time to work: 60.0% less than 15 minutes, 15.5% 15 to 30 minutes, 11.3% 30 to 45 minutes, 7.2% 45 to 60 minutes, 6.0% 60 minutes or more (2000)

DENVER (township). Covers a land area of 35.362 square miles and a water area of 0.426 square miles. Located at 43.59° N. Lat.; 85.99° W. Long.
Population: 1,971 (2000); Race: 96.0% White, 0.3% Black, 0.0% Asian, 1.4% American Indian and Alaska Native, 3.2% Hispanic of any race, 1.3% two or more races (2000); Density: 55.7 persons per square mile (2000); Age: 30.1% under 18, 13.1% over 64 (2000); Marriage status: 18.5% never married, 61.9% now married, 7.7% widowed, 11.9% divorced (2000); Foreign born: 1.0% (2000); Ancestry (includes multiple ancestries): 21.3% German, 11.9% Irish, 11.7% Other groups, 10.6% Dutch, 9.0% English (2000).
Economy: Employment by occupation: 7.1% management, 10.4% professional, 17.1% services, 20.1% sales, 1.5% farming, 12.4% construction, 31.3% production (2000).
Income: Per capita income: $14,746 (2000); Median household income: $33,365 (2000); Poverty rate: 14.1% (2000).
Taxes: Total city taxes per capita: $21 (1997); City property taxes per capita: $21 (1997).

Education: High school graduation rate: 74.2% (2000); College graduation rate: 5.8% (2000).
Housing: Homeownership rate: 83.2% (2000); Median home value: $72,600 (2000); Median rent: $323 per month (2000); Median age of housing: 24 years (2000).
Transportation: Commute to work: 92.0% car, 0.3% public transportation, 1.8% walk, 4.7% work from home (2000); Travel time to work: 21.5% less than 15 minutes, 31.2% 15 to 30 minutes, 14.7% 30 to 45 minutes, 17.7% 45 to 60 minutes, 14.9% 60 minutes or more (2000)

ENSLEY (township). Covers a land area of 35.675 square miles and a water area of 0.414 square miles. Located at 43.33° N. Lat.; 85.63° W. Long.
Population: 2,474 (2000); Race: 95.8% White, 0.4% Black, 0.4% Asian, 0.4% American Indian and Alaska Native, 3.3% Hispanic of any race, 2.1% two or more races (2000); Density: 69.3 persons per square mile (2000); Age: 31.1% under 18, 7.6% over 64 (2000); Marriage status: 18.8% never married, 69.3% now married, 2.6% widowed, 9.3% divorced (2000); Foreign born: 2.2% (2000); Ancestry (includes multiple ancestries): 21.9% German, 16.7% Dutch, 11.7% United States or American, 11.6% Irish, 9.3% English (2000).
Economy: Single-family building permits issued: 16 (2001) / 1 (2000); Multi-family building permits issued: 0 (2001) / 0 (2000); Employment by occupation: 5.5% management, 9.4% professional, 11.7% services, 22.7% sales, 0.0% farming, 15.4% construction, 35.3% production (2000).
Income: Per capita income: $17,845 (2000); Median household income: $47,993 (2000); Poverty rate: 6.5% (2000).
Taxes: Total city taxes per capita: $23 (1997); City property taxes per capita: $16 (1997).
Education: High school graduation rate: 84.5% (2000); College graduation rate: 8.0% (2000).
Housing: Homeownership rate: 95.0% (2000); Median home value: $109,900 (2000); Median rent: $456 per month (2000); Median age of housing: 21 years (2000).
Transportation: Commute to work: 96.0% car, 0.4% public transportation, 1.1% walk, 2.5% work from home (2000); Travel time to work: 14.7% less than 15 minutes, 22.1% 15 to 30 minutes, 33.2% 30 to 45 minutes, 21.5% 45 to 60 minutes, 8.6% 60 minutes or more (2000)

EVERETT (township). Covers a land area of 35.560 square miles and a water area of 0.238 square miles. Located at 43.51° N. Lat.; 85.74° W. Long.
Population: 1,985 (2000); Race: 93.8% White, 2.7% Black, 0.0% Asian, 1.0% American Indian and Alaska Native, 1.6% Hispanic of any race, 1.5% two or more races (2000); Density: 55.8 persons per square mile (2000); Age: 32.4% under 18, 8.6% over 64 (2000); Marriage status: 22.3% never married, 60.1% now married, 4.6% widowed, 13.0% divorced (2000); Foreign born: 0.4% (2000); Ancestry (includes multiple ancestries): 25.4% German, 12.8% Dutch, 11.6% Other groups, 11.6% Irish, 9.4% Polish (2000).
Economy: Employment by occupation: 5.6% management, 10.6% professional, 14.2% services, 22.7% sales, 1.9% farming, 18.2% construction, 26.6% production (2000).
Income: Per capita income: $14,164 (2000); Median household income: $35,000 (2000); Poverty rate: 16.2% (2000).
Taxes: Total city taxes per capita: $32 (1997); City property taxes per capita: $32 (1997).
Education: High school graduation rate: 72.9% (2000); College graduation rate: 6.3% (2000).
Housing: Homeownership rate: 82.1% (2000); Median home value: $77,000 (2000); Median rent: $338 per month (2000); Median age of housing: 26 years (2000).
Transportation: Commute to work: 94.2% car, 0.0% public transportation, 0.9% walk, 3.7% work from home (2000); Travel time to work: 30.9% less than 15 minutes, 24.3% 15 to 30 minutes, 10.9% 30 to 45 minutes, 11.4% 45 to 60 minutes, 22.5% 60 minutes or more (2000)

FREMONT (city). Covers a land area of 3.331 square miles and a water area of 1.282 square miles. Located at 43.46° N. Lat.; 85.94° W. Long. Elevation is 823 feet.
History: Native American village sites and mounds nearby. Settled 1855; incorporated as village 1875, as city 1911.
Population: 4,224 (2000); Race: 96.0% White, 0.3% Black, 1.4% Asian, 0.5% American Indian and Alaska Native, 1.7% Hispanic of any race, 1.0% two or more races (2000); Density: 1,268.3 persons per square mile (2000); Age: 27.5% under 18, 19.6% over 64 (2000); Marriage status: 20.8% never married, 58.8% now married, 11.8% widowed, 8.6% divorced (2000); Foreign born: 2.6% (2000); Ancestry (includes multiple ancestries): 23.2% German, 22.1% Dutch, 14.3% Irish, 14.2% English, 7.7% Other groups (2000).
Economy: Railroad terminus and airport here. In dairying and fruit-growing area; food processing; baby-food processing. Manistee National Forest to West, North, and East. Employment by occupation: 15.0% management, 24.4% professional, 13.6% services, 23.3% sales, 0.4% farming, 5.2% construction, 18.1% production (2000).
Income: Per capita income: $19,475 (2000); Median household income: $32,246 (2000); Poverty rate: 12.2% (2000).
Taxes: Total city taxes per capita: $487 (1997); City property taxes per capita: $487 (1997).
Education: High school graduation rate: 83.3% (2000); College graduation rate: 23.3% (2000).

School District(s)

Fremont Public School District (KG-12)
2000 Enrollment: 2,784 231-924-2350
Housing: Homeownership rate: 70.9% (2000); Median home value: $90,600 (2000); Median rent: $373 per month (2000); Median age of housing: 36 years (2000).
Hospitals: Gerber Memorial Hospital (73 beds)
Safety: Violent crime rate: 14.1 per 10,000 population; Property crime rate: 339.1 per 10,000 population (2001).
Newspapers: Fremont Times-Indicator (1 x week)
Transportation: Commute to work: 92.3% car, 0.3% public transportation, 4.2% walk, 2.7% work from home (2000); Travel time to work: 63.8% less than 15 minutes, 12.9% 15 to 30 minutes, 6.8% 30 to 45 minutes, 6.8% 45 to 60 minutes, 9.7% 60 minutes or more (2000)

Additional Information Contacts

Fremont Chamber of Commerce 231-924-0770
West Central Board of Realtors 231-924-6555

GARFIELD (township). Covers a land area of 32.990 square miles and a water area of 1.050 square miles. Located at 43.42° N. Lat.; 85.84° W. Long.
Population: 2,464 (2000); Race: 93.9% White, 0.0% Black, 1.3% Asian, 0.2% American Indian and Alaska Native, 6.7% Hispanic of any race, 1.6% two or more races (2000); Density: 74.7 persons per square mile (2000); Age: 27.9% under 18, 18.0% over 64 (2000); Marriage status: 18.7% never married, 62.6% now married, 7.3% widowed, 11.4% divorced (2000); Foreign born: 5.8% (2000); Ancestry (includes multiple ancestries): 21.2% German, 12.9% Dutch, 11.1% English, 10.9% Other groups, 9.3% Irish (2000).
Economy: Employment by occupation: 10.0% management, 12.2% professional, 13.7% services, 23.2% sales, 5.7% farming, 12.5% construction, 22.8% production (2000).
Income: Per capita income: $16,410 (2000); Median household income: $38,548 (2000); Poverty rate: 9.8% (2000).
Taxes: Total city taxes per capita: $23 (1997); City property taxes per capita: $19 (1997).
Education: High school graduation rate: 77.5% (2000); College graduation rate: 14.3% (2000).
Housing: Homeownership rate: 81.6% (2000); Median home value: $102,700 (2000); Median rent: $313 per month (2000); Median age of housing: 31 years (2000).
Transportation: Commute to work: 91.9% car, 0.0% public transportation, 2.4% walk, 5.5% work from home (2000); Travel time to work: 38.4% less than 15 minutes, 23.5% 15 to 30 minutes, 11.5% 30 to 45 minutes, 11.9% 45 to 60 minutes, 14.7% 60 minutes or more (2000)

GOODWELL (township). Covers a land area of 35.648 square miles and a water area of 0.095 square miles. Located at 43.60° N. Lat.; 85.63° W. Long.
Population: 551 (2000); Race: 98.1% White, 0.0% Black, 0.0% Asian, 0.4% American Indian and Alaska Native, 1.2% Hispanic of any race, 0.9% two or more races (2000); Density: 15.5 persons per square mile (2000); Age: 34.7% under 18, 6.2% over 64 (2000); Marriage status: 22.6% never married, 64.0% now married, 3.6% widowed, 9.9% divorced (2000); Foreign born: 1.1% (2000); Ancestry (includes multiple ancestries): 29.3% German, 15.9% Irish, 11.5% English, 9.0% Other groups, 6.7% Dutch (2000).
Economy: Employment by occupation: 9.6% management, 11.3% professional, 12.2% services, 17.4% sales, 1.7% farming, 16.1% construction, 31.7% production (2000).
Income: Per capita income: $14,498 (2000); Median household income: $37,813 (2000); Poverty rate: 11.0% (2000).
Taxes: Total city taxes per capita: $133 (1997); City property taxes per capita: $133 (1997).
Education: High school graduation rate: 81.0% (2000); College graduation rate: 9.9% (2000).

Housing: Homeownership rate: 88.4% (2000); Median home value: $48,500 (2000); Median rent: $367 per month (2000); Median age of housing: 30 years (2000).
Transportation: Commute to work: 96.9% car, 0.0% public transportation, 0.0% walk, 3.1% work from home (2000); Travel time to work: 7.8% less than 15 minutes, 39.0% 15 to 30 minutes, 21.1% 30 to 45 minutes, 9.6% 45 to 60 minutes, 22.5% 60 minutes or more (2000)

GRANT (city). Covers a land area of 0.653 square miles and a water area of 0.021 square miles. Located at 43.33° N. Lat.; 85.81° W. Long. Elevation is 835 feet.
History: Andrew J. Squier built a sawmill here in 1882. When the Chicago & Western Michigan Railroad established a station, Squier named it Grant Station, for General Ulysses S. Grant. Grant was incorporated as a village in 1893.
Population: 881 (2000); Race: 93.4% White, 0.5% Black, 0.0% Asian, 0.0% American Indian and Alaska Native, 13.2% Hispanic of any race, 0.9% two or more races (2000); Density: 1,350.1 persons per square mile (2000); Age: 30.2% under 18, 16.0% over 64 (2000); Marriage status: 15.0% never married, 57.2% now married, 12.9% widowed, 15.0% divorced (2000); Foreign born: 5.6% (2000); Ancestry (includes multiple ancestries): 16.0% Other groups, 15.9% United States or American, 13.5% German, 13.3% Dutch, 8.1% English (2000).
Economy: Employment by occupation: 8.9% management, 18.9% professional, 16.9% services, 20.8% sales, 2.7% farming, 9.9% construction, 21.8% production (2000).
Income: Per capita income: $15,308 (2000); Median household income: $30,972 (2000); Poverty rate: 20.8% (2000).
Taxes: Total city taxes per capita: $173 (1997); City property taxes per capita: $172 (1997).
Education: High school graduation rate: 77.5% (2000); College graduation rate: 10.0% (2000).

School District(s)

Grant Public School District (KG-12)
2000 Enrollment: 2,435 231-834-5621
Housing: Homeownership rate: 71.6% (2000); Median home value: $77,700 (2000); Median rent: $290 per month (2000); Median age of housing: 44 years (2000).
Safety: Violent crime rate: 33.9 per 10,000 population; Property crime rate: 327.3 per 10,000 population (2001).
Transportation: Commute to work: 89.9% car, 4.0% public transportation, 4.0% walk, 1.5% work from home (2000); Travel time to work: 34.8% less than 15 minutes, 18.9% 15 to 30 minutes, 22.5% 30 to 45 minutes, 11.0% 45 to 60 minutes, 12.8% 60 minutes or more (2000)

GRANT (township). Covers a land area of 35.906 square miles and a water area of 0.170 square miles. Located at 43.34° N. Lat.; 85.74° W. Long. Elevation is 835 feet.
Population: 3,130 (2000); Race: 91.7% White, 0.1% Black, 0.1% Asian, 0.8% American Indian and Alaska Native, 11.7% Hispanic of any race, 2.0% two or more races (2000); Density: 87.2 persons per square mile (2000); Age: 33.3% under 18, 8.9% over 64 (2000); Marriage status: 23.0% never married, 65.4% now married, 2.7% widowed, 9.0% divorced (2000); Foreign born: 2.5% (2000); Ancestry (includes multiple ancestries): 21.4% German, 18.9% Dutch, 16.2% Other groups, 9.3% Irish, 8.5% United States or American (2000).
Economy: In dairy and fruit region. Manufacturing. Mainistee National Forest to Northeast. Employment by occupation: 8.3% management, 11.2% professional, 11.2% services, 23.0% sales, 3.4% farming, 15.2% construction, 27.8% production (2000).
Income: Per capita income: $15,910 (2000); Median household income: $41,295 (2000); Poverty rate: 4.3% (2000).
Taxes: Total city taxes per capita: $69 (1997); City property taxes per capita: $69 (1997).
Education: High school graduation rate: 79.5% (2000); College graduation rate: 10.7% (2000).
Housing: Homeownership rate: 89.7% (2000); Median home value: $95,200 (2000); Median rent: $434 per month (2000); Median age of housing: 25 years (2000).
Transportation: Commute to work: 93.4% car, 0.0% public transportation, 1.8% walk, 4.1% work from home (2000); Travel time to work: 21.6% less than 15 minutes, 23.7% 15 to 30 minutes, 19.4% 30 to 45 minutes, 26.3% 45 to 60 minutes, 8.9% 60 minutes or more (2000)

HOME (township). Covers a land area of 35.577 square miles and a water area of 0.022 square miles. Located at 43.76° N. Lat.; 85.74° W. Long.
Population: 261 (2000); Race: 99.6% White, 0.0% Black, 0.0% Asian, 0.0% American Indian and Alaska Native, 0.0% Hispanic of any race, 0.4% two or more races (2000); Density: 7.3 persons per square mile (2000); Age: 28.7% under 18, 16.9% over 64 (2000); Marriage status: 22.0% never married, 65.5% now married, 4.5% widowed, 8.1% divorced (2000); Foreign born: 0.0% (2000); Ancestry (includes multiple ancestries): 21.0% German, 11.8% United States or American, 8.5% English, 6.6% Polish, 6.3% Dutch (2000).
Economy: Employment by occupation: 10.2% management, 10.2% professional, 13.9% services, 30.6% sales, 10.2% farming, 4.6% construction, 20.4% production (2000).
Income: Per capita income: $14,244 (2000); Median household income: $31,964 (2000); Poverty rate: 3.7% (2000).
Taxes: Total city taxes per capita: $130 (1997); City property taxes per capita: $113 (1997).
Education: High school graduation rate: 76.1% (2000); College graduation rate: 5.9% (2000).
Housing: Homeownership rate: 87.4% (2000); Median home value: $57,500 (2000); Median rent: $325 per month (2000); Median age of housing: 29 years (2000).
Transportation: Commute to work: 85.8% car, 0.0% public transportation, 2.8% walk, 6.6% work from home (2000); Travel time to work: 16.2% less than 15 minutes, 52.5% 15 to 30 minutes, 18.2% 30 to 45 minutes, 2.0% 45 to 60 minutes, 11.1% 60 minutes or more (2000)

LILLEY (township). Covers a land area of 34.478 square miles and a water area of 1.090 square miles. Located at 43.77° N. Lat.; 85.85° W. Long. Elevation is 865 feet.
Population: 788 (2000); Race: 91.0% White, 5.8% Black, 0.0% Asian, 0.9% American Indian and Alaska Native, 1.0% Hispanic of any race, 2.1% two or more races (2000); Density: 22.9 persons per square mile (2000); Age: 26.2% under 18, 17.9% over 64 (2000); Marriage status: 16.4% never married, 64.9% now married, 7.2% widowed, 11.5% divorced (2000); Foreign born: 0.8% (2000); Ancestry (includes multiple ancestries): 20.3% German, 10.7% English, 10.5% Polish, 10.5% Other groups, 9.2% Irish (2000).
Economy: Employment by occupation: 7.2% management, 7.2% professional, 21.5% services, 22.4% sales, 0.8% farming, 14.8% construction, 26.2% production (2000).
Income: Per capita income: $12,765 (2000); Median household income: $25,870 (2000); Poverty rate: 20.2% (2000).
Taxes: Total city taxes per capita: $186 (1997); City property taxes per capita: $179 (1997).
Education: High school graduation rate: 73.1% (2000); College graduation rate: 7.0% (2000).
Housing: Homeownership rate: 92.6% (2000); Median home value: $69,800 (2000); Median rent: $359 per month (2000); Median age of housing: 33 years (2000).
Transportation: Commute to work: 91.6% car, 0.9% public transportation, 3.1% walk, 4.4% work from home (2000); Travel time to work: 30.0% less than 15 minutes, 30.0% 15 to 30 minutes, 18.9% 30 to 45 minutes, 2.8% 45 to 60 minutes, 18.4% 60 minutes or more (2000)

LINCOLN (township). Covers a land area of 35.100 square miles and a water area of 0.480 square miles. Located at 43.59° N. Lat.; 85.86° W. Long.
Population: 1,338 (2000); Race: 94.8% White, 1.4% Black, 0.0% Asian, 1.3% American Indian and Alaska Native, 1.1% Hispanic of any race, 2.3% two or more races (2000); Density: 38.1 persons per square mile (2000); Age: 27.4% under 18, 13.2% over 64 (2000); Marriage status: 19.0% never married, 61.9% now married, 6.3% widowed, 12.7% divorced (2000); Foreign born: 0.5% (2000); Ancestry (includes multiple ancestries): 24.7% German, 16.8% Irish, 12.7% English, 10.6% Other groups, 7.3% Dutch (2000).
Economy: Employment by occupation: 7.9% management, 9.7% professional, 21.0% services, 19.0% sales, 0.6% farming, 11.9% construction, 29.9% production (2000).
Income: Per capita income: $15,697 (2000); Median household income: $35,739 (2000); Poverty rate: 12.3% (2000).
Taxes: Total city taxes per capita: $41 (1997); City property taxes per capita: $41 (1997).
Education: High school graduation rate: 79.3% (2000); College graduation rate: 8.4% (2000).
Housing: Homeownership rate: 86.1% (2000); Median home value: $80,200 (2000); Median rent: $380 per month (2000); Median age of housing: 28 years (2000).
Transportation: Commute to work: 92.0% car, 0.6% public transportation, 0.0% walk, 4.5% work from home (2000); Travel time to work: 13.5% less

than 15 minutes, 39.7% 15 to 30 minutes, 9.6% 30 to 45 minutes, 7.9% 45 to 60 minutes, 29.3% 60 minutes or more (2000)

MERRILL (township). Covers a land area of 34.913 square miles and a water area of 0.932 square miles. Located at 43.70° N. Lat.; 85.85° W. Long.
Population: 590 (2000); Race: 72.9% White, 18.0% Black, 0.0% Asian, 2.7% American Indian and Alaska Native, 4.4% Hispanic of any race, 6.1% two or more races (2000); Density: 16.9 persons per square mile (2000); Age: 21.7% under 18, 23.5% over 64 (2000); Marriage status: 17.5% never married, 51.9% now married, 11.7% widowed, 18.9% divorced (2000); Foreign born: 0.5% (2000); Ancestry (includes multiple ancestries): 29.9% Other groups, 14.5% German, 11.8% United States or American, 9.2% English, 7.7% Irish (2000).
Economy: Employment by occupation: 4.5% management, 6.0% professional, 24.0% services, 17.0% sales, 2.0% farming, 17.5% construction, 29.0% production (2000).
Income: Per capita income: $13,526 (2000); Median household income: $22,917 (2000); Poverty rate: 19.8% (2000).
Taxes: Total city taxes per capita: $114 (1997); City property taxes per capita: $114 (1997).
Education: High school graduation rate: 64.6% (2000); College graduation rate: 8.8% (2000).
Housing: Homeownership rate: 86.5% (2000); Median home value: $70,300 (2000); Median rent: $313 per month (2000); Median age of housing: 29 years (2000).
Transportation: Commute to work: 94.2% car, 0.0% public transportation, 2.6% walk, 2.1% work from home (2000); Travel time to work: 11.4% less than 15 minutes, 17.3% 15 to 30 minutes, 24.3% 30 to 45 minutes, 18.4% 45 to 60 minutes, 28.6% 60 minutes or more (2000)

MONROE (township). Covers a land area of 35.834 square miles and a water area of 0.171 square miles. Located at 43.69° N. Lat.; 85.73° W. Long.
Population: 324 (2000); Race: 95.1% White, 0.6% Black, 0.0% Asian, 0.6% American Indian and Alaska Native, 0.6% Hispanic of any race, 3.7% two or more races (2000); Density: 9.0 persons per square mile (2000); Age: 20.7% under 18, 23.2% over 64 (2000); Marriage status: 20.1% never married, 64.4% now married, 7.6% widowed, 7.9% divorced (2000); Foreign born: 0.9% (2000); Ancestry (includes multiple ancestries): 25.0% German, 14.6% English, 14.0% Dutch, 13.1% Irish, 12.5% French (except Basque) (2000).
Economy: Employment by occupation: 11.5% management, 19.1% professional, 10.7% services, 16.0% sales, 0.0% farming, 19.8% construction, 22.9% production (2000).
Income: Per capita income: $16,214 (2000); Median household income: $30,156 (2000); Poverty rate: 11.3% (2000).
Taxes: Total city taxes per capita: $90 (1997); City property taxes per capita: $84 (1997).
Education: High school graduation rate: 70.6% (2000); College graduation rate: 11.0% (2000).
Housing: Homeownership rate: 91.5% (2000); Median home value: $85,000 (2000); Median rent: $375 per month (2000); Median age of housing: 25 years (2000).
Transportation: Commute to work: 95.4% car, 1.5% public transportation, 0.0% walk, 3.1% work from home (2000); Travel time to work: 11.8% less than 15 minutes, 34.6% 15 to 30 minutes, 29.9% 30 to 45 minutes, 3.9% 45 to 60 minutes, 19.7% 60 minutes or more (2000)

NEWAYGO (city). Covers a land area of 3.332 square miles and a water area of 0.138 square miles. Located at 43.41° N. Lat.; 85.79° W. Long. Elevation is 633 feet.
History: Newaygo was settled in 1836 and incorporated as a village in 1867. Industries in the early 1900's included a screw factory and a furniture supply factory.
Population: 1,670 (2000); Race: 94.3% White, 0.6% Black, 0.1% Asian, 0.2% American Indian and Alaska Native, 4.7% Hispanic of any race, 1.7% two or more races (2000); Density: 501.2 persons per square mile (2000); Age: 32.4% under 18, 12.1% over 64 (2000); Marriage status: 25.0% never married, 53.3% now married, 6.2% widowed, 15.4% divorced (2000); Foreign born: 1.5% (2000); Ancestry (includes multiple ancestries): 18.9% German, 12.5% English, 11.7% Other groups, 10.8% Dutch, 10.6% United States or American (2000).
Economy: Employment by occupation: 6.3% management, 14.7% professional, 15.7% services, 24.4% sales, 0.7% farming, 12.3% construction, 25.9% production (2000).
Income: Per capita income: $14,643 (2000); Median household income: $32,273 (2000); Poverty rate: 16.5% (2000).
Taxes: Total city taxes per capita: $186 (1997); City property taxes per capita: $179 (1997).
Education: High school graduation rate: 79.4% (2000); College graduation rate: 10.2% (2000).

School District(s)

Newaygo Public School District (KG-12)
2000 Enrollment: 2,083 231-652-6984

Housing: Homeownership rate: 73.9% (2000); Median home value: $74,500 (2000); Median rent: $344 per month (2000); Median age of housing: 44 years (2000).
Safety: Violent crime rate: 77.4 per 10,000 population; Property crime rate: 768.3 per 10,000 population (2001).
Transportation: Commute to work: 94.4% car, 0.0% public transportation, 1.9% walk, 3.3% work from home (2000); Travel time to work: 39.4% less than 15 minutes, 20.8% 15 to 30 minutes, 9.5% 30 to 45 minutes, 15.9% 45 to 60 minutes, 14.4% 60 minutes or more (2000)

Additional Information Contacts

Newaygo Chamber of Commerce 231-652-3068
Newaygo County Tourist Council 231-652-9298

NORWICH (township). Covers a land area of 35.253 square miles and a water area of 0.177 square miles. Located at 43.69° N. Lat.; 85.62° W. Long.
Population: 557 (2000); Race: 97.0% White, 0.0% Black, 0.0% Asian, 0.7% American Indian and Alaska Native, 4.8% Hispanic of any race, 1.1% two or more races (2000); Density: 15.8 persons per square mile (2000); Age: 25.8% under 18, 9.7% over 64 (2000); Marriage status: 24.6% never married, 65.8% now married, 4.2% widowed, 5.4% divorced (2000); Foreign born: 1.1% (2000); Ancestry (includes multiple ancestries): 26.2% German, 13.6% French (except Basque), 11.2% Irish, 11.0% English, 7.6% United States or American (2000).
Economy: Employment by occupation: 9.8% management, 18.9% professional, 23.0% services, 19.6% sales, 2.3% farming, 12.8% construction, 13.6% production (2000).
Income: Per capita income: $17,054 (2000); Median household income: $36,250 (2000); Poverty rate: 13.8% (2000).
Taxes: Total city taxes per capita: $67 (1997); City property taxes per capita: $67 (1997).
Education: High school graduation rate: 86.0% (2000); College graduation rate: 14.9% (2000).
Housing: Homeownership rate: 90.3% (2000); Median home value: $84,200 (2000); Median rent: $338 per month (2000); Median age of housing: 28 years (2000).
Transportation: Commute to work: 90.0% car, 0.0% public transportation, 2.3% walk, 6.1% work from home (2000); Travel time to work: 22.9% less than 15 minutes, 48.6% 15 to 30 minutes, 11.4% 30 to 45 minutes, 4.9% 45 to 60 minutes, 12.2% 60 minutes or more (2000)

SHERIDAN CHARTER (township). Covers a land area of 33.184 square miles and a water area of 0.025 square miles. Located at 43.43° N. Lat.; 85.97° W. Long.
Population: 2,423 (2000); Race: 97.1% White, 0.1% Black, 0.6% Asian, 0.1% American Indian and Alaska Native, 3.2% Hispanic of any race, 0.7% two or more races (2000); Density: 73.0 persons per square mile (2000); Age: 29.1% under 18, 11.4% over 64 (2000); Marriage status: 18.5% never married, 71.6% now married, 3.6% widowed, 6.3% divorced (2000); Foreign born: 1.2% (2000); Ancestry (includes multiple ancestries): 28.5% German, 21.5% Dutch, 10.2% English, 9.3% United States or American, 7.2% Irish (2000).
Economy: Employment by occupation: 9.3% management, 20.0% professional, 13.6% services, 26.3% sales, 1.5% farming, 11.8% construction, 17.6% production (2000).
Income: Per capita income: $21,834 (2000); Median household income: $41,875 (2000); Poverty rate: 7.7% (2000).
Taxes: Total city taxes per capita: $24 (1997); City property taxes per capita: $18 (1997).
Education: High school graduation rate: 86.9% (2000); College graduation rate: 20.9% (2000).
Housing: Homeownership rate: 88.6% (2000); Median home value: $90,500 (2000); Median rent: $373 per month (2000); Median age of housing: 43 years (2000).
Transportation: Commute to work: 91.3% car, 0.4% public transportation, 2.4% walk, 5.6% work from home (2000); Travel time to work: 52.4% less than 15 minutes, 23.7% 15 to 30 minutes, 13.3% 30 to 45 minutes, 4.4% 45 to 60 minutes, 6.2% 60 minutes or more (2000)

SHERMAN (township). Covers a land area of 34.618 square miles and a water area of 1.217 square miles. Located at 43.51° N. Lat.; 85.86° W. Long.
Population: 2,159 (2000); Race: 97.1% White, 0.2% Black, 0.1% Asian, 0.2% American Indian and Alaska Native, 3.0% Hispanic of any race, 1.3% two or more races (2000); Density: 62.4 persons per square mile (2000); Age: 27.1% under 18, 17.6% over 64 (2000); Marriage status: 18.8% never married, 64.6% now married, 8.3% widowed, 8.3% divorced (2000); Foreign born: 0.8% (2000); Ancestry (includes multiple ancestries): 22.8% German, 15.7% Dutch, 10.4% English, 9.9% Irish, 7.1% United States or American (2000).
Economy: Single-family building permits issued: 18 (2001) / 14 (2000); Multi-family building permits issued: 0 (2001) / 0 (2000); Employment by occupation: 10.2% management, 16.6% professional, 17.9% services, 23.2% sales, 0.7% farming, 10.0% construction, 21.3% production (2000).
Income: Per capita income: $16,195 (2000); Median household income: $40,163 (2000); Poverty rate: 10.2% (2000).
Taxes: Total city taxes per capita: $27 (1997); City property taxes per capita: $24 (1997).
Education: High school graduation rate: 80.0% (2000); College graduation rate: 11.5% (2000).
Housing: Homeownership rate: 89.7% (2000); Median home value: $86,100 (2000); Median rent: $339 per month (2000); Median age of housing: 33 years (2000).
Transportation: Commute to work: 94.2% car, 0.0% public transportation, 1.1% walk, 4.2% work from home (2000); Travel time to work: 35.0% less than 15 minutes, 30.3% 15 to 30 minutes, 8.4% 30 to 45 minutes, 9.7% 45 to 60 minutes, 16.6% 60 minutes or more (2000)

TROY (township). Covers a land area of 36.167 square miles and a water area of 0.084 square miles. Located at 43.78° N. Lat.; 85.98° W. Long. Elevation is 833 feet.
Population: 243 (2000); Race: 94.2% White, 0.0% Black, 0.0% Asian, 0.0% American Indian and Alaska Native, 5.8% Hispanic of any race, 0.8% two or more races (2000); Density: 6.7 persons per square mile (2000); Age: 24.7% under 18, 7.8% over 64 (2000); Marriage status: 22.8% never married, 62.4% now married, 1.6% widowed, 13.2% divorced (2000); Foreign born: 0.8% (2000); Ancestry (includes multiple ancestries): 23.0% German, 18.5% Irish, 18.1% United States or American, 10.3% Other groups, 7.8% French Canadian (2000).
Economy: Employment by occupation: 17.0% management, 8.0% professional, 25.9% services, 16.1% sales, 7.1% farming, 11.6% construction, 14.3% production (2000).
Income: Per capita income: $12,665 (2000); Median household income: $26,250 (2000); Poverty rate: 19.8% (2000).
Taxes: Total city taxes per capita: $90 (1997); City property taxes per capita: $90 (1997).
Education: High school graduation rate: 76.6% (2000); College graduation rate: 6.2% (2000).
Housing: Homeownership rate: 77.9% (2000); Median home value: $42,900 (2000); Median rent: $319 per month (2000); Median age of housing: 14 years (2000).
Transportation: Commute to work: 100.0% car, 0.0% public transportation, 0.0% walk, 0.0% work from home (2000); Travel time to work: 31.8% less than 15 minutes, 14.5% 15 to 30 minutes, 27.3% 30 to 45 minutes, 13.6% 45 to 60 minutes, 12.7% 60 minutes or more (2000)

WHITE CLOUD (city). Covers a land area of 1.928 square miles and a water area of 0.070 square miles. Located at 43.55° N. Lat.; 85.77° W. Long. Elevation is 871 feet.
Population: 1,420 (2000); Race: 86.5% White, 8.0% Black, 0.2% Asian, 0.8% American Indian and Alaska Native, 4.5% Hispanic of any race, 2.0% two or more races (2000); Density: 736.7 persons per square mile (2000); Age: 25.6% under 18, 13.5% over 64 (2000); Marriage status: 23.6% never married, 49.7% now married, 7.8% widowed, 18.8% divorced (2000); Foreign born: 2.1% (2000); Ancestry (includes multiple ancestries): 20.1% German, 16.6% Other groups, 11.3% Irish, 10.7% English, 8.3% United States or American (2000).
Economy: In farm area. Manufacturing: lumber, refractory products, fabricated metal products. In Manistee National Forest. Employment by occupation: 7.6% management, 15.0% professional, 19.4% services, 19.9% sales, 0.5% farming, 12.9% construction, 24.7% production (2000).
Income: Per capita income: $12,369 (2000); Median household income: $24,313 (2000); Poverty rate: 21.8% (2000).
Taxes: Total city taxes per capita: $175 (1997); City property taxes per capita: $175 (1997).
Education: High school graduation rate: 75.1% (2000); College graduation rate: 8.5% (2000).

School District(s)

White Cloud Public Schools (KG-12)
2000 Enrollment: 1,564 231-689-6591
Housing: Homeownership rate: 59.0% (2000); Median home value: $67,100 (2000); Median rent: $354 per month (2000); Median age of housing: 37 years (2000).
Safety: Violent crime rate: 70.1 per 10,000 population; Property crime rate: 784.9 per 10,000 population (2001).
Transportation: Commute to work: 89.6% car, 1.2% public transportation, 5.2% walk, 2.8% work from home (2000); Travel time to work: 39.9% less than 15 minutes, 24.1% 15 to 30 minutes, 14.4% 30 to 45 minutes, 7.1% 45 to 60 minutes, 14.6% 60 minutes or more (2000)
Additional Information Contacts
White Cloud Chamber of Commerce..................... 231-689-6607

WILCOX (township). Covers a land area of 33.887 square miles and a water area of 0.090 square miles. Located at 43.60° N. Lat.; 85.74° W. Long.
Population: 1,145 (2000); Race: 95.2% White, 1.7% Black, 0.0% Asian, 1.2% American Indian and Alaska Native, 1.1% Hispanic of any race, 1.6% two or more races (2000); Density: 33.8 persons per square mile (2000); Age: 30.7% under 18, 9.2% over 64 (2000); Marriage status: 20.0% never married, 57.8% now married, 6.3% widowed, 15.9% divorced (2000); Foreign born: 1.1% (2000); Ancestry (includes multiple ancestries): 20.5% German, 14.7% Other groups, 10.9% United States or American, 10.0% Dutch, 9.3% Irish (2000).
Economy: Employment by occupation: 4.9% management, 10.4% professional, 19.7% services, 17.2% sales, 0.7% farming, 18.6% construction, 28.5% production (2000).
Income: Per capita income: $13,564 (2000); Median household income: $32,039 (2000); Poverty rate: 18.1% (2000).
Taxes: Total city taxes per capita: $33 (1997); City property taxes per capita: $33 (1997).
Education: High school graduation rate: 67.6% (2000); College graduation rate: 7.5% (2000).
Housing: Homeownership rate: 82.6% (2000); Median home value: $77,900 (2000); Median rent: $318 per month (2000); Median age of housing: 26 years (2000).
Transportation: Commute to work: 95.0% car, 0.0% public transportation, 1.4% walk, 1.9% work from home (2000); Travel time to work: 31.8% less than 15 minutes, 23.0% 15 to 30 minutes, 13.2% 30 to 45 minutes, 7.6% 45 to 60 minutes, 24.4% 60 minutes or more (2000)

Oakland County

Located in southeastern Michigan; drained by the Shiawassee, Huron, Clinton, and Rogue Rivers; includes many small lakes. Covers a land area of 872.50 square miles, a water area of 35.50 square miles, and is located in the Eastern Time Zone. The county government was organized in 1819. County seat is Pontiac.

Oakland County is part of the Detroit, MI PMSA. The entire metro area includes: Lapeer County; Macomb County; Monroe County; Oakland County; St. Clair County; Wayne County

Weather Station: Pontiac State Hospital — Elevation: 980 feet

	Jan	Feb	Mar	Apr	May	Jun	Jul	Aug	Sep	Oct	Nov	Dec
High	30	33	45	58	71	79	83	81	74	60	46	34
Low	16	17	26	36	47	57	61	60	53	42	32	22
Precip	1.4	1.5	2.3	2.7	2.7	3.1	2.8	3.1	3.0	2.6	2.7	2.3
Snow	9.1	6.3	4.5	1.6	tr	0.0	0.0	0.0	0.0	0.1	2.2	7.5

High and Low temperatures in degrees Fahrenheit; Precipitation and Snow in inches

Population: 1,194,156 (2000); Race: 82.8% White, 10.0% Black, 4.1% Asian, 0.3% American Indian and Alaska Native, 2.5% Hispanic of any race, 2.0% two or more races (2000); Density: 1,368.6 persons per square mile (2000); Age: 25.1% under 18, 11.3% over 64 (2000).
Religion: Five largest groups: 25.3% Catholic Church, 6.4% Jewish estimate, 2.4% The United Methodist Church, 2.1% Lutheran Church—Missouri Synod, 1.4% Presbyterian Church (U.S.A.) (2000).
Economy: Unemployment rate: 4.0% (11/2002); Total civilian labor force: 679,330 (11/2002); Leading industries: 11.7% manufacturing; 10.9% administration, support, waste management, remediation services; 10.8% retail trade (2000); Companies that employ more than 1,000 persons: 49 (2000); Companies that employ more than 100 persons: 1,267 (2000); Farms:

544 totaling 45,366 acres (1997); Minority business ownership rate: 8.6% (1997); Women business ownership rate: 25.9% (1997); Retail sales per capita: $14,175 (1997). Single-family building permits issued: 4,205 (2001) / 4,654 (2000); Multi-family building permits issued: 1,030 (2001) / 805 (2000).
Income: Per capita income: $32,534 (2000); Median household income: $61,907 (2000); Poverty rate: 5.5% (2000); Bankruptcy rate: 3.53% (2001).
Taxes: Total county taxes per capita: $150 (2000); County property taxes per capita: $141 (2000).
Education: High school graduation rate: 89.3% (2000); College graduation rate: 38.2% (2000).
Housing: Homeownership rate: 74.8% (2000); Median home value: $181,200 (2000); Median rent: $643 per month (2000); Median age of housing: 30 years (2000).
Health: Birth rate: 131.8 per 10,000 population (1998); Age adjusted death rate: 84.3 per 10,000 population (1999); Infant mortality rate: 6.9 per 1,000 live births (1998); Age adjusted cancer mortality rate: 207.5 deaths per 100,000 population (1999). Air Quality Index: 80% good, 20% moderate, 0% unhealthy (percent of days in 2000). Number of physicians: 47.4 per 10,000 population (1999); Number of hospital beds: 29.9 per 10,000 population (1999).
Elections: 2000 Presidential election results: 49.3% Gore, 48.1% Bush, 1.8% Nader, 0.1% Buchanan
National and State Parks: Bald Mountain State Recreation Area; Dodge Brothers State Park Number 2; Highland State Recreation Area; Holly State Recreation Area; Pontiac Lake State Recreation Area; Proud Lake State Recreation Area
Additional Information Contacts
Oakland County Government Offices 248-858-1000
Auburn Hills Chamber of Commerce 248-853-7862
Birmingham Chamber of Commerce 248-644-1700
Clarkston Chamber of Commerce 248-625-8055
Detroit Area Commercial Board of Realtors 248-626-0260
Farmington Chamber of Commerce 248-474-3440
Ferndale Chamber of Commerce 248-542-2160
French-American Chamber of Commerce 248-358-1861
Greater Berkley Chamber 248-414-9157
Holly Chamber of Commerce 248-634-1900
Madison Heights Chamber of Commerce 248-542-5010
Metropolitan Consolidated Association of Realtors 248-879-5730
North Oakland County Board of Realtors 248-674-4080
Northville Chamber of Commerce 248-349-7640
Novi Chamber of Commerce 248-349-3743
Novi Convention & Visitors Bureau 248-349-7940
Orion Area Chamber of Commerce 248-693-6300
Oxford Chamber of Commerce 248-628-0410
Pontiac Chamber of Commerce 248-335-9600
Rochester Chamber of Commerce 248-651-6700
Royal Oak Chamber of Commerce 248-547-4000
South Lyon Chamber of Commerce 248-437-3257
Southfield Chamber of Commerce 248-827-1127
Walled Lake Chamber of Commerce 248-624-2826
West Bloomfield Chamber of Commerce 248-626-3636
Western Wayne Oakland County Association of Realtors 248-478-1700

Oakland County Communities

ADDISON (township). Covers a land area of 36.235 square miles and a water area of 0.925 square miles. Located at 42.83° N. Lat.; 83.15° W. Long.
Population: 6,439 (2000); Race: 96.2% White, 1.3% Black, 0.4% Asian, 0.0% American Indian and Alaska Native, 2.5% Hispanic of any race, 1.3% two or more races (2000); Density: 177.7 persons per square mile (2000); Age: 29.0% under 18, 7.5% over 64 (2000); Marriage status: 22.2% never married, 64.8% now married, 4.1% widowed, 9.0% divorced (2000); Foreign born: 4.8% (2000); Ancestry (includes multiple ancestries): 25.1% German, 15.3% Polish, 14.1% Irish, 13.3% English, 10.5% Italian (2000).
Economy: Single-family building permits issued: 24 (2001) / 55 (2000); Multi-family building permits issued: 0 (2001) / 0 (2000); Employment by occupation: 15.9% management, 22.0% professional, 12.0% services, 24.6% sales, 0.0% farming, 10.8% construction, 14.6% production (2000).
Income: Per capita income: $29,350 (2000); Median household income: $69,266 (2000); Poverty rate: 5.7% (2000).
Taxes: Total city taxes per capita: $200 (1997); City property taxes per capita: $178 (1997).
Education: High school graduation rate: 87.1% (2000); College graduation rate: 27.4% (2000).
Housing: Homeownership rate: 92.3% (2000); Median home value: $227,500 (2000); Median rent: $604 per month (2000); Median age of housing: 23 years (2000).
Transportation: Commute to work: 94.5% car, 0.0% public transportation, 0.9% walk, 3.9% work from home (2000); Travel time to work: 11.2% less than 15 minutes, 27.6% 15 to 30 minutes, 32.6% 30 to 45 minutes, 15.9% 45 to 60 minutes, 12.7% 60 minutes or more (2000)

AUBURN HILLS (city). Covers a land area of 16.607 square miles and a water area of 0.017 square miles. Located at 42.66° N. Lat.; 83.24° W. Long. Elevation is 975 feet.
Population: 19,837 (2000); Race: 76.5% White, 12.6% Black, 6.2% Asian, 0.0% American Indian and Alaska Native, 5.0% Hispanic of any race, 2.9% two or more races (2000); Density: 1,194.5 persons per square mile (2000); Age: 20.4% under 18, 7.3% over 64 (2000); Marriage status: 37.2% never married, 47.0% now married, 4.5% widowed, 11.3% divorced (2000); Foreign born: 10.4% (2000); Ancestry (includes multiple ancestries): 28.3% Other groups, 16.8% German, 10.4% English, 9.6% Irish, 7.1% Polish (2000).
Vital Statistics: Birth rate: 147.7 per 10,000 population (1998)
Economy: Site of The Palace, sports complex that is home to the Detroit Pistons National Basketball Association team. Manufacturing includes industrial robotics, consumer goods, transportation equipment, machinery, electronic equipment, tilt tables, tooling and gauges, motor vehicles; machining. Single-family building permits issued: 88 (2001) / 87 (2000); Multi-family building permits issued: 0 (2001) / 43 (2000); Employment by occupation: 14.6% management, 27.2% professional, 13.5% services, 28.1% sales, 0.1% farming, 6.0% construction, 10.6% production (2000).
Income: Per capita income: $25,529 (2000); Median household income: $51,376 (2000); Poverty rate: 6.3% (2000).
Taxes: Total city taxes per capita: $1,112 (1997); City property taxes per capita: $1,059 (1997).
Education: High school graduation rate: 87.9% (2000); College graduation rate: 32.8% (2000).

School District(s)

Avondale School District (KG-12)
2000 Enrollment: 3,774 248-852-4411

Four-year College(s)

Baker College of Auburn Hills (Private, Not-for-profit)
2001 Enrollment: 2,199 248-340-0600
2001 Tuition: In-state $5,580; Out-of-state $5,580

Housing: Homeownership rate: 51.2% (2000); Median home value: $137,200 (2000); Median rent: $693 per month (2000); Median age of housing: 19 years (2000).
Hospitals: Havenwyck Hospital (150 beds)
Safety: Violent crime rate: 29.1 per 10,000 population; Property crime rate: 686.5 per 10,000 population (2001).
Transportation: Commute to work: 93.4% car, 0.7% public transportation, 3.1% walk, 2.1% work from home (2000); Travel time to work: 33.9% less than 15 minutes, 38.2% 15 to 30 minutes, 18.5% 30 to 45 minutes, 5.1% 45 to 60 minutes, 4.3% 60 minutes or more (2000)
Additional Information Contacts
Auburn Hills Chamber of Commerce 248-853-7862

BERKLEY (city). Covers a land area of 2.621 square miles and a water area of 0 square miles. Located at 42.49° N. Lat.; 83.18° W. Long. Elevation is 700 feet.
History: Berkley was incorporated as a village in 1925 and granted a city charter in 1932. The city was established in an area that had been under cultivation until 1913, when it was subdivided by Detroit real estate operators.
Population: 15,531 (2000); Race: 95.8% White, 0.7% Black, 0.9% Asian, 0.2% American Indian and Alaska Native, 1.3% Hispanic of any race, 1.5% two or more races (2000); Density: 5,925.5 persons per square mile (2000); Age: 22.7% under 18, 13.2% over 64 (2000); Marriage status: 27.9% never married, 54.5% now married, 7.2% widowed, 10.4% divorced (2000); Foreign born: 4.2% (2000); Ancestry (includes multiple ancestries): 27.9% German, 19.5% Irish, 14.2% Polish, 13.5% English, 7.9% Italian (2000).
Vital Statistics: Birth rate: 157.1 per 10,000 population (1998)
Economy: Single-family building permits issued: 19 (2001) / 13 (2000); Multi-family building permits issued: 0 (2001) / 0 (2000); Employment by occupation: 16.6% management, 28.3% professional, 9.7% services, 30.0% sales, 0.1% farming, 8.2% construction, 7.1% production (2000).

Income: Per capita income: $27,504 (2000); Median household income: $57,620 (2000); Poverty rate: 3.6% (2000).
Taxes: Total city taxes per capita: $305 (1997); City property taxes per capita: $285 (1997).
Education: High school graduation rate: 90.9% (2000); College graduation rate: 35.6% (2000).

School District(s)

Berkley School District (PK-12)
2000 Enrollment: 4,287 248-414-2268

Housing: Homeownership rate: 85.8% (2000); Median home value: $140,600 (2000); Median rent: $597 per month (2000); Median age of housing: 51 years (2000).
Safety: Violent crime rate: 7.7 per 10,000 population; Property crime rate: 148.6 per 10,000 population (2001).
Transportation: Commute to work: 95.8% car, 0.5% public transportation, 0.9% walk, 2.4% work from home (2000); Travel time to work: 26.8% less than 15 minutes, 45.1% 15 to 30 minutes, 21.6% 30 to 45 minutes, 4.2% 45 to 60 minutes, 2.4% 60 minutes or more (2000)

Additional Information Contacts

Greater Berkley Chamber. 248-414-9157

BEVERLY HILLS (village). Aka Westwood. Covers a land area of 4.009 square miles and a water area of 0.027 square miles. Located at 42.52° N. Lat.; 83.23° W. Long. Elevation is 730 feet.
History: Beverly Hills was incorporated as the village of Westwood in 1958, and renamed the next year to reflect the previous referral to the area as the Beverly Hills Subdivisions.
Population: 10,437 (2000); Race: 93.2% White, 2.5% Black, 1.2% Asian, 0.3% American Indian and Alaska Native, 1.3% Hispanic of any race, 2.2% two or more races (2000); Density: 2,603.6 persons per square mile (2000); Age: 24.5% under 18, 19.6% over 64 (2000); Marriage status: 18.4% never married, 66.2% now married, 7.2% widowed, 8.2% divorced (2000); Foreign born: 7.2% (2000); Ancestry (includes multiple ancestries): 25.8% German, 21.3% Irish, 15.6% English, 11.2% Polish, 7.7% Italian (2000).
Vital Statistics: Birth rate: 90.1 per 10,000 population (1998)
Economy: Single-family building permits issued: 4 (2001) / 7 (2000); Multi-family building permits issued: 0 (2001) / 0 (2000); Employment by occupation: 26.2% management, 35.0% professional, 5.8% services, 25.6% sales, 0.0% farming, 3.8% construction, 3.5% production (2000).
Income: Per capita income: $43,452 (2000); Median household income: $90,341 (2000); Poverty rate: 2.3% (2000).
Taxes: Total city taxes per capita: $399 (1997); City property taxes per capita: $388 (1997).
Education: High school graduation rate: 96.0% (2000); College graduation rate: 62.8% (2000).
Housing: Homeownership rate: 92.3% (2000); Median home value: $270,600 (2000); Median rent: $814 per month (2000); Median age of housing: 42 years (2000).
Safety: Violent crime rate: 6.7 per 10,000 population; Property crime rate: 133.4 per 10,000 population (2001).
Transportation: Commute to work: 95.0% car, 0.2% public transportation, 0.4% walk, 4.0% work from home (2000); Travel time to work: 26.4% less than 15 minutes, 40.8% 15 to 30 minutes, 25.9% 30 to 45 minutes, 5.4% 45 to 60 minutes, 1.6% 60 minutes or more (2000)

BINGHAM FARMS (village). Covers a land area of 1.200 square miles and a water area of 0 square miles. Located at 42.51° N. Lat.; 83.27° W. Long. Elevation is 716 feet.
History: Bingham Farms was founded in 1955, and named for the original owners of the land on which it was established.
Population: 1,030 (2000); Race: 93.4% White, 3.7% Black, 1.4% Asian, 0.0% American Indian and Alaska Native, 0.9% Hispanic of any race, 1.0% two or more races (2000); Density: 858.2 persons per square mile (2000); Age: 15.7% under 18, 28.9% over 64 (2000); Marriage status: 14.4% never married, 72.0% now married, 7.8% widowed, 5.7% divorced (2000); Foreign born: 9.6% (2000); Ancestry (includes multiple ancestries): 19.9% German, 14.5% English, 12.6% Irish, 9.9% Polish, 9.1% Russian (2000).
Economy: Employment by occupation: 28.2% management, 39.3% professional, 4.8% services, 24.2% sales, 0.0% farming, 1.0% construction, 2.5% production (2000).
Income: Per capita income: $74,588 (2000); Median household income: $123,771 (2000); Poverty rate: 0.9% (2000).
Taxes: Total city taxes per capita: $1,070 (2000); City property taxes per capita: $1,064 (2000).
Education: High school graduation rate: 97.8% (2000); College graduation rate: 70.4% (2000).
Housing: Homeownership rate: 96.0% (2000); Median home value: $381,900 (2000); Median rent: $1,375 per month (2000); Median age of housing: 17 years (2000).
Transportation: Commute to work: 90.8% car, 1.5% public transportation, 0.0% walk, 7.3% work from home (2000); Travel time to work: 23.9% less than 15 minutes, 38.1% 15 to 30 minutes, 29.0% 30 to 45 minutes, 3.9% 45 to 60 minutes, 5.1% 60 minutes or more (2000)

BIRMINGHAM (city). Covers a land area of 4.777 square miles and a water area of 0.012 square miles. Located at 42.54° N. Lat.; 83.21° W. Long. Elevation is 777 feet.
History: Birmingham was founded by John and Rufus Hunter, who built a cabin here in 1817. By 1839, Birmingham was a stagecoach stop on the Saginaw Trail, named by Roswell T. Merrill who believed it would become an industrial leader like Birmingham, England. The village was incorporated in 1864, and became a city in 1933.
Population: 19,291 (2000); Race: 96.3% White, 0.8% Black, 1.2% Asian, 0.2% American Indian and Alaska Native, 1.5% Hispanic of any race, 1.3% two or more races (2000); Density: 4,038.4 persons per square mile (2000); Age: 21.4% under 18, 13.9% over 64 (2000); Marriage status: 25.2% never married, 57.7% now married, 5.4% widowed, 11.7% divorced (2000); Foreign born: 7.4% (2000); Ancestry (includes multiple ancestries): 21.6% German, 16.3% English, 16.3% Irish, 9.0% Polish, 6.9% Italian (2000).
Vital Statistics: Birth rate: 150.3 per 10,000 population (1998)
Economy: Single-family building permits issued: 71 (2001) / 67 (2000); Multi-family building permits issued: 0 (2001) / 4 (2000); Employment by occupation: 29.3% management, 34.4% professional, 4.6% services, 25.4% sales, 0.1% farming, 3.8% construction, 2.4% production (2000).
Income: Per capita income: $59,314 (2000); Median household income: $80,861 (2000); Poverty rate: 2.9% (2000).
Taxes: Total city taxes per capita: $919 (2000); City property taxes per capita: $850 (2000).
Education: High school graduation rate: 97.2% (2000); College graduation rate: 67.1% (2000).

School District(s)

Birmingham City School District (KG-12)
2000 Enrollment: 7,620 248-203-3004

Housing: Homeownership rate: 75.8% (2000); Median home value: $318,000 (2000); Median rent: $906 per month (2000); Median age of housing: 47 years (2000).
Safety: Violent crime rate: 7.7 per 10,000 population; Property crime rate: 236.2 per 10,000 population (2001).
Newspapers: Waterford Eccentric (2 x week); Farmington Observer (2 x week); West Bloomfield Eccentric (2 x week); Troy Eccentric (2 x week); Southfield Eccentric (2 x week); Birmingham Eccentric (2 x week); The Rochester Clarion-Eccentric (2 x week); Clarkston Eccentric (2 x week); Northeast Detroiter & The Harper Woods Herald (1 x week); Lake Orion Eccentric (2 x week)
Transportation: Commute to work: 92.4% car, 0.5% public transportation, 1.4% walk, 5.2% work from home (2000); Travel time to work: 30.3% less than 15 minutes, 37.4% 15 to 30 minutes, 23.4% 30 to 45 minutes, 5.7% 45 to 60 minutes, 3.2% 60 minutes or more (2000); Amtrak: Service available.

Additional Information Contacts

Birmingham Chamber of Commerce 248-644-1700

BLOOMFIELD (township). Covers a land area of 24.948 square miles and a water area of 1.093 square miles. Located at 42.57° N. Lat.; 83.26° W. Long.
Population: 43,023 (2000); Race: 87.1% White, 4.4% Black, 6.3% Asian, 0.2% American Indian and Alaska Native, 1.3% Hispanic of any race, 1.4% two or more races (2000); Density: 1,724.5 persons per square mile (2000); Age: 23.8% under 18, 17.9% over 64 (2000); Marriage status: 17.4% never married, 70.0% now married, 6.3% widowed, 6.2% divorced (2000); Foreign born: 14.2% (2000); Ancestry (includes multiple ancestries): 19.3% German, 14.6% Other groups, 14.0% Irish, 13.6% English, 8.3% Polish (2000).
Vital Statistics: Birth rate: 52.5 per 10,000 population (1998)
Economy: Unemployment rate: 1.6% (11/2002); Total civilian labor force: 26,448 (11/2002); Single-family building permits issued: 72 (2001) / 101 (2000); Multi-family building permits issued: 0 (2001) / 0 (2000); Employment by occupation: 28.3% management, 36.5% professional, 4.1% services, 25.7% sales, 0.0% farming, 1.9% construction, 3.6% production (2000).
Income: Per capita income: $62,716 (2000); Median household income: $103,897 (2000); Poverty rate: 2.5% (2000).
Taxes: Total city taxes per capita: $458 (2000); City property taxes per capita: $433 (2000).

Education: High school graduation rate: 96.2% (2000); College graduation rate: 65.8% (2000).
Housing: Homeownership rate: 90.2% (2000); Median home value: $356,800 (2000); Median rent: $842 per month (2000); Median age of housing: 34 years (2000).
Transportation: Commute to work: 93.8% car, 0.2% public transportation, 0.3% walk, 5.4% work from home (2000); Travel time to work: 21.9% less than 15 minutes, 39.9% 15 to 30 minutes, 25.9% 30 to 45 minutes, 8.5% 45 to 60 minutes, 3.7% 60 minutes or more (2000)

BLOOMFIELD HILLS (city). Covers a land area of 4.948 square miles and a water area of 0.048 square miles. Located at 42.57° N. Lat.; 83.24° W. Long. Elevation is 830 feet.
History: Bloomfield Hills was first settled by Amasa Bagley, who came to farm the land. A settlement known as Bagley's Corners grew up, but when Bagley moved away the name was changed to Bloomfield Center. For many years a farming town, it gradually became a residential center for city dwellers who wanted privacy and quiet. The name was changed to Bloomfield Hills, and by 1932 it was incorporated as a city.
Population: 3,940 (2000); Race: 89.3% White, 3.0% Black, 5.6% Asian, 0.0% American Indian and Alaska Native, 0.4% Hispanic of any race, 1.9% two or more races (2000); Density: 796.4 persons per square mile (2000); Age: 19.7% under 18, 23.8% over 64 (2000); Marriage status: 19.8% never married, 69.8% now married, 6.4% widowed, 4.0% divorced (2000); Foreign born: 10.4% (2000); Ancestry (includes multiple ancestries): 16.6% German, 14.6% English, 13.9% Irish, 10.4% Other groups, 10.4% Polish (2000).
Economy: Single-family building permits issued: 11 (2001) / 21 (2000); Multi-family building permits issued: 0 (2001) / 0 (2000); Employment by occupation: 34.6% management, 36.3% professional, 4.9% services, 21.8% sales, 0.0% farming, 0.3% construction, 2.1% production (2000).
Income: Per capita income: $104,920 (2000); Median household income: $170,790 (2000); Poverty rate: 3.8% (2000).
Taxes: Total city taxes per capita: $754 (1997); City property taxes per capita: $713 (1997).
Education: High school graduation rate: 95.4% (2000); College graduation rate: 66.7% (2000).

School District(s)

Bloomfield Hills School District (KG-12)
2000 Enrollment: 6,050 248-645-4500

Four-year College(s)

Cranbrook Academy of Art (Private, Not-for-profit)
2001 Enrollment: 136 248-645-3300

Two-year College(s)

Oakland Community College-Bloomfield Hills Campus (Public)
2001 Enrollment: 23,503 248-341-2000
2001 Tuition: In-state $2,641; Out-of-state $3,705

Housing: Homeownership rate: 91.1% (2000); Median home value: $854,000 (2000); Median rent: $1,388 per month (2000); Median age of housing: 32 years (2000).
Safety: Violent crime rate: 0.0 per 10,000 population; Property crime rate: 42.9 per 10,000 population (2001).
Transportation: Commute to work: 90.1% car, 0.0% public transportation, 2.4% walk, 6.6% work from home (2000); Travel time to work: 29.8% less than 15 minutes, 38.6% 15 to 30 minutes, 21.9% 30 to 45 minutes, 6.9% 45 to 60 minutes, 2.8% 60 minutes or more (2000)

BRANDON (township). Covers a land area of 35.064 square miles and a water area of 0.771 square miles. Located at 42.82° N. Lat.; 83.40° W. Long.
History: Brandon Township was founded in 1837.
Population: 14,765 (2000); Race: 97.6% White, 0.0% Black, 0.8% Asian, 0.3% American Indian and Alaska Native, 2.2% Hispanic of any race, 0.8% two or more races (2000); Density: 421.1 persons per square mile (2000); Age: 30.6% under 18, 5.3% over 64 (2000); Marriage status: 23.2% never married, 64.0% now married, 3.2% widowed, 9.6% divorced (2000); Foreign born: 2.3% (2000); Ancestry (includes multiple ancestries): 24.7% German, 13.2% Irish, 12.9% English, 10.7% Polish, 8.0% Italian (2000).
Economy: Single-family building permits issued: 88 (2001) / 98 (2000); Multi-family building permits issued: 0 (2001) / 0 (2000); Employment by occupation: 12.1% management, 19.3% professional, 13.6% services, 25.6% sales, 0.0% farming, 12.6% construction, 16.8% production (2000).
Income: Per capita income: $25,011 (2000); Median household income: $66,458 (2000); Poverty rate: 4.4% (2000).
Taxes: Total city taxes per capita: $220 (2000); City property taxes per capita: $209 (2000).
Education: High school graduation rate: 89.5% (2000); College graduation rate: 19.9% (2000).
Housing: Homeownership rate: 93.6% (2000); Median home value: $189,600 (2000); Median rent: $587 per month (2000); Median age of housing: 20 years (2000).
Transportation: Commute to work: 96.3% car, 0.0% public transportation, 0.4% walk, 2.6% work from home (2000); Travel time to work: 10.9% less than 15 minutes, 27.0% 15 to 30 minutes, 33.3% 30 to 45 minutes, 15.6% 45 to 60 minutes, 13.2% 60 minutes or more (2000)

CLAWSON (city). Covers a land area of 2.200 square miles and a water area of 0 square miles. Located at 42.53° N. Lat.; 83.15° W. Long. Elevation is 667 feet.
History: Joshua Fay built a house on this land in 1829, and the settlement that grew up around it was called Pumachug or The Corners. When John Lawson applied for a post office, he asked for it to be named Lawson. An error resulted in the name of Clawson.
Population: 12,732 (2000); Race: 96.4% White, 0.9% Black, 1.0% Asian, 0.0% American Indian and Alaska Native, 1.5% Hispanic of any race, 1.4% two or more races (2000); Density: 5,787.0 persons per square mile (2000); Age: 20.7% under 18, 15.1% over 64 (2000); Marriage status: 27.4% never married, 53.6% now married, 7.7% widowed, 11.3% divorced (2000); Foreign born: 5.8% (2000); Ancestry (includes multiple ancestries): 24.8% German, 17.8% Irish, 15.5% English, 12.4% Polish, 8.1% Italian (2000).
Vital Statistics: Birth rate: 124.9 per 10,000 population (1998)
Economy: Single-family building permits issued: 0 (2001) / 4 (2000); Multi-family building permits issued: 9 (2001) / 0 (2000); Employment by occupation: 13.3% management, 22.6% professional, 12.9% services, 31.0% sales, 0.0% farming, 7.9% construction, 12.3% production (2000).
Income: Per capita income: $25,676 (2000); Median household income: $50,929 (2000); Poverty rate: 3.5% (2000).
Taxes: Total city taxes per capita: $308 (1997); City property taxes per capita: $290 (1997).
Education: High school graduation rate: 89.7% (2000); College graduation rate: 26.1% (2000).

School District(s)

Clawson City School District (KG-12)
2000 Enrollment: 1,525 248-435-7500

Housing: Homeownership rate: 75.0% (2000); Median home value: $137,700 (2000); Median rent: $573 per month (2000); Median age of housing: 43 years (2000).
Safety: Violent crime rate: 5.5 per 10,000 population; Property crime rate: 101.6 per 10,000 population (2001).
Transportation: Commute to work: 95.7% car, 0.0% public transportation, 1.6% walk, 2.3% work from home (2000); Travel time to work: 31.4% less than 15 minutes, 39.5% 15 to 30 minutes, 20.5% 30 to 45 minutes, 5.7% 45 to 60 minutes, 2.9% 60 minutes or more (2000)

COMMERCE (township). Covers a land area of 27.567 square miles and a water area of 2.270 square miles. Located at 42.57° N. Lat.; 83.48° W. Long. Elevation is 943 feet.
History: Commerce was settled in the 1830's and named by its early residents in the hope that it would become a business center.
Population: 34,764 (2000); Race: 97.2% White, 0.5% Black, 0.9% Asian, 0.5% American Indian and Alaska Native, 1.0% Hispanic of any race, 0.8% two or more races (2000); Density: 1,261.1 persons per square mile (2000); Age: 29.5% under 18, 7.1% over 64 (2000); Marriage status: 19.8% never married, 67.6% now married, 3.7% widowed, 8.9% divorced (2000); Foreign born: 4.3% (2000); Ancestry (includes multiple ancestries): 24.5% German, 16.5% Irish, 13.5% Polish, 13.2% English, 8.4% Italian (2000).
Economy: Unemployment rate: 2.9% (11/2002); Total civilian labor force: 17,896 (11/2002); Single-family building permits issued: 331 (2001) / 328 (2000); Multi-family building permits issued: 308 (2001) / 0 (2000); Employment by occupation: 18.0% management, 22.0% professional, 9.8% services, 29.7% sales, 0.1% farming, 8.4% construction, 12.0% production (2000).
Income: Per capita income: $33,104 (2000); Median household income: $72,702 (2000); Poverty rate: 3.4% (2000).
Taxes: Total city taxes per capita: $194 (2000); City property taxes per capita: $172 (2000).
Education: High school graduation rate: 92.4% (2000); College graduation rate: 33.7% (2000).
Housing: Homeownership rate: 92.6% (2000); Median home value: $197,600 (2000); Median rent: $689 per month (2000); Median age of housing: 23 years (2000).
Transportation: Commute to work: 96.5% car, 0.1% public transportation, 0.2% walk, 2.7% work from home (2000); Travel time to work: 17.9% less

than 15 minutes, 28.6% 15 to 30 minutes, 29.1% 30 to 45 minutes, 16.3% 45 to 60 minutes, 8.2% 60 minutes or more (2000)

COMMERCE TOWNSHIP (unincorporated postal area, zip code 48382). Covers a land area of 17.285 square miles and a water area of 1.476 square miles. Located at 42.58° N. Lat.; 83.50° W. Long.
Population: 19,018 (2000); Race: 97.7% White, 0.4% Black, 0.7% Asian, 0.5% American Indian and Alaska Native, 0.7% Hispanic of any race, 0.6% two or more races (2000); Density: 1,100.3 persons per square mile (2000); Age: 30.3% under 18, 7.0% over 64 (2000); Marriage status: 18.2% never married, 70.3% now married, 3.8% widowed, 7.7% divorced (2000); Foreign born: 3.8% (2000); Ancestry (includes multiple ancestries): 24.0% German, 15.6% Irish, 13.4% English, 13.2% Polish, 7.8% Italian (2000).
Economy: Employment by occupation: 19.4% management, 22.8% professional, 8.9% services, 30.5% sales, 0.1% farming, 8.8% construction, 9.5% production (2000).
Income: Per capita income: $35,995 (2000); Median household income: $78,982 (2000); Poverty rate: 2.7% (2000).
Education: High school graduation rate: 94.0% (2000); College graduation rate: 36.9% (2000).
Housing: Homeownership rate: 95.9% (2000); Median home value: $210,300 (2000); Median rent: $788 per month (2000); Median age of housing: 25 years (2000).
Transportation: Commute to work: 95.5% car, 0.2% public transportation, 0.2% walk, 3.6% work from home (2000); Travel time to work: 14.2% less than 15 minutes, 28.2% 15 to 30 minutes, 30.9% 30 to 45 minutes, 17.2% 45 to 60 minutes, 9.5% 60 minutes or more (2000)

DAVISBURG (unincorporated postal area, zip code 48350). Covers a land area of 20.075 square miles and a water area of 0.834 square miles. Located at 42.74° N. Lat.; 83.52° W. Long.
Population: 7,080 (2000); Race: 96.1% White, 0.8% Black, 0.1% Asian, 0.7% American Indian and Alaska Native, 1.0% Hispanic of any race, 2.2% two or more races (2000); Density: 352.7 persons per square mile (2000); Age: 29.8% under 18, 7.0% over 64 (2000); Marriage status: 19.1% never married, 66.2% now married, 3.5% widowed, 11.2% divorced (2000); Foreign born: 1.4% (2000); Ancestry (includes multiple ancestries): 22.8% German, 17.8% English, 12.1% Irish, 11.8% Polish, 7.8% French (except Basque) (2000).
Economy: Employment by occupation: 15.8% management, 21.2% professional, 9.9% services, 25.5% sales, 0.3% farming, 12.3% construction, 15.0% production (2000).
Income: Per capita income: $26,562 (2000); Median household income: $66,940 (2000); Poverty rate: 6.8% (2000).
Education: High school graduation rate: 88.8% (2000); College graduation rate: 25.1% (2000).
Housing: Homeownership rate: 92.7% (2000); Median home value: $225,100 (2000); Median rent: $628 per month (2000); Median age of housing: 17 years (2000).
Transportation: Commute to work: 95.9% car, 0.3% public transportation, 1.0% walk, 2.6% work from home (2000); Travel time to work: 10.6% less than 15 minutes, 31.3% 15 to 30 minutes, 32.9% 30 to 45 minutes, 12.5% 45 to 60 minutes, 12.6% 60 minutes or more (2000)

FARMINGTON (city). Covers a land area of 2.670 square miles and a water area of 0 square miles. Located at 42.46° N. Lat.; 83.37° W. Long. Elevation is 750 feet.
History: Farmington was settled by Quakers in 1824, when the area was accessible only by a trail. The town was named for the former home in New York of one of the early settlers, but it was often referred to as Quakertown. Farmington later became a residential community for people working in Detroit.
Population: 10,423 (2000); Race: 86.2% White, 2.2% Black, 10.2% Asian, 0.3% American Indian and Alaska Native, 1.8% Hispanic of any race, 0.6% two or more races (2000); Density: 3,904.4 persons per square mile (2000); Age: 20.0% under 18, 20.1% over 64 (2000); Marriage status: 21.9% never married, 58.5% now married, 9.8% widowed, 9.8% divorced (2000); Foreign born: 16.1% (2000); Ancestry (includes multiple ancestries): 24.2% German, 18.2% Irish, 15.5% Other groups, 14.1% English, 9.1% Polish (2000).
Vital Statistics: Birth rate: 163.1 per 10,000 population (1998)
Economy: Single-family building permits issued: 0 (2001) / 0 (2000); Multi-family building permits issued: 0 (2001) / 0 (2000); Employment by occupation: 19.3% management, 34.7% professional, 9.3% services, 26.9% sales, 0.0% farming, 4.6% construction, 5.2% production (2000).
Income: Per capita income: $32,452 (2000); Median household income: $56,442 (2000); Poverty rate: 3.3% (2000).
Taxes: Total city taxes per capita: $480 (1997); City property taxes per capita: $467 (1997).
Education: High school graduation rate: 91.6% (2000); College graduation rate: 47.9% (2000).

School District(s)

Farmington Public School District (KG-12)
2000 Enrollment: 12,122 248-489-3300

Housing: Homeownership rate: 64.1% (2000); Median home value: $173,900 (2000); Median rent: $690 per month (2000); Median age of housing: 35 years (2000).
Hospitals: Botsford General Hospital (336 beds)
Safety: Violent crime rate: 8.6 per 10,000 population; Property crime rate: 221.4 per 10,000 population (2001).
Transportation: Commute to work: 94.9% car, 0.1% public transportation, 1.2% walk, 3.0% work from home (2000); Travel time to work: 29.4% less than 15 minutes, 35.9% 15 to 30 minutes, 23.0% 30 to 45 minutes, 9.2% 45 to 60 minutes, 2.5% 60 minutes or more (2000)

Additional Information Contacts

Farmington Chamber of Commerce. 248-474-3440
Western Wayne Oakland County Association of Realtors 248-478-1700

FARMINGTON HILLS (city). Covers a land area of 33.292 square miles and a water area of 0 square miles. Located at 42.48° N. Lat.; 83.37° W. Long. Elevation is 800 feet.
Population: 82,111 (2000); Race: 83.0% White, 7.0% Black, 7.0% Asian, 0.1% American Indian and Alaska Native, 1.5% Hispanic of any race, 2.4% two or more races (2000); Density: 2,466.4 persons per square mile (2000); Age: 23.1% under 18, 14.4% over 64 (2000); Marriage status: 25.0% never married, 59.4% now married, 6.9% widowed, 8.7% divorced (2000); Foreign born: 15.7% (2000); Ancestry (includes multiple ancestries): 19.1% Other groups, 17.3% German, 12.1% Irish, 11.0% Polish, 10.1% English (2000).
Vital Statistics: Birth rate: 104.0 per 10,000 population (1998)
Economy: Manufacturing: machinery, transportation equipment, electronics assembly, rubber and plastic products, security control equipment, metal products. Unemployment rate: 2.7% (11/2002); Total civilian labor force: 48,973 (11/2002); Single-family building permits issued: 113 (2001) / 126 (2000); Multi-family building permits issued: 137 (2001) / 40 (2000); Employment by occupation: 21.0% management, 32.3% professional, 8.2% services, 26.6% sales, 0.0% farming, 4.5% construction, 7.4% production (2000).
Income: Per capita income: $36,134 (2000); Median household income: $67,493 (2000); Poverty rate: 4.1% (2000).
Taxes: Total city taxes per capita: $418 (2000); City property taxes per capita: $399 (2000).
Education: High school graduation rate: 91.7% (2000); College graduation rate: 47.9% (2000).

School District(s)

Oakland International Academy (KG-12)
2000 Enrollment: 93 517-249-4623

Four-year College(s)

William Tyndale College (Private, Not-for-profit, Undenominational)
2001 Enrollment: 608 800-483-0707
2001 Tuition: In-state $7,950; Out-of-state $7,950

Housing: Homeownership rate: 66.8% (2000); Median home value: $227,300 (2000); Median rent: $774 per month (2000); Median age of housing: 23 years (2000).
Safety: Violent crime rate: 23.3 per 10,000 population; Property crime rate: 232.6 per 10,000 population (2001).
Transportation: Commute to work: 95.4% car, 0.3% public transportation, 1.0% walk, 2.9% work from home (2000); Travel time to work: 20.9% less than 15 minutes, 37.5% 15 to 30 minutes, 28.9% 30 to 45 minutes, 8.8% 45 to 60 minutes, 3.8% 60 minutes or more (2000)

Additional Information Contacts

Detroit Area Commercial Board of Realtors 248-626-0260

FERNDALE (city). Covers a land area of 3.880 square miles and a water area of 0 square miles. Located at 42.46° N. Lat.; 83.12° W. Long. Elevation is 649 feet.
History: Ferndale was incorporated as a village in 1918, and as a city in 1927.
Population: 22,105 (2000); Race: 90.2% White, 3.3% Black, 1.9% Asian, 0.5% American Indian and Alaska Native, 1.1% Hispanic of any race, 3.3% two or more races (2000); Density: 5,697.9 persons per square mile (2000); Age: 20.4% under 18, 9.6% over 64 (2000); Marriage status: 39.0% never married, 42.1% now married, 5.3% widowed, 13.6% divorced (2000); Foreign born: 5.1% (2000); Ancestry (includes multiple ancestries): 20.0%

German, 16.0% Irish, 12.3% Other groups, 12.1% English, 11.1% Polish (2000).
Vital Statistics: Birth rate: 153.8 per 10,000 population (1998)
Economy: Unemployment rate: 4.8% (11/2002); Total civilian labor force: 15,145 (11/2002); Single-family building permits issued: 3 (2001) / 15 (2000); Multi-family building permits issued: 6 (2001) / 0 (2000); Employment by occupation: 12.3% management, 24.4% professional, 14.1% services, 26.0% sales, 0.2% farming, 8.2% construction, 14.9% production (2000).
Income: Per capita income: $23,133 (2000); Median household income: $45,629 (2000); Poverty rate: 8.2% (2000).
Taxes: Total city taxes per capita: $560 (2000); City property taxes per capita: $546 (2000).
Education: High school graduation rate: 84.9% (2000); College graduation rate: 26.4% (2000).

School District(s)

Academy of Michigan (09-11)
2000 Enrollment: 252 248-370-3050
Edison-Oakland Academy (KG-08)
2000 Enrollment: 846 313-487-2420
Ferndale Public Schools (PK-12)
2000 Enrollment: 4,354 248-586-8691

Housing: Homeownership rate: 70.8% (2000); Median home value: $102,900 (2000); Median rent: $538 per month (2000); Median age of housing: 55 years (2000).
Hospitals: Kingswood Hospital (100 beds)
Safety: Violent crime rate: 36.9 per 10,000 population; Property crime rate: 357.8 per 10,000 population (2001).
Transportation: Commute to work: 94.1% car, 1.2% public transportation, 1.8% walk, 2.2% work from home (2000); Travel time to work: 23.5% less than 15 minutes, 48.8% 15 to 30 minutes, 21.1% 30 to 45 minutes, 4.5% 45 to 60 minutes, 2.1% 60 minutes or more (2000)
Additional Information Contacts
Ferndale Chamber of Commerce 248-542-2160

FRANKLIN (village). Covers a land area of 2.657 square miles and a water area of 0 square miles. Located at 42.52° N. Lat.; 83.30° W. Long. Elevation is 833 feet.
Population: 2,937 (2000); Race: 89.2% White, 5.9% Black, 3.1% Asian, 0.2% American Indian and Alaska Native, 0.6% Hispanic of any race, 0.8% two or more races (2000); Density: 1,105.5 persons per square mile (2000); Age: 28.3% under 18, 13.8% over 64 (2000); Marriage status: 13.8% never married, 75.0% now married, 6.7% widowed, 4.5% divorced (2000); Foreign born: 11.3% (2000); Ancestry (includes multiple ancestries): 14.2% Other groups, 13.9% English, 13.8% German, 11.4% Polish, 9.5% Irish (2000).
Economy: Single-family building permits issued: 13 (2001) / 15 (2000); Multi-family building permits issued: 0 (2001) / 0 (2000); Employment by occupation: 31.4% management, 37.7% professional, 3.7% services, 22.2% sales, 0.0% farming, 1.8% construction, 3.2% production (2000).
Income: Per capita income: $71,033 (2000); Median household income: $124,014 (2000); Poverty rate: 1.0% (2000).
Taxes: Total city taxes per capita: $473 (1997); City property taxes per capita: $406 (1997).
Education: High school graduation rate: 96.3% (2000); College graduation rate: 71.1% (2000).
Housing: Homeownership rate: 97.1% (2000); Median home value: $414,400 (2000); Median rent: $2,000+ per month (2000); Median age of housing: 41 years (2000).
Safety: Violent crime rate: 13.6 per 10,000 population; Property crime rate: 162.6 per 10,000 population (2001).
Transportation: Commute to work: 92.9% car, 0.0% public transportation, 0.0% walk, 6.6% work from home (2000); Travel time to work: 20.8% less than 15 minutes, 47.5% 15 to 30 minutes, 24.5% 30 to 45 minutes, 4.8% 45 to 60 minutes, 2.4% 60 minutes or more (2000)

GROVELAND (township). Covers a land area of 35.534 square miles and a water area of 0.536 square miles. Located at 42.82° N. Lat.; 83.52° W. Long.
Population: 6,150 (2000); Race: 97.2% White, 0.4% Black, 0.0% Asian, 0.2% American Indian and Alaska Native, 1.0% Hispanic of any race, 2.2% two or more races (2000); Density: 173.1 persons per square mile (2000); Age: 27.8% under 18, 5.0% over 64 (2000); Marriage status: 24.2% never married, 66.1% now married, 2.7% widowed, 7.0% divorced (2000); Foreign born: 1.6% (2000); Ancestry (includes multiple ancestries): 20.5% German, 17.2% English, 14.5% Irish, 11.5% Polish, 7.6% French (except Basque) (2000).
Economy: Single-family building permits issued: 27 (2001) / 24 (2000); Multi-family building permits issued: 0 (2001) / 0 (2000); Employment by occupation: 15.2% management, 21.2% professional, 10.0% services, 29.0% sales, 0.7% farming, 11.0% construction, 12.9% production (2000).
Income: Per capita income: $28,574 (2000); Median household income: $72,188 (2000); Poverty rate: 8.3% (2000).
Taxes: Total city taxes per capita: $124 (1997); City property taxes per capita: $111 (1997).
Education: High school graduation rate: 88.8% (2000); College graduation rate: 20.8% (2000).
Housing: Homeownership rate: 95.0% (2000); Median home value: $197,300 (2000); Median rent: $409 per month (2000); Median age of housing: 21 years (2000).
Transportation: Commute to work: 95.6% car, 0.0% public transportation, 1.2% walk, 3.0% work from home (2000); Travel time to work: 16.6% less than 15 minutes, 28.1% 15 to 30 minutes, 28.3% 30 to 45 minutes, 15.7% 45 to 60 minutes, 11.3% 60 minutes or more (2000)

HAZEL PARK (city). Covers a land area of 2.818 square miles and a water area of 0 square miles. Located at 42.45° N. Lat.; 83.09° W. Long. Elevation is 634 feet.
History: The land on which Hazel Park was established was once owned by Anthony Neusius. First called Hazel Slump for the hazelnut bushes and water, it was later incorporated as the city of Hazel Park.
Population: 18,963 (2000); Race: 91.1% White, 1.3% Black, 2.2% Asian, 0.9% American Indian and Alaska Native, 1.9% Hispanic of any race, 3.4% two or more races (2000); Density: 6,728.4 persons per square mile (2000); Age: 27.7% under 18, 11.3% over 64 (2000); Marriage status: 32.8% never married, 46.6% now married, 7.7% widowed, 12.9% divorced (2000); Foreign born: 7.2% (2000); Ancestry (includes multiple ancestries): 18.6% German, 14.8% Irish, 11.9% Other groups, 10.3% Polish, 9.7% English (2000).
Vital Statistics: Birth rate: 145.0 per 10,000 population (1998)
Economy: Single-family building permits issued: 26 (2001) / 5 (2000); Multi-family building permits issued: 0 (2001) / 0 (2000); Employment by occupation: 5.9% management, 12.7% professional, 17.3% services, 25.9% sales, 0.2% farming, 13.3% construction, 24.7% production (2000).
Income: Per capita income: $16,723 (2000); Median household income: $37,045 (2000); Poverty rate: 12.4% (2000).
Taxes: Total city taxes per capita: $224 (1997); City property taxes per capita: $206 (1997).
Education: High school graduation rate: 70.3% (2000); College graduation rate: 8.0% (2000).

School District(s)

Hazel Park City School District (PK-12)
2000 Enrollment: 4,841 248-542-3910

Housing: Homeownership rate: 73.4% (2000); Median home value: $77,000 (2000); Median rent: $502 per month (2000); Median age of housing: 47 years (2000).
Safety: Violent crime rate: 61.9 per 10,000 population; Property crime rate: 387.7 per 10,000 population (2001).
Transportation: Commute to work: 92.1% car, 1.7% public transportation, 4.2% walk, 1.0% work from home (2000); Travel time to work: 30.4% less than 15 minutes, 44.7% 15 to 30 minutes, 17.3% 30 to 45 minutes, 3.7% 45 to 60 minutes, 3.8% 60 minutes or more (2000)

HIGHLAND (township). Covers a land area of 33.619 square miles and a water area of 2.197 square miles. Located at 42.65° N. Lat.; 83.61° W. Long.
Population: 19,169 (2000); Race: 97.3% White, 0.3% Black, 0.6% Asian, 0.6% American Indian and Alaska Native, 1.0% Hispanic of any race, 0.9% two or more races (2000); Density: 570.2 persons per square mile (2000); Age: 29.2% under 18, 7.3% over 64 (2000); Marriage status: 22.7% never married, 64.1% now married, 4.1% widowed, 9.1% divorced (2000); Foreign born: 3.0% (2000); Ancestry (includes multiple ancestries): 24.4% German, 16.8% Irish, 14.1% English, 11.5% Polish, 6.3% Other groups (2000).
Economy: Single-family building permits issued: 116 (2001) / 130 (2000); Multi-family building permits issued: 0 (2001) / 0 (2000); Employment by occupation: 12.9% management, 17.1% professional, 11.7% services, 27.9% sales, 0.5% farming, 16.3% construction, 13.6% production (2000).
Income: Per capita income: $25,484 (2000); Median household income: $62,805 (2000); Poverty rate: 5.8% (2000).
Taxes: Total city taxes per capita: $129 (2000); City property taxes per capita: $106 (2000).
Education: High school graduation rate: 88.9% (2000); College graduation rate: 20.2% (2000).

School District(s)

Huron Valley Schools (PK-12)
2000 Enrollment: 10,829 248-684-8000

Housing: Homeownership rate: 92.8% (2000); Median home value: $171,700 (2000); Median rent: $531 per month (2000); Median age of housing: 25 years (2000).

Transportation: Commute to work: 95.7% car, 0.3% public transportation, 0.6% walk, 2.8% work from home (2000); Travel time to work: 18.7% less than 15 minutes, 24.4% 15 to 30 minutes, 23.3% 30 to 45 minutes, 19.1% 45 to 60 minutes, 14.5% 60 minutes or more (2000)

HOLLY (village). Covers a land area of 2.783 square miles and a water area of 0.292 square miles. Located at 42.79° N. Lat.; 83.62° W. Long. Elevation is 937 feet.

History: Holly grew up around a sawmill and a grist mill built by Ira C. Alger in the mid-1840's. The village may have been named Holly because so much holly grew there, or because one of the early settlers was from Mount Holly, New Jersey. Holly had an early reputation as a flower center, encouraged by the Holly Flower Lovers' Club.

Population: 6,135 (2000); Race: 96.7% White, 1.8% Black, 0.1% Asian, 0.0% American Indian and Alaska Native, 2.9% Hispanic of any race, 1.2% two or more races (2000); Density: 2,204.6 persons per square mile (2000); Age: 27.2% under 18, 11.3% over 64 (2000); Marriage status: 25.4% never married, 55.5% now married, 6.5% widowed, 12.6% divorced (2000); Foreign born: 1.6% (2000); Ancestry (includes multiple ancestries): 20.4% German, 15.8% English, 13.5% Irish, 8.0% United States or American, 6.7% Other groups (2000).

Economy: Single-family building permits issued: 12 (2001) / 16 (2000); Multi-family building permits issued: 4 (2001) / 4 (2000); Employment by occupation: 10.5% management, 14.3% professional, 16.3% services, 25.2% sales, 1.0% farming, 14.2% construction, 18.5% production (2000).

Income: Per capita income: $19,988 (2000); Median household income: $46,436 (2000); Poverty rate: 7.3% (2000).

Taxes: Total city taxes per capita: $202 (1997); City property taxes per capita: $179 (1997).

Education: High school graduation rate: 82.7% (2000); College graduation rate: 11.9% (2000).

School District(s)

Holly Academy (KG-07)
2000 Enrollment: 509 517-774-2100

Holly Area School District (KG-12)
2000 Enrollment: 4,253 248-328-3100

Housing: Homeownership rate: 75.2% (2000); Median home value: $117,700 (2000); Median rent: $465 per month (2000); Median age of housing: 31 years (2000).

Safety: Violent crime rate: 0.0 per 10,000 population; Property crime rate: 97.3 per 10,000 population (2001).

Transportation: Commute to work: 95.9% car, 0.0% public transportation, 2.5% walk, 1.1% work from home (2000); Travel time to work: 24.5% less than 15 minutes, 29.9% 15 to 30 minutes, 25.6% 30 to 45 minutes, 9.6% 45 to 60 minutes, 10.3% 60 minutes or more (2000)

Additional Information Contacts

Holly Chamber of Commerce 248-634-1900

HOLLY (township). Covers a land area of 34.829 square miles and a water area of 1.802 square miles. Located at 42.81° N. Lat.; 83.62° W. Long. Elevation is 937 feet.

History: Settled 1836, incorporated 1865.

Population: 10,037 (2000); Race: 95.3% White, 3.0% Black, 0.5% Asian, 0.0% American Indian and Alaska Native, 2.1% Hispanic of any race, 1.0% two or more races (2000); Density: 288.2 persons per square mile (2000); Age: 26.7% under 18, 10.3% over 64 (2000); Marriage status: 24.3% never married, 58.4% now married, 5.9% widowed, 11.3% divorced (2000); Foreign born: 1.9% (2000); Ancestry (includes multiple ancestries): 21.5% German, 14.9% English, 14.6% Irish, 8.0% Other groups, 7.2% Polish (2000).

Economy: Manufacturing: auto parts, winery, foundry, machinery, automotive tubing, apple cider. Mt. Holly and Pine Knob Ski Areas to East. Single-family building permits issued: 49 (2001) / 138 (2000); Multi-family building permits issued: 0 (2001) / 0 (2000); Employment by occupation: 11.6% management, 16.6% professional, 16.2% services, 21.9% sales, 0.7% farming, 14.0% construction, 18.9% production (2000).

Income: Per capita income: $22,370 (2000); Median household income: $52,865 (2000); Poverty rate: 7.6% (2000).

Taxes: Total city taxes per capita: $67 (2000); City property taxes per capita: $53 (2000).

Education: High school graduation rate: 85.0% (2000); College graduation rate: 16.4% (2000).

Housing: Homeownership rate: 80.7% (2000); Median home value: $130,200 (2000); Median rent: $475 per month (2000); Median age of housing: 30 years (2000).

Transportation: Commute to work: 95.4% car, 0.0% public transportation, 1.5% walk, 2.6% work from home (2000); Travel time to work: 22.0% less than 15 minutes, 30.9% 15 to 30 minutes, 24.6% 30 to 45 minutes, 10.8% 45 to 60 minutes, 11.7% 60 minutes or more (2000)

HUNTINGTON WOODS (city). Covers a land area of 1.466 square miles and a water area of 0.004 square miles. Located at 42.48° N. Lat.; 83.16° W. Long. Elevation is 660 feet.

History: Huntington Woods was established as a residential community in the early 1920's. It was incorporated as a village in 1927 and as a city in 1932.

Population: 6,151 (2000); Race: 96.4% White, 0.1% Black, 1.7% Asian, 0.2% American Indian and Alaska Native, 1.9% Hispanic of any race, 1.5% two or more races (2000); Density: 4,196.0 persons per square mile (2000); Age: 26.5% under 18, 12.7% over 64 (2000); Marriage status: 17.8% never married, 69.0% now married, 5.8% widowed, 7.4% divorced (2000); Foreign born: 8.0% (2000); Ancestry (includes multiple ancestries): 16.7% German, 12.4% Russian, 11.9% Polish, 11.3% English, 11.2% Other groups (2000).

Economy: Single-family building permits issued: 1 (2001) / 3 (2000); Multi-family building permits issued: 0 (2001) / 0 (2000); Employment by occupation: 17.6% management, 50.7% professional, 5.9% services, 19.9% sales, 0.0% farming, 1.9% construction, 4.1% production (2000).

Income: Per capita income: $45,264 (2000); Median household income: $87,086 (2000); Poverty rate: 2.6% (2000).

Taxes: Total city taxes per capita: $602 (1997); City property taxes per capita: $577 (1997).

Education: High school graduation rate: 96.8% (2000); College graduation rate: 72.5% (2000).

Housing: Homeownership rate: 97.4% (2000); Median home value: $245,400 (2000); Median rent: $1,179 per month (2000); Median age of housing: 52 years (2000).

Safety: Violent crime rate: 0.0 per 10,000 population; Property crime rate: 98.7 per 10,000 population (2001).

Transportation: Commute to work: 92.4% car, 0.3% public transportation, 0.8% walk, 6.2% work from home (2000); Travel time to work: 25.6% less than 15 minutes, 48.2% 15 to 30 minutes, 21.2% 30 to 45 minutes, 2.5% 45 to 60 minutes, 2.5% 60 minutes or more (2000)

INDEPENDENCE (township). Covers a land area of 35.199 square miles and a water area of 1.100 square miles. Located at 42.74° N. Lat.; 83.38° W. Long.

History: Independence Township was organized in 1837 and named for Independence, New Jersey, the former home of one of its first settlers.

Population: 32,581 (2000); Race: 96.0% White, 0.6% Black, 1.6% Asian, 0.2% American Indian and Alaska Native, 2.2% Hispanic of any race, 1.3% two or more races (2000); Density: 925.6 persons per square mile (2000); Age: 27.8% under 18, 7.9% over 64 (2000); Marriage status: 21.4% never married, 66.0% now married, 4.0% widowed, 8.6% divorced (2000); Foreign born: 3.7% (2000); Ancestry (includes multiple ancestries): 25.2% German, 15.9% Irish, 15.0% English, 9.7% Polish, 7.6% Other groups (2000).

Economy: Unemployment rate: 3.6% (11/2002); Total civilian labor force: 16,121 (11/2002); Single-family building permits issued: 200 (2001) / 260 (2000); Multi-family building permits issued: 0 (2001) / 0 (2000); Employment by occupation: 19.0% management, 26.8% professional, 12.1% services, 24.9% sales, 0.0% farming, 7.4% construction, 9.9% production (2000).

Income: Per capita income: $33,067 (2000); Median household income: $74,993 (2000); Poverty rate: 2.5% (2000).

Taxes: Total city taxes per capita: $235 (2000); City property taxes per capita: $207 (2000).

Education: High school graduation rate: 92.0% (2000); College graduation rate: 36.2% (2000).

Housing: Homeownership rate: 83.4% (2000); Median home value: $203,600 (2000); Median rent: $741 per month (2000); Median age of housing: 20 years (2000).

Transportation: Commute to work: 95.0% car, 0.3% public transportation, 0.3% walk, 3.9% work from home (2000); Travel time to work: 17.6% less than 15 minutes, 33.5% 15 to 30 minutes, 25.2% 30 to 45 minutes, 12.9% 45 to 60 minutes, 10.7% 60 minutes or more (2000)

KEEGO HARBOR (city). Covers a land area of 0.514 square miles and a water area of 0.034 square miles. Located at 42.60° N. Lat.; 83.34° W. Long. Elevation is 930 feet.
History: In 1902, J.E. Sawyer built a canal connecting Dollar Lake with Cass Lake, thus making Dollar Lake into a harbor which he named Keego Harbor. Keego is the name of a fish.
Population: 2,769 (2000); Race: 93.2% White, 1.2% Black, 0.5% Asian, 1.4% American Indian and Alaska Native, 3.9% Hispanic of any race, 2.5% two or more races (2000); Density: 5,388.9 persons per square mile (2000); Age: 24.6% under 18, 7.5% over 64 (2000); Marriage status: 32.8% never married, 47.5% now married, 2.6% widowed, 17.1% divorced (2000); Foreign born: 7.0% (2000); Ancestry (includes multiple ancestries): 20.7% German, 18.2% Irish, 15.4% Other groups, 11.3% English, 9.6% Polish (2000).
Economy: Single-family building permits issued: 6 (2001) / 10 (2000); Multi-family building permits issued: 0 (2001) / 0 (2000); Employment by occupation: 15.9% management, 14.7% professional, 19.4% services, 29.1% sales, 0.0% farming, 10.8% construction, 10.2% production (2000).
Income: Per capita income: $26,305 (2000); Median household income: $46,552 (2000); Poverty rate: 5.1% (2000).
Taxes: Total city taxes per capita: $332 (1997); City property taxes per capita: $312 (1997).
Education: High school graduation rate: 84.2% (2000); College graduation rate: 23.7% (2000).
Housing: Homeownership rate: 69.1% (2000); Median home value: $117,200 (2000); Median rent: $640 per month (2000); Median age of housing: 43 years (2000).
Safety: Violent crime rate: 10.8 per 10,000 population; Property crime rate: 79.0 per 10,000 population (2001).
Transportation: Commute to work: 95.6% car, 0.0% public transportation, 2.1% walk, 1.4% work from home (2000); Travel time to work: 19.2% less than 15 minutes, 42.1% 15 to 30 minutes, 20.4% 30 to 45 minutes, 11.6% 45 to 60 minutes, 6.6% 60 minutes or more (2000)

LAKE ANGELUS (city). Covers a land area of 1.037 square miles and a water area of 0.580 square miles. Located at 42.69° N. Lat.; 83.32° W. Long.
Population: 326 (2000); Race: 95.7% White, 1.5% Black, 0.0% Asian, 0.0% American Indian and Alaska Native, 3.4% Hispanic of any race, 2.8% two or more races (2000); Density: 314.5 persons per square mile (2000); Age: 21.8% under 18, 23.3% over 64 (2000); Marriage status: 11.0% never married, 79.1% now married, 5.7% widowed, 4.2% divorced (2000); Foreign born: 8.9% (2000); Ancestry (includes multiple ancestries): 22.1% German, 16.6% Polish, 15.6% English, 12.9% Irish, 10.1% United States or American (2000).
Economy: Single-family building permits issued: 1 (2001) / 2 (2000); Multi-family building permits issued: 0 (2001) / 0 (2000); Employment by occupation: 31.6% management, 30.8% professional, 2.6% services, 23.9% sales, 0.0% farming, 4.3% construction, 6.8% production (2000).
Income: Per capita income: $83,792 (2000); Median household income: $114,524 (2000); Poverty rate: 1.2% (2000).
Taxes: Total city taxes per capita: $1,198 (1997); City property taxes per capita: $1,134 (1997).
Education: High school graduation rate: 100.0% (2000); College graduation rate: 63.2% (2000).
Housing: Homeownership rate: 96.2% (2000); Median home value: $814,800 (2000); Median rent: $775 per month (2000); Median age of housing: 35 years (2000).
Transportation: Commute to work: 96.5% car, 0.0% public transportation, 0.0% walk, 3.5% work from home (2000); Travel time to work: 11.7% less than 15 minutes, 37.8% 15 to 30 minutes, 28.8% 30 to 45 minutes, 13.5% 45 to 60 minutes, 8.1% 60 minutes or more (2000)

LAKE ORION (village). Covers a land area of 0.759 square miles and a water area of 0.524 square miles. Located at 42.78° N. Lat.; 83.24° W. Long.
History: Lake Orion developed as a country market center, becoming a popular railroad excursion point after 1872. When an electric interurban railway was built between Detroit and Flint in the early 1900's, Lake Orion became a summer resort.
Population: 2,715 (2000); Race: 98.5% White, 0.2% Black, 0.0% Asian, 0.5% American Indian and Alaska Native, 2.1% Hispanic of any race, 0.7% two or more races (2000); Density: 3,575.4 persons per square mile (2000); Age: 19.4% under 18, 13.2% over 64 (2000); Marriage status: 29.6% never married, 48.9% now married, 6.8% widowed, 14.7% divorced (2000); Foreign born: 1.1% (2000); Ancestry (includes multiple ancestries): 19.8% German, 12.9% English, 10.5% Irish, 8.4% Polish, 7.7% Scottish (2000).
Economy: Single-family building permits issued: 0 (2001) / 0 (2000); Multi-family building permits issued: 0 (2001) / 0 (2000); Employment by occupation: 16.1% management, 24.6% professional, 15.1% services, 20.2% sales, 0.0% farming, 7.9% construction, 16.1% production (2000).
Income: Per capita income: $28,671 (2000); Median household income: $51,311 (2000); Poverty rate: 5.6% (2000).
Taxes: Total city taxes per capita: $337 (1997); City property taxes per capita: $337 (1997).
Education: High school graduation rate: 88.7% (2000); College graduation rate: 29.2% (2000).

School District(s)

Lake Orion Community Schools (PK-12)
2000 Enrollment: 6,854 248-693-5413
Housing: Homeownership rate: 57.4% (2000); Median home value: $164,600 (2000); Median rent: $558 per month (2000); Median age of housing: 48 years (2000).
Safety: Violent crime rate: 22.0 per 10,000 population; Property crime rate: 241.8 per 10,000 population (2001).
Newspapers: The Lake Orion Review (1 x week); Oxford Eccentric (2 x week)
Transportation: Commute to work: 93.8% car, 0.0% public transportation, 2.5% walk, 3.2% work from home (2000); Travel time to work: 28.4% less than 15 minutes, 22.7% 15 to 30 minutes, 27.0% 30 to 45 minutes, 11.6% 45 to 60 minutes, 10.4% 60 minutes or more (2000)
Additional Information Contacts
Orion Area Chamber of Commerce 248-693-6300

LATHRUP VILLAGE (city). Covers a land area of 1.510 square miles and a water area of 0 square miles. Located at 42.49° N. Lat.; 83.22° W. Long. Elevation is 703 feet.
History: Lathrup Village was founded in 1926 by Louise Lathrup, a real estate developer, and promoted by Louise and her husband, Charles D. Kelley, a real estate editor of the Detroit newspaper.
Population: 4,236 (2000); Race: 47.8% White, 50.4% Black, 0.0% Asian, 0.0% American Indian and Alaska Native, 1.0% Hispanic of any race, 1.7% two or more races (2000); Density: 2,806.1 persons per square mile (2000); Age: 24.8% under 18, 12.0% over 64 (2000); Marriage status: 25.2% never married, 61.2% now married, 4.6% widowed, 8.9% divorced (2000); Foreign born: 6.5% (2000); Ancestry (includes multiple ancestries): 44.5% Other groups, 12.0% German, 8.3% English, 8.0% Irish, 7.2% Polish (2000).
Economy: Single-family building permits issued: 1 (2001) / 16 (2000); Multi-family building permits issued: 0 (2001) / 0 (2000); Employment by occupation: 18.5% management, 35.7% professional, 6.1% services, 25.1% sales, 0.0% farming, 3.7% construction, 10.9% production (2000).
Income: Per capita income: $35,998 (2000); Median household income: $89,303 (2000); Poverty rate: 2.7% (2000).
Taxes: Total city taxes per capita: $558 (1997); City property taxes per capita: $535 (1997).
Education: High school graduation rate: 94.8% (2000); College graduation rate: 51.5% (2000).

School District(s)

Academy of Lathrup Village (KG-08)
2000 Enrollment: 592 517-774-2100
Housing: Homeownership rate: 98.5% (2000); Median home value: $187,000 (2000); Median rent: $1,083 per month (2000); Median age of housing: 43 years (2000).
Safety: Violent crime rate: 23.5 per 10,000 population; Property crime rate: 138.6 per 10,000 population (2001).
Transportation: Commute to work: 95.7% car, 0.8% public transportation, 0.3% walk, 3.2% work from home (2000); Travel time to work: 17.4% less than 15 minutes, 40.6% 15 to 30 minutes, 34.5% 30 to 45 minutes, 4.3% 45 to 60 minutes, 3.1% 60 minutes or more (2000)

LEONARD (village). Covers a land area of 0.963 square miles and a water area of 0 square miles. Located at 42.86° N. Lat.; 83.14° W. Long. Elevation is 1,003 feet.
History: Leonard was founded in 1882 by Leonard Rowland, and named for him. The town developed after the Pontiac, Oxford & Northern Railroad arrived.
Population: 332 (2000); Race: 82.1% White, 17.3% Black, 0.0% Asian, 0.0% American Indian and Alaska Native, 19.1% Hispanic of any race, 0.6% two or more races (2000); Density: 344.7 persons per square mile (2000); Age: 30.0% under 18, 16.1% over 64 (2000); Marriage status: 19.7% never married, 62.3% now married, 9.4% widowed, 8.6% divorced (2000); Foreign

born: 7.0% (2000); Ancestry (includes multiple ancestries): 21.8% German, 13.9% English, 10.3% Irish, 7.6% French (except Basque), 6.4% United States or American (2000).
Economy: Single-family building permits issued: 1 (2001) / 0 (2000); Multi-family building permits issued: 0 (2001) / 0 (2000); Employment by occupation: 7.5% management, 8.3% professional, 12.0% services, 28.6% sales, 0.0% farming, 17.3% construction, 26.3% production (2000).
Income: Per capita income: $29,006 (2000); Median household income: $45,625 (2000); Poverty rate: 3.9% (2000).
Taxes: Total city taxes per capita: $128 (1997); City property taxes per capita: $117 (1997).
Education: High school graduation rate: 74.1% (2000); College graduation rate: 7.1% (2000).
Housing: Homeownership rate: 91.5% (2000); Median home value: $118,400 (2000); Median rent: $381 per month (2000); Median age of housing: 60+ years (2000).
Transportation: Commute to work: 97.7% car, 0.0% public transportation, 0.8% walk, 1.5% work from home (2000); Travel time to work: 7.6% less than 15 minutes, 26.7% 15 to 30 minutes, 20.6% 30 to 45 minutes, 16.0% 45 to 60 minutes, 29.0% 60 minutes or more (2000)

LYON (township). Covers a land area of 31.343 square miles and a water area of 0.640 square miles. Located at 42.48° N. Lat.; 83.62° W. Long.
History: Lyon Township was organized in 1832 and named for Lucius Lyon, a member of the state legislature.
Population: 11,041 (2000); Race: 98.1% White, 0.2% Black, 0.2% Asian, 0.6% American Indian and Alaska Native, 2.0% Hispanic of any race, 0.5% two or more races (2000); Density: 352.3 persons per square mile (2000); Age: 29.0% under 18, 6.9% over 64 (2000); Marriage status: 20.8% never married, 66.4% now married, 3.4% widowed, 9.3% divorced (2000); Foreign born: 2.2% (2000); Ancestry (includes multiple ancestries): 27.5% German, 15.8% Irish, 13.7% English, 13.6% Polish, 8.6% Italian (2000).
Economy: Single-family building permits issued: 108 (2001) / 154 (2000); Multi-family building permits issued: 146 (2001) / 109 (2000); Employment by occupation: 16.1% management, 21.0% professional, 9.4% services, 30.2% sales, 0.5% farming, 10.8% construction, 12.0% production (2000).
Income: Per capita income: $27,414 (2000); Median household income: $67,288 (2000); Poverty rate: 4.2% (2000).
Taxes: Total city taxes per capita: $128 (1997); City property taxes per capita: $112 (1997).
Education: High school graduation rate: 89.7% (2000); College graduation rate: 26.0% (2000).
Housing: Homeownership rate: 92.0% (2000); Median home value: $211,700 (2000); Median rent: $588 per month (2000); Median age of housing: 18 years (2000).
Transportation: Commute to work: 96.7% car, 0.4% public transportation, 0.3% walk, 2.4% work from home (2000); Travel time to work: 17.5% less than 15 minutes, 34.7% 15 to 30 minutes, 28.0% 30 to 45 minutes, 12.6% 45 to 60 minutes, 7.2% 60 minutes or more (2000)

MADISON HEIGHTS (city). Covers a land area of 7.164 square miles and a water area of 0 square miles. Located at 42.50° N. Lat.; 83.10° W. Long. Elevation is 633 feet.
History: Incorporated 1955.
Population: 31,101 (2000); Race: 90.6% White, 1.8% Black, 5.1% Asian, 0.4% American Indian and Alaska Native, 1.4% Hispanic of any race, 1.4% two or more races (2000); Density: 4,341.3 persons per square mile (2000); Age: 21.9% under 18, 14.1% over 64 (2000); Marriage status: 27.8% never married, 52.9% now married, 7.6% widowed, 11.7% divorced (2000); Foreign born: 14.4% (2000); Ancestry (includes multiple ancestries): 18.3% German, 13.7% Polish, 11.7% Irish, 11.1% Other groups, 10.7% English (2000).
Vital Statistics: Birth rate: 136.7 per 10,000 population (1998)
Economy: Manufacturing: tool design and prototypes, encoder products, displays, machinery, fabricated metal products, apparel. Unemployment rate: 5.2% (11/2002); Total civilian labor force: 20,309 (11/2002); Single-family building permits issued: 18 (2001) / 23 (2000); Multi-family building permits issued: 0 (2001) / 0 (2000); Employment by occupation: 9.3% management, 20.2% professional, 13.8% services, 28.6% sales, 0.1% farming, 10.9% construction, 17.1% production (2000).
Income: Per capita income: $21,429 (2000); Median household income: $42,326 (2000); Poverty rate: 8.9% (2000).
Taxes: Total city taxes per capita: $578 (2000); City property taxes per capita: $548 (2000).
Education: High school graduation rate: 78.8% (2000); College graduation rate: 18.5% (2000).

School District(s)

Chandler Park Academy (PK-12)
2000 Enrollment: 502 517-790-4000
Lamphere Public Schools (PK-12)
2000 Enrollment: 2,524 248-589-1990
Madison Public Schools (Oakland) (PK-12)
2000 Enrollment: 2,140 248-399-7800

Housing: Homeownership rate: 70.1% (2000); Median home value: $110,600 (2000); Median rent: $548 per month (2000); Median age of housing: 40 years (2000).
Hospitals: Madison Community Hospital (67 beds); Saint John Oakland Hospital (261 beds)
Safety: Violent crime rate: 24.6 per 10,000 population; Property crime rate: 404.6 per 10,000 population (2001).
Transportation: Commute to work: 95.8% car, 0.7% public transportation, 1.1% walk, 2.0% work from home (2000); Travel time to work: 28.2% less than 15 minutes, 42.8% 15 to 30 minutes, 21.5% 30 to 45 minutes, 4.4% 45 to 60 minutes, 3.1% 60 minutes or more (2000)

Additional Information Contacts

Madison Heights Chamber of Commerce 248-542-5010

MILFORD (village). Covers a land area of 2.449 square miles and a water area of 0.064 square miles. Located at 42.58° N. Lat.; 83.59° W. Long. Elevation is 945 feet.
Population: 6,272 (2000); Race: 97.0% White, 0.2% Black, 0.0% Asian, 0.7% American Indian and Alaska Native, 1.1% Hispanic of any race, 1.5% two or more races (2000); Density: 2,560.7 persons per square mile (2000); Age: 27.6% under 18, 10.4% over 64 (2000); Marriage status: 23.8% never married, 57.4% now married, 6.2% widowed, 12.7% divorced (2000); Foreign born: 3.7% (2000); Ancestry (includes multiple ancestries): 26.0% German, 15.8% Irish, 13.5% English, 12.2% Polish, 6.0% Italian (2000).
Economy: Single-family building permits issued: 19 (2001) / 5 (2000); Multi-family building permits issued: 0 (2001) / 0 (2000); Employment by occupation: 16.2% management, 22.0% professional, 12.1% services, 25.9% sales, 0.0% farming, 11.0% construction, 12.8% production (2000).
Income: Per capita income: $26,159 (2000); Median household income: $59,688 (2000); Poverty rate: 7.2% (2000).
Taxes: Total city taxes per capita: $361 (1997); City property taxes per capita: $342 (1997).
Education: High school graduation rate: 90.6% (2000); College graduation rate: 30.2% (2000).
Housing: Homeownership rate: 75.0% (2000); Median home value: $157,300 (2000); Median rent: $540 per month (2000); Median age of housing: 33 years (2000).
Newspapers: Milford Times (1 x week); Highlander (1 x week)
Transportation: Commute to work: 95.7% car, 0.0% public transportation, 1.9% walk, 1.8% work from home (2000); Travel time to work: 26.4% less than 15 minutes, 26.3% 15 to 30 minutes, 24.3% 30 to 45 minutes, 14.8% 45 to 60 minutes, 8.2% 60 minutes or more (2000)

MILFORD (township). Covers a land area of 33.296 square miles and a water area of 1.886 square miles. Located at 42.57° N. Lat.; 83.60° W. Long. Elevation is 945 feet.
History: Incorporated 1869.
Population: 15,271 (2000); Race: 97.4% White, 0.4% Black, 0.3% Asian, 0.4% American Indian and Alaska Native, 1.8% Hispanic of any race, 1.1% two or more races (2000); Density: 458.6 persons per square mile (2000); Age: 28.3% under 18, 9.1% over 64 (2000); Marriage status: 23.0% never married, 62.2% now married, 5.0% widowed, 9.8% divorced (2000); Foreign born: 5.2% (2000); Ancestry (includes multiple ancestries): 24.7% German, 14.3% Irish, 13.9% English, 13.3% Polish, 7.8% Italian (2000).
Economy: Manufacturing: transportation equipment, machinery. General Motors proving ground is nearby. Highland State Recreational Area to North; Proud Lake State Recreational Area to Southeast. Island Lake State Recreational Area and Kennington Metropark to Southwest. Single-family building permits issued: 56 (2001) / 81 (2000); Multi-family building permits issued: 0 (2001) / 0 (2000); Employment by occupation: 15.6% management, 22.7% professional, 10.8% services, 27.2% sales, 0.3% farming, 10.6% construction, 12.8% production (2000).
Income: Per capita income: $29,913 (2000); Median household income: $67,672 (2000); Poverty rate: 5.3% (2000).
Taxes: Total city taxes per capita: $241 (2000); City property taxes per capita: $221 (2000).
Education: High school graduation rate: 91.2% (2000); College graduation rate: 31.4% (2000).

Housing: Homeownership rate: 86.6% (2000); Median home value: $218,200 (2000); Median rent: $537 per month (2000); Median age of housing: 22 years (2000).
Transportation: Commute to work: 95.6% car, 0.1% public transportation, 1.0% walk, 2.9% work from home (2000); Travel time to work: 20.3% less than 15 minutes, 29.1% 15 to 30 minutes, 26.0% 30 to 45 minutes, 15.6% 45 to 60 minutes, 9.0% 60 minutes or more (2000)

NEW HUDSON (unincorporated postal area, zip code 48165). Covers a land area of 9.607 square miles and a water area of 0.016 square miles. Located at 42.50° N. Lat.; 83.62° W. Long. Elevation is 950 feet.
Population: 5,419 (2000); Race: 98.4% White, 0.0% Black, 0.1% Asian, 0.3% American Indian and Alaska Native, 2.3% Hispanic of any race, 0.3% two or more races (2000); Density: 564.1 persons per square mile (2000); Age: 30.6% under 18, 6.6% over 64 (2000); Marriage status: 23.5% never married, 65.9% now married, 2.4% widowed, 8.2% divorced (2000); Foreign born: 1.9% (2000); Ancestry (includes multiple ancestries): 27.5% German, 15.0% Irish, 14.4% Polish, 12.8% English, 7.6% Italian (2000).
Economy: In farm area. Manufacturing: glass products, motor vehicle parts, machinery. Oakland Southwest Airport is here. Island Lake State Recreation Area to West. Employment by occupation: 13.0% management, 21.3% professional, 9.7% services, 32.1% sales, 0.6% farming, 9.2% construction, 14.0% production (2000).
Income: Per capita income: $25,127 (2000); Median household income: $66,875 (2000); Poverty rate: 4.9% (2000).
Education: High school graduation rate: 90.2% (2000); College graduation rate: 24.7% (2000).
Housing: Homeownership rate: 87.6% (2000); Median home value: $192,600 (2000); Median rent: $585 per month (2000); Median age of housing: 17 years (2000).
Transportation: Commute to work: 96.8% car, 0.2% public transportation, 0.2% walk, 2.6% work from home (2000); Travel time to work: 20.3% less than 15 minutes, 39.5% 15 to 30 minutes, 24.0% 30 to 45 minutes, 10.1% 45 to 60 minutes, 6.1% 60 minutes or more (2000)

NORTHVILLE (city). Covers a land area of 1.994 square miles and a water area of 0.013 square miles. Located at 42.43° N. Lat.; 83.48° W. Long.
Population: 6,459 (2000); Race: 96.3% White, 0.1% Black, 2.6% Asian, 0.3% American Indian and Alaska Native, 1.4% Hispanic of any race, 0.5% two or more races (2000); Density: 3,239.1 persons per square mile (2000); Age: 24.3% under 18, 11.9% over 64 (2000); Marriage status: 20.2% never married, 66.0% now married, 6.0% widowed, 7.8% divorced (2000); Foreign born: 7.4% (2000); Ancestry (includes multiple ancestries): 24.5% German, 20.6% Irish, 15.0% English, 13.6% Polish, 9.3% Italian (2000).
Economy: Single-family building permits issued: 6 (2001) / 4 (2000); Multi-family building permits issued: 3 (2001) / 0 (2000); Employment by occupation: 25.4% management, 29.8% professional, 7.9% services, 26.7% sales, 0.0% farming, 4.5% construction, 5.7% production (2000).
Income: Per capita income: $43,454 (2000); Median household income: $83,961 (2000); Poverty rate: 1.6% (2000).
Education: High school graduation rate: 94.0% (2000); College graduation rate: 53.9% (2000).
Housing: Homeownership rate: 76.3% (2000); Median home value: $237,000 (2000); Median rent: $653 per month (2000); Median age of housing: 31 years (2000).
Hospitals: Hawthorn Center (118 beds); Northville Psychiatric Hospital (460 beds)
Safety: Violent crime rate: 1.5 per 10,000 population; Property crime rate: 57.0 per 10,000 population (2001).
Transportation: Commute to work: 92.4% car, 0.2% public transportation, 2.2% walk, 4.7% work from home (2000); Travel time to work: 29.0% less than 15 minutes, 30.9% 15 to 30 minutes, 27.6% 30 to 45 minutes, 10.7% 45 to 60 minutes, 1.9% 60 minutes or more (2000)
Additional Information Contacts
Northville Chamber of Commerce 248-349-7640

NOVI (city). Covers a land area of 30.469 square miles and a water area of 0.858 square miles. Located at 42.48° N. Lat.; 83.47° W. Long. Elevation is 909 feet.
History: Novi was platted and named in 1830 by the board of supervisors. The name of Novi was reportedly suggested by the wife of one of the supervisors.
Population: 47,386 (2000); Race: 87.1% White, 2.0% Black, 8.4% Asian, 0.1% American Indian and Alaska Native, 2.1% Hispanic of any race, 1.6% two or more races (2000); Density: 1,555.2 persons per square mile (2000); Age: 27.4% under 18, 8.2% over 64 (2000); Marriage status: 25.1% never married, 62.0% now married, 4.3% widowed, 8.6% divorced (2000); Foreign born: 12.7% (2000); Ancestry (includes multiple ancestries): 22.7% German, 14.8% Irish, 13.8% Other groups, 12.9% English, 12.5% Polish (2000).
Vital Statistics: Birth rate: 129.2 per 10,000 population (1998)
Economy: Unemployment rate: 3.0% (11/2002); Total civilian labor force: 21,897 (11/2002); Single-family building permits issued: 321 (2001) / 265 (2000); Multi-family building permits issued: 10 (2001) / 279 (2000); Employment by occupation: 24.0% management, 29.0% professional, 8.4% services, 25.8% sales, 0.0% farming, 4.3% construction, 8.5% production (2000).
Income: Per capita income: $35,992 (2000); Median household income: $71,918 (2000); Poverty rate: 2.2% (2000).
Taxes: Total city taxes per capita: $461 (2000); City property taxes per capita: $432 (2000).
Education: High school graduation rate: 94.0% (2000); College graduation rate: 49.1% (2000).

School District(s)
Novi Community School District (PK-12)
2000 Enrollment: 5,832 248-449-1200
Housing: Homeownership rate: 70.9% (2000); Median home value: $236,300 (2000); Median rent: $746 per month (2000); Median age of housing: 15 years (2000).
Safety: Violent crime rate: 10.5 per 10,000 population; Property crime rate: 303.3 per 10,000 population (2001).
Transportation: Commute to work: 96.3% car, 0.3% public transportation, 0.5% walk, 2.5% work from home (2000); Travel time to work: 22.7% less than 15 minutes, 33.8% 15 to 30 minutes, 27.0% 30 to 45 minutes, 12.1% 45 to 60 minutes, 4.4% 60 minutes or more (2000)
Additional Information Contacts
Novi Chamber of Commerce 248-349-3743
Novi Convention & Visitors Bureau 248-349-7940

NOVI (township). Covers a land area of 0.138 square miles and a water area of 0 square miles. Located at 42.45° N. Lat.; 83.48° W. Long. Elevation is 909 feet.
Population: 193 (2000); Race: 100.0% White, 0.0% Black, 0.0% Asian, 0.0% American Indian and Alaska Native, 0.0% Hispanic of any race, 0.0% two or more races (2000); Density: 1,397.8 persons per square mile (2000); Age: 25.8% under 18, 9.1% over 64 (2000); Marriage status: 15.6% never married, 80.3% now married, 4.1% widowed, 0.0% divorced (2000); Foreign born: 5.4% (2000); Ancestry (includes multiple ancestries): 33.3% German, 14.5% English, 13.4% Polish, 11.3% Italian, 10.8% Scottish (2000).
Economy: Heavy manufacturing. Oakland Southwest Airport to Northwest. Employment by occupation: 19.2% management, 27.3% professional, 13.1% services, 29.3% sales, 0.0% farming, 9.1% construction, 2.0% production (2000).
Income: Per capita income: $36,985 (2000); Median household income: $105,172 (2000); Poverty rate: 0.0% (2000).
Taxes: Total city taxes per capita: $906 (1997); City property taxes per capita: $906 (1997).
Education: High school graduation rate: 94.5% (2000); College graduation rate: 56.3% (2000).
Housing: Homeownership rate: 100.0% (2000); Median home value: $318,500 (2000); Median age of housing: 32 years (2000).
Transportation: Commute to work: 98.0% car, 0.0% public transportation, 0.0% walk, 2.0% work from home (2000); Travel time to work: 36.1% less than 15 minutes, 20.6% 15 to 30 minutes, 33.0% 30 to 45 minutes, 10.3% 45 to 60 minutes, 0.0% 60 minutes or more (2000)

OAK PARK (city). Covers a land area of 5.022 square miles and a water area of 0 square miles. Located at 42.46° N. Lat.; 83.18° W. Long. Elevation is 666 feet.
History: Marian Sandweiss born here. Incorporated 1927.
Population: 29,793 (2000); Race: 47.6% White, 45.1% Black, 2.6% Asian, 0.2% American Indian and Alaska Native, 1.2% Hispanic of any race, 3.9% two or more races (2000); Density: 5,932.0 persons per square mile (2000); Age: 28.2% under 18, 12.1% over 64 (2000); Marriage status: 32.2% never married, 48.6% now married, 7.4% widowed, 11.8% divorced (2000); Foreign born: 14.9% (2000); Ancestry (includes multiple ancestries): 48.9% Other groups, 6.3% Assyrian/Chaldean/Syriac, 5.7% Polish, 5.1% German, 4.9% Russian (2000).
Vital Statistics: Birth rate: 136.3 per 10,000 population (1998)
Economy: Residential with some industry. Manufacturing: laser cutting, sheet metal forming; fabricated metal products, foods, textiles. Detroit Zoological Park to Northeast. Unemployment rate: 4.7% (11/2002); Total civilian labor force: 17,513 (11/2002); Single-family building permits issued:

3 (2001) / 17 (2000); Multi-family building permits issued: 0 (2001) / 0 (2000); Employment by occupation: 11.8% management, 23.0% professional, 13.7% services, 30.7% sales, 0.0% farming, 4.9% construction, 15.9% production (2000).
Income: Per capita income: $21,677 (2000); Median household income: $48,697 (2000); Poverty rate: 9.4% (2000).
Taxes: Total city taxes per capita: $442 (2000); City property taxes per capita: $429 (2000).
Education: High school graduation rate: 82.2% (2000); College graduation rate: 27.2% (2000).

School District(s)

Academy of Oak Park (KG-12)
2000 Enrollment: 1,541 517-774-2100
Nsoroma Institute (KG-08)
2000 Enrollment: 224 248-370-3050
Oak Park City School District (KG-12)
2000 Enrollment: 4,081 248-691-8400

Four-year College(s)

Yeshiva Gedolah Rabbinical College (Private, Not-for-profit, Jewish)
2001 Enrollment: 35 248-968-3360
2001 Tuition: In-state $3,400; Out-of-state $3,400
Michigan Jewish Institute (Private, Not-for-profit, Jewish)
2001 Enrollment: 72 248-414-6900
2001 Tuition: In-state $8,400; Out-of-state $8,400
Housing: Homeownership rate: 74.9% (2000); Median home value: $114,400 (2000); Median rent: $653 per month (2000); Median age of housing: 44 years (2000).
Safety: Violent crime rate: 22.7 per 10,000 population; Property crime rate: 289.8 per 10,000 population (2001).
Transportation: Commute to work: 93.9% car, 1.1% public transportation, 2.0% walk, 2.4% work from home (2000); Travel time to work: 19.8% less than 15 minutes, 46.4% 15 to 30 minutes, 26.1% 30 to 45 minutes, 3.9% 45 to 60 minutes, 3.8% 60 minutes or more (2000)

OAKLAND CHARTER (township). Covers a land area of 36.428 square miles and a water area of 0.336 square miles. Located at 42.74° N. Lat.; 83.17° W. Long.
Population: 13,071 (2000); Race: 93.5% White, 2.5% Black, 3.2% Asian, 0.1% American Indian and Alaska Native, 0.6% Hispanic of any race, 0.7% two or more races (2000); Density: 358.8 persons per square mile (2000); Age: 30.2% under 18, 6.7% over 64 (2000); Marriage status: 18.6% never married, 72.7% now married, 2.8% widowed, 5.9% divorced (2000); Foreign born: 8.2% (2000); Ancestry (includes multiple ancestries): 25.8% German, 15.6% English, 13.8% Polish, 10.8% Irish, 10.1% Italian (2000).
Economy: Single-family building permits issued: 139 (2001) / 183 (2000); Multi-family building permits issued: 12 (2001) / 0 (2000); Employment by occupation: 27.5% management, 29.4% professional, 6.9% services, 25.1% sales, 0.1% farming, 4.0% construction, 7.0% production (2000).
Income: Per capita income: $42,616 (2000); Median household income: $102,034 (2000); Poverty rate: 2.6% (2000).
Taxes: Total city taxes per capita: $210 (2000); City property taxes per capita: $143 (2000).
Education: High school graduation rate: 95.1% (2000); College graduation rate: 47.7% (2000).
Housing: Homeownership rate: 98.4% (2000); Median home value: $315,700 (2000); Median rent: $741 per month (2000); Median age of housing: 15 years (2000).
Transportation: Commute to work: 96.4% car, 0.3% public transportation, 0.5% walk, 2.7% work from home (2000); Travel time to work: 11.9% less than 15 minutes, 33.9% 15 to 30 minutes, 28.1% 30 to 45 minutes, 15.0% 45 to 60 minutes, 11.1% 60 minutes or more (2000)

ORCHARD LAKE VILLAGE (city). Aka Orchard Lake. Covers a land area of 2.589 square miles and a water area of 1.512 square miles. Located at 42.58° N. Lat.; 83.38° W. Long.
Population: 2,215 (2000); Race: 94.2% White, 2.3% Black, 2.3% Asian, 0.0% American Indian and Alaska Native, 2.6% Hispanic of any race, 0.8% two or more races (2000); Density: 855.7 persons per square mile (2000); Age: 27.1% under 18, 11.0% over 64 (2000); Marriage status: 20.0% never married, 71.5% now married, 2.9% widowed, 5.6% divorced (2000); Foreign born: 15.3% (2000); Ancestry (includes multiple ancestries): 18.7% German, 15.3% English, 11.3% Irish, 10.9% Assyrian/Chaldean/Syriac, 10.7% Other groups (2000).
Economy: Single-family building permits issued: 11 (2001) / 20 (2000); Multi-family building permits issued: 0 (2001) / 0 (2000); Employment by occupation: 26.8% management, 29.6% professional, 8.3% services, 26.1% sales, 0.0% farming, 3.4% construction, 5.8% production (2000).
Income: Per capita income: $67,881 (2000); Median household income: $121,126 (2000); Poverty rate: 0.5% (2000).
Taxes: Total city taxes per capita: $1,044 (1997); City property taxes per capita: $1,004 (1997).
Education: High school graduation rate: 93.4% (2000); College graduation rate: 61.5% (2000).

Four-year College(s)

Saint Mary's College of Ave Maria University (Private, Not-for-profit, Roman Catholic)
2001 Enrollment: 513 248-683-1757
2001 Tuition: In-state $6,504; Out-of-state $6,504
Saints Cyril and Methodius Seminary (Private, Not-for-profit, Roman Catholic)
2001 Enrollment: n/a 248-683-0310
Housing: Homeownership rate: 97.5% (2000); Median home value: $571,700 (2000); Median rent: $635 per month (2000); Median age of housing: 24 years (2000).
Transportation: Commute to work: 96.7% car, 0.0% public transportation, 0.6% walk, 2.4% work from home (2000); Travel time to work: 11.4% less than 15 minutes, 40.5% 15 to 30 minutes, 27.9% 30 to 45 minutes, 15.2% 45 to 60 minutes, 5.1% 60 minutes or more (2000)

ORION (township). Covers a land area of 33.352 square miles and a water area of 2.580 square miles. Located at 42.76° N. Lat.; 83.26° W. Long.
Population: 33,463 (2000); Race: 95.7% White, 1.4% Black, 1.0% Asian, 0.2% American Indian and Alaska Native, 1.9% Hispanic of any race, 1.3% two or more races (2000); Density: 1,003.3 persons per square mile (2000); Age: 28.6% under 18, 6.2% over 64 (2000); Marriage status: 23.6% never married, 62.5% now married, 4.1% widowed, 9.8% divorced (2000); Foreign born: 4.7% (2000); Ancestry (includes multiple ancestries): 26.7% German, 15.7% Irish, 12.9% English, 11.9% Polish, 8.2% Other groups (2000).
Economy: Manufacturing: electronic equipment, transportation equipment, machinery. Unemployment rate: 4.1% (11/2002); Total civilian labor force: 15,769 (11/2002); Single-family building permits issued: 134 (2001) / 174 (2000); Multi-family building permits issued: 64 (2001) / 72 (2000); Employment by occupation: 19.8% management, 26.1% professional, 11.0% services, 23.3% sales, 0.0% farming, 7.7% construction, 12.2% production (2000).
Income: Per capita income: $30,299 (2000); Median household income: $71,844 (2000); Poverty rate: 3.2% (2000).
Taxes: Total city taxes per capita: $242 (2000); City property taxes per capita: $209 (2000).
Education: High school graduation rate: 92.1% (2000); College graduation rate: 36.3% (2000).
Housing: Homeownership rate: 81.8% (2000); Median home value: $197,000 (2000); Median rent: $634 per month (2000); Median age of housing: 22 years (2000).
Transportation: Commute to work: 95.9% car, 0.1% public transportation, 0.9% walk, 2.7% work from home (2000); Travel time to work: 18.6% less than 15 minutes, 35.2% 15 to 30 minutes, 26.8% 30 to 45 minutes, 11.6% 45 to 60 minutes, 7.9% 60 minutes or more (2000)

ORTONVILLE (village). Covers a land area of 0.993 square miles and a water area of 0.003 square miles. Located at 42.85° N. Lat.; 83.44° W. Long. Elevation is 941 feet.
Population: 1,535 (2000); Race: 97.2% White, 0.0% Black, 0.3% Asian, 1.0% American Indian and Alaska Native, 2.2% Hispanic of any race, 0.2% two or more races (2000); Density: 1,546.2 persons per square mile (2000); Age: 32.7% under 18, 7.5% over 64 (2000); Marriage status: 24.6% never married, 57.4% now married, 6.8% widowed, 11.2% divorced (2000); Foreign born: 1.2% (2000); Ancestry (includes multiple ancestries): 31.7% German, 14.8% Irish, 12.4% English, 8.9% Polish, 7.7% Other groups (2000).
Economy: In farm area. Diverse manufacturing. Ortonville State Recreational Area to North; Mt. Hilly and Pine Knob ski areas to Southwest. Single-family building permits issued: 1 (2001) / 1 (2000); Multi-family building permits issued: 0 (2001) / 4 (2000); Employment by occupation: 10.5% management, 23.0% professional, 15.6% services, 21.4% sales, 0.0% farming, 14.0% construction, 15.5% production (2000).
Income: Per capita income: $24,110 (2000); Median household income: $60,972 (2000); Poverty rate: 4.8% (2000).
Taxes: Total city taxes per capita: $174 (1997); City property taxes per capita: $165 (1997).

Education: High school graduation rate: 88.2% (2000); College graduation rate: 21.1% (2000).

School District(s)

Brandon School District (KG-12)
2000 Enrollment: 3,551 248-627-1802

Housing: Homeownership rate: 69.7% (2000); Median home value: $155,800 (2000); Median rent: $574 per month (2000); Median age of housing: 31 years (2000).

Newspapers: County Line Reminder (1 x week)

Transportation: Commute to work: 93.2% car, 0.0% public transportation, 3.5% walk, 2.8% work from home (2000); Travel time to work: 20.9% less than 15 minutes, 22.6% 15 to 30 minutes, 32.7% 30 to 45 minutes, 15.5% 45 to 60 minutes, 8.3% 60 minutes or more (2000)

OXFORD (village). Covers a land area of 1.232 square miles and a water area of 0.194 square miles. Located at 42.82° N. Lat.; 83.26° W. Long. Elevation is 1,057 feet.

History: Settled 1836; incorporated 1876.

Population: 3,540 (2000); Race: 98.7% White, 0.0% Black, 0.3% Asian, 0.1% American Indian and Alaska Native, 2.8% Hispanic of any race, 0.8% two or more races (2000); Density: 2,873.5 persons per square mile (2000); Age: 29.9% under 18, 7.3% over 64 (2000); Marriage status: 23.1% never married, 61.3% now married, 3.8% widowed, 11.8% divorced (2000); Foreign born: 3.0% (2000); Ancestry (includes multiple ancestries): 27.1% German, 17.0% English, 16.5% Irish, 10.5% Polish, 9.1% French (except Basque) (2000).

Economy: In lake and farm area: cattle; grain. Manufacturing: steel castings, urethane foam systems, plastic products, dies, metal stampings. Gravel pits. Resort. Mt. Grampian Ski Area to East. Single-family building permits issued: 232 (2001) / 12 (2000); Multi-family building permits issued: 0 (2001) / 0 (2000); Employment by occupation: 16.3% management, 20.3% professional, 10.5% services, 26.6% sales, 0.0% farming, 11.6% construction, 14.7% production (2000).

Income: Per capita income: $24,811 (2000); Median household income: $53,885 (2000); Poverty rate: 5.3% (2000).

Taxes: Total city taxes per capita: $258 (1997); City property taxes per capita: $243 (1997).

Education: High school graduation rate: 89.4% (2000); College graduation rate: 29.7% (2000).

School District(s)

Oxford Area Community Schools (PK-12)
2000 Enrollment: 3,879 248-969-5000

Housing: Homeownership rate: 68.1% (2000); Median home value: $165,200 (2000); Median rent: $535 per month (2000); Median age of housing: 29 years (2000).

Safety: Violent crime rate: 11.2 per 10,000 population; Property crime rate: 219.2 per 10,000 population (2001).

Newspapers: Oxford Leader (1 x week); The Advertiser (1 x week); The Citizen (1 x week)

Transportation: Commute to work: 95.8% car, 0.2% public transportation, 1.7% walk, 1.9% work from home (2000); Travel time to work: 19.7% less than 15 minutes, 22.7% 15 to 30 minutes, 31.0% 30 to 45 minutes, 15.3% 45 to 60 minutes, 11.3% 60 minutes or more (2000)

Additional Information Contacts

Oxford Chamber of Commerce 248-628-0410

OXFORD CHARTER (township). Covers a land area of 33.890 square miles and a water area of 1.329 square miles. Located at 42.82° N. Lat.; 83.27° W. Long. Elevation is 1,057 feet.

Population: 16,025 (2000); Race: 96.7% White, 0.3% Black, 0.8% Asian, 0.1% American Indian and Alaska Native, 2.2% Hispanic of any race, 1.4% two or more races (2000); Density: 472.9 persons per square mile (2000); Age: 29.2% under 18, 7.3% over 64 (2000); Marriage status: 23.3% never married, 61.8% now married, 4.7% widowed, 10.2% divorced (2000); Foreign born: 3.5% (2000); Ancestry (includes multiple ancestries): 23.8% German, 16.8% Irish, 15.9% English, 10.2% Polish, 8.2% Other groups (2000).

Economy: Employment by occupation: 17.0% management, 21.2% professional, 11.5% services, 27.0% sales, 0.0% farming, 9.8% construction, 13.5% production (2000).

Income: Per capita income: $26,601 (2000); Median household income: $63,494 (2000); Poverty rate: 4.3% (2000).

Taxes: Total city taxes per capita: $126 (2000); City property taxes per capita: $99 (2000).

Education: High school graduation rate: 89.8% (2000); College graduation rate: 26.9% (2000).

Housing: Homeownership rate: 84.8% (2000); Median home value: $178,400 (2000); Median rent: $537 per month (2000); Median age of housing: 22 years (2000).

Transportation: Commute to work: 96.5% car, 0.0% public transportation, 0.8% walk, 2.5% work from home (2000); Travel time to work: 18.2% less than 15 minutes, 23.6% 15 to 30 minutes, 30.8% 30 to 45 minutes, 15.9% 45 to 60 minutes, 11.4% 60 minutes or more (2000)

PLEASANT RIDGE (city). Covers a land area of 0.568 square miles and a water area of 0 square miles. Located at 42.47° N. Lat.; 83.14° W. Long. Elevation is 650 feet.

History: Pleasant Ridge developed as a suburban residential community. It was incorporated as a village in 1919 and as a city in 1938.

Population: 2,594 (2000); Race: 95.4% White, 1.0% Black, 0.7% Asian, 0.2% American Indian and Alaska Native, 3.6% Hispanic of any race, 1.7% two or more races (2000); Density: 4,563.7 persons per square mile (2000); Age: 22.1% under 18, 11.5% over 64 (2000); Marriage status: 25.5% never married, 59.6% now married, 4.9% widowed, 10.0% divorced (2000); Foreign born: 4.9% (2000); Ancestry (includes multiple ancestries): 24.7% German, 21.0% Irish, 16.7% Polish, 15.1% English, 10.1% Italian (2000).

Economy: Single-family building permits issued: 2 (2001) / 0 (2000); Multi-family building permits issued: 0 (2001) / 0 (2000); Employment by occupation: 18.4% management, 43.9% professional, 5.5% services, 21.1% sales, 0.0% farming, 4.3% construction, 6.9% production (2000).

Income: Per capita income: $40,846 (2000); Median household income: $80,682 (2000); Poverty rate: 2.0% (2000).

Taxes: Total city taxes per capita: $186 (1997); City property taxes per capita: $179 (1997).

Education: High school graduation rate: 96.0% (2000); College graduation rate: 66.5% (2000).

Housing: Homeownership rate: 94.2% (2000); Median home value: $223,800 (2000); Median rent: $629 per month (2000); Median age of housing: 60+ years (2000).

Safety: Violent crime rate: 0.0 per 10,000 population; Property crime rate: 38.3 per 10,000 population (2001).

Transportation: Commute to work: 95.3% car, 0.0% public transportation, 0.9% walk, 3.8% work from home (2000); Travel time to work: 25.6% less than 15 minutes, 50.9% 15 to 30 minutes, 18.2% 30 to 45 minutes, 3.1% 45 to 60 minutes, 2.2% 60 minutes or more (2000)

PONTIAC (city). Covers a land area of 19.992 square miles and a water area of 0.220 square miles. Located at 42.64° N. Lat.; 83.29° W. Long. Elevation is 943 feet.

History: Pontiac was established in 1818 by a group of Detroit businessmen known as the Pontiac Company. It was named for Ottawa chief Pontiac. The Pontiac Spring Wagon Works was founded in the mid-1800's, and until the close of the 1800's, carriage manufacture was the chief industry. The early 1900's brought the Oakland Motor Car Company, the Rapid Motor Truck Company, and other automotive firms, including, eventually, the Pontiac Motor Division of the General Motors Corporation.

Population: 66,337 (2000); Race: 39.5% White, 47.7% Black, 2.3% Asian, 0.6% American Indian and Alaska Native, 12.7% Hispanic of any race, 3.9% two or more races (2000); Density: 3,318.2 persons per square mile (2000); Age: 30.4% under 18, 8.3% over 64 (2000); Marriage status: 39.1% never married, 40.2% now married, 6.5% widowed, 14.2% divorced (2000); Foreign born: 6.2% (2000); Ancestry (includes multiple ancestries): 54.1% Other groups, 6.9% German, 5.0% Irish, 3.9% English, 3.8% United States or American (2000).

Vital Statistics: Birth rate: 197.0 per 10,000 population (1998)

Economy: Unemployment rate: 11.3% (11/2002); Total civilian labor force: 34,773 (11/2002); Single-family building permits issued: 237 (2001) / 210 (2000); Multi-family building permits issued: 0 (2001) / 5 (2000); Employment by occupation: 6.2% management, 12.3% professional, 21.4% services, 25.0% sales, 0.4% farming, 9.5% construction, 25.2% production (2000).

Income: Per capita income: $15,842 (2000); Median household income: $31,207 (2000); Poverty rate: 22.1% (2000).

Taxes: Total city taxes per capita: $745 (2000); City property taxes per capita: $431 (2000).

Education: High school graduation rate: 68.9% (2000); College graduation rate: 10.3% (2000).

School District(s)

Great Lakes Academy (KG-06)
2000 Enrollment: 388 313-487-0252

Pontiac Academy of Excellence (KG-05)
2000 Enrollment: 236 517-790-4000

Pontiac City School District (KG-12)
2000 Enrollment: 12,383 248-857-8123
Pontiac Psa (KG-05)
2000 Enrollment: 0 248-452-9309
Walton Charter Academy (KG-06)
2000 Enrollment: 528 248-371-9300

Housing: Homeownership rate: 52.8% (2000); Median home value: $74,300 (2000); Median rent: $493 per month (2000); Median age of housing: 43 years (2000).
Hospitals: North Oakland Medical Center (380 beds); POH Medical Center (308 beds); Saint Joseph Mercy Oakland (528 beds)
Safety: Violent crime rate: 169.0 per 10,000 population; Property crime rate: 509.1 per 10,000 population (2001).
Newspapers: The Oakland Press (7 x week); Lakeland Reminder (1 x week); Orion/Oxford Reminder (1 x week); In Your Community News (1 x week); West Bloomfield Community News (1 x week)
Transportation: Commute to work: 94.4% car, 1.1% public transportation, 2.2% walk, 1.1% work from home (2000); Travel time to work: 34.3% less than 15 minutes, 40.5% 15 to 30 minutes, 15.0% 30 to 45 minutes, 4.9% 45 to 60 minutes, 5.2% 60 minutes or more (2000); Amtrak: Service available.
Airports: Oakland County International
Additional Information Contacts
Pontiac Chamber of Commerce 248-335-9600

ROCHESTER (city). Covers a land area of 3.861 square miles and a water area of 0 square miles. Located at 42.68° N. Lat.; 83.12° W. Long. Elevation is 749 feet.
History: Rochester was settled in the early 1800's by families from New York, who named it after the New York town of Rochester. Rochester later developed as a residential community for workers in the Pontiac automobile plants. Industries in the early 1900's in Rochester included a foundry, knitting works, and a paper company.
Population: 10,467 (2000); Race: 91.3% White, 2.1% Black, 5.2% Asian, 0.0% American Indian and Alaska Native, 1.0% Hispanic of any race, 1.0% two or more races (2000); Density: 2,710.6 persons per square mile (2000); Age: 23.2% under 18, 10.1% over 64 (2000); Marriage status: 27.2% never married, 58.3% now married, 4.5% widowed, 10.0% divorced (2000); Foreign born: 8.6% (2000); Ancestry (includes multiple ancestries): 25.2% German, 15.1% English, 14.4% Irish, 13.3% Polish, 9.7% Other groups (2000).
Economy: Single-family building permits issued: 78 (2001) / 141 (2000); Multi-family building permits issued: 0 (2001) / 0 (2000); Employment by occupation: 25.5% management, 29.9% professional, 8.5% services, 26.5% sales, 0.0% farming, 3.9% construction, 5.6% production (2000).
Income: Per capita income: $36,989 (2000); Median household income: $65,179 (2000); Poverty rate: 2.7% (2000).
Taxes: Total city taxes per capita: $748 (2000); City property taxes per capita: $693 (2000).
Education: High school graduation rate: 94.1% (2000); College graduation rate: 52.1% (2000).

School District(s)

Oakland U—E T Clark Academy (N -N)
2000 Enrollment: n/a 810-370-2100
Rochester Community School District (KG-12)
2000 Enrollment: 13,862 248-651-6210

Housing: Homeownership rate: 64.2% (2000); Median home value: $260,700 (2000); Median rent: $613 per month (2000); Median age of housing: 28 years (2000).
Hospitals: Crittenton Hospital (290 beds)
Safety: Violent crime rate: 4.8 per 10,000 population; Property crime rate: 194.8 per 10,000 population (2001).
Newspapers: Rochester Community News (1 x week)
Transportation: Commute to work: 93.1% car, 0.4% public transportation, 2.3% walk, 3.7% work from home (2000); Travel time to work: 24.8% less than 15 minutes, 31.3% 15 to 30 minutes, 23.2% 30 to 45 minutes, 11.3% 45 to 60 minutes, 9.3% 60 minutes or more (2000)
Additional Information Contacts
Rochester Chamber of Commerce 248-651-6700

ROCHESTER HILLS (city). Covers a land area of 32.849 square miles and a water area of 0.076 square miles. Located at 42.66° N. Lat.; 83.15° W. Long. Elevation is 810 feet.
History: Oakland University and Michigan Christian College are here.
Population: 68,825 (2000); Race: 88.6% White, 2.1% Black, 6.7% Asian, 0.2% American Indian and Alaska Native, 2.3% Hispanic of any race, 1.8% two or more races (2000); Density: 2,095.2 persons per square mile (2000); Age: 25.9% under 18, 10.4% over 64 (2000); Marriage status: 21.6% never married, 64.9% now married, 5.6% widowed, 8.0% divorced (2000); Foreign born: 12.2% (2000); Ancestry (includes multiple ancestries): 23.0% German, 14.1% Irish, 13.6% Other groups, 13.5% English, 12.3% Polish (2000).
Vital Statistics: Birth rate: 113.8 per 10,000 population (1998)
Economy: Manufacturing: transportation equipment, plastic products, fabricated metal products. Rochester-Utica State Recreation Area to East; Stony Creek Metropark to Northeast. Unemployment rate: 3.1% (11/2002); Total civilian labor force: 38,995 (11/2002); Single-family building permits issued: 173 (2001) / 167 (2000); Multi-family building permits issued: 0 (2001) / 0 (2000); Employment by occupation: 22.7% management, 30.5% professional, 8.1% services, 25.6% sales, 0.1% farming, 5.1% construction, 7.8% production (2000).
Income: Per capita income: $35,070 (2000); Median household income: $74,912 (2000); Poverty rate: 3.4% (2000).
Taxes: Total city taxes per capita: $279 (2000); City property taxes per capita: $254 (2000).
Education: High school graduation rate: 92.7% (2000); College graduation rate: 47.3% (2000).

Four-year College(s)

Rochester College (Private, Not-for-profit, Churches of Christ)
2001 Enrollment: 893 248-218-2000
2001 Tuition: In-state $9,462; Out-of-state $9,462
Oakland University (Public)
2001 Enrollment: 15,875 248-370-2100
2001 Tuition: In-state $4,166; Out-of-state $11,340

Two-year College(s)

Michigan Montessori Teacher Education Center (Private, Not-for-profit)
2001 Enrollment: n/a 248-375-2800

Housing: Homeownership rate: 79.2% (2000); Median home value: $226,200 (2000); Median rent: $733 per month (2000); Median age of housing: 19 years (2000).
Transportation: Commute to work: 95.4% car, 0.1% public transportation, 0.8% walk, 3.2% work from home (2000); Travel time to work: 21.6% less than 15 minutes, 37.3% 15 to 30 minutes, 24.0% 30 to 45 minutes, 10.5% 45 to 60 minutes, 6.6% 60 minutes or more (2000)

ROSE (township). Covers a land area of 35.018 square miles and a water area of 1.346 square miles. Located at 42.74° N. Lat.; 83.62° W. Long.
History: Rose Township was organized in 1837. The village of Rose Center grew up around the Pere Marquette Railroad station.
Population: 6,210 (2000); Race: 97.9% White, 0.1% Black, 0.1% Asian, 0.3% American Indian and Alaska Native, 3.4% Hispanic of any race, 1.0% two or more races (2000); Density: 177.3 persons per square mile (2000); Age: 26.6% under 18, 7.0% over 64 (2000); Marriage status: 22.8% never married, 66.1% now married, 3.0% widowed, 8.1% divorced (2000); Foreign born: 3.6% (2000); Ancestry (includes multiple ancestries): 22.2% German, 15.8% English, 11.7% Irish, 9.0% Polish, 5.5% French (except Basque) (2000).
Economy: Single-family building permits issued: 29 (2001) / 46 (2000); Multi-family building permits issued: 0 (2001) / 0 (2000); Employment by occupation: 12.9% management, 19.4% professional, 13.3% services, 20.9% sales, 0.2% farming, 18.5% construction, 14.9% production (2000).
Income: Per capita income: $24,983 (2000); Median household income: $66,401 (2000); Poverty rate: 4.6% (2000).
Taxes: Total city taxes per capita: $63 (1997); City property taxes per capita: $47 (1997).
Education: High school graduation rate: 88.9% (2000); College graduation rate: 19.5% (2000).
Housing: Homeownership rate: 94.4% (2000); Median home value: $172,000 (2000); Median rent: $704 per month (2000); Median age of housing: 24 years (2000).
Transportation: Commute to work: 96.1% car, 0.8% public transportation, 0.8% walk, 1.8% work from home (2000); Travel time to work: 13.2% less than 15 minutes, 26.9% 15 to 30 minutes, 27.7% 30 to 45 minutes, 18.8% 45 to 60 minutes, 13.3% 60 minutes or more (2000)

ROYAL OAK (city). Covers a land area of 11.816 square miles and a water area of 0.001 square miles. Located at 42.50° N. Lat.; 83.15° W. Long. Elevation is 661 feet.
History: The naming of Royal Oak is said to have been by Governor Lewis Cass, who camped under a large oak tree here and exclaimed that it was indeed a royal oak, reminding him of the Royal Oak in Scotland where Prince Charles the Pretender once hid from his enemies. Settlement began here around 1820. For a time, cow bells and sheep bells were manufactured in Royal Oak.

Population: 60,062 (2000); Race: 94.4% White, 1.8% Black, 1.6% Asian, 0.2% American Indian and Alaska Native, 1.4% Hispanic of any race, 1.5% two or more races (2000); Density: 5,083.0 persons per square mile (2000); Age: 17.8% under 18, 15.0% over 64 (2000); Marriage status: 33.7% never married, 47.9% now married, 6.9% widowed, 11.5% divorced (2000); Foreign born: 6.3% (2000); Ancestry (includes multiple ancestries): 22.9% German, 17.1% Irish, 14.6% English, 11.6% Polish, 7.6% Italian (2000).
Vital Statistics: Birth rate: 133.0 per 10,000 population (1998)
Economy: Manufacturing: motor vehicle and computer parts, metal forging. Detroit Zoological Park is to South in Huntington Woods. Oakland Troy Airport to North. Unemployment rate: 3.3% (11/2002); Total civilian labor force: 42,399 (11/2002); Single-family building permits issued: 3 (2001) / 16 (2000); Multi-family building permits issued: 0 (2001) / 0 (2000); Employment by occupation: 17.7% management, 30.3% professional, 10.7% services, 26.2% sales, 0.1% farming, 6.4% construction, 8.6% production (2000).
Income: Per capita income: $30,990 (2000); Median household income: $52,252 (2000); Poverty rate: 4.3% (2000).
Taxes: Total city taxes per capita: $462 (2000); City property taxes per capita: $408 (2000).
Education: High school graduation rate: 91.5% (2000); College graduation rate: 39.9% (2000).

School District(s)

School District of the City of R (PK-12)
2000 Enrollment: 6,709 248-435-8400

Four-year College(s)

William Beaumont Hospital (Private, Not-for-profit)
2001 Enrollment: n/a 248-551-5000

Housing: Homeownership rate: 70.1% (2000); Median home value: $150,900 (2000); Median rent: $605 per month (2000); Median age of housing: 46 years (2000).
Hospitals: William Beaumont Hospital (937 beds)
Safety: Violent crime rate: 21.4 per 10,000 population; Property crime rate: 257.0 per 10,000 population (2001).
Newspapers: The Daily Tribune (6 x week); Tribune Plus (1 x week); The Mirror of Royal Oak (1 x week); The Mirror of Berkeley/Huntington Woods (1 x week); The Ferndale Pleasant Ridge Mirror (1 x week); The Clawson Mirror (1 x week)
Transportation: Commute to work: 93.8% car, 1.0% public transportation, 1.8% walk, 2.8% work from home (2000); Travel time to work: 26.1% less than 15 minutes, 44.6% 15 to 30 minutes, 22.1% 30 to 45 minutes, 4.4% 45 to 60 minutes, 2.8% 60 minutes or more (2000); Amtrak: Service available.
Additional Information Contacts
Royal Oak Chamber of Commerce 248-547-4000

ROYAL OAK CHARTER (township). Covers a land area of 0.676 square miles and a water area of 0 square miles. Located at 42.45° N. Lat.; 83.16° W. Long. Elevation is 661 feet.
Population: 5,446 (2000); Race: 23.4% White, 70.9% Black, 1.0% Asian, 0.1% American Indian and Alaska Native, 1.0% Hispanic of any race, 4.1% two or more races (2000); Density: 8,055.8 persons per square mile (2000); Age: 25.1% under 18, 17.9% over 64 (2000); Marriage status: 40.9% never married, 30.7% now married, 13.4% widowed, 14.9% divorced (2000); Foreign born: 16.8% (2000); Ancestry (includes multiple ancestries): 67.7% Other groups, 6.1% Russian, 3.1% Ukrainian, 3.0% African, 2.3% United States or American (2000).
Economy: Employment by occupation: 3.5% management, 17.0% professional, 19.2% services, 33.0% sales, 0.0% farming, 5.1% construction, 22.3% production (2000).
Income: Per capita income: $15,027 (2000); Median household income: $23,710 (2000); Poverty rate: 23.5% (2000).
Taxes: Total city taxes per capita: $19 (1997); City property taxes per capita: $19 (1997).
Education: High school graduation rate: 78.9% (2000); College graduation rate: 15.4% (2000).
Housing: Homeownership rate: 17.6% (2000); Median home value: $74,700 (2000); Median rent: $532 per month (2000); Median age of housing: 36 years (2000).
Transportation: Commute to work: 86.5% car, 5.5% public transportation, 6.6% walk, 0.7% work from home (2000); Travel time to work: 29.3% less than 15 minutes, 45.0% 15 to 30 minutes, 18.0% 30 to 45 minutes, 3.2% 45 to 60 minutes, 4.5% 60 minutes or more (2000)

SOUTH LYON (city). Covers a land area of 3.393 square miles and a water area of 0 square miles. Located at 42.46° N. Lat.; 83.65° W. Long. Elevation is 919 feet.
History: South Lyon was first settled in 1832 by the widow Thompson and her son William, who operated a store in a part of their home. First called Thompson's Corners, it was later renamed for Lucius Lyon, a member of the legislature.
Population: 10,036 (2000); Race: 96.9% White, 0.4% Black, 0.6% Asian, 0.5% American Indian and Alaska Native, 1.6% Hispanic of any race, 0.8% two or more races (2000); Density: 2,958.2 persons per square mile (2000); Age: 24.6% under 18, 15.1% over 64 (2000); Marriage status: 21.2% never married, 59.4% now married, 7.8% widowed, 11.5% divorced (2000); Foreign born: 3.7% (2000); Ancestry (includes multiple ancestries): 25.4% German, 15.2% Irish, 14.2% English, 10.5% Polish, 7.3% Other groups (2000).
Economy: Single-family building permits issued: 80 (2001) / 104 (2000); Multi-family building permits issued: 42 (2001) / 80 (2000); Employment by occupation: 15.0% management, 25.9% professional, 9.6% services, 27.4% sales, 0.5% farming, 8.2% construction, 13.5% production (2000).
Income: Per capita income: $26,187 (2000); Median household income: $53,395 (2000); Poverty rate: 5.2% (2000).
Taxes: Total city taxes per capita: $302 (1997); City property taxes per capita: $280 (1997).
Education: High school graduation rate: 89.6% (2000); College graduation rate: 31.3% (2000).

School District(s)

South Lyon Community Schools (KG-12)
2000 Enrollment: 6,107 248-573-8127

Housing: Homeownership rate: 74.7% (2000); Median home value: $160,400 (2000); Median rent: $596 per month (2000); Median age of housing: 18 years (2000).
Safety: Violent crime rate: 17.8 per 10,000 population; Property crime rate: 121.9 per 10,000 population (2001).
Newspapers: South Lyon Herald (1 x week)
Transportation: Commute to work: 95.3% car, 0.0% public transportation, 1.4% walk, 2.6% work from home (2000); Travel time to work: 16.4% less than 15 minutes, 30.8% 15 to 30 minutes, 32.6% 30 to 45 minutes, 13.9% 45 to 60 minutes, 6.4% 60 minutes or more (2000)
Additional Information Contacts
South Lyon Chamber of Commerce. 248-437-3257

SOUTHFIELD (city). Covers a land area of 26.233 square miles and a water area of 0.006 square miles. Located at 42.48° N. Lat.; 83.24° W. Long. Elevation is 684 feet.
History: Southfield was settled in the 1820's by John Daniels. It was incorporated as a city in 1958.
Population: 78,296 (2000); Race: 39.0% White, 53.3% Black, 3.1% Asian, 0.3% American Indian and Alaska Native, 1.3% Hispanic of any race, 3.7% two or more races (2000); Density: 2,984.6 persons per square mile (2000); Age: 21.5% under 18, 15.1% over 64 (2000); Marriage status: 31.9% never married, 47.6% now married, 8.4% widowed, 12.1% divorced (2000); Foreign born: 14.0% (2000); Ancestry (includes multiple ancestries): 53.9% Other groups, 5.1% German, 4.7% Assyrian/Chaldean/Syriac, 4.0% Polish, 3.4% Irish (2000).
Vital Statistics: Birth rate: 115.8 per 10,000 population (1998)
Economy: Unemployment rate: 4.4% (11/2002); Total civilian labor force: 48,635 (11/2002); Single-family building permits issued: 161 (2001) / 125 (2000); Multi-family building permits issued: 0 (2001) / 0 (2000); Employment by occupation: 15.9% management, 28.0% professional, 10.1% services, 28.4% sales, 0.1% farming, 4.9% construction, 12.6% production (2000).
Income: Per capita income: $28,096 (2000); Median household income: $51,802 (2000); Poverty rate: 7.4% (2000).
Taxes: Total city taxes per capita: $648 (2000); City property taxes per capita: $626 (2000).
Education: High school graduation rate: 87.3% (2000); College graduation rate: 36.7% (2000).

School District(s)

Academy of Southfield (KG-07)
2000 Enrollment: 483 517-774-2100
Advanced Technology Academy (11-12)
2000 Enrollment: 71 248-204-2400
Agbu Alex-Marie Manoogian School (KG-12)
2000 Enrollment: 279 517-774-2100
Oasis Academy (KG-08)
2000 Enrollment: 408 517-774-2100
Southfield Public School District (KG-12)
2000 Enrollment: 9,436 248-746-8500

Four-year College(s)

Lawrence Technological University (Private, Not-for-profit)
2001 Enrollment: 4,151 248-204-4000
2001 Tuition: In-state $10,442; Out-of-state $10,442

Two-year College(s)

Elsa Cooper Institute of Court Reporting (Private, For-profit)
2001 Enrollment: 67 248-352-1600
2001 Tuition: In-state $8,970; Out-of-state $8,970

Housing: Homeownership rate: 54.1% (2000); Median home value: $155,400 (2000); Median rent: $734 per month (2000); Median age of housing: 32 years (2000).
Hospitals: Great Lakes Rehabilitation Hospital (101 beds); Providence Hospital (462 beds)
Safety: Violent crime rate: 127.7 per 10,000 population; Property crime rate: 546.1 per 10,000 population (2001).
Newspapers: The Detroit Jewish News (1 x week)
Transportation: Commute to work: 94.5% car, 1.1% public transportation, 1.5% walk, 2.4% work from home (2000); Travel time to work: 21.0% less than 15 minutes, 42.6% 15 to 30 minutes, 27.0% 30 to 45 minutes, 5.9% 45 to 60 minutes, 3.5% 60 minutes or more (2000)
Additional Information Contacts
French-American Chamber of Commerce 248-358-1861
Southfield Chamber of Commerce 248-827-1127

SOUTHFIELD (township). Covers a land area of 8.039 square miles and a water area of 0.027 square miles. Located at 42.52° N. Lat.; 83.25° W. Long. Elevation is 684 feet.
History: Laid out 1817, Incorporated as a city 1958.
Population: 14,430 (2000); Race: 92.4% White, 3.3% Black, 1.6% Asian, 0.2% American Indian and Alaska Native, 1.1% Hispanic of any race, 1.9% two or more races (2000); Density: 1,794.9 persons per square mile (2000); Age: 24.6% under 18, 19.1% over 64 (2000); Marriage status: 17.1% never married, 68.4% now married, 7.1% widowed, 7.3% divorced (2000); Foreign born: 8.2% (2000); Ancestry (includes multiple ancestries): 22.9% German, 18.3% Irish, 15.2% English, 11.2% Polish, 8.9% Other groups (2000).
Economy: Manufacturing includes electronic research, meat processing, printing, plastic products, fabricated metal products, chemicals, transportation equipment, rubber products, wood products and machinery. It is the center of the retail and office industries in the Detroit metropolitan area. Also has varied light manufacturing and a warehousing industry. Employment by occupation: 27.4% management, 35.9% professional, 5.3% services, 24.8% sales, 0.0% farming, 3.2% construction, 3.4% production (2000).
Income: Per capita income: $51,328 (2000); Median household income: $97,719 (2000); Poverty rate: 1.9% (2000).
Taxes: Total city taxes per capita: $33 (1997); City property taxes per capita: $32 (1997).
Education: High school graduation rate: 96.2% (2000); College graduation rate: 65.0% (2000).
Housing: Homeownership rate: 93.5% (2000); Median home value: $299,300 (2000); Median rent: $833 per month (2000); Median age of housing: 41 years (2000).
Transportation: Commute to work: 94.3% car, 0.2% public transportation, 0.3% walk, 4.8% work from home (2000); Travel time to work: 25.2% less than 15 minutes, 41.9% 15 to 30 minutes, 25.8% 30 to 45 minutes, 5.2% 45 to 60 minutes, 2.0% 60 minutes or more (2000)

SPRINGFIELD (township). Covers a land area of 35.590 square miles and a water area of 1.157 square miles. Located at 42.75° N. Lat.; 83.50° W. Long.
History: Springfield Township was organized in 1837, after settlement began here in the early 1830's.
Population: 13,338 (2000); Race: 96.6% White, 0.6% Black, 0.3% Asian, 0.7% American Indian and Alaska Native, 1.7% Hispanic of any race, 1.4% two or more races (2000); Density: 374.8 persons per square mile (2000); Age: 28.5% under 18, 6.0% over 64 (2000); Marriage status: 20.9% never married, 66.4% now married, 3.2% widowed, 9.5% divorced (2000); Foreign born: 1.5% (2000); Ancestry (includes multiple ancestries): 22.5% German, 17.4% English, 13.3% Irish, 10.0% Polish, 7.4% Italian (2000).
Economy: Single-family building permits issued: 100 (2001) / 88 (2000); Multi-family building permits issued: 0 (2001) / 0 (2000); Employment by occupation: 17.0% management, 21.7% professional, 10.6% services, 25.4% sales, 0.0% farming, 11.2% construction, 14.1% production (2000).
Income: Per capita income: $28,247 (2000); Median household income: $71,977 (2000); Poverty rate: 5.9% (2000).
Taxes: Total city taxes per capita: $139 (2000); City property taxes per capita: $123 (2000).
Education: High school graduation rate: 91.5% (2000); College graduation rate: 28.0% (2000).
Housing: Homeownership rate: 91.4% (2000); Median home value: $209,100 (2000); Median rent: $669 per month (2000); Median age of housing: 20 years (2000).
Transportation: Commute to work: 96.0% car, 0.1% public transportation, 0.9% walk, 2.9% work from home (2000); Travel time to work: 14.2% less than 15 minutes, 31.5% 15 to 30 minutes, 31.6% 30 to 45 minutes, 12.6% 45 to 60 minutes, 10.1% 60 minutes or more (2000)

SYLVAN LAKE (city). Covers a land area of 0.525 square miles and a water area of 0.282 square miles. Located at 42.61° N. Lat.; 83.33° W. Long.
History: Sylvan Lake began in 1881 as a station on the Grand Trunk Railroad. A charter commission organized the village in 1921.
Population: 1,735 (2000); Race: 96.8% White, 0.5% Black, 0.5% Asian, 0.9% American Indian and Alaska Native, 0.4% Hispanic of any race, 1.3% two or more races (2000); Density: 3,305.8 persons per square mile (2000); Age: 20.1% under 18, 13.3% over 64 (2000); Marriage status: 20.1% never married, 63.0% now married, 5.9% widowed, 11.0% divorced (2000); Foreign born: 5.7% (2000); Ancestry (includes multiple ancestries): 25.3% German, 17.6% Irish, 16.3% English, 8.8% Other groups, 8.0% French (except Basque) (2000).
Economy: Single-family building permits issued: 2 (2001) / 3 (2000); Multi-family building permits issued: 0 (2001) / 0 (2000); Employment by occupation: 26.4% management, 24.0% professional, 5.1% services, 34.5% sales, 0.0% farming, 6.0% construction, 3.9% production (2000).
Income: Per capita income: $48,744 (2000); Median household income: $71,875 (2000); Poverty rate: 2.0% (2000).
Taxes: Total city taxes per capita: $425 (1997); City property taxes per capita: $397 (1997).
Education: High school graduation rate: 95.2% (2000); College graduation rate: 53.9% (2000).
Housing: Homeownership rate: 86.2% (2000); Median home value: $182,100 (2000); Median rent: $667 per month (2000); Median age of housing: 46 years (2000).
Transportation: Commute to work: 96.5% car, 0.0% public transportation, 0.4% walk, 2.4% work from home (2000); Travel time to work: 21.5% less than 15 minutes, 45.0% 15 to 30 minutes, 19.0% 30 to 45 minutes, 11.9% 45 to 60 minutes, 2.6% 60 minutes or more (2000)

TROY (city). Covers a land area of 33.539 square miles and a water area of 0.102 square miles. Located at 42.58° N. Lat.; 83.14° W. Long. Elevation is 687 feet.
History: Troy contains many historic buildings. Settled 1821; Incorporated 1955.
Population: 80,959 (2000); Race: 82.5% White, 2.3% Black, 12.8% Asian, 0.2% American Indian and Alaska Native, 1.4% Hispanic of any race, 2.0% two or more races (2000); Density: 2,413.9 persons per square mile (2000); Age: 26.1% under 18, 10.2% over 64 (2000); Marriage status: 24.0% never married, 64.1% now married, 4.7% widowed, 7.2% divorced (2000); Foreign born: 19.6% (2000); Ancestry (includes multiple ancestries): 19.3% German, 17.9% Other groups, 12.6% Irish, 11.5% English, 11.0% Polish (2000).
Vital Statistics: Birth rate: 114.0 per 10,000 population (1998)
Economy: Varied manufactures include automobiles and parts, electronics, chemicals, door systems, video and compact discs. Unemployment rate: 2.4% (11/2002); Total civilian labor force: 47,122 (11/2002); Single-family building permits issued: 272 (2001) / 215 (2000); Multi-family building permits issued: 2 (2001) / 76 (2000); Employment by occupation: 21.5% management, 33.3% professional, 8.4% services, 25.3% sales, 0.0% farming, 4.3% construction, 7.2% production (2000).
Income: Per capita income: $35,936 (2000); Median household income: $77,538 (2000); Poverty rate: 2.7% (2000).
Taxes: Total city taxes per capita: $567 (2000); City property taxes per capita: $530 (2000).
Education: High school graduation rate: 92.2% (2000); College graduation rate: 50.0% (2000).

School District(s)

Troy School District (PK-12)
2000 Enrollment: 12,062 248-689-0600

Four-year College(s)

Walsh College of Accountancy and Business Administration (Private, Not-for-profit)
2001 Enrollment: 3,214 248-689-8282
2001 Tuition: In-state $5,232; Out-of-state $5,232
University of Phoenix-Detroit Campus (Private, For-profit)
2001 Enrollment: 3,132 248-925-4100

Two-year College(s)
ITT Technical Institute (Private, For-profit)
2001 Enrollment: 665 248-524-1800
2001 Tuition: In-state $10,548; Out-of-state $10,548

Housing: Homeownership rate: 77.4% (2000); Median home value: $219,800 (2000); Median rent: $760 per month (2000); Median age of housing: 25 years (2000).

Hospitals: William Beaumont Hospital (226 beds)

Safety: Violent crime rate: 11.1 per 10,000 population; Property crime rate: 269.6 per 10,000 population (2001).

Newspapers: Troy-Somerset Gazette (1 x week)

Transportation: Commute to work: 95.6% car, 0.3% public transportation, 0.6% walk, 2.9% work from home (2000); Travel time to work: 24.5% less than 15 minutes, 40.7% 15 to 30 minutes, 22.6% 30 to 45 minutes, 8.2% 45 to 60 minutes, 4.1% 60 minutes or more (2000)

Airports: Oakland/Troy

Additional Information Contacts
Metropolitan Consolidated Association of Realtors 248-879-5730

VILLAGE OF CLARKSTON (city). Aka Clarkston. Covers a land area of 0.457 square miles and a water area of 0.049 square miles. Located at 42.73° N. Lat.; 83.42° W. Long.

Population: 962 (2000); Race: 95.9% White, 0.3% Black, 0.0% Asian, 0.0% American Indian and Alaska Native, 2.0% Hispanic of any race, 3.7% two or more races (2000); Density: 2,106.0 persons per square mile (2000); Age: 25.5% under 18, 12.2% over 64 (2000); Marriage status: 21.9% never married, 59.3% now married, 5.8% widowed, 13.1% divorced (2000); Foreign born: 2.3% (2000); Ancestry (includes multiple ancestries): 24.9% German, 19.9% Irish, 19.5% English, 8.4% Polish, 6.4% Italian (2000).

Economy: Employment by occupation: 19.4% management, 32.9% professional, 7.0% services, 26.9% sales, 0.0% farming, 6.8% construction, 7.0% production (2000).

Income: Per capita income: $36,838 (2000); Median household income: $62,667 (2000); Poverty rate: 3.7% (2000).

Education: High school graduation rate: 89.6% (2000); College graduation rate: 43.7% (2000).

Housing: Homeownership rate: 65.0% (2000); Median home value: $231,300 (2000); Median rent: $633 per month (2000); Median age of housing: 53 years (2000).

Transportation: Commute to work: 90.5% car, 0.4% public transportation, 3.4% walk, 4.5% work from home (2000); Travel time to work: 30.4% less than 15 minutes, 29.7% 15 to 30 minutes, 21.4% 30 to 45 minutes, 11.3% 45 to 60 minutes, 7.2% 60 minutes or more (2000)

WALLED LAKE (city). Covers a land area of 2.270 square miles and a water area of 0.197 square miles. Located at 42.53° N. Lat.; 83.47° W. Long. Elevation is 939 feet.

History: The Walled Lake from which the city took its name was called that because it was bordered by a large row of boulders, piled up along the shore by the pressure of expanding ice.

Population: 6,713 (2000); Race: 94.4% White, 1.0% Black, 2.0% Asian, 0.4% American Indian and Alaska Native, 1.1% Hispanic of any race, 1.7% two or more races (2000); Density: 2,956.9 persons per square mile (2000); Age: 21.4% under 18, 12.1% over 64 (2000); Marriage status: 30.6% never married, 45.7% now married, 8.1% widowed, 15.6% divorced (2000); Foreign born: 9.6% (2000); Ancestry (includes multiple ancestries): 19.3% German, 15.9% Irish, 13.7% English, 10.5% Polish, 8.8% Other groups (2000).

Economy: Single-family building permits issued: 8 (2001) / 1 (2000); Multi-family building permits issued: 14 (2001) / 14 (2000); Employment by occupation: 12.1% management, 17.7% professional, 14.0% services, 33.0% sales, 0.0% farming, 9.9% construction, 13.3% production (2000).

Income: Per capita income: $24,199 (2000); Median household income: $45,386 (2000); Poverty rate: 5.0% (2000).

Taxes: Total city taxes per capita: $433 (1997); City property taxes per capita: $400 (1997).

Education: High school graduation rate: 88.1% (2000); College graduation rate: 25.6% (2000).

School District(s)
Walled Lake Consolidated Schools (PK-12)
2000 Enrollment: 14,438 248-956-2000

Housing: Homeownership rate: 66.7% (2000); Median home value: $130,700 (2000); Median rent: $586 per month (2000); Median age of housing: 21 years (2000).

Safety: Violent crime rate: 20.7 per 10,000 population; Property crime rate: 327.5 per 10,000 population (2001).

Transportation: Commute to work: 96.1% car, 0.2% public transportation, 2.4% walk, 1.3% work from home (2000); Travel time to work: 29.6% less than 15 minutes, 29.2% 15 to 30 minutes, 24.7% 30 to 45 minutes, 11.3% 45 to 60 minutes, 5.2% 60 minutes or more (2000)

Additional Information Contacts
Walled Lake Chamber of Commerce 248-624-2826

WATERFORD (CDP). Covers a land area of 31.337 square miles and a water area of 3.988 square miles. Located at 42.66° N. Lat.; 83.38° W. Long.

Population: 73,150 (2000); Race: 92.3% White, 3.0% Black, 1.2% Asian, 0.4% American Indian and Alaska Native, 3.9% Hispanic of any race, 1.9% two or more races (2000); Density: 2,334.3 persons per square mile (2000); Age: 23.1% under 18, 10.9% over 64 (2000); Marriage status: 24.9% never married, 56.4% now married, 5.9% widowed, 12.8% divorced (2000); Foreign born: 5.0% (2000); Ancestry (includes multiple ancestries): 21.2% German, 14.5% Irish, 13.9% English, 11.7% Other groups, 8.3% Polish (2000).

Vital Statistics: Birth rate: 147.5 per 10,000 population (1998)

Economy: Unemployment rate: 4.7% (11/2002); Total civilian labor force: 43,257 (11/2002); Single-family building permits issued: 154 (2001) / 189 (2000); Multi-family building permits issued: 269 (2001) / 71 (2000); Employment by occupation: 12.1% management, 20.0% professional, 13.9% services, 29.2% sales, 0.2% farming, 10.3% construction, 14.3% production (2000).

Income: Per capita income: $27,432 (2000); Median household income: $55,008 (2000); Poverty rate: 5.1% (2000).

Education: High school graduation rate: 87.2% (2000); College graduation rate: 23.9% (2000).

School District(s)
Waterford School District (KG-12)
2000 Enrollment: 11,842 248-666-2222

Housing: Homeownership rate: 76.2% (2000); Median home value: $144,400 (2000); Median rent: $566 per month (2000); Median age of housing: 32 years (2000).

Safety: Violent crime rate: 18.2 per 10,000 population; Property crime rate: 289.4 per 10,000 population (2001).

Newspapers: Spinal Column Newsweekly (1 x week)

Transportation: Commute to work: 96.1% car, 0.2% public transportation, 0.9% walk, 2.5% work from home (2000); Travel time to work: 21.3% less than 15 minutes, 34.0% 15 to 30 minutes, 25.6% 30 to 45 minutes, 11.3% 45 to 60 minutes, 7.9% 60 minutes or more (2000)

Additional Information Contacts
North Oakland County Board of Realtors 248-674-4080

WEST BLOOMFIELD (township). Covers a land area of 27.317 square miles and a water area of 3.902 square miles. Located at 42.56° N. Lat.; 83.38° W. Long.

Population: 64,860 (2000); Race: 84.5% White, 5.0% Black, 7.7% Asian, 0.1% American Indian and Alaska Native, 2.1% Hispanic of any race, 1.8% two or more races (2000); Density: 2,374.3 persons per square mile (2000); Age: 26.1% under 18, 13.5% over 64 (2000); Marriage status: 19.3% never married, 68.4% now married, 5.9% widowed, 6.3% divorced (2000); Foreign born: 18.9% (2000); Ancestry (includes multiple ancestries): 20.0% Other groups, 11.2% German, 9.4% Russian, 9.2% Polish, 7.5% Assyrian/Chaldean/Syriac (2000).

Vital Statistics: Birth rate: 109.6 per 10,000 population (1998)

Economy: Unemployment rate: 2.7% (11/2002); Total civilian labor force: 34,869 (11/2002); Single-family building permits issued: 278 (2001) / 287 (2000); Multi-family building permits issued: 0 (2001) / 0 (2000); Employment by occupation: 23.1% management, 34.3% professional, 7.5% services, 27.1% sales, 0.0% farming, 3.8% construction, 4.1% production (2000).

Income: Per capita income: $44,885 (2000); Median household income: $91,661 (2000); Poverty rate: 2.7% (2000).

Taxes: Total city taxes per capita: $317 (2000); City property taxes per capita: $286 (2000).

Education: High school graduation rate: 93.3% (2000); College graduation rate: 55.3% (2000).

School District(s)
West Bloomfield School District (KG-12)
2000 Enrollment: 6,281 248-738-3562

Housing: Homeownership rate: 86.9% (2000); Median home value: $264,200 (2000); Median rent: $1,068 per month (2000); Median age of housing: 22 years (2000).

Safety: Violent crime rate: 3.7 per 10,000 population; Property crime rate: 126.4 per 10,000 population (2001).

Transportation: Commute to work: 94.9% car, 0.2% public transportation, 0.5% walk, 4.1% work from home (2000); Travel time to work: 14.2% less than 15 minutes, 35.5% 15 to 30 minutes, 32.1% 30 to 45 minutes, 12.8% 45 to 60 minutes, 5.5% 60 minutes or more (2000)

Additional Information Contacts

West Bloomfield Chamber of Commerce 248-626-3636

WHITE LAKE (township). Covers a land area of 33.662 square miles and a water area of 3.509 square miles. Located at 42.64° N. Lat.; 83.49° W. Long.

Population: 28,219 (2000); Race: 96.8% White, 0.7% Black, 0.6% Asian, 0.2% American Indian and Alaska Native, 1.9% Hispanic of any race, 1.3% two or more races (2000); Density: 838.3 persons per square mile (2000); Age: 27.4% under 18, 7.8% over 64 (2000); Marriage status: 22.8% never married, 63.3% now married, 4.0% widowed, 9.9% divorced (2000); Foreign born: 2.8% (2000); Ancestry (includes multiple ancestries): 25.3% German, 15.6% Irish, 13.5% English, 10.1% Polish, 7.9% Other groups (2000).

Economy: Light manufacturing. Alpine Valley Ski Area and Pontiac Lake State Recreation Area to East. Unemployment rate: 4.8% (11/2002); Total civilian labor force: 14,171 (11/2002); Single-family building permits issued: 158 (2001) / 168 (2000); Multi-family building permits issued: 0 (2001) / 0 (2000); Employment by occupation: 13.5% management, 18.7% professional, 12.4% services, 28.3% sales, 0.2% farming, 12.0% construction, 14.9% production (2000).

Income: Per capita income: $27,916 (2000); Median household income: $65,894 (2000); Poverty rate: 3.1% (2000).

Taxes: Total city taxes per capita: $161 (2000); City property taxes per capita: $140 (2000).

Education: High school graduation rate: 87.9% (2000); College graduation rate: 23.0% (2000).

Housing: Homeownership rate: 91.8% (2000); Median home value: $190,900 (2000); Median rent: $603 per month (2000); Median age of housing: 25 years (2000).

Safety: Violent crime rate: 11.6 per 10,000 population; Property crime rate: 193.2 per 10,000 population (2001).

Transportation: Commute to work: 95.8% car, 0.3% public transportation, 0.5% walk, 3.1% work from home (2000); Travel time to work: 13.3% less than 15 minutes, 27.6% 15 to 30 minutes, 29.0% 30 to 45 minutes, 18.6% 45 to 60 minutes, 11.5% 60 minutes or more (2000)

WIXOM (city). Covers a land area of 9.340 square miles and a water area of 0.122 square miles. Located at 42.53° N. Lat.; 83.53° W. Long. Elevation is 930 feet.

Population: 13,263 (2000); Race: 90.4% White, 3.3% Black, 2.8% Asian, 0.0% American Indian and Alaska Native, 3.2% Hispanic of any race, 1.9% two or more races (2000); Density: 1,420.0 persons per square mile (2000); Age: 24.6% under 18, 5.5% over 64 (2000); Marriage status: 34.3% never married, 52.0% now married, 3.6% widowed, 10.1% divorced (2000); Foreign born: 10.2% (2000); Ancestry (includes multiple ancestries): 23.0% German, 15.4% Irish, 13.3% Other groups, 11.3% Polish, 10.5% English (2000).

Economy: Manufacturing: machinery, cleaning compounds, tools, consumer goods, fabricated metal products. Proud Lake State Recreation Area to North, Island Lake State Recreation Area to West and Kensington Metropark to West. Oakland Southwest Airport to West. Single-family building permits issued: 95 (2001) / 97 (2000); Multi-family building permits issued: 4 (2001) / 4 (2000); Employment by occupation: 15.7% management, 22.6% professional, 12.6% services, 27.9% sales, 0.0% farming, 9.1% construction, 12.0% production (2000).

Income: Per capita income: $27,543 (2000); Median household income: $44,320 (2000); Poverty rate: 5.4% (2000).

Taxes: Total city taxes per capita: $574 (2000); City property taxes per capita: $521 (2000).

Education: High school graduation rate: 93.0% (2000); College graduation rate: 38.1% (2000).

Housing: Homeownership rate: 43.6% (2000); Median home value: $195,000 (2000); Median rent: $480 per month (2000); Median age of housing: 20 years (2000).

Safety: Violent crime rate: 11.3 per 10,000 population; Property crime rate: 327.8 per 10,000 population (2001).

Transportation: Commute to work: 95.8% car, 0.0% public transportation, 1.4% walk, 2.3% work from home (2000); Travel time to work: 23.5% less than 15 minutes, 31.2% 15 to 30 minutes, 26.9% 30 to 45 minutes, 12.3% 45 to 60 minutes, 6.1% 60 minutes or more (2000)

WOLVERINE LAKE (village). Covers a land area of 1.302 square miles and a water area of 0.382 square miles. Located at 42.55° N. Lat.; 83.49° W. Long. Elevation is 946 feet.

Population: 4,415 (2000); Race: 97.1% White, 1.0% Black, 0.3% Asian, 0.3% American Indian and Alaska Native, 1.2% Hispanic of any race, 1.3% two or more races (2000); Density: 3,391.9 persons per square mile (2000); Age: 24.3% under 18, 7.0% over 64 (2000); Marriage status: 22.4% never married, 63.5% now married, 3.7% widowed, 10.5% divorced (2000); Foreign born: 2.1% (2000); Ancestry (includes multiple ancestries): 25.1% German, 17.7% Irish, 17.4% Polish, 16.7% English, 8.3% French (except Basque) (2000).

Economy: Proud Lake State Recreation Area to West and North. Single-family building permits issued: 5 (2001) / 4 (2000); Multi-family building permits issued: 0 (2001) / 0 (2000); Employment by occupation: 13.4% management, 19.5% professional, 10.0% services, 29.8% sales, 0.0% farming, 10.5% construction, 16.8% production (2000).

Income: Per capita income: $30,026 (2000); Median household income: $65,682 (2000); Poverty rate: 2.7% (2000).

Taxes: Total city taxes per capita: $215 (1997); City property taxes per capita: $205 (1997).

Education: High school graduation rate: 89.6% (2000); College graduation rate: 23.3% (2000).

Housing: Homeownership rate: 87.5% (2000); Median home value: $160,900 (2000); Median rent: $519 per month (2000); Median age of housing: 33 years (2000).

Safety: Violent crime rate: 11.3 per 10,000 population; Property crime rate: 99.1 per 10,000 population (2001).

Transportation: Commute to work: 97.8% car, 0.4% public transportation, 0.4% walk, 1.3% work from home (2000); Travel time to work: 22.2% less than 15 minutes, 29.6% 15 to 30 minutes, 27.7% 30 to 45 minutes, 16.0% 45 to 60 minutes, 4.5% 60 minutes or more (2000)

Oceana County

Located in western Michigan; bounded on the west by Lake Michigan; drained by the White and Pentwater Rivers; includes part of Manistee National Forest. Covers a land area of 540.50 square miles, a water area of 766.30 square miles, and is located in the Eastern Time Zone. The county government was organized in 1831. County seat is Hart.

Weather Station: Hart Elevation: 698 feet

	Jan	Feb	Mar	Apr	May	Jun	Jul	Aug	Sep	Oct	Nov	Dec
High	29	32	41	54	67	76	80	78	70	58	45	34
Low	16	16	24	34	44	54	59	58	50	40	31	22
Precip	2.6	1.7	2.4	2.9	2.8	3.3	2.9	4.0	3.8	3.6	3.3	2.6
Snow	31.1	19.0	9.0	2.1	tr	0.0	0.0	0.0	0.0	0.2	5.4	21.7

High and Low temperatures in degrees Fahrenheit; Precipitation and Snow in inches

Population: 26,873 (2000); Race: 90.1% White, 0.3% Black, 0.1% Asian, 1.1% American Indian and Alaska Native, 12.0% Hispanic of any race, 2.3% two or more races (2000); Density: 49.7 persons per square mile (2000); Age: 28.1% under 18, 13.9% over 64 (2000).

Religion: Five largest groups: 10.9% Catholic Church, 4.0% The United Methodist Church, 3.1% The Wesleyan Church, 2.9% General Association of Regular Baptist Churches, 2.1% United Church of Christ (2000).

Economy: Unemployment rate: 8.4% (11/2002); Total civilian labor force: 14,165 (11/2002); Leading industries: 29.4% manufacturing; 17.5% retail trade; 14.5% health care and social assistance (2000); Companies that employ more than 1,000 persons: 0 (2000); Companies that employ more than 100 persons: 6 (2000); Farms: 573 totaling 127,994 acres (1997); Minority business ownership rate: 9.1% (1997); Women business ownership rate: 21.3% (1997); Retail sales per capita: $5,043 (1997). Single-family building permits issued: 135 (2001) / 129 (2000); Multi-family building permits issued: 0 (2001) / 24 (2000).

Income: Per capita income: $15,878 (2000); Median household income: $35,307 (2000); Poverty rate: 14.7% (2000); Bankruptcy rate: 3.27% (2001).

Taxes: Total county taxes per capita: $167 (2000); County property taxes per capita: $165 (2000).

Education: High school graduation rate: 79.8% (2000); College graduation rate: 12.6% (2000).

Housing: Homeownership rate: 82.7% (2000); Median home value: $82,500 (2000); Median rent: $332 per month (2000); Median age of housing: 29 years (2000).

Health: Birth rate: 134.0 per 10,000 population (1998); Age adjusted death rate: 98.9 per 10,000 population (1999); Age adjusted cancer mortality rate:

189.8 deaths per 100,000 population (1999). Number of physicians: 3.3 per 10,000 population (1999); Number of hospital beds: 8.9 per 10,000 population (1999).
Elections: 2000 Presidential election results: 42.7% Gore, 54.9% Bush, 2.0% Nader, 0.0% Buchanan
National and State Parks: Charles Mears State Park; Rentwater River State Game Area; Silver Lake State Park
Additional Information Contacts
Oceana County Government Offices 231-873-4835
Hart Silver Lake Chamber of Commerce. 231-873-2247
Pentwater Chamber of Commerce 231-869-4150

Oceana County Communities

BENONA (township). Covers a land area of 40.768 square miles and a water area of 0.491 square miles. Located at 43.59° N. Lat.; 86.46° W. Long.
Population: 1,520 (2000); Race: 90.6% White, 0.3% Black, 0.0% Asian, 0.5% American Indian and Alaska Native, 12.3% Hispanic of any race, 1.7% two or more races (2000); Density: 37.3 persons per square mile (2000); Age: 24.0% under 18, 15.2% over 64 (2000); Marriage status: 18.4% never married, 63.4% now married, 7.7% widowed, 10.6% divorced (2000); Foreign born: 5.6% (2000); Ancestry (includes multiple ancestries): 30.5% German, 13.1% Irish, 12.5% Other groups, 11.3% English, 10.8% Dutch (2000).
Economy: Employment by occupation: 11.9% management, 20.0% professional, 10.4% services, 17.3% sales, 3.5% farming, 12.8% construction, 24.2% production (2000).
Income: Per capita income: $24,724 (2000); Median household income: $44,375 (2000); Poverty rate: 11.1% (2000).
Taxes: Total city taxes per capita: $98 (1997); City property taxes per capita: $94 (1997).
Education: High school graduation rate: 84.9% (2000); College graduation rate: 21.4% (2000).
Housing: Homeownership rate: 90.9% (2000); Median home value: $110,600 (2000); Median rent: $325 per month (2000); Median age of housing: 27 years (2000).
Transportation: Commute to work: 92.8% car, 0.3% public transportation, 3.4% walk, 3.2% work from home (2000); Travel time to work: 30.9% less than 15 minutes, 29.6% 15 to 30 minutes, 16.6% 30 to 45 minutes, 9.7% 45 to 60 minutes, 13.2% 60 minutes or more (2000)

CLAYBANKS (township). Covers a land area of 23.862 square miles and a water area of 0.147 square miles. Located at 43.52° N. Lat.; 86.44° W. Long.
Population: 831 (2000); Race: 94.6% White, 0.3% Black, 0.0% Asian, 0.8% American Indian and Alaska Native, 5.7% Hispanic of any race, 1.6% two or more races (2000); Density: 34.8 persons per square mile (2000); Age: 25.8% under 18, 16.3% over 64 (2000); Marriage status: 20.4% never married, 66.5% now married, 5.8% widowed, 7.3% divorced (2000); Foreign born: 1.6% (2000); Ancestry (includes multiple ancestries): 37.9% German, 12.3% Dutch, 11.8% Irish, 11.8% English, 9.3% Other groups (2000).
Economy: Employment by occupation: 12.0% management, 13.3% professional, 12.5% services, 18.7% sales, 6.6% farming, 15.2% construction, 21.6% production (2000).
Income: Per capita income: $17,351 (2000); Median household income: $41,319 (2000); Poverty rate: 7.3% (2000).
Taxes: Total city taxes per capita: $55 (1997); City property taxes per capita: $53 (1997).
Education: High school graduation rate: 85.4% (2000); College graduation rate: 16.1% (2000).
Housing: Homeownership rate: 90.2% (2000); Median home value: $101,300 (2000); Median rent: $308 per month (2000); Median age of housing: 38 years (2000).
Transportation: Commute to work: 90.5% car, 0.0% public transportation, 1.3% walk, 8.3% work from home (2000); Travel time to work: 17.8% less than 15 minutes, 41.9% 15 to 30 minutes, 21.6% 30 to 45 minutes, 6.6% 45 to 60 minutes, 12.1% 60 minutes or more (2000)

COLFAX (township). Covers a land area of 35.376 square miles and a water area of 0.560 square miles. Located at 43.75° N. Lat.; 86.09° W. Long. Elevation is 854 feet.
History: Colfax Township was named for Schuyler Colfax, vice president under Ulysses S. Grant.
Population: 574 (2000); Race: 90.6% White, 4.3% Black, 0.0% Asian, 0.4% American Indian and Alaska Native, 10.4% Hispanic of any race, 0.9% two or more races (2000); Density: 16.2 persons per square mile (2000); Age: 32.8% under 18, 15.5% over 64 (2000); Marriage status: 16.4% never married, 68.6% now married, 7.9% widowed, 7.1% divorced (2000); Foreign born: 0.6% (2000); Ancestry (includes multiple ancestries): 10.9% German, 10.6% English, 8.1% Irish, 6.2% Other groups, 5.7% United States or American (2000).
Economy: Employment by occupation: 7.4% management, 9.8% professional, 17.2% services, 15.3% sales, 2.5% farming, 12.9% construction, 35.0% production (2000).
Income: Per capita income: $11,986 (2000); Median household income: $30,417 (2000); Poverty rate: 26.9% (2000).
Taxes: Total city taxes per capita: $48 (1997); City property taxes per capita: $48 (1997).
Education: High school graduation rate: 66.2% (2000); College graduation rate: 2.8% (2000).
Housing: Homeownership rate: 87.5% (2000); Median home value: $81,400 (2000); Median rent: $313 per month (2000); Median age of housing: 22 years (2000).
Transportation: Commute to work: 90.5% car, 0.0% public transportation, 1.3% walk, 7.0% work from home (2000); Travel time to work: 25.2% less than 15 minutes, 19.7% 15 to 30 minutes, 23.1% 30 to 45 minutes, 5.4% 45 to 60 minutes, 26.5% 60 minutes or more (2000)

CRYSTAL (township). Covers a land area of 36.019 square miles and a water area of 0.007 square miles. Located at 43.77° N. Lat.; 86.22° W. Long.
Population: 832 (2000); Race: 81.8% White, 0.2% Black, 0.0% Asian, 0.6% American Indian and Alaska Native, 31.5% Hispanic of any race, 3.0% two or more races (2000); Density: 23.1 persons per square mile (2000); Age: 33.9% under 18, 8.4% over 64 (2000); Marriage status: 17.4% never married, 70.1% now married, 5.4% widowed, 7.1% divorced (2000); Foreign born: 14.0% (2000); Ancestry (includes multiple ancestries): 26.2% Other groups, 12.0% German, 7.5% United States or American, 6.2% English, 5.9% Dutch (2000).
Economy: Employment by occupation: 8.5% management, 11.6% professional, 12.3% services, 13.3% sales, 20.8% farming, 8.9% construction, 24.6% production (2000).
Income: Per capita income: $10,899 (2000); Median household income: $31,719 (2000); Poverty rate: 22.8% (2000).
Taxes: Total city taxes per capita: $25 (1997); City property taxes per capita: $25 (1997).
Education: High school graduation rate: 62.1% (2000); College graduation rate: 3.1% (2000).
Housing: Homeownership rate: 80.7% (2000); Median home value: $67,100 (2000); Median rent: $250 per month (2000); Median age of housing: 28 years (2000).
Transportation: Commute to work: 93.4% car, 0.0% public transportation, 3.1% walk, 3.5% work from home (2000); Travel time to work: 27.8% less than 15 minutes, 36.1% 15 to 30 minutes, 18.8% 30 to 45 minutes, 6.5% 45 to 60 minutes, 10.8% 60 minutes or more (2000)

ELBRIDGE (township). Covers a land area of 36.189 square miles and a water area of 0.076 square miles. Located at 43.67° N. Lat.; 86.22° W. Long.
Population: 1,233 (2000); Race: 76.3% White, 0.0% Black, 0.0% Asian, 3.3% American Indian and Alaska Native, 26.9% Hispanic of any race, 5.7% two or more races (2000); Density: 34.1 persons per square mile (2000); Age: 28.7% under 18, 17.1% over 64 (2000); Marriage status: 29.3% never married, 54.3% now married, 8.2% widowed, 8.1% divorced (2000); Foreign born: 9.5% (2000); Ancestry (includes multiple ancestries): 21.6% Other groups, 17.9% German, 8.0% United States or American, 7.9% English, 7.7% Irish (2000).
Economy: Employment by occupation: 12.0% management, 11.5% professional, 8.9% services, 13.0% sales, 12.7% farming, 12.7% construction, 29.1% production (2000).
Income: Per capita income: $11,755 (2000); Median household income: $31,838 (2000); Poverty rate: 25.4% (2000).
Taxes: Total city taxes per capita: $36 (1997); City property taxes per capita: $36 (1997).
Education: High school graduation rate: 66.9% (2000); College graduation rate: 7.1% (2000).
Housing: Homeownership rate: 82.0% (2000); Median home value: $67,700 (2000); Median rent: $338 per month (2000); Median age of housing: 32 years (2000).
Transportation: Commute to work: 91.7% car, 0.5% public transportation, 0.0% walk, 7.5% work from home (2000); Travel time to work: 28.2% less than 15 minutes, 41.3% 15 to 30 minutes, 17.9% 30 to 45 minutes, 8.7% 45 to 60 minutes, 3.9% 60 minutes or more (2000)

FERRY (township). Covers a land area of 35.996 square miles and a water area of 0.132 square miles. Located at 43.59° N. Lat.; 86.21° W. Long. Elevation is 717 feet.
Population: 1,296 (2000); Race: 91.3% White, 2.2% Black, 0.2% Asian, 2.5% American Indian and Alaska Native, 4.7% Hispanic of any race, 2.0% two or more races (2000); Density: 36.0 persons per square mile (2000); Age: 26.2% under 18, 9.3% over 64 (2000); Marriage status: 19.8% never married, 60.2% now married, 5.8% widowed, 14.2% divorced (2000); Foreign born: 2.3% (2000); Ancestry (includes multiple ancestries): 21.9% German, 15.2% Other groups, 12.1% Irish, 10.0% English, 9.3% United States or American (2000).
Economy: Employment by occupation: 6.2% management, 10.5% professional, 13.0% services, 12.1% sales, 0.9% farming, 15.1% construction, 42.2% production (2000).
Income: Per capita income: $16,212 (2000); Median household income: $35,170 (2000); Poverty rate: 13.5% (2000).
Taxes: Total city taxes per capita: $10 (1997); City property taxes per capita: $9 (1997).
Education: High school graduation rate: 74.0% (2000); College graduation rate: 6.3% (2000).
Housing: Homeownership rate: 89.6% (2000); Median home value: $58,800 (2000); Median rent: $322 per month (2000); Median age of housing: 27 years (2000).
Transportation: Commute to work: 94.5% car, 0.0% public transportation, 0.7% walk, 4.8% work from home (2000); Travel time to work: 10.1% less than 15 minutes, 34.7% 15 to 30 minutes, 27.3% 30 to 45 minutes, 15.5% 45 to 60 minutes, 12.4% 60 minutes or more (2000)

GOLDEN (township). Covers a land area of 33.545 square miles and a water area of 1.453 square miles. Located at 43.67° N. Lat.; 86.46° W. Long.
History: Golden Township was formed in 1864, and named by early settler William J. Haughey. He intended to use his mother's maiden name of Golding, but a clerical error made the name Golden.
Population: 1,810 (2000); Race: 91.2% White, 0.0% Black, 0.0% Asian, 1.1% American Indian and Alaska Native, 11.0% Hispanic of any race, 2.4% two or more races (2000); Density: 54.0 persons per square mile (2000); Age: 24.5% under 18, 15.9% over 64 (2000); Marriage status: 19.3% never married, 67.6% now married, 4.2% widowed, 8.9% divorced (2000); Foreign born: 2.6% (2000); Ancestry (includes multiple ancestries): 23.5% German, 13.6% Other groups, 13.0% English, 12.0% Dutch, 11.6% Irish (2000).
Economy: Employment by occupation: 11.1% management, 10.8% professional, 17.9% services, 22.0% sales, 6.2% farming, 14.6% construction, 17.5% production (2000).
Income: Per capita income: $17,934 (2000); Median household income: $35,878 (2000); Poverty rate: 14.5% (2000).
Taxes: Total city taxes per capita: $169 (1997); City property taxes per capita: $164 (1997).
Education: High school graduation rate: 83.3% (2000); College graduation rate: 12.8% (2000).
Housing: Homeownership rate: 83.0% (2000); Median home value: $111,100 (2000); Median rent: $325 per month (2000); Median age of housing: 20 years (2000).
Transportation: Commute to work: 89.3% car, 0.0% public transportation, 4.7% walk, 5.3% work from home (2000); Travel time to work: 45.0% less than 15 minutes, 27.9% 15 to 30 minutes, 15.5% 30 to 45 minutes, 5.1% 45 to 60 minutes, 6.5% 60 minutes or more (2000)

GRANT (township). Covers a land area of 35.387 square miles and a water area of 0.407 square miles. Located at 43.51° N. Lat.; 86.34° W. Long.
History: Settled in 1851, Grant Township was organized in 1866 and named for General Ulysses S. Grant.
Population: 2,932 (2000); Race: 91.3% White, 0.2% Black, 0.1% Asian, 1.8% American Indian and Alaska Native, 9.1% Hispanic of any race, 1.0% two or more races (2000); Density: 82.9 persons per square mile (2000); Age: 29.5% under 18, 10.8% over 64 (2000); Marriage status: 22.3% never married, 61.3% now married, 5.0% widowed, 11.4% divorced (2000); Foreign born: 2.9% (2000); Ancestry (includes multiple ancestries): 22.7% German, 13.1% Other groups, 12.8% United States or American, 9.7% Dutch, 9.4% Irish (2000).
Economy: Single-family building permits issued: 14 (2001) / 11 (2000); Multi-family building permits issued: 0 (2001) / 0 (2000); Employment by occupation: 7.2% management, 10.0% professional, 15.4% services, 16.0% sales, 0.8% farming, 13.1% construction, 37.7% production (2000).
Income: Per capita income: $15,267 (2000); Median household income: $37,594 (2000); Poverty rate: 15.4% (2000).
Taxes: Total city taxes per capita: $31 (1997); City property taxes per capita: $30 (1997).
Education: High school graduation rate: 80.5% (2000); College graduation rate: 5.9% (2000).
Housing: Homeownership rate: 83.1% (2000); Median home value: $80,100 (2000); Median rent: $335 per month (2000); Median age of housing: 24 years (2000).
Transportation: Commute to work: 94.3% car, 0.6% public transportation, 1.2% walk, 3.6% work from home (2000); Travel time to work: 25.0% less than 15 minutes, 45.7% 15 to 30 minutes, 20.2% 30 to 45 minutes, 4.5% 45 to 60 minutes, 4.6% 60 minutes or more (2000)

GREENWOOD (township). Covers a land area of 35.810 square miles and a water area of 0.159 square miles. Located at 43.51° N. Lat.; 86.09° W. Long.
History: Greenwood Township was organized in 1858, having been settled three years earlier by Henry D. Clark. It was named for its forests.
Population: 1,154 (2000); Race: 97.2% White, 0.0% Black, 0.0% Asian, 0.8% American Indian and Alaska Native, 1.2% Hispanic of any race, 1.8% two or more races (2000); Density: 32.2 persons per square mile (2000); Age: 30.8% under 18, 7.8% over 64 (2000); Marriage status: 25.7% never married, 59.9% now married, 3.3% widowed, 11.0% divorced (2000); Foreign born: 0.6% (2000); Ancestry (includes multiple ancestries): 25.5% German, 10.8% English, 10.2% Dutch, 8.2% Irish, 6.9% Other groups (2000).
Economy: Employment by occupation: 9.0% management, 11.9% professional, 15.5% services, 17.2% sales, 2.5% farming, 17.8% construction, 26.2% production (2000).
Income: Per capita income: $13,910 (2000); Median household income: $36,964 (2000); Poverty rate: 16.7% (2000).
Taxes: Total city taxes per capita: $39 (1997); City property taxes per capita: $39 (1997).
Education: High school graduation rate: 83.8% (2000); College graduation rate: 9.6% (2000).
Housing: Homeownership rate: 88.5% (2000); Median home value: $79,100 (2000); Median rent: $365 per month (2000); Median age of housing: 27 years (2000).
Transportation: Commute to work: 89.2% car, 0.4% public transportation, 4.1% walk, 5.4% work from home (2000); Travel time to work: 23.9% less than 15 minutes, 38.4% 15 to 30 minutes, 19.8% 30 to 45 minutes, 11.6% 45 to 60 minutes, 6.4% 60 minutes or more (2000)

HART (city). Covers a land area of 1.916 square miles and a water area of 0.140 square miles. Located at 43.69° N. Lat.; 86.36° W. Long. Elevation is 655 feet.
History: The town of Hart grew up around a sawmill and grist mill built by Lyman Corbin in the early 1860's. Hart, incorporated as a village in 1885, developed as the center of a region devoted to fruit orchards. It was incorporated as a city in 1946.
Population: 1,950 (2000); Race: 85.9% White, 0.4% Black, 0.3% Asian, 1.3% American Indian and Alaska Native, 17.2% Hispanic of any race, 4.3% two or more races (2000); Density: 1,017.7 persons per square mile (2000); Age: 28.2% under 18, 16.9% over 64 (2000); Marriage status: 23.3% never married, 51.0% now married, 11.8% widowed, 13.9% divorced (2000); Foreign born: 6.2% (2000); Ancestry (includes multiple ancestries): 23.0% German, 22.8% Other groups, 10.8% Irish, 8.9% English, 6.6% Polish (2000).
Economy: Employment by occupation: 6.7% management, 13.5% professional, 19.8% services, 23.9% sales, 2.5% farming, 8.9% construction, 24.7% production (2000).
Income: Per capita income: $13,844 (2000); Median household income: $25,855 (2000); Poverty rate: 20.4% (2000).
Taxes: Total city taxes per capita: $201 (1997); City property taxes per capita: $198 (1997).
Education: High school graduation rate: 76.2% (2000); College graduation rate: 11.4% (2000).

School District(s)

Lakeshore Public Academy (KG-12)
2000 Enrollment: 131 616-895-3029
Housing: Homeownership rate: 61.7% (2000); Median home value: $67,000 (2000); Median rent: $331 per month (2000); Median age of housing: 55 years (2000).
Safety: Violent crime rate: 51.0 per 10,000 population; Property crime rate: 428.6 per 10,000 population (2001).
Newspapers: Oceana's Herald Journal (1 x week)
Transportation: Commute to work: 88.6% car, 0.0% public transportation, 6.0% walk, 4.1% work from home (2000); Travel time to work: 57.4% less

than 15 minutes, 23.2% 15 to 30 minutes, 11.5% 30 to 45 minutes, 5.4% 45 to 60 minutes, 2.5% 60 minutes or more (2000)
Additional Information Contacts
Hart Silver Lake Chamber of Commerce 231-873-2247

HART (township). Covers a land area of 33.917 square miles and a water area of 0.339 square miles. Located at 43.69° N. Lat.; 86.34° W. Long. Elevation is 655 feet.
History: Hart Township was organized in 1858 and named for Wellington Hart, a pioneer settler.
Population: 2,026 (2000); Race: 89.1% White, 0.0% Black, 0.2% Asian, 1.0% American Indian and Alaska Native, 12.8% Hispanic of any race, 3.2% two or more races (2000); Density: 59.7 persons per square mile (2000); Age: 27.8% under 18, 14.9% over 64 (2000); Marriage status: 22.1% never married, 65.8% now married, 5.1% widowed, 7.0% divorced (2000); Foreign born: 5.5% (2000); Ancestry (includes multiple ancestries): 24.6% German, 17.6% Other groups, 10.2% English, 8.1% Irish, 7.5% United States or American (2000).
Economy: Employment by occupation: 14.6% management, 12.5% professional, 20.9% services, 17.0% sales, 5.1% farming, 9.4% construction, 20.4% production (2000).
Income: Per capita income: $15,625 (2000); Median household income: $37,434 (2000); Poverty rate: 14.2% (2000).
Taxes: Total city taxes per capita: $26 (1997); City property taxes per capita: $24 (1997).
Education: High school graduation rate: 78.9% (2000); College graduation rate: 16.2% (2000).
Housing: Homeownership rate: 83.3% (2000); Median home value: $84,400 (2000); Median rent: $302 per month (2000); Median age of housing: 29 years (2000).
Transportation: Commute to work: 90.5% car, 0.8% public transportation, 3.0% walk, 5.1% work from home (2000); Travel time to work: 61.8% less than 15 minutes, 17.5% 15 to 30 minutes, 12.2% 30 to 45 minutes, 3.4% 45 to 60 minutes, 5.2% 60 minutes or more (2000)

HESPERIA (village). Covers a land area of 0.822 square miles and a water area of 0.031 square miles. Located at 43.57° N. Lat.; 86.04° W. Long. Elevation is 773 feet.
History: Hesperia was laid out in 1866 by John P. Cook and Daniel Weaver, who operated a sawmill and a general store. There had been settlers in this area since the mid-1850's, including Alexander McLaren, for whom McLaren Lake was named. Cook's daughter suggested the name of Hesperia for the village.
Population: 954 (2000); Race: 98.9% White, 0.3% Black, 0.0% Asian, 0.4% American Indian and Alaska Native, 1.4% Hispanic of any race, 0.1% two or more races (2000); Density: 1,159.9 persons per square mile (2000); Age: 30.6% under 18, 14.9% over 64 (2000); Marriage status: 20.3% never married, 51.6% now married, 10.7% widowed, 17.4% divorced (2000); Foreign born: 0.5% (2000); Ancestry (includes multiple ancestries): 20.1% German, 12.6% Irish, 10.0% Other groups, 9.0% English, 8.9% Dutch (2000).
Economy: Employment by occupation: 5.3% management, 20.3% professional, 15.3% services, 18.4% sales, 0.8% farming, 10.8% construction, 29.2% production (2000).
Income: Per capita income: $13,704 (2000); Median household income: $27,460 (2000); Poverty rate: 13.8% (2000).
Taxes: Total city taxes per capita: $175 (1997); City property taxes per capita: $175 (1997).
Education: High school graduation rate: 77.2% (2000); College graduation rate: 11.0% (2000).

School District(s)
Hesperia Community Schools (KG-12)
2000 Enrollment: 1,214 231-854-6185
Housing: Homeownership rate: 65.4% (2000); Median home value: $65,900 (2000); Median rent: $310 per month (2000); Median age of housing: 41 years (2000).
Transportation: Commute to work: 90.2% car, 0.0% public transportation, 2.1% walk, 6.9% work from home (2000); Travel time to work: 28.0% less than 15 minutes, 30.6% 15 to 30 minutes, 17.7% 30 to 45 minutes, 12.9% 45 to 60 minutes, 10.9% 60 minutes or more (2000)

LEAVITT (township). Covers a land area of 35.269 square miles and a water area of 0.633 square miles. Located at 43.70° N. Lat.; 86.10° W. Long.
Population: 845 (2000); Race: 86.2% White, 0.2% Black, 0.0% Asian, 1.1% American Indian and Alaska Native, 15.0% Hispanic of any race, 1.7% two or more races (2000); Density: 24.0 persons per square mile (2000); Age: 32.3% under 18, 8.8% over 64 (2000); Marriage status: 27.6% never married, 61.0% now married, 5.2% widowed, 6.2% divorced (2000); Foreign born: 4.3% (2000); Ancestry (includes multiple ancestries): 15.1% German, 14.6% Other groups, 11.2% Irish, 8.6% English, 7.9% United States or American (2000).
Economy: Employment by occupation: 11.9% management, 6.0% professional, 14.8% services, 21.0% sales, 5.2% farming, 16.6% construction, 24.4% production (2000).
Income: Per capita income: $13,570 (2000); Median household income: $30,179 (2000); Poverty rate: 17.8% (2000).
Taxes: Total city taxes per capita: $39 (1997); City property taxes per capita: $39 (1997).
Education: High school graduation rate: 79.9% (2000); College graduation rate: 5.0% (2000).
Housing: Homeownership rate: 81.3% (2000); Median home value: $52,300 (2000); Median rent: $349 per month (2000); Median age of housing: 31 years (2000).
Transportation: Commute to work: 90.6% car, 0.0% public transportation, 6.0% walk, 3.4% work from home (2000); Travel time to work: 42.8% less than 15 minutes, 18.7% 15 to 30 minutes, 21.1% 30 to 45 minutes, 13.6% 45 to 60 minutes, 3.8% 60 minutes or more (2000)

MEARS (unincorporated postal area, zip code 49436). Covers a land area of 34.248 square miles and a water area of 1.373 square miles. Located at 43.67° N. Lat.; 86.46° W. Long.
Population: 1,675 (2000); Race: 90.5% White, 0.0% Black, 0.0% Asian, 0.9% American Indian and Alaska Native, 11.2% Hispanic of any race, 2.5% two or more races (2000); Density: 48.9 persons per square mile (2000); Age: 24.2% under 18, 15.6% over 64 (2000); Marriage status: 19.6% never married, 67.4% now married, 3.8% widowed, 9.2% divorced (2000); Foreign born: 2.9% (2000); Ancestry (includes multiple ancestries): 23.8% German, 14.3% Other groups, 13.9% English, 12.8% Irish, 11.4% Dutch (2000).
Economy: Employment by occupation: 10.0% management, 11.1% professional, 17.5% services, 22.7% sales, 7.0% farming, 14.7% construction, 16.9% production (2000).
Income: Per capita income: $17,613 (2000); Median household income: $36,360 (2000); Poverty rate: 16.2% (2000).
Education: High school graduation rate: 82.8% (2000); College graduation rate: 14.0% (2000).

School District(s)
Hart Public School District (KG-12)
2000 Enrollment: 1,508 231-873-4080
Housing: Homeownership rate: 82.2% (2000); Median home value: $119,200 (2000); Median rent: $327 per month (2000); Median age of housing: 19 years (2000).
Transportation: Commute to work: 89.2% car, 0.0% public transportation, 4.8% walk, 5.5% work from home (2000); Travel time to work: 42.1% less than 15 minutes, 30.0% 15 to 30 minutes, 16.5% 30 to 45 minutes, 5.1% 45 to 60 minutes, 6.3% 60 minutes or more (2000)

NEW ERA (village). Covers a land area of 0.848 square miles and a water area of 0 square miles. Located at 43.56° N. Lat.; 86.34° W. Long. Elevation is 754 feet.
Population: 461 (2000); Race: 94.5% White, 0.0% Black, 0.0% Asian, 0.4% American Indian and Alaska Native, 6.8% Hispanic of any race, 0.2% two or more races (2000); Density: 543.8 persons per square mile (2000); Age: 26.2% under 18, 11.5% over 64 (2000); Marriage status: 22.8% never married, 70.2% now married, 3.8% widowed, 3.3% divorced (2000); Foreign born: 0.0% (2000); Ancestry (includes multiple ancestries): 24.5% Dutch, 23.4% German, 10.2% English, 9.4% Irish, 6.6% Swedish (2000).
Economy: Fruit and vegetable canning. Employment by occupation: 10.1% management, 26.8% professional, 9.2% services, 18.9% sales, 0.0% farming, 11.4% construction, 23.7% production (2000).
Income: Per capita income: $18,417 (2000); Median household income: $45,909 (2000); Poverty rate: 2.8% (2000).
Taxes: Total city taxes per capita: $89 (1997); City property taxes per capita: $89 (1997).
Education: High school graduation rate: 92.9% (2000); College graduation rate: 24.4% (2000).
Housing: Homeownership rate: 88.6% (2000); Median home value: $84,400 (2000); Median rent: $316 per month (2000); Median age of housing: 40 years (2000).
Transportation: Commute to work: 91.9% car, 0.0% public transportation, 3.6% walk, 3.2% work from home (2000); Travel time to work: 36.3% less than 15 minutes, 35.4% 15 to 30 minutes, 21.3% 30 to 45 minutes, 3.8% 45 to 60 minutes, 3.3% 60 minutes or more (2000)

NEWFIELD (township). Covers a land area of 35.057 square miles and a water area of 0.652 square miles. Located at 43.59° N. Lat.; 86.08° W. Long.
Population: 2,483 (2000); Race: 96.7% White, 0.1% Black, 0.0% Asian, 0.3% American Indian and Alaska Native, 2.5% Hispanic of any race, 1.4% two or more races (2000); Density: 70.8 persons per square mile (2000); Age: 29.0% under 18, 12.5% over 64 (2000); Marriage status: 21.3% never married, 56.9% now married, 5.9% widowed, 16.0% divorced (2000); Foreign born: 0.6% (2000); Ancestry (includes multiple ancestries): 21.8% German, 11.8% Irish, 10.4% English, 9.3% Dutch, 7.3% Other groups (2000).
Economy: Employment by occupation: 10.3% management, 11.3% professional, 16.2% services, 18.5% sales, 1.3% farming, 11.1% construction, 31.4% production (2000).
Income: Per capita income: $14,054 (2000); Median household income: $30,547 (2000); Poverty rate: 15.5% (2000).
Taxes: Total city taxes per capita: $27 (1997); City property taxes per capita: $26 (1997).
Education: High school graduation rate: 81.4% (2000); College graduation rate: 9.4% (2000).
Housing: Homeownership rate: 85.0% (2000); Median home value: $78,800 (2000); Median rent: $304 per month (2000); Median age of housing: 30 years (2000).
Transportation: Commute to work: 91.9% car, 0.2% public transportation, 1.0% walk, 4.9% work from home (2000); Travel time to work: 23.5% less than 15 minutes, 35.1% 15 to 30 minutes, 19.0% 30 to 45 minutes, 12.2% 45 to 60 minutes, 10.1% 60 minutes or more (2000)

OTTO (township). Covers a land area of 35.869 square miles and a water area of 0.075 square miles. Located at 43.50° N. Lat.; 86.22° W. Long.
Population: 662 (2000); Race: 97.2% White, 0.0% Black, 1.0% Asian, 0.0% American Indian and Alaska Native, 3.8% Hispanic of any race, 0.3% two or more races (2000); Density: 18.5 persons per square mile (2000); Age: 27.4% under 18, 9.1% over 64 (2000); Marriage status: 20.0% never married, 63.2% now married, 4.0% widowed, 12.7% divorced (2000); Foreign born: 1.4% (2000); Ancestry (includes multiple ancestries): 25.3% German, 14.3% Dutch, 11.1% Irish, 8.2% United States or American, 7.0% English (2000).
Economy: Employment by occupation: 6.7% management, 7.0% professional, 12.7% services, 22.0% sales, 2.0% farming, 12.0% construction, 37.7% production (2000).
Income: Per capita income: $15,606 (2000); Median household income: $36,625 (2000); Poverty rate: 5.8% (2000).
Taxes: Total city taxes per capita: $25 (1997); City property taxes per capita: $25 (1997).
Education: High school graduation rate: 78.4% (2000); College graduation rate: 9.3% (2000).
Housing: Homeownership rate: 95.8% (2000); Median home value: $87,000 (2000); Median rent: $350 per month (2000); Median age of housing: 23 years (2000).
Transportation: Commute to work: 97.2% car, 0.0% public transportation, 0.7% walk, 2.1% work from home (2000); Travel time to work: 7.2% less than 15 minutes, 50.7% 15 to 30 minutes, 27.5% 30 to 45 minutes, 7.2% 45 to 60 minutes, 7.2% 60 minutes or more (2000)

PENTWATER (village). Covers a land area of 1.305 square miles and a water area of 0.327 square miles. Located at 43.78° N. Lat.; 86.43° W. Long. Elevation is 689 feet.
History: Pentwater grew up around a sawmill at the mouth of the Pentwater River on Lake Michigan, and later developed as a shipping point for fruit and berries. Many Mennonite farmers settled in this area, and planted orchards. Charles Mears, a Chicago capitalist, built a tile and brick factory here using the clay from the Pentwater River.
Population: 958 (2000); Race: 96.7% White, 0.0% Black, 0.6% Asian, 0.5% American Indian and Alaska Native, 0.9% Hispanic of any race, 1.2% two or more races (2000); Density: 733.8 persons per square mile (2000); Age: 15.6% under 18, 31.7% over 64 (2000); Marriage status: 17.3% never married, 60.6% now married, 9.8% widowed, 12.2% divorced (2000); Foreign born: 2.5% (2000); Ancestry (includes multiple ancestries): 28.6% German, 25.0% English, 14.2% Irish, 10.5% Dutch, 5.2% Swedish (2000).
Economy: Employment by occupation: 19.7% management, 25.2% professional, 15.6% services, 27.1% sales, 0.0% farming, 8.9% construction, 3.6% production (2000).
Income: Per capita income: $22,783 (2000); Median household income: $38,542 (2000); Poverty rate: 8.4% (2000).
Taxes: Total city taxes per capita: $479 (1997); City property taxes per capita: $468 (1997).
Education: High school graduation rate: 90.2% (2000); College graduation rate: 30.7% (2000).

School District(s)

Pentwater Public School District (KG-12)
2000 Enrollment: 319 231-869-4100
Housing: Homeownership rate: 81.0% (2000); Median home value: $126,200 (2000); Median rent: $342 per month (2000); Median age of housing: 47 years (2000).
Transportation: Commute to work: 82.8% car, 0.5% public transportation, 6.4% walk, 8.4% work from home (2000); Travel time to work: 51.3% less than 15 minutes, 34.4% 15 to 30 minutes, 8.3% 30 to 45 minutes, 3.2% 45 to 60 minutes, 2.7% 60 minutes or more (2000)
Additional Information Contacts
Pentwater Chamber of Commerce 231-869-4150

PENTWATER (township). Covers a land area of 13.419 square miles and a water area of 0.749 square miles. Located at 43.78° N. Lat.; 86.42° W. Long. Elevation is 689 feet.
History: Incorporated 1867.
Population: 1,513 (2000); Race: 96.1% White, 0.0% Black, 0.4% Asian, 0.8% American Indian and Alaska Native, 2.7% Hispanic of any race, 1.1% two or more races (2000); Density: 112.8 persons per square mile (2000); Age: 15.8% under 18, 28.7% over 64 (2000); Marriage status: 15.5% never married, 65.3% now married, 9.3% widowed, 9.9% divorced (2000); Foreign born: 1.7% (2000); Ancestry (includes multiple ancestries): 25.9% German, 20.8% English, 14.1% Irish, 9.5% Dutch, 6.4% Polish (2000).
Economy: In resort and farm area; ships fruit; has fisheries. Manufacturing: store displays. Employment by occupation: 16.8% management, 25.6% professional, 12.4% services, 26.8% sales, 0.0% farming, 11.6% construction, 6.8% production (2000).
Income: Per capita income: $23,837 (2000); Median household income: $42,574 (2000); Poverty rate: 7.4% (2000).
Taxes: Total city taxes per capita: $133 (1997); City property taxes per capita: $132 (1997).
Education: High school graduation rate: 90.5% (2000); College graduation rate: 32.1% (2000).
Housing: Homeownership rate: 83.9% (2000); Median home value: $128,600 (2000); Median rent: $361 per month (2000); Median age of housing: 32 years (2000).
Transportation: Commute to work: 84.2% car, 0.7% public transportation, 4.9% walk, 8.6% work from home (2000); Travel time to work: 43.4% less than 15 minutes, 35.9% 15 to 30 minutes, 10.0% 30 to 45 minutes, 4.4% 45 to 60 minutes, 6.2% 60 minutes or more (2000)

ROTHBURY (village). Covers a land area of 0.989 square miles and a water area of 0 square miles. Located at 43.50° N. Lat.; 86.34° W. Long. Elevation is 690 feet.
Population: 416 (2000); Race: 95.7% White, 1.1% Black, 0.0% Asian, 0.0% American Indian and Alaska Native, 7.3% Hispanic of any race, 0.0% two or more races (2000); Density: 420.8 persons per square mile (2000); Age: 26.6% under 18, 11.3% over 64 (2000); Marriage status: 26.6% never married, 57.3% now married, 5.2% widowed, 10.8% divorced (2000); Foreign born: 0.8% (2000); Ancestry (includes multiple ancestries): 25.5% German, 13.4% Irish, 10.5% Other groups, 10.2% United States or American, 8.9% English (2000).
Economy: Employment by occupation: 3.8% management, 3.8% professional, 14.1% services, 26.3% sales, 0.0% farming, 10.3% construction, 41.7% production (2000).
Income: Per capita income: $14,846 (2000); Median household income: $30,357 (2000); Poverty rate: 15.7% (2000).
Taxes: Total city taxes per capita: $87 (1997); City property taxes per capita: $87 (1997).
Education: High school graduation rate: 79.7% (2000); College graduation rate: 1.8% (2000).
Housing: Homeownership rate: 68.2% (2000); Median home value: $93,800 (2000); Median rent: $331 per month (2000); Median age of housing: 29 years (2000).
Transportation: Commute to work: 98.7% car, 0.0% public transportation, 1.3% walk, 0.0% work from home (2000); Travel time to work: 28.2% less than 15 minutes, 44.9% 15 to 30 minutes, 16.0% 30 to 45 minutes, 4.5% 45 to 60 minutes, 6.4% 60 minutes or more (2000)

SHELBY (village). Covers a land area of 1.742 square miles and a water area of 0 square miles. Located at 43.61° N. Lat.; 86.36° W. Long. Elevation is 810 feet.

History: Shelby was once on the migration path of thousands of passenger pigeons. The annual slaughter of the birds here led to the extinction of the passenger pigeon. The town of Shelby developed as a center for orchards and dairy farms.
Population: 1,914 (2000); Race: 80.5% White, 0.4% Black, 0.0% Asian, 0.7% American Indian and Alaska Native, 28.9% Hispanic of any race, 2.8% two or more races (2000); Density: 1,098.8 persons per square mile (2000); Age: 32.8% under 18, 15.0% over 64 (2000); Marriage status: 21.4% never married, 57.8% now married, 10.6% widowed, 10.2% divorced (2000); Foreign born: 14.0% (2000); Ancestry (includes multiple ancestries): 29.6% Other groups, 21.2% German, 11.1% English, 9.2% Irish, 6.2% Dutch (2000).
Economy: Employment by occupation: 6.1% management, 14.2% professional, 17.0% services, 17.2% sales, 3.4% farming, 10.9% construction, 31.2% production (2000).
Income: Per capita income: $13,468 (2000); Median household income: $28,710 (2000); Poverty rate: 16.7% (2000).
Taxes: Total city taxes per capita: $126 (1997); City property taxes per capita: $126 (1997).
Education: High school graduation rate: 75.2% (2000); College graduation rate: 11.0% (2000).

School District(s)

Shelby Public Schools (KG-12)
2000 Enrollment: 1,806 231-861-5211

Housing: Homeownership rate: 66.1% (2000); Median home value: $63,700 (2000); Median rent: $348 per month (2000); Median age of housing: 47 years (2000).
Hospitals: Lakeshore Community Hospital (35 beds)
Transportation: Commute to work: 90.0% car, 0.0% public transportation, 4.6% walk, 4.9% work from home (2000); Travel time to work: 53.4% less than 15 minutes, 26.8% 15 to 30 minutes, 11.6% 30 to 45 minutes, 2.6% 45 to 60 minutes, 5.7% 60 minutes or more (2000)

SHELBY (township). Covers a land area of 35.990 square miles and a water area of 0.097 square miles. Located at 43.60° N. Lat.; 86.35° W. Long. Elevation is 810 feet.
History: Shelby Township was named for General Isaac Shelby, leader of the Kentucky Rangers in the War of 1812.
Population: 3,951 (2000); Race: 86.3% White, 0.2% Black, 0.1% Asian, 0.5% American Indian and Alaska Native, 20.0% Hispanic of any race, 2.4% two or more races (2000); Density: 109.8 persons per square mile (2000); Age: 30.9% under 18, 13.5% over 64 (2000); Marriage status: 23.1% never married, 61.9% now married, 7.0% widowed, 8.1% divorced (2000); Foreign born: 7.7% (2000); Ancestry (includes multiple ancestries): 23.2% German, 19.9% Other groups, 11.7% Dutch, 10.5% Irish, 9.6% English (2000).
Economy: Employment by occupation: 9.8% management, 19.6% professional, 15.0% services, 18.8% sales, 3.6% farming, 7.1% construction, 26.2% production (2000).
Income: Per capita income: $15,501 (2000); Median household income: $35,078 (2000); Poverty rate: 11.9% (2000).
Taxes: Total city taxes per capita: $13 (1997); City property taxes per capita: $13 (1997).
Education: High school graduation rate: 80.9% (2000); College graduation rate: 15.7% (2000).
Housing: Homeownership rate: 78.7% (2000); Median home value: $71,800 (2000); Median rent: $341 per month (2000); Median age of housing: 43 years (2000).
Transportation: Commute to work: 90.2% car, 0.1% public transportation, 3.8% walk, 4.5% work from home (2000); Travel time to work: 45.9% less than 15 minutes, 30.8% 15 to 30 minutes, 16.0% 30 to 45 minutes, 3.6% 45 to 60 minutes, 3.7% 60 minutes or more (2000)

WALKERVILLE (village). Covers a land area of 1.218 square miles and a water area of 0 square miles. Located at 43.71° N. Lat.; 86.12° W. Long. Elevation is 870 feet.
Population: 254 (2000); Race: 87.1% White, 0.0% Black, 0.0% Asian, 1.7% American Indian and Alaska Native, 20.3% Hispanic of any race, 1.0% two or more races (2000); Density: 208.6 persons per square mile (2000); Age: 37.6% under 18, 8.1% over 64 (2000); Marriage status: 32.4% never married, 57.7% now married, 5.2% widowed, 4.7% divorced (2000); Foreign born: 4.7% (2000); Ancestry (includes multiple ancestries): 13.9% Other groups, 12.9% United States or American, 8.5% German, 8.5% Polish, 8.5% English (2000).
Economy: In orchard and farm area. In Manistee National Forest. Employment by occupation: 12.5% management, 3.1% professional, 22.9% services, 18.8% sales, 4.2% farming, 12.5% construction, 26.0% production (2000).
Income: Per capita income: $9,305 (2000); Median household income: $27,083 (2000); Poverty rate: 32.5% (2000).
Taxes: Total city taxes per capita: $68 (1997); City property taxes per capita: $68 (1997).
Education: High school graduation rate: 74.7% (2000); College graduation rate: 4.7% (2000).

School District(s)

Walkerville Public Schools (PK-12)
2000 Enrollment: 490 231-873-4850

Housing: Homeownership rate: 80.0% (2000); Median home value: $41,700 (2000); Median rent: $343 per month (2000); Median age of housing: 32 years (2000).
Transportation: Commute to work: 85.4% car, 0.0% public transportation, 11.5% walk, 3.1% work from home (2000); Travel time to work: 46.2% less than 15 minutes, 16.1% 15 to 30 minutes, 23.7% 30 to 45 minutes, 14.0% 45 to 60 minutes, 0.0% 60 minutes or more (2000)

WEARE (township). Covers a land area of 36.069 square miles and a water area of 0.003 square miles. Located at 43.77° N. Lat.; 86.34° W. Long. Elevation is 739 feet.
Population: 1,261 (2000); Race: 93.1% White, 0.0% Black, 0.3% Asian, 1.9% American Indian and Alaska Native, 10.6% Hispanic of any race, 3.0% two or more races (2000); Density: 35.0 persons per square mile (2000); Age: 31.9% under 18, 11.5% over 64 (2000); Marriage status: 21.9% never married, 62.0% now married, 6.9% widowed, 9.2% divorced (2000); Foreign born: 3.0% (2000); Ancestry (includes multiple ancestries): 27.4% German, 15.0% Other groups, 12.0% English, 9.7% Irish, 6.5% United States or American (2000).
Economy: Employment by occupation: 10.1% management, 7.5% professional, 16.3% services, 25.0% sales, 4.8% farming, 12.8% construction, 23.5% production (2000).
Income: Per capita income: $14,106 (2000); Median household income: $37,283 (2000); Poverty rate: 13.3% (2000).
Taxes: Total city taxes per capita: $41 (1997); City property taxes per capita: $40 (1997).
Education: High school graduation rate: 77.7% (2000); College graduation rate: 9.2% (2000).
Housing: Homeownership rate: 86.9% (2000); Median home value: $82,900 (2000); Median rent: $370 per month (2000); Median age of housing: 24 years (2000).
Transportation: Commute to work: 86.2% car, 0.0% public transportation, 8.8% walk, 5.0% work from home (2000); Travel time to work: 40.6% less than 15 minutes, 30.1% 15 to 30 minutes, 12.4% 30 to 45 minutes, 6.9% 45 to 60 minutes, 10.0% 60 minutes or more (2000)

Ogemaw County

Located in northeast central Michigan; drained by the Au Gres and Rifle Rivers; includes many small lakes, and part of Huron National Forest. Covers a land area of 564.30 square miles, a water area of 10.30 square miles, and is located in the Eastern Time Zone. The county government was organized in 1875. County seat is West Branch.

Weather Station: West Branch 3 SE — Elevation: 882 feet

	Jan	Feb	Mar	Apr	May	Jun	Jul	Aug	Sep	Oct	Nov	Dec
High	27	31	40	55	68	77	81	79	70	58	44	33
Low	8	10	19	31	42	51	56	54	46	35	27	16
Precip	1.7	1.2	2.0	2.4	2.9	3.1	3.1	3.7	3.6	2.6	2.4	1.9
Snow	14.9	9.4	8.8	2.0	0.1	0.0	0.0	0.0	0.0	0.3	4.9	10.8

High and Low temperatures in degrees Fahrenheit; Precipitation and Snow in inches

Population: 21,645 (2000); Race: 97.3% White, 0.0% Black, 0.4% Asian, 0.5% American Indian and Alaska Native, 1.0% Hispanic of any race, 1.5% two or more races (2000); Density: 38.4 persons per square mile (2000); Age: 23.5% under 18, 18.7% over 64 (2000).
Religion: Five largest groups: 17.8% Catholic Church, 4.6% Lutheran Church—Missouri Synod, 3.5% The United Methodist Church, 1.4% Free Methodist Church of North America, 1.0% Southern Baptist Convention (2000).
Economy: Unemployment rate: 6.9% (11/2002); Total civilian labor force: 9,659 (11/2002); Leading industries: 26.1% retail trade; 18.7% health care and social assistance; 16.3% manufacturing (2000); Companies that employ more than 1,000 persons: 0 (2000); Companies that employ more than 100 persons: 10 (2000); Farms: 261 totaling 73,239 acres (1997); Minority

business ownership rate: 0.0% (1997); Women business ownership rate: 18.5% (1997); Retail sales per capita: $11,018 (1997). Single-family building permits issued: 132 (2001) / 135 (2000); Multi-family building permits issued: 0 (2001) / 0 (2000).
Income: Per capita income: $15,768 (2000); Median household income: $30,474 (2000); Poverty rate: 14.0% (2000); Bankruptcy rate: 4.29% (2001).
Taxes: Total county taxes per capita: $187 (2000); County property taxes per capita: $165 (2000).
Education: High school graduation rate: 75.0% (2000); College graduation rate: 9.6% (2000).
Housing: Homeownership rate: 85.0% (2000); Median home value: $72,900 (2000); Median rent: $340 per month (2000); Median age of housing: 29 years (2000).
Health: Birth rate: 115.5 per 10,000 population (1998); Age adjusted death rate: 98.1 per 10,000 population (1999); Age adjusted cancer mortality rate: 200.1 deaths per 100,000 population (1999). Number of physicians: 11.6 per 10,000 population (1999); Number of hospital beds: 40.7 per 10,000 population (1999).
Elections: 2000 Presidential election results: 49.7% Gore, 47.8% Bush, 1.9% Nader, 0.1% Buchanan
National and State Parks: Ogemaw State Forest; Rifle River State Recreation Area
Additional Information Contacts
Ogemaw County Government Offices 989-345-0215
Prescott Chamber of Commerce. 989-873-4150
West Branch Chamber of Commerce. 989-345-2821

Ogemaw County Communities

CHURCHILL (township). Covers a land area of 35.650 square miles and a water area of 0.292 square miles. Located at 44.27° N. Lat.; 84.07° W. Long.
Population: 1,603 (2000); Race: 96.8% White, 0.0% Black, 0.3% Asian, 0.8% American Indian and Alaska Native, 0.7% Hispanic of any race, 2.1% two or more races (2000); Density: 45.0 persons per square mile (2000); Age: 25.2% under 18, 16.0% over 64 (2000); Marriage status: 17.9% never married, 67.7% now married, 6.6% widowed, 7.8% divorced (2000); Foreign born: 1.1% (2000); Ancestry (includes multiple ancestries): 26.3% German, 13.5% English, 11.5% Irish, 9.4% French (except Basque), 8.0% United States or American (2000).
Economy: Employment by occupation: 13.1% management, 17.9% professional, 15.9% services, 25.4% sales, 2.4% farming, 10.7% construction, 14.5% production (2000).
Income: Per capita income: $17,081 (2000); Median household income: $35,577 (2000); Poverty rate: 8.9% (2000).
Taxes: Total city taxes per capita: $77 (1997); City property taxes per capita: $77 (1997).
Education: High school graduation rate: 80.1% (2000); College graduation rate: 13.4% (2000).
Housing: Homeownership rate: 92.6% (2000); Median home value: $87,800 (2000); Median rent: $353 per month (2000); Median age of housing: 23 years (2000).
Transportation: Commute to work: 91.3% car, 0.2% public transportation, 2.0% walk, 6.5% work from home (2000); Travel time to work: 30.7% less than 15 minutes, 48.1% 15 to 30 minutes, 6.0% 30 to 45 minutes, 6.3% 45 to 60 minutes, 9.0% 60 minutes or more (2000)

CUMMING (township). Covers a land area of 34.684 square miles and a water area of 0.710 square miles. Located at 44.39° N. Lat.; 84.06° W. Long.
Population: 796 (2000); Race: 97.0% White, 0.0% Black, 0.0% Asian, 0.5% American Indian and Alaska Native, 1.6% Hispanic of any race, 2.2% two or more races (2000); Density: 23.0 persons per square mile (2000); Age: 27.3% under 18, 16.8% over 64 (2000); Marriage status: 19.2% never married, 69.4% now married, 5.9% widowed, 5.5% divorced (2000); Foreign born: 0.9% (2000); Ancestry (includes multiple ancestries): 30.4% German, 14.7% English, 13.9% Irish, 12.3% French (except Basque), 8.2% United States or American (2000).
Economy: Employment by occupation: 12.2% management, 13.5% professional, 11.8% services, 26.0% sales, 4.6% farming, 9.2% construction, 22.7% production (2000).
Income: Per capita income: $15,971 (2000); Median household income: $32,143 (2000); Poverty rate: 14.8% (2000).
Taxes: Total city taxes per capita: $144 (1997); City property taxes per capita: $144 (1997).
Education: High school graduation rate: 77.4% (2000); College graduation rate: 5.9% (2000).
Housing: Homeownership rate: 84.3% (2000); Median home value: $66,500 (2000); Median rent: $300 per month (2000); Median age of housing: 29 years (2000).
Transportation: Commute to work: 89.7% car, 0.0% public transportation, 4.0% walk, 5.0% work from home (2000); Travel time to work: 40.1% less than 15 minutes, 35.2% 15 to 30 minutes, 8.4% 30 to 45 minutes, 6.3% 45 to 60 minutes, 10.1% 60 minutes or more (2000)

EDWARDS (township). Covers a land area of 34.983 square miles and a water area of 0.731 square miles. Located at 44.19° N. Lat.; 84.29° W. Long. Elevation is 847 feet.
Population: 1,390 (2000); Race: 98.3% White, 0.3% Black, 0.2% Asian, 0.0% American Indian and Alaska Native, 0.8% Hispanic of any race, 1.0% two or more races (2000); Density: 39.7 persons per square mile (2000); Age: 25.4% under 18, 15.3% over 64 (2000); Marriage status: 18.4% never married, 66.8% now married, 7.8% widowed, 7.0% divorced (2000); Foreign born: 1.7% (2000); Ancestry (includes multiple ancestries): 34.7% German, 11.4% United States or American, 11.4% English, 9.6% Irish, 8.9% French (except Basque) (2000).
Economy: Employment by occupation: 12.4% management, 12.9% professional, 15.7% services, 26.0% sales, 2.8% farming, 13.5% construction, 16.7% production (2000).
Income: Per capita income: $15,031 (2000); Median household income: $30,119 (2000); Poverty rate: 12.3% (2000).
Taxes: Total city taxes per capita: $46 (1997); City property taxes per capita: $46 (1997).
Education: High school graduation rate: 75.2% (2000); College graduation rate: 10.0% (2000).
Housing: Homeownership rate: 91.3% (2000); Median home value: $86,000 (2000); Median rent: $355 per month (2000); Median age of housing: 25 years (2000).
Transportation: Commute to work: 90.2% car, 0.0% public transportation, 1.7% walk, 7.1% work from home (2000); Travel time to work: 39.8% less than 15 minutes, 35.1% 15 to 30 minutes, 9.9% 30 to 45 minutes, 4.7% 45 to 60 minutes, 10.5% 60 minutes or more (2000)

FOSTER (township). Covers a land area of 89.317 square miles and a water area of 0.601 square miles. Located at 44.43° N. Lat.; 84.27° W. Long.
Population: 821 (2000); Race: 99.3% White, 0.2% Black, 0.0% Asian, 0.0% American Indian and Alaska Native, 0.0% Hispanic of any race, 0.5% two or more races (2000); Density: 9.2 persons per square mile (2000); Age: 21.8% under 18, 21.2% over 64 (2000); Marriage status: 15.1% never married, 62.2% now married, 9.7% widowed, 13.0% divorced (2000); Foreign born: 1.5% (2000); Ancestry (includes multiple ancestries): 33.5% German, 19.3% Irish, 10.1% English, 9.0% Polish, 8.0% French (except Basque) (2000).
Economy: Employment by occupation: 9.3% management, 18.6% professional, 13.4% services, 28.3% sales, 0.0% farming, 10.4% construction, 20.1% production (2000).
Income: Per capita income: $17,319 (2000); Median household income: $29,091 (2000); Poverty rate: 13.4% (2000).
Taxes: Total city taxes per capita: $26 (1997); City property taxes per capita: $26 (1997).
Education: High school graduation rate: 76.9% (2000); College graduation rate: 9.4% (2000).
Housing: Homeownership rate: 90.6% (2000); Median home value: $86,100 (2000); Median rent: $367 per month (2000); Median age of housing: 30 years (2000).
Transportation: Commute to work: 90.8% car, 0.8% public transportation, 1.9% walk, 5.0% work from home (2000); Travel time to work: 12.4% less than 15 minutes, 53.8% 15 to 30 minutes, 16.1% 30 to 45 minutes, 3.6% 45 to 60 minutes, 14.1% 60 minutes or more (2000)

GOODAR (township). Covers a land area of 35.317 square miles and a water area of 0.635 square miles. Located at 44.45° N. Lat.; 83.91° W. Long. Elevation is 1,040 feet.
Population: 493 (2000); Race: 98.4% White, 0.0% Black, 0.0% Asian, 0.0% American Indian and Alaska Native, 1.2% Hispanic of any race, 0.8% two or more races (2000); Density: 14.0 persons per square mile (2000); Age: 16.7% under 18, 27.3% over 64 (2000); Marriage status: 12.8% never married, 69.1% now married, 8.4% widowed, 9.7% divorced (2000); Foreign born: 0.4% (2000); Ancestry (includes multiple ancestries): 28.1% German, 16.1% Irish, 11.0% United States or American, 10.4% French (except Basque), 10.4% English (2000).

Economy: Employment by occupation: 9.6% management, 6.0% professional, 12.0% services, 31.1% sales, 1.2% farming, 19.2% construction, 21.0% production (2000).
Income: Per capita income: $14,052 (2000); Median household income: $28,214 (2000); Poverty rate: 14.6% (2000).
Taxes: Total city taxes per capita: $47 (1997); City property taxes per capita: $47 (1997).
Education: High school graduation rate: 67.3% (2000); College graduation rate: 6.5% (2000).
Housing: Homeownership rate: 95.6% (2000); Median home value: $81,400 (2000); Median rent: $338 per month (2000); Median age of housing: 39 years (2000).
Transportation: Commute to work: 92.8% car, 0.0% public transportation, 1.3% walk, 3.9% work from home (2000); Travel time to work: 29.3% less than 15 minutes, 25.2% 15 to 30 minutes, 17.7% 30 to 45 minutes, 13.6% 45 to 60 minutes, 14.3% 60 minutes or more (2000)

HILL (township). Covers a land area of 32.690 square miles and a water area of 3.401 square miles. Located at 44.37° N. Lat.; 83.95° W. Long.
Population: 1,584 (2000); Race: 97.2% White, 0.0% Black, 0.3% Asian, 0.7% American Indian and Alaska Native, 0.6% Hispanic of any race, 1.7% two or more races (2000); Density: 48.5 persons per square mile (2000); Age: 14.8% under 18, 27.1% over 64 (2000); Marriage status: 13.2% never married, 66.4% now married, 9.3% widowed, 11.2% divorced (2000); Foreign born: 1.4% (2000); Ancestry (includes multiple ancestries): 27.4% German, 11.8% English, 10.9% Irish, 10.0% United States or American, 7.3% Polish (2000).
Economy: Employment by occupation: 5.2% management, 17.2% professional, 18.5% services, 21.1% sales, 0.4% farming, 17.5% construction, 20.0% production (2000).
Income: Per capita income: $18,770 (2000); Median household income: $29,821 (2000); Poverty rate: 13.4% (2000).
Taxes: Total city taxes per capita: $52 (1997); City property taxes per capita: $52 (1997).
Education: High school graduation rate: 74.4% (2000); College graduation rate: 10.5% (2000).
Housing: Homeownership rate: 94.8% (2000); Median home value: $85,300 (2000); Median rent: $328 per month (2000); Median age of housing: 36 years (2000).
Transportation: Commute to work: 95.8% car, 0.0% public transportation, 0.2% walk, 3.5% work from home (2000); Travel time to work: 19.2% less than 15 minutes, 37.3% 15 to 30 minutes, 17.6% 30 to 45 minutes, 8.7% 45 to 60 minutes, 17.2% 60 minutes or more (2000)

HORTON (township). Covers a land area of 35.453 square miles and a water area of 0.267 square miles. Located at 44.20° N. Lat.; 84.19° W. Long.
Population: 997 (2000); Race: 97.4% White, 0.0% Black, 1.1% Asian, 0.2% American Indian and Alaska Native, 2.7% Hispanic of any race, 1.3% two or more races (2000); Density: 28.1 persons per square mile (2000); Age: 26.7% under 18, 13.2% over 64 (2000); Marriage status: 22.1% never married, 60.7% now married, 7.7% widowed, 9.5% divorced (2000); Foreign born: 1.4% (2000); Ancestry (includes multiple ancestries): 31.3% German, 14.7% Irish, 11.5% English, 9.7% United States or American, 8.2% French (except Basque) (2000).
Economy: Employment by occupation: 10.1% management, 9.9% professional, 19.8% services, 24.2% sales, 1.0% farming, 10.9% construction, 24.2% production (2000).
Income: Per capita income: $16,230 (2000); Median household income: $33,816 (2000); Poverty rate: 8.8% (2000).
Taxes: Total city taxes per capita: $22 (1997); City property taxes per capita: $18 (1997).
Education: High school graduation rate: 76.6% (2000); College graduation rate: 8.0% (2000).
Housing: Homeownership rate: 80.2% (2000); Median home value: $83,200 (2000); Median rent: $338 per month (2000); Median age of housing: 25 years (2000).
Transportation: Commute to work: 92.8% car, 0.0% public transportation, 3.2% walk, 4.0% work from home (2000); Travel time to work: 46.9% less than 15 minutes, 29.0% 15 to 30 minutes, 11.4% 30 to 45 minutes, 4.9% 45 to 60 minutes, 7.8% 60 minutes or more (2000)

KLACKING (township). Covers a land area of 35.845 square miles and a water area of 0.066 square miles. Located at 44.37° N. Lat.; 84.19° W. Long.
Population: 617 (2000); Race: 95.9% White, 0.0% Black, 0.0% Asian, 0.3% American Indian and Alaska Native, 3.6% Hispanic of any race, 2.4% two or more races (2000); Density: 17.2 persons per square mile (2000); Age: 24.2% under 18, 12.2% over 64 (2000); Marriage status: 19.1% never married, 65.9% now married, 6.9% widowed, 8.1% divorced (2000); Foreign born: 2.6% (2000); Ancestry (includes multiple ancestries): 33.6% German, 11.9% English, 10.6% Irish, 10.4% United States or American, 8.9% Polish (2000).
Economy: Employment by occupation: 12.9% management, 11.2% professional, 11.6% services, 26.1% sales, 3.3% farming, 14.5% construction, 20.3% production (2000).
Income: Per capita income: $16,238 (2000); Median household income: $40,625 (2000); Poverty rate: 8.8% (2000).
Taxes: Total city taxes per capita: $83 (1997); City property taxes per capita: $83 (1997).
Education: High school graduation rate: 81.4% (2000); College graduation rate: 9.4% (2000).
Housing: Homeownership rate: 88.8% (2000); Median home value: $76,200 (2000); Median rent: $375 per month (2000); Median age of housing: 26 years (2000).
Transportation: Commute to work: 94.4% car, 0.0% public transportation, 0.9% walk, 4.7% work from home (2000); Travel time to work: 32.7% less than 15 minutes, 49.8% 15 to 30 minutes, 11.2% 30 to 45 minutes, 0.9% 45 to 60 minutes, 5.4% 60 minutes or more (2000)

LOGAN (township). Covers a land area of 35.252 square miles and a water area of 0.725 square miles. Located at 44.28° N. Lat.; 83.95° W. Long.
Population: 581 (2000); Race: 97.4% White, 0.0% Black, 0.0% Asian, 0.5% American Indian and Alaska Native, 0.5% Hispanic of any race, 2.0% two or more races (2000); Density: 16.5 persons per square mile (2000); Age: 20.1% under 18, 24.7% over 64 (2000); Marriage status: 17.7% never married, 66.9% now married, 9.3% widowed, 6.2% divorced (2000); Foreign born: 2.2% (2000); Ancestry (includes multiple ancestries): 30.4% German, 13.8% English, 10.1% Irish, 8.5% French Canadian, 6.5% French (except Basque) (2000).
Economy: Employment by occupation: 14.3% management, 15.3% professional, 20.1% services, 16.4% sales, 0.0% farming, 15.3% construction, 18.5% production (2000).
Income: Per capita income: $15,372 (2000); Median household income: $22,105 (2000); Poverty rate: 15.9% (2000).
Taxes: Total city taxes per capita: $29 (1997); City property taxes per capita: $29 (1997).
Education: High school graduation rate: 66.7% (2000); College graduation rate: 4.5% (2000).
Housing: Homeownership rate: 92.7% (2000); Median home value: $69,400 (2000); Median rent: $313 per month (2000); Median age of housing: 27 years (2000).
Transportation: Commute to work: 87.7% car, 0.0% public transportation, 5.9% walk, 6.4% work from home (2000); Travel time to work: 25.1% less than 15 minutes, 38.3% 15 to 30 minutes, 16.0% 30 to 45 minutes, 4.6% 45 to 60 minutes, 16.0% 60 minutes or more (2000)

LUPTON (unincorporated postal area, zip code 48635). Covers a land area of 67.052 square miles and a water area of 2.162 square miles. Located at 44.40° N. Lat.; 83.99° W. Long.
History: Lupton was settled by several Quaker families from Ohio in 1880, and was first known as Lane Heights. In 1893, the village was renamed Lupton for Emmor Lupton, one of the first settlers and the first postmaster.
Population: 1,839 (2000); Race: 97.5% White, 0.0% Black, 0.2% Asian, 0.5% American Indian and Alaska Native, 0.9% Hispanic of any race, 1.7% two or more races (2000); Density: 27.4 persons per square mile (2000); Age: 18.6% under 18, 24.0% over 64 (2000); Marriage status: 14.5% never married, 68.2% now married, 7.7% widowed, 9.6% divorced (2000); Foreign born: 1.2% (2000); Ancestry (includes multiple ancestries): 24.1% German, 11.5% English, 11.4% United States or American, 9.7% Irish, 6.9% Other groups (2000).
Economy: Employment by occupation: 10.2% management, 14.0% professional, 18.5% services, 22.3% sales, 1.3% farming, 13.9% construction, 19.7% production (2000).
Income: Per capita income: $18,721 (2000); Median household income: $30,302 (2000); Poverty rate: 12.9% (2000).
Education: High school graduation rate: 73.1% (2000); College graduation rate: 8.9% (2000).
Housing: Homeownership rate: 92.8% (2000); Median home value: $71,700 (2000); Median rent: $311 per month (2000); Median age of housing: 32 years (2000).
Transportation: Commute to work: 93.8% car, 0.0% public transportation, 0.7% walk, 3.4% work from home (2000); Travel time to work: 30.3% less than 15 minutes, 36.5% 15 to 30 minutes, 12.9% 30 to 45 minutes, 8.3% 45 to 60 minutes, 12.0% 60 minutes or more (2000)

MILLS (township). Covers a land area of 34.449 square miles and a water area of 1.133 square miles. Located at 44.20° N. Lat.; 84.06° W. Long.
Population: 4,005 (2000); Race: 96.5% White, 0.0% Black, 0.2% Asian, 1.1% American Indian and Alaska Native, 0.6% Hispanic of any race, 2.1% two or more races (2000); Density: 116.3 persons per square mile (2000); Age: 20.4% under 18, 20.6% over 64 (2000); Marriage status: 20.0% never married, 57.3% now married, 8.5% widowed, 14.1% divorced (2000); Foreign born: 1.0% (2000); Ancestry (includes multiple ancestries): 24.3% German, 12.4% English, 12.2% Irish, 10.8% French (except Basque), 7.3% Polish (2000).
Economy: Employment by occupation: 4.9% management, 8.2% professional, 29.8% services, 22.5% sales, 1.3% farming, 11.9% construction, 21.5% production (2000).
Income: Per capita income: $12,355 (2000); Median household income: $21,703 (2000); Poverty rate: 21.6% (2000).
Taxes: Total city taxes per capita: $55 (1997); City property taxes per capita: $53 (1997).
Education: High school graduation rate: 60.4% (2000); College graduation rate: 3.5% (2000).
Housing: Homeownership rate: 85.0% (2000); Median home value: $49,800 (2000); Median rent: $310 per month (2000); Median age of housing: 30 years (2000).
Transportation: Commute to work: 93.8% car, 0.0% public transportation, 1.6% walk, 2.9% work from home (2000); Travel time to work: 21.1% less than 15 minutes, 34.3% 15 to 30 minutes, 28.1% 30 to 45 minutes, 3.9% 45 to 60 minutes, 12.5% 60 minutes or more (2000)

OGEMAW (township). Covers a land area of 36.389 square miles and a water area of 0.088 square miles. Located at 44.30° N. Lat.; 84.28° W. Long.
Population: 1,118 (2000); Race: 98.1% White, 0.2% Black, 0.4% Asian, 0.2% American Indian and Alaska Native, 0.4% Hispanic of any race, 0.7% two or more races (2000); Density: 30.7 persons per square mile (2000); Age: 26.2% under 18, 14.7% over 64 (2000); Marriage status: 21.6% never married, 64.3% now married, 6.4% widowed, 7.7% divorced (2000); Foreign born: 1.5% (2000); Ancestry (includes multiple ancestries): 26.5% German, 12.6% Irish, 11.2% United States or American, 10.4% English, 6.3% Other groups (2000).
Economy: Employment by occupation: 8.5% management, 17.5% professional, 18.5% services, 25.2% sales, 2.3% farming, 9.1% construction, 18.9% production (2000).
Income: Per capita income: $17,785 (2000); Median household income: $41,000 (2000); Poverty rate: 7.5% (2000).
Taxes: Total city taxes per capita: $47 (1997); City property taxes per capita: $47 (1997).
Education: High school graduation rate: 82.9% (2000); College graduation rate: 10.8% (2000).
Housing: Homeownership rate: 87.4% (2000); Median home value: $79,300 (2000); Median rent: $299 per month (2000); Median age of housing: 28 years (2000).
Transportation: Commute to work: 94.5% car, 0.0% public transportation, 1.2% walk, 4.3% work from home (2000); Travel time to work: 62.9% less than 15 minutes, 19.1% 15 to 30 minutes, 7.4% 30 to 45 minutes, 4.1% 45 to 60 minutes, 6.6% 60 minutes or more (2000)

PRESCOTT (village). Covers a land area of 1.171 square miles and a water area of 0 square miles. Located at 44.19° N. Lat.; 83.93° W. Long. Elevation is 793 feet.
History: Prescott was named for C.H. Prescott, who bought the Lake Huron & Southwestern Railroad in 1879.
Population: 286 (2000); Race: 98.7% White, 0.0% Black, 0.0% Asian, 0.7% American Indian and Alaska Native, 0.7% Hispanic of any race, 0.7% two or more races (2000); Density: 244.2 persons per square mile (2000); Age: 34.9% under 18, 11.3% over 64 (2000); Marriage status: 14.8% never married, 63.2% now married, 12.9% widowed, 9.1% divorced (2000); Foreign born: 0.7% (2000); Ancestry (includes multiple ancestries): 17.9% German, 14.3% English, 13.6% Irish, 12.3% United States or American, 5.6% Italian (2000).
Economy: Employment by occupation: 11.0% management, 19.3% professional, 13.8% services, 14.7% sales, 1.8% farming, 11.0% construction, 28.4% production (2000).
Income: Per capita income: $11,014 (2000); Median household income: $27,188 (2000); Poverty rate: 26.9% (2000).
Taxes: Total city taxes per capita: $51 (1997); City property taxes per capita: $51 (1997).
Education: High school graduation rate: 79.8% (2000); College graduation rate: 8.7% (2000).
Housing: Homeownership rate: 90.2% (2000); Median home value: $52,600 (2000); Median rent: $344 per month (2000); Median age of housing: 42 years (2000).
Transportation: Commute to work: 87.2% car, 0.0% public transportation, 3.7% walk, 9.2% work from home (2000); Travel time to work: 34.3% less than 15 minutes, 22.2% 15 to 30 minutes, 15.2% 30 to 45 minutes, 6.1% 45 to 60 minutes, 22.2% 60 minutes or more (2000)
Additional Information Contacts
Prescott Chamber of Commerce. 989-873-4150

RICHLAND (township). Covers a land area of 34.822 square miles and a water area of 0.898 square miles. Located at 44.19° N. Lat.; 83.94° W. Long.
Population: 956 (2000); Race: 97.0% White, 0.0% Black, 0.0% Asian, 0.7% American Indian and Alaska Native, 2.6% Hispanic of any race, 2.3% two or more races (2000); Density: 27.5 persons per square mile (2000); Age: 29.4% under 18, 16.0% over 64 (2000); Marriage status: 15.3% never married, 67.7% now married, 9.7% widowed, 7.3% divorced (2000); Foreign born: 0.6% (2000); Ancestry (includes multiple ancestries): 24.6% German, 14.8% English, 9.8% Irish, 8.8% United States or American, 7.9% French (except Basque) (2000).
Economy: Employment by occupation: 9.9% management, 16.0% professional, 19.6% services, 19.3% sales, 2.2% farming, 12.4% construction, 20.7% production (2000).
Income: Per capita income: $13,294 (2000); Median household income: $29,000 (2000); Poverty rate: 17.4% (2000).
Taxes: Total city taxes per capita: $52 (1997); City property taxes per capita: $52 (1997).
Education: High school graduation rate: 74.2% (2000); College graduation rate: 6.8% (2000).
Housing: Homeownership rate: 91.3% (2000); Median home value: $63,200 (2000); Median rent: $325 per month (2000); Median age of housing: 35 years (2000).
Transportation: Commute to work: 85.6% car, 0.0% public transportation, 3.7% walk, 9.5% work from home (2000); Travel time to work: 27.7% less than 15 minutes, 27.7% 15 to 30 minutes, 19.1% 30 to 45 minutes, 3.2% 45 to 60 minutes, 22.3% 60 minutes or more (2000)

ROSE (township). Covers a land area of 52.870 square miles and a water area of 0.258 square miles. Located at 44.43° N. Lat.; 84.11° W. Long.
Population: 1,409 (2000); Race: 98.6% White, 0.0% Black, 0.2% Asian, 0.1% American Indian and Alaska Native, 2.1% Hispanic of any race, 0.8% two or more races (2000); Density: 26.7 persons per square mile (2000); Age: 24.9% under 18, 17.5% over 64 (2000); Marriage status: 20.6% never married, 61.4% now married, 9.2% widowed, 8.9% divorced (2000); Foreign born: 0.8% (2000); Ancestry (includes multiple ancestries): 22.5% German, 12.5% United States or American, 12.4% English, 11.7% Irish, 8.1% French (except Basque) (2000).
Economy: Employment by occupation: 9.5% management, 17.4% professional, 15.7% services, 20.4% sales, 0.2% farming, 15.9% construction, 20.9% production (2000).
Income: Per capita income: $17,168 (2000); Median household income: $30,625 (2000); Poverty rate: 11.8% (2000).
Taxes: Total city taxes per capita: $74 (1997); City property taxes per capita: $73 (1997).
Education: High school graduation rate: 78.6% (2000); College graduation rate: 10.2% (2000).
Housing: Homeownership rate: 95.2% (2000); Median home value: $69,800 (2000); Median rent: $346 per month (2000); Median age of housing: 28 years (2000).
Transportation: Commute to work: 91.6% car, 0.0% public transportation, 0.0% walk, 5.6% work from home (2000); Travel time to work: 39.6% less than 15 minutes, 32.0% 15 to 30 minutes, 14.3% 30 to 45 minutes, 6.0% 45 to 60 minutes, 8.1% 60 minutes or more (2000)

ROSE CITY (city). Covers a land area of 1.083 square miles and a water area of 0.011 square miles. Located at 44.42° N. Lat.; 84.11° W. Long. Elevation is 953 feet.
History: Rose City was settled in the 1870's. The French & Rose Lumber Company was founded here by M.S. French, who negotiatied for the railroad to build a line in 1892 so lumber could be shipped out. The settlement was first called Churchill, but the name was changed to Rose City in 1892.
Population: 721 (2000); Race: 97.5% White, 0.0% Black, 0.0% Asian, 1.0% American Indian and Alaska Native, 1.1% Hispanic of any race, 0.4% two or more races (2000); Density: 665.7 persons per square mile (2000); Age:

27.1% under 18, 23.7% over 64 (2000); Marriage status: 21.7% never married, 58.8% now married, 11.0% widowed, 8.5% divorced (2000); Foreign born: 1.4% (2000); Ancestry (includes multiple ancestries): 20.3% German, 13.4% English, 12.8% Irish, 9.1% French (except Basque), 7.1% Other groups (2000).
Economy: Employment by occupation: 6.0% management, 15.1% professional, 27.0% services, 20.2% sales, 0.4% farming, 9.9% construction, 21.4% production (2000).
Income: Per capita income: $10,684 (2000); Median household income: $25,192 (2000); Poverty rate: 24.7% (2000).
Taxes: Total city taxes per capita: $218 (1997); City property taxes per capita: $218 (1997).
Education: High school graduation rate: 75.3% (2000); College graduation rate: 6.3% (2000).
Housing: Homeownership rate: 55.6% (2000); Median home value: $58,600 (2000); Median rent: $341 per month (2000); Median age of housing: 40 years (2000).
Safety: Violent crime rate: 27.6 per 10,000 population; Property crime rate: 179.3 per 10,000 population (2001).
Transportation: Commute to work: 90.5% car, 0.0% public transportation, 3.7% walk, 4.1% work from home (2000); Travel time to work: 47.4% less than 15 minutes, 29.7% 15 to 30 minutes, 15.1% 30 to 45 minutes, 0.9% 45 to 60 minutes, 6.9% 60 minutes or more (2000)

SKIDWAY LAKE (CDP). Covers a land area of 11.327 square miles and a water area of 0.340 square miles. Located at 44.18° N. Lat.; 84.04° W. Long.
Population: 3,147 (2000); Race: 96.0% White, 0.0% Black, 0.2% Asian, 1.3% American Indian and Alaska Native, 0.6% Hispanic of any race, 2.5% two or more races (2000); Density: 277.8 persons per square mile (2000); Age: 20.8% under 18, 20.6% over 64 (2000); Marriage status: 20.8% never married, 53.5% now married, 9.3% widowed, 16.4% divorced (2000); Foreign born: 1.1% (2000); Ancestry (includes multiple ancestries): 23.9% German, 13.2% Irish, 11.1% French (except Basque), 10.4% English, 7.7% Polish (2000).
Economy: Employment by occupation: 4.7% management, 6.2% professional, 35.5% services, 21.2% sales, 1.1% farming, 11.2% construction, 20.0% production (2000).
Income: Per capita income: $11,405 (2000); Median household income: $20,806 (2000); Poverty rate: 25.3% (2000).
Education: High school graduation rate: 55.5% (2000); College graduation rate: 1.6% (2000).
Housing: Homeownership rate: 81.7% (2000); Median home value: $44,100 (2000); Median rent: $309 per month (2000); Median age of housing: 32 years (2000).
Transportation: Commute to work: 94.2% car, 0.0% public transportation, 2.1% walk, 1.9% work from home (2000); Travel time to work: 23.1% less than 15 minutes, 27.4% 15 to 30 minutes, 30.5% 30 to 45 minutes, 4.3% 45 to 60 minutes, 14.7% 60 minutes or more (2000)

SOUTH BRANCH (unincorporated postal area, zip code 48761). Aka Southbranch. Covers a land area of 106.702 square miles and a water area of 0.754 square miles. Located at 44.54° N. Lat.; 83.91° W. Long.
Population: 1,133 (2000); Race: 98.8% White, 0.0% Black, 0.0% Asian, 0.0% American Indian and Alaska Native, 0.7% Hispanic of any race, 0.8% two or more races (2000); Density: 10.6 persons per square mile (2000); Age: 15.8% under 18, 28.6% over 64 (2000); Marriage status: 12.3% never married, 67.7% now married, 9.0% widowed, 11.0% divorced (2000); Foreign born: 0.7% (2000); Ancestry (includes multiple ancestries): 24.0% German, 13.6% Irish, 12.8% English, 12.1% French (except Basque), 11.9% Polish (2000).
Economy: Employment by occupation: 11.4% management, 11.1% professional, 11.4% services, 19.2% sales, 1.5% farming, 15.0% construction, 30.3% production (2000).
Income: Per capita income: $16,008 (2000); Median household income: $26,150 (2000); Poverty rate: 17.4% (2000).
Education: High school graduation rate: 64.3% (2000); College graduation rate: 5.3% (2000).
Housing: Homeownership rate: 92.0% (2000); Median home value: $72,000 (2000); Median rent: $276 per month (2000); Median age of housing: 32 years (2000).
Transportation: Commute to work: 94.6% car, 0.0% public transportation, 0.6% walk, 3.8% work from home (2000); Travel time to work: 15.5% less than 15 minutes, 25.7% 15 to 30 minutes, 34.2% 30 to 45 minutes, 13.5% 45 to 60 minutes, 11.2% 60 minutes or more (2000)

WEST BRANCH (city). Covers a land area of 1.330 square miles and a water area of 0 square miles. Located at 44.27° N. Lat.; 84.23° W. Long. Elevation is 959 feet.
History: West Branch was settled by farmers along the west branch of the Rifle River. Farming remained the chief source of revenue until oil was discovered here in the 1930's.
Population: 1,926 (2000); Race: 94.8% White, 0.0% Black, 2.5% Asian, 0.6% American Indian and Alaska Native, 0.7% Hispanic of any race, 2.1% two or more races (2000); Density: 1,447.6 persons per square mile (2000); Age: 25.8% under 18, 16.4% over 64 (2000); Marriage status: 28.7% never married, 46.6% now married, 10.0% widowed, 14.6% divorced (2000); Foreign born: 1.9% (2000); Ancestry (includes multiple ancestries): 33.1% German, 12.6% English, 8.7% Irish, 8.0% French (except Basque), 5.4% Other groups (2000).
Economy: Employment by occupation: 7.8% management, 23.0% professional, 22.0% services, 25.8% sales, 0.3% farming, 6.7% construction, 14.3% production (2000).
Income: Per capita income: $17,852 (2000); Median household income: $30,132 (2000); Poverty rate: 14.0% (2000).
Taxes: Total city taxes per capita: $295 (1997); City property taxes per capita: $295 (1997).
Education: High school graduation rate: 83.7% (2000); College graduation rate: 18.9% (2000).

School District(s)

West Branch-Rose City Area Schoo (KG-12)
2000 Enrollment: 2,700 517-345-5959
Housing: Homeownership rate: 53.2% (2000); Median home value: $67,200 (2000); Median rent: $361 per month (2000); Median age of housing: 44 years (2000).
Hospitals: West Branch Regional Medical Center (88 beds)
Safety: Violent crime rate: 41.3 per 10,000 population; Property crime rate: 599.2 per 10,000 population (2001).
Newspapers: Ogemaw/Oscoda County Star (1 x week); Ogemaw County Herald (1 x week)
Transportation: Commute to work: 88.0% car, 2.3% public transportation, 4.8% walk, 2.9% work from home (2000); Travel time to work: 73.3% less than 15 minutes, 11.0% 15 to 30 minutes, 5.0% 30 to 45 minutes, 4.7% 45 to 60 minutes, 5.9% 60 minutes or more (2000)
Additional Information Contacts
West Branch Chamber of Commerce. 989-345-2821

WEST BRANCH (township). Covers a land area of 34.169 square miles and a water area of 0.513 square miles. Located at 44.28° N. Lat.; 84.20° W. Long. Elevation is 959 feet.
History: Incorporated as village 1885, as city 1905.
Population: 2,628 (2000); Race: 99.0% White, 0.1% Black, 0.0% Asian, 0.1% American Indian and Alaska Native, 0.2% Hispanic of any race, 0.8% two or more races (2000); Density: 76.9 persons per square mile (2000); Age: 24.9% under 18, 18.8% over 64 (2000); Marriage status: 18.0% never married, 67.8% now married, 6.7% widowed, 7.6% divorced (2000); Foreign born: 0.9% (2000); Ancestry (includes multiple ancestries): 31.5% German, 13.3% Irish, 13.0% United States or American, 12.3% English, 5.9% French (except Basque) (2000).
Economy: In recreation and agricultural area: cattle; grain. Manufacturing: wood and lumber products, automotive parts, garage doors, cutting tools. Annual trout festival held here. Airport to Southeast. Employment by occupation: 10.0% management, 14.9% professional, 22.9% services, 22.6% sales, 2.5% farming, 10.7% construction, 16.4% production (2000).
Income: Per capita income: $17,503 (2000); Median household income: $38,182 (2000); Poverty rate: 9.6% (2000).
Taxes: Total city taxes per capita: $122 (1997); City property taxes per capita: $122 (1997).
Education: High school graduation rate: 84.3% (2000); College graduation rate: 13.9% (2000).
Housing: Homeownership rate: 88.8% (2000); Median home value: $100,800 (2000); Median rent: $385 per month (2000); Median age of housing: 24 years (2000).
Transportation: Commute to work: 92.6% car, 0.0% public transportation, 1.3% walk, 6.1% work from home (2000); Travel time to work: 61.1% less than 15 minutes, 22.1% 15 to 30 minutes, 8.0% 30 to 45 minutes, 1.5% 45 to 60 minutes, 7.3% 60 minutes or more (2000)

Ontonagon County

Located in northwestern Michigan, on the Upper Peninsula; bounded on the north by Lake Superior; drained by the Ontonagon, Iron, and Firesteel Rivers; includes the Porcupine Mountains, and part of Ottawa National Forest and Gogebic Lake. Covers a land area of 1,311.50 square miles, a water area of 2,429.90 square miles, and is located in the Eastern Time Zone. The county government was organized in 1843. County seat is Ontonagon.

Weather Station: Bergland Dam Elevation: 1,299 feet

	Jan	Feb	Mar	Apr	May	Jun	Jul	Aug	Sep	Oct	Nov	Dec
High	20	25	36	50	64	73	78	76	66	53	37	25
Low	-1	0	10	25	37	47	52	50	42	32	21	8
Precip	2.9	1.6	2.4	2.3	3.6	3.9	3.9	4.0	3.8	3.6	3.5	2.9
Snow	44.0	24.5	24.9	9.1	1.4	0.0	0.0	0.0	0.1	3.5	27.7	41.2

High and Low temperatures in degrees Fahrenheit; Precipitation and Snow in inches

Population: 7,818 (2000); Race: 97.1% White, 0.0% Black, 0.2% Asian, 1.2% American Indian and Alaska Native, 0.8% Hispanic of any race, 1.2% two or more races (2000); Density: 6.0 persons per square mile (2000); Age: 20.2% under 18, 21.6% over 64 (2000).
Religion: Five largest groups: 22.3% Catholic Church, 15.8% Evangelical Lutheran Church in America, 6.3% Lutheran Church—Missouri Synod, 4.5% The United Methodist Church, 2.0% Wisconsin Evangelical Lutheran Synod (2000).
Economy: Unemployment rate: 6.3% (11/2002); Total civilian labor force: 2,799 (11/2002); Leading industries: 20.4% retail trade; 19.4% health care and social assistance; 14.9% accommodation & food services (2000); Companies that employ more than 1,000 persons: 0 (2000); Companies that employ more than 100 persons: 2 (2000); Farms: 92 totaling 32,516 acres (1997); Minority business ownership rate: 0.0% (1997); Women business ownership rate: 25.0% (1997); Retail sales per capita: $7,455 (1997). Single-family building permits issued: 16 (2001) / 18 (2000); Multi-family building permits issued: 0 (2001) / 0 (2000).
Income: Per capita income: $16,695 (2000); Median household income: $29,552 (2000); Poverty rate: 10.4% (2000); Bankruptcy rate: 2.09% (2001).
Taxes: Total county taxes per capita: $195 (1997); County property taxes per capita: $194 (1997).
Education: High school graduation rate: 83.8% (2000); College graduation rate: 13.0% (2000).
Housing: Homeownership rate: 84.9% (2000); Median home value: $41,400 (2000); Median rent: $233 per month (2000); Median age of housing: 44 years (2000).
Health: Birth rate: 65.2 per 10,000 population (1998); Age adjusted death rate: 108.8 per 10,000 population (1999); Age adjusted cancer mortality rate: 249.9 deaths per 100,000 population (1999). Number of physicians: 6.4 per 10,000 population (1999); Number of hospital beds: 92.1 per 10,000 population (1999).
Elections: 2000 Presidential election results: 36.5% Gore, 59.6% Bush, 3.3% Nader, 0.1% Buchanan
National and State Parks: North Country National Scenic Trail; Ottawa National Forest; Porcupine Mountains Wilderness State Park
Additional Information Contacts
Ontonagon County Government Offices 906-884-4255
Bergland Chamber of Commerce. 906-842-3611
Lake Gogebic Area Chamber of Commerce 906-575-3265
Ontonagon Chamber of Commerce 906-884-4735

Ontonagon County Communities

BERGLAND (township). Covers a land area of 98.454 square miles and a water area of 9.792 square miles. Located at 46.57° N. Lat.; 89.60° W. Long. Elevation is 1,294 feet.
History: Bergland was founded by Gunlak A. Bergland of Milwaukee, who opened a sawmill here in 1900.
Population: 550 (2000); Race: 99.3% White, 0.0% Black, 0.0% Asian, 0.3% American Indian and Alaska Native, 0.5% Hispanic of any race, 0.3% two or more races (2000); Density: 5.6 persons per square mile (2000); Age: 16.0% under 18, 22.5% over 64 (2000); Marriage status: 21.3% never married, 60.9% now married, 7.1% widowed, 10.7% divorced (2000); Foreign born: 0.9% (2000); Ancestry (includes multiple ancestries): 26.2% Finnish, 24.8% German, 10.0% Swedish, 9.1% Polish, 8.3% English (2000).
Economy: Single-family building permits issued: 0 (2001) / 0 (2000); Multi-family building permits issued: 0 (2001) / 0 (2000); Employment by occupation: 7.7% management, 11.6% professional, 31.8% services, 18.9% sales, 2.6% farming, 12.0% construction, 15.5% production (2000).
Income: Per capita income: $15,573 (2000); Median household income: $28,125 (2000); Poverty rate: 8.6% (2000).
Taxes: Total city taxes per capita: $84 (1997); City property taxes per capita: $76 (1997).
Education: High school graduation rate: 88.6% (2000); College graduation rate: 15.0% (2000).
Housing: Homeownership rate: 89.1% (2000); Median home value: $57,000 (2000); Median rent: $275 per month (2000); Median age of housing: 34 years (2000).
Transportation: Commute to work: 91.7% car, 0.0% public transportation, 6.5% walk, 0.9% work from home (2000); Travel time to work: 36.8% less than 15 minutes, 28.9% 15 to 30 minutes, 16.7% 30 to 45 minutes, 7.9% 45 to 60 minutes, 9.6% 60 minutes or more (2000)
Additional Information Contacts
Bergland Chamber of Commerce. 906-842-3611
Lake Gogebic Area Chamber of Commerce 906-575-3265

BOHEMIA (township). Covers a land area of 91.914 square miles and a water area of 0.452 square miles. Located at 46.83° N. Lat.; 88.94° W. Long.
Population: 77 (2000); Race: 100.0% White, 0.0% Black, 0.0% Asian, 0.0% American Indian and Alaska Native, 0.0% Hispanic of any race, 0.0% two or more races (2000); Density: 0.8 persons per square mile (2000); Age: 9.6% under 18, 16.4% over 64 (2000); Marriage status: 8.8% never married, 67.6% now married, 10.3% widowed, 13.2% divorced (2000); Foreign born: 0.0% (2000); Ancestry (includes multiple ancestries): 53.4% Finnish, 15.1% English, 9.6% United States or American, 9.6% Irish, 8.2% German (2000).
Economy: Single-family building permits issued: 0 (2001) / 0 (2000); Multi-family building permits issued: 0 (2001) / 0 (2000); Employment by occupation: 11.1% management, 19.4% professional, 13.9% services, 19.4% sales, 0.0% farming, 19.4% construction, 16.7% production (2000).
Income: Per capita income: $23,775 (2000); Median household income: $31,875 (2000); Poverty rate: 9.6% (2000).
Taxes: Total city taxes per capita: $126 (1997); City property taxes per capita: $126 (1997).
Education: High school graduation rate: 85.9% (2000); College graduation rate: 10.9% (2000).
Housing: Homeownership rate: 95.0% (2000); Median home value: $28,800 (2000); Median age of housing: 32 years (2000).
Transportation: Commute to work: 76.5% car, 0.0% public transportation, 5.9% walk, 5.9% work from home (2000); Travel time to work: 21.9% less than 15 minutes, 21.9% 15 to 30 minutes, 40.6% 30 to 45 minutes, 12.5% 45 to 60 minutes, 3.1% 60 minutes or more (2000)

BRUCE CROSSING (unincorporated postal area, zip code 49912). Aka Bruce's Crossing. Covers a land area of 136.472 square miles and a water area of 0.246 square miles. Located at 46.46° N. Lat.; 89.15° W. Long. Elevation is 1,144 feet.
History: The community of Bruce Crossing was named for Donald M. Bruce, who operated a store at the crossroads where August Neuman had built a sawmill. The Duluth, South Shore & Atlantic Railroad crossed the old Military Road at this place.
Population: 1,115 (2000); Race: 96.6% White, 0.0% Black, 0.5% Asian, 1.1% American Indian and Alaska Native, 0.0% Hispanic of any race, 1.6% two or more races (2000); Density: 8.2 persons per square mile (2000); Age: 21.0% under 18, 22.4% over 64 (2000); Marriage status: 19.1% never married, 60.3% now married, 8.1% widowed, 12.4% divorced (2000); Foreign born: 1.9% (2000); Ancestry (includes multiple ancestries): 45.3% Finnish, 12.7% German, 6.5% Irish, 6.4% Swedish, 6.3% United States or American (2000).
Economy: Employment by occupation: 10.6% management, 7.1% professional, 22.9% services, 23.6% sales, 2.8% farming, 11.7% construction, 21.3% production (2000).
Income: Per capita income: $15,011 (2000); Median household income: $27,875 (2000); Poverty rate: 13.7% (2000).
Education: High school graduation rate: 75.9% (2000); College graduation rate: 7.9% (2000).
Housing: Homeownership rate: 86.2% (2000); Median home value: $47,700 (2000); Median rent: $233 per month (2000); Median age of housing: 51 years (2000).
Transportation: Commute to work: 81.9% car, 5.0% public transportation, 3.8% walk, 8.8% work from home (2000); Travel time to work: 39.5% less than 15 minutes, 22.3% 15 to 30 minutes, 16.0% 30 to 45 minutes, 7.3% 45 to 60 minutes, 14.9% 60 minutes or more (2000)

CARP LAKE (township). Covers a land area of 225.078 square miles and a water area of 0.794 square miles. Located at 46.73° N. Lat.; 89.62° W. Long.
Population: 891 (2000); Race: 94.0% White, 0.0% Black, 0.0% Asian, 2.9% American Indian and Alaska Native, 0.5% Hispanic of any race, 2.5% two or more races (2000); Density: 4.0 persons per square mile (2000); Age: 18.6% under 18, 23.2% over 64 (2000); Marriage status: 18.3% never married, 65.1% now married, 10.1% widowed, 6.5% divorced (2000); Foreign born: 3.3% (2000); Ancestry (includes multiple ancestries): 22.8% Finnish, 22.7% German, 14.1% English, 12.5% French (except Basque), 10.4% Polish (2000).
Economy: Single-family building permits issued: 3 (2001) / 3 (2000); Multi-family building permits issued: 0 (2001) / 0 (2000); Employment by occupation: 8.1% management, 14.0% professional, 34.4% services, 20.9% sales, 0.6% farming, 11.7% construction, 10.3% production (2000).
Income: Per capita income: $16,333 (2000); Median household income: $26,731 (2000); Poverty rate: 10.3% (2000).
Taxes: Total city taxes per capita: $23 (1997); City property taxes per capita: $22 (1997).
Education: High school graduation rate: 85.8% (2000); College graduation rate: 12.6% (2000).
Housing: Homeownership rate: 85.1% (2000); Median home value: $31,400 (2000); Median rent: $240 per month (2000); Median age of housing: 41 years (2000).
Transportation: Commute to work: 91.3% car, 0.0% public transportation, 6.7% walk, 2.0% work from home (2000); Travel time to work: 46.7% less than 15 minutes, 28.3% 15 to 30 minutes, 5.4% 30 to 45 minutes, 6.8% 45 to 60 minutes, 12.8% 60 minutes or more (2000)

EWEN (unincorporated postal area, zip code 49925). Covers a land area of 125.914 square miles and a water area of 0.024 square miles. Located at 46.55° N. Lat.; 89.34° W. Long. Elevation is 1,134 feet.
Population: 662 (2000); Race: 98.7% White, 0.0% Black, 0.7% Asian, 0.0% American Indian and Alaska Native, 0.0% Hispanic of any race, 0.6% two or more races (2000); Density: 5.3 persons per square mile (2000); Age: 21.3% under 18, 16.7% over 64 (2000); Marriage status: 24.0% never married, 57.4% now married, 8.1% widowed, 10.4% divorced (2000); Foreign born: 1.8% (2000); Ancestry (includes multiple ancestries): 30.6% Finnish, 18.6% German, 13.0% Irish, 8.3% Swedish, 8.0% Norwegian (2000).
Economy: In dairy area. Area surrounded by, but not included in, Ottawa National Forest. Employment by occupation: 9.6% management, 23.1% professional, 25.3% services, 17.1% sales, 0.0% farming, 12.8% construction, 12.1% production (2000).
Income: Per capita income: $15,560 (2000); Median household income: $27,132 (2000); Poverty rate: 11.7% (2000).
Education: High school graduation rate: 86.6% (2000); College graduation rate: 14.9% (2000).

School District(s)

Ewen-Trout Creek Consolidated Sc (KG-12)
2000 Enrollment: 400 906-988-2364

Housing: Homeownership rate: 80.8% (2000); Median home value: $37,000 (2000); Median rent: $184 per month (2000); Median age of housing: 42 years (2000).
Transportation: Commute to work: 85.0% car, 1.5% public transportation, 6.6% walk, 6.2% work from home (2000); Travel time to work: 50.2% less than 15 minutes, 10.9% 15 to 30 minutes, 22.6% 30 to 45 minutes, 10.1% 45 to 60 minutes, 6.2% 60 minutes or more (2000)

GREENLAND (township). Covers a land area of 113.205 square miles and a water area of 0 square miles. Located at 46.77° N. Lat.; 89.06° W. Long. Elevation is 1,138 feet.
History: Greenland was named for Greenland, New Hampshire. A settlement grew up around the mining claim of William W. Spalding, who came here in 1858.
Population: 870 (2000); Race: 97.4% White, 0.0% Black, 0.0% Asian, 0.9% American Indian and Alaska Native, 1.9% Hispanic of any race, 1.4% two or more races (2000); Density: 7.7 persons per square mile (2000); Age: 22.2% under 18, 16.7% over 64 (2000); Marriage status: 23.1% never married, 61.2% now married, 9.6% widowed, 6.1% divorced (2000); Foreign born: 0.3% (2000); Ancestry (includes multiple ancestries): 45.4% Finnish, 12.8% German, 9.9% Irish, 7.5% Swedish, 7.4% English (2000).
Economy: Single-family building permits issued: 0 (2001) / 0 (2000); Multi-family building permits issued: 0 (2001) / 0 (2000); Employment by occupation: 8.5% management, 12.4% professional, 18.4% services, 26.6% sales, 3.3% farming, 9.1% construction, 21.7% production (2000).
Income: Per capita income: $16,152 (2000); Median household income: $31,574 (2000); Poverty rate: 7.4% (2000).
Taxes: Total city taxes per capita: $19 (1997); City property taxes per capita: $16 (1997).
Education: High school graduation rate: 81.0% (2000); College graduation rate: 11.4% (2000).
Housing: Homeownership rate: 89.4% (2000); Median home value: $36,800 (2000); Median rent: $188 per month (2000); Median age of housing: 60+ years (2000).
Transportation: Commute to work: 85.8% car, 0.5% public transportation, 6.0% walk, 7.1% work from home (2000); Travel time to work: 25.6% less than 15 minutes, 37.1% 15 to 30 minutes, 19.1% 30 to 45 minutes, 8.5% 45 to 60 minutes, 9.7% 60 minutes or more (2000)

HAIGHT (township). Covers a land area of 105.805 square miles and a water area of 1.282 square miles. Located at 46.38° N. Lat.; 89.20° W. Long.
History: Haight Township was organized in 1899 and named for Joseph Haight, the chairman of the board of supervisors at that time.
Population: 228 (2000); Race: 96.7% White, 0.0% Black, 0.0% Asian, 0.0% American Indian and Alaska Native, 0.0% Hispanic of any race, 3.3% two or more races (2000); Density: 2.2 persons per square mile (2000); Age: 23.6% under 18, 19.1% over 64 (2000); Marriage status: 20.1% never married, 63.3% now married, 8.0% widowed, 8.5% divorced (2000); Foreign born: 2.0% (2000); Ancestry (includes multiple ancestries): 24.8% Finnish, 13.4% Irish, 7.7% Polish, 7.7% Other groups, 7.3% German (2000).
Economy: Single-family building permits issued: 2 (2001) / 0 (2000); Multi-family building permits issued: 0 (2001) / 0 (2000); Employment by occupation: 2.0% management, 8.0% professional, 26.0% services, 25.0% sales, 0.0% farming, 17.0% construction, 22.0% production (2000).
Income: Per capita income: $14,980 (2000); Median household income: $30,104 (2000); Poverty rate: 11.0% (2000).
Taxes: Total city taxes per capita: $76 (1997); City property taxes per capita: $71 (1997).
Education: High school graduation rate: 76.6% (2000); College graduation rate: 6.3% (2000).
Housing: Homeownership rate: 90.6% (2000); Median home value: $55,000 (2000); Median rent: $350 per month (2000); Median age of housing: 50 years (2000).
Transportation: Commute to work: 80.6% car, 3.2% public transportation, 0.0% walk, 16.1% work from home (2000); Travel time to work: 44.9% less than 15 minutes, 23.1% 15 to 30 minutes, 11.5% 30 to 45 minutes, 9.0% 45 to 60 minutes, 11.5% 60 minutes or more (2000)

INTERIOR (township). Covers a land area of 86.499 square miles and a water area of 2.975 square miles. Located at 46.43° N. Lat.; 89.05° W. Long.
Population: 375 (2000); Race: 93.4% White, 0.0% Black, 0.5% Asian, 4.5% American Indian and Alaska Native, 0.0% Hispanic of any race, 1.1% two or more races (2000); Density: 4.3 persons per square mile (2000); Age: 13.2% under 18, 28.8% over 64 (2000); Marriage status: 22.1% never married, 54.6% now married, 17.2% widowed, 6.0% divorced (2000); Foreign born: 1.3% (2000); Ancestry (includes multiple ancestries): 38.1% Finnish, 10.6% Irish, 9.0% German, 7.1% English, 7.1% United States or American (2000).
Economy: Single-family building permits issued: 0 (2001) / 0 (2000); Multi-family building permits issued: 0 (2001) / 0 (2000); Employment by occupation: 8.1% management, 14.0% professional, 19.8% services, 19.8% sales, 9.3% farming, 9.3% construction, 19.8% production (2000).
Income: Per capita income: $16,906 (2000); Median household income: $27,679 (2000); Poverty rate: 11.4% (2000).
Taxes: Total city taxes per capita: $39 (1997); City property taxes per capita: $33 (1997).
Education: High school graduation rate: 71.8% (2000); College graduation rate: 8.0% (2000).
Housing: Homeownership rate: 92.4% (2000); Median home value: $31,000 (2000); Median rent: $225 per month (2000); Median age of housing: 58 years (2000).
Transportation: Commute to work: 84.2% car, 0.0% public transportation, 4.2% walk, 9.1% work from home (2000); Travel time to work: 25.3% less than 15 minutes, 22.7% 15 to 30 minutes, 26.0% 30 to 45 minutes, 17.3% 45 to 60 minutes, 8.7% 60 minutes or more (2000)

MASS CITY (unincorporated postal area, zip code 49948). Aka Mass. Covers a land area of 96.066 square miles and a water area of 0.444 square miles. Located at 46.73° N. Lat.; 89.02° W. Long. Elevation is 1,065 feet.
Population: 688 (2000); Race: 97.9% White, 0.0% Black, 0.0% Asian, 0.4% American Indian and Alaska Native, 2.3% Hispanic of any race, 1.4% two or more races (2000); Density: 7.2 persons per square mile (2000); Age: 22.7%

under 18, 17.8% over 64 (2000); Marriage status: 22.5% never married, 61.2% now married, 10.7% widowed, 5.7% divorced (2000); Foreign born: 0.4% (2000); Ancestry (includes multiple ancestries): 44.6% Finnish, 14.0% German, 11.5% Irish, 6.3% Swedish, 6.3% English (2000).
Economy: Employment by occupation: 6.0% management, 13.2% professional, 19.2% services, 27.0% sales, 3.2% farming, 9.6% construction, 21.7% production (2000).
Income: Per capita income: $15,400 (2000); Median household income: $30,648 (2000); Poverty rate: 8.7% (2000).
Education: High school graduation rate: 78.7% (2000); College graduation rate: 11.8% (2000).
Housing: Homeownership rate: 88.0% (2000); Median home value: $34,300 (2000); Median rent: $194 per month (2000); Median age of housing: 60 years (2000).
Transportation: Commute to work: 84.8% car, 0.0% public transportation, 5.7% walk, 7.4% work from home (2000); Travel time to work: 26.1% less than 15 minutes, 33.0% 15 to 30 minutes, 21.8% 30 to 45 minutes, 11.1% 45 to 60 minutes, 8.0% 60 minutes or more (2000)

MATCHWOOD (township). Covers a land area of 109.494 square miles and a water area of 0.041 square miles. Located at 46.60° N. Lat.; 89.45° W. Long.
Population: 115 (2000); Race: 100.0% White, 0.0% Black, 0.0% Asian, 0.0% American Indian and Alaska Native, 0.0% Hispanic of any race, 0.0% two or more races (2000); Density: 1.1 persons per square mile (2000); Age: 11.7% under 18, 26.2% over 64 (2000); Marriage status: 14.3% never married, 67.0% now married, 6.6% widowed, 12.1% divorced (2000); Foreign born: 0.0% (2000); Ancestry (includes multiple ancestries): 26.2% German, 16.5% French (except Basque), 9.7% Polish, 9.7% Irish, 7.8% Finnish (2000).
Economy: Employment by occupation: 16.7% management, 22.9% professional, 31.3% services, 10.4% sales, 0.0% farming, 12.5% construction, 6.3% production (2000).
Income: Per capita income: $15,190 (2000); Median household income: $18,125 (2000); Poverty rate: 25.2% (2000).
Taxes: Total city taxes per capita: $495 (1997); City property taxes per capita: $477 (1997).
Education: High school graduation rate: 78.6% (2000); College graduation rate: 11.9% (2000).
Housing: Homeownership rate: 96.3% (2000); Median home value: $20,000 (2000); Median age of housing: 28 years (2000).
Transportation: Commute to work: 74.4% car, 0.0% public transportation, 7.0% walk, 18.6% work from home (2000); Travel time to work: 20.0% less than 15 minutes, 11.4% 15 to 30 minutes, 48.6% 30 to 45 minutes, 20.0% 45 to 60 minutes, 0.0% 60 minutes or more (2000)

MCMILLAN (township). Covers a land area of 70.371 square miles and a water area of 0.072 square miles. Located at 46.52° N. Lat.; 89.28° W. Long.
Population: 601 (2000); Race: 98.2% White, 0.0% Black, 0.8% Asian, 0.0% American Indian and Alaska Native, 0.0% Hispanic of any race, 0.6% two or more races (2000); Density: 8.5 persons per square mile (2000); Age: 24.1% under 18, 14.1% over 64 (2000); Marriage status: 25.4% never married, 56.3% now married, 8.0% widowed, 10.3% divorced (2000); Foreign born: 1.9% (2000); Ancestry (includes multiple ancestries): 35.3% Finnish, 17.8% German, 13.3% Irish, 8.8% Swedish, 8.3% Norwegian (2000).
Economy: Single-family building permits issued: 3 (2001) / 3 (2000); Multi-family building permits issued: 0 (2001) / 0 (2000); Employment by occupation: 7.7% management, 22.8% professional, 23.2% services, 19.5% sales, 0.4% farming, 13.8% construction, 12.6% production (2000).
Income: Per capita income: $15,486 (2000); Median household income: $28,580 (2000); Poverty rate: 10.1% (2000).
Taxes: Total city taxes per capita: $4 (1997); City property taxes per capita: $4 (1997).
Education: High school graduation rate: 88.0% (2000); College graduation rate: 15.5% (2000).
Housing: Homeownership rate: 79.1% (2000); Median home value: $37,500 (2000); Median rent: $184 per month (2000); Median age of housing: 52 years (2000).
Transportation: Commute to work: 87.7% car, 1.6% public transportation, 6.1% walk, 3.7% work from home (2000); Travel time to work: 54.0% less than 15 minutes, 11.5% 15 to 30 minutes, 19.1% 30 to 45 minutes, 8.5% 45 to 60 minutes, 6.8% 60 minutes or more (2000)

ONTONAGON (village). Covers a land area of 3.748 square miles and a water area of 0.130 square miles. Located at 46.87° N. Lat.; 89.31° W. Long. Elevation is 642 feet.
History: Ontonagon was first known for the Ontonagon Boulder, a mass of copper that attracted scientists, authors, and the merely curious from the mid-1600's to the mid-1800's, when the boulder ended up in the Smithsonian Institution in Washington, D.C. Attempts at mining in Ontonagon were not successful, and those who settled here turned to lumbering. The Diamond Match Company was the owner of one of the early sawmills.
Population: 1,769 (2000); Race: 98.0% White, 0.0% Black, 0.1% Asian, 0.9% American Indian and Alaska Native, 1.2% Hispanic of any race, 0.6% two or more races (2000); Density: 472.0 persons per square mile (2000); Age: 21.4% under 18, 27.4% over 64 (2000); Marriage status: 19.2% never married, 58.8% now married, 9.2% widowed, 12.9% divorced (2000); Foreign born: 1.6% (2000); Ancestry (includes multiple ancestries): 26.8% German, 24.5% Finnish, 10.7% French (except Basque), 10.4% English, 8.3% Irish (2000).
Economy: Single-family building permits issued: 2 (2001) / 4 (2000); Multi-family building permits issued: 0 (2001) / 0 (2000); Employment by occupation: 10.0% management, 20.9% professional, 21.2% services, 21.3% sales, 0.6% farming, 9.2% construction, 16.8% production (2000).
Income: Per capita income: $16,293 (2000); Median household income: $28,300 (2000); Poverty rate: 11.8% (2000).
Taxes: Total city taxes per capita: $265 (1997); City property taxes per capita: $265 (1997).
Education: High school graduation rate: 83.8% (2000); College graduation rate: 16.4% (2000).

School District(s)

Ontonagon Area Schools (KG-12)
2000 Enrollment: 655 906-884-4422
Housing: Homeownership rate: 75.6% (2000); Median home value: $42,400 (2000); Median rent: $233 per month (2000); Median age of housing: 51 years (2000).
Hospitals: Ontonagon Memorial Hospital (26 beds)
Newspapers: Ontonagon Herald (1 x week)
Transportation: Commute to work: 82.1% car, 0.3% public transportation, 10.9% walk, 5.0% work from home (2000); Travel time to work: 79.1% less than 15 minutes, 8.2% 15 to 30 minutes, 4.2% 30 to 45 minutes, 2.7% 45 to 60 minutes, 5.7% 60 minutes or more (2000)
Additional Information Contacts
Ontonagon Chamber of Commerce 906-884-4735

ONTONAGON (township). Covers a land area of 192.849 square miles and a water area of 0.766 square miles. Located at 46.85° N. Lat.; 89.29° W. Long. Elevation is 642 feet.
History: The Ontonagon boulder, a huge copper mass, was found near the river, and was moved to the Smithsonian Institution. Established on site of Native American village. Incorporated 1885.
Population: 2,954 (2000); Race: 97.6% White, 0.0% Black, 0.1% Asian, 0.9% American Indian and Alaska Native, 1.2% Hispanic of any race, 1.1% two or more races (2000); Density: 15.3 persons per square mile (2000); Age: 21.5% under 18, 22.1% over 64 (2000); Marriage status: 17.5% never married, 62.4% now married, 7.9% widowed, 12.2% divorced (2000); Foreign born: 1.1% (2000); Ancestry (includes multiple ancestries): 26.3% Finnish, 25.3% German, 10.1% French (except Basque), 10.0% Polish, 9.7% English (2000).
Economy: Railroad terminus and railroad ship transfer point. Manufacturing of paperboard. Shipping center, fishing. Resort. Single-family building permits issued: 6 (2001) / 8 (2000); Multi-family building permits issued: 0 (2001) / 0 (2000); Employment by occupation: 8.6% management, 17.5% professional, 20.4% services, 20.3% sales, 1.8% farming, 12.1% construction, 19.3% production (2000).
Income: Per capita income: $17,802 (2000); Median household income: $32,308 (2000); Poverty rate: 10.1% (2000).
Taxes: Total city taxes per capita: $23 (1997); City property taxes per capita: $22 (1997).
Education: High school graduation rate: 87.1% (2000); College graduation rate: 15.4% (2000).
Housing: Homeownership rate: 81.6% (2000); Median home value: $47,700 (2000); Median rent: $231 per month (2000); Median age of housing: 45 years (2000).
Transportation: Commute to work: 87.0% car, 0.2% public transportation, 7.3% walk, 4.6% work from home (2000); Travel time to work: 73.7% less than 15 minutes, 13.7% 15 to 30 minutes, 4.8% 30 to 45 minutes, 2.5% 45 to 60 minutes, 5.2% 60 minutes or more (2000)

ROCKLAND (township). Covers a land area of 92.799 square miles and a water area of 1.020 square miles. Located at 46.72° N. Lat.; 89.21° W. Long. Elevation is 1,180 feet.
History: A large deposit of pure copper was discovered in the Rockland area in 1856, attracting many Irish and Cornish miners. The village of Rockland was formed in 1864 from the union of Rockland, Rosendale, and Williamsburg. The Minnesota Mining Company was active in this area.
Population: 324 (2000); Race: 98.0% White, 0.0% Black, 0.0% Asian, 1.7% American Indian and Alaska Native, 0.0% Hispanic of any race, 0.3% two or more races (2000); Density: 3.5 persons per square mile (2000); Age: 19.3% under 18, 22.3% over 64 (2000); Marriage status: 21.9% never married, 59.4% now married, 10.8% widowed, 8.0% divorced (2000); Foreign born: 0.7% (2000); Ancestry (includes multiple ancestries): 26.0% Finnish, 24.7% German, 20.0% English, 7.0% French (except Basque), 6.3% Other groups (2000).
Economy: Employment by occupation: 7.2% management, 17.1% professional, 19.8% services, 16.2% sales, 0.0% farming, 11.7% construction, 27.9% production (2000).
Income: Per capita income: $19,319 (2000); Median household income: $32,250 (2000); Poverty rate: 9.0% (2000).
Taxes: Total city taxes per capita: $206 (1997); City property taxes per capita: $195 (1997).
Education: High school graduation rate: 83.5% (2000); College graduation rate: 13.0% (2000).
Housing: Homeownership rate: 86.9% (2000); Median home value: $30,200 (2000); Median rent: $258 per month (2000); Median age of housing: 60+ years (2000).
Transportation: Commute to work: 92.8% car, 1.8% public transportation, 1.8% walk, 3.6% work from home (2000); Travel time to work: 17.8% less than 15 minutes, 54.2% 15 to 30 minutes, 5.6% 30 to 45 minutes, 11.2% 45 to 60 minutes, 11.2% 60 minutes or more (2000)

STANNARD (township). Covers a land area of 125.067 square miles and a water area of 0.029 square miles. Located at 46.56° N. Lat.; 89.14° W. Long.
History: Stannard Township was named for William Stannard, a member of the state legislature.
Population: 833 (2000); Race: 96.3% White, 0.0% Black, 0.8% Asian, 1.5% American Indian and Alaska Native, 0.0% Hispanic of any race, 1.4% two or more races (2000); Density: 6.7 persons per square mile (2000); Age: 19.5% under 18, 24.9% over 64 (2000); Marriage status: 18.8% never married, 59.0% now married, 8.4% widowed, 13.8% divorced (2000); Foreign born: 2.0% (2000); Ancestry (includes multiple ancestries): 51.6% Finnish, 14.6% German, 7.3% Swedish, 6.0% United States or American, 5.8% English (2000).
Economy: Single-family building permits issued: 0 (2001) / 0 (2000); Multi-family building permits issued: 0 (2001) / 0 (2000); Employment by occupation: 14.1% management, 6.1% professional, 23.4% services, 23.4% sales, 3.5% farming, 9.6% construction, 19.9% production (2000).
Income: Per capita income: $14,327 (2000); Median household income: $24,706 (2000); Poverty rate: 14.6% (2000).
Taxes: Total city taxes per capita: $26 (1997); City property taxes per capita: $18 (1997).
Education: High school graduation rate: 74.5% (2000); College graduation rate: 7.6% (2000).
Housing: Homeownership rate: 83.9% (2000); Median home value: $47,700 (2000); Median rent: $200 per month (2000); Median age of housing: 49 years (2000).
Transportation: Commute to work: 80.8% car, 6.0% public transportation, 5.3% walk, 7.3% work from home (2000); Travel time to work: 38.9% less than 15 minutes, 22.1% 15 to 30 minutes, 16.4% 30 to 45 minutes, 5.4% 45 to 60 minutes, 17.1% 60 minutes or more (2000)

TROUT CREEK (unincorporated postal area, zip code 49967). Covers a land area of 172.315 square miles and a water area of 0.560 square miles. Located at 46.46° N. Lat.; 89.00° W. Long. Elevation is 1,115 feet.
Population: 444 (2000); Race: 92.7% White, 0.4% Black, 0.4% Asian, 4.2% American Indian and Alaska Native, 0.0% Hispanic of any race, 1.8% two or more races (2000); Density: 2.6 persons per square mile (2000); Age: 13.7% under 18, 26.8% over 64 (2000); Marriage status: 21.8% never married, 54.7% now married, 14.5% widowed, 9.0% divorced (2000); Foreign born: 1.1% (2000); Ancestry (includes multiple ancestries): 34.8% Finnish, 12.0% Irish, 9.5% German, 7.8% English, 6.9% United States or American (2000).
Economy: Employment by occupation: 8.5% management, 15.4% professional, 20.9% services, 21.4% sales, 9.0% farming, 9.5% construction, 15.4% production (2000).
Income: Per capita income: $16,336 (2000); Median household income: $27,697 (2000); Poverty rate: 14.2% (2000).
Education: High school graduation rate: 72.2% (2000); College graduation rate: 10.7% (2000).
Housing: Homeownership rate: 92.8% (2000); Median home value: $31,200 (2000); Median rent: $225 per month (2000); Median age of housing: 47 years (2000).
Transportation: Commute to work: 83.6% car, 0.0% public transportation, 4.2% walk, 10.1% work from home (2000); Travel time to work: 27.1% less than 15 minutes, 21.8% 15 to 30 minutes, 21.8% 30 to 45 minutes, 18.8% 45 to 60 minutes, 10.6% 60 minutes or more (2000)

Osceola County

Located in central Michigan; crossed by the Muskegon River; drained by the South Branch of the Manistee River; includes part of Manistee National Forest. Covers a land area of 566.00 square miles, a water area of 7.10 square miles, and is located in the Eastern Time Zone. The county government was organized in 1869. County seat is Reed City.
Population: 23,197 (2000); Race: 97.3% White, 0.3% Black, 0.2% Asian, 0.4% American Indian and Alaska Native, 1.0% Hispanic of any race, 1.5% two or more races (2000); Density: 41.0 persons per square mile (2000); Age: 27.1% under 18, 14.1% over 64 (2000).
Religion: Five largest groups: 7.3% Catholic Church, 5.3% The United Methodist Church, 3.7% Evangelical Lutheran Church in America, 2.8% Christian Reformed Church in North America, 1.5% The Wesleyan Church (2000).
Economy: Unemployment rate: 6.3% (11/2002); Total civilian labor force: 11,004 (11/2002); Leading industries: 55.2% manufacturing; 10.5% health care and social assistance; 10.3% retail trade (2000); Companies that employ more than 1,000 persons: 2 (2000); Companies that employ more than 100 persons: 11 (2000); Farms: 496 totaling 108,250 acres (1997); Minority business ownership rate: 0.0% (1997); Women business ownership rate: 19.7% (1997); Retail sales per capita: $4,788 (1997). Single-family building permits issued: 192 (2001) / 204 (2000); Multi-family building permits issued: 0 (2001) / 0 (2000).
Income: Per capita income: $15,632 (2000); Median household income: $34,102 (2000); Poverty rate: 12.7% (2000); Bankruptcy rate: 4.60% (2001).
Taxes: Total county taxes per capita: $141 (1997); County property taxes per capita: $134 (1997).
Education: High school graduation rate: 80.5% (2000); College graduation rate: 11.3% (2000).
Housing: Homeownership rate: 81.3% (2000); Median home value: $70,000 (2000); Median rent: $326 per month (2000); Median age of housing: 28 years (2000).
Health: Birth rate: 118.6 per 10,000 population (1998); Age adjusted death rate: 107.4 per 10,000 population (1999); Age adjusted cancer mortality rate: 237.3 deaths per 100,000 population (1999). Number of physicians: 2.6 per 10,000 population (1999); Number of hospital beds: 31.0 per 10,000 population (1999).
Elections: 2000 Presidential election results: 40.3% Gore, 57.2% Bush, 1.9% Nader, 0.1% Buchanan
National and State Parks: Chippewa River State Forest
Additional Information Contacts
Osceola County Government Offices. 231-832-3261
Reed City Chamber of Commerce 231-832-5431

Osceola County Communities

BURDELL (township). Covers a land area of 37.371 square miles and a water area of 0.208 square miles. Located at 44.11° N. Lat.; 85.49° W. Long.
Population: 1,241 (2000); Race: 98.9% White, 0.0% Black, 0.2% Asian, 0.2% American Indian and Alaska Native, 1.0% Hispanic of any race, 0.8% two or more races (2000); Density: 33.2 persons per square mile (2000); Age: 28.1% under 18, 12.9% over 64 (2000); Marriage status: 21.0% never married, 61.2% now married, 7.5% widowed, 10.3% divorced (2000); Foreign born: 0.9% (2000); Ancestry (includes multiple ancestries): 22.3% German, 13.0% English, 11.9% Swedish, 9.3% Irish, 8.2% United States or American (2000).
Economy: Employment by occupation: 8.7% management, 15.2% professional, 18.6% services, 20.0% sales, 1.1% farming, 11.0% construction, 25.4% production (2000).

Income: Per capita income: $15,375 (2000); Median household income: $35,481 (2000); Poverty rate: 13.4% (2000).
Taxes: Total city taxes per capita: $43 (1997); City property taxes per capita: $43 (1997).
Education: High school graduation rate: 82.0% (2000); College graduation rate: 12.8% (2000).
Housing: Homeownership rate: 87.7% (2000); Median home value: $70,200 (2000); Median rent: $337 per month (2000); Median age of housing: 29 years (2000).
Transportation: Commute to work: 93.5% car, 0.4% public transportation, 2.2% walk, 3.9% work from home (2000); Travel time to work: 22.1% less than 15 minutes, 51.0% 15 to 30 minutes, 17.6% 30 to 45 minutes, 3.4% 45 to 60 minutes, 6.0% 60 minutes or more (2000)

CEDAR (township). Covers a land area of 34.496 square miles and a water area of 0.550 square miles. Located at 43.93° N. Lat.; 85.38° W. Long.
History: Cedar Township was organized in 1871.
Population: 406 (2000); Race: 98.3% White, 0.0% Black, 0.0% Asian, 1.7% American Indian and Alaska Native, 2.4% Hispanic of any race, 0.0% two or more races (2000); Density: 11.8 persons per square mile (2000); Age: 27.1% under 18, 17.1% over 64 (2000); Marriage status: 14.0% never married, 71.3% now married, 3.4% widowed, 11.2% divorced (2000); Foreign born: 0.7% (2000); Ancestry (includes multiple ancestries): 33.1% German, 21.5% English, 12.8% Irish, 8.2% Other groups, 4.6% Polish (2000).
Economy: Employment by occupation: 7.3% management, 22.0% professional, 9.6% services, 11.9% sales, 0.0% farming, 9.6% construction, 39.5% production (2000).
Income: Per capita income: $16,618 (2000); Median household income: $38,500 (2000); Poverty rate: 2.2% (2000).
Taxes: Total city taxes per capita: $68 (1997); City property taxes per capita: $68 (1997).
Education: High school graduation rate: 71.9% (2000); College graduation rate: 14.2% (2000).
Housing: Homeownership rate: 91.2% (2000); Median home value: $68,000 (2000); Median rent: $300 per month (2000); Median age of housing: 16 years (2000).
Transportation: Commute to work: 96.5% car, 1.8% public transportation, 0.0% walk, 1.8% work from home (2000); Travel time to work: 15.6% less than 15 minutes, 38.3% 15 to 30 minutes, 26.9% 30 to 45 minutes, 11.4% 45 to 60 minutes, 7.8% 60 minutes or more (2000)

EVART (city). Covers a land area of 2.005 square miles and a water area of 0.037 square miles. Located at 43.90° N. Lat.; 85.26° W. Long. Elevation is 1,006 feet.
Population: 1,738 (2000); Race: 94.6% White, 1.0% Black, 0.0% Asian, 1.1% American Indian and Alaska Native, 1.5% Hispanic of any race, 3.0% two or more races (2000); Density: 866.8 persons per square mile (2000); Age: 29.6% under 18, 15.4% over 64 (2000); Marriage status: 24.3% never married, 52.1% now married, 10.0% widowed, 13.6% divorced (2000); Foreign born: 0.9% (2000); Ancestry (includes multiple ancestries): 24.5% German, 14.4% Irish, 12.3% English, 8.2% Other groups, 7.6% United States or American (2000).
Economy: Employment by occupation: 4.0% management, 10.8% professional, 22.2% services, 20.6% sales, 0.3% farming, 7.3% construction, 35.0% production (2000).
Income: Per capita income: $12,691 (2000); Median household income: $23,348 (2000); Poverty rate: 24.8% (2000).
Taxes: Total city taxes per capita: $308 (1997); City property taxes per capita: $303 (1997).
Education: High school graduation rate: 79.1% (2000); College graduation rate: 9.0% (2000).

School District(s)

Evart Public Schools (KG-12)
2000 Enrollment: 1,268 231-734-5594
Housing: Homeownership rate: 56.4% (2000); Median home value: $59,300 (2000); Median rent: $327 per month (2000); Median age of housing: 49 years (2000).
Safety: Violent crime rate: 34.3 per 10,000 population; Property crime rate: 360.6 per 10,000 population (2001).
Newspapers: Evart Review (1 x week)
Transportation: Commute to work: 90.3% car, 0.8% public transportation, 5.8% walk, 2.7% work from home (2000); Travel time to work: 57.9% less than 15 minutes, 15.1% 15 to 30 minutes, 12.4% 30 to 45 minutes, 8.4% 45 to 60 minutes, 6.1% 60 minutes or more (2000)

EVART (township). Covers a land area of 32.806 square miles and a water area of 1.403 square miles. Located at 43.84° N. Lat.; 85.27° W. Long. Elevation is 1,006 feet.
History: Indian mounds nearby. Incorporated as village 1872, as city 1938.
Population: 1,513 (2000); Race: 98.3% White, 0.3% Black, 0.1% Asian, 0.4% American Indian and Alaska Native, 0.9% Hispanic of any race, 0.8% two or more races (2000); Density: 46.1 persons per square mile (2000); Age: 25.5% under 18, 15.0% over 64 (2000); Marriage status: 16.5% never married, 67.0% now married, 6.1% widowed, 10.3% divorced (2000); Foreign born: 1.3% (2000); Ancestry (includes multiple ancestries): 24.8% German, 12.8% English, 11.1% Irish, 7.5% Other groups, 6.0% Polish (2000).
Economy: In agricultural area: dairy products; livestock; corn. Manufacturing: automotive parts. Employment by occupation: 10.7% management, 11.0% professional, 11.8% services, 17.1% sales, 1.9% farming, 12.1% construction, 35.4% production (2000).
Income: Per capita income: $15,680 (2000); Median household income: $35,550 (2000); Poverty rate: 8.2% (2000).
Taxes: Total city taxes per capita: $17 (1997); City property taxes per capita: $17 (1997).
Education: High school graduation rate: 79.2% (2000); College graduation rate: 7.3% (2000).
Housing: Homeownership rate: 86.4% (2000); Median home value: $82,000 (2000); Median rent: $333 per month (2000); Median age of housing: 25 years (2000).
Transportation: Commute to work: 89.3% car, 0.0% public transportation, 3.6% walk, 5.0% work from home (2000); Travel time to work: 45.9% less than 15 minutes, 32.0% 15 to 30 minutes, 11.8% 30 to 45 minutes, 5.7% 45 to 60 minutes, 4.6% 60 minutes or more (2000)

HARTWICK (township). Covers a land area of 34.965 square miles and a water area of 0.493 square miles. Located at 44.04° N. Lat.; 85.28° W. Long.
History: Hartwick Township was organized in 1870.
Population: 629 (2000); Race: 99.0% White, 0.0% Black, 0.5% Asian, 0.0% American Indian and Alaska Native, 0.0% Hispanic of any race, 0.5% two or more races (2000); Density: 18.0 persons per square mile (2000); Age: 23.2% under 18, 21.2% over 64 (2000); Marriage status: 16.8% never married, 70.0% now married, 5.7% widowed, 7.6% divorced (2000); Foreign born: 0.5% (2000); Ancestry (includes multiple ancestries): 21.2% German, 11.3% English, 10.4% Irish, 7.5% Dutch, 5.6% United States or American (2000).
Economy: Employment by occupation: 16.6% management, 7.1% professional, 6.6% services, 18.7% sales, 4.6% farming, 11.6% construction, 34.9% production (2000).
Income: Per capita income: $15,262 (2000); Median household income: $34,286 (2000); Poverty rate: 17.4% (2000).
Taxes: Total city taxes per capita: $28 (1997); City property taxes per capita: $28 (1997).
Education: High school graduation rate: 72.9% (2000); College graduation rate: 7.7% (2000).
Housing: Homeownership rate: 89.6% (2000); Median home value: $74,200 (2000); Median rent: $319 per month (2000); Median age of housing: 30 years (2000).
Transportation: Commute to work: 88.2% car, 0.4% public transportation, 1.7% walk, 9.6% work from home (2000); Travel time to work: 18.8% less than 15 minutes, 44.9% 15 to 30 minutes, 20.3% 30 to 45 minutes, 7.2% 45 to 60 minutes, 8.7% 60 minutes or more (2000)

HERSEY (village). Covers a land area of 1.089 square miles and a water area of 0 square miles. Located at 43.85° N. Lat.; 85.44° W. Long. Elevation is 991 feet.
History: Hersey was settled in the early 1850's, and named for Nathan Hersey, a trapper who worked in this area in the 1840's.
Population: 374 (2000); Race: 97.9% White, 0.0% Black, 0.0% Asian, 0.5% American Indian and Alaska Native, 3.2% Hispanic of any race, 1.6% two or more races (2000); Density: 343.4 persons per square mile (2000); Age: 27.0% under 18, 8.3% over 64 (2000); Marriage status: 22.0% never married, 61.9% now married, 4.5% widowed, 11.5% divorced (2000); Foreign born: 0.0% (2000); Ancestry (includes multiple ancestries): 31.3% German, 12.3% English, 10.7% Irish, 9.1% United States or American, 7.0% Other groups (2000).
Economy: Employment by occupation: 5.8% management, 24.8% professional, 17.0% services, 14.6% sales, 1.9% farming, 7.8% construction, 28.2% production (2000).

Income: Per capita income: $15,584 (2000); Median household income: $38,929 (2000); Poverty rate: 12.8% (2000).
Taxes: Total city taxes per capita: $52 (1997); City property taxes per capita: $47 (1997).
Education: High school graduation rate: 91.4% (2000); College graduation rate: 12.3% (2000).
Housing: Homeownership rate: 85.2% (2000); Median home value: $65,000 (2000); Median rent: $388 per month (2000); Median age of housing: 37 years (2000).
Transportation: Commute to work: 91.0% car, 1.0% public transportation, 3.0% walk, 4.0% work from home (2000); Travel time to work: 41.5% less than 15 minutes, 40.9% 15 to 30 minutes, 10.4% 30 to 45 minutes, 5.2% 45 to 60 minutes, 2.1% 60 minutes or more (2000)

HERSEY (township). Covers a land area of 35.272 square miles and a water area of 0.604 square miles. Located at 43.85° N. Lat.; 85.39° W. Long. Elevation is 991 feet.
Population: 1,846 (2000); Race: 96.9% White, 0.3% Black, 0.4% Asian, 0.1% American Indian and Alaska Native, 1.5% Hispanic of any race, 1.9% two or more races (2000); Density: 52.3 persons per square mile (2000); Age: 29.4% under 18, 10.0% over 64 (2000); Marriage status: 18.7% never married, 65.1% now married, 6.3% widowed, 9.9% divorced (2000); Foreign born: 1.0% (2000); Ancestry (includes multiple ancestries): 29.8% German, 11.6% Irish, 10.8% English, 9.8% Other groups, 7.6% United States or American (2000).
Economy: In lake and agricultural area. Single-family building permits issued: 0 (2001) / 102 (2000); Multi-family building permits issued: 0 (2001) / 0 (2000); Employment by occupation: 8.9% management, 13.2% professional, 15.4% services, 18.4% sales, 1.7% farming, 10.3% construction, 32.0% production (2000).
Income: Per capita income: $16,612 (2000); Median household income: $39,706 (2000); Poverty rate: 8.9% (2000).
Taxes: Total city taxes per capita: $67 (1997); City property taxes per capita: $67 (1997).
Education: High school graduation rate: 83.9% (2000); College graduation rate: 14.0% (2000).
Housing: Homeownership rate: 86.3% (2000); Median home value: $77,700 (2000); Median rent: $372 per month (2000); Median age of housing: 25 years (2000).
Transportation: Commute to work: 90.2% car, 0.6% public transportation, 1.4% walk, 7.0% work from home (2000); Travel time to work: 37.2% less than 15 minutes, 44.9% 15 to 30 minutes, 9.6% 30 to 45 minutes, 1.8% 45 to 60 minutes, 6.5% 60 minutes or more (2000)

HIGHLAND (township). Covers a land area of 37.349 square miles and a water area of 0.040 square miles. Located at 44.11° N. Lat.; 85.25° W. Long. Elevation is 1,336 feet.
Population: 1,207 (2000); Race: 97.7% White, 0.0% Black, 0.0% Asian, 0.4% American Indian and Alaska Native, 0.4% Hispanic of any race, 1.7% two or more races (2000); Density: 32.3 persons per square mile (2000); Age: 30.9% under 18, 12.1% over 64 (2000); Marriage status: 18.9% never married, 69.5% now married, 5.0% widowed, 6.6% divorced (2000); Foreign born: 1.0% (2000); Ancestry (includes multiple ancestries): 26.9% Dutch, 18.6% German, 10.6% Irish, 6.9% English, 6.7% United States or American (2000).
Economy: Employment by occupation: 11.2% management, 15.9% professional, 11.2% services, 19.2% sales, 4.9% farming, 13.2% construction, 24.4% production (2000).
Income: Per capita income: $13,741 (2000); Median household income: $32,772 (2000); Poverty rate: 12.0% (2000).
Taxes: Total city taxes per capita: $15 (1997); City property taxes per capita: $15 (1997).
Education: High school graduation rate: 76.6% (2000); College graduation rate: 8.5% (2000).
Housing: Homeownership rate: 82.3% (2000); Median home value: $72,200 (2000); Median rent: $322 per month (2000); Median age of housing: 30 years (2000).
Transportation: Commute to work: 85.1% car, 0.0% public transportation, 3.5% walk, 9.9% work from home (2000); Travel time to work: 33.8% less than 15 minutes, 42.1% 15 to 30 minutes, 15.5% 30 to 45 minutes, 1.9% 45 to 60 minutes, 6.8% 60 minutes or more (2000)

LE ROY (village). Aka Leroy. Covers a land area of 0.970 square miles and a water area of 0 square miles. Located at 44.03° N. Lat.; 85.45° W. Long. Elevation is 1,218 feet.
History: Le Roy was originally settled by a group of Scandinavians, whose immigration was encouraged in the early 1870's by the Grand Rapids & Indiana Railway, which sent an emissary to Norway and Sweden to offer work and free land.
Population: 267 (2000); Race: 94.8% White, 0.3% Black, 0.0% Asian, 0.0% American Indian and Alaska Native, 0.0% Hispanic of any race, 4.1% two or more races (2000); Density: 275.1 persons per square mile (2000); Age: 35.5% under 18, 8.3% over 64 (2000); Marriage status: 18.9% never married, 64.7% now married, 8.0% widowed, 8.5% divorced (2000); Foreign born: 1.0% (2000); Ancestry (includes multiple ancestries): 32.1% German, 14.1% Swedish, 12.4% Other groups, 8.6% English, 8.3% Irish (2000).
Economy: Employment by occupation: 10.6% management, 10.6% professional, 12.1% services, 27.3% sales, 0.0% farming, 12.1% construction, 27.3% production (2000).
Income: Per capita income: $13,434 (2000); Median household income: $32,188 (2000); Poverty rate: 7.9% (2000).
Taxes: Total city taxes per capita: $68 (1997); City property taxes per capita: $68 (1997).
Education: High school graduation rate: 90.0% (2000); College graduation rate: 13.5% (2000).
Housing: Homeownership rate: 90.1% (2000); Median home value: $63,700 (2000); Median rent: $325 per month (2000); Median age of housing: 60+ years (2000).
Transportation: Commute to work: 92.2% car, 0.0% public transportation, 4.7% walk, 3.1% work from home (2000); Travel time to work: 36.3% less than 15 minutes, 33.9% 15 to 30 minutes, 24.2% 30 to 45 minutes, 2.4% 45 to 60 minutes, 3.2% 60 minutes or more (2000)

LE ROY (township). Aka Leroy. Covers a land area of 34.914 square miles and a water area of 0.161 square miles. Located at 44.03° N. Lat.; 85.48° W. Long. Elevation is 1,218 feet.
History: Le Roy Township was named for LeRoy Carr, a federal land agent.
Population: 1,159 (2000); Race: 97.3% White, 0.6% Black, 0.0% Asian, 0.7% American Indian and Alaska Native, 0.7% Hispanic of any race, 1.2% two or more races (2000); Density: 33.2 persons per square mile (2000); Age: 30.3% under 18, 10.3% over 64 (2000); Marriage status: 19.1% never married, 67.2% now married, 6.6% widowed, 7.2% divorced (2000); Foreign born: 1.4% (2000); Ancestry (includes multiple ancestries): 24.0% German, 12.0% Irish, 10.7% English, 10.5% Swedish, 8.0% Other groups (2000).
Economy: Employment by occupation: 9.9% management, 11.6% professional, 14.6% services, 22.5% sales, 0.4% farming, 10.5% construction, 30.6% production (2000).
Income: Per capita income: $15,333 (2000); Median household income: $35,625 (2000); Poverty rate: 10.6% (2000).
Taxes: Total city taxes per capita: $36 (1997); City property taxes per capita: $36 (1997).
Education: High school graduation rate: 84.5% (2000); College graduation rate: 10.4% (2000).
Housing: Homeownership rate: 91.3% (2000); Median home value: $70,600 (2000); Median rent: $300 per month (2000); Median age of housing: 33 years (2000).
Transportation: Commute to work: 96.2% car, 0.0% public transportation, 1.6% walk, 1.8% work from home (2000); Travel time to work: 17.3% less than 15 minutes, 44.4% 15 to 30 minutes, 26.1% 30 to 45 minutes, 5.1% 45 to 60 minutes, 7.0% 60 minutes or more (2000)

LINCOLN (township). Covers a land area of 35.079 square miles and a water area of 0.373 square miles. Located at 43.95° N. Lat.; 85.51° W. Long.
Population: 1,629 (2000); Race: 97.5% White, 0.1% Black, 0.1% Asian, 0.0% American Indian and Alaska Native, 0.4% Hispanic of any race, 2.1% two or more races (2000); Density: 46.4 persons per square mile (2000); Age: 28.5% under 18, 9.7% over 64 (2000); Marriage status: 22.0% never married, 63.1% now married, 4.6% widowed, 10.2% divorced (2000); Foreign born: 1.0% (2000); Ancestry (includes multiple ancestries): 26.7% German, 16.7% English, 10.2% United States or American, 9.5% Irish, 7.5% Other groups (2000).
Economy: Employment by occupation: 6.8% management, 14.6% professional, 14.3% services, 17.2% sales, 0.8% farming, 12.2% construction, 34.1% production (2000).
Income: Per capita income: $15,592 (2000); Median household income: $37,578 (2000); Poverty rate: 9.6% (2000).
Taxes: Total city taxes per capita: $63 (1997); City property taxes per capita: $63 (1997).
Education: High school graduation rate: 82.7% (2000); College graduation rate: 10.2% (2000).

Housing: Homeownership rate: 88.0% (2000); Median home value: $68,200 (2000); Median rent: $377 per month (2000); Median age of housing: 23 years (2000).
Transportation: Commute to work: 91.1% car, 0.0% public transportation, 0.6% walk, 7.7% work from home (2000); Travel time to work: 37.5% less than 15 minutes, 32.9% 15 to 30 minutes, 24.3% 30 to 45 minutes, 2.0% 45 to 60 minutes, 3.4% 60 minutes or more (2000)

MARION (village). Covers a land area of 1.354 square miles and a water area of 0.039 square miles. Located at 44.10° N. Lat.; 85.14° W. Long. Elevation is 1,098 feet.
Population: 836 (2000); Race: 99.3% White, 0.0% Black, 0.0% Asian, 0.2% American Indian and Alaska Native, 1.2% Hispanic of any race, 0.2% two or more races (2000); Density: 617.5 persons per square mile (2000); Age: 23.3% under 18, 17.0% over 64 (2000); Marriage status: 21.9% never married, 55.3% now married, 7.4% widowed, 15.4% divorced (2000); Foreign born: 0.9% (2000); Ancestry (includes multiple ancestries): 14.4% English, 12.4% German, 9.4% Irish, 9.4% United States or American, 9.2% Other groups (2000).
Economy: Employment by occupation: 7.9% management, 17.0% professional, 20.2% services, 19.9% sales, 1.2% farming, 9.4% construction, 24.3% production (2000).
Income: Per capita income: $15,010 (2000); Median household income: $26,467 (2000); Poverty rate: 19.3% (2000).
Taxes: Total city taxes per capita: $208 (1997); City property taxes per capita: $208 (1997).
Education: High school graduation rate: 79.9% (2000); College graduation rate: 9.8% (2000).

School District(s)

Marion Public Schools (KG-12)
2000 Enrollment: 836 231-743-2486
Housing: Homeownership rate: 65.9% (2000); Median home value: $55,200 (2000); Median rent: $300 per month (2000); Median age of housing: 43 years (2000).
Newspapers: The Marion Press (1 x week)
Transportation: Commute to work: 89.9% car, 0.0% public transportation, 6.0% walk, 2.7% work from home (2000); Travel time to work: 39.0% less than 15 minutes, 28.8% 15 to 30 minutes, 21.5% 30 to 45 minutes, 6.4% 45 to 60 minutes, 4.3% 60 minutes or more (2000)

MARION (township). Covers a land area of 37.030 square miles and a water area of 0.039 square miles. Located at 44.10° N. Lat.; 85.14° W. Long. Elevation is 1,098 feet.
Population: 1,580 (2000); Race: 98.8% White, 0.0% Black, 0.0% Asian, 0.7% American Indian and Alaska Native, 1.0% Hispanic of any race, 0.4% two or more races (2000); Density: 42.7 persons per square mile (2000); Age: 25.2% under 18, 14.5% over 64 (2000); Marriage status: 21.8% never married, 56.2% now married, 7.6% widowed, 14.5% divorced (2000); Foreign born: 1.2% (2000); Ancestry (includes multiple ancestries): 17.2% German, 13.4% English, 9.0% Other groups, 8.4% Irish, 8.3% United States or American (2000).
Economy: In farm area. Light manufacturing. Employment by occupation: 7.8% management, 12.3% professional, 16.3% services, 18.6% sales, 2.1% farming, 13.6% construction, 29.3% production (2000).
Income: Per capita income: $16,218 (2000); Median household income: $31,615 (2000); Poverty rate: 17.4% (2000).
Taxes: Total city taxes per capita: $15 (1997); City property taxes per capita: $15 (1997).
Education: High school graduation rate: 82.8% (2000); College graduation rate: 8.4% (2000).
Housing: Homeownership rate: 72.0% (2000); Median home value: $58,200 (2000); Median rent: $313 per month (2000); Median age of housing: 35 years (2000).
Transportation: Commute to work: 87.3% car, 0.0% public transportation, 6.0% walk, 5.7% work from home (2000); Travel time to work: 36.5% less than 15 minutes, 25.7% 15 to 30 minutes, 27.3% 30 to 45 minutes, 4.6% 45 to 60 minutes, 5.9% 60 minutes or more (2000)

MIDDLE BRANCH (township). Covers a land area of 35.506 square miles and a water area of 0.025 square miles. Located at 44.01° N. Lat.; 85.13° W. Long.
Population: 858 (2000); Race: 96.6% White, 0.0% Black, 0.0% Asian, 0.5% American Indian and Alaska Native, 2.0% Hispanic of any race, 2.9% two or more races (2000); Density: 24.2 persons per square mile (2000); Age: 26.6% under 18, 19.1% over 64 (2000); Marriage status: 16.1% never married, 65.9% now married, 6.8% widowed, 11.2% divorced (2000); Foreign born: 0.7% (2000); Ancestry (includes multiple ancestries): 24.8% German, 13.0% English, 9.6% Irish, 8.2% Dutch, 7.1% Other groups (2000).
Economy: Employment by occupation: 6.6% management, 14.4% professional, 15.9% services, 18.7% sales, 3.2% farming, 9.8% construction, 31.4% production (2000).
Income: Per capita income: $13,448 (2000); Median household income: $27,014 (2000); Poverty rate: 18.9% (2000).
Taxes: Total city taxes per capita: $15 (1997); City property taxes per capita: $15 (1997).
Education: High school graduation rate: 78.2% (2000); College graduation rate: 8.1% (2000).
Housing: Homeownership rate: 90.2% (2000); Median home value: $62,300 (2000); Median rent: $358 per month (2000); Median age of housing: 27 years (2000).
Transportation: Commute to work: 91.9% car, 1.2% public transportation, 2.3% walk, 4.6% work from home (2000); Travel time to work: 23.7% less than 15 minutes, 26.4% 15 to 30 minutes, 32.2% 30 to 45 minutes, 8.2% 45 to 60 minutes, 9.4% 60 minutes or more (2000)

ORIENT (township). Covers a land area of 34.820 square miles and a water area of 0.619 square miles. Located at 43.86° N. Lat.; 85.15° W. Long.
Population: 803 (2000); Race: 98.3% White, 0.0% Black, 0.0% Asian, 0.2% American Indian and Alaska Native, 1.6% Hispanic of any race, 1.5% two or more races (2000); Density: 23.1 persons per square mile (2000); Age: 24.8% under 18, 15.1% over 64 (2000); Marriage status: 21.8% never married, 61.0% now married, 7.3% widowed, 9.9% divorced (2000); Foreign born: 1.1% (2000); Ancestry (includes multiple ancestries): 27.3% German, 14.9% English, 10.0% United States or American, 9.3% Irish, 8.8% Dutch (2000).
Economy: Employment by occupation: 11.6% management, 7.1% professional, 9.5% services, 16.9% sales, 3.3% farming, 12.5% construction, 39.2% production (2000).
Income: Per capita income: $14,931 (2000); Median household income: $32,024 (2000); Poverty rate: 14.6% (2000).
Taxes: Total city taxes per capita: $23 (1997); City property taxes per capita: $23 (1997).
Education: High school graduation rate: 73.7% (2000); College graduation rate: 8.5% (2000).
Housing: Homeownership rate: 86.5% (2000); Median home value: $74,300 (2000); Median rent: $304 per month (2000); Median age of housing: 27 years (2000).
Transportation: Commute to work: 91.5% car, 1.8% public transportation, 0.9% walk, 5.8% work from home (2000); Travel time to work: 29.9% less than 15 minutes, 24.8% 15 to 30 minutes, 23.8% 30 to 45 minutes, 10.0% 45 to 60 minutes, 11.6% 60 minutes or more (2000)

OSCEOLA (township). Covers a land area of 34.209 square miles and a water area of 0.257 square miles. Located at 43.92° N. Lat.; 85.25° W. Long.
Population: 1,118 (2000); Race: 96.2% White, 0.9% Black, 1.0% Asian, 0.9% American Indian and Alaska Native, 0.7% Hispanic of any race, 0.9% two or more races (2000); Density: 32.7 persons per square mile (2000); Age: 26.2% under 18, 14.8% over 64 (2000); Marriage status: 23.2% never married, 63.7% now married, 4.4% widowed, 8.7% divorced (2000); Foreign born: 1.4% (2000); Ancestry (includes multiple ancestries): 22.4% German, 13.7% Irish, 9.5% United States or American, 7.7% English, 7.5% French (except Basque) (2000).
Economy: Employment by occupation: 13.5% management, 7.3% professional, 13.5% services, 19.0% sales, 1.6% farming, 6.7% construction, 38.3% production (2000).
Income: Per capita income: $16,236 (2000); Median household income: $36,346 (2000); Poverty rate: 5.0% (2000).
Taxes: Total city taxes per capita: $12 (1997); City property taxes per capita: $12 (1997).
Education: High school graduation rate: 79.0% (2000); College graduation rate: 10.0% (2000).
Housing: Homeownership rate: 87.3% (2000); Median home value: $78,100 (2000); Median rent: $388 per month (2000); Median age of housing: 27 years (2000).
Transportation: Commute to work: 92.1% car, 1.6% public transportation, 3.0% walk, 2.4% work from home (2000); Travel time to work: 61.8% less than 15 minutes, 14.7% 15 to 30 minutes, 13.1% 30 to 45 minutes, 6.4% 45 to 60 minutes, 3.9% 60 minutes or more (2000)

REED CITY (city). Covers a land area of 1.921 square miles and a water area of 0.038 square miles. Located at 43.87° N. Lat.; 85.50° W. Long. Elevation is 1,039 feet.

History: Many of the early residents of Reed City were immigrants from Germany. Considered a good fishing region, in the early 1900's Reed City had a roller mill, flour mill, and a woolen mill furnishing employment to residents.
Population: 2,430 (2000); Race: 96.2% White, 0.7% Black, 0.2% Asian, 0.0% American Indian and Alaska Native, 1.0% Hispanic of any race, 2.8% two or more races (2000); Density: 1,265.3 persons per square mile (2000); Age: 25.6% under 18, 17.8% over 64 (2000); Marriage status: 28.5% never married, 50.6% now married, 9.3% widowed, 11.7% divorced (2000); Foreign born: 0.7% (2000); Ancestry (includes multiple ancestries): 29.2% German, 13.4% English, 11.1% Irish, 5.6% Other groups, 5.0% French (except Basque) (2000).
Economy: Employment by occupation: 9.7% management, 20.4% professional, 14.5% services, 21.4% sales, 0.0% farming, 8.4% construction, 25.6% production (2000).
Income: Per capita income: $15,889 (2000); Median household income: $30,756 (2000); Poverty rate: 17.9% (2000).
Taxes: Total city taxes per capita: $180 (1997); City property taxes per capita: $175 (1997).
Education: High school graduation rate: 83.0% (2000); College graduation rate: 17.1% (2000).

School District(s)

Reed City Area Public Schools (KG-12)
2000 Enrollment: 2,058 231-832-2201
Housing: Homeownership rate: 59.1% (2000); Median home value: $66,500 (2000); Median rent: $315 per month (2000); Median age of housing: 46 years (2000).
Hospitals: Spectrum Health - Reed City Campus (106 beds)
Safety: Violent crime rate: 28.7 per 10,000 population; Property crime rate: 90.1 per 10,000 population (2001).
Newspapers: Herald News (1 x week)
Transportation: Commute to work: 92.7% car, 0.0% public transportation, 4.2% walk, 1.7% work from home (2000); Travel time to work: 40.7% less than 15 minutes, 40.5% 15 to 30 minutes, 10.9% 30 to 45 minutes, 2.6% 45 to 60 minutes, 5.3% 60 minutes or more (2000); Amtrak: Service available.
Additional Information Contacts
Reed City Chamber of Commerce 231-832-5431

RICHMOND (township). Covers a land area of 33.080 square miles and a water area of 0.059 square miles. Located at 43.86° N. Lat.; 85.50° W. Long.
Population: 1,695 (2000); Race: 97.9% White, 0.2% Black, 0.5% Asian, 0.2% American Indian and Alaska Native, 0.4% Hispanic of any race, 0.7% two or more races (2000); Density: 51.2 persons per square mile (2000); Age: 25.2% under 18, 13.1% over 64 (2000); Marriage status: 23.0% never married, 62.0% now married, 5.6% widowed, 9.4% divorced (2000); Foreign born: 1.8% (2000); Ancestry (includes multiple ancestries): 36.7% German, 12.4% English, 11.9% Irish, 7.8% United States or American, 7.4% Dutch (2000).
Economy: Employment by occupation: 8.8% management, 17.3% professional, 13.5% services, 23.1% sales, 0.6% farming, 10.5% construction, 26.3% production (2000).
Income: Per capita income: $18,010 (2000); Median household income: $42,865 (2000); Poverty rate: 7.2% (2000).
Taxes: Total city taxes per capita: $28 (1997); City property taxes per capita: $27 (1997).
Education: High school graduation rate: 87.7% (2000); College graduation rate: 16.1% (2000).
Housing: Homeownership rate: 92.7% (2000); Median home value: $87,100 (2000); Median rent: $270 per month (2000); Median age of housing: 27 years (2000).
Transportation: Commute to work: 94.5% car, 0.0% public transportation, 1.0% walk, 4.4% work from home (2000); Travel time to work: 54.7% less than 15 minutes, 30.9% 15 to 30 minutes, 6.8% 30 to 45 minutes, 2.3% 45 to 60 minutes, 5.2% 60 minutes or more (2000)

ROSE LAKE (township). Covers a land area of 33.610 square miles and a water area of 1.256 square miles. Located at 44.03° N. Lat.; 85.40° W. Long.
Population: 1,231 (2000); Race: 98.8% White, 0.0% Black, 0.3% Asian, 0.3% American Indian and Alaska Native, 1.0% Hispanic of any race, 0.6% two or more races (2000); Density: 36.6 persons per square mile (2000); Age: 24.3% under 18, 16.0% over 64 (2000); Marriage status: 19.3% never married, 65.4% now married, 6.4% widowed, 8.9% divorced (2000); Foreign born: 1.7% (2000); Ancestry (includes multiple ancestries): 24.9% German, 15.1% English, 10.1% Polish, 9.5% Irish, 7.1% Dutch (2000).
Economy: Employment by occupation: 6.4% management, 17.6% professional, 12.2% services, 23.6% sales, 2.6% farming, 12.0% construction, 25.6% production (2000).
Income: Per capita income: $16,731 (2000); Median household income: $34,667 (2000); Poverty rate: 7.6% (2000).
Taxes: Total city taxes per capita: $29 (1997); City property taxes per capita: $26 (1997).
Education: High school graduation rate: 83.0% (2000); College graduation rate: 13.7% (2000).
Housing: Homeownership rate: 92.8% (2000); Median home value: $80,900 (2000); Median rent: $400 per month (2000); Median age of housing: 23 years (2000).
Transportation: Commute to work: 92.6% car, 0.2% public transportation, 1.0% walk, 4.2% work from home (2000); Travel time to work: 24.5% less than 15 minutes, 31.4% 15 to 30 minutes, 29.3% 30 to 45 minutes, 4.4% 45 to 60 minutes, 10.5% 60 minutes or more (2000)

SEARS (unincorporated postal area, zip code 49679). Covers a land area of 45.570 square miles and a water area of 0.712 square miles. Located at 43.87° N. Lat.; 85.15° W. Long.
History: Sears was settled in the late 1860's. It was first called Orient, after its township, but was renamed for a railroad surveyor after the Flint & Pere Marquette Railroad was built here.
Population: 1,110 (2000); Race: 98.0% White, 0.0% Black, 0.0% Asian, 0.6% American Indian and Alaska Native, 0.6% Hispanic of any race, 1.4% two or more races (2000); Density: 24.4 persons per square mile (2000); Age: 23.1% under 18, 16.8% over 64 (2000); Marriage status: 20.4% never married, 62.4% now married, 6.3% widowed, 10.9% divorced (2000); Foreign born: 0.7% (2000); Ancestry (includes multiple ancestries): 23.6% German, 15.5% English, 11.8% United States or American, 9.4% Irish, 7.3% Dutch (2000).
Economy: Employment by occupation: 11.1% management, 8.6% professional, 10.6% services, 18.4% sales, 3.5% farming, 11.8% construction, 35.9% production (2000).
Income: Per capita income: $15,063 (2000); Median household income: $31,198 (2000); Poverty rate: 12.5% (2000).
Education: High school graduation rate: 73.7% (2000); College graduation rate: 8.7% (2000).
Housing: Homeownership rate: 89.2% (2000); Median home value: $72,600 (2000); Median rent: $333 per month (2000); Median age of housing: 26 years (2000).
Transportation: Commute to work: 89.6% car, 1.8% public transportation, 2.5% walk, 5.2% work from home (2000); Travel time to work: 37.9% less than 15 minutes, 24.1% 15 to 30 minutes, 19.1% 30 to 45 minutes, 8.4% 45 to 60 minutes, 10.5% 60 minutes or more (2000)

SHERMAN (township). Covers a land area of 37.053 square miles and a water area of 0.225 square miles. Located at 44.12° N. Lat.; 85.39° W. Long.
Population: 1,081 (2000); Race: 97.3% White, 0.3% Black, 0.0% Asian, 0.2% American Indian and Alaska Native, 0.5% Hispanic of any race, 1.4% two or more races (2000); Density: 29.2 persons per square mile (2000); Age: 28.9% under 18, 11.2% over 64 (2000); Marriage status: 18.7% never married, 62.8% now married, 4.4% widowed, 14.1% divorced (2000); Foreign born: 3.1% (2000); Ancestry (includes multiple ancestries): 24.6% German, 12.4% Irish, 11.3% United States or American, 11.3% English, 7.3% Swedish (2000).
Economy: Employment by occupation: 12.9% management, 14.2% professional, 11.7% services, 16.0% sales, 0.2% farming, 12.5% construction, 32.4% production (2000).
Income: Per capita income: $16,785 (2000); Median household income: $42,569 (2000); Poverty rate: 13.4% (2000).
Taxes: Total city taxes per capita: $39 (1997); City property taxes per capita: $36 (1997).
Education: High school graduation rate: 77.4% (2000); College graduation rate: 12.9% (2000).
Housing: Homeownership rate: 86.4% (2000); Median home value: $70,600 (2000); Median rent: $304 per month (2000); Median age of housing: 24 years (2000).
Transportation: Commute to work: 91.4% car, 0.8% public transportation, 1.3% walk, 6.1% work from home (2000); Travel time to work: 14.1% less than 15 minutes, 57.4% 15 to 30 minutes, 16.5% 30 to 45 minutes, 4.7% 45 to 60 minutes, 7.4% 60 minutes or more (2000)

SYLVAN (township). Covers a land area of 34.496 square miles and a water area of 0.736 square miles. Located at 43.94° N. Lat.; 85.15° W. Long.

Population: 1,033 (2000); Race: 96.6% White, 0.8% Black, 0.0% Asian, 1.0% American Indian and Alaska Native, 0.9% Hispanic of any race, 1.4% two or more races (2000); Density: 29.9 persons per square mile (2000); Age: 26.9% under 18, 16.2% over 64 (2000); Marriage status: 20.7% never married, 60.0% now married, 4.9% widowed, 14.4% divorced (2000); Foreign born: 1.1% (2000); Ancestry (includes multiple ancestries): 20.4% German, 12.0% Irish, 11.3% United States or American, 10.5% English, 7.0% Other groups (2000).
Economy: Employment by occupation: 8.7% management, 8.7% professional, 16.1% services, 19.6% sales, 3.5% farming, 10.6% construction, 32.7% production (2000).
Income: Per capita income: $15,285 (2000); Median household income: $30,833 (2000); Poverty rate: 12.4% (2000).
Taxes: Total city taxes per capita: $16 (1997); City property taxes per capita: $16 (1997).
Education: High school graduation rate: 69.8% (2000); College graduation rate: 5.6% (2000).
Housing: Homeownership rate: 87.9% (2000); Median home value: $66,000 (2000); Median rent: $325 per month (2000); Median age of housing: 27 years (2000).
Transportation: Commute to work: 88.4% car, 0.6% public transportation, 4.7% walk, 3.9% work from home (2000); Travel time to work: 38.2% less than 15 minutes, 36.8% 15 to 30 minutes, 13.2% 30 to 45 minutes, 4.0% 45 to 60 minutes, 7.8% 60 minutes or more (2000)

TUSTIN (village). Covers a land area of 0.386 square miles and a water area of 0 square miles. Located at 44.10° N. Lat.; 85.45° W. Long. Elevation is 1,216 feet.
Population: 237 (2000); Race: 97.6% White, 0.0% Black, 0.0% Asian, 0.0% American Indian and Alaska Native, 1.2% Hispanic of any race, 2.4% two or more races (2000); Density: 613.4 persons per square mile (2000); Age: 33.5% under 18, 13.1% over 64 (2000); Marriage status: 25.1% never married, 41.1% now married, 17.7% widowed, 16.0% divorced (2000); Foreign born: 0.0% (2000); Ancestry (includes multiple ancestries): 20.0% German, 17.6% English, 11.8% Swedish, 9.4% Irish, 6.9% French (except Basque) (2000).
Economy: Manistee National Forest to Northwest. Employment by occupation: 6.9% management, 11.8% professional, 24.5% services, 20.6% sales, 0.0% farming, 2.0% construction, 34.3% production (2000).
Income: Per capita income: $11,390 (2000); Median household income: $29,063 (2000); Poverty rate: 18.6% (2000).
Taxes: Total city taxes per capita: $60 (1997); City property taxes per capita: $60 (1997).
Education: High school graduation rate: 80.3% (2000); College graduation rate: 10.9% (2000).
Housing: Homeownership rate: 72.4% (2000); Median home value: $61,200 (2000); Median rent: $330 per month (2000); Median age of housing: 60+ years (2000).
Transportation: Commute to work: 84.3% car, 2.0% public transportation, 7.8% walk, 5.9% work from home (2000); Travel time to work: 24.0% less than 15 minutes, 54.2% 15 to 30 minutes, 13.5% 30 to 45 minutes, 6.3% 45 to 60 minutes, 2.1% 60 minutes or more (2000)

Oscoda County

Located in northeast central Michigan; crossed by the Au Sable River; drained by the Upper South Branch of the Thunder Bay River; includes several lakes, and part of Huron National Forest. Covers a land area of 565.00 square miles, a water area of 6.60 square miles, and is located in the Eastern Time Zone. The county government was organized in 1840. County seat is Mio.

Weather Station: Mio Hydro Plant — Elevation: 958 feet

	Jan	Feb	Mar	Apr	May	Jun	Jul	Aug	Sep	Oct	Nov	Dec
High	27	31	41	54	68	77	82	79	70	58	44	32
Low	8	9	18	30	41	50	55	53	46	36	27	16
Precip	1.6	1.2	1.8	2.1	2.3	2.6	3.0	3.4	3.0	2.3	1.9	1.7
Snow	15.1	8.1	9.2	2.5	0.3	0.0	0.0	0.0	tr	0.2	4.0	11.0

High and Low temperatures in degrees Fahrenheit; Precipitation and Snow in inches

Population: 9,418 (2000); Race: 97.7% White, 0.1% Black, 0.2% Asian, 0.5% American Indian and Alaska Native, 1.0% Hispanic of any race, 1.2% two or more races (2000); Density: 16.7 persons per square mile (2000); Age: 23.3% under 18, 20.3% over 64 (2000).
Religion: Five largest groups: 5.8% Mennonite Church USA, 5.5% Catholic Church, 2.8% New Testament Association of Independent Baptist Churches and other Fundamental Baptist Associations, 2.3% The United Methodist Church, 2.1% Church of God (Anderso
Economy: Unemployment rate: 12.1% (11/2002); Total civilian labor force: 3,139 (11/2002); Leading industries: 25.2% manufacturing; 19.2% retail trade; 12.8% accommodation & food services (2000); Companies that employ more than 1,000 persons: 0 (2000); Companies that employ more than 100 persons: 2 (2000); Farms: 80 totaling 13,904 acres (1997); Minority business ownership rate: 0.0% (1997); Women business ownership rate: 23.2% (1997); Retail sales per capita: $5,059 (1997). Single-family building permits issued: 73 (2001) / 92 (2000); Multi-family building permits issued: 0 (2001) / 0 (2000).
Income: Per capita income: $15,697 (2000); Median household income: $28,228 (2000); Poverty rate: 14.6% (2000); Bankruptcy rate: 4.32% (2001).
Taxes: Total county taxes per capita: $177 (1997); County property taxes per capita: $166 (1997).
Education: High school graduation rate: 73.7% (2000); College graduation rate: 8.0% (2000).
Housing: Homeownership rate: 85.3% (2000); Median home value: $67,300 (2000); Median rent: $307 per month (2000); Median age of housing: 30 years (2000).
Health: Birth rate: 96.6 per 10,000 population (1998); Age adjusted death rate: 71.1 per 10,000 population (1999); Age adjusted cancer mortality rate: 185.2 deaths per 100,000 population (1999). Number of physicians: n/a (1999); Number of hospital beds: n/a (1999).
Elections: 2000 Presidential election results: 42.0% Gore, 55.3% Bush, 2.2% Nader, 0.0% Buchanan
National and State Parks: Au Sable National Scenic River; Oscoda State Forest
Additional Information Contacts
Oscoda County Chamber of Commerce. 989-826-3331

Oscoda County Communities

BIG CREEK (township). Covers a land area of 141.461 square miles and a water area of 1.669 square miles. Located at 44.61° N. Lat.; 84.22° W. Long.
Population: 3,380 (2000); Race: 97.1% White, 0.1% Black, 0.6% Asian, 0.1% American Indian and Alaska Native, 0.8% Hispanic of any race, 1.5% two or more races (2000); Density: 23.9 persons per square mile (2000); Age: 23.7% under 18, 18.8% over 64 (2000); Marriage status: 16.5% never married, 64.7% now married, 8.2% widowed, 10.6% divorced (2000); Foreign born: 1.8% (2000); Ancestry (includes multiple ancestries): 26.2% German, 13.0% English, 9.3% United States or American, 9.2% Irish, 7.3% Polish (2000).
Economy: Employment by occupation: 6.7% management, 10.3% professional, 22.8% services, 19.1% sales, 0.9% farming, 15.2% construction, 25.1% production (2000).
Income: Per capita income: $15,154 (2000); Median household income: $28,148 (2000); Poverty rate: 17.2% (2000).
Taxes: Total city taxes per capita: $17 (1997); City property taxes per capita: $17 (1997).
Education: High school graduation rate: 73.6% (2000); College graduation rate: 6.7% (2000).
Housing: Homeownership rate: 83.7% (2000); Median home value: $61,300 (2000); Median rent: $324 per month (2000); Median age of housing: 34 years (2000).
Transportation: Commute to work: 91.0% car, 0.0% public transportation, 5.4% walk, 2.8% work from home (2000); Travel time to work: 47.9% less than 15 minutes, 22.1% 15 to 30 minutes, 17.2% 30 to 45 minutes, 4.1% 45 to 60 minutes, 8.8% 60 minutes or more (2000)

CLINTON (township). Covers a land area of 70.302 square miles and a water area of 1.350 square miles. Located at 44.81° N. Lat.; 84.00° W. Long.
Population: 511 (2000); Race: 97.7% White, 0.0% Black, 0.0% Asian, 1.3% American Indian and Alaska Native, 1.0% Hispanic of any race, 1.0% two or more races (2000); Density: 7.3 persons per square mile (2000); Age: 17.5% under 18, 23.3% over 64 (2000); Marriage status: 17.4% never married, 63.7% now married, 7.1% widowed, 11.8% divorced (2000); Foreign born: 0.4% (2000); Ancestry (includes multiple ancestries): 27.2% German, 10.4% English, 10.4% Irish, 9.6% United States or American, 9.2% French (except Basque) (2000).
Economy: Employment by occupation: 9.9% management, 11.4% professional, 16.8% services, 27.7% sales, 1.5% farming, 14.9% construction, 17.8% production (2000).

Income: Per capita income: $23,549 (2000); Median household income: $33,750 (2000); Poverty rate: 6.4% (2000).
Taxes: Total city taxes per capita: $42 (1997); City property taxes per capita: $42 (1997).
Education: High school graduation rate: 82.3% (2000); College graduation rate: 9.5% (2000).
Housing: Homeownership rate: 91.9% (2000); Median home value: $71,000 (2000); Median rent: $264 per month (2000); Median age of housing: 34 years (2000).
Transportation: Commute to work: 95.5% car, 0.0% public transportation, 0.0% walk, 4.5% work from home (2000); Travel time to work: 25.4% less than 15 minutes, 47.6% 15 to 30 minutes, 10.6% 30 to 45 minutes, 5.8% 45 to 60 minutes, 10.6% 60 minutes or more (2000)

COMINS (township). Covers a land area of 70.518 square miles and a water area of 1.326 square miles. Located at 44.73° N. Lat.; 84.01° W. Long.
Population: 2,017 (2000); Race: 98.2% White, 0.1% Black, 0.0% Asian, 1.0% American Indian and Alaska Native, 0.5% Hispanic of any race, 0.6% two or more races (2000); Density: 28.6 persons per square mile (2000); Age: 25.5% under 18, 21.3% over 64 (2000); Marriage status: 17.7% never married, 63.7% now married, 9.3% widowed, 9.3% divorced (2000); Foreign born: 1.2% (2000); Ancestry (includes multiple ancestries): 32.7% German, 11.6% English, 10.3% United States or American, 7.9% Irish, 6.6% French (except Basque) (2000).
Economy: Employment by occupation: 10.3% management, 13.7% professional, 18.7% services, 20.1% sales, 3.5% farming, 9.3% construction, 24.4% production (2000).
Income: Per capita income: $14,813 (2000); Median household income: $28,750 (2000); Poverty rate: 13.2% (2000).
Taxes: Total city taxes per capita: $40 (1997); City property taxes per capita: $39 (1997).
Education: High school graduation rate: 74.9% (2000); College graduation rate: 10.3% (2000).
Housing: Homeownership rate: 78.4% (2000); Median home value: $69,800 (2000); Median rent: $277 per month (2000); Median age of housing: 26 years (2000).
Transportation: Commute to work: 89.4% car, 0.1% public transportation, 2.2% walk, 6.5% work from home (2000); Travel time to work: 59.4% less than 15 minutes, 24.6% 15 to 30 minutes, 5.4% 30 to 45 minutes, 4.5% 45 to 60 minutes, 6.1% 60 minutes or more (2000)

ELMER (township). Covers a land area of 70.779 square miles and a water area of 0.558 square miles. Located at 44.76° N. Lat.; 84.19° W. Long.
Population: 1,095 (2000); Race: 99.3% White, 0.0% Black, 0.0% Asian, 0.4% American Indian and Alaska Native, 0.0% Hispanic of any race, 0.4% two or more races (2000); Density: 15.5 persons per square mile (2000); Age: 30.3% under 18, 12.6% over 64 (2000); Marriage status: 19.8% never married, 67.1% now married, 5.5% widowed, 7.5% divorced (2000); Foreign born: 1.9% (2000); Ancestry (includes multiple ancestries): 30.8% German, 9.0% United States or American, 8.7% Polish, 8.2% Irish, 5.1% English (2000).
Economy: Employment by occupation: 13.1% management, 11.1% professional, 9.8% services, 20.9% sales, 1.3% farming, 13.1% construction, 30.7% production (2000).
Income: Per capita income: $15,273 (2000); Median household income: $27,500 (2000); Poverty rate: 15.2% (2000).
Taxes: Total city taxes per capita: $17 (1997); City property taxes per capita: $17 (1997).
Education: High school graduation rate: 62.7% (2000); College graduation rate: 5.8% (2000).
Housing: Homeownership rate: 90.5% (2000); Median home value: $74,700 (2000); Median rent: $325 per month (2000); Median age of housing: 26 years (2000).
Transportation: Commute to work: 72.8% car, 0.0% public transportation, 2.3% walk, 13.3% work from home (2000); Travel time to work: 43.4% less than 15 minutes, 31.9% 15 to 30 minutes, 11.1% 30 to 45 minutes, 8.1% 45 to 60 minutes, 5.4% 60 minutes or more (2000)

FAIRVIEW (unincorporated postal area, zip code 48621). Covers a land area of 72.882 square miles and a water area of 1.219 square miles. Located at 44.71° N. Lat.; 83.98° W. Long. Elevation is 1,170 feet.
Population: 1,531 (2000); Race: 98.5% White, 0.0% Black, 0.0% Asian, 1.3% American Indian and Alaska Native, 0.3% Hispanic of any race, 0.3% two or more races (2000); Density: 21.0 persons per square mile (2000); Age: 26.7% under 18, 22.5% over 64 (2000); Marriage status: 17.4% never married, 64.9% now married, 10.0% widowed, 7.8% divorced (2000); Foreign born: 1.1% (2000); Ancestry (includes multiple ancestries): 32.2% German, 11.6% English, 10.9% United States or American, 7.7% Irish, 7.4% French (except Basque) (2000).
Economy: Employment by occupation: 10.5% management, 16.2% professional, 20.2% services, 17.5% sales, 3.6% farming, 7.8% construction, 24.1% production (2000).
Income: Per capita income: $14,324 (2000); Median household income: $30,000 (2000); Poverty rate: 11.0% (2000).
Education: High school graduation rate: 77.0% (2000); College graduation rate: 12.9% (2000).

School District(s)

Fairview Area School District (KG-12)
2000 Enrollment: 450 517-848-2480
Housing: Homeownership rate: 77.3% (2000); Median home value: $70,700 (2000); Median rent: $252 per month (2000); Median age of housing: 26 years (2000).
Transportation: Commute to work: 90.5% car, 0.0% public transportation, 2.1% walk, 5.8% work from home (2000); Travel time to work: 61.6% less than 15 minutes, 22.7% 15 to 30 minutes, 5.2% 30 to 45 minutes, 4.5% 45 to 60 minutes, 6.0% 60 minutes or more (2000)

GREENWOOD (township). Covers a land area of 69.873 square miles and a water area of 0.965 square miles. Located at 44.79° N. Lat.; 84.31° W. Long.
Population: 1,195 (2000); Race: 98.8% White, 0.0% Black, 0.0% Asian, 0.0% American Indian and Alaska Native, 2.0% Hispanic of any race, 1.1% two or more races (2000); Density: 17.1 persons per square mile (2000); Age: 17.5% under 18, 26.7% over 64 (2000); Marriage status: 10.8% never married, 69.4% now married, 8.7% widowed, 11.2% divorced (2000); Foreign born: 1.5% (2000); Ancestry (includes multiple ancestries): 33.6% German, 12.5% Irish, 12.4% English, 10.4% Polish, 10.2% French (except Basque) (2000).
Economy: Employment by occupation: 10.4% management, 10.4% professional, 17.0% services, 25.8% sales, 3.0% farming, 13.2% construction, 20.3% production (2000).
Income: Per capita income: $17,083 (2000); Median household income: $28,426 (2000); Poverty rate: 13.1% (2000).
Taxes: Total city taxes per capita: $119 (1997); City property taxes per capita: $119 (1997).
Education: High school graduation rate: 74.3% (2000); College graduation rate: 6.4% (2000).
Housing: Homeownership rate: 92.7% (2000); Median home value: $86,200 (2000); Median rent: $388 per month (2000); Median age of housing: 22 years (2000).
Transportation: Commute to work: 96.9% car, 0.0% public transportation, 0.0% walk, 3.1% work from home (2000); Travel time to work: 37.1% less than 15 minutes, 31.3% 15 to 30 minutes, 12.8% 30 to 45 minutes, 15.4% 45 to 60 minutes, 3.5% 60 minutes or more (2000)

LUZERNE (unincorporated postal area, zip code 48636). Covers a land area of 89.411 square miles and a water area of 0.089 square miles. Located at 44.61° N. Lat.; 84.27° W. Long. Elevation is 1,076 feet.
History: Luzerne was named for Luzerne, Pennsylvania, by Myron B. Hagaman, who came here from Pennsylvania in 1881 and served as the first postmaster.
Population: 1,177 (2000); Race: 98.8% White, 0.0% Black, 0.0% Asian, 0.3% American Indian and Alaska Native, 0.0% Hispanic of any race, 0.9% two or more races (2000); Density: 13.2 persons per square mile (2000); Age: 21.1% under 18, 21.4% over 64 (2000); Marriage status: 13.6% never married, 70.1% now married, 7.5% widowed, 8.8% divorced (2000); Foreign born: 1.5% (2000); Ancestry (includes multiple ancestries): 26.2% German, 9.3% French (except Basque), 8.9% English, 8.3% Polish, 7.8% Other groups (2000).
Economy: Employment by occupation: 4.6% management, 7.8% professional, 24.8% services, 21.8% sales, 1.0% farming, 19.7% construction, 20.3% production (2000).
Income: Per capita income: $18,527 (2000); Median household income: $35,600 (2000); Poverty rate: 14.1% (2000).
Education: High school graduation rate: 74.5% (2000); College graduation rate: 4.4% (2000).
Housing: Homeownership rate: 92.4% (2000); Median home value: $63,200 (2000); Median rent: $350 per month (2000); Median age of housing: 34 years (2000).
Transportation: Commute to work: 95.2% car, 0.0% public transportation, 2.5% walk, 1.8% work from home (2000); Travel time to work: 43.8% less

than 15 minutes, 25.1% 15 to 30 minutes, 18.9% 30 to 45 minutes, 1.8% 45 to 60 minutes, 10.4% 60 minutes or more (2000)

MENTOR (township). Covers a land area of 142.070 square miles and a water area of 0.702 square miles. Located at 44.60° N. Lat.; 84.02° W. Long.
Population: 1,220 (2000); Race: 95.7% White, 0.0% Black, 0.0% Asian, 0.8% American Indian and Alaska Native, 2.5% Hispanic of any race, 2.2% two or more races (2000); Density: 8.6 persons per square mile (2000); Age: 19.9% under 18, 22.7% over 64 (2000); Marriage status: 14.3% never married, 65.6% now married, 8.6% widowed, 11.5% divorced (2000); Foreign born: 1.4% (2000); Ancestry (includes multiple ancestries): 25.7% German, 12.2% Irish, 11.2% French (except Basque), 10.5% Polish, 10.3% English (2000).
Economy: Employment by occupation: 9.1% management, 17.0% professional, 21.8% services, 24.1% sales, 2.3% farming, 6.1% construction, 19.5% production (2000).
Income: Per capita income: $14,392 (2000); Median household income: $26,094 (2000); Poverty rate: 14.1% (2000).
Taxes: Total city taxes per capita: $46 (1997); City property taxes per capita: $44 (1997).
Education: High school graduation rate: 76.2% (2000); College graduation rate: 10.5% (2000).
Housing: Homeownership rate: 85.8% (2000); Median home value: $63,300 (2000); Median rent: $280 per month (2000); Median age of housing: 37 years (2000).
Transportation: Commute to work: 91.3% car, 0.0% public transportation, 4.0% walk, 4.3% work from home (2000); Travel time to work: 48.4% less than 15 minutes, 21.7% 15 to 30 minutes, 8.6% 30 to 45 minutes, 7.2% 45 to 60 minutes, 14.1% 60 minutes or more (2000)

MIO (CDP). Covers a land area of 7.464 square miles and a water area of 0.646 square miles. Located at 44.65° N. Lat.; 84.13° W. Long. Elevation is 1,022 feet.
Population: 2,016 (2000); Race: 95.9% White, 0.2% Black, 0.0% Asian, 0.0% American Indian and Alaska Native, 2.1% Hispanic of any race, 2.4% two or more races (2000); Density: 270.1 persons per square mile (2000); Age: 26.7% under 18, 16.2% over 64 (2000); Marriage status: 21.6% never married, 56.1% now married, 9.9% widowed, 12.4% divorced (2000); Foreign born: 1.3% (2000); Ancestry (includes multiple ancestries): 31.2% German, 14.5% English, 10.2% Irish, 8.9% United States or American, 7.9% Polish (2000).
Economy: Manufacturing: pipe bending, thermocouple alloys. Resort. Surrounded by Huron National Forest on West, South, and East. Mio Mt. Ski Area to South. Employment by occupation: 10.6% management, 13.4% professional, 21.8% services, 20.6% sales, 1.2% farming, 11.2% construction, 21.2% production (2000).
Income: Per capita income: $13,064 (2000); Median household income: $26,831 (2000); Poverty rate: 21.3% (2000).
Education: High school graduation rate: 74.7% (2000); College graduation rate: 10.8% (2000).

School District(s)

Mio-Ausable Schools (KG-12)
2000 Enrollment: 892 517-826-3225

Housing: Homeownership rate: 74.3% (2000); Median home value: $59,900 (2000); Median rent: $294 per month (2000); Median age of housing: 34 years (2000).
Newspapers: Oscoda County Herald (1 x week)
Transportation: Commute to work: 84.1% car, 0.0% public transportation, 8.4% walk, 6.0% work from home (2000); Travel time to work: 63.3% less than 15 minutes, 15.7% 15 to 30 minutes, 8.4% 30 to 45 minutes, 6.2% 45 to 60 minutes, 6.5% 60 minutes or more (2000)
Additional Information Contacts
Oscoda County Chamber of Commerce 989-826-3331

Otsego County

Located in northern Michigan; drained by the Sturgeon and Black Rivers and the North Branch of the Au Sable River; includes many small lakes. Covers a land area of 514.50 square miles, a water area of 11.40 square miles, and is located in the Eastern Time Zone. The county government was organized in 1875. County seat is Gaylord.

Weather Station: Gaylord — Elevation: 1,348 feet

	Jan	Feb	Mar	Apr	May	Jun	Jul	Aug	Sep	Oct	Nov	Dec
High	25	29	39	53	68	76	80	78	68	57	41	30
Low	10	10	18	30	41	51	55	54	47	37	27	16
Precip	3.1	2.0	2.5	2.4	2.8	2.7	3.3	3.7	3.9	3.5	3.3	3.2
Snow	39.0	23.9	19.1	6.9	1.0	0.0	0.0	0.0	tr	2.7	22.1	34.7

High and Low temperatures in degrees Fahrenheit; Precipitation and Snow in inches

Weather Station: Vanderbilt 11 ENE — Elevation: 921 feet

	Jan	Feb	Mar	Apr	May	Jun	Jul	Aug	Sep	Oct	Nov	Dec
High	25	28	38	52	67	76	80	77	68	55	41	30
Low	5	3	13	27	37	46	50	49	41	33	25	14
Precip	2.2	1.4	2.1	2.4	2.9	2.4	3.5	3.5	3.6	2.9	2.4	2.3
Snow	27.5	16.7	12.7	4.9	0.5	0.0	0.0	0.0	tr	0.8	11.6	23.1

High and Low temperatures in degrees Fahrenheit; Precipitation and Snow in inches

Population: 23,301 (2000); Race: 97.3% White, 0.1% Black, 0.6% Asian, 0.8% American Indian and Alaska Native, 0.7% Hispanic of any race, 1.1% two or more races (2000); Density: 45.3 persons per square mile (2000); Age: 26.7% under 18, 13.8% over 64 (2000).
Religion: Five largest groups: 31.2% Catholic Church, 2.7% The United Methodist Church, 2.7% The Evangelical Free Church of America, 1.8% Lutheran Church—Missouri Synod, 1.7% Evangelical Lutheran Church in America (2000).
Economy: Unemployment rate: 6.5% (11/2002); Total civilian labor force: 13,873 (11/2002); Leading industries: 18.1% retail trade; 16.7% manufacturing; 16.1% accommodation & food services (2000); Companies that employ more than 1,000 persons: 0 (2000); Companies that employ more than 100 persons: 14 (2000); Farms: 139 totaling 34,450 acres (1997); Minority business ownership rate: 0.0% (1997); Women business ownership rate: 27.3% (1997); Retail sales per capita: $15,382 (1997). Single-family building permits issued: 303 (2001) / 297 (2000); Multi-family building permits issued: 24 (2001) / 20 (2000).
Income: Per capita income: $19,810 (2000); Median household income: $40,876 (2000); Poverty rate: 6.8% (2000); Bankruptcy rate: 4.47% (2001).
Taxes: Total county taxes per capita: $222 (1997); County property taxes per capita: $204 (1997).
Education: High school graduation rate: 85.5% (2000); College graduation rate: 17.4% (2000).
Housing: Homeownership rate: 81.9% (2000); Median home value: $102,500 (2000); Median rent: $451 per month (2000); Median age of housing: 23 years (2000).
Health: Birth rate: 128.8 per 10,000 population (1998); Age adjusted death rate: 82.1 per 10,000 population (1999); Age adjusted cancer mortality rate: 174.4 deaths per 100,000 population (1999). Number of physicians: 9.9 per 10,000 population (1999); Number of hospital beds: 37.3 per 10,000 population (1999).
Elections: 2000 Presidential election results: 38.4% Gore, 58.1% Bush, 3.0% Nader, 0.1% Buchanan
National and State Parks: Otsego Lake State Park; Pigeon River State Forest
Additional Information Contacts
Otsego County Government Offices 989-732-6484
Gaylord Chamber of Commerce 989-732-4000
Water Wonderland Board of Realtors 989-732-8226

Otsego County Communities

BAGLEY (township). Covers a land area of 28.626 square miles and a water area of 2.677 square miles. Located at 44.98° N. Lat.; 84.67° W. Long.
History: Bagley Township was named for John J. Bagley, a Republican governor of Michigan.
Population: 5,838 (2000); Race: 96.5% White, 0.0% Black, 1.5% Asian, 0.5% American Indian and Alaska Native, 0.7% Hispanic of any race, 1.4% two or more races (2000); Density: 203.9 persons per square mile (2000); Age: 28.5% under 18, 9.0% over 64 (2000); Marriage status: 21.4% never married, 62.5% now married, 4.7% widowed, 11.4% divorced (2000); Foreign born: 2.1% (2000); Ancestry (includes multiple ancestries): 28.6% German, 15.9% Polish, 13.8% English, 12.8% Irish, 7.2% Other groups (2000).
Economy: Employment by occupation: 12.4% management, 18.7% professional, 16.0% services, 26.3% sales, 0.3% farming, 10.6% construction, 15.7% production (2000).
Income: Per capita income: $21,116 (2000); Median household income: $44,205 (2000); Poverty rate: 6.1% (2000).

Education: High school graduation rate: 89.2% (2000); College graduation rate: 20.6% (2000).
Housing: Homeownership rate: 86.2% (2000); Median home value: $101,400 (2000); Median rent: $483 per month (2000); Median age of housing: 24 years (2000).
Transportation: Commute to work: 93.8% car, 0.3% public transportation, 1.4% walk, 4.1% work from home (2000); Travel time to work: 63.9% less than 15 minutes, 22.6% 15 to 30 minutes, 5.9% 30 to 45 minutes, 2.8% 45 to 60 minutes, 4.8% 60 minutes or more (2000)

CHARLTON (township). Covers a land area of 100.341 square miles and a water area of 1.891 square miles. Located at 44.95° N. Lat.; 84.41° W. Long.
Population: 1,330 (2000); Race: 99.1% White, 0.0% Black, 0.0% Asian, 0.5% American Indian and Alaska Native, 0.8% Hispanic of any race, 0.5% two or more races (2000); Density: 13.3 persons per square mile (2000); Age: 20.4% under 18, 17.1% over 64 (2000); Marriage status: 14.7% never married, 70.8% now married, 4.9% widowed, 9.7% divorced (2000); Foreign born: 0.9% (2000); Ancestry (includes multiple ancestries): 24.4% German, 18.7% Polish, 14.4% Irish, 14.2% English, 8.4% French (except Basque) (2000).
Economy: Employment by occupation: 9.6% management, 11.2% professional, 19.7% services, 25.1% sales, 1.6% farming, 11.0% construction, 21.7% production (2000).
Income: Per capita income: $20,211 (2000); Median household income: $36,536 (2000); Poverty rate: 6.5% (2000).
Taxes: Total city taxes per capita: $293 (1997); City property taxes per capita: $293 (1997).
Education: High school graduation rate: 79.2% (2000); College graduation rate: 11.1% (2000).
Housing: Homeownership rate: 89.8% (2000); Median home value: $87,600 (2000); Median rent: $460 per month (2000); Median age of housing: 27 years (2000).
Transportation: Commute to work: 93.8% car, 1.0% public transportation, 2.1% walk, 2.7% work from home (2000); Travel time to work: 20.0% less than 15 minutes, 45.1% 15 to 30 minutes, 22.6% 30 to 45 minutes, 6.3% 45 to 60 minutes, 5.9% 60 minutes or more (2000)

CHESTER (township). Covers a land area of 67.720 square miles and a water area of 1.088 square miles. Located at 44.92° N. Lat.; 84.54° W. Long.
Population: 1,265 (2000); Race: 99.8% White, 0.0% Black, 0.2% Asian, 0.0% American Indian and Alaska Native, 0.0% Hispanic of any race, 0.0% two or more races (2000); Density: 18.7 persons per square mile (2000); Age: 25.8% under 18, 13.6% over 64 (2000); Marriage status: 19.0% never married, 65.8% now married, 5.7% widowed, 9.5% divorced (2000); Foreign born: 1.3% (2000); Ancestry (includes multiple ancestries): 22.1% Polish, 20.2% German, 14.0% United States or American, 11.4% Irish, 9.4% English (2000).
Economy: Employment by occupation: 9.8% management, 12.9% professional, 19.6% services, 29.0% sales, 0.5% farming, 14.2% construction, 13.9% production (2000).
Income: Per capita income: $18,479 (2000); Median household income: $42,368 (2000); Poverty rate: 5.0% (2000).
Taxes: Total city taxes per capita: $84 (1997); City property taxes per capita: $83 (1997).
Education: High school graduation rate: 79.9% (2000); College graduation rate: 12.3% (2000).
Housing: Homeownership rate: 93.4% (2000); Median home value: $98,700 (2000); Median rent: $394 per month (2000); Median age of housing: 23 years (2000).
Transportation: Commute to work: 92.1% car, 0.0% public transportation, 1.9% walk, 5.1% work from home (2000); Travel time to work: 35.5% less than 15 minutes, 48.8% 15 to 30 minutes, 5.7% 30 to 45 minutes, 3.2% 45 to 60 minutes, 6.7% 60 minutes or more (2000)

CORWITH (township). Covers a land area of 107.513 square miles and a water area of 0.573 square miles. Located at 45.15° N. Lat.; 84.57° W. Long.
Population: 1,719 (2000); Race: 96.7% White, 0.2% Black, 0.1% Asian, 1.3% American Indian and Alaska Native, 0.8% Hispanic of any race, 0.9% two or more races (2000); Density: 16.0 persons per square mile (2000); Age: 24.2% under 18, 14.0% over 64 (2000); Marriage status: 20.2% never married, 60.3% now married, 6.5% widowed, 13.0% divorced (2000); Foreign born: 1.3% (2000); Ancestry (includes multiple ancestries): 26.2% German, 15.8% Irish, 13.5% English, 12.3% Polish, 9.8% United States or American (2000).
Economy: Employment by occupation: 7.5% management, 6.2% professional, 20.8% services, 23.8% sales, 0.5% farming, 10.5% construction, 30.6% production (2000).
Income: Per capita income: $15,936 (2000); Median household income: $32,348 (2000); Poverty rate: 11.9% (2000).
Taxes: Total city taxes per capita: $26 (1997); City property taxes per capita: $26 (1997).
Education: High school graduation rate: 78.0% (2000); College graduation rate: 7.8% (2000).
Housing: Homeownership rate: 77.0% (2000); Median home value: $76,700 (2000); Median rent: $372 per month (2000); Median age of housing: 26 years (2000).
Transportation: Commute to work: 91.7% car, 0.8% public transportation, 3.9% walk, 2.6% work from home (2000); Travel time to work: 39.0% less than 15 minutes, 42.5% 15 to 30 minutes, 10.9% 30 to 45 minutes, 2.5% 45 to 60 minutes, 5.1% 60 minutes or more (2000)

DOVER (township). Covers a land area of 35.215 square miles and a water area of 0.044 square miles. Located at 45.06° N. Lat.; 84.55° W. Long.
Population: 614 (2000); Race: 99.7% White, 0.0% Black, 0.0% Asian, 0.3% American Indian and Alaska Native, 0.0% Hispanic of any race, 0.0% two or more races (2000); Density: 17.4 persons per square mile (2000); Age: 33.1% under 18, 8.3% over 64 (2000); Marriage status: 17.5% never married, 73.8% now married, 3.0% widowed, 5.7% divorced (2000); Foreign born: 0.5% (2000); Ancestry (includes multiple ancestries): 21.7% German, 19.8% Polish, 10.2% English, 10.0% Irish, 9.4% United States or American (2000).
Economy: Employment by occupation: 20.3% management, 13.8% professional, 8.6% services, 25.2% sales, 0.0% farming, 16.6% construction, 15.5% production (2000).
Income: Per capita income: $22,739 (2000); Median household income: $45,000 (2000); Poverty rate: 6.4% (2000).
Taxes: Total city taxes per capita: $84 (1997); City property taxes per capita: $84 (1997).
Education: High school graduation rate: 85.9% (2000); College graduation rate: 11.2% (2000).
Housing: Homeownership rate: 88.7% (2000); Median home value: $109,800 (2000); Median rent: $446 per month (2000); Median age of housing: 22 years (2000).
Transportation: Commute to work: 92.2% car, 0.7% public transportation, 1.1% walk, 6.0% work from home (2000); Travel time to work: 29.2% less than 15 minutes, 54.9% 15 to 30 minutes, 11.7% 30 to 45 minutes, 1.9% 45 to 60 minutes, 2.3% 60 minutes or more (2000)

ELMIRA (township). Covers a land area of 35.721 square miles and a water area of 0.454 square miles. Located at 45.06° N. Lat.; 84.82° W. Long. Elevation is 1,228 feet.
Population: 1,598 (2000); Race: 98.1% White, 0.2% Black, 0.0% Asian, 0.9% American Indian and Alaska Native, 1.9% Hispanic of any race, 0.7% two or more races (2000); Density: 44.7 persons per square mile (2000); Age: 31.3% under 18, 11.7% over 64 (2000); Marriage status: 18.6% never married, 71.7% now married, 3.6% widowed, 6.2% divorced (2000); Foreign born: 1.1% (2000); Ancestry (includes multiple ancestries): 26.3% German, 19.7% Polish, 13.5% Irish, 10.2% English, 8.3% United States or American (2000).
Economy: Employment by occupation: 15.2% management, 11.1% professional, 12.5% services, 23.7% sales, 1.3% farming, 17.0% construction, 19.2% production (2000).
Income: Per capita income: $19,286 (2000); Median household income: $45,938 (2000); Poverty rate: 6.9% (2000).
Taxes: Total city taxes per capita: $36 (1997); City property taxes per capita: $36 (1997).
Education: High school graduation rate: 87.9% (2000); College graduation rate: 15.8% (2000).
Housing: Homeownership rate: 93.4% (2000); Median home value: $99,800 (2000); Median rent: $458 per month (2000); Median age of housing: 16 years (2000).
Transportation: Commute to work: 92.8% car, 0.3% public transportation, 1.0% walk, 5.9% work from home (2000); Travel time to work: 35.0% less than 15 minutes, 47.9% 15 to 30 minutes, 10.1% 30 to 45 minutes, 3.2% 45 to 60 minutes, 3.7% 60 minutes or more (2000)

GAYLORD (city). Covers a land area of 3.946 square miles and a water area of 0.009 square miles. Located at 45.02° N. Lat.; 84.67° W. Long. Elevation is 1,349 feet.
History: Gaylord was first called Barnes, but when the Jackson, Lansing & Saginaw Railroad arrived in 1874, the name was changed to Gaylord for a

railroad attorney. Gaylord was incorporated as a village in 1881 and as a city in 1922. It became the seat of Otsego County in 1878.
Population: 3,681 (2000); Race: 96.3% White, 0.4% Black, 0.9% Asian, 0.7% American Indian and Alaska Native, 0.8% Hispanic of any race, 1.7% two or more races (2000); Density: 932.8 persons per square mile (2000); Age: 24.4% under 18, 21.0% over 64 (2000); Marriage status: 26.9% never married, 49.0% now married, 12.7% widowed, 11.5% divorced (2000); Foreign born: 1.4% (2000); Ancestry (includes multiple ancestries): 28.6% German, 19.4% Polish, 12.3% Irish, 10.9% English, 8.0% Other groups (2000).
Economy: Employment by occupation: 13.6% management, 16.6% professional, 17.6% services, 27.0% sales, 0.0% farming, 11.4% construction, 13.8% production (2000).
Income: Per capita income: $17,313 (2000); Median household income: $28,770 (2000); Poverty rate: 9.7% (2000).
Taxes: Total city taxes per capita: $468 (1997); City property taxes per capita: $468 (1997).
Education: High school graduation rate: 81.1% (2000); College graduation rate: 17.7% (2000).

School District(s)

Gaylord Community Schools (KG-12)
2000 Enrollment: 3,464 517-732-6402
Housing: Homeownership rate: 50.5% (2000); Median home value: $92,700 (2000); Median rent: $434 per month (2000); Median age of housing: 29 years (2000).
Hospitals: Otsego Memorial Hospital (53 beds)
Safety: Violent crime rate: 29.7 per 10,000 population; Property crime rate: 848.6 per 10,000 population (2001).
Newspapers: Northern Star (1 x week); Gaylord Herald Times (1 x week)
Transportation: Commute to work: 88.4% car, 0.8% public transportation, 5.3% walk, 5.4% work from home (2000); Travel time to work: 81.1% less than 15 minutes, 13.2% 15 to 30 minutes, 1.1% 30 to 45 minutes, 1.4% 45 to 60 minutes, 3.2% 60 minutes or more (2000)
Airports: Otsego County
Additional Information Contacts
Gaylord Chamber of Commerce 989-732-4000
Water Wonderland Board of Realtors 989-732-8226

HAYES (township). Covers a land area of 68.828 square miles and a water area of 1.627 square miles. Located at 44.94° N. Lat.; 84.79° W. Long.
Population: 2,385 (2000); Race: 96.3% White, 0.2% Black, 0.4% Asian, 1.9% American Indian and Alaska Native, 0.8% Hispanic of any race, 1.0% two or more races (2000); Density: 34.7 persons per square mile (2000); Age: 28.9% under 18, 9.2% over 64 (2000); Marriage status: 18.0% never married, 71.3% now married, 2.9% widowed, 7.9% divorced (2000); Foreign born: 1.5% (2000); Ancestry (includes multiple ancestries): 21.1% German, 13.0% Irish, 11.7% Polish, 11.5% English, 8.0% United States or American (2000).
Economy: Employment by occupation: 8.8% management, 11.5% professional, 19.8% services, 26.6% sales, 0.8% farming, 10.4% construction, 22.0% production (2000).
Income: Per capita income: $17,587 (2000); Median household income: $42,969 (2000); Poverty rate: 5.6% (2000).
Taxes: Total city taxes per capita: $48 (1997); City property taxes per capita: $48 (1997).
Education: High school graduation rate: 87.4% (2000); College graduation rate: 14.5% (2000).
Housing: Homeownership rate: 94.2% (2000); Median home value: $97,400 (2000); Median rent: $455 per month (2000); Median age of housing: 18 years (2000).
Transportation: Commute to work: 92.4% car, 1.7% public transportation, 0.6% walk, 5.1% work from home (2000); Travel time to work: 32.2% less than 15 minutes, 48.8% 15 to 30 minutes, 9.1% 30 to 45 minutes, 4.4% 45 to 60 minutes, 5.5% 60 minutes or more (2000)

JOHANNESBURG (unincorporated postal area, zip code 49751). Covers a land area of 150.242 square miles and a water area of 1.992 square miles. Located at 44.96° N. Lat.; 84.43° W. Long. Elevation is 1,351 feet.
History: The community of Johannesburg grew up around the Johannesburg Manufacturing Company's sawmill.
Population: 1,830 (2000); Race: 99.4% White, 0.0% Black, 0.1% Asian, 0.3% American Indian and Alaska Native, 0.4% Hispanic of any race, 0.2% two or more races (2000); Density: 12.2 persons per square mile (2000); Age: 20.9% under 18, 17.4% over 64 (2000); Marriage status: 16.8% never married, 67.1% now married, 5.9% widowed, 10.2% divorced (2000); Foreign born: 1.2% (2000); Ancestry (includes multiple ancestries): 22.9% German, 15.0% Polish, 13.5% English, 12.8% Irish, 10.8% United States or American (2000).
Economy: Employment by occupation: 9.9% management, 11.3% professional, 17.4% services, 27.9% sales, 1.3% farming, 11.5% construction, 20.7% production (2000).
Income: Per capita income: $19,765 (2000); Median household income: $35,682 (2000); Poverty rate: 5.4% (2000).
Education: High school graduation rate: 76.5% (2000); College graduation rate: 11.5% (2000).

School District(s)

Johannesburg-Lewiston Area Schoo (KG-12)
2000 Enrollment: 875 517-732-1773
Housing: Homeownership rate: 89.9% (2000); Median home value: $84,600 (2000); Median rent: $450 per month (2000); Median age of housing: 27 years (2000).
Transportation: Commute to work: 94.2% car, 0.7% public transportation, 1.2% walk, 3.3% work from home (2000); Travel time to work: 17.8% less than 15 minutes, 49.7% 15 to 30 minutes, 17.7% 30 to 45 minutes, 6.6% 45 to 60 minutes, 8.1% 60 minutes or more (2000)

LIVINGSTON (township). Covers a land area of 33.889 square miles and a water area of 0.332 square miles. Located at 45.06° N. Lat.; 84.67° W. Long.
Population: 2,339 (2000); Race: 97.5% White, 0.0% Black, 0.3% Asian, 0.7% American Indian and Alaska Native, 0.1% Hispanic of any race, 1.5% two or more races (2000); Density: 69.0 persons per square mile (2000); Age: 30.4% under 18, 10.9% over 64 (2000); Marriage status: 21.2% never married, 66.9% now married, 4.3% widowed, 7.6% divorced (2000); Foreign born: 1.3% (2000); Ancestry (includes multiple ancestries): 23.4% German, 22.4% Polish, 14.7% Irish, 8.8% English, 6.5% French (except Basque) (2000).
Economy: Employment by occupation: 14.1% management, 18.2% professional, 13.5% services, 26.3% sales, 0.2% farming, 11.6% construction, 16.2% production (2000).
Income: Per capita income: $21,798 (2000); Median household income: $51,293 (2000); Poverty rate: 2.9% (2000).
Taxes: Total city taxes per capita: $14 (1997); City property taxes per capita: $14 (1997).
Education: High school graduation rate: 89.0% (2000); College graduation rate: 21.8% (2000).
Housing: Homeownership rate: 88.1% (2000); Median home value: $122,000 (2000); Median rent: $529 per month (2000); Median age of housing: 19 years (2000).
Transportation: Commute to work: 93.8% car, 0.3% public transportation, 0.6% walk, 5.2% work from home (2000); Travel time to work: 63.3% less than 15 minutes, 25.9% 15 to 30 minutes, 7.3% 30 to 45 minutes, 1.4% 45 to 60 minutes, 2.0% 60 minutes or more (2000)

OTSEGO LAKE (township). Covers a land area of 32.743 square miles and a water area of 2.746 square miles. Located at 44.90° N. Lat.; 84.66° W. Long. Elevation is 1,274 feet.
Population: 2,532 (2000); Race: 98.5% White, 0.2% Black, 0.1% Asian, 0.7% American Indian and Alaska Native, 0.5% Hispanic of any race, 0.5% two or more races (2000); Density: 77.3 persons per square mile (2000); Age: 21.4% under 18, 22.1% over 64 (2000); Marriage status: 14.6% never married, 71.2% now married, 7.4% widowed, 6.8% divorced (2000); Foreign born: 2.2% (2000); Ancestry (includes multiple ancestries): 27.3% German, 14.7% English, 10.4% Irish, 9.5% Polish, 8.3% United States or American (2000).
Economy: Employment by occupation: 13.1% management, 17.5% professional, 14.3% services, 30.6% sales, 0.4% farming, 10.3% construction, 13.8% production (2000).
Income: Per capita income: $23,350 (2000); Median household income: $44,351 (2000); Poverty rate: 6.5% (2000).
Taxes: Total city taxes per capita: $83 (1997); City property taxes per capita: $83 (1997).
Education: High school graduation rate: 87.8% (2000); College graduation rate: 22.8% (2000).
Housing: Homeownership rate: 90.7% (2000); Median home value: $134,900 (2000); Median rent: $463 per month (2000); Median age of housing: 22 years (2000).
Transportation: Commute to work: 93.4% car, 1.2% public transportation, 0.4% walk, 4.6% work from home (2000); Travel time to work: 29.0% less than 15 minutes, 50.3% 15 to 30 minutes, 10.0% 30 to 45 minutes, 2.5% 45 to 60 minutes, 8.2% 60 minutes or more (2000)

VANDERBILT (village). Covers a land area of 1.106 square miles and a water area of 0 square miles. Located at 45.14° N. Lat.; 84.66° W. Long. Elevation is 1,090 feet.
History: Vanderbilt was founded in 1870 and incorporated in 1901. It was named for the prominent Vanderbilt family. The town once had many mills, but later depended on fishing and hunting for its revenue.
Population: 587 (2000); Race: 95.7% White, 0.3% Black, 0.0% Asian, 2.2% American Indian and Alaska Native, 0.5% Hispanic of any race, 1.2% two or more races (2000); Density: 530.6 persons per square mile (2000); Age: 25.5% under 18, 17.4% over 64 (2000); Marriage status: 24.3% never married, 51.6% now married, 8.4% widowed, 15.7% divorced (2000); Foreign born: 0.9% (2000); Ancestry (includes multiple ancestries): 24.6% German, 15.0% English, 15.0% Irish, 13.8% Polish, 11.2% United States or American (2000).
Economy: Employment by occupation: 6.9% management, 6.5% professional, 28.2% services, 23.4% sales, 0.0% farming, 7.3% construction, 27.8% production (2000).
Income: Per capita income: $11,973 (2000); Median household income: $27,969 (2000); Poverty rate: 6.8% (2000).
Taxes: Total city taxes per capita: $101 (1997); City property taxes per capita: $101 (1997).
Education: High school graduation rate: 72.0% (2000); College graduation rate: 3.2% (2000).

School District(s)

Vanderbilt Area Schools (KG-12)
2000 Enrollment: 291 517-983-4121

Housing: Homeownership rate: 68.9% (2000); Median home value: $67,200 (2000); Median rent: $336 per month (2000); Median age of housing: 26 years (2000).
Transportation: Commute to work: 89.5% car, 1.6% public transportation, 5.6% walk, 2.0% work from home (2000); Travel time to work: 48.1% less than 15 minutes, 42.4% 15 to 30 minutes, 7.0% 30 to 45 minutes, 1.2% 45 to 60 minutes, 1.2% 60 minutes or more (2000)

Ottawa County

Located in southwestern Michigan; bounded on the west by Lake Michigan; drained by the Grand and Black Rivers. Covers a land area of 565.70 square miles, a water area of 1,066.30 square miles, and is located in the Eastern Time Zone. The county government was organized in 1837. County seat is Grand Haven.

Ottawa County is part of the Grand Rapids-Muskegon-Holland, MI MSA. The entire metro area includes: Allegan County; Kent County; Muskegon County; Ottawa County

Weather Station: Grand Haven Fire Dept. Elevation: 620 feet

	Jan	Feb	Mar	Apr	May	Jun	Jul	Aug	Sep	Oct	Nov	Dec
High	31	33	43	55	67	76	80	78	71	60	47	36
Low	19	20	28	38	48	57	63	62	54	44	34	25
Precip	2.0	1.3	2.4	2.8	2.9	3.0	2.5	3.6	3.7	2.7	3.3	2.6
Snow	24.1	13.2	5.8	1.7	tr	0.0	0.0	0.0	0.0	0.2	5.5	19.9

High and Low temperatures in degrees Fahrenheit; Precipitation and Snow in inches

Weather Station: Holland Elevation: 606 feet

	Jan	Feb	Mar	Apr	May	Jun	Jul	Aug	Sep	Oct	Nov	Dec
High	31	35	45	57	70	79	83	81	73	61	48	36
Low	17	19	26	36	46	55	60	59	52	42	33	23
Precip	2.0	1.4	2.1	3.2	3.2	3.7	3.5	3.5	4.0	2.9	3.2	2.9
Snow	28.2	15.5	6.8	1.9	tr	0.0	0.0	0.0	0.0	0.3	5.4	21.3

High and Low temperatures in degrees Fahrenheit; Precipitation and Snow in inches

Population: 238,314 (2000); Race: 91.5% White, 1.0% Black, 2.2% Asian, 0.3% American Indian and Alaska Native, 7.1% Hispanic of any race, 1.7% two or more races (2000); Density: 421.3 persons per square mile (2000); Age: 28.7% under 18, 10.1% over 64 (2000).
Religion: Five largest groups: 15.3% Reformed Church in America, 12.7% Christian Reformed Church in North America, 11.3% Catholic Church, 4.0% The Wesleyan Church, 2.7% Lutheran Church—Missouri Synod (2000).
Economy: Unemployment rate: 4.6% (11/2002); Total civilian labor force: 144,912 (11/2002); Leading industries: 38.4% manufacturing; 11.9% retail trade; 8.7% health care and social assistance (2000); Companies that employ more than 1,000 persons: 6 (2000); Companies that employ more than 100 persons: 162 (2000); Farms: 1,292 totaling 170,627 acres (1997); Minority business ownership rate: 3.6% (1997); Women business ownership rate: 27.3% (1997); Retail sales per capita: $8,709 (1997). Single-family building permits issued: 1,598 (2001) / 1,520 (2000); Multi-family building permits issued: 652 (2001) / 519 (2000).
Income: Per capita income: $21,676 (2000); Median household income: $52,347 (2000); Poverty rate: 5.5% (2000); Bankruptcy rate: 3.32% (2001).
Taxes: Total county taxes per capita: $114 (2000); County property taxes per capita: $108 (2000).
Education: High school graduation rate: 86.6% (2000); College graduation rate: 26.0% (2000).
Housing: Homeownership rate: 80.8% (2000); Median home value: $133,000 (2000); Median rent: $523 per month (2000); Median age of housing: 23 years (2000).
Health: Birth rate: 148.6 per 10,000 population (1998); Age adjusted death rate: 74.9 per 10,000 population (1999); Age adjusted cancer mortality rate: 179.4 deaths per 100,000 population (1999). Air Quality Index: 69% good, 31% moderate, 0% unhealthy (percent of days in 2000). Number of physicians: 10.9 per 10,000 population (1999); Number of hospital beds: 11.7 per 10,000 population (1999).
Elections: 2000 Presidential election results: 26.8% Gore, 71.2% Bush, 1.7% Nader, 0.0% Buchanan
National and State Parks: Grand Haven State Game Area; Grand Haven State Park; Holland State Park
Additional Information Contacts
Ottawa County Government Offices 616-846-8310
Allendale Area Chamber of Commerce 616-895-9444
Coopersville Chamber of Commerce 616-837-9731
Grand Haven Chamber of Commerce 616-842-4910
Holland Area Convention & Visitors Bureau 616-394-0000
Holland Chamber of Commerce. 616-392-2389
Hudsonville Chamber of Commerce 616-896-9020
West Michigan Lakeshore Association of Realtors 616-846-6240
Zeeland Chamber of Commerce. 616-772-2494

Ottawa County Communities

ALLENDALE (township). Covers a land area of 31.295 square miles and a water area of 0.904 square miles. Located at 42.97° N. Lat.; 85.95° W. Long. Elevation is 657 feet.
History: Allendale Township was organized in 1846, and named for Captain Hannibal Allen, son of Ethan Allen. Agnes Allen, Captain Allen's widow, owned land in the township.
Population: 13,042 (2000); Race: 94.8% White, 2.4% Black, 0.6% Asian, 0.5% American Indian and Alaska Native, 2.7% Hispanic of any race, 0.8% two or more races (2000); Density: 416.7 persons per square mile (2000); Age: 21.6% under 18, 4.9% over 64 (2000); Marriage status: 49.5% never married, 45.8% now married, 1.5% widowed, 3.2% divorced (2000); Foreign born: 2.9% (2000); Ancestry (includes multiple ancestries): 28.3% Dutch, 22.1% German, 9.3% Other groups, 8.4% Irish, 7.6% English (2000).
Economy: Single-family building permits issued: 146 (2001) / 121 (2000); Multi-family building permits issued: 128 (2001) / 93 (2000); Employment by occupation: 9.6% management, 16.2% professional, 17.1% services, 29.0% sales, 1.2% farming, 10.1% construction, 16.8% production (2000).
Income: Per capita income: $15,065 (2000); Median household income: $48,669 (2000); Poverty rate: 11.7% (2000).
Taxes: Total city taxes per capita: $35 (2000); City property taxes per capita: $24 (2000).
Education: High school graduation rate: 85.2% (2000); College graduation rate: 17.2% (2000).

School District(s)

Allendale Public School District (PK-12)
2000 Enrollment: 1,832 616-895-4350

Four-year College(s)

Grand Valley State University (Public)
2001 Enrollment: 19,762 616-895-6611
2001 Tuition: In-state $4,660; Out-of-state $10,080

Housing: Homeownership rate: 74.0% (2000); Median home value: $129,500 (2000); Median rent: $522 per month (2000); Median age of housing: 15 years (2000).
Transportation: Commute to work: 85.0% car, 0.1% public transportation, 10.7% walk, 3.2% work from home (2000); Travel time to work: 32.1% less than 15 minutes, 39.3% 15 to 30 minutes, 23.9% 30 to 45 minutes, 3.3% 45 to 60 minutes, 1.5% 60 minutes or more (2000)
Additional Information Contacts
Allendale Area Chamber of Commerce 616-895-9444

BEECHWOOD (CDP). Covers a land area of 1.833 square miles and a water area of 0.867 square miles. Located at 42.79° N. Lat.; 86.12° W. Long.
Population: 2,963 (2000); Race: 90.1% White, 1.9% Black, 4.4% Asian, 0.0% American Indian and Alaska Native, 12.2% Hispanic of any race, 1.1% two or more races (2000); Density: 1,616.3 persons per square mile (2000); Age: 31.9% under 18, 9.7% over 64 (2000); Marriage status: 19.2% never married, 65.6% now married, 5.8% widowed, 9.3% divorced (2000); Foreign born: 7.1% (2000); Ancestry (includes multiple ancestries): 31.1% Dutch, 20.9% Other groups, 17.2% German, 9.8% English, 8.0% United States or American (2000).
Economy: Suburb of Holland. Employment by occupation: 9.4% management, 15.1% professional, 17.1% services, 19.2% sales, 0.5% farming, 10.7% construction, 27.9% production (2000).
Income: Per capita income: $22,968 (2000); Median household income: $46,676 (2000); Poverty rate: 8.1% (2000).
Education: High school graduation rate: 82.9% (2000); College graduation rate: 17.7% (2000).
Housing: Homeownership rate: 71.3% (2000); Median home value: $113,600 (2000); Median rent: $492 per month (2000); Median age of housing: 33 years (2000).
Transportation: Commute to work: 96.8% car, 0.0% public transportation, 0.7% walk, 2.5% work from home (2000); Travel time to work: 52.9% less than 15 minutes, 31.5% 15 to 30 minutes, 8.5% 30 to 45 minutes, 4.8% 45 to 60 minutes, 2.4% 60 minutes or more (2000)

BLENDON (township). Covers a land area of 36.540 square miles and a water area of 0 square miles. Located at 42.90° N. Lat.; 85.95° W. Long.
History: Blendon Township was named for the Blendon Lumber Company, who owned much land here.
Population: 5,721 (2000); Race: 98.8% White, 0.0% Black, 0.4% Asian, 0.0% American Indian and Alaska Native, 0.8% Hispanic of any race, 0.5% two or more races (2000); Density: 156.6 persons per square mile (2000); Age: 32.7% under 18, 6.0% over 64 (2000); Marriage status: 26.1% never married, 68.5% now married, 2.2% widowed, 3.1% divorced (2000); Foreign born: 0.9% (2000); Ancestry (includes multiple ancestries): 57.1% Dutch, 11.8% German, 6.5% United States or American, 5.6% English, 4.4% Irish (2000).
Economy: Single-family building permits issued: 20 (2001) / 19 (2000); Multi-family building permits issued: 0 (2001) / 0 (2000); Employment by occupation: 11.7% management, 12.7% professional, 11.6% services, 19.7% sales, 5.1% farming, 15.9% construction, 23.3% production (2000).
Income: Per capita income: $20,876 (2000); Median household income: $56,094 (2000); Poverty rate: 2.8% (2000).
Taxes: Total city taxes per capita: $58 (1997); City property taxes per capita: $52 (1997).
Education: High school graduation rate: 90.1% (2000); College graduation rate: 16.7% (2000).
Housing: Homeownership rate: 89.0% (2000); Median home value: $140,700 (2000); Median rent: $536 per month (2000); Median age of housing: 25 years (2000).
Transportation: Commute to work: 94.4% car, 0.0% public transportation, 1.2% walk, 4.4% work from home (2000); Travel time to work: 31.2% less than 15 minutes, 41.8% 15 to 30 minutes, 21.7% 30 to 45 minutes, 3.3% 45 to 60 minutes, 2.1% 60 minutes or more (2000)

CHESTER (township). Covers a land area of 35.690 square miles and a water area of 0.165 square miles. Located at 43.16° N. Lat.; 85.85° W. Long.
Population: 2,315 (2000); Race: 95.7% White, 0.4% Black, 0.0% Asian, 0.2% American Indian and Alaska Native, 5.9% Hispanic of any race, 2.4% two or more races (2000); Density: 64.9 persons per square mile (2000); Age: 31.1% under 18, 11.7% over 64 (2000); Marriage status: 25.5% never married, 62.4% now married, 5.5% widowed, 6.6% divorced (2000); Foreign born: 1.6% (2000); Ancestry (includes multiple ancestries): 28.9% German, 22.8% Dutch, 10.7% English, 9.2% Polish, 8.9% Irish (2000).
Economy: Single-family building permits issued: 7 (2001) / 5 (2000); Multi-family building permits issued: 0 (2001) / 0 (2000); Employment by occupation: 12.7% management, 13.1% professional, 12.8% services, 25.9% sales, 2.9% farming, 13.5% construction, 19.2% production (2000).
Income: Per capita income: $18,197 (2000); Median household income: $46,328 (2000); Poverty rate: 10.4% (2000).
Taxes: Total city taxes per capita: $181 (1997); City property taxes per capita: $177 (1997).
Education: High school graduation rate: 81.1% (2000); College graduation rate: 12.5% (2000).
Housing: Homeownership rate: 89.5% (2000); Median home value: $105,200 (2000); Median rent: $430 per month (2000); Median age of housing: 39 years (2000).
Transportation: Commute to work: 89.3% car, 0.0% public transportation, 4.6% walk, 5.6% work from home (2000); Travel time to work: 29.2% less than 15 minutes, 29.4% 15 to 30 minutes, 29.7% 30 to 45 minutes, 9.1% 45 to 60 minutes, 2.7% 60 minutes or more (2000)

CONKLIN (unincorporated postal area, zip code 49403). Covers a land area of 45.210 square miles and a water area of 0.206 square miles. Located at 43.12° N. Lat.; 85.85° W. Long.
History: Conklin grew up around a station on the Grand Rapids & Indiana Railroad, opened in 1886.
Population: 2,495 (2000); Race: 98.3% White, 0.1% Black, 0.3% Asian, 0.1% American Indian and Alaska Native, 3.8% Hispanic of any race, 0.4% two or more races (2000); Density: 55.2 persons per square mile (2000); Age: 30.5% under 18, 9.7% over 64 (2000); Marriage status: 23.8% never married, 66.1% now married, 4.0% widowed, 6.2% divorced (2000); Foreign born: 1.8% (2000); Ancestry (includes multiple ancestries): 37.8% German, 21.4% Dutch, 9.5% Irish, 8.6% English, 8.5% Polish (2000).
Economy: Employment by occupation: 17.1% management, 11.2% professional, 11.4% services, 25.3% sales, 2.8% farming, 11.9% construction, 20.3% production (2000).
Income: Per capita income: $18,349 (2000); Median household income: $51,103 (2000); Poverty rate: 7.4% (2000).
Education: High school graduation rate: 85.9% (2000); College graduation rate: 12.1% (2000).
Housing: Homeownership rate: 90.8% (2000); Median home value: $108,800 (2000); Median rent: $425 per month (2000); Median age of housing: 39 years (2000).
Transportation: Commute to work: 90.9% car, 0.0% public transportation, 1.9% walk, 6.0% work from home (2000); Travel time to work: 27.2% less than 15 minutes, 31.6% 15 to 30 minutes, 28.7% 30 to 45 minutes, 7.7% 45 to 60 minutes, 4.9% 60 minutes or more (2000)

COOPERSVILLE (city). Covers a land area of 4.812 square miles and a water area of 0 square miles. Located at 43.06° N. Lat.; 85.93° W. Long. Elevation is 640 feet.
History: Many of the early residents of Coopersville were of Dutch origin. After first being called Polkton, the town was renamed in 1858 for Benjamin F. Cooper, who gave the land for the railroad station. Industries in the early 1900's included a cannery, a flour mill, and a creamery.
Population: 3,910 (2000); Race: 96.4% White, 0.0% Black, 0.0% Asian, 0.0% American Indian and Alaska Native, 2.9% Hispanic of any race, 1.0% two or more races (2000); Density: 812.5 persons per square mile (2000); Age: 30.0% under 18, 10.2% over 64 (2000); Marriage status: 22.0% never married, 60.0% now married, 6.9% widowed, 11.1% divorced (2000); Foreign born: 2.1% (2000); Ancestry (includes multiple ancestries): 23.3% German, 22.0% Dutch, 9.9% Irish, 9.1% Polish, 8.8% English (2000).
Economy: Single-family building permits issued: 17 (2001) / 23 (2000); Multi-family building permits issued: 48 (2001) / 0 (2000); Employment by occupation: 9.0% management, 12.9% professional, 13.3% services, 26.8% sales, 2.3% farming, 8.9% construction, 26.7% production (2000).
Income: Per capita income: $19,241 (2000); Median household income: $48,875 (2000); Poverty rate: 7.7% (2000).
Taxes: Total city taxes per capita: $415 (1997); City property taxes per capita: $404 (1997).
Education: High school graduation rate: 81.7% (2000); College graduation rate: 16.3% (2000).

School District(s)

Coopersville Public School District (KG-12)
2000 Enrollment: 2,311 616-837-8131
Housing: Homeownership rate: 78.3% (2000); Median home value: $113,500 (2000); Median rent: $434 per month (2000); Median age of housing: 24 years (2000).
Transportation: Commute to work: 93.6% car, 0.3% public transportation, 2.5% walk, 2.5% work from home (2000); Travel time to work: 33.5% less than 15 minutes, 35.6% 15 to 30 minutes, 24.3% 30 to 45 minutes, 4.5% 45 to 60 minutes, 2.1% 60 minutes or more (2000)
Additional Information Contacts
Coopersville Chamber of Commerce 616-837-9731

CROCKERY (township). Covers a land area of 32.707 square miles and a water area of 0.659 square miles. Located at 43.08° N. Lat.; 86.08° W. Long.

Population: 3,782 (2000); Race: 94.6% White, 0.8% Black, 1.0% Asian, 0.0% American Indian and Alaska Native, 3.6% Hispanic of any race, 1.3% two or more races (2000); Density: 115.6 persons per square mile (2000); Age: 27.6% under 18, 9.8% over 64 (2000); Marriage status: 20.5% never married, 64.4% now married, 2.9% widowed, 12.2% divorced (2000); Foreign born: 3.3% (2000); Ancestry (includes multiple ancestries): 27.8% German, 21.8% Dutch, 8.3% Irish, 7.4% English, 7.2% French (except Basque) (2000).
Economy: Single-family building permits issued: 22 (2001) / 24 (2000); Multi-family building permits issued: 0 (2001) / 0 (2000); Employment by occupation: 13.2% management, 12.6% professional, 14.1% services, 22.3% sales, 0.0% farming, 11.5% construction, 26.3% production (2000).
Income: Per capita income: $19,089 (2000); Median household income: $42,399 (2000); Poverty rate: 6.3% (2000).
Taxes: Total city taxes per capita: $43 (1997); City property taxes per capita: $34 (1997).
Education: High school graduation rate: 85.2% (2000); College graduation rate: 14.6% (2000).
Housing: Homeownership rate: 84.9% (2000); Median home value: $105,100 (2000); Median rent: $417 per month (2000); Median age of housing: 32 years (2000).
Transportation: Commute to work: 92.2% car, 0.7% public transportation, 1.0% walk, 5.3% work from home (2000); Travel time to work: 18.3% less than 15 minutes, 52.1% 15 to 30 minutes, 22.5% 30 to 45 minutes, 6.1% 45 to 60 minutes, 1.1% 60 minutes or more (2000)

FERRYSBURG (city). Covers a land area of 2.974 square miles and a water area of 0.590 square miles. Located at 43.08° N. Lat.; 86.21° W. Long. Elevation is 591 feet.
Population: 3,040 (2000); Race: 97.1% White, 0.2% Black, 1.0% Asian, 0.0% American Indian and Alaska Native, 0.8% Hispanic of any race, 1.3% two or more races (2000); Density: 1,022.2 persons per square mile (2000); Age: 23.3% under 18, 13.7% over 64 (2000); Marriage status: 22.2% never married, 61.6% now married, 4.0% widowed, 12.2% divorced (2000); Foreign born: 2.3% (2000); Ancestry (includes multiple ancestries): 25.7% German, 22.6% Dutch, 16.3% English, 14.2% Irish, 7.6% Polish (2000).
Economy: Suburb of Grand Haven, eleven miles South of downtown Muskegon. Manufacturing: boilers. Single-family building permits issued: 8 (2001) / 3 (2000); Multi-family building permits issued: 9 (2001) / 10 (2000); Employment by occupation: 15.9% management, 20.8% professional, 13.7% services, 20.9% sales, 0.4% farming, 6.5% construction, 21.8% production (2000).
Income: Per capita income: $31,254 (2000); Median household income: $53,622 (2000); Poverty rate: 3.5% (2000).
Taxes: Total city taxes per capita: $372 (1997); City property taxes per capita: $352 (1997).
Education: High school graduation rate: 90.8% (2000); College graduation rate: 40.6% (2000).
Housing: Homeownership rate: 82.3% (2000); Median home value: $138,200 (2000); Median rent: $480 per month (2000); Median age of housing: 25 years (2000).
Transportation: Commute to work: 89.7% car, 1.6% public transportation, 2.3% walk, 4.9% work from home (2000); Travel time to work: 41.1% less than 15 minutes, 36.0% 15 to 30 minutes, 9.8% 30 to 45 minutes, 7.8% 45 to 60 minutes, 5.2% 60 minutes or more (2000)

GEORGETOWN (township). Covers a land area of 33.464 square miles and a water area of 0.646 square miles. Located at 42.90° N. Lat.; 85.82° W. Long.
Population: 41,658 (2000); Race: 97.3% White, 0.7% Black, 0.8% Asian, 0.1% American Indian and Alaska Native, 2.0% Hispanic of any race, 0.5% two or more races (2000); Density: 1,244.9 persons per square mile (2000); Age: 29.4% under 18, 10.4% over 64 (2000); Marriage status: 23.9% never married, 68.0% now married, 4.0% widowed, 4.0% divorced (2000); Foreign born: 2.6% (2000); Ancestry (includes multiple ancestries): 42.7% Dutch, 20.2% German, 9.1% English, 8.3% Irish, 6.0% Polish (2000).
Vital Statistics: Birth rate: 120.8 per 10,000 population (1998)
Economy: Unemployment rate: 3.1% (11/2002); Total civilian labor force: 25,312 (11/2002); Single-family building permits issued: 307 (2001) / 273 (2000); Multi-family building permits issued: 54 (2001) / 0 (2000); Employment by occupation: 14.0% management, 21.1% professional, 11.8% services, 29.2% sales, 0.9% farming, 7.4% construction, 15.5% production (2000).
Income: Per capita income: $22,323 (2000); Median household income: $58,936 (2000); Poverty rate: 4.5% (2000).
Taxes: Total city taxes per capita: $59 (2000); City property taxes per capita: $50 (2000).
Education: High school graduation rate: 91.0% (2000); College graduation rate: 28.1% (2000).
Housing: Homeownership rate: 84.1% (2000); Median home value: $137,700 (2000); Median rent: $594 per month (2000); Median age of housing: 20 years (2000).
Transportation: Commute to work: 96.1% car, 0.1% public transportation, 0.8% walk, 2.7% work from home (2000); Travel time to work: 30.5% less than 15 minutes, 44.8% 15 to 30 minutes, 19.7% 30 to 45 minutes, 2.5% 45 to 60 minutes, 2.5% 60 minutes or more (2000)

GRAND HAVEN (city). Covers a land area of 5.806 square miles and a water area of 1.595 square miles. Located at 43.05° N. Lat.; 86.22° W. Long. Elevation is 588 feet.
History: A trading post was established here in 1833, and in 1834 the New Haven Company was formed to promote the area. Grand Haven, established on Spring Lake which is connected to Lake Michigan by the Grand River, developed as a manufacturing and shipping center as well as a resort.
Population: 11,168 (2000); Race: 95.6% White, 0.6% Black, 1.1% Asian, 0.6% American Indian and Alaska Native, 1.3% Hispanic of any race, 1.6% two or more races (2000); Density: 1,923.5 persons per square mile (2000); Age: 19.9% under 18, 20.3% over 64 (2000); Marriage status: 25.1% never married, 53.1% now married, 9.4% widowed, 12.4% divorced (2000); Foreign born: 2.9% (2000); Ancestry (includes multiple ancestries): 24.1% German, 23.2% Dutch, 13.0% Irish, 12.8% English, 6.9% Polish (2000).
Vital Statistics: Birth rate: 122.7 per 10,000 population (1998)
Economy: Single-family building permits issued: 8 (2001) / 7 (2000); Multi-family building permits issued: 0 (2001) / 6 (2000); Employment by occupation: 13.0% management, 21.3% professional, 15.2% services, 24.9% sales, 0.5% farming, 5.2% construction, 20.0% production (2000).
Income: Per capita income: $22,274 (2000); Median household income: $40,322 (2000); Poverty rate: 4.5% (2000).
Taxes: Total city taxes per capita: $533 (2000); City property taxes per capita: $502 (2000).
Education: High school graduation rate: 84.5% (2000); College graduation rate: 26.9% (2000).

School District(s)

Grand Haven Area Public Schools (PK-12)
2000 Enrollment: 6,127 616-850-5015
Housing: Homeownership rate: 67.8% (2000); Median home value: $111,300 (2000); Median rent: $473 per month (2000); Median age of housing: 44 years (2000).
Hospitals: North Ottawa Community Hospital (81 beds)
Safety: Violent crime rate: 21.4 per 10,000 population; Property crime rate: 380.3 per 10,000 population (2001).
Newspapers: Grand Haven Tribune (6 x week); Grand Haven West Michigan News Review (1 x week)
Transportation: Commute to work: 91.5% car, 1.0% public transportation, 4.7% walk, 1.9% work from home (2000); Travel time to work: 60.3% less than 15 minutes, 20.7% 15 to 30 minutes, 11.8% 30 to 45 minutes, 3.8% 45 to 60 minutes, 3.4% 60 minutes or more (2000)
Additional Information Contacts
Grand Haven Chamber of Commerce 616-842-4910
West Michigan Lakeshore Association of Realtors 616-846-6240

GRAND HAVEN (township). Covers a land area of 28.641 square miles and a water area of 7.032 square miles. Located at 43.00° N. Lat.; 86.18° W. Long. Elevation is 588 feet.
History: Tri-City Historical Museum. Incorporated 1867.
Population: 13,278 (2000); Race: 97.4% White, 0.0% Black, 0.6% Asian, 0.2% American Indian and Alaska Native, 2.3% Hispanic of any race, 1.5% two or more races (2000); Density: 463.6 persons per square mile (2000); Age: 30.9% under 18, 8.4% over 64 (2000); Marriage status: 18.6% never married, 70.7% now married, 3.6% widowed, 7.1% divorced (2000); Foreign born: 2.6% (2000); Ancestry (includes multiple ancestries): 30.6% German, 25.3% Dutch, 13.1% English, 9.3% Irish, 6.8% Polish (2000).
Economy: It is a port on Lake Michigan that ships sand and gravel. Manufacturing of fabricated metal products, paper products and consumer goods. Popular resort area. Single-family building permits issued: 120 (2001) / 119 (2000); Multi-family building permits issued: 0 (2001) / 0 (2000); Employment by occupation: 17.8% management, 23.6% professional, 11.3% services, 23.5% sales, 0.1% farming, 6.5% construction, 17.1% production (2000).
Income: Per capita income: $25,025 (2000); Median household income: $62,380 (2000); Poverty rate: 2.2% (2000).

Taxes: Total city taxes per capita: $144 (2000); City property taxes per capita: $118 (2000).
Education: High school graduation rate: 91.2% (2000); College graduation rate: 33.2% (2000).
Housing: Homeownership rate: 92.2% (2000); Median home value: $160,800 (2000); Median rent: $497 per month (2000); Median age of housing: 18 years (2000).
Transportation: Commute to work: 96.6% car, 0.0% public transportation, 0.1% walk, 2.8% work from home (2000); Travel time to work: 42.9% less than 15 minutes, 32.9% 15 to 30 minutes, 14.9% 30 to 45 minutes, 6.6% 45 to 60 minutes, 2.7% 60 minutes or more (2000)

HOLLAND (city). Covers a land area of 16.568 square miles and a water area of 0.620 square miles. Located at 42.77° N. Lat.; 86.10° W. Long. Elevation is 612 feet.
History: Holland was founded by 53 members of the Society of Christians for the Holland Emigration to the United States, led by Dr. A.C. Van Raalte in 1847. More Dutch settlers followed, and in 1868 Holland was incorporated as a city. The Dutch Reformed Church founded both Hope College and the Western Theological Seminary in Holland. Industry and commerce developed here, including the Holland Furnace Company established in 1906.
Population: 35,048 (2000); Race: 78.0% White, 2.5% Black, 3.6% Asian, 0.5% American Indian and Alaska Native, 22.4% Hispanic of any race, 3.1% two or more races (2000); Density: 2,115.3 persons per square mile (2000); Age: 26.2% under 18, 13.5% over 64 (2000); Marriage status: 33.6% never married, 52.4% now married, 6.6% widowed, 7.4% divorced (2000); Foreign born: 10.7% (2000); Ancestry (includes multiple ancestries): 30.0% Dutch, 29.0% Other groups, 15.1% German, 7.5% English, 7.2% Irish (2000).
Vital Statistics: Birth rate: 202.0 per 10,000 population (1998)
Economy: Unemployment rate: 5.6% (11/2002); Total civilian labor force: 22,286 (11/2002); Single-family building permits issued: 41 (2001) / 57 (2000); Multi-family building permits issued: 15 (2001) / 7 (2000); Employment by occupation: 9.9% management, 19.1% professional, 14.7% services, 23.9% sales, 0.7% farming, 5.2% construction, 26.5% production (2000).
Income: Per capita income: $18,823 (2000); Median household income: $42,291 (2000); Poverty rate: 10.6% (2000).
Taxes: Total city taxes per capita: $390 (2000); City property taxes per capita: $382 (2000).
Education: High school graduation rate: 78.5% (2000); College graduation rate: 26.9% (2000).

School District(s)

Black River Public School (04-12)
2000 Enrollment: 292 616-895-3029
Eagle Crest Charter Academy (KG-08)
2000 Enrollment: 500 517-774-2400
Holland City School District (PK-12)
2000 Enrollment: 5,513 616-494-2000
Vanderbilt Charter Academy (KG-08)
2000 Enrollment: 362 616-895-3029
West Ottawa Public School District (KG-12)
2000 Enrollment: 7,545 616-395-2300

Four-year College(s)

Hope College (Private, Not-for-profit, Reformed Church in America)
2001 Enrollment: 2,999 616-395-7000
2001 Tuition: In-state $17,348; Out-of-state $17,348
Western Theological Seminary (Private, Not-for-profit, Reformed Church in America)
2001 Enrollment: 164 616-392-8555
Davenport University-Western Region-Holland (Private, Not-for-profit)
2001 Enrollment: 712 616-395-4600
2001 Tuition: In-state $9,540; Out-of-state $9,540

Housing: Homeownership rate: 67.1% (2000); Median home value: $107,900 (2000); Median rent: $498 per month (2000); Median age of housing: 37 years (2000).
Hospitals: Holland Community Hospital (213 beds)
Safety: Violent crime rate: 42.0 per 10,000 population; Property crime rate: 355.1 per 10,000 population (2001).
Newspapers: The Holland Sentinel (7 x week)
Transportation: Commute to work: 88.0% car, 1.1% public transportation, 7.6% walk, 2.4% work from home (2000); Travel time to work: 63.7% less than 15 minutes, 24.3% 15 to 30 minutes, 7.2% 30 to 45 minutes, 2.7% 45 to 60 minutes, 2.1% 60 minutes or more (2000); Amtrak: Service available.
Additional Information Contacts
Holland Area Convention & Visitors Bureau 616-394-0000
Holland Chamber of Commerce 616-392-2389

HOLLAND (township). Covers a land area of 27.187 square miles and a water area of 0.277 square miles. Located at 42.81° N. Lat.; 86.08° W. Long. Elevation is 612 feet.
Population: 28,911 (2000); Race: 79.4% White, 2.2% Black, 7.8% Asian, 0.7% American Indian and Alaska Native, 15.6% Hispanic of any race, 4.0% two or more races (2000); Density: 1,063.4 persons per square mile (2000); Age: 31.3% under 18, 6.9% over 64 (2000); Marriage status: 24.6% never married, 63.6% now married, 3.4% widowed, 8.5% divorced (2000); Foreign born: 11.7% (2000); Ancestry (includes multiple ancestries): 33.0% Dutch, 24.3% Other groups, 13.9% German, 7.5% Irish, 6.5% English (2000).
Economy: Unemployment rate: 4.6% (11/2002); Total civilian labor force: 14,772 (11/2002); Single-family building permits issued: 318 (2001) / 353 (2000); Multi-family building permits issued: 270 (2001) / 252 (2000); Employment by occupation: 10.7% management, 17.1% professional, 11.8% services, 21.9% sales, 1.1% farming, 7.0% construction, 30.5% production (2000).
Income: Per capita income: $19,671 (2000); Median household income: $49,458 (2000); Poverty rate: 6.3% (2000).
Taxes: Total city taxes per capita: $189 (2000); City property taxes per capita: $171 (2000).
Education: High school graduation rate: 82.4% (2000); College graduation rate: 22.7% (2000).
Housing: Homeownership rate: 71.2% (2000); Median home value: $127,700 (2000); Median rent: $549 per month (2000); Median age of housing: 15 years (2000).
Transportation: Commute to work: 95.0% car, 1.0% public transportation, 0.7% walk, 2.2% work from home (2000); Travel time to work: 53.5% less than 15 minutes, 34.4% 15 to 30 minutes, 6.7% 30 to 45 minutes, 2.8% 45 to 60 minutes, 2.5% 60 minutes or more (2000); Amtrak: Service available.

HUDSONVILLE (city). Covers a land area of 4.141 square miles and a water area of 0 square miles. Located at 42.86° N. Lat.; 85.86° W. Long. Elevation is 630 feet.
History: Hudsonville was named in 1872 for Homer E. Hudson, the first postmaster of the town that had been called South Georgetown. Another Hudson, Horace A., was the station agent when the Chicago & Western Michigan Railroad arrived here in 1874.
Population: 7,160 (2000); Race: 97.6% White, 0.7% Black, 0.4% Asian, 0.1% American Indian and Alaska Native, 2.1% Hispanic of any race, 0.8% two or more races (2000); Density: 1,729.1 persons per square mile (2000); Age: 31.1% under 18, 13.9% over 64 (2000); Marriage status: 20.4% never married, 66.5% now married, 5.5% widowed, 7.5% divorced (2000); Foreign born: 1.8% (2000); Ancestry (includes multiple ancestries): 58.2% Dutch, 15.8% German, 6.0% Irish, 4.7% English, 4.4% United States or American (2000).
Economy: Single-family building permits issued: 5 (2001) / 8 (2000); Multi-family building permits issued: 12 (2001) / 17 (2000); Employment by occupation: 11.1% management, 18.2% professional, 12.8% services, 25.0% sales, 0.4% farming, 9.6% construction, 22.8% production (2000).
Income: Per capita income: $19,286 (2000); Median household income: $46,961 (2000); Poverty rate: 4.6% (2000).
Taxes: Total city taxes per capita: $220 (1997); City property taxes per capita: $212 (1997).
Education: High school graduation rate: 86.1% (2000); College graduation rate: 21.4% (2000).

School District(s)

Hudsonville Public School District (PK-12)
2000 Enrollment: 4,636 616-669-1740

Housing: Homeownership rate: 86.6% (2000); Median home value: $118,200 (2000); Median rent: $529 per month (2000); Median age of housing: 23 years (2000).
Safety: Violent crime rate: 6.9 per 10,000 population; Property crime rate: 169.5 per 10,000 population (2001).
Transportation: Commute to work: 94.8% car, 0.0% public transportation, 1.0% walk, 3.8% work from home (2000); Travel time to work: 29.5% less than 15 minutes, 50.5% 15 to 30 minutes, 16.6% 30 to 45 minutes, 1.7% 45 to 60 minutes, 1.7% 60 minutes or more (2000)
Additional Information Contacts
Hudsonville Chamber of Commerce 616-896-9020

JAMESTOWN CHARTER (township). Covers a land area of 35.595 square miles and a water area of 0.013 square miles. Located at 42.81° N. Lat.; 85.83° W. Long. Elevation is 713 feet.
Population: 5,062 (2000); Race: 97.3% White, 0.0% Black, 1.5% Asian, 0.0% American Indian and Alaska Native, 2.3% Hispanic of any race, 0.8%

two or more races (2000); Density: 142.2 persons per square mile (2000); Age: 35.2% under 18, 6.2% over 64 (2000); Marriage status: 25.4% never married, 70.6% now married, 2.2% widowed, 1.8% divorced (2000); Foreign born: 2.3% (2000); Ancestry (includes multiple ancestries): 61.4% Dutch, 16.4% German, 6.1% English, 5.6% Other groups, 3.6% French (except Basque) (2000).
Economy: Employment by occupation: 16.3% management, 14.0% professional, 12.7% services, 22.2% sales, 2.6% farming, 9.2% construction, 23.0% production (2000).
Income: Per capita income: $21,184 (2000); Median household income: $68,689 (2000); Poverty rate: 1.1% (2000).
Taxes: Total city taxes per capita: $86 (1997); City property taxes per capita: $79 (1997).
Education: High school graduation rate: 87.0% (2000); College graduation rate: 19.8% (2000).
Housing: Homeownership rate: 95.0% (2000); Median home value: $161,800 (2000); Median rent: $448 per month (2000); Median age of housing: 25 years (2000).
Transportation: Commute to work: 92.7% car, 0.2% public transportation, 2.4% walk, 3.4% work from home (2000); Travel time to work: 27.6% less than 15 minutes, 49.8% 15 to 30 minutes, 17.6% 30 to 45 minutes, 1.7% 45 to 60 minutes, 3.4% 60 minutes or more (2000)

JENISON (CDP). Covers a land area of 5.852 square miles and a water area of 0.046 square miles. Located at 42.90° N. Lat.; 85.83° W. Long. Elevation is 608 feet.
History: Jenison grew up around a grist mill built here by Luman and Lucius Jenison in 1864.
Population: 17,211 (2000); Race: 97.7% White, 0.7% Black, 0.4% Asian, 0.0% American Indian and Alaska Native, 2.0% Hispanic of any race, 0.5% two or more races (2000); Density: 2,940.8 persons per square mile (2000); Age: 29.0% under 18, 12.7% over 64 (2000); Marriage status: 20.7% never married, 69.0% now married, 5.8% widowed, 4.6% divorced (2000); Foreign born: 2.8% (2000); Ancestry (includes multiple ancestries): 41.9% Dutch, 20.0% German, 10.0% English, 9.0% Irish, 5.7% Polish (2000).
Economy: Employment by occupation: 11.3% management, 18.5% professional, 11.2% services, 31.7% sales, 0.5% farming, 7.3% construction, 19.6% production (2000).
Income: Per capita income: $21,021 (2000); Median household income: $56,426 (2000); Poverty rate: 2.5% (2000).
Education: High school graduation rate: 89.4% (2000); College graduation rate: 23.5% (2000).

School District(s)

Jenison Public Schools (PK-12)
2000 Enrollment: 4,827 616-457-8890
Housing: Homeownership rate: 91.1% (2000); Median home value: $125,700 (2000); Median rent: $764 per month (2000); Median age of housing: 27 years (2000).
Newspapers: South Advance (1 x week); Wyoming Advance (1 x week); Walker/Westside Advance (1 x week); Sparta/Kent City Advance (1 x week); Rockford/Cedar Springs Advance (1 x week); Ottawa Advance (1 x week); Northfield Advance (1 x week); Kentwood Advance (1 x week); Grand Valley Advance (1 x week); Grand Rapids Advance (1 x week); East Grand Rapids Cadence (1 x week); Ada/Cascade/Forest Hills Advance (1 x week)
Transportation: Commute to work: 96.2% car, 0.1% public transportation, 0.5% walk, 3.0% work from home (2000); Travel time to work: 27.7% less than 15 minutes, 45.1% 15 to 30 minutes, 21.0% 30 to 45 minutes, 2.9% 45 to 60 minutes, 3.3% 60 minutes or more (2000)

MARNE (unincorporated postal area, zip code 49435). Aka Berlin. Covers a land area of 24.341 square miles and a water area of 0.012 square miles. Located at 43.03° N. Lat.; 85.83° W. Long. Elevation is 672 feet.
History: Marne began as a lumber town, but turned to agriculture when the timber was exhausted. The town, first called Berlin, was renamed during World War I.
Population: 3,615 (2000); Race: 93.6% White, 0.7% Black, 0.3% Asian, 0.5% American Indian and Alaska Native, 4.6% Hispanic of any race, 0.9% two or more races (2000); Density: 148.5 persons per square mile (2000); Age: 31.2% under 18, 10.4% over 64 (2000); Marriage status: 23.9% never married, 64.4% now married, 4.9% widowed, 6.7% divorced (2000); Foreign born: 1.6% (2000); Ancestry (includes multiple ancestries): 32.9% Dutch, 23.5% German, 11.9% Polish, 10.6% Irish, 10.1% English (2000).
Economy: Employment by occupation: 14.1% management, 11.7% professional, 7.4% services, 29.5% sales, 1.2% farming, 15.4% construction, 20.7% production (2000).
Income: Per capita income: $19,841 (2000); Median household income: $57,356 (2000); Poverty rate: 6.5% (2000).
Education: High school graduation rate: 86.7% (2000); College graduation rate: 12.4% (2000).
Housing: Homeownership rate: 92.6% (2000); Median home value: $125,900 (2000); Median rent: $555 per month (2000); Median age of housing: 34 years (2000).
Transportation: Commute to work: 94.4% car, 1.2% public transportation, 1.6% walk, 2.6% work from home (2000); Travel time to work: 28.4% less than 15 minutes, 42.9% 15 to 30 minutes, 23.8% 30 to 45 minutes, 2.3% 45 to 60 minutes, 2.6% 60 minutes or more (2000)

NUNICA (unincorporated postal area, zip code 49448). Covers a land area of 32.562 square miles and a water area of 0.084 square miles. Located at 43.09° N. Lat.; 86.07° W. Long.
Population: 3,251 (2000); Race: 95.0% White, 0.7% Black, 0.8% Asian, 0.0% American Indian and Alaska Native, 3.2% Hispanic of any race, 2.0% two or more races (2000); Density: 99.8 persons per square mile (2000); Age: 27.0% under 18, 9.2% over 64 (2000); Marriage status: 21.2% never married, 63.5% now married, 2.7% widowed, 12.6% divorced (2000); Foreign born: 2.6% (2000); Ancestry (includes multiple ancestries): 27.8% German, 21.7% Dutch, 9.5% English, 7.9% Irish, 7.3% Other groups (2000).
Economy: Employment by occupation: 12.7% management, 12.0% professional, 15.7% services, 22.1% sales, 0.0% farming, 13.3% construction, 24.2% production (2000).
Income: Per capita income: $19,883 (2000); Median household income: $46,019 (2000); Poverty rate: 4.5% (2000).
Education: High school graduation rate: 84.5% (2000); College graduation rate: 15.3% (2000).
Housing: Homeownership rate: 88.0% (2000); Median home value: $102,800 (2000); Median rent: $421 per month (2000); Median age of housing: 33 years (2000).
Transportation: Commute to work: 93.7% car, 0.4% public transportation, 1.1% walk, 4.5% work from home (2000); Travel time to work: 19.7% less than 15 minutes, 50.5% 15 to 30 minutes, 22.2% 30 to 45 minutes, 6.2% 45 to 60 minutes, 1.4% 60 minutes or more (2000)

OLIVE (township). Covers a land area of 36.203 square miles and a water area of 0.017 square miles. Located at 42.90° N. Lat.; 86.09° W. Long.
Population: 4,691 (2000); Race: 87.9% White, 1.9% Black, 1.1% Asian, 1.8% American Indian and Alaska Native, 12.9% Hispanic of any race, 0.6% two or more races (2000); Density: 129.6 persons per square mile (2000); Age: 34.0% under 18, 6.4% over 64 (2000); Marriage status: 21.6% never married, 67.8% now married, 3.9% widowed, 6.6% divorced (2000); Foreign born: 7.1% (2000); Ancestry (includes multiple ancestries): 39.2% Dutch, 17.0% Other groups, 16.4% German, 7.1% English, 6.3% Irish (2000).
Economy: Single-family building permits issued: 12 (2001) / 12 (2000); Multi-family building permits issued: 0 (2001) / 0 (2000); Employment by occupation: 10.9% management, 11.3% professional, 13.8% services, 15.4% sales, 4.5% farming, 15.1% construction, 29.0% production (2000).
Income: Per capita income: $17,023 (2000); Median household income: $48,526 (2000); Poverty rate: 7.5% (2000).
Taxes: Total city taxes per capita: $168 (1997); City property taxes per capita: $154 (1997).
Education: High school graduation rate: 78.1% (2000); College graduation rate: 8.2% (2000).
Housing: Homeownership rate: 88.8% (2000); Median home value: $138,400 (2000); Median rent: $475 per month (2000); Median age of housing: 20 years (2000).
Transportation: Commute to work: 91.5% car, 3.3% public transportation, 2.4% walk, 2.8% work from home (2000); Travel time to work: 29.8% less than 15 minutes, 51.3% 15 to 30 minutes, 13.8% 30 to 45 minutes, 3.5% 45 to 60 minutes, 1.5% 60 minutes or more (2000)

PARK (township). Covers a land area of 19.276 square miles and a water area of 2.046 square miles. Located at 42.79° N. Lat.; 86.18° W. Long.
Population: 17,579 (2000); Race: 93.7% White, 0.3% Black, 2.6% Asian, 0.2% American Indian and Alaska Native, 5.3% Hispanic of any race, 1.0% two or more races (2000); Density: 912.0 persons per square mile (2000); Age: 30.8% under 18, 7.7% over 64 (2000); Marriage status: 19.1% never married, 71.2% now married, 2.9% widowed, 6.8% divorced (2000); Foreign born: 4.5% (2000); Ancestry (includes multiple ancestries): 35.6% Dutch, 21.0% German, 11.3% English, 9.7% Irish, 9.4% Other groups (2000).
Economy: Single-family building permits issued: 140 (2001) / 120 (2000); Multi-family building permits issued: 0 (2001) / 0 (2000); Employment by

occupation: 20.8% management, 21.3% professional, 11.7% services, 22.4% sales, 0.2% farming, 6.5% construction, 17.0% production (2000).
Income: Per capita income: $28,777 (2000); Median household income: $65,328 (2000); Poverty rate: 2.6% (2000).
Taxes: Total city taxes per capita: $101 (2000); City property taxes per capita: $91 (2000).
Education: High school graduation rate: 92.7% (2000); College graduation rate: 39.7% (2000).
Housing: Homeownership rate: 90.1% (2000); Median home value: $162,200 (2000); Median rent: $540 per month (2000); Median age of housing: 22 years (2000).
Transportation: Commute to work: 95.7% car, 0.0% public transportation, 0.3% walk, 3.6% work from home (2000); Travel time to work: 36.4% less than 15 minutes, 48.1% 15 to 30 minutes, 7.4% 30 to 45 minutes, 5.6% 45 to 60 minutes, 2.5% 60 minutes or more (2000)

POLKTON (township). Covers a land area of 39.237 square miles and a water area of 0.422 square miles. Located at 43.07° N. Lat.; 85.97° W. Long.
Population: 2,335 (2000); Race: 96.1% White, 0.3% Black, 0.0% Asian, 0.4% American Indian and Alaska Native, 5.4% Hispanic of any race, 1.2% two or more races (2000); Density: 59.5 persons per square mile (2000); Age: 28.8% under 18, 10.6% over 64 (2000); Marriage status: 23.3% never married, 68.7% now married, 2.2% widowed, 5.8% divorced (2000); Foreign born: 3.8% (2000); Ancestry (includes multiple ancestries): 39.0% Dutch, 21.9% German, 10.4% English, 6.6% Irish, 6.5% Other groups (2000).
Economy: Single-family building permits issued: 21 (2001) / 13 (2000); Multi-family building permits issued: 0 (2001) / 0 (2000); Employment by occupation: 12.5% management, 16.7% professional, 10.8% services, 22.3% sales, 3.5% farming, 12.1% construction, 22.1% production (2000).
Income: Per capita income: $22,868 (2000); Median household income: $53,929 (2000); Poverty rate: 5.4% (2000).
Taxes: Total city taxes per capita: $59 (1997); City property taxes per capita: $57 (1997).
Education: High school graduation rate: 83.6% (2000); College graduation rate: 17.9% (2000).
Housing: Homeownership rate: 88.3% (2000); Median home value: $126,900 (2000); Median rent: $500 per month (2000); Median age of housing: 34 years (2000).
Transportation: Commute to work: 91.0% car, 1.0% public transportation, 2.2% walk, 4.8% work from home (2000); Travel time to work: 32.7% less than 15 minutes, 31.8% 15 to 30 minutes, 27.9% 30 to 45 minutes, 4.3% 45 to 60 minutes, 3.3% 60 minutes or more (2000)

PORT SHELDON (township). Covers a land area of 22.357 square miles and a water area of 0.292 square miles. Located at 42.90° N. Lat.; 86.17° W. Long.
Population: 4,503 (2000); Race: 94.5% White, 0.1% Black, 1.5% Asian, 0.0% American Indian and Alaska Native, 5.5% Hispanic of any race, 3.3% two or more races (2000); Density: 201.4 persons per square mile (2000); Age: 28.0% under 18, 7.1% over 64 (2000); Marriage status: 15.3% never married, 72.9% now married, 2.2% widowed, 9.6% divorced (2000); Foreign born: 3.3% (2000); Ancestry (includes multiple ancestries): 35.7% Dutch, 19.6% German, 11.2% Other groups, 8.3% English, 8.1% Irish (2000).
Economy: Single-family building permits issued: 32 (2001) / 30 (2000); Multi-family building permits issued: 0 (2001) / 0 (2000); Employment by occupation: 14.4% management, 15.4% professional, 12.9% services, 24.8% sales, 0.0% farming, 7.6% construction, 24.9% production (2000).
Income: Per capita income: $26,854 (2000); Median household income: $63,604 (2000); Poverty rate: 1.8% (2000).
Taxes: Total city taxes per capita: $151 (2000); City property taxes per capita: $135 (2000).
Education: High school graduation rate: 87.8% (2000); College graduation rate: 29.2% (2000).
Housing: Homeownership rate: 94.4% (2000); Median home value: $192,100 (2000); Median rent: $675 per month (2000); Median age of housing: 17 years (2000).
Transportation: Commute to work: 94.7% car, 0.0% public transportation, 0.8% walk, 3.9% work from home (2000); Travel time to work: 18.5% less than 15 minutes, 58.1% 15 to 30 minutes, 13.5% 30 to 45 minutes, 4.7% 45 to 60 minutes, 5.2% 60 minutes or more (2000)

ROBINSON (township). Covers a land area of 38.615 square miles and a water area of 0.830 square miles. Located at 42.99° N. Lat.; 86.08° W. Long. Elevation is 628 feet.
History: Robinson was settled by the four Robinson brothers (Ira, John, Lucas, and Rodney) in 1835.
Population: 5,588 (2000); Race: 92.6% White, 0.2% Black, 3.0% Asian, 0.5% American Indian and Alaska Native, 3.9% Hispanic of any race, 1.3% two or more races (2000); Density: 144.7 persons per square mile (2000); Age: 28.6% under 18, 4.3% over 64 (2000); Marriage status: 15.9% never married, 72.7% now married, 4.6% widowed, 6.7% divorced (2000); Foreign born: 3.1% (2000); Ancestry (includes multiple ancestries): 26.4% Dutch, 25.4% German, 9.5% Other groups, 8.6% English, 8.0% United States or American (2000).
Economy: Single-family building permits issued: 64 (2001) / 59 (2000); Multi-family building permits issued: 0 (2001) / 0 (2000); Employment by occupation: 10.1% management, 14.6% professional, 14.4% services, 18.6% sales, 0.8% farming, 12.1% construction, 29.6% production (2000).
Income: Per capita income: $19,603 (2000); Median household income: $57,110 (2000); Poverty rate: 4.2% (2000).
Taxes: Total city taxes per capita: $58 (1997); City property taxes per capita: $44 (1997).
Education: High school graduation rate: 84.6% (2000); College graduation rate: 16.1% (2000).
Housing: Homeownership rate: 92.5% (2000); Median home value: $127,000 (2000); Median rent: $460 per month (2000); Median age of housing: 17 years (2000).
Transportation: Commute to work: 95.7% car, 0.0% public transportation, 0.0% walk, 3.5% work from home (2000); Travel time to work: 16.4% less than 15 minutes, 46.1% 15 to 30 minutes, 25.1% 30 to 45 minutes, 8.4% 45 to 60 minutes, 4.1% 60 minutes or more (2000)

SPRING LAKE (village). Covers a land area of 1.060 square miles and a water area of 0.056 square miles. Located at 43.07° N. Lat.; 86.19° W. Long. Elevation is 594 feet.
History: Spring Lake changed from a milling center, established in 1837 as Hopkins Mill, to a shipping point for fruit. Mineral springs here were popular from 1870 to 1900, attracting visitors seeking cures. The town continued as a resort center.
Population: 2,514 (2000); Race: 98.5% White, 0.0% Black, 0.0% Asian, 0.0% American Indian and Alaska Native, 2.6% Hispanic of any race, 0.5% two or more races (2000); Density: 2,372.4 persons per square mile (2000); Age: 19.0% under 18, 26.8% over 64 (2000); Marriage status: 21.0% never married, 58.5% now married, 11.8% widowed, 8.7% divorced (2000); Foreign born: 3.9% (2000); Ancestry (includes multiple ancestries): 31.5% Dutch, 22.8% German, 11.0% Irish, 10.3% English, 5.0% Italian (2000).
Economy: Single-family building permits issued: 3 (2001) / 0 (2000); Multi-family building permits issued: 0 (2001) / 0 (2000); Employment by occupation: 14.9% management, 24.1% professional, 12.4% services, 24.6% sales, 0.8% farming, 5.5% construction, 17.7% production (2000).
Income: Per capita income: $26,372 (2000); Median household income: $37,889 (2000); Poverty rate: 6.1% (2000).
Taxes: Total city taxes per capita: $381 (1997); City property taxes per capita: $364 (1997).
Education: High school graduation rate: 89.0% (2000); College graduation rate: 31.5% (2000).

School District(s)

Spring Lake Public Schools (PK-12)
2000 Enrollment: 2,121 616-847-7919
Walden Green Day School (KG-09)
2000 Enrollment: 105 517-774-2100
West Mi Academy of Arts & Academ (KG-08)
2000 Enrollment: 286 616-895-3029

Housing: Homeownership rate: 71.1% (2000); Median home value: $106,800 (2000); Median rent: $385 per month (2000); Median age of housing: 43 years (2000).
Transportation: Commute to work: 94.0% car, 1.4% public transportation, 1.8% walk, 2.8% work from home (2000); Travel time to work: 41.2% less than 15 minutes, 31.0% 15 to 30 minutes, 17.9% 30 to 45 minutes, 6.9% 45 to 60 minutes, 3.0% 60 minutes or more (2000)

SPRING LAKE (township). Covers a land area of 16.532 square miles and a water area of 3.415 square miles. Located at 43.08° N. Lat.; 86.18° W. Long. Elevation is 594 feet.
History: Native American mounds nearby. Incorporated 1869.
Population: 13,140 (2000); Race: 97.6% White, 0.0% Black, 0.5% Asian, 0.0% American Indian and Alaska Native, 2.6% Hispanic of any race, 0.9% two or more races (2000); Density: 794.8 persons per square mile (2000); Age: 25.4% under 18, 14.5% over 64 (2000); Marriage status: 18.9% never married, 66.9% now married, 6.1% widowed, 8.2% divorced (2000); Foreign born: 2.4% (2000); Ancestry (includes multiple ancestries): 22.7% German,

22.2% Dutch, 15.0% English, 11.5% Irish, 5.9% United States or American (2000).
Economy: Resort and shipping point for orchard (apples) and farm area (poultry). Manufacturing: furniture, marine instruments, display cases, metal products. Single-family building permits issued: 109 (2001) / 77 (2000); Multi-family building permits issued: 108 (2001) / 118 (2000); Employment by occupation: 18.3% management, 24.4% professional, 13.5% services, 22.8% sales, 0.2% farming, 5.8% construction, 15.0% production (2000).
Income: Per capita income: $27,548 (2000); Median household income: $50,648 (2000); Poverty rate: 4.1% (2000).
Taxes: Total city taxes per capita: $95 (2000); City property taxes per capita: $73 (2000).
Education: High school graduation rate: 92.3% (2000); College graduation rate: 35.7% (2000).
Housing: Homeownership rate: 77.5% (2000); Median home value: $143,200 (2000); Median rent: $516 per month (2000); Median age of housing: 23 years (2000).
Transportation: Commute to work: 94.3% car, 0.5% public transportation, 1.0% walk, 3.8% work from home (2000); Travel time to work: 32.3% less than 15 minutes, 40.8% 15 to 30 minutes, 16.8% 30 to 45 minutes, 6.8% 45 to 60 minutes, 3.3% 60 minutes or more (2000)

TALLMADGE (township). Covers a land area of 32.418 square miles and a water area of 0.582 square miles. Located at 42.99° N. Lat.; 85.82° W. Long.
Population: 6,881 (2000); Race: 98.1% White, 0.7% Black, 0.5% Asian, 0.1% American Indian and Alaska Native, 0.4% Hispanic of any race, 0.5% two or more races (2000); Density: 212.3 persons per square mile (2000); Age: 29.4% under 18, 9.4% over 64 (2000); Marriage status: 23.1% never married, 66.8% now married, 3.3% widowed, 6.9% divorced (2000); Foreign born: 1.4% (2000); Ancestry (includes multiple ancestries): 35.0% Dutch, 21.7% German, 13.0% Polish, 13.0% Irish, 9.6% English (2000).
Economy: Single-family building permits issued: 41 (2001) / 29 (2000); Multi-family building permits issued: 0 (2001) / 0 (2000); Employment by occupation: 15.5% management, 14.1% professional, 9.5% services, 28.0% sales, 0.0% farming, 12.0% construction, 20.9% production (2000).
Income: Per capita income: $23,957 (2000); Median household income: $59,205 (2000); Poverty rate: 5.0% (2000).
Taxes: Total city taxes per capita: $29 (1997); City property taxes per capita: $24 (1997).
Education: High school graduation rate: 88.2% (2000); College graduation rate: 18.3% (2000).
Housing: Homeownership rate: 91.6% (2000); Median home value: $139,000 (2000); Median rent: $517 per month (2000); Median age of housing: 25 years (2000).
Transportation: Commute to work: 92.8% car, 1.5% public transportation, 1.3% walk, 4.4% work from home (2000); Travel time to work: 27.8% less than 15 minutes, 46.6% 15 to 30 minutes, 21.6% 30 to 45 minutes, 2.4% 45 to 60 minutes, 1.6% 60 minutes or more (2000)

WEST OLIVE (unincorporated postal area, zip code 49460). Covers a land area of 51.660 square miles and a water area of 0.062 square miles. Located at 42.93° N. Lat.; 86.14° W. Long.
Population: 7,697 (2000); Race: 93.4% White, 0.7% Black, 2.4% Asian, 0.1% American Indian and Alaska Native, 9.4% Hispanic of any race, 1.6% two or more races (2000); Density: 149.0 persons per square mile (2000); Age: 27.7% under 18, 8.1% over 64 (2000); Marriage status: 15.7% never married, 69.7% now married, 5.5% widowed, 9.1% divorced (2000); Foreign born: 4.6% (2000); Ancestry (includes multiple ancestries): 29.9% Dutch, 17.8% German, 14.7% Other groups, 9.2% English, 6.3% Irish (2000).
Economy: Employment by occupation: 10.7% management, 13.9% professional, 12.6% services, 20.2% sales, 0.2% farming, 13.0% construction, 29.4% production (2000).
Income: Per capita income: $20,967 (2000); Median household income: $54,503 (2000); Poverty rate: 5.0% (2000).
Education: High school graduation rate: 80.7% (2000); College graduation rate: 18.2% (2000).
Housing: Homeownership rate: 92.6% (2000); Median home value: $154,100 (2000); Median rent: $474 per month (2000); Median age of housing: 14 years (2000).
Transportation: Commute to work: 96.0% car, 0.0% public transportation, 0.4% walk, 2.8% work from home (2000); Travel time to work: 15.0% less than 15 minutes, 53.9% 15 to 30 minutes, 23.7% 30 to 45 minutes, 4.1% 45 to 60 minutes, 3.3% 60 minutes or more (2000)

WRIGHT (township). Covers a land area of 36.168 square miles and a water area of 0.138 square miles. Located at 43.06° N. Lat.; 85.83° W. Long. Elevation is 870 feet.
Population: 3,286 (2000); Race: 93.5% White, 0.2% Black, 0.9% Asian, 0.9% American Indian and Alaska Native, 4.5% Hispanic of any race, 0.3% two or more races (2000); Density: 90.9 persons per square mile (2000); Age: 29.0% under 18, 11.5% over 64 (2000); Marriage status: 22.0% never married, 66.3% now married, 5.1% widowed, 6.6% divorced (2000); Foreign born: 1.5% (2000); Ancestry (includes multiple ancestries): 29.3% German, 22.1% Dutch, 11.0% English, 9.5% Polish, 8.8% Irish (2000).
Economy: Single-family building permits issued: 13 (2001) / 18 (2000); Multi-family building permits issued: 0 (2001) / 0 (2000); Employment by occupation: 11.9% management, 12.5% professional, 11.4% services, 24.5% sales, 1.9% farming, 13.4% construction, 24.5% production (2000).
Income: Per capita income: $18,183 (2000); Median household income: $51,023 (2000); Poverty rate: 4.2% (2000).
Taxes: Total city taxes per capita: $86 (1997); City property taxes per capita: $85 (1997).
Education: High school graduation rate: 84.9% (2000); College graduation rate: 10.3% (2000).
Housing: Homeownership rate: 91.7% (2000); Median home value: $118,300 (2000); Median rent: $402 per month (2000); Median age of housing: 41 years (2000).
Transportation: Commute to work: 93.5% car, 0.5% public transportation, 1.9% walk, 3.0% work from home (2000); Travel time to work: 29.8% less than 15 minutes, 35.2% 15 to 30 minutes, 26.5% 30 to 45 minutes, 1.8% 45 to 60 minutes, 6.6% 60 minutes or more (2000)

ZEELAND (city). Covers a land area of 3.011 square miles and a water area of 0.008 square miles. Located at 42.81° N. Lat.; 86.01° W. Long. Elevation is 646 feet.
History: The site of Zeeland was purchased in 1847 by Johannes Vander Luyster, and named for the Netherlands province of Zeeland, the former home of Vander Luyster and his colony of Dutch immigrants. Zeeland was incorporated in 1904, and became the center of a baby chick industry.
Population: 5,805 (2000); Race: 95.2% White, 0.2% Black, 0.9% Asian, 0.3% American Indian and Alaska Native, 4.5% Hispanic of any race, 1.7% two or more races (2000); Density: 1,927.7 persons per square mile (2000); Age: 27.8% under 18, 22.3% over 64 (2000); Marriage status: 21.3% never married, 60.3% now married, 12.5% widowed, 5.9% divorced (2000); Foreign born: 3.2% (2000); Ancestry (includes multiple ancestries): 58.6% Dutch, 18.2% German, 10.0% Other groups, 5.3% English, 5.2% Irish (2000).
Economy: Single-family building permits issued: 102 (2001) / 6 (2000); Multi-family building permits issued: 0 (2001) / 12 (2000); Employment by occupation: 9.7% management, 17.4% professional, 14.3% services, 26.7% sales, 0.0% farming, 7.2% construction, 24.6% production (2000).
Income: Per capita income: $20,801 (2000); Median household income: $45,611 (2000); Poverty rate: 4.6% (2000).
Taxes: Total city taxes per capita: $663 (2000); City property taxes per capita: $650 (2000).
Education: High school graduation rate: 81.8% (2000); College graduation rate: 22.0% (2000).

School District(s)

Zeeland Public Schools (KG-12)
2000 Enrollment: 4,753 616-748-3000
Housing: Homeownership rate: 76.6% (2000); Median home value: $116,900 (2000); Median rent: $526 per month (2000); Median age of housing: 41 years (2000).
Hospitals: Zeeland Community Hospital (57 beds)
Safety: Violent crime rate: 3.4 per 10,000 population; Property crime rate: 20.6 per 10,000 population (2001).
Newspapers: Zeeland Record (1 x week)
Transportation: Commute to work: 90.6% car, 2.1% public transportation, 2.7% walk, 4.3% work from home (2000); Travel time to work: 52.3% less than 15 minutes, 35.2% 15 to 30 minutes, 10.2% 30 to 45 minutes, 1.0% 45 to 60 minutes, 1.2% 60 minutes or more (2000)
Additional Information Contacts
Zeeland Chamber of Commerce. 616-772-2494

ZEELAND CHARTER (township). Covers a land area of 34.432 square miles and a water area of 0.023 square miles. Located at 42.81° N. Lat.; 85.97° W. Long. Elevation is 646 feet.
History: Located in Dutch heritage area, Dutch village to northwest. Settled 1847 by Dutch; Incorporated as village 1875, as city 1907.

Population: 7,613 (2000); Race: 90.3% White, 0.2% Black, 2.1% Asian, 0.2% American Indian and Alaska Native, 7.9% Hispanic of any race, 1.8% two or more races (2000); Density: 221.1 persons per square mile (2000); Age: 34.7% under 18, 8.0% over 64 (2000); Marriage status: 21.8% never married, 70.0% now married, 2.4% widowed, 5.8% divorced (2000); Foreign born: 3.5% (2000); Ancestry (includes multiple ancestries): 52.0% Dutch, 14.4% Other groups, 13.2% German, 6.9% United States or American, 5.3% Irish (2000).
Economy: In farm area. Livestock, fruit, grain, corn, hay and dairy products. Major poultry area. Manufacturing includes meat and fish processing, infant formulas, garment hangers, metal stampings, window frames, office furniture, plastics, metal and floor clocks, chemicals and powdered metal parts. Employment by occupation: 11.1% management, 13.0% professional, 10.8% services, 25.0% sales, 2.0% farming, 10.3% construction, 27.8% production (2000).
Income: Per capita income: $19,295 (2000); Median household income: $52,079 (2000); Poverty rate: 6.3% (2000).
Taxes: Total city taxes per capita: $208 (1997); City property taxes per capita: $191 (1997).
Education: High school graduation rate: 83.8% (2000); College graduation rate: 18.8% (2000).
Housing: Homeownership rate: 94.9% (2000); Median home value: $151,800 (2000); Median rent: $524 per month (2000); Median age of housing: 12 years (2000).
Transportation: Commute to work: 96.2% car, 0.0% public transportation, 0.3% walk, 3.0% work from home (2000); Travel time to work: 46.3% less than 15 minutes, 42.3% 15 to 30 minutes, 7.9% 30 to 45 minutes, 2.2% 45 to 60 minutes, 1.3% 60 minutes or more (2000)

Presque Isle County

Located in northeastern Michigan; bounded on the northeast by Lake Huron; drained by the Black, Rainy, Ocqueoc, and North Branch of the Thunder Bay Rivers. Covers a land area of 660.10 square miles, a water area of 1,912.70 square miles, and is located in the Eastern Time Zone. The county government was organized in 1840. County seat is Rogers City.

Weather Station: Onaway State Park Elevation: 688 feet

	Jan	Feb	Mar	Apr	May	Jun	Jul	Aug	Sep	Oct	Nov	Dec
High	27	31	40	54	69	77	82	79	71	59	44	33
Low	10	10	18	31	42	51	57	55	48	39	29	19
Precip	1.9	1.3	2.1	2.5	2.8	2.7	3.3	3.3	3.6	2.8	2.3	2.1
Snow	25.4	16.4	15.0	5.0	0.2	0.0	0.0	0.0	0.0	0.3	10.0	20.6

High and Low temperatures in degrees Fahrenheit; Precipitation and Snow in inches

Population: 14,411 (2000); Race: 98.3% White, 0.1% Black, 0.0% Asian, 0.6% American Indian and Alaska Native, 0.4% Hispanic of any race, 0.8% two or more races (2000); Density: 21.8 persons per square mile (2000); Age: 20.9% under 18, 22.5% over 64 (2000).
Religion: Five largest groups: 38.0% Catholic Church, 14.2% Lutheran Church—Missouri Synod, 2.5% Evangelical Lutheran Church in America, 2.2% The United Methodist Church, 1.8% Presbyterian Church (U.S.A.) (2000).
Economy: Unemployment rate: 8.0% (11/2002); Total civilian labor force: 6,226 (11/2002); Leading industries: 25.3% retail trade; 9.6% health care and social assistance; 8.5% administration, support, waste management, remediation services (2000); Companies that employ more than 1,000 persons: 0 (2000); Companies that employ more than 100 persons: 6 (2000); Farms: 296 totaling 82,466 acres (1997); Minority business ownership rate: 0.0% (1997); Women business ownership rate: 18.1% (1997); Retail sales per capita: $8,528 (1997). Single-family building permits issued: 125 (2001) / 134 (2000); Multi-family building permits issued: 0 (2001) / 0 (2000).
Income: Per capita income: $17,363 (2000); Median household income: $31,656 (2000); Poverty rate: 10.3% (2000); Bankruptcy rate: 2.66% (2001).
Taxes: Total county taxes per capita: $136 (1997); County property taxes per capita: $129 (1997).
Education: High school graduation rate: 77.0% (2000); College graduation rate: 11.5% (2000).
Housing: Homeownership rate: 85.5% (2000); Median home value: $77,800 (2000); Median rent: $288 per month (2000); Median age of housing: 32 years (2000).
Health: Birth rate: 93.7 per 10,000 population (1998); Age adjusted death rate: 77.2 per 10,000 population (1999); Age adjusted cancer mortality rate: 184.8 deaths per 100,000 population (1999). Number of physicians: 3.5 per 10,000 population (1999); Number of hospital beds: 11.8 per 10,000 population (1999).
Elections: 2000 Presidential election results: 45.8% Gore, 51.7% Bush, 1.9% Nader, 0.0% Buchanan
National and State Parks: Onaway State Park; P H Hoeft State Park
Additional Information Contacts
Presque Isle County Government Offices 517-734-3288
Onaway Chamber of Commerce 989-733-2874
Presque Isle County Tourism 989-734-2577
Rogers City Chamber of Commerce 989-734-2535

Presque Isle County Communities

ALLIS (township). Covers a land area of 64.547 square miles and a water area of 1.417 square miles. Located at 45.26° N. Lat.; 84.19° W. Long.
Population: 1,035 (2000); Race: 96.5% White, 0.0% Black, 0.0% Asian, 2.2% American Indian and Alaska Native, 0.9% Hispanic of any race, 1.3% two or more races (2000); Density: 16.0 persons per square mile (2000); Age: 23.6% under 18, 14.4% over 64 (2000); Marriage status: 19.4% never married, 65.4% now married, 7.3% widowed, 7.9% divorced (2000); Foreign born: 0.0% (2000); Ancestry (includes multiple ancestries): 23.3% German, 15.7% English, 10.8% United States or American, 10.0% Irish, 8.3% French (except Basque) (2000).
Economy: Employment by occupation: 10.3% management, 8.9% professional, 21.6% services, 18.8% sales, 1.0% farming, 15.4% construction, 24.0% production (2000).
Income: Per capita income: $14,419 (2000); Median household income: $31,477 (2000); Poverty rate: 12.0% (2000).
Taxes: Total city taxes per capita: $28 (2000); City property taxes per capita: $28 (2000).
Education: High school graduation rate: 76.8% (2000); College graduation rate: 5.6% (2000).
Housing: Homeownership rate: 86.8% (2000); Median home value: $59,100 (2000); Median rent: $313 per month (2000); Median age of housing: 29 years (2000).
Transportation: Commute to work: 92.8% car, 0.0% public transportation, 0.5% walk, 5.7% work from home (2000); Travel time to work: 44.6% less than 15 minutes, 21.0% 15 to 30 minutes, 12.3% 30 to 45 minutes, 8.1% 45 to 60 minutes, 13.9% 60 minutes or more (2000)

BEARINGER (township). Covers a land area of 61.474 square miles and a water area of 2.107 square miles. Located at 45.53° N. Lat.; 84.20° W. Long.
Population: 329 (2000); Race: 98.2% White, 0.0% Black, 0.0% Asian, 0.3% American Indian and Alaska Native, 2.3% Hispanic of any race, 1.5% two or more races (2000); Density: 5.4 persons per square mile (2000); Age: 13.2% under 18, 34.3% over 64 (2000); Marriage status: 12.5% never married, 75.4% now married, 6.6% widowed, 5.6% divorced (2000); Foreign born: 2.9% (2000); Ancestry (includes multiple ancestries): 29.6% German, 14.4% English, 12.3% Irish, 9.7% Polish, 8.8% French (except Basque) (2000).
Economy: Employment by occupation: 13.2% management, 12.3% professional, 18.9% services, 24.5% sales, 0.0% farming, 16.0% construction, 15.1% production (2000).
Income: Per capita income: $29,780 (2000); Median household income: $35,962 (2000); Poverty rate: 10.9% (2000).
Taxes: Total city taxes per capita: $171 (1997); City property taxes per capita: $171 (1997).
Education: High school graduation rate: 77.8% (2000); College graduation rate: 15.8% (2000).
Housing: Homeownership rate: 91.7% (2000); Median home value: $96,900 (2000); Median rent: $400 per month (2000); Median age of housing: 27 years (2000).
Transportation: Commute to work: 93.2% car, 0.0% public transportation, 0.0% walk, 6.8% work from home (2000); Travel time to work: 32.3% less than 15 minutes, 25.0% 15 to 30 minutes, 19.8% 30 to 45 minutes, 9.4% 45 to 60 minutes, 13.5% 60 minutes or more (2000)

BELKNAP (township). Covers a land area of 35.807 square miles and a water area of 0.016 square miles. Located at 45.34° N. Lat.; 83.81° W. Long. Elevation is 824 feet.
Population: 854 (2000); Race: 98.8% White, 0.0% Black, 0.0% Asian, 1.0% American Indian and Alaska Native, 0.5% Hispanic of any race, 0.2% two or more races (2000); Density: 23.9 persons per square mile (2000); Age: 21.2% under 18, 21.6% over 64 (2000); Marriage status: 22.1% never married, 62.0% now married, 9.1% widowed, 6.8% divorced (2000); Foreign born: 0.5% (2000); Ancestry (includes multiple ancestries): 59.1% German, 31.5% Polish, 5.7% English, 3.6% Irish, 3.3% French (except Basque) (2000).

Economy: Employment by occupation: 13.9% management, 17.8% professional, 11.9% services, 18.4% sales, 2.8% farming, 12.7% construction, 22.4% production (2000).
Income: Per capita income: $14,409 (2000); Median household income: $31,875 (2000); Poverty rate: 7.7% (2000).
Taxes: Total city taxes per capita: $15 (1997); City property taxes per capita: $15 (1997).
Education: High school graduation rate: 70.8% (2000); College graduation rate: 6.1% (2000).
Housing: Homeownership rate: 92.5% (2000); Median home value: $67,200 (2000); Median rent: $250 per month (2000); Median age of housing: 39 years (2000).
Transportation: Commute to work: 86.0% car, 0.0% public transportation, 3.4% walk, 10.6% work from home (2000); Travel time to work: 48.4% less than 15 minutes, 32.7% 15 to 30 minutes, 12.5% 30 to 45 minutes, 4.2% 45 to 60 minutes, 2.2% 60 minutes or more (2000)

BISMARCK (township). Covers a land area of 67.639 square miles and a water area of 2.233 square miles. Located at 45.29° N. Lat.; 83.96° W. Long.
Population: 408 (2000); Race: 98.7% White, 0.0% Black, 0.8% Asian, 0.0% American Indian and Alaska Native, 0.0% Hispanic of any race, 0.5% two or more races (2000); Density: 6.0 persons per square mile (2000); Age: 16.9% under 18, 26.5% over 64 (2000); Marriage status: 14.7% never married, 69.4% now married, 8.6% widowed, 7.3% divorced (2000); Foreign born: 1.9% (2000); Ancestry (includes multiple ancestries): 49.1% German, 17.7% Polish, 10.7% English, 9.4% Irish, 6.2% Other groups (2000).
Economy: Employment by occupation: 8.9% management, 10.6% professional, 17.9% services, 19.5% sales, 4.9% farming, 15.4% construction, 22.8% production (2000).
Income: Per capita income: $16,713 (2000); Median household income: $31,477 (2000); Poverty rate: 8.6% (2000).
Taxes: Total city taxes per capita: $56 (1997); City property taxes per capita: $56 (1997).
Education: High school graduation rate: 74.3% (2000); College graduation rate: 7.9% (2000).
Housing: Homeownership rate: 89.0% (2000); Median home value: $71,300 (2000); Median rent: $308 per month (2000); Median age of housing: 29 years (2000).
Transportation: Commute to work: 85.0% car, 0.0% public transportation, 1.7% walk, 13.3% work from home (2000); Travel time to work: 31.7% less than 15 minutes, 52.9% 15 to 30 minutes, 6.7% 30 to 45 minutes, 0.0% 45 to 60 minutes, 8.7% 60 minutes or more (2000)

CASE (township). Covers a land area of 67.354 square miles and a water area of 0.891 square miles. Located at 45.31° N. Lat.; 84.06° W. Long.
History: Case Township was named for Charles E. Case, an early resident.
Population: 942 (2000); Race: 98.6% White, 0.0% Black, 0.0% Asian, 0.0% American Indian and Alaska Native, 0.0% Hispanic of any race, 1.4% two or more races (2000); Density: 14.0 persons per square mile (2000); Age: 23.5% under 18, 18.5% over 64 (2000); Marriage status: 17.7% never married, 59.6% now married, 9.9% widowed, 12.8% divorced (2000); Foreign born: 0.4% (2000); Ancestry (includes multiple ancestries): 25.9% German, 17.5% Irish, 13.1% English, 9.1% French (except Basque), 9.0% Polish (2000).
Economy: Employment by occupation: 10.9% management, 7.8% professional, 16.4% services, 24.4% sales, 0.0% farming, 18.7% construction, 21.8% production (2000).
Income: Per capita income: $15,466 (2000); Median household income: $30,188 (2000); Poverty rate: 14.1% (2000).
Taxes: Total city taxes per capita: $44 (1997); City property taxes per capita: $44 (1997).
Education: High school graduation rate: 73.4% (2000); College graduation rate: 7.2% (2000).
Housing: Homeownership rate: 86.5% (2000); Median home value: $69,600 (2000); Median rent: $302 per month (2000); Median age of housing: 27 years (2000).
Transportation: Commute to work: 92.4% car, 0.9% public transportation, 0.6% walk, 5.9% work from home (2000); Travel time to work: 31.6% less than 15 minutes, 26.9% 15 to 30 minutes, 11.3% 30 to 45 minutes, 6.6% 45 to 60 minutes, 23.8% 60 minutes or more (2000)

HAWKS (unincorporated postal area, zip code 49743). Aka La Rocque. Covers a land area of 86.250 square miles and a water area of 1.389 square miles. Located at 45.28° N. Lat.; 83.93° W. Long. Elevation is 842 feet.
History: Hawks was established in 1895 as a station on the Detroit & Mackinaw Railroad, and named for James Dudley Hawks, president of the railroad company.
Population: 860 (2000); Race: 98.7% White, 0.0% Black, 0.4% Asian, 0.7% American Indian and Alaska Native, 0.2% Hispanic of any race, 0.2% two or more races (2000); Density: 10.0 persons per square mile (2000); Age: 21.8% under 18, 22.5% over 64 (2000); Marriage status: 19.8% never married, 63.9% now married, 10.9% widowed, 5.4% divorced (2000); Foreign born: 1.3% (2000); Ancestry (includes multiple ancestries): 46.2% German, 36.2% Polish, 7.0% English, 5.2% French (except Basque), 5.2% United States or American (2000).
Economy: Employment by occupation: 12.1% management, 16.4% professional, 12.1% services, 20.3% sales, 3.6% farming, 14.2% construction, 21.2% production (2000).
Income: Per capita income: $15,543 (2000); Median household income: $32,102 (2000); Poverty rate: 8.5% (2000).
Education: High school graduation rate: 70.3% (2000); College graduation rate: 6.4% (2000).
Housing: Homeownership rate: 93.7% (2000); Median home value: $74,200 (2000); Median rent: $283 per month (2000); Median age of housing: 32 years (2000).
Transportation: Commute to work: 86.5% car, 0.0% public transportation, 1.5% walk, 12.0% work from home (2000); Travel time to work: 31.4% less than 15 minutes, 44.3% 15 to 30 minutes, 13.2% 30 to 45 minutes, 6.6% 45 to 60 minutes, 4.5% 60 minutes or more (2000)

KRAKOW (township). Covers a land area of 55.804 square miles and a water area of 4.969 square miles. Located at 45.27° N. Lat.; 83.55° W. Long.
Population: 622 (2000); Race: 99.2% White, 0.0% Black, 0.0% Asian, 0.5% American Indian and Alaska Native, 0.0% Hispanic of any race, 0.3% two or more races (2000); Density: 11.1 persons per square mile (2000); Age: 16.0% under 18, 30.0% over 64 (2000); Marriage status: 11.9% never married, 67.8% now married, 11.2% widowed, 9.0% divorced (2000); Foreign born: 2.2% (2000); Ancestry (includes multiple ancestries): 45.6% Polish, 25.5% German, 11.8% Irish, 9.9% English, 7.5% French (except Basque) (2000).
Economy: Employment by occupation: 16.5% management, 14.6% professional, 10.4% services, 21.2% sales, 2.8% farming, 17.9% construction, 16.5% production (2000).
Income: Per capita income: $20,979 (2000); Median household income: $31,111 (2000); Poverty rate: 6.9% (2000).
Taxes: Total city taxes per capita: $63 (1997); City property taxes per capita: $62 (1997).
Education: High school graduation rate: 73.9% (2000); College graduation rate: 11.7% (2000).
Housing: Homeownership rate: 94.6% (2000); Median home value: $122,800 (2000); Median rent: $413 per month (2000); Median age of housing: 28 years (2000).
Transportation: Commute to work: 96.2% car, 1.9% public transportation, 0.0% walk, 1.4% work from home (2000); Travel time to work: 19.1% less than 15 minutes, 43.1% 15 to 30 minutes, 32.1% 30 to 45 minutes, 0.0% 45 to 60 minutes, 5.7% 60 minutes or more (2000)

METZ (township). Covers a land area of 35.801 square miles and a water area of 0.011 square miles. Located at 45.25° N. Lat.; 83.81° W. Long. Elevation is 829 feet.
Population: 331 (2000); Race: 99.4% White, 0.0% Black, 0.0% Asian, 0.6% American Indian and Alaska Native, 0.0% Hispanic of any race, 0.0% two or more races (2000); Density: 9.2 persons per square mile (2000); Age: 21.7% under 18, 22.8% over 64 (2000); Marriage status: 25.3% never married, 58.6% now married, 8.8% widowed, 7.4% divorced (2000); Foreign born: 0.6% (2000); Ancestry (includes multiple ancestries): 64.4% Polish, 21.7% German, 6.5% English, 6.2% French (except Basque), 3.9% Irish (2000).
Economy: Employment by occupation: 3.9% management, 7.1% professional, 11.0% services, 22.8% sales, 4.7% farming, 27.6% construction, 22.8% production (2000).
Income: Per capita income: $14,191 (2000); Median household income: $28,611 (2000); Poverty rate: 13.6% (2000).
Taxes: Total city taxes per capita: $23 (1997); City property taxes per capita: $23 (1997).
Education: High school graduation rate: 64.4% (2000); College graduation rate: 5.5% (2000).
Housing: Homeownership rate: 94.8% (2000); Median home value: $70,600 (2000); Median age of housing: 34 years (2000).
Transportation: Commute to work: 94.3% car, 0.0% public transportation, 1.6% walk, 3.3% work from home (2000); Travel time to work: 25.4% less than 15 minutes, 35.6% 15 to 30 minutes, 20.3% 30 to 45 minutes, 13.6% 45 to 60 minutes, 5.1% 60 minutes or more (2000)

MILLERSBURG (village). Covers a land area of 1.023 square miles and a water area of 0 square miles. Located at 45.33° N. Lat.; 84.06° W. Long. Elevation is 786 feet.
Population: 263 (2000); Race: 95.8% White, 0.0% Black, 0.0% Asian, 0.0% American Indian and Alaska Native, 0.0% Hispanic of any race, 4.2% two or more races (2000); Density: 257.1 persons per square mile (2000); Age: 31.3% under 18, 14.5% over 64 (2000); Marriage status: 21.6% never married, 57.2% now married, 10.3% widowed, 10.8% divorced (2000); Foreign born: 0.0% (2000); Ancestry (includes multiple ancestries): 25.2% German, 21.8% Irish, 14.9% English, 10.7% French (except Basque), 10.7% United States or American (2000).
Economy: In farm area. Lumber. Employment by occupation: 6.0% management, 6.0% professional, 24.1% services, 13.3% sales, 0.0% farming, 28.9% construction, 21.7% production (2000).
Income: Per capita income: $11,890 (2000); Median household income: $24,063 (2000); Poverty rate: 19.8% (2000).
Taxes: Total city taxes per capita: $57 (1997); City property taxes per capita: $57 (1997).
Education: High school graduation rate: 72.1% (2000); College graduation rate: 9.1% (2000).
Housing: Homeownership rate: 80.9% (2000); Median home value: $38,800 (2000); Median rent: $292 per month (2000); Median age of housing: 40 years (2000).
Transportation: Commute to work: 87.0% car, 0.0% public transportation, 0.0% walk, 13.0% work from home (2000); Travel time to work: 31.3% less than 15 minutes, 23.9% 15 to 30 minutes, 7.5% 30 to 45 minutes, 10.4% 45 to 60 minutes, 26.9% 60 minutes or more (2000)

MOLTKE (township). Covers a land area of 33.950 square miles and a water area of 0.006 square miles. Located at 45.39° N. Lat.; 83.96° W. Long. Elevation is 919 feet.
Population: 352 (2000); Race: 100.0% White, 0.0% Black, 0.0% Asian, 0.0% American Indian and Alaska Native, 0.0% Hispanic of any race, 0.0% two or more races (2000); Density: 10.4 persons per square mile (2000); Age: 22.7% under 18, 19.5% over 64 (2000); Marriage status: 17.6% never married, 68.1% now married, 11.0% widowed, 3.3% divorced (2000); Foreign born: 0.0% (2000); Ancestry (includes multiple ancestries): 58.4% German, 20.1% Polish, 6.5% Irish, 4.7% United States or American, 3.5% French (except Basque) (2000).
Economy: Employment by occupation: 20.0% management, 14.8% professional, 6.5% services, 27.1% sales, 3.2% farming, 10.3% construction, 18.1% production (2000).
Income: Per capita income: $16,272 (2000); Median household income: $32,083 (2000); Poverty rate: 11.8% (2000).
Taxes: Total city taxes per capita: $45 (1997); City property taxes per capita: $45 (1997).
Education: High school graduation rate: 74.0% (2000); College graduation rate: 14.8% (2000).
Housing: Homeownership rate: 95.7% (2000); Median home value: $63,900 (2000); Median rent: $225 per month (2000); Median age of housing: 30 years (2000).
Transportation: Commute to work: 78.1% car, 0.0% public transportation, 4.5% walk, 17.4% work from home (2000); Travel time to work: 43.8% less than 15 minutes, 35.9% 15 to 30 minutes, 3.1% 30 to 45 minutes, 7.8% 45 to 60 minutes, 9.4% 60 minutes or more (2000)

NORTH ALLIS (township). Covers a land area of 32.688 square miles and a water area of 1.596 square miles. Located at 45.41° N. Lat.; 84.19° W. Long.
Population: 618 (2000); Race: 98.0% White, 1.2% Black, 0.0% Asian, 0.0% American Indian and Alaska Native, 1.7% Hispanic of any race, 0.5% two or more races (2000); Density: 18.9 persons per square mile (2000); Age: 23.8% under 18, 17.6% over 64 (2000); Marriage status: 18.8% never married, 63.9% now married, 10.8% widowed, 6.5% divorced (2000); Foreign born: 0.6% (2000); Ancestry (includes multiple ancestries): 26.6% German, 17.1% English, 9.8% Polish, 9.8% French (except Basque), 6.1% Italian (2000).
Economy: Employment by occupation: 14.5% management, 10.5% professional, 17.3% services, 19.1% sales, 1.4% farming, 17.3% construction, 20.0% production (2000).
Income: Per capita income: $14,489 (2000); Median household income: $30,583 (2000); Poverty rate: 9.5% (2000).
Taxes: Total city taxes per capita: $24 (1997); City property taxes per capita: $24 (1997).
Education: High school graduation rate: 80.8% (2000); College graduation rate: 6.7% (2000).
Housing: Homeownership rate: 92.7% (2000); Median home value: $78,200 (2000); Median rent: $338 per month (2000); Median age of housing: 29 years (2000).
Transportation: Commute to work: 87.8% car, 0.0% public transportation, 2.8% walk, 8.5% work from home (2000); Travel time to work: 41.5% less than 15 minutes, 24.6% 15 to 30 minutes, 16.4% 30 to 45 minutes, 6.7% 45 to 60 minutes, 10.8% 60 minutes or more (2000)

OCQUEOC (township). Covers a land area of 52.333 square miles and a water area of 0.308 square miles. Located at 45.45° N. Lat.; 84.06° W. Long.
Population: 634 (2000); Race: 98.3% White, 0.3% Black, 0.0% Asian, 0.0% American Indian and Alaska Native, 0.3% Hispanic of any race, 1.4% two or more races (2000); Density: 12.1 persons per square mile (2000); Age: 18.1% under 18, 31.1% over 64 (2000); Marriage status: 12.3% never married, 67.3% now married, 13.4% widowed, 7.0% divorced (2000); Foreign born: 2.4% (2000); Ancestry (includes multiple ancestries): 38.2% German, 12.1% Irish, 11.8% Polish, 11.2% English, 7.1% French (except Basque) (2000).
Economy: Employment by occupation: 14.0% management, 17.0% professional, 17.5% services, 17.0% sales, 2.9% farming, 22.8% construction, 8.8% production (2000).
Income: Per capita income: $15,432 (2000); Median household income: $28,125 (2000); Poverty rate: 14.5% (2000).
Taxes: Total city taxes per capita: $110 (1997); City property taxes per capita: $110 (1997).
Education: High school graduation rate: 73.5% (2000); College graduation rate: 14.8% (2000).
Housing: Homeownership rate: 93.1% (2000); Median home value: $89,500 (2000); Median rent: $415 per month (2000); Median age of housing: 28 years (2000).
Transportation: Commute to work: 87.4% car, 0.0% public transportation, 3.0% walk, 6.6% work from home (2000); Travel time to work: 28.8% less than 15 minutes, 35.3% 15 to 30 minutes, 17.9% 30 to 45 minutes, 9.6% 45 to 60 minutes, 8.3% 60 minutes or more (2000)

ONAWAY (city). Covers a land area of 1.696 square miles and a water area of 0 square miles. Located at 45.35° N. Lat.; 84.22° W. Long. Elevation is 895 feet.
History: Onaway was founded in 1881 as Shaw Post Office. The town developed as a resort center, depending on tourist trade after its wood-rim plant was destroyed by fire in 1926.
Population: 993 (2000); Race: 93.2% White, 1.0% Black, 0.0% Asian, 3.5% American Indian and Alaska Native, 2.0% Hispanic of any race, 2.2% two or more races (2000); Density: 585.6 persons per square mile (2000); Age: 26.2% under 18, 19.4% over 64 (2000); Marriage status: 32.5% never married, 37.3% now married, 15.8% widowed, 14.4% divorced (2000); Foreign born: 1.1% (2000); Ancestry (includes multiple ancestries): 23.2% German, 11.9% English, 11.1% Irish, 9.8% United States or American, 8.8% French (except Basque) (2000).
Economy: Employment by occupation: 3.8% management, 10.6% professional, 23.7% services, 26.0% sales, 2.9% farming, 11.5% construction, 21.5% production (2000).
Income: Per capita income: $13,552 (2000); Median household income: $20,787 (2000); Poverty rate: 26.9% (2000).
Taxes: Total city taxes per capita: $182 (1997); City property taxes per capita: $181 (1997).
Education: High school graduation rate: 69.2% (2000); College graduation rate: 8.0% (2000).

School District(s)

Onaway Area Community School District (KG-12)
2000 Enrollment: 917 517-733-8423
Presque Isle Academy II (09-12)
2000 Enrollment: 3 989-734-0709

Housing: Homeownership rate: 61.9% (2000); Median home value: $46,000 (2000); Median rent: $239 per month (2000); Median age of housing: 42 years (2000).
Safety: Violent crime rate: 20.0 per 10,000 population; Property crime rate: 450.9 per 10,000 population (2001).
Newspapers: Onaway Outlook (1 x week)
Transportation: Commute to work: 89.5% car, 0.7% public transportation, 6.8% walk, 3.1% work from home (2000); Travel time to work: 52.1% less than 15 minutes, 11.9% 15 to 30 minutes, 14.7% 30 to 45 minutes, 8.7% 45 to 60 minutes, 12.6% 60 minutes or more (2000)
Additional Information Contacts
Onaway Chamber of Commerce 989-733-2874

POSEN (village). Covers a land area of 1.001 square miles and a water area of 0 square miles. Located at 45.26° N. Lat.; 83.69° W. Long. Elevation is 793 feet.
History: Many of the early residents of Posen were of Polish ancestry, who settled here about 1870 when it was a thriving lumber town. When the timber was gone, the people turned to farming.
Population: 292 (2000); Race: 100.0% White, 0.0% Black, 0.0% Asian, 0.0% American Indian and Alaska Native, 0.0% Hispanic of any race, 0.0% two or more races (2000); Density: 291.6 persons per square mile (2000); Age: 26.5% under 18, 15.0% over 64 (2000); Marriage status: 26.9% never married, 59.7% now married, 6.7% widowed, 6.7% divorced (2000); Foreign born: 1.6% (2000); Ancestry (includes multiple ancestries): 56.1% Polish, 15.3% German, 7.8% United States or American, 3.1% French (except Basque), 2.5% English (2000).
Economy: Employment by occupation: 6.2% management, 17.7% professional, 9.7% services, 15.9% sales, 6.2% farming, 8.0% construction, 36.3% production (2000).
Income: Per capita income: $12,708 (2000); Median household income: $27,969 (2000); Poverty rate: 19.3% (2000).
Taxes: Total city taxes per capita: $43 (1997); City property taxes per capita: $43 (1997).
Education: High school graduation rate: 66.7% (2000); College graduation rate: 5.0% (2000).

School District(s)

Posen Consolidated School District (KG-12)
2000 Enrollment: 359 517-766-2573

Housing: Homeownership rate: 72.6% (2000); Median home value: $69,200 (2000); Median rent: $258 per month (2000); Median age of housing: 46 years (2000).
Transportation: Commute to work: 94.7% car, 0.0% public transportation, 0.0% walk, 5.3% work from home (2000); Travel time to work: 35.5% less than 15 minutes, 25.2% 15 to 30 minutes, 19.6% 30 to 45 minutes, 3.7% 45 to 60 minutes, 15.9% 60 minutes or more (2000)

POSEN (township). Covers a land area of 35.306 square miles and a water area of 0.223 square miles. Located at 45.24° N. Lat.; 83.69° W. Long. Elevation is 793 feet.
History: Posen Township was settled in 1870 by a group of Polish immigrants led by Lawrence Kowalski. They named Posen for the province of Poznan in Poland.
Population: 959 (2000); Race: 100.0% White, 0.0% Black, 0.0% Asian, 0.0% American Indian and Alaska Native, 0.0% Hispanic of any race, 0.0% two or more races (2000); Density: 27.2 persons per square mile (2000); Age: 23.4% under 18, 16.5% over 64 (2000); Marriage status: 23.0% never married, 64.0% now married, 7.8% widowed, 5.2% divorced (2000); Foreign born: 1.3% (2000); Ancestry (includes multiple ancestries): 65.4% Polish, 16.9% German, 4.0% United States or American, 3.5% Irish, 3.4% English (2000).
Economy: Employment by occupation: 8.3% management, 15.3% professional, 10.7% services, 22.4% sales, 4.6% farming, 12.4% construction, 26.3% production (2000).
Income: Per capita income: $15,259 (2000); Median household income: $31,912 (2000); Poverty rate: 9.7% (2000).
Taxes: Total city taxes per capita: $34 (1997); City property taxes per capita: $34 (1997).
Education: High school graduation rate: 73.9% (2000); College graduation rate: 7.3% (2000).
Housing: Homeownership rate: 85.1% (2000); Median home value: $72,900 (2000); Median rent: $250 per month (2000); Median age of housing: 34 years (2000).
Transportation: Commute to work: 93.5% car, 0.0% public transportation, 2.3% walk, 4.3% work from home (2000); Travel time to work: 29.8% less than 15 minutes, 24.3% 15 to 30 minutes, 33.4% 30 to 45 minutes, 3.4% 45 to 60 minutes, 9.1% 60 minutes or more (2000)

PRESQUE ISLE (township). Covers a land area of 35.591 square miles and a water area of 11.585 square miles. Located at 45.28° N. Lat.; 83.47° W. Long. Elevation is 606 feet.
History: Lighthouse nearby.
Population: 1,691 (2000); Race: 99.1% White, 0.1% Black, 0.1% Asian, 0.0% American Indian and Alaska Native, 0.0% Hispanic of any race, 0.7% two or more races (2000); Density: 47.5 persons per square mile (2000); Age: 17.1% under 18, 24.0% over 64 (2000); Marriage status: 14.2% never married, 74.5% now married, 5.1% widowed, 6.1% divorced (2000); Foreign born: 1.2% (2000); Ancestry (includes multiple ancestries): 30.4% German, 25.4% Polish, 13.9% English, 10.6% Irish, 10.1% French (except Basque) (2000).
Economy: Employment by occupation: 14.1% management, 26.1% professional, 11.7% services, 28.0% sales, 0.2% farming, 9.9% construction, 10.1% production (2000).
Income: Per capita income: $23,938 (2000); Median household income: $41,705 (2000); Poverty rate: 3.9% (2000).
Taxes: Total city taxes per capita: $84 (1997); City property taxes per capita: $82 (1997).
Education: High school graduation rate: 91.7% (2000); College graduation rate: 23.7% (2000).
Housing: Homeownership rate: 95.3% (2000); Median home value: $130,700 (2000); Median rent: $408 per month (2000); Median age of housing: 29 years (2000).
Transportation: Commute to work: 95.5% car, 0.3% public transportation, 0.8% walk, 1.9% work from home (2000); Travel time to work: 16.6% less than 15 minutes, 52.0% 15 to 30 minutes, 23.0% 30 to 45 minutes, 2.0% 45 to 60 minutes, 6.4% 60 minutes or more (2000)

PULAWSKI (township). Covers a land area of 41.926 square miles and a water area of 1.903 square miles. Located at 45.38° N. Lat.; 83.71° W. Long.
Population: 372 (2000); Race: 96.4% White, 0.0% Black, 0.0% Asian, 0.0% American Indian and Alaska Native, 0.0% Hispanic of any race, 3.6% two or more races (2000); Density: 8.9 persons per square mile (2000); Age: 26.8% under 18, 17.7% over 64 (2000); Marriage status: 20.3% never married, 64.8% now married, 8.4% widowed, 6.5% divorced (2000); Foreign born: 3.6% (2000); Ancestry (includes multiple ancestries): 65.7% Polish, 21.6% German, 6.8% French (except Basque), 3.6% Jordanian, 3.4% United States or American (2000).
Economy: Employment by occupation: 9.9% management, 16.4% professional, 12.5% services, 18.4% sales, 4.6% farming, 9.9% construction, 28.3% production (2000).
Income: Per capita income: $13,496 (2000); Median household income: $35,192 (2000); Poverty rate: 10.6% (2000).
Taxes: Total city taxes per capita: $81 (1997); City property taxes per capita: $81 (1997).
Education: High school graduation rate: 67.3% (2000); College graduation rate: 3.1% (2000).
Housing: Homeownership rate: 88.6% (2000); Median home value: $62,800 (2000); Median rent: $344 per month (2000); Median age of housing: 29 years (2000).
Transportation: Commute to work: 86.8% car, 0.0% public transportation, 1.4% walk, 11.8% work from home (2000); Travel time to work: 41.7% less than 15 minutes, 19.7% 15 to 30 minutes, 18.1% 30 to 45 minutes, 11.8% 45 to 60 minutes, 8.7% 60 minutes or more (2000)

ROGERS (township). Covers a land area of 33.588 square miles and a water area of 0.060 square miles. Located at 45.41° N. Lat.; 83.85° W. Long.
Population: 949 (2000); Race: 99.6% White, 0.0% Black, 0.0% Asian, 0.0% American Indian and Alaska Native, 0.0% Hispanic of any race, 0.4% two or more races (2000); Density: 28.3 persons per square mile (2000); Age: 22.8% under 18, 17.1% over 64 (2000); Marriage status: 16.7% never married, 72.3% now married, 5.2% widowed, 5.7% divorced (2000); Foreign born: 1.2% (2000); Ancestry (includes multiple ancestries): 38.6% German, 33.4% Polish, 10.0% English, 7.4% Irish, 6.1% Italian (2000).
Economy: Employment by occupation: 8.0% management, 14.2% professional, 14.2% services, 25.1% sales, 3.1% farming, 13.7% construction, 21.5% production (2000).
Income: Per capita income: $18,157 (2000); Median household income: $39,205 (2000); Poverty rate: 9.5% (2000).
Taxes: Total city taxes per capita: $26 (1997); City property taxes per capita: $26 (1997).
Education: High school graduation rate: 81.4% (2000); College graduation rate: 14.6% (2000).
Housing: Homeownership rate: 94.0% (2000); Median home value: $89,700 (2000); Median rent: $317 per month (2000); Median age of housing: 26 years (2000).
Transportation: Commute to work: 88.2% car, 0.5% public transportation, 3.4% walk, 2.9% work from home (2000); Travel time to work: 58.0% less than 15 minutes, 19.0% 15 to 30 minutes, 10.0% 30 to 45 minutes, 4.3% 45 to 60 minutes, 8.7% 60 minutes or more (2000)

ROGERS CITY (city). Covers a land area of 4.568 square miles and a water area of 3.865 square miles. Located at 45.41° N. Lat.; 83.81° W. Long. Elevation is 605 feet.

History: Rogers City began when Albert Molitor built a dock and mill at this place on Lake Huron. The village that grew up around the mill was named for William E. Rogers, who had come to the area with Molitor. A limestone quarry provided Rogers City with its source of revenue in the early 1900's. The limestone was shipped from the nearby port named Calcite.
Population: 3,322 (2000); Race: 98.7% White, 0.0% Black, 0.0% Asian, 0.6% American Indian and Alaska Native, 0.2% Hispanic of any race, 0.7% two or more races (2000); Density: 727.2 persons per square mile (2000); Age: 19.4% under 18, 26.7% over 64 (2000); Marriage status: 19.2% never married, 59.9% now married, 12.2% widowed, 8.7% divorced (2000); Foreign born: 1.2% (2000); Ancestry (includes multiple ancestries): 37.4% German, 28.9% Polish, 10.9% Irish, 8.6% English, 8.0% French (except Basque) (2000).
Economy: Employment by occupation: 9.7% management, 15.0% professional, 26.3% services, 25.2% sales, 2.7% farming, 12.7% construction, 8.4% production (2000).
Income: Per capita income: $17,750 (2000); Median household income: $29,531 (2000); Poverty rate: 7.6% (2000).
Taxes: Total city taxes per capita: $214 (1997); City property taxes per capita: $213 (1997).
Education: High school graduation rate: 77.0% (2000); College graduation rate: 11.6% (2000).

School District(s)

Presque Isle Academy I (09-12)
2000 Enrollment: 10 989-734-0709
Rogers City Area Schools (KG-12)
2000 Enrollment: 733 517-734-4013

Housing: Homeownership rate: 75.6% (2000); Median home value: $65,200 (2000); Median rent: $293 per month (2000); Median age of housing: 48 years (2000).
Hospitals: Tendercare Health Center (89 beds)
Safety: Violent crime rate: 0.0 per 10,000 population; Property crime rate: 47.9 per 10,000 population (2001).
Newspapers: Presque Isle County Advance (1 x week)
Transportation: Commute to work: 93.3% car, 0.0% public transportation, 1.7% walk, 3.9% work from home (2000); Travel time to work: 77.5% less than 15 minutes, 7.3% 15 to 30 minutes, 8.0% 30 to 45 minutes, 4.5% 45 to 60 minutes, 2.8% 60 minutes or more (2000)

Additional Information Contacts

Presque Isle County Tourism 989-734-2577
Rogers City Chamber of Commerce 989-734-2535

Roscommon County

Located in north central Michigan; drained by the Muskegon River and branches of the Tittabawassee and Au Sable Rivers; includes Houghton and Higgins Lakes and Lake St. Helen. Covers a land area of 521.40 square miles, a water area of 58.40 square miles, and is located in the Eastern Time Zone. The county government was organized in 1875. County seat is Roscommon.

Weather Station: Houghton Lake Airport — Elevation: 1,148 feet

	Jan	Feb	Mar	Apr	May	Jun	Jul	Aug	Sep	Oct	Nov	Dec
High	26	29	39	53	67	75	80	77	68	56	42	31
Low	9	10	19	32	43	51	56	54	47	37	28	17
Precip	1.6	1.2	2.1	2.3	2.5	3.0	2.7	3.7	3.2	2.3	2.2	1.8
Snow	19.1	12.8	11.5	4.1	0.3	0.0	tr	tr	tr	0.6	9.5	15.7

High and Low temperatures in degrees Fahrenheit; Precipitation and Snow in inches

Population: 25,469 (2000); Race: 98.0% White, 0.2% Black, 0.4% Asian, 0.5% American Indian and Alaska Native, 0.9% Hispanic of any race, 0.7% two or more races (2000); Density: 48.8 persons per square mile (2000); Age: 19.9% under 18, 23.7% over 64 (2000).
Religion: Five largest groups: 15.6% Catholic Church, 3.0% Lutheran Church—Missouri Synod, 2.4% The United Methodist Church, 2.0% American Baptist Churches in the USA, 1.2% Episcopal Church (2000).
Economy: Unemployment rate: 6.8% (11/2002); Total civilian labor force: 8,805 (11/2002); Leading industries: 31.5% retail trade; 19.7% accommodation & food services; 10.5% health care and social assistance (2000); Companies that employ more than 1,000 persons: 0 (2000); Companies that employ more than 100 persons: 3 (2000); Farms: 36 totaling 4,139 acres (1997); Minority business ownership rate: 0.0% (1997); Women business ownership rate: 25.1% (1997); Retail sales per capita: $11,503 (1997). Single-family building permits issued: 366 (2001) / 373 (2000); Multi-family building permits issued: 0 (2001) / 0 (2000).
Income: Per capita income: $17,837 (2000); Median household income: $30,029 (2000); Poverty rate: 12.4% (2000); Bankruptcy rate: 4.47% (2001).
Taxes: Total county taxes per capita: $197 (2000); County property taxes per capita: $190 (2000).
Education: High school graduation rate: 79.5% (2000); College graduation rate: 10.9% (2000).
Housing: Homeownership rate: 85.8% (2000); Median home value: $78,900 (2000); Median rent: $337 per month (2000); Median age of housing: 29 years (2000).
Health: Birth rate: 79.3 per 10,000 population (1998); Age adjusted death rate: 107.6 per 10,000 population (1999); Age adjusted cancer mortality rate: 276.8 deaths per 100,000 population (1999). Number of physicians: 11.0 per 10,000 population (1999); Number of hospital beds: n/a (1999).
Elections: 2000 Presidential election results: 49.8% Gore, 47.9% Bush, 2.0% Nader, 0.1% Buchanan
National and State Parks: Backus Creek State Game Area; Higgins Lake State Park; Houghton Lake State Forest

Additional Information Contacts

Roscommon County Government Offices 989-275-5923
Higgins Lake-Roscommon Chamber 989-275-8760
Houghton Lake Chamber of Commerce 989-366-5644
St. Helen Chamber of Commerce 989-389-3725

Roscommon County Communities

AU SABLE (township). Covers a land area of 35.759 square miles and a water area of 0.025 square miles. Located at 44.45° N. Lat.; 84.44° W. Long.
Population: 281 (2000); Race: 100.0% White, 0.0% Black, 0.0% Asian, 0.0% American Indian and Alaska Native, 0.0% Hispanic of any race, 0.0% two or more races (2000); Density: 7.9 persons per square mile (2000); Age: 24.6% under 18, 14.1% over 64 (2000); Marriage status: 17.9% never married, 67.0% now married, 3.6% widowed, 11.6% divorced (2000); Foreign born: 2.1% (2000); Ancestry (includes multiple ancestries): 32.7% German, 13.0% United States or American, 11.3% English, 8.1% Irish, 4.6% Other groups (2000).
Economy: Single-family building permits issued: 30 (2001) / 30 (2000); Multi-family building permits issued: 0 (2001) / 0 (2000); Employment by occupation: 15.5% management, 15.5% professional, 25.2% services, 17.5% sales, 0.0% farming, 11.7% construction, 14.6% production (2000).
Income: Per capita income: $13,651 (2000); Median household income: $30,000 (2000); Poverty rate: 23.9% (2000).
Taxes: Total city taxes per capita: $64 (1997); City property taxes per capita: $64 (1997).
Education: High school graduation rate: 75.4% (2000); College graduation rate: 11.1% (2000).
Housing: Homeownership rate: 84.4% (2000); Median home value: $81,300 (2000); Median rent: $442 per month (2000); Median age of housing: 28 years (2000).
Transportation: Commute to work: 100.0% car, 0.0% public transportation, 0.0% walk, 0.0% work from home (2000); Travel time to work: 23.3% less than 15 minutes, 39.8% 15 to 30 minutes, 28.2% 30 to 45 minutes, 6.8% 45 to 60 minutes, 1.9% 60 minutes or more (2000)

BACKUS (township). Covers a land area of 34.293 square miles and a water area of 1.582 square miles. Located at 44.29° N. Lat.; 84.57° W. Long.
Population: 350 (2000); Race: 98.3% White, 0.0% Black, 0.0% Asian, 1.1% American Indian and Alaska Native, 2.5% Hispanic of any race, 0.6% two or more races (2000); Density: 10.2 persons per square mile (2000); Age: 25.7% under 18, 12.7% over 64 (2000); Marriage status: 16.0% never married, 68.4% now married, 5.8% widowed, 9.8% divorced (2000); Foreign born: 1.7% (2000); Ancestry (includes multiple ancestries): 27.4% German, 13.6% United States or American, 10.5% Polish, 9.9% Irish, 8.8% Other groups (2000).
Economy: Employment by occupation: 12.5% management, 18.8% professional, 16.4% services, 24.2% sales, 0.0% farming, 15.6% construction, 12.5% production (2000).
Income: Per capita income: $15,836 (2000); Median household income: $32,222 (2000); Poverty rate: 17.5% (2000).
Taxes: Total city taxes per capita: $97 (1997); City property taxes per capita: $82 (1997).
Education: High school graduation rate: 80.6% (2000); College graduation rate: 8.3% (2000).
Housing: Homeownership rate: 89.0% (2000); Median home value: $84,400 (2000); Median rent: $392 per month (2000); Median age of housing: 27 years (2000).
Transportation: Commute to work: 78.9% car, 0.0% public transportation, 1.6% walk, 13.8% work from home (2000); Travel time to work: 28.3% less

than 15 minutes, 36.8% 15 to 30 minutes, 20.8% 30 to 45 minutes, 0.0% 45 to 60 minutes, 14.2% 60 minutes or more (2000)

DENTON (township). Covers a land area of 26.372 square miles and a water area of 9.638 square miles. Located at 44.29° N. Lat.; 84.66° W. Long.
Population: 5,817 (2000); Race: 99.2% White, 0.2% Black, 0.3% Asian, 0.0% American Indian and Alaska Native, 1.2% Hispanic of any race, 0.1% two or more races (2000); Density: 220.6 persons per square mile (2000); Age: 19.4% under 18, 25.2% over 64 (2000); Marriage status: 16.2% never married, 65.4% now married, 7.9% widowed, 10.5% divorced (2000); Foreign born: 1.8% (2000); Ancestry (includes multiple ancestries): 25.7% German, 17.2% English, 13.6% Irish, 10.7% Polish, 6.9% French (except Basque) (2000).
Economy: Employment by occupation: 11.1% management, 15.9% professional, 19.2% services, 31.1% sales, 0.0% farming, 11.0% construction, 11.6% production (2000).
Income: Per capita income: $18,946 (2000); Median household income: $29,397 (2000); Poverty rate: 10.2% (2000).
Taxes: Total city taxes per capita: $183 (2000); City property taxes per capita: $168 (2000).
Education: High school graduation rate: 81.4% (2000); College graduation rate: 11.5% (2000).
Housing: Homeownership rate: 81.9% (2000); Median home value: $87,800 (2000); Median rent: $330 per month (2000); Median age of housing: 28 years (2000).
Safety: Violent crime rate: 6.8 per 10,000 population; Property crime rate: 183.0 per 10,000 population (2001).
Transportation: Commute to work: 92.4% car, 0.8% public transportation, 2.9% walk, 2.8% work from home (2000); Travel time to work: 56.6% less than 15 minutes, 22.7% 15 to 30 minutes, 11.7% 30 to 45 minutes, 1.7% 45 to 60 minutes, 7.3% 60 minutes or more (2000)

GERRISH (township). Covers a land area of 27.636 square miles and a water area of 9.595 square miles. Located at 44.46° N. Lat.; 84.68° W. Long.
Population: 3,072 (2000); Race: 97.4% White, 0.2% Black, 1.1% Asian, 0.6% American Indian and Alaska Native, 0.1% Hispanic of any race, 0.8% two or more races (2000); Density: 111.2 persons per square mile (2000); Age: 19.9% under 18, 24.8% over 64 (2000); Marriage status: 14.7% never married, 71.0% now married, 7.4% widowed, 6.9% divorced (2000); Foreign born: 2.3% (2000); Ancestry (includes multiple ancestries): 31.0% German, 16.8% English, 15.4% Irish, 9.9% Polish, 7.5% French (except Basque) (2000).
Economy: Single-family building permits issued: 45 (2001) / 33 (2000); Multi-family building permits issued: 0 (2001) / 0 (2000); Employment by occupation: 10.9% management, 27.5% professional, 15.1% services, 25.0% sales, 0.0% farming, 9.3% construction, 12.2% production (2000).
Income: Per capita income: $19,877 (2000); Median household income: $37,147 (2000); Poverty rate: 6.8% (2000).
Taxes: Total city taxes per capita: $298 (1997); City property taxes per capita: $278 (1997).
Education: High school graduation rate: 86.9% (2000); College graduation rate: 22.1% (2000).
Housing: Homeownership rate: 91.4% (2000); Median home value: $106,000 (2000); Median rent: $443 per month (2000); Median age of housing: 28 years (2000).
Safety: Violent crime rate: 0.0 per 10,000 population; Property crime rate: 139.2 per 10,000 population (2001).
Transportation: Commute to work: 94.9% car, 0.5% public transportation, 1.5% walk, 3.1% work from home (2000); Travel time to work: 40.5% less than 15 minutes, 32.6% 15 to 30 minutes, 12.1% 30 to 45 minutes, 4.5% 45 to 60 minutes, 10.4% 60 minutes or more (2000)

HIGGINS (township). Covers a land area of 70.473 square miles and a water area of 2.844 square miles. Located at 44.45° N. Lat.; 84.58° W. Long.
Population: 2,061 (2000); Race: 96.0% White, 0.3% Black, 0.3% Asian, 0.1% American Indian and Alaska Native, 0.3% Hispanic of any race, 2.8% two or more races (2000); Density: 29.2 persons per square mile (2000); Age: 21.9% under 18, 21.3% over 64 (2000); Marriage status: 22.5% never married, 53.4% now married, 10.6% widowed, 13.5% divorced (2000); Foreign born: 1.2% (2000); Ancestry (includes multiple ancestries): 22.6% German, 14.6% Irish, 11.3% English, 9.6% Other groups, 7.9% Polish (2000).
Economy: Single-family building permits issued: 12 (2001) / 20 (2000); Multi-family building permits issued: 0 (2001) / 0 (2000); Employment by occupation: 12.2% management, 19.3% professional, 19.9% services, 24.1% sales, 0.3% farming, 8.9% construction, 15.3% production (2000).
Income: Per capita income: $15,529 (2000); Median household income: $29,801 (2000); Poverty rate: 17.8% (2000).
Taxes: Total city taxes per capita: $88 (2000); City property taxes per capita: $85 (2000).
Education: High school graduation rate: 78.9% (2000); College graduation rate: 15.2% (2000).
Housing: Homeownership rate: 71.5% (2000); Median home value: $65,300 (2000); Median rent: $301 per month (2000); Median age of housing: 31 years (2000).
Transportation: Commute to work: 93.3% car, 0.0% public transportation, 3.6% walk, 2.9% work from home (2000); Travel time to work: 48.4% less than 15 minutes, 32.0% 15 to 30 minutes, 9.1% 30 to 45 minutes, 4.8% 45 to 60 minutes, 5.8% 60 minutes or more (2000)

HOUGHTON LAKE (CDP). Aka The Heights. Covers a land area of 5.917 square miles and a water area of 1.625 square miles. Located at 44.30° N. Lat.; 84.74° W. Long. Elevation is 1,162 feet.
History: Houghton Lake was named for Douglass Houghton, a pioneer geologist in Michigan. The community developed in the 1870's around the lumber operations of S.C. Hall. It later became a resort area.
Population: 3,749 (2000); Race: 98.5% White, 0.0% Black, 0.2% Asian, 0.3% American Indian and Alaska Native, 1.1% Hispanic of any race, 0.4% two or more races (2000); Density: 633.6 persons per square mile (2000); Age: 19.7% under 18, 23.9% over 64 (2000); Marriage status: 19.9% never married, 56.3% now married, 8.3% widowed, 15.6% divorced (2000); Foreign born: 0.9% (2000); Ancestry (includes multiple ancestries): 22.1% German, 18.0% English, 11.4% Irish, 8.2% Polish, 6.9% United States or American (2000).
Economy: Employment by occupation: 6.1% management, 14.8% professional, 28.4% services, 28.7% sales, 1.0% farming, 8.3% construction, 12.8% production (2000).
Income: Per capita income: $16,862 (2000); Median household income: $27,443 (2000); Poverty rate: 16.0% (2000).
Education: High school graduation rate: 76.8% (2000); College graduation rate: 7.7% (2000).

School District(s)

Houghton Lake Community Schools (PK-12)
2000 Enrollment: 2,248 517-366-2000

Housing: Homeownership rate: 76.6% (2000); Median home value: $71,800 (2000); Median rent: $339 per month (2000); Median age of housing: 37 years (2000).
Newspapers: The Houghton Lake Resorter (1 x week)
Transportation: Commute to work: 91.7% car, 1.1% public transportation, 2.6% walk, 2.8% work from home (2000); Travel time to work: 56.1% less than 15 minutes, 19.0% 15 to 30 minutes, 15.7% 30 to 45 minutes, 3.8% 45 to 60 minutes, 5.4% 60 minutes or more (2000)
Airports: Roscommon County
Additional Information Contacts
Houghton Lake Chamber of Commerce 989-366-5644

LAKE (township). Covers a land area of 23.806 square miles and a water area of 11.787 square miles. Located at 44.37° N. Lat.; 84.79° W. Long.
Population: 1,351 (2000); Race: 97.8% White, 0.3% Black, 0.1% Asian, 0.6% American Indian and Alaska Native, 1.3% Hispanic of any race, 0.3% two or more races (2000); Density: 56.8 persons per square mile (2000); Age: 12.8% under 18, 29.0% over 64 (2000); Marriage status: 14.2% never married, 62.2% now married, 11.5% widowed, 12.0% divorced (2000); Foreign born: 1.7% (2000); Ancestry (includes multiple ancestries): 22.4% German, 13.8% English, 10.7% Irish, 8.4% French (except Basque), 7.9% United States or American (2000).
Economy: Employment by occupation: 9.4% management, 13.0% professional, 26.0% services, 24.9% sales, 1.6% farming, 11.0% construction, 14.1% production (2000).
Income: Per capita income: $20,793 (2000); Median household income: $29,242 (2000); Poverty rate: 14.3% (2000).
Taxes: Total city taxes per capita: $321 (2000); City property taxes per capita: $301 (2000).
Education: High school graduation rate: 76.9% (2000); College graduation rate: 8.7% (2000).
Housing: Homeownership rate: 88.4% (2000); Median home value: $108,400 (2000); Median rent: $383 per month (2000); Median age of housing: 31 years (2000).
Transportation: Commute to work: 90.1% car, 0.9% public transportation, 4.1% walk, 4.8% work from home (2000); Travel time to work: 35.7% less than 15 minutes, 39.1% 15 to 30 minutes, 9.9% 30 to 45 minutes, 4.6% 45 to 60 minutes, 10.6% 60 minutes or more (2000)

LYON (township). Covers a land area of 29.982 square miles and a water area of 6.501 square miles. Located at 44.47° N. Lat.; 84.77° W. Long.
Population: 1,462 (2000); Race: 97.4% White, 0.2% Black, 0.0% Asian, 0.4% American Indian and Alaska Native, 2.1% Hispanic of any race, 1.8% two or more races (2000); Density: 48.8 persons per square mile (2000); Age: 16.2% under 18, 27.7% over 64 (2000); Marriage status: 15.2% never married, 69.8% now married, 7.0% widowed, 8.0% divorced (2000); Foreign born: 1.2% (2000); Ancestry (includes multiple ancestries): 23.8% German, 18.9% English, 10.9% Irish, 9.9% French (except Basque), 8.5% Polish (2000).
Economy: Single-family building permits issued: 24 (2001) / 23 (2000); Multi-family building permits issued: 0 (2001) / 0 (2000); Employment by occupation: 10.2% management, 18.8% professional, 17.4% services, 24.1% sales, 0.4% farming, 13.7% construction, 15.5% production (2000).
Income: Per capita income: $19,232 (2000); Median household income: $33,226 (2000); Poverty rate: 10.8% (2000).
Taxes: Total city taxes per capita: $195 (1997); City property taxes per capita: $176 (1997).
Education: High school graduation rate: 86.8% (2000); College graduation rate: 12.3% (2000).
Housing: Homeownership rate: 91.6% (2000); Median home value: $86,400 (2000); Median rent: $406 per month (2000); Median age of housing: 37 years (2000).
Transportation: Commute to work: 91.6% car, 0.0% public transportation, 2.2% walk, 5.9% work from home (2000); Travel time to work: 23.0% less than 15 minutes, 52.4% 15 to 30 minutes, 10.5% 30 to 45 minutes, 4.5% 45 to 60 minutes, 9.6% 60 minutes or more (2000)

MARKEY (township). Covers a land area of 28.912 square miles and a water area of 7.264 square miles. Located at 44.38° N. Lat.; 84.67° W. Long.
Population: 2,424 (2000); Race: 97.9% White, 0.1% Black, 0.7% Asian, 0.4% American Indian and Alaska Native, 1.0% Hispanic of any race, 0.6% two or more races (2000); Density: 83.8 persons per square mile (2000); Age: 16.4% under 18, 28.3% over 64 (2000); Marriage status: 13.4% never married, 66.7% now married, 11.0% widowed, 9.0% divorced (2000); Foreign born: 2.5% (2000); Ancestry (includes multiple ancestries): 24.1% German, 14.5% English, 13.4% Irish, 9.8% Polish, 8.8% United States or American (2000).
Economy: Employment by occupation: 10.2% management, 13.4% professional, 19.6% services, 28.2% sales, 0.7% farming, 12.4% construction, 15.5% production (2000).
Income: Per capita income: $18,213 (2000); Median household income: $29,505 (2000); Poverty rate: 9.4% (2000).
Taxes: Total city taxes per capita: $165 (1997); City property taxes per capita: $147 (1997).
Education: High school graduation rate: 80.7% (2000); College graduation rate: 9.8% (2000).
Housing: Homeownership rate: 94.3% (2000); Median home value: $80,000 (2000); Median rent: $375 per month (2000); Median age of housing: 26 years (2000).
Transportation: Commute to work: 94.3% car, 0.6% public transportation, 1.4% walk, 3.2% work from home (2000); Travel time to work: 22.0% less than 15 minutes, 50.0% 15 to 30 minutes, 10.4% 30 to 45 minutes, 6.1% 45 to 60 minutes, 11.5% 60 minutes or more (2000)

NESTER (township). Covers a land area of 71.330 square miles and a water area of 0.852 square miles. Located at 44.19° N. Lat.; 84.49° W. Long.
Population: 263 (2000); Race: 99.1% White, 0.0% Black, 0.9% Asian, 0.0% American Indian and Alaska Native, 0.0% Hispanic of any race, 0.0% two or more races (2000); Density: 3.7 persons per square mile (2000); Age: 20.0% under 18, 20.0% over 64 (2000); Marriage status: 8.2% never married, 78.6% now married, 6.1% widowed, 7.1% divorced (2000); Foreign born: 5.5% (2000); Ancestry (includes multiple ancestries): 20.4% English, 19.6% German, 14.9% Irish, 13.2% United States or American, 11.1% French (except Basque) (2000).
Economy: Single-family building permits issued: 8 (2001) / 0 (2000); Multi-family building permits issued: 0 (2001) / 0 (2000); Employment by occupation: 2.7% management, 24.3% professional, 17.6% services, 36.5% sales, 2.7% farming, 6.8% construction, 9.5% production (2000).
Income: Per capita income: $14,645 (2000); Median household income: $31,250 (2000); Poverty rate: 15.3% (2000).
Taxes: Total city taxes per capita: $205 (1997); City property taxes per capita: $197 (1997).
Education: High school graduation rate: 74.3% (2000); College graduation rate: 6.4% (2000).
Housing: Homeownership rate: 100.0% (2000); Median home value: $85,900 (2000); Median age of housing: 26 years (2000).
Transportation: Commute to work: 83.8% car, 0.0% public transportation, 0.0% walk, 12.2% work from home (2000); Travel time to work: 12.3% less than 15 minutes, 30.8% 15 to 30 minutes, 15.4% 30 to 45 minutes, 23.1% 45 to 60 minutes, 18.5% 60 minutes or more (2000)

PRUDENVILLE (CDP). Covers a land area of 2.801 square miles and a water area of 0.848 square miles. Located at 44.29° N. Lat.; 84.65° W. Long.
History: Prudenville was founded in 1875 by John Pruden.
Population: 1,737 (2000); Race: 97.9% White, 0.7% Black, 1.0% Asian, 0.0% American Indian and Alaska Native, 0.4% Hispanic of any race, 0.4% two or more races (2000); Density: 620.1 persons per square mile (2000); Age: 19.9% under 18, 27.1% over 64 (2000); Marriage status: 17.4% never married, 63.4% now married, 9.9% widowed, 9.3% divorced (2000); Foreign born: 1.3% (2000); Ancestry (includes multiple ancestries): 25.4% German, 12.7% Irish, 12.0% Polish, 10.8% English, 8.7% United States or American (2000).
Economy: Employment by occupation: 12.6% management, 17.5% professional, 16.6% services, 34.4% sales, 0.0% farming, 11.1% construction, 7.7% production (2000).
Income: Per capita income: $19,018 (2000); Median household income: $29,821 (2000); Poverty rate: 11.6% (2000).
Education: High school graduation rate: 83.9% (2000); College graduation rate: 10.2% (2000).
Housing: Homeownership rate: 83.9% (2000); Median home value: $79,500 (2000); Median rent: $409 per month (2000); Median age of housing: 29 years (2000).
Newspapers: Roscommon County Star (1 x week)
Transportation: Commute to work: 91.5% car, 1.4% public transportation, 3.1% walk, 3.6% work from home (2000); Travel time to work: 53.1% less than 15 minutes, 24.2% 15 to 30 minutes, 11.3% 30 to 45 minutes, 3.0% 45 to 60 minutes, 8.3% 60 minutes or more (2000)

RICHFIELD (township). Covers a land area of 68.906 square miles and a water area of 4.006 square miles. Located at 44.35° N. Lat.; 84.42° W. Long.
Population: 4,139 (2000); Race: 98.3% White, 0.0% Black, 0.4% Asian, 1.1% American Indian and Alaska Native, 0.7% Hispanic of any race, 0.2% two or more races (2000); Density: 60.1 persons per square mile (2000); Age: 19.5% under 18, 24.1% over 64 (2000); Marriage status: 13.5% never married, 58.2% now married, 12.3% widowed, 16.0% divorced (2000); Foreign born: 1.6% (2000); Ancestry (includes multiple ancestries): 26.9% German, 13.5% English, 13.3% Irish, 8.8% Polish, 8.2% French (except Basque) (2000).
Economy: Single-family building permits issued: 21 (2001) / 30 (2000); Multi-family building permits issued: 0 (2001) / 0 (2000); Employment by occupation: 11.7% management, 13.6% professional, 15.8% services, 25.3% sales, 0.4% farming, 14.0% construction, 19.1% production (2000).
Income: Per capita income: $17,282 (2000); Median household income: $26,806 (2000); Poverty rate: 15.9% (2000).
Taxes: Total city taxes per capita: $160 (2000); City property taxes per capita: $152 (2000).
Education: High school graduation rate: 70.6% (2000); College graduation rate: 5.9% (2000).
Housing: Homeownership rate: 87.9% (2000); Median home value: $57,400 (2000); Median rent: $328 per month (2000); Median age of housing: 32 years (2000).
Safety: Violent crime rate: 0.0 per 10,000 population; Property crime rate: 158.6 per 10,000 population (2001).
Transportation: Commute to work: 93.2% car, 0.0% public transportation, 0.9% walk, 3.4% work from home (2000); Travel time to work: 25.1% less than 15 minutes, 43.5% 15 to 30 minutes, 18.8% 30 to 45 minutes, 3.8% 45 to 60 minutes, 8.8% 60 minutes or more (2000)

ROSCOMMON (village). Covers a land area of 1.630 square miles and a water area of 0 square miles. Located at 44.49° N. Lat.; 84.59° W. Long. Elevation is 1,130 feet.
History: Roscommon was founded in 1845 by George C. Robinson of Detroit. It was named for the county, which had been named for a county in Ireland. Roscommon, once a lumber town with one hotel and 14 saloons, became a vacation and resort center.
Population: 1,133 (2000); Race: 96.8% White, 0.5% Black, 0.3% Asian, 0.3% American Indian and Alaska Native, 0.0% Hispanic of any race, 1.4% two or more races (2000); Density: 695.1 persons per square mile (2000); Age: 25.5% under 18, 20.7% over 64 (2000); Marriage status: 26.2% never

married, 43.3% now married, 13.8% widowed, 16.7% divorced (2000); Foreign born: 0.8% (2000); Ancestry (includes multiple ancestries): 23.8% German, 16.1% Irish, 11.5% Other groups, 8.9% French (except Basque), 8.1% United States or American (2000).
Economy: Single-family building permits issued: 0 (2001) / 2 (2000); Multi-family building permits issued: 0 (2001) / 0 (2000); Employment by occupation: 11.6% management, 17.0% professional, 19.9% services, 26.7% sales, 0.0% farming, 7.0% construction, 17.8% production (2000).
Income: Per capita income: $14,746 (2000); Median household income: $28,229 (2000); Poverty rate: 21.2% (2000).
Taxes: Total city taxes per capita: $205 (1997); City property taxes per capita: $197 (1997).
Education: High school graduation rate: 75.9% (2000); College graduation rate: 11.6% (2000).

School District(s)

Gerrish-Higgins School District (KG-12)
2000 Enrollment: 1,898 517-275-6600

Two-year College(s)

Kirtland Community College (Public)
2001 Enrollment: 1,409 517-275-5000
2001 Tuition: In-state $2,424; Out-of-state $3,144
Housing: Homeownership rate: 57.5% (2000); Median home value: $57,600 (2000); Median rent: $294 per month (2000); Median age of housing: 36 years (2000).
Newspapers: Roscommon County Herald-News (1 x week)
Transportation: Commute to work: 92.1% car, 0.0% public transportation, 3.1% walk, 4.2% work from home (2000); Travel time to work: 50.3% less than 15 minutes, 32.9% 15 to 30 minutes, 7.4% 30 to 45 minutes, 5.0% 45 to 60 minutes, 4.4% 60 minutes or more (2000)
Additional Information Contacts
Higgins Lake-Roscommon Chamber 989-275-8760

ROSCOMMON (township). Covers a land area of 103.932 square miles and a water area of 4.349 square miles. Located at 44.24° N. Lat.; 84.71° W. Long. Elevation is 1,130 feet.
Population: 4,249 (2000); Race: 97.8% White, 0.4% Black, 0.1% Asian, 0.9% American Indian and Alaska Native, 1.0% Hispanic of any race, 0.6% two or more races (2000); Density: 40.9 persons per square mile (2000); Age: 24.7% under 18, 18.0% over 64 (2000); Marriage status: 18.0% never married, 60.2% now married, 7.3% widowed, 14.4% divorced (2000); Foreign born: 0.9% (2000); Ancestry (includes multiple ancestries): 21.5% German, 13.9% English, 12.0% Irish, 8.0% Polish, 7.7% United States or American (2000).
Economy: Trade center for resort and farm area: cattle, forage and crops. Manufacturing of transportation equipment. Employment by occupation: 5.4% management, 15.8% professional, 24.4% services, 28.9% sales, 0.9% farming, 13.1% construction, 11.4% production (2000).
Income: Per capita income: $15,508 (2000); Median household income: $28,805 (2000); Poverty rate: 13.9% (2000).
Taxes: Total city taxes per capita: $173 (2000); City property taxes per capita: $151 (2000).
Education: High school graduation rate: 78.3% (2000); College graduation rate: 5.9% (2000).
Housing: Homeownership rate: 82.1% (2000); Median home value: $74,200 (2000); Median rent: $329 per month (2000); Median age of housing: 27 years (2000).
Transportation: Commute to work: 92.5% car, 1.5% public transportation, 1.5% walk, 2.8% work from home (2000); Travel time to work: 51.9% less than 15 minutes, 21.2% 15 to 30 minutes, 14.5% 30 to 45 minutes, 4.2% 45 to 60 minutes, 8.2% 60 minutes or more (2000)

SAINT HELEN (CDP). Aka Saint Helens. Covers a land area of 5.042 square miles and a water area of 0.880 square miles. Located at 44.36° N. Lat.; 84.41° W. Long.
History: St. Helen was settled in 1870 as a service center for lumbermen working the vast timberlands here. The village was first owned by the Henry L. Stevens & Company lumber firm. It later became a market center for a summer colony.
Population: 2,993 (2000); Race: 99.0% White, 0.0% Black, 0.0% Asian, 0.7% American Indian and Alaska Native, 0.9% Hispanic of any race, 0.3% two or more races (2000); Density: 593.6 persons per square mile (2000); Age: 20.5% under 18, 23.4% over 64 (2000); Marriage status: 13.2% never married, 53.5% now married, 15.0% widowed, 18.4% divorced (2000); Foreign born: 1.1% (2000); Ancestry (includes multiple ancestries): 25.4% German, 14.0% Irish, 10.3% English, 8.8% Polish, 8.2% Other groups (2000).
Economy: Employment by occupation: 11.2% management, 13.8% professional, 16.1% services, 24.2% sales, 0.5% farming, 14.7% construction, 19.4% production (2000).
Income: Per capita income: $17,198 (2000); Median household income: $24,104 (2000); Poverty rate: 19.5% (2000).
Education: High school graduation rate: 69.8% (2000); College graduation rate: 6.3% (2000).
Housing: Homeownership rate: 85.3% (2000); Median home value: $52,400 (2000); Median rent: $322 per month (2000); Median age of housing: 33 years (2000).
Transportation: Commute to work: 93.5% car, 0.0% public transportation, 1.0% walk, 3.4% work from home (2000); Travel time to work: 24.0% less than 15 minutes, 44.8% 15 to 30 minutes, 20.0% 30 to 45 minutes, 3.8% 45 to 60 minutes, 7.5% 60 minutes or more (2000)
Additional Information Contacts
St. Helen Chamber of Commerce. 989-389-3725

Saginaw County

Located in east central Michigan; drained by the Saginaw, Cass, Flint, Shiawassee, Bad, and Tittabawassee Rivers. Covers a land area of 808.90 square miles, a water area of 6.80 square miles, and is located in the Eastern Time Zone. The county government was organized in 1835. County seat is Saginaw.

Saginaw County is part of the Saginaw-Bay City-Midland, MI MSA. The entire metro area includes: Bay County; Midland County; Saginaw County

Weather Station: Saginaw Tri City Int'l Airport — Elevation: 659 feet

	Jan	Feb	Mar	Apr	May	Jun	Jul	Aug	Sep	Oct	Nov	Dec
High	28	30	41	55	68	77	82	79	71	59	45	33
Low	15	16	25	36	47	56	61	58	51	40	31	21
Precip	1.7	1.5	2.5	2.8	2.8	3.0	2.5	3.3	4.0	2.6	2.7	2.1
Snow	11.4	8.0	8.4	2.2	tr	tr	tr	tr	tr	0.2	3.6	11.0

High and Low temperatures in degrees Fahrenheit; Precipitation and Snow in inches

Population: 210,039 (2000); Race: 75.2% White, 18.4% Black, 0.8% Asian, 0.4% American Indian and Alaska Native, 6.7% Hispanic of any race, 2.1% two or more races (2000); Density: 259.6 persons per square mile (2000); Age: 26.6% under 18, 13.4% over 64 (2000).
Religion: Five largest groups: 20.0% Catholic Church, 8.3% Lutheran Church—Missouri Synod, 4.0% New Testament Association of Independent Baptist Churches and other Fundamental Baptist Associations, 3.3% Evangelical Lutheran Church in America, 2.8%
Economy: Unemployment rate: 6.6% (11/2002); Total civilian labor force: 100,787 (11/2002); Leading industries: 22.1% manufacturing; 16.2% retail trade; 15.5% health care and social assistance (2000); Companies that employ more than 1,000 persons: 7 (2000); Companies that employ more than 100 persons: 124 (2000); Farms: 1,163 totaling 297,842 acres (1997); Minority business ownership rate: 9.3% (1997); Women business ownership rate: 28.1% (1997); Retail sales per capita: $11,753 (1997). Single-family building permits issued: 490 (2001) / 630 (2000); Multi-family building permits issued: 40 (2001) / 342 (2000).
Income: Per capita income: $19,438 (2000); Median household income: $38,637 (2000); Poverty rate: 13.9% (2000); Bankruptcy rate: 5.11% (2001).
Taxes: Total county taxes per capita: $130 (2000); County property taxes per capita: $119 (2000).
Education: High school graduation rate: 81.6% (2000); College graduation rate: 15.9% (2000).
Housing: Homeownership rate: 73.8% (2000); Median home value: $85,200 (2000); Median rent: $406 per month (2000); Median age of housing: 38 years (2000).
Health: Birth rate: 137.1 per 10,000 population (1998); Age adjusted death rate: 87.2 per 10,000 population (1999); Age adjusted cancer mortality rate: 201.2 deaths per 100,000 population (1999). Number of physicians: 21.9 per 10,000 population (1999); Number of hospital beds: 57.3 per 10,000 population (1999).
Elections: 2000 Presidential election results: 54.2% Gore, 43.9% Bush, 1.5% Nader, 0.0% Buchanan
National and State Parks: Crow Island State Game Area; Gratiot - Saginaw State Game Management Area; Shiawassee National Wildlife Refuge; Shiawassee River State Game Area
Additional Information Contacts
Saginaw County Government Offices 989-790-5210
Bridgeport Chamber of Commerce 989-777-6041
Chesaning Chamber of Commerce. 989-845-4252

Frankenmuth Chamber of Commerce 989-652-6106
Freeland Area Chamber of Commerce. 989-695-6620
Saginaw Board of Realtors. 989-793-6332
Saginaw Chamber of Commerce 989-752-7161
Saginaw County Convention Bureau 989-752-7164
St. Charles Chamber of Commerce 989-865-8635

Saginaw County Communities

ALBEE (township). Covers a land area of 36.105 square miles and a water area of 0.047 square miles. Located at 43.26° N. Lat.; 83.98° W. Long.
History: Albee Township was organized in 1863 and named for William C. Albee, who had settled here in 1855.
Population: 2,338 (2000); Race: 92.7% White, 0.9% Black, 0.3% Asian, 2.0% American Indian and Alaska Native, 6.1% Hispanic of any race, 1.8% two or more races (2000); Density: 64.8 persons per square mile (2000); Age: 30.6% under 18, 7.9% over 64 (2000); Marriage status: 22.5% never married, 61.0% now married, 5.9% widowed, 10.6% divorced (2000); Foreign born: 1.2% (2000); Ancestry (includes multiple ancestries): 27.0% German, 14.7% United States or American, 10.9% Other groups, 7.7% Irish, 7.3% French (except Basque) (2000).
Economy: Single-family building permits issued: 6 (2001) / 8 (2000); Multi-family building permits issued: 0 (2001) / 0 (2000); Employment by occupation: 6.2% management, 10.4% professional, 19.3% services, 20.7% sales, 0.7% farming, 15.4% construction, 27.2% production (2000).
Income: Per capita income: $16,415 (2000); Median household income: $42,000 (2000); Poverty rate: 9.2% (2000).
Taxes: Total city taxes per capita: $38 (1997); City property taxes per capita: $32 (1997).
Education: High school graduation rate: 74.5% (2000); College graduation rate: 7.7% (2000).
Housing: Homeownership rate: 92.5% (2000); Median home value: $79,700 (2000); Median rent: $406 per month (2000); Median age of housing: 34 years (2000).
Transportation: Commute to work: 96.3% car, 0.9% public transportation, 0.7% walk, 1.5% work from home (2000); Travel time to work: 11.6% less than 15 minutes, 48.1% 15 to 30 minutes, 25.6% 30 to 45 minutes, 8.4% 45 to 60 minutes, 6.4% 60 minutes or more (2000)

BIRCH RUN (village). Covers a land area of 1.919 square miles and a water area of 0 square miles. Located at 43.25° N. Lat.; 83.79° W. Long. Elevation is 635 feet.
History: Birch Run was founded when the Pere Marquette Railroad needed a station here in 1852. This was first a bean-raising area. Oil was discovered here in 1925.
Population: 1,653 (2000); Race: 95.1% White, 0.8% Black, 0.6% Asian, 0.2% American Indian and Alaska Native, 3.6% Hispanic of any race, 2.2% two or more races (2000); Density: 861.5 persons per square mile (2000); Age: 26.9% under 18, 11.2% over 64 (2000); Marriage status: 22.1% never married, 55.5% now married, 7.9% widowed, 14.5% divorced (2000); Foreign born: 1.4% (2000); Ancestry (includes multiple ancestries): 33.1% German, 13.7% Irish, 11.9% English, 10.3% Polish, 8.7% French (except Basque) (2000).
Economy: Single-family building permits issued: 0 (2001) / 31 (2000); Multi-family building permits issued: 0 (2001) / 16 (2000); Employment by occupation: 12.0% management, 15.4% professional, 11.3% services, 34.4% sales, 0.0% farming, 8.7% construction, 18.3% production (2000).
Income: Per capita income: $20,631 (2000); Median household income: $41,685 (2000); Poverty rate: 4.8% (2000).
Taxes: Total city taxes per capita: $749 (1997); City property taxes per capita: $669 (1997).
Education: High school graduation rate: 88.1% (2000); College graduation rate: 16.8% (2000).

School District(s)

Birch Run Area School District (KG-12)
2000 Enrollment: 1,941 517-624-9307
Housing: Homeownership rate: 62.8% (2000); Median home value: $99,900 (2000); Median rent: $483 per month (2000); Median age of housing: 16 years (2000).
Safety: Violent crime rate: 78.2 per 10,000 population; Property crime rate: 2,791.8 per 10,000 population (2001).
Transportation: Commute to work: 95.9% car, 0.0% public transportation, 2.0% walk, 1.7% work from home (2000); Travel time to work: 27.2% less than 15 minutes, 43.1% 15 to 30 minutes, 19.9% 30 to 45 minutes, 2.9% 45 to 60 minutes, 6.9% 60 minutes or more (2000)

BIRCH RUN (township). Covers a land area of 35.600 square miles and a water area of 0 square miles. Located at 43.25° N. Lat.; 83.77° W. Long. Elevation is 635 feet.
Population: 6,191 (2000); Race: 96.1% White, 0.2% Black, 0.3% Asian, 0.2% American Indian and Alaska Native, 3.0% Hispanic of any race, 1.3% two or more races (2000); Density: 173.9 persons per square mile (2000); Age: 27.0% under 18, 11.4% over 64 (2000); Marriage status: 21.3% never married, 64.7% now married, 4.8% widowed, 9.2% divorced (2000); Foreign born: 2.0% (2000); Ancestry (includes multiple ancestries): 36.6% German, 12.7% Polish, 10.2% English, 10.0% Irish, 7.4% United States or American (2000).
Economy: In agricultural area; steel fabricating. Single-family building permits issued: 18 (2001) / 12 (2000); Multi-family building permits issued: 0 (2001) / 0 (2000); Employment by occupation: 10.7% management, 16.2% professional, 14.1% services, 26.2% sales, 0.0% farming, 11.4% construction, 21.3% production (2000).
Income: Per capita income: $20,984 (2000); Median household income: $47,538 (2000); Poverty rate: 4.9% (2000).
Taxes: Total city taxes per capita: $52 (1997); City property taxes per capita: $39 (1997).
Education: High school graduation rate: 85.1% (2000); College graduation rate: 16.3% (2000).
Housing: Homeownership rate: 82.2% (2000); Median home value: $108,300 (2000); Median rent: $465 per month (2000); Median age of housing: 28 years (2000).
Transportation: Commute to work: 93.8% car, 0.0% public transportation, 1.1% walk, 4.8% work from home (2000); Travel time to work: 31.8% less than 15 minutes, 37.7% 15 to 30 minutes, 20.2% 30 to 45 minutes, 4.7% 45 to 60 minutes, 5.5% 60 minutes or more (2000)

BLUMFIELD (township). Covers a land area of 35.637 square miles and a water area of 0.003 square miles. Located at 43.43° N. Lat.; 83.77° W. Long.
History: Blumfield Township was organized in 1853 by Germans who fled from the 1848 political turmoil in Germany. It was named for Robert Blum, a political offender who had been killed in 1848.
Population: 2,014 (2000); Race: 98.2% White, 0.0% Black, 0.8% Asian, 0.0% American Indian and Alaska Native, 1.7% Hispanic of any race, 0.8% two or more races (2000); Density: 56.5 persons per square mile (2000); Age: 26.5% under 18, 12.8% over 64 (2000); Marriage status: 19.0% never married, 71.1% now married, 4.4% widowed, 5.5% divorced (2000); Foreign born: 1.0% (2000); Ancestry (includes multiple ancestries): 63.5% German, 9.5% English, 8.3% Polish, 8.3% French (except Basque), 7.1% Irish (2000).
Economy: Single-family building permits issued: 3 (2001) / 3 (2000); Multi-family building permits issued: 0 (2001) / 0 (2000); Employment by occupation: 14.9% management, 16.5% professional, 13.5% services, 26.2% sales, 0.7% farming, 12.9% construction, 15.4% production (2000).
Income: Per capita income: $22,514 (2000); Median household income: $53,182 (2000); Poverty rate: 3.9% (2000).
Taxes: Total city taxes per capita: $85 (1997); City property taxes per capita: $72 (1997).
Education: High school graduation rate: 86.0% (2000); College graduation rate: 13.4% (2000).
Housing: Homeownership rate: 90.4% (2000); Median home value: $122,800 (2000); Median rent: $458 per month (2000); Median age of housing: 39 years (2000).
Transportation: Commute to work: 95.3% car, 0.2% public transportation, 0.8% walk, 3.5% work from home (2000); Travel time to work: 33.7% less than 15 minutes, 48.9% 15 to 30 minutes, 13.0% 30 to 45 minutes, 3.3% 45 to 60 minutes, 1.1% 60 minutes or more (2000)

BRADY (township). Covers a land area of 36.746 square miles and a water area of 0.028 square miles. Located at 43.16° N. Lat.; 84.22° W. Long.
History: Brady Township was organized in 1856 and named for General Hugh Brady of Detroit.
Population: 2,344 (2000); Race: 98.3% White, 0.0% Black, 0.0% Asian, 0.1% American Indian and Alaska Native, 1.8% Hispanic of any race, 0.9% two or more races (2000); Density: 63.8 persons per square mile (2000); Age: 27.3% under 18, 11.3% over 64 (2000); Marriage status: 24.1% never married, 61.4% now married, 6.6% widowed, 7.9% divorced (2000); Foreign born: 0.7% (2000); Ancestry (includes multiple ancestries): 38.6% German, 11.7% Irish, 10.2% English, 6.7% United States or American, 5.9% Polish (2000).
Economy: Single-family building permits issued: 0 (2001) / 0 (2000); Multi-family building permits issued: 0 (2001) / 0 (2000); Employment by

occupation: 5.3% management, 11.5% professional, 20.0% services, 23.0% sales, 0.7% farming, 12.5% construction, 26.9% production (2000).
Income: Per capita income: $16,723 (2000); Median household income: $40,565 (2000); Poverty rate: 6.1% (2000).
Taxes: Total city taxes per capita: $19 (1997); City property taxes per capita: $14 (1997).
Education: High school graduation rate: 81.3% (2000); College graduation rate: 6.3% (2000).
Housing: Homeownership rate: 87.4% (2000); Median home value: $90,100 (2000); Median rent: $396 per month (2000); Median age of housing: 31 years (2000).
Transportation: Commute to work: 96.4% car, 0.0% public transportation, 1.3% walk, 2.1% work from home (2000); Travel time to work: 26.6% less than 15 minutes, 26.9% 15 to 30 minutes, 19.9% 30 to 45 minutes, 14.6% 45 to 60 minutes, 12.0% 60 minutes or more (2000)

BRANT (township). Covers a land area of 37.066 square miles and a water area of 0.014 square miles. Located at 43.26° N. Lat.; 84.22° W. Long. Elevation is 613 feet.
History: Brant Township was founded in 1858.
Population: 2,023 (2000); Race: 98.0% White, 0.0% Black, 0.0% Asian, 0.0% American Indian and Alaska Native, 2.4% Hispanic of any race, 1.7% two or more races (2000); Density: 54.6 persons per square mile (2000); Age: 28.5% under 18, 9.4% over 64 (2000); Marriage status: 20.1% never married, 68.1% now married, 5.2% widowed, 6.6% divorced (2000); Foreign born: 1.0% (2000); Ancestry (includes multiple ancestries): 36.8% German, 12.4% English, 11.6% Irish, 9.6% Polish, 9.6% French (except Basque) (2000).
Economy: Single-family building permits issued: 12 (2001) / 15 (2000); Multi-family building permits issued: 0 (2001) / 0 (2000); Employment by occupation: 8.2% management, 11.9% professional, 13.9% services, 23.3% sales, 0.4% farming, 17.2% construction, 25.1% production (2000).
Income: Per capita income: $19,400 (2000); Median household income: $46,157 (2000); Poverty rate: 8.3% (2000).
Taxes: Total city taxes per capita: $29 (1997); City property taxes per capita: $27 (1997).
Education: High school graduation rate: 80.6% (2000); College graduation rate: 7.9% (2000).
Housing: Homeownership rate: 94.2% (2000); Median home value: $94,500 (2000); Median rent: $378 per month (2000); Median age of housing: 26 years (2000).
Transportation: Commute to work: 95.3% car, 0.4% public transportation, 0.0% walk, 2.9% work from home (2000); Travel time to work: 14.8% less than 15 minutes, 24.4% 15 to 30 minutes, 34.0% 30 to 45 minutes, 18.0% 45 to 60 minutes, 8.8% 60 minutes or more (2000)

BRIDGEPORT (CDP). Covers a land area of 8.337 square miles and a water area of 0 square miles. Located at 43.37° N. Lat.; 83.89° W. Long.
Population: 7,849 (2000); Race: 63.3% White, 29.3% Black, 0.6% Asian, 0.3% American Indian and Alaska Native, 9.7% Hispanic of any race, 3.0% two or more races (2000); Density: 941.4 persons per square mile (2000); Age: 25.8% under 18, 12.0% over 64 (2000); Marriage status: 26.2% never married, 55.3% now married, 6.6% widowed, 12.0% divorced (2000); Foreign born: 0.9% (2000); Ancestry (includes multiple ancestries): 41.4% Other groups, 22.0% German, 8.0% Polish, 6.8% Irish, 5.4% French (except Basque) (2000).
Economy: In farm area. Manufacturing: machinery, battery-operated vehicles, medical supplies, pickles and sauerkraut, gauges and dies. Employment by occupation: 5.8% management, 12.4% professional, 23.7% services, 25.3% sales, 0.1% farming, 10.2% construction, 22.4% production (2000).
Income: Per capita income: $19,797 (2000); Median household income: $37,515 (2000); Poverty rate: 11.3% (2000).
Education: High school graduation rate: 78.1% (2000); College graduation rate: 11.2% (2000).

School District(s)

Bridgeport-Spaulding Community S (KG-12)
2000 Enrollment: 2,499 517-777-1770

Housing: Homeownership rate: 72.0% (2000); Median home value: $72,000 (2000); Median rent: $390 per month (2000); Median age of housing: 35 years (2000).
Transportation: Commute to work: 95.2% car, 0.9% public transportation, 0.7% walk, 2.0% work from home (2000); Travel time to work: 33.3% less than 15 minutes, 44.2% 15 to 30 minutes, 15.1% 30 to 45 minutes, 2.8% 45 to 60 minutes, 4.6% 60 minutes or more (2000)

Additional Information Contacts

Bridgeport Chamber of Commerce 989-777-6041

BRIDGEPORT CHARTER (township). Covers a land area of 34.628 square miles and a water area of 0.079 square miles. Located at 43.36° N. Lat.; 83.88° W. Long. Elevation is 610 feet.
Population: 11,709 (2000); Race: 73.7% White, 20.4% Black, 0.4% Asian, 0.3% American Indian and Alaska Native, 8.4% Hispanic of any race, 2.4% two or more races (2000); Density: 338.1 persons per square mile (2000); Age: 25.0% under 18, 12.6% over 64 (2000); Marriage status: 24.9% never married, 58.2% now married, 6.3% widowed, 10.6% divorced (2000); Foreign born: 0.9% (2000); Ancestry (includes multiple ancestries): 32.5% Other groups, 27.9% German, 9.2% Polish, 7.8% Irish, 6.2% French (except Basque) (2000).
Economy: Single-family building permits issued: 15 (2001) / 15 (2000); Multi-family building permits issued: 0 (2001) / 0 (2000); Employment by occupation: 6.6% management, 12.6% professional, 21.0% services, 24.7% sales, 0.4% farming, 11.8% construction, 22.9% production (2000).
Income: Per capita income: $19,760 (2000); Median household income: $39,765 (2000); Poverty rate: 9.4% (2000).
Taxes: Total city taxes per capita: $146 (2000); City property taxes per capita: $141 (2000).
Education: High school graduation rate: 79.1% (2000); College graduation rate: 10.2% (2000).
Housing: Homeownership rate: 78.2% (2000); Median home value: $76,100 (2000); Median rent: $384 per month (2000); Median age of housing: 35 years (2000).
Transportation: Commute to work: 95.3% car, 0.5% public transportation, 1.4% walk, 1.9% work from home (2000); Travel time to work: 33.8% less than 15 minutes, 44.0% 15 to 30 minutes, 14.3% 30 to 45 minutes, 2.7% 45 to 60 minutes, 5.3% 60 minutes or more (2000)

BUENA VISTA (CDP). Covers a land area of 4.481 square miles and a water area of 0 square miles. Located at 43.41° N. Lat.; 83.90° W. Long.
Population: 7,845 (2000); Race: 21.8% White, 68.7% Black, 0.4% Asian, 0.1% American Indian and Alaska Native, 9.8% Hispanic of any race, 3.2% two or more races (2000); Density: 1,750.6 persons per square mile (2000); Age: 30.9% under 18, 12.4% over 64 (2000); Marriage status: 36.4% never married, 39.8% now married, 8.1% widowed, 15.7% divorced (2000); Foreign born: 0.4% (2000); Ancestry (includes multiple ancestries): 70.1% Other groups, 6.5% German, 4.1% African, 2.8% Irish, 2.3% English (2000).
Economy: Employment by occupation: 8.4% management, 10.9% professional, 25.2% services, 24.4% sales, 0.0% farming, 4.9% construction, 26.1% production (2000).
Income: Per capita income: $14,243 (2000); Median household income: $26,689 (2000); Poverty rate: 22.9% (2000).
Education: High school graduation rate: 74.1% (2000); College graduation rate: 7.6% (2000).
Housing: Homeownership rate: 71.2% (2000); Median home value: $37,400 (2000); Median rent: $374 per month (2000); Median age of housing: 42 years (2000).
Safety: Violent crime rate: 89.7 per 10,000 population; Property crime rate: 691.3 per 10,000 population (2001).
Transportation: Commute to work: 92.5% car, 2.0% public transportation, 1.2% walk, 2.7% work from home (2000); Travel time to work: 43.1% less than 15 minutes, 37.0% 15 to 30 minutes, 12.0% 30 to 45 minutes, 3.4% 45 to 60 minutes, 4.5% 60 minutes or more (2000)

BUENA VISTA CHARTER (township). Covers a land area of 35.993 square miles and a water area of 0.232 square miles. Located at 43.43° N. Lat.; 83.88° W. Long.
Population: 10,318 (2000); Race: 36.6% White, 55.3% Black, 0.3% Asian, 0.1% American Indian and Alaska Native, 9.0% Hispanic of any race, 2.6% two or more races (2000); Density: 286.7 persons per square mile (2000); Age: 30.3% under 18, 12.3% over 64 (2000); Marriage status: 34.0% never married, 43.6% now married, 7.2% widowed, 15.2% divorced (2000); Foreign born: 0.4% (2000); Ancestry (includes multiple ancestries): 57.3% Other groups, 14.7% German, 4.0% Polish, 3.8% English, 3.3% Irish (2000).
Economy: Single-family building permits issued: 0 (2001) / 0 (2000); Multi-family building permits issued: 0 (2001) / 0 (2000); Employment by occupation: 8.5% management, 11.6% professional, 24.1% services, 24.7% sales, 0.3% farming, 6.8% construction, 24.1% production (2000).
Income: Per capita income: $15,636 (2000); Median household income: $30,339 (2000); Poverty rate: 20.4% (2000).
Taxes: Total city taxes per capita: $208 (2000); City property taxes per capita: $188 (2000).
Education: High school graduation rate: 76.0% (2000); College graduation rate: 7.4% (2000).

Housing: Homeownership rate: 76.5% (2000); Median home value: $42,700 (2000); Median rent: $379 per month (2000); Median age of housing: 41 years (2000).
Transportation: Commute to work: 94.2% car, 1.4% public transportation, 0.9% walk, 2.3% work from home (2000); Travel time to work: 38.9% less than 15 minutes, 42.6% 15 to 30 minutes, 11.8% 30 to 45 minutes, 2.5% 45 to 60 minutes, 4.2% 60 minutes or more (2000)

BURT (CDP). Covers a land area of 4.536 square miles and a water area of 0 square miles. Located at 43.24° N. Lat.; 83.91° W. Long.
History: Burt developed around a station on the Cincinnati, Saginaw & Mackinaw Railroad.
Population: 1,122 (2000); Race: 90.1% White, 0.4% Black, 1.9% Asian, 0.6% American Indian and Alaska Native, 8.7% Hispanic of any race, 6.7% two or more races (2000); Density: 247.4 persons per square mile (2000); Age: 32.3% under 18, 4.6% over 64 (2000); Marriage status: 25.9% never married, 66.3% now married, 1.7% widowed, 6.1% divorced (2000); Foreign born: 1.9% (2000); Ancestry (includes multiple ancestries): 30.7% German, 24.3% Other groups, 10.1% French (except Basque), 10.1% Polish, 8.9% English (2000).
Economy: Employment by occupation: 2.3% management, 8.2% professional, 14.8% services, 35.3% sales, 0.0% farming, 15.9% construction, 23.5% production (2000).
Income: Per capita income: $15,997 (2000); Median household income: $47,250 (2000); Poverty rate: 8.3% (2000).
Education: High school graduation rate: 81.7% (2000); College graduation rate: 7.6% (2000).
Housing: Homeownership rate: 88.5% (2000); Median home value: $92,400 (2000); Median rent: $344 per month (2000); Median age of housing: 29 years (2000).
Transportation: Commute to work: 94.8% car, 0.0% public transportation, 3.3% walk, 1.9% work from home (2000); Travel time to work: 22.0% less than 15 minutes, 28.1% 15 to 30 minutes, 36.2% 30 to 45 minutes, 8.7% 45 to 60 minutes, 5.0% 60 minutes or more (2000)

CARROLLTON (CDP). Covers a land area of 3.211 square miles and a water area of 0.212 square miles. Located at 43.45° N. Lat.; 83.94° W. Long.
Population: 6,602 (2000); Race: 82.3% White, 8.7% Black, 1.3% Asian, 0.1% American Indian and Alaska Native, 10.7% Hispanic of any race, 3.9% two or more races (2000); Density: 2,056.2 persons per square mile (2000); Age: 27.6% under 18, 14.7% over 64 (2000); Marriage status: 27.4% never married, 56.3% now married, 7.6% widowed, 8.7% divorced (2000); Foreign born: 1.2% (2000); Ancestry (includes multiple ancestries): 29.4% German, 23.4% Other groups, 16.5% Polish, 12.4% English, 10.6% Irish (2000).
Economy: Beet sugar refining. Manufacturing of asphalt mixes. Single-family building permits issued: 7 (2001) / 5 (2000); Multi-family building permits issued: 0 (2001) / 0 (2000); Employment by occupation: 8.5% management, 16.1% professional, 19.7% services, 30.7% sales, 0.0% farming, 9.4% construction, 15.8% production (2000).
Income: Per capita income: $16,377 (2000); Median household income: $38,405 (2000); Poverty rate: 8.9% (2000).
Education: High school graduation rate: 80.3% (2000); College graduation rate: 10.8% (2000).

School District(s)

Carrollton School District (KG-12)
2000 Enrollment: 1,448 517-754-1475
Housing: Homeownership rate: 74.6% (2000); Median home value: $68,100 (2000); Median rent: $432 per month (2000); Median age of housing: 41 years (2000).
Safety: Violent crime rate: 13.6 per 10,000 population; Property crime rate: 262.2 per 10,000 population (2001).
Transportation: Commute to work: 94.8% car, 0.4% public transportation, 1.6% walk, 3.2% work from home (2000); Travel time to work: 49.0% less than 15 minutes, 33.7% 15 to 30 minutes, 7.7% 30 to 45 minutes, 3.2% 45 to 60 minutes, 6.4% 60 minutes or more (2000)

CHAPIN (township). Covers a land area of 24.671 square miles and a water area of 0 square miles. Located at 43.16° N. Lat.; 84.31° W. Long.
History: Chapin Township was organized in 1867 and named for Austin Chapin, one of the organizers.
Population: 1,045 (2000); Race: 93.5% White, 0.5% Black, 0.3% Asian, 1.9% American Indian and Alaska Native, 2.3% Hispanic of any race, 2.7% two or more races (2000); Density: 42.4 persons per square mile (2000); Age: 27.7% under 18, 7.8% over 64 (2000); Marriage status: 22.4% never married, 63.7% now married, 4.7% widowed, 9.2% divorced (2000); Foreign born: 0.6% (2000); Ancestry (includes multiple ancestries): 28.8% German, 10.9% Irish, 10.2% Other groups, 8.8% English, 6.3% United States or American (2000).
Economy: Single-family building permits issued: 0 (2001) / 0 (2000); Multi-family building permits issued: 0 (2001) / 0 (2000); Employment by occupation: 7.9% management, 9.2% professional, 16.7% services, 16.0% sales, 2.3% farming, 12.4% construction, 35.6% production (2000).
Income: Per capita income: $16,599 (2000); Median household income: $36,375 (2000); Poverty rate: 13.6% (2000).
Taxes: Total city taxes per capita: $30 (1997); City property taxes per capita: $27 (1997).
Education: High school graduation rate: 75.2% (2000); College graduation rate: 4.7% (2000).
Housing: Homeownership rate: 80.2% (2000); Median home value: $78,900 (2000); Median rent: $367 per month (2000); Median age of housing: 30 years (2000).
Transportation: Commute to work: 94.9% car, 0.0% public transportation, 1.2% walk, 3.9% work from home (2000); Travel time to work: 6.0% less than 15 minutes, 34.1% 15 to 30 minutes, 32.0% 30 to 45 minutes, 13.5% 45 to 60 minutes, 14.4% 60 minutes or more (2000)

CHESANING (village). Covers a land area of 3.114 square miles and a water area of 0 square miles. Located at 43.18° N. Lat.; 84.11° W. Long. Elevation is 636 feet.
History: Chesaning was settled in 1839 by Thomas W. Wright and his family. First called Northampton, the village was renamed Chesaning when the township was renamed.
Population: 2,548 (2000); Race: 96.4% White, 0.9% Black, 0.7% Asian, 0.0% American Indian and Alaska Native, 6.2% Hispanic of any race, 1.4% two or more races (2000); Density: 818.2 persons per square mile (2000); Age: 23.8% under 18, 16.7% over 64 (2000); Marriage status: 25.1% never married, 56.5% now married, 10.1% widowed, 8.3% divorced (2000); Foreign born: 1.7% (2000); Ancestry (includes multiple ancestries): 36.5% German, 16.1% Irish, 11.4% English, 9.3% Other groups, 6.1% Polish (2000).
Economy: Single-family building permits issued: 3 (2001) / 3 (2000); Multi-family building permits issued: 0 (2001) / 0 (2000); Employment by occupation: 13.0% management, 16.8% professional, 16.1% services, 24.6% sales, 0.0% farming, 8.0% construction, 21.4% production (2000).
Income: Per capita income: $19,408 (2000); Median household income: $34,952 (2000); Poverty rate: 9.7% (2000).
Taxes: Total city taxes per capita: $233 (1997); City property taxes per capita: $231 (1997).
Education: High school graduation rate: 82.0% (2000); College graduation rate: 13.7% (2000).

School District(s)

Chesaning Union Schools (KG-12)
2000 Enrollment: 2,189 517-845-7020
Housing: Homeownership rate: 64.8% (2000); Median home value: $89,000 (2000); Median rent: $332 per month (2000); Median age of housing: 46 years (2000).
Newspapers: Chesaning Tri-County Citizen (1 x week)
Transportation: Commute to work: 92.2% car, 0.0% public transportation, 5.7% walk, 2.1% work from home (2000); Travel time to work: 41.5% less than 15 minutes, 17.8% 15 to 30 minutes, 19.8% 30 to 45 minutes, 12.4% 45 to 60 minutes, 8.5% 60 minutes or more (2000)

Additional Information Contacts

Chesaning Chamber of Commerce. 989-845-4252

CHESANING (township). Covers a land area of 34.689 square miles and a water area of 0 square miles. Located at 43.18° N. Lat.; 84.11° W. Long. Elevation is 636 feet.
History: Chesaning Township began as Northampton Township in 1846. It was renamed in 1853. The name is of Indian origin meaning "big rock."
Population: 4,861 (2000); Race: 97.3% White, 0.5% Black, 0.5% Asian, 0.0% American Indian and Alaska Native, 4.8% Hispanic of any race, 0.7% two or more races (2000); Density: 140.1 persons per square mile (2000); Age: 24.4% under 18, 15.7% over 64 (2000); Marriage status: 22.8% never married, 61.4% now married, 8.6% widowed, 7.3% divorced (2000); Foreign born: 1.4% (2000); Ancestry (includes multiple ancestries): 37.0% German, 14.5% Irish, 13.6% English, 7.5% Other groups, 7.4% Polish (2000).
Economy: Single-family building permits issued: 17 (2001) / 17 (2000); Multi-family building permits issued: 0 (2001) / 0 (2000); Employment by occupation: 11.5% management, 15.1% professional, 16.0% services, 24.3% sales, 0.4% farming, 11.7% construction, 21.0% production (2000).
Income: Per capita income: $19,839 (2000); Median household income: $40,254 (2000); Poverty rate: 6.2% (2000).

Taxes: Total city taxes per capita: $47 (2000); City property taxes per capita: $42 (2000).
Education: High school graduation rate: 81.9% (2000); College graduation rate: 13.4% (2000).
Housing: Homeownership rate: 77.2% (2000); Median home value: $91,400 (2000); Median rent: $339 per month (2000); Median age of housing: 40 years (2000).
Transportation: Commute to work: 93.2% car, 0.0% public transportation, 4.0% walk, 2.5% work from home (2000); Travel time to work: 38.8% less than 15 minutes, 16.2% 15 to 30 minutes, 22.1% 30 to 45 minutes, 12.0% 45 to 60 minutes, 10.8% 60 minutes or more (2000)

FRANKENMUTH (city). Covers a land area of 2.728 square miles and a water area of 0.059 square miles. Located at 43.33° N. Lat.; 83.74° W. Long. Elevation is 625 feet.
History: Frankenmuth was settled by German immigrants, and became known for its Frankenmuth beer. It was established in 1845 by a group from Bavaria, who were joined by refugees from the German revolution of 1848.
Population: 4,838 (2000); Race: 99.2% White, 0.0% Black, 0.0% Asian, 0.2% American Indian and Alaska Native, 0.4% Hispanic of any race, 0.6% two or more races (2000); Density: 1,773.6 persons per square mile (2000); Age: 20.4% under 18, 28.7% over 64 (2000); Marriage status: 16.3% never married, 61.6% now married, 15.6% widowed, 6.5% divorced (2000); Foreign born: 1.9% (2000); Ancestry (includes multiple ancestries): 52.9% German, 13.2% English, 9.5% Irish, 7.9% Polish, 6.0% French (except Basque) (2000).
Economy: Single-family building permits issued: 8 (2001) / 10 (2000); Multi-family building permits issued: 4 (2001) / 6 (2000); Employment by occupation: 21.0% management, 23.4% professional, 10.6% services, 33.3% sales, 0.2% farming, 2.3% construction, 9.2% production (2000).
Income: Per capita income: $30,479 (2000); Median household income: $51,153 (2000); Poverty rate: 4.9% (2000).
Taxes: Total city taxes per capita: $359 (1997); City property taxes per capita: $349 (1997).
Education: High school graduation rate: 88.4% (2000); College graduation rate: 31.8% (2000).

School District(s)

Frankenmuth School District (KG-12)
2000 Enrollment: 1,259 517-652-9958
Housing: Homeownership rate: 67.3% (2000); Median home value: $146,700 (2000); Median rent: $524 per month (2000); Median age of housing: 26 years (2000).
Safety: Violent crime rate: 18.5 per 10,000 population; Property crime rate: 187.1 per 10,000 population (2001).
Newspapers: Frankenmuth News (1 x week)
Transportation: Commute to work: 92.8% car, 0.3% public transportation, 3.9% walk, 2.4% work from home (2000); Travel time to work: 50.9% less than 15 minutes, 27.0% 15 to 30 minutes, 16.9% 30 to 45 minutes, 2.7% 45 to 60 minutes, 2.5% 60 minutes or more (2000)
Additional Information Contacts
Frankenmuth Chamber of Commerce 989-652-6106

FRANKENMUTH (township). Covers a land area of 32.496 square miles and a water area of 0.162 square miles. Located at 43.34° N. Lat.; 83.75° W. Long. Elevation is 625 feet.
History: Historical Museum, Military and Space Museum, antique-arts village, flour mill (1847), Covered bridge on Cass River, famous German Glockenspiel, 35-bell carillon. Settled 1845 by German Bavarians; incorporated 1904.
Population: 2,049 (2000); Race: 98.4% White, 0.0% Black, 0.8% Asian, 0.0% American Indian and Alaska Native, 1.8% Hispanic of any race, 0.2% two or more races (2000); Density: 63.1 persons per square mile (2000); Age: 27.1% under 18, 13.2% over 64 (2000); Marriage status: 19.4% never married, 71.3% now married, 5.2% widowed, 4.1% divorced (2000); Foreign born: 1.5% (2000); Ancestry (includes multiple ancestries): 65.8% German, 13.3% English, 7.5% Irish, 6.5% United States or American, 6.4% French (except Basque) (2000).
Economy: In farm area; wineries; brewery. Manufacturing: printing, food processing, machine tools; tourism. Single-family building permits issued: 6 (2001) / 6 (2000); Multi-family building permits issued: 0 (2001) / 0 (2000); Employment by occupation: 17.7% management, 22.2% professional, 13.4% services, 25.7% sales, 1.0% farming, 9.0% construction, 11.1% production (2000).
Income: Per capita income: $25,833 (2000); Median household income: $61,480 (2000); Poverty rate: 3.5% (2000).
Taxes: Total city taxes per capita: $89 (1997); City property taxes per capita: $86 (1997).
Education: High school graduation rate: 88.3% (2000); College graduation rate: 26.1% (2000).
Housing: Homeownership rate: 89.8% (2000); Median home value: $155,300 (2000); Median rent: $447 per month (2000); Median age of housing: 37 years (2000).
Transportation: Commute to work: 93.0% car, 0.5% public transportation, 1.7% walk, 4.8% work from home (2000); Travel time to work: 49.2% less than 15 minutes, 31.9% 15 to 30 minutes, 13.0% 30 to 45 minutes, 2.1% 45 to 60 minutes, 3.8% 60 minutes or more (2000)

FREELAND (CDP). Covers a land area of 6.687 square miles and a water area of 0.028 square miles. Located at 43.52° N. Lat.; 84.12° W. Long. Elevation is 635 feet.
Population: 5,147 (2000); Race: 82.0% White, 12.7% Black, 0.2% Asian, 0.8% American Indian and Alaska Native, 4.3% Hispanic of any race, 2.9% two or more races (2000); Density: 769.7 persons per square mile (2000); Age: 21.3% under 18, 6.4% over 64 (2000); Marriage status: 31.5% never married, 52.4% now married, 4.0% widowed, 12.2% divorced (2000); Foreign born: 4.5% (2000); Ancestry (includes multiple ancestries): 31.2% German, 14.2% Other groups, 11.9% English, 8.5% Polish, 8.1% Irish (2000).
Economy: Employment by occupation: 11.9% management, 27.2% professional, 11.3% services, 30.6% sales, 0.4% farming, 10.4% construction, 8.3% production (2000).
Income: Per capita income: $20,470 (2000); Median household income: $55,455 (2000); Poverty rate: 2.6% (2000).
Education: High school graduation rate: 88.4% (2000); College graduation rate: 23.3% (2000).

School District(s)

Freeland Community School District (KG-12)
2000 Enrollment: 1,596 517-695-5527
Housing: Homeownership rate: 82.6% (2000); Median home value: $119,200 (2000); Median rent: $468 per month (2000); Median age of housing: 27 years (2000).
Transportation: Commute to work: 96.7% car, 0.0% public transportation, 0.2% walk, 2.8% work from home (2000); Travel time to work: 18.6% less than 15 minutes, 56.9% 15 to 30 minutes, 16.4% 30 to 45 minutes, 3.9% 45 to 60 minutes, 4.3% 60 minutes or more (2000)
Additional Information Contacts
Freeland Area Chamber of Commerce 989-695-6620

FREMONT (township). Covers a land area of 36.752 square miles and a water area of 0 square miles. Located at 43.34° N. Lat.; 84.22° W. Long.
Population: 2,099 (2000); Race: 97.0% White, 0.1% Black, 0.7% Asian, 0.7% American Indian and Alaska Native, 1.6% Hispanic of any race, 1.3% two or more races (2000); Density: 57.1 persons per square mile (2000); Age: 27.4% under 18, 8.7% over 64 (2000); Marriage status: 20.5% never married, 66.4% now married, 6.0% widowed, 7.1% divorced (2000); Foreign born: 1.0% (2000); Ancestry (includes multiple ancestries): 39.7% German, 12.7% Irish, 11.0% English, 10.8% Polish, 8.0% French (except Basque) (2000).
Economy: Single-family building permits issued: 11 (2001) / 9 (2000); Multi-family building permits issued: 0 (2001) / 0 (2000); Employment by occupation: 12.5% management, 16.8% professional, 14.9% services, 19.6% sales, 1.4% farming, 12.8% construction, 22.1% production (2000).
Income: Per capita income: $19,210 (2000); Median household income: $47,841 (2000); Poverty rate: 9.9% (2000).
Taxes: Total city taxes per capita: $30 (1997); City property taxes per capita: $28 (1997).
Education: High school graduation rate: 88.2% (2000); College graduation rate: 12.7% (2000).
Housing: Homeownership rate: 92.4% (2000); Median home value: $97,700 (2000); Median rent: $356 per month (2000); Median age of housing: 27 years (2000).
Transportation: Commute to work: 94.1% car, 0.2% public transportation, 0.8% walk, 4.9% work from home (2000); Travel time to work: 13.1% less than 15 minutes, 32.2% 15 to 30 minutes, 34.0% 30 to 45 minutes, 11.6% 45 to 60 minutes, 9.2% 60 minutes or more (2000)

HEMLOCK (CDP). Covers a land area of 2.540 square miles and a water area of 0 square miles. Located at 43.41° N. Lat.; 84.23° W. Long. Elevation is 653 feet.
History: Hemlock developed around a sawmill built here in 1868 by W.S. Gillespie. The settlement grew when the Saginaw Valley & St. Louis

Railroad arrived in 1869. The town was named for the quantity of hemlock trees in the area.
Population: 1,585 (2000); Race: 98.4% White, 0.0% Black, 0.0% Asian, 0.0% American Indian and Alaska Native, 6.6% Hispanic of any race, 0.0% two or more races (2000); Density: 624.1 persons per square mile (2000); Age: 28.3% under 18, 13.9% over 64 (2000); Marriage status: 25.1% never married, 55.5% now married, 6.2% widowed, 13.3% divorced (2000); Foreign born: 1.8% (2000); Ancestry (includes multiple ancestries): 34.5% German, 15.4% Irish, 9.8% Polish, 9.6% Other groups, 6.9% United States or American (2000).
Economy: Employment by occupation: 8.1% management, 15.9% professional, 16.4% services, 30.9% sales, 1.1% farming, 8.5% construction, 19.1% production (2000).
Income: Per capita income: $18,085 (2000); Median household income: $40,846 (2000); Poverty rate: 9.9% (2000).
Education: High school graduation rate: 85.1% (2000); College graduation rate: 13.6% (2000).

School District(s)

Hemlock Public School District (PK-12)
2000 Enrollment: 1,495 517-642-5282
Housing: Homeownership rate: 77.7% (2000); Median home value: $86,800 (2000); Median rent: $344 per month (2000); Median age of housing: 36 years (2000).
Transportation: Commute to work: 97.4% car, 0.0% public transportation, 1.0% walk, 0.8% work from home (2000); Travel time to work: 25.0% less than 15 minutes, 32.6% 15 to 30 minutes, 32.5% 30 to 45 minutes, 3.5% 45 to 60 minutes, 6.4% 60 minutes or more (2000)

JAMES (township). Covers a land area of 18.156 square miles and a water area of 1.355 square miles. Located at 43.35° N. Lat.; 84.05° W. Long.
History: James Township, also known as Jimtown, was organized in 1875 and named for James Murphy, who began making bricks here in 1865.
Population: 1,930 (2000); Race: 96.4% White, 0.1% Black, 0.0% Asian, 0.6% American Indian and Alaska Native, 2.3% Hispanic of any race, 1.8% two or more races (2000); Density: 106.3 persons per square mile (2000); Age: 23.4% under 18, 10.7% over 64 (2000); Marriage status: 19.2% never married, 67.5% now married, 4.5% widowed, 8.9% divorced (2000); Foreign born: 0.7% (2000); Ancestry (includes multiple ancestries): 45.2% German, 13.0% Irish, 10.4% French (except Basque), 10.3% Polish, 9.6% English (2000).
Economy: Single-family building permits issued: 11 (2001) / 9 (2000); Multi-family building permits issued: 0 (2001) / 0 (2000); Employment by occupation: 11.6% management, 14.9% professional, 12.2% services, 26.0% sales, 0.5% farming, 15.4% construction, 19.3% production (2000).
Income: Per capita income: $22,340 (2000); Median household income: $54,286 (2000); Poverty rate: 3.7% (2000).
Taxes: Total city taxes per capita: $59 (1997); City property taxes per capita: $49 (1997).
Education: High school graduation rate: 85.4% (2000); College graduation rate: 11.2% (2000).
Housing: Homeownership rate: 93.6% (2000); Median home value: $95,100 (2000); Median rent: $446 per month (2000); Median age of housing: 40 years (2000).
Transportation: Commute to work: 95.8% car, 0.2% public transportation, 1.4% walk, 2.0% work from home (2000); Travel time to work: 31.7% less than 15 minutes, 48.3% 15 to 30 minutes, 12.8% 30 to 45 minutes, 1.9% 45 to 60 minutes, 5.3% 60 minutes or more (2000)

JONESFIELD (township). Covers a land area of 25.198 square miles and a water area of 0 square miles. Located at 43.41° N. Lat.; 84.33° W. Long.
History: The Jonesfield Township was organized in 1873 after the Saginaw Valley & St. Louis Railroad was built here.
Population: 1,710 (2000); Race: 98.2% White, 0.0% Black, 0.1% Asian, 0.4% American Indian and Alaska Native, 1.9% Hispanic of any race, 0.6% two or more races (2000); Density: 67.9 persons per square mile (2000); Age: 24.7% under 18, 15.8% over 64 (2000); Marriage status: 21.6% never married, 62.8% now married, 7.8% widowed, 7.9% divorced (2000); Foreign born: 0.5% (2000); Ancestry (includes multiple ancestries): 33.7% German, 12.8% Irish, 12.0% French (except Basque), 8.7% English, 7.4% Polish (2000).
Economy: Single-family building permits issued: 5 (2001) / 5 (2000); Multi-family building permits issued: 0 (2001) / 0 (2000); Employment by occupation: 7.7% management, 12.3% professional, 12.7% services, 30.7% sales, 0.5% farming, 12.2% construction, 23.9% production (2000).
Income: Per capita income: $19,348 (2000); Median household income: $41,992 (2000); Poverty rate: 7.7% (2000).
Taxes: Total city taxes per capita: $60 (1997); City property taxes per capita: $59 (1997).
Education: High school graduation rate: 87.4% (2000); College graduation rate: 9.3% (2000).
Housing: Homeownership rate: 86.3% (2000); Median home value: $75,100 (2000); Median rent: $388 per month (2000); Median age of housing: 46 years (2000).
Transportation: Commute to work: 94.7% car, 0.0% public transportation, 2.7% walk, 1.8% work from home (2000); Travel time to work: 20.8% less than 15 minutes, 23.8% 15 to 30 minutes, 38.7% 30 to 45 minutes, 10.5% 45 to 60 minutes, 6.2% 60 minutes or more (2000)

KOCHVILLE (township). Covers a land area of 18.795 square miles and a water area of 0 square miles. Located at 43.50° N. Lat.; 83.96° W. Long.
History: Kochville Township was organized in 1856 and named for Frederick Charles Koch, who had settled here in 1849.
Population: 3,241 (2000); Race: 88.8% White, 6.9% Black, 2.0% Asian, 0.0% American Indian and Alaska Native, 2.6% Hispanic of any race, 1.5% two or more races (2000); Density: 172.4 persons per square mile (2000); Age: 16.1% under 18, 8.2% over 64 (2000); Marriage status: 42.7% never married, 41.4% now married, 9.1% widowed, 6.8% divorced (2000); Foreign born: 3.4% (2000); Ancestry (includes multiple ancestries): 26.0% German, 9.8% United States or American, 8.7% Polish, 7.4% Other groups, 6.9% Irish (2000).
Economy: Single-family building permits issued: 5 (2001) / 11 (2000); Multi-family building permits issued: 0 (2001) / 0 (2000); Employment by occupation: 7.1% management, 19.8% professional, 21.7% services, 33.6% sales, 0.3% farming, 8.9% construction, 8.6% production (2000).
Income: Per capita income: $16,312 (2000); Median household income: $42,545 (2000); Poverty rate: 15.9% (2000).
Taxes: Total city taxes per capita: $61 (1997); City property taxes per capita: $51 (1997).
Education: High school graduation rate: 91.4% (2000); College graduation rate: 15.4% (2000).
Housing: Homeownership rate: 79.6% (2000); Median home value: $101,000 (2000); Median rent: $420 per month (2000); Median age of housing: 33 years (2000).
Transportation: Commute to work: 81.9% car, 0.5% public transportation, 14.7% walk, 0.7% work from home (2000); Travel time to work: 57.1% less than 15 minutes, 30.9% 15 to 30 minutes, 8.4% 30 to 45 minutes, 2.0% 45 to 60 minutes, 1.6% 60 minutes or more (2000)

LAKEFIELD (township). Covers a land area of 24.108 square miles and a water area of 0 square miles. Located at 43.34° N. Lat.; 84.34° W. Long. Elevation is 669 feet.
Population: 1,030 (2000); Race: 95.8% White, 0.0% Black, 0.2% Asian, 0.2% American Indian and Alaska Native, 5.5% Hispanic of any race, 2.0% two or more races (2000); Density: 42.7 persons per square mile (2000); Age: 24.4% under 18, 11.8% over 64 (2000); Marriage status: 22.0% never married, 68.8% now married, 4.8% widowed, 4.4% divorced (2000); Foreign born: 1.3% (2000); Ancestry (includes multiple ancestries): 37.3% German, 10.5% Irish, 10.0% English, 9.5% United States or American, 7.3% French (except Basque) (2000).
Economy: Single-family building permits issued: 9 (2001) / 10 (2000); Multi-family building permits issued: 0 (2001) / 0 (2000); Employment by occupation: 8.2% management, 14.3% professional, 9.2% services, 27.1% sales, 0.8% farming, 18.3% construction, 22.1% production (2000).
Income: Per capita income: $22,265 (2000); Median household income: $44,500 (2000); Poverty rate: 5.9% (2000).
Taxes: Total city taxes per capita: $89 (1997); City property taxes per capita: $86 (1997).
Education: High school graduation rate: 86.2% (2000); College graduation rate: 11.6% (2000).
Housing: Homeownership rate: 94.8% (2000); Median home value: $90,700 (2000); Median rent: $313 per month (2000); Median age of housing: 29 years (2000).
Transportation: Commute to work: 94.6% car, 0.0% public transportation, 0.2% walk, 4.5% work from home (2000); Travel time to work: 16.4% less than 15 minutes, 18.7% 15 to 30 minutes, 44.4% 30 to 45 minutes, 11.5% 45 to 60 minutes, 9.0% 60 minutes or more (2000)

MAPLE GROVE (township). Covers a land area of 35.640 square miles and a water area of 1.029 square miles. Located at 43.18° N. Lat.; 83.97° W. Long.

Population: 2,640 (2000); Race: 98.6% White, 0.7% Black, 0.0% Asian, 0.0% American Indian and Alaska Native, 0.8% Hispanic of any race, 0.2% two or more races (2000); Density: 74.1 persons per square mile (2000); Age: 23.2% under 18, 12.1% over 64 (2000); Marriage status: 23.0% never married, 65.4% now married, 5.1% widowed, 6.5% divorced (2000); Foreign born: 0.3% (2000); Ancestry (includes multiple ancestries): 48.2% German, 10.8% United States or American, 9.0% English, 8.9% Irish, 7.2% French (except Basque) (2000).
Economy: Single-family building permits issued: 8 (2001) / 13 (2000); Multi-family building permits issued: 0 (2001) / 0 (2000); Employment by occupation: 7.1% management, 17.6% professional, 13.7% services, 21.7% sales, 0.5% farming, 17.4% construction, 22.1% production (2000).
Income: Per capita income: $24,506 (2000); Median household income: $56,111 (2000); Poverty rate: 6.7% (2000).
Taxes: Total city taxes per capita: $21 (1997); City property taxes per capita: $16 (1997).
Education: High school graduation rate: 84.1% (2000); College graduation rate: 9.0% (2000).
Housing: Homeownership rate: 89.1% (2000); Median home value: $108,100 (2000); Median rent: $381 per month (2000); Median age of housing: 30 years (2000).
Transportation: Commute to work: 95.2% car, 0.2% public transportation, 0.9% walk, 3.0% work from home (2000); Travel time to work: 21.5% less than 15 minutes, 23.3% 15 to 30 minutes, 37.8% 30 to 45 minutes, 9.9% 45 to 60 minutes, 7.5% 60 minutes or more (2000)

MARION (township). Covers a land area of 24.639 square miles and a water area of 0 square miles. Located at 43.26° N. Lat.; 84.31° W. Long.
Population: 925 (2000); Race: 97.0% White, 0.4% Black, 0.0% Asian, 1.5% American Indian and Alaska Native, 0.0% Hispanic of any race, 1.1% two or more races (2000); Density: 37.5 persons per square mile (2000); Age: 28.5% under 18, 8.0% over 64 (2000); Marriage status: 24.5% never married, 63.0% now married, 5.5% widowed, 6.9% divorced (2000); Foreign born: 0.9% (2000); Ancestry (includes multiple ancestries): 38.9% German, 10.7% Irish, 6.1% English, 5.3% Polish, 5.2% Other groups (2000).
Economy: Single-family building permits issued: 6 (2001) / 12 (2000); Multi-family building permits issued: 0 (2001) / 0 (2000); Employment by occupation: 8.3% management, 10.1% professional, 9.9% services, 21.0% sales, 1.3% farming, 21.0% construction, 28.3% production (2000).
Income: Per capita income: $16,703 (2000); Median household income: $38,333 (2000); Poverty rate: 14.3% (2000).
Taxes: Total city taxes per capita: $67 (1997); City property taxes per capita: $62 (1997).
Education: High school graduation rate: 78.9% (2000); College graduation rate: 6.5% (2000).
Housing: Homeownership rate: 84.6% (2000); Median home value: $87,900 (2000); Median rent: $350 per month (2000); Median age of housing: 25 years (2000).
Transportation: Commute to work: 96.2% car, 0.0% public transportation, 0.0% walk, 3.8% work from home (2000); Travel time to work: 9.2% less than 15 minutes, 27.3% 15 to 30 minutes, 33.7% 30 to 45 minutes, 22.6% 45 to 60 minutes, 7.2% 60 minutes or more (2000)

MERRILL (village). Covers a land area of 0.685 square miles and a water area of 0 square miles. Located at 43.41° N. Lat.; 84.33° W. Long. Elevation is 671 feet.
History: Merrill was named for a railroad engineer who assisted the residents of the town in 1881 when a forest fire threatened their community. The town grew up around a wheat, beans, and sugar beet growing area.
Population: 782 (2000); Race: 97.2% White, 0.0% Black, 0.0% Asian, 0.8% American Indian and Alaska Native, 4.3% Hispanic of any race, 0.3% two or more races (2000); Density: 1,141.4 persons per square mile (2000); Age: 27.7% under 18, 16.8% over 64 (2000); Marriage status: 20.6% never married, 59.1% now married, 9.2% widowed, 11.1% divorced (2000); Foreign born: 0.3% (2000); Ancestry (includes multiple ancestries): 32.6% German, 10.4% Irish, 10.2% Polish, 8.0% Other groups, 6.7% English (2000).
Economy: Single-family building permits issued: 3 (2001) / 4 (2000); Multi-family building permits issued: 0 (2001) / 0 (2000); Employment by occupation: 9.4% management, 10.3% professional, 13.8% services, 27.2% sales, 1.3% farming, 11.6% construction, 26.6% production (2000).
Income: Per capita income: $19,312 (2000); Median household income: $36,167 (2000); Poverty rate: 8.0% (2000).
Taxes: Total city taxes per capita: $167 (1997); City property taxes per capita: $161 (1997).
Education: High school graduation rate: 87.5% (2000); College graduation rate: 10.1% (2000).

School District(s)

Merrill Community Schools (KG-12)
2000 Enrollment: 943 517-643-7261
Housing: Homeownership rate: 82.0% (2000); Median home value: $64,000 (2000); Median rent: $339 per month (2000); Median age of housing: 54 years (2000).
Transportation: Commute to work: 95.2% car, 0.0% public transportation, 4.2% walk, 0.6% work from home (2000); Travel time to work: 21.1% less than 15 minutes, 23.4% 15 to 30 minutes, 37.0% 30 to 45 minutes, 12.7% 45 to 60 minutes, 5.8% 60 minutes or more (2000)

OAKLEY (village). Covers a land area of 1.020 square miles and a water area of 0 square miles. Located at 43.14° N. Lat.; 84.16° W. Long. Elevation is 602 feet.
Population: 339 (2000); Race: 93.2% White, 0.0% Black, 0.0% Asian, 0.9% American Indian and Alaska Native, 7.1% Hispanic of any race, 4.5% two or more races (2000); Density: 332.5 persons per square mile (2000); Age: 22.3% under 18, 16.1% over 64 (2000); Marriage status: 27.7% never married, 53.2% now married, 9.7% widowed, 9.4% divorced (2000); Foreign born: 1.5% (2000); Ancestry (includes multiple ancestries): 33.0% German, 14.3% Irish, 13.4% Other groups, 8.9% English, 8.3% United States or American (2000).
Economy: Lumber. Single-family building permits issued: 0 (2001) / 2 (2000); Multi-family building permits issued: 0 (2001) / 0 (2000); Employment by occupation: 8.2% management, 5.7% professional, 23.3% services, 18.9% sales, 0.0% farming, 9.4% construction, 34.6% production (2000).
Income: Per capita income: $17,403 (2000); Median household income: $32,159 (2000); Poverty rate: 9.5% (2000).
Taxes: Total city taxes per capita: $76 (1997); City property taxes per capita: $76 (1997).
Education: High school graduation rate: 80.2% (2000); College graduation rate: 4.7% (2000).
Housing: Homeownership rate: 64.7% (2000); Median home value: $62,100 (2000); Median rent: $427 per month (2000); Median age of housing: 52 years (2000).
Transportation: Commute to work: 92.1% car, 0.0% public transportation, 6.6% walk, 0.0% work from home (2000); Travel time to work: 35.1% less than 15 minutes, 32.5% 15 to 30 minutes, 12.6% 30 to 45 minutes, 6.6% 45 to 60 minutes, 13.2% 60 minutes or more (2000)

RICHLAND (township). Covers a land area of 37.084 square miles and a water area of 0 square miles. Located at 43.41° N. Lat.; 84.22° W. Long.
History: Richland Township was first settled in 1857 by Lemuel Cone. The township was organized in 1862, and named by Cone.
Population: 4,281 (2000); Race: 98.2% White, 0.0% Black, 0.7% Asian, 0.1% American Indian and Alaska Native, 3.3% Hispanic of any race, 0.4% two or more races (2000); Density: 115.4 persons per square mile (2000); Age: 27.8% under 18, 11.7% over 64 (2000); Marriage status: 24.5% never married, 64.0% now married, 4.6% widowed, 6.9% divorced (2000); Foreign born: 1.4% (2000); Ancestry (includes multiple ancestries): 43.0% German, 12.3% Irish, 9.0% Polish, 8.8% Other groups, 6.3% English (2000).
Economy: Single-family building permits issued: 14 (2001) / 23 (2000); Multi-family building permits issued: 0 (2001) / 0 (2000); Employment by occupation: 11.7% management, 18.3% professional, 15.3% services, 25.8% sales, 1.2% farming, 10.6% construction, 17.1% production (2000).
Income: Per capita income: $19,362 (2000); Median household income: $45,580 (2000); Poverty rate: 5.9% (2000).
Taxes: Total city taxes per capita: $94 (1997); City property taxes per capita: $88 (1997).
Education: High school graduation rate: 87.1% (2000); College graduation rate: 15.2% (2000).
Housing: Homeownership rate: 86.9% (2000); Median home value: $96,700 (2000); Median rent: $372 per month (2000); Median age of housing: 31 years (2000).
Transportation: Commute to work: 91.8% car, 0.0% public transportation, 1.5% walk, 5.2% work from home (2000); Travel time to work: 21.2% less than 15 minutes, 37.4% 15 to 30 minutes, 31.9% 30 to 45 minutes, 4.7% 45 to 60 minutes, 4.9% 60 minutes or more (2000)

ROBIN GLEN-INDIANTOWN (CDP). Covers a land area of 2.142 square miles and a water area of 0 square miles. Located at 43.44° N. Lat.; 83.83° W. Long.

Population: 1,158 (2000); Race: 94.0% White, 0.0% Black, 0.0% Asian, 0.5% American Indian and Alaska Native, 7.7% Hispanic of any race, 0.7% two or more races (2000); Density: 540.7 persons per square mile (2000); Age: 33.7% under 18, 6.0% over 64 (2000); Marriage status: 27.7% never married, 44.6% now married, 3.9% widowed, 23.8% divorced (2000); Foreign born: 0.6% (2000); Ancestry (includes multiple ancestries): 39.0% German, 11.3% Polish, 9.8% English, 9.7% Other groups, 9.3% United States or American (2000).
Economy: Employment by occupation: 9.0% management, 12.8% professional, 18.7% services, 28.1% sales, 1.1% farming, 7.6% construction, 22.6% production (2000).
Income: Per capita income: $19,145 (2000); Median household income: $31,613 (2000); Poverty rate: 14.9% (2000).
Education: High school graduation rate: 86.3% (2000); College graduation rate: 5.3% (2000).
Housing: Homeownership rate: 89.9% (2000); Median home value: $71,200 (2000); Median rent: $453 per month (2000); Median age of housing: 22 years (2000).
Transportation: Commute to work: 98.7% car, 0.0% public transportation, 0.0% walk, 1.3% work from home (2000); Travel time to work: 15.5% less than 15 minutes, 62.4% 15 to 30 minutes, 20.2% 30 to 45 minutes, 1.0% 45 to 60 minutes, 1.0% 60 minutes or more (2000)

SAGINAW (city). Covers a land area of 17.443 square miles and a water area of 0.724 square miles. Located at 43.42° N. Lat.; 83.95° W. Long. Elevation is 610 feet.
History: In 1816 a fur trading post was built here by Louis Campau of Canada, followed in 1819 by Fort Saginaw, abandoned in 1823. A settlement grew up around the American Fur Company's operation, and was incorporated as the village of Saginaw in 1837. Lumberjacks and steam sawmills became numerous along the Saginaw River, until coal was discovered in the late 1880's. Rivalry between the communities of East and West Saginaw ended in 1889 when the two were united as the City of Saginaw. Saginaw became the center of a large agricultural area, storing and shipping beans, grains, and sugar beets.
Population: 61,799 (2000); Race: 46.7% White, 43.2% Black, 0.3% Asian, 0.5% American Indian and Alaska Native, 11.9% Hispanic of any race, 2.9% two or more races (2000); Density: 3,542.9 persons per square mile (2000); Age: 31.6% under 18, 11.3% over 64 (2000); Marriage status: 37.6% never married, 42.0% now married, 8.0% widowed, 12.4% divorced (2000); Foreign born: 1.6% (2000); Ancestry (includes multiple ancestries): 50.3% Other groups, 15.9% German, 5.1% Irish, 5.0% Polish, 4.8% English (2000).
Vital Statistics: Birth rate: 208.6 per 10,000 population (1998)
Economy: Unemployment rate: 11.5% (11/2002); Total civilian labor force: 27,692 (11/2002); Single-family building permits issued: 3 (2001) / 5 (2000); Multi-family building permits issued: 0 (2001) / 0 (2000); Employment by occupation: 5.8% management, 15.5% professional, 26.0% services, 26.0% sales, 0.5% farming, 7.2% construction, 19.1% production (2000).
Income: Per capita income: $13,816 (2000); Median household income: $26,485 (2000); Poverty rate: 28.5% (2000).
Taxes: Total city taxes per capita: $368 (2000); City property taxes per capita: $103 (2000).
Education: High school graduation rate: 73.1% (2000); College graduation rate: 10.4% (2000).

School District(s)

Academy for Technology & Enterpr (11-12)
2000 Enrollment: 434 517-799-4736
Benito Juarez Academy (09-12)
2000 Enrollment: 37 517-774-2100
Buena Vista School District (PK-12)
2000 Enrollment: 1,566 517-755-2184
Francis Reh Psa (KG-08)
2000 Enrollment: 256 616-592-2300
Mosaica Academy of Saginaw (PK-08)
2000 Enrollment: 424 517-790-4000
North Saginaw Charter Academy (KG-06)
2000 Enrollment: 410 517-774-2100
Saginaw City School District (PK-12)
2000 Enrollment: 12,103 517-759-2200
Saginaw County Transition Academ (07-12)
2000 Enrollment: 16 517-799-4736
Saginaw Township Community Schoo (PK-12)
2000 Enrollment: 4,823 517-797-1800
Swan Valley School District (KG-12)
2000 Enrollment: 1,596 517-921-3701

Housing: Homeownership rate: 63.6% (2000); Median home value: $46,800 (2000); Median rent: $347 per month (2000); Median age of housing: 53 years (2000).
Hospitals: Aleda E. Lutz VA Medical Center (238 beds); Covenant Health Care (709 beds); Covenant HealthCare (709 beds); HealthSource Saginaw (317 beds); Saint Mary's (268 beds)
Safety: Violent crime rate: 201.2 per 10,000 population; Property crime rate: 503.7 per 10,000 population (2001).
Newspapers: Saginaw News (7 x week); Catholic Weekly (1 x week); The Township Times (1 x week); The Saginaw Press (1 x week)
Transportation: Commute to work: 92.9% car, 1.5% public transportation, 2.0% walk, 2.5% work from home (2000); Travel time to work: 47.3% less than 15 minutes, 37.0% 15 to 30 minutes, 9.7% 30 to 45 minutes, 2.5% 45 to 60 minutes, 3.6% 60 minutes or more (2000)
Airports: Mbs International (primary service)

Additional Information Contacts

Saginaw Board of Realtors 989-793-6332
Saginaw Chamber of Commerce 989-752-7161
Saginaw County Convention Bureau 989-752-7164

SAGINAW CHARTER (township). Covers a land area of 24.649 square miles and a water area of 0.139 square miles. Located at 43.44° N. Lat.; 84.01° W. Long. Elevation is 610 feet.
History: Native American trails once crossed the site, and local Native American villages were abundant. Lewis Cass negotiated a treaty here (1819) with the indigenous groups, who ceded much of what is now Michigan to the U.S. Fur trade was followed by a great pine-lumbering industry, which thrived until about 1890. The old Schuch Hotel (1868) has an interesting collection of antiques. Saginaw Valley State University. Historical Museum. Settled 1816, Incorporated 1857.
Population: 39,657 (2000); Race: 88.4% White, 5.1% Black, 2.6% Asian, 0.4% American Indian and Alaska Native, 4.1% Hispanic of any race, 1.7% two or more races (2000); Density: 1,608.9 persons per square mile (2000); Age: 21.2% under 18, 19.0% over 64 (2000); Marriage status: 23.9% never married, 57.8% now married, 9.0% widowed, 9.2% divorced (2000); Foreign born: 4.7% (2000); Ancestry (includes multiple ancestries): 34.9% German, 14.1% Other groups, 11.5% Irish, 11.2% Polish, 10.3% English (2000).
Vital Statistics: Birth rate: 96.8 per 10,000 population (1998)
Economy: Railroad junction. Situated in an extensive agricultural area, Saginaw is also a port of entry with diversified industries. Manufacturing includes machinery, animal feeds, fabricated metal products, automobile parts, food processing, concrete and electrical equipment. Nearby are major salt, coal and oil deposits. Unemployment rate: 3.5% (11/2002); Total civilian labor force: 20,486 (11/2002); Single-family building permits issued: 131 (2001) / 141 (2000); Multi-family building permits issued: 20 (2001) / 168 (2000); Employment by occupation: 12.9% management, 25.9% professional, 11.8% services, 28.9% sales, 0.0% farming, 6.5% construction, 13.9% production (2000).
Income: Per capita income: $25,759 (2000); Median household income: $45,147 (2000); Poverty rate: 6.6% (2000).
Taxes: Total city taxes per capita: $150 (2000); City property taxes per capita: $139 (2000).
Education: High school graduation rate: 88.1% (2000); College graduation rate: 28.4% (2000).
Housing: Homeownership rate: 65.3% (2000); Median home value: $121,800 (2000); Median rent: $515 per month (2000); Median age of housing: 28 years (2000).
Safety: Violent crime rate: 21.8 per 10,000 population; Property crime rate: 328.3 per 10,000 population (2001).
Transportation: Commute to work: 96.3% car, 0.4% public transportation, 0.6% walk, 2.4% work from home (2000); Travel time to work: 43.3% less than 15 minutes, 41.0% 15 to 30 minutes, 8.7% 30 to 45 minutes, 2.7% 45 to 60 minutes, 4.3% 60 minutes or more (2000)

SAGINAW TOWNSHIP NORTH (CDP). Covers a land area of 13.499 square miles and a water area of 0 square miles. Located at 43.45° N. Lat.; 84.00° W. Long.
Population: 24,994 (2000); Race: 87.7% White, 5.3% Black, 3.3% Asian, 0.4% American Indian and Alaska Native, 3.7% Hispanic of any race, 1.8% two or more races (2000); Density: 1,851.5 persons per square mile (2000); Age: 20.9% under 18, 19.5% over 64 (2000); Marriage status: 25.1% never married, 56.1% now married, 9.6% widowed, 9.3% divorced (2000); Foreign born: 5.0% (2000); Ancestry (includes multiple ancestries): 34.7% German, 14.6% Other groups, 11.4% Polish, 10.7% Irish, 10.5% English (2000).

Economy: Employment by occupation: 12.3% management, 24.9% professional, 13.0% services, 29.3% sales, 0.0% farming, 6.6% construction, 13.7% production (2000).
Income: Per capita income: $24,466 (2000); Median household income: $42,481 (2000); Poverty rate: 7.1% (2000).
Education: High school graduation rate: 87.7% (2000); College graduation rate: 28.0% (2000).
Housing: Homeownership rate: 61.7% (2000); Median home value: $117,800 (2000); Median rent: $519 per month (2000); Median age of housing: 26 years (2000).
Transportation: Commute to work: 96.5% car, 0.5% public transportation, 0.5% walk, 2.1% work from home (2000); Travel time to work: 45.8% less than 15 minutes, 39.1% 15 to 30 minutes, 7.6% 30 to 45 minutes, 2.8% 45 to 60 minutes, 4.8% 60 minutes or more (2000)

SAGINAW TOWNSHIP SOUTH (CDP). Covers a land area of 6.904 square miles and a water area of 0.139 square miles. Located at 43.42° N. Lat.; 84.01° W. Long.
Population: 13,801 (2000); Race: 89.7% White, 5.2% Black, 1.2% Asian, 0.4% American Indian and Alaska Native, 4.8% Hispanic of any race, 1.6% two or more races (2000); Density: 1,999.1 persons per square mile (2000); Age: 21.7% under 18, 18.5% over 64 (2000); Marriage status: 21.9% never married, 60.3% now married, 8.4% widowed, 9.3% divorced (2000); Foreign born: 4.1% (2000); Ancestry (includes multiple ancestries): 35.7% German, 13.2% Irish, 13.0% Other groups, 10.4% English, 10.4% Polish (2000).
Economy: Employment by occupation: 14.3% management, 27.8% professional, 9.8% services, 28.0% sales, 0.1% farming, 5.9% construction, 14.1% production (2000).
Income: Per capita income: $28,012 (2000); Median household income: $48,605 (2000); Poverty rate: 6.0% (2000).
Education: High school graduation rate: 88.7% (2000); College graduation rate: 29.8% (2000).
Housing: Homeownership rate: 70.0% (2000); Median home value: $128,700 (2000); Median rent: $507 per month (2000); Median age of housing: 32 years (2000).
Transportation: Commute to work: 96.2% car, 0.2% public transportation, 0.5% walk, 2.8% work from home (2000); Travel time to work: 39.7% less than 15 minutes, 43.1% 15 to 30 minutes, 10.7% 30 to 45 minutes, 2.8% 45 to 60 minutes, 3.7% 60 minutes or more (2000)

SAINT CHARLES (village). Covers a land area of 2.441 square miles and a water area of 0 square miles. Located at 43.29° N. Lat.; 84.14° W. Long. Elevation is 593 feet.
History: St. Charles was established in the 1850's on the Bad River, and named for Charles Kimberly who was nicknamed "Saint" Charles.
Population: 2,215 (2000); Race: 95.0% White, 0.5% Black, 0.7% Asian, 0.1% American Indian and Alaska Native, 4.2% Hispanic of any race, 1.7% two or more races (2000); Density: 907.4 persons per square mile (2000); Age: 29.3% under 18, 14.2% over 64 (2000); Marriage status: 24.6% never married, 57.9% now married, 7.4% widowed, 10.0% divorced (2000); Foreign born: 0.5% (2000); Ancestry (includes multiple ancestries): 30.2% German, 11.6% Polish, 10.5% Irish, 9.0% French (except Basque), 8.7% United States or American (2000).
Economy: Employment by occupation: 7.9% management, 13.0% professional, 19.8% services, 23.4% sales, 0.0% farming, 14.6% construction, 21.3% production (2000).
Income: Per capita income: $17,126 (2000); Median household income: $39,909 (2000); Poverty rate: 11.5% (2000).
Education: High school graduation rate: 77.9% (2000); College graduation rate: 8.8% (2000).

School District(s)

Saint Charles Community Schools (KG-12)
2000 Enrollment: 1,255 517-865-9961

Housing: Homeownership rate: 75.6% (2000); Median home value: $76,100 (2000); Median rent: $347 per month (2000); Median age of housing: 45 years (2000).
Transportation: Commute to work: 95.1% car, 0.0% public transportation, 0.8% walk, 3.6% work from home (2000); Travel time to work: 26.9% less than 15 minutes, 24.3% 15 to 30 minutes, 36.0% 30 to 45 minutes, 4.0% 45 to 60 minutes, 8.8% 60 minutes or more (2000)

Additional Information Contacts

St. Charles Chamber of Commerce 989-865-8635

SAINT CHARLES (township). Covers a land area of 36.961 square miles and a water area of 0.229 square miles. Located at 43.27° N. Lat.; 84.13° W. Long. Elevation is 593 feet.
Population: 3,393 (2000); Race: 96.1% White, 0.4% Black, 0.5% Asian, 0.1% American Indian and Alaska Native, 3.2% Hispanic of any race, 1.5% two or more races (2000); Density: 91.8 persons per square mile (2000); Age: 27.8% under 18, 11.8% over 64 (2000); Marriage status: 24.2% never married, 61.9% now married, 5.8% widowed, 8.1% divorced (2000); Foreign born: 0.6% (2000); Ancestry (includes multiple ancestries): 32.6% German, 9.9% Polish, 9.7% French (except Basque), 9.2% English, 8.8% Irish (2000).
Economy: Single-family building permits issued: 7 (2001) / 4 (2000); Multi-family building permits issued: 0 (2001) / 0 (2000); Employment by occupation: 7.9% management, 12.4% professional, 19.5% services, 24.5% sales, 0.5% farming, 13.1% construction, 22.1% production (2000).
Income: Per capita income: $17,818 (2000); Median household income: $40,726 (2000); Poverty rate: 8.0% (2000).
Education: High school graduation rate: 80.9% (2000); College graduation rate: 9.3% (2000).
Housing: Homeownership rate: 79.1% (2000); Median home value: $78,500 (2000); Median rent: $353 per month (2000); Median age of housing: 43 years (2000).
Transportation: Commute to work: 94.2% car, 0.0% public transportation, 0.5% walk, 4.9% work from home (2000); Travel time to work: 29.8% less than 15 minutes, 23.7% 15 to 30 minutes, 32.0% 30 to 45 minutes, 5.7% 45 to 60 minutes, 8.8% 60 minutes or more (2000)

SHIELDS (CDP). Covers a land area of 6.538 square miles and a water area of 0.068 square miles. Located at 43.41° N. Lat.; 84.07° W. Long. Elevation is 590 feet.
Population: 6,590 (2000); Race: 96.5% White, 0.7% Black, 0.3% Asian, 0.3% American Indian and Alaska Native, 2.4% Hispanic of any race, 1.4% two or more races (2000); Density: 1,007.9 persons per square mile (2000); Age: 24.0% under 18, 13.9% over 64 (2000); Marriage status: 23.0% never married, 62.1% now married, 5.9% widowed, 9.0% divorced (2000); Foreign born: 2.2% (2000); Ancestry (includes multiple ancestries): 39.1% German, 11.7% Irish, 11.3% English, 10.1% Polish, 7.2% French (except Basque) (2000).
Economy: Employment by occupation: 8.9% management, 20.5% professional, 15.7% services, 28.5% sales, 0.3% farming, 10.7% construction, 15.5% production (2000).
Income: Per capita income: $23,519 (2000); Median household income: $49,859 (2000); Poverty rate: 3.7% (2000).
Education: High school graduation rate: 87.9% (2000); College graduation rate: 19.8% (2000).
Housing: Homeownership rate: 86.4% (2000); Median home value: $106,600 (2000); Median rent: $442 per month (2000); Median age of housing: 30 years (2000).
Transportation: Commute to work: 95.5% car, 0.2% public transportation, 0.7% walk, 3.3% work from home (2000); Travel time to work: 32.2% less than 15 minutes, 48.0% 15 to 30 minutes, 11.2% 30 to 45 minutes, 2.1% 45 to 60 minutes, 6.6% 60 minutes or more (2000)

SPAULDING (township). Covers a land area of 26.562 square miles and a water area of 0.811 square miles. Located at 43.35° N. Lat.; 83.97° W. Long.
History: Spaulding Township was organized in 1858 and named for Phineas Spaulding, who had come here from New Hampshire in 1835.
Population: 2,399 (2000); Race: 80.6% White, 10.5% Black, 1.1% Asian, 1.1% American Indian and Alaska Native, 12.4% Hispanic of any race, 4.6% two or more races (2000); Density: 90.3 persons per square mile (2000); Age: 25.4% under 18, 13.5% over 64 (2000); Marriage status: 21.1% never married, 66.7% now married, 7.2% widowed, 5.0% divorced (2000); Foreign born: 1.5% (2000); Ancestry (includes multiple ancestries): 27.0% German, 25.7% Other groups, 9.5% Irish, 7.5% Polish, 7.2% English (2000).
Economy: Single-family building permits issued: 5 (2001) / 1 (2000); Multi-family building permits issued: 0 (2001) / 0 (2000); Employment by occupation: 9.5% management, 10.8% professional, 19.0% services, 25.2% sales, 0.7% farming, 8.5% construction, 26.4% production (2000).
Income: Per capita income: $17,910 (2000); Median household income: $36,791 (2000); Poverty rate: 9.3% (2000).
Taxes: Total city taxes per capita: $38 (1997); City property taxes per capita: $35 (1997).
Education: High school graduation rate: 76.2% (2000); College graduation rate: 6.0% (2000).
Housing: Homeownership rate: 89.7% (2000); Median home value: $61,900 (2000); Median rent: $384 per month (2000); Median age of housing: 45 years (2000).
Transportation: Commute to work: 93.5% car, 0.0% public transportation, 0.9% walk, 5.3% work from home (2000); Travel time to work: 27.5% less

than 15 minutes, 48.2% 15 to 30 minutes, 11.1% 30 to 45 minutes, 6.0% 45 to 60 minutes, 7.2% 60 minutes or more (2000)

SWAN CREEK (township). Covers a land area of 23.156 square miles and a water area of 0.464 square miles. Located at 43.35° N. Lat.; 84.12° W. Long. Elevation is 594 feet.
History: Swan Creek Township was organized in 1860 and named for the stream that traversed it.
Population: 2,536 (2000); Race: 99.0% White, 0.0% Black, 0.2% Asian, 0.1% American Indian and Alaska Native, 2.7% Hispanic of any race, 0.2% two or more races (2000); Density: 109.5 persons per square mile (2000); Age: 23.9% under 18, 12.7% over 64 (2000); Marriage status: 19.5% never married, 68.0% now married, 6.0% widowed, 6.5% divorced (2000); Foreign born: 0.7% (2000); Ancestry (includes multiple ancestries): 43.0% German, 13.8% Irish, 11.6% Polish, 10.1% French (except Basque), 7.9% English (2000).
Economy: Single-family building permits issued: 7 (2001) / 14 (2000); Multi-family building permits issued: 0 (2001) / 0 (2000); Employment by occupation: 7.0% management, 15.7% professional, 15.5% services, 27.3% sales, 0.5% farming, 12.8% construction, 21.2% production (2000).
Income: Per capita income: $23,129 (2000); Median household income: $45,887 (2000); Poverty rate: 4.3% (2000).
Taxes: Total city taxes per capita: $100 (1997); City property taxes per capita: $90 (1997).
Education: High school graduation rate: 86.0% (2000); College graduation rate: 10.1% (2000).
Housing: Homeownership rate: 94.6% (2000); Median home value: $99,800 (2000); Median rent: $386 per month (2000); Median age of housing: 30 years (2000).
Transportation: Commute to work: 94.9% car, 0.0% public transportation, 0.4% walk, 4.7% work from home (2000); Travel time to work: 17.8% less than 15 minutes, 39.0% 15 to 30 minutes, 34.3% 30 to 45 minutes, 5.5% 45 to 60 minutes, 3.4% 60 minutes or more (2000)

TAYMOUTH (township). Covers a land area of 35.561 square miles and a water area of 0.119 square miles. Located at 43.26° N. Lat.; 83.86° W. Long.
Population: 4,624 (2000); Race: 94.5% White, 0.2% Black, 0.6% Asian, 0.8% American Indian and Alaska Native, 3.7% Hispanic of any race, 3.7% two or more races (2000); Density: 130.0 persons per square mile (2000); Age: 28.2% under 18, 7.9% over 64 (2000); Marriage status: 23.6% never married, 64.6% now married, 4.4% widowed, 7.4% divorced (2000); Foreign born: 0.6% (2000); Ancestry (includes multiple ancestries): 31.5% German, 11.7% Other groups, 10.6% Polish, 10.5% French (except Basque), 10.2% English (2000).
Economy: Single-family building permits issued: 19 (2001) / 20 (2000); Multi-family building permits issued: 0 (2001) / 0 (2000); Employment by occupation: 6.2% management, 10.6% professional, 13.3% services, 30.5% sales, 0.7% farming, 14.1% construction, 24.6% production (2000).
Income: Per capita income: $18,054 (2000); Median household income: $46,581 (2000); Poverty rate: 9.2% (2000).
Taxes: Total city taxes per capita: $46 (1997); City property taxes per capita: $40 (1997).
Education: High school graduation rate: 81.3% (2000); College graduation rate: 8.8% (2000).
Housing: Homeownership rate: 91.8% (2000); Median home value: $96,500 (2000); Median rent: $326 per month (2000); Median age of housing: 29 years (2000).
Transportation: Commute to work: 94.4% car, 0.0% public transportation, 0.8% walk, 4.8% work from home (2000); Travel time to work: 21.5% less than 15 minutes, 35.8% 15 to 30 minutes, 32.1% 30 to 45 minutes, 3.7% 45 to 60 minutes, 6.9% 60 minutes or more (2000)

THOMAS (township). Covers a land area of 31.516 square miles and a water area of 0.420 square miles. Located at 43.42° N. Lat.; 84.10° W. Long.
Population: 11,877 (2000); Race: 96.9% White, 0.5% Black, 0.7% Asian, 0.3% American Indian and Alaska Native, 2.2% Hispanic of any race, 0.8% two or more races (2000); Density: 376.9 persons per square mile (2000); Age: 24.3% under 18, 13.6% over 64 (2000); Marriage status: 20.3% never married, 65.8% now married, 6.1% widowed, 7.7% divorced (2000); Foreign born: 1.9% (2000); Ancestry (includes multiple ancestries): 39.1% German, 12.7% Irish, 10.9% English, 10.7% Polish, 7.6% French (except Basque) (2000).
Economy: Single-family building permits issued: 63 (2001) / 73 (2000); Multi-family building permits issued: 0 (2001) / 150 (2000); Employment by occupation: 9.9% management, 19.0% professional, 14.9% services, 30.5% sales, 0.2% farming, 10.7% construction, 14.8% production (2000).
Income: Per capita income: $25,700 (2000); Median household income: $52,536 (2000); Poverty rate: 3.5% (2000).
Taxes: Total city taxes per capita: $125 (2000); City property taxes per capita: $115 (2000).
Education: High school graduation rate: 87.6% (2000); College graduation rate: 18.8% (2000).
Housing: Homeownership rate: 90.6% (2000); Median home value: $116,300 (2000); Median rent: $430 per month (2000); Median age of housing: 26 years (2000).
Safety: Violent crime rate: 15.1 per 10,000 population; Property crime rate: 266.3 per 10,000 population (2001).
Transportation: Commute to work: 95.7% car, 0.1% public transportation, 0.4% walk, 3.5% work from home (2000); Travel time to work: 27.0% less than 15 minutes, 50.7% 15 to 30 minutes, 14.3% 30 to 45 minutes, 2.6% 45 to 60 minutes, 5.3% 60 minutes or more (2000)

TITTABAWASSEE (township). Covers a land area of 35.190 square miles and a water area of 0.309 square miles. Located at 43.52° N. Lat.; 84.12° W. Long.
Population: 7,706 (2000); Race: 87.0% White, 8.4% Black, 0.2% Asian, 0.9% American Indian and Alaska Native, 3.1% Hispanic of any race, 2.7% two or more races (2000); Density: 219.0 persons per square mile (2000); Age: 23.8% under 18, 7.3% over 64 (2000); Marriage status: 28.0% never married, 57.7% now married, 4.1% widowed, 10.2% divorced (2000); Foreign born: 3.2% (2000); Ancestry (includes multiple ancestries): 33.8% German, 11.4% English, 11.4% Other groups, 8.0% Polish, 7.8% French (except Basque) (2000).
Economy: Single-family building permits issued: 82 (2001) / 140 (2000); Multi-family building permits issued: 16 (2001) / 0 (2000); Employment by occupation: 11.6% management, 24.6% professional, 13.2% services, 28.4% sales, 0.4% farming, 13.0% construction, 8.9% production (2000).
Income: Per capita income: $20,554 (2000); Median household income: $54,980 (2000); Poverty rate: 4.7% (2000).
Taxes: Total city taxes per capita: $114 (2000); City property taxes per capita: $100 (2000).
Education: High school graduation rate: 89.2% (2000); College graduation rate: 24.1% (2000).
Housing: Homeownership rate: 86.4% (2000); Median home value: $126,600 (2000); Median rent: $460 per month (2000); Median age of housing: 26 years (2000).
Transportation: Commute to work: 95.1% car, 0.0% public transportation, 1.0% walk, 3.6% work from home (2000); Travel time to work: 22.5% less than 15 minutes, 51.9% 15 to 30 minutes, 16.8% 30 to 45 minutes, 3.7% 45 to 60 minutes, 5.2% 60 minutes or more (2000)

ZILWAUKEE (city). Covers a land area of 2.219 square miles and a water area of 0.088 square miles. Located at 43.47° N. Lat.; 83.92° W. Long.
Population: 1,799 (2000); Race: 94.0% White, 0.8% Black, 0.1% Asian, 0.6% American Indian and Alaska Native, 6.8% Hispanic of any race, 0.6% two or more races (2000); Density: 810.7 persons per square mile (2000); Age: 22.5% under 18, 15.2% over 64 (2000); Marriage status: 22.3% never married, 60.0% now married, 8.5% widowed, 9.2% divorced (2000); Foreign born: 1.4% (2000); Ancestry (includes multiple ancestries): 37.5% German, 13.1% French (except Basque), 12.6% Other groups, 12.3% Irish, 10.9% Polish (2000).
Economy: Single-family building permits issued: 3 (2001) / 3 (2000); Multi-family building permits issued: 0 (2001) / 0 (2000); Employment by occupation: 8.9% management, 12.7% professional, 15.8% services, 28.8% sales, 0.0% farming, 11.4% construction, 22.3% production (2000).
Income: Per capita income: $19,491 (2000); Median household income: $42,014 (2000); Poverty rate: 6.4% (2000).
Taxes: Total city taxes per capita: $176 (1997); City property taxes per capita: $169 (1997).
Education: High school graduation rate: 84.6% (2000); College graduation rate: 8.6% (2000).
Housing: Homeownership rate: 87.1% (2000); Median home value: $71,800 (2000); Median rent: $427 per month (2000); Median age of housing: 44 years (2000).
Safety: Violent crime rate: 11.1 per 10,000 population; Property crime rate: 94.0 per 10,000 population (2001).
Transportation: Commute to work: 95.8% car, 0.2% public transportation, 2.9% walk, 1.1% work from home (2000); Travel time to work: 43.5% less than 15 minutes, 42.1% 15 to 30 minutes, 8.2% 30 to 45 minutes, 1.1% 45 to 60 minutes, 5.1% 60 minutes or more (2000)

ZILWAUKEE (township). Covers a land area of 5.734 square miles and a water area of 0.326 square miles. Located at 43.50° N. Lat.; 83.89° W. Long.
Population: 61 (2000); Race: 100.0% White, 0.0% Black, 0.0% Asian, 0.0% American Indian and Alaska Native, 0.0% Hispanic of any race, 0.0% two or more races (2000); Density: 10.6 persons per square mile (2000); Age: 33.3% under 18, 10.0% over 64 (2000); Marriage status: 15.9% never married, 75.0% now married, 4.5% widowed, 4.5% divorced (2000); Foreign born: 0.0% (2000); Ancestry (includes multiple ancestries): 38.3% German, 16.7% United States or American, 11.7% Dutch, 8.3% Canadian, 8.3% Scottish (2000).
Economy: Single-family building permits issued: 0 (2001) / 0 (2000); Multi-family building permits issued: 0 (2001) / 0 (2000); Employment by occupation: 17.4% management, 21.7% professional, 0.0% services, 21.7% sales, 0.0% farming, 26.1% construction, 13.0% production (2000).
Income: Per capita income: $21,268 (2000); Median household income: $50,625 (2000); Poverty rate: 0.0% (2000).
Taxes: Total city taxes per capita: $450 (1997); City property taxes per capita: $450 (1997).
Education: High school graduation rate: 75.7% (2000); College graduation rate: 24.3% (2000).
Housing: Homeownership rate: 80.0% (2000); Median home value: $115,600 (2000); Median rent: $325 per month (2000); Median age of housing: 52 years (2000).
Transportation: Commute to work: 100.0% car, 0.0% public transportation, 0.0% walk, 0.0% work from home (2000); Travel time to work: 39.1% less than 15 minutes, 30.4% 15 to 30 minutes, 21.7% 30 to 45 minutes, 0.0% 45 to 60 minutes, 8.7% 60 minutes or more (2000)

Saint Clair County

Located in eastern Michigan; bounded on the east by Lake Huron and the St. Clair River, and on the south by Lake St. Clair; drained by the Belle and Black Rivers. Covers a land area of 724.40 square miles, a water area of 112.30 square miles, and is located in the Eastern Time Zone. The county government was organized in 1820. County seat is Port Huron.

Saint Clair County is part of the Detroit, MI PMSA. The entire metro area includes: Lapeer County; Macomb County; Monroe County; Oakland County; St. Clair County; Wayne County

Weather Station: Port Huron — Elevation: 587 feet

	Jan	Feb	Mar	Apr	May	Jun	Jul	Aug	Sep	Oct	Nov	Dec
High	30	33	42	55	67	77	82	80	73	60	47	36
Low	16	18	26	35	46	56	62	61	53	42	32	22
Precip	1.8	1.6	2.3	3.0	2.7	3.2	2.8	3.0	3.4	2.5	2.9	2.1
Snow	10.0	8.3	4.7	1.3	tr	0.0	0.0	0.0	0.0	0.5	1.5	7.9

High and Low temperatures in degrees Fahrenheit; Precipitation and Snow in inches

Population: 164,235 (2000); Race: 94.9% White, 2.2% Black, 0.3% Asian, 0.5% American Indian and Alaska Native, 2.2% Hispanic of any race, 1.3% two or more races (2000); Density: 226.7 persons per square mile (2000); Age: 26.6% under 18, 12.3% over 64 (2000).
Religion: Five largest groups: 25.2% Catholic Church, 2.5% Evangelical Lutheran Church in America, 2.4% Lutheran Church—Missouri Synod, 2.1% The United Methodist Church, 1.1% Muslim estimate (2000).
Economy: Unemployment rate: 7.0% (11/2002); Total civilian labor force: 82,385 (11/2002); Leading industries: 26.7% manufacturing; 16.7% retail trade; 14.2% health care and social assistance (2000); Companies that employ more than 1,000 persons: 2 (2000); Companies that employ more than 100 persons: 80 (2000); Farms: 940 totaling 162,887 acres (1997); Minority business ownership rate: 3.2% (1997); Women business ownership rate: 27.1% (1997); Retail sales per capita: $8,350 (1997). Single-family building permits issued: 803 (2001) / 936 (2000); Multi-family building permits issued: 23 (2001) / 140 (2000).
Income: Per capita income: $21,582 (2000); Median household income: $46,313 (2000); Poverty rate: 7.8% (2000); Bankruptcy rate: 4.88% (2001).
Taxes: Total county taxes per capita: $182 (2000); County property taxes per capita: $177 (2000).
Education: High school graduation rate: 82.8% (2000); College graduation rate: 12.6% (2000).
Housing: Homeownership rate: 79.6% (2000); Median home value: $125,200 (2000); Median rent: $453 per month (2000); Median age of housing: 33 years (2000).
Health: Birth rate: 126.4 per 10,000 population (1998); Age adjusted death rate: 97.6 per 10,000 population (1999); Age adjusted cancer mortality rate: 242.7 deaths per 100,000 population (1999). Air Quality Index: 78% good, 22% moderate, 1% unhealthy (percent of days in 2000). Number of physicians: 11.8 per 10,000 population (1999); Number of hospital beds: 21.9 per 10,000 population (1999).
Elections: 2000 Presidential election results: 48.2% Gore, 49.0% Bush, 2.0% Nader, 0.1% Buchanan
National and State Parks: Algonac State Park; Lakeport State Park; Port Huron State Game Area; Saint Clair Flats State Wildlife Area
Additional Information Contacts
St. Clair County Government Offices 810-985-2001
Clay Chamber of Commerce 810-794-5511
Eastern Thumb Association of Realtors 810-982-6889
Marine City Chamber of Commerce 810-765-4501
Marysville Chamber of Commerce 810-364-6180
Port Huron Chamber of Commerce 810-985-7101
St. Clair Chamber of Commerce 810-329-2962

Saint Clair County Communities

ALGONAC (city). Covers a land area of 1.401 square miles and a water area of 0.001 square miles. Located at 42.62° N. Lat.; 82.53° W. Long. Elevation is 584 feet.
History: The first settler in Algonac was John Martin, who came in 1805 and called the place Pointe du Chene (Oak Point). After being known as Plainfield and Clay, the town was renamed Algonac, taken from the name of the Algonquin Indians. Algonac developed as a shipbuilding center, with the Chris Craft plant that lead the racing world with its line of "Miss Americas" located here.
Population: 4,613 (2000); Race: 97.5% White, 0.0% Black, 0.1% Asian, 0.5% American Indian and Alaska Native, 0.7% Hispanic of any race, 1.6% two or more races (2000); Density: 3,291.7 persons per square mile (2000); Age: 25.7% under 18, 13.2% over 64 (2000); Marriage status: 23.7% never married, 57.7% now married, 8.9% widowed, 9.7% divorced (2000); Foreign born: 2.1% (2000); Ancestry (includes multiple ancestries): 29.9% German, 12.8% Polish, 11.5% Irish, 11.4% French (except Basque), 7.9% English (2000).
Economy: Single-family building permits issued: 10 (2001) / 15 (2000); Multi-family building permits issued: 12 (2001) / 0 (2000); Employment by occupation: 5.4% management, 16.7% professional, 17.3% services, 20.0% sales, 0.0% farming, 15.3% construction, 25.2% production (2000).
Income: Per capita income: $22,441 (2000); Median household income: $42,133 (2000); Poverty rate: 9.4% (2000).
Taxes: Total city taxes per capita: $235 (1997); City property taxes per capita: $226 (1997).
Education: High school graduation rate: 79.2% (2000); College graduation rate: 10.0% (2000).

School District(s)
Algonac Community School District (KG-12)
2000 Enrollment: 2,546 810-794-9364
Blue Water Learning Academy (07-12)
2000 Enrollment: 19 810-794-4911

Housing: Homeownership rate: 74.8% (2000); Median home value: $113,500 (2000); Median rent: $420 per month (2000); Median age of housing: 36 years (2000).
Safety: Violent crime rate: 17.3 per 10,000 population; Property crime rate: 224.3 per 10,000 population (2001).
Transportation: Commute to work: 95.6% car, 0.8% public transportation, 1.3% walk, 2.1% work from home (2000); Travel time to work: 28.2% less than 15 minutes, 15.3% 15 to 30 minutes, 21.1% 30 to 45 minutes, 15.5% 45 to 60 minutes, 19.8% 60 minutes or more (2000)

ALLENTON (unincorporated postal area, zip code 48002). Covers a land area of 37.132 square miles and a water area of 0 square miles. Located at 42.93° N. Lat.; 82.91° W. Long.
History: Allenton was founded about 1844 by Herkimer Smith, who operated an inn and a stagecoach. The place was called Smith's when the Pere Marquette Railroad built a station here. In 1910 it was renamed Allenton for Darius and Jesse Allen, leaders in the village.
Population: 3,162 (2000); Race: 97.2% White, 0.1% Black, 0.5% Asian, 0.7% American Indian and Alaska Native, 4.6% Hispanic of any race, 0.9% two or more races (2000); Density: 85.2 persons per square mile (2000); Age: 28.6% under 18, 7.8% over 64 (2000); Marriage status: 23.0% never married, 66.8% now married, 3.9% widowed, 6.3% divorced (2000); Foreign born:

3.7% (2000); Ancestry (includes multiple ancestries): 32.7% German, 13.0% Polish, 11.2% Irish, 9.4% United States or American, 8.6% English (2000).
Economy: Employment by occupation: 11.1% management, 12.2% professional, 12.8% services, 18.4% sales, 0.3% farming, 15.8% construction, 29.4% production (2000).
Income: Per capita income: $21,412 (2000); Median household income: $61,157 (2000); Poverty rate: 6.9% (2000).
Education: High school graduation rate: 83.4% (2000); College graduation rate: 8.3% (2000).
Housing: Homeownership rate: 91.0% (2000); Median home value: $139,800 (2000); Median rent: $593 per month (2000); Median age of housing: 25 years (2000).
Transportation: Commute to work: 93.0% car, 0.0% public transportation, 1.5% walk, 4.9% work from home (2000); Travel time to work: 11.1% less than 15 minutes, 24.5% 15 to 30 minutes, 29.4% 30 to 45 minutes, 20.4% 45 to 60 minutes, 14.6% 60 minutes or more (2000)

AVOCA (unincorporated postal area, zip code 48006). Covers a land area of 72.087 square miles and a water area of 0.150 square miles. Located at 43.06° N. Lat.; 82.69° W. Long. Elevation is 765 feet.
History: Avoca was founded about 1884, and developed around the Pere Marquette Railroad station built in 1889. The village was named for the Avoca River in County Wicklow, Ireland.
Population: 3,791 (2000); Race: 96.9% White, 1.2% Black, 0.2% Asian, 0.2% American Indian and Alaska Native, 1.4% Hispanic of any race, 0.5% two or more races (2000); Density: 52.6 persons per square mile (2000); Age: 28.1% under 18, 9.5% over 64 (2000); Marriage status: 20.4% never married, 67.4% now married, 5.3% widowed, 7.0% divorced (2000); Foreign born: 2.2% (2000); Ancestry (includes multiple ancestries): 27.5% German, 17.1% Irish, 11.8% Polish, 11.2% English, 9.5% French (except Basque) (2000).
Economy: Employment by occupation: 9.9% management, 11.7% professional, 13.0% services, 21.9% sales, 0.5% farming, 17.1% construction, 26.0% production (2000).
Income: Per capita income: $21,255 (2000); Median household income: $53,821 (2000); Poverty rate: 3.3% (2000).
Education: High school graduation rate: 84.0% (2000); College graduation rate: 6.8% (2000).
Housing: Homeownership rate: 93.0% (2000); Median home value: $132,100 (2000); Median rent: $418 per month (2000); Median age of housing: 25 years (2000).
Transportation: Commute to work: 94.5% car, 0.1% public transportation, 1.2% walk, 4.1% work from home (2000); Travel time to work: 8.3% less than 15 minutes, 32.7% 15 to 30 minutes, 26.4% 30 to 45 minutes, 12.0% 45 to 60 minutes, 20.6% 60 minutes or more (2000)

BERLIN (township). Covers a land area of 37.132 square miles and a water area of 0 square miles. Located at 42.93° N. Lat.; 82.91° W. Long.
Population: 3,162 (2000); Race: 97.2% White, 0.1% Black, 0.5% Asian, 0.7% American Indian and Alaska Native, 4.6% Hispanic of any race, 0.9% two or more races (2000); Density: 85.2 persons per square mile (2000); Age: 28.6% under 18, 7.8% over 64 (2000); Marriage status: 23.0% never married, 66.8% now married, 3.9% widowed, 6.3% divorced (2000); Foreign born: 3.7% (2000); Ancestry (includes multiple ancestries): 32.7% German, 13.0% Polish, 11.2% Irish, 9.4% United States or American, 8.6% English (2000).
Economy: Single-family building permits issued: 21 (2001) / 30 (2000); Multi-family building permits issued: 0 (2001) / 0 (2000); Employment by occupation: 11.1% management, 12.2% professional, 12.8% services, 18.4% sales, 0.3% farming, 15.8% construction, 29.4% production (2000).
Income: Per capita income: $21,412 (2000); Median household income: $61,157 (2000); Poverty rate: 6.9% (2000).
Taxes: Total city taxes per capita: $42 (1997); City property taxes per capita: $31 (1997).
Education: High school graduation rate: 83.4% (2000); College graduation rate: 8.3% (2000).
Housing: Homeownership rate: 91.0% (2000); Median home value: $139,800 (2000); Median rent: $593 per month (2000); Median age of housing: 25 years (2000).
Transportation: Commute to work: 93.0% car, 0.0% public transportation, 1.5% walk, 4.9% work from home (2000); Travel time to work: 11.1% less than 15 minutes, 24.5% 15 to 30 minutes, 29.4% 30 to 45 minutes, 20.4% 45 to 60 minutes, 14.6% 60 minutes or more (2000)

BROCKWAY (township). Covers a land area of 33.874 square miles and a water area of 0 square miles. Located at 43.12° N. Lat.; 82.80° W. Long.
History: Brockway Township was organized in 1848 and named for Lewis Brockway, who built a grist mill and sawmill here in 1840.
Population: 1,900 (2000); Race: 95.8% White, 0.2% Black, 0.7% Asian, 0.6% American Indian and Alaska Native, 1.8% Hispanic of any race, 1.3% two or more races (2000); Density: 56.1 persons per square mile (2000); Age: 28.7% under 18, 9.2% over 64 (2000); Marriage status: 20.8% never married, 68.3% now married, 5.2% widowed, 5.7% divorced (2000); Foreign born: 1.8% (2000); Ancestry (includes multiple ancestries): 26.0% German, 15.4% Irish, 14.4% Polish, 11.9% English, 5.8% Other groups (2000).
Economy: Single-family building permits issued: 21 (2001) / 14 (2000); Multi-family building permits issued: 0 (2001) / 0 (2000); Employment by occupation: 6.4% management, 13.1% professional, 13.9% services, 20.2% sales, 1.1% farming, 17.9% construction, 27.5% production (2000).
Income: Per capita income: $19,268 (2000); Median household income: $52,361 (2000); Poverty rate: 8.0% (2000).
Taxes: Total city taxes per capita: $53 (1997); City property taxes per capita: $49 (1997).
Education: High school graduation rate: 81.5% (2000); College graduation rate: 8.0% (2000).
Housing: Homeownership rate: 90.8% (2000); Median home value: $130,200 (2000); Median rent: $494 per month (2000); Median age of housing: 28 years (2000).
Transportation: Commute to work: 95.9% car, 0.2% public transportation, 1.0% walk, 2.9% work from home (2000); Travel time to work: 24.1% less than 15 minutes, 13.8% 15 to 30 minutes, 19.5% 30 to 45 minutes, 18.1% 45 to 60 minutes, 24.6% 60 minutes or more (2000)

BURTCHVILLE (township). Covers a land area of 15.614 square miles and a water area of 0.022 square miles. Located at 43.11° N. Lat.; 82.50° W. Long.
History: Burtchville Township was named for lumberman Jonathan Burtch, who settled here in 1840. The township was organized in 1862.
Population: 3,956 (2000); Race: 97.6% White, 0.2% Black, 0.5% Asian, 0.1% American Indian and Alaska Native, 1.4% Hispanic of any race, 1.6% two or more races (2000); Density: 253.4 persons per square mile (2000); Age: 24.7% under 18, 12.3% over 64 (2000); Marriage status: 22.2% never married, 59.2% now married, 6.9% widowed, 11.7% divorced (2000); Foreign born: 2.9% (2000); Ancestry (includes multiple ancestries): 28.2% German, 16.1% Irish, 15.2% English, 12.7% Polish, 7.0% Other groups (2000).
Economy: Single-family building permits issued: 27 (2001) / 14 (2000); Multi-family building permits issued: 0 (2001) / 0 (2000); Employment by occupation: 8.2% management, 14.7% professional, 10.5% services, 27.4% sales, 1.5% farming, 13.0% construction, 24.7% production (2000).
Income: Per capita income: $22,782 (2000); Median household income: $43,830 (2000); Poverty rate: 6.4% (2000).
Taxes: Total city taxes per capita: $57 (1997); City property taxes per capita: $49 (1997).
Education: High school graduation rate: 81.6% (2000); College graduation rate: 16.1% (2000).
Housing: Homeownership rate: 85.7% (2000); Median home value: $116,100 (2000); Median rent: $438 per month (2000); Median age of housing: 26 years (2000).
Transportation: Commute to work: 94.9% car, 0.7% public transportation, 1.7% walk, 2.4% work from home (2000); Travel time to work: 19.8% less than 15 minutes, 43.8% 15 to 30 minutes, 19.5% 30 to 45 minutes, 5.3% 45 to 60 minutes, 11.7% 60 minutes or more (2000)

CAPAC (village). Covers a land area of 1.619 square miles and a water area of 0 square miles. Located at 43.01° N. Lat.; 82.92° W. Long. Elevation is 814 feet.
History: Capac was founded in 1857 and named for Manco Capac, considered to be the founder of the Inca dynasty in South America. The village was incorporated in 1873.
Population: 1,775 (2000); Race: 92.1% White, 0.0% Black, 0.0% Asian, 0.8% American Indian and Alaska Native, 16.7% Hispanic of any race, 2.4% two or more races (2000); Density: 1,096.5 persons per square mile (2000); Age: 33.4% under 18, 8.6% over 64 (2000); Marriage status: 24.8% never married, 59.7% now married, 7.3% widowed, 8.2% divorced (2000); Foreign born: 8.2% (2000); Ancestry (includes multiple ancestries): 29.4% German, 19.3% Other groups, 11.4% Irish, 10.9% English, 9.9% Polish (2000).
Economy: Employment by occupation: 6.8% management, 11.7% professional, 15.5% services, 20.9% sales, 0.5% farming, 13.7% construction, 30.8% production (2000).
Income: Per capita income: $16,297 (2000); Median household income: $42,105 (2000); Poverty rate: 10.9% (2000).
Taxes: Total city taxes per capita: $289 (1997); City property taxes per capita: $286 (1997).

Education: High school graduation rate: 76.2% (2000); College graduation rate: 10.1% (2000).

School District(s)

Capac Community School District (KG-12)
2000 Enrollment: 1,822 810-395-4321

Housing: Homeownership rate: 73.5% (2000); Median home value: $105,100 (2000); Median rent: $407 per month (2000); Median age of housing: 48 years (2000).
Safety: Violent crime rate: 50.4 per 10,000 population; Property crime rate: 308.3 per 10,000 population (2001).
Transportation: Commute to work: 94.4% car, 0.0% public transportation, 2.6% walk, 1.8% work from home (2000); Travel time to work: 25.4% less than 15 minutes, 24.2% 15 to 30 minutes, 21.9% 30 to 45 minutes, 16.2% 45 to 60 minutes, 12.4% 60 minutes or more (2000)

CASCO (township). Covers a land area of 37.101 square miles and a water area of 0.029 square miles. Located at 42.77° N. Lat.; 82.67° W. Long. Elevation is 639 feet.
Population: 4,747 (2000); Race: 96.2% White, 0.2% Black, 1.2% Asian, 0.4% American Indian and Alaska Native, 0.0% Hispanic of any race, 1.6% two or more races (2000); Density: 127.9 persons per square mile (2000); Age: 30.5% under 18, 5.7% over 64 (2000); Marriage status: 25.8% never married, 62.1% now married, 5.2% widowed, 6.9% divorced (2000); Foreign born: 2.7% (2000); Ancestry (includes multiple ancestries): 38.0% German, 18.7% Polish, 11.9% Irish, 10.7% English, 9.2% French (except Basque) (2000).
Economy: Single-family building permits issued: 14 (2001) / 19 (2000); Multi-family building permits issued: 0 (2001) / 0 (2000); Employment by occupation: 11.8% management, 14.3% professional, 14.8% services, 18.5% sales, 1.1% farming, 16.7% construction, 22.7% production (2000).
Income: Per capita income: $22,299 (2000); Median household income: $52,961 (2000); Poverty rate: 1.6% (2000).
Taxes: Total city taxes per capita: $29 (1997); City property taxes per capita: $21 (1997).
Education: High school graduation rate: 88.7% (2000); College graduation rate: 11.9% (2000).
Housing: Homeownership rate: 94.1% (2000); Median home value: $149,100 (2000); Median rent: $534 per month (2000); Median age of housing: 24 years (2000).
Transportation: Commute to work: 98.0% car, 0.0% public transportation, 0.0% walk, 2.0% work from home (2000); Travel time to work: 14.1% less than 15 minutes, 29.5% 15 to 30 minutes, 21.2% 30 to 45 minutes, 19.2% 45 to 60 minutes, 16.1% 60 minutes or more (2000)

CHINA (township). Covers a land area of 34.368 square miles and a water area of 0 square miles. Located at 42.77° N. Lat.; 82.54° W. Long.
History: A dam and a grist mill were built in China Township in 1825. It was named by Captain John Clarke, an early resident, for China Township in Maine where he had previously lived.
Population: 3,340 (2000); Race: 95.6% White, 0.3% Black, 0.4% Asian, 1.5% American Indian and Alaska Native, 1.4% Hispanic of any race, 1.3% two or more races (2000); Density: 97.2 persons per square mile (2000); Age: 29.2% under 18, 8.8% over 64 (2000); Marriage status: 20.5% never married, 69.2% now married, 4.0% widowed, 6.3% divorced (2000); Foreign born: 1.9% (2000); Ancestry (includes multiple ancestries): 36.6% German, 13.2% French (except Basque), 12.7% Polish, 11.4% Irish, 8.9% English (2000).
Economy: Single-family building permits issued: 28 (2001) / 37 (2000); Multi-family building permits issued: 0 (2001) / 0 (2000); Employment by occupation: 11.4% management, 16.0% professional, 11.2% services, 20.2% sales, 0.5% farming, 15.0% construction, 25.7% production (2000).
Income: Per capita income: $22,674 (2000); Median household income: $62,194 (2000); Poverty rate: 2.0% (2000).
Taxes: Total city taxes per capita: $272 (1997); City property taxes per capita: $261 (1997).
Education: High school graduation rate: 85.1% (2000); College graduation rate: 13.5% (2000).
Housing: Homeownership rate: 94.2% (2000); Median home value: $169,500 (2000); Median rent: $612 per month (2000); Median age of housing: 28 years (2000).
Transportation: Commute to work: 94.4% car, 0.0% public transportation, 0.4% walk, 5.0% work from home (2000); Travel time to work: 20.9% less than 15 minutes, 28.2% 15 to 30 minutes, 20.8% 30 to 45 minutes, 12.5% 45 to 60 minutes, 17.6% 60 minutes or more (2000)

CLAY (township). Covers a land area of 35.460 square miles and a water area of 47.056 square miles. Located at 42.61° N. Lat.; 82.59° W. Long.
Population: 9,822 (2000); Race: 98.0% White, 0.2% Black, 0.5% Asian, 0.5% American Indian and Alaska Native, 1.0% Hispanic of any race, 0.7% two or more races (2000); Density: 277.0 persons per square mile (2000); Age: 22.0% under 18, 14.0% over 64 (2000); Marriage status: 19.9% never married, 62.2% now married, 6.8% widowed, 11.2% divorced (2000); Foreign born: 2.6% (2000); Ancestry (includes multiple ancestries): 27.1% German, 18.7% Polish, 12.9% Irish, 9.7% French (except Basque), 9.1% English (2000).
Economy: Single-family building permits issued: 61 (2001) / 50 (2000); Multi-family building permits issued: 0 (2001) / 14 (2000); Employment by occupation: 9.1% management, 15.1% professional, 12.9% services, 25.2% sales, 0.1% farming, 14.2% construction, 23.4% production (2000).
Income: Per capita income: $27,169 (2000); Median household income: $55,059 (2000); Poverty rate: 4.7% (2000).
Taxes: Total city taxes per capita: $194 (2000); City property taxes per capita: $182 (2000).
Education: High school graduation rate: 84.3% (2000); College graduation rate: 11.6% (2000).
Housing: Homeownership rate: 92.5% (2000); Median home value: $162,400 (2000); Median rent: $466 per month (2000); Median age of housing: 35 years (2000).
Safety: Violent crime rate: 4.1 per 10,000 population; Property crime rate: 43.5 per 10,000 population (2001).
Transportation: Commute to work: 96.1% car, 0.0% public transportation, 0.5% walk, 2.7% work from home (2000); Travel time to work: 14.7% less than 15 minutes, 19.4% 15 to 30 minutes, 19.4% 30 to 45 minutes, 18.7% 45 to 60 minutes, 27.9% 60 minutes or more (2000)

Additional Information Contacts

Clay Chamber of Commerce 810-794-5511

CLYDE (township). Covers a land area of 35.881 square miles and a water area of 0.122 square miles. Located at 43.03° N. Lat.; 82.58° W. Long.
Population: 5,523 (2000); Race: 98.8% White, 0.0% Black, 0.0% Asian, 0.3% American Indian and Alaska Native, 1.5% Hispanic of any race, 0.5% two or more races (2000); Density: 153.9 persons per square mile (2000); Age: 26.4% under 18, 9.1% over 64 (2000); Marriage status: 20.0% never married, 68.8% now married, 5.0% widowed, 6.3% divorced (2000); Foreign born: 1.4% (2000); Ancestry (includes multiple ancestries): 30.3% German, 16.4% English, 16.2% Irish, 9.9% Polish, 6.8% French (except Basque) (2000).
Economy: Single-family building permits issued: 24 (2001) / 34 (2000); Multi-family building permits issued: 0 (2001) / 0 (2000); Employment by occupation: 10.8% management, 16.2% professional, 11.2% services, 25.6% sales, 0.0% farming, 11.5% construction, 24.7% production (2000).
Income: Per capita income: $22,882 (2000); Median household income: $53,986 (2000); Poverty rate: 4.9% (2000).
Taxes: Total city taxes per capita: $27 (1997); City property taxes per capita: $13 (1997).
Education: High school graduation rate: 87.1% (2000); College graduation rate: 14.7% (2000).
Housing: Homeownership rate: 91.8% (2000); Median home value: $138,800 (2000); Median rent: $459 per month (2000); Median age of housing: 26 years (2000).
Transportation: Commute to work: 97.3% car, 0.6% public transportation, 0.0% walk, 1.8% work from home (2000); Travel time to work: 20.9% less than 15 minutes, 50.4% 15 to 30 minutes, 11.6% 30 to 45 minutes, 5.5% 45 to 60 minutes, 11.5% 60 minutes or more (2000)

COLUMBUS (township). Covers a land area of 37.103 square miles and a water area of 0.136 square miles. Located at 42.85° N. Lat.; 82.68° W. Long. Elevation is 676 feet.
History: Columbus Township was organized in 1837 and named for Christopher Columbus.
Population: 4,615 (2000); Race: 96.8% White, 0.0% Black, 0.0% Asian, 1.1% American Indian and Alaska Native, 2.1% Hispanic of any race, 1.4% two or more races (2000); Density: 124.4 persons per square mile (2000); Age: 29.2% under 18, 7.8% over 64 (2000); Marriage status: 18.5% never married, 71.1% now married, 3.1% widowed, 7.3% divorced (2000); Foreign born: 4.1% (2000); Ancestry (includes multiple ancestries): 32.1% German, 18.9% Polish, 16.0% Irish, 10.9% Italian, 9.6% English (2000).
Economy: Single-family building permits issued: 22 (2001) / 27 (2000); Multi-family building permits issued: 0 (2001) / 0 (2000); Employment by occupation: 9.1% management, 15.5% professional, 12.8% services, 25.0% sales, 0.0% farming, 13.8% construction, 23.8% production (2000).
Income: Per capita income: $21,767 (2000); Median household income: $61,063 (2000); Poverty rate: 3.7% (2000).

Taxes: Total city taxes per capita: $37 (1997); City property taxes per capita: $21 (1997).
Education: High school graduation rate: 82.9% (2000); College graduation rate: 11.8% (2000).
Housing: Homeownership rate: 95.9% (2000); Median home value: $165,200 (2000); Median rent: $509 per month (2000); Median age of housing: 19 years (2000).
Transportation: Commute to work: 95.0% car, 0.4% public transportation, 1.9% walk, 2.3% work from home (2000); Travel time to work: 15.6% less than 15 minutes, 25.5% 15 to 30 minutes, 31.1% 30 to 45 minutes, 17.1% 45 to 60 minutes, 10.7% 60 minutes or more (2000)

COTTRELLVILLE (township). Covers a land area of 21.193 square miles and a water area of 1.183 square miles. Located at 42.69° N. Lat.; 82.53° W. Long.
History: Cottrellville Township was organized in 1822 and named for county commissioner George Cottrell.
Population: 3,814 (2000); Race: 99.2% White, 0.0% Black, 0.0% Asian, 0.0% American Indian and Alaska Native, 1.4% Hispanic of any race, 0.4% two or more races (2000); Density: 180.0 persons per square mile (2000); Age: 27.6% under 18, 10.4% over 64 (2000); Marriage status: 23.9% never married, 61.1% now married, 6.5% widowed, 8.5% divorced (2000); Foreign born: 0.8% (2000); Ancestry (includes multiple ancestries): 33.9% German, 15.8% French (except Basque), 13.0% Irish, 11.3% Polish, 9.9% English (2000).
Economy: Single-family building permits issued: 12 (2001) / 32 (2000); Multi-family building permits issued: 0 (2001) / 0 (2000); Employment by occupation: 8.3% management, 11.5% professional, 12.8% services, 22.1% sales, 0.0% farming, 16.9% construction, 28.4% production (2000).
Income: Per capita income: $24,510 (2000); Median household income: $47,396 (2000); Poverty rate: 2.6% (2000).
Taxes: Total city taxes per capita: $24 (1997); City property taxes per capita: $15 (1997).
Education: High school graduation rate: 83.2% (2000); College graduation rate: 8.2% (2000).
Housing: Homeownership rate: 90.8% (2000); Median home value: $164,600 (2000); Median rent: $426 per month (2000); Median age of housing: 29 years (2000).
Transportation: Commute to work: 96.3% car, 0.0% public transportation, 1.0% walk, 1.9% work from home (2000); Travel time to work: 24.1% less than 15 minutes, 27.6% 15 to 30 minutes, 18.1% 30 to 45 minutes, 14.2% 45 to 60 minutes, 15.9% 60 minutes or more (2000)

EAST CHINA (township). Covers a land area of 6.686 square miles and a water area of 1.147 square miles. Located at 42.77° N. Lat.; 82.48° W. Long.
Population: 3,630 (2000); Race: 99.1% White, 0.0% Black, 0.0% Asian, 0.4% American Indian and Alaska Native, 0.4% Hispanic of any race, 0.5% two or more races (2000); Density: 542.9 persons per square mile (2000); Age: 20.5% under 18, 19.9% over 64 (2000); Marriage status: 18.4% never married, 64.5% now married, 9.2% widowed, 7.8% divorced (2000); Foreign born: 1.1% (2000); Ancestry (includes multiple ancestries): 31.7% German, 15.3% English, 13.4% Irish, 13.0% French (except Basque), 9.0% Polish (2000).
Economy: Single-family building permits issued: 19 (2001) / 36 (2000); Multi-family building permits issued: 0 (2001) / 0 (2000); Employment by occupation: 10.5% management, 15.7% professional, 12.5% services, 24.3% sales, 0.7% farming, 13.8% construction, 22.5% production (2000).
Income: Per capita income: $26,792 (2000); Median household income: $51,652 (2000); Poverty rate: 4.6% (2000).
Taxes: Total city taxes per capita: $384 (1997); City property taxes per capita: $373 (1997).
Education: High school graduation rate: 79.6% (2000); College graduation rate: 15.3% (2000).

School District(s)

East China School District (PK-12)
2000 Enrollment: 5,642 810-765-1753
Housing: Homeownership rate: 79.0% (2000); Median home value: $155,200 (2000); Median rent: $422 per month (2000); Median age of housing: 27 years (2000).
Hospitals: River District Hospital (68 beds)
Transportation: Commute to work: 96.9% car, 0.0% public transportation, 1.0% walk, 0.8% work from home (2000); Travel time to work: 31.8% less than 15 minutes, 15.8% 15 to 30 minutes, 22.0% 30 to 45 minutes, 11.7% 45 to 60 minutes, 18.7% 60 minutes or more (2000)

EMMETT (village). Covers a land area of 1.491 square miles and a water area of 0 square miles. Located at 42.99° N. Lat.; 82.76° W. Long. Elevation is 775 feet.
Population: 251 (2000); Race: 99.2% White, 0.0% Black, 0.8% Asian, 0.0% American Indian and Alaska Native, 0.0% Hispanic of any race, 0.0% two or more races (2000); Density: 168.4 persons per square mile (2000); Age: 28.8% under 18, 10.1% over 64 (2000); Marriage status: 28.8% never married, 66.7% now married, 1.5% widowed, 3.0% divorced (2000); Foreign born: 0.8% (2000); Ancestry (includes multiple ancestries): 29.2% Irish, 12.1% English, 9.7% Scottish, 8.6% Polish, 7.4% German (2000).
Economy: Employment by occupation: 4.3% management, 18.1% professional, 18.1% services, 15.5% sales, 1.7% farming, 26.7% construction, 15.5% production (2000).
Income: Per capita income: $16,500 (2000); Median household income: $50,536 (2000); Poverty rate: 1.2% (2000).
Taxes: Total city taxes per capita: $67 (1997); City property taxes per capita: $67 (1997).
Education: High school graduation rate: 97.3% (2000); College graduation rate: 12.1% (2000).
Housing: Homeownership rate: 89.4% (2000); Median home value: $97,800 (2000); Median rent: $515 per month (2000); Median age of housing: 50 years (2000).
Transportation: Commute to work: 93.1% car, 0.0% public transportation, 0.0% walk, 6.9% work from home (2000); Travel time to work: 15.7% less than 15 minutes, 24.1% 15 to 30 minutes, 26.9% 30 to 45 minutes, 3.7% 45 to 60 minutes, 29.6% 60 minutes or more (2000)

EMMETT (township). Covers a land area of 35.302 square miles and a water area of 0 square miles. Located at 43.01° N. Lat.; 82.79° W. Long. Elevation is 775 feet.
Population: 2,506 (2000); Race: 95.4% White, 1.1% Black, 0.4% Asian, 0.2% American Indian and Alaska Native, 3.8% Hispanic of any race, 0.4% two or more races (2000); Density: 71.0 persons per square mile (2000); Age: 31.1% under 18, 7.9% over 64 (2000); Marriage status: 20.6% never married, 68.7% now married, 4.2% widowed, 6.5% divorced (2000); Foreign born: 2.6% (2000); Ancestry (includes multiple ancestries): 27.9% German, 19.8% Irish, 15.9% Polish, 11.0% French (except Basque), 8.1% Italian (2000).
Economy: In agricultural area. Single-family building permits issued: 23 (2001) / 32 (2000); Multi-family building permits issued: 0 (2001) / 0 (2000); Employment by occupation: 7.4% management, 15.9% professional, 12.8% services, 20.0% sales, 0.9% farming, 20.1% construction, 22.9% production (2000).
Income: Per capita income: $18,430 (2000); Median household income: $53,452 (2000); Poverty rate: 5.8% (2000).
Taxes: Total city taxes per capita: $32 (1997); City property taxes per capita: $14 (1997).
Education: High school graduation rate: 86.1% (2000); College graduation rate: 6.2% (2000).
Housing: Homeownership rate: 93.3% (2000); Median home value: $142,300 (2000); Median rent: $521 per month (2000); Median age of housing: 22 years (2000).
Transportation: Commute to work: 95.2% car, 0.0% public transportation, 0.3% walk, 3.9% work from home (2000); Travel time to work: 12.9% less than 15 minutes, 22.5% 15 to 30 minutes, 26.3% 30 to 45 minutes, 14.3% 45 to 60 minutes, 24.0% 60 minutes or more (2000)

FAIR HAVEN (unincorporated postal area, zip code 48023). Covers a land area of 16.605 square miles and a water area of 0.042 square miles. Located at 42.70° N. Lat.; 82.66° W. Long.
History: Fair Haven began as a timber town, later developing into a market center for farmers. Many Detroiters built summer homes here in the early 1900's, where Anchor Bay is protected from the wind.
Population: 6,984 (2000); Race: 96.9% White, 0.4% Black, 0.1% Asian, 1.0% American Indian and Alaska Native, 0.9% Hispanic of any race, 1.5% two or more races (2000); Density: 420.6 persons per square mile (2000); Age: 27.3% under 18, 10.0% over 64 (2000); Marriage status: 23.6% never married, 54.0% now married, 6.6% widowed, 15.8% divorced (2000); Foreign born: 3.6% (2000); Ancestry (includes multiple ancestries): 30.8% German, 14.4% Irish, 14.2% Polish, 7.7% Italian, 7.1% French (except Basque) (2000).
Economy: Employment by occupation: 11.7% management, 10.9% professional, 13.4% services, 18.9% sales, 0.2% farming, 17.0% construction, 27.8% production (2000).
Income: Per capita income: $22,091 (2000); Median household income: $45,625 (2000); Poverty rate: 9.4% (2000).

Education: High school graduation rate: 81.6% (2000); College graduation rate: 9.0% (2000).
Housing: Homeownership rate: 89.0% (2000); Median home value: $166,700 (2000); Median rent: $529 per month (2000); Median age of housing: 21 years (2000).
Transportation: Commute to work: 95.4% car, 0.0% public transportation, 1.6% walk, 1.6% work from home (2000); Travel time to work: 19.7% less than 15 minutes, 24.6% 15 to 30 minutes, 30.3% 30 to 45 minutes, 14.0% 45 to 60 minutes, 11.4% 60 minutes or more (2000)

FORT GRATIOT (township). Covers a land area of 16.083 square miles and a water area of 0.028 square miles. Located at 43.03° N. Lat.; 82.47° W. Long.
Population: 10,691 (2000); Race: 95.8% White, 2.8% Black, 0.2% Asian, 0.4% American Indian and Alaska Native, 1.5% Hispanic of any race, 0.2% two or more races (2000); Density: 664.7 persons per square mile (2000); Age: 23.7% under 18, 15.3% over 64 (2000); Marriage status: 19.9% never married, 63.3% now married, 7.7% widowed, 9.0% divorced (2000); Foreign born: 3.5% (2000); Ancestry (includes multiple ancestries): 27.8% German, 17.0% Irish, 14.8% English, 7.4% Polish, 7.2% French (except Basque) (2000).
Economy: Single-family building permits issued: 42 (2001) / 49 (2000); Multi-family building permits issued: 0 (2001) / 0 (2000); Employment by occupation: 10.7% management, 19.9% professional, 14.2% services, 29.0% sales, 0.1% farming, 9.6% construction, 16.6% production (2000).
Income: Per capita income: $25,485 (2000); Median household income: $50,736 (2000); Poverty rate: 5.7% (2000).
Taxes: Total city taxes per capita: $73 (2000); City property taxes per capita: $45 (2000).
Education: High school graduation rate: 88.2% (2000); College graduation rate: 21.8% (2000).
Housing: Homeownership rate: 80.5% (2000); Median home value: $138,500 (2000); Median rent: $501 per month (2000); Median age of housing: 27 years (2000).
Transportation: Commute to work: 95.1% car, 0.3% public transportation, 0.7% walk, 3.6% work from home (2000); Travel time to work: 40.4% less than 15 minutes, 37.1% 15 to 30 minutes, 8.4% 30 to 45 minutes, 5.9% 45 to 60 minutes, 8.2% 60 minutes or more (2000)

GOODELLS (unincorporated postal area, zip code 48027). Covers a land area of 37.363 square miles and a water area of 0.024 square miles. Located at 42.95° N. Lat.; 82.68° W. Long. Elevation is 707 feet.
History: Goodells developed in the mid-1860's when the Grand Trunk Railroad built a station here. The community was named for John Goodell.
Population: 2,986 (2000); Race: 94.7% White, 2.7% Black, 0.2% Asian, 0.6% American Indian and Alaska Native, 1.2% Hispanic of any race, 1.4% two or more races (2000); Density: 79.9 persons per square mile (2000); Age: 28.2% under 18, 9.1% over 64 (2000); Marriage status: 20.6% never married, 68.1% now married, 4.7% widowed, 6.5% divorced (2000); Foreign born: 1.9% (2000); Ancestry (includes multiple ancestries): 33.2% German, 16.9% Polish, 16.1% Irish, 12.9% English, 7.3% Other groups (2000).
Economy: Employment by occupation: 8.7% management, 13.0% professional, 11.6% services, 21.0% sales, 1.1% farming, 16.7% construction, 27.9% production (2000).
Income: Per capita income: $20,817 (2000); Median household income: $51,716 (2000); Poverty rate: 6.4% (2000).
Education: High school graduation rate: 86.9% (2000); College graduation rate: 9.7% (2000).
Housing: Homeownership rate: 91.5% (2000); Median home value: $134,500 (2000); Median rent: $465 per month (2000); Median age of housing: 26 years (2000).
Transportation: Commute to work: 95.6% car, 0.0% public transportation, 1.2% walk, 2.8% work from home (2000); Travel time to work: 12.9% less than 15 minutes, 32.8% 15 to 30 minutes, 20.0% 30 to 45 minutes, 16.2% 45 to 60 minutes, 18.2% 60 minutes or more (2000)

GRANT (township). Covers a land area of 29.839 square miles and a water area of 0.005 square miles. Located at 43.12° N. Lat.; 82.59° W. Long.
Population: 1,667 (2000); Race: 97.4% White, 0.0% Black, 0.5% Asian, 0.2% American Indian and Alaska Native, 2.6% Hispanic of any race, 0.7% two or more races (2000); Density: 55.9 persons per square mile (2000); Age: 29.9% under 18, 7.1% over 64 (2000); Marriage status: 22.8% never married, 64.5% now married, 5.7% widowed, 7.1% divorced (2000); Foreign born: 2.8% (2000); Ancestry (includes multiple ancestries): 28.0% German, 17.3% English, 13.6% Irish, 9.9% Polish, 7.4% French (except Basque) (2000).
Economy: Single-family building permits issued: 18 (2001) / 9 (2000); Multi-family building permits issued: 0 (2001) / 0 (2000); Employment by occupation: 10.9% management, 10.8% professional, 16.1% services, 23.9% sales, 1.4% farming, 15.4% construction, 21.5% production (2000).
Income: Per capita income: $20,729 (2000); Median household income: $58,603 (2000); Poverty rate: 4.2% (2000).
Taxes: Total city taxes per capita: $166 (1997); City property taxes per capita: $164 (1997).
Education: High school graduation rate: 86.9% (2000); College graduation rate: 11.5% (2000).
Housing: Homeownership rate: 91.2% (2000); Median home value: $125,600 (2000); Median rent: $363 per month (2000); Median age of housing: 22 years (2000).
Transportation: Commute to work: 95.3% car, 0.0% public transportation, 1.2% walk, 3.0% work from home (2000); Travel time to work: 7.8% less than 15 minutes, 46.1% 15 to 30 minutes, 22.0% 30 to 45 minutes, 7.3% 45 to 60 minutes, 16.9% 60 minutes or more (2000)

GREENWOOD (township). Covers a land area of 35.751 square miles and a water area of 0.136 square miles. Located at 43.12° N. Lat.; 82.69° W. Long.
Population: 1,373 (2000); Race: 96.4% White, 1.0% Black, 0.5% Asian, 0.3% American Indian and Alaska Native, 0.8% Hispanic of any race, 1.3% two or more races (2000); Density: 38.4 persons per square mile (2000); Age: 28.4% under 18, 10.5% over 64 (2000); Marriage status: 22.4% never married, 63.4% now married, 5.2% widowed, 8.9% divorced (2000); Foreign born: 2.4% (2000); Ancestry (includes multiple ancestries): 29.6% German, 14.7% English, 14.3% Irish, 11.5% Polish, 7.1% Other groups (2000).
Economy: Single-family building permits issued: 13 (2001) / 23 (2000); Multi-family building permits issued: 0 (2001) / 0 (2000); Employment by occupation: 7.7% management, 15.9% professional, 10.5% services, 22.4% sales, 0.0% farming, 20.6% construction, 22.8% production (2000).
Income: Per capita income: $22,050 (2000); Median household income: $52,604 (2000); Poverty rate: 1.8% (2000).
Taxes: Total city taxes per capita: $200 (1997); City property taxes per capita: $195 (1997).
Education: High school graduation rate: 83.7% (2000); College graduation rate: 8.8% (2000).
Housing: Homeownership rate: 92.3% (2000); Median home value: $117,600 (2000); Median rent: $363 per month (2000); Median age of housing: 28 years (2000).
Transportation: Commute to work: 94.7% car, 0.3% public transportation, 1.3% walk, 3.4% work from home (2000); Travel time to work: 12.6% less than 15 minutes, 25.4% 15 to 30 minutes, 27.6% 30 to 45 minutes, 11.0% 45 to 60 minutes, 23.3% 60 minutes or more (2000)

HARSENS ISLAND (unincorporated postal area, zip code 48028). Aka Sans Souci. Covers a land area of 19.004 square miles and a water area of 0.477 square miles. Located at 42.56° N. Lat.; 82.62° W. Long.
History: James Harsen and Isaac Graveraet came to the island in the late 1770's and purchased the land.
Population: 1,285 (2000); Race: 96.0% White, 0.0% Black, 0.0% Asian, 4.0% American Indian and Alaska Native, 0.0% Hispanic of any race, 0.0% two or more races (2000); Density: 67.6 persons per square mile (2000); Age: 10.5% under 18, 24.9% over 64 (2000); Marriage status: 13.6% never married, 63.7% now married, 10.2% widowed, 12.5% divorced (2000); Foreign born: 2.9% (2000); Ancestry (includes multiple ancestries): 23.7% German, 15.8% Polish, 13.7% English, 12.3% Irish, 10.8% French (except Basque) (2000).
Economy: Employment by occupation: 18.0% management, 15.0% professional, 5.4% services, 35.5% sales, 0.0% farming, 13.5% construction, 12.6% production (2000).
Income: Per capita income: $34,578 (2000); Median household income: $55,720 (2000); Poverty rate: 5.0% (2000).
Education: High school graduation rate: 82.8% (2000); College graduation rate: 19.0% (2000).
Housing: Homeownership rate: 98.8% (2000); Median home value: $170,500 (2000); Median age of housing: 43 years (2000).
Transportation: Commute to work: 94.5% car, 0.0% public transportation, 1.1% walk, 2.9% work from home (2000); Travel time to work: 10.4% less than 15 minutes, 13.7% 15 to 30 minutes, 13.3% 30 to 45 minutes, 11.2% 45 to 60 minutes, 51.4% 60 minutes or more (2000)

IRA (township). Covers a land area of 16.951 square miles and a water area of 4.616 square miles. Located at 42.69° N. Lat.; 82.66° W. Long.

History: Ira Township was organized in 1837 and named for Ira Marks, an early settler here.
Population: 6,966 (2000); Race: 96.9% White, 0.4% Black, 0.1% Asian, 1.0% American Indian and Alaska Native, 0.9% Hispanic of any race, 1.5% two or more races (2000); Density: 411.0 persons per square mile (2000); Age: 27.3% under 18, 10.0% over 64 (2000); Marriage status: 23.6% never married, 53.9% now married, 6.7% widowed, 15.8% divorced (2000); Foreign born: 3.6% (2000); Ancestry (includes multiple ancestries): 30.9% German, 14.5% Irish, 14.1% Polish, 7.8% Italian, 7.1% French (except Basque) (2000).
Economy: Single-family building permits issued: 17 (2001) / 40 (2000); Multi-family building permits issued: 0 (2001) / 4 (2000); Employment by occupation: 11.8% management, 11.0% professional, 13.5% services, 18.9% sales, 0.2% farming, 17.1% construction, 27.6% production (2000).
Income: Per capita income: $22,115 (2000); Median household income: $45,525 (2000); Poverty rate: 9.4% (2000).
Taxes: Total city taxes per capita: $65 (2000); City property taxes per capita: $51 (2000).
Education: High school graduation rate: 81.6% (2000); College graduation rate: 9.0% (2000).
Housing: Homeownership rate: 88.9% (2000); Median home value: $167,500 (2000); Median rent: $529 per month (2000); Median age of housing: 21 years (2000).
Transportation: Commute to work: 95.4% car, 0.0% public transportation, 1.6% walk, 1.6% work from home (2000); Travel time to work: 19.8% less than 15 minutes, 24.7% 15 to 30 minutes, 30.4% 30 to 45 minutes, 13.8% 45 to 60 minutes, 11.4% 60 minutes or more (2000)

JEDDO (unincorporated postal area, zip code 48032). Covers a land area of 38.983 square miles and a water area of 0.028 square miles. Located at 43.12° N. Lat.; 82.59° W. Long.
History: Jeddo grew up around Potter's Corners, named for A.S. Potter, the first settler here.
Population: 2,070 (2000); Race: 97.7% White, 0.0% Black, 0.5% Asian, 0.2% American Indian and Alaska Native, 2.2% Hispanic of any race, 0.6% two or more races (2000); Density: 53.1 persons per square mile (2000); Age: 27.7% under 18, 9.2% over 64 (2000); Marriage status: 20.7% never married, 66.1% now married, 5.5% widowed, 7.7% divorced (2000); Foreign born: 2.5% (2000); Ancestry (includes multiple ancestries): 26.0% German, 16.8% English, 13.8% Irish, 11.4% Polish, 7.7% United States or American (2000).
Economy: Employment by occupation: 10.9% management, 11.6% professional, 15.1% services, 23.2% sales, 1.5% farming, 16.1% construction, 21.6% production (2000).
Income: Per capita income: $20,003 (2000); Median household income: $51,927 (2000); Poverty rate: 4.2% (2000).
Education: High school graduation rate: 84.6% (2000); College graduation rate: 10.0% (2000).
Housing: Homeownership rate: 92.5% (2000); Median home value: $118,300 (2000); Median rent: $388 per month (2000); Median age of housing: 23 years (2000).
Transportation: Commute to work: 95.6% car, 0.0% public transportation, 1.1% walk, 2.9% work from home (2000); Travel time to work: 8.8% less than 15 minutes, 43.6% 15 to 30 minutes, 23.2% 30 to 45 minutes, 8.1% 45 to 60 minutes, 16.3% 60 minutes or more (2000)

KENOCKEE (township). Covers a land area of 35.825 square miles and a water area of 0.014 square miles. Located at 43.02° N. Lat.; 82.69° W. Long.
History: Kenockee Township was organized in 1855. The name is of Chippewa origin, meaning "long-legged."
Population: 2,423 (2000); Race: 97.2% White, 1.2% Black, 0.0% Asian, 0.2% American Indian and Alaska Native, 1.8% Hispanic of any race, 0.0% two or more races (2000); Density: 67.6 persons per square mile (2000); Age: 28.0% under 18, 8.9% over 64 (2000); Marriage status: 19.2% never married, 69.6% now married, 5.3% widowed, 5.9% divorced (2000); Foreign born: 2.1% (2000); Ancestry (includes multiple ancestries): 26.5% German, 18.6% Irish, 11.9% Polish, 10.9% French (except Basque), 9.1% English (2000).
Economy: Single-family building permits issued: 19 (2001) / 27 (2000); Multi-family building permits issued: 0 (2001) / 0 (2000); Employment by occupation: 11.1% management, 9.3% professional, 14.3% services, 21.1% sales, 0.7% farming, 15.2% construction, 28.1% production (2000).
Income: Per capita income: $20,764 (2000); Median household income: $54,293 (2000); Poverty rate: 4.2% (2000).
Taxes: Total city taxes per capita: $52 (1997); City property taxes per capita: $42 (1997).
Education: High school graduation rate: 83.9% (2000); College graduation rate: 5.7% (2000).
Housing: Homeownership rate: 93.4% (2000); Median home value: $139,300 (2000); Median rent: $457 per month (2000); Median age of housing: 23 years (2000).
Transportation: Commute to work: 94.7% car, 0.0% public transportation, 1.2% walk, 4.1% work from home (2000); Travel time to work: 6.2% less than 15 minutes, 36.3% 15 to 30 minutes, 25.8% 30 to 45 minutes, 12.6% 45 to 60 minutes, 19.1% 60 minutes or more (2000)

KIMBALL (township). Covers a land area of 37.254 square miles and a water area of 0.264 square miles. Located at 42.94° N. Lat.; 82.57° W. Long. Elevation is 637 feet.
History: Barzillai Wheeler and John S. Kimball settled here about 1840. Kimball Township was organized in 1855 and named for John Kimball.
Population: 8,628 (2000); Race: 97.2% White, 1.0% Black, 0.3% Asian, 0.2% American Indian and Alaska Native, 1.7% Hispanic of any race, 1.2% two or more races (2000); Density: 231.6 persons per square mile (2000); Age: 26.7% under 18, 10.4% over 64 (2000); Marriage status: 24.2% never married, 58.3% now married, 6.2% widowed, 11.3% divorced (2000); Foreign born: 1.8% (2000); Ancestry (includes multiple ancestries): 24.5% German, 12.6% English, 11.2% Irish, 8.8% Polish, 7.5% United States or American (2000).
Economy: Single-family building permits issued: 88 (2001) / 103 (2000); Multi-family building permits issued: 0 (2001) / 4 (2000); Employment by occupation: 9.7% management, 10.4% professional, 16.2% services, 19.7% sales, 0.5% farming, 12.0% construction, 31.5% production (2000).
Income: Per capita income: $19,253 (2000); Median household income: $47,627 (2000); Poverty rate: 7.8% (2000).
Taxes: Total city taxes per capita: $53 (2000); City property taxes per capita: $17 (2000).
Education: High school graduation rate: 78.4% (2000); College graduation rate: 7.2% (2000).

School District(s)

Landmark Academy (KG-08)
2000 Enrollment: 219 517-249-4623

Housing: Homeownership rate: 87.8% (2000); Median home value: $100,500 (2000); Median rent: $445 per month (2000); Median age of housing: 29 years (2000).
Transportation: Commute to work: 96.8% car, 0.0% public transportation, 0.7% walk, 2.0% work from home (2000); Travel time to work: 31.1% less than 15 minutes, 39.3% 15 to 30 minutes, 8.9% 30 to 45 minutes, 7.9% 45 to 60 minutes, 12.7% 60 minutes or more (2000)

LYNN (township). Covers a land area of 36.067 square miles and a water area of 0 square miles. Located at 43.11° N. Lat.; 82.92° W. Long.
History: Lynn Township was organized in 1850 and named for Edward J. Lynn, a lumber foreman. The settlement grew up around a sawmill established here in 1840.
Population: 1,187 (2000); Race: 94.8% White, 2.0% Black, 0.0% Asian, 0.7% American Indian and Alaska Native, 6.3% Hispanic of any race, 0.5% two or more races (2000); Density: 32.9 persons per square mile (2000); Age: 30.8% under 18, 9.2% over 64 (2000); Marriage status: 22.4% never married, 69.0% now married, 3.1% widowed, 5.5% divorced (2000); Foreign born: 3.3% (2000); Ancestry (includes multiple ancestries): 32.4% German, 14.7% Irish, 12.2% English, 10.4% Polish, 9.8% Other groups (2000).
Economy: Employment by occupation: 15.3% management, 10.1% professional, 15.8% services, 17.7% sales, 1.5% farming, 17.5% construction, 22.2% production (2000).
Income: Per capita income: $20,250 (2000); Median household income: $52,250 (2000); Poverty rate: 5.8% (2000).
Taxes: Total city taxes per capita: $24 (1997); City property taxes per capita: $24 (1997).
Education: High school graduation rate: 81.7% (2000); College graduation rate: 10.1% (2000).
Housing: Homeownership rate: 92.7% (2000); Median home value: $130,400 (2000); Median rent: $488 per month (2000); Median age of housing: 28 years (2000).
Transportation: Commute to work: 90.3% car, 0.0% public transportation, 2.7% walk, 6.3% work from home (2000); Travel time to work: 14.9% less than 15 minutes, 14.1% 15 to 30 minutes, 14.3% 30 to 45 minutes, 22.4% 45 to 60 minutes, 34.1% 60 minutes or more (2000)

MARINE CITY (city). Covers a land area of 2.194 square miles and a water area of 0.279 square miles. Located at 42.71° N. Lat.; 82.49° W. Long. Elevation is 588 feet.

History: Marine City began as a lumber town, but turned to shipping from its port on the St. Clair River.
Population: 4,652 (2000); Race: 98.6% White, 0.1% Black, 0.2% Asian, 0.4% American Indian and Alaska Native, 1.9% Hispanic of any race, 0.3% two or more races (2000); Density: 2,120.8 persons per square mile (2000); Age: 28.3% under 18, 13.9% over 64 (2000); Marriage status: 26.2% never married, 54.1% now married, 8.6% widowed, 11.1% divorced (2000); Foreign born: 1.6% (2000); Ancestry (includes multiple ancestries): 30.6% German, 16.1% Irish, 12.4% French (except Basque), 11.9% Polish, 9.4% Other groups (2000).
Economy: Single-family building permits issued: 1 (2001) / 4 (2000); Multi-family building permits issued: 0 (2001) / 0 (2000); Employment by occupation: 9.0% management, 11.6% professional, 16.9% services, 18.6% sales, 0.0% farming, 19.4% construction, 24.5% production (2000).
Income: Per capita income: $19,722 (2000); Median household income: $40,146 (2000); Poverty rate: 8.9% (2000).
Taxes: Total city taxes per capita: $431 (1997); City property taxes per capita: $420 (1997).
Education: High school graduation rate: 81.8% (2000); College graduation rate: 9.3% (2000).
Housing: Homeownership rate: 71.0% (2000); Median home value: $105,200 (2000); Median rent: $442 per month (2000); Median age of housing: 51 years (2000).
Safety: Violent crime rate: 6.4 per 10,000 population; Property crime rate: 228.8 per 10,000 population (2001).
Transportation: Commute to work: 93.6% car, 0.0% public transportation, 4.8% walk, 1.6% work from home (2000); Travel time to work: 32.0% less than 15 minutes, 21.0% 15 to 30 minutes, 21.4% 30 to 45 minutes, 13.0% 45 to 60 minutes, 12.6% 60 minutes or more (2000)
Additional Information Contacts
Marine City Chamber of Commerce 810-765-4501

MARYSVILLE (city). Covers a land area of 6.939 square miles and a water area of 1.004 square miles. Located at 42.91° N. Lat.; 82.48° W. Long. Elevation is 587 feet.
History: A sawmill was operating in Marysville in 1780, and more sawmills began in 1805, supplying lumber for the growing town of Detroit. Salt beds beneath Marysville provided the material for a Morton Salt Works plant. In 1930, the Gar Wood Boat Works began operations here, founded by Garfield Arthur Wood, speedboat racing champion and inventor of the hydraulic hoist that revolutionized dump trucks.
Population: 9,684 (2000); Race: 98.3% White, 0.4% Black, 0.1% Asian, 0.3% American Indian and Alaska Native, 0.6% Hispanic of any race, 0.8% two or more races (2000); Density: 1,395.6 persons per square mile (2000); Age: 23.4% under 18, 17.6% over 64 (2000); Marriage status: 18.9% never married, 64.6% now married, 8.2% widowed, 8.3% divorced (2000); Foreign born: 3.4% (2000); Ancestry (includes multiple ancestries): 28.0% German, 12.3% Irish, 11.6% English, 9.5% Polish, 8.8% United States or American (2000).
Economy: Single-family building permits issued: 55 (2001) / 61 (2000); Multi-family building permits issued: 0 (2001) / 0 (2000); Employment by occupation: 9.6% management, 21.1% professional, 14.4% services, 25.8% sales, 0.2% farming, 11.8% construction, 17.1% production (2000).
Income: Per capita income: $23,443 (2000); Median household income: $49,299 (2000); Poverty rate: 4.6% (2000).
Taxes: Total city taxes per capita: $574 (1997); City property taxes per capita: $550 (1997).
Education: High school graduation rate: 89.4% (2000); College graduation rate: 19.3% (2000).

School District(s)

Marysville Public Schools (PK-12)
2000 Enrollment: 2,662 810-364-7731
Housing: Homeownership rate: 84.0% (2000); Median home value: $129,700 (2000); Median rent: $444 per month (2000); Median age of housing: 25 years (2000).
Safety: Violent crime rate: 8.2 per 10,000 population; Property crime rate: 231.1 per 10,000 population (2001).
Transportation: Commute to work: 97.1% car, 0.0% public transportation, 0.9% walk, 1.4% work from home (2000); Travel time to work: 42.3% less than 15 minutes, 34.0% 15 to 30 minutes, 6.8% 30 to 45 minutes, 7.7% 45 to 60 minutes, 9.2% 60 minutes or more (2000)
Additional Information Contacts
Marysville Chamber of Commerce 810-364-6180

MUSSEY (township). Covers a land area of 35.966 square miles and a water area of 0 square miles. Located at 43.01° N. Lat.; 82.92° W. Long.
Population: 3,740 (2000); Race: 93.8% White, 0.2% Black, 0.0% Asian, 0.5% American Indian and Alaska Native, 10.2% Hispanic of any race, 1.6% two or more races (2000); Density: 104.0 persons per square mile (2000); Age: 31.5% under 18, 8.5% over 64 (2000); Marriage status: 24.2% never married, 63.2% now married, 6.1% widowed, 6.5% divorced (2000); Foreign born: 4.4% (2000); Ancestry (includes multiple ancestries): 30.3% German, 14.3% Other groups, 12.6% Irish, 11.3% English, 10.6% United States or American (2000).
Economy: Single-family building permits issued: 29 (2001) / 47 (2000); Multi-family building permits issued: 0 (2001) / 0 (2000); Employment by occupation: 8.1% management, 12.0% professional, 12.3% services, 21.0% sales, 0.8% farming, 17.7% construction, 28.0% production (2000).
Income: Per capita income: $18,568 (2000); Median household income: $46,618 (2000); Poverty rate: 7.5% (2000).
Taxes: Total city taxes per capita: $42 (1997); City property taxes per capita: $41 (1997).
Education: High school graduation rate: 82.1% (2000); College graduation rate: 9.8% (2000).
Housing: Homeownership rate: 82.2% (2000); Median home value: $114,800 (2000); Median rent: $405 per month (2000); Median age of housing: 33 years (2000).
Transportation: Commute to work: 94.6% car, 0.0% public transportation, 1.5% walk, 2.6% work from home (2000); Travel time to work: 21.7% less than 15 minutes, 19.6% 15 to 30 minutes, 22.6% 30 to 45 minutes, 19.5% 45 to 60 minutes, 16.7% 60 minutes or more (2000)

NORTH STREET (unincorporated postal area, zip code 48049). Covers a land area of 34.732 square miles and a water area of 0.122 square miles. Located at 43.03° N. Lat.; 82.59° W. Long.
Population: 5,765 (2000); Race: 98.3% White, 0.5% Black, 0.0% Asian, 0.3% American Indian and Alaska Native, 1.5% Hispanic of any race, 0.5% two or more races (2000); Density: 166.0 persons per square mile (2000); Age: 26.2% under 18, 8.8% over 64 (2000); Marriage status: 19.8% never married, 69.3% now married, 5.0% widowed, 6.0% divorced (2000); Foreign born: 1.4% (2000); Ancestry (includes multiple ancestries): 30.8% German, 15.7% Irish, 15.5% English, 9.6% Polish, 6.4% French (except Basque) (2000).
Economy: Employment by occupation: 10.2% management, 17.0% professional, 11.1% services, 25.1% sales, 0.0% farming, 11.6% construction, 25.0% production (2000).
Income: Per capita income: $23,056 (2000); Median household income: $57,031 (2000); Poverty rate: 5.1% (2000).
Education: High school graduation rate: 88.1% (2000); College graduation rate: 14.8% (2000).
Housing: Homeownership rate: 92.2% (2000); Median home value: $139,300 (2000); Median rent: $459 per month (2000); Median age of housing: 26 years (2000).
Transportation: Commute to work: 97.2% car, 0.5% public transportation, 0.0% walk, 2.0% work from home (2000); Travel time to work: 20.5% less than 15 minutes, 49.0% 15 to 30 minutes, 11.8% 30 to 45 minutes, 6.5% 45 to 60 minutes, 12.2% 60 minutes or more (2000)

PEARL BEACH (CDP). Covers a land area of 2.129 square miles and a water area of 0.951 square miles. Located at 42.62° N. Lat.; 82.59° W. Long. Elevation is 581 feet.
History: Pearl Beach was settled in the late 1700's. Since the time of the French traders, the village has attracted duck hunters.
Population: 3,224 (2000); Race: 99.3% White, 0.0% Black, 0.0% Asian, 0.0% American Indian and Alaska Native, 0.2% Hispanic of any race, 0.5% two or more races (2000); Density: 1,514.7 persons per square mile (2000); Age: 15.5% under 18, 16.4% over 64 (2000); Marriage status: 16.5% never married, 64.3% now married, 7.6% widowed, 11.5% divorced (2000); Foreign born: 1.9% (2000); Ancestry (includes multiple ancestries): 28.1% German, 21.5% Polish, 14.5% Irish, 9.2% French (except Basque), 8.8% Italian (2000).
Economy: Employment by occupation: 9.4% management, 18.6% professional, 13.3% services, 27.8% sales, 0.4% farming, 9.2% construction, 21.1% production (2000).
Income: Per capita income: $32,320 (2000); Median household income: $55,186 (2000); Poverty rate: 3.2% (2000).
Education: High school graduation rate: 87.9% (2000); College graduation rate: 13.0% (2000).
Housing: Homeownership rate: 93.2% (2000); Median home value: $188,700 (2000); Median rent: $466 per month (2000); Median age of housing: 36 years (2000).

Transportation: Commute to work: 95.9% car, 0.0% public transportation, 1.1% walk, 2.2% work from home (2000); Travel time to work: 15.9% less than 15 minutes, 18.8% 15 to 30 minutes, 16.3% 30 to 45 minutes, 23.2% 45 to 60 minutes, 25.8% 60 minutes or more (2000)

PORT HURON (city). Covers a land area of 8.081 square miles and a water area of 4.163 square miles. Located at 42.98° N. Lat.; 82.43° W. Long. Elevation is 586 feet.
History: Fort St. Joseph, the second fortified post in lower Michigan, was built here in 1686 to protect the French fur trade from English aggression. A permanent colony was founded in 1790, when Frenchman Anselm Petit settled near the mouth of the Black River. In 1814, Fort Gratiot was built on the site of old Fort St. Joseph. It was in 1826, when the Fort Gratiot Turnpike was constructed from Detroit, that the four villages of Peru, Desmond, Huron, and Gratiot, sprang up. They united in 1837 to form the village of Port Huron. Incorporated as a village in 1849 and chartered as a city in 1857, Port Huron became the seat of St. Clair County in 1871. Its location on Lake Huron and the St. Clair River made Port Huron an important port, with access to the Canadian city across the river.
Population: 32,338 (2000); Race: 86.6% White, 7.9% Black, 0.4% Asian, 0.8% American Indian and Alaska Native, 4.1% Hispanic of any race, 3.0% two or more races (2000); Density: 4,001.9 persons per square mile (2000); Age: 26.8% under 18, 14.1% over 64 (2000); Marriage status: 29.1% never married, 47.2% now married, 8.7% widowed, 15.0% divorced (2000); Foreign born: 3.2% (2000); Ancestry (includes multiple ancestries): 24.4% German, 15.1% Other groups, 12.6% Irish, 10.6% English, 6.4% Polish (2000).
Vital Statistics: Birth rate: 161.7 per 10,000 population (1998)
Economy: Unemployment rate: 9.2% (11/2002); Total civilian labor force: 17,450 (11/2002); Single-family building permits issued: 40 (2001) / 37 (2000); Multi-family building permits issued: 4 (2001) / 112 (2000); Employment by occupation: 6.6% management, 13.9% professional, 18.6% services, 25.1% sales, 0.0% farming, 8.1% construction, 27.5% production (2000).
Income: Per capita income: $17,100 (2000); Median household income: $31,327 (2000); Poverty rate: 16.9% (2000).
Taxes: Total city taxes per capita: $527 (1997); City property taxes per capita: $348 (1997).
Education: High school graduation rate: 76.8% (2000); College graduation rate: 11.3% (2000).

School District(s)

Academy for Plastics Mfg. Techno (11-12)
2000 Enrollment: 0 810-364-8990
Health Career Academy of Saint Cla (11-12)
2000 Enrollment: 0 810-364-8990
Hospitality Academy of Saint Clair (11-12)
2000 Enrollment: 0 810-364-8990
Information Technology Academy (11-12)
2000 Enrollment: 0 810-364-8990
Port Huron Area School District (PK-12)
2000 Enrollment: 12,081 810-984-3101
Saint Clair County Learning Academ (06-12)
2000 Enrollment: 21 810-364-8990

Four-year College(s)

Baker College of Port Huron (Private, Not-for-profit)
2001 Enrollment: 1,329 810-985-7000
2001 Tuition: In-state $5,580; Out-of-state $5,580

Two-year College(s)

Port Huron Hospital School of Radiologic Techn (Public)
2001 Enrollment: n/a 313-987-5000
Saint Clair County Community College (Public)
2001 Enrollment: 4,061 810-984-3881
2001 Tuition: In-state $2,790; Out-of-state $3,759

Housing: Homeownership rate: 57.1% (2000); Median home value: $84,400 (2000); Median rent: $444 per month (2000); Median age of housing: 50 years (2000).
Hospitals: Mercy Hospital (119 beds); Port Huron Hospital (186 beds)
Safety: Violent crime rate: 61.5 per 10,000 population; Property crime rate: 417.4 per 10,000 population (2001).
Newspapers: The Times Herald (7 x week)
Transportation: Commute to work: 89.2% car, 1.7% public transportation, 3.8% walk, 3.4% work from home (2000); Travel time to work: 54.0% less than 15 minutes, 27.9% 15 to 30 minutes, 7.2% 30 to 45 minutes, 3.7% 45 to 60 minutes, 7.2% 60 minutes or more (2000); Amtrak: Service available.
Additional Information Contacts
Eastern Thumb Association of Realtors. 810-982-6889
Port Huron Chamber of Commerce 810-985-7101

PORT HURON (township). Covers a land area of 12.925 square miles and a water area of 0.176 square miles. Located at 42.96° N. Lat.; 82.47° W. Long. Elevation is 586 feet.
History: The earliest European settlement began (1686) with the French fort, St. Joseph. The town grew after the building (1826) of Fort Gratiot Turnpike (between Port Huron and Detroit), ushering in a lumbering era. Local deposits of salt, oil, and natural gas were developed. The old Fort Gratiot lighthouse marks the St. Clair straits off Port Huron. Thomas Edison grew up here. Incorporated 1857.
Population: 8,615 (2000); Race: 93.5% White, 3.8% Black, 0.0% Asian, 0.9% American Indian and Alaska Native, 1.9% Hispanic of any race, 1.1% two or more races (2000); Density: 666.6 persons per square mile (2000); Age: 25.7% under 18, 12.4% over 64 (2000); Marriage status: 22.7% never married, 60.1% now married, 5.6% widowed, 11.6% divorced (2000); Foreign born: 2.0% (2000); Ancestry (includes multiple ancestries): 27.3% German, 12.8% Irish, 12.7% English, 9.0% Other groups, 7.3% Polish (2000).
Economy: Railroad junction and railroad ship transfer. A shipping center with railroad shops. Manufacturing includes transportation equipment, building materials, machinery, salt, fabricated metal products, paper products, chemicals, machinery, consumer goods, electrical equipment and electroplating. Single-family building permits issued: 60 (2001) / 57 (2000); Multi-family building permits issued: 0 (2001) / 6 (2000); Employment by occupation: 10.4% management, 13.9% professional, 13.9% services, 23.6% sales, 0.0% farming, 12.3% construction, 25.9% production (2000).
Income: Per capita income: $21,583 (2000); Median household income: $43,978 (2000); Poverty rate: 7.4% (2000).
Taxes: Total city taxes per capita: $235 (2000); City property taxes per capita: $207 (2000).
Education: High school graduation rate: 80.5% (2000); College graduation rate: 10.5% (2000).
Housing: Homeownership rate: 77.5% (2000); Median home value: $124,300 (2000); Median rent: $497 per month (2000); Median age of housing: 35 years (2000).
Transportation: Commute to work: 96.5% car, 0.7% public transportation, 1.1% walk, 1.2% work from home (2000); Travel time to work: 38.8% less than 15 minutes, 33.9% 15 to 30 minutes, 10.7% 30 to 45 minutes, 5.9% 45 to 60 minutes, 10.8% 60 minutes or more (2000); Amtrak: Service available.

RILEY (township). Covers a land area of 38.273 square miles and a water area of 0.018 square miles. Located at 42.94° N. Lat.; 82.80° W. Long.
History: Riley Township was organized in 1841 and named for John Riley, a Chippewa who owned land here.
Population: 3,046 (2000); Race: 96.3% White, 0.0% Black, 0.4% Asian, 0.3% American Indian and Alaska Native, 2.1% Hispanic of any race, 2.3% two or more races (2000); Density: 79.6 persons per square mile (2000); Age: 29.5% under 18, 7.9% over 64 (2000); Marriage status: 21.6% never married, 66.7% now married, 4.9% widowed, 6.7% divorced (2000); Foreign born: 1.8% (2000); Ancestry (includes multiple ancestries): 39.7% German, 15.8% Polish, 13.6% Irish, 12.2% English, 10.2% Italian (2000).
Economy: Single-family building permits issued: 29 (2001) / 33 (2000); Multi-family building permits issued: 0 (2001) / 0 (2000); Employment by occupation: 7.6% management, 15.6% professional, 13.8% services, 21.1% sales, 0.8% farming, 15.7% construction, 25.4% production (2000).
Income: Per capita income: $22,381 (2000); Median household income: $63,790 (2000); Poverty rate: 3.4% (2000).
Taxes: Total city taxes per capita: $31 (1997); City property taxes per capita: $20 (1997).
Education: High school graduation rate: 83.7% (2000); College graduation rate: 7.0% (2000).
Housing: Homeownership rate: 94.6% (2000); Median home value: $162,600 (2000); Median rent: $356 per month (2000); Median age of housing: 21 years (2000).
Transportation: Commute to work: 96.0% car, 0.6% public transportation, 0.1% walk, 3.3% work from home (2000); Travel time to work: 14.2% less than 15 minutes, 22.0% 15 to 30 minutes, 23.9% 30 to 45 minutes, 20.1% 45 to 60 minutes, 19.7% 60 minutes or more (2000)

SAINT CLAIR (city). Covers a land area of 2.771 square miles and a water area of 0.648 square miles. Located at 42.82° N. Lat.; 82.49° W. Long. Elevation is 589 feet.
History: St. Clair was laid out in 1818, and a post office was established here in 1826. The name probably came from LaSalle, who entered the lake in 1679 on the feast day of Saint Claire. The name was later applied to the lake, the

river, and the village. Between LaSalle and the 19th-century village, a British officer named Patrick Sinclair erected Fort Sinclair as a supply depot in the area. The St. Clair name may have come from him.
Population: 5,802 (2000); Race: 98.0% White, 0.0% Black, 0.3% Asian, 0.1% American Indian and Alaska Native, 1.6% Hispanic of any race, 1.4% two or more races (2000); Density: 2,093.7 persons per square mile (2000); Age: 28.1% under 18, 15.1% over 64 (2000); Marriage status: 20.9% never married, 62.3% now married, 7.2% widowed, 9.7% divorced (2000); Foreign born: 3.5% (2000); Ancestry (includes multiple ancestries): 30.9% German, 12.6% Irish, 10.7% French (except Basque), 10.4% English, 10.2% Polish (2000).
Economy: Single-family building permits issued: 34 (2001) / 8 (2000); Multi-family building permits issued: 7 (2001) / 0 (2000); Employment by occupation: 11.0% management, 19.3% professional, 14.7% services, 22.3% sales, 0.3% farming, 11.4% construction, 21.1% production (2000).
Income: Per capita income: $25,180 (2000); Median household income: $52,957 (2000); Poverty rate: 4.1% (2000).
Education: High school graduation rate: 89.1% (2000); College graduation rate: 20.8% (2000).
Housing: Homeownership rate: 70.7% (2000); Median home value: $137,100 (2000); Median rent: $491 per month (2000); Median age of housing: 42 years (2000).
Safety: Violent crime rate: 12.0 per 10,000 population; Property crime rate: 185.2 per 10,000 population (2001).
Transportation: Commute to work: 91.3% car, 0.0% public transportation, 4.4% walk, 3.0% work from home (2000); Travel time to work: 44.9% less than 15 minutes, 22.4% 15 to 30 minutes, 12.8% 30 to 45 minutes, 7.6% 45 to 60 minutes, 12.3% 60 minutes or more (2000)
Additional Information Contacts
St. Clair Chamber of Commerce 810-329-2962

SAINT CLAIR (township). Covers a land area of 38.953 square miles and a water area of 0.640 square miles. Located at 42.86° N. Lat.; 82.54° W. Long. Elevation is 589 feet.
Population: 6,423 (2000); Race: 97.5% White, 1.2% Black, 0.0% Asian, 0.2% American Indian and Alaska Native, 1.4% Hispanic of any race, 0.6% two or more races (2000); Density: 164.9 persons per square mile (2000); Age: 27.7% under 18, 9.4% over 64 (2000); Marriage status: 19.7% never married, 72.1% now married, 2.7% widowed, 5.5% divorced (2000); Foreign born: 2.1% (2000); Ancestry (includes multiple ancestries): 31.7% German, 12.3% English, 11.7% Polish, 9.9% Irish, 8.8% French (except Basque) (2000).
Economy: Single-family building permits issued: 37 (2001) / 57 (2000); Multi-family building permits issued: 0 (2001) / 0 (2000); Employment by occupation: 12.3% management, 14.7% professional, 11.8% services, 24.9% sales, 0.2% farming, 11.4% construction, 24.7% production (2000).
Income: Per capita income: $24,705 (2000); Median household income: $58,711 (2000); Poverty rate: 3.2% (2000).
Education: High school graduation rate: 89.7% (2000); College graduation rate: 17.8% (2000).
Housing: Homeownership rate: 91.6% (2000); Median home value: $154,300 (2000); Median rent: $550 per month (2000); Median age of housing: 21 years (2000).
Transportation: Commute to work: 97.2% car, 0.0% public transportation, 0.0% walk, 2.0% work from home (2000); Travel time to work: 26.4% less than 15 minutes, 32.7% 15 to 30 minutes, 15.4% 30 to 45 minutes, 11.2% 45 to 60 minutes, 14.4% 60 minutes or more (2000)

SMITHS CREEK (unincorporated postal area, zip code 48074). Covers a land area of 37.246 square miles and a water area of 0.264 square miles. Located at 42.94° N. Lat.; 82.57° W. Long.
History: The village of Smith's Creek was named for Elisha Smith, who owned land here. A post office was established in Smith's Creek in 1861, and Smith's Creek Station on the Grand Trunk Railroad was built in 1865. Smith's Creek served as the seat of St. Clair County from 1869 to 1871.
Population: 8,623 (2000); Race: 97.2% White, 1.0% Black, 0.3% Asian, 0.2% American Indian and Alaska Native, 1.7% Hispanic of any race, 1.2% two or more races (2000); Density: 231.5 persons per square mile (2000); Age: 26.7% under 18, 10.4% over 64 (2000); Marriage status: 24.2% never married, 58.3% now married, 6.2% widowed, 11.3% divorced (2000); Foreign born: 1.8% (2000); Ancestry (includes multiple ancestries): 24.5% German, 12.6% English, 11.2% Irish, 8.8% Polish, 7.5% United States or American (2000).
Economy: Employment by occupation: 9.7% management, 10.4% professional, 16.2% services, 19.8% sales, 0.5% farming, 11.9% construction, 31.5% production (2000).
Income: Per capita income: $19,244 (2000); Median household income: $47,585 (2000); Poverty rate: 7.8% (2000).
Education: High school graduation rate: 78.3% (2000); College graduation rate: 7.2% (2000).
Housing: Homeownership rate: 87.8% (2000); Median home value: $100,300 (2000); Median rent: $445 per month (2000); Median age of housing: 29 years (2000).
Transportation: Commute to work: 96.8% car, 0.0% public transportation, 0.7% walk, 2.0% work from home (2000); Travel time to work: 31.1% less than 15 minutes, 39.4% 15 to 30 minutes, 9.0% 30 to 45 minutes, 7.9% 45 to 60 minutes, 12.6% 60 minutes or more (2000)

WALES (township). Covers a land area of 37.354 square miles and a water area of 0.024 square miles. Located at 42.95° N. Lat.; 82.68° W. Long.
Population: 2,986 (2000); Race: 94.7% White, 2.7% Black, 0.2% Asian, 0.6% American Indian and Alaska Native, 1.2% Hispanic of any race, 1.4% two or more races (2000); Density: 79.9 persons per square mile (2000); Age: 28.2% under 18, 9.1% over 64 (2000); Marriage status: 20.6% never married, 68.1% now married, 4.7% widowed, 6.5% divorced (2000); Foreign born: 1.9% (2000); Ancestry (includes multiple ancestries): 33.2% German, 16.9% Polish, 16.1% Irish, 12.9% English, 7.3% Other groups (2000).
Economy: Single-family building permits issued: 39 (2001) / 38 (2000); Multi-family building permits issued: 0 (2001) / 0 (2000); Employment by occupation: 8.7% management, 13.0% professional, 11.6% services, 21.0% sales, 1.1% farming, 16.7% construction, 27.9% production (2000).
Income: Per capita income: $20,817 (2000); Median household income: $51,716 (2000); Poverty rate: 6.4% (2000).
Taxes: Total city taxes per capita: $30 (1997); City property taxes per capita: $19 (1997).
Education: High school graduation rate: 86.9% (2000); College graduation rate: 9.7% (2000).
Housing: Homeownership rate: 91.5% (2000); Median home value: $134,500 (2000); Median rent: $465 per month (2000); Median age of housing: 26 years (2000).
Transportation: Commute to work: 95.6% car, 0.0% public transportation, 1.2% walk, 2.8% work from home (2000); Travel time to work: 12.9% less than 15 minutes, 32.8% 15 to 30 minutes, 20.0% 30 to 45 minutes, 16.2% 45 to 60 minutes, 18.2% 60 minutes or more (2000)

YALE (city). Covers a land area of 1.290 square miles and a water area of 0 square miles. Located at 43.13° N. Lat.; 82.79° W. Long. Elevation is 802 feet.
History: Settled 1859; incorporated as village 1885, as city 1905.
Population: 2,063 (2000); Race: 98.2% White, 0.1% Black, 0.0% Asian, 1.3% American Indian and Alaska Native, 1.2% Hispanic of any race, 0.1% two or more races (2000); Density: 1,599.2 persons per square mile (2000); Age: 29.5% under 18, 17.1% over 64 (2000); Marriage status: 24.0% never married, 53.4% now married, 11.8% widowed, 10.8% divorced (2000); Foreign born: 2.0% (2000); Ancestry (includes multiple ancestries): 25.8% German, 15.6% Irish, 11.0% English, 7.9% Polish, 7.3% United States or American (2000).
Economy: In grain-growing and dairy, poultry, livestock farming area; some manufacturing. Single-family building permits issued: 0 (2001) / 3 (2000); Multi-family building permits issued: 0 (2001) / 0 (2000); Employment by occupation: 5.0% management, 12.5% professional, 17.4% services, 23.9% sales, 0.1% farming, 13.1% construction, 27.9% production (2000).
Income: Per capita income: $17,054 (2000); Median household income: $38,375 (2000); Poverty rate: 6.1% (2000).
Taxes: Total city taxes per capita: $150 (1997); City property taxes per capita: $147 (1997).
Education: High school graduation rate: 76.3% (2000); College graduation rate: 7.9% (2000).

School District(s)

Yale Public Schools (KG-12)
2000 Enrollment: 2,078 810-387-4274
Housing: Homeownership rate: 71.7% (2000); Median home value: $88,800 (2000); Median rent: $402 per month (2000); Median age of housing: 52 years (2000).
Safety: Violent crime rate: 57.9 per 10,000 population; Property crime rate: 202.5 per 10,000 population (2001).
Newspapers: The Yale Expositor (1 x week)
Transportation: Commute to work: 89.0% car, 0.0% public transportation, 7.4% walk, 3.3% work from home (2000); Travel time to work: 34.4% less than 15 minutes, 10.5% 15 to 30 minutes, 27.3% 30 to 45 minutes, 13.0% 45 to 60 minutes, 14.8% 60 minutes or more (2000)

Saint Joseph County

Located in southwestern Michigan; bounded on the south by Indiana; drained by the St. Joseph River; includes several lakes. Covers a land area of 503.70 square miles, a water area of 17.40 square miles, and is located in the Eastern Time Zone. The county government was organized in 1829. County seat is Centreville.

Weather Station: Three Rivers — Elevation: 807 feet

	Jan	Feb	Mar	Apr	May	Jun	Jul	Aug	Sep	Oct	Nov	Dec
High	31	35	46	59	72	81	84	82	75	63	48	36
Low	15	17	26	36	47	56	60	58	51	40	31	22
Precip	1.9	1.6	2.6	3.3	3.6	3.6	4.0	3.8	3.6	3.0	2.9	2.5
Snow	8.9	5.7	5.4	1.5	tr	0.0	0.0	0.0	0.0	0.4	3.4	7.3

High and Low temperatures in degrees Fahrenheit; Precipitation and Snow in inches

Population: 62,422 (2000); Race: 93.1% White, 2.5% Black, 0.5% Asian, 0.4% American Indian and Alaska Native, 3.8% Hispanic of any race, 2.0% two or more races (2000); Density: 123.9 persons per square mile (2000); Age: 27.4% under 18, 13.0% over 64 (2000).
Religion: Five largest groups: 11.8% Catholic Church, 3.6% The United Methodist Church, 3.5% Lutheran Church—Missouri Synod, 1.9% The Wesleyan Church, 1.8% Presbyterian Church (U.S.A.) (2000).
Economy: Unemployment rate: 5.1% (11/2002); Total civilian labor force: 33,779 (11/2002); Leading industries: 49.3% manufacturing; 14.0% retail trade; 8.8% health care and social assistance (2000); Companies that employ more than 1,000 persons: 0 (2000); Companies that employ more than 100 persons: 41 (2000); Farms: 791 totaling 217,345 acres (1997); Minority business ownership rate: 2.6% (1997); Women business ownership rate: 28.5% (1997); Retail sales per capita: $6,535 (1997). Single-family building permits issued: 166 (2001) / 232 (2000); Multi-family building permits issued: 12 (2001) / 8 (2000).
Income: Per capita income: $18,247 (2000); Median household income: $40,355 (2000); Poverty rate: 11.3% (2000); Bankruptcy rate: 5.86% (2001).
Taxes: Total county taxes per capita: $113 (2000); County property taxes per capita: $109 (2000).
Education: High school graduation rate: 78.6% (2000); College graduation rate: 12.7% (2000).
Housing: Homeownership rate: 76.9% (2000); Median home value: $85,000 (2000); Median rent: $396 per month (2000); Median age of housing: 38 years (2000).
Health: Birth rate: 136.0 per 10,000 population (1998); Age adjusted death rate: 92.0 per 10,000 population (1999); Age adjusted cancer mortality rate: 244.8 deaths per 100,000 population (1999). Number of physicians: 8.0 per 10,000 population (1999); Number of hospital beds: 20.3 per 10,000 population (1999).
Elections: 2000 Presidential election results: 38.9% Gore, 58.6% Bush, 2.0% Nader, 0.0% Buchanan

Additional Information Contacts

St. Joseph County Government Offices 616-467-5500
St. Joseph County Association of Realtors 616-467-6261
Sturgis Area Chamber of Commerce 616-651-5758
Three Rivers Chamber of Commerce..................... 616-278-8193

Saint Joseph County Communities

BURR OAK (village). Covers a land area of 1.003 square miles and a water area of 0 square miles. Located at 41.84° N. Lat.; 85.31° W. Long. Elevation is 883 feet.
History: Named for the burr oak trees in the area, Burr Oak was platted in 1851 by William Lock and Henry Weaver. It was first called Lock's Station when the railroad arrived, but was renamed in 1857.
Population: 797 (2000); Race: 98.7% White, 0.0% Black, 0.0% Asian, 0.3% American Indian and Alaska Native, 0.6% Hispanic of any race, 1.0% two or more races (2000); Density: 794.4 persons per square mile (2000); Age: 29.1% under 18, 12.5% over 64 (2000); Marriage status: 26.9% never married, 52.5% now married, 8.1% widowed, 12.5% divorced (2000); Foreign born: 0.3% (2000); Ancestry (includes multiple ancestries): 21.5% German, 12.5% United States or American, 11.1% English, 9.3% Other groups, 8.2% Irish (2000).
Economy: Single-family building permits issued: 0 (2001) / 0 (2000); Multi-family building permits issued: 0 (2001) / 0 (2000); Employment by occupation: 6.7% management, 10.1% professional, 14.9% services, 21.6% sales, 0.5% farming, 11.6% construction, 34.5% production (2000).
Income: Per capita income: $17,463 (2000); Median household income: $34,792 (2000); Poverty rate: 8.5% (2000).
Taxes: Total city taxes per capita: $84 (1997); City property taxes per capita: $83 (1997).
Education: High school graduation rate: 82.0% (2000); College graduation rate: 9.4% (2000).

School District(s)

Burr Oak Community School District (KG-12)
2000 Enrollment: 353 616-489-2213

Housing: Homeownership rate: 71.0% (2000); Median home value: $60,000 (2000); Median rent: $397 per month (2000); Median age of housing: 60+ years (2000).
Safety: Violent crime rate: 12.5 per 10,000 population; Property crime rate: 212.2 per 10,000 population (2001).
Transportation: Commute to work: 92.1% car, 0.0% public transportation, 5.8% walk, 1.6% work from home (2000); Travel time to work: 34.3% less than 15 minutes, 43.2% 15 to 30 minutes, 15.0% 30 to 45 minutes, 2.7% 45 to 60 minutes, 4.8% 60 minutes or more (2000)

BURR OAK (township). Covers a land area of 35.571 square miles and a water area of 0.487 square miles. Located at 41.85° N. Lat.; 85.34° W. Long. Elevation is 883 feet.
Population: 2,739 (2000); Race: 98.2% White, 0.8% Black, 0.0% Asian, 0.3% American Indian and Alaska Native, 1.1% Hispanic of any race, 0.4% two or more races (2000); Density: 77.0 persons per square mile (2000); Age: 28.1% under 18, 11.1% over 64 (2000); Marriage status: 23.6% never married, 61.5% now married, 5.5% widowed, 9.4% divorced (2000); Foreign born: 0.4% (2000); Ancestry (includes multiple ancestries): 26.5% German, 12.7% United States or American, 11.4% English, 7.6% Irish, 6.1% Other groups (2000).
Economy: In diversified agricultural area: wheat, potatoes, corn. Manufacturing of plastics. Single-family building permits issued: 11 (2001) / 11 (2000); Multi-family building permits issued: 0 (2001) / 0 (2000); Employment by occupation: 11.0% management, 8.6% professional, 9.7% services, 22.0% sales, 0.4% farming, 11.7% construction, 36.6% production (2000).
Income: Per capita income: $18,266 (2000); Median household income: $44,875 (2000); Poverty rate: 6.9% (2000).
Taxes: Total city taxes per capita: $16 (1997); City property taxes per capita: $11 (1997).
Education: High school graduation rate: 79.8% (2000); College graduation rate: 9.7% (2000).
Housing: Homeownership rate: 80.5% (2000); Median home value: $76,100 (2000); Median rent: $402 per month (2000); Median age of housing: 40 years (2000).
Transportation: Commute to work: 92.8% car, 0.0% public transportation, 2.5% walk, 4.0% work from home (2000); Travel time to work: 32.6% less than 15 minutes, 41.9% 15 to 30 minutes, 15.7% 30 to 45 minutes, 5.5% 45 to 60 minutes, 4.3% 60 minutes or more (2000)

CENTREVILLE (village). Aka Centerville. Covers a land area of 1.414 square miles and a water area of 0 square miles. Located at 41.92° N. Lat.; 85.52° W. Long. Elevation is 826 feet.
History: In Centreville in 1878, the famous Dr. Denton Sleeping Garment Mill had its beginning. The village was settled in the late 1820's, and incorporated in 1837.
Population: 1,579 (2000); Race: 95.2% White, 3.3% Black, 0.2% Asian, 0.3% American Indian and Alaska Native, 0.6% Hispanic of any race, 0.4% two or more races (2000); Density: 1,116.9 persons per square mile (2000); Age: 27.8% under 18, 12.6% over 64 (2000); Marriage status: 28.7% never married, 51.0% now married, 6.6% widowed, 13.8% divorced (2000); Foreign born: 0.3% (2000); Ancestry (includes multiple ancestries): 31.2% German, 12.1% United States or American, 10.8% English, 10.3% Other groups, 8.9% Irish (2000).
Economy: Single-family building permits issued: 2 (2001) / 2 (2000); Multi-family building permits issued: 0 (2001) / 0 (2000); Employment by occupation: 4.6% management, 13.6% professional, 17.0% services, 21.1% sales, 0.9% farming, 6.6% construction, 36.3% production (2000).
Income: Per capita income: $15,472 (2000); Median household income: $33,929 (2000); Poverty rate: 7.9% (2000).
Taxes: Total city taxes per capita: $137 (1997); City property taxes per capita: $135 (1997).
Education: High school graduation rate: 83.0% (2000); College graduation rate: 11.8% (2000).

School District(s)

Centreville Public Schools (KG-12)
2000 Enrollment: 906 616-467-5220

Two-year College(s)

Glen Oaks Community College (Public)
2001 Enrollment: 1,894 616-467-9945
2001 Tuition: In-state $2,074; Out-of-state $2,652

Housing: Homeownership rate: 72.2% (2000); Median home value: $79,700 (2000); Median rent: $342 per month (2000); Median age of housing: 47 years (2000).

Transportation: Commute to work: 92.8% car, 1.1% public transportation, 2.7% walk, 3.1% work from home (2000); Travel time to work: 38.8% less than 15 minutes, 37.7% 15 to 30 minutes, 14.4% 30 to 45 minutes, 6.2% 45 to 60 minutes, 3.0% 60 minutes or more (2000)

Additional Information Contacts

St. Joseph County Association of Realtors 616-467-6261

COLON (village). Covers a land area of 1.391 square miles and a water area of 0.318 square miles. Located at 41.95° N. Lat.; 85.32° W. Long. Elevation is 844 feet.

Population: 1,227 (2000); Race: 97.2% White, 0.0% Black, 0.4% Asian, 0.0% American Indian and Alaska Native, 0.2% Hispanic of any race, 2.1% two or more races (2000); Density: 882.0 persons per square mile (2000); Age: 29.1% under 18, 17.5% over 64 (2000); Marriage status: 26.5% never married, 52.9% now married, 9.0% widowed, 11.6% divorced (2000); Foreign born: 1.2% (2000); Ancestry (includes multiple ancestries): 26.8% German, 13.8% United States or American, 10.8% English, 9.2% Other groups, 8.9% Irish (2000).

Economy: Single-family building permits issued: 0 (2001) / 0 (2000); Multi-family building permits issued: 0 (2001) / 0 (2000); Employment by occupation: 6.3% management, 10.7% professional, 12.0% services, 19.2% sales, 1.3% farming, 8.3% construction, 42.4% production (2000).

Income: Per capita income: $14,502 (2000); Median household income: $29,417 (2000); Poverty rate: 15.1% (2000).

Taxes: Total city taxes per capita: $164 (1997); City property taxes per capita: $157 (1997).

Education: High school graduation rate: 78.3% (2000); College graduation rate: 10.8% (2000).

School District(s)

Colon Community School District (PK-12)
2000 Enrollment: 895 616-432-3442

Housing: Homeownership rate: 70.8% (2000); Median home value: $72,200 (2000); Median rent: $294 per month (2000); Median age of housing: 54 years (2000).

Safety: Violent crime rate: 16.2 per 10,000 population; Property crime rate: 413.6 per 10,000 population (2001).

Newspapers: The Express (1 x week)

Transportation: Commute to work: 92.1% car, 0.2% public transportation, 4.7% walk, 0.6% work from home (2000); Travel time to work: 37.2% less than 15 minutes, 33.9% 15 to 30 minutes, 15.6% 30 to 45 minutes, 8.2% 45 to 60 minutes, 5.1% 60 minutes or more (2000)

COLON (township). Covers a land area of 34.575 square miles and a water area of 1.795 square miles. Located at 41.94° N. Lat.; 85.33° W. Long. Elevation is 844 feet.

Population: 3,405 (2000); Race: 97.2% White, 0.0% Black, 0.8% Asian, 0.0% American Indian and Alaska Native, 0.4% Hispanic of any race, 2.0% two or more races (2000); Density: 98.5 persons per square mile (2000); Age: 26.0% under 18, 15.8% over 64 (2000); Marriage status: 21.7% never married, 61.0% now married, 7.5% widowed, 9.8% divorced (2000); Foreign born: 0.8% (2000); Ancestry (includes multiple ancestries): 26.9% German, 15.4% United States or American, 10.4% Irish, 8.9% English, 8.6% Dutch (2000).

Economy: In mint-growing area. Manufacturing: apparel, transportation equipment. Lake resort. Single-family building permits issued: 1 (2001) / 6 (2000); Multi-family building permits issued: 0 (2001) / 0 (2000); Employment by occupation: 10.4% management, 10.6% professional, 11.9% services, 16.6% sales, 1.0% farming, 13.1% construction, 36.4% production (2000).

Income: Per capita income: $16,904 (2000); Median household income: $34,890 (2000); Poverty rate: 10.4% (2000).

Taxes: Total city taxes per capita: $21 (1997); City property taxes per capita: $17 (1997).

Education: High school graduation rate: 72.9% (2000); College graduation rate: 9.4% (2000).

Housing: Homeownership rate: 79.8% (2000); Median home value: $85,000 (2000); Median rent: $338 per month (2000); Median age of housing: 41 years (2000).

Transportation: Commute to work: 85.2% car, 0.1% public transportation, 2.4% walk, 9.6% work from home (2000); Travel time to work: 28.5% less than 15 minutes, 39.7% 15 to 30 minutes, 16.1% 30 to 45 minutes, 9.2% 45 to 60 minutes, 6.5% 60 minutes or more (2000)

CONSTANTINE (village). Covers a land area of 1.622 square miles and a water area of 0.102 square miles. Located at 41.84° N. Lat.; 85.66° W. Long. Elevation is 815 feet.

History: Constantine grew up in 1830 around a sawmill and gristmill built by Judge William Meek, when the community was known as Meek's Mills. The name was changed in 1835 to honor Constantine the Great. The Constantine Cooperative Creamery was organized here in 1915.

Population: 2,095 (2000); Race: 97.3% White, 0.5% Black, 0.0% Asian, 0.1% American Indian and Alaska Native, 0.8% Hispanic of any race, 1.3% two or more races (2000); Density: 1,291.9 persons per square mile (2000); Age: 29.6% under 18, 9.8% over 64 (2000); Marriage status: 25.5% never married, 54.2% now married, 6.6% widowed, 13.8% divorced (2000); Foreign born: 0.6% (2000); Ancestry (includes multiple ancestries): 31.7% German, 13.0% Irish, 11.7% English, 10.9% United States or American, 8.7% Other groups (2000).

Economy: Single-family building permits issued: 3 (2001) / 3 (2000); Multi-family building permits issued: 6 (2001) / 6 (2000); Employment by occupation: 5.5% management, 9.9% professional, 13.9% services, 24.4% sales, 0.3% farming, 8.7% construction, 37.1% production (2000).

Income: Per capita income: $15,542 (2000); Median household income: $40,428 (2000); Poverty rate: 15.5% (2000).

Taxes: Total city taxes per capita: $277 (1997); City property taxes per capita: $275 (1997).

Education: High school graduation rate: 79.8% (2000); College graduation rate: 7.2% (2000).

School District(s)

Constantine Public School District (KG-12)
2000 Enrollment: 1,640 616-435-2015

Housing: Homeownership rate: 72.0% (2000); Median home value: $74,600 (2000); Median rent: $396 per month (2000); Median age of housing: 55 years (2000).

Safety: Violent crime rate: 61.7 per 10,000 population; Property crime rate: 417.9 per 10,000 population (2001).

Transportation: Commute to work: 94.1% car, 0.0% public transportation, 3.1% walk, 2.1% work from home (2000); Travel time to work: 33.4% less than 15 minutes, 41.7% 15 to 30 minutes, 15.4% 30 to 45 minutes, 5.7% 45 to 60 minutes, 3.8% 60 minutes or more (2000)

CONSTANTINE (township). Covers a land area of 34.556 square miles and a water area of 1.067 square miles. Located at 41.84° N. Lat.; 85.67° W. Long. Elevation is 815 feet.

History: Settled 1828; incorporated 1837.

Population: 4,181 (2000); Race: 96.7% White, 0.2% Black, 0.5% Asian, 0.7% American Indian and Alaska Native, 0.5% Hispanic of any race, 1.0% two or more races (2000); Density: 121.0 persons per square mile (2000); Age: 27.8% under 18, 11.1% over 64 (2000); Marriage status: 24.4% never married, 57.7% now married, 6.3% widowed, 11.6% divorced (2000); Foreign born: 0.9% (2000); Ancestry (includes multiple ancestries): 28.1% German, 12.2% Irish, 10.7% English, 10.6% United States or American, 9.3% Other groups (2000).

Economy: In agricultural area: grain, vegetables; livestock, poultry; dairy products. Manufacturing: paper and plastic products. Single-family building permits issued: 2 (2001) / 2 (2000); Multi-family building permits issued: 0 (2001) / 0 (2000); Employment by occupation: 8.4% management, 12.2% professional, 10.2% services, 19.9% sales, 0.1% farming, 9.7% construction, 39.5% production (2000).

Income: Per capita income: $16,909 (2000); Median household income: $43,125 (2000); Poverty rate: 11.8% (2000).

Taxes: Total city taxes per capita: $25 (1997); City property taxes per capita: $24 (1997).

Education: High school graduation rate: 82.1% (2000); College graduation rate: 9.5% (2000).

Housing: Homeownership rate: 81.7% (2000); Median home value: $83,300 (2000); Median rent: $401 per month (2000); Median age of housing: 39 years (2000).

Transportation: Commute to work: 95.0% car, 0.2% public transportation, 1.7% walk, 2.8% work from home (2000); Travel time to work: 33.4% less than 15 minutes, 40.4% 15 to 30 minutes, 16.6% 30 to 45 minutes, 5.8% 45 to 60 minutes, 3.9% 60 minutes or more (2000)

FABIUS (township). Covers a land area of 32.347 square miles and a water area of 2.984 square miles. Located at 41.94° N. Lat.; 85.70° W. Long. Elevation is 889 feet.

Population: 3,285 (2000); Race: 96.3% White, 0.5% Black, 0.3% Asian, 0.1% American Indian and Alaska Native, 0.2% Hispanic of any race, 2.0% two or more races (2000); Density: 101.6 persons per square mile (2000); Age: 23.6% under 18, 15.5% over 64 (2000); Marriage status: 15.5% never married, 74.0% now married, 3.7% widowed, 6.7% divorced (2000); Foreign born: 2.4% (2000); Ancestry (includes multiple ancestries): 28.9% German, 14.1% English, 11.2% Irish, 8.5% United States or American, 8.5% Dutch (2000).

Economy: Single-family building permits issued: 12 (2001) / 16 (2000); Multi-family building permits issued: 0 (2001) / 0 (2000); Employment by occupation: 11.4% management, 20.6% professional, 11.4% services, 20.0% sales, 0.0% farming, 10.7% construction, 25.9% production (2000).

Income: Per capita income: $23,474 (2000); Median household income: $50,888 (2000); Poverty rate: 3.6% (2000).

Taxes: Total city taxes per capita: $20 (1997); City property taxes per capita: $14 (1997).

Education: High school graduation rate: 90.1% (2000); College graduation rate: 26.4% (2000).

Housing: Homeownership rate: 86.8% (2000); Median home value: $115,800 (2000); Median rent: $466 per month (2000); Median age of housing: 30 years (2000).

Transportation: Commute to work: 95.1% car, 0.0% public transportation, 1.4% walk, 3.6% work from home (2000); Travel time to work: 44.0% less than 15 minutes, 24.4% 15 to 30 minutes, 19.8% 30 to 45 minutes, 8.1% 45 to 60 minutes, 3.7% 60 minutes or more (2000)

FAWN RIVER (township). Covers a land area of 19.501 square miles and a water area of 0.366 square miles. Located at 41.78° N. Lat.; 85.36° W. Long.

Population: 1,648 (2000); Race: 94.4% White, 2.1% Black, 0.0% Asian, 0.1% American Indian and Alaska Native, 3.2% Hispanic of any race, 1.3% two or more races (2000); Density: 84.5 persons per square mile (2000); Age: 28.6% under 18, 10.3% over 64 (2000); Marriage status: 22.7% never married, 61.2% now married, 5.6% widowed, 10.5% divorced (2000); Foreign born: 2.6% (2000); Ancestry (includes multiple ancestries): 30.8% German, 12.5% United States or American, 12.2% Irish, 11.3% Other groups, 6.5% English (2000).

Economy: Single-family building permits issued: 3 (2001) / 10 (2000); Multi-family building permits issued: 0 (2001) / 0 (2000); Employment by occupation: 9.9% management, 9.9% professional, 10.9% services, 20.6% sales, 1.8% farming, 9.6% construction, 37.4% production (2000).

Income: Per capita income: $17,533 (2000); Median household income: $41,852 (2000); Poverty rate: 7.3% (2000).

Taxes: Total city taxes per capita: $10 (1997); City property taxes per capita: $0 (1997).

Education: High school graduation rate: 83.9% (2000); College graduation rate: 10.9% (2000).

Housing: Homeownership rate: 86.6% (2000); Median home value: $88,500 (2000); Median rent: $391 per month (2000); Median age of housing: 33 years (2000).

Transportation: Commute to work: 93.4% car, 0.0% public transportation, 1.5% walk, 3.4% work from home (2000); Travel time to work: 53.1% less than 15 minutes, 31.0% 15 to 30 minutes, 8.3% 30 to 45 minutes, 3.2% 45 to 60 minutes, 4.3% 60 minutes or more (2000)

FLORENCE (township). Covers a land area of 33.563 square miles and a water area of 0.191 square miles. Located at 41.86° N. Lat.; 85.60° W. Long.

Population: 1,436 (2000); Race: 95.4% White, 0.7% Black, 0.0% Asian, 1.0% American Indian and Alaska Native, 5.1% Hispanic of any race, 2.1% two or more races (2000); Density: 42.8 persons per square mile (2000); Age: 33.0% under 18, 7.8% over 64 (2000); Marriage status: 23.4% never married, 63.1% now married, 3.8% widowed, 9.7% divorced (2000); Foreign born: 2.0% (2000); Ancestry (includes multiple ancestries): 30.4% German, 10.7% Irish, 10.5% United States or American, 9.0% Other groups, 8.5% English (2000).

Economy: Single-family building permits issued: 0 (2001) / 0 (2000); Multi-family building permits issued: 0 (2001) / 0 (2000); Employment by occupation: 10.8% management, 9.7% professional, 12.0% services, 18.1% sales, 2.7% farming, 12.8% construction, 33.9% production (2000).

Income: Per capita income: $19,086 (2000); Median household income: $45,288 (2000); Poverty rate: 9.6% (2000).

Taxes: Total city taxes per capita: $18 (1997); City property taxes per capita: $18 (1997).

Education: High school graduation rate: 76.9% (2000); College graduation rate: 7.9% (2000).

Housing: Homeownership rate: 85.4% (2000); Median home value: $83,500 (2000); Median rent: $386 per month (2000); Median age of housing: 37 years (2000).

Transportation: Commute to work: 92.0% car, 0.3% public transportation, 1.3% walk, 6.2% work from home (2000); Travel time to work: 34.9% less than 15 minutes, 45.3% 15 to 30 minutes, 9.2% 30 to 45 minutes, 7.1% 45 to 60 minutes, 3.6% 60 minutes or more (2000)

FLOWERFIELD (township). Covers a land area of 35.805 square miles and a water area of 0.049 square miles. Located at 42.03° N. Lat.; 85.71° W. Long.

Population: 1,592 (2000); Race: 96.1% White, 0.8% Black, 0.4% Asian, 0.9% American Indian and Alaska Native, 1.4% Hispanic of any race, 0.9% two or more races (2000); Density: 44.5 persons per square mile (2000); Age: 26.6% under 18, 9.9% over 64 (2000); Marriage status: 21.0% never married, 65.4% now married, 4.1% widowed, 9.5% divorced (2000); Foreign born: 2.5% (2000); Ancestry (includes multiple ancestries): 30.5% German, 13.1% Dutch, 12.4% English, 10.9% United States or American, 10.1% Irish (2000).

Economy: Single-family building permits issued: 12 (2001) / 15 (2000); Multi-family building permits issued: 0 (2001) / 0 (2000); Employment by occupation: 9.9% management, 14.3% professional, 11.3% services, 24.7% sales, 0.8% farming, 12.8% construction, 26.4% production (2000).

Income: Per capita income: $19,969 (2000); Median household income: $46,897 (2000); Poverty rate: 7.8% (2000).

Taxes: Total city taxes per capita: $14 (1997); City property taxes per capita: $12 (1997).

Education: High school graduation rate: 81.4% (2000); College graduation rate: 12.4% (2000).

Housing: Homeownership rate: 87.8% (2000); Median home value: $100,400 (2000); Median rent: $433 per month (2000); Median age of housing: 25 years (2000).

Transportation: Commute to work: 93.3% car, 0.0% public transportation, 0.5% walk, 5.8% work from home (2000); Travel time to work: 25.5% less than 15 minutes, 35.4% 15 to 30 minutes, 27.0% 30 to 45 minutes, 6.0% 45 to 60 minutes, 6.0% 60 minutes or more (2000)

LEONIDAS (township). Covers a land area of 35.710 square miles and a water area of 0.500 square miles. Located at 42.02° N. Lat.; 85.35° W. Long. Elevation is 869 feet.

History: Leonidas Township was named for a king of ancient Sparta.

Population: 1,239 (2000); Race: 100.0% White, 0.0% Black, 0.0% Asian, 0.0% American Indian and Alaska Native, 0.2% Hispanic of any race, 0.0% two or more races (2000); Density: 34.7 persons per square mile (2000); Age: 31.1% under 18, 10.2% over 64 (2000); Marriage status: 23.6% never married, 63.8% now married, 3.8% widowed, 8.7% divorced (2000); Foreign born: 0.4% (2000); Ancestry (includes multiple ancestries): 29.1% German, 18.5% United States or American, 12.1% Irish, 7.7% English, 7.0% Dutch (2000).

Economy: Single-family building permits issued: 0 (2001) / 0 (2000); Multi-family building permits issued: 0 (2001) / 0 (2000); Employment by occupation: 7.4% management, 8.9% professional, 12.5% services, 17.8% sales, 3.3% farming, 13.7% construction, 36.4% production (2000).

Income: Per capita income: $14,983 (2000); Median household income: $42,417 (2000); Poverty rate: 9.6% (2000).

Taxes: Total city taxes per capita: $37 (1997); City property taxes per capita: $27 (1997).

Education: High school graduation rate: 71.8% (2000); College graduation rate: 9.7% (2000).

Housing: Homeownership rate: 86.1% (2000); Median home value: $78,700 (2000); Median rent: $362 per month (2000); Median age of housing: 53 years (2000).

Transportation: Commute to work: 88.8% car, 1.2% public transportation, 1.8% walk, 7.0% work from home (2000); Travel time to work: 22.8% less than 15 minutes, 39.1% 15 to 30 minutes, 25.1% 30 to 45 minutes, 8.3% 45 to 60 minutes, 4.7% 60 minutes or more (2000)

LOCKPORT (township). Covers a land area of 29.600 square miles and a water area of 1.660 square miles. Located at 41.94° N. Lat.; 85.58° W. Long.

Population: 3,814 (2000); Race: 86.3% White, 10.4% Black, 0.8% Asian, 0.4% American Indian and Alaska Native, 0.3% Hispanic of any race, 2.2% two or more races (2000); Density: 128.8 persons per square mile (2000);

Age: 27.1% under 18, 12.3% over 64 (2000); Marriage status: 16.6% never married, 65.1% now married, 6.9% widowed, 11.3% divorced (2000); Foreign born: 0.8% (2000); Ancestry (includes multiple ancestries): 30.5% German, 15.4% Other groups, 12.5% English, 8.5% Irish, 8.5% Dutch (2000).
Economy: Single-family building permits issued: 18 (2001) / 25 (2000); Multi-family building permits issued: 0 (2001) / 0 (2000); Employment by occupation: 7.0% management, 17.9% professional, 10.2% services, 26.4% sales, 0.9% farming, 8.1% construction, 29.6% production (2000).
Income: Per capita income: $21,184 (2000); Median household income: $43,931 (2000); Poverty rate: 9.9% (2000).
Taxes: Total city taxes per capita: $30 (1997); City property taxes per capita: $17 (1997).
Education: High school graduation rate: 81.9% (2000); College graduation rate: 16.6% (2000).
Housing: Homeownership rate: 80.3% (2000); Median home value: $93,700 (2000); Median rent: $330 per month (2000); Median age of housing: 29 years (2000).
Transportation: Commute to work: 93.2% car, 0.6% public transportation, 0.6% walk, 4.5% work from home (2000); Travel time to work: 41.6% less than 15 minutes, 27.7% 15 to 30 minutes, 17.0% 30 to 45 minutes, 9.6% 45 to 60 minutes, 4.1% 60 minutes or more (2000)

MENDON (village). Covers a land area of 0.753 square miles and a water area of 0.007 square miles. Located at 42.00° N. Lat.; 85.45° W. Long. Elevation is 852 feet.
History: A fur-trading post was established here in 1831. Patrice Marantette, a Frenchman, bought the property in 1833 and built a large home on a hill nearby.
Population: 917 (2000); Race: 98.6% White, 0.0% Black, 0.0% Asian, 0.6% American Indian and Alaska Native, 1.1% Hispanic of any race, 0.9% two or more races (2000); Density: 1,217.1 persons per square mile (2000); Age: 31.9% under 18, 10.4% over 64 (2000); Marriage status: 23.2% never married, 62.1% now married, 4.4% widowed, 10.3% divorced (2000); Foreign born: 0.6% (2000); Ancestry (includes multiple ancestries): 28.3% German, 13.2% Irish, 11.4% United States or American, 9.3% Dutch, 8.3% Other groups (2000).
Economy: Single-family building permits issued: 4 (2001) / 4 (2000); Multi-family building permits issued: 0 (2001) / 0 (2000); Employment by occupation: 10.6% management, 14.6% professional, 11.8% services, 17.7% sales, 0.7% farming, 11.8% construction, 32.8% production (2000).
Income: Per capita income: $17,266 (2000); Median household income: $40,000 (2000); Poverty rate: 5.9% (2000).
Taxes: Total city taxes per capita: $234 (1997); City property taxes per capita: $227 (1997).
Education: High school graduation rate: 83.5% (2000); College graduation rate: 10.8% (2000).

School District(s)

Mendon Community School District (KG-12)
2000 Enrollment: 788 616-496-8491
Housing: Homeownership rate: 83.3% (2000); Median home value: $80,200 (2000); Median rent: $444 per month (2000); Median age of housing: 59 years (2000).
Transportation: Commute to work: 89.3% car, 0.0% public transportation, 3.8% walk, 5.8% work from home (2000); Travel time to work: 37.4% less than 15 minutes, 38.4% 15 to 30 minutes, 18.7% 30 to 45 minutes, 3.1% 45 to 60 minutes, 2.4% 60 minutes or more (2000)

MENDON (township). Covers a land area of 34.976 square miles and a water area of 1.244 square miles. Located at 42.01° N. Lat.; 85.47° W. Long. Elevation is 852 feet.
Population: 2,775 (2000); Race: 97.8% White, 0.5% Black, 0.0% Asian, 0.8% American Indian and Alaska Native, 0.6% Hispanic of any race, 0.7% two or more races (2000); Density: 79.3 persons per square mile (2000); Age: 26.9% under 18, 15.3% over 64 (2000); Marriage status: 18.5% never married, 67.4% now married, 5.5% widowed, 8.6% divorced (2000); Foreign born: 1.3% (2000); Ancestry (includes multiple ancestries): 27.7% German, 14.0% United States or American, 11.4% Irish, 9.9% English, 9.2% Dutch (2000).
Economy: Rich farm area. Manufacturing: plastic products. Single-family building permits issued: 6 (2001) / 8 (2000); Multi-family building permits issued: 0 (2001) / 0 (2000); Employment by occupation: 8.3% management, 10.6% professional, 12.5% services, 21.5% sales, 1.1% farming, 11.4% construction, 34.5% production (2000).
Income: Per capita income: $17,600 (2000); Median household income: $41,324 (2000); Poverty rate: 8.2% (2000).
Taxes: Total city taxes per capita: $59 (1997); City property taxes per capita: $56 (1997).
Education: High school graduation rate: 82.4% (2000); College graduation rate: 7.6% (2000).
Housing: Homeownership rate: 87.1% (2000); Median home value: $87,200 (2000); Median rent: $382 per month (2000); Median age of housing: 28 years (2000).
Transportation: Commute to work: 91.7% car, 0.0% public transportation, 2.5% walk, 5.1% work from home (2000); Travel time to work: 33.0% less than 15 minutes, 36.6% 15 to 30 minutes, 22.5% 30 to 45 minutes, 2.8% 45 to 60 minutes, 5.0% 60 minutes or more (2000)

MOTTVILLE (township). Covers a land area of 19.572 square miles and a water area of 0.393 square miles. Located at 41.78° N. Lat.; 85.73° W. Long.
History: The Mottville area developed around a sawmill erected on the St. Joseph River in the 1820's. The shipping business on the river brought warehoues and businesses, reaching its greatest volume in the 1840's. Mottville declined when the railroad replaced the river as the primary shipping route.
Population: 1,499 (2000); Race: 98.2% White, 0.0% Black, 0.0% Asian, 0.8% American Indian and Alaska Native, 1.2% Hispanic of any race, 0.7% two or more races (2000); Density: 76.6 persons per square mile (2000); Age: 27.7% under 18, 10.8% over 64 (2000); Marriage status: 18.5% never married, 60.5% now married, 5.2% widowed, 15.8% divorced (2000); Foreign born: 0.6% (2000); Ancestry (includes multiple ancestries): 31.8% German, 13.7% Irish, 10.8% Other groups, 9.3% United States or American, 8.8% English (2000).
Economy: Employment by occupation: 10.5% management, 7.7% professional, 10.1% services, 19.0% sales, 0.4% farming, 8.9% construction, 43.3% production (2000).
Income: Per capita income: $17,917 (2000); Median household income: $43,421 (2000); Poverty rate: 10.0% (2000).
Taxes: Total city taxes per capita: $16 (1997); City property taxes per capita: $16 (1997).
Education: High school graduation rate: 72.2% (2000); College graduation rate: 5.7% (2000).
Housing: Homeownership rate: 85.4% (2000); Median home value: $83,300 (2000); Median rent: $450 per month (2000); Median age of housing: 31 years (2000).
Transportation: Commute to work: 94.0% car, 0.4% public transportation, 2.0% walk, 2.3% work from home (2000); Travel time to work: 33.5% less than 15 minutes, 43.1% 15 to 30 minutes, 17.8% 30 to 45 minutes, 3.1% 45 to 60 minutes, 2.4% 60 minutes or more (2000)

NOTTAWA (township). Covers a land area of 35.791 square miles and a water area of 1.813 square miles. Located at 41.93° N. Lat.; 85.48° W. Long. Elevation is 841 feet.
History: Nottawa Township was settled by a group of Amish colonists, who came from Ohio in 1847. The name of Nottawa comes from that of the Potawatomi chief, Nottawaseepe.
Population: 3,999 (2000); Race: 96.7% White, 2.1% Black, 0.2% Asian, 0.0% American Indian and Alaska Native, 0.4% Hispanic of any race, 0.9% two or more races (2000); Density: 111.7 persons per square mile (2000); Age: 29.2% under 18, 12.1% over 64 (2000); Marriage status: 24.7% never married, 61.7% now married, 5.4% widowed, 8.2% divorced (2000); Foreign born: 1.0% (2000); Ancestry (includes multiple ancestries): 28.2% German, 12.4% United States or American, 10.9% English, 7.6% Irish, 7.1% Other groups (2000).
Economy: Single-family building permits issued: 14 (2001) / 27 (2000); Multi-family building permits issued: 0 (2001) / 0 (2000); Employment by occupation: 9.9% management, 12.8% professional, 12.7% services, 15.5% sales, 2.1% farming, 12.1% construction, 35.0% production (2000).
Income: Per capita income: $16,814 (2000); Median household income: $41,875 (2000); Poverty rate: 10.1% (2000).
Taxes: Total city taxes per capita: $41 (1997); City property taxes per capita: $38 (1997).
Education: High school graduation rate: 75.3% (2000); College graduation rate: 12.4% (2000).
Housing: Homeownership rate: 82.5% (2000); Median home value: $88,700 (2000); Median rent: $363 per month (2000); Median age of housing: 30 years (2000).
Transportation: Commute to work: 89.5% car, 0.4% public transportation, 2.1% walk, 7.6% work from home (2000); Travel time to work: 24.9% less than 15 minutes, 46.6% 15 to 30 minutes, 15.2% 30 to 45 minutes, 8.3% 45 to 60 minutes, 5.2% 60 minutes or more (2000)

PARK (township). Covers a land area of 35.107 square miles and a water area of 0.669 square miles. Located at 42.02° N. Lat.; 85.58° W. Long.
Population: 2,699 (2000); Race: 91.4% White, 2.7% Black, 0.0% Asian, 0.4% American Indian and Alaska Native, 3.4% Hispanic of any race, 5.3% two or more races (2000); Density: 76.9 persons per square mile (2000); Age: 25.1% under 18, 16.8% over 64 (2000); Marriage status: 18.2% never married, 66.0% now married, 7.8% widowed, 8.0% divorced (2000); Foreign born: 2.5% (2000); Ancestry (includes multiple ancestries): 22.8% German, 13.4% English, 12.6% Other groups, 11.8% Irish, 9.0% United States or American (2000).
Economy: Single-family building permits issued: 17 (2001) / 17 (2000); Multi-family building permits issued: 0 (2001) / 0 (2000); Employment by occupation: 15.1% management, 14.5% professional, 10.7% services, 22.2% sales, 0.6% farming, 10.6% construction, 26.3% production (2000).
Income: Per capita income: $21,045 (2000); Median household income: $48,173 (2000); Poverty rate: 7.4% (2000).
Taxes: Total city taxes per capita: $22 (1997); City property taxes per capita: $22 (1997).
Education: High school graduation rate: 84.0% (2000); College graduation rate: 14.3% (2000).
Housing: Homeownership rate: 90.0% (2000); Median home value: $104,000 (2000); Median rent: $470 per month (2000); Median age of housing: 35 years (2000).
Transportation: Commute to work: 95.7% car, 0.0% public transportation, 0.9% walk, 3.0% work from home (2000); Travel time to work: 31.8% less than 15 minutes, 36.2% 15 to 30 minutes, 19.7% 30 to 45 minutes, 4.5% 45 to 60 minutes, 7.8% 60 minutes or more (2000)

SHERMAN (township). Covers a land area of 33.103 square miles and a water area of 1.872 square miles. Located at 41.85° N. Lat.; 85.45° W. Long.
History: Sherman Township was settled in the 1830's, and named for Colonel Benjamin Sherman, an early settler.
Population: 3,248 (2000); Race: 96.1% White, 0.2% Black, 1.5% Asian, 0.4% American Indian and Alaska Native, 2.0% Hispanic of any race, 1.8% two or more races (2000); Density: 98.1 persons per square mile (2000); Age: 26.1% under 18, 13.4% over 64 (2000); Marriage status: 23.0% never married, 62.7% now married, 3.1% widowed, 11.1% divorced (2000); Foreign born: 4.4% (2000); Ancestry (includes multiple ancestries): 34.4% German, 13.1% English, 12.5% Irish, 9.5% Other groups, 8.5% United States or American (2000).
Economy: Single-family building permits issued: 34 (2001) / 34 (2000); Multi-family building permits issued: 0 (2001) / 0 (2000); Employment by occupation: 16.1% management, 14.4% professional, 10.0% services, 22.3% sales, 0.9% farming, 10.5% construction, 25.8% production (2000).
Income: Per capita income: $20,904 (2000); Median household income: $47,727 (2000); Poverty rate: 6.8% (2000).
Taxes: Total city taxes per capita: $46 (1997); City property taxes per capita: $40 (1997).
Education: High school graduation rate: 82.0% (2000); College graduation rate: 17.5% (2000).
Housing: Homeownership rate: 86.5% (2000); Median home value: $107,600 (2000); Median rent: $378 per month (2000); Median age of housing: 33 years (2000).
Transportation: Commute to work: 90.9% car, 0.9% public transportation, 2.2% walk, 5.0% work from home (2000); Travel time to work: 41.2% less than 15 minutes, 42.0% 15 to 30 minutes, 10.2% 30 to 45 minutes, 1.9% 45 to 60 minutes, 4.8% 60 minutes or more (2000)

STURGIS (city). Covers a land area of 5.957 square miles and a water area of 0 square miles. Located at 41.79° N. Lat.; 85.41° W. Long. Elevation is 918 feet.
History: Sturgis grew up at the junction of the Great Sauk Trail and the Nottawaseepe Trail. Settlement began here in 1827, and the village was established about 1833, named for Judge John Sturgis, the first settler. The manufacture of furniture was an early industry in Sturgis.
Population: 11,285 (2000); Race: 89.9% White, 1.5% Black, 0.8% Asian, 0.5% American Indian and Alaska Native, 13.0% Hispanic of any race, 2.3% two or more races (2000); Density: 1,894.5 persons per square mile (2000); Age: 28.2% under 18, 13.6% over 64 (2000); Marriage status: 27.5% never married, 50.8% now married, 8.5% widowed, 13.2% divorced (2000); Foreign born: 10.2% (2000); Ancestry (includes multiple ancestries): 26.3% German, 16.3% Other groups, 9.8% United States or American, 9.4% Irish, 9.0% English (2000).
Vital Statistics: Birth rate: 172.8 per 10,000 population (1998)
Economy: Single-family building permits issued: 4 (2001) / 14 (2000); Multi-family building permits issued: 6 (2001) / 2 (2000); Employment by occupation: 6.0% management, 12.6% professional, 14.2% services, 19.6% sales, 1.3% farming, 9.3% construction, 37.1% production (2000).
Income: Per capita income: $15,990 (2000); Median household income: $33,838 (2000); Poverty rate: 16.2% (2000).
Taxes: Total city taxes per capita: $233 (2000); City property taxes per capita: $231 (2000).
Education: High school graduation rate: 74.3% (2000); College graduation rate: 13.7% (2000).

School District(s)

Nottawa Community School (KG-08)
2000 Enrollment: 167 616-467-7153
Sturgis Public Schools (KG-12)
2000 Enrollment: 3,113 616-659-1500

Housing: Homeownership rate: 58.0% (2000); Median home value: $76,100 (2000); Median rent: $407 per month (2000); Median age of housing: 46 years (2000).
Hospitals: Sturgis Hospital (94 beds)
Safety: Violent crime rate: 22.9 per 10,000 population; Property crime rate: 364.1 per 10,000 population (2001).
Newspapers: The Sturgis Journal (6 x week)
Transportation: Commute to work: 91.5% car, 0.6% public transportation, 3.2% walk, 2.0% work from home (2000); Travel time to work: 59.3% less than 15 minutes, 24.0% 15 to 30 minutes, 10.6% 30 to 45 minutes, 3.4% 45 to 60 minutes, 2.7% 60 minutes or more (2000)
Additional Information Contacts
Sturgis Area Chamber of Commerce 616-651-5758

STURGIS (township). Covers a land area of 17.940 square miles and a water area of 0.073 square miles. Located at 41.78° N. Lat.; 85.45° W. Long. Elevation is 918 feet.
History: Settled 1827; incorporated as village 1855, as city 1895.
Population: 2,403 (2000); Race: 95.5% White, 0.5% Black, 0.0% Asian, 0.0% American Indian and Alaska Native, 5.0% Hispanic of any race, 1.4% two or more races (2000); Density: 133.9 persons per square mile (2000); Age: 27.3% under 18, 13.5% over 64 (2000); Marriage status: 19.0% never married, 65.5% now married, 6.0% widowed, 9.5% divorced (2000); Foreign born: 4.0% (2000); Ancestry (includes multiple ancestries): 28.8% German, 11.3% Other groups, 9.8% United States or American, 9.1% English, 7.8% Irish (2000).
Economy: Manufacturing: food, fabricated metal products, plastic products; printing and publishing. Single-family building permits issued: 1 (2001) / 1 (2000); Multi-family building permits issued: 0 (2001) / 0 (2000); Employment by occupation: 8.2% management, 12.0% professional, 12.5% services, 17.0% sales, 0.8% farming, 13.2% construction, 36.3% production (2000).
Income: Per capita income: $18,367 (2000); Median household income: $40,982 (2000); Poverty rate: 4.1% (2000).
Taxes: Total city taxes per capita: $3 (1997); City property taxes per capita: $0 (1997).
Education: High school graduation rate: 76.9% (2000); College graduation rate: 9.6% (2000).
Housing: Homeownership rate: 92.0% (2000); Median home value: $96,800 (2000); Median rent: $416 per month (2000); Median age of housing: 24 years (2000).
Transportation: Commute to work: 96.6% car, 0.0% public transportation, 1.8% walk, 0.7% work from home (2000); Travel time to work: 53.5% less than 15 minutes, 28.7% 15 to 30 minutes, 8.4% 30 to 45 minutes, 3.3% 45 to 60 minutes, 6.1% 60 minutes or more (2000)

THREE RIVERS (city). Covers a land area of 4.507 square miles and a water area of 0.237 square miles. Located at 41.94° N. Lat.; 85.63° W. Long. Elevation is 814 feet.
History: Three Rivers was established on the site of a 17th-century Jesuit mission.
Population: 7,328 (2000); Race: 83.9% White, 9.6% Black, 0.6% Asian, 0.2% American Indian and Alaska Native, 3.3% Hispanic of any race, 4.2% two or more races (2000); Density: 1,625.8 persons per square mile (2000); Age: 28.6% under 18, 13.3% over 64 (2000); Marriage status: 29.5% never married, 43.5% now married, 9.4% widowed, 17.5% divorced (2000); Foreign born: 3.0% (2000); Ancestry (includes multiple ancestries): 22.7% German, 20.4% Other groups, 10.5% English, 9.9% Irish, 6.5% United States or American (2000).
Economy: Single-family building permits issued: 0 (2001) / 0 (2000); Multi-family building permits issued: 0 (2001) / 0 (2000); Employment by

occupation: 6.9% management, 12.0% professional, 15.9% services, 23.0% sales, 0.5% farming, 7.0% construction, 34.7% production (2000).
Income: Per capita income: $16,279 (2000); Median household income: $32,460 (2000); Poverty rate: 19.3% (2000).
Taxes: Total city taxes per capita: $325 (1997); City property taxes per capita: $320 (1997).
Education: High school graduation rate: 75.9% (2000); College graduation rate: 9.7% (2000).

School District(s)

Three Rivers Community Schools (PK-12)
2000 Enrollment: 3,128 616-279-1100
Housing: Homeownership rate: 64.7% (2000); Median home value: $63,400 (2000); Median rent: $397 per month (2000); Median age of housing: 53 years (2000).
Hospitals: Three Rivers Area Hospital (60 beds)
Safety: Violent crime rate: 85.5 per 10,000 population; Property crime rate: 746.6 per 10,000 population (2001).
Newspapers: Three Rivers Commercial-News (6 x week); Penny Saver (1 x week)
Transportation: Commute to work: 91.7% car, 0.2% public transportation, 4.9% walk, 1.8% work from home (2000); Travel time to work: 47.3% less than 15 minutes, 23.7% 15 to 30 minutes, 20.9% 30 to 45 minutes, 3.9% 45 to 60 minutes, 4.2% 60 minutes or more (2000)
Additional Information Contacts
Three Rivers Chamber of Commerce. 616-278-8193

WHITE PIGEON (village). Covers a land area of 1.405 square miles and a water area of 0.010 square miles. Located at 41.79° N. Lat.; 85.64° W. Long. Elevation is 830 feet.
History: White Pigeon was named for an Indian chief who, according to legend, saved the village from destruction in 1830. The village was settled in 1827, platted in 1830, and incorporated in 1837. The post office was first called Millville, then White Pigeon Prairie, and later shortened to White Pigeon.
Population: 1,627 (2000); Race: 95.9% White, 0.0% Black, 0.1% Asian, 0.5% American Indian and Alaska Native, 2.7% Hispanic of any race, 1.3% two or more races (2000); Density: 1,157.8 persons per square mile (2000); Age: 30.1% under 18, 10.0% over 64 (2000); Marriage status: 26.2% never married, 52.7% now married, 5.8% widowed, 15.3% divorced (2000); Foreign born: 1.5% (2000); Ancestry (includes multiple ancestries): 26.9% German, 17.2% Irish, 11.0% Other groups, 10.5% English, 10.3% United States or American (2000).
Economy: Single-family building permits issued: 2 (2001) / 3 (2000); Multi-family building permits issued: 0 (2001) / 0 (2000); Employment by occupation: 6.8% management, 7.9% professional, 11.9% services, 20.7% sales, 0.9% farming, 9.2% construction, 42.7% production (2000).
Income: Per capita income: $16,895 (2000); Median household income: $41,292 (2000); Poverty rate: 13.1% (2000).
Taxes: Total city taxes per capita: $140 (1997); City property taxes per capita: $135 (1997).
Education: High school graduation rate: 76.3% (2000); College graduation rate: 5.6% (2000).

School District(s)

White Pigeon Community Schools (KG-12)
2000 Enrollment: 1,124 616-483-7676
Housing: Homeownership rate: 76.3% (2000); Median home value: $68,100 (2000); Median rent: $408 per month (2000); Median age of housing: 46 years (2000).
Safety: Violent crime rate: 18.3 per 10,000 population; Property crime rate: 287.3 per 10,000 population (2001).
Transportation: Commute to work: 91.7% car, 0.0% public transportation, 5.1% walk, 1.0% work from home (2000); Travel time to work: 41.3% less than 15 minutes, 40.7% 15 to 30 minutes, 12.5% 30 to 45 minutes, 3.1% 45 to 60 minutes, 2.3% 60 minutes or more (2000)

WHITE PIGEON (township). Covers a land area of 25.540 square miles and a water area of 2.031 square miles. Located at 41.79° N. Lat.; 85.61° W. Long. Elevation is 830 feet.
History: Settled c.1827, incorporated 1837.
Population: 3,847 (2000); Race: 96.5% White, 0.0% Black, 0.3% Asian, 0.9% American Indian and Alaska Native, 1.5% Hispanic of any race, 1.3% two or more races (2000); Density: 150.6 persons per square mile (2000); Age: 23.6% under 18, 12.7% over 64 (2000); Marriage status: 20.1% never married, 61.4% now married, 6.6% widowed, 11.9% divorced (2000); Foreign born: 1.5% (2000); Ancestry (includes multiple ancestries): 26.4% German, 15.3% English, 14.9% United States or American, 12.2% Irish, 7.4% Other groups (2000).
Economy: Railroad junction. Manufacturing: paper products, mobile homes, transportation equipment, building products. Poultry; dairying; soybeans. Single-family building permits issued: 20 (2001) / 34 (2000); Multi-family building permits issued: 0 (2001) / 0 (2000); Employment by occupation: 14.7% management, 10.3% professional, 13.1% services, 16.8% sales, 0.5% farming, 7.7% construction, 36.8% production (2000).
Income: Per capita income: $22,441 (2000); Median household income: $42,908 (2000); Poverty rate: 11.6% (2000).
Taxes: Total city taxes per capita: $33 (1997); City property taxes per capita: $28 (1997).
Education: High school graduation rate: 77.9% (2000); College graduation rate: 14.9% (2000).
Housing: Homeownership rate: 80.2% (2000); Median home value: $89,000 (2000); Median rent: $377 per month (2000); Median age of housing: 37 years (2000).
Transportation: Commute to work: 93.1% car, 0.0% public transportation, 2.3% walk, 3.7% work from home (2000); Travel time to work: 31.3% less than 15 minutes, 49.3% 15 to 30 minutes, 12.8% 30 to 45 minutes, 2.8% 45 to 60 minutes, 3.7% 60 minutes or more (2000)

Sanilac County

Located in eastern Michigan; bounded on the east by Lake Huron; drained by the Black and Cass Rivers. Covers a land area of 963.80 square miles, a water area of 626.40 square miles, and is located in the Eastern Time Zone. The county government was organized in 1848. County seat is Sandusky.
Population: 44,547 (2000); Race: 97.0% White, 0.3% Black, 0.3% Asian, 0.3% American Indian and Alaska Native, 2.6% Hispanic of any race, 1.0% two or more races (2000); Density: 46.2 persons per square mile (2000); Age: 26.9% under 18, 15.4% over 64 (2000).
Religion: Five largest groups: 14.4% Catholic Church, 5.3% The United Methodist Church, 4.6% Lutheran Church—Missouri Synod, 1.8% Presbyterian Church (U.S.A.), 1.5% The Missionary Church (2000).
Economy: Unemployment rate: 7.6% (11/2002); Total civilian labor force: 20,728 (11/2002); Leading industries: 41.2% manufacturing; 16.1% retail trade; 12.5% health care and social assistance (2000); Companies that employ more than 1,000 persons: 0 (2000); Companies that employ more than 100 persons: 19 (2000); Farms: 1,448 totaling 429,706 acres (1997); Minority business ownership rate: 4.3% (1997); Women business ownership rate: 18.3% (1997); Retail sales per capita: $6,733 (1997). Single-family building permits issued: 218 (2001) / 226 (2000); Multi-family building permits issued: 0 (2001) / 0 (2000).
Income: Per capita income: $17,089 (2000); Median household income: $36,870 (2000); Poverty rate: 10.4% (2000); Bankruptcy rate: 3.81% (2001).
Taxes: Total county taxes per capita: $217 (2000); County property taxes per capita: $205 (2000).
Education: High school graduation rate: 79.7% (2000); College graduation rate: 10.0% (2000).
Housing: Homeownership rate: 81.9% (2000); Median home value: $88,900 (2000); Median rent: $375 per month (2000); Median age of housing: 37 years (2000).
Health: Birth rate: 118.3 per 10,000 population (1998); Age adjusted death rate: 97.8 per 10,000 population (1999); Age adjusted cancer mortality rate: 219.7 deaths per 100,000 population (1999). Number of physicians: 6.3 per 10,000 population (1999); Number of hospital beds: 29.9 per 10,000 population (1999).
Elections: 2000 Presidential election results: 38.5% Gore, 59.1% Bush, 1.7% Nader, 0.2% Buchanan
National and State Parks: Minden City State Game Area
Additional Information Contacts
Sanilac County Government Offices 810-648-2933
Lexington Chamber of Commerce. 810-359-2262
Sandusky Chamber of Commerce 810-648-4445

Sanilac County Communities

APPLEGATE (village). Covers a land area of 0.989 square miles and a water area of 0 square miles. Located at 43.35° N. Lat.; 82.64° W. Long. Elevation is 747 feet.
History: Applegate developed around a sawmill built in 1856 by George Pack. The post office department named the community for Jesse Applegate, leader of the group that opened a route to Oregon in 1845. Applegate was incorporated as a village in 1903.

Population: 287 (2000); Race: 94.3% White, 0.0% Black, 0.0% Asian, 0.0% American Indian and Alaska Native, 3.9% Hispanic of any race, 3.6% two or more races (2000); Density: 290.1 persons per square mile (2000); Age: 32.6% under 18, 13.3% over 64 (2000); Marriage status: 22.0% never married, 57.4% now married, 8.1% widowed, 12.4% divorced (2000); Foreign born: 3.6% (2000); Ancestry (includes multiple ancestries): 17.9% German, 14.7% Irish, 9.3% English, 8.2% Other groups, 7.5% Dutch (2000).
Economy: Employment by occupation: 0.0% management, 4.6% professional, 15.6% services, 22.9% sales, 0.0% farming, 6.4% construction, 50.5% production (2000).
Income: Per capita income: $12,977 (2000); Median household income: $32,188 (2000); Poverty rate: 3.9% (2000).
Taxes: Total city taxes per capita: $61 (1997); City property taxes per capita: $61 (1997).
Education: High school graduation rate: 66.1% (2000); College graduation rate: 3.5% (2000).
Housing: Homeownership rate: 86.9% (2000); Median home value: $65,000 (2000); Median rent: $350 per month (2000); Median age of housing: 60+ years (2000).
Transportation: Commute to work: 95.0% car, 3.0% public transportation, 0.0% walk, 2.0% work from home (2000); Travel time to work: 29.6% less than 15 minutes, 25.5% 15 to 30 minutes, 17.3% 30 to 45 minutes, 13.3% 45 to 60 minutes, 14.3% 60 minutes or more (2000)

ARGYLE (township). Covers a land area of 36.325 square miles and a water area of 0.015 square miles. Located at 43.54° N. Lat.; 82.92° W. Long.
History: Argyle Township was organized in 1872 and given its Scottish name by the early residents, who were mostly Scots from Ontario with names like McLachlin, McLean, McIntyre. Alexander McLachlin was the first township supervisor and the first postmaster.
Population: 770 (2000); Race: 97.1% White, 0.0% Black, 0.0% Asian, 0.9% American Indian and Alaska Native, 0.4% Hispanic of any race, 2.0% two or more races (2000); Density: 21.2 persons per square mile (2000); Age: 27.7% under 18, 10.1% over 64 (2000); Marriage status: 26.5% never married, 61.4% now married, 7.5% widowed, 4.6% divorced (2000); Foreign born: 1.1% (2000); Ancestry (includes multiple ancestries): 39.7% German, 16.3% Polish, 15.2% English, 10.8% United States or American, 7.4% Irish (2000).
Economy: Employment by occupation: 13.6% management, 6.8% professional, 10.8% services, 17.3% sales, 2.8% farming, 12.5% construction, 36.1% production (2000).
Income: Per capita income: $17,012 (2000); Median household income: $35,341 (2000); Poverty rate: 7.5% (2000).
Taxes: Total city taxes per capita: $46 (1997); City property taxes per capita: $46 (1997).
Education: High school graduation rate: 74.7% (2000); College graduation rate: 2.5% (2000).
Housing: Homeownership rate: 84.8% (2000); Median home value: $62,500 (2000); Median rent: $306 per month (2000); Median age of housing: 44 years (2000).
Transportation: Commute to work: 86.1% car, 0.0% public transportation, 3.5% walk, 10.4% work from home (2000); Travel time to work: 14.5% less than 15 minutes, 50.0% 15 to 30 minutes, 17.4% 30 to 45 minutes, 2.9% 45 to 60 minutes, 15.2% 60 minutes or more (2000)

AUSTIN (township). Covers a land area of 36.225 square miles and a water area of 0 square miles. Located at 43.64° N. Lat.; 82.94° W. Long.
History: Austin Township was organized in 1851 and named for William Austin, who had settled here about 1844.
Population: 673 (2000); Race: 98.8% White, 0.0% Black, 0.0% Asian, 0.9% American Indian and Alaska Native, 0.4% Hispanic of any race, 0.3% two or more races (2000); Density: 18.6 persons per square mile (2000); Age: 25.3% under 18, 14.9% over 64 (2000); Marriage status: 21.2% never married, 62.3% now married, 8.6% widowed, 7.9% divorced (2000); Foreign born: 0.0% (2000); Ancestry (includes multiple ancestries): 39.5% Polish, 33.2% German, 10.5% Irish, 7.9% French (except Basque), 7.4% United States or American (2000).
Economy: Employment by occupation: 12.5% management, 7.4% professional, 13.2% services, 20.9% sales, 4.8% farming, 9.0% construction, 32.2% production (2000).
Income: Per capita income: $15,041 (2000); Median household income: $35,139 (2000); Poverty rate: 11.1% (2000).
Taxes: Total city taxes per capita: $55 (1997); City property taxes per capita: $55 (1997).
Education: High school graduation rate: 74.8% (2000); College graduation rate: 7.0% (2000).
Housing: Homeownership rate: 86.2% (2000); Median home value: $69,300 (2000); Median rent: $238 per month (2000); Median age of housing: 47 years (2000).
Transportation: Commute to work: 79.9% car, 4.6% public transportation, 2.0% walk, 12.8% work from home (2000); Travel time to work: 17.7% less than 15 minutes, 40.8% 15 to 30 minutes, 23.0% 30 to 45 minutes, 4.2% 45 to 60 minutes, 14.3% 60 minutes or more (2000)

BRIDGEHAMPTON (township). Covers a land area of 36.203 square miles and a water area of 0.028 square miles. Located at 43.46° N. Lat.; 82.70° W. Long.
Population: 911 (2000); Race: 98.6% White, 0.0% Black, 0.5% Asian, 0.3% American Indian and Alaska Native, 0.9% Hispanic of any race, 0.0% two or more races (2000); Density: 25.2 persons per square mile (2000); Age: 26.8% under 18, 15.6% over 64 (2000); Marriage status: 25.4% never married, 58.7% now married, 7.9% widowed, 8.0% divorced (2000); Foreign born: 0.3% (2000); Ancestry (includes multiple ancestries): 25.6% German, 16.4% English, 10.4% Irish, 8.9% Polish, 7.6% United States or American (2000).
Economy: Employment by occupation: 9.4% management, 9.1% professional, 8.8% services, 26.5% sales, 5.2% farming, 11.7% construction, 29.4% production (2000).
Income: Per capita income: $14,580 (2000); Median household income: $32,604 (2000); Poverty rate: 11.0% (2000).
Taxes: Total city taxes per capita: $39 (1997); City property taxes per capita: $38 (1997).
Education: High school graduation rate: 80.8% (2000); College graduation rate: 7.0% (2000).
Housing: Homeownership rate: 78.7% (2000); Median home value: $67,800 (2000); Median rent: $375 per month (2000); Median age of housing: 44 years (2000).
Transportation: Commute to work: 89.4% car, 0.5% public transportation, 2.6% walk, 6.6% work from home (2000); Travel time to work: 33.4% less than 15 minutes, 38.0% 15 to 30 minutes, 11.3% 30 to 45 minutes, 4.0% 45 to 60 minutes, 13.3% 60 minutes or more (2000)

BROWN CITY (city). Covers a land area of 1.070 square miles and a water area of 0 square miles. Located at 43.21° N. Lat.; 82.98° W. Long. Elevation is 813 feet.
History: Brown City was settled by a group of Mennonites when the Port Huron & Northwestern Railroad established a station here. The village was founded by Robert G. and John M. Brown on land belonging to Robert.
Population: 1,334 (2000); Race: 98.7% White, 0.1% Black, 0.0% Asian, 0.0% American Indian and Alaska Native, 3.2% Hispanic of any race, 0.6% two or more races (2000); Density: 1,247.3 persons per square mile (2000); Age: 28.6% under 18, 13.3% over 64 (2000); Marriage status: 21.6% never married, 61.2% now married, 5.8% widowed, 11.4% divorced (2000); Foreign born: 1.5% (2000); Ancestry (includes multiple ancestries): 24.7% German, 13.2% United States or American, 11.4% Irish, 11.3% English, 7.6% Polish (2000).
Economy: Employment by occupation: 9.0% management, 12.9% professional, 17.9% services, 19.6% sales, 1.0% farming, 15.1% construction, 24.4% production (2000).
Income: Per capita income: $15,929 (2000); Median household income: $33,906 (2000); Poverty rate: 11.7% (2000).
Taxes: Total city taxes per capita: $202 (1997); City property taxes per capita: $199 (1997).
Education: High school graduation rate: 80.5% (2000); College graduation rate: 10.6% (2000).

School District(s)

Brown City Community Schools (KG-12)
2000 Enrollment: 1,230 810-346-2781
Housing: Homeownership rate: 72.8% (2000); Median home value: $91,500 (2000); Median rent: $367 per month (2000); Median age of housing: 43 years (2000).
Safety: Violent crime rate: 37.3 per 10,000 population; Property crime rate: 290.8 per 10,000 population (2001).
Newspapers: Brown City Banner (1 x week)
Transportation: Commute to work: 90.9% car, 0.3% public transportation, 3.8% walk, 3.8% work from home (2000); Travel time to work: 34.0% less than 15 minutes, 24.2% 15 to 30 minutes, 13.8% 30 to 45 minutes, 7.6% 45 to 60 minutes, 20.4% 60 minutes or more (2000)

BUEL (township). Covers a land area of 37.699 square miles and a water area of 0 square miles. Located at 43.28° N. Lat.; 82.72° W. Long.
Population: 1,237 (2000); Race: 95.9% White, 0.0% Black, 0.0% Asian, 0.6% American Indian and Alaska Native, 2.5% Hispanic of any race, 3.3%

two or more races (2000); Density: 32.8 persons per square mile (2000); Age: 27.3% under 18, 12.9% over 64 (2000); Marriage status: 20.5% never married, 65.6% now married, 4.8% widowed, 9.0% divorced (2000); Foreign born: 1.0% (2000); Ancestry (includes multiple ancestries): 26.7% German, 13.9% English, 9.3% United States or American, 8.9% Other groups, 8.8% Irish (2000).
Economy: Employment by occupation: 9.8% management, 10.0% professional, 14.3% services, 18.7% sales, 0.4% farming, 12.3% construction, 34.6% production (2000).
Income: Per capita income: $17,158 (2000); Median household income: $39,828 (2000); Poverty rate: 10.6% (2000).
Taxes: Total city taxes per capita: $33 (1997); City property taxes per capita: $30 (1997).
Education: High school graduation rate: 82.3% (2000); College graduation rate: 7.3% (2000).
Housing: Homeownership rate: 92.8% (2000); Median home value: $87,900 (2000); Median rent: $375 per month (2000); Median age of housing: 26 years (2000).
Transportation: Commute to work: 93.1% car, 0.0% public transportation, 1.1% walk, 3.7% work from home (2000); Travel time to work: 30.2% less than 15 minutes, 26.5% 15 to 30 minutes, 14.6% 30 to 45 minutes, 9.1% 45 to 60 minutes, 19.6% 60 minutes or more (2000)

CARSONVILLE (village). Covers a land area of 1.133 square miles and a water area of 0 square miles. Located at 43.42° N. Lat.; 82.67° W. Long. Elevation is 823 feet.
History: Carsonville was first called Hall's Corners for Silas C. Hall, who operated a store. The name was changed to honor another storekeeper, Arthur Carson, who built a store here in 1874 and a grain elevator in 1880.
Population: 502 (2000); Race: 97.6% White, 0.0% Black, 1.3% Asian, 0.6% American Indian and Alaska Native, 0.4% Hispanic of any race, 0.6% two or more races (2000); Density: 443.1 persons per square mile (2000); Age: 28.7% under 18, 13.7% over 64 (2000); Marriage status: 26.2% never married, 55.0% now married, 9.0% widowed, 9.9% divorced (2000); Foreign born: 1.5% (2000); Ancestry (includes multiple ancestries): 26.2% German, 11.6% United States or American, 9.9% Irish, 9.4% English, 9.2% Other groups (2000).
Economy: Employment by occupation: 5.4% management, 10.4% professional, 13.6% services, 20.4% sales, 1.4% farming, 16.7% construction, 32.1% production (2000).
Income: Per capita income: $13,304 (2000); Median household income: $25,795 (2000); Poverty rate: 15.2% (2000).
Taxes: Total city taxes per capita: $117 (1997); City property taxes per capita: $117 (1997).
Education: High school graduation rate: 79.2% (2000); College graduation rate: 8.2% (2000).

School District(s)

Carsonville-Port Sanilac School (KG-12)
2000 Enrollment: 659 810-657-9393
Housing: Homeownership rate: 81.5% (2000); Median home value: $62,400 (2000); Median rent: $354 per month (2000); Median age of housing: 52 years (2000).
Safety: Violent crime rate: 0.0 per 10,000 population; Property crime rate: 59.4 per 10,000 population (2001).
Transportation: Commute to work: 94.4% car, 0.9% public transportation, 1.9% walk, 1.9% work from home (2000); Travel time to work: 24.6% less than 15 minutes, 44.5% 15 to 30 minutes, 5.7% 30 to 45 minutes, 7.6% 45 to 60 minutes, 17.5% 60 minutes or more (2000)

CROSWELL (city). Covers a land area of 2.284 square miles and a water area of 0 square miles. Located at 43.27° N. Lat.; 82.62° W. Long. Elevation is 736 feet.
History: Croswell grew up around a sawmill built by Ephraim Pierce in 1845 on the Black River. The town was named in 1877 for Charles M. Croswell, governor of Michigan.
Population: 2,467 (2000); Race: 92.9% White, 0.0% Black, 0.2% Asian, 0.1% American Indian and Alaska Native, 9.3% Hispanic of any race, 0.7% two or more races (2000); Density: 1,080.1 persons per square mile (2000); Age: 31.2% under 18, 11.2% over 64 (2000); Marriage status: 32.0% never married, 50.2% now married, 8.7% widowed, 9.2% divorced (2000); Foreign born: 0.8% (2000); Ancestry (includes multiple ancestries): 22.1% German, 14.5% Other groups, 11.1% English, 11.1% Irish, 8.1% United States or American (2000).
Economy: Single-family building permits issued: 8 (2001) / 8 (2000); Multi-family building permits issued: 0 (2001) / 0 (2000); Employment by occupation: 4.1% management, 11.9% professional, 14.9% services, 17.9% sales, 0.7% farming, 10.5% construction, 40.1% production (2000).
Income: Per capita income: $12,686 (2000); Median household income: $30,379 (2000); Poverty rate: 12.6% (2000).
Taxes: Total city taxes per capita: $254 (1997); City property taxes per capita: $249 (1997).
Education: High school graduation rate: 70.7% (2000); College graduation rate: 8.5% (2000).

School District(s)

Croswell-Lexington Community Sch (KG-12)
2000 Enrollment: 2,536 810-679-1000
Housing: Homeownership rate: 73.3% (2000); Median home value: $79,400 (2000); Median rent: $384 per month (2000); Median age of housing: 46 years (2000).
Safety: Violent crime rate: 12.1 per 10,000 population; Property crime rate: 262.1 per 10,000 population (2001).
Transportation: Commute to work: 92.1% car, 0.3% public transportation, 3.7% walk, 2.5% work from home (2000); Travel time to work: 45.3% less than 15 minutes, 16.4% 15 to 30 minutes, 15.0% 30 to 45 minutes, 10.1% 45 to 60 minutes, 13.2% 60 minutes or more (2000)

CUSTER (township). Covers a land area of 35.334 square miles and a water area of 0.012 square miles. Located at 43.46° N. Lat.; 82.81° W. Long.
Population: 1,036 (2000); Race: 98.1% White, 0.0% Black, 0.0% Asian, 0.4% American Indian and Alaska Native, 3.7% Hispanic of any race, 0.5% two or more races (2000); Density: 29.3 persons per square mile (2000); Age: 26.6% under 18, 16.1% over 64 (2000); Marriage status: 21.6% never married, 60.6% now married, 10.3% widowed, 7.4% divorced (2000); Foreign born: 1.4% (2000); Ancestry (includes multiple ancestries): 37.4% German, 13.2% English, 11.9% Irish, 7.3% Other groups, 6.7% Polish (2000).
Economy: Employment by occupation: 13.9% management, 13.9% professional, 11.6% services, 18.0% sales, 1.8% farming, 12.0% construction, 28.8% production (2000).
Income: Per capita income: $15,562 (2000); Median household income: $35,000 (2000); Poverty rate: 13.8% (2000).
Taxes: Total city taxes per capita: $42 (1997); City property taxes per capita: $41 (1997).
Education: High school graduation rate: 83.8% (2000); College graduation rate: 10.8% (2000).
Housing: Homeownership rate: 87.8% (2000); Median home value: $102,200 (2000); Median rent: $388 per month (2000); Median age of housing: 29 years (2000).
Transportation: Commute to work: 90.0% car, 0.0% public transportation, 1.3% walk, 7.9% work from home (2000); Travel time to work: 51.1% less than 15 minutes, 28.1% 15 to 30 minutes, 10.6% 30 to 45 minutes, 2.5% 45 to 60 minutes, 7.7% 60 minutes or more (2000)

DECKER (unincorporated postal area, zip code 48426). Covers a land area of 37.292 square miles and a water area of 0 square miles. Located at 43.50° N. Lat.; 83.06° W. Long.
Population: 1,117 (2000); Race: 97.0% White, 0.3% Black, 0.0% Asian, 0.4% American Indian and Alaska Native, 2.1% Hispanic of any race, 2.0% two or more races (2000); Density: 30.0 persons per square mile (2000); Age: 26.8% under 18, 12.8% over 64 (2000); Marriage status: 26.3% never married, 59.4% now married, 5.7% widowed, 8.7% divorced (2000); Foreign born: 0.8% (2000); Ancestry (includes multiple ancestries): 22.3% German, 12.6% English, 11.4% United States or American, 9.8% Polish, 7.4% Irish (2000).
Economy: In farm area: livestock, poultry; grain; dairy products. Manufacturing: transportation equipment, plastic, chrome, and rubber products. Railroad junction to North at Palms. Employment by occupation: 12.2% management, 11.8% professional, 13.9% services, 17.0% sales, 7.0% farming, 12.0% construction, 26.1% production (2000).
Income: Per capita income: $18,737 (2000); Median household income: $40,167 (2000); Poverty rate: 8.7% (2000).
Education: High school graduation rate: 75.9% (2000); College graduation rate: 8.9% (2000).
Housing: Homeownership rate: 82.5% (2000); Median home value: $86,000 (2000); Median rent: $341 per month (2000); Median age of housing: 37 years (2000).
Transportation: Commute to work: 87.8% car, 0.0% public transportation, 1.7% walk, 9.8% work from home (2000); Travel time to work: 23.7% less than 15 minutes, 32.5% 15 to 30 minutes, 22.0% 30 to 45 minutes, 5.1% 45 to 60 minutes, 16.7% 60 minutes or more (2000)

DECKERVILLE (village). Covers a land area of 1.278 square miles and a water area of 0 square miles. Located at 43.52° N. Lat.; 82.73° W. Long. Elevation is 786 feet.
Population: 944 (2000); Race: 95.2% White, 0.0% Black, 0.0% Asian, 1.0% American Indian and Alaska Native, 5.5% Hispanic of any race, 0.9% two or more races (2000); Density: 738.5 persons per square mile (2000); Age: 24.0% under 18, 20.7% over 64 (2000); Marriage status: 22.0% never married, 51.6% now married, 10.9% widowed, 15.6% divorced (2000); Foreign born: 1.3% (2000); Ancestry (includes multiple ancestries): 30.2% German, 12.1% English, 10.4% Polish, 9.6% Irish, 9.1% Other groups (2000).
Economy: Employment by occupation: 9.3% management, 14.7% professional, 17.7% services, 20.9% sales, 1.1% farming, 7.7% construction, 28.6% production (2000).
Income: Per capita income: $18,791 (2000); Median household income: $30,083 (2000); Poverty rate: 14.0% (2000).
Taxes: Total city taxes per capita: $257 (1997); City property taxes per capita: $253 (1997).
Education: High school graduation rate: 74.8% (2000); College graduation rate: 10.1% (2000).

School District(s)

Deckerville Community School District (KG-12)
2000 Enrollment: 916 810-376-3615
Housing: Homeownership rate: 71.9% (2000); Median home value: $72,200 (2000); Median rent: $362 per month (2000); Median age of housing: 49 years (2000).
Newspapers: The Deckerville Recorder (1 x week)
Transportation: Commute to work: 83.8% car, 0.0% public transportation, 10.3% walk, 4.9% work from home (2000); Travel time to work: 65.9% less than 15 minutes, 21.5% 15 to 30 minutes, 7.4% 30 to 45 minutes, 1.5% 45 to 60 minutes, 3.7% 60 minutes or more (2000)

DELAWARE (township). Covers a land area of 46.556 square miles and a water area of 0.010 square miles. Located at 43.65° N. Lat.; 82.64° W. Long.
Population: 930 (2000); Race: 97.3% White, 0.0% Black, 0.0% Asian, 0.0% American Indian and Alaska Native, 2.4% Hispanic of any race, 1.9% two or more races (2000); Density: 20.0 persons per square mile (2000); Age: 26.9% under 18, 18.8% over 64 (2000); Marriage status: 20.0% never married, 64.8% now married, 8.5% widowed, 6.7% divorced (2000); Foreign born: 1.0% (2000); Ancestry (includes multiple ancestries): 54.4% German, 14.4% Polish, 9.0% Irish, 7.0% Other groups, 6.7% English (2000).
Economy: Employment by occupation: 19.1% management, 8.1% professional, 10.3% services, 15.4% sales, 8.1% farming, 13.6% construction, 25.4% production (2000).
Income: Per capita income: $15,451 (2000); Median household income: $35,568 (2000); Poverty rate: 11.4% (2000).
Taxes: Total city taxes per capita: $107 (1997); City property taxes per capita: $107 (1997).
Education: High school graduation rate: 76.2% (2000); College graduation rate: 7.6% (2000).
Housing: Homeownership rate: 90.3% (2000); Median home value: $77,900 (2000); Median rent: $275 per month (2000); Median age of housing: 40 years (2000).
Transportation: Commute to work: 81.8% car, 0.0% public transportation, 4.3% walk, 12.3% work from home (2000); Travel time to work: 29.7% less than 15 minutes, 35.3% 15 to 30 minutes, 19.5% 30 to 45 minutes, 5.2% 45 to 60 minutes, 10.2% 60 minutes or more (2000)

ELK (township). Covers a land area of 35.697 square miles and a water area of 0 square miles. Located at 43.28° N. Lat.; 82.82° W. Long.
Population: 1,584 (2000); Race: 96.0% White, 0.5% Black, 1.4% Asian, 0.3% American Indian and Alaska Native, 1.3% Hispanic of any race, 1.9% two or more races (2000); Density: 44.4 persons per square mile (2000); Age: 28.0% under 18, 13.8% over 64 (2000); Marriage status: 21.9% never married, 62.8% now married, 6.5% widowed, 8.8% divorced (2000); Foreign born: 1.6% (2000); Ancestry (includes multiple ancestries): 29.1% German, 14.5% English, 12.9% Irish, 8.1% United States or American, 7.5% Polish (2000).
Economy: Employment by occupation: 11.8% management, 12.4% professional, 14.4% services, 18.3% sales, 1.3% farming, 12.8% construction, 29.0% production (2000).
Income: Per capita income: $15,818 (2000); Median household income: $38,550 (2000); Poverty rate: 9.6% (2000).
Education: High school graduation rate: 81.4% (2000); College graduation rate: 6.4% (2000).
Housing: Homeownership rate: 82.3% (2000); Median home value: $82,800 (2000); Median rent: $375 per month (2000); Median age of housing: 42 years (2000).
Transportation: Commute to work: 89.5% car, 0.0% public transportation, 6.4% walk, 3.7% work from home (2000); Travel time to work: 27.0% less than 15 minutes, 38.5% 15 to 30 minutes, 10.6% 30 to 45 minutes, 9.2% 45 to 60 minutes, 14.8% 60 minutes or more (2000)

ELMER (township). Covers a land area of 36.301 square miles and a water area of 0 square miles. Located at 43.37° N. Lat.; 82.93° W. Long.
Population: 790 (2000); Race: 98.8% White, 0.0% Black, 0.0% Asian, 0.0% American Indian and Alaska Native, 0.7% Hispanic of any race, 1.2% two or more races (2000); Density: 21.8 persons per square mile (2000); Age: 31.2% under 18, 12.2% over 64 (2000); Marriage status: 22.5% never married, 66.8% now married, 4.7% widowed, 6.0% divorced (2000); Foreign born: 0.3% (2000); Ancestry (includes multiple ancestries): 37.1% German, 11.6% Irish, 11.3% English, 9.1% United States or American, 4.6% Polish (2000).
Economy: Employment by occupation: 15.7% management, 14.4% professional, 11.8% services, 19.2% sales, 2.4% farming, 12.9% construction, 23.6% production (2000).
Income: Per capita income: $15,023 (2000); Median household income: $41,563 (2000); Poverty rate: 12.9% (2000).
Taxes: Total city taxes per capita: $51 (1997); City property taxes per capita: $50 (1997).
Education: High school graduation rate: 84.8% (2000); College graduation rate: 11.9% (2000).
Housing: Homeownership rate: 86.2% (2000); Median home value: $85,700 (2000); Median rent: $334 per month (2000); Median age of housing: 42 years (2000).
Transportation: Commute to work: 87.8% car, 0.5% public transportation, 1.9% walk, 9.0% work from home (2000); Travel time to work: 34.4% less than 15 minutes, 41.1% 15 to 30 minutes, 10.5% 30 to 45 minutes, 2.3% 45 to 60 minutes, 11.7% 60 minutes or more (2000)

EVERGREEN (township). Covers a land area of 35.374 square miles and a water area of 0 square miles. Located at 43.54° N. Lat.; 83.05° W. Long.
Population: 995 (2000); Race: 97.4% White, 0.3% Black, 0.0% Asian, 0.3% American Indian and Alaska Native, 0.4% Hispanic of any race, 1.6% two or more races (2000); Density: 28.1 persons per square mile (2000); Age: 26.8% under 18, 12.4% over 64 (2000); Marriage status: 27.1% never married, 55.3% now married, 6.8% widowed, 10.8% divorced (2000); Foreign born: 0.4% (2000); Ancestry (includes multiple ancestries): 20.4% German, 13.2% English, 12.4% Polish, 10.4% United States or American, 7.5% Irish (2000).
Economy: Employment by occupation: 16.0% management, 10.2% professional, 11.6% services, 17.6% sales, 3.1% farming, 12.5% construction, 29.0% production (2000).
Income: Per capita income: $15,814 (2000); Median household income: $36,202 (2000); Poverty rate: 8.2% (2000).
Taxes: Total city taxes per capita: $28 (1997); City property taxes per capita: $28 (1997).
Education: High school graduation rate: 74.5% (2000); College graduation rate: 9.4% (2000).
Housing: Homeownership rate: 86.0% (2000); Median home value: $86,000 (2000); Median rent: $288 per month (2000); Median age of housing: 30 years (2000).
Transportation: Commute to work: 81.7% car, 0.0% public transportation, 3.2% walk, 12.2% work from home (2000); Travel time to work: 23.4% less than 15 minutes, 37.0% 15 to 30 minutes, 22.1% 30 to 45 minutes, 3.6% 45 to 60 minutes, 13.9% 60 minutes or more (2000)

FLYNN (township). Covers a land area of 35.762 square miles and a water area of 0 square miles. Located at 43.28° N. Lat.; 82.92° W. Long.
Population: 1,040 (2000); Race: 99.8% White, 0.0% Black, 0.0% Asian, 0.2% American Indian and Alaska Native, 1.2% Hispanic of any race, 0.0% two or more races (2000); Density: 29.1 persons per square mile (2000); Age: 33.3% under 18, 9.7% over 64 (2000); Marriage status: 26.6% never married, 60.6% now married, 4.9% widowed, 7.8% divorced (2000); Foreign born: 1.5% (2000); Ancestry (includes multiple ancestries): 30.3% German, 16.7% English, 11.5% Irish, 6.0% United States or American, 6.0% Polish (2000).
Economy: Employment by occupation: 11.8% management, 9.5% professional, 15.7% services, 16.9% sales, 6.2% farming, 11.8% construction, 28.2% production (2000).

Income: Per capita income: $14,026 (2000); Median household income: $40,850 (2000); Poverty rate: 17.4% (2000).
Taxes: Total city taxes per capita: $11 (1997); City property taxes per capita: $11 (1997).
Education: High school graduation rate: 74.6% (2000); College graduation rate: 5.8% (2000).
Housing: Homeownership rate: 82.0% (2000); Median home value: $107,100 (2000); Median rent: $367 per month (2000); Median age of housing: 31 years (2000).
Transportation: Commute to work: 81.8% car, 0.0% public transportation, 1.2% walk, 16.1% work from home (2000); Travel time to work: 34.9% less than 15 minutes, 24.5% 15 to 30 minutes, 16.6% 30 to 45 minutes, 3.7% 45 to 60 minutes, 20.3% 60 minutes or more (2000)

FORESTER (township). Covers a land area of 25.271 square miles and a water area of 0.031 square miles. Located at 43.52° N. Lat.; 82.59° W. Long.
Population: 1,108 (2000); Race: 97.3% White, 0.0% Black, 0.0% Asian, 0.4% American Indian and Alaska Native, 2.5% Hispanic of any race, 1.3% two or more races (2000); Density: 43.8 persons per square mile (2000); Age: 20.7% under 18, 25.0% over 64 (2000); Marriage status: 17.9% never married, 68.1% now married, 8.3% widowed, 5.8% divorced (2000); Foreign born: 2.4% (2000); Ancestry (includes multiple ancestries): 27.0% German, 16.4% English, 12.4% Polish, 12.4% Irish, 6.4% Other groups (2000).
Economy: Employment by occupation: 13.8% management, 16.8% professional, 13.4% services, 23.4% sales, 0.7% farming, 15.4% construction, 16.6% production (2000).
Income: Per capita income: $19,573 (2000); Median household income: $32,614 (2000); Poverty rate: 8.5% (2000).
Taxes: Total city taxes per capita: $39 (1997); City property taxes per capita: $38 (1997).
Education: High school graduation rate: 81.9% (2000); College graduation rate: 11.9% (2000).
Housing: Homeownership rate: 90.2% (2000); Median home value: $105,900 (2000); Median rent: $395 per month (2000); Median age of housing: 37 years (2000).
Transportation: Commute to work: 91.7% car, 0.0% public transportation, 2.1% walk, 5.8% work from home (2000); Travel time to work: 27.2% less than 15 minutes, 32.6% 15 to 30 minutes, 11.3% 30 to 45 minutes, 10.3% 45 to 60 minutes, 18.6% 60 minutes or more (2000)

FORESTVILLE (village). Covers a land area of 0.829 square miles and a water area of 0 square miles. Located at 43.66° N. Lat.; 82.61° W. Long. Elevation is 635 feet.
History: Forestville was settled in 1835 as a seaport on Lake Huron.
Population: 127 (2000); Race: 93.6% White, 0.0% Black, 0.0% Asian, 0.0% American Indian and Alaska Native, 1.8% Hispanic of any race, 4.5% two or more races (2000); Density: 153.2 persons per square mile (2000); Age: 14.5% under 18, 30.0% over 64 (2000); Marriage status: 24.2% never married, 55.6% now married, 17.2% widowed, 3.0% divorced (2000); Foreign born: 2.7% (2000); Ancestry (includes multiple ancestries): 45.5% German, 35.5% Polish, 9.1% United States or American, 7.3% Irish, 5.5% Other groups (2000).
Economy: Employment by occupation: 10.7% management, 17.9% professional, 5.4% services, 14.3% sales, 0.0% farming, 8.9% construction, 42.9% production (2000).
Income: Per capita income: $21,130 (2000); Median household income: $45,625 (2000); Poverty rate: 10.0% (2000).
Taxes: Total city taxes per capita: $124 (1997); City property taxes per capita: $124 (1997).
Education: High school graduation rate: 63.0% (2000); College graduation rate: 14.8% (2000).
Housing: Homeownership rate: 96.1% (2000); Median home value: $63,800 (2000); Median rent: <$100 per month (2000); Median age of housing: 46 years (2000).
Transportation: Commute to work: 100.0% car, 0.0% public transportation, 0.0% walk, 0.0% work from home (2000); Travel time to work: 14.8% less than 15 minutes, 42.6% 15 to 30 minutes, 22.2% 30 to 45 minutes, 3.7% 45 to 60 minutes, 16.7% 60 minutes or more (2000)

FREMONT (township). Covers a land area of 35.006 square miles and a water area of 0.029 square miles. Located at 43.19° N. Lat.; 82.71° W. Long.
Population: 913 (2000); Race: 96.4% White, 0.0% Black, 0.2% Asian, 1.6% American Indian and Alaska Native, 1.9% Hispanic of any race, 1.0% two or more races (2000); Density: 26.1 persons per square mile (2000); Age: 29.2% under 18, 8.7% over 64 (2000); Marriage status: 18.1% never married, 70.2% now married, 3.6% widowed, 8.1% divorced (2000); Foreign born: 2.5% (2000); Ancestry (includes multiple ancestries): 31.6% German, 13.7% Irish, 12.0% English, 11.3% Polish, 10.0% United States or American (2000).
Economy: Employment by occupation: 15.2% management, 8.7% professional, 13.8% services, 22.0% sales, 3.0% farming, 11.9% construction, 25.3% production (2000).
Income: Per capita income: $15,934 (2000); Median household income: $44,250 (2000); Poverty rate: 10.0% (2000).
Taxes: Total city taxes per capita: $50 (1997); City property taxes per capita: $50 (1997).
Education: High school graduation rate: 78.5% (2000); College graduation rate: 6.4% (2000).
Housing: Homeownership rate: 86.6% (2000); Median home value: $98,200 (2000); Median rent: $454 per month (2000); Median age of housing: 34 years (2000).
Transportation: Commute to work: 92.5% car, 0.0% public transportation, 2.6% walk, 4.8% work from home (2000); Travel time to work: 21.0% less than 15 minutes, 27.8% 15 to 30 minutes, 23.5% 30 to 45 minutes, 10.6% 45 to 60 minutes, 17.2% 60 minutes or more (2000)

GREENLEAF (township). Covers a land area of 35.887 square miles and a water area of 0.009 square miles. Located at 43.63° N. Lat.; 83.06° W. Long.
Population: 804 (2000); Race: 99.8% White, 0.0% Black, 0.0% Asian, 0.0% American Indian and Alaska Native, 1.2% Hispanic of any race, 0.0% two or more races (2000); Density: 22.4 persons per square mile (2000); Age: 30.1% under 18, 13.7% over 64 (2000); Marriage status: 21.2% never married, 68.4% now married, 3.5% widowed, 6.9% divorced (2000); Foreign born: 1.1% (2000); Ancestry (includes multiple ancestries): 28.1% German, 14.9% Polish, 12.4% United States or American, 10.8% English, 10.4% Irish (2000).
Economy: Employment by occupation: 14.6% management, 14.6% professional, 11.9% services, 15.2% sales, 2.7% farming, 14.6% construction, 26.4% production (2000).
Income: Per capita income: $14,067 (2000); Median household income: $34,643 (2000); Poverty rate: 13.9% (2000).
Taxes: Total city taxes per capita: $58 (1997); City property taxes per capita: $58 (1997).
Education: High school graduation rate: 74.8% (2000); College graduation rate: 9.1% (2000).
Housing: Homeownership rate: 90.3% (2000); Median home value: $77,500 (2000); Median rent: $308 per month (2000); Median age of housing: 30 years (2000).
Transportation: Commute to work: 93.2% car, 0.0% public transportation, 0.3% walk, 6.5% work from home (2000); Travel time to work: 25.9% less than 15 minutes, 39.5% 15 to 30 minutes, 16.9% 30 to 45 minutes, 3.7% 45 to 60 minutes, 14.0% 60 minutes or more (2000)

LAMOTTE (township). Covers a land area of 35.486 square miles and a water area of 0 square miles. Located at 43.46° N. Lat.; 83.05° W. Long.
History: Lamotte Township was organized in 1870. The area had been settled in the late 1850's.
Population: 981 (2000); Race: 96.6% White, 1.4% Black, 0.0% Asian, 0.0% American Indian and Alaska Native, 2.5% Hispanic of any race, 1.7% two or more races (2000); Density: 27.6 persons per square mile (2000); Age: 26.9% under 18, 14.4% over 64 (2000); Marriage status: 22.2% never married, 66.2% now married, 5.1% widowed, 6.5% divorced (2000); Foreign born: 0.3% (2000); Ancestry (includes multiple ancestries): 26.9% German, 13.5% United States or American, 10.7% English, 8.5% Irish, 8.2% Polish (2000).
Economy: Employment by occupation: 11.8% management, 11.5% professional, 13.7% services, 18.2% sales, 9.3% farming, 10.9% construction, 24.6% production (2000).
Income: Per capita income: $18,651 (2000); Median household income: $42,614 (2000); Poverty rate: 9.0% (2000).
Taxes: Total city taxes per capita: $61 (1997); City property taxes per capita: $61 (1997).
Education: High school graduation rate: 79.9% (2000); College graduation rate: 6.4% (2000).
Housing: Homeownership rate: 82.0% (2000); Median home value: $88,800 (2000); Median rent: $392 per month (2000); Median age of housing: 41 years (2000).
Transportation: Commute to work: 91.1% car, 0.0% public transportation, 0.4% walk, 7.4% work from home (2000); Travel time to work: 27.2% less than 15 minutes, 37.3% 15 to 30 minutes, 12.8% 30 to 45 minutes, 5.8% 45 to 60 minutes, 16.9% 60 minutes or more (2000)

LEXINGTON (village). Covers a land area of 0.929 square miles and a water area of 0 square miles. Located at 43.26° N. Lat.; 82.53° W. Long. Elevation is 623 feet.
Population: 1,104 (2000); Race: 98.4% White, 0.0% Black, 0.5% Asian, 0.0% American Indian and Alaska Native, 2.2% Hispanic of any race, 1.0% two or more races (2000); Density: 1,188.3 persons per square mile (2000); Age: 20.0% under 18, 25.2% over 64 (2000); Marriage status: 16.9% never married, 59.6% now married, 10.2% widowed, 13.3% divorced (2000); Foreign born: 2.3% (2000); Ancestry (includes multiple ancestries): 24.7% German, 17.1% Irish, 13.5% English, 12.3% Polish, 9.7% French (except Basque) (2000).
Economy: Employment by occupation: 10.9% management, 21.3% professional, 13.1% services, 24.6% sales, 0.0% farming, 10.4% construction, 19.7% production (2000).
Income: Per capita income: $22,218 (2000); Median household income: $30,792 (2000); Poverty rate: 9.4% (2000).
Taxes: Total city taxes per capita: $499 (1997); City property taxes per capita: $485 (1997).
Education: High school graduation rate: 82.7% (2000); College graduation rate: 15.6% (2000).
Housing: Homeownership rate: 69.6% (2000); Median home value: $104,400 (2000); Median rent: $411 per month (2000); Median age of housing: 21 years (2000).
Safety: Violent crime rate: 9.0 per 10,000 population; Property crime rate: 252.3 per 10,000 population (2001).
Transportation: Commute to work: 93.1% car, 0.0% public transportation, 4.3% walk, 1.8% work from home (2000); Travel time to work: 46.5% less than 15 minutes, 12.1% 15 to 30 minutes, 23.0% 30 to 45 minutes, 8.0% 45 to 60 minutes, 10.5% 60 minutes or more (2000)
Additional Information Contacts
Lexington Chamber of Commerce 810-359-2262

LEXINGTON (township). Covers a land area of 36.214 square miles and a water area of 0 square miles. Located at 43.29° N. Lat.; 82.56° W. Long. Elevation is 623 feet.
Population: 3,688 (2000); Race: 97.6% White, 0.1% Black, 0.2% Asian, 0.0% American Indian and Alaska Native, 3.3% Hispanic of any race, 0.4% two or more races (2000); Density: 101.8 persons per square mile (2000); Age: 24.7% under 18, 18.6% over 64 (2000); Marriage status: 17.8% never married, 61.4% now married, 8.8% widowed, 12.0% divorced (2000); Foreign born: 2.2% (2000); Ancestry (includes multiple ancestries): 38.4% German, 22.5% Irish, 12.8% English, 9.4% Polish, 6.9% French (except Basque) (2000).
Economy: Fisheries; lumber; tourism, resorts; light manufacturing. Employment by occupation: 15.0% management, 15.9% professional, 10.4% services, 23.1% sales, 0.1% farming, 12.5% construction, 23.0% production (2000).
Income: Per capita income: $22,027 (2000); Median household income: $39,241 (2000); Poverty rate: 5.6% (2000).
Taxes: Total city taxes per capita: $26 (1997); City property taxes per capita: $24 (1997).
Education: High school graduation rate: 82.3% (2000); College graduation rate: 13.6% (2000).
Housing: Homeownership rate: 82.9% (2000); Median home value: $121,400 (2000); Median rent: $420 per month (2000); Median age of housing: 28 years (2000).
Transportation: Commute to work: 93.6% car, 0.0% public transportation, 1.5% walk, 4.6% work from home (2000); Travel time to work: 38.1% less than 15 minutes, 18.6% 15 to 30 minutes, 21.2% 30 to 45 minutes, 9.3% 45 to 60 minutes, 12.9% 60 minutes or more (2000)

MAPLE VALLEY (township). Covers a land area of 34.516 square miles and a water area of 0 square miles. Located at 43.19° N. Lat.; 82.93° W. Long.
Population: 1,114 (2000); Race: 99.4% White, 0.2% Black, 0.0% Asian, 0.4% American Indian and Alaska Native, 0.4% Hispanic of any race, 0.0% two or more races (2000); Density: 32.3 persons per square mile (2000); Age: 31.2% under 18, 11.2% over 64 (2000); Marriage status: 23.6% never married, 63.5% now married, 5.8% widowed, 7.2% divorced (2000); Foreign born: 2.0% (2000); Ancestry (includes multiple ancestries): 27.1% German, 12.8% English, 9.3% Irish, 8.9% United States or American, 7.0% Polish (2000).
Economy: Employment by occupation: 13.5% management, 11.8% professional, 9.7% services, 18.7% sales, 4.4% farming, 15.6% construction, 26.3% production (2000).
Income: Per capita income: $16,418 (2000); Median household income: $41,058 (2000); Poverty rate: 10.1% (2000).
Taxes: Total city taxes per capita: $30 (1997); City property taxes per capita: $30 (1997).
Education: High school graduation rate: 77.3% (2000); College graduation rate: 8.7% (2000).
Housing: Homeownership rate: 89.0% (2000); Median home value: $110,300 (2000); Median rent: $342 per month (2000); Median age of housing: 41 years (2000).
Transportation: Commute to work: 82.1% car, 0.0% public transportation, 6.8% walk, 9.2% work from home (2000); Travel time to work: 35.9% less than 15 minutes, 15.5% 15 to 30 minutes, 17.8% 30 to 45 minutes, 8.0% 45 to 60 minutes, 22.8% 60 minutes or more (2000)

MARION (township). Covers a land area of 36.128 square miles and a water area of 0.005 square miles. Located at 43.55° N. Lat.; 82.70° W. Long.
Population: 1,803 (2000); Race: 96.2% White, 0.0% Black, 0.4% Asian, 0.5% American Indian and Alaska Native, 4.6% Hispanic of any race, 1.0% two or more races (2000); Density: 49.9 persons per square mile (2000); Age: 25.0% under 18, 17.3% over 64 (2000); Marriage status: 21.9% never married, 58.9% now married, 8.0% widowed, 11.2% divorced (2000); Foreign born: 1.4% (2000); Ancestry (includes multiple ancestries): 29.0% German, 18.2% English, 11.7% Irish, 8.7% Polish, 7.7% Other groups (2000).
Economy: Employment by occupation: 13.7% management, 14.9% professional, 15.1% services, 18.8% sales, 1.7% farming, 8.7% construction, 27.1% production (2000).
Income: Per capita income: $17,964 (2000); Median household income: $34,803 (2000); Poverty rate: 11.5% (2000).
Taxes: Total city taxes per capita: $30 (1997); City property taxes per capita: $30 (1997).
Education: High school graduation rate: 79.9% (2000); College graduation rate: 12.2% (2000).
Housing: Homeownership rate: 80.4% (2000); Median home value: $75,500 (2000); Median rent: $362 per month (2000); Median age of housing: 44 years (2000).
Transportation: Commute to work: 85.8% car, 0.6% public transportation, 6.7% walk, 5.5% work from home (2000); Travel time to work: 54.4% less than 15 minutes, 28.1% 15 to 30 minutes, 9.3% 30 to 45 minutes, 2.3% 45 to 60 minutes, 5.9% 60 minutes or more (2000)

MARLETTE (city). Covers a land area of 1.647 square miles and a water area of 0 square miles. Located at 43.32° N. Lat.; 83.07° W. Long. Elevation is 838 feet.
History: Marlette grew up as the center of a livestock, feed, and dairy products region.
Population: 2,104 (2000); Race: 93.6% White, 2.8% Black, 0.4% Asian, 0.1% American Indian and Alaska Native, 2.9% Hispanic of any race, 1.6% two or more races (2000); Density: 1,277.3 persons per square mile (2000); Age: 30.2% under 18, 16.3% over 64 (2000); Marriage status: 25.8% never married, 51.8% now married, 10.3% widowed, 12.1% divorced (2000); Foreign born: 0.6% (2000); Ancestry (includes multiple ancestries): 24.7% German, 13.1% English, 11.4% Irish, 10.6% Other groups, 7.4% United States or American (2000).
Economy: Employment by occupation: 6.9% management, 15.0% professional, 16.9% services, 19.8% sales, 2.4% farming, 8.6% construction, 30.3% production (2000).
Income: Per capita income: $15,592 (2000); Median household income: $30,938 (2000); Poverty rate: 10.9% (2000).
Taxes: Total city taxes per capita: $249 (1997); City property taxes per capita: $243 (1997).
Education: High school graduation rate: 76.7% (2000); College graduation rate: 11.3% (2000).
School District(s)
Marlette Community Schools (KG-12)
2000 Enrollment: 1,332 517-635-7425
Housing: Homeownership rate: 61.2% (2000); Median home value: $83,400 (2000); Median rent: $397 per month (2000); Median age of housing: 44 years (2000).
Hospitals: Marlette Community Hospital (100 beds)
Safety: Violent crime rate: 56.7 per 10,000 population; Property crime rate: 321.5 per 10,000 population (2001).
Newspapers: The Marlette Leader (1 x week)
Transportation: Commute to work: 89.7% car, 1.1% public transportation, 4.1% walk, 4.0% work from home (2000); Travel time to work: 53.8% less

than 15 minutes, 15.4% 15 to 30 minutes, 10.8% 30 to 45 minutes, 8.0% 45 to 60 minutes, 11.9% 60 minutes or more (2000)

MARLETTE (township). Covers a land area of 52.495 square miles and a water area of 0 square miles. Located at 43.35° N. Lat.; 83.05° W. Long. Elevation is 838 feet.
History: Incorporated 1881.
Population: 2,051 (2000); Race: 96.4% White, 0.0% Black, 0.0% Asian, 0.4% American Indian and Alaska Native, 2.9% Hispanic of any race, 1.3% two or more races (2000); Density: 39.1 persons per square mile (2000); Age: 28.9% under 18, 12.6% over 64 (2000); Marriage status: 24.4% never married, 65.1% now married, 5.9% widowed, 4.6% divorced (2000); Foreign born: 1.3% (2000); Ancestry (includes multiple ancestries): 27.5% German, 16.1% English, 11.2% United States or American, 9.0% Polish, 9.0% Irish (2000).
Economy: In farm area: grain, sugar beets, apples; livestock; dairy products. Manufacturing: building materials, hose clamps, transportation equipment; grain elevators. Employment by occupation: 15.3% management, 13.2% professional, 12.6% services, 19.2% sales, 3.9% farming, 12.3% construction, 23.5% production (2000).
Income: Per capita income: $17,556 (2000); Median household income: $44,907 (2000); Poverty rate: 14.7% (2000).
Taxes: Total city taxes per capita: $34 (1997); City property taxes per capita: $32 (1997).
Education: High school graduation rate: 82.9% (2000); College graduation rate: 12.2% (2000).
Housing: Homeownership rate: 85.5% (2000); Median home value: $94,500 (2000); Median rent: $403 per month (2000); Median age of housing: 39 years (2000).
Transportation: Commute to work: 82.1% car, 2.0% public transportation, 4.0% walk, 10.5% work from home (2000); Travel time to work: 47.4% less than 15 minutes, 20.1% 15 to 30 minutes, 13.4% 30 to 45 minutes, 7.9% 45 to 60 minutes, 11.2% 60 minutes or more (2000)

MELVIN (village). Covers a land area of 0.988 square miles and a water area of 0 square miles. Located at 43.18° N. Lat.; 82.86° W. Long.
Population: 160 (2000); Race: 100.0% White, 0.0% Black, 0.0% Asian, 0.0% American Indian and Alaska Native, 0.0% Hispanic of any race, 0.0% two or more races (2000); Density: 162.0 persons per square mile (2000); Age: 19.0% under 18, 24.1% over 64 (2000); Marriage status: 16.7% never married, 60.5% now married, 7.9% widowed, 14.9% divorced (2000); Foreign born: 0.0% (2000); Ancestry (includes multiple ancestries): 32.8% German, 24.8% English, 17.5% Irish, 15.3% Polish, 13.9% French (except Basque) (2000).
Economy: In farm area. Employment by occupation: 6.1% management, 4.1% professional, 28.6% services, 20.4% sales, 0.0% farming, 18.4% construction, 22.4% production (2000).
Income: Per capita income: $13,646 (2000); Median household income: $28,333 (2000); Poverty rate: 12.4% (2000).
Taxes: Total city taxes per capita: $46 (1997); City property taxes per capita: $46 (1997).
Education: High school graduation rate: 80.4% (2000); College graduation rate: 0.0% (2000).
Housing: Homeownership rate: 90.5% (2000); Median home value: $72,500 (2000); Median rent: $450 per month (2000); Median age of housing: 48 years (2000).
Transportation: Commute to work: 95.6% car, 0.0% public transportation, 4.4% walk, 0.0% work from home (2000); Travel time to work: 17.8% less than 15 minutes, 13.3% 15 to 30 minutes, 31.1% 30 to 45 minutes, 24.4% 45 to 60 minutes, 13.3% 60 minutes or more (2000)

MINDEN (township). Covers a land area of 36.121 square miles and a water area of 0.013 square miles. Located at 43.65° N. Lat.; 82.80° W. Long.
History: Also called Minden.
Population: 633 (2000); Race: 96.6% White, 0.0% Black, 0.0% Asian, 0.0% American Indian and Alaska Native, 3.4% Hispanic of any race, 0.3% two or more races (2000); Density: 17.5 persons per square mile (2000); Age: 28.5% under 18, 15.1% over 64 (2000); Marriage status: 30.4% never married, 50.4% now married, 10.6% widowed, 8.6% divorced (2000); Foreign born: 0.5% (2000); Ancestry (includes multiple ancestries): 41.4% German, 35.0% Polish, 14.2% Irish, 7.3% English, 5.5% Other groups (2000).
Economy: In farm area. Light manufacturing. Employment by occupation: 14.6% management, 5.2% professional, 13.9% services, 20.5% sales, 6.6% farming, 16.0% construction, 23.3% production (2000).
Income: Per capita income: $14,770 (2000); Median household income: $30,227 (2000); Poverty rate: 12.8% (2000).
Taxes: Total city taxes per capita: $53 (1997); City property taxes per capita: $53 (1997).
Education: High school graduation rate: 72.1% (2000); College graduation rate: 3.7% (2000).
Housing: Homeownership rate: 85.7% (2000); Median home value: $62,400 (2000); Median rent: $322 per month (2000); Median age of housing: 53 years (2000).
Transportation: Commute to work: 83.1% car, 0.0% public transportation, 1.4% walk, 14.1% work from home (2000); Travel time to work: 29.9% less than 15 minutes, 36.1% 15 to 30 minutes, 21.7% 30 to 45 minutes, 3.7% 45 to 60 minutes, 8.6% 60 minutes or more (2000)

MINDEN CITY (village). Covers a land area of 1.118 square miles and a water area of 0 square miles. Located at 43.67° N. Lat.; 82.77° W. Long. Elevation is 829 feet.
Population: 242 (2000); Race: 99.1% White, 0.0% Black, 0.0% Asian, 0.0% American Indian and Alaska Native, 0.0% Hispanic of any race, 0.9% two or more races (2000); Density: 216.5 persons per square mile (2000); Age: 21.8% under 18, 17.3% over 64 (2000); Marriage status: 37.5% never married, 41.3% now married, 13.0% widowed, 8.2% divorced (2000); Foreign born: 1.3% (2000); Ancestry (includes multiple ancestries): 41.8% German, 24.9% Polish, 12.4% Irish, 7.6% French (except Basque), 7.6% Other groups (2000).
Economy: Employment by occupation: 4.1% management, 6.1% professional, 21.4% services, 12.2% sales, 10.2% farming, 12.2% construction, 33.7% production (2000).
Income: Per capita income: $14,980 (2000); Median household income: $24,375 (2000); Poverty rate: 16.9% (2000).
Taxes: Total city taxes per capita: $137 (1997); City property taxes per capita: $137 (1997).
Education: High school graduation rate: 69.5% (2000); College graduation rate: 4.3% (2000).
Housing: Homeownership rate: 79.1% (2000); Median home value: $54,000 (2000); Median rent: $316 per month (2000); Median age of housing: 58 years (2000).
Newspapers: The Minden City Herald (1 x week)
Transportation: Commute to work: 88.5% car, 0.0% public transportation, 2.1% walk, 9.4% work from home (2000); Travel time to work: 21.8% less than 15 minutes, 46.0% 15 to 30 minutes, 27.6% 30 to 45 minutes, 0.0% 45 to 60 minutes, 4.6% 60 minutes or more (2000)

MOORE (township). Covers a land area of 36.277 square miles and a water area of 0 square miles. Located at 43.47° N. Lat.; 82.95° W. Long.
Population: 1,262 (2000); Race: 97.0% White, 0.0% Black, 0.0% Asian, 0.6% American Indian and Alaska Native, 2.0% Hispanic of any race, 2.0% two or more races (2000); Density: 34.8 persons per square mile (2000); Age: 28.0% under 18, 11.4% over 64 (2000); Marriage status: 22.3% never married, 64.4% now married, 6.3% widowed, 7.0% divorced (2000); Foreign born: 0.6% (2000); Ancestry (includes multiple ancestries): 33.2% German, 10.5% English, 10.1% Irish, 10.0% Polish, 9.6% United States or American (2000).
Economy: Employment by occupation: 14.2% management, 9.4% professional, 14.2% services, 24.1% sales, 1.2% farming, 13.7% construction, 23.2% production (2000).
Income: Per capita income: $19,424 (2000); Median household income: $39,792 (2000); Poverty rate: 9.4% (2000).
Taxes: Total city taxes per capita: $72 (1997); City property taxes per capita: $72 (1997).
Education: High school graduation rate: 78.3% (2000); College graduation rate: 7.0% (2000).
Housing: Homeownership rate: 81.1% (2000); Median home value: $79,700 (2000); Median rent: $345 per month (2000); Median age of housing: 50 years (2000).
Transportation: Commute to work: 88.7% car, 0.9% public transportation, 3.3% walk, 6.6% work from home (2000); Travel time to work: 34.3% less than 15 minutes, 38.4% 15 to 30 minutes, 9.1% 30 to 45 minutes, 6.2% 45 to 60 minutes, 11.9% 60 minutes or more (2000)

PALMS (unincorporated postal area, zip code 48465). Covers a land area of 39.677 square miles and a water area of 0.010 square miles. Located at 43.61° N. Lat.; 82.68° W. Long.
History: Palms was founded about 1859 and named for its founder, a Mr. Palm. The Port Huron & Northwestern Railroad established a station here in 1880.
Population: 629 (2000); Race: 94.5% White, 0.0% Black, 0.0% Asian, 1.2% American Indian and Alaska Native, 7.5% Hispanic of any race, 0.7% two or

more races (2000); Density: 15.9 persons per square mile (2000); Age: 22.7% under 18, 16.9% over 64 (2000); Marriage status: 27.5% never married, 58.5% now married, 7.8% widowed, 6.2% divorced (2000); Foreign born: 0.7% (2000); Ancestry (includes multiple ancestries): 51.5% German, 16.9% Polish, 10.1% Irish, 9.9% English, 9.2% Other groups (2000).
Economy: Employment by occupation: 17.8% management, 6.3% professional, 10.0% services, 13.8% sales, 9.3% farming, 13.4% construction, 29.4% production (2000).
Income: Per capita income: $16,777 (2000); Median household income: $35,875 (2000); Poverty rate: 10.1% (2000).
Education: High school graduation rate: 76.8% (2000); College graduation rate: 7.1% (2000).
Housing: Homeownership rate: 93.2% (2000); Median home value: $95,300 (2000); Median rent: $365 per month (2000); Median age of housing: 37 years (2000).
Transportation: Commute to work: 80.4% car, 0.0% public transportation, 5.6% walk, 11.9% work from home (2000); Travel time to work: 39.1% less than 15 minutes, 28.6% 15 to 30 minutes, 13.0% 30 to 45 minutes, 5.0% 45 to 60 minutes, 14.3% 60 minutes or more (2000)

PECK (village). Covers a land area of 1.010 square miles and a water area of 0 square miles. Located at 43.25° N. Lat.; 82.81° W. Long. Elevation is 789 feet.
History: Peck had its beginnings when Nathaniel Vannest built the Globe Hotel here in 1859, followed by a store in 1868. Peck was incorporated as a village in 1903.
Population: 599 (2000); Race: 94.8% White, 0.5% Black, 0.7% Asian, 0.2% American Indian and Alaska Native, 0.3% Hispanic of any race, 3.8% two or more races (2000); Density: 593.0 persons per square mile (2000); Age: 25.3% under 18, 17.2% over 64 (2000); Marriage status: 22.5% never married, 56.5% now married, 8.6% widowed, 12.4% divorced (2000); Foreign born: 3.3% (2000); Ancestry (includes multiple ancestries): 21.7% German, 15.7% Irish, 11.4% Other groups, 10.2% English, 8.6% Polish (2000).
Economy: Employment by occupation: 6.3% management, 17.1% professional, 15.5% services, 20.2% sales, 0.0% farming, 12.7% construction, 28.2% production (2000).
Income: Per capita income: $14,622 (2000); Median household income: $29,063 (2000); Poverty rate: 12.5% (2000).
Taxes: Total city taxes per capita: $115 (1997); City property taxes per capita: $115 (1997).
Education: High school graduation rate: 79.3% (2000); College graduation rate: 6.1% (2000).

School District(s)

Peck Community School District (KG-12)
2000 Enrollment: 605 810-378-5171
Housing: Homeownership rate: 73.0% (2000); Median home value: $71,300 (2000); Median rent: $368 per month (2000); Median age of housing: 42 years (2000).
Transportation: Commute to work: 93.1% car, 0.0% public transportation, 5.3% walk, 1.6% work from home (2000); Travel time to work: 32.1% less than 15 minutes, 34.2% 15 to 30 minutes, 13.6% 30 to 45 minutes, 6.6% 45 to 60 minutes, 13.6% 60 minutes or more (2000)

PORT SANILAC (village). Covers a land area of 0.724 square miles and a water area of 0 square miles. Located at 43.43° N. Lat.; 82.54° W. Long. Elevation is 606 feet.
History: Port Sanilac was first settled in 1844, when it was known as Bark Shanty Point. For a time, the "Bark Shanty Times" utilized an unusual method of producing its daily newspaper edition, when large sheets of paper were placed on the storekeeper's counter, along with a supply of lead pencils. Customers were invited to write down their news, which was then available for others to read throughout the day. Daily issues were bound and preserved.
Population: 658 (2000); Race: 96.5% White, 0.0% Black, 0.0% Asian, 0.3% American Indian and Alaska Native, 2.3% Hispanic of any race, 1.5% two or more races (2000); Density: 908.8 persons per square mile (2000); Age: 19.9% under 18, 30.1% over 64 (2000); Marriage status: 16.6% never married, 59.9% now married, 13.7% widowed, 9.8% divorced (2000); Foreign born: 4.3% (2000); Ancestry (includes multiple ancestries): 37.7% German, 19.5% Irish, 18.1% English, 9.9% French (except Basque), 9.3% Polish (2000).
Economy: Employment by occupation: 10.7% management, 20.2% professional, 11.1% services, 27.6% sales, 1.2% farming, 10.3% construction, 18.9% production (2000).
Income: Per capita income: $18,153 (2000); Median household income: $28,409 (2000); Poverty rate: 7.8% (2000).
Taxes: Total city taxes per capita: $380 (1997); City property taxes per capita: $380 (1997).
Education: High school graduation rate: 80.0% (2000); College graduation rate: 17.4% (2000).
Housing: Homeownership rate: 70.8% (2000); Median home value: $104,800 (2000); Median rent: $339 per month (2000); Median age of housing: 37 years (2000).
Transportation: Commute to work: 86.6% car, 2.1% public transportation, 7.5% walk, 3.8% work from home (2000); Travel time to work: 27.8% less than 15 minutes, 30.0% 15 to 30 minutes, 14.3% 30 to 45 minutes, 14.8% 45 to 60 minutes, 13.0% 60 minutes or more (2000)

SANDUSKY (city). Covers a land area of 1.898 square miles and a water area of 0 square miles. Located at 43.42° N. Lat.; 82.83° W. Long. Elevation is 774 feet.
History: Sandusky was founded in 1870 by Wildman Mills and named for his former home of Sandusky, Ohio. Sandusky developed as the center of a livestock area, and as the seat of Sanilac County. For a time it was called Sanilac Center, but was renamed Sandusky when it was incorporated as a city in 1905.
Population: 2,745 (2000); Race: 94.7% White, 0.7% Black, 1.9% Asian, 0.5% American Indian and Alaska Native, 3.2% Hispanic of any race, 1.3% two or more races (2000); Density: 1,446.3 persons per square mile (2000); Age: 23.5% under 18, 18.6% over 64 (2000); Marriage status: 24.3% never married, 49.5% now married, 12.1% widowed, 14.1% divorced (2000); Foreign born: 2.3% (2000); Ancestry (includes multiple ancestries): 27.0% German, 15.6% English, 14.1% Irish, 9.3% Other groups, 7.9% Polish (2000).
Economy: Employment by occupation: 7.8% management, 18.4% professional, 18.4% services, 21.8% sales, 0.8% farming, 5.0% construction, 27.8% production (2000).
Income: Per capita income: $17,639 (2000); Median household income: $33,667 (2000); Poverty rate: 11.0% (2000).
Taxes: Total city taxes per capita: $338 (1997); City property taxes per capita: $338 (1997).
Education: High school graduation rate: 82.0% (2000); College graduation rate: 12.4% (2000).

School District(s)

Sandusky Community School District (KG-12)
2000 Enrollment: 1,451 810-648-3400
Housing: Homeownership rate: 57.3% (2000); Median home value: $81,400 (2000); Median rent: $345 per month (2000); Median age of housing: 33 years (2000).
Hospitals: McKenzie Memorial Hospital (37 beds)
Safety: Violent crime rate: 18.1 per 10,000 population; Property crime rate: 409.6 per 10,000 population (2001).
Newspapers: Sanilac County News (1 x week); Bargain Hunter (1 x week)
Transportation: Commute to work: 91.3% car, 0.7% public transportation, 3.1% walk, 4.0% work from home (2000); Travel time to work: 59.2% less than 15 minutes, 20.2% 15 to 30 minutes, 6.4% 30 to 45 minutes, 5.6% 45 to 60 minutes, 8.6% 60 minutes or more (2000)
Additional Information Contacts
Sandusky Chamber of Commerce 810-648-4445

SANILAC (township). Covers a land area of 40.939 square miles and a water area of 0 square miles. Located at 43.40° N. Lat.; 82.55° W. Long.
Population: 2,609 (2000); Race: 98.0% White, 0.0% Black, 0.0% Asian, 0.7% American Indian and Alaska Native, 1.0% Hispanic of any race, 0.6% two or more races (2000); Density: 63.7 persons per square mile (2000); Age: 22.4% under 18, 22.2% over 64 (2000); Marriage status: 18.1% never married, 63.9% now married, 11.4% widowed, 6.7% divorced (2000); Foreign born: 2.2% (2000); Ancestry (includes multiple ancestries): 35.5% German, 20.4% English, 16.4% Irish, 9.5% Polish, 7.5% French (except Basque) (2000).
Economy: Employment by occupation: 11.7% management, 14.4% professional, 11.7% services, 23.3% sales, 2.8% farming, 12.1% construction, 24.1% production (2000).
Income: Per capita income: $17,963 (2000); Median household income: $37,180 (2000); Poverty rate: 8.1% (2000).
Taxes: Total city taxes per capita: $37 (1997); City property taxes per capita: $36 (1997).
Education: High school graduation rate: 84.8% (2000); College graduation rate: 14.2% (2000).
Housing: Homeownership rate: 85.9% (2000); Median home value: $99,000 (2000); Median rent: $350 per month (2000); Median age of housing: 30 years (2000).

Transportation: Commute to work: 91.5% car, 0.9% public transportation, 3.1% walk, 4.5% work from home (2000); Travel time to work: 21.2% less than 15 minutes, 39.3% 15 to 30 minutes, 15.8% 30 to 45 minutes, 10.2% 45 to 60 minutes, 13.4% 60 minutes or more (2000)

SNOVER (unincorporated postal area, zip code 48472). Covers a land area of 80.365 square miles and a water area of 0.015 square miles. Located at 43.51° N. Lat.; 82.96° W. Long. Elevation is 773 feet.
History: Snover was named for Horace G. Snover, who served from 1895 to 1898 as the district's representative in congress.
Population: 2,042 (2000); Race: 96.4% White, 0.7% Black, 0.0% Asian, 0.7% American Indian and Alaska Native, 1.3% Hispanic of any race, 2.0% two or more races (2000); Density: 25.4 persons per square mile (2000); Age: 28.8% under 18, 11.5% over 64 (2000); Marriage status: 25.0% never married, 61.8% now married, 5.9% widowed, 7.3% divorced (2000); Foreign born: 0.8% (2000); Ancestry (includes multiple ancestries): 35.0% German, 12.6% English, 12.1% Polish, 10.0% United States or American, 9.1% Irish (2000).
Economy: Employment by occupation: 16.0% management, 8.7% professional, 11.7% services, 18.9% sales, 3.1% farming, 11.6% construction, 30.0% production (2000).
Income: Per capita income: $16,204 (2000); Median household income: $36,379 (2000); Poverty rate: 13.3% (2000).
Education: High school graduation rate: 76.4% (2000); College graduation rate: 5.2% (2000).
Housing: Homeownership rate: 81.7% (2000); Median home value: $75,800 (2000); Median rent: $323 per month (2000); Median age of housing: 49 years (2000).
Transportation: Commute to work: 86.3% car, 0.5% public transportation, 3.0% walk, 9.6% work from home (2000); Travel time to work: 22.3% less than 15 minutes, 46.8% 15 to 30 minutes, 12.2% 30 to 45 minutes, 4.2% 45 to 60 minutes, 14.5% 60 minutes or more (2000)

SPEAKER (township). Covers a land area of 34.590 square miles and a water area of 0 square miles. Located at 43.19° N. Lat.; 82.82° W. Long.
History: Speaker Township was organized in 1858.
Population: 1,408 (2000); Race: 98.1% White, 0.0% Black, 0.0% Asian, 0.4% American Indian and Alaska Native, 0.6% Hispanic of any race, 1.2% two or more races (2000); Density: 40.7 persons per square mile (2000); Age: 29.0% under 18, 12.1% over 64 (2000); Marriage status: 20.3% never married, 65.8% now married, 4.9% widowed, 9.0% divorced (2000); Foreign born: 0.8% (2000); Ancestry (includes multiple ancestries): 27.4% German, 15.0% Irish, 12.6% English, 9.4% Polish, 7.1% United States or American (2000).
Economy: Employment by occupation: 14.4% management, 10.0% professional, 15.5% services, 18.7% sales, 1.1% farming, 14.8% construction, 25.5% production (2000).
Income: Per capita income: $17,583 (2000); Median household income: $41,250 (2000); Poverty rate: 6.5% (2000).
Taxes: Total city taxes per capita: $39 (1997); City property taxes per capita: $39 (1997).
Education: High school graduation rate: 78.4% (2000); College graduation rate: 6.7% (2000).
Housing: Homeownership rate: 90.7% (2000); Median home value: $99,600 (2000); Median rent: $436 per month (2000); Median age of housing: 32 years (2000).
Transportation: Commute to work: 94.8% car, 0.0% public transportation, 1.3% walk, 3.9% work from home (2000); Travel time to work: 23.2% less than 15 minutes, 19.6% 15 to 30 minutes, 18.9% 30 to 45 minutes, 12.8% 45 to 60 minutes, 25.6% 60 minutes or more (2000)

WASHINGTON (township). Covers a land area of 36.132 square miles and a water area of 0 square miles. Located at 43.38° N. Lat.; 82.68° W. Long.
Population: 1,636 (2000); Race: 97.0% White, 0.1% Black, 0.5% Asian, 0.2% American Indian and Alaska Native, 1.2% Hispanic of any race, 1.7% two or more races (2000); Density: 45.3 persons per square mile (2000); Age: 28.2% under 18, 14.1% over 64 (2000); Marriage status: 19.7% never married, 63.7% now married, 6.7% widowed, 9.9% divorced (2000); Foreign born: 2.8% (2000); Ancestry (includes multiple ancestries): 26.7% German, 14.1% English, 10.7% Irish, 7.5% Polish, 6.9% Other groups (2000).
Economy: Employment by occupation: 7.2% management, 10.7% professional, 13.5% services, 21.1% sales, 0.3% farming, 13.9% construction, 33.3% production (2000).
Income: Per capita income: $16,015 (2000); Median household income: $35,602 (2000); Poverty rate: 10.0% (2000).
Taxes: Total city taxes per capita: $26 (1997); City property taxes per capita: $26 (1997).
Education: High school graduation rate: 77.4% (2000); College graduation rate: 7.5% (2000).
Housing: Homeownership rate: 87.0% (2000); Median home value: $71,000 (2000); Median rent: $350 per month (2000); Median age of housing: 40 years (2000).
Transportation: Commute to work: 91.8% car, 0.6% public transportation, 1.2% walk, 5.6% work from home (2000); Travel time to work: 23.6% less than 15 minutes, 36.7% 15 to 30 minutes, 10.6% 30 to 45 minutes, 9.4% 45 to 60 minutes, 19.8% 60 minutes or more (2000)

WATERTOWN (township). Covers a land area of 35.255 square miles and a water area of 0 square miles. Located at 43.37° N. Lat.; 82.81° W. Long.
Population: 1,376 (2000); Race: 97.5% White, 0.3% Black, 1.3% Asian, 0.4% American Indian and Alaska Native, 1.8% Hispanic of any race, 0.6% two or more races (2000); Density: 39.0 persons per square mile (2000); Age: 28.1% under 18, 12.5% over 64 (2000); Marriage status: 20.5% never married, 66.8% now married, 6.2% widowed, 6.6% divorced (2000); Foreign born: 1.7% (2000); Ancestry (includes multiple ancestries): 30.6% German, 18.5% English, 12.6% Irish, 8.4% Polish, 6.6% United States or American (2000).
Economy: Employment by occupation: 11.4% management, 18.5% professional, 14.5% services, 22.9% sales, 1.0% farming, 11.2% construction, 20.4% production (2000).
Income: Per capita income: $17,145 (2000); Median household income: $40,000 (2000); Poverty rate: 9.7% (2000).
Taxes: Total city taxes per capita: $59 (1997); City property taxes per capita: $59 (1997).
Education: High school graduation rate: 86.4% (2000); College graduation rate: 12.6% (2000).
Housing: Homeownership rate: 89.9% (2000); Median home value: $99,300 (2000); Median rent: $403 per month (2000); Median age of housing: 34 years (2000).
Transportation: Commute to work: 90.8% car, 0.0% public transportation, 2.6% walk, 6.3% work from home (2000); Travel time to work: 53.3% less than 15 minutes, 27.5% 15 to 30 minutes, 7.0% 30 to 45 minutes, 3.8% 45 to 60 minutes, 8.4% 60 minutes or more (2000)

WHEATLAND (township). Covers a land area of 36.376 square miles and a water area of 0.049 square miles. Located at 43.54° N. Lat.; 82.80° W. Long.
Population: 530 (2000); Race: 95.9% White, 0.0% Black, 0.4% Asian, 1.1% American Indian and Alaska Native, 2.6% Hispanic of any race, 1.5% two or more races (2000); Density: 14.6 persons per square mile (2000); Age: 34.5% under 18, 11.7% over 64 (2000); Marriage status: 26.4% never married, 60.5% now married, 5.2% widowed, 7.9% divorced (2000); Foreign born: 1.9% (2000); Ancestry (includes multiple ancestries): 42.1% German, 18.6% Polish, 10.2% Irish, 9.1% Other groups, 7.4% English (2000).
Economy: Employment by occupation: 18.4% management, 9.7% professional, 18.4% services, 15.7% sales, 1.8% farming, 14.3% construction, 21.7% production (2000).
Income: Per capita income: $13,919 (2000); Median household income: $33,750 (2000); Poverty rate: 4.3% (2000).
Taxes: Total city taxes per capita: $73 (1997); City property taxes per capita: $73 (1997).
Education: High school graduation rate: 80.8% (2000); College graduation rate: 6.5% (2000).
Housing: Homeownership rate: 83.0% (2000); Median home value: $76,900 (2000); Median rent: $325 per month (2000); Median age of housing: 39 years (2000).
Transportation: Commute to work: 86.5% car, 0.0% public transportation, 0.9% walk, 12.6% work from home (2000); Travel time to work: 39.4% less than 15 minutes, 39.9% 15 to 30 minutes, 10.1% 30 to 45 minutes, 5.3% 45 to 60 minutes, 5.3% 60 minutes or more (2000)

WORTH (township). Covers a land area of 38.747 square miles and a water area of 0.024 square miles. Located at 43.21° N. Lat.; 82.53° W. Long.
Population: 4,021 (2000); Race: 99.3% White, 0.0% Black, 0.1% Asian, 0.1% American Indian and Alaska Native, 3.0% Hispanic of any race, 0.3% two or more races (2000); Density: 103.8 persons per square mile (2000); Age: 22.0% under 18, 19.0% over 64 (2000); Marriage status: 16.2% never married, 67.3% now married, 7.7% widowed, 8.8% divorced (2000); Foreign born: 3.1% (2000); Ancestry (includes multiple ancestries): 23.5% German,

16.3% Polish, 12.0% English, 9.5% Irish, 9.3% United States or American (2000).
Economy: Employment by occupation: 10.5% management, 12.7% professional, 14.3% services, 23.8% sales, 1.0% farming, 12.8% construction, 24.8% production (2000).
Income: Per capita income: $18,955 (2000); Median household income: $37,129 (2000); Poverty rate: 12.2% (2000).
Taxes: Total city taxes per capita: $36 (1997); City property taxes per capita: $31 (1997).
Education: High school graduation rate: 79.1% (2000); College graduation rate: 10.4% (2000).
Housing: Homeownership rate: 88.1% (2000); Median home value: $100,700 (2000); Median rent: $482 per month (2000); Median age of housing: 40 years (2000).
Transportation: Commute to work: 96.0% car, 0.0% public transportation, 0.6% walk, 3.4% work from home (2000); Travel time to work: 20.3% less than 15 minutes, 31.1% 15 to 30 minutes, 24.8% 30 to 45 minutes, 10.2% 45 to 60 minutes, 13.7% 60 minutes or more (2000)

Schoolcraft County

Located in northwestern Michigan on the Upper Peninsula; bounded on the south by Lake Michigan; drained by the Indian and Manistique Rivers; includes Indian Lake, and parts of Hiawatha National Forest. Covers a land area of 1,178.10 square miles, a water area of 705.60 square miles, and is located in the Eastern Time Zone. The county government was organized in 1843. County seat is Manistique.

Weather Station: Seney Wildlife Refuge — Elevation: 708 feet

	Jan	Feb	Mar	Apr	May	Jun	Jul	Aug	Sep	Oct	Nov	Dec
High	25	29	38	52	66	75	80	77	68	56	42	30
Low	6	7	16	30	41	49	54	53	47	37	27	16
Precip	2.0	1.2	1.9	1.9	2.7	3.0	3.8	3.2	3.4	3.1	2.5	2.0
Snow	30.0	17.6	14.4	3.4	0.3	0.0	0.0	0.0	tr	1.1	10.8	23.6

High and Low temperatures in degrees Fahrenheit; Precipitation and Snow in inches

Population: 8,903 (2000); Race: 88.8% White, 1.5% Black, 0.3% Asian, 6.2% American Indian and Alaska Native, 0.8% Hispanic of any race, 2.4% two or more races (2000); Density: 7.6 persons per square mile (2000); Age: 22.9% under 18, 18.6% over 64 (2000).
Religion: Five largest groups: 22.0% Catholic Church, 8.6% Evangelical Lutheran Church in America, 3.8% American Baptist Churches in the USA, 1.8% The United Methodist Church, 1.6% National Association of Congregational Christian Churches (2000).
Economy: Unemployment rate: 6.6% (11/2002); Total civilian labor force: 4,213 (11/2002); Leading industries: 23.6% retail trade; 15.8% health care and social assistance; 13.7% manufacturing (2000); Companies that employ more than 1,000 persons: 0 (2000); Companies that employ more than 100 persons: 2 (2000); Farms: 45 totaling 15,742 acres (1997); Minority business ownership rate: 0.0% (1997); Women business ownership rate: 42.7% (1997); Retail sales per capita: $9,042 (1997). Single-family building permits issued: 66 (2001) / 59 (2000); Multi-family building permits issued: 0 (2001) / 0 (2000).
Income: Per capita income: $17,137 (2000); Median household income: $31,140 (2000); Poverty rate: 12.2% (2000); Bankruptcy rate: 2.95% (2001).
Taxes: Total county taxes per capita: $169 (1997); County property taxes per capita: $165 (1997).
Education: High school graduation rate: 79.4% (2000); College graduation rate: 11.3% (2000).
Housing: Homeownership rate: 81.8% (2000); Median home value: $64,900 (2000); Median rent: $299 per month (2000); Median age of housing: 37 years (2000).
Health: Birth rate: 100.0 per 10,000 population (1998); Age adjusted death rate: 96.6 per 10,000 population (1999); Age adjusted cancer mortality rate: 225.3 deaths per 100,000 population (1999). Number of physicians: 7.9 per 10,000 population (1999); Number of hospital beds: 28.1 per 10,000 population (1999).
Elections: 2000 Presidential election results: 48.5% Gore, 49.7% Bush, 1.3% Nader, 0.0% Buchanan
National and State Parks: Grand Sable State Forest; Indian Lake State Park; Palms Book State Park; Seney National Wildlife Refuge
Additional Information Contacts
Schoolcraft County Government Offices 906-341-5532
Manistique Chamber of Commerce 906-341-5010

Schoolcraft County Communities

COOKS (unincorporated postal area, zip code 49817). Covers a land area of 64.472 square miles and a water area of 0.134 square miles. Located at 45.92° N. Lat.; 86.45° W. Long.
Population: 572 (2000); Race: 88.1% White, 0.0% Black, 1.3% Asian, 6.6% American Indian and Alaska Native, 0.0% Hispanic of any race, 4.0% two or more races (2000); Density: 8.9 persons per square mile (2000); Age: 28.9% under 18, 16.4% over 64 (2000); Marriage status: 19.2% never married, 71.9% now married, 6.0% widowed, 2.9% divorced (2000); Foreign born: 1.3% (2000); Ancestry (includes multiple ancestries): 26.2% German, 17.2% French (except Basque), 14.4% Irish, 11.4% Other groups, 11.2% English (2000).
Economy: Employment by occupation: 7.4% management, 19.9% professional, 20.4% services, 17.6% sales, 3.7% farming, 19.4% construction, 11.6% production (2000).
Income: Per capita income: $13,899 (2000); Median household income: $29,219 (2000); Poverty rate: 12.8% (2000).
Education: High school graduation rate: 82.6% (2000); College graduation rate: 10.3% (2000).

School District(s)
Big Bay De Noc School District (KG-12)
2000 Enrollment: 360 906-644-2773
Housing: Homeownership rate: 90.5% (2000); Median home value: $68,200 (2000); Median rent: $231 per month (2000); Median age of housing: 30 years (2000).
Transportation: Commute to work: 82.5% car, 0.5% public transportation, 5.3% walk, 9.7% work from home (2000); Travel time to work: 18.3% less than 15 minutes, 64.0% 15 to 30 minutes, 6.5% 30 to 45 minutes, 2.2% 45 to 60 minutes, 9.1% 60 minutes or more (2000)

DOYLE (township). Covers a land area of 147.371 square miles and a water area of 6.661 square miles. Located at 46.11° N. Lat.; 86.03° W. Long.
Population: 630 (2000); Race: 92.2% White, 0.0% Black, 0.0% Asian, 5.3% American Indian and Alaska Native, 0.0% Hispanic of any race, 2.6% two or more races (2000); Density: 4.3 persons per square mile (2000); Age: 22.3% under 18, 16.4% over 64 (2000); Marriage status: 17.5% never married, 72.4% now married, 4.9% widowed, 5.2% divorced (2000); Foreign born: 1.1% (2000); Ancestry (includes multiple ancestries): 17.5% German, 15.7% English, 13.9% French (except Basque), 8.7% Irish, 8.0% French Canadian (2000).
Economy: Employment by occupation: 7.7% management, 17.9% professional, 19.7% services, 24.8% sales, 4.4% farming, 14.2% construction, 11.3% production (2000).
Income: Per capita income: $18,740 (2000); Median household income: $36,250 (2000); Poverty rate: 8.5% (2000).
Taxes: Total city taxes per capita: $42 (1997); City property taxes per capita: $42 (1997).
Education: High school graduation rate: 78.8% (2000); College graduation rate: 11.9% (2000).
Housing: Homeownership rate: 91.7% (2000); Median home value: $104,000 (2000); Median rent: $313 per month (2000); Median age of housing: 26 years (2000).
Transportation: Commute to work: 87.5% car, 0.7% public transportation, 3.0% walk, 8.9% work from home (2000); Travel time to work: 25.9% less than 15 minutes, 56.3% 15 to 30 minutes, 4.5% 30 to 45 minutes, 5.3% 45 to 60 minutes, 8.1% 60 minutes or more (2000)

GERMFASK (township). Covers a land area of 67.761 square miles and a water area of 3.886 square miles. Located at 46.24° N. Lat.; 85.93° W. Long. Elevation is 710 feet.
History: Germfask Township was settled in 1881. The name came from using the first letter of the names of the eight families who founded the town: John Grant, Matthew Edge, George Robinson, Thaddeus Mead, Dr. W.W. French, Ezekiel Ackley, Oscar Shepard, Hezekiah Knaggs.
Population: 491 (2000); Race: 94.4% White, 0.0% Black, 0.0% Asian, 5.4% American Indian and Alaska Native, 0.0% Hispanic of any race, 0.2% two or more races (2000); Density: 7.2 persons per square mile (2000); Age: 17.9% under 18, 23.3% over 64 (2000); Marriage status: 14.1% never married, 68.2% now married, 9.4% widowed, 8.2% divorced (2000); Foreign born: 0.0% (2000); Ancestry (includes multiple ancestries): 14.4% United States or American, 13.8% Irish, 13.5% German, 9.4% English, 8.3% Other groups (2000).

Economy: Employment by occupation: 8.4% management, 6.6% professional, 25.9% services, 15.1% sales, 3.6% farming, 16.9% construction, 23.5% production (2000).
Income: Per capita income: $14,648 (2000); Median household income: $27,625 (2000); Poverty rate: 11.3% (2000).
Taxes: Total city taxes per capita: $62 (1997); City property taxes per capita: $60 (1997).
Education: High school graduation rate: 68.7% (2000); College graduation rate: 3.9% (2000).
Housing: Homeownership rate: 93.0% (2000); Median home value: $52,500 (2000); Median rent: $235 per month (2000); Median age of housing: 33 years (2000).
Transportation: Commute to work: 89.4% car, 0.0% public transportation, 5.0% walk, 4.3% work from home (2000); Travel time to work: 29.9% less than 15 minutes, 16.9% 15 to 30 minutes, 24.0% 30 to 45 minutes, 13.0% 45 to 60 minutes, 16.2% 60 minutes or more (2000)

GULLIVER (unincorporated postal area, zip code 49840). Covers a land area of 112.709 square miles and a water area of 5.223 square miles. Located at 46.00° N. Lat.; 85.99° W. Long.
Population: 843 (2000); Race: 91.3% White, 0.0% Black, 0.0% Asian, 6.1% American Indian and Alaska Native, 1.7% Hispanic of any race, 2.7% two or more races (2000); Density: 7.5 persons per square mile (2000); Age: 21.2% under 18, 18.2% over 64 (2000); Marriage status: 17.1% never married, 72.3% now married, 4.8% widowed, 5.8% divorced (2000); Foreign born: 0.2% (2000); Ancestry (includes multiple ancestries): 19.7% German, 12.1% English, 12.0% French (except Basque), 8.8% Other groups, 8.3% Irish (2000).
Economy: Employment by occupation: 7.7% management, 15.4% professional, 21.4% services, 23.4% sales, 5.7% farming, 15.1% construction, 11.1% production (2000).
Income: Per capita income: $18,945 (2000); Median household income: $34,844 (2000); Poverty rate: 8.1% (2000).
Education: High school graduation rate: 76.1% (2000); College graduation rate: 10.1% (2000).
Housing: Homeownership rate: 92.3% (2000); Median home value: $87,200 (2000); Median rent: $285 per month (2000); Median age of housing: 30 years (2000).
Transportation: Commute to work: 88.4% car, 0.6% public transportation, 2.3% walk, 7.0% work from home (2000); Travel time to work: 25.0% less than 15 minutes, 52.8% 15 to 30 minutes, 7.5% 30 to 45 minutes, 4.1% 45 to 60 minutes, 10.6% 60 minutes or more (2000)

HIAWATHA (township). Covers a land area of 278.457 square miles and a water area of 12.282 square miles. Located at 46.23° N. Lat.; 86.32° W. Long.
Population: 1,328 (2000); Race: 93.0% White, 0.2% Black, 0.0% Asian, 5.0% American Indian and Alaska Native, 0.6% Hispanic of any race, 1.7% two or more races (2000); Density: 4.8 persons per square mile (2000); Age: 22.4% under 18, 17.6% over 64 (2000); Marriage status: 18.3% never married, 66.1% now married, 8.7% widowed, 6.9% divorced (2000); Foreign born: 1.0% (2000); Ancestry (includes multiple ancestries): 20.3% German, 15.8% French (except Basque), 15.5% Swedish, 12.8% English, 9.5% Other groups (2000).
Economy: Employment by occupation: 11.4% management, 19.7% professional, 18.8% services, 21.2% sales, 3.5% farming, 13.1% construction, 12.2% production (2000).
Income: Per capita income: $20,385 (2000); Median household income: $40,156 (2000); Poverty rate: 6.0% (2000).
Education: High school graduation rate: 86.8% (2000); College graduation rate: 16.8% (2000).
Housing: Homeownership rate: 93.2% (2000); Median home value: $95,200 (2000); Median rent: $307 per month (2000); Median age of housing: 31 years (2000).
Transportation: Commute to work: 94.2% car, 0.7% public transportation, 1.7% walk, 2.4% work from home (2000); Travel time to work: 55.3% less than 15 minutes, 26.3% 15 to 30 minutes, 7.1% 30 to 45 minutes, 4.8% 45 to 60 minutes, 6.5% 60 minutes or more (2000)

INWOOD (township). Covers a land area of 120.300 square miles and a water area of 6.242 square miles. Located at 46.10° N. Lat.; 86.48° W. Long.
Population: 722 (2000); Race: 90.4% White, 0.0% Black, 1.0% Asian, 5.2% American Indian and Alaska Native, 1.3% Hispanic of any race, 2.7% two or more races (2000); Density: 6.0 persons per square mile (2000); Age: 26.1% under 18, 17.5% over 64 (2000); Marriage status: 15.6% never married, 75.7% now married, 5.6% widowed, 3.2% divorced (2000); Foreign born: 1.0% (2000); Ancestry (includes multiple ancestries): 27.2% German, 15.1% French (except Basque), 12.6% Irish, 10.8% Other groups, 10.0% English (2000).
Economy: Employment by occupation: 8.2% management, 19.1% professional, 22.1% services, 19.1% sales, 3.7% farming, 16.9% construction, 10.9% production (2000).
Income: Per capita income: $15,386 (2000); Median household income: $32,500 (2000); Poverty rate: 11.8% (2000).
Taxes: Total city taxes per capita: $44 (1997); City property taxes per capita: $44 (1997).
Education: High school graduation rate: 83.6% (2000); College graduation rate: 13.5% (2000).
Housing: Homeownership rate: 89.6% (2000); Median home value: $80,900 (2000); Median rent: $231 per month (2000); Median age of housing: 35 years (2000).
Transportation: Commute to work: 82.6% car, 0.4% public transportation, 5.1% walk, 10.7% work from home (2000); Travel time to work: 15.9% less than 15 minutes, 57.1% 15 to 30 minutes, 11.9% 30 to 45 minutes, 2.2% 45 to 60 minutes, 12.8% 60 minutes or more (2000)

MANISTIQUE (city). Covers a land area of 3.188 square miles and a water area of 0.316 square miles. Located at 45.95° N. Lat.; 86.25° W. Long. Elevation is 613 feet.
History: Manistique began as a lumber town in 1860 and became one of the largest operations on the Upper Peninsula. Around 1900 the supply of pine was gone, and a tannery, chemical factory, lime kilns, and iron furnaces replaced the lumber industry. These were eventually replaced by papermaking, hardwood manufacture, shipping, and commercial fishing.
Population: 3,583 (2000); Race: 86.7% White, 3.6% Black, 0.2% Asian, 5.7% American Indian and Alaska Native, 1.1% Hispanic of any race, 2.7% two or more races (2000); Density: 1,124.0 persons per square mile (2000); Age: 23.4% under 18, 20.2% over 64 (2000); Marriage status: 25.1% never married, 49.4% now married, 10.4% widowed, 15.1% divorced (2000); Foreign born: 0.7% (2000); Ancestry (includes multiple ancestries): 21.7% German, 12.4% Swedish, 12.4% French (except Basque), 11.3% Irish, 10.5% Other groups (2000).
Economy: Employment by occupation: 7.2% management, 14.1% professional, 26.8% services, 20.7% sales, 0.9% farming, 13.3% construction, 17.0% production (2000).
Income: Per capita income: $14,986 (2000); Median household income: $24,295 (2000); Poverty rate: 15.7% (2000).
Taxes: Total city taxes per capita: $454 (2000); City property taxes per capita: $454 (2000).
Education: High school graduation rate: 79.3% (2000); College graduation rate: 7.7% (2000).

School District(s)

Manistique Area Schools (PK-12)
2000 Enrollment: 1,179 906-341-4300

Housing: Homeownership rate: 67.6% (2000); Median home value: $46,500 (2000); Median rent: $303 per month (2000); Median age of housing: 58 years (2000).
Hospitals: Schoolcraft Memorial Hospital (38 beds)
Newspapers: Pioneer-Tribune (1 x week)
Transportation: Commute to work: 86.8% car, 1.6% public transportation, 6.9% walk, 4.6% work from home (2000); Travel time to work: 72.2% less than 15 minutes, 16.1% 15 to 30 minutes, 2.9% 30 to 45 minutes, 2.4% 45 to 60 minutes, 6.4% 60 minutes or more (2000)
Additional Information Contacts
Manistique Chamber of Commerce 906-341-5010

MANISTIQUE (township). Covers a land area of 150.283 square miles and a water area of 3.371 square miles. Located at 46.06° N. Lat.; 86.17° W. Long. Elevation is 613 feet.
History: Incorporated as village 1885, as city 1901.
Population: 1,053 (2000); Race: 84.7% White, 0.0% Black, 0.7% Asian, 11.1% American Indian and Alaska Native, 0.0% Hispanic of any race, 2.8% two or more races (2000); Density: 7.0 persons per square mile (2000); Age: 27.3% under 18, 11.2% over 64 (2000); Marriage status: 19.7% never married, 65.0% now married, 6.0% widowed, 9.3% divorced (2000); Foreign born: 2.9% (2000); Ancestry (includes multiple ancestries): 23.0% German, 14.0% Other groups, 10.9% French (except Basque), 10.5% English, 8.8% Irish (2000).
Economy: Manufacturing of wood products, paper and building materials. Resort, industrial and shipping center. Lumber and paper milling, processing of hardwood products. Limestone quarrying nearby. Thunder Bowl Ski Area in northwest. Employment by occupation: 12.2% management, 16.2%

professional, 20.1% services, 16.4% sales, 2.3% farming, 14.8% construction, 18.0% production (2000).
Income: Per capita income: $18,127 (2000); Median household income: $40,000 (2000); Poverty rate: 12.5% (2000).
Taxes: Total city taxes per capita: $47 (1997); City property taxes per capita: $41 (1997).
Education: High school graduation rate: 78.8% (2000); College graduation rate: 15.7% (2000).
Housing: Homeownership rate: 86.3% (2000); Median home value: $84,800 (2000); Median rent: $313 per month (2000); Median age of housing: 23 years (2000).
Transportation: Commute to work: 91.8% car, 0.0% public transportation, 3.4% walk, 4.3% work from home (2000); Travel time to work: 54.0% less than 15 minutes, 34.4% 15 to 30 minutes, 3.5% 30 to 45 minutes, 1.0% 45 to 60 minutes, 7.0% 60 minutes or more (2000)

MUELLER (township). Covers a land area of 83.890 square miles and a water area of 4.081 square miles. Located at 46.05° N. Lat.; 85.92° W. Long.
Population: 245 (2000); Race: 89.4% White, 0.0% Black, 0.0% Asian, 7.8% American Indian and Alaska Native, 6.9% Hispanic of any race, 2.8% two or more races (2000); Density: 2.9 persons per square mile (2000); Age: 16.1% under 18, 29.8% over 64 (2000); Marriage status: 9.4% never married, 79.1% now married, 3.7% widowed, 7.9% divorced (2000); Foreign born: 0.0% (2000); Ancestry (includes multiple ancestries): 21.6% German, 13.3% Polish, 11.9% Other groups, 11.9% English, 10.6% Irish (2000).
Economy: Employment by occupation: 7.8% management, 9.1% professional, 27.3% services, 24.7% sales, 9.1% farming, 11.7% construction, 10.4% production (2000).
Income: Per capita income: $18,507 (2000); Median household income: $33,571 (2000); Poverty rate: 6.0% (2000).
Taxes: Total city taxes per capita: $290 (1997); City property taxes per capita: $290 (1997).
Education: High school graduation rate: 69.8% (2000); College graduation rate: 8.4% (2000).
Housing: Homeownership rate: 92.7% (2000); Median home value: $70,000 (2000); Median rent: $192 per month (2000); Median age of housing: 34 years (2000).
Transportation: Commute to work: 91.9% car, 0.0% public transportation, 0.0% walk, 0.0% work from home (2000); Travel time to work: 24.3% less than 15 minutes, 36.5% 15 to 30 minutes, 17.6% 30 to 45 minutes, 2.7% 45 to 60 minutes, 18.9% 60 minutes or more (2000)

SENEY (township). Covers a land area of 213.914 square miles and a water area of 1.716 square miles. Located at 46.42° N. Lat.; 86.01° W. Long. Elevation is 730 feet.
History: Seney was named for George R. Seney, a railroad director. The township was organized about 1882 around the logging activities of the Alger, Smith Company. Tales of corruption and abuse in Seney made newspaper headlines in the 1880's.
Population: 180 (2000); Race: 96.8% White, 0.0% Black, 0.0% Asian, 0.0% American Indian and Alaska Native, 1.3% Hispanic of any race, 1.9% two or more races (2000); Density: 0.8 persons per square mile (2000); Age: 22.4% under 18, 14.1% over 64 (2000); Marriage status: 13.7% never married, 71.0% now married, 5.6% widowed, 9.7% divorced (2000); Foreign born: 1.3% (2000); Ancestry (includes multiple ancestries): 22.4% German, 17.3% English, 9.6% Irish, 6.4% Polish, 5.8% Dutch (2000).
Economy: Employment by occupation: 14.6% management, 12.2% professional, 29.3% services, 29.3% sales, 0.0% farming, 0.0% construction, 14.6% production (2000).
Income: Per capita income: $10,855 (2000); Median household income: $30,625 (2000); Poverty rate: 33.1% (2000).
Taxes: Total city taxes per capita: $106 (2000); City property taxes per capita: $106 (2000).
Education: High school graduation rate: 59.5% (2000); College graduation rate: 12.9% (2000).
Housing: Homeownership rate: 91.5% (2000); Median home value: $45,000 (2000); Median rent: $250 per month (2000); Median age of housing: 19 years (2000).
Transportation: Commute to work: 51.2% car, 0.0% public transportation, 12.2% walk, 26.8% work from home (2000); Travel time to work: 66.7% less than 15 minutes, 33.3% 15 to 30 minutes, 0.0% 30 to 45 minutes, 0.0% 45 to 60 minutes, 0.0% 60 minutes or more (2000)

THOMPSON (township). Covers a land area of 112.946 square miles and a water area of 5.428 square miles. Located at 45.97° N. Lat.; 86.36° W. Long. Elevation is 597 feet.
History: Thompson Township was named for E.L. Thompson of Detroit, president of the Delta Lumber Company which had a mill here. The village of Thompson was first settled by fishermen.
Population: 671 (2000); Race: 87.3% White, 0.9% Black, 0.3% Asian, 8.0% American Indian and Alaska Native, 0.0% Hispanic of any race, 3.1% two or more races (2000); Density: 5.9 persons per square mile (2000); Age: 16.9% under 18, 20.4% over 64 (2000); Marriage status: 13.3% never married, 73.1% now married, 4.3% widowed, 9.3% divorced (2000); Foreign born: 1.2% (2000); Ancestry (includes multiple ancestries): 21.0% German, 13.2% French (except Basque), 13.1% English, 11.5% Other groups, 9.7% Irish (2000).
Economy: Employment by occupation: 13.4% management, 7.5% professional, 20.1% services, 20.5% sales, 2.8% farming, 16.9% construction, 18.9% production (2000).
Income: Per capita income: $24,045 (2000); Median household income: $38,750 (2000); Poverty rate: 8.8% (2000).
Taxes: Total city taxes per capita: $70 (1997); City property taxes per capita: $70 (1997).
Education: High school graduation rate: 78.4% (2000); College graduation rate: 15.8% (2000).
Housing: Homeownership rate: 94.0% (2000); Median home value: $103,900 (2000); Median rent: $300 per month (2000); Median age of housing: 35 years (2000).
Transportation: Commute to work: 87.1% car, 0.0% public transportation, 5.2% walk, 4.4% work from home (2000); Travel time to work: 42.6% less than 15 minutes, 32.1% 15 to 30 minutes, 7.6% 30 to 45 minutes, 3.4% 45 to 60 minutes, 14.3% 60 minutes or more (2000)

Shiawassee County

Located in south central Michigan; drained by the Shiawassee, Maple, and Lookingglass Rivers. Covers a land area of 538.70 square miles, a water area of 2.00 square miles, and is located in the Eastern Time Zone. The county government was organized in 1822. County seat is Corunna.
Population: 71,687 (2000); Race: 97.3% White, 0.2% Black, 0.2% Asian, 0.5% American Indian and Alaska Native, 1.8% Hispanic of any race, 1.4% two or more races (2000); Density: 133.1 persons per square mile (2000); Age: 26.8% under 18, 12.0% over 64 (2000).
Religion: Five largest groups: 18.7% Catholic Church, 4.1% The United Methodist Church, 2.6% Wisconsin Evangelical Lutheran Synod, 2.0% Church of the Nazarene, 1.5% The Wesleyan Church (2000).
Economy: Unemployment rate: 5.3% (11/2002); Total civilian labor force: 36,209 (11/2002); Leading industries: 24.4% manufacturing; 18.3% retail trade; 15.4% health care and social assistance (2000); Companies that employ more than 1,000 persons: 1 (2000); Companies that employ more than 100 persons: 24 (2000); Farms: 915 totaling 214,153 acres (1997); Minority business ownership rate: 3.4% (1997); Women business ownership rate: 27.3% (1997); Retail sales per capita: $7,902 (1997). Single-family building permits issued: 266 (2001) / 281 (2000); Multi-family building permits issued: 18 (2001) / 61 (2000).
Income: Per capita income: $19,229 (2000); Median household income: $42,553 (2000); Poverty rate: 7.8% (2000); Bankruptcy rate: 5.37% (2001).
Taxes: Total county taxes per capita: $115 (2000); County property taxes per capita: $110 (2000).
Education: High school graduation rate: 84.4% (2000); College graduation rate: 13.7% (2000).
Housing: Homeownership rate: 80.1% (2000); Median home value: $95,900 (2000); Median rent: $409 per month (2000); Median age of housing: 37 years (2000).
Health: Birth rate: 133.6 per 10,000 population (1998); Age adjusted death rate: 87.5 per 10,000 population (1999); Age adjusted cancer mortality rate: 235.5 deaths per 100,000 population (1999). Number of physicians: 7.3 per 10,000 population (1999); Number of hospital beds: 18.3 per 10,000 population (1999).
Elections: 2000 Presidential election results: 48.2% Gore, 49.1% Bush, 2.0% Nader, 0.1% Buchanan
Additional Information Contacts
Shiawassee County Government Offices 989-743-2222
Durand Chamber of Commerce 989-288-3715
Owosso Chamber of Commerce 989-723-5149
Perry/Morrice Area Chamber of Commerce 517-625-8122
Shiawassee Regional Board of Realtors 989-723-4672

Shiawassee County Communities

ANTRIM (township). Covers a land area of 36.517 square miles and a water area of 0.249 square miles. Located at 42.83° N. Lat.; 84.09° W. Long.
Population: 2,050 (2000); Race: 97.0% White, 0.0% Black, 1.0% Asian, 0.0% American Indian and Alaska Native, 1.3% Hispanic of any race, 1.4% two or more races (2000); Density: 56.1 persons per square mile (2000); Age: 27.6% under 18, 9.6% over 64 (2000); Marriage status: 22.6% never married, 65.9% now married, 4.7% widowed, 6.8% divorced (2000); Foreign born: 1.9% (2000); Ancestry (includes multiple ancestries): 25.2% German, 17.9% English, 14.5% Irish, 9.3% Other groups, 9.1% United States or American (2000).
Economy: Employment by occupation: 7.7% management, 10.5% professional, 13.7% services, 26.2% sales, 1.7% farming, 18.6% construction, 21.6% production (2000).
Income: Per capita income: $20,806 (2000); Median household income: $53,092 (2000); Poverty rate: 4.6% (2000).
Taxes: Total city taxes per capita: $43 (1997); City property taxes per capita: $43 (1997).
Education: High school graduation rate: 88.6% (2000); College graduation rate: 11.1% (2000).
Housing: Homeownership rate: 94.5% (2000); Median home value: $117,000 (2000); Median rent: $442 per month (2000); Median age of housing: 26 years (2000).
Transportation: Commute to work: 95.2% car, 0.0% public transportation, 0.7% walk, 3.7% work from home (2000); Travel time to work: 12.3% less than 15 minutes, 25.8% 15 to 30 minutes, 32.5% 30 to 45 minutes, 15.4% 45 to 60 minutes, 14.0% 60 minutes or more (2000)

BANCROFT (village). Covers a land area of 0.587 square miles and a water area of 0 square miles. Located at 42.87° N. Lat.; 84.06° W. Long. Elevation is 854 feet.
History: Bancroft became a station on the Chicago & Lake Huron Railroad in 1877. It was incorporated as a village in 1883.
Population: 616 (2000); Race: 96.7% White, 0.0% Black, 0.0% Asian, 0.6% American Indian and Alaska Native, 0.0% Hispanic of any race, 2.3% two or more races (2000); Density: 1,049.4 persons per square mile (2000); Age: 31.9% under 18, 9.2% over 64 (2000); Marriage status: 26.0% never married, 57.7% now married, 4.4% widowed, 11.9% divorced (2000); Foreign born: 0.3% (2000); Ancestry (includes multiple ancestries): 23.1% German, 18.8% English, 11.1% Irish, 7.3% French (except Basque), 7.2% United States or American (2000).
Economy: Employment by occupation: 3.7% management, 6.7% professional, 18.1% services, 18.9% sales, 0.0% farming, 11.9% construction, 40.7% production (2000).
Income: Per capita income: $15,451 (2000); Median household income: $41,538 (2000); Poverty rate: 10.3% (2000).
Taxes: Total city taxes per capita: $89 (1997); City property taxes per capita: $85 (1997).
Education: High school graduation rate: 77.3% (2000); College graduation rate: 4.5% (2000).
Housing: Homeownership rate: 83.8% (2000); Median home value: $82,400 (2000); Median rent: $400 per month (2000); Median age of housing: 60+ years (2000).
Transportation: Commute to work: 96.2% car, 0.0% public transportation, 2.7% walk, 1.1% work from home (2000); Travel time to work: 18.6% less than 15 minutes, 24.0% 15 to 30 minutes, 37.6% 30 to 45 minutes, 10.1% 45 to 60 minutes, 9.7% 60 minutes or more (2000)

BENNINGTON (township). Covers a land area of 36.473 square miles and a water area of 0.317 square miles. Located at 42.91° N. Lat.; 84.21° W. Long. Elevation is 792 feet.
History: Bennington Township was organized in 1838 and named for Bennington, Vermont, the former home of some of the first settlers.
Population: 3,017 (2000); Race: 97.5% White, 0.0% Black, 0.0% Asian, 0.1% American Indian and Alaska Native, 3.0% Hispanic of any race, 1.6% two or more races (2000); Density: 82.7 persons per square mile (2000); Age: 25.8% under 18, 10.2% over 64 (2000); Marriage status: 17.2% never married, 73.8% now married, 3.8% widowed, 5.2% divorced (2000); Foreign born: 1.3% (2000); Ancestry (includes multiple ancestries): 29.9% German, 17.6% English, 14.6% Irish, 10.7% United States or American, 6.6% Other groups (2000).
Economy: Employment by occupation: 12.7% management, 18.8% professional, 10.7% services, 21.9% sales, 0.6% farming, 14.4% construction, 20.8% production (2000).
Income: Per capita income: $21,841 (2000); Median household income: $54,786 (2000); Poverty rate: 3.1% (2000).
Taxes: Total city taxes per capita: $31 (1997); City property taxes per capita: $30 (1997).
Education: High school graduation rate: 89.2% (2000); College graduation rate: 18.5% (2000).
Housing: Homeownership rate: 95.1% (2000); Median home value: $124,200 (2000); Median rent: $553 per month (2000); Median age of housing: 29 years (2000).
Transportation: Commute to work: 95.7% car, 0.0% public transportation, 0.7% walk, 2.5% work from home (2000); Travel time to work: 22.1% less than 15 minutes, 27.2% 15 to 30 minutes, 28.3% 30 to 45 minutes, 13.8% 45 to 60 minutes, 8.6% 60 minutes or more (2000)

BURNS (township). Covers a land area of 35.485 square miles and a water area of 0.220 square miles. Located at 42.82° N. Lat.; 83.98° W. Long.
Population: 3,500 (2000); Race: 97.6% White, 0.0% Black, 0.0% Asian, 0.3% American Indian and Alaska Native, 2.2% Hispanic of any race, 1.6% two or more races (2000); Density: 98.6 persons per square mile (2000); Age: 29.4% under 18, 9.2% over 64 (2000); Marriage status: 20.2% never married, 68.7% now married, 4.7% widowed, 6.4% divorced (2000); Foreign born: 1.1% (2000); Ancestry (includes multiple ancestries): 20.2% German, 19.6% English, 15.5% United States or American, 11.6% Irish, 6.6% Other groups (2000).
Economy: Employment by occupation: 9.1% management, 15.1% professional, 11.2% services, 16.2% sales, 0.4% farming, 14.1% construction, 33.8% production (2000).
Income: Per capita income: $19,622 (2000); Median household income: $49,671 (2000); Poverty rate: 5.5% (2000).
Taxes: Total city taxes per capita: $29 (1997); City property taxes per capita: $28 (1997).
Education: High school graduation rate: 89.0% (2000); College graduation rate: 13.2% (2000).
Housing: Homeownership rate: 90.1% (2000); Median home value: $119,300 (2000); Median rent: $358 per month (2000); Median age of housing: 27 years (2000).
Transportation: Commute to work: 93.0% car, 0.0% public transportation, 0.9% walk, 5.9% work from home (2000); Travel time to work: 12.4% less than 15 minutes, 31.1% 15 to 30 minutes, 32.8% 30 to 45 minutes, 8.9% 45 to 60 minutes, 14.9% 60 minutes or more (2000)

BYRON (village). Covers a land area of 0.738 square miles and a water area of 0.019 square miles. Located at 42.82° N. Lat.; 83.94° W. Long. Elevation is 848 feet.
History: The village of Byron was founded by Judge Samuel W. Dexter in 1824, and was incorporated in 1873.
Population: 595 (2000); Race: 95.1% White, 0.0% Black, 0.0% Asian, 0.3% American Indian and Alaska Native, 4.4% Hispanic of any race, 4.5% two or more races (2000); Density: 806.2 persons per square mile (2000); Age: 32.6% under 18, 9.4% over 64 (2000); Marriage status: 27.5% never married, 59.3% now married, 6.4% widowed, 6.8% divorced (2000); Foreign born: 1.8% (2000); Ancestry (includes multiple ancestries): 21.1% German, 10.9% Other groups, 9.7% United States or American, 9.6% English, 7.6% Irish (2000).
Economy: Single-family building permits issued: 0 (2001) / 1 (2000); Multi-family building permits issued: 0 (2001) / 0 (2000); Employment by occupation: 10.9% management, 6.2% professional, 16.7% services, 17.8% sales, 1.6% farming, 22.5% construction, 24.4% production (2000).
Income: Per capita income: $17,137 (2000); Median household income: $39,167 (2000); Poverty rate: 6.7% (2000).
Taxes: Total city taxes per capita: $133 (1997); City property taxes per capita: $126 (1997).
Education: High school graduation rate: 86.0% (2000); College graduation rate: 7.6% (2000).

School District(s)

Byron Area Schools (KG-12)
2000 Enrollment: 1,270 810-266-4881

Housing: Homeownership rate: 69.2% (2000); Median home value: $98,300 (2000); Median rent: $364 per month (2000); Median age of housing: 60 years (2000).
Transportation: Commute to work: 94.5% car, 0.0% public transportation, 0.4% walk, 3.9% work from home (2000); Travel time to work: 10.6% less than 15 minutes, 31.0% 15 to 30 minutes, 31.8% 30 to 45 minutes, 9.0% 45 to 60 minutes, 17.6% 60 minutes or more (2000)

CALEDONIA (township). Covers a land area of 31.662 square miles and a water area of 0.123 square miles. Located at 42.99° N. Lat.; 84.12° W. Long.
Population: 4,427 (2000); Race: 97.8% White, 0.2% Black, 0.1% Asian, 0.0% American Indian and Alaska Native, 1.8% Hispanic of any race, 1.4% two or more races (2000); Density: 139.8 persons per square mile (2000); Age: 23.2% under 18, 13.9% over 64 (2000); Marriage status: 19.3% never married, 66.6% now married, 5.6% widowed, 8.5% divorced (2000); Foreign born: 1.5% (2000); Ancestry (includes multiple ancestries): 27.0% German, 12.9% English, 12.8% Irish, 10.2% United States or American, 8.0% Other groups (2000).
Economy: Single-family building permits issued: 22 (2001) / 18 (2000); Multi-family building permits issued: 0 (2001) / 2 (2000); Employment by occupation: 8.7% management, 13.8% professional, 16.2% services, 23.2% sales, 0.0% farming, 10.5% construction, 27.5% production (2000).
Income: Per capita income: $19,385 (2000); Median household income: $42,139 (2000); Poverty rate: 5.7% (2000).
Taxes: Total city taxes per capita: $23 (1997); City property taxes per capita: $18 (1997).
Education: High school graduation rate: 82.3% (2000); College graduation rate: 10.4% (2000).
Housing: Homeownership rate: 86.4% (2000); Median home value: $99,300 (2000); Median rent: $354 per month (2000); Median age of housing: 38 years (2000).
Transportation: Commute to work: 94.6% car, 0.2% public transportation, 1.4% walk, 3.6% work from home (2000); Travel time to work: 44.8% less than 15 minutes, 20.5% 15 to 30 minutes, 14.4% 30 to 45 minutes, 10.2% 45 to 60 minutes, 10.1% 60 minutes or more (2000)

CORUNNA (city). Covers a land area of 3.088 square miles and a water area of 0.044 square miles. Located at 42.98° N. Lat.; 84.11° W. Long. Elevation is 757 feet.
History: Corunna was settled in 1836 around a flour mill, and platted by the Shiawassee County Seat Company in 1837. Industries in the early 1900's included a furniture factory, cigar factory, and some active coal mines.
Population: 3,381 (2000); Race: 95.4% White, 1.5% Black, 0.1% Asian, 1.2% American Indian and Alaska Native, 1.8% Hispanic of any race, 1.5% two or more races (2000); Density: 1,095.0 persons per square mile (2000); Age: 23.6% under 18, 15.0% over 64 (2000); Marriage status: 24.6% never married, 52.9% now married, 7.1% widowed, 15.4% divorced (2000); Foreign born: 2.5% (2000); Ancestry (includes multiple ancestries): 22.2% German, 11.5% English, 9.9% United States or American, 9.8% Irish, 9.7% Other groups (2000).
Economy: Single-family building permits issued: 0 (2001) / 5 (2000); Multi-family building permits issued: 0 (2001) / 23 (2000); Employment by occupation: 9.2% management, 14.7% professional, 15.1% services, 26.6% sales, 0.4% farming, 10.0% construction, 24.0% production (2000).
Income: Per capita income: $17,053 (2000); Median household income: $29,831 (2000); Poverty rate: 12.0% (2000).
Taxes: Total city taxes per capita: $240 (1997); City property taxes per capita: $228 (1997).
Education: High school graduation rate: 75.7% (2000); College graduation rate: 11.3% (2000).

School District(s)

Corunna Public School District (KG-12)
2000 Enrollment: 2,126 517-743-6338
Housing: Homeownership rate: 49.8% (2000); Median home value: $84,800 (2000); Median rent: $464 per month (2000); Median age of housing: 36 years (2000).
Safety: Violent crime rate: 11.8 per 10,000 population; Property crime rate: 250.1 per 10,000 population (2001).
Transportation: Commute to work: 94.9% car, 0.0% public transportation, 2.0% walk, 1.5% work from home (2000); Travel time to work: 49.4% less than 15 minutes, 19.9% 15 to 30 minutes, 15.4% 30 to 45 minutes, 6.8% 45 to 60 minutes, 8.6% 60 minutes or more (2000)

DURAND (city). Covers a land area of 1.967 square miles and a water area of 0 square miles. Located at 42.91° N. Lat.; 83.98° W. Long. Elevation is 796 feet.
History: Incorporated as village 1887, as city 1933.
Population: 3,933 (2000); Race: 98.5% White, 0.2% Black, 0.0% Asian, 0.0% American Indian and Alaska Native, 1.0% Hispanic of any race, 1.0% two or more races (2000); Density: 1,999.6 persons per square mile (2000); Age: 25.9% under 18, 16.1% over 64 (2000); Marriage status: 21.6% never married, 53.8% now married, 12.0% widowed, 12.7% divorced (2000); Foreign born: 0.9% (2000); Ancestry (includes multiple ancestries): 21.6% German, 18.0% English, 16.0% United States or American, 12.4% Irish, 6.7% French (except Basque) (2000).
Economy: Railroad junction in farm area: beans, corn, wheat, soybeans; light manufacturing. Employment by occupation: 11.1% management, 14.6% professional, 13.1% services, 20.6% sales, 0.6% farming, 8.6% construction, 31.3% production (2000).
Income: Per capita income: $17,273 (2000); Median household income: $36,563 (2000); Poverty rate: 11.3% (2000).
Taxes: Total city taxes per capita: $262 (1997); City property taxes per capita: $255 (1997).
Education: High school graduation rate: 85.9% (2000); College graduation rate: 13.7% (2000).

School District(s)

Durand Area Schools (PK-12)
2000 Enrollment: 2,089 517-288-2681
Housing: Homeownership rate: 66.8% (2000); Median home value: $82,300 (2000); Median rent: $400 per month (2000); Median age of housing: 51 years (2000).
Safety: Violent crime rate: 35.4 per 10,000 population; Property crime rate: 237.7 per 10,000 population (2001).
Newspapers: The Express (1 x week)
Transportation: Commute to work: 93.5% car, 0.0% public transportation, 4.3% walk, 1.8% work from home (2000); Travel time to work: 30.7% less than 15 minutes, 20.4% 15 to 30 minutes, 24.7% 30 to 45 minutes, 13.8% 45 to 60 minutes, 10.4% 60 minutes or more (2000); Amtrak: Service available.
Additional Information Contacts
Durand Chamber of Commerce 989-288-3715

FAIRFIELD (township). Covers a land area of 25.105 square miles and a water area of 0.004 square miles. Located at 43.07° N. Lat.; 84.33° W. Long.
Population: 745 (2000); Race: 99.2% White, 0.0% Black, 0.0% Asian, 0.5% American Indian and Alaska Native, 1.8% Hispanic of any race, 0.0% two or more races (2000); Density: 29.7 persons per square mile (2000); Age: 28.4% under 18, 14.1% over 64 (2000); Marriage status: 21.3% never married, 63.2% now married, 7.3% widowed, 8.2% divorced (2000); Foreign born: 1.3% (2000); Ancestry (includes multiple ancestries): 27.5% German, 16.5% English, 15.2% United States or American, 9.6% Irish, 5.6% Other groups (2000).
Economy: Employment by occupation: 10.7% management, 9.6% professional, 15.3% services, 13.6% sales, 3.7% farming, 11.6% construction, 35.6% production (2000).
Income: Per capita income: $16,327 (2000); Median household income: $42,188 (2000); Poverty rate: 10.2% (2000).
Taxes: Total city taxes per capita: $58 (1997); City property taxes per capita: $58 (1997).
Education: High school graduation rate: 82.7% (2000); College graduation rate: 7.0% (2000).
Housing: Homeownership rate: 85.9% (2000); Median home value: $79,600 (2000); Median rent: $458 per month (2000); Median age of housing: 56 years (2000).
Transportation: Commute to work: 90.6% car, 0.0% public transportation, 2.8% walk, 6.5% work from home (2000); Travel time to work: 25.2% less than 15 minutes, 35.0% 15 to 30 minutes, 20.4% 30 to 45 minutes, 14.9% 45 to 60 minutes, 4.6% 60 minutes or more (2000)

HAZELTON (township). Covers a land area of 37.268 square miles and a water area of 0.026 square miles. Located at 43.09° N. Lat.; 83.98° W. Long.
Population: 2,206 (2000); Race: 98.4% White, 0.0% Black, 0.0% Asian, 0.6% American Indian and Alaska Native, 0.2% Hispanic of any race, 0.9% two or more races (2000); Density: 59.2 persons per square mile (2000); Age: 25.1% under 18, 11.9% over 64 (2000); Marriage status: 21.6% never married, 66.6% now married, 4.3% widowed, 7.5% divorced (2000); Foreign born: 0.9% (2000); Ancestry (includes multiple ancestries): 32.6% German, 13.9% Irish, 12.1% English, 6.3% United States or American, 5.4% French (except Basque) (2000).
Economy: Employment by occupation: 12.1% management, 13.8% professional, 11.3% services, 25.6% sales, 0.9% farming, 10.9% construction, 25.5% production (2000).
Income: Per capita income: $21,960 (2000); Median household income: $47,358 (2000); Poverty rate: 5.5% (2000).
Taxes: Total city taxes per capita: $41 (1997); City property taxes per capita: $41 (1997).
Education: High school graduation rate: 89.4% (2000); College graduation rate: 12.9% (2000).

Housing: Homeownership rate: 85.0% (2000); Median home value: $98,100 (2000); Median rent: $336 per month (2000); Median age of housing: 39 years (2000).
Transportation: Commute to work: 90.8% car, 0.0% public transportation, 1.2% walk, 7.3% work from home (2000); Travel time to work: 15.4% less than 15 minutes, 35.1% 15 to 30 minutes, 33.3% 30 to 45 minutes, 10.1% 45 to 60 minutes, 6.1% 60 minutes or more (2000)

HENDERSON (unincorporated postal area, zip code 48841). Covers a land area of 23.460 square miles and a water area of 0.012 square miles. Located at 43.10° N. Lat.; 84.23° W. Long.
History: Henderson grew up around a store operated in 1868 by John Henderson. The village was platted in 1879.
Population: 860 (2000); Race: 97.8% White, 0.0% Black, 0.0% Asian, 1.6% American Indian and Alaska Native, 1.4% Hispanic of any race, 0.3% two or more races (2000); Density: 36.7 persons per square mile (2000); Age: 29.0% under 18, 12.7% over 64 (2000); Marriage status: 21.6% never married, 65.7% now married, 4.8% widowed, 7.9% divorced (2000); Foreign born: 0.3% (2000); Ancestry (includes multiple ancestries): 26.2% German, 16.3% English, 16.3% Irish, 8.3% United States or American, 7.3% Other groups (2000).
Economy: Employment by occupation: 5.5% management, 13.7% professional, 15.2% services, 18.4% sales, 0.7% farming, 14.4% construction, 32.1% production (2000).
Income: Per capita income: $16,753 (2000); Median household income: $41,477 (2000); Poverty rate: 4.2% (2000).
Education: High school graduation rate: 78.4% (2000); College graduation rate: 7.0% (2000).
Housing: Homeownership rate: 93.7% (2000); Median home value: $80,000 (2000); Median rent: $400 per month (2000); Median age of housing: 55 years (2000).
Transportation: Commute to work: 94.5% car, 0.3% public transportation, 1.0% walk, 4.3% work from home (2000); Travel time to work: 10.8% less than 15 minutes, 53.0% 15 to 30 minutes, 14.2% 30 to 45 minutes, 11.8% 45 to 60 minutes, 10.2% 60 minutes or more (2000)

LAINGSBURG (city). Covers a land area of 1.667 square miles and a water area of 0.006 square miles. Located at 42.89° N. Lat.; 84.35° W. Long. Elevation is 835 feet.
History: Laingsburg was founded in 1836 by Dr. Peter Laing, who operated a tavern here. The village was platted in 1860 when the railroad arrived.
Population: 1,223 (2000); Race: 98.5% White, 0.0% Black, 0.3% Asian, 0.2% American Indian and Alaska Native, 0.7% Hispanic of any race, 0.8% two or more races (2000); Density: 733.6 persons per square mile (2000); Age: 31.4% under 18, 10.5% over 64 (2000); Marriage status: 22.3% never married, 58.7% now married, 6.8% widowed, 12.2% divorced (2000); Foreign born: 1.1% (2000); Ancestry (includes multiple ancestries): 31.9% German, 17.6% Irish, 11.4% English, 8.4% Other groups, 6.7% Dutch (2000).
Economy: Employment by occupation: 8.7% management, 18.2% professional, 18.9% services, 21.2% sales, 0.3% farming, 14.9% construction, 17.8% production (2000).
Income: Per capita income: $16,083 (2000); Median household income: $39,063 (2000); Poverty rate: 6.7% (2000).
Taxes: Total city taxes per capita: $172 (1997); City property taxes per capita: $163 (1997).
Education: High school graduation rate: 87.7% (2000); College graduation rate: 11.4% (2000).

School District(s)

Laingsburg Community School District (KG-12)
2000 Enrollment: 1,282 517-651-2705
Housing: Homeownership rate: 68.9% (2000); Median home value: $92,700 (2000); Median rent: $389 per month (2000); Median age of housing: 58 years (2000).
Transportation: Commute to work: 92.1% car, 0.4% public transportation, 5.4% walk, 1.8% work from home (2000); Travel time to work: 20.3% less than 15 minutes, 25.8% 15 to 30 minutes, 42.7% 30 to 45 minutes, 6.6% 45 to 60 minutes, 4.6% 60 minutes or more (2000)

LENNON (village). Covers a land area of 0.922 square miles and a water area of 0 square miles. Located at 42.98° N. Lat.; 83.93° W. Long.
History: Lennon was founded by Peter Lennon, Sr., who built a grain elevator here and persuaded the Grand Trunk Railroad to run its line through the town.
Population: 517 (2000); Race: 99.6% White, 0.0% Black, 0.0% Asian, 0.0% American Indian and Alaska Native, 0.2% Hispanic of any race, 0.4% two or more races (2000); Density: 560.7 persons per square mile (2000); Age: 27.6% under 18, 16.1% over 64 (2000); Marriage status: 18.8% never married, 67.0% now married, 7.9% widowed, 6.3% divorced (2000); Foreign born: 0.6% (2000); Ancestry (includes multiple ancestries): 17.9% United States or American, 13.6% German, 10.4% English, 10.2% Irish, 6.0% Polish (2000).
Economy: Single-family building permits issued: 0 (2001) / 2 (2000); Multi-family building permits issued: 0 (2001) / 0 (2000); Employment by occupation: 5.7% management, 15.7% professional, 19.2% services, 16.2% sales, 0.0% farming, 15.7% construction, 27.5% production (2000).
Income: Per capita income: $17,148 (2000); Median household income: $48,583 (2000); Poverty rate: 5.2% (2000).
Taxes: Total city taxes per capita: $111 (1997); City property taxes per capita: $109 (1997).
Education: High school graduation rate: 87.3% (2000); College graduation rate: 8.3% (2000).
Housing: Homeownership rate: 92.7% (2000); Median home value: $92,600 (2000); Median rent: $429 per month (2000); Median age of housing: 43 years (2000).
Safety: Violent crime rate: 0.0 per 10,000 population; Property crime rate: 96.2 per 10,000 population (2001).
Transportation: Commute to work: 85.9% car, 0.0% public transportation, 8.0% walk, 6.1% work from home (2000); Travel time to work: 20.5% less than 15 minutes, 43.5% 15 to 30 minutes, 21.5% 30 to 45 minutes, 8.0% 45 to 60 minutes, 6.5% 60 minutes or more (2000)

MIDDLEBURY (township). Covers a land area of 24.711 square miles and a water area of 0.046 square miles. Located at 42.99° N. Lat.; 84.33° W. Long.
Population: 1,491 (2000); Race: 98.1% White, 0.1% Black, 0.1% Asian, 0.1% American Indian and Alaska Native, 1.2% Hispanic of any race, 1.0% two or more races (2000); Density: 60.3 persons per square mile (2000); Age: 26.3% under 18, 10.5% over 64 (2000); Marriage status: 19.0% never married, 65.1% now married, 4.9% widowed, 11.0% divorced (2000); Foreign born: 0.9% (2000); Ancestry (includes multiple ancestries): 30.7% German, 18.0% English, 13.7% Irish, 6.3% French (except Basque), 6.3% Other groups (2000).
Economy: Employment by occupation: 11.0% management, 15.1% professional, 13.0% services, 21.7% sales, 2.2% farming, 10.2% construction, 26.8% production (2000).
Income: Per capita income: $18,398 (2000); Median household income: $45,313 (2000); Poverty rate: 2.4% (2000).
Taxes: Total city taxes per capita: $20 (1997); City property taxes per capita: $18 (1997).
Education: High school graduation rate: 87.1% (2000); College graduation rate: 12.7% (2000).
Housing: Homeownership rate: 89.5% (2000); Median home value: $97,000 (2000); Median rent: $350 per month (2000); Median age of housing: 32 years (2000).
Transportation: Commute to work: 93.7% car, 0.3% public transportation, 0.6% walk, 4.6% work from home (2000); Travel time to work: 29.2% less than 15 minutes, 28.1% 15 to 30 minutes, 20.6% 30 to 45 minutes, 14.6% 45 to 60 minutes, 7.5% 60 minutes or more (2000)

MIDDLETOWN (CDP). Covers a land area of 0.490 square miles and a water area of 0 square miles. Located at 42.98° N. Lat.; 84.14° W. Long.
Population: 966 (2000); Race: 96.2% White, 0.8% Black, 0.0% Asian, 0.0% American Indian and Alaska Native, 1.8% Hispanic of any race, 2.3% two or more races (2000); Density: 1,973.3 persons per square mile (2000); Age: 22.0% under 18, 12.6% over 64 (2000); Marriage status: 18.9% never married, 60.9% now married, 5.5% widowed, 14.6% divorced (2000); Foreign born: 2.8% (2000); Ancestry (includes multiple ancestries): 29.1% German, 16.4% Irish, 13.1% Other groups, 6.7% United States or American, 6.4% English (2000).
Economy: Employment by occupation: 7.1% management, 15.1% professional, 22.2% services, 11.8% sales, 0.0% farming, 14.4% construction, 29.3% production (2000).
Income: Per capita income: $16,500 (2000); Median household income: $32,891 (2000); Poverty rate: 7.7% (2000).
Education: High school graduation rate: 76.3% (2000); College graduation rate: 6.6% (2000).
Housing: Homeownership rate: 80.1% (2000); Median home value: $67,600 (2000); Median rent: $357 per month (2000); Median age of housing: 48 years (2000).
Transportation: Commute to work: 94.1% car, 0.0% public transportation, 0.0% walk, 5.9% work from home (2000); Travel time to work: 50.8% less

than 15 minutes, 12.1% 15 to 30 minutes, 16.9% 30 to 45 minutes, 11.1% 45 to 60 minutes, 9.0% 60 minutes or more (2000)

MORRICE (village). Covers a land area of 1.053 square miles and a water area of 0 square miles. Located at 42.83° N. Lat.; 84.17° W. Long.
Population: 882 (2000); Race: 91.2% White, 0.0% Black, 0.8% Asian, 1.7% American Indian and Alaska Native, 1.9% Hispanic of any race, 5.1% two or more races (2000); Density: 837.4 persons per square mile (2000); Age: 30.1% under 18, 6.0% over 64 (2000); Marriage status: 22.9% never married, 59.8% now married, 4.2% widowed, 13.1% divorced (2000); Foreign born: 1.4% (2000); Ancestry (includes multiple ancestries): 20.5% German, 17.1% United States or American, 11.0% Other groups, 10.9% English, 8.8% Irish (2000).
Economy: In agricultural area. Employment by occupation: 8.0% management, 10.8% professional, 11.9% services, 21.1% sales, 1.9% farming, 14.7% construction, 31.7% production (2000).
Income: Per capita income: $17,423 (2000); Median household income: $40,417 (2000); Poverty rate: 5.1% (2000).
Taxes: Total city taxes per capita: $128 (1997); City property taxes per capita: $125 (1997).
Education: High school graduation rate: 87.1% (2000); College graduation rate: 9.6% (2000).

School District(s)

Morrice Area Schools (KG-12)
2000 Enrollment: 727 517-625-3142
Housing: Homeownership rate: 90.5% (2000); Median home value: $85,000 (2000); Median rent: $433 per month (2000); Median age of housing: 33 years (2000).
Transportation: Commute to work: 94.1% car, 0.4% public transportation, 2.6% walk, 1.8% work from home (2000); Travel time to work: 11.8% less than 15 minutes, 32.1% 15 to 30 minutes, 32.6% 30 to 45 minutes, 11.4% 45 to 60 minutes, 12.1% 60 minutes or more (2000)

NEW HAVEN (township). Covers a land area of 35.693 square miles and a water area of 0.030 square miles. Located at 43.09° N. Lat.; 84.11° W. Long.
Population: 1,293 (2000); Race: 99.1% White, 0.0% Black, 0.0% Asian, 0.0% American Indian and Alaska Native, 0.2% Hispanic of any race, 0.5% two or more races (2000); Density: 36.2 persons per square mile (2000); Age: 24.1% under 18, 13.3% over 64 (2000); Marriage status: 17.8% never married, 70.4% now married, 5.3% widowed, 6.5% divorced (2000); Foreign born: 0.5% (2000); Ancestry (includes multiple ancestries): 35.8% German, 13.7% English, 12.6% Irish, 9.6% Czech, 9.3% United States or American (2000).
Economy: Employment by occupation: 9.3% management, 20.4% professional, 14.8% services, 22.0% sales, 0.7% farming, 10.8% construction, 21.9% production (2000).
Income: Per capita income: $21,757 (2000); Median household income: $46,420 (2000); Poverty rate: 2.9% (2000).
Taxes: Total city taxes per capita: $85 (1997); City property taxes per capita: $85 (1997).
Education: High school graduation rate: 89.1% (2000); College graduation rate: 14.7% (2000).
Housing: Homeownership rate: 89.9% (2000); Median home value: $100,500 (2000); Median rent: $400 per month (2000); Median age of housing: 51 years (2000).
Transportation: Commute to work: 93.4% car, 0.2% public transportation, 1.5% walk, 4.3% work from home (2000); Travel time to work: 22.0% less than 15 minutes, 34.9% 15 to 30 minutes, 15.3% 30 to 45 minutes, 13.4% 45 to 60 minutes, 14.4% 60 minutes or more (2000)

NEW LOTHROP (village). Covers a land area of 0.788 square miles and a water area of 0.003 square miles. Located at 43.11° N. Lat.; 83.96° W. Long.
Population: 603 (2000); Race: 96.0% White, 0.0% Black, 0.0% Asian, 2.3% American Indian and Alaska Native, 0.2% Hispanic of any race, 1.5% two or more races (2000); Density: 765.0 persons per square mile (2000); Age: 28.8% under 18, 10.5% over 64 (2000); Marriage status: 24.6% never married, 61.0% now married, 5.6% widowed, 8.8% divorced (2000); Foreign born: 0.0% (2000); Ancestry (includes multiple ancestries): 37.3% German, 15.1% English, 13.9% Irish, 7.2% United States or American, 6.9% French (except Basque) (2000).
Economy: Employment by occupation: 5.2% management, 23.8% professional, 14.3% services, 27.0% sales, 0.0% farming, 9.9% construction, 19.8% production (2000).
Income: Per capita income: $21,056 (2000); Median household income: $40,227 (2000); Poverty rate: 10.0% (2000).
Taxes: Total city taxes per capita: $152 (1997); City property taxes per capita: $147 (1997).
Education: High school graduation rate: 88.8% (2000); College graduation rate: 17.2% (2000).

School District(s)

New Lothrop Area Public Schools (PK-12)
2000 Enrollment: 813 810-638-5091
Housing: Homeownership rate: 71.9% (2000); Median home value: $96,000 (2000); Median rent: $334 per month (2000); Median age of housing: 48 years (2000).
Transportation: Commute to work: 93.1% car, 0.0% public transportation, 2.0% walk, 2.0% work from home (2000); Travel time to work: 18.2% less than 15 minutes, 29.3% 15 to 30 minutes, 38.4% 30 to 45 minutes, 5.0% 45 to 60 minutes, 9.1% 60 minutes or more (2000)

OWOSSO (city). Covers a land area of 4.950 square miles and a water area of 0.015 square miles. Located at 42.99° N. Lat.; 84.17° W. Long. Elevation is 740 feet.
History: Owosso, established on the Shiawassee River, began as a lumber town. Diversified industry replaced lumbering at the turn of the century. Owosso was the home of writer James Oliver Curwood, whose studio and home were both of architectural interest.
Population: 15,713 (2000); Race: 96.3% White, 0.2% Black, 0.2% Asian, 0.8% American Indian and Alaska Native, 2.8% Hispanic of any race, 1.7% two or more races (2000); Density: 3,174.5 persons per square mile (2000); Age: 27.2% under 18, 13.1% over 64 (2000); Marriage status: 25.9% never married, 52.4% now married, 8.6% widowed, 13.0% divorced (2000); Foreign born: 1.2% (2000); Ancestry (includes multiple ancestries): 27.2% German, 14.3% English, 14.3% Irish, 9.8% Other groups, 9.1% United States or American (2000).
Vital Statistics: Birth rate: 173.7 per 10,000 population (1998)
Economy: Single-family building permits issued: 6 (2001) / 9 (2000); Multi-family building permits issued: 2 (2001) / 36 (2000); Employment by occupation: 7.6% management, 13.6% professional, 19.1% services, 24.0% sales, 0.7% farming, 11.3% construction, 23.7% production (2000).
Income: Per capita income: $16,764 (2000); Median household income: $32,576 (2000); Poverty rate: 13.2% (2000).
Taxes: Total city taxes per capita: $193 (2000); City property taxes per capita: $186 (2000).
Education: High school graduation rate: 80.8% (2000); College graduation rate: 12.3% (2000).

School District(s)

Owosso Public Schools (KG-12)
2000 Enrollment: 4,219 517-723-8131

Four-year College(s)

Baker College of Owosso (Private, Not-for-profit)
2001 Enrollment: 2,067 517-729-3300
2001 Tuition: In-state $5,580; Out-of-state $5,580
Housing: Homeownership rate: 66.0% (2000); Median home value: $81,700 (2000); Median rent: $402 per month (2000); Median age of housing: 56 years (2000).
Hospitals: Memorial Healthcare Center (131 beds)
Safety: Violent crime rate: 31.0 per 10,000 population; Property crime rate: 345.7 per 10,000 population (2001).
Newspapers: The Argus-Press (7 x week); The Sunday Independent (1 x week)
Transportation: Commute to work: 91.9% car, 0.1% public transportation, 3.8% walk, 3.0% work from home (2000); Travel time to work: 54.0% less than 15 minutes, 16.3% 15 to 30 minutes, 10.6% 30 to 45 minutes, 11.3% 45 to 60 minutes, 7.8% 60 minutes or more (2000)
Additional Information Contacts
Owosso Chamber of Commerce. 989-723-5149
Shiawassee Regional Board of Realtors. 989-723-4672

OWOSSO (township). Covers a land area of 32.371 square miles and a water area of 0.028 square miles. Located at 42.99° N. Lat.; 84.21° W. Long. Elevation is 740 feet.
History: Thomas E. Dewey born here. Incorporated 1859.
Population: 4,670 (2000); Race: 98.7% White, 0.2% Black, 0.1% Asian, 0.0% American Indian and Alaska Native, 0.7% Hispanic of any race, 1.0% two or more races (2000); Density: 144.3 persons per square mile (2000); Age: 24.7% under 18, 17.3% over 64 (2000); Marriage status: 20.2% never married, 63.6% now married, 6.0% widowed, 10.2% divorced (2000); Foreign born: 1.3% (2000); Ancestry (includes multiple ancestries): 28.6%

German, 12.2% English, 10.7% Irish, 8.6% United States or American, 7.4% French (except Basque) (2000).
Economy: Railroad junction. Airport to Northeast. Manufacturing: printing, building materials, auto parts, corrugated containers, boats, auto seats, machinery; grain, soybeans; livestock. Single-family building permits issued: 69 (2001) / 68 (2000); Multi-family building permits issued: 0 (2001) / 0 (2000); Employment by occupation: 10.3% management, 17.6% professional, 12.2% services, 21.8% sales, 0.8% farming, 10.2% construction, 27.1% production (2000).
Income: Per capita income: $19,772 (2000); Median household income: $41,500 (2000); Poverty rate: 6.7% (2000).
Taxes: Total city taxes per capita: $64 (2000); City property taxes per capita: $54 (2000).
Education: High school graduation rate: 84.0% (2000); College graduation rate: 13.1% (2000).
Housing: Homeownership rate: 84.9% (2000); Median home value: $112,900 (2000); Median rent: $414 per month (2000); Median age of housing: 29 years (2000).
Transportation: Commute to work: 93.8% car, 0.2% public transportation, 1.0% walk, 3.9% work from home (2000); Travel time to work: 43.3% less than 15 minutes, 26.1% 15 to 30 minutes, 13.5% 30 to 45 minutes, 9.4% 45 to 60 minutes, 7.7% 60 minutes or more (2000)

PERRY (city). Covers a land area of 2.852 square miles and a water area of 0.062 square miles. Located at 42.82° N. Lat.; 84.22° W. Long. Elevation is 889 feet.
History: Perry was founded in 1850 by William P. Laing, who opened a store here. The village was named for Oliver Hazard Perry, American naval hero.
Population: 2,065 (2000); Race: 98.0% White, 0.1% Black, 0.0% Asian, 0.8% American Indian and Alaska Native, 1.1% Hispanic of any race, 1.0% two or more races (2000); Density: 724.1 persons per square mile (2000); Age: 32.6% under 18, 8.2% over 64 (2000); Marriage status: 22.2% never married, 60.3% now married, 6.2% widowed, 11.4% divorced (2000); Foreign born: 0.6% (2000); Ancestry (includes multiple ancestries): 26.7% German, 13.8% English, 11.8% United States or American, 10.4% Irish, 6.7% Other groups (2000).
Economy: Employment by occupation: 9.4% management, 12.6% professional, 17.7% services, 24.4% sales, 1.0% farming, 15.6% construction, 19.3% production (2000).
Income: Per capita income: $16,769 (2000); Median household income: $45,179 (2000); Poverty rate: 5.7% (2000).
Taxes: Total city taxes per capita: $179 (1997); City property taxes per capita: $175 (1997).
Education: High school graduation rate: 88.4% (2000); College graduation rate: 11.4% (2000).

School District(s)

Perry Public School District (PK-12)
2000 Enrollment: 1,962 517-625-3108
Housing: Homeownership rate: 76.3% (2000); Median home value: $90,900 (2000); Median rent: $409 per month (2000); Median age of housing: 43 years (2000).
Safety: Violent crime rate: 14.5 per 10,000 population; Property crime rate: 380.5 per 10,000 population (2001).
Transportation: Commute to work: 92.3% car, 0.0% public transportation, 3.2% walk, 4.1% work from home (2000); Travel time to work: 16.0% less than 15 minutes, 24.2% 15 to 30 minutes, 39.2% 30 to 45 minutes, 10.7% 45 to 60 minutes, 10.0% 60 minutes or more (2000)
Additional Information Contacts
Perry/Morrice Area Chamber of Commerce 517-625-8122

PERRY (township). Covers a land area of 31.836 square miles and a water area of 0.065 square miles. Located at 42.83° N. Lat.; 84.22° W. Long. Elevation is 889 feet.
Population: 4,438 (2000); Race: 96.4% White, 0.1% Black, 0.5% Asian, 0.6% American Indian and Alaska Native, 2.3% Hispanic of any race, 1.6% two or more races (2000); Density: 139.4 persons per square mile (2000); Age: 29.0% under 18, 7.7% over 64 (2000); Marriage status: 22.4% never married, 64.4% now married, 4.2% widowed, 9.0% divorced (2000); Foreign born: 1.4% (2000); Ancestry (includes multiple ancestries): 22.4% German, 13.4% English, 12.3% Irish, 10.8% United States or American, 8.1% Other groups (2000).
Economy: In farm area: livestock, oats, soy beans, grain, beans; dairy products. Employment by occupation: 9.1% management, 16.3% professional, 13.8% services, 22.4% sales, 1.4% farming, 13.8% construction, 23.2% production (2000).
Income: Per capita income: $20,744 (2000); Median household income: $50,783 (2000); Poverty rate: 5.9% (2000).
Taxes: Total city taxes per capita: $37 (1997); City property taxes per capita: $36 (1997).
Education: High school graduation rate: 86.1% (2000); College graduation rate: 19.1% (2000).
Housing: Homeownership rate: 90.1% (2000); Median home value: $120,000 (2000); Median rent: $514 per month (2000); Median age of housing: 24 years (2000).
Transportation: Commute to work: 95.2% car, 0.1% public transportation, 0.9% walk, 3.6% work from home (2000); Travel time to work: 15.0% less than 15 minutes, 31.6% 15 to 30 minutes, 34.1% 30 to 45 minutes, 10.3% 45 to 60 minutes, 9.0% 60 minutes or more (2000)

RUSH (township). Covers a land area of 35.207 square miles and a water area of 0.012 square miles. Located at 43.08° N. Lat.; 84.22° W. Long.
History: Rush was named for Henry Rush, a settler in the area in the 1840's. The township was organized in 1850.
Population: 1,409 (2000); Race: 99.4% White, 0.1% Black, 0.0% Asian, 0.3% American Indian and Alaska Native, 0.9% Hispanic of any race, 0.1% two or more races (2000); Density: 40.0 persons per square mile (2000); Age: 25.5% under 18, 12.8% over 64 (2000); Marriage status: 20.7% never married, 65.0% now married, 6.3% widowed, 7.9% divorced (2000); Foreign born: 0.6% (2000); Ancestry (includes multiple ancestries): 28.7% German, 17.2% English, 12.4% Irish, 6.5% United States or American, 6.1% Other groups (2000).
Economy: Employment by occupation: 11.7% management, 19.4% professional, 11.4% services, 18.5% sales, 0.8% farming, 11.9% construction, 26.3% production (2000).
Income: Per capita income: $20,053 (2000); Median household income: $47,232 (2000); Poverty rate: 3.7% (2000).
Taxes: Total city taxes per capita: $49 (1997); City property taxes per capita: $49 (1997).
Education: High school graduation rate: 86.4% (2000); College graduation rate: 15.6% (2000).
Housing: Homeownership rate: 91.8% (2000); Median home value: $106,500 (2000); Median rent: $408 per month (2000); Median age of housing: 47 years (2000).
Transportation: Commute to work: 91.3% car, 0.0% public transportation, 1.0% walk, 7.7% work from home (2000); Travel time to work: 27.5% less than 15 minutes, 41.4% 15 to 30 minutes, 12.0% 30 to 45 minutes, 11.6% 45 to 60 minutes, 7.5% 60 minutes or more (2000)

SCIOTA (township). Covers a land area of 26.708 square miles and a water area of 0.073 square miles. Located at 42.90° N. Lat.; 84.32° W. Long.
Population: 1,801 (2000); Race: 97.2% White, 1.0% Black, 0.0% Asian, 0.5% American Indian and Alaska Native, 0.9% Hispanic of any race, 1.0% two or more races (2000); Density: 67.4 persons per square mile (2000); Age: 28.2% under 18, 10.3% over 64 (2000); Marriage status: 19.8% never married, 67.7% now married, 3.6% widowed, 8.9% divorced (2000); Foreign born: 0.9% (2000); Ancestry (includes multiple ancestries): 27.1% German, 16.5% English, 11.0% Irish, 9.4% United States or American, 5.3% Other groups (2000).
Economy: Employment by occupation: 10.6% management, 20.4% professional, 11.3% services, 23.1% sales, 1.7% farming, 13.9% construction, 19.0% production (2000).
Income: Per capita income: $20,502 (2000); Median household income: $55,375 (2000); Poverty rate: 8.5% (2000).
Taxes: Total city taxes per capita: $26 (1997); City property taxes per capita: $26 (1997).
Education: High school graduation rate: 90.6% (2000); College graduation rate: 18.4% (2000).
Housing: Homeownership rate: 93.5% (2000); Median home value: $116,000 (2000); Median rent: $450 per month (2000); Median age of housing: 26 years (2000).
Transportation: Commute to work: 93.7% car, 0.0% public transportation, 1.3% walk, 4.8% work from home (2000); Travel time to work: 11.5% less than 15 minutes, 32.1% 15 to 30 minutes, 40.0% 30 to 45 minutes, 7.0% 45 to 60 minutes, 9.5% 60 minutes or more (2000)

SHIAWASSEE (township). Covers a land area of 36.705 square miles and a water area of 0.192 square miles. Located at 42.90° N. Lat.; 84.08° W. Long.
History: The name of Shiawassee is an Indian word for "the river that twists about." Settlement began here in the 1830's when Charles Bacon of Ohio formed a company to sell land.

Population: 2,907 (2000); Race: 96.9% White, 0.0% Black, 0.0% Asian, 0.7% American Indian and Alaska Native, 1.4% Hispanic of any race, 1.8% two or more races (2000); Density: 79.2 persons per square mile (2000); Age: 27.8% under 18, 9.1% over 64 (2000); Marriage status: 22.3% never married, 63.2% now married, 4.1% widowed, 10.5% divorced (2000); Foreign born: 0.7% (2000); Ancestry (includes multiple ancestries): 23.3% German, 19.0% English, 9.4% Irish, 7.6% Other groups, 7.1% United States or American (2000).
Economy: Employment by occupation: 11.0% management, 16.1% professional, 13.7% services, 19.9% sales, 1.2% farming, 14.1% construction, 24.0% production (2000).
Income: Per capita income: $19,713 (2000); Median household income: $48,220 (2000); Poverty rate: 6.1% (2000).
Taxes: Total city taxes per capita: $28 (1997); City property taxes per capita: $28 (1997).
Education: High school graduation rate: 85.1% (2000); College graduation rate: 10.8% (2000).
Housing: Homeownership rate: 89.2% (2000); Median home value: $104,500 (2000); Median rent: $385 per month (2000); Median age of housing: 41 years (2000).
Transportation: Commute to work: 94.5% car, 0.2% public transportation, 3.3% walk, 2.0% work from home (2000); Travel time to work: 25.9% less than 15 minutes, 27.2% 15 to 30 minutes, 28.2% 30 to 45 minutes, 10.4% 45 to 60 minutes, 8.3% 60 minutes or more (2000)

VENICE (township). Covers a land area of 37.456 square miles and a water area of <.001 square miles. Located at 42.99° N. Lat.; 83.96° W. Long.
Population: 2,588 (2000); Race: 96.9% White, 0.1% Black, 0.0% Asian, 0.0% American Indian and Alaska Native, 2.1% Hispanic of any race, 2.0% two or more races (2000); Density: 69.1 persons per square mile (2000); Age: 27.2% under 18, 13.0% over 64 (2000); Marriage status: 17.2% never married, 68.2% now married, 8.4% widowed, 6.3% divorced (2000); Foreign born: 1.3% (2000); Ancestry (includes multiple ancestries): 20.8% German, 18.9% English, 15.1% United States or American, 7.6% Irish, 6.2% Other groups (2000).
Economy: Employment by occupation: 10.3% management, 14.3% professional, 14.6% services, 18.2% sales, 0.5% farming, 14.5% construction, 27.6% production (2000).
Income: Per capita income: $19,119 (2000); Median household income: $45,833 (2000); Poverty rate: 4.4% (2000).
Taxes: Total city taxes per capita: $19 (1997); City property taxes per capita: $18 (1997).
Education: High school graduation rate: 82.0% (2000); College graduation rate: 6.5% (2000).
Housing: Homeownership rate: 90.0% (2000); Median home value: $91,700 (2000); Median rent: $413 per month (2000); Median age of housing: 36 years (2000).
Transportation: Commute to work: 91.6% car, 0.0% public transportation, 2.1% walk, 5.7% work from home (2000); Travel time to work: 20.7% less than 15 minutes, 39.5% 15 to 30 minutes, 19.3% 30 to 45 minutes, 9.0% 45 to 60 minutes, 11.4% 60 minutes or more (2000)

VERNON (village). Covers a land area of 0.718 square miles and a water area of 0 square miles. Located at 42.93° N. Lat.; 84.03° W. Long.
Population: 847 (2000); Race: 98.9% White, 0.0% Black, 0.0% Asian, 0.1% American Indian and Alaska Native, 1.1% Hispanic of any race, 0.7% two or more races (2000); Density: 1,180.0 persons per square mile (2000); Age: 28.9% under 18, 9.9% over 64 (2000); Marriage status: 20.9% never married, 61.3% now married, 5.3% widowed, 12.5% divorced (2000); Foreign born: 1.0% (2000); Ancestry (includes multiple ancestries): 24.5% German, 17.6% English, 14.3% Irish, 9.9% Polish, 9.1% United States or American (2000).
Economy: Single-family building permits issued: 0 (2001) / 1 (2000); Multi-family building permits issued: 0 (2001) / 0 (2000); Employment by occupation: 4.6% management, 15.3% professional, 15.8% services, 23.6% sales, 0.0% farming, 12.1% construction, 28.7% production (2000).
Income: Per capita income: $16,337 (2000); Median household income: $47,875 (2000); Poverty rate: 4.8% (2000).
Taxes: Total city taxes per capita: $137 (1997); City property taxes per capita: $129 (1997).
Education: High school graduation rate: 86.8% (2000); College graduation rate: 10.6% (2000).
Housing: Homeownership rate: 89.4% (2000); Median home value: $85,700 (2000); Median rent: $430 per month (2000); Median age of housing: 53 years (2000).
Transportation: Commute to work: 93.4% car, 0.0% public transportation, 3.3% walk, 3.3% work from home (2000); Travel time to work: 18.8% less than 15 minutes, 35.3% 15 to 30 minutes, 19.7% 30 to 45 minutes, 14.0% 45 to 60 minutes, 12.3% 60 minutes or more (2000)

VERNON (township). Covers a land area of 33.898 square miles and a water area of 0.171 square miles. Located at 42.92° N. Lat.; 83.99° W. Long.
Population: 4,980 (2000); Race: 96.9% White, 0.2% Black, 0.0% Asian, 0.5% American Indian and Alaska Native, 1.8% Hispanic of any race, 1.9% two or more races (2000); Density: 146.9 persons per square mile (2000); Age: 27.3% under 18, 10.7% over 64 (2000); Marriage status: 19.6% never married, 63.9% now married, 4.9% widowed, 11.6% divorced (2000); Foreign born: 0.4% (2000); Ancestry (includes multiple ancestries): 22.8% German, 15.0% English, 14.3% United States or American, 13.2% Irish, 8.8% Other groups (2000).
Economy: In farm area. Employment by occupation: 8.9% management, 14.2% professional, 12.5% services, 22.4% sales, 0.9% farming, 13.2% construction, 27.8% production (2000).
Income: Per capita income: $18,990 (2000); Median household income: $47,339 (2000); Poverty rate: 7.2% (2000).
Taxes: Total city taxes per capita: $37 (1997); City property taxes per capita: $32 (1997).
Education: High school graduation rate: 82.8% (2000); College graduation rate: 9.9% (2000).
Housing: Homeownership rate: 89.0% (2000); Median home value: $107,900 (2000); Median rent: $409 per month (2000); Median age of housing: 24 years (2000).
Transportation: Commute to work: 94.8% car, 0.0% public transportation, 1.5% walk, 3.5% work from home (2000); Travel time to work: 25.5% less than 15 minutes, 31.1% 15 to 30 minutes, 21.5% 30 to 45 minutes, 11.5% 45 to 60 minutes, 10.3% 60 minutes or more (2000)

WOODHULL (township). Covers a land area of 27.113 square miles and a water area of 0.316 square miles. Located at 42.81° N. Lat.; 84.32° W. Long.
Population: 3,850 (2000); Race: 97.3% White, 0.2% Black, 1.2% Asian, 0.6% American Indian and Alaska Native, 0.7% Hispanic of any race, 0.7% two or more races (2000); Density: 142.0 persons per square mile (2000); Age: 26.9% under 18, 8.1% over 64 (2000); Marriage status: 19.5% never married, 68.5% now married, 4.6% widowed, 7.4% divorced (2000); Foreign born: 1.5% (2000); Ancestry (includes multiple ancestries): 30.9% German, 21.1% English, 14.4% Irish, 6.2% United States or American, 5.8% Dutch (2000).
Economy: Employment by occupation: 14.9% management, 21.4% professional, 16.1% services, 24.2% sales, 1.0% farming, 9.8% construction, 12.6% production (2000).
Income: Per capita income: $27,310 (2000); Median household income: $60,658 (2000); Poverty rate: 4.6% (2000).
Taxes: Total city taxes per capita: $34 (1997); City property taxes per capita: $33 (1997).
Education: High school graduation rate: 86.2% (2000); College graduation rate: 31.3% (2000).
Housing: Homeownership rate: 91.6% (2000); Median home value: $142,200 (2000); Median rent: $502 per month (2000); Median age of housing: 25 years (2000).
Transportation: Commute to work: 94.9% car, 0.5% public transportation, 0.2% walk, 4.4% work from home (2000); Travel time to work: 14.5% less than 15 minutes, 39.6% 15 to 30 minutes, 33.0% 30 to 45 minutes, 6.0% 45 to 60 minutes, 6.9% 60 minutes or more (2000)

Tuscola County

Located in eastern Michigan; bounded on the northwest by Saginaw Bay; drained by the Cass River and its affluents. Covers a land area of 812.40 square miles, a water area of 101.40 square miles, and is located in the Eastern Time Zone. The county government was organized in 1840. County seat is Caro.

Weather Station: Caro Regional Center — Elevation: 669 feet

	Jan	Feb	Mar	Apr	May	Jun	Jul	Aug	Sep	Oct	Nov	Dec
High	29	32	43	58	71	80	84	81	73	61	46	34
Low	14	15	24	34	44	53	58	56	49	39	31	21
Precip	1.7	1.2	2.4	2.8	2.9	3.3	2.9	3.3	4.3	2.6	2.7	2.0
Snow	11.1	6.6	5.5	1.1	tr	0.0	0.0	0.0	0.0	tr	2.5	9.0

High and Low temperatures in degrees Fahrenheit; Precipitation and Snow in inches

Population: 58,266 (2000); Race: 95.9% White, 1.1% Black, 0.3% Asian, 0.6% American Indian and Alaska Native, 2.1% Hispanic of any race, 1.5%

two or more races (2000); Density: 71.7 persons per square mile (2000); Age: 26.9% under 18, 12.8% over 64 (2000).
Religion: Five largest groups: 12.0% Lutheran Church—Missouri Synod, 11.0% Catholic Church, 5.7% The United Methodist Church, 1.8% Wisconsin Evangelical Lutheran Synod, 1.3% Presbyterian Church (U.S.A.) (2000).
Economy: Unemployment rate: 7.2% (11/2002); Total civilian labor force: 28,295 (11/2002); Leading industries: 22.1% health care and social assistance; 22.1% manufacturing; 18.7% retail trade (2000); Companies that employ more than 1,000 persons: 0 (2000); Companies that employ more than 100 persons: 20 (2000); Farms: 1,140 totaling 333,099 acres (1997); Minority business ownership rate: 2.9% (1997); Women business ownership rate: 32.8% (1997); Retail sales per capita: $7,119 (1997). Single-family building permits issued: 174 (2001) / 168 (2000); Multi-family building permits issued: 2 (2001) / 4 (2000).
Income: Per capita income: $17,985 (2000); Median household income: $40,174 (2000); Poverty rate: 8.2% (2000); Bankruptcy rate: 4.33% (2001).
Taxes: Total county taxes per capita: $146 (2000); County property taxes per capita: $134 (2000).
Education: High school graduation rate: 81.2% (2000); College graduation rate: 10.6% (2000).
Housing: Homeownership rate: 84.1% (2000); Median home value: $87,100 (2000); Median rent: $359 per month (2000); Median age of housing: 35 years (2000).
Health: Birth rate: 114.7 per 10,000 population (1998); Age adjusted death rate: 89.8 per 10,000 population (1999); Age adjusted cancer mortality rate: 198.3 deaths per 100,000 population (1999). Number of physicians: 8.4 per 10,000 population (1999); Number of hospital beds: 41.0 per 10,000 population (1999).
Elections: 2000 Presidential election results: 44.0% Gore, 53.6% Bush, 1.8% Nader, 0.1% Buchanan
National and State Parks: Deford State Game Area; Murphy Lake State Game Area; Tuscola State Game Area; Vassar State Game Area
Additional Information Contacts
Tuscola County Government Offices........................989-672-3700
Caro Chamber of Commerce........................989-673-5211
Cass City Chamber of Commerce........................989-872-4618
Vassar Chamber of Commerce........................989-823-2601

Tuscola County Communities

AKRON (village). Covers a land area of 0.954 square miles and a water area of 0 square miles. Located at 43.56° N. Lat.; 83.51° W. Long. Elevation is 646 feet.
History: Akron was settled by Charles H. Beach in 1854, and first called Beach's Corners. When the post office was established, it was called Akron, after the township, which had been named for Akron, Ohio. The village was platted in 1882.
Population: 461 (2000); Race: 98.1% White, 0.0% Black, 0.0% Asian, 0.5% American Indian and Alaska Native, 6.3% Hispanic of any race, 0.7% two or more races (2000); Density: 483.5 persons per square mile (2000); Age: 30.8% under 18, 11.8% over 64 (2000); Marriage status: 25.2% never married, 55.9% now married, 7.8% widowed, 11.2% divorced (2000); Foreign born: 0.0% (2000); Ancestry (includes multiple ancestries): 38.9% German, 14.4% Irish, 13.0% Other groups, 12.0% French (except Basque), 10.9% Polish (2000).
Economy: Employment by occupation: 6.3% management, 9.2% professional, 13.8% services, 21.3% sales, 0.0% farming, 17.8% construction, 31.6% production (2000).
Income: Per capita income: $14,570 (2000); Median household income: $35,208 (2000); Poverty rate: 17.1% (2000).
Taxes: Total city taxes per capita: $114 (1997); City property taxes per capita: $114 (1997).
Education: High school graduation rate: 87.0% (2000); College graduation rate: 3.0% (2000).
Housing: Homeownership rate: 76.6% (2000); Median home value: $56,100 (2000); Median rent: $397 per month (2000); Median age of housing: 58 years (2000).
Transportation: Commute to work: 95.3% car, 0.0% public transportation, 2.4% walk, 2.4% work from home (2000); Travel time to work: 14.5% less than 15 minutes, 38.2% 15 to 30 minutes, 21.8% 30 to 45 minutes, 12.1% 45 to 60 minutes, 13.3% 60 minutes or more (2000)

AKRON (township). Covers a land area of 52.903 square miles and a water area of 4.006 square miles. Located at 43.63° N. Lat.; 83.52° W. Long. Elevation is 646 feet.
Population: 1,589 (2000); Race: 96.3% White, 0.2% Black, 0.2% Asian, 0.1% American Indian and Alaska Native, 3.2% Hispanic of any race, 2.0% two or more races (2000); Density: 30.0 persons per square mile (2000); Age: 26.1% under 18, 15.6% over 64 (2000); Marriage status: 21.2% never married, 61.7% now married, 9.8% widowed, 7.3% divorced (2000); Foreign born: 2.2% (2000); Ancestry (includes multiple ancestries): 43.0% German, 9.1% English, 8.9% Irish, 6.9% United States or American, 6.7% Other groups (2000).
Economy: In agricultural area. Employment by occupation: 9.6% management, 10.7% professional, 14.8% services, 21.7% sales, 0.7% farming, 17.7% construction, 24.8% production (2000).
Income: Per capita income: $16,487 (2000); Median household income: $36,891 (2000); Poverty rate: 11.7% (2000).
Taxes: Total city taxes per capita: $131 (1997); City property taxes per capita: $131 (1997).
Education: High school graduation rate: 80.4% (2000); College graduation rate: 5.8% (2000).
Housing: Homeownership rate: 84.5% (2000); Median home value: $68,500 (2000); Median rent: $406 per month (2000); Median age of housing: 51 years (2000).
Transportation: Commute to work: 93.1% car, 0.8% public transportation, 0.3% walk, 5.6% work from home (2000); Travel time to work: 21.3% less than 15 minutes, 31.5% 15 to 30 minutes, 26.1% 30 to 45 minutes, 11.9% 45 to 60 minutes, 9.1% 60 minutes or more (2000)

ALMER (township). Covers a land area of 34.620 square miles and a water area of 0.018 square miles. Located at 43.53° N. Lat.; 83.40° W. Long.
Population: 3,023 (2000); Race: 97.1% White, 0.0% Black, 0.1% Asian, 0.4% American Indian and Alaska Native, 4.8% Hispanic of any race, 1.3% two or more races (2000); Density: 87.3 persons per square mile (2000); Age: 26.7% under 18, 17.9% over 64 (2000); Marriage status: 21.0% never married, 60.7% now married, 7.6% widowed, 10.7% divorced (2000); Foreign born: 1.4% (2000); Ancestry (includes multiple ancestries): 30.7% German, 12.7% English, 12.2% Irish, 11.8% Polish, 7.6% French (except Basque) (2000).
Economy: Employment by occupation: 6.7% management, 22.5% professional, 23.3% services, 18.1% sales, 0.0% farming, 10.4% construction, 19.0% production (2000).
Income: Per capita income: $19,464 (2000); Median household income: $39,491 (2000); Poverty rate: 6.9% (2000).
Taxes: Total city taxes per capita: $47 (1997); City property taxes per capita: $46 (1997).
Education: High school graduation rate: 81.3% (2000); College graduation rate: 17.2% (2000).
Housing: Homeownership rate: 80.2% (2000); Median home value: $96,100 (2000); Median rent: $335 per month (2000); Median age of housing: 28 years (2000).
Transportation: Commute to work: 95.2% car, 0.6% public transportation, 1.2% walk, 3.0% work from home (2000); Travel time to work: 56.2% less than 15 minutes, 18.0% 15 to 30 minutes, 12.4% 30 to 45 minutes, 7.6% 45 to 60 minutes, 5.8% 60 minutes or more (2000)

ARBELA (township). Covers a land area of 33.417 square miles and a water area of 0.041 square miles. Located at 43.26° N. Lat.; 83.64° W. Long.
Population: 3,219 (2000); Race: 96.8% White, 0.9% Black, 0.2% Asian, 0.5% American Indian and Alaska Native, 1.3% Hispanic of any race, 1.3% two or more races (2000); Density: 96.3 persons per square mile (2000); Age: 28.1% under 18, 10.3% over 64 (2000); Marriage status: 20.6% never married, 67.0% now married, 5.1% widowed, 7.2% divorced (2000); Foreign born: 0.7% (2000); Ancestry (includes multiple ancestries): 29.4% German, 10.4% Other groups, 10.1% English, 9.7% United States or American, 8.8% Irish (2000).
Economy: Single-family building permits issued: 22 (2001) / 14 (2000); Multi-family building permits issued: 0 (2001) / 0 (2000); Employment by occupation: 7.6% management, 9.3% professional, 17.4% services, 22.4% sales, 0.5% farming, 15.9% construction, 27.0% production (2000).
Income: Per capita income: $17,519 (2000); Median household income: $44,840 (2000); Poverty rate: 4.6% (2000).
Taxes: Total city taxes per capita: $101 (1997); City property taxes per capita: $97 (1997).
Education: High school graduation rate: 76.6% (2000); College graduation rate: 5.4% (2000).

Housing: Homeownership rate: 91.7% (2000); Median home value: $95,900 (2000); Median rent: $307 per month (2000); Median age of housing: 30 years (2000).
Transportation: Commute to work: 95.3% car, 0.0% public transportation, 0.9% walk, 2.9% work from home (2000); Travel time to work: 16.7% less than 15 minutes, 29.8% 15 to 30 minutes, 29.7% 30 to 45 minutes, 10.8% 45 to 60 minutes, 13.0% 60 minutes or more (2000)

CARO (village). Covers a land area of 2.374 square miles and a water area of 0.015 square miles. Located at 43.49° N. Lat.; 83.39° W. Long. Elevation is 711 feet.
History: Caro began as a logging camp in 1847. First called Centervillle and later Tuscola Center, the name of Caro was suggested as a form of Egypt's Cairo. Caro developed as the center of an area producing sugar beets, potatoes, and grain. A beet-sugar refinery was opened here.
Population: 4,145 (2000); Race: 95.5% White, 0.5% Black, 0.1% Asian, 0.1% American Indian and Alaska Native, 4.4% Hispanic of any race, 2.3% two or more races (2000); Density: 1,746.0 persons per square mile (2000); Age: 24.7% under 18, 16.5% over 64 (2000); Marriage status: 29.2% never married, 48.6% now married, 8.9% widowed, 13.2% divorced (2000); Foreign born: 1.7% (2000); Ancestry (includes multiple ancestries): 30.6% German, 12.3% Polish, 12.2% Irish, 12.0% Other groups, 9.9% English (2000).
Economy: Employment by occupation: 8.6% management, 17.2% professional, 23.9% services, 22.2% sales, 0.0% farming, 10.7% construction, 17.4% production (2000).
Income: Per capita income: $17,152 (2000); Median household income: $31,226 (2000); Poverty rate: 11.1% (2000).
Taxes: Total city taxes per capita: $252 (1997); City property taxes per capita: $252 (1997).
Education: High school graduation rate: 82.7% (2000); College graduation rate: 16.6% (2000).

School District(s)

Caro Community Schools (KG-12)
2000 Enrollment: 2,355 517-673-3166

Housing: Homeownership rate: 63.3% (2000); Median home value: $78,500 (2000); Median rent: $323 per month (2000); Median age of housing: 48 years (2000).
Hospitals: Caro Center (180 beds); Caro Community Hospital (50 beds)
Safety: Violent crime rate: 14.4 per 10,000 population; Property crime rate: 499.2 per 10,000 population (2001).
Newspapers: The Tuscola County Advertiser (2 x week); Shoppers Advantage (1 x week)
Transportation: Commute to work: 91.5% car, 1.1% public transportation, 3.8% walk, 2.0% work from home (2000); Travel time to work: 53.8% less than 15 minutes, 17.9% 15 to 30 minutes, 10.6% 30 to 45 minutes, 12.6% 45 to 60 minutes, 5.2% 60 minutes or more (2000)

Additional Information Contacts

Caro Chamber of Commerce 989-673-5211

CASS CITY (village). Covers a land area of 1.735 square miles and a water area of 0 square miles. Located at 43.59° N. Lat.; 83.17° W. Long. Elevation is 743 feet.
History: Cass City grew up around a lumber mill started in the early 1850's. The town was named for the Cass River, which had been named for General Lewis Cass, territorial governor of Michigan.
Population: 2,643 (2000); Race: 94.1% White, 0.0% Black, 1.1% Asian, 1.6% American Indian and Alaska Native, 2.0% Hispanic of any race, 2.6% two or more races (2000); Density: 1,523.7 persons per square mile (2000); Age: 25.3% under 18, 19.8% over 64 (2000); Marriage status: 22.4% never married, 58.1% now married, 9.4% widowed, 10.1% divorced (2000); Foreign born: 3.6% (2000); Ancestry (includes multiple ancestries): 28.1% German, 15.0% English, 11.7% Polish, 11.5% Other groups, 7.7% French (except Basque) (2000).
Economy: Employment by occupation: 10.7% management, 17.7% professional, 16.0% services, 22.1% sales, 0.6% farming, 5.0% construction, 27.9% production (2000).
Income: Per capita income: $17,159 (2000); Median household income: $33,397 (2000); Poverty rate: 10.8% (2000).
Taxes: Total city taxes per capita: $334 (1997); City property taxes per capita: $327 (1997).
Education: High school graduation rate: 80.9% (2000); College graduation rate: 15.3% (2000).

School District(s)

Cass City Public Schools (PK-12)
2000 Enrollment: 1,634 517-872-2200

Housing: Homeownership rate: 77.1% (2000); Median home value: $85,900 (2000); Median rent: $349 per month (2000); Median age of housing: 37 years (2000).
Hospitals: Hills and Dales General Hospital (65 beds)
Safety: Violent crime rate: 7.5 per 10,000 population; Property crime rate: 207.0 per 10,000 population (2001).
Newspapers: Cass City Chronicle (1 x week)
Transportation: Commute to work: 91.1% car, 0.0% public transportation, 6.5% walk, 2.2% work from home (2000); Travel time to work: 52.5% less than 15 minutes, 21.9% 15 to 30 minutes, 16.4% 30 to 45 minutes, 1.9% 45 to 60 minutes, 7.3% 60 minutes or more (2000)

Additional Information Contacts

Cass City Chamber of Commerce 989-872-4618

COLUMBIA (township). Covers a land area of 36.053 square miles and a water area of 0 square miles. Located at 43.63° N. Lat.; 83.42° W. Long.
Population: 1,419 (2000); Race: 96.7% White, 0.0% Black, 0.7% Asian, 0.6% American Indian and Alaska Native, 1.4% Hispanic of any race, 0.7% two or more races (2000); Density: 39.4 persons per square mile (2000); Age: 26.6% under 18, 14.7% over 64 (2000); Marriage status: 20.6% never married, 66.2% now married, 6.3% widowed, 6.9% divorced (2000); Foreign born: 1.5% (2000); Ancestry (includes multiple ancestries): 49.6% German, 9.7% English, 7.5% French (except Basque), 6.5% Polish, 5.8% Other groups (2000).
Economy: Employment by occupation: 11.7% management, 16.1% professional, 14.6% services, 21.2% sales, 2.6% farming, 9.8% construction, 24.0% production (2000).
Income: Per capita income: $17,026 (2000); Median household income: $39,375 (2000); Poverty rate: 10.5% (2000).
Taxes: Total city taxes per capita: $94 (1997); City property taxes per capita: $94 (1997).
Education: High school graduation rate: 85.4% (2000); College graduation rate: 11.5% (2000).
Housing: Homeownership rate: 86.0% (2000); Median home value: $73,400 (2000); Median rent: $372 per month (2000); Median age of housing: 60+ years (2000).
Transportation: Commute to work: 92.2% car, 0.0% public transportation, 1.3% walk, 6.0% work from home (2000); Travel time to work: 28.8% less than 15 minutes, 27.9% 15 to 30 minutes, 22.0% 30 to 45 minutes, 11.6% 45 to 60 minutes, 9.7% 60 minutes or more (2000)

DAYTON (township). Covers a land area of 35.811 square miles and a water area of 0.337 square miles. Located at 43.37° N. Lat.; 83.27° W. Long. Elevation is 739 feet.
Population: 1,869 (2000); Race: 94.6% White, 2.5% Black, 0.3% Asian, 0.3% American Indian and Alaska Native, 2.2% Hispanic of any race, 1.7% two or more races (2000); Density: 52.2 persons per square mile (2000); Age: 26.8% under 18, 12.7% over 64 (2000); Marriage status: 21.1% never married, 63.9% now married, 4.9% widowed, 10.2% divorced (2000); Foreign born: 1.2% (2000); Ancestry (includes multiple ancestries): 28.6% German, 15.9% English, 15.7% Irish, 8.1% Polish, 7.2% Other groups (2000).
Economy: Employment by occupation: 9.0% management, 13.5% professional, 11.2% services, 18.3% sales, 2.8% farming, 18.3% construction, 27.0% production (2000).
Income: Per capita income: $18,890 (2000); Median household income: $42,000 (2000); Poverty rate: 10.5% (2000).
Taxes: Total city taxes per capita: $83 (1997); City property taxes per capita: $82 (1997).
Education: High school graduation rate: 83.8% (2000); College graduation rate: 9.3% (2000).
Housing: Homeownership rate: 90.3% (2000); Median home value: $96,800 (2000); Median rent: $377 per month (2000); Median age of housing: 29 years (2000).
Transportation: Commute to work: 92.7% car, 0.0% public transportation, 0.9% walk, 6.1% work from home (2000); Travel time to work: 17.0% less than 15 minutes, 22.3% 15 to 30 minutes, 22.2% 30 to 45 minutes, 13.4% 45 to 60 minutes, 25.1% 60 minutes or more (2000)

DEFORD (unincorporated postal area, zip code 48729). Covers a land area of 39.437 square miles and a water area of 0 square miles. Located at 43.49° N. Lat.; 83.17° W. Long.
Population: 1,611 (2000); Race: 98.4% White, 0.0% Black, 0.0% Asian, 0.5% American Indian and Alaska Native, 0.4% Hispanic of any race, 1.1% two or more races (2000); Density: 40.9 persons per square mile (2000); Age: 26.8% under 18, 10.7% over 64 (2000); Marriage status: 26.7% never

married, 58.0% now married, 5.6% widowed, 9.8% divorced (2000); Foreign born: 0.5% (2000); Ancestry (includes multiple ancestries): 32.0% German, 14.6% English, 10.4% Irish, 9.9% Polish, 8.4% Other groups (2000).
Economy: Employment by occupation: 11.7% management, 7.6% professional, 9.1% services, 17.0% sales, 1.5% farming, 17.2% construction, 35.8% production (2000).
Income: Per capita income: $17,520 (2000); Median household income: $40,809 (2000); Poverty rate: 10.4% (2000).
Education: High school graduation rate: 75.6% (2000); College graduation rate: 5.1% (2000).
Housing: Homeownership rate: 89.2% (2000); Median home value: $71,200 (2000); Median rent: $343 per month (2000); Median age of housing: 30 years (2000).
Transportation: Commute to work: 91.3% car, 0.0% public transportation, 1.6% walk, 5.5% work from home (2000); Travel time to work: 19.4% less than 15 minutes, 40.3% 15 to 30 minutes, 16.5% 30 to 45 minutes, 8.2% 45 to 60 minutes, 15.6% 60 minutes or more (2000)

DENMARK (township). Covers a land area of 35.264 square miles and a water area of 0 square miles. Located at 43.42° N. Lat.; 83.66° W. Long.
Population: 3,249 (2000); Race: 98.1% White, 0.0% Black, 0.6% Asian, 0.3% American Indian and Alaska Native, 2.6% Hispanic of any race, 0.9% two or more races (2000); Density: 92.1 persons per square mile (2000); Age: 24.3% under 18, 14.3% over 64 (2000); Marriage status: 19.6% never married, 65.8% now married, 6.9% widowed, 7.7% divorced (2000); Foreign born: 1.3% (2000); Ancestry (includes multiple ancestries): 56.2% German, 9.8% English, 9.1% Polish, 7.5% Irish, 6.5% French (except Basque) (2000).
Economy: Employment by occupation: 14.0% management, 16.2% professional, 16.3% services, 21.6% sales, 0.6% farming, 10.0% construction, 21.3% production (2000).
Income: Per capita income: $19,782 (2000); Median household income: $41,366 (2000); Poverty rate: 4.8% (2000).
Taxes: Total city taxes per capita: $75 (2000); City property taxes per capita: $74 (2000).
Education: High school graduation rate: 84.3% (2000); College graduation rate: 14.1% (2000).
Housing: Homeownership rate: 86.7% (2000); Median home value: $104,600 (2000); Median rent: $365 per month (2000); Median age of housing: 36 years (2000).
Transportation: Commute to work: 96.0% car, 0.0% public transportation, 1.1% walk, 2.8% work from home (2000); Travel time to work: 18.4% less than 15 minutes, 48.0% 15 to 30 minutes, 20.5% 30 to 45 minutes, 6.0% 45 to 60 minutes, 7.1% 60 minutes or more (2000)

ELKLAND (township). Covers a land area of 35.582 square miles and a water area of 0.001 square miles. Located at 43.61° N. Lat.; 83.17° W. Long.
Population: 3,659 (2000); Race: 94.1% White, 0.1% Black, 1.2% Asian, 1.3% American Indian and Alaska Native, 1.5% Hispanic of any race, 2.7% two or more races (2000); Density: 102.8 persons per square mile (2000); Age: 25.2% under 18, 19.1% over 64 (2000); Marriage status: 22.4% never married, 58.9% now married, 8.4% widowed, 10.3% divorced (2000); Foreign born: 3.2% (2000); Ancestry (includes multiple ancestries): 33.2% German, 16.0% English, 11.4% Polish, 10.0% Other groups, 7.6% Irish (2000).
Economy: Employment by occupation: 10.0% management, 16.2% professional, 15.0% services, 21.0% sales, 1.4% farming, 7.8% construction, 28.4% production (2000).
Income: Per capita income: $16,837 (2000); Median household income: $33,532 (2000); Poverty rate: 11.0% (2000).
Taxes: Total city taxes per capita: $54 (1997); City property taxes per capita: $53 (1997).
Education: High school graduation rate: 80.7% (2000); College graduation rate: 13.4% (2000).
Housing: Homeownership rate: 80.0% (2000); Median home value: $86,800 (2000); Median rent: $349 per month (2000); Median age of housing: 41 years (2000).
Transportation: Commute to work: 89.9% car, 0.0% public transportation, 5.0% walk, 3.0% work from home (2000); Travel time to work: 50.3% less than 15 minutes, 22.2% 15 to 30 minutes, 16.0% 30 to 45 minutes, 2.1% 45 to 60 minutes, 9.4% 60 minutes or more (2000)

ELLINGTON (township). Covers a land area of 35.699 square miles and a water area of 0.006 square miles. Located at 43.54° N. Lat.; 83.30° W. Long. Elevation is 788 feet.
Population: 1,304 (2000); Race: 99.1% White, 0.0% Black, 0.0% Asian, 0.3% American Indian and Alaska Native, 0.5% Hispanic of any race, 0.6% two or more races (2000); Density: 36.5 persons per square mile (2000); Age: 25.1% under 18, 7.3% over 64 (2000); Marriage status: 20.8% never married, 63.2% now married, 4.9% widowed, 11.0% divorced (2000); Foreign born: 0.5% (2000); Ancestry (includes multiple ancestries): 33.4% German, 14.4% English, 12.1% Irish, 9.2% United States or American, 7.0% Polish (2000).
Economy: Employment by occupation: 8.8% management, 17.9% professional, 13.1% services, 17.4% sales, 0.8% farming, 15.4% construction, 26.5% production (2000).
Income: Per capita income: $18,677 (2000); Median household income: $43,750 (2000); Poverty rate: 8.3% (2000).
Taxes: Total city taxes per capita: $73 (1997); City property taxes per capita: $73 (1997).
Education: High school graduation rate: 83.1% (2000); College graduation rate: 12.5% (2000).
Housing: Homeownership rate: 87.3% (2000); Median home value: $86,100 (2000); Median rent: $354 per month (2000); Median age of housing: 29 years (2000).
Transportation: Commute to work: 94.5% car, 0.0% public transportation, 0.8% walk, 4.4% work from home (2000); Travel time to work: 35.3% less than 15 minutes, 28.6% 15 to 30 minutes, 8.9% 30 to 45 minutes, 11.9% 45 to 60 minutes, 15.2% 60 minutes or more (2000)

ELMWOOD (township). Covers a land area of 35.525 square miles and a water area of 0 square miles. Located at 43.63° N. Lat.; 83.28° W. Long. Elevation is 771 feet.
Population: 1,213 (2000); Race: 97.6% White, 0.0% Black, 0.0% Asian, 0.7% American Indian and Alaska Native, 2.4% Hispanic of any race, 1.2% two or more races (2000); Density: 34.1 persons per square mile (2000); Age: 24.9% under 18, 15.1% over 64 (2000); Marriage status: 22.4% never married, 63.9% now married, 6.1% widowed, 7.6% divorced (2000); Foreign born: 0.5% (2000); Ancestry (includes multiple ancestries): 36.5% German, 11.0% Irish, 9.8% English, 9.0% Polish, 8.5% Other groups (2000).
Economy: Employment by occupation: 6.8% management, 12.2% professional, 17.6% services, 18.3% sales, 1.3% farming, 12.7% construction, 31.1% production (2000).
Income: Per capita income: $18,317 (2000); Median household income: $37,583 (2000); Poverty rate: 10.8% (2000).
Taxes: Total city taxes per capita: $70 (1997); City property taxes per capita: $55 (1997).
Education: High school graduation rate: 80.0% (2000); College graduation rate: 7.5% (2000).
Housing: Homeownership rate: 83.2% (2000); Median home value: $68,100 (2000); Median rent: $320 per month (2000); Median age of housing: 49 years (2000).
Transportation: Commute to work: 91.8% car, 0.0% public transportation, 3.3% walk, 2.0% work from home (2000); Travel time to work: 30.3% less than 15 minutes, 39.2% 15 to 30 minutes, 11.2% 30 to 45 minutes, 8.2% 45 to 60 minutes, 11.2% 60 minutes or more (2000)

FAIRGROVE (village). Covers a land area of 1.096 square miles and a water area of 0 square miles. Located at 43.52° N. Lat.; 83.54° W. Long. Elevation is 659 feet.
Population: 627 (2000); Race: 96.5% White, 0.3% Black, 0.7% Asian, 0.0% American Indian and Alaska Native, 4.3% Hispanic of any race, 0.0% two or more races (2000); Density: 572.1 persons per square mile (2000); Age: 25.4% under 18, 12.4% over 64 (2000); Marriage status: 22.1% never married, 58.4% now married, 8.2% widowed, 11.3% divorced (2000); Foreign born: 4.1% (2000); Ancestry (includes multiple ancestries): 27.2% German, 10.5% Other groups, 9.1% United States or American, 7.9% English, 7.6% Polish (2000).
Economy: Employment by occupation: 7.9% management, 9.4% professional, 14.8% services, 20.6% sales, 2.2% farming, 12.6% construction, 32.5% production (2000).
Income: Per capita income: $17,741 (2000); Median household income: $35,391 (2000); Poverty rate: 7.8% (2000).
Taxes: Total city taxes per capita: $105 (1997); City property taxes per capita: $105 (1997).
Education: High school graduation rate: 72.5% (2000); College graduation rate: 6.3% (2000).

School District(s)

Akron-Fairgrove Schools (KG-12)
2000 Enrollment: 469 517-693-6163
Housing: Homeownership rate: 82.3% (2000); Median home value: $68,600 (2000); Median rent: $370 per month (2000); Median age of housing: 44 years (2000).

Transportation: Commute to work: 89.9% car, 1.5% public transportation, 4.5% walk, 4.1% work from home (2000); Travel time to work: 21.1% less than 15 minutes, 36.3% 15 to 30 minutes, 23.8% 30 to 45 minutes, 10.2% 45 to 60 minutes, 8.6% 60 minutes or more (2000)

FAIRGROVE (township). Covers a land area of 35.332 square miles and a water area of 0 square miles. Located at 43.52° N. Lat.; 83.52° W. Long. Elevation is 659 feet.
Population: 1,749 (2000); Race: 97.1% White, 0.1% Black, 0.3% Asian, 0.3% American Indian and Alaska Native, 3.1% Hispanic of any race, 1.1% two or more races (2000); Density: 49.5 persons per square mile (2000); Age: 24.9% under 18, 16.2% over 64 (2000); Marriage status: 21.9% never married, 60.4% now married, 8.6% widowed, 9.1% divorced (2000); Foreign born: 1.6% (2000); Ancestry (includes multiple ancestries): 35.9% German, 12.1% English, 9.7% Polish, 9.7% United States or American, 8.1% Other groups (2000).
Economy: In agricultural area. Employment by occupation: 12.1% management, 11.8% professional, 12.1% services, 23.1% sales, 1.7% farming, 13.0% construction, 26.1% production (2000).
Income: Per capita income: $20,511 (2000); Median household income: $39,653 (2000); Poverty rate: 5.8% (2000).
Taxes: Total city taxes per capita: $106 (1997); City property taxes per capita: $106 (1997).
Education: High school graduation rate: 81.6% (2000); College graduation rate: 10.7% (2000).
Housing: Homeownership rate: 84.4% (2000); Median home value: $70,400 (2000); Median rent: $370 per month (2000); Median age of housing: 50 years (2000).
Transportation: Commute to work: 91.0% car, 0.5% public transportation, 4.2% walk, 4.3% work from home (2000); Travel time to work: 27.3% less than 15 minutes, 31.6% 15 to 30 minutes, 24.2% 30 to 45 minutes, 9.8% 45 to 60 minutes, 7.0% 60 minutes or more (2000)

FOSTORIA (unincorporated postal area, zip code 48435). Covers a land area of 26.965 square miles and a water area of 0.025 square miles. Located at 43.23° N. Lat.; 83.36° W. Long.
Population: 2,231 (2000); Race: 97.2% White, 0.4% Black, 0.0% Asian, 0.8% American Indian and Alaska Native, 0.7% Hispanic of any race, 1.6% two or more races (2000); Density: 82.7 persons per square mile (2000); Age: 26.1% under 18, 12.8% over 64 (2000); Marriage status: 21.0% never married, 65.0% now married, 7.7% widowed, 6.3% divorced (2000); Foreign born: 0.2% (2000); Ancestry (includes multiple ancestries): 21.9% German, 14.8% Irish, 13.2% English, 11.8% United States or American, 7.0% Polish (2000).
Economy: Employment by occupation: 10.0% management, 11.5% professional, 13.5% services, 24.9% sales, 0.5% farming, 12.8% construction, 26.9% production (2000).
Income: Per capita income: $21,589 (2000); Median household income: $46,935 (2000); Poverty rate: 8.9% (2000).
Education: High school graduation rate: 79.5% (2000); College graduation rate: 8.3% (2000).
Housing: Homeownership rate: 89.0% (2000); Median home value: $101,000 (2000); Median rent: $427 per month (2000); Median age of housing: 27 years (2000).
Transportation: Commute to work: 97.8% car, 0.0% public transportation, 1.2% walk, 0.5% work from home (2000); Travel time to work: 10.8% less than 15 minutes, 33.1% 15 to 30 minutes, 21.1% 30 to 45 minutes, 8.3% 45 to 60 minutes, 26.6% 60 minutes or more (2000)

FREMONT (township). Covers a land area of 35.943 square miles and a water area of 0.189 square miles. Located at 43.35° N. Lat.; 83.38° W. Long.
Population: 3,559 (2000); Race: 97.1% White, 0.1% Black, 0.4% Asian, 0.7% American Indian and Alaska Native, 1.1% Hispanic of any race, 1.7% two or more races (2000); Density: 99.0 persons per square mile (2000); Age: 28.4% under 18, 12.7% over 64 (2000); Marriage status: 19.4% never married, 62.3% now married, 8.5% widowed, 9.8% divorced (2000); Foreign born: 0.9% (2000); Ancestry (includes multiple ancestries): 31.4% German, 13.4% English, 10.8% Irish, 10.3% Polish, 7.2% French (except Basque) (2000).
Economy: Employment by occupation: 4.9% management, 17.6% professional, 14.0% services, 17.3% sales, 1.9% farming, 14.2% construction, 30.2% production (2000).
Income: Per capita income: $16,355 (2000); Median household income: $38,909 (2000); Poverty rate: 9.7% (2000).
Taxes: Total city taxes per capita: $19 (1997); City property taxes per capita: $18 (1997).
Education: High school graduation rate: 77.7% (2000); College graduation rate: 8.7% (2000).
Housing: Homeownership rate: 85.0% (2000); Median home value: $88,300 (2000); Median rent: $350 per month (2000); Median age of housing: 30 years (2000).
Transportation: Commute to work: 93.5% car, 0.0% public transportation, 3.0% walk, 3.2% work from home (2000); Travel time to work: 19.7% less than 15 minutes, 27.0% 15 to 30 minutes, 23.9% 30 to 45 minutes, 14.7% 45 to 60 minutes, 14.8% 60 minutes or more (2000)

GAGETOWN (village). Covers a land area of 0.957 square miles and a water area of 0 square miles. Located at 43.65° N. Lat.; 83.24° W. Long.
History: Gagetown grew up around a mill and store operated by Joseph Gage in 1869. Gage platted the village in 1871, and it was named for him.
Population: 389 (2000); Race: 93.5% White, 0.0% Black, 0.0% Asian, 2.4% American Indian and Alaska Native, 4.0% Hispanic of any race, 3.5% two or more races (2000); Density: 406.3 persons per square mile (2000); Age: 27.2% under 18, 16.4% over 64 (2000); Marriage status: 26.8% never married, 54.0% now married, 10.1% widowed, 9.1% divorced (2000); Foreign born: 0.5% (2000); Ancestry (includes multiple ancestries): 30.1% German, 14.0% Other groups, 10.8% French (except Basque), 9.9% Irish, 8.9% English (2000).
Economy: Employment by occupation: 2.0% management, 6.6% professional, 17.8% services, 16.4% sales, 2.0% farming, 19.1% construction, 36.2% production (2000).
Income: Per capita income: $14,165 (2000); Median household income: $28,750 (2000); Poverty rate: 14.9% (2000).
Taxes: Total city taxes per capita: $112 (1997); City property taxes per capita: $109 (1997).
Education: High school graduation rate: 74.9% (2000); College graduation rate: 2.8% (2000).
Housing: Homeownership rate: 74.3% (2000); Median home value: $40,500 (2000); Median rent: $300 per month (2000); Median age of housing: 53 years (2000).
Transportation: Commute to work: 88.4% car, 0.0% public transportation, 8.8% walk, 1.4% work from home (2000); Travel time to work: 45.5% less than 15 minutes, 39.3% 15 to 30 minutes, 6.2% 30 to 45 minutes, 2.1% 45 to 60 minutes, 6.9% 60 minutes or more (2000)

GILFORD (township). Covers a land area of 34.793 square miles and a water area of 0 square miles. Located at 43.53° N. Lat.; 83.65° W. Long.
Population: 833 (2000); Race: 98.5% White, 0.2% Black, 0.0% Asian, 0.0% American Indian and Alaska Native, 3.7% Hispanic of any race, 0.6% two or more races (2000); Density: 23.9 persons per square mile (2000); Age: 27.8% under 18, 13.8% over 64 (2000); Marriage status: 23.0% never married, 65.7% now married, 7.5% widowed, 3.9% divorced (2000); Foreign born: 0.0% (2000); Ancestry (includes multiple ancestries): 45.0% German, 17.6% French (except Basque), 11.3% Polish, 9.9% English, 8.5% Other groups (2000).
Economy: Employment by occupation: 14.2% management, 13.2% professional, 12.2% services, 24.1% sales, 2.0% farming, 14.5% construction, 19.8% production (2000).
Income: Per capita income: $17,778 (2000); Median household income: $40,288 (2000); Poverty rate: 8.1% (2000).
Taxes: Total city taxes per capita: $102 (1997); City property taxes per capita: $102 (1997).
Education: High school graduation rate: 85.3% (2000); College graduation rate: 6.9% (2000).
Housing: Homeownership rate: 86.8% (2000); Median home value: $82,600 (2000); Median rent: $375 per month (2000); Median age of housing: 59 years (2000).
Transportation: Commute to work: 93.2% car, 0.0% public transportation, 0.5% walk, 6.3% work from home (2000); Travel time to work: 18.3% less than 15 minutes, 47.2% 15 to 30 minutes, 27.5% 30 to 45 minutes, 1.7% 45 to 60 minutes, 5.3% 60 minutes or more (2000)

INDIANFIELDS (township). Covers a land area of 34.740 square miles and a water area of 0.484 square miles. Located at 43.47° N. Lat.; 83.40° W. Long.
History: Indianfields Township was organized in 1852 and so named because the earliest inhabitants had used the area to raise corn and potatoes.
Population: 6,392 (2000); Race: 91.8% White, 3.1% Black, 0.1% Asian, 0.7% American Indian and Alaska Native, 4.6% Hispanic of any race, 2.1% two or more races (2000); Density: 184.0 persons per square mile (2000); Age: 24.1% under 18, 14.3% over 64 (2000); Marriage status: 27.6% never married, 52.0% now married, 7.4% widowed, 13.0% divorced (2000);

Foreign born: 1.2% (2000); Ancestry (includes multiple ancestries): 29.7% German, 14.9% Other groups, 12.3% Irish, 10.3% Polish, 10.2% English (2000).
Economy: Employment by occupation: 8.0% management, 16.8% professional, 19.6% services, 23.4% sales, 0.0% farming, 10.3% construction, 21.9% production (2000).
Income: Per capita income: $16,511 (2000); Median household income: $33,155 (2000); Poverty rate: 12.0% (2000).
Taxes: Total city taxes per capita: $24 (1997); City property taxes per capita: $24 (1997).
Education: High school graduation rate: 80.5% (2000); College graduation rate: 12.7% (2000).
Housing: Homeownership rate: 73.2% (2000); Median home value: $81,700 (2000); Median rent: $338 per month (2000); Median age of housing: 40 years (2000).
Transportation: Commute to work: 93.3% car, 0.4% public transportation, 2.2% walk, 2.7% work from home (2000); Travel time to work: 49.0% less than 15 minutes, 20.9% 15 to 30 minutes, 11.8% 30 to 45 minutes, 11.2% 45 to 60 minutes, 7.1% 60 minutes or more (2000)

JUNIATA (township). Covers a land area of 35.265 square miles and a water area of 0 square miles. Located at 43.44° N. Lat.; 83.51° W. Long. Elevation is 747 feet.
Population: 1,673 (2000); Race: 93.2% White, 2.2% Black, 0.0% Asian, 1.5% American Indian and Alaska Native, 2.9% Hispanic of any race, 1.1% two or more races (2000); Density: 47.4 persons per square mile (2000); Age: 29.3% under 18, 10.9% over 64 (2000); Marriage status: 22.2% never married, 64.5% now married, 5.5% widowed, 7.8% divorced (2000); Foreign born: 1.0% (2000); Ancestry (includes multiple ancestries): 33.9% German, 12.6% Other groups, 12.1% United States or American, 11.3% English, 10.2% Polish (2000).
Economy: Employment by occupation: 9.5% management, 14.1% professional, 16.2% services, 21.6% sales, 1.7% farming, 14.0% construction, 23.0% production (2000).
Income: Per capita income: $18,210 (2000); Median household income: $44,286 (2000); Poverty rate: 9.9% (2000).
Taxes: Total city taxes per capita: $64 (1997); City property taxes per capita: $63 (1997).
Education: High school graduation rate: 83.7% (2000); College graduation rate: 12.5% (2000).
Housing: Homeownership rate: 91.4% (2000); Median home value: $91,600 (2000); Median rent: $389 per month (2000); Median age of housing: 28 years (2000).
Transportation: Commute to work: 93.0% car, 0.6% public transportation, 1.7% walk, 4.8% work from home (2000); Travel time to work: 30.3% less than 15 minutes, 28.9% 15 to 30 minutes, 22.5% 30 to 45 minutes, 9.0% 45 to 60 minutes, 9.3% 60 minutes or more (2000)

KINGSTON (village). Covers a land area of 0.841 square miles and a water area of 0 square miles. Located at 43.41° N. Lat.; 83.18° W. Long. Elevation is 787 feet.
History: Alanson K. King settled here in 1857 on the only dry land in an area known as Tag Alder Swamp. First known as Newburg, the settlement was renamed Kingston in 1871, in honor of Alanson King.
Population: 450 (2000); Race: 94.2% White, 0.8% Black, 0.0% Asian, 0.0% American Indian and Alaska Native, 0.2% Hispanic of any race, 5.0% two or more races (2000); Density: 534.9 persons per square mile (2000); Age: 31.3% under 18, 11.6% over 64 (2000); Marriage status: 18.8% never married, 64.3% now married, 5.5% widowed, 11.4% divorced (2000); Foreign born: 0.0% (2000); Ancestry (includes multiple ancestries): 32.7% German, 22.4% English, 18.2% Irish, 14.1% Other groups, 11.8% Polish (2000).
Economy: Employment by occupation: 5.4% management, 17.6% professional, 22.2% services, 17.2% sales, 0.9% farming, 14.5% construction, 22.2% production (2000).
Income: Per capita income: $14,753 (2000); Median household income: $32,813 (2000); Poverty rate: 6.5% (2000).
Taxes: Total city taxes per capita: $138 (1997); City property taxes per capita: $129 (1997).
Education: High school graduation rate: 87.8% (2000); College graduation rate: 11.8% (2000).

School District(s)

Kingston Community School District (KG-12)
2000 Enrollment: 739 517-683-2294

Housing: Homeownership rate: 66.1% (2000); Median home value: $75,200 (2000); Median rent: $350 per month (2000); Median age of housing: 52 years (2000).
Transportation: Commute to work: 89.6% car, 0.0% public transportation, 5.4% walk, 5.0% work from home (2000); Travel time to work: 26.2% less than 15 minutes, 33.8% 15 to 30 minutes, 13.3% 30 to 45 minutes, 11.4% 45 to 60 minutes, 15.2% 60 minutes or more (2000)

KINGSTON (township). Covers a land area of 35.861 square miles and a water area of 0 square miles. Located at 43.44° N. Lat.; 83.17° W. Long. Elevation is 787 feet.
Population: 1,615 (2000); Race: 96.7% White, 0.3% Black, 0.0% Asian, 0.0% American Indian and Alaska Native, 0.9% Hispanic of any race, 2.7% two or more races (2000); Density: 45.0 persons per square mile (2000); Age: 28.1% under 18, 11.8% over 64 (2000); Marriage status: 23.0% never married, 59.8% now married, 6.2% widowed, 11.1% divorced (2000); Foreign born: 0.8% (2000); Ancestry (includes multiple ancestries): 27.5% German, 17.1% English, 14.4% Polish, 12.9% Irish, 10.4% Other groups (2000).
Economy: In agricultural area. Employment by occupation: 9.2% management, 12.9% professional, 11.4% services, 18.8% sales, 1.3% farming, 15.2% construction, 31.1% production (2000).
Income: Per capita income: $16,804 (2000); Median household income: $40,000 (2000); Poverty rate: 5.7% (2000).
Taxes: Total city taxes per capita: $48 (1997); City property taxes per capita: $47 (1997).
Education: High school graduation rate: 80.8% (2000); College graduation rate: 8.0% (2000).
Housing: Homeownership rate: 82.7% (2000); Median home value: $78,800 (2000); Median rent: $367 per month (2000); Median age of housing: 32 years (2000).
Transportation: Commute to work: 93.3% car, 0.0% public transportation, 1.8% walk, 3.7% work from home (2000); Travel time to work: 15.9% less than 15 minutes, 37.6% 15 to 30 minutes, 17.4% 30 to 45 minutes, 12.6% 45 to 60 minutes, 16.6% 60 minutes or more (2000)

KOYLTON (township). Covers a land area of 36.070 square miles and a water area of 0.082 square miles. Located at 43.37° N. Lat.; 83.16° W. Long.
History: Koylton Township was organized in 1859 and named for several settlers of that name who had come here in 1856 and 1857.
Population: 1,579 (2000); Race: 97.0% White, 0.0% Black, 0.5% Asian, 0.3% American Indian and Alaska Native, 1.5% Hispanic of any race, 2.0% two or more races (2000); Density: 43.8 persons per square mile (2000); Age: 30.3% under 18, 10.6% over 64 (2000); Marriage status: 20.3% never married, 65.5% now married, 5.2% widowed, 9.0% divorced (2000); Foreign born: 1.1% (2000); Ancestry (includes multiple ancestries): 25.6% German, 12.1% English, 10.7% Irish, 9.2% Other groups, 8.6% Polish (2000).
Economy: Employment by occupation: 7.1% management, 13.2% professional, 12.5% services, 16.5% sales, 1.8% farming, 21.2% construction, 27.6% production (2000).
Income: Per capita income: $17,179 (2000); Median household income: $41,667 (2000); Poverty rate: 6.2% (2000).
Taxes: Total city taxes per capita: $23 (1997); City property taxes per capita: $23 (1997).
Education: High school graduation rate: 82.6% (2000); College graduation rate: 10.3% (2000).
Housing: Homeownership rate: 86.0% (2000); Median home value: $95,900 (2000); Median rent: $409 per month (2000); Median age of housing: 28 years (2000).
Transportation: Commute to work: 95.9% car, 0.0% public transportation, 1.1% walk, 2.3% work from home (2000); Travel time to work: 26.7% less than 15 minutes, 22.3% 15 to 30 minutes, 16.4% 30 to 45 minutes, 14.9% 45 to 60 minutes, 19.7% 60 minutes or more (2000)

MAYVILLE (village). Covers a land area of 1.025 square miles and a water area of 0 square miles. Located at 43.33° N. Lat.; 83.35° W. Long. Elevation is 900 feet.
Population: 1,055 (2000); Race: 96.5% White, 0.4% Black, 0.0% Asian, 0.7% American Indian and Alaska Native, 1.3% Hispanic of any race, 2.1% two or more races (2000); Density: 1,028.9 persons per square mile (2000); Age: 29.5% under 18, 12.3% over 64 (2000); Marriage status: 24.8% never married, 56.3% now married, 6.6% widowed, 12.3% divorced (2000); Foreign born: 0.7% (2000); Ancestry (includes multiple ancestries): 30.8% German, 12.6% English, 10.2% Irish, 7.7% Other groups, 6.7% Polish (2000).

Economy: In agricultural area. Manufacturing: calcium chloride; machining. Employment by occupation: 5.6% management, 14.6% professional, 15.3% services, 23.1% sales, 1.4% farming, 15.5% construction, 24.5% production (2000).
Income: Per capita income: $15,281 (2000); Median household income: $33,375 (2000); Poverty rate: 11.3% (2000).
Taxes: Total city taxes per capita: $132 (1997); City property taxes per capita: $131 (1997).
Education: High school graduation rate: 80.3% (2000); College graduation rate: 8.3% (2000).

School District(s)

Mayville Community School District (KG-12)
2000 Enrollment: 1,192 517-843-6115
Housing: Homeownership rate: 69.8% (2000); Median home value: $79,600 (2000); Median rent: $350 per month (2000); Median age of housing: 55 years (2000).
Safety: Violent crime rate: 47.1 per 10,000 population; Property crime rate: 329.9 per 10,000 population (2001).
Newspapers: Mayville Monitor (1 x week)
Transportation: Commute to work: 89.9% car, 0.0% public transportation, 5.9% walk, 3.4% work from home (2000); Travel time to work: 26.1% less than 15 minutes, 26.7% 15 to 30 minutes, 19.1% 30 to 45 minutes, 13.0% 45 to 60 minutes, 15.0% 60 minutes or more (2000)

MILLINGTON (village). Covers a land area of 1.031 square miles and a water area of 0 square miles. Located at 43.28° N. Lat.; 83.52° W. Long. Elevation is 757 feet.
Population: 1,137 (2000); Race: 98.8% White, 0.4% Black, 0.6% Asian, 0.0% American Indian and Alaska Native, 1.9% Hispanic of any race, 0.0% two or more races (2000); Density: 1,102.7 persons per square mile (2000); Age: 24.2% under 18, 16.8% over 64 (2000); Marriage status: 26.9% never married, 50.3% now married, 10.3% widowed, 12.4% divorced (2000); Foreign born: 2.1% (2000); Ancestry (includes multiple ancestries): 29.5% German, 14.2% English, 9.7% United States or American, 7.5% Other groups, 7.1% French (except Basque) (2000).
Economy: Employment by occupation: 7.3% management, 13.1% professional, 15.0% services, 30.4% sales, 0.0% farming, 6.4% construction, 27.9% production (2000).
Income: Per capita income: $17,195 (2000); Median household income: $35,223 (2000); Poverty rate: 10.2% (2000).
Taxes: Total city taxes per capita: $174 (1997); City property taxes per capita: $174 (1997).
Education: High school graduation rate: 82.2% (2000); College graduation rate: 10.5% (2000).

School District(s)

Millington Community Schools (KG-12)
2000 Enrollment: 1,772 517-871-5201
Housing: Homeownership rate: 63.9% (2000); Median home value: $76,300 (2000); Median rent: $350 per month (2000); Median age of housing: 52 years (2000).
Transportation: Commute to work: 92.5% car, 0.0% public transportation, 5.5% walk, 1.9% work from home (2000); Travel time to work: 27.6% less than 15 minutes, 23.9% 15 to 30 minutes, 27.4% 30 to 45 minutes, 12.2% 45 to 60 minutes, 8.9% 60 minutes or more (2000)

MILLINGTON (township). Covers a land area of 35.768 square miles and a water area of 0.246 square miles. Located at 43.27° N. Lat.; 83.52° W. Long. Elevation is 757 feet.
Population: 4,459 (2000); Race: 98.6% White, 0.5% Black, 0.2% Asian, 0.0% American Indian and Alaska Native, 0.5% Hispanic of any race, 0.6% two or more races (2000); Density: 124.7 persons per square mile (2000); Age: 26.9% under 18, 9.8% over 64 (2000); Marriage status: 23.3% never married, 63.3% now married, 5.5% widowed, 7.9% divorced (2000); Foreign born: 0.8% (2000); Ancestry (includes multiple ancestries): 33.4% German, 13.7% English, 12.4% Irish, 8.4% French (except Basque), 8.3% Polish (2000).
Economy: In agricultural area: potatoes, beans, wheat, corn, soybeans, sugar beets; poultry, hogs. Manufacturing: fiberglass products, steel fabrication. Employment by occupation: 9.3% management, 12.1% professional, 14.0% services, 25.5% sales, 0.4% farming, 14.7% construction, 24.0% production (2000).
Income: Per capita income: $19,698 (2000); Median household income: $48,365 (2000); Poverty rate: 6.1% (2000).
Taxes: Total city taxes per capita: $41 (1997); City property taxes per capita: $41 (1997).
Education: High school graduation rate: 85.8% (2000); College graduation rate: 12.2% (2000).
Housing: Homeownership rate: 85.5% (2000); Median home value: $96,700 (2000); Median rent: $360 per month (2000); Median age of housing: 35 years (2000).
Transportation: Commute to work: 92.2% car, 0.0% public transportation, 3.6% walk, 4.3% work from home (2000); Travel time to work: 22.2% less than 15 minutes, 24.5% 15 to 30 minutes, 25.9% 30 to 45 minutes, 14.5% 45 to 60 minutes, 12.9% 60 minutes or more (2000)

NOVESTA (township). Covers a land area of 35.927 square miles and a water area of 0 square miles. Located at 43.54° N. Lat.; 83.17° W. Long.
Population: 1,606 (2000); Race: 97.4% White, 0.2% Black, 0.0% Asian, 0.9% American Indian and Alaska Native, 1.4% Hispanic of any race, 1.1% two or more races (2000); Density: 44.7 persons per square mile (2000); Age: 27.8% under 18, 10.9% over 64 (2000); Marriage status: 26.8% never married, 60.1% now married, 4.7% widowed, 8.4% divorced (2000); Foreign born: 0.7% (2000); Ancestry (includes multiple ancestries): 33.9% German, 13.1% English, 10.8% Irish, 9.8% Polish, 6.9% Other groups (2000).
Economy: Employment by occupation: 9.1% management, 10.1% professional, 12.9% services, 16.6% sales, 1.9% farming, 14.7% construction, 34.7% production (2000).
Income: Per capita income: $15,624 (2000); Median household income: $38,583 (2000); Poverty rate: 11.4% (2000).
Taxes: Total city taxes per capita: $59 (1997); City property taxes per capita: $52 (1997).
Education: High school graduation rate: 71.3% (2000); College graduation rate: 6.9% (2000).
Housing: Homeownership rate: 85.9% (2000); Median home value: $75,200 (2000); Median rent: $342 per month (2000); Median age of housing: 31 years (2000).
Transportation: Commute to work: 90.6% car, 0.4% public transportation, 1.2% walk, 6.8% work from home (2000); Travel time to work: 27.0% less than 15 minutes, 34.6% 15 to 30 minutes, 17.8% 30 to 45 minutes, 6.7% 45 to 60 minutes, 13.7% 60 minutes or more (2000)

REESE (village). Covers a land area of 1.150 square miles and a water area of 0 square miles. Located at 43.45° N. Lat.; 83.69° W. Long. Elevation is 628 feet.
History: Reese was settled in the mid-1860's. First called Gates for A.W. Gates, who was responsible for the town receiving a post office in 1871, the town was renamed for G.W. Reese, railroad superintendent, when the Detroit & Bay City Railroad built a station here in 1873.
Population: 1,375 (2000); Race: 98.4% White, 0.0% Black, 0.0% Asian, 0.3% American Indian and Alaska Native, 2.8% Hispanic of any race, 1.0% two or more races (2000); Density: 1,195.8 persons per square mile (2000); Age: 22.6% under 18, 14.9% over 64 (2000); Marriage status: 21.8% never married, 60.5% now married, 8.5% widowed, 9.2% divorced (2000); Foreign born: 0.7% (2000); Ancestry (includes multiple ancestries): 49.2% German, 9.8% Polish, 8.8% English, 8.7% French (except Basque), 7.9% Irish (2000).
Economy: Employment by occupation: 9.6% management, 19.4% professional, 15.4% services, 28.4% sales, 0.3% farming, 8.3% construction, 18.8% production (2000).
Income: Per capita income: $22,498 (2000); Median household income: $40,469 (2000); Poverty rate: 4.6% (2000).
Taxes: Total city taxes per capita: $132 (1997); City property taxes per capita: $131 (1997).
Education: High school graduation rate: 88.3% (2000); College graduation rate: 17.3% (2000).

School District(s)

Reese Public Schools (PK-12)
2000 Enrollment: 1,101 517-868-9864
Housing: Homeownership rate: 82.7% (2000); Median home value: $104,600 (2000); Median rent: $363 per month (2000); Median age of housing: 30 years (2000).
Safety: Violent crime rate: 0.0 per 10,000 population; Property crime rate: 79.6 per 10,000 population (2001).
Transportation: Commute to work: 97.4% car, 0.0% public transportation, 1.5% walk, 0.8% work from home (2000); Travel time to work: 21.8% less than 15 minutes, 48.2% 15 to 30 minutes, 18.3% 30 to 45 minutes, 3.8% 45 to 60 minutes, 7.9% 60 minutes or more (2000)

TUSCOLA (township). Covers a land area of 32.960 square miles and a water area of 0.092 square miles. Located at 43.34° N. Lat.; 83.63° W. Long. Elevation is 635 feet.

Population: 2,152 (2000); Race: 99.1% White, 0.0% Black, 0.0% Asian, 0.0% American Indian and Alaska Native, 1.0% Hispanic of any race, 0.2% two or more races (2000); Density: 65.3 persons per square mile (2000); Age: 31.0% under 18, 10.1% over 64 (2000); Marriage status: 20.0% never married, 69.0% now married, 5.4% widowed, 5.6% divorced (2000); Foreign born: 0.7% (2000); Ancestry (includes multiple ancestries): 50.3% German, 11.3% Irish, 9.1% French (except Basque), 8.9% English, 7.7% Polish (2000).
Economy: Employment by occupation: 12.0% management, 14.3% professional, 16.1% services, 23.7% sales, 1.0% farming, 12.5% construction, 20.4% production (2000).
Income: Per capita income: $18,986 (2000); Median household income: $49,130 (2000); Poverty rate: 4.4% (2000).
Taxes: Total city taxes per capita: $73 (1997); City property taxes per capita: $73 (1997).
Education: High school graduation rate: 87.4% (2000); College graduation rate: 12.0% (2000).
Housing: Homeownership rate: 88.9% (2000); Median home value: $98,900 (2000); Median rent: $440 per month (2000); Median age of housing: 39 years (2000).
Transportation: Commute to work: 93.4% car, 0.0% public transportation, 2.1% walk, 4.5% work from home (2000); Travel time to work: 38.9% less than 15 minutes, 28.3% 15 to 30 minutes, 21.1% 30 to 45 minutes, 6.4% 45 to 60 minutes, 5.3% 60 minutes or more (2000)

UNIONVILLE (village). Covers a land area of 0.928 square miles and a water area of 0 square miles. Located at 43.65° N. Lat.; 83.46° W. Long. Elevation is 620 feet.
History: Many of the early residents of Unionville were of German ancestry. The early economy here was based on sugar-beet production, and on coal mining.
Population: 605 (2000); Race: 97.4% White, 0.0% Black, 0.8% Asian, 0.0% American Indian and Alaska Native, 2.7% Hispanic of any race, 0.0% two or more races (2000); Density: 652.2 persons per square mile (2000); Age: 26.2% under 18, 13.9% over 64 (2000); Marriage status: 21.1% never married, 63.8% now married, 7.1% widowed, 8.1% divorced (2000); Foreign born: 2.1% (2000); Ancestry (includes multiple ancestries): 46.7% German, 9.0% English, 7.4% Polish, 7.3% Other groups, 6.8% French (except Basque) (2000).
Economy: Employment by occupation: 7.1% management, 16.6% professional, 18.0% services, 22.0% sales, 0.0% farming, 7.1% construction, 29.2% production (2000).
Income: Per capita income: $18,490 (2000); Median household income: $37,500 (2000); Poverty rate: 11.8% (2000).
Taxes: Total city taxes per capita: $124 (1997); City property taxes per capita: $124 (1997).
Education: High school graduation rate: 86.9% (2000); College graduation rate: 13.4% (2000).
Housing: Homeownership rate: 83.1% (2000); Median home value: $64,300 (2000); Median rent: $373 per month (2000); Median age of housing: 58 years (2000).
Transportation: Commute to work: 93.9% car, 0.0% public transportation, 2.0% walk, 4.1% work from home (2000); Travel time to work: 36.7% less than 15 minutes, 21.4% 15 to 30 minutes, 26.7% 30 to 45 minutes, 10.3% 45 to 60 minutes, 5.0% 60 minutes or more (2000)

VASSAR (city). Covers a land area of 2.230 square miles and a water area of 0 square miles. Located at 43.37° N. Lat.; 83.58° W. Long. Elevation is 640 feet.
History: Vassar was settled in 1849 on the Cass River, and named for Matthew Vassar, an uncle of one of the early settlers and the founder of Vassar College at Poughkeepsie, New York.
Population: 2,823 (2000); Race: 88.9% White, 7.3% Black, 0.0% Asian, 0.4% American Indian and Alaska Native, 3.1% Hispanic of any race, 2.4% two or more races (2000); Density: 1,266.2 persons per square mile (2000); Age: 34.0% under 18, 11.8% over 64 (2000); Marriage status: 34.3% never married, 50.5% now married, 5.8% widowed, 9.3% divorced (2000); Foreign born: 0.2% (2000); Ancestry (includes multiple ancestries): 28.8% German, 12.3% Other groups, 11.3% English, 11.0% Irish, 5.7% United States or American (2000).
Economy: Employment by occupation: 3.1% management, 18.4% professional, 18.9% services, 19.7% sales, 0.0% farming, 11.4% construction, 28.6% production (2000).
Income: Per capita income: $15,029 (2000); Median household income: $38,087 (2000); Poverty rate: 9.2% (2000).
Taxes: Total city taxes per capita: $360 (2000); City property taxes per capita: $357 (2000).
Education: High school graduation rate: 82.8% (2000); College graduation rate: 13.5% (2000).

School District(s)

Vassar Public Schools (PK-12)
2000 Enrollment: 2,001 517-823-8535

Housing: Homeownership rate: 68.6% (2000); Median home value: $69,000 (2000); Median rent: $378 per month (2000); Median age of housing: 49 years (2000).
Safety: Violent crime rate: 7.0 per 10,000 population; Property crime rate: 109.2 per 10,000 population (2001).
Newspapers: The Vassar Pioneer Times (1 x week)
Transportation: Commute to work: 93.8% car, 0.0% public transportation, 4.0% walk, 1.5% work from home (2000); Travel time to work: 39.0% less than 15 minutes, 27.1% 15 to 30 minutes, 19.4% 30 to 45 minutes, 5.7% 45 to 60 minutes, 8.7% 60 minutes or more (2000)
Additional Information Contacts
Vassar Chamber of Commerce. 989-823-2601

VASSAR (township). Covers a land area of 35.219 square miles and a water area of 0.121 square miles. Located at 43.34° N. Lat.; 83.53° W. Long. Elevation is 640 feet.
History: Settled 1849, incorporated 1871 as village, as city 1945.
Population: 4,356 (2000); Race: 96.7% White, 1.2% Black, 0.0% Asian, 0.6% American Indian and Alaska Native, 1.0% Hispanic of any race, 1.4% two or more races (2000); Density: 123.7 persons per square mile (2000); Age: 27.8% under 18, 8.0% over 64 (2000); Marriage status: 20.9% never married, 64.8% now married, 4.1% widowed, 10.2% divorced (2000); Foreign born: 0.8% (2000); Ancestry (includes multiple ancestries): 29.1% German, 12.5% French (except Basque), 11.7% English, 10.3% Irish, 6.4% Polish (2000).
Economy: Major railroad junction. Manufacturing of iron castings. Lumber. Agriculture: potatoes, sugar beets, grain, beans; poultry. Employment by occupation: 3.7% management, 11.8% professional, 17.0% services, 22.7% sales, 0.9% farming, 13.7% construction, 30.1% production (2000).
Income: Per capita income: $18,697 (2000); Median household income: $42,152 (2000); Poverty rate: 4.6% (2000).
Taxes: Total city taxes per capita: $73 (1997); City property taxes per capita: $49 (1997).
Education: High school graduation rate: 79.8% (2000); College graduation rate: 6.8% (2000).
Housing: Homeownership rate: 89.6% (2000); Median home value: $89,600 (2000); Median rent: $375 per month (2000); Median age of housing: 23 years (2000).
Transportation: Commute to work: 98.9% car, 0.0% public transportation, 0.0% walk, 1.1% work from home (2000); Travel time to work: 30.5% less than 15 minutes, 22.9% 15 to 30 minutes, 23.0% 30 to 45 minutes, 13.4% 45 to 60 minutes, 10.1% 60 minutes or more (2000)

WATERTOWN (township). Covers a land area of 32.664 square miles and a water area of 0.250 square miles. Located at 43.27° N. Lat.; 83.40° W. Long.
Population: 2,231 (2000); Race: 96.7% White, 0.4% Black, 0.4% Asian, 0.7% American Indian and Alaska Native, 1.2% Hispanic of any race, 1.8% two or more races (2000); Density: 68.3 persons per square mile (2000); Age: 27.1% under 18, 11.9% over 64 (2000); Marriage status: 20.3% never married, 66.5% now married, 5.4% widowed, 7.8% divorced (2000); Foreign born: 0.4% (2000); Ancestry (includes multiple ancestries): 24.2% German, 13.9% English, 11.6% Irish, 10.3% Other groups, 8.5% United States or American (2000).
Economy: Employment by occupation: 12.1% management, 11.5% professional, 14.2% services, 21.6% sales, 0.5% farming, 14.7% construction, 25.4% production (2000).
Income: Per capita income: $20,398 (2000); Median household income: $46,875 (2000); Poverty rate: 7.6% (2000).
Taxes: Total city taxes per capita: $17 (1997); City property taxes per capita: $17 (1997).
Education: High school graduation rate: 81.8% (2000); College graduation rate: 9.3% (2000).
Housing: Homeownership rate: 90.1% (2000); Median home value: $93,300 (2000); Median rent: $356 per month (2000); Median age of housing: 30 years (2000).
Transportation: Commute to work: 95.8% car, 0.0% public transportation, 0.0% walk, 3.0% work from home (2000); Travel time to work: 11.4% less

than 15 minutes, 23.6% 15 to 30 minutes, 25.1% 30 to 45 minutes, 10.9% 45 to 60 minutes, 29.0% 60 minutes or more (2000)

WELLS (township). Covers a land area of 35.417 square miles and a water area of 0.006 square miles. Located at 43.45° N. Lat.; 83.29° W. Long.
Population: 1,946 (2000); Race: 94.8% White, 1.8% Black, 0.0% Asian, 1.7% American Indian and Alaska Native, 1.3% Hispanic of any race, 0.9% two or more races (2000); Density: 54.9 persons per square mile (2000); Age: 22.9% under 18, 10.7% over 64 (2000); Marriage status: 25.6% never married, 58.9% now married, 5.3% widowed, 10.2% divorced (2000); Foreign born: 0.7% (2000); Ancestry (includes multiple ancestries): 27.7% German, 14.5% Polish, 10.4% English, 9.3% Other groups, 6.9% Irish (2000).
Economy: Employment by occupation: 9.3% management, 15.7% professional, 15.7% services, 21.2% sales, 0.6% farming, 12.1% construction, 25.2% production (2000).
Income: Per capita income: $18,986 (2000); Median household income: $43,200 (2000); Poverty rate: 9.8% (2000).
Taxes: Total city taxes per capita: $20 (1997); City property taxes per capita: $19 (1997).
Education: High school graduation rate: 74.7% (2000); College graduation rate: 7.3% (2000).
Housing: Homeownership rate: 93.3% (2000); Median home value: $87,900 (2000); Median rent: $378 per month (2000); Median age of housing: 25 years (2000).
Transportation: Commute to work: 95.5% car, 0.5% public transportation, 0.8% walk, 3.2% work from home (2000); Travel time to work: 21.5% less than 15 minutes, 35.2% 15 to 30 minutes, 13.0% 30 to 45 minutes, 10.7% 45 to 60 minutes, 19.6% 60 minutes or more (2000)

WISNER (township). Covers a land area of 19.365 square miles and a water area of 6.286 square miles. Located at 43.60° N. Lat.; 83.63° W. Long.
Population: 749 (2000); Race: 97.3% White, 0.0% Black, 0.3% Asian, 0.3% American Indian and Alaska Native, 3.3% Hispanic of any race, 1.1% two or more races (2000); Density: 38.7 persons per square mile (2000); Age: 17.7% under 18, 17.5% over 64 (2000); Marriage status: 16.3% never married, 66.2% now married, 9.0% widowed, 8.5% divorced (2000); Foreign born: 1.2% (2000); Ancestry (includes multiple ancestries): 32.5% German, 12.0% Irish, 12.0% English, 11.7% Polish, 10.6% French (except Basque) (2000).
Economy: Employment by occupation: 7.1% management, 14.1% professional, 10.9% services, 23.4% sales, 1.3% farming, 16.7% construction, 26.6% production (2000).
Income: Per capita income: $20,153 (2000); Median household income: $35,250 (2000); Poverty rate: 13.0% (2000).
Taxes: Total city taxes per capita: $28 (1997); City property taxes per capita: $28 (1997).
Education: High school graduation rate: 75.7% (2000); College graduation rate: 5.3% (2000).
Housing: Homeownership rate: 91.9% (2000); Median home value: $63,900 (2000); Median rent: $325 per month (2000); Median age of housing: 40 years (2000).
Transportation: Commute to work: 91.1% car, 0.0% public transportation, 1.6% walk, 6.6% work from home (2000); Travel time to work: 11.6% less than 15 minutes, 37.5% 15 to 30 minutes, 29.1% 30 to 45 minutes, 15.1% 45 to 60 minutes, 6.7% 60 minutes or more (2000)

Van Buren County

Located in southwestern Michigan; bounded on the west by Lake Michigan; drained by the Paw Paw and Black Rivers. Covers a land area of 610.90 square miles, a water area of 479.30 square miles, and is located in the Eastern Time Zone. The county government was organized in 1829. County seat is Paw Paw.

Van Buren County is part of the Kalamazoo-Battle Creek, MI MSA. The entire metro area includes: Calhoun County; Kalamazoo County; Van Buren County

Weather Station: Bloomingdale — Elevation: 725 feet

	Jan	Feb	Mar	Apr	May	Jun	Jul	Aug	Sep	Oct	Nov	Dec
High	30	34	44	57	69	79	83	81	73	61	47	36
Low	15	16	24	35	45	54	58	56	49	38	30	21
Precip	2.6	1.8	2.7	3.6	3.4	3.6	4.0	3.6	4.4	3.1	3.6	3.3
Snow	29.9	14.3	7.4	1.5	tr	0.0	0.0	0.0	0.0	0.4	8.1	22.8

High and Low temperatures in degrees Fahrenheit; Precipitation and Snow in inches

Weather Station: South Haven — Elevation: 620 feet

	Jan	Feb	Mar	Apr	May	Jun	Jul	Aug	Sep	Oct	Nov	Dec
High	32	35	44	55	66	75	79	78	72	62	48	37
Low	19	21	29	38	48	57	63	62	55	45	35	25
Precip	2.1	1.5	2.1	3.3	3.1	3.2	3.5	3.6	4.1	2.9	3.4	2.7
Snow	na	na	4.0	1.2	0.0	0.0	0.0	0.0	0.0	0.2	2.3	na

High and Low temperatures in degrees Fahrenheit; Precipitation and Snow in inches

Population: 76,263 (2000); Race: 87.8% White, 5.4% Black, 0.3% Asian, 0.8% American Indian and Alaska Native, 7.6% Hispanic of any race, 2.5% two or more races (2000); Density: 124.8 persons per square mile (2000); Age: 28.1% under 18, 12.3% over 64 (2000).
Religion: Five largest groups: 12.5% Catholic Church, 2.9% The United Methodist Church, 1.7% Lutheran Church—Missouri Synod, 1.4% Reformed Church in America, 1.0% Seventh-day Adventist Church (2000).
Economy: Unemployment rate: 5.4% (11/2002); Total civilian labor force: 37,917 (11/2002); Leading industries: 28.9% manufacturing; 16.0% retail trade; 11.9% health care and social assistance (2000); Companies that employ more than 1,000 persons: 0 (2000); Companies that employ more than 100 persons: 23 (2000); Farms: 1,059 totaling 177,360 acres (1997); Minority business ownership rate: 4.9% (1997); Women business ownership rate: 36.8% (1997); Retail sales per capita: $6,686 (1997). Single-family building permits issued: 397 (2001) / 412 (2000); Multi-family building permits issued: 0 (2001) / 35 (2000).
Income: Per capita income: $17,878 (2000); Median household income: $39,365 (2000); Poverty rate: 11.1% (2000); Bankruptcy rate: 5.38% (2001).
Taxes: Total county taxes per capita: $142 (2000); County property taxes per capita: $136 (2000).
Education: High school graduation rate: 78.9% (2000); College graduation rate: 14.3% (2000).
Housing: Homeownership rate: 79.5% (2000); Median home value: $94,200 (2000); Median rent: $374 per month (2000); Median age of housing: 31 years (2000).
Health: Birth rate: 137.4 per 10,000 population (1998); Age adjusted death rate: 89.1 per 10,000 population (1999); Age adjusted cancer mortality rate: 199.8 deaths per 100,000 population (1999). Number of physicians: 8.7 per 10,000 population (1999); Number of hospital beds: 29.6 per 10,000 population (1999).
Elections: 2000 Presidential election results: 46.8% Gore, 50.2% Bush, 2.3% Nader, 0.1% Buchanan
Additional Information Contacts
Van Buren County Government Offices 616-657-8253
Paw Paw Chamber of Commerce. 616-657-5395
South Haven Chamber of Commerce. 616-637-5171

Van Buren County Communities

ALMENA (township). Covers a land area of 34.477 square miles and a water area of 0.324 square miles. Located at 42.28° N. Lat.; 85.82° W. Long.
History: Almena Township was organized in 1842, and named by F.C. Annable for an Indian princess of whom he had heard.
Population: 4,226 (2000); Race: 96.9% White, 1.6% Black, 0.0% Asian, 0.0% American Indian and Alaska Native, 2.0% Hispanic of any race, 0.4% two or more races (2000); Density: 122.6 persons per square mile (2000); Age: 26.6% under 18, 9.6% over 64 (2000); Marriage status: 21.1% never married, 69.6% now married, 2.1% widowed, 7.2% divorced (2000); Foreign born: 1.3% (2000); Ancestry (includes multiple ancestries): 26.6% German, 17.2% English, 14.7% Irish, 14.2% Dutch, 7.9% United States or American (2000).
Economy: Single-family building permits issued: 60 (2001) / 60 (2000); Multi-family building permits issued: 0 (2001) / 0 (2000); Employment by occupation: 15.9% management, 18.3% professional, 11.6% services, 23.6% sales, 1.0% farming, 10.3% construction, 19.3% production (2000).
Income: Per capita income: $20,733 (2000); Median household income: $51,027 (2000); Poverty rate: 5.3% (2000).
Taxes: Total city taxes per capita: $27 (1997); City property taxes per capita: $27 (1997).
Education: High school graduation rate: 87.4% (2000); College graduation rate: 23.8% (2000).
Housing: Homeownership rate: 93.3% (2000); Median home value: $118,500 (2000); Median rent: $355 per month (2000); Median age of housing: 20 years (2000).
Transportation: Commute to work: 97.6% car, 0.0% public transportation, 0.5% walk, 1.4% work from home (2000); Travel time to work: 24.2% less than 15 minutes, 47.5% 15 to 30 minutes, 18.6% 30 to 45 minutes, 5.5% 45 to 60 minutes, 4.2% 60 minutes or more (2000)

ANTWERP (township). Covers a land area of 34.893 square miles and a water area of 0.194 square miles. Located at 42.19° N. Lat.; 85.82° W. Long.
History: Antwerp Township was organized in 1837 and named by its oldest inhabitant at the time, Harmon Van Antwerp, for Antwerp, Belgium.
Population: 10,813 (2000); Race: 93.9% White, 1.1% Black, 0.4% Asian, 0.4% American Indian and Alaska Native, 4.8% Hispanic of any race, 3.0% two or more races (2000); Density: 309.9 persons per square mile (2000); Age: 29.9% under 18, 9.7% over 64 (2000); Marriage status: 22.1% never married, 61.5% now married, 6.0% widowed, 10.4% divorced (2000); Foreign born: 2.2% (2000); Ancestry (includes multiple ancestries): 24.6% German, 13.4% Irish, 11.7% English, 11.3% Other groups, 11.2% Dutch (2000).
Economy: Single-family building permits issued: 71 (2001) / 71 (2000); Multi-family building permits issued: 0 (2001) / 0 (2000); Employment by occupation: 13.6% management, 17.9% professional, 15.6% services, 23.5% sales, 0.4% farming, 10.1% construction, 18.9% production (2000).
Income: Per capita income: $19,418 (2000); Median household income: $50,556 (2000); Poverty rate: 5.4% (2000).
Taxes: Total city taxes per capita: $48 (1997); City property taxes per capita: $41 (1997).
Education: High school graduation rate: 85.8% (2000); College graduation rate: 21.1% (2000).
Housing: Homeownership rate: 85.0% (2000); Median home value: $110,200 (2000); Median rent: $396 per month (2000); Median age of housing: 23 years (2000).
Transportation: Commute to work: 94.8% car, 0.3% public transportation, 2.1% walk, 2.0% work from home (2000); Travel time to work: 27.6% less than 15 minutes, 44.6% 15 to 30 minutes, 19.8% 30 to 45 minutes, 3.9% 45 to 60 minutes, 4.1% 60 minutes or more (2000)

ARLINGTON (township). Covers a land area of 34.501 square miles and a water area of 0.470 square miles. Located at 42.29° N. Lat.; 86.04° W. Long.
History: Arlington Township was organized in 1842 and named for the town in Vermont.
Population: 2,075 (2000); Race: 91.2% White, 4.7% Black, 0.1% Asian, 0.1% American Indian and Alaska Native, 7.7% Hispanic of any race, 0.5% two or more races (2000); Density: 60.1 persons per square mile (2000); Age: 27.4% under 18, 12.2% over 64 (2000); Marriage status: 23.6% never married, 59.2% now married, 6.1% widowed, 11.1% divorced (2000); Foreign born: 3.0% (2000); Ancestry (includes multiple ancestries): 25.2% German, 15.7% Other groups, 12.0% Irish, 11.2% English, 8.2% United States or American (2000).
Economy: Single-family building permits issued: 10 (2001) / 15 (2000); Multi-family building permits issued: 0 (2001) / 0 (2000); Employment by occupation: 9.0% management, 12.7% professional, 14.8% services, 19.8% sales, 1.5% farming, 13.0% construction, 29.2% production (2000).
Income: Per capita income: $16,349 (2000); Median household income: $36,847 (2000); Poverty rate: 11.2% (2000).
Taxes: Total city taxes per capita: $64 (1997); City property taxes per capita: $61 (1997).
Education: High school graduation rate: 77.5% (2000); College graduation rate: 8.8% (2000).
Housing: Homeownership rate: 88.5% (2000); Median home value: $84,100 (2000); Median rent: $350 per month (2000); Median age of housing: 35 years (2000).
Transportation: Commute to work: 89.5% car, 0.2% public transportation, 3.6% walk, 4.4% work from home (2000); Travel time to work: 28.2% less than 15 minutes, 30.5% 15 to 30 minutes, 23.7% 30 to 45 minutes, 10.1% 45 to 60 minutes, 7.5% 60 minutes or more (2000)

BANGOR (city). Covers a land area of 1.942 square miles and a water area of 0 square miles. Located at 42.31° N. Lat.; 86.11° W. Long. Elevation is 658 feet.
History: The city of Bangor was settled by Charles U. Cross in 1837 and, with the township, was named for Bangor, Maine. Bangor was incorporated as a village in 1877.
Population: 1,933 (2000); Race: 76.6% White, 13.0% Black, 0.0% Asian, 0.8% American Indian and Alaska Native, 12.7% Hispanic of any race, 2.6% two or more races (2000); Density: 995.4 persons per square mile (2000); Age: 30.8% under 18, 13.8% over 64 (2000); Marriage status: 26.6% never married, 49.3% now married, 9.1% widowed, 14.9% divorced (2000); Foreign born: 5.9% (2000); Ancestry (includes multiple ancestries): 28.2% Other groups, 17.7% German, 11.2% Irish, 11.0% English, 9.4% United States or American (2000).
Economy: Single-family building permits issued: 2 (2001) / 2 (2000); Multi-family building permits issued: 0 (2001) / 0 (2000); Employment by occupation: 5.0% management, 9.7% professional, 18.4% services, 22.8% sales, 2.9% farming, 7.4% construction, 33.8% production (2000).
Income: Per capita income: $14,925 (2000); Median household income: $28,165 (2000); Poverty rate: 16.3% (2000).
Taxes: Total city taxes per capita: $181 (1997); City property taxes per capita: $170 (1997).
Education: High school graduation rate: 66.7% (2000); College graduation rate: 8.2% (2000).

School District(s)

Bangor Public Schools (Van Buren (KG-12)
2000 Enrollment: 1,623 616-427-6800
Bangor Township School District #8 (KG-08)
2000 Enrollment: 19 616-427-8562

Housing: Homeownership rate: 64.4% (2000); Median home value: $60,600 (2000); Median rent: $330 per month (2000); Median age of housing: 45 years (2000).
Safety: Violent crime rate: 97.8 per 10,000 population; Property crime rate: 756.6 per 10,000 population (2001).
Transportation: Commute to work: 93.4% car, 0.0% public transportation, 4.6% walk, 0.7% work from home (2000); Travel time to work: 37.7% less than 15 minutes, 32.6% 15 to 30 minutes, 12.6% 30 to 45 minutes, 10.3% 45 to 60 minutes, 6.8% 60 minutes or more (2000); Amtrak: Service available.

BANGOR (township). Covers a land area of 33.718 square miles and a water area of 0.744 square miles. Located at 42.28° N. Lat.; 86.17° W. Long. Elevation is 658 feet.
History: Bangor Township was organized in 1854 and named for Bangor, Maine.
Population: 2,121 (2000); Race: 89.3% White, 2.1% Black, 0.2% Asian, 2.0% American Indian and Alaska Native, 13.2% Hispanic of any race, 1.2% two or more races (2000); Density: 62.9 persons per square mile (2000); Age: 28.2% under 18, 11.8% over 64 (2000); Marriage status: 20.6% never married, 65.8% now married, 4.6% widowed, 9.0% divorced (2000); Foreign born: 5.2% (2000); Ancestry (includes multiple ancestries): 24.4% German, 22.3% Other groups, 11.8% Irish, 9.8% English, 5.2% United States or American (2000).
Economy: Single-family building permits issued: 23 (2001) / 14 (2000); Multi-family building permits issued: 0 (2001) / 0 (2000); Employment by occupation: 11.4% management, 10.2% professional, 15.7% services, 19.7% sales, 3.4% farming, 14.5% construction, 25.2% production (2000).
Income: Per capita income: $16,759 (2000); Median household income: $35,375 (2000); Poverty rate: 11.6% (2000).
Taxes: Total city taxes per capita: $80 (1997); City property taxes per capita: $77 (1997).
Education: High school graduation rate: 74.5% (2000); College graduation rate: 7.0% (2000).
Housing: Homeownership rate: 80.7% (2000); Median home value: $81,800 (2000); Median rent: $363 per month (2000); Median age of housing: 33 years (2000).
Transportation: Commute to work: 95.0% car, 0.1% public transportation, 2.5% walk, 2.4% work from home (2000); Travel time to work: 33.0% less than 15 minutes, 35.7% 15 to 30 minutes, 13.0% 30 to 45 minutes, 11.8% 45 to 60 minutes, 6.5% 60 minutes or more (2000); Amtrak: Service available.

BLOOMINGDALE (village). Covers a land area of 1.125 square miles and a water area of 0 square miles. Located at 42.38° N. Lat.; 85.95° W. Long.
History: Bloomingdale was founded in 1855 by two men who came from Ohio. It was incorporated in 1881.
Population: 528 (2000); Race: 94.2% White, 2.2% Black, 0.0% Asian, 0.4% American Indian and Alaska Native, 2.6% Hispanic of any race, 2.4% two or more races (2000); Density: 469.5 persons per square mile (2000); Age: 28.6% under 18, 7.7% over 64 (2000); Marriage status: 25.9% never married, 53.7% now married, 5.1% widowed, 15.2% divorced (2000); Foreign born: 1.0% (2000); Ancestry (includes multiple ancestries): 18.1% United States or American, 15.3% German, 11.7% English, 10.5% Other groups, 6.9% Irish (2000).
Economy: Employment by occupation: 7.4% management, 16.2% professional, 11.6% services, 17.1% sales, 1.9% farming, 19.4% construction, 26.4% production (2000).
Income: Per capita income: $15,705 (2000); Median household income: $35,714 (2000); Poverty rate: 13.2% (2000).
Taxes: Total city taxes per capita: $66 (1997); City property taxes per capita: $66 (1997).

Education: High school graduation rate: 78.9% (2000); College graduation rate: 9.7% (2000).

School District(s)

Bloomingdale Public School District (KG-12)
2000 Enrollment: 1,355 616-521-3900

Housing: Homeownership rate: 76.7% (2000); Median home value: $70,800 (2000); Median rent: $330 per month (2000); Median age of housing: 60+ years (2000).

Safety: Violent crime rate: 75.3 per 10,000 population; Property crime rate: 753.3 per 10,000 population (2001).

Transportation: Commute to work: 90.7% car, 0.0% public transportation, 5.1% walk, 3.7% work from home (2000); Travel time to work: 22.3% less than 15 minutes, 29.6% 15 to 30 minutes, 26.2% 30 to 45 minutes, 21.8% 45 to 60 minutes, 0.0% 60 minutes or more (2000)

BLOOMINGDALE (township). Covers a land area of 34.070 square miles and a water area of 1.025 square miles. Located at 42.38° N. Lat.; 85.94° W. Long.

Population: 3,364 (2000); Race: 93.0% White, 1.9% Black, 0.0% Asian, 0.6% American Indian and Alaska Native, 5.7% Hispanic of any race, 1.5% two or more races (2000); Density: 98.7 persons per square mile (2000); Age: 28.2% under 18, 12.9% over 64 (2000); Marriage status: 23.2% never married, 58.4% now married, 6.8% widowed, 11.6% divorced (2000); Foreign born: 1.7% (2000); Ancestry (includes multiple ancestries): 23.6% German, 15.1% Other groups, 10.9% English, 10.8% Dutch, 10.8% Irish (2000).

Economy: Manufacturing of motor vehicle stampings. Single-family building permits issued: 18 (2001) / 21 (2000); Multi-family building permits issued: 0 (2001) / 0 (2000); Employment by occupation: 6.8% management, 16.3% professional, 10.5% services, 21.3% sales, 1.4% farming, 13.2% construction, 30.5% production (2000).

Income: Per capita income: $16,337 (2000); Median household income: $40,488 (2000); Poverty rate: 12.3% (2000).

Taxes: Total city taxes per capita: $73 (1997); City property taxes per capita: $66 (1997).

Education: High school graduation rate: 79.1% (2000); College graduation rate: 8.7% (2000).

Housing: Homeownership rate: 81.8% (2000); Median home value: $89,400 (2000); Median rent: $378 per month (2000); Median age of housing: 26 years (2000).

Transportation: Commute to work: 90.7% car, 0.0% public transportation, 2.9% walk, 4.7% work from home (2000); Travel time to work: 24.6% less than 15 minutes, 26.8% 15 to 30 minutes, 30.7% 30 to 45 minutes, 13.7% 45 to 60 minutes, 4.3% 60 minutes or more (2000)

BREEDSVILLE (village). Covers a land area of 0.670 square miles and a water area of 0 square miles. Located at 42.34° N. Lat.; 86.07° W. Long.

History: Breedsville was named for Silas Breed who built a sawmill here in 1835. The village was incorporated in 1883.

Population: 235 (2000); Race: 84.0% White, 0.8% Black, 0.0% Asian, 7.0% American Indian and Alaska Native, 10.7% Hispanic of any race, 0.8% two or more races (2000); Density: 350.7 persons per square mile (2000); Age: 30.7% under 18, 9.4% over 64 (2000); Marriage status: 28.5% never married, 56.4% now married, 4.5% widowed, 10.6% divorced (2000); Foreign born: 6.6% (2000); Ancestry (includes multiple ancestries): 43.9% Other groups, 9.8% United States or American, 7.0% English, 6.1% German, 3.7% Polish (2000).

Economy: Single-family building permits issued: 0 (2001) / 0 (2000); Multi-family building permits issued: 0 (2001) / 0 (2000); Employment by occupation: 9.0% management, 7.9% professional, 14.6% services, 23.6% sales, 0.0% farming, 14.6% construction, 30.3% production (2000).

Income: Per capita income: $11,741 (2000); Median household income: $32,917 (2000); Poverty rate: 28.0% (2000).

Taxes: Total city taxes per capita: $52 (1997); City property taxes per capita: $47 (1997).

Education: High school graduation rate: 61.2% (2000); College graduation rate: 6.1% (2000).

Housing: Homeownership rate: 83.6% (2000); Median home value: $43,300 (2000); Median rent: $513 per month (2000); Median age of housing: 58 years (2000).

Transportation: Commute to work: 96.6% car, 0.0% public transportation, 0.0% walk, 3.4% work from home (2000); Travel time to work: 23.8% less than 15 minutes, 36.9% 15 to 30 minutes, 15.5% 30 to 45 minutes, 23.8% 45 to 60 minutes, 0.0% 60 minutes or more (2000)

COLUMBIA (township). Covers a land area of 34.108 square miles and a water area of 1.348 square miles. Located at 42.37° N. Lat.; 86.04° W. Long.

Population: 2,714 (2000); Race: 88.6% White, 3.1% Black, 0.0% Asian, 1.2% American Indian and Alaska Native, 9.9% Hispanic of any race, 1.4% two or more races (2000); Density: 79.6 persons per square mile (2000); Age: 29.2% under 18, 12.4% over 64 (2000); Marriage status: 23.4% never married, 59.7% now married, 5.8% widowed, 11.1% divorced (2000); Foreign born: 4.5% (2000); Ancestry (includes multiple ancestries): 29.6% Other groups, 15.0% German, 9.8% Irish, 8.4% English, 6.6% Polish (2000).

Economy: Single-family building permits issued: 11 (2001) / 25 (2000); Multi-family building permits issued: 0 (2001) / 0 (2000); Employment by occupation: 8.6% management, 11.2% professional, 17.1% services, 17.7% sales, 3.7% farming, 11.5% construction, 30.1% production (2000).

Income: Per capita income: $15,015 (2000); Median household income: $34,389 (2000); Poverty rate: 18.0% (2000).

Taxes: Total city taxes per capita: $39 (1997); City property taxes per capita: $33 (1997).

Education: High school graduation rate: 71.5% (2000); College graduation rate: 9.8% (2000).

Housing: Homeownership rate: 86.8% (2000); Median home value: $73,200 (2000); Median rent: $401 per month (2000); Median age of housing: 31 years (2000).

Transportation: Commute to work: 97.1% car, 0.0% public transportation, 0.0% walk, 2.5% work from home (2000); Travel time to work: 16.6% less than 15 minutes, 32.9% 15 to 30 minutes, 24.6% 30 to 45 minutes, 17.0% 45 to 60 minutes, 8.9% 60 minutes or more (2000)

COVERT (township). Covers a land area of 34.988 square miles and a water area of 0 square miles. Located at 42.29° N. Lat.; 86.28° W. Long. Elevation is 690 feet.

Population: 3,141 (2000); Race: 51.2% White, 36.1% Black, 0.0% Asian, 1.5% American Indian and Alaska Native, 15.7% Hispanic of any race, 4.6% two or more races (2000); Density: 89.8 persons per square mile (2000); Age: 31.7% under 18, 12.5% over 64 (2000); Marriage status: 25.6% never married, 51.6% now married, 10.7% widowed, 12.2% divorced (2000); Foreign born: 7.1% (2000); Ancestry (includes multiple ancestries): 50.6% Other groups, 9.0% Irish, 8.7% German, 4.2% United States or American, 3.4% English (2000).

Economy: Single-family building permits issued: 13 (2001) / 13 (2000); Multi-family building permits issued: 0 (2001) / 0 (2000); Employment by occupation: 7.3% management, 6.7% professional, 20.0% services, 17.8% sales, 3.6% farming, 15.1% construction, 29.5% production (2000).

Income: Per capita income: $12,156 (2000); Median household income: $22,829 (2000); Poverty rate: 32.4% (2000).

Taxes: Total city taxes per capita: $327 (2000); City property taxes per capita: $323 (2000).

Education: High school graduation rate: 63.3% (2000); College graduation rate: 7.6% (2000).

School District(s)

Covert Public Schools (KG-12)
2000 Enrollment: 696 616-764-0201

Housing: Homeownership rate: 68.7% (2000); Median home value: $63,800 (2000); Median rent: $304 per month (2000); Median age of housing: 34 years (2000).

Safety: Violent crime rate: 72.8 per 10,000 population; Property crime rate: 380.0 per 10,000 population (2001).

Transportation: Commute to work: 92.2% car, 0.0% public transportation, 1.3% walk, 4.0% work from home (2000); Travel time to work: 23.3% less than 15 minutes, 40.8% 15 to 30 minutes, 20.1% 30 to 45 minutes, 9.4% 45 to 60 minutes, 6.5% 60 minutes or more (2000)

DECATUR (village). Covers a land area of 1.149 square miles and a water area of 0 square miles. Located at 42.11° N. Lat.; 85.97° W. Long. Elevation is 781 feet.

Population: 1,838 (2000); Race: 84.3% White, 9.4% Black, 0.1% Asian, 1.7% American Indian and Alaska Native, 2.1% Hispanic of any race, 3.3% two or more races (2000); Density: 1,599.1 persons per square mile (2000); Age: 26.0% under 18, 17.0% over 64 (2000); Marriage status: 26.8% never married, 46.9% now married, 10.7% widowed, 15.7% divorced (2000); Foreign born: 1.8% (2000); Ancestry (includes multiple ancestries): 25.0% German, 18.9% Other groups, 14.4% Irish, 12.4% Dutch, 7.1% Polish (2000).

Economy: Single-family building permits issued: 4 (2001) / 3 (2000); Multi-family building permits issued: 0 (2001) / 0 (2000); Employment by occupation: 3.4% management, 10.6% professional, 19.6% services, 30.2% sales, 3.1% farming, 6.9% construction, 26.3% production (2000).

Income: Per capita income: $14,098 (2000); Median household income: $30,550 (2000); Poverty rate: 20.9% (2000).
Taxes: Total city taxes per capita: $143 (1997); City property taxes per capita: $139 (1997).
Education: High school graduation rate: 73.0% (2000); College graduation rate: 7.9% (2000).

School District(s)

Decatur Public Schools (KG-12)
2000 Enrollment: 1,128 616-423-6111
Housing: Homeownership rate: 66.1% (2000); Median home value: $65,800 (2000); Median rent: $340 per month (2000); Median age of housing: 60 years (2000).
Safety: Violent crime rate: 70.3 per 10,000 population; Property crime rate: 633.1 per 10,000 population (2001).
Newspapers: Decatur Republican (1 x week)
Transportation: Commute to work: 96.1% car, 0.0% public transportation, 3.1% walk, 0.4% work from home (2000); Travel time to work: 31.1% less than 15 minutes, 37.9% 15 to 30 minutes, 16.1% 30 to 45 minutes, 11.3% 45 to 60 minutes, 3.5% 60 minutes or more (2000)

DECATUR (township). Covers a land area of 35.191 square miles and a water area of 0.349 square miles. Located at 42.11° N. Lat.; 85.95° W. Long. Elevation is 781 feet.
History: Incorporated 1861.
Population: 3,916 (2000); Race: 88.0% White, 5.6% Black, 0.4% Asian, 1.1% American Indian and Alaska Native, 4.1% Hispanic of any race, 2.0% two or more races (2000); Density: 111.3 persons per square mile (2000); Age: 27.3% under 18, 13.4% over 64 (2000); Marriage status: 25.4% never married, 52.9% now married, 8.3% widowed, 13.4% divorced (2000); Foreign born: 2.5% (2000); Ancestry (includes multiple ancestries): 22.4% German, 14.3% Other groups, 12.6% United States or American, 11.0% Irish, 9.6% Dutch (2000).
Economy: In farm area: grains, vegetables, fruit; livestock; light manufacturing. Small (resort) lakes nearby, especially Southeast. Single-family building permits issued: 11 (2001) / 11 (2000); Multi-family building permits issued: 0 (2001) / 0 (2000); Employment by occupation: 8.1% management, 8.5% professional, 19.4% services, 24.2% sales, 2.3% farming, 8.2% construction, 29.3% production (2000).
Income: Per capita income: $16,912 (2000); Median household income: $35,754 (2000); Poverty rate: 14.2% (2000).
Taxes: Total city taxes per capita: $49 (1997); City property taxes per capita: $48 (1997).
Education: High school graduation rate: 74.3% (2000); College graduation rate: 7.2% (2000).
Housing: Homeownership rate: 74.9% (2000); Median home value: $69,800 (2000); Median rent: $358 per month (2000); Median age of housing: 45 years (2000).
Transportation: Commute to work: 96.1% car, 0.0% public transportation, 1.4% walk, 2.0% work from home (2000); Travel time to work: 30.0% less than 15 minutes, 39.6% 15 to 30 minutes, 18.1% 30 to 45 minutes, 9.1% 45 to 60 minutes, 3.3% 60 minutes or more (2000)

GENEVA (township). Covers a land area of 35.322 square miles and a water area of 0.019 square miles. Located at 42.37° N. Lat.; 86.18° W. Long.
Population: 3,975 (2000); Race: 82.3% White, 11.1% Black, 0.2% Asian, 1.4% American Indian and Alaska Native, 5.6% Hispanic of any race, 2.6% two or more races (2000); Density: 112.5 persons per square mile (2000); Age: 28.9% under 18, 11.7% over 64 (2000); Marriage status: 20.9% never married, 57.9% now married, 8.0% widowed, 13.3% divorced (2000); Foreign born: 2.5% (2000); Ancestry (includes multiple ancestries): 29.3% Other groups, 18.1% German, 8.4% Irish, 7.7% English, 6.9% Polish (2000).
Economy: Single-family building permits issued: 22 (2001) / 23 (2000); Multi-family building permits issued: 0 (2001) / 0 (2000); Employment by occupation: 8.2% management, 10.1% professional, 17.1% services, 23.0% sales, 2.3% farming, 9.2% construction, 29.9% production (2000).
Income: Per capita income: $16,499 (2000); Median household income: $34,900 (2000); Poverty rate: 10.4% (2000).
Taxes: Total city taxes per capita: $96 (1997); City property taxes per capita: $91 (1997).
Education: High school graduation rate: 80.1% (2000); College graduation rate: 10.3% (2000).
Housing: Homeownership rate: 86.1% (2000); Median home value: $97,800 (2000); Median rent: $347 per month (2000); Median age of housing: 19 years (2000).
Transportation: Commute to work: 96.1% car, 0.0% public transportation, 0.8% walk, 2.7% work from home (2000); Travel time to work: 41.7% less than 15 minutes, 34.5% 15 to 30 minutes, 10.8% 30 to 45 minutes, 7.3% 45 to 60 minutes, 5.6% 60 minutes or more (2000)

GOBLES (city). Covers a land area of 1.036 square miles and a water area of 0 square miles. Located at 42.36° N. Lat.; 85.87° W. Long. Elevation is 815 feet.
History: Gobles was named for the Gobles. John Goble built a hotel here in the mid-1860's; Hiram E. Goble platted the village in 1870; Warren Goble made an addition to the plat in 1872, when Hiram Goble became the postmaster. Gobles was incorporated as a village in 1893, and as a city in 1957.
Population: 815 (2000); Race: 92.3% White, 0.1% Black, 0.0% Asian, 3.1% American Indian and Alaska Native, 4.5% Hispanic of any race, 4.0% two or more races (2000); Density: 786.9 persons per square mile (2000); Age: 29.9% under 18, 13.3% over 64 (2000); Marriage status: 29.3% never married, 47.2% now married, 8.4% widowed, 15.1% divorced (2000); Foreign born: 0.9% (2000); Ancestry (includes multiple ancestries): 20.0% German, 13.4% Irish, 13.1% Other groups, 12.9% English, 10.9% Dutch (2000).
Economy: Single-family building permits issued: 2 (2001) / 2 (2000); Multi-family building permits issued: 0 (2001) / 0 (2000); Employment by occupation: 6.3% management, 11.1% professional, 17.8% services, 21.1% sales, 0.6% farming, 8.7% construction, 34.3% production (2000).
Income: Per capita income: $12,804 (2000); Median household income: $26,917 (2000); Poverty rate: 18.3% (2000).
Taxes: Total city taxes per capita: $202 (1997); City property taxes per capita: $198 (1997).
Education: High school graduation rate: 79.4% (2000); College graduation rate: 6.0% (2000).

School District(s)

Gobles Public School District (KG-12)
2000 Enrollment: 1,035 616-628-5618
Housing: Homeownership rate: 62.6% (2000); Median home value: $69,000 (2000); Median rent: $364 per month (2000); Median age of housing: 48 years (2000).
Transportation: Commute to work: 92.2% car, 0.0% public transportation, 5.3% walk, 1.2% work from home (2000); Travel time to work: 24.9% less than 15 minutes, 43.5% 15 to 30 minutes, 22.1% 30 to 45 minutes, 4.4% 45 to 60 minutes, 5.0% 60 minutes or more (2000)

GRAND JUNCTION (unincorporated postal area, zip code 49056). Covers a land area of 53.822 square miles and a water area of 1.656 square miles. Located at 42.39° N. Lat.; 86.05° W. Long. Elevation is 682 feet.
History: Grand Junction, at the junction of two railroads, was first settled by David Young, who built an inn here in 1869.
Population: 4,107 (2000); Race: 85.7% White, 5.9% Black, 0.0% Asian, 0.7% American Indian and Alaska Native, 10.1% Hispanic of any race, 1.6% two or more races (2000); Density: 76.3 persons per square mile (2000); Age: 28.7% under 18, 11.9% over 64 (2000); Marriage status: 24.1% never married, 58.4% now married, 5.4% widowed, 12.0% divorced (2000); Foreign born: 3.7% (2000); Ancestry (includes multiple ancestries): 26.7% Other groups, 14.5% German, 9.0% Irish, 8.7% English, 7.2% United States or American (2000).
Economy: Employment by occupation: 7.3% management, 9.8% professional, 16.4% services, 16.0% sales, 3.7% farming, 10.8% construction, 36.0% production (2000).
Income: Per capita income: $13,923 (2000); Median household income: $32,276 (2000); Poverty rate: 19.3% (2000).
Education: High school graduation rate: 73.0% (2000); College graduation rate: 7.1% (2000).
Housing: Homeownership rate: 81.9% (2000); Median home value: $77,600 (2000); Median rent: $366 per month (2000); Median age of housing: 30 years (2000).
Transportation: Commute to work: 96.4% car, 0.3% public transportation, 0.6% walk, 2.1% work from home (2000); Travel time to work: 12.3% less than 15 minutes, 41.4% 15 to 30 minutes, 22.4% 30 to 45 minutes, 13.5% 45 to 60 minutes, 10.4% 60 minutes or more (2000)

HAMILTON (township). Covers a land area of 34.465 square miles and a water area of 1.128 square miles. Located at 42.10° N. Lat.; 86.05° W. Long.
History: Hamilton Township was first settled in the early 1830's. When it was organized in 1839, it was called Alpina, but was renamed in 1840 to honor Alexander Hamilton, American statesman.
Population: 1,797 (2000); Race: 85.2% White, 1.9% Black, 0.3% Asian, 1.3% American Indian and Alaska Native, 21.1% Hispanic of any race, 5.8%

two or more races (2000); Density: 52.1 persons per square mile (2000); Age: 30.9% under 18, 12.3% over 64 (2000); Marriage status: 18.7% never married, 65.2% now married, 6.4% widowed, 9.8% divorced (2000); Foreign born: 7.8% (2000); Ancestry (includes multiple ancestries): 23.7% Other groups, 22.3% German, 11.7% Irish, 9.4% English, 8.4% Dutch (2000).
Economy: Single-family building permits issued: 14 (2001) / 14 (2000); Multi-family building permits issued: 0 (2001) / 0 (2000); Employment by occupation: 9.5% management, 10.5% professional, 12.2% services, 21.1% sales, 9.1% farming, 10.6% construction, 27.0% production (2000).
Income: Per capita income: $16,169 (2000); Median household income: $37,434 (2000); Poverty rate: 13.5% (2000).
Taxes: Total city taxes per capita: $71 (1997); City property taxes per capita: $70 (1997).
Education: High school graduation rate: 65.8% (2000); College graduation rate: 10.0% (2000).
Housing: Homeownership rate: 86.1% (2000); Median home value: $88,600 (2000); Median rent: $363 per month (2000); Median age of housing: 27 years (2000).
Transportation: Commute to work: 91.9% car, 0.8% public transportation, 5.1% walk, 1.2% work from home (2000); Travel time to work: 29.1% less than 15 minutes, 35.1% 15 to 30 minutes, 16.7% 30 to 45 minutes, 13.4% 45 to 60 minutes, 5.7% 60 minutes or more (2000)

HARTFORD (city). Covers a land area of 1.371 square miles and a water area of 0 square miles. Located at 42.20° N. Lat.; 86.16° W. Long. Elevation is 664 feet.
History: Hartford developed as a shipping center for the fruits and vegetables grown in the area. An industry in Hartford was a foliage factory, where natural foliage was preserved for use in garlands and wreaths.
Population: 2,476 (2000); Race: 83.8% White, 0.4% Black, 0.4% Asian, 2.1% American Indian and Alaska Native, 14.9% Hispanic of any race, 5.2% two or more races (2000); Density: 1,805.6 persons per square mile (2000); Age: 29.6% under 18, 10.6% over 64 (2000); Marriage status: 27.0% never married, 50.7% now married, 7.5% widowed, 14.8% divorced (2000); Foreign born: 3.8% (2000); Ancestry (includes multiple ancestries): 31.4% Other groups, 15.8% German, 15.4% Irish, 7.8% English, 6.1% United States or American (2000).
Economy: Single-family building permits issued: 5 (2001) / 2 (2000); Multi-family building permits issued: 0 (2001) / 0 (2000); Employment by occupation: 7.8% management, 7.8% professional, 14.2% services, 24.3% sales, 2.3% farming, 8.0% construction, 35.7% production (2000).
Income: Per capita income: $14,181 (2000); Median household income: $32,879 (2000); Poverty rate: 16.1% (2000).
Taxes: Total city taxes per capita: $157 (1997); City property taxes per capita: $154 (1997).
Education: High school graduation rate: 68.9% (2000); College graduation rate: 6.4% (2000).

School District(s)

Hartford Public School District (KG-12)
2000 Enrollment: 1,440 616-621-2441
Housing: Homeownership rate: 67.0% (2000); Median home value: $62,600 (2000); Median rent: $351 per month (2000); Median age of housing: 45 years (2000).
Safety: Violent crime rate: 88.4 per 10,000 population; Property crime rate: 630.8 per 10,000 population (2001).
Transportation: Commute to work: 91.3% car, 0.0% public transportation, 6.0% walk, 1.9% work from home (2000); Travel time to work: 32.6% less than 15 minutes, 38.7% 15 to 30 minutes, 22.1% 30 to 45 minutes, 3.8% 45 to 60 minutes, 2.7% 60 minutes or more (2000)

HARTFORD (township). Covers a land area of 33.721 square miles and a water area of 0.118 square miles. Located at 42.20° N. Lat.; 86.17° W. Long. Elevation is 664 feet.
History: Hartford Township was settled in 1837 and organized in 1840 under the name of Hartland, for the home town in New York of Ferdino Olds, the first settler here. Since there was already a Hartland in Michigan, the name was changed to Hartford.
Population: 3,159 (2000); Race: 87.7% White, 0.8% Black, 0.1% Asian, 0.5% American Indian and Alaska Native, 13.9% Hispanic of any race, 3.6% two or more races (2000); Density: 93.7 persons per square mile (2000); Age: 28.5% under 18, 11.0% over 64 (2000); Marriage status: 24.2% never married, 61.4% now married, 6.3% widowed, 8.1% divorced (2000); Foreign born: 7.6% (2000); Ancestry (includes multiple ancestries): 21.6% Other groups, 14.8% German, 12.5% Irish, 10.7% English, 8.1% United States or American (2000).
Economy: Single-family building permits issued: 12 (2001) / 12 (2000); Multi-family building permits issued: 0 (2001) / 0 (2000); Employment by occupation: 5.8% management, 11.4% professional, 12.6% services, 24.9% sales, 2.2% farming, 13.7% construction, 29.4% production (2000).
Income: Per capita income: $14,801 (2000); Median household income: $35,741 (2000); Poverty rate: 12.8% (2000).
Taxes: Total city taxes per capita: $38 (2000); City property taxes per capita: $35 (2000).
Education: High school graduation rate: 70.1% (2000); College graduation rate: 8.8% (2000).
Housing: Homeownership rate: 79.4% (2000); Median home value: $79,900 (2000); Median rent: $371 per month (2000); Median age of housing: 28 years (2000).
Transportation: Commute to work: 94.1% car, 0.0% public transportation, 1.3% walk, 3.4% work from home (2000); Travel time to work: 28.0% less than 15 minutes, 36.4% 15 to 30 minutes, 24.0% 30 to 45 minutes, 6.2% 45 to 60 minutes, 5.3% 60 minutes or more (2000)

KEELER (township). Covers a land area of 34.008 square miles and a water area of 1.014 square miles. Located at 42.10° N. Lat.; 86.17° W. Long. Elevation is 806 feet.
History: Keeler Township was organized about 1835, and named for Eleazer H. Keeler, tavern operator who became the first postmaster.
Population: 2,601 (2000); Race: 87.8% White, 0.0% Black, 0.2% Asian, 1.7% American Indian and Alaska Native, 23.7% Hispanic of any race, 4.2% two or more races (2000); Density: 76.5 persons per square mile (2000); Age: 29.0% under 18, 12.0% over 64 (2000); Marriage status: 23.3% never married, 62.0% now married, 6.5% widowed, 8.2% divorced (2000); Foreign born: 7.6% (2000); Ancestry (includes multiple ancestries): 18.7% Other groups, 17.0% German, 12.6% Irish, 10.0% English, 6.7% United States or American (2000).
Economy: Single-family building permits issued: 6 (2001) / 6 (2000); Multi-family building permits issued: 0 (2001) / 0 (2000); Employment by occupation: 14.0% management, 10.3% professional, 9.2% services, 24.3% sales, 8.2% farming, 10.4% construction, 23.6% production (2000).
Income: Per capita income: $19,989 (2000); Median household income: $42,955 (2000); Poverty rate: 16.4% (2000).
Taxes: Total city taxes per capita: $93 (1997); City property taxes per capita: $81 (1997).
Education: High school graduation rate: 71.4% (2000); College graduation rate: 9.8% (2000).
Housing: Homeownership rate: 80.1% (2000); Median home value: $85,900 (2000); Median rent: $339 per month (2000); Median age of housing: 40 years (2000).
Transportation: Commute to work: 89.6% car, 0.6% public transportation, 2.2% walk, 5.1% work from home (2000); Travel time to work: 22.2% less than 15 minutes, 45.5% 15 to 30 minutes, 21.7% 30 to 45 minutes, 4.0% 45 to 60 minutes, 6.6% 60 minutes or more (2000)

LAWRENCE (village). Covers a land area of 1.764 square miles and a water area of 0 square miles. Located at 42.21° N. Lat.; 86.05° W. Long. Elevation is 686 feet.
History: Lawrence, founded in 1835 by John Allen, once served as a loading point for flatboats on the Paw Paw River. First known as Mason (for Governor Stevens T. Mason) and later as Brush Creek (for the stream through it), the name of Lawrence was established in 1844. The area produced a variety of fruits and vegetables.
Population: 1,059 (2000); Race: 80.5% White, 2.9% Black, 1.0% Asian, 0.0% American Indian and Alaska Native, 21.0% Hispanic of any race, 5.0% two or more races (2000); Density: 600.4 persons per square mile (2000); Age: 29.9% under 18, 9.0% over 64 (2000); Marriage status: 25.4% never married, 52.1% now married, 9.7% widowed, 12.7% divorced (2000); Foreign born: 9.5% (2000); Ancestry (includes multiple ancestries): 33.1% Other groups, 18.5% German, 11.0% English, 10.6% Irish, 7.3% Dutch (2000).
Economy: Single-family building permits issued: 2 (2001) / 1 (2000); Multi-family building permits issued: 0 (2001) / 0 (2000); Employment by occupation: 5.6% management, 13.7% professional, 13.7% services, 19.5% sales, 3.6% farming, 11.4% construction, 32.5% production (2000).
Income: Per capita income: $13,169 (2000); Median household income: $29,583 (2000); Poverty rate: 19.1% (2000).
Taxes: Total city taxes per capita: $154 (1997); City property taxes per capita: $150 (1997).
Education: High school graduation rate: 66.0% (2000); College graduation rate: 9.0% (2000).

School District(s)

Lawrence Public School District (KG-12)
2000 Enrollment: 859 616-674-8233

Housing: Homeownership rate: 63.6% (2000); Median home value: $70,600 (2000); Median rent: $300 per month (2000); Median age of housing: 45 years (2000).

Safety: Violent crime rate: 56.3 per 10,000 population; Property crime rate: 863.8 per 10,000 population (2001).

Transportation: Commute to work: 93.1% car, 0.0% public transportation, 4.4% walk, 2.1% work from home (2000); Travel time to work: 27.7% less than 15 minutes, 28.9% 15 to 30 minutes, 23.9% 30 to 45 minutes, 7.7% 45 to 60 minutes, 11.7% 60 minutes or more (2000)

LAWRENCE (township). Covers a land area of 35.008 square miles and a water area of 0.866 square miles. Located at 42.20° N. Lat.; 86.04° W. Long. Elevation is 686 feet.

Population: 3,341 (2000); Race: 83.3% White, 4.1% Black, 0.3% Asian, 0.0% American Indian and Alaska Native, 13.8% Hispanic of any race, 5.7% two or more races (2000); Density: 95.4 persons per square mile (2000); Age: 28.7% under 18, 12.5% over 64 (2000); Marriage status: 23.3% never married, 61.0% now married, 7.4% widowed, 8.3% divorced (2000); Foreign born: 6.3% (2000); Ancestry (includes multiple ancestries): 23.8% Other groups, 22.5% German, 11.2% Irish, 10.1% English, 7.2% United States or American (2000).

Economy: Agriculture: vegetables, fruit; hogs, poultry. Manufacturing: food processing, walk-in coolers and freezers, canned and frozen fruits and vegetables, electroplating, molded plastic products. Single-family building permits issued: 17 (2001) / 14 (2000); Multi-family building permits issued: 0 (2001) / 0 (2000); Employment by occupation: 7.8% management, 15.2% professional, 12.9% services, 23.4% sales, 4.3% farming, 10.0% construction, 26.5% production (2000).

Income: Per capita income: $16,246 (2000); Median household income: $36,944 (2000); Poverty rate: 12.8% (2000).

Taxes: Total city taxes per capita: $25 (1997); City property taxes per capita: $21 (1997).

Education: High school graduation rate: 72.3% (2000); College graduation rate: 11.8% (2000).

Housing: Homeownership rate: 80.4% (2000); Median home value: $82,200 (2000); Median rent: $339 per month (2000); Median age of housing: 35 years (2000).

Transportation: Commute to work: 95.1% car, 0.3% public transportation, 2.0% walk, 2.1% work from home (2000); Travel time to work: 29.0% less than 15 minutes, 32.0% 15 to 30 minutes, 23.7% 30 to 45 minutes, 8.5% 45 to 60 minutes, 6.8% 60 minutes or more (2000)

LAWTON (village). Covers a land area of 2.259 square miles and a water area of 0 square miles. Located at 42.16° N. Lat.; 85.84° W. Long.

History: Lawton developed as a wine making center, surrounded by vineyards. The village was named for Nathan Lawton, who donated land for a railroad depot in 1848.

Population: 1,859 (2000); Race: 90.0% White, 2.1% Black, 0.0% Asian, 0.6% American Indian and Alaska Native, 10.3% Hispanic of any race, 4.0% two or more races (2000); Density: 823.0 persons per square mile (2000); Age: 27.6% under 18, 19.6% over 64 (2000); Marriage status: 22.8% never married, 50.3% now married, 14.5% widowed, 12.4% divorced (2000); Foreign born: 2.8% (2000); Ancestry (includes multiple ancestries): 20.1% German, 14.6% Other groups, 11.5% English, 10.8% Irish, 10.7% United States or American (2000).

Economy: Single-family building permits issued: 5 (2001) / 5 (2000); Multi-family building permits issued: 0 (2001) / 0 (2000); Employment by occupation: 10.8% management, 10.8% professional, 19.4% services, 19.5% sales, 0.8% farming, 10.5% construction, 28.2% production (2000).

Income: Per capita income: $15,600 (2000); Median household income: $36,250 (2000); Poverty rate: 11.5% (2000).

Taxes: Total city taxes per capita: $214 (1997); City property taxes per capita: $206 (1997).

Education: High school graduation rate: 76.2% (2000); College graduation rate: 12.3% (2000).

School District(s)

Lawton Community School District (KG-12)
2000 Enrollment: 1,192 616-624-4931

Housing: Homeownership rate: 68.7% (2000); Median home value: $84,300 (2000); Median rent: $371 per month (2000); Median age of housing: 52 years (2000).

Safety: Violent crime rate: 32.1 per 10,000 population; Property crime rate: 363.8 per 10,000 population (2001).

Transportation: Commute to work: 87.8% car, 0.0% public transportation, 6.2% walk, 4.0% work from home (2000); Travel time to work: 40.8% less than 15 minutes, 25.2% 15 to 30 minutes, 25.5% 30 to 45 minutes, 5.8% 45 to 60 minutes, 2.7% 60 minutes or more (2000)

MATTAWAN (village). Covers a land area of 4.121 square miles and a water area of 0.019 square miles. Located at 42.21° N. Lat.; 85.79° W. Long.

Population: 2,536 (2000); Race: 93.2% White, 2.9% Black, 0.0% Asian, 0.6% American Indian and Alaska Native, 4.4% Hispanic of any race, 3.1% two or more races (2000); Density: 615.4 persons per square mile (2000); Age: 29.1% under 18, 8.0% over 64 (2000); Marriage status: 24.1% never married, 55.9% now married, 4.6% widowed, 15.3% divorced (2000); Foreign born: 1.0% (2000); Ancestry (includes multiple ancestries): 25.5% German, 14.3% Other groups, 13.6% Irish, 13.2% Dutch, 11.9% English (2000).

Economy: Single-family building permits issued: 30 (2001) / 30 (2000); Multi-family building permits issued: 0 (2001) / 0 (2000); Employment by occupation: 10.9% management, 14.5% professional, 17.2% services, 26.2% sales, 0.0% farming, 7.0% construction, 24.2% production (2000).

Income: Per capita income: $17,971 (2000); Median household income: $42,241 (2000); Poverty rate: 3.8% (2000).

Taxes: Total city taxes per capita: $67 (1997); City property taxes per capita: $57 (1997).

Education: High school graduation rate: 86.8% (2000); College graduation rate: 15.4% (2000).

School District(s)

Mattawan Consolidated School (KG-12)
2000 Enrollment: 3,261 616-668-3361

Housing: Homeownership rate: 81.7% (2000); Median home value: $95,700 (2000); Median rent: $425 per month (2000); Median age of housing: 20 years (2000).

Safety: Violent crime rate: 3.9 per 10,000 population; Property crime rate: 302.1 per 10,000 population (2001).

Transportation: Commute to work: 93.5% car, 0.1% public transportation, 3.1% walk, 2.6% work from home (2000); Travel time to work: 25.2% less than 15 minutes, 51.8% 15 to 30 minutes, 18.0% 30 to 45 minutes, 2.1% 45 to 60 minutes, 2.8% 60 minutes or more (2000)

PAW PAW (village). Covers a land area of 2.664 square miles and a water area of 0.212 square miles. Located at 42.21° N. Lat.; 85.89° W. Long. Elevation is 739 feet.

History: Paw Paw, first settled in 1832, developed as the center of a grape-growing area. The Paw Paw River, as well as the village, was named for the trees that grew along its banks. Paw Paw became the seat of Van Buren County in 1838, and was incorporated as a village in 1859.

Population: 3,363 (2000); Race: 94.6% White, 1.5% Black, 0.0% Asian, 0.0% American Indian and Alaska Native, 3.9% Hispanic of any race, 0.7% two or more races (2000); Density: 1,262.5 persons per square mile (2000); Age: 21.1% under 18, 16.6% over 64 (2000); Marriage status: 22.8% never married, 50.5% now married, 9.1% widowed, 17.6% divorced (2000); Foreign born: 2.3% (2000); Ancestry (includes multiple ancestries): 21.9% German, 14.8% English, 13.6% Irish, 7.3% Other groups, 6.7% Dutch (2000).

Economy: Employment by occupation: 10.6% management, 25.1% professional, 21.7% services, 17.6% sales, 0.0% farming, 8.8% construction, 16.3% production (2000).

Income: Per capita income: $21,859 (2000); Median household income: $38,750 (2000); Poverty rate: 5.7% (2000).

Taxes: Total city taxes per capita: $284 (1997); City property taxes per capita: $264 (1997).

Education: High school graduation rate: 78.9% (2000); College graduation rate: 19.4% (2000).

School District(s)

Paw Paw Public School District (KG-12)
2000 Enrollment: 2,298 616-657-8800

Housing: Homeownership rate: 59.5% (2000); Median home value: $86,800 (2000); Median rent: $372 per month (2000); Median age of housing: 45 years (2000).

Hospitals: LakeView Community Hospital Authority (174 beds)

Safety: Violent crime rate: 35.5 per 10,000 population; Property crime rate: 641.8 per 10,000 population (2001).

Newspapers: Courier-Leader (1 x week)

Transportation: Commute to work: 94.2% car, 0.0% public transportation, 3.1% walk, 1.2% work from home (2000); Travel time to work: 39.9% less than 15 minutes, 26.3% 15 to 30 minutes, 26.4% 30 to 45 minutes, 4.1% 45 to 60 minutes, 3.3% 60 minutes or more (2000)

Additional Information Contacts
Paw Paw Chamber of Commerce. 616-657-5395

PAW PAW (township). Covers a land area of 35.215 square miles and a water area of 1.797 square miles. Located at 42.21° N. Lat.; 85.91° W. Long. Elevation is 739 feet.
History: Paw Paw Township was organized in 1836. It was first called Lafayette, but changed to the name of Paw Paw in 1867.
Population: 7,091 (2000); Race: 93.0% White, 2.5% Black, 0.6% Asian, 0.0% American Indian and Alaska Native, 3.6% Hispanic of any race, 1.6% two or more races (2000); Density: 201.4 persons per square mile (2000); Age: 26.0% under 18, 13.4% over 64 (2000); Marriage status: 23.7% never married, 57.2% now married, 6.8% widowed, 12.3% divorced (2000); Foreign born: 2.9% (2000); Ancestry (includes multiple ancestries): 23.4% German, 12.2% Irish, 12.2% English, 10.6% Other groups, 10.1% Dutch (2000).
Economy: Single-family building permits issued: 15 (2001) / 9 (2000); Multi-family building permits issued: 0 (2001) / 0 (2000); Employment by occupation: 11.3% management, 20.9% professional, 18.5% services, 19.9% sales, 0.6% farming, 10.2% construction, 18.6% production (2000).
Income: Per capita income: $20,549 (2000); Median household income: $43,802 (2000); Poverty rate: 7.0% (2000).
Taxes: Total city taxes per capita: $30 (1997); City property taxes per capita: $24 (1997).
Education: High school graduation rate: 83.2% (2000); College graduation rate: 19.3% (2000).
Housing: Homeownership rate: 70.8% (2000); Median home value: $98,500 (2000); Median rent: $390 per month (2000); Median age of housing: 37 years (2000).
Transportation: Commute to work: 96.4% car, 0.0% public transportation, 1.9% walk, 1.0% work from home (2000); Travel time to work: 33.5% less than 15 minutes, 29.3% 15 to 30 minutes, 29.7% 30 to 45 minutes, 5.0% 45 to 60 minutes, 2.4% 60 minutes or more (2000)

PINE GROVE (township). Covers a land area of 34.437 square miles and a water area of 0.566 square miles. Located at 42.37° N. Lat.; 85.82° W. Long. Elevation is 796 feet.
Population: 2,773 (2000); Race: 95.1% White, 0.7% Black, 0.7% Asian, 1.8% American Indian and Alaska Native, 2.0% Hispanic of any race, 1.5% two or more races (2000); Density: 80.5 persons per square mile (2000); Age: 27.4% under 18, 10.9% over 64 (2000); Marriage status: 19.5% never married, 65.3% now married, 3.7% widowed, 11.5% divorced (2000); Foreign born: 1.3% (2000); Ancestry (includes multiple ancestries): 29.4% German, 15.8% Dutch, 14.9% English, 14.4% Irish, 9.2% Other groups (2000).
Economy: Single-family building permits issued: 19 (2001) / 19 (2000); Multi-family building permits issued: 0 (2001) / 0 (2000); Employment by occupation: 12.3% management, 14.0% professional, 14.7% services, 18.9% sales, 1.7% farming, 14.9% construction, 23.5% production (2000).
Income: Per capita income: $22,270 (2000); Median household income: $47,060 (2000); Poverty rate: 4.4% (2000).
Taxes: Total city taxes per capita: $103 (1997); City property taxes per capita: $93 (1997).
Education: High school graduation rate: 87.5% (2000); College graduation rate: 14.4% (2000).
Housing: Homeownership rate: 90.0% (2000); Median home value: $106,000 (2000); Median rent: $416 per month (2000); Median age of housing: 28 years (2000).
Transportation: Commute to work: 95.5% car, 0.0% public transportation, 0.4% walk, 3.9% work from home (2000); Travel time to work: 16.4% less than 15 minutes, 43.0% 15 to 30 minutes, 27.0% 30 to 45 minutes, 6.7% 45 to 60 minutes, 6.9% 60 minutes or more (2000)

PORTER (township). Covers a land area of 33.299 square miles and a water area of 2.077 square miles. Located at 42.10° N. Lat.; 85.83° W. Long.
History: Porter Township was organized in 1845 and named for Commodore David Porter, American naval hero in the early 1800's.
Population: 2,406 (2000); Race: 95.8% White, 0.0% Black, 0.0% Asian, 0.1% American Indian and Alaska Native, 4.9% Hispanic of any race, 0.3% two or more races (2000); Density: 72.3 persons per square mile (2000); Age: 25.5% under 18, 12.3% over 64 (2000); Marriage status: 20.3% never married, 65.9% now married, 5.3% widowed, 8.5% divorced (2000); Foreign born: 2.2% (2000); Ancestry (includes multiple ancestries): 24.2% German, 16.3% English, 13.8% Dutch, 13.0% Irish, 7.8% Other groups (2000).
Economy: Single-family building permits issued: 12 (2001) / 14 (2000); Multi-family building permits issued: 0 (2001) / 0 (2000); Employment by occupation: 12.8% management, 16.0% professional, 15.5% services, 18.9% sales, 0.6% farming, 15.4% construction, 20.7% production (2000).
Income: Per capita income: $23,104 (2000); Median household income: $48,491 (2000); Poverty rate: 5.5% (2000).
Taxes: Total city taxes per capita: $64 (1997); City property taxes per capita: $58 (1997).
Education: High school graduation rate: 86.8% (2000); College graduation rate: 18.3% (2000).
Housing: Homeownership rate: 89.1% (2000); Median home value: $141,900 (2000); Median rent: $428 per month (2000); Median age of housing: 32 years (2000).
Transportation: Commute to work: 96.1% car, 0.0% public transportation, 0.6% walk, 3.3% work from home (2000); Travel time to work: 21.2% less than 15 minutes, 36.2% 15 to 30 minutes, 26.0% 30 to 45 minutes, 10.3% 45 to 60 minutes, 6.2% 60 minutes or more (2000)

SOUTH HAVEN (city). Covers a land area of 3.457 square miles and a water area of 0.036 square miles. Located at 42.39° N. Lat.; 86.27° W. Long. Elevation is 618 feet.
History: South Haven was laid out in 1851 and named for its location south of Grand Haven. South Haven developed as a port on Lake Michigan, and as a manufacturing city and supply center for resorts on the many small lakes nearby. Peach orchards were planted in South Haven as early as 1826, and continued to be a primary crop.
Population: 5,021 (2000); Race: 81.8% White, 12.5% Black, 0.4% Asian, 0.2% American Indian and Alaska Native, 3.3% Hispanic of any race, 2.8% two or more races (2000); Density: 1,452.3 persons per square mile (2000); Age: 23.4% under 18, 21.4% over 64 (2000); Marriage status: 19.6% never married, 56.5% now married, 11.1% widowed, 12.8% divorced (2000); Foreign born: 3.3% (2000); Ancestry (includes multiple ancestries): 19.7% German, 14.8% Other groups, 13.4% Irish, 9.6% Dutch, 8.3% English (2000).
Economy: Single-family building permits issued: 12 (2001) / 21 (2000); Multi-family building permits issued: 0 (2001) / 11 (2000); Employment by occupation: 14.3% management, 20.4% professional, 11.9% services, 19.7% sales, 0.6% farming, 11.6% construction, 21.5% production (2000).
Income: Per capita income: $19,396 (2000); Median household income: $35,885 (2000); Poverty rate: 9.8% (2000).
Taxes: Total city taxes per capita: $710 (2000); City property taxes per capita: $685 (2000).
Education: High school graduation rate: 81.5% (2000); College graduation rate: 22.2% (2000).

School District(s)

South Haven Public Schools (KG-12)
2000 Enrollment: 2,552 616-637-0520
Housing: Homeownership rate: 70.2% (2000); Median home value: $123,000 (2000); Median rent: $425 per month (2000); Median age of housing: 48 years (2000).
Hospitals: South Haven Community Hospital (82 beds)
Safety: Violent crime rate: 77.3 per 10,000 population; Property crime rate: 816.3 per 10,000 population (2001).
Newspapers: South Haven Tribune (1 x week)
Transportation: Commute to work: 94.6% car, 0.1% public transportation, 2.1% walk, 2.9% work from home (2000); Travel time to work: 61.1% less than 15 minutes, 19.3% 15 to 30 minutes, 11.7% 30 to 45 minutes, 4.8% 45 to 60 minutes, 3.1% 60 minutes or more (2000)
Airports: South Haven Area Regional
Additional Information Contacts
South Haven Chamber of Commerce. 616-637-5171

SOUTH HAVEN CHARTER (township). Covers a land area of 17.535 square miles and a water area of 0 square miles. Located at 42.37° N. Lat.; 86.26° W. Long. Elevation is 618 feet.
History: Maritime Museum. Settled before 1840; Incorporated as village 1869, as city 1902.
Population: 4,046 (2000); Race: 83.5% White, 12.8% Black, 0.0% Asian, 0.6% American Indian and Alaska Native, 4.0% Hispanic of any race, 1.8% two or more races (2000); Density: 230.7 persons per square mile (2000); Age: 27.3% under 18, 12.9% over 64 (2000); Marriage status: 21.1% never married, 59.4% now married, 6.4% widowed, 13.1% divorced (2000); Foreign born: 2.4% (2000); Ancestry (includes multiple ancestries): 24.7% Other groups, 20.0% German, 14.4% English, 8.6% Irish, 7.8% United States or American (2000).
Economy: Port of entry and supply center for resort and fruit-growing area: fruits and vegetables, poultry and dairying. Manufacturing includes food, paper and rubber products, plastic products, glass products, pulleys and belts,

dairy products, electrical products and chemicals and fisheries. Employment by occupation: 14.2% management, 11.9% professional, 15.4% services, 20.9% sales, 0.8% farming, 11.8% construction, 25.0% production (2000).
Income: Per capita income: $17,097 (2000); Median household income: $35,000 (2000); Poverty rate: 11.8% (2000).
Taxes: Total city taxes per capita: $117 (1997); City property taxes per capita: $113 (1997).
Education: High school graduation rate: 80.1% (2000); College graduation rate: 14.0% (2000).
Housing: Homeownership rate: 73.0% (2000); Median home value: $88,300 (2000); Median rent: $372 per month (2000); Median age of housing: 30 years (2000).
Transportation: Commute to work: 95.2% car, 0.8% public transportation, 1.2% walk, 1.5% work from home (2000); Travel time to work: 56.6% less than 15 minutes, 19.0% 15 to 30 minutes, 15.3% 30 to 45 minutes, 6.1% 45 to 60 minutes, 3.0% 60 minutes or more (2000)

WAVERLY (township). Covers a land area of 34.141 square miles and a water area of 0.248 square miles. Located at 42.27° N. Lat.; 85.92° W. Long.
Population: 2,467 (2000); Race: 94.7% White, 0.9% Black, 0.6% Asian, 1.3% American Indian and Alaska Native, 3.4% Hispanic of any race, 0.7% two or more races (2000); Density: 72.3 persons per square mile (2000); Age: 27.9% under 18, 7.8% over 64 (2000); Marriage status: 22.2% never married, 63.9% now married, 2.5% widowed, 11.4% divorced (2000); Foreign born: 3.1% (2000); Ancestry (includes multiple ancestries): 25.4% German, 12.5% Dutch, 11.7% English, 9.8% Other groups, 9.0% United States or American (2000).
Economy: Employment by occupation: 9.6% management, 13.7% professional, 14.6% services, 19.9% sales, 0.6% farming, 17.2% construction, 24.3% production (2000).
Income: Per capita income: $18,443 (2000); Median household income: $51,100 (2000); Poverty rate: 9.0% (2000).
Taxes: Total city taxes per capita: $62 (1997); City property taxes per capita: $56 (1997).
Education: High school graduation rate: 87.0% (2000); College graduation rate: 14.4% (2000).
Housing: Homeownership rate: 88.8% (2000); Median home value: $99,100 (2000); Median rent: $441 per month (2000); Median age of housing: 25 years (2000).
Transportation: Commute to work: 95.4% car, 0.0% public transportation, 0.0% walk, 4.4% work from home (2000); Travel time to work: 18.9% less than 15 minutes, 36.1% 15 to 30 minutes, 25.2% 30 to 45 minutes, 10.0% 45 to 60 minutes, 9.8% 60 minutes or more (2000)

Washtenaw County

Located in southeastern Michigan; drained by the Huron and Raisin Rivers. Covers a land area of 709.90 square miles, a water area of 12.60 square miles, and is located in the Eastern Time Zone. The county government was organized in 1826. County seat is Ann Arbor.

Washtenaw County is part of the Ann Arbor, MI PMSA. The entire metro area includes: Lenawee County; Livingston County; Washtenaw County

Weather Station: Ann Arbor Univ. of Michigan — Elevation: 898 feet

	Jan	Feb	Mar	Apr	May	Jun	Jul	Aug	Sep	Oct	Nov	Dec
High	30	34	45	59	71	80	83	81	74	62	47	35
Low	17	19	27	37	48	58	62	61	53	42	33	23
Precip	2.2	2.0	2.8	3.3	2.9	3.3	3.2	3.6	3.3	2.5	3.0	2.7
Snow	14.6	10.2	8.4	2.4	tr	0.0	0.0	0.0	tr	0.3	3.6	12.4

High and Low temperatures in degrees Fahrenheit; Precipitation and Snow in inches

Population: 322,895 (2000); Race: 77.6% White, 12.0% Black, 6.2% Asian, 0.4% American Indian and Alaska Native, 2.8% Hispanic of any race, 2.9% two or more races (2000); Density: 454.8 persons per square mile (2000); Age: 22.0% under 18, 8.0% over 64 (2000).
Religion: Five largest groups: 12.9% Catholic Church, 2.1% The United Methodist Church, 2.1% Jewish estimate, 1.7% Evangelical Lutheran Church in America, 1.5% United Church of Christ (2000).
Economy: Unemployment rate: 2.3% (11/2002); Total civilian labor force: 181,177 (11/2002); Leading industries: 18.4% manufacturing; 17.3% health care and social assistance; 12.1% retail trade (2000); Companies that employ more than 1,000 persons: 11 (2000); Companies that employ more than 100 persons: 226 (2000); Farms: 1,030 totaling 180,223 acres (1997); Minority business ownership rate: 10.4% (1997); Women business ownership rate: 29.4% (1997); Retail sales per capita: $11,267 (1997). Single-family building permits issued: 1,813 (2001) / 1,863 (2000); Multi-family building permits issued: 292 (2001) / 117 (2000).
Income: Per capita income: $27,173 (2000); Median household income: $51,990 (2000); Poverty rate: 11.1% (2000); Bankruptcy rate: 3.10% (2001).
Taxes: Total county taxes per capita: $154 (2000); County property taxes per capita: $138 (2000).
Education: High school graduation rate: 91.5% (2000); College graduation rate: 48.1% (2000).
Housing: Homeownership rate: 59.7% (2000); Median home value: $174,300 (2000); Median rent: $633 per month (2000); Median age of housing: 29 years (2000).
Health: Birth rate: 123.4 per 10,000 population (1998); Age adjusted death rate: 81.6 per 10,000 population (1999); Infant mortality rate: 4.3 per 1,000 live births (1998); Age adjusted cancer mortality rate: 200.9 deaths per 100,000 population (1999). Air Quality Index: 67% good, 33% moderate, 1% unhealthy (percent of days in 2000). Number of physicians: 91.6 per 10,000 population (1999); Number of hospital beds: 47.4 per 10,000 population (1999).
Elections: 2000 Presidential election results: 59.8% Gore, 36.2% Bush, 3.3% Nader, 0.0% Buchanan
National and State Parks: Chelsea State Game Area; Pinckney State Recreation Area
Additional Information Contacts
Washtenaw County Government Offices.................. 734-994-2400
Ann Arbor Area Board of Realtors 734-761-7340
Ann Arbor Area Chamber of Commerce.................. 734-665-4433
Ann Arbor Convention & Vistors Bureau 734-995-7281
Ann Arbor Convention Vistor 734-995-7281
Chelsea Chamber of Commerce.................. 734-475-1145
Dexter Area Chamber of Commerce 734-426-0887
Manchester Chamber of Commerce.................. 734-428-6222
Milan Chamber of Commerce 734-439-7932
Saline Area Chamber of Commerce.................. 734-429-4494
Ypsilanti Chamber of Commerce.................. 734-482-4920

Washtenaw County Communities

ANN ARBOR (city). Covers a land area of 27.013 square miles and a water area of 0.665 square miles. Located at 42.27° N. Lat.; 83.73° W. Long. Elevation is 802 feet.
History: The first homes in Ann Arbor were those of John and Ann Allen from Virginia, and Elisha and Ann Rumsey from New York, who settled here in 1824. One version of the naming of the town says that they built an arbor with wild grapevines growing over it, and named the settlement Anns' Arbor for the two wives. Another story attributes the name to a woman named Ann d'Arbeur, who was a wilderness guide in this area in the early 1800's. Allen set up a gristmill when he arrived, and soon other settlers and other mills, a tannery, and a general store followed. In 1837 the young town was successful in its bid to have the University of Michigan moved here from Detroit. One of the early industries in Ann Arbor was the making of watches, followed by the making of organs and pianos. Later industries produced baling machinery, steel balls, radios, and cameras.
Population: 114,024 (2000); Race: 74.9% White, 8.6% Black, 11.7% Asian, 0.4% American Indian and Alaska Native, 3.2% Hispanic of any race, 3.0% two or more races (2000); Density: 4,221.1 persons per square mile (2000); Age: 16.6% under 18, 7.9% over 64 (2000); Marriage status: 50.3% never married, 39.4% now married, 3.2% widowed, 7.1% divorced (2000); Foreign born: 16.6% (2000); Ancestry (includes multiple ancestries): 25.6% Other groups, 19.8% German, 11.8% English, 11.1% Irish, 6.4% Polish (2000).
Vital Statistics: Birth rate: 120.9 per 10,000 population (1998)
Economy: Unemployment rate: 2.0% (11/2002); Total civilian labor force: 71,012 (11/2002); Single-family building permits issued: 126 (2001) / 279 (2000); Multi-family building permits issued: 226 (2001) / 73 (2000); Employment by occupation: 14.0% management, 46.9% professional, 12.4% services, 19.7% sales, 0.2% farming, 2.7% construction, 4.0% production (2000).
Income: Per capita income: $26,419 (2000); Median household income: $46,299 (2000); Poverty rate: 16.6% (2000).
Taxes: Total city taxes per capita: $523 (2000); City property taxes per capita: $487 (2000).
Education: High school graduation rate: 95.7% (2000); College graduation rate: 69.3% (2000).

School District(s)

Ann Arbor Learning Community (KG-08)
2000 Enrollment: 102 313-487-2420

Ann Arbor Public Schools (PK-12)
2000 Enrollment: 16,539 734-994-2230
Central Academy (KG-12)
2000 Enrollment: 279 517-774-2100
Honey Creek Community School (KG-05)
2000 Enrollment: 89 734-994-8100
Washtenaw Technical Middle Colle (10-12)
2000 Enrollment: 227 313-973-3300

Four-year College(s)

Cleary College (Private, Not-for-profit)
2001 Enrollment: 632 734-332-4477
2001 Tuition: In-state $13,800; Out-of-state $13,800
Concordia College (Private, Not-for-profit, Lutheran Church - Missouri Synod)
2001 Enrollment: 568 734-995-7300
2001 Tuition: In-state $14,250; Out-of-state $14,250
University of Michigan-Ann Arbor (Public)
2001 Enrollment: 38,248 734-764-1817
2001 Tuition: In-state $6,750; Out-of-state $21,460

Two-year College(s)

Washtenaw Community College (Public)
2001 Enrollment: 11,171 734-973-3543
2001 Tuition: In-state $2,844; Out-of-state $3,636

Housing: Homeownership rate: 45.2% (2000); Median home value: $181,400 (2000); Median rent: $696 per month (2000); Median age of housing: 34 years (2000).
Hospitals: Saint Joseph Mercy Hospital (530 beds); University of Michigan Medical Center (872 beds); Veterans Affairs Medical Center (132 beds)
Safety: Violent crime rate: 30.7 per 10,000 population; Property crime rate: 307.8 per 10,000 population (2001).
Newspapers: The Ann Arbor News (7 x week); The Michigan Daily (5 x week)
Transportation: Commute to work: 70.5% car, 6.6% public transportation, 15.8% walk, 4.4% work from home (2000); Travel time to work: 44.1% less than 15 minutes, 35.8% 15 to 30 minutes, 11.0% 30 to 45 minutes, 5.6% 45 to 60 minutes, 3.5% 60 minutes or more (2000); Amtrak: Service available.
Airports: Ann Arbor Municipal
Additional Information Contacts
Ann Arbor Area Board of Realtors 734-761-7340
Ann Arbor Area Chamber of Commerce 734-665-4433
Ann Arbor Convention & Vistors Bureau 734-995-7281
Ann Arbor Convention Vistor 734-995-7281

ANN ARBOR (township). Covers a land area of 17.648 square miles and a water area of 0.090 square miles. Located at 42.29° N. Lat.; 83.72° W. Long. Elevation is 802 feet.
History: Cobblestone Farm, 19th-century farmhouse, 1837 cabin, gardens. Incorporated 1851.
Population: 4,720 (2000); Race: 80.0% White, 2.0% Black, 13.5% Asian, 0.0% American Indian and Alaska Native, 2.0% Hispanic of any race, 3.7% two or more races (2000); Density: 267.5 persons per square mile (2000); Age: 20.3% under 18, 14.9% over 64 (2000); Marriage status: 22.8% never married, 65.7% now married, 4.0% widowed, 7.6% divorced (2000); Foreign born: 20.4% (2000); Ancestry (includes multiple ancestries): 21.0% Other groups, 20.1% German, 13.9% English, 12.9% Irish, 4.5% Polish (2000).
Economy: Railroad junction, research and educational center, with a large number of government and industrial research and development firms, many in high-technology fields such as aerospace and nuclear research. Manufacturing includes printing and publishing, electronic, medical and transportation equipment and precision machinery. Municipal airport to south. Single-family building permits issued: 11 (2001) / 17 (2000); Multi-family building permits issued: 0 (2001) / 0 (2000); Employment by occupation: 19.7% management, 55.0% professional, 5.1% services, 15.0% sales, 0.0% farming, 1.9% construction, 3.4% production (2000).
Income: Per capita income: $56,084 (2000); Median household income: $86,797 (2000); Poverty rate: 3.2% (2000).
Taxes: Total city taxes per capita: $280 (1997); City property taxes per capita: $235 (1997).
Education: High school graduation rate: 97.1% (2000); College graduation rate: 79.0% (2000).
Housing: Homeownership rate: 69.9% (2000); Median home value: $325,300 (2000); Median rent: $931 per month (2000); Median age of housing: 18 years (2000).
Transportation: Commute to work: 89.2% car, 0.4% public transportation, 2.1% walk, 6.7% work from home (2000); Travel time to work: 34.8% less than 15 minutes, 39.7% 15 to 30 minutes, 12.0% 30 to 45 minutes, 7.8% 45 to 60 minutes, 5.6% 60 minutes or more (2000); Amtrak: Service available.

AUGUSTA (township). Covers a land area of 36.740 square miles and a water area of 0 square miles. Located at 42.12° N. Lat.; 83.60° W. Long.
Population: 4,813 (2000); Race: 92.4% White, 5.1% Black, 0.1% Asian, 0.1% American Indian and Alaska Native, 0.5% Hispanic of any race, 2.2% two or more races (2000); Density: 131.0 persons per square mile (2000); Age: 24.8% under 18, 10.7% over 64 (2000); Marriage status: 20.2% never married, 65.1% now married, 6.5% widowed, 8.3% divorced (2000); Foreign born: 2.3% (2000); Ancestry (includes multiple ancestries): 20.1% German, 14.1% Irish, 11.6% United States or American, 11.0% English, 9.4% Other groups (2000).
Economy: Employment by occupation: 11.4% management, 18.8% professional, 12.2% services, 23.8% sales, 0.5% farming, 12.0% construction, 21.3% production (2000).
Income: Per capita income: $27,509 (2000); Median household income: $65,033 (2000); Poverty rate: 5.4% (2000).
Taxes: Total city taxes per capita: $99 (2000); City property taxes per capita: $91(2000).
Education: High school graduation rate: 83.8% (2000); College graduation rate: 13.6% (2000).
Housing: Homeownership rate: 91.6% (2000); Median home value: $159,200 (2000); Median rent: $523 per month (2000); Median age of housing: 35 years (2000).
Transportation: Commute to work: 96.1% car, 0.3% public transportation, 0.7% walk, 2.7% work from home (2000); Travel time to work: 13.5% less than 15 minutes, 39.7% 15 to 30 minutes, 34.6% 30 to 45 minutes, 7.8% 45 to 60 minutes, 4.4% 60 minutes or more (2000)

BARTON HILLS (village). Covers a land area of 0.801 square miles and a water area of 0 square miles. Located at 42.31° N. Lat.; 83.75° W. Long.
Population: 335 (2000); Race: 87.1% White, 2.6% Black, 8.3% Asian, 0.0% American Indian and Alaska Native, 2.0% Hispanic of any race, 2.0% two or more races (2000); Density: 418.2 persons per square mile (2000); Age: 18.1% under 18, 16.7% over 64 (2000); Marriage status: 12.8% never married, 80.9% now married, 2.3% widowed, 3.9% divorced (2000); Foreign born: 10.6% (2000); Ancestry (includes multiple ancestries): 28.4% German, 18.7% English, 16.4% Other groups, 14.4% Irish, 8.6% Scottish (2000).
Economy: Single-family building permits issued: 0 (2001) / 0 (2000); Multi-family building permits issued: 0 (2001) / 0 (2000); Employment by occupation: 31.7% management, 48.1% professional, 5.5% services, 8.2% sales, 0.0% farming, 1.1% construction, 5.5% production (2000).
Income: Per capita income: $110,683 (2000); Median household income: $149,056 (2000); Poverty rate: 0.6% (2000).
Taxes: Total city taxes per capita: $1,038 (1997); City property taxes per capita: $1,033 (1997).
Education: High school graduation rate: 97.5% (2000); College graduation rate: 83.5% (2000).
Housing: Homeownership rate: 90.1% (2000); Median home value: $710,400 (2000); Median rent: $1,625 per month (2000); Median age of housing: 45 years (2000).
Transportation: Commute to work: 88.0% car, 1.6% public transportation, 3.3% walk, 5.5% work from home (2000); Travel time to work: 30.6% less than 15 minutes, 47.4% 15 to 30 minutes, 10.4% 30 to 45 minutes, 5.8% 45 to 60 minutes, 5.8% 60 minutes or more (2000)

BRIDGEWATER (township). Covers a land area of 36.572 square miles and a water area of 0.285 square miles. Located at 42.13° N. Lat.; 83.96° W. Long. Elevation is 910 feet.
History: Bridgewater Township was first named Hixon for Colonel Daniel Hixon, who settled here in 1829. It was renamed in 1833.
Population: 1,646 (2000); Race: 99.1% White, 0.0% Black, 0.2% Asian, 0.1% American Indian and Alaska Native, 0.8% Hispanic of any race, 0.5% two or more races (2000); Density: 45.0 persons per square mile (2000); Age: 25.2% under 18, 9.8% over 64 (2000); Marriage status: 16.6% never married, 69.7% now married, 4.1% widowed, 9.6% divorced (2000); Foreign born: 1.2% (2000); Ancestry (includes multiple ancestries): 37.2% German, 19.5% English, 16.2% Irish, 8.7% Polish, 7.2% United States or American (2000).
Economy: Single-family building permits issued: 14 (2001) / 9 (2000); Multi-family building permits issued: 0 (2001) / 0 (2000); Employment by occupation: 13.1% management, 16.8% professional, 12.9% services, 21.9% sales, 0.9% farming, 13.7% construction, 20.6% production (2000).
Income: Per capita income: $27,120 (2000); Median household income: $68,011 (2000); Poverty rate: 3.6% (2000).

Taxes: Total city taxes per capita: $50 (1997); City property taxes per capita: $32 (1997).
Education: High school graduation rate: 89.4% (2000); College graduation rate: 21.5% (2000).
Housing: Homeownership rate: 90.7% (2000); Median home value: $158,800 (2000); Median rent: $575 per month (2000); Median age of housing: 33 years (2000).
Transportation: Commute to work: 94.7% car, 0.0% public transportation, 1.0% walk, 4.0% work from home (2000); Travel time to work: 17.2% less than 15 minutes, 23.2% 15 to 30 minutes, 36.9% 30 to 45 minutes, 11.9% 45 to 60 minutes, 10.8% 60 minutes or more (2000)

CHELSEA (village). Covers a land area of 3.344 square miles and a water area of 0.055 square miles. Located at 42.31° N. Lat.; 84.01° W. Long. Elevation is 913 feet.
History: Chelsea came into existence when the Michigan Central Railroad built a station here in 1850. The village was once a leading shipper of wool, as well as the market center for farm produce.
Population: 4,398 (2000); Race: 96.3% White, 1.5% Black, 0.1% Asian, 1.0% American Indian and Alaska Native, 0.8% Hispanic of any race, 0.4% two or more races (2000); Density: 1,315.3 persons per square mile (2000); Age: 23.3% under 18, 24.1% over 64 (2000); Marriage status: 20.4% never married, 55.9% now married, 13.4% widowed, 10.3% divorced (2000); Foreign born: 1.6% (2000); Ancestry (includes multiple ancestries): 32.1% German, 15.7% Irish, 14.8% English, 7.6% Other groups, 4.9% French (except Basque) (2000).
Economy: Employment by occupation: 12.6% management, 35.9% professional, 14.1% services, 20.8% sales, 0.0% farming, 8.6% construction, 7.9% production (2000).
Income: Per capita income: $27,608 (2000); Median household income: $51,132 (2000); Poverty rate: 4.3% (2000).
Taxes: Total city taxes per capita: $485 (1997); City property taxes per capita: $480 (1997).
Education: High school graduation rate: 92.0% (2000); College graduation rate: 40.6% (2000).

School District(s)

Chelsea School District (KG-12)
2000 Enrollment: 2,940 734-433-2208
Housing: Homeownership rate: 66.9% (2000); Median home value: $159,800 (2000); Median rent: $614 per month (2000); Median age of housing: 42 years (2000).
Hospitals: Chelsea Community Hospital (113 beds)
Safety: Violent crime rate: 9.0 per 10,000 population; Property crime rate: 438.8 per 10,000 population (2001).
Newspapers: The Chelsea Standard (1 x week); The Dexter Leader (1 x week)
Transportation: Commute to work: 90.9% car, 0.2% public transportation, 4.7% walk, 3.0% work from home (2000); Travel time to work: 34.0% less than 15 minutes, 22.8% 15 to 30 minutes, 30.7% 30 to 45 minutes, 8.5% 45 to 60 minutes, 3.9% 60 minutes or more (2000)
Additional Information Contacts
Chelsea Chamber of Commerce. 734-475-1145

DEXTER (village). Covers a land area of 1.891 square miles and a water area of 0 square miles. Located at 42.33° N. Lat.; 83.88° W. Long. Elevation is 862 feet.
History: Dexter was named for Judge Samuel W. Dexter, who built a home here in the early 1840's.
Population: 2,338 (2000); Race: 97.0% White, 0.3% Black, 0.7% Asian, 0.0% American Indian and Alaska Native, 1.2% Hispanic of any race, 1.7% two or more races (2000); Density: 1,236.7 persons per square mile (2000); Age: 24.9% under 18, 9.0% over 64 (2000); Marriage status: 27.1% never married, 54.2% now married, 6.1% widowed, 12.7% divorced (2000); Foreign born: 3.7% (2000); Ancestry (includes multiple ancestries): 27.7% German, 14.8% English, 14.0% Irish, 7.9% Other groups, 6.9% French (except Basque) (2000).
Economy: Employment by occupation: 11.4% management, 30.4% professional, 15.9% services, 24.9% sales, 0.4% farming, 8.4% construction, 8.6% production (2000).
Income: Per capita income: $27,974 (2000); Median household income: $50,510 (2000); Poverty rate: 4.5% (2000).
Taxes: Total city taxes per capita: $474 (1997); City property taxes per capita: $429 (1997).
Education: High school graduation rate: 92.0% (2000); College graduation rate: 38.4% (2000).

School District(s)

Dexter Community School District (KG-12)
2000 Enrollment: 3,090 734-426-4623
Housing: Homeownership rate: 61.7% (2000); Median home value: $160,300 (2000); Median rent: $590 per month (2000); Median age of housing: 40 years (2000).
Transportation: Commute to work: 89.8% car, 1.1% public transportation, 4.3% walk, 3.8% work from home (2000); Travel time to work: 29.3% less than 15 minutes, 41.3% 15 to 30 minutes, 18.2% 30 to 45 minutes, 5.0% 45 to 60 minutes, 6.3% 60 minutes or more (2000)
Additional Information Contacts
Dexter Area Chamber of Commerce 734-426-0887

DEXTER (township). Covers a land area of 30.766 square miles and a water area of 2.508 square miles. Located at 42.40° N. Lat.; 83.95° W. Long. Elevation is 862 feet.
History: Settled 1823; incorporated 1855.
Population: 5,248 (2000); Race: 97.3% White, 0.7% Black, 0.3% Asian, 0.0% American Indian and Alaska Native, 1.1% Hispanic of any race, 0.5% two or more races (2000); Density: 170.6 persons per square mile (2000); Age: 28.1% under 18, 8.1% over 64 (2000); Marriage status: 20.3% never married, 69.5% now married, 4.2% widowed, 6.1% divorced (2000); Foreign born: 1.6% (2000); Ancestry (includes multiple ancestries): 32.9% German, 17.4% Irish, 15.8% English, 9.1% Italian, 6.7% Polish (2000).
Economy: In agricultural area: fruit; poultry, livestock; dairying; lumbering. Manufacturing: machinery, printing and publishing, fabricated metal products. Employment by occupation: 16.1% management, 28.3% professional, 10.6% services, 24.0% sales, 0.7% farming, 9.6% construction, 10.7% production (2000).
Income: Per capita income: $30,164 (2000); Median household income: $75,085 (2000); Poverty rate: 1.8% (2000).
Taxes: Total city taxes per capita: $67 (2000); City property taxes per capita: $62 (2000).
Education: High school graduation rate: 93.5% (2000); College graduation rate: 38.2% (2000).
Housing: Homeownership rate: 91.4% (2000); Median home value: $206,800 (2000); Median rent: $750 per month (2000); Median age of housing: 27 years (2000).
Transportation: Commute to work: 96.0% car, 0.1% public transportation, 0.0% walk, 3.7% work from home (2000); Travel time to work: 11.5% less than 15 minutes, 42.3% 15 to 30 minutes, 27.9% 30 to 45 minutes, 11.5% 45 to 60 minutes, 6.8% 60 minutes or more (2000)

FREEDOM (township). Covers a land area of 35.461 square miles and a water area of 0.320 square miles. Located at 42.21° N. Lat.; 83.94° W. Long.
Population: 1,562 (2000); Race: 90.8% White, 0.1% Black, 0.0% Asian, 0.4% American Indian and Alaska Native, 9.2% Hispanic of any race, 1.4% two or more races (2000); Density: 44.0 persons per square mile (2000); Age: 23.1% under 18, 9.6% over 64 (2000); Marriage status: 21.6% never married, 66.2% now married, 4.2% widowed, 8.1% divorced (2000); Foreign born: 6.4% (2000); Ancestry (includes multiple ancestries): 37.0% German, 12.4% English, 12.2% Irish, 11.3% Other groups, 5.4% United States or American (2000).
Economy: Single-family building permits issued: 4 (2001) / 3 (2000); Multi-family building permits issued: 0 (2001) / 0 (2000); Employment by occupation: 14.3% management, 20.8% professional, 9.8% services, 17.7% sales, 13.5% farming, 9.7% construction, 14.3% production (2000).
Income: Per capita income: $26,397 (2000); Median household income: $62,321 (2000); Poverty rate: 5.2% (2000).
Taxes: Total city taxes per capita: $46 (2000); City property taxes per capita: $36 (2000).
Education: High school graduation rate: 85.1% (2000); College graduation rate: 27.0% (2000).
Housing: Homeownership rate: 83.8% (2000); Median home value: $203,600 (2000); Median rent: $432 per month (2000); Median age of housing: 43 years (2000).
Transportation: Commute to work: 90.1% car, 0.0% public transportation, 2.1% walk, 7.4% work from home (2000); Travel time to work: 30.2% less than 15 minutes, 33.9% 15 to 30 minutes, 25.3% 30 to 45 minutes, 5.4% 45 to 60 minutes, 5.2% 60 minutes or more (2000)

LIMA (township). Covers a land area of 36.221 square miles and a water area of 0.562 square miles. Located at 42.29° N. Lat.; 83.96° W. Long.
Population: 3,224 (2000); Race: 96.1% White, 0.3% Black, 2.0% Asian, 0.9% American Indian and Alaska Native, 0.0% Hispanic of any race, 0.7% two or more races (2000); Density: 89.0 persons per square mile (2000); Age:

26.8% under 18, 12.5% over 64 (2000); Marriage status: 17.7% never married, 72.5% now married, 4.1% widowed, 5.8% divorced (2000); Foreign born: 2.7% (2000); Ancestry (includes multiple ancestries): 39.4% German, 20.2% English, 14.6% Irish, 5.9% Polish, 5.6% Other groups (2000).
Economy: Employment by occupation: 16.5% management, 25.9% professional, 14.3% services, 23.4% sales, 0.0% farming, 10.8% construction, 9.1% production (2000).
Income: Per capita income: $30,220 (2000); Median household income: $68,531 (2000); Poverty rate: 2.3% (2000).
Taxes: Total city taxes per capita: $34 (1997); City property taxes per capita: $29 (1997).
Education: High school graduation rate: 92.9% (2000); College graduation rate: 44.6% (2000).
Housing: Homeownership rate: 86.2% (2000); Median home value: $187,900 (2000); Median rent: $435 per month (2000); Median age of housing: 28 years (2000).
Transportation: Commute to work: 94.1% car, 0.3% public transportation, 0.9% walk, 4.4% work from home (2000); Travel time to work: 26.0% less than 15 minutes, 30.9% 15 to 30 minutes, 29.7% 30 to 45 minutes, 8.7% 45 to 60 minutes, 4.8% 60 minutes or more (2000)

LODI (township). Covers a land area of 33.712 square miles and a water area of 0.075 square miles. Located at 42.20° N. Lat.; 83.81° W. Long.
History: Lodi Township was settled in 1825, and named for Lodi in the Finger Lakes region of New York, the former home of many of the early residents.
Population: 5,710 (2000); Race: 94.2% White, 2.6% Black, 1.4% Asian, 0.5% American Indian and Alaska Native, 1.5% Hispanic of any race, 1.2% two or more races (2000); Density: 169.4 persons per square mile (2000); Age: 29.0% under 18, 9.2% over 64 (2000); Marriage status: 19.7% never married, 71.7% now married, 3.3% widowed, 5.3% divorced (2000); Foreign born: 5.3% (2000); Ancestry (includes multiple ancestries): 29.8% German, 15.9% English, 11.4% Irish, 8.4% Other groups, 6.5% Polish (2000).
Economy: Employment by occupation: 22.5% management, 29.9% professional, 8.1% services, 24.4% sales, 0.1% farming, 5.3% construction, 9.7% production (2000).
Income: Per capita income: $37,516 (2000); Median household income: $88,419 (2000); Poverty rate: 3.3% (2000).
Taxes: Total city taxes per capita: $63 (1997); City property taxes per capita: $60 (1997).
Education: High school graduation rate: 92.3% (2000); College graduation rate: 50.5% (2000).
Housing: Homeownership rate: 94.5% (2000); Median home value: $255,900 (2000); Median rent: $588 per month (2000); Median age of housing: 16 years (2000).
Transportation: Commute to work: 95.8% car, 0.7% public transportation, 0.7% walk, 2.7% work from home (2000); Travel time to work: 23.8% less than 15 minutes, 48.3% 15 to 30 minutes, 14.1% 30 to 45 minutes, 9.9% 45 to 60 minutes, 4.0% 60 minutes or more (2000)

LYNDON (township). Covers a land area of 32.066 square miles and a water area of 2.898 square miles. Located at 42.38° N. Lat.; 84.07° W. Long.
Population: 2,728 (2000); Race: 90.4% White, 6.5% Black, 0.4% Asian, 0.8% American Indian and Alaska Native, 2.5% Hispanic of any race, 1.2% two or more races (2000); Density: 85.1 persons per square mile (2000); Age: 23.1% under 18, 7.3% over 64 (2000); Marriage status: 28.2% never married, 60.8% now married, 3.5% widowed, 7.5% divorced (2000); Foreign born: 1.1% (2000); Ancestry (includes multiple ancestries): 26.4% German, 16.6% English, 13.1% Other groups, 10.9% Irish, 8.8% United States or American (2000).
Economy: Employment by occupation: 11.4% management, 25.8% professional, 12.5% services, 24.8% sales, 0.3% farming, 12.5% construction, 12.6% production (2000).
Income: Per capita income: $26,297 (2000); Median household income: $71,595 (2000); Poverty rate: 1.8% (2000).
Taxes: Total city taxes per capita: $23 (1997); City property taxes per capita: $22 (1997).
Education: High school graduation rate: 92.7% (2000); College graduation rate: 31.6% (2000).
Housing: Homeownership rate: 92.4% (2000); Median home value: $176,000 (2000); Median rent: $596 per month (2000); Median age of housing: 27 years (2000).
Transportation: Commute to work: 94.9% car, 0.0% public transportation, 0.3% walk, 4.4% work from home (2000); Travel time to work: 12.9% less than 15 minutes, 22.1% 15 to 30 minutes, 35.0% 30 to 45 minutes, 19.3% 45 to 60 minutes, 10.7% 60 minutes or more (2000)

MANCHESTER (village). Covers a land area of 1.797 square miles and a water area of 0.099 square miles. Located at 42.14° N. Lat.; 84.03° W. Long. Elevation is 918 feet.
Population: 2,160 (2000); Race: 99.1% White, 0.4% Black, 0.3% Asian, 0.0% American Indian and Alaska Native, 1.1% Hispanic of any race, 0.3% two or more races (2000); Density: 1,201.8 persons per square mile (2000); Age: 27.2% under 18, 13.9% over 64 (2000); Marriage status: 25.3% never married, 53.7% now married, 8.5% widowed, 12.5% divorced (2000); Foreign born: 0.2% (2000); Ancestry (includes multiple ancestries): 36.9% German, 19.0% Irish, 14.7% English, 6.1% United States or American, 6.1% Italian (2000).
Economy: Single-family building permits issued: 15 (2001) / 4 (2000); Multi-family building permits issued: 0 (2001) / 0 (2000); Employment by occupation: 11.1% management, 17.5% professional, 15.5% services, 27.9% sales, 0.4% farming, 11.1% construction, 16.5% production (2000).
Income: Per capita income: $24,113 (2000); Median household income: $46,974 (2000); Poverty rate: 5.2% (2000).
Taxes: Total city taxes per capita: $484 (1997); City property taxes per capita: $465 (1997).
Education: High school graduation rate: 86.0% (2000); College graduation rate: 21.3% (2000).

School District(s)

Manchester Community Schools (KG-12)
2000 Enrollment: 1,262 734-428-9711
Housing: Homeownership rate: 73.2% (2000); Median home value: $140,900 (2000); Median rent: $533 per month (2000); Median age of housing: 45 years (2000).
Newspapers: The Manchester Enterprise (1 x week)
Transportation: Commute to work: 95.3% car, 0.0% public transportation, 2.7% walk, 1.9% work from home (2000); Travel time to work: 26.4% less than 15 minutes, 23.9% 15 to 30 minutes, 35.4% 30 to 45 minutes, 9.3% 45 to 60 minutes, 5.0% 60 minutes or more (2000)
Additional Information Contacts
Manchester Chamber of Commerce 734-428-6222

MANCHESTER (township). Covers a land area of 38.035 square miles and a water area of 0.569 square miles. Located at 42.12° N. Lat.; 84.04° W. Long. Elevation is 918 feet.
History: Incorporated 1867.
Population: 4,102 (2000); Race: 98.1% White, 0.2% Black, 0.7% Asian, 0.0% American Indian and Alaska Native, 1.5% Hispanic of any race, 0.6% two or more races (2000); Density: 107.8 persons per square mile (2000); Age: 26.2% under 18, 11.9% over 64 (2000); Marriage status: 21.1% never married, 61.2% now married, 6.9% widowed, 10.8% divorced (2000); Foreign born: 1.3% (2000); Ancestry (includes multiple ancestries): 34.2% German, 17.4% Irish, 15.5% English, 8.0% United States or American, 5.3% Other groups (2000).
Economy: In diversified agricultural area; feed milling. Manufacturing: machinery, fabricated metal products, transportation equipment. Single-family building permits issued: 32 (2001) / 35 (2000); Multi-family building permits issued: 0 (2001) / 0 (2000); Employment by occupation: 13.0% management, 20.9% professional, 13.5% services, 21.9% sales, 0.9% farming, 13.5% construction, 16.3% production (2000).
Income: Per capita income: $27,038 (2000); Median household income: $55,847 (2000); Poverty rate: 4.3% (2000).
Taxes: Total city taxes per capita: $53 (1997); City property taxes per capita: $47 (1997).
Education: High school graduation rate: 88.5% (2000); College graduation rate: 23.4% (2000).
Housing: Homeownership rate: 82.1% (2000); Median home value: $147,600 (2000); Median rent: $525 per month (2000); Median age of housing: 31 years (2000).
Transportation: Commute to work: 94.7% car, 0.0% public transportation, 1.4% walk, 3.9% work from home (2000); Travel time to work: 19.5% less than 15 minutes, 20.2% 15 to 30 minutes, 36.1% 30 to 45 minutes, 14.9% 45 to 60 minutes, 9.3% 60 minutes or more (2000)

MILAN (city). Covers a land area of 2.245 square miles and a water area of 0.079 square miles. Located at 42.08° N. Lat.; 83.68° W. Long. Elevation is 693 feet.
Population: 4,775 (2000); Race: 96.4% White, 1.8% Black, 0.1% Asian, 0.0% American Indian and Alaska Native, 3.4% Hispanic of any race, 0.7% two or more races (2000); Density: 2,127.4 persons per square mile (2000); Age: 26.1% under 18, 12.4% over 64 (2000); Marriage status: 22.7% never married, 57.1% now married, 6.7% widowed, 13.5% divorced (2000);

Foreign born: 1.3% (2000); Ancestry (includes multiple ancestries): 26.4% German, 13.5% Irish, 12.9% English, 9.9% Other groups, 5.7% French (except Basque) (2000).
Economy: Single-family building permits issued: 9 (2001) / 18 (2000); Multi-family building permits issued: 6 (2001) / 0 (2000); Employment by occupation: 8.8% management, 17.6% professional, 23.5% services, 22.5% sales, 0.6% farming, 11.3% construction, 15.9% production (2000).
Income: Per capita income: $23,895 (2000); Median household income: $48,510 (2000); Poverty rate: 4.9% (2000).
Taxes: Total city taxes per capita: $556 (1997); City property taxes per capita: $539 (1997).
Education: High school graduation rate: 87.2% (2000); College graduation rate: 20.0% (2000).

School District(s)

Milan Area Schools (PK-12)
2000 Enrollment: 2,184 734-439-5050

Housing: Homeownership rate: 69.1% (2000); Median home value: $125,500 (2000); Median rent: $577 per month (2000); Median age of housing: 37 years (2000).
Safety: Violent crime rate: 52.1 per 10,000 population; Property crime rate: 341.7 per 10,000 population (2001).
Transportation: Commute to work: 90.3% car, 1.1% public transportation, 4.0% walk, 3.2% work from home (2000); Travel time to work: 27.9% less than 15 minutes, 39.9% 15 to 30 minutes, 23.7% 30 to 45 minutes, 4.6% 45 to 60 minutes, 4.0% 60 minutes or more (2000)

Additional Information Contacts

Milan Chamber of Commerce 734-439-7932

NORTHFIELD (township). Covers a land area of 36.285 square miles and a water area of 0.825 square miles. Located at 42.40° N. Lat.; 83.74° W. Long.
Population: 8,252 (2000); Race: 96.4% White, 1.0% Black, 1.1% Asian, 0.0% American Indian and Alaska Native, 1.4% Hispanic of any race, 1.4% two or more races (2000); Density: 227.4 persons per square mile (2000); Age: 26.2% under 18, 7.5% over 64 (2000); Marriage status: 22.7% never married, 62.3% now married, 3.5% widowed, 11.5% divorced (2000); Foreign born: 4.1% (2000); Ancestry (includes multiple ancestries): 22.8% German, 12.0% Irish, 10.8% Polish, 9.9% English, 7.0% Other groups (2000).
Economy: Single-family building permits issued: 58 (2001) / 76 (2000); Multi-family building permits issued: 0 (2001) / 0 (2000); Employment by occupation: 14.1% management, 20.6% professional, 12.5% services, 26.6% sales, 0.2% farming, 11.2% construction, 14.8% production (2000).
Income: Per capita income: $25,543 (2000); Median household income: $58,396 (2000); Poverty rate: 4.1% (2000).
Taxes: Total city taxes per capita: $493 (2000); City property taxes per capita: $335 (2000).
Education: High school graduation rate: 89.6% (2000); College graduation rate: 28.2% (2000).
Housing: Homeownership rate: 83.3% (2000); Median home value: $171,600 (2000); Median rent: $649 per month (2000); Median age of housing: 18 years (2000).
Safety: Violent crime rate: 36.2 per 10,000 population; Property crime rate: 282.1 per 10,000 population (2001).
Transportation: Commute to work: 97.8% car, 0.3% public transportation, 0.4% walk, 1.5% work from home (2000); Travel time to work: 14.0% less than 15 minutes, 44.7% 15 to 30 minutes, 24.5% 30 to 45 minutes, 9.8% 45 to 60 minutes, 7.0% 60 minutes or more (2000)

PITTSFIELD CHARTER (township). Covers a land area of 27.540 square miles and a water area of 0 square miles. Located at 42.22° N. Lat.; 83.71° W. Long.
History: Settlement began in the 1820's in Pittsfield, which was named for William Pitt, the English prime minister.
Population: 30,167 (2000); Race: 71.3% White, 13.5% Black, 9.2% Asian, 0.2% American Indian and Alaska Native, 4.3% Hispanic of any race, 4.5% two or more races (2000); Density: 1,095.4 persons per square mile (2000); Age: 24.2% under 18, 5.3% over 64 (2000); Marriage status: 33.9% never married, 53.0% now married, 3.9% widowed, 9.2% divorced (2000); Foreign born: 16.7% (2000); Ancestry (includes multiple ancestries): 26.6% Other groups, 17.1% German, 10.3% Irish, 9.8% English, 5.8% Polish (2000).
Economy: Single-family building permits issued: 239 (2001) / 257 (2000); Multi-family building permits issued: 0 (2001) / 0 (2000); Employment by occupation: 18.2% management, 34.2% professional, 12.8% services, 22.7% sales, 0.1% farming, 3.8% construction, 8.2% production (2000).
Income: Per capita income: $29,645 (2000); Median household income: $61,262 (2000); Poverty rate: 9.1% (2000).
Taxes: Total city taxes per capita: $203 (2000); City property taxes per capita: $170 (2000).
Education: High school graduation rate: 89.5% (2000); College graduation rate: 52.3% (2000).
Housing: Homeownership rate: 56.7% (2000); Median home value: $220,700 (2000); Median rent: $667 per month (2000); Median age of housing: 14 years (2000).
Safety: Violent crime rate: 22.4 per 10,000 population; Property crime rate: 329.4 per 10,000 population (2001).
Transportation: Commute to work: 93.4% car, 2.0% public transportation, 0.9% walk, 2.9% work from home (2000); Travel time to work: 29.2% less than 15 minutes, 43.3% 15 to 30 minutes, 17.2% 30 to 45 minutes, 6.3% 45 to 60 minutes, 4.0% 60 minutes or more (2000)

SALEM (township). Covers a land area of 34.298 square miles and a water area of 0.003 square miles. Located at 42.39° N. Lat.; 83.59° W. Long. Elevation is 938 feet.
History: Salem was settled in the mid-1820's and named for Salem, Massachusetts, the former home of some of the early residents.
Population: 5,562 (2000); Race: 95.1% White, 1.4% Black, 0.9% Asian, 0.0% American Indian and Alaska Native, 1.1% Hispanic of any race, 2.5% two or more races (2000); Density: 162.2 persons per square mile (2000); Age: 27.0% under 18, 9.0% over 64 (2000); Marriage status: 21.9% never married, 67.4% now married, 2.8% widowed, 7.9% divorced (2000); Foreign born: 3.4% (2000); Ancestry (includes multiple ancestries): 24.9% German, 17.4% Polish, 15.9% Irish, 13.9% English, 9.3% Other groups (2000).
Economy: Single-family building permits issued: 30 (2001) / 33 (2000); Multi-family building permits issued: 0 (2001) / 0 (2000); Employment by occupation: 16.2% management, 22.4% professional, 9.9% services, 27.2% sales, 0.0% farming, 11.6% construction, 12.7% production (2000).
Income: Per capita income: $29,450 (2000); Median household income: $69,258 (2000); Poverty rate: 2.2% (2000).
Taxes: Total city taxes per capita: $27 (1997); City property taxes per capita: $3 (1997).
Education: High school graduation rate: 91.3% (2000); College graduation rate: 26.3% (2000).
Housing: Homeownership rate: 93.9% (2000); Median home value: $231,800 (2000); Median rent: $596 per month (2000); Median age of housing: 16 years (2000).
Transportation: Commute to work: 90.9% car, 0.0% public transportation, 3.7% walk, 4.4% work from home (2000); Travel time to work: 16.3% less than 15 minutes, 42.6% 15 to 30 minutes, 25.7% 30 to 45 minutes, 8.4% 45 to 60 minutes, 7.0% 60 minutes or more (2000)

SALINE (city). Covers a land area of 4.627 square miles and a water area of 0.033 square miles. Located at 42.17° N. Lat.; 83.78° W. Long. Elevation is 816 feet.
History: Saline was settled in the mid-1820's and named for the salt springs here, on the Saline River. The old Saline gristmill, built in the 1840's, was purchased by Henry Ford in the early 1900's, who used it to extract oil from soy beans to be used in finishing Ford cars. The Ford Company provided the seed to farmers willing to raise soy beans for this purpose.
Population: 8,034 (2000); Race: 95.3% White, 0.7% Black, 1.2% Asian, 0.2% American Indian and Alaska Native, 2.2% Hispanic of any race, 1.8% two or more races (2000); Density: 1,736.3 persons per square mile (2000); Age: 28.6% under 18, 11.1% over 64 (2000); Marriage status: 21.0% never married, 59.1% now married, 7.5% widowed, 12.3% divorced (2000); Foreign born: 4.3% (2000); Ancestry (includes multiple ancestries): 31.4% German, 18.0% English, 15.4% Irish, 7.3% Other groups, 7.0% Polish (2000).
Economy: Single-family building permits issued: 111 (2001) / 76 (2000); Multi-family building permits issued: 0 (2001) / 0 (2000); Employment by occupation: 14.4% management, 29.1% professional, 12.3% services, 26.6% sales, 0.2% farming, 6.5% construction, 10.8% production (2000).
Income: Per capita income: $26,208 (2000); Median household income: $59,382 (2000); Poverty rate: 4.0% (2000).
Taxes: Total city taxes per capita: $537 (1997); City property taxes per capita: $517 (1997).
Education: High school graduation rate: 93.5% (2000); College graduation rate: 40.4% (2000).

School District(s)

Saline Area Schools (PK-12)
2000 Enrollment: 4,982 734-429-8000

Housing: Homeownership rate: 71.7% (2000); Median home value: $169,200 (2000); Median rent: $547 per month (2000); Median age of housing: 28 years (2000).
Hospitals: Saline Community Hospital (82 beds)
Safety: Violent crime rate: 19.8 per 10,000 population; Property crime rate: 257.6 per 10,000 population (2001).
Newspapers: The Milan News-Leader (1 x week); The Saline Reporter (1 x week)
Transportation: Commute to work: 95.5% car, 0.0% public transportation, 1.3% walk, 3.0% work from home (2000); Travel time to work: 31.9% less than 15 minutes, 40.8% 15 to 30 minutes, 17.0% 30 to 45 minutes, 5.8% 45 to 60 minutes, 4.5% 60 minutes or more (2000)
Additional Information Contacts
Saline Area Chamber of Commerce....................... 734-429-4494

SALINE (township). Covers a land area of 34.858 square miles and a water area of 0.043 square miles. Located at 42.11° N. Lat.; 83.82° W. Long. Elevation is 816 feet.
History: Settled 1824; incorporated as city 1931.
Population: 1,302 (2000); Race: 96.6% White, 0.9% Black, 0.5% Asian, 0.0% American Indian and Alaska Native, 0.7% Hispanic of any race, 1.8% two or more races (2000); Density: 37.4 persons per square mile (2000); Age: 25.4% under 18, 11.8% over 64 (2000); Marriage status: 22.4% never married, 66.0% now married, 5.6% widowed, 6.0% divorced (2000); Foreign born: 3.6% (2000); Ancestry (includes multiple ancestries): 41.8% German, 11.3% Other groups, 9.8% Irish, 9.5% English, 9.2% Polish (2000).
Economy: In diversified farm area: corn, wheat, apples; dairying. Manufacturing: sheet metal doors, machinery, bulk publishing, cutting machine tools, industrial microcomputers. Ann Arbor Municipal Airport to Northeast. Cooperative Saline Valley Farms nearby. Employment by occupation: 18.4% management, 20.4% professional, 10.6% services, 20.0% sales, 0.4% farming, 13.4% construction, 16.8% production (2000).
Income: Per capita income: $30,630 (2000); Median household income: $77,024 (2000); Poverty rate: 2.5% (2000).
Taxes: Total city taxes per capita: $42 (1997); City property taxes per capita: $35 (1997).
Education: High school graduation rate: 90.4% (2000); College graduation rate: 28.3% (2000).
Housing: Homeownership rate: 89.5% (2000); Median home value: $211,400 (2000); Median rent: $450 per month (2000); Median age of housing: 30 years (2000).
Transportation: Commute to work: 92.0% car, 0.0% public transportation, 0.3% walk, 7.7% work from home (2000); Travel time to work: 21.6% less than 15 minutes, 36.6% 15 to 30 minutes, 21.6% 30 to 45 minutes, 12.7% 45 to 60 minutes, 7.4% 60 minutes or more (2000)

SCIO (township). Covers a land area of 34.035 square miles and a water area of 0.264 square miles. Located at 42.30° N. Lat.; 83.83° W. Long. Elevation is 852 feet.
History: Scio was settled in the 1830's. The name is Latin for "I know."
Population: 15,759 (2000); Race: 88.6% White, 4.5% Black, 3.9% Asian, 0.4% American Indian and Alaska Native, 1.1% Hispanic of any race, 2.3% two or more races (2000); Density: 463.0 persons per square mile (2000); Age: 27.1% under 18, 8.6% over 64 (2000); Marriage status: 23.7% never married, 63.3% now married, 4.0% widowed, 9.0% divorced (2000); Foreign born: 5.8% (2000); Ancestry (includes multiple ancestries): 28.7% German, 16.6% English, 14.0% Other groups, 13.6% Irish, 8.4% Polish (2000).
Economy: Employment by occupation: 18.9% management, 36.6% professional, 9.7% services, 21.7% sales, 0.1% farming, 4.9% construction, 8.0% production (2000).
Income: Per capita income: $36,837 (2000); Median household income: $73,705 (2000); Poverty rate: 2.9% (2000).
Taxes: Total city taxes per capita: $221 (2000); City property taxes per capita: $216 (2000).
Education: High school graduation rate: 95.1% (2000); College graduation rate: 55.5% (2000).
Housing: Homeownership rate: 78.9% (2000); Median home value: $258,200 (2000); Median rent: $646 per month (2000); Median age of housing: 15 years (2000).
Transportation: Commute to work: 92.4% car, 0.5% public transportation, 1.1% walk, 5.2% work from home (2000); Travel time to work: 26.3% less than 15 minutes, 50.4% 15 to 30 minutes, 14.3% 30 to 45 minutes, 4.3% 45 to 60 minutes, 4.7% 60 minutes or more (2000)

SHARON (township). Covers a land area of 37.627 square miles and a water area of 0.009 square miles. Located at 42.20° N. Lat.; 84.08° W. Long.
History: Settlement began in the 1830's and was known as Peppergrass. The township of Sharon was organized in 1834 and named for Sharon, Connecticut.
Population: 1,678 (2000); Race: 99.0% White, 0.1% Black, 0.1% Asian, 0.1% American Indian and Alaska Native, 2.0% Hispanic of any race, 0.5% two or more races (2000); Density: 44.6 persons per square mile (2000); Age: 24.2% under 18, 9.4% over 64 (2000); Marriage status: 17.4% never married, 72.3% now married, 3.9% widowed, 6.4% divorced (2000); Foreign born: 0.8% (2000); Ancestry (includes multiple ancestries): 33.3% German, 16.7% English, 13.2% Irish, 8.7% Polish, 8.3% United States or American (2000).
Economy: Employment by occupation: 14.9% management, 20.9% professional, 11.6% services, 19.6% sales, 3.2% farming, 15.1% construction, 14.7% production (2000).
Income: Per capita income: $28,304 (2000); Median household income: $75,979 (2000); Poverty rate: 3.4% (2000).
Taxes: Total city taxes per capita: $44 (1997); City property taxes per capita: $34 (1997).
Education: High school graduation rate: 93.0% (2000); College graduation rate: 28.8% (2000).
Housing: Homeownership rate: 91.0% (2000); Median home value: $170,900 (2000); Median rent: $638 per month (2000); Median age of housing: 27 years (2000).
Transportation: Commute to work: 94.6% car, 0.0% public transportation, 0.2% walk, 5.0% work from home (2000); Travel time to work: 16.3% less than 15 minutes, 27.0% 15 to 30 minutes, 29.9% 30 to 45 minutes, 16.7% 45 to 60 minutes, 10.1% 60 minutes or more (2000)

SUPERIOR (township). Covers a land area of 35.363 square miles and a water area of 0.232 square miles. Located at 42.29° N. Lat.; 83.60° W. Long.
Population: 10,740 (2000); Race: 62.9% White, 28.7% Black, 3.8% Asian, 0.3% American Indian and Alaska Native, 2.5% Hispanic of any race, 3.3% two or more races (2000); Density: 303.7 persons per square mile (2000); Age: 28.7% under 18, 6.7% over 64 (2000); Marriage status: 28.1% never married, 57.2% now married, 3.9% widowed, 10.8% divorced (2000); Foreign born: 5.1% (2000); Ancestry (includes multiple ancestries): 32.4% Other groups, 16.4% German, 10.8% Irish, 10.3% English, 6.3% Polish (2000).
Economy: Single-family building permits issued: 107 (2001) / 57 (2000); Multi-family building permits issued: 0 (2001) / 0 (2000); Employment by occupation: 15.1% management, 27.2% professional, 13.0% services, 23.6% sales, 0.4% farming, 5.9% construction, 14.7% production (2000).
Income: Per capita income: $31,093 (2000); Median household income: $56,622 (2000); Poverty rate: 9.6% (2000).
Taxes: Total city taxes per capita: $153 (2000); City property taxes per capita: $136 (2000).
Education: High school graduation rate: 90.3% (2000); College graduation rate: 35.9% (2000).
Housing: Homeownership rate: 81.7% (2000); Median home value: $140,700 (2000); Median rent: $327 per month (2000); Median age of housing: 24 years (2000).
Transportation: Commute to work: 92.1% car, 2.7% public transportation, 0.8% walk, 3.5% work from home (2000); Travel time to work: 18.2% less than 15 minutes, 51.3% 15 to 30 minutes, 18.8% 30 to 45 minutes, 7.5% 45 to 60 minutes, 4.2% 60 minutes or more (2000)

SYLVAN (township). Aka Sylvan Center. Covers a land area of 35.158 square miles and a water area of 0.826 square miles. Located at 42.30° N. Lat.; 84.05° W. Long.
Population: 6,425 (2000); Race: 96.9% White, 1.2% Black, 0.6% Asian, 0.5% American Indian and Alaska Native, 1.5% Hispanic of any race, 0.3% two or more races (2000); Density: 182.7 persons per square mile (2000); Age: 24.5% under 18, 18.0% over 64 (2000); Marriage status: 22.2% never married, 57.5% now married, 9.6% widowed, 10.8% divorced (2000); Foreign born: 2.3% (2000); Ancestry (includes multiple ancestries): 28.5% German, 16.9% English, 13.8% Irish, 7.0% Other groups, 5.9% Polish (2000).
Economy: Employment by occupation: 14.5% management, 31.8% professional, 12.4% services, 20.3% sales, 0.2% farming, 10.1% construction, 10.6% production (2000).
Income: Per capita income: $28,781 (2000); Median household income: $56,519 (2000); Poverty rate: 3.0% (2000).
Taxes: Total city taxes per capita: $32 (1997); City property taxes per capita: $31 (1997).
Education: High school graduation rate: 91.3% (2000); College graduation rate: 37.8% (2000).

Housing: Homeownership rate: 76.8% (2000); Median home value: $172,100 (2000); Median rent: $655 per month (2000); Median age of housing: 35 years (2000).
Transportation: Commute to work: 92.6% car, 0.2% public transportation, 3.0% walk, 3.4% work from home (2000); Travel time to work: 32.2% less than 15 minutes, 26.9% 15 to 30 minutes, 30.8% 30 to 45 minutes, 6.6% 45 to 60 minutes, 3.5% 60 minutes or more (2000)

WEBSTER (township). Covers a land area of 35.262 square miles and a water area of 0.616 square miles. Located at 42.37° N. Lat.; 83.83° W. Long. Elevation is 902 feet.
Population: 5,198 (2000); Race: 97.2% White, 0.5% Black, 1.0% Asian, 0.0% American Indian and Alaska Native, 1.0% Hispanic of any race, 1.4% two or more races (2000); Density: 147.4 persons per square mile (2000); Age: 30.7% under 18, 6.9% over 64 (2000); Marriage status: 18.4% never married, 72.1% now married, 2.7% widowed, 6.8% divorced (2000); Foreign born: 2.1% (2000); Ancestry (includes multiple ancestries): 31.1% German, 18.9% English, 16.4% Irish, 10.8% Polish, 5.9% Other groups (2000).
Economy: Employment by occupation: 19.8% management, 35.9% professional, 7.1% services, 22.9% sales, 0.0% farming, 8.2% construction, 6.2% production (2000).
Income: Per capita income: $35,883 (2000); Median household income: $90,830 (2000); Poverty rate: 0.8% (2000).
Taxes: Total city taxes per capita: $47 (1997); City property taxes per capita: $46 (1997).
Education: High school graduation rate: 96.2% (2000); College graduation rate: 51.6% (2000).
Housing: Homeownership rate: 94.2% (2000); Median home value: $254,300 (2000); Median rent: $804 per month (2000); Median age of housing: 19 years (2000).
Transportation: Commute to work: 96.3% car, 0.0% public transportation, 0.4% walk, 3.1% work from home (2000); Travel time to work: 13.5% less than 15 minutes, 43.3% 15 to 30 minutes, 26.0% 30 to 45 minutes, 10.2% 45 to 60 minutes, 7.0% 60 minutes or more (2000)

WILLIS (unincorporated postal area, zip code 48191). Covers a land area of 16.537 square miles and a water area of 0 square miles. Located at 42.12° N. Lat.; 83.57° W. Long. Elevation is 688 feet.
Population: 2,616 (2000); Race: 91.6% White, 7.9% Black, 0.0% Asian, 0.2% American Indian and Alaska Native, 0.4% Hispanic of any race, 0.2% two or more races (2000); Density: 158.2 persons per square mile (2000); Age: 22.7% under 18, 9.5% over 64 (2000); Marriage status: 18.4% never married, 62.3% now married, 8.2% widowed, 11.1% divorced (2000); Foreign born: 2.6% (2000); Ancestry (includes multiple ancestries): 18.3% German, 13.0% Irish, 11.9% English, 10.8% Other groups, 10.6% United States or American (2000).
Economy: Employment by occupation: 12.1% management, 14.7% professional, 11.2% services, 22.8% sales, 0.4% farming, 14.6% construction, 24.3% production (2000).
Income: Per capita income: $29,033 (2000); Median household income: $69,180 (2000); Poverty rate: 5.1% (2000).
Education: High school graduation rate: 85.3% (2000); College graduation rate: 9.8% (2000).
Housing: Homeownership rate: 93.4% (2000); Median home value: $155,800 (2000); Median rent: $580 per month (2000); Median age of housing: 35 years (2000).
Transportation: Commute to work: 96.5% car, 0.0% public transportation, 1.5% walk, 2.0% work from home (2000); Travel time to work: 13.0% less than 15 minutes, 41.2% 15 to 30 minutes, 32.8% 30 to 45 minutes, 8.6% 45 to 60 minutes, 4.4% 60 minutes or more (2000)

YORK CHARTER (township). Covers a land area of 35.167 square miles and a water area of 0.025 square miles. Located at 42.13° N. Lat.; 83.71° W. Long.
Population: 7,392 (2000); Race: 82.8% White, 14.2% Black, 0.8% Asian, 1.1% American Indian and Alaska Native, 3.9% Hispanic of any race, 0.8% two or more races (2000); Density: 210.2 persons per square mile (2000); Age: 22.7% under 18, 5.7% over 64 (2000); Marriage status: 26.4% never married, 64.2% now married, 2.4% widowed, 6.9% divorced (2000); Foreign born: 4.6% (2000); Ancestry (includes multiple ancestries): 24.1% German, 11.2% English, 10.4% Irish, 5.8% Other groups, 5.3% Polish (2000).
Economy: Employment by occupation: 19.4% management, 25.4% professional, 10.6% services, 23.4% sales, 0.0% farming, 8.6% construction, 12.5% production (2000).
Income: Per capita income: $25,528 (2000); Median household income: $84,232 (2000); Poverty rate: 3.8% (2000).
Taxes: Total city taxes per capita: $48 (1997); City property taxes per capita: $24 (1997).
Education: High school graduation rate: 85.4% (2000); College graduation rate: 27.9% (2000).
Housing: Homeownership rate: 93.2% (2000); Median home value: $214,600 (2000); Median rent: $694 per month (2000); Median age of housing: 24 years (2000).
Transportation: Commute to work: 92.2% car, 0.2% public transportation, 1.3% walk, 5.5% work from home (2000); Travel time to work: 25.2% less than 15 minutes, 40.4% 15 to 30 minutes, 22.2% 30 to 45 minutes, 7.4% 45 to 60 minutes, 4.7% 60 minutes or more (2000)

YPSILANTI (city). Covers a land area of 4.401 square miles and a water area of 0.105 square miles. Located at 42.24° N. Lat.; 83.61° W. Long. Elevation is 713 feet.
History: In 1809 Ypsilanti was a French trading post. Settlement around it began in 1823, and grew after the railroad arrived in 1838. The city was named by Augustus Woodward, first Chief Justice of the Territorial Supreme Court, for General Demetrios Ypsilanti, a young Greek hero of the early 1800's. The Ypsilanti Monument recognizing the hero was made in Athens by Christopher Natsos, who also designed the Greek monument to the Unknown Soldier.
Population: 22,362 (2000); Race: 61.0% White, 30.7% Black, 3.5% Asian, 0.5% American Indian and Alaska Native, 2.2% Hispanic of any race, 3.4% two or more races (2000); Density: 5,081.5 persons per square mile (2000); Age: 15.6% under 18, 6.9% over 64 (2000); Marriage status: 63.3% never married, 24.6% now married, 3.9% widowed, 8.3% divorced (2000); Foreign born: 5.9% (2000); Ancestry (includes multiple ancestries): 35.5% Other groups, 16.2% German, 8.6% Irish, 8.0% English, 6.0% Polish (2000).
Vital Statistics: Birth rate: 310.8 per 10,000 population (1998)
Economy: Single-family building permits issued: 46 (2001) / 59 (2000); Multi-family building permits issued: 24 (2001) / 40 (2000); Employment by occupation: 7.9% management, 21.9% professional, 22.8% services, 32.4% sales, 0.2% farming, 4.6% construction, 10.2% production (2000).
Income: Per capita income: $16,692 (2000); Median household income: $28,610 (2000); Poverty rate: 25.8% (2000).
Taxes: Total city taxes per capita: $663 (1997); City property taxes per capita: $645 (1997).
Education: High school graduation rate: 87.3% (2000); College graduation rate: 35.4% (2000).

School District(s)

Lincoln Consolidated School District (PK-12)
2000 Enrollment: 4,426 734-484-7001
New Beginnings Academy (KG-05)
2000 Enrollment: 95 517-774-2100
School District of Ypsilanti (KG-12)
2000 Enrollment: 4,641 734-482-9388
South Arbor Charter Academy (KG-06)
2000 Enrollment: 374 517-774-2100
Willow Run Community Schools (PK-12)
2000 Enrollment: 3,099 734-481-8200

Four-year College(s)

Eastern Michigan University (Public)
2001 Enrollment: 24,287 313-487-1849
2001 Tuition: In-state $3,622; Out-of-state $11,250
High Scope Educational Research Foundation (Private, Not-for-profit)
2001 Enrollment: n/a 313-485-2000
Ave Maria College (Private, Not-for-profit)
2001 Enrollment: 187 734-482-4519
2001 Tuition: In-state $7,000; Out-of-state $7,000

Housing: Homeownership rate: 32.9% (2000); Median home value: $117,500 (2000); Median rent: $481 per month (2000); Median age of housing: 45 years (2000).
Safety: Violent crime rate: 103.6 per 10,000 population; Property crime rate: 546.7 per 10,000 population (2001).
Newspapers: Ypsilanti Courier (1 x week)
Transportation: Commute to work: 77.1% car, 4.5% public transportation, 15.3% walk, 2.3% work from home (2000); Travel time to work: 37.3% less than 15 minutes, 40.8% 15 to 30 minutes, 13.9% 30 to 45 minutes, 4.3% 45 to 60 minutes, 3.7% 60 minutes or more (2000)
Additional Information Contacts
Ypsilanti Chamber of Commerce. 734-482-4920

YPSILANTI (township). Covers a land area of 30.147 square miles and a water area of 1.604 square miles. Located at 42.22° N. Lat.; 83.59° W. Long. Elevation is 713 feet.

History: Native American trails once crossed this site, and a Native American village and a French trading post (1809—c.1819) were here. Eastern Michigan University and Cleary College are here; Historical Museum, Depot Town, pastoral historic district with parks. Incorporated 1832.
Population: 49,182 (2000); Race: 68.3% White, 24.7% Black, 1.7% Asian, 0.6% American Indian and Alaska Native, 3.0% Hispanic of any race, 3.9% two or more races (2000); Density: 1,631.4 persons per square mile (2000); Age: 26.3% under 18, 7.1% over 64 (2000); Marriage status: 33.2% never married, 49.6% now married, 4.9% widowed, 12.4% divorced (2000); Foreign born: 6.3% (2000); Ancestry (includes multiple ancestries): 31.4% Other groups, 16.0% German, 10.3% Irish, 10.0% English, 6.3% United States or American (2000).
Vital Statistics: Birth rate: 115.7 per 10,000 population (1998)
Economy: A residential, commercial and farm-trade center. Light industry includes motor-vehicle parts and specialty printing. Unemployment rate: 3.3% (11/2002); Total civilian labor force: 28,892 (11/2002); Single-family building permits issued: 428 (2001) / 294 (2000); Multi-family building permits issued: 36 (2001) / 0 (2000); Employment by occupation: 10.3% management, 21.9% professional, 16.1% services, 23.7% sales, 0.1% farming, 8.2% construction, 19.6% production (2000).
Income: Per capita income: $22,970 (2000); Median household income: $46,460 (2000); Poverty rate: 10.5% (2000).
Taxes: Total city taxes per capita: $208 (2000); City property taxes per capita: $189 (2000).
Education: High school graduation rate: 85.7% (2000); College graduation rate: 27.0% (2000).
Housing: Homeownership rate: 59.9% (2000); Median home value: $117,300 (2000); Median rent: $567 per month (2000); Median age of housing: 28 years (2000).
Transportation: Commute to work: 95.6% car, 1.5% public transportation, 0.8% walk, 1.6% work from home (2000); Travel time to work: 25.8% less than 15 minutes, 46.7% 15 to 30 minutes, 17.7% 30 to 45 minutes, 5.9% 45 to 60 minutes, 3.9% 60 minutes or more (2000)

Wayne County

Located in southeastern Michigan; bounded on the east by the Detroit River, Lakes St. Clair and Erie, and the Canadian province of Ontario; drained by the Huron River and the River Rogue. Covers a land area of 614.20 square miles, a water area of 58.10 square miles, and is located in the Eastern Time Zone. The county government was organized in 1796. County seat is Detroit.

Wayne County is part of the Detroit, MI PMSA. The entire metro area includes: Lapeer County; Macomb County; Monroe County; Oakland County; St. Clair County; Wayne County

Weather Station: Dearborn — Elevation: 603 feet

	Jan	Feb	Mar	Apr	May	Jun	Jul	Aug	Sep	Oct	Nov	Dec
High	31	35	45	58	71	80	84	83	75	62	49	37
Low	16	18	27	37	48	57	62	60	52	41	32	23
Precip	1.9	1.9	2.7	3.3	2.9	3.6	3.1	2.8	3.4	2.5	2.8	2.5
Snow	10.8	7.6	4.8	0.8	0.0	0.0	0.0	0.0	0.0	tr	1.7	7.3

High and Low temperatures in degrees Fahrenheit; Precipitation and Snow in inches

Weather Station: Detroit City Airport — Elevation: 623 feet

	Jan	Feb	Mar	Apr	May	Jun	Jul	Aug	Sep	Oct	Nov	Dec
High	31	33	44	57	70	79	83	81	73	61	48	36
Low	19	21	29	39	51	60	66	64	56	45	36	25
Precip	na	na	na	na	na	na	na	na	na	na	na	na
Snow	na	na	na	na	na	na	na	na	na	na	na	na

High and Low temperatures in degrees Fahrenheit; Precipitation and Snow in inches

Weather Station: Detroit Metropolitan Airport — Elevation: 629 feet

	Jan	Feb	Mar	Apr	May	Jun	Jul	Aug	Sep	Oct	Nov	Dec
High	31	34	45	58	70	79	84	82	74	61	48	36
Low	17	19	27	37	48	58	62	61	53	42	33	23
Precip	1.9	1.9	2.6	3.0	3.0	3.5	3.1	3.0	3.1	2.2	2.7	2.5
Snow	11.9	9.2	7.3	1.7	tr	0.0	0.0	0.0	tr	0.2	2.8	10.1

High and Low temperatures in degrees Fahrenheit; Precipitation and Snow in inches

Weather Station: Detroit WBAP Willow — Elevation: 777 feet

	Jan	Feb	Mar	Apr	May	Jun	Jul	Aug	Sep	Oct	Nov	Dec
High	31	35	46	59	72	81	84	82	75	62	48	36
Low	17	20	28	38	49	59	63	61	54	43	33	24
Precip	1.8	1.6	2.5	3.1	3.1	3.2	3.0	3.2	3.4	2.3	2.8	2.4
Snow	10.8	7.0	5.5	1.1	tr	0.0	0.0	0.0	0.0	tr	2.1	9.0

High and Low temperatures in degrees Fahrenheit; Precipitation and Snow in inches

Weather Station: Grosse Pointe Farms — Elevation: 610 feet

	Jan	Feb	Mar	Apr	May	Jun	Jul	Aug	Sep	Oct	Nov	Dec
High	32	35	45	58	70	80	84	81	74	62	49	37
Low	18	20	28	38	49	58	64	63	56	44	34	25
Precip	1.8	1.8	2.5	3.2	2.9	3.4	3.4	3.5	3.4	2.6	2.9	2.4
Snow	9.2	6.7	2.9	0.7	tr	0.0	0.0	0.0	0.0	tr	1.0	5.9

High and Low temperatures in degrees Fahrenheit; Precipitation and Snow in inches

Population: 2,061,162 (2000); Race: 51.6% White, 42.0% Black, 1.7% Asian, 0.4% American Indian and Alaska Native, 3.8% Hispanic of any race, 2.6% two or more races (2000); Density: 3,356.1 persons per square mile (2000); Age: 28.0% under 18, 12.1% over 64 (2000).
Religion: Five largest groups: 21.8% Catholic Church, 2.2% Muslim estimate, 1.4% Lutheran Church—Missouri Synod, 1.2% American Baptist Churches in the USA, 1.0% The United Methodist Church (2000).
Economy: Unemployment rate: 6.3% (11/2002); Total civilian labor force: 965,298 (11/2002); Leading industries: 17.2% manufacturing; 12.6% health care and social assistance; 11.2% retail trade (2000); Companies that employ more than 1,000 persons: 64 (2000); Companies that employ more than 100 persons: 1,145 (2000); Farms: 303 totaling 39,102 acres (1997); Minority business ownership rate: 18.6% (1997); Women business ownership rate: 27.3% (1997); Retail sales per capita: $7,449 (1997). Single-family building permits issued: 3,006 (2001) / 2,939 (2000); Multi-family building permits issued: 1,255 (2001) / 1,143 (2000).
Income: Per capita income: $20,058 (2000); Median household income: $40,776 (2000); Poverty rate: 16.4% (2000); Bankruptcy rate: 6.20% (2001).
Taxes: Total county taxes per capita: $143 (2000); County property taxes per capita: $137 (2000).
Education: High school graduation rate: 77.0% (2000); College graduation rate: 17.2% (2000).
Housing: Homeownership rate: 66.6% (2000); Median home value: $99,400 (2000); Median rent: $428 per month (2000); Median age of housing: 46 years (2000).
Health: Birth rate: 152.8 per 10,000 population (1998); Age adjusted death rate: 99.9 per 10,000 population (1999); Infant mortality rate: 10.5 per 1,000 live births (1998); Age adjusted cancer mortality rate: 216.5 deaths per 100,000 population (1999). Air Quality Index: 69% good, 31% moderate, 0% unhealthy (percent of days in 2000). Number of physicians: 22.3 per 10,000 population (1999); Number of hospital beds: 33.6 per 10,000 population (1999).
Elections: 2000 Presidential election results: 69.0% Gore, 29.0% Bush, 1.5% Nader, 0.0% Buchanan
National and State Parks: Wyandotte National Wildlife Refuge
Additional Information Contacts
Wayne County Government Offices 313-224-0903
Allen Park Chamber of Commerce 313-382-7303
Belleville Area Chamber of Commerce 734-697-7151
Canton Chamber of Commerce 734-453-4040
Dearborn Board of Realtors 313-278-2220
Dearborn Chamber of Commerce 313-584-6100
Dearborn Heights Chamber of Commerce 313-274-7480
Detroit Association of Realtors 313-962-1313
Detroit Chamber of Commerce 313-875-7877
Down River Association of Realtors 734-287-8060
Garden City Chamber of Commerce 734-422-4448
Grosse Pointe Board of Realtors 313-882-8000
Highland Park Chamber of Commerce 313-868-6420
Livonia Chamber of Commerce 734-427-2122
New Boston Chamber of Commerce 734-753-4220
Plymouth Chamber of Commerce 734-453-1540
Redford Chamber of Commerce 313-535-0960
Romulus Chamber of Commerce 734-326-4290
Taylor Chamber of Commerce 734-284-6000
Wayne Chamber of Commerce 734-721-0100
Westland Chamber of Commerce 734-326-7222

Wayne County Communities

ALLEN PARK (city). Covers a land area of 7.012 square miles and a water area of 0 square miles. Located at 42.25° N. Lat.; 83.21° W. Long. Elevation is 598 feet.

History: Allen Park was incorporated as a village in 1927 and as a city in 1957. It was named for Lewis Allen, a lawyer and lumberman who came to the area as a child in 1819, and later owned the land on which Allen Park was established.

Population: 29,376 (2000); Race: 95.1% White, 0.8% Black, 1.0% Asian, 0.5% American Indian and Alaska Native, 4.6% Hispanic of any race, 1.1% two or more races (2000); Density: 4,189.7 persons per square mile (2000); Age: 22.1% under 18, 21.1% over 64 (2000); Marriage status: 21.5% never married, 59.1% now married, 9.8% widowed, 9.5% divorced (2000); Foreign born: 4.7% (2000); Ancestry (includes multiple ancestries): 19.6% German, 16.8% Polish, 15.1% Irish, 10.4% English, 10.2% Italian (2000).

Vital Statistics: Birth rate: 101.4 per 10,000 population (1998)

Economy: Unemployment rate: 2.7% (11/2002); Total civilian labor force: 15,281 (11/2002); Single-family building permits issued: 8 (2001) / 3 (2000); Multi-family building permits issued: 0 (2001) / 0 (2000); Employment by occupation: 11.7% management, 21.9% professional, 12.3% services, 28.4% sales, 0.0% farming, 9.6% construction, 16.0% production (2000).

Income: Per capita income: $24,980 (2000); Median household income: $51,992 (2000); Poverty rate: 3.2% (2000).

Taxes: Total city taxes per capita: $382 (1997); City property taxes per capita: $362 (1997).

Education: High school graduation rate: 87.3% (2000); College graduation rate: 19.7% (2000).

School District(s)

Allen Park Public Schools (KG-12)
2000 Enrollment: 3,298 313-928-4667

Four-year College(s)

Detroit Baptist Theological Seminary (Private, Not-for-profit, Baptist)
2001 Enrollment: n/a 313-381-0111

Housing: Homeownership rate: 87.9% (2000); Median home value: $118,700 (2000); Median rent: $551 per month (2000); Median age of housing: 45 years (2000).

Safety: Violent crime rate: 14.2 per 10,000 population; Property crime rate: 217.4 per 10,000 population (2001).

Transportation: Commute to work: 96.7% car, 0.5% public transportation, 1.2% walk, 1.2% work from home (2000); Travel time to work: 32.0% less than 15 minutes, 40.0% 15 to 30 minutes, 17.8% 30 to 45 minutes, 6.4% 45 to 60 minutes, 3.8% 60 minutes or more (2000)

Additional Information Contacts

Allen Park Chamber of Commerce 313-382-7303

BELLEVILLE (city). Covers a land area of 1.135 square miles and a water area of 0.039 square miles. Located at 42.20° N. Lat.; 83.48° W. Long. Elevation is 695 feet.

History: Belleville was first settled in 1826. The village was platted in 1848, and incorporated in 1905. In 1946 it received city status.

Population: 3,997 (2000); Race: 89.2% White, 5.8% Black, 0.6% Asian, 0.8% American Indian and Alaska Native, 3.9% Hispanic of any race, 2.5% two or more races (2000); Density: 3,520.3 persons per square mile (2000); Age: 22.0% under 18, 14.9% over 64 (2000); Marriage status: 22.9% never married, 50.9% now married, 8.5% widowed, 17.7% divorced (2000); Foreign born: 2.4% (2000); Ancestry (includes multiple ancestries): 18.3% German, 15.5% Other groups, 14.2% English, 13.3% Polish, 11.9% Irish (2000).

Economy: Single-family building permits issued: 0 (2001) / 0 (2000); Multi-family building permits issued: 8 (2001) / 0 (2000); Employment by occupation: 11.4% management, 23.5% professional, 15.8% services, 19.7% sales, 0.0% farming, 7.8% construction, 21.8% production (2000).

Income: Per capita income: $25,927 (2000); Median household income: $44,196 (2000); Poverty rate: 6.0% (2000).

Taxes: Total city taxes per capita: $315 (1997); City property taxes per capita: $268 (1997).

Education: High school graduation rate: 82.7% (2000); College graduation rate: 24.2% (2000).

School District(s)

Van Buren Public Schools (PK-12)
2000 Enrollment: 6,247 734-697-9123

Two-year College(s)

Michigan Institute of Aeronautics (Private, For-profit)
2001 Enrollment: 400 734-483-3758

Housing: Homeownership rate: 71.5% (2000); Median home value: $160,600 (2000); Median rent: $464 per month (2000); Median age of housing: 25 years (2000).

Safety: Violent crime rate: 10.0 per 10,000 population; Property crime rate: 176.7 per 10,000 population (2001).

Newspapers: The View (1 x week)

Transportation: Commute to work: 97.0% car, 0.0% public transportation, 1.1% walk, 1.2% work from home (2000); Travel time to work: 22.1% less than 15 minutes, 42.7% 15 to 30 minutes, 23.8% 30 to 45 minutes, 6.8% 45 to 60 minutes, 4.6% 60 minutes or more (2000)

Additional Information Contacts

Belleville Area Chamber of Commerce 734-697-7151

BROWNSTOWN (township). Covers a land area of 22.449 square miles and a water area of 8.081 square miles. Located at 42.12° N. Lat.; 83.25° W. Long.

History: Brownstown Township was named for Adam Brown, adopted by a group of Virginia Indians as a child, who later became a chief when the group migrated to Michigan.

Population: 22,989 (2000); Race: 88.6% White, 4.4% Black, 4.0% Asian, 0.3% American Indian and Alaska Native, 3.4% Hispanic of any race, 2.0% two or more races (2000); Density: 1,024.0 persons per square mile (2000); Age: 28.5% under 18, 5.8% over 64 (2000); Marriage status: 25.4% never married, 60.3% now married, 4.7% widowed, 9.6% divorced (2000); Foreign born: 5.2% (2000); Ancestry (includes multiple ancestries): 19.1% German, 16.7% Other groups, 13.5% Irish, 12.6% Polish, 8.8% English (2000).

Economy: Single-family building permits issued: 413 (2001) / 330 (2000); Multi-family building permits issued: 64 (2001) / 96 (2000); Employment by occupation: 10.4% management, 16.2% professional, 14.0% services, 27.1% sales, 0.1% farming, 11.8% construction, 20.5% production (2000).

Income: Per capita income: $22,523 (2000); Median household income: $55,239 (2000); Poverty rate: 6.9% (2000).

Taxes: Total city taxes per capita: $235 (2000); City property taxes per capita: $186 (2000).

Education: High school graduation rate: 85.1% (2000); College graduation rate: 15.7% (2000).

School District(s)

Woodhaven-Brownstown School District (KG-12)
2000 Enrollment: 4,841 734-783-3300

Housing: Homeownership rate: 75.7% (2000); Median home value: $147,200 (2000); Median rent: $482 per month (2000); Median age of housing: 23 years (2000).

Safety: Violent crime rate: 31.6 per 10,000 population; Property crime rate: 285.6 per 10,000 population (2001).

Transportation: Commute to work: 97.1% car, 0.4% public transportation, 0.7% walk, 1.3% work from home (2000); Travel time to work: 25.8% less than 15 minutes, 38.2% 15 to 30 minutes, 23.2% 30 to 45 minutes, 8.1% 45 to 60 minutes, 4.7% 60 minutes or more (2000)

CANTON (CDP). Covers a land area of 35.996 square miles and a water area of 0.004 square miles. Located at 42.31° N. Lat.; 83.47° W. Long.

Population: 76,366 (2000); Race: 83.7% White, 4.7% Black, 8.6% Asian, 0.3% American Indian and Alaska Native, 2.3% Hispanic of any race, 2.2% two or more races (2000); Density: 2,121.5 persons per square mile (2000); Age: 29.0% under 18, 6.0% over 64 (2000); Marriage status: 24.9% never married, 63.9% now married, 3.8% widowed, 7.4% divorced (2000); Foreign born: 10.6% (2000); Ancestry (includes multiple ancestries): 22.2% German, 18.2% Other groups, 14.4% Irish, 13.8% Polish, 10.8% English (2000).

Vital Statistics: Birth rate: 149.2 per 10,000 population (1998)

Economy: Unemployment rate: 2.3% (11/2002); Total civilian labor force: 33,272 (11/2002); Single-family building permits issued: 645 (2001) / 631 (2000); Multi-family building permits issued: 474 (2001) / 101 (2000); Employment by occupation: 17.0% management, 28.1% professional, 10.8% services, 26.2% sales, 0.1% farming, 6.2% construction, 11.6% production (2000).

Income: Per capita income: $28,609 (2000); Median household income: $72,495 (2000); Poverty rate: 3.7% (2000).

Education: High school graduation rate: 92.0% (2000); College graduation rate: 39.4% (2000).

School District(s)

Canton Charter Academy (KG-05)
2000 Enrollment: 294 734-453-9517

Housing: Homeownership rate: 79.2% (2000); Median home value: $194,100 (2000); Median rent: $617 per month (2000); Median age of housing: 20 years (2000).

Safety: Violent crime rate: 11.3 per 10,000 population; Property crime rate: 224.4 per 10,000 population (2001).
Transportation: Commute to work: 96.7% car, 0.3% public transportation, 0.5% walk, 2.2% work from home (2000); Travel time to work: 20.4% less than 15 minutes, 37.8% 15 to 30 minutes, 28.8% 30 to 45 minutes, 8.4% 45 to 60 minutes, 4.7% 60 minutes or more (2000)
Additional Information Contacts
Canton Chamber of Commerce 734-453-4040

DEARBORN (city). Covers a land area of 24.363 square miles and a water area of 0.088 square miles. Located at 42.31° N. Lat.; 83.21° W. Long. Elevation is 604 feet.
History: Among the first to settle in Dearborn were A.J. Bucklin and the Thomas brothers from Ohio, whose homesteads later became part of the Ford estate. Pekin Township, established when many settlers came after the War of 1812, later became Dearborn, renamed to honor General Henry Dearborn (1751-1829), secretary of war under President Andrew Jackson. Dearborn later encompassed Greenfield and Springwells Townships as well. A local legend claims that Michigan's nickname of the Wolverine State originated at Conrad "Old Coon" Ten Eyck's Tavern in Dearborn, where visitors were told they had been served wolf steaks and were then wolverines. Henry Ford was born in Dearborn in 1863. When he founded a plant to build small iron ships here on the River Rouge in 1917, his Ford Motor Company had already made him wealthy. Soon the entire plant was moved from Highland Park, and the City of Springwells was incorporated. Its name was changed to Fordson in 1925, and in 1928 Fordson and Dearborn were united as one municipality.
Population: 97,775 (2000); Race: 86.5% White, 1.2% Black, 1.4% Asian, 0.4% American Indian and Alaska Native, 3.0% Hispanic of any race, 9.3% two or more races (2000); Density: 4,013.2 persons per square mile (2000); Age: 27.7% under 18, 15.6% over 64 (2000); Marriage status: 26.0% never married, 56.8% now married, 8.9% widowed, 8.4% divorced (2000); Foreign born: 25.4% (2000); Ancestry (includes multiple ancestries): 17.7% Lebanese, 13.7% German, 11.8% Polish, 9.4% Irish, 7.7% Other groups (2000).
Vital Statistics: Birth rate: 177.8 per 10,000 population (1998)
Economy: Unemployment rate: 3.1% (11/2002); Total civilian labor force: 43,106 (11/2002); Single-family building permits issued: 91 (2001) / 57 (2000); Multi-family building permits issued: 4 (2001) / 246 (2000); Employment by occupation: 12.6% management, 25.2% professional, 13.3% services, 26.9% sales, 0.1% farming, 7.3% construction, 14.7% production (2000).
Income: Per capita income: $21,488 (2000); Median household income: $44,560 (2000); Poverty rate: 16.1% (2000).
Taxes: Total city taxes per capita: $654 (2000); City property taxes per capita: $620 (2000).
Education: High school graduation rate: 78.0% (2000); College graduation rate: 26.4% (2000).

School District(s)
Dearborn Academy (KG-08)
2000 Enrollment: 489 517-774-2100
Dearborn City School District (KG-12)
2000 Enrollment: 17,129 313-730-0224
Henry Ford Academy of Mfg., Arts (09-12)
2000 Enrollment: 416 734-334-1300
West Village Academy (KG-07)
2000 Enrollment: 375 517-774-2100

Four-year College(s)
Davenport University-Eastern Region-Dearborn (Private, Not-for-profit)
2001 Enrollment: 3,138 313-581-4400
2001 Tuition: In-state $7,344; Out-of-state $7,344
University of Michigan-Dearborn (Public)
2001 Enrollment: 8,144 313-593-5000
2001 Tuition: In-state $4,915; Out-of-state $11,883

Two-year College(s)
Henry Ford Community College (Public)
2001 Enrollment: n/a 313-845-9615
2001 Tuition: In-state $2,208; Out-of-state $2,544
Detroit Barber College Inc (Private, For-profit)
2001 Enrollment: n/a 313-581-3210
Housing: Homeownership rate: 73.5% (2000); Median home value: $129,300 (2000); Median rent: $546 per month (2000); Median age of housing: 50 years (2000).
Hospitals: Oakwood Hospital & Medical Center (615 beds); Oakwood Hospital Merriman Center (119 beds)
Safety: Violent crime rate: 99.3 per 10,000 population; Property crime rate: 499.2 per 10,000 population (2001).
Newspapers: Dearborn Heights Times-Herald (1 x week); Dearborn Times-Herald (1 x week); Dearborn Press & Guide (2 x week); Sunday Times (1 x week)
Transportation: Commute to work: 94.6% car, 1.2% public transportation, 1.9% walk, 1.6% work from home (2000); Travel time to work: 35.1% less than 15 minutes, 37.3% 15 to 30 minutes, 18.3% 30 to 45 minutes, 4.9% 45 to 60 minutes, 4.4% 60 minutes or more (2000); Amtrak: Service available.
Additional Information Contacts
Dearborn Board of Realtors 313-278-2220
Dearborn Chamber of Commerce 313-584-6100

DEARBORN HEIGHTS (city). Covers a land area of 11.716 square miles and a water area of 0 square miles. Located at 42.31° N. Lat.; 83.28° W. Long. Elevation is 623 feet.
Population: 58,264 (2000); Race: 91.5% White, 2.1% Black, 2.0% Asian, 0.6% American Indian and Alaska Native, 3.9% Hispanic of any race, 2.7% two or more races (2000); Density: 4,973.1 persons per square mile (2000); Age: 22.5% under 18, 18.7% over 64 (2000); Marriage status: 24.0% never married, 56.6% now married, 9.5% widowed, 9.9% divorced (2000); Foreign born: 12.4% (2000); Ancestry (includes multiple ancestries): 20.7% Polish, 15.8% German, 12.3% Irish, 11.1% Other groups, 8.4% Italian (2000).
Vital Statistics: Birth rate: 122.0 per 10,000 population (1998)
Economy: Gerrymandered corporate limits surround West end of city of Dearborn. Light manufacturing. Unemployment rate: 2.9% (11/2002); Total civilian labor force: 31,331 (11/2002); Single-family building permits issued: 39 (2001) / 52 (2000); Multi-family building permits issued: 0 (2001) / 0 (2000); Employment by occupation: 10.5% management, 17.6% professional, 13.8% services, 29.9% sales, 0.0% farming, 11.0% construction, 17.2% production (2000).
Income: Per capita income: $22,829 (2000); Median household income: $48,222 (2000); Poverty rate: 6.1% (2000).
Taxes: Total city taxes per capita: $371 (2000); City property taxes per capita: $343 (2000).
Education: High school graduation rate: 79.0% (2000); College graduation rate: 16.7% (2000).

School District(s)
Academy for Business & Technolog (06-12)
2000 Enrollment: 350 313-487-0252
Crestwood School District (PK-12)
2000 Enrollment: 3,227 313-278-0903
Dearborn Heights School District (KG-12)
2000 Enrollment: 2,508 313-278-1900
Westwood Community Schools (KG-12)
2000 Enrollment: 2,206 313-565-1900
Housing: Homeownership rate: 85.4% (2000); Median home value: $110,800 (2000); Median rent: $619 per month (2000); Median age of housing: 43 years (2000).
Safety: Violent crime rate: 21.2 per 10,000 population; Property crime rate: 256.4 per 10,000 population (2001).
Transportation: Commute to work: 96.3% car, 0.4% public transportation, 1.1% walk, 1.8% work from home (2000); Travel time to work: 27.0% less than 15 minutes, 44.5% 15 to 30 minutes, 19.2% 30 to 45 minutes, 5.6% 45 to 60 minutes, 3.7% 60 minutes or more (2000)
Additional Information Contacts
Dearborn Heights Chamber of Commerce 313-274-7480

DETROIT (city). Covers a land area of 138.769 square miles and a water area of 4.177 square miles. Located at 42.38° N. Lat.; 83.10° W. Long. Elevation is 600 feet.
History: Detroit began as a trading post founded in 1701 by Antoine de la Mothe Cadillac, in the service of Louis XIV of France. The post became an important fur depot and a military site for the British, who acquired it at the end of the French and Indian War and held it until 1796. The settlement that then came under American rule was named for the river, "detroit" being French for "the strait." Growth in Detroit was slowed by political dissension and reports of the swampy and sandy soil, which discouraged settlers until after the Erie Canal was completed. Between 1830 and 1860 the town grew rapidly, becoming an industrial center that continued to expand after the Civil War. The automobile changed Detroit as it changed America. Not only Ford came to Detroit, but also Buick, Durant, R.E. Olds, the Fisher brothers, and numerous others connected with the automobile industry.
Population: 951,270 (2000); Race: 12.4% White, 81.4% Black, 1.0% Asian, 0.3% American Indian and Alaska Native, 5.0% Hispanic of any race, 2.3% two or more races (2000); Density: 6,855.1 persons per square mile (2000); Age: 31.1% under 18, 10.5% over 64 (2000); Marriage status: 43.6% never married, 35.4% now married, 8.3% widowed, 12.7% divorced (2000);

Foreign born: 4.8% (2000); Ancestry (includes multiple ancestries): 70.1% Other groups, 2.0% Polish, 1.8% German, 1.5% Irish, 1.5% African (2000).
Vital Statistics: Birth rate: 172.7 per 10,000 population (1998)
Economy: Unemployment rate: 10.5% (11/2002); Total civilian labor force: 401,590 (11/2002); Single-family building permits issued: 56 (2001) / 72 (2000); Multi-family building permits issued: 81 (2001) / 294 (2000); Employment by occupation: 7.5% management, 14.1% professional, 21.6% services, 26.8% sales, 0.2% farming, 7.2% construction, 22.5% production (2000).
Income: Per capita income: $14,717 (2000); Median household income: $29,526 (2000); Poverty rate: 26.1% (2000).
Taxes: Total city taxes per capita: $949 (2000); City property taxes per capita: $412 (2000).
Education: High school graduation rate: 69.6% (2000); College graduation rate: 11.0% (2000).

School District(s)

Academy of Detroit-West (KG-07)
2000 Enrollment: 580 517-774-2100
Aisha Shule/Web Dubois Prep. Sch (KG-12)
2000 Enrollment: 210 313-494-1399
Allen Academy (KG-12)
2000 Enrollment: 457 231-591-5802
Beacon International Academy (KG-05)
2000 Enrollment: 313 231-591-5802
Benjamin Carson Academy (UG-UG)
2000 Enrollment: 169 313-467-1300
Center for Literacy and Creativi (KG-08)
2000 Enrollment: 165 313-494-1399
Cesar Chavez Academy (KG-08)
2000 Enrollment: 765 517-790-4000
Charlotte Forten Academy (05-12)
2000 Enrollment: 151 313-467-1300
Colin Powell Academy (KG-09)
2000 Enrollment: 352 517-774-2100
Commonwealth Community Devel. Ac (KG-08)
2000 Enrollment: 690 313-487-2420
David Ellis Academy (KG-08)
2000 Enrollment: 233 313-494-1399
Detroit Academy of Arts and Scie (KG-10)
2000 Enrollment: 868 517-774-2100
Detroit Advantage Academy (KG-05)
2000 Enrollment: 571 313-933-3963
Detroit City School District (PK-12)
2000 Enrollment: 162,194 313-494-1075
Detroit Community High School (KG-12)
2000 Enrollment: 320 517-790-4000
Detroit Ps—New Horizon Academ (N -N)
2000 Enrollment: n/a 313-494-1399
Detroit School of Industrial Art (09-12)
2000 Enrollment: 340 517-774-2100
Dove Academy of Detroit (KG-05)
2000 Enrollment: 323 248-370-3050
Edison Public School Academy (KG-08)
2000 Enrollment: 1,108 248-370-3050
George Crockett Academy (KG-12)
2000 Enrollment: 353 616-592-2300
Heart Academy (09-12)
2000 Enrollment: 85 517-790-4000
Hope Academy (KG-05)
2000 Enrollment: 418 313-487-2420
Hope of Detroit Academy (KG-12)
2000 Enrollment: 394 231-591-5802
Joy Preparatory Academy (KG-08)
2000 Enrollment: 109 231-591-5802
M.L. King Jr. Education Center (KG-06)
2000 Enrollment: 191 313-494-1399
Marilyn F. Lundy Academy (05-12)
2000 Enrollment: 0 313-369-1270
Mi Institute for Construction Tr (09-12)
2000 Enrollment: 142 313-494-1399
Michigan Automotive Academy (KG-12)
2000 Enrollment: 350 517-774-2100
Ml Winans Academy of Performing (KG-08)
2000 Enrollment: 432 517-790-4000
Nataki Talibah School of Detroit (KG-06)
2000 Enrollment: 326 517-774-2100
Old Redford Academy (KG-08)
2000 Enrollment: 342 517-774-2100
Pierre Toussaint Academy (KG-12)
2000 Enrollment: 367 616-592-2300
Plymouth Educational Center (KG-07)
2000 Enrollment: 718 517-774-2100
Ross Hill Academy (KG-08)
2000 Enrollment: 287 313-494-1399
Sankore Marine Immersion HS Acad (09-12)
2000 Enrollment: 357 313-467-1300
Ser Casa Environ./Tech. Academy (07-12)
2000 Enrollment: 89 313-467-1402
Star International Academy (KG-07)
2000 Enrollment: 421 248-370-3050
Timbuktu Academy of Science & Te (KG-12)
2000 Enrollment: 233 313-494-1097
Universal Academy (08-09)
2000 Enrollment: 102 313-494-1399
University Preparatory Academy (06-12)
2000 Enrollment: 113 313-831-0116
University Public School (06-08)
2000 Enrollment: 523 313-964-1600
Voyageur Academy (KG-12)
2000 Enrollment: 316 616-592-2300
Warrendale Charter Academy (KG-05)
2000 Enrollment: 0 313-564-0924
Weston Technical Academy (06-11)
2000 Enrollment: 384 248-370-3050
Woodward Academy (KG-08)
2000 Enrollment: 715 517-774-2100
Ymca Service Learning Academy (KG-08)
2000 Enrollment: 1,079 906-635-2211

Four-year College(s)

Center for Humanistic Studies (Private, Not-for-profit)
2001 Enrollment: 87 313-875-7440
Center for Creative Studies College of Art and Design (Private, Not-for-profit)
2001 Enrollment: 1,152 313-664-7400
2001 Tuition: In-state $16,560; Out-of-state $16,560
University of Detroit Mercy (Private, Not-for-profit, Roman Catholic)
2001 Enrollment: 5,843 313-993-1000
2001 Tuition: In-state $15,900; Out-of-state $15,900
Marygrove College (Private, Not-for-profit, Roman Catholic)
2001 Enrollment: 6,097 313-927-1200
2001 Tuition: In-state $10,500; Out-of-state $10,500
Sacred Heart Major Seminary (Private, Not-for-profit, Roman Catholic)
2001 Enrollment: 420 313-883-8500
2001 Tuition: In-state $6,792; Out-of-state $6,792
Wayne State University (Public)
2001 Enrollment: 31,040 313-577-2424
2001 Tuition: In-state $3,110; Out-of-state $7,128
Ecumenical Theological Seminary (Private, Not-for-profit)
2001 Enrollment: 108 313-831-5200
Detroit Health Department Nutrition Division (Public)
2001 Enrollment: n/a 313-876-4090

Two-year College(s)

Henry Ford Hospital School of Radiologic Techn (Private, Not-for-profit)
2001 Enrollment: n/a 313-916-2600
Krainz Woods Academy of Medical Laboratory Tech (Private, For-profit)
2001 Enrollment: n/a 313-366-5204
Lewis College of Business (Private, Not-for-profit, Historically black)
2001 Enrollment: 358 313-862-6300
2001 Tuition: In-state $6,738; Out-of-state $6,738
Michigan Barber School Inc (Private, Not-for-profit)
2001 Enrollment: 200 313-894-2300
Saint John Hospital and Medical Center School of Rad Techn (Private, Not-for-profit, Roman Catholic)
2001 Enrollment: n/a 313-343-4000
Wayne County Community College District (Public)
2001 Enrollment: 10,433 313-496-2600
2001 Tuition: In-state $2,250; Out-of-state $2,858
SJ Williams School of Religion (Private, Not-for-profit, Baptist)
2001 Enrollment: n/a 313-924-7544

Housing: Homeownership rate: 54.9% (2000); Median home value: $63,600 (2000); Median rent: $383 per month (2000); Median age of housing: 52 years (2000).

Hospitals: Children's Hospital of Michigan (245 beds); DMC Hutzel Hospital (244 beds); Detroit Receiving Hospital & University Health Center (305 beds); Harper Hospital (658 beds); Henry Ford Cottage Hospital (185 beds); Henry Ford Hospital (903 beds); Kindred Hospital-Metro Detroit (240 beds); Rehabilitation Institute of Michigan (94 beds); Sinai-Grace Hospital (440 beds); Saint John NorthEast Community Hospital (295 beds); Saint John's Hospital and Medical Center (607 beds); Saint Johns Detroit Riverview Hospital (262 beds); Veterans Affairs Medical Center (372 beds)
Safety: Violent crime rate: 219.0 per 10,000 population; Property crime rate: 724.1 per 10,000 population (2001).
Newspapers: The Detroit News and Free Press; Detroit Legal News (5 x week); The Detroit News (7 x week); Detroit Free Press (7 x week); Michigan Chronicle (1 x week); Michigan Catholic Newspaper (1 x week); The Metro Times (1 x week); Michigan Chronicle-Oakland County Edition (1 x week); El Central (1 x week)
Transportation: Commute to work: 85.7% car, 8.7% public transportation, 2.8% walk, 1.8% work from home (2000); Travel time to work: 17.2% less than 15 minutes, 43.2% 15 to 30 minutes, 24.3% 30 to 45 minutes, 7.2% 45 to 60 minutes, 8.1% 60 minutes or more (2000); Amtrak: Service available.
Airports: Detroit Metropolitan Wayne County (primary service/large hub); Willow Run (primary service/large hub); Grosse Ile Municipal (primary service/large hub); Detroit City (primary service/large hub); Berz-Macomb (primary service/large hub)
Additional Information Contacts
Detroit Association of Realtors 313-962-1313
Detroit Chamber of Commerce 313-875-7877

ECORSE (city). Covers a land area of 2.690 square miles and a water area of 0.926 square miles. Located at 42.25° N. Lat.; 83.14° W. Long. Elevation is 583 feet.
History: First called Grandport, the village of Ecorse was established at the mouth of a stream known to the French as the Riviere Aux Ecorses. The French who first settled here were descendants of the early fur trappers and traders. During prohibition times, Ecorse was known as a rumrunners' paradise, outside the control of the Detroit authorities and with the river islands giving hiding places from the Federal authorities.
Population: 11,229 (2000); Race: 50.6% White, 41.1% Black, 0.2% Asian, 0.6% American Indian and Alaska Native, 9.4% Hispanic of any race, 4.0% two or more races (2000); Density: 4,175.1 persons per square mile (2000); Age: 27.8% under 18, 12.2% over 64 (2000); Marriage status: 37.2% never married, 39.2% now married, 8.6% widowed, 15.1% divorced (2000); Foreign born: 3.5% (2000); Ancestry (includes multiple ancestries): 48.3% Other groups, 7.2% Irish, 7.1% German, 7.0% United States or American, 4.2% French (except Basque) (2000).
Vital Statistics: Birth rate: 174.6 per 10,000 population (1998)
Economy: Single-family building permits issued: 16 (2001) / 5 (2000); Multi-family building permits issued: 37 (2001) / 0 (2000); Employment by occupation: 5.4% management, 6.9% professional, 21.5% services, 27.6% sales, 0.0% farming, 12.8% construction, 25.8% production (2000).
Income: Per capita income: $14,468 (2000); Median household income: $27,142 (2000); Poverty rate: 22.6% (2000).
Taxes: Total city taxes per capita: $614 (1997); City property taxes per capita: $601 (1997).
Education: High school graduation rate: 64.1% (2000); College graduation rate: 4.7% (2000).

School District(s)
Ecorse Public School District (KG-12)
2000 Enrollment: 1,134 313-382-6320
Housing: Homeownership rate: 61.5% (2000); Median home value: $44,300 (2000); Median rent: $368 per month (2000); Median age of housing: 49 years (2000).
Newspapers: Ecorse Telegram (1 x week)
Transportation: Commute to work: 91.0% car, 2.6% public transportation, 3.9% walk, 1.3% work from home (2000); Travel time to work: 24.2% less than 15 minutes, 45.7% 15 to 30 minutes, 18.4% 30 to 45 minutes, 6.2% 45 to 60 minutes, 5.4% 60 minutes or more (2000)

FLAT ROCK (city). Covers a land area of 6.700 square miles and a water area of 0.102 square miles. Located at 42.10° N. Lat.; 83.27° W. Long. Elevation is 629 feet.
History: A community was first settled here in 1824, and later grew around a branch plant of the Ford Motor Company where headlights and taillights were manufactured. The name of Flat Rock came from the smooth rock bed of the Huron River at this point.
Population: 8,488 (2000); Race: 94.6% White, 2.1% Black, 0.7% Asian, 0.3% American Indian and Alaska Native, 2.6% Hispanic of any race, 1.7% two or more races (2000); Density: 1,266.9 persons per square mile (2000); Age: 28.9% under 18, 9.4% over 64 (2000); Marriage status: 26.8% never married, 55.1% now married, 6.0% widowed, 12.1% divorced (2000); Foreign born: 2.3% (2000); Ancestry (includes multiple ancestries): 25.2% German, 14.6% Polish, 14.5% Irish, 11.1% Other groups, 9.8% French (except Basque) (2000).
Economy: Single-family building permits issued: 71 (2001) / 51 (2000); Multi-family building permits issued: 0 (2001) / 0 (2000); Employment by occupation: 6.3% management, 14.4% professional, 17.8% services, 23.9% sales, 0.0% farming, 11.5% construction, 26.1% production (2000).
Income: Per capita income: $21,256 (2000); Median household income: $44,084 (2000); Poverty rate: 8.8% (2000).
Taxes: Total city taxes per capita: $338 (1997); City property taxes per capita: $316 (1997).
Education: High school graduation rate: 83.5% (2000); College graduation rate: 12.0% (2000).

School District(s)
Flat Rock Community Schools (KG-12)
2000 Enrollment: 1,723 734-782-2451
Summit Academy (KG-12)
2000 Enrollment: 579 517-774-2100
Housing: Homeownership rate: 72.4% (2000); Median home value: $121,700 (2000); Median rent: $417 per month (2000); Median age of housing: 29 years (2000).
Safety: Violent crime rate: 30.5 per 10,000 population; Property crime rate: 334.0 per 10,000 population (2001).
Transportation: Commute to work: 95.8% car, 0.2% public transportation, 2.1% walk, 1.4% work from home (2000); Travel time to work: 29.1% less than 15 minutes, 35.3% 15 to 30 minutes, 21.4% 30 to 45 minutes, 7.6% 45 to 60 minutes, 6.6% 60 minutes or more (2000)

GARDEN CITY (city). Covers a land area of 5.864 square miles and a water area of 0 square miles. Located at 42.32° N. Lat.; 83.33° W. Long. Elevation is 636 feet.
History: Garden City was laid out in 1921, with the plots purposely being large enough so that each owner could have a vegetable garden.
Population: 30,047 (2000); Race: 96.4% White, 1.1% Black, 0.8% Asian, 0.3% American Indian and Alaska Native, 1.9% Hispanic of any race, 1.2% two or more races (2000); Density: 5,124.0 persons per square mile (2000); Age: 25.0% under 18, 13.5% over 64 (2000); Marriage status: 24.5% never married, 57.9% now married, 7.0% widowed, 10.6% divorced (2000); Foreign born: 3.3% (2000); Ancestry (includes multiple ancestries): 23.0% German, 17.1% Irish, 16.7% Polish, 11.8% English, 8.6% Other groups (2000).
Vital Statistics: Birth rate: 131.1 per 10,000 population (1998)
Economy: Unemployment rate: 2.9% (11/2002); Total civilian labor force: 17,463 (11/2002); Single-family building permits issued: 30 (2001) / 19 (2000); Multi-family building permits issued: 0 (2001) / 0 (2000); Employment by occupation: 9.0% management, 13.6% professional, 13.7% services, 29.1% sales, 0.0% farming, 12.9% construction, 21.6% production (2000).
Income: Per capita income: $21,651 (2000); Median household income: $51,841 (2000); Poverty rate: 4.5% (2000).
Taxes: Total city taxes per capita: $315 (2000); City property taxes per capita: $294 (2000).
Education: High school graduation rate: 81.1% (2000); College graduation rate: 9.0% (2000).

School District(s)
Garden City School District (PK-12)
2000 Enrollment: 5,349 734-762-8300
Housing: Homeownership rate: 86.3% (2000); Median home value: $110,700 (2000); Median rent: $513 per month (2000); Median age of housing: 44 years (2000).
Safety: Violent crime rate: 22.5 per 10,000 population; Property crime rate: 204.9 per 10,000 population (2001).
Transportation: Commute to work: 96.8% car, 0.2% public transportation, 1.4% walk, 0.9% work from home (2000); Travel time to work: 24.6% less than 15 minutes, 43.0% 15 to 30 minutes, 20.5% 30 to 45 minutes, 6.9% 45 to 60 minutes, 5.0% 60 minutes or more (2000)
Additional Information Contacts
Garden City Chamber of Commerce 734-422-4448

GIBRALTAR (city). Covers a land area of 3.845 square miles and a water area of 0.498 square miles. Located at 42.09° N. Lat.; 83.19° W. Long. Elevation is 584 feet.

History: Gibraltar was first settled in 1811. The settlement was platted in 1837, but prospered only after the suburban growth of Wayne County in the 1900's.
Population: 4,264 (2000); Race: 97.2% White, 0.4% Black, 0.3% Asian, 0.0% American Indian and Alaska Native, 1.3% Hispanic of any race, 1.8% two or more races (2000); Density: 1,109.1 persons per square mile (2000); Age: 23.7% under 18, 8.9% over 64 (2000); Marriage status: 20.4% never married, 62.4% now married, 5.1% widowed, 12.1% divorced (2000); Foreign born: 4.1% (2000); Ancestry (includes multiple ancestries): 26.0% German, 16.4% Polish, 15.1% Irish, 11.6% English, 9.9% French (except Basque) (2000).
Economy: Single-family building permits issued: 6 (2001) / 7 (2000); Multi-family building permits issued: 0 (2001) / 0 (2000); Employment by occupation: 10.9% management, 17.1% professional, 14.2% services, 25.3% sales, 0.0% farming, 14.0% construction, 18.5% production (2000).
Income: Per capita income: $28,528 (2000); Median household income: $58,167 (2000); Poverty rate: 2.7% (2000).
Taxes: Total city taxes per capita: $383 (1997); City property taxes per capita: $361 (1997).
Education: High school graduation rate: 85.3% (2000); College graduation rate: 16.3% (2000).
Housing: Homeownership rate: 73.4% (2000); Median home value: $147,700 (2000); Median rent: $525 per month (2000); Median age of housing: 33 years (2000).
Safety: Violent crime rate: 11.7 per 10,000 population; Property crime rate: 210.0 per 10,000 population (2001).
Transportation: Commute to work: 97.9% car, 0.0% public transportation, 0.0% walk, 1.5% work from home (2000); Travel time to work: 18.9% less than 15 minutes, 35.8% 15 to 30 minutes, 29.7% 30 to 45 minutes, 11.6% 45 to 60 minutes, 4.0% 60 minutes or more (2000)

GROSSE ILE (CDP). Covers a land area of 9.608 square miles and a water area of 8.718 square miles. Located at 42.13° N. Lat.; 83.16° W. Long.
History: Grosse Ile, the largest of the islands in the Detroit River, attracted attention from the times of earliest exploration here. Title to the land on the island was transferred to Alexander and William Macomb, merchants from Detroit, in 1776. Though disputed, the title was later confirmed to the Macomb heirs by President James Madison. The township developed in the 1900's as an exclusive residential area.
Population: 10,894 (2000); Race: 95.3% White, 0.5% Black, 2.3% Asian, 0.4% American Indian and Alaska Native, 1.6% Hispanic of any race, 1.5% two or more races (2000); Density: 1,133.9 persons per square mile (2000); Age: 24.7% under 18, 12.0% over 64 (2000); Marriage status: 17.5% never married, 71.4% now married, 5.7% widowed, 5.4% divorced (2000); Foreign born: 6.5% (2000); Ancestry (includes multiple ancestries): 26.2% German, 17.3% Polish, 16.4% Irish, 11.8% English, 9.8% Italian (2000).
Economy: Single-family building permits issued: 33 (2001) / 29 (2000); Multi-family building permits issued: 50 (2001) / 0 (2000); Employment by occupation: 22.5% management, 31.5% professional, 9.3% services, 21.2% sales, 0.0% farming, 7.9% construction, 7.6% production (2000).
Income: Per capita income: $42,150 (2000); Median household income: $87,062 (2000); Poverty rate: 2.6% (2000).
Education: High school graduation rate: 94.4% (2000); College graduation rate: 45.1% (2000).

School District(s)

Grosse Ile Township Schools (KG-12)
2000 Enrollment: 2,067 734-362-2555
Housing: Homeownership rate: 93.9% (2000); Median home value: $248,800 (2000); Median rent: $825 per month (2000); Median age of housing: 32 years (2000).
Safety: Violent crime rate: 0.9 per 10,000 population; Property crime rate: 73.1 per 10,000 population (2001).
Newspapers: The Ile Camera (1 x week)
Transportation: Commute to work: 96.6% car, 0.0% public transportation, 0.7% walk, 1.9% work from home (2000); Travel time to work: 22.1% less than 15 minutes, 31.8% 15 to 30 minutes, 25.2% 30 to 45 minutes, 11.9% 45 to 60 minutes, 9.0% 60 minutes or more (2000)
Airports: Grosse Ile Municipal

GROSSE POINTE (city). Covers a land area of 1.070 square miles and a water area of 1.209 square miles. Located at 42.39° N. Lat.; 82.91° W. Long. Elevation is 592 feet.
History: Grosse Pointe developed as one of the Gold Coast communities along the shore of Lake St. Clair.
Population: 5,670 (2000); Race: 95.8% White, 1.3% Black, 1.7% Asian, 0.3% American Indian and Alaska Native, 0.7% Hispanic of any race, 0.9% two or more races (2000); Density: 5,297.9 persons per square mile (2000); Age: 25.2% under 18, 15.6% over 64 (2000); Marriage status: 19.3% never married, 61.4% now married, 8.9% widowed, 10.4% divorced (2000); Foreign born: 5.5% (2000); Ancestry (includes multiple ancestries): 28.3% German, 20.7% Irish, 18.9% English, 11.5% Polish, 8.8% Italian (2000).
Economy: Single-family building permits issued: 5 (2001) / 0 (2000); Multi-family building permits issued: 0 (2001) / 2 (2000); Employment by occupation: 26.8% management, 40.1% professional, 5.3% services, 21.8% sales, 0.0% farming, 2.6% construction, 3.4% production (2000).
Income: Per capita income: $53,942 (2000); Median household income: $81,111 (2000); Poverty rate: 2.5% (2000).
Taxes: Total city taxes per capita: $687 (2000); City property taxes per capita: $680 (2000).
Education: High school graduation rate: 97.0% (2000); College graduation rate: 68.9% (2000).

School District(s)

Grosse Pointe Public Schools (KG-12)
2000 Enrollment: 8,637 313-343-2000
Housing: Homeownership rate: 81.9% (2000); Median home value: $288,400 (2000); Median rent: $844 per month (2000); Median age of housing: 60+ years (2000).
Hospitals: Bon Secours Cottage Health Services (313 beds)
Safety: Violent crime rate: 0.0 per 10,000 population; Property crime rate: 249.1 per 10,000 population (2001).
Newspapers: Grosse Pointe News (1 x week)
Transportation: Commute to work: 91.0% car, 2.3% public transportation, 1.4% walk, 4.6% work from home (2000); Travel time to work: 23.7% less than 15 minutes, 37.1% 15 to 30 minutes, 23.5% 30 to 45 minutes, 10.7% 45 to 60 minutes, 5.0% 60 minutes or more (2000)
Additional Information Contacts
Grosse Pointe Board of Realtors 313-882-8000

GROSSE POINTE (township). Covers a land area of 0.986 square miles and a water area of 17.608 square miles. Located at 42.43° N. Lat.; 82.88° W. Long. Elevation is 592 feet.
History: The area was originally settled, and called Grosse Pointe Park, by the French along the lake shore c.1712. Farms clustered there became organized as Grosse Pointe township c.1846. As the nearby city of Detroit boomed with the auto industry, many wealthy industrialists established large estates in the outlying area. Henry Ford's family, including his son Edsel, built their homes there.
Population: 2,743 (2000); Race: 93.4% White, 0.8% Black, 4.0% Asian, 0.0% American Indian and Alaska Native, 1.1% Hispanic of any race, 1.5% two or more races (2000); Density: 2,781.3 persons per square mile (2000); Age: 23.2% under 18, 24.1% over 64 (2000); Marriage status: 18.7% never married, 72.0% now married, 6.7% widowed, 2.5% divorced (2000); Foreign born: 12.8% (2000); Ancestry (includes multiple ancestries): 26.2% German, 14.1% Irish, 13.0% English, 12.4% Italian, 8.7% Polish (2000).
Economy: Employment by occupation: 28.6% management, 40.1% professional, 2.1% services, 24.1% sales, 0.0% farming, 1.5% construction, 3.6% production (2000).
Income: Per capita income: $69,731 (2000); Median household income: $114,863 (2000); Poverty rate: 3.0% (2000).
Taxes: Total city taxes per capita: $77 (1997); City property taxes per capita: $77 (1997).
Education: High school graduation rate: 93.9% (2000); College graduation rate: 62.1% (2000).
Housing: Homeownership rate: 97.5% (2000); Median home value: $597,900 (2000); Median rent: $1,150 per month (2000); Median age of housing: 42 years (2000).
Transportation: Commute to work: 92.8% car, 1.1% public transportation, 2.2% walk, 3.4% work from home (2000); Travel time to work: 33.7% less than 15 minutes, 30.2% 15 to 30 minutes, 26.9% 30 to 45 minutes, 6.9% 45 to 60 minutes, 2.4% 60 minutes or more (2000)

GROSSE POINTE FARMS (city). Covers a land area of 2.698 square miles and a water area of 9.630 square miles. Located at 42.40° N. Lat.; 82.90° W. Long. Elevation is 585 feet.
History: Grosse Pointe Farms was the first settled of the Gold Coast communities. Captain Alexander Grant, Commodore of the British Navy on the Great Lakes, purchased land here during the time of English occupation, and erected a large home known as Grant's Castle, a gathering place for British officers and Detroit society of the day. Grosse Pointe Farms was incorporated as a village in 1879.
Population: 9,764 (2000); Race: 96.4% White, 0.9% Black, 1.3% Asian, 0.4% American Indian and Alaska Native, 0.7% Hispanic of any race, 0.5%

two or more races (2000); Density: 3,618.8 persons per square mile (2000); Age: 26.2% under 18, 17.7% over 64 (2000); Marriage status: 16.6% never married, 69.9% now married, 6.8% widowed, 6.7% divorced (2000); Foreign born: 5.0% (2000); Ancestry (includes multiple ancestries): 24.7% German, 18.3% Irish, 18.1% English, 10.3% Italian, 9.6% Polish (2000).
Vital Statistics: Birth rate: 106.5 per 10,000 population (1998)
Economy: Single-family building permits issued: 1 (2001) / 3 (2000); Multi-family building permits issued: 0 (2001) / 0 (2000); Employment by occupation: 28.8% management, 38.6% professional, 4.7% services, 23.3% sales, 0.0% farming, 1.2% construction, 3.5% production (2000).
Income: Per capita income: $54,846 (2000); Median household income: $100,153 (2000); Poverty rate: 2.1% (2000).
Taxes: Total city taxes per capita: $663 (1997); City property taxes per capita: $645 (1997).
Education: High school graduation rate: 97.7% (2000); College graduation rate: 68.1% (2000).
Housing: Homeownership rate: 96.8% (2000); Median home value: $295,100 (2000); Median rent: $778 per month (2000); Median age of housing: 53 years (2000).
Safety: Violent crime rate: 5.1 per 10,000 population; Property crime rate: 190.5 per 10,000 population (2001).
Transportation: Commute to work: 93.7% car, 0.6% public transportation, 0.7% walk, 5.0% work from home (2000); Travel time to work: 25.9% less than 15 minutes, 34.1% 15 to 30 minutes, 26.1% 30 to 45 minutes, 10.7% 45 to 60 minutes, 3.2% 60 minutes or more (2000)

GROSSE POINTE PARK (city). Covers a land area of 2.156 square miles and a water area of 1.542 square miles. Located at 42.38° N. Lat.; 82.93° W. Long. Elevation is 585 feet.
History: Grosse Pointe Park grew as the Gold Coast community closest to the industrial outskirts of Detroit.
Population: 12,443 (2000); Race: 93.4% White, 3.1% Black, 1.1% Asian, 0.3% American Indian and Alaska Native, 2.3% Hispanic of any race, 1.8% two or more races (2000); Density: 5,772.6 persons per square mile (2000); Age: 27.2% under 18, 10.7% over 64 (2000); Marriage status: 26.9% never married, 60.4% now married, 4.4% widowed, 8.4% divorced (2000); Foreign born: 9.1% (2000); Ancestry (includes multiple ancestries): 24.8% German, 20.1% Irish, 12.5% English, 10.6% Polish, 9.2% Other groups (2000).
Vital Statistics: Birth rate: 112.5 per 10,000 population (1998)
Economy: Single-family building permits issued: 1 (2001) / 3 (2000); Multi-family building permits issued: 2 (2001) / 2 (2000); Employment by occupation: 24.1% management, 35.9% professional, 9.4% services, 23.2% sales, 0.0% farming, 3.5% construction, 3.9% production (2000).
Income: Per capita income: $42,051 (2000); Median household income: $80,485 (2000); Poverty rate: 4.0% (2000).
Taxes: Total city taxes per capita: $596 (2000); City property taxes per capita: $576 (2000).
Education: High school graduation rate: 96.1% (2000); College graduation rate: 59.5% (2000).

Two-year College(s)
Detroit Institute of Ophthalmology (Private, Not-for-profit)
2001 Enrollment: n/a 313-824-4710

Housing: Homeownership rate: 71.1% (2000); Median home value: $331,200 (2000); Median rent: $597 per month (2000); Median age of housing: 60+ years (2000).
Safety: Violent crime rate: 9.6 per 10,000 population; Property crime rate: 253.4 per 10,000 population (2001).
Transportation: Commute to work: 92.3% car, 1.4% public transportation, 1.2% walk, 4.9% work from home (2000); Travel time to work: 23.4% less than 15 minutes, 40.0% 15 to 30 minutes, 23.3% 30 to 45 minutes, 8.5% 45 to 60 minutes, 4.9% 60 minutes or more (2000)

GROSSE POINTE SHORES (village). Covers a land area of 1.143 square miles and a water area of 18.094 square miles. Located at 42.43° N. Lat.; 82.88° W. Long. Elevation is 586 feet.
History: Grosse Pointe Shores was incorporated as a village in 1911. The Edsel Ford Estate was among those that made this area known as Detroit's Gold Coast.
Population: 2,823 (2000); Race: 93.5% White, 0.8% Black, 3.9% Asian, 0.0% American Indian and Alaska Native, 1.0% Hispanic of any race, 1.5% two or more races (2000); Density: 2,470.6 persons per square mile (2000); Age: 23.0% under 18, 24.5% over 64 (2000); Marriage status: 18.4% never married, 71.9% now married, 7.2% widowed, 2.5% divorced (2000); Foreign born: 12.8% (2000); Ancestry (includes multiple ancestries): 26.0% German, 14.0% Irish, 13.0% English, 12.2% Italian, 8.9% Polish (2000).
Economy: Single-family building permits issued: 4 (2001) / 4 (2000); Multi-family building permits issued: 0 (2001) / 0 (2000); Employment by occupation: 28.4% management, 40.1% professional, 2.1% services, 24.4% sales, 0.0% farming, 1.4% construction, 3.5% production (2000).
Income: Per capita income: $69,639 (2000); Median household income: $113,882 (2000); Poverty rate: 3.0% (2000).
Taxes: Total city taxes per capita: $1,108 (1997); City property taxes per capita: $1,103 (1997).
Education: High school graduation rate: 93.8% (2000); College graduation rate: 61.7% (2000).
Housing: Homeownership rate: 97.4% (2000); Median home value: $594,200 (2000); Median rent: $1,143 per month (2000); Median age of housing: 42 years (2000).
Safety: Violent crime rate: 0.0 per 10,000 population; Property crime rate: 35.2 per 10,000 population (2001).
Transportation: Commute to work: 93.0% car, 1.1% public transportation, 2.2% walk, 3.3% work from home (2000); Travel time to work: 33.5% less than 15 minutes, 30.6% 15 to 30 minutes, 26.8% 30 to 45 minutes, 6.8% 45 to 60 minutes, 2.4% 60 minutes or more (2000)

GROSSE POINTE WOODS (city). Covers a land area of 3.261 square miles and a water area of 0 square miles. Located at 42.43° N. Lat.; 82.89° W. Long. Elevation is 587 feet.
History: Grosse Pointe Woods was first known as the village of Lochmoor. It was incorporated as Grosse Pointe Woods in 1939, becoming part of the Gold Coast development.
Population: 17,080 (2000); Race: 95.9% White, 0.5% Black, 2.2% Asian, 0.1% American Indian and Alaska Native, 1.0% Hispanic of any race, 1.0% two or more races (2000); Density: 5,237.3 persons per square mile (2000); Age: 26.1% under 18, 18.2% over 64 (2000); Marriage status: 20.9% never married, 65.2% now married, 7.8% widowed, 6.1% divorced (2000); Foreign born: 6.6% (2000); Ancestry (includes multiple ancestries): 26.1% German, 15.2% Italian, 14.9% Irish, 12.0% Polish, 10.6% English (2000).
Vital Statistics: Birth rate: 107.1 per 10,000 population (1998)
Economy: Single-family building permits issued: 3 (2001) / 2 (2000); Multi-family building permits issued: 0 (2001) / 0 (2000); Employment by occupation: 23.3% management, 33.1% professional, 5.9% services, 28.5% sales, 0.0% farming, 4.0% construction, 5.2% production (2000).
Income: Per capita income: $38,653 (2000); Median household income: $78,558 (2000); Poverty rate: 2.4% (2000).
Taxes: Total city taxes per capita: $594 (1997); City property taxes per capita: $576 (1997).
Education: High school graduation rate: 94.8% (2000); College graduation rate: 51.2% (2000).
Housing: Homeownership rate: 94.8% (2000); Median home value: $233,100 (2000); Median rent: $793 per month (2000); Median age of housing: 47 years (2000).
Transportation: Commute to work: 95.5% car, 0.5% public transportation, 0.5% walk, 3.1% work from home (2000); Travel time to work: 31.0% less than 15 minutes, 33.9% 15 to 30 minutes, 22.6% 30 to 45 minutes, 9.1% 45 to 60 minutes, 3.5% 60 minutes or more (2000)

HAMTRAMCK (city). Covers a land area of 2.108 square miles and a water area of 0 square miles. Located at 42.39° N. Lat.; 83.05° W. Long. Elevation is 627 feet.
History: Hamtramck Township was named for Colonel John Francis Hamtramck, a German-French Canadian who became General Anthony Wayne's strategist after the Revolutionary War, and the first military commander of Detroit. In 1901 Hamtramck was organized as a village settled by German-American farmers. The Dodge Brothers Company established an automobile plant here in 1910, which attracted the Polish migration to Hamtramck. It was incorporated as a city in 1922. Though surrounded by Detroit, Hamtramck has maintained its city status, partly because the large number of Polish residents relished political autonomy.
Population: 22,976 (2000); Race: 61.5% White, 14.5% Black, 10.3% Asian, 0.7% American Indian and Alaska Native, 1.5% Hispanic of any race, 12.2% two or more races (2000); Density: 10,900.5 persons per square mile (2000); Age: 27.7% under 18, 12.2% over 64 (2000); Marriage status: 35.0% never married, 46.1% now married, 9.7% widowed, 9.2% divorced (2000); Foreign born: 41.1% (2000); Ancestry (includes multiple ancestries): 23.5% Other groups, 22.9% Polish, 10.5% Yugoslavian, 5.6% Arab/Arabic, 3.2% Ukrainian (2000).
Vital Statistics: Birth rate: 168.0 per 10,000 population (1998)
Economy: Single-family building permits issued: 0 (2001) / 0 (2000); Multi-family building permits issued: 0 (2001) / 0 (2000); Employment by

occupation: 4.6% management, 13.2% professional, 18.7% services, 21.8% sales, 0.1% farming, 9.0% construction, 32.6% production (2000).
Income: Per capita income: $12,691 (2000); Median household income: $26,616 (2000); Poverty rate: 27.0% (2000).
Taxes: Total city taxes per capita: $391 (1997); City property taxes per capita: $268 (1997).
Education: High school graduation rate: 62.2% (2000); College graduation rate: 11.5% (2000).

School District(s)

Hamtramck Public Schools (KG-12)
2000 Enrollment: 3,743 313-872-9270

Housing: Homeownership rate: 50.0% (2000); Median home value: $71,200 (2000); Median rent: $378 per month (2000); Median age of housing: 60+ years (2000).
Newspapers: The Citizen (1 x week)
Transportation: Commute to work: 89.3% car, 3.6% public transportation, 4.9% walk, 0.8% work from home (2000); Travel time to work: 23.9% less than 15 minutes, 38.4% 15 to 30 minutes, 25.5% 30 to 45 minutes, 6.5% 45 to 60 minutes, 5.7% 60 minutes or more (2000)

HARPER WOODS (city). Covers a land area of 2.582 square miles and a water area of 0 square miles. Located at 42.43° N. Lat.; 82.92° W. Long. Elevation is 590 feet.
History: There was settlement in the Harper Woods area in the 1850's, and a plat was recorded in 1920 calling it Manchester Park. After the 1929 depression, however, the area returned to wilderness. A new community was developed in 1934 by subdividers, who named it Harper Woods.
Population: 14,254 (2000); Race: 86.5% White, 9.8% Black, 1.5% Asian, 0.7% American Indian and Alaska Native, 1.9% Hispanic of any race, 1.3% two or more races (2000); Density: 5,521.1 persons per square mile (2000); Age: 22.1% under 18, 19.8% over 64 (2000); Marriage status: 26.4% never married, 51.4% now married, 10.0% widowed, 12.2% divorced (2000); Foreign born: 6.0% (2000); Ancestry (includes multiple ancestries): 19.9% German, 16.1% Irish, 15.0% Polish, 14.2% Italian, 14.0% Other groups (2000).
Vital Statistics: Birth rate: 131.2 per 10,000 population (1998)
Economy: Single-family building permits issued: 0 (2001) / 0 (2000); Multi-family building permits issued: 0 (2001) / 0 (2000); Employment by occupation: 15.8% management, 25.3% professional, 12.1% services, 27.9% sales, 0.0% farming, 6.4% construction, 12.4% production (2000).
Income: Per capita income: $24,900 (2000); Median household income: $46,769 (2000); Poverty rate: 5.1% (2000).
Taxes: Total city taxes per capita: $520 (1997); City property taxes per capita: $506 (1997).
Education: High school graduation rate: 84.9% (2000); College graduation rate: 28.0% (2000).

School District(s)

City of Harper Woods Schools (KG-12)
2000 Enrollment: 1,096 313-839-1296

Housing: Homeownership rate: 82.2% (2000); Median home value: $108,600 (2000); Median rent: $625 per month (2000); Median age of housing: 46 years (2000).
Transportation: Commute to work: 96.0% car, 1.1% public transportation, 1.1% walk, 1.7% work from home (2000); Travel time to work: 24.2% less than 15 minutes, 36.0% 15 to 30 minutes, 26.3% 30 to 45 minutes, 9.6% 45 to 60 minutes, 3.9% 60 minutes or more (2000)

HIGHLAND PARK (city). Covers a land area of 2.978 square miles and a water area of 0 square miles. Located at 42.40° N. Lat.; 83.10° W. Long. Elevation is 636 feet.
History: About a hundred years before Henry Ford brought prosperity to Highland Park with his Ford Motor Company plant in 1909, another Ford, Richard (not related to Henry) had settled here. He built his farm on the ridge, since leveled, that was the "highland" for which the town was named. Several attempts at creating a town failed, until 1887 when Captain William H. Stevens, who had made a fortune in the Colorado silver mines, attracted investors in a promotional scheme. The village of Highland Park was organized in 1889, and in 1918 it was incorporated as a city. When Ford moved his plant to Dearborn in 1920, Highland Park's population declined, but later grew as it became a residential suburb for Detroit.
Population: 16,746 (2000); Race: 4.4% White, 93.7% Black, 0.4% Asian, 0.2% American Indian and Alaska Native, 0.7% Hispanic of any race, 1.1% two or more races (2000); Density: 5,622.9 persons per square mile (2000); Age: 29.1% under 18, 14.5% over 64 (2000); Marriage status: 45.9% never married, 28.6% now married, 11.1% widowed, 14.4% divorced (2000); Foreign born: 1.2% (2000); Ancestry (includes multiple ancestries): 71.1% Other groups, 1.7% African, 1.4% German, 0.7% Polish, 0.7% United States or American (2000).
Vital Statistics: Birth rate: 170.8 per 10,000 population (1998)
Economy: Unemployment rate: 17.9% (11/2002); Total civilian labor force: 6,591 (11/2002); Single-family building permits issued: 0 (2001) / 0 (2000); Multi-family building permits issued: 5 (2001) / 5 (2000); Employment by occupation: 6.4% management, 13.8% professional, 27.5% services, 29.3% sales, 0.1% farming, 5.5% construction, 17.4% production (2000).
Income: Per capita income: $12,121 (2000); Median household income: $17,737 (2000); Poverty rate: 38.3% (2000).
Taxes: Total city taxes per capita: $554 (2000); City property taxes per capita: $534 (2000).
Education: High school graduation rate: 63.9% (2000); College graduation rate: 6.1% (2000).

School District(s)

Blanche Kelso Bruce Academy (05-12)
2000 Enrollment: 0 313-852-7506
George Washington Carver Academy (KG-06)
2000 Enrollment: 572 517-774-2100
Highland Park City Schools (KG-12)
2000 Enrollment: 3,887 313-252-0440

Housing: Homeownership rate: 38.6% (2000); Median home value: $49,800 (2000); Median rent: $320 per month (2000); Median age of housing: 56 years (2000).
Newspapers: Michigan Citizen (1 x week)
Transportation: Commute to work: 73.2% car, 19.5% public transportation, 4.0% walk, 1.8% work from home (2000); Travel time to work: 17.9% less than 15 minutes, 36.0% 15 to 30 minutes, 22.2% 30 to 45 minutes, 11.2% 45 to 60 minutes, 12.8% 60 minutes or more (2000)

Additional Information Contacts

Highland Park Chamber of Commerce 313-868-6420

HURON CHARTER (township). Covers a land area of 35.573 square miles and a water area of 0.464 square miles. Located at 42.13° N. Lat.; 83.36° W. Long.
Population: 13,737 (2000); Race: 95.8% White, 1.1% Black, 0.2% Asian, 1.0% American Indian and Alaska Native, 2.4% Hispanic of any race, 1.5% two or more races (2000); Density: 386.2 persons per square mile (2000); Age: 28.4% under 18, 7.7% over 64 (2000); Marriage status: 23.7% never married, 60.2% now married, 4.4% widowed, 11.7% divorced (2000); Foreign born: 1.6% (2000); Ancestry (includes multiple ancestries): 25.0% German, 14.2% Polish, 13.9% Irish, 10.8% Other groups, 9.6% English (2000).
Economy: Single-family building permits issued: 92 (2001) / 86 (2000); Multi-family building permits issued: 41 (2001) / 13 (2000); Employment by occupation: 10.4% management, 15.1% professional, 10.4% services, 23.1% sales, 0.0% farming, 18.3% construction, 22.7% production (2000).
Income: Per capita income: $23,497 (2000); Median household income: $59,890 (2000); Poverty rate: 5.7% (2000).
Taxes: Total city taxes per capita: $158 (1997); City property taxes per capita: $134 (1997).
Education: High school graduation rate: 81.4% (2000); College graduation rate: 11.8% (2000).
Housing: Homeownership rate: 93.5% (2000); Median home value: $168,500 (2000); Median rent: $436 per month (2000); Median age of housing: 24 years (2000).
Transportation: Commute to work: 96.2% car, 0.1% public transportation, 1.1% walk, 2.1% work from home (2000); Travel time to work: 14.5% less than 15 minutes, 44.9% 15 to 30 minutes, 27.6% 30 to 45 minutes, 8.2% 45 to 60 minutes, 4.9% 60 minutes or more (2000)

INKSTER (city). Covers a land area of 6.263 square miles and a water area of 0 square miles. Located at 42.29° N. Lat.; 83.31° W. Long. Elevation is 628 feet.
History: A post office was established here in 1857, when it was known as Moulin Rouge. In the early 1860's, Robert Inkster operated a steam sawmill in the area, and the name was changed to Inkster. Inkster grew in the 1900's as a residential community for workers in the factories of neighboring Dearborn and Detroit. The economic depression of the early 1930's had a disastrous effect here.
Population: 30,115 (2000); Race: 25.2% White, 66.3% Black, 3.8% Asian, 0.5% American Indian and Alaska Native, 1.8% Hispanic of any race, 3.1% two or more races (2000); Density: 4,808.1 persons per square mile (2000); Age: 29.9% under 18, 10.6% over 64 (2000); Marriage status: 36.6% never married, 42.1% now married, 7.6% widowed, 13.6% divorced (2000);

Foreign born: 5.4% (2000); Ancestry (includes multiple ancestries): 64.7% Other groups, 4.8% German, 4.1% Irish, 3.8% Polish, 2.5% English (2000).
Vital Statistics: Birth rate: 162.7 per 10,000 population (1998)
Economy: Unemployment rate: 7.1% (11/2002); Total civilian labor force: 13,851 (11/2002); Single-family building permits issued: 28 (2001) / 13 (2000); Multi-family building permits issued: 0 (2001) / 8 (2000); Employment by occupation: 7.8% management, 13.7% professional, 20.0% services, 25.2% sales, 0.1% farming, 8.7% construction, 24.4% production (2000).
Income: Per capita income: $16,711 (2000); Median household income: $35,950 (2000); Poverty rate: 19.5% (2000).
Taxes: Total city taxes per capita: $204 (1997); City property taxes per capita: $193 (1997).
Education: High school graduation rate: 74.3% (2000); College graduation rate: 12.1% (2000).

School District(s)

Academy of Inkster (09-12)
2000 Enrollment: 99 517-774-2100
Cherry Hill School of Performing (KG-12)
2000 Enrollment: 1,259 517-774-2100
Gaudior Academy (KG-08)
2000 Enrollment: 202 734-487-3036
Inkster-Edison Public Schools (KG-12)
2000 Enrollment: 1,781 734-722-5310
King Academy (KG-06)
2000 Enrollment: 226 313-722-5310
Thomas-Gist Academy (KG-08)
2000 Enrollment: 393 517-774-2100

Housing: Homeownership rate: 57.9% (2000); Median home value: $68,000 (2000); Median rent: $449 per month (2000); Median age of housing: 41 years (2000).
Safety: Violent crime rate: 134.1 per 10,000 population; Property crime rate: 419.5 per 10,000 population (2001).
Transportation: Commute to work: 93.6% car, 2.2% public transportation, 2.2% walk, 0.8% work from home (2000); Travel time to work: 23.3% less than 15 minutes, 43.9% 15 to 30 minutes, 21.0% 30 to 45 minutes, 7.0% 45 to 60 minutes, 4.8% 60 minutes or more (2000)

LINCOLN PARK (city). Covers a land area of 5.854 square miles and a water area of 0 square miles. Located at 42.24° N. Lat.; 83.18° W. Long. Elevation is 587 feet.
History: Lincoln Park developed as a residential suburb for workers in the Ford Motor Company's Dearborn plant or in the other industries in the south section of Detroit. The town was laid out in 1906, incorporated as a village in 1921 and as a city in 1925.
Population: 40,008 (2000); Race: 93.8% White, 2.0% Black, 0.4% Asian, 0.5% American Indian and Alaska Native, 6.3% Hispanic of any race, 2.1% two or more races (2000); Density: 6,834.9 persons per square mile (2000); Age: 24.2% under 18, 14.2% over 64 (2000); Marriage status: 26.6% never married, 51.5% now married, 7.6% widowed, 14.3% divorced (2000); Foreign born: 4.0% (2000); Ancestry (includes multiple ancestries): 19.5% German, 14.8% Irish, 14.2% Other groups, 14.1% Polish, 8.1% English (2000).
Vital Statistics: Birth rate: 146.0 per 10,000 population (1998)
Economy: Unemployment rate: 3.9% (11/2002); Total civilian labor force: 20,958 (11/2002); Single-family building permits issued: 8 (2001) / 5 (2000); Multi-family building permits issued: 0 (2001) / 0 (2000); Employment by occupation: 6.7% management, 10.8% professional, 15.6% services, 28.9% sales, 0.1% farming, 13.1% construction, 25.0% production (2000).
Income: Per capita income: $20,140 (2000); Median household income: $42,515 (2000); Poverty rate: 7.7% (2000).
Taxes: Total city taxes per capita: $383 (2000); City property taxes per capita: $363 (2000).
Education: High school graduation rate: 74.7% (2000); College graduation rate: 6.9% (2000).

School District(s)

Lincoln Park Public Schools (KG-12)
2000 Enrollment: 5,490 313-389-0200

Housing: Homeownership rate: 79.1% (2000); Median home value: $84,100 (2000); Median rent: $452 per month (2000); Median age of housing: 47 years (2000).
Hospitals: Vencor Hospital - Detroit (72 beds)
Safety: Violent crime rate: 34.1 per 10,000 population; Property crime rate: 440.8 per 10,000 population (2001).
Transportation: Commute to work: 96.0% car, 0.8% public transportation, 1.5% walk, 1.2% work from home (2000); Travel time to work: 28.6% less than 15 minutes, 44.5% 15 to 30 minutes, 17.8% 30 to 45 minutes, 5.0% 45 to 60 minutes, 4.0% 60 minutes or more (2000)

LIVONIA (city). Covers a land area of 35.718 square miles and a water area of 0.119 square miles. Located at 42.39° N. Lat.; 83.36° W. Long. Elevation is 638 feet.
History: Livonia was named for Livonia, New York, the former home of several of the early residents. The area was first settled in 1832, and was incorporated as the city of Livonia in 1950.
Population: 100,545 (2000); Race: 95.4% White, 0.8% Black, 2.1% Asian, 0.2% American Indian and Alaska Native, 1.8% Hispanic of any race, 1.1% two or more races (2000); Density: 2,815.0 persons per square mile (2000); Age: 23.9% under 18, 16.9% over 64 (2000); Marriage status: 23.0% never married, 61.7% now married, 7.6% widowed, 7.7% divorced (2000); Foreign born: 6.7% (2000); Ancestry (includes multiple ancestries): 22.7% German, 18.0% Polish, 16.3% Irish, 11.9% English, 9.2% Italian (2000).
Vital Statistics: Birth rate: 110.8 per 10,000 population (1998)
Economy: Unemployment rate: 2.2% (11/2002); Total civilian labor force: 56,285 (11/2002); Single-family building permits issued: 166 (2001) / 117 (2000); Multi-family building permits issued: 0 (2001) / 0 (2000); Employment by occupation: 15.5% management, 25.6% professional, 11.1% services, 27.6% sales, 0.0% farming, 8.2% construction, 12.0% production (2000).
Income: Per capita income: $27,923 (2000); Median household income: $63,018 (2000); Poverty rate: 3.2% (2000).
Taxes: Total city taxes per capita: $415 (2000); City property taxes per capita: $390 (2000).
Education: High school graduation rate: 88.8% (2000); College graduation rate: 29.7% (2000).

School District(s)

Clarenceville School District (KG-12)
2000 Enrollment: 1,926 248-473-8900
Livonia Public Schools (KG-12)
2000 Enrollment: 18,347 734-523-8800

Four-year College(s)

Madonna University (Private, Not-for-profit, Roman Catholic)
2001 Enrollment: 3,821 734-432-5300
2001 Tuition: In-state $7,560; Out-of-state $7,560

Two-year College(s)

Schoolcraft College (Public)
2001 Enrollment: 9,530 734-462-4400
2001 Tuition: In-state $1,968; Out-of-state $2,928

Housing: Homeownership rate: 88.8% (2000); Median home value: $161,800 (2000); Median rent: $672 per month (2000); Median age of housing: 37 years (2000).
Hospitals: Saint Mary Mercy Hospital (304 beds)
Safety: Violent crime rate: 20.3 per 10,000 population; Property crime rate: 287.7 per 10,000 population (2001).
Newspapers: Westland Observer (2 x week); Redford Observer (2 x week); Plymouth Observer (2 x week); Garden City Observer (2 x week); Canton Observer (2 x week); Livonia Observer (2 x week)
Transportation: Commute to work: 96.1% car, 0.4% public transportation, 1.1% walk, 2.1% work from home (2000); Travel time to work: 28.4% less than 15 minutes, 39.7% 15 to 30 minutes, 23.2% 30 to 45 minutes, 5.6% 45 to 60 minutes, 3.1% 60 minutes or more (2000)
Additional Information Contacts
Livonia Chamber of Commerce 734-427-2122

MELVINDALE (city). Covers a land area of 2.769 square miles and a water area of 0 square miles. Located at 42.28° N. Lat.; 83.18° W. Long. Elevation is 591 feet.
History: Melvindale grew up as a residential suburb for workers in the Dearborn and Detroit factories.
Population: 10,735 (2000); Race: 86.5% White, 5.2% Black, 0.8% Asian, 0.8% American Indian and Alaska Native, 8.9% Hispanic of any race, 4.2% two or more races (2000); Density: 3,876.9 persons per square mile (2000); Age: 24.5% under 18, 13.5% over 64 (2000); Marriage status: 28.3% never married, 46.8% now married, 8.6% widowed, 16.2% divorced (2000); Foreign born: 6.2% (2000); Ancestry (includes multiple ancestries): 21.7% Other groups, 15.9% German, 12.0% Irish, 10.3% Polish, 6.6% English (2000).
Vital Statistics: Birth rate: 138.8 per 10,000 population (1998)
Economy: Single-family building permits issued: 6 (2001) / 5 (2000); Multi-family building permits issued: 0 (2001) / 0 (2000); Employment by occupation: 7.8% management, 11.3% professional, 15.7% services, 25.1% sales, 0.0% farming, 13.1% construction, 27.0% production (2000).

Income: Per capita income: $19,011 (2000); Median household income: $37,954 (2000); Poverty rate: 11.4% (2000).
Taxes: Total city taxes per capita: $357 (1997); City property taxes per capita: $339 (1997).
Education: High school graduation rate: 71.9% (2000); College graduation rate: 5.8% (2000).

School District(s)

Melvindale-North Allen Park School (KG-12)
2000 Enrollment: 2,323 313-389-3300

Housing: Homeownership rate: 67.6% (2000); Median home value: $78,500 (2000); Median rent: $451 per month (2000); Median age of housing: 47 years (2000).
Safety: Violent crime rate: 31.5 per 10,000 population; Property crime rate: 466.1 per 10,000 population (2001).
Transportation: Commute to work: 94.0% car, 1.1% public transportation, 3.0% walk, 1.1% work from home (2000); Travel time to work: 33.6% less than 15 minutes, 43.9% 15 to 30 minutes, 14.2% 30 to 45 minutes, 4.2% 45 to 60 minutes, 4.1% 60 minutes or more (2000)

NEW BOSTON (unincorporated postal area, zip code 48164). Covers a land area of 27.436 square miles and a water area of 0 square miles. Located at 42.12° N. Lat.; 83.38° W. Long. Elevation is 635 feet.
Population: 7,792 (2000); Race: 94.2% White, 3.6% Black, 0.2% Asian, 1.2% American Indian and Alaska Native, 1.3% Hispanic of any race, 0.8% two or more races (2000); Density: 284.0 persons per square mile (2000); Age: 27.4% under 18, 9.1% over 64 (2000); Marriage status: 20.9% never married, 65.2% now married, 5.4% widowed, 8.6% divorced (2000); Foreign born: 2.4% (2000); Ancestry (includes multiple ancestries): 20.7% German, 15.0% Polish, 12.2% Irish, 10.2% Other groups, 8.9% English (2000).
Economy: Manufacturing: concrete, steel, plastic products. Detroit Metropolitan Wayne County Airport to Northeast. Lower Huron Metropark along river. Employment by occupation: 10.7% management, 18.6% professional, 10.2% services, 21.6% sales, 0.0% farming, 17.7% construction, 21.2% production (2000).
Income: Per capita income: $25,435 (2000); Median household income: $65,308 (2000); Poverty rate: 5.7% (2000).
Education: High school graduation rate: 83.0% (2000); College graduation rate: 15.3% (2000).

School District(s)

Huron School District (KG-12)
2000 Enrollment: 1,993 734-782-2441
Summit Academy North (KG-12)
2000 Enrollment: 850 248-370-3050

Housing: Homeownership rate: 90.8% (2000); Median home value: $166,600 (2000); Median rent: $458 per month (2000); Median age of housing: 33 years (2000).
Transportation: Commute to work: 95.3% car, 0.0% public transportation, 1.4% walk, 3.0% work from home (2000); Travel time to work: 15.4% less than 15 minutes, 44.5% 15 to 30 minutes, 28.5% 30 to 45 minutes, 8.5% 45 to 60 minutes, 3.2% 60 minutes or more (2000)
Additional Information Contacts
New Boston Chamber of Commerce 734-753-4220

NORTHVILLE (township). Covers a land area of 16.454 square miles and a water area of 0.157 square miles. Located at 42.41° N. Lat.; 83.46° W. Long. Elevation is 829 feet.
Population: 21,036 (2000); Race: 88.8% White, 4.2% Black, 4.4% Asian, 0.3% American Indian and Alaska Native, 1.9% Hispanic of any race, 1.4% two or more races (2000); Density: 1,278.5 persons per square mile (2000); Age: 21.2% under 18, 13.9% over 64 (2000); Marriage status: 24.2% never married, 61.4% now married, 6.3% widowed, 8.1% divorced (2000); Foreign born: 9.6% (2000); Ancestry (includes multiple ancestries): 22.3% German, 16.3% Irish, 14.4% Polish, 13.8% English, 11.5% Other groups (2000).
Vital Statistics: Birth rate: 41.4 per 10,000 population (1998)
Economy: Single-family building permits issued: 290 (2001) / 333 (2000); Multi-family building permits issued: 100 (2001) / 81 (2000); Employment by occupation: 25.0% management, 32.2% professional, 8.1% services, 24.3% sales, 0.0% farming, 3.1% construction, 7.3% production (2000).
Income: Per capita income: $40,258 (2000); Median household income: $81,541 (2000); Poverty rate: 2.5% (2000).
Taxes: Total city taxes per capita: $280 (2000); City property taxes per capita: $234 (2000).
Education: High school graduation rate: 91.7% (2000); College graduation rate: 48.1% (2000).

School District(s)

Northville Public Schools (KG-12)
2000 Enrollment: 5,542 248-349-3400

Housing: Homeownership rate: 73.6% (2000); Median home value: $282,500 (2000); Median rent: $764 per month (2000); Median age of housing: 19 years (2000).
Safety: Violent crime rate: 3.3 per 10,000 population; Property crime rate: 106.9 per 10,000 population (2001).
Newspapers: The Novi News (1 x week); Northville Record (1 x week)
Transportation: Commute to work: 95.6% car, 0.2% public transportation, 0.7% walk, 3.2% work from home (2000); Travel time to work: 22.5% less than 15 minutes, 31.3% 15 to 30 minutes, 33.4% 30 to 45 minutes, 9.0% 45 to 60 minutes, 3.7% 60 minutes or more (2000)

PLYMOUTH (city). Covers a land area of 2.228 square miles and a water area of 0.008 square miles. Located at 42.37° N. Lat.; 83.46° W. Long. Elevation is 741 feet.
History: Plymouth was settled in 1825 by descendants of the Pilgrims, who named it for the landing place in Massachusetts. It developed as an industrial town around two air rifle factories.
Population: 9,022 (2000); Race: 96.0% White, 0.7% Black, 1.1% Asian, 0.1% American Indian and Alaska Native, 1.3% Hispanic of any race, 1.6% two or more races (2000); Density: 4,048.6 persons per square mile (2000); Age: 19.0% under 18, 16.4% over 64 (2000); Marriage status: 25.3% never married, 52.8% now married, 8.1% widowed, 13.8% divorced (2000); Foreign born: 3.7% (2000); Ancestry (includes multiple ancestries): 25.4% German, 18.5% Irish, 16.2% English, 11.8% Polish, 8.3% Italian (2000).
Economy: Diversified manufacturing. Single-family building permits issued: 111 (2001) / 3 (2000); Multi-family building permits issued: 0 (2001) / 0 (2000); Employment by occupation: 16.7% management, 30.0% professional, 12.7% services, 24.1% sales, 0.3% farming, 7.6% construction, 8.7% production (2000).
Income: Per capita income: $33,222 (2000); Median household income: $51,535 (2000); Poverty rate: 3.3% (2000).
Taxes: Total city taxes per capita: $425 (1997); City property taxes per capita: $405 (1997).
Education: High school graduation rate: 89.9% (2000); College graduation rate: 40.7% (2000).

School District(s)

Plymouth-Canton Community School (KG-12)
2000 Enrollment: 16,518 734-416-3045

Four-year College(s)

Michigan Theological Seminary (Private, Not-for-profit)
2001 Enrollment: 152 734-207-9581

Housing: Homeownership rate: 65.7% (2000); Median home value: $178,700 (2000); Median rent: $533 per month (2000); Median age of housing: 44 years (2000).
Safety: Violent crime rate: 2.2 per 10,000 population; Property crime rate: 115.8 per 10,000 population (2001).
Newspapers: The Community Crier (1 x week)
Transportation: Commute to work: 94.9% car, 0.0% public transportation, 2.2% walk, 2.2% work from home (2000); Travel time to work: 29.2% less than 15 minutes, 31.8% 15 to 30 minutes, 28.6% 30 to 45 minutes, 6.5% 45 to 60 minutes, 3.8% 60 minutes or more (2000)
Additional Information Contacts
Plymouth Chamber of Commerce 734-453-1540

PLYMOUTH TOWNSHIP (CDP). Covers a land area of 15.918 square miles and a water area of 0.040 square miles. Located at 42.37° N. Lat.; 83.48° W. Long. Elevation is 741 feet.
Population: 27,798 (2000); Race: 91.6% White, 3.2% Black, 2.7% Asian, 0.2% American Indian and Alaska Native, 1.3% Hispanic of any race, 1.7% two or more races (2000); Density: 1,746.3 persons per square mile (2000); Age: 22.6% under 18, 12.1% over 64 (2000); Marriage status: 22.0% never married, 64.5% now married, 5.2% widowed, 8.3% divorced (2000); Foreign born: 6.0% (2000); Ancestry (includes multiple ancestries): 24.6% German, 19.1% Irish, 15.5% Polish, 13.2% English, 8.1% Other groups (2000).
Vital Statistics: Birth rate: 70.5 per 10,000 population (1998)
Economy: Unemployment rate: 1.9% (11/2002); Total civilian labor force: 14,059 (11/2002); Employment by occupation: 20.7% management, 27.3% professional, 8.8% services, 26.0% sales, 0.1% farming, 6.2% construction, 10.9% production (2000).
Income: Per capita income: $37,081 (2000); Median household income: $74,738 (2000); Poverty rate: 1.8% (2000).
Education: High school graduation rate: 92.6% (2000); College graduation rate: 42.0% (2000).

Housing: Homeownership rate: 83.5% (2000); Median home value: $218,500 (2000); Median rent: $603 per month (2000); Median age of housing: 25 years (2000).
Safety: Violent crime rate: 8.9 per 10,000 population; Property crime rate: 171.8 per 10,000 population (2001).
Transportation: Commute to work: 95.8% car, 0.1% public transportation, 0.7% walk, 3.1% work from home (2000); Travel time to work: 25.9% less than 15 minutes, 35.4% 15 to 30 minutes, 28.7% 30 to 45 minutes, 6.1% 45 to 60 minutes, 3.9% 60 minutes or more (2000)

REDFORD (CDP). Covers a land area of 11.229 square miles and a water area of 0 square miles. Located at 42.39° N. Lat.; 83.29° W. Long. Elevation is 621 feet.
History: The name of Redford came from a crossing place on the River Rouge, first known as Rouge Ford. A portion of Redford Township, including the village of Redford, was annexed by the city of Detroit in 1926.
Population: 51,622 (2000); Race: 88.3% White, 8.5% Black, 0.6% Asian, 0.5% American Indian and Alaska Native, 2.1% Hispanic of any race, 1.6% two or more races (2000); Density: 4,597.4 persons per square mile (2000); Age: 25.4% under 18, 15.2% over 64 (2000); Marriage status: 26.0% never married, 53.9% now married, 9.0% widowed, 11.0% divorced (2000); Foreign born: 4.0% (2000); Ancestry (includes multiple ancestries): 21.4% German, 16.4% Irish, 15.1% Polish, 13.0% Other groups, 10.7% English (2000).
Vital Statistics: Birth rate: 132.1 per 10,000 population (1998)
Economy: Unemployment rate: 2.6% (11/2002); Total civilian labor force: 28,422 (11/2002); Single-family building permits issued: 13 (2001) / 13 (2000); Multi-family building permits issued: 0 (2001) / 0 (2000); Employment by occupation: 11.2% management, 17.1% professional, 13.1% services, 29.0% sales, 0.0% farming, 10.6% construction, 19.0% production (2000).
Income: Per capita income: $22,263 (2000); Median household income: $49,522 (2000); Poverty rate: 5.1% (2000).
Education: High school graduation rate: 86.1% (2000); College graduation rate: 16.1% (2000).

School District(s)

Redford Union School District (KG-12)
2000 Enrollment: 4,773 313-592-3304
South Redford School District (KG-12)
2000 Enrollment: 3,488 313-535-4000
Housing: Homeownership rate: 90.1% (2000); Median home value: $104,800 (2000); Median rent: $563 per month (2000); Median age of housing: 46 years (2000).
Safety: Violent crime rate: 36.4 per 10,000 population; Property crime rate: 350.1 per 10,000 population (2001).
Transportation: Commute to work: 96.8% car, 0.6% public transportation, 1.1% walk, 1.2% work from home (2000); Travel time to work: 21.9% less than 15 minutes, 46.2% 15 to 30 minutes, 23.2% 30 to 45 minutes, 4.8% 45 to 60 minutes, 4.0% 60 minutes or more (2000)
Additional Information Contacts
Redford Chamber of Commerce 313-535-0960

RIVER ROUGE (city). Covers a land area of 2.670 square miles and a water area of 0.737 square miles. Located at 42.27° N. Lat.; 83.13° W. Long. Elevation is 584 feet.
History: The River Rouge area was settled by French immigrant farmers in the late 1700's. River Rouge became a village in 1899, and was incorporated as a city in 1921. It developed as an industrial area, particularly influenced by the Ford Motor Company and by the Great Lakes Engineering Works (formerly S.F. Hodge & Company), builders of machinery and marine engines.
Population: 9,917 (2000); Race: 52.2% White, 41.8% Black, 0.1% Asian, 0.8% American Indian and Alaska Native, 5.2% Hispanic of any race, 3.6% two or more races (2000); Density: 3,713.9 persons per square mile (2000); Age: 31.2% under 18, 10.7% over 64 (2000); Marriage status: 40.9% never married, 38.2% now married, 8.7% widowed, 12.2% divorced (2000); Foreign born: 1.9% (2000); Ancestry (includes multiple ancestries): 46.9% Other groups, 6.4% Irish, 6.1% French (except Basque), 6.1% German, 5.8% Polish (2000).
Vital Statistics: Birth rate: 175.5 per 10,000 population (1998)
Economy: Single-family building permits issued: 1 (2001) / 1 (2000); Multi-family building permits issued: 0 (2001) / 0 (2000); Employment by occupation: 3.4% management, 9.6% professional, 25.7% services, 26.2% sales, 0.0% farming, 9.4% construction, 25.7% production (2000).
Income: Per capita income: $13,728 (2000); Median household income: $29,214 (2000); Poverty rate: 22.0% (2000).
Taxes: Total city taxes per capita: $721 (1997); City property taxes per capita: $701 (1997).
Education: High school graduation rate: 69.5% (2000); College graduation rate: 5.6% (2000).

School District(s)

River Rouge School District (KG-12)
2000 Enrollment: 2,855 313-297-9600
Housing: Homeownership rate: 58.0% (2000); Median home value: $45,500 (2000); Median rent: $358 per month (2000); Median age of housing: 55 years (2000).
Transportation: Commute to work: 89.4% car, 4.4% public transportation, 4.5% walk, 1.7% work from home (2000); Travel time to work: 27.9% less than 15 minutes, 40.9% 15 to 30 minutes, 19.9% 30 to 45 minutes, 6.9% 45 to 60 minutes, 4.3% 60 minutes or more (2000)

RIVERVIEW (city). Covers a land area of 4.406 square miles and a water area of 0.121 square miles. Located at 42.17° N. Lat.; 83.18° W. Long. Elevation is 594 feet.
History: Riverview came into existence in 1906 when the Detroit, Monroe & Toledo Railroad built a station here. The river that was in view was the Detroit River.
Population: 13,272 (2000); Race: 93.3% White, 2.4% Black, 1.3% Asian, 0.7% American Indian and Alaska Native, 2.7% Hispanic of any race, 1.4% two or more races (2000); Density: 3,012.6 persons per square mile (2000); Age: 21.5% under 18, 20.2% over 64 (2000); Marriage status: 23.6% never married, 56.1% now married, 10.9% widowed, 9.4% divorced (2000); Foreign born: 5.3% (2000); Ancestry (includes multiple ancestries): 20.8% German, 15.0% Irish, 13.3% Polish, 10.6% English, 9.4% Italian (2000).
Vital Statistics: Birth rate: 81.4 per 10,000 population (1998)
Economy: Single-family building permits issued: 9 (2001) / 10 (2000); Multi-family building permits issued: 0 (2001) / 0 (2000); Employment by occupation: 11.0% management, 18.1% professional, 15.3% services, 27.6% sales, 0.0% farming, 10.7% construction, 17.2% production (2000).
Income: Per capita income: $25,460 (2000); Median household income: $47,623 (2000); Poverty rate: 4.7% (2000).
Taxes: Total city taxes per capita: $286 (1997); City property taxes per capita: $280 (1997).
Education: High school graduation rate: 80.9% (2000); College graduation rate: 17.6% (2000).

School District(s)

Riverview Community School District (KG-12)
2000 Enrollment: 2,279 734-285-9660
Housing: Homeownership rate: 64.5% (2000); Median home value: $144,300 (2000); Median rent: $537 per month (2000); Median age of housing: 32 years (2000).
Safety: Violent crime rate: 9.0 per 10,000 population; Property crime rate: 224.9 per 10,000 population (2001).
Transportation: Commute to work: 97.2% car, 0.6% public transportation, 0.4% walk, 1.5% work from home (2000); Travel time to work: 33.2% less than 15 minutes, 35.4% 15 to 30 minutes, 21.3% 30 to 45 minutes, 6.1% 45 to 60 minutes, 4.0% 60 minutes or more (2000)

ROCKWOOD (city). Covers a land area of 2.704 square miles and a water area of 0 square miles. Located at 42.07° N. Lat.; 83.24° W. Long. Elevation is 576 feet.
History: Incorporated 1926.
Population: 3,442 (2000); Race: 92.7% White, 2.4% Black, 2.3% Asian, 0.0% American Indian and Alaska Native, 0.8% Hispanic of any race, 1.7% two or more races (2000); Density: 1,272.9 persons per square mile (2000); Age: 24.9% under 18, 9.1% over 64 (2000); Marriage status: 25.0% never married, 57.7% now married, 5.1% widowed, 12.2% divorced (2000); Foreign born: 3.2% (2000); Ancestry (includes multiple ancestries): 20.0% German, 11.9% Irish, 10.7% English, 9.3% French (except Basque), 7.9% Other groups (2000).
Economy: In farm area. Light manufacturing. Single-family building permits issued: 12 (2001) / 19 (2000); Multi-family building permits issued: 0 (2001) / 0 (2000); Employment by occupation: 8.6% management, 15.8% professional, 12.2% services, 21.4% sales, 0.8% farming, 17.4% construction, 23.8% production (2000).
Income: Per capita income: $23,563 (2000); Median household income: $55,987 (2000); Poverty rate: 4.0% (2000).
Taxes: Total city taxes per capita: $327 (1997); City property taxes per capita: $306 (1997).
Education: High school graduation rate: 82.1% (2000); College graduation rate: 10.5% (2000).

Housing: Homeownership rate: 73.2% (2000); Median home value: $114,500 (2000); Median rent: $499 per month (2000); Median age of housing: 33 years (2000).
Safety: Violent crime rate: 11.6 per 10,000 population; Property crime rate: 271.7 per 10,000 population (2001).
Transportation: Commute to work: 97.5% car, 0.0% public transportation, 1.7% walk, 0.5% work from home (2000); Travel time to work: 25.7% less than 15 minutes, 31.7% 15 to 30 minutes, 27.1% 30 to 45 minutes, 10.0% 45 to 60 minutes, 5.5% 60 minutes or more (2000)

ROMULUS (city). Covers a land area of 35.910 square miles and a water area of 0.012 square miles. Located at 42.23° N. Lat.; 83.37° W. Long. Elevation is 658 feet.
History: Romulus was named for Romulus, New York, the former home of Samuel McMath whose family settled here in the 1820's.
Population: 22,979 (2000); Race: 65.5% White, 29.8% Black, 0.8% Asian, 0.4% American Indian and Alaska Native, 2.0% Hispanic of any race, 2.6% two or more races (2000); Density: 639.9 persons per square mile (2000); Age: 29.1% under 18, 7.7% over 64 (2000); Marriage status: 27.7% never married, 52.7% now married, 6.1% widowed, 13.5% divorced (2000); Foreign born: 1.9% (2000); Ancestry (includes multiple ancestries): 33.4% Other groups, 16.3% German, 9.0% Polish, 8.9% Irish, 5.4% United States or American (2000).
Vital Statistics: Birth rate: 174.1 per 10,000 population (1998)
Economy: Unemployment rate: 4.8% (11/2002); Total civilian labor force: 11,502 (11/2002); Single-family building permits issued: 166 (2001) / 170 (2000); Multi-family building permits issued: 20 (2001) / 112 (2000); Employment by occupation: 7.9% management, 9.8% professional, 17.2% services, 25.2% sales, 0.3% farming, 12.4% construction, 27.2% production (2000).
Income: Per capita income: $19,679 (2000); Median household income: $45,088 (2000); Poverty rate: 12.6% (2000).
Taxes: Total city taxes per capita: $485 (1997); City property taxes per capita: $453 (1997).
Education: High school graduation rate: 76.4% (2000); College graduation rate: 8.1% (2000).

School District(s)

Metro Charter Academy (KG-05)
2000 Enrollment: 371 734-941-6082
Romulus Community Schools (PK-12)
2000 Enrollment: 4,084 313-941-1600

Housing: Homeownership rate: 70.5% (2000); Median home value: $97,300 (2000); Median rent: $447 per month (2000); Median age of housing: 32 years (2000).
Safety: Violent crime rate: 47.6 per 10,000 population; Property crime rate: 522.1 per 10,000 population (2001).
Transportation: Commute to work: 95.3% car, 0.4% public transportation, 1.7% walk, 2.0% work from home (2000); Travel time to work: 30.8% less than 15 minutes, 41.4% 15 to 30 minutes, 18.4% 30 to 45 minutes, 5.1% 45 to 60 minutes, 4.3% 60 minutes or more (2000)
Additional Information Contacts
Romulus Chamber of Commerce 734-326-4290

SOUTHGATE (city). Covers a land area of 6.856 square miles and a water area of 0 square miles. Located at 42.20° N. Lat.; 83.19° W. Long. Elevation is 591 feet.
History: Pierre Michel Campau settled here in 1795. The village later became a gateway to the metropolitan Detroit area, and was incorporated in the 1950's.
Population: 30,136 (2000); Race: 92.9% White, 2.0% Black, 1.6% Asian, 0.8% American Indian and Alaska Native, 3.9% Hispanic of any race, 2.1% two or more races (2000); Density: 4,395.8 persons per square mile (2000); Age: 21.5% under 18, 16.3% over 64 (2000); Marriage status: 23.9% never married, 55.6% now married, 9.0% widowed, 11.6% divorced (2000); Foreign born: 5.7% (2000); Ancestry (includes multiple ancestries): 18.5% German, 15.2% Polish, 15.0% Irish, 11.6% Other groups, 8.8% English (2000).
Vital Statistics: Birth rate: 109.2 per 10,000 population (1998)
Economy: Unemployment rate: 3.0% (11/2002); Total civilian labor force: 16,676 (11/2002); Single-family building permits issued: 54 (2001) / 83 (2000); Multi-family building permits issued: 0 (2001) / 40 (2000); Employment by occupation: 10.1% management, 17.2% professional, 14.0% services, 28.2% sales, 0.0% farming, 11.9% construction, 18.6% production (2000).
Income: Per capita income: $23,219 (2000); Median household income: $46,927 (2000); Poverty rate: 4.6% (2000).
Taxes: Total city taxes per capita: $369 (1997); City property taxes per capita: $350 (1997).
Education: High school graduation rate: 80.5% (2000); College graduation rate: 12.7% (2000).

School District(s)

Creative Montessori Academy (KG-08)
2000 Enrollment: 0 734-284-5600
Michigan Health Academy (09-12)
2000 Enrollment: 46 517-790-4000
Southgate Community School District (KG-12)
2000 Enrollment: 4,611 734-246-4600

Housing: Homeownership rate: 70.8% (2000); Median home value: $109,200 (2000); Median rent: $553 per month (2000); Median age of housing: 40 years (2000).
Safety: Violent crime rate: 33.3 per 10,000 population; Property crime rate: 425.8 per 10,000 population (2001).
Newspapers: The News-Herald Wednesday (2 x week); Heritage Sunday (2 x week); Heritage Sunday - Dearborn & Dearborn Heights Edition (1 x week)
Transportation: Commute to work: 96.2% car, 1.0% public transportation, 1.2% walk, 1.0% work from home (2000); Travel time to work: 30.6% less than 15 minutes, 40.2% 15 to 30 minutes, 17.1% 30 to 45 minutes, 7.9% 45 to 60 minutes, 4.2% 60 minutes or more (2000)

SUMPTER (township). Covers a land area of 37.566 square miles and a water area of 0.006 square miles. Located at 42.13° N. Lat.; 83.49° W. Long.
Population: 11,856 (2000); Race: 83.8% White, 12.7% Black, 0.3% Asian, 0.1% American Indian and Alaska Native, 1.3% Hispanic of any race, 2.6% two or more races (2000); Density: 315.6 persons per square mile (2000); Age: 29.3% under 18, 7.4% over 64 (2000); Marriage status: 23.1% never married, 60.2% now married, 4.5% widowed, 12.3% divorced (2000); Foreign born: 0.8% (2000); Ancestry (includes multiple ancestries): 19.6% German, 17.8% Other groups, 15.3% Irish, 9.0% Polish, 8.5% English (2000).
Economy: Single-family building permits issued: 58 (2001) / 59 (2000); Multi-family building permits issued: 0 (2001) / 0 (2000); Employment by occupation: 9.5% management, 11.1% professional, 15.0% services, 20.5% sales, 0.2% farming, 16.7% construction, 27.1% production (2000).
Income: Per capita income: $19,323 (2000); Median household income: $48,680 (2000); Poverty rate: 10.0% (2000).
Taxes: Total city taxes per capita: $96 (2000); City property taxes per capita: $79 (2000).
Education: High school graduation rate: 79.3% (2000); College graduation rate: 9.3% (2000).
Housing: Homeownership rate: 92.6% (2000); Median home value: $139,400 (2000); Median rent: $435 per month (2000); Median age of housing: 25 years (2000).
Safety: Violent crime rate: 18.5 per 10,000 population; Property crime rate: 262.6 per 10,000 population (2001).
Transportation: Commute to work: 97.0% car, 0.0% public transportation, 0.4% walk, 2.4% work from home (2000); Travel time to work: 11.7% less than 15 minutes, 37.7% 15 to 30 minutes, 32.2% 30 to 45 minutes, 12.5% 45 to 60 minutes, 5.9% 60 minutes or more (2000)

TAYLOR (city). Covers a land area of 23.610 square miles and a water area of 0 square miles. Located at 42.23° N. Lat.; 83.26° W. Long. Elevation is 615 feet.
History: A small rural village until World War II, it grew from a population of c.5,000 to its present size. Its growth has been commercial as well as residential. Founded 1847 as a township, incorporated as a city 1968.
Population: 65,868 (2000); Race: 85.8% White, 8.9% Black, 1.4% Asian, 0.6% American Indian and Alaska Native, 3.3% Hispanic of any race, 2.4% two or more races (2000); Density: 2,789.8 persons per square mile (2000); Age: 27.2% under 18, 11.0% over 64 (2000); Marriage status: 27.4% never married, 53.3% now married, 6.8% widowed, 12.4% divorced (2000); Foreign born: 4.0% (2000); Ancestry (includes multiple ancestries): 19.1% Other groups, 18.4% German, 13.6% Irish, 10.8% Polish, 8.2% English (2000).
Vital Statistics: Birth rate: 149.2 per 10,000 population (1998)
Economy: Manufacturing includes adhesives, building materials, furniture, sheet metal, motor vehicle parts, motorcycles, metal stampings. Unemployment rate: 4.4% (11/2002); Total civilian labor force: 35,801 (11/2002); Single-family building permits issued: 60 (2001) / 102 (2000); Multi-family building permits issued: 0 (2001) / 0 (2000); Employment by occupation: 7.3% management, 10.2% professional, 16.6% services, 26.8% sales, 0.1% farming, 13.3% construction, 25.7% production (2000).

Income: Per capita income: $19,638 (2000); Median household income: $42,944 (2000); Poverty rate: 10.8% (2000).
Taxes: Total city taxes per capita: $574 (2000); City property taxes per capita: $556 (2000).
Education: High school graduation rate: 75.2% (2000); College graduation rate: 7.0% (2000).

School District(s)

Taylor School District (PK-12)
2000 Enrollment: 10,877 734-374-1200
Housing: Homeownership rate: 70.8% (2000); Median home value: $93,000 (2000); Median rent: $515 per month (2000); Median age of housing: 38 years (2000).
Hospitals: Oakwood Hospital Heritage Center (271 beds)
Safety: Violent crime rate: 52.0 per 10,000 population; Property crime rate: 490.2 per 10,000 population (2001).
Transportation: Commute to work: 96.7% car, 0.3% public transportation, 0.9% walk, 1.2% work from home (2000); Travel time to work: 29.8% less than 15 minutes, 42.2% 15 to 30 minutes, 17.9% 30 to 45 minutes, 5.5% 45 to 60 minutes, 4.6% 60 minutes or more (2000)
Additional Information Contacts
Down River Association of Realtors 734-287-8060
Taylor Chamber of Commerce 734-284-6000

TRENTON (city). Covers a land area of 7.300 square miles and a water area of 0.200 square miles. Located at 42.14° N. Lat.; 83.19° W. Long. Elevation is 600 feet.
History: The site of Trenton was acquired by Major Caleb Truax, who came from New York in 1816. He built a sawmill, church, and store, and platted a village in 1827 with the name of Truaxton. Truaxton became a shipping and shipbuilding center in the days of wooden vessels. With the opening of the Erie Canal in 1825,industry in Truaxton expanded to include commercial fishing and the production of lime and building stone from quarries nearby. In 1875, Truaxton was incorporated as a village and the name was changed to Trenton.
Population: 19,584 (2000); Race: 96.2% White, 0.4% Black, 0.7% Asian, 0.3% American Indian and Alaska Native, 2.2% Hispanic of any race, 2.1% two or more races (2000); Density: 2,682.8 persons per square mile (2000); Age: 23.4% under 18, 19.7% over 64 (2000); Marriage status: 20.8% never married, 60.7% now married, 8.5% widowed, 9.9% divorced (2000); Foreign born: 4.0% (2000); Ancestry (includes multiple ancestries): 21.9% German, 16.0% Polish, 15.7% Irish, 12.9% English, 9.5% French (except Basque) (2000).
Vital Statistics: Birth rate: 133.8 per 10,000 population (1998)
Economy: Single-family building permits issued: 9 (2001) / 11 (2000); Multi-family building permits issued: 67 (2001) / 44 (2000); Employment by occupation: 10.1% management, 20.2% professional, 13.9% services, 27.8% sales, 0.0% farming, 11.0% construction, 17.0% production (2000).
Income: Per capita income: $25,288 (2000); Median household income: $49,566 (2000); Poverty rate: 5.1% (2000).
Taxes: Total city taxes per capita: $745 (2000); City property taxes per capita: $727 (2000).
Education: High school graduation rate: 86.4% (2000); College graduation rate: 20.0% (2000).

School District(s)

Trenton Public Schools (PK-12)
2000 Enrollment: 3,202 734-676-8600
Housing: Homeownership rate: 80.8% (2000); Median home value: $137,800 (2000); Median rent: $453 per month (2000); Median age of housing: 41 years (2000).
Hospitals: Oakwood Hospital Seaway Center (203 beds); Riverside Osteopathic Hospital (162 beds)
Safety: Violent crime rate: 11.2 per 10,000 population; Property crime rate: 168.1 per 10,000 population (2001).
Transportation: Commute to work: 96.5% car, 0.3% public transportation, 1.3% walk, 1.3% work from home (2000); Travel time to work: 36.8% less than 15 minutes, 30.7% 15 to 30 minutes, 19.6% 30 to 45 minutes, 7.9% 45 to 60 minutes, 5.0% 60 minutes or more (2000)

VAN BUREN (township). Covers a land area of 33.903 square miles and a water area of 1.890 square miles. Located at 42.22° N. Lat.; 83.48° W. Long.
Population: 23,559 (2000); Race: 82.2% White, 11.5% Black, 2.4% Asian, 0.5% American Indian and Alaska Native, 1.8% Hispanic of any race, 3.0% two or more races (2000); Density: 694.9 persons per square mile (2000); Age: 23.8% under 18, 6.6% over 64 (2000); Marriage status: 30.2% never married, 53.1% now married, 4.2% widowed, 12.4% divorced (2000); Foreign born: 4.7% (2000); Ancestry (includes multiple ancestries): 20.1% Other groups, 19.2% German, 12.0% Irish, 10.2% Polish, 10.1% English (2000).
Economy: Unemployment rate: 3.1% (11/2002); Total civilian labor force: 12,101 (11/2002); Single-family building permits issued: 317 (2001) / 195 (2000); Multi-family building permits issued: 180 (2001) / 35 (2000); Employment by occupation: 9.3% management, 18.8% professional, 15.8% services, 23.0% sales, 0.2% farming, 11.4% construction, 21.6% production (2000).
Income: Per capita income: $24,820 (2000); Median household income: $50,984 (2000); Poverty rate: 6.3% (2000).
Taxes: Total city taxes per capita: $271 (2000); City property taxes per capita: $243 (2000).
Education: High school graduation rate: 86.2% (2000); College graduation rate: 20.1% (2000).
Housing: Homeownership rate: 60.7% (2000); Median home value: $143,100 (2000); Median rent: $637 per month (2000); Median age of housing: 23 years (2000).
Safety: Violent crime rate: 8.9 per 10,000 population; Property crime rate: 263.5 per 10,000 population (2001).
Transportation: Commute to work: 96.5% car, 0.1% public transportation, 0.8% walk, 2.0% work from home (2000); Travel time to work: 23.6% less than 15 minutes, 46.3% 15 to 30 minutes, 19.8% 30 to 45 minutes, 6.1% 45 to 60 minutes, 4.2% 60 minutes or more (2000)

WAYNE (city). Covers a land area of 6.019 square miles and a water area of 0 square miles. Located at 42.27° N. Lat.; 83.37° W. Long. Elevation is 658 feet.
History: Wayne was settled in 1836 and named for General "Mad Anthony" Wayne, the Revolutionary War hero. Situated near the highly industrialized west-side corridor of Dearborn and Detroit, Wayne developed several industries of its own, including an aircraft plant.
Population: 19,051 (2000); Race: 85.5% White, 10.6% Black, 1.4% Asian, 0.8% American Indian and Alaska Native, 2.4% Hispanic of any race, 1.2% two or more races (2000); Density: 3,165.2 persons per square mile (2000); Age: 26.6% under 18, 11.7% over 64 (2000); Marriage status: 26.6% never married, 52.3% now married, 7.0% widowed, 14.1% divorced (2000); Foreign born: 3.1% (2000); Ancestry (includes multiple ancestries): 19.5% German, 17.0% Other groups, 13.4% Irish, 10.3% English, 9.3% Polish (2000).
Vital Statistics: Birth rate: 158.0 per 10,000 population (1998)
Economy: Single-family building permits issued: 29 (2001) / 20 (2000); Multi-family building permits issued: 24 (2001) / 64 (2000); Employment by occupation: 7.2% management, 12.5% professional, 15.4% services, 27.2% sales, 0.2% farming, 12.0% construction, 25.6% production (2000).
Income: Per capita income: $21,326 (2000); Median household income: $46,397 (2000); Poverty rate: 9.1% (2000).
Taxes: Total city taxes per capita: $453 (1997); City property taxes per capita: $437 (1997).
Education: High school graduation rate: 78.0% (2000); College graduation rate: 12.1% (2000).

Two-year College(s)

Annapolis Hospital School of X-ray Technology (Private, Not-for-profit)
2001 Enrollment: n/a 734-467-4196
Housing: Homeownership rate: 64.8% (2000); Median home value: $94,900 (2000); Median rent: $444 per month (2000); Median age of housing: 43 years (2000).
Hospitals: Oakwood Annapolic Hospital (296 beds)
Safety: Violent crime rate: 56.4 per 10,000 population; Property crime rate: 446.5 per 10,000 population (2001).
Newspapers: The Westland Eagle (2 x week); The Canton Eagle (2 x week); The Belleville Enterprise (2 x week); The Wayne Eagle (2 x week); The Romulus Roman (2 x week); The Inkster Ledger-Star (2 x week); Eye Witness (1 x week)
Transportation: Commute to work: 95.6% car, 0.4% public transportation, 2.3% walk, 1.0% work from home (2000); Travel time to work: 30.5% less than 15 minutes, 40.8% 15 to 30 minutes, 20.1% 30 to 45 minutes, 4.9% 45 to 60 minutes, 3.7% 60 minutes or more (2000)
Additional Information Contacts
Wayne Chamber of Commerce 734-721-0100

WESTLAND (city). Covers a land area of 20.450 square miles and a water area of 0.005 square miles. Located at 42.31° N. Lat.; 83.37° W. Long. Elevation is 668 feet.
Population: 86,602 (2000); Race: 87.1% White, 6.4% Black, 2.7% Asian, 0.5% American Indian and Alaska Native, 2.5% Hispanic of any race, 2.5%

two or more races (2000); Density: 4,234.9 persons per square mile (2000); Age: 23.2% under 18, 13.2% over 64 (2000); Marriage status: 27.5% never married, 51.7% now married, 8.1% widowed, 12.6% divorced (2000); Foreign born: 6.8% (2000); Ancestry (includes multiple ancestries): 20.2% German, 16.4% Other groups, 14.8% Irish, 13.7% Polish, 9.7% English (2000).
Vital Statistics: Birth rate: 141.6 per 10,000 population (1998)
Economy: Manufacturing of fabricated metal products, transportation equipment, plastic products, electrical equipment. Unemployment rate: 3.1% (11/2002); Total civilian labor force: 48,514 (11/2002); Single-family building permits issued: 81 (2001) / 93 (2000); Multi-family building permits issued: 48 (2001) / 0 (2000); Employment by occupation: 11.0% management, 16.1% professional, 14.5% services, 27.6% sales, 0.1% farming, 10.0% construction, 20.8% production (2000).
Income: Per capita income: $22,615 (2000); Median household income: $46,308 (2000); Poverty rate: 6.8% (2000).
Taxes: Total city taxes per capita: $275 (2000); City property taxes per capita: $263 (2000).
Education: High school graduation rate: 81.1% (2000); College graduation rate: 16.1% (2000).

School District(s)

Academy of Westland (KG-10)
2000 Enrollment: 342 517-774-2100
Wayne-Westland Community School (KG-12)
2000 Enrollment: 14,503 734-595-2000

Housing: Homeownership rate: 62.7% (2000); Median home value: $118,500 (2000); Median rent: $574 per month (2000); Median age of housing: 33 years (2000).
Hospitals: Walter P. Reuther Psychiatric Hospital (220 beds)
Safety: Violent crime rate: 33.1 per 10,000 population; Property crime rate: 324.4 per 10,000 population (2001).
Transportation: Commute to work: 96.4% car, 0.4% public transportation, 1.2% walk, 1.3% work from home (2000); Travel time to work: 23.3% less than 15 minutes, 44.9% 15 to 30 minutes, 20.3% 30 to 45 minutes, 7.0% 45 to 60 minutes, 4.4% 60 minutes or more (2000)
Additional Information Contacts
Westland Chamber of Commerce 734-326-7222

WOODHAVEN (city). Covers a land area of 6.470 square miles and a water area of 0 square miles. Located at 42.13° N. Lat.; 83.23° W. Long. Elevation is 598 feet.
Population: 12,530 (2000); Race: 92.6% White, 2.1% Black, 2.3% Asian, 0.6% American Indian and Alaska Native, 3.5% Hispanic of any race, 1.2% two or more races (2000); Density: 1,936.6 persons per square mile (2000); Age: 24.6% under 18, 7.0% over 64 (2000); Marriage status: 26.0% never married, 59.9% now married, 4.5% widowed, 9.6% divorced (2000); Foreign born: 5.3% (2000); Ancestry (includes multiple ancestries): 19.9% German, 16.6% Polish, 13.1% Irish, 12.1% Other groups, 11.2% Italian (2000).
Vital Statistics: Birth rate: 126.1 per 10,000 population (1998)
Economy: Manufacturing includes wood products, metal fabrication. Single-family building permits issued: 44 (2001) / 41 (2000); Multi-family building permits issued: 38 (2001) / 0 (2000); Employment by occupation: 10.9% management, 19.4% professional, 12.8% services, 25.4% sales, 0.0% farming, 12.7% construction, 18.8% production (2000).
Income: Per capita income: $27,759 (2000); Median household income: $64,954 (2000); Poverty rate: 3.3% (2000).
Taxes: Total city taxes per capita: $544 (1997); City property taxes per capita: $505 (1997).
Education: High school graduation rate: 87.3% (2000); College graduation rate: 20.1% (2000).

School District(s)

Gibraltar School District (PK-12)
2000 Enrollment: 2,929 734-692-4002

Housing: Homeownership rate: 72.6% (2000); Median home value: $154,300 (2000); Median rent: $539 per month (2000); Median age of housing: 24 years (2000).
Safety: Violent crime rate: 15.1 per 10,000 population; Property crime rate: 341.4 per 10,000 population (2001).
Transportation: Commute to work: 97.5% car, 0.8% public transportation, 0.8% walk, 0.5% work from home (2000); Travel time to work: 28.4% less than 15 minutes, 36.2% 15 to 30 minutes, 24.6% 30 to 45 minutes, 6.6% 45 to 60 minutes, 4.3% 60 minutes or more (2000)

WYANDOTTE (city). Covers a land area of 5.306 square miles and a water area of 1.659 square miles. Located at 42.20° N. Lat.; 83.16° W. Long. Elevation is 590 feet.
History: Major John Biddle purchased land and settled here in 1818. In 1853, Captain Eber B. Ward purchased the Biddle estate and founded the Eureka Iron and Steel Company, with a blast furnace and rolling mill. The settlement of Wyandotte was platted then, and grew up around the steel plant. It was incorporated as a city in 1867. In 1891, salt replaced steel in Wyandotte, and many products such as baking soda, soaps, and cleaners were developed from the soda ash mined here.
Population: 28,006 (2000); Race: 95.8% White, 0.7% Black, 0.5% Asian, 0.4% American Indian and Alaska Native, 2.3% Hispanic of any race, 2.1% two or more races (2000); Density: 5,278.1 persons per square mile (2000); Age: 22.6% under 18, 15.8% over 64 (2000); Marriage status: 27.2% never married, 51.6% now married, 8.9% widowed, 12.2% divorced (2000); Foreign born: 3.6% (2000); Ancestry (includes multiple ancestries): 22.5% Polish, 21.9% German, 17.5% Irish, 9.0% English, 8.9% Other groups (2000).
Vital Statistics: Birth rate: 126.0 per 10,000 population (1998)
Economy: Unemployment rate: 4.0% (11/2002); Total civilian labor force: 14,842 (11/2002); Single-family building permits issued: 26 (2001) / 16 (2000); Multi-family building permits issued: 4 (2001) / 0 (2000); Employment by occupation: 8.0% management, 14.9% professional, 15.7% services, 28.6% sales, 0.1% farming, 12.7% construction, 20.1% production (2000).
Income: Per capita income: $22,185 (2000); Median household income: $43,740 (2000); Poverty rate: 6.2% (2000).
Taxes: Total city taxes per capita: $622 (2000); City property taxes per capita: $603 (2000).
Education: High school graduation rate: 79.7% (2000); College graduation rate: 12.7% (2000).

School District(s)

Wyandotte City School District (KG-12)
2000 Enrollment: 4,780 734-246-1000

Housing: Homeownership rate: 73.1% (2000); Median home value: $101,700 (2000); Median rent: $464 per month (2000); Median age of housing: 52 years (2000).
Hospitals: Henry Ford Wyandotte Hospital (302 beds)
Safety: Violent crime rate: 12.1 per 10,000 population; Property crime rate: 278.4 per 10,000 population (2001).
Transportation: Commute to work: 96.3% car, 0.2% public transportation, 1.9% walk, 1.1% work from home (2000); Travel time to work: 32.4% less than 15 minutes, 37.2% 15 to 30 minutes, 17.5% 30 to 45 minutes, 8.6% 45 to 60 minutes, 4.4% 60 minutes or more (2000)

Wexford County

Located in northwestern Michigan; crossed by the Manistee River; drained by the Clam River; includes Lakes Mitchell and Cadillac, and part of Manistee National Forest. Covers a land area of 565.50 square miles, a water area of 10.30 square miles, and is located in the Eastern Time Zone. The county government was organized in 1840. County seat is Cadillac.

Weather Station: Cadillac — Elevation: 1,292 feet

	Jan	Feb	Mar	Apr	May	Jun	Jul	Aug	Sep	Oct	Nov	Dec
High	26	29	38	52	66	75	79	76	68	56	42	31
Low	9	9	17	30	40	50	55	53	45	36	27	16
Precip	1.8	1.3	2.1	2.7	2.8	3.0	3.1	3.8	4.1	3.2	2.7	2.0
Snow	25.7	na	13.1	3.2	tr	0.0	0.0	0.0	tr	0.5	8.5	20.9

High and Low temperatures in degrees Fahrenheit; Precipitation and Snow in inches

Population: 30,484 (2000); Race: 97.2% White, 0.2% Black, 0.6% Asian, 0.5% American Indian and Alaska Native, 1.1% Hispanic of any race, 1.1% two or more races (2000); Density: 53.9 persons per square mile (2000); Age: 26.8% under 18, 14.0% over 64 (2000).
Religion: Five largest groups: 12.0% Catholic Church, 4.1% American Baptist Churches in the USA, 3.2% The United Methodist Church, 2.2% Church of the Nazarene, 1.9% Evangelical Lutheran Church in America (2000).
Economy: Unemployment rate: 7.1% (11/2002); Total civilian labor force: 14,854 (11/2002); Leading industries: 34.4% manufacturing; 17.4% retail trade; 10.9% health care and social assistance (2000); Companies that employ more than 1,000 persons: 0 (2000); Companies that employ more than 100 persons: 24 (2000); Farms: 251 totaling 43,321 acres (1997); Minority business ownership rate: 0.0% (1997); Women business ownership rate: 22.0% (1997); Retail sales per capita: $12,330 (1997). Single-family building permits issued: 172 (2001) / 164 (2000); Multi-family building permits issued: 42 (2001) / 62 (2000).

Income: Per capita income: $17,144 (2000); Median household income: $35,363 (2000); Poverty rate: 10.3% (2000); Bankruptcy rate: 5.97% (2001).
Taxes: Total county taxes per capita: $168 (2000); County property taxes per capita: $164 (2000).
Education: High school graduation rate: 82.0% (2000); College graduation rate: 15.3% (2000).
Housing: Homeownership rate: 79.2% (2000); Median home value: $79,900 (2000); Median rent: $369 per month (2000); Median age of housing: 28 years (2000).
Health: Birth rate: 133.2 per 10,000 population (1998); Age adjusted death rate: 92.7 per 10,000 population (1999); Age adjusted cancer mortality rate: 232.3 deaths per 100,000 population (1999). Number of physicians: 16.1 per 10,000 population (1999); Number of hospital beds: 25.6 per 10,000 population (1999).
Elections: 2000 Presidential election results: 41.0% Gore, 55.6% Bush, 2.7% Nader, 0.1% Buchanan
National and State Parks: William Mitchell State Park
Additional Information Contacts
Wexford County Government Offices 231-779-9453
Cadillac Area Chamber of Commerce 231-775-9776
Manton Area Chamber of Commerce 231-824-4158
Mesick Chamber of Commerce 231-885-2679
Paul Bunyan Board of Realtors 231-775-2660

Wexford County Communities

ANTIOCH (township). Covers a land area of 35.230 square miles and a water area of 0.052 square miles. Located at 44.38° N. Lat.; 85.64° W. Long.
Population: 810 (2000); Race: 97.4% White, 0.0% Black, 0.0% Asian, 1.2% American Indian and Alaska Native, 0.7% Hispanic of any race, 1.2% two or more races (2000); Density: 23.0 persons per square mile (2000); Age: 24.4% under 18, 13.9% over 64 (2000); Marriage status: 20.2% never married, 61.9% now married, 6.5% widowed, 11.5% divorced (2000); Foreign born: 0.9% (2000); Ancestry (includes multiple ancestries): 20.8% German, 10.9% English, 10.8% Irish, 9.9% United States or American, 7.8% Other groups (2000).
Economy: Employment by occupation: 8.2% management, 10.8% professional, 17.8% services, 24.5% sales, 2.9% farming, 16.0% construction, 19.8% production (2000).
Income: Per capita income: $15,387 (2000); Median household income: $32,679 (2000); Poverty rate: 9.7% (2000).
Taxes: Total city taxes per capita: $4 (1997); City property taxes per capita: $4 (1997).
Education: High school graduation rate: 78.0% (2000); College graduation rate: 9.6% (2000).
Housing: Homeownership rate: 89.5% (2000); Median home value: $62,900 (2000); Median rent: $347 per month (2000); Median age of housing: 24 years (2000).
Transportation: Commute to work: 95.6% car, 1.2% public transportation, 0.0% walk, 2.9% work from home (2000); Travel time to work: 26.1% less than 15 minutes, 34.5% 15 to 30 minutes, 24.5% 30 to 45 minutes, 9.7% 45 to 60 minutes, 5.2% 60 minutes or more (2000)

BOON (township). Covers a land area of 36.034 square miles and a water area of 0 square miles. Located at 44.30° N. Lat.; 85.64° W. Long. Elevation is 1,376 feet.
Population: 670 (2000); Race: 98.2% White, 0.0% Black, 0.0% Asian, 0.3% American Indian and Alaska Native, 0.3% Hispanic of any race, 1.5% two or more races (2000); Density: 18.6 persons per square mile (2000); Age: 28.0% under 18, 11.2% over 64 (2000); Marriage status: 25.1% never married, 58.6% now married, 6.7% widowed, 9.6% divorced (2000); Foreign born: 0.7% (2000); Ancestry (includes multiple ancestries): 20.5% English, 20.0% German, 10.0% Irish, 8.7% Dutch, 6.3% French (except Basque) (2000).
Economy: Employment by occupation: 11.4% management, 9.8% professional, 17.4% services, 22.7% sales, 0.6% farming, 8.8% construction, 29.3% production (2000).
Income: Per capita income: $16,294 (2000); Median household income: $41,042 (2000); Poverty rate: 7.2% (2000).
Taxes: Total city taxes per capita: $27 (1997); City property taxes per capita: $27 (1997).
Education: High school graduation rate: 78.2% (2000); College graduation rate: 10.3% (2000).
Housing: Homeownership rate: 87.4% (2000); Median home value: $57,500 (2000); Median rent: $340 per month (2000); Median age of housing: 28 years (2000).
Transportation: Commute to work: 93.9% car, 0.0% public transportation, 1.3% walk, 4.8% work from home (2000); Travel time to work: 12.9% less than 15 minutes, 64.1% 15 to 30 minutes, 11.5% 30 to 45 minutes, 8.5% 45 to 60 minutes, 3.1% 60 minutes or more (2000)

BUCKLEY (village). Covers a land area of 1.777 square miles and a water area of 0.063 square miles. Located at 44.50° N. Lat.; 85.67° W. Long. Elevation is 1,040 feet.
History: Buckley was founded in 1905 by G.A. Brigham and named for the Buckley & Douglas Lumber Company.
Population: 550 (2000); Race: 93.6% White, 1.0% Black, 0.3% Asian, 0.2% American Indian and Alaska Native, 3.4% Hispanic of any race, 3.4% two or more races (2000); Density: 309.4 persons per square mile (2000); Age: 30.7% under 18, 7.4% over 64 (2000); Marriage status: 26.5% never married, 57.0% now married, 2.0% widowed, 14.6% divorced (2000); Foreign born: 4.4% (2000); Ancestry (includes multiple ancestries): 23.6% German, 11.6% Polish, 10.7% Irish, 7.5% Other groups, 7.2% French Canadian (2000).
Economy: Employment by occupation: 2.7% management, 12.6% professional, 21.9% services, 27.9% sales, 0.0% farming, 13.6% construction, 21.3% production (2000).
Income: Per capita income: $14,258 (2000); Median household income: $36,667 (2000); Poverty rate: 7.3% (2000).
Taxes: Total city taxes per capita: $87 (1997); City property taxes per capita: $87 (1997).
Education: High school graduation rate: 79.4% (2000); College graduation rate: 7.0% (2000).

School District(s)
Buckley Community School District (KG-12)
2000 Enrollment: 403 231-269-3325
Housing: Homeownership rate: 76.1% (2000); Median home value: $81,600 (2000); Median rent: $475 per month (2000); Median age of housing: 26 years (2000).
Transportation: Commute to work: 92.2% car, 0.0% public transportation, 6.5% walk, 0.7% work from home (2000); Travel time to work: 17.5% less than 15 minutes, 25.4% 15 to 30 minutes, 45.0% 30 to 45 minutes, 6.2% 45 to 60 minutes, 5.8% 60 minutes or more (2000); Amtrak: Service available.

CADILLAC (city). Covers a land area of 6.821 square miles and a water area of 1.780 square miles. Located at 44.25° N. Lat.; 85.41° W. Long. Elevation is 1,328 feet.
History: Cadillac was settled by timber operators, and incorporated in 1877. It was named for Antoine de la Mothe Cadillac, the founder of Detroit. When two railroad lines were built through Cadillac, it developed as an industrial center.
Population: 10,000 (2000); Race: 96.2% White, 0.2% Black, 1.4% Asian, 0.6% American Indian and Alaska Native, 1.4% Hispanic of any race, 0.9% two or more races (2000); Density: 1,466.0 persons per square mile (2000); Age: 25.8% under 18, 16.7% over 64 (2000); Marriage status: 24.3% never married, 51.1% now married, 9.2% widowed, 15.4% divorced (2000); Foreign born: 2.7% (2000); Ancestry (includes multiple ancestries): 22.2% German, 13.8% English, 11.3% Irish, 8.9% Dutch, 8.9% Other groups (2000).
Vital Statistics: Birth rate: 160.0 per 10,000 population (1998)
Economy: Single-family building permits issued: 7 (2001) / 8 (2000); Multi-family building permits issued: 42 (2001) / 62 (2000); Employment by occupation: 8.4% management, 16.3% professional, 18.2% services, 23.4% sales, 0.3% farming, 5.4% construction, 27.8% production (2000).
Income: Per capita income: $16,801 (2000); Median household income: $29,899 (2000); Poverty rate: 13.7% (2000).
Taxes: Total city taxes per capita: $247 (1997); City property taxes per capita: $237 (1997).
Education: High school graduation rate: 81.3% (2000); College graduation rate: 17.6% (2000).

School District(s)
Cadillac Area Public Schools (KG-12)
2000 Enrollment: 3,638 231-876-5002

Four-year College(s)
Baker College of Cadillac (Private, Not-for-profit)
2001 Enrollment: 1,024 231-876-3101
2001 Tuition: In-state $7,440; Out-of-state $7,440
Housing: Homeownership rate: 64.6% (2000); Median home value: $72,500 (2000); Median rent: $364 per month (2000); Median age of housing: 46 years (2000).
Hospitals: Mercy Hospital (174 beds)
Safety: Violent crime rate: 41.8 per 10,000 population; Property crime rate: 496.4 per 10,000 population (2001).

Newspapers: Cadillac News (6 x week); Northern Michigan News (1 x week)
Transportation: Commute to work: 90.7% car, 0.4% public transportation, 5.2% walk, 2.5% work from home (2000); Travel time to work: 71.5% less than 15 minutes, 14.7% 15 to 30 minutes, 2.7% 30 to 45 minutes, 4.6% 45 to 60 minutes, 6.4% 60 minutes or more (2000); Amtrak: Service available.
Airports: Wexford County
Additional Information Contacts
Cadillac Area Chamber of Commerce 231-775-9776
Paul Bunyan Board of Realtors 231-775-2660

CEDAR CREEK (township). Covers a land area of 34.174 square miles and a water area of 0.023 square miles. Located at 44.39° N. Lat.; 85.40° W. Long.
Population: 1,489 (2000); Race: 97.5% White, 0.0% Black, 0.0% Asian, 0.7% American Indian and Alaska Native, 1.2% Hispanic of any race, 1.6% two or more races (2000); Density: 43.6 persons per square mile (2000); Age: 31.5% under 18, 8.3% over 64 (2000); Marriage status: 20.2% never married, 64.7% now married, 3.6% widowed, 11.5% divorced (2000); Foreign born: 0.6% (2000); Ancestry (includes multiple ancestries): 20.3% German, 13.8% Irish, 11.8% English, 8.9% Other groups, 6.0% United States or American (2000).
Economy: Employment by occupation: 7.1% management, 19.7% professional, 13.1% services, 18.4% sales, 2.1% farming, 13.1% construction, 26.6% production (2000).
Income: Per capita income: $15,645 (2000); Median household income: $37,566 (2000); Poverty rate: 10.9% (2000).
Taxes: Total city taxes per capita: $17 (1997); City property taxes per capita: $12 (1997).
Education: High school graduation rate: 80.6% (2000); College graduation rate: 10.1% (2000).
Housing: Homeownership rate: 87.7% (2000); Median home value: $76,800 (2000); Median rent: $361 per month (2000); Median age of housing: 21 years (2000).
Transportation: Commute to work: 88.9% car, 0.0% public transportation, 0.9% walk, 7.7% work from home (2000); Travel time to work: 25.8% less than 15 minutes, 52.7% 15 to 30 minutes, 9.0% 30 to 45 minutes, 7.5% 45 to 60 minutes, 5.1% 60 minutes or more (2000)

CHERRY GROVE (township). Covers a land area of 33.362 square miles and a water area of 2.810 square miles. Located at 44.19° N. Lat.; 85.50° W. Long.
Population: 2,328 (2000); Race: 97.3% White, 0.5% Black, 0.5% Asian, 0.6% American Indian and Alaska Native, 0.7% Hispanic of any race, 0.9% two or more races (2000); Density: 69.8 persons per square mile (2000); Age: 25.4% under 18, 12.1% over 64 (2000); Marriage status: 18.1% never married, 69.7% now married, 4.0% widowed, 8.2% divorced (2000); Foreign born: 1.8% (2000); Ancestry (includes multiple ancestries): 21.5% German, 14.5% English, 14.5% Irish, 6.7% Swedish, 6.2% Dutch (2000).
Economy: Employment by occupation: 15.9% management, 23.8% professional, 13.4% services, 24.7% sales, 0.6% farming, 5.9% construction, 15.6% production (2000).
Income: Per capita income: $22,798 (2000); Median household income: $51,190 (2000); Poverty rate: 5.9% (2000).
Taxes: Total city taxes per capita: $39 (1997); City property taxes per capita: $37 (1997).
Education: High school graduation rate: 89.5% (2000); College graduation rate: 28.5% (2000).
Housing: Homeownership rate: 89.7% (2000); Median home value: $139,300 (2000); Median rent: $429 per month (2000); Median age of housing: 25 years (2000).
Transportation: Commute to work: 95.2% car, 0.5% public transportation, 2.0% walk, 2.1% work from home (2000); Travel time to work: 35.1% less than 15 minutes, 47.8% 15 to 30 minutes, 6.5% 30 to 45 minutes, 4.9% 45 to 60 minutes, 5.7% 60 minutes or more (2000)

CLAM LAKE (township). Covers a land area of 30.851 square miles and a water area of 0.268 square miles. Located at 44.20° N. Lat.; 85.40° W. Long.
Population: 2,238 (2000); Race: 98.4% White, 0.0% Black, 0.2% Asian, 0.1% American Indian and Alaska Native, 1.5% Hispanic of any race, 1.3% two or more races (2000); Density: 72.5 persons per square mile (2000); Age: 26.7% under 18, 12.4% over 64 (2000); Marriage status: 19.5% never married, 68.6% now married, 4.0% widowed, 7.9% divorced (2000); Foreign born: 1.9% (2000); Ancestry (includes multiple ancestries): 30.3% German, 14.7% English, 14.3% Irish, 11.3% Swedish, 7.1% Dutch (2000).
Economy: Employment by occupation: 14.1% management, 21.7% professional, 11.2% services, 26.1% sales, 0.0% farming, 9.2% construction, 17.8% production (2000).
Income: Per capita income: $21,062 (2000); Median household income: $47,102 (2000); Poverty rate: 3.8% (2000).
Taxes: Total city taxes per capita: $60 (1997); City property taxes per capita: $58 (1997).
Education: High school graduation rate: 91.7% (2000); College graduation rate: 25.8% (2000).
Housing: Homeownership rate: 86.2% (2000); Median home value: $106,300 (2000); Median rent: $400 per month (2000); Median age of housing: 25 years (2000).
Transportation: Commute to work: 93.9% car, 0.4% public transportation, 0.4% walk, 4.8% work from home (2000); Travel time to work: 56.7% less than 15 minutes, 34.9% 15 to 30 minutes, 3.6% 30 to 45 minutes, 0.5% 45 to 60 minutes, 4.4% 60 minutes or more (2000)

COLFAX (township). Covers a land area of 35.323 square miles and a water area of 0.137° square miles. Located at 44.37° N. Lat.; 85.52° W. Long.
History: Colfax County was named for Schuyler Colfax, vice president under Ulysses S. Grant.
Population: 763 (2000); Race: 98.8% White, 0.0% Black, 0.2% Asian, 0.0% American Indian and Alaska Native, 0.0% Hispanic of any race, 1.0% two or more races (2000); Density: 21.6 persons per square mile (2000); Age: 28.2% under 18, 10.0% over 64 (2000); Marriage status: 15.8% never married, 68.2% now married, 3.2% widowed, 12.7% divorced (2000); Foreign born: 1.3% (2000); Ancestry (includes multiple ancestries): 19.7% German, 17.2% English, 16.0% Irish, 9.0% United States or American, 8.2% Dutch (2000).
Economy: Employment by occupation: 13.1% management, 11.0% professional, 14.4% services, 26.7% sales, 4.0% farming, 9.6% construction, 21.1% production (2000).
Income: Per capita income: $16,082 (2000); Median household income: $39,135 (2000); Poverty rate: 7.6% (2000).
Taxes: Total city taxes per capita: $43 (1997); City property taxes per capita: $37 (1997).
Education: High school graduation rate: 84.8% (2000); College graduation rate: 7.2% (2000).
Housing: Homeownership rate: 97.3% (2000); Median home value: $82,500 (2000); Median rent: $175 per month (2000); Median age of housing: 24 years (2000).
Transportation: Commute to work: 88.0% car, 0.5% public transportation, 2.7% walk, 8.7% work from home (2000); Travel time to work: 18.3% less than 15 minutes, 45.8% 15 to 30 minutes, 19.5% 30 to 45 minutes, 12.0% 45 to 60 minutes, 4.5% 60 minutes or more (2000)

GREENWOOD (township). Covers a land area of 35.334 square miles and a water area of 0.040 square miles. Located at 44.46° N. Lat.; 85.52° W. Long.
Population: 542 (2000); Race: 97.6% White, 0.0% Black, 0.0% Asian, 1.4% American Indian and Alaska Native, 0.4% Hispanic of any race, 0.5% two or more races (2000); Density: 15.3 persons per square mile (2000); Age: 30.9% under 18, 9.8% over 64 (2000); Marriage status: 16.1% never married, 67.7% now married, 3.4% widowed, 12.7% divorced (2000); Foreign born: 0.0% (2000); Ancestry (includes multiple ancestries): 29.3% German, 12.1% Irish, 11.6% English, 8.0% United States or American, 7.6% French (except Basque) (2000).
Economy: Employment by occupation: 5.5% management, 14.1% professional, 19.5% services, 24.5% sales, 2.3% farming, 16.4% construction, 17.7% production (2000).
Income: Per capita income: $15,009 (2000); Median household income: $37,083 (2000); Poverty rate: 12.3% (2000).
Taxes: Total city taxes per capita: $18 (1997); City property taxes per capita: $18 (1997).
Education: High school graduation rate: 77.1% (2000); College graduation rate: 9.5% (2000).
Housing: Homeownership rate: 91.7% (2000); Median home value: $77,500 (2000); Median rent: $232 per month (2000); Median age of housing: 23 years (2000).
Transportation: Commute to work: 90.8% car, 0.0% public transportation, 0.0% walk, 8.3% work from home (2000); Travel time to work: 14.0% less than 15 minutes, 29.5% 15 to 30 minutes, 38.0% 30 to 45 minutes, 10.0% 45 to 60 minutes, 8.5% 60 minutes or more (2000)

HANOVER (township). Covers a land area of 36.036 square miles and a water area of 0.171 square miles. Located at 44.47° N. Lat.; 85.64° W. Long.

Population: 1,200 (2000); Race: 95.2% White, 0.7% Black, 0.3% Asian, 0.4% American Indian and Alaska Native, 1.9% Hispanic of any race, 2.3% two or more races (2000); Density: 33.3 persons per square mile (2000); Age: 27.7% under 18, 10.9% over 64 (2000); Marriage status: 21.8% never married, 59.7% now married, 4.5% widowed, 14.0% divorced (2000); Foreign born: 2.7% (2000); Ancestry (includes multiple ancestries): 22.1% German, 11.2% Irish, 9.9% English, 9.9% United States or American, 9.2% Other groups (2000).
Economy: Employment by occupation: 6.7% management, 11.9% professional, 19.5% services, 26.6% sales, 0.0% farming, 15.7% construction, 19.5% production (2000).
Income: Per capita income: $15,271 (2000); Median household income: $36,850 (2000); Poverty rate: 5.8% (2000).
Taxes: Total city taxes per capita: $21 (1997); City property taxes per capita: $21 (1997).
Education: High school graduation rate: 78.6% (2000); College graduation rate: 8.3% (2000).
Housing: Homeownership rate: 83.2% (2000); Median home value: $88,300 (2000); Median rent: $435 per month (2000); Median age of housing: 21 years (2000).
Transportation: Commute to work: 94.6% car, 0.0% public transportation, 3.5% walk, 1.5% work from home (2000); Travel time to work: 15.5% less than 15 minutes, 27.0% 15 to 30 minutes, 42.1% 30 to 45 minutes, 7.7% 45 to 60 minutes, 7.7% 60 minutes or more (2000)

HARING (township). Covers a land area of 32.507 square miles and a water area of 0.449 square miles. Located at 44.28° N. Lat.; 85.39° W. Long. Elevation is 1,328 feet.
Population: 2,962 (2000); Race: 98.8% White, 0.1% Black, 0.0% Asian, 0.5% American Indian and Alaska Native, 0.8% Hispanic of any race, 0.4% two or more races (2000); Density: 91.1 persons per square mile (2000); Age: 28.5% under 18, 12.9% over 64 (2000); Marriage status: 23.3% never married, 61.9% now married, 4.7% widowed, 10.2% divorced (2000); Foreign born: 1.5% (2000); Ancestry (includes multiple ancestries): 17.7% German, 12.3% English, 10.6% Dutch, 9.3% United States or American, 9.2% Irish (2000).
Economy: Employment by occupation: 11.4% management, 17.0% professional, 12.5% services, 24.0% sales, 0.3% farming, 6.8% construction, 28.0% production (2000).
Income: Per capita income: $17,001 (2000); Median household income: $40,265 (2000); Poverty rate: 7.2% (2000).
Taxes: Total city taxes per capita: $48 (1997); City property taxes per capita: $43 (1997).
Education: High school graduation rate: 82.4% (2000); College graduation rate: 14.7% (2000).
Housing: Homeownership rate: 90.0% (2000); Median home value: $86,700 (2000); Median rent: $393 per month (2000); Median age of housing: 22 years (2000).
Transportation: Commute to work: 93.5% car, 1.0% public transportation, 0.7% walk, 4.0% work from home (2000); Travel time to work: 62.3% less than 15 minutes, 25.2% 15 to 30 minutes, 4.7% 30 to 45 minutes, 3.0% 45 to 60 minutes, 4.8% 60 minutes or more (2000)

HARRIETTA (village). Covers a land area of 0.928 square miles and a water area of 0 square miles. Located at 44.30° N. Lat.; 85.69° W. Long. Elevation is 1,112 feet.
History: There was a post office here as early as 1874, called Springdale. The village of Harrietta was platted in 1889 by James M. Ashley and named by combining his father's name of Harry and his fiancee's name of Henriette.
Population: 169 (2000); Race: 97.9% White, 0.0% Black, 0.0% Asian, 0.0% American Indian and Alaska Native, 1.4% Hispanic of any race, 2.1% two or more races (2000); Density: 182.0 persons per square mile (2000); Age: 25.0% under 18, 20.8% over 64 (2000); Marriage status: 26.7% never married, 50.8% now married, 9.2% widowed, 13.3% divorced (2000); Foreign born: 1.4% (2000); Ancestry (includes multiple ancestries): 27.8% German, 20.8% English, 13.9% Other groups, 12.5% Dutch, 11.8% Slovene (2000).
Economy: Employment by occupation: 16.7% management, 3.3% professional, 18.3% services, 25.0% sales, 0.0% farming, 5.0% construction, 31.7% production (2000).
Income: Per capita income: $15,258 (2000); Median household income: $33,500 (2000); Poverty rate: 6.9% (2000).
Taxes: Total city taxes per capita: $50 (1997); City property taxes per capita: $50 (1997).
Education: High school graduation rate: 74.2% (2000); College graduation rate: 9.3% (2000).
Housing: Homeownership rate: 89.3% (2000); Median home value: $56,000 (2000); Median rent: $400 per month (2000); Median age of housing: 33 years (2000).
Transportation: Commute to work: 95.0% car, 0.0% public transportation, 0.0% walk, 5.0% work from home (2000); Travel time to work: 0.0% less than 15 minutes, 75.4% 15 to 30 minutes, 7.0% 30 to 45 minutes, 12.3% 45 to 60 minutes, 5.3% 60 minutes or more (2000)

HENDERSON (township). Covers a land area of 36.148 square miles and a water area of <.001 square miles. Located at 44.20° N. Lat.; 85.65° W. Long.
Population: 176 (2000); Race: 100.0% White, 0.0% Black, 0.0% Asian, 0.0% American Indian and Alaska Native, 0.0% Hispanic of any race, 0.0% two or more races (2000); Density: 4.9 persons per square mile (2000); Age: 14.3% under 18, 11.8% over 64 (2000); Marriage status: 16.0% never married, 69.4% now married, 4.2% widowed, 10.4% divorced (2000); Foreign born: 3.1% (2000); Ancestry (includes multiple ancestries): 29.2% German, 13.7% French (except Basque), 9.9% United States or American, 8.7% English, 8.1% French Canadian (2000).
Economy: Employment by occupation: 12.3% management, 14.8% professional, 13.6% services, 27.2% sales, 2.5% farming, 19.8% construction, 9.9% production (2000).
Income: Per capita income: $18,877 (2000); Median household income: $32,000 (2000); Poverty rate: 6.2% (2000).
Taxes: Total city taxes per capita: $16 (1997); City property taxes per capita: $16 (1997).
Education: High school graduation rate: 76.5% (2000); College graduation rate: 15.7% (2000).
Housing: Homeownership rate: 97.1% (2000); Median home value: $56,700 (2000); Median age of housing: 31 years (2000).
Transportation: Commute to work: 93.8% car, 0.0% public transportation, 2.5% walk, 1.2% work from home (2000); Travel time to work: 7.5% less than 15 minutes, 47.5% 15 to 30 minutes, 32.5% 30 to 45 minutes, 2.5% 45 to 60 minutes, 10.0% 60 minutes or more (2000)

LIBERTY (township). Covers a land area of 36.523 square miles and a water area of 0.017 square miles. Located at 44.46° N. Lat.; 85.40° W. Long.
Population: 800 (2000); Race: 95.6% White, 0.0% Black, 0.0% Asian, 1.1% American Indian and Alaska Native, 1.6% Hispanic of any race, 3.3% two or more races (2000); Density: 21.9 persons per square mile (2000); Age: 26.6% under 18, 14.1% over 64 (2000); Marriage status: 22.1% never married, 59.8% now married, 7.2% widowed, 10.9% divorced (2000); Foreign born: 1.4% (2000); Ancestry (includes multiple ancestries): 21.4% German, 12.3% Irish, 11.2% English, 10.4% Other groups, 7.5% French (except Basque) (2000).
Economy: Employment by occupation: 6.7% management, 12.2% professional, 13.7% services, 22.6% sales, 1.0% farming, 14.7% construction, 29.1% production (2000).
Income: Per capita income: $17,612 (2000); Median household income: $36,979 (2000); Poverty rate: 9.2% (2000).
Taxes: Total city taxes per capita: $23 (1997); City property taxes per capita: $23 (1997).
Education: High school graduation rate: 79.1% (2000); College graduation rate: 7.7% (2000).
Housing: Homeownership rate: 86.1% (2000); Median home value: $78,800 (2000); Median rent: $389 per month (2000); Median age of housing: 23 years (2000).
Transportation: Commute to work: 95.6% car, 0.0% public transportation, 0.5% walk, 2.3% work from home (2000); Travel time to work: 29.4% less than 15 minutes, 38.1% 15 to 30 minutes, 20.2% 30 to 45 minutes, 7.9% 45 to 60 minutes, 4.5% 60 minutes or more (2000)

MANTON (city). Covers a land area of 1.557 square miles and a water area of 0.059 square miles. Located at 44.41° N. Lat.; 85.40° W. Long. Elevation is 1,127 feet.
History: Manton was settled in 1871. It developed as a lumber town with a sawmill and planing mill.
Population: 1,221 (2000); Race: 98.7% White, 0.0% Black, 0.0% Asian, 0.1% American Indian and Alaska Native, 0.3% Hispanic of any race, 1.2% two or more races (2000); Density: 784.2 persons per square mile (2000); Age: 27.0% under 18, 15.8% over 64 (2000); Marriage status: 24.0% never married, 49.7% now married, 7.9% widowed, 18.3% divorced (2000); Foreign born: 0.5% (2000); Ancestry (includes multiple ancestries): 22.4% German, 13.7% English, 9.5% Irish, 8.2% United States or American, 6.1% Other groups (2000).

Economy: Employment by occupation: 6.3% management, 13.6% professional, 16.5% services, 20.9% sales, 0.0% farming, 8.9% construction, 33.9% production (2000).
Income: Per capita income: $13,528 (2000); Median household income: $27,339 (2000); Poverty rate: 14.2% (2000).
Taxes: Total city taxes per capita: $190 (1997); City property taxes per capita: $185 (1997).
Education: High school graduation rate: 78.7% (2000); College graduation rate: 9.7% (2000).

School District(s)

Manton Consolidated Schools (KG-12)
2000 Enrollment: 1,033 231-824-6411

Housing: Homeownership rate: 69.2% (2000); Median home value: $60,300 (2000); Median rent: $372 per month (2000); Median age of housing: 45 years (2000).
Safety: Violent crime rate: 8.1 per 10,000 population; Property crime rate: 236.3 per 10,000 population (2001).
Transportation: Commute to work: 89.9% car, 0.0% public transportation, 4.8% walk, 3.4% work from home (2000); Travel time to work: 27.0% less than 15 minutes, 46.0% 15 to 30 minutes, 14.2% 30 to 45 minutes, 9.0% 45 to 60 minutes, 3.8% 60 minutes or more (2000)

Additional Information Contacts

Manton Area Chamber of Commerce 231-824-4158

MESICK (village). Covers a land area of 1.138 square miles and a water area of 0.005 square miles. Located at 44.40° N. Lat.; 85.72° W. Long. Elevation is 903 feet.
History: Annual mushroom festival.
Population: 447 (2000); Race: 97.5% White, 1.5% Black, 0.0% Asian, 0.0% American Indian and Alaska Native, 0.5% Hispanic of any race, 1.0% two or more races (2000); Density: 392.9 persons per square mile (2000); Age: 31.1% under 18, 15.2% over 64 (2000); Marriage status: 23.5% never married, 49.3% now married, 13.2% widowed, 13.9% divorced (2000); Foreign born: 1.0% (2000); Ancestry (includes multiple ancestries): 16.2% German, 14.5% English, 8.1% French (except Basque), 7.8% Polish, 7.1% Irish (2000).
Economy: Manufacturing: tool and die; machining. Manistee National Forest to South. Employment by occupation: 6.3% management, 15.3% professional, 16.0% services, 20.8% sales, 1.4% farming, 15.3% construction, 25.0% production (2000).
Income: Per capita income: $10,600 (2000); Median household income: $24,375 (2000); Poverty rate: 21.9% (2000).
Taxes: Total city taxes per capita: $92 (1997); City property taxes per capita: $92 (1997).
Education: High school graduation rate: 77.7% (2000); College graduation rate: 7.6% (2000).

School District(s)

Mesick Consolidated Schools (KG-12)
2000 Enrollment: 948 231-885-2727

Housing: Homeownership rate: 72.0% (2000); Median home value: $52,800 (2000); Median rent: $315 per month (2000); Median age of housing: 38 years (2000).
Transportation: Commute to work: 81.2% car, 0.0% public transportation, 8.7% walk, 10.1% work from home (2000); Travel time to work: 25.0% less than 15 minutes, 29.0% 15 to 30 minutes, 38.7% 30 to 45 minutes, 2.4% 45 to 60 minutes, 4.8% 60 minutes or more (2000); Amtrak: Service available.

Additional Information Contacts

Mesick Chamber of Commerce 231-885-2679

SELMA (township). Covers a land area of 34.439 square miles and a water area of 1.619 square miles. Located at 44.29° N. Lat.; 85.51° W. Long.
Population: 1,915 (2000); Race: 98.5% White, 0.1% Black, 0.2% Asian, 0.4% American Indian and Alaska Native, 0.4% Hispanic of any race, 0.6% two or more races (2000); Density: 55.6 persons per square mile (2000); Age: 24.7% under 18, 14.0% over 64 (2000); Marriage status: 21.0% never married, 61.7% now married, 6.2% widowed, 11.2% divorced (2000); Foreign born: 1.2% (2000); Ancestry (includes multiple ancestries): 26.6% German, 12.3% English, 11.7% Irish, 7.9% Dutch, 7.4% Swedish (2000).
Economy: Employment by occupation: 9.8% management, 13.4% professional, 17.2% services, 23.3% sales, 0.4% farming, 8.2% construction, 27.7% production (2000).
Income: Per capita income: $19,873 (2000); Median household income: $37,287 (2000); Poverty rate: 8.1% (2000).
Taxes: Total city taxes per capita: $40 (1997); City property taxes per capita: $39 (1997).
Education: High school graduation rate: 83.0% (2000); College graduation rate: 13.7% (2000).
Housing: Homeownership rate: 87.9% (2000); Median home value: $97,200 (2000); Median rent: $398 per month (2000); Median age of housing: 23 years (2000).
Transportation: Commute to work: 93.9% car, 1.2% public transportation, 0.7% walk, 3.5% work from home (2000); Travel time to work: 39.6% less than 15 minutes, 46.4% 15 to 30 minutes, 6.0% 30 to 45 minutes, 4.7% 45 to 60 minutes, 3.2% 60 minutes or more (2000)

SLAGLE (township). Covers a land area of 35.813 square miles and a water area of 0 square miles. Located at 44.29° N. Lat.; 85.76° W. Long.
Population: 569 (2000); Race: 96.3% White, 0.0% Black, 0.0% Asian, 0.9% American Indian and Alaska Native, 1.1% Hispanic of any race, 2.6% two or more races (2000); Density: 15.9 persons per square mile (2000); Age: 23.6% under 18, 21.5% over 64 (2000); Marriage status: 13.1% never married, 65.7% now married, 5.8% widowed, 15.4% divorced (2000); Foreign born: 0.2% (2000); Ancestry (includes multiple ancestries): 25.4% German, 13.8% Irish, 10.3% English, 9.6% Other groups, 8.1% Polish (2000).
Economy: Employment by occupation: 6.7% management, 12.4% professional, 8.2% services, 20.6% sales, 2.6% farming, 21.6% construction, 27.8% production (2000).
Income: Per capita income: $14,069 (2000); Median household income: $29,250 (2000); Poverty rate: 17.2% (2000).
Taxes: Total city taxes per capita: $22 (1997); City property taxes per capita: $22 (1997).
Education: High school graduation rate: 72.7% (2000); College graduation rate: 7.6% (2000).
Housing: Homeownership rate: 87.3% (2000); Median home value: $70,300 (2000); Median rent: $383 per month (2000); Median age of housing: 24 years (2000).
Transportation: Commute to work: 93.5% car, 0.0% public transportation, 2.7% walk, 2.2% work from home (2000); Travel time to work: 20.3% less than 15 minutes, 30.2% 15 to 30 minutes, 26.4% 30 to 45 minutes, 11.0% 45 to 60 minutes, 12.1% 60 minutes or more (2000)

SOUTH BRANCH (township). Covers a land area of 36.097 square miles and a water area of 0.019 square miles. Located at 44.21° N. Lat.; 85.76° W. Long.
Population: 330 (2000); Race: 98.0% White, 0.0% Black, 0.0% Asian, 0.0% American Indian and Alaska Native, 1.5% Hispanic of any race, 1.5% two or more races (2000); Density: 9.1 persons per square mile (2000); Age: 22.1% under 18, 23.3% over 64 (2000); Marriage status: 18.1% never married, 62.1% now married, 8.1% widowed, 11.7% divorced (2000); Foreign born: 2.6% (2000); Ancestry (includes multiple ancestries): 20.1% German, 15.1% Dutch, 9.6% English, 7.8% Irish, 7.3% French (except Basque) (2000).
Economy: Employment by occupation: 7.1% management, 12.1% professional, 20.7% services, 21.4% sales, 1.4% farming, 10.7% construction, 26.4% production (2000).
Income: Per capita income: $16,620 (2000); Median household income: $31,667 (2000); Poverty rate: 9.5% (2000).
Taxes: Total city taxes per capita: $134 (1997); City property taxes per capita: $134 (1997).
Education: High school graduation rate: 81.4% (2000); College graduation rate: 9.9% (2000).
Housing: Homeownership rate: 90.9% (2000); Median home value: $80,000 (2000); Median rent: $175 per month (2000); Median age of housing: 29 years (2000).
Transportation: Commute to work: 89.6% car, 0.0% public transportation, 0.0% walk, 7.5% work from home (2000); Travel time to work: 17.7% less than 15 minutes, 23.4% 15 to 30 minutes, 41.9% 30 to 45 minutes, 5.6% 45 to 60 minutes, 11.3% 60 minutes or more (2000)

SPRINGVILLE (township). Covers a land area of 32.725 square miles and a water area of 2.901 square miles. Located at 44.38° N. Lat.; 85.74° W. Long.
Population: 1,673 (2000); Race: 96.4% White, 0.5% Black, 0.5% Asian, 0.6% American Indian and Alaska Native, 1.0% Hispanic of any race, 1.6% two or more races (2000); Density: 51.1 persons per square mile (2000); Age: 29.4% under 18, 12.7% over 64 (2000); Marriage status: 19.0% never married, 58.7% now married, 6.4% widowed, 16.0% divorced (2000); Foreign born: 1.6% (2000); Ancestry (includes multiple ancestries): 16.7% German, 14.9% English, 10.3% United States or American, 8.8% Irish, 8.0% Other groups (2000).

Economy: Employment by occupation: 6.2% management, 7.7% professional, 15.7% services, 20.8% sales, 0.5% farming, 16.3% construction, 33.0% production (2000).
Income: Per capita income: $12,857 (2000); Median household income: $28,821 (2000); Poverty rate: 14.4% (2000).
Taxes: Total city taxes per capita: $23 (1997); City property taxes per capita: $22 (1997).
Education: High school graduation rate: 73.4% (2000); College graduation rate: 5.5% (2000).
Housing: Homeownership rate: 83.3% (2000); Median home value: $59,100 (2000); Median rent: $323 per month (2000); Median age of housing: 28 years (2000).
Transportation: Commute to work: 92.6% car, 0.0% public transportation, 2.8% walk, 4.3% work from home (2000); Travel time to work: 24.5% less than 15 minutes, 20.7% 15 to 30 minutes, 36.1% 30 to 45 minutes, 12.5% 45 to 60 minutes, 6.2% 60 minutes or more (2000)

WEXFORD (township). Covers a land area of 36.519 square miles and a water area of 0.003 square miles. Located at 44.46° N. Lat.; 85.74° W. Long.
Population: 798 (2000); Race: 98.6% White, 0.0% Black, 0.4% Asian, 0.8% American Indian and Alaska Native, 0.6% Hispanic of any race, 0.3% two or more races (2000); Density: 21.9 persons per square mile (2000); Age: 30.7% under 18, 10.9% over 64 (2000); Marriage status: 19.5% never married, 62.9% now married, 5.5% widowed, 12.0% divorced (2000); Foreign born: 0.9% (2000); Ancestry (includes multiple ancestries): 27.3% German, 14.3% Irish, 10.3% Other groups, 9.3% English, 8.3% Polish (2000).
Economy: Employment by occupation: 7.0% management, 10.5% professional, 13.7% services, 23.0% sales, 2.3% farming, 18.3% construction, 25.3% production (2000).
Income: Per capita income: $14,331 (2000); Median household income: $35,083 (2000); Poverty rate: 11.3% (2000).
Taxes: Total city taxes per capita: $5 (1997); City property taxes per capita: $5 (1997).
Education: High school graduation rate: 81.2% (2000); College graduation rate: 8.1% (2000).
Housing: Homeownership rate: 89.0% (2000); Median home value: $88,100 (2000); Median rent: $325 per month (2000); Median age of housing: 24 years (2000).
Transportation: Commute to work: 90.4% car, 0.0% public transportation, 0.0% walk, 8.7% work from home (2000); Travel time to work: 20.7% less than 15 minutes, 18.0% 15 to 30 minutes, 44.3% 30 to 45 minutes, 8.2% 45 to 60 minutes, 8.9% 60 minutes or more (2000)

Minnesota

The North Star State

MINNESOTA –Metropolitan Areas, Counties, and Central Cities

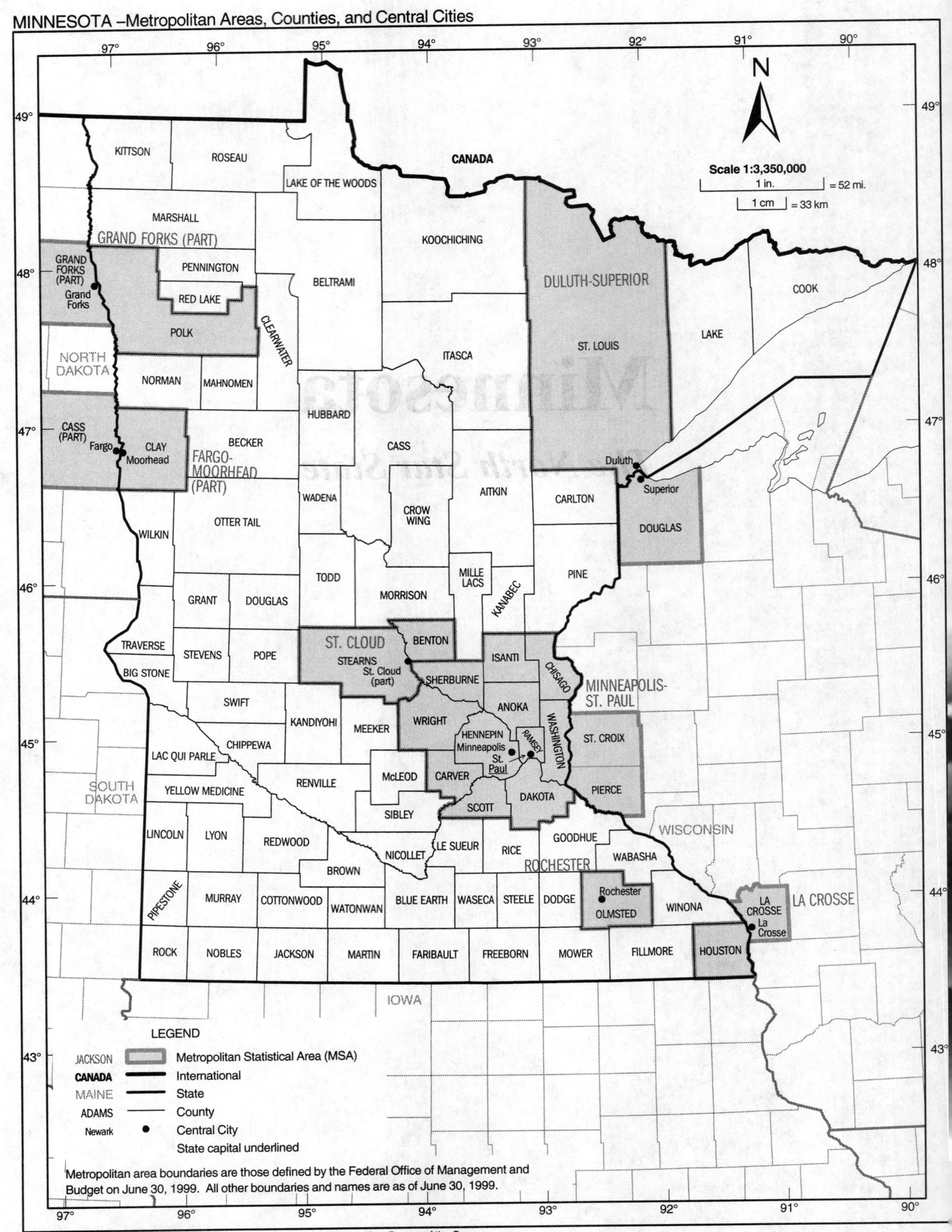

Metropolitan area boundaries are those defined by the Federal Office of Management and Budget on June 30, 1999. All other boundaries and names are as of June 30, 1999.

A

B

CDP = Census Designated Place

C

CDP = Census Designated Place

D

E

CDP = Census Designated Place

CDP = Census Designated Place

L

CDP = Census Designated Place

O

P

CDP = Census Designated Place

CDP = Census Designated Place

T

CDP = Census Designated Place

CDP = Census Designated Place

Y

Z

Aitkin County

Located in east central Minnesota; drained by the Mississippi River and watered in the southwest by part of Mille Lacs Lake. Covers a land area of 1,819.30 square miles, a water area of 176.00 square miles, and is located in the Central Time Zone. The county government was organized in 1857. County seat is Aitkin.

Weather Station: Isle 12 N Elevation: 1,282 feet

	Jan	Feb	Mar	Apr	May	Jun	Jul	Aug	Sep	Oct	Nov	Dec
High	17	25	36	52	66	75	79	77	67	54	36	22
Low	-5	2	15	29	42	52	57	55	46	34	20	3
Precip	0.6	0.5	1.2	2.0	2.8	4.4	4.9	3.8	2.9	2.3	1.5	0.7
Snow	12.0	6.1	na	2.2	tr	0.0	0.0	0.0	0.0	0.7	5.2	6.4

High and Low temperatures in degrees Fahrenheit; Precipitation and Snow in inches

Weather Station: Sandy Lake Dam Libby Elevation: 1,233 feet

	Jan	Feb	Mar	Apr	May	Jun	Jul	Aug	Sep	Oct	Nov	Dec
High	19	27	38	54	68	76	80	78	68	56	na	na
Low	-4	3	16	30	42	52	57	55	46	35	na	3
Precip	0.9	0.5	1.2	1.8	2.9	4.5	4.5	3.8	3.1	2.5	1.3	0.7
Snow	15.6	8.3	9.7	3.1	0.2	0.0	0.0	0.0	tr	1.0	8.3	10.8

High and Low temperatures in degrees Fahrenheit; Precipitation and Snow in inches

Population: 15,301 (2000); Race: 96.3% White, 0.2% Black, 0.3% Asian, 2.3% American Indian and Alaska Native, 0.7% Hispanic of any race, 0.8% two or more races (2000); Density: 8.4 persons per square mile (2000); Age: 20.9% under 18, 23.0% over 64 (2000).
Religion: Five largest groups: 34.8% Evangelical Lutheran Church in America, 18.4% Catholic Church, 6.6% Lutheran Church—Missouri Synod, 4.4% The United Methodist Church, 1.4% Assemblies of God (2000).
Economy: Unemployment rate: 6.1% (11/2002); Total civilian labor force: 6,329 (11/2002); Leading industries: 18.2% health care and social assistance; 17.8% retail trade; 16.0% accommodation & food services (2000); Companies that employ more than 1,000 persons: 0 (2000); Companies that employ more than 100 persons: 2 (2000); Farms: 587 totaling 163,523 acres (1997); Minority business ownership rate: 0.0% (1997); Women business ownership rate: 23.1% (1997); Retail sales per capita: $5,611 (1997). Single-family building permits issued: 303 (2001) / 157 (2000); Multi-family building permits issued: 0 (2001) / 26 (2000).
Income: Per capita income: $17,848 (2000); Median household income: $31,139 (2000); Poverty rate: 11.6% (2000); Bankruptcy rate: 2.50% (2001).
Taxes: Total county taxes per capita: $430 (1997); County property taxes per capita: $423 (1997).
Education: High school graduation rate: 80.4% (2000); College graduation rate: 11.3% (2000).
Housing: Homeownership rate: 85.3% (2000); Median home value: $93,200 (2000); Median rent: $321 per month (2000); Median age of housing: 28 years (2000).
Health: Birth rate: 86.3 per 10,000 population (1998); Age adjusted death rate: 80.3 per 10,000 population (1999); Age adjusted cancer mortality rate: 184.2 deaths per 100,000 population (1999). Number of physicians: 6.5 per 10,000 population (1999); Number of hospital beds: 41.2 per 10,000 population (1999).
Elections: 2000 Presidential election results: 46.4% Gore, 45.5% Bush, 4.9% Nader, 2.7% Buchanan
National and State Parks: Cedar State Wildlife Management Area; Farm Island State Wildlife Management Area; Grayling State Wildlife Management Area; Hill River State Forest; Kimberly State Wildlife Management Area; Little Willow State Wildlife Management Area; Newstrom State Wildlife Management Area; Rice Lake National Wildlife Refuge; Ripple River State Wildlife Management Area; Salo Marsh State Wildlife Management Area; Savanna Portage State Park; Savanna State Forest; Solana State Forest; Swamp Lake State Wildlife Management Area; Wealthwood State Forest
Additional Information Contacts
Aitkin County Government Offices 218-927-7283
Aitkin Chamber of Commerce 218-927-2316
Mc Gregor Chamber of Commerce 218-768-3692

Aitkin County Communities

AITKIN (city). Covers a land area of 1.725 square miles and a water area of 0 square miles. Located at 46.53° N. Lat.; 93.70° W. Long. Elevation is 1,217 feet.
History: Aitkin developed as a shipping center for dairy products, turkeys, and fruit. The fertile soil in this region is attributed to the prehistoric Lake Aitkin, which covered a large area to the north and left many bogs and swamps behind when it disappeared.
Population: 1,984 (2000); Race: 98.1% White, 0.0% Black, 0.3% Asian, 0.1% American Indian and Alaska Native, 0.4% Hispanic of any race, 1.3% two or more races (2000); Density: 1,150.3 persons per square mile (2000); Age: 19.9% under 18, 34.3% over 64 (2000); Marriage status: 21.9% never married, 46.4% now married, 21.5% widowed, 10.3% divorced (2000); Foreign born: 0.7% (2000); Ancestry (includes multiple ancestries): 28.8% German, 15.9% Swedish, 13.4% Norwegian, 9.9% Irish, 7.2% English (2000).
Economy: Single-family building permits issued: 2 (2001) / 5 (2000); Multi-family building permits issued: 0 (2001) / 26 (2000); Employment by occupation: 11.0% management, 17.6% professional, 23.9% services, 24.1% sales, 0.6% farming, 7.3% construction, 15.5% production (2000).
Income: Per capita income: $17,471 (2000); Median household income: $24,574 (2000); Poverty rate: 14.2% (2000).
Taxes: Total city taxes per capita: $101 (1997); City property taxes per capita: $95 (1997).
Education: High school graduation rate: 74.7% (2000); College graduation rate: 14.6% (2000).

School District(s)

Aitkin (PK-12)
2000 Enrollment: 1,369 218-927-2115
Housing: Homeownership rate: 56.3% (2000); Median home value: $69,900 (2000); Median rent: $364 per month (2000); Median age of housing: 44 years (2000).
Hospitals: Riverwood HealthCare Center (36 beds)
Newspapers: Aitkin Independent Age (1 x week)
Transportation: Commute to work: 80.4% car, 0.0% public transportation, 12.7% walk, 6.3% work from home (2000); Travel time to work: 71.6% less than 15 minutes, 14.7% 15 to 30 minutes, 8.6% 30 to 45 minutes, 1.3% 45 to 60 minutes, 3.7% 60 minutes or more (2000)
Additional Information Contacts
Aitkin Chamber of Commerce 218-927-2316

AITKIN (township). Covers a land area of 32.462 square miles and a water area of 2.266 square miles. Located at 46.53° N. Lat.; 93.76° W. Long. Elevation is 1,217 feet.
History: Settled 1870.
Population: 642 (2000); Race: 98.8% White, 0.0% Black, 0.0% Asian, 1.2% American Indian and Alaska Native, 0.7% Hispanic of any race, 0.0% two or more races (2000); Density: 19.8 persons per square mile (2000); Age: 25.9% under 18, 16.9% over 64 (2000); Marriage status: 20.7% never married, 60.9% now married, 7.1% widowed, 11.2% divorced (2000); Foreign born: 0.3% (2000); Ancestry (includes multiple ancestries): 40.5% German, 13.2% Swedish, 13.2% Irish, 10.0% Norwegian, 8.5% French (except Basque) (2000).
Economy: Timber; hay; wild rice. Printing and publishing industries; manufactures concrete, wood containers. Resort area. Employment by occupation: 13.8% management, 17.2% professional, 17.5% services, 25.6% sales, 1.3% farming, 13.8% construction, 10.8% production (2000).
Income: Per capita income: $18,896 (2000); Median household income: $34,250 (2000); Poverty rate: 7.1% (2000).
Taxes: Total city taxes per capita: $64 (1997); City property taxes per capita: $64 (1997).
Education: High school graduation rate: 83.6% (2000); College graduation rate: 13.3% (2000).
Housing: Homeownership rate: 83.7% (2000); Median home value: $118,400 (2000); Median rent: $133 per month (2000); Median age of housing: 28 years (2000).
Transportation: Commute to work: 91.8% car, 0.0% public transportation, 0.7% walk, 6.5% work from home (2000); Travel time to work: 60.8% less than 15 minutes, 16.8% 15 to 30 minutes, 12.5% 30 to 45 minutes, 4.8% 45 to 60 minutes, 5.1% 60 minutes or more (2000)

BALL BLUFF (township). Covers a land area of 33.855 square miles and a water area of 1.419 square miles. Located at 46.99° N. Lat.; 93.26° W. Long. Elevation is 1,247 feet.
Population: 300 (2000); Race: 97.3% White, 0.3% Black, 0.0% Asian, 1.2% American Indian and Alaska Native, 0.0% Hispanic of any race, 1.2% two or more races (2000); Density: 8.9 persons per square mile (2000); Age: 21.6% under 18, 11.6% over 64 (2000); Marriage status: 26.1% never married, 60.4% now married, 1.9% widowed, 11.6% divorced (2000); Foreign born:

0.6% (2000); Ancestry (includes multiple ancestries): 36.9% German, 21.6% Swedish, 14.3% Finnish, 13.4% Norwegian, 8.5% English (2000).
Economy: Employment by occupation: 9.2% management, 10.6% professional, 10.6% services, 23.4% sales, 1.4% farming, 17.0% construction, 27.7% production (2000).
Income: Per capita income: $16,602 (2000); Median household income: $33,750 (2000); Poverty rate: 28.4% (2000).
Taxes: Total city taxes per capita: $49 (1997); City property taxes per capita: $49 (1997).
Education: High school graduation rate: 80.7% (2000); College graduation rate: 4.6% (2000).
Housing: Homeownership rate: 94.5% (2000); Median home value: $59,000 (2000); Median rent: $142 per month (2000); Median age of housing: 23 years (2000).
Transportation: Commute to work: 85.8% car, 1.4% public transportation, 0.0% walk, 9.9% work from home (2000); Travel time to work: 15.0% less than 15 minutes, 22.8% 15 to 30 minutes, 37.0% 30 to 45 minutes, 10.2% 45 to 60 minutes, 15.0% 60 minutes or more (2000)

BALSAM (township). Covers a land area of 36.089 square miles and a water area of 0.753 square miles. Located at 46.78° N. Lat.; 93.14° W. Long. Elevation is 1,238 feet.
Population: 34 (2000); Race: 100.0% White, 0.0% Black, 0.0% Asian, 0.0% American Indian and Alaska Native, 0.0% Hispanic of any race, 0.0% two or more races (2000); Density: 0.9 persons per square mile (2000); Age: 0.0% under 18, 40.9% over 64 (2000); Marriage status: 22.7% never married, 77.3% now married, 0.0% widowed, 0.0% divorced (2000); Foreign born: 0.0% (2000); Ancestry (includes multiple ancestries): 36.4% Swedish, 22.7% Scotch-Irish, 13.6% Norwegian, 9.1% German, 9.1% Danish (2000).
Economy: Employment by occupation: 0.0% management, 0.0% professional, 18.2% services, 63.6% sales, 0.0% farming, 0.0% construction, 18.2% production (2000).
Income: Per capita income: $8,973 (2000); Median household income: $18,250 (2000); Poverty rate: 13.6% (2000).
Taxes: Total city taxes per capita: $40 (1997); City property taxes per capita: $40 (1997).
Education: High school graduation rate: 86.4% (2000); College graduation rate: 13.6% (2000).
Housing: Homeownership rate: 80.0% (2000); Median home value: $95,000 (2000); Median rent: $425 per month (2000); Median age of housing: 29 years (2000).
Transportation: Commute to work: 100.0% car, 0.0% public transportation, 0.0% walk, 0.0% work from home (2000); Travel time to work: 18.2% less than 15 minutes, 18.2% 15 to 30 minutes, 63.6% 30 to 45 minutes, 0.0% 45 to 60 minutes, 0.0% 60 minutes or more (2000)

BEAVER (township). Covers a land area of 35.277 square miles and a water area of 0 square miles. Located at 46.43° N. Lat.; 93.14° W. Long.
Population: 76 (2000); Race: 97.7% White, 0.0% Black, 0.0% Asian, 2.3% American Indian and Alaska Native, 0.0% Hispanic of any race, 0.0% two or more races (2000); Density: 2.2 persons per square mile (2000); Age: 18.4% under 18, 11.5% over 64 (2000); Marriage status: 28.6% never married, 58.4% now married, 6.5% widowed, 6.5% divorced (2000); Foreign born: 0.0% (2000); Ancestry (includes multiple ancestries): 21.8% Finnish, 20.7% Norwegian, 17.2% Swedish, 17.2% German, 14.9% Irish (2000).
Economy: Employment by occupation: 7.5% management, 17.0% professional, 34.0% services, 15.1% sales, 3.8% farming, 3.8% construction, 18.9% production (2000).
Income: Per capita income: $15,039 (2000); Median household income: $30,000 (2000); Poverty rate: 10.3% (2000).
Taxes: Total city taxes per capita: $92 (1997); City property taxes per capita: $92 (1997).
Education: High school graduation rate: 85.9% (2000); College graduation rate: 15.6% (2000).
Housing: Homeownership rate: 84.2% (2000); Median home value: $112,500 (2000); Median rent: $325 per month (2000); Median age of housing: 30 years (2000).
Transportation: Commute to work: 79.2% car, 0.0% public transportation, 3.8% walk, 3.8% work from home (2000); Travel time to work: 25.5% less than 15 minutes, 72.5% 15 to 30 minutes, 0.0% 30 to 45 minutes, 2.0% 45 to 60 minutes, 0.0% 60 minutes or more (2000)

CLARK (township). Covers a land area of 31.699 square miles and a water area of 0.519 square miles. Located at 46.62° N. Lat.; 93.13° W. Long.
Population: 148 (2000); Race: 97.6% White, 0.0% Black, 0.0% Asian, 0.0% American Indian and Alaska Native, 0.8% Hispanic of any race, 2.4% two or more races (2000); Density: 4.7 persons per square mile (2000); Age: 14.2% under 18, 20.5% over 64 (2000); Marriage status: 19.6% never married, 60.7% now married, 11.6% widowed, 8.0% divorced (2000); Foreign born: 0.0% (2000); Ancestry (includes multiple ancestries): 40.9% German, 24.4% Finnish, 16.5% Swedish, 15.7% Norwegian, 11.8% French Canadian (2000).
Economy: Employment by occupation: 12.9% management, 8.1% professional, 17.7% services, 21.0% sales, 4.8% farming, 11.3% construction, 24.2% production (2000).
Income: Per capita income: $13,591 (2000); Median household income: $26,250 (2000); Poverty rate: 23.6% (2000).
Taxes: Total city taxes per capita: $42 (1997); City property taxes per capita: $42 (1997).
Education: High school graduation rate: 79.0% (2000); College graduation rate: 8.0% (2000).
Housing: Homeownership rate: 96.6% (2000); Median home value: $55,000 (2000); Median rent: $375 per month (2000); Median age of housing: 28 years (2000).
Transportation: Commute to work: 81.5% car, 0.0% public transportation, 0.0% walk, 18.5% work from home (2000); Travel time to work: 25.0% less than 15 minutes, 29.5% 15 to 30 minutes, 13.6% 30 to 45 minutes, 11.4% 45 to 60 minutes, 20.5% 60 minutes or more (2000)

CORNISH (township). Covers a land area of 34.330 square miles and a water area of 1.528 square miles. Located at 46.89° N. Lat.; 93.28° W. Long.
Population: 27 (2000); Race: 100.0% White, 0.0% Black, 0.0% Asian, 0.0% American Indian and Alaska Native, 0.0% Hispanic of any race, 0.0% two or more races (2000); Density: 0.8 persons per square mile (2000); Age: 0.0% under 18, 42.4% over 64 (2000); Marriage status: 9.1% never married, 69.7% now married, 9.1% widowed, 12.1% divorced (2000); Foreign born: 0.0% (2000); Ancestry (includes multiple ancestries): 57.6% German, 12.1% Finnish, 6.1% French (except Basque), 6.1% Irish, 3.0% Welsh (2000).
Economy: Employment by occupation: 0.0% management, 0.0% professional, 50.0% services, 0.0% sales, 0.0% farming, 25.0% construction, 25.0% production (2000).
Income: Per capita income: $16,188 (2000); Median household income: $28,500 (2000); Poverty rate: 0.0% (2000).
Taxes: Total city taxes per capita: $524 (1997); City property taxes per capita: $524 (1997).
Education: High school graduation rate: 82.8% (2000); College graduation rate: 3.4% (2000).
Housing: Homeownership rate: 100.0% (2000); Median age of housing: 22 years (2000).
Transportation: Commute to work: 75.0% car, 0.0% public transportation, 0.0% walk, 25.0% work from home (2000); Travel time to work: 0.0% less than 15 minutes, 0.0% 15 to 30 minutes, 33.3% 30 to 45 minutes, 33.3% 45 to 60 minutes, 33.3% 60 minutes or more (2000)

FARM ISLAND (township). Covers a land area of 28.065 square miles and a water area of 7.620 square miles. Located at 46.44° N. Lat.; 93.73° W. Long.
Population: 1,071 (2000); Race: 98.4% White, 0.0% Black, 0.5% Asian, 0.5% American Indian and Alaska Native, 0.8% Hispanic of any race, 0.0% two or more races (2000); Density: 38.2 persons per square mile (2000); Age: 22.6% under 18, 17.1% over 64 (2000); Marriage status: 14.7% never married, 71.1% now married, 5.0% widowed, 9.2% divorced (2000); Foreign born: 1.5% (2000); Ancestry (includes multiple ancestries): 41.9% German, 22.0% Norwegian, 15.7% Swedish, 10.3% Irish, 5.9% French (except Basque) (2000).
Economy: Employment by occupation: 10.5% management, 16.4% professional, 19.9% services, 24.3% sales, 1.1% farming, 11.4% construction, 16.4% production (2000).
Income: Per capita income: $20,067 (2000); Median household income: $40,882 (2000); Poverty rate: 7.0% (2000).
Taxes: Total city taxes per capita: $109 (2000); City property taxes per capita: $109 (2000).
Education: High school graduation rate: 86.0% (2000); College graduation rate: 13.1% (2000).
Housing: Homeownership rate: 93.0% (2000); Median home value: $127,400 (2000); Median rent: $513 per month (2000); Median age of housing: 18 years (2000).
Transportation: Commute to work: 88.5% car, 0.0% public transportation, 3.4% walk, 7.7% work from home (2000); Travel time to work: 41.2% less than 15 minutes, 27.1% 15 to 30 minutes, 16.6% 30 to 45 minutes, 6.8% 45 to 60 minutes, 8.3% 60 minutes or more (2000)

FLEMING (township). Covers a land area of 33.543 square miles and a water area of 2.645 square miles. Located at 46.63° N. Lat.; 93.51° W. Long.
Population: 327 (2000); Race: 98.9% White, 0.0% Black, 0.0% Asian, 0.6% American Indian and Alaska Native, 0.6% Hispanic of any race, 0.6% two or more races (2000); Density: 9.7 persons per square mile (2000); Age: 15.7% under 18, 26.2% over 64 (2000); Marriage status: 17.1% never married, 71.9% now married, 3.9% widowed, 7.1% divorced (2000); Foreign born: 0.9% (2000); Ancestry (includes multiple ancestries): 31.1% German, 15.7% Norwegian, 13.4% Irish, 12.0% Swedish, 8.8% English (2000).
Economy: Employment by occupation: 10.7% management, 13.2% professional, 25.8% services, 25.8% sales, 3.1% farming, 10.1% construction, 11.3% production (2000).
Income: Per capita income: $24,298 (2000); Median household income: $37,500 (2000); Poverty rate: 1.7% (2000).
Taxes: Total city taxes per capita: $177 (1997); City property taxes per capita: $177 (1997).
Education: High school graduation rate: 84.9% (2000); College graduation rate: 7.9% (2000).
Housing: Homeownership rate: 89.5% (2000); Median home value: $97,500 (2000); Median rent: $225 per month (2000); Median age of housing: 26 years (2000).
Transportation: Commute to work: 84.3% car, 0.0% public transportation, 3.9% walk, 7.8% work from home (2000); Travel time to work: 19.9% less than 15 minutes, 48.2% 15 to 30 minutes, 13.5% 30 to 45 minutes, 6.4% 45 to 60 minutes, 12.1% 60 minutes or more (2000)

GLEN (township). Covers a land area of 33.784 square miles and a water area of 2.813 square miles. Located at 46.45° N. Lat.; 93.49° W. Long. Elevation is 1,302 feet.
Population: 442 (2000); Race: 98.8% White, 0.0% Black, 1.2% Asian, 0.0% American Indian and Alaska Native, 0.0% Hispanic of any race, 0.0% two or more races (2000); Density: 13.1 persons per square mile (2000); Age: 20.0% under 18, 26.8% over 64 (2000); Marriage status: 9.9% never married, 73.5% now married, 8.1% widowed, 8.4% divorced (2000); Foreign born: 1.7% (2000); Ancestry (includes multiple ancestries): 38.0% German, 23.3% Swedish, 22.3% Norwegian, 8.6% Irish, 6.4% English (2000).
Economy: Employment by occupation: 22.9% management, 12.7% professional, 12.1% services, 21.0% sales, 3.2% farming, 10.8% construction, 17.2% production (2000).
Income: Per capita income: $21,908 (2000); Median household income: $32,500 (2000); Poverty rate: 6.5% (2000).
Taxes: Total city taxes per capita: $155 (1997); City property taxes per capita: $155 (1997).
Education: High school graduation rate: 79.9% (2000); College graduation rate: 10.1% (2000).
Housing: Homeownership rate: 93.7% (2000); Median home value: $120,800 (2000); Median rent: $250 per month (2000); Median age of housing: 30 years (2000).
Transportation: Commute to work: 88.2% car, 0.0% public transportation, 0.0% walk, 11.8% work from home (2000); Travel time to work: 12.6% less than 15 minutes, 43.0% 15 to 30 minutes, 21.5% 30 to 45 minutes, 11.9% 45 to 60 minutes, 11.1% 60 minutes or more (2000)

HAUGEN (township). Covers a land area of 35.748 square miles and a water area of 0.578 square miles. Located at 46.72° N. Lat.; 93.14° W. Long.
Population: 163 (2000); Race: 100.0% White, 0.0% Black, 0.0% Asian, 0.0% American Indian and Alaska Native, 0.0% Hispanic of any race, 0.0% two or more races (2000); Density: 4.6 persons per square mile (2000); Age: 2.5% under 18, 37.7% over 64 (2000); Marriage status: 4.2% never married, 74.8% now married, 12.6% widowed, 8.4% divorced (2000); Foreign born: 0.0% (2000); Ancestry (includes multiple ancestries): 19.7% German, 18.0% Norwegian, 15.6% Swedish, 15.6% Finnish, 10.7% Irish (2000).
Economy: Employment by occupation: 9.8% management, 24.6% professional, 31.1% services, 9.8% sales, 3.3% farming, 11.5% construction, 9.8% production (2000).
Income: Per capita income: $20,246 (2000); Median household income: $36,250 (2000); Poverty rate: 8.2% (2000).
Taxes: Total city taxes per capita: $117 (1997); City property taxes per capita: $117 (1997).
Education: High school graduation rate: 79.8% (2000); College graduation rate: 12.3% (2000).
Housing: Homeownership rate: 96.8% (2000); Median home value: $187,500 (2000); Median rent: $325 per month (2000); Median age of housing: 28 years (2000).
Transportation: Commute to work: 88.5% car, 0.0% public transportation, 3.3% walk, 8.2% work from home (2000); Travel time to work: 23.2% less than 15 minutes, 44.6% 15 to 30 minutes, 8.9% 30 to 45 minutes, 14.3% 45 to 60 minutes, 8.9% 60 minutes or more (2000)

HAZELTON (township). Covers a land area of 28.121 square miles and a water area of 42.653 square miles. Located at 46.36° N. Lat.; 93.77° W. Long.
Population: 712 (2000); Race: 94.4% White, 0.0% Black, 0.0% Asian, 4.7% American Indian and Alaska Native, 0.0% Hispanic of any race, 0.9% two or more races (2000); Density: 25.3 persons per square mile (2000); Age: 15.2% under 18, 29.1% over 64 (2000); Marriage status: 13.7% never married, 69.3% now married, 7.8% widowed, 9.2% divorced (2000); Foreign born: 0.4% (2000); Ancestry (includes multiple ancestries): 33.6% German, 20.6% Swedish, 18.6% Norwegian, 10.7% Irish, 6.4% English (2000).
Economy: Employment by occupation: 6.4% management, 12.7% professional, 24.7% services, 28.1% sales, 0.0% farming, 19.1% construction, 9.0% production (2000).
Income: Per capita income: $20,731 (2000); Median household income: $33,056 (2000); Poverty rate: 10.4% (2000).
Taxes: Total city taxes per capita: $255 (1997); City property taxes per capita: $255 (1997).
Education: High school graduation rate: 86.7% (2000); College graduation rate: 11.7% (2000).
Housing: Homeownership rate: 88.3% (2000); Median home value: $109,900 (2000); Median rent: $494 per month (2000); Median age of housing: 34 years (2000).
Transportation: Commute to work: 86.7% car, 0.0% public transportation, 7.6% walk, 5.7% work from home (2000); Travel time to work: 25.8% less than 15 minutes, 38.3% 15 to 30 minutes, 20.2% 30 to 45 minutes, 7.3% 45 to 60 minutes, 8.5% 60 minutes or more (2000)

HILL CITY (city). Covers a land area of 1.086 square miles and a water area of 0.237 square miles. Located at 46.98° N. Lat.; 93.59° W. Long. Elevation is 1,357 feet.
Population: 479 (2000); Race: 96.0% White, 0.4% Black, 0.0% Asian, 3.5% American Indian and Alaska Native, 1.1% Hispanic of any race, 0.0% two or more races (2000); Density: 441.1 persons per square mile (2000); Age: 18.9% under 18, 14.3% over 64 (2000); Marriage status: 23.9% never married, 48.1% now married, 11.4% widowed, 16.6% divorced (2000); Foreign born: 0.4% (2000); Ancestry (includes multiple ancestries): 28.8% German, 13.6% Norwegian, 9.5% Irish, 7.9% Swedish, 6.6% Other groups (2000).
Economy: Alfalfa, hay, wild rice. Manufacturing: machinery, building materials. Single-family building permits issued: 1 (2001) / 1 (2000); Multi-family building permits issued: 0 (2001) / 0 (2000); Employment by occupation: 7.7% management, 3.6% professional, 20.4% services, 35.2% sales, 0.0% farming, 11.7% construction, 21.4% production (2000).
Income: Per capita income: $15,742 (2000); Median household income: $22,308 (2000); Poverty rate: 14.8% (2000).
Taxes: Total city taxes per capita: $379 (1997); City property taxes per capita: $340 (1997).
Education: High school graduation rate: 82.6% (2000); College graduation rate: 9.7% (2000).

School District(s)

Hill City (PK-12)
2000 Enrollment: 376 218-697-2394

Housing: Homeownership rate: 72.7% (2000); Median home value: $39,200 (2000); Median rent: $318 per month (2000); Median age of housing: 28 years (2000).
Transportation: Commute to work: 88.2% car, 0.0% public transportation, 9.6% walk, 2.1% work from home (2000); Travel time to work: 39.3% less than 15 minutes, 35.0% 15 to 30 minutes, 20.8% 30 to 45 minutes, 4.9% 45 to 60 minutes, 0.0% 60 minutes or more (2000)

HILL LAKE (township). Covers a land area of 33.374 square miles and a water area of 1.212 square miles. Located at 46.97° N. Lat.; 93.61° W. Long.
Population: 447 (2000); Race: 97.4% White, 0.0% Black, 0.0% Asian, 1.5% American Indian and Alaska Native, 0.4% Hispanic of any race, 1.1% two or more races (2000); Density: 13.4 persons per square mile (2000); Age: 25.6% under 18, 16.1% over 64 (2000); Marriage status: 22.8% never married, 66.1% now married, 4.1% widowed, 7.0% divorced (2000); Foreign born: 0.4% (2000); Ancestry (includes multiple ancestries): 27.3% German, 11.7% Norwegian, 9.3% Swedish, 7.4% Irish, 5.0% Polish (2000).

Economy: Employment by occupation: 14.4% management, 20.2% professional, 16.8% services, 16.8% sales, 1.0% farming, 15.9% construction, 14.9% production (2000).
Income: Per capita income: $16,915 (2000); Median household income: $40,000 (2000); Poverty rate: 5.4% (2000).
Taxes: Total city taxes per capita: $55 (1997); City property taxes per capita: $55 (1997).
Education: High school graduation rate: 88.5% (2000); College graduation rate: 17.0% (2000).
Housing: Homeownership rate: 93.7% (2000); Median home value: $106,700 (2000); Median rent: $275 per month (2000); Median age of housing: 27 years (2000).
Transportation: Commute to work: 90.0% car, 0.0% public transportation, 3.3% walk, 4.3% work from home (2000); Travel time to work: 25.9% less than 15 minutes, 37.3% 15 to 30 minutes, 21.4% 30 to 45 minutes, 9.0% 45 to 60 minutes, 6.5% 60 minutes or more (2000)

IDUN (township). Covers a land area of 36.617 square miles and a water area of 0.608 square miles. Located at 46.22° N. Lat.; 93.37° W. Long.
Population: 235 (2000); Race: 97.9% White, 0.0% Black, 0.0% Asian, 0.0% American Indian and Alaska Native, 3.1% Hispanic of any race, 2.1% two or more races (2000); Density: 6.4 persons per square mile (2000); Age: 28.9% under 18, 16.0% over 64 (2000); Marriage status: 25.3% never married, 63.3% now married, 3.6% widowed, 7.7% divorced (2000); Foreign born: 0.0% (2000); Ancestry (includes multiple ancestries): 27.2% German, 16.7% Norwegian, 13.9% Polish, 11.1% Irish, 7.7% Swedish (2000).
Economy: Employment by occupation: 5.6% management, 15.9% professional, 9.5% services, 25.4% sales, 1.6% farming, 10.3% construction, 31.7% production (2000).
Income: Per capita income: $15,193 (2000); Median household income: $29,063 (2000); Poverty rate: 13.3% (2000).
Taxes: Total city taxes per capita: $94 (1997); City property taxes per capita: $94 (1997).
Education: High school graduation rate: 72.7% (2000); College graduation rate: 12.8% (2000).
Housing: Homeownership rate: 98.0% (2000); Median home value: $55,000 (2000); Median age of housing: 33 years (2000).
Transportation: Commute to work: 87.7% car, 0.0% public transportation, 0.0% walk, 12.3% work from home (2000); Travel time to work: 22.4% less than 15 minutes, 22.4% 15 to 30 minutes, 30.8% 30 to 45 minutes, 8.4% 45 to 60 minutes, 15.9% 60 minutes or more (2000)

JACOBSON (unincorporated postal area, zip code 55752). Covers a land area of 171.279 square miles and a water area of 2.318 square miles. Located at 46.97° N. Lat.; 93.26° W. Long. Elevation is 1,255 feet.
Population: 390 (2000); Race: 97.1% White, 0.2% Black, 0.0% Asian, 1.7% American Indian and Alaska Native, 0.0% Hispanic of any race, 1.0% two or more races (2000); Density: 2.3 persons per square mile (2000); Age: 17.3% under 18, 15.6% over 64 (2000); Marriage status: 23.1% never married, 62.4% now married, 2.8% widowed, 11.7% divorced (2000); Foreign born: 0.5% (2000); Ancestry (includes multiple ancestries): 38.9% German, 20.9% Swedish, 14.1% Norwegian, 12.4% Finnish, 10.2% English (2000).
Economy: Employment by occupation: 8.7% management, 10.5% professional, 12.8% services, 23.8% sales, 3.5% farming, 15.7% construction, 25.0% production (2000).
Income: Per capita income: $16,833 (2000); Median household income: $32,143 (2000); Poverty rate: 24.1% (2000).
Education: High school graduation rate: 81.7% (2000); College graduation rate: 6.0% (2000).
Housing: Homeownership rate: 94.7% (2000); Median home value: $65,000 (2000); Median rent: $142 per month (2000); Median age of housing: 23 years (2000).
Transportation: Commute to work: 77.9% car, 1.2% public transportation, 3.5% walk, 15.1% work from home (2000); Travel time to work: 15.8% less than 15 minutes, 21.2% 15 to 30 minutes, 34.9% 30 to 45 minutes, 13.7% 45 to 60 minutes, 14.4% 60 minutes or more (2000)

JEVNE (township). Covers a land area of 34.117 square miles and a water area of 1.743 square miles. Located at 46.64° N. Lat.; 93.37° W. Long.
Population: 321 (2000); Race: 99.0% White, 0.0% Black, 1.0% Asian, 0.0% American Indian and Alaska Native, 0.0% Hispanic of any race, 0.0% two or more races (2000); Density: 9.4 persons per square mile (2000); Age: 25.8% under 18, 20.6% over 64 (2000); Marriage status: 14.2% never married, 66.1% now married, 6.9% widowed, 12.9% divorced (2000); Foreign born: 2.1% (2000); Ancestry (includes multiple ancestries): 33.3% German, 15.1% Swedish, 12.7% Norwegian, 12.4% Irish, 5.8% English (2000).
Economy: Employment by occupation: 7.1% management, 18.8% professional, 16.1% services, 21.4% sales, 4.5% farming, 12.5% construction, 19.6% production (2000).
Income: Per capita income: $15,689 (2000); Median household income: $33,333 (2000); Poverty rate: 15.9% (2000).
Taxes: Total city taxes per capita: $102 (1997); City property taxes per capita: $102 (1997).
Education: High school graduation rate: 69.1% (2000); College graduation rate: 8.2% (2000).
Housing: Homeownership rate: 93.6% (2000); Median home value: $96,400 (2000); Median rent: $308 per month (2000); Median age of housing: 25 years (2000).
Transportation: Commute to work: 91.7% car, 0.0% public transportation, 2.8% walk, 1.9% work from home (2000); Travel time to work: 52.8% less than 15 minutes, 25.5% 15 to 30 minutes, 6.6% 30 to 45 minutes, 5.7% 45 to 60 minutes, 9.4% 60 minutes or more (2000)

KIMBERLY (township). Covers a land area of 35.905 square miles and a water area of 1.113 square miles. Located at 46.55° N. Lat.; 93.49° W. Long. Elevation is 1,240 feet.
Population: 245 (2000); Race: 98.2% White, 1.8% Black, 0.0% Asian, 0.0% American Indian and Alaska Native, 0.0% Hispanic of any race, 0.0% two or more races (2000); Density: 6.8 persons per square mile (2000); Age: 19.8% under 18, 20.3% over 64 (2000); Marriage status: 18.7% never married, 65.8% now married, 6.7% widowed, 8.8% divorced (2000); Foreign born: 0.0% (2000); Ancestry (includes multiple ancestries): 28.2% German, 22.9% Norwegian, 14.5% Irish, 11.9% United States or American, 9.7% Swedish (2000).
Economy: Employment by occupation: 10.7% management, 0.0% professional, 20.4% services, 24.3% sales, 0.0% farming, 12.6% construction, 32.0% production (2000).
Income: Per capita income: $16,161 (2000); Median household income: $32,500 (2000); Poverty rate: 15.4% (2000).
Taxes: Total city taxes per capita: $155 (1997); City property taxes per capita: $155 (1997).
Education: High school graduation rate: 88.3% (2000); College graduation rate: 8.2% (2000).
Housing: Homeownership rate: 94.8% (2000); Median home value: $92,500 (2000); Median rent: $325 per month (2000); Median age of housing: 39 years (2000).
Transportation: Commute to work: 87.4% car, 0.0% public transportation, 1.9% walk, 7.8% work from home (2000); Travel time to work: 20.0% less than 15 minutes, 46.3% 15 to 30 minutes, 24.2% 30 to 45 minutes, 7.4% 45 to 60 minutes, 2.1% 60 minutes or more (2000)

LAKESIDE (township). Covers a land area of 29.093 square miles and a water area of 7.766 square miles. Located at 46.28° N. Lat.; 93.52° W. Long.
Population: 495 (2000); Race: 96.2% White, 0.0% Black, 2.2% Asian, 0.0% American Indian and Alaska Native, 0.6% Hispanic of any race, 1.0% two or more races (2000); Density: 17.0 persons per square mile (2000); Age: 11.5% under 18, 28.8% over 64 (2000); Marriage status: 15.1% never married, 65.1% now married, 7.3% widowed, 12.5% divorced (2000); Foreign born: 3.6% (2000); Ancestry (includes multiple ancestries): 40.2% German, 22.1% Swedish, 14.5% Irish, 11.5% Norwegian, 5.6% English (2000).
Economy: Employment by occupation: 21.6% management, 4.1% professional, 19.6% services, 24.2% sales, 2.6% farming, 11.3% construction, 16.5% production (2000).
Income: Per capita income: $19,908 (2000); Median household income: $28,462 (2000); Poverty rate: 9.3% (2000).
Taxes: Total city taxes per capita: $117 (1997); City property taxes per capita: $117 (1997).
Education: High school graduation rate: 78.2% (2000); College graduation rate: 9.9% (2000).
Housing: Homeownership rate: 93.8% (2000); Median home value: $129,200 (2000); Median rent: $200 per month (2000); Median age of housing: 24 years (2000).
Transportation: Commute to work: 89.4% car, 0.0% public transportation, 3.2% walk, 7.4% work from home (2000); Travel time to work: 20.1% less than 15 minutes, 32.8% 15 to 30 minutes, 19.5% 30 to 45 minutes, 12.6% 45 to 60 minutes, 14.9% 60 minutes or more (2000)

LEE (township). Covers a land area of 34.469 square miles and a water area of 1.204 square miles. Located at 46.49° N. Lat.; 93.35° W. Long.
Population: 54 (2000); Race: 100.0% White, 0.0% Black, 0.0% Asian, 0.0% American Indian and Alaska Native, 0.0% Hispanic of any race, 0.0% two or more races (2000); Density: 1.6 persons per square mile (2000); Age: 25.0%

under 18, 10.3% over 64 (2000); Marriage status: 9.3% never married, 85.2% now married, 0.0% widowed, 5.6% divorced (2000); Foreign born: 5.9% (2000); Ancestry (includes multiple ancestries): 26.5% German, 22.1% Norwegian, 16.2% Swedish, 10.3% English, 8.8% United States or American (2000).
Economy: Employment by occupation: 14.3% management, 17.9% professional, 32.1% services, 35.7% sales, 0.0% farming, 0.0% construction, 0.0% production (2000).
Income: Per capita income: $19,319 (2000); Median household income: $28,750 (2000); Poverty rate: 5.9% (2000).
Education: High school graduation rate: 87.8% (2000); College graduation rate: 6.1% (2000).
Housing: Homeownership rate: 92.0% (2000); Median home value: $162,500 (2000); Median age of housing: 27 years (2000).
Transportation: Commute to work: 100.0% car, 0.0% public transportation, 0.0% walk, 0.0% work from home (2000); Travel time to work: 24.0% less than 15 minutes, 28.0% 15 to 30 minutes, 40.0% 30 to 45 minutes, 0.0% 45 to 60 minutes, 8.0% 60 minutes or more (2000)

LIBBY (township). Covers a land area of 34.676 square miles and a water area of 1.432 square miles. Located at 46.79° N. Lat.; 93.35° W. Long. Elevation is 1,229 feet.
Population: 47 (2000); Race: 100.0% White, 0.0% Black, 0.0% Asian, 0.0% American Indian and Alaska Native, 0.0% Hispanic of any race, 0.0% two or more races (2000); Density: 1.4 persons per square mile (2000); Age: 3.6% under 18, 32.1% over 64 (2000); Marriage status: 11.1% never married, 66.7% now married, 7.4% widowed, 14.8% divorced (2000); Foreign born: 0.0% (2000); Ancestry (includes multiple ancestries): 53.6% German, 35.7% Norwegian, 25.0% English, 10.7% Irish, 7.1% Scotch-Irish (2000).
Economy: Employment by occupation: 0.0% management, 20.0% professional, 50.0% services, 20.0% sales, 10.0% farming, 0.0% construction, 0.0% production (2000).
Income: Per capita income: $25,971 (2000); Median household income: $23,750 (2000); Poverty rate: 21.4% (2000).
Taxes: Total city taxes per capita: $250 (1997); City property taxes per capita: $250 (1997).
Education: High school graduation rate: 77.8% (2000); College graduation rate: 37.0% (2000).
Housing: Homeownership rate: 100.0% (2000); Median home value: $47,500 (2000); Median age of housing: 52 years (2000).
Transportation: Commute to work: 80.0% car, 0.0% public transportation, 0.0% walk, 20.0% work from home (2000); Travel time to work: 12.5% less than 15 minutes, 87.5% 15 to 30 minutes, 0.0% 30 to 45 minutes, 0.0% 45 to 60 minutes, 0.0% 60 minutes or more (2000)

LOGAN (township). Covers a land area of 35.162 square miles and a water area of 0.554 square miles. Located at 46.71° N. Lat.; 93.48° W. Long.
Population: 231 (2000); Race: 98.0% White, 0.8% Black, 0.0% Asian, 0.0% American Indian and Alaska Native, 3.1% Hispanic of any race, 1.2% two or more races (2000); Density: 6.6 persons per square mile (2000); Age: 22.4% under 18, 20.5% over 64 (2000); Marriage status: 24.6% never married, 57.3% now married, 10.0% widowed, 8.1% divorced (2000); Foreign born: 0.0% (2000); Ancestry (includes multiple ancestries): 29.5% German, 16.1% Swedish, 13.0% Norwegian, 7.9% English, 6.3% Yugoslavian (2000).
Economy: Employment by occupation: 9.7% management, 12.6% professional, 23.3% services, 16.5% sales, 3.9% farming, 12.6% construction, 21.4% production (2000).
Income: Per capita income: $15,404 (2000); Median household income: $34,444 (2000); Poverty rate: 10.8% (2000).
Taxes: Total city taxes per capita: $94 (1997); City property taxes per capita: $94 (1997).
Education: High school graduation rate: 74.3% (2000); College graduation rate: 5.3% (2000).
Housing: Homeownership rate: 100.0% (2000); Median home value: $77,900 (2000); Median age of housing: 23 years (2000).
Transportation: Commute to work: 85.4% car, 0.0% public transportation, 6.8% walk, 5.8% work from home (2000); Travel time to work: 30.9% less than 15 minutes, 20.6% 15 to 30 minutes, 33.0% 30 to 45 minutes, 0.0% 45 to 60 minutes, 15.5% 60 minutes or more (2000)

MACVILLE (township). Covers a land area of 36.174 square miles and a water area of 0.314 square miles. Located at 46.89° N. Lat.; 93.64° W. Long.
Population: 204 (2000); Race: 98.2% White, 0.0% Black, 0.0% Asian, 1.8% American Indian and Alaska Native, 0.9% Hispanic of any race, 0.0% two or more races (2000); Density: 5.6 persons per square mile (2000); Age: 33.5% under 18, 11.3% over 64 (2000); Marriage status: 27.8% never married, 56.2% now married, 5.9% widowed, 10.1% divorced (2000); Foreign born: 0.0% (2000); Ancestry (includes multiple ancestries): 23.1% German, 11.8% Norwegian, 11.8% Polish, 11.8% English, 11.3% Swedish (2000).
Economy: Employment by occupation: 5.1% management, 8.9% professional, 20.3% services, 22.8% sales, 3.8% farming, 10.1% construction, 29.1% production (2000).
Income: Per capita income: $13,859 (2000); Median household income: $28,750 (2000); Poverty rate: 28.5% (2000).
Taxes: Total city taxes per capita: $54 (1997); City property taxes per capita: $54 (1997).
Education: High school graduation rate: 77.7% (2000); College graduation rate: 3.8% (2000).
Housing: Homeownership rate: 94.7% (2000); Median home value: $20,000 (2000); Median age of housing: 36 years (2000).
Transportation: Commute to work: 82.3% car, 0.0% public transportation, 5.1% walk, 5.1% work from home (2000); Travel time to work: 30.7% less than 15 minutes, 6.7% 15 to 30 minutes, 44.0% 30 to 45 minutes, 10.7% 45 to 60 minutes, 8.0% 60 minutes or more (2000)

MALMO (township). Covers a land area of 32.955 square miles and a water area of 2.749 square miles. Located at 46.36° N. Lat.; 93.50° W. Long. Elevation is 1,260 feet.
Population: 332 (2000); Race: 91.6% White, 0.0% Black, 0.0% Asian, 6.8% American Indian and Alaska Native, 0.0% Hispanic of any race, 1.6% two or more races (2000); Density: 10.1 persons per square mile (2000); Age: 21.4% under 18, 20.8% over 64 (2000); Marriage status: 19.0% never married, 70.4% now married, 6.3% widowed, 4.3% divorced (2000); Foreign born: 0.6% (2000); Ancestry (includes multiple ancestries): 32.8% German, 26.6% Swedish, 11.0% Norwegian, 7.8% Irish, 7.1% United States or American (2000).
Economy: Employment by occupation: 9.6% management, 8.1% professional, 12.5% services, 23.5% sales, 2.2% farming, 22.8% construction, 21.3% production (2000).
Income: Per capita income: $16,737 (2000); Median household income: $31,161 (2000); Poverty rate: 9.2% (2000).
Taxes: Total city taxes per capita: $118 (1997); City property taxes per capita: $118 (1997).
Education: High school graduation rate: 83.0% (2000); College graduation rate: 8.0% (2000).
Housing: Homeownership rate: 92.2% (2000); Median home value: $80,000 (2000); Median rent: $375 per month (2000); Median age of housing: 30 years (2000).
Transportation: Commute to work: 88.1% car, 0.0% public transportation, 0.0% walk, 11.9% work from home (2000); Travel time to work: 20.7% less than 15 minutes, 41.4% 15 to 30 minutes, 20.7% 30 to 45 minutes, 11.7% 45 to 60 minutes, 5.4% 60 minutes or more (2000)

MCGRATH (city). Covers a land area of 0.371 square miles and a water area of 0 square miles. Located at 46.24° N. Lat.; 93.27° W. Long. Elevation is 1,240 feet.
Population: 65 (2000); Race: 98.2% White, 0.0% Black, 0.0% Asian, 0.0% American Indian and Alaska Native, 0.0% Hispanic of any race, 1.8% two or more races (2000); Density: 175.1 persons per square mile (2000); Age: 34.5% under 18, 1.8% over 64 (2000); Marriage status: 34.1% never married, 46.3% now married, 7.3% widowed, 12.2% divorced (2000); Foreign born: 0.0% (2000); Ancestry (includes multiple ancestries): 72.7% German, 18.2% Norwegian, 12.7% Danish, 7.3% English, 5.5% Czech (2000).
Economy: Employment by occupation: 17.2% management, 13.8% professional, 37.9% services, 0.0% sales, 0.0% farming, 17.2% construction, 13.8% production (2000).
Income: Per capita income: $9,540 (2000); Median household income: $24,250 (2000); Poverty rate: 12.7% (2000).
Taxes: Total city taxes per capita: $57 (1997); City property taxes per capita: $43 (1997).
Education: High school graduation rate: 81.8% (2000); College graduation rate: 12.1% (2000).
Housing: Homeownership rate: 72.0% (2000); Median home value: $70,000 (2000); Median rent: $275 per month (2000); Median age of housing: 35 years (2000).
Transportation: Commute to work: 72.4% car, 0.0% public transportation, 10.3% walk, 17.2% work from home (2000); Travel time to work: 33.3% less than 15 minutes, 8.3% 15 to 30 minutes, 29.2% 30 to 45 minutes, 8.3% 45 to 60 minutes, 20.8% 60 minutes or more (2000)

MCGREGOR (city). Covers a land area of 1.966 square miles and a water area of 0.126 square miles. Located at 46.60° N. Lat.; 93.30° W. Long. Elevation is 1,233 feet.
Population: 404 (2000); Race: 96.3% White, 0.0% Black, 0.0% Asian, 2.8% American Indian and Alaska Native, 0.2% Hispanic of any race, 0.7% two or more races (2000); Density: 205.5 persons per square mile (2000); Age: 21.3% under 18, 22.7% over 64 (2000); Marriage status: 24.2% never married, 54.7% now married, 9.4% widowed, 11.7% divorced (2000); Foreign born: 0.5% (2000); Ancestry (includes multiple ancestries): 32.3% German, 16.2% Norwegian, 12.5% Finnish, 9.0% Swedish, 7.7% Irish (2000).
Economy: Single-family building permits issued: 1 (2001) / 1 (2000); Multi-family building permits issued: 0 (2001) / 0 (2000); Employment by occupation: 6.6% management, 24.7% professional, 24.7% services, 14.6% sales, 0.0% farming, 4.0% construction, 25.3% production (2000).
Income: Per capita income: $13,167 (2000); Median household income: $24,318 (2000); Poverty rate: 13.7% (2000).
Taxes: Total city taxes per capita: $163 (1997); City property taxes per capita: $148 (1997).
Education: High school graduation rate: 65.6% (2000); College graduation rate: 7.9% (2000).

School District(s)

Mcgregor (PK-12)
2000 Enrollment: 546 218-768-2111

Housing: Homeownership rate: 56.7% (2000); Median home value: $57,300 (2000); Median rent: $252 per month (2000); Median age of housing: 33 years (2000).
Transportation: Commute to work: 75.3% car, 0.0% public transportation, 14.2% walk, 10.5% work from home (2000); Travel time to work: 67.6% less than 15 minutes, 7.6% 15 to 30 minutes, 18.8% 30 to 45 minutes, 1.8% 45 to 60 minutes, 4.1% 60 minutes or more (2000)
Additional Information Contacts
Mc Gregor Chamber of Commerce 218-768-3692

MCGREGOR (township). Covers a land area of 32.721 square miles and a water area of 1.491 square miles. Located at 46.62° N. Lat.; 93.26° W. Long. Elevation is 1,233 feet.
History: Sandy Lake Fur Post (1794) to North.
Population: 116 (2000); Race: 96.3% White, 0.0% Black, 0.0% Asian, 3.7% American Indian and Alaska Native, 0.0% Hispanic of any race, 0.0% two or more races (2000); Density: 3.5 persons per square mile (2000); Age: 20.4% under 18, 13.9% over 64 (2000); Marriage status: 27.4% never married, 52.6% now married, 10.5% widowed, 9.5% divorced (2000); Foreign born: 0.0% (2000); Ancestry (includes multiple ancestries): 12.0% German, 10.2% Irish, 8.3% Norwegian, 7.4% French (except Basque), 7.4% Finnish (2000).
Economy: Manufacturing: motor vehicle parts, wood products, machinery. Rice Lake National Wildlife Refuge to South. Employment by occupation: 25.7% management, 8.6% professional, 22.9% services, 11.4% sales, 0.0% farming, 14.3% construction, 17.1% production (2000).
Income: Per capita income: $13,003 (2000); Median household income: $28,542 (2000); Poverty rate: 0.0% (2000).
Taxes: Total city taxes per capita: $52 (1997); City property taxes per capita: $52 (1997).
Education: High school graduation rate: 63.2% (2000); College graduation rate: 6.6% (2000).
Housing: Homeownership rate: 91.5% (2000); Median home value: $153,100 (2000); Median age of housing: 23 years (2000).
Transportation: Commute to work: 88.6% car, 0.0% public transportation, 5.7% walk, 5.7% work from home (2000); Travel time to work: 72.7% less than 15 minutes, 9.1% 15 to 30 minutes, 9.1% 30 to 45 minutes, 9.1% 45 to 60 minutes, 0.0% 60 minutes or more (2000)

MILLWARD (township). Covers a land area of 71.350 square miles and a water area of 0.049 square miles. Located at 46.36° N. Lat.; 93.12° W. Long.
Population: 69 (2000); Race: 85.0% White, 8.3% Black, 0.0% Asian, 3.3% American Indian and Alaska Native, 0.0% Hispanic of any race, 3.3% two or more races (2000); Density: 1.0 persons per square mile (2000); Age: 10.0% under 18, 20.0% over 64 (2000); Marriage status: 9.1% never married, 74.5% now married, 0.0% widowed, 16.4% divorced (2000); Foreign born: 11.7% (2000); Ancestry (includes multiple ancestries): 26.7% German, 25.0% Norwegian, 11.7% Jamaican, 8.3% French (except Basque), 8.3% Other groups (2000).
Economy: Employment by occupation: 12.9% management, 12.9% professional, 12.9% services, 25.8% sales, 3.2% farming, 16.1% construction, 16.1% production (2000).
Income: Per capita income: $14,060 (2000); Median household income: $21,250 (2000); Poverty rate: 16.7% (2000).
Taxes: Total city taxes per capita: $174 (1997); City property taxes per capita: $174 (1997).
Education: High school graduation rate: 71.2% (2000); College graduation rate: 7.7% (2000).
Housing: Homeownership rate: 100.0% (2000); Median age of housing: 19 years (2000).
Transportation: Commute to work: 100.0% car, 0.0% public transportation, 0.0% walk, 0.0% work from home (2000); Travel time to work: 12.9% less than 15 minutes, 25.8% 15 to 30 minutes, 38.7% 30 to 45 minutes, 6.5% 45 to 60 minutes, 16.1% 60 minutes or more (2000)

MORRISON (township). Covers a land area of 35.985 square miles and a water area of 0.696 square miles. Located at 46.64° N. Lat.; 93.61° W. Long.
Population: 186 (2000); Race: 92.6% White, 1.9% Black, 0.0% Asian, 3.1% American Indian and Alaska Native, 0.0% Hispanic of any race, 0.0% two or more races (2000); Density: 5.2 persons per square mile (2000); Age: 27.8% under 18, 18.5% over 64 (2000); Marriage status: 16.4% never married, 66.4% now married, 0.0% widowed, 17.2% divorced (2000); Foreign born: 0.0% (2000); Ancestry (includes multiple ancestries): 22.8% German, 17.3% Irish, 14.8% United States or American, 13.0% Swedish, 8.0% Norwegian (2000).
Economy: Employment by occupation: 9.3% management, 12.0% professional, 16.0% services, 29.3% sales, 0.0% farming, 9.3% construction, 24.0% production (2000).
Income: Per capita income: $13,984 (2000); Median household income: $25,750 (2000); Poverty rate: 15.4% (2000).
Taxes: Total city taxes per capita: $90 (1997); City property taxes per capita: $90 (1997).
Education: High school graduation rate: 78.1% (2000); College graduation rate: 6.1% (2000).
Housing: Homeownership rate: 83.6% (2000); Median home value: $65,000 (2000); Median age of housing: 40 years (2000).
Transportation: Commute to work: 86.7% car, 2.7% public transportation, 4.0% walk, 6.7% work from home (2000); Travel time to work: 21.4% less than 15 minutes, 44.3% 15 to 30 minutes, 12.9% 30 to 45 minutes, 15.7% 45 to 60 minutes, 5.7% 60 minutes or more (2000)

NORDLAND (township). Covers a land area of 31.258 square miles and a water area of 5.418 square miles. Located at 46.47° N. Lat.; 93.62° W. Long.
Population: 853 (2000); Race: 97.3% White, 0.0% Black, 0.3% Asian, 2.0% American Indian and Alaska Native, 0.0% Hispanic of any race, 0.3% two or more races (2000); Density: 27.3 persons per square mile (2000); Age: 17.7% under 18, 23.6% over 64 (2000); Marriage status: 10.6% never married, 76.5% now married, 5.8% widowed, 7.1% divorced (2000); Foreign born: 0.6% (2000); Ancestry (includes multiple ancestries): 38.7% German, 25.0% Norwegian, 19.2% Swedish, 9.7% Irish, 8.3% English (2000).
Economy: Employment by occupation: 9.0% management, 15.5% professional, 17.7% services, 29.3% sales, 0.8% farming, 16.3% construction, 11.3% production (2000).
Income: Per capita income: $18,742 (2000); Median household income: $41,172 (2000); Poverty rate: 7.6% (2000).
Taxes: Total city taxes per capita: $35 (1997); City property taxes per capita: $35 (1997).
Education: High school graduation rate: 88.7% (2000); College graduation rate: 15.0% (2000).
Housing: Homeownership rate: 92.7% (2000); Median home value: $124,000 (2000); Median rent: $525 per month (2000); Median age of housing: 24 years (2000).
Transportation: Commute to work: 90.4% car, 0.0% public transportation, 1.4% walk, 7.5% work from home (2000); Travel time to work: 32.9% less than 15 minutes, 43.3% 15 to 30 minutes, 14.1% 30 to 45 minutes, 5.3% 45 to 60 minutes, 4.4% 60 minutes or more (2000)

PALISADE (city). Covers a land area of 0.454 square miles and a water area of 0 square miles. Located at 46.71° N. Lat.; 93.48° W. Long.
Population: 118 (2000); Race: 100.0% White, 0.0% Black, 0.0% Asian, 0.0% American Indian and Alaska Native, 0.0% Hispanic of any race, 0.0% two or more races (2000); Density: 259.9 persons per square mile (2000); Age: 20.3% under 18, 26.6% over 64 (2000); Marriage status: 24.5% never married, 56.6% now married, 13.2% widowed, 5.7% divorced (2000);

Foreign born: 0.0% (2000); Ancestry (includes multiple ancestries): 15.6% German, 14.1% Swedish, 12.5% Norwegian, 7.8% Irish, 6.3% French (except Basque) (2000).
Economy: Manufacturing: industrial furnaces. Employment by occupation: 0.0% management, 0.0% professional, 0.0% services, 61.1% sales, 0.0% farming, 0.0% construction, 38.9% production (2000).
Income: Per capita income: $11,702 (2000); Median household income: $27,083 (2000); Poverty rate: 12.5% (2000).
Taxes: Total city taxes per capita: $76 (2000); City property taxes per capita: $68 (2000).
Education: High school graduation rate: 60.5% (2000); College graduation rate: 0.0% (2000).
Housing: Homeownership rate: 88.9% (2000); Median home value: $61,300 (2000); Median age of housing: 22 years (2000).
Transportation: Commute to work: 77.8% car, 22.2% public transportation, 0.0% walk, 0.0% work from home (2000); Travel time to work: 44.4% less than 15 minutes, 27.8% 15 to 30 minutes, 0.0% 30 to 45 minutes, 27.8% 45 to 60 minutes, 0.0% 60 minutes or more (2000)

PLINY (township). Covers a land area of 36.375 square miles and a water area of 0.040 square miles. Located at 46.27° N. Lat.; 93.26° W. Long.
Population: 120 (2000); Race: 100.0% White, 0.0% Black, 0.0% Asian, 0.0% American Indian and Alaska Native, 1.7% Hispanic of any race, 0.0% two or more races (2000); Density: 3.3 persons per square mile (2000); Age: 31.7% under 18, 15.0% over 64 (2000); Marriage status: 37.1% never married, 38.1% now married, 10.3% widowed, 14.4% divorced (2000); Foreign born: 0.0% (2000); Ancestry (includes multiple ancestries): 23.3% German, 20.8% Scottish, 17.5% Norwegian, 14.2% English, 9.2% Swedish (2000).
Economy: Employment by occupation: 22.0% management, 0.0% professional, 19.5% services, 17.1% sales, 0.0% farming, 22.0% construction, 19.5% production (2000).
Income: Per capita income: $11,306 (2000); Median household income: $22,386 (2000); Poverty rate: 19.5% (2000).
Taxes: Total city taxes per capita: $46 (1997); City property taxes per capita: $46 (1997).
Education: High school graduation rate: 87.5% (2000); College graduation rate: 0.0% (2000).
Housing: Homeownership rate: 95.3% (2000); Median home value: $52,500 (2000); Median rent: $325 per month (2000); Median age of housing: 41 years (2000).
Transportation: Commute to work: 70.7% car, 7.3% public transportation, 0.0% walk, 22.0% work from home (2000); Travel time to work: 15.6% less than 15 minutes, 18.8% 15 to 30 minutes, 53.1% 30 to 45 minutes, 6.3% 45 to 60 minutes, 6.3% 60 minutes or more (2000)

RICE RIVER (township). Covers a land area of 36.063 square miles and a water area of 0 square miles. Located at 46.46° N. Lat.; 93.23° W. Long.
Population: 158 (2000); Race: 86.7% White, 1.8% Black, 7.2% Asian, 0.0% American Indian and Alaska Native, 21.7% Hispanic of any race, 4.2% two or more races (2000); Density: 4.4 persons per square mile (2000); Age: 28.9% under 18, 26.5% over 64 (2000); Marriage status: 13.6% never married, 67.2% now married, 12.0% widowed, 7.2% divorced (2000); Foreign born: 6.6% (2000); Ancestry (includes multiple ancestries): 34.3% Finnish, 11.4% Norwegian, 11.4% German, 9.0% Other groups, 7.2% Irish (2000).
Economy: Employment by occupation: 7.7% management, 25.0% professional, 13.5% services, 9.6% sales, 15.4% farming, 7.7% construction, 21.2% production (2000).
Income: Per capita income: $20,205 (2000); Median household income: $28,000 (2000); Poverty rate: 13.9% (2000).
Taxes: Total city taxes per capita: $76 (1997); City property taxes per capita: $76 (1997).
Education: High school graduation rate: 73.1% (2000); College graduation rate: 9.6% (2000).
Housing: Homeownership rate: 93.5% (2000); Median home value: $32,500 (2000); Median age of housing: 49 years (2000).
Transportation: Commute to work: 69.2% car, 15.4% public transportation, 3.8% walk, 5.8% work from home (2000); Travel time to work: 26.5% less than 15 minutes, 46.9% 15 to 30 minutes, 8.2% 30 to 45 minutes, 6.1% 45 to 60 minutes, 12.2% 60 minutes or more (2000)

SALO (township). Covers a land area of 35.480 square miles and a water area of 0.128 square miles. Located at 46.54° N. Lat.; 93.16° W. Long.
Population: 119 (2000); Race: 100.0% White, 0.0% Black, 0.0% Asian, 0.0% American Indian and Alaska Native, 0.0% Hispanic of any race, 0.0% two or more races (2000); Density: 3.4 persons per square mile (2000); Age: 14.9% under 18, 27.0% over 64 (2000); Marriage status: 16.7% never married, 68.2% now married, 9.1% widowed, 6.1% divorced (2000); Foreign born: 0.0% (2000); Ancestry (includes multiple ancestries): 50.0% Finnish, 28.4% German, 14.9% Norwegian, 13.5% Irish, 12.2% Swedish (2000).
Economy: Employment by occupation: 22.2% management, 0.0% professional, 11.1% services, 25.0% sales, 0.0% farming, 27.8% construction, 13.9% production (2000).
Income: Per capita income: $16,047 (2000); Median household income: $23,542 (2000); Poverty rate: 5.4% (2000).
Taxes: Total city taxes per capita: $92 (2000); City property taxes per capita: $92 (2000).
Education: High school graduation rate: 64.9% (2000); College graduation rate: 0.0% (2000).
Housing: Homeownership rate: 84.6% (2000); Median home value: $93,000 (2000); Median rent: $175 per month (2000); Median age of housing: 43 years (2000).
Transportation: Commute to work: 72.2% car, 0.0% public transportation, 5.6% walk, 22.2% work from home (2000); Travel time to work: 28.6% less than 15 minutes, 35.7% 15 to 30 minutes, 17.9% 30 to 45 minutes, 0.0% 45 to 60 minutes, 17.9% 60 minutes or more (2000)

SEAVEY (township). Covers a land area of 36.323 square miles and a water area of 0 square miles. Located at 46.27° N. Lat.; 93.37° W. Long.
Population: 64 (2000); Race: 100.0% White, 0.0% Black, 0.0% Asian, 0.0% American Indian and Alaska Native, 0.0% Hispanic of any race, 0.0% two or more races (2000); Density: 1.8 persons per square mile (2000); Age: 9.9% under 18, 29.6% over 64 (2000); Marriage status: 12.5% never married, 65.6% now married, 3.1% widowed, 18.8% divorced (2000); Foreign born: 0.0% (2000); Ancestry (includes multiple ancestries): 14.1% German, 12.7% Other groups, 12.7% Norwegian, 11.3% Swedish, 7.0% United States or American (2000).
Economy: Employment by occupation: 20.0% management, 13.3% professional, 6.7% services, 0.0% sales, 0.0% farming, 26.7% construction, 33.3% production (2000).
Income: Per capita income: $24,582 (2000); Median household income: $30,000 (2000); Poverty rate: 21.1% (2000).
Taxes: Total city taxes per capita: $127 (1997); City property taxes per capita: $127 (1997).
Education: High school graduation rate: 73.0% (2000); College graduation rate: 9.5% (2000).
Housing: Homeownership rate: 89.5% (2000); Median age of housing: 36 years (2000).
Transportation: Commute to work: 66.7% car, 0.0% public transportation, 6.7% walk, 20.0% work from home (2000); Travel time to work: 54.2% less than 15 minutes, 0.0% 15 to 30 minutes, 25.0% 30 to 45 minutes, 0.0% 45 to 60 minutes, 20.8% 60 minutes or more (2000)

SHAMROCK (township). Covers a land area of 24.496 square miles and a water area of 11.109 square miles. Located at 46.72° N. Lat.; 93.27° W. Long.
Population: 1,172 (2000); Race: 94.0% White, 0.2% Black, 0.0% Asian, 4.3% American Indian and Alaska Native, 0.5% Hispanic of any race, 1.5% two or more races (2000); Density: 47.8 persons per square mile (2000); Age: 18.8% under 18, 30.9% over 64 (2000); Marriage status: 13.3% never married, 64.1% now married, 11.7% widowed, 10.8% divorced (2000); Foreign born: 0.2% (2000); Ancestry (includes multiple ancestries): 30.4% German, 16.3% Swedish, 16.3% Norwegian, 12.7% Irish, 8.0% Other groups (2000).
Economy: Employment by occupation: 11.8% management, 17.4% professional, 22.6% services, 19.7% sales, 1.6% farming, 14.5% construction, 12.4% production (2000).
Income: Per capita income: $18,485 (2000); Median household income: $29,688 (2000); Poverty rate: 11.6% (2000).
Taxes: Total city taxes per capita: $142 (2000); City property taxes per capita: $142 (2000).
Education: High school graduation rate: 80.5% (2000); College graduation rate: 12.9% (2000).
Housing: Homeownership rate: 93.5% (2000); Median home value: $113,300 (2000); Median rent: $322 per month (2000); Median age of housing: 31 years (2000).
Transportation: Commute to work: 90.9% car, 0.0% public transportation, 3.6% walk, 4.4% work from home (2000); Travel time to work: 34.8% less than 15 minutes, 37.6% 15 to 30 minutes, 12.4% 30 to 45 minutes, 8.6% 45 to 60 minutes, 6.6% 60 minutes or more (2000)

SPALDING (township). Covers a land area of 36.816 square miles and a water area of 0.358 square miles. Located at 46.54° N. Lat.; 93.25° W. Long.
Population: 237 (2000); Race: 56.9% White, 0.0% Black, 0.0% Asian, 39.4% American Indian and Alaska Native, 0.4% Hispanic of any race, 3.7% two or more races (2000); Density: 6.4 persons per square mile (2000); Age: 43.9% under 18, 12.6% over 64 (2000); Marriage status: 25.6% never married, 60.3% now married, 5.1% widowed, 9.0% divorced (2000); Foreign born: 1.2% (2000); Ancestry (includes multiple ancestries): 35.4% Other groups, 26.4% German, 14.2% Finnish, 11.8% Swedish, 7.7% Polish (2000).
Economy: Employment by occupation: 17.8% management, 21.9% professional, 8.2% services, 19.2% sales, 0.0% farming, 19.2% construction, 13.7% production (2000).
Income: Per capita income: $10,260 (2000); Median household income: $24,000 (2000); Poverty rate: 32.9% (2000).
Taxes: Total city taxes per capita: $49 (1997); City property taxes per capita: $49 (1997).
Education: High school graduation rate: 76.7% (2000); College graduation rate: 7.0% (2000).
Housing: Homeownership rate: 88.5% (2000); Median home value: $67,000 (2000); Median rent: $217 per month (2000); Median age of housing: 31 years (2000).
Transportation: Commute to work: 88.7% car, 0.0% public transportation, 2.8% walk, 8.5% work from home (2000); Travel time to work: 32.3% less than 15 minutes, 15.4% 15 to 30 minutes, 35.4% 30 to 45 minutes, 0.0% 45 to 60 minutes, 16.9% 60 minutes or more (2000)

SPENCER (township). Covers a land area of 36.899 square miles and a water area of 0.811 square miles. Located at 46.53° N. Lat.; 93.63° W. Long.
Population: 602 (2000); Race: 96.1% White, 0.0% Black, 0.0% Asian, 3.6% American Indian and Alaska Native, 0.3% Hispanic of any race, 0.3% two or more races (2000); Density: 16.3 persons per square mile (2000); Age: 28.2% under 18, 10.3% over 64 (2000); Marriage status: 20.3% never married, 65.5% now married, 5.0% widowed, 9.2% divorced (2000); Foreign born: 0.4% (2000); Ancestry (includes multiple ancestries): 25.2% German, 21.0% Swedish, 14.5% Norwegian, 8.7% Irish, 8.1% United States or American (2000).
Economy: Employment by occupation: 16.2% management, 18.0% professional, 14.5% services, 26.1% sales, 0.9% farming, 12.2% construction, 12.2% production (2000).
Income: Per capita income: $17,396 (2000); Median household income: $43,542 (2000); Poverty rate: 8.7% (2000).
Taxes: Total city taxes per capita: $45 (1997); City property taxes per capita: $45 (1997).
Education: High school graduation rate: 87.2% (2000); College graduation rate: 15.8% (2000).
Housing: Homeownership rate: 97.5% (2000); Median home value: $85,600 (2000); Median rent: $250 per month (2000); Median age of housing: 27 years (2000).
Transportation: Commute to work: 90.0% car, 0.0% public transportation, 4.7% walk, 4.7% work from home (2000); Travel time to work: 64.9% less than 15 minutes, 12.3% 15 to 30 minutes, 13.5% 30 to 45 minutes, 5.5% 45 to 60 minutes, 3.7% 60 minutes or more (2000)

SWATARA (unincorporated postal area, zip code 55785). Covers a land area of 87.432 square miles and a water area of 2.803 square miles. Located at 46.87° N. Lat.; 93.70° W. Long. Elevation is 1,296 feet.
Population: 237 (2000); Race: 98.4% White, 0.0% Black, 0.0% Asian, 1.6% American Indian and Alaska Native, 0.0% Hispanic of any race, 0.0% two or more races (2000); Density: 2.7 persons per square mile (2000); Age: 35.7% under 18, 12.0% over 64 (2000); Marriage status: 19.5% never married, 68.6% now married, 6.5% widowed, 5.4% divorced (2000); Foreign born: 0.0% (2000); Ancestry (includes multiple ancestries): 28.3% German, 14.7% Norwegian, 14.0% Irish, 8.9% English, 7.8% Polish (2000).
Economy: Employment by occupation: 6.3% management, 4.2% professional, 18.8% services, 25.0% sales, 3.1% farming, 6.3% construction, 36.5% production (2000).
Income: Per capita income: $12,000 (2000); Median household income: $28,333 (2000); Poverty rate: 13.2% (2000).
Education: High school graduation rate: 75.9% (2000); College graduation rate: 3.7% (2000).
Housing: Homeownership rate: 84.3% (2000); Median home value: $20,000 (2000); Median age of housing: 24 years (2000).
Transportation: Commute to work: 95.8% car, 0.0% public transportation, 0.0% walk, 4.2% work from home (2000); Travel time to work: 20.7% less than 15 minutes, 30.4% 15 to 30 minutes, 27.2% 30 to 45 minutes, 17.4% 45 to 60 minutes, 4.3% 60 minutes or more (2000)

TAMARACK (city). Covers a land area of 3.598 square miles and a water area of 0 square miles. Located at 46.64° N. Lat.; 93.12° W. Long. Elevation is 1,269 feet.
Population: 59 (2000); Race: 100.0% White, 0.0% Black, 0.0% Asian, 0.0% American Indian and Alaska Native, 0.0% Hispanic of any race, 0.0% two or more races (2000); Density: 16.4 persons per square mile (2000); Age: 10.6% under 18, 33.3% over 64 (2000); Marriage status: 18.0% never married, 73.8% now married, 3.3% widowed, 4.9% divorced (2000); Foreign born: 7.6% (2000); Ancestry (includes multiple ancestries): 30.3% Norwegian, 21.2% Swedish, 18.2% Finnish, 16.7% Irish, 12.1% German (2000).
Economy: In lake resort region. Employment by occupation: 12.9% management, 6.5% professional, 22.6% services, 29.0% sales, 6.5% farming, 6.5% construction, 16.1% production (2000).
Income: Per capita income: $35,197 (2000); Median household income: $20,625 (2000); Poverty rate: 10.6% (2000).
Taxes: Total city taxes per capita: $133 (1997); City property taxes per capita: $100 (1997).
Education: High school graduation rate: 78.9% (2000); College graduation rate: 14.0% (2000).
Housing: Homeownership rate: 91.4% (2000); Median home value: $43,300 (2000); Median age of housing: 45 years (2000).
Transportation: Commute to work: 65.5% car, 0.0% public transportation, 10.3% walk, 24.1% work from home (2000); Travel time to work: 31.8% less than 15 minutes, 18.2% 15 to 30 minutes, 40.9% 30 to 45 minutes, 0.0% 45 to 60 minutes, 9.1% 60 minutes or more (2000)

TURNER (township). Covers a land area of 29.765 square miles and a water area of 5.982 square miles. Located at 46.78° N. Lat.; 93.26° W. Long.
Population: 144 (2000); Race: 80.9% White, 0.0% Black, 0.0% Asian, 15.3% American Indian and Alaska Native, 0.0% Hispanic of any race, 3.8% two or more races (2000); Density: 4.8 persons per square mile (2000); Age: 14.5% under 18, 19.8% over 64 (2000); Marriage status: 9.6% never married, 62.6% now married, 10.4% widowed, 17.4% divorced (2000); Foreign born: 0.0% (2000); Ancestry (includes multiple ancestries): 29.8% German, 20.6% Swedish, 11.5% Other groups, 11.5% English, 9.2% Irish (2000).
Economy: Employment by occupation: 7.4% management, 14.8% professional, 14.8% services, 14.8% sales, 3.7% farming, 16.7% construction, 27.8% production (2000).
Income: Per capita income: $18,766 (2000); Median household income: $28,333 (2000); Poverty rate: 17.5% (2000).
Taxes: Total city taxes per capita: $77 (1997); City property taxes per capita: $77 (1997).
Education: High school graduation rate: 75.5% (2000); College graduation rate: 14.5% (2000).
Housing: Homeownership rate: 89.4% (2000); Median home value: $121,900 (2000); Median rent: $225 per month (2000); Median age of housing: 32 years (2000).
Transportation: Commute to work: 76.0% car, 8.0% public transportation, 4.0% walk, 12.0% work from home (2000); Travel time to work: 9.1% less than 15 minutes, 29.5% 15 to 30 minutes, 15.9% 30 to 45 minutes, 4.5% 45 to 60 minutes, 40.9% 60 minutes or more (2000)

VERDON (township). Covers a land area of 35.688 square miles and a water area of 0.524 square miles. Located at 46.88° N. Lat.; 93.36° W. Long.
Population: 44 (2000); Race: 93.5% White, 0.0% Black, 0.0% Asian, 6.5% American Indian and Alaska Native, 0.0% Hispanic of any race, 0.0% two or more races (2000); Density: 1.2 persons per square mile (2000); Age: 0.0% under 18, 39.1% over 64 (2000); Marriage status: 21.7% never married, 65.2% now married, 0.0% widowed, 13.0% divorced (2000); Foreign born: 0.0% (2000); Ancestry (includes multiple ancestries): 34.8% German, 28.3% Swedish, 26.1% English, 26.1% Norwegian, 19.6% Irish (2000).
Economy: Employment by occupation: 9.5% management, 14.3% professional, 14.3% services, 28.6% sales, 9.5% farming, 4.8% construction, 19.0% production (2000).
Income: Per capita income: $20,226 (2000); Median household income: $39,375 (2000); Poverty rate: 13.0% (2000).
Taxes: Total city taxes per capita: $50 (1997); City property taxes per capita: $50 (1997).
Education: High school graduation rate: 84.8% (2000); College graduation rate: 23.9% (2000).
Housing: Homeownership rate: 91.7% (2000); Median home value: $72,500 (2000); Median age of housing: 17 years (2000).

Transportation: Commute to work: 14.3% car, 0.0% public transportation, 19.0% walk, 66.7% work from home (2000); Travel time to work: 28.6% less than 15 minutes, 28.6% 15 to 30 minutes, 28.6% 30 to 45 minutes, 14.3% 45 to 60 minutes, 0.0% 60 minutes or more (2000)

WAGNER (township). Covers a land area of 35.008 square miles and a water area of 0.858 square miles. Located at 46.20° N. Lat.; 93.09° W. Long.
Population: 320 (2000); Race: 96.4% White, 0.9% Black, 0.6% Asian, 0.0% American Indian and Alaska Native, 0.6% Hispanic of any race, 2.1% two or more races (2000); Density: 9.1 persons per square mile (2000); Age: 19.1% under 18, 14.6% over 64 (2000); Marriage status: 20.0% never married, 60.0% now married, 7.5% widowed, 12.5% divorced (2000); Foreign born: 1.2% (2000); Ancestry (includes multiple ancestries): 41.3% German, 19.1% Norwegian, 12.8% Swedish, 8.5% United States or American, 6.4% Irish (2000).
Economy: Employment by occupation: 16.9% management, 14.0% professional, 19.8% services, 22.1% sales, 2.9% farming, 9.3% construction, 15.1% production (2000).
Income: Per capita income: $18,968 (2000); Median household income: $38,438 (2000); Poverty rate: 15.9% (2000).
Taxes: Total city taxes per capita: $91 (1997); City property taxes per capita: $91 (1997).
Education: High school graduation rate: 85.6% (2000); College graduation rate: 8.6% (2000).
Housing: Homeownership rate: 91.7% (2000); Median home value: $127,500 (2000); Median rent: $263 per month (2000); Median age of housing: 35 years (2000).
Transportation: Commute to work: 75.3% car, 0.0% public transportation, 2.4% walk, 20.5% work from home (2000); Travel time to work: 18.2% less than 15 minutes, 28.0% 15 to 30 minutes, 34.8% 30 to 45 minutes, 4.5% 45 to 60 minutes, 14.4% 60 minutes or more (2000)

WAUKENABO (township). Covers a land area of 32.939 square miles and a water area of 3.195 square miles. Located at 46.71° N. Lat.; 93.64° W. Long. Elevation is 1,249 feet.
Population: 340 (2000); Race: 99.2% White, 0.0% Black, 0.8% Asian, 0.0% American Indian and Alaska Native, 0.0% Hispanic of any race, 0.0% two or more races (2000); Density: 10.3 persons per square mile (2000); Age: 26.1% under 18, 24.0% over 64 (2000); Marriage status: 17.9% never married, 66.2% now married, 6.0% widowed, 9.9% divorced (2000); Foreign born: 1.3% (2000); Ancestry (includes multiple ancestries): 38.8% German, 15.6% Irish, 11.9% Norwegian, 10.3% Swedish, 6.3% English (2000).
Economy: Employment by occupation: 14.9% management, 12.7% professional, 12.7% services, 22.4% sales, 5.2% farming, 9.0% construction, 23.1% production (2000).
Income: Per capita income: $13,621 (2000); Median household income: $29,643 (2000); Poverty rate: 13.6% (2000).
Taxes: Total city taxes per capita: $169 (1997); City property taxes per capita: $169 (1997).
Education: High school graduation rate: 76.7% (2000); College graduation rate: 10.7% (2000).
Housing: Homeownership rate: 88.8% (2000); Median home value: $105,000 (2000); Median rent: $308 per month (2000); Median age of housing: 16 years (2000).
Transportation: Commute to work: 90.8% car, 0.0% public transportation, 2.3% walk, 6.9% work from home (2000); Travel time to work: 17.2% less than 15 minutes, 40.2% 15 to 30 minutes, 24.6% 30 to 45 minutes, 7.4% 45 to 60 minutes, 10.7% 60 minutes or more (2000)

WEALTHWOOD (township). Covers a land area of 23.201 square miles and a water area of 49.412 square miles. Located at 46.36° N. Lat.; 93.61° W. Long. Elevation is 1,274 feet.
Population: 262 (2000); Race: 98.4% White, 0.0% Black, 0.0% Asian, 1.6% American Indian and Alaska Native, 0.0% Hispanic of any race, 0.0% two or more races (2000); Density: 11.3 persons per square mile (2000); Age: 4.8% under 18, 44.8% over 64 (2000); Marriage status: 12.8% never married, 67.5% now married, 6.6% widowed, 13.2% divorced (2000); Foreign born: 0.8% (2000); Ancestry (includes multiple ancestries): 34.9% German, 17.9% English, 15.1% Norwegian, 11.5% Swedish, 10.3% Irish (2000).
Economy: Employment by occupation: 12.9% management, 10.6% professional, 22.4% services, 17.6% sales, 0.0% farming, 16.5% construction, 20.0% production (2000).
Income: Per capita income: $25,423 (2000); Median household income: $35,227 (2000); Poverty rate: 6.7% (2000).
Taxes: Total city taxes per capita: $110 (1997); City property taxes per capita: $110 (1997).
Education: High school graduation rate: 74.3% (2000); College graduation rate: 8.9% (2000).
Housing: Homeownership rate: 86.9% (2000); Median home value: $107,500 (2000); Median rent: $565 per month (2000); Median age of housing: 29 years (2000).
Transportation: Commute to work: 79.0% car, 0.0% public transportation, 2.5% walk, 18.5% work from home (2000); Travel time to work: 21.2% less than 15 minutes, 33.3% 15 to 30 minutes, 21.2% 30 to 45 minutes, 3.0% 45 to 60 minutes, 21.2% 60 minutes or more (2000)

WHITE PINE (township). Covers a land area of 36.615 square miles and a water area of 0.032 square miles. Located at 46.36° N. Lat.; 93.26° W. Long.
Population: 34 (2000); Race: 100.0% White, 0.0% Black, 0.0% Asian, 0.0% American Indian and Alaska Native, 0.0% Hispanic of any race, 0.0% two or more races (2000); Density: 0.9 persons per square mile (2000); Age: 8.3% under 18, 54.2% over 64 (2000); Marriage status: 18.2% never married, 31.8% now married, 31.8% widowed, 18.2% divorced (2000); Foreign born: 0.0% (2000); Ancestry (includes multiple ancestries): 20.8% German, 16.7% English, 8.3% Danish, 8.3% Swedish (2000).
Economy: Employment by occupation: 57.1% management, 0.0% professional, 0.0% services, 28.6% sales, 0.0% farming, 14.3% construction, 0.0% production (2000).
Income: Per capita income: $16,163 (2000); Median household income: $17,500 (2000); Poverty rate: 8.3% (2000).
Taxes: Total city taxes per capita: $21 (1997); City property taxes per capita: $21 (1997).
Education: High school graduation rate: 50.0% (2000); College graduation rate: 0.0% (2000).
Housing: Homeownership rate: 82.4% (2000); Median home value: $17,500 (2000); Median age of housing: 50 years (2000).
Transportation: Commute to work: 71.4% car, 0.0% public transportation, 0.0% walk, 28.6% work from home (2000); Travel time to work: 20.0% less than 15 minutes, 0.0% 15 to 30 minutes, 40.0% 30 to 45 minutes, 40.0% 45 to 60 minutes, 0.0% 60 minutes or more (2000)

WILLIAMS (township). Covers a land area of 35.866 square miles and a water area of 0.022 square miles. Located at 46.21° N. Lat.; 93.24° W. Long.
Population: 153 (2000); Race: 100.0% White, 0.0% Black, 0.0% Asian, 0.0% American Indian and Alaska Native, 0.0% Hispanic of any race, 0.0% two or more races (2000); Density: 4.3 persons per square mile (2000); Age: 28.0% under 18, 12.7% over 64 (2000); Marriage status: 20.9% never married, 65.2% now married, 2.6% widowed, 11.3% divorced (2000); Foreign born: 0.0% (2000); Ancestry (includes multiple ancestries): 28.0% German, 24.8% Norwegian, 12.1% Irish, 10.8% French (except Basque), 6.4% United States or American (2000).
Economy: Employment by occupation: 10.7% management, 0.0% professional, 23.2% services, 17.9% sales, 0.0% farming, 19.6% construction, 28.6% production (2000).
Income: Per capita income: $20,566 (2000); Median household income: $39,375 (2000); Poverty rate: 22.9% (2000).
Taxes: Total city taxes per capita: $79 (1997); City property taxes per capita: $79 (1997).
Education: High school graduation rate: 78.0% (2000); College graduation rate: 0.0% (2000).
Housing: Homeownership rate: 76.1% (2000); Median home value: $36,300 (2000); Median rent: $242 per month (2000); Median age of housing: 31 years (2000).
Transportation: Commute to work: 96.4% car, 0.0% public transportation, 0.0% walk, 3.6% work from home (2000); Travel time to work: 13.0% less than 15 minutes, 22.2% 15 to 30 minutes, 25.9% 30 to 45 minutes, 16.7% 45 to 60 minutes, 22.2% 60 minutes or more (2000)

WORKMAN (township). Covers a land area of 32.799 square miles and a water area of 2.860 square miles. Located at 46.73° N. Lat.; 93.37° W. Long.
Population: 194 (2000); Race: 96.4% White, 0.0% Black, 0.0% Asian, 2.6% American Indian and Alaska Native, 0.0% Hispanic of any race, 1.0% two or more races (2000); Density: 5.9 persons per square mile (2000); Age: 14.9% under 18, 23.1% over 64 (2000); Marriage status: 14.2% never married, 69.2% now married, 5.3% widowed, 11.2% divorced (2000); Foreign born: 0.0% (2000); Ancestry (includes multiple ancestries): 32.3% German, 17.9% Norwegian, 11.8% Swedish, 10.3% Irish, 6.2% Other groups (2000).
Economy: Employment by occupation: 12.0% management, 2.4% professional, 26.5% services, 22.9% sales, 4.8% farming, 16.9% construction, 14.5% production (2000).

Income: Per capita income: $18,518 (2000); Median household income: $35,833 (2000); Poverty rate: 6.2% (2000).
Taxes: Total city taxes per capita: $123 (1997); City property taxes per capita: $123 (1997).
Education: High school graduation rate: 82.6% (2000); College graduation rate: 14.8% (2000).
Housing: Homeownership rate: 88.0% (2000); Median home value: $79,200 (2000); Median rent: $325 per month (2000); Median age of housing: 24 years (2000).
Transportation: Commute to work: 80.0% car, 0.0% public transportation, 2.4% walk, 17.6% work from home (2000); Travel time to work: 30.0% less than 15 minutes, 35.7% 15 to 30 minutes, 8.6% 30 to 45 minutes, 4.3% 45 to 60 minutes, 21.4% 60 minutes or more (2000)

Anoka County

Located in eastern Minnesota; bounded on the southwest by the Mississippi River. Covers a land area of 423.60 square miles, a water area of 22.60 square miles, and is located in the Central Time Zone. The county government was organized in 1857. County seat is Anoka.

Anoka County is part of the Minneapolis-St. Paul, MN-WI MSA. The entire metro area includes: Anoka County, MN; Carver County, MN; Chisago County, MN; Dakota County, MN; Hennepin County, MN; Isanti County, MN; Ramsey County, MN; Scott County, MN; Sherburne County, MN; Washington County, MN; Wright County, MN; Pierce County, WI; St. Croix County, WI

Weather Station: Cedar — Elevation: 905 feet

	Jan	Feb	Mar	Apr	May	Jun	Jul	Aug	Sep	Oct	Nov	Dec
High	21	29	40	58	71	79	83	80	71	59	40	26
Low	1	8	20	34	46	55	60	58	49	37	23	9
Precip	1.1	0.7	1.8	2.5	3.6	4.2	4.3	4.8	3.4	2.6	2.1	0.9
Snow	13.2	7.3	10.5	2.9	tr	0.0	0.0	0.0	tr	0.5	9.9	9.1

High and Low temperatures in degrees Fahrenheit; Precipitation and Snow in inches

Population: 298,084 (2000); Race: 93.4% White, 1.5% Black, 1.7% Asian, 0.8% American Indian and Alaska Native, 1.6% Hispanic of any race, 1.8% two or more races (2000); Density: 703.7 persons per square mile (2000); Age: 28.9% under 18, 7.0% over 64 (2000).
Religion: Five largest groups: 24.0% Catholic Church, 14.1% Evangelical Lutheran Church in America, 3.1% Lutheran Church—Missouri Synod, 2.5% Assemblies of God, 1.4% The United Methodist Church (2000).
Economy: Unemployment rate: 3.5% (11/2002); Total civilian labor force: 191,201 (11/2002); Leading industries: 23.5% manufacturing; 14.1% retail trade; 11.5% health care and social assistance (2000); Companies that employ more than 1,000 persons: 8 (2000); Companies that employ more than 100 persons: 169 (2000); Farms: 473 totaling 57,313 acres (1997); Minority business ownership rate: 2.5% (1997); Women business ownership rate: 28.8% (1997); Retail sales per capita: $7,789 (1997). Single-family building permits issued: 2,081 (2001) / 1,983 (2000); Multi-family building permits issued: 313 (2001) / 64 (2000).
Income: Per capita income: $23,297 (2000); Median household income: $57,754 (2000); Poverty rate: 4.2% (2000); Bankruptcy rate: 4.74% (2001).
Taxes: Total county taxes per capita: $211 (2000); County property taxes per capita: $210 (2000).
Education: High school graduation rate: 91.0% (2000); College graduation rate: 21.3% (2000).
Housing: Homeownership rate: 83.4% (2000); Median home value: $131,300 (2000); Median rent: $611 per month (2000); Median age of housing: 22 years (2000).
Health: Birth rate: 141.4 per 10,000 population (1998); Age adjusted death rate: 67.2 per 10,000 population (1999); Age adjusted cancer mortality rate: 166.6 deaths per 100,000 population (1999). Air Quality Index: 86% good, 14% moderate, <1% unhealthy (percent of days in 2000). Number of physicians: 11.6 per 10,000 population (1999); Number of hospital beds: 22.4 per 10,000 population (1999).
Elections: 2000 Presidential election results: 46.7% Gore, 47.6% Bush, 4.5% Nader, 0.7% Buchanan
National and State Parks: Bethel State Wildlife Management Area; Carlos Avery State Wildlife Management Area
Additional Information Contacts
Anoka County Government Offices 763-421-4760
Anoka Chamber of Commerce 763-421-7130
Coon Rapids Chamber of Commerce 763-783-3553
Fridley Chamber of Commerce 763-571-9781
Ham Lake Chamber of Commerce 763-434-3011
North Metro Realtors Association 763-757-7230

Anoka County Communities

ANDOVER (city). Covers a land area of 34.106 square miles and a water area of 0.875 square miles. Located at 45.25° N. Lat.; 93.33° W. Long. Elevation is 891 feet.
Population: 26,588 (2000); Race: 96.1% White, 0.3% Black, 0.9% Asian, 0.7% American Indian and Alaska Native, 1.0% Hispanic of any race, 1.5% two or more races (2000); Density: 779.6 persons per square mile (2000); Age: 35.5% under 18, 2.7% over 64 (2000); Marriage status: 20.3% never married, 72.9% now married, 2.2% widowed, 4.6% divorced (2000); Foreign born: 2.5% (2000); Ancestry (includes multiple ancestries): 36.5% German, 17.5% Norwegian, 13.6% Swedish, 12.9% Irish, 8.4% Polish (2000).
Vital Statistics: Birth rate: 147.8 per 10,000 population (1998)
Economy: Manufacturing: furniture, transportation equipment, Christmas ornaments. Agriculture: alfalfa, rye. Unemployment rate: 3.1% (11/2002); Total civilian labor force: 15,709 (11/2002); Single-family building permits issued: 285 (2001) / 342 (2000); Multi-family building permits issued: 0 (2001) / 0 (2000); Employment by occupation: 17.0% management, 19.9% professional, 10.5% services, 28.6% sales, 0.1% farming, 10.0% construction, 13.8% production (2000).
Income: Per capita income: $26,317 (2000); Median household income: $76,241 (2000); Poverty rate: 2.0% (2000).
Taxes: Total city taxes per capita: $186 (2000); City property taxes per capita: $163 (2000).
Education: High school graduation rate: 94.5% (2000); College graduation rate: 28.0% (2000).
Housing: Homeownership rate: 95.9% (2000); Median home value: $158,400 (2000); Median rent: $666 per month (2000); Median age of housing: 11 years (2000).
Safety: Violent crime rate: 13.8 per 10,000 population; Property crime rate: 219.2 per 10,000 population (2001).
Transportation: Commute to work: 93.3% car, 2.2% public transportation, 0.6% walk, 3.6% work from home (2000); Travel time to work: 15.8% less than 15 minutes, 31.6% 15 to 30 minutes, 29.3% 30 to 45 minutes, 16.1% 45 to 60 minutes, 7.1% 60 minutes or more (2000)

ANOKA (city). Covers a land area of 6.673 square miles and a water area of 0.501 square miles. Located at 45.20° N. Lat.; 93.38° W. Long. Elevation is 879 feet.
History: Anoka was settled at a site on the old Red River Trail. The town was platted in the early 1850's, and thought by some to be the best suited by location to become the metropolitan center of the state. Its position on the Rum and Mississippi Rivers made it an early milling center, but the development of electrical power at Minneapolis left Anoka behind.
Population: 18,076 (2000); Race: 92.6% White, 2.2% Black, 1.3% Asian, 1.2% American Indian and Alaska Native, 2.3% Hispanic of any race, 1.5% two or more races (2000); Density: 2,709.0 persons per square mile (2000); Age: 24.5% under 18, 11.7% over 64 (2000); Marriage status: 28.9% never married, 51.8% now married, 6.7% widowed, 12.5% divorced (2000); Foreign born: 3.0% (2000); Ancestry (includes multiple ancestries): 33.0% German, 17.1% Norwegian, 12.8% Swedish, 11.2% Irish, 8.8% Other groups (2000).
Vital Statistics: Birth rate: 182.0 per 10,000 population (1998)
Economy: Single-family building permits issued: 17 (2001) / 9 (2000); Multi-family building permits issued: 0 (2001) / 0 (2000); Employment by occupation: 10.3% management, 17.0% professional, 14.1% services, 28.2% sales, 0.1% farming, 11.0% construction, 19.3% production (2000).
Income: Per capita income: $21,367 (2000); Median household income: $42,659 (2000); Poverty rate: 6.8% (2000).
Taxes: Total city taxes per capita: $372 (2000); City property taxes per capita: $299 (2000).
Education: High school graduation rate: 87.9% (2000); College graduation rate: 17.8% (2000).

School District(s)

Pact Charter School (KG-12)
2000 Enrollment: 317 763-421-8475

Two-year College(s)

Anoka-Hennepin Technical College (Public)
2001 Enrollment: 2,409 763-576-4700
2001 Tuition: In-state $2,452; Out-of-state $4,905

Housing: Homeownership rate: 56.3% (2000); Median home value: $119,000 (2000); Median rent: $562 per month (2000); Median age of housing: 29 years (2000).

Hospitals: Anoka-Metro Regional Treatment Center (347 beds)
Safety: Violent crime rate: 18.6 per 10,000 population; Property crime rate: 423.6 per 10,000 population (2001).
Newspapers: Blaine-Spring Lake Park Life (1 x week); Anoka County Union (1 x week)
Transportation: Commute to work: 90.7% car, 3.2% public transportation, 2.9% walk, 2.8% work from home (2000); Travel time to work: 30.7% less than 15 minutes, 30.9% 15 to 30 minutes, 22.7% 30 to 45 minutes, 9.4% 45 to 60 minutes, 6.4% 60 minutes or more (2000)
Additional Information Contacts
Anoka Chamber of Commerce.......................... 763-421-7130

BETHEL (city). Covers a land area of 0.862 square miles and a water area of 0.056 square miles. Located at 45.40° N. Lat.; 93.26° W. Long. Elevation is 929 feet.
Population: 443 (2000); Race: 88.7% White, 0.5% Black, 0.5% Asian, 0.5% American Indian and Alaska Native, 2.2% Hispanic of any race, 8.6% two or more races (2000); Density: 514.1 persons per square mile (2000); Age: 37.0% under 18, 5.4% over 64 (2000); Marriage status: 24.8% never married, 62.2% now married, 2.2% widowed, 10.7% divorced (2000); Foreign born: 0.5% (2000); Ancestry (includes multiple ancestries): 32.1% German, 14.5% Swedish, 14.5% Irish, 12.5% Norwegian, 10.0% Other groups (2000).
Economy: Agricultural area: dairying; poultry; rye, alfalfa. Manufacturing: machining parts, trophies. Single-family building permits issued: 2 (2001) / 3 (2000); Multi-family building permits issued: 0 (2001) / 0 (2000); Employment by occupation: 3.2% management, 13.7% professional, 10.5% services, 20.5% sales, 0.0% farming, 18.4% construction, 33.7% production (2000).
Income: Per capita income: $16,399 (2000); Median household income: $45,125 (2000); Poverty rate: 6.4% (2000).
Taxes: Total city taxes per capita: $320 (1997); City property taxes per capita: $293 (1997).
Education: High school graduation rate: 87.9% (2000); College graduation rate: 9.0% (2000).
Housing: Homeownership rate: 81.8% (2000); Median home value: $102,900 (2000); Median rent: $408 per month (2000); Median age of housing: 22 years (2000).
Transportation: Commute to work: 90.4% car, 0.0% public transportation, 4.8% walk, 4.8% work from home (2000); Travel time to work: 30.9% less than 15 minutes, 9.0% 15 to 30 minutes, 19.1% 30 to 45 minutes, 18.5% 45 to 60 minutes, 22.5% 60 minutes or more (2000)

BLAINE (city). Covers a land area of 33.851 square miles and a water area of 0.172 square miles. Located at 45.15° N. Lat.; 93.22° W. Long. Elevation is 900 feet.
History: The area was organized as a township in 1877 and was named in honor of James G. Blaine, then senator from Maine. Settled 1862, Incorporated 1964.
Population: 44,942 (2000); Race: 93.4% White, 0.9% Black, 2.1% Asian, 0.9% American Indian and Alaska Native, 1.9% Hispanic of any race, 1.8% two or more races (2000); Density: 1,327.6 persons per square mile (2000); Age: 29.2% under 18, 5.1% over 64 (2000); Marriage status: 26.9% never married, 60.3% now married, 3.0% widowed, 9.9% divorced (2000); Foreign born: 3.4% (2000); Ancestry (includes multiple ancestries): 38.3% German, 17.6% Norwegian, 12.6% Irish, 12.5% Swedish, 7.1% Other groups (2000).
Vital Statistics: Birth rate: 137.7 per 10,000 population (1998)
Economy: Manufacturing includes medical equipment, gun parts, optical components, beauty products, fabricated metal products, building materials, furniture, prototype models, apparel, countertops, machinery, consumer goods. Unemployment rate: 3.7% (11/2002); Total civilian labor force: 30,593 (11/2002); Single-family building permits issued: 667 (2001) / 564 (2000); Multi-family building permits issued: 0 (2001) / 0 (2000); Employment by occupation: 13.2% management, 17.7% professional, 11.8% services, 28.9% sales, 0.1% farming, 9.3% construction, 19.0% production (2000).
Income: Per capita income: $22,777 (2000); Median household income: $59,219 (2000); Poverty rate: 3.0% (2000).
Taxes: Total city taxes per capita: $233 (2000); City property taxes per capita: $183 (2000).
Education: High school graduation rate: 91.2% (2000); College graduation rate: 19.7% (2000).
Housing: Homeownership rate: 90.6% (2000); Median home value: $125,600 (2000); Median rent: $661 per month (2000); Median age of housing: 19 years (2000).
Newspapers: Blaine Banner (1 x month)
Transportation: Commute to work: 93.0% car, 2.5% public transportation, 0.8% walk, 2.8% work from home (2000); Travel time to work: 18.7% less than 15 minutes, 39.3% 15 to 30 minutes, 27.8% 30 to 45 minutes, 9.3% 45 to 60 minutes, 5.0% 60 minutes or more (2000)

BURNS (township). Covers a land area of 33.789 square miles and a water area of 1.395 square miles. Located at 45.33° N. Lat.; 93.44° W. Long.
Population: 3,557 (2000); Race: 99.1% White, 0.0% Black, 0.0% Asian, 0.7% American Indian and Alaska Native, 0.4% Hispanic of any race, 0.2% two or more races (2000); Density: 105.3 persons per square mile (2000); Age: 33.2% under 18, 5.0% over 64 (2000); Marriage status: 20.4% never married, 72.4% now married, 2.2% widowed, 4.9% divorced (2000); Foreign born: 0.7% (2000); Ancestry (includes multiple ancestries): 40.6% German, 19.8% Norwegian, 13.2% Swedish, 9.4% Irish, 6.4% Polish (2000).
Economy: Single-family building permits issued: 33 (2001) / 30 (2000); Multi-family building permits issued: 0 (2001) / 0 (2000); Employment by occupation: 13.6% management, 17.2% professional, 8.5% services, 24.1% sales, 0.9% farming, 16.5% construction, 19.2% production (2000).
Income: Per capita income: $21,569 (2000); Median household income: $63,819 (2000); Poverty rate: 4.6% (2000).
Taxes: Total city taxes per capita: $114 (2000); City property taxes per capita: $77 (2000).
Education: High school graduation rate: 91.1% (2000); College graduation rate: 15.6% (2000).
Housing: Homeownership rate: 98.1% (2000); Median home value: $157,500 (2000); Median rent: $525 per month (2000); Median age of housing: 16 years (2000).
Transportation: Commute to work: 90.0% car, 1.2% public transportation, 1.0% walk, 7.2% work from home (2000); Travel time to work: 14.7% less than 15 minutes, 26.1% 15 to 30 minutes, 29.5% 30 to 45 minutes, 20.9% 45 to 60 minutes, 8.8% 60 minutes or more (2000)

CEDAR (unincorporated postal area, zip code 55011). Covers a land area of 42.021 square miles and a water area of 1.913 square miles. Located at 45.33° N. Lat.; 93.27° W. Long. Elevation is 910 feet.
Population: 8,696 (2000); Race: 96.6% White, 0.1% Black, 1.1% Asian, 0.4% American Indian and Alaska Native, 0.1% Hispanic of any race, 1.6% two or more races (2000); Density: 206.9 persons per square mile (2000); Age: 30.7% under 18, 3.5% over 64 (2000); Marriage status: 26.4% never married, 62.1% now married, 1.1% widowed, 10.4% divorced (2000); Foreign born: 1.1% (2000); Ancestry (includes multiple ancestries): 38.9% German, 17.0% Norwegian, 16.0% Swedish, 14.4% Irish, 8.6% Polish (2000).
Economy: Employment by occupation: 13.6% management, 16.8% professional, 11.9% services, 25.4% sales, 0.3% farming, 12.7% construction, 19.2% production (2000).
Income: Per capita income: $21,801 (2000); Median household income: $62,275 (2000); Poverty rate: 2.7% (2000).
Education: High school graduation rate: 92.7% (2000); College graduation rate: 13.3% (2000).
Housing: Homeownership rate: 98.9% (2000); Median home value: $140,500 (2000); Median rent: $533 per month (2000); Median age of housing: 18 years (2000).
Transportation: Commute to work: 92.8% car, 0.7% public transportation, 0.8% walk, 5.3% work from home (2000); Travel time to work: 9.3% less than 15 minutes, 27.6% 15 to 30 minutes, 31.1% 30 to 45 minutes, 18.1% 45 to 60 minutes, 13.9% 60 minutes or more (2000)

CENTERVILLE (city). Covers a land area of 2.154 square miles and a water area of 0.256 square miles. Located at 45.16° N. Lat.; 93.05° W. Long. Elevation is 933 feet.
Population: 3,202 (2000); Race: 96.1% White, 0.9% Black, 0.1% Asian, 0.4% American Indian and Alaska Native, 1.1% Hispanic of any race, 1.4% two or more races (2000); Density: 1,486.5 persons per square mile (2000); Age: 33.2% under 18, 3.1% over 64 (2000); Marriage status: 16.3% never married, 75.3% now married, 1.9% widowed, 6.6% divorced (2000); Foreign born: 1.3% (2000); Ancestry (includes multiple ancestries): 46.7% German, 17.6% Irish, 12.9% Norwegian, 11.2% Swedish, 7.1% Italian (2000).
Economy: Grain. Manufacturing: machining. Single-family building permits issued: 43 (2001) / 55 (2000); Multi-family building permits issued: 0 (2001) / 0 (2000); Employment by occupation: 13.1% management, 21.0% professional, 14.5% services, 28.9% sales, 0.0% farming, 9.2% construction, 13.4% production (2000).
Income: Per capita income: $23,113 (2000); Median household income: $63,696 (2000); Poverty rate: 2.4% (2000).

Taxes: Total city taxes per capita: $322 (1997); City property taxes per capita: $278 (1997).
Education: High school graduation rate: 94.4% (2000); College graduation rate: 31.2% (2000).
Housing: Homeownership rate: 93.5% (2000); Median home value: $142,400 (2000); Median rent: $525 per month (2000); Median age of housing: 8 years (2000).
Transportation: Commute to work: 93.2% car, 0.7% public transportation, 1.1% walk, 3.9% work from home (2000); Travel time to work: 14.5% less than 15 minutes, 42.9% 15 to 30 minutes, 30.0% 30 to 45 minutes, 10.0% 45 to 60 minutes, 2.5% 60 minutes or more (2000)

CIRCLE PINES (city). Covers a land area of 1.753 square miles and a water area of 0.194 square miles. Located at 45.14° N. Lat.; 93.15° W. Long. Elevation is 915 feet.
Population: 4,663 (2000); Race: 96.2% White, 0.1% Black, 2.1% Asian, 0.7% American Indian and Alaska Native, 0.7% Hispanic of any race, 0.7% two or more races (2000); Density: 2,660.7 persons per square mile (2000); Age: 27.9% under 18, 9.2% over 64 (2000); Marriage status: 23.7% never married, 62.4% now married, 3.8% widowed, 10.1% divorced (2000); Foreign born: 3.9% (2000); Ancestry (includes multiple ancestries): 44.8% German, 18.3% Norwegian, 16.3% Irish, 13.9% Swedish, 8.4% English (2000).
Economy: Manufacturing: printing and publishing, industrial engraving; electronic equipment. Single-family building permits issued: 0 (2001) / 0 (2000); Multi-family building permits issued: 0 (2001) / 4 (2000); Employment by occupation: 19.9% management, 17.7% professional, 10.6% services, 29.6% sales, 0.0% farming, 9.0% construction, 13.2% production (2000).
Income: Per capita income: $25,438 (2000); Median household income: $60,469 (2000); Poverty rate: 2.3% (2000).
Taxes: Total city taxes per capita: $227 (2000); City property taxes per capita: $216 (2000).
Education: High school graduation rate: 93.7% (2000); College graduation rate: 31.5% (2000).

School District(s)

Centennial (KG-12)
2000 Enrollment: 6,946 763-792-6000

Housing: Homeownership rate: 93.2% (2000); Median home value: $116,300 (2000); Median rent: $569 per month (2000); Median age of housing: 27 years (2000).
Transportation: Commute to work: 91.6% car, 3.1% public transportation, 0.8% walk, 4.5% work from home (2000); Travel time to work: 18.2% less than 15 minutes, 44.2% 15 to 30 minutes, 27.2% 30 to 45 minutes, 6.2% 45 to 60 minutes, 4.2% 60 minutes or more (2000)

COLUMBIA HEIGHTS (city). Covers a land area of 3.450 square miles and a water area of 0.098 square miles. Located at 45.04° N. Lat.; 93.24° W. Long. Elevation is 950 feet.
History: Incorporated 1921.
Population: 18,520 (2000); Race: 87.8% White, 3.5% Black, 3.6% Asian, 1.5% American Indian and Alaska Native, 2.8% Hispanic of any race, 2.7% two or more races (2000); Density: 5,368.7 persons per square mile (2000); Age: 20.8% under 18, 18.9% over 64 (2000); Marriage status: 28.8% never married, 50.3% now married, 9.7% widowed, 11.1% divorced (2000); Foreign born: 8.4% (2000); Ancestry (includes multiple ancestries): 30.3% German, 16.3% Norwegian, 12.4% Irish, 12.1% Swedish, 11.3% Polish (2000).
Vital Statistics: Birth rate: 105.8 per 10,000 population (1998)
Economy: Manufacturing. Single-family building permits issued: 8 (2001) / 6 (2000); Multi-family building permits issued: 90 (2001) / 4 (2000); Employment by occupation: 12.3% management, 15.7% professional, 16.1% services, 31.3% sales, 0.1% farming, 7.1% construction, 17.3% production (2000).
Income: Per capita income: $21,368 (2000); Median household income: $40,562 (2000); Poverty rate: 6.4% (2000).
Taxes: Total city taxes per capita: $222 (1997); City property taxes per capita: $205 (1997).
Education: High school graduation rate: 84.2% (2000); College graduation rate: 17.6% (2000).

School District(s)

Columbia Heights (PK-12)
2000 Enrollment: 3,018 763-586-4505

Two-year College(s)

Nei College of Technology (Private, Not-for-profit)
2001 Enrollment: 451 763-781-4881
2001 Tuition: In-state $13,749; Out-of-state $13,749

Housing: Homeownership rate: 71.5% (2000); Median home value: $103,000 (2000); Median rent: $525 per month (2000); Median age of housing: 40 years (2000).
Newspapers: Focus News - Blaine/Spring Lake Park (1 x week); Focus News - Mounds View/New Brighton/Saint Anthony (1 x week); Focus News - Roseville/Arden Hills/Falcon Heights (1 x week); Focus News - Fridley/Columbia Heights (1 x week)
Transportation: Commute to work: 88.1% car, 6.5% public transportation, 2.8% walk, 2.0% work from home (2000); Travel time to work: 26.3% less than 15 minutes, 47.9% 15 to 30 minutes, 19.8% 30 to 45 minutes, 4.0% 45 to 60 minutes, 2.0% 60 minutes or more (2000)

COLUMBUS (township). Covers a land area of 44.879 square miles and a water area of 2.931 square miles. Located at 45.27° N. Lat.; 93.06° W. Long.
Population: 3,957 (2000); Race: 96.7% White, 0.8% Black, 0.3% Asian, 0.2% American Indian and Alaska Native, 0.9% Hispanic of any race, 1.5% two or more races (2000); Density: 88.2 persons per square mile (2000); Age: 27.3% under 18, 6.2% over 64 (2000); Marriage status: 23.3% never married, 64.6% now married, 3.5% widowed, 8.6% divorced (2000); Foreign born: 1.1% (2000); Ancestry (includes multiple ancestries): 40.9% German, 14.6% Swedish, 11.9% Norwegian, 9.7% Irish, 7.1% English (2000).
Economy: Single-family building permits issued: 14 (2001) / 10 (2000); Multi-family building permits issued: 0 (2001) / 0 (2000); Employment by occupation: 13.2% management, 18.9% professional, 10.8% services, 28.2% sales, 0.0% farming, 13.0% construction, 15.9% production (2000).
Income: Per capita income: $24,479 (2000); Median household income: $67,500 (2000); Poverty rate: 3.8% (2000).
Taxes: Total city taxes per capita: $234 (2000); City property taxes per capita: $212 (2000).
Education: High school graduation rate: 93.6% (2000); College graduation rate: 16.5% (2000).
Housing: Homeownership rate: 98.0% (2000); Median home value: $154,600 (2000); Median rent: $832 per month (2000); Median age of housing: 24 years (2000).
Transportation: Commute to work: 94.5% car, 0.3% public transportation, 0.2% walk, 4.9% work from home (2000); Travel time to work: 18.6% less than 15 minutes, 21.6% 15 to 30 minutes, 41.3% 30 to 45 minutes, 13.1% 45 to 60 minutes, 5.4% 60 minutes or more (2000)

COON RAPIDS (city). Aka Coon Creek. Covers a land area of 22.665 square miles and a water area of 0.674 square miles. Located at 45.17° N. Lat.; 93.30° W. Long. Elevation is 875 feet.
History: Incorporated 1952.
Population: 61,607 (2000); Race: 93.3% White, 1.9% Black, 1.5% Asian, 0.7% American Indian and Alaska Native, 1.5% Hispanic of any race, 2.0% two or more races (2000); Density: 2,718.1 persons per square mile (2000); Age: 28.6% under 18, 7.1% over 64 (2000); Marriage status: 27.2% never married, 58.5% now married, 3.9% widowed, 10.4% divorced (2000); Foreign born: 3.7% (2000); Ancestry (includes multiple ancestries): 36.4% German, 18.1% Norwegian, 13.0% Swedish, 12.4% Irish, 7.1% Other groups (2000).
Vital Statistics: Birth rate: 143.7 per 10,000 population (1998)
Economy: Railroad junction. Manufacturing: transportation equipment, fabricated metal products, medical equipment, consumer goods, printing and publishing, machinery. Unemployment rate: 3.2% (11/2002); Total civilian labor force: 41,363 (11/2002); Single-family building permits issued: 152 (2001) / 135 (2000); Multi-family building permits issued: 165 (2001) / 13 (2000); Employment by occupation: 13.2% management, 19.7% professional, 12.0% services, 29.1% sales, 0.1% farming, 9.8% construction, 16.2% production (2000).
Income: Per capita income: $22,915 (2000); Median household income: $55,550 (2000); Poverty rate: 4.8% (2000).
Taxes: Total city taxes per capita: $235 (2000); City property taxes per capita: $188 (2000).
Education: High school graduation rate: 91.9% (2000); College graduation rate: 21.4% (2000).

School District(s)

Anoka-Hennepin (PK-12)
2000 Enrollment: 41,314 763-506-1000
Coon Rapids Learning Center (10-12)
2000 Enrollment: 112 763-862-9223

Two-year College(s)

Anoka-Ramsey Community College (Public)
2001 Enrollment: 5,978 763-427-2600
2001 Tuition: In-state $2,362; Out-of-state $4,725

Housing: Homeownership rate: 80.3% (2000); Median home value: $124,600 (2000); Median rent: $689 per month (2000); Median age of housing: 18 years (2000).

Newspapers: Coon Rapids Herald (1 x week)

Transportation: Commute to work: 92.6% car, 3.5% public transportation, 0.8% walk, 2.7% work from home (2000); Travel time to work: 21.6% less than 15 minutes, 37.9% 15 to 30 minutes, 25.8% 30 to 45 minutes, 9.8% 45 to 60 minutes, 4.8% 60 minutes or more (2000)

Additional Information Contacts

Coon Rapids Chamber of Commerce. 763-783-3553
North Metro Realtors Association 763-757-7230

EAST BETHEL (city). Covers a land area of 44.851 square miles and a water area of 3.201 square miles. Located at 45.32° N. Lat.; 93.21° W. Long.

Population: 10,941 (2000); Race: 96.7% White, 0.3% Black, 0.9% Asian, 1.0% American Indian and Alaska Native, 0.6% Hispanic of any race, 0.9% two or more races (2000); Density: 243.9 persons per square mile (2000); Age: 32.1% under 18, 4.1% over 64 (2000); Marriage status: 24.5% never married, 63.8% now married, 1.7% widowed, 9.9% divorced (2000); Foreign born: 0.9% (2000); Ancestry (includes multiple ancestries): 37.1% German, 16.9% Norwegian, 15.1% Swedish, 10.9% Irish, 9.4% Polish (2000).

Economy: Manufacturing: trophies. Agriculture: alfalfa, rye, dairying, poultry. Single-family building permits issued: 95 (2001) / 93 (2000); Multi-family building permits issued: 0 (2001) / 0 (2000); Employment by occupation: 13.0% management, 16.7% professional, 11.9% services, 25.6% sales, 0.1% farming, 14.0% construction, 18.7% production (2000).

Income: Per capita income: $21,087 (2000); Median household income: $57,880 (2000); Poverty rate: 3.8% (2000).

Taxes: Total city taxes per capita: $163 (1997); City property taxes per capita: $142 (1997).

Education: High school graduation rate: 91.7% (2000); College graduation rate: 13.9% (2000).

Housing: Homeownership rate: 98.7% (2000); Median home value: $138,300 (2000); Median rent: $575 per month (2000); Median age of housing: 18 years (2000).

Safety: Violent crime rate: 14.5 per 10,000 population; Property crime rate: 307.5 per 10,000 population (2001).

Transportation: Commute to work: 94.7% car, 0.2% public transportation, 0.5% walk, 4.5% work from home (2000); Travel time to work: 10.0% less than 15 minutes, 26.1% 15 to 30 minutes, 32.4% 30 to 45 minutes, 17.5% 45 to 60 minutes, 14.1% 60 minutes or more (2000)

FRIDLEY (city). Covers a land area of 10.161 square miles and a water area of 0.727 square miles. Located at 45.08° N. Lat.; 93.26° W. Long. Elevation is 844 feet.

History: Settled 1847, incorporated as a city 1957.

Population: 27,449 (2000); Race: 88.0% White, 3.6% Black, 3.0% Asian, 0.7% American Indian and Alaska Native, 2.2% Hispanic of any race, 3.3% two or more races (2000); Density: 2,701.3 persons per square mile (2000); Age: 22.5% under 18, 11.8% over 64 (2000); Marriage status: 28.1% never married, 53.7% now married, 5.3% widowed, 12.9% divorced (2000); Foreign born: 7.2% (2000); Ancestry (includes multiple ancestries): 32.0% German, 16.1% Norwegian, 12.6% Swedish, 11.1% Irish, 9.9% Other groups (2000).

Vital Statistics: Birth rate: 128.2 per 10,000 population (1998)

Economy: A distribution center with railroad yards and warehouses. Manufacturing: rubber and plastic products, electrical products, electroplating, machinery, aircraft, cosmetics, computers, X-ray equipment, ordnance and weapons systems. Unemployment rate: 3.6% (11/2002); Total civilian labor force: 19,216 (11/2002); Single-family building permits issued: 31 (2001) / 16 (2000); Multi-family building permits issued: 12 (2001) / 4 (2000); Employment by occupation: 13.1% management, 18.4% professional, 11.8% services, 29.5% sales, 0.2% farming, 9.2% construction, 17.7% production (2000).

Income: Per capita income: $23,022 (2000); Median household income: $48,372 (2000); Poverty rate: 7.3% (2000).

Taxes: Total city taxes per capita: $293 (2000); City property taxes per capita: $259 (2000).

Education: High school graduation rate: 89.4% (2000); College graduation rate: 24.4% (2000).

School District(s)

Fridley (PK-12)
2000 Enrollment: 2,554 763-502-5000

Housing: Homeownership rate: 67.7% (2000); Median home value: $120,300 (2000); Median rent: $608 per month (2000); Median age of housing: 33 years (2000).

Transportation: Commute to work: 91.9% car, 3.8% public transportation, 1.2% walk, 2.4% work from home (2000); Travel time to work: 29.1% less than 15 minutes, 41.5% 15 to 30 minutes, 21.6% 30 to 45 minutes, 4.7% 45 to 60 minutes, 3.0% 60 minutes or more (2000)

Additional Information Contacts

Fridley Chamber of Commerce 763-571-9781

HAM LAKE (city). Covers a land area of 34.452 square miles and a water area of 1.253 square miles. Located at 45.25° N. Lat.; 93.21° W. Long. Elevation is 911 feet.

Population: 12,710 (2000); Race: 96.1% White, 0.7% Black, 0.8% Asian, 0.1% American Indian and Alaska Native, 1.6% Hispanic of any race, 1.2% two or more races (2000); Density: 368.9 persons per square mile (2000); Age: 31.6% under 18, 4.0% over 64 (2000); Marriage status: 22.9% never married, 67.8% now married, 2.3% widowed, 7.0% divorced (2000); Foreign born: 2.1% (2000); Ancestry (includes multiple ancestries): 37.4% German, 20.3% Norwegian, 16.0% Swedish, 13.5% Irish, 8.3% Polish (2000).

Economy: Manufacturing: commercial fixtures, building materials, wood products; machining. Single-family building permits issued: 158 (2001) / 164 (2000); Multi-family building permits issued: 10 (2001) / 12 (2000); Employment by occupation: 15.1% management, 17.0% professional, 11.2% services, 25.1% sales, 0.2% farming, 12.4% construction, 19.0% production (2000).

Income: Per capita income: $24,329 (2000); Median household income: $67,750 (2000); Poverty rate: 2.1% (2000).

Taxes: Total city taxes per capita: $113 (1997); City property taxes per capita: $89 (1997).

Education: High school graduation rate: 92.7% (2000); College graduation rate: 20.8% (2000).

Housing: Homeownership rate: 94.2% (2000); Median home value: $150,300 (2000); Median rent: $601 per month (2000); Median age of housing: 19 years (2000).

Safety: Violent crime rate: 7.0 per 10,000 population; Property crime rate: 312.9 per 10,000 population (2001).

Transportation: Commute to work: 93.8% car, 0.8% public transportation, 0.6% walk, 4.1% work from home (2000); Travel time to work: 12.1% less than 15 minutes, 36.8% 15 to 30 minutes, 30.7% 30 to 45 minutes, 14.6% 45 to 60 minutes, 5.8% 60 minutes or more (2000)

Additional Information Contacts

Ham Lake Chamber of Commerce. 763-434-3011

HILLTOP (city). Covers a land area of 0.125 square miles and a water area of 0 square miles. Located at 45.05° N. Lat.; 93.24° W. Long. Elevation is 1,013 feet.

Population: 766 (2000); Race: 87.6% White, 5.6% Black, 3.9% Asian, 0.0% American Indian and Alaska Native, 5.2% Hispanic of any race, 2.5% two or more races (2000); Density: 6,111.3 persons per square mile (2000); Age: 20.2% under 18, 7.5% over 64 (2000); Marriage status: 37.6% never married, 30.7% now married, 3.6% widowed, 28.0% divorced (2000); Foreign born: 7.5% (2000); Ancestry (includes multiple ancestries): 22.2% German, 15.6% Norwegian, 14.6% Other groups, 8.9% Irish, 7.5% Swedish (2000).

Economy: Single-family building permits issued: 0 (2001) / 0 (2000); Multi-family building permits issued: 0 (2001) / 0 (2000); Employment by occupation: 4.6% management, 11.6% professional, 21.9% services, 30.7% sales, 0.0% farming, 5.9% construction, 25.3% production (2000).

Income: Per capita income: $16,576 (2000); Median household income: $26,528 (2000); Poverty rate: 21.4% (2000).

Taxes: Total city taxes per capita: $461 (1997); City property taxes per capita: $425 (1997).

Education: High school graduation rate: 73.0% (2000); College graduation rate: 8.1% (2000).

Housing: Homeownership rate: 63.2% (2000); Median home value: $55,000 (2000); Median rent: $477 per month (2000); Median age of housing: 27 years (2000).

Safety: Violent crime rate: 142.1 per 10,000 population; Property crime rate: 788.1 per 10,000 population (2001).

Transportation: Commute to work: 70.9% car, 15.2% public transportation, 7.1% walk, 5.8% work from home (2000); Travel time to work: 27.2% less than 15 minutes, 37.5% 15 to 30 minutes, 11.7% 30 to 45 minutes, 7.8% 45 to 60 minutes, 15.8% 60 minutes or more (2000)

LEXINGTON (city). Covers a land area of 0.693 square miles and a water area of 0 square miles. Located at 45.13° N. Lat.; 93.17° W. Long. Elevation is 910 feet.
Population: 2,214 (2000); Race: 91.9% White, 0.9% Black, 1.1% Asian, 1.9% American Indian and Alaska Native, 1.7% Hispanic of any race, 2.0% two or more races (2000); Density: 3,196.1 persons per square mile (2000); Age: 29.3% under 18, 5.4% over 64 (2000); Marriage status: 34.8% never married, 46.4% now married, 4.0% widowed, 14.8% divorced (2000); Foreign born: 3.5% (2000); Ancestry (includes multiple ancestries): 37.3% German, 14.5% Norwegian, 13.2% Irish, 9.8% Swedish, 7.6% Polish (2000).
Economy: Light manufacturing. Single-family building permits issued: 0 (2001) / 1 (2000); Multi-family building permits issued: 0 (2001) / 0 (2000); Employment by occupation: 8.7% management, 14.9% professional, 13.5% services, 28.6% sales, 0.6% farming, 13.8% construction, 19.8% production (2000).
Income: Per capita income: $18,944 (2000); Median household income: $41,618 (2000); Poverty rate: 10.7% (2000).
Taxes: Total city taxes per capita: $180 (1997); City property taxes per capita: $170 (1997).
Education: High school graduation rate: 85.4% (2000); College graduation rate: 10.8% (2000).
Housing: Homeownership rate: 70.8% (2000); Median home value: $104,100 (2000); Median rent: $525 per month (2000); Median age of housing: 32 years (2000).
Transportation: Commute to work: 91.3% car, 1.3% public transportation, 4.1% walk, 2.8% work from home (2000); Travel time to work: 26.2% less than 15 minutes, 45.7% 15 to 30 minutes, 19.3% 30 to 45 minutes, 5.7% 45 to 60 minutes, 3.1% 60 minutes or more (2000)

LINO LAKES (city). Covers a land area of 28.217 square miles and a water area of 4.994 square miles. Located at 45.16° N. Lat.; 93.09° W. Long. Elevation is 905 feet.
Population: 16,791 (2000); Race: 92.8% White, 2.3% Black, 1.6% Asian, 0.9% American Indian and Alaska Native, 1.4% Hispanic of any race, 1.8% two or more races (2000); Density: 595.1 persons per square mile (2000); Age: 34.0% under 18, 3.4% over 64 (2000); Marriage status: 22.4% never married, 69.9% now married, 2.0% widowed, 5.7% divorced (2000); Foreign born: 3.0% (2000); Ancestry (includes multiple ancestries): 43.1% German, 16.3% Norwegian, 14.0% Irish, 11.3% Swedish, 7.1% English (2000).
Economy: Manufacturing: plastic products, machining, building materials, corrosion inhibiting products, electrical products. Minnesota Correctional Facility to West. Single-family building permits issued: 201 (2001) / 240 (2000); Multi-family building permits issued: 0 (2001) / 0 (2000); Employment by occupation: 20.0% management, 23.4% professional, 10.2% services, 26.3% sales, 0.0% farming, 8.7% construction, 11.3% production (2000).
Income: Per capita income: $25,419 (2000); Median household income: $75,708 (2000); Poverty rate: 3.0% (2000).
Taxes: Total city taxes per capita: $326 (2000); City property taxes per capita: $272 (2000).
Education: High school graduation rate: 93.3% (2000); College graduation rate: 33.5% (2000).
Housing: Homeownership rate: 96.2% (2000); Median home value: $162,700 (2000); Median rent: $696 per month (2000); Median age of housing: 10 years (2000).
Transportation: Commute to work: 95.4% car, 1.3% public transportation, 0.1% walk, 2.9% work from home (2000); Travel time to work: 17.2% less than 15 minutes, 39.4% 15 to 30 minutes, 32.0% 30 to 45 minutes, 7.0% 45 to 60 minutes, 4.4% 60 minutes or more (2000)

LINWOOD (township). Covers a land area of 33.369 square miles and a water area of 2.535 square miles. Located at 45.38° N. Lat.; 93.08° W. Long.
Population: 4,668 (2000); Race: 97.6% White, 1.2% Black, 0.2% Asian, 0.8% American Indian and Alaska Native, 0.2% Hispanic of any race, 0.2% two or more races (2000); Density: 139.9 persons per square mile (2000); Age: 30.1% under 18, 4.5% over 64 (2000); Marriage status: 24.5% never married, 64.4% now married, 1.5% widowed, 9.5% divorced (2000); Foreign born: 0.7% (2000); Ancestry (includes multiple ancestries): 35.6% German, 12.6% Swedish, 12.2% Norwegian, 11.4% Irish, 6.6% United States or American (2000).
Economy: Single-family building permits issued: 42 (2001) / 17 (2000); Multi-family building permits issued: 0 (2001) / 0 (2000); Employment by occupation: 14.4% management, 15.3% professional, 10.6% services, 22.6% sales, 0.6% farming, 14.2% construction, 22.3% production (2000).
Income: Per capita income: $23,690 (2000); Median household income: $58,596 (2000); Poverty rate: 3.5% (2000).
Taxes: Total city taxes per capita: $103 (2000); City property taxes per capita: $94 (2000).
Education: High school graduation rate: 91.6% (2000); College graduation rate: 11.7% (2000).
Housing: Homeownership rate: 98.0% (2000); Median home value: $135,200 (2000); Median rent: $442 per month (2000); Median age of housing: 21 years (2000).
Transportation: Commute to work: 95.3% car, 0.3% public transportation, 1.5% walk, 3.0% work from home (2000); Travel time to work: 9.9% less than 15 minutes, 26.3% 15 to 30 minutes, 29.9% 30 to 45 minutes, 24.8% 45 to 60 minutes, 9.0% 60 minutes or more (2000)

OAK GROVE (city). Covers a land area of 33.695 square miles and a water area of 1.315 square miles. Located at 45.33° N. Lat.; 93.33° W. Long. Elevation is 915 feet.
Population: 6,903 (2000); Race: 97.3% White, 0.5% Black, 0.2% Asian, 0.6% American Indian and Alaska Native, 0.2% Hispanic of any race, 1.5% two or more races (2000); Density: 204.9 persons per square mile (2000); Age: 32.3% under 18, 3.6% over 64 (2000); Marriage status: 23.7% never married, 67.3% now married, 1.7% widowed, 7.4% divorced (2000); Foreign born: 0.8% (2000); Ancestry (includes multiple ancestries): 40.8% German, 20.5% Swedish, 20.3% Norwegian, 13.8% Irish, 7.5% Polish (2000).
Economy: Single-family building permits issued: 77 (2001) / 43 (2000); Multi-family building permits issued: 0 (2001) / 0 (2000); Employment by occupation: 14.1% management, 17.7% professional, 9.5% services, 25.7% sales, 0.4% farming, 15.4% construction, 17.1% production (2000).
Income: Per capita income: $23,693 (2000); Median household income: $70,169 (2000); Poverty rate: 1.5% (2000).
Taxes: Total city taxes per capita: $210 (1997); City property taxes per capita: $191 (1997).
Education: High school graduation rate: 92.6% (2000); College graduation rate: 16.3% (2000).
Housing: Homeownership rate: 97.6% (2000); Median home value: $151,100 (2000); Median rent: $619 per month (2000); Median age of housing: 18 years (2000).
Transportation: Commute to work: 92.9% car, 1.0% public transportation, 0.6% walk, 4.7% work from home (2000); Travel time to work: 8.6% less than 15 minutes, 25.4% 15 to 30 minutes, 30.3% 30 to 45 minutes, 19.9% 45 to 60 minutes, 15.8% 60 minutes or more (2000)

RAMSEY (city). Covers a land area of 28.789 square miles and a water area of 0.953 square miles. Located at 45.26° N. Lat.; 93.44° W. Long. Elevation is 870 feet.
Population: 18,510 (2000); Race: 96.2% White, 0.1% Black, 1.5% Asian, 0.4% American Indian and Alaska Native, 1.0% Hispanic of any race, 1.1% two or more races (2000); Density: 642.9 persons per square mile (2000); Age: 32.1% under 18, 3.1% over 64 (2000); Marriage status: 20.3% never married, 71.2% now married, 1.3% widowed, 7.2% divorced (2000); Foreign born: 1.6% (2000); Ancestry (includes multiple ancestries): 40.8% German, 19.4% Norwegian, 13.0% Swedish, 12.1% Irish, 9.1% Polish (2000).
Vital Statistics: Birth rate: 146.4 per 10,000 population (1998)
Economy: Manufacturing: abrasives, athletic exercise equipment, Easter products, diverse light manufacturing. Agriculture includes alfalfa, rye; dairying. Gateway North Industrial Airport in South. Single-family building permits issued: 102 (2001) / 108 (2000); Multi-family building permits issued: 12 (2001) / 0 (2000); Employment by occupation: 15.7% management, 18.9% professional, 10.2% services, 27.7% sales, 0.3% farming, 10.6% construction, 16.5% production (2000).
Income: Per capita income: $26,057 (2000); Median household income: $68,988 (2000); Poverty rate: 1.6% (2000).
Taxes: Total city taxes per capita: $260 (2000); City property taxes per capita: $243 (2000).
Education: High school graduation rate: 94.0% (2000); College graduation rate: 21.1% (2000).
Housing: Homeownership rate: 97.4% (2000); Median home value: $143,500 (2000); Median rent: $864 per month (2000); Median age of housing: 16 years (2000).
Transportation: Commute to work: 92.8% car, 1.6% public transportation, 0.4% walk, 4.9% work from home (2000); Travel time to work: 18.2% less than 15 minutes, 32.8% 15 to 30 minutes, 28.1% 30 to 45 minutes, 13.6% 45 to 60 minutes, 7.3% 60 minutes or more (2000)

SAINT FRANCIS (city). Covers a land area of 23.318 square miles and a water area of 0.411 square miles. Located at 45.39° N. Lat.; 93.38° W. Long. Elevation is 918 feet.
Population: 4,910 (2000); Race: 96.5% White, 0.0% Black, 0.4% Asian, 1.0% American Indian and Alaska Native, 0.0% Hispanic of any race, 1.4% two or more races (2000); Density: 210.6 persons per square mile (2000); Age: 33.8% under 18, 2.9% over 64 (2000); Marriage status: 24.9% never married, 60.4% now married, 2.8% widowed, 11.8% divorced (2000); Foreign born: 1.2% (2000); Ancestry (includes multiple ancestries): 36.6% German, 14.8% Norwegian, 12.3% Irish, 8.1% Swedish, 6.5% English (2000).
Economy: Single-family building permits issued: 137 (2001) / 147 (2000); Multi-family building permits issued: 12 (2001) / 22 (2000); Employment by occupation: 6.8% management, 15.4% professional, 13.4% services, 22.5% sales, 0.2% farming, 17.4% construction, 24.3% production (2000).
Income: Per capita income: $19,957 (2000); Median household income: $51,982 (2000); Poverty rate: 4.8% (2000).
Education: High school graduation rate: 89.6% (2000); College graduation rate: 9.9% (2000).

School District(s)

Saint Francis (PK-12)
2000 Enrollment: 5,963 763-753-7059

Housing: Homeownership rate: 87.2% (2000); Median home value: $128,500 (2000); Median rent: $575 per month (2000); Median age of housing: 9 years (2000).
Transportation: Commute to work: 94.6% car, 1.2% public transportation, 1.8% walk, 1.7% work from home (2000); Travel time to work: 13.2% less than 15 minutes, 24.6% 15 to 30 minutes, 28.2% 30 to 45 minutes, 20.9% 45 to 60 minutes, 13.0% 60 minutes or more (2000)

SPRING LAKE PARK (city). Covers a land area of 1.985 square miles and a water area of 0.108 square miles. Located at 45.11° N. Lat.; 93.24° W. Long. Elevation is 903 feet.
Population: 6,772 (2000); Race: 90.6% White, 1.8% Black, 2.5% Asian, 0.6% American Indian and Alaska Native, 3.7% Hispanic of any race, 1.2% two or more races (2000); Density: 3,411.0 persons per square mile (2000); Age: 21.3% under 18, 12.6% over 64 (2000); Marriage status: 28.7% never married, 51.5% now married, 8.1% widowed, 11.6% divorced (2000); Foreign born: 6.9% (2000); Ancestry (includes multiple ancestries): 33.3% German, 17.2% Norwegian, 12.8% Swedish, 12.4% Irish, 8.7% Polish (2000).
Economy: Single-family building permits issued: 17 (2001) / 0 (2000); Multi-family building permits issued: 12 (2001) / 5 (2000); Employment by occupation: 9.8% management, 15.0% professional, 16.3% services, 29.1% sales, 0.1% farming, 12.7% construction, 17.0% production (2000).
Income: Per capita income: $21,932 (2000); Median household income: $46,646 (2000); Poverty rate: 5.1% (2000).
Taxes: Total city taxes per capita: $198 (1997); City property taxes per capita: $168 (1997).
Education: High school graduation rate: 87.4% (2000); College graduation rate: 16.7% (2000).

School District(s)

Spring Lake Park (PK-12)
2000 Enrollment: 4,234 763-786-5570

Housing: Homeownership rate: 74.6% (2000); Median home value: $120,000 (2000); Median rent: $644 per month (2000); Median age of housing: 30 years (2000).
Transportation: Commute to work: 89.3% car, 3.8% public transportation, 2.2% walk, 3.8% work from home (2000); Travel time to work: 28.0% less than 15 minutes, 37.9% 15 to 30 minutes, 22.1% 30 to 45 minutes, 7.6% 45 to 60 minutes, 4.5% 60 minutes or more (2000)

Becker County

Located in western Minnesota; includes White Earth Lake in the north, and Detroit and Cormorant Lakes in the southwest. Covers a land area of 1,310.40 square miles, a water area of 134.70 square miles, and is located in the Central Time Zone. The county government was organized in 1858. County seat is Detroit Lakes.
Population: 30,000 (2000); Race: 89.5% White, 0.3% Black, 0.5% Asian, 7.4% American Indian and Alaska Native, 0.5% Hispanic of any race, 2.2% two or more races (2000); Density: 22.9 persons per square mile (2000); Age: 26.6% under 18, 16.3% over 64 (2000).
Religion: Five largest groups: 25.3% Evangelical Lutheran Church in America, 24.4% Catholic Church, 12.3% Lutheran Church—Missouri Synod, 2.2% The United Methodist Church, 2.1% Episcopal Church (2000).
Economy: Unemployment rate: 4.8% (11/2002); Total civilian labor force: 15,025 (11/2002); Leading industries: 12.0% retail trade; 10.8% manufacturing; 9.7% health care and social assistance (2000); Companies that employ more than 1,000 persons: 1 (2000); Companies that employ more than 100 persons: 20 (2000); Farms: 1,084 totaling 388,733 acres (1997); Minority business ownership rate: 0.0% (1997); Women business ownership rate: 18.1% (1997); Retail sales per capita: $8,822 (1997). Single-family building permits issued: 205 (2001) / 191 (2000); Multi-family building permits issued: 28 (2001) / 8 (2000).
Income: Per capita income: $17,085 (2000); Median household income: $34,797 (2000); Poverty rate: 12.2% (2000); Bankruptcy rate: 2.56% (2001).
Taxes: Total county taxes per capita: $201 (2000); County property taxes per capita: $196 (2000).
Education: High school graduation rate: 82.9% (2000); College graduation rate: 16.7% (2000).
Housing: Homeownership rate: 80.4% (2000); Median home value: $87,400 (2000); Median rent: $315 per month (2000); Median age of housing: 29 years (2000).
Health: Birth rate: 119.7 per 10,000 population (1998); Age adjusted death rate: 82.9 per 10,000 population (1999); Age adjusted cancer mortality rate: 222.6 deaths per 100,000 population (1999). Number of physicians: 10.0 per 10,000 population (1999); Number of hospital beds: 55.0 per 10,000 population (1999).
Elections: 2000 Presidential election results: 36.7% Gore, 56.9% Bush, 4.1% Nader, 1.8% Buchanan
National and State Parks: Atlanta State Wildlife Management Area; Callaway State Wildlife Management Area; Coburn State Wildlife Management Area; Cuba State Wildlife Management Area; Linbom Lake State Wildlife Management Area; Lunde State Wildlife Management Area; Melbye State Wildlife Management Area; Ogema Springs State Wildlife Management Area; Pednor State Wildlife Management Area; Riparia State Wildlife Management Area; Smoky Hills State Forest; Spring Creek State Wildlife Management Area; Tamarac National Wildlife Refuge; Teiken-Dalve State Wildlife Management Area; Two Inlets State Forest; White Earth State Wildlife Management Area
Additional Information Contacts
Becker County Government Offices 218-846-7201
Detroit Lakes Park Rapids Board of Realtors 218-847-1950
Detroit Lakes Regional Chamber 218-847-9202
Elbow Lake Chamber of Commerce 218-685-5380

Becker County Communities

ATLANTA (township). Covers a land area of 35.572 square miles and a water area of 0.546 square miles. Located at 47.02° N. Lat.; 96.11° W. Long.
Population: 113 (2000); Race: 100.0% White, 0.0% Black, 0.0% Asian, 0.0% American Indian and Alaska Native, 0.0% Hispanic of any race, 0.0% two or more races (2000); Density: 3.2 persons per square mile (2000); Age: 33.3% under 18, 13.2% over 64 (2000); Marriage status: 16.3% never married, 62.0% now married, 4.3% widowed, 17.4% divorced (2000); Foreign born: 0.0% (2000); Ancestry (includes multiple ancestries): 51.9% Norwegian, 20.2% German, 6.2% Irish, 5.4% Swedish, 5.4% Other groups (2000).
Economy: Employment by occupation: 18.5% management, 3.7% professional, 35.2% services, 11.1% sales, 0.0% farming, 14.8% construction, 16.7% production (2000).
Income: Per capita income: $11,453 (2000); Median household income: $28,393 (2000); Poverty rate: 8.5% (2000).
Taxes: Total city taxes per capita: $242 (1997); City property taxes per capita: $242 (1997).
Education: High school graduation rate: 67.5% (2000); College graduation rate: 5.2% (2000).
Housing: Homeownership rate: 84.8% (2000); Median home value: $46,300 (2000); Median age of housing: 47 years (2000).
Transportation: Commute to work: 100.0% car, 0.0% public transportation, 0.0% walk, 0.0% work from home (2000); Travel time to work: 17.3% less than 15 minutes, 17.3% 15 to 30 minutes, 40.4% 30 to 45 minutes, 17.3% 45 to 60 minutes, 7.7% 60 minutes or more (2000)

AUDUBON (city). Covers a land area of 0.582 square miles and a water area of 0.006 square miles. Located at 46.86° N. Lat.; 95.97° W. Long. Elevation is 1,312 feet.

History: Audubon was named for the ornithologist John James Audubon (1780-1851), at the suggestion of his niece who once camped in the vicinity.
Population: 445 (2000); Race: 94.4% White, 0.0% Black, 0.0% Asian, 2.8% American Indian and Alaska Native, 0.4% Hispanic of any race, 2.8% two or more races (2000); Density: 764.0 persons per square mile (2000); Age: 33.7% under 18, 10.3% over 64 (2000); Marriage status: 27.2% never married, 56.9% now married, 7.8% widowed, 8.1% divorced (2000); Foreign born: 0.6% (2000); Ancestry (includes multiple ancestries): 35.9% German, 34.1% Norwegian, 10.5% Other groups, 7.3% Swedish, 4.2% Irish (2000).
Economy: Employment by occupation: 11.4% management, 12.3% professional, 14.2% services, 27.4% sales, 1.8% farming, 8.2% construction, 24.7% production (2000).
Income: Per capita income: $13,435 (2000); Median household income: $35,729 (2000); Poverty rate: 18.2% (2000).
Taxes: Total city taxes per capita: $190 (1997); City property taxes per capita: $188 (1997).
Education: High school graduation rate: 77.6% (2000); College graduation rate: 6.6% (2000).

School District(s)

Lake Agassiz Special Education Coop (PK-PK)
2000 Enrollment: 17 218-439-6876

Housing: Homeownership rate: 55.8% (2000); Median home value: $65,600 (2000); Median rent: $398 per month (2000); Median age of housing: 28 years (2000).
Transportation: Commute to work: 86.4% car, 0.0% public transportation, 7.7% walk, 5.0% work from home (2000); Travel time to work: 51.4% less than 15 minutes, 24.3% 15 to 30 minutes, 5.2% 30 to 45 minutes, 10.5% 45 to 60 minutes, 8.6% 60 minutes or more (2000)

AUDUBON (township). Covers a land area of 32.354 square miles and a water area of 3.041 square miles. Located at 46.85° N. Lat.; 95.99° W. Long. Elevation is 1,312 feet.
Population: 416 (2000); Race: 99.5% White, 0.0% Black, 0.0% Asian, 0.0% American Indian and Alaska Native, 0.0% Hispanic of any race, 0.5% two or more races (2000); Density: 12.9 persons per square mile (2000); Age: 25.4% under 18, 12.7% over 64 (2000); Marriage status: 22.2% never married, 65.3% now married, 5.5% widowed, 7.0% divorced (2000); Foreign born: 0.5% (2000); Ancestry (includes multiple ancestries): 48.7% German, 40.6% Norwegian, 10.4% Swedish, 9.6% Irish, 7.6% English (2000).
Economy: Dairying; poultry; sunflowers, grain, sugar beets, beans. Manufacturing: machining; cabinets. Employment by occupation: 11.5% management, 11.5% professional, 10.0% services, 28.2% sales, 0.0% farming, 9.6% construction, 29.2% production (2000).
Income: Per capita income: $20,650 (2000); Median household income: $40,000 (2000); Poverty rate: 9.3% (2000).
Taxes: Total city taxes per capita: $79 (1997); City property taxes per capita: $79 (1997).
Education: High school graduation rate: 88.4% (2000); College graduation rate: 9.0% (2000).
Housing: Homeownership rate: 95.8% (2000); Median home value: $101,100 (2000); Median rent: $408 per month (2000); Median age of housing: 24 years (2000).
Transportation: Commute to work: 83.9% car, 1.0% public transportation, 2.9% walk, 12.2% work from home (2000); Travel time to work: 25.6% less than 15 minutes, 45.6% 15 to 30 minutes, 7.8% 30 to 45 minutes, 9.4% 45 to 60 minutes, 11.7% 60 minutes or more (2000)

BURLINGTON (township). Covers a land area of 33.360 square miles and a water area of 2.168 square miles. Located at 46.74° N. Lat.; 95.74° W. Long.
Population: 1,304 (2000); Race: 97.3% White, 0.0% Black, 0.2% Asian, 0.4% American Indian and Alaska Native, 0.0% Hispanic of any race, 2.2% two or more races (2000); Density: 39.1 persons per square mile (2000); Age: 27.5% under 18, 11.4% over 64 (2000); Marriage status: 21.4% never married, 68.2% now married, 3.5% widowed, 6.9% divorced (2000); Foreign born: 0.4% (2000); Ancestry (includes multiple ancestries): 47.8% German, 23.0% Norwegian, 10.9% Swedish, 8.4% Irish, 5.4% French (except Basque) (2000).
Economy: Employment by occupation: 9.8% management, 16.0% professional, 15.9% services, 20.0% sales, 1.0% farming, 13.0% construction, 24.3% production (2000).
Income: Per capita income: $17,003 (2000); Median household income: $43,295 (2000); Poverty rate: 7.7% (2000).
Taxes: Total city taxes per capita: $36 (1997); City property taxes per capita: $36 (1997).
Education: High school graduation rate: 82.5% (2000); College graduation rate: 14.0% (2000).
Housing: Homeownership rate: 93.6% (2000); Median home value: $89,200 (2000); Median rent: $405 per month (2000); Median age of housing: 25 years (2000).
Transportation: Commute to work: 91.5% car, 0.3% public transportation, 1.3% walk, 5.0% work from home (2000); Travel time to work: 45.9% less than 15 minutes, 36.5% 15 to 30 minutes, 7.2% 30 to 45 minutes, 3.4% 45 to 60 minutes, 7.1% 60 minutes or more (2000)

CALLAWAY (city). Covers a land area of 0.631 square miles and a water area of 0.002 square miles. Located at 46.98° N. Lat.; 95.90° W. Long. Elevation is 1,370 feet.
Population: 200 (2000); Race: 56.5% White, 0.0% Black, 5.6% Asian, 27.1% American Indian and Alaska Native, 3.7% Hispanic of any race, 10.7% two or more races (2000); Density: 316.9 persons per square mile (2000); Age: 33.6% under 18, 8.4% over 64 (2000); Marriage status: 32.1% never married, 59.6% now married, 5.8% widowed, 2.6% divorced (2000); Foreign born: 5.6% (2000); Ancestry (includes multiple ancestries): 38.3% Other groups, 34.1% German, 7.0% Swedish, 4.7% Polish, 4.2% Norwegian (2000).
Economy: Single-family building permits issued: 2 (2001) / 0 (2000); Multi-family building permits issued: 0 (2001) / 0 (2000); Employment by occupation: 4.3% management, 21.5% professional, 20.4% services, 21.5% sales, 0.0% farming, 11.8% construction, 20.4% production (2000).
Income: Per capita income: $12,151 (2000); Median household income: $33,750 (2000); Poverty rate: 9.3% (2000).
Taxes: Total city taxes per capita: $70 (1997); City property taxes per capita: $70 (1997).
Education: High school graduation rate: 87.7% (2000); College graduation rate: 13.8% (2000).
Housing: Homeownership rate: 84.7% (2000); Median home value: $40,000 (2000); Median rent: $325 per month (2000); Median age of housing: 36 years (2000).
Transportation: Commute to work: 73.1% car, 0.0% public transportation, 9.7% walk, 17.2% work from home (2000); Travel time to work: 20.8% less than 15 minutes, 45.5% 15 to 30 minutes, 23.4% 30 to 45 minutes, 5.2% 45 to 60 minutes, 5.2% 60 minutes or more (2000)

CALLAWAY (township). Covers a land area of 33.866 square miles and a water area of 1.410 square miles. Located at 47.01° N. Lat.; 95.87° W. Long. Elevation is 1,370 feet.
Population: 260 (2000); Race: 60.5% White, 0.0% Black, 0.0% Asian, 22.2% American Indian and Alaska Native, 2.3% Hispanic of any race, 17.2% two or more races (2000); Density: 7.7 persons per square mile (2000); Age: 28.0% under 18, 13.8% over 64 (2000); Marriage status: 27.9% never married, 59.2% now married, 6.5% widowed, 6.5% divorced (2000); Foreign born: 0.8% (2000); Ancestry (includes multiple ancestries): 31.8% German, 28.4% Other groups, 16.5% United States or American, 8.8% French (except Basque), 7.3% Norwegian (2000).
Economy: Grain, wild rice, alfalfa; livestock; dairying. Manufacturing: wild rice milling; timber. Employment by occupation: 14.3% management, 10.1% professional, 25.2% services, 14.3% sales, 0.0% farming, 14.3% construction, 21.8% production (2000).
Income: Per capita income: $14,020 (2000); Median household income: $33,542 (2000); Poverty rate: 13.8% (2000).
Taxes: Total city taxes per capita: $31 (1997); City property taxes per capita: $31 (1997).
Education: High school graduation rate: 82.6% (2000); College graduation rate: 10.8% (2000).
Housing: Homeownership rate: 87.5% (2000); Median home value: $70,000 (2000); Median age of housing: 31 years (2000).
Transportation: Commute to work: 78.2% car, 0.0% public transportation, 0.0% walk, 17.6% work from home (2000); Travel time to work: 11.2% less than 15 minutes, 29.6% 15 to 30 minutes, 19.4% 30 to 45 minutes, 9.2% 45 to 60 minutes, 30.6% 60 minutes or more (2000)

CARSONVILLE (township). Covers a land area of 35.061 square miles and a water area of 0.735 square miles. Located at 46.94° N. Lat.; 95.35° W. Long.
Population: 252 (2000); Race: 83.2% White, 0.0% Black, 0.0% Asian, 16.8% American Indian and Alaska Native, 0.0% Hispanic of any race, 0.0% two or more races (2000); Density: 7.2 persons per square mile (2000); Age: 23.4% under 18, 12.1% over 64 (2000); Marriage status: 12.2% never married, 75.6% now married, 7.6% widowed, 4.7% divorced (2000); Foreign

born: 0.0% (2000); Ancestry (includes multiple ancestries): 29.4% German, 26.6% Finnish, 16.8% Other groups, 12.1% Norwegian, 8.4% English (2000).
Economy: Employment by occupation: 12.5% management, 17.3% professional, 16.3% services, 24.0% sales, 1.9% farming, 16.3% construction, 11.5% production (2000).
Income: Per capita income: $15,768 (2000); Median household income: $35,000 (2000); Poverty rate: 10.7% (2000).
Taxes: Total city taxes per capita: $28 (2000); City property taxes per capita: $28 (2000).
Education: High school graduation rate: 86.8% (2000); College graduation rate: 13.8% (2000).
Housing: Homeownership rate: 91.6% (2000); Median home value: $57,000 (2000); Median rent: $275 per month (2000); Median age of housing: 26 years (2000).
Transportation: Commute to work: 81.7% car, 0.0% public transportation, 4.8% walk, 13.5% work from home (2000); Travel time to work: 24.4% less than 15 minutes, 28.9% 15 to 30 minutes, 38.9% 30 to 45 minutes, 2.2% 45 to 60 minutes, 5.6% 60 minutes or more (2000)

CORMORANT (township). Covers a land area of 26.345 square miles and a water area of 9.917 square miles. Located at 46.76° N. Lat.; 96.10° W. Long. Elevation is 1,350 feet.
Population: 965 (2000); Race: 98.8% White, 0.1% Black, 0.0% Asian, 0.3% American Indian and Alaska Native, 0.5% Hispanic of any race, 0.7% two or more races (2000); Density: 36.6 persons per square mile (2000); Age: 16.2% under 18, 23.0% over 64 (2000); Marriage status: 14.4% never married, 70.6% now married, 6.5% widowed, 8.5% divorced (2000); Foreign born: 0.3% (2000); Ancestry (includes multiple ancestries): 43.6% Norwegian, 31.8% German, 14.8% Swedish, 6.5% English, 5.2% Irish (2000).
Economy: Employment by occupation: 19.2% management, 15.9% professional, 11.5% services, 25.9% sales, 0.7% farming, 12.8% construction, 13.9% production (2000).
Income: Per capita income: $24,016 (2000); Median household income: $47,560 (2000); Poverty rate: 4.7% (2000).
Taxes: Total city taxes per capita: $171 (1997); City property taxes per capita: $171 (1997).
Education: High school graduation rate: 86.2% (2000); College graduation rate: 23.4% (2000).
Housing: Homeownership rate: 94.1% (2000); Median home value: $161,300 (2000); Median rent: $459 per month (2000); Median age of housing: 25 years (2000).
Transportation: Commute to work: 91.6% car, 0.0% public transportation, 0.0% walk, 7.5% work from home (2000); Travel time to work: 9.3% less than 15 minutes, 29.4% 15 to 30 minutes, 23.3% 30 to 45 minutes, 28.4% 45 to 60 minutes, 9.6% 60 minutes or more (2000)

CUBA (township). Covers a land area of 34.165 square miles and a water area of 1.380 square miles. Located at 46.92° N. Lat.; 96.09° W. Long.
Population: 208 (2000); Race: 98.9% White, 0.0% Black, 0.0% Asian, 0.0% American Indian and Alaska Native, 0.5% Hispanic of any race, 1.1% two or more races (2000); Density: 6.1 persons per square mile (2000); Age: 16.6% under 18, 27.8% over 64 (2000); Marriage status: 22.5% never married, 67.5% now married, 5.6% widowed, 4.4% divorced (2000); Foreign born: 1.6% (2000); Ancestry (includes multiple ancestries): 47.1% Norwegian, 42.2% German, 13.4% Swedish, 10.7% Irish, 3.7% Other groups (2000).
Economy: Employment by occupation: 22.7% management, 5.2% professional, 11.3% services, 22.7% sales, 15.5% farming, 10.3% construction, 12.4% production (2000).
Income: Per capita income: $19,991 (2000); Median household income: $39,167 (2000); Poverty rate: 6.4% (2000).
Taxes: Total city taxes per capita: $83 (1997); City property taxes per capita: $83 (1997).
Education: High school graduation rate: 89.8% (2000); College graduation rate: 7.5% (2000).
Housing: Homeownership rate: 86.6% (2000); Median home value: $63,300 (2000); Median rent: $350 per month (2000); Median age of housing: 60+ years (2000).
Transportation: Commute to work: 89.2% car, 0.0% public transportation, 7.5% walk, 3.2% work from home (2000); Travel time to work: 37.8% less than 15 minutes, 34.4% 15 to 30 minutes, 4.4% 30 to 45 minutes, 11.1% 45 to 60 minutes, 12.2% 60 minutes or more (2000)

DETROIT (township). Covers a land area of 25.923 square miles and a water area of 4.751 square miles. Located at 46.84° N. Lat.; 95.86° W. Long.
Population: 2,359 (2000); Race: 94.2% White, 0.0% Black, 0.5% Asian, 3.4% American Indian and Alaska Native, 0.0% Hispanic of any race, 1.9% two or more races (2000); Density: 91.0 persons per square mile (2000); Age: 24.3% under 18, 12.8% over 64 (2000); Marriage status: 20.0% never married, 66.5% now married, 4.0% widowed, 9.5% divorced (2000); Foreign born: 1.3% (2000); Ancestry (includes multiple ancestries): 38.6% German, 35.2% Norwegian, 10.0% Swedish, 8.1% Irish, 6.9% English (2000).
Economy: Employment by occupation: 10.8% management, 16.2% professional, 16.3% services, 23.8% sales, 2.3% farming, 14.1% construction, 16.4% production (2000).
Income: Per capita income: $20,529 (2000); Median household income: $42,644 (2000); Poverty rate: 6.4% (2000).
Taxes: Total city taxes per capita: $48 (2000); City property taxes per capita: $48 (2000).
Education: High school graduation rate: 85.6% (2000); College graduation rate: 19.0% (2000).
Housing: Homeownership rate: 90.6% (2000); Median home value: $106,300 (2000); Median rent: $341 per month (2000); Median age of housing: 27 years (2000).
Transportation: Commute to work: 91.6% car, 0.3% public transportation, 0.6% walk, 7.1% work from home (2000); Travel time to work: 67.9% less than 15 minutes, 16.5% 15 to 30 minutes, 2.1% 30 to 45 minutes, 6.5% 45 to 60 minutes, 7.1% 60 minutes or more (2000)

DETROIT LAKES (city). Covers a land area of 7.495 square miles and a water area of 4.837 square miles. Located at 46.81° N. Lat.; 95.84° W. Long. Elevation is 1,353 feet.
History: The name of Detroit Lakes is from the French "detroit," meaning a strait or narrows. It was given to this place in the 1700's by a French missionary. The "Lakes" part of the name was added to attract vacationers to the more than 400 lakes in the vicinity. The discovery of an ancient stone tablet, swords and axes, and mooring stones indicates that Vikings visited this area in the 1300's.
Population: 7,348 (2000); Race: 91.5% White, 0.6% Black, 0.7% Asian, 5.5% American Indian and Alaska Native, 0.3% Hispanic of any race, 1.3% two or more races (2000); Density: 980.4 persons per square mile (2000); Age: 23.3% under 18, 23.6% over 64 (2000); Marriage status: 22.6% never married, 53.7% now married, 14.3% widowed, 9.4% divorced (2000); Foreign born: 1.5% (2000); Ancestry (includes multiple ancestries): 39.1% German, 31.4% Norwegian, 8.9% Swedish, 8.9% Other groups, 7.8% Irish (2000).
Economy: Single-family building permits issued: 19 (2001) / 17 (2000); Multi-family building permits issued: 28 (2001) / 8 (2000); Employment by occupation: 11.7% management, 20.7% professional, 19.7% services, 24.0% sales, 1.7% farming, 8.8% construction, 13.2% production (2000).
Income: Per capita income: $18,509 (2000); Median household income: $29,264 (2000); Poverty rate: 15.0% (2000).
Taxes: Total city taxes per capita: $213 (1997); City property taxes per capita: $194 (1997).
Education: High school graduation rate: 83.7% (2000); College graduation rate: 24.1% (2000).

School District(s)

Detroit Lakes (PK-12)
2000 Enrollment: 2,896 218-847-9271

Two-year College(s)

Northwest Technical College-Detroit Lakes (Public)
2001 Enrollment: n/a 218-846-7444

Housing: Homeownership rate: 64.8% (2000); Median home value: $83,400 (2000); Median rent: $319 per month (2000); Median age of housing: 39 years (2000).
Hospitals: Saint Mary's Regional Health Center (187 beds)
Newspapers: The Detroit Lakes Tribune (1 x week); The Becker County Record (1 x week); Lake Area Press (1 x week)
Transportation: Commute to work: 90.2% car, 0.4% public transportation, 3.8% walk, 4.5% work from home (2000); Travel time to work: 64.5% less than 15 minutes, 19.5% 15 to 30 minutes, 5.9% 30 to 45 minutes, 5.2% 45 to 60 minutes, 4.8% 60 minutes or more (2000); Amtrak: Service available.
Airports: Detroit Lakes-Wething Field
Additional Information Contacts
Detroit Lakes Park Rapids Board of Realtors 218-847-1950
Detroit Lakes Regional Chamber. 218-847-9202

EAGLE VIEW (township). Covers a land area of 31.332 square miles and a water area of 4.910 square miles. Located at 47.12° N. Lat.; 95.59° W. Long.
Population: 165 (2000); Race: 26.5% White, 0.0% Black, 0.0% Asian, 73.5% American Indian and Alaska Native, 0.0% Hispanic of any race, 0.0% two or more races (2000); Density: 5.3 persons per square mile (2000); Age:

40.0% under 18, 12.2% over 64 (2000); Marriage status: 26.1% never married, 64.7% now married, 5.9% widowed, 3.3% divorced (2000); Foreign born: 0.0% (2000); Ancestry (includes multiple ancestries): 66.1% Other groups, 18.7% German, 8.7% Norwegian, 4.8% Swedish, 4.8% Irish (2000).
Economy: Employment by occupation: 6.8% management, 20.3% professional, 35.6% services, 28.8% sales, 0.0% farming, 3.4% construction, 5.1% production (2000).
Income: Per capita income: $8,728 (2000); Median household income: $19,318 (2000); Poverty rate: 21.7% (2000).
Taxes: Total city taxes per capita: $156 (1997); City property taxes per capita: $156 (1997).
Education: High school graduation rate: 77.3% (2000); College graduation rate: 8.3% (2000).
Housing: Homeownership rate: 67.1% (2000); Median home value: $59,400 (2000); Median rent: $157 per month (2000); Median age of housing: 23 years (2000).
Transportation: Commute to work: 100.0% car, 0.0% public transportation, 0.0% walk, 0.0% work from home (2000); Travel time to work: 15.3% less than 15 minutes, 6.8% 15 to 30 minutes, 42.4% 30 to 45 minutes, 11.9% 45 to 60 minutes, 23.7% 60 minutes or more (2000)

ELBOW LAKE (CDP). Covers a land area of 1.212 square miles and a water area of 0 square miles. Located at 47.14° N. Lat.; 95.54° W. Long.
Population: 104 (2000); Race: 14.1% White, 0.0% Black, 0.0% Asian, 85.9% American Indian and Alaska Native, 0.0% Hispanic of any race, 0.0% two or more races (2000); Density: 85.8 persons per square mile (2000); Age: 48.3% under 18, 6.7% over 64 (2000); Marriage status: 32.6% never married, 58.7% now married, 5.4% widowed, 3.3% divorced (2000); Foreign born: 0.0% (2000); Ancestry (includes multiple ancestries): 84.6% Other groups, 5.4% German, 5.4% Norwegian, 4.0% United States or American, 1.3% Danish (2000).
Economy: Employment by occupation: 8.0% management, 16.0% professional, 44.0% services, 22.0% sales, 0.0% farming, 4.0% construction, 6.0% production (2000).
Income: Per capita income: $6,713 (2000); Median household income: $17,708 (2000); Poverty rate: 24.2% (2000).
Education: High school graduation rate: 66.2% (2000); College graduation rate: 2.7% (2000).
Housing: Homeownership rate: 60.4% (2000); Median home value: $45,000 (2000); Median rent: $157 per month (2000); Median age of housing: 22 years (2000).
Transportation: Commute to work: 90.0% car, 0.0% public transportation, 10.0% walk, 0.0% work from home (2000); Travel time to work: 32.0% less than 15 minutes, 0.0% 15 to 30 minutes, 50.0% 30 to 45 minutes, 12.0% 45 to 60 minutes, 6.0% 60 minutes or more (2000)
Additional Information Contacts
Elbow Lake Chamber of Commerce 218-685-5380

ERIE (township). Covers a land area of 32.089 square miles and a water area of 4.255 square miles. Located at 46.86° N. Lat.; 95.71° W. Long.
Population: 1,621 (2000); Race: 96.9% White, 0.0% Black, 0.0% Asian, 1.5% American Indian and Alaska Native, 0.2% Hispanic of any race, 1.5% two or more races (2000); Density: 50.5 persons per square mile (2000); Age: 31.4% under 18, 11.1% over 64 (2000); Marriage status: 20.4% never married, 67.8% now married, 4.7% widowed, 7.1% divorced (2000); Foreign born: 1.2% (2000); Ancestry (includes multiple ancestries): 43.5% German, 36.5% Norwegian, 11.3% Swedish, 5.9% Irish, 5.4% English (2000).
Economy: Employment by occupation: 10.1% management, 20.0% professional, 15.7% services, 21.8% sales, 1.9% farming, 13.3% construction, 17.2% production (2000).
Income: Per capita income: $18,837 (2000); Median household income: $43,024 (2000); Poverty rate: 4.2% (2000).
Taxes: Total city taxes per capita: $19 (1997); City property taxes per capita: $19 (1997).
Education: High school graduation rate: 90.8% (2000); College graduation rate: 18.9% (2000).
Housing: Homeownership rate: 95.5% (2000); Median home value: $98,900 (2000); Median rent: $315 per month (2000); Median age of housing: 27 years (2000).
Transportation: Commute to work: 91.0% car, 0.6% public transportation, 1.0% walk, 6.8% work from home (2000); Travel time to work: 36.1% less than 15 minutes, 42.0% 15 to 30 minutes, 7.8% 30 to 45 minutes, 2.8% 45 to 60 minutes, 11.2% 60 minutes or more (2000)

EVERGREEN (township). Covers a land area of 36.231 square miles and a water area of 0.136 square miles. Located at 46.76° N. Lat.; 95.47° W. Long. Elevation is 1,548 feet.
Population: 290 (2000); Race: 99.4% White, 0.0% Black, 0.0% Asian, 0.0% American Indian and Alaska Native, 1.6% Hispanic of any race, 0.6% two or more races (2000); Density: 8.0 persons per square mile (2000); Age: 27.4% under 18, 10.9% over 64 (2000); Marriage status: 28.0% never married, 62.6% now married, 5.4% widowed, 3.9% divorced (2000); Foreign born: 0.6% (2000); Ancestry (includes multiple ancestries): 56.4% German, 15.6% Irish, 15.0% Norwegian, 8.1% Polish, 6.5% English (2000).
Economy: Employment by occupation: 16.4% management, 15.8% professional, 12.3% services, 8.2% sales, 10.5% farming, 17.0% construction, 19.9% production (2000).
Income: Per capita income: $14,993 (2000); Median household income: $32,692 (2000); Poverty rate: 9.7% (2000).
Taxes: Total city taxes per capita: $59 (2000); City property taxes per capita: $59 (2000).
Education: High school graduation rate: 76.7% (2000); College graduation rate: 4.5% (2000).
Housing: Homeownership rate: 82.0% (2000); Median home value: $97,500 (2000); Median rent: $263 per month (2000); Median age of housing: 57 years (2000).
Transportation: Commute to work: 77.3% car, 0.0% public transportation, 2.5% walk, 19.0% work from home (2000); Travel time to work: 24.2% less than 15 minutes, 40.9% 15 to 30 minutes, 30.3% 30 to 45 minutes, 0.0% 45 to 60 minutes, 4.5% 60 minutes or more (2000)

FOREST (township). Covers a land area of 32.370 square miles and a water area of 3.606 square miles. Located at 47.12° N. Lat.; 95.38° W. Long.
Population: 58 (2000); Race: 100.0% White, 0.0% Black, 0.0% Asian, 0.0% American Indian and Alaska Native, 0.0% Hispanic of any race, 0.0% two or more races (2000); Density: 1.8 persons per square mile (2000); Age: 0.0% under 18, 69.4% over 64 (2000); Marriage status: 3.2% never married, 74.2% now married, 8.1% widowed, 14.5% divorced (2000); Foreign born: 3.2% (2000); Ancestry (includes multiple ancestries): 41.9% German, 32.3% Norwegian, 16.1% United States or American, 16.1% Irish, 11.3% English (2000).
Economy: Employment by occupation: 16.7% management, 44.4% professional, 11.1% services, 11.1% sales, 16.7% farming, 0.0% construction, 0.0% production (2000).
Income: Per capita income: $30,232 (2000); Median household income: $49,167 (2000); Poverty rate: 6.5% (2000).
Taxes: Total city taxes per capita: $211 (1997); City property taxes per capita: $211 (1997).
Education: High school graduation rate: 87.1% (2000); College graduation rate: 41.9% (2000).
Housing: Homeownership rate: 91.4% (2000); Median home value: $205,400 (2000); Median age of housing: 24 years (2000).
Transportation: Commute to work: 61.1% car, 0.0% public transportation, 27.8% walk, 11.1% work from home (2000); Travel time to work: 31.3% less than 15 minutes, 0.0% 15 to 30 minutes, 43.8% 30 to 45 minutes, 0.0% 45 to 60 minutes, 25.0% 60 minutes or more (2000)

FRAZEE (city). Covers a land area of 0.864 square miles and a water area of 0.054 square miles. Located at 46.72° N. Lat.; 95.70° W. Long. Elevation is 1,390 feet.
History: Frazee developed in the heart of the park region, with many summer resorts.
Population: 1,377 (2000); Race: 92.2% White, 0.7% Black, 0.0% Asian, 4.3% American Indian and Alaska Native, 1.1% Hispanic of any race, 2.5% two or more races (2000); Density: 1,593.2 persons per square mile (2000); Age: 28.6% under 18, 19.9% over 64 (2000); Marriage status: 26.5% never married, 52.3% now married, 10.1% widowed, 11.1% divorced (2000); Foreign born: 0.3% (2000); Ancestry (includes multiple ancestries): 47.2% German, 23.3% Norwegian, 9.2% Irish, 8.7% Other groups, 5.6% Swedish (2000).
Economy: Single-family building permits issued: 1 (2001) / 1 (2000); Multi-family building permits issued: 0 (2001) / 0 (2000); Employment by occupation: 7.0% management, 13.2% professional, 23.0% services, 17.3% sales, 1.8% farming, 12.5% construction, 25.3% production (2000).
Income: Per capita income: $12,257 (2000); Median household income: $26,150 (2000); Poverty rate: 19.0% (2000).
Taxes: Total city taxes per capita: $131 (1997); City property taxes per capita: $128 (1997).

Education: High school graduation rate: 69.8% (2000); College graduation rate: 7.5% (2000).

School District(s)

Frazee (PK-12)
2000 Enrollment: 1,244 218-334-3181

Housing: Homeownership rate: 62.7% (2000); Median home value: $51,100 (2000); Median rent: $331 per month (2000); Median age of housing: 42 years (2000).

Newspapers: Frazee Forum (1 x week)

Transportation: Commute to work: 88.4% car, 0.0% public transportation, 4.9% walk, 4.5% work from home (2000); Travel time to work: 40.5% less than 15 minutes, 42.0% 15 to 30 minutes, 7.8% 30 to 45 minutes, 3.0% 45 to 60 minutes, 6.7% 60 minutes or more (2000)

GREEN VALLEY (township). Covers a land area of 35.439 square miles and a water area of 0.517 square miles. Located at 46.83° N. Lat.; 95.21° W. Long.

Population: 346 (2000); Race: 97.9% White, 0.0% Black, 0.0% Asian, 0.0% American Indian and Alaska Native, 2.1% Hispanic of any race, 0.0% two or more races (2000); Density: 9.8 persons per square mile (2000); Age: 27.8% under 18, 10.2% over 64 (2000); Marriage status: 21.9% never married, 65.6% now married, 8.4% widowed, 4.2% divorced (2000); Foreign born: 0.0% (2000); Ancestry (includes multiple ancestries): 33.1% Finnish, 22.5% German, 11.6% Norwegian, 8.5% English, 8.5% Swedish (2000).

Economy: Employment by occupation: 23.4% management, 10.3% professional, 16.6% services, 23.4% sales, 2.1% farming, 4.8% construction, 19.3% production (2000).

Income: Per capita income: $15,149 (2000); Median household income: $40,417 (2000); Poverty rate: 13.7% (2000).

Taxes: Total city taxes per capita: $39 (1997); City property taxes per capita: $39 (1997).

Education: High school graduation rate: 80.2% (2000); College graduation rate: 12.3% (2000).

Housing: Homeownership rate: 98.1% (2000); Median home value: $187,500 (2000); Median age of housing: 28 years (2000).

Transportation: Commute to work: 90.3% car, 2.8% public transportation, 4.1% walk, 2.8% work from home (2000); Travel time to work: 17.0% less than 15 minutes, 58.9% 15 to 30 minutes, 9.9% 30 to 45 minutes, 5.7% 45 to 60 minutes, 8.5% 60 minutes or more (2000)

HAMDEN (township). Covers a land area of 33.983 square miles and a water area of 1.468 square miles. Located at 46.95° N. Lat.; 95.99° W. Long.

Population: 220 (2000); Race: 97.4% White, 0.0% Black, 0.0% Asian, 0.9% American Indian and Alaska Native, 0.0% Hispanic of any race, 1.7% two or more races (2000); Density: 6.5 persons per square mile (2000); Age: 26.1% under 18, 9.4% over 64 (2000); Marriage status: 26.6% never married, 63.0% now married, 3.6% widowed, 6.8% divorced (2000); Foreign born: 0.0% (2000); Ancestry (includes multiple ancestries): 46.2% German, 45.7% Norwegian, 12.4% Swedish, 7.7% Irish, 5.6% Other groups (2000).

Economy: Employment by occupation: 21.4% management, 20.6% professional, 13.5% services, 18.3% sales, 3.2% farming, 12.7% construction, 10.3% production (2000).

Income: Per capita income: $19,353 (2000); Median household income: $43,333 (2000); Poverty rate: 6.9% (2000).

Taxes: Total city taxes per capita: $142 (1997); City property taxes per capita: $142 (1997).

Education: High school graduation rate: 84.3% (2000); College graduation rate: 20.3% (2000).

Housing: Homeownership rate: 97.7% (2000); Median home value: $72,500 (2000); Median age of housing: 45 years (2000).

Transportation: Commute to work: 88.1% car, 0.0% public transportation, 0.0% walk, 11.9% work from home (2000); Travel time to work: 7.2% less than 15 minutes, 46.8% 15 to 30 minutes, 16.2% 30 to 45 minutes, 24.3% 45 to 60 minutes, 5.4% 60 minutes or more (2000)

HEIGHT OF LAND (township). Covers a land area of 58.024 square miles and a water area of 13.475 square miles. Located at 46.90° N. Lat.; 95.61° W. Long.

Population: 639 (2000); Race: 97.4% White, 0.0% Black, 0.7% Asian, 0.0% American Indian and Alaska Native, 0.5% Hispanic of any race, 2.0% two or more races (2000); Density: 11.0 persons per square mile (2000); Age: 25.0% under 18, 9.3% over 64 (2000); Marriage status: 22.0% never married, 68.5% now married, 3.0% widowed, 6.5% divorced (2000); Foreign born: 1.7% (2000); Ancestry (includes multiple ancestries): 51.9% German, 30.6% Norwegian, 10.4% Swedish, 8.1% English, 5.6% Dutch (2000).

Economy: Employment by occupation: 15.4% management, 9.7% professional, 9.4% services, 23.5% sales, 1.3% farming, 14.4% construction, 26.3% production (2000).

Income: Per capita income: $16,973 (2000); Median household income: $36,154 (2000); Poverty rate: 8.1% (2000).

Taxes: Total city taxes per capita: $49 (1997); City property taxes per capita: $49 (1997).

Education: High school graduation rate: 81.3% (2000); College graduation rate: 14.3% (2000).

Housing: Homeownership rate: 93.2% (2000); Median home value: $83,100 (2000); Median age of housing: 28 years (2000).

Transportation: Commute to work: 86.6% car, 0.0% public transportation, 2.2% walk, 8.9% work from home (2000); Travel time to work: 12.6% less than 15 minutes, 49.7% 15 to 30 minutes, 24.8% 30 to 45 minutes, 4.9% 45 to 60 minutes, 8.0% 60 minutes or more (2000)

HOLMESVILLE (township). Covers a land area of 28.066 square miles and a water area of 8.064 square miles. Located at 46.93° N. Lat.; 95.72° W. Long.

Population: 457 (2000); Race: 95.3% White, 0.0% Black, 0.0% Asian, 2.4% American Indian and Alaska Native, 0.0% Hispanic of any race, 2.4% two or more races (2000); Density: 16.3 persons per square mile (2000); Age: 25.0% under 18, 15.1% over 64 (2000); Marriage status: 19.9% never married, 63.0% now married, 7.4% widowed, 9.6% divorced (2000); Foreign born: 1.3% (2000); Ancestry (includes multiple ancestries): 51.7% German, 31.7% Norwegian, 12.9% Swedish, 7.5% Irish, 5.2% French (except Basque) (2000).

Economy: Employment by occupation: 11.5% management, 9.6% professional, 14.8% services, 24.9% sales, 2.4% farming, 14.4% construction, 22.5% production (2000).

Income: Per capita income: $18,366 (2000); Median household income: $32,500 (2000); Poverty rate: 11.6% (2000).

Taxes: Total city taxes per capita: $72 (1997); City property taxes per capita: $72 (1997).

Education: High school graduation rate: 79.3% (2000); College graduation rate: 10.8% (2000).

Housing: Homeownership rate: 94.7% (2000); Median home value: $81,700 (2000); Median rent: $325 per month (2000); Median age of housing: 33 years (2000).

Transportation: Commute to work: 87.8% car, 0.0% public transportation, 1.5% walk, 8.8% work from home (2000); Travel time to work: 3.7% less than 15 minutes, 79.1% 15 to 30 minutes, 10.2% 30 to 45 minutes, 1.6% 45 to 60 minutes, 5.3% 60 minutes or more (2000)

LAKE EUNICE (township). Covers a land area of 30.031 square miles and a water area of 5.959 square miles. Located at 46.76° N. Lat.; 95.97° W. Long.

Population: 1,198 (2000); Race: 98.3% White, 0.3% Black, 0.0% Asian, 0.6% American Indian and Alaska Native, 0.2% Hispanic of any race, 0.8% two or more races (2000); Density: 39.9 persons per square mile (2000); Age: 21.9% under 18, 15.6% over 64 (2000); Marriage status: 15.4% never married, 70.1% now married, 4.8% widowed, 9.7% divorced (2000); Foreign born: 0.7% (2000); Ancestry (includes multiple ancestries): 40.5% Norwegian, 37.2% German, 12.1% Swedish, 8.2% Irish, 6.5% French (except Basque) (2000).

Economy: Employment by occupation: 13.6% management, 20.7% professional, 13.0% services, 23.7% sales, 0.0% farming, 11.7% construction, 17.4% production (2000).

Income: Per capita income: $18,756 (2000); Median household income: $34,688 (2000); Poverty rate: 11.2% (2000).

Taxes: Total city taxes per capita: $126 (2000); City property taxes per capita: $126 (2000).

Education: High school graduation rate: 87.9% (2000); College graduation rate: 18.4% (2000).

Housing: Homeownership rate: 90.8% (2000); Median home value: $124,700 (2000); Median rent: $398 per month (2000); Median age of housing: 22 years (2000).

Transportation: Commute to work: 92.8% car, 0.4% public transportation, 1.4% walk, 5.5% work from home (2000); Travel time to work: 24.8% less than 15 minutes, 47.1% 15 to 30 minutes, 8.7% 30 to 45 minutes, 12.2% 45 to 60 minutes, 7.2% 60 minutes or more (2000)

LAKE PARK (city). Covers a land area of 0.978 square miles and a water area of 0 square miles. Located at 46.88° N. Lat.; 96.09° W. Long. Elevation is 1,320 feet.

Population: 782 (2000); Race: 95.6% White, 0.0% Black, 0.0% Asian, 1.0% American Indian and Alaska Native, 0.0% Hispanic of any race, 3.3% two or more races (2000); Density: 799.4 persons per square mile (2000); Age: 31.8% under 18, 13.6% over 64 (2000); Marriage status: 23.8% never married, 58.8% now married, 10.6% widowed, 6.8% divorced (2000); Foreign born: 0.6% (2000); Ancestry (includes multiple ancestries): 49.7% Norwegian, 32.1% German, 15.9% Swedish, 6.9% Irish, 4.9% French (except Basque) (2000).
Economy: Single-family building permits issued: 5 (2001) / 5 (2000); Multi-family building permits issued: 0 (2001) / 0 (2000); Employment by occupation: 5.2% management, 14.4% professional, 19.9% services, 25.6% sales, 0.5% farming, 11.4% construction, 22.9% production (2000).
Income: Per capita income: $14,307 (2000); Median household income: $32,857 (2000); Poverty rate: 10.1% (2000).
Taxes: Total city taxes per capita: $115 (1997); City property taxes per capita: $113 (1997).
Education: High school graduation rate: 82.0% (2000); College graduation rate: 9.4% (2000).

School District(s)

Lake Park Audubon District (PK-12)
2000 Enrollment: 661 218-238-5914
Housing: Homeownership rate: 73.5% (2000); Median home value: $63,800 (2000); Median rent: $319 per month (2000); Median age of housing: 35 years (2000).
Transportation: Commute to work: 89.2% car, 0.0% public transportation, 5.0% walk, 5.0% work from home (2000); Travel time to work: 43.6% less than 15 minutes, 28.8% 15 to 30 minutes, 14.5% 30 to 45 minutes, 10.5% 45 to 60 minutes, 2.6% 60 minutes or more (2000)

LAKE PARK (township). Covers a land area of 30.693 square miles and a water area of 4.327 square miles. Located at 46.86° N. Lat.; 96.11° W. Long. Elevation is 1,320 feet.
Population: 418 (2000); Race: 100.0% White, 0.0% Black, 0.0% Asian, 0.0% American Indian and Alaska Native, 3.2% Hispanic of any race, 0.0% two or more races (2000); Density: 13.6 persons per square mile (2000); Age: 17.0% under 18, 26.2% over 64 (2000); Marriage status: 19.5% never married, 65.7% now married, 7.4% widowed, 7.4% divorced (2000); Foreign born: 0.5% (2000); Ancestry (includes multiple ancestries): 49.3% Norwegian, 28.9% German, 17.2% Swedish, 7.3% Irish, 4.1% English (2000).
Economy: Agriculture: grain, sugar beets, sunflowers; livestock, poultry; dairying. Manufacturing: fishing tackle. Employment by occupation: 14.2% management, 19.3% professional, 8.5% services, 26.7% sales, 1.7% farming, 10.2% construction, 19.3% production (2000).
Income: Per capita income: $20,983 (2000); Median household income: $40,972 (2000); Poverty rate: 1.1% (2000).
Taxes: Total city taxes per capita: $18 (1997); City property taxes per capita: $18 (1997).
Education: High school graduation rate: 74.8% (2000); College graduation rate: 17.4% (2000).
Housing: Homeownership rate: 96.1% (2000); Median home value: $76,000 (2000); Median age of housing: 38 years (2000).
Transportation: Commute to work: 86.8% car, 0.0% public transportation, 1.7% walk, 11.5% work from home (2000); Travel time to work: 29.9% less than 15 minutes, 37.0% 15 to 30 minutes, 14.9% 30 to 45 minutes, 14.3% 45 to 60 minutes, 3.9% 60 minutes or more (2000)

LAKE VIEW (township). Covers a land area of 21.648 square miles and a water area of 7.883 square miles. Located at 46.75° N. Lat.; 95.87° W. Long.
Population: 1,730 (2000); Race: 95.2% White, 0.1% Black, 0.0% Asian, 2.0% American Indian and Alaska Native, 0.6% Hispanic of any race, 2.2% two or more races (2000); Density: 79.9 persons per square mile (2000); Age: 27.8% under 18, 12.8% over 64 (2000); Marriage status: 20.8% never married, 66.7% now married, 4.6% widowed, 7.9% divorced (2000); Foreign born: 0.6% (2000); Ancestry (includes multiple ancestries): 35.6% German, 33.0% Norwegian, 10.1% Swedish, 10.0% Irish, 6.4% Other groups (2000).
Economy: Employment by occupation: 12.1% management, 19.4% professional, 14.6% services, 26.9% sales, 1.0% farming, 13.8% construction, 12.1% production (2000).
Income: Per capita income: $20,025 (2000); Median household income: $44,125 (2000); Poverty rate: 10.0% (2000).
Taxes: Total city taxes per capita: $143 (1997); City property taxes per capita: $131 (1997).
Education: High school graduation rate: 86.9% (2000); College graduation rate: 21.1% (2000).
Housing: Homeownership rate: 88.2% (2000); Median home value: $125,900 (2000); Median rent: $333 per month (2000); Median age of housing: 34 years (2000).
Transportation: Commute to work: 93.0% car, 0.0% public transportation, 1.6% walk, 4.6% work from home (2000); Travel time to work: 47.9% less than 15 minutes, 33.8% 15 to 30 minutes, 5.4% 30 to 45 minutes, 5.8% 45 to 60 minutes, 7.1% 60 minutes or more (2000)

MAPLE GROVE (township). Covers a land area of 27.702 square miles and a water area of 8.004 square miles. Located at 47.10° N. Lat.; 95.76° W. Long.
Population: 405 (2000); Race: 37.6% White, 0.0% Black, 3.0% Asian, 47.2% American Indian and Alaska Native, 3.0% Hispanic of any race, 12.1% two or more races (2000); Density: 14.6 persons per square mile (2000); Age: 29.5% under 18, 13.9% over 64 (2000); Marriage status: 24.1% never married, 54.5% now married, 5.4% widowed, 16.1% divorced (2000); Foreign born: 2.3% (2000); Ancestry (includes multiple ancestries): 56.6% Other groups, 18.4% German, 7.8% Irish, 7.6% Norwegian, 4.0% French Canadian (2000).
Economy: Employment by occupation: 5.9% management, 10.5% professional, 20.4% services, 23.0% sales, 5.3% farming, 20.4% construction, 14.5% production (2000).
Income: Per capita income: $14,359 (2000); Median household income: $37,667 (2000); Poverty rate: 16.2% (2000).
Taxes: Total city taxes per capita: $209 (1997); City property taxes per capita: $209 (1997).
Education: High school graduation rate: 76.8% (2000); College graduation rate: 5.1% (2000).
Housing: Homeownership rate: 85.6% (2000); Median home value: $94,300 (2000); Median rent: $225 per month (2000); Median age of housing: 23 years (2000).
Transportation: Commute to work: 97.9% car, 0.0% public transportation, 2.1% walk, 0.0% work from home (2000); Travel time to work: 22.1% less than 15 minutes, 26.2% 15 to 30 minutes, 40.0% 30 to 45 minutes, 4.1% 45 to 60 minutes, 7.6% 60 minutes or more (2000)

OGEMA (city). Covers a land area of 1.217 square miles and a water area of 0.066 square miles. Located at 47.10° N. Lat.; 95.92° W. Long. Elevation is 1,269 feet.
Population: 143 (2000); Race: 66.3% White, 0.0% Black, 1.2% Asian, 30.1% American Indian and Alaska Native, 0.0% Hispanic of any race, 2.4% two or more races (2000); Density: 117.5 persons per square mile (2000); Age: 24.1% under 18, 22.9% over 64 (2000); Marriage status: 23.5% never married, 53.0% now married, 13.6% widowed, 9.8% divorced (2000); Foreign born: 1.2% (2000); Ancestry (includes multiple ancestries): 41.6% Other groups, 31.9% German, 12.7% United States or American, 10.8% Norwegian, 8.4% Danish (2000).
Economy: Dairying; grain, wild rice. Employment by occupation: 15.0% management, 15.0% professional, 17.5% services, 21.3% sales, 3.8% farming, 8.8% construction, 18.8% production (2000).
Income: Per capita income: $14,622 (2000); Median household income: $27,083 (2000); Poverty rate: 7.8% (2000).
Taxes: Total city taxes per capita: $80 (1997); City property taxes per capita: $80 (1997).
Education: High school graduation rate: 75.9% (2000); College graduation rate: 10.2% (2000).
Housing: Homeownership rate: 88.0% (2000); Median home value: $35,500 (2000); Median rent: $325 per month (2000); Median age of housing: 40 years (2000).
Transportation: Commute to work: 85.0% car, 0.0% public transportation, 8.8% walk, 2.5% work from home (2000); Travel time to work: 35.9% less than 15 minutes, 25.6% 15 to 30 minutes, 6.4% 30 to 45 minutes, 0.0% 45 to 60 minutes, 32.1% 60 minutes or more (2000)

OSAGE (township). Covers a land area of 34.914 square miles and a water area of 0.924 square miles. Located at 46.92° N. Lat.; 95.23° W. Long. Elevation is 1,493 feet.
Population: 774 (2000); Race: 98.4% White, 0.0% Black, 0.0% Asian, 1.0% American Indian and Alaska Native, 1.3% Hispanic of any race, 0.6% two or more races (2000); Density: 22.2 persons per square mile (2000); Age: 30.3% under 18, 14.4% over 64 (2000); Marriage status: 20.2% never married, 68.5% now married, 7.7% widowed, 3.6% divorced (2000); Foreign born: 0.2% (2000); Ancestry (includes multiple ancestries): 40.9% German, 16.9% Norwegian, 12.7% English, 10.1% Finnish, 9.2% Irish (2000).

Economy: Employment by occupation: 9.0% management, 20.9% professional, 13.8% services, 18.0% sales, 2.9% farming, 19.3% construction, 16.1% production (2000).
Income: Per capita income: $14,788 (2000); Median household income: $37,500 (2000); Poverty rate: 6.2% (2000).
Taxes: Total city taxes per capita: $69 (1997); City property taxes per capita: $69 (1997).
Education: High school graduation rate: 87.3% (2000); College graduation rate: 11.8% (2000).
Housing: Homeownership rate: 87.0% (2000); Median home value: $90,400 (2000); Median rent: $303 per month (2000); Median age of housing: 24 years (2000).
Transportation: Commute to work: 89.4% car, 0.8% public transportation, 2.1% walk, 6.6% work from home (2000); Travel time to work: 28.6% less than 15 minutes, 49.3% 15 to 30 minutes, 7.9% 30 to 45 minutes, 1.1% 45 to 60 minutes, 13.0% 60 minutes or more (2000)

PINE POINT (township). Covers a land area of 34.436 square miles and a water area of 1.407 square miles. Located at 47.02° N. Lat.; 95.37° W. Long. Elevation is 1,538 feet.
Population: 419 (2000); Race: 21.1% White, 0.0% Black, 0.0% Asian, 78.9% American Indian and Alaska Native, 0.0% Hispanic of any race, 0.0% two or more races (2000); Density: 12.2 persons per square mile (2000); Age: 39.8% under 18, 4.6% over 64 (2000); Marriage status: 50.0% never married, 34.2% now married, 4.4% widowed, 11.4% divorced (2000); Foreign born: 0.0% (2000); Ancestry (includes multiple ancestries): 62.7% Other groups, 7.0% Norwegian, 3.4% German, 1.8% Finnish, 1.2% United States or American (2000).
Economy: Employment by occupation: 7.2% management, 10.3% professional, 18.6% services, 16.5% sales, 4.1% farming, 11.3% construction, 32.0% production (2000).
Income: Per capita income: $9,210 (2000); Median household income: $21,250 (2000); Poverty rate: 35.5% (2000).
Taxes: Total city taxes per capita: $16 (1997); City property taxes per capita: $16 (1997).
Education: High school graduation rate: 78.4% (2000); College graduation rate: 6.8% (2000).
Housing: Homeownership rate: 61.1% (2000); Median home value: $57,500 (2000); Median rent: <$100 per month (2000); Median age of housing: 18 years (2000).
Transportation: Commute to work: 89.5% car, 6.3% public transportation, 4.2% walk, 0.0% work from home (2000); Travel time to work: 27.4% less than 15 minutes, 15.8% 15 to 30 minutes, 45.3% 30 to 45 minutes, 5.3% 45 to 60 minutes, 6.3% 60 minutes or more (2000)

PONSFORD (unincorporated postal area, zip code 56575). Covers a land area of 145.403 square miles and a water area of 10.056 square miles. Located at 47.04° N. Lat.; 95.43° W. Long. Elevation is 1,536 feet.
Population: 721 (2000); Race: 39.0% White, 0.0% Black, 4.1% Asian, 56.9% American Indian and Alaska Native, 0.0% Hispanic of any race, 0.0% two or more races (2000); Density: 5.0 persons per square mile (2000); Age: 32.9% under 18, 16.6% over 64 (2000); Marriage status: 29.3% never married, 53.8% now married, 6.4% widowed, 10.5% divorced (2000); Foreign born: 4.5% (2000); Ancestry (includes multiple ancestries): 52.7% Other groups, 11.3% German, 10.8% Norwegian, 3.4% English, 3.0% Irish (2000).
Economy: Employment by occupation: 12.2% management, 16.6% professional, 17.6% services, 15.1% sales, 3.4% farming, 11.7% construction, 23.4% production (2000).
Income: Per capita income: $12,725 (2000); Median household income: $27,250 (2000); Poverty rate: 25.2% (2000).
Education: High school graduation rate: 77.5% (2000); College graduation rate: 15.8% (2000).

School District(s)

Pine Point (PK-08)
2000 Enrollment: 63 218-573-3550
Housing: Homeownership rate: 74.2% (2000); Median home value: $80,000 (2000); Median rent: $153 per month (2000); Median age of housing: 23 years (2000).
Transportation: Commute to work: 82.3% car, 3.0% public transportation, 10.8% walk, 3.9% work from home (2000); Travel time to work: 30.3% less than 15 minutes, 21.5% 15 to 30 minutes, 36.9% 30 to 45 minutes, 4.1% 45 to 60 minutes, 7.2% 60 minutes or more (2000)

RICEVILLE (township). Covers a land area of 37.041 square miles and a water area of 0.505 square miles. Located at 47.01° N. Lat.; 95.99° W. Long.
Population: 103 (2000); Race: 100.0% White, 0.0% Black, 0.0% Asian, 0.0% American Indian and Alaska Native, 0.0% Hispanic of any race, 0.0% two or more races (2000); Density: 2.8 persons per square mile (2000); Age: 35.0% under 18, 14.6% over 64 (2000); Marriage status: 22.1% never married, 69.1% now married, 5.9% widowed, 2.9% divorced (2000); Foreign born: 1.9% (2000); Ancestry (includes multiple ancestries): 40.8% German, 27.2% Norwegian, 14.6% United States or American, 14.6% Irish, 9.7% Czech (2000).
Economy: Employment by occupation: 40.0% management, 15.0% professional, 25.0% services, 5.0% sales, 0.0% farming, 0.0% construction, 15.0% production (2000).
Income: Per capita income: $10,999 (2000); Median household income: $35,625 (2000); Poverty rate: 17.5% (2000).
Taxes: Total city taxes per capita: $101 (1997); City property taxes per capita: $101 (1997).
Education: High school graduation rate: 75.8% (2000); College graduation rate: 3.2% (2000).
Housing: Homeownership rate: 94.1% (2000); Median home value: $50,000 (2000); Median rent: $225 per month (2000); Median age of housing: 43 years (2000).
Transportation: Commute to work: 70.0% car, 2.5% public transportation, 0.0% walk, 27.5% work from home (2000); Travel time to work: 3.4% less than 15 minutes, 20.7% 15 to 30 minutes, 0.0% 30 to 45 minutes, 6.9% 45 to 60 minutes, 69.0% 60 minutes or more (2000)

RICHWOOD (township). Covers a land area of 34.101 square miles and a water area of 1.881 square miles. Located at 46.94° N. Lat.; 95.84° W. Long. Elevation is 1,476 feet.
Population: 610 (2000); Race: 91.2% White, 1.3% Black, 0.0% Asian, 5.9% American Indian and Alaska Native, 0.2% Hispanic of any race, 1.6% two or more races (2000); Density: 17.9 persons per square mile (2000); Age: 28.3% under 18, 8.2% over 64 (2000); Marriage status: 27.2% never married, 63.3% now married, 3.4% widowed, 6.1% divorced (2000); Foreign born: 0.5% (2000); Ancestry (includes multiple ancestries): 38.9% German, 31.7% Norwegian, 10.7% Swedish, 7.5% Other groups, 6.4% Irish (2000).
Economy: Employment by occupation: 20.8% management, 13.6% professional, 13.9% services, 23.1% sales, 3.6% farming, 12.5% construction, 12.5% production (2000).
Income: Per capita income: $18,149 (2000); Median household income: $43,125 (2000); Poverty rate: 14.6% (2000).
Taxes: Total city taxes per capita: $25 (1997); City property taxes per capita: $25 (1997).
Education: High school graduation rate: 87.5% (2000); College graduation rate: 15.8% (2000).
Housing: Homeownership rate: 92.4% (2000); Median home value: $97,300 (2000); Median age of housing: 27 years (2000).
Transportation: Commute to work: 87.8% car, 0.9% public transportation, 3.0% walk, 8.4% work from home (2000); Travel time to work: 30.3% less than 15 minutes, 55.0% 15 to 30 minutes, 4.2% 30 to 45 minutes, 3.6% 45 to 60 minutes, 6.8% 60 minutes or more (2000)

ROCHERT (unincorporated postal area, zip code 56578). Covers a land area of 57.279 square miles and a water area of 10.868 square miles. Located at 46.92° N. Lat.; 95.66° W. Long. Elevation is 1,450 feet.
Population: 842 (2000); Race: 98.6% White, 0.0% Black, 0.0% Asian, 0.7% American Indian and Alaska Native, 0.0% Hispanic of any race, 0.7% two or more races (2000); Density: 14.7 persons per square mile (2000); Age: 24.8% under 18, 13.2% over 64 (2000); Marriage status: 18.7% never married, 65.8% now married, 6.9% widowed, 8.7% divorced (2000); Foreign born: 1.0% (2000); Ancestry (includes multiple ancestries): 47.7% German, 34.9% Norwegian, 11.4% Swedish, 5.9% Dutch, 5.3% Irish (2000).
Economy: Employment by occupation: 14.1% management, 16.5% professional, 13.4% services, 23.0% sales, 1.9% farming, 14.4% construction, 16.5% production (2000).
Income: Per capita income: $19,723 (2000); Median household income: $39,444 (2000); Poverty rate: 9.4% (2000).
Education: High school graduation rate: 83.3% (2000); College graduation rate: 21.3% (2000).
Housing: Homeownership rate: 95.4% (2000); Median home value: $109,700 (2000); Median rent: $325 per month (2000); Median age of housing: 41 years (2000).
Transportation: Commute to work: 88.8% car, 0.0% public transportation, 2.0% walk, 7.6% work from home (2000); Travel time to work: 16.9% less than 15 minutes, 50.8% 15 to 30 minutes, 16.4% 30 to 45 minutes, 3.7% 45 to 60 minutes, 12.2% 60 minutes or more (2000)

ROUND LAKE (township). Covers a land area of 64.067 square miles and a water area of 8.506 square miles. Located at 47.06° N. Lat.; 95.52° W. Long.
Population: 157 (2000); Race: 48.2% White, 0.0% Black, 0.0% Asian, 51.8% American Indian and Alaska Native, 0.0% Hispanic of any race, 0.0% two or more races (2000); Density: 2.5 persons per square mile (2000); Age: 25.0% under 18, 22.0% over 64 (2000); Marriage status: 7.8% never married, 76.6% now married, 4.7% widowed, 10.9% divorced (2000); Foreign born: 4.8% (2000); Ancestry (includes multiple ancestries): 58.3% Other groups, 14.9% German, 9.5% Norwegian, 6.0% English, 3.0% Canadian (2000).
Economy: Employment by occupation: 19.7% management, 14.8% professional, 16.4% services, 16.4% sales, 0.0% farming, 14.8% construction, 18.0% production (2000).
Income: Per capita income: $12,996 (2000); Median household income: $23,500 (2000); Poverty rate: 18.1% (2000).
Taxes: Total city taxes per capita: $122 (1997); City property taxes per capita: $122 (1997).
Education: High school graduation rate: 78.0% (2000); College graduation rate: 17.1% (2000).
Housing: Homeownership rate: 76.0% (2000); Median home value: $75,000 (2000); Median rent: $250 per month (2000); Median age of housing: 23 years (2000).
Transportation: Commute to work: 54.1% car, 0.0% public transportation, 34.4% walk, 11.5% work from home (2000); Travel time to work: 48.1% less than 15 minutes, 16.7% 15 to 30 minutes, 13.0% 30 to 45 minutes, 16.7% 45 to 60 minutes, 5.6% 60 minutes or more (2000)

RUNEBERG (township). Covers a land area of 35.708 square miles and a water area of 0.023 square miles. Located at 46.76° N. Lat.; 95.21° W. Long.
Population: 387 (2000); Race: 93.6% White, 0.5% Black, 0.0% Asian, 6.0% American Indian and Alaska Native, 0.7% Hispanic of any race, 0.0% two or more races (2000); Density: 10.8 persons per square mile (2000); Age: 32.6% under 18, 11.5% over 64 (2000); Marriage status: 29.8% never married, 63.4% now married, 2.2% widowed, 4.6% divorced (2000); Foreign born: 0.2% (2000); Ancestry (includes multiple ancestries): 39.9% Finnish, 31.0% German, 12.4% Norwegian, 6.4% Other groups, 4.4% English (2000).
Economy: Employment by occupation: 13.7% management, 13.7% professional, 18.3% services, 11.4% sales, 7.3% farming, 14.6% construction, 21.0% production (2000).
Income: Per capita income: $13,747 (2000); Median household income: $36,500 (2000); Poverty rate: 10.4% (2000).
Taxes: Total city taxes per capita: $58 (1997); City property taxes per capita: $58 (1997).
Education: High school graduation rate: 79.1% (2000); College graduation rate: 9.2% (2000).
Housing: Homeownership rate: 89.7% (2000); Median home value: $27,500 (2000); Median rent: $338 per month (2000); Median age of housing: 53 years (2000).
Transportation: Commute to work: 86.6% car, 0.0% public transportation, 0.0% walk, 13.4% work from home (2000); Travel time to work: 14.9% less than 15 minutes, 46.3% 15 to 30 minutes, 25.0% 30 to 45 minutes, 1.1% 45 to 60 minutes, 12.8% 60 minutes or more (2000)

SAVANNAH (township). Covers a land area of 34.329 square miles and a water area of 2.221 square miles. Located at 47.10° N. Lat.; 95.21° W. Long.
Population: 162 (2000); Race: 100.0% White, 0.0% Black, 0.0% Asian, 0.0% American Indian and Alaska Native, 0.0% Hispanic of any race, 0.0% two or more races (2000); Density: 4.7 persons per square mile (2000); Age: 26.8% under 18, 8.3% over 64 (2000); Marriage status: 15.6% never married, 81.1% now married, 3.3% widowed, 0.0% divorced (2000); Foreign born: 0.0% (2000); Ancestry (includes multiple ancestries): 47.1% German, 14.0% Norwegian, 12.1% United States or American, 7.6% Czech, 7.0% Swedish (2000).
Economy: Employment by occupation: 3.1% management, 21.5% professional, 10.8% services, 35.4% sales, 3.1% farming, 12.3% construction, 13.8% production (2000).
Income: Per capita income: $13,880 (2000); Median household income: $32,813 (2000); Poverty rate: 20.4% (2000).
Taxes: Total city taxes per capita: $88 (1997); City property taxes per capita: $88 (1997).
Education: High school graduation rate: 96.0% (2000); College graduation rate: 21.8% (2000).
Housing: Homeownership rate: 96.4% (2000); Median home value: $143,800 (2000); Median age of housing: 20 years (2000).
Transportation: Commute to work: 80.6% car, 0.0% public transportation, 0.0% walk, 19.4% work from home (2000); Travel time to work: 10.0% less than 15 minutes, 66.0% 15 to 30 minutes, 16.0% 30 to 45 minutes, 0.0% 45 to 60 minutes, 8.0% 60 minutes or more (2000)

SHELL LAKE (township). Covers a land area of 28.476 square miles and a water area of 7.405 square miles. Located at 46.91° N. Lat.; 95.47° W. Long.
Population: 314 (2000); Race: 96.4% White, 0.0% Black, 0.0% Asian, 3.0% American Indian and Alaska Native, 0.0% Hispanic of any race, 0.6% two or more races (2000); Density: 11.0 persons per square mile (2000); Age: 24.7% under 18, 10.7% over 64 (2000); Marriage status: 25.6% never married, 64.1% now married, 1.9% widowed, 8.4% divorced (2000); Foreign born: 0.0% (2000); Ancestry (includes multiple ancestries): 30.7% German, 24.7% Norwegian, 18.5% Finnish, 14.9% Swedish, 5.7% Other groups (2000).
Economy: Employment by occupation: 9.9% management, 18.0% professional, 13.0% services, 18.6% sales, 4.3% farming, 10.6% construction, 25.5% production (2000).
Income: Per capita income: $16,107 (2000); Median household income: $34,375 (2000); Poverty rate: 9.8% (2000).
Taxes: Total city taxes per capita: $73 (1997); City property taxes per capita: $73 (1997).
Education: High school graduation rate: 79.6% (2000); College graduation rate: 7.7% (2000).
Housing: Homeownership rate: 100.0% (2000); Median home value: $80,700 (2000); Median age of housing: 27 years (2000).
Transportation: Commute to work: 87.6% car, 0.0% public transportation, 0.0% walk, 12.4% work from home (2000); Travel time to work: 5.7% less than 15 minutes, 34.0% 15 to 30 minutes, 37.6% 30 to 45 minutes, 9.2% 45 to 60 minutes, 13.5% 60 minutes or more (2000)

SILVER LEAF (township). Covers a land area of 35.023 square miles and a water area of 1.180 square miles. Located at 46.73° N. Lat.; 95.60° W. Long.
Population: 493 (2000); Race: 99.8% White, 0.0% Black, 0.0% Asian, 0.0% American Indian and Alaska Native, 0.2% Hispanic of any race, 0.2% two or more races (2000); Density: 14.1 persons per square mile (2000); Age: 28.8% under 18, 12.5% over 64 (2000); Marriage status: 18.4% never married, 74.5% now married, 4.7% widowed, 2.4% divorced (2000); Foreign born: 0.0% (2000); Ancestry (includes multiple ancestries): 58.4% German, 19.1% Norwegian, 10.3% Polish, 7.6% Swedish, 5.2% Irish (2000).
Economy: Employment by occupation: 15.2% management, 8.8% professional, 17.2% services, 19.2% sales, 1.6% farming, 12.0% construction, 26.0% production (2000).
Income: Per capita income: $13,905 (2000); Median household income: $36,458 (2000); Poverty rate: 5.8% (2000).
Taxes: Total city taxes per capita: $21 (1997); City property taxes per capita: $21 (1997).
Education: High school graduation rate: 80.6% (2000); College graduation rate: 7.5% (2000).
Housing: Homeownership rate: 83.9% (2000); Median home value: $74,000 (2000); Median rent: $200 per month (2000); Median age of housing: 28 years (2000).
Transportation: Commute to work: 89.9% car, 0.0% public transportation, 0.8% walk, 9.3% work from home (2000); Travel time to work: 27.1% less than 15 minutes, 49.8% 15 to 30 minutes, 16.0% 30 to 45 minutes, 3.6% 45 to 60 minutes, 3.6% 60 minutes or more (2000)

SPRING CREEK (township). Covers a land area of 37.176 square miles and a water area of 0.554 square miles. Located at 47.09° N. Lat.; 95.98° W. Long.
Population: 120 (2000); Race: 76.8% White, 0.0% Black, 0.0% Asian, 11.1% American Indian and Alaska Native, 0.0% Hispanic of any race, 12.1% two or more races (2000); Density: 3.2 persons per square mile (2000); Age: 29.3% under 18, 10.1% over 64 (2000); Marriage status: 15.3% never married, 77.8% now married, 4.2% widowed, 2.8% divorced (2000); Foreign born: 0.0% (2000); Ancestry (includes multiple ancestries): 59.6% German, 26.3% Other groups, 18.2% Czech, 10.1% Irish, 10.1% Norwegian (2000).
Economy: Employment by occupation: 25.0% management, 0.0% professional, 22.9% services, 18.8% sales, 4.2% farming, 16.7% construction, 12.5% production (2000).
Income: Per capita income: $17,456 (2000); Median household income: $37,750 (2000); Poverty rate: 11.1% (2000).

Taxes: Total city taxes per capita: $112 (1997); City property taxes per capita: $112 (1997).
Education: High school graduation rate: 77.3% (2000); College graduation rate: 0.0% (2000).
Housing: Homeownership rate: 94.7% (2000); Median home value: $39,200 (2000); Median age of housing: 29 years (2000).
Transportation: Commute to work: 75.0% car, 0.0% public transportation, 16.7% walk, 6.3% work from home (2000); Travel time to work: 40.0% less than 15 minutes, 20.0% 15 to 30 minutes, 24.4% 30 to 45 minutes, 0.0% 45 to 60 minutes, 15.6% 60 minutes or more (2000)

SPRUCE GROVE (township). Covers a land area of 35.555 square miles and a water area of 0.108 square miles. Located at 46.76° N. Lat.; 95.36° W. Long.
Population: 358 (2000); Race: 100.0% White, 0.0% Black, 0.0% Asian, 0.0% American Indian and Alaska Native, 0.5% Hispanic of any race, 0.0% two or more races (2000); Density: 10.1 persons per square mile (2000); Age: 29.2% under 18, 16.9% over 64 (2000); Marriage status: 21.9% never married, 65.4% now married, 9.2% widowed, 3.5% divorced (2000); Foreign born: 1.6% (2000); Ancestry (includes multiple ancestries): 43.1% Finnish, 21.8% German, 19.1% Norwegian, 13.6% Swedish, 5.7% Irish (2000).
Economy: Employment by occupation: 24.5% management, 9.8% professional, 10.4% services, 17.2% sales, 9.8% farming, 16.6% construction, 11.7% production (2000).
Income: Per capita income: $12,135 (2000); Median household income: $25,341 (2000); Poverty rate: 4.7% (2000).
Taxes: Total city taxes per capita: $46 (1997); City property taxes per capita: $46 (1997).
Education: High school graduation rate: 74.5% (2000); College graduation rate: 9.8% (2000).
Housing: Homeownership rate: 83.5% (2000); Median home value: $61,000 (2000); Median rent: $313 per month (2000); Median age of housing: 45 years (2000).
Transportation: Commute to work: 82.2% car, 0.0% public transportation, 3.7% walk, 13.5% work from home (2000); Travel time to work: 29.1% less than 15 minutes, 25.5% 15 to 30 minutes, 28.4% 30 to 45 minutes, 12.8% 45 to 60 minutes, 4.3% 60 minutes or more (2000)

SUGAR BUSH (township). Covers a land area of 65.286 square miles and a water area of 7.342 square miles. Located at 47.03° N. Lat.; 95.65° W. Long.
Population: 537 (2000); Race: 61.1% White, 0.0% Black, 4.4% Asian, 24.2% American Indian and Alaska Native, 1.9% Hispanic of any race, 8.2% two or more races (2000); Density: 8.2 persons per square mile (2000); Age: 37.9% under 18, 10.4% over 64 (2000); Marriage status: 29.1% never married, 57.9% now married, 5.1% widowed, 7.8% divorced (2000); Foreign born: 4.1% (2000); Ancestry (includes multiple ancestries): 30.9% Other groups, 27.3% German, 8.7% Norwegian, 7.7% Irish, 5.1% United States or American (2000).
Economy: Employment by occupation: 11.2% management, 12.9% professional, 21.4% services, 11.6% sales, 2.2% farming, 17.9% construction, 22.8% production (2000).
Income: Per capita income: $11,486 (2000); Median household income: $25,500 (2000); Poverty rate: 21.8% (2000).
Taxes: Total city taxes per capita: $30 (1997); City property taxes per capita: $30 (1997).
Education: High school graduation rate: 75.0% (2000); College graduation rate: 7.1% (2000).
Housing: Homeownership rate: 94.9% (2000); Median home value: $78,000 (2000); Median rent: $175 per month (2000); Median age of housing: 24 years (2000).
Transportation: Commute to work: 88.9% car, 0.0% public transportation, 4.9% walk, 6.2% work from home (2000); Travel time to work: 16.5% less than 15 minutes, 31.6% 15 to 30 minutes, 33.0% 30 to 45 minutes, 9.4% 45 to 60 minutes, 9.4% 60 minutes or more (2000)

TOAD LAKE (township). Covers a land area of 32.572 square miles and a water area of 3.715 square miles. Located at 46.85° N. Lat.; 95.48° W. Long.
Population: 465 (2000); Race: 95.9% White, 1.0% Black, 0.7% Asian, 1.0% American Indian and Alaska Native, 0.7% Hispanic of any race, 0.7% two or more races (2000); Density: 14.3 persons per square mile (2000); Age: 24.3% under 18, 18.8% over 64 (2000); Marriage status: 21.6% never married, 69.2% now married, 5.9% widowed, 3.3% divorced (2000); Foreign born: 0.7% (2000); Ancestry (includes multiple ancestries): 43.5% German, 22.1% Norwegian, 16.1% Finnish, 7.2% Irish, 6.5% English (2000).
Economy: Employment by occupation: 26.3% management, 9.5% professional, 15.8% services, 9.5% sales, 6.8% farming, 11.1% construction, 21.1% production (2000).
Income: Per capita income: $13,315 (2000); Median household income: $35,703 (2000); Poverty rate: 15.1% (2000).
Taxes: Total city taxes per capita: $99 (1997); City property taxes per capita: $99 (1997).
Education: High school graduation rate: 79.1% (2000); College graduation rate: 9.1% (2000).
Housing: Homeownership rate: 85.5% (2000); Median home value: $120,000 (2000); Median rent: $375 per month (2000); Median age of housing: 25 years (2000).
Transportation: Commute to work: 74.1% car, 0.0% public transportation, 1.1% walk, 22.7% work from home (2000); Travel time to work: 11.2% less than 15 minutes, 33.6% 15 to 30 minutes, 32.9% 30 to 45 minutes, 2.1% 45 to 60 minutes, 20.3% 60 minutes or more (2000)

TWO INLETS (township). Covers a land area of 34.060 square miles and a water area of 1.878 square miles. Located at 47.02° N. Lat.; 95.20° W. Long. Elevation is 1,486 feet.
Population: 237 (2000); Race: 100.0% White, 0.0% Black, 0.0% Asian, 0.0% American Indian and Alaska Native, 0.0% Hispanic of any race, 0.0% two or more races (2000); Density: 7.0 persons per square mile (2000); Age: 13.6% under 18, 35.8% over 64 (2000); Marriage status: 16.1% never married, 67.1% now married, 13.4% widowed, 3.4% divorced (2000); Foreign born: 0.0% (2000); Ancestry (includes multiple ancestries): 59.9% German, 21.6% Norwegian, 8.6% Irish, 5.6% Swedish, 4.3% Czechoslovakian (2000).
Economy: Employment by occupation: 5.8% management, 10.1% professional, 11.6% services, 34.8% sales, 4.3% farming, 11.6% construction, 21.7% production (2000).
Income: Per capita income: $15,946 (2000); Median household income: $31,429 (2000); Poverty rate: 3.1% (2000).
Taxes: Total city taxes per capita: $131 (1997); City property taxes per capita: $131 (1997).
Education: High school graduation rate: 72.7% (2000); College graduation rate: 12.9% (2000).
Housing: Homeownership rate: 90.8% (2000); Median home value: $130,000 (2000); Median rent: $225 per month (2000); Median age of housing: 16 years (2000).
Transportation: Commute to work: 94.2% car, 2.9% public transportation, 0.0% walk, 2.9% work from home (2000); Travel time to work: 38.8% less than 15 minutes, 49.3% 15 to 30 minutes, 11.9% 30 to 45 minutes, 0.0% 45 to 60 minutes, 0.0% 60 minutes or more (2000)

WALWORTH (township). Covers a land area of 36.137 square miles and a water area of 0.127 square miles. Located at 47.12° N. Lat.; 96.14° W. Long.
Population: 88 (2000); Race: 100.0% White, 0.0% Black, 0.0% Asian, 0.0% American Indian and Alaska Native, 0.0% Hispanic of any race, 0.0% two or more races (2000); Density: 2.4 persons per square mile (2000); Age: 24.0% under 18, 24.0% over 64 (2000); Marriage status: 26.7% never married, 62.8% now married, 2.3% widowed, 8.1% divorced (2000); Foreign born: 0.0% (2000); Ancestry (includes multiple ancestries): 49.0% Norwegian, 25.0% German, 18.0% Swedish, 14.0% Czech, 8.0% United States or American (2000).
Economy: Employment by occupation: 14.3% management, 23.8% professional, 23.8% services, 0.0% sales, 0.0% farming, 4.8% construction, 33.3% production (2000).
Income: Per capita income: $18,440 (2000); Median household income: $34,167 (2000); Poverty rate: 0.0% (2000).
Taxes: Total city taxes per capita: $129 (1997); City property taxes per capita: $129 (1997).
Education: High school graduation rate: 87.1% (2000); College graduation rate: 14.5% (2000).
Housing: Homeownership rate: 81.0% (2000); Median home value: $95,000 (2000); Median rent: $275 per month (2000); Median age of housing: 58 years (2000).
Transportation: Commute to work: 73.8% car, 0.0% public transportation, 0.0% walk, 26.2% work from home (2000); Travel time to work: 45.2% less than 15 minutes, 16.1% 15 to 30 minutes, 12.9% 30 to 45 minutes, 25.8% 45 to 60 minutes, 0.0% 60 minutes or more (2000)

WHITE EARTH (township). Covers a land area of 32.251 square miles and a water area of 2.600 square miles. Located at 47.09° N. Lat.; 95.85° W. Long. Elevation is 1,572 feet.

Population: 799 (2000); Race: 26.6% White, 0.0% Black, 2.5% Asian, 59.3% American Indian and Alaska Native, 1.4% Hispanic of any race, 11.6% two or more races (2000); Density: 24.8 persons per square mile (2000); Age: 38.9% under 18, 8.8% over 64 (2000); Marriage status: 43.4% never married, 39.3% now married, 7.7% widowed, 9.6% divorced (2000); Foreign born: 1.3% (2000); Ancestry (includes multiple ancestries): 67.0% Other groups, 17.9% German, 6.6% Norwegian, 6.3% Czech, 3.6% French (except Basque) (2000).
Economy: Hospital and mission school are here. Tamarac National Wildlife Refuge to Southeast. Employment by occupation: 13.8% management, 15.1% professional, 23.4% services, 15.1% sales, 3.2% farming, 18.3% construction, 11.0% production (2000).
Income: Per capita income: $10,225 (2000); Median household income: $21,094 (2000); Poverty rate: 32.8% (2000).
Taxes: Total city taxes per capita: $16 (1997); City property taxes per capita: $16 (1997).
Education: High school graduation rate: 75.1% (2000); College graduation rate: 7.7% (2000).
Housing: Homeownership rate: 61.4% (2000); Median home value: $53,100 (2000); Median rent: $176 per month (2000); Median age of housing: 21 years (2000).
Newspapers: Anishinaabeg Today (2 x month)
Transportation: Commute to work: 76.6% car, 0.5% public transportation, 6.5% walk, 14.5% work from home (2000); Travel time to work: 37.7% less than 15 minutes, 30.6% 15 to 30 minutes, 13.7% 30 to 45 minutes, 4.9% 45 to 60 minutes, 13.1% 60 minutes or more (2000)

WOLF LAKE (city). Covers a land area of 0.142 square miles and a water area of 0 square miles. Located at 46.80° N. Lat.; 95.35° W. Long. Elevation is 1,573 feet.
Population: 31 (2000); Race: 94.9% White, 0.0% Black, 0.0% Asian, 5.1% American Indian and Alaska Native, 0.0% Hispanic of any race, 0.0% two or more races (2000); Density: 218.9 persons per square mile (2000); Age: 23.1% under 18, 7.7% over 64 (2000); Marriage status: 26.7% never married, 63.3% now married, 3.3% widowed, 6.7% divorced (2000); Foreign born: 0.0% (2000); Ancestry (includes multiple ancestries): 74.4% Finnish, 17.9% German, 10.3% Other groups, 5.1% Danish, 5.1% United States or American (2000).
Economy: Single-family building permits issued: 0 (2001) / 0 (2000); Multi-family building permits issued: 0 (2001) / 0 (2000); Employment by occupation: 8.7% management, 17.4% professional, 0.0% services, 17.4% sales, 21.7% farming, 26.1% construction, 8.7% production (2000).
Income: Per capita income: $13,569 (2000); Median household income: $22,083 (2000); Poverty rate: 7.7% (2000).
Taxes: Total city taxes per capita: $29 (1997); City property taxes per capita: $29 (1997).
Education: High school graduation rate: 90.5% (2000); College graduation rate: 0.0% (2000).
Housing: Homeownership rate: 100.0% (2000); Median home value: $35,800 (2000); Median age of housing: 60+ years (2000).
Transportation: Commute to work: 78.3% car, 0.0% public transportation, 8.7% walk, 0.0% work from home (2000); Travel time to work: 47.8% less than 15 minutes, 8.7% 15 to 30 minutes, 30.4% 30 to 45 minutes, 0.0% 45 to 60 minutes, 13.0% 60 minutes or more (2000)

WOLF LAKE (township). Covers a land area of 33.123 square miles and a water area of 2.796 square miles. Located at 46.84° N. Lat.; 95.36° W. Long. Elevation is 1,573 feet.
Population: 227 (2000); Race: 94.2% White, 0.0% Black, 0.0% Asian, 2.9% American Indian and Alaska Native, 0.0% Hispanic of any race, 2.9% two or more races (2000); Density: 6.9 persons per square mile (2000); Age: 38.9% under 18, 11.5% over 64 (2000); Marriage status: 30.6% never married, 51.7% now married, 11.6% widowed, 6.1% divorced (2000); Foreign born: 0.0% (2000); Ancestry (includes multiple ancestries): 61.1% Finnish, 13.0% German, 9.1% Norwegian, 8.7% Other groups, 3.4% French (except Basque) (2000).
Economy: Agriculture: dairying; grain. Employment by occupation: 29.5% management, 14.8% professional, 8.0% services, 20.5% sales, 8.0% farming, 4.5% construction, 14.8% production (2000).
Income: Per capita income: $10,622 (2000); Median household income: $25,250 (2000); Poverty rate: 41.0% (2000).
Taxes: Total city taxes per capita: $39 (1997); City property taxes per capita: $39 (1997).
Education: High school graduation rate: 86.8% (2000); College graduation rate: 20.2% (2000).
Housing: Homeownership rate: 93.0% (2000); Median home value: $33,100 (2000); Median age of housing: 37 years (2000).
Transportation: Commute to work: 83.0% car, 0.0% public transportation, 0.0% walk, 17.0% work from home (2000); Travel time to work: 30.1% less than 15 minutes, 26.0% 15 to 30 minutes, 23.3% 30 to 45 minutes, 12.3% 45 to 60 minutes, 8.2% 60 minutes or more (2000)

Beltrami County

Located in northwestern Minnesota; drained by Upper and Lower Red Lakes and by the headwaters of the Mississippi River. Covers a land area of 2,505.30 square miles, a water area of 550.30 square miles, and is located in the Central Time Zone. The county government was organized in 1866. County seat is Bemidji.

Weather Station: Red Lake Indian Agency — Elevation: 1,217 feet

	Jan	Feb	Mar	Apr	May	Jun	Jul	Aug	Sep	Oct	Nov	Dec
High	14	22	33	50	65	73	78	76	65	53	34	20
Low	-7	-1	12	28	43	53	58	55	45	33	18	1
Precip	0.6	0.4	0.8	1.2	2.5	3.7	4.2	3.3	2.6	2.1	0.8	0.4
Snow	10.6	5.9	6.6	2.2	tr	0.0	0.0	0.0	0.0	1.1	8.0	7.7

High and Low temperatures in degrees Fahrenheit; Precipitation and Snow in inches

Population: 39,650 (2000); Race: 76.7% White, 0.4% Black, 1.3% Asian, 19.4% American Indian and Alaska Native, 1.0% Hispanic of any race, 2.0% two or more races (2000); Density: 15.8 persons per square mile (2000); Age: 28.7% under 18, 11.6% over 64 (2000).
Religion: Five largest groups: 18.1% Catholic Church, 14.8% Evangelical Lutheran Church in America, 2.2% Lutheran Church—Missouri Synod, 1.5% Presbyterian Church (U.S.A.), 1.5% The Evangelical Free Church of America (2000).
Economy: Unemployment rate: 4.0% (11/2002); Total civilian labor force: 21,293 (11/2002); Leading industries: 19.8% health care and social assistance; 19.6% retail trade; 11.6% accommodation & food services (2000); Companies that employ more than 1,000 persons: 0 (2000); Companies that employ more than 100 persons: 21 (2000); Farms: 656 totaling 224,898 acres (1997); Minority business ownership rate: 3.3% (1997); Women business ownership rate: 22.6% (1997); Retail sales per capita: $9,454 (1997). Single-family building permits issued: 75 (2001) / 77 (2000); Multi-family building permits issued: 47 (2001) / 8 (2000).
Income: Per capita income: $15,497 (2000); Median household income: $33,392 (2000); Poverty rate: 17.6% (2000); Bankruptcy rate: 2.49% (2001).
Taxes: Total county taxes per capita: $289 (2000); County property taxes per capita: $282 (2000).
Education: High school graduation rate: 83.4% (2000); College graduation rate: 23.5% (2000).
Housing: Homeownership rate: 74.5% (2000); Median home value: $79,800 (2000); Median rent: $369 per month (2000); Median age of housing: 25 years (2000).
Health: Birth rate: 146.5 per 10,000 population (1998); Age adjusted death rate: 92.7 per 10,000 population (1999); Age adjusted cancer mortality rate: 188.3 deaths per 100,000 population (1999). Number of physicians: 15.4 per 10,000 population (1999); Number of hospital beds: 48.2 per 10,000 population (1999).
Elections: 2000 Presidential election results: 42.4% Gore, 48.5% Bush, 7.4% Nader, 1.2% Buchanan
National and State Parks: Beltrami Island State Forest; Blackduck State Forest; Buena Vista State Forest; Buena Vista State Forest; Carmelee State Wildlife Management Area; Gimmer Lake State Waterfowl Refuge; Hamre State Wildlife Management Area; Lake Bemidji State Park; Long Lake State Wildlife Management Area; Mississippi Headwaters State Forest; Norris Camp State Game Refuge; Northwood State Wildlife Management Area; Pine Tree State Park; Red Lake State Forest; Red Lake State Wildlife Management Area; Shooks State Wildlife Management Area; Shotley State Wildlife Management Area; Steenerson State Wildlife Management Area
Additional Information Contacts
Beltrami County Government Offices 218-759-4109
Bemidji Board of Realtors 218-751-6048
Bemidji Chamber of Commerce. 218-751-3541
Bemidji Visitor & Convention & Visitors Bureau. 218-759-0164

Beltrami County Communities

ALASKA (township). Covers a land area of 32.242 square miles and a water area of 3.150 square miles. Located at 47.78° N. Lat.; 95.09° W. Long.

Population: 197 (2000); Race: 91.9% White, 0.0% Black, 0.0% Asian, 5.2% American Indian and Alaska Native, 0.0% Hispanic of any race, 2.9% two or more races (2000); Density: 6.1 persons per square mile (2000); Age: 23.3% under 18, 16.2% over 64 (2000); Marriage status: 21.8% never married, 60.3% now married, 10.1% widowed, 7.8% divorced (2000); Foreign born: 1.4% (2000); Ancestry (includes multiple ancestries): 34.8% Norwegian, 19.0% German, 16.7% Swedish, 13.8% Irish, 8.6% English (2000).
Economy: Employment by occupation: 9.7% management, 15.5% professional, 9.7% services, 12.6% sales, 1.9% farming, 22.3% construction, 28.2% production (2000).
Income: Per capita income: $16,990 (2000); Median household income: $40,313 (2000); Poverty rate: 13.8% (2000).
Taxes: Total city taxes per capita: $39 (1997); City property taxes per capita: $39 (1997).
Education: High school graduation rate: 86.8% (2000); College graduation rate: 11.1% (2000).
Housing: Homeownership rate: 87.8% (2000); Median home value: $81,700 (2000); Median rent: $375 per month (2000); Median age of housing: 42 years (2000).
Transportation: Commute to work: 89.3% car, 0.0% public transportation, 1.9% walk, 8.7% work from home (2000); Travel time to work: 14.9% less than 15 minutes, 23.4% 15 to 30 minutes, 43.6% 30 to 45 minutes, 7.4% 45 to 60 minutes, 10.6% 60 minutes or more (2000)

BATTLE (township). Covers a land area of 13.724 square miles and a water area of 0.028 square miles. Located at 47.95° N. Lat.; 94.70° W. Long.
Population: 60 (2000); Race: 100.0% White, 0.0% Black, 0.0% Asian, 0.0% American Indian and Alaska Native, 0.0% Hispanic of any race, 0.0% two or more races (2000); Density: 4.4 persons per square mile (2000); Age: 24.2% under 18, 13.6% over 64 (2000); Marriage status: 30.4% never married, 50.0% now married, 12.5% widowed, 7.1% divorced (2000); Foreign born: 0.0% (2000); Ancestry (includes multiple ancestries): 37.9% Norwegian, 24.2% United States or American, 9.1% Swedish, 7.6% French Canadian, 7.6% Irish (2000).
Economy: Employment by occupation: 33.3% management, 0.0% professional, 12.1% services, 6.1% sales, 9.1% farming, 15.2% construction, 24.2% production (2000).
Income: Per capita income: $18,980 (2000); Median household income: $23,750 (2000); Poverty rate: 36.4% (2000).
Taxes: Total city taxes per capita: $17 (1997); City property taxes per capita: $17 (1997).
Education: High school graduation rate: 93.3% (2000); College graduation rate: 15.6% (2000).
Housing: Homeownership rate: 78.3% (2000); Median home value: $27,500 (2000); Median rent: $125 per month (2000); Median age of housing: 60+ years (2000).
Transportation: Commute to work: 66.7% car, 0.0% public transportation, 0.0% walk, 33.3% work from home (2000); Travel time to work: 68.2% less than 15 minutes, 18.2% 15 to 30 minutes, 13.6% 30 to 45 minutes, 0.0% 45 to 60 minutes, 0.0% 60 minutes or more (2000)

BEMIDJI (city). Covers a land area of 11.778 square miles and a water area of 1.176 square miles. Located at 47.47° N. Lat.; 94.87° W. Long. Elevation is 1,343 feet.
History: Bemidji, established in one of the last areas along the Mississippi River to be opened to settlement, developed in the 1890's. The first land purchasers thought that quartzite pebbles found on the shore of Lake Itasca were diamonds. The lumber boom of the early 1900's brought more wealth than the stones, and many sawmills began operations. When lumbering declined, the sawmills were replaced by woodworking plants and dairy creameries. Bemidji was named for Chippewa chief Bemidji.
Population: 11,917 (2000); Race: 84.5% White, 0.8% Black, 2.0% Asian, 10.4% American Indian and Alaska Native, 0.7% Hispanic of any race, 1.9% two or more races (2000); Density: 1,011.8 persons per square mile (2000); Age: 21.5% under 18, 15.4% over 64 (2000); Marriage status: 42.2% never married, 40.3% now married, 8.4% widowed, 9.2% divorced (2000); Foreign born: 2.9% (2000); Ancestry (includes multiple ancestries): 28.8% German, 22.6% Norwegian, 13.1% Other groups, 8.8% Swedish, 8.6% Irish (2000).
Vital Statistics: Birth rate: 154.4 per 10,000 population (1998)
Economy: Single-family building permits issued: 35 (2001) / 34 (2000); Multi-family building permits issued: 47 (2001) / 8 (2000); Employment by occupation: 9.1% management, 23.8% professional, 22.3% services, 25.8% sales, 0.4% farming, 5.8% construction, 12.9% production (2000).
Income: Per capita income: $15,264 (2000); Median household income: $28,072 (2000); Poverty rate: 19.2% (2000).
Taxes: Total city taxes per capita: $120 (1997); City property taxes per capita: $107 (1997).
Education: High school graduation rate: 84.9% (2000); College graduation rate: 28.8% (2000).

School District(s)

Bemidji (PK-12)
2000 Enrollment: 5,398 218-759-3110
Schoolcraft Learning Community Chtr (01-08)
2000 Enrollment: 147 218-586-3284

Four-year College(s)

Bemidji State University (Public)
2001 Enrollment: 4,664 800-475-2001
2001 Tuition: In-state $3,470; Out-of-state $7,360
Oak Hills Christian College (Private, Not-for-profit, Interdenominational)
2001 Enrollment: 174 218-751-8670
2001 Tuition: In-state $9,450; Out-of-state $9,450

Two-year College(s)

Northwest Technical College-Bemidji (Public)
2001 Enrollment: 4,865 218-755-4270
2001 Tuition: In-state $2,550; Out-of-state $5,100

Housing: Homeownership rate: 54.3% (2000); Median home value: $69,800 (2000); Median rent: $396 per month (2000); Median age of housing: 33 years (2000).
Hospitals: North Country Regional Hospital (98 beds)
Safety: Violent crime rate: 28.2 per 10,000 population; Property crime rate: 898.3 per 10,000 population (2001).
Newspapers: The Pioneer/Advertiser (6 x week); Buy Line (2 x week)
Transportation: Commute to work: 81.7% car, 0.9% public transportation, 12.5% walk, 3.9% work from home (2000); Travel time to work: 65.4% less than 15 minutes, 20.5% 15 to 30 minutes, 7.8% 30 to 45 minutes, 2.3% 45 to 60 minutes, 3.9% 60 minutes or more (2000)
Airports: Bemidji-Beltrami County (primary service)
Additional Information Contacts
Bemidji Board of Realtors 218-751-6048
Bemidji Chamber of Commerce.......... 218-751-3541
Bemidji Visitor & Convention & Visitors Bureau.......... 218-759-0164

BEMIDJI (township). Covers a land area of 21.114 square miles and a water area of 4.536 square miles. Located at 47.44° N. Lat.; 94.86° W. Long. Elevation is 1,343 feet.
History: On the lakeshore stands an 18-foot statue of legendary Paul Bunyan and his blue ox. Incorporated 1896.
Population: 2,934 (2000); Race: 87.3% White, 0.4% Black, 0.7% Asian, 7.9% American Indian and Alaska Native, 1.5% Hispanic of any race, 2.8% two or more races (2000); Density: 139.0 persons per square mile (2000); Age: 27.7% under 18, 9.0% over 64 (2000); Marriage status: 27.5% never married, 57.8% now married, 4.1% widowed, 10.6% divorced (2000); Foreign born: 2.2% (2000); Ancestry (includes multiple ancestries): 32.2% German, 26.4% Norwegian, 11.0% Irish, 9.6% Other groups, 8.3% Swedish (2000).
Economy: Resort area; tourism is the major industry. Also a trade and marketing center for the dairy farms of the region; grain, sunflowers; livestock, poultry; timber. Manufacturing includes printing and publishing; building materials, textiles, trusses, beverages, consumer goods, lumber, wire harnesses, computer equipment, garage doors, crating materials.
Single-family building permits issued: 18 (2001) / 19 (2000); Multi-family building permits issued: 0 (2001) / 0 (2000); Employment by occupation: 9.9% management, 23.1% professional, 18.1% services, 29.6% sales, 0.3% farming, 10.6% construction, 8.3% production (2000).
Income: Per capita income: $18,218 (2000); Median household income: $41,279 (2000); Poverty rate: 10.5% (2000).
Taxes: Total city taxes per capita: $31 (1997); City property taxes per capita: $30 (1997).
Education: High school graduation rate: 90.0% (2000); College graduation rate: 32.2% (2000).
Housing: Homeownership rate: 81.1% (2000); Median home value: $96,900 (2000); Median rent: $409 per month (2000); Median age of housing: 22 years (2000).
Transportation: Commute to work: 86.8% car, 1.0% public transportation, 6.0% walk, 6.1% work from home (2000); Travel time to work: 57.4% less than 15 minutes, 27.8% 15 to 30 minutes, 8.1% 30 to 45 minutes, 3.8% 45 to 60 minutes, 3.0% 60 minutes or more (2000)
Airports: Bemidji-Beltrami County (primary service)

BENVILLE (township). Covers a land area of 34.516 square miles and a water area of 0 square miles. Located at 48.31° N. Lat.; 95.55° W. Long.

Population: 65 (2000); Race: 100.0% White, 0.0% Black, 0.0% Asian, 0.0% American Indian and Alaska Native, 0.0% Hispanic of any race, 0.0% two or more races (2000); Density: 1.9 persons per square mile (2000); Age: 29.5% under 18, 10.3% over 64 (2000); Marriage status: 10.5% never married, 78.9% now married, 0.0% widowed, 10.5% divorced (2000); Foreign born: 0.0% (2000); Ancestry (includes multiple ancestries): 56.4% Norwegian, 23.1% German, 10.3% Swedish, 5.1% Ukrainian, 5.1% Polish (2000).
Economy: Employment by occupation: 29.4% management, 20.6% professional, 5.9% services, 11.8% sales, 0.0% farming, 5.9% construction, 26.5% production (2000).
Income: Per capita income: $15,667 (2000); Median household income: $28,750 (2000); Poverty rate: 5.1% (2000).
Taxes: Total city taxes per capita: $37 (1997); City property taxes per capita: $37 (1997).
Education: High school graduation rate: 89.1% (2000); College graduation rate: 7.3% (2000).
Housing: Homeownership rate: 93.9% (2000); Median home value: $60,000 (2000); Median age of housing: 36 years (2000).
Transportation: Commute to work: 70.6% car, 0.0% public transportation, 8.8% walk, 14.7% work from home (2000); Travel time to work: 44.8% less than 15 minutes, 24.1% 15 to 30 minutes, 0.0% 30 to 45 minutes, 0.0% 45 to 60 minutes, 31.0% 60 minutes or more (2000)

BIRCH (township). Covers a land area of 34.144 square miles and a water area of 1.997 square miles. Located at 47.60° N. Lat.; 94.50° W. Long.
Population: 116 (2000); Race: 100.0% White, 0.0% Black, 0.0% Asian, 0.0% American Indian and Alaska Native, 0.0% Hispanic of any race, 0.0% two or more races (2000); Density: 3.4 persons per square mile (2000); Age: 33.6% under 18, 16.0% over 64 (2000); Marriage status: 21.1% never married, 65.3% now married, 6.3% widowed, 7.4% divorced (2000); Foreign born: 0.0% (2000); Ancestry (includes multiple ancestries): 40.5% German, 19.1% Norwegian, 16.0% Swedish, 11.5% Finnish, 9.2% United States or American (2000).
Economy: Employment by occupation: 9.8% management, 11.5% professional, 8.2% services, 23.0% sales, 19.7% farming, 9.8% construction, 18.0% production (2000).
Income: Per capita income: $18,474 (2000); Median household income: $41,250 (2000); Poverty rate: 1.5% (2000).
Taxes: Total city taxes per capita: $32 (1997); City property taxes per capita: $32 (1997).
Education: High school graduation rate: 88.2% (2000); College graduation rate: 22.4% (2000).
Housing: Homeownership rate: 92.9% (2000); Median home value: $158,300 (2000); Median rent: $475 per month (2000); Median age of housing: 19 years (2000).
Transportation: Commute to work: 96.4% car, 0.0% public transportation, 0.0% walk, 3.6% work from home (2000); Travel time to work: 32.1% less than 15 minutes, 43.4% 15 to 30 minutes, 17.0% 30 to 45 minutes, 3.8% 45 to 60 minutes, 3.8% 60 minutes or more (2000)

BLACKDUCK (city). Covers a land area of 1.494 square miles and a water area of 0.035 square miles. Located at 47.73° N. Lat.; 94.54° W. Long. Elevation is 1,383 feet.
Population: 696 (2000); Race: 92.8% White, 0.3% Black, 0.7% Asian, 2.5% American Indian and Alaska Native, 0.4% Hispanic of any race, 3.2% two or more races (2000); Density: 465.8 persons per square mile (2000); Age: 23.8% under 18, 27.0% over 64 (2000); Marriage status: 22.0% never married, 50.9% now married, 14.1% widowed, 13.0% divorced (2000); Foreign born: 1.9% (2000); Ancestry (includes multiple ancestries): 25.9% German, 19.1% Norwegian, 7.5% Swedish, 6.4% Irish, 6.4% Other groups (2000).
Economy: Manufacturing: draperies and bedspreads; sawmill. Single-family building permits issued: 7 (2001) / 10 (2000); Multi-family building permits issued: 0 (2001) / 0 (2000); Employment by occupation: 6.7% management, 18.2% professional, 11.6% services, 27.4% sales, 1.4% farming, 7.7% construction, 27.0% production (2000).
Income: Per capita income: $12,536 (2000); Median household income: $21,848 (2000); Poverty rate: 16.9% (2000).
Taxes: Total city taxes per capita: $161 (1997); City property taxes per capita: $159 (1997).
Education: High school graduation rate: 82.1% (2000); College graduation rate: 15.3% (2000).

School District(s)

Blackduck (PK-12)
2000 Enrollment: 866 218-835-5200

Housing: Homeownership rate: 66.4% (2000); Median home value: $50,000 (2000); Median rent: $339 per month (2000); Median age of housing: 33 years (2000).
Newspapers: The American (1 x week); The Blackduck Shopper (1 x week)
Transportation: Commute to work: 79.8% car, 0.0% public transportation, 12.9% walk, 4.0% work from home (2000); Travel time to work: 79.3% less than 15 minutes, 5.7% 15 to 30 minutes, 11.9% 30 to 45 minutes, 1.9% 45 to 60 minutes, 1.1% 60 minutes or more (2000)

BUZZLE (township). Covers a land area of 34.866 square miles and a water area of 1.291 square miles. Located at 47.62° N. Lat.; 95.11° W. Long.
Population: 286 (2000); Race: 98.2% White, 1.8% Black, 0.0% Asian, 0.0% American Indian and Alaska Native, 1.8% Hispanic of any race, 0.0% two or more races (2000); Density: 8.2 persons per square mile (2000); Age: 21.4% under 18, 16.1% over 64 (2000); Marriage status: 21.8% never married, 64.1% now married, 6.8% widowed, 7.3% divorced (2000); Foreign born: 0.0% (2000); Ancestry (includes multiple ancestries): 43.6% Norwegian, 33.2% German, 13.9% Swedish, 6.8% Irish, 6.4% English (2000).
Economy: Employment by occupation: 11.4% management, 13.8% professional, 26.0% services, 17.1% sales, 1.6% farming, 8.1% construction, 22.0% production (2000).
Income: Per capita income: $17,151 (2000); Median household income: $25,000 (2000); Poverty rate: 25.7% (2000).
Taxes: Total city taxes per capita: $42 (1997); City property taxes per capita: $42 (1997).
Education: High school graduation rate: 71.5% (2000); College graduation rate: 16.1% (2000).
Housing: Homeownership rate: 100.0% (2000); Median home value: $42,700 (2000); Median age of housing: 28 years (2000).
Transportation: Commute to work: 85.0% car, 0.0% public transportation, 1.7% walk, 13.3% work from home (2000); Travel time to work: 9.6% less than 15 minutes, 50.0% 15 to 30 minutes, 36.5% 30 to 45 minutes, 3.8% 45 to 60 minutes, 0.0% 60 minutes or more (2000)

CORMANT (township). Covers a land area of 36.435 square miles and a water area of 0 square miles. Located at 47.87° N. Lat.; 94.59° W. Long.
Population: 207 (2000); Race: 100.0% White, 0.0% Black, 0.0% Asian, 0.0% American Indian and Alaska Native, 0.0% Hispanic of any race, 0.0% two or more races (2000); Density: 5.7 persons per square mile (2000); Age: 34.4% under 18, 11.2% over 64 (2000); Marriage status: 14.3% never married, 77.3% now married, 5.8% widowed, 2.6% divorced (2000); Foreign born: 0.0% (2000); Ancestry (includes multiple ancestries): 40.6% Norwegian, 36.2% German, 24.6% Swedish, 8.9% French (except Basque), 8.0% Irish (2000).
Economy: Employment by occupation: 9.5% management, 18.9% professional, 8.1% services, 17.6% sales, 2.7% farming, 16.2% construction, 27.0% production (2000).
Income: Per capita income: $10,537 (2000); Median household income: $25,625 (2000); Poverty rate: 29.0% (2000).
Taxes: Total city taxes per capita: $9 (1997); City property taxes per capita: $9 (1997).
Education: High school graduation rate: 87.6% (2000); College graduation rate: 15.3% (2000).
Housing: Homeownership rate: 88.8% (2000); Median rent: $225 per month (2000); Median age of housing: 27 years (2000).
Transportation: Commute to work: 85.1% car, 0.0% public transportation, 0.0% walk, 12.2% work from home (2000); Travel time to work: 7.7% less than 15 minutes, 35.4% 15 to 30 minutes, 18.5% 30 to 45 minutes, 21.5% 45 to 60 minutes, 16.9% 60 minutes or more (2000)

DURAND (township). Covers a land area of 15.096 square miles and a water area of 3.249 square miles. Located at 47.68° N. Lat.; 94.88° W. Long.
Population: 175 (2000); Race: 92.0% White, 0.0% Black, 0.7% Asian, 7.3% American Indian and Alaska Native, 0.0% Hispanic of any race, 0.0% two or more races (2000); Density: 11.6 persons per square mile (2000); Age: 12.7% under 18, 13.3% over 64 (2000); Marriage status: 13.4% never married, 68.7% now married, 6.0% widowed, 11.9% divorced (2000); Foreign born: 0.7% (2000); Ancestry (includes multiple ancestries): 28.7% Norwegian, 22.0% German, 12.0% Irish, 8.0% Other groups, 7.3% Swedish (2000).
Economy: Employment by occupation: 11.7% management, 20.2% professional, 20.2% services, 19.1% sales, 3.2% farming, 9.6% construction, 16.0% production (2000).
Income: Per capita income: $22,886 (2000); Median household income: $39,375 (2000); Poverty rate: 7.3% (2000).
Taxes: Total city taxes per capita: $60 (1997); City property taxes per capita: $60 (1997).

Education: High school graduation rate: 82.2% (2000); College graduation rate: 30.5% (2000).
Housing: Homeownership rate: 94.5% (2000); Median home value: $67,500 (2000); Median age of housing: 27 years (2000).
Transportation: Commute to work: 84.0% car, 0.0% public transportation, 0.0% walk, 6.4% work from home (2000); Travel time to work: 12.5% less than 15 minutes, 43.2% 15 to 30 minutes, 29.5% 30 to 45 minutes, 10.2% 45 to 60 minutes, 4.5% 60 minutes or more (2000)

ECKLES (township). Covers a land area of 31.643 square miles and a water area of 0.614 square miles. Located at 47.52° N. Lat.; 94.99° W. Long.
Population: 1,033 (2000); Race: 84.2% White, 0.2% Black, 0.2% Asian, 10.6% American Indian and Alaska Native, 0.0% Hispanic of any race, 4.7% two or more races (2000); Density: 32.6 persons per square mile (2000); Age: 33.0% under 18, 8.6% over 64 (2000); Marriage status: 27.2% never married, 59.3% now married, 2.6% widowed, 10.9% divorced (2000); Foreign born: 0.2% (2000); Ancestry (includes multiple ancestries): 28.0% Norwegian, 24.2% German, 14.4% Other groups, 7.9% Swedish, 7.4% Irish (2000).
Economy: Employment by occupation: 10.4% management, 15.1% professional, 18.6% services, 25.6% sales, 1.9% farming, 12.2% construction, 16.2% production (2000).
Income: Per capita income: $13,462 (2000); Median household income: $29,000 (2000); Poverty rate: 17.1% (2000).
Taxes: Total city taxes per capita: $43 (1997); City property taxes per capita: $43 (1997).
Education: High school graduation rate: 83.3% (2000); College graduation rate: 12.4% (2000).
Housing: Homeownership rate: 74.5% (2000); Median home value: $72,000 (2000); Median rent: $402 per month (2000); Median age of housing: 22 years (2000).
Transportation: Commute to work: 93.5% car, 1.1% public transportation, 0.6% walk, 4.3% work from home (2000); Travel time to work: 38.3% less than 15 minutes, 41.7% 15 to 30 minutes, 16.4% 30 to 45 minutes, 1.4% 45 to 60 minutes, 2.3% 60 minutes or more (2000)

FROHN (township). Covers a land area of 32.547 square miles and a water area of 3.913 square miles. Located at 47.44° N. Lat.; 94.72° W. Long.
Population: 1,408 (2000); Race: 91.3% White, 0.0% Black, 0.1% Asian, 6.1% American Indian and Alaska Native, 0.4% Hispanic of any race, 2.0% two or more races (2000); Density: 43.3 persons per square mile (2000); Age: 30.6% under 18, 6.3% over 64 (2000); Marriage status: 22.4% never married, 67.7% now married, 2.8% widowed, 7.1% divorced (2000); Foreign born: 0.6% (2000); Ancestry (includes multiple ancestries): 33.1% German, 27.4% Norwegian, 11.3% Swedish, 10.0% Irish, 8.3% Other groups (2000).
Economy: Single-family building permits issued: 5 (2001) / 5 (2000); Multi-family building permits issued: 0 (2001) / 0 (2000); Employment by occupation: 14.3% management, 21.1% professional, 14.6% services, 23.4% sales, 1.1% farming, 11.9% construction, 13.5% production (2000).
Income: Per capita income: $17,988 (2000); Median household income: $47,788 (2000); Poverty rate: 7.4% (2000).
Taxes: Total city taxes per capita: $57 (1997); City property taxes per capita: $56 (1997).
Education: High school graduation rate: 91.6% (2000); College graduation rate: 28.3% (2000).
Housing: Homeownership rate: 94.0% (2000); Median home value: $99,000 (2000); Median rent: $397 per month (2000); Median age of housing: 21 years (2000).
Transportation: Commute to work: 89.9% car, 0.1% public transportation, 2.7% walk, 6.5% work from home (2000); Travel time to work: 23.4% less than 15 minutes, 63.1% 15 to 30 minutes, 9.8% 30 to 45 minutes, 2.0% 45 to 60 minutes, 1.8% 60 minutes or more (2000)

FUNKLEY (city). Covers a land area of 0.386 square miles and a water area of 0 square miles. Located at 47.78° N. Lat.; 94.43° W. Long. Elevation is 1,391 feet.
Population: 15 (2000); Race: 100.0% White, 0.0% Black, 0.0% Asian, 0.0% American Indian and Alaska Native, 0.0% Hispanic of any race, 0.0% two or more races (2000); Density: 38.9 persons per square mile (2000); Age: 20.8% under 18, 33.3% over 64 (2000); Marriage status: 0.0% never married, 94.7% now married, 0.0% widowed, 5.3% divorced (2000); Foreign born: 0.0% (2000); Ancestry (includes multiple ancestries): 58.3% German, 20.8% Norwegian, 20.8% Irish, 8.3% Polish, 8.3% English (2000).
Economy: Grain; livestock. Chippewa National Forest to East and South. Single-family building permits issued: 0 (2001) / 0 (2000); Multi-family building permits issued: 0 (2001) / 0 (2000); Employment by occupation: 33.3% management, 0.0% professional, 0.0% services, 22.2% sales, 0.0% farming, 0.0% construction, 44.4% production (2000).
Income: Per capita income: $15,521 (2000); Median household income: $26,250 (2000); Poverty rate: 0.0% (2000).
Taxes: Total city taxes per capita: $125 (1997); City property taxes per capita: $125 (1997).
Education: High school graduation rate: 63.2% (2000); College graduation rate: 0.0% (2000).
Housing: Homeownership rate: 100.0% (2000); Median home value: $22,500 (2000); Median age of housing: 24 years (2000).
Transportation: Commute to work: 55.6% car, 0.0% public transportation, 0.0% walk, 44.4% work from home (2000); Travel time to work: 40.0% less than 15 minutes, 60.0% 15 to 30 minutes, 0.0% 30 to 45 minutes, 0.0% 45 to 60 minutes, 0.0% 60 minutes or more (2000)

GRANT VALLEY (township). Covers a land area of 34.074 square miles and a water area of 1.875 square miles. Located at 47.46° N. Lat.; 94.97° W. Long.
Population: 1,450 (2000); Race: 91.9% White, 0.7% Black, 0.7% Asian, 3.4% American Indian and Alaska Native, 0.0% Hispanic of any race, 3.0% two or more races (2000); Density: 42.6 persons per square mile (2000); Age: 31.0% under 18, 7.9% over 64 (2000); Marriage status: 20.6% never married, 66.8% now married, 3.1% widowed, 9.5% divorced (2000); Foreign born: 1.0% (2000); Ancestry (includes multiple ancestries): 32.4% German, 24.8% Norwegian, 10.8% Swedish, 8.5% Other groups, 6.8% Irish (2000).
Economy: Employment by occupation: 11.5% management, 18.5% professional, 15.2% services, 25.5% sales, 0.1% farming, 14.7% construction, 14.4% production (2000).
Income: Per capita income: $18,020 (2000); Median household income: $40,595 (2000); Poverty rate: 8.8% (2000).
Taxes: Total city taxes per capita: $97 (1997); City property taxes per capita: $97 (1997).
Education: High school graduation rate: 84.1% (2000); College graduation rate: 16.4% (2000).
Housing: Homeownership rate: 87.5% (2000); Median home value: $95,200 (2000); Median rent: $395 per month (2000); Median age of housing: 19 years (2000).
Transportation: Commute to work: 89.9% car, 2.7% public transportation, 1.7% walk, 4.6% work from home (2000); Travel time to work: 49.2% less than 15 minutes, 36.4% 15 to 30 minutes, 10.3% 30 to 45 minutes, 1.6% 45 to 60 minutes, 2.5% 60 minutes or more (2000)

HAGALI (township). Covers a land area of 33.255 square miles and a water area of 3.116 square miles. Located at 47.70° N. Lat.; 94.75° W. Long.
Population: 319 (2000); Race: 96.5% White, 0.0% Black, 0.6% Asian, 0.3% American Indian and Alaska Native, 6.9% Hispanic of any race, 2.5% two or more races (2000); Density: 9.6 persons per square mile (2000); Age: 28.0% under 18, 11.3% over 64 (2000); Marriage status: 14.6% never married, 72.4% now married, 6.9% widowed, 6.1% divorced (2000); Foreign born: 2.2% (2000); Ancestry (includes multiple ancestries): 23.6% German, 21.1% Norwegian, 14.5% Irish, 13.5% Other groups, 10.7% English (2000).
Economy: Employment by occupation: 8.1% management, 16.9% professional, 25.0% services, 16.2% sales, 3.4% farming, 11.5% construction, 18.9% production (2000).
Income: Per capita income: $13,672 (2000); Median household income: $38,000 (2000); Poverty rate: 11.6% (2000).
Taxes: Total city taxes per capita: $43 (1997); City property taxes per capita: $43 (1997).
Education: High school graduation rate: 82.6% (2000); College graduation rate: 15.0% (2000).
Housing: Homeownership rate: 98.3% (2000); Median home value: $103,600 (2000); Median age of housing: 17 years (2000).
Transportation: Commute to work: 89.8% car, 0.0% public transportation, 0.0% walk, 10.2% work from home (2000); Travel time to work: 12.1% less than 15 minutes, 56.1% 15 to 30 minutes, 26.5% 30 to 45 minutes, 3.0% 45 to 60 minutes, 2.3% 60 minutes or more (2000)

HAMRE (township). Covers a land area of 35.919 square miles and a water area of 0.016 square miles. Located at 48.24° N. Lat.; 95.39° W. Long.
Population: 15 (2000); Race: 100.0% White, 0.0% Black, 0.0% Asian, 0.0% American Indian and Alaska Native, 0.0% Hispanic of any race, 0.0% two or more races (2000); Density: 0.4 persons per square mile (2000); Age: 23.5% under 18, 23.5% over 64 (2000); Marriage status: 0.0% never married, 76.9% now married, 15.4% widowed, 7.7% divorced (2000); Foreign born: 0.0% (2000); Ancestry (includes multiple ancestries): 29.4% Norwegian, 29.4% German, 17.6% English, 11.8% Polish (2000).

Economy: Employment by occupation: 0.0% management, 0.0% professional, 33.3% services, 33.3% sales, 0.0% farming, 11.1% construction, 22.2% production (2000).
Income: Per capita income: $8,476 (2000); Median household income: $16,875 (2000); Poverty rate: 11.8% (2000).
Taxes: Total city taxes per capita: $33 (1997); City property taxes per capita: $33 (1997).
Education: High school graduation rate: 84.6% (2000); College graduation rate: 7.7% (2000).
Housing: Homeownership rate: 57.1% (2000); Median age of housing: 33 years (2000).
Transportation: Commute to work: 100.0% car, 0.0% public transportation, 0.0% walk, 0.0% work from home (2000); Travel time to work: 0.0% less than 15 minutes, 44.4% 15 to 30 minutes, 0.0% 30 to 45 minutes, 0.0% 45 to 60 minutes, 55.6% 60 minutes or more (2000)

HINES (township). Covers a land area of 30.506 square miles and a water area of 4.671 square miles. Located at 47.70° N. Lat.; 94.61° W. Long. Elevation is 1,404 feet.
Population: 674 (2000); Race: 95.9% White, 0.2% Black, 0.0% Asian, 4.0% American Indian and Alaska Native, 1.1% Hispanic of any race, 0.0% two or more races (2000); Density: 22.1 persons per square mile (2000); Age: 29.2% under 18, 12.5% over 64 (2000); Marriage status: 23.7% never married, 64.4% now married, 5.8% widowed, 6.2% divorced (2000); Foreign born: 0.5% (2000); Ancestry (includes multiple ancestries): 36.4% German, 26.2% Norwegian, 14.5% Swedish, 8.4% Irish, 8.1% English (2000).
Economy: Employment by occupation: 8.5% management, 13.2% professional, 18.0% services, 18.6% sales, 6.3% farming, 14.2% construction, 21.1% production (2000).
Income: Per capita income: $17,342 (2000); Median household income: $42,292 (2000); Poverty rate: 9.3% (2000).
Taxes: Total city taxes per capita: $24 (1997); City property taxes per capita: $24 (1997).
Education: High school graduation rate: 81.9% (2000); College graduation rate: 15.2% (2000).
Housing: Homeownership rate: 94.3% (2000); Median home value: $71,700 (2000); Median rent: $338 per month (2000); Median age of housing: 28 years (2000).
Transportation: Commute to work: 91.7% car, 1.3% public transportation, 0.7% walk, 5.6% work from home (2000); Travel time to work: 49.3% less than 15 minutes, 17.8% 15 to 30 minutes, 21.0% 30 to 45 minutes, 4.9% 45 to 60 minutes, 7.0% 60 minutes or more (2000)

HORNET (township). Covers a land area of 35.782 square miles and a water area of 0.036 square miles. Located at 47.80° N. Lat.; 94.52° W. Long.
Population: 227 (2000); Race: 94.0% White, 0.0% Black, 0.0% Asian, 0.0% American Indian and Alaska Native, 0.0% Hispanic of any race, 6.0% two or more races (2000); Density: 6.3 persons per square mile (2000); Age: 27.2% under 18, 11.5% over 64 (2000); Marriage status: 18.2% never married, 66.3% now married, 5.5% widowed, 9.9% divorced (2000); Foreign born: 1.7% (2000); Ancestry (includes multiple ancestries): 32.3% German, 13.6% Irish, 13.6% Swedish, 13.6% Norwegian, 10.2% English (2000).
Economy: Employment by occupation: 19.1% management, 4.3% professional, 15.7% services, 17.4% sales, 11.3% farming, 10.4% construction, 21.7% production (2000).
Income: Per capita income: $14,578 (2000); Median household income: $36,250 (2000); Poverty rate: 22.6% (2000).
Taxes: Total city taxes per capita: $32 (1997); City property taxes per capita: $32 (1997).
Education: High school graduation rate: 76.8% (2000); College graduation rate: 3.9% (2000).
Housing: Homeownership rate: 97.5% (2000); Median home value: $65,000 (2000); Median age of housing: 25 years (2000).
Transportation: Commute to work: 73.0% car, 0.0% public transportation, 8.1% walk, 18.9% work from home (2000); Travel time to work: 52.2% less than 15 minutes, 24.4% 15 to 30 minutes, 8.9% 30 to 45 minutes, 6.7% 45 to 60 minutes, 7.8% 60 minutes or more (2000)

JONES (township). Covers a land area of 35.389 square miles and a water area of 0.619 square miles. Located at 47.46° N. Lat.; 95.12° W. Long.
Population: 277 (2000); Race: 92.8% White, 0.7% Black, 0.0% Asian, 4.0% American Indian and Alaska Native, 0.0% Hispanic of any race, 2.5% two or more races (2000); Density: 7.8 persons per square mile (2000); Age: 35.7% under 18, 9.0% over 64 (2000); Marriage status: 21.3% never married, 63.5% now married, 4.1% widowed, 11.2% divorced (2000); Foreign born: 0.4% (2000); Ancestry (includes multiple ancestries): 42.2% Norwegian, 29.6% German, 11.9% Swedish, 10.8% Irish, 5.1% English (2000).
Economy: Employment by occupation: 12.5% management, 25.0% professional, 12.5% services, 22.8% sales, 1.5% farming, 8.8% construction, 16.9% production (2000).
Income: Per capita income: $13,612 (2000); Median household income: $38,750 (2000); Poverty rate: 7.3% (2000).
Taxes: Total city taxes per capita: $63 (1997); City property taxes per capita: $63 (1997).
Education: High school graduation rate: 81.4% (2000); College graduation rate: 26.1% (2000).
Housing: Homeownership rate: 97.7% (2000); Median home value: $78,800 (2000); Median rent: $175 per month (2000); Median age of housing: 18 years (2000).
Transportation: Commute to work: 92.4% car, 0.8% public transportation, 0.8% walk, 4.5% work from home (2000); Travel time to work: 23.0% less than 15 minutes, 57.9% 15 to 30 minutes, 14.3% 30 to 45 minutes, 2.4% 45 to 60 minutes, 2.4% 60 minutes or more (2000)

KELLIHER (city). Covers a land area of 2.086 square miles and a water area of 0.058 square miles. Located at 47.94° N. Lat.; 94.44° W. Long. Elevation is 1,361 feet.
Population: 294 (2000); Race: 92.5% White, 0.0% Black, 0.0% Asian, 7.5% American Indian and Alaska Native, 0.0% Hispanic of any race, 0.0% two or more races (2000); Density: 140.9 persons per square mile (2000); Age: 31.1% under 18, 24.3% over 64 (2000); Marriage status: 20.4% never married, 51.7% now married, 18.7% widowed, 9.1% divorced (2000); Foreign born: 0.0% (2000); Ancestry (includes multiple ancestries): 29.5% German, 26.6% Norwegian, 7.9% Other groups, 7.2% Swedish, 6.9% Polish (2000).
Economy: Single-family building permits issued: 1 (2001) / 1 (2000); Multi-family building permits issued: 0 (2001) / 0 (2000); Employment by occupation: 13.2% management, 17.0% professional, 15.1% services, 20.8% sales, 3.8% farming, 10.4% construction, 19.8% production (2000).
Income: Per capita income: $13,386 (2000); Median household income: $20,625 (2000); Poverty rate: 19.6% (2000).
Taxes: Total city taxes per capita: $39 (1997); City property taxes per capita: $37 (1997).
Education: High school graduation rate: 68.7% (2000); College graduation rate: 8.2% (2000).

School District(s)

Kelliher (KG-12)
2000 Enrollment: 268 218-647-8286

Housing: Homeownership rate: 71.2% (2000); Median home value: $30,800 (2000); Median rent: $216 per month (2000); Median age of housing: 39 years (2000).
Transportation: Commute to work: 83.2% car, 0.0% public transportation, 9.9% walk, 6.9% work from home (2000); Travel time to work: 51.1% less than 15 minutes, 22.3% 15 to 30 minutes, 10.6% 30 to 45 minutes, 9.6% 45 to 60 minutes, 6.4% 60 minutes or more (2000)

KELLIHER (township). Covers a land area of 33.539 square miles and a water area of 0.035 square miles. Located at 47.93° N. Lat.; 94.49° W. Long. Elevation is 1,361 feet.
Population: 150 (2000); Race: 100.0% White, 0.0% Black, 0.0% Asian, 0.0% American Indian and Alaska Native, 0.0% Hispanic of any race, 0.0% two or more races (2000); Density: 4.5 persons per square mile (2000); Age: 27.8% under 18, 9.9% over 64 (2000); Marriage status: 30.5% never married, 55.7% now married, 5.3% widowed, 8.4% divorced (2000); Foreign born: 0.0% (2000); Ancestry (includes multiple ancestries): 38.4% German, 13.2% Norwegian, 12.6% English, 11.3% Polish, 9.9% French (except Basque) (2000).
Economy: Grain, sunflowers; livestock; dairying. Manufacturing: hardwood lumber. Employment by occupation: 12.0% management, 17.3% professional, 21.3% services, 22.7% sales, 2.7% farming, 8.0% construction, 16.0% production (2000).
Income: Per capita income: $12,613 (2000); Median household income: $21,250 (2000); Poverty rate: 32.5% (2000).
Taxes: Total city taxes per capita: $45 (1997); City property taxes per capita: $45 (1997).
Education: High school graduation rate: 87.8% (2000); College graduation rate: 12.2% (2000).
Housing: Homeownership rate: 100.0% (2000); Median home value: $91,700 (2000); Median age of housing: 27 years (2000).
Transportation: Commute to work: 76.0% car, 0.0% public transportation, 6.7% walk, 17.3% work from home (2000); Travel time to work: 41.9% less

than 15 minutes, 17.7% 15 to 30 minutes, 27.4% 30 to 45 minutes, 0.0% 45 to 60 minutes, 12.9% 60 minutes or more (2000)

LAMMERS (township). Covers a land area of 34.792 square miles and a water area of 0.267 square miles. Located at 47.53° N. Lat.; 95.10° W. Long.
Population: 492 (2000); Race: 95.3% White, 0.0% Black, 0.6% Asian, 0.0% American Indian and Alaska Native, 2.4% Hispanic of any race, 4.0% two or more races (2000); Density: 14.1 persons per square mile (2000); Age: 29.1% under 18, 10.5% over 64 (2000); Marriage status: 28.6% never married, 54.5% now married, 6.5% widowed, 10.4% divorced (2000); Foreign born: 0.6% (2000); Ancestry (includes multiple ancestries): 33.0% Norwegian, 30.2% German, 17.6% Swedish, 10.3% Irish, 6.9% Other groups (2000).
Economy: Employment by occupation: 7.1% management, 18.4% professional, 17.4% services, 22.7% sales, 3.5% farming, 12.1% construction, 18.8% production (2000).
Income: Per capita income: $16,894 (2000); Median household income: $43,375 (2000); Poverty rate: 12.1% (2000).
Taxes: Total city taxes per capita: $146 (1997); City property taxes per capita: $146 (1997).
Education: High school graduation rate: 90.5% (2000); College graduation rate: 14.1% (2000).
Housing: Homeownership rate: 90.7% (2000); Median home value: $82,500 (2000); Median rent: $432 per month (2000); Median age of housing: 23 years (2000).
Transportation: Commute to work: 86.5% car, 0.0% public transportation, 1.4% walk, 12.1% work from home (2000); Travel time to work: 23.4% less than 15 minutes, 54.4% 15 to 30 minutes, 17.3% 30 to 45 minutes, 0.8% 45 to 60 minutes, 4.0% 60 minutes or more (2000)

LANGOR (township). Covers a land area of 36.158 square miles and a water area of 0.038 square miles. Located at 47.78° N. Lat.; 94.58° W. Long. Elevation is 1,326 feet.
Population: 186 (2000); Race: 96.9% White, 0.0% Black, 0.0% Asian, 1.9% American Indian and Alaska Native, 0.0% Hispanic of any race, 1.2% two or more races (2000); Density: 5.1 persons per square mile (2000); Age: 25.3% under 18, 15.4% over 64 (2000); Marriage status: 35.8% never married, 58.4% now married, 1.5% widowed, 4.4% divorced (2000); Foreign born: 1.2% (2000); Ancestry (includes multiple ancestries): 37.7% German, 18.5% Norwegian, 14.8% Irish, 9.3% Other groups, 8.0% Swedish (2000).
Economy: Employment by occupation: 13.7% management, 9.5% professional, 18.9% services, 15.8% sales, 2.1% farming, 14.7% construction, 25.3% production (2000).
Income: Per capita income: $17,662 (2000); Median household income: $41,000 (2000); Poverty rate: 3.8% (2000).
Taxes: Total city taxes per capita: $19 (1997); City property taxes per capita: $19 (1997).
Education: High school graduation rate: 78.4% (2000); College graduation rate: 6.9% (2000).
Housing: Homeownership rate: 96.9% (2000); Median age of housing: 21 years (2000).
Transportation: Commute to work: 78.9% car, 0.0% public transportation, 7.4% walk, 11.6% work from home (2000); Travel time to work: 36.9% less than 15 minutes, 28.6% 15 to 30 minutes, 14.3% 30 to 45 minutes, 15.5% 45 to 60 minutes, 4.8% 60 minutes or more (2000)

LEE (township). Covers a land area of 36.170 square miles and a water area of 0.198 square miles. Located at 48.24° N. Lat.; 95.51° W. Long.
Population: 36 (2000); Race: 100.0% White, 0.0% Black, 0.0% Asian, 0.0% American Indian and Alaska Native, 0.0% Hispanic of any race, 0.0% two or more races (2000); Density: 1.0 persons per square mile (2000); Age: 29.7% under 18, 16.2% over 64 (2000); Marriage status: 23.1% never married, 69.2% now married, 7.7% widowed, 0.0% divorced (2000); Foreign born: 0.0% (2000); Ancestry (includes multiple ancestries): 64.9% Norwegian, 29.7% German, 8.1% Swedish, 5.4% French Canadian, 5.4% Danish (2000).
Economy: Employment by occupation: 36.8% management, 21.1% professional, 15.8% services, 0.0% sales, 10.5% farming, 0.0% construction, 15.8% production (2000).
Income: Per capita income: $8,370 (2000); Median household income: $24,167 (2000); Poverty rate: 5.4% (2000).
Education: High school graduation rate: 77.3% (2000); College graduation rate: 27.3% (2000).
Housing: Homeownership rate: 85.7% (2000); Median home value: $55,000 (2000); Median age of housing: 35 years (2000).
Transportation: Commute to work: 73.7% car, 0.0% public transportation, 10.5% walk, 15.8% work from home (2000); Travel time to work: 0.0% less than 15 minutes, 37.5% 15 to 30 minutes, 18.8% 30 to 45 minutes, 18.8% 45 to 60 minutes, 25.0% 60 minutes or more (2000)

LIBERTY (township). Covers a land area of 32.947 square miles and a water area of 3.395 square miles. Located at 47.64° N. Lat.; 94.99° W. Long.
Population: 623 (2000); Race: 96.7% White, 0.0% Black, 0.3% Asian, 2.2% American Indian and Alaska Native, 0.3% Hispanic of any race, 0.8% two or more races (2000); Density: 18.9 persons per square mile (2000); Age: 30.9% under 18, 7.9% over 64 (2000); Marriage status: 26.4% never married, 60.0% now married, 2.8% widowed, 10.8% divorced (2000); Foreign born: 1.1% (2000); Ancestry (includes multiple ancestries): 43.9% German, 25.3% Norwegian, 10.5% Swedish, 10.2% English, 8.2% Irish (2000).
Economy: Employment by occupation: 6.2% management, 18.5% professional, 19.1% services, 18.5% sales, 2.1% farming, 18.8% construction, 17.0% production (2000).
Income: Per capita income: $18,482 (2000); Median household income: $45,391 (2000); Poverty rate: 4.4% (2000).
Taxes: Total city taxes per capita: $50 (1997); City property taxes per capita: $50 (1997).
Education: High school graduation rate: 84.3% (2000); College graduation rate: 19.6% (2000).
Housing: Homeownership rate: 93.2% (2000); Median home value: $80,500 (2000); Median rent: $290 per month (2000); Median age of housing: 18 years (2000).
Transportation: Commute to work: 92.0% car, 0.6% public transportation, 0.6% walk, 5.9% work from home (2000); Travel time to work: 13.8% less than 15 minutes, 64.6% 15 to 30 minutes, 16.9% 30 to 45 minutes, 2.5% 45 to 60 minutes, 2.2% 60 minutes or more (2000)

LITTLE ROCK (CDP). Covers a land area of 13.043 square miles and a water area of 0.664 square miles. Located at 47.86° N. Lat.; 95.07° W. Long.
Population: 1,055 (2000); Race: 1.9% White, 0.0% Black, 6.9% Asian, 90.8% American Indian and Alaska Native, 4.7% Hispanic of any race, 0.5% two or more races (2000); Density: 80.9 persons per square mile (2000); Age: 46.3% under 18, 5.9% over 64 (2000); Marriage status: 54.9% never married, 29.5% now married, 5.1% widowed, 10.4% divorced (2000); Foreign born: 1.4% (2000); Ancestry (includes multiple ancestries): 93.7% Other groups, 0.4% Norwegian (2000).
Economy: Employment by occupation: 5.7% management, 7.8% professional, 35.9% services, 27.3% sales, 1.6% farming, 9.0% construction, 12.7% production (2000).
Income: Per capita income: $8,668 (2000); Median household income: $25,688 (2000); Poverty rate: 31.8% (2000).
Education: High school graduation rate: 57.2% (2000); College graduation rate: 0.9% (2000).
Housing: Homeownership rate: 62.0% (2000); Median home value: $60,400 (2000); Median rent: $149 per month (2000); Median age of housing: 18 years (2000).
Transportation: Commute to work: 88.3% car, 5.4% public transportation, 4.6% walk, 0.0% work from home (2000); Travel time to work: 41.7% less than 15 minutes, 25.4% 15 to 30 minutes, 8.8% 30 to 45 minutes, 4.6% 45 to 60 minutes, 19.6% 60 minutes or more (2000)

MAPLE RIDGE (township). Covers a land area of 34.162 square miles and a water area of 2.305 square miles. Located at 47.69° N. Lat.; 94.98° W. Long.
Population: 108 (2000); Race: 96.6% White, 0.0% Black, 0.0% Asian, 3.4% American Indian and Alaska Native, 0.0% Hispanic of any race, 0.0% two or more races (2000); Density: 3.2 persons per square mile (2000); Age: 20.2% under 18, 28.1% over 64 (2000); Marriage status: 14.7% never married, 61.3% now married, 10.7% widowed, 13.3% divorced (2000); Foreign born: 0.0% (2000); Ancestry (includes multiple ancestries): 23.6% Norwegian, 21.3% Swedish, 20.2% German, 14.6% United States or American, 13.5% Irish (2000).
Economy: Employment by occupation: 15.2% management, 10.9% professional, 8.7% services, 4.3% sales, 0.0% farming, 28.3% construction, 32.6% production (2000).
Income: Per capita income: $13,615 (2000); Median household income: $30,625 (2000); Poverty rate: 13.5% (2000).
Taxes: Total city taxes per capita: $38 (1997); City property taxes per capita: $38 (1997).
Education: High school graduation rate: 67.7% (2000); College graduation rate: 12.3% (2000).
Housing: Homeownership rate: 90.0% (2000); Median home value: $45,000 (2000); Median rent: $275 per month (2000); Median age of housing: 30 years (2000).

Transportation: Commute to work: 89.1% car, 0.0% public transportation, 0.0% walk, 10.9% work from home (2000); Travel time to work: 9.8% less than 15 minutes, 36.6% 15 to 30 minutes, 41.5% 30 to 45 minutes, 7.3% 45 to 60 minutes, 4.9% 60 minutes or more (2000)

MINNIE (township). Covers a land area of 34.867 square miles and a water area of 0 square miles. Located at 48.33° N. Lat.; 95.26° W. Long.
Population: 19 (2000); Race: 100.0% White, 0.0% Black, 0.0% Asian, 0.0% American Indian and Alaska Native, 0.0% Hispanic of any race, 0.0% two or more races (2000); Density: 0.5 persons per square mile (2000); Age: 0.0% under 18, 66.7% over 64 (2000); Marriage status: 16.7% never married, 33.3% now married, 33.3% widowed, 16.7% divorced (2000); Foreign born: 0.0% (2000); Ancestry (includes multiple ancestries): 66.7% German, 50.0% Norwegian, 16.7% Danish, 16.7% Swedish, 16.7% English (2000).
Economy: Employment by occupation: 0.0% management, 0.0% professional, 100.0% services, 0.0% sales, 0.0% farming, 0.0% construction, 0.0% production (2000).
Income: Per capita income: $42,900 (2000); Median household income: $46,250 (2000); Poverty rate: 0.0% (2000).
Taxes: Total city taxes per capita: $300 (1997); City property taxes per capita: $300 (1997).
Education: High school graduation rate: 50.0% (2000); College graduation rate: 16.7% (2000).
Housing: Homeownership rate: 100.0% (2000); Median home value: $32,500 (2000); Median age of housing: 29 years (2000).
Transportation: Commute to work: 100.0% car, 0.0% public transportation, 0.0% walk, 0.0% work from home (2000); Travel time to work: 0.0% less than 15 minutes, 100.0% 15 to 30 minutes, 0.0% 30 to 45 minutes, 0.0% 45 to 60 minutes, 0.0% 60 minutes or more (2000)

MOOSE LAKE (township). Covers a land area of 30.857 square miles and a water area of 5.293 square miles. Located at 47.54° N. Lat.; 94.49° W. Long.
Population: 205 (2000); Race: 100.0% White, 0.0% Black, 0.0% Asian, 0.0% American Indian and Alaska Native, 0.0% Hispanic of any race, 0.0% two or more races (2000); Density: 6.6 persons per square mile (2000); Age: 25.4% under 18, 15.0% over 64 (2000); Marriage status: 20.6% never married, 68.8% now married, 2.8% widowed, 7.8% divorced (2000); Foreign born: 0.0% (2000); Ancestry (includes multiple ancestries): 33.5% German, 9.8% Norwegian, 8.7% Irish, 8.1% Other groups, 7.5% Swedish (2000).
Economy: Employment by occupation: 17.5% management, 8.8% professional, 28.1% services, 10.5% sales, 0.0% farming, 12.3% construction, 22.8% production (2000).
Income: Per capita income: $13,527 (2000); Median household income: $24,271 (2000); Poverty rate: 20.8% (2000).
Taxes: Total city taxes per capita: $5 (1997); City property taxes per capita: $5 (1997).
Education: High school graduation rate: 75.2% (2000); College graduation rate: 6.6% (2000).
Housing: Homeownership rate: 95.9% (2000); Median home value: $68,800 (2000); Median rent: $188 per month (2000); Median age of housing: 27 years (2000).
Transportation: Commute to work: 96.5% car, 0.0% public transportation, 0.0% walk, 3.5% work from home (2000); Travel time to work: 9.1% less than 15 minutes, 27.3% 15 to 30 minutes, 20.0% 30 to 45 minutes, 9.1% 45 to 60 minutes, 34.5% 60 minutes or more (2000)

NEBISH (township). Covers a land area of 34.296 square miles and a water area of 1.601 square miles. Located at 47.76° N. Lat.; 94.85° W. Long.
Population: 318 (2000); Race: 98.9% White, 0.0% Black, 0.0% Asian, 1.1% American Indian and Alaska Native, 0.6% Hispanic of any race, 0.0% two or more races (2000); Density: 9.3 persons per square mile (2000); Age: 32.5% under 18, 13.3% over 64 (2000); Marriage status: 21.5% never married, 59.4% now married, 4.2% widowed, 14.9% divorced (2000); Foreign born: 0.0% (2000); Ancestry (includes multiple ancestries): 28.8% German, 18.9% Norwegian, 14.4% Irish, 9.0% United States or American, 8.2% English (2000).
Economy: Employment by occupation: 9.6% management, 17.8% professional, 11.0% services, 21.9% sales, 6.2% farming, 5.5% construction, 28.1% production (2000).
Income: Per capita income: $13,204 (2000); Median household income: $40,833 (2000); Poverty rate: 15.0% (2000).
Taxes: Total city taxes per capita: $51 (1997); City property taxes per capita: $51 (1997).
Education: High school graduation rate: 75.3% (2000); College graduation rate: 6.8% (2000).
Housing: Homeownership rate: 92.1% (2000); Median home value: $40,000 (2000); Median rent: $325 per month (2000); Median age of housing: 20 years (2000).
Transportation: Commute to work: 90.0% car, 0.0% public transportation, 3.6% walk, 5.0% work from home (2000); Travel time to work: 13.5% less than 15 minutes, 39.1% 15 to 30 minutes, 33.8% 30 to 45 minutes, 6.8% 45 to 60 minutes, 6.8% 60 minutes or more (2000)

NORTHERN (township). Covers a land area of 27.526 square miles and a water area of 7.266 square miles. Located at 47.52° N. Lat.; 94.87° W. Long.
Population: 4,021 (2000); Race: 91.3% White, 0.0% Black, 1.9% Asian, 3.7% American Indian and Alaska Native, 0.6% Hispanic of any race, 3.2% two or more races (2000); Density: 146.1 persons per square mile (2000); Age: 29.9% under 18, 10.0% over 64 (2000); Marriage status: 25.3% never married, 61.7% now married, 4.7% widowed, 8.4% divorced (2000); Foreign born: 2.3% (2000); Ancestry (includes multiple ancestries): 34.5% German, 26.7% Norwegian, 9.1% Swedish, 9.0% Irish, 8.1% Other groups (2000).
Economy: Employment by occupation: 15.2% management, 27.3% professional, 13.8% services, 22.5% sales, 1.9% farming, 7.3% construction, 12.0% production (2000).
Income: Per capita income: $18,843 (2000); Median household income: $44,535 (2000); Poverty rate: 7.1% (2000).
Taxes: Total city taxes per capita: $57 (2000); City property taxes per capita: $54 (2000).
Education: High school graduation rate: 93.1% (2000); College graduation rate: 36.2% (2000).
Housing: Homeownership rate: 87.9% (2000); Median home value: $99,700 (2000); Median rent: $417 per month (2000); Median age of housing: 24 years (2000).
Transportation: Commute to work: 93.0% car, 0.2% public transportation, 2.1% walk, 4.5% work from home (2000); Travel time to work: 50.8% less than 15 minutes, 38.1% 15 to 30 minutes, 5.4% 30 to 45 minutes, 2.1% 45 to 60 minutes, 3.5% 60 minutes or more (2000)

O'BRIEN (township). Covers a land area of 35.930 square miles and a water area of 0.028 square miles. Located at 47.80° N. Lat.; 94.71° W. Long.
Population: 56 (2000); Race: 100.0% White, 0.0% Black, 0.0% Asian, 0.0% American Indian and Alaska Native, 27.1% Hispanic of any race, 0.0% two or more races (2000); Density: 1.6 persons per square mile (2000); Age: 31.4% under 18, 15.7% over 64 (2000); Marriage status: 28.1% never married, 57.9% now married, 10.5% widowed, 3.5% divorced (2000); Foreign born: 0.0% (2000); Ancestry (includes multiple ancestries): 28.6% German, 27.1% Other groups, 11.4% Irish, 11.4% Swedish, 4.3% Norwegian (2000).
Economy: Employment by occupation: 35.7% management, 14.3% professional, 21.4% services, 7.1% sales, 0.0% farming, 7.1% construction, 14.3% production (2000).
Income: Per capita income: $12,509 (2000); Median household income: $12,083 (2000); Poverty rate: 35.7% (2000).
Education: High school graduation rate: 76.7% (2000); College graduation rate: 0.0% (2000).
Housing: Homeownership rate: 92.6% (2000); Median home value: <$10,000 (2000); Median rent: $325 per month (2000); Median age of housing: 28 years (2000).
Transportation: Commute to work: 78.6% car, 0.0% public transportation, 0.0% walk, 21.4% work from home (2000); Travel time to work: 9.1% less than 15 minutes, 81.8% 15 to 30 minutes, 9.1% 30 to 45 minutes, 0.0% 45 to 60 minutes, 0.0% 60 minutes or more (2000)

PENNINGTON (unincorporated postal area, zip code 56663). Covers a land area of 27.557 square miles and a water area of 0.596 square miles. Located at 47.46° N. Lat.; 94.44° W. Long. Elevation is 1,320 feet.
Population: 188 (2000); Race: 81.9% White, 0.0% Black, 0.0% Asian, 18.1% American Indian and Alaska Native, 10.3% Hispanic of any race, 0.0% two or more races (2000); Density: 6.8 persons per square mile (2000); Age: 11.0% under 18, 29.7% over 64 (2000); Marriage status: 12.6% never married, 66.2% now married, 11.9% widowed, 9.3% divorced (2000); Foreign born: 0.0% (2000); Ancestry (includes multiple ancestries): 34.8% Other groups, 11.6% German, 7.7% English, 5.2% Swedish, 4.5% Irish (2000).
Economy: Employment by occupation: 27.0% management, 2.2% professional, 3.4% services, 20.2% sales, 10.1% farming, 28.1% construction, 9.0% production (2000).
Income: Per capita income: $14,668 (2000); Median household income: $21,146 (2000); Poverty rate: 22.6% (2000).

Education: High school graduation rate: 42.8% (2000); College graduation rate: 1.4% (2000).
Housing: Homeownership rate: 90.0% (2000); Median home value: $18,400 (2000); Median rent: $125 per month (2000); Median age of housing: 21 years (2000).
Transportation: Commute to work: 71.9% car, 0.0% public transportation, 0.0% walk, 10.1% work from home (2000); Travel time to work: 11.3% less than 15 minutes, 67.5% 15 to 30 minutes, 3.8% 30 to 45 minutes, 3.8% 45 to 60 minutes, 13.8% 60 minutes or more (2000)

PONEMAH (CDP). Covers a land area of 19.600 square miles and a water area of 0 square miles. Located at 48.02° N. Lat.; 94.92° W. Long. Elevation is 1,192 feet.
Population: 874 (2000); Race: 2.0% White, 0.0% Black, 0.3% Asian, 96.5% American Indian and Alaska Native, 1.9% Hispanic of any race, 0.2% two or more races (2000); Density: 44.6 persons per square mile (2000); Age: 51.9% under 18, 1.3% over 64 (2000); Marriage status: 64.1% never married, 24.4% now married, 4.7% widowed, 6.8% divorced (2000); Foreign born: 1.1% (2000); Ancestry (includes multiple ancestries): 83.7% Other groups, 0.6% Canadian, 0.4% African, 0.3% United States or American (2000).
Economy: Employment by occupation: 5.0% management, 27.9% professional, 25.7% services, 15.7% sales, 3.6% farming, 9.3% construction, 12.9% production (2000).
Income: Per capita income: $4,000 (2000); Median household income: $13,571 (2000); Poverty rate: 52.3% (2000).
Education: High school graduation rate: 58.0% (2000); College graduation rate: 0.0% (2000).
Housing: Homeownership rate: 57.1% (2000); Median home value: $39,500 (2000); Median rent: $135 per month (2000); Median age of housing: 17 years (2000).
Transportation: Commute to work: 100.0% car, 0.0% public transportation, 0.0% walk, 0.0% work from home (2000); Travel time to work: 21.1% less than 15 minutes, 22.6% 15 to 30 minutes, 27.1% 30 to 45 minutes, 12.8% 45 to 60 minutes, 16.5% 60 minutes or more (2000)

PORT HOPE (township). Covers a land area of 28.426 square miles and a water area of 4.075 square miles. Located at 47.61° N. Lat.; 94.74° W. Long.
Population: 590 (2000); Race: 96.9% White, 0.0% Black, 0.4% Asian, 2.7% American Indian and Alaska Native, 0.0% Hispanic of any race, 0.0% two or more races (2000); Density: 20.8 persons per square mile (2000); Age: 26.9% under 18, 8.1% over 64 (2000); Marriage status: 23.2% never married, 66.1% now married, 3.4% widowed, 7.3% divorced (2000); Foreign born: 0.4% (2000); Ancestry (includes multiple ancestries): 32.0% German, 20.3% Norwegian, 16.3% United States or American, 15.4% Irish, 9.0% English (2000).
Economy: Employment by occupation: 8.7% management, 17.0% professional, 24.6% services, 21.8% sales, 0.7% farming, 16.6% construction, 10.7% production (2000).
Income: Per capita income: $18,960 (2000); Median household income: $41,154 (2000); Poverty rate: 9.2% (2000).
Taxes: Total city taxes per capita: $45 (1997); City property taxes per capita: $45 (1997).
Education: High school graduation rate: 88.6% (2000); College graduation rate: 25.3% (2000).
Housing: Homeownership rate: 90.6% (2000); Median home value: $93,800 (2000); Median rent: $375 per month (2000); Median age of housing: 20 years (2000).
Transportation: Commute to work: 94.4% car, 0.0% public transportation, 2.5% walk, 2.1% work from home (2000); Travel time to work: 13.3% less than 15 minutes, 62.4% 15 to 30 minutes, 11.8% 30 to 45 minutes, 4.3% 45 to 60 minutes, 8.2% 60 minutes or more (2000)

PUPOSKY (unincorporated postal area, zip code 56667). Covers a land area of 87.923 square miles and a water area of 8.073 square miles. Located at 47.75° N. Lat.; 94.91° W. Long.
Population: 670 (2000); Race: 97.1% White, 0.0% Black, 0.1% Asian, 2.5% American Indian and Alaska Native, 0.3% Hispanic of any race, 0.3% two or more races (2000); Density: 7.6 persons per square mile (2000); Age: 25.4% under 18, 13.5% over 64 (2000); Marriage status: 19.4% never married, 61.9% now married, 6.4% widowed, 12.3% divorced (2000); Foreign born: 0.1% (2000); Ancestry (includes multiple ancestries): 25.0% German, 24.7% Norwegian, 14.9% Irish, 7.0% English, 6.9% Swedish (2000).
Economy: Employment by occupation: 10.8% management, 15.6% professional, 13.5% services, 16.2% sales, 3.6% farming, 15.0% construction, 25.2% production (2000).
Income: Per capita income: $15,755 (2000); Median household income: $38,977 (2000); Poverty rate: 12.4% (2000).
Education: High school graduation rate: 78.5% (2000); College graduation rate: 13.9% (2000).
Housing: Homeownership rate: 92.6% (2000); Median home value: $51,500 (2000); Median rent: $325 per month (2000); Median age of housing: 22 years (2000).
Transportation: Commute to work: 87.2% car, 0.0% public transportation, 2.1% walk, 7.3% work from home (2000); Travel time to work: 13.9% less than 15 minutes, 32.0% 15 to 30 minutes, 39.3% 30 to 45 minutes, 7.6% 45 to 60 minutes, 7.3% 60 minutes or more (2000)

QUIRING (township). Covers a land area of 23.911 square miles and a water area of 0.016 square miles. Located at 47.87° N. Lat.; 94.71° W. Long. Elevation is 1,206 feet.
Population: 85 (2000); Race: 87.8% White, 9.8% Black, 0.0% Asian, 2.4% American Indian and Alaska Native, 0.0% Hispanic of any race, 0.0% two or more races (2000); Density: 3.6 persons per square mile (2000); Age: 22.0% under 18, 28.0% over 64 (2000); Marriage status: 28.1% never married, 54.7% now married, 14.1% widowed, 3.1% divorced (2000); Foreign born: 0.0% (2000); Ancestry (includes multiple ancestries): 22.0% German, 15.9% Irish, 11.0% Norwegian, 9.8% Other groups, 7.3% Swedish (2000).
Economy: Employment by occupation: 22.6% management, 0.0% professional, 6.5% services, 19.4% sales, 6.5% farming, 29.0% construction, 16.1% production (2000).
Income: Per capita income: $9,218 (2000); Median household income: $19,167 (2000); Poverty rate: 18.3% (2000).
Taxes: Total city taxes per capita: $36 (1997); City property taxes per capita: $36 (1997).
Education: High school graduation rate: 78.3% (2000); College graduation rate: 0.0% (2000).
Housing: Homeownership rate: 86.5% (2000); Median home value: $90,000 (2000); Median age of housing: 26 years (2000).
Transportation: Commute to work: 83.9% car, 0.0% public transportation, 6.5% walk, 9.7% work from home (2000); Travel time to work: 14.3% less than 15 minutes, 39.3% 15 to 30 minutes, 21.4% 30 to 45 minutes, 14.3% 45 to 60 minutes, 10.7% 60 minutes or more (2000)

RED LAKE (CDP). Aka Redlake. Covers a land area of 12.981 square miles and a water area of 0.414 square miles. Located at 47.87° N. Lat.; 95.01° W. Long. Elevation is 1,216 feet.
Population: 1,430 (2000); Race: 1.9% White, 0.0% Black, 2.2% Asian, 93.9% American Indian and Alaska Native, 1.8% Hispanic of any race, 2.1% two or more races (2000); Density: 110.2 persons per square mile (2000); Age: 40.9% under 18, 5.1% over 64 (2000); Marriage status: 48.2% never married, 36.7% now married, 6.4% widowed, 8.7% divorced (2000); Foreign born: 1.7% (2000); Ancestry (includes multiple ancestries): 90.9% Other groups, 1.1% Scandinavian, 0.7% United States or American, 0.5% German, 0.4% Norwegian (2000).
Economy: Native American school and reservation headquarters are here. Employment by occupation: 8.1% management, 19.0% professional, 35.7% services, 15.5% sales, 4.0% farming, 13.3% construction, 4.3% production (2000).
Income: Per capita income: $8,787 (2000); Median household income: $23,224 (2000); Poverty rate: 36.4% (2000).
Education: High school graduation rate: 60.8% (2000); College graduation rate: 4.6% (2000).

School District(s)

Red Lake (PK-12)
2000 Enrollment: 1,406 218-679-3353
Housing: Homeownership rate: 61.0% (2000); Median home value: $49,300 (2000); Median rent: $179 per month (2000); Median age of housing: 18 years (2000).
Hospitals: USPHS Cherokee Indian Hospital (23 beds)
Transportation: Commute to work: 85.9% car, 5.6% public transportation, 5.6% walk, 1.7% work from home (2000); Travel time to work: 65.1% less than 15 minutes, 11.1% 15 to 30 minutes, 2.5% 30 to 45 minutes, 2.2% 45 to 60 minutes, 19.1% 60 minutes or more (2000)

REDBY (CDP). Covers a land area of 11.667 square miles and a water area of 0.480 square miles. Located at 47.87° N. Lat.; 94.92° W. Long. Elevation is 1,205 feet.
Population: 957 (2000); Race: 1.0% White, 0.0% Black, 0.0% Asian, 98.1% American Indian and Alaska Native, 3.6% Hispanic of any race, 0.9% two or more races (2000); Density: 82.0 persons per square mile (2000); Age: 44.9% under 18, 5.4% over 64 (2000); Marriage status: 54.3% never married, 30.9%

now married, 7.9% widowed, 6.9% divorced (2000); Foreign born: 0.0% (2000); Ancestry (includes multiple ancestries): 90.6% Other groups, 1.9% Swedish, 1.9% Dutch, 0.9% French (except Basque), 0.4% Polish (2000).
Economy: Manufacturing: freshwater-fish processing, forest products, landscape materials, docks, and pallets. Agriculture: livestock, grain; fish; timber. Employment by occupation: 12.2% management, 19.0% professional, 23.5% services, 16.1% sales, 2.3% farming, 17.7% construction, 9.3% production (2000).
Income: Per capita income: $9,886 (2000); Median household income: $30,000 (2000); Poverty rate: 36.9% (2000).
Education: High school graduation rate: 67.9% (2000); College graduation rate: 1.8% (2000).
Housing: Homeownership rate: 65.3% (2000); Median home value: $56,900 (2000); Median rent: $172 per month (2000); Median age of housing: 16 years (2000).
Transportation: Commute to work: 93.7% car, 1.0% public transportation, 1.7% walk, 0.0% work from home (2000); Travel time to work: 68.1% less than 15 minutes, 17.3% 15 to 30 minutes, 7.3% 30 to 45 minutes, 1.3% 45 to 60 minutes, 6.0% 60 minutes or more (2000)

ROOSEVELT (township). Covers a land area of 34.058 square miles and a water area of 1.876 square miles. Located at 47.73° N. Lat.; 95.13° W. Long.
Population: 219 (2000); Race: 94.3% White, 0.0% Black, 0.0% Asian, 0.0% American Indian and Alaska Native, 0.0% Hispanic of any race, 4.8% two or more races (2000); Density: 6.4 persons per square mile (2000); Age: 16.5% under 18, 19.1% over 64 (2000); Marriage status: 19.2% never married, 52.5% now married, 10.6% widowed, 17.7% divorced (2000); Foreign born: 0.9% (2000); Ancestry (includes multiple ancestries): 46.1% Norwegian, 19.6% German, 11.7% Swedish, 7.8% French Canadian, 7.4% Dutch (2000).
Economy: Employment by occupation: 18.9% management, 21.7% professional, 17.9% services, 7.5% sales, 8.5% farming, 12.3% construction, 13.2% production (2000).
Income: Per capita income: $14,057 (2000); Median household income: $25,893 (2000); Poverty rate: 19.5% (2000).
Taxes: Total city taxes per capita: $367 (1997); City property taxes per capita: $367 (1997).
Education: High school graduation rate: 81.7% (2000); College graduation rate: 16.0% (2000).
Housing: Homeownership rate: 87.9% (2000); Median home value: $45,000 (2000); Median rent: $317 per month (2000); Median age of housing: 33 years (2000).
Transportation: Commute to work: 89.3% car, 0.0% public transportation, 0.0% walk, 10.7% work from home (2000); Travel time to work: 9.8% less than 15 minutes, 31.5% 15 to 30 minutes, 50.0% 30 to 45 minutes, 4.3% 45 to 60 minutes, 4.3% 60 minutes or more (2000)

SHOOKS (township). Covers a land area of 36.481 square miles and a water area of 0.013 square miles. Located at 47.88° N. Lat.; 94.47° W. Long. Elevation is 1,358 feet.
Population: 190 (2000); Race: 91.0% White, 0.0% Black, 0.0% Asian, 1.6% American Indian and Alaska Native, 0.0% Hispanic of any race, 7.4% two or more races (2000); Density: 5.2 persons per square mile (2000); Age: 33.0% under 18, 11.2% over 64 (2000); Marriage status: 23.5% never married, 68.2% now married, 6.8% widowed, 1.5% divorced (2000); Foreign born: 0.0% (2000); Ancestry (includes multiple ancestries): 36.7% German, 10.6% Norwegian, 8.0% Other groups, 7.4% Polish, 6.4% Croatian (2000).
Economy: Employment by occupation: 21.1% management, 18.4% professional, 11.8% services, 25.0% sales, 6.6% farming, 7.9% construction, 9.2% production (2000).
Income: Per capita income: $10,554 (2000); Median household income: $21,500 (2000); Poverty rate: 28.6% (2000).
Taxes: Total city taxes per capita: $29 (1997); City property taxes per capita: $29 (1997).
Education: High school graduation rate: 76.5% (2000); College graduation rate: 9.2% (2000).
Housing: Homeownership rate: 82.0% (2000); Median home value: $14,200 (2000); Median rent: $306 per month (2000); Median age of housing: 25 years (2000).
Transportation: Commute to work: 71.1% car, 0.0% public transportation, 14.5% walk, 14.5% work from home (2000); Travel time to work: 56.9% less than 15 minutes, 23.1% 15 to 30 minutes, 15.4% 30 to 45 minutes, 0.0% 45 to 60 minutes, 4.6% 60 minutes or more (2000)

SHOTLEY (township). Covers a land area of 32.787 square miles and a water area of 14.015 square miles. Located at 48.07° N. Lat.; 94.63° W. Long. Elevation is 1,210 feet.
Population: 54 (2000); Race: 100.0% White, 0.0% Black, 0.0% Asian, 0.0% American Indian and Alaska Native, 0.0% Hispanic of any race, 0.0% two or more races (2000); Density: 1.6 persons per square mile (2000); Age: 0.0% under 18, 38.1% over 64 (2000); Marriage status: 7.1% never married, 78.6% now married, 9.5% widowed, 4.8% divorced (2000); Foreign born: 0.0% (2000); Ancestry (includes multiple ancestries): 23.8% English, 21.4% United States or American, 19.0% German, 14.3% Norwegian, 11.9% Danish (2000).
Economy: Employment by occupation: 30.0% management, 20.0% professional, 0.0% services, 20.0% sales, 10.0% farming, 20.0% construction, 0.0% production (2000).
Income: Per capita income: $17,802 (2000); Median household income: $21,458 (2000); Poverty rate: 9.5% (2000).
Taxes: Total city taxes per capita: $95 (1997); City property taxes per capita: $95 (1997).
Education: High school graduation rate: 81.0% (2000); College graduation rate: 21.4% (2000).
Housing: Homeownership rate: 100.0% (2000); Median home value: $80,000 (2000); Median age of housing: 32 years (2000).
Transportation: Commute to work: 100.0% car, 0.0% public transportation, 0.0% walk, 0.0% work from home (2000); Travel time to work: 20.0% less than 15 minutes, 40.0% 15 to 30 minutes, 0.0% 30 to 45 minutes, 0.0% 45 to 60 minutes, 40.0% 60 minutes or more (2000)

SOLWAY (city). Covers a land area of 1.028 square miles and a water area of 0 square miles. Located at 47.52° N. Lat.; 95.13° W. Long.
Population: 69 (2000); Race: 92.6% White, 0.0% Black, 0.0% Asian, 2.9% American Indian and Alaska Native, 0.0% Hispanic of any race, 4.4% two or more races (2000); Density: 67.1 persons per square mile (2000); Age: 29.4% under 18, 7.4% over 64 (2000); Marriage status: 11.5% never married, 63.5% now married, 7.7% widowed, 17.3% divorced (2000); Foreign born: 0.0% (2000); Ancestry (includes multiple ancestries): 30.9% Norwegian, 27.9% German, 8.8% English, 8.8% Swedish, 7.4% European (2000).
Economy: Grain; dairying; timber. Manufacturing: wood products and pulpwood. Employment by occupation: 23.1% management, 12.8% professional, 5.1% services, 25.6% sales, 0.0% farming, 10.3% construction, 23.1% production (2000).
Income: Per capita income: $19,912 (2000); Median household income: $25,625 (2000); Poverty rate: 29.4% (2000).
Taxes: Total city taxes per capita: $86 (1997); City property taxes per capita: $62 (1997).
Education: High school graduation rate: 68.2% (2000); College graduation rate: 22.7% (2000).
Housing: Homeownership rate: 84.8% (2000); Median home value: $53,100 (2000); Median rent: $375 per month (2000); Median age of housing: 40 years (2000).
Transportation: Commute to work: 80.0% car, 0.0% public transportation, 14.3% walk, 5.7% work from home (2000); Travel time to work: 51.5% less than 15 minutes, 48.5% 15 to 30 minutes, 0.0% 30 to 45 minutes, 0.0% 45 to 60 minutes, 0.0% 60 minutes or more (2000)

SPRUCE GROVE (township). Covers a land area of 34.596 square miles and a water area of 0 square miles. Located at 48.31° N. Lat.; 95.41° W. Long.
Population: 63 (2000); Race: 100.0% White, 0.0% Black, 0.0% Asian, 0.0% American Indian and Alaska Native, 0.0% Hispanic of any race, 0.0% two or more races (2000); Density: 1.8 persons per square mile (2000); Age: 19.6% under 18, 21.7% over 64 (2000); Marriage status: 27.0% never married, 64.9% now married, 5.4% widowed, 2.7% divorced (2000); Foreign born: 0.0% (2000); Ancestry (includes multiple ancestries): 54.3% Norwegian, 39.1% Swedish, 28.3% German, 10.9% United States or American, 4.3% Other groups (2000).
Economy: Employment by occupation: 10.0% management, 10.0% professional, 10.0% services, 30.0% sales, 0.0% farming, 10.0% construction, 30.0% production (2000).
Income: Per capita income: $10,498 (2000); Median household income: $28,333 (2000); Poverty rate: 8.7% (2000).
Taxes: Total city taxes per capita: $22 (1997); City property taxes per capita: $22 (1997).
Education: High school graduation rate: 81.3% (2000); College graduation rate: 3.1% (2000).

Housing: Homeownership rate: 100.0% (2000); Median home value: $34,200 (2000); Median age of housing: 24 years (2000).
Transportation: Commute to work: 100.0% car, 0.0% public transportation, 0.0% walk, 0.0% work from home (2000); Travel time to work: 0.0% less than 15 minutes, 44.4% 15 to 30 minutes, 0.0% 30 to 45 minutes, 22.2% 45 to 60 minutes, 33.3% 60 minutes or more (2000)

STEENERSON (township). Covers a land area of 36.291 square miles and a water area of 0.004 square miles. Located at 48.24° N. Lat.; 95.28° W. Long.
Population: 28 (2000); Race: 100.0% White, 0.0% Black, 0.0% Asian, 0.0% American Indian and Alaska Native, 0.0% Hispanic of any race, 0.0% two or more races (2000); Density: 0.8 persons per square mile (2000); Age: 28.6% under 18, 32.1% over 64 (2000); Marriage status: 26.1% never married, 56.5% now married, 17.4% widowed, 0.0% divorced (2000); Foreign born: 0.0% (2000); Ancestry (includes multiple ancestries): 53.6% Norwegian, 46.4% German, 14.3% Swedish (2000).
Economy: Employment by occupation: 22.2% management, 0.0% professional, 0.0% services, 55.6% sales, 0.0% farming, 0.0% construction, 22.2% production (2000).
Income: Per capita income: $10,075 (2000); Median household income: $13,750 (2000); Poverty rate: 0.0% (2000).
Taxes: Total city taxes per capita: $63 (1997); City property taxes per capita: $63 (1997).
Education: High school graduation rate: 30.0% (2000); College graduation rate: 0.0% (2000).
Housing: Homeownership rate: 100.0% (2000); Median age of housing: 27 years (2000).
Transportation: Commute to work: 71.4% car, 0.0% public transportation, 0.0% walk, 28.6% work from home (2000); Travel time to work: 0.0% less than 15 minutes, 100.0% 15 to 30 minutes, 0.0% 30 to 45 minutes, 0.0% 45 to 60 minutes, 0.0% 60 minutes or more (2000)

SUGAR BUSH (township). Covers a land area of 29.562 square miles and a water area of 5.523 square miles. Located at 47.54° N. Lat.; 94.60° W. Long.
Population: 193 (2000); Race: 63.3% White, 0.0% Black, 0.0% Asian, 36.7% American Indian and Alaska Native, 0.0% Hispanic of any race, 0.0% two or more races (2000); Density: 6.5 persons per square mile (2000); Age: 35.8% under 18, 3.1% over 64 (2000); Marriage status: 30.0% never married, 56.3% now married, 0.0% widowed, 13.8% divorced (2000); Foreign born: 0.9% (2000); Ancestry (includes multiple ancestries): 36.7% Other groups, 19.0% German, 16.8% Norwegian, 10.2% English, 9.3% Irish (2000).
Economy: Employment by occupation: 12.0% management, 28.3% professional, 17.4% services, 17.4% sales, 0.0% farming, 13.0% construction, 12.0% production (2000).
Income: Per capita income: $10,082 (2000); Median household income: $28,542 (2000); Poverty rate: 29.1% (2000).
Taxes: Total city taxes per capita: $104 (1997); City property taxes per capita: $104 (1997).
Education: High school graduation rate: 79.8% (2000); College graduation rate: 21.8% (2000).
Housing: Homeownership rate: 91.8% (2000); Median home value: $84,000 (2000); Median age of housing: 24 years (2000).
Transportation: Commute to work: 87.5% car, 0.0% public transportation, 3.4% walk, 9.1% work from home (2000); Travel time to work: 5.0% less than 15 minutes, 57.5% 15 to 30 minutes, 21.3% 30 to 45 minutes, 12.5% 45 to 60 minutes, 3.8% 60 minutes or more (2000)

SUMMIT (township). Covers a land area of 34.999 square miles and a water area of 0.190 square miles. Located at 47.71° N. Lat.; 94.48° W. Long.
Population: 259 (2000); Race: 100.0% White, 0.0% Black, 0.0% Asian, 0.0% American Indian and Alaska Native, 0.0% Hispanic of any race, 0.0% two or more races (2000); Density: 7.4 persons per square mile (2000); Age: 22.1% under 18, 14.6% over 64 (2000); Marriage status: 14.7% never married, 67.9% now married, 9.2% widowed, 8.2% divorced (2000); Foreign born: 0.4% (2000); Ancestry (includes multiple ancestries): 45.1% German, 25.7% Norwegian, 16.4% Swedish, 8.4% English, 6.2% Polish (2000).
Economy: Employment by occupation: 8.9% management, 18.7% professional, 13.8% services, 22.0% sales, 9.8% farming, 9.8% construction, 17.1% production (2000).
Income: Per capita income: $18,208 (2000); Median household income: $36,250 (2000); Poverty rate: 5.3% (2000).
Taxes: Total city taxes per capita: $15 (1997); City property taxes per capita: $15 (1997).
Education: High school graduation rate: 88.1% (2000); College graduation rate: 20.8% (2000).
Housing: Homeownership rate: 91.8% (2000); Median home value: $46,700 (2000); Median rent: $125 per month (2000); Median age of housing: 24 years (2000).
Transportation: Commute to work: 96.7% car, 0.0% public transportation, 1.7% walk, 1.7% work from home (2000); Travel time to work: 58.5% less than 15 minutes, 12.7% 15 to 30 minutes, 15.3% 30 to 45 minutes, 6.8% 45 to 60 minutes, 6.8% 60 minutes or more (2000)

TAYLOR (township). Covers a land area of 32.163 square miles and a water area of 2.064 square miles. Located at 47.61° N. Lat.; 94.61° W. Long.
Population: 108 (2000); Race: 95.2% White, 0.0% Black, 0.0% Asian, 0.0% American Indian and Alaska Native, 0.0% Hispanic of any race, 4.8% two or more races (2000); Density: 3.4 persons per square mile (2000); Age: 16.2% under 18, 4.8% over 64 (2000); Marriage status: 29.3% never married, 60.6% now married, 0.0% widowed, 10.1% divorced (2000); Foreign born: 0.0% (2000); Ancestry (includes multiple ancestries): 21.9% Norwegian, 21.0% German, 15.2% Swedish, 11.4% Irish, 11.4% United States or American (2000).
Economy: Single-family building permits issued: 2 (2001) / 2 (2000); Multi-family building permits issued: 0 (2001) / 0 (2000); Employment by occupation: 14.8% management, 29.5% professional, 11.5% services, 8.2% sales, 3.3% farming, 23.0% construction, 9.8% production (2000).
Income: Per capita income: $18,946 (2000); Median household income: $39,722 (2000); Poverty rate: 15.2% (2000).
Taxes: Total city taxes per capita: $50 (1997); City property taxes per capita: $50 (1997).
Education: High school graduation rate: 91.9% (2000); College graduation rate: 25.7% (2000).
Housing: Homeownership rate: 92.2% (2000); Median home value: $112,500 (2000); Median age of housing: 22 years (2000).
Transportation: Commute to work: 90.2% car, 0.0% public transportation, 0.0% walk, 9.8% work from home (2000); Travel time to work: 16.4% less than 15 minutes, 34.5% 15 to 30 minutes, 29.1% 30 to 45 minutes, 14.5% 45 to 60 minutes, 5.5% 60 minutes or more (2000)

TEN LAKE (township). Covers a land area of 22.715 square miles and a water area of 13.254 square miles. Located at 47.45° N. Lat.; 94.61° W. Long.
Population: 1,005 (2000); Race: 32.2% White, 0.0% Black, 0.0% Asian, 66.3% American Indian and Alaska Native, 0.2% Hispanic of any race, 1.5% two or more races (2000); Density: 44.2 persons per square mile (2000); Age: 37.8% under 18, 6.3% over 64 (2000); Marriage status: 41.3% never married, 45.3% now married, 4.1% widowed, 9.3% divorced (2000); Foreign born: 1.7% (2000); Ancestry (includes multiple ancestries): 61.0% Other groups, 10.1% German, 8.7% Norwegian, 3.3% Irish, 2.4% Swedish (2000).
Economy: Single-family building permits issued: 2 (2001) / 2 (2000); Multi-family building permits issued: 0 (2001) / 0 (2000); Employment by occupation: 12.6% management, 17.9% professional, 21.6% services, 23.5% sales, 0.0% farming, 12.9% construction, 11.5% production (2000).
Income: Per capita income: $11,853 (2000); Median household income: $33,906 (2000); Poverty rate: 21.6% (2000).
Taxes: Total city taxes per capita: $80 (1997); City property taxes per capita: $79 (1997).
Education: High school graduation rate: 86.5% (2000); College graduation rate: 13.3% (2000).
Housing: Homeownership rate: 82.3% (2000); Median home value: $83,300 (2000); Median rent: $189 per month (2000); Median age of housing: 22 years (2000).
Transportation: Commute to work: 89.2% car, 2.8% public transportation, 3.4% walk, 2.8% work from home (2000); Travel time to work: 38.1% less than 15 minutes, 35.5% 15 to 30 minutes, 19.6% 30 to 45 minutes, 1.8% 45 to 60 minutes, 5.0% 60 minutes or more (2000)

TENSTRIKE (city). Covers a land area of 3.278 square miles and a water area of 1.177 square miles. Located at 47.66° N. Lat.; 94.68° W. Long. Elevation is 1,403 feet.
Population: 195 (2000); Race: 93.9% White, 0.0% Black, 0.0% Asian, 3.7% American Indian and Alaska Native, 0.9% Hispanic of any race, 2.3% two or more races (2000); Density: 59.5 persons per square mile (2000); Age: 27.6% under 18, 13.6% over 64 (2000); Marriage status: 19.9% never married, 63.9% now married, 6.6% widowed, 9.6% divorced (2000); Foreign born: 2.8% (2000); Ancestry (includes multiple ancestries): 19.6% United States or American, 19.2% Norwegian, 19.2% German, 12.1% Irish, 8.9% French (except Basque) (2000).

Economy: Resort village. Grain; timber. Manufacturing of treated lumber. Chippewa National Forest to East. Employment by occupation: 9.3% management, 11.6% professional, 22.1% services, 15.1% sales, 8.1% farming, 10.5% construction, 23.3% production (2000).
Income: Per capita income: $18,415 (2000); Median household income: $35,000 (2000); Poverty rate: 8.9% (2000).
Taxes: Total city taxes per capita: $78 (1997); City property taxes per capita: $63 (1997).
Education: High school graduation rate: 74.3% (2000); College graduation rate: 12.8% (2000).
Housing: Homeownership rate: 92.1% (2000); Median home value: $62,500 (2000); Median rent: $575 per month (2000); Median age of housing: 27 years (2000).
Transportation: Commute to work: 95.3% car, 0.0% public transportation, 3.5% walk, 0.0% work from home (2000); Travel time to work: 27.9% less than 15 minutes, 32.6% 15 to 30 minutes, 24.4% 30 to 45 minutes, 4.7% 45 to 60 minutes, 10.5% 60 minutes or more (2000)

TURTLE LAKE (township). Covers a land area of 28.683 square miles and a water area of 7.530 square miles. Located at 47.61° N. Lat.; 94.85° W. Long.
Population: 1,122 (2000); Race: 94.0% White, 0.2% Black, 1.0% Asian, 3.7% American Indian and Alaska Native, 0.0% Hispanic of any race, 1.2% two or more races (2000); Density: 39.1 persons per square mile (2000); Age: 25.4% under 18, 12.4% over 64 (2000); Marriage status: 20.3% never married, 70.9% now married, 3.8% widowed, 4.9% divorced (2000); Foreign born: 1.9% (2000); Ancestry (includes multiple ancestries): 33.0% German, 22.3% Norwegian, 10.7% Swedish, 9.8% Irish, 7.6% English (2000).
Economy: Employment by occupation: 13.5% management, 27.9% professional, 14.8% services, 22.1% sales, 0.9% farming, 9.0% construction, 11.8% production (2000).
Income: Per capita income: $23,770 (2000); Median household income: $52,857 (2000); Poverty rate: 6.6% (2000).
Taxes: Total city taxes per capita: $77 (1997); City property taxes per capita: $77 (1997).
Education: High school graduation rate: 92.0% (2000); College graduation rate: 43.0% (2000).
Housing: Homeownership rate: 91.7% (2000); Median home value: $152,900 (2000); Median rent: $431 per month (2000); Median age of housing: 23 years (2000).
Transportation: Commute to work: 93.6% car, 0.0% public transportation, 0.9% walk, 4.7% work from home (2000); Travel time to work: 22.1% less than 15 minutes, 59.2% 15 to 30 minutes, 11.3% 30 to 45 minutes, 2.3% 45 to 60 minutes, 5.2% 60 minutes or more (2000)

TURTLE RIVER (city). Covers a land area of 1.117 square miles and a water area of 0 square miles. Located at 47.59° N. Lat.; 94.76° W. Long. Elevation is 1,367 feet.
Population: 75 (2000); Race: 100.0% White, 0.0% Black, 0.0% Asian, 0.0% American Indian and Alaska Native, 0.0% Hispanic of any race, 0.0% two or more races (2000); Density: 67.2 persons per square mile (2000); Age: 18.5% under 18, 9.2% over 64 (2000); Marriage status: 21.8% never married, 49.1% now married, 7.3% widowed, 21.8% divorced (2000); Foreign born: 0.0% (2000); Ancestry (includes multiple ancestries): 30.8% Norwegian, 26.2% German, 21.5% United States or American, 12.3% Swedish, 12.3% English (2000).
Economy: Employment by occupation: 0.0% management, 5.8% professional, 36.5% services, 7.7% sales, 0.0% farming, 21.2% construction, 28.8% production (2000).
Income: Per capita income: $22,102 (2000); Median household income: $38,333 (2000); Poverty rate: 3.3% (2000).
Taxes: Total city taxes per capita: $103 (1997); City property taxes per capita: $29 (1997).
Education: High school graduation rate: 91.8% (2000); College graduation rate: 6.1% (2000).
Housing: Homeownership rate: 80.6% (2000); Median home value: $90,000 (2000); Median rent: $238 per month (2000); Median age of housing: 28 years (2000).
Transportation: Commute to work: 78.8% car, 0.0% public transportation, 15.4% walk, 5.8% work from home (2000); Travel time to work: 34.7% less than 15 minutes, 49.0% 15 to 30 minutes, 12.2% 30 to 45 minutes, 0.0% 45 to 60 minutes, 4.1% 60 minutes or more (2000)

TURTLE RIVER (township). Covers a land area of 31.476 square miles and a water area of 4.369 square miles. Located at 47.53° N. Lat.; 94.73° W. Long. Elevation is 1,367 feet.
Population: 1,098 (2000); Race: 93.7% White, 0.0% Black, 1.7% Asian, 3.4% American Indian and Alaska Native, 0.0% Hispanic of any race, 1.2% two or more races (2000); Density: 34.9 persons per square mile (2000); Age: 27.9% under 18, 10.2% over 64 (2000); Marriage status: 23.2% never married, 65.7% now married, 3.7% widowed, 7.5% divorced (2000); Foreign born: 2.5% (2000); Ancestry (includes multiple ancestries): 32.9% German, 25.4% Norwegian, 12.9% Irish, 9.5% Swedish, 7.8% English (2000).
Economy: Single-family building permits issued: 5 (2001) / 4 (2000); Multi-family building permits issued: 0 (2001) / 0 (2000); Employment by occupation: 12.7% management, 26.5% professional, 11.3% services, 26.0% sales, 1.7% farming, 8.8% construction, 13.0% production (2000).
Income: Per capita income: $23,704 (2000); Median household income: $53,571 (2000); Poverty rate: 8.2% (2000).
Taxes: Total city taxes per capita: $58 (2000); City property taxes per capita: $57 (2000).
Education: High school graduation rate: 87.3% (2000); College graduation rate: 41.8% (2000).
Housing: Homeownership rate: 90.3% (2000); Median home value: $119,300 (2000); Median rent: $363 per month (2000); Median age of housing: 22 years (2000).
Transportation: Commute to work: 92.2% car, 1.6% public transportation, 2.0% walk, 4.3% work from home (2000); Travel time to work: 15.6% less than 15 minutes, 62.8% 15 to 30 minutes, 13.3% 30 to 45 minutes, 5.2% 45 to 60 minutes, 3.1% 60 minutes or more (2000)

WASKISH (township). Covers a land area of 65.031 square miles and a water area of 6.976 square miles. Located at 48.16° N. Lat.; 94.51° W. Long.
Population: 116 (2000); Race: 100.0% White, 0.0% Black, 0.0% Asian, 0.0% American Indian and Alaska Native, 0.0% Hispanic of any race, 0.0% two or more races (2000); Density: 1.8 persons per square mile (2000); Age: 14.6% under 18, 28.5% over 64 (2000); Marriage status: 12.8% never married, 66.1% now married, 15.6% widowed, 5.5% divorced (2000); Foreign born: 0.0% (2000); Ancestry (includes multiple ancestries): 28.5% German, 26.8% Swedish, 18.7% Norwegian, 8.9% Irish, 8.1% Czech (2000).
Economy: Employment by occupation: 22.6% management, 29.0% professional, 6.5% services, 19.4% sales, 6.5% farming, 6.5% construction, 9.7% production (2000).
Income: Per capita income: $19,489 (2000); Median household income: $25,000 (2000); Poverty rate: 26.8% (2000).
Taxes: Total city taxes per capita: $57 (1997); City property taxes per capita: $57 (1997).
Education: High school graduation rate: 73.3% (2000); College graduation rate: 7.9% (2000).
Housing: Homeownership rate: 95.1% (2000); Median home value: $78,800 (2000); Median rent: $263 per month (2000); Median age of housing: 27 years (2000).
Transportation: Commute to work: 72.4% car, 0.0% public transportation, 0.0% walk, 27.6% work from home (2000); Travel time to work: 0.0% less than 15 minutes, 57.1% 15 to 30 minutes, 19.0% 30 to 45 minutes, 9.5% 45 to 60 minutes, 14.3% 60 minutes or more (2000)

WILTON (city). Covers a land area of 2.322 square miles and a water area of 0.043 square miles. Located at 47.50° N. Lat.; 94.99° W. Long. Elevation is 1,383 feet.
Population: 186 (2000); Race: 93.7% White, 0.0% Black, 0.0% Asian, 1.1% American Indian and Alaska Native, 3.2% Hispanic of any race, 5.3% two or more races (2000); Density: 80.1 persons per square mile (2000); Age: 27.4% under 18, 10.5% over 64 (2000); Marriage status: 40.5% never married, 43.7% now married, 4.4% widowed, 11.4% divorced (2000); Foreign born: 0.0% (2000); Ancestry (includes multiple ancestries): 44.2% German, 30.5% Norwegian, 9.5% Irish, 7.4% English, 5.8% Swedish (2000).
Economy: Railroad junction. Livestock; dairying; timber. Employment by occupation: 14.6% management, 8.7% professional, 13.6% services, 27.2% sales, 1.9% farming, 8.7% construction, 25.2% production (2000).
Income: Per capita income: $13,432 (2000); Median household income: $33,750 (2000); Poverty rate: 14.7% (2000).
Taxes: Total city taxes per capita: $57 (1997); City property taxes per capita: $21 (1997).
Education: High school graduation rate: 81.4% (2000); College graduation rate: 21.2% (2000).
Housing: Homeownership rate: 84.9% (2000); Median home value: $78,600 (2000); Median rent: $213 per month (2000); Median age of housing: 27 years (2000).
Transportation: Commute to work: 94.2% car, 0.0% public transportation, 3.9% walk, 1.9% work from home (2000); Travel time to work: 57.4% less

than 15 minutes, 23.8% 15 to 30 minutes, 3.0% 30 to 45 minutes, 4.0% 45 to 60 minutes, 11.9% 60 minutes or more (2000)

WOODROW (township). Covers a land area of 35.929 square miles and a water area of 0 square miles. Located at 47.97° N. Lat.; 94.61° W. Long.
Population: 74 (2000); Race: 100.0% White, 0.0% Black, 0.0% Asian, 0.0% American Indian and Alaska Native, 0.0% Hispanic of any race, 0.0% two or more races (2000); Density: 2.1 persons per square mile (2000); Age: 32.1% under 18, 15.5% over 64 (2000); Marriage status: 22.6% never married, 61.3% now married, 6.5% widowed, 9.7% divorced (2000); Foreign born: 0.0% (2000); Ancestry (includes multiple ancestries): 45.2% German, 21.4% United States or American, 20.2% Norwegian, 13.1% Irish, 6.0% English (2000).
Economy: Employment by occupation: 22.2% management, 5.6% professional, 5.6% services, 8.3% sales, 16.7% farming, 11.1% construction, 30.6% production (2000).
Income: Per capita income: $8,540 (2000); Median household income: $15,250 (2000); Poverty rate: 59.5% (2000).
Taxes: Total city taxes per capita: $37 (1997); City property taxes per capita: $37 (1997).
Education: High school graduation rate: 75.9% (2000); College graduation rate: 7.4% (2000).
Housing: Homeownership rate: 93.8% (2000); Median home value: $22,500 (2000); Median age of housing: 35 years (2000).
Transportation: Commute to work: 50.0% car, 0.0% public transportation, 11.1% walk, 38.9% work from home (2000); Travel time to work: 31.8% less than 15 minutes, 40.9% 15 to 30 minutes, 18.2% 30 to 45 minutes, 9.1% 45 to 60 minutes, 0.0% 60 minutes or more (2000)

Benton County

Located in central Minnesota; bounded on the west by the Mississippi River. Covers a land area of 408.30 square miles, a water area of 4.70 square miles, and is located in the Central Time Zone. The county government was organized in 1849. County seat is Foley.

Benton County is part of the St. Cloud, MN MSA. The entire metro area includes: Benton County; Stearns County

Population: 34,226 (2000); Race: 95.7% White, 0.6% Black, 1.4% Asian, 0.4% American Indian and Alaska Native, 1.0% Hispanic of any race, 1.4% two or more races (2000); Density: 83.8 persons per square mile (2000); Age: 27.0% under 18, 11.1% over 64 (2000).
Religion: Five largest groups: 38.2% Catholic Church, 7.0% Lutheran Church—Missouri Synod, 3.5% Evangelical Lutheran Church in America, 1.8% Presbyterian Church (U.S.A.), 1.4% The Church of Jesus Christ of Latter-day Saints (2000).
Economy: Unemployment rate: 3.9% (11/2002); Total civilian labor force: 21,875 (11/2002); Leading industries: 25.9% manufacturing; 16.0% retail trade; 11.4% construction (2000); Companies that employ more than 1,000 persons: 0 (2000); Companies that employ more than 100 persons: 19 (2000); Farms: 834 totaling 176,330 acres (1997); Minority business ownership rate: 0.0% (1997); Women business ownership rate: 23.1% (1997); Retail sales per capita: $5,543 (1997). Single-family building permits issued: 344 (2001) / 276 (2000); Multi-family building permits issued: 76 (2001) / 120 (2000).
Income: Per capita income: $19,008 (2000); Median household income: $41,968 (2000); Poverty rate: 7.1% (2000); Bankruptcy rate: 2.59% (2001).
Taxes: Total county taxes per capita: $281 (2000); County property taxes per capita: $278 (2000).
Education: High school graduation rate: 84.9% (2000); College graduation rate: 17.2% (2000).
Housing: Homeownership rate: 67.1% (2000); Median home value: $99,100 (2000); Median rent: $450 per month (2000); Median age of housing: 24 years (2000).
Health: Birth rate: 150.2 per 10,000 population (1998); Age adjusted death rate: 93.0 per 10,000 population (1999); Age adjusted cancer mortality rate: 195.2 deaths per 100,000 population (1999). Number of physicians: 3.8 per 10,000 population (1999); Number of hospital beds: n/a (1999).
Elections: 2000 Presidential election results: 40.3% Gore, 51.4% Bush, 5.8% Nader, 1.9% Buchanan
National and State Parks: Benlacs State Wildlife Management Area; Bibles State Wildlife Management Area; Sartell State Wildlife Management Area; Wisneski State Wildlife Management Area
Additional Information Contacts
Benton County Government Offices 320-968-5000

Benton County Communities

ALBERTA (township). Covers a land area of 36.288 square miles and a water area of 0 square miles. Located at 45.77° N. Lat.; 93.94° W. Long.
Population: 772 (2000); Race: 99.4% White, 0.0% Black, 0.0% Asian, 0.2% American Indian and Alaska Native, 0.0% Hispanic of any race, 0.4% two or more races (2000); Density: 21.3 persons per square mile (2000); Age: 32.2% under 18, 11.2% over 64 (2000); Marriage status: 31.4% never married, 61.2% now married, 4.0% widowed, 3.5% divorced (2000); Foreign born: 0.0% (2000); Ancestry (includes multiple ancestries): 48.8% Polish, 45.4% German, 5.2% Norwegian, 4.4% United States or American, 3.5% Irish (2000).
Economy: Employment by occupation: 15.9% management, 6.3% professional, 15.6% services, 18.5% sales, 3.2% farming, 12.7% construction, 27.8% production (2000).
Income: Per capita income: $17,027 (2000); Median household income: $48,958 (2000); Poverty rate: 7.8% (2000).
Taxes: Total city taxes per capita: $30 (1997); City property taxes per capita: $30 (1997).
Education: High school graduation rate: 70.5% (2000); College graduation rate: 5.6% (2000).
Housing: Homeownership rate: 93.4% (2000); Median home value: $97,900 (2000); Median rent: $100 per month (2000); Median age of housing: 29 years (2000).
Transportation: Commute to work: 83.7% car, 0.0% public transportation, 1.5% walk, 12.8% work from home (2000); Travel time to work: 15.3% less than 15 minutes, 20.9% 15 to 30 minutes, 37.6% 30 to 45 minutes, 15.5% 45 to 60 minutes, 10.7% 60 minutes or more (2000)

FOLEY (city). Covers a land area of 1.875 square miles and a water area of 0 square miles. Located at 45.66° N. Lat.; 93.91° W. Long. Elevation is 1,132 feet.
Population: 2,154 (2000); Race: 96.1% White, 1.2% Black, 0.8% Asian, 0.7% American Indian and Alaska Native, 1.6% Hispanic of any race, 0.6% two or more races (2000); Density: 1,148.6 persons per square mile (2000); Age: 28.4% under 18, 17.5% over 64 (2000); Marriage status: 24.0% never married, 56.7% now married, 10.5% widowed, 8.8% divorced (2000); Foreign born: 2.1% (2000); Ancestry (includes multiple ancestries): 45.6% German, 18.7% Polish, 10.0% Norwegian, 8.4% Irish, 7.4% Swedish (2000).
Economy: Grain, soybeans; livestock; dairying. Manufacturing: plastic products, cabinets, other light manufacturing. Single-family building permits issued: 58 (2001) / 20 (2000); Multi-family building permits issued: 0 (2001) / 18 (2000); Employment by occupation: 7.3% management, 16.5% professional, 13.6% services, 24.3% sales, 1.3% farming, 11.3% construction, 25.7% production (2000).
Income: Per capita income: $17,168 (2000); Median household income: $38,393 (2000); Poverty rate: 9.4% (2000).
Taxes: Total city taxes per capita: $195 (1997); City property taxes per capita: $188 (1997).
Education: High school graduation rate: 74.7% (2000); College graduation rate: 16.3% (2000).

School District(s)

Foley (PK-12)
2000 Enrollment: 1,749 320-968-7175
Housing: Homeownership rate: 71.6% (2000); Median home value: $83,600 (2000); Median rent: $322 per month (2000); Median age of housing: 29 years (2000).
Newspapers: Benton County News (1 x week)
Transportation: Commute to work: 90.1% car, 0.0% public transportation, 6.7% walk, 2.4% work from home (2000); Travel time to work: 41.1% less than 15 minutes, 31.8% 15 to 30 minutes, 15.0% 30 to 45 minutes, 4.1% 45 to 60 minutes, 8.0% 60 minutes or more (2000)

GILMAN (city). Covers a land area of 0.519 square miles and a water area of 0 square miles. Located at 45.73° N. Lat.; 93.94° W. Long.
Population: 215 (2000); Race: 99.1% White, 0.0% Black, 0.0% Asian, 0.0% American Indian and Alaska Native, 0.0% Hispanic of any race, 0.9% two or more races (2000); Density: 414.4 persons per square mile (2000); Age: 24.7% under 18, 11.7% over 64 (2000); Marriage status: 22.3% never married, 62.6% now married, 10.1% widowed, 5.0% divorced (2000); Foreign born: 0.0% (2000); Ancestry (includes multiple ancestries): 59.6% German, 51.1% Polish, 7.2% Norwegian, 3.6% Irish, 2.7% Czech (2000).
Economy: Manufacturing of feeds. Agriculture: grains, soybeans, alfalfa, livestock, dairying. Employment by occupation: 14.6% management, 8.1%

professional, 14.6% services, 19.5% sales, 1.6% farming, 9.8% construction, 31.7% production (2000).
Income: Per capita income: $17,641 (2000); Median household income: $49,063 (2000); Poverty rate: 9.9% (2000).
Taxes: Total city taxes per capita: $20 (1997); City property taxes per capita: $20 (1997).
Education: High school graduation rate: 70.8% (2000); College graduation rate: 8.4% (2000).
Housing: Homeownership rate: 74.2% (2000); Median home value: $70,000 (2000); Median rent: $171 per month (2000); Median age of housing: 29 years (2000).
Transportation: Commute to work: 85.1% car, 0.0% public transportation, 1.7% walk, 13.2% work from home (2000); Travel time to work: 25.7% less than 15 minutes, 29.5% 15 to 30 minutes, 22.9% 30 to 45 minutes, 13.3% 45 to 60 minutes, 8.6% 60 minutes or more (2000)

GILMANTON (township). Covers a land area of 34.273 square miles and a water area of 0 square miles. Located at 45.67° N. Lat.; 93.95° W. Long.
Population: 769 (2000); Race: 98.9% White, 0.0% Black, 0.0% Asian, 0.3% American Indian and Alaska Native, 0.0% Hispanic of any race, 0.9% two or more races (2000); Density: 22.4 persons per square mile (2000); Age: 26.8% under 18, 15.8% over 64 (2000); Marriage status: 25.0% never married, 63.3% now married, 5.4% widowed, 6.3% divorced (2000); Foreign born: 0.3% (2000); Ancestry (includes multiple ancestries): 43.5% German, 34.7% Polish, 8.8% Swedish, 7.5% Norwegian, 6.6% Irish (2000).
Economy: Employment by occupation: 19.1% management, 15.1% professional, 8.5% services, 21.7% sales, 2.3% farming, 12.5% construction, 20.8% production (2000).
Income: Per capita income: $20,432 (2000); Median household income: $45,893 (2000); Poverty rate: 7.5% (2000).
Taxes: Total city taxes per capita: $47 (1997); City property taxes per capita: $47 (1997).
Education: High school graduation rate: 82.0% (2000); College graduation rate: 16.9% (2000).
Housing: Homeownership rate: 91.6% (2000); Median home value: $86,800 (2000); Median rent: $325 per month (2000); Median age of housing: 44 years (2000).
Transportation: Commute to work: 82.6% car, 0.0% public transportation, 4.0% walk, 12.8% work from home (2000); Travel time to work: 26.1% less than 15 minutes, 44.8% 15 to 30 minutes, 22.5% 30 to 45 minutes, 0.7% 45 to 60 minutes, 5.9% 60 minutes or more (2000)

GLENDORADO (township). Covers a land area of 36.435 square miles and a water area of 0.054 square miles. Located at 45.59° N. Lat.; 93.81° W. Long.
Population: 785 (2000); Race: 100.0% White, 0.0% Black, 0.0% Asian, 0.0% American Indian and Alaska Native, 0.0% Hispanic of any race, 0.0% two or more races (2000); Density: 21.5 persons per square mile (2000); Age: 32.3% under 18, 8.5% over 64 (2000); Marriage status: 28.5% never married, 64.4% now married, 3.6% widowed, 3.5% divorced (2000); Foreign born: 0.0% (2000); Ancestry (includes multiple ancestries): 53.5% German, 20.3% Polish, 15.2% Norwegian, 13.9% Swedish, 11.8% Irish (2000).
Economy: Employment by occupation: 16.5% management, 12.2% professional, 13.8% services, 21.4% sales, 3.7% farming, 11.3% construction, 21.0% production (2000).
Income: Per capita income: $16,494 (2000); Median household income: $49,643 (2000); Poverty rate: 4.2% (2000).
Taxes: Total city taxes per capita: $46 (1997); City property taxes per capita: $46 (1997).
Education: High school graduation rate: 87.9% (2000); College graduation rate: 12.7% (2000).
Housing: Homeownership rate: 94.9% (2000); Median home value: $98,000 (2000); Median rent: $325 per month (2000); Median age of housing: 29 years (2000).
Transportation: Commute to work: 89.0% car, 0.0% public transportation, 4.1% walk, 6.4% work from home (2000); Travel time to work: 27.2% less than 15 minutes, 30.7% 15 to 30 minutes, 24.5% 30 to 45 minutes, 4.9% 45 to 60 minutes, 12.8% 60 minutes or more (2000)

GRAHAM (township). Covers a land area of 36.662 square miles and a water area of 0.012 square miles. Located at 45.78° N. Lat.; 94.06° W. Long.
Population: 567 (2000); Race: 98.8% White, 0.0% Black, 0.4% Asian, 0.0% American Indian and Alaska Native, 0.7% Hispanic of any race, 0.9% two or more races (2000); Density: 15.5 persons per square mile (2000); Age: 37.0% under 18, 7.9% over 64 (2000); Marriage status: 24.6% never married, 67.1% now married, 2.5% widowed, 5.9% divorced (2000); Foreign born: 0.4% (2000); Ancestry (includes multiple ancestries): 62.5% German, 27.7% Polish, 5.4% Swedish, 4.6% French (except Basque), 3.0% Other groups (2000).
Economy: Employment by occupation: 20.6% management, 10.1% professional, 11.2% services, 17.1% sales, 5.2% farming, 7.7% construction, 28.0% production (2000).
Income: Per capita income: $14,709 (2000); Median household income: $41,389 (2000); Poverty rate: 9.8% (2000).
Taxes: Total city taxes per capita: $53 (1997); City property taxes per capita: $53 (1997).
Education: High school graduation rate: 87.7% (2000); College graduation rate: 8.2% (2000).
Housing: Homeownership rate: 91.7% (2000); Median home value: $107,500 (2000); Median rent: $325 per month (2000); Median age of housing: 26 years (2000).
Transportation: Commute to work: 78.0% car, 0.0% public transportation, 2.4% walk, 19.6% work from home (2000); Travel time to work: 15.2% less than 15 minutes, 37.0% 15 to 30 minutes, 28.3% 30 to 45 minutes, 10.0% 45 to 60 minutes, 9.6% 60 minutes or more (2000)

GRANITE LEDGE (township). Covers a land area of 35.240 square miles and a water area of 0.008 square miles. Located at 45.78° N. Lat.; 93.82° W. Long.
Population: 685 (2000); Race: 98.3% White, 0.3% Black, 0.5% Asian, 0.3% American Indian and Alaska Native, 0.0% Hispanic of any race, 0.5% two or more races (2000); Density: 19.4 persons per square mile (2000); Age: 29.3% under 18, 10.6% over 64 (2000); Marriage status: 23.9% never married, 65.1% now married, 4.4% widowed, 6.6% divorced (2000); Foreign born: 1.2% (2000); Ancestry (includes multiple ancestries): 42.2% German, 33.9% Polish, 8.3% Norwegian, 7.1% Swedish, 4.9% English (2000).
Economy: Employment by occupation: 10.2% management, 12.6% professional, 13.8% services, 20.7% sales, 0.6% farming, 16.8% construction, 25.2% production (2000).
Income: Per capita income: $17,188 (2000); Median household income: $44,063 (2000); Poverty rate: 9.0% (2000).
Taxes: Total city taxes per capita: $22 (1997); City property taxes per capita: $22 (1997).
Education: High school graduation rate: 77.9% (2000); College graduation rate: 9.6% (2000).
Housing: Homeownership rate: 93.2% (2000); Median home value: $112,500 (2000); Median rent: <$100 per month (2000); Median age of housing: 28 years (2000).
Transportation: Commute to work: 92.4% car, 0.0% public transportation, 0.0% walk, 6.9% work from home (2000); Travel time to work: 11.9% less than 15 minutes, 28.8% 15 to 30 minutes, 26.8% 30 to 45 minutes, 16.6% 45 to 60 minutes, 15.9% 60 minutes or more (2000)

LANGOLA (township). Covers a land area of 39.693 square miles and a water area of 1.470 square miles. Located at 45.78° N. Lat.; 94.23° W. Long.
Population: 916 (2000); Race: 99.7% White, 0.0% Black, 0.0% Asian, 0.0% American Indian and Alaska Native, 0.0% Hispanic of any race, 0.3% two or more races (2000); Density: 23.1 persons per square mile (2000); Age: 30.2% under 18, 9.6% over 64 (2000); Marriage status: 25.0% never married, 68.2% now married, 2.9% widowed, 3.9% divorced (2000); Foreign born: 0.2% (2000); Ancestry (includes multiple ancestries): 58.3% German, 31.0% Polish, 8.8% Norwegian, 8.1% Irish, 6.9% Swedish (2000).
Economy: Employment by occupation: 13.6% management, 15.5% professional, 8.5% services, 21.7% sales, 3.9% farming, 15.3% construction, 21.4% production (2000).
Income: Per capita income: $18,753 (2000); Median household income: $52,667 (2000); Poverty rate: 4.4% (2000).
Taxes: Total city taxes per capita: $84 (1997); City property taxes per capita: $84 (1997).
Education: High school graduation rate: 90.9% (2000); College graduation rate: 10.8% (2000).
Housing: Homeownership rate: 94.7% (2000); Median home value: $127,000 (2000); Median rent: $325 per month (2000); Median age of housing: 21 years (2000).
Transportation: Commute to work: 89.8% car, 0.0% public transportation, 1.2% walk, 7.5% work from home (2000); Travel time to work: 21.2% less than 15 minutes, 52.0% 15 to 30 minutes, 19.7% 30 to 45 minutes, 3.4% 45 to 60 minutes, 3.6% 60 minutes or more (2000)

MAYHEW LAKE (township). Covers a land area of 36.861 square miles and a water area of 0.232 square miles. Located at 45.68° N. Lat.; 94.04° W. Long.
Population: 804 (2000); Race: 99.5% White, 0.0% Black, 0.0% Asian, 0.0% American Indian and Alaska Native, 1.3% Hispanic of any race, 0.5% two or more races (2000); Density: 21.8 persons per square mile (2000); Age: 30.2% under 18, 7.4% over 64 (2000); Marriage status: 30.0% never married, 63.1% now married, 3.2% widowed, 3.8% divorced (2000); Foreign born: 0.0% (2000); Ancestry (includes multiple ancestries): 64.0% German, 24.4% Polish, 6.3% French (except Basque), 5.5% United States or American, 4.7% Norwegian (2000).
Economy: Employment by occupation: 22.6% management, 11.5% professional, 8.8% services, 21.9% sales, 2.2% farming, 12.8% construction, 20.1% production (2000).
Income: Per capita income: $18,553 (2000); Median household income: $48,750 (2000); Poverty rate: 5.1% (2000).
Taxes: Total city taxes per capita: $38 (1997); City property taxes per capita: $38 (1997).
Education: High school graduation rate: 78.4% (2000); College graduation rate: 12.2% (2000).
Housing: Homeownership rate: 90.9% (2000); Median home value: $108,300 (2000); Median rent: $308 per month (2000); Median age of housing: 27 years (2000).
Transportation: Commute to work: 79.1% car, 0.0% public transportation, 1.1% walk, 19.3% work from home (2000); Travel time to work: 14.7% less than 15 minutes, 55.3% 15 to 30 minutes, 16.7% 30 to 45 minutes, 3.1% 45 to 60 minutes, 10.3% 60 minutes or more (2000)

MAYWOOD (township). Covers a land area of 35.287 square miles and a water area of 0 square miles. Located at 45.69° N. Lat.; 93.81° W. Long.
Population: 860 (2000); Race: 98.2% White, 0.0% Black, 0.0% Asian, 0.3% American Indian and Alaska Native, 0.7% Hispanic of any race, 1.3% two or more races (2000); Density: 24.4 persons per square mile (2000); Age: 30.5% under 18, 9.1% over 64 (2000); Marriage status: 24.6% never married, 65.0% now married, 3.8% widowed, 6.6% divorced (2000); Foreign born: 0.0% (2000); Ancestry (includes multiple ancestries): 44.2% German, 15.5% Polish, 12.7% Swedish, 11.8% Norwegian, 6.6% Irish (2000).
Economy: Employment by occupation: 9.4% management, 14.6% professional, 13.4% services, 16.7% sales, 3.1% farming, 11.1% construction, 31.7% production (2000).
Income: Per capita income: $17,911 (2000); Median household income: $47,500 (2000); Poverty rate: 5.6% (2000).
Taxes: Total city taxes per capita: $32 (1997); City property taxes per capita: $32 (1997).
Education: High school graduation rate: 76.6% (2000); College graduation rate: 10.2% (2000).
Housing: Homeownership rate: 91.9% (2000); Median home value: $80,300 (2000); Median rent: $238 per month (2000); Median age of housing: 44 years (2000).
Transportation: Commute to work: 91.5% car, 0.0% public transportation, 0.6% walk, 7.7% work from home (2000); Travel time to work: 25.2% less than 15 minutes, 32.4% 15 to 30 minutes, 24.5% 30 to 45 minutes, 4.4% 45 to 60 minutes, 13.4% 60 minutes or more (2000)

MINDEN (township). Covers a land area of 36.327 square miles and a water area of 0.117 square miles. Located at 45.58° N. Lat.; 94.08° W. Long.
Population: 1,790 (2000); Race: 96.7% White, 0.0% Black, 1.1% Asian, 1.9% American Indian and Alaska Native, 0.9% Hispanic of any race, 0.4% two or more races (2000); Density: 49.3 persons per square mile (2000); Age: 27.8% under 18, 8.4% over 64 (2000); Marriage status: 21.8% never married, 69.7% now married, 2.4% widowed, 6.0% divorced (2000); Foreign born: 0.6% (2000); Ancestry (includes multiple ancestries): 54.5% German, 16.9% Polish, 10.6% Norwegian, 9.7% Irish, 6.6% United States or American (2000).
Economy: Employment by occupation: 13.2% management, 13.2% professional, 9.3% services, 31.1% sales, 1.0% farming, 10.3% construction, 22.1% production (2000).
Income: Per capita income: $21,130 (2000); Median household income: $58,854 (2000); Poverty rate: 3.8% (2000).
Taxes: Total city taxes per capita: $53 (1997); City property taxes per capita: $53 (1997).
Education: High school graduation rate: 88.7% (2000); College graduation rate: 17.2% (2000).
Housing: Homeownership rate: 94.3% (2000); Median home value: $118,000 (2000); Median rent: $421 per month (2000); Median age of housing: 27 years (2000).
Transportation: Commute to work: 94.5% car, 0.0% public transportation, 2.2% walk, 3.2% work from home (2000); Travel time to work: 34.6% less than 15 minutes, 45.7% 15 to 30 minutes, 11.7% 30 to 45 minutes, 3.0% 45 to 60 minutes, 5.0% 60 minutes or more (2000)

OAK PARK (unincorporated postal area, zip code 56357). Aka Oaks. Covers a land area of 33.156 square miles and a water area of 0 square miles. Located at 45.70° N. Lat.; 93.80° W. Long. Elevation is 1,130 feet.
Population: 822 (2000); Race: 98.0% White, 0.0% Black, 0.0% Asian, 0.4% American Indian and Alaska Native, 0.5% Hispanic of any race, 1.4% two or more races (2000); Density: 24.8 persons per square mile (2000); Age: 29.4% under 18, 9.4% over 64 (2000); Marriage status: 22.6% never married, 66.7% now married, 4.1% widowed, 6.6% divorced (2000); Foreign born: 0.0% (2000); Ancestry (includes multiple ancestries): 44.0% German, 18.8% Polish, 16.3% Swedish, 9.5% Norwegian, 5.5% Irish (2000).
Economy: Employment by occupation: 8.3% management, 11.1% professional, 13.0% services, 22.0% sales, 2.8% farming, 10.6% construction, 32.2% production (2000).
Income: Per capita income: $17,254 (2000); Median household income: $46,111 (2000); Poverty rate: 8.2% (2000).
Education: High school graduation rate: 71.6% (2000); College graduation rate: 7.5% (2000).
Housing: Homeownership rate: 94.7% (2000); Median home value: $83,200 (2000); Median rent: $525 per month (2000); Median age of housing: 40 years (2000).
Transportation: Commute to work: 91.0% car, 0.0% public transportation, 0.7% walk, 8.1% work from home (2000); Travel time to work: 17.6% less than 15 minutes, 34.8% 15 to 30 minutes, 26.1% 30 to 45 minutes, 8.0% 45 to 60 minutes, 13.6% 60 minutes or more (2000)

RICE (city). Covers a land area of 5.986 square miles and a water area of 0.112 square miles. Located at 45.75° N. Lat.; 94.22° W. Long. Elevation is 1,068 feet.
Population: 711 (2000); Race: 97.5% White, 0.0% Black, 0.0% Asian, 0.0% American Indian and Alaska Native, 2.2% Hispanic of any race, 0.3% two or more races (2000); Density: 118.8 persons per square mile (2000); Age: 35.3% under 18, 2.6% over 64 (2000); Marriage status: 26.6% never married, 65.4% now married, 2.1% widowed, 5.9% divorced (2000); Foreign born: 0.3% (2000); Ancestry (includes multiple ancestries): 67.2% German, 21.8% Polish, 7.0% Norwegian, 6.7% Swedish, 6.0% Irish (2000).
Economy: Dairying; light manufacturing. Single-family building permits issued: 13 (2001) / 11 (2000); Multi-family building permits issued: 0 (2001) / 0 (2000); Employment by occupation: 13.4% management, 12.4% professional, 11.6% services, 23.5% sales, 2.3% farming, 11.1% construction, 25.6% production (2000).
Income: Per capita income: $16,882 (2000); Median household income: $48,173 (2000); Poverty rate: 6.3% (2000).
Taxes: Total city taxes per capita: $389 (1997); City property taxes per capita: $349 (1997).
Education: High school graduation rate: 92.5% (2000); College graduation rate: 20.3% (2000).
Housing: Homeownership rate: 85.4% (2000); Median home value: $91,500 (2000); Median rent: $389 per month (2000); Median age of housing: 22 years (2000).
Transportation: Commute to work: 92.8% car, 0.0% public transportation, 4.5% walk, 2.7% work from home (2000); Travel time to work: 19.5% less than 15 minutes, 53.7% 15 to 30 minutes, 21.9% 30 to 45 minutes, 1.4% 45 to 60 minutes, 3.6% 60 minutes or more (2000)

RONNEBY (city). Covers a land area of 0.248 square miles and a water area of 0 square miles. Located at 45.68° N. Lat.; 93.86° W. Long.
Population: 16 (2000); Race: 100.0% White, 0.0% Black, 0.0% Asian, 0.0% American Indian and Alaska Native, 0.0% Hispanic of any race, 0.0% two or more races (2000); Density: 64.5 persons per square mile (2000); Age: 33.3% under 18, 41.7% over 64 (2000); Marriage status: 0.0% never married, 37.5% now married, 62.5% widowed, 0.0% divorced (2000); Foreign born: 0.0% (2000); Ancestry (includes multiple ancestries): 66.7% Irish, 58.3% German, 25.0% Dutch (2000).
Economy: In grain and livestock area. Single-family building permits issued: 0 (2001) / 0 (2000); Multi-family building permits issued: 0 (2001) / 4 (2000); Employment by occupation: 0.0% management, 33.3% professional, 0.0% services, 0.0% sales, 0.0% farming, 0.0% construction, 66.7% production (2000).

Income: Per capita income: $11,700 (2000); Median household income: $40,625 (2000); Poverty rate: 0.0% (2000).
Taxes: Total city taxes per capita: $89 (1997); City property taxes per capita: $89 (1997).
Education: High school graduation rate: 75.0% (2000); College graduation rate: 0.0% (2000).
Housing: Homeownership rate: 100.0% (2000); Median home value: $75,000 (2000); Median age of housing: 60+ years (2000).
Transportation: Commute to work: 100.0% car, 0.0% public transportation, 0.0% walk, 0.0% work from home (2000); Travel time to work: 83.3% less than 15 minutes, 0.0% 15 to 30 minutes, 16.7% 30 to 45 minutes, 0.0% 45 to 60 minutes, 0.0% 60 minutes or more (2000)

SAINT GEORGE (township). Covers a land area of 36.701 square miles and a water area of 0.071 square miles. Located at 45.59° N. Lat.; 93.93° W. Long.
Population: 924 (2000); Race: 98.9% White, 0.0% Black, 0.4% Asian, 0.7% American Indian and Alaska Native, 0.0% Hispanic of any race, 0.0% two or more races (2000); Density: 25.2 persons per square mile (2000); Age: 26.4% under 18, 13.6% over 64 (2000); Marriage status: 22.4% never married, 69.4% now married, 2.9% widowed, 5.2% divorced (2000); Foreign born: 0.4% (2000); Ancestry (includes multiple ancestries): 57.2% German, 20.1% Polish, 10.3% Irish, 9.3% Norwegian, 6.4% French (except Basque) (2000).
Economy: Employment by occupation: 17.2% management, 12.2% professional, 12.0% services, 22.2% sales, 1.8% farming, 13.0% construction, 21.8% production (2000).
Income: Per capita income: $20,857 (2000); Median household income: $50,694 (2000); Poverty rate: 4.8% (2000).
Education: High school graduation rate: 84.8% (2000); College graduation rate: 12.8% (2000).
Housing: Homeownership rate: 91.5% (2000); Median home value: $118,900 (2000); Median rent: $383 per month (2000); Median age of housing: 30 years (2000).
Transportation: Commute to work: 85.7% car, 0.6% public transportation, 1.2% walk, 9.2% work from home (2000); Travel time to work: 29.3% less than 15 minutes, 44.5% 15 to 30 minutes, 20.1% 30 to 45 minutes, 2.5% 45 to 60 minutes, 3.6% 60 minutes or more (2000)

SAUK RAPIDS (city). Covers a land area of 4.571 square miles and a water area of 0.239 square miles. Located at 45.59° N. Lat.; 94.16° W. Long. Elevation is 1,008 feet.
History: Sauk Rapids became the northern terminal of the Northern Pacific and Great Northern Railways, and as such was an important junction for rail and ox-cart traffic. After a beginning as a sawmill town, Sauk Rapids suffered a devastating cyclone in 1886. The town emerged from the disaster to become a flour milling center.
Population: 10,213 (2000); Race: 95.5% White, 0.7% Black, 0.7% Asian, 0.1% American Indian and Alaska Native, 1.0% Hispanic of any race, 2.5% two or more races (2000); Density: 2,234.1 persons per square mile (2000); Age: 28.1% under 18, 11.4% over 64 (2000); Marriage status: 27.7% never married, 56.4% now married, 7.4% widowed, 8.4% divorced (2000); Foreign born: 2.0% (2000); Ancestry (includes multiple ancestries): 55.4% German, 12.6% Polish, 11.4% Norwegian, 9.2% Irish, 5.0% English (2000).
Economy: Single-family building permits issued: 174 (2001) / 158 (2000); Multi-family building permits issued: 76 (2001) / 98 (2000); Employment by occupation: 11.5% management, 17.4% professional, 12.1% services, 28.2% sales, 0.0% farming, 9.0% construction, 21.7% production (2000).
Income: Per capita income: $19,510 (2000); Median household income: $45,857 (2000); Poverty rate: 4.9% (2000).
Taxes: Total city taxes per capita: $258 (1997); City property taxes per capita: $242 (1997).
Education: High school graduation rate: 87.8% (2000); College graduation rate: 20.8% (2000).

School District(s)

Sauk Rapids (PK-12)
2000 Enrollment: 3,466 320-253-4703

Housing: Homeownership rate: 66.0% (2000); Median home value: $103,600 (2000); Median rent: $441 per month (2000); Median age of housing: 20 years (2000).
Safety: Violent crime rate: 15.5 per 10,000 population; Property crime rate: 269.3 per 10,000 population (2001).
Newspapers: Sauk Rapids Herald (1 x week)
Transportation: Commute to work: 94.2% car, 1.6% public transportation, 0.7% walk, 2.8% work from home (2000); Travel time to work: 50.8% less than 15 minutes, 34.8% 15 to 30 minutes, 6.3% 30 to 45 minutes, 3.0% 45 to 60 minutes, 5.1% 60 minutes or more (2000)

SAUK RAPIDS (township). Covers a land area of 8.182 square miles and a water area of 0.164 square miles. Located at 45.61° N. Lat.; 94.16° W. Long. Elevation is 1,008 feet.
History: Plotted 1851, incorporated 1881.
Population: 723 (2000); Race: 99.3% White, 0.7% Black, 0.0% Asian, 0.0% American Indian and Alaska Native, 0.0% Hispanic of any race, 0.0% two or more races (2000); Density: 88.4 persons per square mile (2000); Age: 25.8% under 18, 8.1% over 64 (2000); Marriage status: 28.8% never married, 62.2% now married, 2.4% widowed, 6.6% divorced (2000); Foreign born: 0.5% (2000); Ancestry (includes multiple ancestries): 53.7% German, 16.0% Norwegian, 15.3% Polish, 13.0% Irish, 7.1% English (2000).
Economy: Agriculture: dairy products, flour. Manufacturing: fishing boats, electric signs, urethane foam fixtures flotation products, ophthalmic lenses. Granite quarries nearby. Employment by occupation: 10.8% management, 20.4% professional, 12.5% services, 24.6% sales, 0.4% farming, 11.0% construction, 20.2% production (2000).
Income: Per capita income: $24,421 (2000); Median household income: $61,161 (2000); Poverty rate: 2.2% (2000).
Taxes: Total city taxes per capita: $26 (1997); City property taxes per capita: $26 (1997).
Education: High school graduation rate: 93.2% (2000); College graduation rate: 22.4% (2000).
Housing: Homeownership rate: 72.7% (2000); Median home value: $115,300 (2000); Median rent: $604 per month (2000); Median age of housing: 22 years (2000).
Transportation: Commute to work: 94.0% car, 0.0% public transportation, 0.4% walk, 4.7% work from home (2000); Travel time to work: 47.4% less than 15 minutes, 37.7% 15 to 30 minutes, 7.0% 30 to 45 minutes, 2.5% 45 to 60 minutes, 5.4% 60 minutes or more (2000)

WATAB (township). Covers a land area of 20.309 square miles and a water area of 2.063 square miles. Located at 45.69° N. Lat.; 94.18° W. Long. Elevation is 1,046 feet.
Population: 2,920 (2000); Race: 98.8% White, 0.0% Black, 0.2% Asian, 0.8% American Indian and Alaska Native, 0.2% Hispanic of any race, 0.1% two or more races (2000); Density: 143.8 persons per square mile (2000); Age: 30.1% under 18, 7.7% over 64 (2000); Marriage status: 21.0% never married, 67.9% now married, 3.0% widowed, 8.2% divorced (2000); Foreign born: 1.1% (2000); Ancestry (includes multiple ancestries): 60.4% German, 17.4% Polish, 12.9% Norwegian, 7.8% Swedish, 6.6% Irish (2000).
Economy: Employment by occupation: 7.8% management, 12.6% professional, 8.6% services, 31.6% sales, 0.9% farming, 14.5% construction, 24.0% production (2000).
Income: Per capita income: $20,554 (2000); Median household income: $50,604 (2000); Poverty rate: 6.1% (2000).
Taxes: Total city taxes per capita: $51 (1997); City property taxes per capita: $51 (1997).
Education: High school graduation rate: 88.8% (2000); College graduation rate: 12.5% (2000).
Housing: Homeownership rate: 95.2% (2000); Median home value: $111,800 (2000); Median rent: $488 per month (2000); Median age of housing: 20 years (2000).
Transportation: Commute to work: 96.6% car, 0.0% public transportation, 1.3% walk, 2.0% work from home (2000); Travel time to work: 22.0% less than 15 minutes, 62.3% 15 to 30 minutes, 8.6% 30 to 45 minutes, 1.9% 45 to 60 minutes, 5.1% 60 minutes or more (2000)

Big Stone County

Located in western Minnesota; bounded on the west by Big Stone Lake and the South Dakota border. Covers a land area of 496.90 square miles, a water area of 30.90 square miles, and is located in the Central Time Zone. The county government was organized in 1862. County seat is Ortonville.

Weather Station: Artichoke Lake — Elevation: 1,072 feet

	Jan	Feb	Mar	Apr	May	Jun	Jul	Aug	Sep	Oct	Nov	Dec
High	20	26	37	55	69	78	82	80	70	58	38	25
Low	-0	7	20	34	47	57	61	59	49	37	21	7
Precip	0.9	0.6	1.5	2.1	2.5	3.7	3.9	3.0	2.0	2.2	1.2	0.5
Snow	10.0	6.6	8.0	2.5	tr	0.0	0.0	0.0	tr	0.9	6.6	5.4

High and Low temperatures in degrees Fahrenheit; Precipitation and Snow in inches

Population: 5,820 (2000); Race: 98.6% White, 0.1% Black, 0.0% Asian, 0.5% American Indian and Alaska Native, 0.2% Hispanic of any race, 0.7%

two or more races (2000); Density: 11.7 persons per square mile (2000); Age: 24.9% under 18, 24.2% over 64 (2000).
Religion: Five largest groups: 33.6% Evangelical Lutheran Church in America, 32.2% Catholic Church, 18.5% Lutheran Church—Missouri Synod, 7.3% The United Methodist Church, 4.8% The Association of Free Lutheran Congregations (2000).
Economy: Unemployment rate: 2.6% (11/2002); Total civilian labor force: 2,854 (11/2002); Leading industries: 28.0% health care and social assistance; 23.9% retail trade; 9.7% accommodation & food services (2000); Companies that employ more than 1,000 persons: 0 (2000); Companies that employ more than 100 persons: 2 (2000); Farms: 420 totaling 253,988 acres (1997); Minority business ownership rate: 0.0% (1997); Women business ownership rate: 0.0% (1997); Retail sales per capita: $4,745 (1997). Single-family building permits issued: 11 (2001) / 10 (2000); Multi-family building permits issued: 2 (2001) / 0 (2000).
Income: Per capita income: $15,708 (2000); Median household income: $30,721 (2000); Poverty rate: 12.0% (2000); Bankruptcy rate: 1.61% (2001).
Taxes: Total county taxes per capita: $303 (1997); County property taxes per capita: $301 (1997).
Education: High school graduation rate: 79.0% (2000); College graduation rate: 11.4% (2000).
Housing: Homeownership rate: 85.1% (2000); Median home value: $41,900 (2000); Median rent: $181 per month (2000); Median age of housing: 48 years (2000).
Health: Birth rate: 96.2 per 10,000 population (1998); Age adjusted death rate: 92.0 per 10,000 population (1999); Age adjusted cancer mortality rate: 224.8 deaths per 100,000 population (1999). Number of physicians: 12.0 per 10,000 population (1999); Number of hospital beds: 338.5 per 10,000 population (1999).
Elections: 2000 Presidential election results: 48.0% Gore, 46.0% Bush, 3.7% Nader, 2.0% Buchanan
National and State Parks: Allen State Wildlife Management Area; Big Stone Lake State Park; Dismal Swamp State Wildlife Management Area; Finberg State Wildlife Management Area; Freed State Wildlife Management Area; Klages State Wildlife Management Areas; Lac Qui Parle State Wildlife Management Area; Lindquist State Wildlife Management Area; Mallard Hole State Wildlife Management Area; Otrey State Wildlife Management Area; Prairie State Wildlife Management Area; Reisdorph State Wildlife Management Area; Skoog State Wildlife Management Area; Taffe State Wildlife Management Area; Thomson State Wildlife Management Area; Victor State Wildlife Management Area
Additional Information Contacts
Big Stone County Government Offices 320-839-2525

Big Stone County Communities

AKRON (township). Covers a land area of 48.619 square miles and a water area of 4.680 square miles. Located at 45.26° N. Lat.; 96.17° W. Long.
Population: 196 (2000); Race: 96.4% White, 0.5% Black, 0.0% Asian, 0.0% American Indian and Alaska Native, 0.0% Hispanic of any race, 3.1% two or more races (2000); Density: 4.0 persons per square mile (2000); Age: 24.4% under 18, 21.8% over 64 (2000); Marriage status: 16.2% never married, 74.0% now married, 6.5% widowed, 3.2% divorced (2000); Foreign born: 0.5% (2000); Ancestry (includes multiple ancestries): 64.2% German, 43.5% Norwegian, 10.9% Swedish, 4.7% Scandinavian, 3.6% French (except Basque) (2000).
Economy: Employment by occupation: 30.1% management, 9.7% professional, 13.3% services, 19.5% sales, 6.2% farming, 6.2% construction, 15.0% production (2000).
Income: Per capita income: $15,473 (2000); Median household income: $29,750 (2000); Poverty rate: 18.7% (2000).
Taxes: Total city taxes per capita: $69 (1997); City property taxes per capita: $69 (1997).
Education: High school graduation rate: 89.7% (2000); College graduation rate: 11.8% (2000).
Housing: Homeownership rate: 86.1% (2000); Median home value: $55,000 (2000); Median rent: $175 per month (2000); Median age of housing: 57 years (2000).
Transportation: Commute to work: 64.0% car, 0.0% public transportation, 2.7% walk, 33.3% work from home (2000); Travel time to work: 31.1% less than 15 minutes, 45.9% 15 to 30 minutes, 10.8% 30 to 45 minutes, 9.5% 45 to 60 minutes, 2.7% 60 minutes or more (2000)

ALMOND (township). Covers a land area of 33.186 square miles and a water area of 1.610 square miles. Located at 45.45° N. Lat.; 96.43° W. Long.
Population: 190 (2000); Race: 97.4% White, 0.0% Black, 0.0% Asian, 2.6% American Indian and Alaska Native, 1.3% Hispanic of any race, 0.0% two or more races (2000); Density: 5.7 persons per square mile (2000); Age: 22.4% under 18, 25.6% over 64 (2000); Marriage status: 13.0% never married, 61.8% now married, 14.6% widowed, 10.6% divorced (2000); Foreign born: 0.0% (2000); Ancestry (includes multiple ancestries): 39.7% German, 23.7% Norwegian, 18.6% Swedish, 9.0% Irish, 7.7% English (2000).
Economy: Employment by occupation: 28.3% management, 16.7% professional, 15.0% services, 15.0% sales, 3.3% farming, 8.3% construction, 13.3% production (2000).
Income: Per capita income: $16,141 (2000); Median household income: $43,750 (2000); Poverty rate: 8.0% (2000).
Taxes: Total city taxes per capita: $156 (1997); City property taxes per capita: $156 (1997).
Education: High school graduation rate: 79.8% (2000); College graduation rate: 20.2% (2000).
Housing: Homeownership rate: 82.0% (2000); Median home value: $57,000 (2000); Median rent: <$100 per month (2000); Median age of housing: 37 years (2000).
Transportation: Commute to work: 84.5% car, 0.0% public transportation, 0.0% walk, 15.5% work from home (2000); Travel time to work: 46.9% less than 15 minutes, 40.8% 15 to 30 minutes, 4.1% 30 to 45 minutes, 8.2% 45 to 60 minutes, 0.0% 60 minutes or more (2000)

ARTICHOKE (township). Covers a land area of 32.227 square miles and a water area of 3.337 square miles. Located at 45.38° N. Lat.; 96.17° W. Long. Elevation is 1,096 feet.
Population: 84 (2000); Race: 100.0% White, 0.0% Black, 0.0% Asian, 0.0% American Indian and Alaska Native, 0.0% Hispanic of any race, 0.0% two or more races (2000); Density: 2.6 persons per square mile (2000); Age: 27.9% under 18, 17.6% over 64 (2000); Marriage status: 22.0% never married, 68.0% now married, 4.0% widowed, 6.0% divorced (2000); Foreign born: 0.0% (2000); Ancestry (includes multiple ancestries): 48.5% Norwegian, 47.1% German, 7.4% Dutch, 5.9% Swedish, 4.4% United States or American (2000).
Economy: Employment by occupation: 60.7% management, 0.0% professional, 14.3% services, 10.7% sales, 0.0% farming, 0.0% construction, 14.3% production (2000).
Income: Per capita income: $12,471 (2000); Median household income: $27,500 (2000); Poverty rate: 13.2% (2000).
Taxes: Total city taxes per capita: $143 (2000); City property taxes per capita: $143 (2000).
Education: High school graduation rate: 100.0% (2000); College graduation rate: 2.2% (2000).
Housing: Homeownership rate: 76.9% (2000); Median home value: $95,000 (2000); Median age of housing: 60+ years (2000).
Transportation: Commute to work: 71.4% car, 0.0% public transportation, 0.0% walk, 28.6% work from home (2000); Travel time to work: 50.0% less than 15 minutes, 50.0% 15 to 30 minutes, 0.0% 30 to 45 minutes, 0.0% 45 to 60 minutes, 0.0% 60 minutes or more (2000)

BARRY (city). Covers a land area of 0.247 square miles and a water area of 0 square miles. Located at 45.55° N. Lat.; 96.56° W. Long.
Population: 25 (2000); Race: 100.0% White, 0.0% Black, 0.0% Asian, 0.0% American Indian and Alaska Native, 0.0% Hispanic of any race, 0.0% two or more races (2000); Density: 101.3 persons per square mile (2000); Age: 23.8% under 18, 38.1% over 64 (2000); Marriage status: 26.3% never married, 52.6% now married, 21.1% widowed, 0.0% divorced (2000); Foreign born: 0.0% (2000); Ancestry (includes multiple ancestries): 61.9% German, 14.3% Dutch, 14.3% Norwegian, 14.3% Swedish, 9.5% Irish (2000).
Economy: Grain area. Single-family building permits issued: 0 (2001) / 0 (2000); Multi-family building permits issued: 0 (2001) / 0 (2000); Employment by occupation: 0.0% management, 100.0% professional, 0.0% services, 0.0% sales, 0.0% farming, 0.0% construction, 0.0% production (2000).
Income: Per capita income: $7,124 (2000); Median household income: $18,250 (2000); Poverty rate: 19.0% (2000).
Taxes: Total city taxes per capita: $158 (1997); City property taxes per capita: $158 (1997).
Education: High school graduation rate: 81.3% (2000); College graduation rate: 0.0% (2000).
Housing: Homeownership rate: 81.8% (2000); Median home value: $21,300 (2000); Median age of housing: 60+ years (2000).
Transportation: Commute to work: 100.0% car, 0.0% public transportation, 0.0% walk, 0.0% work from home (2000); Travel time to work: 0.0% less

than 15 minutes, 100.0% 15 to 30 minutes, 0.0% 30 to 45 minutes, 0.0% 45 to 60 minutes, 0.0% 60 minutes or more (2000)

BEARDSLEY (city). Covers a land area of 0.474 square miles and a water area of 0.003 square miles. Located at 45.55° N. Lat.; 96.71° W. Long. Elevation is 1,098 feet.
Population: 262 (2000); Race: 99.3% White, 0.0% Black, 0.0% Asian, 0.0% American Indian and Alaska Native, 0.0% Hispanic of any race, 0.7% two or more races (2000); Density: 552.5 persons per square mile (2000); Age: 25.9% under 18, 24.8% over 64 (2000); Marriage status: 13.5% never married, 63.3% now married, 19.2% widowed, 3.9% divorced (2000); Foreign born: 1.7% (2000); Ancestry (includes multiple ancestries): 53.1% German, 12.2% Norwegian, 8.4% Irish, 7.0% Swedish, 5.2% English (2000).
Economy: Grain, soybeans; livestock. Single-family building permits issued: 0 (2001) / 0 (2000); Multi-family building permits issued: 0 (2001) / 0 (2000); Employment by occupation: 18.7% management, 9.3% professional, 11.2% services, 36.4% sales, 4.7% farming, 5.6% construction, 14.0% production (2000).
Income: Per capita income: $16,106 (2000); Median household income: $26,429 (2000); Poverty rate: 12.2% (2000).
Taxes: Total city taxes per capita: $123 (1997); City property taxes per capita: $119 (1997).
Education: High school graduation rate: 72.5% (2000); College graduation rate: 8.0% (2000).
Housing: Homeownership rate: 87.1% (2000); Median home value: $15,000 (2000); Median rent: $155 per month (2000); Median age of housing: 60+ years (2000).
Transportation: Commute to work: 99.0% car, 0.0% public transportation, 0.0% walk, 1.0% work from home (2000); Travel time to work: 58.4% less than 15 minutes, 20.8% 15 to 30 minutes, 12.9% 30 to 45 minutes, 4.0% 45 to 60 minutes, 4.0% 60 minutes or more (2000)

BIG STONE (township). Covers a land area of 30.261 square miles and a water area of 4.139 square miles. Located at 45.37° N. Lat.; 96.44° W. Long.
Population: 253 (2000); Race: 100.0% White, 0.0% Black, 0.0% Asian, 0.0% American Indian and Alaska Native, 0.0% Hispanic of any race, 0.0% two or more races (2000); Density: 8.4 persons per square mile (2000); Age: 22.0% under 18, 20.9% over 64 (2000); Marriage status: 17.4% never married, 71.5% now married, 3.9% widowed, 7.2% divorced (2000); Foreign born: 3.1% (2000); Ancestry (includes multiple ancestries): 43.3% German, 28.0% Norwegian, 16.9% Swedish, 13.0% Irish, 5.9% English (2000).
Economy: Employment by occupation: 29.1% management, 15.7% professional, 11.9% services, 11.9% sales, 0.0% farming, 16.4% construction, 14.9% production (2000).
Income: Per capita income: $17,856 (2000); Median household income: $38,750 (2000); Poverty rate: 5.5% (2000).
Taxes: Total city taxes per capita: $67 (1997); City property taxes per capita: $67 (1997).
Education: High school graduation rate: 87.2% (2000); College graduation rate: 8.9% (2000).
Housing: Homeownership rate: 89.7% (2000); Median home value: $77,500 (2000); Median rent: $475 per month (2000); Median age of housing: 44 years (2000).
Transportation: Commute to work: 81.3% car, 0.0% public transportation, 1.5% walk, 17.2% work from home (2000); Travel time to work: 56.8% less than 15 minutes, 23.4% 15 to 30 minutes, 12.6% 30 to 45 minutes, 3.6% 45 to 60 minutes, 3.6% 60 minutes or more (2000)

BROWNS VALLEY (township). Covers a land area of 47.584 square miles and a water area of 1.306 square miles. Located at 45.54° N. Lat.; 96.70° W. Long.
Population: 438 (2000); Race: 99.1% White, 0.0% Black, 0.0% Asian, 0.4% American Indian and Alaska Native, 0.0% Hispanic of any race, 0.4% two or more races (2000); Density: 9.2 persons per square mile (2000); Age: 29.3% under 18, 21.8% over 64 (2000); Marriage status: 18.9% never married, 62.7% now married, 14.2% widowed, 4.1% divorced (2000); Foreign born: 1.1% (2000); Ancestry (includes multiple ancestries): 56.1% German, 18.1% Norwegian, 6.8% Irish, 5.5% Swedish, 4.4% Polish (2000).
Economy: Employment by occupation: 27.6% management, 10.1% professional, 10.6% services, 27.1% sales, 2.5% farming, 9.0% construction, 13.1% production (2000).
Income: Per capita income: $15,312 (2000); Median household income: $28,571 (2000); Poverty rate: 14.7% (2000).
Taxes: Total city taxes per capita: $50 (1997); City property taxes per capita: $50 (1997).
Education: High school graduation rate: 79.5% (2000); College graduation rate: 8.6% (2000).
Housing: Homeownership rate: 88.8% (2000); Median home value: $19,300 (2000); Median rent: $155 per month (2000); Median age of housing: 60+ years (2000).
Transportation: Commute to work: 80.4% car, 0.0% public transportation, 6.2% walk, 12.4% work from home (2000); Travel time to work: 56.5% less than 15 minutes, 22.9% 15 to 30 minutes, 11.8% 30 to 45 minutes, 2.4% 45 to 60 minutes, 6.5% 60 minutes or more (2000)

CLINTON (city). Covers a land area of 0.962 square miles and a water area of 0.078 square miles. Located at 45.46° N. Lat.; 96.43° W. Long. Elevation is 850 feet.
Population: 453 (2000); Race: 97.5% White, 0.0% Black, 0.0% Asian, 2.1% American Indian and Alaska Native, 0.0% Hispanic of any race, 0.4% two or more races (2000); Density: 471.0 persons per square mile (2000); Age: 26.3% under 18, 19.5% over 64 (2000); Marriage status: 24.8% never married, 62.4% now married, 9.1% widowed, 3.7% divorced (2000); Foreign born: 0.6% (2000); Ancestry (includes multiple ancestries): 40.3% German, 32.1% Norwegian, 18.3% Swedish, 12.8% Irish, 4.0% United States or American (2000).
Economy: Agricultural area: grain, alfalfa, soybeans; hogs. Manufacturing: fertilizers. Single-family building permits issued: 0 (2001) / 0 (2000); Multi-family building permits issued: 0 (2001) / 0 (2000); Employment by occupation: 9.0% management, 19.5% professional, 19.9% services, 20.8% sales, 2.3% farming, 11.8% construction, 16.7% production (2000).
Income: Per capita income: $17,469 (2000); Median household income: $31,591 (2000); Poverty rate: 13.9% (2000).
Taxes: Total city taxes per capita: $49 (1997); City property taxes per capita: $47 (1997).
Education: High school graduation rate: 78.1% (2000); College graduation rate: 18.1% (2000).

School District(s)

Clinton-Graceville-Beardsley (PK-12)
2000 Enrollment: 545 320-325-5282

Housing: Homeownership rate: 83.3% (2000); Median home value: $29,300 (2000); Median rent: $113 per month (2000); Median age of housing: 40 years (2000).
Newspapers: Northern Star (1 x week)
Transportation: Commute to work: 87.2% car, 0.0% public transportation, 10.0% walk, 2.7% work from home (2000); Travel time to work: 60.6% less than 15 minutes, 21.6% 15 to 30 minutes, 9.4% 30 to 45 minutes, 7.5% 45 to 60 minutes, 0.9% 60 minutes or more (2000)

CORRELL (city). Covers a land area of 0.367 square miles and a water area of 0 square miles. Located at 45.23° N. Lat.; 96.16° W. Long. Elevation is 973 feet.
Population: 47 (2000); Race: 96.1% White, 0.0% Black, 0.0% Asian, 0.0% American Indian and Alaska Native, 3.9% Hispanic of any race, 0.0% two or more races (2000); Density: 128.2 persons per square mile (2000); Age: 19.6% under 18, 27.5% over 64 (2000); Marriage status: 26.1% never married, 63.0% now married, 6.5% widowed, 4.3% divorced (2000); Foreign born: 0.0% (2000); Ancestry (includes multiple ancestries): 68.6% German, 17.6% Norwegian, 11.8% Irish, 7.8% Dutch, 5.9% English (2000).
Economy: Employment by occupation: 0.0% management, 0.0% professional, 18.5% services, 37.0% sales, 0.0% farming, 37.0% construction, 7.4% production (2000).
Income: Per capita income: $12,920 (2000); Median household income: $19,375 (2000); Poverty rate: 15.7% (2000).
Taxes: Total city taxes per capita: $86 (1997); City property taxes per capita: $69 (1997).
Education: High school graduation rate: 82.1% (2000); College graduation rate: 0.0% (2000).
Housing: Homeownership rate: 100.0% (2000); Median home value: $22,500 (2000); Median age of housing: 52 years (2000).
Transportation: Commute to work: 88.9% car, 0.0% public transportation, 0.0% walk, 11.1% work from home (2000); Travel time to work: 37.5% less than 15 minutes, 45.8% 15 to 30 minutes, 8.3% 30 to 45 minutes, 8.3% 45 to 60 minutes, 0.0% 60 minutes or more (2000)

FOSTER (township). Covers a land area of 30.057 square miles and a water area of 3.131 square miles. Located at 45.46° N. Lat.; 96.67° W. Long.
Population: 123 (2000); Race: 100.0% White, 0.0% Black, 0.0% Asian, 0.0% American Indian and Alaska Native, 0.0% Hispanic of any race, 0.0% two or more races (2000); Density: 4.1 persons per square mile (2000); Age: 16.8% under 18, 23.2% over 64 (2000); Marriage status: 19.4% never

married, 74.1% now married, 3.7% widowed, 2.8% divorced (2000); Foreign born: 0.0% (2000); Ancestry (includes multiple ancestries): 57.6% German, 34.4% Norwegian, 15.2% Swedish, 8.0% Irish, 5.6% Other groups (2000).
Economy: Employment by occupation: 25.0% management, 10.7% professional, 23.2% services, 25.0% sales, 5.4% farming, 7.1% construction, 3.6% production (2000).
Income: Per capita income: $16,178 (2000); Median household income: $31,875 (2000); Poverty rate: 18.4% (2000).
Taxes: Total city taxes per capita: $122 (1997); City property taxes per capita: $122 (1997).
Education: High school graduation rate: 84.5% (2000); College graduation rate: 15.5% (2000).
Housing: Homeownership rate: 93.1% (2000); Median home value: $131,300 (2000); Median rent: $175 per month (2000); Median age of housing: 38 years (2000).
Transportation: Commute to work: 78.6% car, 0.0% public transportation, 5.4% walk, 16.1% work from home (2000); Travel time to work: 27.7% less than 15 minutes, 51.1% 15 to 30 minutes, 4.3% 30 to 45 minutes, 8.5% 45 to 60 minutes, 8.5% 60 minutes or more (2000)

GRACEVILLE (city). Covers a land area of 0.600 square miles and a water area of 0 square miles. Located at 45.56° N. Lat.; 96.43° W. Long. Elevation is 1,116 feet.
Population: 605 (2000); Race: 99.4% White, 0.0% Black, 0.0% Asian, 0.6% American Indian and Alaska Native, 0.2% Hispanic of any race, 0.0% two or more races (2000); Density: 1,007.7 persons per square mile (2000); Age: 21.2% under 18, 33.0% over 64 (2000); Marriage status: 18.1% never married, 65.6% now married, 12.4% widowed, 3.9% divorced (2000); Foreign born: 0.6% (2000); Ancestry (includes multiple ancestries): 50.6% German, 11.3% Irish, 10.8% Norwegian, 6.3% Swedish, 6.1% Danish (2000).
Economy: Single-family building permits issued: 2 (2001) / 1 (2000); Multi-family building permits issued: 0 (2001) / 0 (2000); Employment by occupation: 9.1% management, 18.1% professional, 16.5% services, 26.0% sales, 4.7% farming, 15.0% construction, 10.6% production (2000).
Income: Per capita income: $15,451 (2000); Median household income: $27,143 (2000); Poverty rate: 8.6% (2000).
Taxes: Total city taxes per capita: $126 (1997); City property taxes per capita: $125 (1997).
Education: High school graduation rate: 78.1% (2000); College graduation rate: 11.5% (2000).
Housing: Homeownership rate: 82.6% (2000); Median home value: $44,600 (2000); Median rent: $203 per month (2000); Median age of housing: 52 years (2000).
Hospitals: Holy Trinity Hospital (32 beds)
Transportation: Commute to work: 87.8% car, 0.4% public transportation, 5.9% walk, 5.5% work from home (2000); Travel time to work: 65.4% less than 15 minutes, 24.6% 15 to 30 minutes, 8.3% 30 to 45 minutes, 0.0% 45 to 60 minutes, 1.7% 60 minutes or more (2000)

GRACEVILLE (township). Covers a land area of 32.892 square miles and a water area of 2.046 square miles. Located at 45.54° N. Lat.; 96.42° W. Long. Elevation is 1,116 feet.
Population: 205 (2000); Race: 100.0% White, 0.0% Black, 0.0% Asian, 0.0% American Indian and Alaska Native, 0.0% Hispanic of any race, 0.0% two or more races (2000); Density: 6.2 persons per square mile (2000); Age: 38.2% under 18, 11.3% over 64 (2000); Marriage status: 25.7% never married, 71.6% now married, 1.4% widowed, 1.4% divorced (2000); Foreign born: 2.4% (2000); Ancestry (includes multiple ancestries): 65.1% German, 9.4% Swedish, 9.0% United States or American, 8.0% Norwegian, 6.6% Irish (2000).
Economy: Agricultural area: grain, soybeans, alfalfa; hogs. Employment by occupation: 27.8% management, 3.7% professional, 22.2% services, 11.1% sales, 0.0% farming, 13.0% construction, 22.2% production (2000).
Income: Per capita income: $7,826 (2000); Median household income: $25,833 (2000); Poverty rate: 43.9% (2000).
Taxes: Total city taxes per capita: $88 (1997); City property taxes per capita: $88 (1997).
Education: High school graduation rate: 45.3% (2000); College graduation rate: 0.0% (2000).
Housing: Homeownership rate: 71.9% (2000); Median home value: $45,000 (2000); Median age of housing: 19 years (2000).
Transportation: Commute to work: 82.0% car, 0.0% public transportation, 0.0% walk, 18.0% work from home (2000); Travel time to work: 43.9% less than 15 minutes, 34.1% 15 to 30 minutes, 12.2% 30 to 45 minutes, 4.9% 45 to 60 minutes, 4.9% 60 minutes or more (2000)

JOHNSON (city). Covers a land area of 0.308 square miles and a water area of 0 square miles. Located at 45.57° N. Lat.; 96.29° W. Long.
Population: 32 (2000); Race: 100.0% White, 0.0% Black, 0.0% Asian, 0.0% American Indian and Alaska Native, 0.0% Hispanic of any race, 0.0% two or more races (2000); Density: 103.7 persons per square mile (2000); Age: 16.2% under 18, 5.4% over 64 (2000); Marriage status: 34.3% never married, 54.3% now married, 5.7% widowed, 5.7% divorced (2000); Foreign born: 0.0% (2000); Ancestry (includes multiple ancestries): 37.8% German, 10.8% Irish, 10.8% Swedish, 5.4% Norwegian (2000).
Economy: Grain. Manufacturing: feeds. Single-family building permits issued: 0 (2001) / 0 (2000); Multi-family building permits issued: 0 (2001) / 0 (2000); Employment by occupation: 19.0% management, 9.5% professional, 0.0% services, 33.3% sales, 0.0% farming, 19.0% construction, 19.0% production (2000).
Income: Per capita income: $20,759 (2000); Median household income: $38,125 (2000); Poverty rate: 5.4% (2000).
Taxes: Total city taxes per capita: $116 (1997); City property taxes per capita: $70 (1997).
Education: High school graduation rate: 65.5% (2000); College graduation rate: 0.0% (2000).
Housing: Homeownership rate: 100.0% (2000); Median home value: $27,500 (2000); Median age of housing: 60+ years (2000).
Transportation: Commute to work: 100.0% car, 0.0% public transportation, 0.0% walk, 0.0% work from home (2000); Travel time to work: 47.6% less than 15 minutes, 0.0% 15 to 30 minutes, 42.9% 30 to 45 minutes, 9.5% 45 to 60 minutes, 0.0% 60 minutes or more (2000)

MALTA (township). Covers a land area of 36.287 square miles and a water area of 0.864 square miles. Located at 45.44° N. Lat.; 96.31° W. Long.
Population: 90 (2000); Race: 100.0% White, 0.0% Black, 0.0% Asian, 0.0% American Indian and Alaska Native, 0.0% Hispanic of any race, 0.0% two or more races (2000); Density: 2.5 persons per square mile (2000); Age: 43.8% under 18, 9.0% over 64 (2000); Marriage status: 24.1% never married, 72.4% now married, 0.0% widowed, 3.4% divorced (2000); Foreign born: 0.0% (2000); Ancestry (includes multiple ancestries): 43.8% German, 27.0% Swedish, 18.0% Norwegian, 10.1% United States or American, 9.0% English (2000).
Economy: Employment by occupation: 30.4% management, 21.7% professional, 10.9% services, 8.7% sales, 0.0% farming, 15.2% construction, 13.0% production (2000).
Income: Per capita income: $11,949 (2000); Median household income: $43,750 (2000); Poverty rate: 2.2% (2000).
Taxes: Total city taxes per capita: $173 (1997); City property taxes per capita: $173 (1997).
Education: High school graduation rate: 100.0% (2000); College graduation rate: 8.3% (2000).
Housing: Homeownership rate: 100.0% (2000); Median home value: $82,500 (2000); Median age of housing: 57 years (2000).
Transportation: Commute to work: 88.6% car, 0.0% public transportation, 6.8% walk, 4.5% work from home (2000); Travel time to work: 52.4% less than 15 minutes, 33.3% 15 to 30 minutes, 14.3% 30 to 45 minutes, 0.0% 45 to 60 minutes, 0.0% 60 minutes or more (2000)

MOONSHINE (township). Covers a land area of 37.539 square miles and a water area of 0.035 square miles. Located at 45.54° N. Lat.; 96.29° W. Long.
Population: 150 (2000); Race: 95.2% White, 0.0% Black, 0.0% Asian, 0.0% American Indian and Alaska Native, 0.0% Hispanic of any race, 4.8% two or more races (2000); Density: 4.0 persons per square mile (2000); Age: 22.4% under 18, 18.2% over 64 (2000); Marriage status: 19.7% never married, 74.5% now married, 4.4% widowed, 1.5% divorced (2000); Foreign born: 0.0% (2000); Ancestry (includes multiple ancestries): 47.9% German, 13.9% Irish, 13.3% Swedish, 10.3% Norwegian, 4.8% Other groups (2000).
Economy: Employment by occupation: 25.7% management, 11.4% professional, 8.6% services, 21.4% sales, 5.7% farming, 8.6% construction, 18.6% production (2000).
Income: Per capita income: $15,313 (2000); Median household income: $37,500 (2000); Poverty rate: 10.9% (2000).
Taxes: Total city taxes per capita: $120 (1997); City property taxes per capita: $120 (1997).
Education: High school graduation rate: 86.8% (2000); College graduation rate: 5.0% (2000).
Housing: Homeownership rate: 96.9% (2000); Median home value: $30,000 (2000); Median rent: $275 per month (2000); Median age of housing: 53 years (2000).

Transportation: Commute to work: 77.1% car, 0.0% public transportation, 5.7% walk, 17.1% work from home (2000); Travel time to work: 55.2% less than 15 minutes, 5.2% 15 to 30 minutes, 19.0% 30 to 45 minutes, 3.4% 45 to 60 minutes, 17.2% 60 minutes or more (2000)

ODESSA (city). Covers a land area of 0.756 square miles and a water area of 0 square miles. Located at 45.26° N. Lat.; 96.32° W. Long. Elevation is 995 feet.
Population: 113 (2000); Race: 100.0% White, 0.0% Black, 0.0% Asian, 0.0% American Indian and Alaska Native, 0.0% Hispanic of any race, 0.0% two or more races (2000); Density: 149.4 persons per square mile (2000); Age: 13.8% under 18, 40.4% over 64 (2000); Marriage status: 13.4% never married, 54.6% now married, 16.5% widowed, 15.5% divorced (2000); Foreign born: 0.0% (2000); Ancestry (includes multiple ancestries): 45.9% German, 39.4% Norwegian, 10.1% Swedish, 3.7% Polish, 3.7% Dutch (2000).
Economy: Employment by occupation: 10.5% management, 26.3% professional, 13.2% services, 18.4% sales, 0.0% farming, 21.1% construction, 10.5% production (2000).
Income: Per capita income: $13,905 (2000); Median household income: $23,125 (2000); Poverty rate: 11.0% (2000).
Taxes: Total city taxes per capita: $50 (1997); City property taxes per capita: $36 (1997).
Education: High school graduation rate: 68.5% (2000); College graduation rate: 7.6% (2000).
Housing: Homeownership rate: 96.2% (2000); Median home value: $21,700 (2000); Median rent: <$100 per month (2000); Median age of housing: 60+ years (2000).
Transportation: Commute to work: 88.9% car, 0.0% public transportation, 0.0% walk, 11.1% work from home (2000); Travel time to work: 50.0% less than 15 minutes, 31.3% 15 to 30 minutes, 6.3% 30 to 45 minutes, 12.5% 45 to 60 minutes, 0.0% 60 minutes or more (2000)

ODESSA (township). Covers a land area of 35.555 square miles and a water area of 0.773 square miles. Located at 45.28° N. Lat.; 96.30° W. Long. Elevation is 995 feet.
Population: 147 (2000); Race: 98.7% White, 0.0% Black, 0.0% Asian, 0.0% American Indian and Alaska Native, 1.3% Hispanic of any race, 1.3% two or more races (2000); Density: 4.1 persons per square mile (2000); Age: 22.7% under 18, 15.6% over 64 (2000); Marriage status: 14.4% never married, 80.0% now married, 2.4% widowed, 3.2% divorced (2000); Foreign born: 2.6% (2000); Ancestry (includes multiple ancestries): 48.1% German, 28.6% Norwegian, 9.7% Swedish, 9.1% United States or American, 6.5% English (2000).
Economy: Grain. Employment by occupation: 20.5% management, 6.8% professional, 10.2% services, 33.0% sales, 2.3% farming, 15.9% construction, 11.4% production (2000).
Income: Per capita income: $17,174 (2000); Median household income: $36,429 (2000); Poverty rate: 2.6% (2000).
Taxes: Total city taxes per capita: $35 (1997); City property taxes per capita: $35 (1997).
Education: High school graduation rate: 85.0% (2000); College graduation rate: 5.3% (2000).
Housing: Homeownership rate: 93.7% (2000); Median home value: $51,700 (2000); Median rent: $175 per month (2000); Median age of housing: 60+ years (2000).
Transportation: Commute to work: 88.6% car, 0.0% public transportation, 4.5% walk, 6.8% work from home (2000); Travel time to work: 41.5% less than 15 minutes, 39.0% 15 to 30 minutes, 9.8% 30 to 45 minutes, 2.4% 45 to 60 minutes, 7.3% 60 minutes or more (2000)

ORTONVILLE (city). Covers a land area of 3.394 square miles and a water area of 0.051 square miles. Located at 45.30° N. Lat.; 96.44° W. Long. Elevation is 984 feet.
History: Ortonville was named for C.K. Orton, who settled here in 1872 and laid out the town in 1873 around his trading post. Ortonville flourished as a western outpost, with grain and other farm produce shipped down the Big Stone Lake to the town. Early industries included the quarrying of ruby-red granite, and the Big Stone Canning Company which processed corn.
Population: 2,158 (2000); Race: 98.2% White, 0.1% Black, 0.0% Asian, 0.3% American Indian and Alaska Native, 0.1% Hispanic of any race, 0.9% two or more races (2000); Density: 635.8 persons per square mile (2000); Age: 24.2% under 18, 25.9% over 64 (2000); Marriage status: 21.2% never married, 62.4% now married, 10.3% widowed, 6.1% divorced (2000); Foreign born: 0.6% (2000); Ancestry (includes multiple ancestries): 48.5% German, 26.6% Norwegian, 11.5% Swedish, 11.0% Irish, 4.2% English (2000).
Economy: Single-family building permits issued: 5 (2001) / 5 (2000); Multi-family building permits issued: 0 (2001) / 0 (2000); Employment by occupation: 10.2% management, 19.7% professional, 21.2% services, 21.2% sales, 0.8% farming, 11.1% construction, 15.7% production (2000).
Income: Per capita income: $17,132 (2000); Median household income: $30,614 (2000); Poverty rate: 9.2% (2000).
Taxes: Total city taxes per capita: $179 (1997); City property taxes per capita: $165 (1997).
Education: High school graduation rate: 77.3% (2000); College graduation rate: 14.2% (2000).

School District(s)

Ortonville (PK-12)
2000 Enrollment: 683 320-839-6181

Housing: Homeownership rate: 81.5% (2000); Median home value: $45,000 (2000); Median rent: $188 per month (2000); Median age of housing: 48 years (2000).
Hospitals: Ortonville Area Health Services (105 beds)
Safety: Violent crime rate: 13.8 per 10,000 population; Property crime rate: 133.0 per 10,000 population (2001).
Newspapers: The Ortonville Independent (1 x week)
Transportation: Commute to work: 87.3% car, 1.2% public transportation, 7.0% walk, 3.7% work from home (2000); Travel time to work: 78.9% less than 15 minutes, 11.1% 15 to 30 minutes, 6.8% 30 to 45 minutes, 0.0% 45 to 60 minutes, 3.1% 60 minutes or more (2000)

ORTONVILLE (township). Covers a land area of 17.445 square miles and a water area of 1.146 square miles. Located at 45.30° N. Lat.; 96.44° W. Long. Elevation is 984 feet.
History: Settled 1872, laid out 1873.
Population: 2,287 (2000); Race: 98.3% White, 0.1% Black, 0.0% Asian, 0.3% American Indian and Alaska Native, 0.1% Hispanic of any race, 0.9% two or more races (2000); Density: 131.1 persons per square mile (2000); Age: 23.8% under 18, 26.7% over 64 (2000); Marriage status: 21.2% never married, 62.7% now married, 9.9% widowed, 6.2% divorced (2000); Foreign born: 0.6% (2000); Ancestry (includes multiple ancestries): 47.8% German, 25.6% Norwegian, 11.3% Swedish, 10.4% Irish, 4.4% English (2000).
Economy: Manufacturing: fertilizer, soft drinks, printing and publishing. Granite quarries nearby. Employment by occupation: 10.8% management, 19.3% professional, 21.4% services, 20.9% sales, 0.7% farming, 10.7% construction, 16.1% production (2000).
Income: Per capita income: $16,873 (2000); Median household income: $30,000 (2000); Poverty rate: 9.3% (2000).
Taxes: Total city taxes per capita: $5 (1997); City property taxes per capita: $5 (1997).
Education: High school graduation rate: 76.6% (2000); College graduation rate: 13.5% (2000).
Housing: Homeownership rate: 82.5% (2000); Median home value: $45,600 (2000); Median rent: $188 per month (2000); Median age of housing: 48 years (2000).
Transportation: Commute to work: 87.0% car, 1.2% public transportation, 7.3% walk, 3.8% work from home (2000); Travel time to work: 78.6% less than 15 minutes, 10.8% 15 to 30 minutes, 7.1% 30 to 45 minutes, 0.0% 45 to 60 minutes, 3.5% 60 minutes or more (2000)

OTREY (township). Covers a land area of 34.086 square miles and a water area of 3.055 square miles. Located at 45.36° N. Lat.; 96.31° W. Long.
Population: 104 (2000); Race: 100.0% White, 0.0% Black, 0.0% Asian, 0.0% American Indian and Alaska Native, 0.0% Hispanic of any race, 0.0% two or more races (2000); Density: 3.1 persons per square mile (2000); Age: 29.0% under 18, 27.1% over 64 (2000); Marriage status: 25.6% never married, 67.4% now married, 2.3% widowed, 4.7% divorced (2000); Foreign born: 1.9% (2000); Ancestry (includes multiple ancestries): 57.0% German, 42.1% Norwegian, 12.1% Swedish, 9.3% French (except Basque), 7.5% Irish (2000).
Economy: Employment by occupation: 45.6% management, 10.5% professional, 21.1% services, 8.8% sales, 0.0% farming, 0.0% construction, 14.0% production (2000).
Income: Per capita income: $11,589 (2000); Median household income: $32,143 (2000); Poverty rate: 3.7% (2000).
Taxes: Total city taxes per capita: $72 (1997); City property taxes per capita: $72 (1997).
Education: High school graduation rate: 91.5% (2000); College graduation rate: 5.6% (2000).

Housing: Homeownership rate: 86.5% (2000); Median home value: $65,000 (2000); Median age of housing: 60+ years (2000).
Transportation: Commute to work: 61.8% car, 0.0% public transportation, 7.3% walk, 27.3% work from home (2000); Travel time to work: 27.5% less than 15 minutes, 47.5% 15 to 30 minutes, 12.5% 30 to 45 minutes, 0.0% 45 to 60 minutes, 12.5% 60 minutes or more (2000)

PRIOR (township). Covers a land area of 44.515 square miles and a water area of 3.387 square miles. Located at 45.44° N. Lat.; 96.54° W. Long.
Population: 223 (2000); Race: 100.0% White, 0.0% Black, 0.0% Asian, 0.0% American Indian and Alaska Native, 0.0% Hispanic of any race, 0.0% two or more races (2000); Density: 5.0 persons per square mile (2000); Age: 26.5% under 18, 15.0% over 64 (2000); Marriage status: 25.6% never married, 64.4% now married, 4.4% widowed, 5.6% divorced (2000); Foreign born: 0.0% (2000); Ancestry (includes multiple ancestries): 42.0% German, 16.0% Norwegian, 15.0% United States or American, 9.5% Swedish, 5.0% Dutch (2000).
Economy: Employment by occupation: 29.5% management, 3.8% professional, 19.2% services, 19.2% sales, 3.8% farming, 11.5% construction, 12.8% production (2000).
Income: Per capita income: $11,741 (2000); Median household income: $31,667 (2000); Poverty rate: 21.5% (2000).
Taxes: Total city taxes per capita: $165 (1997); City property taxes per capita: $165 (1997).
Education: High school graduation rate: 84.3% (2000); College graduation rate: 6.7% (2000).
Housing: Homeownership rate: 87.7% (2000); Median home value: $80,000 (2000); Median age of housing: 45 years (2000).
Transportation: Commute to work: 70.5% car, 0.0% public transportation, 9.0% walk, 20.5% work from home (2000); Travel time to work: 50.0% less than 15 minutes, 25.8% 15 to 30 minutes, 21.0% 30 to 45 minutes, 0.0% 45 to 60 minutes, 3.2% 60 minutes or more (2000)

TOQUA (township). Covers a land area of 33.762 square miles and a water area of 1.348 square miles. Located at 45.55° N. Lat.; 96.57° W. Long.
Population: 87 (2000); Race: 100.0% White, 0.0% Black, 0.0% Asian, 0.0% American Indian and Alaska Native, 0.0% Hispanic of any race, 0.0% two or more races (2000); Density: 2.6 persons per square mile (2000); Age: 41.0% under 18, 15.4% over 64 (2000); Marriage status: 19.2% never married, 61.5% now married, 19.2% widowed, 0.0% divorced (2000); Foreign born: 0.0% (2000); Ancestry (includes multiple ancestries): 39.7% German, 21.8% Irish, 14.1% Other groups, 12.8% Swedish, 11.5% Polish (2000).
Economy: Employment by occupation: 56.3% management, 12.5% professional, 15.6% services, 3.1% sales, 6.3% farming, 0.0% construction, 6.3% production (2000).
Income: Per capita income: $16,155 (2000); Median household income: $38,333 (2000); Poverty rate: 17.9% (2000).
Taxes: Total city taxes per capita: $182 (1997); City property taxes per capita: $182 (1997).
Education: High school graduation rate: 91.1% (2000); College graduation rate: 0.0% (2000).
Housing: Homeownership rate: 92.3% (2000); Median home value: $21,300 (2000); Median age of housing: 60+ years (2000).
Transportation: Commute to work: 53.3% car, 0.0% public transportation, 40.0% walk, 6.7% work from home (2000); Travel time to work: 60.7% less than 15 minutes, 39.3% 15 to 30 minutes, 0.0% 30 to 45 minutes, 0.0% 45 to 60 minutes, 0.0% 60 minutes or more (2000)

Blue Earth County

Located in southern Minnesota; bounded on the north by the Minnesota River. Covers a land area of 752.40 square miles, a water area of 13.50 square miles, and is located in the Central Time Zone. The county government was organized in 1853. County seat is Mankato.
Population: 55,941 (2000); Race: 95.3% White, 1.4% Black, 1.6% Asian, 0.2% American Indian and Alaska Native, 1.5% Hispanic of any race, 1.0% two or more races (2000); Density: 74.4 persons per square mile (2000); Age: 21.3% under 18, 12.1% over 64 (2000).
Religion: Five largest groups: 21.7% Catholic Church, 16.8% Evangelical Lutheran Church in America, 9.0% Lutheran Church—Missouri Synod, 3.3% The United Methodist Church, 2.8% Presbyterian Church (U.S.A.) (2000).
Economy: Unemployment rate: 2.5% (11/2002); Total civilian labor force: 35,472 (11/2002); Leading industries: 20.8% retail trade; 17.8% health care and social assistance; 16.2% manufacturing (2000); Companies that employ more than 1,000 persons: 1 (2000); Companies that employ more than 100 persons: 63 (2000); Farms: 1,037 totaling 403,362 acres (1997); Minority business ownership rate: 0.0% (1997); Women business ownership rate: 22.3% (1997); Retail sales per capita: $13,868 (1997). Single-family building permits issued: 313 (2001) / 212 (2000); Multi-family building permits issued: 120 (2001) / 119 (2000).
Income: Per capita income: $18,712 (2000); Median household income: $38,940 (2000); Poverty rate: 12.9% (2000); Bankruptcy rate: 2.69% (2001).
Taxes: Total county taxes per capita: $271 (2000); County property taxes per capita: $261 (2000).
Education: High school graduation rate: 87.7% (2000); College graduation rate: 26.6% (2000).
Housing: Homeownership rate: 66.4% (2000); Median home value: $98,200 (2000); Median rent: $441 per month (2000); Median age of housing: 37 years (2000).
Health: Birth rate: 116.4 per 10,000 population (1998); Age adjusted death rate: 74.7 per 10,000 population (1999); Age adjusted cancer mortality rate: 168.0 deaths per 100,000 population (1999). Number of physicians: 19.3 per 10,000 population (1999); Number of hospital beds: 28.1 per 10,000 population (1999).
Elections: 2000 Presidential election results: 45.0% Gore, 47.2% Bush, 6.4% Nader, 0.9% Buchanan
National and State Parks: Gage State Wildlife Management Area; Hobza State Wildlife Management Area; Lost Marsh State Wildlife Management Area; Minneopa State Park; Pick State Wildlife Management Area
Additional Information Contacts
Blue Earth County Government Offices 507-389-8100
Lake Crystal Chamber of Commerce 507-726-6088
Mankato Area Chamber of Commerce 507-345-4519
Mapleton Area Chamber of Commerce 507-524-4756
Realtor Association of Southern Minnesota. 507-345-6018

Blue Earth County Communities

AMBOY (city). Covers a land area of 0.313 square miles and a water area of 0 square miles. Located at 43.88° N. Lat.; 94.15° W. Long. Elevation is 1,044 feet.
Population: 575 (2000); Race: 99.7% White, 0.0% Black, 0.0% Asian, 0.0% American Indian and Alaska Native, 0.0% Hispanic of any race, 0.3% two or more races (2000); Density: 1,838.9 persons per square mile (2000); Age: 27.0% under 18, 19.9% over 64 (2000); Marriage status: 22.3% never married, 62.6% now married, 8.4% widowed, 6.7% divorced (2000); Foreign born: 0.0% (2000); Ancestry (includes multiple ancestries): 58.5% German, 12.1% Norwegian, 9.4% English, 6.0% Dutch, 5.6% French (except Basque) (2000).
Economy: Agriculture: grain, soybeans, alfalfa; livestock. Manufactures fertilizers, horse stalls. Single-family building permits issued: 0 (2001) / 1 (2000); Multi-family building permits issued: 0 (2001) / 0 (2000); Employment by occupation: 12.7% management, 12.7% professional, 12.7% services, 22.8% sales, 4.7% farming, 13.8% construction, 20.7% production (2000).
Income: Per capita income: $15,658 (2000); Median household income: $35,595 (2000); Poverty rate: 13.0% (2000).
Taxes: Total city taxes per capita: $165 (1997); City property taxes per capita: $159 (1997).
Education: High school graduation rate: 84.4% (2000); College graduation rate: 11.3% (2000).
Housing: Homeownership rate: 85.5% (2000); Median home value: $60,100 (2000); Median rent: $213 per month (2000); Median age of housing: 56 years (2000).
Transportation: Commute to work: 90.0% car, 0.0% public transportation, 7.7% walk, 2.2% work from home (2000); Travel time to work: 50.2% less than 15 minutes, 13.2% 15 to 30 minutes, 29.1% 30 to 45 minutes, 3.0% 45 to 60 minutes, 4.5% 60 minutes or more (2000)

BEAUFORD (township). Covers a land area of 35.554 square miles and a water area of 0.315 square miles. Located at 43.99° N. Lat.; 93.93° W. Long. Elevation is 1,011 feet.
Population: 442 (2000); Race: 98.7% White, 0.0% Black, 0.0% Asian, 0.0% American Indian and Alaska Native, 0.6% Hispanic of any race, 1.3% two or more races (2000); Density: 12.4 persons per square mile (2000); Age: 31.0% under 18, 11.9% over 64 (2000); Marriage status: 21.0% never married, 65.3% now married, 9.9% widowed, 3.8% divorced (2000); Foreign born: 0.8% (2000); Ancestry (includes multiple ancestries): 61.6% German, 9.3% Norwegian, 9.3% Irish, 7.2% Swedish, 3.2% Danish (2000).

Economy: Employment by occupation: 32.1% management, 12.5% professional, 13.8% services, 22.1% sales, 3.3% farming, 5.8% construction, 10.4% production (2000).
Income: Per capita income: $18,029 (2000); Median household income: $43,542 (2000); Poverty rate: 5.5% (2000).
Taxes: Total city taxes per capita: $100 (1997); City property taxes per capita: $100 (1997).
Education: High school graduation rate: 81.7% (2000); College graduation rate: 18.7% (2000).
Housing: Homeownership rate: 89.9% (2000); Median home value: $99,400 (2000); Median rent: $350 per month (2000); Median age of housing: 60+ years (2000).
Transportation: Commute to work: 80.0% car, 0.0% public transportation, 4.6% walk, 15.4% work from home (2000); Travel time to work: 23.6% less than 15 minutes, 46.3% 15 to 30 minutes, 20.7% 30 to 45 minutes, 1.5% 45 to 60 minutes, 7.9% 60 minutes or more (2000)

BUTTERNUT VALLEY (township). Covers a land area of 35.388 square miles and a water area of 0.647 square miles. Located at 44.15° N. Lat.; 94.31° W. Long.
Population: 382 (2000); Race: 96.1% White, 3.9% Black, 0.0% Asian, 0.0% American Indian and Alaska Native, 0.0% Hispanic of any race, 0.0% two or more races (2000); Density: 10.8 persons per square mile (2000); Age: 25.7% under 18, 14.6% over 64 (2000); Marriage status: 23.4% never married, 68.5% now married, 3.7% widowed, 4.4% divorced (2000); Foreign born: 0.0% (2000); Ancestry (includes multiple ancestries): 48.9% German, 21.0% Norwegian, 10.5% Welsh, 8.3% Irish, 7.5% English (2000).
Economy: Employment by occupation: 22.0% management, 11.5% professional, 16.8% services, 15.2% sales, 0.0% farming, 7.3% construction, 27.2% production (2000).
Income: Per capita income: $16,797 (2000); Median household income: $41,136 (2000); Poverty rate: 8.6% (2000).
Taxes: Total city taxes per capita: $63 (1997); City property taxes per capita: $63 (1997).
Education: High school graduation rate: 88.6% (2000); College graduation rate: 15.9% (2000).
Housing: Homeownership rate: 84.0% (2000); Median home value: $84,600 (2000); Median rent: $331 per month (2000); Median age of housing: 60+ years (2000).
Transportation: Commute to work: 75.7% car, 0.0% public transportation, 1.7% walk, 22.7% work from home (2000); Travel time to work: 23.6% less than 15 minutes, 50.7% 15 to 30 minutes, 17.1% 30 to 45 minutes, 4.3% 45 to 60 minutes, 4.3% 60 minutes or more (2000)

CAMBRIA (township). Covers a land area of 19.659 square miles and a water area of 0.040 square miles. Located at 44.22° N. Lat.; 94.32° W. Long.
Population: 271 (2000); Race: 100.0% White, 0.0% Black, 0.0% Asian, 0.0% American Indian and Alaska Native, 0.0% Hispanic of any race, 0.0% two or more races (2000); Density: 13.8 persons per square mile (2000); Age: 26.1% under 18, 11.7% over 64 (2000); Marriage status: 22.4% never married, 65.2% now married, 7.6% widowed, 4.8% divorced (2000); Foreign born: 1.6% (2000); Ancestry (includes multiple ancestries): 54.4% German, 13.7% Welsh, 12.4% Norwegian, 9.1% United States or American, 7.2% Irish (2000).
Economy: Employment by occupation: 16.9% management, 12.2% professional, 11.0% services, 20.9% sales, 1.7% farming, 8.1% construction, 29.1% production (2000).
Income: Per capita income: $21,900 (2000); Median household income: $40,625 (2000); Poverty rate: 1.3% (2000).
Taxes: Total city taxes per capita: $84 (1997); City property taxes per capita: $84 (1997).
Education: High school graduation rate: 87.0% (2000); College graduation rate: 15.0% (2000).
Housing: Homeownership rate: 89.5% (2000); Median home value: $72,800 (2000); Median rent: $135 per month (2000); Median age of housing: 44 years (2000).
Transportation: Commute to work: 83.7% car, 0.0% public transportation, 0.0% walk, 16.3% work from home (2000); Travel time to work: 20.8% less than 15 minutes, 54.9% 15 to 30 minutes, 15.3% 30 to 45 minutes, 3.5% 45 to 60 minutes, 5.6% 60 minutes or more (2000)

CERESCO (township). Covers a land area of 35.829 square miles and a water area of 0.083 square miles. Located at 43.96° N. Lat.; 94.31° W. Long.
Population: 255 (2000); Race: 99.1% White, 0.0% Black, 0.0% Asian, 0.0% American Indian and Alaska Native, 0.0% Hispanic of any race, 0.9% two or more races (2000); Density: 7.1 persons per square mile (2000); Age: 28.9% under 18, 20.2% over 64 (2000); Marriage status: 15.3% never married, 74.7% now married, 7.6% widowed, 2.4% divorced (2000); Foreign born: 1.8% (2000); Ancestry (includes multiple ancestries): 64.0% German, 13.2% Irish, 9.2% English, 7.0% Norwegian, 7.0% Swedish (2000).
Economy: Employment by occupation: 23.5% management, 23.5% professional, 11.8% services, 13.7% sales, 3.9% farming, 8.8% construction, 14.7% production (2000).
Income: Per capita income: $15,412 (2000); Median household income: $38,750 (2000); Poverty rate: 7.9% (2000).
Taxes: Total city taxes per capita: $67 (1997); City property taxes per capita: $67 (1997).
Education: High school graduation rate: 75.0% (2000); College graduation rate: 21.5% (2000).
Housing: Homeownership rate: 78.0% (2000); Median home value: $75,000 (2000); Median rent: $325 per month (2000); Median age of housing: 60+ years (2000).
Transportation: Commute to work: 78.0% car, 0.0% public transportation, 3.0% walk, 16.0% work from home (2000); Travel time to work: 29.8% less than 15 minutes, 48.8% 15 to 30 minutes, 15.5% 30 to 45 minutes, 3.6% 45 to 60 minutes, 2.4% 60 minutes or more (2000)

DANVILLE (township). Covers a land area of 35.836 square miles and a water area of 0.262 square miles. Located at 43.89° N. Lat.; 93.84° W. Long.
Population: 262 (2000); Race: 100.0% White, 0.0% Black, 0.0% Asian, 0.0% American Indian and Alaska Native, 0.0% Hispanic of any race, 0.0% two or more races (2000); Density: 7.3 persons per square mile (2000); Age: 26.2% under 18, 20.2% over 64 (2000); Marriage status: 22.4% never married, 66.2% now married, 9.5% widowed, 2.0% divorced (2000); Foreign born: 0.4% (2000); Ancestry (includes multiple ancestries): 71.4% German, 13.9% Norwegian, 9.1% Polish, 8.3% Irish, 5.2% Dutch (2000).
Economy: Employment by occupation: 34.6% management, 3.0% professional, 9.8% services, 24.8% sales, 3.0% farming, 12.8% construction, 12.0% production (2000).
Income: Per capita income: $21,527 (2000); Median household income: $41,250 (2000); Poverty rate: 12.3% (2000).
Taxes: Total city taxes per capita: $236 (1997); City property taxes per capita: $236 (1997).
Education: High school graduation rate: 80.0% (2000); College graduation rate: 12.9% (2000).
Housing: Homeownership rate: 95.8% (2000); Median home value: $98,000 (2000); Median rent: $325 per month (2000); Median age of housing: 50 years (2000).
Transportation: Commute to work: 75.9% car, 0.0% public transportation, 0.0% walk, 24.1% work from home (2000); Travel time to work: 51.5% less than 15 minutes, 21.8% 15 to 30 minutes, 26.7% 30 to 45 minutes, 0.0% 45 to 60 minutes, 0.0% 60 minutes or more (2000)

DECORIA (township). Covers a land area of 35.809 square miles and a water area of 0 square miles. Located at 44.07° N. Lat.; 93.96° W. Long.
Population: 922 (2000); Race: 99.8% White, 0.0% Black, 0.0% Asian, 0.0% American Indian and Alaska Native, 1.0% Hispanic of any race, 0.2% two or more races (2000); Density: 25.7 persons per square mile (2000); Age: 28.2% under 18, 9.4% over 64 (2000); Marriage status: 19.5% never married, 71.1% now married, 4.5% widowed, 4.9% divorced (2000); Foreign born: 0.3% (2000); Ancestry (includes multiple ancestries): 60.0% German, 16.1% Norwegian, 8.4% Irish, 6.8% Swedish, 6.6% English (2000).
Economy: Employment by occupation: 16.1% management, 12.2% professional, 19.3% services, 26.3% sales, 0.4% farming, 8.0% construction, 17.8% production (2000).
Income: Per capita income: $20,996 (2000); Median household income: $52,639 (2000); Poverty rate: 2.6% (2000).
Taxes: Total city taxes per capita: $77 (1997); City property taxes per capita: $77 (1997).
Education: High school graduation rate: 90.2% (2000); College graduation rate: 26.1% (2000).
Housing: Homeownership rate: 89.5% (2000); Median home value: $122,500 (2000); Median rent: $435 per month (2000); Median age of housing: 33 years (2000).
Transportation: Commute to work: 92.4% car, 0.0% public transportation, 1.3% walk, 5.9% work from home (2000); Travel time to work: 27.0% less than 15 minutes, 62.9% 15 to 30 minutes, 5.2% 30 to 45 minutes, 2.0% 45 to 60 minutes, 2.8% 60 minutes or more (2000)

EAGLE LAKE (city). Covers a land area of 1.203 square miles and a water area of 0 square miles. Located at 44.16° N. Lat.; 93.88° W. Long. Elevation is 1,014 feet.

Population: 1,787 (2000); Race: 95.5% White, 1.1% Black, 1.5% Asian, 0.0% American Indian and Alaska Native, 1.4% Hispanic of any race, 1.0% two or more races (2000); Density: 1,485.0 persons per square mile (2000); Age: 31.3% under 18, 5.1% over 64 (2000); Marriage status: 26.6% never married, 62.6% now married, 2.4% widowed, 8.4% divorced (2000); Foreign born: 3.2% (2000); Ancestry (includes multiple ancestries): 54.6% German, 19.5% Norwegian, 8.6% Irish, 5.2% Other groups, 5.2% Swedish (2000).
Economy: Agricultural area: corn, oats, alfalfa, soybeans; livestock. Manufacturing: livestock equipment. Single-family building permits issued: 16 (2001) / 25 (2000); Multi-family building permits issued: 0 (2001) / 4 (2000); Employment by occupation: 10.9% management, 14.8% professional, 12.3% services, 32.3% sales, 0.6% farming, 10.7% construction, 18.3% production (2000).
Income: Per capita income: $17,574 (2000); Median household income: $46,413 (2000); Poverty rate: 6.9% (2000).
Taxes: Total city taxes per capita: $82 (1997); City property taxes per capita: $71 (1997).
Education: High school graduation rate: 90.5% (2000); College graduation rate: 26.3% (2000).
Housing: Homeownership rate: 84.2% (2000); Median home value: $110,200 (2000); Median rent: $402 per month (2000); Median age of housing: 23 years (2000).
Transportation: Commute to work: 93.8% car, 0.2% public transportation, 1.8% walk, 3.9% work from home (2000); Travel time to work: 42.5% less than 15 minutes, 49.0% 15 to 30 minutes, 4.6% 30 to 45 minutes, 1.0% 45 to 60 minutes, 2.9% 60 minutes or more (2000)

GARDEN CITY (township). Covers a land area of 33.093 square miles and a water area of 1.822 square miles. Located at 44.06° N. Lat.; 94.19° W. Long. Elevation is 963 feet.
Population: 700 (2000); Race: 98.5% White, 0.0% Black, 0.0% Asian, 0.0% American Indian and Alaska Native, 0.8% Hispanic of any race, 1.2% two or more races (2000); Density: 21.2 persons per square mile (2000); Age: 26.5% under 18, 12.0% over 64 (2000); Marriage status: 24.4% never married, 67.4% now married, 3.4% widowed, 4.9% divorced (2000); Foreign born: 0.7% (2000); Ancestry (includes multiple ancestries): 53.5% German, 12.6% Norwegian, 8.4% Irish, 5.5% English, 4.7% Swedish (2000).
Economy: Employment by occupation: 13.2% management, 12.5% professional, 12.7% services, 27.4% sales, 1.0% farming, 12.5% construction, 20.8% production (2000).
Income: Per capita income: $20,191 (2000); Median household income: $51,750 (2000); Poverty rate: 2.2% (2000).
Taxes: Total city taxes per capita: $58 (1997); City property taxes per capita: $58 (1997).
Education: High school graduation rate: 90.8% (2000); College graduation rate: 20.2% (2000).
Housing: Homeownership rate: 90.5% (2000); Median home value: $106,500 (2000); Median rent: $450 per month (2000); Median age of housing: 42 years (2000).
Transportation: Commute to work: 90.7% car, 0.0% public transportation, 3.4% walk, 5.9% work from home (2000); Travel time to work: 26.0% less than 15 minutes, 56.6% 15 to 30 minutes, 12.7% 30 to 45 minutes, 1.6% 45 to 60 minutes, 3.1% 60 minutes or more (2000)

GOOD THUNDER (city). Covers a land area of 0.626 square miles and a water area of 0 square miles. Located at 44.00° N. Lat.; 94.06° W. Long. Elevation is 979 feet.
Population: 592 (2000); Race: 96.2% White, 0.0% Black, 0.0% Asian, 0.0% American Indian and Alaska Native, 0.0% Hispanic of any race, 3.8% two or more races (2000); Density: 945.7 persons per square mile (2000); Age: 34.5% under 18, 9.4% over 64 (2000); Marriage status: 19.0% never married, 65.9% now married, 6.2% widowed, 9.0% divorced (2000); Foreign born: 0.3% (2000); Ancestry (includes multiple ancestries): 57.4% German, 14.5% Irish, 10.1% Norwegian, 7.3% English, 6.6% Swedish (2000).
Economy: Grain, alfalfa, soybeans; hogs, cattle, sheep. Manufacturing: meat processing. Single-family building permits issued: 2 (2001) / 1 (2000); Multi-family building permits issued: 0 (2001) / 0 (2000); Employment by occupation: 9.5% management, 8.6% professional, 8.2% services, 23.7% sales, 2.0% farming, 13.5% construction, 34.5% production (2000).
Income: Per capita income: $14,524 (2000); Median household income: $42,500 (2000); Poverty rate: 13.0% (2000).
Taxes: Total city taxes per capita: $201 (1997); City property taxes per capita: $197 (1997).
Education: High school graduation rate: 89.4% (2000); College graduation rate: 8.2% (2000).
Housing: Homeownership rate: 81.5% (2000); Median home value: $71,500 (2000); Median rent: $378 per month (2000); Median age of housing: 60+ years (2000).
Transportation: Commute to work: 90.0% car, 0.0% public transportation, 4.3% walk, 5.7% work from home (2000); Travel time to work: 18.7% less than 15 minutes, 56.2% 15 to 30 minutes, 17.0% 30 to 45 minutes, 2.1% 45 to 60 minutes, 6.0% 60 minutes or more (2000)

JAMESTOWN (township). Covers a land area of 15.337 square miles and a water area of 2.202 square miles. Located at 44.22° N. Lat.; 93.82° W. Long.
Population: 628 (2000); Race: 100.0% White, 0.0% Black, 0.0% Asian, 0.0% American Indian and Alaska Native, 1.0% Hispanic of any race, 0.0% two or more races (2000); Density: 40.9 persons per square mile (2000); Age: 27.0% under 18, 10.1% over 64 (2000); Marriage status: 24.2% never married, 67.7% now married, 5.2% widowed, 2.9% divorced (2000); Foreign born: 0.5% (2000); Ancestry (includes multiple ancestries): 57.4% German, 17.7% Irish, 15.3% Norwegian, 5.8% Swedish, 5.8% French (except Basque) (2000).
Economy: Employment by occupation: 14.0% management, 11.8% professional, 6.5% services, 32.8% sales, 1.1% farming, 17.5% construction, 16.4% production (2000).
Income: Per capita income: $26,014 (2000); Median household income: $56,875 (2000); Poverty rate: 3.6% (2000).
Taxes: Total city taxes per capita: $81 (1997); City property taxes per capita: $81 (1997).
Education: High school graduation rate: 94.4% (2000); College graduation rate: 21.5% (2000).
Housing: Homeownership rate: 90.9% (2000); Median home value: $149,600 (2000); Median rent: $325 per month (2000); Median age of housing: 27 years (2000).
Transportation: Commute to work: 91.6% car, 0.5% public transportation, 0.0% walk, 6.5% work from home (2000); Travel time to work: 14.5% less than 15 minutes, 69.6% 15 to 30 minutes, 10.1% 30 to 45 minutes, 1.7% 45 to 60 minutes, 4.1% 60 minutes or more (2000)

JUDSON (township). Covers a land area of 36.629 square miles and a water area of 0.595 square miles. Located at 44.15° N. Lat.; 94.19° W. Long. Elevation is 803 feet.
Population: 591 (2000); Race: 99.3% White, 0.0% Black, 0.0% Asian, 0.0% American Indian and Alaska Native, 0.0% Hispanic of any race, 0.7% two or more races (2000); Density: 16.1 persons per square mile (2000); Age: 23.8% under 18, 16.7% over 64 (2000); Marriage status: 24.0% never married, 61.6% now married, 5.6% widowed, 8.8% divorced (2000); Foreign born: 0.5% (2000); Ancestry (includes multiple ancestries): 47.8% German, 17.2% Norwegian, 12.7% Welsh, 12.2% Swedish, 6.9% English (2000).
Economy: Employment by occupation: 15.9% management, 10.0% professional, 12.6% services, 24.4% sales, 2.1% farming, 10.6% construction, 24.4% production (2000).
Income: Per capita income: $19,917 (2000); Median household income: $46,071 (2000); Poverty rate: 3.8% (2000).
Taxes: Total city taxes per capita: $73 (1997); City property taxes per capita: $73 (1997).
Education: High school graduation rate: 88.9% (2000); College graduation rate: 14.6% (2000).
Housing: Homeownership rate: 88.0% (2000); Median home value: $92,300 (2000); Median rent: $334 per month (2000); Median age of housing: 48 years (2000).
Transportation: Commute to work: 88.1% car, 0.0% public transportation, 2.1% walk, 9.9% work from home (2000); Travel time to work: 22.8% less than 15 minutes, 66.6% 15 to 30 minutes, 7.9% 30 to 45 minutes, 0.3% 45 to 60 minutes, 2.3% 60 minutes or more (2000)

LAKE CRYSTAL (city). Covers a land area of 1.778 square miles and a water area of 0 square miles. Located at 44.10° N. Lat.; 94.21° W. Long. Elevation is 1,000 feet.
History: Plotted 1857; incorporated as village 1870; as city 1930.
Population: 2,420 (2000); Race: 99.2% White, 0.0% Black, 0.2% Asian, 0.4% American Indian and Alaska Native, 0.2% Hispanic of any race, 0.0% two or more races (2000); Density: 1,361.3 persons per square mile (2000); Age: 27.0% under 18, 17.9% over 64 (2000); Marriage status: 22.9% never married, 60.5% now married, 8.8% widowed, 7.8% divorced (2000); Foreign born: 0.5% (2000); Ancestry (includes multiple ancestries): 45.3% German, 18.6% Norwegian, 9.4% Irish, 7.6% English, 6.3% Swedish (2000).
Economy: Resort. Agricultural trading point: corn, oats, soybeans, peas, hogs; sheep, cattle. Manufacturing: fertilizers, dump bodies, metal

fabricating. Single-family building permits issued: 17 (2001) / 17 (2000); Multi-family building permits issued: 0 (2001) / 0 (2000); Employment by occupation: 10.2% management, 14.7% professional, 14.1% services, 26.3% sales, 0.2% farming, 10.7% construction, 23.8% production (2000).
Income: Per capita income: $17,454 (2000); Median household income: $39,912 (2000); Poverty rate: 5.4% (2000).
Taxes: Total city taxes per capita: $165 (1997); City property taxes per capita: $136 (1997).
Education: High school graduation rate: 83.1% (2000); College graduation rate: 18.0% (2000).

School District(s)

Lake Crystal-Wellcome Memorial (PK-12)
2000 Enrollment: 1,004 507-726-2323

Housing: Homeownership rate: 79.8% (2000); Median home value: $83,300 (2000); Median rent: $329 per month (2000); Median age of housing: 39 years (2000).
Newspapers: Tribune (1 x week)
Transportation: Commute to work: 93.4% car, 0.2% public transportation, 4.0% walk, 1.8% work from home (2000); Travel time to work: 32.4% less than 15 minutes, 51.8% 15 to 30 minutes, 7.7% 30 to 45 minutes, 2.2% 45 to 60 minutes, 5.9% 60 minutes or more (2000)

Additional Information Contacts

Lake Crystal Chamber of Commerce 507-726-6088

LE RAY (township). Covers a land area of 32.543 square miles and a water area of 2.519 square miles. Located at 44.15° N. Lat.; 93.82° W. Long.
Population: 846 (2000); Race: 97.9% White, 0.8% Black, 0.8% Asian, 0.0% American Indian and Alaska Native, 0.3% Hispanic of any race, 0.1% two or more races (2000); Density: 26.0 persons per square mile (2000); Age: 29.3% under 18, 10.6% over 64 (2000); Marriage status: 28.1% never married, 62.9% now married, 6.1% widowed, 3.0% divorced (2000); Foreign born: 1.4% (2000); Ancestry (includes multiple ancestries): 58.8% German, 10.6% Irish, 8.4% Norwegian, 6.2% Swedish, 4.7% United States or American (2000).
Economy: Employment by occupation: 17.8% management, 12.2% professional, 11.6% services, 24.7% sales, 0.4% farming, 15.3% construction, 18.0% production (2000).
Income: Per capita income: $19,848 (2000); Median household income: $52,188 (2000); Poverty rate: 3.6% (2000).
Taxes: Total city taxes per capita: $122 (1997); City property taxes per capita: $122 (1997).
Education: High school graduation rate: 88.5% (2000); College graduation rate: 21.3% (2000).
Housing: Homeownership rate: 91.2% (2000); Median home value: $124,600 (2000); Median rent: $425 per month (2000); Median age of housing: 41 years (2000).
Transportation: Commute to work: 87.7% car, 0.0% public transportation, 2.2% walk, 9.6% work from home (2000); Travel time to work: 26.6% less than 15 minutes, 57.3% 15 to 30 minutes, 12.2% 30 to 45 minutes, 1.2% 45 to 60 minutes, 2.7% 60 minutes or more (2000)

LIME (township). Covers a land area of 16.002 square miles and a water area of 1.029 square miles. Located at 44.22° N. Lat.; 93.96° W. Long.
Population: 1,314 (2000); Race: 98.7% White, 0.0% Black, 0.3% Asian, 0.8% American Indian and Alaska Native, 1.0% Hispanic of any race, 0.2% two or more races (2000); Density: 82.1 persons per square mile (2000); Age: 23.1% under 18, 9.0% over 64 (2000); Marriage status: 24.1% never married, 61.7% now married, 4.2% widowed, 10.1% divorced (2000); Foreign born: 0.8% (2000); Ancestry (includes multiple ancestries): 59.2% German, 13.3% Norwegian, 12.7% Irish, 7.5% English, 6.5% Swedish (2000).
Economy: Employment by occupation: 14.0% management, 15.6% professional, 11.6% services, 26.9% sales, 0.2% farming, 9.5% construction, 22.1% production (2000).
Income: Per capita income: $26,615 (2000); Median household income: $49,412 (2000); Poverty rate: 2.1% (2000).
Taxes: Total city taxes per capita: $104 (1997); City property taxes per capita: $104 (1997).
Education: High school graduation rate: 90.8% (2000); College graduation rate: 22.0% (2000).
Housing: Homeownership rate: 90.5% (2000); Median home value: $153,600 (2000); Median rent: $321 per month (2000); Median age of housing: 24 years (2000).
Transportation: Commute to work: 92.9% car, 0.0% public transportation, 1.4% walk, 5.0% work from home (2000); Travel time to work: 64.6% less than 15 minutes, 29.9% 15 to 30 minutes, 2.5% 30 to 45 minutes, 1.2% 45 to 60 minutes, 1.8% 60 minutes or more (2000)

LINCOLN (township). Covers a land area of 35.962 square miles and a water area of 0 square miles. Located at 44.06° N. Lat.; 94.30° W. Long.
Population: 227 (2000); Race: 99.0% White, 0.0% Black, 0.0% Asian, 1.0% American Indian and Alaska Native, 1.0% Hispanic of any race, 0.0% two or more races (2000); Density: 6.3 persons per square mile (2000); Age: 24.2% under 18, 18.7% over 64 (2000); Marriage status: 14.1% never married, 74.4% now married, 9.0% widowed, 2.6% divorced (2000); Foreign born: 0.0% (2000); Ancestry (includes multiple ancestries): 48.5% German, 26.3% Norwegian, 11.1% Swedish, 11.1% English, 9.1% United States or American (2000).
Economy: Employment by occupation: 26.3% management, 14.0% professional, 11.4% services, 13.2% sales, 0.0% farming, 9.6% construction, 25.4% production (2000).
Income: Per capita income: $23,559 (2000); Median household income: $43,125 (2000); Poverty rate: 5.1% (2000).
Taxes: Total city taxes per capita: $116 (1997); City property taxes per capita: $116 (1997).
Education: High school graduation rate: 92.3% (2000); College graduation rate: 18.9% (2000).
Housing: Homeownership rate: 92.5% (2000); Median home value: $96,300 (2000); Median rent: <$100 per month (2000); Median age of housing: 51 years (2000).
Transportation: Commute to work: 82.7% car, 0.0% public transportation, 0.0% walk, 17.3% work from home (2000); Travel time to work: 14.3% less than 15 minutes, 54.9% 15 to 30 minutes, 17.6% 30 to 45 minutes, 4.4% 45 to 60 minutes, 8.8% 60 minutes or more (2000)

LYRA (township). Covers a land area of 35.386 square miles and a water area of 0.021 square miles. Located at 43.99° N. Lat.; 94.08° W. Long.
Population: 378 (2000); Race: 99.4% White, 0.0% Black, 0.0% Asian, 0.0% American Indian and Alaska Native, 3.7% Hispanic of any race, 0.6% two or more races (2000); Density: 10.7 persons per square mile (2000); Age: 25.3% under 18, 20.1% over 64 (2000); Marriage status: 18.1% never married, 72.7% now married, 7.8% widowed, 1.4% divorced (2000); Foreign born: 0.0% (2000); Ancestry (includes multiple ancestries): 69.0% German, 14.4% Irish, 10.6% Norwegian, 10.3% English, 4.3% Swedish (2000).
Economy: Employment by occupation: 21.1% management, 11.1% professional, 9.9% services, 23.4% sales, 7.6% farming, 12.9% construction, 14.0% production (2000).
Income: Per capita income: $14,795 (2000); Median household income: $34,219 (2000); Poverty rate: 8.0% (2000).
Taxes: Total city taxes per capita: $101 (1997); City property taxes per capita: $101 (1997).
Education: High school graduation rate: 82.0% (2000); College graduation rate: 9.0% (2000).
Housing: Homeownership rate: 87.8% (2000); Median home value: $96,800 (2000); Median rent: $292 per month (2000); Median age of housing: 57 years (2000).
Transportation: Commute to work: 80.7% car, 0.0% public transportation, 2.3% walk, 15.8% work from home (2000); Travel time to work: 34.0% less than 15 minutes, 39.6% 15 to 30 minutes, 18.1% 30 to 45 minutes, 2.1% 45 to 60 minutes, 6.3% 60 minutes or more (2000)

MADISON LAKE (city). Covers a land area of 0.466 square miles and a water area of 0.003 square miles. Located at 44.20° N. Lat.; 93.81° W. Long. Elevation is 1,150 feet.
Population: 837 (2000); Race: 97.8% White, 0.0% Black, 0.2% Asian, 0.0% American Indian and Alaska Native, 2.7% Hispanic of any race, 1.9% two or more races (2000); Density: 1,794.4 persons per square mile (2000); Age: 29.3% under 18, 10.0% over 64 (2000); Marriage status: 25.4% never married, 60.9% now married, 4.3% widowed, 9.3% divorced (2000); Foreign born: 2.4% (2000); Ancestry (includes multiple ancestries): 55.0% German, 16.8% Norwegian, 15.6% Irish, 6.9% Other groups, 5.5% Swedish (2000).
Economy: Grain; livestock. Light manufacturing. Single-family building permits issued: 9 (2001) / 4 (2000); Multi-family building permits issued: 2 (2001) / 4 (2000); Employment by occupation: 5.6% management, 16.2% professional, 14.0% services, 29.1% sales, 0.0% farming, 7.0% construction, 28.2% production (2000).
Income: Per capita income: $18,312 (2000); Median household income: $44,659 (2000); Poverty rate: 4.0% (2000).
Taxes: Total city taxes per capita: $209 (2000); City property taxes per capita: $173 (2000).
Education: High school graduation rate: 90.2% (2000); College graduation rate: 19.2% (2000).

Housing: Homeownership rate: 76.1% (2000); Median home value: $101,900 (2000); Median rent: $376 per month (2000); Median age of housing: 30 years (2000).
Newspapers: Lake Region Times (1 x week)
Transportation: Commute to work: 93.7% car, 0.9% public transportation, 1.1% walk, 3.4% work from home (2000); Travel time to work: 13.8% less than 15 minutes, 63.8% 15 to 30 minutes, 7.7% 30 to 45 minutes, 3.0% 45 to 60 minutes, 11.7% 60 minutes or more (2000)

MANKATO (city). Covers a land area of 15.206 square miles and a water area of 0.191 square miles. Located at 44.16° N. Lat.; 93.99° W. Long. Elevation is 785 feet.
History: Mankato was founded in 1852 by Henry Jackson, Parsons K. Johnson, and Daniel Williams, who had made the six-day trip over the prairies from St. Paul. The name of Mankato is a Sioux word for the blue earth found along the Minnesota River, which early French explorers thought held copper. Mankato developed rapidly as a frontier settlement, soon becoming a trade center for southwestern Minnesota and parts of nearby states. Limestone quarries joined the factories, which produced a diversity of products, and agriculture to form the economic base.
Population: 32,427 (2000); Race: 93.1% White, 2.2% Black, 2.5% Asian, 0.3% American Indian and Alaska Native, 1.9% Hispanic of any race, 1.3% two or more races (2000); Density: 2,132.5 persons per square mile (2000); Age: 16.8% under 18, 11.2% over 64 (2000); Marriage status: 48.4% never married, 39.3% now married, 5.1% widowed, 7.2% divorced (2000); Foreign born: 4.3% (2000); Ancestry (includes multiple ancestries): 45.7% German, 17.4% Norwegian, 11.1% Irish, 7.7% Other groups, 6.0% English (2000).
Economy: Unemployment rate: 3.1% (11/2002); Total civilian labor force: 21,653 (11/2002); Employment by occupation: 9.2% management, 20.9% professional, 19.1% services, 28.0% sales, 0.5% farming, 5.7% construction, 16.6% production (2000).
Income: Per capita income: $17,652 (2000); Median household income: $33,956 (2000); Poverty rate: 19.0% (2000).
Taxes: Total city taxes per capita: $384 (2000); City property taxes per capita: $263 (2000).
Education: High school graduation rate: 88.1% (2000); College graduation rate: 32.2% (2000).

School District(s)

Mankato (PK-12)
2000 Enrollment: 6,991 507-387-1868
Riverbend Academy Charter School (07-12)
2000 Enrollment: 151 507-625-9331

Four-year College(s)

Minnesota State University-Mankato (Public)
2001 Enrollment: 13,275 507-389-6767
2001 Tuition: In-state $3,050; Out-of-state $6,468

Two-year College(s)

Bethany Lutheran College (Private, Not-for-profit, Seventh Day Adventists)
2001 Enrollment: 401 507-344-7000
2001 Tuition: In-state $11,132; Out-of-state $11,132
Rasmussen College-Mankato (Private, For-profit)
2001 Enrollment: 313 507-625-6556
2001 Tuition: In-state $12,600; Out-of-state $12,600

Housing: Homeownership rate: 52.9% (2000); Median home value: $97,400 (2000); Median rent: $460 per month (2000); Median age of housing: 37 years (2000).
Hospitals: Immanuel Saint Joseph's - Mayo Health System (272 beds)
Newspapers: Free Press (6 x week)
Transportation: Commute to work: 85.8% car, 2.7% public transportation, 8.0% walk, 2.4% work from home (2000); Travel time to work: 69.0% less than 15 minutes, 21.5% 15 to 30 minutes, 3.8% 30 to 45 minutes, 2.0% 45 to 60 minutes, 3.7% 60 minutes or more (2000)
Additional Information Contacts
Mankato Area Chamber of Commerce 507-345-4519
Realtor Association of Southern Minnesota. 507-345-6018

MANKATO (township). Covers a land area of 28.904 square miles and a water area of 0.608 square miles. Located at 44.14° N. Lat.; 93.95° W. Long. Elevation is 785 feet.
History: Mankato stone has been quarried here for more than 100 years. Seat of Mankato State University and Bethany College. Sibley Park in Mankato was the site of Camp Lincoln, where more than 300 Sioux were held and 38 of them hanged, after their revolt in1862. Incorporated 1865.
Population: 1,833 (2000); Race: 99.6% White, 0.0% Black, 0.4% Asian, 0.0% American Indian and Alaska Native, 0.0% Hispanic of any race, 0.0% two or more races (2000); Density: 63.4 persons per square mile (2000); Age: 29.5% under 18, 9.7% over 64 (2000); Marriage status: 21.4% never married, 70.3% now married, 3.8% widowed, 4.4% divorced (2000); Foreign born: 1.1% (2000); Ancestry (includes multiple ancestries): 52.0% German, 17.4% Irish, 15.7% Norwegian, 6.6% English, 5.1% United States or American (2000).
Economy: Trade and processing center for a farm region: grain, alfalfa, livestock, dairying. Manufacturing includes soybean processing, dairy products, oilseed processing, printing and publishing, flour, feeds, building materials, computer equipment, machinery, paper products, fabricated metal products, consumer goods, lumber, electronic equipment and plastic products. Mankato stone has been quarried here for more than 100 years. Mankato Municipal Airport. Single-family building permits issued: 10 (2001) / 13 (2000); Multi-family building permits issued: 0 (2001) / 0 (2000); Employment by occupation: 16.7% management, 19.9% professional, 11.5% services, 28.0% sales, 0.0% farming, 11.5% construction, 12.3% production (2000).
Income: Per capita income: $27,189 (2000); Median household income: $64,471 (2000); Poverty rate: 3.7% (2000).
Taxes: Total city taxes per capita: $81 (1997); City property taxes per capita: $81 (1997).
Education: High school graduation rate: 92.7% (2000); College graduation rate: 37.0% (2000).
Housing: Homeownership rate: 91.9% (2000); Median home value: $149,200 (2000); Median rent: $453 per month (2000); Median age of housing: 27 years (2000).
Transportation: Commute to work: 94.1% car, 0.0% public transportation, 0.5% walk, 5.5% work from home (2000); Travel time to work: 50.2% less than 15 minutes, 41.0% 15 to 30 minutes, 3.2% 30 to 45 minutes, 2.5% 45 to 60 minutes, 3.2% 60 minutes or more (2000)

MAPLETON (city). Covers a land area of 1.501 square miles and a water area of 0 square miles. Located at 43.92° N. Lat.; 93.95° W. Long. Elevation is 1,036 feet.
Population: 1,678 (2000); Race: 97.8% White, 0.1% Black, 0.0% Asian, 0.7% American Indian and Alaska Native, 2.1% Hispanic of any race, 1.4% two or more races (2000); Density: 1,117.8 persons per square mile (2000); Age: 27.1% under 18, 20.4% over 64 (2000); Marriage status: 20.2% never married, 63.7% now married, 9.0% widowed, 7.1% divorced (2000); Foreign born: 0.5% (2000); Ancestry (includes multiple ancestries): 52.4% German, 14.9% Norwegian, 10.0% Irish, 6.4% Swedish, 4.8% French (except Basque) (2000).
Economy: Single-family building permits issued: 5 (2001) / 2 (2000); Multi-family building permits issued: 0 (2001) / 4 (2000); Employment by occupation: 7.0% management, 16.5% professional, 17.3% services, 31.6% sales, 2.1% farming, 10.3% construction, 15.2% production (2000).
Income: Per capita income: $18,375 (2000); Median household income: $38,790 (2000); Poverty rate: 3.7% (2000).
Taxes: Total city taxes per capita: $89 (1997); City property taxes per capita: $86 (1997).
Education: High school graduation rate: 83.4% (2000); College graduation rate: 17.5% (2000).

School District(s)

Maple River (PK-12)
2000 Enrollment: 1,308 507-524-3915

Housing: Homeownership rate: 77.6% (2000); Median home value: $81,500 (2000); Median rent: $316 per month (2000); Median age of housing: 46 years (2000).
Newspapers: Maple River Messenger (1 x week)
Transportation: Commute to work: 86.0% car, 0.2% public transportation, 7.2% walk, 6.1% work from home (2000); Travel time to work: 35.3% less than 15 minutes, 33.0% 15 to 30 minutes, 21.4% 30 to 45 minutes, 4.7% 45 to 60 minutes, 5.5% 60 minutes or more (2000)
Additional Information Contacts
Mapleton Area Chamber of Commerce 507-524-4756

MAPLETON (township). Covers a land area of 34.121 square miles and a water area of 0.263 square miles. Located at 43.89° N. Lat.; 93.95° W. Long. Elevation is 1,036 feet.
History: Laid out and incorporated 1878.
Population: 310 (2000); Race: 98.1% White, 0.0% Black, 1.3% Asian, 0.0% American Indian and Alaska Native, 0.6% Hispanic of any race, 0.0% two or more races (2000); Density: 9.1 persons per square mile (2000); Age: 22.3% under 18, 14.9% over 64 (2000); Marriage status: 18.5% never married, 70.4% now married, 5.4% widowed, 5.8% divorced (2000); Foreign born: 1.9% (2000); Ancestry (includes multiple ancestries): 54.0% German, 16.2% Irish, 12.9% Norwegian, 8.4% English, 7.4% Scottish (2000).

Economy: Grain; livestock; light manufacturing. Employment by occupation: 20.0% management, 9.7% professional, 13.8% services, 22.6% sales, 3.6% farming, 9.7% construction, 20.5% production (2000).
Income: Per capita income: $22,557 (2000); Median household income: $50,000 (2000); Poverty rate: 9.7% (2000).
Taxes: Total city taxes per capita: $165 (1997); City property taxes per capita: $165 (1997).
Education: High school graduation rate: 86.9% (2000); College graduation rate: 15.3% (2000).
Housing: Homeownership rate: 92.0% (2000); Median home value: $95,600 (2000); Median age of housing: 60+ years (2000).
Transportation: Commute to work: 78.2% car, 0.0% public transportation, 1.6% walk, 15.5% work from home (2000); Travel time to work: 43.6% less than 15 minutes, 26.4% 15 to 30 minutes, 22.7% 30 to 45 minutes, 3.7% 45 to 60 minutes, 3.7% 60 minutes or more (2000)

MCPHERSON (township). Covers a land area of 34.985 square miles and a water area of 0.404 square miles. Located at 44.06° N. Lat.; 93.83° W. Long.
Population: 470 (2000); Race: 99.6% White, 0.4% Black, 0.0% Asian, 0.0% American Indian and Alaska Native, 1.0% Hispanic of any race, 0.0% two or more races (2000); Density: 13.4 persons per square mile (2000); Age: 32.4% under 18, 8.7% over 64 (2000); Marriage status: 28.4% never married, 61.4% now married, 3.4% widowed, 6.8% divorced (2000); Foreign born: 1.2% (2000); Ancestry (includes multiple ancestries): 64.7% German, 16.7% Irish, 14.4% Norwegian, 8.0% English, 5.4% French (except Basque) (2000).
Economy: Employment by occupation: 14.2% management, 15.8% professional, 7.7% services, 25.4% sales, 2.7% farming, 9.2% construction, 25.0% production (2000).
Income: Per capita income: $17,610 (2000); Median household income: $45,804 (2000); Poverty rate: 5.1% (2000).
Taxes: Total city taxes per capita: $105 (1997); City property taxes per capita: $105 (1997).
Education: High school graduation rate: 88.0% (2000); College graduation rate: 14.9% (2000).
Housing: Homeownership rate: 91.7% (2000); Median home value: $107,500 (2000); Median rent: $388 per month (2000); Median age of housing: 52 years (2000).
Transportation: Commute to work: 88.8% car, 0.0% public transportation, 0.0% walk, 11.2% work from home (2000); Travel time to work: 18.8% less than 15 minutes, 61.1% 15 to 30 minutes, 16.2% 30 to 45 minutes, 0.9% 45 to 60 minutes, 3.1% 60 minutes or more (2000)

MEDO (township). Covers a land area of 34.965 square miles and a water area of 0.749 square miles. Located at 43.98° N. Lat.; 93.81° W. Long.
Population: 374 (2000); Race: 98.7% White, 0.0% Black, 0.0% Asian, 0.0% American Indian and Alaska Native, 0.5% Hispanic of any race, 0.8% two or more races (2000); Density: 10.7 persons per square mile (2000); Age: 27.4% under 18, 18.2% over 64 (2000); Marriage status: 22.0% never married, 64.2% now married, 2.9% widowed, 10.9% divorced (2000); Foreign born: 0.0% (2000); Ancestry (includes multiple ancestries): 51.5% German, 19.5% Norwegian, 7.9% United States or American, 7.2% Irish, 6.2% English (2000).
Economy: Employment by occupation: 11.5% management, 6.7% professional, 15.9% services, 32.7% sales, 2.9% farming, 14.9% construction, 15.4% production (2000).
Income: Per capita income: $16,418 (2000); Median household income: $42,159 (2000); Poverty rate: 10.8% (2000).
Taxes: Total city taxes per capita: $238 (2000); City property taxes per capita: $238 (2000).
Education: High school graduation rate: 81.0% (2000); College graduation rate: 15.2% (2000).
Housing: Homeownership rate: 82.4% (2000); Median home value: $111,700 (2000); Median rent: $275 per month (2000); Median age of housing: 60+ years (2000).
Transportation: Commute to work: 84.4% car, 0.0% public transportation, 3.9% walk, 11.7% work from home (2000); Travel time to work: 17.1% less than 15 minutes, 43.1% 15 to 30 minutes, 26.0% 30 to 45 minutes, 5.0% 45 to 60 minutes, 8.8% 60 minutes or more (2000)

PEMBERTON (city). Covers a land area of 0.206 square miles and a water area of 0 square miles. Located at 44.00° N. Lat.; 93.78° W. Long. Elevation is 1,044 feet.
Population: 246 (2000); Race: 100.0% White, 0.0% Black, 0.0% Asian, 0.0% American Indian and Alaska Native, 0.0% Hispanic of any race, 0.0% two or more races (2000); Density: 1,196.4 persons per square mile (2000); Age: 25.6% under 18, 8.5% over 64 (2000); Marriage status: 29.0% never married, 58.5% now married, 4.0% widowed, 8.5% divorced (2000); Foreign born: 1.3% (2000); Ancestry (includes multiple ancestries): 63.7% German, 20.2% Norwegian, 8.1% Irish, 6.7% Other groups, 5.4% Swedish (2000).
Economy: Dairying; livestock; corn, alfalfa. Manufacturing: feed and fertilizer. Single-family building permits issued: 3 (2001) / 3 (2000); Multi-family building permits issued: 0 (2001) / 0 (2000); Employment by occupation: 6.0% management, 6.8% professional, 19.5% services, 20.3% sales, 0.0% farming, 19.5% construction, 27.8% production (2000).
Income: Per capita income: $17,640 (2000); Median household income: $39,167 (2000); Poverty rate: 4.1% (2000).
Taxes: Total city taxes per capita: $165 (1997); City property taxes per capita: $161 (1997).
Education: High school graduation rate: 88.4% (2000); College graduation rate: 9.3% (2000).
Housing: Homeownership rate: 94.1% (2000); Median home value: $72,500 (2000); Median rent: $625 per month (2000); Median age of housing: 31 years (2000).
Transportation: Commute to work: 93.9% car, 0.0% public transportation, 3.1% walk, 1.5% work from home (2000); Travel time to work: 17.8% less than 15 minutes, 48.1% 15 to 30 minutes, 25.6% 30 to 45 minutes, 6.2% 45 to 60 minutes, 2.3% 60 minutes or more (2000)

PLEASANT MOUND (township). Covers a land area of 35.971 square miles and a water area of 0 square miles. Located at 43.89° N. Lat.; 94.29° W. Long.
Population: 235 (2000); Race: 100.0% White, 0.0% Black, 0.0% Asian, 0.0% American Indian and Alaska Native, 0.0% Hispanic of any race, 0.0% two or more races (2000); Density: 6.5 persons per square mile (2000); Age: 31.0% under 18, 14.2% over 64 (2000); Marriage status: 22.8% never married, 70.7% now married, 1.4% widowed, 5.1% divorced (2000); Foreign born: 0.0% (2000); Ancestry (includes multiple ancestries): 74.5% German, 9.5% Norwegian, 4.7% Scottish, 3.6% United States or American, 3.6% Swedish (2000).
Economy: Employment by occupation: 21.6% management, 12.9% professional, 9.4% services, 23.7% sales, 6.5% farming, 7.9% construction, 18.0% production (2000).
Income: Per capita income: $13,614 (2000); Median household income: $30,000 (2000); Poverty rate: 17.9% (2000).
Taxes: Total city taxes per capita: $204 (2000); City property taxes per capita: $204 (2000).
Education: High school graduation rate: 82.7% (2000); College graduation rate: 10.6% (2000).
Housing: Homeownership rate: 82.7% (2000); Median home value: $79,300 (2000); Median rent: $375 per month (2000); Median age of housing: 60+ years (2000).
Transportation: Commute to work: 77.6% car, 0.0% public transportation, 7.5% walk, 14.9% work from home (2000); Travel time to work: 43.9% less than 15 minutes, 32.5% 15 to 30 minutes, 17.5% 30 to 45 minutes, 6.1% 45 to 60 minutes, 0.0% 60 minutes or more (2000)

RAPIDAN (township). Covers a land area of 35.693 square miles and a water area of 0 square miles. Located at 44.05° N. Lat.; 94.05° W. Long. Elevation is 986 feet.
Population: 1,061 (2000); Race: 98.4% White, 0.2% Black, 0.3% Asian, 0.2% American Indian and Alaska Native, 0.7% Hispanic of any race, 0.6% two or more races (2000); Density: 29.7 persons per square mile (2000); Age: 25.4% under 18, 9.7% over 64 (2000); Marriage status: 18.8% never married, 70.4% now married, 4.9% widowed, 5.9% divorced (2000); Foreign born: 1.1% (2000); Ancestry (includes multiple ancestries): 55.7% German, 19.0% Norwegian, 14.3% Irish, 8.1% Swedish, 6.1% United States or American (2000).
Economy: Employment by occupation: 16.5% management, 17.4% professional, 9.6% services, 24.0% sales, 1.5% farming, 14.9% construction, 16.2% production (2000).
Income: Per capita income: $24,856 (2000); Median household income: $53,839 (2000); Poverty rate: 3.2% (2000).
Taxes: Total city taxes per capita: $109 (1997); City property taxes per capita: $109 (1997).
Education: High school graduation rate: 88.2% (2000); College graduation rate: 22.4% (2000).
Housing: Homeownership rate: 86.4% (2000); Median home value: $108,200 (2000); Median rent: $475 per month (2000); Median age of housing: 43 years (2000).
Transportation: Commute to work: 88.2% car, 0.0% public transportation, 1.5% walk, 9.0% work from home (2000); Travel time to work: 22.4% less

than 15 minutes, 65.6% 15 to 30 minutes, 6.4% 30 to 45 minutes, 0.9% 45 to 60 minutes, 4.7% 60 minutes or more (2000)

SAINT CLAIR (city). Covers a land area of 0.554 square miles and a water area of 0 square miles. Located at 44.08° N. Lat.; 93.85° W. Long. Elevation is 985 feet.
Population: 827 (2000); Race: 98.5% White, 0.6% Black, 0.5% Asian, 0.0% American Indian and Alaska Native, 1.2% Hispanic of any race, 0.0% two or more races (2000); Density: 1,492.1 persons per square mile (2000); Age: 29.3% under 18, 11.7% over 64 (2000); Marriage status: 20.5% never married, 64.8% now married, 7.3% widowed, 7.3% divorced (2000); Foreign born: 0.7% (2000); Ancestry (includes multiple ancestries): 56.1% German, 16.8% Norwegian, 9.5% Irish, 5.6% English, 3.9% Other groups (2000).
Economy: Single-family building permits issued: 0 (2001) / 4 (2000); Multi-family building permits issued: 0 (2001) / 0 (2000); Employment by occupation: 11.3% management, 19.6% professional, 12.2% services, 27.0% sales, 0.7% farming, 9.5% construction, 19.6% production (2000).
Income: Per capita income: $19,512 (2000); Median household income: $43,854 (2000); Poverty rate: 7.2% (2000).
Education: High school graduation rate: 87.7% (2000); College graduation rate: 16.7% (2000).

School District(s)

Saint Clair (PK-12)
2000 Enrollment: 675 507-245-3501
Housing: Homeownership rate: 84.3% (2000); Median home value: $96,700 (2000); Median rent: $333 per month (2000); Median age of housing: 27 years (2000).
Transportation: Commute to work: 92.1% car, 0.0% public transportation, 3.0% walk, 4.4% work from home (2000); Travel time to work: 25.2% less than 15 minutes, 56.6% 15 to 30 minutes, 10.4% 30 to 45 minutes, 2.7% 45 to 60 minutes, 5.1% 60 minutes or more (2000)

SHELBY (township). Covers a land area of 35.563 square miles and a water area of 0.193 square miles. Located at 43.88° N. Lat.; 94.19° W. Long.
Population: 294 (2000); Race: 100.0% White, 0.0% Black, 0.0% Asian, 0.0% American Indian and Alaska Native, 0.0% Hispanic of any race, 0.0% two or more races (2000); Density: 8.3 persons per square mile (2000); Age: 28.7% under 18, 17.8% over 64 (2000); Marriage status: 18.2% never married, 68.4% now married, 6.7% widowed, 6.7% divorced (2000); Foreign born: 0.0% (2000); Ancestry (includes multiple ancestries): 65.4% German, 28.3% Norwegian, 13.6% English, 7.3% Irish, 5.9% Swedish (2000).
Economy: Employment by occupation: 32.6% management, 18.4% professional, 6.4% services, 22.0% sales, 0.0% farming, 10.6% construction, 9.9% production (2000).
Income: Per capita income: $21,355 (2000); Median household income: $48,125 (2000); Poverty rate: 2.4% (2000).
Taxes: Total city taxes per capita: $127 (1997); City property taxes per capita: $127 (1997).
Education: High school graduation rate: 91.9% (2000); College graduation rate: 18.3% (2000).
Housing: Homeownership rate: 77.2% (2000); Median home value: $95,600 (2000); Median rent: $265 per month (2000); Median age of housing: 59 years (2000).
Transportation: Commute to work: 78.1% car, 0.0% public transportation, 8.8% walk, 13.1% work from home (2000); Travel time to work: 32.8% less than 15 minutes, 24.4% 15 to 30 minutes, 31.9% 30 to 45 minutes, 1.7% 45 to 60 minutes, 9.2% 60 minutes or more (2000)

SKYLINE (city). Covers a land area of 0.188 square miles and a water area of 0 square miles. Located at 44.14° N. Lat.; 94.03° W. Long.
Population: 330 (2000); Race: 99.7% White, 0.0% Black, 0.3% Asian, 0.0% American Indian and Alaska Native, 0.5% Hispanic of any race, 0.0% two or more races (2000); Density: 1,752.5 persons per square mile (2000); Age: 30.5% under 18, 16.4% over 64 (2000); Marriage status: 13.3% never married, 79.0% now married, 4.4% widowed, 3.3% divorced (2000); Foreign born: 1.1% (2000); Ancestry (includes multiple ancestries): 45.0% German, 17.0% Norwegian, 13.5% Irish, 9.4% Swedish, 8.1% English (2000).
Economy: Employment by occupation: 21.6% management, 29.7% professional, 13.0% services, 24.3% sales, 0.0% farming, 3.2% construction, 8.1% production (2000).
Income: Per capita income: $25,778 (2000); Median household income: $59,583 (2000); Poverty rate: 0.3% (2000).
Taxes: Total city taxes per capita: $64 (1997); City property taxes per capita: $61 (1997).
Education: High school graduation rate: 93.4% (2000); College graduation rate: 51.5% (2000).
Housing: Homeownership rate: 97.1% (2000); Median home value: $128,400 (2000); Median rent: $500 per month (2000); Median age of housing: 41 years (2000).
Transportation: Commute to work: 94.0% car, 0.0% public transportation, 0.0% walk, 6.0% work from home (2000); Travel time to work: 69.8% less than 15 minutes, 26.2% 15 to 30 minutes, 1.2% 30 to 45 minutes, 0.0% 45 to 60 minutes, 2.9% 60 minutes or more (2000)

SOUTH BEND (township). Covers a land area of 16.912 square miles and a water area of 0 square miles. Located at 44.14° N. Lat.; 94.08° W. Long.
Population: 1,491 (2000); Race: 95.5% White, 1.7% Black, 0.5% Asian, 0.0% American Indian and Alaska Native, 3.3% Hispanic of any race, 1.6% two or more races (2000); Density: 88.2 persons per square mile (2000); Age: 23.6% under 18, 17.9% over 64 (2000); Marriage status: 30.4% never married, 51.4% now married, 10.8% widowed, 7.5% divorced (2000); Foreign born: 0.9% (2000); Ancestry (includes multiple ancestries): 51.7% German, 15.1% Norwegian, 9.5% Other groups, 9.5% Irish, 7.6% Swedish (2000).
Economy: Employment by occupation: 10.5% management, 16.0% professional, 17.5% services, 20.9% sales, 0.6% farming, 11.3% construction, 23.4% production (2000).
Income: Per capita income: $18,038 (2000); Median household income: $42,083 (2000); Poverty rate: 7.2% (2000).
Taxes: Total city taxes per capita: $52 (2000); City property taxes per capita: $52 (2000).
Education: High school graduation rate: 76.9% (2000); College graduation rate: 21.2% (2000).
Housing: Homeownership rate: 79.8% (2000); Median home value: $85,300 (2000); Median rent: $390 per month (2000); Median age of housing: 40 years (2000).
Transportation: Commute to work: 93.3% car, 0.0% public transportation, 2.0% walk, 3.6% work from home (2000); Travel time to work: 56.0% less than 15 minutes, 34.6% 15 to 30 minutes, 5.3% 30 to 45 minutes, 1.0% 45 to 60 minutes, 3.1% 60 minutes or more (2000)

STERLING (township). Covers a land area of 34.409 square miles and a water area of 1.615 square miles. Located at 43.89° N. Lat.; 94.06° W. Long.
Population: 276 (2000); Race: 99.6% White, 0.0% Black, 0.4% Asian, 0.0% American Indian and Alaska Native, 0.7% Hispanic of any race, 0.0% two or more races (2000); Density: 8.0 persons per square mile (2000); Age: 26.8% under 18, 15.4% over 64 (2000); Marriage status: 11.6% never married, 78.3% now married, 6.8% widowed, 3.4% divorced (2000); Foreign born: 1.1% (2000); Ancestry (includes multiple ancestries): 55.9% German, 17.3% Norwegian, 13.6% Irish, 8.1% Scottish, 6.6% English (2000).
Economy: Employment by occupation: 31.3% management, 12.7% professional, 9.7% services, 18.7% sales, 6.7% farming, 6.0% construction, 14.9% production (2000).
Income: Per capita income: $20,442 (2000); Median household income: $49,091 (2000); Poverty rate: 2.6% (2000).
Taxes: Total city taxes per capita: $118 (1997); City property taxes per capita: $118 (1997).
Education: High school graduation rate: 88.8% (2000); College graduation rate: 23.5% (2000).
Housing: Homeownership rate: 89.1% (2000); Median home value: $95,000 (2000); Median rent: $200 per month (2000); Median age of housing: 49 years (2000).
Transportation: Commute to work: 73.8% car, 0.0% public transportation, 2.3% walk, 23.8% work from home (2000); Travel time to work: 30.3% less than 15 minutes, 12.1% 15 to 30 minutes, 39.4% 30 to 45 minutes, 6.1% 45 to 60 minutes, 12.1% 60 minutes or more (2000)

VERNON CENTER (city). Covers a land area of 0.494 square miles and a water area of 0 square miles. Located at 43.96° N. Lat.; 94.16° W. Long. Elevation is 1,025 feet.
Population: 359 (2000); Race: 96.6% White, 0.0% Black, 0.0% Asian, 0.0% American Indian and Alaska Native, 0.6% Hispanic of any race, 3.4% two or more races (2000); Density: 727.2 persons per square mile (2000); Age: 20.2% under 18, 17.5% over 64 (2000); Marriage status: 15.1% never married, 69.9% now married, 8.1% widowed, 7.0% divorced (2000); Foreign born: 1.8% (2000); Ancestry (includes multiple ancestries): 50.9% German, 8.3% Other groups, 7.7% English, 6.4% Irish, 5.2% Norwegian (2000).
Economy: Single-family building permits issued: 0 (2001) / 0 (2000); Multi-family building permits issued: 0 (2001) / 0 (2000); Employment by occupation: 17.3% management, 14.5% professional, 0.6% services, 22.9% sales, 3.4% farming, 11.2% construction, 30.2% production (2000).

Income: Per capita income: $20,693 (2000); Median household income: $50,703 (2000); Poverty rate: 1.5% (2000).
Taxes: Total city taxes per capita: $238 (1997); City property taxes per capita: $232 (1997).
Education: High school graduation rate: 87.1% (2000); College graduation rate: 6.9% (2000).
Housing: Homeownership rate: 90.6% (2000); Median home value: $64,400 (2000); Median rent: $260 per month (2000); Median age of housing: 60+ years (2000).
Transportation: Commute to work: 96.0% car, 0.0% public transportation, 0.0% walk, 4.0% work from home (2000); Travel time to work: 28.9% less than 15 minutes, 36.7% 15 to 30 minutes, 25.9% 30 to 45 minutes, 1.2% 45 to 60 minutes, 7.2% 60 minutes or more (2000)

VERNON CENTER (township). Covers a land area of 35.529 square miles and a water area of 0 square miles. Located at 43.97° N. Lat.; 94.19° W. Long. Elevation is 1,025 feet.
Population: 301 (2000); Race: 100.0% White, 0.0% Black, 0.0% Asian, 0.0% American Indian and Alaska Native, 0.0% Hispanic of any race, 0.0% two or more races (2000); Density: 8.5 persons per square mile (2000); Age: 27.1% under 18, 12.4% over 64 (2000); Marriage status: 23.0% never married, 71.3% now married, 1.5% widowed, 4.2% divorced (2000); Foreign born: 2.6% (2000); Ancestry (includes multiple ancestries): 52.9% German, 13.8% Dutch, 9.4% Irish, 8.8% Norwegian, 6.5% English (2000).
Economy: In grain and livestock area. Manufacturing of fertilizer. Employment by occupation: 20.7% management, 18.8% professional, 7.5% services, 18.3% sales, 9.9% farming, 7.5% construction, 17.4% production (2000).
Income: Per capita income: $20,729 (2000); Median household income: $44,375 (2000); Poverty rate: 10.1% (2000).
Taxes: Total city taxes per capita: $182 (1997); City property taxes per capita: $182 (1997).
Education: High school graduation rate: 97.3% (2000); College graduation rate: 15.9% (2000).
Housing: Homeownership rate: 85.6% (2000); Median home value: $105,000 (2000); Median rent: $225 per month (2000); Median age of housing: 52 years (2000).
Transportation: Commute to work: 77.0% car, 0.0% public transportation, 4.7% walk, 18.3% work from home (2000); Travel time to work: 35.1% less than 15 minutes, 19.5% 15 to 30 minutes, 31.6% 30 to 45 minutes, 9.2% 45 to 60 minutes, 4.6% 60 minutes or more (2000)

Brown County

Located in southern Minnesota; bounded on the north by the Minnesota River. Covers a land area of 610.90 square miles, a water area of 7.70 square miles, and is located in the Central Time Zone. The county government was organized in 1855. County seat is New Ulm.

Weather Station: New Ulm 2 SE — Elevation: 859 feet

	Jan	Feb	Mar	Apr	May	Jun	Jul	Aug	Sep	Oct	Nov	Dec
High	23	30	41	59	72	81	84	81	73	61	41	27
Low	4	11	23	36	48	58	62	59	50	38	25	11
Precip	0.7	0.6	2.1	2.7	3.2	4.4	4.0	3.9	2.9	2.3	1.8	0.8
Snow	9.6	6.3	8.8	2.2	tr	0.0	0.0	0.0	tr	0.5	7.3	7.9

High and Low temperatures in degrees Fahrenheit; Precipitation and Snow in inches

Weather Station: Springfield 1 NW — Elevation: 1,062 feet

	Jan	Feb	Mar	Apr	May	Jun	Jul	Aug	Sep	Oct	Nov	Dec
High	21	28	39	56	71	81	83	80	73	60	40	27
Low	2	9	22	34	47	57	60	57	47	36	22	9
Precip	0.6	0.6	2.0	2.8	3.1	3.9	3.5	3.3	2.6	2.1	1.7	0.6
Snow	9.1	5.9	9.5	3.0	tr	0.0	0.0	0.0	tr	0.7	7.7	7.9

High and Low temperatures in degrees Fahrenheit; Precipitation and Snow in inches

Population: 26,911 (2000); Race: 97.7% White, 0.3% Black, 0.3% Asian, 0.4% American Indian and Alaska Native, 2.2% Hispanic of any race, 0.6% two or more races (2000); Density: 44.1 persons per square mile (2000); Age: 25.3% under 18, 17.5% over 64 (2000).
Religion: Five largest groups: 44.3% Catholic Church, 21.0% Evangelical Lutheran Church in America, 13.6% Wisconsin Evangelical Lutheran Synod, 4.5% The United Methodist Church, 3.1% Lutheran Church—Missouri Synod (2000).
Economy: Unemployment rate: 3.4% (11/2002); Total civilian labor force: 14,612 (11/2002); Leading industries: 30.8% manufacturing; 14.9% health care and social assistance; 14.7% retail trade (2000); Companies that employ more than 1,000 persons: 0 (2000); Companies that employ more than 100 persons: 21 (2000); Farms: 1,054 totaling 350,398 acres (1997); Minority business ownership rate: 0.0% (1997); Women business ownership rate: 18.9% (1997); Retail sales per capita: $8,618 (1997). Single-family building permits issued: 64 (2001) / 37 (2000); Multi-family building permits issued: 12 (2001) / 2 (2000).
Income: Per capita income: $19,535 (2000); Median household income: $39,800 (2000); Poverty rate: 6.4% (2000); Bankruptcy rate: 2.10% (2001).
Taxes: Total county taxes per capita: $204 (1997); County property taxes per capita: $204 (1997).
Education: High school graduation rate: 81.7% (2000); College graduation rate: 16.5% (2000).
Housing: Homeownership rate: 80.1% (2000); Median home value: $85,400 (2000); Median rent: $353 per month (2000); Median age of housing: 45 years (2000).
Health: Birth rate: 97.7 per 10,000 population (1998); Age adjusted death rate: 81.0 per 10,000 population (1999); Age adjusted cancer mortality rate: 209.7 deaths per 100,000 population (1999). Number of physicians: 11.5 per 10,000 population (1999); Number of hospital beds: 33.8 per 10,000 population (1999).
Elections: 2000 Presidential election results: 36.2% Gore, 57.4% Bush, 4.4% Nader, 1.6% Buchanan
National and State Parks: Bashaw State Wildlife Management Area; Flandrau State Park; Sleepy Eye State Park
Additional Information Contacts
Brown County Government Offices. 507-233-6660
New Ulm Chamber of Commerce 507-233-4300
Sleepy Eye Chamber of Commerce 507-794-4731

Brown County Communities

ALBIN (township). Covers a land area of 34.369 square miles and a water area of 1.212 square miles. Located at 44.14° N. Lat.; 94.68° W. Long.
Population: 329 (2000); Race: 98.4% White, 0.0% Black, 0.0% Asian, 1.6% American Indian and Alaska Native, 0.0% Hispanic of any race, 0.0% two or more races (2000); Density: 9.6 persons per square mile (2000); Age: 30.6% under 18, 14.3% over 64 (2000); Marriage status: 17.8% never married, 69.1% now married, 7.2% widowed, 5.9% divorced (2000); Foreign born: 0.6% (2000); Ancestry (includes multiple ancestries): 66.9% German, 22.9% Norwegian, 5.4% Irish, 4.5% Belgian, 3.8% Polish (2000).
Economy: Employment by occupation: 35.1% management, 6.0% professional, 9.5% services, 14.3% sales, 3.6% farming, 9.5% construction, 22.0% production (2000).
Income: Per capita income: $15,830 (2000); Median household income: $36,111 (2000); Poverty rate: 13.7% (2000).
Taxes: Total city taxes per capita: $41 (1997); City property taxes per capita: $41 (1997).
Education: High school graduation rate: 81.7% (2000); College graduation rate: 4.0% (2000).
Housing: Homeownership rate: 86.7% (2000); Median home value: $71,300 (2000); Median rent: $188 per month (2000); Median age of housing: 56 years (2000).
Transportation: Commute to work: 65.7% car, 0.0% public transportation, 2.4% walk, 31.9% work from home (2000); Travel time to work: 18.6% less than 15 minutes, 48.7% 15 to 30 minutes, 25.7% 30 to 45 minutes, 1.8% 45 to 60 minutes, 5.3% 60 minutes or more (2000)

BASHAW (township). Covers a land area of 35.753 square miles and a water area of 0.006 square miles. Located at 44.15° N. Lat.; 94.92° W. Long.
Population: 255 (2000); Race: 100.0% White, 0.0% Black, 0.0% Asian, 0.0% American Indian and Alaska Native, 0.0% Hispanic of any race, 0.0% two or more races (2000); Density: 7.1 persons per square mile (2000); Age: 26.8% under 18, 15.6% over 64 (2000); Marriage status: 22.3% never married, 70.6% now married, 5.2% widowed, 1.9% divorced (2000); Foreign born: 0.0% (2000); Ancestry (includes multiple ancestries): 58.0% German, 14.9% Norwegian, 8.2% Swedish, 6.3% United States or American, 2.6% Danish (2000).
Economy: Employment by occupation: 30.5% management, 14.5% professional, 2.3% services, 17.6% sales, 8.4% farming, 12.2% construction, 14.5% production (2000).
Income: Per capita income: $16,604 (2000); Median household income: $39,500 (2000); Poverty rate: 3.3% (2000).
Education: High school graduation rate: 87.4% (2000); College graduation rate: 10.9% (2000).

Housing: Homeownership rate: 84.0% (2000); Median home value: $75,000 (2000); Median rent: $233 per month (2000); Median age of housing: 60+ years (2000).
Transportation: Commute to work: 74.2% car, 0.0% public transportation, 0.0% walk, 25.8% work from home (2000); Travel time to work: 37.9% less than 15 minutes, 42.1% 15 to 30 minutes, 12.6% 30 to 45 minutes, 7.4% 45 to 60 minutes, 0.0% 60 minutes or more (2000)

BURNSTOWN (township). Covers a land area of 34.697 square miles and a water area of 0.211 square miles. Located at 44.24° N. Lat.; 94.92° W. Long.
Population: 260 (2000); Race: 100.0% White, 0.0% Black, 0.0% Asian, 0.0% American Indian and Alaska Native, 0.0% Hispanic of any race, 0.0% two or more races (2000); Density: 7.5 persons per square mile (2000); Age: 27.8% under 18, 12.0% over 64 (2000); Marriage status: 18.2% never married, 71.7% now married, 6.1% widowed, 4.0% divorced (2000); Foreign born: 0.8% (2000); Ancestry (includes multiple ancestries): 68.3% German, 13.5% Norwegian, 6.6% Swedish, 5.0% Irish, 4.2% English (2000).
Economy: Employment by occupation: 29.2% management, 20.8% professional, 7.7% services, 13.1% sales, 1.5% farming, 17.7% construction, 10.0% production (2000).
Income: Per capita income: $18,919 (2000); Median household income: $34,375 (2000); Poverty rate: 5.5% (2000).
Taxes: Total city taxes per capita: $90 (1997); City property taxes per capita: $90 (1997).
Education: High school graduation rate: 82.3% (2000); College graduation rate: 11.4% (2000).
Housing: Homeownership rate: 84.8% (2000); Median home value: $88,800 (2000); Median rent: $288 per month (2000); Median age of housing: 58 years (2000).
Transportation: Commute to work: 78.4% car, 0.0% public transportation, 4.0% walk, 15.2% work from home (2000); Travel time to work: 65.1% less than 15 minutes, 15.1% 15 to 30 minutes, 6.6% 30 to 45 minutes, 11.3% 45 to 60 minutes, 1.9% 60 minutes or more (2000)

COBDEN (city). Covers a land area of 0.958 square miles and a water area of 0 square miles. Located at 44.28° N. Lat.; 94.84° W. Long. Elevation is 1,050 feet.
Population: 61 (2000); Race: 97.4% White, 0.0% Black, 0.0% Asian, 0.0% American Indian and Alaska Native, 0.0% Hispanic of any race, 2.6% two or more races (2000); Density: 63.7 persons per square mile (2000); Age: 27.6% under 18, 14.5% over 64 (2000); Marriage status: 13.8% never married, 86.2% now married, 0.0% widowed, 0.0% divorced (2000); Foreign born: 0.0% (2000); Ancestry (includes multiple ancestries): 78.9% German, 10.5% United States or American, 5.3% Irish, 2.6% Norwegian (2000).
Economy: Grain; livestock; dairying. Employment by occupation: 4.7% management, 0.0% professional, 9.3% services, 16.3% sales, 7.0% farming, 18.6% construction, 44.2% production (2000).
Income: Per capita income: $15,179 (2000); Median household income: $43,750 (2000); Poverty rate: 6.6% (2000).
Taxes: Total city taxes per capita: $63 (1997); City property taxes per capita: $16 (1997).
Education: High school graduation rate: 68.9% (2000); College graduation rate: 4.4% (2000).
Housing: Homeownership rate: 84.6% (2000); Median home value: $37,500 (2000); Median rent: $375 per month (2000); Median age of housing: 50 years (2000).
Transportation: Commute to work: 94.7% car, 0.0% public transportation, 0.0% walk, 5.3% work from home (2000); Travel time to work: 19.4% less than 15 minutes, 52.8% 15 to 30 minutes, 13.9% 30 to 45 minutes, 0.0% 45 to 60 minutes, 13.9% 60 minutes or more (2000)

COMFREY (city). Covers a land area of 0.421 square miles and a water area of 0 square miles. Located at 44.10° N. Lat.; 94.90° W. Long. Elevation is 1,301 feet.
Population: 367 (2000); Race: 99.5% White, 0.0% Black, 0.0% Asian, 0.5% American Indian and Alaska Native, 0.5% Hispanic of any race, 0.0% two or more races (2000); Density: 871.9 persons per square mile (2000); Age: 23.4% under 18, 30.9% over 64 (2000); Marriage status: 16.2% never married, 70.6% now married, 9.4% widowed, 3.9% divorced (2000); Foreign born: 0.5% (2000); Ancestry (includes multiple ancestries): 56.7% German, 15.3% Swedish, 11.0% Norwegian, 5.9% Irish, 4.6% Other groups (2000).
Economy: Agricultural area: grain, soybeans, peas; dairying; poultry, livestock. Manufacturing: machinery. Single-family building permits issued: 1 (2001) / 1 (2000); Multi-family building permits issued: 0 (2001) / 2 (2000); Employment by occupation: 17.2% management, 9.7% professional, 11.0% services, 27.6% sales, 3.4% farming, 11.7% construction, 19.3% production (2000).
Income: Per capita income: $14,878 (2000); Median household income: $30,938 (2000); Poverty rate: 10.8% (2000).
Taxes: Total city taxes per capita: $179 (1997); City property taxes per capita: $175 (1997).
Education: High school graduation rate: 79.0% (2000); College graduation rate: 4.3% (2000).

School District(s)

Comfrey (PK-12)
2000 Enrollment: 170 507-877-3491
Housing: Homeownership rate: 89.8% (2000); Median home value: $45,900 (2000); Median rent: $240 per month (2000); Median age of housing: 45 years (2000).
Newspapers: The Comfrey Times (1 x week)
Transportation: Commute to work: 88.7% car, 0.0% public transportation, 11.3% walk, 0.0% work from home (2000); Travel time to work: 57.0% less than 15 minutes, 26.1% 15 to 30 minutes, 11.3% 30 to 45 minutes, 2.8% 45 to 60 minutes, 2.8% 60 minutes or more (2000)

COTTONWOOD (township). Covers a land area of 35.366 square miles and a water area of 0.031 square miles. Located at 44.26° N. Lat.; 94.43° W. Long.
Population: 938 (2000); Race: 99.4% White, 0.0% Black, 0.4% Asian, 0.0% American Indian and Alaska Native, 1.2% Hispanic of any race, 0.0% two or more races (2000); Density: 26.5 persons per square mile (2000); Age: 28.6% under 18, 12.3% over 64 (2000); Marriage status: 28.8% never married, 62.9% now married, 3.3% widowed, 5.0% divorced (2000); Foreign born: 1.2% (2000); Ancestry (includes multiple ancestries): 77.5% German, 6.9% Norwegian, 5.0% Swedish, 3.9% United States or American, 3.1% Irish (2000).
Economy: Employment by occupation: 16.7% management, 13.0% professional, 11.1% services, 22.9% sales, 1.6% farming, 10.9% construction, 23.9% production (2000).
Income: Per capita income: $21,299 (2000); Median household income: $48,750 (2000); Poverty rate: 6.9% (2000).
Taxes: Total city taxes per capita: $41 (1997); City property taxes per capita: $41 (1997).
Education: High school graduation rate: 83.4% (2000); College graduation rate: 11.0% (2000).
Housing: Homeownership rate: 90.3% (2000); Median home value: $115,500 (2000); Median rent: $292 per month (2000); Median age of housing: 30 years (2000).
Transportation: Commute to work: 90.6% car, 0.0% public transportation, 1.8% walk, 7.6% work from home (2000); Travel time to work: 49.3% less than 15 minutes, 35.3% 15 to 30 minutes, 13.1% 30 to 45 minutes, 1.3% 45 to 60 minutes, 1.1% 60 minutes or more (2000)

EDEN (township). Covers a land area of 41.323 square miles and a water area of 0.211 square miles. Located at 44.42° N. Lat.; 94.81° W. Long.
Population: 321 (2000); Race: 100.0% White, 0.0% Black, 0.0% Asian, 0.0% American Indian and Alaska Native, 0.0% Hispanic of any race, 0.0% two or more races (2000); Density: 7.8 persons per square mile (2000); Age: 19.2% under 18, 21.1% over 64 (2000); Marriage status: 33.7% never married, 55.9% now married, 3.8% widowed, 6.5% divorced (2000); Foreign born: 0.0% (2000); Ancestry (includes multiple ancestries): 70.0% German, 12.1% Danish, 11.2% Norwegian, 5.8% Czech, 4.5% Swedish (2000).
Economy: Employment by occupation: 26.4% management, 21.3% professional, 8.0% services, 13.2% sales, 5.7% farming, 13.8% construction, 11.5% production (2000).
Income: Per capita income: $22,425 (2000); Median household income: $53,036 (2000); Poverty rate: 3.2% (2000).
Taxes: Total city taxes per capita: $63 (1997); City property taxes per capita: $63 (1997).
Education: High school graduation rate: 81.6% (2000); College graduation rate: 14.5% (2000).
Housing: Homeownership rate: 89.0% (2000); Median home value: $65,000 (2000); Median rent: $463 per month (2000); Median age of housing: 60+ years (2000).
Transportation: Commute to work: 68.4% car, 0.0% public transportation, 4.6% walk, 27.0% work from home (2000); Travel time to work: 24.4% less than 15 minutes, 44.1% 15 to 30 minutes, 18.9% 30 to 45 minutes, 4.7% 45 to 60 minutes, 7.9% 60 minutes or more (2000)

EVAN (city). Covers a land area of 1.004 square miles and a water area of 0 square miles. Located at 44.35° N. Lat.; 94.84° W. Long. Elevation is 1,025 feet.
Population: 91 (2000); Race: 95.7% White, 0.0% Black, 0.0% Asian, 0.0% American Indian and Alaska Native, 2.6% Hispanic of any race, 4.3% two or more races (2000); Density: 90.6 persons per square mile (2000); Age: 31.9% under 18, 12.9% over 64 (2000); Marriage status: 19.0% never married, 65.5% now married, 7.1% widowed, 8.3% divorced (2000); Foreign born: 0.0% (2000); Ancestry (includes multiple ancestries): 56.9% German, 22.4% Norwegian, 6.0% Czech, 5.2% Russian, 5.2% United States or American (2000).
Economy: Dairying; livestock; grain. Employment by occupation: 13.2% management, 26.4% professional, 20.8% services, 17.0% sales, 0.0% farming, 7.5% construction, 15.1% production (2000).
Income: Per capita income: $13,670 (2000); Median household income: $45,000 (2000); Poverty rate: 4.5% (2000).
Taxes: Total city taxes per capita: $63 (1997); City property taxes per capita: $50 (1997).
Education: High school graduation rate: 82.9% (2000); College graduation rate: 19.7% (2000).
Housing: Homeownership rate: 90.2% (2000); Median home value: $35,000 (2000); Median rent: $175 per month (2000); Median age of housing: 60+ years (2000).
Transportation: Commute to work: 90.6% car, 0.0% public transportation, 3.8% walk, 5.7% work from home (2000); Travel time to work: 18.0% less than 15 minutes, 54.0% 15 to 30 minutes, 24.0% 30 to 45 minutes, 0.0% 45 to 60 minutes, 4.0% 60 minutes or more (2000)

HANSKA (city). Covers a land area of 0.239 square miles and a water area of 0 square miles. Located at 44.15° N. Lat.; 94.49° W. Long. Elevation is 1,009 feet.
Population: 443 (2000); Race: 98.5% White, 0.0% Black, 0.0% Asian, 0.9% American Indian and Alaska Native, 0.0% Hispanic of any race, 0.7% two or more races (2000); Density: 1,856.5 persons per square mile (2000); Age: 25.1% under 18, 17.9% over 64 (2000); Marriage status: 22.6% never married, 60.9% now married, 7.3% widowed, 9.2% divorced (2000); Foreign born: 0.0% (2000); Ancestry (includes multiple ancestries): 50.5% German, 50.1% Norwegian, 6.1% Swedish, 3.3% Irish, 2.8% English (2000).
Economy: Grain, soybeans, peas; livestock, poultry; dairying. Manufacturing: fertilizers and feeds. Single-family building permits issued: 1 (2001) / 0 (2000); Multi-family building permits issued: 0 (2001) / 0 (2000); Employment by occupation: 10.6% management, 15.0% professional, 12.6% services, 21.1% sales, 0.0% farming, 10.2% construction, 30.5% production (2000).
Income: Per capita income: $16,803 (2000); Median household income: $40,114 (2000); Poverty rate: 3.1% (2000).
Taxes: Total city taxes per capita: $170 (1997); City property taxes per capita: $167 (1997).
Education: High school graduation rate: 84.1% (2000); College graduation rate: 12.6% (2000).

School District(s)

Hanska Charter School (KG-06)
2000 Enrollment: 46 507-439-6225
Housing: Homeownership rate: 84.0% (2000); Median home value: $60,500 (2000); Median rent: $275 per month (2000); Median age of housing: 57 years (2000).
Newspapers: The Hanska Herald (1 x week)
Transportation: Commute to work: 89.5% car, 0.0% public transportation, 6.7% walk, 1.7% work from home (2000); Travel time to work: 22.1% less than 15 minutes, 61.7% 15 to 30 minutes, 11.5% 30 to 45 minutes, 1.7% 45 to 60 minutes, 3.0% 60 minutes or more (2000)

HOME (township). Covers a land area of 52.349 square miles and a water area of 0.148 square miles. Located at 44.33° N. Lat.; 94.69° W. Long.
Population: 800 (2000); Race: 99.7% White, 0.0% Black, 0.0% Asian, 0.0% American Indian and Alaska Native, 0.0% Hispanic of any race, 0.3% two or more races (2000); Density: 15.3 persons per square mile (2000); Age: 25.6% under 18, 26.1% over 64 (2000); Marriage status: 18.8% never married, 69.8% now married, 10.2% widowed, 1.3% divorced (2000); Foreign born: 0.0% (2000); Ancestry (includes multiple ancestries): 58.2% German, 9.1% United States or American, 8.2% Norwegian, 3.7% Irish, 1.9% Swedish (2000).
Economy: Employment by occupation: 17.7% management, 10.4% professional, 9.0% services, 21.3% sales, 10.7% farming, 14.3% construction, 16.6% production (2000).
Income: Per capita income: $19,139 (2000); Median household income: $53,750 (2000); Poverty rate: 4.8% (2000).
Taxes: Total city taxes per capita: $94 (1997); City property taxes per capita: $94 (1997).
Education: High school graduation rate: 77.0% (2000); College graduation rate: 11.6% (2000).
Housing: Homeownership rate: 84.8% (2000); Median home value: $119,200 (2000); Median rent: $225 per month (2000); Median age of housing: 49 years (2000).
Transportation: Commute to work: 79.5% car, 0.0% public transportation, 4.8% walk, 15.7% work from home (2000); Travel time to work: 51.0% less than 15 minutes, 39.5% 15 to 30 minutes, 7.1% 30 to 45 minutes, 1.0% 45 to 60 minutes, 1.4% 60 minutes or more (2000)

LAKE HANSKA (township). Covers a land area of 36.729 square miles and a water area of 2.058 square miles. Located at 44.14° N. Lat.; 94.55° W. Long.
Population: 322 (2000); Race: 99.1% White, 0.0% Black, 0.6% Asian, 0.0% American Indian and Alaska Native, 1.5% Hispanic of any race, 0.0% two or more races (2000); Density: 8.8 persons per square mile (2000); Age: 26.2% under 18, 17.1% over 64 (2000); Marriage status: 26.3% never married, 63.7% now married, 4.2% widowed, 5.7% divorced (2000); Foreign born: 1.8% (2000); Ancestry (includes multiple ancestries): 60.1% German, 43.0% Norwegian, 5.2% Swedish, 4.6% Irish, 3.4% Polish (2000).
Economy: Employment by occupation: 25.9% management, 10.6% professional, 9.4% services, 24.7% sales, 1.2% farming, 13.5% construction, 14.7% production (2000).
Income: Per capita income: $17,652 (2000); Median household income: $36,786 (2000); Poverty rate: 1.2% (2000).
Taxes: Total city taxes per capita: $55 (1997); City property taxes per capita: $55 (1997).
Education: High school graduation rate: 87.4% (2000); College graduation rate: 11.3% (2000).
Housing: Homeownership rate: 87.6% (2000); Median home value: $125,000 (2000); Median rent: $375 per month (2000); Median age of housing: 60+ years (2000).
Transportation: Commute to work: 67.7% car, 0.0% public transportation, 8.4% walk, 22.8% work from home (2000); Travel time to work: 27.9% less than 15 minutes, 56.6% 15 to 30 minutes, 11.6% 30 to 45 minutes, 3.1% 45 to 60 minutes, 0.8% 60 minutes or more (2000)

LEAVENWORTH (township). Covers a land area of 35.112 square miles and a water area of 0.267 square miles. Located at 44.25° N. Lat.; 94.81° W. Long.
Population: 336 (2000); Race: 97.9% White, 0.0% Black, 0.0% Asian, 0.0% American Indian and Alaska Native, 1.2% Hispanic of any race, 0.9% two or more races (2000); Density: 9.6 persons per square mile (2000); Age: 28.8% under 18, 9.8% over 64 (2000); Marriage status: 24.2% never married, 65.2% now married, 7.0% widowed, 3.5% divorced (2000); Foreign born: 1.2% (2000); Ancestry (includes multiple ancestries): 70.2% German, 4.9% Irish, 4.6% Norwegian, 4.6% Polish, 4.3% United States or American (2000).
Economy: Employment by occupation: 25.7% management, 8.2% professional, 9.3% services, 20.8% sales, 5.5% farming, 8.7% construction, 21.9% production (2000).
Income: Per capita income: $19,796 (2000); Median household income: $40,313 (2000); Poverty rate: 7.4% (2000).
Taxes: Total city taxes per capita: $122 (1997); City property taxes per capita: $122 (1997).
Education: High school graduation rate: 76.1% (2000); College graduation rate: 8.7% (2000).
Housing: Homeownership rate: 89.0% (2000); Median home value: $87,500 (2000); Median rent: $356 per month (2000); Median age of housing: 60+ years (2000).
Transportation: Commute to work: 65.9% car, 0.0% public transportation, 1.1% walk, 33.0% work from home (2000); Travel time to work: 39.3% less than 15 minutes, 39.3% 15 to 30 minutes, 13.1% 30 to 45 minutes, 2.5% 45 to 60 minutes, 5.7% 60 minutes or more (2000)

LINDEN (township). Covers a land area of 35.190 square miles and a water area of 0.837 square miles. Located at 44.15° N. Lat.; 94.42° W. Long. Elevation is 995 feet.
Population: 343 (2000); Race: 100.0% White, 0.0% Black, 0.0% Asian, 0.0% American Indian and Alaska Native, 0.6% Hispanic of any race, 0.0% two or more races (2000); Density: 9.7 persons per square mile (2000); Age: 25.4% under 18, 13.3% over 64 (2000); Marriage status: 30.0% never married, 64.4% now married, 1.5% widowed, 4.1% divorced (2000); Foreign

born: 1.2% (2000); Ancestry (includes multiple ancestries): 58.3% German, 42.0% Norwegian, 3.6% Swiss, 3.6% Swedish, 3.3% Irish (2000).
Economy: Employment by occupation: 25.8% management, 10.3% professional, 7.7% services, 20.6% sales, 2.6% farming, 7.2% construction, 25.8% production (2000).
Income: Per capita income: $22,939 (2000); Median household income: $63,125 (2000); Poverty rate: 1.2% (2000).
Taxes: Total city taxes per capita: $110 (1997); City property taxes per capita: $110 (1997).
Education: High school graduation rate: 92.1% (2000); College graduation rate: 17.3% (2000).
Housing: Homeownership rate: 84.3% (2000); Median home value: $98,100 (2000); Median rent: $219 per month (2000); Median age of housing: 60+ years (2000).
Transportation: Commute to work: 77.8% car, 0.0% public transportation, 3.1% walk, 18.6% work from home (2000); Travel time to work: 25.9% less than 15 minutes, 60.8% 15 to 30 minutes, 8.9% 30 to 45 minutes, 0.0% 45 to 60 minutes, 4.4% 60 minutes or more (2000)

MILFORD (township). Covers a land area of 39.193 square miles and a water area of 0.383 square miles. Located at 44.31° N. Lat.; 94.56° W. Long.
Population: 793 (2000); Race: 98.4% White, 0.0% Black, 0.0% Asian, 0.0% American Indian and Alaska Native, 1.8% Hispanic of any race, 0.4% two or more races (2000); Density: 20.2 persons per square mile (2000); Age: 31.2% under 18, 9.7% over 64 (2000); Marriage status: 22.2% never married, 73.5% now married, 1.8% widowed, 2.6% divorced (2000); Foreign born: 1.2% (2000); Ancestry (includes multiple ancestries): 74.0% German, 7.8% Norwegian, 6.8% Swedish, 3.2% Irish, 2.5% Danish (2000).
Economy: Employment by occupation: 17.7% management, 12.0% professional, 12.0% services, 22.0% sales, 0.4% farming, 12.4% construction, 23.5% production (2000).
Income: Per capita income: $20,417 (2000); Median household income: $57,813 (2000); Poverty rate: 3.2% (2000).
Taxes: Total city taxes per capita: $76 (1997); City property taxes per capita: $76 (1997).
Education: High school graduation rate: 89.0% (2000); College graduation rate: 13.3% (2000).
Housing: Homeownership rate: 89.5% (2000); Median home value: $121,500 (2000); Median rent: $300 per month (2000); Median age of housing: 35 years (2000).
Transportation: Commute to work: 85.1% car, 0.5% public transportation, 3.8% walk, 10.6% work from home (2000); Travel time to work: 56.9% less than 15 minutes, 31.7% 15 to 30 minutes, 3.3% 30 to 45 minutes, 3.0% 45 to 60 minutes, 5.0% 60 minutes or more (2000)

MULLIGAN (township). Covers a land area of 35.887 square miles and a water area of 0.404 square miles. Located at 44.15° N. Lat.; 94.80° W. Long.
Population: 245 (2000); Race: 100.0% White, 0.0% Black, 0.0% Asian, 0.0% American Indian and Alaska Native, 0.0% Hispanic of any race, 0.0% two or more races (2000); Density: 6.8 persons per square mile (2000); Age: 28.2% under 18, 16.1% over 64 (2000); Marriage status: 28.1% never married, 62.3% now married, 7.5% widowed, 2.0% divorced (2000); Foreign born: 0.0% (2000); Ancestry (includes multiple ancestries): 83.1% German, 8.1% Austrian, 7.3% Norwegian, 4.0% Irish, 3.6% Swedish (2000).
Economy: Employment by occupation: 37.5% management, 15.2% professional, 3.6% services, 12.5% sales, 5.4% farming, 8.9% construction, 17.0% production (2000).
Income: Per capita income: $15,939 (2000); Median household income: $37,188 (2000); Poverty rate: 10.9% (2000).
Taxes: Total city taxes per capita: $69 (1997); City property taxes per capita: $69 (1997).
Education: High school graduation rate: 73.0% (2000); College graduation rate: 8.0% (2000).
Housing: Homeownership rate: 81.1% (2000); Median home value: $87,500 (2000); Median rent: $150 per month (2000); Median age of housing: 60+ years (2000).
Transportation: Commute to work: 62.7% car, 0.0% public transportation, 0.0% walk, 37.3% work from home (2000); Travel time to work: 20.3% less than 15 minutes, 43.5% 15 to 30 minutes, 26.1% 30 to 45 minutes, 10.1% 45 to 60 minutes, 0.0% 60 minutes or more (2000)

NEW ULM (city). Covers a land area of 8.780 square miles and a water area of 0.205 square miles. Located at 44.31° N. Lat.; 94.46° W. Long. Elevation is 837 feet.
History: New Ulm was founded in 1854 by representatives of a German land society in Chicago, and named for the cathedral city of Ulm in Wurttemberg, Germany. Most of the early residents were of German ancestry. New Ulm was an early milling center, with flour production as its leading industry. Author and illustrator Wanda Gag, who wrote "Millions of Cats," was born in New Ulm.
Population: 13,594 (2000); Race: 97.5% White, 0.4% Black, 0.1% Asian, 0.8% American Indian and Alaska Native, 1.4% Hispanic of any race, 0.8% two or more races (2000); Density: 1,548.3 persons per square mile (2000); Age: 23.0% under 18, 16.6% over 64 (2000); Marriage status: 27.6% never married, 58.7% now married, 7.2% widowed, 6.6% divorced (2000); Foreign born: 1.0% (2000); Ancestry (includes multiple ancestries): 65.9% German, 11.8% Norwegian, 5.7% Irish, 5.0% Swedish, 3.8% United States or American (2000).
Vital Statistics: Birth rate: 81.7 per 10,000 population (1998)
Economy: Single-family building permits issued: 27 (2001) / 16 (2000); Multi-family building permits issued: 4 (2001) / 0 (2000); Employment by occupation: 9.1% management, 16.9% professional, 16.8% services, 24.4% sales, 0.7% farming, 7.4% construction, 24.7% production (2000).
Income: Per capita income: $20,308 (2000); Median household income: $40,044 (2000); Poverty rate: 6.2% (2000).
Taxes: Total city taxes per capita: $212 (1997); City property taxes per capita: $205 (1997).
Education: High school graduation rate: 83.3% (2000); College graduation rate: 21.4% (2000).

School District(s)

New Ulm (PK-12)
2000 Enrollment: 2,582 507-359-8401
River Bend Ed. Dist. (PK-12)
2000 Enrollment: 110 507-359-8700

Four-year College(s)

Martin Luther College (Private, Not-for-profit, Wisconsin Evangelical Lutheran Synod)
2001 Enrollment: 1,060 507-354-8221
2001 Tuition: In-state $4,750; Out-of-state $4,750

Housing: Homeownership rate: 77.1% (2000); Median home value: $89,600 (2000); Median rent: $384 per month (2000); Median age of housing: 41 years (2000).
Hospitals: New Ulm Medical Center (85 beds)
Safety: Violent crime rate: 8.7 per 10,000 population; Property crime rate: 243.1 per 10,000 population (2001).
Newspapers: Prairie Catholic (1 x month); The Journal (7 x week); New Ulm Shopper/Post-Review (1 x week)
Transportation: Commute to work: 87.5% car, 1.0% public transportation, 6.6% walk, 3.7% work from home (2000); Travel time to work: 78.4% less than 15 minutes, 12.3% 15 to 30 minutes, 5.7% 30 to 45 minutes, 1.2% 45 to 60 minutes, 2.3% 60 minutes or more (2000)
Airports: New Ulm Municipal
Additional Information Contacts
New Ulm Chamber of Commerce 507-233-4300

NORTH STAR (township). Covers a land area of 35.362 square miles and a water area of 0.010 square miles. Located at 44.22° N. Lat.; 95.05° W. Long.
Population: 325 (2000); Race: 100.0% White, 0.0% Black, 0.0% Asian, 0.0% American Indian and Alaska Native, 0.0% Hispanic of any race, 0.0% two or more races (2000); Density: 9.2 persons per square mile (2000); Age: 29.7% under 18, 10.6% over 64 (2000); Marriage status: 21.8% never married, 74.5% now married, 2.1% widowed, 1.6% divorced (2000); Foreign born: 0.0% (2000); Ancestry (includes multiple ancestries): 63.5% German, 9.4% United States or American, 6.5% Irish, 5.5% Scandinavian, 4.2% Norwegian (2000).
Economy: Employment by occupation: 14.6% management, 12.2% professional, 15.2% services, 28.0% sales, 7.9% farming, 7.3% construction, 14.6% production (2000).
Income: Per capita income: $20,308 (2000); Median household income: $45,938 (2000); Poverty rate: 5.5% (2000).
Taxes: Total city taxes per capita: $57 (1997); City property taxes per capita: $57 (1997).
Education: High school graduation rate: 85.8% (2000); College graduation rate: 8.8% (2000).
Housing: Homeownership rate: 85.7% (2000); Median home value: $75,600 (2000); Median rent: $356 per month (2000); Median age of housing: 54 years (2000).
Transportation: Commute to work: 85.8% car, 0.0% public transportation, 0.0% walk, 14.2% work from home (2000); Travel time to work: 47.5% less than 15 minutes, 30.9% 15 to 30 minutes, 14.4% 30 to 45 minutes, 0.0% 45 to 60 minutes, 7.2% 60 minutes or more (2000)

PRAIRIEVILLE (township). Covers a land area of 34.349 square miles and a water area of 0.007 square miles. Located at 44.31° N. Lat.; 94.81° W. Long.
Population: 346 (2000); Race: 100.0% White, 0.0% Black, 0.0% Asian, 0.0% American Indian and Alaska Native, 0.0% Hispanic of any race, 0.0% two or more races (2000); Density: 10.1 persons per square mile (2000); Age: 28.8% under 18, 13.0% over 64 (2000); Marriage status: 24.4% never married, 68.3% now married, 4.6% widowed, 2.7% divorced (2000); Foreign born: 0.0% (2000); Ancestry (includes multiple ancestries): 78.0% German, 13.9% Norwegian, 9.9% Danish, 5.9% Irish, 5.0% English (2000).
Economy: Employment by occupation: 22.8% management, 9.4% professional, 15.4% services, 24.2% sales, 0.0% farming, 8.7% construction, 19.5% production (2000).
Income: Per capita income: $16,206 (2000); Median household income: $33,542 (2000); Poverty rate: 6.8% (2000).
Taxes: Total city taxes per capita: $76 (1997); City property taxes per capita: $76 (1997).
Education: High school graduation rate: 86.7% (2000); College graduation rate: 5.2% (2000).
Housing: Homeownership rate: 81.7% (2000); Median home value: $88,800 (2000); Median rent: $300 per month (2000); Median age of housing: 60+ years (2000).
Transportation: Commute to work: 78.8% car, 0.0% public transportation, 1.4% walk, 19.2% work from home (2000); Travel time to work: 49.2% less than 15 minutes, 43.2% 15 to 30 minutes, 3.4% 30 to 45 minutes, 0.0% 45 to 60 minutes, 4.2% 60 minutes or more (2000)

SIGEL (township). Covers a land area of 38.761 square miles and a water area of 0.848 square miles. Located at 44.23° N. Lat.; 94.56° W. Long.
Population: 432 (2000); Race: 99.5% White, 0.0% Black, 0.5% Asian, 0.0% American Indian and Alaska Native, 0.7% Hispanic of any race, 0.0% two or more races (2000); Density: 11.1 persons per square mile (2000); Age: 28.1% under 18, 12.0% over 64 (2000); Marriage status: 20.4% never married, 72.0% now married, 3.5% widowed, 4.1% divorced (2000); Foreign born: 1.4% (2000); Ancestry (includes multiple ancestries): 73.4% German, 6.5% Norwegian, 5.3% Czech, 2.6% United States or American, 2.4% Other groups (2000).
Economy: Employment by occupation: 28.0% management, 8.9% professional, 7.6% services, 16.0% sales, 4.4% farming, 14.7% construction, 20.4% production (2000).
Income: Per capita income: $17,051 (2000); Median household income: $43,472 (2000); Poverty rate: 3.1% (2000).
Taxes: Total city taxes per capita: $48 (1997); City property taxes per capita: $48 (1997).
Education: High school graduation rate: 77.3% (2000); College graduation rate: 11.2% (2000).
Housing: Homeownership rate: 94.4% (2000); Median home value: $89,500 (2000); Median rent: $575 per month (2000); Median age of housing: 57 years (2000).
Transportation: Commute to work: 77.3% car, 0.0% public transportation, 4.0% walk, 18.7% work from home (2000); Travel time to work: 31.1% less than 15 minutes, 59.6% 15 to 30 minutes, 7.1% 30 to 45 minutes, 0.0% 45 to 60 minutes, 2.2% 60 minutes or more (2000)

SLEEPY EYE (city). Covers a land area of 1.674 square miles and a water area of 0.282 square miles. Located at 44.29° N. Lat.; 94.72° W. Long. Elevation is 1,030 feet.
History: Sleepy Eye was named for the Indian chief Isk-Irk-Ha-Ba, whose named was translated "sleepy eye." The chief was reportedly buried beneath a monument near the railroad station.
Population: 3,515 (2000); Race: 94.1% White, 0.5% Black, 1.0% Asian, 0.0% American Indian and Alaska Native, 7.9% Hispanic of any race, 0.7% two or more races (2000); Density: 2,099.9 persons per square mile (2000); Age: 27.8% under 18, 19.5% over 64 (2000); Marriage status: 20.8% never married, 58.5% now married, 12.3% widowed, 8.5% divorced (2000); Foreign born: 3.3% (2000); Ancestry (includes multiple ancestries): 60.5% German, 10.2% Other groups, 8.3% Norwegian, 6.5% Irish, 5.3% United States or American (2000).
Economy: Single-family building permits issued: 2 (2001) / 7 (2000); Multi-family building permits issued: 0 (2001) / 0 (2000); Employment by occupation: 9.7% management, 16.2% professional, 18.4% services, 17.8% sales, 2.7% farming, 11.0% construction, 24.3% production (2000).
Income: Per capita income: $20,175 (2000); Median household income: $37,123 (2000); Poverty rate: 8.1% (2000).
Taxes: Total city taxes per capita: $110 (1997); City property taxes per capita: $85 (1997).
Education: High school graduation rate: 75.3% (2000); College graduation rate: 12.4% (2000).

School District(s)

Sleepy Eye (PK-12)
2000 Enrollment: 709 507-794-7903
Housing: Homeownership rate: 75.7% (2000); Median home value: $78,300 (2000); Median rent: $321 per month (2000); Median age of housing: 49 years (2000).
Hospitals: Sleepy Eye Municipal Hospital (25 beds)
Newspapers: Sleepy Eye Herald Dispatch (1 x week)
Transportation: Commute to work: 85.1% car, 0.9% public transportation, 9.8% walk, 3.2% work from home (2000); Travel time to work: 70.8% less than 15 minutes, 22.1% 15 to 30 minutes, 1.6% 30 to 45 minutes, 1.9% 45 to 60 minutes, 3.7% 60 minutes or more (2000)
Additional Information Contacts
Sleepy Eye Chamber of Commerce 507-794-4731

SPRINGFIELD (city). Covers a land area of 1.810 square miles and a water area of 0 square miles. Located at 44.23° N. Lat.; 94.97° W. Long. Elevation is 1,026 feet.
History: Springfield was platted in 1877, when it was called Burns. The name was later changed for a nearby spring.
Population: 2,215 (2000); Race: 98.7% White, 0.0% Black, 0.5% Asian, 0.0% American Indian and Alaska Native, 3.4% Hispanic of any race, 0.1% two or more races (2000); Density: 1,223.9 persons per square mile (2000); Age: 26.0% under 18, 27.6% over 64 (2000); Marriage status: 18.1% never married, 63.2% now married, 13.0% widowed, 5.7% divorced (2000); Foreign born: 1.7% (2000); Ancestry (includes multiple ancestries): 63.2% German, 10.4% Norwegian, 9.4% Irish, 4.5% Swedish, 3.9% English (2000).
Economy: Single-family building permits issued: 1 (2001) / 3 (2000); Multi-family building permits issued: 8 (2001) / 0 (2000); Employment by occupation: 11.4% management, 15.4% professional, 18.2% services, 20.1% sales, 1.6% farming, 9.2% construction, 24.1% production (2000).
Income: Per capita income: $16,977 (2000); Median household income: $34,643 (2000); Poverty rate: 6.5% (2000).
Taxes: Total city taxes per capita: $244 (1997); City property taxes per capita: $243 (1997).
Education: High school graduation rate: 78.6% (2000); College graduation rate: 14.3% (2000).

School District(s)

Springfield (PK-12)
2000 Enrollment: 737 507-723-4283
Housing: Homeownership rate: 84.2% (2000); Median home value: $55,100 (2000); Median rent: $264 per month (2000); Median age of housing: 49 years (2000).
Hospitals: Springfield Medical Center - Mayo Health System (24 beds)
Newspapers: Springfield Advance-Press (1 x week)
Transportation: Commute to work: 88.4% car, 0.0% public transportation, 8.7% walk, 2.2% work from home (2000); Travel time to work: 66.6% less than 15 minutes, 13.7% 15 to 30 minutes, 12.3% 30 to 45 minutes, 0.9% 45 to 60 minutes, 6.5% 60 minutes or more (2000)

STARK (township). Covers a land area of 35.585 square miles and a water area of 0.536 square miles. Located at 44.24° N. Lat.; 94.68° W. Long.
Population: 384 (2000); Race: 100.0% White, 0.0% Black, 0.0% Asian, 0.0% American Indian and Alaska Native, 0.0% Hispanic of any race, 0.0% two or more races (2000); Density: 10.8 persons per square mile (2000); Age: 34.8% under 18, 11.7% over 64 (2000); Marriage status: 23.0% never married, 66.6% now married, 2.7% widowed, 7.8% divorced (2000); Foreign born: 0.0% (2000); Ancestry (includes multiple ancestries): 70.5% German, 6.7% Norwegian, 5.2% United States or American, 3.1% Czech, 2.6% Irish (2000).
Economy: Employment by occupation: 24.9% management, 12.4% professional, 6.2% services, 17.7% sales, 9.6% farming, 10.0% construction, 19.1% production (2000).
Income: Per capita income: $14,716 (2000); Median household income: $36,705 (2000); Poverty rate: 8.3% (2000).
Taxes: Total city taxes per capita: $47 (1997); City property taxes per capita: $47 (1997).
Education: High school graduation rate: 86.3% (2000); College graduation rate: 5.0% (2000).
Housing: Homeownership rate: 88.4% (2000); Median home value: $100,000 (2000); Median rent: $250 per month (2000); Median age of housing: 60+ years (2000).

Transportation: Commute to work: 71.7% car, 0.0% public transportation, 2.9% walk, 25.4% work from home (2000); Travel time to work: 37.9% less than 15 minutes, 54.9% 15 to 30 minutes, 2.6% 30 to 45 minutes, 1.3% 45 to 60 minutes, 3.3% 60 minutes or more (2000)

STATELY (township). Covers a land area of 35.961 square miles and a water area of 0.083 square miles. Located at 44.15° N. Lat.; 95.03° W. Long.
Population: 206 (2000); Race: 99.0% White, 0.0% Black, 0.0% Asian, 0.0% American Indian and Alaska Native, 0.0% Hispanic of any race, 1.0% two or more races (2000); Density: 5.7 persons per square mile (2000); Age: 33.2% under 18, 8.7% over 64 (2000); Marriage status: 26.2% never married, 70.5% now married, 1.3% widowed, 2.0% divorced (2000); Foreign born: 0.0% (2000); Ancestry (includes multiple ancestries): 71.2% German, 15.4% Norwegian, 9.6% Swedish, 4.8% United States or American, 3.8% English (2000).
Economy: Employment by occupation: 23.9% management, 16.5% professional, 14.7% services, 15.6% sales, 1.8% farming, 9.2% construction, 18.3% production (2000).
Income: Per capita income: $20,458 (2000); Median household income: $39,583 (2000); Poverty rate: 14.1% (2000).
Taxes: Total city taxes per capita: $31 (1997); City property taxes per capita: $31 (1997).
Education: High school graduation rate: 74.8% (2000); College graduation rate: 13.4% (2000).
Housing: Homeownership rate: 80.9% (2000); Median home value: $81,300 (2000); Median rent: $175 per month (2000); Median age of housing: 59 years (2000).
Transportation: Commute to work: 77.1% car, 0.0% public transportation, 5.5% walk, 17.4% work from home (2000); Travel time to work: 37.8% less than 15 minutes, 33.3% 15 to 30 minutes, 25.6% 30 to 45 minutes, 2.2% 45 to 60 minutes, 1.1% 60 minutes or more (2000)

Carlton County

Located in eastern Minnesota; bounded on the east by Wisconsin; drained by the St. Louis River. Covers a land area of 860.30 square miles, a water area of 14.90 square miles, and is located in the Central Time Zone. The county government was organized in 1857. County seat is Carlton.

Weather Station: Cloquet — Elevation: 1,263 feet

	Jan	Feb	Mar	Apr	May	Jun	Jul	Aug	Sep	Oct	Nov	Dec
High	18	26	37	53	68	76	80	77	67	54	36	23
Low	-1	4	16	28	39	48	54	53	45	34	21	6
Precip	1.2	0.8	1.7	2.1	3.3	4.2	4.3	4.3	4.1	2.8	2.1	1.1
Snow	16.1	9.9	10.6	3.6	0.1	0.0	0.0	0.0	tr	0.8	11.0	13.3

High and Low temperatures in degrees Fahrenheit; Precipitation and Snow in inches

Weather Station: Moose Lake 1 SSE — Elevation: 1,108 feet

	Jan	Feb	Mar	Apr	May	Jun	Jul	Aug	Sep	Oct	Nov	Dec
High	19	27	38	54	68	76	81	78	68	56	37	24
Low	-3	3	16	28	39	48	54	53	44	34	20	5
Precip	0.9	0.6	1.5	2.0	3.1	4.4	4.3	4.0	3.6	2.6	1.9	0.9
Snow	9.5	5.3	7.2	3.4	tr	0.0	0.0	0.0	0.0	0.7	7.2	7.2

High and Low temperatures in degrees Fahrenheit; Precipitation and Snow in inches

Weather Station: Wright 4 NW — Elevation: 1,292 feet

	Jan	Feb	Mar	Apr	May	Jun	Jul	Aug	Sep	Oct	Nov	Dec
High	18	26	37	53	67	75	79	77	67	54	36	22
Low	-4	3	15	28	40	48	54	52	44	34	19	4
Precip	1.0	0.6	1.4	2.1	3.2	4.3	4.2	4.0	3.4	2.7	1.7	0.9
Snow	14.1	7.7	9.7	4.6	0.3	0.0	0.0	0.0	tr	1.6	11.0	10.2

High and Low temperatures in degrees Fahrenheit; Precipitation and Snow in inches

Population: 31,671 (2000); Race: 91.8% White, 0.8% Black, 0.4% Asian, 5.0% American Indian and Alaska Native, 1.0% Hispanic of any race, 1.6% two or more races (2000); Density: 36.8 persons per square mile (2000); Age: 25.4% under 18, 15.1% over 64 (2000).
Religion: Five largest groups: 21.0% Catholic Church, 18.4% Evangelical Lutheran Church in America, 5.6% Lutheran Church—Missouri Synod, 2.5% The Association of Free Lutheran Congregations, 1.5% The United Methodist Church (2000).
Economy: Unemployment rate: 4.7% (11/2002); Total civilian labor force: 16,500 (11/2002); Leading industries: 24.1% manufacturing; 15.8% retail trade; 13.6% health care and social assistance (2000); Companies that employ more than 1,000 persons: 1 (2000); Companies that employ more than 100 persons: 12 (2000); Farms: 527 totaling 107,166 acres (1997); Minority business ownership rate: 0.0% (1997); Women business ownership rate: 30.8% (1997); Retail sales per capita: $7,344 (1997). Single-family building permits issued: 222 (2001) / 226 (2000); Multi-family building permits issued: 7 (2001) / 78 (2000).
Income: Per capita income: $18,073 (2000); Median household income: $40,021 (2000); Poverty rate: 7.9% (2000); Bankruptcy rate: 3.17% (2001).
Taxes: Total county taxes per capita: $342 (2000); County property taxes per capita: $339 (2000).
Education: High school graduation rate: 84.3% (2000); College graduation rate: 14.9% (2000).
Housing: Homeownership rate: 82.0% (2000); Median home value: $85,400 (2000); Median rent: $346 per month (2000); Median age of housing: 36 years (2000).
Health: Birth rate: 121.6 per 10,000 population (1998); Age adjusted death rate: 81.3 per 10,000 population (1999); Age adjusted cancer mortality rate: 155.5 deaths per 100,000 population (1999). Air Quality Index: 94% good, 6% moderate, 0% unhealthy (percent of days in 2000). Number of physicians: 8.8 per 10,000 population (1999); Number of hospital beds: 72.0 per 10,000 population (1999).
Elections: 2000 Presidential election results: 57.2% Gore, 37.0% Bush, 4.2% Nader, 1.2% Buchanan
National and State Parks: Dye State Wildlife Management Area; Fond du Lac State Forest; Jay Cooke State Park; Kettle Lake State Wildlife Management Area; Mervin State Wildlife Management Area; Moose Lake State Recreation Area; Sawyer State Wildlife Management Area
Additional Information Contacts
Carlton County Government Offices 218-384-4281
Cloquet Chamber of Commerce. 218-879-1551
Moose Lake Chamber of Commerce 218-485-4145

Carlton County Communities

ATKINSON (township). Covers a land area of 17.370 square miles and a water area of 0.788 square miles. Located at 46.59° N. Lat.; 92.61° W. Long. Elevation is 1,147 feet.
Population: 319 (2000); Race: 97.4% White, 0.0% Black, 1.2% Asian, 0.0% American Indian and Alaska Native, 0.0% Hispanic of any race, 1.5% two or more races (2000); Density: 18.4 persons per square mile (2000); Age: 26.0% under 18, 14.9% over 64 (2000); Marriage status: 25.2% never married, 63.1% now married, 5.0% widowed, 6.7% divorced (2000); Foreign born: 0.6% (2000); Ancestry (includes multiple ancestries): 29.2% Swedish, 27.2% German, 17.8% Norwegian, 11.1% French (except Basque), 10.2% Finnish (2000).
Economy: Employment by occupation: 9.0% management, 16.8% professional, 14.8% services, 16.8% sales, 3.9% farming, 17.4% construction, 21.3% production (2000).
Income: Per capita income: $18,479 (2000); Median household income: $49,375 (2000); Poverty rate: 0.6% (2000).
Taxes: Total city taxes per capita: $57 (1997); City property taxes per capita: $57 (1997).
Education: High school graduation rate: 84.9% (2000); College graduation rate: 20.7% (2000).
Housing: Homeownership rate: 96.7% (2000); Median home value: $63,800 (2000); Median age of housing: 25 years (2000).
Transportation: Commute to work: 97.4% car, 0.0% public transportation, 2.6% walk, 0.0% work from home (2000); Travel time to work: 17.8% less than 15 minutes, 58.6% 15 to 30 minutes, 19.7% 30 to 45 minutes, 3.9% 45 to 60 minutes, 0.0% 60 minutes or more (2000)

AUTOMBA (township). Covers a land area of 36.389 square miles and a water area of 0.013 square miles. Located at 46.54° N. Lat.; 92.98° W. Long. Elevation is 1,284 feet.
Population: 137 (2000); Race: 98.6% White, 0.0% Black, 0.0% Asian, 0.0% American Indian and Alaska Native, 0.0% Hispanic of any race, 1.4% two or more races (2000); Density: 3.8 persons per square mile (2000); Age: 18.8% under 18, 20.8% over 64 (2000); Marriage status: 39.0% never married, 55.3% now married, 4.1% widowed, 1.6% divorced (2000); Foreign born: 0.0% (2000); Ancestry (includes multiple ancestries): 31.9% Finnish, 18.1% Polish, 16.0% German, 15.3% Norwegian, 6.3% United States or American (2000).
Economy: Employment by occupation: 7.0% management, 19.3% professional, 10.5% services, 17.5% sales, 0.0% farming, 33.3% construction, 12.3% production (2000).
Income: Per capita income: $17,524 (2000); Median household income: $36,000 (2000); Poverty rate: 10.4% (2000).

Taxes: Total city taxes per capita: $83 (1997); City property taxes per capita: $83 (1997).
Education: High school graduation rate: 78.4% (2000); College graduation rate: 12.7% (2000).
Housing: Homeownership rate: 85.5% (2000); Median home value: $25,000 (2000); Median rent: $225 per month (2000); Median age of housing: 33 years (2000).
Transportation: Commute to work: 92.7% car, 0.0% public transportation, 0.0% walk, 3.6% work from home (2000); Travel time to work: 0.0% less than 15 minutes, 50.9% 15 to 30 minutes, 9.4% 30 to 45 minutes, 17.0% 45 to 60 minutes, 22.6% 60 minutes or more (2000)

BARNUM (city). Covers a land area of 1.010 square miles and a water area of 0 square miles. Located at 46.50° N. Lat.; 92.69° W. Long. Elevation is 1,103 feet.
History: Barnum began as a lumber town, but turned to farming when the timber was gone. The area was known for fine Guernsey cattle and white Leghorn chickens. Potatoes and red clover were the early crops.
Population: 525 (2000); Race: 97.4% White, 0.0% Black, 0.0% Asian, 1.1% American Indian and Alaska Native, 0.0% Hispanic of any race, 1.5% two or more races (2000); Density: 519.7 persons per square mile (2000); Age: 31.4% under 18, 16.4% over 64 (2000); Marriage status: 24.9% never married, 51.2% now married, 10.0% widowed, 13.9% divorced (2000); Foreign born: 0.4% (2000); Ancestry (includes multiple ancestries): 24.6% German, 18.2% Norwegian, 13.5% Swedish, 9.8% United States or American, 7.3% Finnish (2000).
Economy: Single-family building permits issued: 2 (2001) / 6 (2000); Multi-family building permits issued: 5 (2001) / 0 (2000); Employment by occupation: 5.8% management, 14.6% professional, 31.1% services, 18.9% sales, 1.0% farming, 15.5% construction, 13.1% production (2000).
Income: Per capita income: $14,621 (2000); Median household income: $31,518 (2000); Poverty rate: 9.4% (2000).
Taxes: Total city taxes per capita: $200 (1997); City property taxes per capita: $194 (1997).
Education: High school graduation rate: 83.9% (2000); College graduation rate: 11.8% (2000).

School District(s)

Barnum (PK-12)
2000 Enrollment: 664 218-389-6978
Housing: Homeownership rate: 67.0% (2000); Median home value: $63,300 (2000); Median rent: $281 per month (2000); Median age of housing: 40 years (2000).
Transportation: Commute to work: 92.1% car, 0.0% public transportation, 3.0% walk, 4.9% work from home (2000); Travel time to work: 35.8% less than 15 minutes, 26.4% 15 to 30 minutes, 23.3% 30 to 45 minutes, 11.9% 45 to 60 minutes, 2.6% 60 minutes or more (2000)

BARNUM (township). Covers a land area of 44.983 square miles and a water area of 1.194 square miles. Located at 46.49° N. Lat.; 92.65° W. Long. Elevation is 1,103 feet.
Population: 978 (2000); Race: 98.0% White, 0.0% Black, 0.3% Asian, 0.4% American Indian and Alaska Native, 1.4% Hispanic of any race, 0.8% two or more races (2000); Density: 21.7 persons per square mile (2000); Age: 25.0% under 18, 12.5% over 64 (2000); Marriage status: 23.2% never married, 64.9% now married, 4.5% widowed, 7.4% divorced (2000); Foreign born: 0.6% (2000); Ancestry (includes multiple ancestries): 32.4% German, 22.9% Swedish, 17.5% Norwegian, 13.7% Finnish, 9.4% Irish (2000).
Economy: Dairying; poultry; oats, alfalfa. Light manufacturing. Employment by occupation: 7.5% management, 15.2% professional, 20.5% services, 19.9% sales, 0.8% farming, 16.3% construction, 19.9% production (2000).
Income: Per capita income: $18,776 (2000); Median household income: $42,679 (2000); Poverty rate: 7.9% (2000).
Taxes: Total city taxes per capita: $78 (1997); City property taxes per capita: $78 (1997).
Education: High school graduation rate: 87.1% (2000); College graduation rate: 15.4% (2000).
Housing: Homeownership rate: 94.9% (2000); Median home value: $98,200 (2000); Median rent: $408 per month (2000); Median age of housing: 25 years (2000).
Transportation: Commute to work: 91.8% car, 0.4% public transportation, 1.4% walk, 6.0% work from home (2000); Travel time to work: 28.5% less than 15 minutes, 34.6% 15 to 30 minutes, 20.0% 30 to 45 minutes, 10.8% 45 to 60 minutes, 6.2% 60 minutes or more (2000)

BESEMAN (township). Covers a land area of 35.984 square miles and a water area of 0.030 square miles. Located at 46.70° N. Lat.; 93.02° W. Long.
Population: 149 (2000); Race: 100.0% White, 0.0% Black, 0.0% Asian, 0.0% American Indian and Alaska Native, 0.0% Hispanic of any race, 0.0% two or more races (2000); Density: 4.1 persons per square mile (2000); Age: 34.3% under 18, 6.7% over 64 (2000); Marriage status: 26.5% never married, 67.4% now married, 3.0% widowed, 3.0% divorced (2000); Foreign born: 0.0% (2000); Ancestry (includes multiple ancestries): 25.3% Finnish, 22.5% German, 21.3% Swedish, 12.9% United States or American, 10.7% Norwegian (2000).
Economy: Employment by occupation: 5.7% management, 14.8% professional, 26.1% services, 13.6% sales, 2.3% farming, 22.7% construction, 14.8% production (2000).
Income: Per capita income: $14,767 (2000); Median household income: $39,583 (2000); Poverty rate: 19.1% (2000).
Taxes: Total city taxes per capita: $164 (1997); City property taxes per capita: $164 (1997).
Education: High school graduation rate: 86.1% (2000); College graduation rate: 13.0% (2000).
Housing: Homeownership rate: 96.7% (2000); Median home value: $95,000 (2000); Median rent: $225 per month (2000); Median age of housing: 29 years (2000).
Transportation: Commute to work: 85.4% car, 0.0% public transportation, 6.1% walk, 8.5% work from home (2000); Travel time to work: 34.7% less than 15 minutes, 17.3% 15 to 30 minutes, 28.0% 30 to 45 minutes, 0.0% 45 to 60 minutes, 20.0% 60 minutes or more (2000)

BLACKHOOF (township). Covers a land area of 35.979 square miles and a water area of 0.453 square miles. Located at 46.53° N. Lat.; 92.50° W. Long. Elevation is 968 feet.
Population: 753 (2000); Race: 97.1% White, 0.0% Black, 0.0% Asian, 0.8% American Indian and Alaska Native, 1.9% Hispanic of any race, 2.1% two or more races (2000); Density: 20.9 persons per square mile (2000); Age: 28.9% under 18, 7.7% over 64 (2000); Marriage status: 19.0% never married, 70.0% now married, 2.1% widowed, 8.9% divorced (2000); Foreign born: 0.0% (2000); Ancestry (includes multiple ancestries): 29.5% German, 21.5% Swedish, 11.9% Norwegian, 11.3% Finnish, 7.5% Polish (2000).
Economy: Employment by occupation: 9.5% management, 22.9% professional, 14.2% services, 20.2% sales, 0.5% farming, 10.4% construction, 22.3% production (2000).
Income: Per capita income: $22,021 (2000); Median household income: $44,125 (2000); Poverty rate: 5.6% (2000).
Taxes: Total city taxes per capita: $42 (1997); City property taxes per capita: $42 (1997).
Education: High school graduation rate: 89.7% (2000); College graduation rate: 16.6% (2000).
Housing: Homeownership rate: 91.2% (2000); Median home value: $88,900 (2000); Median rent: $481 per month (2000); Median age of housing: 25 years (2000).
Transportation: Commute to work: 90.9% car, 0.0% public transportation, 3.3% walk, 5.2% work from home (2000); Travel time to work: 5.8% less than 15 minutes, 51.9% 15 to 30 minutes, 22.0% 30 to 45 minutes, 13.9% 45 to 60 minutes, 6.4% 60 minutes or more (2000)

CARLTON (city). Covers a land area of 2.057 square miles and a water area of 0.201 square miles. Located at 46.66° N. Lat.; 92.42° W. Long. Elevation is 1,091 feet.
History: When the building of the Northern Pacific Railway was begun, Carlton had the distinction of having the first spike driven here.
Population: 810 (2000); Race: 93.7% White, 0.0% Black, 1.1% Asian, 3.4% American Indian and Alaska Native, 0.7% Hispanic of any race, 1.9% two or more races (2000); Density: 393.8 persons per square mile (2000); Age: 25.1% under 18, 27.2% over 64 (2000); Marriage status: 20.8% never married, 53.3% now married, 14.4% widowed, 11.4% divorced (2000); Foreign born: 1.2% (2000); Ancestry (includes multiple ancestries): 26.1% German, 16.2% Norwegian, 11.6% Finnish, 10.2% Swedish, 9.2% Polish (2000).
Economy: Single-family building permits issued: 1 (2001) / 0 (2000); Multi-family building permits issued: 0 (2001) / 0 (2000); Employment by occupation: 6.8% management, 14.9% professional, 17.4% services, 29.2% sales, 0.3% farming, 9.3% construction, 22.0% production (2000).
Income: Per capita income: $15,586 (2000); Median household income: $31,477 (2000); Poverty rate: 9.7% (2000).
Taxes: Total city taxes per capita: $120 (1997); City property taxes per capita: $113 (1997).
Education: High school graduation rate: 77.0% (2000); College graduation rate: 8.1% (2000).

School District(s)

Carlton (PK-12)
2000 Enrollment: 732 218-384-4225

Housing: Homeownership rate: 68.5% (2000); Median home value: $69,300 (2000); Median rent: $439 per month (2000); Median age of housing: 46 years (2000).

Transportation: Commute to work: 91.9% car, 0.0% public transportation, 4.7% walk, 1.9% work from home (2000); Travel time to work: 53.5% less than 15 minutes, 28.0% 15 to 30 minutes, 11.1% 30 to 45 minutes, 1.9% 45 to 60 minutes, 5.4% 60 minutes or more (2000)

CLOQUET (city). Covers a land area of 35.236 square miles and a water area of 0.737 square miles. Located at 46.71° N. Lat.; 92.46° W. Long. Elevation is 1,204 feet.

History: Cloquet is built on the ashes of its predecessor, which was the victim of a devastating forest fire in 1918. The manufacture of wood products and the paper industry resumed when the residents returned and rebuilt the town.

Population: 11,201 (2000); Race: 88.6% White, 0.0% Black, 0.5% Asian, 8.0% American Indian and Alaska Native, 0.8% Hispanic of any race, 2.7% two or more races (2000); Density: 317.9 persons per square mile (2000); Age: 25.4% under 18, 17.7% over 64 (2000); Marriage status: 26.0% never married, 54.5% now married, 9.0% widowed, 10.4% divorced (2000); Foreign born: 2.4% (2000); Ancestry (includes multiple ancestries): 21.5% German, 15.8% Norwegian, 15.7% Finnish, 15.5% Swedish, 9.5% Other groups (2000).

Vital Statistics: Birth rate: 137.5 per 10,000 population (1998)

Economy: Single-family building permits issued: 24 (2001) / 22 (2000); Multi-family building permits issued: 2 (2001) / 76 (2000); Employment by occupation: 9.5% management, 17.4% professional, 19.4% services, 24.2% sales, 1.0% farming, 9.6% construction, 19.0% production (2000).

Income: Per capita income: $17,812 (2000); Median household income: $35,675 (2000); Poverty rate: 9.9% (2000).

Taxes: Total city taxes per capita: $298 (2000); City property taxes per capita: $278 (2000).

Education: High school graduation rate: 82.3% (2000); College graduation rate: 14.7% (2000).

School District(s)

Cloquet (PK-12)
2000 Enrollment: 2,447 218-879-6721

Two-year College(s)

Fond Du Lac Tribal and Community College (Public)
2001 Enrollment: 1,023 218-879-0800
2001 Tuition: In-state $2,332; Out-of-state $4,664

Housing: Homeownership rate: 73.7% (2000); Median home value: $80,100 (2000); Median rent: $348 per month (2000); Median age of housing: 45 years (2000).

Hospitals: Community Memorial Hospital Association (36 beds)

Safety: Violent crime rate: 27.4 per 10,000 population; Property crime rate: 342.7 per 10,000 population (2001).

Newspapers: The Pine Knot (2 x week); Cloquet Journal (1 x week)

Transportation: Commute to work: 93.6% car, 0.3% public transportation, 3.2% walk, 2.2% work from home (2000); Travel time to work: 58.2% less than 15 minutes, 22.1% 15 to 30 minutes, 15.4% 30 to 45 minutes, 2.0% 45 to 60 minutes, 2.3% 60 minutes or more (2000)

Airports: Cloquet Carlton County

Additional Information Contacts

Cloquet Chamber of Commerce 218-879-1551

CROMWELL (city). Covers a land area of 1.817 square miles and a water area of 0.188 square miles. Located at 46.68° N. Lat.; 92.87° W. Long. Elevation is 1,311 feet.

Population: 143 (2000); Race: 96.9% White, 0.0% Black, 0.8% Asian, 2.3% American Indian and Alaska Native, 0.0% Hispanic of any race, 0.0% two or more races (2000); Density: 78.7 persons per square mile (2000); Age: 23.4% under 18, 29.7% over 64 (2000); Marriage status: 23.6% never married, 55.7% now married, 10.4% widowed, 10.4% divorced (2000); Foreign born: 0.0% (2000); Ancestry (includes multiple ancestries): 33.6% Finnish, 28.9% German, 14.8% Norwegian, 11.7% Swedish, 8.6% Other groups (2000).

Economy: Dairying; poultry; oats, alfalfa. Manufacturing: furniture. Single-family building permits issued: 2 (2001) / 1 (2000); Multi-family building permits issued: 0 (2001) / 0 (2000); Employment by occupation: 0.0% management, 5.0% professional, 10.0% services, 25.0% sales, 12.5% farming, 15.0% construction, 32.5% production (2000).

Income: Per capita income: $16,605 (2000); Median household income: $25,000 (2000); Poverty rate: 20.3% (2000).

Taxes: Total city taxes per capita: $178 (1997); City property taxes per capita: $178 (1997).

Education: High school graduation rate: 70.2% (2000); College graduation rate: 6.4% (2000).

School District(s)

Cromwell (PK-12)
2000 Enrollment: 336 218-644-3737

Housing: Homeownership rate: 73.0% (2000); Median home value: $63,800 (2000); Median rent: $270 per month (2000); Median age of housing: 56 years (2000).

Transportation: Commute to work: 100.0% car, 0.0% public transportation, 0.0% walk, 0.0% work from home (2000); Travel time to work: 21.1% less than 15 minutes, 26.3% 15 to 30 minutes, 39.5% 30 to 45 minutes, 13.2% 45 to 60 minutes, 0.0% 60 minutes or more (2000)

EAGLE (township). Covers a land area of 34.613 square miles and a water area of 1.106 square miles. Located at 46.64° N. Lat.; 92.88° W. Long.

Population: 565 (2000); Race: 99.2% White, 0.0% Black, 0.4% Asian, 0.0% American Indian and Alaska Native, 0.0% Hispanic of any race, 0.4% two or more races (2000); Density: 16.3 persons per square mile (2000); Age: 18.5% under 18, 23.0% over 64 (2000); Marriage status: 22.1% never married, 63.6% now married, 6.8% widowed, 7.5% divorced (2000); Foreign born: 0.8% (2000); Ancestry (includes multiple ancestries): 38.7% Finnish, 21.4% Swedish, 16.3% Norwegian, 14.8% German, 7.8% Irish (2000).

Economy: Employment by occupation: 14.8% management, 16.0% professional, 16.0% services, 21.5% sales, 2.5% farming, 10.1% construction, 19.0% production (2000).

Income: Per capita income: $19,078 (2000); Median household income: $36,071 (2000); Poverty rate: 9.7% (2000).

Taxes: Total city taxes per capita: $32 (1997); City property taxes per capita: $32 (1997).

Education: High school graduation rate: 87.8% (2000); College graduation rate: 11.9% (2000).

Housing: Homeownership rate: 93.9% (2000); Median home value: $99,000 (2000); Median rent: $225 per month (2000); Median age of housing: 35 years (2000).

Transportation: Commute to work: 91.3% car, 0.0% public transportation, 1.7% walk, 6.9% work from home (2000); Travel time to work: 21.4% less than 15 minutes, 8.8% 15 to 30 minutes, 38.1% 30 to 45 minutes, 17.7% 45 to 60 minutes, 14.0% 60 minutes or more (2000)

ESKO (unincorporated postal area, zip code 55733). Covers a land area of 35.385 square miles and a water area of 0.052 square miles. Located at 46.70° N. Lat.; 92.36° W. Long. Elevation is 1,170 feet.

History: Esko was established by immigrants from Finland, and grew around a dairy industry.

Population: 4,106 (2000); Race: 98.0% White, 0.0% Black, 0.5% Asian, 1.4% American Indian and Alaska Native, 0.6% Hispanic of any race, 0.2% two or more races (2000); Density: 116.0 persons per square mile (2000); Age: 29.1% under 18, 9.5% over 64 (2000); Marriage status: 22.2% never married, 68.1% now married, 3.0% widowed, 6.6% divorced (2000); Foreign born: 1.2% (2000); Ancestry (includes multiple ancestries): 24.9% Finnish, 21.2% German, 18.5% Swedish, 17.7% Norwegian, 10.0% Irish (2000).

Economy: Employment by occupation: 8.8% management, 22.4% professional, 16.3% services, 25.0% sales, 0.2% farming, 10.6% construction, 16.7% production (2000).

Income: Per capita income: $20,165 (2000); Median household income: $53,136 (2000); Poverty rate: 5.5% (2000).

Education: High school graduation rate: 92.2% (2000); College graduation rate: 20.6% (2000).

School District(s)

Esko (PK-12)
2000 Enrollment: 1,044 218-879-2969

Housing: Homeownership rate: 95.8% (2000); Median home value: $104,400 (2000); Median rent: $431 per month (2000); Median age of housing: 32 years (2000).

Transportation: Commute to work: 94.7% car, 0.2% public transportation, 1.0% walk, 3.4% work from home (2000); Travel time to work: 34.9% less than 15 minutes, 50.4% 15 to 30 minutes, 11.6% 30 to 45 minutes, 0.8% 45 to 60 minutes, 2.3% 60 minutes or more (2000)

HOLYOKE (township). Covers a land area of 37.914 square miles and a water area of 0.066 square miles. Located at 46.47° N. Lat.; 92.36° W. Long. Elevation is 1,037 feet.

Population: 179 (2000); Race: 100.0% White, 0.0% Black, 0.0% Asian, 0.0% American Indian and Alaska Native, 0.0% Hispanic of any race, 0.0%

two or more races (2000); Density: 4.7 persons per square mile (2000); Age: 21.4% under 18, 9.9% over 64 (2000); Marriage status: 25.5% never married, 54.2% now married, 6.5% widowed, 13.7% divorced (2000); Foreign born: 3.3% (2000); Ancestry (includes multiple ancestries): 33.0% German, 14.8% Swedish, 12.1% Polish, 9.9% Irish, 7.7% Dutch (2000).
Economy: Employment by occupation: 14.3% management, 22.6% professional, 17.9% services, 15.5% sales, 0.0% farming, 16.7% construction, 13.1% production (2000).
Income: Per capita income: $19,805 (2000); Median household income: $41,563 (2000); Poverty rate: 7.7% (2000).
Taxes: Total city taxes per capita: $133 (1997); City property taxes per capita: $133 (1997).
Education: High school graduation rate: 89.8% (2000); College graduation rate: 22.6% (2000).
Housing: Homeownership rate: 90.6% (2000); Median home value: $75,000 (2000); Median age of housing: 29 years (2000).
Transportation: Commute to work: 97.6% car, 0.0% public transportation, 0.0% walk, 2.4% work from home (2000); Travel time to work: 1.2% less than 15 minutes, 4.8% 15 to 30 minutes, 59.0% 30 to 45 minutes, 26.5% 45 to 60 minutes, 8.4% 60 minutes or more (2000)

KALEVALA (township). Covers a land area of 35.800 square miles and a water area of 0 square miles. Located at 46.54° N. Lat.; 92.89° W. Long.
Population: 302 (2000); Race: 100.0% White, 0.0% Black, 0.0% Asian, 0.0% American Indian and Alaska Native, 3.4% Hispanic of any race, 0.0% two or more races (2000); Density: 8.4 persons per square mile (2000); Age: 22.1% under 18, 17.9% over 64 (2000); Marriage status: 23.7% never married, 63.3% now married, 4.9% widowed, 8.2% divorced (2000); Foreign born: 3.1% (2000); Ancestry (includes multiple ancestries): 36.6% Finnish, 24.5% German, 16.6% Norwegian, 11.0% Polish, 8.3% Swedish (2000).
Economy: Employment by occupation: 17.8% management, 10.4% professional, 22.2% services, 16.3% sales, 1.5% farming, 18.5% construction, 13.3% production (2000).
Income: Per capita income: $17,144 (2000); Median household income: $33,333 (2000); Poverty rate: 4.5% (2000).
Taxes: Total city taxes per capita: $45 (1997); City property taxes per capita: $45 (1997).
Education: High school graduation rate: 77.1% (2000); College graduation rate: 7.0% (2000).
Housing: Homeownership rate: 89.5% (2000); Median home value: $38,800 (2000); Median rent: $525 per month (2000); Median age of housing: 36 years (2000).
Transportation: Commute to work: 92.5% car, 0.0% public transportation, 1.5% walk, 6.0% work from home (2000); Travel time to work: 19.2% less than 15 minutes, 43.2% 15 to 30 minutes, 27.2% 30 to 45 minutes, 1.6% 45 to 60 minutes, 8.8% 60 minutes or more (2000)

KETTLE RIVER (city). Covers a land area of 0.385 square miles and a water area of 0 square miles. Located at 46.48° N. Lat.; 92.87° W. Long. Elevation is 1,182 feet.
Population: 168 (2000); Race: 97.0% White, 0.0% Black, 0.0% Asian, 0.0% American Indian and Alaska Native, 0.0% Hispanic of any race, 3.0% two or more races (2000); Density: 436.4 persons per square mile (2000); Age: 21.8% under 18, 17.0% over 64 (2000); Marriage status: 31.4% never married, 47.9% now married, 7.1% widowed, 13.6% divorced (2000); Foreign born: 0.0% (2000); Ancestry (includes multiple ancestries): 34.5% Finnish, 27.9% German, 14.5% Irish, 12.1% Polish, 10.3% Norwegian (2000).
Economy: Agriculture: poultry; oats, alfalfa; dairying. Manufacturing: Indian pottery, feeds. Sandstone quarries in area. Single-family building permits issued: 1 (2001) / 0 (2000); Multi-family building permits issued: 0 (2001) / 0 (2000); Employment by occupation: 4.5% management, 13.5% professional, 33.7% services, 10.1% sales, 6.7% farming, 16.9% construction, 14.6% production (2000).
Income: Per capita income: $15,620 (2000); Median household income: $24,750 (2000); Poverty rate: 7.9% (2000).
Taxes: Total city taxes per capita: $186 (1997); City property taxes per capita: $170 (1997).
Education: High school graduation rate: 83.2% (2000); College graduation rate: 7.1% (2000).
Housing: Homeownership rate: 75.0% (2000); Median home value: $46,000 (2000); Median rent: $208 per month (2000); Median age of housing: 47 years (2000).
Transportation: Commute to work: 87.2% car, 0.0% public transportation, 9.3% walk, 3.5% work from home (2000); Travel time to work: 36.1% less than 15 minutes, 15.7% 15 to 30 minutes, 25.3% 30 to 45 minutes, 3.6% 45 to 60 minutes, 19.3% 60 minutes or more (2000)

LAKEVIEW (township). Covers a land area of 33.411 square miles and a water area of 0.965 square miles. Located at 46.64° N. Lat.; 93.04° W. Long.
Population: 194 (2000); Race: 99.0% White, 0.0% Black, 0.0% Asian, 0.0% American Indian and Alaska Native, 0.0% Hispanic of any race, 1.0% two or more races (2000); Density: 5.8 persons per square mile (2000); Age: 21.8% under 18, 28.2% over 64 (2000); Marriage status: 21.6% never married, 66.5% now married, 5.4% widowed, 6.6% divorced (2000); Foreign born: 0.0% (2000); Ancestry (includes multiple ancestries): 29.7% German, 24.3% Finnish, 11.4% Swedish, 6.9% Norwegian, 6.4% Polish (2000).
Economy: Employment by occupation: 11.4% management, 11.4% professional, 19.3% services, 13.6% sales, 2.3% farming, 23.9% construction, 18.2% production (2000).
Income: Per capita income: $17,822 (2000); Median household income: $29,545 (2000); Poverty rate: 10.9% (2000).
Taxes: Total city taxes per capita: $172 (1997); City property taxes per capita: $172 (1997).
Education: High school graduation rate: 86.5% (2000); College graduation rate: 14.2% (2000).
Housing: Homeownership rate: 91.7% (2000); Median home value: $81,300 (2000); Median age of housing: 38 years (2000).
Transportation: Commute to work: 90.5% car, 0.0% public transportation, 4.8% walk, 4.8% work from home (2000); Travel time to work: 21.3% less than 15 minutes, 3.8% 15 to 30 minutes, 28.7% 30 to 45 minutes, 8.8% 45 to 60 minutes, 37.5% 60 minutes or more (2000)

MAHTOWA (township). Covers a land area of 23.816 square miles and a water area of 0.338 square miles. Located at 46.57° N. Lat.; 92.62° W. Long. Elevation is 1,152 feet.
Population: 494 (2000); Race: 96.8% White, 0.0% Black, 0.4% Asian, 1.6% American Indian and Alaska Native, 0.0% Hispanic of any race, 1.2% two or more races (2000); Density: 20.7 persons per square mile (2000); Age: 26.4% under 18, 13.6% over 64 (2000); Marriage status: 26.7% never married, 61.5% now married, 5.7% widowed, 6.2% divorced (2000); Foreign born: 2.0% (2000); Ancestry (includes multiple ancestries): 32.0% Swedish, 26.8% German, 22.5% Norwegian, 11.6% Finnish, 11.2% Irish (2000).
Economy: Employment by occupation: 13.7% management, 13.3% professional, 16.4% services, 19.9% sales, 1.6% farming, 14.8% construction, 20.3% production (2000).
Income: Per capita income: $17,832 (2000); Median household income: $43,750 (2000); Poverty rate: 4.1% (2000).
Taxes: Total city taxes per capita: $105 (1997); City property taxes per capita: $105 (1997).
Education: High school graduation rate: 90.2% (2000); College graduation rate: 14.3% (2000).
Housing: Homeownership rate: 94.4% (2000); Median home value: $68,300 (2000); Median age of housing: 34 years (2000).
Transportation: Commute to work: 92.5% car, 0.0% public transportation, 1.2% walk, 6.3% work from home (2000); Travel time to work: 10.6% less than 15 minutes, 44.5% 15 to 30 minutes, 26.3% 30 to 45 minutes, 13.6% 45 to 60 minutes, 5.1% 60 minutes or more (2000)

MOOSE LAKE (city). Covers a land area of 2.760 square miles and a water area of 0.368 square miles. Located at 46.45° N. Lat.; 92.76° W. Long. Elevation is 1,062 feet.
History: Moose Lake began in the early 1860's as an overnight stage stop on the road between Superior and St. Paul. The citizens moved their community about three miles west when the Lake Superior Mississippi River Railroad was built in the early 1870's. This was logging country, with white pine floated down the lake to the sawmill.
Population: 2,239 (2000); Race: 80.6% White, 11.0% Black, 0.3% Asian, 4.2% American Indian and Alaska Native, 4.3% Hispanic of any race, 1.6% two or more races (2000); Density: 811.1 persons per square mile (2000); Age: 11.9% under 18, 18.5% over 64 (2000); Marriage status: 21.3% never married, 55.6% now married, 12.1% widowed, 11.1% divorced (2000); Foreign born: 2.4% (2000); Ancestry (includes multiple ancestries): 17.2% German, 9.2% Swedish, 8.1% Norwegian, 7.9% Other groups, 6.9% Finnish (2000).
Economy: Single-family building permits issued: 5 (2001) / 4 (2000); Multi-family building permits issued: 0 (2001) / 0 (2000); Employment by occupation: 6.9% management, 21.8% professional, 26.7% services, 25.9% sales, 1.2% farming, 7.1% construction, 10.4% production (2000).
Income: Per capita income: $14,128 (2000); Median household income: $27,130 (2000); Poverty rate: 10.1% (2000).

Taxes: Total city taxes per capita: $136 (1997); City property taxes per capita: $111 (1997).
Education: High school graduation rate: 75.1% (2000); College graduation rate: 10.9% (2000).

School District(s)

Moose Lake (PK-12)
2000 Enrollment: 791 218-485-4435

Housing: Homeownership rate: 56.2% (2000); Median home value: $76,300 (2000); Median rent: $346 per month (2000); Median age of housing: 41 years (2000).
Hospitals: Mercy Hospital (31 beds)
Safety: Violent crime rate: 4.4 per 10,000 population; Property crime rate: 366.8 per 10,000 population (2001).
Newspapers: Star Gazette (1 x week); Arrowhead Leader (1 x week)
Transportation: Commute to work: 83.2% car, 0.0% public transportation, 9.7% walk, 6.3% work from home (2000); Travel time to work: 61.2% less than 15 minutes, 14.1% 15 to 30 minutes, 11.7% 30 to 45 minutes, 10.3% 45 to 60 minutes, 2.7% 60 minutes or more (2000)
Additional Information Contacts
Moose Lake Chamber of Commerce 218-485-4145

MOOSE LAKE (township). Covers a land area of 32.699 square miles and a water area of 0.808 square miles. Located at 46.44° N. Lat.; 92.74° W. Long. Elevation is 1,062 feet.
History: Founded as lumber town before 1875, rebuilt after destruction by forest fire, 1918.
Population: 956 (2000); Race: 98.6% White, 0.0% Black, 0.2% Asian, 0.4% American Indian and Alaska Native, 0.7% Hispanic of any race, 0.0% two or more races (2000); Density: 29.2 persons per square mile (2000); Age: 27.7% under 18, 14.3% over 64 (2000); Marriage status: 16.1% never married, 70.7% now married, 5.5% widowed, 7.7% divorced (2000); Foreign born: 1.4% (2000); Ancestry (includes multiple ancestries): 32.7% German, 24.2% Swedish, 17.8% Norwegian, 12.7% Finnish, 11.7% Irish (2000).
Economy: Oats, alfalfa; timber; poultry; dairying. Manufacturing: feeds, fishing tackles. Employment by occupation: 7.8% management, 22.8% professional, 23.4% services, 24.5% sales, 0.7% farming, 6.7% construction, 14.1% production (2000).
Income: Per capita income: $17,505 (2000); Median household income: $42,946 (2000); Poverty rate: 6.3% (2000).
Taxes: Total city taxes per capita: $51 (1997); City property taxes per capita: $51 (1997).
Education: High school graduation rate: 84.0% (2000); College graduation rate: 21.9% (2000).
Housing: Homeownership rate: 93.3% (2000); Median home value: $96,100 (2000); Median rent: $343 per month (2000); Median age of housing: 29 years (2000).
Transportation: Commute to work: 94.9% car, 0.0% public transportation, 1.1% walk, 3.7% work from home (2000); Travel time to work: 62.8% less than 15 minutes, 11.9% 15 to 30 minutes, 12.1% 30 to 45 minutes, 9.4% 45 to 60 minutes, 3.9% 60 minutes or more (2000)

PERCH LAKE (township). Covers a land area of 34.647 square miles and a water area of 1.903 square miles. Located at 46.71° N. Lat.; 92.62° W. Long.
Population: 998 (2000); Race: 74.4% White, 0.0% Black, 0.6% Asian, 22.5% American Indian and Alaska Native, 1.1% Hispanic of any race, 1.7% two or more races (2000); Density: 28.8 persons per square mile (2000); Age: 27.8% under 18, 12.9% over 64 (2000); Marriage status: 21.7% never married, 61.3% now married, 4.8% widowed, 12.2% divorced (2000); Foreign born: 0.6% (2000); Ancestry (includes multiple ancestries): 24.5% German, 22.4% Other groups, 17.0% Finnish, 14.4% Swedish, 11.3% Norwegian (2000).
Economy: Employment by occupation: 7.6% management, 15.9% professional, 21.8% services, 18.0% sales, 2.3% farming, 12.9% construction, 21.6% production (2000).
Income: Per capita income: $16,794 (2000); Median household income: $34,028 (2000); Poverty rate: 9.8% (2000).
Taxes: Total city taxes per capita: $131 (1997); City property taxes per capita: $131 (1997).
Education: High school graduation rate: 86.4% (2000); College graduation rate: 10.1% (2000).
Housing: Homeownership rate: 82.6% (2000); Median home value: $106,500 (2000); Median rent: $131 per month (2000); Median age of housing: 26 years (2000).
Transportation: Commute to work: 92.1% car, 0.0% public transportation, 0.9% walk, 3.9% work from home (2000); Travel time to work: 21.9% less than 15 minutes, 49.3% 15 to 30 minutes, 18.3% 30 to 45 minutes, 4.0% 45 to 60 minutes, 6.5% 60 minutes or more (2000)

SAWYER (unincorporated postal area, zip code 55780). Covers a land area of 10.408 square miles and a water area of 0.397 square miles. Located at 46.67° N. Lat.; 92.69° W. Long. Elevation is 1,330 feet.
Population: 132 (2000); Race: 55.3% White, 0.0% Black, 0.0% Asian, 42.4% American Indian and Alaska Native, 0.0% Hispanic of any race, 2.3% two or more races (2000); Density: 12.7 persons per square mile (2000); Age: 47.7% under 18, 5.3% over 64 (2000); Marriage status: 16.7% never married, 79.2% now married, 2.8% widowed, 1.4% divorced (2000); Foreign born: 0.0% (2000); Ancestry (includes multiple ancestries): 39.4% Other groups, 28.0% Finnish, 12.1% Swedish, 9.8% Norwegian, 6.1% Polish (2000).
Economy: Employment by occupation: 5.8% management, 11.5% professional, 23.1% services, 15.4% sales, 5.8% farming, 23.1% construction, 15.4% production (2000).
Income: Per capita income: $10,255 (2000); Median household income: $35,625 (2000); Poverty rate: 11.4% (2000).
Education: High school graduation rate: 90.2% (2000); College graduation rate: 14.8% (2000).
Housing: Homeownership rate: 66.7% (2000); Median home value: $80,000 (2000); Median rent: $165 per month (2000); Median age of housing: 23 years (2000).
Transportation: Commute to work: 93.9% car, 0.0% public transportation, 0.0% walk, 6.1% work from home (2000); Travel time to work: 4.3% less than 15 minutes, 60.9% 15 to 30 minutes, 28.3% 30 to 45 minutes, 6.5% 45 to 60 minutes, 0.0% 60 minutes or more (2000)

SCANLON (city). Covers a land area of 0.841 square miles and a water area of 0 square miles. Located at 46.70° N. Lat.; 92.43° W. Long. Elevation is 1,134 feet.
Population: 838 (2000); Race: 95.6% White, 0.7% Black, 0.2% Asian, 3.4% American Indian and Alaska Native, 0.2% Hispanic of any race, 0.0% two or more races (2000); Density: 996.8 persons per square mile (2000); Age: 19.5% under 18, 18.1% over 64 (2000); Marriage status: 18.6% never married, 61.7% now married, 7.4% widowed, 12.3% divorced (2000); Foreign born: 2.7% (2000); Ancestry (includes multiple ancestries): 25.7% German, 19.5% Norwegian, 16.4% Finnish, 14.0% Swedish, 8.1% English (2000).
Economy: Agriculture: dairying; poultry; oats, alfalfa. Single-family building permits issued: 1 (2001) / 1 (2000); Multi-family building permits issued: 0 (2001) / 0 (2000); Employment by occupation: 10.1% management, 14.7% professional, 15.1% services, 25.0% sales, 0.7% farming, 10.3% construction, 24.0% production (2000).
Income: Per capita income: $19,590 (2000); Median household income: $42,857 (2000); Poverty rate: 3.9% (2000).
Taxes: Total city taxes per capita: $101 (1997); City property taxes per capita: $80 (1997).
Education: High school graduation rate: 85.0% (2000); College graduation rate: 16.9% (2000).
Housing: Homeownership rate: 90.5% (2000); Median home value: $80,400 (2000); Median rent: $538 per month (2000); Median age of housing: 45 years (2000).
Safety: Violent crime rate: 11.8 per 10,000 population; Property crime rate: 106.3 per 10,000 population (2001).
Transportation: Commute to work: 93.8% car, 0.7% public transportation, 2.7% walk, 2.7% work from home (2000); Travel time to work: 63.5% less than 15 minutes, 21.2% 15 to 30 minutes, 13.0% 30 to 45 minutes, 1.0% 45 to 60 minutes, 1.3% 60 minutes or more (2000)

SILVER (township). Covers a land area of 35.050 square miles and a water area of 0.042 square miles. Located at 46.47° N. Lat.; 92.86° W. Long.
Population: 389 (2000); Race: 100.0% White, 0.0% Black, 0.0% Asian, 0.0% American Indian and Alaska Native, 2.4% Hispanic of any race, 0.0% two or more races (2000); Density: 11.1 persons per square mile (2000); Age: 27.3% under 18, 12.4% over 64 (2000); Marriage status: 22.7% never married, 64.9% now married, 4.1% widowed, 8.2% divorced (2000); Foreign born: 0.0% (2000); Ancestry (includes multiple ancestries): 24.3% Finnish, 19.2% German, 15.1% Polish, 15.1% Swedish, 14.3% Norwegian (2000).
Economy: Employment by occupation: 15.7% management, 8.1% professional, 17.8% services, 25.4% sales, 10.3% farming, 12.4% construction, 10.3% production (2000).
Income: Per capita income: $15,505 (2000); Median household income: $36,833 (2000); Poverty rate: 4.9% (2000).
Taxes: Total city taxes per capita: $35 (1997); City property taxes per capita: $35 (1997).

Education: High school graduation rate: 90.2% (2000); College graduation rate: 10.2% (2000).
Housing: Homeownership rate: 89.4% (2000); Median home value: $57,500 (2000); Median rent: $425 per month (2000); Median age of housing: 29 years (2000).
Transportation: Commute to work: 93.0% car, 0.0% public transportation, 1.1% walk, 5.9% work from home (2000); Travel time to work: 60.9% less than 15 minutes, 13.2% 15 to 30 minutes, 16.7% 30 to 45 minutes, 8.0% 45 to 60 minutes, 1.1% 60 minutes or more (2000)

SILVER BROOK (township). Covers a land area of 20.018 square miles and a water area of 0.037 square miles. Located at 46.60° N. Lat.; 92.37° W. Long.
Population: 609 (2000); Race: 97.7% White, 0.3% Black, 0.0% Asian, 1.0% American Indian and Alaska Native, 0.0% Hispanic of any race, 1.0% two or more races (2000); Density: 30.4 persons per square mile (2000); Age: 29.4% under 18, 9.5% over 64 (2000); Marriage status: 17.5% never married, 76.1% now married, 2.3% widowed, 4.1% divorced (2000); Foreign born: 0.3% (2000); Ancestry (includes multiple ancestries): 27.6% German, 21.3% Norwegian, 21.0% Swedish, 9.4% Finnish, 8.4% Polish (2000).
Economy: Employment by occupation: 8.7% management, 15.7% professional, 20.6% services, 12.9% sales, 1.7% farming, 14.7% construction, 25.5% production (2000).
Income: Per capita income: $18,535 (2000); Median household income: $51,875 (2000); Poverty rate: 2.5% (2000).
Taxes: Total city taxes per capita: $128 (1997); City property taxes per capita: $128 (1997).
Education: High school graduation rate: 86.7% (2000); College graduation rate: 14.3% (2000).
Housing: Homeownership rate: 95.8% (2000); Median home value: $90,000 (2000); Median rent: $358 per month (2000); Median age of housing: 27 years (2000).
Transportation: Commute to work: 93.0% car, 0.7% public transportation, 2.4% walk, 3.8% work from home (2000); Travel time to work: 22.2% less than 15 minutes, 43.3% 15 to 30 minutes, 23.6% 30 to 45 minutes, 6.5% 45 to 60 minutes, 4.4% 60 minutes or more (2000)

SKELTON (township). Covers a land area of 34.973 square miles and a water area of 0.026 square miles. Located at 46.55° N. Lat.; 92.73° W. Long.
Population: 372 (2000); Race: 97.5% White, 0.0% Black, 0.0% Asian, 0.0% American Indian and Alaska Native, 0.0% Hispanic of any race, 0.5% two or more races (2000); Density: 10.6 persons per square mile (2000); Age: 30.1% under 18, 8.7% over 64 (2000); Marriage status: 18.5% never married, 75.5% now married, 3.4% widowed, 2.7% divorced (2000); Foreign born: 1.2% (2000); Ancestry (includes multiple ancestries): 24.9% German, 15.2% Norwegian, 12.2% Polish, 11.2% Swedish, 9.5% Finnish (2000).
Economy: Employment by occupation: 16.2% management, 17.8% professional, 13.6% services, 10.5% sales, 5.2% farming, 7.3% construction, 29.3% production (2000).
Income: Per capita income: $15,571 (2000); Median household income: $45,568 (2000); Poverty rate: 4.1% (2000).
Taxes: Total city taxes per capita: $53 (1997); City property taxes per capita: $53 (1997).
Education: High school graduation rate: 85.7% (2000); College graduation rate: 18.7% (2000).
Housing: Homeownership rate: 95.5% (2000); Median home value: $92,500 (2000); Median rent: $225 per month (2000); Median age of housing: 30 years (2000).
Transportation: Commute to work: 88.3% car, 0.0% public transportation, 1.6% walk, 10.1% work from home (2000); Travel time to work: 26.6% less than 15 minutes, 34.9% 15 to 30 minutes, 26.6% 30 to 45 minutes, 5.3% 45 to 60 minutes, 6.5% 60 minutes or more (2000)

SPLIT ROCK (township). Covers a land area of 36.597 square miles and a water area of 0 square miles. Located at 46.45° N. Lat.; 92.97° W. Long.
Population: 124 (2000); Race: 100.0% White, 0.0% Black, 0.0% Asian, 0.0% American Indian and Alaska Native, 0.0% Hispanic of any race, 0.0% two or more races (2000); Density: 3.4 persons per square mile (2000); Age: 31.6% under 18, 19.1% over 64 (2000); Marriage status: 18.4% never married, 52.4% now married, 15.5% widowed, 13.6% divorced (2000); Foreign born: 0.0% (2000); Ancestry (includes multiple ancestries): 27.9% Polish, 27.2% German, 25.0% Finnish, 11.8% Irish, 9.6% United States or American (2000).
Economy: Employment by occupation: 20.0% management, 10.9% professional, 16.4% services, 23.6% sales, 0.0% farming, 25.5% construction, 3.6% production (2000).
Income: Per capita income: $17,677 (2000); Median household income: $26,250 (2000); Poverty rate: 17.3% (2000).
Taxes: Total city taxes per capita: $105 (1997); City property taxes per capita: $105 (1997).
Education: High school graduation rate: 87.1% (2000); College graduation rate: 7.1% (2000).
Housing: Homeownership rate: 96.4% (2000); Median home value: $62,500 (2000); Median age of housing: 40 years (2000).
Transportation: Commute to work: 73.6% car, 0.0% public transportation, 0.0% walk, 26.4% work from home (2000); Travel time to work: 30.8% less than 15 minutes, 35.9% 15 to 30 minutes, 12.8% 30 to 45 minutes, 0.0% 45 to 60 minutes, 20.5% 60 minutes or more (2000)

THOMSON (city). Covers a land area of 1.882 square miles and a water area of 0.340 square miles. Located at 46.66° N. Lat.; 92.39° W. Long.
Population: 153 (2000); Race: 99.4% White, 0.0% Black, 0.0% Asian, 0.6% American Indian and Alaska Native, 0.0% Hispanic of any race, 0.0% two or more races (2000); Density: 81.3 persons per square mile (2000); Age: 15.3% under 18, 11.5% over 64 (2000); Marriage status: 22.3% never married, 57.6% now married, 10.8% widowed, 9.4% divorced (2000); Foreign born: 0.0% (2000); Ancestry (includes multiple ancestries): 33.8% German, 17.2% Irish, 16.6% Finnish, 15.9% Norwegian, 10.2% Swedish (2000).
Economy: Single-family building permits issued: 1 (2001) / 3 (2000); Multi-family building permits issued: 0 (2001) / 0 (2000); Employment by occupation: 6.0% management, 15.7% professional, 25.3% services, 19.3% sales, 0.0% farming, 7.2% construction, 26.5% production (2000).
Income: Per capita income: $24,290 (2000); Median household income: $48,438 (2000); Poverty rate: 5.7% (2000).
Taxes: Total city taxes per capita: $405 (1997); City property taxes per capita: $405 (1997).
Education: High school graduation rate: 79.2% (2000); College graduation rate: 3.3% (2000).
Housing: Homeownership rate: 100.0% (2000); Median home value: $64,200 (2000); Median age of housing: 40 years (2000).
Transportation: Commute to work: 100.0% car, 0.0% public transportation, 0.0% walk, 0.0% work from home (2000); Travel time to work: 30.1% less than 15 minutes, 50.6% 15 to 30 minutes, 16.9% 30 to 45 minutes, 0.0% 45 to 60 minutes, 2.4% 60 minutes or more (2000)

THOMSON (township). Covers a land area of 39.655 square miles and a water area of 0.247 square miles. Located at 46.71° N. Lat.; 92.36° W. Long.
Population: 4,361 (2000); Race: 98.0% White, 0.0% Black, 0.4% Asian, 1.4% American Indian and Alaska Native, 0.7% Hispanic of any race, 0.2% two or more races (2000); Density: 110.0 persons per square mile (2000); Age: 29.5% under 18, 9.3% over 64 (2000); Marriage status: 22.4% never married, 68.3% now married, 2.8% widowed, 6.4% divorced (2000); Foreign born: 1.1% (2000); Ancestry (includes multiple ancestries): 25.4% Finnish, 20.4% German, 19.1% Swedish, 17.9% Norwegian, 9.2% Irish (2000).
Economy: Agriculture: dairying; poultry; oats, alfalfa. Single-family building permits issued: 37 (2001) / 31 (2000); Multi-family building permits issued: 0 (2001) / 2 (2000); Employment by occupation: 9.2% management, 22.2% professional, 15.7% services, 24.7% sales, 0.5% farming, 11.6% construction, 16.2% production (2000).
Income: Per capita income: $20,045 (2000); Median household income: $53,026 (2000); Poverty rate: 5.4% (2000).
Taxes: Total city taxes per capita: $96 (2000); City property taxes per capita: $92 (2000).
Education: High school graduation rate: 92.9% (2000); College graduation rate: 21.2% (2000).
Housing: Homeownership rate: 95.1% (2000); Median home value: $105,900 (2000); Median rent: $425 per month (2000); Median age of housing: 31 years (2000).
Transportation: Commute to work: 94.7% car, 0.2% public transportation, 0.9% walk, 3.5% work from home (2000); Travel time to work: 34.4% less than 15 minutes, 51.2% 15 to 30 minutes, 11.2% 30 to 45 minutes, 1.1% 45 to 60 minutes, 2.1% 60 minutes or more (2000)

TWIN LAKES (township). Covers a land area of 42.763 square miles and a water area of 2.046 square miles. Located at 46.65° N. Lat.; 92.47° W. Long.
Population: 1,912 (2000); Race: 95.4% White, 0.7% Black, 0.2% Asian, 2.6% American Indian and Alaska Native, 0.9% Hispanic of any race, 0.8% two or more races (2000); Density: 44.7 persons per square mile (2000); Age: 25.2% under 18, 10.6% over 64 (2000); Marriage status: 18.5% never married, 68.9% now married, 1.5% widowed, 11.1% divorced (2000); Foreign born: 0.4% (2000); Ancestry (includes multiple ancestries): 26.7%

German, 24.4% Swedish, 18.2% Norwegian, 13.2% Finnish, 7.5% Irish (2000).
Economy: Employment by occupation: 12.5% management, 16.7% professional, 20.9% services, 17.5% sales, 1.0% farming, 13.0% construction, 18.5% production (2000).
Income: Per capita income: $20,265 (2000); Median household income: $48,565 (2000); Poverty rate: 6.4% (2000).
Taxes: Total city taxes per capita: $147 (2000); City property taxes per capita: $147 (2000).
Education: High school graduation rate: 86.6% (2000); College graduation rate: 18.0% (2000).
Housing: Homeownership rate: 92.1% (2000); Median home value: $110,300 (2000); Median rent: $386 per month (2000); Median age of housing: 27 years (2000).
Transportation: Commute to work: 94.9% car, 0.2% public transportation, 0.6% walk, 3.6% work from home (2000); Travel time to work: 37.3% less than 15 minutes, 39.1% 15 to 30 minutes, 17.9% 30 to 45 minutes, 2.1% 45 to 60 minutes, 3.6% 60 minutes or more (2000)

WRENSHALL (city). Covers a land area of 1.507 square miles and a water area of 0 square miles. Located at 46.62° N. Lat.; 92.38° W. Long. Elevation is 1,041 feet.
Population: 308 (2000); Race: 92.5% White, 0.0% Black, 0.0% Asian, 4.2% American Indian and Alaska Native, 0.0% Hispanic of any race, 1.9% two or more races (2000); Density: 204.3 persons per square mile (2000); Age: 33.4% under 18, 8.4% over 64 (2000); Marriage status: 24.4% never married, 62.7% now married, 4.4% widowed, 8.4% divorced (2000); Foreign born: 0.0% (2000); Ancestry (includes multiple ancestries): 26.0% German, 20.1% Finnish, 18.2% Norwegian, 17.2% Swedish, 12.0% Polish (2000).
Economy: Single-family building permits issued: 1 (2001) / 4 (2000); Multi-family building permits issued: 0 (2001) / 0 (2000); Employment by occupation: 5.6% management, 16.1% professional, 21.7% services, 23.1% sales, 0.0% farming, 8.4% construction, 25.2% production (2000).
Income: Per capita income: $21,510 (2000); Median household income: $39,643 (2000); Poverty rate: 2.6% (2000).
Taxes: Total city taxes per capita: $55 (2000); City property taxes per capita: $52 (2000).
Education: High school graduation rate: 88.8% (2000); College graduation rate: 11.8% (2000).

School District(s)

Wrenshall (PK-12)
2000 Enrollment: 390 218-384-4274
Housing: Homeownership rate: 88.2% (2000); Median home value: $81,900 (2000); Median rent: $313 per month (2000); Median age of housing: 26 years (2000).
Transportation: Commute to work: 87.4% car, 0.0% public transportation, 5.6% walk, 7.0% work from home (2000); Travel time to work: 33.8% less than 15 minutes, 42.1% 15 to 30 minutes, 18.0% 30 to 45 minutes, 6.0% 45 to 60 minutes, 0.0% 60 minutes or more (2000)

WRENSHALL (township). Covers a land area of 37.865 square miles and a water area of 0 square miles. Located at 46.53° N. Lat.; 92.38° W. Long. Elevation is 1,041 feet.
Population: 326 (2000); Race: 89.8% White, 0.0% Black, 0.6% Asian, 0.6% American Indian and Alaska Native, 0.6% Hispanic of any race, 8.4% two or more races (2000); Density: 8.6 persons per square mile (2000); Age: 27.3% under 18, 6.5% over 64 (2000); Marriage status: 27.2% never married, 60.6% now married, 3.7% widowed, 8.5% divorced (2000); Foreign born: 0.0% (2000); Ancestry (includes multiple ancestries): 28.3% German, 15.5% Swedish, 11.8% Norwegian, 11.2% Other groups, 7.8% French (except Basque) (2000).
Economy: Agriculture includes dairying; poultry; oats, alfalfa. Manufacturing of liquid gasses. Employment by occupation: 11.0% management, 10.4% professional, 15.9% services, 23.8% sales, 1.2% farming, 19.5% construction, 18.3% production (2000).
Income: Per capita income: $25,067 (2000); Median household income: $44,219 (2000); Poverty rate: 4.7% (2000).
Taxes: Total city taxes per capita: $27 (1997); City property taxes per capita: $27 (1997).
Education: High school graduation rate: 86.4% (2000); College graduation rate: 16.5% (2000).
Housing: Homeownership rate: 95.2% (2000); Median home value: $76,000 (2000); Median age of housing: 24 years (2000).
Transportation: Commute to work: 94.2% car, 0.0% public transportation, 1.3% walk, 4.5% work from home (2000); Travel time to work: 14.9% less than 15 minutes, 45.3% 15 to 30 minutes, 25.7% 30 to 45 minutes, 6.8% 45 to 60 minutes, 7.4% 60 minutes or more (2000)

WRIGHT (city). Covers a land area of 1.549 square miles and a water area of 0 square miles. Located at 46.67° N. Lat.; 93.00° W. Long. Elevation is 1,303 feet.
Population: 93 (2000); Race: 100.0% White, 0.0% Black, 0.0% Asian, 0.0% American Indian and Alaska Native, 0.0% Hispanic of any race, 0.0% two or more races (2000); Density: 60.1 persons per square mile (2000); Age: 31.9% under 18, 15.5% over 64 (2000); Marriage status: 27.8% never married, 46.7% now married, 13.3% widowed, 12.2% divorced (2000); Foreign born: 0.0% (2000); Ancestry (includes multiple ancestries): 29.3% Swedish, 25.0% German, 16.4% Finnish, 12.1% Irish, 9.5% Other groups (2000).
Economy: Agriculture: dairying; poultry; oats. Manufacturing of outdoor stoves. Employment by occupation: 5.7% management, 3.8% professional, 13.2% services, 22.6% sales, 0.0% farming, 11.3% construction, 43.4% production (2000).
Income: Per capita income: $14,715 (2000); Median household income: $39,375 (2000); Poverty rate: 3.6% (2000).
Taxes: Total city taxes per capita: $110 (1997); City property taxes per capita: $97 (1997).
Education: High school graduation rate: 84.9% (2000); College graduation rate: 11.0% (2000).
Housing: Homeownership rate: 84.4% (2000); Median home value: $39,600 (2000); Median rent: $375 per month (2000); Median age of housing: 36 years (2000).
Transportation: Commute to work: 100.0% car, 0.0% public transportation, 0.0% walk, 0.0% work from home (2000); Travel time to work: 37.7% less than 15 minutes, 0.0% 15 to 30 minutes, 28.3% 30 to 45 minutes, 13.2% 45 to 60 minutes, 20.8% 60 minutes or more (2000)

Carver County

Located in south central Minnesota; bounded on the southeast by the Minnesota River. Covers a land area of 357.00 square miles, a water area of 19.10 square miles, and is located in the Central Time Zone. The county government was organized in 1855. County seat is Chaska.

Carver County is part of the Minneapolis-St. Paul, MN-WI MSA. The entire metro area includes: Anoka County, MN; Carver County, MN; Chisago County, MN; Dakota County, MN; Hennepin County, MN; Isanti County, MN; Ramsey County, MN; Scott County, MN; Sherburne County, MN; Washington County, MN; Wright County, MN; Pierce County, WI; St. Croix County, WI

Weather Station: Chaska Elevation: 718 feet

	Jan	Feb	Mar	Apr	May	Jun	Jul	Aug	Sep	Oct	Nov	Dec
High	24	31	42	60	73	82	85	82	73	61	41	28
Low	4	11	23	36	48	57	62	60	50	39	25	11
Precip	0.9	0.6	1.8	2.5	3.7	4.2	4.5	4.5	3.1	2.3	2.1	0.8
Snow	11.0	6.3	8.6	2.1	tr	0.0	0.0	0.0	tr	0.1	7.5	8.0

High and Low temperatures in degrees Fahrenheit; Precipitation and Snow in inches

Population: 70,205 (2000); Race: 96.1% White, 0.6% Black, 1.5% Asian, 0.2% American Indian and Alaska Native, 2.6% Hispanic of any race, 0.9% two or more races (2000); Density: 196.6 persons per square mile (2000); Age: 31.6% under 18, 7.3% over 64 (2000).
Religion: Five largest groups: 28.3% Catholic Church, 14.7% Lutheran Church—Missouri Synod, 11.1% Evangelical Lutheran Church in America, 1.9% Baptist General Conference, 1.0% Moravian Church in America—Northern Province (2000).
Economy: Unemployment rate: 3.1% (11/2002); Total civilian labor force: 42,526 (11/2002); Leading industries: 35.1% manufacturing; 10.9% health care and social assistance; 10.3% retail trade (2000); Companies that employ more than 1,000 persons: 3 (2000); Companies that employ more than 100 persons: 43 (2000); Farms: 779 totaling 153,223 acres (1997); Minority business ownership rate: 4.8% (1997); Women business ownership rate: 25.6% (1997); Retail sales per capita: $6,554 (1997). Single-family building permits issued: 849 (2001) / 900 (2000); Multi-family building permits issued: 334 (2001) / 475 (2000).
Income: Per capita income: $28,486 (2000); Median household income: $65,540 (2000); Poverty rate: 3.5% (2000); Bankruptcy rate: 2.47% (2001).
Taxes: Total county taxes per capita: $359 (2000); County property taxes per capita: $353 (2000).
Education: High school graduation rate: 91.4% (2000); College graduation rate: 34.3% (2000).

Housing: Homeownership rate: 83.5% (2000); Median home value: $170,200 (2000); Median rent: $596 per month (2000); Median age of housing: 18 years (2000).
Health: Birth rate: 149.9 per 10,000 population (1998); Age adjusted death rate: 66.4 per 10,000 population (1999); Age adjusted cancer mortality rate: 161.6 deaths per 100,000 population (1999). Number of physicians: 13.5 per 10,000 population (1999); Number of hospital beds: 13.8 per 10,000 population (1999).
Elections: 2000 Presidential election results: 35.6% Gore, 59.4% Bush, 3.9% Nader, 0.6% Buchanan
National and State Parks: Assumption State Wildlife Management Area; Gravel Pit State Wildlife Management Area; Schneewind State Wildlife Management Area; Waconia State Wildlife Management Area
Additional Information Contacts
Carver County Government Offices. 612-361-1648
Chanhassen Chamber of Commerce 952-934-3903
Chaska Chamber of Commerce 952-448-5000
Waconia Chamber of Commerce. 952-442-5812

Carver County Communities

BENTON (township). Covers a land area of 33.964 square miles and a water area of 0.896 square miles. Located at 44.76° N. Lat.; 93.81° W. Long.
Population: 939 (2000); Race: 97.8% White, 0.0% Black, 0.8% Asian, 0.0% American Indian and Alaska Native, 1.9% Hispanic of any race, 0.0% two or more races (2000); Density: 27.6 persons per square mile (2000); Age: 27.7% under 18, 12.3% over 64 (2000); Marriage status: 32.2% never married, 61.3% now married, 4.2% widowed, 2.4% divorced (2000); Foreign born: 1.5% (2000); Ancestry (includes multiple ancestries): 69.6% German, 6.9% Norwegian, 4.8% Swedish, 4.3% Irish, 3.6% Dutch (2000).
Economy: Employment by occupation: 18.3% management, 9.6% professional, 10.2% services, 26.7% sales, 2.8% farming, 10.2% construction, 22.1% production (2000).
Income: Per capita income: $22,652 (2000); Median household income: $62,574 (2000); Poverty rate: 2.6% (2000).
Taxes: Total city taxes per capita: $59 (1997); City property taxes per capita: $59 (1997).
Education: High school graduation rate: 87.0% (2000); College graduation rate: 11.6% (2000).
Housing: Homeownership rate: 83.8% (2000); Median home value: $146,500 (2000); Median rent: $425 per month (2000); Median age of housing: 47 years (2000).
Transportation: Commute to work: 82.6% car, 0.0% public transportation, 3.1% walk, 13.6% work from home (2000); Travel time to work: 28.6% less than 15 minutes, 36.1% 15 to 30 minutes, 21.3% 30 to 45 minutes, 10.2% 45 to 60 minutes, 3.8% 60 minutes or more (2000)

CAMDEN (township). Covers a land area of 33.922 square miles and a water area of 0.625 square miles. Located at 44.86° N. Lat.; 93.96° W. Long.
Population: 955 (2000); Race: 98.1% White, 0.0% Black, 0.7% Asian, 0.0% American Indian and Alaska Native, 0.8% Hispanic of any race, 1.1% two or more races (2000); Density: 28.2 persons per square mile (2000); Age: 27.8% under 18, 10.8% over 64 (2000); Marriage status: 25.1% never married, 67.4% now married, 3.8% widowed, 3.8% divorced (2000); Foreign born: 1.6% (2000); Ancestry (includes multiple ancestries): 66.6% German, 10.7% Norwegian, 8.3% Swedish, 6.0% Irish, 5.1% English (2000).
Economy: Employment by occupation: 17.0% management, 15.9% professional, 13.1% services, 18.0% sales, 2.0% farming, 14.6% construction, 19.3% production (2000).
Income: Per capita income: $23,502 (2000); Median household income: $60,563 (2000); Poverty rate: 2.9% (2000).
Taxes: Total city taxes per capita: $88 (2000); City property taxes per capita: $87 (2000).
Education: High school graduation rate: 87.1% (2000); College graduation rate: 10.4% (2000).
Housing: Homeownership rate: 94.0% (2000); Median home value: $160,700 (2000); Median rent: $563 per month (2000); Median age of housing: 37 years (2000).
Transportation: Commute to work: 87.9% car, 0.0% public transportation, 2.5% walk, 9.7% work from home (2000); Travel time to work: 22.4% less than 15 minutes, 32.1% 15 to 30 minutes, 21.2% 30 to 45 minutes, 13.8% 45 to 60 minutes, 10.5% 60 minutes or more (2000)

CARVER (city). Covers a land area of 3.852 square miles and a water area of 0.173 square miles. Located at 44.76° N. Lat.; 93.62° W. Long.
Population: 1,266 (2000); Race: 98.0% White, 0.0% Black, 0.3% Asian, 0.1% American Indian and Alaska Native, 2.1% Hispanic of any race, 0.5% two or more races (2000); Density: 328.6 persons per square mile (2000); Age: 27.3% under 18, 5.5% over 64 (2000); Marriage status: 23.3% never married, 64.3% now married, 2.4% widowed, 10.0% divorced (2000); Foreign born: 2.0% (2000); Ancestry (includes multiple ancestries): 52.2% German, 16.1% Norwegian, 9.8% Irish, 8.6% Swedish, 6.2% English (2000).
Economy: Agricultural area: dairying, poultry. Manufacturing: wood products, furniture. Single-family building permits issued: 84 (2001) / 78 (2000); Multi-family building permits issued: 0 (2001) / 0 (2000); Employment by occupation: 14.9% management, 22.6% professional, 13.4% services, 22.7% sales, 0.4% farming, 9.3% construction, 16.8% production (2000).
Income: Per capita income: $25,020 (2000); Median household income: $65,083 (2000); Poverty rate: 2.0% (2000).
Taxes: Total city taxes per capita: $374 (1997); City property taxes per capita: $314 (1997).
Education: High school graduation rate: 92.2% (2000); College graduation rate: 30.3% (2000).
Housing: Homeownership rate: 85.0% (2000); Median home value: $152,500 (2000); Median rent: $547 per month (2000); Median age of housing: 19 years (2000).
Transportation: Commute to work: 91.8% car, 2.1% public transportation, 1.4% walk, 4.5% work from home (2000); Travel time to work: 18.5% less than 15 minutes, 41.5% 15 to 30 minutes, 23.9% 30 to 45 minutes, 9.3% 45 to 60 minutes, 6.7% 60 minutes or more (2000)

CHANHASSEN (city). Covers a land area of 20.776 square miles and a water area of 2.120 square miles. Located at 44.86° N. Lat.; 93.55° W. Long. Elevation is 976 feet.
Population: 20,321 (2000); Race: 95.0% White, 0.6% Black, 2.8% Asian, 0.2% American Indian and Alaska Native, 1.9% Hispanic of any race, 1.2% two or more races (2000); Density: 978.1 persons per square mile (2000); Age: 34.6% under 18, 4.4% over 64 (2000); Marriage status: 18.7% never married, 71.9% now married, 2.3% widowed, 7.1% divorced (2000); Foreign born: 5.0% (2000); Ancestry (includes multiple ancestries): 41.4% German, 18.1% Norwegian, 13.0% Irish, 12.0% Swedish, 9.0% English (2000).
Vital Statistics: Birth rate: 147.1 per 10,000 population (1998)
Economy: Manufacturing: millwork, furniture, machinery, medical equipment, consumer goods, electronics; printing. University of Minnesota Landscape Arboretum is here. Single-family building permits issued: 115 (2001) / 157 (2000); Multi-family building permits issued: 114 (2001) / 162 (2000); Employment by occupation: 28.7% management, 24.5% professional, 7.8% services, 27.3% sales, 0.1% farming, 5.0% construction, 6.6% production (2000).
Income: Per capita income: $36,008 (2000); Median household income: $84,215 (2000); Poverty rate: 1.9% (2000).
Taxes: Total city taxes per capita: $666 (2000); City property taxes per capita: $562 (2000).
Education: High school graduation rate: 96.7% (2000); College graduation rate: 53.1% (2000).
Housing: Homeownership rate: 89.6% (2000); Median home value: $210,700 (2000); Median rent: $626 per month (2000); Median age of housing: 12 years (2000).
Safety: Violent crime rate: 8.8 per 10,000 population; Property crime rate: 170.4 per 10,000 population (2001).
Newspapers: Chanhassen Villager (1 x week)
Transportation: Commute to work: 92.0% car, 1.1% public transportation, 1.1% walk, 5.3% work from home (2000); Travel time to work: 21.3% less than 15 minutes, 41.9% 15 to 30 minutes, 27.7% 30 to 45 minutes, 6.5% 45 to 60 minutes, 2.5% 60 minutes or more (2000)
Additional Information Contacts
Chanhassen Chamber of Commerce 952-934-3903

CHASKA (city). Covers a land area of 13.732 square miles and a water area of 0.607 square miles. Located at 44.81° N. Lat.; 93.59° W. Long. Elevation is 728 feet.
History: Chaska was named for a Sioux chief who lived near the town. Many of the early residents of Chaska were of German ancestry. The town developed around the production of sugar beets.
Population: 17,449 (2000); Race: 94.6% White, 1.2% Black, 1.1% Asian, 0.3% American Indian and Alaska Native, 6.0% Hispanic of any race, 0.9% two or more races (2000); Density: 1,270.7 persons per square mile (2000); Age: 32.9% under 18, 5.5% over 64 (2000); Marriage status: 25.1% never married, 62.5% now married, 3.8% widowed, 8.6% divorced (2000); Foreign

born: 5.0% (2000); Ancestry (includes multiple ancestries): 44.9% German, 15.5% Norwegian, 12.9% Irish, 8.6% Swedish, 8.4% Other groups (2000).
Vital Statistics: Birth rate: 176.5 per 10,000 population (1998)
Economy: Single-family building permits issued: 176 (2001) / 140 (2000); Multi-family building permits issued: 208 (2001) / 305 (2000); Employment by occupation: 17.1% management, 21.2% professional, 12.1% services, 27.4% sales, 0.1% farming, 7.3% construction, 14.9% production (2000).
Income: Per capita income: $25,368 (2000); Median household income: $60,325 (2000); Poverty rate: 4.7% (2000).
Taxes: Total city taxes per capita: $528 (2000); City property taxes per capita: $411 (2000).
Education: High school graduation rate: 91.6% (2000); College graduation rate: 32.1% (2000).

School District(s)

Carver-Scott Educational Coop. (01-12)
2000 Enrollment: 396 952-368-8800
Chaska (PK-12)
2000 Enrollment: 7,104 952-556-6100
World Learner Charter School (01-06)
2000 Enrollment: 82 952-368-7398

Housing: Homeownership rate: 75.3% (2000); Median home value: $161,000 (2000); Median rent: $646 per month (2000); Median age of housing: 17 years (2000).
Safety: Violent crime rate: 20.4 per 10,000 population; Property crime rate: 182.0 per 10,000 population (2001).
Newspapers: Chaska Herald (1 x week)
Transportation: Commute to work: 93.5% car, 0.6% public transportation, 1.5% walk, 4.1% work from home (2000); Travel time to work: 28.1% less than 15 minutes, 33.6% 15 to 30 minutes, 26.1% 30 to 45 minutes, 8.0% 45 to 60 minutes, 4.2% 60 minutes or more (2000)
Additional Information Contacts
Chaska Chamber of Commerce 952-448-5000

CHASKA (township). Covers a land area of 2.862 square miles and a water area of 0.008 square miles. Located at 44.79° N. Lat.; 93.62° W. Long. Elevation is 728 feet.
History: Prehistoric Native American mounds in city park. Settled 1853, incorporated as village 1871, as city 1891.
Population: 154 (2000); Race: 100.0% White, 0.0% Black, 0.0% Asian, 0.0% American Indian and Alaska Native, 0.0% Hispanic of any race, 0.0% two or more races (2000); Density: 53.8 persons per square mile (2000); Age: 24.2% under 18, 21.6% over 64 (2000); Marriage status: 15.0% never married, 71.7% now married, 5.8% widowed, 7.5% divorced (2000); Foreign born: 0.0% (2000); Ancestry (includes multiple ancestries): 62.7% German, 15.7% Swedish, 10.5% Irish, 7.2% Norwegian, 2.6% Dutch (2000).
Economy: Trade and shipping point in agricultural area. Manufacturing: electronic equipment, chemicals, food processing, furniture, feeds, paper products. Employment by occupation: 10.5% management, 18.6% professional, 9.3% services, 43.0% sales, 2.3% farming, 4.7% construction, 11.6% production (2000).
Income: Per capita income: $23,548 (2000); Median household income: $54,375 (2000); Poverty rate: 2.0% (2000).
Taxes: Total city taxes per capita: $41 (1997); City property taxes per capita: $41 (1997).
Education: High school graduation rate: 88.4% (2000); College graduation rate: 17.9% (2000).
Housing: Homeownership rate: 90.9% (2000); Median home value: $162,500 (2000); Median rent: $525 per month (2000); Median age of housing: 36 years (2000).
Transportation: Commute to work: 83.7% car, 0.0% public transportation, 0.0% walk, 16.3% work from home (2000); Travel time to work: 18.1% less than 15 minutes, 45.8% 15 to 30 minutes, 26.4% 30 to 45 minutes, 9.7% 45 to 60 minutes, 0.0% 60 minutes or more (2000)

COLOGNE (city). Covers a land area of 0.753 square miles and a water area of 0.104 square miles. Located at 44.77° N. Lat.; 93.78° W. Long. Elevation is 948 feet.
History: Cologne, settled by German immigrants, was named for the city on the Rhine River in Germany.
Population: 1,012 (2000); Race: 98.0% White, 0.0% Black, 1.4% Asian, 0.2% American Indian and Alaska Native, 1.5% Hispanic of any race, 0.2% two or more races (2000); Density: 1,343.5 persons per square mile (2000); Age: 28.2% under 18, 7.9% over 64 (2000); Marriage status: 22.0% never married, 64.7% now married, 4.8% widowed, 8.6% divorced (2000); Foreign born: 3.0% (2000); Ancestry (includes multiple ancestries): 53.2% German, 14.3% Irish, 12.6% Norwegian, 7.6% Swedish, 5.8% Other groups (2000).
Economy: Single-family building permits issued: 8 (2001) / 23 (2000); Multi-family building permits issued: 6 (2001) / 0 (2000); Employment by occupation: 11.4% management, 12.9% professional, 11.1% services, 28.1% sales, 0.0% farming, 15.2% construction, 21.3% production (2000).
Income: Per capita income: $20,955 (2000); Median household income: $54,583 (2000); Poverty rate: 1.9% (2000).
Taxes: Total city taxes per capita: $255 (1997); City property taxes per capita: $209 (1997).
Education: High school graduation rate: 90.1% (2000); College graduation rate: 12.3% (2000).
Housing: Homeownership rate: 87.1% (2000); Median home value: $129,000 (2000); Median rent: $350 per month (2000); Median age of housing: 22 years (2000).
Transportation: Commute to work: 92.2% car, 0.7% public transportation, 1.7% walk, 5.4% work from home (2000); Travel time to work: 24.5% less than 15 minutes, 32.6% 15 to 30 minutes, 26.0% 30 to 45 minutes, 9.7% 45 to 60 minutes, 7.1% 60 minutes or more (2000)

DAHLGREN (township). Covers a land area of 35.478 square miles and a water area of 0.442 square miles. Located at 44.76° N. Lat.; 93.71° W. Long. Elevation is 979 feet.
Population: 1,453 (2000); Race: 99.3% White, 0.0% Black, 0.3% Asian, 0.0% American Indian and Alaska Native, 0.5% Hispanic of any race, 0.3% two or more races (2000); Density: 41.0 persons per square mile (2000); Age: 30.5% under 18, 8.4% over 64 (2000); Marriage status: 24.1% never married, 67.9% now married, 2.9% widowed, 5.0% divorced (2000); Foreign born: 0.4% (2000); Ancestry (includes multiple ancestries): 69.6% German, 11.8% Norwegian, 11.7% Swedish, 8.7% Irish, 4.0% English (2000).
Economy: Employment by occupation: 19.5% management, 14.8% professional, 15.1% services, 20.2% sales, 0.9% farming, 17.3% construction, 12.3% production (2000).
Income: Per capita income: $23,747 (2000); Median household income: $63,224 (2000); Poverty rate: 2.6% (2000).
Taxes: Total city taxes per capita: $100 (2000); City property taxes per capita: $100 (2000).
Education: High school graduation rate: 89.6% (2000); College graduation rate: 18.2% (2000).
Housing: Homeownership rate: 88.2% (2000); Median home value: $174,600 (2000); Median rent: $400 per month (2000); Median age of housing: 35 years (2000).
Transportation: Commute to work: 87.3% car, 0.5% public transportation, 2.8% walk, 8.4% work from home (2000); Travel time to work: 20.2% less than 15 minutes, 41.0% 15 to 30 minutes, 23.4% 30 to 45 minutes, 8.7% 45 to 60 minutes, 6.6% 60 minutes or more (2000)

HAMBURG (city). Covers a land area of 0.199 square miles and a water area of 0 square miles. Located at 44.73° N. Lat.; 93.96° W. Long. Elevation is 999 feet.
Population: 538 (2000); Race: 98.8% White, 0.7% Black, 0.0% Asian, 0.0% American Indian and Alaska Native, 2.3% Hispanic of any race, 0.0% two or more races (2000); Density: 2,697.0 persons per square mile (2000); Age: 25.5% under 18, 16.9% over 64 (2000); Marriage status: 20.8% never married, 64.5% now married, 7.5% widowed, 7.1% divorced (2000); Foreign born: 0.4% (2000); Ancestry (includes multiple ancestries): 76.4% German, 9.5% Norwegian, 6.3% Irish, 6.2% English, 4.9% French (except Basque) (2000).
Economy: Poultry, livestock; soybeans, alfalfa; dairying. Manufacturing: feeds, fertilizers. Single-family building permits issued: 0 (2001) / 1 (2000); Multi-family building permits issued: 0 (2001) / 0 (2000); Employment by occupation: 8.7% management, 15.7% professional, 12.9% services, 23.3% sales, 0.0% farming, 11.5% construction, 27.9% production (2000).
Income: Per capita income: $21,221 (2000); Median household income: $47,578 (2000); Poverty rate: 5.6% (2000).
Taxes: Total city taxes per capita: $210 (1997); City property taxes per capita: $193 (1997).
Education: High school graduation rate: 81.9% (2000); College graduation rate: 12.6% (2000).
Housing: Homeownership rate: 78.1% (2000); Median home value: $114,200 (2000); Median rent: $325 per month (2000); Median age of housing: 40 years (2000).
Transportation: Commute to work: 97.1% car, 0.0% public transportation, 1.4% walk, 1.4% work from home (2000); Travel time to work: 28.7% less than 15 minutes, 26.5% 15 to 30 minutes, 26.2% 30 to 45 minutes, 13.5% 45 to 60 minutes, 5.1% 60 minutes or more (2000)

HANCOCK (township). Covers a land area of 17.729 square miles and a water area of 0.173 square miles. Located at 44.69° N. Lat.; 93.82° W. Long.
Population: 367 (2000); Race: 98.9% White, 0.0% Black, 0.0% Asian, 0.0% American Indian and Alaska Native, 0.0% Hispanic of any race, 1.1% two or more races (2000); Density: 20.7 persons per square mile (2000); Age: 31.2% under 18, 10.5% over 64 (2000); Marriage status: 24.9% never married, 67.4% now married, 4.8% widowed, 2.9% divorced (2000); Foreign born: 0.5% (2000); Ancestry (includes multiple ancestries): 68.3% German, 12.6% Norwegian, 7.5% Dutch, 5.6% Irish, 5.6% Swedish (2000).
Economy: Employment by occupation: 22.0% management, 15.6% professional, 10.8% services, 26.3% sales, 3.8% farming, 8.6% construction, 12.9% production (2000).
Income: Per capita income: $20,568 (2000); Median household income: $58,750 (2000); Poverty rate: 9.1% (2000).
Taxes: Total city taxes per capita: $78 (1997); City property taxes per capita: $78 (1997).
Education: High school graduation rate: 83.5% (2000); College graduation rate: 8.2% (2000).
Housing: Homeownership rate: 89.7% (2000); Median home value: $175,000 (2000); Median rent: $675 per month (2000); Median age of housing: 48 years (2000).
Transportation: Commute to work: 80.2% car, 0.0% public transportation, 2.2% walk, 17.6% work from home (2000); Travel time to work: 25.3% less than 15 minutes, 35.3% 15 to 30 minutes, 21.3% 30 to 45 minutes, 15.3% 45 to 60 minutes, 2.7% 60 minutes or more (2000)

HOLLYWOOD (township). Covers a land area of 35.966 square miles and a water area of 0.128 square miles. Located at 44.93° N. Lat.; 93.94° W. Long. Elevation is 976 feet.
Population: 1,102 (2000); Race: 99.6% White, 0.0% Black, 0.0% Asian, 0.0% American Indian and Alaska Native, 0.0% Hispanic of any race, 0.4% two or more races (2000); Density: 30.6 persons per square mile (2000); Age: 26.7% under 18, 10.6% over 64 (2000); Marriage status: 27.7% never married, 64.4% now married, 4.0% widowed, 4.0% divorced (2000); Foreign born: 0.7% (2000); Ancestry (includes multiple ancestries): 64.6% German, 13.4% Irish, 6.1% Polish, 6.0% United States or American, 5.6% Swedish (2000).
Economy: Employment by occupation: 21.5% management, 11.6% professional, 13.4% services, 20.4% sales, 3.9% farming, 10.1% construction, 19.0% production (2000).
Income: Per capita income: $22,664 (2000); Median household income: $52,833 (2000); Poverty rate: 3.2% (2000).
Taxes: Total city taxes per capita: $105 (2000); City property taxes per capita: $104 (2000).
Education: High school graduation rate: 82.5% (2000); College graduation rate: 12.1% (2000).
Housing: Homeownership rate: 87.6% (2000); Median home value: $141,900 (2000); Median rent: $550 per month (2000); Median age of housing: 45 years (2000).
Transportation: Commute to work: 81.4% car, 0.0% public transportation, 2.6% walk, 16.1% work from home (2000); Travel time to work: 25.4% less than 15 minutes, 19.9% 15 to 30 minutes, 29.4% 30 to 45 minutes, 18.4% 45 to 60 minutes, 6.9% 60 minutes or more (2000)

LAKETOWN (township). Covers a land area of 27.675 square miles and a water area of 2.697 square miles. Located at 44.84° N. Lat.; 93.70° W. Long.
Population: 2,331 (2000); Race: 97.7% White, 0.1% Black, 0.9% Asian, 0.1% American Indian and Alaska Native, 0.9% Hispanic of any race, 1.0% two or more races (2000); Density: 84.2 persons per square mile (2000); Age: 22.2% under 18, 6.3% over 64 (2000); Marriage status: 21.5% never married, 71.7% now married, 2.4% widowed, 4.3% divorced (2000); Foreign born: 2.9% (2000); Ancestry (includes multiple ancestries): 50.6% German, 10.0% Norwegian, 7.8% Swedish, 7.6% Irish, 6.9% English (2000).
Economy: Employment by occupation: 18.2% management, 15.8% professional, 15.7% services, 27.1% sales, 0.3% farming, 10.1% construction, 12.8% production (2000).
Income: Per capita income: $27,543 (2000); Median household income: $75,000 (2000); Poverty rate: 1.8% (2000).
Taxes: Total city taxes per capita: $152 (2000); City property taxes per capita: $151 (2000).
Education: High school graduation rate: 92.2% (2000); College graduation rate: 33.8% (2000).
Housing: Homeownership rate: 95.0% (2000); Median home value: $180,800 (2000); Median rent: $288 per month (2000); Median age of housing: 28 years (2000).
Transportation: Commute to work: 85.1% car, 0.5% public transportation, 6.3% walk, 7.5% work from home (2000); Travel time to work: 32.3% less than 15 minutes, 30.7% 15 to 30 minutes, 21.0% 30 to 45 minutes, 11.5% 45 to 60 minutes, 4.5% 60 minutes or more (2000)

MAYER (city). Covers a land area of 0.969 square miles and a water area of 0.009 square miles. Located at 44.88° N. Lat.; 93.89° W. Long. Elevation is 979 feet.
Population: 554 (2000); Race: 97.8% White, 0.0% Black, 2.2% Asian, 0.0% American Indian and Alaska Native, 1.1% Hispanic of any race, 0.0% two or more races (2000); Density: 572.0 persons per square mile (2000); Age: 29.8% under 18, 9.3% over 64 (2000); Marriage status: 20.9% never married, 68.4% now married, 5.6% widowed, 5.1% divorced (2000); Foreign born: 1.5% (2000); Ancestry (includes multiple ancestries): 65.1% German, 14.2% Norwegian, 9.6% Polish, 9.1% Swedish, 4.2% Irish (2000).
Economy: Dairying; poultry; grain, soybeans, alfalfa. Single-family building permits issued: 26 (2001) / 2 (2000); Multi-family building permits issued: 0 (2001) / 0 (2000); Employment by occupation: 10.0% management, 19.3% professional, 9.7% services, 27.0% sales, 0.0% farming, 19.0% construction, 15.0% production (2000).
Income: Per capita income: $18,547 (2000); Median household income: $48,125 (2000); Poverty rate: 2.0% (2000).
Taxes: Total city taxes per capita: $165 (1997); City property taxes per capita: $134 (1997).
Education: High school graduation rate: 89.2% (2000); College graduation rate: 15.8% (2000).
Housing: Homeownership rate: 86.1% (2000); Median home value: $116,500 (2000); Median rent: $408 per month (2000); Median age of housing: 31 years (2000).
Transportation: Commute to work: 90.3% car, 0.0% public transportation, 4.7% walk, 4.0% work from home (2000); Travel time to work: 25.4% less than 15 minutes, 23.7% 15 to 30 minutes, 28.9% 30 to 45 minutes, 15.0% 45 to 60 minutes, 7.0% 60 minutes or more (2000)

NEW GERMANY (city). Covers a land area of 0.654 square miles and a water area of 0 square miles. Located at 44.88° N. Lat.; 93.96° W. Long. Elevation is 986 feet.
Population: 346 (2000); Race: 95.9% White, 2.1% Black, 0.0% Asian, 0.6% American Indian and Alaska Native, 0.6% Hispanic of any race, 1.5% two or more races (2000); Density: 528.9 persons per square mile (2000); Age: 21.2% under 18, 22.6% over 64 (2000); Marriage status: 19.5% never married, 57.4% now married, 16.6% widowed, 6.5% divorced (2000); Foreign born: 0.0% (2000); Ancestry (includes multiple ancestries): 67.9% German, 9.4% Swedish, 8.5% Norwegian, 8.5% Irish, 3.5% Other groups (2000).
Economy: Grain, soybeans, alfalfa; livestock; dairying; light manufacturing. Single-family building permits issued: 0 (2001) / 0 (2000); Multi-family building permits issued: 0 (2001) / 0 (2000); Employment by occupation: 9.8% management, 12.7% professional, 23.1% services, 19.7% sales, 0.0% farming, 12.1% construction, 22.5% production (2000).
Income: Per capita income: $16,314 (2000); Median household income: $36,094 (2000); Poverty rate: 14.4% (2000).
Taxes: Total city taxes per capita: $142 (1997); City property taxes per capita: $117 (1997).
Education: High school graduation rate: 73.2% (2000); College graduation rate: 11.5% (2000).
Housing: Homeownership rate: 74.0% (2000); Median home value: $89,800 (2000); Median rent: $370 per month (2000); Median age of housing: 37 years (2000).
Transportation: Commute to work: 86.0% car, 0.0% public transportation, 7.0% walk, 7.0% work from home (2000); Travel time to work: 17.0% less than 15 minutes, 32.1% 15 to 30 minutes, 29.6% 30 to 45 minutes, 17.6% 45 to 60 minutes, 3.8% 60 minutes or more (2000)

NORWOOD YOUNG AMERICA (city). Covers a land area of 1.675 square miles and a water area of 0 square miles. Located at 44.77° N. Lat.; 93.92° W. Long.
Population: 3,108 (2000); Race: 96.6% White, 0.1% Black, 2.3% Asian, 0.2% American Indian and Alaska Native, 2.4% Hispanic of any race, 0.8% two or more races (2000); Density: 1,855.8 persons per square mile (2000); Age: 30.0% under 18, 11.4% over 64 (2000); Marriage status: 28.9% never married, 56.7% now married, 5.9% widowed, 8.5% divorced (2000); Foreign born: 2.5% (2000); Ancestry (includes multiple ancestries): 61.5% German,

8.4% Irish, 7.9% Norwegian, 6.5% Swedish, 4.3% United States or American (2000).
Economy: Single-family building permits issued: 8 (2001) / 16 (2000); Multi-family building permits issued: 2 (2001) / 0 (2000); Employment by occupation: 8.6% management, 13.1% professional, 15.0% services, 27.0% sales, 0.5% farming, 11.3% construction, 24.4% production (2000).
Income: Per capita income: $18,431 (2000); Median household income: $46,152 (2000); Poverty rate: 5.6% (2000).
Education: High school graduation rate: 85.4% (2000); College graduation rate: 9.5% (2000).

School District(s)

Norwood (PK-12)
2000 Enrollment: 1,181 952-467-7000
Housing: Homeownership rate: 73.3% (2000); Median home value: $111,300 (2000); Median rent: $459 per month (2000); Median age of housing: 31 years (2000).
Transportation: Commute to work: 91.0% car, 0.2% public transportation, 3.0% walk, 4.8% work from home (2000); Travel time to work: 36.6% less than 15 minutes, 21.7% 15 to 30 minutes, 21.6% 30 to 45 minutes, 15.3% 45 to 60 minutes, 4.8% 60 minutes or more (2000)

SAN FRANCISCO (township). Covers a land area of 23.148 square miles and a water area of 0.880 square miles. Located at 44.70° N. Lat.; 93.71° W. Long.
Population: 888 (2000); Race: 98.4% White, 0.0% Black, 0.3% Asian, 0.2% American Indian and Alaska Native, 1.2% Hispanic of any race, 0.7% two or more races (2000); Density: 38.4 persons per square mile (2000); Age: 32.7% under 18, 6.7% over 64 (2000); Marriage status: 21.5% never married, 70.1% now married, 3.0% widowed, 5.4% divorced (2000); Foreign born: 0.9% (2000); Ancestry (includes multiple ancestries): 50.2% German, 14.7% Norwegian, 12.8% Irish, 10.6% Swedish, 5.4% English (2000).
Economy: Employment by occupation: 18.1% management, 11.7% professional, 12.1% services, 22.7% sales, 1.9% farming, 15.8% construction, 17.7% production (2000).
Income: Per capita income: $24,734 (2000); Median household income: $68,889 (2000); Poverty rate: 0.5% (2000).
Taxes: Total city taxes per capita: $79 (1997); City property taxes per capita: $77 (1997).
Education: High school graduation rate: 91.0% (2000); College graduation rate: 17.2% (2000).
Housing: Homeownership rate: 95.2% (2000); Median home value: $192,400 (2000); Median rent: $675 per month (2000); Median age of housing: 20 years (2000).
Transportation: Commute to work: 88.9% car, 0.0% public transportation, 1.3% walk, 9.8% work from home (2000); Travel time to work: 16.3% less than 15 minutes, 34.7% 15 to 30 minutes, 28.8% 30 to 45 minutes, 15.6% 45 to 60 minutes, 4.7% 60 minutes or more (2000)

VICTORIA (city). Covers a land area of 6.995 square miles and a water area of 1.534 square miles. Located at 44.86° N. Lat.; 93.64° W. Long.
Population: 4,025 (2000); Race: 98.0% White, 0.2% Black, 1.0% Asian, 0.1% American Indian and Alaska Native, 1.0% Hispanic of any race, 0.1% two or more races (2000); Density: 575.4 persons per square mile (2000); Age: 32.6% under 18, 6.7% over 64 (2000); Marriage status: 16.2% never married, 76.4% now married, 2.6% widowed, 4.7% divorced (2000); Foreign born: 1.9% (2000); Ancestry (includes multiple ancestries): 44.6% German, 19.9% Norwegian, 13.1% Swedish, 9.8% Irish, 8.3% English (2000).
Economy: Manufacturing: candy, electronic components, cabinets, boathouses. Single-family building permits issued: 150 (2001) / 140 (2000); Multi-family building permits issued: 0 (2001) / 6 (2000); Employment by occupation: 27.1% management, 24.5% professional, 9.9% services, 27.7% sales, 0.1% farming, 4.4% construction, 6.3% production (2000).
Income: Per capita income: $38,929 (2000); Median household income: $86,772 (2000); Poverty rate: 2.3% (2000).
Taxes: Total city taxes per capita: $318 (1997); City property taxes per capita: $266 (1997).
Education: High school graduation rate: 95.9% (2000); College graduation rate: 45.8% (2000).
Housing: Homeownership rate: 92.3% (2000); Median home value: $228,700 (2000); Median rent: $659 per month (2000); Median age of housing: 11 years (2000).
Transportation: Commute to work: 90.7% car, 1.9% public transportation, 1.9% walk, 5.0% work from home (2000); Travel time to work: 21.7% less than 15 minutes, 28.5% 15 to 30 minutes, 31.5% 30 to 45 minutes, 9.6% 45 to 60 minutes, 8.7% 60 minutes or more (2000)

WACONIA (city). Covers a land area of 2.802 square miles and a water area of 0.041 square miles. Located at 44.84° N. Lat.; 93.79° W. Long. Elevation is 991 feet.
Population: 6,814 (2000); Race: 96.5% White, 0.7% Black, 0.9% Asian, 0.0% American Indian and Alaska Native, 1.2% Hispanic of any race, 1.4% two or more races (2000); Density: 2,432.0 persons per square mile (2000); Age: 29.9% under 18, 12.6% over 64 (2000); Marriage status: 20.0% never married, 66.6% now married, 6.5% widowed, 7.0% divorced (2000); Foreign born: 1.5% (2000); Ancestry (includes multiple ancestries): 55.1% German, 14.0% Norwegian, 8.8% Irish, 8.6% Swedish, 5.5% English (2000).
Economy: Single-family building permits issued: 153 (2001) / 215 (2000); Multi-family building permits issued: 0 (2001) / 0 (2000); Employment by occupation: 17.6% management, 18.3% professional, 13.8% services, 28.2% sales, 0.5% farming, 8.0% construction, 13.6% production (2000).
Income: Per capita income: $26,996 (2000); Median household income: $55,705 (2000); Poverty rate: 3.8% (2000).
Taxes: Total city taxes per capita: $349 (2000); City property taxes per capita: $254 (2000).
Education: High school graduation rate: 87.4% (2000); College graduation rate: 29.4% (2000).

School District(s)

Waconia (PK-12)
2000 Enrollment: 2,144 952-442-6600
Housing: Homeownership rate: 76.3% (2000); Median home value: $151,500 (2000); Median rent: $615 per month (2000); Median age of housing: 13 years (2000).
Safety: Violent crime rate: 4.4 per 10,000 population; Property crime rate: 264.3 per 10,000 population (2001).
Newspapers: The Waconia Patriot (1 x week); Gold Miner (1 x week)
Transportation: Commute to work: 93.6% car, 0.3% public transportation, 1.6% walk, 4.0% work from home (2000); Travel time to work: 25.7% less than 15 minutes, 27.9% 15 to 30 minutes, 26.6% 30 to 45 minutes, 14.7% 45 to 60 minutes, 5.0% 60 minutes or more (2000)
Additional Information Contacts
Waconia Chamber of Commerce 952-442-5812

WACONIA (township). Covers a land area of 27.110 square miles and a water area of 5.391 square miles. Located at 44.84° N. Lat.; 93.83° W. Long. Elevation is 991 feet.
History: Incorporated 1921.
Population: 1,284 (2000); Race: 98.1% White, 0.0% Black, 1.0% Asian, 0.0% American Indian and Alaska Native, 0.0% Hispanic of any race, 0.9% two or more races (2000); Density: 47.4 persons per square mile (2000); Age: 31.7% under 18, 7.0% over 64 (2000); Marriage status: 21.6% never married, 67.9% now married, 2.7% widowed, 7.8% divorced (2000); Foreign born: 1.0% (2000); Ancestry (includes multiple ancestries): 61.1% German, 11.4% Norwegian, 7.9% Irish, 5.4% English, 5.1% Swedish (2000).
Economy: In poultry, livestock; grain area. Dairy products, hard disk drives, valves, kitchen cabinets, printed circuit boards, printing, fertilizer. Employment by occupation: 15.1% management, 23.7% professional, 9.3% services, 27.4% sales, 0.7% farming, 8.0% construction, 15.7% production (2000).
Income: Per capita income: $27,437 (2000); Median household income: $76,113 (2000); Poverty rate: 2.9% (2000).
Taxes: Total city taxes per capita: $100 (2000); City property taxes per capita: $100 (2000).
Education: High school graduation rate: 91.5% (2000); College graduation rate: 24.3% (2000).
Housing: Homeownership rate: 92.4% (2000); Median home value: $187,500 (2000); Median rent: $642 per month (2000); Median age of housing: 29 years (2000).
Transportation: Commute to work: 91.7% car, 0.0% public transportation, 2.0% walk, 5.1% work from home (2000); Travel time to work: 28.4% less than 15 minutes, 26.1% 15 to 30 minutes, 23.5% 30 to 45 minutes, 17.3% 45 to 60 minutes, 4.8% 60 minutes or more (2000)

WATERTOWN (city). Covers a land area of 1.675 square miles and a water area of 0.042 square miles. Located at 44.96° N. Lat.; 93.84° W. Long.
Population: 3,029 (2000); Race: 97.4% White, 0.1% Black, 0.3% Asian, 0.3% American Indian and Alaska Native, 1.7% Hispanic of any race, 1.3% two or more races (2000); Density: 1,808.0 persons per square mile (2000); Age: 28.3% under 18, 13.8% over 64 (2000); Marriage status: 26.9% never married, 57.1% now married, 8.2% widowed, 7.9% divorced (2000); Foreign born: 1.1% (2000); Ancestry (includes multiple ancestries): 51.1% German, 15.8% Norwegian, 13.0% Swedish, 10.9% Irish, 5.9% Polish (2000).

Economy: Single-family building permits issued: 81 (2001) / 80 (2000); Multi-family building permits issued: 4 (2001) / 2 (2000); Employment by occupation: 11.0% management, 16.8% professional, 16.0% services, 23.9% sales, 0.6% farming, 10.9% construction, 20.8% production (2000).
Income: Per capita income: $18,918 (2000); Median household income: $47,500 (2000); Poverty rate: 6.3% (2000).
Taxes: Total city taxes per capita: $160 (1997); City property taxes per capita: $141 (1997).
Education: High school graduation rate: 81.0% (2000); College graduation rate: 17.9% (2000).

School District(s)

Watertown-Mayer (PK-12)
2000 Enrollment: 1,377 952-955-0200
Housing: Homeownership rate: 80.4% (2000); Median home value: $125,200 (2000); Median rent: $425 per month (2000); Median age of housing: 23 years (2000).
Newspapers: Carver County News (1 x week)
Transportation: Commute to work: 92.2% car, 0.9% public transportation, 3.1% walk, 3.5% work from home (2000); Travel time to work: 22.3% less than 15 minutes, 30.6% 15 to 30 minutes, 24.3% 30 to 45 minutes, 17.6% 45 to 60 minutes, 5.1% 60 minutes or more (2000)

WATERTOWN (township). Covers a land area of 32.554 square miles and a water area of 1.935 square miles. Located at 44.94° N. Lat.; 93.82° W. Long.
Population: 1,432 (2000); Race: 98.6% White, 0.0% Black, 1.4% Asian, 0.0% American Indian and Alaska Native, 0.4% Hispanic of any race, 0.0% two or more races (2000); Density: 44.0 persons per square mile (2000); Age: 29.2% under 18, 8.6% over 64 (2000); Marriage status: 24.4% never married, 67.3% now married, 3.4% widowed, 5.0% divorced (2000); Foreign born: 0.6% (2000); Ancestry (includes multiple ancestries): 57.2% German, 14.5% Norwegian, 12.1% Swedish, 9.5% Irish, 7.1% Polish (2000).
Economy: Agriculture includes livestock, poultry; dairying; grain, soybeans, alfalfa. Manufacturing includes printing and publishing, light manufacturing. Employment by occupation: 15.5% management, 19.3% professional, 10.6% services, 28.5% sales, 2.2% farming, 12.0% construction, 12.0% production (2000).
Income: Per capita income: $24,005 (2000); Median household income: $61,083 (2000); Poverty rate: 6.2% (2000).
Taxes: Total city taxes per capita: $101 (2000); City property taxes per capita: $101 (2000).
Education: High school graduation rate: 85.2% (2000); College graduation rate: 21.6% (2000).
Housing: Homeownership rate: 89.5% (2000); Median home value: $179,600 (2000); Median rent: $463 per month (2000); Median age of housing: 30 years (2000).
Transportation: Commute to work: 86.7% car, 1.1% public transportation, 3.7% walk, 8.2% work from home (2000); Travel time to work: 24.2% less than 15 minutes, 29.6% 15 to 30 minutes, 22.4% 30 to 45 minutes, 14.8% 45 to 60 minutes, 9.1% 60 minutes or more (2000)

YOUNG AMERICA (township). Covers a land area of 32.783 square miles and a water area of 1.305 square miles. Located at 44.77° N. Lat.; 93.94° W. Long.
Population: 838 (2000); Race: 100.0% White, 0.0% Black, 0.0% Asian, 0.0% American Indian and Alaska Native, 0.6% Hispanic of any race, 0.0% two or more races (2000); Density: 25.6 persons per square mile (2000); Age: 25.6% under 18, 9.6% over 64 (2000); Marriage status: 29.7% never married, 66.4% now married, 2.2% widowed, 1.7% divorced (2000); Foreign born: 0.0% (2000); Ancestry (includes multiple ancestries): 75.4% German, 11.2% Norwegian, 7.1% Irish, 7.0% Swedish, 2.7% English (2000).
Economy: Agriculture: grain, soybeans, corn; dairying; livestock. Manufacturing: irrigation systems. Employment by occupation: 17.7% management, 17.5% professional, 10.7% services, 19.7% sales, 2.0% farming, 10.3% construction, 22.1% production (2000).
Income: Per capita income: $23,216 (2000); Median household income: $65,000 (2000); Poverty rate: 3.0% (2000).
Taxes: Total city taxes per capita: $62 (1997); City property taxes per capita: $62 (1997).
Education: High school graduation rate: 87.1% (2000); College graduation rate: 21.1% (2000).
Housing: Homeownership rate: 96.1% (2000); Median home value: $157,900 (2000); Median rent: $375 per month (2000); Median age of housing: 57 years (2000).
Transportation: Commute to work: 84.8% car, 0.0% public transportation, 1.4% walk, 13.0% work from home (2000); Travel time to work: 32.7% less than 15 minutes, 20.8% 15 to 30 minutes, 24.8% 30 to 45 minutes, 12.6% 45 to 60 minutes, 9.1% 60 minutes or more (2000)

Cass County

Located in north central Minnesota; bounded on the south by the Crow Wing River, and on the north by the Mississippi River; includes part of Chippewa National Forest. Covers a land area of 2,017.60 square miles, a water area of 396.60 square miles, and is located in the Central Time Zone. The county government was organized in 1851. County seat is Walker.

Weather Station: Cass Lake — Elevation: 1,295 feet

	Jan	Feb	Mar	Apr	May	Jun	Jul	Aug	Sep	Oct	Nov	Dec
High	16	24	36	52	67	75	79	77	66	53	35	21
Low	-10	-3	12	27	40	51	55	53	44	32	16	-1
Precip	0.8	0.6	1.3	1.9	2.6	3.9	4.3	3.2	2.8	2.6	1.3	0.7
Snow	11.3	7.2	8.7	3.0	tr	0.0	0.0	0.0	0.0	0.7	8.2	8.6

High and Low temperatures in degrees Fahrenheit; Precipitation and Snow in inches

Weather Station: Gull Lake Dam — Elevation: 1,213 feet

	Jan	Feb	Mar	Apr	May	Jun	Jul	Aug	Sep	Oct	Nov	Dec
High	18	26	37	54	68	76	80	78	68	55	36	23
Low	-3	4	16	30	43	54	59	57	47	35	21	5
Precip	0.8	0.5	1.4	1.8	3.0	4.2	3.9	3.7	2.6	2.7	1.3	0.6
Snow	na	na	9.6	2.8	0.2	0.0	0.0	0.0	0.0	0.6	na	na

High and Low temperatures in degrees Fahrenheit; Precipitation and Snow in inches

Weather Station: Leech Lake Dam — Elevation: 1,299 feet

	Jan	Feb	Mar	Apr	May	Jun	Jul	Aug	Sep	Oct	Nov	Dec
High	17	27	38	54	68	76	80	78	68	55	35	22
Low	-5	2	15	29	42	52	57	55	46	34	20	4
Precip	0.8	0.5	1.0	1.6	2.6	3.8	4.4	3.6	2.8	2.6	1.1	0.7
Snow	12.3	6.8	7.9	2.7	tr	0.0	0.0	0.0	tr	0.8	6.9	9.1

High and Low temperatures in degrees Fahrenheit; Precipitation and Snow in inches

Weather Station: Walker Ah Gwah Ching — Elevation: 1,407 feet

	Jan	Feb	Mar	Apr	May	Jun	Jul	Aug	Sep	Oct	Nov	Dec
High	17	25	36	53	67	75	79	77	66	54	35	22
Low	-3	4	17	31	44	53	58	56	46	36	20	5
Precip	0.8	0.6	1.3	2.1	2.9	4.0	4.1	3.5	2.9	2.8	1.3	0.8
Snow	11.3	6.6	8.4	2.0	tr	0.0	0.0	0.0	tr	0.5	7.7	8.9

High and Low temperatures in degrees Fahrenheit; Precipitation and Snow in inches

Population: 27,150 (2000); Race: 86.9% White, 0.1% Black, 0.3% Asian, 11.0% American Indian and Alaska Native, 0.8% Hispanic of any race, 1.5% two or more races (2000); Density: 13.5 persons per square mile (2000); Age: 25.1% under 18, 18.0% over 64 (2000).
Religion: Five largest groups: 15.0% Evangelical Lutheran Church in America, 11.3% Catholic Church, 2.2% Lutheran Church—Missouri Synod, 2.1% United Church of Christ, 1.8% Episcopal Church (2000).
Economy: Unemployment rate: 6.4% (11/2002); Total civilian labor force: 13,832 (11/2002); Leading industries: 19.4% retail trade; 15.5% arts, entertainment & recreation; 12.5% health care and social assistance (2000); Companies that employ more than 1,000 persons: 0 (2000); Companies that employ more than 100 persons: 4 (2000); Farms: 598 totaling 191,847 acres (1997); Minority business ownership rate: 0.0% (1997); Women business ownership rate: 12.2% (1997); Retail sales per capita: $6,368 (1997). Single-family building permits issued: 466 (2001) / 383 (2000); Multi-family building permits issued: 19 (2001) / 9 (2000).
Income: Per capita income: $17,189 (2000); Median household income: $34,332 (2000); Poverty rate: 13.6% (2000); Bankruptcy rate: 2.05% (2001).
Taxes: Total county taxes per capita: $437 (2000); County property taxes per capita: $435 (2000).
Education: High school graduation rate: 83.9% (2000); College graduation rate: 16.6% (2000).
Housing: Homeownership rate: 86.0% (2000); Median home value: $105,900 (2000); Median rent: $296 per month (2000); Median age of housing: 25 years (2000).
Health: Birth rate: 106.8 per 10,000 population (1998); Age adjusted death rate: 89.6 per 10,000 population (1999); Age adjusted cancer mortality rate: 186.2 deaths per 100,000 population (1999). Number of physicians: 3.7 per 10,000 population (1999); Number of hospital beds: 4.8 per 10,000 population (1999).
Elections: 2000 Presidential election results: 40.7% Gore, 52.5% Bush, 4.9% Nader, 1.5% Buchanan
National and State Parks: Battleground State Forest; Bowstring State Forest; Foot Hills State Forest; Land O'Lakes State Forest; Pillsbury State

Forest; Remer State Forest; School Craft State Recreation Area; Schoolcraft State Recreation Area; Welsh Lake State Forest

Additional Information Contacts

Cass County Government Offices 218-547-1488
Cass Lake Chamber of Commerce. 218-335-6723
Leech Lake Area Chamber of Commerce 218-547-1313
Longville Chamber of Commerce 218-363-2630
Pine River Chamber of Commerce 218-587-4000
Remer Area Chamber of Commerce 218-566-1680

Cass County Communities

ANSEL (township). Covers a land area of 35.311 square miles and a water area of 0.427 square miles. Located at 46.67° N. Lat.; 94.73° W. Long.
Population: 101 (2000); Race: 98.2% White, 0.0% Black, 0.0% Asian, 0.0% American Indian and Alaska Native, 0.0% Hispanic of any race, 1.8% two or more races (2000); Density: 2.9 persons per square mile (2000); Age: 27.5% under 18, 6.4% over 64 (2000); Marriage status: 19.1% never married, 75.3% now married, 0.0% widowed, 5.6% divorced (2000); Foreign born: 0.0% (2000); Ancestry (includes multiple ancestries): 45.9% German, 15.6% English, 13.8% United States or American, 12.8% Irish, 4.6% Czech (2000).
Economy: Single-family building permits issued: 0 (2001) / 0 (2000); Multi-family building permits issued: 0 (2001) / 0 (2000); Employment by occupation: 8.3% management, 0.0% professional, 16.7% services, 26.4% sales, 22.2% farming, 0.0% construction, 26.4% production (2000).
Income: Per capita income: $14,102 (2000); Median household income: $40,000 (2000); Poverty rate: 13.8% (2000).
Taxes: Total city taxes per capita: $70 (1997); City property taxes per capita: $70 (1997).
Education: High school graduation rate: 84.7% (2000); College graduation rate: 0.0% (2000).
Housing: Homeownership rate: 100.0% (2000); Median home value: $65,000 (2000); Median age of housing: 27 years (2000).
Transportation: Commute to work: 70.8% car, 0.0% public transportation, 5.6% walk, 23.6% work from home (2000); Travel time to work: 16.4% less than 15 minutes, 18.2% 15 to 30 minutes, 32.7% 30 to 45 minutes, 16.4% 45 to 60 minutes, 16.4% 60 minutes or more (2000)

BACKUS (city). Covers a land area of 0.599 square miles and a water area of 0 square miles. Located at 46.82° N. Lat.; 94.51° W. Long. Elevation is 1,337 feet.
Population: 311 (2000); Race: 99.4% White, 0.0% Black, 0.0% Asian, 0.0% American Indian and Alaska Native, 0.0% Hispanic of any race, 0.6% two or more races (2000); Density: 518.9 persons per square mile (2000); Age: 31.9% under 18, 17.9% over 64 (2000); Marriage status: 30.6% never married, 44.2% now married, 10.3% widowed, 14.9% divorced (2000); Foreign born: 1.6% (2000); Ancestry (includes multiple ancestries): 28.4% German, 14.7% United States or American, 9.6% Irish, 9.3% Norwegian, 8.6% English (2000).
Economy: Dairying; cattle, sheep; oats, alfalfa. Manufacturing: motor vehicles. Single-family building permits issued: 1 (2001) / 0 (2000); Multi-family building permits issued: 0 (2001) / 0 (2000); Employment by occupation: 4.6% management, 16.7% professional, 25.9% services, 20.4% sales, 0.0% farming, 6.5% construction, 25.9% production (2000).
Income: Per capita income: $12,077 (2000); Median household income: $26,875 (2000); Poverty rate: 23.0% (2000).
Taxes: Total city taxes per capita: $144 (1997); City property taxes per capita: $133 (1997).
Education: High school graduation rate: 83.1% (2000); College graduation rate: 9.0% (2000).
Housing: Homeownership rate: 77.9% (2000); Median home value: $47,300 (2000); Median rent: $269 per month (2000); Median age of housing: 37 years (2000).
Transportation: Commute to work: 98.1% car, 0.0% public transportation, 0.0% walk, 1.9% work from home (2000); Travel time to work: 32.0% less than 15 minutes, 30.1% 15 to 30 minutes, 20.4% 30 to 45 minutes, 14.6% 45 to 60 minutes, 2.9% 60 minutes or more (2000)
Airports: Backus Municipal

BARCLAY (township). Covers a land area of 13.966 square miles and a water area of 1.060 square miles. Located at 46.75° N. Lat.; 94.37° W. Long.
Population: 516 (2000); Race: 96.3% White, 1.2% Black, 0.0% Asian, 1.6% American Indian and Alaska Native, 0.0% Hispanic of any race, 1.0% two or more races (2000); Density: 36.9 persons per square mile (2000); Age: 27.5% under 18, 15.8% over 64 (2000); Marriage status: 19.6% never married, 64.5% now married, 6.8% widowed, 9.0% divorced (2000); Foreign born: 0.4% (2000); Ancestry (includes multiple ancestries): 32.0% German, 15.4% Swedish, 12.5% Norwegian, 11.7% Irish, 7.6% English (2000).
Economy: Employment by occupation: 11.3% management, 21.8% professional, 14.6% services, 20.5% sales, 4.2% farming, 19.2% construction, 8.4% production (2000).
Income: Per capita income: $15,215 (2000); Median household income: $32,039 (2000); Poverty rate: 8.0% (2000).
Taxes: Total city taxes per capita: $47 (1997); City property taxes per capita: $47 (1997).
Education: High school graduation rate: 85.3% (2000); College graduation rate: 19.1% (2000).
Housing: Homeownership rate: 91.4% (2000); Median home value: $76,500 (2000); Median rent: $363 per month (2000); Median age of housing: 28 years (2000).
Transportation: Commute to work: 87.3% car, 0.8% public transportation, 3.8% walk, 6.3% work from home (2000); Travel time to work: 47.7% less than 15 minutes, 26.1% 15 to 30 minutes, 20.3% 30 to 45 minutes, 1.4% 45 to 60 minutes, 4.5% 60 minutes or more (2000)

BECKER (township). Covers a land area of 36.291 square miles and a water area of 0.987 square miles. Located at 46.41° N. Lat.; 94.72° W. Long.
Population: 485 (2000); Race: 96.3% White, 0.0% Black, 0.8% Asian, 1.0% American Indian and Alaska Native, 0.0% Hispanic of any race, 1.9% two or more races (2000); Density: 13.4 persons per square mile (2000); Age: 35.0% under 18, 5.1% over 64 (2000); Marriage status: 24.8% never married, 60.1% now married, 2.2% widowed, 12.9% divorced (2000); Foreign born: 0.4% (2000); Ancestry (includes multiple ancestries): 47.7% German, 19.3% Norwegian, 11.5% Irish, 11.1% United States or American, 6.2% Swedish (2000).
Economy: Employment by occupation: 10.2% management, 15.3% professional, 11.4% services, 23.7% sales, 1.7% farming, 11.4% construction, 26.3% production (2000).
Income: Per capita income: $14,025 (2000); Median household income: $35,795 (2000); Poverty rate: 14.6% (2000).
Taxes: Total city taxes per capita: $52 (1997); City property taxes per capita: $52 (1997).
Education: High school graduation rate: 86.3% (2000); College graduation rate: 9.7% (2000).
Housing: Homeownership rate: 90.2% (2000); Median home value: $85,600 (2000); Median rent: $175 per month (2000); Median age of housing: 22 years (2000).
Transportation: Commute to work: 91.9% car, 0.0% public transportation, 0.0% walk, 3.4% work from home (2000); Travel time to work: 59.7% less than 15 minutes, 14.6% 15 to 30 minutes, 11.1% 30 to 45 minutes, 6.2% 45 to 60 minutes, 8.4% 60 minutes or more (2000)

BENA (city). Covers a land area of 0.505 square miles and a water area of 0 square miles. Located at 47.34° N. Lat.; 94.20° W. Long. Elevation is 1,304 feet.
Population: 110 (2000); Race: 29.6% White, 3.7% Black, 0.0% Asian, 66.7% American Indian and Alaska Native, 0.0% Hispanic of any race, 0.0% two or more races (2000); Density: 218.0 persons per square mile (2000); Age: 24.7% under 18, 18.5% over 64 (2000); Marriage status: 54.5% never married, 25.8% now married, 12.1% widowed, 7.6% divorced (2000); Foreign born: 2.5% (2000); Ancestry (includes multiple ancestries): 40.7% Other groups, 7.4% Irish, 4.9% Norwegian, 4.9% German, 2.5% Polish (2000).
Economy: Cattle; dairying; alfalfa, oats. Employment by occupation: 26.7% management, 0.0% professional, 6.7% services, 13.3% sales, 20.0% farming, 20.0% construction, 13.3% production (2000).
Income: Per capita income: $7,619 (2000); Median household income: $11,563 (2000); Poverty rate: 58.0% (2000).
Taxes: Total city taxes per capita: $23 (1997); City property taxes per capita: $23 (1997).
Education: High school graduation rate: 33.3% (2000); College graduation rate: 0.0% (2000).
Housing: Homeownership rate: 85.7% (2000); Median home value: $30,600 (2000); Median rent: $250 per month (2000); Median age of housing: 48 years (2000).
Transportation: Commute to work: 73.3% car, 6.7% public transportation, 0.0% walk, 20.0% work from home (2000); Travel time to work: 8.3% less than 15 minutes, 33.3% 15 to 30 minutes, 25.0% 30 to 45 minutes, 16.7% 45 to 60 minutes, 16.7% 60 minutes or more (2000)

BEULAH (township). Covers a land area of 34.645 square miles and a water area of 1.067 square miles. Located at 46.85° N. Lat.; 93.84° W. Long.
Population: 57 (2000); Race: 100.0% White, 0.0% Black, 0.0% Asian, 0.0% American Indian and Alaska Native, 0.0% Hispanic of any race, 0.0% two or more races (2000); Density: 1.6 persons per square mile (2000); Age: 6.3% under 18, 31.7% over 64 (2000); Marriage status: 15.0% never married, 73.3% now married, 3.3% widowed, 8.3% divorced (2000); Foreign born: 0.0% (2000); Ancestry (includes multiple ancestries): 36.5% German, 23.8% Polish, 15.9% French (except Basque), 15.9% Irish, 11.1% Swedish (2000).
Economy: Employment by occupation: 0.0% management, 17.6% professional, 41.2% services, 11.8% sales, 0.0% farming, 0.0% construction, 29.4% production (2000).
Income: Per capita income: $16,613 (2000); Median household income: $26,875 (2000); Poverty rate: 15.9% (2000).
Taxes: Total city taxes per capita: $125 (1997); City property taxes per capita: $125 (1997).
Education: High school graduation rate: 76.3% (2000); College graduation rate: 5.1% (2000).
Housing: Homeownership rate: 100.0% (2000); Median home value: $133,300 (2000); Median age of housing: 30 years (2000).
Transportation: Commute to work: 100.0% car, 0.0% public transportation, 0.0% walk, 0.0% work from home (2000); Travel time to work: 33.3% less than 15 minutes, 13.3% 15 to 30 minutes, 20.0% 30 to 45 minutes, 33.3% 45 to 60 minutes, 0.0% 60 minutes or more (2000)

BIRCH LAKE (township). Covers a land area of 28.726 square miles and a water area of 6.629 square miles. Located at 46.93° N. Lat.; 94.48° W. Long.
Population: 573 (2000); Race: 98.9% White, 0.0% Black, 0.5% Asian, 0.0% American Indian and Alaska Native, 0.3% Hispanic of any race, 0.3% two or more races (2000); Density: 19.9 persons per square mile (2000); Age: 19.3% under 18, 21.2% over 64 (2000); Marriage status: 11.3% never married, 79.3% now married, 5.3% widowed, 4.1% divorced (2000); Foreign born: 0.5% (2000); Ancestry (includes multiple ancestries): 39.0% German, 15.5% Norwegian, 14.9% Swedish, 13.0% Irish, 9.0% English (2000).
Economy: Employment by occupation: 13.8% management, 20.1% professional, 13.4% services, 20.5% sales, 0.0% farming, 15.5% construction, 16.7% production (2000).
Income: Per capita income: $18,687 (2000); Median household income: $36,042 (2000); Poverty rate: 5.4% (2000).
Taxes: Total city taxes per capita: $176 (1997); City property taxes per capita: $176 (1997).
Education: High school graduation rate: 87.8% (2000); College graduation rate: 19.3% (2000).
Housing: Homeownership rate: 93.4% (2000); Median home value: $145,200 (2000); Median rent: $238 per month (2000); Median age of housing: 24 years (2000).
Transportation: Commute to work: 90.6% car, 0.0% public transportation, 2.7% walk, 6.7% work from home (2000); Travel time to work: 43.8% less than 15 minutes, 27.4% 15 to 30 minutes, 13.0% 30 to 45 minutes, 5.3% 45 to 60 minutes, 10.6% 60 minutes or more (2000)

BLIND LAKE (township). Covers a land area of 34.016 square miles and a water area of 1.333 square miles. Located at 46.83° N. Lat.; 94.23° W. Long.
Population: 88 (2000); Race: 88.3% White, 0.0% Black, 0.0% Asian, 0.0% American Indian and Alaska Native, 0.0% Hispanic of any race, 11.7% two or more races (2000); Density: 2.6 persons per square mile (2000); Age: 49.5% under 18, 5.8% over 64 (2000); Marriage status: 28.4% never married, 62.7% now married, 3.0% widowed, 6.0% divorced (2000); Foreign born: 0.0% (2000); Ancestry (includes multiple ancestries): 21.4% United States or American, 16.5% German, 14.6% Norwegian, 14.6% Swedish, 7.8% French (except Basque) (2000).
Economy: Employment by occupation: 23.5% management, 5.9% professional, 5.9% services, 17.6% sales, 0.0% farming, 5.9% construction, 41.2% production (2000).
Income: Per capita income: $6,420 (2000); Median household income: $19,250 (2000); Poverty rate: 20.4% (2000).
Taxes: Total city taxes per capita: $114 (1997); City property taxes per capita: $114 (1997).
Education: High school graduation rate: 94.2% (2000); College graduation rate: 7.7% (2000).
Housing: Homeownership rate: 93.3% (2000); Median home value: $55,000 (2000); Median age of housing: 32 years (2000).
Transportation: Commute to work: 76.5% car, 0.0% public transportation, 0.0% walk, 23.5% work from home (2000); Travel time to work: 0.0% less than 15 minutes, 53.8% 15 to 30 minutes, 23.1% 30 to 45 minutes, 15.4% 45 to 60 minutes, 7.7% 60 minutes or more (2000)

BOY LAKE (township). Covers a land area of 27.597 square miles and a water area of 8.719 square miles. Located at 47.09° N. Lat.; 94.19° W. Long.
Population: 132 (2000); Race: 80.2% White, 0.0% Black, 0.0% Asian, 6.9% American Indian and Alaska Native, 0.0% Hispanic of any race, 12.9% two or more races (2000); Density: 4.8 persons per square mile (2000); Age: 13.8% under 18, 12.9% over 64 (2000); Marriage status: 18.6% never married, 64.7% now married, 7.8% widowed, 8.8% divorced (2000); Foreign born: 0.0% (2000); Ancestry (includes multiple ancestries): 44.0% German, 20.7% Other groups, 14.7% Norwegian, 8.6% Swedish, 7.8% English (2000).
Economy: Employment by occupation: 33.9% management, 12.5% professional, 14.3% services, 12.5% sales, 0.0% farming, 12.5% construction, 14.3% production (2000).
Income: Per capita income: $20,070 (2000); Median household income: $37,500 (2000); Poverty rate: 26.7% (2000).
Taxes: Total city taxes per capita: $224 (1997); City property taxes per capita: $224 (1997).
Education: High school graduation rate: 92.5% (2000); College graduation rate: 11.8% (2000).
Housing: Homeownership rate: 86.0% (2000); Median home value: $137,500 (2000); Median age of housing: 28 years (2000).
Transportation: Commute to work: 64.3% car, 0.0% public transportation, 5.4% walk, 26.8% work from home (2000); Travel time to work: 12.2% less than 15 minutes, 53.7% 15 to 30 minutes, 4.9% 30 to 45 minutes, 0.0% 45 to 60 minutes, 29.3% 60 minutes or more (2000)

BOY RIVER (city). Covers a land area of 0.427 square miles and a water area of <.001 square miles. Located at 47.16° N. Lat.; 94.12° W. Long. Elevation is 1,329 feet.
Population: 38 (2000); Race: 100.0% White, 0.0% Black, 0.0% Asian, 0.0% American Indian and Alaska Native, 0.0% Hispanic of any race, 0.0% two or more races (2000); Density: 89.0 persons per square mile (2000); Age: 28.0% under 18, 28.0% over 64 (2000); Marriage status: 0.0% never married, 57.9% now married, 26.3% widowed, 15.8% divorced (2000); Foreign born: 0.0% (2000); Ancestry (includes multiple ancestries): 48.0% German, 36.0% Irish, 20.0% Swedish, 12.0% Norwegian (2000).
Economy: Employment by occupation: 0.0% management, 0.0% professional, 0.0% services, 40.0% sales, 0.0% farming, 60.0% construction, 0.0% production (2000).
Income: Per capita income: $10,556 (2000); Median household income: $13,125 (2000); Poverty rate: 24.0% (2000).
Taxes: Total city taxes per capita: $80 (1997); City property taxes per capita: $40 (1997).
Education: High school graduation rate: 50.0% (2000); College graduation rate: 0.0% (2000).
Housing: Homeownership rate: 100.0% (2000); Median home value: $21,300 (2000); Median age of housing: 30 years (2000).
Transportation: Commute to work: 60.0% car, 0.0% public transportation, 0.0% walk, 40.0% work from home (2000); Travel time to work: 0.0% less than 15 minutes, 100.0% 15 to 30 minutes, 0.0% 30 to 45 minutes, 0.0% 45 to 60 minutes, 0.0% 60 minutes or more (2000)

BOY RIVER (township). Covers a land area of 35.619 square miles and a water area of 0.274 square miles. Located at 47.18° N. Lat.; 94.12° W. Long. Elevation is 1,329 feet.
Population: 100 (2000); Race: 88.6% White, 0.0% Black, 0.0% Asian, 11.4% American Indian and Alaska Native, 0.0% Hispanic of any race, 0.0% two or more races (2000); Density: 2.8 persons per square mile (2000); Age: 25.0% under 18, 15.9% over 64 (2000); Marriage status: 13.4% never married, 56.7% now married, 20.9% widowed, 9.0% divorced (2000); Foreign born: 0.0% (2000); Ancestry (includes multiple ancestries): 34.1% German, 17.0% English, 13.6% Swedish, 11.4% Other groups, 8.0% Norwegian (2000).
Economy: Dairying; oats. Employment by occupation: 17.6% management, 23.5% professional, 26.5% services, 0.0% sales, 5.9% farming, 26.5% construction, 0.0% production (2000).
Income: Per capita income: $13,025 (2000); Median household income: $19,500 (2000); Poverty rate: 33.3% (2000).
Taxes: Total city taxes per capita: $39 (1997); City property taxes per capita: $39 (1997).
Education: High school graduation rate: 76.2% (2000); College graduation rate: 6.3% (2000).

Housing: Homeownership rate: 89.5% (2000); Median home value: $91,300 (2000); Median rent: $625 per month (2000); Median age of housing: 25 years (2000).
Transportation: Commute to work: 81.3% car, 0.0% public transportation, 0.0% walk, 12.5% work from home (2000); Travel time to work: 21.4% less than 15 minutes, 25.0% 15 to 30 minutes, 28.6% 30 to 45 minutes, 17.9% 45 to 60 minutes, 7.1% 60 minutes or more (2000)

BULL MOOSE (township). Covers a land area of 34.301 square miles and a water area of 1.667 square miles. Located at 46.75° N. Lat.; 94.58° W. Long.
Population: 107 (2000); Race: 100.0% White, 0.0% Black, 0.0% Asian, 0.0% American Indian and Alaska Native, 0.0% Hispanic of any race, 0.0% two or more races (2000); Density: 3.1 persons per square mile (2000); Age: 23.9% under 18, 14.1% over 64 (2000); Marriage status: 16.7% never married, 76.4% now married, 4.2% widowed, 2.8% divorced (2000); Foreign born: 0.0% (2000); Ancestry (includes multiple ancestries): 29.3% Norwegian, 22.8% German, 16.3% English, 16.3% Swedish, 6.5% Irish (2000).
Economy: Employment by occupation: 3.4% management, 10.2% professional, 6.8% services, 39.0% sales, 10.2% farming, 13.6% construction, 16.9% production (2000).
Income: Per capita income: $12,596 (2000); Median household income: $31,563 (2000); Poverty rate: 9.8% (2000).
Taxes: Total city taxes per capita: $50 (1997); City property taxes per capita: $50 (1997).
Education: High school graduation rate: 82.8% (2000); College graduation rate: 3.1% (2000).
Housing: Homeownership rate: 89.5% (2000); Median home value: $95,000 (2000); Median age of housing: 21 years (2000).
Transportation: Commute to work: 96.6% car, 0.0% public transportation, 0.0% walk, 3.4% work from home (2000); Travel time to work: 38.6% less than 15 minutes, 36.8% 15 to 30 minutes, 7.0% 30 to 45 minutes, 17.5% 45 to 60 minutes, 0.0% 60 minutes or more (2000)

BUNGO (township). Covers a land area of 34.610 square miles and a water area of 1.311 square miles. Located at 46.67° N. Lat.; 94.57° W. Long.
Population: 111 (2000); Race: 99.1% White, 0.0% Black, 0.0% Asian, 0.0% American Indian and Alaska Native, 0.0% Hispanic of any race, 0.9% two or more races (2000); Density: 3.2 persons per square mile (2000); Age: 29.9% under 18, 14.0% over 64 (2000); Marriage status: 27.2% never married, 69.1% now married, 3.7% widowed, 0.0% divorced (2000); Foreign born: 0.0% (2000); Ancestry (includes multiple ancestries): 42.1% German, 28.0% Swedish, 19.6% Irish, 10.3% United States or American, 10.3% Scottish (2000).
Economy: Employment by occupation: 24.0% management, 14.0% professional, 4.0% services, 26.0% sales, 12.0% farming, 4.0% construction, 16.0% production (2000).
Income: Per capita income: $9,993 (2000); Median household income: $29,375 (2000); Poverty rate: 32.7% (2000).
Taxes: Total city taxes per capita: $84 (1997); City property taxes per capita: $84 (1997).
Education: High school graduation rate: 88.4% (2000); College graduation rate: 0.0% (2000).
Housing: Homeownership rate: 100.0% (2000); Median home value: $275,000 (2000); Median age of housing: 38 years (2000).
Transportation: Commute to work: 73.9% car, 0.0% public transportation, 17.4% walk, 8.7% work from home (2000); Travel time to work: 19.0% less than 15 minutes, 42.9% 15 to 30 minutes, 31.0% 30 to 45 minutes, 7.1% 45 to 60 minutes, 0.0% 60 minutes or more (2000)

BYRON (township). Covers a land area of 35.730 square miles and a water area of 0.182 square miles. Located at 46.50° N. Lat.; 94.71° W. Long.
Population: 118 (2000); Race: 100.0% White, 0.0% Black, 0.0% Asian, 0.0% American Indian and Alaska Native, 0.0% Hispanic of any race, 0.0% two or more races (2000); Density: 3.3 persons per square mile (2000); Age: 29.0% under 18, 20.2% over 64 (2000); Marriage status: 23.2% never married, 65.7% now married, 7.1% widowed, 4.0% divorced (2000); Foreign born: 0.0% (2000); Ancestry (includes multiple ancestries): 50.8% German, 30.6% Norwegian, 20.2% English, 9.7% Danish, 8.9% Swedish (2000).
Economy: Employment by occupation: 27.3% management, 1.8% professional, 18.2% services, 16.4% sales, 5.5% farming, 3.6% construction, 27.3% production (2000).
Income: Per capita income: $13,077 (2000); Median household income: $29,500 (2000); Poverty rate: 6.5% (2000).
Taxes: Total city taxes per capita: $25 (1997); City property taxes per capita: $25 (1997).
Education: High school graduation rate: 78.6% (2000); College graduation rate: 2.4% (2000).
Housing: Homeownership rate: 93.3% (2000); Median home value: $32,500 (2000); Median age of housing: 37 years (2000).
Transportation: Commute to work: 78.8% car, 0.0% public transportation, 5.8% walk, 15.4% work from home (2000); Travel time to work: 11.4% less than 15 minutes, 52.3% 15 to 30 minutes, 20.5% 30 to 45 minutes, 15.9% 45 to 60 minutes, 0.0% 60 minutes or more (2000)

CASS LAKE (city). Covers a land area of 1.142 square miles and a water area of 0 square miles. Located at 47.37° N. Lat.; 94.60° W. Long. Elevation is 1,330 feet.
History: A fur trading post and a mission preceded the settlement of Cass Lake, on the lake of the same name. Cass Lake was named for Lewis Cass, who led an expedition through the area in 1820.
Population: 860 (2000); Race: 27.3% White, 0.0% Black, 0.5% Asian, 69.3% American Indian and Alaska Native, 1.7% Hispanic of any race, 2.9% two or more races (2000); Density: 753.2 persons per square mile (2000); Age: 36.6% under 18, 16.4% over 64 (2000); Marriage status: 37.2% never married, 32.4% now married, 14.5% widowed, 15.9% divorced (2000); Foreign born: 1.7% (2000); Ancestry (includes multiple ancestries): 68.0% Other groups, 10.3% German, 7.6% Norwegian, 4.5% English, 2.5% Irish (2000).
Economy: Single-family building permits issued: 0 (2001) / 0 (2000); Multi-family building permits issued: 0 (2001) / 0 (2000); Employment by occupation: 7.7% management, 12.5% professional, 36.5% services, 30.3% sales, 0.0% farming, 8.5% construction, 4.4% production (2000).
Income: Per capita income: $9,569 (2000); Median household income: $20,583 (2000); Poverty rate: 29.0% (2000).
Taxes: Total city taxes per capita: $93 (1997); City property taxes per capita: $85 (1997).
Education: High school graduation rate: 70.7% (2000); College graduation rate: 6.9% (2000).

School District(s)

Cass Lake (PK-12)
2000 Enrollment: 1,163 218-335-2204

Two-year College(s)

Leech Lake Tribal College (Public)
2001 Enrollment: 174 218-335-4200
2001 Tuition: In-state $2,100; Out-of-state $2,100

Housing: Homeownership rate: 53.5% (2000); Median home value: $32,700 (2000); Median rent: $241 per month (2000); Median age of housing: 49 years (2000).
Newspapers: Times (1 x week)
Transportation: Commute to work: 84.9% car, 5.0% public transportation, 6.9% walk, 0.0% work from home (2000); Travel time to work: 68.7% less than 15 minutes, 16.6% 15 to 30 minutes, 10.0% 30 to 45 minutes, 3.5% 45 to 60 minutes, 1.2% 60 minutes or more (2000)
Additional Information Contacts
Cass Lake Chamber of Commerce. 218-335-6723

CHICKAMAW BEACH (city). Covers a land area of 2.186 square miles and a water area of 0.369 square miles. Located at 46.74° N. Lat.; 94.40° W. Long.
Population: 148 (2000); Race: 100.0% White, 0.0% Black, 0.0% Asian, 0.0% American Indian and Alaska Native, 0.0% Hispanic of any race, 0.0% two or more races (2000); Density: 67.7 persons per square mile (2000); Age: 26.8% under 18, 20.1% over 64 (2000); Marriage status: 17.7% never married, 65.5% now married, 6.2% widowed, 10.6% divorced (2000); Foreign born: 1.3% (2000); Ancestry (includes multiple ancestries): 30.2% German, 20.8% Norwegian, 14.8% Irish, 13.4% Polish, 12.8% French (except Basque) (2000).
Economy: Resort area. Single-family building permits issued: 0 (2001) / 0 (2000); Multi-family building permits issued: 0 (2001) / 0 (2000); Employment by occupation: 9.8% management, 33.3% professional, 9.8% services, 5.9% sales, 0.0% farming, 23.5% construction, 17.6% production (2000).
Income: Per capita income: $20,223 (2000); Median household income: $28,750 (2000); Poverty rate: 5.4% (2000).
Taxes: Total city taxes per capita: $65 (1997); City property taxes per capita: $65 (1997).
Education: High school graduation rate: 86.0% (2000); College graduation rate: 21.0% (2000).

Housing: Homeownership rate: 100.0% (2000); Median home value: $97,500 (2000); Median age of housing: 44 years (2000).
Transportation: Commute to work: 92.2% car, 0.0% public transportation, 5.9% walk, 2.0% work from home (2000); Travel time to work: 40.0% less than 15 minutes, 18.0% 15 to 30 minutes, 38.0% 30 to 45 minutes, 0.0% 45 to 60 minutes, 4.0% 60 minutes or more (2000)

CROOKED LAKE (township). Covers a land area of 30.044 square miles and a water area of 6.049 square miles. Located at 46.85° N. Lat.; 93.95° W. Long.
Population: 498 (2000); Race: 99.3% White, 0.0% Black, 0.0% Asian, 0.7% American Indian and Alaska Native, 0.0% Hispanic of any race, 0.0% two or more races (2000); Density: 16.6 persons per square mile (2000); Age: 13.0% under 18, 26.7% over 64 (2000); Marriage status: 10.7% never married, 71.2% now married, 8.4% widowed, 9.7% divorced (2000); Foreign born: 0.0% (2000); Ancestry (includes multiple ancestries): 29.0% German, 17.6% Swedish, 16.0% Norwegian, 10.2% English, 6.5% Irish (2000).
Economy: Employment by occupation: 16.3% management, 8.7% professional, 14.5% services, 30.2% sales, 1.2% farming, 10.5% construction, 18.6% production (2000).
Income: Per capita income: $21,294 (2000); Median household income: $32,708 (2000); Poverty rate: 6.3% (2000).
Taxes: Total city taxes per capita: $207 (1997); City property taxes per capita: $207 (1997).
Education: High school graduation rate: 82.0% (2000); College graduation rate: 16.3% (2000).
Housing: Homeownership rate: 96.1% (2000); Median home value: $128,100 (2000); Median rent: $315 per month (2000); Median age of housing: 25 years (2000).
Transportation: Commute to work: 79.6% car, 3.0% public transportation, 4.8% walk, 10.2% work from home (2000); Travel time to work: 42.7% less than 15 minutes, 16.7% 15 to 30 minutes, 22.0% 30 to 45 minutes, 8.0% 45 to 60 minutes, 10.7% 60 minutes or more (2000)

DEERFIELD (township). Covers a land area of 32.382 square miles and a water area of 3.539 square miles. Located at 46.83° N. Lat.; 94.56° W. Long.
Population: 154 (2000); Race: 100.0% White, 0.0% Black, 0.0% Asian, 0.0% American Indian and Alaska Native, 0.0% Hispanic of any race, 0.0% two or more races (2000); Density: 4.8 persons per square mile (2000); Age: 24.8% under 18, 25.5% over 64 (2000); Marriage status: 9.2% never married, 80.8% now married, 5.8% widowed, 4.2% divorced (2000); Foreign born: 0.0% (2000); Ancestry (includes multiple ancestries): 26.2% German, 18.8% United States or American, 16.8% French (except Basque), 16.8% Norwegian, 13.4% Dutch (2000).
Economy: Employment by occupation: 14.1% management, 23.4% professional, 15.6% services, 21.9% sales, 0.0% farming, 0.0% construction, 25.0% production (2000).
Income: Per capita income: $13,681 (2000); Median household income: $31,944 (2000); Poverty rate: 9.4% (2000).
Taxes: Total city taxes per capita: $38 (1997); City property taxes per capita: $38 (1997).
Education: High school graduation rate: 84.4% (2000); College graduation rate: 11.9% (2000).
Housing: Homeownership rate: 100.0% (2000); Median home value: $101,300 (2000); Median age of housing: 27 years (2000).
Transportation: Commute to work: 85.9% car, 0.0% public transportation, 0.0% walk, 14.1% work from home (2000); Travel time to work: 32.7% less than 15 minutes, 32.7% 15 to 30 minutes, 16.4% 30 to 45 minutes, 12.7% 45 to 60 minutes, 5.5% 60 minutes or more (2000)

EAST GULL LAKE (city). Covers a land area of 7.915 square miles and a water area of 6.915 square miles. Located at 46.39° N. Lat.; 94.36° W. Long. Elevation is 1,252 feet.
Population: 978 (2000); Race: 98.1% White, 0.5% Black, 0.3% Asian, 0.0% American Indian and Alaska Native, 1.2% Hispanic of any race, 1.1% two or more races (2000); Density: 123.6 persons per square mile (2000); Age: 25.9% under 18, 12.3% over 64 (2000); Marriage status: 18.3% never married, 73.8% now married, 2.3% widowed, 5.6% divorced (2000); Foreign born: 1.2% (2000); Ancestry (includes multiple ancestries): 37.3% German, 20.8% Norwegian, 14.2% Swedish, 12.7% Irish, 8.5% English (2000).
Economy: Timber; dairying; poultry, cattle, sheep; oats, alfalfa; resort area. Single-family building permits issued: 6 (2001) / 8 (2000); Multi-family building permits issued: 0 (2001) / 0 (2000); Employment by occupation: 18.5% management, 20.2% professional, 11.4% services, 31.5% sales, 0.0% farming, 5.8% construction, 12.7% production (2000).
Income: Per capita income: $27,329 (2000); Median household income: $55,750 (2000); Poverty rate: 8.7% (2000).
Taxes: Total city taxes per capita: $268 (1997); City property taxes per capita: $252 (1997).
Education: High school graduation rate: 96.1% (2000); College graduation rate: 37.3% (2000).
Housing: Homeownership rate: 91.0% (2000); Median home value: $194,400 (2000); Median rent: $463 per month (2000); Median age of housing: 22 years (2000).
Transportation: Commute to work: 91.8% car, 0.0% public transportation, 1.3% walk, 6.5% work from home (2000); Travel time to work: 23.9% less than 15 minutes, 63.1% 15 to 30 minutes, 7.7% 30 to 45 minutes, 0.5% 45 to 60 minutes, 4.9% 60 minutes or more (2000)

FAIRVIEW (township). Covers a land area of 35.725 square miles and a water area of 4.125 square miles. Located at 46.39° N. Lat.; 94.43° W. Long.
Population: 567 (2000); Race: 97.3% White, 0.0% Black, 0.6% Asian, 0.6% American Indian and Alaska Native, 1.4% Hispanic of any race, 1.5% two or more races (2000); Density: 15.9 persons per square mile (2000); Age: 22.8% under 18, 13.1% over 64 (2000); Marriage status: 14.6% never married, 74.4% now married, 2.6% widowed, 8.4% divorced (2000); Foreign born: 0.0% (2000); Ancestry (includes multiple ancestries): 28.2% German, 26.1% Norwegian, 17.2% Swedish, 12.2% Irish, 9.1% French (except Basque) (2000).
Economy: Employment by occupation: 17.8% management, 20.4% professional, 12.2% services, 27.8% sales, 0.7% farming, 13.3% construction, 7.8% production (2000).
Income: Per capita income: $29,871 (2000); Median household income: $55,000 (2000); Poverty rate: 3.5% (2000).
Taxes: Total city taxes per capita: $164 (2000); City property taxes per capita: $164 (2000).
Education: High school graduation rate: 94.7% (2000); College graduation rate: 34.6% (2000).
Housing: Homeownership rate: 93.5% (2000); Median home value: $310,600 (2000); Median rent: $475 per month (2000); Median age of housing: 20 years (2000).
Transportation: Commute to work: 92.2% car, 0.0% public transportation, 0.7% walk, 7.1% work from home (2000); Travel time to work: 17.7% less than 15 minutes, 53.8% 15 to 30 minutes, 19.7% 30 to 45 minutes, 1.6% 45 to 60 minutes, 7.2% 60 minutes or more (2000)

FEDERAL DAM (city). Covers a land area of 1.896 square miles and a water area of 0.019 square miles. Located at 47.24° N. Lat.; 94.21° W. Long. Elevation is 1,310 feet.
Population: 101 (2000); Race: 85.0% White, 0.0% Black, 0.0% Asian, 11.2% American Indian and Alaska Native, 0.0% Hispanic of any race, 3.7% two or more races (2000); Density: 53.3 persons per square mile (2000); Age: 32.7% under 18, 27.1% over 64 (2000); Marriage status: 21.0% never married, 50.6% now married, 8.6% widowed, 19.8% divorced (2000); Foreign born: 0.0% (2000); Ancestry (includes multiple ancestries): 43.9% Norwegian, 19.6% Other groups, 14.0% German, 10.3% English, 9.3% Irish (2000).
Economy: Dairying; cattle, sheep; oats; timber. Employment by occupation: 15.4% management, 5.1% professional, 5.1% services, 33.3% sales, 0.0% farming, 30.8% construction, 10.3% production (2000).
Income: Per capita income: $12,414 (2000); Median household income: $22,917 (2000); Poverty rate: 28.0% (2000).
Taxes: Total city taxes per capita: $60 (1997); City property taxes per capita: $23 (1997).
Education: High school graduation rate: 72.1% (2000); College graduation rate: 8.8% (2000).
Housing: Homeownership rate: 96.0% (2000); Median home value: $38,300 (2000); Median age of housing: 50 years (2000).
Transportation: Commute to work: 76.9% car, 0.0% public transportation, 12.8% walk, 7.7% work from home (2000); Travel time to work: 19.4% less than 15 minutes, 25.0% 15 to 30 minutes, 11.1% 30 to 45 minutes, 44.4% 45 to 60 minutes, 0.0% 60 minutes or more (2000)

GOULD (township). Covers a land area of 33.411 square miles and a water area of 10.829 square miles. Located at 47.19° N. Lat.; 94.23° W. Long.
Population: 249 (2000); Race: 45.5% White, 0.0% Black, 1.4% Asian, 46.8% American Indian and Alaska Native, 0.0% Hispanic of any race, 6.3% two or more races (2000); Density: 7.5 persons per square mile (2000); Age: 30.6% under 18, 17.1% over 64 (2000); Marriage status: 35.5% never married, 44.4% now married, 7.1% widowed, 13.0% divorced (2000);

Foreign born: 1.4% (2000); Ancestry (includes multiple ancestries): 52.3% Other groups, 23.0% German, 5.9% English, 5.4% Swedish, 5.4% Polish (2000).
Economy: Employment by occupation: 23.6% management, 8.3% professional, 18.1% services, 25.0% sales, 0.0% farming, 15.3% construction, 9.7% production (2000).
Income: Per capita income: $9,813 (2000); Median household income: $17,813 (2000); Poverty rate: 42.8% (2000).
Taxes: Total city taxes per capita: $34 (1997); City property taxes per capita: $34 (1997).
Education: High school graduation rate: 81.0% (2000); College graduation rate: 9.2% (2000).
Housing: Homeownership rate: 75.6% (2000); Median home value: $72,900 (2000); Median rent: $231 per month (2000); Median age of housing: 23 years (2000).
Transportation: Commute to work: 65.3% car, 0.0% public transportation, 4.2% walk, 9.7% work from home (2000); Travel time to work: 18.5% less than 15 minutes, 20.0% 15 to 30 minutes, 40.0% 30 to 45 minutes, 9.2% 45 to 60 minutes, 12.3% 60 minutes or more (2000)

HACKENSACK (city). Covers a land area of 0.711 square miles and a water area of 0.013 square miles. Located at 46.92° N. Lat.; 94.52° W. Long. Elevation is 1,389 feet.
Population: 285 (2000); Race: 93.5% White, 0.0% Black, 0.0% Asian, 1.8% American Indian and Alaska Native, 0.0% Hispanic of any race, 4.7% two or more races (2000); Density: 400.6 persons per square mile (2000); Age: 21.4% under 18, 23.6% over 64 (2000); Marriage status: 27.9% never married, 46.3% now married, 16.2% widowed, 9.6% divorced (2000); Foreign born: 1.4% (2000); Ancestry (includes multiple ancestries): 44.6% German, 27.5% Norwegian, 13.4% English, 12.0% Irish, 5.1% Swedish (2000).
Economy: In wooded lakes region. Poultry; oats, wild rice; dairying; timber. Manufacturing: signs, septic tanks. Chippewa National Forest to North. Single-family building permits issued: 2 (2001) / 3 (2000); Multi-family building permits issued: 0 (2001) / 0 (2000); Employment by occupation: 5.0% management, 11.0% professional, 37.0% services, 20.0% sales, 0.0% farming, 18.0% construction, 9.0% production (2000).
Income: Per capita income: $12,768 (2000); Median household income: $24,375 (2000); Poverty rate: 10.5% (2000).
Taxes: Total city taxes per capita: $227 (1997); City property taxes per capita: $210 (1997).
Education: High school graduation rate: 84.8% (2000); College graduation rate: 23.0% (2000).
Housing: Homeownership rate: 63.6% (2000); Median home value: $78,800 (2000); Median rent: $360 per month (2000); Median age of housing: 40 years (2000).
Transportation: Commute to work: 88.8% car, 0.0% public transportation, 6.1% walk, 5.1% work from home (2000); Travel time to work: 39.8% less than 15 minutes, 43.0% 15 to 30 minutes, 8.6% 30 to 45 minutes, 0.0% 45 to 60 minutes, 8.6% 60 minutes or more (2000)

HIRAM (township). Covers a land area of 27.094 square miles and a water area of 8.506 square miles. Located at 46.94° N. Lat.; 94.58° W. Long.
Population: 334 (2000); Race: 100.0% White, 0.0% Black, 0.0% Asian, 0.0% American Indian and Alaska Native, 0.0% Hispanic of any race, 0.0% two or more races (2000); Density: 12.3 persons per square mile (2000); Age: 13.0% under 18, 29.6% over 64 (2000); Marriage status: 5.8% never married, 80.1% now married, 8.6% widowed, 5.5% divorced (2000); Foreign born: 0.0% (2000); Ancestry (includes multiple ancestries): 32.6% German, 22.7% Norwegian, 15.4% Swedish, 10.9% English, 9.1% Irish (2000).
Economy: Employment by occupation: 5.6% management, 23.4% professional, 7.3% services, 36.3% sales, 0.0% farming, 9.7% construction, 17.7% production (2000).
Income: Per capita income: $22,217 (2000); Median household income: $34,000 (2000); Poverty rate: 13.6% (2000).
Taxes: Total city taxes per capita: $261 (1997); City property taxes per capita: $261 (1997).
Education: High school graduation rate: 85.3% (2000); College graduation rate: 21.6% (2000).
Housing: Homeownership rate: 97.4% (2000); Median home value: $165,600 (2000); Median age of housing: 28 years (2000).
Transportation: Commute to work: 93.3% car, 2.5% public transportation, 0.0% walk, 4.2% work from home (2000); Travel time to work: 39.1% less than 15 minutes, 33.9% 15 to 30 minutes, 13.0% 30 to 45 minutes, 2.6% 45 to 60 minutes, 11.3% 60 minutes or more (2000)

HOME BROOK (township). Covers a land area of 36.038 square miles and a water area of 0.219 square miles. Located at 46.49° N. Lat.; 94.45° W. Long.
Population: 191 (2000); Race: 96.3% White, 0.0% Black, 1.3% Asian, 1.7% American Indian and Alaska Native, 3.3% Hispanic of any race, 0.8% two or more races (2000); Density: 5.3 persons per square mile (2000); Age: 30.8% under 18, 12.9% over 64 (2000); Marriage status: 35.4% never married, 46.0% now married, 8.5% widowed, 10.1% divorced (2000); Foreign born: 2.1% (2000); Ancestry (includes multiple ancestries): 31.7% German, 21.7% Norwegian, 12.5% Swedish, 10.0% Irish, 8.8% United States or American (2000).
Economy: Employment by occupation: 7.3% management, 7.3% professional, 28.5% services, 13.0% sales, 7.3% farming, 19.5% construction, 17.1% production (2000).
Income: Per capita income: $16,303 (2000); Median household income: $34,375 (2000); Poverty rate: 13.6% (2000).
Taxes: Total city taxes per capita: $75 (1997); City property taxes per capita: $75 (1997).
Education: High school graduation rate: 72.4% (2000); College graduation rate: 10.5% (2000).
Housing: Homeownership rate: 97.5% (2000); Median age of housing: 22 years (2000).
Transportation: Commute to work: 83.7% car, 2.4% public transportation, 0.0% walk, 9.8% work from home (2000); Travel time to work: 2.7% less than 15 minutes, 64.0% 15 to 30 minutes, 19.8% 30 to 45 minutes, 7.2% 45 to 60 minutes, 6.3% 60 minutes or more (2000)

INGUADONA (township). Covers a land area of 34.625 square miles and a water area of 3.518 square miles. Located at 47.01° N. Lat.; 94.07° W. Long. Elevation is 1,310 feet.
Population: 190 (2000); Race: 97.9% White, 0.0% Black, 0.0% Asian, 0.5% American Indian and Alaska Native, 0.0% Hispanic of any race, 1.6% two or more races (2000); Density: 5.5 persons per square mile (2000); Age: 13.8% under 18, 41.8% over 64 (2000); Marriage status: 16.7% never married, 70.7% now married, 5.2% widowed, 7.5% divorced (2000); Foreign born: 0.0% (2000); Ancestry (includes multiple ancestries): 25.4% German, 21.2% Norwegian, 12.7% Swedish, 10.1% Irish, 9.0% English (2000).
Economy: Employment by occupation: 9.3% management, 20.0% professional, 37.3% services, 10.7% sales, 6.7% farming, 16.0% construction, 0.0% production (2000).
Income: Per capita income: $29,501 (2000); Median household income: $34,375 (2000); Poverty rate: 5.9% (2000).
Taxes: Total city taxes per capita: $135 (1997); City property taxes per capita: $135 (1997).
Education: High school graduation rate: 87.5% (2000); College graduation rate: 10.6% (2000).
Housing: Homeownership rate: 95.7% (2000); Median home value: $150,700 (2000); Median age of housing: 22 years (2000).
Transportation: Commute to work: 90.7% car, 0.0% public transportation, 6.7% walk, 2.7% work from home (2000); Travel time to work: 32.9% less than 15 minutes, 38.4% 15 to 30 minutes, 13.7% 30 to 45 minutes, 9.6% 45 to 60 minutes, 5.5% 60 minutes or more (2000)

KEGO (township). Covers a land area of 31.577 square miles and a water area of 4.638 square miles. Located at 47.00° N. Lat.; 94.21° W. Long.
Population: 465 (2000); Race: 83.5% White, 0.0% Black, 0.0% Asian, 15.9% American Indian and Alaska Native, 0.0% Hispanic of any race, 0.6% two or more races (2000); Density: 14.7 persons per square mile (2000); Age: 24.4% under 18, 20.3% over 64 (2000); Marriage status: 17.1% never married, 68.9% now married, 7.5% widowed, 6.5% divorced (2000); Foreign born: 0.6% (2000); Ancestry (includes multiple ancestries): 33.4% German, 15.9% Other groups, 10.4% Norwegian, 8.4% Irish, 7.7% Swedish (2000).
Economy: Employment by occupation: 9.8% management, 6.7% professional, 15.5% services, 22.2% sales, 3.6% farming, 24.7% construction, 17.5% production (2000).
Income: Per capita income: $15,598 (2000); Median household income: $30,750 (2000); Poverty rate: 16.2% (2000).
Taxes: Total city taxes per capita: $100 (1997); City property taxes per capita: $100 (1997).
Education: High school graduation rate: 84.7% (2000); College graduation rate: 8.8% (2000).
Housing: Homeownership rate: 92.2% (2000); Median home value: $142,800 (2000); Median rent: $300 per month (2000); Median age of housing: 22 years (2000).

Transportation: Commute to work: 90.2% car, 1.5% public transportation, 1.5% walk, 6.7% work from home (2000); Travel time to work: 58.0% less than 15 minutes, 21.0% 15 to 30 minutes, 11.6% 30 to 45 minutes, 3.9% 45 to 60 minutes, 5.5% 60 minutes or more (2000)

LAKE SHORE (city). Covers a land area of 12.793 square miles and a water area of 5.361 square miles. Located at 46.50° N. Lat.; 94.35° W. Long. Elevation is 1,242 feet.
Population: 966 (2000); Race: 98.9% White, 0.0% Black, 0.2% Asian, 0.9% American Indian and Alaska Native, 0.0% Hispanic of any race, 0.0% two or more races (2000); Density: 75.5 persons per square mile (2000); Age: 16.3% under 18, 20.6% over 64 (2000); Marriage status: 13.1% never married, 75.0% now married, 4.3% widowed, 7.6% divorced (2000); Foreign born: 0.5% (2000); Ancestry (includes multiple ancestries): 38.0% German, 22.9% Norwegian, 12.7% Swedish, 8.4% Irish, 7.9% English (2000).
Economy: Resorts. Dairying; poultry; oats, alfalfa. Employment by occupation: 17.7% management, 18.1% professional, 10.2% services, 33.8% sales, 0.0% farming, 10.4% construction, 9.8% production (2000).
Income: Per capita income: $33,387 (2000); Median household income: $51,500 (2000); Poverty rate: 4.5% (2000).
Taxes: Total city taxes per capita: $343 (1997); City property taxes per capita: $323 (1997).
Education: High school graduation rate: 91.7% (2000); College graduation rate: 28.0% (2000).
Housing: Homeownership rate: 92.9% (2000); Median home value: $238,400 (2000); Median rent: $475 per month (2000); Median age of housing: 24 years (2000).
Transportation: Commute to work: 91.2% car, 0.4% public transportation, 0.4% walk, 6.7% work from home (2000); Travel time to work: 27.4% less than 15 minutes, 42.2% 15 to 30 minutes, 23.3% 30 to 45 minutes, 1.6% 45 to 60 minutes, 5.5% 60 minutes or more (2000)

LEECH LAKE (township). Covers a land area of 23.179 square miles and a water area of 12.081 square miles. Located at 47.18° N. Lat.; 94.59° W. Long.
Population: 384 (2000); Race: 80.3% White, 0.0% Black, 2.1% Asian, 17.6% American Indian and Alaska Native, 2.7% Hispanic of any race, 0.0% two or more races (2000); Density: 16.6 persons per square mile (2000); Age: 24.7% under 18, 18.8% over 64 (2000); Marriage status: 17.6% never married, 64.6% now married, 8.6% widowed, 9.2% divorced (2000); Foreign born: 1.1% (2000); Ancestry (includes multiple ancestries): 34.3% German, 21.1% Other groups, 17.8% Norwegian, 12.4% Irish, 12.4% Swedish (2000).
Economy: Employment by occupation: 18.3% management, 12.9% professional, 11.8% services, 33.9% sales, 2.2% farming, 10.2% construction, 10.8% production (2000).
Income: Per capita income: $17,112 (2000); Median household income: $38,125 (2000); Poverty rate: 14.4% (2000).
Taxes: Total city taxes per capita: $128 (2000); City property taxes per capita: $128 (2000).
Education: High school graduation rate: 88.3% (2000); College graduation rate: 17.7% (2000).
Housing: Homeownership rate: 87.1% (2000); Median home value: $166,000 (2000); Median rent: $263 per month (2000); Median age of housing: 17 years (2000).
Transportation: Commute to work: 83.3% car, 0.0% public transportation, 8.6% walk, 2.7% work from home (2000); Travel time to work: 56.9% less than 15 minutes, 25.4% 15 to 30 minutes, 13.3% 30 to 45 minutes, 4.4% 45 to 60 minutes, 0.0% 60 minutes or more (2000)

LIMA (township). Covers a land area of 35.423 square miles and a water area of 0.566 square miles. Located at 47.03° N. Lat.; 93.85° W. Long.
Population: 111 (2000); Race: 100.0% White, 0.0% Black, 0.0% Asian, 0.0% American Indian and Alaska Native, 4.4% Hispanic of any race, 0.0% two or more races (2000); Density: 3.1 persons per square mile (2000); Age: 34.3% under 18, 21.2% over 64 (2000); Marriage status: 19.2% never married, 76.8% now married, 0.0% widowed, 4.0% divorced (2000); Foreign born: 0.0% (2000); Ancestry (includes multiple ancestries): 48.9% German, 20.4% Irish, 15.3% Norwegian, 13.1% English, 13.1% Swedish (2000).
Economy: Employment by occupation: 3.3% management, 10.0% professional, 33.3% services, 25.0% sales, 0.0% farming, 11.7% construction, 16.7% production (2000).
Income: Per capita income: $11,462 (2000); Median household income: $26,250 (2000); Poverty rate: 8.0% (2000).
Taxes: Total city taxes per capita: $7 (1997); City property taxes per capita: $7 (1997).
Education: High school graduation rate: 81.4% (2000); College graduation rate: 2.3% (2000).
Housing: Homeownership rate: 100.0% (2000); Median home value: $48,300 (2000); Median age of housing: 25 years (2000).
Transportation: Commute to work: 86.7% car, 0.0% public transportation, 0.0% walk, 3.3% work from home (2000); Travel time to work: 53.4% less than 15 minutes, 3.4% 15 to 30 minutes, 41.4% 30 to 45 minutes, 1.7% 45 to 60 minutes, 0.0% 60 minutes or more (2000)

LONGVILLE (city). Covers a land area of 0.597 square miles and a water area of 0.021 square miles. Located at 46.98° N. Lat.; 94.21° W. Long. Elevation is 1,340 feet.
Population: 180 (2000); Race: 100.0% White, 0.0% Black, 0.0% Asian, 0.0% American Indian and Alaska Native, 0.0% Hispanic of any race, 0.0% two or more races (2000); Density: 301.7 persons per square mile (2000); Age: 8.6% under 18, 53.6% over 64 (2000); Marriage status: 9.8% never married, 59.4% now married, 18.9% widowed, 11.9% divorced (2000); Foreign born: 0.0% (2000); Ancestry (includes multiple ancestries): 33.1% German, 15.9% Norwegian, 12.6% English, 12.6% Polish, 7.9% United States or American (2000).
Economy: Dairying; livestock; oats; timber. Single-family building permits issued: 1 (2001) / 0 (2000); Multi-family building permits issued: 0 (2001) / 0 (2000); Employment by occupation: 16.7% management, 0.0% professional, 19.0% services, 23.8% sales, 0.0% farming, 16.7% construction, 23.8% production (2000).
Income: Per capita income: $26,524 (2000); Median household income: $26,818 (2000); Poverty rate: 5.3% (2000).
Taxes: Total city taxes per capita: $172 (1997); City property taxes per capita: $161 (1997).
Education: High school graduation rate: 76.2% (2000); College graduation rate: 7.7% (2000).
Housing: Homeownership rate: 89.9% (2000); Median home value: $86,500 (2000); Median rent: $392 per month (2000); Median age of housing: 26 years (2000).
Newspapers: Pine Cone Press-Citizen (1 x week)
Transportation: Commute to work: 78.6% car, 0.0% public transportation, 0.0% walk, 9.5% work from home (2000); Travel time to work: 47.4% less than 15 minutes, 13.2% 15 to 30 minutes, 26.3% 30 to 45 minutes, 0.0% 45 to 60 minutes, 13.2% 60 minutes or more (2000)
Additional Information Contacts
Longville Chamber of Commerce 218-363-2630

LOON LAKE (township). Covers a land area of 17.374 square miles and a water area of 0.592 square miles. Located at 46.59° N. Lat.; 94.36° W. Long.
Population: 376 (2000); Race: 97.9% White, 0.0% Black, 0.0% Asian, 0.0% American Indian and Alaska Native, 0.0% Hispanic of any race, 2.1% two or more races (2000); Density: 21.6 persons per square mile (2000); Age: 28.3% under 18, 10.4% over 64 (2000); Marriage status: 22.7% never married, 67.9% now married, 2.7% widowed, 6.7% divorced (2000); Foreign born: 0.5% (2000); Ancestry (includes multiple ancestries): 44.4% German, 22.7% Norwegian, 15.2% Irish, 13.9% Swedish, 5.9% English (2000).
Economy: Employment by occupation: 15.0% management, 14.0% professional, 21.2% services, 21.2% sales, 2.6% farming, 17.6% construction, 8.3% production (2000).
Income: Per capita income: $16,489 (2000); Median household income: $37,750 (2000); Poverty rate: 13.1% (2000).
Taxes: Total city taxes per capita: $89 (1997); City property taxes per capita: $89 (1997).
Education: High school graduation rate: 85.5% (2000); College graduation rate: 18.2% (2000).
Housing: Homeownership rate: 94.2% (2000); Median home value: $86,300 (2000); Median rent: $375 per month (2000); Median age of housing: 23 years (2000).
Transportation: Commute to work: 90.2% car, 0.0% public transportation, 1.0% walk, 7.8% work from home (2000); Travel time to work: 38.2% less than 15 minutes, 26.4% 15 to 30 minutes, 30.9% 30 to 45 minutes, 2.8% 45 to 60 minutes, 1.7% 60 minutes or more (2000)

MAPLE (township). Covers a land area of 36.250 square miles and a water area of 0.307 square miles. Located at 46.59° N. Lat.; 94.42° W. Long.
Population: 291 (2000); Race: 96.9% White, 1.4% Black, 0.7% Asian, 1.0% American Indian and Alaska Native, 0.0% Hispanic of any race, 0.0% two or more races (2000); Density: 8.0 persons per square mile (2000); Age: 32.1% under 18, 10.2% over 64 (2000); Marriage status: 22.8% never married, 63.6% now married, 3.9% widowed, 9.6% divorced (2000); Foreign born:

0.0% (2000); Ancestry (includes multiple ancestries): 38.9% German, 24.9% Norwegian, 18.8% Swedish, 5.8% Other groups, 5.5% French (except Basque) (2000).
Economy: Single-family building permits issued: 0 (2001) / 0 (2000); Multi-family building permits issued: 0 (2001) / 0 (2000); Employment by occupation: 19.7% management, 14.5% professional, 15.8% services, 23.0% sales, 2.6% farming, 12.5% construction, 11.8% production (2000).
Income: Per capita income: $14,583 (2000); Median household income: $36,250 (2000); Poverty rate: 8.5% (2000).
Taxes: Total city taxes per capita: $78 (1997); City property taxes per capita: $78 (1997).
Education: High school graduation rate: 85.6% (2000); College graduation rate: 8.6% (2000).
Housing: Homeownership rate: 96.2% (2000); Median home value: $95,000 (2000); Median age of housing: 24 years (2000).
Transportation: Commute to work: 78.7% car, 0.0% public transportation, 2.7% walk, 18.7% work from home (2000); Travel time to work: 19.7% less than 15 minutes, 39.3% 15 to 30 minutes, 23.0% 30 to 45 minutes, 11.5% 45 to 60 minutes, 6.6% 60 minutes or more (2000)

MAY (township). Covers a land area of 59.979 square miles and a water area of 0.596 square miles. Located at 46.37° N. Lat.; 94.59° W. Long.
Population: 730 (2000); Race: 96.7% White, 0.1% Black, 0.8% Asian, 0.7% American Indian and Alaska Native, 0.7% Hispanic of any race, 1.7% two or more races (2000); Density: 12.2 persons per square mile (2000); Age: 28.0% under 18, 11.5% over 64 (2000); Marriage status: 20.6% never married, 67.6% now married, 2.9% widowed, 8.9% divorced (2000); Foreign born: 1.7% (2000); Ancestry (includes multiple ancestries): 36.6% German, 16.0% Irish, 14.8% Norwegian, 9.8% Swedish, 7.3% Other groups (2000).
Economy: Employment by occupation: 7.5% management, 10.0% professional, 14.1% services, 26.0% sales, 0.0% farming, 11.1% construction, 31.3% production (2000).
Income: Per capita income: $14,854 (2000); Median household income: $36,875 (2000); Poverty rate: 7.2% (2000).
Taxes: Total city taxes per capita: $103 (2000); City property taxes per capita: $103 (2000).
Education: High school graduation rate: 76.2% (2000); College graduation rate: 7.6% (2000).
Housing: Homeownership rate: 88.9% (2000); Median home value: $85,200 (2000); Median rent: $300 per month (2000); Median age of housing: 27 years (2000).
Transportation: Commute to work: 95.0% car, 0.0% public transportation, 1.9% walk, 2.2% work from home (2000); Travel time to work: 29.1% less than 15 minutes, 39.3% 15 to 30 minutes, 20.5% 30 to 45 minutes, 3.1% 45 to 60 minutes, 8.0% 60 minutes or more (2000)

MCKINLEY (township). Covers a land area of 36.063 square miles and a water area of 0.268 square miles. Located at 46.75° N. Lat.; 94.71° W. Long.
Population: 130 (2000); Race: 98.5% White, 0.0% Black, 0.0% Asian, 1.5% American Indian and Alaska Native, 0.0% Hispanic of any race, 0.0% two or more races (2000); Density: 3.6 persons per square mile (2000); Age: 27.0% under 18, 8.8% over 64 (2000); Marriage status: 32.4% never married, 64.0% now married, 1.8% widowed, 1.8% divorced (2000); Foreign born: 0.0% (2000); Ancestry (includes multiple ancestries): 23.4% Norwegian, 19.0% English, 13.1% German, 12.4% French (except Basque), 10.9% United States or American (2000).
Economy: Employment by occupation: 13.7% management, 3.9% professional, 27.5% services, 17.6% sales, 7.8% farming, 11.8% construction, 17.6% production (2000).
Income: Per capita income: $11,005 (2000); Median household income: $35,750 (2000); Poverty rate: 21.9% (2000).
Taxes: Total city taxes per capita: $64 (1997); City property taxes per capita: $64 (1997).
Education: High school graduation rate: 80.2% (2000); College graduation rate: 11.6% (2000).
Housing: Homeownership rate: 90.0% (2000); Median home value: $53,000 (2000); Median age of housing: 44 years (2000).
Transportation: Commute to work: 70.6% car, 0.0% public transportation, 17.6% walk, 9.8% work from home (2000); Travel time to work: 30.4% less than 15 minutes, 13.0% 15 to 30 minutes, 39.1% 30 to 45 minutes, 6.5% 45 to 60 minutes, 10.9% 60 minutes or more (2000)

MEADOW BROOK (township). Covers a land area of 38.565 square miles and a water area of 0.351 square miles. Located at 46.51° N. Lat.; 94.55° W. Long.
Population: 183 (2000); Race: 94.8% White, 0.0% Black, 0.9% Asian, 0.0% American Indian and Alaska Native, 0.0% Hispanic of any race, 4.2% two or more races (2000); Density: 4.7 persons per square mile (2000); Age: 21.7% under 18, 12.7% over 64 (2000); Marriage status: 24.3% never married, 59.9% now married, 5.6% widowed, 10.2% divorced (2000); Foreign born: 0.0% (2000); Ancestry (includes multiple ancestries): 26.9% German, 19.3% Norwegian, 17.5% United States or American, 7.1% Irish, 4.7% French (except Basque) (2000).
Economy: Employment by occupation: 14.9% management, 10.6% professional, 17.0% services, 11.7% sales, 3.2% farming, 2.1% construction, 40.4% production (2000).
Income: Per capita income: $14,869 (2000); Median household income: $35,278 (2000); Poverty rate: 22.2% (2000).
Taxes: Total city taxes per capita: $74 (1997); City property taxes per capita: $74 (1997).
Education: High school graduation rate: 79.0% (2000); College graduation rate: 1.4% (2000).
Housing: Homeownership rate: 93.2% (2000); Median home value: $22,500 (2000); Median rent: $225 per month (2000); Median age of housing: 24 years (2000).
Transportation: Commute to work: 84.8% car, 0.0% public transportation, 0.0% walk, 15.2% work from home (2000); Travel time to work: 5.1% less than 15 minutes, 25.6% 15 to 30 minutes, 41.0% 30 to 45 minutes, 19.2% 45 to 60 minutes, 9.0% 60 minutes or more (2000)

MOOSE LAKE (township). Covers a land area of 37.496 square miles and a water area of 1.210 square miles. Located at 46.59° N. Lat.; 94.56° W. Long.
Population: 142 (2000); Race: 89.2% White, 0.0% Black, 0.0% Asian, 0.8% American Indian and Alaska Native, 5.4% Hispanic of any race, 10.0% two or more races (2000); Density: 3.8 persons per square mile (2000); Age: 30.8% under 18, 8.5% over 64 (2000); Marriage status: 38.5% never married, 47.9% now married, 6.3% widowed, 7.3% divorced (2000); Foreign born: 2.3% (2000); Ancestry (includes multiple ancestries): 29.2% German, 14.6% French (except Basque), 13.8% Scotch-Irish, 13.8% Irish, 10.0% Norwegian (2000).
Economy: Employment by occupation: 15.0% management, 5.0% professional, 15.0% services, 5.0% sales, 1.7% farming, 18.3% construction, 40.0% production (2000).
Income: Per capita income: $15,687 (2000); Median household income: $43,333 (2000); Poverty rate: 22.3% (2000).
Taxes: Total city taxes per capita: $40 (1997); City property taxes per capita: $40 (1997).
Education: High school graduation rate: 79.7% (2000); College graduation rate: 12.5% (2000).
Housing: Homeownership rate: 79.1% (2000); Median home value: $85,000 (2000); Median rent: $225 per month (2000); Median age of housing: 35 years (2000).
Transportation: Commute to work: 94.7% car, 0.0% public transportation, 3.5% walk, 1.8% work from home (2000); Travel time to work: 3.6% less than 15 minutes, 41.1% 15 to 30 minutes, 25.0% 30 to 45 minutes, 16.1% 45 to 60 minutes, 14.3% 60 minutes or more (2000)

OTTER TAIL PENINSULA (township). Covers a land area of 64.287 square miles and a water area of 10.803 square miles. Located at 47.28° N. Lat.; 94.40° W. Long.
Population: 43 (2000); Race: 91.4% White, 0.0% Black, 0.0% Asian, 8.6% American Indian and Alaska Native, 0.0% Hispanic of any race, 0.0% two or more races (2000); Density: 0.7 persons per square mile (2000); Age: 8.6% under 18, 11.4% over 64 (2000); Marriage status: 15.6% never married, 68.8% now married, 9.4% widowed, 6.3% divorced (2000); Foreign born: 0.0% (2000); Ancestry (includes multiple ancestries): 71.4% German, 17.1% Irish, 14.3% Italian, 14.3% English, 11.4% Norwegian (2000).
Economy: Employment by occupation: 42.1% management, 15.8% professional, 10.5% services, 31.6% sales, 0.0% farming, 0.0% construction, 0.0% production (2000).
Income: Per capita income: $30,869 (2000); Median household income: $31,875 (2000); Poverty rate: 0.0% (2000).
Taxes: Total city taxes per capita: $1,047 (2000); City property taxes per capita: $1,023 (2000).
Education: High school graduation rate: 80.6% (2000); College graduation rate: 19.4% (2000).
Housing: Homeownership rate: 81.0% (2000); Median home value: $162,500 (2000); Median age of housing: 27 years (2000).
Transportation: Commute to work: 36.8% car, 0.0% public transportation, 0.0% walk, 63.2% work from home (2000); Travel time to work: 0.0% less

than 15 minutes, 100.0% 15 to 30 minutes, 0.0% 30 to 45 minutes, 0.0% 45 to 60 minutes, 0.0% 60 minutes or more (2000)

OUTING (unincorporated postal area, zip code 56662). Covers a land area of 97.448 square miles and a water area of 3.918 square miles. Located at 46.85° N. Lat.; 93.94° W. Long. Elevation is 1,325 feet.
Population: 532 (2000); Race: 99.3% White, 0.0% Black, 0.0% Asian, 0.7% American Indian and Alaska Native, 0.0% Hispanic of any race, 0.0% two or more races (2000); Density: 5.5 persons per square mile (2000); Age: 13.1% under 18, 21.6% over 64 (2000); Marriage status: 11.5% never married, 72.4% now married, 6.6% widowed, 9.5% divorced (2000); Foreign born: 0.0% (2000); Ancestry (includes multiple ancestries): 32.5% German, 16.5% Swedish, 11.8% Norwegian, 8.2% Polish, 7.3% French (except Basque) (2000).
Economy: Employment by occupation: 15.4% management, 9.9% professional, 17.0% services, 26.4% sales, 1.1% farming, 11.0% construction, 19.2% production (2000).
Income: Per capita income: $19,155 (2000); Median household income: $29,000 (2000); Poverty rate: 8.2% (2000).
Education: High school graduation rate: 82.2% (2000); College graduation rate: 14.9% (2000).
Housing: Homeownership rate: 96.2% (2000); Median home value: $127,200 (2000); Median rent: $315 per month (2000); Median age of housing: 28 years (2000).
Transportation: Commute to work: 82.3% car, 1.1% public transportation, 4.6% walk, 9.7% work from home (2000); Travel time to work: 41.8% less than 15 minutes, 19.6% 15 to 30 minutes, 19.6% 30 to 45 minutes, 8.9% 45 to 60 minutes, 10.1% 60 minutes or more (2000)

PIKE BAY (township). Covers a land area of 22.320 square miles and a water area of 12.432 square miles. Located at 47.37° N. Lat.; 94.60° W. Long.
Population: 1,643 (2000); Race: 30.1% White, 0.1% Black, 0.3% Asian, 64.6% American Indian and Alaska Native, 3.5% Hispanic of any race, 3.8% two or more races (2000); Density: 73.6 persons per square mile (2000); Age: 37.7% under 18, 6.7% over 64 (2000); Marriage status: 38.5% never married, 44.2% now married, 3.5% widowed, 13.8% divorced (2000); Foreign born: 0.9% (2000); Ancestry (includes multiple ancestries): 65.9% Other groups, 10.5% German, 6.5% Norwegian, 3.7% Irish, 2.5% Swedish (2000).
Economy: Employment by occupation: 6.9% management, 16.2% professional, 26.2% services, 23.8% sales, 2.5% farming, 13.3% construction, 11.1% production (2000).
Income: Per capita income: $10,589 (2000); Median household income: $28,792 (2000); Poverty rate: 24.1% (2000).
Taxes: Total city taxes per capita: $38 (1997); City property taxes per capita: $38 (1997).
Education: High school graduation rate: 83.1% (2000); College graduation rate: 9.4% (2000).
Housing: Homeownership rate: 71.7% (2000); Median home value: $58,700 (2000); Median rent: $165 per month (2000); Median age of housing: 23 years (2000).
Transportation: Commute to work: 82.6% car, 4.1% public transportation, 4.4% walk, 8.2% work from home (2000); Travel time to work: 62.1% less than 15 minutes, 19.6% 15 to 30 minutes, 9.9% 30 to 45 minutes, 4.0% 45 to 60 minutes, 4.4% 60 minutes or more (2000)

PILLAGER (city). Covers a land area of 0.641 square miles and a water area of 0.029 square miles. Located at 46.32° N. Lat.; 94.47° W. Long. Elevation is 1,209 feet.
Population: 420 (2000); Race: 97.9% White, 0.0% Black, 1.6% Asian, 0.5% American Indian and Alaska Native, 0.8% Hispanic of any race, 0.0% two or more races (2000); Density: 655.3 persons per square mile (2000); Age: 21.4% under 18, 16.9% over 64 (2000); Marriage status: 29.4% never married, 44.4% now married, 9.6% widowed, 16.6% divorced (2000); Foreign born: 1.0% (2000); Ancestry (includes multiple ancestries): 40.1% German, 15.4% Norwegian, 10.4% Irish, 7.8% Swedish, 5.5% Other groups (2000).
Economy: Dairying; poultry, cattle; oats, alfalfa, timber; light manufacturing. Camp Ripley Military Reserve to SE. Single-family building permits issued: 6 (2001) / 4 (2000); Multi-family building permits issued: 0 (2001) / 0 (2000); Employment by occupation: 10.1% management, 16.4% professional, 12.7% services, 23.3% sales, 1.1% farming, 9.5% construction, 27.0% production (2000).
Income: Per capita income: $14,291 (2000); Median household income: $29,375 (2000); Poverty rate: 8.0% (2000).
Taxes: Total city taxes per capita: $160 (1997); City property taxes per capita: $138 (1997).
Education: High school graduation rate: 73.7% (2000); College graduation rate: 10.6% (2000).

School District(s)

Peaks Charter School-Pillager (09-12)
2000 Enrollment: 49 218-746-4060
Pillager (PK-12)
2000 Enrollment: 710 218-746-3772

Housing: Homeownership rate: 73.5% (2000); Median home value: $56,500 (2000); Median rent: $375 per month (2000); Median age of housing: 41 years (2000).
Transportation: Commute to work: 85.2% car, 3.7% public transportation, 7.4% walk, 2.6% work from home (2000); Travel time to work: 28.3% less than 15 minutes, 48.4% 15 to 30 minutes, 17.4% 30 to 45 minutes, 5.4% 45 to 60 minutes, 0.5% 60 minutes or more (2000)

PINE LAKE (township). Covers a land area of 28.439 square miles and a water area of 5.963 square miles. Located at 47.03° N. Lat.; 94.34° W. Long.
Population: 170 (2000); Race: 72.8% White, 0.0% Black, 2.9% Asian, 9.2% American Indian and Alaska Native, 0.0% Hispanic of any race, 15.0% two or more races (2000); Density: 6.0 persons per square mile (2000); Age: 19.1% under 18, 17.9% over 64 (2000); Marriage status: 14.2% never married, 66.7% now married, 7.1% widowed, 12.1% divorced (2000); Foreign born: 1.2% (2000); Ancestry (includes multiple ancestries): 26.0% Irish, 25.4% Other groups, 19.7% Norwegian, 18.5% German, 11.0% English (2000).
Economy: Employment by occupation: 15.1% management, 16.4% professional, 11.0% services, 39.7% sales, 0.0% farming, 12.3% construction, 5.5% production (2000).
Income: Per capita income: $22,201 (2000); Median household income: $41,250 (2000); Poverty rate: 15.0% (2000).
Taxes: Total city taxes per capita: $75 (1997); City property taxes per capita: $75 (1997).
Education: High school graduation rate: 87.9% (2000); College graduation rate: 16.7% (2000).
Housing: Homeownership rate: 95.8% (2000); Median home value: $98,300 (2000); Median age of housing: 19 years (2000).
Transportation: Commute to work: 83.1% car, 0.0% public transportation, 4.2% walk, 7.0% work from home (2000); Travel time to work: 31.8% less than 15 minutes, 43.9% 15 to 30 minutes, 12.1% 30 to 45 minutes, 0.0% 45 to 60 minutes, 12.1% 60 minutes or more (2000)

PINE RIVER (city). Covers a land area of 1.112 square miles and a water area of 0.039 square miles. Located at 46.72° N. Lat.; 94.40° W. Long. Elevation is 1,296 feet.
Population: 928 (2000); Race: 98.2% White, 0.0% Black, 0.0% Asian, 0.2% American Indian and Alaska Native, 1.3% Hispanic of any race, 1.5% two or more races (2000); Density: 834.6 persons per square mile (2000); Age: 24.5% under 18, 30.9% over 64 (2000); Marriage status: 20.5% never married, 49.2% now married, 17.5% widowed, 12.8% divorced (2000); Foreign born: 1.4% (2000); Ancestry (includes multiple ancestries): 28.4% German, 11.9% English, 11.9% Swedish, 11.5% Norwegian, 7.3% Irish (2000).
Economy: Single-family building permits issued: 0 (2001) / 1 (2000); Multi-family building permits issued: 12 (2001) / 0 (2000); Employment by occupation: 4.7% management, 18.0% professional, 27.6% services, 23.6% sales, 0.0% farming, 11.5% construction, 14.6% production (2000).
Income: Per capita income: $14,571 (2000); Median household income: $23,480 (2000); Poverty rate: 16.7% (2000).
Taxes: Total city taxes per capita: $178 (1997); City property taxes per capita: $174 (1997).
Education: High school graduation rate: 76.9% (2000); College graduation rate: 15.4% (2000).

School District(s)

Pine River-Backus (PK-12)
2000 Enrollment: 1,266 218-587-4720

Housing: Homeownership rate: 58.0% (2000); Median home value: $60,600 (2000); Median rent: $268 per month (2000); Median age of housing: 30 years (2000).
Newspapers: Piper Shopper (1 x week); Pine River Journal (1 x week)
Transportation: Commute to work: 83.3% car, 0.0% public transportation, 14.1% walk, 0.0% work from home (2000); Travel time to work: 53.6% less than 15 minutes, 24.2% 15 to 30 minutes, 12.7% 30 to 45 minutes, 2.3% 45 to 60 minutes, 7.2% 60 minutes or more (2000)
Additional Information Contacts

Pine River Chamber of Commerce 218-587-4000

PINE RIVER (township). Covers a land area of 34.853 square miles and a water area of 1.118 square miles. Located at 46.75° N. Lat.; 94.46° W. Long. Elevation is 1,296 feet.
Population: 1,061 (2000); Race: 96.9% White, 0.2% Black, 0.7% Asian, 1.3% American Indian and Alaska Native, 0.9% Hispanic of any race, 0.9% two or more races (2000); Density: 30.4 persons per square mile (2000); Age: 30.7% under 18, 15.2% over 64 (2000); Marriage status: 22.6% never married, 62.8% now married, 4.7% widowed, 9.9% divorced (2000); Foreign born: 1.2% (2000); Ancestry (includes multiple ancestries): 29.4% German, 13.7% Norwegian, 11.6% United States or American, 10.3% English, 9.0% Irish (2000).
Economy: Manufacturing: lumber, wood products. Livestock, poultry; dairying; oats, alfalfa; cattle, sheep. Employment by occupation: 11.8% management, 13.0% professional, 18.6% services, 19.3% sales, 1.0% farming, 20.5% construction, 15.7% production (2000).
Income: Per capita income: $14,910 (2000); Median household income: $37,212 (2000); Poverty rate: 9.4% (2000).
Taxes: Total city taxes per capita: $48 (1997); City property taxes per capita: $48 (1997).
Education: High school graduation rate: 86.3% (2000); College graduation rate: 9.2% (2000).
Housing: Homeownership rate: 91.9% (2000); Median home value: $75,700 (2000); Median rent: $390 per month (2000); Median age of housing: 20 years (2000).
Transportation: Commute to work: 93.0% car, 0.0% public transportation, 0.4% walk, 5.7% work from home (2000); Travel time to work: 38.0% less than 15 minutes, 27.6% 15 to 30 minutes, 22.7% 30 to 45 minutes, 5.8% 45 to 60 minutes, 5.8% 60 minutes or more (2000)

PONTO LAKE (township). Covers a land area of 29.617 square miles and a water area of 6.762 square miles. Located at 46.84° N. Lat.; 94.34° W. Long.
Population: 530 (2000); Race: 97.1% White, 0.0% Black, 0.0% Asian, 1.9% American Indian and Alaska Native, 0.6% Hispanic of any race, 1.0% two or more races (2000); Density: 17.9 persons per square mile (2000); Age: 9.1% under 18, 31.3% over 64 (2000); Marriage status: 10.5% never married, 70.1% now married, 12.4% widowed, 7.0% divorced (2000); Foreign born: 2.3% (2000); Ancestry (includes multiple ancestries): 36.3% German, 13.2% English, 12.4% Norwegian, 10.9% Swedish, 10.7% Irish (2000).
Economy: Employment by occupation: 1.5% management, 19.9% professional, 21.9% services, 28.9% sales, 3.5% farming, 10.0% construction, 14.4% production (2000).
Income: Per capita income: $17,642 (2000); Median household income: $27,105 (2000); Poverty rate: 9.5% (2000).
Taxes: Total city taxes per capita: $93 (1997); City property taxes per capita: $93 (1997).
Education: High school graduation rate: 83.6% (2000); College graduation rate: 18.5% (2000).
Housing: Homeownership rate: 94.4% (2000); Median home value: $118,900 (2000); Median rent: $350 per month (2000); Median age of housing: 29 years (2000).
Transportation: Commute to work: 88.2% car, 0.5% public transportation, 0.0% walk, 11.2% work from home (2000); Travel time to work: 13.9% less than 15 minutes, 57.8% 15 to 30 minutes, 17.5% 30 to 45 minutes, 9.0% 45 to 60 minutes, 1.8% 60 minutes or more (2000)

POPLAR (township). Covers a land area of 35.514 square miles and a water area of 0.012 square miles. Located at 46.59° N. Lat.; 94.70° W. Long. Elevation is 1,359 feet.
Population: 173 (2000); Race: 98.7% White, 0.0% Black, 0.0% Asian, 0.0% American Indian and Alaska Native, 0.0% Hispanic of any race, 1.3% two or more races (2000); Density: 4.9 persons per square mile (2000); Age: 24.2% under 18, 19.1% over 64 (2000); Marriage status: 20.8% never married, 61.6% now married, 1.6% widowed, 16.0% divorced (2000); Foreign born: 0.0% (2000); Ancestry (includes multiple ancestries): 38.9% German, 17.2% Norwegian, 8.9% Irish, 6.4% Polish, 5.7% French (except Basque) (2000).
Economy: Employment by occupation: 17.1% management, 12.9% professional, 5.7% services, 10.0% sales, 15.7% farming, 7.1% construction, 31.4% production (2000).
Income: Per capita income: $11,915 (2000); Median household income: $36,875 (2000); Poverty rate: 3.8% (2000).
Taxes: Total city taxes per capita: $30 (1997); City property taxes per capita: $30 (1997).
Education: High school graduation rate: 72.4% (2000); College graduation rate: 5.7% (2000).
Housing: Homeownership rate: 96.4% (2000); Median home value: $23,800 (2000); Median rent: $175 per month (2000); Median age of housing: 33 years (2000).
Transportation: Commute to work: 80.0% car, 0.0% public transportation, 0.0% walk, 20.0% work from home (2000); Travel time to work: 5.4% less than 15 minutes, 42.9% 15 to 30 minutes, 23.2% 30 to 45 minutes, 8.9% 45 to 60 minutes, 19.6% 60 minutes or more (2000)

POWERS (township). Covers a land area of 28.677 square miles and a water area of 6.648 square miles. Located at 46.84° N. Lat.; 94.47° W. Long.
Population: 918 (2000); Race: 99.6% White, 0.0% Black, 0.0% Asian, 0.0% American Indian and Alaska Native, 0.0% Hispanic of any race, 0.4% two or more races (2000); Density: 32.0 persons per square mile (2000); Age: 20.6% under 18, 26.5% over 64 (2000); Marriage status: 17.1% never married, 62.3% now married, 10.6% widowed, 10.0% divorced (2000); Foreign born: 0.0% (2000); Ancestry (includes multiple ancestries): 37.0% German, 17.5% Norwegian, 11.8% Irish, 10.4% Swedish, 7.0% English (2000).
Economy: Employment by occupation: 6.2% management, 12.6% professional, 18.0% services, 35.7% sales, 2.1% farming, 9.8% construction, 15.7% production (2000).
Income: Per capita income: $16,140 (2000); Median household income: $40,547 (2000); Poverty rate: 13.6% (2000).
Taxes: Total city taxes per capita: $107 (1997); City property taxes per capita: $107 (1997).
Education: High school graduation rate: 79.0% (2000); College graduation rate: 13.8% (2000).
Housing: Homeownership rate: 89.9% (2000); Median home value: $101,300 (2000); Median rent: $292 per month (2000); Median age of housing: 27 years (2000).
Transportation: Commute to work: 93.6% car, 0.5% public transportation, 1.5% walk, 4.4% work from home (2000); Travel time to work: 42.3% less than 15 minutes, 31.3% 15 to 30 minutes, 12.1% 30 to 45 minutes, 4.6% 45 to 60 minutes, 9.7% 60 minutes or more (2000)

REMER (city). Covers a land area of 1.135 square miles and a water area of 0 square miles. Located at 47.05° N. Lat.; 93.91° W. Long. Elevation is 1,340 feet.
Population: 372 (2000); Race: 95.2% White, 0.0% Black, 0.0% Asian, 3.4% American Indian and Alaska Native, 0.0% Hispanic of any race, 1.4% two or more races (2000); Density: 327.8 persons per square mile (2000); Age: 27.8% under 18, 22.4% over 64 (2000); Marriage status: 22.3% never married, 50.6% now married, 15.3% widowed, 11.8% divorced (2000); Foreign born: 0.7% (2000); Ancestry (includes multiple ancestries): 19.9% German, 19.9% United States or American, 16.3% Norwegian, 6.8% English, 6.6% Irish (2000).
Economy: Employment by occupation: 7.6% management, 17.4% professional, 25.0% services, 17.4% sales, 2.8% farming, 14.6% construction, 15.3% production (2000).
Income: Per capita income: $11,674 (2000); Median household income: $19,583 (2000); Poverty rate: 34.5% (2000).
Taxes: Total city taxes per capita: $110 (1997); City property taxes per capita: $110 (1997).
Education: High school graduation rate: 75.5% (2000); College graduation rate: 16.2% (2000).

School District(s)

Northland Community Schools (PK-12)
2000 Enrollment: 641 218-566-2351

Housing: Homeownership rate: 75.0% (2000); Median home value: $50,700 (2000); Median rent: $215 per month (2000); Median age of housing: 41 years (2000).
Transportation: Commute to work: 86.8% car, 0.0% public transportation, 11.1% walk, 0.7% work from home (2000); Travel time to work: 62.2% less than 15 minutes, 13.3% 15 to 30 minutes, 16.1% 30 to 45 minutes, 5.6% 45 to 60 minutes, 2.8% 60 minutes or more (2000)

Additional Information Contacts

Remer Area Chamber of Commerce 218-566-1680

REMER (township). Covers a land area of 29.152 square miles and a water area of 5.931 square miles. Located at 47.04° N. Lat.; 93.97° W. Long. Elevation is 1,340 feet.
Population: 183 (2000); Race: 96.8% White, 0.0% Black, 1.1% Asian, 2.1% American Indian and Alaska Native, 0.0% Hispanic of any race, 0.0% two or more races (2000); Density: 6.3 persons per square mile (2000); Age: 24.3% under 18, 14.3% over 64 (2000); Marriage status: 22.3% never married,

52.9% now married, 7.0% widowed, 17.8% divorced (2000); Foreign born: 2.6% (2000); Ancestry (includes multiple ancestries): 54.5% German, 21.7% Irish, 15.3% Swedish, 12.7% Norwegian, 7.4% English (2000).
Economy: In Chippewa National Forest. Wild rice, oats; poultry, cattle, sheep; dairying; light manufacturing. Employment by occupation: 11.1% management, 22.2% professional, 16.2% services, 22.2% sales, 0.0% farming, 19.2% construction, 9.1% production (2000).
Income: Per capita income: $17,006 (2000); Median household income: $35,000 (2000); Poverty rate: 19.0% (2000).
Taxes: Total city taxes per capita: $39 (1997); City property taxes per capita: $39 (1997).
Education: High school graduation rate: 88.2% (2000); College graduation rate: 13.4% (2000).
Housing: Homeownership rate: 94.8% (2000); Median home value: $85,700 (2000); Median rent: $325 per month (2000); Median age of housing: 24 years (2000).
Transportation: Commute to work: 80.8% car, 0.0% public transportation, 0.0% walk, 19.2% work from home (2000); Travel time to work: 61.3% less than 15 minutes, 6.3% 15 to 30 minutes, 22.5% 30 to 45 minutes, 10.0% 45 to 60 minutes, 0.0% 60 minutes or more (2000)

ROGERS (township). Covers a land area of 30.848 square miles and a water area of 5.451 square miles. Located at 47.09° N. Lat.; 94.09° W. Long.
Population: 43 (2000); Race: 100.0% White, 0.0% Black, 0.0% Asian, 0.0% American Indian and Alaska Native, 0.0% Hispanic of any race, 0.0% two or more races (2000); Density: 1.4 persons per square mile (2000); Age: 0.0% under 18, 51.1% over 64 (2000); Marriage status: 4.4% never married, 80.0% now married, 15.6% widowed, 0.0% divorced (2000); Foreign born: 8.9% (2000); Ancestry (includes multiple ancestries): 31.1% Swedish, 26.7% German, 15.6% English, 13.3% Norwegian, 8.9% Canadian (2000).
Economy: Employment by occupation: 17.6% management, 35.3% professional, 23.5% services, 23.5% sales, 0.0% farming, 0.0% construction, 0.0% production (2000).
Income: Per capita income: $28,367 (2000); Median household income: $36,667 (2000); Poverty rate: 11.1% (2000).
Taxes: Total city taxes per capita: $342 (1997); City property taxes per capita: $342 (1997).
Education: High school graduation rate: 88.9% (2000); College graduation rate: 33.3% (2000).
Housing: Homeownership rate: 92.3% (2000); Median home value: $165,300 (2000); Median age of housing: 24 years (2000).
Transportation: Commute to work: 100.0% car, 0.0% public transportation, 0.0% walk, 0.0% work from home (2000); Travel time to work: 14.3% less than 15 minutes, 35.7% 15 to 30 minutes, 35.7% 30 to 45 minutes, 0.0% 45 to 60 minutes, 14.3% 60 minutes or more (2000)

SALEM (township). Covers a land area of 35.100 square miles and a water area of 1.288 square miles. Located at 47.16° N. Lat.; 93.98° W. Long.
Population: 78 (2000); Race: 96.8% White, 0.0% Black, 0.0% Asian, 2.2% American Indian and Alaska Native, 0.0% Hispanic of any race, 1.1% two or more races (2000); Density: 2.2 persons per square mile (2000); Age: 23.7% under 18, 8.6% over 64 (2000); Marriage status: 31.2% never married, 62.3% now married, 6.5% widowed, 0.0% divorced (2000); Foreign born: 0.0% (2000); Ancestry (includes multiple ancestries): 47.3% German, 41.9% Norwegian, 8.6% Scottish, 7.5% English, 6.5% Dutch (2000).
Economy: Employment by occupation: 5.9% management, 17.6% professional, 9.8% services, 19.6% sales, 0.0% farming, 0.0% construction, 47.1% production (2000).
Income: Per capita income: $18,322 (2000); Median household income: $52,500 (2000); Poverty rate: 0.0% (2000).
Taxes: Total city taxes per capita: $24 (1997); City property taxes per capita: $24 (1997).
Education: High school graduation rate: 92.7% (2000); College graduation rate: 10.9% (2000).
Housing: Homeownership rate: 100.0% (2000); Median home value: $85,000 (2000); Median age of housing: 19 years (2000).
Transportation: Commute to work: 72.5% car, 0.0% public transportation, 0.0% walk, 11.8% work from home (2000); Travel time to work: 8.9% less than 15 minutes, 44.4% 15 to 30 minutes, 15.6% 30 to 45 minutes, 31.1% 45 to 60 minutes, 0.0% 60 minutes or more (2000)

SHINGOBEE (township). Covers a land area of 53.711 square miles and a water area of 18.064 square miles. Located at 47.07° N. Lat.; 94.57° W. Long.
Population: 1,745 (2000); Race: 84.3% White, 0.2% Black, 0.3% Asian, 13.7% American Indian and Alaska Native, 0.3% Hispanic of any race, 1.0% two or more races (2000); Density: 32.5 persons per square mile (2000); Age: 21.7% under 18, 20.9% over 64 (2000); Marriage status: 20.4% never married, 62.5% now married, 6.4% widowed, 10.7% divorced (2000); Foreign born: 0.9% (2000); Ancestry (includes multiple ancestries): 30.9% German, 19.2% Norwegian, 13.5% Other groups, 11.5% Swedish, 9.2% Irish (2000).
Economy: Employment by occupation: 13.6% management, 22.6% professional, 17.8% services, 27.0% sales, 0.0% farming, 12.8% construction, 6.1% production (2000).
Income: Per capita income: $20,407 (2000); Median household income: $41,818 (2000); Poverty rate: 13.0% (2000).
Taxes: Total city taxes per capita: $143 (2000); City property taxes per capita: $141 (2000).
Education: High school graduation rate: 83.0% (2000); College graduation rate: 27.0% (2000).
Housing: Homeownership rate: 88.8% (2000); Median home value: $158,700 (2000); Median rent: $388 per month (2000); Median age of housing: 24 years (2000).
Transportation: Commute to work: 90.5% car, 1.1% public transportation, 4.5% walk, 3.9% work from home (2000); Travel time to work: 65.8% less than 15 minutes, 19.1% 15 to 30 minutes, 6.5% 30 to 45 minutes, 3.6% 45 to 60 minutes, 4.9% 60 minutes or more (2000)

SLATER (township). Covers a land area of 33.888 square miles and a water area of 2.803 square miles. Located at 47.11° N. Lat.; 93.93° W. Long.
Population: 249 (2000); Race: 89.2% White, 0.0% Black, 0.0% Asian, 0.9% American Indian and Alaska Native, 5.2% Hispanic of any race, 4.7% two or more races (2000); Density: 7.3 persons per square mile (2000); Age: 22.0% under 18, 17.7% over 64 (2000); Marriage status: 19.6% never married, 62.3% now married, 9.3% widowed, 8.8% divorced (2000); Foreign born: 2.6% (2000); Ancestry (includes multiple ancestries): 34.1% German, 13.4% Norwegian, 12.9% Other groups, 12.5% English, 8.2% United States or American (2000).
Economy: Employment by occupation: 9.2% management, 18.4% professional, 18.4% services, 10.3% sales, 0.0% farming, 20.7% construction, 23.0% production (2000).
Income: Per capita income: $13,941 (2000); Median household income: $26,932 (2000); Poverty rate: 23.5% (2000).
Taxes: Total city taxes per capita: $38 (1997); City property taxes per capita: $38 (1997).
Education: High school graduation rate: 80.7% (2000); College graduation rate: 5.6% (2000).
Housing: Homeownership rate: 95.7% (2000); Median home value: $92,500 (2000); Median rent: $175 per month (2000); Median age of housing: 28 years (2000).
Transportation: Commute to work: 85.0% car, 0.0% public transportation, 5.0% walk, 10.0% work from home (2000); Travel time to work: 29.2% less than 15 minutes, 25.0% 15 to 30 minutes, 31.9% 30 to 45 minutes, 11.1% 45 to 60 minutes, 2.8% 60 minutes or more (2000)

SMOKY HOLLOW (township). Covers a land area of 34.808 square miles and a water area of 1.267 square miles. Located at 46.94° N. Lat.; 93.85° W. Long.
Population: 61 (2000); Race: 100.0% White, 0.0% Black, 0.0% Asian, 0.0% American Indian and Alaska Native, 0.0% Hispanic of any race, 0.0% two or more races (2000); Density: 1.8 persons per square mile (2000); Age: 8.3% under 18, 33.3% over 64 (2000); Marriage status: 20.5% never married, 50.0% now married, 9.1% widowed, 20.5% divorced (2000); Foreign born: 0.0% (2000); Ancestry (includes multiple ancestries): 27.1% Swedish, 16.7% Irish, 10.4% German, 10.4% Norwegian, 8.3% Ukrainian (2000).
Economy: Employment by occupation: 0.0% management, 53.8% professional, 0.0% services, 30.8% sales, 0.0% farming, 15.4% construction, 0.0% production (2000).
Income: Per capita income: $15,042 (2000); Median household income: $21,875 (2000); Poverty rate: 10.4% (2000).
Taxes: Total city taxes per capita: $169 (1997); City property taxes per capita: $169 (1997).
Education: High school graduation rate: 84.1% (2000); College graduation rate: 13.6% (2000).
Housing: Homeownership rate: 100.0% (2000); Median home value: $54,000 (2000); Median age of housing: 35 years (2000).
Transportation: Commute to work: 33.3% car, 0.0% public transportation, 0.0% walk, 66.7% work from home (2000); Travel time to work: 100.0% less than 15 minutes, 0.0% 15 to 30 minutes, 0.0% 30 to 45 minutes, 0.0% 45 to 60 minutes, 0.0% 60 minutes or more (2000)

SYLVAN (township). Covers a land area of 30.791 square miles and a water area of 3.905 square miles. Located at 46.33° N. Lat.; 94.41° W. Long. Elevation is 1,206 feet.
Population: 1,965 (2000); Race: 98.7% White, 0.1% Black, 0.0% Asian, 0.2% American Indian and Alaska Native, 0.5% Hispanic of any race, 1.1% two or more races (2000); Density: 63.8 persons per square mile (2000); Age: 28.8% under 18, 10.3% over 64 (2000); Marriage status: 19.3% never married, 67.7% now married, 3.6% widowed, 9.4% divorced (2000); Foreign born: 0.5% (2000); Ancestry (includes multiple ancestries): 38.3% German, 16.3% Norwegian, 12.1% Swedish, 11.0% Irish, 7.5% United States or American (2000).
Economy: Employment by occupation: 10.1% management, 14.6% professional, 19.6% services, 24.3% sales, 0.8% farming, 12.9% construction, 17.8% production (2000).
Income: Per capita income: $17,493 (2000); Median household income: $43,173 (2000); Poverty rate: 7.1% (2000).
Taxes: Total city taxes per capita: $144 (2000); City property taxes per capita: $144 (2000).
Education: High school graduation rate: 85.9% (2000); College graduation rate: 19.2% (2000).
Housing: Homeownership rate: 91.7% (2000); Median home value: $102,100 (2000); Median rent: $370 per month (2000); Median age of housing: 21 years (2000).
Transportation: Commute to work: 93.5% car, 0.5% public transportation, 0.6% walk, 4.6% work from home (2000); Travel time to work: 24.3% less than 15 minutes, 54.2% 15 to 30 minutes, 14.5% 30 to 45 minutes, 3.4% 45 to 60 minutes, 3.6% 60 minutes or more (2000)

THUNDER LAKE (township). Covers a land area of 32.246 square miles and a water area of 4.202 square miles. Located at 46.94° N. Lat.; 93.96° W. Long.
Population: 262 (2000); Race: 95.5% White, 0.0% Black, 0.0% Asian, 4.5% American Indian and Alaska Native, 0.0% Hispanic of any race, 0.0% two or more races (2000); Density: 8.1 persons per square mile (2000); Age: 11.7% under 18, 30.1% over 64 (2000); Marriage status: 10.0% never married, 72.1% now married, 6.3% widowed, 11.7% divorced (2000); Foreign born: 1.1% (2000); Ancestry (includes multiple ancestries): 34.6% German, 23.3% Norwegian, 16.5% Swedish, 15.8% Irish, 8.6% English (2000).
Economy: Employment by occupation: 9.9% management, 11.9% professional, 20.8% services, 31.7% sales, 0.0% farming, 16.8% construction, 8.9% production (2000).
Income: Per capita income: $20,111 (2000); Median household income: $32,083 (2000); Poverty rate: 8.6% (2000).
Taxes: Total city taxes per capita: $190 (1997); City property taxes per capita: $190 (1997).
Education: High school graduation rate: 90.4% (2000); College graduation rate: 17.0% (2000).
Housing: Homeownership rate: 88.7% (2000); Median home value: $181,300 (2000); Median rent: $325 per month (2000); Median age of housing: 21 years (2000).
Transportation: Commute to work: 85.9% car, 0.0% public transportation, 2.0% walk, 10.1% work from home (2000); Travel time to work: 30.3% less than 15 minutes, 49.4% 15 to 30 minutes, 10.1% 30 to 45 minutes, 5.6% 45 to 60 minutes, 4.5% 60 minutes or more (2000)

TORREY (township). Covers a land area of 31.816 square miles and a water area of 2.393 square miles. Located at 47.18° N. Lat.; 93.84° W. Long.
Population: 122 (2000); Race: 100.0% White, 0.0% Black, 0.0% Asian, 0.0% American Indian and Alaska Native, 3.7% Hispanic of any race, 0.0% two or more races (2000); Density: 3.8 persons per square mile (2000); Age: 19.4% under 18, 15.7% over 64 (2000); Marriage status: 9.4% never married, 76.0% now married, 7.3% widowed, 7.3% divorced (2000); Foreign born: 2.8% (2000); Ancestry (includes multiple ancestries): 26.9% Norwegian, 23.1% German, 13.9% English, 9.3% Polish, 7.4% Other groups (2000).
Economy: Employment by occupation: 14.0% management, 4.0% professional, 32.0% services, 24.0% sales, 0.0% farming, 18.0% construction, 8.0% production (2000).
Income: Per capita income: $18,231 (2000); Median household income: $35,714 (2000); Poverty rate: 3.7% (2000).
Taxes: Total city taxes per capita: $69 (1997); City property taxes per capita: $69 (1997).
Education: High school graduation rate: 81.6% (2000); College graduation rate: 9.2% (2000).
Housing: Homeownership rate: 100.0% (2000); Median home value: $107,500 (2000); Median age of housing: 29 years (2000).
Transportation: Commute to work: 100.0% car, 0.0% public transportation, 0.0% walk, 0.0% work from home (2000); Travel time to work: 4.0% less than 15 minutes, 62.0% 15 to 30 minutes, 30.0% 30 to 45 minutes, 0.0% 45 to 60 minutes, 4.0% 60 minutes or more (2000)

TRELIPE (township). Covers a land area of 66.762 square miles and a water area of 4.113 square miles. Located at 46.90° N. Lat.; 94.07° W. Long.
Population: 174 (2000); Race: 100.0% White, 0.0% Black, 0.0% Asian, 0.0% American Indian and Alaska Native, 0.0% Hispanic of any race, 0.0% two or more races (2000); Density: 2.6 persons per square mile (2000); Age: 16.6% under 18, 20.9% over 64 (2000); Marriage status: 23.7% never married, 55.4% now married, 13.7% widowed, 7.2% divorced (2000); Foreign born: 1.8% (2000); Ancestry (includes multiple ancestries): 27.6% German, 14.7% Swedish, 11.0% Norwegian, 10.4% French (except Basque), 9.8% Irish (2000).
Economy: Employment by occupation: 14.7% management, 10.3% professional, 19.1% services, 25.0% sales, 2.9% farming, 11.8% construction, 16.2% production (2000).
Income: Per capita income: $16,671 (2000); Median household income: $30,208 (2000); Poverty rate: 14.1% (2000).
Taxes: Total city taxes per capita: $65 (1997); City property taxes per capita: $65 (1997).
Education: High school graduation rate: 83.3% (2000); College graduation rate: 9.5% (2000).
Housing: Homeownership rate: 94.9% (2000); Median home value: $146,900 (2000); Median rent: $300 per month (2000); Median age of housing: 32 years (2000).
Transportation: Commute to work: 92.6% car, 0.0% public transportation, 0.0% walk, 7.4% work from home (2000); Travel time to work: 20.6% less than 15 minutes, 36.5% 15 to 30 minutes, 22.2% 30 to 45 minutes, 9.5% 45 to 60 minutes, 11.1% 60 minutes or more (2000)

TURTLE LAKE (township). Covers a land area of 48.673 square miles and a water area of 23.319 square miles. Located at 47.07° N. Lat.; 94.48° W. Long.
Population: 699 (2000); Race: 62.9% White, 0.0% Black, 0.7% Asian, 34.2% American Indian and Alaska Native, 1.9% Hispanic of any race, 0.9% two or more races (2000); Density: 14.4 persons per square mile (2000); Age: 26.0% under 18, 16.3% over 64 (2000); Marriage status: 25.9% never married, 59.3% now married, 4.9% widowed, 9.9% divorced (2000); Foreign born: 1.2% (2000); Ancestry (includes multiple ancestries): 37.4% Other groups, 20.8% German, 11.0% Irish, 8.3% Norwegian, 7.0% Swedish (2000).
Economy: Employment by occupation: 19.1% management, 15.5% professional, 25.1% services, 19.8% sales, 0.0% farming, 13.8% construction, 6.7% production (2000).
Income: Per capita income: $17,049 (2000); Median household income: $38,750 (2000); Poverty rate: 8.2% (2000).
Taxes: Total city taxes per capita: $109 (1997); City property taxes per capita: $109 (1997).
Education: High school graduation rate: 86.2% (2000); College graduation rate: 10.1% (2000).
Housing: Homeownership rate: 83.3% (2000); Median home value: $110,400 (2000); Median rent: $168 per month (2000); Median age of housing: 22 years (2000).
Transportation: Commute to work: 81.0% car, 3.3% public transportation, 10.0% walk, 5.6% work from home (2000); Travel time to work: 54.3% less than 15 minutes, 24.8% 15 to 30 minutes, 5.5% 30 to 45 minutes, 5.9% 45 to 60 minutes, 9.4% 60 minutes or more (2000)

WABEDO (township). Covers a land area of 24.649 square miles and a water area of 10.679 square miles. Located at 46.93° N. Lat.; 94.22° W. Long. Elevation is 1,316 feet.
Population: 375 (2000); Race: 100.0% White, 0.0% Black, 0.0% Asian, 0.0% American Indian and Alaska Native, 0.0% Hispanic of any race, 0.0% two or more races (2000); Density: 15.2 persons per square mile (2000); Age: 9.8% under 18, 28.5% over 64 (2000); Marriage status: 7.7% never married, 79.3% now married, 7.1% widowed, 6.0% divorced (2000); Foreign born: 1.8% (2000); Ancestry (includes multiple ancestries): 29.0% German, 16.6% Norwegian, 13.0% Irish, 9.6% English, 9.6% Swedish (2000).
Economy: Employment by occupation: 8.7% management, 15.2% professional, 3.6% services, 50.7% sales, 0.0% farming, 12.3% construction, 9.4% production (2000).
Income: Per capita income: $21,022 (2000); Median household income: $36,979 (2000); Poverty rate: 3.4% (2000).
Taxes: Total city taxes per capita: $212 (1997); City property taxes per capita: $212 (1997).

Education: High school graduation rate: 88.1% (2000); College graduation rate: 24.4% (2000).
Housing: Homeownership rate: 94.1% (2000); Median home value: $127,100 (2000); Median rent: $350 per month (2000); Median age of housing: 26 years (2000).
Transportation: Commute to work: 91.7% car, 0.0% public transportation, 3.8% walk, 4.5% work from home (2000); Travel time to work: 44.4% less than 15 minutes, 22.2% 15 to 30 minutes, 19.0% 30 to 45 minutes, 6.3% 45 to 60 minutes, 7.9% 60 minutes or more (2000)

WALDEN (township). Covers a land area of 36.149 square miles and a water area of 0.042 square miles. Located at 46.67° N. Lat.; 94.45° W. Long.
Population: 405 (2000); Race: 98.1% White, 0.7% Black, 0.0% Asian, 0.0% American Indian and Alaska Native, 0.5% Hispanic of any race, 1.2% two or more races (2000); Density: 11.2 persons per square mile (2000); Age: 31.4% under 18, 10.6% over 64 (2000); Marriage status: 23.9% never married, 61.3% now married, 4.7% widowed, 10.1% divorced (2000); Foreign born: 0.5% (2000); Ancestry (includes multiple ancestries): 38.4% German, 22.3% Norwegian, 11.8% Irish, 10.1% Swedish, 5.8% Finnish (2000).
Economy: Employment by occupation: 15.8% management, 6.5% professional, 20.7% services, 22.8% sales, 3.3% farming, 16.3% construction, 14.7% production (2000).
Income: Per capita income: $13,678 (2000); Median household income: $34,063 (2000); Poverty rate: 15.8% (2000).
Taxes: Total city taxes per capita: $42 (1997); City property taxes per capita: $42 (1997).
Education: High school graduation rate: 79.5% (2000); College graduation rate: 6.2% (2000).
Housing: Homeownership rate: 88.2% (2000); Median home value: $95,000 (2000); Median age of housing: 22 years (2000).
Transportation: Commute to work: 86.9% car, 0.0% public transportation, 2.2% walk, 9.3% work from home (2000); Travel time to work: 34.3% less than 15 minutes, 31.3% 15 to 30 minutes, 17.5% 30 to 45 minutes, 12.7% 45 to 60 minutes, 4.2% 60 minutes or more (2000)

WALKER (city). Covers a land area of 1.456 square miles and a water area of 0.002 square miles. Located at 47.10° N. Lat.; 94.58° W. Long. Elevation is 1,358 feet.
History: Walker was named for Thomas Barlow Walker, a pioneer lumberman and landowner.
Population: 1,069 (2000); Race: 90.8% White, 0.0% Black, 0.0% Asian, 7.9% American Indian and Alaska Native, 0.8% Hispanic of any race, 1.3% two or more races (2000); Density: 734.3 persons per square mile (2000); Age: 23.8% under 18, 23.8% over 64 (2000); Marriage status: 22.7% never married, 54.0% now married, 13.8% widowed, 9.5% divorced (2000); Foreign born: 1.3% (2000); Ancestry (includes multiple ancestries): 32.4% German, 26.0% Norwegian, 9.9% Irish, 9.8% English, 9.2% Swedish (2000).
Economy: Single-family building permits issued: 2 (2001) / 2 (2000); Multi-family building permits issued: 7 (2001) / 7 (2000); Employment by occupation: 16.4% management, 24.4% professional, 20.7% services, 22.7% sales, 0.6% farming, 6.3% construction, 8.9% production (2000).
Income: Per capita income: $17,079 (2000); Median household income: $33,125 (2000); Poverty rate: 12.4% (2000).
Taxes: Total city taxes per capita: $242 (1997); City property taxes per capita: $232 (1997).
Education: High school graduation rate: 90.1% (2000); College graduation rate: 24.7% (2000).

School District(s)

Walker-Hackensack-Akeley (PK-12)
2000 Enrollment: 1,043 218-547-4201
Housing: Homeownership rate: 67.3% (2000); Median home value: $90,000 (2000); Median rent: $321 per month (2000); Median age of housing: 41 years (2000).
Newspapers: The Pilot-Independent (1 x week)
Transportation: Commute to work: 75.5% car, 0.2% public transportation, 13.7% walk, 8.9% work from home (2000); Travel time to work: 77.4% less than 15 minutes, 11.9% 15 to 30 minutes, 4.3% 30 to 45 minutes, 1.2% 45 to 60 minutes, 5.2% 60 minutes or more (2000)
Additional Information Contacts
Leech Lake Area Chamber of Commerce 218-547-1313

WILKINSON (township). Covers a land area of 30.715 square miles and a water area of 5.324 square miles. Located at 47.28° N. Lat.; 94.62° W. Long. Elevation is 1,310 feet.
Population: 270 (2000); Race: 64.8% White, 0.0% Black, 0.0% Asian, 32.4% American Indian and Alaska Native, 0.0% Hispanic of any race, 1.2% two or more races (2000); Density: 8.8 persons per square mile (2000); Age: 23.1% under 18, 12.6% over 64 (2000); Marriage status: 27.6% never married, 53.3% now married, 4.3% widowed, 14.8% divorced (2000); Foreign born: 0.8% (2000); Ancestry (includes multiple ancestries): 33.6% German, 31.6% Other groups, 11.7% Norwegian, 10.9% Swedish, 6.5% English (2000).
Economy: Employment by occupation: 5.3% management, 14.2% professional, 23.9% services, 25.7% sales, 0.0% farming, 15.9% construction, 15.0% production (2000).
Income: Per capita income: $15,628 (2000); Median household income: $30,750 (2000); Poverty rate: 10.5% (2000).
Taxes: Total city taxes per capita: $79 (1997); City property taxes per capita: $79 (1997).
Education: High school graduation rate: 86.0% (2000); College graduation rate: 15.1% (2000).
Housing: Homeownership rate: 92.0% (2000); Median home value: $112,500 (2000); Median rent: $175 per month (2000); Median age of housing: 21 years (2000).
Transportation: Commute to work: 87.6% car, 8.8% public transportation, 0.0% walk, 1.8% work from home (2000); Travel time to work: 26.1% less than 15 minutes, 58.6% 15 to 30 minutes, 12.6% 30 to 45 minutes, 0.9% 45 to 60 minutes, 1.8% 60 minutes or more (2000)

WILSON (township). Covers a land area of 17.737 square miles and a water area of 0.124 square miles. Located at 46.69° N. Lat.; 94.37° W. Long.
Population: 551 (2000); Race: 98.6% White, 0.0% Black, 0.0% Asian, 0.0% American Indian and Alaska Native, 1.4% Hispanic of any race, 1.4% two or more races (2000); Density: 31.1 persons per square mile (2000); Age: 29.4% under 18, 13.8% over 64 (2000); Marriage status: 23.0% never married, 63.6% now married, 6.2% widowed, 7.3% divorced (2000); Foreign born: 0.0% (2000); Ancestry (includes multiple ancestries): 26.1% German, 23.2% Norwegian, 13.7% Irish, 12.6% English, 6.7% Polish (2000).
Economy: Employment by occupation: 14.0% management, 14.0% professional, 13.3% services, 25.3% sales, 2.8% farming, 18.6% construction, 11.9% production (2000).
Income: Per capita income: $12,945 (2000); Median household income: $30,833 (2000); Poverty rate: 18.9% (2000).
Taxes: Total city taxes per capita: $24 (1997); City property taxes per capita: $24 (1997).
Education: High school graduation rate: 82.0% (2000); College graduation rate: 9.9% (2000).
Housing: Homeownership rate: 91.8% (2000); Median home value: $82,100 (2000); Median rent: $420 per month (2000); Median age of housing: 26 years (2000).
Transportation: Commute to work: 78.9% car, 0.0% public transportation, 6.0% walk, 11.6% work from home (2000); Travel time to work: 49.2% less than 15 minutes, 23.0% 15 to 30 minutes, 17.1% 30 to 45 minutes, 6.0% 45 to 60 minutes, 4.8% 60 minutes or more (2000)

WOODROW (township). Covers a land area of 25.060 square miles and a water area of 11.715 square miles. Located at 46.93° N. Lat.; 94.34° W. Long.
Population: 667 (2000); Race: 99.5% White, 0.0% Black, 0.0% Asian, 0.0% American Indian and Alaska Native, 0.0% Hispanic of any race, 0.5% two or more races (2000); Density: 26.6 persons per square mile (2000); Age: 10.1% under 18, 32.2% over 64 (2000); Marriage status: 9.1% never married, 75.2% now married, 7.5% widowed, 8.2% divorced (2000); Foreign born: 0.0% (2000); Ancestry (includes multiple ancestries): 39.8% German, 18.7% Swedish, 18.2% Norwegian, 13.1% English, 7.8% Irish (2000).
Economy: Employment by occupation: 12.8% management, 24.5% professional, 4.1% services, 32.1% sales, 1.0% farming, 9.7% construction, 15.8% production (2000).
Income: Per capita income: $23,201 (2000); Median household income: $35,987 (2000); Poverty rate: 6.6% (2000).
Taxes: Total city taxes per capita: $122 (1997); City property taxes per capita: $122 (1997).
Education: High school graduation rate: 91.1% (2000); College graduation rate: 26.2% (2000).
Housing: Homeownership rate: 95.1% (2000); Median home value: $140,900 (2000); Median rent: $313 per month (2000); Median age of housing: 26 years (2000).
Transportation: Commute to work: 75.3% car, 1.1% public transportation, 6.8% walk, 16.8% work from home (2000); Travel time to work: 25.9% less than 15 minutes, 41.1% 15 to 30 minutes, 26.6% 30 to 45 minutes, 0.0% 45 to 60 minutes, 6.3% 60 minutes or more (2000)

Chippewa County

Located in southwestern Minnesota; bounded on the west by the Minnesota River; drained by the Chippewa River. Covers a land area of 582.80 square miles, a water area of 5.00 square miles, and is located in the Central Time Zone. The county government was organized in 1870. County seat is Montevideo.

Weather Station: Milan 1 NW — Elevation: 1,017 feet

	Jan	Feb	Mar	Apr	May	Jun	Jul	Aug	Sep	Oct	Nov	Dec
High	21	28	40	58	72	80	85	82	73	60	40	26
Low	-0	7	20	34	46	55	59	57	47	35	20	7
Precip	0.7	0.6	1.5	2.2	2.7	3.9	3.9	3.1	2.4	2.3	1.2	0.4
Snow	11.2	7.9	9.1	2.6	tr	0.0	0.0	0.0	tr	0.7	6.7	6.6

High and Low temperatures in degrees Fahrenheit; Precipitation and Snow in inches

Population: 13,088 (2000); Race: 96.9% White, 0.2% Black, 0.2% Asian, 1.2% American Indian and Alaska Native, 1.7% Hispanic of any race, 0.7% two or more races (2000); Density: 22.5 persons per square mile (2000); Age: 25.3% under 18, 20.0% over 64 (2000).
Religion: Five largest groups: 53.5% Evangelical Lutheran Church in America, 11.5% Catholic Church, 8.0% Reformed Church in America, 6.1% Lutheran Church—Missouri Synod, 3.7% Christian Reformed Church in North America (2000).
Economy: Unemployment rate: 3.5% (11/2002); Total civilian labor force: 7,271 (11/2002); Leading industries: 20.3% manufacturing; 18.2% retail trade; 15.9% health care and social assistance (2000); Companies that employ more than 1,000 persons: 0 (2000); Companies that employ more than 100 persons: 9 (2000); Farms: 618 totaling 318,472 acres (1997); Minority business ownership rate: 0.0% (1997); Women business ownership rate: 12.1% (1997); Retail sales per capita: $9,629 (1997). Single-family building permits issued: 13 (2001) / 40 (2000); Multi-family building permits issued: 14 (2001) / 5 (2000).
Income: Per capita income: $18,039 (2000); Median household income: $35,582 (2000); Poverty rate: 8.6% (2000); Bankruptcy rate: 2.74% (2001).
Taxes: Total county taxes per capita: $307 (2000); County property taxes per capita: $306 (2000).
Education: High school graduation rate: 81.6% (2000); College graduation rate: 13.7% (2000).
Housing: Homeownership rate: 76.5% (2000); Median home value: $62,200 (2000); Median rent: $320 per month (2000); Median age of housing: 47 years (2000).
Health: Birth rate: 100.1 per 10,000 population (1998); Age adjusted death rate: 68.3 per 10,000 population (1999); Age adjusted cancer mortality rate: 143.0 deaths per 100,000 population (1999). Number of physicians: 7.6 per 10,000 population (1999); Number of hospital beds: 22.2 per 10,000 population (1999).
Elections: 2000 Presidential election results: 46.5% Gore, 46.9% Bush, 4.2% Nader, 1.8% Buchanan
National and State Parks: Boike State Wildlife Management Area; Franko State Wildlife Management Area; Spartan State Wildlife Management Area
Additional Information Contacts
Chippewa County Government Offices 320-269-7216
Montevideo Chamber of Commerce 320-269-5527

Chippewa County Communities

BIG BEND (township). Covers a land area of 35.744 square miles and a water area of 0.038 square miles. Located at 45.12° N. Lat.; 95.78° W. Long.
Population: 257 (2000); Race: 100.0% White, 0.0% Black, 0.0% Asian, 0.0% American Indian and Alaska Native, 0.0% Hispanic of any race, 0.0% two or more races (2000); Density: 7.2 persons per square mile (2000); Age: 24.5% under 18, 18.9% over 64 (2000); Marriage status: 16.8% never married, 69.0% now married, 9.1% widowed, 5.1% divorced (2000); Foreign born: 0.0% (2000); Ancestry (includes multiple ancestries): 72.7% Norwegian, 27.3% German, 4.0% Swedish, 2.8% Czech, 2.4% Irish (2000).
Economy: Employment by occupation: 23.5% management, 10.9% professional, 12.6% services, 16.8% sales, 4.2% farming, 16.0% construction, 16.0% production (2000).
Income: Per capita income: $18,435 (2000); Median household income: $39,375 (2000); Poverty rate: 4.8% (2000).
Taxes: Total city taxes per capita: $52 (1997); City property taxes per capita: $52 (1997).
Education: High school graduation rate: 91.0% (2000); College graduation rate: 13.0% (2000).
Housing: Homeownership rate: 82.9% (2000); Median home value: $61,400 (2000); Median rent: $258 per month (2000); Median age of housing: 60+ years (2000).
Transportation: Commute to work: 88.2% car, 0.0% public transportation, 0.0% walk, 11.8% work from home (2000); Travel time to work: 28.6% less than 15 minutes, 46.7% 15 to 30 minutes, 15.2% 30 to 45 minutes, 5.7% 45 to 60 minutes, 3.8% 60 minutes or more (2000)

CLARA CITY (city). Covers a land area of 1.911 square miles and a water area of 0 square miles. Located at 44.95° N. Lat.; 95.36° W. Long. Elevation is 1,062 feet.
Population: 1,393 (2000); Race: 98.3% White, 0.0% Black, 0.1% Asian, 0.0% American Indian and Alaska Native, 2.9% Hispanic of any race, 0.0% two or more races (2000); Density: 729.0 persons per square mile (2000); Age: 19.5% under 18, 30.8% over 64 (2000); Marriage status: 20.6% never married, 59.2% now married, 14.6% widowed, 5.6% divorced (2000); Foreign born: 1.4% (2000); Ancestry (includes multiple ancestries): 58.1% German, 20.3% Norwegian, 10.6% Dutch, 4.6% Irish, 4.1% Swedish (2000).
Economy: Grain, soybeans, sugar beets; hogs, sheep. Manufacturing: fertilizer, tool and die, cereal products, machinery. Single-family building permits issued: 1 (2001) / 2 (2000); Multi-family building permits issued: 0 (2001) / 5 (2000); Employment by occupation: 10.0% management, 18.3% professional, 19.0% services, 22.0% sales, 0.8% farming, 9.5% construction, 20.3% production (2000).
Income: Per capita income: $17,639 (2000); Median household income: $34,306 (2000); Poverty rate: 7.3% (2000).
Taxes: Total city taxes per capita: $98 (1997); City property taxes per capita: $92 (1997).
Education: High school graduation rate: 68.3% (2000); College graduation rate: 8.5% (2000).

School District(s)

M.A.C.C.R.A.Y. (PK-12)
2000 Enrollment: 967 320-847-2154
Housing: Homeownership rate: 80.8% (2000); Median home value: $58,500 (2000); Median rent: $291 per month (2000); Median age of housing: 44 years (2000).
Newspapers: The Clara City Herald (1 x week)
Transportation: Commute to work: 89.3% car, 0.0% public transportation, 6.8% walk, 3.6% work from home (2000); Travel time to work: 57.7% less than 15 minutes, 24.9% 15 to 30 minutes, 14.3% 30 to 45 minutes, 1.8% 45 to 60 minutes, 1.4% 60 minutes or more (2000)

CRATE (township). Covers a land area of 35.851 square miles and a water area of 0.008 square miles. Located at 45.01° N. Lat.; 95.43° W. Long.
Population: 247 (2000); Race: 96.2% White, 0.0% Black, 0.0% Asian, 2.3% American Indian and Alaska Native, 0.0% Hispanic of any race, 1.5% two or more races (2000); Density: 6.9 persons per square mile (2000); Age: 34.6% under 18, 10.8% over 64 (2000); Marriage status: 25.0% never married, 63.0% now married, 5.7% widowed, 6.3% divorced (2000); Foreign born: 0.0% (2000); Ancestry (includes multiple ancestries): 70.4% German, 20.0% Norwegian, 10.4% Swedish, 9.6% Dutch, 6.5% Other groups (2000).
Economy: Employment by occupation: 22.4% management, 6.9% professional, 12.1% services, 20.7% sales, 7.8% farming, 6.0% construction, 24.1% production (2000).
Income: Per capita income: $16,532 (2000); Median household income: $40,000 (2000); Poverty rate: 3.1% (2000).
Taxes: Total city taxes per capita: $81 (1997); City property taxes per capita: $81 (1997).
Education: High school graduation rate: 82.8% (2000); College graduation rate: 6.4% (2000).
Housing: Homeownership rate: 89.8% (2000); Median home value: $75,600 (2000); Median rent: $125 per month (2000); Median age of housing: 56 years (2000).
Transportation: Commute to work: 80.7% car, 0.0% public transportation, 0.0% walk, 19.3% work from home (2000); Travel time to work: 33.7% less than 15 minutes, 23.9% 15 to 30 minutes, 32.6% 30 to 45 minutes, 5.4% 45 to 60 minutes, 4.3% 60 minutes or more (2000)

GRACE (township). Covers a land area of 35.853 square miles and a water area of 0.022 square miles. Located at 45.11° N. Lat.; 95.54° W. Long.
Population: 134 (2000); Race: 100.0% White, 0.0% Black, 0.0% Asian, 0.0% American Indian and Alaska Native, 0.0% Hispanic of any race, 0.0% two or more races (2000); Density: 3.7 persons per square mile (2000); Age: 28.8% under 18, 10.2% over 64 (2000); Marriage status: 19.1% never married, 71.9% now married, 3.4% widowed, 5.6% divorced (2000); Foreign born: 0.0% (2000); Ancestry (includes multiple ancestries): 45.8%

Norwegian, 33.1% German, 14.4% Swedish, 13.6% Irish, 5.9% Dutch (2000).
Economy: Employment by occupation: 37.1% management, 21.0% professional, 11.3% services, 16.1% sales, 3.2% farming, 3.2% construction, 8.1% production (2000).
Income: Per capita income: $19,552 (2000); Median household income: $61,667 (2000); Poverty rate: 8.5% (2000).
Taxes: Total city taxes per capita: $216 (1997); City property taxes per capita: $216 (1997).
Education: High school graduation rate: 84.0% (2000); College graduation rate: 25.9% (2000).
Housing: Homeownership rate: 84.0% (2000); Median home value: $100,000 (2000); Median age of housing: 49 years (2000).
Transportation: Commute to work: 69.4% car, 0.0% public transportation, 6.5% walk, 24.2% work from home (2000); Travel time to work: 23.4% less than 15 minutes, 40.4% 15 to 30 minutes, 29.8% 30 to 45 minutes, 6.4% 45 to 60 minutes, 0.0% 60 minutes or more (2000)

GRANITE FALLS (township). Covers a land area of 31.457 square miles and a water area of 0.320 square miles. Located at 44.85° N. Lat.; 95.54° W. Long.
Population: 222 (2000); Race: 92.2% White, 1.1% Black, 0.0% Asian, 5.0% American Indian and Alaska Native, 1.7% Hispanic of any race, 0.0% two or more races (2000); Density: 7.1 persons per square mile (2000); Age: 18.4% under 18, 18.4% over 64 (2000); Marriage status: 20.9% never married, 66.9% now married, 6.1% widowed, 6.1% divorced (2000); Foreign born: 2.2% (2000); Ancestry (includes multiple ancestries): 46.9% Norwegian, 44.1% German, 12.3% Swedish, 6.7% Dutch, 6.7% Other groups (2000).
Economy: Employment by occupation: 23.5% management, 18.4% professional, 9.2% services, 24.5% sales, 0.0% farming, 6.1% construction, 18.4% production (2000).
Income: Per capita income: $20,762 (2000); Median household income: $32,273 (2000); Poverty rate: 7.0% (2000).
Taxes: Total city taxes per capita: $127 (1997); City property taxes per capita: $127 (1997).
Education: High school graduation rate: 86.7% (2000); College graduation rate: 14.7% (2000).
Housing: Homeownership rate: 91.5% (2000); Median home value: $94,300 (2000); Median rent: $525 per month (2000); Median age of housing: 47 years (2000).
Transportation: Commute to work: 81.6% car, 0.0% public transportation, 2.0% walk, 16.3% work from home (2000); Travel time to work: 68.3% less than 15 minutes, 14.6% 15 to 30 minutes, 12.2% 30 to 45 minutes, 2.4% 45 to 60 minutes, 2.4% 60 minutes or more (2000)

HAVELOCK (township). Covers a land area of 35.759 square miles and a water area of 0 square miles. Located at 45.02° N. Lat.; 95.54° W. Long.
Population: 189 (2000); Race: 95.5% White, 0.0% Black, 0.0% Asian, 0.0% American Indian and Alaska Native, 4.5% Hispanic of any race, 0.0% two or more races (2000); Density: 5.3 persons per square mile (2000); Age: 22.9% under 18, 13.4% over 64 (2000); Marriage status: 22.1% never married, 74.4% now married, 1.7% widowed, 1.7% divorced (2000); Foreign born: 2.0% (2000); Ancestry (includes multiple ancestries): 57.7% German, 36.3% Norwegian, 8.0% Swedish, 7.5% English, 4.5% United States or American (2000).
Economy: Employment by occupation: 21.4% management, 5.1% professional, 12.0% services, 32.5% sales, 0.9% farming, 5.1% construction, 23.1% production (2000).
Income: Per capita income: $17,012 (2000); Median household income: $42,500 (2000); Poverty rate: 7.5% (2000).
Taxes: Total city taxes per capita: $25 (1997); City property taxes per capita: $25 (1997).
Education: High school graduation rate: 86.9% (2000); College graduation rate: 6.6% (2000).
Housing: Homeownership rate: 91.9% (2000); Median home value: $52,500 (2000); Median rent: $225 per month (2000); Median age of housing: 50 years (2000).
Transportation: Commute to work: 80.0% car, 0.0% public transportation, 3.5% walk, 16.5% work from home (2000); Travel time to work: 21.9% less than 15 minutes, 55.2% 15 to 30 minutes, 20.8% 30 to 45 minutes, 0.0% 45 to 60 minutes, 2.1% 60 minutes or more (2000)

KRAGERO (township). Covers a land area of 41.484 square miles and a water area of 3.225 square miles. Located at 45.09° N. Lat.; 95.90° W. Long.
Population: 164 (2000); Race: 100.0% White, 0.0% Black, 0.0% Asian, 0.0% American Indian and Alaska Native, 0.0% Hispanic of any race, 0.0% two or more races (2000); Density: 4.0 persons per square mile (2000); Age: 22.6% under 18, 13.8% over 64 (2000); Marriage status: 17.5% never married, 73.0% now married, 4.4% widowed, 5.1% divorced (2000); Foreign born: 0.0% (2000); Ancestry (includes multiple ancestries): 73.0% Norwegian, 23.9% German, 16.4% Swedish, 4.4% Dutch, 3.1% Irish (2000).
Economy: Employment by occupation: 23.2% management, 13.1% professional, 8.1% services, 27.3% sales, 5.1% farming, 11.1% construction, 12.1% production (2000).
Income: Per capita income: $17,119 (2000); Median household income: $42,292 (2000); Poverty rate: 2.5% (2000).
Taxes: Total city taxes per capita: $128 (1997); City property taxes per capita: $128 (1997).
Education: High school graduation rate: 92.0% (2000); College graduation rate: 25.0% (2000).
Housing: Homeownership rate: 85.1% (2000); Median home value: $80,000 (2000); Median rent: $150 per month (2000); Median age of housing: 60+ years (2000).
Transportation: Commute to work: 83.2% car, 0.0% public transportation, 6.3% walk, 10.5% work from home (2000); Travel time to work: 52.9% less than 15 minutes, 23.5% 15 to 30 minutes, 10.6% 30 to 45 minutes, 10.6% 45 to 60 minutes, 2.4% 60 minutes or more (2000)

LEENTHROP (township). Covers a land area of 35.699 square miles and a water area of 0.006 square miles. Located at 44.92° N. Lat.; 95.54° W. Long.
Population: 396 (2000); Race: 100.0% White, 0.0% Black, 0.0% Asian, 0.0% American Indian and Alaska Native, 0.0% Hispanic of any race, 0.0% two or more races (2000); Density: 11.1 persons per square mile (2000); Age: 23.3% under 18, 35.0% over 64 (2000); Marriage status: 18.5% never married, 49.1% now married, 25.4% widowed, 6.9% divorced (2000); Foreign born: 2.6% (2000); Ancestry (includes multiple ancestries): 44.8% Norwegian, 30.2% German, 7.9% Swedish, 4.8% Irish, 4.6% English (2000).
Economy: Employment by occupation: 27.3% management, 5.2% professional, 12.3% services, 24.0% sales, 0.6% farming, 10.4% construction, 20.1% production (2000).
Income: Per capita income: $13,738 (2000); Median household income: $46,250 (2000); Poverty rate: 4.3% (2000).
Taxes: Total city taxes per capita: $89 (1997); City property taxes per capita: $89 (1997).
Education: High school graduation rate: 69.0% (2000); College graduation rate: 5.0% (2000).
Housing: Homeownership rate: 93.4% (2000); Median home value: $76,300 (2000); Median age of housing: 60+ years (2000).
Transportation: Commute to work: 88.5% car, 0.0% public transportation, 0.0% walk, 11.5% work from home (2000); Travel time to work: 38.2% less than 15 minutes, 47.3% 15 to 30 minutes, 6.9% 30 to 45 minutes, 2.3% 45 to 60 minutes, 5.3% 60 minutes or more (2000)

LONE TREE (township). Covers a land area of 36.232 square miles and a water area of 0 square miles. Located at 45.02° N. Lat.; 95.31° W. Long.
Population: 256 (2000); Race: 94.7% White, 0.0% Black, 0.9% Asian, 0.0% American Indian and Alaska Native, 8.8% Hispanic of any race, 0.0% two or more races (2000); Density: 7.1 persons per square mile (2000); Age: 28.3% under 18, 12.4% over 64 (2000); Marriage status: 20.7% never married, 79.3% now married, 0.0% widowed, 0.0% divorced (2000); Foreign born: 2.7% (2000); Ancestry (includes multiple ancestries): 49.6% German, 15.9% Dutch, 14.2% Norwegian, 11.9% Other groups, 6.2% United States or American (2000).
Economy: Employment by occupation: 34.5% management, 14.3% professional, 9.2% services, 17.6% sales, 6.7% farming, 8.4% construction, 9.2% production (2000).
Income: Per capita income: $20,397 (2000); Median household income: $46,250 (2000); Poverty rate: 12.4% (2000).
Taxes: Total city taxes per capita: $111 (1997); City property taxes per capita: $111 (1997).
Education: High school graduation rate: 78.4% (2000); College graduation rate: 6.5% (2000).
Housing: Homeownership rate: 82.3% (2000); Median home value: $98,300 (2000); Median rent: $188 per month (2000); Median age of housing: 40 years (2000).
Transportation: Commute to work: 75.4% car, 0.0% public transportation, 1.8% walk, 22.8% work from home (2000); Travel time to work: 35.2% less than 15 minutes, 34.1% 15 to 30 minutes, 28.4% 30 to 45 minutes, 2.3% 45 to 60 minutes, 0.0% 60 minutes or more (2000)

LOURISTON (township). Covers a land area of 35.615 square miles and a water area of 0.478 square miles. Located at 45.11° N. Lat.; 95.44° W. Long. Elevation is 1,050 feet.

Population: 211 (2000); Race: 98.2% White, 1.8% Black, 0.0% Asian, 0.0% American Indian and Alaska Native, 0.0% Hispanic of any race, 0.0% two or more races (2000); Density: 5.9 persons per square mile (2000); Age: 34.7% under 18, 13.5% over 64 (2000); Marriage status: 23.9% never married, 66.0% now married, 3.8% widowed, 6.3% divorced (2000); Foreign born: 0.0% (2000); Ancestry (includes multiple ancestries): 49.1% German, 30.2% Norwegian, 17.6% Swedish, 10.8% Dutch, 7.2% Danish (2000).
Economy: Employment by occupation: 29.5% management, 11.4% professional, 17.1% services, 21.0% sales, 5.7% farming, 5.7% construction, 9.5% production (2000).
Income: Per capita income: $20,876 (2000); Median household income: $41,250 (2000); Poverty rate: 10.4% (2000).
Taxes: Total city taxes per capita: $98 (1997); City property taxes per capita: $98 (1997).
Education: High school graduation rate: 92.2% (2000); College graduation rate: 17.2% (2000).
Housing: Homeownership rate: 85.7% (2000); Median home value: $70,000 (2000); Median rent: $175 per month (2000); Median age of housing: 41 years (2000).
Transportation: Commute to work: 78.1% car, 0.0% public transportation, 9.5% walk, 12.4% work from home (2000); Travel time to work: 26.1% less than 15 minutes, 37.0% 15 to 30 minutes, 29.3% 30 to 45 minutes, 7.6% 45 to 60 minutes, 0.0% 60 minutes or more (2000)

MANDT (township). Covers a land area of 35.495 square miles and a water area of 0.031 square miles. Located at 45.10° N. Lat.; 95.68° W. Long.
Population: 175 (2000); Race: 98.9% White, 0.0% Black, 0.0% Asian, 1.1% American Indian and Alaska Native, 0.0% Hispanic of any race, 0.0% two or more races (2000); Density: 4.9 persons per square mile (2000); Age: 21.8% under 18, 25.7% over 64 (2000); Marriage status: 16.6% never married, 76.6% now married, 2.8% widowed, 4.1% divorced (2000); Foreign born: 0.0% (2000); Ancestry (includes multiple ancestries): 63.1% Norwegian, 35.8% German, 11.2% Swedish, 3.9% Danish, 3.4% English (2000).
Economy: Employment by occupation: 25.6% management, 25.6% professional, 7.0% services, 18.6% sales, 5.8% farming, 10.5% construction, 7.0% production (2000).
Income: Per capita income: $17,376 (2000); Median household income: $33,125 (2000); Poverty rate: 7.3% (2000).
Taxes: Total city taxes per capita: $106 (1997); City property taxes per capita: $106 (1997).
Education: High school graduation rate: 81.5% (2000); College graduation rate: 13.7% (2000).
Housing: Homeownership rate: 81.6% (2000); Median home value: $61,700 (2000); Median age of housing: 60+ years (2000).
Transportation: Commute to work: 79.8% car, 0.0% public transportation, 3.6% walk, 16.7% work from home (2000); Travel time to work: 14.3% less than 15 minutes, 51.4% 15 to 30 minutes, 24.3% 30 to 45 minutes, 7.1% 45 to 60 minutes, 2.9% 60 minutes or more (2000)

MAYNARD (city). Covers a land area of 0.649 square miles and a water area of 0 square miles. Located at 44.90° N. Lat.; 95.46° W. Long. Elevation is 1,029 feet.
Population: 388 (2000); Race: 96.5% White, 0.0% Black, 0.5% Asian, 0.0% American Indian and Alaska Native, 3.5% Hispanic of any race, 0.0% two or more races (2000); Density: 597.6 persons per square mile (2000); Age: 23.2% under 18, 19.7% over 64 (2000); Marriage status: 21.3% never married, 66.8% now married, 9.0% widowed, 3.0% divorced (2000); Foreign born: 3.5% (2000); Ancestry (includes multiple ancestries): 46.4% German, 38.5% Norwegian, 6.2% Other groups, 5.7% Swedish, 4.3% Irish (2000).
Economy: Grain, soybeans, sugar beets; hogs, sheep. Manufacturing: plastic products. Single-family building permits issued: 1 (2001) / 0 (2000); Multi-family building permits issued: 0 (2001) / 0 (2000); Employment by occupation: 9.7% management, 10.7% professional, 18.9% services, 15.8% sales, 2.6% farming, 7.1% construction, 35.2% production (2000).
Income: Per capita income: $14,285 (2000); Median household income: $28,571 (2000); Poverty rate: 7.8% (2000).
Taxes: Total city taxes per capita: $256 (1997); City property taxes per capita: $256 (1997).
Education: High school graduation rate: 78.6% (2000); College graduation rate: 4.0% (2000).
Housing: Homeownership rate: 81.8% (2000); Median home value: $35,600 (2000); Median rent: $320 per month (2000); Median age of housing: 57 years (2000).
Transportation: Commute to work: 87.8% car, 0.0% public transportation, 8.2% walk, 3.1% work from home (2000); Travel time to work: 52.1% less than 15 minutes, 25.8% 15 to 30 minutes, 14.7% 30 to 45 minutes, 7.4% 45 to 60 minutes, 0.0% 60 minutes or more (2000)

MILAN (city). Covers a land area of 0.979 square miles and a water area of 0 square miles. Located at 45.11° N. Lat.; 95.91° W. Long. Elevation is 1,005 feet.
Population: 326 (2000); Race: 92.7% White, 0.0% Black, 0.0% Asian, 0.0% American Indian and Alaska Native, 6.1% Hispanic of any race, 1.2% two or more races (2000); Density: 333.0 persons per square mile (2000); Age: 24.9% under 18, 30.4% over 64 (2000); Marriage status: 16.3% never married, 63.6% now married, 9.5% widowed, 10.6% divorced (2000); Foreign born: 4.0% (2000); Ancestry (includes multiple ancestries): 57.1% Norwegian, 30.4% German, 4.9% Swedish, 4.9% Other groups, 3.0% English (2000).
Economy: Grain, soybeans, sugar beets. Manufacturing of dolls. Employment by occupation: 10.6% management, 15.5% professional, 11.3% services, 30.3% sales, 3.5% farming, 7.7% construction, 21.1% production (2000).
Income: Per capita income: $17,338 (2000); Median household income: $31,000 (2000); Poverty rate: 12.8% (2000).
Taxes: Total city taxes per capita: $194 (1997); City property taxes per capita: $194 (1997).
Education: High school graduation rate: 85.5% (2000); College graduation rate: 18.1% (2000).
Housing: Homeownership rate: 78.9% (2000); Median home value: $29,200 (2000); Median rent: $362 per month (2000); Median age of housing: 60+ years (2000).
Newspapers: The Milan Standard-Watson Journal (1 x week)
Transportation: Commute to work: 80.3% car, 0.0% public transportation, 15.3% walk, 4.4% work from home (2000); Travel time to work: 53.4% less than 15 minutes, 32.8% 15 to 30 minutes, 7.6% 30 to 45 minutes, 1.5% 45 to 60 minutes, 4.6% 60 minutes or more (2000)

MONTEVIDEO (city). Covers a land area of 4.491 square miles and a water area of 0.046 square miles. Located at 44.94° N. Lat.; 95.72° W. Long. Elevation is 923 feet.
History: Montevideo was settled on a bluff at the junction of the Minnesota and Chippewa Rivers. The town was named for the capital of Uruguay in South America. Many of the early residents of the Montevideo area were farmers of Scandinavian or German heritage.
Population: 5,346 (2000); Race: 97.8% White, 0.0% Black, 0.3% Asian, 0.4% American Indian and Alaska Native, 1.4% Hispanic of any race, 1.3% two or more races (2000); Density: 1,190.5 persons per square mile (2000); Age: 24.7% under 18, 20.9% over 64 (2000); Marriage status: 21.1% never married, 57.6% now married, 12.2% widowed, 9.1% divorced (2000); Foreign born: 1.5% (2000); Ancestry (includes multiple ancestries): 44.5% Norwegian, 36.8% German, 9.2% Swedish, 6.9% Irish, 4.3% Other groups (2000).
Economy: Single-family building permits issued: 5 (2001) / 26 (2000); Multi-family building permits issued: 14 (2001) / 0 (2000); Employment by occupation: 9.0% management, 16.3% professional, 19.4% services, 22.0% sales, 1.2% farming, 12.0% construction, 20.2% production (2000).
Income: Per capita income: $18,025 (2000); Median household income: $32,447 (2000); Poverty rate: 10.1% (2000).
Taxes: Total city taxes per capita: $257 (2000); City property taxes per capita: $234 (2000).
Education: High school graduation rate: 82.4% (2000); College graduation rate: 16.0% (2000).

School District(s)

Minnesota River Valley Ed. Dist. (07-12)
2000 Enrollment: 82 320-269-9297
Montevideo (PK-12)
2000 Enrollment: 1,596 320-269-8833

Housing: Homeownership rate: 71.0% (2000); Median home value: $62,500 (2000); Median rent: $325 per month (2000); Median age of housing: 46 years (2000).
Hospitals: Chippewa County Montevideo Hospital (35 beds)
Safety: Violent crime rate: 16.7 per 10,000 population; Property crime rate: 261.0 per 10,000 population (2001).
Transportation: Commute to work: 92.3% car, 0.3% public transportation, 2.7% walk, 3.9% work from home (2000); Travel time to work: 80.2% less

than 15 minutes, 10.7% 15 to 30 minutes, 3.3% 30 to 45 minutes, 2.0% 45 to 60 minutes, 3.7% 60 minutes or more (2000)
Airports: Montevideo-Chippewa County
Additional Information Contacts
Montevideo Chamber of Commerce 320-269-5527

RHEIDERLAND (township). Covers a land area of 34.765 square miles and a water area of 0 square miles. Located at 44.93° N. Lat.; 95.32° W. Long.
Population: 328 (2000); Race: 99.5% White, 0.5% Black, 0.0% Asian, 0.0% American Indian and Alaska Native, 0.0% Hispanic of any race, 0.0% two or more races (2000); Density: 9.4 persons per square mile (2000); Age: 41.0% under 18, 10.1% over 64 (2000); Marriage status: 20.0% never married, 76.3% now married, 3.7% widowed, 0.0% divorced (2000); Foreign born: 0.0% (2000); Ancestry (includes multiple ancestries): 70.5% German, 19.1% Dutch, 6.9% Swedish, 5.3% Norwegian, 2.7% United States or American (2000).
Economy: Employment by occupation: 22.6% management, 18.9% professional, 13.2% services, 16.4% sales, 5.0% farming, 14.5% construction, 9.4% production (2000).
Income: Per capita income: $11,951 (2000); Median household income: $36,250 (2000); Poverty rate: 6.1% (2000).
Taxes: Total city taxes per capita: $90 (1997); City property taxes per capita: $90 (1997).
Education: High school graduation rate: 85.1% (2000); College graduation rate: 15.4% (2000).
Housing: Homeownership rate: 87.1% (2000); Median home value: $95,000 (2000); Median rent: $125 per month (2000); Median age of housing: 56 years (2000).
Transportation: Commute to work: 78.3% car, 0.0% public transportation, 5.1% walk, 15.3% work from home (2000); Travel time to work: 48.1% less than 15 minutes, 28.6% 15 to 30 minutes, 18.8% 30 to 45 minutes, 4.5% 45 to 60 minutes, 0.0% 60 minutes or more (2000)

ROSEWOOD (township). Covers a land area of 35.691 square miles and a water area of 0.080 square miles. Located at 45.03° N. Lat.; 95.67° W. Long.
Population: 303 (2000); Race: 100.0% White, 0.0% Black, 0.0% Asian, 0.0% American Indian and Alaska Native, 0.0% Hispanic of any race, 0.0% two or more races (2000); Density: 8.5 persons per square mile (2000); Age: 23.5% under 18, 18.7% over 64 (2000); Marriage status: 23.1% never married, 69.7% now married, 3.8% widowed, 3.4% divorced (2000); Foreign born: 0.0% (2000); Ancestry (includes multiple ancestries): 46.3% German, 39.1% Norwegian, 7.8% United States or American, 7.8% Dutch, 3.4% Irish (2000).
Economy: Employment by occupation: 23.3% management, 13.3% professional, 6.7% services, 16.7% sales, 0.0% farming, 22.0% construction, 18.0% production (2000).
Income: Per capita income: $15,811 (2000); Median household income: $36,250 (2000); Poverty rate: 8.2% (2000).
Taxes: Total city taxes per capita: $61 (1997); City property taxes per capita: $61 (1997).
Education: High school graduation rate: 84.1% (2000); College graduation rate: 12.3% (2000).
Housing: Homeownership rate: 93.8% (2000); Median home value: $81,900 (2000); Median age of housing: 49 years (2000).
Transportation: Commute to work: 75.3% car, 0.0% public transportation, 1.3% walk, 22.0% work from home (2000); Travel time to work: 49.6% less than 15 minutes, 37.6% 15 to 30 minutes, 6.0% 30 to 45 minutes, 1.7% 45 to 60 minutes, 5.1% 60 minutes or more (2000)

SPARTA (township). Covers a land area of 39.280 square miles and a water area of 0.346 square miles. Located at 44.94° N. Lat.; 95.69° W. Long.
Population: 814 (2000); Race: 98.9% White, 0.0% Black, 0.0% Asian, 0.7% American Indian and Alaska Native, 0.6% Hispanic of any race, 0.0% two or more races (2000); Density: 20.7 persons per square mile (2000); Age: 26.4% under 18, 10.1% over 64 (2000); Marriage status: 21.0% never married, 68.9% now married, 3.5% widowed, 6.6% divorced (2000); Foreign born: 0.4% (2000); Ancestry (includes multiple ancestries): 46.7% Norwegian, 42.9% German, 5.7% Swedish, 4.4% Irish, 4.0% Other groups (2000).
Economy: Employment by occupation: 15.3% management, 20.3% professional, 13.3% services, 24.7% sales, 1.7% farming, 10.5% construction, 14.2% production (2000).
Income: Per capita income: $19,392 (2000); Median household income: $46,042 (2000); Poverty rate: 7.5% (2000).
Taxes: Total city taxes per capita: $113 (2000); City property taxes per capita: $112 (2000).
Education: High school graduation rate: 92.2% (2000); College graduation rate: 19.8% (2000).
Housing: Homeownership rate: 89.9% (2000); Median home value: $87,700 (2000); Median rent: $243 per month (2000); Median age of housing: 37 years (2000).
Transportation: Commute to work: 87.6% car, 0.0% public transportation, 3.8% walk, 8.6% work from home (2000); Travel time to work: 69.9% less than 15 minutes, 17.5% 15 to 30 minutes, 6.1% 30 to 45 minutes, 2.4% 45 to 60 minutes, 4.1% 60 minutes or more (2000)

STONEHAM (township). Covers a land area of 34.734 square miles and a water area of 0.039 square miles. Located at 44.92° N. Lat.; 95.43° W. Long.
Population: 260 (2000); Race: 100.0% White, 0.0% Black, 0.0% Asian, 0.0% American Indian and Alaska Native, 2.4% Hispanic of any race, 0.0% two or more races (2000); Density: 7.5 persons per square mile (2000); Age: 25.6% under 18, 16.9% over 64 (2000); Marriage status: 22.5% never married, 64.0% now married, 10.0% widowed, 3.5% divorced (2000); Foreign born: 0.0% (2000); Ancestry (includes multiple ancestries): 66.9% German, 31.1% Norwegian, 4.7% United States or American, 4.3% Danish, 3.1% Swedish (2000).
Economy: Employment by occupation: 25.4% management, 14.6% professional, 11.5% services, 20.0% sales, 0.0% farming, 12.3% construction, 16.2% production (2000).
Income: Per capita income: $16,581 (2000); Median household income: $38,500 (2000); Poverty rate: 6.7% (2000).
Taxes: Total city taxes per capita: $99 (1997); City property taxes per capita: $99 (1997).
Education: High school graduation rate: 79.9% (2000); College graduation rate: 8.5% (2000).
Housing: Homeownership rate: 76.5% (2000); Median home value: $86,400 (2000); Median rent: $283 per month (2000); Median age of housing: 52 years (2000).
Transportation: Commute to work: 76.6% car, 2.3% public transportation, 0.8% walk, 20.3% work from home (2000); Travel time to work: 49.0% less than 15 minutes, 35.3% 15 to 30 minutes, 15.7% 30 to 45 minutes, 0.0% 45 to 60 minutes, 0.0% 60 minutes or more (2000)

TUNSBERG (township). Covers a land area of 33.021 square miles and a water area of 0.276 square miles. Located at 45.03° N. Lat.; 95.78° W. Long.
Population: 183 (2000); Race: 100.0% White, 0.0% Black, 0.0% Asian, 0.0% American Indian and Alaska Native, 0.0% Hispanic of any race, 0.0% two or more races (2000); Density: 5.5 persons per square mile (2000); Age: 27.1% under 18, 10.2% over 64 (2000); Marriage status: 19.6% never married, 76.9% now married, 0.0% widowed, 3.5% divorced (2000); Foreign born: 0.0% (2000); Ancestry (includes multiple ancestries): 50.3% Norwegian, 30.5% German, 11.3% English, 9.0% Swedish, 3.4% United States or American (2000).
Economy: Employment by occupation: 33.0% management, 16.0% professional, 7.0% services, 18.0% sales, 5.0% farming, 9.0% construction, 12.0% production (2000).
Income: Per capita income: $24,303 (2000); Median household income: $55,417 (2000); Poverty rate: 0.0% (2000).
Taxes: Total city taxes per capita: $87 (1997); City property taxes per capita: $87 (1997).
Education: High school graduation rate: 98.3% (2000); College graduation rate: 21.8% (2000).
Housing: Homeownership rate: 90.5% (2000); Median home value: $118,800 (2000); Median age of housing: 60+ years (2000).
Transportation: Commute to work: 84.7% car, 0.0% public transportation, 0.0% walk, 15.3% work from home (2000); Travel time to work: 27.7% less than 15 minutes, 47.0% 15 to 30 minutes, 10.8% 30 to 45 minutes, 0.0% 45 to 60 minutes, 14.5% 60 minutes or more (2000)

WATSON (city). Covers a land area of 0.176 square miles and a water area of 0 square miles. Located at 45.01° N. Lat.; 95.80° W. Long. Elevation is 1,031 feet.
Population: 209 (2000); Race: 100.0% White, 0.0% Black, 0.0% Asian, 0.0% American Indian and Alaska Native, 0.0% Hispanic of any race, 0.0% two or more races (2000); Density: 1,186.3 persons per square mile (2000); Age: 29.2% under 18, 11.1% over 64 (2000); Marriage status: 27.5% never married, 52.1% now married, 11.4% widowed, 9.0% divorced (2000); Foreign born: 0.4% (2000); Ancestry (includes multiple ancestries): 47.8%

Norwegian, 29.6% German, 8.8% Swedish, 8.0% Polish, 7.5% United States or American (2000).
Economy: Agricultural area: grain, soybeans, sugar beets; hogs, sheep. Single-family building permits issued: 0 (2001) / 0 (2000); Multi-family building permits issued: 0 (2001) / 0 (2000); Employment by occupation: 9.7% management, 6.2% professional, 25.7% services, 7.1% sales, 0.0% farming, 22.1% construction, 29.2% production (2000).
Income: Per capita income: $14,617 (2000); Median household income: $34,688 (2000); Poverty rate: 13.0% (2000).
Taxes: Total city taxes per capita: $246 (1997); City property taxes per capita: $236 (1997).
Education: High school graduation rate: 78.5% (2000); College graduation rate: 0.0% (2000).
Housing: Homeownership rate: 75.6% (2000); Median home value: $35,000 (2000); Median rent: $180 per month (2000); Median age of housing: 60+ years (2000).
Transportation: Commute to work: 92.9% car, 0.0% public transportation, 3.5% walk, 3.5% work from home (2000); Travel time to work: 26.6% less than 15 minutes, 45.9% 15 to 30 minutes, 5.5% 30 to 45 minutes, 9.2% 45 to 60 minutes, 12.8% 60 minutes or more (2000)

WOODS (township). Covers a land area of 36.178 square miles and a water area of 0.015 square miles. Located at 45.11° N. Lat.; 95.31° W. Long.
Population: 242 (2000); Race: 93.6% White, 0.9% Black, 0.0% Asian, 0.0% American Indian and Alaska Native, 5.5% Hispanic of any race, 0.9% two or more races (2000); Density: 6.7 persons per square mile (2000); Age: 31.5% under 18, 8.9% over 64 (2000); Marriage status: 18.5% never married, 76.8% now married, 1.2% widowed, 3.6% divorced (2000); Foreign born: 3.8% (2000); Ancestry (includes multiple ancestries): 47.2% German, 18.3% Norwegian, 12.8% Swedish, 9.8% Other groups, 7.7% Dutch (2000).
Economy: Employment by occupation: 23.6% management, 9.8% professional, 8.9% services, 26.0% sales, 5.7% farming, 6.5% construction, 19.5% production (2000).
Income: Per capita income: $39,374 (2000); Median household income: $44,375 (2000); Poverty rate: 6.8% (2000).
Taxes: Total city taxes per capita: $158 (1997); City property taxes per capita: $158 (1997).
Education: High school graduation rate: 82.7% (2000); College graduation rate: 8.6% (2000).
Housing: Homeownership rate: 66.2% (2000); Median home value: $73,800 (2000); Median rent: $392 per month (2000); Median age of housing: 59 years (2000).
Transportation: Commute to work: 74.0% car, 0.0% public transportation, 0.0% walk, 24.4% work from home (2000); Travel time to work: 9.7% less than 15 minutes, 65.6% 15 to 30 minutes, 18.3% 30 to 45 minutes, 2.2% 45 to 60 minutes, 4.3% 60 minutes or more (2000)

Chisago County

Located in eastern Minnesota; bounded on the east by the St. Croix River and the Wisconsin border; watered in the south by many small lakes. Covers a land area of 417.60 square miles, a water area of 24.90 square miles, and is located in the Central Time Zone. The county government was organized in 1851. County seat is Center City.

Chisago County is part of the Minneapolis-St. Paul, MN-WI MSA. The entire metro area includes: Anoka County, MN; Carver County, MN; Chisago County, MN; Dakota County, MN; Hennepin County, MN; Isanti County, MN; Ramsey County, MN; Scott County, MN; Sherburne County, MN; Washington County, MN; Wright County, MN; Pierce County, WI; St. Croix County, WI

Weather Station: Forest Lake 5 NE — Elevation: 958 feet

	Jan	Feb	Mar	Apr	May	Jun	Jul	Aug	Sep	Oct	Nov	Dec
High	22	29	41	57	71	78	82	80	71	59	40	27
Low	2	9	21	35	47	57	61	60	50	39	24	10
Precip	1.0	0.8	1.6	2.4	3.5	4.6	4.5	4.6	3.3	2.7	1.9	1.0
Snow	10.4	6.5	8.9	3.0	tr	0.0	0.0	0.0	tr	0.3	8.6	8.9

High and Low temperatures in degrees Fahrenheit; Precipitation and Snow in inches

Population: 41,101 (2000); Race: 96.7% White, 0.4% Black, 0.7% Asian, 1.0% American Indian and Alaska Native, 0.9% Hispanic of any race, 0.9% two or more races (2000); Density: 98.4 persons per square mile (2000); Age: 30.1% under 18, 9.8% over 64 (2000).
Religion: Five largest groups: 23.2% Evangelical Lutheran Church in America, 15.4% Catholic Church, 2.3% The United Methodist Church, 2.0% Lutheran Church—Missouri Synod, 1.7% The Evangelical Free Church of America (2000).
Economy: Unemployment rate: 4.4% (11/2002); Total civilian labor force: 22,930 (11/2002); Leading industries: 24.5% health care and social assistance; 20.0% manufacturing; 16.6% retail trade (2000); Companies that employ more than 1,000 persons: 0 (2000); Companies that employ more than 100 persons: 13 (2000); Farms: 762 totaling 121,527 acres (1997); Minority business ownership rate: 0.0% (1997); Women business ownership rate: 20.9% (1997); Retail sales per capita: $5,609 (1997). Single-family building permits issued: 683 (2001) / 635 (2000); Multi-family building permits issued: 4 (2001) / 24 (2000).
Income: Per capita income: $21,013 (2000); Median household income: $52,012 (2000); Poverty rate: 5.1% (2000); Bankruptcy rate: 4.29% (2001).
Taxes: Total county taxes per capita: $316 (2000); County property taxes per capita: $302 (2000).
Education: High school graduation rate: 88.7% (2000); College graduation rate: 15.3% (2000).
Housing: Homeownership rate: 87.0% (2000); Median home value: $132,500 (2000); Median rent: $450 per month (2000); Median age of housing: 20 years (2000).
Health: Birth rate: 139.9 per 10,000 population (1998); Age adjusted death rate: 79.7 per 10,000 population (1999); Age adjusted cancer mortality rate: 207.0 deaths per 100,000 population (1999). Number of physicians: 7.8 per 10,000 population (1999); Number of hospital beds: 9.2 per 10,000 population (1999).
Elections: 2000 Presidential election results: 43.6% Gore, 49.7% Bush, 5.1% Nader, 1.1% Buchanan
National and State Parks: Interstate State Park; Saint Croix National Scenic River; Saint Croix Wild River State Park
Additional Information Contacts
Chisago County Government Offices 651-257-1300
North Branch Chamber of Cmmrc 651-674-4077
Rush City Chamber of Commerce 320-358-4743
Taylors Falls Chamber of Commerce 651-465-6661

Chisago County Communities

AMADOR (township). Covers a land area of 29.938 square miles and a water area of 0.645 square miles. Located at 45.50° N. Lat.; 92.76° W. Long.
Population: 744 (2000); Race: 98.3% White, 0.7% Black, 0.0% Asian, 0.3% American Indian and Alaska Native, 0.7% Hispanic of any race, 0.3% two or more races (2000); Density: 24.9 persons per square mile (2000); Age: 28.4% under 18, 7.9% over 64 (2000); Marriage status: 24.5% never married, 62.8% now married, 4.1% widowed, 8.6% divorced (2000); Foreign born: 0.6% (2000); Ancestry (includes multiple ancestries): 37.5% Swedish, 35.2% German, 14.8% Norwegian, 7.6% French (except Basque), 7.2% Irish (2000).
Economy: Employment by occupation: 18.8% management, 12.8% professional, 11.7% services, 17.8% sales, 0.0% farming, 20.4% construction, 18.5% production (2000).
Income: Per capita income: $22,759 (2000); Median household income: $55,000 (2000); Poverty rate: 2.5% (2000).
Education: High school graduation rate: 87.2% (2000); College graduation rate: 11.7% (2000).
Housing: Homeownership rate: 96.1% (2000); Median home value: $94,100 (2000); Median rent: $625 per month (2000); Median age of housing: 54 years (2000).
Transportation: Commute to work: 85.0% car, 0.5% public transportation, 3.5% walk, 9.4% work from home (2000); Travel time to work: 18.3% less than 15 minutes, 34.5% 15 to 30 minutes, 11.2% 30 to 45 minutes, 15.6% 45 to 60 minutes, 20.4% 60 minutes or more (2000)

CENTER CITY (city). Covers a land area of 0.469 square miles and a water area of 0.010 square miles. Located at 45.39° N. Lat.; 92.81° W. Long. Elevation is 901 feet.
History: Important Swedish settlement.
Population: 582 (2000); Race: 93.2% White, 1.4% Black, 0.0% Asian, 4.4% American Indian and Alaska Native, 0.6% Hispanic of any race, 1.1% two or more races (2000); Density: 1,240.8 persons per square mile (2000); Age: 25.5% under 18, 13.7% over 64 (2000); Marriage status: 30.1% never married, 61.0% now married, 1.4% widowed, 7.6% divorced (2000); Foreign born: 2.3% (2000); Ancestry (includes multiple ancestries): 32.8% German, 16.4% Swedish, 15.8% Norwegian, 12.6% Irish, 4.1% Italian (2000).
Economy: In region of resorts and lakes; grain; cattle, poultry; dairying. Manufacturing: cheese. Single-family building permits issued: 0 (2001) / 1 (2000); Multi-family building permits issued: 0 (2001) / 0 (2000);

Employment by occupation: 12.1% management, 18.2% professional, 15.8% services, 24.2% sales, 1.0% farming, 9.4% construction, 19.2% production (2000).
Income: Per capita income: $17,774 (2000); Median household income: $48,594 (2000); Poverty rate: 5.5% (2000).
Taxes: Total city taxes per capita: $147 (1997); City property taxes per capita: $101 (1997).
Education: High school graduation rate: 82.1% (2000); College graduation rate: 18.8% (2000).

Four-year College(s)

Hazelden Foundation (Private, Not-for-profit)
2001 Enrollment: n/a 651-213-4000
Housing: Homeownership rate: 92.2% (2000); Median home value: $140,100 (2000); Median rent: $388 per month (2000); Median age of housing: 44 years (2000).
Transportation: Commute to work: 95.9% car, 0.0% public transportation, 0.7% walk, 2.0% work from home (2000); Travel time to work: 28.6% less than 15 minutes, 21.0% 15 to 30 minutes, 12.8% 30 to 45 minutes, 20.0% 45 to 60 minutes, 17.6% 60 minutes or more (2000)

CHISAGO CITY (city). Covers a land area of 1.973 square miles and a water area of 0.045 square miles. Located at 45.36° N. Lat.; 92.88° W. Long.
History: Settlement of the Chisago area began in 1850. The first settlers came from Illinois and Missouri, but they were followed by an influx of immigrants from Sweden, and the area became the center of Swedish culture and religion in Minnesota.
Population: 2,622 (2000); Race: 96.5% White, 0.4% Black, 0.6% Asian, 0.6% American Indian and Alaska Native, 0.9% Hispanic of any race, 1.5% two or more races (2000); Density: 1,329.0 persons per square mile (2000); Age: 23.9% under 18, 23.0% over 64 (2000); Marriage status: 24.1% never married, 51.3% now married, 15.7% widowed, 8.8% divorced (2000); Foreign born: 1.2% (2000); Ancestry (includes multiple ancestries): 38.8% German, 20.0% Swedish, 14.0% Norwegian, 13.2% Irish, 7.4% French (except Basque) (2000).
Economy: Single-family building permits issued: 60 (2001) / 48 (2000); Multi-family building permits issued: 0 (2001) / 0 (2000); Employment by occupation: 10.9% management, 17.6% professional, 18.3% services, 25.4% sales, 0.8% farming, 7.3% construction, 19.7% production (2000).
Income: Per capita income: $22,321 (2000); Median household income: $38,352 (2000); Poverty rate: 6.0% (2000).
Taxes: Total city taxes per capita: $272 (1997); City property taxes per capita: $224 (1997).
Education: High school graduation rate: 83.5% (2000); College graduation rate: 15.9% (2000).

School District(s)

Summit School for the Arts (N -N)
2000 Enrollment: n/a 651-257-6369
Housing: Homeownership rate: 60.3% (2000); Median home value: $127,200 (2000); Median rent: $556 per month (2000); Median age of housing: 19 years (2000).
Transportation: Commute to work: 92.3% car, 0.0% public transportation, 1.6% walk, 3.3% work from home (2000); Travel time to work: 29.3% less than 15 minutes, 24.2% 15 to 30 minutes, 19.0% 30 to 45 minutes, 17.2% 45 to 60 minutes, 10.3% 60 minutes or more (2000)

CHISAGO LAKE (township). Covers a land area of 46.216 square miles and a water area of 8.316 square miles. Located at 45.39° N. Lat.; 92.85° W. Long.
Population: 3,276 (2000); Race: 98.7% White, 0.4% Black, 0.1% Asian, 0.4% American Indian and Alaska Native, 0.9% Hispanic of any race, 0.4% two or more races (2000); Density: 70.9 persons per square mile (2000); Age: 31.8% under 18, 7.2% over 64 (2000); Marriage status: 16.1% never married, 73.0% now married, 2.9% widowed, 8.1% divorced (2000); Foreign born: 0.5% (2000); Ancestry (includes multiple ancestries): 42.7% German, 25.0% Swedish, 16.0% Norwegian, 11.7% Irish, 7.5% English (2000).
Economy: Employment by occupation: 22.1% management, 17.5% professional, 10.2% services, 23.2% sales, 0.3% farming, 12.1% construction, 14.6% production (2000).
Income: Per capita income: $23,019 (2000); Median household income: $65,858 (2000); Poverty rate: 1.8% (2000).
Taxes: Total city taxes per capita: $87 (2000); City property taxes per capita: $86 (2000).
Education: High school graduation rate: 94.8% (2000); College graduation rate: 23.0% (2000).
Housing: Homeownership rate: 95.5% (2000); Median home value: $172,100 (2000); Median rent: $506 per month (2000); Median age of housing: 21 years (2000).
Transportation: Commute to work: 93.2% car, 0.5% public transportation, 0.2% walk, 4.9% work from home (2000); Travel time to work: 16.2% less than 15 minutes, 20.6% 15 to 30 minutes, 21.8% 30 to 45 minutes, 29.6% 45 to 60 minutes, 11.9% 60 minutes or more (2000)

FISH LAKE (township). Covers a land area of 32.345 square miles and a water area of 2.319 square miles. Located at 45.60° N. Lat.; 93.08° W. Long.
Population: 1,723 (2000); Race: 98.5% White, 0.2% Black, 0.0% Asian, 0.6% American Indian and Alaska Native, 0.9% Hispanic of any race, 0.7% two or more races (2000); Density: 53.3 persons per square mile (2000); Age: 27.8% under 18, 10.0% over 64 (2000); Marriage status: 22.6% never married, 66.0% now married, 3.0% widowed, 8.3% divorced (2000); Foreign born: 1.0% (2000); Ancestry (includes multiple ancestries): 34.8% German, 29.1% Swedish, 16.5% Norwegian, 9.5% Irish, 6.5% English (2000).
Economy: Employment by occupation: 10.6% management, 16.2% professional, 13.5% services, 21.5% sales, 0.0% farming, 18.7% construction, 19.5% production (2000).
Income: Per capita income: $22,051 (2000); Median household income: $54,297 (2000); Poverty rate: 4.1% (2000).
Taxes: Total city taxes per capita: $64 (1997); City property taxes per capita: $64 (1997).
Education: High school graduation rate: 86.4% (2000); College graduation rate: 12.7% (2000).
Housing: Homeownership rate: 93.5% (2000); Median home value: $122,600 (2000); Median rent: $450 per month (2000); Median age of housing: 25 years (2000).
Transportation: Commute to work: 94.1% car, 0.2% public transportation, 2.1% walk, 3.0% work from home (2000); Travel time to work: 16.2% less than 15 minutes, 26.0% 15 to 30 minutes, 11.6% 30 to 45 minutes, 20.3% 45 to 60 minutes, 25.8% 60 minutes or more (2000)

FRANCONIA (township). Covers a land area of 30.537 square miles and a water area of 1.418 square miles. Located at 45.35° N. Lat.; 92.75° W. Long.
Population: 1,128 (2000); Race: 98.8% White, 0.0% Black, 0.0% Asian, 0.8% American Indian and Alaska Native, 0.7% Hispanic of any race, 0.4% two or more races (2000); Density: 36.9 persons per square mile (2000); Age: 32.4% under 18, 6.2% over 64 (2000); Marriage status: 24.7% never married, 57.8% now married, 1.3% widowed, 16.2% divorced (2000); Foreign born: 0.7% (2000); Ancestry (includes multiple ancestries): 42.8% German, 15.8% Swedish, 14.2% Norwegian, 12.7% Irish, 7.4% French (except Basque) (2000).
Economy: Employment by occupation: 18.5% management, 19.8% professional, 11.6% services, 19.7% sales, 0.0% farming, 17.4% construction, 13.0% production (2000).
Income: Per capita income: $25,233 (2000); Median household income: $68,125 (2000); Poverty rate: 0.9% (2000).
Taxes: Total city taxes per capita: $91 (1997); City property taxes per capita: $91 (1997).
Education: High school graduation rate: 95.4% (2000); College graduation rate: 25.8% (2000).
Housing: Homeownership rate: 92.6% (2000); Median home value: $177,300 (2000); Median rent: $458 per month (2000); Median age of housing: 21 years (2000).
Transportation: Commute to work: 89.6% car, 0.6% public transportation, 1.4% walk, 8.5% work from home (2000); Travel time to work: 16.5% less than 15 minutes, 13.5% 15 to 30 minutes, 25.2% 30 to 45 minutes, 32.3% 45 to 60 minutes, 12.5% 60 minutes or more (2000)

HARRIS (city). Covers a land area of 19.767 square miles and a water area of 0.084 square miles. Located at 45.59° N. Lat.; 92.98° W. Long. Elevation is 902 feet.
Population: 1,121 (2000); Race: 97.4% White, 0.0% Black, 0.0% Asian, 1.2% American Indian and Alaska Native, 1.4% Hispanic of any race, 1.3% two or more races (2000); Density: 56.7 persons per square mile (2000); Age: 31.9% under 18, 8.0% over 64 (2000); Marriage status: 26.1% never married, 59.2% now married, 3.5% widowed, 11.3% divorced (2000); Foreign born: 0.4% (2000); Ancestry (includes multiple ancestries): 37.4% German, 29.5% Swedish, 17.2% Norwegian, 10.8% Irish, 4.9% French (except Basque) (2000).
Economy: Employment by occupation: 11.3% management, 12.7% professional, 16.6% services, 18.7% sales, 1.4% farming, 15.1% construction, 24.3% production (2000).

Income: Per capita income: $18,258 (2000); Median household income: $49,545 (2000); Poverty rate: 4.9% (2000).
Taxes: Total city taxes per capita: $146 (1997); City property taxes per capita: $118 (1997).
Education: High school graduation rate: 86.5% (2000); College graduation rate: 9.1% (2000).
Housing: Homeownership rate: 90.2% (2000); Median home value: $107,100 (2000); Median rent: $213 per month (2000); Median age of housing: 25 years (2000).
Transportation: Commute to work: 92.4% car, 0.0% public transportation, 0.9% walk, 5.2% work from home (2000); Travel time to work: 29.6% less than 15 minutes, 24.0% 15 to 30 minutes, 13.8% 30 to 45 minutes, 19.3% 45 to 60 minutes, 13.3% 60 minutes or more (2000)

LENT (township). Covers a land area of 33.233 square miles and a water area of 2.203 square miles. Located at 45.41° N. Lat.; 92.96° W. Long.
Population: 1,992 (2000); Race: 97.9% White, 0.0% Black, 0.4% Asian, 0.3% American Indian and Alaska Native, 1.3% Hispanic of any race, 1.3% two or more races (2000); Density: 59.9 persons per square mile (2000); Age: 31.5% under 18, 3.2% over 64 (2000); Marriage status: 24.7% never married, 68.3% now married, 1.3% widowed, 5.6% divorced (2000); Foreign born: 1.1% (2000); Ancestry (includes multiple ancestries): 39.0% German, 16.4% Swedish, 14.2% Irish, 13.8% Norwegian, 7.1% French (except Basque) (2000).
Economy: Employment by occupation: 10.4% management, 12.1% professional, 12.0% services, 27.4% sales, 0.0% farming, 15.3% construction, 22.7% production (2000).
Income: Per capita income: $22,089 (2000); Median household income: $61,163 (2000); Poverty rate: 1.2% (2000).
Taxes: Total city taxes per capita: $145 (2000); City property taxes per capita: $137 (2000).
Education: High school graduation rate: 93.5% (2000); College graduation rate: 12.0% (2000).
Housing: Homeownership rate: 96.4% (2000); Median home value: $147,100 (2000); Median rent: $375 per month (2000); Median age of housing: 16 years (2000).
Transportation: Commute to work: 95.6% car, 0.0% public transportation, 0.3% walk, 3.9% work from home (2000); Travel time to work: 18.8% less than 15 minutes, 18.7% 15 to 30 minutes, 30.4% 30 to 45 minutes, 20.5% 45 to 60 minutes, 11.5% 60 minutes or more (2000)

LINDSTROM (city). Covers a land area of 2.263 square miles and a water area of 0.046 square miles. Located at 45.38° N. Lat.; 92.84° W. Long.
History: Early Swedish settlement.
Population: 3,015 (2000); Race: 98.9% White, 0.0% Black, 0.0% Asian, 0.2% American Indian and Alaska Native, 0.3% Hispanic of any race, 0.6% two or more races (2000); Density: 1,332.1 persons per square mile (2000); Age: 25.3% under 18, 17.5% over 64 (2000); Marriage status: 23.1% never married, 65.1% now married, 4.8% widowed, 7.0% divorced (2000); Foreign born: 0.3% (2000); Ancestry (includes multiple ancestries): 34.5% German, 23.7% Swedish, 16.7% Norwegian, 9.8% Irish, 9.3% French (except Basque) (2000).
Economy: Agricultural area: grain; cattle, poultry, dairying. Manufacturing: food products, plastic products, consumer goods, printing and publishing. Single-family building permits issued: 89 (2001) / 58 (2000); Multi-family building permits issued: 0 (2001) / 0 (2000); Employment by occupation: 12.5% management, 22.6% professional, 17.4% services, 23.6% sales, 0.0% farming, 8.3% construction, 15.6% production (2000).
Income: Per capita income: $21,195 (2000); Median household income: $44,980 (2000); Poverty rate: 8.0% (2000).
Taxes: Total city taxes per capita: $165 (1997); City property taxes per capita: $147 (1997).
Education: High school graduation rate: 89.5% (2000); College graduation rate: 17.9% (2000).

School District(s)

Chisago Lakes (PK-12)
2000 Enrollment: 3,578 651-213-2000

Housing: Homeownership rate: 84.9% (2000); Median home value: $124,400 (2000); Median rent: $443 per month (2000); Median age of housing: 25 years (2000).
Safety: Violent crime rate: 23.0 per 10,000 population; Property crime rate: 328.2 per 10,000 population (2001).
Newspapers: Chisago County Press (1 x week); Search Shopping Guide (1 x week)
Transportation: Commute to work: 94.2% car, 0.0% public transportation, 1.3% walk, 2.1% work from home (2000); Travel time to work: 30.8% less than 15 minutes, 18.5% 15 to 30 minutes, 14.6% 30 to 45 minutes, 22.8% 45 to 60 minutes, 13.2% 60 minutes or more (2000)

NESSEL (township). Covers a land area of 38.112 square miles and a water area of 5.070 square miles. Located at 45.68° N. Lat.; 93.07° W. Long.
Population: 1,765 (2000); Race: 98.8% White, 0.0% Black, 0.3% Asian, 0.5% American Indian and Alaska Native, 0.5% Hispanic of any race, 0.4% two or more races (2000); Density: 46.3 persons per square mile (2000); Age: 25.7% under 18, 15.3% over 64 (2000); Marriage status: 20.1% never married, 66.5% now married, 4.4% widowed, 9.1% divorced (2000); Foreign born: 0.9% (2000); Ancestry (includes multiple ancestries): 41.5% German, 22.0% Swedish, 14.6% Norwegian, 13.1% Irish, 6.4% English (2000).
Economy: Employment by occupation: 12.6% management, 13.9% professional, 9.9% services, 28.4% sales, 2.1% farming, 13.1% construction, 20.0% production (2000).
Income: Per capita income: $20,953 (2000); Median household income: $47,578 (2000); Poverty rate: 5.3% (2000).
Taxes: Total city taxes per capita: $75 (1997); City property taxes per capita: $75 (1997).
Education: High school graduation rate: 87.4% (2000); College graduation rate: 13.0% (2000).
Housing: Homeownership rate: 96.2% (2000); Median home value: $128,700 (2000); Median rent: $438 per month (2000); Median age of housing: 32 years (2000).
Transportation: Commute to work: 91.9% car, 0.2% public transportation, 0.5% walk, 6.2% work from home (2000); Travel time to work: 22.1% less than 15 minutes, 21.5% 15 to 30 minutes, 11.3% 30 to 45 minutes, 16.5% 45 to 60 minutes, 28.6% 60 minutes or more (2000)

NORTH BRANCH (city). Covers a land area of 35.676 square miles and a water area of 0.336 square miles. Located at 45.51° N. Lat.; 92.98° W. Long. Elevation is 896 feet.
Population: 8,023 (2000); Race: 95.7% White, 0.3% Black, 1.2% Asian, 1.9% American Indian and Alaska Native, 0.7% Hispanic of any race, 0.6% two or more races (2000); Density: 224.9 persons per square mile (2000); Age: 32.6% under 18, 8.1% over 64 (2000); Marriage status: 21.0% never married, 63.3% now married, 5.0% widowed, 10.7% divorced (2000); Foreign born: 1.6% (2000); Ancestry (includes multiple ancestries): 30.8% German, 21.6% Swedish, 13.0% Norwegian, 9.8% Irish, 6.4% Other groups (2000).
Economy: Grain; cattle, poultry; dairying. Manufacturing: metal stampings, feed ingredients, concrete, mops, tool and die, physical training devices; grain mill. Single-family building permits issued: 156 (2001) / 184 (2000); Multi-family building permits issued: 0 (2001) / 16 (2000); Employment by occupation: 11.6% management, 15.6% professional, 13.3% services, 27.4% sales, 0.5% farming, 11.1% construction, 20.6% production (2000).
Income: Per capita income: $20,875 (2000); Median household income: $50,294 (2000); Poverty rate: 5.0% (2000).
Taxes: Total city taxes per capita: $466 (1997); City property taxes per capita: $383 (1997).
Education: High school graduation rate: 88.6% (2000); College graduation rate: 12.8% (2000).

School District(s)

North Branch (PK-12)
2000 Enrollment: 3,746 651-674-1000

Housing: Homeownership rate: 87.0% (2000); Median home value: $124,500 (2000); Median rent: $423 per month (2000); Median age of housing: 11 years (2000).
Newspapers: ECM Post Review (1 x week)
Transportation: Commute to work: 95.8% car, 0.0% public transportation, 0.7% walk, 3.1% work from home (2000); Travel time to work: 28.2% less than 15 minutes, 20.8% 15 to 30 minutes, 20.1% 30 to 45 minutes, 19.9% 45 to 60 minutes, 11.1% 60 minutes or more (2000)
Additional Information Contacts
North Branch Chamber of Cmmrc 651-674-4077

RUSH CITY (city). Covers a land area of 3.048 square miles and a water area of 0.008 square miles. Located at 45.68° N. Lat.; 92.96° W. Long. Elevation is 917 feet.
History: Settled before 1873.
Population: 2,102 (2000); Race: 89.6% White, 2.7% Black, 1.1% Asian, 3.4% American Indian and Alaska Native, 2.6% Hispanic of any race, 0.9% two or more races (2000); Density: 689.6 persons per square mile (2000); Age: 25.9% under 18, 13.5% over 64 (2000); Marriage status: 29.5% never married, 45.7% now married, 8.3% widowed, 16.5% divorced (2000); Foreign born: 3.5% (2000); Ancestry (includes multiple ancestries): 36.7%

German, 19.9% Swedish, 11.2% Norwegian, 10.9% Irish, 8.2% Other groups (2000).
Economy: In agricultural region: grain; cattle, poultry; dairying. Manufacturing: printed circuit boards, plastic molds. St. Croix National Scenic Riverway to East. Employment by occupation: 7.4% management, 14.0% professional, 14.2% services, 25.3% sales, 0.3% farming, 13.4% construction, 25.2% production (2000).
Income: Per capita income: $14,668 (2000); Median household income: $34,219 (2000); Poverty rate: 11.6% (2000).
Taxes: Total city taxes per capita: $360 (1997); City property taxes per capita: $353 (1997).
Education: High school graduation rate: 78.8% (2000); College graduation rate: 9.0% (2000).

School District(s)

Rush City (PK-12)
2000 Enrollment: 974 320-358-4855
Housing: Homeownership rate: 64.1% (2000); Median home value: $83,800 (2000); Median rent: $403 per month (2000); Median age of housing: 29 years (2000).
Hospitals: Rush City Hospital & Clinic (29 beds)
Transportation: Commute to work: 91.0% car, 0.0% public transportation, 5.3% walk, 3.3% work from home (2000); Travel time to work: 42.1% less than 15 minutes, 23.2% 15 to 30 minutes, 11.6% 30 to 45 minutes, 9.8% 45 to 60 minutes, 13.3% 60 minutes or more (2000)
Additional Information Contacts
Rush City Chamber of Commerce 320-358-4743

RUSHSEBA (township). Covers a land area of 30.783 square miles and a water area of 0.419 square miles. Located at 45.68° N. Lat.; 92.93° W. Long.
Population: 769 (2000); Race: 99.0% White, 0.0% Black, 0.1% Asian, 0.0% American Indian and Alaska Native, 1.5% Hispanic of any race, 0.1% two or more races (2000); Density: 25.0 persons per square mile (2000); Age: 27.8% under 18, 11.1% over 64 (2000); Marriage status: 22.5% never married, 66.1% now married, 4.0% widowed, 7.5% divorced (2000); Foreign born: 0.3% (2000); Ancestry (includes multiple ancestries): 41.2% German, 24.7% Swedish, 17.8% Norwegian, 6.2% Irish, 5.3% French (except Basque) (2000).
Economy: Employment by occupation: 13.9% management, 14.4% professional, 16.8% services, 20.6% sales, 5.1% farming, 12.2% construction, 17.0% production (2000).
Income: Per capita income: $19,727 (2000); Median household income: $47,917 (2000); Poverty rate: 5.6% (2000).
Taxes: Total city taxes per capita: $54 (1997); City property taxes per capita: $54 (1997).
Education: High school graduation rate: 90.0% (2000); College graduation rate: 11.0% (2000).
Housing: Homeownership rate: 93.5% (2000); Median home value: $107,200 (2000); Median rent: $375 per month (2000); Median age of housing: 38 years (2000).
Transportation: Commute to work: 86.6% car, 0.0% public transportation, 0.4% walk, 12.9% work from home (2000); Travel time to work: 32.8% less than 15 minutes, 16.9% 15 to 30 minutes, 16.7% 30 to 45 minutes, 6.9% 45 to 60 minutes, 26.7% 60 minutes or more (2000)

SHAFER (city). Covers a land area of 0.634 square miles and a water area of 0 square miles. Located at 45.38° N. Lat.; 92.74° W. Long.
Population: 343 (2000); Race: 96.9% White, 0.0% Black, 0.0% Asian, 0.6% American Indian and Alaska Native, 2.6% Hispanic of any race, 2.0% two or more races (2000); Density: 540.7 persons per square mile (2000); Age: 33.7% under 18, 5.1% over 64 (2000); Marriage status: 33.6% never married, 53.0% now married, 2.0% widowed, 11.5% divorced (2000); Foreign born: 0.0% (2000); Ancestry (includes multiple ancestries): 41.7% German, 18.3% Norwegian, 17.4% Swedish, 10.3% Polish, 8.9% Irish (2000).
Economy: Employment by occupation: 5.2% management, 13.4% professional, 20.1% services, 15.5% sales, 0.5% farming, 16.0% construction, 29.4% production (2000).
Income: Per capita income: $17,561 (2000); Median household income: $41,667 (2000); Poverty rate: 9.1% (2000).
Taxes: Total city taxes per capita: $262 (1997); City property taxes per capita: $249 (1997).
Education: High school graduation rate: 78.5% (2000); College graduation rate: 5.9% (2000).
Housing: Homeownership rate: 90.5% (2000); Median home value: $105,000 (2000); Median rent: $410 per month (2000); Median age of housing: 22 years (2000).
Transportation: Commute to work: 91.6% car, 2.1% public transportation, 2.1% walk, 0.0% work from home (2000); Travel time to work: 32.6% less than 15 minutes, 19.5% 15 to 30 minutes, 13.2% 30 to 45 minutes, 15.8% 45 to 60 minutes, 18.9% 60 minutes or more (2000)

SHAFER (township). Covers a land area of 29.967 square miles and a water area of 0.300 square miles. Located at 45.42° N. Lat.; 92.70° W. Long.
Population: 646 (2000); Race: 98.4% White, 0.0% Black, 0.7% Asian, 0.0% American Indian and Alaska Native, 0.3% Hispanic of any race, 0.9% two or more races (2000); Density: 21.6 persons per square mile (2000); Age: 29.9% under 18, 9.9% over 64 (2000); Marriage status: 22.6% never married, 67.7% now married, 3.9% widowed, 5.8% divorced (2000); Foreign born: 1.2% (2000); Ancestry (includes multiple ancestries): 37.8% German, 30.5% Swedish, 11.2% Norwegian, 9.1% English, 8.8% French (except Basque) (2000).
Economy: Agriculture: dairying; poultry, cattle; grain. Manufacturing: plastic coatings, electronic subassembly. Employment by occupation: 16.0% management, 16.0% professional, 14.8% services, 22.5% sales, 0.3% farming, 10.8% construction, 19.7% production (2000).
Income: Per capita income: $20,983 (2000); Median household income: $59,375 (2000); Poverty rate: 1.9% (2000).
Taxes: Total city taxes per capita: $73 (1997); City property taxes per capita: $73 (1997).
Education: High school graduation rate: 89.5% (2000); College graduation rate: 13.6% (2000).
Housing: Homeownership rate: 96.9% (2000); Median home value: $152,100 (2000); Median rent: $563 per month (2000); Median age of housing: 27 years (2000).
Transportation: Commute to work: 91.1% car, 0.3% public transportation, 0.0% walk, 6.6% work from home (2000); Travel time to work: 26.7% less than 15 minutes, 26.4% 15 to 30 minutes, 10.4% 30 to 45 minutes, 21.5% 45 to 60 minutes, 15.0% 60 minutes or more (2000)

STACY (city). Covers a land area of 1.103 square miles and a water area of 0.046 square miles. Located at 45.39° N. Lat.; 92.98° W. Long. Elevation is 928 feet.
Population: 1,278 (2000); Race: 94.5% White, 1.1% Black, 0.2% Asian, 1.6% American Indian and Alaska Native, 0.7% Hispanic of any race, 2.6% two or more races (2000); Density: 1,159.0 persons per square mile (2000); Age: 33.0% under 18, 6.8% over 64 (2000); Marriage status: 31.6% never married, 50.6% now married, 5.8% widowed, 12.0% divorced (2000); Foreign born: 0.4% (2000); Ancestry (includes multiple ancestries): 34.0% German, 16.2% Norwegian, 12.4% Swedish, 10.6% Irish, 7.5% Other groups (2000).
Economy: Employment by occupation: 8.5% management, 9.1% professional, 14.6% services, 25.9% sales, 0.5% farming, 12.5% construction, 28.9% production (2000).
Income: Per capita income: $16,893 (2000); Median household income: $42,026 (2000); Poverty rate: 9.4% (2000).
Taxes: Total city taxes per capita: $47 (1997); City property taxes per capita: $42 (1997).
Education: High school graduation rate: 84.3% (2000); College graduation rate: 8.5% (2000).
Housing: Homeownership rate: 90.2% (2000); Median home value: $118,800 (2000); Median rent: $438 per month (2000); Median age of housing: 20 years (2000).
Transportation: Commute to work: 97.3% car, 0.3% public transportation, 0.5% walk, 1.2% work from home (2000); Travel time to work: 14.1% less than 15 minutes, 28.4% 15 to 30 minutes, 36.1% 30 to 45 minutes, 12.4% 45 to 60 minutes, 8.9% 60 minutes or more (2000)

SUNRISE (township). Covers a land area of 45.338 square miles and a water area of 0.594 square miles. Located at 45.54° N. Lat.; 92.88° W. Long. Elevation is 811 feet.
Population: 1,594 (2000); Race: 98.1% White, 0.9% Black, 0.2% Asian, 0.0% American Indian and Alaska Native, 0.2% Hispanic of any race, 0.7% two or more races (2000); Density: 35.2 persons per square mile (2000); Age: 30.1% under 18, 7.0% over 64 (2000); Marriage status: 22.2% never married, 69.3% now married, 2.9% widowed, 5.6% divorced (2000); Foreign born: 0.7% (2000); Ancestry (includes multiple ancestries): 37.1% German, 26.0% Swedish, 15.9% Norwegian, 13.4% Irish, 8.5% English (2000).
Economy: Employment by occupation: 9.1% management, 13.7% professional, 13.7% services, 24.1% sales, 1.2% farming, 16.2% construction, 22.0% production (2000).
Income: Per capita income: $22,336 (2000); Median household income: $60,223 (2000); Poverty rate: 4.2% (2000).

Taxes: Total city taxes per capita: $86 (2000); City property taxes per capita: $82 (2000).
Education: High school graduation rate: 90.5% (2000); College graduation rate: 14.4% (2000).
Housing: Homeownership rate: 95.4% (2000); Median home value: $131,700 (2000); Median rent: $392 per month (2000); Median age of housing: 24 years (2000).
Transportation: Commute to work: 90.1% car, 0.2% public transportation, 1.7% walk, 6.9% work from home (2000); Travel time to work: 16.1% less than 15 minutes, 25.9% 15 to 30 minutes, 20.3% 30 to 45 minutes, 19.8% 45 to 60 minutes, 17.9% 60 minutes or more (2000)

TAYLORS FALLS (city). Covers a land area of 3.721 square miles and a water area of 0.311 square miles. Located at 45.40° N. Lat.; 92.65° W. Long. Elevation is 744 feet.
History: Taylors Falls was named for Jesse Taylor, who came in 1838 to establish timber claims.
Population: 951 (2000); Race: 85.2% White, 0.0% Black, 11.2% Asian, 0.5% American Indian and Alaska Native, 1.9% Hispanic of any race, 1.2% two or more races (2000); Density: 255.6 persons per square mile (2000); Age: 29.9% under 18, 16.1% over 64 (2000); Marriage status: 28.0% never married, 52.5% now married, 7.7% widowed, 11.8% divorced (2000); Foreign born: 7.5% (2000); Ancestry (includes multiple ancestries): 28.2% German, 26.0% Swedish, 14.1% Norwegian, 12.4% Other groups, 9.1% Irish (2000).
Economy: Employment by occupation: 8.3% management, 17.7% professional, 18.9% services, 22.8% sales, 0.0% farming, 12.2% construction, 20.0% production (2000).
Income: Per capita income: $17,615 (2000); Median household income: $35,250 (2000); Poverty rate: 20.0% (2000).
Taxes: Total city taxes per capita: $298 (1997); City property taxes per capita: $284 (1997).
Education: High school graduation rate: 86.9% (2000); College graduation rate: 21.8% (2000).
Housing: Homeownership rate: 71.5% (2000); Median home value: $100,700 (2000); Median rent: $417 per month (2000); Median age of housing: 29 years (2000).
Transportation: Commute to work: 88.7% car, 0.0% public transportation, 4.6% walk, 6.7% work from home (2000); Travel time to work: 30.3% less than 15 minutes, 28.0% 15 to 30 minutes, 15.6% 30 to 45 minutes, 8.9% 45 to 60 minutes, 17.1% 60 minutes or more (2000)
Additional Information Contacts
Taylors Falls Chamber of Commerce 651-465-6661

WYOMING (city). Covers a land area of 2.849 square miles and a water area of 0.038 square miles. Located at 45.33° N. Lat.; 92.99° W. Long. Elevation is 905 feet.
Population: 3,048 (2000); Race: 98.6% White, 0.2% Black, 0.1% Asian, 0.1% American Indian and Alaska Native, 0.6% Hispanic of any race, 0.8% two or more races (2000); Density: 1,069.8 persons per square mile (2000); Age: 29.6% under 18, 6.6% over 64 (2000); Marriage status: 23.2% never married, 65.1% now married, 3.0% widowed, 8.6% divorced (2000); Foreign born: 0.6% (2000); Ancestry (includes multiple ancestries): 41.8% German, 16.9% Norwegian, 12.0% Swedish, 11.8% Irish, 9.5% English (2000).
Economy: Single-family building permits issued: 91 (2001) / 92 (2000); Multi-family building permits issued: 0 (2001) / 0 (2000); Employment by occupation: 13.7% management, 14.9% professional, 13.4% services, 31.9% sales, 0.0% farming, 11.9% construction, 14.2% production (2000).
Income: Per capita income: $20,290 (2000); Median household income: $56,192 (2000); Poverty rate: 5.5% (2000).
Taxes: Total city taxes per capita: $240 (1997); City property taxes per capita: $188 (1997).
Education: High school graduation rate: 88.7% (2000); College graduation rate: 18.4% (2000).
Housing: Homeownership rate: 80.8% (2000); Median home value: $136,900 (2000); Median rent: $385 per month (2000); Median age of housing: 15 years (2000).
Transportation: Commute to work: 94.9% car, 0.5% public transportation, 0.5% walk, 3.8% work from home (2000); Travel time to work: 23.4% less than 15 minutes, 22.9% 15 to 30 minutes, 35.0% 30 to 45 minutes, 14.5% 45 to 60 minutes, 4.2% 60 minutes or more (2000)

WYOMING (township). Covers a land area of 29.659 square miles and a water area of 2.649 square miles. Located at 45.33° N. Lat.; 92.95° W. Long. Elevation is 905 feet.
Population: 4,379 (2000); Race: 97.5% White, 0.1% Black, 0.2% Asian, 0.5% American Indian and Alaska Native, 0.8% Hispanic of any race, 1.4% two or more races (2000); Density: 147.6 persons per square mile (2000); Age: 34.3% under 18, 5.5% over 64 (2000); Marriage status: 17.9% never married, 73.2% now married, 2.7% widowed, 6.2% divorced (2000); Foreign born: 0.6% (2000); Ancestry (includes multiple ancestries): 42.2% German, 16.3% Swedish, 14.1% Irish, 10.5% Norwegian, 8.9% Polish (2000).
Economy: Agriculture: grain; cattle, poultry; dairying. Manufacturing: fabricated metal products, machinery, fiberglass products, transportation equipment, plastic products, fixtures. Single-family building permits issued: 35 (2001) / 19 (2000); Multi-family building permits issued: 0 (2001) / 0 (2000); Employment by occupation: 15.9% management, 16.7% professional, 12.7% services, 24.1% sales, 0.4% farming, 15.0% construction, 15.2% production (2000).
Income: Per capita income: $23,204 (2000); Median household income: $67,598 (2000); Poverty rate: 1.8% (2000).
Taxes: Total city taxes per capita: $142 (2000); City property taxes per capita: $95 (2000).
Education: High school graduation rate: 92.6% (2000); College graduation rate: 17.6% (2000).
Housing: Homeownership rate: 97.9% (2000); Median home value: $165,800 (2000); Median rent: $1,029 per month (2000); Median age of housing: 10 years (2000).
Transportation: Commute to work: 95.2% car, 0.0% public transportation, 0.8% walk, 3.7% work from home (2000); Travel time to work: 21.5% less than 15 minutes, 18.3% 15 to 30 minutes, 35.2% 30 to 45 minutes, 19.4% 45 to 60 minutes, 5.6% 60 minutes or more (2000)

Clay County

Located in western Minnesota; bounded on the west by the Red River of the North and the North Dakota border; drained by the Buffalo River. Covers a land area of 1,045.20 square miles, a water area of 7.50 square miles, and is located in the Central Time Zone. The county government was organized in 1862. County seat is Moorhead.

Clay County is part of the Fargo-Moorhead, ND-MN MSA. The entire metro area includes: Clay County, MN; Cass County, ND

Population: 51,229 (2000); Race: 93.9% White, 0.5% Black, 0.8% Asian, 1.3% American Indian and Alaska Native, 3.6% Hispanic of any race, 1.9% two or more races (2000); Density: 49.0 persons per square mile (2000); Age: 25.0% under 18, 13.0% over 64 (2000).
Religion: Five largest groups: 34.7% Evangelical Lutheran Church in America, 19.3% Catholic Church, 3.1% Lutheran Church—Missouri Synod, 1.8% United Church of Christ, 1.3% The United Methodist Church (2000).
Economy: Unemployment rate: 1.9% (11/2002); Total civilian labor force: 31,636 (11/2002); Leading industries: 20.0% retail trade; 13.5% health care and social assistance; 9.6% accommodation & food services (2000); Companies that employ more than 1,000 persons: 1 (2000); Companies that employ more than 100 persons: 20 (2000); Farms: 887 totaling 581,226 acres (1997); Minority business ownership rate: 0.0% (1997); Women business ownership rate: 33.6% (1997); Retail sales per capita: $8,867 (1997). Single-family building permits issued: 216 (2001) / 181 (2000); Multi-family building permits issued: 26 (2001) / 44 (2000).
Income: Per capita income: $17,557 (2000); Median household income: $37,889 (2000); Poverty rate: 13.2% (2000); Bankruptcy rate: 1.91% (2001).
Taxes: Total county taxes per capita: $262 (2000); County property taxes per capita: $261 (2000).
Education: High school graduation rate: 86.7% (2000); College graduation rate: 24.7% (2000).
Housing: Homeownership rate: 71.6% (2000); Median home value: $85,400 (2000); Median rent: $372 per month (2000); Median age of housing: 32 years (2000).
Health: Birth rate: 125.7 per 10,000 population (1998); Age adjusted death rate: 77.1 per 10,000 population (1999); Age adjusted cancer mortality rate: 197.7 deaths per 100,000 population (1999). Number of physicians: 3.3 per 10,000 population (1999); Number of hospital beds: n/a (1999).
Elections: 2000 Presidential election results: 43.4% Gore, 50.1% Bush, 4.1% Nader, 1.8% Buchanan
National and State Parks: Aspen State Wildlife Management Area; Barnesville State Wildlife Management Area; Bjornson State Wildlife Management Area; Buffalo River State Park; Clay County State Wildlife Management Area; Cromwell State Wildlife Management Area; Felton State Wildlife Management Area; Goose Prairie State Wildlife Management Area;

Gruhl State Wildlife Management Area; Hawley State Wildlife Management Area; Hay Creek State Wildlife Management Area; Highland State Wildlife Management Area; Hitterdal State Wildlife Management Area; Janssen State Wildlife Management Area; Jeral State Wildlife Management Area; Magnusson State Wildlife Management Area; Skree State Wildlife Management Area; Ulen State Wildlife Management Area

Additional Information Contacts

Clay County Government Offices 218-299-5002
Moorhead Chamber of Commerce 218-233-1100

Clay County Communities

ALLIANCE (township). Covers a land area of 36.329 square miles and a water area of 0 square miles. Located at 46.67° N. Lat.; 96.60° W. Long.
Population: 246 (2000); Race: 100.0% White, 0.0% Black, 0.0% Asian, 0.0% American Indian and Alaska Native, 0.0% Hispanic of any race, 0.0% two or more races (2000); Density: 6.8 persons per square mile (2000); Age: 19.9% under 18, 19.5% over 64 (2000); Marriage status: 12.0% never married, 78.1% now married, 1.0% widowed, 8.9% divorced (2000); Foreign born: 0.0% (2000); Ancestry (includes multiple ancestries): 54.5% German, 27.3% Norwegian, 10.8% English, 8.2% French (except Basque), 7.4% Irish (2000).
Economy: Employment by occupation: 23.7% management, 14.4% professional, 7.6% services, 28.8% sales, 4.2% farming, 5.9% construction, 15.3% production (2000).
Income: Per capita income: $17,867 (2000); Median household income: $45,000 (2000); Poverty rate: 4.8% (2000).
Taxes: Total city taxes per capita: $60 (1997); City property taxes per capita: $60 (1997).
Education: High school graduation rate: 82.4% (2000); College graduation rate: 9.7% (2000).
Housing: Homeownership rate: 97.7% (2000); Median home value: $81,700 (2000); Median age of housing: 47 years (2000).
Transportation: Commute to work: 85.7% car, 0.0% public transportation, 0.0% walk, 14.3% work from home (2000); Travel time to work: 10.4% less than 15 minutes, 53.1% 15 to 30 minutes, 27.1% 30 to 45 minutes, 5.2% 45 to 60 minutes, 4.2% 60 minutes or more (2000)

BAKER (unincorporated postal area, zip code 56513). Covers a land area of 20.567 square miles and a water area of 0.064 square miles. Located at 46.72° N. Lat.; 96.54° W. Long. Elevation is 936 feet.
Population: 194 (2000); Race: 100.0% White, 0.0% Black, 0.0% Asian, 0.0% American Indian and Alaska Native, 0.0% Hispanic of any race, 0.0% two or more races (2000); Density: 9.4 persons per square mile (2000); Age: 28.3% under 18, 14.4% over 64 (2000); Marriage status: 15.9% never married, 64.5% now married, 5.1% widowed, 14.5% divorced (2000); Foreign born: 0.0% (2000); Ancestry (includes multiple ancestries): 48.3% German, 38.9% Norwegian, 10.6% Irish, 10.0% English, 9.4% Polish (2000).
Economy: Employment by occupation: 26.3% management, 18.8% professional, 12.5% services, 17.5% sales, 2.5% farming, 7.5% construction, 15.0% production (2000).
Income: Per capita income: $17,054 (2000); Median household income: $50,625 (2000); Poverty rate: 1.1% (2000).
Education: High school graduation rate: 87.0% (2000); College graduation rate: 12.2% (2000).
Housing: Homeownership rate: 96.8% (2000); Median home value: $107,300 (2000); Median age of housing: 44 years (2000).
Transportation: Commute to work: 88.8% car, 0.0% public transportation, 3.8% walk, 7.5% work from home (2000); Travel time to work: 24.3% less than 15 minutes, 41.9% 15 to 30 minutes, 33.8% 30 to 45 minutes, 0.0% 45 to 60 minutes, 0.0% 60 minutes or more (2000)

BARNESVILLE (city). Covers a land area of 2.104 square miles and a water area of 0.017 square miles. Located at 46.65° N. Lat.; 96.41° W. Long. Elevation is 1,020 feet.
Population: 2,173 (2000); Race: 98.3% White, 0.0% Black, 0.0% Asian, 1.0% American Indian and Alaska Native, 0.8% Hispanic of any race, 0.0% two or more races (2000); Density: 1,032.8 persons per square mile (2000); Age: 26.6% under 18, 19.4% over 64 (2000); Marriage status: 18.8% never married, 61.5% now married, 9.3% widowed, 10.5% divorced (2000); Foreign born: 0.8% (2000); Ancestry (includes multiple ancestries): 43.8% German, 41.4% Norwegian, 10.0% Swedish, 7.0% Polish, 5.7% Irish (2000).
Economy: Single-family building permits issued: 18 (2001) / 13 (2000); Multi-family building permits issued: 10 (2001) / 0 (2000); Employment by occupation: 8.3% management, 22.7% professional, 15.0% services, 26.9% sales, 0.0% farming, 14.5% construction, 12.6% production (2000).
Income: Per capita income: $18,373 (2000); Median household income: $35,814 (2000); Poverty rate: 6.7% (2000).
Taxes: Total city taxes per capita: $78 (1997); City property taxes per capita: $73 (1997).
Education: High school graduation rate: 79.8% (2000); College graduation rate: 20.0% (2000).

School District(s)

Barnesville (KG-12)
2000 Enrollment: 766 218-354-2217
Housing: Homeownership rate: 81.9% (2000); Median home value: $76,100 (2000); Median rent: $248 per month (2000); Median age of housing: 30 years (2000).
Newspapers: Record Review (1 x week)
Transportation: Commute to work: 93.3% car, 0.9% public transportation, 4.0% walk, 1.4% work from home (2000); Travel time to work: 38.2% less than 15 minutes, 9.9% 15 to 30 minutes, 43.5% 30 to 45 minutes, 5.5% 45 to 60 minutes, 2.9% 60 minutes or more (2000)

BARNESVILLE (township). Covers a land area of 35.509 square miles and a water area of 0 square miles. Located at 46.67° N. Lat.; 96.47° W. Long. Elevation is 1,020 feet.
Population: 149 (2000); Race: 100.0% White, 0.0% Black, 0.0% Asian, 0.0% American Indian and Alaska Native, 0.0% Hispanic of any race, 0.0% two or more races (2000); Density: 4.2 persons per square mile (2000); Age: 23.5% under 18, 15.4% over 64 (2000); Marriage status: 18.5% never married, 71.4% now married, 3.4% widowed, 6.7% divorced (2000); Foreign born: 1.5% (2000); Ancestry (includes multiple ancestries): 46.3% Norwegian, 40.4% German, 7.4% Irish, 7.4% Swedish, 5.9% Scandinavian (2000).
Economy: Shipping point for agricultural area: grain, potatoes; livestock; dairying. Manufacturing: concrete. Railroad shops. Employment by occupation: 21.1% management, 11.3% professional, 9.9% services, 23.9% sales, 0.0% farming, 22.5% construction, 11.3% production (2000).
Income: Per capita income: $16,317 (2000); Median household income: $46,750 (2000); Poverty rate: 2.9% (2000).
Taxes: Total city taxes per capita: $112 (1997); City property taxes per capita: $112 (1997).
Education: High school graduation rate: 83.0% (2000); College graduation rate: 12.8% (2000).
Housing: Homeownership rate: 96.5% (2000); Median home value: $83,000 (2000); Median age of housing: 51 years (2000).
Transportation: Commute to work: 91.5% car, 0.0% public transportation, 5.6% walk, 2.8% work from home (2000); Travel time to work: 44.9% less than 15 minutes, 10.1% 15 to 30 minutes, 36.2% 30 to 45 minutes, 8.7% 45 to 60 minutes, 0.0% 60 minutes or more (2000)

COMSTOCK (city). Covers a land area of 0.216 square miles and a water area of 0 square miles. Located at 46.66° N. Lat.; 96.74° W. Long. Elevation is 920 feet.
Population: 123 (2000); Race: 94.8% White, 0.0% Black, 0.0% Asian, 2.2% American Indian and Alaska Native, 2.2% Hispanic of any race, 3.0% two or more races (2000); Density: 570.5 persons per square mile (2000); Age: 24.6% under 18, 23.9% over 64 (2000); Marriage status: 22.5% never married, 70.3% now married, 4.5% widowed, 2.7% divorced (2000); Foreign born: 0.0% (2000); Ancestry (includes multiple ancestries): 50.0% Norwegian, 16.4% German, 7.5% Scottish, 7.5% Swedish, 7.5% Irish (2000).
Economy: Grain; dairying. Manufacturing: fertilizers. Employment by occupation: 7.6% management, 9.1% professional, 28.8% services, 27.3% sales, 0.0% farming, 19.7% construction, 7.6% production (2000).
Income: Per capita income: $19,781 (2000); Median household income: $37,917 (2000); Poverty rate: 2.2% (2000).
Taxes: Total city taxes per capita: $49 (2000); City property taxes per capita: $41 (2000).
Education: High school graduation rate: 77.4% (2000); College graduation rate: 8.6% (2000).
Housing: Homeownership rate: 100.0% (2000); Median home value: $61,300 (2000); Median age of housing: 60+ years (2000).
Transportation: Commute to work: 84.8% car, 0.0% public transportation, 7.6% walk, 7.6% work from home (2000); Travel time to work: 14.8% less than 15 minutes, 55.7% 15 to 30 minutes, 29.5% 30 to 45 minutes, 0.0% 45 to 60 minutes, 0.0% 60 minutes or more (2000)

CROMWELL (township). Covers a land area of 33.296 square miles and a water area of 0.422 square miles. Located at 46.94° N. Lat.; 96.35° W. Long.

Population: 323 (2000); Race: 96.4% White, 0.0% Black, 0.0% Asian, 1.6% American Indian and Alaska Native, 2.3% Hispanic of any race, 1.3% two or more races (2000); Density: 9.7 persons per square mile (2000); Age: 27.3% under 18, 9.2% over 64 (2000); Marriage status: 17.8% never married, 74.8% now married, 3.7% widowed, 3.7% divorced (2000); Foreign born: 0.0% (2000); Ancestry (includes multiple ancestries): 56.3% Norwegian, 44.4% German, 12.5% Swedish, 6.9% English, 5.9% Irish (2000).

Economy: Employment by occupation: 10.4% management, 12.2% professional, 11.6% services, 35.4% sales, 2.4% farming, 17.7% construction, 10.4% production (2000).

Income: Per capita income: $20,993 (2000); Median household income: $47,292 (2000); Poverty rate: 4.3% (2000).

Taxes: Total city taxes per capita: $58 (1997); City property taxes per capita: $58 (1997).

Education: High school graduation rate: 90.7% (2000); College graduation rate: 14.1% (2000).

Housing: Homeownership rate: 96.4% (2000); Median home value: $84,400 (2000); Median age of housing: 32 years (2000).

Transportation: Commute to work: 97.5% car, 0.0% public transportation, 0.0% walk, 2.5% work from home (2000); Travel time to work: 20.1% less than 15 minutes, 13.8% 15 to 30 minutes, 39.0% 30 to 45 minutes, 24.5% 45 to 60 minutes, 2.5% 60 minutes or more (2000)

DILWORTH (city). Covers a land area of 1.987 square miles and a water area of 0 square miles. Located at 46.87° N. Lat.; 96.70° W. Long.

Population: 3,001 (2000); Race: 90.0% White, 0.3% Black, 0.3% Asian, 3.2% American Indian and Alaska Native, 7.9% Hispanic of any race, 3.3% two or more races (2000); Density: 1,510.6 persons per square mile (2000); Age: 32.2% under 18, 10.6% over 64 (2000); Marriage status: 23.3% never married, 59.1% now married, 6.4% widowed, 11.1% divorced (2000); Foreign born: 3.0% (2000); Ancestry (includes multiple ancestries): 34.9% Norwegian, 31.5% German, 13.5% Other groups, 7.1% Irish, 7.1% French (except Basque) (2000).

Economy: Corn, wheat, barley, potatoes, sugar beets, beans, sunflowers; cattle, sheep, hogs, poultry; dairying. Manufacturing: fertilizers. Single-family building permits issued: 17 (2001) / 20 (2000); Multi-family building permits issued: 10 (2001) / 0 (2000); Employment by occupation: 6.0% management, 12.9% professional, 19.1% services, 28.7% sales, 0.7% farming, 12.2% construction, 20.4% production (2000).

Income: Per capita income: $14,726 (2000); Median household income: $34,571 (2000); Poverty rate: 16.1% (2000).

Taxes: Total city taxes per capita: $129 (1997); City property taxes per capita: $123 (1997).

Education: High school graduation rate: 86.2% (2000); College graduation rate: 14.9% (2000).

Housing: Homeownership rate: 71.6% (2000); Median home value: $77,100 (2000); Median rent: $360 per month (2000); Median age of housing: 27 years (2000).

Safety: Violent crime rate: 39.6 per 10,000 population; Property crime rate: 451.7 per 10,000 population (2001).

Transportation: Commute to work: 93.8% car, 0.0% public transportation, 3.6% walk, 2.6% work from home (2000); Travel time to work: 36.2% less than 15 minutes, 52.8% 15 to 30 minutes, 6.7% 30 to 45 minutes, 1.3% 45 to 60 minutes, 3.1% 60 minutes or more (2000)

EGLON (township). Covers a land area of 34.014 square miles and a water area of 1.943 square miles. Located at 46.85° N. Lat.; 96.23° W. Long.

Population: 440 (2000); Race: 98.7% White, 0.4% Black, 0.0% Asian, 0.4% American Indian and Alaska Native, 0.4% Hispanic of any race, 0.0% two or more races (2000); Density: 12.9 persons per square mile (2000); Age: 32.0% under 18, 9.1% over 64 (2000); Marriage status: 20.2% never married, 72.1% now married, 1.2% widowed, 6.5% divorced (2000); Foreign born: 1.7% (2000); Ancestry (includes multiple ancestries): 61.5% Norwegian, 34.3% German, 13.9% Swedish, 4.1% Irish, 3.5% United States or American (2000).

Economy: Employment by occupation: 14.0% management, 19.3% professional, 8.3% services, 19.7% sales, 5.3% farming, 21.1% construction, 12.3% production (2000).

Income: Per capita income: $17,356 (2000); Median household income: $49,318 (2000); Poverty rate: 0.4% (2000).

Taxes: Total city taxes per capita: $38 (1997); City property taxes per capita: $38 (1997).

Education: High school graduation rate: 91.2% (2000); College graduation rate: 16.5% (2000).

Housing: Homeownership rate: 95.3% (2000); Median home value: $83,900 (2000); Median rent: $375 per month (2000); Median age of housing: 40 years (2000).

Transportation: Commute to work: 90.7% car, 0.9% public transportation, 0.9% walk, 6.7% work from home (2000); Travel time to work: 46.2% less than 15 minutes, 18.1% 15 to 30 minutes, 24.8% 30 to 45 minutes, 7.6% 45 to 60 minutes, 3.3% 60 minutes or more (2000)

ELKTON (township). Covers a land area of 36.103 square miles and a water area of 0.064 square miles. Located at 46.75° N. Lat.; 96.49° W. Long.

Population: 283 (2000); Race: 100.0% White, 0.0% Black, 0.0% Asian, 0.0% American Indian and Alaska Native, 0.0% Hispanic of any race, 0.0% two or more races (2000); Density: 7.8 persons per square mile (2000); Age: 25.1% under 18, 9.3% over 64 (2000); Marriage status: 24.2% never married, 68.7% now married, 2.6% widowed, 4.4% divorced (2000); Foreign born: 0.0% (2000); Ancestry (includes multiple ancestries): 40.5% German, 35.1% Norwegian, 12.9% Swedish, 9.3% English, 6.1% United States or American (2000).

Economy: Employment by occupation: 25.9% management, 17.5% professional, 14.7% services, 17.5% sales, 3.5% farming, 14.0% construction, 7.0% production (2000).

Income: Per capita income: $24,312 (2000); Median household income: $52,500 (2000); Poverty rate: 6.8% (2000).

Taxes: Total city taxes per capita: $57 (1997); City property taxes per capita: $57 (1997).

Education: High school graduation rate: 92.4% (2000); College graduation rate: 17.9% (2000).

Housing: Homeownership rate: 96.2% (2000); Median home value: $104,200 (2000); Median age of housing: 29 years (2000).

Transportation: Commute to work: 85.3% car, 0.0% public transportation, 2.9% walk, 10.3% work from home (2000); Travel time to work: 25.4% less than 15 minutes, 43.4% 15 to 30 minutes, 23.8% 30 to 45 minutes, 2.5% 45 to 60 minutes, 4.9% 60 minutes or more (2000)

ELMWOOD (township). Covers a land area of 35.685 square miles and a water area of 0 square miles. Located at 46.76° N. Lat.; 96.60° W. Long.

Population: 371 (2000); Race: 100.0% White, 0.0% Black, 0.0% Asian, 0.0% American Indian and Alaska Native, 0.0% Hispanic of any race, 0.0% two or more races (2000); Density: 10.4 persons per square mile (2000); Age: 29.8% under 18, 11.7% over 64 (2000); Marriage status: 17.9% never married, 72.4% now married, 5.8% widowed, 3.8% divorced (2000); Foreign born: 0.5% (2000); Ancestry (includes multiple ancestries): 57.5% German, 38.4% Norwegian, 9.3% Swedish, 6.6% Polish, 4.6% English (2000).

Economy: Employment by occupation: 20.0% management, 9.2% professional, 11.8% services, 29.2% sales, 1.5% farming, 11.3% construction, 16.9% production (2000).

Income: Per capita income: $19,666 (2000); Median household income: $58,929 (2000); Poverty rate: 0.0% (2000).

Taxes: Total city taxes per capita: $56 (1997); City property taxes per capita: $56 (1997).

Education: High school graduation rate: 89.9% (2000); College graduation rate: 9.4% (2000).

Housing: Homeownership rate: 95.5% (2000); Median home value: $99,700 (2000); Median age of housing: 34 years (2000).

Transportation: Commute to work: 91.8% car, 0.0% public transportation, 5.1% walk, 3.1% work from home (2000); Travel time to work: 21.7% less than 15 minutes, 53.4% 15 to 30 minutes, 23.8% 30 to 45 minutes, 1.1% 45 to 60 minutes, 0.0% 60 minutes or more (2000)

FELTON (city). Covers a land area of 1.024 square miles and a water area of 0 square miles. Located at 47.07° N. Lat.; 96.50° W. Long. Elevation is 910 feet.

Population: 216 (2000); Race: 93.9% White, 0.0% Black, 0.0% Asian, 0.0% American Indian and Alaska Native, 1.9% Hispanic of any race, 6.1% two or more races (2000); Density: 211.0 persons per square mile (2000); Age: 26.8% under 18, 18.3% over 64 (2000); Marriage status: 24.4% never married, 58.5% now married, 10.4% widowed, 6.7% divorced (2000); Foreign born: 0.0% (2000); Ancestry (includes multiple ancestries): 51.6% Norwegian, 26.8% German, 11.3% Other groups, 9.9% Swedish, 5.6% Irish (2000).

Economy: Single-family building permits issued: 0 (2001) / 1 (2000); Multi-family building permits issued: 0 (2001) / 0 (2000); Employment by occupation: 9.4% management, 12.5% professional, 17.7% services, 33.3% sales, 5.2% farming, 10.4% construction, 11.5% production (2000).

Income: Per capita income: $15,321 (2000); Median household income: $26,477 (2000); Poverty rate: 16.9% (2000).
Taxes: Total city taxes per capita: $63 (1997); City property taxes per capita: $54 (1997).
Education: High school graduation rate: 78.2% (2000); College graduation rate: 9.5% (2000).
Housing: Homeownership rate: 82.4% (2000); Median home value: $43,800 (2000); Median rent: $213 per month (2000); Median age of housing: 32 years (2000).
Transportation: Commute to work: 90.3% car, 0.0% public transportation, 5.4% walk, 4.3% work from home (2000); Travel time to work: 20.2% less than 15 minutes, 12.4% 15 to 30 minutes, 50.6% 30 to 45 minutes, 10.1% 45 to 60 minutes, 6.7% 60 minutes or more (2000)

FELTON (township). Covers a land area of 35.268 square miles and a water area of 0 square miles. Located at 47.11° N. Lat.; 96.51° W. Long. Elevation is 910 feet.
Population: 108 (2000); Race: 100.0% White, 0.0% Black, 0.0% Asian, 0.0% American Indian and Alaska Native, 5.9% Hispanic of any race, 0.0% two or more races (2000); Density: 3.1 persons per square mile (2000); Age: 23.8% under 18, 9.9% over 64 (2000); Marriage status: 34.1% never married, 52.9% now married, 2.4% widowed, 10.6% divorced (2000); Foreign born: 0.0% (2000); Ancestry (includes multiple ancestries): 49.5% Norwegian, 41.6% German, 12.9% United States or American, 9.9% Danish, 5.9% Other groups (2000).
Economy: Agriculture: grain, sunflowers; dairying; poultry, livestock. Manufacturing: fertilizers. Employment by occupation: 43.5% management, 8.7% professional, 0.0% services, 28.3% sales, 0.0% farming, 6.5% construction, 13.0% production (2000).
Income: Per capita income: $21,187 (2000); Median household income: $43,750 (2000); Poverty rate: 7.9% (2000).
Taxes: Total city taxes per capita: $170 (1997); City property taxes per capita: $170 (1997).
Education: High school graduation rate: 91.2% (2000); College graduation rate: 4.4% (2000).
Housing: Homeownership rate: 77.8% (2000); Median home value: $84,000 (2000); Median rent: $225 per month (2000); Median age of housing: 46 years (2000).
Transportation: Commute to work: 90.7% car, 0.0% public transportation, 0.0% walk, 9.3% work from home (2000); Travel time to work: 30.8% less than 15 minutes, 10.3% 15 to 30 minutes, 25.6% 30 to 45 minutes, 33.3% 45 to 60 minutes, 0.0% 60 minutes or more (2000)

FLOWING (township). Covers a land area of 35.921 square miles and a water area of 0.024 square miles. Located at 47.02° N. Lat.; 96.51° W. Long.
Population: 97 (2000); Race: 99.2% White, 0.0% Black, 0.0% Asian, 0.8% American Indian and Alaska Native, 0.0% Hispanic of any race, 0.0% two or more races (2000); Density: 2.7 persons per square mile (2000); Age: 35.5% under 18, 9.7% over 64 (2000); Marriage status: 29.3% never married, 66.3% now married, 3.3% widowed, 1.1% divorced (2000); Foreign born: 2.4% (2000); Ancestry (includes multiple ancestries): 54.0% Norwegian, 24.2% German, 12.1% Danish, 8.1% Irish, 4.8% Swedish (2000).
Economy: Employment by occupation: 21.0% management, 14.5% professional, 6.5% services, 24.2% sales, 6.5% farming, 11.3% construction, 16.1% production (2000).
Income: Per capita income: $24,326 (2000); Median household income: $66,875 (2000); Poverty rate: 0.0% (2000).
Taxes: Total city taxes per capita: $142 (1997); City property taxes per capita: $142 (1997).
Education: High school graduation rate: 84.3% (2000); College graduation rate: 12.9% (2000).
Housing: Homeownership rate: 92.1% (2000); Median home value: $87,800 (2000); Median rent: $175 per month (2000); Median age of housing: 60+ years (2000).
Transportation: Commute to work: 82.3% car, 0.0% public transportation, 0.0% walk, 17.7% work from home (2000); Travel time to work: 0.0% less than 15 minutes, 3.9% 15 to 30 minutes, 92.2% 30 to 45 minutes, 0.0% 45 to 60 minutes, 3.9% 60 minutes or more (2000)

GEORGETOWN (city). Covers a land area of 1.003 square miles and a water area of 0 square miles. Located at 47.07° N. Lat.; 96.79° W. Long. Elevation is 886 feet.
Population: 125 (2000); Race: 98.3% White, 0.0% Black, 0.0% Asian, 0.0% American Indian and Alaska Native, 0.0% Hispanic of any race, 1.7% two or more races (2000); Density: 124.7 persons per square mile (2000); Age: 22.6% under 18, 13.0% over 64 (2000); Marriage status: 18.8% never married, 72.9% now married, 4.2% widowed, 4.2% divorced (2000); Foreign born: 0.0% (2000); Ancestry (includes multiple ancestries): 60.0% German, 44.3% Norwegian, 6.1% Swedish, 6.1% Irish, 2.6% Scottish (2000).
Economy: Single-family building permits issued: 0 (2001) / 0 (2000); Multi-family building permits issued: 0 (2001) / 0 (2000); Employment by occupation: 0.0% management, 7.6% professional, 21.2% services, 25.8% sales, 0.0% farming, 16.7% construction, 28.8% production (2000).
Income: Per capita income: $17,043 (2000); Median household income: $35,625 (2000); Poverty rate: 1.7% (2000).
Taxes: Total city taxes per capita: $72 (1997); City property taxes per capita: $63 (1997).
Education: High school graduation rate: 86.5% (2000); College graduation rate: 10.8% (2000).
Housing: Homeownership rate: 91.7% (2000); Median home value: $54,400 (2000); Median rent: $213 per month (2000); Median age of housing: 26 years (2000).
Transportation: Commute to work: 95.5% car, 0.0% public transportation, 0.0% walk, 4.5% work from home (2000); Travel time to work: 7.9% less than 15 minutes, 36.5% 15 to 30 minutes, 44.4% 30 to 45 minutes, 7.9% 45 to 60 minutes, 3.2% 60 minutes or more (2000)

GEORGETOWN (township). Covers a land area of 36.856 square miles and a water area of 0 square miles. Located at 47.10° N. Lat.; 96.76° W. Long. Elevation is 886 feet.
Population: 188 (2000); Race: 96.9% White, 0.0% Black, 1.5% Asian, 1.5% American Indian and Alaska Native, 5.2% Hispanic of any race, 0.0% two or more races (2000); Density: 5.1 persons per square mile (2000); Age: 30.4% under 18, 15.5% over 64 (2000); Marriage status: 19.4% never married, 66.2% now married, 9.4% widowed, 5.0% divorced (2000); Foreign born: 0.0% (2000); Ancestry (includes multiple ancestries): 45.9% German, 18.0% Irish, 15.5% Norwegian, 11.9% Swedish, 8.8% Polish (2000).
Economy: Grain, potatoes, sugar beets, beans; livestock; dairying. Employment by occupation: 28.2% management, 2.8% professional, 8.5% services, 18.3% sales, 15.5% farming, 8.5% construction, 18.3% production (2000).
Income: Per capita income: $17,178 (2000); Median household income: $40,000 (2000); Poverty rate: 14.4% (2000).
Taxes: Total city taxes per capita: $107 (1997); City property taxes per capita: $107 (1997).
Education: High school graduation rate: 81.9% (2000); College graduation rate: 13.4% (2000).
Housing: Homeownership rate: 92.8% (2000); Median home value: $85,600 (2000); Median age of housing: 41 years (2000).
Transportation: Commute to work: 78.3% car, 0.0% public transportation, 11.6% walk, 7.2% work from home (2000); Travel time to work: 28.1% less than 15 minutes, 18.8% 15 to 30 minutes, 45.3% 30 to 45 minutes, 3.1% 45 to 60 minutes, 4.7% 60 minutes or more (2000)

GLYNDON (city). Covers a land area of 1.513 square miles and a water area of 0 square miles. Located at 46.87° N. Lat.; 96.58° W. Long. Elevation is 922 feet.
History: Glyndon was established in 1872 around a railway station.
Population: 1,049 (2000); Race: 94.6% White, 0.2% Black, 0.0% Asian, 0.8% American Indian and Alaska Native, 7.1% Hispanic of any race, 2.2% two or more races (2000); Density: 693.5 persons per square mile (2000); Age: 34.2% under 18, 5.7% over 64 (2000); Marriage status: 19.7% never married, 70.1% now married, 2.5% widowed, 7.8% divorced (2000); Foreign born: 1.8% (2000); Ancestry (includes multiple ancestries): 41.9% Norwegian, 41.6% German, 9.3% Other groups, 4.8% Irish, 4.5% Swedish (2000).
Economy: Single-family building permits issued: 17 (2001) / 10 (2000); Multi-family building permits issued: 0 (2001) / 0 (2000); Employment by occupation: 12.6% management, 16.3% professional, 17.7% services, 26.5% sales, 0.0% farming, 11.8% construction, 15.1% production (2000).
Income: Per capita income: $17,922 (2000); Median household income: $44,028 (2000); Poverty rate: 9.7% (2000).
Taxes: Total city taxes per capita: $161 (1997); City property taxes per capita: $150 (1997).
Education: High school graduation rate: 84.0% (2000); College graduation rate: 15.6% (2000).

School District(s)

Dilworth-Glyndon-Felton (PK-12)
2000 Enrollment: 1,277 218-287-2371

Housing: Homeownership rate: 86.1% (2000); Median home value: $78,800 (2000); Median rent: $313 per month (2000); Median age of housing: 28 years (2000).

Transportation: Commute to work: 94.4% car, 0.0% public transportation, 2.0% walk, 3.2% work from home (2000); Travel time to work: 18.5% less than 15 minutes, 66.1% 15 to 30 minutes, 10.5% 30 to 45 minutes, 1.0% 45 to 60 minutes, 3.9% 60 minutes or more (2000)

GLYNDON (township). Covers a land area of 33.956 square miles and a water area of 0.027 square miles. Located at 46.85° N. Lat.; 96.61° W. Long. Elevation is 922 feet.

Population: 281 (2000); Race: 92.9% White, 0.0% Black, 0.8% Asian, 1.3% American Indian and Alaska Native, 0.0% Hispanic of any race, 5.0% two or more races (2000); Density: 8.3 persons per square mile (2000); Age: 16.7% under 18, 12.1% over 64 (2000); Marriage status: 16.0% never married, 74.8% now married, 6.3% widowed, 2.9% divorced (2000); Foreign born: 1.3% (2000); Ancestry (includes multiple ancestries): 41.3% German, 26.3% Norwegian, 10.8% Swedish, 8.8% Other groups, 7.9% French (except Basque) (2000).

Economy: Railroad junction. Grain. Employment by occupation: 18.5% management, 19.3% professional, 10.9% services, 31.9% sales, 1.7% farming, 5.0% construction, 12.6% production (2000).

Income: Per capita income: $21,309 (2000); Median household income: $46,250 (2000); Poverty rate: 3.3% (2000).

Taxes: Total city taxes per capita: $73 (1997); City property taxes per capita: $73 (1997).

Education: High school graduation rate: 79.4% (2000); College graduation rate: 14.4% (2000).

Housing: Homeownership rate: 83.5% (2000); Median home value: $92,500 (2000); Median rent: $517 per month (2000); Median age of housing: 37 years (2000).

Transportation: Commute to work: 94.1% car, 0.0% public transportation, 4.2% walk, 1.7% work from home (2000); Travel time to work: 23.1% less than 15 minutes, 61.5% 15 to 30 minutes, 15.4% 30 to 45 minutes, 0.0% 45 to 60 minutes, 0.0% 60 minutes or more (2000)

GOOSE PRAIRIE (township). Covers a land area of 34.819 square miles and a water area of 0.759 square miles. Located at 47.01° N. Lat.; 96.25° W. Long.

Population: 199 (2000); Race: 98.0% White, 0.0% Black, 0.0% Asian, 2.0% American Indian and Alaska Native, 0.0% Hispanic of any race, 0.0% two or more races (2000); Density: 5.7 persons per square mile (2000); Age: 31.8% under 18, 11.4% over 64 (2000); Marriage status: 19.9% never married, 67.1% now married, 6.8% widowed, 6.2% divorced (2000); Foreign born: 0.0% (2000); Ancestry (includes multiple ancestries): 58.7% Norwegian, 15.4% Swedish, 12.9% German, 8.0% United States or American, 4.5% English (2000).

Economy: Employment by occupation: 19.6% management, 9.8% professional, 10.9% services, 25.0% sales, 4.3% farming, 8.7% construction, 21.7% production (2000).

Income: Per capita income: $13,285 (2000); Median household income: $37,083 (2000); Poverty rate: 17.4% (2000).

Taxes: Total city taxes per capita: $102 (1997); City property taxes per capita: $102 (1997).

Education: High school graduation rate: 81.5% (2000); College graduation rate: 12.1% (2000).

Housing: Homeownership rate: 91.0% (2000); Median home value: $55,000 (2000); Median rent: $175 per month (2000); Median age of housing: 42 years (2000).

Transportation: Commute to work: 91.1% car, 0.0% public transportation, 0.0% walk, 8.9% work from home (2000); Travel time to work: 15.9% less than 15 minutes, 24.4% 15 to 30 minutes, 17.1% 30 to 45 minutes, 37.8% 45 to 60 minutes, 4.9% 60 minutes or more (2000)

HAGEN (township). Covers a land area of 32.459 square miles and a water area of 0.021 square miles. Located at 47.11° N. Lat.; 96.39° W. Long.

Population: 153 (2000); Race: 100.0% White, 0.0% Black, 0.0% Asian, 0.0% American Indian and Alaska Native, 0.0% Hispanic of any race, 0.0% two or more races (2000); Density: 4.7 persons per square mile (2000); Age: 24.7% under 18, 12.0% over 64 (2000); Marriage status: 17.2% never married, 73.8% now married, 5.7% widowed, 3.3% divorced (2000); Foreign born: 0.0% (2000); Ancestry (includes multiple ancestries): 48.7% Norwegian, 20.0% German, 8.7% Swedish, 8.7% United States or American, 5.3% European (2000).

Economy: Employment by occupation: 30.7% management, 9.3% professional, 26.7% services, 10.7% sales, 2.7% farming, 14.7% construction, 5.3% production (2000).

Income: Per capita income: $16,186 (2000); Median household income: $37,500 (2000); Poverty rate: 0.0% (2000).

Taxes: Total city taxes per capita: $30 (1997); City property taxes per capita: $30 (1997).

Education: High school graduation rate: 80.4% (2000); College graduation rate: 16.8% (2000).

Housing: Homeownership rate: 100.0% (2000); Median home value: $90,000 (2000); Median age of housing: 38 years (2000).

Transportation: Commute to work: 64.0% car, 0.0% public transportation, 2.7% walk, 33.3% work from home (2000); Travel time to work: 14.0% less than 15 minutes, 30.0% 15 to 30 minutes, 14.0% 30 to 45 minutes, 32.0% 45 to 60 minutes, 10.0% 60 minutes or more (2000)

HAWLEY (city). Covers a land area of 2.461 square miles and a water area of 0.004 square miles. Located at 46.88° N. Lat.; 96.31° W. Long. Elevation is 1,154 feet.

History: Hawley was settled in 1871 by a group of English colonists.

Population: 1,882 (2000); Race: 98.0% White, 0.0% Black, 0.3% Asian, 0.8% American Indian and Alaska Native, 0.5% Hispanic of any race, 0.7% two or more races (2000); Density: 764.8 persons per square mile (2000); Age: 26.6% under 18, 20.1% over 64 (2000); Marriage status: 21.6% never married, 59.0% now married, 11.5% widowed, 7.9% divorced (2000); Foreign born: 0.8% (2000); Ancestry (includes multiple ancestries): 58.3% Norwegian, 31.4% German, 10.8% Swedish, 5.5% Irish, 4.7% English (2000).

Economy: Single-family building permits issued: 6 (2001) / 1 (2000); Multi-family building permits issued: 0 (2001) / 0 (2000); Employment by occupation: 9.5% management, 20.8% professional, 16.4% services, 27.5% sales, 0.5% farming, 10.7% construction, 14.7% production (2000).

Income: Per capita income: $17,178 (2000); Median household income: $35,652 (2000); Poverty rate: 8.5% (2000).

Taxes: Total city taxes per capita: $163 (1997); City property taxes per capita: $90 (1997).

Education: High school graduation rate: 83.2% (2000); College graduation rate: 23.4% (2000).

School District(s)

Hawley (KG-12)
2000 Enrollment: 914 218-483-4647

Housing: Homeownership rate: 71.0% (2000); Median home value: $75,400 (2000); Median rent: $341 per month (2000); Median age of housing: 32 years (2000).

Newspapers: The Hawley Herald (1 x week)

Transportation: Commute to work: 92.1% car, 0.8% public transportation, 2.5% walk, 4.2% work from home (2000); Travel time to work: 35.6% less than 15 minutes, 19.3% 15 to 30 minutes, 36.3% 30 to 45 minutes, 6.7% 45 to 60 minutes, 2.1% 60 minutes or more (2000)

HAWLEY (township). Covers a land area of 30.713 square miles and a water area of 0.524 square miles. Located at 46.85° N. Lat.; 96.36° W. Long. Elevation is 1,154 feet.

History: Settled c.1870.

Population: 459 (2000); Race: 97.1% White, 0.0% Black, 0.0% Asian, 1.7% American Indian and Alaska Native, 0.4% Hispanic of any race, 1.2% two or more races (2000); Density: 14.9 persons per square mile (2000); Age: 34.4% under 18, 7.4% over 64 (2000); Marriage status: 24.0% never married, 68.8% now married, 3.5% widowed, 3.7% divorced (2000); Foreign born: 0.8% (2000); Ancestry (includes multiple ancestries): 57.3% Norwegian, 42.9% German, 9.7% Swedish, 8.9% Irish, 5.2% French (except Basque) (2000).

Economy: Manufacturing: printing and publishing; foods, machinery. Employment by occupation: 16.1% management, 19.0% professional, 8.0% services, 27.4% sales, 1.5% farming, 15.3% construction, 12.8% production (2000).

Income: Per capita income: $18,252 (2000); Median household income: $54,886 (2000); Poverty rate: 7.8% (2000).

Taxes: Total city taxes per capita: $40 (1997); City property taxes per capita: $40 (1997).

Education: High school graduation rate: 92.9% (2000); College graduation rate: 21.8% (2000).

Housing: Homeownership rate: 95.0% (2000); Median home value: $111,700 (2000); Median age of housing: 25 years (2000).

Transportation: Commute to work: 95.3% car, 0.0% public transportation, 0.0% walk, 4.7% work from home (2000); Travel time to work: 27.2% less than 15 minutes, 28.4% 15 to 30 minutes, 36.8% 30 to 45 minutes, 4.2% 45 to 60 minutes, 3.4% 60 minutes or more (2000)

HIGHLAND GROVE (township). Covers a land area of 34.342 square miles and a water area of 0.625 square miles. Located at 46.92° N. Lat.; 96.24° W. Long.

Population: 304 (2000); Race: 99.3% White, 0.0% Black, 0.0% Asian, 0.7% American Indian and Alaska Native, 0.7% Hispanic of any race, 0.0% two or more races (2000); Density: 8.9 persons per square mile (2000); Age: 35.0% under 18, 11.8% over 64 (2000); Marriage status: 23.7% never married, 65.2% now married, 5.1% widowed, 6.1% divorced (2000); Foreign born: 1.4% (2000); Ancestry (includes multiple ancestries): 55.7% Norwegian, 32.1% German, 17.9% Swedish, 11.4% Czech, 9.6% Irish (2000).
Economy: Employment by occupation: 19.9% management, 14.7% professional, 11.0% services, 25.0% sales, 1.5% farming, 14.7% construction, 13.2% production (2000).
Income: Per capita income: $15,339 (2000); Median household income: $42,917 (2000); Poverty rate: 10.8% (2000).
Taxes: Total city taxes per capita: $60 (1997); City property taxes per capita: $60 (1997).
Education: High school graduation rate: 85.9% (2000); College graduation rate: 16.5% (2000).
Housing: Homeownership rate: 95.7% (2000); Median home value: $72,700 (2000); Median rent: $125 per month (2000); Median age of housing: 55 years (2000).
Transportation: Commute to work: 85.0% car, 0.0% public transportation, 0.0% walk, 15.0% work from home (2000); Travel time to work: 15.9% less than 15 minutes, 15.9% 15 to 30 minutes, 46.0% 30 to 45 minutes, 18.6% 45 to 60 minutes, 3.5% 60 minutes or more (2000)

HITTERDAL (city). Covers a land area of 0.806 square miles and a water area of 0.073 square miles. Located at 46.97° N. Lat.; 96.25° W. Long. Elevation is 1,254 feet.
Population: 201 (2000); Race: 100.0% White, 0.0% Black, 0.0% Asian, 0.0% American Indian and Alaska Native, 0.0% Hispanic of any race, 0.0% two or more races (2000); Density: 249.3 persons per square mile (2000); Age: 31.5% under 18, 17.8% over 64 (2000); Marriage status: 22.4% never married, 61.2% now married, 10.6% widowed, 5.9% divorced (2000); Foreign born: 0.0% (2000); Ancestry (includes multiple ancestries): 63.0% Norwegian, 24.2% German, 9.1% Swedish, 6.4% Danish, 5.0% Polish (2000).
Economy: Grain, beans, sugar beets; dairying. Employment by occupation: 2.0% management, 12.9% professional, 25.7% services, 18.8% sales, 2.0% farming, 14.9% construction, 23.8% production (2000).
Income: Per capita income: $13,737 (2000); Median household income: $32,500 (2000); Poverty rate: 12.3% (2000).
Taxes: Total city taxes per capita: $56 (1997); City property taxes per capita: $56 (1997).
Education: High school graduation rate: 81.6% (2000); College graduation rate: 6.6% (2000).
Housing: Homeownership rate: 87.5% (2000); Median home value: $40,800 (2000); Median rent: $175 per month (2000); Median age of housing: 42 years (2000).
Transportation: Commute to work: 93.9% car, 0.0% public transportation, 4.0% walk, 2.0% work from home (2000); Travel time to work: 26.8% less than 15 minutes, 29.9% 15 to 30 minutes, 25.8% 30 to 45 minutes, 16.5% 45 to 60 minutes, 1.0% 60 minutes or more (2000)

HOLY CROSS (township). Covers a land area of 33.252 square miles and a water area of 0 square miles. Located at 46.67° N. Lat.; 96.73° W. Long.
Population: 129 (2000); Race: 100.0% White, 0.0% Black, 0.0% Asian, 0.0% American Indian and Alaska Native, 0.0% Hispanic of any race, 0.0% two or more races (2000); Density: 3.9 persons per square mile (2000); Age: 28.4% under 18, 19.4% over 64 (2000); Marriage status: 10.0% never married, 87.0% now married, 3.0% widowed, 0.0% divorced (2000); Foreign born: 1.5% (2000); Ancestry (includes multiple ancestries): 56.0% Norwegian, 39.6% German, 15.7% Irish, 11.9% Swedish, 6.7% Dutch (2000).
Economy: Employment by occupation: 17.6% management, 17.6% professional, 3.9% services, 31.4% sales, 3.9% farming, 17.6% construction, 7.8% production (2000).
Income: Per capita income: $15,863 (2000); Median household income: $45,313 (2000); Poverty rate: 7.5% (2000).
Taxes: Total city taxes per capita: $66 (1997); City property taxes per capita: $66 (1997).
Education: High school graduation rate: 91.4% (2000); College graduation rate: 14.0% (2000).
Housing: Homeownership rate: 89.1% (2000); Median home value: $112,500 (2000); Median age of housing: 41 years (2000).
Transportation: Commute to work: 72.5% car, 0.0% public transportation, 0.0% walk, 27.5% work from home (2000); Travel time to work: 16.2% less than 15 minutes, 59.5% 15 to 30 minutes, 24.3% 30 to 45 minutes, 0.0% 45 to 60 minutes, 0.0% 60 minutes or more (2000)

HUMBOLDT (township). Covers a land area of 33.043 square miles and a water area of 0.038 square miles. Located at 46.66° N. Lat.; 96.37° W. Long.
Population: 239 (2000); Race: 98.4% White, 0.0% Black, 0.0% Asian, 0.8% American Indian and Alaska Native, 0.8% Hispanic of any race, 0.0% two or more races (2000); Density: 7.2 persons per square mile (2000); Age: 28.0% under 18, 16.0% over 64 (2000); Marriage status: 19.8% never married, 70.1% now married, 4.3% widowed, 5.9% divorced (2000); Foreign born: 0.8% (2000); Ancestry (includes multiple ancestries): 65.0% Norwegian, 35.0% German, 8.2% Irish, 5.3% Polish, 4.9% Swedish (2000).
Economy: Employment by occupation: 27.5% management, 23.3% professional, 11.7% services, 15.8% sales, 0.0% farming, 9.2% construction, 12.5% production (2000).
Income: Per capita income: $21,303 (2000); Median household income: $51,806 (2000); Poverty rate: 2.5% (2000).
Taxes: Total city taxes per capita: $77 (1997); City property taxes per capita: $77 (1997).
Education: High school graduation rate: 89.6% (2000); College graduation rate: 23.3% (2000).
Housing: Homeownership rate: 94.0% (2000); Median home value: $93,800 (2000); Median rent: $525 per month (2000); Median age of housing: 40 years (2000).
Transportation: Commute to work: 80.0% car, 2.5% public transportation, 1.7% walk, 15.8% work from home (2000); Travel time to work: 26.7% less than 15 minutes, 13.9% 15 to 30 minutes, 41.6% 30 to 45 minutes, 12.9% 45 to 60 minutes, 5.0% 60 minutes or more (2000)

KEENE (township). Covers a land area of 32.358 square miles and a water area of 0.178 square miles. Located at 47.01° N. Lat.; 96.37° W. Long.
Population: 128 (2000); Race: 100.0% White, 0.0% Black, 0.0% Asian, 0.0% American Indian and Alaska Native, 0.0% Hispanic of any race, 0.0% two or more races (2000); Density: 4.0 persons per square mile (2000); Age: 26.8% under 18, 19.7% over 64 (2000); Marriage status: 22.4% never married, 66.3% now married, 5.1% widowed, 6.1% divorced (2000); Foreign born: 0.0% (2000); Ancestry (includes multiple ancestries): 75.6% Norwegian, 15.0% German, 3.9% Italian, 3.9% Czech, 3.1% English (2000).
Economy: Employment by occupation: 10.4% management, 14.6% professional, 20.8% services, 25.0% sales, 4.2% farming, 12.5% construction, 12.5% production (2000).
Income: Per capita income: $16,748 (2000); Median household income: $40,625 (2000); Poverty rate: 11.8% (2000).
Taxes: Total city taxes per capita: $36 (1997); City property taxes per capita: $36 (1997).
Education: High school graduation rate: 76.9% (2000); College graduation rate: 8.8% (2000).
Housing: Homeownership rate: 91.8% (2000); Median home value: $80,000 (2000); Median rent: $325 per month (2000); Median age of housing: 52 years (2000).
Transportation: Commute to work: 81.3% car, 0.0% public transportation, 0.0% walk, 18.8% work from home (2000); Travel time to work: 17.9% less than 15 minutes, 15.4% 15 to 30 minutes, 48.7% 30 to 45 minutes, 12.8% 45 to 60 minutes, 5.1% 60 minutes or more (2000)

KRAGNES (township). Covers a land area of 38.178 square miles and a water area of 0 square miles. Located at 47.01° N. Lat.; 96.76° W. Long. Elevation is 890 feet.
Population: 319 (2000); Race: 99.4% White, 0.0% Black, 0.0% Asian, 0.0% American Indian and Alaska Native, 3.8% Hispanic of any race, 0.6% two or more races (2000); Density: 8.4 persons per square mile (2000); Age: 31.3% under 18, 10.3% over 64 (2000); Marriage status: 18.3% never married, 75.4% now married, 2.5% widowed, 3.8% divorced (2000); Foreign born: 0.6% (2000); Ancestry (includes multiple ancestries): 53.9% Norwegian, 39.8% German, 12.2% Swedish, 9.7% English, 7.2% French (except Basque) (2000).
Economy: Employment by occupation: 22.2% management, 13.1% professional, 12.4% services, 30.1% sales, 3.3% farming, 6.5% construction, 12.4% production (2000).
Income: Per capita income: $21,006 (2000); Median household income: $53,571 (2000); Poverty rate: 4.7% (2000).
Taxes: Total city taxes per capita: $38 (1997); City property taxes per capita: $38 (1997).
Education: High school graduation rate: 91.2% (2000); College graduation rate: 24.9% (2000).

Housing: Homeownership rate: 97.3% (2000); Median home value: $91,100 (2000); Median age of housing: 34 years (2000).
Transportation: Commute to work: 88.2% car, 0.0% public transportation, 3.3% walk, 8.5% work from home (2000); Travel time to work: 22.9% less than 15 minutes, 58.6% 15 to 30 minutes, 7.9% 30 to 45 minutes, 5.0% 45 to 60 minutes, 5.7% 60 minutes or more (2000)

KURTZ (township). Covers a land area of 32.453 square miles and a water area of 0 square miles. Located at 46.77° N. Lat.; 96.74° W. Long.
Population: 288 (2000); Race: 95.9% White, 0.0% Black, 0.0% Asian, 2.4% American Indian and Alaska Native, 1.7% Hispanic of any race, 0.0% two or more races (2000); Density: 8.9 persons per square mile (2000); Age: 30.7% under 18, 11.7% over 64 (2000); Marriage status: 25.0% never married, 68.8% now married, 1.8% widowed, 4.5% divorced (2000); Foreign born: 3.8% (2000); Ancestry (includes multiple ancestries): 50.0% Norwegian, 39.0% German, 6.9% English, 6.2% Irish, 5.9% Swedish (2000).
Economy: Employment by occupation: 16.1% management, 24.5% professional, 10.3% services, 28.4% sales, 1.3% farming, 8.4% construction, 11.0% production (2000).
Income: Per capita income: $23,501 (2000); Median household income: $62,750 (2000); Poverty rate: 1.4% (2000).
Taxes: Total city taxes per capita: $87 (1997); City property taxes per capita: $87 (1997).
Education: High school graduation rate: 92.8% (2000); College graduation rate: 31.1% (2000).
Housing: Homeownership rate: 98.0% (2000); Median home value: $137,500 (2000); Median age of housing: 30 years (2000).
Transportation: Commute to work: 88.8% car, 0.0% public transportation, 0.7% walk, 10.5% work from home (2000); Travel time to work: 16.9% less than 15 minutes, 64.7% 15 to 30 minutes, 15.4% 30 to 45 minutes, 0.0% 45 to 60 minutes, 2.9% 60 minutes or more (2000)

MOLAND (township). Covers a land area of 35.119 square miles and a water area of 0.013 square miles. Located at 46.92° N. Lat.; 96.60° W. Long.
Population: 340 (2000); Race: 95.9% White, 0.0% Black, 0.0% Asian, 0.0% American Indian and Alaska Native, 4.1% Hispanic of any race, 0.0% two or more races (2000); Density: 9.7 persons per square mile (2000); Age: 30.7% under 18, 7.9% over 64 (2000); Marriage status: 13.8% never married, 73.6% now married, 2.4% widowed, 10.2% divorced (2000); Foreign born: 3.2% (2000); Ancestry (includes multiple ancestries): 42.4% Norwegian, 38.6% German, 11.4% Irish, 7.0% Swedish, 4.7% Other groups (2000).
Economy: Employment by occupation: 24.4% management, 12.2% professional, 12.2% services, 29.7% sales, 0.0% farming, 11.6% construction, 9.9% production (2000).
Income: Per capita income: $28,200 (2000); Median household income: $52,083 (2000); Poverty rate: 3.8% (2000).
Taxes: Total city taxes per capita: $42 (1997); City property taxes per capita: $42 (1997).
Education: High school graduation rate: 93.5% (2000); College graduation rate: 14.3% (2000).
Housing: Homeownership rate: 85.5% (2000); Median home value: $92,000 (2000); Median rent: $292 per month (2000); Median age of housing: 42 years (2000).
Transportation: Commute to work: 91.8% car, 0.0% public transportation, 0.0% walk, 7.1% work from home (2000); Travel time to work: 10.1% less than 15 minutes, 74.7% 15 to 30 minutes, 11.4% 30 to 45 minutes, 3.8% 45 to 60 minutes, 0.0% 60 minutes or more (2000)

MOORHEAD (city). Covers a land area of 13.439 square miles and a water area of 0 square miles. Located at 46.86° N. Lat.; 96.75° W. Long. Elevation is 906 feet.
History: A settlement grew up at Moorhead because it was a transportation junction for trails and river traffic, and later for the railroad. The town was named in 1871 in honor of Dr. William G. Moorhead, a director of the Northern Pacific Railraod. Early settlers failed to realize the fertility of the prairie land for crops, but Moorhead later became the center of a prosperous farming region, with potatoes and sugar beets as leaders. Concordia College was established in 1891 in Moorhead.
Population: 32,177 (2000); Race: 92.3% White, 0.7% Black, 1.1% Asian, 1.5% American Indian and Alaska Native, 4.4% Hispanic of any race, 2.4% two or more races (2000); Density: 2,394.3 persons per square mile (2000); Age: 22.6% under 18, 12.8% over 64 (2000); Marriage status: 40.2% never married, 46.2% now married, 6.0% widowed, 7.6% divorced (2000); Foreign born: 3.4% (2000); Ancestry (includes multiple ancestries): 40.0% Norwegian, 35.4% German, 9.2% Swedish, 8.2% Other groups, 7.6% Irish (2000).
Vital Statistics: Birth rate: 127.7 per 10,000 population (1998)
Economy: Unemployment rate: 1.4% (11/2002); Total civilian labor force: 20,907 (11/2002); Single-family building permits issued: 116 (2001) / 100 (2000); Multi-family building permits issued: 6 (2001) / 44 (2000); Employment by occupation: 11.4% management, 21.3% professional, 18.9% services, 28.9% sales, 0.2% farming, 7.8% construction, 11.5% production (2000).
Income: Per capita income: $17,150 (2000); Median household income: $34,781 (2000); Poverty rate: 16.3% (2000).
Taxes: Total city taxes per capita: $122 (2000); City property taxes per capita: $105 (2000).
Education: High school graduation rate: 87.7% (2000); College graduation rate: 29.5% (2000).

School District(s)

Moorhead (PK-12)
2000 Enrollment: 5,698 218-236-6400

Four-year College(s)

Concordia College at Moorhead (Private, Not-for-profit, Evangelical Lutheran Church)
2001 Enrollment: 2,707 218-299-4100
Minnesota State University-Moorhead (Public)
2001 Enrollment: 7,431 218-236-2011
2001 Tuition: In-state $2,874; Out-of-state $6,444

Two-year College(s)

Northwest Technical College-Moorhead (Public)
2001 Enrollment: n/a 218-236-6277

Housing: Homeownership rate: 63.7% (2000); Median home value: $86,100 (2000); Median rent: $379 per month (2000); Median age of housing: 33 years (2000).
Safety: Violent crime rate: 16.3 per 10,000 population; Property crime rate: 348.4 per 10,000 population (2001).
Transportation: Commute to work: 85.7% car, 1.0% public transportation, 9.8% walk, 2.6% work from home (2000); Travel time to work: 57.4% less than 15 minutes, 35.9% 15 to 30 minutes, 2.5% 30 to 45 minutes, 1.3% 45 to 60 minutes, 2.9% 60 minutes or more (2000)

Additional Information Contacts

Moorhead Chamber of Commerce 218-233-1100

MOORHEAD (township). Covers a land area of 18.934 square miles and a water area of 0 square miles. Located at 46.84° N. Lat.; 96.71° W. Long. Elevation is 906 feet.
History: Seat of Moorhead State University and Concordia College. The Plains Art Museum is here. Incorporated 1881.
Population: 442 (2000); Race: 99.7% White, 0.0% Black, 0.0% Asian, 0.0% American Indian and Alaska Native, 0.0% Hispanic of any race, 0.3% two or more races (2000); Density: 23.3 persons per square mile (2000); Age: 21.1% under 18, 18.3% over 64 (2000); Marriage status: 20.4% never married, 67.5% now married, 5.3% widowed, 6.8% divorced (2000); Foreign born: 2.3% (2000); Ancestry (includes multiple ancestries): 49.1% Norwegian, 36.1% German, 9.2% Irish, 7.9% Scandinavian, 7.6% Swedish (2000).
Economy: Railroad junction. Shipping and processing center for an agricultural area: cattle, poultry, sheep, hogs, dairying. Manufacturing includes sugar and molasses, barley malt, soft drinks, printing and publishing, dairy bottles and fiberglass tanks. Employment by occupation: 13.7% management, 14.7% professional, 9.0% services, 38.9% sales, 0.0% farming, 10.9% construction, 12.8% production (2000).
Income: Per capita income: $27,591 (2000); Median household income: $54,286 (2000); Poverty rate: 1.0% (2000).
Taxes: Total city taxes per capita: $38 (1997); City property taxes per capita: $38 (1997).
Education: High school graduation rate: 84.8% (2000); College graduation rate: 21.7% (2000).
Housing: Homeownership rate: 96.4% (2000); Median home value: $109,800 (2000); Median rent: $408 per month (2000); Median age of housing: 32 years (2000).
Transportation: Commute to work: 90.3% car, 1.0% public transportation, 0.0% walk, 8.7% work from home (2000); Travel time to work: 52.7% less than 15 minutes, 42.0% 15 to 30 minutes, 1.1% 30 to 45 minutes, 0.0% 45 to 60 minutes, 4.3% 60 minutes or more (2000)

MORKEN (township). Covers a land area of 35.875 square miles and a water area of 0 square miles. Located at 47.01° N. Lat.; 96.63° W. Long.
Population: 203 (2000); Race: 100.0% White, 0.0% Black, 0.0% Asian, 0.0% American Indian and Alaska Native, 0.0% Hispanic of any race, 0.0% two or more races (2000); Density: 5.7 persons per square mile (2000); Age: 22.7% under 18, 17.4% over 64 (2000); Marriage status: 22.1% never

married, 74.3% now married, 0.0% widowed, 3.6% divorced (2000); Foreign born: 0.0% (2000); Ancestry (includes multiple ancestries): 44.2% Norwegian, 40.1% German, 20.9% Swedish, 7.6% Dutch, 4.7% French (except Basque) (2000).
Economy: Employment by occupation: 18.5% management, 13.8% professional, 24.6% services, 6.2% sales, 4.6% farming, 7.7% construction, 24.6% production (2000).
Income: Per capita income: $17,130 (2000); Median household income: $46,250 (2000); Poverty rate: 8.7% (2000).
Taxes: Total city taxes per capita: $122 (1997); City property taxes per capita: $122 (1997).
Education: High school graduation rate: 86.7% (2000); College graduation rate: 15.0% (2000).
Housing: Homeownership rate: 87.7% (2000); Median home value: $94,200 (2000); Median rent: $275 per month (2000); Median age of housing: 40 years (2000).
Transportation: Commute to work: 82.8% car, 0.0% public transportation, 6.3% walk, 10.9% work from home (2000); Travel time to work: 10.5% less than 15 minutes, 43.9% 15 to 30 minutes, 45.6% 30 to 45 minutes, 0.0% 45 to 60 minutes, 0.0% 60 minutes or more (2000)

OAKPORT (township). Covers a land area of 29.175 square miles and a water area of 0 square miles. Located at 46.94° N. Lat.; 96.75° W. Long.
Population: 1,689 (2000); Race: 98.7% White, 0.4% Black, 0.0% Asian, 0.0% American Indian and Alaska Native, 1.0% Hispanic of any race, 0.7% two or more races (2000); Density: 57.9 persons per square mile (2000); Age: 30.7% under 18, 7.4% over 64 (2000); Marriage status: 18.7% never married, 73.4% now married, 2.4% widowed, 5.5% divorced (2000); Foreign born: 0.6% (2000); Ancestry (includes multiple ancestries): 46.4% Norwegian, 40.7% German, 9.7% Swedish, 7.8% Irish, 5.1% Polish (2000).
Economy: Employment by occupation: 13.1% management, 22.6% professional, 13.7% services, 26.2% sales, 0.3% farming, 11.9% construction, 12.1% production (2000).
Income: Per capita income: $21,570 (2000); Median household income: $60,400 (2000); Poverty rate: 4.5% (2000).
Taxes: Total city taxes per capita: $62 (2000); City property taxes per capita: $62 (2000).
Education: High school graduation rate: 93.6% (2000); College graduation rate: 27.5% (2000).
Housing: Homeownership rate: 96.0% (2000); Median home value: $112,700 (2000); Median rent: $135 per month (2000); Median age of housing: 26 years (2000).
Transportation: Commute to work: 94.4% car, 0.0% public transportation, 0.4% walk, 5.0% work from home (2000); Travel time to work: 30.6% less than 15 minutes, 60.1% 15 to 30 minutes, 6.4% 30 to 45 minutes, 0.8% 45 to 60 minutes, 2.1% 60 minutes or more (2000)

PARKE (township). Covers a land area of 34.110 square miles and a water area of 1.921 square miles. Located at 46.77° N. Lat.; 96.22° W. Long.
Population: 450 (2000); Race: 99.5% White, 0.5% Black, 0.0% Asian, 0.0% American Indian and Alaska Native, 0.0% Hispanic of any race, 0.0% two or more races (2000); Density: 13.2 persons per square mile (2000); Age: 28.3% under 18, 8.9% over 64 (2000); Marriage status: 19.9% never married, 71.6% now married, 3.5% widowed, 5.0% divorced (2000); Foreign born: 0.5% (2000); Ancestry (includes multiple ancestries): 55.3% Norwegian, 38.6% German, 11.9% Swedish, 9.1% Irish, 5.7% Dutch (2000).
Economy: Employment by occupation: 18.9% management, 22.5% professional, 10.1% services, 18.5% sales, 3.5% farming, 12.3% construction, 14.1% production (2000).
Income: Per capita income: $22,207 (2000); Median household income: $51,094 (2000); Poverty rate: 3.7% (2000).
Taxes: Total city taxes per capita: $49 (1997); City property taxes per capita: $49 (1997).
Education: High school graduation rate: 93.8% (2000); College graduation rate: 21.3% (2000).
Housing: Homeownership rate: 95.7% (2000); Median home value: $112,500 (2000); Median rent: $292 per month (2000); Median age of housing: 22 years (2000).
Transportation: Commute to work: 92.9% car, 0.9% public transportation, 0.0% walk, 5.3% work from home (2000); Travel time to work: 8.5% less than 15 minutes, 24.9% 15 to 30 minutes, 39.4% 30 to 45 minutes, 22.5% 45 to 60 minutes, 4.7% 60 minutes or more (2000)

RIVERTON (township). Covers a land area of 35.767 square miles and a water area of 0.033 square miles. Located at 46.85° N. Lat.; 96.50° W. Long.
Population: 462 (2000); Race: 98.6% White, 0.5% Black, 0.0% Asian, 0.0% American Indian and Alaska Native, 0.0% Hispanic of any race, 0.9% two or more races (2000); Density: 12.9 persons per square mile (2000); Age: 29.7% under 18, 4.0% over 64 (2000); Marriage status: 29.2% never married, 62.3% now married, 2.4% widowed, 6.1% divorced (2000); Foreign born: 0.0% (2000); Ancestry (includes multiple ancestries): 44.0% German, 39.8% Norwegian, 10.1% Swedish, 9.8% English, 6.1% French (except Basque) (2000).
Economy: Employment by occupation: 11.2% management, 15.2% professional, 14.8% services, 22.8% sales, 2.0% farming, 16.8% construction, 17.2% production (2000).
Income: Per capita income: $17,670 (2000); Median household income: $51,042 (2000); Poverty rate: 8.5% (2000).
Taxes: Total city taxes per capita: $60 (1997); City property taxes per capita: $60 (1997).
Education: High school graduation rate: 84.8% (2000); College graduation rate: 16.7% (2000).
Housing: Homeownership rate: 96.6% (2000); Median home value: $100,000 (2000); Median rent: $175 per month (2000); Median age of housing: 24 years (2000).
Transportation: Commute to work: 90.7% car, 0.0% public transportation, 2.8% walk, 6.5% work from home (2000); Travel time to work: 6.1% less than 15 minutes, 64.9% 15 to 30 minutes, 24.7% 30 to 45 minutes, 0.0% 45 to 60 minutes, 4.3% 60 minutes or more (2000)

SABIN (city). Covers a land area of 0.303 square miles and a water area of 0 square miles. Located at 46.77° N. Lat.; 96.65° W. Long. Elevation is 932 feet.
Population: 421 (2000); Race: 97.9% White, 1.3% Black, 0.0% Asian, 0.4% American Indian and Alaska Native, 0.9% Hispanic of any race, 0.0% two or more races (2000); Density: 1,390.5 persons per square mile (2000); Age: 32.1% under 18, 6.2% over 64 (2000); Marriage status: 18.6% never married, 67.7% now married, 5.1% widowed, 8.7% divorced (2000); Foreign born: 0.0% (2000); Ancestry (includes multiple ancestries): 53.4% German, 43.0% Norwegian, 9.8% Swedish, 6.0% Dutch, 6.0% Irish (2000).
Economy: Grain, potatoes, sugar beets; livestock; dairying. Single-family building permits issued: 0 (2001) / 0 (2000); Multi-family building permits issued: 0 (2001) / 0 (2000); Employment by occupation: 10.2% management, 15.7% professional, 16.5% services, 30.6% sales, 0.8% farming, 14.5% construction, 11.8% production (2000).
Income: Per capita income: $15,776 (2000); Median household income: $43,523 (2000); Poverty rate: 6.4% (2000).
Taxes: Total city taxes per capita: $35 (1997); City property taxes per capita: $25 (1997).
Education: High school graduation rate: 93.6% (2000); College graduation rate: 16.3% (2000).
Housing: Homeownership rate: 90.7% (2000); Median home value: $72,400 (2000); Median rent: $250 per month (2000); Median age of housing: 35 years (2000).
Transportation: Commute to work: 89.6% car, 3.2% public transportation, 2.4% walk, 4.0% work from home (2000); Travel time to work: 13.4% less than 15 minutes, 69.9% 15 to 30 minutes, 14.2% 30 to 45 minutes, 0.0% 45 to 60 minutes, 2.5% 60 minutes or more (2000)

SKREE (township). Covers a land area of 33.566 square miles and a water area of 0.277 square miles. Located at 46.75° N. Lat.; 96.37° W. Long.
Population: 166 (2000); Race: 100.0% White, 0.0% Black, 0.0% Asian, 0.0% American Indian and Alaska Native, 0.0% Hispanic of any race, 0.0% two or more races (2000); Density: 4.9 persons per square mile (2000); Age: 32.5% under 18, 10.1% over 64 (2000); Marriage status: 23.6% never married, 63.8% now married, 7.1% widowed, 5.5% divorced (2000); Foreign born: 0.0% (2000); Ancestry (includes multiple ancestries): 43.8% Norwegian, 30.8% German, 7.1% United States or American, 6.5% Swedish, 5.9% Czech (2000).
Economy: Employment by occupation: 21.5% management, 10.1% professional, 6.3% services, 24.1% sales, 7.6% farming, 7.6% construction, 22.8% production (2000).
Income: Per capita income: $15,174 (2000); Median household income: $46,250 (2000); Poverty rate: 8.3% (2000).
Taxes: Total city taxes per capita: $96 (1997); City property taxes per capita: $96 (1997).
Education: High school graduation rate: 93.3% (2000); College graduation rate: 12.4% (2000).
Housing: Homeownership rate: 90.5% (2000); Median home value: $112,500 (2000); Median age of housing: 38 years (2000).

Transportation: Commute to work: 82.7% car, 0.0% public transportation, 2.7% walk, 14.7% work from home (2000); Travel time to work: 23.4% less than 15 minutes, 23.4% 15 to 30 minutes, 37.5% 30 to 45 minutes, 15.6% 45 to 60 minutes, 0.0% 60 minutes or more (2000)

SPRING PRAIRIE (township). Covers a land area of 35.645 square miles and a water area of 0.015 square miles. Located at 46.93° N. Lat.; 96.48° W. Long.
Population: 364 (2000); Race: 98.6% White, 0.0% Black, 0.0% Asian, 0.0% American Indian and Alaska Native, 1.4% Hispanic of any race, 0.0% two or more races (2000); Density: 10.2 persons per square mile (2000); Age: 34.6% under 18, 7.1% over 64 (2000); Marriage status: 27.6% never married, 63.8% now married, 1.2% widowed, 7.4% divorced (2000); Foreign born: 2.0% (2000); Ancestry (includes multiple ancestries): 54.0% German, 24.0% Norwegian, 9.7% Swedish, 4.3% Irish, 3.4% Danish (2000).
Economy: Employment by occupation: 26.7% management, 12.7% professional, 12.0% services, 14.7% sales, 2.7% farming, 19.3% construction, 12.0% production (2000).
Income: Per capita income: $13,731 (2000); Median household income: $44,167 (2000); Poverty rate: 29.1% (2000).
Taxes: Total city taxes per capita: $45 (1997); City property taxes per capita: $45 (1997).
Education: High school graduation rate: 61.9% (2000); College graduation rate: 5.7% (2000).
Housing: Homeownership rate: 84.7% (2000); Median home value: $100,000 (2000); Median age of housing: 26 years (2000).
Transportation: Commute to work: 69.3% car, 0.0% public transportation, 4.7% walk, 26.0% work from home (2000); Travel time to work: 9.9% less than 15 minutes, 41.4% 15 to 30 minutes, 43.2% 30 to 45 minutes, 3.6% 45 to 60 minutes, 1.8% 60 minutes or more (2000)

TANSEM (township). Covers a land area of 35.595 square miles and a water area of 0.517 square miles. Located at 46.65° N. Lat.; 96.22° W. Long.
Population: 222 (2000); Race: 98.2% White, 0.9% Black, 0.0% Asian, 0.0% American Indian and Alaska Native, 1.8% Hispanic of any race, 0.9% two or more races (2000); Density: 6.2 persons per square mile (2000); Age: 23.2% under 18, 15.8% over 64 (2000); Marriage status: 12.7% never married, 83.4% now married, 2.2% widowed, 1.7% divorced (2000); Foreign born: 0.0% (2000); Ancestry (includes multiple ancestries): 50.0% Norwegian, 38.2% German, 7.9% Other groups, 6.6% English, 5.7% French (except Basque) (2000).
Economy: Employment by occupation: 23.4% management, 16.8% professional, 5.6% services, 24.3% sales, 1.9% farming, 15.9% construction, 12.1% production (2000).
Income: Per capita income: $18,917 (2000); Median household income: $43,750 (2000); Poverty rate: 16.2% (2000).
Taxes: Total city taxes per capita: $62 (1997); City property taxes per capita: $62 (1997).
Education: High school graduation rate: 93.5% (2000); College graduation rate: 27.4% (2000).
Housing: Homeownership rate: 90.6% (2000); Median home value: $75,000 (2000); Median age of housing: 52 years (2000).
Transportation: Commute to work: 84.1% car, 0.0% public transportation, 2.8% walk, 13.1% work from home (2000); Travel time to work: 3.2% less than 15 minutes, 19.4% 15 to 30 minutes, 23.7% 30 to 45 minutes, 45.2% 45 to 60 minutes, 8.6% 60 minutes or more (2000)

ULEN (city). Covers a land area of 1.088 square miles and a water area of 0 square miles. Located at 47.07° N. Lat.; 96.26° W. Long. Elevation is 1,158 feet.
Population: 532 (2000); Race: 98.9% White, 0.0% Black, 0.7% Asian, 0.4% American Indian and Alaska Native, 0.0% Hispanic of any race, 0.0% two or more races (2000); Density: 488.9 persons per square mile (2000); Age: 22.5% under 18, 34.1% over 64 (2000); Marriage status: 16.7% never married, 63.6% now married, 12.6% widowed, 7.1% divorced (2000); Foreign born: 1.5% (2000); Ancestry (includes multiple ancestries): 65.9% Norwegian, 21.6% German, 3.2% Swedish, 3.2% Irish, 2.6% Danish (2000).
Economy: Single-family building permits issued: 3 (2001) / 0 (2000); Multi-family building permits issued: 0 (2001) / 0 (2000); Employment by occupation: 13.6% management, 18.1% professional, 27.6% services, 15.6% sales, 1.5% farming, 8.0% construction, 15.6% production (2000).
Income: Per capita income: $16,593 (2000); Median household income: $27,813 (2000); Poverty rate: 8.5% (2000).
Taxes: Total city taxes per capita: $66 (1997); City property taxes per capita: $64 (1997).
Education: High school graduation rate: 65.4% (2000); College graduation rate: 8.5% (2000).

School District(s)

Ulen-Hitterdal (KG-12)
2000 Enrollment: 301 218-596-8853

Housing: Homeownership rate: 72.5% (2000); Median home value: $41,300 (2000); Median rent: $335 per month (2000); Median age of housing: 39 years (2000).
Newspapers: Ulen Union (1 x week)
Transportation: Commute to work: 79.6% car, 0.0% public transportation, 12.8% walk, 3.6% work from home (2000); Travel time to work: 49.2% less than 15 minutes, 18.5% 15 to 30 minutes, 9.0% 30 to 45 minutes, 16.9% 45 to 60 minutes, 6.3% 60 minutes or more (2000)

ULEN (township). Covers a land area of 35.225 square miles and a water area of 0 square miles. Located at 47.10° N. Lat.; 96.24° W. Long. Elevation is 1,158 feet.
Population: 163 (2000); Race: 95.7% White, 0.0% Black, 4.3% Asian, 0.0% American Indian and Alaska Native, 0.0% Hispanic of any race, 0.0% two or more races (2000); Density: 4.6 persons per square mile (2000); Age: 32.7% under 18, 14.8% over 64 (2000); Marriage status: 27.5% never married, 55.0% now married, 4.2% widowed, 13.3% divorced (2000); Foreign born: 4.3% (2000); Ancestry (includes multiple ancestries): 41.4% Norwegian, 22.8% German, 8.0% French (except Basque), 8.0% Danish, 3.7% English (2000).
Economy: Terminus of railroad spur. Agriculture includes wheat, potatoes, sugar beets, sunflowers; livestock, poultry; dairying. Employment by occupation: 12.3% management, 18.5% professional, 16.9% services, 10.8% sales, 3.1% farming, 18.5% construction, 20.0% production (2000).
Income: Per capita income: $14,318 (2000); Median household income: $37,500 (2000); Poverty rate: 21.3% (2000).
Taxes: Total city taxes per capita: $105 (1997); City property taxes per capita: $105 (1997).
Education: High school graduation rate: 63.6% (2000); College graduation rate: 10.1% (2000).
Housing: Homeownership rate: 88.5% (2000); Median home value: $53,300 (2000); Median age of housing: 54 years (2000).
Transportation: Commute to work: 92.3% car, 0.0% public transportation, 0.0% walk, 7.7% work from home (2000); Travel time to work: 50.0% less than 15 minutes, 11.7% 15 to 30 minutes, 10.0% 30 to 45 minutes, 20.0% 45 to 60 minutes, 8.3% 60 minutes or more (2000)

VIDING (township). Covers a land area of 35.737 square miles and a water area of 0 square miles. Located at 47.10° N. Lat.; 96.63° W. Long.
Population: 124 (2000); Race: 100.0% White, 0.0% Black, 0.0% Asian, 0.0% American Indian and Alaska Native, 0.0% Hispanic of any race, 0.0% two or more races (2000); Density: 3.5 persons per square mile (2000); Age: 27.7% under 18, 16.9% over 64 (2000); Marriage status: 14.9% never married, 67.0% now married, 6.4% widowed, 11.7% divorced (2000); Foreign born: 1.5% (2000); Ancestry (includes multiple ancestries): 48.5% German, 34.6% Norwegian, 17.7% English, 9.2% Dutch, 9.2% Swedish (2000).
Economy: Employment by occupation: 39.7% management, 15.5% professional, 8.6% services, 12.1% sales, 3.4% farming, 5.2% construction, 15.5% production (2000).
Income: Per capita income: $19,637 (2000); Median household income: $42,083 (2000); Poverty rate: 0.0% (2000).
Taxes: Total city taxes per capita: $165 (1997); City property taxes per capita: $165 (1997).
Education: High school graduation rate: 87.2% (2000); College graduation rate: 18.6% (2000).
Housing: Homeownership rate: 80.8% (2000); Median home value: $87,500 (2000); Median rent: $508 per month (2000); Median age of housing: 50 years (2000).
Transportation: Commute to work: 79.3% car, 0.0% public transportation, 0.0% walk, 20.7% work from home (2000); Travel time to work: 21.7% less than 15 minutes, 39.1% 15 to 30 minutes, 34.8% 30 to 45 minutes, 4.3% 45 to 60 minutes, 0.0% 60 minutes or more (2000)

Clearwater County

Located in northwestern Minnesota; drained by the Clearwater River and headwaters of the Mississippi River. Covers a land area of 994.70 square miles, a water area of 35.10 square miles, and is located in the Central Time Zone. The county government was organized in 1902. County seat is Bagley.

Weather Station: Itasca Univ. of Minnesota Elevation: 1,489 feet

	Jan	Feb	Mar	Apr	May	Jun	Jul	Aug	Sep	Oct	Nov	Dec
High	16	25	36	53	68	76	80	78	67	54	34	21
Low	-7	-1	13	27	40	50	55	53	43	32	17	1
Precip	0.9	0.6	1.3	1.8	2.8	4.2	3.9	3.6	3.0	2.6	1.3	0.8
Snow	11.8	7.0	9.2	3.2	tr	0.0	0.0	0.0	tr	1.3	8.7	8.5

High and Low temperatures in degrees Fahrenheit; Precipitation and Snow in inches

Population: 8,423 (2000); Race: 90.4% White, 0.1% Black, 0.4% Asian, 7.2% American Indian and Alaska Native, 0.6% Hispanic of any race, 1.8% two or more races (2000); Density: 8.5 persons per square mile (2000); Age: 26.1% under 18, 17.3% over 64 (2000).
Religion: Five largest groups: 29.2% Evangelical Lutheran Church in America, 6.5% Catholic Church, 6.3% The Association of Free Lutheran Congregations, 3.4% Episcopal Church, 1.8% Assemblies of God (2000).
Economy: Unemployment rate: 8.3% (11/2002); Total civilian labor force: 4,669 (11/2002); Leading industries: 25.4% health care and social assistance; 23.0% manufacturing; 16.2% retail trade (2000); Companies that employ more than 1,000 persons: 0 (2000); Companies that employ more than 100 persons: 3 (2000); Farms: 570 totaling 212,285 acres (1997); Minority business ownership rate: 0.0% (1997); Women business ownership rate: 33.9% (1997); Retail sales per capita: $4,170 (1997). Single-family building permits issued: 5 (2001) / 5 (2000); Multi-family building permits issued: 0 (2001) / 0 (2000).
Income: Per capita income: $15,694 (2000); Median household income: $30,517 (2000); Poverty rate: 15.1% (2000); Bankruptcy rate: 1.96% (2001).
Taxes: Total county taxes per capita: $451 (1997); County property taxes per capita: $449 (1997).
Education: High school graduation rate: 76.4% (2000); College graduation rate: 14.7% (2000).
Housing: Homeownership rate: 81.6% (2000); Median home value: $51,300 (2000); Median rent: $268 per month (2000); Median age of housing: 32 years (2000).
Health: Birth rate: 85.5 per 10,000 population (1998); Age adjusted death rate: 95.7 per 10,000 population (1999); Age adjusted cancer mortality rate: 186.5 deaths per 100,000 population (1999). Number of physicians: 9.5 per 10,000 population (1999); Number of hospital beds: 111.6 per 10,000 population (1999).
Elections: 2000 Presidential election results: 38.3% Gore, 55.9% Bush, 3.5% Nader, 1.8% Buchanan
National and State Parks: Bagley Lake State Wildlife Management Area; Clearwater State Wildlife Management Area; Itasca State Park; Jackson Lake State Wildlife Management Area; Le Blanc State Wildlife Management Area; Little Pine State Wildlife Management Are; Lower Rice Lake State Wildlife Management Ar; Old Red Lake Trail State Wildlife Management; Upper Rice Lake State Wildlife Management Ar; White Earth State Forest
Additional Information Contacts
Clearwater County Government Offices 218-694-6520

Clearwater County Communities

BAGLEY (city). Covers a land area of 1.832 square miles and a water area of 0.058 square miles. Located at 47.52° N. Lat.; 95.40° W. Long. Elevation is 1,441 feet.
History: Settled 1898, incorporated 1900.
Population: 1,235 (2000); Race: 90.2% White, 0.4% Black, 1.5% Asian, 7.1% American Indian and Alaska Native, 0.6% Hispanic of any race, 0.9% two or more races (2000); Density: 674.1 persons per square mile (2000); Age: 20.7% under 18, 28.7% over 64 (2000); Marriage status: 20.8% never married, 50.8% now married, 17.2% widowed, 11.2% divorced (2000); Foreign born: 2.5% (2000); Ancestry (includes multiple ancestries): 48.1% Norwegian, 18.4% German, 9.5% Other groups, 8.7% Swedish, 7.7% Irish (2000).
Economy: Dairying; poultry, eggs, cattle, sheep; grain, sunflowers, alfalfa. Manufacturing: hardwood products, pulpwood, concrete products, wooden pallets. Single-family building permits issued: 4 (2001) / 4 (2000); Multi-family building permits issued: 0 (2001) / 0 (2000); Employment by occupation: 6.5% management, 22.4% professional, 19.0% services, 22.0% sales, 1.9% farming, 12.7% construction, 15.5% production (2000).
Income: Per capita income: $15,472 (2000); Median household income: $23,125 (2000); Poverty rate: 20.7% (2000).
Taxes: Total city taxes per capita: $132 (1997); City property taxes per capita: $129 (1997).
Education: High school graduation rate: 71.7% (2000); College graduation rate: 16.3% (2000).

School District(s)

Bagley (PK-12)
2000 Enrollment: 1,127 218-694-6184
Housing: Homeownership rate: 58.6% (2000); Median home value: $42,600 (2000); Median rent: $314 per month (2000); Median age of housing: 48 years (2000).
Hospitals: Clearwater Health Services (40 beds)
Newspapers: Farmers Independent (1 x week)
Transportation: Commute to work: 83.1% car, 0.4% public transportation, 12.4% walk, 3.4% work from home (2000); Travel time to work: 63.6% less than 15 minutes, 13.1% 15 to 30 minutes, 14.0% 30 to 45 minutes, 4.2% 45 to 60 minutes, 5.1% 60 minutes or more (2000)

BEAR CREEK (township). Covers a land area of 30.317 square miles and a water area of 1.708 square miles. Located at 47.36° N. Lat.; 95.23° W. Long.
Population: 107 (2000); Race: 84.9% White, 0.0% Black, 5.8% Asian, 0.0% American Indian and Alaska Native, 7.0% Hispanic of any race, 2.3% two or more races (2000); Density: 3.5 persons per square mile (2000); Age: 31.4% under 18, 9.3% over 64 (2000); Marriage status: 16.2% never married, 73.5% now married, 0.0% widowed, 10.3% divorced (2000); Foreign born: 5.8% (2000); Ancestry (includes multiple ancestries): 19.8% German, 19.8% United States or American, 12.8% Other groups, 11.6% Irish, 9.3% Norwegian (2000).
Economy: Employment by occupation: 8.7% management, 23.9% professional, 21.7% services, 6.5% sales, 13.0% farming, 8.7% construction, 17.4% production (2000).
Income: Per capita income: $17,842 (2000); Median household income: $47,500 (2000); Poverty rate: 3.5% (2000).
Taxes: Total city taxes per capita: $98 (1997); City property taxes per capita: $98 (1997).
Education: High school graduation rate: 88.1% (2000); College graduation rate: 15.3% (2000).
Housing: Homeownership rate: 100.0% (2000); Median home value: $65,000 (2000); Median age of housing: 36 years (2000).
Transportation: Commute to work: 86.4% car, 0.0% public transportation, 0.0% walk, 9.1% work from home (2000); Travel time to work: 5.0% less than 15 minutes, 22.5% 15 to 30 minutes, 52.5% 30 to 45 minutes, 7.5% 45 to 60 minutes, 12.5% 60 minutes or more (2000)

CLEARBROOK (city). Covers a land area of 0.445 square miles and a water area of 0 square miles. Located at 47.69° N. Lat.; 95.42° W. Long. Elevation is 1,355 feet.
Population: 551 (2000); Race: 98.4% White, 0.4% Black, 0.0% Asian, 0.0% American Indian and Alaska Native, 0.2% Hispanic of any race, 1.3% two or more races (2000); Density: 1,239.6 persons per square mile (2000); Age: 21.8% under 18, 34.3% over 64 (2000); Marriage status: 23.8% never married, 44.9% now married, 20.9% widowed, 10.4% divorced (2000); Foreign born: 0.5% (2000); Ancestry (includes multiple ancestries): 46.1% Norwegian, 17.6% German, 15.1% Swedish, 6.5% English, 4.5% European (2000).
Economy: Agriculture: dairying, poultry, cattle, sheep, sunflowers, grain, alfalfa. Single-family building permits issued: 1 (2001) / 1 (2000); Multi-family building permits issued: 0 (2001) / 0 (2000); Employment by occupation: 4.9% management, 31.5% professional, 24.6% services, 13.8% sales, 2.0% farming, 11.3% construction, 11.8% production (2000).
Income: Per capita income: $13,052 (2000); Median household income: $19,091 (2000); Poverty rate: 10.5% (2000).
Taxes: Total city taxes per capita: $94 (1997); City property taxes per capita: $94 (1997).
Education: High school graduation rate: 71.7% (2000); College graduation rate: 10.7% (2000).

School District(s)

Clearbrook-Gonvick (PK-12)
2000 Enrollment: 633 218-776-3112
Housing: Homeownership rate: 60.0% (2000); Median home value: $41,600 (2000); Median rent: $272 per month (2000); Median age of housing: 48 years (2000).
Transportation: Commute to work: 79.7% car, 0.0% public transportation, 20.3% walk, 0.0% work from home (2000); Travel time to work: 60.4% less than 15 minutes, 19.3% 15 to 30 minutes, 8.1% 30 to 45 minutes, 8.1% 45 to 60 minutes, 4.1% 60 minutes or more (2000)

CLOVER (township). Covers a land area of 17.064 square miles and a water area of 0.588 square miles. Located at 47.77° N. Lat.; 95.23° W. Long.

Population: 116 (2000); Race: 98.6% White, 0.0% Black, 0.0% Asian, 0.0% American Indian and Alaska Native, 0.0% Hispanic of any race, 1.4% two or more races (2000); Density: 6.8 persons per square mile (2000); Age: 36.2% under 18, 7.8% over 64 (2000); Marriage status: 16.0% never married, 67.0% now married, 2.1% widowed, 14.9% divorced (2000); Foreign born: 0.0% (2000); Ancestry (includes multiple ancestries): 39.7% Norwegian, 14.9% Swedish, 11.3% German, 6.4% United States or American, 3.5% French (except Basque) (2000).
Economy: Employment by occupation: 0.0% management, 22.0% professional, 19.5% services, 4.9% sales, 7.3% farming, 31.7% construction, 14.6% production (2000).
Income: Per capita income: $16,248 (2000); Median household income: $32,083 (2000); Poverty rate: 27.0% (2000).
Taxes: Total city taxes per capita: $17 (1997); City property taxes per capita: $17 (1997).
Education: High school graduation rate: 86.0% (2000); College graduation rate: 12.8% (2000).
Housing: Homeownership rate: 95.9% (2000); Median age of housing: 18 years (2000).
Transportation: Commute to work: 100.0% car, 0.0% public transportation, 0.0% walk, 0.0% work from home (2000); Travel time to work: 8.1% less than 15 minutes, 18.9% 15 to 30 minutes, 62.2% 30 to 45 minutes, 0.0% 45 to 60 minutes, 10.8% 60 minutes or more (2000)

COPLEY (township). Covers a land area of 33.805 square miles and a water area of 0.198 square miles. Located at 47.52° N. Lat.; 95.38° W. Long.
Population: 859 (2000); Race: 94.4% White, 0.0% Black, 0.0% Asian, 3.6% American Indian and Alaska Native, 0.0% Hispanic of any race, 2.0% two or more races (2000); Density: 25.4 persons per square mile (2000); Age: 28.1% under 18, 10.7% over 64 (2000); Marriage status: 22.0% never married, 65.7% now married, 5.7% widowed, 6.6% divorced (2000); Foreign born: 1.2% (2000); Ancestry (includes multiple ancestries): 41.1% Norwegian, 22.9% German, 12.7% Swedish, 7.6% United States or American, 5.4% Other groups (2000).
Economy: Employment by occupation: 14.4% management, 23.5% professional, 15.4% services, 18.0% sales, 1.6% farming, 10.4% construction, 16.7% production (2000).
Income: Per capita income: $19,302 (2000); Median household income: $46,324 (2000); Poverty rate: 8.0% (2000).
Taxes: Total city taxes per capita: $30 (1997); City property taxes per capita: $30 (1997).
Education: High school graduation rate: 81.8% (2000); College graduation rate: 28.1% (2000).
Housing: Homeownership rate: 90.9% (2000); Median home value: $88,200 (2000); Median rent: $379 per month (2000); Median age of housing: 27 years (2000).
Transportation: Commute to work: 91.5% car, 0.5% public transportation, 1.3% walk, 6.6% work from home (2000); Travel time to work: 62.0% less than 15 minutes, 16.4% 15 to 30 minutes, 12.5% 30 to 45 minutes, 6.2% 45 to 60 minutes, 2.8% 60 minutes or more (2000)

DUDLEY (township). Covers a land area of 29.635 square miles and a water area of 1.664 square miles. Located at 47.63° N. Lat.; 95.25° W. Long.
Population: 365 (2000); Race: 100.0% White, 0.0% Black, 0.0% Asian, 0.0% American Indian and Alaska Native, 0.0% Hispanic of any race, 0.0% two or more races (2000); Density: 12.3 persons per square mile (2000); Age: 37.9% under 18, 9.0% over 64 (2000); Marriage status: 22.6% never married, 67.7% now married, 3.6% widowed, 6.1% divorced (2000); Foreign born: 0.0% (2000); Ancestry (includes multiple ancestries): 34.4% Norwegian, 28.7% German, 14.5% United States or American, 10.0% Swedish, 7.6% English (2000).
Economy: Employment by occupation: 6.3% management, 8.8% professional, 14.4% services, 23.8% sales, 13.1% farming, 12.5% construction, 21.3% production (2000).
Income: Per capita income: $12,049 (2000); Median household income: $32,813 (2000); Poverty rate: 18.5% (2000).
Taxes: Total city taxes per capita: $32 (1997); City property taxes per capita: $32 (1997).
Education: High school graduation rate: 70.3% (2000); College graduation rate: 3.0% (2000).
Housing: Homeownership rate: 94.7% (2000); Median home value: $35,000 (2000); Median rent: $175 per month (2000); Median age of housing: 28 years (2000).
Transportation: Commute to work: 86.3% car, 0.0% public transportation, 5.2% walk, 5.2% work from home (2000); Travel time to work: 14.5% less than 15 minutes, 51.7% 15 to 30 minutes, 25.5% 30 to 45 minutes, 4.1% 45 to 60 minutes, 4.1% 60 minutes or more (2000)

EDDY (township). Covers a land area of 34.841 square miles and a water area of 0.772 square miles. Located at 47.63° N. Lat.; 95.48° W. Long.
Population: 322 (2000); Race: 99.4% White, 0.0% Black, 0.0% Asian, 0.6% American Indian and Alaska Native, 0.0% Hispanic of any race, 0.0% two or more races (2000); Density: 9.2 persons per square mile (2000); Age: 28.0% under 18, 17.5% over 64 (2000); Marriage status: 13.8% never married, 72.0% now married, 7.8% widowed, 6.5% divorced (2000); Foreign born: 0.6% (2000); Ancestry (includes multiple ancestries): 58.0% Norwegian, 26.4% German, 20.7% Swedish, 4.8% Dutch, 4.5% English (2000).
Economy: Employment by occupation: 13.9% management, 16.6% professional, 13.2% services, 19.2% sales, 4.6% farming, 19.2% construction, 13.2% production (2000).
Income: Per capita income: $20,293 (2000); Median household income: $30,357 (2000); Poverty rate: 7.3% (2000).
Taxes: Total city taxes per capita: $38 (1997); City property taxes per capita: $38 (1997).
Education: High school graduation rate: 76.4% (2000); College graduation rate: 18.9% (2000).
Housing: Homeownership rate: 89.0% (2000); Median home value: $75,000 (2000); Median rent: $275 per month (2000); Median age of housing: 56 years (2000).
Transportation: Commute to work: 90.5% car, 0.0% public transportation, 2.0% walk, 7.4% work from home (2000); Travel time to work: 37.2% less than 15 minutes, 43.8% 15 to 30 minutes, 7.3% 30 to 45 minutes, 8.8% 45 to 60 minutes, 2.9% 60 minutes or more (2000)

FALK (township). Covers a land area of 36.264 square miles and a water area of 0.266 square miles. Located at 47.47° N. Lat.; 95.48° W. Long.
Population: 261 (2000); Race: 61.0% White, 0.0% Black, 0.0% Asian, 30.5% American Indian and Alaska Native, 1.9% Hispanic of any race, 8.6% two or more races (2000); Density: 7.2 persons per square mile (2000); Age: 37.5% under 18, 8.2% over 64 (2000); Marriage status: 31.1% never married, 58.9% now married, 6.3% widowed, 3.7% divorced (2000); Foreign born: 0.0% (2000); Ancestry (includes multiple ancestries): 28.6% Other groups, 14.1% Norwegian, 8.6% German, 8.2% United States or American, 6.3% French (except Basque) (2000).
Economy: Employment by occupation: 8.7% management, 9.6% professional, 25.0% services, 13.5% sales, 7.7% farming, 19.2% construction, 16.3% production (2000).
Income: Per capita income: $9,554 (2000); Median household income: $20,313 (2000); Poverty rate: 32.7% (2000).
Taxes: Total city taxes per capita: $89 (1997); City property taxes per capita: $89 (1997).
Education: High school graduation rate: 70.7% (2000); College graduation rate: 2.1% (2000).
Housing: Homeownership rate: 92.6% (2000); Median home value: $80,000 (2000); Median rent: $175 per month (2000); Median age of housing: 27 years (2000).
Transportation: Commute to work: 81.7% car, 0.0% public transportation, 8.7% walk, 9.6% work from home (2000); Travel time to work: 18.1% less than 15 minutes, 27.7% 15 to 30 minutes, 25.5% 30 to 45 minutes, 17.0% 45 to 60 minutes, 11.7% 60 minutes or more (2000)

GONVICK (city). Covers a land area of 1.313 square miles and a water area of 0 square miles. Located at 47.73° N. Lat.; 95.51° W. Long. Elevation is 1,271 feet.
Population: 294 (2000); Race: 93.4% White, 0.0% Black, 0.0% Asian, 3.2% American Indian and Alaska Native, 0.0% Hispanic of any race, 3.5% two or more races (2000); Density: 223.9 persons per square mile (2000); Age: 26.2% under 18, 18.9% over 64 (2000); Marriage status: 28.6% never married, 54.1% now married, 13.7% widowed, 3.5% divorced (2000); Foreign born: 1.3% (2000); Ancestry (includes multiple ancestries): 53.9% Norwegian, 17.0% Swedish, 10.7% German, 4.4% Other groups, 3.5% Polish (2000).
Economy: Grain, potatoes; poultry, cattle, sheep; dairying. Manufacturing: printing; food processing. Employment by occupation: 7.7% management, 20.8% professional, 17.7% services, 15.4% sales, 0.8% farming, 18.5% construction, 19.2% production (2000).
Income: Per capita income: $14,650 (2000); Median household income: $24,722 (2000); Poverty rate: 12.0% (2000).
Taxes: Total city taxes per capita: $164 (1997); City property taxes per capita: $164 (1997).

Education: High school graduation rate: 73.9% (2000); College graduation rate: 11.8% (2000).
Housing: Homeownership rate: 81.0% (2000); Median home value: $39,400 (2000); Median rent: $150 per month (2000); Median age of housing: 45 years (2000).
Newspapers: McIntosh Times (1 x week); Leader Record (1 x week)
Transportation: Commute to work: 88.7% car, 0.0% public transportation, 11.3% walk, 0.0% work from home (2000); Travel time to work: 58.9% less than 15 minutes, 26.6% 15 to 30 minutes, 7.3% 30 to 45 minutes, 3.2% 45 to 60 minutes, 4.0% 60 minutes or more (2000)

GREENWOOD (township). Covers a land area of 23.714 square miles and a water area of 0 square miles. Located at 47.80° N. Lat.; 95.38° W. Long.
Population: 96 (2000); Race: 95.5% White, 0.0% Black, 0.0% Asian, 0.9% American Indian and Alaska Native, 0.0% Hispanic of any race, 3.6% two or more races (2000); Density: 4.0 persons per square mile (2000); Age: 23.4% under 18, 27.9% over 64 (2000); Marriage status: 24.8% never married, 68.3% now married, 5.0% widowed, 2.0% divorced (2000); Foreign born: 0.0% (2000); Ancestry (includes multiple ancestries): 27.0% Norwegian, 18.9% United States or American, 15.3% German, 9.9% Swedish, 4.5% English (2000).
Economy: Employment by occupation: 22.2% management, 16.7% professional, 25.0% services, 13.9% sales, 5.6% farming, 5.6% construction, 11.1% production (2000).
Income: Per capita income: $10,259 (2000); Median household income: $23,125 (2000); Poverty rate: 32.4% (2000).
Taxes: Total city taxes per capita: $84 (1997); City property taxes per capita: $84 (1997).
Education: High school graduation rate: 68.4% (2000); College graduation rate: 0.0% (2000).
Housing: Homeownership rate: 84.6% (2000); Median home value: $30,000 (2000); Median age of housing: 45 years (2000).
Transportation: Commute to work: 80.0% car, 0.0% public transportation, 0.0% walk, 13.3% work from home (2000); Travel time to work: 19.2% less than 15 minutes, 15.4% 15 to 30 minutes, 38.5% 30 to 45 minutes, 15.4% 45 to 60 minutes, 11.5% 60 minutes or more (2000)

HANGAARD (township). Covers a land area of 21.988 square miles and a water area of 0 square miles. Located at 47.86° N. Lat.; 95.54° W. Long.
Population: 8 (2000); Race: 100.0% White, 0.0% Black, 0.0% Asian, 0.0% American Indian and Alaska Native, 0.0% Hispanic of any race, 0.0% two or more races (2000); Density: 0.4 persons per square mile (2000); Age: 0.0% under 18, 0.0% over 64 (2000); Marriage status: 40.0% never married, 0.0% now married, 0.0% widowed, 60.0% divorced (2000); Foreign born: 0.0% (2000); Ancestry (includes multiple ancestries): 60.0% Swedish, 60.0% Yugoslavian, 40.0% Norwegian (2000).
Economy: Employment by occupation: 100.0% management, 0.0% professional, 0.0% services, 0.0% sales, 0.0% farming, 0.0% construction, 0.0% production (2000).
Income: Per capita income: $30,000 (2000); Median household income: $50,417 (2000); Poverty rate: 40.0% (2000).
Taxes: Total city taxes per capita: $294 (1997); City property taxes per capita: $294 (1997).
Education: High school graduation rate: 100.0% (2000); College graduation rate: 0.0% (2000).
Housing: Homeownership rate: 50.0% (2000); Median age of housing: 35 years (2000).
Transportation: Commute to work: 60.0% car, 0.0% public transportation, 0.0% walk, 40.0% work from home (2000); Travel time to work: 100.0% less than 15 minutes, 0.0% 15 to 30 minutes, 0.0% 30 to 45 minutes, 0.0% 45 to 60 minutes, 0.0% 60 minutes or more (2000)

HOLST (township). Covers a land area of 35.131 square miles and a water area of 0.482 square miles. Located at 47.62° N. Lat.; 95.37° W. Long.
Population: 316 (2000); Race: 100.0% White, 0.0% Black, 0.0% Asian, 0.0% American Indian and Alaska Native, 0.0% Hispanic of any race, 0.0% two or more races (2000); Density: 9.0 persons per square mile (2000); Age: 16.9% under 18, 14.4% over 64 (2000); Marriage status: 28.4% never married, 62.1% now married, 5.3% widowed, 4.1% divorced (2000); Foreign born: 0.7% (2000); Ancestry (includes multiple ancestries): 41.4% Norwegian, 28.1% German, 16.5% Swedish, 9.4% English, 9.0% Irish (2000).
Economy: Employment by occupation: 13.1% management, 23.8% professional, 8.5% services, 18.5% sales, 3.1% farming, 18.5% construction, 14.6% production (2000).
Income: Per capita income: $17,427 (2000); Median household income: $35,313 (2000); Poverty rate: 3.3% (2000).
Taxes: Total city taxes per capita: $46 (1997); City property taxes per capita: $46 (1997).
Education: High school graduation rate: 82.4% (2000); College graduation rate: 17.1% (2000).
Housing: Homeownership rate: 93.6% (2000); Median home value: $72,500 (2000); Median rent: $225 per month (2000); Median age of housing: 34 years (2000).
Transportation: Commute to work: 85.4% car, 0.0% public transportation, 1.5% walk, 10.8% work from home (2000); Travel time to work: 48.3% less than 15 minutes, 28.4% 15 to 30 minutes, 11.2% 30 to 45 minutes, 2.6% 45 to 60 minutes, 9.5% 60 minutes or more (2000)

ITASCA (township). Covers a land area of 34.373 square miles and a water area of 1.478 square miles. Located at 47.28° N. Lat.; 95.24° W. Long.
Population: 136 (2000); Race: 92.0% White, 0.0% Black, 1.4% Asian, 1.4% American Indian and Alaska Native, 1.4% Hispanic of any race, 3.6% two or more races (2000); Density: 4.0 persons per square mile (2000); Age: 27.5% under 18, 17.4% over 64 (2000); Marriage status: 10.7% never married, 69.9% now married, 8.7% widowed, 10.7% divorced (2000); Foreign born: 0.0% (2000); Ancestry (includes multiple ancestries): 41.3% Norwegian, 26.8% German, 17.4% Swedish, 11.6% Scottish, 8.0% Other groups (2000).
Economy: Employment by occupation: 16.7% management, 11.1% professional, 11.1% services, 16.7% sales, 7.4% farming, 27.8% construction, 9.3% production (2000).
Income: Per capita income: $14,296 (2000); Median household income: $28,750 (2000); Poverty rate: 8.7% (2000).
Taxes: Total city taxes per capita: $107 (1997); City property taxes per capita: $107 (1997).
Education: High school graduation rate: 79.8% (2000); College graduation rate: 12.8% (2000).
Housing: Homeownership rate: 89.5% (2000); Median home value: $50,000 (2000); Median age of housing: 25 years (2000).
Transportation: Commute to work: 91.1% car, 0.0% public transportation, 0.0% walk, 8.9% work from home (2000); Travel time to work: 7.3% less than 15 minutes, 9.8% 15 to 30 minutes, 56.1% 30 to 45 minutes, 17.1% 45 to 60 minutes, 9.8% 60 minutes or more (2000)

LA PRAIRIE (township). Covers a land area of 99.567 square miles and a water area of 7.478 square miles. Located at 47.29° N. Lat.; 95.46° W. Long.
Population: 371 (2000); Race: 19.5% White, 0.0% Black, 0.0% Asian, 73.8% American Indian and Alaska Native, 5.4% Hispanic of any race, 5.4% two or more races (2000); Density: 3.7 persons per square mile (2000); Age: 35.1% under 18, 8.6% over 64 (2000); Marriage status: 46.8% never married, 36.7% now married, 5.9% widowed, 10.5% divorced (2000); Foreign born: 0.0% (2000); Ancestry (includes multiple ancestries): 73.2% Other groups, 8.9% German, 5.8% Norwegian, 3.8% Irish, 3.8% Czech (2000).
Economy: Employment by occupation: 7.5% management, 13.2% professional, 21.7% services, 17.9% sales, 2.8% farming, 16.0% construction, 20.8% production (2000).
Income: Per capita income: $11,949 (2000); Median household income: $22,500 (2000); Poverty rate: 43.1% (2000).
Taxes: Total city taxes per capita: $29 (1997); City property taxes per capita: $29 (1997).
Education: High school graduation rate: 72.9% (2000); College graduation rate: 7.2% (2000).
Housing: Homeownership rate: 66.7% (2000); Median home value: $50,000 (2000); Median rent: <$100 per month (2000); Median age of housing: 24 years (2000).
Transportation: Commute to work: 73.6% car, 3.8% public transportation, 7.5% walk, 5.7% work from home (2000); Travel time to work: 15.0% less than 15 minutes, 30.0% 15 to 30 minutes, 43.0% 30 to 45 minutes, 9.0% 45 to 60 minutes, 3.0% 60 minutes or more (2000)

LEON (township). Covers a land area of 35.384 square miles and a water area of 0.367 square miles. Located at 47.71° N. Lat.; 95.39° W. Long.
Population: 345 (2000); Race: 99.7% White, 0.0% Black, 0.0% Asian, 0.0% American Indian and Alaska Native, 0.0% Hispanic of any race, 0.3% two or more races (2000); Density: 9.8 persons per square mile (2000); Age: 21.9% under 18, 21.9% over 64 (2000); Marriage status: 11.6% never married, 77.2% now married, 7.9% widowed, 3.4% divorced (2000); Foreign born: 0.6% (2000); Ancestry (includes multiple ancestries): 46.7% Norwegian, 22.3% German, 13.2% Swedish, 9.1% English, 8.5% Scandinavian (2000).

Economy: Dairying. Employment by occupation: 22.1% management, 25.0% professional, 9.3% services, 15.7% sales, 2.1% farming, 12.1% construction, 13.6% production (2000).
Income: Per capita income: $15,669 (2000); Median household income: $31,250 (2000); Poverty rate: 8.5% (2000).
Taxes: Total city taxes per capita: $126 (1997); City property taxes per capita: $126 (1997).
Education: High school graduation rate: 81.6% (2000); College graduation rate: 16.3% (2000).
Housing: Homeownership rate: 87.5% (2000); Median home value: $54,200 (2000); Median rent: $325 per month (2000); Median age of housing: 33 years (2000).
Transportation: Commute to work: 86.4% car, 0.0% public transportation, 0.7% walk, 12.9% work from home (2000); Travel time to work: 53.3% less than 15 minutes, 18.0% 15 to 30 minutes, 19.7% 30 to 45 minutes, 4.9% 45 to 60 minutes, 4.1% 60 minutes or more (2000)

LEONARD (city). Covers a land area of 0.453 square miles and a water area of 0 square miles. Located at 47.65° N. Lat.; 95.26° W. Long. Elevation is 1,449 feet.
Population: 29 (2000); Race: 100.0% White, 0.0% Black, 0.0% Asian, 0.0% American Indian and Alaska Native, 0.0% Hispanic of any race, 0.0% two or more races (2000); Density: 64.0 persons per square mile (2000); Age: 12.8% under 18, 38.5% over 64 (2000); Marriage status: 33.3% never married, 43.6% now married, 15.4% widowed, 7.7% divorced (2000); Foreign born: 0.0% (2000); Ancestry (includes multiple ancestries): 61.5% Norwegian, 43.6% Swedish, 17.9% English, 10.3% German, 7.7% Irish (2000).
Economy: Employment by occupation: 0.0% management, 0.0% professional, 50.0% services, 27.3% sales, 0.0% farming, 0.0% construction, 22.7% production (2000).
Income: Per capita income: $17,005 (2000); Median household income: $31,250 (2000); Poverty rate: 7.7% (2000).
Taxes: Total city taxes per capita: $115 (1997); City property taxes per capita: $38 (1997).
Education: High school graduation rate: 100.0% (2000); College graduation rate: 16.1% (2000).
Housing: Homeownership rate: 90.0% (2000); Median home value: $52,500 (2000); Median rent: <$100 per month (2000); Median age of housing: 60+ years (2000).
Transportation: Commute to work: 77.3% car, 0.0% public transportation, 0.0% walk, 9.1% work from home (2000); Travel time to work: 40.0% less than 15 minutes, 35.0% 15 to 30 minutes, 25.0% 30 to 45 minutes, 0.0% 45 to 60 minutes, 0.0% 60 minutes or more (2000)

MINERVA (township). Covers a land area of 34.521 square miles and a water area of 1.623 square miles. Located at 47.36° N. Lat.; 95.37° W. Long. Elevation is 1,515 feet.
Population: 283 (2000); Race: 92.3% White, 0.3% Black, 0.6% Asian, 3.7% American Indian and Alaska Native, 0.3% Hispanic of any race, 3.1% two or more races (2000); Density: 8.2 persons per square mile (2000); Age: 26.2% under 18, 11.4% over 64 (2000); Marriage status: 23.0% never married, 65.2% now married, 2.3% widowed, 9.4% divorced (2000); Foreign born: 1.2% (2000); Ancestry (includes multiple ancestries): 42.8% Norwegian, 23.4% German, 10.2% Irish, 9.2% Swedish, 6.2% Other groups (2000).
Economy: Employment by occupation: 15.7% management, 13.0% professional, 24.3% services, 17.4% sales, 0.9% farming, 13.9% construction, 14.8% production (2000).
Income: Per capita income: $15,561 (2000); Median household income: $39,167 (2000); Poverty rate: 17.6% (2000).
Taxes: Total city taxes per capita: $34 (1997); City property taxes per capita: $34 (1997).
Education: High school graduation rate: 69.9% (2000); College graduation rate: 18.4% (2000).
Housing: Homeownership rate: 83.2% (2000); Median home value: $55,000 (2000); Median rent: $275 per month (2000); Median age of housing: 32 years (2000).
Transportation: Commute to work: 87.5% car, 0.0% public transportation, 6.3% walk, 6.3% work from home (2000); Travel time to work: 12.4% less than 15 minutes, 48.6% 15 to 30 minutes, 28.6% 30 to 45 minutes, 4.8% 45 to 60 minutes, 5.7% 60 minutes or more (2000)

MOOSE CREEK (township). Covers a land area of 31.696 square miles and a water area of 0.499 square miles. Located at 47.47° N. Lat.; 95.23° W. Long.
Population: 227 (2000); Race: 100.0% White, 0.0% Black, 0.0% Asian, 0.0% American Indian and Alaska Native, 0.4% Hispanic of any race, 0.0% two or more races (2000); Density: 7.2 persons per square mile (2000); Age: 24.6% under 18, 15.6% over 64 (2000); Marriage status: 21.4% never married, 66.5% now married, 8.8% widowed, 3.3% divorced (2000); Foreign born: 0.0% (2000); Ancestry (includes multiple ancestries): 36.6% Norwegian, 30.8% German, 16.1% Swedish, 10.3% Irish, 4.0% Dutch (2000).
Economy: Employment by occupation: 13.9% management, 20.8% professional, 7.9% services, 16.8% sales, 3.0% farming, 20.8% construction, 16.8% production (2000).
Income: Per capita income: $18,725 (2000); Median household income: $42,500 (2000); Poverty rate: 8.1% (2000).
Taxes: Total city taxes per capita: $50 (1997); City property taxes per capita: $50 (1997).
Education: High school graduation rate: 83.7% (2000); College graduation rate: 17.0% (2000).
Housing: Homeownership rate: 94.8% (2000); Median home value: $63,300 (2000); Median age of housing: 20 years (2000).
Transportation: Commute to work: 97.0% car, 0.0% public transportation, 1.0% walk, 0.0% work from home (2000); Travel time to work: 11.1% less than 15 minutes, 54.5% 15 to 30 minutes, 21.2% 30 to 45 minutes, 8.1% 45 to 60 minutes, 5.1% 60 minutes or more (2000)

NORA (township). Covers a land area of 35.778 square miles and a water area of 0.296 square miles. Located at 47.45° N. Lat.; 95.35° W. Long.
Population: 408 (2000); Race: 97.2% White, 0.0% Black, 0.0% Asian, 0.3% American Indian and Alaska Native, 0.0% Hispanic of any race, 2.5% two or more races (2000); Density: 11.4 persons per square mile (2000); Age: 27.9% under 18, 15.7% over 64 (2000); Marriage status: 23.2% never married, 62.9% now married, 7.0% widowed, 7.0% divorced (2000); Foreign born: 0.0% (2000); Ancestry (includes multiple ancestries): 54.1% Norwegian, 20.3% German, 15.0% Irish, 9.4% English, 7.1% French (except Basque) (2000).
Economy: Employment by occupation: 18.1% management, 13.8% professional, 17.6% services, 19.1% sales, 1.6% farming, 15.4% construction, 14.4% production (2000).
Income: Per capita income: $15,197 (2000); Median household income: $31,477 (2000); Poverty rate: 12.7% (2000).
Taxes: Total city taxes per capita: $26 (1997); City property taxes per capita: $26 (1997).
Education: High school graduation rate: 79.0% (2000); College graduation rate: 7.9% (2000).
Housing: Homeownership rate: 89.3% (2000); Median home value: $70,000 (2000); Median rent: $285 per month (2000); Median age of housing: 28 years (2000).
Transportation: Commute to work: 88.8% car, 2.7% public transportation, 0.5% walk, 6.9% work from home (2000); Travel time to work: 47.4% less than 15 minutes, 28.0% 15 to 30 minutes, 13.7% 30 to 45 minutes, 4.6% 45 to 60 minutes, 6.3% 60 minutes or more (2000)

PINE LAKE (township). Covers a land area of 31.783 square miles and a water area of 2.499 square miles. Located at 47.71° N. Lat.; 95.51° W. Long.
Population: 324 (2000); Race: 99.4% White, 0.0% Black, 0.0% Asian, 0.6% American Indian and Alaska Native, 0.0% Hispanic of any race, 0.0% two or more races (2000); Density: 10.2 persons per square mile (2000); Age: 23.1% under 18, 12.2% over 64 (2000); Marriage status: 22.5% never married, 64.7% now married, 4.7% widowed, 8.1% divorced (2000); Foreign born: 0.0% (2000); Ancestry (includes multiple ancestries): 61.5% Norwegian, 17.6% Swedish, 8.7% German, 4.2% United States or American, 4.2% French (except Basque) (2000).
Economy: Employment by occupation: 17.1% management, 19.7% professional, 20.4% services, 15.1% sales, 3.9% farming, 7.2% construction, 16.4% production (2000).
Income: Per capita income: $17,815 (2000); Median household income: $32,500 (2000); Poverty rate: 15.7% (2000).
Taxes: Total city taxes per capita: $62 (1997); City property taxes per capita: $62 (1997).
Education: High school graduation rate: 78.7% (2000); College graduation rate: 18.2% (2000).
Housing: Homeownership rate: 91.4% (2000); Median home value: $47,900 (2000); Median rent: $325 per month (2000); Median age of housing: 36 years (2000).
Transportation: Commute to work: 85.5% car, 0.0% public transportation, 0.7% walk, 11.2% work from home (2000); Travel time to work: 45.9% less than 15 minutes, 23.0% 15 to 30 minutes, 9.6% 30 to 45 minutes, 11.1% 45 to 60 minutes, 10.4% 60 minutes or more (2000)

POPPLE (township). Covers a land area of 34.858 square miles and a water area of 0.913 square miles. Located at 47.53° N. Lat.; 95.48° W. Long.
Population: 564 (2000); Race: 90.9% White, 0.5% Black, 0.0% Asian, 5.9% American Indian and Alaska Native, 0.9% Hispanic of any race, 2.7% two or more races (2000); Density: 16.2 persons per square mile (2000); Age: 30.2% under 18, 10.7% over 64 (2000); Marriage status: 23.1% never married, 61.2% now married, 4.3% widowed, 11.4% divorced (2000); Foreign born: 1.6% (2000); Ancestry (includes multiple ancestries): 43.6% Norwegian, 19.3% German, 9.7% Other groups, 7.5% United States or American, 6.8% Swedish (2000).
Economy: Employment by occupation: 13.4% management, 23.0% professional, 15.2% services, 17.0% sales, 3.2% farming, 16.6% construction, 11.7% production (2000).
Income: Per capita income: $14,611 (2000); Median household income: $35,795 (2000); Poverty rate: 12.5% (2000).
Taxes: Total city taxes per capita: $32 (1997); City property taxes per capita: $32 (1997).
Education: High school graduation rate: 82.7% (2000); College graduation rate: 19.0% (2000).
Housing: Homeownership rate: 87.6% (2000); Median home value: $48,800 (2000); Median rent: $175 per month (2000); Median age of housing: 27 years (2000).
Transportation: Commute to work: 88.6% car, 1.8% public transportation, 1.5% walk, 8.1% work from home (2000); Travel time to work: 40.2% less than 15 minutes, 34.1% 15 to 30 minutes, 16.1% 30 to 45 minutes, 4.8% 45 to 60 minutes, 4.8% 60 minutes or more (2000)

RICE (township). Covers a land area of 34.905 square miles and a water area of 1.149 square miles. Located at 47.27° N. Lat.; 95.37° W. Long.
Population: 134 (2000); Race: 83.5% White, 0.0% Black, 0.0% Asian, 14.6% American Indian and Alaska Native, 0.0% Hispanic of any race, 1.9% two or more races (2000); Density: 3.8 persons per square mile (2000); Age: 24.1% under 18, 20.9% over 64 (2000); Marriage status: 13.6% never married, 76.0% now married, 4.8% widowed, 5.6% divorced (2000); Foreign born: 0.0% (2000); Ancestry (includes multiple ancestries): 32.9% Norwegian, 14.6% German, 12.0% Other groups, 7.6% Swedish, 7.0% Irish (2000).
Economy: Employment by occupation: 14.8% management, 3.3% professional, 24.6% services, 34.4% sales, 8.2% farming, 9.8% construction, 4.9% production (2000).
Income: Per capita income: $10,349 (2000); Median household income: $19,583 (2000); Poverty rate: 34.2% (2000).
Taxes: Total city taxes per capita: $64 (1997); City property taxes per capita: $64 (1997).
Education: High school graduation rate: 70.4% (2000); College graduation rate: 10.2% (2000).
Housing: Homeownership rate: 84.8% (2000); Median home value: $72,500 (2000); Median rent: $192 per month (2000); Median age of housing: 22 years (2000).
Transportation: Commute to work: 94.8% car, 0.0% public transportation, 0.0% walk, 5.2% work from home (2000); Travel time to work: 18.2% less than 15 minutes, 18.2% 15 to 30 minutes, 50.9% 30 to 45 minutes, 7.3% 45 to 60 minutes, 5.5% 60 minutes or more (2000)

SHEVLIN (city). Covers a land area of 0.796 square miles and a water area of 0 square miles. Located at 47.53° N. Lat.; 95.26° W. Long. Elevation is 1,449 feet.
Population: 160 (2000); Race: 96.9% White, 0.0% Black, 0.0% Asian, 1.9% American Indian and Alaska Native, 0.0% Hispanic of any race, 1.3% two or more races (2000); Density: 201.1 persons per square mile (2000); Age: 20.1% under 18, 7.5% over 64 (2000); Marriage status: 26.3% never married, 51.1% now married, 5.1% widowed, 17.5% divorced (2000); Foreign born: 0.0% (2000); Ancestry (includes multiple ancestries): 44.0% Norwegian, 20.1% German, 8.2% Swedish, 6.3% United States or American, 6.3% Other groups (2000).
Economy: Employment by occupation: 6.5% management, 9.8% professional, 8.7% services, 33.7% sales, 3.3% farming, 19.6% construction, 18.5% production (2000).
Income: Per capita income: $20,015 (2000); Median household income: $30,000 (2000); Poverty rate: 12.6% (2000).
Taxes: Total city taxes per capita: $63 (1997); City property taxes per capita: $38 (1997).
Education: High school graduation rate: 74.1% (2000); College graduation rate: 9.8% (2000).
Housing: Homeownership rate: 97.1% (2000); Median home value: $32,300 (2000); Median rent: $125 per month (2000); Median age of housing: 37 years (2000).
Transportation: Commute to work: 75.9% car, 0.0% public transportation, 16.1% walk, 4.6% work from home (2000); Travel time to work: 43.4% less than 15 minutes, 22.9% 15 to 30 minutes, 12.0% 30 to 45 minutes, 16.9% 45 to 60 minutes, 4.8% 60 minutes or more (2000)

SHEVLIN (township). Covers a land area of 31.034 square miles and a water area of 0.026 square miles. Located at 47.53° N. Lat.; 95.24° W. Long. Elevation is 1,449 feet.
Population: 434 (2000); Race: 98.5% White, 0.0% Black, 0.6% Asian, 0.4% American Indian and Alaska Native, 0.4% Hispanic of any race, 0.4% two or more races (2000); Density: 14.0 persons per square mile (2000); Age: 30.3% under 18, 13.0% over 64 (2000); Marriage status: 20.3% never married, 68.0% now married, 2.8% widowed, 8.9% divorced (2000); Foreign born: 1.5% (2000); Ancestry (includes multiple ancestries): 44.5% Norwegian, 37.6% German, 7.4% Swedish, 7.1% Irish, 6.5% English (2000).
Economy: Dairying; livestock; grain. Employment by occupation: 15.6% management, 14.7% professional, 22.3% services, 17.4% sales, 3.6% farming, 10.7% construction, 15.6% production (2000).
Income: Per capita income: $16,534 (2000); Median household income: $31,389 (2000); Poverty rate: 9.7% (2000).
Taxes: Total city taxes per capita: $87 (1997); City property taxes per capita: $87 (1997).
Education: High school graduation rate: 72.7% (2000); College graduation rate: 9.9% (2000).
Housing: Homeownership rate: 90.6% (2000); Median home value: $44,200 (2000); Median rent: $392 per month (2000); Median age of housing: 27 years (2000).
Transportation: Commute to work: 87.8% car, 0.0% public transportation, 0.0% walk, 11.3% work from home (2000); Travel time to work: 16.2% less than 15 minutes, 56.9% 15 to 30 minutes, 18.8% 30 to 45 minutes, 3.0% 45 to 60 minutes, 5.1% 60 minutes or more (2000)

SINCLAIR (township). Covers a land area of 34.518 square miles and a water area of 1.727 square miles. Located at 47.73° N. Lat.; 95.24° W. Long.
Population: 175 (2000); Race: 100.0% White, 0.0% Black, 0.0% Asian, 0.0% American Indian and Alaska Native, 0.0% Hispanic of any race, 0.0% two or more races (2000); Density: 5.1 persons per square mile (2000); Age: 10.7% under 18, 30.2% over 64 (2000); Marriage status: 20.8% never married, 59.1% now married, 11.7% widowed, 8.4% divorced (2000); Foreign born: 0.0% (2000); Ancestry (includes multiple ancestries): 58.6% Norwegian, 18.9% Swedish, 13.0% German, 8.3% English, 3.0% United States or American (2000).
Economy: Employment by occupation: 13.9% management, 19.0% professional, 5.1% services, 17.7% sales, 6.3% farming, 20.3% construction, 17.7% production (2000).
Income: Per capita income: $22,163 (2000); Median household income: $40,000 (2000); Poverty rate: 11.8% (2000).
Taxes: Total city taxes per capita: $89 (1997); City property taxes per capita: $89 (1997).
Education: High school graduation rate: 80.0% (2000); College graduation rate: 14.5% (2000).
Housing: Homeownership rate: 89.4% (2000); Median home value: $87,500 (2000); Median rent: $175 per month (2000); Median age of housing: 41 years (2000).
Transportation: Commute to work: 94.6% car, 0.0% public transportation, 0.0% walk, 5.4% work from home (2000); Travel time to work: 17.1% less than 15 minutes, 42.9% 15 to 30 minutes, 17.1% 30 to 45 minutes, 7.1% 45 to 60 minutes, 15.7% 60 minutes or more (2000)

WINSOR (township). Covers a land area of 35.730 square miles and a water area of 0.135 square miles. Located at 47.78° N. Lat.; 95.49° W. Long.
Population: 146 (2000); Race: 100.0% White, 0.0% Black, 0.0% Asian, 0.0% American Indian and Alaska Native, 0.0% Hispanic of any race, 0.0% two or more races (2000); Density: 4.1 persons per square mile (2000); Age: 20.5% under 18, 14.5% over 64 (2000); Marriage status: 24.2% never married, 59.6% now married, 6.1% widowed, 10.1% divorced (2000); Foreign born: 0.0% (2000); Ancestry (includes multiple ancestries): 82.1% Norwegian, 26.5% Swedish, 10.3% German, 2.6% United States or American, 2.6% Scandinavian (2000).
Economy: Employment by occupation: 24.4% management, 2.4% professional, 22.0% services, 22.0% sales, 0.0% farming, 24.4% construction, 4.9% production (2000).

Income: Per capita income: $15,375 (2000); Median household income: $29,107 (2000); Poverty rate: 1.7% (2000).
Taxes: Total city taxes per capita: $130 (1997); City property taxes per capita: $130 (1997).
Education: High school graduation rate: 74.7% (2000); College graduation rate: 8.4% (2000).
Housing: Homeownership rate: 92.0% (2000); Median home value: $71,700 (2000); Median rent: $125 per month (2000); Median age of housing: 43 years (2000).
Transportation: Commute to work: 87.8% car, 0.0% public transportation, 9.8% walk, 2.4% work from home (2000); Travel time to work: 22.5% less than 15 minutes, 27.5% 15 to 30 minutes, 30.0% 30 to 45 minutes, 7.5% 45 to 60 minutes, 12.5% 60 minutes or more (2000)

Cook County

Located in northeastern Minnesota; bounded on the south by Lake Superior, and on the north by Chain of Lakes and the Canadian province of Ontario; includes part of Superior National Forest. Covers a land area of 1,450.60 square miles, a water area of 1,889.10 square miles, and is located in the Central Time Zone. The county government was organized in 1874. County seat is Grand Marais.

Weather Station: Grand Marais — Elevation: 610 feet

	Jan	Feb	Mar	Apr	May	Jun	Jul	Aug	Sep	Oct	Nov	Dec
High	22	27	35	46	55	63	70	71	62	51	38	27
Low	5	9	19	30	38	44	51	54	47	37	25	12
Precip	0.8	0.6	1.1	1.4	2.6	3.4	3.5	3.0	3.5	2.8	1.7	0.8
Snow	17.5	7.9	7.7	1.8	tr	0.0	0.0	0.0	0.0	0.2	3.9	12.6

High and Low temperatures in degrees Fahrenheit; Precipitation and Snow in inches

Population: 5,168 (2000); Race: 89.5% White, 0.1% Black, 0.3% Asian, 7.0% American Indian and Alaska Native, 0.5% Hispanic of any race, 2.5% two or more races (2000); Density: 3.6 persons per square mile (2000); Age: 20.1% under 18, 17.3% over 64 (2000).
Religion: Five largest groups: 21.3% Evangelical Lutheran Church in America, 10.3% Catholic Church, 6.5% United Church of Christ, 3.8% New Testament Association of Independent Baptist Churches and other Fundamental Baptist Associations, 2.9% The Evangelical Free Church
Economy: Unemployment rate: 4.4% (11/2002); Total civilian labor force: 2,813 (11/2002); Leading industries: 39.6% accommodation & food services; 15.1% retail trade; 7.3% health care and social assistance (2000); Companies that employ more than 1,000 persons: 0 (2000); Companies that employ more than 100 persons: 4 (2000); Farms: 11 (1997); Minority business ownership rate: 0.0% (1997); Women business ownership rate: 32.0% (1997); Retail sales per capita: $9,302 (1997). Single-family building permits issued: 110 (2001) / 106 (2000); Multi-family building permits issued: 8 (2001) / 11 (2000).
Income: Per capita income: $21,775 (2000); Median household income: $36,640 (2000); Poverty rate: 10.1% (2000); Bankruptcy rate: 2.91% (2001).
Taxes: Total county taxes per capita: $882 (2000); County property taxes per capita: $655 (2000).
Education: High school graduation rate: 88.7% (2000); College graduation rate: 28.8% (2000).
Housing: Homeownership rate: 78.2% (2000); Median home value: $107,700 (2000); Median rent: $373 per month (2000); Median age of housing: 25 years (2000).
Health: Birth rate: 96.8 per 10,000 population (1998); Age adjusted death rate: 88.1 per 10,000 population (1999); Age adjusted cancer mortality rate: 151.3 (Unreliable figure as per CDC) deaths per 100,000 population (1999). Number of physicians: 9.7 per 10,000 population (1999); Number of hospital beds: 121.9 per 10,000 population (1999).
Elections: 2000 Presidential election results: 41.5% Gore, 45.9% Bush, 10.3% Nader, 0.9% Buchanan
National and State Parks: Cascade River State Park Recreation Site; Grand Portage National Monument; Grand Portage State Forest; Grand Portage State Park; Judge C R Magney State Park; Kadunce River State Park; North Shore State Trail; Pat Bayle State Forest; Temperance River State Park
Additional Information Contacts
Cook County Government Offices. 218-387-3000

Cook County Communities

GRAND MARAIS (city). Covers a land area of 2.670 square miles and a water area of 0 square miles. Located at 47.75° N. Lat.; 90.33° W. Long. Elevation is 688 feet.
History: Grand Marais developed on the north shore of Lake Superior as a year-round sports and recreation center for Minnesota's "arrowhead" country.
Population: 1,353 (2000); Race: 95.2% White, 0.0% Black, 0.0% Asian, 3.2% American Indian and Alaska Native, 0.0% Hispanic of any race, 1.5% two or more races (2000); Density: 506.7 persons per square mile (2000); Age: 18.4% under 18, 27.2% over 64 (2000); Marriage status: 22.6% never married, 54.8% now married, 12.4% widowed, 10.2% divorced (2000); Foreign born: 1.2% (2000); Ancestry (includes multiple ancestries): 26.0% German, 24.7% Norwegian, 17.3% Swedish, 10.1% Irish, 8.9% English (2000).
Economy: Single-family building permits issued: 11 (2001) / 4 (2000); Multi-family building permits issued: 2 (2001) / 0 (2000); Employment by occupation: 13.9% management, 18.3% professional, 22.7% services, 20.4% sales, 1.4% farming, 13.4% construction, 9.9% production (2000).
Income: Per capita income: $21,863 (2000); Median household income: $33,493 (2000); Poverty rate: 10.0% (2000).
Taxes: Total city taxes per capita: $346 (1997); City property taxes per capita: $265 (1997).
Education: High school graduation rate: 88.0% (2000); College graduation rate: 30.1% (2000).

School District(s)

Cook County (PK-12)
2000 Enrollment: 741 218-387-2271
Housing: Homeownership rate: 66.4% (2000); Median home value: $99,800 (2000); Median rent: $340 per month (2000); Median age of housing: 40 years (2000).
Newspapers: Cook County News-Herald (1 x week)
Transportation: Commute to work: 80.1% car, 0.0% public transportation, 12.1% walk, 7.0% work from home (2000); Travel time to work: 72.0% less than 15 minutes, 14.1% 15 to 30 minutes, 8.7% 30 to 45 minutes, 2.9% 45 to 60 minutes, 2.3% 60 minutes or more (2000)
Airports: Grand Marais/Cook County

GRAND PORTAGE (unincorporated postal area, zip code 55605). Covers a land area of 74.233 square miles and a water area of 0.768 square miles. Located at 47.96° N. Lat.; 89.73° W. Long. Elevation is 700 feet.
History: Fishing center. Was busy fur-trading point in 18th century and central depot for North West Company It was east terminus of the Grand Portage, 9 mile overland link between Lake Superior and Pigeon River; the route of the old trail, long used by Native Americans, explorers, and traders. Grand Portage National Monument adjacent to village. Dedicated 1951 as a national historic site, now a national monument.
Population: 557 (2000); Race: 32.0% White, 0.6% Black, 1.5% Asian, 56.1% American Indian and Alaska Native, 1.3% Hispanic of any race, 9.5% two or more races (2000); Density: 7.5 persons per square mile (2000); Age: 29.0% under 18, 5.9% over 64 (2000); Marriage status: 39.1% never married, 40.3% now married, 3.0% widowed, 17.7% divorced (2000); Foreign born: 4.6% (2000); Ancestry (includes multiple ancestries): 69.7% Other groups, 8.7% Irish, 7.6% Swedish, 7.2% German, 4.1% Norwegian (2000).
Economy: Port of entry on Grand Portage Bay, Lake Superior. Fishing center. Employment by occupation: 17.1% management, 12.3% professional, 38.4% services, 15.4% sales, 0.7% farming, 11.0% construction, 5.1% production (2000).
Income: Per capita income: $15,782 (2000); Median household income: $30,326 (2000); Poverty rate: 21.7% (2000).
Education: High school graduation rate: 78.0% (2000); College graduation rate: 10.6% (2000).
Housing: Homeownership rate: 65.7% (2000); Median home value: $68,000 (2000); Median rent: $347 per month (2000); Median age of housing: 10 years (2000).
Transportation: Commute to work: 86.1% car, 0.0% public transportation, 8.0% walk, 3.8% work from home (2000); Travel time to work: 78.3% less than 15 minutes, 6.9% 15 to 30 minutes, 9.4% 30 to 45 minutes, 1.8% 45 to 60 minutes, 3.6% 60 minutes or more (2000)

HOVLAND (unincorporated postal area, zip code 55606). Covers a land area of 130.084 square miles and a water area of 3.714 square miles. Located at 47.94° N. Lat.; 90.01° W. Long. Elevation is 660 feet.
Population: 272 (2000); Race: 95.8% White, 0.0% Black, 0.0% Asian, 0.0% American Indian and Alaska Native, 0.0% Hispanic of any race, 2.0% two or more races (2000); Density: 2.1 persons per square mile (2000); Age: 26.7% under 18, 7.2% over 64 (2000); Marriage status: 5.2% never married, 69.8% now married, 3.0% widowed, 22.0% divorced (2000); Foreign born: 2.3% (2000); Ancestry (includes multiple ancestries): 42.7% German, 20.8% Norwegian, 16.6% Irish, 11.4% Swedish, 9.4% United States or American (2000).

Economy: Employment by occupation: 12.5% management, 10.2% professional, 25.8% services, 22.7% sales, 5.5% farming, 18.0% construction, 5.5% production (2000).
Income: Per capita income: $20,865 (2000); Median household income: $51,500 (2000); Poverty rate: 9.8% (2000).
Education: High school graduation rate: 95.5% (2000); College graduation rate: 25.0% (2000).
Housing: Homeownership rate: 94.9% (2000); Median home value: $189,600 (2000); Median rent: $475 per month (2000); Median age of housing: 21 years (2000).
Transportation: Commute to work: 95.3% car, 0.0% public transportation, 0.0% walk, 0.0% work from home (2000); Travel time to work: 20.3% less than 15 minutes, 21.1% 15 to 30 minutes, 34.4% 30 to 45 minutes, 10.9% 45 to 60 minutes, 13.3% 60 minutes or more (2000)

LUTSEN (township). Covers a land area of 97.891 square miles and a water area of 7.859 square miles. Located at 47.72° N. Lat.; 90.69° W. Long. Elevation is 671 feet.
Population: 360 (2000); Race: 97.5% White, 0.0% Black, 0.6% Asian, 0.6% American Indian and Alaska Native, 0.0% Hispanic of any race, 1.4% two or more races (2000); Density: 3.7 persons per square mile (2000); Age: 20.9% under 18, 9.3% over 64 (2000); Marriage status: 23.4% never married, 65.0% now married, 3.5% widowed, 8.0% divorced (2000); Foreign born: 2.0% (2000); Ancestry (includes multiple ancestries): 32.5% German, 26.8% Norwegian, 13.0% English, 12.1% Swedish, 11.0% Irish (2000).
Economy: Resort community on Lake Superior, in Superior National Forest. Manufacturing of draperies and upholstery. Lutsen Ski Area to North. Lutsen Mountains Resort to Southwest. Employment by occupation: 21.6% management, 16.4% professional, 15.5% services, 23.5% sales, 0.0% farming, 14.6% construction, 8.5% production (2000).
Income: Per capita income: $29,249 (2000); Median household income: $44,167 (2000); Poverty rate: 0.0% (2000).
Education: High school graduation rate: 94.4% (2000); College graduation rate: 38.3% (2000).
Housing: Homeownership rate: 82.2% (2000); Median home value: $148,200 (2000); Median rent: $450 per month (2000); Median age of housing: 22 years (2000).
Transportation: Commute to work: 81.4% car, 0.0% public transportation, 5.7% walk, 11.0% work from home (2000); Travel time to work: 44.9% less than 15 minutes, 37.4% 15 to 30 minutes, 10.2% 30 to 45 minutes, 1.1% 45 to 60 minutes, 6.4% 60 minutes or more (2000)

SCHROEDER (township). Covers a land area of 149.909 square miles and a water area of 9.139 square miles. Located at 47.65° N. Lat.; 90.95° W. Long. Elevation is 650 feet.
Population: 187 (2000); Race: 91.9% White, 0.9% Black, 1.4% Asian, 2.4% American Indian and Alaska Native, 0.0% Hispanic of any race, 3.3% two or more races (2000); Density: 1.2 persons per square mile (2000); Age: 19.9% under 18, 17.1% over 64 (2000); Marriage status: 18.7% never married, 72.5% now married, 4.1% widowed, 4.7% divorced (2000); Foreign born: 4.7% (2000); Ancestry (includes multiple ancestries): 23.7% Norwegian, 22.7% German, 14.7% Swedish, 11.8% Irish, 10.4% English (2000).
Economy: Employment by occupation: 18.5% management, 11.3% professional, 21.0% services, 21.0% sales, 4.8% farming, 21.0% construction, 2.4% production (2000).
Income: Per capita income: $19,853 (2000); Median household income: $33,250 (2000); Poverty rate: 6.6% (2000).
Taxes: Total city taxes per capita: $5 (1997); City property taxes per capita: $5 (1997).
Education: High school graduation rate: 89.7% (2000); College graduation rate: 32.1% (2000).
Housing: Homeownership rate: 89.4% (2000); Median home value: $138,600 (2000); Median rent: $275 per month (2000); Median age of housing: 14 years (2000).
Transportation: Commute to work: 75.9% car, 2.6% public transportation, 12.1% walk, 9.5% work from home (2000); Travel time to work: 45.7% less than 15 minutes, 34.3% 15 to 30 minutes, 8.6% 30 to 45 minutes, 0.0% 45 to 60 minutes, 11.4% 60 minutes or more (2000)

TOFTE (township). Covers a land area of 154.556 square miles and a water area of 8.002 square miles. Located at 47.76° N. Lat.; 90.84° W. Long. Elevation is 629 feet.
Population: 226 (2000); Race: 97.5% White, 0.0% Black, 0.8% Asian, 1.2% American Indian and Alaska Native, 0.4% Hispanic of any race, 0.0% two or more races (2000); Density: 1.5 persons per square mile (2000); Age: 19.5% under 18, 17.8% over 64 (2000); Marriage status: 18.0% never married, 72.2% now married, 1.0% widowed, 8.8% divorced (2000); Foreign born: 2.5% (2000); Ancestry (includes multiple ancestries): 22.8% German, 21.2% English, 14.5% Norwegian, 11.2% Swedish, 9.1% Irish (2000).
Economy: Employment by occupation: 23.1% management, 11.2% professional, 14.2% services, 23.9% sales, 0.0% farming, 18.7% construction, 9.0% production (2000).
Income: Per capita income: $23,120 (2000); Median household income: $47,188 (2000); Poverty rate: 1.2% (2000).
Taxes: Total city taxes per capita: $74 (1997); City property taxes per capita: $74 (1997).
Education: High school graduation rate: 80.9% (2000); College graduation rate: 19.7% (2000).
Housing: Homeownership rate: 88.5% (2000); Median home value: $147,900 (2000); Median rent: $420 per month (2000); Median age of housing: 20 years (2000).
Transportation: Commute to work: 70.5% car, 0.0% public transportation, 23.5% walk, 4.5% work from home (2000); Travel time to work: 76.2% less than 15 minutes, 6.3% 15 to 30 minutes, 15.9% 30 to 45 minutes, 0.0% 45 to 60 minutes, 1.6% 60 minutes or more (2000)

Cottonwood County

Located in southwestern Minnesota; watered by the Des Moines River. Covers a land area of 640.00 square miles, a water area of 8.90 square miles, and is located in the Central Time Zone. The county government was organized in 1857. County seat is Windom.

Weather Station: Windom — Elevation: 1,374 feet

	Jan	Feb	Mar	Apr	May	Jun	Jul	Aug	Sep	Oct	Nov	Dec
High	23	29	41	57	71	80	84	81	73	60	41	27
Low	3	10	22	34	47	57	61	59	49	36	23	10
Precip	0.8	0.6	2.1	2.9	3.5	4.4	4.0	3.5	2.8	2.0	1.8	0.8
Snow	9.3	5.8	9.4	3.2	0.0	0.0	0.0	0.0	tr	0.9	6.9	7.6

High and Low temperatures in degrees Fahrenheit; Precipitation and Snow in inches

Population: 12,167 (2000); Race: 95.4% White, 0.1% Black, 1.6% Asian, 0.1% American Indian and Alaska Native, 2.5% Hispanic of any race, 1.2% two or more races (2000); Density: 19.0 persons per square mile (2000); Age: 25.0% under 18, 22.0% over 64 (2000).
Religion: Five largest groups: 32.5% Evangelical Lutheran Church in America, 10.9% Lutheran Church—Missouri Synod, 10.8% Catholic Church, 9.1% The United Methodist Church, 6.8% Mennonite Church USA (2000).
Economy: Unemployment rate: 3.2% (11/2002); Total civilian labor force: 5,953 (11/2002); Leading industries: 30.1% manufacturing; 21.1% health care and social assistance; 17.9% retail trade (2000); Companies that employ more than 1,000 persons: 0 (2000); Companies that employ more than 100 persons: 4 (2000); Farms: 784 totaling 368,346 acres (1997); Minority business ownership rate: 0.0% (1997); Women business ownership rate: 29.2% (1997); Retail sales per capita: $8,501 (1997). Single-family building permits issued: 35 (2001) / 13 (2000); Multi-family building permits issued: 4 (2001) / 4 (2000).
Income: Per capita income: $16,647 (2000); Median household income: $31,943 (2000); Poverty rate: 11.7% (2000); Bankruptcy rate: 1.42% (2001).
Taxes: Total county taxes per capita: $371 (2000); County property taxes per capita: $371 (2000).
Education: High school graduation rate: 80.4% (2000); College graduation rate: 14.2% (2000).
Housing: Homeownership rate: 80.4% (2000); Median home value: $50,600 (2000); Median rent: $245 per month (2000); Median age of housing: 48 years (2000).
Health: Birth rate: 111.8 per 10,000 population (1998); Age adjusted death rate: 85.2 per 10,000 population (1999); Age adjusted cancer mortality rate: 209.1 deaths per 100,000 population (1999). Number of physicians: 8.2 per 10,000 population (1999); Number of hospital beds: 33.7 per 10,000 population (1999).
Elections: 2000 Presidential election results: 40.5% Gore, 54.5% Bush, 3.4% Nader, 1.2% Buchanan
National and State Parks: Banks State Wildlife Management Area; Bennett State Wildlife Management Area; Delft State Wildlife Management Area; Hurricane State Wildlife Management Area; Little Swan Lake State Wildlife Management A; Mountain Lake State Wildlife Management Area; Regehr State Wildlife Management Area; Talcot Lake State Wildlife Management Area

Additional Information Contacts
Cottonwood County Government Offices 507-831-5520
Mountain Lake Chamber of Commerce 507-427-3002

Windom Chamber of Commerce 507-831-2752

Cottonwood County Communities

AMBOY (township). Covers a land area of 35.632 square miles and a water area of 0 square miles. Located at 44.05° N. Lat.; 95.15° W. Long.
Population: 172 (2000); Race: 100.0% White, 0.0% Black, 0.0% Asian, 0.0% American Indian and Alaska Native, 0.0% Hispanic of any race, 0.0% two or more races (2000); Density: 4.8 persons per square mile (2000); Age: 23.4% under 18, 20.1% over 64 (2000); Marriage status: 17.8% never married, 69.8% now married, 9.3% widowed, 3.1% divorced (2000); Foreign born: 0.0% (2000); Ancestry (includes multiple ancestries): 74.7% German, 23.4% Norwegian, 7.1% Irish, 5.8% Dutch, 5.2% English (2000).
Economy: Employment by occupation: 31.7% management, 17.1% professional, 8.5% services, 17.1% sales, 0.0% farming, 7.3% construction, 18.3% production (2000).
Income: Per capita income: $20,877 (2000); Median household income: $35,250 (2000); Poverty rate: 7.8% (2000).
Taxes: Total city taxes per capita: $37 (1997); City property taxes per capita: $37 (1997).
Education: High school graduation rate: 91.0% (2000); College graduation rate: 12.6% (2000).
Housing: Homeownership rate: 81.2% (2000); Median home value: $54,400 (2000); Median rent: $225 per month (2000); Median age of housing: 56 years (2000).
Transportation: Commute to work: 83.5% car, 0.0% public transportation, 3.8% walk, 12.7% work from home (2000); Travel time to work: 44.9% less than 15 minutes, 37.7% 15 to 30 minutes, 10.1% 30 to 45 minutes, 1.4% 45 to 60 minutes, 5.8% 60 minutes or more (2000)

AMO (township). Covers a land area of 35.138 square miles and a water area of 0.706 square miles. Located at 43.98° N. Lat.; 95.27° W. Long.
Population: 140 (2000); Race: 100.0% White, 0.0% Black, 0.0% Asian, 0.0% American Indian and Alaska Native, 0.0% Hispanic of any race, 0.0% two or more races (2000); Density: 4.0 persons per square mile (2000); Age: 31.3% under 18, 5.6% over 64 (2000); Marriage status: 28.6% never married, 66.7% now married, 4.8% widowed, 0.0% divorced (2000); Foreign born: 0.0% (2000); Ancestry (includes multiple ancestries): 64.6% German, 25.0% Norwegian, 11.1% Dutch, 10.4% Danish, 9.7% Luxemburger (2000).
Economy: Employment by occupation: 40.2% management, 9.8% professional, 6.5% services, 16.3% sales, 2.2% farming, 4.3% construction, 20.7% production (2000).
Income: Per capita income: $25,945 (2000); Median household income: $55,625 (2000); Poverty rate: 13.5% (2000).
Education: High school graduation rate: 94.0% (2000); College graduation rate: 20.2% (2000).
Housing: Homeownership rate: 72.5% (2000); Median home value: $60,000 (2000); Median rent: $100 per month (2000); Median age of housing: 60+ years (2000).
Transportation: Commute to work: 67.4% car, 0.0% public transportation, 2.2% walk, 30.4% work from home (2000); Travel time to work: 34.4% less than 15 minutes, 59.4% 15 to 30 minutes, 6.3% 30 to 45 minutes, 0.0% 45 to 60 minutes, 0.0% 60 minutes or more (2000)

ANN (township). Covers a land area of 36.165 square miles and a water area of 0.001 square miles. Located at 44.14° N. Lat.; 95.39° W. Long.
Population: 191 (2000); Race: 100.0% White, 0.0% Black, 0.0% Asian, 0.0% American Indian and Alaska Native, 0.0% Hispanic of any race, 0.0% two or more races (2000); Density: 5.3 persons per square mile (2000); Age: 21.8% under 18, 22.3% over 64 (2000); Marriage status: 16.4% never married, 80.5% now married, 3.1% widowed, 0.0% divorced (2000); Foreign born: 0.0% (2000); Ancestry (includes multiple ancestries): 61.7% Norwegian, 41.5% German, 10.9% Swedish, 7.8% Danish, 3.6% Hungarian (2000).
Economy: Employment by occupation: 32.7% management, 15.8% professional, 15.8% services, 14.9% sales, 0.0% farming, 9.9% construction, 10.9% production (2000).
Income: Per capita income: $20,134 (2000); Median household income: $40,000 (2000); Poverty rate: 4.2% (2000).
Education: High school graduation rate: 94.2% (2000); College graduation rate: 17.3% (2000).
Housing: Homeownership rate: 87.5% (2000); Median home value: $32,500 (2000); Median age of housing: 59 years (2000).
Transportation: Commute to work: 70.4% car, 0.0% public transportation, 3.1% walk, 26.5% work from home (2000); Travel time to work: 33.3% less than 15 minutes, 40.3% 15 to 30 minutes, 15.3% 30 to 45 minutes, 8.3% 45 to 60 minutes, 2.8% 60 minutes or more (2000)

BINGHAM LAKE (city). Covers a land area of 0.778 square miles and a water area of 0 square miles. Located at 43.90° N. Lat.; 95.04° W. Long.
Population: 167 (2000); Race: 80.7% White, 1.8% Black, 11.4% Asian, 0.0% American Indian and Alaska Native, 1.8% Hispanic of any race, 4.8% two or more races (2000); Density: 214.7 persons per square mile (2000); Age: 33.7% under 18, 8.4% over 64 (2000); Marriage status: 25.7% never married, 61.9% now married, 2.7% widowed, 9.7% divorced (2000); Foreign born: 9.6% (2000); Ancestry (includes multiple ancestries): 39.8% German, 24.7% Other groups, 19.9% Norwegian, 14.5% Irish, 8.4% Swedish (2000).
Economy: Livestock; grain, soybeans. Manufacturing: medical equipment. Single-family building permits issued: 0 (2001) / 2 (2000); Multi-family building permits issued: 0 (2001) / 0 (2000); Employment by occupation: 9.7% management, 18.1% professional, 12.5% services, 13.9% sales, 0.0% farming, 9.7% construction, 36.1% production (2000).
Income: Per capita income: $11,820 (2000); Median household income: $33,750 (2000); Poverty rate: 14.5% (2000).
Taxes: Total city taxes per capita: $285 (1997); City property taxes per capita: $285 (1997).
Education: High school graduation rate: 82.9% (2000); College graduation rate: 7.6% (2000).
Housing: Homeownership rate: 85.2% (2000); Median home value: $37,500 (2000); Median rent: $375 per month (2000); Median age of housing: 45 years (2000).
Transportation: Commute to work: 85.3% car, 4.4% public transportation, 8.8% walk, 1.5% work from home (2000); Travel time to work: 83.6% less than 15 minutes, 4.5% 15 to 30 minutes, 6.0% 30 to 45 minutes, 6.0% 45 to 60 minutes, 0.0% 60 minutes or more (2000)

CARSON (township). Covers a land area of 35.233 square miles and a water area of 0.639 square miles. Located at 43.98° N. Lat.; 95.05° W. Long.
Population: 311 (2000); Race: 100.0% White, 0.0% Black, 0.0% Asian, 0.0% American Indian and Alaska Native, 1.3% Hispanic of any race, 0.0% two or more races (2000); Density: 8.8 persons per square mile (2000); Age: 30.7% under 18, 13.9% over 64 (2000); Marriage status: 21.1% never married, 67.2% now married, 4.3% widowed, 7.3% divorced (2000); Foreign born: 0.0% (2000); Ancestry (includes multiple ancestries): 66.3% German, 10.0% Dutch, 7.8% Norwegian, 5.8% Swedish, 5.2% Irish (2000).
Economy: Employment by occupation: 26.2% management, 12.2% professional, 10.4% services, 15.2% sales, 2.4% farming, 11.0% construction, 22.6% production (2000).
Income: Per capita income: $14,597 (2000); Median household income: $38,250 (2000); Poverty rate: 6.2% (2000).
Taxes: Total city taxes per capita: $95 (1997); City property taxes per capita: $95 (1997).
Education: High school graduation rate: 87.6% (2000); College graduation rate: 19.7% (2000).
Housing: Homeownership rate: 86.4% (2000); Median home value: $55,000 (2000); Median rent: $208 per month (2000); Median age of housing: 60+ years (2000).
Transportation: Commute to work: 73.8% car, 0.0% public transportation, 0.0% walk, 21.9% work from home (2000); Travel time to work: 24.0% less than 15 minutes, 57.6% 15 to 30 minutes, 8.0% 30 to 45 minutes, 2.4% 45 to 60 minutes, 8.0% 60 minutes or more (2000)

DALE (township). Covers a land area of 35.594 square miles and a water area of 0.460 square miles. Located at 43.99° N. Lat.; 95.17° W. Long.
Population: 154 (2000); Race: 100.0% White, 0.0% Black, 0.0% Asian, 0.0% American Indian and Alaska Native, 0.0% Hispanic of any race, 0.0% two or more races (2000); Density: 4.3 persons per square mile (2000); Age: 16.1% under 18, 35.0% over 64 (2000); Marriage status: 17.1% never married, 69.1% now married, 11.4% widowed, 2.4% divorced (2000); Foreign born: 4.4% (2000); Ancestry (includes multiple ancestries): 46.0% German, 19.7% Norwegian, 10.2% United States or American, 8.8% English, 4.4% Danish (2000).
Economy: Employment by occupation: 38.6% management, 12.3% professional, 14.0% services, 17.5% sales, 0.0% farming, 7.0% construction, 10.5% production (2000).
Income: Per capita income: $20,131 (2000); Median household income: $41,250 (2000); Poverty rate: 10.2% (2000).
Taxes: Total city taxes per capita: $229 (1997); City property taxes per capita: $229 (1997).
Education: High school graduation rate: 83.0% (2000); College graduation rate: 2.8% (2000).

Housing: Homeownership rate: 89.4% (2000); Median home value: $92,500 (2000); Median rent: $225 per month (2000); Median age of housing: 58 years (2000).
Transportation: Commute to work: 66.7% car, 0.0% public transportation, 3.5% walk, 29.8% work from home (2000); Travel time to work: 37.5% less than 15 minutes, 45.0% 15 to 30 minutes, 17.5% 30 to 45 minutes, 0.0% 45 to 60 minutes, 0.0% 60 minutes or more (2000)

DELTON (township). Covers a land area of 35.728 square miles and a water area of 0.012 square miles. Located at 44.07° N. Lat.; 95.04° W. Long.
Population: 146 (2000); Race: 100.0% White, 0.0% Black, 0.0% Asian, 0.0% American Indian and Alaska Native, 4.7% Hispanic of any race, 0.0% two or more races (2000); Density: 4.1 persons per square mile (2000); Age: 17.4% under 18, 16.1% over 64 (2000); Marriage status: 27.9% never married, 62.0% now married, 5.4% widowed, 4.7% divorced (2000); Foreign born: 0.0% (2000); Ancestry (includes multiple ancestries): 62.4% German, 20.1% Norwegian, 8.1% Swedish, 6.7% United States or American, 6.0% Danish (2000).
Economy: Employment by occupation: 52.5% management, 12.5% professional, 6.3% services, 6.3% sales, 3.8% farming, 2.5% construction, 16.3% production (2000).
Income: Per capita income: $20,666 (2000); Median household income: $41,563 (2000); Poverty rate: 12.8% (2000).
Taxes: Total city taxes per capita: $157 (1997); City property taxes per capita: $157 (1997).
Education: High school graduation rate: 86.9% (2000); College graduation rate: 12.1% (2000).
Housing: Homeownership rate: 83.9% (2000); Median home value: $48,800 (2000); Median rent: <$100 per month (2000); Median age of housing: 60+ years (2000).
Transportation: Commute to work: 71.3% car, 0.0% public transportation, 5.0% walk, 23.8% work from home (2000); Travel time to work: 44.3% less than 15 minutes, 24.6% 15 to 30 minutes, 9.8% 30 to 45 minutes, 9.8% 45 to 60 minutes, 11.5% 60 minutes or more (2000)

GERMANTOWN (township). Covers a land area of 35.840 square miles and a water area of 0.008 square miles. Located at 44.15° N. Lat.; 95.17° W. Long.
Population: 224 (2000); Race: 100.0% White, 0.0% Black, 0.0% Asian, 0.0% American Indian and Alaska Native, 0.0% Hispanic of any race, 0.0% two or more races (2000); Density: 6.2 persons per square mile (2000); Age: 34.1% under 18, 16.8% over 64 (2000); Marriage status: 12.6% never married, 80.8% now married, 4.2% widowed, 2.4% divorced (2000); Foreign born: 0.0% (2000); Ancestry (includes multiple ancestries): 62.5% German, 7.8% English, 7.8% Swedish, 7.3% Dutch, 6.5% Norwegian (2000).
Economy: Employment by occupation: 38.5% management, 14.7% professional, 17.4% services, 12.8% sales, 5.5% farming, 6.4% construction, 4.6% production (2000).
Income: Per capita income: $19,071 (2000); Median household income: $35,893 (2000); Poverty rate: 3.9% (2000).
Taxes: Total city taxes per capita: $61 (1997); City property taxes per capita: $61 (1997).
Education: High school graduation rate: 83.7% (2000); College graduation rate: 9.5% (2000).
Housing: Homeownership rate: 95.0% (2000); Median home value: $106,300 (2000); Median age of housing: 51 years (2000).
Transportation: Commute to work: 64.5% car, 0.0% public transportation, 2.8% walk, 32.7% work from home (2000); Travel time to work: 40.3% less than 15 minutes, 34.7% 15 to 30 minutes, 22.2% 30 to 45 minutes, 2.8% 45 to 60 minutes, 0.0% 60 minutes or more (2000)

GREAT BEND (township). Covers a land area of 31.592 square miles and a water area of 0.702 square miles. Located at 43.88° N. Lat.; 95.14° W. Long.
Population: 326 (2000); Race: 98.2% White, 0.0% Black, 0.6% Asian, 0.0% American Indian and Alaska Native, 0.3% Hispanic of any race, 1.2% two or more races (2000); Density: 10.3 persons per square mile (2000); Age: 31.4% under 18, 15.0% over 64 (2000); Marriage status: 21.3% never married, 68.1% now married, 5.5% widowed, 5.1% divorced (2000); Foreign born: 0.6% (2000); Ancestry (includes multiple ancestries): 40.4% German, 15.3% Norwegian, 12.3% Irish, 7.5% English, 7.5% Dutch (2000).
Economy: Employment by occupation: 21.2% management, 14.0% professional, 13.4% services, 24.0% sales, 0.0% farming, 7.8% construction, 19.6% production (2000).
Income: Per capita income: $16,134 (2000); Median household income: $36,406 (2000); Poverty rate: 12.2% (2000).
Taxes: Total city taxes per capita: $31 (1997); City property taxes per capita: $31 (1997).
Education: High school graduation rate: 82.4% (2000); College graduation rate: 13.4% (2000).
Housing: Homeownership rate: 79.8% (2000); Median home value: $102,800 (2000); Median rent: $296 per month (2000); Median age of housing: 60 years (2000).
Transportation: Commute to work: 92.1% car, 0.0% public transportation, 4.0% walk, 4.0% work from home (2000); Travel time to work: 71.2% less than 15 minutes, 18.2% 15 to 30 minutes, 5.3% 30 to 45 minutes, 2.4% 45 to 60 minutes, 2.9% 60 minutes or more (2000)

HIGHWATER (township). Covers a land area of 35.938 square miles and a water area of 0.233 square miles. Located at 44.14° N. Lat.; 95.28° W. Long.
Population: 169 (2000); Race: 97.0% White, 0.0% Black, 0.0% Asian, 0.0% American Indian and Alaska Native, 3.0% Hispanic of any race, 1.2% two or more races (2000); Density: 4.7 persons per square mile (2000); Age: 16.1% under 18, 10.1% over 64 (2000); Marriage status: 16.8% never married, 80.5% now married, 1.3% widowed, 1.3% divorced (2000); Foreign born: 0.0% (2000); Ancestry (includes multiple ancestries): 49.4% Norwegian, 37.5% German, 6.5% United States or American, 6.5% Danish, 4.2% Irish (2000).
Economy: Employment by occupation: 25.2% management, 10.3% professional, 14.0% services, 15.0% sales, 13.1% farming, 4.7% construction, 17.8% production (2000).
Income: Per capita income: $16,858 (2000); Median household income: $45,625 (2000); Poverty rate: 10.7% (2000).
Taxes: Total city taxes per capita: $108 (1997); City property taxes per capita: $108 (1997).
Education: High school graduation rate: 87.9% (2000); College graduation rate: 12.9% (2000).
Housing: Homeownership rate: 85.3% (2000); Median home value: $82,500 (2000); Median rent: $200 per month (2000); Median age of housing: 58 years (2000).
Transportation: Commute to work: 70.5% car, 1.9% public transportation, 10.5% walk, 17.1% work from home (2000); Travel time to work: 56.3% less than 15 minutes, 27.6% 15 to 30 minutes, 9.2% 30 to 45 minutes, 1.1% 45 to 60 minutes, 5.7% 60 minutes or more (2000)

JEFFERS (city). Covers a land area of 0.386 square miles and a water area of 0 square miles. Located at 44.05° N. Lat.; 95.19° W. Long. Elevation is 1,477 feet.
Population: 396 (2000); Race: 98.2% White, 0.0% Black, 0.0% Asian, 0.0% American Indian and Alaska Native, 0.8% Hispanic of any race, 1.8% two or more races (2000); Density: 1,025.0 persons per square mile (2000); Age: 20.6% under 18, 26.8% over 64 (2000); Marriage status: 15.6% never married, 60.3% now married, 14.1% widowed, 10.0% divorced (2000); Foreign born: 0.0% (2000); Ancestry (includes multiple ancestries): 53.6% German, 16.7% Norwegian, 7.8% Dutch, 5.5% English, 5.2% Danish (2000).
Economy: Agriculture: grain, soybeans; livestock. Manufacturing: hydraulic cylinders, carts. Single-family building permits issued: 1 (2001) / 0 (2000); Multi-family building permits issued: 0 (2001) / 0 (2000); Employment by occupation: 7.8% management, 9.6% professional, 17.4% services, 16.2% sales, 2.4% farming, 21.0% construction, 25.7% production (2000).
Income: Per capita income: $16,649 (2000); Median household income: $29,286 (2000); Poverty rate: 9.9% (2000).
Taxes: Total city taxes per capita: $97 (1997); City property taxes per capita: $88 (1997).
Education: High school graduation rate: 70.2% (2000); College graduation rate: 8.7% (2000).
Housing: Homeownership rate: 81.8% (2000); Median home value: $23,900 (2000); Median rent: $192 per month (2000); Median age of housing: 54 years (2000).
Transportation: Commute to work: 94.4% car, 0.0% public transportation, 2.5% walk, 1.9% work from home (2000); Travel time to work: 43.0% less than 15 minutes, 39.2% 15 to 30 minutes, 10.1% 30 to 45 minutes, 5.1% 45 to 60 minutes, 2.5% 60 minutes or more (2000)

LAKESIDE (township). Covers a land area of 33.504 square miles and a water area of 1.769 square miles. Located at 43.89° N. Lat.; 95.04° W. Long.
Population: 255 (2000); Race: 99.2% White, 0.0% Black, 0.0% Asian, 0.0% American Indian and Alaska Native, 0.0% Hispanic of any race, 0.8% two or more races (2000); Density: 7.6 persons per square mile (2000); Age: 25.1% under 18, 9.4% over 64 (2000); Marriage status: 15.7% never married, 81.2% now married, 1.5% widowed, 1.5% divorced (2000); Foreign born: 0.4%

(2000); Ancestry (includes multiple ancestries): 47.8% German, 31.0% Norwegian, 9.8% United States or American, 8.6% English, 4.7% European (2000).
Economy: Employment by occupation: 10.4% management, 18.8% professional, 13.6% services, 27.3% sales, 3.9% farming, 12.3% construction, 13.6% production (2000).
Income: Per capita income: $20,758 (2000); Median household income: $39,688 (2000); Poverty rate: 19.2% (2000).
Taxes: Total city taxes per capita: $64 (1997); City property taxes per capita: $64 (1997).
Education: High school graduation rate: 95.5% (2000); College graduation rate: 18.4% (2000).
Housing: Homeownership rate: 89.8% (2000); Median home value: $67,200 (2000); Median rent: $425 per month (2000); Median age of housing: 52 years (2000).
Transportation: Commute to work: 74.8% car, 0.0% public transportation, 3.3% walk, 19.9% work from home (2000); Travel time to work: 66.1% less than 15 minutes, 19.8% 15 to 30 minutes, 7.4% 30 to 45 minutes, 3.3% 45 to 60 minutes, 3.3% 60 minutes or more (2000)

MIDWAY (township). Covers a land area of 34.263 square miles and a water area of 0.362 square miles. Located at 43.97° N. Lat.; 94.91° W. Long.
Population: 297 (2000); Race: 98.7% White, 0.0% Black, 0.0% Asian, 0.0% American Indian and Alaska Native, 0.0% Hispanic of any race, 0.0% two or more races (2000); Density: 8.7 persons per square mile (2000); Age: 25.2% under 18, 23.3% over 64 (2000); Marriage status: 14.5% never married, 76.9% now married, 6.6% widowed, 2.1% divorced (2000); Foreign born: 2.0% (2000); Ancestry (includes multiple ancestries): 72.1% German, 15.3% Norwegian, 4.7% Dutch, 4.3% Swedish, 4.3% Irish (2000).
Economy: Employment by occupation: 28.9% management, 10.6% professional, 10.6% services, 16.2% sales, 4.9% farming, 12.7% construction, 16.2% production (2000).
Income: Per capita income: $19,818 (2000); Median household income: $38,750 (2000); Poverty rate: 7.3% (2000).
Taxes: Total city taxes per capita: $115 (1997); City property taxes per capita: $115 (1997).
Education: High school graduation rate: 87.3% (2000); College graduation rate: 19.5% (2000).
Housing: Homeownership rate: 88.6% (2000); Median home value: $61,400 (2000); Median rent: $165 per month (2000); Median age of housing: 60+ years (2000).
Transportation: Commute to work: 88.0% car, 0.0% public transportation, 4.9% walk, 7.0% work from home (2000); Travel time to work: 65.9% less than 15 minutes, 22.0% 15 to 30 minutes, 4.5% 30 to 45 minutes, 5.3% 45 to 60 minutes, 2.3% 60 minutes or more (2000)

MOUNTAIN LAKE (city). Covers a land area of 1.352 square miles and a water area of 0.020 square miles. Located at 43.94° N. Lat.; 94.93° W. Long. Elevation is 1,305 feet.
Population: 2,082 (2000); Race: 82.0% White, 0.0% Black, 7.0% Asian, 0.2% American Indian and Alaska Native, 8.2% Hispanic of any race, 4.5% two or more races (2000); Density: 1,540.3 persons per square mile (2000); Age: 26.3% under 18, 26.7% over 64 (2000); Marriage status: 19.6% never married, 61.0% now married, 13.2% widowed, 6.2% divorced (2000); Foreign born: 7.9% (2000); Ancestry (includes multiple ancestries): 46.9% German, 16.9% Other groups, 7.7% Norwegian, 7.3% Dutch, 3.5% English (2000).
Economy: Single-family building permits issued: 3 (2001) / 2 (2000); Multi-family building permits issued: 0 (2001) / 0 (2000); Employment by occupation: 6.8% management, 18.2% professional, 21.0% services, 18.6% sales, 2.6% farming, 6.8% construction, 26.0% production (2000).
Income: Per capita income: $13,845 (2000); Median household income: $29,146 (2000); Poverty rate: 13.0% (2000).
Taxes: Total city taxes per capita: $167 (1997); City property taxes per capita: $164 (1997).
Education: High school graduation rate: 74.5% (2000); College graduation rate: 16.0% (2000).

School District(s)

Mountain Lake (PK-12)
2000 Enrollment: 519 507-427-2325
Housing: Homeownership rate: 79.7% (2000); Median home value: $42,800 (2000); Median rent: $259 per month (2000); Median age of housing: 50 years (2000).
Safety: Violent crime rate: 19.0 per 10,000 population; Property crime rate: 332.7 per 10,000 population (2001).
Newspapers: Mountain Lake Observer - Advocate (1 x week)
Transportation: Commute to work: 86.7% car, 0.0% public transportation, 8.4% walk, 3.7% work from home (2000); Travel time to work: 69.6% less than 15 minutes, 18.1% 15 to 30 minutes, 7.5% 30 to 45 minutes, 1.3% 45 to 60 minutes, 3.5% 60 minutes or more (2000)
Additional Information Contacts
Mountain Lake Chamber of Commerce 507-427-3002

MOUNTAIN LAKE (township). Covers a land area of 35.708 square miles and a water area of 0.060 square miles. Located at 43.89° N. Lat.; 94.93° W. Long. Elevation is 1,305 feet.
History: Laid out 1872, settled by Mennonites.
Population: 442 (2000); Race: 97.7% White, 0.5% Black, 0.7% Asian, 0.0% American Indian and Alaska Native, 3.0% Hispanic of any race, 0.0% two or more races (2000); Density: 12.4 persons per square mile (2000); Age: 48.1% under 18, 13.8% over 64 (2000); Marriage status: 28.6% never married, 67.9% now married, 1.1% widowed, 2.5% divorced (2000); Foreign born: 2.8% (2000); Ancestry (includes multiple ancestries): 54.0% German, 11.7% Dutch, 5.8% English, 5.1% United States or American, 4.9% Swedish (2000).
Economy: Grain, soybeans; livestock. Manufacturing: slurry pumps, oak furniture, light manufacturing. Employment by occupation: 32.3% management, 12.8% professional, 10.5% services, 9.0% sales, 6.0% farming, 6.0% construction, 23.3% production (2000).
Income: Per capita income: $8,240 (2000); Median household income: $27,143 (2000); Poverty rate: 49.8% (2000).
Taxes: Total city taxes per capita: $121 (1997); City property taxes per capita: $121 (1997).
Education: High school graduation rate: 66.5% (2000); College graduation rate: 7.4% (2000).
Housing: Homeownership rate: 66.3% (2000); Median home value: $58,900 (2000); Median rent: $200 per month (2000); Median age of housing: 60+ years (2000).
Transportation: Commute to work: 76.5% car, 0.0% public transportation, 4.5% walk, 18.9% work from home (2000); Travel time to work: 57.9% less than 15 minutes, 31.8% 15 to 30 minutes, 7.5% 30 to 45 minutes, 2.8% 45 to 60 minutes, 0.0% 60 minutes or more (2000)

ROSE HILL (township). Covers a land area of 35.739 square miles and a water area of 0.797 square miles. Located at 43.98° N. Lat.; 95.39° W. Long.
Population: 189 (2000); Race: 100.0% White, 0.0% Black, 0.0% Asian, 0.0% American Indian and Alaska Native, 0.0% Hispanic of any race, 0.0% two or more races (2000); Density: 5.3 persons per square mile (2000); Age: 30.3% under 18, 14.1% over 64 (2000); Marriage status: 11.6% never married, 81.9% now married, 1.4% widowed, 5.1% divorced (2000); Foreign born: 1.1% (2000); Ancestry (includes multiple ancestries): 73.0% German, 26.5% Norwegian, 11.9% United States or American, 8.6% Czech, 7.6% Swedish (2000).
Economy: Employment by occupation: 28.7% management, 16.8% professional, 10.9% services, 17.8% sales, 5.0% farming, 4.0% construction, 16.8% production (2000).
Income: Per capita income: $14,594 (2000); Median household income: $39,688 (2000); Poverty rate: 7.0% (2000).
Education: High school graduation rate: 82.5% (2000); College graduation rate: 21.4% (2000).
Housing: Homeownership rate: 88.4% (2000); Median home value: $27,500 (2000); Median rent: $125 per month (2000); Median age of housing: 60+ years (2000).
Transportation: Commute to work: 74.3% car, 0.0% public transportation, 0.0% walk, 24.8% work from home (2000); Travel time to work: 30.3% less than 15 minutes, 32.9% 15 to 30 minutes, 25.0% 30 to 45 minutes, 6.6% 45 to 60 minutes, 5.3% 60 minutes or more (2000)

SELMA (township). Covers a land area of 36.058 square miles and a water area of 0 square miles. Located at 44.06° N. Lat.; 94.93° W. Long.
Population: 204 (2000); Race: 98.5% White, 1.5% Black, 0.0% Asian, 0.0% American Indian and Alaska Native, 1.5% Hispanic of any race, 0.0% two or more races (2000); Density: 5.7 persons per square mile (2000); Age: 25.6% under 18, 25.1% over 64 (2000); Marriage status: 19.1% never married, 75.9% now married, 4.3% widowed, 0.6% divorced (2000); Foreign born: 1.0% (2000); Ancestry (includes multiple ancestries): 71.9% German, 14.3% Swedish, 9.4% Norwegian, 7.4% Irish, 6.4% Czech (2000).
Economy: Employment by occupation: 29.9% management, 15.6% professional, 7.8% services, 16.9% sales, 11.7% farming, 5.2% construction, 13.0% production (2000).
Income: Per capita income: $15,551 (2000); Median household income: $37,250 (2000); Poverty rate: 10.8% (2000).

Taxes: Total city taxes per capita: $125 (1997); City property taxes per capita: $125 (1997).
Education: High school graduation rate: 84.8% (2000); College graduation rate: 6.9% (2000).
Housing: Homeownership rate: 97.5% (2000); Median home value: $78,300 (2000); Median age of housing: 54 years (2000).
Transportation: Commute to work: 75.3% car, 0.0% public transportation, 0.0% walk, 24.7% work from home (2000); Travel time to work: 32.8% less than 15 minutes, 34.5% 15 to 30 minutes, 8.6% 30 to 45 minutes, 13.8% 45 to 60 minutes, 10.3% 60 minutes or more (2000)

SOUTHBROOK (township). Covers a land area of 34.258 square miles and a water area of 2.096 square miles. Located at 43.88° N. Lat.; 95.39° W. Long.
Population: 112 (2000); Race: 100.0% White, 0.0% Black, 0.0% Asian, 0.0% American Indian and Alaska Native, 0.0% Hispanic of any race, 0.0% two or more races (2000); Density: 3.3 persons per square mile (2000); Age: 33.8% under 18, 5.3% over 64 (2000); Marriage status: 22.9% never married, 68.6% now married, 6.7% widowed, 1.9% divorced (2000); Foreign born: 0.0% (2000); Ancestry (includes multiple ancestries): 57.1% German, 28.6% Dutch, 17.3% Norwegian, 9.0% Belgian, 6.8% Swedish (2000).
Economy: Employment by occupation: 28.9% management, 10.5% professional, 17.1% services, 18.4% sales, 11.8% farming, 10.5% construction, 2.6% production (2000).
Income: Per capita income: $14,154 (2000); Median household income: $41,250 (2000); Poverty rate: 6.0% (2000).
Taxes: Total city taxes per capita: $165 (1997); City property taxes per capita: $165 (1997).
Education: High school graduation rate: 90.6% (2000); College graduation rate: 5.9% (2000).
Housing: Homeownership rate: 90.7% (2000); Median home value: $85,000 (2000); Median age of housing: 45 years (2000).
Transportation: Commute to work: 66.7% car, 0.0% public transportation, 2.7% walk, 28.0% work from home (2000); Travel time to work: 29.6% less than 15 minutes, 51.9% 15 to 30 minutes, 3.7% 30 to 45 minutes, 0.0% 45 to 60 minutes, 14.8% 60 minutes or more (2000)

SPRINGFIELD (township). Covers a land area of 36.080 square miles and a water area of 0.034 square miles. Located at 43.89° N. Lat.; 95.27° W. Long.
Population: 161 (2000); Race: 98.7% White, 0.0% Black, 0.0% Asian, 1.3% American Indian and Alaska Native, 0.0% Hispanic of any race, 0.0% two or more races (2000); Density: 4.5 persons per square mile (2000); Age: 19.0% under 18, 13.1% over 64 (2000); Marriage status: 23.1% never married, 72.4% now married, 4.5% widowed, 0.0% divorced (2000); Foreign born: 0.0% (2000); Ancestry (includes multiple ancestries): 62.7% German, 17.0% Dutch, 15.0% Norwegian, 7.8% Swedish, 4.6% Finnish (2000).
Economy: Employment by occupation: 27.8% management, 11.1% professional, 7.8% services, 16.7% sales, 0.0% farming, 10.0% construction, 26.7% production (2000).
Income: Per capita income: $15,175 (2000); Median household income: $39,286 (2000); Poverty rate: 1.3% (2000).
Taxes: Total city taxes per capita: $135 (1997); City property taxes per capita: $135 (1997).
Education: High school graduation rate: 89.7% (2000); College graduation rate: 15.9% (2000).
Housing: Homeownership rate: 85.5% (2000); Median home value: $53,100 (2000); Median rent: $125 per month (2000); Median age of housing: 53 years (2000).
Transportation: Commute to work: 80.0% car, 0.0% public transportation, 5.6% walk, 14.4% work from home (2000); Travel time to work: 39.0% less than 15 minutes, 40.3% 15 to 30 minutes, 10.4% 30 to 45 minutes, 6.5% 45 to 60 minutes, 3.9% 60 minutes or more (2000)

STORDEN (city). Covers a land area of 0.214 square miles and a water area of 0 square miles. Located at 44.03° N. Lat.; 95.31° W. Long. Elevation is 1,405 feet.
Population: 274 (2000); Race: 94.7% White, 0.0% Black, 0.0% Asian, 0.0% American Indian and Alaska Native, 6.5% Hispanic of any race, 0.0% two or more races (2000); Density: 1,279.5 persons per square mile (2000); Age: 26.7% under 18, 18.0% over 64 (2000); Marriage status: 24.1% never married, 63.0% now married, 6.2% widowed, 6.6% divorced (2000); Foreign born: 1.9% (2000); Ancestry (includes multiple ancestries): 43.2% German, 42.5% Norwegian, 8.4% Irish, 7.8% Other groups, 5.3% Italian (2000).
Economy: Single-family building permits issued: 0 (2001) / 1 (2000); Multi-family building permits issued: 0 (2001) / 0 (2000); Employment by occupation: 11.5% management, 12.2% professional, 26.9% services, 17.3% sales, 0.0% farming, 8.3% construction, 23.7% production (2000).
Income: Per capita income: $15,134 (2000); Median household income: $30,694 (2000); Poverty rate: 14.7% (2000).
Taxes: Total city taxes per capita: $361 (2000); City property taxes per capita: $358 (2000).
Education: High school graduation rate: 76.7% (2000); College graduation rate: 12.6% (2000).
Housing: Homeownership rate: 88.3% (2000); Median home value: $24,600 (2000); Median rent: $192 per month (2000); Median age of housing: 60 years (2000).
Newspapers: Storden-Jeffers Times/Review (1 x week)
Transportation: Commute to work: 86.3% car, 0.0% public transportation, 0.0% walk, 9.2% work from home (2000); Travel time to work: 35.3% less than 15 minutes, 50.4% 15 to 30 minutes, 9.4% 30 to 45 minutes, 5.0% 45 to 60 minutes, 0.0% 60 minutes or more (2000)

STORDEN (township). Covers a land area of 35.733 square miles and a water area of 0.104 square miles. Located at 44.06° N. Lat.; 95.29° W. Long. Elevation is 1,405 feet.
Population: 198 (2000); Race: 100.0% White, 0.0% Black, 0.0% Asian, 0.0% American Indian and Alaska Native, 0.0% Hispanic of any race, 0.0% two or more races (2000); Density: 5.5 persons per square mile (2000); Age: 10.2% under 18, 23.7% over 64 (2000); Marriage status: 12.1% never married, 71.5% now married, 12.1% widowed, 4.2% divorced (2000); Foreign born: 0.0% (2000); Ancestry (includes multiple ancestries): 41.2% Norwegian, 40.7% German, 5.6% English, 2.3% United States or American, 2.3% Welsh (2000).
Economy: Grain, soybeans; livestock. Manufacturing of bins. Employment by occupation: 42.9% management, 4.4% professional, 13.2% services, 13.2% sales, 1.1% farming, 12.1% construction, 13.2% production (2000).
Income: Per capita income: $37,695 (2000); Median household income: $38,750 (2000); Poverty rate: 4.5% (2000).
Taxes: Total city taxes per capita: $119 (1997); City property taxes per capita: $119 (1997).
Education: High school graduation rate: 84.7% (2000); College graduation rate: 9.0% (2000).
Housing: Homeownership rate: 77.2% (2000); Median home value: $32,500 (2000); Median rent: $213 per month (2000); Median age of housing: 60+ years (2000).
Transportation: Commute to work: 76.9% car, 0.0% public transportation, 0.0% walk, 23.1% work from home (2000); Travel time to work: 60.0% less than 15 minutes, 25.7% 15 to 30 minutes, 5.7% 30 to 45 minutes, 5.7% 45 to 60 minutes, 2.9% 60 minutes or more (2000)

WESTBROOK (city). Covers a land area of 0.775 square miles and a water area of 0 square miles. Located at 44.04° N. Lat.; 95.43° W. Long. Elevation is 1,422 feet.
Population: 755 (2000); Race: 97.6% White, 0.4% Black, 0.7% Asian, 0.7% American Indian and Alaska Native, 1.2% Hispanic of any race, 0.0% two or more races (2000); Density: 974.7 persons per square mile (2000); Age: 21.4% under 18, 36.1% over 64 (2000); Marriage status: 15.8% never married, 57.0% now married, 18.8% widowed, 8.4% divorced (2000); Foreign born: 1.7% (2000); Ancestry (includes multiple ancestries): 46.2% German, 33.2% Norwegian, 6.3% Swedish, 6.2% Danish, 4.6% Irish (2000).
Economy: Single-family building permits issued: 0 (2001) / 0 (2000); Multi-family building permits issued: 0 (2001) / 0 (2000); Employment by occupation: 9.7% management, 18.3% professional, 18.6% services, 24.5% sales, 2.4% farming, 11.7% construction, 14.8% production (2000).
Income: Per capita income: $15,919 (2000); Median household income: $24,063 (2000); Poverty rate: 13.5% (2000).
Taxes: Total city taxes per capita: $84 (1997); City property taxes per capita: $77 (1997).
Education: High school graduation rate: 74.9% (2000); College graduation rate: 13.2% (2000).

School District(s)

Westbrook (PK-12)
2000 Enrollment: 251 507-274-5450

Housing: Homeownership rate: 82.5% (2000); Median home value: $29,600 (2000); Median rent: $231 per month (2000); Median age of housing: 53 years (2000).
Hospitals: Westbrook Health Center (13 beds)
Newspapers: Westbrook Sentinel & Tribune (1 x week)
Transportation: Commute to work: 82.1% car, 0.0% public transportation, 11.4% walk, 4.1% work from home (2000); Travel time to work: 61.2% less

than 15 minutes, 15.5% 15 to 30 minutes, 12.2% 30 to 45 minutes, 9.4% 45 to 60 minutes, 1.8% 60 minutes or more (2000)

WESTBROOK (township). Covers a land area of 34.723 square miles and a water area of 0.720 square miles. Located at 44.05° N. Lat.; 95.39° W. Long. Elevation is 1,422 feet.
Population: 302 (2000); Race: 100.0% White, 0.0% Black, 0.0% Asian, 0.0% American Indian and Alaska Native, 0.0% Hispanic of any race, 0.0% two or more races (2000); Density: 8.7 persons per square mile (2000); Age: 17.4% under 18, 31.4% over 64 (2000); Marriage status: 12.5% never married, 68.8% now married, 15.6% widowed, 3.1% divorced (2000); Foreign born: 0.0% (2000); Ancestry (includes multiple ancestries): 44.0% German, 39.2% Norwegian, 12.6% Danish, 5.5% Swedish, 5.5% Irish (2000).
Economy: Diversified-farming area: grain, soybeans, alfalfa; livestock. Employment by occupation: 16.2% management, 16.9% professional, 16.9% services, 19.6% sales, 2.7% farming, 10.1% construction, 17.6% production (2000).
Income: Per capita income: $19,905 (2000); Median household income: $40,000 (2000); Poverty rate: 3.2% (2000).
Taxes: Total city taxes per capita: $139 (1997); City property taxes per capita: $139 (1997).
Education: High school graduation rate: 71.0% (2000); College graduation rate: 12.5% (2000).
Housing: Homeownership rate: 93.0% (2000); Median home value: $72,000 (2000); Median rent: $175 per month (2000); Median age of housing: 60+ years (2000).
Transportation: Commute to work: 84.0% car, 0.0% public transportation, 2.1% walk, 13.9% work from home (2000); Travel time to work: 46.8% less than 15 minutes, 15.3% 15 to 30 minutes, 24.2% 30 to 45 minutes, 9.7% 45 to 60 minutes, 4.0% 60 minutes or more (2000)

WINDOM (city). Covers a land area of 3.553 square miles and a water area of 0.191 square miles. Located at 43.86° N. Lat.; 95.11° W. Long. Elevation is 1,364 feet.
History: Windom was named for William Windom (1829-1894), a statesman and member of the cabinets of Presidents Garfield and Harrison.
Population: 4,490 (2000); Race: 98.4% White, 0.2% Black, 0.3% Asian, 0.0% American Indian and Alaska Native, 1.3% Hispanic of any race, 0.8% two or more races (2000); Density: 1,263.6 persons per square mile (2000); Age: 22.9% under 18, 21.7% over 64 (2000); Marriage status: 22.7% never married, 59.0% now married, 10.3% widowed, 8.0% divorced (2000); Foreign born: 0.9% (2000); Ancestry (includes multiple ancestries): 49.1% German, 20.8% Norwegian, 7.1% Dutch, 6.7% Swedish, 5.0% English (2000).
Economy: Single-family building permits issued: 24 (2001) / 6 (2000); Multi-family building permits issued: 4 (2001) / 4 (2000); Employment by occupation: 10.6% management, 14.1% professional, 19.2% services, 26.2% sales, 0.5% farming, 7.5% construction, 21.9% production (2000).
Income: Per capita income: $17,155 (2000); Median household income: $30,744 (2000); Poverty rate: 9.6% (2000).
Taxes: Total city taxes per capita: $143 (1997); City property taxes per capita: $141 (1997).
Education: High school graduation rate: 81.5% (2000); College graduation rate: 15.2% (2000).

School District(s)

Windom (PK-12)
2000 Enrollment: 1,112 507-831-6901
Housing: Homeownership rate: 75.7% (2000); Median home value: $63,600 (2000); Median rent: $255 per month (2000); Median age of housing: 41 years (2000).
Hospitals: Windom Area Hospital (35 beds)
Safety: Violent crime rate: 2.2 per 10,000 population; Property crime rate: 271.0 per 10,000 population (2001).
Newspapers: Windom Shopper (1 x week); Southern Minnesota Peach (1 x week); Cottonwood County Citizen (1 x week)
Transportation: Commute to work: 88.4% car, 1.0% public transportation, 6.2% walk, 3.5% work from home (2000); Travel time to work: 80.1% less than 15 minutes, 11.0% 15 to 30 minutes, 5.5% 30 to 45 minutes, 1.3% 45 to 60 minutes, 2.1% 60 minutes or more (2000)
Additional Information Contacts
Windom Chamber of Commerce 507-831-2752

Crow Wing County

Located in central Minnesota; drained by the Mississippi River. Covers a land area of 996.60 square miles, a water area of 160.00 square miles, and is located in the Central Time Zone. The county government was organized in 1857. County seat is Brainerd.

Weather Station: Brainerd — Elevation: 1,177 feet

	Jan	Feb	Mar	Apr	May	Jun	Jul	Aug	Sep	Oct	Nov	Dec
High	19	27	37	54	68	76	81	78	68	55	37	23
Low	-7	-0	14	30	43	52	56	54	44	32	18	2
Precip	0.8	0.6	1.4	2.1	3.1	4.2	4.0	3.5	2.8	2.7	1.6	0.7
Snow	13.3	6.0	9.7	2.1	tr	0.0	0.0	0.0	0.0	0.5	7.1	8.1

High and Low temperatures in degrees Fahrenheit; Precipitation and Snow in inches

Weather Station: Pine River Dam — Elevation: 1,250 feet

	Jan	Feb	Mar	Apr	May	Jun	Jul	Aug	Sep	Oct	Nov	Dec
High	19	27	38	55	70	78	82	79	69	57	38	24
Low	-5	2	15	29	42	52	57	55	45	34	20	4
Precip	1.0	0.6	1.7	2.1	3.1	4.2	4.3	3.5	2.8	2.8	1.8	0.8
Snow	12.3	6.8	8.1	2.8	0.3	0.0	0.0	0.0	tr	0.5	na	7.6

High and Low temperatures in degrees Fahrenheit; Precipitation and Snow in inches

Population: 55,099 (2000); Race: 97.7% White, 0.1% Black, 0.4% Asian, 0.8% American Indian and Alaska Native, 0.7% Hispanic of any race, 0.8% two or more races (2000); Density: 55.3 persons per square mile (2000); Age: 24.8% under 18, 17.1% over 64 (2000).
Religion: Five largest groups: 29.7% Catholic Church, 20.3% Evangelical Lutheran Church in America, 4.8% Lutheran Church—Missouri Synod, 2.1% The United Methodist Church, 1.9% The Evangelical Free Church of America (2000).
Economy: Unemployment rate: 5.1% (11/2002); Total civilian labor force: 30,946 (11/2002); Leading industries: 20.3% retail trade; 16.9% health care and social assistance; 14.1% manufacturing (2000); Companies that employ more than 1,000 persons: 0 (2000); Companies that employ more than 100 persons: 31 (2000); Farms: 593 totaling 135,322 acres (1997); Minority business ownership rate: 3.7% (1997); Women business ownership rate: 20.7% (1997); Retail sales per capita: $13,861 (1997). Single-family building permits issued: 786 (2001) / 793 (2000); Multi-family building permits issued: 48 (2001) / 24 (2000).
Income: Per capita income: $19,174 (2000); Median household income: $37,589 (2000); Poverty rate: 9.8% (2000); Bankruptcy rate: 2.90% (2001).
Taxes: Total county taxes per capita: $284 (2000); County property taxes per capita: $273 (2000).
Education: High school graduation rate: 86.3% (2000); College graduation rate: 18.4% (2000).
Housing: Homeownership rate: 79.6% (2000); Median home value: $107,500 (2000); Median rent: $407 per month (2000); Median age of housing: 26 years (2000).
Health: Birth rate: 112.7 per 10,000 population (1998); Age adjusted death rate: 78.0 per 10,000 population (1999); Age adjusted cancer mortality rate: 183.5 deaths per 100,000 population (1999). Air Quality Index: 100% good, 0% moderate, 0% unhealthy (percent of days in 2000). Number of physicians: 18.9 per 10,000 population (1999); Number of hospital beds: 108.7 per 10,000 population (1999).
Elections: 2000 Presidential election results: 40.0% Gore, 53.5% Bush, 4.7% Nader, 1.4% Buchanan
National and State Parks: Birchdale State Wildlife Management Area; Cooks State Wildlife Management Area; Crow Wing State Forest; Duck Lake State Wildlife Management Area; Emily State Forest; Loerch State Wildlife Management Area; Upper Dean State Wildlife Management Area
Additional Information Contacts
Crow Wing County Government Offices. 218-824-1045
Brainerd Lakes Chamber of Commerce 218-829-2838
Crosslake Chamber of Commerce 218-692-4027
Greater Lakes Association of Realtors. 218-828-4567
Ironton Chamber of Commerce 218-546-8131
Nisswa Chamber of Commerce 218-963-2620
Pequot Lakes Chamber of Commerce 218-568-8911

Crow Wing County Communities

BAXTER (city). Covers a land area of 17.320 square miles and a water area of 2.351 square miles. Located at 46.34° N. Lat.; 94.26° W. Long. Elevation is 1,208 feet.
History: Incorporated 1939.

Population: 5,555 (2000); Race: 98.5% White, 0.0% Black, 0.9% Asian, 0.1% American Indian and Alaska Native, 1.2% Hispanic of any race, 0.0% two or more races (2000); Density: 320.7 persons per square mile (2000); Age: 31.3% under 18, 10.1% over 64 (2000); Marriage status: 18.7% never married, 70.7% now married, 4.4% widowed, 6.2% divorced (2000); Foreign born: 1.6% (2000); Ancestry (includes multiple ancestries): 42.0% German, 18.6% Norwegian, 14.6% Swedish, 9.6% Irish, 6.7% English (2000).
Economy: Cattle, poultry; dairying; oats, alfalfa. Manufacturing: concrete. Employment by occupation: 10.2% management, 25.3% professional, 18.0% services, 26.5% sales, 0.8% farming, 7.5% construction, 11.7% production (2000).
Income: Per capita income: $19,772 (2000); Median household income: $52,289 (2000); Poverty rate: 5.0% (2000).
Taxes: Total city taxes per capita: $256 (1997); City property taxes per capita: $232 (1997).
Education: High school graduation rate: 94.0% (2000); College graduation rate: 30.8% (2000).
Housing: Homeownership rate: 90.6% (2000); Median home value: $121,600 (2000); Median rent: $513 per month (2000); Median age of housing: 14 years (2000).
Safety: Violent crime rate: 16.0 per 10,000 population; Property crime rate: 648.3 per 10,000 population (2001).
Transportation: Commute to work: 96.1% car, 0.2% public transportation, 0.5% walk, 3.2% work from home (2000); Travel time to work: 58.8% less than 15 minutes, 28.2% 15 to 30 minutes, 4.3% 30 to 45 minutes, 3.7% 45 to 60 minutes, 4.9% 60 minutes or more (2000)

BAY LAKE (township). Covers a land area of 27.026 square miles and a water area of 9.239 square miles. Located at 46.37° N. Lat.; 93.87° W. Long. Elevation is 1,288 feet.
Population: 923 (2000); Race: 98.6% White, 0.0% Black, 0.4% Asian, 0.0% American Indian and Alaska Native, 0.0% Hispanic of any race, 1.0% two or more races (2000); Density: 34.2 persons per square mile (2000); Age: 18.7% under 18, 24.5% over 64 (2000); Marriage status: 11.9% never married, 73.3% now married, 6.6% widowed, 8.2% divorced (2000); Foreign born: 0.9% (2000); Ancestry (includes multiple ancestries): 39.9% German, 21.7% Norwegian, 12.7% Swedish, 10.6% Irish, 9.4% English (2000).
Economy: Employment by occupation: 11.2% management, 22.7% professional, 14.5% services, 27.6% sales, 0.0% farming, 10.2% construction, 13.8% production (2000).
Income: Per capita income: $26,194 (2000); Median household income: $42,596 (2000); Poverty rate: 7.9% (2000).
Taxes: Total city taxes per capita: $160 (2000); City property taxes per capita: $158 (2000).
Education: High school graduation rate: 87.0% (2000); College graduation rate: 24.3% (2000).
Housing: Homeownership rate: 94.6% (2000); Median home value: $146,400 (2000); Median rent: $625 per month (2000); Median age of housing: 27 years (2000).
Transportation: Commute to work: 93.3% car, 0.0% public transportation, 2.3% walk, 4.4% work from home (2000); Travel time to work: 18.9% less than 15 minutes, 51.8% 15 to 30 minutes, 21.8% 30 to 45 minutes, 1.6% 45 to 60 minutes, 5.9% 60 minutes or more (2000)

BRAINERD (city). Covers a land area of 7.973 square miles and a water area of 0.468 square miles. Located at 46.35° N. Lat.; 94.19° W. Long. Elevation is 1,210 feet.
History: Brainerd was established in 1870 when the Northern Pacific Railway reached the area. The town was named for Ann Eliza Brainerd Smith, the wife of the railroad president. First a lumber town, Brainerd later became a gateway to the lakes and resorts of Minnesota's north, calling itself the "Capital of the Paul Bunyan playground."
Population: 13,178 (2000); Race: 96.1% White, 0.1% Black, 0.6% Asian, 1.6% American Indian and Alaska Native, 0.8% Hispanic of any race, 1.3% two or more races (2000); Density: 1,652.8 persons per square mile (2000); Age: 25.1% under 18, 18.6% over 64 (2000); Marriage status: 28.5% never married, 46.1% now married, 11.9% widowed, 13.5% divorced (2000); Foreign born: 1.6% (2000); Ancestry (includes multiple ancestries): 33.3% German, 16.8% Norwegian, 10.6% Irish, 10.2% Swedish, 7.1% English (2000).
Vital Statistics: Birth rate: 156.3 per 10,000 population (1998)
Economy: Single-family building permits issued: 38 (2001) / 52 (2000); Multi-family building permits issued: 4 (2001) / 12 (2000); Employment by occupation: 8.1% management, 18.6% professional, 21.7% services, 25.7% sales, 0.0% farming, 7.9% construction, 17.9% production (2000).
Income: Per capita income: $15,744 (2000); Median household income: $26,901 (2000); Poverty rate: 17.6% (2000).
Taxes: Total city taxes per capita: $185 (2000); City property taxes per capita: $156 (2000).
Education: High school graduation rate: 83.7% (2000); College graduation rate: 14.1% (2000).

School District(s)

Brainerd (PK-12)
2000 Enrollment: 7,258 218-828-5300

Two-year College(s)

Central Lakes College-Brainerd (Public)
2001 Enrollment: 3,104 218-855-8000
2001 Tuition: In-state $2,345; Out-of-state $4,689

Housing: Homeownership rate: 53.8% (2000); Median home value: $70,800 (2000); Median rent: $400 per month (2000); Median age of housing: 42 years (2000).
Hospitals: Brainerd Regional Human Services Center (708 beds); Saint Joseph's Medical Center (162 beds)
Newspapers: Brainerd Daily Dispatch (6 x week)
Transportation: Commute to work: 90.2% car, 1.4% public transportation, 4.9% walk, 2.4% work from home (2000); Travel time to work: 63.1% less than 15 minutes, 20.9% 15 to 30 minutes, 9.9% 30 to 45 minutes, 3.3% 45 to 60 minutes, 2.8% 60 minutes or more (2000)
Airports: Brainerd Lakes Regional (primary service)
Additional Information Contacts
Brainerd Lakes Chamber of Commerce 218-829-2838
Greater Lakes Association of Realtors 218-828-4567

BREEZY POINT (city). Aka Pelican Lakes. Covers a land area of 13.110 square miles and a water area of 3.378 square miles. Located at 46.60° N. Lat.; 94.21° W. Long.
History: Formerly called Pelican Lakes.
Population: 979 (2000); Race: 98.2% White, 0.0% Black, 0.4% Asian, 0.2% American Indian and Alaska Native, 0.0% Hispanic of any race, 1.2% two or more races (2000); Density: 74.7 persons per square mile (2000); Age: 22.0% under 18, 19.6% over 64 (2000); Marriage status: 17.8% never married, 65.3% now married, 5.5% widowed, 11.4% divorced (2000); Foreign born: 1.1% (2000); Ancestry (includes multiple ancestries): 42.1% German, 20.2% Norwegian, 11.9% Swedish, 9.2% Irish, 7.5% Polish (2000).
Economy: Agriculture: dairying; poultry; oats, alfalfa. Single-family building permits issued: 70 (2001) / 70 (2000); Multi-family building permits issued: 0 (2001) / 0 (2000); Employment by occupation: 20.8% management, 15.3% professional, 9.5% services, 33.9% sales, 0.0% farming, 9.3% construction, 11.2% production (2000).
Income: Per capita income: $21,959 (2000); Median household income: $44,000 (2000); Poverty rate: 6.2% (2000).
Taxes: Total city taxes per capita: $1,176 (1997); City property taxes per capita: $1,115 (1997).
Education: High school graduation rate: 91.4% (2000); College graduation rate: 24.1% (2000).
Housing: Homeownership rate: 93.0% (2000); Median home value: $134,400 (2000); Median rent: $503 per month (2000); Median age of housing: 23 years (2000).
Transportation: Commute to work: 94.0% car, 0.0% public transportation, 0.6% walk, 4.3% work from home (2000); Travel time to work: 41.3% less than 15 minutes, 31.2% 15 to 30 minutes, 19.0% 30 to 45 minutes, 3.2% 45 to 60 minutes, 5.4% 60 minutes or more (2000)

CENTER (township). Covers a land area of 17.753 square miles and a water area of 3.956 square miles. Located at 46.51° N. Lat.; 94.11° W. Long.
Population: 808 (2000); Race: 97.8% White, 0.0% Black, 0.0% Asian, 0.6% American Indian and Alaska Native, 0.6% Hispanic of any race, 1.6% two or more races (2000); Density: 45.5 persons per square mile (2000); Age: 22.8% under 18, 15.2% over 64 (2000); Marriage status: 21.2% never married, 65.9% now married, 4.9% widowed, 8.1% divorced (2000); Foreign born: 0.0% (2000); Ancestry (includes multiple ancestries): 37.2% German, 16.5% Norwegian, 11.1% Swedish, 9.2% English, 8.9% Irish (2000).
Economy: Employment by occupation: 12.9% management, 17.0% professional, 12.2% services, 27.0% sales, 0.7% farming, 11.2% construction, 19.0% production (2000).
Income: Per capita income: $19,940 (2000); Median household income: $40,000 (2000); Poverty rate: 5.3% (2000).
Taxes: Total city taxes per capita: $59 (1997); City property taxes per capita: $59 (1997).
Education: High school graduation rate: 85.4% (2000); College graduation rate: 12.6% (2000).

Housing: Homeownership rate: 91.9% (2000); Median home value: $132,300 (2000); Median rent: $483 per month (2000); Median age of housing: 26 years (2000).
Transportation: Commute to work: 89.2% car, 0.0% public transportation, 0.0% walk, 9.1% work from home (2000); Travel time to work: 14.6% less than 15 minutes, 59.3% 15 to 30 minutes, 16.4% 30 to 45 minutes, 3.5% 45 to 60 minutes, 6.2% 60 minutes or more (2000)

CROSBY (city). Covers a land area of 3.045 square miles and a water area of 0.616 square miles. Located at 46.48° N. Lat.; 93.95° W. Long. Elevation is 1,261 feet.
History: Crosby developed at the eastern end of the Cuyuna Iron Range, where the first iron ore was shipped in 1911.
Population: 2,299 (2000); Race: 96.9% White, 0.0% Black, 0.0% Asian, 2.0% American Indian and Alaska Native, 1.6% Hispanic of any race, 0.5% two or more races (2000); Density: 755.0 persons per square mile (2000); Age: 24.4% under 18, 24.9% over 64 (2000); Marriage status: 21.8% never married, 53.8% now married, 12.5% widowed, 11.9% divorced (2000); Foreign born: 0.9% (2000); Ancestry (includes multiple ancestries): 28.2% German, 13.9% Norwegian, 12.7% Swedish, 10.0% Irish, 9.5% English (2000).
Economy: Single-family building permits issued: 4 (2001) / 6 (2000); Multi-family building permits issued: 0 (2001) / 0 (2000); Employment by occupation: 6.6% management, 12.1% professional, 27.2% services, 25.4% sales, 0.0% farming, 11.1% construction, 17.6% production (2000).
Income: Per capita income: $15,465 (2000); Median household income: $24,053 (2000); Poverty rate: 16.9% (2000).
Taxes: Total city taxes per capita: $236 (1997); City property taxes per capita: $229 (1997).
Education: High school graduation rate: 77.7% (2000); College graduation rate: 9.1% (2000).

School District(s)

Crosby-Ironton (PK-12)
2000 Enrollment: 1,515 218-546-5165

Housing: Homeownership rate: 71.1% (2000); Median home value: $57,000 (2000); Median rent: $337 per month (2000); Median age of housing: 47 years (2000).
Hospitals: Cuyuna Regional Medical Center (42 beds)
Safety: Violent crime rate: 12.9 per 10,000 population; Property crime rate: 671.3 per 10,000 population (2001).
Newspapers: Crosby-Ironton Courier (1 x week)
Transportation: Commute to work: 85.7% car, 0.0% public transportation, 10.2% walk, 4.0% work from home (2000); Travel time to work: 56.8% less than 15 minutes, 24.3% 15 to 30 minutes, 12.0% 30 to 45 minutes, 4.1% 45 to 60 minutes, 2.9% 60 minutes or more (2000)

CROSSLAKE (city). Covers a land area of 25.640 square miles and a water area of 11.285 square miles. Located at 46.67° N. Lat.; 94.10° W. Long.
Population: 1,893 (2000); Race: 99.9% White, 0.0% Black, 0.0% Asian, 0.1% American Indian and Alaska Native, 0.3% Hispanic of any race, 0.0% two or more races (2000); Density: 73.8 persons per square mile (2000); Age: 12.9% under 18, 32.6% over 64 (2000); Marriage status: 13.1% never married, 70.7% now married, 7.6% widowed, 8.7% divorced (2000); Foreign born: 0.6% (2000); Ancestry (includes multiple ancestries): 35.9% German, 23.1% Norwegian, 18.6% Swedish, 10.3% Irish, 9.6% English (2000).
Economy: Single-family building permits issued: 49 (2001) / 67 (2000); Multi-family building permits issued: 8 (2001) / 0 (2000); Employment by occupation: 13.6% management, 18.3% professional, 12.3% services, 33.5% sales, 0.3% farming, 11.3% construction, 10.8% production (2000).
Income: Per capita income: $27,227 (2000); Median household income: $41,125 (2000); Poverty rate: 4.5% (2000).
Taxes: Total city taxes per capita: $623 (1997); City property taxes per capita: $588 (1997).
Education: High school graduation rate: 90.7% (2000); College graduation rate: 24.7% (2000).

School District(s)

Crosslake Community Charter School (KG-06)
2000 Enrollment: 40 218-692-3156

Housing: Homeownership rate: 92.2% (2000); Median home value: $199,500 (2000); Median rent: $397 per month (2000); Median age of housing: 16 years (2000).
Transportation: Commute to work: 90.6% car, 0.0% public transportation, 1.7% walk, 7.1% work from home (2000); Travel time to work: 38.4% less than 15 minutes, 29.0% 15 to 30 minutes, 24.2% 30 to 45 minutes, 1.8% 45 to 60 minutes, 6.7% 60 minutes or more (2000)

Additional Information Contacts
Crosslake Chamber of Commerce 218-692-4027

CROW WING (township). Covers a land area of 30.504 square miles and a water area of 0.320 square miles. Located at 46.29° N. Lat.; 94.25° W. Long. Elevation is 1,194 feet.
Population: 1,212 (2000); Race: 97.0% White, 0.7% Black, 0.2% Asian, 1.6% American Indian and Alaska Native, 0.4% Hispanic of any race, 0.5% two or more races (2000); Density: 39.7 persons per square mile (2000); Age: 32.6% under 18, 6.2% over 64 (2000); Marriage status: 27.5% never married, 57.1% now married, 3.7% widowed, 11.7% divorced (2000); Foreign born: 1.2% (2000); Ancestry (includes multiple ancestries): 43.3% German, 12.4% Norwegian, 11.7% Irish, 8.0% Swedish, 7.7% French (except Basque) (2000).
Economy: Employment by occupation: 6.9% management, 11.0% professional, 19.0% services, 25.4% sales, 0.0% farming, 13.0% construction, 24.6% production (2000).
Income: Per capita income: $16,139 (2000); Median household income: $39,417 (2000); Poverty rate: 9.3% (2000).
Taxes: Total city taxes per capita: $69 (1997); City property taxes per capita: $69 (1997).
Education: High school graduation rate: 83.0% (2000); College graduation rate: 12.3% (2000).
Housing: Homeownership rate: 93.0% (2000); Median home value: $97,000 (2000); Median rent: $444 per month (2000); Median age of housing: 17 years (2000).
Transportation: Commute to work: 95.0% car, 1.1% public transportation, 1.3% walk, 1.6% work from home (2000); Travel time to work: 31.3% less than 15 minutes, 46.9% 15 to 30 minutes, 14.1% 30 to 45 minutes, 2.5% 45 to 60 minutes, 5.3% 60 minutes or more (2000)

CUYUNA (city). Covers a land area of 3.273 square miles and a water area of 0.232 square miles. Located at 46.51° N. Lat.; 93.92° W. Long.
Population: 231 (2000); Race: 100.0% White, 0.0% Black, 0.0% Asian, 0.0% American Indian and Alaska Native, 0.0% Hispanic of any race, 0.0% two or more races (2000); Density: 70.6 persons per square mile (2000); Age: 27.3% under 18, 16.5% over 64 (2000); Marriage status: 25.0% never married, 53.8% now married, 4.3% widowed, 16.8% divorced (2000); Foreign born: 0.0% (2000); Ancestry (includes multiple ancestries): 38.1% German, 12.1% Swedish, 11.3% French (except Basque), 10.0% United States or American, 9.5% Norwegian (2000).
Economy: Located at center of Cuyuna Iron Range, iron mining district. Single-family building permits issued: 5 (2001) / 5 (2000); Multi-family building permits issued: 0 (2001) / 0 (2000); Employment by occupation: 2.5% management, 17.5% professional, 24.2% services, 27.5% sales, 0.0% farming, 18.3% construction, 10.0% production (2000).
Income: Per capita income: $17,838 (2000); Median household income: $44,107 (2000); Poverty rate: 10.0% (2000).
Taxes: Total city taxes per capita: $100 (1997); City property taxes per capita: $81 (1997).
Education: High school graduation rate: 89.2% (2000); College graduation rate: 8.9% (2000).
Housing: Homeownership rate: 95.4% (2000); Median home value: $117,200 (2000); Median rent: $325 per month (2000); Median age of housing: 22 years (2000).
Transportation: Commute to work: 95.8% car, 0.0% public transportation, 0.0% walk, 0.0% work from home (2000); Travel time to work: 40.8% less than 15 minutes, 25.0% 15 to 30 minutes, 30.0% 30 to 45 minutes, 1.7% 45 to 60 minutes, 2.5% 60 minutes or more (2000)

DAGGETT BROOK (township). Covers a land area of 36.318 square miles and a water area of 0.076 square miles. Located at 46.20° N. Lat.; 94.11° W. Long.
Population: 448 (2000); Race: 98.1% White, 0.7% Black, 0.0% Asian, 0.0% American Indian and Alaska Native, 1.2% Hispanic of any race, 0.5% two or more races (2000); Density: 12.3 persons per square mile (2000); Age: 30.3% under 18, 10.6% over 64 (2000); Marriage status: 21.7% never married, 66.9% now married, 4.8% widowed, 6.7% divorced (2000); Foreign born: 1.7% (2000); Ancestry (includes multiple ancestries): 32.5% German, 17.5% Swedish, 16.1% Norwegian, 11.8% Polish, 4.8% Irish (2000).
Economy: Employment by occupation: 10.2% management, 9.3% professional, 19.4% services, 25.9% sales, 0.9% farming, 19.0% construction, 15.3% production (2000).
Income: Per capita income: $17,820 (2000); Median household income: $46,250 (2000); Poverty rate: 12.3% (2000).

Taxes: Total city taxes per capita: $43 (1997); City property taxes per capita: $43 (1997).
Education: High school graduation rate: 80.1% (2000); College graduation rate: 7.0% (2000).
Housing: Homeownership rate: 89.9% (2000); Median home value: $62,500 (2000); Median rent: $475 per month (2000); Median age of housing: 28 years (2000).
Transportation: Commute to work: 90.6% car, 0.0% public transportation, 0.0% walk, 8.5% work from home (2000); Travel time to work: 11.3% less than 15 minutes, 57.9% 15 to 30 minutes, 20.5% 30 to 45 minutes, 2.6% 45 to 60 minutes, 7.7% 60 minutes or more (2000)

DEERWOOD (city). Covers a land area of 1.368 square miles and a water area of 0.670 square miles. Located at 46.47° N. Lat.; 93.90° W. Long. Elevation is 1,277 feet.
Population: 590 (2000); Race: 98.2% White, 0.0% Black, 0.0% Asian, 1.8% American Indian and Alaska Native, 0.0% Hispanic of any race, 0.0% two or more races (2000); Density: 431.1 persons per square mile (2000); Age: 28.6% under 18, 20.9% over 64 (2000); Marriage status: 20.4% never married, 53.8% now married, 15.8% widowed, 10.0% divorced (2000); Foreign born: 0.7% (2000); Ancestry (includes multiple ancestries): 34.1% German, 16.4% Norwegian, 10.4% Irish, 8.7% Swedish, 8.4% English (2000).
Economy: Single-family building permits issued: 1 (2001) / 2 (2000); Multi-family building permits issued: 0 (2001) / 0 (2000); Employment by occupation: 9.5% management, 14.9% professional, 20.4% services, 24.9% sales, 0.0% farming, 5.0% construction, 25.3% production (2000).
Income: Per capita income: $15,697 (2000); Median household income: $30,069 (2000); Poverty rate: 13.7% (2000).
Taxes: Total city taxes per capita: $398 (1997); City property taxes per capita: $386 (1997).
Education: High school graduation rate: 81.5% (2000); College graduation rate: 12.4% (2000).
Housing: Homeownership rate: 61.4% (2000); Median home value: $98,500 (2000); Median rent: $278 per month (2000); Median age of housing: 30 years (2000).
Transportation: Commute to work: 93.2% car, 0.0% public transportation, 1.8% walk, 4.1% work from home (2000); Travel time to work: 43.8% less than 15 minutes, 27.6% 15 to 30 minutes, 22.4% 30 to 45 minutes, 1.9% 45 to 60 minutes, 4.3% 60 minutes or more (2000)

DEERWOOD (township). Covers a land area of 28.397 square miles and a water area of 5.105 square miles. Located at 46.46° N. Lat.; 93.86° W. Long. Elevation is 1,277 feet.
Population: 1,244 (2000); Race: 98.5% White, 0.0% Black, 0.0% Asian, 0.8% American Indian and Alaska Native, 0.0% Hispanic of any race, 0.7% two or more races (2000); Density: 43.8 persons per square mile (2000); Age: 20.7% under 18, 20.9% over 64 (2000); Marriage status: 13.8% never married, 71.8% now married, 7.3% widowed, 7.1% divorced (2000); Foreign born: 0.6% (2000); Ancestry (includes multiple ancestries): 32.9% German, 20.6% Norwegian, 14.8% Swedish, 10.3% Irish, 8.1% English (2000).
Economy: In Cuyuna Iron Range mining district. Manufacturing: machinery, lumber, food. Employment by occupation: 10.9% management, 24.7% professional, 14.4% services, 24.9% sales, 0.7% farming, 11.7% construction, 12.8% production (2000).
Income: Per capita income: $21,403 (2000); Median household income: $46,429 (2000); Poverty rate: 7.3% (2000).
Taxes: Total city taxes per capita: $74 (1997); City property taxes per capita: $74 (1997).
Education: High school graduation rate: 89.4% (2000); College graduation rate: 18.8% (2000).
Housing: Homeownership rate: 94.8% (2000); Median home value: $150,000 (2000); Median rent: $525 per month (2000); Median age of housing: 28 years (2000).
Transportation: Commute to work: 93.6% car, 0.4% public transportation, 0.5% walk, 5.5% work from home (2000); Travel time to work: 42.8% less than 15 minutes, 35.1% 15 to 30 minutes, 16.1% 30 to 45 minutes, 3.0% 45 to 60 minutes, 3.0% 60 minutes or more (2000)

EMILY (city). Covers a land area of 29.997 square miles and a water area of 6.102 square miles. Located at 46.77° N. Lat.; 93.97° W. Long. Elevation is 1,290 feet.
Population: 847 (2000); Race: 97.1% White, 0.5% Black, 0.0% Asian, 0.0% American Indian and Alaska Native, 2.5% Hispanic of any race, 1.0% two or more races (2000); Density: 28.2 persons per square mile (2000); Age: 20.7% under 18, 24.2% over 64 (2000); Marriage status: 14.8% never married, 65.0% now married, 9.9% widowed, 10.2% divorced (2000); Foreign born: 2.7% (2000); Ancestry (includes multiple ancestries): 29.8% German, 11.0% Norwegian, 10.3% Irish, 9.9% Swedish, 9.4% English (2000).
Economy: Light manufacturing; agriculture: dairying; poultry; oats, alfalfa. Single-family building permits issued: 24 (2001) / 24 (2000); Multi-family building permits issued: 0 (2001) / 0 (2000); Employment by occupation: 10.0% management, 15.2% professional, 19.7% services, 22.1% sales, 2.1% farming, 16.7% construction, 14.2% production (2000).
Income: Per capita income: $17,854 (2000); Median household income: $34,276 (2000); Poverty rate: 7.7% (2000).
Taxes: Total city taxes per capita: $341 (1997); City property taxes per capita: $321 (1997).
Education: High school graduation rate: 84.8% (2000); College graduation rate: 12.9% (2000).

School District(s)

Emily Charter School (PK-06)
2000 Enrollment: 85 218-763-3401

Housing: Homeownership rate: 89.2% (2000); Median home value: $118,500 (2000); Median rent: $338 per month (2000); Median age of housing: 16 years (2000).
Transportation: Commute to work: 86.7% car, 0.9% public transportation, 5.6% walk, 6.8% work from home (2000); Travel time to work: 35.1% less than 15 minutes, 19.9% 15 to 30 minutes, 22.8% 30 to 45 minutes, 18.2% 45 to 60 minutes, 4.0% 60 minutes or more (2000)

FAIRFIELD (township). Covers a land area of 33.548 square miles and a water area of 2.362 square miles. Located at 46.67° N. Lat.; 93.96° W. Long.
Population: 275 (2000); Race: 97.3% White, 0.0% Black, 2.7% Asian, 0.0% American Indian and Alaska Native, 0.0% Hispanic of any race, 0.0% two or more races (2000); Density: 8.2 persons per square mile (2000); Age: 20.5% under 18, 25.4% over 64 (2000); Marriage status: 17.4% never married, 67.0% now married, 7.6% widowed, 8.0% divorced (2000); Foreign born: 2.7% (2000); Ancestry (includes multiple ancestries): 43.9% German, 17.4% Swedish, 10.6% English, 9.8% Norwegian, 6.4% Irish (2000).
Economy: Employment by occupation: 2.6% management, 14.1% professional, 26.9% services, 19.2% sales, 0.0% farming, 23.1% construction, 14.1% production (2000).
Income: Per capita income: $16,670 (2000); Median household income: $29,375 (2000); Poverty rate: 14.6% (2000).
Taxes: Total city taxes per capita: $84 (1997); City property taxes per capita: $84 (1997).
Education: High school graduation rate: 74.2% (2000); College graduation rate: 8.8% (2000).
Housing: Homeownership rate: 94.0% (2000); Median home value: $143,100 (2000); Median age of housing: 18 years (2000).
Transportation: Commute to work: 91.7% car, 0.0% public transportation, 5.6% walk, 2.8% work from home (2000); Travel time to work: 44.3% less than 15 minutes, 12.9% 15 to 30 minutes, 18.6% 30 to 45 minutes, 17.1% 45 to 60 minutes, 7.1% 60 minutes or more (2000)

FIFTY LAKES (city). Covers a land area of 29.029 square miles and a water area of 4.149 square miles. Located at 46.74° N. Lat.; 94.07° W. Long.
Population: 392 (2000); Race: 98.9% White, 0.0% Black, 0.0% Asian, 0.0% American Indian and Alaska Native, 1.1% Hispanic of any race, 0.0% two or more races (2000); Density: 13.5 persons per square mile (2000); Age: 9.7% under 18, 31.9% over 64 (2000); Marriage status: 8.9% never married, 77.4% now married, 7.1% widowed, 6.5% divorced (2000); Foreign born: 1.7% (2000); Ancestry (includes multiple ancestries): 34.4% German, 26.9% Norwegian, 16.4% Swedish, 11.9% Irish, 11.1% English (2000).
Economy: Resort area; dairying; cattle, poultry; alfalfa. Single-family building permits issued: 12 (2001) / 5 (2000); Multi-family building permits issued: 0 (2001) / 0 (2000); Employment by occupation: 12.1% management, 17.2% professional, 16.4% services, 24.1% sales, 0.0% farming, 19.0% construction, 11.2% production (2000).
Income: Per capita income: $23,575 (2000); Median household income: $34,773 (2000); Poverty rate: 3.9% (2000).
Taxes: Total city taxes per capita: $427 (1997); City property taxes per capita: $402 (1997).
Education: High school graduation rate: 83.5% (2000); College graduation rate: 14.6% (2000).
Housing: Homeownership rate: 92.2% (2000); Median home value: $140,800 (2000); Median rent: $335 per month (2000); Median age of housing: 21 years (2000).
Transportation: Commute to work: 86.5% car, 0.0% public transportation, 0.0% walk, 13.5% work from home (2000); Travel time to work: 40.6% less

than 15 minutes, 24.0% 15 to 30 minutes, 20.8% 30 to 45 minutes, 12.5% 45 to 60 minutes, 2.1% 60 minutes or more (2000)

FORT RIPLEY (city). Covers a land area of 1.331 square miles and a water area of 0.112 square miles. Located at 46.17° N. Lat.; 94.36° W. Long. Elevation is 1,170 feet.
Population: 74 (2000); Race: 97.3% White, 0.0% Black, 0.0% Asian, 2.7% American Indian and Alaska Native, 0.0% Hispanic of any race, 0.0% two or more races (2000); Density: 55.6 persons per square mile (2000); Age: 12.3% under 18, 12.3% over 64 (2000); Marriage status: 22.4% never married, 68.7% now married, 9.0% widowed, 0.0% divorced (2000); Foreign born: 0.0% (2000); Ancestry (includes multiple ancestries): 38.4% German, 15.1% Irish, 13.7% French (except Basque), 11.0% Norwegian, 9.6% Other groups (2000).
Economy: Single-family building permits issued: 0 (2001) / 0 (2000); Multi-family building permits issued: 0 (2001) / 0 (2000); Employment by occupation: 7.7% management, 9.6% professional, 28.8% services, 23.1% sales, 0.0% farming, 9.6% construction, 21.2% production (2000).
Income: Per capita income: $18,559 (2000); Median household income: $37,250 (2000); Poverty rate: 6.8% (2000).
Taxes: Total city taxes per capita: $73 (1997); City property taxes per capita: $42 (1997).
Education: High school graduation rate: 81.7% (2000); College graduation rate: 8.3% (2000).
Housing: Homeownership rate: 93.9% (2000); Median home value: $91,000 (2000); Median rent: $325 per month (2000); Median age of housing: 29 years (2000).
Transportation: Commute to work: 94.2% car, 0.0% public transportation, 5.8% walk, 0.0% work from home (2000); Travel time to work: 5.8% less than 15 minutes, 51.9% 15 to 30 minutes, 23.1% 30 to 45 minutes, 15.4% 45 to 60 minutes, 3.8% 60 minutes or more (2000)

FORT RIPLEY (township). Covers a land area of 22.162 square miles and a water area of 1.716 square miles. Located at 46.20° N. Lat.; 94.35° W. Long. Elevation is 1,170 feet.
History: Ruins of Old Fort Ripley (1850-1878) here.
Population: 600 (2000); Race: 98.3% White, 0.0% Black, 0.3% Asian, 1.4% American Indian and Alaska Native, 0.0% Hispanic of any race, 0.0% two or more races (2000); Density: 27.1 persons per square mile (2000); Age: 20.6% under 18, 18.4% over 64 (2000); Marriage status: 20.1% never married, 67.3% now married, 6.7% widowed, 5.9% divorced (2000); Foreign born: 0.0% (2000); Ancestry (includes multiple ancestries): 39.1% German, 16.2% Norwegian, 9.1% Irish, 9.1% French (except Basque), 8.6% Swedish (2000).
Economy: Grain, potatoes; manufacturing: exercise equipment. Camp Ripley Military Reservation, used by Minnesota National Guard, to West. Employment by occupation: 6.8% management, 11.0% professional, 20.2% services, 27.1% sales, 1.7% farming, 14.7% construction, 18.5% production (2000).
Income: Per capita income: $16,076 (2000); Median household income: $35,500 (2000); Poverty rate: 6.1% (2000).
Taxes: Total city taxes per capita: $80 (2000); City property taxes per capita: $80 (2000).
Education: High school graduation rate: 80.2% (2000); College graduation rate: 9.2% (2000).
Housing: Homeownership rate: 94.2% (2000); Median home value: $108,300 (2000); Median rent: $225 per month (2000); Median age of housing: 21 years (2000).
Transportation: Commute to work: 96.2% car, 0.3% public transportation, 0.7% walk, 1.4% work from home (2000); Travel time to work: 7.4% less than 15 minutes, 59.2% 15 to 30 minutes, 27.1% 30 to 45 minutes, 2.1% 45 to 60 minutes, 4.2% 60 minutes or more (2000)

GAIL LAKE (township). Covers a land area of 16.687 square miles and a water area of 1.397 square miles. Located at 46.77° N. Lat.; 94.31° W. Long.
Population: 92 (2000); Race: 91.3% White, 0.0% Black, 0.0% Asian, 3.3% American Indian and Alaska Native, 0.0% Hispanic of any race, 5.4% two or more races (2000); Density: 5.5 persons per square mile (2000); Age: 22.8% under 18, 14.1% over 64 (2000); Marriage status: 20.0% never married, 72.0% now married, 4.0% widowed, 4.0% divorced (2000); Foreign born: 0.0% (2000); Ancestry (includes multiple ancestries): 39.1% German, 15.2% Norwegian, 15.2% Swedish, 14.1% Irish, 10.9% English (2000).
Economy: Employment by occupation: 0.0% management, 0.0% professional, 15.9% services, 52.3% sales, 4.5% farming, 15.9% construction, 11.4% production (2000).
Income: Per capita income: $15,721 (2000); Median household income: $30,625 (2000); Poverty rate: 7.6% (2000).
Taxes: Total city taxes per capita: $69 (1997); City property taxes per capita: $69 (1997).
Education: High school graduation rate: 80.6% (2000); College graduation rate: 8.1% (2000).
Housing: Homeownership rate: 83.3% (2000); Median home value: $90,000 (2000); Median age of housing: 30 years (2000).
Transportation: Commute to work: 90.9% car, 0.0% public transportation, 4.5% walk, 4.5% work from home (2000); Travel time to work: 26.2% less than 15 minutes, 35.7% 15 to 30 minutes, 28.6% 30 to 45 minutes, 4.8% 45 to 60 minutes, 4.8% 60 minutes or more (2000)

GARRISON (city). Covers a land area of 1.071 square miles and a water area of 0.014 square miles. Located at 46.29° N. Lat.; 93.82° W. Long. Elevation is 1,259 feet.
Population: 213 (2000); Race: 96.9% White, 0.0% Black, 0.0% Asian, 0.0% American Indian and Alaska Native, 0.0% Hispanic of any race, 3.1% two or more races (2000); Density: 198.9 persons per square mile (2000); Age: 10.4% under 18, 28.8% over 64 (2000); Marriage status: 21.6% never married, 47.3% now married, 10.8% widowed, 20.3% divorced (2000); Foreign born: 1.8% (2000); Ancestry (includes multiple ancestries): 37.4% German, 12.3% Swedish, 10.4% Norwegian, 7.4% English, 6.1% Scottish (2000).
Economy: Single-family building permits issued: 0 (2001) / 0 (2000); Multi-family building permits issued: 0 (2001) / 0 (2000); Employment by occupation: 13.9% management, 13.9% professional, 20.8% services, 23.6% sales, 0.0% farming, 19.4% construction, 8.3% production (2000).
Income: Per capita income: $19,447 (2000); Median household income: $23,750 (2000); Poverty rate: 14.7% (2000).
Taxes: Total city taxes per capita: $305 (1997); City property taxes per capita: $225 (1997).
Education: High school graduation rate: 72.9% (2000); College graduation rate: 10.9% (2000).
Housing: Homeownership rate: 77.2% (2000); Median home value: $101,300 (2000); Median rent: $419 per month (2000); Median age of housing: 16 years (2000).
Transportation: Commute to work: 88.6% car, 0.0% public transportation, 8.6% walk, 2.9% work from home (2000); Travel time to work: 48.5% less than 15 minutes, 29.4% 15 to 30 minutes, 13.2% 30 to 45 minutes, 2.9% 45 to 60 minutes, 5.9% 60 minutes or more (2000)

GARRISON (township). Covers a land area of 29.307 square miles and a water area of 6.128 square miles. Located at 46.28° N. Lat.; 93.85° W. Long. Elevation is 1,259 feet.
History: Mille Lacs Indian Museum.
Population: 796 (2000); Race: 93.7% White, 0.3% Black, 0.8% Asian, 2.6% American Indian and Alaska Native, 0.0% Hispanic of any race, 1.3% two or more races (2000); Density: 27.2 persons per square mile (2000); Age: 17.8% under 18, 22.1% over 64 (2000); Marriage status: 15.7% never married, 67.3% now married, 5.0% widowed, 12.0% divorced (2000); Foreign born: 1.4% (2000); Ancestry (includes multiple ancestries): 40.5% German, 17.1% Irish, 16.1% Norwegian, 12.7% Swedish, 7.1% French (except Basque) (2000).
Economy: Resort area; light manufacturing. Employment by occupation: 10.6% management, 13.2% professional, 17.2% services, 27.2% sales, 0.6% farming, 16.0% construction, 15.2% production (2000).
Income: Per capita income: $19,004 (2000); Median household income: $33,421 (2000); Poverty rate: 7.8% (2000).
Taxes: Total city taxes per capita: $113 (1997); City property taxes per capita: $113 (1997).
Education: High school graduation rate: 77.4% (2000); College graduation rate: 11.5% (2000).
Housing: Homeownership rate: 92.0% (2000); Median home value: $109,400 (2000); Median rent: $417 per month (2000); Median age of housing: 23 years (2000).
Transportation: Commute to work: 89.5% car, 0.0% public transportation, 2.9% walk, 6.7% work from home (2000); Travel time to work: 22.1% less than 15 minutes, 39.3% 15 to 30 minutes, 23.4% 30 to 45 minutes, 4.0% 45 to 60 minutes, 11.2% 60 minutes or more (2000)

IDEAL (township). Covers a land area of 19.616 square miles and a water area of 15.428 square miles. Located at 46.67° N. Lat.; 94.22° W. Long.
Population: 950 (2000); Race: 99.2% White, 0.0% Black, 0.0% Asian, 0.0% American Indian and Alaska Native, 0.0% Hispanic of any race, 0.8% two or more races (2000); Density: 48.4 persons per square mile (2000); Age: 19.3%

under 18, 28.5% over 64 (2000); Marriage status: 11.3% never married, 74.2% now married, 5.7% widowed, 8.8% divorced (2000); Foreign born: 0.5% (2000); Ancestry (includes multiple ancestries): 43.3% German, 19.3% Norwegian, 14.5% Irish, 13.0% English, 11.4% Swedish (2000).
Economy: Employment by occupation: 22.9% management, 16.9% professional, 13.0% services, 27.3% sales, 0.5% farming, 10.1% construction, 9.4% production (2000).
Income: Per capita income: $29,697 (2000); Median household income: $46,607 (2000); Poverty rate: 5.0% (2000).
Taxes: Total city taxes per capita: $362 (2000); City property taxes per capita: $362 (2000).
Education: High school graduation rate: 91.0% (2000); College graduation rate: 31.7% (2000).
Housing: Homeownership rate: 95.8% (2000); Median home value: $220,600 (2000); Median rent: $330 per month (2000); Median age of housing: 21 years (2000).
Transportation: Commute to work: 83.3% car, 0.5% public transportation, 5.8% walk, 9.5% work from home (2000); Travel time to work: 38.0% less than 15 minutes, 33.3% 15 to 30 minutes, 17.8% 30 to 45 minutes, 2.3% 45 to 60 minutes, 8.5% 60 minutes or more (2000)

IRONDALE (township). Covers a land area of 27.838 square miles and a water area of 3.247 square miles. Located at 46.47° N. Lat.; 94.00° W. Long.
Population: 1,113 (2000); Race: 97.0% White, 1.2% Black, 0.0% Asian, 0.1% American Indian and Alaska Native, 0.0% Hispanic of any race, 1.5% two or more races (2000); Density: 40.0 persons per square mile (2000); Age: 25.3% under 18, 16.3% over 64 (2000); Marriage status: 20.8% never married, 65.0% now married, 6.5% widowed, 7.6% divorced (2000); Foreign born: 0.2% (2000); Ancestry (includes multiple ancestries): 33.2% German, 14.7% Swedish, 14.5% Norwegian, 9.7% Irish, 6.4% English (2000).
Economy: Employment by occupation: 6.7% management, 12.4% professional, 21.6% services, 21.6% sales, 1.0% farming, 16.7% construction, 20.0% production (2000).
Income: Per capita income: $17,968 (2000); Median household income: $40,625 (2000); Poverty rate: 4.0% (2000).
Taxes: Total city taxes per capita: $55 (1997); City property taxes per capita: $51 (1997).
Education: High school graduation rate: 81.2% (2000); College graduation rate: 14.5% (2000).
Housing: Homeownership rate: 91.6% (2000); Median home value: $100,300 (2000); Median rent: $434 per month (2000); Median age of housing: 30 years (2000).
Transportation: Commute to work: 91.5% car, 0.0% public transportation, 1.0% walk, 6.1% work from home (2000); Travel time to work: 42.2% less than 15 minutes, 31.0% 15 to 30 minutes, 14.7% 30 to 45 minutes, 5.0% 45 to 60 minutes, 7.1% 60 minutes or more (2000)

IRONTON (city). Covers a land area of 1.495 square miles and a water area of 0.479 square miles. Located at 46.47° N. Lat.; 93.98° W. Long. Elevation is 1,245 feet.
Population: 498 (2000); Race: 98.9% White, 0.0% Black, 1.1% Asian, 0.0% American Indian and Alaska Native, 0.0% Hispanic of any race, 0.0% two or more races (2000); Density: 333.2 persons per square mile (2000); Age: 24.8% under 18, 26.2% over 64 (2000); Marriage status: 14.6% never married, 64.3% now married, 14.3% widowed, 6.9% divorced (2000); Foreign born: 1.6% (2000); Ancestry (includes multiple ancestries): 44.9% United States or American, 16.6% German, 10.0% Swedish, 9.6% Irish, 8.9% Norwegian (2000).
Economy: Grain, oats, alfalfa; dairying; poultry. Manufacturing: machining, signs; iron-mining district. In lake and forest area. Single-family building permits issued: 4 (2001) / 1 (2000); Multi-family building permits issued: 0 (2001) / 12 (2000); Employment by occupation: 3.9% management, 13.4% professional, 32.4% services, 21.2% sales, 0.0% farming, 18.4% construction, 10.6% production (2000).
Income: Per capita income: $12,949 (2000); Median household income: $22,813 (2000); Poverty rate: 17.5% (2000).
Taxes: Total city taxes per capita: $164 (1997); City property taxes per capita: $154 (1997).
Education: High school graduation rate: 80.6% (2000); College graduation rate: 5.3% (2000).
Housing: Homeownership rate: 72.8% (2000); Median home value: $57,200 (2000); Median rent: $278 per month (2000); Median age of housing: 48 years (2000).
Transportation: Commute to work: 81.0% car, 0.0% public transportation, 6.7% walk, 10.6% work from home (2000); Travel time to work: 51.2% less than 15 minutes, 28.7% 15 to 30 minutes, 10.6% 30 to 45 minutes, 7.5% 45 to 60 minutes, 1.9% 60 minutes or more (2000)
Additional Information Contacts
Ironton Chamber of Commerce 218-546-8131

JENKINS (city). Covers a land area of 4.254 square miles and a water area of 0.028 square miles. Located at 46.64° N. Lat.; 94.33° W. Long. Elevation is 1,270 feet.
Population: 287 (2000); Race: 99.3% White, 0.0% Black, 0.7% Asian, 0.0% American Indian and Alaska Native, 0.0% Hispanic of any race, 0.0% two or more races (2000); Density: 67.5 persons per square mile (2000); Age: 26.2% under 18, 8.6% over 64 (2000); Marriage status: 25.8% never married, 55.5% now married, 3.8% widowed, 14.8% divorced (2000); Foreign born: 0.7% (2000); Ancestry (includes multiple ancestries): 34.8% German, 20.6% Norwegian, 10.5% Swedish, 8.6% English, 5.2% Finnish (2000).
Economy: Single-family building permits issued: 2 (2001) / 3 (2000); Multi-family building permits issued: 0 (2001) / 0 (2000); Employment by occupation: 5.8% management, 8.4% professional, 28.6% services, 20.8% sales, 0.0% farming, 21.4% construction, 14.9% production (2000).
Income: Per capita income: $14,198 (2000); Median household income: $34,167 (2000); Poverty rate: 10.1% (2000).
Taxes: Total city taxes per capita: $110 (1997); City property taxes per capita: $103 (1997).
Education: High school graduation rate: 94.4% (2000); College graduation rate: 3.4% (2000).
Housing: Homeownership rate: 89.7% (2000); Median home value: $69,600 (2000); Median rent: $525 per month (2000); Median age of housing: 24 years (2000).
Transportation: Commute to work: 90.7% car, 0.0% public transportation, 2.0% walk, 7.3% work from home (2000); Travel time to work: 51.8% less than 15 minutes, 30.9% 15 to 30 minutes, 15.1% 30 to 45 minutes, 0.7% 45 to 60 minutes, 1.4% 60 minutes or more (2000)

JENKINS (township). Covers a land area of 11.844 square miles and a water area of 2.085 square miles. Located at 46.67° N. Lat.; 94.29° W. Long. Elevation is 1,270 feet.
Population: 425 (2000); Race: 99.6% White, 0.4% Black, 0.0% Asian, 0.0% American Indian and Alaska Native, 0.0% Hispanic of any race, 0.0% two or more races (2000); Density: 35.9 persons per square mile (2000); Age: 23.5% under 18, 21.6% over 64 (2000); Marriage status: 14.1% never married, 70.7% now married, 5.4% widowed, 9.8% divorced (2000); Foreign born: 0.9% (2000); Ancestry (includes multiple ancestries): 37.4% German, 16.6% Norwegian, 11.0% Swedish, 10.8% Irish, 9.7% French (except Basque) (2000).
Economy: Dairying; poultry; oats, alfalfa. Employment by occupation: 16.2% management, 15.1% professional, 14.6% services, 26.5% sales, 1.1% farming, 14.1% construction, 12.4% production (2000).
Income: Per capita income: $18,498 (2000); Median household income: $40,208 (2000); Poverty rate: 10.3% (2000).
Taxes: Total city taxes per capita: $119 (1997); City property taxes per capita: $119 (1997).
Education: High school graduation rate: 88.0% (2000); College graduation rate: 13.7% (2000).
Housing: Homeownership rate: 89.8% (2000); Median home value: $184,000 (2000); Median rent: $517 per month (2000); Median age of housing: 23 years (2000).
Transportation: Commute to work: 94.1% car, 0.0% public transportation, 1.1% walk, 4.9% work from home (2000); Travel time to work: 31.3% less than 15 minutes, 33.5% 15 to 30 minutes, 22.2% 30 to 45 minutes, 3.4% 45 to 60 minutes, 9.7% 60 minutes or more (2000)

LAKE EDWARDS (township). Covers a land area of 25.424 square miles and a water area of 10.806 square miles. Located at 46.49° N. Lat.; 94.19° W. Long.
Population: 1,995 (2000); Race: 98.4% White, 0.3% Black, 0.0% Asian, 0.0% American Indian and Alaska Native, 0.4% Hispanic of any race, 1.2% two or more races (2000); Density: 78.5 persons per square mile (2000); Age: 23.7% under 18, 13.6% over 64 (2000); Marriage status: 17.5% never married, 70.1% now married, 4.0% widowed, 8.4% divorced (2000); Foreign born: 0.8% (2000); Ancestry (includes multiple ancestries): 38.4% German, 18.9% Norwegian, 13.0% Swedish, 9.0% Irish, 6.8% English (2000).
Economy: Employment by occupation: 12.7% management, 16.4% professional, 15.3% services, 27.9% sales, 0.2% farming, 10.6% construction, 17.0% production (2000).
Income: Per capita income: $19,714 (2000); Median household income: $43,274 (2000); Poverty rate: 8.9% (2000).

Taxes: Total city taxes per capita: $71 (1997); City property taxes per capita: $71 (1997).
Education: High school graduation rate: 85.7% (2000); College graduation rate: 19.9% (2000).
Housing: Homeownership rate: 93.6% (2000); Median home value: $134,900 (2000); Median rent: $475 per month (2000); Median age of housing: 32 years (2000).
Transportation: Commute to work: 94.5% car, 0.0% public transportation, 0.8% walk, 4.5% work from home (2000); Travel time to work: 18.2% less than 15 minutes, 62.9% 15 to 30 minutes, 13.5% 30 to 45 minutes, 2.0% 45 to 60 minutes, 3.4% 60 minutes or more (2000)

LITTLE PINE (township). Covers a land area of 34.502 square miles and a water area of 1.300 square miles. Located at 46.75° N. Lat.; 93.83° W. Long. Elevation is 1,276 feet.
Population: 86 (2000); Race: 100.0% White, 0.0% Black, 0.0% Asian, 0.0% American Indian and Alaska Native, 0.0% Hispanic of any race, 0.0% two or more races (2000); Density: 2.5 persons per square mile (2000); Age: 32.0% under 18, 11.3% over 64 (2000); Marriage status: 18.7% never married, 74.7% now married, 0.0% widowed, 6.7% divorced (2000); Foreign born: 2.1% (2000); Ancestry (includes multiple ancestries): 27.8% Irish, 26.8% German, 20.6% English, 6.2% Ukrainian, 5.2% Dutch (2000).
Economy: Employment by occupation: 10.0% management, 7.5% professional, 30.0% services, 25.0% sales, 5.0% farming, 17.5% construction, 5.0% production (2000).
Income: Per capita income: $12,602 (2000); Median household income: $24,375 (2000); Poverty rate: 44.3% (2000).
Taxes: Total city taxes per capita: $158 (1997); City property taxes per capita: $158 (1997).
Education: High school graduation rate: 95.1% (2000); College graduation rate: 11.5% (2000).
Housing: Homeownership rate: 91.9% (2000); Median home value: $137,500 (2000); Median age of housing: 16 years (2000).
Transportation: Commute to work: 78.4% car, 10.8% public transportation, 5.4% walk, 5.4% work from home (2000); Travel time to work: 11.4% less than 15 minutes, 28.6% 15 to 30 minutes, 31.4% 30 to 45 minutes, 11.4% 45 to 60 minutes, 17.1% 60 minutes or more (2000)

LONG LAKE (township). Covers a land area of 34.165 square miles and a water area of 2.240 square miles. Located at 46.28° N. Lat.; 94.12° W. Long.
Population: 1,025 (2000); Race: 98.5% White, 0.0% Black, 1.0% Asian, 0.2% American Indian and Alaska Native, 1.5% Hispanic of any race, 0.2% two or more races (2000); Density: 30.0 persons per square mile (2000); Age: 24.7% under 18, 15.4% over 64 (2000); Marriage status: 19.0% never married, 70.1% now married, 3.9% widowed, 6.9% divorced (2000); Foreign born: 2.8% (2000); Ancestry (includes multiple ancestries): 44.2% German, 16.9% Norwegian, 12.8% Swedish, 10.7% Irish, 6.5% Polish (2000).
Economy: Employment by occupation: 9.3% management, 16.0% professional, 15.6% services, 20.1% sales, 0.7% farming, 16.0% construction, 22.3% production (2000).
Income: Per capita income: $24,136 (2000); Median household income: $44,297 (2000); Poverty rate: 4.0% (2000).
Taxes: Total city taxes per capita: $57 (1997); City property taxes per capita: $57 (1997).
Education: High school graduation rate: 85.4% (2000); College graduation rate: 13.9% (2000).
Housing: Homeownership rate: 94.3% (2000); Median home value: $108,800 (2000); Median rent: $492 per month (2000); Median age of housing: 27 years (2000).
Transportation: Commute to work: 92.2% car, 0.8% public transportation, 0.9% walk, 4.7% work from home (2000); Travel time to work: 21.9% less than 15 minutes, 53.7% 15 to 30 minutes, 13.5% 30 to 45 minutes, 3.2% 45 to 60 minutes, 7.8% 60 minutes or more (2000)

MANHATTAN BEACH (city). Covers a land area of 1.513 square miles and a water area of 0.271 square miles. Located at 46.72° N. Lat.; 94.13° W. Long.
Population: 50 (2000); Race: 100.0% White, 0.0% Black, 0.0% Asian, 0.0% American Indian and Alaska Native, 0.0% Hispanic of any race, 0.0% two or more races (2000); Density: 33.1 persons per square mile (2000); Age: 14.3% under 18, 20.6% over 64 (2000); Marriage status: 17.9% never married, 78.6% now married, 3.6% widowed, 0.0% divorced (2000); Foreign born: 0.0% (2000); Ancestry (includes multiple ancestries): 41.3% German, 41.3% Norwegian, 17.5% Swedish, 12.7% Irish, 7.9% Polish (2000).
Economy: Single-family building permits issued: 0 (2001) / 0 (2000); Multi-family building permits issued: 0 (2001) / 0 (2000); Employment by occupation: 16.7% management, 10.0% professional, 0.0% services, 50.0% sales, 0.0% farming, 16.7% construction, 6.7% production (2000).
Income: Per capita income: $29,268 (2000); Median household income: $51,250 (2000); Poverty rate: 0.0% (2000).
Taxes: Total city taxes per capita: $238 (1997); City property taxes per capita: $190 (1997).
Education: High school graduation rate: 71.7% (2000); College graduation rate: 10.9% (2000).
Housing: Homeownership rate: 92.3% (2000); Median home value: $325,000 (2000); Median age of housing: 14 years (2000).
Transportation: Commute to work: 90.0% car, 0.0% public transportation, 0.0% walk, 10.0% work from home (2000); Travel time to work: 29.6% less than 15 minutes, 37.0% 15 to 30 minutes, 7.4% 30 to 45 minutes, 7.4% 45 to 60 minutes, 18.5% 60 minutes or more (2000)

MAPLE GROVE (township). Covers a land area of 34.326 square miles and a water area of 1.626 square miles. Located at 46.29° N. Lat.; 94.01° W. Long.
Population: 665 (2000); Race: 98.6% White, 0.0% Black, 0.4% Asian, 0.6% American Indian and Alaska Native, 0.3% Hispanic of any race, 0.4% two or more races (2000); Density: 19.4 persons per square mile (2000); Age: 29.6% under 18, 9.7% over 64 (2000); Marriage status: 17.4% never married, 70.4% now married, 5.1% widowed, 7.2% divorced (2000); Foreign born: 1.3% (2000); Ancestry (includes multiple ancestries): 42.2% German, 20.9% Norwegian, 13.8% Swedish, 8.6% United States or American, 6.3% Irish (2000).
Economy: Employment by occupation: 17.3% management, 18.8% professional, 17.9% services, 24.1% sales, 0.0% farming, 11.0% construction, 11.0% production (2000).
Income: Per capita income: $20,552 (2000); Median household income: $50,833 (2000); Poverty rate: 5.4% (2000).
Taxes: Total city taxes per capita: $89 (1997); City property taxes per capita: $89 (1997).
Education: High school graduation rate: 84.8% (2000); College graduation rate: 17.2% (2000).
Housing: Homeownership rate: 95.1% (2000); Median home value: $121,600 (2000); Median rent: $475 per month (2000); Median age of housing: 23 years (2000).
Transportation: Commute to work: 89.1% car, 0.0% public transportation, 0.6% walk, 9.4% work from home (2000); Travel time to work: 10.4% less than 15 minutes, 66.2% 15 to 30 minutes, 18.7% 30 to 45 minutes, 2.3% 45 to 60 minutes, 2.3% 60 minutes or more (2000)

MERRIFIELD (unincorporated postal area, zip code 56465). Covers a land area of 32.712 square miles and a water area of 7.406 square miles. Located at 46.52° N. Lat.; 94.11° W. Long. Elevation is 1,219 feet.
Population: 1,727 (2000); Race: 98.1% White, 0.0% Black, 0.0% Asian, 0.3% American Indian and Alaska Native, 0.3% Hispanic of any race, 1.6% two or more races (2000); Density: 52.8 persons per square mile (2000); Age: 23.8% under 18, 16.5% over 64 (2000); Marriage status: 22.1% never married, 64.5% now married, 4.8% widowed, 8.6% divorced (2000); Foreign born: 0.2% (2000); Ancestry (includes multiple ancestries): 37.6% German, 17.3% Norwegian, 14.6% Swedish, 10.3% Irish, 8.1% English (2000).
Economy: Manufacturing: fabricated metal products, consumer goods, electronic products. Agriculture: cattle; dairying; oats. Timber. Employment by occupation: 12.3% management, 15.7% professional, 15.1% services, 27.3% sales, 0.6% farming, 10.3% construction, 18.7% production (2000).
Income: Per capita income: $20,355 (2000); Median household income: $39,598 (2000); Poverty rate: 5.9% (2000).
Education: High school graduation rate: 87.8% (2000); College graduation rate: 16.1% (2000).
Housing: Homeownership rate: 91.5% (2000); Median home value: $139,100 (2000); Median rent: $492 per month (2000); Median age of housing: 25 years (2000).
Transportation: Commute to work: 90.5% car, 0.0% public transportation, 1.8% walk, 6.8% work from home (2000); Travel time to work: 20.2% less than 15 minutes, 49.3% 15 to 30 minutes, 20.9% 30 to 45 minutes, 2.5% 45 to 60 minutes, 7.2% 60 minutes or more (2000)

MISSION (township). Covers a land area of 29.572 square miles and a water area of 5.094 square miles. Located at 46.58° N. Lat.; 94.09° W. Long.
Population: 733 (2000); Race: 96.9% White, 0.4% Black, 0.0% Asian, 0.4% American Indian and Alaska Native, 0.0% Hispanic of any race, 2.2% two or more races (2000); Density: 24.8 persons per square mile (2000); Age: 17.8%

under 18, 23.2% over 64 (2000); Marriage status: 14.4% never married, 73.8% now married, 5.1% widowed, 6.7% divorced (2000); Foreign born: 0.4% (2000); Ancestry (includes multiple ancestries): 36.8% German, 19.4% Swedish, 17.1% Norwegian, 10.1% Irish, 8.8% English (2000).
Economy: Employment by occupation: 14.9% management, 19.3% professional, 12.7% services, 27.2% sales, 1.3% farming, 11.4% construction, 13.3% production (2000).
Income: Per capita income: $26,503 (2000); Median household income: $41,750 (2000); Poverty rate: 3.8% (2000).
Taxes: Total city taxes per capita: $242 (1997); City property taxes per capita: $242 (1997).
Education: High school graduation rate: 90.8% (2000); College graduation rate: 20.6% (2000).
Housing: Homeownership rate: 94.8% (2000); Median home value: $198,400 (2000); Median rent: $525 per month (2000); Median age of housing: 22 years (2000).
Transportation: Commute to work: 90.1% car, 0.0% public transportation, 4.2% walk, 5.8% work from home (2000); Travel time to work: 30.6% less than 15 minutes, 28.6% 15 to 30 minutes, 30.3% 30 to 45 minutes, 1.4% 45 to 60 minutes, 9.2% 60 minutes or more (2000)

NISSWA (city). Covers a land area of 10.877 square miles and a water area of 7.512 square miles. Located at 46.50° N. Lat.; 94.29° W. Long. Elevation is 1,231 feet.
Population: 1,953 (2000); Race: 99.1% White, 0.2% Black, 0.4% Asian, 0.0% American Indian and Alaska Native, 0.2% Hispanic of any race, 0.4% two or more races (2000); Density: 179.5 persons per square mile (2000); Age: 24.5% under 18, 18.1% over 64 (2000); Marriage status: 17.9% never married, 65.1% now married, 7.7% widowed, 9.3% divorced (2000); Foreign born: 1.5% (2000); Ancestry (includes multiple ancestries): 44.1% German, 20.7% Norwegian, 16.2% Swedish, 10.1% English, 10.0% Irish (2000).
Economy: Resort area. Dairying; poultry; oats, alfalfa. Manufacturing: boat lifts and docks, labels. Single-family building permits issued: 30 (2001) / 28 (2000); Multi-family building permits issued: 2 (2001) / 0 (2000); Employment by occupation: 18.5% management, 21.4% professional, 9.6% services, 30.9% sales, 0.6% farming, 9.3% construction, 9.7% production (2000).
Income: Per capita income: $26,265 (2000); Median household income: $48,306 (2000); Poverty rate: 4.9% (2000).
Taxes: Total city taxes per capita: $415 (1997); City property taxes per capita: $401 (1997).
Education: High school graduation rate: 91.0% (2000); College graduation rate: 30.0% (2000).
Housing: Homeownership rate: 87.2% (2000); Median home value: $149,100 (2000); Median rent: $566 per month (2000); Median age of housing: 26 years (2000).
Transportation: Commute to work: 88.6% car, 0.6% public transportation, 2.4% walk, 7.5% work from home (2000); Travel time to work: 35.0% less than 15 minutes, 45.0% 15 to 30 minutes, 14.7% 30 to 45 minutes, 1.5% 45 to 60 minutes, 3.7% 60 minutes or more (2000)
Additional Information Contacts
Nisswa Chamber of Commerce 218-963-2620

NOKAY LAKE (township). Covers a land area of 33.133 square miles and a water area of 2.769 square miles. Located at 46.38° N. Lat.; 93.98° W. Long.
Population: 681 (2000); Race: 98.7% White, 0.0% Black, 0.0% Asian, 0.3% American Indian and Alaska Native, 0.7% Hispanic of any race, 1.0% two or more races (2000); Density: 20.6 persons per square mile (2000); Age: 27.2% under 18, 11.4% over 64 (2000); Marriage status: 20.1% never married, 65.6% now married, 4.5% widowed, 9.8% divorced (2000); Foreign born: 0.1% (2000); Ancestry (includes multiple ancestries): 40.3% German, 24.5% Norwegian, 15.8% Swedish, 7.3% Irish, 6.8% Polish (2000).
Economy: Employment by occupation: 9.3% management, 14.7% professional, 21.8% services, 17.7% sales, 0.3% farming, 15.5% construction, 20.7% production (2000).
Income: Per capita income: $15,393 (2000); Median household income: $35,809 (2000); Poverty rate: 12.4% (2000).
Taxes: Total city taxes per capita: $69 (1997); City property taxes per capita: $69 (1997).
Education: High school graduation rate: 84.1% (2000); College graduation rate: 11.2% (2000).
Housing: Homeownership rate: 88.8% (2000); Median home value: $90,900 (2000); Median rent: $375 per month (2000); Median age of housing: 31 years (2000).
Transportation: Commute to work: 90.7% car, 0.0% public transportation, 1.7% walk, 6.2% work from home (2000); Travel time to work: 15.9% less than 15 minutes, 59.6% 15 to 30 minutes, 14.7% 30 to 45 minutes, 1.2% 45 to 60 minutes, 8.7% 60 minutes or more (2000)

OAK LAWN (township). Covers a land area of 35.092 square miles and a water area of 2.389 square miles. Located at 46.38° N. Lat.; 94.12° W. Long.
Population: 1,793 (2000); Race: 96.8% White, 0.5% Black, 0.4% Asian, 1.2% American Indian and Alaska Native, 0.3% Hispanic of any race, 1.1% two or more races (2000); Density: 51.1 persons per square mile (2000); Age: 25.0% under 18, 12.7% over 64 (2000); Marriage status: 27.9% never married, 57.4% now married, 5.2% widowed, 9.6% divorced (2000); Foreign born: 0.8% (2000); Ancestry (includes multiple ancestries): 36.3% German, 18.8% Norwegian, 11.6% Swedish, 9.8% Irish, 6.0% French (except Basque) (2000).
Economy: Employment by occupation: 10.9% management, 17.9% professional, 15.1% services, 26.8% sales, 0.2% farming, 10.8% construction, 18.2% production (2000).
Income: Per capita income: $16,599 (2000); Median household income: $45,388 (2000); Poverty rate: 5.0% (2000).
Taxes: Total city taxes per capita: $87 (2000); City property taxes per capita: $86 (2000).
Education: High school graduation rate: 82.9% (2000); College graduation rate: 16.1% (2000).
Housing: Homeownership rate: 88.3% (2000); Median home value: $100,500 (2000); Median rent: $468 per month (2000); Median age of housing: 26 years (2000).
Transportation: Commute to work: 94.7% car, 0.6% public transportation, 0.5% walk, 3.9% work from home (2000); Travel time to work: 44.0% less than 15 minutes, 42.0% 15 to 30 minutes, 8.7% 30 to 45 minutes, 2.3% 45 to 60 minutes, 2.9% 60 minutes or more (2000)

PELICAN (township). Covers a land area of 7.966 square miles and a water area of 11.395 square miles. Located at 46.57° N. Lat.; 94.20° W. Long.
Population: 400 (2000); Race: 98.7% White, 0.0% Black, 0.0% Asian, 0.8% American Indian and Alaska Native, 0.0% Hispanic of any race, 0.5% two or more races (2000); Density: 50.2 persons per square mile (2000); Age: 15.9% under 18, 23.6% over 64 (2000); Marriage status: 13.1% never married, 67.3% now married, 7.6% widowed, 11.9% divorced (2000); Foreign born: 0.0% (2000); Ancestry (includes multiple ancestries): 35.5% German, 15.9% Norwegian, 14.9% Irish, 11.7% Swedish, 8.5% English (2000).
Economy: Employment by occupation: 16.9% management, 15.5% professional, 11.3% services, 34.7% sales, 0.0% farming, 9.9% construction, 11.7% production (2000).
Income: Per capita income: $24,495 (2000); Median household income: $51,250 (2000); Poverty rate: 7.7% (2000).
Education: High school graduation rate: 95.0% (2000); College graduation rate: 27.0% (2000).
Housing: Homeownership rate: 93.4% (2000); Median home value: $170,400 (2000); Median rent: $475 per month (2000); Median age of housing: 32 years (2000).
Transportation: Commute to work: 91.4% car, 0.0% public transportation, 0.0% walk, 7.1% work from home (2000); Travel time to work: 28.2% less than 15 minutes, 37.9% 15 to 30 minutes, 28.2% 30 to 45 minutes, 1.0% 45 to 60 minutes, 4.6% 60 minutes or more (2000)

PEQUOT LAKES (city). Covers a land area of 1.449 square miles and a water area of 0.233 square miles. Located at 46.60° N. Lat.; 94.31° W. Long. Elevation is 1,280 feet.
History: Known as Pequot until 1939.
Population: 947 (2000); Race: 98.4% White, 0.0% Black, 0.7% Asian, 0.5% American Indian and Alaska Native, 0.8% Hispanic of any race, 0.4% two or more races (2000); Density: 653.8 persons per square mile (2000); Age: 24.5% under 18, 23.4% over 64 (2000); Marriage status: 23.0% never married, 49.2% now married, 13.3% widowed, 14.6% divorced (2000); Foreign born: 1.1% (2000); Ancestry (includes multiple ancestries): 41.1% German, 18.3% Norwegian, 12.6% Irish, 9.5% Swedish, 7.9% English (2000).
Economy: Dairying; poultry; oats, alfalfa. Manufacturing: chapel cabinets, candles, tool and die, steel docks. Single-family building permits issued: 4 (2001) / 3 (2000); Multi-family building permits issued: 2 (2001) / 0 (2000); Employment by occupation: 9.0% management, 20.5% professional, 19.8% services, 25.4% sales, 0.0% farming, 10.8% construction, 14.4% production (2000).

Income: Per capita income: $16,275 (2000); Median household income: $23,813 (2000); Poverty rate: 14.8% (2000).
Taxes: Total city taxes per capita: $237 (1997); City property taxes per capita: $199 (1997).
Education: High school graduation rate: 81.7% (2000); College graduation rate: 17.5% (2000).

School District(s)

Pequot Lakes (PK-12)
2000 Enrollment: 1,334 218-568-4996

Housing: Homeownership rate: 51.5% (2000); Median home value: $82,400 (2000); Median rent: $363 per month (2000); Median age of housing: 26 years (2000).
Newspapers: The Lake Country Echo (1 x week)
Transportation: Commute to work: 90.0% car, 0.0% public transportation, 6.3% walk, 1.8% work from home (2000); Travel time to work: 57.4% less than 15 minutes, 20.2% 15 to 30 minutes, 18.6% 30 to 45 minutes, 1.5% 45 to 60 minutes, 2.3% 60 minutes or more (2000)

Additional Information Contacts

Pequot Lakes Chamber of Commerce 218-568-8911

PERRY LAKE (township). Covers a land area of 30.850 square miles and a water area of 1.713 square miles. Located at 46.57° N. Lat.; 93.94° W. Long.
Population: 237 (2000); Race: 96.1% White, 0.0% Black, 2.1% Asian, 1.8% American Indian and Alaska Native, 1.8% Hispanic of any race, 0.0% two or more races (2000); Density: 7.7 persons per square mile (2000); Age: 32.3% under 18, 11.6% over 64 (2000); Marriage status: 13.7% never married, 82.8% now married, 1.0% widowed, 2.5% divorced (2000); Foreign born: 4.2% (2000); Ancestry (includes multiple ancestries): 25.3% German, 18.9% Norwegian, 16.1% Swedish, 11.6% Irish, 8.1% Other groups (2000).
Economy: Employment by occupation: 9.4% management, 17.3% professional, 7.9% services, 28.3% sales, 3.9% farming, 14.2% construction, 18.9% production (2000).
Income: Per capita income: $16,728 (2000); Median household income: $46,563 (2000); Poverty rate: 11.9% (2000).
Taxes: Total city taxes per capita: $85 (1997); City property taxes per capita: $85 (1997).
Education: High school graduation rate: 81.1% (2000); College graduation rate: 14.4% (2000).
Housing: Homeownership rate: 96.8% (2000); Median home value: $96,800 (2000); Median rent: $375 per month (2000); Median age of housing: 21 years (2000).
Transportation: Commute to work: 92.0% car, 0.0% public transportation, 0.0% walk, 8.0% work from home (2000); Travel time to work: 27.0% less than 15 minutes, 40.0% 15 to 30 minutes, 26.1% 30 to 45 minutes, 3.5% 45 to 60 minutes, 3.5% 60 minutes or more (2000)

PLATTE LAKE (township). Covers a land area of 35.651 square miles and a water area of 0.324 square miles. Located at 46.19° N. Lat.; 94.01° W. Long.
Population: 305 (2000); Race: 99.0% White, 0.0% Black, 0.0% Asian, 0.0% American Indian and Alaska Native, 0.3% Hispanic of any race, 1.0% two or more races (2000); Density: 8.6 persons per square mile (2000); Age: 21.0% under 18, 9.8% over 64 (2000); Marriage status: 28.5% never married, 57.0% now married, 4.8% widowed, 9.6% divorced (2000); Foreign born: 1.0% (2000); Ancestry (includes multiple ancestries): 50.5% German, 23.7% Polish, 10.2% Irish, 8.8% Swedish, 8.1% Norwegian (2000).
Economy: Employment by occupation: 15.2% management, 10.3% professional, 17.6% services, 14.5% sales, 4.8% farming, 15.8% construction, 21.8% production (2000).
Income: Per capita income: $14,899 (2000); Median household income: $32,857 (2000); Poverty rate: 10.2% (2000).
Taxes: Total city taxes per capita: $56 (1997); City property taxes per capita: $56 (1997).
Education: High school graduation rate: 77.1% (2000); College graduation rate: 5.4% (2000).
Housing: Homeownership rate: 95.7% (2000); Median home value: $52,500 (2000); Median rent: $325 per month (2000); Median age of housing: 31 years (2000).
Transportation: Commute to work: 78.8% car, 0.0% public transportation, 5.5% walk, 15.8% work from home (2000); Travel time to work: 16.5% less than 15 minutes, 35.3% 15 to 30 minutes, 38.8% 30 to 45 minutes, 2.2% 45 to 60 minutes, 7.2% 60 minutes or more (2000)

RABBIT LAKE (township). Covers a land area of 21.997 square miles and a water area of 2.113 square miles. Located at 46.53° N. Lat.; 93.89° W. Long.
Population: 348 (2000); Race: 100.0% White, 0.0% Black, 0.0% Asian, 0.0% American Indian and Alaska Native, 0.0% Hispanic of any race, 0.0% two or more races (2000); Density: 15.8 persons per square mile (2000); Age: 29.1% under 18, 9.3% over 64 (2000); Marriage status: 16.7% never married, 77.8% now married, 1.8% widowed, 3.6% divorced (2000); Foreign born: 0.0% (2000); Ancestry (includes multiple ancestries): 47.5% German, 16.9% Norwegian, 12.7% Swedish, 10.7% Irish, 5.9% Polish (2000).
Economy: Employment by occupation: 13.0% management, 26.0% professional, 5.3% services, 30.2% sales, 0.0% farming, 12.4% construction, 13.0% production (2000).
Income: Per capita income: $20,041 (2000); Median household income: $57,500 (2000); Poverty rate: 3.7% (2000).
Taxes: Total city taxes per capita: $103 (1997); City property taxes per capita: $103 (1997).
Education: High school graduation rate: 93.2% (2000); College graduation rate: 22.2% (2000).
Housing: Homeownership rate: 94.1% (2000); Median home value: $150,000 (2000); Median age of housing: 22 years (2000).
Transportation: Commute to work: 93.6% car, 0.0% public transportation, 0.0% walk, 6.4% work from home (2000); Travel time to work: 32.3% less than 15 minutes, 41.0% 15 to 30 minutes, 17.4% 30 to 45 minutes, 9.3% 45 to 60 minutes, 0.0% 60 minutes or more (2000)

RIVERTON (city). Covers a land area of 0.785 square miles and a water area of 0.071 square miles. Located at 46.46° N. Lat.; 94.04° W. Long. Elevation is 1,228 feet.
Population: 115 (2000); Race: 98.2% White, 0.0% Black, 1.8% Asian, 0.0% American Indian and Alaska Native, 0.0% Hispanic of any race, 0.0% two or more races (2000); Density: 146.5 persons per square mile (2000); Age: 15.9% under 18, 13.3% over 64 (2000); Marriage status: 33.3% never married, 39.4% now married, 12.1% widowed, 15.2% divorced (2000); Foreign born: 0.0% (2000); Ancestry (includes multiple ancestries): 38.9% German, 25.7% Norwegian, 15.0% Swedish, 7.1% United States or American, 6.2% French (except Basque) (2000).
Economy: Cuyuna Iron Range mining district to Northeast. Single-family building permits issued: 0 (2001) / 0 (2000); Multi-family building permits issued: 0 (2001) / 0 (2000); Employment by occupation: 8.1% management, 29.7% professional, 14.9% services, 9.5% sales, 0.0% farming, 12.2% construction, 25.7% production (2000).
Income: Per capita income: $19,406 (2000); Median household income: $35,000 (2000); Poverty rate: 8.0% (2000).
Taxes: Total city taxes per capita: $102 (1997); City property taxes per capita: $102 (1997).
Education: High school graduation rate: 97.4% (2000); College graduation rate: 20.5% (2000).
Housing: Homeownership rate: 89.1% (2000); Median home value: $71,400 (2000); Median rent: $375 per month (2000); Median age of housing: 46 years (2000).
Transportation: Commute to work: 97.3% car, 0.0% public transportation, 0.0% walk, 2.7% work from home (2000); Travel time to work: 37.5% less than 15 minutes, 34.7% 15 to 30 minutes, 6.9% 30 to 45 minutes, 2.8% 45 to 60 minutes, 18.1% 60 minutes or more (2000)

ROOSEVELT (township). Covers a land area of 31.125 square miles and a water area of 5.237 square miles. Located at 46.19° N. Lat.; 93.87° W. Long.
Population: 534 (2000); Race: 93.4% White, 0.5% Black, 0.0% Asian, 4.7% American Indian and Alaska Native, 0.0% Hispanic of any race, 1.4% two or more races (2000); Density: 17.2 persons per square mile (2000); Age: 22.4% under 18, 18.5% over 64 (2000); Marriage status: 17.4% never married, 65.7% now married, 5.9% widowed, 11.1% divorced (2000); Foreign born: 0.4% (2000); Ancestry (includes multiple ancestries): 31.1% German, 20.3% Norwegian, 12.0% Polish, 11.5% Swedish, 8.3% Irish (2000).
Economy: Employment by occupation: 7.7% management, 22.5% professional, 28.8% services, 16.7% sales, 1.4% farming, 10.8% construction, 12.2% production (2000).
Income: Per capita income: $18,417 (2000); Median household income: $32,500 (2000); Poverty rate: 14.7% (2000).
Taxes: Total city taxes per capita: $161 (1997); City property taxes per capita: $161 (1997).
Education: High school graduation rate: 83.7% (2000); College graduation rate: 12.3% (2000).

Housing: Homeownership rate: 93.1% (2000); Median home value: $93,500 (2000); Median rent: $444 per month (2000); Median age of housing: 39 years (2000).
Transportation: Commute to work: 90.9% car, 1.4% public transportation, 3.2% walk, 4.5% work from home (2000); Travel time to work: 17.1% less than 15 minutes, 35.2% 15 to 30 minutes, 26.7% 30 to 45 minutes, 7.6% 45 to 60 minutes, 13.3% 60 minutes or more (2000)

ROSS LAKE (township). Covers a land area of 33.362 square miles and a water area of 2.848 square miles. Located at 46.66° N. Lat.; 93.85° W. Long.
Population: 134 (2000); Race: 100.0% White, 0.0% Black, 0.0% Asian, 0.0% American Indian and Alaska Native, 0.0% Hispanic of any race, 0.0% two or more races (2000); Density: 4.0 persons per square mile (2000); Age: 15.0% under 18, 31.0% over 64 (2000); Marriage status: 9.2% never married, 74.5% now married, 9.2% widowed, 7.1% divorced (2000); Foreign born: 0.0% (2000); Ancestry (includes multiple ancestries): 39.8% German, 25.7% Swedish, 11.5% English, 11.5% Irish, 10.6% French (except Basque) (2000).
Economy: Employment by occupation: 7.7% management, 20.5% professional, 5.1% services, 23.1% sales, 5.1% farming, 25.6% construction, 12.8% production (2000).
Income: Per capita income: $15,906 (2000); Median household income: $32,500 (2000); Poverty rate: 2.7% (2000).
Taxes: Total city taxes per capita: $199 (1997); City property taxes per capita: $199 (1997).
Education: High school graduation rate: 57.4% (2000); College graduation rate: 3.2% (2000).
Housing: Homeownership rate: 100.0% (2000); Median home value: $95,500 (2000); Median age of housing: 13 years (2000).
Transportation: Commute to work: 100.0% car, 0.0% public transportation, 0.0% walk, 0.0% work from home (2000); Travel time to work: 11.4% less than 15 minutes, 34.3% 15 to 30 minutes, 25.7% 30 to 45 minutes, 11.4% 45 to 60 minutes, 17.1% 60 minutes or more (2000)

SAINT MATHIAS (township). Covers a land area of 35.567 square miles and a water area of 0.478 square miles. Located at 46.21° N. Lat.; 94.24° W. Long.
Population: 490 (2000); Race: 100.0% White, 0.0% Black, 0.0% Asian, 0.0% American Indian and Alaska Native, 1.3% Hispanic of any race, 0.0% two or more races (2000); Density: 13.8 persons per square mile (2000); Age: 32.5% under 18, 9.9% over 64 (2000); Marriage status: 20.0% never married, 72.8% now married, 0.5% widowed, 6.7% divorced (2000); Foreign born: 0.9% (2000); Ancestry (includes multiple ancestries): 48.2% German, 11.2% Norwegian, 10.1% French (except Basque), 8.6% Irish, 8.4% United States or American (2000).
Economy: Employment by occupation: 12.2% management, 13.7% professional, 13.3% services, 21.7% sales, 1.5% farming, 15.6% construction, 22.1% production (2000).
Income: Per capita income: $15,761 (2000); Median household income: $43,462 (2000); Poverty rate: 3.0% (2000).
Education: High school graduation rate: 82.3% (2000); College graduation rate: 11.1% (2000).
Housing: Homeownership rate: 93.7% (2000); Median home value: $83,800 (2000); Median rent: $125 per month (2000); Median age of housing: 28 years (2000).
Transportation: Commute to work: 80.5% car, 0.0% public transportation, 3.4% walk, 16.1% work from home (2000); Travel time to work: 13.2% less than 15 minutes, 67.1% 15 to 30 minutes, 11.0% 30 to 45 minutes, 0.0% 45 to 60 minutes, 8.7% 60 minutes or more (2000)

SIBLEY (township). Covers a land area of 14.895 square miles and a water area of 1.569 square miles. Located at 46.57° N. Lat.; 94.30° W. Long.
Population: 855 (2000); Race: 98.4% White, 0.0% Black, 0.3% Asian, 0.1% American Indian and Alaska Native, 0.9% Hispanic of any race, 0.5% two or more races (2000); Density: 57.4 persons per square mile (2000); Age: 25.4% under 18, 15.7% over 64 (2000); Marriage status: 18.4% never married, 69.2% now married, 5.1% widowed, 7.4% divorced (2000); Foreign born: 1.6% (2000); Ancestry (includes multiple ancestries): 33.4% German, 25.9% Norwegian, 12.6% Swedish, 11.1% Irish, 8.0% English (2000).
Economy: Employment by occupation: 10.1% management, 20.0% professional, 12.2% services, 30.4% sales, 0.0% farming, 13.5% construction, 13.8% production (2000).
Income: Per capita income: $17,175 (2000); Median household income: $39,559 (2000); Poverty rate: 8.9% (2000).
Taxes: Total city taxes per capita: $98 (1997); City property taxes per capita: $98 (1997).
Education: High school graduation rate: 92.8% (2000); College graduation rate: 19.1% (2000).
Housing: Homeownership rate: 90.6% (2000); Median home value: $123,000 (2000); Median rent: $375 per month (2000); Median age of housing: 32 years (2000).
Transportation: Commute to work: 95.8% car, 0.0% public transportation, 1.1% walk, 3.2% work from home (2000); Travel time to work: 38.9% less than 15 minutes, 35.1% 15 to 30 minutes, 18.8% 30 to 45 minutes, 4.3% 45 to 60 minutes, 3.0% 60 minutes or more (2000)

TIMOTHY (township). Covers a land area of 34.131 square miles and a water area of 1.469 square miles. Located at 46.74° N. Lat.; 94.18° W. Long.
Population: 147 (2000); Race: 94.6% White, 0.0% Black, 0.0% Asian, 0.0% American Indian and Alaska Native, 0.0% Hispanic of any race, 2.4% two or more races (2000); Density: 4.3 persons per square mile (2000); Age: 22.0% under 18, 15.5% over 64 (2000); Marriage status: 18.0% never married, 66.9% now married, 7.2% widowed, 7.9% divorced (2000); Foreign born: 3.0% (2000); Ancestry (includes multiple ancestries): 25.6% German, 21.4% Norwegian, 20.2% English, 17.3% Swedish, 13.1% Irish (2000).
Economy: Employment by occupation: 18.1% management, 9.7% professional, 18.1% services, 25.0% sales, 0.0% farming, 6.9% construction, 22.2% production (2000).
Income: Per capita income: $36,103 (2000); Median household income: $37,273 (2000); Poverty rate: 9.5% (2000).
Taxes: Total city taxes per capita: $125 (1997); City property taxes per capita: $125 (1997).
Education: High school graduation rate: 87.0% (2000); College graduation rate: 22.0% (2000).
Housing: Homeownership rate: 94.1% (2000); Median home value: $275,000 (2000); Median rent: $525 per month (2000); Median age of housing: 19 years (2000).
Transportation: Commute to work: 80.6% car, 0.0% public transportation, 5.6% walk, 9.7% work from home (2000); Travel time to work: 24.6% less than 15 minutes, 49.2% 15 to 30 minutes, 10.8% 30 to 45 minutes, 0.0% 45 to 60 minutes, 15.4% 60 minutes or more (2000)

TROMMALD (city). Covers a land area of 3.701 square miles and a water area of 0.234 square miles. Located at 46.50° N. Lat.; 94.01° W. Long.
Population: 125 (2000); Race: 93.4% White, 0.0% Black, 0.0% Asian, 0.0% American Indian and Alaska Native, 6.6% Hispanic of any race, 0.0% two or more races (2000); Density: 33.8 persons per square mile (2000); Age: 38.7% under 18, 8.0% over 64 (2000); Marriage status: 21.8% never married, 51.5% now married, 9.9% widowed, 16.8% divorced (2000); Foreign born: 3.6% (2000); Ancestry (includes multiple ancestries): 21.9% German, 21.2% Norwegian, 13.9% Irish, 9.5% Other groups, 8.0% Polish (2000).
Economy: In Cuyuna Iron Range, iron mining district. Single-family building permits issued: 0 (2001) / 2 (2000); Multi-family building permits issued: 0 (2001) / 0 (2000); Employment by occupation: 4.4% management, 6.7% professional, 11.1% services, 24.4% sales, 0.0% farming, 22.2% construction, 31.1% production (2000).
Income: Per capita income: $14,714 (2000); Median household income: $21,500 (2000); Poverty rate: 16.0% (2000).
Taxes: Total city taxes per capita: $147 (1997); City property taxes per capita: $126 (1997).
Education: High school graduation rate: 81.1% (2000); College graduation rate: 0.0% (2000).
Housing: Homeownership rate: 84.0% (2000); Median home value: $36,300 (2000); Median rent: $450 per month (2000); Median age of housing: 31 years (2000).
Transportation: Commute to work: 95.2% car, 0.0% public transportation, 0.0% walk, 0.0% work from home (2000); Travel time to work: 23.8% less than 15 minutes, 40.5% 15 to 30 minutes, 14.3% 30 to 45 minutes, 4.8% 45 to 60 minutes, 16.7% 60 minutes or more (2000)

WOLFORD (township). Covers a land area of 14.606 square miles and a water area of 2.364 square miles. Located at 46.52° N. Lat.; 93.98° W. Long.
Population: 326 (2000); Race: 98.6% White, 0.0% Black, 0.0% Asian, 1.4% American Indian and Alaska Native, 0.0% Hispanic of any race, 0.0% two or more races (2000); Density: 22.3 persons per square mile (2000); Age: 26.8% under 18, 15.1% over 64 (2000); Marriage status: 19.0% never married, 72.5% now married, 4.9% widowed, 3.5% divorced (2000); Foreign born: 1.1% (2000); Ancestry (includes multiple ancestries): 41.3% German, 11.5% Norwegian, 8.9% Irish, 8.4% English, 8.1% Swedish (2000).
Economy: Employment by occupation: 9.8% management, 22.6% professional, 20.1% services, 22.0% sales, 0.0% farming, 11.6% construction, 14.0% production (2000).

Income: Per capita income: $17,179 (2000); Median household income: $50,833 (2000); Poverty rate: 6.7% (2000).
Taxes: Total city taxes per capita: $124 (1997); City property taxes per capita: $124 (1997).
Education: High school graduation rate: 91.6% (2000); College graduation rate: 18.9% (2000).
Housing: Homeownership rate: 91.6% (2000); Median home value: $153,900 (2000); Median rent: $192 per month (2000); Median age of housing: 21 years (2000).
Transportation: Commute to work: 93.0% car, 0.0% public transportation, 0.0% walk, 5.1% work from home (2000); Travel time to work: 50.7% less than 15 minutes, 25.3% 15 to 30 minutes, 16.0% 30 to 45 minutes, 4.7% 45 to 60 minutes, 3.3% 60 minutes or more (2000)

Dakota County

Located in southeastern Minnesota; bounded on the north and northeast by the Mississippi River, and on the northwest by the Minnesota River. Covers a land area of 569.60 square miles, a water area of 16.80 square miles, and is located in the Central Time Zone. The county government was organized in 1849. County seat is Hastings.

Dakota County is part of the Minneapolis-St. Paul, MN-WI MSA. The entire metro area includes: Anoka County, MN; Carver County, MN; Chisago County, MN; Dakota County, MN; Hennepin County, MN; Isanti County, MN; Ramsey County, MN; Scott County, MN; Sherburne County, MN; Washington County, MN; Wright County, MN; Pierce County, WI; St. Croix County, WI

Weather Station: Farmington 3 NW — Elevation: 977 feet

	Jan	Feb	Mar	Apr	May	Jun	Jul	Aug	Sep	Oct	Nov	Dec
High	21	28	40	58	71	80	83	80	72	59	40	27
Low	3	10	22	36	48	57	61	58	50	38	24	10
Precip	0.9	0.7	2.0	2.7	3.7	4.4	4.0	4.4	3.3	2.4	2.1	1.0
Snow	10.6	7.1	9.0	3.1	tr	0.0	0.0	0.0	tr	0.2	7.9	8.0

High and Low temperatures in degrees Fahrenheit; Precipitation and Snow in inches

Weather Station: Rosemount Agr. Exp. Station — Elevation: 948 feet

	Jan	Feb	Mar	Apr	May	Jun	Jul	Aug	Sep	Oct	Nov	Dec
High	22	29	41	58	72	80	84	81	73	60	41	27
Low	2	9	21	34	47	56	61	58	50	38	24	10
Precip	1.2	0.8	2.3	2.9	4.0	4.6	4.6	4.6	3.7	2.7	2.3	1.1
Snow	10.8	6.3	9.2	2.1	tr	0.0	0.0	0.0	0.0	0.2	7.3	8.3

High and Low temperatures in degrees Fahrenheit; Precipitation and Snow in inches

Population: 355,904 (2000); Race: 91.3% White, 2.3% Black, 2.6% Asian, 0.4% American Indian and Alaska Native, 2.9% Hispanic of any race, 2.0% two or more races (2000); Density: 624.9 persons per square mile (2000); Age: 29.1% under 18, 7.4% over 64 (2000).
Religion: Five largest groups: 26.5% Catholic Church, 13.3% Evangelical Lutheran Church in America, 2.3% Lutheran Church—Missouri Synod, 1.8% The United Methodist Church, 1.2% Independent, Non-Charismatic Churches (2000).
Economy: Unemployment rate: 2.9% (11/2002); Total civilian labor force: 226,749 (11/2002); Leading industries: 15.0% retail trade; 11.7% transportation & warehousing; 11.6% manufacturing (2000); Companies that employ more than 1,000 persons: 5 (2000); Companies that employ more than 100 persons: 245 (2000); Farms: 890 totaling 221,316 acres (1997); Minority business ownership rate: 3.9% (1997); Women business ownership rate: 28.8% (1997); Retail sales per capita: $11,981 (1997). Single-family building permits issued: 2,274 (2001) / 2,383 (2000); Multi-family building permits issued: 897 (2001) / 783 (2000).
Income: Per capita income: $27,008 (2000); Median household income: $61,863 (2000); Poverty rate: 3.6% (2000); Bankruptcy rate: 3.99% (2001).
Taxes: Total county taxes per capita: $232 (2000); County property taxes per capita: $230 (2000).
Education: High school graduation rate: 93.2% (2000); College graduation rate: 34.9% (2000).
Housing: Homeownership rate: 78.2% (2000); Median home value: $152,400 (2000); Median rent: $681 per month (2000); Median age of housing: 19 years (2000).
Health: Birth rate: 148.9 per 10,000 population (1998); Age adjusted death rate: 75.4 per 10,000 population (1999); Infant mortality rate: 4.3 per 1,000 live births (1998); Age adjusted cancer mortality rate: 189.2 deaths per 100,000 population (1999). Air Quality Index: 88% good, 12% moderate, 0% unhealthy (percent of days in 2000). Number of physicians: 13.5 per 10,000 population (1999); Number of hospital beds: 6.9 per 10,000 population (1999).
Elections: 2000 Presidential election results: 46.9% Gore, 47.9% Bush, 4.3% Nader, 0.5% Buchanan

Additional Information Contacts

Dakota County Government Offices 651-437-3191
Apple Valley Chamber of Commerce 952-432-8422
Burnsville Chamber of Commerce. 952-435-6000
Burnsville Convention Bureau. 952-898-5646
Eagan Convention & Visitors Bureau 651-452-4188
Farmington Area Chamber of Commerce 651-460-6444
Farmington Chamber of Commerce. 651-460-2221
Hastings Chamber of Commerce 651-437-6775
Hastings Tourism Bureau. 651-437-7740
Lakeville Area Chamber of Commerce 952-469-2020
Northern Dakota County Chambers. 651-452-9872
River Heights Chamber of Commerce 651-451-2266
Southern Twin Cities Association of Realtors 651-452-6611

Dakota County Communities

APPLE VALLEY (city). Covers a land area of 17.340 square miles and a water area of 0.381 square miles. Located at 44.74° N. Lat.; 93.20° W. Long. Elevation is 955 feet.
Population: 45,527 (2000); Race: 91.6% White, 1.9% Black, 3.3% Asian, 0.3% American Indian and Alaska Native, 1.9% Hispanic of any race, 2.2% two or more races (2000); Density: 2,625.5 persons per square mile (2000); Age: 29.7% under 18, 5.5% over 64 (2000); Marriage status: 24.8% never married, 64.1% now married, 3.0% widowed, 8.2% divorced (2000); Foreign born: 5.4% (2000); Ancestry (includes multiple ancestries): 37.7% German, 17.2% Norwegian, 14.3% Irish, 9.8% Swedish, 9.0% Other groups (2000).
Vital Statistics: Birth rate: 137.1 per 10,000 population (1998)
Economy: Manufactures concrete, hand tools. Agriculture: grain, soybeans; livestock, dairying, poultry. Unemployment rate: 2.6% (11/2002); Total civilian labor force: 30,080 (11/2002); Single-family building permits issued: 226 (2001) / 184 (2000); Multi-family building permits issued: 376 (2001) / 451 (2000); Employment by occupation: 18.3% management, 22.3% professional, 11.2% services, 32.0% sales, 0.1% farming, 6.8% construction, 9.3% production (2000).
Income: Per capita income: $29,477 (2000); Median household income: $69,752 (2000); Poverty rate: 2.1% (2000).
Taxes: Total city taxes per capita: $288 (2000); City property taxes per capita: $242 (2000).
Education: High school graduation rate: 95.4% (2000); College graduation rate: 41.0% (2000).
Housing: Homeownership rate: 87.9% (2000); Median home value: $154,300 (2000); Median rent: $694 per month (2000); Median age of housing: 16 years (2000).
Safety: Violent crime rate: 9.3 per 10,000 population; Property crime rate: 289.9 per 10,000 population (2001).
Transportation: Commute to work: 91.7% car, 3.1% public transportation, 0.6% walk, 3.8% work from home (2000); Travel time to work: 22.7% less than 15 minutes, 43.1% 15 to 30 minutes, 25.6% 30 to 45 minutes, 5.8% 45 to 60 minutes, 2.8% 60 minutes or more (2000)

Additional Information Contacts

Apple Valley Chamber of Commerce 952-432-8422

BURNSVILLE (city). Covers a land area of 24.874 square miles and a water area of 1.862 square miles. Located at 44.75° N. Lat.; 93.28° W. Long. Elevation is 975 feet.
Population: 60,220 (2000); Race: 87.9% White, 3.6% Black, 3.4% Asian, 0.7% American Indian and Alaska Native, 3.0% Hispanic of any race, 2.6% two or more races (2000); Density: 2,421.0 persons per square mile (2000); Age: 26.3% under 18, 7.3% over 64 (2000); Marriage status: 29.1% never married, 57.1% now married, 3.5% widowed, 10.4% divorced (2000); Foreign born: 7.4% (2000); Ancestry (includes multiple ancestries): 35.2% German, 17.6% Norwegian, 15.2% Irish, 11.7% Other groups, 10.0% Swedish (2000).
Vital Statistics: Birth rate: 144.6 per 10,000 population (1998)
Economy: Manufacturing: machinery, labels, electronic equipment, pharmaceutical supplies, security cards and keys, computer equipment, bird food, machinery, aerospace parts, cigarettes, trade show displays, furniture; printing and publishing. Unemployment rate: 2.9% (11/2002); Total civilian labor force: 42,150 (11/2002); Single-family building permits issued: 128 (2001) / 118 (2000); Multi-family building permits issued: 0 (2001) / 41

(2000); Employment by occupation: 18.6% management, 20.8% professional, 13.0% services, 31.5% sales, 0.0% farming, 6.7% construction, 9.4% production (2000).
Income: Per capita income: $27,093 (2000); Median household income: $57,965 (2000); Poverty rate: 5.1% (2000).
Taxes: Total city taxes per capita: $368 (2000); City property taxes per capita: $327 (2000).
Education: High school graduation rate: 93.9% (2000); College graduation rate: 36.8% (2000).

School District(s)

Burnsville (PK-12)
2000 Enrollment: 11,529 952-707-2000

Housing: Homeownership rate: 68.3% (2000); Median home value: $155,900 (2000); Median rent: $737 per month (2000); Median age of housing: 20 years (2000).
Hospitals: Fairview Ridges Hospital (150 beds)
Safety: Violent crime rate: 7.4 per 10,000 population; Property crime rate: 192.7 per 10,000 population (2001).
Newspapers: Farmington This Week (1 x week); Rosemount This Week (1 x week); Eagan This Week (1 x week); Lakeville This Week (1 x week); Apple Valley This Week (1 x week); Eagan Sun-Current (1 x week); Dakota County Tribune (1 x week); Burnsville-Lakeville Sun Current (1 x week); Apple Valley-Rosemount-Sun-Current (1 x week); Burnsville This Week (1 x week)
Transportation: Commute to work: 91.7% car, 2.9% public transportation, 1.0% walk, 3.7% work from home (2000); Travel time to work: 27.0% less than 15 minutes, 41.5% 15 to 30 minutes, 23.7% 30 to 45 minutes, 5.3% 45 to 60 minutes, 2.5% 60 minutes or more (2000)

Additional Information Contacts

Burnsville Chamber of Commerce 952-435-6000
Burnsville Convention Bureau 952-898-5646

CASTLE ROCK (township). Covers a land area of 35.766 square miles and a water area of 0 square miles. Located at 44.58° N. Lat.; 93.10° W. Long.
Population: 1,495 (2000); Race: 97.9% White, 0.1% Black, 0.3% Asian, 0.1% American Indian and Alaska Native, 0.3% Hispanic of any race, 1.3% two or more races (2000); Density: 41.8 persons per square mile (2000); Age: 28.7% under 18, 8.1% over 64 (2000); Marriage status: 24.5% never married, 65.4% now married, 2.6% widowed, 7.5% divorced (2000); Foreign born: 1.1% (2000); Ancestry (includes multiple ancestries): 48.0% German, 19.9% Norwegian, 12.9% Irish, 7.6% English, 7.2% Swedish (2000).
Economy: Single-family building permits issued: 3 (2001) / 2 (2000); Multi-family building permits issued: 0 (2001) / 0 (2000); Employment by occupation: 14.3% management, 13.9% professional, 12.7% services, 28.2% sales, 1.6% farming, 14.2% construction, 15.1% production (2000).
Income: Per capita income: $23,334 (2000); Median household income: $59,479 (2000); Poverty rate: 5.3% (2000).
Taxes: Total city taxes per capita: $151 (1997); City property taxes per capita: $138 (1997).
Education: High school graduation rate: 91.5% (2000); College graduation rate: 16.5% (2000).
Housing: Homeownership rate: 89.9% (2000); Median home value: $178,100 (2000); Median rent: $508 per month (2000); Median age of housing: 28 years (2000).
Transportation: Commute to work: 87.9% car, 0.7% public transportation, 1.6% walk, 9.6% work from home (2000); Travel time to work: 28.6% less than 15 minutes, 31.7% 15 to 30 minutes, 23.5% 30 to 45 minutes, 11.0% 45 to 60 minutes, 5.1% 60 minutes or more (2000)

COATES (city). Covers a land area of 1.395 square miles and a water area of 0 square miles. Located at 44.71° N. Lat.; 93.03° W. Long. Elevation is 890 feet.
Population: 163 (2000); Race: 96.7% White, 0.0% Black, 0.0% Asian, 0.0% American Indian and Alaska Native, 2.0% Hispanic of any race, 3.3% two or more races (2000); Density: 116.9 persons per square mile (2000); Age: 19.9% under 18, 6.6% over 64 (2000); Marriage status: 40.9% never married, 47.4% now married, 5.8% widowed, 5.8% divorced (2000); Foreign born: 0.0% (2000); Ancestry (includes multiple ancestries): 53.0% German, 17.2% Irish, 14.6% Norwegian, 8.6% Polish, 7.3% Swedish (2000).
Economy: Agricultural area: grains, livestock; dairying. Mississippi River to Northeast. Single-family building permits issued: 0 (2001) / 0 (2000); Multi-family building permits issued: 0 (2001) / 0 (2000); Employment by occupation: 6.6% management, 1.9% professional, 6.6% services, 27.4% sales, 0.0% farming, 20.8% construction, 36.8% production (2000).
Income: Per capita income: $20,348 (2000); Median household income: $48,958 (2000); Poverty rate: 7.9% (2000).
Taxes: Total city taxes per capita: $121 (1997); City property taxes per capita: $115 (1997).
Education: High school graduation rate: 87.9% (2000); College graduation rate: 7.7% (2000).
Housing: Homeownership rate: 63.5% (2000); Median home value: $109,700 (2000); Median rent: $470 per month (2000); Median age of housing: 44 years (2000).
Transportation: Commute to work: 80.6% car, 0.0% public transportation, 8.2% walk, 8.2% work from home (2000); Travel time to work: 23.3% less than 15 minutes, 31.1% 15 to 30 minutes, 21.1% 30 to 45 minutes, 5.6% 45 to 60 minutes, 18.9% 60 minutes or more (2000)

DOUGLAS (township). Covers a land area of 33.898 square miles and a water area of 0 square miles. Located at 44.59° N. Lat.; 92.84° W. Long.
Population: 760 (2000); Race: 98.5% White, 0.0% Black, 0.0% Asian, 1.5% American Indian and Alaska Native, 0.0% Hispanic of any race, 0.0% two or more races (2000); Density: 22.4 persons per square mile (2000); Age: 33.8% under 18, 10.3% over 64 (2000); Marriage status: 21.6% never married, 66.9% now married, 5.0% widowed, 6.5% divorced (2000); Foreign born: 0.5% (2000); Ancestry (includes multiple ancestries): 67.6% German, 18.1% Irish, 12.0% Swedish, 9.7% Norwegian, 5.2% English (2000).
Economy: Single-family building permits issued: 3 (2001) / 5 (2000); Multi-family building permits issued: 0 (2001) / 0 (2000); Employment by occupation: 20.1% management, 15.7% professional, 10.6% services, 19.5% sales, 5.1% farming, 11.9% construction, 17.1% production (2000).
Income: Per capita income: $22,319 (2000); Median household income: $60,536 (2000); Poverty rate: 3.7% (2000).
Taxes: Total city taxes per capita: $92 (1997); City property taxes per capita: $91 (1997).
Education: High school graduation rate: 85.9% (2000); College graduation rate: 14.7% (2000).
Housing: Homeownership rate: 90.8% (2000); Median home value: $172,900 (2000); Median rent: $575 per month (2000); Median age of housing: 25 years (2000).
Transportation: Commute to work: 79.6% car, 0.5% public transportation, 4.1% walk, 15.8% work from home (2000); Travel time to work: 30.7% less than 15 minutes, 31.7% 15 to 30 minutes, 21.4% 30 to 45 minutes, 7.4% 45 to 60 minutes, 8.7% 60 minutes or more (2000)

EAGAN (city). Covers a land area of 32.302 square miles and a water area of 1.126 square miles. Located at 44.81° N. Lat.; 93.16° W. Long. Elevation is 955 feet.
Population: 63,557 (2000); Race: 87.6% White, 3.9% Black, 4.9% Asian, 0.4% American Indian and Alaska Native, 2.1% Hispanic of any race, 2.2% two or more races (2000); Density: 1,967.6 persons per square mile (2000); Age: 29.7% under 18, 4.1% over 64 (2000); Marriage status: 26.6% never married, 62.1% now married, 2.0% widowed, 9.3% divorced (2000); Foreign born: 7.7% (2000); Ancestry (includes multiple ancestries): 36.5% German, 15.0% Norwegian, 14.0% Irish, 13.0% Other groups, 9.7% Swedish (2000).
Vital Statistics: Birth rate: 160.6 per 10,000 population (1998)
Economy: Manufacturing: consumer goods, construction materials, printing and publishing, computers, fixtures; steel fabricating. Minnesota Zoo to South. Unemployment rate: 2.7% (11/2002); Total civilian labor force: 42,305 (11/2002); Single-family building permits issued: 216 (2001) / 259 (2000); Multi-family building permits issued: 19 (2001) / 73 (2000); Employment by occupation: 22.0% management, 27.0% professional, 9.6% services, 27.7% sales, 0.1% farming, 5.3% construction, 8.4% production (2000).
Income: Per capita income: $30,167 (2000); Median household income: $67,388 (2000); Poverty rate: 2.9% (2000).
Taxes: Total city taxes per capita: $243 (2000); City property taxes per capita: $214 (2000).
Education: High school graduation rate: 96.0% (2000); College graduation rate: 47.7% (2000).

Two-year College(s)

Rasmussen College-Eagan (Private, For-profit)
2001 Enrollment: 351 651-687-9000
2001 Tuition: In-state $7,380; Out-of-state $7,380

Housing: Homeownership rate: 74.8% (2000); Median home value: $164,500 (2000); Median rent: $760 per month (2000); Median age of housing: 15 years (2000).
Safety: Violent crime rate: 8.1 per 10,000 population; Property crime rate: 286.1 per 10,000 population (2001).
Transportation: Commute to work: 92.4% car, 2.2% public transportation, 1.0% walk, 4.0% work from home (2000); Travel time to work: 27.9% less

than 15 minutes, 41.7% 15 to 30 minutes, 23.4% 30 to 45 minutes, 4.3% 45 to 60 minutes, 2.7% 60 minutes or more (2000)
Additional Information Contacts
Eagan Convention & Visitors Bureau 651-452-4188
Northern Dakota County Chambers 651-452-9872
Southern Twin Cities Association of Realtors 651-452-6611

EMPIRE (township). Aka Empire City. Covers a land area of 33.756 square miles and a water area of 0 square miles. Located at 44.67° N. Lat.; 93.09° W. Long. Elevation is 859 feet.
Population: 1,638 (2000); Race: 99.0% White, 0.0% Black, 0.0% Asian, 0.0% American Indian and Alaska Native, 0.8% Hispanic of any race, 1.0% two or more races (2000); Density: 48.5 persons per square mile (2000); Age: 32.0% under 18, 3.8% over 64 (2000); Marriage status: 23.0% never married, 68.8% now married, 4.1% widowed, 4.1% divorced (2000); Foreign born: 1.9% (2000); Ancestry (includes multiple ancestries): 36.3% German, 29.0% Norwegian, 16.1% Irish, 6.3% English, 5.7% French (except Basque) (2000).
Economy: Single-family building permits issued: 18 (2001) / 7 (2000); Multi-family building permits issued: 0 (2001) / 0 (2000); Employment by occupation: 12.4% management, 15.9% professional, 14.0% services, 25.5% sales, 3.5% farming, 14.6% construction, 14.0% production (2000).
Income: Per capita income: $21,802 (2000); Median household income: $68,500 (2000); Poverty rate: 6.6% (2000).
Taxes: Total city taxes per capita: $221 (2000); City property taxes per capita: $189 (2000).
Education: High school graduation rate: 91.5% (2000); College graduation rate: 18.3% (2000).
Housing: Homeownership rate: 90.7% (2000); Median home value: $159,600 (2000); Median rent: $696 per month (2000); Median age of housing: 23 years (2000).
Transportation: Commute to work: 94.6% car, 0.0% public transportation, 1.8% walk, 2.8% work from home (2000); Travel time to work: 33.6% less than 15 minutes, 26.3% 15 to 30 minutes, 24.7% 30 to 45 minutes, 12.8% 45 to 60 minutes, 2.6% 60 minutes or more (2000)

EUREKA (township). Covers a land area of 35.353 square miles and a water area of 0.511 square miles. Located at 44.58° N. Lat.; 93.22° W. Long.
Population: 1,490 (2000); Race: 97.6% White, 0.0% Black, 0.7% Asian, 0.3% American Indian and Alaska Native, 1.1% Hispanic of any race, 0.3% two or more races (2000); Density: 42.1 persons per square mile (2000); Age: 29.5% under 18, 6.5% over 64 (2000); Marriage status: 22.8% never married, 67.5% now married, 3.5% widowed, 6.1% divorced (2000); Foreign born: 1.4% (2000); Ancestry (includes multiple ancestries): 43.3% German, 23.0% Norwegian, 11.2% Irish, 8.8% Swedish, 5.6% English (2000).
Economy: Single-family building permits issued: 13 (2001) / 11 (2000); Multi-family building permits issued: 0 (2001) / 0 (2000); Employment by occupation: 14.0% management, 15.6% professional, 13.8% services, 29.8% sales, 0.7% farming, 14.0% construction, 12.1% production (2000).
Income: Per capita income: $26,636 (2000); Median household income: $66,875 (2000); Poverty rate: 1.3% (2000).
Taxes: Total city taxes per capita: $112 (1997); City property taxes per capita: $107 (1997).
Education: High school graduation rate: 93.5% (2000); College graduation rate: 21.3% (2000).
Housing: Homeownership rate: 93.2% (2000); Median home value: $197,400 (2000); Median rent: $681 per month (2000); Median age of housing: 26 years (2000).
Transportation: Commute to work: 88.0% car, 1.5% public transportation, 0.9% walk, 8.5% work from home (2000); Travel time to work: 28.1% less than 15 minutes, 33.6% 15 to 30 minutes, 27.3% 30 to 45 minutes, 6.9% 45 to 60 minutes, 4.1% 60 minutes or more (2000)

FARMINGTON (city). Covers a land area of 12.541 square miles and a water area of 0 square miles. Located at 44.64° N. Lat.; 93.15° W. Long. Elevation is 904 feet.
Population: 12,365 (2000); Race: 96.4% White, 1.0% Black, 0.9% Asian, 0.0% American Indian and Alaska Native, 2.5% Hispanic of any race, 1.0% two or more races (2000); Density: 986.0 persons per square mile (2000); Age: 33.3% under 18, 5.8% over 64 (2000); Marriage status: 21.2% never married, 67.4% now married, 3.4% widowed, 8.0% divorced (2000); Foreign born: 2.6% (2000); Ancestry (includes multiple ancestries): 42.1% German, 16.6% Norwegian, 13.1% Irish, 7.4% Swedish, 6.3% Other groups (2000).
Economy: Shipping point for agricultural area on South fringe of Twin Cities region: dairying; grain, soybeans; poultry, livestock. Manufacturing: electrical equipment, plastic products. Single-family building permits issued: 362 (2001) / 302 (2000); Multi-family building permits issued: 122 (2001) / 50 (2000); Employment by occupation: 13.8% management, 18.2% professional, 11.3% services, 26.7% sales, 0.4% farming, 13.0% construction, 16.8% production (2000).
Income: Per capita income: $22,281 (2000); Median household income: $61,864 (2000); Poverty rate: 2.4% (2000).
Taxes: Total city taxes per capita: $318 (1997); City property taxes per capita: $237 (1997).
Education: High school graduation rate: 90.4% (2000); College graduation rate: 23.6% (2000).

School District(s)
Farmington (PK-12)
2000 Enrollment: 4,792 651-463-5001
Housing: Homeownership rate: 87.9% (2000); Median home value: $146,200 (2000); Median rent: $541 per month (2000); Median age of housing: 10 years (2000).
Hospitals: Trinity Hospital (112 beds)
Safety: Violent crime rate: 12.0 per 10,000 population; Property crime rate: 188.8 per 10,000 population (2001).
Newspapers: Rosemount Town Pages (1 x week); Farmington Independent (1 x week)
Transportation: Commute to work: 94.7% car, 0.9% public transportation, 1.3% walk, 2.5% work from home (2000); Travel time to work: 24.4% less than 15 minutes, 33.2% 15 to 30 minutes, 28.3% 30 to 45 minutes, 11.0% 45 to 60 minutes, 3.0% 60 minutes or more (2000)
Additional Information Contacts
Farmington Area Chamber of Commerce 651-460-6444
Farmington Chamber of Commerce 651-460-2221

GREENVALE (township). Covers a land area of 29.715 square miles and a water area of 0.012 square miles. Located at 44.51° N. Lat.; 93.21° W. Long.
Population: 684 (2000); Race: 99.3% White, 0.0% Black, 0.0% Asian, 0.0% American Indian and Alaska Native, 0.0% Hispanic of any race, 0.7% two or more races (2000); Density: 23.0 persons per square mile (2000); Age: 30.6% under 18, 4.9% over 64 (2000); Marriage status: 24.3% never married, 68.6% now married, 1.5% widowed, 5.6% divorced (2000); Foreign born: 1.5% (2000); Ancestry (includes multiple ancestries): 41.7% German, 30.6% Norwegian, 19.2% Irish, 8.3% Czech, 7.0% Swedish (2000).
Economy: Single-family building permits issued: 5 (2001) / 10 (2000); Multi-family building permits issued: 0 (2001) / 0 (2000); Employment by occupation: 13.8% management, 18.3% professional, 14.3% services, 27.1% sales, 1.3% farming, 13.0% construction, 12.3% production (2000).
Income: Per capita income: $23,398 (2000); Median household income: $66,818 (2000); Poverty rate: 2.9% (2000).
Taxes: Total city taxes per capita: $116 (1997); City property taxes per capita: $94 (1997).
Education: High school graduation rate: 91.0% (2000); College graduation rate: 25.4% (2000).
Housing: Homeownership rate: 92.4% (2000); Median home value: $203,300 (2000); Median rent: $313 per month (2000); Median age of housing: 30 years (2000).
Transportation: Commute to work: 87.8% car, 0.5% public transportation, 2.1% walk, 9.6% work from home (2000); Travel time to work: 25.0% less than 15 minutes, 35.3% 15 to 30 minutes, 24.1% 30 to 45 minutes, 10.9% 45 to 60 minutes, 4.6% 60 minutes or more (2000)

HAMPTON (city). Covers a land area of 1.343 square miles and a water area of 0 square miles. Located at 44.61° N. Lat.; 92.99° W. Long. Elevation is 980 feet.
Population: 434 (2000); Race: 99.2% White, 0.0% Black, 0.0% Asian, 0.0% American Indian and Alaska Native, 1.2% Hispanic of any race, 0.4% two or more races (2000); Density: 323.2 persons per square mile (2000); Age: 36.8% under 18, 10.4% over 64 (2000); Marriage status: 26.9% never married, 64.0% now married, 3.9% widowed, 5.1% divorced (2000); Foreign born: 0.4% (2000); Ancestry (includes multiple ancestries): 50.3% German, 13.9% Norwegian, 11.9% Irish, 9.4% Swedish, 6.3% Scandinavian (2000).
Economy: Single-family building permits issued: 60 (2001) / 0 (2000); Multi-family building permits issued: 0 (2001) / 0 (2000); Employment by occupation: 12.3% management, 11.0% professional, 22.9% services, 16.5% sales, 0.0% farming, 20.8% construction, 16.5% production (2000).
Income: Per capita income: $17,121 (2000); Median household income: $53,438 (2000); Poverty rate: 5.8% (2000).
Taxes: Total city taxes per capita: $143 (1997); City property taxes per capita: $113 (1997).
Education: High school graduation rate: 86.2% (2000); College graduation rate: 11.6% (2000).

Housing: Homeownership rate: 83.6% (2000); Median home value: $120,300 (2000); Median rent: $450 per month (2000); Median age of housing: 43 years (2000).
Transportation: Commute to work: 93.1% car, 0.0% public transportation, 3.0% walk, 1.7% work from home (2000); Travel time to work: 16.2% less than 15 minutes, 41.7% 15 to 30 minutes, 31.1% 30 to 45 minutes, 7.0% 45 to 60 minutes, 3.9% 60 minutes or more (2000)

HAMPTON (township). Covers a land area of 34.279 square miles and a water area of 0 square miles. Located at 44.60° N. Lat.; 92.98° W. Long. Elevation is 980 feet.
Population: 986 (2000); Race: 97.6% White, 0.2% Black, 0.0% Asian, 1.9% American Indian and Alaska Native, 1.1% Hispanic of any race, 0.3% two or more races (2000); Density: 28.8 persons per square mile (2000); Age: 29.8% under 18, 9.1% over 64 (2000); Marriage status: 21.7% never married, 71.1% now married, 1.4% widowed, 5.8% divorced (2000); Foreign born: 1.0% (2000); Ancestry (includes multiple ancestries): 60.6% German, 13.9% Irish, 10.3% Norwegian, 9.6% Swedish, 6.8% Polish (2000).
Economy: Grain, soybeans; livestock, poultry; dairying. Manufacturing: meat processing; fertilizers. Single-family building permits issued: 11 (2001) / 3 (2000); Multi-family building permits issued: 0 (2001) / 0 (2000); Employment by occupation: 21.4% management, 12.9% professional, 9.5% services, 26.0% sales, 0.0% farming, 14.0% construction, 16.3% production (2000).
Income: Per capita income: $25,576 (2000); Median household income: $62,292 (2000); Poverty rate: 2.2% (2000).
Taxes: Total city taxes per capita: $112 (1997); City property taxes per capita: $103 (1997).
Education: High school graduation rate: 87.0% (2000); College graduation rate: 14.3% (2000).
Housing: Homeownership rate: 89.0% (2000); Median home value: $201,200 (2000); Median rent: $563 per month (2000); Median age of housing: 25 years (2000).
Transportation: Commute to work: 90.5% car, 0.0% public transportation, 1.7% walk, 6.9% work from home (2000); Travel time to work: 13.5% less than 15 minutes, 41.3% 15 to 30 minutes, 30.8% 30 to 45 minutes, 11.0% 45 to 60 minutes, 3.5% 60 minutes or more (2000)

HASTINGS (city). Covers a land area of 10.123 square miles and a water area of 0.867 square miles. Located at 44.73° N. Lat.; 92.85° W. Long. Elevation is 730 feet.
History: Hastings was first called Oliver's Grove for Lieutenant William G. Oliver, whose troops camped here in 1819. One of the soldiers, Joseph R. Brown, came back in 1833 to establish a trading post.
Population: 18,204 (2000); Race: 96.9% White, 0.7% Black, 0.6% Asian, 0.3% American Indian and Alaska Native, 1.0% Hispanic of any race, 1.1% two or more races (2000); Density: 1,798.2 persons per square mile (2000); Age: 26.9% under 18, 12.1% over 64 (2000); Marriage status: 25.4% never married, 59.1% now married, 5.5% widowed, 10.0% divorced (2000); Foreign born: 1.5% (2000); Ancestry (includes multiple ancestries): 46.8% German, 15.9% Norwegian, 15.6% Irish, 9.6% Swedish, 5.2% English (2000).
Economy: Single-family building permits issued: 111 (2001) / 115 (2000); Multi-family building permits issued: 197 (2001) / 20 (2000); Employment by occupation: 11.6% management, 19.3% professional, 14.6% services, 26.1% sales, 0.4% farming, 12.7% construction, 15.4% production (2000).
Income: Per capita income: $22,075 (2000); Median household income: $53,145 (2000); Poverty rate: 4.9% (2000).
Taxes: Total city taxes per capita: $304 (1997); City property taxes per capita: $281 (1997).
Education: High school graduation rate: 87.7% (2000); College graduation rate: 20.2% (2000).

School District(s)

Hastings (PK-12)
2000 Enrollment: 5,187 651-437-6111
Housing: Homeownership rate: 76.5% (2000); Median home value: $131,700 (2000); Median rent: $546 per month (2000); Median age of housing: 28 years (2000).
Hospitals: Regina Medical Center (57 beds)
Newspapers: Hastings Star Gazette (1 x week); The Free Press (1 x week)
Transportation: Commute to work: 93.2% car, 0.5% public transportation, 2.3% walk, 2.9% work from home (2000); Travel time to work: 40.5% less than 15 minutes, 23.9% 15 to 30 minutes, 24.3% 30 to 45 minutes, 7.4% 45 to 60 minutes, 4.0% 60 minutes or more (2000)
Additional Information Contacts
Hastings Chamber of Commerce 651-437-6775
Hastings Tourism Bureau 651-437-7740

INVER GROVE HEIGHTS (city). Aka Inver Grove. Covers a land area of 28.639 square miles and a water area of 1.485 square miles. Located at 44.83° N. Lat.; 93.05° W. Long. Elevation is 850 feet.
Population: 29,751 (2000); Race: 91.5% White, 2.1% Black, 1.5% Asian, 0.6% American Indian and Alaska Native, 4.1% Hispanic of any race, 2.3% two or more races (2000); Density: 1,038.8 persons per square mile (2000); Age: 27.3% under 18, 7.9% over 64 (2000); Marriage status: 27.0% never married, 59.4% now married, 4.1% widowed, 9.5% divorced (2000); Foreign born: 4.4% (2000); Ancestry (includes multiple ancestries): 39.9% German, 15.3% Irish, 15.3% Norwegian, 9.9% Other groups, 7.9% Swedish (2000).
Vital Statistics: Birth rate: 138.5 per 10,000 population (1998)
Economy: Has benefited from the industrial and cultural growth of the greater Minneapolis-St. Paul area. Manufacturing: motor-vehicle and aircraft parts, asphalt, feeds, consumer goods, building materials, paper products, medical equipment. South St. Paul Airport to Northeast. Unemployment rate: 2.6% (11/2002); Total civilian labor force: 19,557 (11/2002); Single-family building permits issued: 159 (2001) / 204 (2000); Multi-family building permits issued: 159 (2001) / 4 (2000); Employment by occupation: 15.4% management, 22.7% professional, 11.5% services, 29.4% sales, 0.1% farming, 9.1% construction, 11.9% production (2000).
Income: Per capita income: $25,493 (2000); Median household income: $59,090 (2000); Poverty rate: 4.2% (2000).
Taxes: Total city taxes per capita: $287 (2000); City property taxes per capita: $256 (2000).
Education: High school graduation rate: 92.0% (2000); College graduation rate: 29.6% (2000).

School District(s)

Inver Grove (PK-12)
2000 Enrollment: 4,047 651-306-7825

Two-year College(s)

Inver Hills Community College (Public)
2001 Enrollment: 4,545 651-450-8500
2001 Tuition: In-state $2,473; Out-of-state $4,946
Housing: Homeownership rate: 77.4% (2000); Median home value: $144,800 (2000); Median rent: $731 per month (2000); Median age of housing: 17 years (2000).
Safety: Violent crime rate: 21.9 per 10,000 population; Property crime rate: 321.6 per 10,000 population (2001).
Transportation: Commute to work: 94.4% car, 2.2% public transportation, 0.7% walk, 2.3% work from home (2000); Travel time to work: 26.8% less than 15 minutes, 46.1% 15 to 30 minutes, 19.3% 30 to 45 minutes, 4.9% 45 to 60 minutes, 2.8% 60 minutes or more (2000)

LAKEVILLE (city). Covers a land area of 36.169 square miles and a water area of 1.367 square miles. Located at 44.69° N. Lat.; 93.24° W. Long. Elevation is 974 feet.
Population: 43,128 (2000); Race: 94.5% White, 1.0% Black, 1.8% Asian, 0.4% American Indian and Alaska Native, 1.3% Hispanic of any race, 1.6% two or more races (2000); Density: 1,192.4 persons per square mile (2000); Age: 36.1% under 18, 3.0% over 64 (2000); Marriage status: 20.3% never married, 70.5% now married, 1.4% widowed, 7.7% divorced (2000); Foreign born: 3.0% (2000); Ancestry (includes multiple ancestries): 41.2% German, 19.6% Norwegian, 15.3% Irish, 10.0% Swedish, 7.9% English (2000).
Vital Statistics: Birth rate: 130.3 per 10,000 population (1998)
Economy: Agricultural area: grain, soybeans; livestock, poultry; dairying. Manufacturing: patterns and prototypes, machinery, paper products, building materials, plastic products, furniture; millwork, food and beverage processing, printing and publishing. Airlake Park Airport to South. Unemployment rate: 2.1% (11/2002); Total civilian labor force: 26,146 (11/2002); Single-family building permits issued: 513 (2001) / 592 (2000); Multi-family building permits issued: 20 (2001) / 21 (2000); Employment by occupation: 18.9% management, 19.0% professional, 9.2% services, 32.1% sales, 0.2% farming, 9.1% construction, 11.4% production (2000).
Income: Per capita income: $26,492 (2000); Median household income: $72,404 (2000); Poverty rate: 2.0% (2000).
Taxes: Total city taxes per capita: $207 (2000); City property taxes per capita: $152 (2000).
Education: High school graduation rate: 95.6% (2000); College graduation rate: 35.7% (2000).

School District(s)

Lakeville (PK-12)
2000 Enrollment: 9,481 952-469-7100

Housing: Homeownership rate: 91.4% (2000); Median home value: $170,400 (2000); Median rent: $765 per month (2000); Median age of housing: 11 years (2000).
Safety: Violent crime rate: 5.7 per 10,000 population; Property crime rate: 198.0 per 10,000 population (2001).
Transportation: Commute to work: 93.3% car, 1.5% public transportation, 0.6% walk, 3.9% work from home (2000); Travel time to work: 22.9% less than 15 minutes, 40.3% 15 to 30 minutes, 26.7% 30 to 45 minutes, 6.6% 45 to 60 minutes, 3.6% 60 minutes or more (2000)
Additional Information Contacts
Lakeville Area Chamber of Commerce 952-469-2020

LILYDALE (city). Covers a land area of 0.730 square miles and a water area of 0.183 square miles. Located at 44.90° N. Lat.; 93.13° W. Long. Elevation is 700 feet.
Population: 552 (2000); Race: 85.3% White, 0.0% Black, 12.4% Asian, 1.1% American Indian and Alaska Native, 1.9% Hispanic of any race, 0.0% two or more races (2000); Density: 756.4 persons per square mile (2000); Age: 8.6% under 18, 39.1% over 64 (2000); Marriage status: 23.0% never married, 55.4% now married, 15.1% widowed, 6.6% divorced (2000); Foreign born: 16.4% (2000); Ancestry (includes multiple ancestries): 22.8% German, 19.6% Other groups, 17.9% Irish, 10.7% Norwegian, 10.7% Swedish (2000).
Economy: Single-family building permits issued: 20 (2001) / 15 (2000); Multi-family building permits issued: 4 (2001) / 0 (2000); Employment by occupation: 24.2% management, 29.5% professional, 14.9% services, 27.8% sales, 0.0% farming, 1.7% construction, 2.0% production (2000).
Income: Per capita income: $42,724 (2000); Median household income: $54,792 (2000); Poverty rate: 2.9% (2000).
Taxes: Total city taxes per capita: $363 (1997); City property taxes per capita: $330 (1997).
Education: High school graduation rate: 96.5% (2000); College graduation rate: 47.6% (2000).
Housing: Homeownership rate: 64.7% (2000); Median home value: $245,500 (2000); Median rent: $1,114 per month (2000); Median age of housing: 20 years (2000).
Transportation: Commute to work: 88.4% car, 0.0% public transportation, 0.7% walk, 10.3% work from home (2000); Travel time to work: 38.4% less than 15 minutes, 39.1% 15 to 30 minutes, 17.7% 30 to 45 minutes, 1.5% 45 to 60 minutes, 3.3% 60 minutes or more (2000)

MARSHAN (township). Covers a land area of 34.504 square miles and a water area of 0 square miles. Located at 44.68° N. Lat.; 92.86° W. Long.
Population: 1,263 (2000); Race: 99.1% White, 0.3% Black, 0.4% Asian, 0.0% American Indian and Alaska Native, 0.2% Hispanic of any race, 0.2% two or more races (2000); Density: 36.6 persons per square mile (2000); Age: 35.0% under 18, 5.2% over 64 (2000); Marriage status: 24.3% never married, 67.6% now married, 2.1% widowed, 5.9% divorced (2000); Foreign born: 1.7% (2000); Ancestry (includes multiple ancestries): 52.0% German, 16.1% Irish, 14.7% Norwegian, 9.0% Swedish, 4.3% French (except Basque) (2000).
Economy: Single-family building permits issued: 5 (2001) / 4 (2000); Multi-family building permits issued: 0 (2001) / 0 (2000); Employment by occupation: 17.8% management, 16.1% professional, 14.1% services, 23.2% sales, 2.1% farming, 11.1% construction, 15.6% production (2000).
Income: Per capita income: $26,278 (2000); Median household income: $62,171 (2000); Poverty rate: 6.6% (2000).
Taxes: Total city taxes per capita: $75 (1997); City property taxes per capita: $72 (1997).
Education: High school graduation rate: 89.5% (2000); College graduation rate: 22.7% (2000).
Housing: Homeownership rate: 87.9% (2000); Median home value: $198,500 (2000); Median rent: $428 per month (2000); Median age of housing: 24 years (2000).
Transportation: Commute to work: 87.8% car, 0.0% public transportation, 4.4% walk, 6.5% work from home (2000); Travel time to work: 30.7% less than 15 minutes, 30.7% 15 to 30 minutes, 18.0% 30 to 45 minutes, 16.6% 45 to 60 minutes, 4.0% 60 minutes or more (2000)

MENDOTA (city). Covers a land area of 0.188 square miles and a water area of 0 square miles. Located at 44.88° N. Lat.; 93.16° W. Long. Elevation is 719 feet.
History: The site of Mendota was chosen for settlement in the early 1800's. First known as St. Peter's, it served as a meeting place for traders and trappers. Jean Baptiste Faribault moved his family to the settlement in 1822. In 1837 the name was changed to Mendota, meaning "meeting of the waters," referring to the Mississippi and Minnesota Rivers which meet here.
Population: 197 (2000); Race: 87.7% White, 0.0% Black, 1.9% Asian, 4.5% American Indian and Alaska Native, 1.3% Hispanic of any race, 3.9% two or more races (2000); Density: 1,045.8 persons per square mile (2000); Age: 18.2% under 18, 9.7% over 64 (2000); Marriage status: 29.4% never married, 46.8% now married, 7.1% widowed, 16.7% divorced (2000); Foreign born: 3.2% (2000); Ancestry (includes multiple ancestries): 26.0% German, 16.9% Irish, 13.0% Swedish, 11.7% Other groups, 10.4% United States or American (2000).
Economy: Single-family building permits issued: 1 (2001) / 0 (2000); Multi-family building permits issued: 0 (2001) / 0 (2000); Employment by occupation: 3.9% management, 19.5% professional, 20.8% services, 35.1% sales, 0.0% farming, 9.1% construction, 11.7% production (2000).
Income: Per capita income: $26,745 (2000); Median household income: $45,938 (2000); Poverty rate: 1.3% (2000).
Taxes: Total city taxes per capita: $374 (1997); City property taxes per capita: $319 (1997).
Education: High school graduation rate: 87.6% (2000); College graduation rate: 10.6% (2000).
Housing: Homeownership rate: 81.2% (2000); Median home value: $101,300 (2000); Median rent: $509 per month (2000); Median age of housing: 50 years (2000).
Transportation: Commute to work: 88.3% car, 0.0% public transportation, 6.5% walk, 0.0% work from home (2000); Travel time to work: 53.2% less than 15 minutes, 27.3% 15 to 30 minutes, 11.7% 30 to 45 minutes, 5.2% 45 to 60 minutes, 2.6% 60 minutes or more (2000)

MENDOTA HEIGHTS (city). Covers a land area of 9.355 square miles and a water area of 0.713 square miles. Located at 44.88° N. Lat.; 93.13° W. Long. Elevation is 900 feet.
Population: 11,434 (2000); Race: 95.3% White, 0.6% Black, 2.1% Asian, 0.1% American Indian and Alaska Native, 2.2% Hispanic of any race, 1.0% two or more races (2000); Density: 1,222.2 persons per square mile (2000); Age: 27.7% under 18, 14.3% over 64 (2000); Marriage status: 21.3% never married, 68.1% now married, 4.8% widowed, 5.8% divorced (2000); Foreign born: 3.8% (2000); Ancestry (includes multiple ancestries): 36.3% German, 21.7% Irish, 10.4% Norwegian, 10.1% English, 7.6% Swedish (2000).
Economy: Railroad junction. Manufacturing: rubber products, concrete, printing, medical equipment, food, pharmaceuticals, machinery. Single-family building permits issued: 36 (2001) / 25 (2000); Multi-family building permits issued: 0 (2001) / 24 (2000); Employment by occupation: 24.5% management, 29.9% professional, 9.1% services, 26.0% sales, 0.2% farming, 4.6% construction, 5.7% production (2000).
Income: Per capita income: $39,407 (2000); Median household income: $81,155 (2000); Poverty rate: 1.9% (2000).
Taxes: Total city taxes per capita: $426 (2000); City property taxes per capita: $407 (2000).
Education: High school graduation rate: 96.4% (2000); College graduation rate: 55.0% (2000).

School District(s)
West Saint Paul-Mendota Hts.-Eagan (PK-12)
2000 Enrollment: 4,837 651-681-2396

Two-year College(s)
Brown Institute Ltd (Private, For-profit)
2001 Enrollment: 2,420 612-905-3400

Housing: Homeownership rate: 92.4% (2000); Median home value: $209,000 (2000); Median rent: $788 per month (2000); Median age of housing: 21 years (2000).
Safety: Violent crime rate: 4.3 per 10,000 population; Property crime rate: 129.8 per 10,000 population (2001).
Transportation: Commute to work: 92.8% car, 1.7% public transportation, 0.3% walk, 4.8% work from home (2000); Travel time to work: 34.8% less than 15 minutes, 47.8% 15 to 30 minutes, 12.3% 30 to 45 minutes, 2.4% 45 to 60 minutes, 2.7% 60 minutes or more (2000)

MIESVILLE (city). Covers a land area of 1.804 square miles and a water area of 0 square miles. Located at 44.59° N. Lat.; 92.80° W. Long. Elevation is 945 feet.
Population: 135 (2000); Race: 100.0% White, 0.0% Black, 0.0% Asian, 0.0% American Indian and Alaska Native, 0.0% Hispanic of any race, 0.0% two or more races (2000); Density: 74.8 persons per square mile (2000); Age: 24.4% under 18, 8.4% over 64 (2000); Marriage status: 21.9% never married, 68.6% now married, 2.9% widowed, 6.7% divorced (2000); Foreign born: 0.0% (2000); Ancestry (includes multiple ancestries): 77.1% German, 21.4%

Irish, 6.1% French (except Basque), 4.6% United States or American, 3.8% Norwegian (2000).
Economy: Agriculture: grain; livestock; dairying. Single-family building permits issued: 1 (2001) / 0 (2000); Multi-family building permits issued: 0 (2001) / 0 (2000); Employment by occupation: 22.4% management, 10.5% professional, 22.4% services, 28.9% sales, 0.0% farming, 7.9% construction, 7.9% production (2000).
Income: Per capita income: $19,931 (2000); Median household income: $53,750 (2000); Poverty rate: 9.9% (2000).
Taxes: Total city taxes per capita: $138 (1997); City property taxes per capita: $116 (1997).
Education: High school graduation rate: 94.4% (2000); College graduation rate: 4.5% (2000).
Housing: Homeownership rate: 81.8% (2000); Median home value: $141,700 (2000); Median rent: $375 per month (2000); Median age of housing: 38 years (2000).
Transportation: Commute to work: 79.4% car, 0.0% public transportation, 8.8% walk, 11.8% work from home (2000); Travel time to work: 45.0% less than 15 minutes, 30.0% 15 to 30 minutes, 5.0% 30 to 45 minutes, 5.0% 45 to 60 minutes, 15.0% 60 minutes or more (2000)

NEW TRIER (city). Covers a land area of 0.196 square miles and a water area of 0 square miles. Located at 44.60° N. Lat.; 92.93° W. Long. Elevation is 980 feet.
Population: 116 (2000); Race: 100.0% White, 0.0% Black, 0.0% Asian, 0.0% American Indian and Alaska Native, 0.0% Hispanic of any race, 0.0% two or more races (2000); Density: 592.0 persons per square mile (2000); Age: 32.8% under 18, 9.0% over 64 (2000); Marriage status: 41.3% never married, 54.3% now married, 0.0% widowed, 4.3% divorced (2000); Foreign born: 0.0% (2000); Ancestry (includes multiple ancestries): 79.5% German, 26.2% Irish, 10.7% Polish, 7.4% English, 6.6% Norwegian (2000).
Economy: Agricultural area: grain; livestock; dairying. Single-family building permits issued: 1 (2001) / 0 (2000); Multi-family building permits issued: 0 (2001) / 0 (2000); Employment by occupation: 2.9% management, 21.4% professional, 18.6% services, 25.7% sales, 0.0% farming, 11.4% construction, 20.0% production (2000).
Income: Per capita income: $18,427 (2000); Median household income: $59,583 (2000); Poverty rate: 2.5% (2000).
Taxes: Total city taxes per capita: $120 (1997); City property taxes per capita: $60 (1997).
Education: High school graduation rate: 86.8% (2000); College graduation rate: 25.0% (2000).
Housing: Homeownership rate: 88.2% (2000); Median home value: $122,900 (2000); Median rent: $450 per month (2000); Median age of housing: 49 years (2000).
Transportation: Commute to work: 82.9% car, 0.0% public transportation, 2.9% walk, 11.4% work from home (2000); Travel time to work: 19.4% less than 15 minutes, 38.7% 15 to 30 minutes, 32.3% 30 to 45 minutes, 3.2% 45 to 60 minutes, 6.5% 60 minutes or more (2000)

NININGER (township). Covers a land area of 13.343 square miles and a water area of 3.869 square miles. Located at 44.74° N. Lat.; 92.92° W. Long.
Population: 865 (2000); Race: 97.8% White, 0.0% Black, 0.0% Asian, 0.0% American Indian and Alaska Native, 2.3% Hispanic of any race, 1.9% two or more races (2000); Density: 64.8 persons per square mile (2000); Age: 28.3% under 18, 8.1% over 64 (2000); Marriage status: 21.3% never married, 65.8% now married, 3.2% widowed, 9.6% divorced (2000); Foreign born: 0.6% (2000); Ancestry (includes multiple ancestries): 56.5% German, 13.4% Norwegian, 11.8% Irish, 8.5% French (except Basque), 5.5% English (2000).
Economy: Single-family building permits issued: 5 (2001) / 9 (2000); Multi-family building permits issued: 0 (2001) / 0 (2000); Employment by occupation: 14.3% management, 17.7% professional, 15.8% services, 26.0% sales, 2.3% farming, 12.6% construction, 11.1% production (2000).
Income: Per capita income: $27,337 (2000); Median household income: $72,955 (2000); Poverty rate: 2.8% (2000).
Taxes: Total city taxes per capita: $153 (1997); City property taxes per capita: $138 (1997).
Education: High school graduation rate: 94.0% (2000); College graduation rate: 21.3% (2000).
Housing: Homeownership rate: 93.0% (2000); Median home value: $176,600 (2000); Median rent: $450 per month (2000); Median age of housing: 26 years (2000).
Transportation: Commute to work: 90.9% car, 0.0% public transportation, 4.3% walk, 4.3% work from home (2000); Travel time to work: 31.5% less than 15 minutes, 32.9% 15 to 30 minutes, 20.6% 30 to 45 minutes, 12.7% 45 to 60 minutes, 2.2% 60 minutes or more (2000)

RANDOLPH (city). Covers a land area of 0.994 square miles and a water area of 0.039 square miles. Located at 44.52° N. Lat.; 93.01° W. Long. Elevation is 877 feet.
Population: 318 (2000); Race: 99.3% White, 0.0% Black, 0.7% Asian, 0.0% American Indian and Alaska Native, 0.7% Hispanic of any race, 0.0% two or more races (2000); Density: 320.1 persons per square mile (2000); Age: 33.0% under 18, 12.2% over 64 (2000); Marriage status: 21.4% never married, 64.1% now married, 5.0% widowed, 9.5% divorced (2000); Foreign born: 0.7% (2000); Ancestry (includes multiple ancestries): 59.4% German, 23.4% Norwegian, 18.8% Irish, 6.6% French (except Basque), 5.6% Other groups (2000).
Economy: Single-family building permits issued: 2 (2001) / 1 (2000); Multi-family building permits issued: 0 (2001) / 0 (2000); Employment by occupation: 9.2% management, 14.9% professional, 18.4% services, 22.0% sales, 1.4% farming, 19.1% construction, 14.9% production (2000).
Income: Per capita income: $16,947 (2000); Median household income: $42,750 (2000); Poverty rate: 4.3% (2000).
Taxes: Total city taxes per capita: $88 (1997); City property taxes per capita: $71 (1997).
Education: High school graduation rate: 79.0% (2000); College graduation rate: 18.8% (2000).

School District(s)

Randolph (PK-12)
2000 Enrollment: 424 507-263-2151
Housing: Homeownership rate: 87.2% (2000); Median home value: $103,100 (2000); Median rent: $475 per month (2000); Median age of housing: 51 years (2000).
Transportation: Commute to work: 93.6% car, 0.0% public transportation, 5.7% walk, 0.0% work from home (2000); Travel time to work: 27.7% less than 15 minutes, 41.8% 15 to 30 minutes, 18.4% 30 to 45 minutes, 6.4% 45 to 60 minutes, 5.7% 60 minutes or more (2000)

RANDOLPH (township). Covers a land area of 9.407 square miles and a water area of 1.213 square miles. Located at 44.52° N. Lat.; 92.96° W. Long. Elevation is 877 feet.
Population: 536 (2000); Race: 98.1% White, 0.0% Black, 0.0% Asian, 0.3% American Indian and Alaska Native, 2.6% Hispanic of any race, 1.2% two or more races (2000); Density: 57.0 persons per square mile (2000); Age: 25.6% under 18, 8.5% over 64 (2000); Marriage status: 21.1% never married, 69.3% now married, 3.9% widowed, 5.7% divorced (2000); Foreign born: 0.3% (2000); Ancestry (includes multiple ancestries): 44.3% German, 27.0% Norwegian, 17.0% Swedish, 11.0% Irish, 8.9% English (2000).
Economy: In grain, livestock area. Single-family building permits issued: 6 (2001) / 15 (2000); Multi-family building permits issued: 0 (2001) / 0 (2000); Employment by occupation: 12.9% management, 14.0% professional, 11.0% services, 30.1% sales, 3.6% farming, 12.3% construction, 16.2% production (2000).
Income: Per capita income: $28,277 (2000); Median household income: $62,222 (2000); Poverty rate: 3.1% (2000).
Taxes: Total city taxes per capita: $75 (1997); City property taxes per capita: $65 (1997).
Education: High school graduation rate: 92.4% (2000); College graduation rate: 20.4% (2000).
Housing: Homeownership rate: 93.3% (2000); Median home value: $185,800 (2000); Median rent: $725 per month (2000); Median age of housing: 29 years (2000).
Transportation: Commute to work: 93.5% car, 0.0% public transportation, 2.5% walk, 3.4% work from home (2000); Travel time to work: 30.5% less than 15 minutes, 23.5% 15 to 30 minutes, 22.7% 30 to 45 minutes, 14.0% 45 to 60 minutes, 9.3% 60 minutes or more (2000)

RAVENNA (township). Covers a land area of 20.606 square miles and a water area of 1.257 square miles. Located at 44.67° N. Lat.; 92.76° W. Long.
Population: 2,355 (2000); Race: 98.0% White, 0.7% Black, 0.0% Asian, 0.8% American Indian and Alaska Native, 0.8% Hispanic of any race, 0.4% two or more races (2000); Density: 114.3 persons per square mile (2000); Age: 30.8% under 18, 3.9% over 64 (2000); Marriage status: 21.0% never married, 71.3% now married, 2.2% widowed, 5.6% divorced (2000); Foreign born: 1.3% (2000); Ancestry (includes multiple ancestries): 47.1% German, 16.4% Norwegian, 15.5% Irish, 9.9% Swedish, 7.3% English (2000).
Economy: Single-family building permits issued: 14 (2001) / 5 (2000); Multi-family building permits issued: 0 (2001) / 0 (2000); Employment by occupation: 8.6% management, 20.3% professional, 12.5% services, 23.1% sales, 0.5% farming, 16.2% construction, 18.8% production (2000).

Income: Per capita income: $23,987 (2000); Median household income: $74,286 (2000); Poverty rate: 1.4% (2000).
Taxes: Total city taxes per capita: $104 (2000); City property taxes per capita: $88 (2000).
Education: High school graduation rate: 95.3% (2000); College graduation rate: 19.7% (2000).
Housing: Homeownership rate: 98.4% (2000); Median home value: $173,900 (2000); Median rent: $775 per month (2000); Median age of housing: 20 years (2000).
Transportation: Commute to work: 93.9% car, 0.2% public transportation, 0.4% walk, 4.7% work from home (2000); Travel time to work: 18.9% less than 15 minutes, 30.9% 15 to 30 minutes, 24.1% 30 to 45 minutes, 18.3% 45 to 60 minutes, 7.8% 60 minutes or more (2000)

ROSEMOUNT (city). Covers a land area of 33.671 square miles and a water area of 1.465 square miles. Located at 44.74° N. Lat.; 93.12° W. Long. Elevation is 970 feet.
History: Seat of Dakota County Technical College.
Population: 14,619 (2000); Race: 92.5% White, 2.7% Black, 0.2% Asian, 0.4% American Indian and Alaska Native, 2.0% Hispanic of any race, 3.3% two or more races (2000); Density: 434.2 persons per square mile (2000); Age: 35.6% under 18, 5.5% over 64 (2000); Marriage status: 21.0% never married, 68.3% now married, 3.0% widowed, 7.7% divorced (2000); Foreign born: 2.5% (2000); Ancestry (includes multiple ancestries): 42.4% German, 16.8% Norwegian, 15.9% Irish, 8.1% Other groups, 8.0% English (2000).
Economy: Railroad junction. Agricultural area to South: grain, soybeans; livestock; dairying. Manufacturing: concrete products, plastic laminating, multiwall paper bags, weather strips, mats. Single-family building permits issued: 295 (2001) / 285 (2000); Multi-family building permits issued: 0 (2001) / 0 (2000); Employment by occupation: 15.5% management, 21.7% professional, 11.2% services, 29.8% sales, 0.3% farming, 8.4% construction, 13.0% production (2000).
Income: Per capita income: $23,116 (2000); Median household income: $65,916 (2000); Poverty rate: 3.3% (2000).
Taxes: Total city taxes per capita: $389 (2000); City property taxes per capita: $338 (2000).
Education: High school graduation rate: 94.1% (2000); College graduation rate: 29.3% (2000).

School District(s)

Intermediate School District 917 (PK-12)
2000 Enrollment: 607 651-423-8214
Rosemount-Apple Valley-Eagan (PK-12)
2000 Enrollment: 28,330 651-423-7700

Two-year College(s)

Dakota County Technical College (Public)
2001 Enrollment: 2,788 651-423-8000
2001 Tuition: In-state $2,454; Out-of-state $4,908

Housing: Homeownership rate: 88.1% (2000); Median home value: $154,100 (2000); Median rent: $579 per month (2000); Median age of housing: 12 years (2000).
Safety: Violent crime rate: 12.9 per 10,000 population; Property crime rate: 343.1 per 10,000 population (2001).
Transportation: Commute to work: 94.2% car, 2.3% public transportation, 0.5% walk, 2.3% work from home (2000); Travel time to work: 23.9% less than 15 minutes, 39.5% 15 to 30 minutes, 25.0% 30 to 45 minutes, 8.5% 45 to 60 minutes, 3.1% 60 minutes or more (2000)

SCIOTA (township). Covers a land area of 14.956 square miles and a water area of 0 square miles. Located at 44.50° N. Lat.; 93.05° W. Long.
Population: 285 (2000); Race: 97.3% White, 0.0% Black, 0.0% Asian, 0.0% American Indian and Alaska Native, 0.7% Hispanic of any race, 0.0% two or more races (2000); Density: 19.1 persons per square mile (2000); Age: 28.5% under 18, 8.5% over 64 (2000); Marriage status: 20.2% never married, 73.5% now married, 3.1% widowed, 3.1% divorced (2000); Foreign born: 1.4% (2000); Ancestry (includes multiple ancestries): 64.4% German, 22.4% Norwegian, 8.8% Swedish, 7.8% English, 7.8% Irish (2000).
Economy: Single-family building permits issued: 11 (2001) / 9 (2000); Multi-family building permits issued: 0 (2001) / 0 (2000); Employment by occupation: 20.9% management, 11.0% professional, 11.6% services, 19.2% sales, 1.7% farming, 16.9% construction, 18.6% production (2000).
Income: Per capita income: $23,181 (2000); Median household income: $63,125 (2000); Poverty rate: 9.5% (2000).
Taxes: Total city taxes per capita: $114 (1997); City property taxes per capita: $104 (1997).
Education: High school graduation rate: 88.8% (2000); College graduation rate: 17.9% (2000).
Housing: Homeownership rate: 87.6% (2000); Median home value: $165,900 (2000); Median rent: $500 per month (2000); Median age of housing: 23 years (2000).
Transportation: Commute to work: 84.1% car, 0.0% public transportation, 2.4% walk, 13.5% work from home (2000); Travel time to work: 32.7% less than 15 minutes, 37.4% 15 to 30 minutes, 18.4% 30 to 45 minutes, 4.1% 45 to 60 minutes, 7.5% 60 minutes or more (2000)

SOUTH SAINT PAUL (city). Covers a land area of 5.736 square miles and a water area of 0.405 square miles. Located at 44.88° N. Lat.; 93.04° W. Long. Elevation is 827 feet.
History: South St. Paul developed as a livestock market, with packing houses and tanneries surrounding a stockyards opened in 1888 by A.B. Stickney, president of the Chicago Great Western Railroad.
Population: 20,167 (2000); Race: 93.2% White, 1.1% Black, 1.0% Asian, 0.3% American Indian and Alaska Native, 6.1% Hispanic of any race, 1.6% two or more races (2000); Density: 3,515.9 persons per square mile (2000); Age: 25.5% under 18, 12.9% over 64 (2000); Marriage status: 29.0% never married, 52.7% now married, 6.4% widowed, 11.9% divorced (2000); Foreign born: 3.9% (2000); Ancestry (includes multiple ancestries): 39.8% German, 15.6% Irish, 11.7% Norwegian, 10.4% Other groups, 8.3% Swedish (2000).
Vital Statistics: Birth rate: 145.3 per 10,000 population (1998)
Economy: Single-family building permits issued: 29 (2001) / 25 (2000); Multi-family building permits issued: 0 (2001) / 2 (2000); Employment by occupation: 11.3% management, 16.1% professional, 15.9% services, 31.3% sales, 0.2% farming, 8.1% construction, 17.1% production (2000).
Income: Per capita income: $21,396 (2000); Median household income: $45,216 (2000); Poverty rate: 6.1% (2000).
Taxes: Total city taxes per capita: $295 (2000); City property taxes per capita: $250 (2000).
Education: High school graduation rate: 86.6% (2000); College graduation rate: 16.1% (2000).

School District(s)

South Saint Paul (PK-12)
2000 Enrollment: 3,533 651-457-9400

Housing: Homeownership rate: 72.1% (2000); Median home value: $110,300 (2000); Median rent: $519 per month (2000); Median age of housing: 45 years (2000).
Safety: Violent crime rate: 18.2 per 10,000 population; Property crime rate: 330.7 per 10,000 population (2001).
Transportation: Commute to work: 92.3% car, 3.1% public transportation, 1.2% walk, 2.5% work from home (2000); Travel time to work: 34.9% less than 15 minutes, 43.3% 15 to 30 minutes, 16.5% 30 to 45 minutes, 3.0% 45 to 60 minutes, 2.4% 60 minutes or more (2000)
Airports: South St Paul Municipal-Richard E Flemin
Additional Information Contacts
River Heights Chamber of Commerce 651-451-2266

SUNFISH LAKE (city). Covers a land area of 1.580 square miles and a water area of 0.119 square miles. Located at 44.86° N. Lat.; 93.09° W. Long. Elevation is 1,010 feet.
Population: 504 (2000); Race: 96.6% White, 0.0% Black, 2.8% Asian, 0.0% American Indian and Alaska Native, 2.4% Hispanic of any race, 0.6% two or more races (2000); Density: 319.0 persons per square mile (2000); Age: 27.5% under 18, 13.8% over 64 (2000); Marriage status: 21.9% never married, 69.1% now married, 3.3% widowed, 5.8% divorced (2000); Foreign born: 4.7% (2000); Ancestry (includes multiple ancestries): 33.0% Irish, 30.0% German, 13.6% Norwegian, 10.1% Swedish, 7.9% English (2000).
Economy: Single-family building permits issued: 1 (2001) / 8 (2000); Multi-family building permits issued: 0 (2001) / 0 (2000); Employment by occupation: 26.0% management, 41.3% professional, 6.6% services, 16.3% sales, 0.0% farming, 1.0% construction, 8.7% production (2000).
Income: Per capita income: $82,347 (2000); Median household income: $148,410 (2000); Poverty rate: 2.4% (2000).
Taxes: Total city taxes per capita: $384 (1997); City property taxes per capita: $346 (1997).
Education: High school graduation rate: 97.6% (2000); College graduation rate: 62.5% (2000).
Housing: Homeownership rate: 94.8% (2000); Median home value: $538,800 (2000); Median rent: $275 per month (2000); Median age of housing: 28 years (2000).
Transportation: Commute to work: 93.9% car, 1.0% public transportation, 0.0% walk, 2.6% work from home (2000); Travel time to work: 32.5% less than 15 minutes, 46.6% 15 to 30 minutes, 18.3% 30 to 45 minutes, 2.6% 45 to 60 minutes, 0.0% 60 minutes or more (2000)

VERMILLION (city). Covers a land area of 0.996 square miles and a water area of 0 square miles. Located at 44.67° N. Lat.; 92.96° W. Long.
Population: 437 (2000); Race: 97.7% White, 0.0% Black, 0.0% Asian, 0.0% American Indian and Alaska Native, 2.5% Hispanic of any race, 0.0% two or more races (2000); Density: 438.6 persons per square mile (2000); Age: 22.0% under 18, 13.2% over 64 (2000); Marriage status: 23.6% never married, 63.3% now married, 6.4% widowed, 6.7% divorced (2000); Foreign born: 0.0% (2000); Ancestry (includes multiple ancestries): 70.5% German, 11.6% Irish, 10.2% Norwegian, 8.4% Swedish, 5.2% Luxemburger (2000).
Economy: Single-family building permits issued: 0 (2001) / 2 (2000); Multi-family building permits issued: 0 (2001) / 0 (2000); Employment by occupation: 9.4% management, 16.9% professional, 12.0% services, 30.5% sales, 0.0% farming, 14.7% construction, 16.5% production (2000).
Income: Per capita income: $22,552 (2000); Median household income: $61,667 (2000); Poverty rate: 0.9% (2000).
Taxes: Total city taxes per capita: $190 (1997); City property taxes per capita: $180 (1997).
Education: High school graduation rate: 84.6% (2000); College graduation rate: 9.4% (2000).
Housing: Homeownership rate: 89.4% (2000); Median home value: $123,600 (2000); Median rent: $511 per month (2000); Median age of housing: 29 years (2000).
Transportation: Commute to work: 93.2% car, 1.5% public transportation, 0.0% walk, 4.6% work from home (2000); Travel time to work: 22.3% less than 15 minutes, 49.0% 15 to 30 minutes, 18.3% 30 to 45 minutes, 6.4% 45 to 60 minutes, 4.0% 60 minutes or more (2000)

VERMILLION (township). Covers a land area of 34.127 square miles and a water area of 0 square miles. Located at 44.66° N. Lat.; 92.99° W. Long.
Population: 1,243 (2000); Race: 96.1% White, 0.0% Black, 0.1% Asian, 0.0% American Indian and Alaska Native, 1.9% Hispanic of any race, 2.4% two or more races (2000); Density: 36.4 persons per square mile (2000); Age: 30.7% under 18, 7.0% over 64 (2000); Marriage status: 26.3% never married, 64.3% now married, 3.2% widowed, 6.2% divorced (2000); Foreign born: 0.5% (2000); Ancestry (includes multiple ancestries): 54.3% German, 15.9% Irish, 12.0% Norwegian, 6.0% English, 5.9% Swedish (2000).
Economy: Agriculture: grain; livestock, poultry. Single-family building permits issued: 5 (2001) / 2 (2000); Multi-family building permits issued: 0 (2001) / 0 (2000); Employment by occupation: 16.6% management, 17.2% professional, 13.4% services, 19.1% sales, 2.1% farming, 16.8% construction, 14.8% production (2000).
Income: Per capita income: $24,783 (2000); Median household income: $64,118 (2000); Poverty rate: 3.1% (2000).
Taxes: Total city taxes per capita: $140 (1997); City property taxes per capita: $135 (1997).
Education: High school graduation rate: 88.2% (2000); College graduation rate: 15.6% (2000).
Housing: Homeownership rate: 89.8% (2000); Median home value: $163,400 (2000); Median rent: $511 per month (2000); Median age of housing: 28 years (2000).
Transportation: Commute to work: 89.6% car, 0.0% public transportation, 1.0% walk, 8.3% work from home (2000); Travel time to work: 27.0% less than 15 minutes, 39.2% 15 to 30 minutes, 24.5% 30 to 45 minutes, 5.2% 45 to 60 minutes, 4.1% 60 minutes or more (2000)

WATERFORD (township). Covers a land area of 14.749 square miles and a water area of 0 square miles. Located at 44.50° N. Lat.; 93.13° W. Long.
Population: 517 (2000); Race: 100.0% White, 0.0% Black, 0.0% Asian, 0.0% American Indian and Alaska Native, 0.0% Hispanic of any race, 0.0% two or more races (2000); Density: 35.1 persons per square mile (2000); Age: 29.8% under 18, 8.9% over 64 (2000); Marriage status: 25.4% never married, 62.2% now married, 4.8% widowed, 7.7% divorced (2000); Foreign born: 1.6% (2000); Ancestry (includes multiple ancestries): 36.4% German, 23.5% Norwegian, 9.3% English, 8.3% Czech, 7.7% French (except Basque) (2000).
Economy: Single-family building permits issued: 2 (2001) / 3 (2000); Multi-family building permits issued: 0 (2001) / 0 (2000); Employment by occupation: 12.3% management, 14.8% professional, 16.6% services, 23.1% sales, 0.0% farming, 13.4% construction, 19.9% production (2000).
Income: Per capita income: $22,570 (2000); Median household income: $51,563 (2000); Poverty rate: 1.4% (2000).
Taxes: Total city taxes per capita: $99 (2000); City property taxes per capita: $83 (2000).
Education: High school graduation rate: 92.3% (2000); College graduation rate: 18.4% (2000).
Housing: Homeownership rate: 87.2% (2000); Median home value: $132,100 (2000); Median rent: $400 per month (2000); Median age of housing: 41 years (2000).
Transportation: Commute to work: 93.3% car, 0.7% public transportation, 0.0% walk, 5.9% work from home (2000); Travel time to work: 47.0% less than 15 minutes, 14.6% 15 to 30 minutes, 17.4% 30 to 45 minutes, 9.9% 45 to 60 minutes, 11.1% 60 minutes or more (2000)

WEST SAINT PAUL (city). Covers a land area of 5.009 square miles and a water area of 0.024 square miles. Located at 44.90° N. Lat.; 93.08° W. Long. Elevation is 991 feet.
Population: 19,405 (2000); Race: 86.4% White, 2.7% Black, 2.5% Asian, 0.4% American Indian and Alaska Native, 10.2% Hispanic of any race, 2.9% two or more races (2000); Density: 3,874.2 persons per square mile (2000); Age: 21.2% under 18, 19.3% over 64 (2000); Marriage status: 27.8% never married, 51.2% now married, 10.4% widowed, 10.6% divorced (2000); Foreign born: 5.9% (2000); Ancestry (includes multiple ancestries): 37.8% German, 15.5% Other groups, 15.0% Irish, 9.6% Norwegian, 7.2% Swedish (2000).
Vital Statistics: Birth rate: 128.8 per 10,000 population (1998)
Economy: Single-family building permits issued: 12 (2001) / 163 (2000); Multi-family building permits issued: 0 (2001) / 97 (2000); Employment by occupation: 13.1% management, 20.7% professional, 13.7% services, 32.5% sales, 0.2% farming, 7.4% construction, 12.4% production (2000).
Income: Per capita income: $23,558 (2000); Median household income: $41,103 (2000); Poverty rate: 5.9% (2000).
Taxes: Total city taxes per capita: $221 (1997); City property taxes per capita: $179 (1997).
Education: High school graduation rate: 87.7% (2000); College graduation rate: 23.9% (2000).
Housing: Homeownership rate: 58.5% (2000); Median home value: $124,100 (2000); Median rent: $590 per month (2000); Median age of housing: 35 years (2000).
Safety: Violent crime rate: 29.1 per 10,000 population; Property crime rate: 443.6 per 10,000 population (2001).
Newspapers: La Voz Latina (1 x month); The Lowertown News (1 x month); The Saint Paul Voice (1 x month)
Transportation: Commute to work: 89.9% car, 4.5% public transportation, 1.7% walk, 2.5% work from home (2000); Travel time to work: 33.0% less than 15 minutes, 45.4% 15 to 30 minutes, 15.8% 30 to 45 minutes, 3.7% 45 to 60 minutes, 2.1% 60 minutes or more (2000)

Dodge County

Located in southeastern Minnesota; drained by branches of the Zumbro River. Covers a land area of 439.50 square miles, a water area of 0.10 square miles, and is located in the Central Time Zone. The county government was organized in 1855. County seat is Mantorville.
Population: 17,731 (2000); Race: 96.5% White, 0.2% Black, 0.4% Asian, 0.1% American Indian and Alaska Native, 3.1% Hispanic of any race, 0.7% two or more races (2000); Density: 40.3 persons per square mile (2000); Age: 30.3% under 18, 12.1% over 64 (2000).
Religion: Five largest groups: 32.1% Evangelical Lutheran Church in America, 20.4% Catholic Church, 5.3% The United Methodist Church, 3.4% Presbyterian Church (U.S.A.), 2.6% Lutheran Church—Missouri Synod (2000).
Economy: Unemployment rate: 3.3% (11/2002); Total civilian labor force: 9,472 (11/2002); Leading industries: 32.5% manufacturing; 15.0% retail trade; 10.1% accommodation & food services (2000); Companies that employ more than 1,000 persons: 0 (2000); Companies that employ more than 100 persons: 5 (2000); Farms: 674 totaling 246,818 acres (1997); Minority business ownership rate: 0.0% (1997); Women business ownership rate: 18.3% (1997); Retail sales per capita: $4,133 (1997). Single-family building permits issued: 206 (2001) / 175 (2000); Multi-family building permits issued: 4 (2001) / 6 (2000).
Income: Per capita income: $19,259 (2000); Median household income: $47,437 (2000); Poverty rate: 5.8% (2000); Bankruptcy rate: 1.87% (2001).
Taxes: Total county taxes per capita: $305 (1997); County property taxes per capita: $298 (1997).
Education: High school graduation rate: 86.7% (2000); College graduation rate: 17.1% (2000).

Housing: Homeownership rate: 84.4% (2000); Median home value: $97,100 (2000); Median rent: $337 per month (2000); Median age of housing: 31 years (2000).
Health: Birth rate: 138.7 per 10,000 population (1998); Age adjusted death rate: 76.8 per 10,000 population (1999); Age adjusted cancer mortality rate: 155.3 deaths per 100,000 population (1999). Number of physicians: 5.1 per 10,000 population (1999); Number of hospital beds: n/a (1999).
Elections: 2000 Presidential election results: 41.9% Gore, 52.3% Bush, 4.1% Nader, 1.2% Buchanan
Additional Information Contacts
Dodge County Government Offices....................... 507-635-6239

Dodge County Communities

ASHLAND (township). Covers a land area of 37.372 square miles and a water area of 0 square miles. Located at 43.98° N. Lat.; 92.86° W. Long.
Population: 367 (2000); Race: 97.9% White, 0.0% Black, 0.0% Asian, 0.8% American Indian and Alaska Native, 1.1% Hispanic of any race, 0.8% two or more races (2000); Density: 9.8 persons per square mile (2000); Age: 26.0% under 18, 11.5% over 64 (2000); Marriage status: 27.8% never married, 63.2% now married, 1.0% widowed, 7.9% divorced (2000); Foreign born: 3.2% (2000); Ancestry (includes multiple ancestries): 46.6% German, 28.2% Norwegian, 9.9% United States or American, 8.0% Swedish, 6.2% English (2000).
Economy: Employment by occupation: 22.5% management, 10.1% professional, 9.6% services, 22.5% sales, 3.2% farming, 13.8% construction, 18.3% production (2000).
Income: Per capita income: $18,806 (2000); Median household income: $54,375 (2000); Poverty rate: 8.6% (2000).
Taxes: Total city taxes per capita: $78 (1997); City property taxes per capita: $78 (1997).
Education: High school graduation rate: 87.1% (2000); College graduation rate: 10.7% (2000).
Housing: Homeownership rate: 86.5% (2000); Median home value: $110,400 (2000); Median rent: $375 per month (2000); Median age of housing: 36 years (2000).
Transportation: Commute to work: 79.7% car, 1.8% public transportation, 4.1% walk, 14.3% work from home (2000); Travel time to work: 37.6% less than 15 minutes, 26.3% 15 to 30 minutes, 28.5% 30 to 45 minutes, 0.0% 45 to 60 minutes, 7.5% 60 minutes or more (2000)

CANISTEO (township). Covers a land area of 35.887 square miles and a water area of 0 square miles. Located at 43.98° N. Lat.; 92.73° W. Long.
Population: 662 (2000); Race: 99.4% White, 0.0% Black, 0.3% Asian, 0.0% American Indian and Alaska Native, 1.4% Hispanic of any race, 0.3% two or more races (2000); Density: 18.4 persons per square mile (2000); Age: 26.9% under 18, 9.0% over 64 (2000); Marriage status: 22.2% never married, 71.0% now married, 3.3% widowed, 3.5% divorced (2000); Foreign born: 0.3% (2000); Ancestry (includes multiple ancestries): 41.4% Norwegian, 35.8% German, 8.3% Irish, 7.1% Danish, 7.1% United States or American (2000).
Economy: Employment by occupation: 12.6% management, 23.2% professional, 8.8% services, 22.4% sales, 4.4% farming, 15.2% construction, 13.4% production (2000).
Income: Per capita income: $21,889 (2000); Median household income: $53,750 (2000); Poverty rate: 3.2% (2000).
Taxes: Total city taxes per capita: $78 (1997); City property taxes per capita: $78 (1997).
Education: High school graduation rate: 89.0% (2000); College graduation rate: 16.2% (2000).
Housing: Homeownership rate: 93.7% (2000); Median home value: $125,000 (2000); Median age of housing: 60+ years (2000).
Transportation: Commute to work: 85.6% car, 1.3% public transportation, 2.3% walk, 10.7% work from home (2000); Travel time to work: 25.4% less than 15 minutes, 51.8% 15 to 30 minutes, 17.5% 30 to 45 minutes, 2.0% 45 to 60 minutes, 3.2% 60 minutes or more (2000)

CLAREMONT (city). Covers a land area of 1.153 square miles and a water area of 0 square miles. Located at 44.04° N. Lat.; 92.99° W. Long.
History: Claremont was settled in the 1850's by New Englanders.
Population: 620 (2000); Race: 85.8% White, 0.0% Black, 0.0% Asian, 0.0% American Indian and Alaska Native, 15.5% Hispanic of any race, 2.0% two or more races (2000); Density: 537.6 persons per square mile (2000); Age: 29.7% under 18, 13.5% over 64 (2000); Marriage status: 23.5% never married, 61.8% now married, 6.5% widowed, 8.2% divorced (2000); Foreign born: 5.4% (2000); Ancestry (includes multiple ancestries): 34.3% German, 18.6% Norwegian, 16.8% Other groups, 8.9% Irish, 6.9% English (2000).
Economy: Single-family building permits issued: 2 (2001) / 0 (2000); Multi-family building permits issued: 0 (2001) / 0 (2000); Employment by occupation: 5.3% management, 10.2% professional, 15.2% services, 20.1% sales, 2.3% farming, 17.8% construction, 29.0% production (2000).
Income: Per capita income: $15,498 (2000); Median household income: $35,987 (2000); Poverty rate: 10.5% (2000).
Taxes: Total city taxes per capita: $130 (1997); City property taxes per capita: $125 (1997).
Education: High school graduation rate: 78.0% (2000); College graduation rate: 6.5% (2000).
Housing: Homeownership rate: 80.4% (2000); Median home value: $74,500 (2000); Median rent: $372 per month (2000); Median age of housing: 44 years (2000).
Transportation: Commute to work: 91.1% car, 1.0% public transportation, 4.4% walk, 2.0% work from home (2000); Travel time to work: 23.3% less than 15 minutes, 47.7% 15 to 30 minutes, 16.7% 30 to 45 minutes, 3.5% 45 to 60 minutes, 8.7% 60 minutes or more (2000)

CLAREMONT (township). Covers a land area of 34.800 square miles and a water area of 0.052 square miles. Located at 44.05° N. Lat.; 92.97° W. Long.
Population: 468 (2000); Race: 99.4% White, 0.6% Black, 0.0% Asian, 0.0% American Indian and Alaska Native, 0.0% Hispanic of any race, 0.0% two or more races (2000); Density: 13.4 persons per square mile (2000); Age: 27.7% under 18, 8.9% over 64 (2000); Marriage status: 28.7% never married, 63.7% now married, 2.6% widowed, 5.0% divorced (2000); Foreign born: 2.7% (2000); Ancestry (includes multiple ancestries): 52.0% German, 19.3% Norwegian, 17.3% United States or American, 9.1% English, 7.7% Czech (2000).
Economy: Corn, soybeans, peas; livestock, poultry; dairying; light manufacturing. Employment by occupation: 16.8% management, 14.9% professional, 7.8% services, 19.4% sales, 6.0% farming, 13.8% construction, 21.3% production (2000).
Income: Per capita income: $20,532 (2000); Median household income: $63,125 (2000); Poverty rate: 6.3% (2000).
Taxes: Total city taxes per capita: $75 (1997); City property taxes per capita: $75 (1997).
Education: High school graduation rate: 86.8% (2000); College graduation rate: 12.8% (2000).
Housing: Homeownership rate: 84.8% (2000); Median home value: $102,800 (2000); Median rent: $392 per month (2000); Median age of housing: 40 years (2000).
Transportation: Commute to work: 84.6% car, 0.8% public transportation, 4.1% walk, 9.8% work from home (2000); Travel time to work: 23.3% less than 15 minutes, 43.3% 15 to 30 minutes, 25.0% 30 to 45 minutes, 5.8% 45 to 60 minutes, 2.5% 60 minutes or more (2000)

CONCORD (township). Covers a land area of 36.866 square miles and a water area of 0.009 square miles. Located at 44.15° N. Lat.; 92.85° W. Long.
Population: 587 (2000); Race: 95.3% White, 0.0% Black, 0.3% Asian, 0.0% American Indian and Alaska Native, 1.9% Hispanic of any race, 3.0% two or more races (2000); Density: 15.9 persons per square mile (2000); Age: 27.8% under 18, 11.6% over 64 (2000); Marriage status: 20.2% never married, 65.7% now married, 6.3% widowed, 7.8% divorced (2000); Foreign born: 1.7% (2000); Ancestry (includes multiple ancestries): 40.6% German, 34.5% Norwegian, 12.6% Irish, 7.1% English, 4.4% Swedish (2000).
Economy: Agriculture includes grains, soybeans, peas; livestock, poultry; dairying; manufacturing of feeds. Employment by occupation: 14.4% management, 19.0% professional, 10.5% services, 21.6% sales, 1.0% farming, 9.8% construction, 23.6% production (2000).
Income: Per capita income: $16,895 (2000); Median household income: $45,588 (2000); Poverty rate: 8.6% (2000).
Taxes: Total city taxes per capita: $66 (1997); City property taxes per capita: $66 (1997).
Education: High school graduation rate: 88.0% (2000); College graduation rate: 13.1% (2000).
Housing: Homeownership rate: 87.9% (2000); Median home value: $102,300 (2000); Median rent: $400 per month (2000); Median age of housing: 60+ years (2000).
Transportation: Commute to work: 85.5% car, 1.7% public transportation, 3.6% walk, 9.2% work from home (2000); Travel time to work: 20.0% less than 15 minutes, 26.9% 15 to 30 minutes, 32.7% 30 to 45 minutes, 13.1% 45 to 60 minutes, 7.3% 60 minutes or more (2000)

DODGE CENTER (city). Covers a land area of 1.896 square miles and a water area of 0 square miles. Located at 44.02° N. Lat.; 92.85° W. Long. Elevation is 1,293 feet.
History: Settled 1853, incorporated 1872.
Population: 2,226 (2000); Race: 90.7% White, 0.5% Black, 0.3% Asian, 0.1% American Indian and Alaska Native, 8.4% Hispanic of any race, 1.9% two or more races (2000); Density: 1,173.8 persons per square mile (2000); Age: 30.9% under 18, 13.8% over 64 (2000); Marriage status: 23.4% never married, 57.8% now married, 9.3% widowed, 9.5% divorced (2000); Foreign born: 5.5% (2000); Ancestry (includes multiple ancestries): 34.6% German, 21.9% Norwegian, 9.1% Other groups, 8.7% Irish, 8.2% United States or American (2000).
Economy: Shipping point for agricultural area: livestock, poultry; dairying; grain, soybeans, peas. Manufacturing: concrete mixers, printing and publishing. Single-family building permits issued: 18 (2001) / 20 (2000); Multi-family building permits issued: 0 (2001) / 0 (2000); Employment by occupation: 8.3% management, 14.6% professional, 17.6% services, 22.1% sales, 1.2% farming, 11.5% construction, 24.7% production (2000).
Income: Per capita income: $16,858 (2000); Median household income: $39,453 (2000); Poverty rate: 9.3% (2000).
Taxes: Total city taxes per capita: $396 (1997); City property taxes per capita: $372 (1997).
Education: High school graduation rate: 80.0% (2000); College graduation rate: 11.7% (2000).

School District(s)

Triton (PK-12)
2000 Enrollment: 1,224 507-374-2192

Housing: Homeownership rate: 75.5% (2000); Median home value: $80,200 (2000); Median rent: $307 per month (2000); Median age of housing: 33 years (2000).
Newspapers: Dodge Center Star-Record (1 x week)
Transportation: Commute to work: 92.1% car, 0.9% public transportation, 3.7% walk, 2.4% work from home (2000); Travel time to work: 42.2% less than 15 minutes, 26.7% 15 to 30 minutes, 21.2% 30 to 45 minutes, 3.7% 45 to 60 minutes, 6.1% 60 minutes or more (2000)

ELLINGTON (township). Covers a land area of 36.024 square miles and a water area of 0 square miles. Located at 44.15° N. Lat.; 92.99° W. Long.
Population: 278 (2000); Race: 100.0% White, 0.0% Black, 0.0% Asian, 0.0% American Indian and Alaska Native, 0.0% Hispanic of any race, 0.0% two or more races (2000); Density: 7.7 persons per square mile (2000); Age: 31.9% under 18, 15.4% over 64 (2000); Marriage status: 21.3% never married, 69.7% now married, 6.2% widowed, 2.8% divorced (2000); Foreign born: 0.0% (2000); Ancestry (includes multiple ancestries): 43.5% German, 29.5% Norwegian, 13.3% Irish, 11.9% United States or American, 10.2% Czech (2000).
Economy: Employment by occupation: 27.2% management, 18.4% professional, 4.4% services, 16.9% sales, 8.1% farming, 3.7% construction, 21.3% production (2000).
Income: Per capita income: $17,594 (2000); Median household income: $45,208 (2000); Poverty rate: 5.7% (2000).
Taxes: Total city taxes per capita: $110 (1997); City property taxes per capita: $110 (1997).
Education: High school graduation rate: 83.5% (2000); College graduation rate: 19.2% (2000).
Housing: Homeownership rate: 82.7% (2000); Median home value: $93,100 (2000); Median rent: $250 per month (2000); Median age of housing: 55 years (2000).
Transportation: Commute to work: 77.3% car, 3.0% public transportation, 7.6% walk, 10.6% work from home (2000); Travel time to work: 28.0% less than 15 minutes, 18.6% 15 to 30 minutes, 26.3% 30 to 45 minutes, 8.5% 45 to 60 minutes, 18.6% 60 minutes or more (2000)

HAYFIELD (city). Covers a land area of 1.262 square miles and a water area of 0 square miles. Located at 43.88° N. Lat.; 92.84° W. Long. Elevation is 1,319 feet.
Population: 1,325 (2000); Race: 97.0% White, 0.0% Black, 1.1% Asian, 0.2% American Indian and Alaska Native, 0.5% Hispanic of any race, 1.5% two or more races (2000); Density: 1,049.6 persons per square mile (2000); Age: 27.5% under 18, 20.5% over 64 (2000); Marriage status: 23.4% never married, 60.9% now married, 10.2% widowed, 5.4% divorced (2000); Foreign born: 1.6% (2000); Ancestry (includes multiple ancestries): 42.8% German, 31.9% Norwegian, 9.3% Irish, 5.6% English, 3.9% Other groups (2000).
Economy: Single-family building permits issued: 9 (2001) / 20 (2000); Multi-family building permits issued: 0 (2001) / 0 (2000); Employment by occupation: 6.9% management, 20.6% professional, 20.7% services, 22.0% sales, 1.3% farming, 9.8% construction, 18.8% production (2000).
Income: Per capita income: $17,201 (2000); Median household income: $38,214 (2000); Poverty rate: 4.4% (2000).
Taxes: Total city taxes per capita: $277 (1997); City property taxes per capita: $268 (1997).
Education: High school graduation rate: 82.5% (2000); College graduation rate: 14.4% (2000).

School District(s)

Hayfield (PK-12)
2000 Enrollment: 971 507-477-3235

Housing: Homeownership rate: 79.6% (2000); Median home value: $83,700 (2000); Median rent: $328 per month (2000); Median age of housing: 37 years (2000).
Newspapers: The Hayfield Herald (1 x week)
Transportation: Commute to work: 89.6% car, 0.0% public transportation, 6.4% walk, 3.3% work from home (2000); Travel time to work: 38.8% less than 15 minutes, 15.4% 15 to 30 minutes, 33.7% 30 to 45 minutes, 7.7% 45 to 60 minutes, 4.4% 60 minutes or more (2000)

HAYFIELD (township). Covers a land area of 36.583 square miles and a water area of 0 square miles. Located at 43.88° N. Lat.; 92.85° W. Long. Elevation is 1,319 feet.
Population: 445 (2000); Race: 98.9% White, 0.0% Black, 0.9% Asian, 0.0% American Indian and Alaska Native, 1.8% Hispanic of any race, 0.0% two or more races (2000); Density: 12.2 persons per square mile (2000); Age: 39.1% under 18, 10.8% over 64 (2000); Marriage status: 22.9% never married, 68.6% now married, 4.2% widowed, 4.2% divorced (2000); Foreign born: 1.8% (2000); Ancestry (includes multiple ancestries): 46.5% German, 33.7% Norwegian, 11.2% English, 9.7% Czech, 8.3% Swedish (2000).
Economy: Agricultural area: poultry, livestock; grain, soybeans, peas; dairying. Manufacturing: windows and doors, feeds, fiber cans. Employment by occupation: 23.1% management, 19.6% professional, 11.1% services, 23.6% sales, 3.6% farming, 8.9% construction, 10.2% production (2000).
Income: Per capita income: $15,587 (2000); Median household income: $48,438 (2000); Poverty rate: 9.2% (2000).
Taxes: Total city taxes per capita: $53 (1997); City property taxes per capita: $53 (1997).
Education: High school graduation rate: 88.8% (2000); College graduation rate: 15.3% (2000).
Housing: Homeownership rate: 90.6% (2000); Median home value: $95,000 (2000); Median rent: $425 per month (2000); Median age of housing: 60+ years (2000).
Transportation: Commute to work: 81.3% car, 0.0% public transportation, 0.9% walk, 16.9% work from home (2000); Travel time to work: 34.6% less than 15 minutes, 24.2% 15 to 30 minutes, 31.9% 30 to 45 minutes, 6.6% 45 to 60 minutes, 2.7% 60 minutes or more (2000)

KASSON (city). Covers a land area of 2.026 square miles and a water area of 0 square miles. Located at 44.03° N. Lat.; 92.75° W. Long. Elevation is 1,242 feet.
History: Kasson developed as a commerce and trading center for the dairy farms in the surrounding area.
Population: 4,398 (2000); Race: 97.1% White, 0.3% Black, 0.5% Asian, 0.0% American Indian and Alaska Native, 2.8% Hispanic of any race, 0.0% two or more races (2000); Density: 2,170.4 persons per square mile (2000); Age: 30.6% under 18, 11.9% over 64 (2000); Marriage status: 21.9% never married, 62.0% now married, 7.3% widowed, 8.7% divorced (2000); Foreign born: 2.8% (2000); Ancestry (includes multiple ancestries): 43.0% German, 28.0% Norwegian, 11.1% Irish, 8.6% English, 4.7% Other groups (2000).
Economy: Single-family building permits issued: 86 (2001) / 88 (2000); Multi-family building permits issued: 0 (2001) / 0 (2000); Employment by occupation: 8.8% management, 22.9% professional, 13.0% services, 29.3% sales, 1.4% farming, 8.3% construction, 16.3% production (2000).
Income: Per capita income: $19,249 (2000); Median household income: $49,022 (2000); Poverty rate: 4.2% (2000).
Taxes: Total city taxes per capita: $129 (1997); City property taxes per capita: $123 (1997).
Education: High school graduation rate: 88.9% (2000); College graduation rate: 19.0% (2000).

School District(s)

Kasson-Mantorville (PK-12)
2000 Enrollment: 1,781 507-634-1100

Housing: Homeownership rate: 81.4% (2000); Median home value: $107,400 (2000); Median rent: $342 per month (2000); Median age of housing: 21 years (2000).
Safety: Violent crime rate: 2.2 per 10,000 population; Property crime rate: 128.2 per 10,000 population (2001).
Newspapers: Dodge County Independent (1 x week)
Transportation: Commute to work: 92.5% car, 1.2% public transportation, 2.9% walk, 3.2% work from home (2000); Travel time to work: 33.4% less than 15 minutes, 46.3% 15 to 30 minutes, 16.4% 30 to 45 minutes, 1.5% 45 to 60 minutes, 2.3% 60 minutes or more (2000)

MANTORVILLE (city). Covers a land area of 1.422 square miles and a water area of 0 square miles. Located at 44.06° N. Lat.; 92.75° W. Long. Elevation is 1,150 feet.
History: Mantorville grew up around the stone quarries, from which came building material for many of the structures in Rochester. The settlement began in the 1850's, but missed out on the railroad in the 1880's, when many of the residents moved to the new town of Kasson.
Population: 1,054 (2000); Race: 99.2% White, 0.0% Black, 0.0% Asian, 0.6% American Indian and Alaska Native, 1.2% Hispanic of any race, 0.2% two or more races (2000); Density: 741.3 persons per square mile (2000); Age: 31.2% under 18, 8.2% over 64 (2000); Marriage status: 17.1% never married, 70.7% now married, 4.7% widowed, 7.5% divorced (2000); Foreign born: 1.9% (2000); Ancestry (includes multiple ancestries): 40.2% German, 30.7% Norwegian, 9.0% Irish, 7.4% English, 5.1% United States or American (2000).
Economy: Single-family building permits issued: 11 (2001) / 15 (2000); Multi-family building permits issued: 4 (2001) / 6 (2000); Employment by occupation: 11.3% management, 25.7% professional, 11.3% services, 20.4% sales, 0.7% farming, 16.2% construction, 14.3% production (2000).
Income: Per capita income: $20,853 (2000); Median household income: $55,735 (2000); Poverty rate: 6.4% (2000).
Taxes: Total city taxes per capita: $102 (1997); City property taxes per capita: $96 (1997).
Education: High school graduation rate: 90.6% (2000); College graduation rate: 22.7% (2000).
Housing: Homeownership rate: 91.2% (2000); Median home value: $110,300 (2000); Median rent: $363 per month (2000); Median age of housing: 23 years (2000).
Transportation: Commute to work: 94.1% car, 0.9% public transportation, 1.8% walk, 3.2% work from home (2000); Travel time to work: 31.0% less than 15 minutes, 42.8% 15 to 30 minutes, 21.8% 30 to 45 minutes, 1.5% 45 to 60 minutes, 2.9% 60 minutes or more (2000)

MANTORVILLE (township). Covers a land area of 32.444 square miles and a water area of 0.011 square miles. Located at 44.05° N. Lat.; 92.73° W. Long. Elevation is 1,150 feet.
Population: 1,610 (2000); Race: 97.8% White, 0.0% Black, 0.6% Asian, 0.2% American Indian and Alaska Native, 1.1% Hispanic of any race, 0.7% two or more races (2000); Density: 49.6 persons per square mile (2000); Age: 35.1% under 18, 5.4% over 64 (2000); Marriage status: 18.7% never married, 73.3% now married, 3.5% widowed, 4.5% divorced (2000); Foreign born: 1.4% (2000); Ancestry (includes multiple ancestries): 41.9% German, 27.4% Norwegian, 10.7% English, 10.3% Irish, 5.1% Swedish (2000).
Economy: Grain, soybeans, peas; livestock, poultry; dairying. Employment by occupation: 14.9% management, 27.2% professional, 12.1% services, 23.3% sales, 2.6% farming, 10.1% construction, 9.9% production (2000).
Income: Per capita income: $25,557 (2000); Median household income: $62,891 (2000); Poverty rate: 2.0% (2000).
Taxes: Total city taxes per capita: $88 (1997); City property taxes per capita: $88 (1997).
Education: High school graduation rate: 94.2% (2000); College graduation rate: 31.6% (2000).
Housing: Homeownership rate: 93.3% (2000); Median home value: $167,700 (2000); Median rent: $231 per month (2000); Median age of housing: 23 years (2000).
Transportation: Commute to work: 90.8% car, 0.9% public transportation, 1.7% walk, 6.6% work from home (2000); Travel time to work: 29.6% less than 15 minutes, 50.1% 15 to 30 minutes, 16.7% 30 to 45 minutes, 1.9% 45 to 60 minutes, 1.7% 60 minutes or more (2000)

MILTON (township). Covers a land area of 36.002 square miles and a water area of 0.050 square miles. Located at 44.15° N. Lat.; 92.74° W. Long.
Population: 692 (2000); Race: 97.6% White, 0.0% Black, 0.0% Asian, 0.0% American Indian and Alaska Native, 2.1% Hispanic of any race, 0.9% two or more races (2000); Density: 19.2 persons per square mile (2000); Age: 26.7% under 18, 12.4% over 64 (2000); Marriage status: 26.0% never married, 61.9% now married, 5.5% widowed, 6.6% divorced (2000); Foreign born: 2.7% (2000); Ancestry (includes multiple ancestries): 39.9% German, 25.7% Norwegian, 11.3% Swiss, 11.3% Irish, 8.1% English (2000).
Economy: Employment by occupation: 14.9% management, 19.3% professional, 12.2% services, 22.4% sales, 5.0% farming, 10.2% construction, 16.0% production (2000).
Income: Per capita income: $20,209 (2000); Median household income: $50,000 (2000); Poverty rate: 7.9% (2000).
Taxes: Total city taxes per capita: $119 (1997); City property taxes per capita: $119 (1997).
Education: High school graduation rate: 86.5% (2000); College graduation rate: 16.9% (2000).
Housing: Homeownership rate: 85.9% (2000); Median home value: $150,000 (2000); Median rent: $433 per month (2000); Median age of housing: 57 years (2000).
Transportation: Commute to work: 85.2% car, 0.6% public transportation, 3.6% walk, 10.6% work from home (2000); Travel time to work: 27.3% less than 15 minutes, 34.2% 15 to 30 minutes, 27.3% 30 to 45 minutes, 5.3% 45 to 60 minutes, 6.0% 60 minutes or more (2000)

RIPLEY (township). Covers a land area of 36.152 square miles and a water area of 0 square miles. Located at 43.99° N. Lat.; 92.97° W. Long.
Population: 212 (2000); Race: 98.5% White, 0.0% Black, 0.0% Asian, 1.5% American Indian and Alaska Native, 0.0% Hispanic of any race, 0.0% two or more races (2000); Density: 5.9 persons per square mile (2000); Age: 31.6% under 18, 16.0% over 64 (2000); Marriage status: 17.4% never married, 73.8% now married, 4.7% widowed, 4.0% divorced (2000); Foreign born: 0.0% (2000); Ancestry (includes multiple ancestries): 45.6% German, 20.4% Norwegian, 12.1% English, 10.7% French (except Basque), 8.3% Irish (2000).
Economy: Employment by occupation: 24.5% management, 15.3% professional, 17.3% services, 17.3% sales, 3.1% farming, 9.2% construction, 13.3% production (2000).
Income: Per capita income: $18,240 (2000); Median household income: $42,500 (2000); Poverty rate: 9.0% (2000).
Taxes: Total city taxes per capita: $126 (1997); City property taxes per capita: $126 (1997).
Education: High school graduation rate: 83.2% (2000); College graduation rate: 19.0% (2000).
Housing: Homeownership rate: 87.3% (2000); Median home value: $107,500 (2000); Median age of housing: 38 years (2000).
Transportation: Commute to work: 75.0% car, 0.0% public transportation, 0.0% walk, 25.0% work from home (2000); Travel time to work: 23.2% less than 15 minutes, 44.9% 15 to 30 minutes, 23.2% 30 to 45 minutes, 4.3% 45 to 60 minutes, 4.3% 60 minutes or more (2000)

VERNON (township). Covers a land area of 36.198 square miles and a water area of 0 square miles. Located at 43.88° N. Lat.; 92.72° W. Long.
Population: 567 (2000); Race: 100.0% White, 0.0% Black, 0.0% Asian, 0.0% American Indian and Alaska Native, 0.0% Hispanic of any race, 0.0% two or more races (2000); Density: 15.7 persons per square mile (2000); Age: 29.7% under 18, 11.0% over 64 (2000); Marriage status: 17.5% never married, 75.2% now married, 5.2% widowed, 2.1% divorced (2000); Foreign born: 0.0% (2000); Ancestry (includes multiple ancestries): 49.5% Norwegian, 47.6% German, 6.5% Irish, 4.6% English, 3.3% French (except Basque) (2000).
Economy: Employment by occupation: 21.3% management, 20.7% professional, 9.5% services, 20.4% sales, 2.1% farming, 11.3% construction, 14.6% production (2000).
Income: Per capita income: $21,206 (2000); Median household income: $56,042 (2000); Poverty rate: 1.7% (2000).
Taxes: Total city taxes per capita: $72 (2000); City property taxes per capita: $72 (2000).
Education: High school graduation rate: 92.2% (2000); College graduation rate: 21.8% (2000).
Housing: Homeownership rate: 88.9% (2000); Median home value: $111,500 (2000); Median rent: $300 per month (2000); Median age of housing: 60+ years (2000).
Transportation: Commute to work: 81.4% car, 0.0% public transportation, 2.5% walk, 14.9% work from home (2000); Travel time to work: 22.9% less than 15 minutes, 34.9% 15 to 30 minutes, 33.5% 30 to 45 minutes, 5.5% 45 to 60 minutes, 3.3% 60 minutes or more (2000)

WASIOJA (township). Covers a land area of 36.095 square miles and a water area of 0 square miles. Located at 44.06° N. Lat.; 92.85° W. Long.

Population: 963 (2000); Race: 98.1% White, 0.0% Black, 0.0% Asian, 0.0% American Indian and Alaska Native, 1.1% Hispanic of any race, 0.9% two or more races (2000); Density: 26.7 persons per square mile (2000); Age: 30.5% under 18, 10.3% over 64 (2000); Marriage status: 22.1% never married, 70.6% now married, 2.3% widowed, 5.0% divorced (2000); Foreign born: 0.6% (2000); Ancestry (includes multiple ancestries): 40.0% German, 27.0% Norwegian, 7.9% English, 7.1% Irish, 5.0% United States or American (2000).
Economy: Employment by occupation: 15.2% management, 15.2% professional, 13.4% services, 23.6% sales, 3.0% farming, 12.1% construction, 17.5% production (2000).
Income: Per capita income: $19,834 (2000); Median household income: $55,714 (2000); Poverty rate: 6.3% (2000).
Taxes: Total city taxes per capita: $72 (1997); City property taxes per capita: $72 (1997).
Education: High school graduation rate: 88.4% (2000); College graduation rate: 14.0% (2000).
Housing: Homeownership rate: 89.7% (2000); Median home value: $112,200 (2000); Median rent: $544 per month (2000); Median age of housing: 38 years (2000).
Transportation: Commute to work: 86.0% car, 0.0% public transportation, 1.9% walk, 11.7% work from home (2000); Travel time to work: 40.7% less than 15 minutes, 24.2% 15 to 30 minutes, 25.7% 30 to 45 minutes, 4.8% 45 to 60 minutes, 4.6% 60 minutes or more (2000)

WEST CONCORD (city). Covers a land area of 1.066 square miles and a water area of 0 square miles. Located at 44.15° N. Lat.; 92.90° W. Long. Elevation is 1,230 feet.
Population: 836 (2000); Race: 95.7% White, 0.0% Black, 1.1% Asian, 0.0% American Indian and Alaska Native, 5.4% Hispanic of any race, 0.4% two or more races (2000); Density: 784.0 persons per square mile (2000); Age: 27.8% under 18, 17.8% over 64 (2000); Marriage status: 20.0% never married, 62.3% now married, 9.8% widowed, 7.9% divorced (2000); Foreign born: 3.3% (2000); Ancestry (includes multiple ancestries): 41.3% German, 25.4% Norwegian, 13.1% Irish, 11.1% United States or American, 7.6% English (2000).
Economy: Single-family building permits issued: 2 (2001) / 2 (2000); Multi-family building permits issued: 0 (2001) / 0 (2000); Employment by occupation: 7.4% management, 16.5% professional, 15.5% services, 26.5% sales, 0.5% farming, 14.0% construction, 19.7% production (2000).
Income: Per capita income: $16,958 (2000); Median household income: $39,453 (2000); Poverty rate: 7.9% (2000).
Taxes: Total city taxes per capita: $283 (2000); City property taxes per capita: $276 (2000).
Education: High school graduation rate: 80.5% (2000); College graduation rate: 11.9% (2000).
Housing: Homeownership rate: 85.2% (2000); Median home value: $69,000 (2000); Median rent: $168 per month (2000); Median age of housing: 55 years (2000).
Newspapers: West Concord Enterprise (1 x week); Claremont News (1 x week)
Transportation: Commute to work: 87.0% car, 1.5% public transportation, 8.8% walk, 1.7% work from home (2000); Travel time to work: 30.9% less than 15 minutes, 20.2% 15 to 30 minutes, 39.9% 30 to 45 minutes, 5.5% 45 to 60 minutes, 3.5% 60 minutes or more (2000)

WESTFIELD (township). Covers a land area of 36.187 square miles and a water area of 0 square miles. Located at 43.89° N. Lat.; 92.98° W. Long.
Population: 421 (2000); Race: 99.5% White, 0.0% Black, 0.0% Asian, 0.0% American Indian and Alaska Native, 0.9% Hispanic of any race, 0.0% two or more races (2000); Density: 11.6 persons per square mile (2000); Age: 27.4% under 18, 11.7% over 64 (2000); Marriage status: 18.4% never married, 74.1% now married, 2.4% widowed, 5.1% divorced (2000); Foreign born: 0.0% (2000); Ancestry (includes multiple ancestries): 43.3% German, 41.7% Norwegian, 7.0% Irish, 5.4% Danish, 4.7% English (2000).
Economy: Employment by occupation: 25.6% management, 12.0% professional, 16.2% services, 15.4% sales, 2.1% farming, 12.0% construction, 16.7% production (2000).
Income: Per capita income: $18,807 (2000); Median household income: $48,333 (2000); Poverty rate: 5.6% (2000).
Taxes: Total city taxes per capita: $60 (1997); City property taxes per capita: $60 (1997).
Education: High school graduation rate: 83.7% (2000); College graduation rate: 10.3% (2000).
Housing: Homeownership rate: 91.4% (2000); Median home value: $108,300 (2000); Median rent: $508 per month (2000); Median age of housing: 60+ years (2000).
Transportation: Commute to work: 86.6% car, 0.0% public transportation, 1.7% walk, 11.6% work from home (2000); Travel time to work: 30.2% less than 15 minutes, 29.3% 15 to 30 minutes, 28.3% 30 to 45 minutes, 9.3% 45 to 60 minutes, 2.9% 60 minutes or more (2000)

Douglas County

Located in western Minnesota; watered by Long Prairie River and numerous lakes. Covers a land area of 634.30 square miles, a water area of 85.60 square miles, and is located in the Central Time Zone. The county government was organized in 1858. County seat is Alexandria.

Weather Station: Alexandria Chandler Field — Elevation: 1,414 feet

	Jan	Feb	Mar	Apr	May	Jun	Jul	Aug	Sep	Oct	Nov	Dec
High	18	24	36	54	68	76	81	79	68	55	36	22
Low	-1	5	19	33	47	56	61	59	48	36	22	6
Precip	0.9	0.7	1.5	2.1	3.0	4.3	3.2	3.6	2.7	2.2	1.2	0.6
Snow	10.1	6.7	9.2	2.9	tr	tr	0.0	tr	tr	0.8	7.0	6.0

High and Low temperatures in degrees Fahrenheit; Precipitation and Snow in inches

Population: 32,821 (2000); Race: 98.6% White, 0.3% Black, 0.2% Asian, 0.2% American Indian and Alaska Native, 0.5% Hispanic of any race, 0.6% two or more races (2000); Density: 51.7 persons per square mile (2000); Age: 24.0% under 18, 17.9% over 64 (2000).
Religion: Five largest groups: 30.1% Evangelical Lutheran Church in America, 23.8% Catholic Church, 7.1% Lutheran Church—Missouri Synod, 2.0% The United Methodist Church, 1.9% The Evangelical Covenant Church (2000).
Economy: Unemployment rate: 3.0% (11/2002); Total civilian labor force: 17,518 (11/2002); Leading industries: 19.6% retail trade; 19.5% manufacturing; 15.8% health care and social assistance (2000); Companies that employ more than 1,000 persons: 0 (2000); Companies that employ more than 100 persons: 22 (2000); Farms: 1,042 totaling 267,875 acres (1997); Minority business ownership rate: 0.0% (1997); Women business ownership rate: 16.0% (1997); Retail sales per capita: $12,005 (1997). Single-family building permits issued: 498 (2001) / 326 (2000); Multi-family building permits issued: 40 (2001) / 30 (2000).
Income: Per capita income: $18,850 (2000); Median household income: $37,703 (2000); Poverty rate: 8.5% (2000); Bankruptcy rate: 3.08% (2001).
Taxes: Total county taxes per capita: $324 (2000); County property taxes per capita: $317 (2000).
Education: High school graduation rate: 85.6% (2000); College graduation rate: 17.3% (2000).
Housing: Homeownership rate: 77.2% (2000); Median home value: $102,300 (2000); Median rent: $364 per month (2000); Median age of housing: 28 years (2000).
Health: Birth rate: 119.7 per 10,000 population (1998); Age adjusted death rate: 68.5 per 10,000 population (1999); Age adjusted cancer mortality rate: 178.8 deaths per 100,000 population (1999). Air Quality Index: 100% good, 0% moderate, 0% unhealthy (percent of days in 2000). Number of physicians: 17.1 per 10,000 population (1999); Number of hospital beds: 30.2 per 10,000 population (1999).
Elections: 2000 Presidential election results: 36.9% Gore, 57.0% Bush, 4.3% Nader, 1.3% Buchanan
National and State Parks: Anderson State Wildlife Management Area; Balgaard State Wildlife Management Area; Belle River State Wildlife Management Area; Big Spruce State Wildlife Management Area; Chermak State Wildlife Management Area; Eng Lake State Wildlife Management Area; Hartfiel State Wildlife Management Area; Hegg Lake State Wildlife Management Area; Herberger Lake State Wildlife Management Are; Kensington State Wildlife Management Area; LaGrand State Wildlife Management Area; Lake Carlos State Park; Lake Carlos State Park; Pioneer Trail State Wildlife Management Area; Red Rock State Wildlife Management Area; Schnepf State Wildlife Management Area; Spruce Creek State Wildlife Management Area; Thornberg State Wildlife Management Area; Urness State Wildlife Management Area
Additional Information Contacts
Douglas County Government Offices 320-762-2381
Alexandria Lakes Chamber of Commerce 320-763-3161
Greater Alexandria Area Association of Realtors 320-762-2022

Douglas County Communities

ALEXANDRIA (city). Covers a land area of 8.887 square miles and a water area of 0.474 square miles. Located at 45.88° N. Lat.; 95.37° W. Long. Elevation is 1,392 feet.
History: The Alexandria area was settled in the 1850's, and organized as a township in 1866. It was named for Alexander Kinkaid, who with his brother, William, claimed a tract of land here in 1857. The St. Paul, Minneapolis & Manitoba Railroad reached Alexandria in 1878.
Population: 8,820 (2000); Race: 98.9% White, 0.6% Black, 0.1% Asian, 0.2% American Indian and Alaska Native, 0.3% Hispanic of any race, 0.2% two or more races (2000); Density: 992.5 persons per square mile (2000); Age: 19.7% under 18, 23.8% over 64 (2000); Marriage status: 31.2% never married, 45.2% now married, 11.7% widowed, 11.9% divorced (2000); Foreign born: 1.1% (2000); Ancestry (includes multiple ancestries): 40.6% German, 26.8% Norwegian, 13.1% Swedish, 7.7% Irish, 4.3% United States or American (2000).
Economy: Single-family building permits issued: 154 (2001) / 41 (2000); Multi-family building permits issued: 40 (2001) / 30 (2000); Employment by occupation: 10.1% management, 11.8% professional, 20.1% services, 24.9% sales, 0.4% farming, 9.2% construction, 23.4% production (2000).
Income: Per capita income: $16,085 (2000); Median household income: $26,851 (2000); Poverty rate: 13.3% (2000).
Taxes: Total city taxes per capita: $255 (2000); City property taxes per capita: $229 (2000).
Education: High school graduation rate: 80.0% (2000); College graduation rate: 15.5% (2000).

School District(s)

Alexandria (PK-12)
2000 Enrollment: 4,179 320-762-2141
Runestone Area Ed. Dist. (02-12)
2000 Enrollment: 123 320-763-5559

Two-year College(s)

Alexandria Technical College (Public)
2001 Enrollment: 2,320 320-762-0221
2001 Tuition: In-state $2,686; Out-of-state $5,372

Housing: Homeownership rate: 51.1% (2000); Median home value: $85,100 (2000); Median rent: $368 per month (2000); Median age of housing: 31 years (2000).
Hospitals: Douglas County Hospital (127 beds)
Newspapers: Echo Press (2 x week); Vacationer; The Lakeland Shopping Guide (1 x week)
Transportation: Commute to work: 89.2% car, 0.7% public transportation, 4.8% walk, 4.4% work from home (2000); Travel time to work: 73.0% less than 15 minutes, 15.1% 15 to 30 minutes, 5.3% 30 to 45 minutes, 1.8% 45 to 60 minutes, 4.8% 60 minutes or more (2000)
Additional Information Contacts
Alexandria Lakes Chamber of Commerce 320-763-3161
Greater Alexandria Area Association of Realtors 320-762-2022

ALEXANDRIA (township). Covers a land area of 24.620 square miles and a water area of 4.590 square miles. Located at 45.90° N. Lat.; 95.34° W. Long. Elevation is 1,392 feet.
History: Settled 1857, laid out 1865.
Population: 4,760 (2000); Race: 97.8% White, 0.0% Black, 0.4% Asian, 0.6% American Indian and Alaska Native, 1.0% Hispanic of any race, 1.2% two or more races (2000); Density: 193.3 persons per square mile (2000); Age: 25.7% under 18, 14.6% over 64 (2000); Marriage status: 22.4% never married, 66.8% now married, 5.3% widowed, 5.5% divorced (2000); Foreign born: 1.3% (2000); Ancestry (includes multiple ancestries): 47.9% German, 32.4% Norwegian, 11.3% Swedish, 7.7% English, 5.5% Irish (2000).
Economy: RR junction. Resort; tourist and trade center; grain, soybeans, alfalfa; livestock, poultry; dairying. Manufactures dairy products, concrete, machinery, electronics, furniture. Employment by occupation: 14.2% management, 20.3% professional, 13.2% services, 28.5% sales, 0.0% farming, 10.7% construction, 13.1% production (2000).
Income: Per capita income: $24,514 (2000); Median household income: $48,846 (2000); Poverty rate: 5.4% (2000).
Taxes: Total city taxes per capita: $93 (2000); City property taxes per capita: $93 (2000).
Education: High school graduation rate: 91.4% (2000); College graduation rate: 23.2% (2000).
Housing: Homeownership rate: 91.6% (2000); Median home value: $123,800 (2000); Median rent: $403 per month (2000); Median age of housing: 24 years (2000).
Transportation: Commute to work: 90.9% car, 0.3% public transportation, 1.1% walk, 7.7% work from home (2000); Travel time to work: 66.5% less than 15 minutes, 26.4% 15 to 30 minutes, 2.7% 30 to 45 minutes, 2.2% 45 to 60 minutes, 2.3% 60 minutes or more (2000)

BELLE RIVER (township). Covers a land area of 35.765 square miles and a water area of 0.193 square miles. Located at 45.98° N. Lat.; 95.20° W. Long. Elevation is 1,362 feet.
Population: 350 (2000); Race: 98.2% White, 0.0% Black, 0.0% Asian, 0.0% American Indian and Alaska Native, 0.0% Hispanic of any race, 1.8% two or more races (2000); Density: 9.8 persons per square mile (2000); Age: 28.3% under 18, 7.6% over 64 (2000); Marriage status: 18.4% never married, 70.3% now married, 3.2% widowed, 8.1% divorced (2000); Foreign born: 0.0% (2000); Ancestry (includes multiple ancestries): 56.8% German, 15.2% Irish, 11.0% Swedish, 9.7% Norwegian, 4.5% French (except Basque) (2000).
Economy: Employment by occupation: 15.9% management, 16.8% professional, 9.6% services, 9.1% sales, 6.3% farming, 16.3% construction, 26.0% production (2000).
Income: Per capita income: $14,630 (2000); Median household income: $36,875 (2000); Poverty rate: 8.4% (2000).
Taxes: Total city taxes per capita: $17 (1997); City property taxes per capita: $17 (1997).
Education: High school graduation rate: 86.9% (2000); College graduation rate: 5.7% (2000).
Housing: Homeownership rate: 87.7% (2000); Median home value: $83,300 (2000); Median rent: $325 per month (2000); Median age of housing: 60+ years (2000).
Transportation: Commute to work: 82.4% car, 0.0% public transportation, 1.0% walk, 16.1% work from home (2000); Travel time to work: 22.1% less than 15 minutes, 48.3% 15 to 30 minutes, 22.7% 30 to 45 minutes, 2.9% 45 to 60 minutes, 4.1% 60 minutes or more (2000)

BRANDON (city). Covers a land area of 0.402 square miles and a water area of 0.008 square miles. Located at 45.96° N. Lat.; 95.59° W. Long. Elevation is 1,387 feet.
History: The town site of Brandon was laid out by Mary Griffin of Minneapolis in 1879, when the Great Northern tracks reached the area. The nearby town of Chippewa was moved to the new site near the railroad. Brandon was named for Brandon, Vermont, the birthplace of Stephen A. Douglas, for whom the county was named.
Population: 450 (2000); Race: 99.0% White, 0.0% Black, 0.5% Asian, 0.0% American Indian and Alaska Native, 0.0% Hispanic of any race, 0.5% two or more races (2000); Density: 1,120.2 persons per square mile (2000); Age: 28.9% under 18, 15.3% over 64 (2000); Marriage status: 22.5% never married, 61.9% now married, 6.9% widowed, 8.8% divorced (2000); Foreign born: 0.5% (2000); Ancestry (includes multiple ancestries): 41.3% German, 27.4% Norwegian, 18.9% Swedish, 7.9% Irish, 5.5% Polish (2000).
Economy: Single-family building permits issued: 0 (2001) / 0 (2000); Multi-family building permits issued: 0 (2001) / 0 (2000); Employment by occupation: 7.2% management, 19.8% professional, 12.6% services, 25.1% sales, 1.0% farming, 13.5% construction, 20.8% production (2000).
Income: Per capita income: $15,088 (2000); Median household income: $28,750 (2000); Poverty rate: 11.7% (2000).
Taxes: Total city taxes per capita: $107 (1997); City property taxes per capita: $107 (1997).
Education: High school graduation rate: 85.7% (2000); College graduation rate: 10.2% (2000).

School District(s)

Brandon (PK-12)
2000 Enrollment: 338 320-524-2263

Housing: Homeownership rate: 74.4% (2000); Median home value: $70,800 (2000); Median rent: $285 per month (2000); Median age of housing: 43 years (2000).
Transportation: Commute to work: 87.8% car, 0.0% public transportation, 6.8% walk, 2.0% work from home (2000); Travel time to work: 38.8% less than 15 minutes, 43.8% 15 to 30 minutes, 10.4% 30 to 45 minutes, 1.5% 45 to 60 minutes, 5.5% 60 minutes or more (2000)

BRANDON (township). Covers a land area of 30.412 square miles and a water area of 5.146 square miles. Located at 45.98° N. Lat.; 95.59° W. Long. Elevation is 1,387 feet.
Population: 641 (2000); Race: 98.5% White, 0.0% Black, 0.0% Asian, 0.0% American Indian and Alaska Native, 0.0% Hispanic of any race, 1.5% two or more races (2000); Density: 21.1 persons per square mile (2000); Age: 22.0% under 18, 15.1% over 64 (2000); Marriage status: 21.1% never married, 71.1% now married, 3.2% widowed, 4.6% divorced (2000); Foreign born:

0.0% (2000); Ancestry (includes multiple ancestries): 48.0% German, 26.3% Norwegian, 13.3% Swedish, 9.7% Irish, 8.8% Polish (2000).
Economy: Grain; livestock, poultry; dairying (butter). Manufacturing: fertilizer, pontoons. Employment by occupation: 17.5% management, 13.7% professional, 12.2% services, 23.3% sales, 1.2% farming, 17.8% construction, 14.3% production (2000).
Income: Per capita income: $21,735 (2000); Median household income: $44,875 (2000); Poverty rate: 5.4% (2000).
Taxes: Total city taxes per capita: $102 (1997); City property taxes per capita: $102 (1997).
Education: High school graduation rate: 86.5% (2000); College graduation rate: 12.4% (2000).
Housing: Homeownership rate: 96.9% (2000); Median home value: $123,400 (2000); Median rent: $325 per month (2000); Median age of housing: 25 years (2000).
Transportation: Commute to work: 86.0% car, 0.0% public transportation, 1.5% walk, 12.5% work from home (2000); Travel time to work: 31.0% less than 15 minutes, 53.7% 15 to 30 minutes, 8.4% 30 to 45 minutes, 3.1% 45 to 60 minutes, 3.8% 60 minutes or more (2000)

CARLOS (city). Covers a land area of 0.468 square miles and a water area of 0 square miles. Located at 45.97° N. Lat.; 95.29° W. Long. Elevation is 1,370 feet.
Population: 329 (2000); Race: 98.6% White, 1.4% Black, 0.0% Asian, 0.0% American Indian and Alaska Native, 0.0% Hispanic of any race, 0.0% two or more races (2000); Density: 702.3 persons per square mile (2000); Age: 20.5% under 18, 16.5% over 64 (2000); Marriage status: 22.9% never married, 54.9% now married, 5.1% widowed, 17.2% divorced (2000); Foreign born: 0.6% (2000); Ancestry (includes multiple ancestries): 54.9% German, 14.5% Norwegian, 9.5% Swedish, 7.2% English, 6.6% United States or American (2000).
Economy: Single-family building permits issued: 9 (2001) / 4 (2000); Multi-family building permits issued: 0 (2001) / 0 (2000); Employment by occupation: 12.1% management, 12.6% professional, 14.6% services, 21.6% sales, 0.0% farming, 10.6% construction, 28.6% production (2000).
Income: Per capita income: $21,495 (2000); Median household income: $38,125 (2000); Poverty rate: 4.4% (2000).
Taxes: Total city taxes per capita: $71 (1997); City property taxes per capita: $63 (1997).
Education: High school graduation rate: 81.4% (2000); College graduation rate: 11.0% (2000).
Housing: Homeownership rate: 85.9% (2000); Median home value: $61,600 (2000); Median rent: $250 per month (2000); Median age of housing: 41 years (2000).
Transportation: Commute to work: 93.5% car, 0.0% public transportation, 1.0% walk, 4.5% work from home (2000); Travel time to work: 34.2% less than 15 minutes, 57.9% 15 to 30 minutes, 2.6% 30 to 45 minutes, 0.0% 45 to 60 minutes, 5.3% 60 minutes or more (2000)

CARLOS (township). Covers a land area of 30.119 square miles and a water area of 5.266 square miles. Located at 45.97° N. Lat.; 95.33° W. Long. Elevation is 1,370 feet.
Population: 1,912 (2000); Race: 98.0% White, 0.0% Black, 0.9% Asian, 0.0% American Indian and Alaska Native, 1.2% Hispanic of any race, 0.4% two or more races (2000); Density: 63.5 persons per square mile (2000); Age: 27.2% under 18, 13.9% over 64 (2000); Marriage status: 17.7% never married, 73.9% now married, 4.1% widowed, 4.3% divorced (2000); Foreign born: 1.4% (2000); Ancestry (includes multiple ancestries): 44.8% German, 25.7% Norwegian, 14.6% Swedish, 9.6% Irish, 6.5% English (2000).
Economy: Agricultural area: dairying; poultry, livestock; grain. Employment by occupation: 16.3% management, 19.6% professional, 11.2% services, 28.4% sales, 0.2% farming, 8.4% construction, 15.9% production (2000).
Income: Per capita income: $23,282 (2000); Median household income: $53,009 (2000); Poverty rate: 3.9% (2000).
Taxes: Total city taxes per capita: $107 (1997); City property taxes per capita: $107 (1997).
Education: High school graduation rate: 93.1% (2000); College graduation rate: 24.6% (2000).
Housing: Homeownership rate: 92.8% (2000); Median home value: $155,800 (2000); Median rent: $475 per month (2000); Median age of housing: 27 years (2000).
Transportation: Commute to work: 92.2% car, 0.0% public transportation, 1.2% walk, 6.4% work from home (2000); Travel time to work: 25.5% less than 15 minutes, 61.3% 15 to 30 minutes, 6.3% 30 to 45 minutes, 0.9% 45 to 60 minutes, 6.0% 60 minutes or more (2000)

EVANSVILLE (city). Covers a land area of 0.697 square miles and a water area of 0.006 square miles. Located at 46.00° N. Lat.; 95.68° W. Long. Elevation is 1,359 feet.
History: Evansville began in the 1850's as a stage station on the route from St. Cloud to Fort Abercrombie, North Dakota. It later became a shipping center for dairy products and livestock.
Population: 566 (2000); Race: 99.1% White, 0.4% Black, 0.0% Asian, 0.0% American Indian and Alaska Native, 0.0% Hispanic of any race, 0.5% two or more races (2000); Density: 811.8 persons per square mile (2000); Age: 19.8% under 18, 34.5% over 64 (2000); Marriage status: 19.0% never married, 54.1% now married, 19.2% widowed, 7.7% divorced (2000); Foreign born: 0.7% (2000); Ancestry (includes multiple ancestries): 41.9% Norwegian, 30.0% German, 23.7% Swedish, 8.1% Irish, 2.5% United States or American (2000).
Economy: Single-family building permits issued: 3 (2001) / 1 (2000); Multi-family building permits issued: 0 (2001) / 0 (2000); Employment by occupation: 6.0% management, 15.7% professional, 19.0% services, 27.3% sales, 0.9% farming, 9.3% construction, 21.8% production (2000).
Income: Per capita income: $17,021 (2000); Median household income: $24,219 (2000); Poverty rate: 10.0% (2000).
Taxes: Total city taxes per capita: $121 (1997); City property taxes per capita: $114 (1997).
Education: High school graduation rate: 74.9% (2000); College graduation rate: 11.2% (2000).

School District(s)

Evansville (KG-12)
2000 Enrollment: 256 218-948-2241
Housing: Homeownership rate: 70.5% (2000); Median home value: $56,900 (2000); Median rent: $245 per month (2000); Median age of housing: 33 years (2000).
Newspapers: West Douglas County Record (1 x week)
Transportation: Commute to work: 86.2% car, 0.0% public transportation, 7.6% walk, 3.8% work from home (2000); Travel time to work: 50.5% less than 15 minutes, 28.2% 15 to 30 minutes, 18.3% 30 to 45 minutes, 0.0% 45 to 60 minutes, 3.0% 60 minutes or more (2000)

EVANSVILLE (township). Covers a land area of 32.618 square miles and a water area of 2.744 square miles. Located at 45.98° N. Lat.; 95.69° W. Long. Elevation is 1,359 feet.
Population: 244 (2000); Race: 100.0% White, 0.0% Black, 0.0% Asian, 0.0% American Indian and Alaska Native, 0.0% Hispanic of any race, 0.0% two or more races (2000); Density: 7.5 persons per square mile (2000); Age: 30.8% under 18, 8.0% over 64 (2000); Marriage status: 21.7% never married, 74.1% now married, 2.1% widowed, 2.1% divorced (2000); Foreign born: 0.8% (2000); Ancestry (includes multiple ancestries): 53.2% Norwegian, 43.5% German, 29.5% Swedish, 8.4% Irish, 5.5% United States or American (2000).
Economy: Dairying; poultry; grain, soybeans, alfalfa. Employment by occupation: 33.3% management, 10.0% professional, 12.0% services, 24.0% sales, 4.7% farming, 6.0% construction, 10.0% production (2000).
Income: Per capita income: $17,601 (2000); Median household income: $48,750 (2000); Poverty rate: 14.3% (2000).
Taxes: Total city taxes per capita: $63 (1997); City property taxes per capita: $63 (1997).
Education: High school graduation rate: 91.2% (2000); College graduation rate: 12.2% (2000).
Housing: Homeownership rate: 91.7% (2000); Median home value: $78,900 (2000); Median rent: $275 per month (2000); Median age of housing: 60+ years (2000).
Transportation: Commute to work: 78.3% car, 0.0% public transportation, 4.9% walk, 16.8% work from home (2000); Travel time to work: 19.3% less than 15 minutes, 48.7% 15 to 30 minutes, 28.6% 30 to 45 minutes, 1.7% 45 to 60 minutes, 1.7% 60 minutes or more (2000)

FORADA (city). Covers a land area of 0.532 square miles and a water area of 0.007 square miles. Located at 45.79° N. Lat.; 95.35° W. Long. Elevation is 1,414 feet.
Population: 197 (2000); Race: 100.0% White, 0.0% Black, 0.0% Asian, 0.0% American Indian and Alaska Native, 0.0% Hispanic of any race, 0.0% two or more races (2000); Density: 370.5 persons per square mile (2000); Age: 24.6% under 18, 15.0% over 64 (2000); Marriage status: 21.6% never married, 61.4% now married, 5.3% widowed, 11.7% divorced (2000); Foreign born: 1.0% (2000); Ancestry (includes multiple ancestries): 43.5% German, 35.7% Norwegian, 13.0% Czech, 13.0% Swedish, 9.2% English (2000).

Economy: Grain; poultry; dairying. Single-family building permits issued: 1 (2001) / 1 (2000); Multi-family building permits issued: 0 (2001) / 0 (2000); Employment by occupation: 7.2% management, 13.4% professional, 21.6% services, 21.6% sales, 6.2% farming, 4.1% construction, 25.8% production (2000).
Income: Per capita income: $16,736 (2000); Median household income: $33,393 (2000); Poverty rate: 5.4% (2000).
Taxes: Total city taxes per capita: $99 (1997); City property taxes per capita: $58 (1997).
Education: High school graduation rate: 92.4% (2000); College graduation rate: 11.1% (2000).
Housing: Homeownership rate: 89.7% (2000); Median home value: $75,900 (2000); Median rent: $525 per month (2000); Median age of housing: 32 years (2000).
Transportation: Commute to work: 91.8% car, 0.0% public transportation, 3.1% walk, 5.2% work from home (2000); Travel time to work: 23.9% less than 15 minutes, 65.2% 15 to 30 minutes, 5.4% 30 to 45 minutes, 2.2% 45 to 60 minutes, 3.3% 60 minutes or more (2000)

GARFIELD (city). Covers a land area of 0.771 square miles and a water area of 0.007 square miles. Located at 45.94° N. Lat.; 95.49° W. Long. Elevation is 1,416 feet.
Population: 281 (2000); Race: 93.8% White, 1.0% Black, 0.0% Asian, 0.0% American Indian and Alaska Native, 0.0% Hispanic of any race, 3.6% two or more races (2000); Density: 364.6 persons per square mile (2000); Age: 32.8% under 18, 10.4% over 64 (2000); Marriage status: 31.1% never married, 49.1% now married, 4.5% widowed, 15.3% divorced (2000); Foreign born: 0.0% (2000); Ancestry (includes multiple ancestries): 47.1% German, 23.1% Norwegian, 13.0% Swedish, 11.7% Irish, 3.9% Other groups (2000).
Economy: Grain; poultry; dairying. Manufacturing: fertilizer, plastic sheets, wood trusses. Single-family building permits issued: 1 (2001) / 2 (2000); Multi-family building permits issued: 0 (2001) / 0 (2000); Employment by occupation: 2.5% management, 17.1% professional, 22.2% services, 29.7% sales, 0.0% farming, 4.4% construction, 24.1% production (2000).
Income: Per capita income: $12,847 (2000); Median household income: $30,000 (2000); Poverty rate: 15.6% (2000).
Taxes: Total city taxes per capita: $104 (1997); City property taxes per capita: $96 (1997).
Education: High school graduation rate: 84.7% (2000); College graduation rate: 7.4% (2000).
Housing: Homeownership rate: 76.6% (2000); Median home value: $67,300 (2000); Median rent: $479 per month (2000); Median age of housing: 41 years (2000).
Transportation: Commute to work: 84.0% car, 0.0% public transportation, 10.9% walk, 2.6% work from home (2000); Travel time to work: 32.9% less than 15 minutes, 59.9% 15 to 30 minutes, 2.0% 30 to 45 minutes, 3.9% 45 to 60 minutes, 1.3% 60 minutes or more (2000)

HOLMES CITY (township). Covers a land area of 30.375 square miles and a water area of 6.008 square miles. Located at 45.82° N. Lat.; 95.57° W. Long. Elevation is 1,406 feet.
Population: 737 (2000); Race: 97.6% White, 0.0% Black, 0.0% Asian, 0.4% American Indian and Alaska Native, 1.1% Hispanic of any race, 0.3% two or more races (2000); Density: 24.3 persons per square mile (2000); Age: 30.5% under 18, 12.4% over 64 (2000); Marriage status: 18.5% never married, 70.1% now married, 5.2% widowed, 6.2% divorced (2000); Foreign born: 1.6% (2000); Ancestry (includes multiple ancestries): 41.0% German, 33.4% Norwegian, 18.8% Swedish, 5.5% Czech, 5.3% English (2000).
Economy: Employment by occupation: 18.3% management, 16.9% professional, 13.8% services, 24.4% sales, 1.7% farming, 6.3% construction, 18.6% production (2000).
Income: Per capita income: $17,411 (2000); Median household income: $35,000 (2000); Poverty rate: 4.2% (2000).
Taxes: Total city taxes per capita: $66 (1997); City property taxes per capita: $66 (1997).
Education: High school graduation rate: 84.9% (2000); College graduation rate: 13.9% (2000).
Housing: Homeownership rate: 89.7% (2000); Median home value: $122,400 (2000); Median rent: $311 per month (2000); Median age of housing: 26 years (2000).
Transportation: Commute to work: 84.6% car, 0.6% public transportation, 2.0% walk, 12.2% work from home (2000); Travel time to work: 18.2% less than 15 minutes, 67.5% 15 to 30 minutes, 8.6% 30 to 45 minutes, 2.0% 45 to 60 minutes, 3.6% 60 minutes or more (2000)

HUDSON (township). Covers a land area of 33.078 square miles and a water area of 2.020 square miles. Located at 45.80° N. Lat.; 95.34° W. Long.
Population: 686 (2000); Race: 99.7% White, 0.0% Black, 0.0% Asian, 0.3% American Indian and Alaska Native, 0.0% Hispanic of any race, 0.0% two or more races (2000); Density: 20.7 persons per square mile (2000); Age: 21.9% under 18, 17.3% over 64 (2000); Marriage status: 21.7% never married, 61.1% now married, 5.9% widowed, 11.4% divorced (2000); Foreign born: 0.5% (2000); Ancestry (includes multiple ancestries): 46.7% German, 27.7% Norwegian, 9.3% Irish, 9.2% English, 8.4% Swedish (2000).
Economy: Employment by occupation: 20.3% management, 19.4% professional, 9.3% services, 20.0% sales, 2.8% farming, 11.8% construction, 16.3% production (2000).
Income: Per capita income: $20,897 (2000); Median household income: $40,972 (2000); Poverty rate: 5.9% (2000).
Taxes: Total city taxes per capita: $115 (1997); City property taxes per capita: $115 (1997).
Education: High school graduation rate: 84.6% (2000); College graduation rate: 22.8% (2000).
Housing: Homeownership rate: 90.4% (2000); Median home value: $130,300 (2000); Median rent: $369 per month (2000); Median age of housing: 26 years (2000).
Transportation: Commute to work: 90.9% car, 0.0% public transportation, 1.2% walk, 7.0% work from home (2000); Travel time to work: 43.7% less than 15 minutes, 45.6% 15 to 30 minutes, 3.8% 30 to 45 minutes, 1.3% 45 to 60 minutes, 5.7% 60 minutes or more (2000)

IDA (township). Covers a land area of 27.944 square miles and a water area of 7.644 square miles. Located at 45.97° N. Lat.; 95.45° W. Long.
Population: 1,057 (2000); Race: 96.3% White, 0.0% Black, 1.0% Asian, 0.0% American Indian and Alaska Native, 1.4% Hispanic of any race, 1.4% two or more races (2000); Density: 37.8 persons per square mile (2000); Age: 24.0% under 18, 14.8% over 64 (2000); Marriage status: 17.4% never married, 71.7% now married, 4.3% widowed, 6.6% divorced (2000); Foreign born: 1.0% (2000); Ancestry (includes multiple ancestries): 44.9% German, 22.4% Norwegian, 11.5% Swedish, 7.8% Irish, 7.0% English (2000).
Economy: Employment by occupation: 17.2% management, 14.5% professional, 11.7% services, 25.0% sales, 1.6% farming, 9.6% construction, 20.4% production (2000).
Income: Per capita income: $19,221 (2000); Median household income: $45,208 (2000); Poverty rate: 5.1% (2000).
Education: High school graduation rate: 90.5% (2000); College graduation rate: 20.0% (2000).
Housing: Homeownership rate: 93.2% (2000); Median home value: $143,600 (2000); Median rent: $467 per month (2000); Median age of housing: 23 years (2000).
Transportation: Commute to work: 86.5% car, 0.0% public transportation, 2.4% walk, 9.1% work from home (2000); Travel time to work: 31.9% less than 15 minutes, 60.6% 15 to 30 minutes, 3.7% 30 to 45 minutes, 0.7% 45 to 60 minutes, 3.1% 60 minutes or more (2000)

KENSINGTON (city). Covers a land area of 0.261 square miles and a water area of 0 square miles. Located at 45.77° N. Lat.; 95.69° W. Long. Elevation is 1,318 feet.
History: Kensington Rune Stone, with ancient inscription describing journey of Swedish and Norwegian explorers, was found nearby in 1989.
Population: 286 (2000); Race: 95.3% White, 1.3% Black, 0.0% Asian, 0.0% American Indian and Alaska Native, 0.0% Hispanic of any race, 3.3% two or more races (2000); Density: 1,093.9 persons per square mile (2000); Age: 21.7% under 18, 21.1% over 64 (2000); Marriage status: 22.4% never married, 54.4% now married, 9.1% widowed, 14.1% divorced (2000); Foreign born: 0.0% (2000); Ancestry (includes multiple ancestries): 41.1% German, 32.8% Norwegian, 18.7% Swedish, 8.7% Irish, 4.0% Other groups (2000).
Economy: Dairying; poultry; alfalfa, soybeans, grain. Manufacturing: feeds. Single-family building permits issued: 0 (2001) / 0 (2000); Multi-family building permits issued: 0 (2001) / 0 (2000); Employment by occupation: 9.6% management, 15.1% professional, 11.6% services, 12.3% sales, 0.0% farming, 17.1% construction, 34.2% production (2000).
Income: Per capita income: $14,932 (2000); Median household income: $31,979 (2000); Poverty rate: 14.8% (2000).
Taxes: Total city taxes per capita: $98 (1997); City property taxes per capita: $98 (1997).
Education: High school graduation rate: 75.0% (2000); College graduation rate: 8.5% (2000).

Housing: Homeownership rate: 78.5% (2000); Median home value: $37,500 (2000); Median rent: $145 per month (2000); Median age of housing: 46 years (2000).
Transportation: Commute to work: 81.3% car, 0.0% public transportation, 13.2% walk, 1.4% work from home (2000); Travel time to work: 37.3% less than 15 minutes, 36.6% 15 to 30 minutes, 21.1% 30 to 45 minutes, 1.4% 45 to 60 minutes, 3.5% 60 minutes or more (2000)

LA GRAND (township). Covers a land area of 26.398 square miles and a water area of 6.514 square miles. Located at 45.89° N. Lat.; 95.43° W. Long.
Population: 4,056 (2000); Race: 99.2% White, 0.4% Black, 0.0% Asian, 0.0% American Indian and Alaska Native, 0.2% Hispanic of any race, 0.4% two or more races (2000); Density: 153.6 persons per square mile (2000); Age: 26.1% under 18, 14.3% over 64 (2000); Marriage status: 19.0% never married, 72.1% now married, 4.1% widowed, 4.8% divorced (2000); Foreign born: 0.8% (2000); Ancestry (includes multiple ancestries): 48.6% German, 28.5% Norwegian, 17.0% Swedish, 9.5% Irish, 6.2% English (2000).
Economy: Employment by occupation: 11.8% management, 19.9% professional, 12.6% services, 30.8% sales, 1.1% farming, 8.5% construction, 15.2% production (2000).
Income: Per capita income: $20,837 (2000); Median household income: $52,500 (2000); Poverty rate: 4.4% (2000).
Taxes: Total city taxes per capita: $122 (2000); City property taxes per capita: $122 (2000).
Education: High school graduation rate: 91.8% (2000); College graduation rate: 27.1% (2000).
Housing: Homeownership rate: 92.3% (2000); Median home value: $129,100 (2000); Median rent: $419 per month (2000); Median age of housing: 25 years (2000).
Transportation: Commute to work: 91.0% car, 0.4% public transportation, 1.9% walk, 5.5% work from home (2000); Travel time to work: 68.4% less than 15 minutes, 20.7% 15 to 30 minutes, 6.0% 30 to 45 minutes, 1.9% 45 to 60 minutes, 3.0% 60 minutes or more (2000)

LAKE MARY (township). Covers a land area of 28.730 square miles and a water area of 6.461 square miles. Located at 45.80° N. Lat.; 95.45° W. Long.
Population: 997 (2000); Race: 99.5% White, 0.3% Black, 0.0% Asian, 0.0% American Indian and Alaska Native, 0.4% Hispanic of any race, 0.2% two or more races (2000); Density: 34.7 persons per square mile (2000); Age: 24.7% under 18, 16.1% over 64 (2000); Marriage status: 17.9% never married, 75.3% now married, 3.0% widowed, 3.7% divorced (2000); Foreign born: 0.2% (2000); Ancestry (includes multiple ancestries): 41.6% German, 23.8% Norwegian, 18.4% Czech, 13.4% Swedish, 7.0% Irish (2000).
Economy: Employment by occupation: 17.5% management, 18.3% professional, 10.6% services, 25.3% sales, 0.4% farming, 10.2% construction, 17.7% production (2000).
Income: Per capita income: $19,621 (2000); Median household income: $45,515 (2000); Poverty rate: 3.4% (2000).
Taxes: Total city taxes per capita: $69 (1997); City property taxes per capita: $69 (1997).
Education: High school graduation rate: 86.0% (2000); College graduation rate: 14.5% (2000).
Housing: Homeownership rate: 92.2% (2000); Median home value: $113,500 (2000); Median rent: $425 per month (2000); Median age of housing: 24 years (2000).
Transportation: Commute to work: 88.7% car, 0.0% public transportation, 0.0% walk, 10.9% work from home (2000); Travel time to work: 38.6% less than 15 minutes, 51.7% 15 to 30 minutes, 3.2% 30 to 45 minutes, 3.9% 45 to 60 minutes, 2.5% 60 minutes or more (2000)

LEAF VALLEY (township). Covers a land area of 33.432 square miles and a water area of 2.795 square miles. Located at 46.05° N. Lat.; 95.44° W. Long.
Population: 484 (2000); Race: 100.0% White, 0.0% Black, 0.0% Asian, 0.0% American Indian and Alaska Native, 1.0% Hispanic of any race, 0.0% two or more races (2000); Density: 14.5 persons per square mile (2000); Age: 22.6% under 18, 17.5% over 64 (2000); Marriage status: 22.9% never married, 65.4% now married, 6.3% widowed, 5.4% divorced (2000); Foreign born: 0.0% (2000); Ancestry (includes multiple ancestries): 67.8% German, 10.4% Norwegian, 10.2% Polish, 7.7% Irish, 6.7% Swedish (2000).
Economy: Employment by occupation: 25.7% management, 10.5% professional, 9.7% services, 18.7% sales, 2.7% farming, 8.2% construction, 24.5% production (2000).
Income: Per capita income: $18,310 (2000); Median household income: $41,500 (2000); Poverty rate: 8.8% (2000).
Taxes: Total city taxes per capita: $96 (1997); City property taxes per capita: $96 (1997).
Education: High school graduation rate: 82.9% (2000); College graduation rate: 12.3% (2000).
Housing: Homeownership rate: 87.6% (2000); Median home value: $149,300 (2000); Median rent: $375 per month (2000); Median age of housing: 28 years (2000).
Transportation: Commute to work: 82.0% car, 0.0% public transportation, 4.3% walk, 13.7% work from home (2000); Travel time to work: 24.4% less than 15 minutes, 54.3% 15 to 30 minutes, 14.5% 30 to 45 minutes, 0.9% 45 to 60 minutes, 5.9% 60 minutes or more (2000)

LUND (township). Covers a land area of 28.221 square miles and a water area of 7.794 square miles. Located at 46.07° N. Lat.; 95.71° W. Long.
Population: 355 (2000); Race: 98.7% White, 0.0% Black, 0.0% Asian, 0.0% American Indian and Alaska Native, 0.0% Hispanic of any race, 1.3% two or more races (2000); Density: 12.6 persons per square mile (2000); Age: 31.8% under 18, 11.2% over 64 (2000); Marriage status: 25.7% never married, 64.5% now married, 3.3% widowed, 6.6% divorced (2000); Foreign born: 0.5% (2000); Ancestry (includes multiple ancestries): 48.6% Norwegian, 34.9% German, 26.2% Swedish, 6.4% United States or American, 5.6% Irish (2000).
Economy: Employment by occupation: 15.2% management, 19.7% professional, 12.4% services, 20.8% sales, 2.2% farming, 13.5% construction, 16.3% production (2000).
Income: Per capita income: $15,567 (2000); Median household income: $40,417 (2000); Poverty rate: 5.9% (2000).
Taxes: Total city taxes per capita: $69 (1997); City property taxes per capita: $69 (1997).
Education: High school graduation rate: 82.8% (2000); College graduation rate: 10.9% (2000).
Housing: Homeownership rate: 87.0% (2000); Median home value: $77,500 (2000); Median rent: $300 per month (2000); Median age of housing: 33 years (2000).
Transportation: Commute to work: 82.1% car, 0.0% public transportation, 5.2% walk, 11.6% work from home (2000); Travel time to work: 41.2% less than 15 minutes, 25.5% 15 to 30 minutes, 28.8% 30 to 45 minutes, 0.7% 45 to 60 minutes, 3.9% 60 minutes or more (2000)

MILLERVILLE (city). Covers a land area of 0.872 square miles and a water area of 0 square miles. Located at 46.06° N. Lat.; 95.56° W. Long. Elevation is 1,392 feet.
Population: 115 (2000); Race: 96.0% White, 0.0% Black, 0.0% Asian, 0.0% American Indian and Alaska Native, 0.0% Hispanic of any race, 4.0% two or more races (2000); Density: 131.9 persons per square mile (2000); Age: 29.6% under 18, 14.4% over 64 (2000); Marriage status: 29.0% never married, 54.0% now married, 11.0% widowed, 6.0% divorced (2000); Foreign born: 0.0% (2000); Ancestry (includes multiple ancestries): 72.0% German, 15.2% Polish, 7.2% Swedish, 7.2% Other groups, 7.2% Norwegian (2000).
Economy: Employment by occupation: 21.4% management, 10.7% professional, 23.2% services, 26.8% sales, 0.0% farming, 3.6% construction, 14.3% production (2000).
Income: Per capita income: $13,322 (2000); Median household income: $29,063 (2000); Poverty rate: 12.2% (2000).
Education: High school graduation rate: 71.1% (2000); College graduation rate: 13.2% (2000).
Housing: Homeownership rate: 70.6% (2000); Median home value: $50,000 (2000); Median rent: $195 per month (2000); Median age of housing: 60 years (2000).
Transportation: Commute to work: 75.0% car, 0.0% public transportation, 0.0% walk, 25.0% work from home (2000); Travel time to work: 31.0% less than 15 minutes, 57.1% 15 to 30 minutes, 11.9% 30 to 45 minutes, 0.0% 45 to 60 minutes, 0.0% 60 minutes or more (2000)

MILLERVILLE (township). Covers a land area of 31.871 square miles and a water area of 3.366 square miles. Located at 46.05° N. Lat.; 95.60° W. Long. Elevation is 1,392 feet.
Population: 350 (2000); Race: 100.0% White, 0.0% Black, 0.0% Asian, 0.0% American Indian and Alaska Native, 0.0% Hispanic of any race, 0.0% two or more races (2000); Density: 11.0 persons per square mile (2000); Age: 32.5% under 18, 9.8% over 64 (2000); Marriage status: 27.0% never married, 66.4% now married, 3.3% widowed, 3.3% divorced (2000); Foreign born: 0.0% (2000); Ancestry (includes multiple ancestries): 64.4% German, 12.6% Irish, 12.3% Norwegian, 11.7% Polish, 4.9% Swedish (2000).

Economy: Grain; livestock; dairying. Employment by occupation: 34.1% management, 9.1% professional, 9.1% services, 17.7% sales, 4.9% farming, 7.3% construction, 17.7% production (2000).
Income: Per capita income: $14,366 (2000); Median household income: $36,500 (2000); Poverty rate: 16.3% (2000).
Taxes: Total city taxes per capita: $71 (1997); City property taxes per capita: $71 (1997).
Education: High school graduation rate: 86.5% (2000); College graduation rate: 4.3% (2000).
Housing: Homeownership rate: 87.5% (2000); Median home value: $109,400 (2000); Median rent: $375 per month (2000); Median age of housing: 30 years (2000).
Transportation: Commute to work: 61.0% car, 1.2% public transportation, 2.4% walk, 35.4% work from home (2000); Travel time to work: 20.8% less than 15 minutes, 60.4% 15 to 30 minutes, 12.3% 30 to 45 minutes, 4.7% 45 to 60 minutes, 1.9% 60 minutes or more (2000)

MILTONA (city). Covers a land area of 0.531 square miles and a water area of 0 square miles. Located at 46.04° N. Lat.; 95.29° W. Long. Elevation is 1,399 feet.
Population: 279 (2000); Race: 99.3% White, 0.0% Black, 0.0% Asian, 0.0% American Indian and Alaska Native, 1.1% Hispanic of any race, 0.7% two or more races (2000); Density: 525.3 persons per square mile (2000); Age: 25.9% under 18, 19.1% over 64 (2000); Marriage status: 16.4% never married, 65.7% now married, 9.4% widowed, 8.5% divorced (2000); Foreign born: 0.0% (2000); Ancestry (includes multiple ancestries): 68.8% German, 20.6% Norwegian, 11.0% Irish, 8.5% Danish, 6.0% Swedish (2000).
Economy: Single-family building permits issued: 2 (2001) / 1 (2000); Multi-family building permits issued: 0 (2001) / 0 (2000); Employment by occupation: 11.0% management, 18.5% professional, 11.6% services, 19.2% sales, 0.0% farming, 17.1% construction, 22.6% production (2000).
Income: Per capita income: $13,845 (2000); Median household income: $28,333 (2000); Poverty rate: 20.2% (2000).
Taxes: Total city taxes per capita: $115 (1997); City property taxes per capita: $100 (1997).
Education: High school graduation rate: 82.1% (2000); College graduation rate: 7.6% (2000).
Housing: Homeownership rate: 81.0% (2000); Median home value: $74,600 (2000); Median rent: $375 per month (2000); Median age of housing: 28 years (2000).
Transportation: Commute to work: 92.7% car, 0.0% public transportation, 4.4% walk, 1.5% work from home (2000); Travel time to work: 29.6% less than 15 minutes, 54.1% 15 to 30 minutes, 11.9% 30 to 45 minutes, 1.5% 45 to 60 minutes, 3.0% 60 minutes or more (2000)

MILTONA (township). Covers a land area of 27.114 square miles and a water area of 8.723 square miles. Located at 46.05° N. Lat.; 95.31° W. Long. Elevation is 1,399 feet.
Population: 814 (2000); Race: 99.6% White, 0.0% Black, 0.0% Asian, 0.4% American Indian and Alaska Native, 0.0% Hispanic of any race, 0.0% two or more races (2000); Density: 30.0 persons per square mile (2000); Age: 17.5% under 18, 18.7% over 64 (2000); Marriage status: 16.9% never married, 73.9% now married, 4.9% widowed, 4.3% divorced (2000); Foreign born: 0.4% (2000); Ancestry (includes multiple ancestries): 52.9% German, 23.8% Norwegian, 15.7% Swedish, 8.6% Irish, 5.2% English (2000).
Economy: Grain; poultry; dairying. Manufacturing: concrete, golf course repair tools. Employment by occupation: 15.2% management, 20.2% professional, 12.9% services, 21.4% sales, 1.2% farming, 8.5% construction, 20.5% production (2000).
Income: Per capita income: $20,773 (2000); Median household income: $38,083 (2000); Poverty rate: 8.1% (2000).
Taxes: Total city taxes per capita: $122 (1997); City property taxes per capita: $122 (1997).
Education: High school graduation rate: 86.9% (2000); College graduation rate: 14.2% (2000).
Housing: Homeownership rate: 93.7% (2000); Median home value: $137,900 (2000); Median rent: $475 per month (2000); Median age of housing: 27 years (2000).
Transportation: Commute to work: 81.8% car, 0.0% public transportation, 3.8% walk, 13.8% work from home (2000); Travel time to work: 24.8% less than 15 minutes, 54.4% 15 to 30 minutes, 17.0% 30 to 45 minutes, 0.7% 45 to 60 minutes, 3.1% 60 minutes or more (2000)

MOE (township). Covers a land area of 30.326 square miles and a water area of 5.585 square miles. Located at 45.88° N. Lat.; 95.56° W. Long.
Population: 683 (2000); Race: 99.7% White, 0.0% Black, 0.0% Asian, 0.0% American Indian and Alaska Native, 0.6% Hispanic of any race, 0.3% two or more races (2000); Density: 22.5 persons per square mile (2000); Age: 21.2% under 18, 14.6% over 64 (2000); Marriage status: 16.5% never married, 76.3% now married, 2.8% widowed, 4.3% divorced (2000); Foreign born: 1.2% (2000); Ancestry (includes multiple ancestries): 39.5% German, 32.2% Norwegian, 13.6% Swedish, 6.6% Irish, 4.8% Polish (2000).
Economy: Employment by occupation: 12.9% management, 14.8% professional, 15.9% services, 23.4% sales, 2.2% farming, 14.8% construction, 15.9% production (2000).
Income: Per capita income: $19,917 (2000); Median household income: $43,828 (2000); Poverty rate: 4.9% (2000).
Education: High school graduation rate: 88.7% (2000); College graduation rate: 15.0% (2000).
Housing: Homeownership rate: 93.5% (2000); Median home value: $141,200 (2000); Median rent: $408 per month (2000); Median age of housing: 19 years (2000).
Transportation: Commute to work: 94.2% car, 0.0% public transportation, 0.6% walk, 5.3% work from home (2000); Travel time to work: 16.7% less than 15 minutes, 64.8% 15 to 30 minutes, 10.3% 30 to 45 minutes, 2.9% 45 to 60 minutes, 5.3% 60 minutes or more (2000)

NELSON (city). Covers a land area of 0.729 square miles and a water area of 0 square miles. Located at 45.88° N. Lat.; 95.26° W. Long.
Population: 172 (2000); Race: 93.6% White, 0.0% Black, 1.3% Asian, 0.0% American Indian and Alaska Native, 1.3% Hispanic of any race, 0.0% two or more races (2000); Density: 235.8 persons per square mile (2000); Age: 28.8% under 18, 14.7% over 64 (2000); Marriage status: 34.2% never married, 53.8% now married, 8.5% widowed, 3.4% divorced (2000); Foreign born: 0.0% (2000); Ancestry (includes multiple ancestries): 45.5% German, 26.9% Norwegian, 12.8% Swedish, 10.3% United States or American, 7.7% Other groups (2000).
Economy: Poultry, livestock; grain; dairying. Manufacturing of wood products, dairy products. Employment by occupation: 0.0% management, 10.0% professional, 14.3% services, 15.7% sales, 0.0% farming, 30.0% construction, 30.0% production (2000).
Income: Per capita income: $13,419 (2000); Median household income: $34,375 (2000); Poverty rate: 23.1% (2000).
Taxes: Total city taxes per capita: $72 (1997); City property taxes per capita: $36 (1997).
Education: High school graduation rate: 86.7% (2000); College graduation rate: 7.8% (2000).
Housing: Homeownership rate: 65.6% (2000); Median home value: $65,000 (2000); Median rent: $380 per month (2000); Median age of housing: 60+ years (2000).
Transportation: Commute to work: 97.1% car, 0.0% public transportation, 2.9% walk, 0.0% work from home (2000); Travel time to work: 45.7% less than 15 minutes, 47.1% 15 to 30 minutes, 2.9% 30 to 45 minutes, 4.3% 45 to 60 minutes, 0.0% 60 minutes or more (2000)

ORANGE (township). Covers a land area of 34.456 square miles and a water area of 1.415 square miles. Located at 45.80° N. Lat.; 95.19° W. Long.
Population: 324 (2000); Race: 95.5% White, 1.4% Black, 0.0% Asian, 3.1% American Indian and Alaska Native, 0.0% Hispanic of any race, 0.0% two or more races (2000); Density: 9.4 persons per square mile (2000); Age: 29.5% under 18, 10.5% over 64 (2000); Marriage status: 22.3% never married, 74.0% now married, 2.6% widowed, 1.1% divorced (2000); Foreign born: 1.4% (2000); Ancestry (includes multiple ancestries): 60.2% German, 18.5% Irish, 14.5% Norwegian, 4.8% Other groups, 4.8% English (2000).
Economy: Employment by occupation: 15.1% management, 14.5% professional, 17.9% services, 19.0% sales, 1.7% farming, 12.3% construction, 19.6% production (2000).
Income: Per capita income: $15,837 (2000); Median household income: $46,250 (2000); Poverty rate: 7.4% (2000).
Taxes: Total city taxes per capita: $63 (1997); City property taxes per capita: $63 (1997).
Education: High school graduation rate: 84.6% (2000); College graduation rate: 5.9% (2000).
Housing: Homeownership rate: 87.1% (2000); Median home value: $102,500 (2000); Median age of housing: 28 years (2000).
Transportation: Commute to work: 79.9% car, 2.2% public transportation, 0.6% walk, 16.2% work from home (2000); Travel time to work: 19.3% less than 15 minutes, 48.0% 15 to 30 minutes, 26.0% 30 to 45 minutes, 2.7% 45 to 60 minutes, 4.0% 60 minutes or more (2000)

OSAKIS (city). Covers a land area of 2.011 square miles and a water area of 0.122 square miles. Located at 45.86° N. Lat.; 95.14° W. Long. Elevation is 1,345 feet.
History: Osakis was established on the lake of the same name, which is of Indian origin meaning "danger." The community developed as a popular fishing and summer resort.
Population: 1,567 (2000); Race: 97.8% White, 0.4% Black, 1.1% Asian, 0.3% American Indian and Alaska Native, 0.3% Hispanic of any race, 0.4% two or more races (2000); Density: 779.4 persons per square mile (2000); Age: 22.7% under 18, 28.4% over 64 (2000); Marriage status: 20.2% never married, 61.6% now married, 11.5% widowed, 6.7% divorced (2000); Foreign born: 1.4% (2000); Ancestry (includes multiple ancestries): 42.0% German, 21.8% Norwegian, 9.7% Irish, 9.3% Swedish, 6.9% United States or American (2000).
Economy: Single-family building permits issued: 16 (2001) / 7 (2000); Multi-family building permits issued: 0 (2001) / 0 (2000); Employment by occupation: 7.6% management, 16.9% professional, 17.5% services, 22.2% sales, 0.7% farming, 7.2% construction, 28.0% production (2000).
Income: Per capita income: $15,212 (2000); Median household income: $29,833 (2000); Poverty rate: 9.1% (2000).
Taxes: Total city taxes per capita: $167 (1997); City property taxes per capita: $145 (1997).
Education: High school graduation rate: 76.1% (2000); College graduation rate: 10.2% (2000).

School District(s)

Osakis (PK-12)
2000 Enrollment: 652 320-859-2191
Peaks-Alexandria (09-12)
2000 Enrollment: 60 320-859-5302

Housing: Homeownership rate: 72.7% (2000); Median home value: $64,300 (2000); Median rent: $287 per month (2000); Median age of housing: 43 years (2000).
Newspapers: Osakis Review (1 x week)
Transportation: Commute to work: 85.6% car, 0.0% public transportation, 7.0% walk, 6.5% work from home (2000); Travel time to work: 36.6% less than 15 minutes, 46.6% 15 to 30 minutes, 8.2% 30 to 45 minutes, 0.9% 45 to 60 minutes, 7.7% 60 minutes or more (2000)

OSAKIS (township). Covers a land area of 31.371 square miles and a water area of 2.755 square miles. Located at 45.89° N. Lat.; 95.19° W. Long. Elevation is 1,345 feet.
Population: 584 (2000); Race: 99.7% White, 0.0% Black, 0.0% Asian, 0.0% American Indian and Alaska Native, 0.0% Hispanic of any race, 0.3% two or more races (2000); Density: 18.6 persons per square mile (2000); Age: 30.1% under 18, 11.1% over 64 (2000); Marriage status: 18.4% never married, 70.0% now married, 3.0% widowed, 8.6% divorced (2000); Foreign born: 0.0% (2000); Ancestry (includes multiple ancestries): 49.3% German, 15.6% Irish, 15.4% Norwegian, 11.9% Swedish, 6.4% French (except Basque) (2000).
Economy: Employment by occupation: 23.6% management, 10.9% professional, 14.1% services, 17.9% sales, 4.8% farming, 9.3% construction, 19.5% production (2000).
Income: Per capita income: $16,130 (2000); Median household income: $35,909 (2000); Poverty rate: 11.4% (2000).
Taxes: Total city taxes per capita: $99 (1997); City property taxes per capita: $99 (1997).
Education: High school graduation rate: 87.5% (2000); College graduation rate: 8.2% (2000).
Housing: Homeownership rate: 93.5% (2000); Median home value: $93,000 (2000); Median rent: $138 per month (2000); Median age of housing: 29 years (2000).
Transportation: Commute to work: 80.2% car, 0.0% public transportation, 4.3% walk, 14.9% work from home (2000); Travel time to work: 38.8% less than 15 minutes, 46.5% 15 to 30 minutes, 9.7% 30 to 45 minutes, 0.8% 45 to 60 minutes, 4.3% 60 minutes or more (2000)

SOLEM (township). Covers a land area of 33.918 square miles and a water area of 1.940 square miles. Located at 45.80° N. Lat.; 95.68° W. Long.
Population: 239 (2000); Race: 100.0% White, 0.0% Black, 0.0% Asian, 0.0% American Indian and Alaska Native, 0.0% Hispanic of any race, 0.0% two or more races (2000); Density: 7.0 persons per square mile (2000); Age: 29.0% under 18, 19.8% over 64 (2000); Marriage status: 17.9% never married, 68.4% now married, 6.3% widowed, 7.4% divorced (2000); Foreign born: 1.2% (2000); Ancestry (includes multiple ancestries): 34.5% Norwegian, 29.8% German, 19.4% Swedish, 9.1% English, 5.6% Irish (2000).
Economy: Employment by occupation: 29.7% management, 9.3% professional, 8.5% services, 16.9% sales, 4.2% farming, 9.3% construction, 22.0% production (2000).
Income: Per capita income: $18,016 (2000); Median household income: $34,688 (2000); Poverty rate: 4.8% (2000).
Taxes: Total city taxes per capita: $45 (1997); City property taxes per capita: $45 (1997).
Education: High school graduation rate: 86.2% (2000); College graduation rate: 15.0% (2000).
Housing: Homeownership rate: 94.6% (2000); Median home value: $85,000 (2000); Median rent: $225 per month (2000); Median age of housing: 50 years (2000).
Transportation: Commute to work: 71.3% car, 0.0% public transportation, 5.2% walk, 23.5% work from home (2000); Travel time to work: 45.5% less than 15 minutes, 36.4% 15 to 30 minutes, 5.7% 30 to 45 minutes, 4.5% 45 to 60 minutes, 8.0% 60 minutes or more (2000)

SPRUCE HILL (township). Covers a land area of 35.833 square miles and a water area of 0.299 square miles. Located at 46.07° N. Lat.; 95.21° W. Long.
Population: 395 (2000); Race: 99.6% White, 0.0% Black, 0.4% Asian, 0.0% American Indian and Alaska Native, 0.0% Hispanic of any race, 0.0% two or more races (2000); Density: 11.0 persons per square mile (2000); Age: 30.3% under 18, 10.3% over 64 (2000); Marriage status: 23.2% never married, 68.3% now married, 4.1% widowed, 4.4% divorced (2000); Foreign born: 0.0% (2000); Ancestry (includes multiple ancestries): 47.6% German, 19.3% Swedish, 16.6% Norwegian, 8.5% United States or American, 4.9% Irish (2000).
Economy: Employment by occupation: 23.0% management, 8.6% professional, 7.8% services, 18.4% sales, 4.1% farming, 13.9% construction, 24.2% production (2000).
Income: Per capita income: $14,583 (2000); Median household income: $37,292 (2000); Poverty rate: 15.3% (2000).
Taxes: Total city taxes per capita: $19 (1997); City property taxes per capita: $19 (1997).
Education: High school graduation rate: 85.1% (2000); College graduation rate: 6.8% (2000).
Housing: Homeownership rate: 89.6% (2000); Median home value: $98,800 (2000); Median rent: $250 per month (2000); Median age of housing: 60+ years (2000).
Transportation: Commute to work: 75.0% car, 2.1% public transportation, 1.7% walk, 18.8% work from home (2000); Travel time to work: 25.6% less than 15 minutes, 34.9% 15 to 30 minutes, 37.4% 30 to 45 minutes, 1.0% 45 to 60 minutes, 1.0% 60 minutes or more (2000)

URNESS (township). Covers a land area of 31.915 square miles and a water area of 3.817 square miles. Located at 45.88° N. Lat.; 95.68° W. Long.
Population: 266 (2000); Race: 99.2% White, 0.0% Black, 0.8% Asian, 0.0% American Indian and Alaska Native, 2.7% Hispanic of any race, 0.0% two or more races (2000); Density: 8.3 persons per square mile (2000); Age: 19.2% under 18, 16.1% over 64 (2000); Marriage status: 25.8% never married, 62.9% now married, 5.7% widowed, 5.7% divorced (2000); Foreign born: 2.4% (2000); Ancestry (includes multiple ancestries): 32.5% Norwegian, 31.0% German, 14.5% Swedish, 11.8% United States or American, 4.7% Irish (2000).
Economy: Employment by occupation: 16.8% management, 14.7% professional, 9.1% services, 20.3% sales, 6.3% farming, 4.9% construction, 28.0% production (2000).
Income: Per capita income: $17,054 (2000); Median household income: $39,583 (2000); Poverty rate: 8.3% (2000).
Taxes: Total city taxes per capita: $114 (1997); City property taxes per capita: $114 (1997).
Education: High school graduation rate: 86.4% (2000); College graduation rate: 16.4% (2000).
Housing: Homeownership rate: 93.0% (2000); Median home value: $94,400 (2000); Median rent: $325 per month (2000); Median age of housing: 23 years (2000).
Transportation: Commute to work: 92.9% car, 0.0% public transportation, 2.8% walk, 4.3% work from home (2000); Travel time to work: 17.8% less than 15 minutes, 43.7% 15 to 30 minutes, 34.8% 30 to 45 minutes, 1.5% 45 to 60 minutes, 2.2% 60 minutes or more (2000)

Faribault County

Located in southern Minnesota; bounded on the south by Iowa; drained by the Blue Earth River. Covers a land area of 713.60 square miles, a water area of 8.00 square miles, and is located in the Central Time Zone. The county government was organized in 1855. County seat is Blue Earth.

Weather Station: Winnebago Elevation: 1,108 feet

	Jan	Feb	Mar	Apr	May	Jun	Jul	Aug	Sep	Oct	Nov	Dec
High	21	27	39	55	69	79	82	80	72	59	40	26
Low	2	10	21	34	47	57	61	59	49	37	23	9
Precip	0.9	0.6	1.9	3.0	3.9	4.5	4.1	4.1	2.8	2.5	1.8	1.0
Snow	11.1	6.2	8.2	3.1	tr	0.0	0.0	0.0	0.0	0.4	6.7	9.4

High and Low temperatures in degrees Fahrenheit; Precipitation and Snow in inches

Population: 16,181 (2000); Race: 96.5% White, 0.2% Black, 0.3% Asian, 0.7% American Indian and Alaska Native, 3.7% Hispanic of any race, 0.8% two or more races (2000); Density: 22.7 persons per square mile (2000); Age: 24.4% under 18, 22.3% over 64 (2000).
Religion: Five largest groups: 32.7% Evangelical Lutheran Church in America, 28.9% Catholic Church, 11.8% The United Methodist Church, 10.3% Lutheran Church—Missouri Synod, 2.8% United Church of Christ (2000).
Economy: Unemployment rate: 3.4% (11/2002); Total civilian labor force: 7,844 (11/2002); Leading industries: 31.3% manufacturing; 16.8% health care and social assistance; 13.5% retail trade (2000); Companies that employ more than 1,000 persons: 0 (2000); Companies that employ more than 100 persons: 7 (2000); Farms: 878 totaling 413,409 acres (1997); Minority business ownership rate: 0.0% (1997); Women business ownership rate: 16.2% (1997); Retail sales per capita: $4,903 (1997). Single-family building permits issued: 18 (2001) / 18 (2000); Multi-family building permits issued: 0 (2001) / 0 (2000).
Income: Per capita income: $17,193 (2000); Median household income: $34,440 (2000); Poverty rate: 8.6% (2000); Bankruptcy rate: 2.70% (2001).
Taxes: Total county taxes per capita: $291 (2000); County property taxes per capita: $291 (2000).
Education: High school graduation rate: 83.6% (2000); College graduation rate: 13.8% (2000).
Housing: Homeownership rate: 80.6% (2000); Median home value: $50,300 (2000); Median rent: $264 per month (2000); Median age of housing: 56 years (2000).
Health: Birth rate: 95.8 per 10,000 population (1998); Age adjusted death rate: 72.0 per 10,000 population (1999); Age adjusted cancer mortality rate: 161.3 deaths per 100,000 population (1999). Number of physicians: 3.7 per 10,000 population (1999); Number of hospital beds: 29.7 per 10,000 population (1999).
Elections: 2000 Presidential election results: 43.0% Gore, 51.5% Bush, 3.7% Nader, 1.3% Buchanan
National and State Parks: Walnut Lake State Wildlife Management Area
Additional Information Contacts
Faribault County Government Offices.................... 507-526-6225
Blue Earth Chamber of Commerce 507-526-2916
Wells Chamber of Commerce 507-553-6450
Winnebago Chamber of Commerce....................... 507-893-3217

Faribault County Communities

BARBER (township). Covers a land area of 36.042 square miles and a water area of 0 square miles. Located at 43.72° N. Lat.; 93.94° W. Long.
Population: 278 (2000); Race: 100.0% White, 0.0% Black, 0.0% Asian, 0.0% American Indian and Alaska Native, 0.0% Hispanic of any race, 0.0% two or more races (2000); Density: 7.7 persons per square mile (2000); Age: 29.8% under 18, 17.4% over 64 (2000); Marriage status: 19.7% never married, 75.1% now married, 3.5% widowed, 1.7% divorced (2000); Foreign born: 0.0% (2000); Ancestry (includes multiple ancestries): 62.3% German, 16.4% Polish, 15.1% Irish, 12.8% Norwegian, 3.9% United States or American (2000).
Economy: Employment by occupation: 21.9% management, 9.4% professional, 16.3% services, 28.1% sales, 5.0% farming, 10.0% construction, 9.4% production (2000).
Income: Per capita income: $14,399 (2000); Median household income: $37,500 (2000); Poverty rate: 0.7% (2000).
Taxes: Total city taxes per capita: $152 (1997); City property taxes per capita: $152 (1997).
Education: High school graduation rate: 92.0% (2000); College graduation rate: 14.1% (2000).
Housing: Homeownership rate: 87.4% (2000); Median home value: $93,100 (2000); Median rent: $225 per month (2000); Median age of housing: 53 years (2000).
Transportation: Commute to work: 75.0% car, 0.0% public transportation, 11.9% walk, 13.1% work from home (2000); Travel time to work: 26.6% less than 15 minutes, 59.0% 15 to 30 minutes, 10.1% 30 to 45 minutes, 0.0% 45 to 60 minutes, 4.3% 60 minutes or more (2000)

BLUE EARTH (city). Covers a land area of 3.185 square miles and a water area of 0 square miles. Located at 43.64° N. Lat.; 94.09° W. Long. Elevation is 1,095 feet.
History: The city of Blue Earth, as well as the river on which it was established, was named for the blue-gren clay in the rocks of the river gorge. One of the founders of the town was James B. Wakefield, who served as lieutenant governor of Minnesota. One of Blue Earth's early industries, an ice cream factory, brought the town the claim of originating the ice cream sandwich. Blue Earth is also home to the Jolly Green Giant, an outgrowth of an early vegetable packing plant.
Population: 3,621 (2000); Race: 96.3% White, 0.0% Black, 0.0% Asian, 1.8% American Indian and Alaska Native, 4.6% Hispanic of any race, 0.6% two or more races (2000); Density: 1,137.0 persons per square mile (2000); Age: 23.1% under 18, 26.0% over 64 (2000); Marriage status: 19.8% never married, 61.6% now married, 11.5% widowed, 7.0% divorced (2000); Foreign born: 0.9% (2000); Ancestry (includes multiple ancestries): 43.8% German, 25.3% Norwegian, 8.5% Irish, 6.3% English, 5.4% Swedish (2000).
Economy: Single-family building permits issued: 6 (2001) / 2 (2000); Multi-family building permits issued: 0 (2001) / 0 (2000); Employment by occupation: 9.7% management, 16.1% professional, 18.6% services, 25.6% sales, 0.8% farming, 8.2% construction, 21.1% production (2000).
Income: Per capita income: $18,037 (2000); Median household income: $34,940 (2000); Poverty rate: 8.0% (2000).
Taxes: Total city taxes per capita: $234 (1997); City property taxes per capita: $224 (1997).
Education: High school graduation rate: 83.9% (2000); College graduation rate: 16.2% (2000).

School District(s)
Blue Earth Area Public School (KG-12)
2000 Enrollment: 1,506 507-526-3188
Housing: Homeownership rate: 74.1% (2000); Median home value: $62,500 (2000); Median rent: $292 per month (2000); Median age of housing: 51 years (2000).
Hospitals: United Hospital District (43 beds)
Safety: Violent crime rate: 2.7 per 10,000 population; Property crime rate: 448.1 per 10,000 population (2001).
Newspapers: Scuttlebutt Magazine (9 x year); The Faribault County Register (1 x week)
Transportation: Commute to work: 87.1% car, 2.3% public transportation, 6.6% walk, 3.1% work from home (2000); Travel time to work: 75.2% less than 15 minutes, 13.0% 15 to 30 minutes, 4.2% 30 to 45 minutes, 3.1% 45 to 60 minutes, 4.5% 60 minutes or more (2000)
Additional Information Contacts
Blue Earth Chamber of Commerce 507-526-2916

BLUE EARTH CITY (township). Covers a land area of 32.919 square miles and a water area of 0.017 square miles. Located at 43.63° N. Lat.; 94.07° W. Long.
Population: 454 (2000); Race: 100.0% White, 0.0% Black, 0.0% Asian, 0.0% American Indian and Alaska Native, 0.0% Hispanic of any race, 0.0% two or more races (2000); Density: 13.8 persons per square mile (2000); Age: 24.7% under 18, 15.8% over 64 (2000); Marriage status: 19.8% never married, 75.4% now married, 3.6% widowed, 1.2% divorced (2000); Foreign born: 0.7% (2000); Ancestry (includes multiple ancestries): 48.4% German, 26.7% Norwegian, 12.1% Irish, 7.4% English, 5.7% United States or American (2000).
Economy: Employment by occupation: 24.1% management, 15.9% professional, 7.8% services, 23.3% sales, 3.4% farming, 12.5% construction, 12.9% production (2000).
Income: Per capita income: $21,517 (2000); Median household income: $52,500 (2000); Poverty rate: 5.4% (2000).
Taxes: Total city taxes per capita: $33 (1997); City property taxes per capita: $33 (1997).
Education: High school graduation rate: 92.8% (2000); College graduation rate: 19.2% (2000).
Housing: Homeownership rate: 87.3% (2000); Median home value: $89,600 (2000); Median rent: $275 per month (2000); Median age of housing: 52 years (2000).

Transportation: Commute to work: 88.4% car, 0.0% public transportation, 0.9% walk, 10.3% work from home (2000); Travel time to work: 64.9% less than 15 minutes, 19.7% 15 to 30 minutes, 7.7% 30 to 45 minutes, 1.9% 45 to 60 minutes, 5.8% 60 minutes or more (2000)

BRICELYN (city). Covers a land area of 0.295 square miles and a water area of 0 square miles. Located at 43.56° N. Lat.; 93.81° W. Long. Elevation is 1,177 feet.
Population: 379 (2000); Race: 94.0% White, 0.0% Black, 0.0% Asian, 0.0% American Indian and Alaska Native, 6.9% Hispanic of any race, 1.5% two or more races (2000); Density: 1,283.9 persons per square mile (2000); Age: 23.1% under 18, 30.8% over 64 (2000); Marriage status: 17.4% never married, 65.5% now married, 10.2% widowed, 6.8% divorced (2000); Foreign born: 2.7% (2000); Ancestry (includes multiple ancestries): 46.7% Norwegian, 36.2% German, 9.4% Other groups, 5.7% Irish, 4.7% United States or American (2000).
Economy: Railroad junction. Corn, oats, soybeans; livestock. Single-family building permits issued: 0 (2001) / 0 (2000); Multi-family building permits issued: 0 (2001) / 0 (2000); Employment by occupation: 9.6% management, 13.2% professional, 14.4% services, 15.0% sales, 3.0% farming, 12.0% construction, 32.9% production (2000).
Income: Per capita income: $15,340 (2000); Median household income: $29,375 (2000); Poverty rate: 10.2% (2000).
Taxes: Total city taxes per capita: $178 (1997); City property taxes per capita: $176 (1997).
Education: High school graduation rate: 81.3% (2000); College graduation rate: 8.7% (2000).
Housing: Homeownership rate: 82.0% (2000); Median home value: $27,900 (2000); Median rent: $306 per month (2000); Median age of housing: 60+ years (2000).
Transportation: Commute to work: 81.9% car, 0.0% public transportation, 11.9% walk, 3.8% work from home (2000); Travel time to work: 39.0% less than 15 minutes, 31.8% 15 to 30 minutes, 16.9% 30 to 45 minutes, 5.2% 45 to 60 minutes, 7.1% 60 minutes or more (2000)

BRUSH CREEK (township). Covers a land area of 35.128 square miles and a water area of 0.954 square miles. Located at 43.63° N. Lat.; 93.81° W. Long. Elevation is 1,134 feet.
Population: 241 (2000); Race: 100.0% White, 0.0% Black, 0.0% Asian, 0.0% American Indian and Alaska Native, 0.7% Hispanic of any race, 0.0% two or more races (2000); Density: 6.9 persons per square mile (2000); Age: 33.8% under 18, 14.5% over 64 (2000); Marriage status: 21.6% never married, 70.1% now married, 1.5% widowed, 6.7% divorced (2000); Foreign born: 0.0% (2000); Ancestry (includes multiple ancestries): 49.5% Norwegian, 42.5% German, 9.1% Swedish, 8.7% English, 7.3% Polish (2000).
Economy: Employment by occupation: 33.0% management, 7.0% professional, 10.4% services, 19.1% sales, 4.3% farming, 13.9% construction, 12.2% production (2000).
Income: Per capita income: $14,469 (2000); Median household income: $44,063 (2000); Poverty rate: 2.2% (2000).
Taxes: Total city taxes per capita: $135 (1997); City property taxes per capita: $135 (1997).
Education: High school graduation rate: 93.4% (2000); College graduation rate: 10.8% (2000).
Housing: Homeownership rate: 92.2% (2000); Median home value: $70,000 (2000); Median age of housing: 60+ years (2000).
Transportation: Commute to work: 80.5% car, 1.8% public transportation, 0.0% walk, 17.7% work from home (2000); Travel time to work: 41.9% less than 15 minutes, 34.4% 15 to 30 minutes, 10.8% 30 to 45 minutes, 3.2% 45 to 60 minutes, 9.7% 60 minutes or more (2000)

CLARK (township). Covers a land area of 34.625 square miles and a water area of 0 square miles. Located at 43.72° N. Lat.; 93.71° W. Long.
Population: 459 (2000); Race: 100.0% White, 0.0% Black, 0.0% Asian, 0.0% American Indian and Alaska Native, 1.5% Hispanic of any race, 0.0% two or more races (2000); Density: 13.3 persons per square mile (2000); Age: 32.0% under 18, 13.9% over 64 (2000); Marriage status: 29.9% never married, 64.7% now married, 2.6% widowed, 2.8% divorced (2000); Foreign born: 1.5% (2000); Ancestry (includes multiple ancestries): 61.4% German, 18.5% Norwegian, 13.6% Polish, 9.7% Irish, 6.8% Danish (2000).
Economy: Employment by occupation: 31.7% management, 13.5% professional, 18.8% services, 9.7% sales, 5.0% farming, 8.2% construction, 13.2% production (2000).
Income: Per capita income: $14,655 (2000); Median household income: $41,944 (2000); Poverty rate: 13.2% (2000).
Taxes: Total city taxes per capita: $104 (1997); City property taxes per capita: $104 (1997).
Education: High school graduation rate: 89.4% (2000); College graduation rate: 15.7% (2000).
Housing: Homeownership rate: 81.6% (2000); Median home value: $80,000 (2000); Median rent: $156 per month (2000); Median age of housing: 57 years (2000).
Transportation: Commute to work: 79.7% car, 0.0% public transportation, 6.0% walk, 13.0% work from home (2000); Travel time to work: 74.5% less than 15 minutes, 10.6% 15 to 30 minutes, 8.0% 30 to 45 minutes, 4.0% 45 to 60 minutes, 2.9% 60 minutes or more (2000)

DELAVAN (city). Covers a land area of 1.062 square miles and a water area of 0 square miles. Located at 43.76° N. Lat.; 94.01° W. Long. Elevation is 1,063 feet.
Population: 223 (2000); Race: 95.3% White, 0.0% Black, 0.0% Asian, 0.0% American Indian and Alaska Native, 4.7% Hispanic of any race, 0.0% two or more races (2000); Density: 209.9 persons per square mile (2000); Age: 17.2% under 18, 27.0% over 64 (2000); Marriage status: 16.8% never married, 65.2% now married, 11.4% widowed, 6.5% divorced (2000); Foreign born: 0.0% (2000); Ancestry (includes multiple ancestries): 39.5% German, 13.0% English, 13.0% Norwegian, 8.8% Other groups, 6.5% Irish (2000).
Economy: Employment by occupation: 9.7% management, 14.2% professional, 15.9% services, 10.6% sales, 5.3% farming, 12.4% construction, 31.9% production (2000).
Income: Per capita income: $18,144 (2000); Median household income: $38,125 (2000); Poverty rate: 4.7% (2000).
Taxes: Total city taxes per capita: $256 (1997); City property taxes per capita: $256 (1997).
Education: High school graduation rate: 81.4% (2000); College graduation rate: 13.7% (2000).
Housing: Homeownership rate: 87.7% (2000); Median home value: $18,800 (2000); Median rent: $275 per month (2000); Median age of housing: 60+ years (2000).
Transportation: Commute to work: 91.7% car, 0.0% public transportation, 6.4% walk, 1.8% work from home (2000); Travel time to work: 28.0% less than 15 minutes, 42.1% 15 to 30 minutes, 9.3% 30 to 45 minutes, 15.0% 45 to 60 minutes, 5.6% 60 minutes or more (2000)

DELAVAN (township). Covers a land area of 33.269 square miles and a water area of 2.226 square miles. Located at 43.79° N. Lat.; 94.05° W. Long. Elevation is 1,063 feet.
Population: 275 (2000); Race: 96.4% White, 0.0% Black, 0.9% Asian, 0.0% American Indian and Alaska Native, 0.0% Hispanic of any race, 2.7% two or more races (2000); Density: 8.3 persons per square mile (2000); Age: 14.1% under 18, 23.2% over 64 (2000); Marriage status: 10.3% never married, 77.9% now married, 6.2% widowed, 5.6% divorced (2000); Foreign born: 0.9% (2000); Ancestry (includes multiple ancestries): 50.0% German, 18.6% Norwegian, 10.0% English, 8.6% Irish, 8.2% Other groups (2000).
Economy: Grain, soybeans; livestock. Manufacturing: feed, fertilizers. Employment by occupation: 33.3% management, 7.0% professional, 5.4% services, 21.7% sales, 2.3% farming, 8.5% construction, 21.7% production (2000).
Income: Per capita income: $24,100 (2000); Median household income: $40,893 (2000); Poverty rate: 4.5% (2000).
Taxes: Total city taxes per capita: $255 (1997); City property taxes per capita: $255 (1997).
Education: High school graduation rate: 93.5% (2000); College graduation rate: 11.8% (2000).
Housing: Homeownership rate: 86.0% (2000); Median home value: $73,800 (2000); Median rent: $181 per month (2000); Median age of housing: 48 years (2000).
Transportation: Commute to work: 79.8% car, 0.0% public transportation, 1.6% walk, 18.6% work from home (2000); Travel time to work: 20.0% less than 15 minutes, 39.0% 15 to 30 minutes, 17.1% 30 to 45 minutes, 16.2% 45 to 60 minutes, 7.6% 60 minutes or more (2000)

DUNBAR (township). Covers a land area of 35.891 square miles and a water area of 0 square miles. Located at 43.79° N. Lat.; 93.71° W. Long.
Population: 312 (2000); Race: 98.1% White, 0.0% Black, 0.6% Asian, 0.0% American Indian and Alaska Native, 1.9% Hispanic of any race, 1.3% two or more races (2000); Density: 8.7 persons per square mile (2000); Age: 29.9% under 18, 11.3% over 64 (2000); Marriage status: 26.3% never married, 64.8% now married, 3.2% widowed, 5.7% divorced (2000); Foreign born:

2.2% (2000); Ancestry (includes multiple ancestries): 64.2% German, 22.0% Polish, 13.5% Norwegian, 6.6% Irish, 2.8% Danish (2000).
Economy: Employment by occupation: 17.2% management, 16.6% professional, 15.3% services, 17.8% sales, 5.7% farming, 7.0% construction, 20.4% production (2000).
Income: Per capita income: $20,805 (2000); Median household income: $46,563 (2000); Poverty rate: 5.3% (2000).
Taxes: Total city taxes per capita: $62 (1997); City property taxes per capita: $62 (1997).
Education: High school graduation rate: 89.1% (2000); College graduation rate: 17.7% (2000).
Housing: Homeownership rate: 87.6% (2000); Median home value: $87,500 (2000); Median rent: $300 per month (2000); Median age of housing: 53 years (2000).
Transportation: Commute to work: 78.9% car, 0.0% public transportation, 2.0% walk, 19.1% work from home (2000); Travel time to work: 50.4% less than 15 minutes, 24.4% 15 to 30 minutes, 18.7% 30 to 45 minutes, 6.5% 45 to 60 minutes, 0.0% 60 minutes or more (2000)

EASTON (city). Covers a land area of 0.943 square miles and a water area of 0 square miles. Located at 43.76° N. Lat.; 93.90° W. Long. Elevation is 1,060 feet.
Population: 214 (2000); Race: 100.0% White, 0.0% Black, 0.0% Asian, 0.0% American Indian and Alaska Native, 0.0% Hispanic of any race, 0.0% two or more races (2000); Density: 227.0 persons per square mile (2000); Age: 17.3% under 18, 22.0% over 64 (2000); Marriage status: 30.8% never married, 53.5% now married, 7.0% widowed, 8.7% divorced (2000); Foreign born: 0.0% (2000); Ancestry (includes multiple ancestries): 44.0% German, 13.6% Irish, 12.6% Norwegian, 5.8% Polish, 4.7% United States or American (2000).
Economy: Livestock; soybeans, grain. Single-family building permits issued: 0 (2001) / 0 (2000); Multi-family building permits issued: 0 (2001) / 0 (2000); Employment by occupation: 11.2% management, 5.6% professional, 15.7% services, 11.2% sales, 5.6% farming, 20.2% construction, 30.3% production (2000).
Income: Per capita income: $17,095 (2000); Median household income: $28,125 (2000); Poverty rate: 14.7% (2000).
Taxes: Total city taxes per capita: $210 (1997); City property taxes per capita: $201 (1997).
Education: High school graduation rate: 81.8% (2000); College graduation rate: 5.1% (2000).
Housing: Homeownership rate: 93.4% (2000); Median home value: $42,200 (2000); Median rent: $150 per month (2000); Median age of housing: 45 years (2000).
Transportation: Commute to work: 91.7% car, 0.0% public transportation, 0.0% walk, 0.0% work from home (2000); Travel time to work: 44.0% less than 15 minutes, 22.6% 15 to 30 minutes, 16.7% 30 to 45 minutes, 11.9% 45 to 60 minutes, 4.8% 60 minutes or more (2000)

ELMORE (city). Covers a land area of 0.901 square miles and a water area of 0 square miles. Located at 43.50° N. Lat.; 94.08° W. Long. Elevation is 1,128 feet.
History: Elmore was settled in 1855 by Crawford W. Wilson, who came to farm the land. The town that grew up was first called Dobson, for James Dobson. In 1862 the name was changed to Elmore to honor Andrew E. Elmore of Wisconsin, a friend of several early settlers.
Population: 735 (2000); Race: 92.2% White, 0.7% Black, 2.0% Asian, 1.3% American Indian and Alaska Native, 5.6% Hispanic of any race, 2.0% two or more races (2000); Density: 815.9 persons per square mile (2000); Age: 27.2% under 18, 19.9% over 64 (2000); Marriage status: 23.5% never married, 58.2% now married, 8.9% widowed, 9.3% divorced (2000); Foreign born: 2.4% (2000); Ancestry (includes multiple ancestries): 42.0% German, 27.6% Norwegian, 11.8% Irish, 11.0% Other groups, 3.8% Polish (2000).
Economy: Single-family building permits issued: 0 (2001) / 0 (2000); Multi-family building permits issued: 0 (2001) / 0 (2000); Employment by occupation: 5.8% management, 10.4% professional, 15.9% services, 24.6% sales, 2.3% farming, 7.5% construction, 33.3% production (2000).
Income: Per capita income: $15,761 (2000); Median household income: $26,146 (2000); Poverty rate: 11.8% (2000).
Taxes: Total city taxes per capita: $150 (1997); City property taxes per capita: $144 (1997).
Education: High school graduation rate: 78.0% (2000); College graduation rate: 10.0% (2000).
Housing: Homeownership rate: 84.4% (2000); Median home value: $25,400 (2000); Median rent: $256 per month (2000); Median age of housing: 55 years (2000).
Transportation: Commute to work: 93.0% car, 0.0% public transportation, 4.1% walk, 1.8% work from home (2000); Travel time to work: 42.6% less than 15 minutes, 38.7% 15 to 30 minutes, 8.6% 30 to 45 minutes, 2.7% 45 to 60 minutes, 7.4% 60 minutes or more (2000)

ELMORE (township). Covers a land area of 35.026 square miles and a water area of 0 square miles. Located at 43.53° N. Lat.; 94.07° W. Long. Elevation is 1,128 feet.
Population: 203 (2000); Race: 98.5% White, 1.5% Black, 0.0% Asian, 0.0% American Indian and Alaska Native, 0.0% Hispanic of any race, 0.0% two or more races (2000); Density: 5.8 persons per square mile (2000); Age: 18.2% under 18, 28.6% over 64 (2000); Marriage status: 11.6% never married, 80.2% now married, 8.1% widowed, 0.0% divorced (2000); Foreign born: 0.0% (2000); Ancestry (includes multiple ancestries): 58.1% German, 26.1% Norwegian, 7.9% Irish, 6.4% English, 5.9% Swedish (2000).
Economy: Grain, soybeans; livestock. Manufacturing: grain processing. Employment by occupation: 30.7% management, 13.9% professional, 12.9% services, 23.8% sales, 0.0% farming, 8.9% construction, 9.9% production (2000).
Income: Per capita income: $25,557 (2000); Median household income: $31,806 (2000); Poverty rate: 8.6% (2000).
Taxes: Total city taxes per capita: $267 (1997); City property taxes per capita: $267 (1997).
Education: High school graduation rate: 92.5% (2000); College graduation rate: 11.2% (2000).
Housing: Homeownership rate: 89.8% (2000); Median home value: $82,500 (2000); Median rent: $175 per month (2000); Median age of housing: 60+ years (2000).
Transportation: Commute to work: 74.0% car, 0.0% public transportation, 0.0% walk, 25.0% work from home (2000); Travel time to work: 55.6% less than 15 minutes, 33.3% 15 to 30 minutes, 4.2% 30 to 45 minutes, 4.2% 45 to 60 minutes, 2.8% 60 minutes or more (2000)

EMERALD (township). Covers a land area of 35.802 square miles and a water area of 0 square miles. Located at 43.64° N. Lat.; 93.94° W. Long.
Population: 228 (2000); Race: 100.0% White, 0.0% Black, 0.0% Asian, 0.0% American Indian and Alaska Native, 0.0% Hispanic of any race, 0.0% two or more races (2000); Density: 6.4 persons per square mile (2000); Age: 23.1% under 18, 12.7% over 64 (2000); Marriage status: 10.1% never married, 79.8% now married, 7.3% widowed, 2.8% divorced (2000); Foreign born: 0.0% (2000); Ancestry (includes multiple ancestries): 50.7% German, 47.1% Norwegian, 10.9% English, 6.8% Swedish, 4.5% Irish (2000).
Economy: Employment by occupation: 39.0% management, 14.0% professional, 0.0% services, 20.6% sales, 5.9% farming, 11.0% construction, 9.6% production (2000).
Income: Per capita income: $18,127 (2000); Median household income: $41,806 (2000); Poverty rate: 7.2% (2000).
Taxes: Total city taxes per capita: $129 (1997); City property taxes per capita: $129 (1997).
Education: High school graduation rate: 92.0% (2000); College graduation rate: 23.5% (2000).
Housing: Homeownership rate: 84.1% (2000); Median home value: $66,400 (2000); Median rent: $275 per month (2000); Median age of housing: 60+ years (2000).
Transportation: Commute to work: 71.6% car, 0.0% public transportation, 2.2% walk, 24.6% work from home (2000); Travel time to work: 56.4% less than 15 minutes, 27.7% 15 to 30 minutes, 6.9% 30 to 45 minutes, 5.0% 45 to 60 minutes, 4.0% 60 minutes or more (2000)

FOSTER (township). Covers a land area of 35.424 square miles and a water area of 0.433 square miles. Located at 43.63° N. Lat.; 93.70° W. Long.
Population: 314 (2000); Race: 100.0% White, 0.0% Black, 0.0% Asian, 0.0% American Indian and Alaska Native, 3.8% Hispanic of any race, 0.0% two or more races (2000); Density: 8.9 persons per square mile (2000); Age: 27.8% under 18, 12.8% over 64 (2000); Marriage status: 22.1% never married, 62.5% now married, 8.2% widowed, 7.2% divorced (2000); Foreign born: 0.0% (2000); Ancestry (includes multiple ancestries): 60.5% German, 30.1% Norwegian, 9.0% Danish, 6.4% Other groups, 4.9% Swedish (2000).
Economy: Employment by occupation: 21.4% management, 6.1% professional, 9.2% services, 26.0% sales, 3.1% farming, 11.5% construction, 22.9% production (2000).
Income: Per capita income: $16,224 (2000); Median household income: $40,833 (2000); Poverty rate: 3.8% (2000).
Taxes: Total city taxes per capita: $106 (1997); City property taxes per capita: $106 (1997).

Education: High school graduation rate: 83.7% (2000); College graduation rate: 14.0% (2000).
Housing: Homeownership rate: 92.2% (2000); Median home value: $78,100 (2000); Median age of housing: 60+ years (2000).
Transportation: Commute to work: 77.2% car, 0.0% public transportation, 0.0% walk, 22.8% work from home (2000); Travel time to work: 17.3% less than 15 minutes, 43.9% 15 to 30 minutes, 29.6% 30 to 45 minutes, 5.1% 45 to 60 minutes, 4.1% 60 minutes or more (2000)

FROST (city). Covers a land area of 0.527 square miles and a water area of 0 square miles. Located at 43.58° N. Lat.; 93.92° W. Long. Elevation is 1,136 feet.
Population: 251 (2000); Race: 94.5% White, 3.7% Black, 0.0% Asian, 0.0% American Indian and Alaska Native, 0.9% Hispanic of any race, 0.9% two or more races (2000); Density: 476.7 persons per square mile (2000); Age: 24.7% under 18, 25.1% over 64 (2000); Marriage status: 21.7% never married, 54.9% now married, 15.2% widowed, 8.2% divorced (2000); Foreign born: 2.7% (2000); Ancestry (includes multiple ancestries): 48.4% Norwegian, 41.1% German, 7.3% Irish, 5.0% Polish, 3.7% African (2000).
Economy: Livestock; grain, soybeans. Single-family building permits issued: 0 (2001) / 0 (2000); Multi-family building permits issued: 0 (2001) / 0 (2000); Employment by occupation: 8.0% management, 10.2% professional, 18.2% services, 29.5% sales, 6.8% farming, 4.5% construction, 22.7% production (2000).
Income: Per capita income: $14,756 (2000); Median household income: $26,389 (2000); Poverty rate: 12.8% (2000).
Taxes: Total city taxes per capita: $280 (1997); City property taxes per capita: $280 (1997).
Education: High school graduation rate: 85.5% (2000); College graduation rate: 9.9% (2000).
Housing: Homeownership rate: 76.1% (2000); Median home value: $30,600 (2000); Median rent: $271 per month (2000); Median age of housing: 56 years (2000).
Transportation: Commute to work: 89.8% car, 2.3% public transportation, 4.5% walk, 3.4% work from home (2000); Travel time to work: 36.5% less than 15 minutes, 49.4% 15 to 30 minutes, 8.2% 30 to 45 minutes, 1.2% 45 to 60 minutes, 4.7% 60 minutes or more (2000)

JO DAVIESS (township). Covers a land area of 35.937 square miles and a water area of 0.041 square miles. Located at 43.63° N. Lat.; 94.19° W. Long.
Population: 281 (2000); Race: 86.6% White, 0.0% Black, 0.0% Asian, 2.0% American Indian and Alaska Native, 16.7% Hispanic of any race, 7.0% two or more races (2000); Density: 7.8 persons per square mile (2000); Age: 33.8% under 18, 12.0% over 64 (2000); Marriage status: 27.0% never married, 63.5% now married, 6.3% widowed, 3.2% divorced (2000); Foreign born: 5.0% (2000); Ancestry (includes multiple ancestries): 56.2% German, 20.1% Other groups, 19.1% Irish, 15.1% Norwegian, 4.7% English (2000).
Economy: Employment by occupation: 14.3% management, 18.6% professional, 10.7% services, 15.7% sales, 2.1% farming, 15.7% construction, 22.9% production (2000).
Income: Per capita income: $13,220 (2000); Median household income: $33,750 (2000); Poverty rate: 12.4% (2000).
Taxes: Total city taxes per capita: $167 (1997); City property taxes per capita: $167 (1997).
Education: High school graduation rate: 84.0% (2000); College graduation rate: 12.2% (2000).
Housing: Homeownership rate: 77.8% (2000); Median home value: $53,300 (2000); Median rent: $175 per month (2000); Median age of housing: 60+ years (2000).
Transportation: Commute to work: 91.9% car, 0.0% public transportation, 0.0% walk, 8.1% work from home (2000); Travel time to work: 41.6% less than 15 minutes, 49.6% 15 to 30 minutes, 2.4% 30 to 45 minutes, 4.8% 45 to 60 minutes, 1.6% 60 minutes or more (2000)

KIESTER (city). Covers a land area of 0.444 square miles and a water area of 0 square miles. Located at 43.53° N. Lat.; 93.71° W. Long. Elevation is 1,265 feet.
Population: 540 (2000); Race: 97.9% White, 0.4% Black, 0.0% Asian, 0.0% American Indian and Alaska Native, 3.5% Hispanic of any race, 0.4% two or more races (2000); Density: 1,217.0 persons per square mile (2000); Age: 24.1% under 18, 23.9% over 64 (2000); Marriage status: 20.8% never married, 63.0% now married, 9.1% widowed, 7.1% divorced (2000); Foreign born: 0.7% (2000); Ancestry (includes multiple ancestries): 45.3% German, 44.1% Norwegian, 5.6% Danish, 4.6% Dutch, 3.7% Other groups (2000).
Economy: Single-family building permits issued: 0 (2001) / 1 (2000); Multi-family building permits issued: 0 (2001) / 0 (2000); Employment by occupation: 8.9% management, 17.8% professional, 13.3% services, 17.8% sales, 3.3% farming, 15.2% construction, 23.7% production (2000).
Income: Per capita income: $16,098 (2000); Median household income: $32,768 (2000); Poverty rate: 9.3% (2000).
Taxes: Total city taxes per capita: $91 (1997); City property taxes per capita: $91 (1997).
Education: High school graduation rate: 87.7% (2000); College graduation rate: 12.8% (2000).
Housing: Homeownership rate: 78.5% (2000); Median home value: $32,800 (2000); Median rent: $170 per month (2000); Median age of housing: 49 years (2000).
Newspapers: Courier-Sentinel (1 x week)
Transportation: Commute to work: 83.5% car, 0.0% public transportation, 12.0% walk, 3.0% work from home (2000); Travel time to work: 41.9% less than 15 minutes, 28.3% 15 to 30 minutes, 20.9% 30 to 45 minutes, 0.8% 45 to 60 minutes, 8.1% 60 minutes or more (2000)

KIESTER (township). Covers a land area of 35.826 square miles and a water area of 0 square miles. Located at 43.54° N. Lat.; 93.71° W. Long. Elevation is 1,265 feet.
Population: 320 (2000); Race: 99.0% White, 0.0% Black, 0.0% Asian, 0.0% American Indian and Alaska Native, 0.0% Hispanic of any race, 1.0% two or more races (2000); Density: 8.9 persons per square mile (2000); Age: 23.2% under 18, 18.5% over 64 (2000); Marriage status: 19.5% never married, 70.1% now married, 4.6% widowed, 5.8% divorced (2000); Foreign born: 0.0% (2000); Ancestry (includes multiple ancestries): 59.4% German, 36.9% Norwegian, 7.7% Irish, 5.7% United States or American, 4.4% Danish (2000).
Economy: Agricultural area: grain, soybeans; livestock. Manufacturing: feeds. Employment by occupation: 20.4% management, 11.5% professional, 13.4% services, 15.3% sales, 3.2% farming, 5.1% construction, 31.2% production (2000).
Income: Per capita income: $17,258 (2000); Median household income: $37,188 (2000); Poverty rate: 7.7% (2000).
Taxes: Total city taxes per capita: $89 (1997); City property taxes per capita: $89 (1997).
Education: High school graduation rate: 89.0% (2000); College graduation rate: 15.5% (2000).
Housing: Homeownership rate: 89.7% (2000); Median home value: $46,100 (2000); Median rent: $125 per month (2000); Median age of housing: 60+ years (2000).
Transportation: Commute to work: 81.3% car, 0.0% public transportation, 1.9% walk, 14.8% work from home (2000); Travel time to work: 32.6% less than 15 minutes, 17.4% 15 to 30 minutes, 33.3% 30 to 45 minutes, 9.8% 45 to 60 minutes, 6.8% 60 minutes or more (2000)

LURA (township). Covers a land area of 35.154 square miles and a water area of 0 square miles. Located at 43.80° N. Lat.; 93.95° W. Long.
Population: 217 (2000); Race: 100.0% White, 0.0% Black, 0.0% Asian, 0.0% American Indian and Alaska Native, 0.0% Hispanic of any race, 0.0% two or more races (2000); Density: 6.2 persons per square mile (2000); Age: 30.1% under 18, 15.3% over 64 (2000); Marriage status: 24.3% never married, 62.7% now married, 6.2% widowed, 6.8% divorced (2000); Foreign born: 0.0% (2000); Ancestry (includes multiple ancestries): 46.2% German, 21.6% Polish, 17.4% Norwegian, 5.9% Irish, 5.5% English (2000).
Economy: Employment by occupation: 25.0% management, 19.8% professional, 9.5% services, 18.1% sales, 1.7% farming, 16.4% construction, 9.5% production (2000).
Income: Per capita income: $17,344 (2000); Median household income: $40,625 (2000); Poverty rate: 15.3% (2000).
Taxes: Total city taxes per capita: $145 (1997); City property taxes per capita: $145 (1997).
Education: High school graduation rate: 91.1% (2000); College graduation rate: 20.4% (2000).
Housing: Homeownership rate: 80.7% (2000); Median home value: $65,500 (2000); Median rent: $325 per month (2000); Median age of housing: 60+ years (2000).
Transportation: Commute to work: 78.4% car, 0.0% public transportation, 2.6% walk, 19.0% work from home (2000); Travel time to work: 13.8% less than 15 minutes, 41.5% 15 to 30 minutes, 18.1% 30 to 45 minutes, 12.8% 45 to 60 minutes, 13.8% 60 minutes or more (2000)

MINNESOTA LAKE (city). Covers a land area of 1.578 square miles and a water area of 0.488 square miles. Located at 43.84° N. Lat.; 93.83° W. Long. Elevation is 1,050 feet.

Population: 681 (2000); Race: 98.7% White, 0.4% Black, 0.0% Asian, 0.0% American Indian and Alaska Native, 0.0% Hispanic of any race, 0.9% two or more races (2000); Density: 431.6 persons per square mile (2000); Age: 22.0% under 18, 20.5% over 64 (2000); Marriage status: 20.0% never married, 63.7% now married, 10.1% widowed, 6.2% divorced (2000); Foreign born: 0.4% (2000); Ancestry (includes multiple ancestries): 55.9% German, 13.8% Norwegian, 8.8% Polish, 7.2% French (except Basque), 6.9% Irish (2000).

Economy: Single-family building permits issued: 3 (2001) / 0 (2000); Multi-family building permits issued: 0 (2001) / 0 (2000); Employment by occupation: 12.5% management, 8.2% professional, 12.2% services, 28.8% sales, 0.0% farming, 13.0% construction, 25.3% production (2000).

Income: Per capita income: $18,609 (2000); Median household income: $34,896 (2000); Poverty rate: 4.3% (2000).

Taxes: Total city taxes per capita: $107 (1997); City property taxes per capita: $104 (1997).

Education: High school graduation rate: 83.4% (2000); College graduation rate: 12.7% (2000).

Housing: Homeownership rate: 83.1% (2000); Median home value: $55,900 (2000); Median rent: $263 per month (2000); Median age of housing: 47 years (2000).

Newspapers: Minnesota Lake Tribune (1 x week)

Transportation: Commute to work: 92.9% car, 0.0% public transportation, 4.6% walk, 2.5% work from home (2000); Travel time to work: 37.8% less than 15 minutes, 18.5% 15 to 30 minutes, 32.2% 30 to 45 minutes, 5.0% 45 to 60 minutes, 6.4% 60 minutes or more (2000)

MINNESOTA LAKE (township). Covers a land area of 31.428 square miles and a water area of 2.588 square miles. Located at 43.80° N. Lat.; 93.83° W. Long. Elevation is 1,050 feet.

Population: 237 (2000); Race: 95.4% White, 0.0% Black, 0.9% Asian, 0.0% American Indian and Alaska Native, 2.8% Hispanic of any race, 2.8% two or more races (2000); Density: 7.5 persons per square mile (2000); Age: 33.0% under 18, 14.7% over 64 (2000); Marriage status: 21.8% never married, 66.7% now married, 4.8% widowed, 6.7% divorced (2000); Foreign born: 5.5% (2000); Ancestry (includes multiple ancestries): 61.9% German, 22.0% Polish, 15.6% Norwegian, 15.6% Irish, 8.7% English (2000).

Economy: Corn, oats, peas, soybeans; livestock, poultry. Employment by occupation: 21.9% management, 24.0% professional, 4.2% services, 33.3% sales, 2.1% farming, 7.3% construction, 7.3% production (2000).

Income: Per capita income: $23,788 (2000); Median household income: $41,250 (2000); Poverty rate: 10.6% (2000).

Taxes: Total city taxes per capita: $181 (1997); City property taxes per capita: $181 (1997).

Education: High school graduation rate: 84.0% (2000); College graduation rate: 22.2% (2000).

Housing: Homeownership rate: 79.3% (2000); Median home value: $60,000 (2000); Median rent: $250 per month (2000); Median age of housing: 55 years (2000).

Transportation: Commute to work: 76.8% car, 0.0% public transportation, 2.1% walk, 16.8% work from home (2000); Travel time to work: 55.7% less than 15 minutes, 22.8% 15 to 30 minutes, 12.7% 30 to 45 minutes, 8.9% 45 to 60 minutes, 0.0% 60 minutes or more (2000)

PILOT GROVE (township). Covers a land area of 35.979 square miles and a water area of 0 square miles. Located at 43.53° N. Lat.; 94.19° W. Long. Elevation is 1,128 feet.

Population: 182 (2000); Race: 100.0% White, 0.0% Black, 0.0% Asian, 0.0% American Indian and Alaska Native, 0.0% Hispanic of any race, 0.0% two or more races (2000); Density: 5.1 persons per square mile (2000); Age: 30.3% under 18, 23.1% over 64 (2000); Marriage status: 23.4% never married, 67.6% now married, 5.5% widowed, 3.4% divorced (2000); Foreign born: 2.6% (2000); Ancestry (includes multiple ancestries): 36.4% German, 35.9% Norwegian, 10.3% English, 7.7% Irish, 7.2% Swedish (2000).

Economy: Employment by occupation: 28.1% management, 18.0% professional, 13.5% services, 20.2% sales, 3.4% farming, 5.6% construction, 11.2% production (2000).

Income: Per capita income: $16,876 (2000); Median household income: $42,500 (2000); Poverty rate: 5.3% (2000).

Taxes: Total city taxes per capita: $217 (1997); City property taxes per capita: $217 (1997).

Education: High school graduation rate: 83.6% (2000); College graduation rate: 14.2% (2000).

Housing: Homeownership rate: 84.0% (2000); Median home value: $50,000 (2000); Median rent: $250 per month (2000); Median age of housing: 60+ years (2000).

Transportation: Commute to work: 84.3% car, 0.0% public transportation, 0.0% walk, 15.7% work from home (2000); Travel time to work: 28.0% less than 15 minutes, 62.7% 15 to 30 minutes, 6.7% 30 to 45 minutes, 0.0% 45 to 60 minutes, 2.7% 60 minutes or more (2000)

PRESCOTT (township). Covers a land area of 35.933 square miles and a water area of 0.175 square miles. Located at 43.71° N. Lat.; 94.06° W. Long.

Population: 222 (2000); Race: 99.2% White, 0.0% Black, 0.0% Asian, 0.0% American Indian and Alaska Native, 1.2% Hispanic of any race, 0.8% two or more races (2000); Density: 6.2 persons per square mile (2000); Age: 32.5% under 18, 14.5% over 64 (2000); Marriage status: 18.6% never married, 75.4% now married, 1.1% widowed, 4.9% divorced (2000); Foreign born: 0.8% (2000); Ancestry (includes multiple ancestries): 59.4% German, 13.7% Irish, 12.4% French Canadian, 8.0% English, 6.0% Norwegian (2000).

Economy: Employment by occupation: 30.6% management, 9.7% professional, 8.9% services, 27.4% sales, 4.0% farming, 13.7% construction, 5.6% production (2000).

Income: Per capita income: $16,986 (2000); Median household income: $48,571 (2000); Poverty rate: 8.4% (2000).

Taxes: Total city taxes per capita: $220 (1997); City property taxes per capita: $220 (1997).

Education: High school graduation rate: 93.1% (2000); College graduation rate: 15.0% (2000).

Housing: Homeownership rate: 69.9% (2000); Median home value: $77,500 (2000); Median rent: $263 per month (2000); Median age of housing: 60+ years (2000).

Transportation: Commute to work: 75.0% car, 0.0% public transportation, 1.6% walk, 23.4% work from home (2000); Travel time to work: 52.6% less than 15 minutes, 34.7% 15 to 30 minutes, 4.2% 30 to 45 minutes, 5.3% 45 to 60 minutes, 3.2% 60 minutes or more (2000)

ROME (township). Covers a land area of 35.733 square miles and a water area of 0 square miles. Located at 43.55° N. Lat.; 93.94° W. Long.

Population: 172 (2000); Race: 100.0% White, 0.0% Black, 0.0% Asian, 0.0% American Indian and Alaska Native, 1.9% Hispanic of any race, 0.0% two or more races (2000); Density: 4.8 persons per square mile (2000); Age: 24.2% under 18, 15.9% over 64 (2000); Marriage status: 24.4% never married, 65.1% now married, 4.7% widowed, 5.8% divorced (2000); Foreign born: 1.9% (2000); Ancestry (includes multiple ancestries): 54.6% Norwegian, 39.6% German, 7.7% Irish, 5.8% Swedish, 3.9% Dutch (2000).

Economy: Employment by occupation: 28.7% management, 7.9% professional, 7.9% services, 25.7% sales, 15.8% farming, 5.9% construction, 7.9% production (2000).

Income: Per capita income: $19,896 (2000); Median household income: $37,500 (2000); Poverty rate: 6.3% (2000).

Taxes: Total city taxes per capita: $189 (1997); City property taxes per capita: $189 (1997).

Education: High school graduation rate: 92.5% (2000); College graduation rate: 19.4% (2000).

Housing: Homeownership rate: 81.0% (2000); Median home value: $42,500 (2000); Median rent: $125 per month (2000); Median age of housing: 60+ years (2000).

Transportation: Commute to work: 78.2% car, 0.0% public transportation, 3.0% walk, 18.8% work from home (2000); Travel time to work: 39.0% less than 15 minutes, 39.0% 15 to 30 minutes, 13.4% 30 to 45 minutes, 7.3% 45 to 60 minutes, 1.2% 60 minutes or more (2000)

SEELY (township). Covers a land area of 36.050 square miles and a water area of 0 square miles. Located at 43.55° N. Lat.; 93.83° W. Long.

Population: 210 (2000); Race: 100.0% White, 0.0% Black, 0.0% Asian, 0.0% American Indian and Alaska Native, 2.3% Hispanic of any race, 0.0% two or more races (2000); Density: 5.8 persons per square mile (2000); Age: 18.4% under 18, 23.0% over 64 (2000); Marriage status: 17.5% never married, 73.4% now married, 6.5% widowed, 2.6% divorced (2000); Foreign born: 0.0% (2000); Ancestry (includes multiple ancestries): 66.1% Norwegian, 42.0% German, 6.3% Swedish, 5.2% Dutch, 4.0% English (2000).

Economy: Employment by occupation: 44.3% management, 18.6% professional, 10.0% services, 18.6% sales, 1.4% farming, 2.9% construction, 4.3% production (2000).

Income: Per capita income: $19,555 (2000); Median household income: $31,250 (2000); Poverty rate: 1.1% (2000).
Taxes: Total city taxes per capita: $143 (1997); City property taxes per capita: $143 (1997).
Education: High school graduation rate: 89.1% (2000); College graduation rate: 26.4% (2000).
Housing: Homeownership rate: 92.0% (2000); Median home value: $65,000 (2000); Median rent: $125 per month (2000); Median age of housing: 60+ years (2000).
Transportation: Commute to work: 77.1% car, 0.0% public transportation, 11.4% walk, 11.4% work from home (2000); Travel time to work: 50.0% less than 15 minutes, 27.4% 15 to 30 minutes, 21.0% 30 to 45 minutes, 0.0% 45 to 60 minutes, 1.6% 60 minutes or more (2000)

VERONA (township). Covers a land area of 35.461 square miles and a water area of 0.008 square miles. Located at 43.72° N. Lat.; 94.19° W. Long.
Population: 391 (2000); Race: 100.0% White, 0.0% Black, 0.0% Asian, 0.0% American Indian and Alaska Native, 0.3% Hispanic of any race, 0.0% two or more races (2000); Density: 11.0 persons per square mile (2000); Age: 20.9% under 18, 19.3% over 64 (2000); Marriage status: 18.4% never married, 73.1% now married, 6.1% widowed, 2.3% divorced (2000); Foreign born: 0.0% (2000); Ancestry (includes multiple ancestries): 51.7% German, 20.4% Norwegian, 16.4% Irish, 8.8% English, 4.6% United States or American (2000).
Economy: Employment by occupation: 26.2% management, 13.6% professional, 15.0% services, 16.0% sales, 4.9% farming, 5.3% construction, 18.9% production (2000).
Income: Per capita income: $19,690 (2000); Median household income: $42,750 (2000); Poverty rate: 12.6% (2000).
Taxes: Total city taxes per capita: $122 (1997); City property taxes per capita: $122 (1997).
Education: High school graduation rate: 90.2% (2000); College graduation rate: 17.4% (2000).
Housing: Homeownership rate: 80.0% (2000); Median home value: $47,900 (2000); Median rent: $188 per month (2000); Median age of housing: 60+ years (2000).
Transportation: Commute to work: 81.9% car, 1.0% public transportation, 3.9% walk, 11.8% work from home (2000); Travel time to work: 45.0% less than 15 minutes, 45.0% 15 to 30 minutes, 4.4% 30 to 45 minutes, 2.2% 45 to 60 minutes, 3.3% 60 minutes or more (2000)

WALNUT LAKE (township). Covers a land area of 34.906 square miles and a water area of 1.006 square miles. Located at 43.71° N. Lat.; 93.83° W. Long.
Population: 251 (2000); Race: 93.5% White, 0.0% Black, 0.0% Asian, 0.0% American Indian and Alaska Native, 6.5% Hispanic of any race, 0.0% two or more races (2000); Density: 7.2 persons per square mile (2000); Age: 28.1% under 18, 15.6% over 64 (2000); Marriage status: 24.3% never married, 65.5% now married, 4.9% widowed, 5.3% divorced (2000); Foreign born: 0.0% (2000); Ancestry (includes multiple ancestries): 54.0% German, 9.9% Polish, 9.5% Norwegian, 8.0% United States or American, 7.6% Irish (2000).
Economy: Employment by occupation: 26.1% management, 14.2% professional, 9.7% services, 24.6% sales, 7.5% farming, 8.2% construction, 9.7% production (2000).
Income: Per capita income: $16,632 (2000); Median household income: $39,375 (2000); Poverty rate: 5.8% (2000).
Taxes: Total city taxes per capita: $103 (1997); City property taxes per capita: $103 (1997).
Education: High school graduation rate: 85.6% (2000); College graduation rate: 16.8% (2000).
Housing: Homeownership rate: 87.9% (2000); Median home value: $76,700 (2000); Median rent: $125 per month (2000); Median age of housing: 57 years (2000).
Transportation: Commute to work: 77.6% car, 0.0% public transportation, 3.0% walk, 19.4% work from home (2000); Travel time to work: 37.0% less than 15 minutes, 23.1% 15 to 30 minutes, 22.2% 30 to 45 minutes, 3.7% 45 to 60 minutes, 13.9% 60 minutes or more (2000)

WALTERS (city). Covers a land area of 0.200 square miles and a water area of 0 square miles. Located at 43.60° N. Lat.; 93.67° W. Long.
Population: 88 (2000); Race: 100.0% White, 0.0% Black, 0.0% Asian, 0.0% American Indian and Alaska Native, 4.6% Hispanic of any race, 0.0% two or more races (2000); Density: 440.2 persons per square mile (2000); Age: 34.5% under 18, 21.8% over 64 (2000); Marriage status: 20.3% never married, 53.1% now married, 4.7% widowed, 21.9% divorced (2000); Foreign born: 0.0% (2000); Ancestry (includes multiple ancestries): 43.7% Norwegian, 20.7% German, 6.9% French (except Basque), 5.7% Irish, 3.4% Scandinavian (2000).
Economy: Agricultural area: grain, soybeans; livestock. Manufacturing of agricultural equipment. Single-family building permits issued: 0 (2001) / 0 (2000); Multi-family building permits issued: 0 (2001) / 0 (2000); Employment by occupation: 6.5% management, 0.0% professional, 9.7% services, 22.6% sales, 0.0% farming, 16.1% construction, 45.2% production (2000).
Income: Per capita income: $10,472 (2000); Median household income: $28,750 (2000); Poverty rate: 22.9% (2000).
Taxes: Total city taxes per capita: $73 (1997); City property taxes per capita: $61 (1997).
Education: High school graduation rate: 66.7% (2000); College graduation rate: 3.5% (2000).
Housing: Homeownership rate: 86.1% (2000); Median home value: $13,200 (2000); Median rent: $125 per month (2000); Median age of housing: 60+ years (2000).
Transportation: Commute to work: 100.0% car, 0.0% public transportation, 0.0% walk, 0.0% work from home (2000); Travel time to work: 6.5% less than 15 minutes, 32.3% 15 to 30 minutes, 38.7% 30 to 45 minutes, 22.6% 45 to 60 minutes, 0.0% 60 minutes or more (2000)

WELLS (city). Covers a land area of 1.351 square miles and a water area of 0 square miles. Located at 43.74° N. Lat.; 93.72° W. Long. Elevation is 1,162 feet.
History: Settled before 1870.
Population: 2,494 (2000); Race: 92.8% White, 0.7% Black, 0.8% Asian, 0.3% American Indian and Alaska Native, 5.4% Hispanic of any race, 1.2% two or more races (2000); Density: 1,846.5 persons per square mile (2000); Age: 22.6% under 18, 27.1% over 64 (2000); Marriage status: 18.7% never married, 61.5% now married, 13.5% widowed, 6.3% divorced (2000); Foreign born: 4.6% (2000); Ancestry (includes multiple ancestries): 52.2% German, 15.5% Norwegian, 13.5% Polish, 7.8% Other groups, 5.7% Irish (2000).
Economy: Railroad junction. Agricultural trade center: corn, oats, peas, soybeans: livestock, poultry. Manufacturing includes feeds, machining, canned peas and corn, chicken and turkey products, prestressed concrete. Single-family building permits issued: 2 (2001) / 6 (2000); Multi-family building permits issued: 0 (2001) / 0 (2000); Employment by occupation: 7.8% management, 16.3% professional, 17.1% services, 21.0% sales, 3.1% farming, 15.4% construction, 19.3% production (2000).
Income: Per capita income: $15,614 (2000); Median household income: $26,463 (2000); Poverty rate: 9.8% (2000).
Taxes: Total city taxes per capita: $136 (1997); City property taxes per capita: $133 (1997).
Education: High school graduation rate: 73.1% (2000); College graduation rate: 10.6% (2000).

School District(s)

United South Central (PK-12)
2000 Enrollment: 1,013 507-553-3134

Housing: Homeownership rate: 80.2% (2000); Median home value: $49,000 (2000); Median rent: $259 per month (2000); Median age of housing: 53 years (2000).
Newspapers: Wells Shopper (1 x week); Wells Mirror (1 x week)
Transportation: Commute to work: 84.6% car, 0.0% public transportation, 8.7% walk, 5.3% work from home (2000); Travel time to work: 67.6% less than 15 minutes, 8.5% 15 to 30 minutes, 9.0% 30 to 45 minutes, 8.6% 45 to 60 minutes, 6.3% 60 minutes or more (2000)
Additional Information Contacts
Wells Chamber of Commerce 507-553-6450

WINNEBAGO (city). Covers a land area of 2.201 square miles and a water area of 0.008 square miles. Located at 43.76° N. Lat.; 94.16° W. Long. Elevation is 1,111 feet.
History: Winnebago developed as a business center for a farming region, with canneries, hatcheries, and a cooperative creamery. Scottish settlers here are said to have introduced the game of curling to Minnesota in the 1850's, using their wives' flatirons.
Population: 1,487 (2000); Race: 96.6% White, 0.0% Black, 0.1% Asian, 1.1% American Indian and Alaska Native, 5.4% Hispanic of any race, 0.7% two or more races (2000); Density: 675.5 persons per square mile (2000); Age: 21.1% under 18, 27.2% over 64 (2000); Marriage status: 19.3% never married, 58.6% now married, 12.7% widowed, 9.3% divorced (2000); Foreign born: 0.8% (2000); Ancestry (includes multiple ancestries): 46.9% German, 15.8% Norwegian, 9.9% English, 9.8% Irish, 7.2% Other groups (2000).

Economy: Single-family building permits issued: 1 (2001) / 3 (2000); Multi-family building permits issued: 0 (2001) / 0 (2000); Employment by occupation: 9.4% management, 14.9% professional, 12.8% services, 20.0% sales, 0.8% farming, 13.4% construction, 28.7% production (2000).
Income: Per capita income: $16,435 (2000); Median household income: $32,321 (2000); Poverty rate: 9.5% (2000).
Taxes: Total city taxes per capita: $227 (1997); City property taxes per capita: $218 (1997).
Education: High school graduation rate: 81.1% (2000); College graduation rate: 10.6% (2000).
Housing: Homeownership rate: 79.1% (2000); Median home value: $40,600 (2000); Median rent: $252 per month (2000); Median age of housing: 53 years (2000).
Transportation: Commute to work: 86.1% car, 0.3% public transportation, 7.0% walk, 5.7% work from home (2000); Travel time to work: 55.1% less than 15 minutes, 27.4% 15 to 30 minutes, 8.1% 30 to 45 minutes, 5.2% 45 to 60 minutes, 4.2% 60 minutes or more (2000)
Additional Information Contacts
Winnebago Chamber of Commerce........................507-893-3217

WINNEBAGO CITY (township). Covers a land area of 34.428 square miles and a water area of 0.039 square miles. Located at 43.78° N. Lat.; 94.19° W. Long.
Population: 221 (2000); Race: 99.6% White, 0.0% Black, 0.0% Asian, 0.0% American Indian and Alaska Native, 0.0% Hispanic of any race, 0.4% two or more races (2000); Density: 6.4 persons per square mile (2000); Age: 29.8% under 18, 10.1% over 64 (2000); Marriage status: 25.3% never married, 55.8% now married, 4.2% widowed, 14.7% divorced (2000); Foreign born: 0.0% (2000); Ancestry (includes multiple ancestries): 29.8% German, 23.4% Norwegian, 8.9% Swedish, 8.9% English, 6.5% Czech (2000).
Economy: Employment by occupation: 21.6% management, 14.4% professional, 10.4% services, 18.4% sales, 6.4% farming, 12.0% construction, 16.8% production (2000).
Income: Per capita income: $14,458 (2000); Median household income: $39,375 (2000); Poverty rate: 13.1% (2000).
Taxes: Total city taxes per capita: $93 (1997); City property taxes per capita: $93 (1997).
Education: High school graduation rate: 92.6% (2000); College graduation rate: 14.2% (2000).
Housing: Homeownership rate: 81.4% (2000); Median home value: $68,000 (2000); Median rent: $200 per month (2000); Median age of housing: 60+ years (2000).
Transportation: Commute to work: 88.0% car, 0.0% public transportation, 0.0% walk, 12.0% work from home (2000); Travel time to work: 31.8% less than 15 minutes, 41.8% 15 to 30 minutes, 17.3% 30 to 45 minutes, 7.3% 45 to 60 minutes, 1.8% 60 minutes or more (2000)

Fillmore County

Located in southeastern Minnesota; bounded on the south by Iowa; watered by the Root River. Covers a land area of 861.30 square miles, a water area of 0.90 square miles, and is located in the Central Time Zone. The county government was organized in 1853. County seat is Preston.

Weather Station: Preston — Elevation: 928 feet

	Jan	Feb	Mar	Apr	May	Jun	Jul	Aug	Sep	Oct	Nov	Dec
High	24	30	42	57	69	79	83	81	73	61	43	29
Low	3	9	21	33	44	54	58	56	47	36	23	10
Precip	1.0	0.8	1.9	3.3	3.9	4.3	4.7	4.6	3.7	2.4	2.1	1.3
Snow	11.1	6.7	7.1	2.1	tr	0.0	0.0	0.0	0.0	tr	4.6	10.0

High and Low temperatures in degrees Fahrenheit; Precipitation and Snow in inches

Population: 21,122 (2000); Race: 98.9% White, 0.2% Black, 0.1% Asian, 0.1% American Indian and Alaska Native, 0.5% Hispanic of any race, 0.4% two or more races (2000); Density: 24.5 persons per square mile (2000); Age: 26.1% under 18, 19.3% over 64 (2000).
Religion: Five largest groups: 51.7% Evangelical Lutheran Church in America, 13.7% Catholic Church, 10.6% The United Methodist Church, 7.1% Lutheran Church—Missouri Synod, 1.7% Old Order Amish Church (2000).
Economy: Unemployment rate: 3.2% (11/2002); Total civilian labor force: 9,828 (11/2002); Leading industries: 22.1% manufacturing; 18.6% health care and social assistance; 16.1% retail trade (2000); Companies that employ more than 1,000 persons: 0 (2000); Companies that employ more than 100 persons: 9 (2000); Farms: 1,546 totaling 434,581 acres (1997); Minority business ownership rate: 0.0% (1997); Women business ownership rate: 17.9% (1997); Retail sales per capita: $7,210 (1997). Single-family building permits issued: 135 (2001) / 108 (2000); Multi-family building permits issued: 56 (2001) / 20 (2000).
Income: Per capita income: $17,067 (2000); Median household income: $36,651 (2000); Poverty rate: 10.1% (2000); Bankruptcy rate: 1.87% (2001).
Taxes: Total county taxes per capita: $194 (2000); County property taxes per capita: $190 (2000).
Education: High school graduation rate: 81.7% (2000); College graduation rate: 15.1% (2000).
Housing: Homeownership rate: 80.7% (2000); Median home value: $74,400 (2000); Median rent: $291 per month (2000); Median age of housing: 56 years (2000).
Health: Birth rate: 124.5 per 10,000 population (1998); Age adjusted death rate: 76.9 per 10,000 population (1999); Age adjusted cancer mortality rate: 172.5 deaths per 100,000 population (1999). Number of physicians: 6.2 per 10,000 population (1999); Number of hospital beds: n/a (1999).
Elections: 2000 Presidential election results: 49.1% Gore, 45.5% Bush, 4.0% Nader, 0.9% Buchanan
National and State Parks: Minnesota Memorial Hardwood State Forest
Additional Information Contacts
Fillmore County Government Offices....................507-765-2144
Spring Valley Chamber of Commerce...................507-346-1015

Fillmore County Communities

AMHERST (township). Covers a land area of 35.841 square miles and a water area of 0 square miles. Located at 43.62° N. Lat.; 91.91° W. Long. Elevation is 1,049 feet.
Population: 405 (2000); Race: 98.6% White, 0.0% Black, 0.0% Asian, 0.0% American Indian and Alaska Native, 0.0% Hispanic of any race, 1.4% two or more races (2000); Density: 11.3 persons per square mile (2000); Age: 34.2% under 18, 15.6% over 64 (2000); Marriage status: 24.3% never married, 67.6% now married, 5.0% widowed, 3.1% divorced (2000); Foreign born: 0.6% (2000); Ancestry (includes multiple ancestries): 38.1% German, 38.1% Norwegian, 8.6% Irish, 6.1% English, 4.7% United States or American (2000).
Economy: Employment by occupation: 33.1% management, 16.5% professional, 5.0% services, 10.8% sales, 7.2% farming, 13.7% construction, 13.7% production (2000).
Income: Per capita income: $11,539 (2000); Median household income: $27,500 (2000); Poverty rate: 25.3% (2000).
Taxes: Total city taxes per capita: $62 (1997); City property taxes per capita: $62 (1997).
Education: High school graduation rate: 70.1% (2000); College graduation rate: 12.4% (2000).
Housing: Homeownership rate: 75.6% (2000); Median home value: $61,700 (2000); Median rent: $300 per month (2000); Median age of housing: 60+ years (2000).
Transportation: Commute to work: 72.3% car, 2.9% public transportation, 2.9% walk, 19.0% work from home (2000); Travel time to work: 30.6% less than 15 minutes, 36.0% 15 to 30 minutes, 9.0% 30 to 45 minutes, 13.5% 45 to 60 minutes, 10.8% 60 minutes or more (2000)

ARENDAHL (township). Covers a land area of 35.680 square miles and a water area of 0.118 square miles. Located at 43.80° N. Lat.; 91.89° W. Long. Elevation is 1,190 feet.
Population: 333 (2000); Race: 100.0% White, 0.0% Black, 0.0% Asian, 0.0% American Indian and Alaska Native, 0.0% Hispanic of any race, 0.0% two or more races (2000); Density: 9.3 persons per square mile (2000); Age: 23.7% under 18, 20.6% over 64 (2000); Marriage status: 28.0% never married, 65.5% now married, 4.5% widowed, 1.9% divorced (2000); Foreign born: 0.6% (2000); Ancestry (includes multiple ancestries): 60.1% Norwegian, 22.2% German, 7.0% English, 4.4% Polish, 4.1% Irish (2000).
Economy: Employment by occupation: 26.6% management, 14.1% professional, 11.3% services, 19.8% sales, 4.0% farming, 8.5% construction, 15.8% production (2000).
Income: Per capita income: $16,915 (2000); Median household income: $42,500 (2000); Poverty rate: 10.1% (2000).
Taxes: Total city taxes per capita: $94 (1997); City property taxes per capita: $94 (1997).
Education: High school graduation rate: 84.5% (2000); College graduation rate: 20.0% (2000).
Housing: Homeownership rate: 84.4% (2000); Median home value: $110,700 (2000); Median rent: $400 per month (2000); Median age of housing: 60+ years (2000).

Transportation: Commute to work: 76.2% car, 1.2% public transportation, 2.3% walk, 19.8% work from home (2000); Travel time to work: 34.8% less than 15 minutes, 31.9% 15 to 30 minutes, 15.2% 30 to 45 minutes, 6.5% 45 to 60 minutes, 11.6% 60 minutes or more (2000)

BEAVER (township). Covers a land area of 36.063 square miles and a water area of 0 square miles. Located at 43.53° N. Lat.; 92.40° W. Long.
Population: 243 (2000); Race: 100.0% White, 0.0% Black, 0.0% Asian, 0.0% American Indian and Alaska Native, 1.6% Hispanic of any race, 0.0% two or more races (2000); Density: 6.7 persons per square mile (2000); Age: 31.1% under 18, 14.6% over 64 (2000); Marriage status: 13.4% never married, 75.3% now married, 5.9% widowed, 5.4% divorced (2000); Foreign born: 0.0% (2000); Ancestry (includes multiple ancestries): 30.3% German, 27.2% Norwegian, 11.4% Irish, 10.2% English, 8.3% Scottish (2000).
Economy: Employment by occupation: 21.1% management, 17.1% professional, 14.6% services, 16.3% sales, 3.3% farming, 13.8% construction, 13.8% production (2000).
Income: Per capita income: $16,007 (2000); Median household income: $40,625 (2000); Poverty rate: 9.1% (2000).
Taxes: Total city taxes per capita: $196 (1997); City property taxes per capita: $196 (1997).
Education: High school graduation rate: 86.6% (2000); College graduation rate: 7.6% (2000).
Housing: Homeownership rate: 90.5% (2000); Median home value: $70,000 (2000); Median rent: $200 per month (2000); Median age of housing: 53 years (2000).
Transportation: Commute to work: 70.7% car, 6.5% public transportation, 0.0% walk, 22.8% work from home (2000); Travel time to work: 23.2% less than 15 minutes, 15.8% 15 to 30 minutes, 7.4% 30 to 45 minutes, 40.0% 45 to 60 minutes, 13.7% 60 minutes or more (2000)

BLOOMFIELD (township). Covers a land area of 35.681 square miles and a water area of 0.030 square miles. Located at 43.62° N. Lat.; 92.39° W. Long.
Population: 414 (2000); Race: 100.0% White, 0.0% Black, 0.0% Asian, 0.0% American Indian and Alaska Native, 0.0% Hispanic of any race, 0.0% two or more races (2000); Density: 11.6 persons per square mile (2000); Age: 29.2% under 18, 13.6% over 64 (2000); Marriage status: 17.9% never married, 75.4% now married, 4.0% widowed, 2.7% divorced (2000); Foreign born: 0.0% (2000); Ancestry (includes multiple ancestries): 46.3% German, 31.8% Norwegian, 8.6% English, 5.8% Dutch, 5.6% Irish (2000).
Economy: Employment by occupation: 19.0% management, 8.3% professional, 19.8% services, 26.4% sales, 2.5% farming, 11.2% construction, 12.8% production (2000).
Income: Per capita income: $20,577 (2000); Median household income: $47,813 (2000); Poverty rate: 5.4% (2000).
Taxes: Total city taxes per capita: $77 (1997); City property taxes per capita: $77 (1997).
Education: High school graduation rate: 88.3% (2000); College graduation rate: 9.3% (2000).
Housing: Homeownership rate: 85.1% (2000); Median home value: $92,500 (2000); Median rent: $288 per month (2000); Median age of housing: 52 years (2000).
Transportation: Commute to work: 89.6% car, 0.8% public transportation, 0.8% walk, 8.8% work from home (2000); Travel time to work: 26.5% less than 15 minutes, 23.7% 15 to 30 minutes, 26.0% 30 to 45 minutes, 14.6% 45 to 60 minutes, 9.1% 60 minutes or more (2000)

BRISTOL (township). Covers a land area of 36.030 square miles and a water area of 0 square miles. Located at 43.53° N. Lat.; 92.14° W. Long. Elevation is 1,334 feet.
Population: 499 (2000); Race: 99.4% White, 0.0% Black, 0.0% Asian, 0.0% American Indian and Alaska Native, 0.0% Hispanic of any race, 0.6% two or more races (2000); Density: 13.8 persons per square mile (2000); Age: 41.9% under 18, 8.9% over 64 (2000); Marriage status: 29.1% never married, 60.4% now married, 4.5% widowed, 6.0% divorced (2000); Foreign born: 0.4% (2000); Ancestry (includes multiple ancestries): 38.4% German, 27.6% Norwegian, 16.7% Dutch, 8.7% Irish, 4.4% English (2000).
Economy: Employment by occupation: 22.3% management, 14.5% professional, 10.3% services, 19.0% sales, 6.6% farming, 11.2% construction, 16.1% production (2000).
Income: Per capita income: $12,854 (2000); Median household income: $33,250 (2000); Poverty rate: 31.9% (2000).
Taxes: Total city taxes per capita: $144 (2000); City property taxes per capita: $144 (2000).
Education: High school graduation rate: 77.0% (2000); College graduation rate: 16.9% (2000).
Housing: Homeownership rate: 77.0% (2000); Median home value: $46,400 (2000); Median rent: $175 per month (2000); Median age of housing: 60+ years (2000).
Transportation: Commute to work: 67.9% car, 0.0% public transportation, 5.4% walk, 22.9% work from home (2000); Travel time to work: 40.5% less than 15 minutes, 31.4% 15 to 30 minutes, 8.6% 30 to 45 minutes, 8.1% 45 to 60 minutes, 11.4% 60 minutes or more (2000)

CANTON (city). Covers a land area of 1.003 square miles and a water area of 0 square miles. Located at 43.53° N. Lat.; 91.93° W. Long. Elevation is 1,345 feet.
Population: 343 (2000); Race: 100.0% White, 0.0% Black, 0.0% Asian, 0.0% American Indian and Alaska Native, 0.0% Hispanic of any race, 0.0% two or more races (2000); Density: 341.9 persons per square mile (2000); Age: 22.3% under 18, 26.0% over 64 (2000); Marriage status: 23.4% never married, 56.2% now married, 9.7% widowed, 10.7% divorced (2000); Foreign born: 0.0% (2000); Ancestry (includes multiple ancestries): 48.9% Norwegian, 37.1% German, 14.9% Irish, 10.9% English, 3.7% Danish (2000).
Economy: Single-family building permits issued: 0 (2001) / 1 (2000); Multi-family building permits issued: 0 (2001) / 0 (2000); Employment by occupation: 9.0% management, 9.7% professional, 19.3% services, 17.9% sales, 2.8% farming, 18.6% construction, 22.8% production (2000).
Income: Per capita income: $14,373 (2000); Median household income: $23,409 (2000); Poverty rate: 13.2% (2000).
Taxes: Total city taxes per capita: $74 (1997); City property taxes per capita: $71 (1997).
Education: High school graduation rate: 85.6% (2000); College graduation rate: 8.6% (2000).
Housing: Homeownership rate: 88.3% (2000); Median home value: $43,300 (2000); Median rent: $242 per month (2000); Median age of housing: 50 years (2000).
Transportation: Commute to work: 86.6% car, 2.1% public transportation, 4.2% walk, 4.9% work from home (2000); Travel time to work: 40.7% less than 15 minutes, 24.4% 15 to 30 minutes, 16.3% 30 to 45 minutes, 1.5% 45 to 60 minutes, 17.0% 60 minutes or more (2000)

CANTON (township). Covers a land area of 35.114 square miles and a water area of 0 square miles. Located at 43.54° N. Lat.; 91.92° W. Long. Elevation is 1,345 feet.
Population: 684 (2000); Race: 98.4% White, 0.3% Black, 0.0% Asian, 0.0% American Indian and Alaska Native, 1.3% Hispanic of any race, 0.4% two or more races (2000); Density: 19.5 persons per square mile (2000); Age: 42.0% under 18, 9.0% over 64 (2000); Marriage status: 31.0% never married, 62.1% now married, 3.9% widowed, 3.0% divorced (2000); Foreign born: 0.9% (2000); Ancestry (includes multiple ancestries): 35.6% German, 21.4% Norwegian, 12.1% Irish, 3.3% United States or American, 3.3% Pennsylvania German (2000).
Economy: Agriculture: corn, oats, soybeans; livestock, poultry; dairying. Employment by occupation: 15.3% management, 10.5% professional, 11.9% services, 15.9% sales, 13.9% farming, 9.5% construction, 23.1% production (2000).
Income: Per capita income: $9,594 (2000); Median household income: $31,429 (2000); Poverty rate: 37.1% (2000).
Taxes: Total city taxes per capita: $94 (2000); City property taxes per capita: $94 (2000).
Education: High school graduation rate: 58.7% (2000); College graduation rate: 9.0% (2000).
Housing: Homeownership rate: 85.0% (2000); Median home value: $67,000 (2000); Median rent: $208 per month (2000); Median age of housing: 60+ years (2000).
Transportation: Commute to work: 53.1% car, 0.7% public transportation, 5.2% walk, 40.3% work from home (2000); Travel time to work: 36.0% less than 15 minutes, 32.0% 15 to 30 minutes, 15.7% 30 to 45 minutes, 7.0% 45 to 60 minutes, 9.3% 60 minutes or more (2000)

CARIMONA (township). Covers a land area of 35.618 square miles and a water area of 0 square miles. Located at 43.62° N. Lat.; 92.12° W. Long.
Population: 272 (2000); Race: 100.0% White, 0.0% Black, 0.0% Asian, 0.0% American Indian and Alaska Native, 0.0% Hispanic of any race, 0.0% two or more races (2000); Density: 7.6 persons per square mile (2000); Age: 21.6% under 18, 16.7% over 64 (2000); Marriage status: 16.3% never married, 71.6% now married, 4.7% widowed, 7.4% divorced (2000); Foreign

born: 0.0% (2000); Ancestry (includes multiple ancestries): 43.9% German, 32.6% Norwegian, 17.8% Dutch, 8.3% Irish, 5.3% English (2000).
Economy: Employment by occupation: 34.3% management, 17.1% professional, 9.3% services, 12.9% sales, 5.7% farming, 13.6% construction, 7.1% production (2000).
Income: Per capita income: $18,278 (2000); Median household income: $39,792 (2000); Poverty rate: 8.7% (2000).
Taxes: Total city taxes per capita: $107 (1997); City property taxes per capita: $107 (1997).
Education: High school graduation rate: 89.7% (2000); College graduation rate: 15.9% (2000).
Housing: Homeownership rate: 81.5% (2000); Median home value: $85,000 (2000); Median rent: $475 per month (2000); Median age of housing: 60+ years (2000).
Transportation: Commute to work: 70.3% car, 0.7% public transportation, 1.4% walk, 27.5% work from home (2000); Travel time to work: 35.0% less than 15 minutes, 31.0% 15 to 30 minutes, 9.0% 30 to 45 minutes, 15.0% 45 to 60 minutes, 10.0% 60 minutes or more (2000)

CARROLTON (township). Covers a land area of 37.794 square miles and a water area of 0.122 square miles. Located at 43.72° N. Lat.; 92.01° W. Long.
Population: 321 (2000); Race: 97.9% White, 0.0% Black, 0.0% Asian, 0.0% American Indian and Alaska Native, 0.0% Hispanic of any race, 2.1% two or more races (2000); Density: 8.5 persons per square mile (2000); Age: 31.8% under 18, 12.2% over 64 (2000); Marriage status: 18.9% never married, 74.7% now married, 2.4% widowed, 4.0% divorced (2000); Foreign born: 1.2% (2000); Ancestry (includes multiple ancestries): 46.3% Norwegian, 30.0% German, 10.1% Irish, 8.9% English, 7.4% Danish (2000).
Economy: Employment by occupation: 21.5% management, 17.2% professional, 17.2% services, 21.5% sales, 4.3% farming, 10.2% construction, 8.1% production (2000).
Income: Per capita income: $18,404 (2000); Median household income: $47,981 (2000); Poverty rate: 4.2% (2000).
Taxes: Total city taxes per capita: $147 (1997); City property taxes per capita: $147 (1997).
Education: High school graduation rate: 90.4% (2000); College graduation rate: 17.8% (2000).
Housing: Homeownership rate: 87.6% (2000); Median home value: $66,400 (2000); Median age of housing: 60+ years (2000).
Transportation: Commute to work: 73.7% car, 2.2% public transportation, 5.9% walk, 18.3% work from home (2000); Travel time to work: 38.2% less than 15 minutes, 19.7% 15 to 30 minutes, 7.9% 30 to 45 minutes, 25.0% 45 to 60 minutes, 9.2% 60 minutes or more (2000)

CHATFIELD (city). Covers a land area of 1.992 square miles and a water area of 0 square miles. Located at 43.84° N. Lat.; 92.18° W. Long. Elevation is 976 feet.
History: Chatfield served for a time as the seat of Fillmore County, and was named for Judge Andrew Chatfield, who presided over the county's first court.
Population: 2,394 (2000); Race: 95.8% White, 0.6% Black, 0.2% Asian, 0.0% American Indian and Alaska Native, 3.5% Hispanic of any race, 0.6% two or more races (2000); Density: 1,201.8 persons per square mile (2000); Age: 25.6% under 18, 20.5% over 64 (2000); Marriage status: 20.3% never married, 63.9% now married, 9.6% widowed, 6.2% divorced (2000); Foreign born: 2.1% (2000); Ancestry (includes multiple ancestries): 36.5% German, 28.2% Norwegian, 15.8% Irish, 11.8% English, 6.0% Other groups (2000).
Economy: Single-family building permits issued: 20 (2001) / 8 (2000); Multi-family building permits issued: 4 (2001) / 2 (2000); Employment by occupation: 10.8% management, 20.9% professional, 17.2% services, 28.7% sales, 1.0% farming, 7.9% construction, 13.5% production (2000).
Income: Per capita income: $20,145 (2000); Median household income: $44,023 (2000); Poverty rate: 6.5% (2000).
Taxes: Total city taxes per capita: $205 (1997); City property taxes per capita: $195 (1997).
Education: High school graduation rate: 87.4% (2000); College graduation rate: 18.0% (2000).

School District(s)

Chatfield (PK-12)
2000 Enrollment: 924 507-867-4210

Housing: Homeownership rate: 78.5% (2000); Median home value: $95,300 (2000); Median rent: $340 per month (2000); Median age of housing: 35 years (2000).
Newspapers: Chatfield News (1 x week)
Transportation: Commute to work: 88.6% car, 2.6% public transportation, 5.4% walk, 3.2% work from home (2000); Travel time to work: 35.3% less than 15 minutes, 28.1% 15 to 30 minutes, 30.2% 30 to 45 minutes, 2.5% 45 to 60 minutes, 3.9% 60 minutes or more (2000)

CHATFIELD (township). Covers a land area of 34.556 square miles and a water area of 0 square miles. Located at 43.79° N. Lat.; 92.14° W. Long. Elevation is 976 feet.
Population: 489 (2000); Race: 99.2% White, 0.0% Black, 0.0% Asian, 0.0% American Indian and Alaska Native, 0.4% Hispanic of any race, 0.8% two or more races (2000); Density: 14.2 persons per square mile (2000); Age: 26.7% under 18, 10.9% over 64 (2000); Marriage status: 12.4% never married, 77.9% now married, 2.6% widowed, 7.1% divorced (2000); Foreign born: 0.4% (2000); Ancestry (includes multiple ancestries): 39.8% German, 34.5% Norwegian, 13.3% Irish, 8.7% English, 3.2% Danish (2000).
Economy: Employment by occupation: 22.4% management, 21.3% professional, 16.1% services, 18.5% sales, 3.5% farming, 7.0% construction, 11.2% production (2000).
Income: Per capita income: $20,317 (2000); Median household income: $48,182 (2000); Poverty rate: 7.3% (2000).
Taxes: Total city taxes per capita: $85 (1997); City property taxes per capita: $85 (1997).
Education: High school graduation rate: 88.4% (2000); College graduation rate: 18.0% (2000).
Housing: Homeownership rate: 95.6% (2000); Median home value: $142,500 (2000); Median rent: $400 per month (2000); Median age of housing: 35 years (2000).
Transportation: Commute to work: 77.5% car, 3.2% public transportation, 1.4% walk, 18.0% work from home (2000); Travel time to work: 30.0% less than 15 minutes, 13.7% 15 to 30 minutes, 44.6% 30 to 45 minutes, 8.2% 45 to 60 minutes, 3.4% 60 minutes or more (2000)

FILLMORE (township). Covers a land area of 34.868 square miles and a water area of 0 square miles. Located at 43.72° N. Lat.; 92.28° W. Long.
Population: 485 (2000); Race: 100.0% White, 0.0% Black, 0.0% Asian, 0.0% American Indian and Alaska Native, 0.0% Hispanic of any race, 0.0% two or more races (2000); Density: 13.9 persons per square mile (2000); Age: 24.6% under 18, 13.5% over 64 (2000); Marriage status: 22.5% never married, 68.4% now married, 4.4% widowed, 4.7% divorced (2000); Foreign born: 1.1% (2000); Ancestry (includes multiple ancestries): 44.8% German, 15.4% Norwegian, 10.9% English, 7.6% Irish, 7.4% Dutch (2000).
Economy: Employment by occupation: 16.1% management, 14.0% professional, 13.3% services, 25.4% sales, 7.2% farming, 11.1% construction, 12.9% production (2000).
Income: Per capita income: $18,431 (2000); Median household income: $40,417 (2000); Poverty rate: 4.9% (2000).
Taxes: Total city taxes per capita: $102 (1997); City property taxes per capita: $102 (1997).
Education: High school graduation rate: 84.0% (2000); College graduation rate: 13.5% (2000).
Housing: Homeownership rate: 83.3% (2000); Median home value: $82,500 (2000); Median rent: $283 per month (2000); Median age of housing: 60+ years (2000).
Transportation: Commute to work: 74.1% car, 3.3% public transportation, 8.4% walk, 14.2% work from home (2000); Travel time to work: 37.4% less than 15 minutes, 20.0% 15 to 30 minutes, 25.1% 30 to 45 minutes, 14.0% 45 to 60 minutes, 3.4% 60 minutes or more (2000)

FORESTVILLE (township). Covers a land area of 36.154 square miles and a water area of 0 square miles. Located at 43.62° N. Lat.; 92.28° W. Long.
Population: 386 (2000); Race: 99.3% White, 0.7% Black, 0.0% Asian, 0.0% American Indian and Alaska Native, 2.0% Hispanic of any race, 0.0% two or more races (2000); Density: 10.7 persons per square mile (2000); Age: 28.9% under 18, 13.6% over 64 (2000); Marriage status: 10.7% never married, 77.9% now married, 3.3% widowed, 8.1% divorced (2000); Foreign born: 0.0% (2000); Ancestry (includes multiple ancestries): 47.9% German, 25.2% Dutch, 19.8% Norwegian, 12.1% Irish, 5.2% English (2000).
Economy: Employment by occupation: 28.0% management, 16.9% professional, 10.7% services, 19.6% sales, 2.7% farming, 10.2% construction, 12.0% production (2000).
Income: Per capita income: $17,559 (2000); Median household income: $38,125 (2000); Poverty rate: 12.6% (2000).
Taxes: Total city taxes per capita: $102 (1997); City property taxes per capita: $102 (1997).

Education: High school graduation rate: 88.2% (2000); College graduation rate: 16.1% (2000).
Housing: Homeownership rate: 93.5% (2000); Median home value: $81,300 (2000); Median rent: $275 per month (2000); Median age of housing: 60+ years (2000).
Transportation: Commute to work: 83.6% car, 3.6% public transportation, 3.2% walk, 9.5% work from home (2000); Travel time to work: 29.6% less than 15 minutes, 28.6% 15 to 30 minutes, 20.6% 30 to 45 minutes, 11.6% 45 to 60 minutes, 9.5% 60 minutes or more (2000)

FOUNTAIN (city). Covers a land area of 0.830 square miles and a water area of 0 square miles. Located at 43.74° N. Lat.; 92.13° W. Long. Elevation is 1,305 feet.
Population: 343 (2000); Race: 100.0% White, 0.0% Black, 0.0% Asian, 0.0% American Indian and Alaska Native, 0.0% Hispanic of any race, 0.0% two or more races (2000); Density: 413.4 persons per square mile (2000); Age: 26.6% under 18, 13.8% over 64 (2000); Marriage status: 33.3% never married, 59.6% now married, 6.0% widowed, 1.1% divorced (2000); Foreign born: 0.6% (2000); Ancestry (includes multiple ancestries): 42.8% German, 37.9% Norwegian, 9.2% Irish, 8.3% Dutch, 3.7% English (2000).
Economy: Employment by occupation: 7.7% management, 12.3% professional, 13.8% services, 25.6% sales, 1.0% farming, 10.8% construction, 28.7% production (2000).
Income: Per capita income: $18,085 (2000); Median household income: $40,250 (2000); Poverty rate: 3.4% (2000).
Taxes: Total city taxes per capita: $222 (1997); City property taxes per capita: $219 (1997).
Education: High school graduation rate: 92.0% (2000); College graduation rate: 10.0% (2000).
Housing: Homeownership rate: 82.8% (2000); Median home value: $86,300 (2000); Median rent: $333 per month (2000); Median age of housing: 49 years (2000).
Transportation: Commute to work: 88.0% car, 5.2% public transportation, 5.2% walk, 1.0% work from home (2000); Travel time to work: 65.1% less than 15 minutes, 16.4% 15 to 30 minutes, 10.6% 30 to 45 minutes, 6.3% 45 to 60 minutes, 1.6% 60 minutes or more (2000)

FOUNTAIN (township). Covers a land area of 34.936 square miles and a water area of 0 square miles. Located at 43.72° N. Lat.; 92.14° W. Long. Elevation is 1,305 feet.
Population: 316 (2000); Race: 98.1% White, 0.0% Black, 0.0% Asian, 1.2% American Indian and Alaska Native, 0.0% Hispanic of any race, 0.6% two or more races (2000); Density: 9.0 persons per square mile (2000); Age: 31.3% under 18, 18.3% over 64 (2000); Marriage status: 24.5% never married, 66.7% now married, 3.6% widowed, 5.2% divorced (2000); Foreign born: 1.5% (2000); Ancestry (includes multiple ancestries): 44.6% German, 25.1% Norwegian, 15.2% English, 11.1% Irish, 8.7% Dutch (2000).
Economy: Poultry, livestock; grain, soybeans; dairying; timber. Employment by occupation: 17.0% management, 11.7% professional, 12.3% services, 28.7% sales, 8.2% farming, 9.9% construction, 12.3% production (2000).
Income: Per capita income: $17,518 (2000); Median household income: $50,250 (2000); Poverty rate: 5.6% (2000).
Taxes: Total city taxes per capita: $98 (1997); City property taxes per capita: $98 (1997).
Education: High school graduation rate: 81.7% (2000); College graduation rate: 6.1% (2000).
Housing: Homeownership rate: 81.9% (2000); Median home value: $86,000 (2000); Median rent: $425 per month (2000); Median age of housing: 58 years (2000).
Transportation: Commute to work: 77.2% car, 2.9% public transportation, 8.8% walk, 11.1% work from home (2000); Travel time to work: 59.9% less than 15 minutes, 14.5% 15 to 30 minutes, 13.8% 30 to 45 minutes, 8.6% 45 to 60 minutes, 3.3% 60 minutes or more (2000)

HARMONY (city). Covers a land area of 1.138 square miles and a water area of 0 square miles. Located at 43.55° N. Lat.; 92.00° W. Long. Elevation is 1,336 feet.
Population: 1,080 (2000); Race: 99.5% White, 0.2% Black, 0.2% Asian, 0.0% American Indian and Alaska Native, 0.1% Hispanic of any race, 0.0% two or more races (2000); Density: 948.9 persons per square mile (2000); Age: 20.7% under 18, 30.3% over 64 (2000); Marriage status: 16.4% never married, 59.4% now married, 15.9% widowed, 8.4% divorced (2000); Foreign born: 0.7% (2000); Ancestry (includes multiple ancestries): 45.9% Norwegian, 28.6% German, 13.4% Irish, 6.7% English, 3.5% Dutch (2000).
Economy: Single-family building permits issued: 4 (2001) / 6 (2000); Multi-family building permits issued: 34 (2001) / 0 (2000); Employment by occupation: 9.6% management, 22.3% professional, 17.6% services, 24.8% sales, 2.3% farming, 10.0% construction, 13.3% production (2000).
Income: Per capita income: $16,859 (2000); Median household income: $30,260 (2000); Poverty rate: 9.8% (2000).
Taxes: Total city taxes per capita: $269 (1997); City property taxes per capita: $269 (1997).
Education: High school graduation rate: 80.7% (2000); College graduation rate: 19.6% (2000).

School District(s)

Fillmore Central (PK-12)
2000 Enrollment: 808 507-886-6464

Housing: Homeownership rate: 78.3% (2000); Median home value: $63,900 (2000); Median rent: $278 per month (2000); Median age of housing: 53 years (2000).
Transportation: Commute to work: 83.6% car, 2.5% public transportation, 8.8% walk, 5.0% work from home (2000); Travel time to work: 49.2% less than 15 minutes, 20.3% 15 to 30 minutes, 9.7% 30 to 45 minutes, 5.7% 45 to 60 minutes, 15.0% 60 minutes or more (2000)

HARMONY (township). Covers a land area of 34.757 square miles and a water area of 0 square miles. Located at 43.55° N. Lat.; 92.02° W. Long. Elevation is 1,336 feet.
Population: 396 (2000); Race: 100.0% White, 0.0% Black, 0.0% Asian, 0.0% American Indian and Alaska Native, 0.0% Hispanic of any race, 0.0% two or more races (2000); Density: 11.4 persons per square mile (2000); Age: 31.4% under 18, 14.4% over 64 (2000); Marriage status: 30.3% never married, 67.1% now married, 1.7% widowed, 0.9% divorced (2000); Foreign born: 0.0% (2000); Ancestry (includes multiple ancestries): 38.7% Norwegian, 28.0% German, 8.4% English, 6.2% Dutch, 5.9% Irish (2000).
Economy: Grain, soybeans; livestock, poultry; dairying. Manufacturing: machinery, feeds, transportation equipment. Hammervold Landing Field to North. Employment by occupation: 26.9% management, 8.7% professional, 8.7% services, 16.0% sales, 7.3% farming, 14.6% construction, 17.8% production (2000).
Income: Per capita income: $14,531 (2000); Median household income: $42,083 (2000); Poverty rate: 14.1% (2000).
Taxes: Total city taxes per capita: $93 (1997); City property taxes per capita: $93 (1997).
Education: High school graduation rate: 82.3% (2000); College graduation rate: 11.0% (2000).
Housing: Homeownership rate: 87.0% (2000); Median home value: $80,000 (2000); Median age of housing: 60+ years (2000).
Transportation: Commute to work: 57.7% car, 0.5% public transportation, 5.6% walk, 34.3% work from home (2000); Travel time to work: 45.7% less than 15 minutes, 25.7% 15 to 30 minutes, 9.3% 30 to 45 minutes, 9.3% 45 to 60 minutes, 10.0% 60 minutes or more (2000)

HOLT (township). Covers a land area of 32.785 square miles and a water area of 0.185 square miles. Located at 43.71° N. Lat.; 91.90° W. Long.
Population: 307 (2000); Race: 99.4% White, 0.0% Black, 0.0% Asian, 0.0% American Indian and Alaska Native, 0.0% Hispanic of any race, 0.6% two or more races (2000); Density: 9.4 persons per square mile (2000); Age: 30.7% under 18, 8.0% over 64 (2000); Marriage status: 22.3% never married, 65.7% now married, 2.6% widowed, 9.4% divorced (2000); Foreign born: 0.6% (2000); Ancestry (includes multiple ancestries): 50.5% Norwegian, 27.5% German, 10.2% Irish, 5.4% English, 4.5% Dutch (2000).
Economy: Employment by occupation: 29.7% management, 13.2% professional, 9.3% services, 13.2% sales, 7.1% farming, 6.6% construction, 20.9% production (2000).
Income: Per capita income: $16,113 (2000); Median household income: $37,083 (2000); Poverty rate: 13.8% (2000).
Taxes: Total city taxes per capita: $117 (1997); City property taxes per capita: $117 (1997).
Education: High school graduation rate: 92.4% (2000); College graduation rate: 19.3% (2000).
Housing: Homeownership rate: 82.7% (2000); Median home value: $90,000 (2000); Median rent: $182 per month (2000); Median age of housing: 57 years (2000).
Transportation: Commute to work: 69.5% car, 0.0% public transportation, 0.0% walk, 30.5% work from home (2000); Travel time to work: 31.4% less than 15 minutes, 47.1% 15 to 30 minutes, 11.6% 30 to 45 minutes, 5.8% 45 to 60 minutes, 4.1% 60 minutes or more (2000)

JORDAN (township). Covers a land area of 35.973 square miles and a water area of 0 square miles. Located at 43.80° N. Lat.; 92.27° W. Long.

Population: 412 (2000); Race: 99.3% White, 0.0% Black, 0.0% Asian, 0.0% American Indian and Alaska Native, 0.5% Hispanic of any race, 0.7% two or more races (2000); Density: 11.5 persons per square mile (2000); Age: 31.7% under 18, 9.3% over 64 (2000); Marriage status: 22.7% never married, 67.5% now married, 3.4% widowed, 6.4% divorced (2000); Foreign born: 0.7% (2000); Ancestry (includes multiple ancestries): 37.3% German, 27.6% Norwegian, 10.2% English, 7.7% Irish, 5.4% United States or American (2000).
Economy: Employment by occupation: 20.5% management, 14.7% professional, 14.7% services, 26.4% sales, 3.1% farming, 8.5% construction, 12.0% production (2000).
Income: Per capita income: $16,843 (2000); Median household income: $47,019 (2000); Poverty rate: 7.5% (2000).
Taxes: Total city taxes per capita: $97 (1997); City property taxes per capita: $97 (1997).
Education: High school graduation rate: 89.1% (2000); College graduation rate: 14.1% (2000).
Housing: Homeownership rate: 82.8% (2000); Median home value: $121,900 (2000); Median rent: $408 per month (2000); Median age of housing: 47 years (2000).
Transportation: Commute to work: 80.2% car, 0.8% public transportation, 2.7% walk, 16.3% work from home (2000); Travel time to work: 14.8% less than 15 minutes, 31.0% 15 to 30 minutes, 45.4% 30 to 45 minutes, 6.5% 45 to 60 minutes, 2.3% 60 minutes or more (2000)

LANESBORO (city). Covers a land area of 1.324 square miles and a water area of 0 square miles. Located at 43.71° N. Lat.; 91.97° W. Long. Elevation is 846 feet.
History: It was in Lanesboro in the late 1800's that Norwegian naturalist Dr. John C. Hvoslef carried on his work in ornithology.
Population: 788 (2000); Race: 98.6% White, 0.1% Black, 0.0% Asian, 0.0% American Indian and Alaska Native, 1.0% Hispanic of any race, 0.5% two or more races (2000); Density: 595.4 persons per square mile (2000); Age: 18.1% under 18, 22.3% over 64 (2000); Marriage status: 23.0% never married, 59.8% now married, 10.7% widowed, 6.5% divorced (2000); Foreign born: 0.8% (2000); Ancestry (includes multiple ancestries): 59.5% Norwegian, 25.2% German, 7.8% Irish, 5.7% Swedish, 5.4% English (2000).
Economy: Single-family building permits issued: 6 (2001) / 2 (2000); Multi-family building permits issued: 2 (2001) / 0 (2000); Employment by occupation: 10.7% management, 19.9% professional, 14.3% services, 21.4% sales, 2.8% farming, 9.2% construction, 21.8% production (2000).
Income: Per capita income: $18,311 (2000); Median household income: $32,206 (2000); Poverty rate: 10.2% (2000).
Taxes: Total city taxes per capita: $212 (1997); City property taxes per capita: $181 (1997).
Education: High school graduation rate: 83.2% (2000); College graduation rate: 21.8% (2000).

School District(s)

Lanesboro (PK-12)
2000 Enrollment: 362 507-467-2229
Housing: Homeownership rate: 73.4% (2000); Median home value: $77,400 (2000); Median rent: $256 per month (2000); Median age of housing: 60+ years (2000).
Transportation: Commute to work: 75.8% car, 1.9% public transportation, 12.7% walk, 9.0% work from home (2000); Travel time to work: 50.2% less than 15 minutes, 18.9% 15 to 30 minutes, 11.8% 30 to 45 minutes, 10.4% 45 to 60 minutes, 8.7% 60 minutes or more (2000)

MABEL (city). Covers a land area of 0.473 square miles and a water area of 0 square miles. Located at 43.52° N. Lat.; 91.76° W. Long. Elevation is 1,134 feet.
History: Richard J. Dorer Memorial Hardwood State Forest to North.
Population: 766 (2000); Race: 98.8% White, 0.0% Black, 0.0% Asian, 0.0% American Indian and Alaska Native, 1.0% Hispanic of any race, 1.2% two or more races (2000); Density: 1,618.4 persons per square mile (2000); Age: 19.8% under 18, 35.6% over 64 (2000); Marriage status: 18.6% never married, 57.6% now married, 14.6% widowed, 9.2% divorced (2000); Foreign born: 0.0% (2000); Ancestry (includes multiple ancestries): 58.0% Norwegian, 22.5% German, 10.1% Irish, 6.9% English, 2.9% United States or American (2000).
Economy: Grain, soybeans; livestock, poultry; dairying. Single-family building permits issued: 2 (2001) / 1 (2000); Multi-family building permits issued: 0 (2001) / 0 (2000); Employment by occupation: 7.2% management, 16.0% professional, 22.5% services, 17.3% sales, 0.0% farming, 12.7% construction, 24.2% production (2000).
Income: Per capita income: $15,496 (2000); Median household income: $27,228 (2000); Poverty rate: 10.7% (2000).
Taxes: Total city taxes per capita: $88 (1997); City property taxes per capita: $83 (1997).
Education: High school graduation rate: 71.5% (2000); College graduation rate: 13.9% (2000).

School District(s)

Mabel-Canton (KG-12)
2000 Enrollment: 393 507-493-5423
Housing: Homeownership rate: 83.7% (2000); Median home value: $57,000 (2000); Median rent: $154 per month (2000); Median age of housing: 57 years (2000).
Newspapers: News Record (1 x week)
Transportation: Commute to work: 80.6% car, 0.3% public transportation, 11.2% walk, 6.3% work from home (2000); Travel time to work: 44.9% less than 15 minutes, 22.5% 15 to 30 minutes, 18.9% 30 to 45 minutes, 0.7% 45 to 60 minutes, 13.0% 60 minutes or more (2000)

NEWBURG (township). Covers a land area of 35.395 square miles and a water area of 0 square miles. Located at 43.55° N. Lat.; 91.78° W. Long.
Population: 444 (2000); Race: 99.3% White, 0.0% Black, 0.0% Asian, 0.0% American Indian and Alaska Native, 0.0% Hispanic of any race, 0.7% two or more races (2000); Density: 12.5 persons per square mile (2000); Age: 29.8% under 18, 16.1% over 64 (2000); Marriage status: 24.1% never married, 60.1% now married, 8.9% widowed, 6.9% divorced (2000); Foreign born: 1.5% (2000); Ancestry (includes multiple ancestries): 63.7% Norwegian, 27.2% German, 14.8% Irish, 8.3% English, 5.0% Swedish (2000).
Economy: Employment by occupation: 25.7% management, 10.5% professional, 11.0% services, 19.5% sales, 3.8% farming, 9.5% construction, 20.0% production (2000).
Income: Per capita income: $16,960 (2000); Median household income: $32,083 (2000); Poverty rate: 5.1% (2000).
Taxes: Total city taxes per capita: $118 (1997); City property taxes per capita: $118 (1997).
Education: High school graduation rate: 79.3% (2000); College graduation rate: 10.0% (2000).
Housing: Homeownership rate: 81.3% (2000); Median home value: $76,000 (2000); Median rent: $303 per month (2000); Median age of housing: 60+ years (2000).
Transportation: Commute to work: 81.4% car, 0.0% public transportation, 4.3% walk, 13.3% work from home (2000); Travel time to work: 37.9% less than 15 minutes, 26.4% 15 to 30 minutes, 19.2% 30 to 45 minutes, 5.5% 45 to 60 minutes, 11.0% 60 minutes or more (2000)

NORWAY (township). Covers a land area of 35.800 square miles and a water area of 0 square miles. Located at 43.70° N. Lat.; 91.81° W. Long.
Population: 335 (2000); Race: 96.9% White, 0.6% Black, 1.1% Asian, 0.0% American Indian and Alaska Native, 0.0% Hispanic of any race, 1.4% two or more races (2000); Density: 9.4 persons per square mile (2000); Age: 30.4% under 18, 11.9% over 64 (2000); Marriage status: 22.4% never married, 72.6% now married, 1.9% widowed, 3.1% divorced (2000); Foreign born: 0.9% (2000); Ancestry (includes multiple ancestries): 69.3% Norwegian, 26.7% German, 6.8% Other groups, 6.8% Polish, 3.7% Irish (2000).
Economy: Employment by occupation: 27.5% management, 18.5% professional, 10.0% services, 15.0% sales, 2.0% farming, 13.5% construction, 13.5% production (2000).
Income: Per capita income: $14,826 (2000); Median household income: $37,000 (2000); Poverty rate: 5.7% (2000).
Taxes: Total city taxes per capita: $76 (1997); City property taxes per capita: $76 (1997).
Education: High school graduation rate: 85.5% (2000); College graduation rate: 13.1% (2000).
Housing: Homeownership rate: 73.6% (2000); Median home value: $72,500 (2000); Median rent: $288 per month (2000); Median age of housing: 60+ years (2000).
Transportation: Commute to work: 73.2% car, 0.0% public transportation, 3.0% walk, 23.7% work from home (2000); Travel time to work: 19.2% less than 15 minutes, 29.8% 15 to 30 minutes, 14.6% 30 to 45 minutes, 17.9% 45 to 60 minutes, 18.5% 60 minutes or more (2000)

OSTRANDER (city). Covers a land area of 0.351 square miles and a water area of 0 square miles. Located at 43.61° N. Lat.; 92.42° W. Long. Elevation is 1,338 feet.
Population: 212 (2000); Race: 99.0% White, 0.0% Black, 0.0% Asian, 0.0% American Indian and Alaska Native, 2.0% Hispanic of any race, 0.0% two or more races (2000); Density: 604.1 persons per square mile (2000); Age:

18.3% under 18, 33.7% over 64 (2000); Marriage status: 12.6% never married, 56.6% now married, 18.9% widowed, 12.0% divorced (2000); Foreign born: 1.0% (2000); Ancestry (includes multiple ancestries): 37.6% Norwegian, 32.2% German, 6.9% Dutch, 6.4% Irish, 4.5% Other groups (2000).
Economy: Grain, soybeans; livestock, poultry; dairying. Employment by occupation: 4.3% management, 23.7% professional, 15.1% services, 21.5% sales, 0.0% farming, 19.4% construction, 16.1% production (2000).
Income: Per capita income: $20,214 (2000); Median household income: $41,875 (2000); Poverty rate: 5.0% (2000).
Taxes: Total city taxes per capita: $235 (1997); City property taxes per capita: $231 (1997).
Education: High school graduation rate: 79.1% (2000); College graduation rate: 12.7% (2000).
Housing: Homeownership rate: 78.4% (2000); Median home value: $55,000 (2000); Median rent: $275 per month (2000); Median age of housing: 53 years (2000).
Transportation: Commute to work: 80.2% car, 4.4% public transportation, 12.1% walk, 3.3% work from home (2000); Travel time to work: 22.7% less than 15 minutes, 21.6% 15 to 30 minutes, 30.7% 30 to 45 minutes, 19.3% 45 to 60 minutes, 5.7% 60 minutes or more (2000)

PETERSON (city). Covers a land area of 0.483 square miles and a water area of 0.022 square miles. Located at 43.78° N. Lat.; 91.83° W. Long. Elevation is 763 feet.
Population: 269 (2000); Race: 100.0% White, 0.0% Black, 0.0% Asian, 0.0% American Indian and Alaska Native, 0.0% Hispanic of any race, 0.0% two or more races (2000); Density: 557.5 persons per square mile (2000); Age: 20.2% under 18, 36.8% over 64 (2000); Marriage status: 18.1% never married, 55.6% now married, 19.9% widowed, 6.5% divorced (2000); Foreign born: 0.0% (2000); Ancestry (includes multiple ancestries): 46.1% Norwegian, 22.5% German, 10.5% United States or American, 7.0% Polish, 5.8% Other groups (2000).
Economy: Manufacturing of wood specialty products; dairying, poultry, grain, soybeans. Employment by occupation: 8.4% management, 12.1% professional, 11.2% services, 16.8% sales, 4.7% farming, 10.3% construction, 36.4% production (2000).
Income: Per capita income: $14,728 (2000); Median household income: $35,781 (2000); Poverty rate: 12.4% (2000).
Taxes: Total city taxes per capita: $93 (1997); City property taxes per capita: $93 (1997).
Education: High school graduation rate: 72.1% (2000); College graduation rate: 13.4% (2000).
Housing: Homeownership rate: 80.2% (2000); Median home value: $61,400 (2000); Median rent: $322 per month (2000); Median age of housing: 60+ years (2000).
Transportation: Commute to work: 94.4% car, 0.0% public transportation, 1.9% walk, 3.7% work from home (2000); Travel time to work: 63.1% less than 15 minutes, 8.7% 15 to 30 minutes, 11.7% 30 to 45 minutes, 9.7% 45 to 60 minutes, 6.8% 60 minutes or more (2000)

PILOT MOUND (township). Covers a land area of 34.209 square miles and a water area of 0.061 square miles. Located at 43.81° N. Lat.; 92.03° W. Long.
Population: 364 (2000); Race: 98.4% White, 0.0% Black, 1.6% Asian, 0.0% American Indian and Alaska Native, 0.0% Hispanic of any race, 0.0% two or more races (2000); Density: 10.6 persons per square mile (2000); Age: 29.8% under 18, 7.1% over 64 (2000); Marriage status: 28.6% never married, 58.8% now married, 5.0% widowed, 7.6% divorced (2000); Foreign born: 1.6% (2000); Ancestry (includes multiple ancestries): 32.7% Norwegian, 27.2% German, 16.2% Irish, 3.4% Dutch, 2.6% United States or American (2000).
Economy: Employment by occupation: 23.5% management, 16.1% professional, 15.2% services, 11.3% sales, 6.5% farming, 12.6% construction, 14.8% production (2000).
Income: Per capita income: $16,877 (2000); Median household income: $45,625 (2000); Poverty rate: 7.1% (2000).
Taxes: Total city taxes per capita: $71 (1997); City property taxes per capita: $71 (1997).
Education: High school graduation rate: 89.5% (2000); College graduation rate: 19.3% (2000).
Housing: Homeownership rate: 75.0% (2000); Median home value: $63,800 (2000); Median rent: $367 per month (2000); Median age of housing: 43 years (2000).
Transportation: Commute to work: 74.6% car, 1.3% public transportation, 3.1% walk, 21.1% work from home (2000); Travel time to work: 15.0% less than 15 minutes, 24.4% 15 to 30 minutes, 31.7% 30 to 45 minutes, 21.7% 45 to 60 minutes, 7.2% 60 minutes or more (2000)

PREBLE (township). Covers a land area of 35.811 square miles and a water area of 0 square miles. Located at 43.63° N. Lat.; 91.80° W. Long.
Population: 272 (2000); Race: 99.3% White, 0.0% Black, 0.7% Asian, 0.0% American Indian and Alaska Native, 0.0% Hispanic of any race, 0.0% two or more races (2000); Density: 7.6 persons per square mile (2000); Age: 26.1% under 18, 16.8% over 64 (2000); Marriage status: 19.3% never married, 66.5% now married, 8.0% widowed, 6.1% divorced (2000); Foreign born: 1.5% (2000); Ancestry (includes multiple ancestries): 61.9% Norwegian, 20.9% German, 7.1% English, 4.1% Other groups, 3.4% Irish (2000).
Economy: Employment by occupation: 22.3% management, 18.5% professional, 6.2% services, 15.4% sales, 7.7% farming, 14.6% construction, 15.4% production (2000).
Income: Per capita income: $16,182 (2000); Median household income: $36,875 (2000); Poverty rate: 5.6% (2000).
Taxes: Total city taxes per capita: $53 (1997); City property taxes per capita: $53 (1997).
Education: High school graduation rate: 84.2% (2000); College graduation rate: 16.9% (2000).
Housing: Homeownership rate: 84.2% (2000); Median home value: $53,800 (2000); Median rent: $213 per month (2000); Median age of housing: 58 years (2000).
Transportation: Commute to work: 71.5% car, 6.9% public transportation, 0.8% walk, 20.8% work from home (2000); Travel time to work: 10.7% less than 15 minutes, 45.6% 15 to 30 minutes, 10.7% 30 to 45 minutes, 14.6% 45 to 60 minutes, 18.4% 60 minutes or more (2000)

PRESTON (city). Covers a land area of 2.352 square miles and a water area of 0 square miles. Located at 43.67° N. Lat.; 92.08° W. Long. Elevation is 925 feet.
Population: 1,426 (2000); Race: 99.1% White, 0.0% Black, 0.1% Asian, 0.4% American Indian and Alaska Native, 0.0% Hispanic of any race, 0.3% two or more races (2000); Density: 606.3 persons per square mile (2000); Age: 22.3% under 18, 24.5% over 64 (2000); Marriage status: 22.7% never married, 58.0% now married, 11.2% widowed, 8.1% divorced (2000); Foreign born: 0.4% (2000); Ancestry (includes multiple ancestries): 44.2% German, 36.2% Norwegian, 10.9% Irish, 6.1% Dutch, 5.9% English (2000).
Economy: Employment by occupation: 10.4% management, 17.8% professional, 19.2% services, 24.4% sales, 1.7% farming, 11.3% construction, 15.2% production (2000).
Income: Per capita income: $18,578 (2000); Median household income: $37,016 (2000); Poverty rate: 8.3% (2000).
Taxes: Total city taxes per capita: $185 (1997); City property taxes per capita: $182 (1997).
Education: High school graduation rate: 81.1% (2000); College graduation rate: 15.6% (2000).
Housing: Homeownership rate: 79.2% (2000); Median home value: $72,900 (2000); Median rent: $310 per month (2000); Median age of housing: 52 years (2000).
Newspapers: Republican Leader (1 x week); Fillmore County Journal (1 x week)
Transportation: Commute to work: 84.5% car, 3.5% public transportation, 8.2% walk, 3.5% work from home (2000); Travel time to work: 57.6% less than 15 minutes, 16.2% 15 to 30 minutes, 5.8% 30 to 45 minutes, 13.6% 45 to 60 minutes, 6.8% 60 minutes or more (2000)

PRESTON (township). Covers a land area of 34.499 square miles and a water area of 0.006 square miles. Located at 43.64° N. Lat.; 92.00° W. Long. Elevation is 925 feet.
History: Courthouse built 1863.
Population: 374 (2000); Race: 99.5% White, 0.0% Black, 0.0% Asian, 0.5% American Indian and Alaska Native, 0.0% Hispanic of any race, 0.0% two or more races (2000); Density: 10.8 persons per square mile (2000); Age: 43.3% under 18, 7.6% over 64 (2000); Marriage status: 29.6% never married, 62.6% now married, 1.6% widowed, 6.2% divorced (2000); Foreign born: 0.0% (2000); Ancestry (includes multiple ancestries): 35.0% Norwegian, 25.8% German, 7.6% Irish, 3.7% Dutch, 3.7% Scandinavian (2000).
Economy: Livestock-shipping point in diversified-farming area; grain, soybeans; poultry; dairying. Manufacturing: lumber, wood products; packaging and assembly. Employment by occupation: 23.4% management, 13.7% professional, 17.1% services, 12.0% sales, 4.6% farming, 10.3% construction, 18.9% production (2000).
Income: Per capita income: $14,134 (2000); Median household income: $46,250 (2000); Poverty rate: 18.1% (2000).

Taxes: Total city taxes per capita: $94 (1997); City property taxes per capita: $94 (1997).
Education: High school graduation rate: 78.0% (2000); College graduation rate: 10.8% (2000).
Housing: Homeownership rate: 79.8% (2000); Median home value: $100,000 (2000); Median rent: $275 per month (2000); Median age of housing: 60+ years (2000).
Transportation: Commute to work: 61.1% car, 2.3% public transportation, 3.4% walk, 22.3% work from home (2000); Travel time to work: 48.5% less than 15 minutes, 22.8% 15 to 30 minutes, 8.8% 30 to 45 minutes, 14.0% 45 to 60 minutes, 5.9% 60 minutes or more (2000)

RUSHFORD (city). Covers a land area of 1.716 square miles and a water area of 0.021 square miles. Located at 43.81° N. Lat.; 91.75° W. Long. Elevation is 726 feet.
History: Settled before 1854.
Population: 1,696 (2000); Race: 98.5% White, 0.5% Black, 0.0% Asian, 0.0% American Indian and Alaska Native, 0.1% Hispanic of any race, 0.9% two or more races (2000); Density: 988.5 persons per square mile (2000); Age: 23.4% under 18, 25.5% over 64 (2000); Marriage status: 20.3% never married, 59.3% now married, 13.8% widowed, 6.7% divorced (2000); Foreign born: 0.8% (2000); Ancestry (includes multiple ancestries): 59.4% Norwegian, 31.8% German, 10.4% Irish, 4.3% English, 3.6% Polish (2000).
Economy: Trade and shipping center for agricultural area: feed. Manufacturing: composite materials, panels and switches. Single-family building permits issued: 5 (2001) / 14 (2000); Multi-family building permits issued: 8 (2001) / 14 (2000); Employment by occupation: 11.9% management, 17.9% professional, 16.5% services, 18.4% sales, 1.0% farming, 10.9% construction, 23.4% production (2000).
Income: Per capita income: $16,508 (2000); Median household income: $37,159 (2000); Poverty rate: 6.2% (2000).
Taxes: Total city taxes per capita: $252 (1997); City property taxes per capita: $246 (1997).
Education: High school graduation rate: 77.0% (2000); College graduation rate: 16.4% (2000).

School District(s)

Rushford-Peterson (PK-12)
2000 Enrollment: 728 507-864-7785

Housing: Homeownership rate: 75.8% (2000); Median home value: $78,400 (2000); Median rent: $314 per month (2000); Median age of housing: 42 years (2000).
Newspapers: Tri-County Record (1 x week)
Transportation: Commute to work: 90.9% car, 0.0% public transportation, 6.0% walk, 2.3% work from home (2000); Travel time to work: 53.7% less than 15 minutes, 14.2% 15 to 30 minutes, 21.2% 30 to 45 minutes, 4.9% 45 to 60 minutes, 6.0% 60 minutes or more (2000)

RUSHFORD VILLAGE (city). Covers a land area of 33.412 square miles and a water area of 0.242 square miles. Located at 43.80° N. Lat.; 91.78° W. Long.
Population: 714 (2000); Race: 98.7% White, 0.0% Black, 0.0% Asian, 0.0% American Indian and Alaska Native, 0.9% Hispanic of any race, 0.4% two or more races (2000); Density: 21.4 persons per square mile (2000); Age: 26.4% under 18, 13.5% over 64 (2000); Marriage status: 17.9% never married, 73.4% now married, 4.0% widowed, 4.7% divorced (2000); Foreign born: 0.4% (2000); Ancestry (includes multiple ancestries): 60.5% Norwegian, 37.7% German, 6.1% Irish, 4.6% English, 2.7% Swedish (2000).
Economy: Single-family building permits issued: 4 (2001) / 7 (2000); Multi-family building permits issued: 0 (2001) / 0 (2000); Employment by occupation: 18.2% management, 14.9% professional, 8.3% services, 23.7% sales, 2.8% farming, 9.8% construction, 22.2% production (2000).
Income: Per capita income: $18,042 (2000); Median household income: $43,125 (2000); Poverty rate: 8.0% (2000).
Taxes: Total city taxes per capita: $155 (1997); City property taxes per capita: $152 (1997).
Education: High school graduation rate: 88.4% (2000); College graduation rate: 17.7% (2000).
Housing: Homeownership rate: 92.5% (2000); Median home value: $84,500 (2000); Median rent: $331 per month (2000); Median age of housing: 36 years (2000).
Transportation: Commute to work: 88.3% car, 0.0% public transportation, 2.1% walk, 9.1% work from home (2000); Travel time to work: 53.8% less than 15 minutes, 17.4% 15 to 30 minutes, 16.8% 30 to 45 minutes, 6.0% 45 to 60 minutes, 6.0% 60 minutes or more (2000)

SPRING VALLEY (city). Covers a land area of 2.510 square miles and a water area of 0 square miles. Located at 43.68° N. Lat.; 92.39° W. Long. Elevation is 1,316 feet.
History: Spring Valley was named for the many springs, coming from underground rivers and limestone caves left by prehistoric seas. Richard Sears, one of the founders of Sears, Roebuck & Company, was from Spring Valley.
Population: 2,518 (2000); Race: 98.0% White, 0.7% Black, 0.3% Asian, 0.2% American Indian and Alaska Native, 0.6% Hispanic of any race, 0.6% two or more races (2000); Density: 1,003.3 persons per square mile (2000); Age: 25.6% under 18, 19.9% over 64 (2000); Marriage status: 23.6% never married, 57.8% now married, 7.9% widowed, 10.8% divorced (2000); Foreign born: 1.7% (2000); Ancestry (includes multiple ancestries): 41.0% German, 28.4% Norwegian, 10.7% Irish, 8.1% English, 5.9% Dutch (2000).
Economy: Single-family building permits issued: 17 (2001) / 11 (2000); Multi-family building permits issued: 0 (2001) / 4 (2000); Employment by occupation: 11.8% management, 15.2% professional, 18.8% services, 26.2% sales, 2.5% farming, 8.8% construction, 16.7% production (2000).
Income: Per capita income: $16,735 (2000); Median household income: $32,688 (2000); Poverty rate: 8.6% (2000).
Taxes: Total city taxes per capita: $181 (1997); City property taxes per capita: $175 (1997).
Education: High school graduation rate: 79.4% (2000); College graduation rate: 17.9% (2000).
Housing: Homeownership rate: 77.0% (2000); Median home value: $76,200 (2000); Median rent: $300 per month (2000); Median age of housing: 51 years (2000).
Newspapers: Spring Valley Tribune (1 x week); River Valley Reader (1 x week)
Transportation: Commute to work: 83.9% car, 3.2% public transportation, 8.3% walk, 4.5% work from home (2000); Travel time to work: 43.3% less than 15 minutes, 14.6% 15 to 30 minutes, 24.1% 30 to 45 minutes, 13.1% 45 to 60 minutes, 4.8% 60 minutes or more (2000)

Additional Information Contacts

Spring Valley Chamber of Commerce 507-346-1015

SPRING VALLEY (township). Covers a land area of 32.062 square miles and a water area of 0.018 square miles. Located at 43.70° N. Lat.; 92.38° W. Long. Elevation is 1,316 feet.
History: Forestville Mystery Cave State Park to East, area noted for its karst topography. Settled 1855, incorporated 1856.
Population: 590 (2000); Race: 99.5% White, 0.0% Black, 0.0% Asian, 0.5% American Indian and Alaska Native, 0.3% Hispanic of any race, 0.0% two or more races (2000); Density: 18.4 persons per square mile (2000); Age: 23.7% under 18, 10.5% over 64 (2000); Marriage status: 20.4% never married, 71.1% now married, 4.0% widowed, 4.5% divorced (2000); Foreign born: 1.0% (2000); Ancestry (includes multiple ancestries): 43.4% German, 31.3% Norwegian, 8.3% Irish, 6.9% English, 6.0% Dutch (2000).
Economy: Trade center for agricultural area: dairying; poultry; grain, soybeans. Manufacturing: cheese; printing and publishing. Employment by occupation: 14.9% management, 15.5% professional, 14.3% services, 29.7% sales, 2.9% farming, 10.2% construction, 12.5% production (2000).
Income: Per capita income: $20,224 (2000); Median household income: $47,250 (2000); Poverty rate: 5.9% (2000).
Taxes: Total city taxes per capita: $88 (1997); City property taxes per capita: $88 (1997).
Education: High school graduation rate: 91.4% (2000); College graduation rate: 14.8% (2000).
Housing: Homeownership rate: 88.1% (2000); Median home value: $107,700 (2000); Median rent: $275 per month (2000); Median age of housing: 36 years (2000).
Transportation: Commute to work: 87.2% car, 2.7% public transportation, 0.6% walk, 9.2% work from home (2000); Travel time to work: 37.9% less than 15 minutes, 17.6% 15 to 30 minutes, 27.8% 30 to 45 minutes, 13.1% 45 to 60 minutes, 3.6% 60 minutes or more (2000)

SUMNER (township). Covers a land area of 37.519 square miles and a water area of 0 square miles. Located at 43.79° N. Lat.; 92.37° W. Long.
Population: 436 (2000); Race: 100.0% White, 0.0% Black, 0.0% Asian, 0.0% American Indian and Alaska Native, 0.0% Hispanic of any race, 0.0% two or more races (2000); Density: 11.6 persons per square mile (2000); Age: 23.7% under 18, 13.6% over 64 (2000); Marriage status: 19.9% never married, 66.9% now married, 5.5% widowed, 7.7% divorced (2000); Foreign born: 0.0% (2000); Ancestry (includes multiple ancestries): 50.1% German, 28.1% Norwegian, 14.3% Irish, 9.6% English, 7.4% Dutch (2000).

Economy: Employment by occupation: 23.5% management, 15.5% professional, 13.1% services, 19.5% sales, 4.0% farming, 12.0% construction, 12.4% production (2000).
Income: Per capita income: $19,549 (2000); Median household income: $44,583 (2000); Poverty rate: 5.2% (2000).
Taxes: Total city taxes per capita: $125 (1997); City property taxes per capita: $125 (1997).
Education: High school graduation rate: 88.6% (2000); College graduation rate: 10.7% (2000).
Housing: Homeownership rate: 81.8% (2000); Median home value: $125,000 (2000); Median rent: $283 per month (2000); Median age of housing: 60+ years (2000).
Transportation: Commute to work: 72.0% car, 1.2% public transportation, 2.9% walk, 22.6% work from home (2000); Travel time to work: 18.1% less than 15 minutes, 41.0% 15 to 30 minutes, 36.2% 30 to 45 minutes, 1.6% 45 to 60 minutes, 3.2% 60 minutes or more (2000)

WHALAN (city). Covers a land area of 0.284 square miles and a water area of 0.020 square miles. Located at 43.73° N. Lat.; 91.92° W. Long. Elevation is 793 feet.
Population: 64 (2000); Race: 100.0% White, 0.0% Black, 0.0% Asian, 0.0% American Indian and Alaska Native, 0.0% Hispanic of any race, 0.0% two or more races (2000); Density: 225.4 persons per square mile (2000); Age: 13.8% under 18, 30.8% over 64 (2000); Marriage status: 22.8% never married, 49.1% now married, 10.5% widowed, 17.5% divorced (2000); Foreign born: 0.0% (2000); Ancestry (includes multiple ancestries): 75.4% Norwegian, 10.8% German, 7.7% Danish, 6.2% French (except Basque), 6.2% Irish (2000).
Economy: Agriculture includes corn, soybeans; livestock, poultry. Employment by occupation: 26.3% management, 13.2% professional, 5.3% services, 26.3% sales, 0.0% farming, 13.2% construction, 15.8% production (2000).
Income: Per capita income: $17,680 (2000); Median household income: $28,750 (2000); Poverty rate: 0.0% (2000).
Taxes: Total city taxes per capita: $118 (1997); City property taxes per capita: $118 (1997).
Education: High school graduation rate: 72.2% (2000); College graduation rate: 7.4% (2000).
Housing: Homeownership rate: 94.4% (2000); Median home value: $45,000 (2000); Median rent: $325 per month (2000); Median age of housing: 60+ years (2000).
Transportation: Commute to work: 89.2% car, 5.4% public transportation, 0.0% walk, 5.4% work from home (2000); Travel time to work: 17.1% less than 15 minutes, 54.3% 15 to 30 minutes, 0.0% 30 to 45 minutes, 17.1% 45 to 60 minutes, 11.4% 60 minutes or more (2000)

WYKOFF (city). Covers a land area of 0.950 square miles and a water area of 0 square miles. Located at 43.70° N. Lat.; 92.26° W. Long. Elevation is 1,322 feet.
Population: 460 (2000); Race: 98.9% White, 0.0% Black, 0.0% Asian, 1.1% American Indian and Alaska Native, 0.6% Hispanic of any race, 0.0% two or more races (2000); Density: 484.0 persons per square mile (2000); Age: 22.1% under 18, 24.5% over 64 (2000); Marriage status: 23.4% never married, 60.6% now married, 8.1% widowed, 7.9% divorced (2000); Foreign born: 0.4% (2000); Ancestry (includes multiple ancestries): 50.9% German, 13.9% Norwegian, 7.9% Dutch, 6.4% United States or American, 6.2% English (2000).
Economy: Agriculture: grain; livestock, poultry; dairying. Timber. Manufacturing: lumber. Employment by occupation: 10.8% management, 7.6% professional, 15.7% services, 25.7% sales, 4.4% farming, 7.6% construction, 28.1% production (2000).
Income: Per capita income: $17,956 (2000); Median household income: $30,625 (2000); Poverty rate: 6.4% (2000).
Taxes: Total city taxes per capita: $92 (1997); City property taxes per capita: $88 (1997).
Education: High school graduation rate: 74.2% (2000); College graduation rate: 4.3% (2000).

School District(s)

Kingsland (PK-12)
2000 Enrollment: 987 507-352-4341

Housing: Homeownership rate: 85.4% (2000); Median home value: $63,000 (2000); Median rent: $300 per month (2000); Median age of housing: 60+ years (2000).
Transportation: Commute to work: 84.6% car, 0.0% public transportation, 9.3% walk, 2.0% work from home (2000); Travel time to work: 38.0% less than 15 minutes, 23.6% 15 to 30 minutes, 20.2% 30 to 45 minutes, 12.8% 45 to 60 minutes, 5.4% 60 minutes or more (2000)

YORK (township). Covers a land area of 36.064 square miles and a water area of 0.054 square miles. Located at 43.54° N. Lat.; 92.27° W. Long.
Population: 409 (2000); Race: 99.5% White, 0.0% Black, 0.5% Asian, 0.0% American Indian and Alaska Native, 0.8% Hispanic of any race, 0.0% two or more races (2000); Density: 11.3 persons per square mile (2000); Age: 23.6% under 18, 18.0% over 64 (2000); Marriage status: 20.2% never married, 66.6% now married, 8.3% widowed, 5.0% divorced (2000); Foreign born: 1.1% (2000); Ancestry (includes multiple ancestries): 41.8% German, 23.1% Norwegian, 17.7% Dutch, 4.8% Irish, 4.3% United States or American (2000).
Economy: Employment by occupation: 20.1% management, 13.4% professional, 14.9% services, 16.0% sales, 5.2% farming, 12.4% construction, 18.0% production (2000).
Income: Per capita income: $21,055 (2000); Median household income: $37,250 (2000); Poverty rate: 9.4% (2000).
Taxes: Total city taxes per capita: $187 (1997); City property taxes per capita: $187 (1997).
Education: High school graduation rate: 78.3% (2000); College graduation rate: 14.5% (2000).
Housing: Homeownership rate: 91.8% (2000); Median home value: $50,900 (2000); Median rent: $225 per month (2000); Median age of housing: 60+ years (2000).
Transportation: Commute to work: 85.4% car, 1.0% public transportation, 3.1% walk, 9.4% work from home (2000); Travel time to work: 21.3% less than 15 minutes, 35.1% 15 to 30 minutes, 12.1% 30 to 45 minutes, 12.6% 45 to 60 minutes, 19.0% 60 minutes or more (2000)

Freeborn County

Located in southern Minnesota; bounded on the south by Iowa. Covers a land area of 707.60 square miles, a water area of 15.00 square miles, and is located in the Central Time Zone. The county government was organized in 1855. County seat is Albert Lea.

Weather Station: Albert Lea 3 SE — Elevation: 1,227 feet

	Jan	Feb	Mar	Apr	May	Jun	Jul	Aug	Sep	Oct	Nov	Dec
High	21	28	39	55	69	79	83	80	72	59	41	27
Low	3	9	22	35	47	57	61	59	49	37	23	10
Precip	0.8	0.6	2.0	3.4	4.1	4.7	4.2	4.4	3.2	2.7	1.9	1.0
Snow	10.6	6.0	6.9	3.4	tr	0.0	0.0	0.0	0.0	0.5	4.8	8.5

High and Low temperatures in degrees Fahrenheit; Precipitation and Snow in inches

Population: 32,584 (2000); Race: 95.4% White, 0.4% Black, 0.3% Asian, 0.1% American Indian and Alaska Native, 6.6% Hispanic of any race, 0.9% two or more races (2000); Density: 46.0 persons per square mile (2000); Age: 23.9% under 18, 18.9% over 64 (2000).
Religion: Five largest groups: 46.4% Evangelical Lutheran Church in America, 11.2% Catholic Church, 3.8% The United Methodist Church, 3.5% American Baptist Churches in the USA, 2.9% Lutheran Church—Missouri Synod (2000).
Economy: Unemployment rate: 4.1% (11/2002); Total civilian labor force: 15,817 (11/2002); Leading industries: 26.6% manufacturing; 16.8% retail trade; 16.3% health care and social assistance (2000); Companies that employ more than 1,000 persons: 0 (2000); Companies that employ more than 100 persons: 21 (2000); Farms: 1,151 totaling 379,580 acres (1997); Minority business ownership rate: 0.0% (1997); Women business ownership rate: 26.6% (1997); Retail sales per capita: $9,838 (1997). Single-family building permits issued: 44 (2001) / 64 (2000); Multi-family building permits issued: 0 (2001) / 42 (2000).
Income: Per capita income: $18,325 (2000); Median household income: $36,964 (2000); Poverty rate: 8.4% (2000); Bankruptcy rate: 2.83% (2001).
Taxes: Total county taxes per capita: $248 (2000); County property taxes per capita: $242 (2000).
Education: High school graduation rate: 81.2% (2000); College graduation rate: 12.8% (2000).
Housing: Homeownership rate: 78.7% (2000); Median home value: $71,400 (2000); Median rent: $300 per month (2000); Median age of housing: 46 years (2000).
Health: Birth rate: 102.5 per 10,000 population (1998); Age adjusted death rate: 84.0 per 10,000 population (1999); Age adjusted cancer mortality rate: 177.1 deaths per 100,000 population (1999). Number of physicians: 11.7 per 10,000 population (1999); Number of hospital beds: 39.6 per 10,000 population (1999).

Elections: 2000 Presidential election results: 52.8% Gore, 42.4% Bush, 3.4% Nader, 0.9% Buchanan
National and State Parks: Bear Lake State Wildlife Management Area; Carey State Wildlife Management Area; Halls Lake State Wildlife Area; Myre Big Island State Park
Additional Information Contacts
Freeborn County Government Offices 507-377-5299
Albert Lea Chamber of Commerce 507-373-3938

Freeborn County Communities

ALBERT LEA (city). Covers a land area of 10.782 square miles and a water area of 1.777 square miles. Located at 43.65° N. Lat.; 93.36° W. Long. Elevation is 1,225 feet.
History: Albert Lea was named for Colonel Albert Lea (1808-1891), who surveyed the area in 1835. The town developed at a railroad junction. It was a horse race that made Albert Lea the seat of Freeborn County. The main street of Albert Lea was part of a race course laid out by the villagers, who liked to bet on their favorite local horses. In 1859, when neighboring Itasca vied with Albert Lea for the courthouse, the challenge was given for a horse race. Sheriff Heath's Old Tom was pitted against Itasca's Itasca Fly. When Old Tom won handily, Itasca was convinced to support Albert Lea as the county seat.
Population: 18,356 (2000); Race: 93.0% White, 0.6% Black, 0.5% Asian, 0.2% American Indian and Alaska Native, 9.8% Hispanic of any race, 1.2% two or more races (2000); Density: 1,702.5 persons per square mile (2000); Age: 22.6% under 18, 21.5% over 64 (2000); Marriage status: 23.5% never married, 56.4% now married, 9.9% widowed, 10.2% divorced (2000); Foreign born: 4.6% (2000); Ancestry (includes multiple ancestries): 34.7% Norwegian, 30.6% German, 12.5% Other groups, 8.3% Danish, 8.3% Irish (2000).
Vital Statistics: Birth rate: 117.1 per 10,000 population (1998)
Economy: Single-family building permits issued: 0 (2001) / 15 (2000); Multi-family building permits issued: 0 (2001) / 36 (2000); Employment by occupation: 8.6% management, 15.2% professional, 17.5% services, 23.4% sales, 0.6% farming, 6.1% construction, 28.5% production (2000).
Income: Per capita income: $17,979 (2000); Median household income: $32,841 (2000); Poverty rate: 10.2% (2000).
Taxes: Total city taxes per capita: $202 (1997); City property taxes per capita: $115 (1997).
Education: High school graduation rate: 78.0% (2000); College graduation rate: 13.8% (2000).

School District(s)

Albert Lea (PK-12)
2000 Enrollment: 3,968 507-379-4800
Housing: Homeownership rate: 72.9% (2000); Median home value: $69,700 (2000); Median rent: $308 per month (2000); Median age of housing: 44 years (2000).
Hospitals: Naeve Hospital - Mayo Health System (115 beds)
Safety: Violent crime rate: 16.2 per 10,000 population; Property crime rate: 259.3 per 10,000 population (2001).
Newspapers: Albert Lea Tribune (6 x week)
Transportation: Commute to work: 92.8% car, 0.5% public transportation, 3.0% walk, 2.6% work from home (2000); Travel time to work: 68.3% less than 15 minutes, 16.7% 15 to 30 minutes, 9.1% 30 to 45 minutes, 2.3% 45 to 60 minutes, 3.5% 60 minutes or more (2000)
Additional Information Contacts
Albert Lea Chamber of Commerce 507-373-3938

ALBERT LEA (township). Covers a land area of 23.350 square miles and a water area of 2.849 square miles. Located at 43.62° N. Lat.; 93.35° W. Long. Elevation is 1,225 feet.
History: Incorporated 1878.
Population: 808 (2000); Race: 99.5% White, 0.0% Black, 0.0% Asian, 0.2% American Indian and Alaska Native, 7.8% Hispanic of any race, 0.0% two or more races (2000); Density: 34.6 persons per square mile (2000); Age: 27.6% under 18, 13.7% over 64 (2000); Marriage status: 21.5% never married, 65.8% now married, 7.0% widowed, 5.8% divorced (2000); Foreign born: 0.2% (2000); Ancestry (includes multiple ancestries): 45.1% Norwegian, 30.8% German, 12.6% Danish, 9.3% Other groups, 6.9% Irish (2000).
Economy: Railroad junction and manufacturing and marketing center in agricultural area includes poultry, cattle, sheep, hogs; dairying; corn, soybeans, potatoes. Manufacturing includes construction materials, printing and publishing, food products, machineryand consumer goods. Municipal airport to north. Albert Lea Vocational Technical School here. Employment by occupation: 12.6% management, 16.4% professional, 15.4% services, 22.8% sales, 0.5% farming, 15.7% construction, 16.6% production (2000).
Income: Per capita income: $18,628 (2000); Median household income: $42,500 (2000); Poverty rate: 10.1% (2000).
Taxes: Total city taxes per capita: $58 (1997); City property taxes per capita: $58 (1997).
Education: High school graduation rate: 89.5% (2000); College graduation rate: 15.4% (2000).
Housing: Homeownership rate: 87.7% (2000); Median home value: $102,400 (2000); Median rent: $356 per month (2000); Median age of housing: 45 years (2000).
Transportation: Commute to work: 90.6% car, 0.0% public transportation, 1.7% walk, 7.0% work from home (2000); Travel time to work: 57.8% less than 15 minutes, 31.1% 15 to 30 minutes, 3.4% 30 to 45 minutes, 4.9% 45 to 60 minutes, 2.8% 60 minutes or more (2000)

ALDEN (city). Covers a land area of 0.959 square miles and a water area of 0.026 square miles. Located at 43.67° N. Lat.; 93.57° W. Long. Elevation is 1,266 feet.
History: Alden was established in 1869. An early industry here was an alfalfa mill, one of the few in the country, which produced meal used as poultry feed.
Population: 652 (2000); Race: 97.6% White, 0.0% Black, 0.8% Asian, 0.0% American Indian and Alaska Native, 4.0% Hispanic of any race, 0.0% two or more races (2000); Density: 680.1 persons per square mile (2000); Age: 24.4% under 18, 20.9% over 64 (2000); Marriage status: 18.4% never married, 65.2% now married, 10.1% widowed, 6.3% divorced (2000); Foreign born: 0.9% (2000); Ancestry (includes multiple ancestries): 40.0% German, 34.7% Norwegian, 11.4% Danish, 7.5% Irish, 7.3% Swedish (2000).
Economy: Employment by occupation: 7.2% management, 17.2% professional, 13.1% services, 20.0% sales, 3.8% farming, 11.6% construction, 27.2% production (2000).
Income: Per capita income: $17,689 (2000); Median household income: $40,000 (2000); Poverty rate: 6.0% (2000).
Taxes: Total city taxes per capita: $172 (1997); City property taxes per capita: $170 (1997).
Education: High school graduation rate: 82.6% (2000); College graduation rate: 16.7% (2000).

School District(s)

Alden (PK-12)
2000 Enrollment: 429 507-874-3240
Housing: Homeownership rate: 85.5% (2000); Median home value: $65,400 (2000); Median rent: $271 per month (2000); Median age of housing: 46 years (2000).
Newspapers: Alden Advance (1 x week)
Transportation: Commute to work: 94.6% car, 0.0% public transportation, 2.6% walk, 2.6% work from home (2000); Travel time to work: 27.9% less than 15 minutes, 58.0% 15 to 30 minutes, 8.2% 30 to 45 minutes, 1.6% 45 to 60 minutes, 4.3% 60 minutes or more (2000)

ALDEN (township). Covers a land area of 35.355 square miles and a water area of 0 square miles. Located at 43.63° N. Lat.; 93.57° W. Long. Elevation is 1,266 feet.
Population: 338 (2000); Race: 100.0% White, 0.0% Black, 0.0% Asian, 0.0% American Indian and Alaska Native, 0.0% Hispanic of any race, 0.0% two or more races (2000); Density: 9.6 persons per square mile (2000); Age: 22.8% under 18, 12.7% over 64 (2000); Marriage status: 19.2% never married, 73.6% now married, 5.7% widowed, 1.5% divorced (2000); Foreign born: 0.0% (2000); Ancestry (includes multiple ancestries): 54.0% German, 27.8% Norwegian, 12.0% Danish, 8.0% Swedish, 4.9% Polish (2000).
Economy: Livestock; grain, soybeans, alfalfa; dairying; manufactures feeds, fertilizers. Employment by occupation: 14.1% management, 13.0% professional, 18.9% services, 24.9% sales, 1.1% farming, 7.0% construction, 21.1% production (2000).
Income: Per capita income: $17,800 (2000); Median household income: $45,417 (2000); Poverty rate: 1.6% (2000).
Taxes: Total city taxes per capita: $105 (1997); City property taxes per capita: $105 (1997).
Education: High school graduation rate: 87.2% (2000); College graduation rate: 8.7% (2000).
Housing: Homeownership rate: 89.3% (2000); Median home value: $87,100 (2000); Median rent: $288 per month (2000); Median age of housing: 60+ years (2000).
Transportation: Commute to work: 82.1% car, 0.0% public transportation, 4.9% walk, 13.0% work from home (2000); Travel time to work: 26.9% less

than 15 minutes, 59.4% 15 to 30 minutes, 5.6% 30 to 45 minutes, 4.4% 45 to 60 minutes, 3.8% 60 minutes or more (2000)

BANCROFT (township). Covers a land area of 33.670 square miles and a water area of 0.006 square miles. Located at 43.71° N. Lat.; 93.36° W. Long. Elevation is 1,236 feet.
Population: 1,065 (2000); Race: 99.5% White, 0.0% Black, 0.2% Asian, 0.0% American Indian and Alaska Native, 1.0% Hispanic of any race, 0.3% two or more races (2000); Density: 31.6 persons per square mile (2000); Age: 25.7% under 18, 14.5% over 64 (2000); Marriage status: 16.0% never married, 78.0% now married, 2.8% widowed, 3.2% divorced (2000); Foreign born: 0.6% (2000); Ancestry (includes multiple ancestries): 43.0% Norwegian, 37.9% German, 13.1% Danish, 8.1% Irish, 6.1% Swedish (2000).
Economy: Employment by occupation: 15.4% management, 18.4% professional, 13.4% services, 26.3% sales, 1.0% farming, 12.4% construction, 13.1% production (2000).
Income: Per capita income: $22,744 (2000); Median household income: $47,102 (2000); Poverty rate: 2.5% (2000).
Taxes: Total city taxes per capita: $63 (1997); City property taxes per capita: $63 (1997).
Education: High school graduation rate: 89.7% (2000); College graduation rate: 16.2% (2000).
Housing: Homeownership rate: 93.3% (2000); Median home value: $103,600 (2000); Median rent: $313 per month (2000); Median age of housing: 38 years (2000).
Transportation: Commute to work: 91.5% car, 0.9% public transportation, 1.0% walk, 6.1% work from home (2000); Travel time to work: 47.1% less than 15 minutes, 36.2% 15 to 30 minutes, 8.2% 30 to 45 minutes, 2.2% 45 to 60 minutes, 6.4% 60 minutes or more (2000)

BATH (township). Covers a land area of 35.710 square miles and a water area of 0.105 square miles. Located at 43.80° N. Lat.; 93.33° W. Long. Elevation is 1,262 feet.
Population: 479 (2000); Race: 98.3% White, 0.7% Black, 0.0% Asian, 0.0% American Indian and Alaska Native, 0.2% Hispanic of any race, 1.1% two or more races (2000); Density: 13.4 persons per square mile (2000); Age: 29.6% under 18, 13.0% over 64 (2000); Marriage status: 21.4% never married, 67.1% now married, 2.5% widowed, 8.9% divorced (2000); Foreign born: 0.4% (2000); Ancestry (includes multiple ancestries): 46.1% Norwegian, 36.1% German, 16.1% Danish, 11.1% Irish, 6.3% Dutch (2000).
Economy: Employment by occupation: 14.5% management, 15.7% professional, 12.1% services, 19.0% sales, 2.4% farming, 11.7% construction, 24.6% production (2000).
Income: Per capita income: $16,835 (2000); Median household income: $34,773 (2000); Poverty rate: 3.5% (2000).
Taxes: Total city taxes per capita: $85 (1997); City property taxes per capita: $85 (1997).
Education: High school graduation rate: 86.8% (2000); College graduation rate: 7.6% (2000).
Housing: Homeownership rate: 87.8% (2000); Median home value: $95,000 (2000); Median rent: $338 per month (2000); Median age of housing: 60+ years (2000).
Transportation: Commute to work: 87.1% car, 0.0% public transportation, 2.1% walk, 10.8% work from home (2000); Travel time to work: 24.8% less than 15 minutes, 47.2% 15 to 30 minutes, 15.4% 30 to 45 minutes, 1.9% 45 to 60 minutes, 10.7% 60 minutes or more (2000)

CARLSTON (township). Covers a land area of 33.093 square miles and a water area of 2.887 square miles. Located at 43.71° N. Lat.; 93.59° W. Long.
Population: 332 (2000); Race: 100.0% White, 0.0% Black, 0.0% Asian, 0.0% American Indian and Alaska Native, 0.6% Hispanic of any race, 0.0% two or more races (2000); Density: 10.0 persons per square mile (2000); Age: 25.0% under 18, 11.0% over 64 (2000); Marriage status: 19.5% never married, 70.3% now married, 7.5% widowed, 2.6% divorced (2000); Foreign born: 0.0% (2000); Ancestry (includes multiple ancestries): 36.0% German, 31.5% Norwegian, 13.4% Danish, 8.9% Polish, 5.1% Irish (2000).
Economy: Employment by occupation: 23.0% management, 15.7% professional, 12.6% services, 17.3% sales, 3.1% farming, 13.1% construction, 15.2% production (2000).
Income: Per capita income: $21,218 (2000); Median household income: $47,500 (2000); Poverty rate: 1.2% (2000).
Taxes: Total city taxes per capita: $65 (1997); City property taxes per capita: $65 (1997).
Education: High school graduation rate: 95.5% (2000); College graduation rate: 9.1% (2000).
Housing: Homeownership rate: 80.0% (2000); Median home value: $97,100 (2000); Median rent: $313 per month (2000); Median age of housing: 59 years (2000).
Transportation: Commute to work: 89.5% car, 0.0% public transportation, 1.6% walk, 8.9% work from home (2000); Travel time to work: 27.0% less than 15 minutes, 51.1% 15 to 30 minutes, 6.3% 30 to 45 minutes, 4.6% 45 to 60 minutes, 10.9% 60 minutes or more (2000)

CLARKS GROVE (city). Covers a land area of 0.427 square miles and a water area of 0 square miles. Located at 43.76° N. Lat.; 93.33° W. Long.
Population: 734 (2000); Race: 99.2% White, 0.3% Black, 0.0% Asian, 0.0% American Indian and Alaska Native, 7.8% Hispanic of any race, 0.6% two or more races (2000); Density: 1,717.4 persons per square mile (2000); Age: 29.7% under 18, 12.7% over 64 (2000); Marriage status: 27.5% never married, 57.2% now married, 5.5% widowed, 9.8% divorced (2000); Foreign born: 2.6% (2000); Ancestry (includes multiple ancestries): 33.1% Norwegian, 29.0% German, 11.3% Danish, 9.9% Irish, 7.9% English (2000).
Economy: Agricultural area: poultry, cattle, hogs, sheep; corn, oats, alfalfa, soybeans; dairying. Manufacturing: concrete. Single-family building permits issued: 2 (2001) / 0 (2000); Multi-family building permits issued: 0 (2001) / 0 (2000); Employment by occupation: 9.6% management, 9.3% professional, 19.8% services, 26.3% sales, 2.5% farming, 11.0% construction, 21.5% production (2000).
Income: Per capita income: $16,491 (2000); Median household income: $40,179 (2000); Poverty rate: 6.7% (2000).
Taxes: Total city taxes per capita: $57 (1997); City property taxes per capita: $56 (1997).
Education: High school graduation rate: 82.5% (2000); College graduation rate: 11.1% (2000).
Housing: Homeownership rate: 88.5% (2000); Median home value: $63,000 (2000); Median rent: $270 per month (2000); Median age of housing: 32 years (2000).
Transportation: Commute to work: 94.6% car, 0.0% public transportation, 2.3% walk, 3.1% work from home (2000); Travel time to work: 29.7% less than 15 minutes, 53.5% 15 to 30 minutes, 12.6% 30 to 45 minutes, 0.0% 45 to 60 minutes, 4.1% 60 minutes or more (2000)

CONGER (city). Covers a land area of 0.117 square miles and a water area of 0 square miles. Located at 43.61° N. Lat.; 93.53° W. Long. Elevation is 1,289 feet.
Population: 133 (2000); Race: 97.6% White, 0.0% Black, 0.0% Asian, 0.0% American Indian and Alaska Native, 2.4% Hispanic of any race, 0.0% two or more races (2000); Density: 1,133.0 persons per square mile (2000); Age: 20.1% under 18, 23.1% over 64 (2000); Marriage status: 15.4% never married, 65.7% now married, 9.8% widowed, 9.1% divorced (2000); Foreign born: 2.4% (2000); Ancestry (includes multiple ancestries): 61.5% German, 26.0% Norwegian, 10.7% Czech, 7.7% Danish, 4.1% European (2000).
Economy: Grain; poultry; dairying. Manufacturing. Employment by occupation: 3.6% management, 8.4% professional, 15.7% services, 16.9% sales, 0.0% farming, 20.5% construction, 34.9% production (2000).
Income: Per capita income: $17,944 (2000); Median household income: $32,500 (2000); Poverty rate: 4.1% (2000).
Taxes: Total city taxes per capita: $83 (1997); City property taxes per capita: $83 (1997).
Education: High school graduation rate: 74.8% (2000); College graduation rate: 0.0% (2000).
Housing: Homeownership rate: 97.1% (2000); Median home value: $43,900 (2000); Median age of housing: 50 years (2000).
Transportation: Commute to work: 100.0% car, 0.0% public transportation, 0.0% walk, 0.0% work from home (2000); Travel time to work: 19.3% less than 15 minutes, 62.7% 15 to 30 minutes, 14.5% 30 to 45 minutes, 3.6% 45 to 60 minutes, 0.0% 60 minutes or more (2000)

EMMONS (city). Covers a land area of 0.802 square miles and a water area of 0.003 square miles. Located at 43.50° N. Lat.; 93.48° W. Long. Elevation is 1,281 feet.
Population: 432 (2000); Race: 98.4% White, 0.0% Black, 0.0% Asian, 0.0% American Indian and Alaska Native, 6.2% Hispanic of any race, 1.6% two or more races (2000); Density: 538.6 persons per square mile (2000); Age: 27.5% under 18, 12.4% over 64 (2000); Marriage status: 22.5% never married, 60.4% now married, 8.1% widowed, 9.0% divorced (2000); Foreign born: 1.1% (2000); Ancestry (includes multiple ancestries): 60.1% Norwegian, 32.8% German, 8.0% Irish, 6.9% Other groups, 6.7% Danish (2000).
Economy: Agriculture: grain, soybeans, alfalfa; livestock, poultry; dairying. Manufacturing: agricultural equipment. Single-family building permits

issued: 0 (2001) / 2 (2000); Multi-family building permits issued: 0 (2001) / 0 (2000); Employment by occupation: 10.3% management, 15.4% professional, 12.8% services, 20.1% sales, 1.3% farming, 6.8% construction, 33.3% production (2000).
Income: Per capita income: $16,825 (2000); Median household income: $37,083 (2000); Poverty rate: 8.0% (2000).
Taxes: Total city taxes per capita: $34 (1997); City property taxes per capita: $31 (1997).
Education: High school graduation rate: 85.2% (2000); College graduation rate: 9.9% (2000).
Housing: Homeownership rate: 83.2% (2000); Median home value: $54,500 (2000); Median rent: $267 per month (2000); Median age of housing: 43 years (2000).
Transportation: Commute to work: 92.2% car, 0.0% public transportation, 4.3% walk, 3.5% work from home (2000); Travel time to work: 34.2% less than 15 minutes, 45.5% 15 to 30 minutes, 13.1% 30 to 45 minutes, 1.4% 45 to 60 minutes, 5.9% 60 minutes or more (2000)

FREEBORN (city). Covers a land area of 0.179 square miles and a water area of 0 square miles. Located at 43.76° N. Lat.; 93.56° W. Long.
Population: 305 (2000); Race: 97.6% White, 0.0% Black, 0.0% Asian, 0.7% American Indian and Alaska Native, 0.7% Hispanic of any race, 1.7% two or more races (2000); Density: 1,706.2 persons per square mile (2000); Age: 20.6% under 18, 21.7% over 64 (2000); Marriage status: 22.1% never married, 62.5% now married, 9.2% widowed, 6.3% divorced (2000); Foreign born: 0.0% (2000); Ancestry (includes multiple ancestries): 38.1% Norwegian, 36.4% German, 12.6% Danish, 8.4% Swedish, 4.2% English (2000).
Economy: Employment by occupation: 7.2% management, 18.7% professional, 11.5% services, 20.9% sales, 2.2% farming, 12.9% construction, 26.6% production (2000).
Income: Per capita income: $18,149 (2000); Median household income: $38,500 (2000); Poverty rate: 6.3% (2000).
Taxes: Total city taxes per capita: $127 (1997); City property taxes per capita: $120 (1997).
Education: High school graduation rate: 88.6% (2000); College graduation rate: 14.8% (2000).
Housing: Homeownership rate: 91.2% (2000); Median home value: $42,000 (2000); Median rent: $194 per month (2000); Median age of housing: 49 years (2000).
Transportation: Commute to work: 87.8% car, 0.0% public transportation, 10.1% walk, 2.2% work from home (2000); Travel time to work: 27.2% less than 15 minutes, 51.5% 15 to 30 minutes, 9.6% 30 to 45 minutes, 9.6% 45 to 60 minutes, 2.2% 60 minutes or more (2000)

FREEBORN (township). Covers a land area of 35.648 square miles and a water area of 0.459 square miles. Located at 43.80° N. Lat.; 93.58° W. Long.
Population: 327 (2000); Race: 100.0% White, 0.0% Black, 0.0% Asian, 0.0% American Indian and Alaska Native, 0.0% Hispanic of any race, 0.0% two or more races (2000); Density: 9.2 persons per square mile (2000); Age: 29.3% under 18, 15.4% over 64 (2000); Marriage status: 19.4% never married, 67.2% now married, 5.5% widowed, 7.9% divorced (2000); Foreign born: 0.0% (2000); Ancestry (includes multiple ancestries): 42.9% German, 23.1% Norwegian, 13.3% Polish, 11.2% Irish, 8.3% Danish (2000).
Economy: Manufacturing of feeds and fertilizers. Agriculture: dairying, poultry, livestock, grain, soybeans, alfalfa. Employment by occupation: 24.1% management, 11.8% professional, 12.9% services, 24.1% sales, 1.8% farming, 12.4% construction, 12.9% production (2000).
Income: Per capita income: $17,882 (2000); Median household income: $40,179 (2000); Poverty rate: 3.9% (2000).
Taxes: Total city taxes per capita: $110 (1997); City property taxes per capita: $110 (1997).
Education: High school graduation rate: 90.0% (2000); College graduation rate: 9.0% (2000).
Housing: Homeownership rate: 90.3% (2000); Median home value: $74,500 (2000); Median rent: $235 per month (2000); Median age of housing: 59 years (2000).
Transportation: Commute to work: 71.8% car, 0.0% public transportation, 0.0% walk, 28.2% work from home (2000); Travel time to work: 22.1% less than 15 minutes, 47.5% 15 to 30 minutes, 18.0% 30 to 45 minutes, 8.2% 45 to 60 minutes, 4.1% 60 minutes or more (2000)

FREEMAN (township). Covers a land area of 35.891 square miles and a water area of 0.029 square miles. Located at 43.54° N. Lat.; 93.34° W. Long.
Population: 528 (2000); Race: 100.0% White, 0.0% Black, 0.0% Asian, 0.0% American Indian and Alaska Native, 1.2% Hispanic of any race, 0.0% two or more races (2000); Density: 14.7 persons per square mile (2000); Age: 25.4% under 18, 21.2% over 64 (2000); Marriage status: 21.6% never married, 67.5% now married, 3.7% widowed, 7.2% divorced (2000); Foreign born: 0.0% (2000); Ancestry (includes multiple ancestries): 48.6% Norwegian, 34.3% German, 7.9% Danish, 5.2% United States or American, 5.0% Swedish (2000).
Economy: Employment by occupation: 10.5% management, 7.8% professional, 16.3% services, 24.8% sales, 3.1% farming, 12.2% construction, 25.2% production (2000).
Income: Per capita income: $16,813 (2000); Median household income: $42,292 (2000); Poverty rate: 8.9% (2000).
Taxes: Total city taxes per capita: $39 (1997); City property taxes per capita: $39 (1997).
Education: High school graduation rate: 82.2% (2000); College graduation rate: 6.6% (2000).
Housing: Homeownership rate: 98.5% (2000); Median home value: $85,500 (2000); Median age of housing: 49 years (2000).
Transportation: Commute to work: 91.3% car, 0.0% public transportation, 0.0% walk, 8.0% work from home (2000); Travel time to work: 32.1% less than 15 minutes, 50.9% 15 to 30 minutes, 6.8% 30 to 45 minutes, 2.3% 45 to 60 minutes, 7.9% 60 minutes or more (2000)

GENEVA (city). Covers a land area of 0.409 square miles and a water area of 0 square miles. Located at 43.82° N. Lat.; 93.26° W. Long.
Population: 449 (2000); Race: 100.0% White, 0.0% Black, 0.0% Asian, 0.0% American Indian and Alaska Native, 0.4% Hispanic of any race, 0.0% two or more races (2000); Density: 1,097.3 persons per square mile (2000); Age: 30.0% under 18, 12.4% over 64 (2000); Marriage status: 18.3% never married, 65.8% now married, 8.1% widowed, 7.8% divorced (2000); Foreign born: 0.0% (2000); Ancestry (includes multiple ancestries): 34.1% German, 23.8% Norwegian, 12.0% Danish, 9.3% Irish, 8.7% English (2000).
Economy: Single-family building permits issued: 4 (2001) / 3 (2000); Multi-family building permits issued: 0 (2001) / 0 (2000); Employment by occupation: 9.1% management, 13.7% professional, 12.9% services, 25.9% sales, 2.7% farming, 8.4% construction, 27.4% production (2000).
Income: Per capita income: $17,129 (2000); Median household income: $39,375 (2000); Poverty rate: 5.2% (2000).
Taxes: Total city taxes per capita: $99 (1997); City property taxes per capita: $88 (1997).
Education: High school graduation rate: 78.9% (2000); College graduation rate: 7.4% (2000).
Housing: Homeownership rate: 89.1% (2000); Median home value: $85,500 (2000); Median rent: $250 per month (2000); Median age of housing: 36 years (2000).
Transportation: Commute to work: 91.4% car, 0.8% public transportation, 3.9% walk, 3.5% work from home (2000); Travel time to work: 26.6% less than 15 minutes, 49.2% 15 to 30 minutes, 20.2% 30 to 45 minutes, 1.2% 45 to 60 minutes, 2.8% 60 minutes or more (2000)

GENEVA (township). Covers a land area of 33.053 square miles and a water area of 2.579 square miles. Located at 43.79° N. Lat.; 93.23° W. Long.
Population: 439 (2000); Race: 98.8% White, 0.0% Black, 0.0% Asian, 0.0% American Indian and Alaska Native, 1.2% Hispanic of any race, 0.5% two or more races (2000); Density: 13.3 persons per square mile (2000); Age: 27.5% under 18, 13.5% over 64 (2000); Marriage status: 23.1% never married, 66.9% now married, 4.7% widowed, 5.3% divorced (2000); Foreign born: 0.5% (2000); Ancestry (includes multiple ancestries): 33.3% German, 27.1% Norwegian, 14.0% Dutch, 11.8% Danish, 9.4% Irish (2000).
Economy: Dairying; poultry, cattle, hogs, sheep; corn, oats, soybeans. Manufacturing: crates. Employment by occupation: 19.7% management, 12.2% professional, 9.9% services, 19.2% sales, 3.8% farming, 11.3% construction, 23.9% production (2000).
Income: Per capita income: $16,674 (2000); Median household income: $46,563 (2000); Poverty rate: 5.3% (2000).
Taxes: Total city taxes per capita: $87 (1997); City property taxes per capita: $87 (1997).
Education: High school graduation rate: 82.5% (2000); College graduation rate: 10.2% (2000).
Housing: Homeownership rate: 88.4% (2000); Median home value: $81,100 (2000); Median rent: $325 per month (2000); Median age of housing: 58 years (2000).
Transportation: Commute to work: 88.5% car, 0.0% public transportation, 2.0% walk, 9.5% work from home (2000); Travel time to work: 32.0% less than 15 minutes, 45.3% 15 to 30 minutes, 16.0% 30 to 45 minutes, 1.7% 45 to 60 minutes, 5.0% 60 minutes or more (2000)

GLENVILLE (city). Covers a land area of 2.179 square miles and a water area of 0.020 square miles. Located at 43.57° N. Lat.; 93.27° W. Long. Elevation is 1,235 feet.
Population: 720 (2000); Race: 99.1% White, 0.4% Black, 0.0% Asian, 0.0% American Indian and Alaska Native, 0.4% Hispanic of any race, 0.5% two or more races (2000); Density: 330.4 persons per square mile (2000); Age: 24.8% under 18, 16.6% over 64 (2000); Marriage status: 20.1% never married, 62.5% now married, 7.9% widowed, 9.5% divorced (2000); Foreign born: 0.3% (2000); Ancestry (includes multiple ancestries): 49.4% Norwegian, 32.7% German, 9.9% Irish, 9.5% Czech, 5.7% Danish (2000).
Economy: Railroad junction. Livestock, poultry; grain, soybeans, alfalfa; dairying. Employment by occupation: 9.1% management, 7.6% professional, 19.9% services, 25.5% sales, 0.0% farming, 6.4% construction, 31.6% production (2000).
Income: Per capita income: $17,663 (2000); Median household income: $37,813 (2000); Poverty rate: 9.4% (2000).
Taxes: Total city taxes per capita: $87 (1997); City property taxes per capita: $79 (1997).
Education: High school graduation rate: 79.7% (2000); College graduation rate: 9.5% (2000).

School District(s)

Glenville-Emmons (PK-12)
2000 Enrollment: 532 507-448-3623

Housing: Homeownership rate: 81.1% (2000); Median home value: $62,900 (2000); Median rent: $251 per month (2000); Median age of housing: 42 years (2000).
Transportation: Commute to work: 90.6% car, 0.0% public transportation, 3.0% walk, 5.2% work from home (2000); Travel time to work: 40.5% less than 15 minutes, 45.2% 15 to 30 minutes, 7.0% 30 to 45 minutes, 2.3% 45 to 60 minutes, 5.0% 60 minutes or more (2000)

HARTLAND (city). Covers a land area of 0.274 square miles and a water area of 0 square miles. Located at 43.80° N. Lat.; 93.48° W. Long. Elevation is 1,252 feet.
Population: 288 (2000); Race: 100.0% White, 0.0% Black, 0.0% Asian, 0.0% American Indian and Alaska Native, 2.3% Hispanic of any race, 0.0% two or more races (2000); Density: 1,052.0 persons per square mile (2000); Age: 17.0% under 18, 20.8% over 64 (2000); Marriage status: 20.9% never married, 61.8% now married, 9.8% widowed, 7.6% divorced (2000); Foreign born: 0.8% (2000); Ancestry (includes multiple ancestries): 49.6% Norwegian, 43.2% German, 17.0% Irish, 6.8% Swedish, 5.3% French (except Basque) (2000).
Economy: Employment by occupation: 5.3% management, 16.6% professional, 10.6% services, 31.8% sales, 0.0% farming, 13.2% construction, 22.5% production (2000).
Income: Per capita income: $22,429 (2000); Median household income: $37,500 (2000); Poverty rate: 3.8% (2000).
Taxes: Total city taxes per capita: $36 (1997); City property taxes per capita: $28 (1997).
Education: High school graduation rate: 89.1% (2000); College graduation rate: 8.5% (2000).
Housing: Homeownership rate: 79.5% (2000); Median home value: $63,100 (2000); Median rent: $261 per month (2000); Median age of housing: 52 years (2000).
Transportation: Commute to work: 90.7% car, 0.0% public transportation, 6.0% walk, 2.0% work from home (2000); Travel time to work: 35.8% less than 15 minutes, 33.8% 15 to 30 minutes, 12.8% 30 to 45 minutes, 10.1% 45 to 60 minutes, 7.4% 60 minutes or more (2000)

HARTLAND (township). Covers a land area of 35.873 square miles and a water area of 0.030 square miles. Located at 43.78° N. Lat.; 93.47° W. Long. Elevation is 1,252 feet.
Population: 298 (2000); Race: 98.6% White, 0.0% Black, 0.0% Asian, 0.0% American Indian and Alaska Native, 0.7% Hispanic of any race, 1.4% two or more races (2000); Density: 8.3 persons per square mile (2000); Age: 24.6% under 18, 19.7% over 64 (2000); Marriage status: 22.6% never married, 66.5% now married, 5.9% widowed, 5.0% divorced (2000); Foreign born: 0.0% (2000); Ancestry (includes multiple ancestries): 47.5% Norwegian, 31.0% German, 9.2% Danish, 8.5% Irish, 7.4% Polish (2000).
Economy: Dairying; poultry; grain. Employment by occupation: 15.2% management, 12.9% professional, 14.4% services, 15.2% sales, 1.5% farming, 21.2% construction, 19.7% production (2000).
Income: Per capita income: $15,913 (2000); Median household income: $38,125 (2000); Poverty rate: 9.5% (2000).
Taxes: Total city taxes per capita: $101 (1997); City property taxes per capita: $101 (1997).
Education: High school graduation rate: 93.1% (2000); College graduation rate: 9.5% (2000).
Housing: Homeownership rate: 91.8% (2000); Median home value: $72,200 (2000); Median rent: $325 per month (2000); Median age of housing: 60+ years (2000).
Transportation: Commute to work: 84.6% car, 0.0% public transportation, 0.0% walk, 15.4% work from home (2000); Travel time to work: 25.5% less than 15 minutes, 46.4% 15 to 30 minutes, 14.5% 30 to 45 minutes, 8.2% 45 to 60 minutes, 5.5% 60 minutes or more (2000)

HAYWARD (city). Covers a land area of 0.622 square miles and a water area of 0 square miles. Located at 43.64° N. Lat.; 93.24° W. Long. Elevation is 1,254 feet.
Population: 249 (2000); Race: 96.2% White, 0.0% Black, 0.0% Asian, 0.0% American Indian and Alaska Native, 4.6% Hispanic of any race, 0.0% two or more races (2000); Density: 400.4 persons per square mile (2000); Age: 19.7% under 18, 19.3% over 64 (2000); Marriage status: 16.3% never married, 64.3% now married, 14.8% widowed, 4.6% divorced (2000); Foreign born: 2.1% (2000); Ancestry (includes multiple ancestries): 39.1% Norwegian, 38.7% German, 7.1% Danish, 6.3% Other groups, 5.5% Dutch (2000).
Economy: Employment by occupation: 2.9% management, 15.2% professional, 18.8% services, 23.9% sales, 0.0% farming, 3.6% construction, 35.5% production (2000).
Income: Per capita income: $19,750 (2000); Median household income: $33,750 (2000); Poverty rate: 5.0% (2000).
Taxes: Total city taxes per capita: $126 (1997); City property taxes per capita: $117 (1997).
Education: High school graduation rate: 75.6% (2000); College graduation rate: 8.0% (2000).
Housing: Homeownership rate: 77.4% (2000); Median home value: $54,300 (2000); Median rent: $319 per month (2000); Median age of housing: 49 years (2000).
Transportation: Commute to work: 90.6% car, 0.0% public transportation, 9.4% walk, 0.0% work from home (2000); Travel time to work: 38.4% less than 15 minutes, 50.0% 15 to 30 minutes, 8.7% 30 to 45 minutes, 0.0% 45 to 60 minutes, 2.9% 60 minutes or more (2000)

HAYWARD (township). Covers a land area of 34.600 square miles and a water area of 0.985 square miles. Located at 43.63° N. Lat.; 93.23° W. Long. Elevation is 1,254 feet.
Population: 438 (2000); Race: 98.1% White, 0.0% Black, 0.4% Asian, 0.0% American Indian and Alaska Native, 0.0% Hispanic of any race, 1.5% two or more races (2000); Density: 12.7 persons per square mile (2000); Age: 31.9% under 18, 13.5% over 64 (2000); Marriage status: 24.4% never married, 66.9% now married, 1.9% widowed, 6.8% divorced (2000); Foreign born: 1.9% (2000); Ancestry (includes multiple ancestries): 49.9% Norwegian, 30.2% German, 13.5% Danish, 11.6% Irish, 9.7% Czech (2000).
Economy: Dairying. Manufacturing: steel fabrication; machine tools. Dodge Center Airport to Southeast. Employment by occupation: 22.7% management, 11.2% professional, 15.9% services, 25.3% sales, 1.3% farming, 6.9% construction, 16.7% production (2000).
Income: Per capita income: $17,064 (2000); Median household income: $45,833 (2000); Poverty rate: 5.3% (2000).
Taxes: Total city taxes per capita: $111 (1997); City property taxes per capita: $111 (1997).
Education: High school graduation rate: 86.3% (2000); College graduation rate: 11.8% (2000).
Housing: Homeownership rate: 89.1% (2000); Median home value: $92,500 (2000); Median rent: $275 per month (2000); Median age of housing: 49 years (2000).
Transportation: Commute to work: 87.3% car, 0.0% public transportation, 4.8% walk, 7.9% work from home (2000); Travel time to work: 41.4% less than 15 minutes, 51.0% 15 to 30 minutes, 3.3% 30 to 45 minutes, 1.0% 45 to 60 minutes, 3.3% 60 minutes or more (2000)

HOLLANDALE (city). Covers a land area of 0.431 square miles and a water area of 0 square miles. Located at 43.76° N. Lat.; 93.20° W. Long.
Population: 292 (2000); Race: 97.0% White, 0.0% Black, 0.0% Asian, 0.0% American Indian and Alaska Native, 7.2% Hispanic of any race, 1.1% two or more races (2000); Density: 677.0 persons per square mile (2000); Age: 18.5% under 18, 32.1% over 64 (2000); Marriage status: 14.3% never married, 72.2% now married, 8.5% widowed, 4.9% divorced (2000); Foreign

born: 8.7% (2000); Ancestry (includes multiple ancestries): 38.1% Dutch, 17.4% German, 11.3% Other groups, 9.4% Norwegian, 9.4% Irish (2000).
Economy: Grain, soybeans; livestock, poultry; dairying; light manufacturing. Employment by occupation: 12.0% management, 16.0% professional, 15.2% services, 8.8% sales, 8.8% farming, 14.4% construction, 24.8% production (2000).
Income: Per capita income: $15,972 (2000); Median household income: $26,250 (2000); Poverty rate: 15.2% (2000).
Taxes: Total city taxes per capita: $125 (1997); City property taxes per capita: $117 (1997).
Education: High school graduation rate: 72.0% (2000); College graduation rate: 7.0% (2000).
Housing: Homeownership rate: 72.2% (2000); Median home value: $74,200 (2000); Median rent: $281 per month (2000); Median age of housing: 50 years (2000).
Transportation: Commute to work: 84.0% car, 0.0% public transportation, 11.2% walk, 4.8% work from home (2000); Travel time to work: 35.3% less than 15 minutes, 36.1% 15 to 30 minutes, 17.6% 30 to 45 minutes, 0.0% 45 to 60 minutes, 10.9% 60 minutes or more (2000)

LONDON (township). Covers a land area of 36.146 square miles and a water area of 0 square miles. Located at 43.54° N. Lat.; 93.10° W. Long. Elevation is 1,199 feet.
Population: 334 (2000); Race: 98.1% White, 0.0% Black, 1.9% Asian, 0.0% American Indian and Alaska Native, 0.0% Hispanic of any race, 0.0% two or more races (2000); Density: 9.2 persons per square mile (2000); Age: 24.3% under 18, 17.4% over 64 (2000); Marriage status: 18.0% never married, 69.8% now married, 7.8% widowed, 4.3% divorced (2000); Foreign born: 1.9% (2000); Ancestry (includes multiple ancestries): 41.7% Norwegian, 41.4% German, 10.9% Czech, 6.5% Irish, 6.2% Danish (2000).
Economy: Employment by occupation: 18.6% management, 11.4% professional, 15.6% services, 22.2% sales, 3.0% farming, 13.8% construction, 15.6% production (2000).
Income: Per capita income: $16,882 (2000); Median household income: $37,500 (2000); Poverty rate: 1.2% (2000).
Taxes: Total city taxes per capita: $111 (1997); City property taxes per capita: $111 (1997).
Education: High school graduation rate: 84.1% (2000); College graduation rate: 13.7% (2000).
Housing: Homeownership rate: 82.6% (2000); Median home value: $61,100 (2000); Median rent: $225 per month (2000); Median age of housing: 60+ years (2000).
Transportation: Commute to work: 81.8% car, 0.0% public transportation, 0.0% walk, 16.4% work from home (2000); Travel time to work: 16.7% less than 15 minutes, 51.4% 15 to 30 minutes, 28.3% 30 to 45 minutes, 2.2% 45 to 60 minutes, 1.4% 60 minutes or more (2000)

MANCHESTER (city). Covers a land area of 0.089 square miles and a water area of 0 square miles. Located at 43.72° N. Lat.; 93.45° W. Long. Elevation is 1,283 feet.
Population: 81 (2000); Race: 94.4% White, 0.0% Black, 0.0% Asian, 0.0% American Indian and Alaska Native, 0.0% Hispanic of any race, 5.6% two or more races (2000); Density: 910.2 persons per square mile (2000); Age: 28.9% under 18, 14.4% over 64 (2000); Marriage status: 36.4% never married, 37.9% now married, 10.6% widowed, 15.2% divorced (2000); Foreign born: 0.0% (2000); Ancestry (includes multiple ancestries): 37.8% Norwegian, 17.8% German, 2.2% English, 2.2% Other groups, 1.1% Scottish (2000).
Economy: Single-family building permits issued: 0 (2001) / 0 (2000); Multi-family building permits issued: 0 (2001) / 0 (2000); Employment by occupation: 14.0% management, 2.3% professional, 16.3% services, 9.3% sales, 4.7% farming, 2.3% construction, 51.2% production (2000).
Income: Per capita income: $15,392 (2000); Median household income: $26,786 (2000); Poverty rate: 15.6% (2000).
Taxes: Total city taxes per capita: $63 (1997); City property taxes per capita: $31 (1997).
Education: High school graduation rate: 79.2% (2000); College graduation rate: 0.0% (2000).
Housing: Homeownership rate: 63.2% (2000); Median home value: $27,500 (2000); Median rent: $307 per month (2000); Median age of housing: 60+ years (2000).
Transportation: Commute to work: 95.3% car, 0.0% public transportation, 4.7% walk, 0.0% work from home (2000); Travel time to work: 37.2% less than 15 minutes, 25.6% 15 to 30 minutes, 34.9% 30 to 45 minutes, 0.0% 45 to 60 minutes, 2.3% 60 minutes or more (2000)

MANCHESTER (township). Covers a land area of 35.659 square miles and a water area of 0.293 square miles. Located at 43.71° N. Lat.; 93.45° W. Long. Elevation is 1,283 feet.
Population: 469 (2000); Race: 99.6% White, 0.0% Black, 0.0% Asian, 0.0% American Indian and Alaska Native, 0.4% Hispanic of any race, 0.4% two or more races (2000); Density: 13.2 persons per square mile (2000); Age: 27.9% under 18, 12.2% over 64 (2000); Marriage status: 23.2% never married, 72.4% now married, 2.8% widowed, 1.5% divorced (2000); Foreign born: 0.0% (2000); Ancestry (includes multiple ancestries): 48.8% Norwegian, 31.3% German, 13.9% Danish, 6.0% Irish, 5.8% English (2000).
Economy: Dairying. Manufacturing: fabricated metal products. Employment by occupation: 17.5% management, 10.2% professional, 23.5% services, 19.6% sales, 3.9% farming, 9.8% construction, 15.4% production (2000).
Income: Per capita income: $18,910 (2000); Median household income: $48,281 (2000); Poverty rate: 4.0% (2000).
Taxes: Total city taxes per capita: $76 (1997); City property taxes per capita: $76 (1997).
Education: High school graduation rate: 93.3% (2000); College graduation rate: 17.9% (2000).
Housing: Homeownership rate: 89.7% (2000); Median home value: $88,900 (2000); Median rent: $238 per month (2000); Median age of housing: 52 years (2000).
Transportation: Commute to work: 87.0% car, 0.0% public transportation, 3.2% walk, 9.8% work from home (2000); Travel time to work: 30.7% less than 15 minutes, 52.9% 15 to 30 minutes, 7.4% 30 to 45 minutes, 5.8% 45 to 60 minutes, 3.1% 60 minutes or more (2000)

MANSFIELD (township). Covers a land area of 36.124 square miles and a water area of 0.019 square miles. Located at 43.54° N. Lat.; 93.58° W. Long. Elevation is 1,247 feet.
Population: 289 (2000); Race: 100.0% White, 0.0% Black, 0.0% Asian, 0.0% American Indian and Alaska Native, 0.0% Hispanic of any race, 0.0% two or more races (2000); Density: 8.0 persons per square mile (2000); Age: 19.4% under 18, 22.3% over 64 (2000); Marriage status: 12.8% never married, 73.1% now married, 9.7% widowed, 4.4% divorced (2000); Foreign born: 0.0% (2000); Ancestry (includes multiple ancestries): 48.0% Norwegian, 33.7% German, 6.6% Swedish, 5.5% Czech, 5.1% Danish (2000).
Economy: Employment by occupation: 20.7% management, 8.3% professional, 11.0% services, 18.6% sales, 7.6% farming, 13.1% construction, 20.7% production (2000).
Income: Per capita income: $16,960 (2000); Median household income: $40,714 (2000); Poverty rate: 7.0% (2000).
Taxes: Total city taxes per capita: $51 (1997); City property taxes per capita: $51 (1997).
Education: High school graduation rate: 86.5% (2000); College graduation rate: 5.5% (2000).
Housing: Homeownership rate: 83.9% (2000); Median home value: $67,500 (2000); Median rent: $225 per month (2000); Median age of housing: 60 years (2000).
Transportation: Commute to work: 75.2% car, 0.0% public transportation, 12.4% walk, 12.4% work from home (2000); Travel time to work: 29.1% less than 15 minutes, 51.2% 15 to 30 minutes, 12.6% 30 to 45 minutes, 3.9% 45 to 60 minutes, 3.1% 60 minutes or more (2000)

MOSCOW (township). Covers a land area of 36.113 square miles and a water area of 0.135 square miles. Located at 43.72° N. Lat.; 93.12° W. Long.
Population: 605 (2000); Race: 98.9% White, 0.0% Black, 0.0% Asian, 0.0% American Indian and Alaska Native, 3.4% Hispanic of any race, 0.0% two or more races (2000); Density: 16.8 persons per square mile (2000); Age: 26.7% under 18, 14.7% over 64 (2000); Marriage status: 21.8% never married, 63.7% now married, 6.1% widowed, 8.4% divorced (2000); Foreign born: 1.8% (2000); Ancestry (includes multiple ancestries): 41.1% Norwegian, 32.4% German, 8.4% Danish, 4.7% Czech, 4.4% Irish (2000).
Economy: Employment by occupation: 13.1% management, 13.4% professional, 17.6% services, 19.7% sales, 3.0% farming, 10.4% construction, 22.7% production (2000).
Income: Per capita income: $20,442 (2000); Median household income: $38,472 (2000); Poverty rate: 9.4% (2000).
Taxes: Total city taxes per capita: $88 (1997); City property taxes per capita: $88 (1997).
Education: High school graduation rate: 86.2% (2000); College graduation rate: 7.0% (2000).

Housing: Homeownership rate: 92.4% (2000); Median home value: $76,500 (2000); Median rent: $335 per month (2000); Median age of housing: 60+ years (2000).
Transportation: Commute to work: 93.3% car, 0.3% public transportation, 0.0% walk, 6.4% work from home (2000); Travel time to work: 19.2% less than 15 minutes, 62.9% 15 to 30 minutes, 7.2% 30 to 45 minutes, 3.3% 45 to 60 minutes, 7.5% 60 minutes or more (2000)

MYRTLE (city). Covers a land area of 0.104 square miles and a water area of 0 square miles. Located at 43.56° N. Lat.; 93.16° W. Long.
Population: 63 (2000); Race: 100.0% White, 0.0% Black, 0.0% Asian, 0.0% American Indian and Alaska Native, 0.0% Hispanic of any race, 0.0% two or more races (2000); Density: 606.2 persons per square mile (2000); Age: 15.9% under 18, 15.9% over 64 (2000); Marriage status: 33.3% never married, 35.9% now married, 17.9% widowed, 12.8% divorced (2000); Foreign born: 0.0% (2000); Ancestry (includes multiple ancestries): 29.5% Norwegian, 25.0% German, 20.5% English, 13.6% Swedish, 13.6% Czech (2000).
Economy: Dairying. Employment by occupation: 0.0% management, 12.0% professional, 32.0% services, 8.0% sales, 0.0% farming, 8.0% construction, 40.0% production (2000).
Income: Per capita income: $13,164 (2000); Median household income: $23,125 (2000); Poverty rate: 0.0% (2000).
Taxes: Total city taxes per capita: $87 (1997); City property taxes per capita: $72 (1997).
Education: High school graduation rate: 96.8% (2000); College graduation rate: 0.0% (2000).
Housing: Homeownership rate: 56.0% (2000); Median home value: $17,500 (2000); Median rent: $167 per month (2000); Median age of housing: 60+ years (2000).
Transportation: Commute to work: 100.0% car, 0.0% public transportation, 0.0% walk, 0.0% work from home (2000); Travel time to work: 13.0% less than 15 minutes, 43.5% 15 to 30 minutes, 30.4% 30 to 45 minutes, 0.0% 45 to 60 minutes, 13.0% 60 minutes or more (2000)

NEWRY (township). Covers a land area of 36.082 square miles and a water area of 0 square miles. Located at 43.79° N. Lat.; 93.11° W. Long.
Population: 500 (2000); Race: 93.9% White, 0.0% Black, 0.0% Asian, 0.0% American Indian and Alaska Native, 5.4% Hispanic of any race, 1.3% two or more races (2000); Density: 13.9 persons per square mile (2000); Age: 23.0% under 18, 15.8% over 64 (2000); Marriage status: 19.8% never married, 70.7% now married, 4.0% widowed, 5.5% divorced (2000); Foreign born: 1.7% (2000); Ancestry (includes multiple ancestries): 30.6% Norwegian, 30.6% German, 12.8% Dutch, 11.7% Irish, 7.2% English (2000).
Economy: Employment by occupation: 17.1% management, 12.0% professional, 16.7% services, 17.1% sales, 1.7% farming, 11.1% construction, 24.4% production (2000).
Income: Per capita income: $18,151 (2000); Median household income: $47,321 (2000); Poverty rate: 2.6% (2000).
Taxes: Total city taxes per capita: $82 (1997); City property taxes per capita: $82 (1997).
Education: High school graduation rate: 81.4% (2000); College graduation rate: 9.5% (2000).
Housing: Homeownership rate: 87.4% (2000); Median home value: $55,400 (2000); Median rent: $163 per month (2000); Median age of housing: 57 years (2000).
Transportation: Commute to work: 82.3% car, 0.0% public transportation, 4.7% walk, 12.9% work from home (2000); Travel time to work: 36.1% less than 15 minutes, 30.7% 15 to 30 minutes, 16.8% 30 to 45 minutes, 9.4% 45 to 60 minutes, 6.9% 60 minutes or more (2000)

NUNDA (township). Covers a land area of 32.914 square miles and a water area of 1.858 square miles. Located at 43.54° N. Lat.; 93.45° W. Long.
Population: 318 (2000); Race: 97.8% White, 0.6% Black, 0.0% Asian, 0.0% American Indian and Alaska Native, 0.0% Hispanic of any race, 1.6% two or more races (2000); Density: 9.7 persons per square mile (2000); Age: 19.4% under 18, 20.6% over 64 (2000); Marriage status: 18.6% never married, 69.0% now married, 7.3% widowed, 5.1% divorced (2000); Foreign born: 0.6% (2000); Ancestry (includes multiple ancestries): 54.4% Norwegian, 39.1% German, 4.7% English, 3.4% United States or American, 3.1% Other groups (2000).
Economy: Employment by occupation: 23.8% management, 18.8% professional, 9.4% services, 14.4% sales, 2.8% farming, 15.5% construction, 15.5% production (2000).
Income: Per capita income: $23,644 (2000); Median household income: $42,917 (2000); Poverty rate: 2.2% (2000).
Taxes: Total city taxes per capita: $99 (1997); City property taxes per capita: $99 (1997).
Education: High school graduation rate: 85.8% (2000); College graduation rate: 7.7% (2000).
Housing: Homeownership rate: 88.8% (2000); Median home value: $67,500 (2000); Median rent: $288 per month (2000); Median age of housing: 58 years (2000).
Transportation: Commute to work: 84.8% car, 0.0% public transportation, 2.2% walk, 12.9% work from home (2000); Travel time to work: 28.4% less than 15 minutes, 58.1% 15 to 30 minutes, 5.2% 30 to 45 minutes, 4.5% 45 to 60 minutes, 3.9% 60 minutes or more (2000)

OAKLAND (township). Covers a land area of 35.997 square miles and a water area of 0 square miles. Located at 43.64° N. Lat.; 93.12° W. Long. Elevation is 1,264 feet.
Population: 430 (2000); Race: 94.5% White, 0.0% Black, 0.0% Asian, 0.0% American Indian and Alaska Native, 5.9% Hispanic of any race, 0.6% two or more races (2000); Density: 11.9 persons per square mile (2000); Age: 27.6% under 18, 11.8% over 64 (2000); Marriage status: 18.6% never married, 75.0% now married, 1.9% widowed, 4.4% divorced (2000); Foreign born: 3.4% (2000); Ancestry (includes multiple ancestries): 34.7% Norwegian, 33.7% German, 10.7% Irish, 6.3% Other groups, 5.3% English (2000).
Economy: Employment by occupation: 19.9% management, 19.6% professional, 10.1% services, 16.3% sales, 2.9% farming, 4.3% construction, 26.8% production (2000).
Income: Per capita income: $17,611 (2000); Median household income: $49,063 (2000); Poverty rate: 7.8% (2000).
Taxes: Total city taxes per capita: $154 (1997); City property taxes per capita: $154 (1997).
Education: High school graduation rate: 85.7% (2000); College graduation rate: 12.3% (2000).
Housing: Homeownership rate: 82.4% (2000); Median home value: $96,100 (2000); Median rent: $321 per month (2000); Median age of housing: 49 years (2000).
Transportation: Commute to work: 81.0% car, 0.7% public transportation, 0.7% walk, 17.5% work from home (2000); Travel time to work: 23.9% less than 15 minutes, 54.0% 15 to 30 minutes, 15.0% 30 to 45 minutes, 2.2% 45 to 60 minutes, 4.9% 60 minutes or more (2000)

PICKEREL LAKE (township). Covers a land area of 34.756 square miles and a water area of 0.887 square miles. Located at 43.63° N. Lat.; 93.46° W. Long.
Population: 746 (2000); Race: 99.0% White, 0.0% Black, 0.0% Asian, 0.0% American Indian and Alaska Native, 0.7% Hispanic of any race, 0.3% two or more races (2000); Density: 21.5 persons per square mile (2000); Age: 24.5% under 18, 13.2% over 64 (2000); Marriage status: 20.7% never married, 71.6% now married, 4.2% widowed, 3.5% divorced (2000); Foreign born: 1.3% (2000); Ancestry (includes multiple ancestries): 43.3% German, 43.0% Norwegian, 14.8% Irish, 9.4% Danish, 5.1% English (2000).
Economy: Employment by occupation: 16.5% management, 20.9% professional, 9.4% services, 21.6% sales, 5.2% farming, 11.1% construction, 15.3% production (2000).
Income: Per capita income: $26,346 (2000); Median household income: $54,063 (2000); Poverty rate: 3.3% (2000).
Taxes: Total city taxes per capita: $52 (1997); City property taxes per capita: $52 (1997).
Education: High school graduation rate: 90.6% (2000); College graduation rate: 26.1% (2000).
Housing: Homeownership rate: 86.8% (2000); Median home value: $128,700 (2000); Median rent: $325 per month (2000); Median age of housing: 48 years (2000).
Transportation: Commute to work: 88.2% car, 0.5% public transportation, 2.6% walk, 8.7% work from home (2000); Travel time to work: 49.2% less than 15 minutes, 35.0% 15 to 30 minutes, 9.6% 30 to 45 minutes, 0.0% 45 to 60 minutes, 6.2% 60 minutes or more (2000)

RICELAND (township). Covers a land area of 36.052 square miles and a water area of 0 square miles. Located at 43.72° N. Lat.; 93.21° W. Long.
Population: 489 (2000); Race: 97.3% White, 0.0% Black, 0.0% Asian, 0.0% American Indian and Alaska Native, 2.7% Hispanic of any race, 0.0% two or more races (2000); Density: 13.6 persons per square mile (2000); Age: 27.9% under 18, 11.8% over 64 (2000); Marriage status: 21.0% never married, 68.2% now married, 4.8% widowed, 6.1% divorced (2000); Foreign born: 3.3% (2000); Ancestry (includes multiple ancestries): 39.5% Norwegian, 20.7% German, 14.7% Dutch, 13.2% Danish, 10.3% Irish (2000).

Economy: Employment by occupation: 16.4% management, 13.7% professional, 9.9% services, 25.2% sales, 2.7% farming, 13.7% construction, 18.3% production (2000).
Income: Per capita income: $17,884 (2000); Median household income: $44,063 (2000); Poverty rate: 8.3% (2000).
Taxes: Total city taxes per capita: $76 (1997); City property taxes per capita: $76 (1997).
Education: High school graduation rate: 84.6% (2000); College graduation rate: 11.1% (2000).
Housing: Homeownership rate: 88.5% (2000); Median home value: $73,300 (2000); Median rent: $344 per month (2000); Median age of housing: 60+ years (2000).
Transportation: Commute to work: 85.1% car, 0.0% public transportation, 0.0% walk, 14.1% work from home (2000); Travel time to work: 25.3% less than 15 minutes, 54.7% 15 to 30 minutes, 13.3% 30 to 45 minutes, 1.8% 45 to 60 minutes, 4.9% 60 minutes or more (2000)

SHELL ROCK (township). Covers a land area of 33.702 square miles and a water area of 0.008 square miles. Located at 43.55° N. Lat.; 93.24° W. Long.
Population: 430 (2000); Race: 98.6% White, 0.0% Black, 0.2% Asian, 0.0% American Indian and Alaska Native, 1.7% Hispanic of any race, 0.0% two or more races (2000); Density: 12.8 persons per square mile (2000); Age: 21.1% under 18, 14.9% over 64 (2000); Marriage status: 20.9% never married, 60.2% now married, 10.4% widowed, 8.5% divorced (2000); Foreign born: 1.9% (2000); Ancestry (includes multiple ancestries): 49.3% Norwegian, 43.4% German, 5.9% Irish, 5.7% Czech, 4.0% Danish (2000).
Economy: Employment by occupation: 16.8% management, 8.6% professional, 15.2% services, 29.5% sales, 0.0% farming, 4.9% construction, 25.0% production (2000).
Income: Per capita income: $18,867 (2000); Median household income: $39,219 (2000); Poverty rate: 5.5% (2000).
Taxes: Total city taxes per capita: $66 (1997); City property taxes per capita: $66 (1997).
Education: High school graduation rate: 83.7% (2000); College graduation rate: 7.7% (2000).
Housing: Homeownership rate: 81.5% (2000); Median home value: $56,400 (2000); Median rent: $267 per month (2000); Median age of housing: 60+ years (2000).
Transportation: Commute to work: 85.5% car, 0.0% public transportation, 4.5% walk, 9.1% work from home (2000); Travel time to work: 25.9% less than 15 minutes, 60.5% 15 to 30 minutes, 10.5% 30 to 45 minutes, 1.8% 45 to 60 minutes, 1.4% 60 minutes or more (2000)

TWIN LAKES (city). Covers a land area of 0.479 square miles and a water area of 0.035 square miles. Located at 43.56° N. Lat.; 93.42° W. Long. Elevation is 1,256 feet.
Population: 168 (2000); Race: 95.4% White, 0.0% Black, 0.0% Asian, 0.0% American Indian and Alaska Native, 4.6% Hispanic of any race, 2.6% two or more races (2000); Density: 350.4 persons per square mile (2000); Age: 22.2% under 18, 13.7% over 64 (2000); Marriage status: 24.6% never married, 54.1% now married, 13.1% widowed, 8.2% divorced (2000); Foreign born: 0.0% (2000); Ancestry (includes multiple ancestries): 39.2% German, 28.8% Norwegian, 9.2% Danish, 7.8% Other groups, 7.2% Italian (2000).
Economy: Employment by occupation: 6.8% management, 6.8% professional, 11.4% services, 15.9% sales, 0.0% farming, 18.2% construction, 40.9% production (2000).
Income: Per capita income: $16,258 (2000); Median household income: $31,250 (2000); Poverty rate: 15.2% (2000).
Taxes: Total city taxes per capita: $80 (1997); City property taxes per capita: $73 (1997).
Education: High school graduation rate: 73.5% (2000); College graduation rate: 10.8% (2000).
Housing: Homeownership rate: 83.8% (2000); Median home value: $32,500 (2000); Median rent: $206 per month (2000); Median age of housing: 38 years (2000).
Transportation: Commute to work: 97.7% car, 0.0% public transportation, 2.3% walk, 0.0% work from home (2000); Travel time to work: 33.3% less than 15 minutes, 52.9% 15 to 30 minutes, 0.0% 30 to 45 minutes, 9.2% 45 to 60 minutes, 4.6% 60 minutes or more (2000)

Goodhue County

Located in southeastern Minnesota; bounded on the northeast by the Mississippi River and the Wisconsin border; drained by the Cannon River. Covers a land area of 758.30 square miles, a water area of 22.20 square miles, and is located in the Central Time Zone. The county government was organized in 1853. County seat is Red Wing.

Weather Station: Zumbrota Elevation: 984 feet

	Jan	Feb	Mar	Apr	May	Jun	Jul	Aug	Sep	Oct	Nov	Dec
High	23	29	42	58	71	80	84	81	73	61	42	28
Low	3	8	21	34	45	55	59	57	48	37	24	10
Precip	1.0	0.7	2.0	3.3	4.0	4.3	4.4	4.2	3.5	2.7	2.2	1.0
Snow	10.7	6.7	7.8	3.0	0.0	0.0	0.0	0.0	0.0	0.5	5.9	8.4

High and Low temperatures in degrees Fahrenheit; Precipitation and Snow in inches

Population: 44,127 (2000); Race: 96.5% White, 0.6% Black, 0.4% Asian, 1.4% American Indian and Alaska Native, 1.0% Hispanic of any race, 0.7% two or more races (2000); Density: 58.2 persons per square mile (2000); Age: 26.4% under 18, 15.0% over 64 (2000).
Religion: Five largest groups: 39.1% Evangelical Lutheran Church in America, 19.8% Catholic Church, 7.7% Wisconsin Evangelical Lutheran Synod, 3.1% The United Methodist Church, 2.2% Lutheran Church—Missouri Synod (2000).
Economy: Unemployment rate: 3.7% (11/2002); Total civilian labor force: 24,234 (11/2002); Leading industries: 25.3% manufacturing; 14.8% health care and social assistance; 12.8% retail trade (2000); Companies that employ more than 1,000 persons: 2 (2000); Companies that employ more than 100 persons: 34 (2000); Farms: 1,489 totaling 384,565 acres (1997); Minority business ownership rate: 0.0% (1997); Women business ownership rate: 27.3% (1997); Retail sales per capita: $7,888 (1997). Single-family building permits issued: 308 (2001) / 238 (2000); Multi-family building permits issued: 26 (2001) / 69 (2000).
Income: Per capita income: $21,934 (2000); Median household income: $46,972 (2000); Poverty rate: 5.7% (2000); Bankruptcy rate: 3.29% (2001).
Taxes: Total county taxes per capita: $349 (2000); County property taxes per capita: $345 (2000).
Education: High school graduation rate: 86.7% (2000); College graduation rate: 19.1% (2000).
Housing: Homeownership rate: 78.9% (2000); Median home value: $116,000 (2000); Median rent: $414 per month (2000); Median age of housing: 35 years (2000).
Health: Birth rate: 112.2 per 10,000 population (1998); Age adjusted death rate: 83.6 per 10,000 population (1999); Age adjusted cancer mortality rate: 177.3 deaths per 100,000 population (1999). Number of physicians: 17.7 per 10,000 population (1999); Number of hospital beds: 40.3 per 10,000 population (1999).
Elections: 2000 Presidential election results: 44.8% Gore, 48.8% Bush, 4.9% Nader, 1.1% Buchanan
National and State Parks: Frontenac State Park; Richard J Dorer Memorial Hardwood State Forest
Additional Information Contacts
Goodhue County Government Offices.......................651-385-3000
Cannon Falls Chamber of Commerce 507-263-2289
Red Wing Chamber of Commerce...........................651-388-4719

Goodhue County Communities

BELLE CREEK (township). Covers a land area of 35.626 square miles and a water area of 0 square miles. Located at 44.42° N. Lat.; 92.74° W. Long.
Population: 437 (2000); Race: 97.6% White, 0.0% Black, 0.0% Asian, 0.4% American Indian and Alaska Native, 0.0% Hispanic of any race, 2.0% two or more races (2000); Density: 12.3 persons per square mile (2000); Age: 32.7% under 18, 12.4% over 64 (2000); Marriage status: 16.2% never married, 74.1% now married, 5.9% widowed, 3.7% divorced (2000); Foreign born: 1.8% (2000); Ancestry (includes multiple ancestries): 44.6% German, 22.1% Norwegian, 16.3% Irish, 14.8% Swedish, 4.2% English (2000).
Economy: Employment by occupation: 23.3% management, 9.8% professional, 13.9% services, 17.1% sales, 4.5% farming, 17.1% construction, 14.3% production (2000).
Income: Per capita income: $20,226 (2000); Median household income: $52,188 (2000); Poverty rate: 7.6% (2000).
Taxes: Total city taxes per capita: $102 (1997); City property taxes per capita: $102 (1997).

Education: High school graduation rate: 92.1% (2000); College graduation rate: 16.6% (2000).
Housing: Homeownership rate: 85.0% (2000); Median home value: $115,600 (2000); Median rent: $421 per month (2000); Median age of housing: 60+ years (2000).
Transportation: Commute to work: 81.9% car, 0.0% public transportation, 3.3% walk, 14.0% work from home (2000); Travel time to work: 18.7% less than 15 minutes, 38.3% 15 to 30 minutes, 23.4% 30 to 45 minutes, 15.8% 45 to 60 minutes, 3.8% 60 minutes or more (2000)

BELLECHESTER (city). Covers a land area of 0.316 square miles and a water area of 0 square miles. Located at 44.37° N. Lat.; 92.51° W. Long. Elevation is 1,116 feet.
Population: 172 (2000); Race: 96.5% White, 0.0% Black, 0.0% Asian, 3.5% American Indian and Alaska Native, 0.0% Hispanic of any race, 0.0% two or more races (2000); Density: 543.6 persons per square mile (2000); Age: 21.4% under 18, 20.2% over 64 (2000); Marriage status: 21.8% never married, 55.6% now married, 14.1% widowed, 8.5% divorced (2000); Foreign born: 0.0% (2000); Ancestry (includes multiple ancestries): 45.7% German, 16.2% Irish, 12.1% Norwegian, 8.1% United States or American, 6.9% Other groups (2000).
Economy: Single-family building permits issued: 2 (2001) / 1 (2000); Multi-family building permits issued: 0 (2001) / 0 (2000); Employment by occupation: 7.7% management, 14.3% professional, 24.2% services, 14.3% sales, 4.4% farming, 9.9% construction, 25.3% production (2000).
Income: Per capita income: $19,927 (2000); Median household income: $33,333 (2000); Poverty rate: 5.2% (2000).
Taxes: Total city taxes per capita: $65 (1997); City property taxes per capita: $52 (1997).
Education: High school graduation rate: 81.4% (2000); College graduation rate: 6.2% (2000).
Housing: Homeownership rate: 90.6% (2000); Median home value: $66,500 (2000); Median rent: $317 per month (2000); Median age of housing: 51 years (2000).
Transportation: Commute to work: 90.7% car, 0.0% public transportation, 4.7% walk, 4.7% work from home (2000); Travel time to work: 17.1% less than 15 minutes, 36.6% 15 to 30 minutes, 31.7% 30 to 45 minutes, 11.0% 45 to 60 minutes, 3.7% 60 minutes or more (2000)

BELVIDERE (township). Covers a land area of 35.605 square miles and a water area of 0 square miles. Located at 44.42° N. Lat.; 92.49° W. Long.
Population: 458 (2000); Race: 100.0% White, 0.0% Black, 0.0% Asian, 0.0% American Indian and Alaska Native, 0.0% Hispanic of any race, 0.0% two or more races (2000); Density: 12.9 persons per square mile (2000); Age: 33.8% under 18, 9.6% over 64 (2000); Marriage status: 25.3% never married, 67.0% now married, 3.4% widowed, 4.3% divorced (2000); Foreign born: 0.0% (2000); Ancestry (includes multiple ancestries): 72.1% German, 20.0% Norwegian, 11.8% Irish, 7.5% Swedish, 4.4% English (2000).
Economy: Employment by occupation: 25.5% management, 9.5% professional, 11.3% services, 19.0% sales, 11.3% farming, 7.4% construction, 16.0% production (2000).
Income: Per capita income: $18,317 (2000); Median household income: $50,972 (2000); Poverty rate: 11.0% (2000).
Taxes: Total city taxes per capita: $109 (2000); City property taxes per capita: $109 (2000).
Education: High school graduation rate: 90.4% (2000); College graduation rate: 17.5% (2000).
Housing: Homeownership rate: 80.0% (2000); Median home value: $90,000 (2000); Median rent: $313 per month (2000); Median age of housing: 52 years (2000).
Transportation: Commute to work: 74.2% car, 0.0% public transportation, 4.9% walk, 20.0% work from home (2000); Travel time to work: 28.9% less than 15 minutes, 41.1% 15 to 30 minutes, 22.8% 30 to 45 minutes, 2.2% 45 to 60 minutes, 5.0% 60 minutes or more (2000)

CANNON FALLS (city). Covers a land area of 4.010 square miles and a water area of 0.064 square miles. Located at 44.51° N. Lat.; 92.90° W. Long. Elevation is 838 feet.
History: Cannon Falls was named for the falls on the Cannon River, though the original name of the river, given by the early French explorers, was Canot, meaning "canoe." English traders misunderstood and marked it the Cannon River on their maps.
Population: 3,795 (2000); Race: 96.5% White, 0.8% Black, 0.7% Asian, 1.0% American Indian and Alaska Native, 1.1% Hispanic of any race, 1.0% two or more races (2000); Density: 946.4 persons per square mile (2000); Age: 25.5% under 18, 17.4% over 64 (2000); Marriage status: 25.4% never married, 57.2% now married, 8.4% widowed, 9.0% divorced (2000); Foreign born: 1.2% (2000); Ancestry (includes multiple ancestries): 40.7% German, 27.2% Norwegian, 17.9% Swedish, 9.4% Irish, 7.8% English (2000).
Economy: Single-family building permits issued: 8 (2001) / 6 (2000); Multi-family building permits issued: 0 (2001) / 3 (2000); Employment by occupation: 8.8% management, 16.4% professional, 12.7% services, 27.5% sales, 1.3% farming, 10.3% construction, 23.1% production (2000).
Income: Per capita income: $20,820 (2000); Median household income: $40,721 (2000); Poverty rate: 5.6% (2000).
Taxes: Total city taxes per capita: $386 (1997); City property taxes per capita: $379 (1997).
Education: High school graduation rate: 84.2% (2000); College graduation rate: 14.3% (2000).

School District(s)

Cannon Falls (PK-12)
2000 Enrollment: 1,519 507-263-3562
Goodhue County Ed. Dist. (PK-11)
2000 Enrollment: 18 507-263-5570

Housing: Homeownership rate: 74.0% (2000); Median home value: $124,400 (2000); Median rent: $395 per month (2000); Median age of housing: 29 years (2000).
Hospitals: Community Hospital (21 beds)
Safety: Violent crime rate: 18.2 per 10,000 population; Property crime rate: 552.7 per 10,000 population (2001).
Newspapers: The Cannon Falls Beacon (1 x week); Cannon Falls Shopper (1 x week)
Transportation: Commute to work: 95.5% car, 0.0% public transportation, 2.5% walk, 1.9% work from home (2000); Travel time to work: 49.5% less than 15 minutes, 20.0% 15 to 30 minutes, 18.7% 30 to 45 minutes, 9.6% 45 to 60 minutes, 2.4% 60 minutes or more (2000)
Additional Information Contacts
Cannon Falls Chamber of Commerce 507-263-2289

CANNON FALLS (township). Covers a land area of 33.903 square miles and a water area of 0 square miles. Located at 44.49° N. Lat.; 92.87° W. Long. Elevation is 838 feet.
Population: 1,236 (2000); Race: 99.4% White, 0.0% Black, 0.0% Asian, 0.2% American Indian and Alaska Native, 0.9% Hispanic of any race, 0.5% two or more races (2000); Density: 36.5 persons per square mile (2000); Age: 29.8% under 18, 8.6% over 64 (2000); Marriage status: 24.2% never married, 69.3% now married, 1.8% widowed, 4.6% divorced (2000); Foreign born: 1.3% (2000); Ancestry (includes multiple ancestries): 41.7% German, 24.8% Norwegian, 16.3% Swedish, 14.4% Irish, 7.5% English (2000).
Economy: Farm trading point: grain, soybeans; livestock, poultry; dairying. Manufacturing: construction materials, machinery, apparel, printing and publishing. Hydroelectric plant. Employment by occupation: 11.8% management, 17.8% professional, 10.3% services, 23.8% sales, 1.6% farming, 13.3% construction, 21.4% production (2000).
Income: Per capita income: $29,568 (2000); Median household income: $66,250 (2000); Poverty rate: 1.5% (2000).
Taxes: Total city taxes per capita: $73 (1997); City property taxes per capita: $72 (1997).
Education: High school graduation rate: 92.7% (2000); College graduation rate: 21.6% (2000).
Housing: Homeownership rate: 92.8% (2000); Median home value: $173,800 (2000); Median rent: $725 per month (2000); Median age of housing: 27 years (2000).
Transportation: Commute to work: 91.7% car, 0.0% public transportation, 1.7% walk, 6.4% work from home (2000); Travel time to work: 38.1% less than 15 minutes, 15.7% 15 to 30 minutes, 16.8% 30 to 45 minutes, 21.3% 45 to 60 minutes, 8.1% 60 minutes or more (2000)

CHERRY GROVE (township). Covers a land area of 38.273 square miles and a water area of 0 square miles. Located at 44.23° N. Lat.; 92.85° W. Long.
Population: 430 (2000); Race: 100.0% White, 0.0% Black, 0.0% Asian, 0.0% American Indian and Alaska Native, 0.5% Hispanic of any race, 0.0% two or more races (2000); Density: 11.2 persons per square mile (2000); Age: 27.3% under 18, 16.0% over 64 (2000); Marriage status: 23.5% never married, 68.0% now married, 2.9% widowed, 5.6% divorced (2000); Foreign born: 0.0% (2000); Ancestry (includes multiple ancestries): 42.1% German, 32.5% Norwegian, 12.5% Irish, 9.2% English, 7.1% Swedish (2000).
Economy: Employment by occupation: 24.7% management, 12.6% professional, 9.2% services, 18.4% sales, 4.6% farming, 12.1% construction, 18.4% production (2000).

Income: Per capita income: $20,093 (2000); Median household income: $52,898 (2000); Poverty rate: 3.8% (2000).
Taxes: Total city taxes per capita: $193 (2000); City property taxes per capita: $191 (2000).
Education: High school graduation rate: 87.9% (2000); College graduation rate: 15.3% (2000).
Housing: Homeownership rate: 94.0% (2000); Median home value: $117,700 (2000); Median rent: $625 per month (2000); Median age of housing: 60+ years (2000).
Transportation: Commute to work: 81.0% car, 0.0% public transportation, 1.3% walk, 17.7% work from home (2000); Travel time to work: 33.3% less than 15 minutes, 20.0% 15 to 30 minutes, 28.2% 30 to 45 minutes, 10.3% 45 to 60 minutes, 8.2% 60 minutes or more (2000)

DENNISON (city). Covers a land area of 1.269 square miles and a water area of 0 square miles. Located at 44.40° N. Lat.; 93.03° W. Long. Elevation is 969 feet.
Population: 168 (2000); Race: 100.0% White, 0.0% Black, 0.0% Asian, 0.0% American Indian and Alaska Native, 0.0% Hispanic of any race, 0.0% two or more races (2000); Density: 132.3 persons per square mile (2000); Age: 25.0% under 18, 7.7% over 64 (2000); Marriage status: 34.6% never married, 52.8% now married, 1.6% widowed, 11.0% divorced (2000); Foreign born: 0.0% (2000); Ancestry (includes multiple ancestries): 47.4% German, 46.2% Norwegian, 8.3% Irish, 7.7% United States or American, 6.4% Polish (2000).
Economy: Employment by occupation: 9.5% management, 11.4% professional, 14.3% services, 26.7% sales, 0.0% farming, 10.5% construction, 27.6% production (2000).
Income: Per capita income: $19,038 (2000); Median household income: $51,667 (2000); Poverty rate: 1.3% (2000).
Taxes: Total city taxes per capita: $164 (1997); City property taxes per capita: $129 (1997).
Education: High school graduation rate: 87.8% (2000); College graduation rate: 11.2% (2000).
Housing: Homeownership rate: 86.0% (2000); Median home value: $105,600 (2000); Median rent: $475 per month (2000); Median age of housing: 60+ years (2000).
Transportation: Commute to work: 99.0% car, 0.0% public transportation, 0.0% walk, 1.0% work from home (2000); Travel time to work: 19.6% less than 15 minutes, 51.0% 15 to 30 minutes, 15.7% 30 to 45 minutes, 13.7% 45 to 60 minutes, 0.0% 60 minutes or more (2000)

FEATHERSTONE (township). Covers a land area of 35.888 square miles and a water area of 0 square miles. Located at 44.48° N. Lat.; 92.60° W. Long.
Population: 785 (2000); Race: 99.5% White, 0.0% Black, 0.3% Asian, 0.0% American Indian and Alaska Native, 0.0% Hispanic of any race, 0.3% two or more races (2000); Density: 21.9 persons per square mile (2000); Age: 25.1% under 18, 12.6% over 64 (2000); Marriage status: 23.0% never married, 69.8% now married, 2.9% widowed, 4.3% divorced (2000); Foreign born: 0.3% (2000); Ancestry (includes multiple ancestries): 55.5% German, 20.8% Norwegian, 16.6% Irish, 15.6% Swedish, 5.6% English (2000).
Economy: Employment by occupation: 18.6% management, 21.5% professional, 16.8% services, 16.8% sales, 2.2% farming, 7.5% construction, 16.6% production (2000).
Income: Per capita income: $24,489 (2000); Median household income: $56,136 (2000); Poverty rate: 1.8% (2000).
Taxes: Total city taxes per capita: $71 (1997); City property taxes per capita: $71 (1997).
Education: High school graduation rate: 88.6% (2000); College graduation rate: 24.1% (2000).
Housing: Homeownership rate: 91.4% (2000); Median home value: $141,200 (2000); Median rent: $425 per month (2000); Median age of housing: 33 years (2000).
Transportation: Commute to work: 87.3% car, 0.0% public transportation, 1.3% walk, 10.5% work from home (2000); Travel time to work: 42.8% less than 15 minutes, 40.3% 15 to 30 minutes, 5.7% 30 to 45 minutes, 5.2% 45 to 60 minutes, 6.0% 60 minutes or more (2000)

FLORENCE (township). Covers a land area of 34.926 square miles and a water area of 5.629 square miles. Located at 44.51° N. Lat.; 92.35° W. Long.
Population: 1,450 (2000); Race: 98.5% White, 0.6% Black, 0.1% Asian, 0.3% American Indian and Alaska Native, 0.1% Hispanic of any race, 0.4% two or more races (2000); Density: 41.5 persons per square mile (2000); Age: 22.0% under 18, 20.0% over 64 (2000); Marriage status: 17.4% never married, 70.5% now married, 5.0% widowed, 7.1% divorced (2000); Foreign born: 0.8% (2000); Ancestry (includes multiple ancestries): 49.1% German, 15.0% Norwegian, 8.7% Swedish, 8.0% Irish, 7.5% English (2000).
Economy: Employment by occupation: 9.3% management, 17.8% professional, 13.7% services, 21.9% sales, 0.6% farming, 12.8% construction, 24.0% production (2000).
Income: Per capita income: $24,276 (2000); Median household income: $53,971 (2000); Poverty rate: 4.4% (2000).
Taxes: Total city taxes per capita: $116 (1997); City property taxes per capita: $115 (1997).
Education: High school graduation rate: 82.0% (2000); College graduation rate: 17.9% (2000).
Housing: Homeownership rate: 93.7% (2000); Median home value: $127,200 (2000); Median rent: $456 per month (2000); Median age of housing: 32 years (2000).
Transportation: Commute to work: 92.3% car, 0.9% public transportation, 1.6% walk, 5.2% work from home (2000); Travel time to work: 37.9% less than 15 minutes, 36.1% 15 to 30 minutes, 13.7% 30 to 45 minutes, 5.6% 45 to 60 minutes, 6.6% 60 minutes or more (2000)

FRONTENAC (unincorporated postal area, zip code 55026). Aka Frontenac Station. Covers a land area of 1.455 square miles and a water area of 0.098 square miles. Located at 44.52° N. Lat.; 92.33° W. Long. Elevation is 717 feet.
History: Frontenac was named for Louis de Buade, Comte de Frontenac (1622-1698), a French Colonial Governor of Canada.
Population: 387 (2000); Race: 99.2% White, 0.0% Black, 0.0% Asian, 0.3% American Indian and Alaska Native, 0.0% Hispanic of any race, 0.5% two or more races (2000); Density: 265.9 persons per square mile (2000); Age: 28.2% under 18, 13.4% over 64 (2000); Marriage status: 20.8% never married, 64.7% now married, 6.7% widowed, 7.8% divorced (2000); Foreign born: 0.5% (2000); Ancestry (includes multiple ancestries): 50.4% German, 14.8% Norwegian, 9.0% English, 7.9% Irish, 6.8% Swedish (2000).
Economy: Employment by occupation: 11.1% management, 21.1% professional, 15.6% services, 17.1% sales, 2.5% farming, 13.6% construction, 19.1% production (2000).
Income: Per capita income: $20,629 (2000); Median household income: $45,781 (2000); Poverty rate: 4.9% (2000).
Education: High school graduation rate: 86.7% (2000); College graduation rate: 19.3% (2000).
Housing: Homeownership rate: 91.4% (2000); Median home value: $109,100 (2000); Median rent: $425 per month (2000); Median age of housing: 51 years (2000).
Transportation: Commute to work: 92.0% car, 0.5% public transportation, 3.0% walk, 4.5% work from home (2000); Travel time to work: 36.3% less than 15 minutes, 41.1% 15 to 30 minutes, 12.6% 30 to 45 minutes, 4.2% 45 to 60 minutes, 5.8% 60 minutes or more (2000)

GOODHUE (city). Covers a land area of 0.911 square miles and a water area of 0 square miles. Located at 44.40° N. Lat.; 92.62° W. Long. Elevation is 1,119 feet.
Population: 778 (2000); Race: 95.8% White, 0.2% Black, 0.0% Asian, 0.0% American Indian and Alaska Native, 4.6% Hispanic of any race, 0.0% two or more races (2000); Density: 853.8 persons per square mile (2000); Age: 33.0% under 18, 12.8% over 64 (2000); Marriage status: 29.1% never married, 59.0% now married, 4.9% widowed, 7.0% divorced (2000); Foreign born: 3.5% (2000); Ancestry (includes multiple ancestries): 57.7% German, 18.8% Irish, 17.2% Norwegian, 9.0% Swedish, 5.0% Other groups (2000).
Economy: Single-family building permits issued: 13 (2001) / 2 (2000); Multi-family building permits issued: 0 (2001) / 0 (2000); Employment by occupation: 7.1% management, 13.0% professional, 14.7% services, 23.9% sales, 5.9% farming, 10.6% construction, 24.8% production (2000).
Income: Per capita income: $15,873 (2000); Median household income: $43,250 (2000); Poverty rate: 3.4% (2000).
Taxes: Total city taxes per capita: $255 (1997); City property taxes per capita: $240 (1997).
Education: High school graduation rate: 82.6% (2000); College graduation rate: 8.2% (2000).

School District(s)

Goodhue (PK-12)
2000 Enrollment: 571 651-923-4447
Housing: Homeownership rate: 84.4% (2000); Median home value: $97,400 (2000); Median rent: $353 per month (2000); Median age of housing: 35 years (2000).
Transportation: Commute to work: 86.7% car, 0.0% public transportation, 8.1% walk, 4.8% work from home (2000); Travel time to work: 30.4% less

than 15 minutes, 47.1% 15 to 30 minutes, 10.7% 30 to 45 minutes, 5.0% 45 to 60 minutes, 6.7% 60 minutes or more (2000)

GOODHUE (township). Covers a land area of 34.981 square miles and a water area of 0 square miles. Located at 44.42° N. Lat.; 92.61° W. Long. Elevation is 1,119 feet.
Population: 530 (2000); Race: 100.0% White, 0.0% Black, 0.0% Asian, 0.0% American Indian and Alaska Native, 0.6% Hispanic of any race, 0.0% two or more races (2000); Density: 15.2 persons per square mile (2000); Age: 26.7% under 18, 10.1% over 64 (2000); Marriage status: 22.4% never married, 70.4% now married, 3.9% widowed, 3.4% divorced (2000); Foreign born: 0.0% (2000); Ancestry (includes multiple ancestries): 62.8% German, 18.3% Norwegian, 11.5% Swedish, 9.0% Irish, 3.5% Finnish (2000).
Economy: Grain, alfalfa; poultry, livestock; dairying. Manufacturing: feeds, calf huts. Employment by occupation: 20.0% management, 14.3% professional, 11.7% services, 19.7% sales, 10.5% farming, 10.2% construction, 13.7% production (2000).
Income: Per capita income: $19,786 (2000); Median household income: $49,500 (2000); Poverty rate: 2.7% (2000).
Taxes: Total city taxes per capita: $192 (2000); City property taxes per capita: $192 (2000).
Education: High school graduation rate: 87.3% (2000); College graduation rate: 9.8% (2000).
Housing: Homeownership rate: 84.3% (2000); Median home value: $121,600 (2000); Median rent: $369 per month (2000); Median age of housing: 60+ years (2000).
Transportation: Commute to work: 72.8% car, 0.0% public transportation, 2.9% walk, 24.3% work from home (2000); Travel time to work: 48.5% less than 15 minutes, 35.0% 15 to 30 minutes, 9.7% 30 to 45 minutes, 3.0% 45 to 60 minutes, 3.8% 60 minutes or more (2000)

HAY CREEK (township). Covers a land area of 34.334 square miles and a water area of 0 square miles. Located at 44.49° N. Lat.; 92.49° W. Long. Elevation is 832 feet.
Population: 862 (2000); Race: 97.1% White, 0.0% Black, 0.7% Asian, 2.0% American Indian and Alaska Native, 1.0% Hispanic of any race, 0.0% two or more races (2000); Density: 25.1 persons per square mile (2000); Age: 30.3% under 18, 8.5% over 64 (2000); Marriage status: 20.9% never married, 70.1% now married, 3.0% widowed, 6.1% divorced (2000); Foreign born: 1.0% (2000); Ancestry (includes multiple ancestries): 58.9% German, 14.2% Swedish, 13.8% Irish, 13.0% Norwegian, 5.6% English (2000).
Economy: Employment by occupation: 18.3% management, 19.7% professional, 15.1% services, 19.2% sales, 3.1% farming, 7.6% construction, 17.0% production (2000).
Income: Per capita income: $24,034 (2000); Median household income: $63,594 (2000); Poverty rate: 3.8% (2000).
Taxes: Total city taxes per capita: $127 (1997); City property taxes per capita: $127 (1997).
Education: High school graduation rate: 89.8% (2000); College graduation rate: 25.0% (2000).
Housing: Homeownership rate: 93.7% (2000); Median home value: $206,600 (2000); Median rent: $538 per month (2000); Median age of housing: 26 years (2000).
Transportation: Commute to work: 90.0% car, 0.0% public transportation, 4.8% walk, 4.8% work from home (2000); Travel time to work: 32.8% less than 15 minutes, 44.5% 15 to 30 minutes, 8.7% 30 to 45 minutes, 4.4% 45 to 60 minutes, 9.6% 60 minutes or more (2000)

HOLDEN (township). Covers a land area of 35.925 square miles and a water area of 0 square miles. Located at 44.33° N. Lat.; 92.97° W. Long.
Population: 457 (2000); Race: 97.4% White, 0.0% Black, 2.2% Asian, 0.0% American Indian and Alaska Native, 0.0% Hispanic of any race, 0.4% two or more races (2000); Density: 12.7 persons per square mile (2000); Age: 31.1% under 18, 4.2% over 64 (2000); Marriage status: 22.3% never married, 65.5% now married, 3.0% widowed, 9.2% divorced (2000); Foreign born: 3.1% (2000); Ancestry (includes multiple ancestries): 44.2% Norwegian, 40.0% German, 8.2% Swedish, 7.1% English, 6.0% Irish (2000).
Economy: Employment by occupation: 25.2% management, 21.1% professional, 13.4% services, 20.3% sales, 0.0% farming, 6.9% construction, 13.0% production (2000).
Income: Per capita income: $17,806 (2000); Median household income: $51,563 (2000); Poverty rate: 12.7% (2000).
Taxes: Total city taxes per capita: $118 (1997); City property taxes per capita: $118 (1997).
Education: High school graduation rate: 93.5% (2000); College graduation rate: 33.2% (2000).
Housing: Homeownership rate: 84.4% (2000); Median home value: $149,000 (2000); Median rent: $425 per month (2000); Median age of housing: 60+ years (2000).
Transportation: Commute to work: 79.8% car, 0.0% public transportation, 4.1% walk, 15.3% work from home (2000); Travel time to work: 23.9% less than 15 minutes, 35.1% 15 to 30 minutes, 18.5% 30 to 45 minutes, 10.7% 45 to 60 minutes, 11.7% 60 minutes or more (2000)

KENYON (city). Covers a land area of 2.255 square miles and a water area of 0 square miles. Located at 44.27° N. Lat.; 92.98° W. Long. Elevation is 1,159 feet.
Population: 1,661 (2000); Race: 95.9% White, 0.1% Black, 0.4% Asian, 1.0% American Indian and Alaska Native, 3.6% Hispanic of any race, 0.3% two or more races (2000); Density: 736.6 persons per square mile (2000); Age: 23.2% under 18, 22.3% over 64 (2000); Marriage status: 24.0% never married, 55.9% now married, 12.1% widowed, 8.0% divorced (2000); Foreign born: 1.9% (2000); Ancestry (includes multiple ancestries): 43.5% Norwegian, 38.0% German, 9.5% Irish, 6.1% Swedish, 5.9% Other groups (2000).
Economy: Single-family building permits issued: 12 (2001) / 0 (2000); Multi-family building permits issued: 0 (2001) / 4 (2000); Employment by occupation: 9.3% management, 15.2% professional, 14.5% services, 28.0% sales, 1.5% farming, 11.3% construction, 20.1% production (2000).
Income: Per capita income: $19,569 (2000); Median household income: $41,786 (2000); Poverty rate: 5.2% (2000).
Taxes: Total city taxes per capita: $303 (2000); City property taxes per capita: $296 (2000).
Education: High school graduation rate: 86.4% (2000); College graduation rate: 17.1% (2000).

School District(s)

Kenyon-Wanamingo (PK-12)
2000 Enrollment: 1,022 507-789-5283
Housing: Homeownership rate: 82.7% (2000); Median home value: $87,600 (2000); Median rent: $344 per month (2000); Median age of housing: 55 years (2000).
Newspapers: The Kenyon Leader (1 x week)
Transportation: Commute to work: 88.0% car, 0.7% public transportation, 7.4% walk, 2.6% work from home (2000); Travel time to work: 32.7% less than 15 minutes, 28.0% 15 to 30 minutes, 21.6% 30 to 45 minutes, 9.9% 45 to 60 minutes, 7.8% 60 minutes or more (2000)

KENYON (township). Covers a land area of 33.730 square miles and a water area of 0 square miles. Located at 44.24° N. Lat.; 92.97° W. Long. Elevation is 1,159 feet.
History: Settled 1856, incorporated 1885.
Population: 437 (2000); Race: 96.3% White, 0.0% Black, 0.5% Asian, 0.0% American Indian and Alaska Native, 3.2% Hispanic of any race, 0.0% two or more races (2000); Density: 13.0 persons per square mile (2000); Age: 30.6% under 18, 8.3% over 64 (2000); Marriage status: 19.6% never married, 72.4% now married, 1.9% widowed, 6.2% divorced (2000); Foreign born: 2.1% (2000); Ancestry (includes multiple ancestries): 40.9% Norwegian, 37.7% German, 9.0% English, 7.8% Irish, 7.1% Swedish (2000).
Economy: Grain, soybeans; livestock, poultry; dairying. Light manufacturing. Employment by occupation: 18.5% management, 16.1% professional, 10.1% services, 22.2% sales, 1.2% farming, 15.7% construction, 16.1% production (2000).
Income: Per capita income: $23,620 (2000); Median household income: $51,250 (2000); Poverty rate: 3.0% (2000).
Taxes: Total city taxes per capita: $177 (1997); City property taxes per capita: $177 (1997).
Education: High school graduation rate: 94.0% (2000); College graduation rate: 21.3% (2000).
Housing: Homeownership rate: 90.4% (2000); Median home value: $102,500 (2000); Median rent: $488 per month (2000); Median age of housing: 55 years (2000).
Transportation: Commute to work: 82.7% car, 0.0% public transportation, 1.6% walk, 13.3% work from home (2000); Travel time to work: 33.5% less than 15 minutes, 27.4% 15 to 30 minutes, 23.3% 30 to 45 minutes, 7.9% 45 to 60 minutes, 7.9% 60 minutes or more (2000)

LEON (township). Covers a land area of 37.789 square miles and a water area of 0.041 square miles. Located at 44.40° N. Lat.; 92.86° W. Long.
Population: 942 (2000); Race: 97.5% White, 0.3% Black, 0.0% Asian, 0.4% American Indian and Alaska Native, 0.7% Hispanic of any race, 0.9% two or more races (2000); Density: 24.9 persons per square mile (2000); Age: 28.6% under 18, 8.3% over 64 (2000); Marriage status: 18.5% never married, 72.8%

now married, 2.1% widowed, 6.5% divorced (2000); Foreign born: 0.4% (2000); Ancestry (includes multiple ancestries): 38.9% German, 29.8% Norwegian, 21.3% Swedish, 10.0% English, 9.6% Irish (2000).
Economy: Employment by occupation: 16.5% management, 20.6% professional, 12.2% services, 20.4% sales, 3.7% farming, 12.2% construction, 14.3% production (2000).
Income: Per capita income: $25,756 (2000); Median household income: $61,094 (2000); Poverty rate: 3.8% (2000).
Taxes: Total city taxes per capita: $82 (1997); City property taxes per capita: $80 (1997).
Education: High school graduation rate: 93.6% (2000); College graduation rate: 22.0% (2000).
Housing: Homeownership rate: 92.6% (2000); Median home value: $150,000 (2000); Median rent: $525 per month (2000); Median age of housing: 37 years (2000).
Transportation: Commute to work: 89.9% car, 0.0% public transportation, 1.5% walk, 8.6% work from home (2000); Travel time to work: 31.3% less than 15 minutes, 24.0% 15 to 30 minutes, 17.7% 30 to 45 minutes, 20.0% 45 to 60 minutes, 6.9% 60 minutes or more (2000)

MINNEOLA (township). Covers a land area of 33.859 square miles and a water area of 0.008 square miles. Located at 44.32° N. Lat.; 92.73° W. Long.
Population: 657 (2000); Race: 98.4% White, 0.0% Black, 0.0% Asian, 0.3% American Indian and Alaska Native, 0.3% Hispanic of any race, 1.2% two or more races (2000); Density: 19.4 persons per square mile (2000); Age: 28.7% under 18, 10.5% over 64 (2000); Marriage status: 24.6% never married, 67.7% now married, 2.8% widowed, 5.0% divorced (2000); Foreign born: 0.9% (2000); Ancestry (includes multiple ancestries): 51.8% German, 37.3% Norwegian, 11.2% Swedish, 6.4% Irish, 6.2% English (2000).
Economy: Employment by occupation: 21.0% management, 22.6% professional, 9.3% services, 18.3% sales, 3.0% farming, 9.5% construction, 16.3% production (2000).
Income: Per capita income: $23,329 (2000); Median household income: $50,000 (2000); Poverty rate: 0.0% (2000).
Taxes: Total city taxes per capita: $114 (1997); City property taxes per capita: $114 (1997).
Education: High school graduation rate: 93.0% (2000); College graduation rate: 24.5% (2000).
Housing: Homeownership rate: 87.3% (2000); Median home value: $140,600 (2000); Median rent: $450 per month (2000); Median age of housing: 44 years (2000).
Transportation: Commute to work: 83.9% car, 3.1% public transportation, 2.2% walk, 10.8% work from home (2000); Travel time to work: 37.7% less than 15 minutes, 15.6% 15 to 30 minutes, 32.4% 30 to 45 minutes, 8.4% 45 to 60 minutes, 5.9% 60 minutes or more (2000)

PINE ISLAND (city). Covers a land area of 2.930 square miles and a water area of 0.023 square miles. Located at 44.20° N. Lat.; 92.64° W. Long. Elevation is 998 feet.
History: Pine Island was settled by many Swiss immigrants, who brought their skill in cheese making. The town was once known as the Cheese Center of Minnesota, having entered a 6,000-pound cheese in the state fair at St. Paul.
Population: 2,337 (2000); Race: 98.1% White, 0.0% Black, 0.1% Asian, 0.0% American Indian and Alaska Native, 1.0% Hispanic of any race, 1.3% two or more races (2000); Density: 797.5 persons per square mile (2000); Age: 28.8% under 18, 14.9% over 64 (2000); Marriage status: 22.7% never married, 58.1% now married, 10.9% widowed, 8.3% divorced (2000); Foreign born: 0.3% (2000); Ancestry (includes multiple ancestries): 45.3% German, 26.1% Norwegian, 13.9% Irish, 6.0% English, 5.4% Swedish (2000).
Economy: Single-family building permits issued: 75 (2001) / 44 (2000); Multi-family building permits issued: 24 (2001) / 58 (2000); Employment by occupation: 10.8% management, 19.8% professional, 14.0% services, 26.6% sales, 1.2% farming, 11.6% construction, 16.1% production (2000).
Income: Per capita income: $20,370 (2000); Median household income: $47,500 (2000); Poverty rate: 5.6% (2000).
Taxes: Total city taxes per capita: $308 (1997); City property taxes per capita: $292 (1997).
Education: High school graduation rate: 87.5% (2000); College graduation rate: 18.8% (2000).

School District(s)

Pine Island (PK-12)
2000 Enrollment: 1,243 507-356-8326

Housing: Homeownership rate: 80.9% (2000); Median home value: $107,200 (2000); Median rent: $328 per month (2000); Median age of housing: 32 years (2000).
Transportation: Commute to work: 88.1% car, 2.1% public transportation, 6.7% walk, 2.7% work from home (2000); Travel time to work: 33.0% less than 15 minutes, 44.1% 15 to 30 minutes, 16.6% 30 to 45 minutes, 3.2% 45 to 60 minutes, 3.1% 60 minutes or more (2000)

PINE ISLAND (township). Covers a land area of 32.734 square miles and a water area of 0.010 square miles. Located at 44.23° N. Lat.; 92.62° W. Long. Elevation is 998 feet.
History: Settled 1854, incorporated 1878.
Population: 628 (2000); Race: 98.7% White, 0.0% Black, 0.0% Asian, 1.0% American Indian and Alaska Native, 0.0% Hispanic of any race, 0.0% two or more races (2000); Density: 19.2 persons per square mile (2000); Age: 28.4% under 18, 9.9% over 64 (2000); Marriage status: 19.3% never married, 69.8% now married, 5.3% widowed, 5.7% divorced (2000); Foreign born: 1.2% (2000); Ancestry (includes multiple ancestries): 59.1% German, 30.4% Norwegian, 9.6% Irish, 6.7% Swedish, 5.0% English (2000).
Economy: Dairying; poultry, livestock; grain, soybeans. Manufacturing: fabricated metal products, food. Employment by occupation: 20.8% management, 21.4% professional, 8.6% services, 20.5% sales, 3.3% farming, 12.5% construction, 12.8% production (2000).
Income: Per capita income: $22,193 (2000); Median household income: $59,063 (2000); Poverty rate: 3.2% (2000).
Taxes: Total city taxes per capita: $49 (2000); City property taxes per capita: $48 (2000).
Education: High school graduation rate: 85.8% (2000); College graduation rate: 15.7% (2000).
Housing: Homeownership rate: 85.4% (2000); Median home value: $158,300 (2000); Median rent: $425 per month (2000); Median age of housing: 35 years (2000).
Transportation: Commute to work: 86.7% car, 2.1% public transportation, 2.1% walk, 9.1% work from home (2000); Travel time to work: 30.6% less than 15 minutes, 38.9% 15 to 30 minutes, 21.9% 30 to 45 minutes, 2.7% 45 to 60 minutes, 6.0% 60 minutes or more (2000)

RED WING (city). Covers a land area of 35.394 square miles and a water area of 5.975 square miles. Located at 44.56° N. Lat.; 92.56° W. Long. Elevation is 750 feet.
History: Red Wing began as one of the three posts established by a Swiss Protestant missionary society in 1836. The city that developed here was named for the Dakota chief Whoo-pa-doo-to, whose name meant "wing of scarlet." Industries that supported Red Wing and took its name are shoes and pottery.
Population: 16,116 (2000); Race: 94.9% White, 1.0% Black, 0.4% Asian, 3.0% American Indian and Alaska Native, 1.1% Hispanic of any race, 0.4% two or more races (2000); Density: 455.3 persons per square mile (2000); Age: 24.6% under 18, 16.6% over 64 (2000); Marriage status: 24.1% never married, 57.5% now married, 7.6% widowed, 10.8% divorced (2000); Foreign born: 1.3% (2000); Ancestry (includes multiple ancestries): 42.6% German, 20.1% Norwegian, 12.7% Swedish, 11.7% Irish, 5.3% Other groups (2000).
Vital Statistics: Birth rate: 112.9 per 10,000 population (1998)
Economy: Single-family building permits issued: 65 (2001) / 55 (2000); Multi-family building permits issued: 0 (2001) / 0 (2000); Employment by occupation: 10.2% management, 17.0% professional, 18.0% services, 23.4% sales, 0.5% farming, 9.1% construction, 21.8% production (2000).
Income: Per capita income: $21,678 (2000); Median household income: $43,674 (2000); Poverty rate: 6.8% (2000).
Taxes: Total city taxes per capita: $636 (2000); City property taxes per capita: $612 (2000).
Education: High school graduation rate: 85.8% (2000); College graduation rate: 19.7% (2000).

School District(s)

Correctional Facility - Red Wing (KG-12)
2000 Enrollment: 0 651-388-7154
Red Wing (PK-12)
2000 Enrollment: 3,350 651-385-4500

Two-year College(s)

Minnesota State College-Southeast Technical-Red Wing (Public)
2001 Enrollment: 1,705 651-385-6300
2001 Tuition: In-state $2,556; Out-of-state $5,111
Housing: Homeownership rate: 71.6% (2000); Median home value: $112,800 (2000); Median rent: $445 per month (2000); Median age of housing: 37 years (2000).

Hospitals: Fairview Red Wing Hospital (96 beds)
Safety: Violent crime rate: 29.5 per 10,000 population; Property crime rate: 472.1 per 10,000 population (2001).
Newspapers: Republican-Eagle (6 x week); Hiawatha Valley Shopper (1 x week)
Transportation: Commute to work: 91.0% car, 1.6% public transportation, 3.6% walk, 3.0% work from home (2000); Travel time to work: 60.1% less than 15 minutes, 23.3% 15 to 30 minutes, 6.8% 30 to 45 minutes, 3.7% 45 to 60 minutes, 6.1% 60 minutes or more (2000); Amtrak: Service available.
Additional Information Contacts
Red Wing Chamber of Commerce 651-388-4719

ROSCOE (township). Aka Roscoe Center. Covers a land area of 35.760 square miles and a water area of 0.012 square miles. Located at 44.24° N. Lat.; 92.72° W. Long.
Population: 784 (2000); Race: 99.4% White, 0.2% Black, 0.4% Asian, 0.0% American Indian and Alaska Native, 0.2% Hispanic of any race, 0.0% two or more races (2000); Density: 21.9 persons per square mile (2000); Age: 31.6% under 18, 8.1% over 64 (2000); Marriage status: 22.0% never married, 72.2% now married, 2.1% widowed, 3.6% divorced (2000); Foreign born: 0.9% (2000); Ancestry (includes multiple ancestries): 48.3% German, 35.1% Norwegian, 8.6% Irish, 4.9% English, 4.4% Swiss (2000).
Economy: Employment by occupation: 12.2% management, 21.3% professional, 15.9% services, 24.2% sales, 3.1% farming, 13.0% construction, 10.3% production (2000).
Income: Per capita income: $20,472 (2000); Median household income: $56,719 (2000); Poverty rate: 3.1% (2000).
Taxes: Total city taxes per capita: $87 (1997); City property taxes per capita: $87 (1997).
Education: High school graduation rate: 89.6% (2000); College graduation rate: 21.6% (2000).
Housing: Homeownership rate: 93.5% (2000); Median home value: $152,500 (2000); Median rent: $338 per month (2000); Median age of housing: 35 years (2000).
Transportation: Commute to work: 86.7% car, 0.4% public transportation, 4.0% walk, 8.9% work from home (2000); Travel time to work: 32.4% less than 15 minutes, 29.5% 15 to 30 minutes, 29.9% 30 to 45 minutes, 2.5% 45 to 60 minutes, 5.7% 60 minutes or more (2000)

STANTON (township). Covers a land area of 22.725 square miles and a water area of 1.132 square miles. Located at 44.48° N. Lat.; 92.96° W. Long. Elevation is 917 feet.
Population: 1,080 (2000); Race: 98.0% White, 0.3% Black, 0.4% Asian, 0.2% American Indian and Alaska Native, 0.0% Hispanic of any race, 1.1% two or more races (2000); Density: 47.5 persons per square mile (2000); Age: 30.3% under 18, 7.9% over 64 (2000); Marriage status: 20.0% never married, 71.6% now married, 2.5% widowed, 5.8% divorced (2000); Foreign born: 1.0% (2000); Ancestry (includes multiple ancestries): 46.8% German, 19.1% Norwegian, 15.8% Swedish, 12.2% Irish, 11.7% English (2000).
Economy: Employment by occupation: 12.7% management, 14.8% professional, 11.4% services, 26.1% sales, 2.0% farming, 14.0% construction, 19.1% production (2000).
Income: Per capita income: $23,473 (2000); Median household income: $60,972 (2000); Poverty rate: 2.8% (2000).
Taxes: Total city taxes per capita: $94 (1997); City property taxes per capita: $91 (1997).
Education: High school graduation rate: 91.3% (2000); College graduation rate: 18.2% (2000).
Housing: Homeownership rate: 93.6% (2000); Median home value: $165,500 (2000); Median rent: $338 per month (2000); Median age of housing: 26 years (2000).
Transportation: Commute to work: 91.4% car, 0.7% public transportation, 1.2% walk, 6.3% work from home (2000); Travel time to work: 34.1% less than 15 minutes, 19.5% 15 to 30 minutes, 25.3% 30 to 45 minutes, 16.9% 45 to 60 minutes, 4.2% 60 minutes or more (2000)

VASA (township). Covers a land area of 40.960 square miles and a water area of 0.200 square miles. Located at 44.50° N. Lat.; 92.73° W. Long.
Population: 872 (2000); Race: 99.2% White, 0.0% Black, 0.0% Asian, 0.2% American Indian and Alaska Native, 0.6% Hispanic of any race, 0.6% two or more races (2000); Density: 21.3 persons per square mile (2000); Age: 29.5% under 18, 13.2% over 64 (2000); Marriage status: 24.5% never married, 62.6% now married, 5.0% widowed, 7.9% divorced (2000); Foreign born: 0.7% (2000); Ancestry (includes multiple ancestries): 44.5% German, 37.8% Swedish, 19.7% Norwegian, 9.0% Irish, 4.2% French (except Basque) (2000).
Economy: Employment by occupation: 13.1% management, 13.1% professional, 18.8% services, 15.1% sales, 4.8% farming, 10.3% construction, 24.9% production (2000).
Income: Per capita income: $23,629 (2000); Median household income: $53,281 (2000); Poverty rate: 4.9% (2000).
Taxes: Total city taxes per capita: $90 (1997); City property taxes per capita: $90 (1997).
Education: High school graduation rate: 85.2% (2000); College graduation rate: 12.2% (2000).
Housing: Homeownership rate: 88.1% (2000); Median home value: $133,900 (2000); Median rent: $221 per month (2000); Median age of housing: 37 years (2000).
Transportation: Commute to work: 84.5% car, 0.0% public transportation, 1.1% walk, 14.3% work from home (2000); Travel time to work: 19.1% less than 15 minutes, 50.8% 15 to 30 minutes, 17.3% 30 to 45 minutes, 5.7% 45 to 60 minutes, 7.2% 60 minutes or more (2000)

WACOUTA (township). Covers a land area of 4.162 square miles and a water area of 5.594 square miles. Located at 44.54° N. Lat.; 92.45° W. Long. Elevation is 709 feet.
Population: 410 (2000); Race: 97.3% White, 0.2% Black, 0.0% Asian, 2.2% American Indian and Alaska Native, 2.0% Hispanic of any race, 0.2% two or more races (2000); Density: 98.5 persons per square mile (2000); Age: 27.9% under 18, 13.5% over 64 (2000); Marriage status: 19.8% never married, 68.6% now married, 7.1% widowed, 4.5% divorced (2000); Foreign born: 1.1% (2000); Ancestry (includes multiple ancestries): 49.7% German, 14.6% Norwegian, 14.2% Irish, 13.5% English, 11.7% Swedish (2000).
Economy: Employment by occupation: 11.7% management, 17.8% professional, 17.8% services, 27.0% sales, 1.7% farming, 8.3% construction, 15.7% production (2000).
Income: Per capita income: $29,281 (2000); Median household income: $63,958 (2000); Poverty rate: 2.9% (2000).
Taxes: Total city taxes per capita: $141 (1997); City property taxes per capita: $139 (1997).
Education: High school graduation rate: 92.3% (2000); College graduation rate: 28.0% (2000).
Housing: Homeownership rate: 88.7% (2000); Median home value: $173,900 (2000); Median rent: $667 per month (2000); Median age of housing: 30 years (2000).
Transportation: Commute to work: 95.2% car, 0.0% public transportation, 0.9% walk, 3.5% work from home (2000); Travel time to work: 47.0% less than 15 minutes, 35.2% 15 to 30 minutes, 5.0% 30 to 45 minutes, 0.9% 45 to 60 minutes, 11.9% 60 minutes or more (2000)

WANAMINGO (city). Covers a land area of 1.095 square miles and a water area of 0 square miles. Located at 44.30° N. Lat.; 92.79° W. Long. Elevation is 1,030 feet.
Population: 1,007 (2000); Race: 97.0% White, 0.4% Black, 0.0% Asian, 0.0% American Indian and Alaska Native, 0.0% Hispanic of any race, 2.0% two or more races (2000); Density: 919.4 persons per square mile (2000); Age: 26.1% under 18, 19.7% over 64 (2000); Marriage status: 17.9% never married, 66.9% now married, 8.5% widowed, 6.7% divorced (2000); Foreign born: 0.4% (2000); Ancestry (includes multiple ancestries): 43.7% Norwegian, 30.1% German, 8.7% Swedish, 7.1% Irish, 4.2% United States or American (2000).
Economy: Single-family building permits issued: 8 (2001) / 2 (2000); Multi-family building permits issued: 0 (2001) / 4 (2000); Employment by occupation: 11.0% management, 15.6% professional, 15.4% services, 25.2% sales, 1.2% farming, 12.1% construction, 19.5% production (2000).
Income: Per capita income: $18,466 (2000); Median household income: $40,000 (2000); Poverty rate: 8.8% (2000).
Taxes: Total city taxes per capita: $193 (1997); City property taxes per capita: $189 (1997).
Education: High school graduation rate: 81.6% (2000); College graduation rate: 15.9% (2000).
Housing: Homeownership rate: 81.8% (2000); Median home value: $93,800 (2000); Median rent: $429 per month (2000); Median age of housing: 32 years (2000).
Transportation: Commute to work: 90.9% car, 1.5% public transportation, 3.8% walk, 3.8% work from home (2000); Travel time to work: 39.2% less than 15 minutes, 20.8% 15 to 30 minutes, 24.5% 30 to 45 minutes, 11.4% 45 to 60 minutes, 4.2% 60 minutes or more (2000)

WANAMINGO (township). Covers a land area of 37.582 square miles and a water area of 0.006 square miles. Located at 44.33° N. Lat.; 92.84° W. Long. Elevation is 1,030 feet.

Population: 504 (2000); Race: 98.6% White, 0.0% Black, 1.0% Asian, 0.0% American Indian and Alaska Native, 1.8% Hispanic of any race, 0.4% two or more races (2000); Density: 13.4 persons per square mile (2000); Age: 32.1% under 18, 9.8% over 64 (2000); Marriage status: 26.2% never married, 62.6% now married, 4.2% widowed, 7.0% divorced (2000); Foreign born: 0.8% (2000); Ancestry (includes multiple ancestries): 57.1% Norwegian, 40.6% German, 10.6% Swedish, 3.9% Irish, 3.7% United States or American (2000).
Economy: Agriculture includes grains, soybeans, peas; livestock, poultry; dairying. Manufacturing: feeds and fertilizers, cabinets. Employment by occupation: 17.6% management, 8.8% professional, 12.1% services, 24.9% sales, 2.6% farming, 14.3% construction, 19.8% production (2000).
Income: Per capita income: $18,714 (2000); Median household income: $42,500 (2000); Poverty rate: 5.9% (2000).
Taxes: Total city taxes per capita: $111 (1997); City property taxes per capita: $111 (1997).
Education: High school graduation rate: 89.7% (2000); College graduation rate: 14.4% (2000).
Housing: Homeownership rate: 80.3% (2000); Median home value: $122,800 (2000); Median rent: $404 per month (2000); Median age of housing: 56 years (2000).
Transportation: Commute to work: 88.2% car, 1.5% public transportation, 1.5% walk, 8.9% work from home (2000); Travel time to work: 28.3% less than 15 minutes, 35.2% 15 to 30 minutes, 17.4% 30 to 45 minutes, 11.3% 45 to 60 minutes, 7.7% 60 minutes or more (2000)

WARSAW (township). Covers a land area of 34.560 square miles and a water area of 0 square miles. Located at 44.41° N. Lat.; 92.97° W. Long.
Population: 603 (2000); Race: 95.1% White, 1.5% Black, 0.0% Asian, 0.3% American Indian and Alaska Native, 1.5% Hispanic of any race, 2.3% two or more races (2000); Density: 17.4 persons per square mile (2000); Age: 30.6% under 18, 7.5% over 64 (2000); Marriage status: 21.3% never married, 69.2% now married, 2.7% widowed, 6.8% divorced (2000); Foreign born: 0.6% (2000); Ancestry (includes multiple ancestries): 35.2% German, 30.8% Norwegian, 16.2% Irish, 10.2% English, 6.2% Swedish (2000).
Economy: Employment by occupation: 18.3% management, 19.9% professional, 10.1% services, 17.4% sales, 1.7% farming, 9.8% construction, 22.8% production (2000).
Income: Per capita income: $26,520 (2000); Median household income: $65,179 (2000); Poverty rate: 2.3% (2000).
Taxes: Total city taxes per capita: $186 (1997); City property taxes per capita: $185 (1997).
Education: High school graduation rate: 91.0% (2000); College graduation rate: 23.6% (2000).
Housing: Homeownership rate: 95.3% (2000); Median home value: $138,500 (2000); Median rent: $125 per month (2000); Median age of housing: 31 years (2000).
Transportation: Commute to work: 85.2% car, 0.0% public transportation, 2.6% walk, 12.2% work from home (2000); Travel time to work: 18.4% less than 15 minutes, 37.2% 15 to 30 minutes, 14.6% 30 to 45 minutes, 19.7% 45 to 60 minutes, 10.0% 60 minutes or more (2000)

WELCH (township). Covers a land area of 39.302 square miles and a water area of 3.429 square miles. Located at 44.63° N. Lat.; 92.72° W. Long.
Population: 697 (2000); Race: 98.1% White, 0.0% Black, 0.3% Asian, 1.1% American Indian and Alaska Native, 0.4% Hispanic of any race, 0.4% two or more races (2000); Density: 17.7 persons per square mile (2000); Age: 24.2% under 18, 9.3% over 64 (2000); Marriage status: 22.9% never married, 67.3% now married, 3.0% widowed, 6.7% divorced (2000); Foreign born: 1.3% (2000); Ancestry (includes multiple ancestries): 42.2% German, 22.7% Norwegian, 21.5% Swedish, 8.4% Irish, 4.9% United States or American (2000).
Economy: Employment by occupation: 15.6% management, 15.8% professional, 16.9% services, 18.4% sales, 3.6% farming, 13.8% construction, 15.8% production (2000).
Income: Per capita income: $23,023 (2000); Median household income: $60,536 (2000); Poverty rate: 5.6% (2000).
Taxes: Total city taxes per capita: $90 (1997); City property taxes per capita: $89 (1997).
Education: High school graduation rate: 90.0% (2000); College graduation rate: 16.9% (2000).
Housing: Homeownership rate: 79.8% (2000); Median home value: $173,600 (2000); Median rent: $430 per month (2000); Median age of housing: 27 years (2000).
Transportation: Commute to work: 89.6% car, 0.0% public transportation, 0.5% walk, 8.8% work from home (2000); Travel time to work: 20.1% less than 15 minutes, 39.1% 15 to 30 minutes, 15.5% 30 to 45 minutes, 14.0% 45 to 60 minutes, 11.4% 60 minutes or more (2000)

ZUMBROTA (city). Covers a land area of 1.974 square miles and a water area of 0.005 square miles. Located at 44.29° N. Lat.; 92.67° W. Long. Elevation is 1,005 feet.
Population: 2,789 (2000); Race: 95.8% White, 1.0% Black, 0.4% Asian, 0.1% American Indian and Alaska Native, 0.4% Hispanic of any race, 1.7% two or more races (2000); Density: 1,412.6 persons per square mile (2000); Age: 26.4% under 18, 18.3% over 64 (2000); Marriage status: 25.1% never married, 57.0% now married, 9.8% widowed, 8.2% divorced (2000); Foreign born: 1.1% (2000); Ancestry (includes multiple ancestries): 44.8% German, 33.5% Norwegian, 8.6% Irish, 6.3% Swedish, 5.5% English (2000).
Economy: Single-family building permits issued: 28 (2001) / 43 (2000); Multi-family building permits issued: 2 (2001) / 0 (2000); Employment by occupation: 10.2% management, 20.7% professional, 14.0% services, 28.7% sales, 0.3% farming, 9.7% construction, 16.4% production (2000).
Income: Per capita income: $22,786 (2000); Median household income: $41,678 (2000); Poverty rate: 8.0% (2000).
Taxes: Total city taxes per capita: $226 (1997); City property taxes per capita: $211 (1997).
Education: High school graduation rate: 84.8% (2000); College graduation rate: 24.3% (2000).
Housing: Homeownership rate: 76.8% (2000); Median home value: $99,100 (2000); Median rent: $365 per month (2000); Median age of housing: 32 years (2000).
Hospitals: Zumbrota Health Care (19 beds)
Safety: Violent crime rate: 17.7 per 10,000 population; Property crime rate: 358.3 per 10,000 population (2001).
Newspapers: News-Record (1 x week); The Country Shopper (1 x week)
Transportation: Commute to work: 87.8% car, 1.6% public transportation, 6.3% walk, 3.2% work from home (2000); Travel time to work: 43.3% less than 15 minutes, 22.6% 15 to 30 minutes, 25.8% 30 to 45 minutes, 4.4% 45 to 60 minutes, 3.9% 60 minutes or more (2000)

ZUMBROTA (township). Covers a land area of 34.841 square miles and a water area of <.001 square miles. Located at 44.33° N. Lat.; 92.62° W. Long. Elevation is 1,005 feet.
Population: 591 (2000); Race: 96.1% White, 0.0% Black, 0.2% Asian, 0.0% American Indian and Alaska Native, 0.5% Hispanic of any race, 2.9% two or more races (2000); Density: 17.0 persons per square mile (2000); Age: 27.9% under 18, 11.9% over 64 (2000); Marriage status: 19.5% never married, 74.2% now married, 3.5% widowed, 2.7% divorced (2000); Foreign born: 1.4% (2000); Ancestry (includes multiple ancestries): 63.6% German, 24.7% Norwegian, 6.6% Irish, 4.7% United States or American, 3.7% Swedish (2000).
Economy: Grain, soybeans; livestock, poultry; dairying. Manufacturing: cheese, spiral staircases; printing and publishing. Employment by occupation: 16.5% management, 21.3% professional, 9.0% services, 23.9% sales, 6.1% farming, 11.4% construction, 11.7% production (2000).
Income: Per capita income: $21,372 (2000); Median household income: $62,188 (2000); Poverty rate: 6.6% (2000).
Taxes: Total city taxes per capita: $102 (1997); City property taxes per capita: $102 (1997).
Education: High school graduation rate: 87.6% (2000); College graduation rate: 19.4% (2000).
Housing: Homeownership rate: 91.6% (2000); Median home value: $130,800 (2000); Median rent: $513 per month (2000); Median age of housing: 52 years (2000).
Transportation: Commute to work: 82.1% car, 2.7% public transportation, 3.5% walk, 11.0% work from home (2000); Travel time to work: 42.6% less than 15 minutes, 18.9% 15 to 30 minutes, 25.5% 30 to 45 minutes, 10.2% 45 to 60 minutes, 2.7% 60 minutes or more (2000)

Grant County

Located in western Minnesota; drained by the Mustinka and Pomme de Terre Rivers. Covers a land area of 546.40 square miles, a water area of 28.80 square miles, and is located in the Central Time Zone. The county government was organized in 1868. County seat is Elbow Lake.
Population: 6,289 (2000); Race: 98.8% White, 0.0% Black, 0.2% Asian, 0.1% American Indian and Alaska Native, 0.7% Hispanic of any race, 0.5% two or more races (2000); Density: 11.5 persons per square mile (2000); Age: 23.7% under 18, 23.0% over 64 (2000).

Religion: Five largest groups: 58.4% Evangelical Lutheran Church in America, 9.9% Catholic Church, 9.1% Lutheran Church—Missouri Synod, 5.5% Presbyterian Church (U.S.A.), 4.4% The United Methodist Church (2000).
Economy: Unemployment rate: 4.8% (11/2002); Total civilian labor force: 2,708 (11/2002); Leading industries: 21.5% retail trade; 18.8% health care and social assistance; 15.3% manufacturing (2000); Companies that employ more than 1,000 persons: 0 (2000); Companies that employ more than 100 persons: 0 (2000); Farms: 468 totaling 278,495 acres (1997); Minority business ownership rate: 0.0% (1997); Women business ownership rate: 22.7% (1997); Retail sales per capita: $8,665 (1997). Single-family building permits issued: 3 (2001) / 11 (2000); Multi-family building permits issued: 0 (2001) / 0 (2000).
Income: Per capita income: $17,131 (2000); Median household income: $33,775 (2000); Poverty rate: 8.4% (2000); Bankruptcy rate: 3.28% (2001).
Taxes: Total county taxes per capita: $336 (1997); County property taxes per capita: $325 (1997).
Education: High school graduation rate: 83.5% (2000); College graduation rate: 15.7% (2000).
Housing: Homeownership rate: 82.2% (2000); Median home value: $52,900 (2000); Median rent: $286 per month (2000); Median age of housing: 48 years (2000).
Health: Birth rate: 85.9 per 10,000 population (1998); Age adjusted death rate: 90.6 per 10,000 population (1999); Age adjusted cancer mortality rate: 199.1 deaths per 100,000 population (1999). Number of physicians: 4.8 per 10,000 population (1999); Number of hospital beds: 23.9 per 10,000 population (1999).
Elections: 2000 Presidential election results: 41.6% Gore, 49.8% Bush, 5.9% Nader, 2.2% Buchanan
National and State Parks: Alvstad State Wildlife Management Area; Bergerud State Wildlife Management Area; Berskow State Wildlife Management Area; Chippewa State Wildlife Management Area; Helsene State Wildlife Management Area; Isaacson State Wildlife Management Area; Kube-swift State Wildlife Management Areas; Marple State Wildlife Management Area; Mustinka State Wildlife Management Area; Pomme de Terre State Wildlife Management Area; Shuck State Wildlife Management Area; Storm-bordson State Wildlife Management Area
Additional Information Contacts
Grant County Government Offices 218-685-4520

Grant County Communities

ASHBY (city). Covers a land area of 0.534 square miles and a water area of 0.038 square miles. Located at 46.09° N. Lat.; 95.81° W. Long. Elevation is 1,298 feet.
Population: 472 (2000); Race: 97.6% White, 0.0% Black, 0.0% Asian, 0.4% American Indian and Alaska Native, 0.6% Hispanic of any race, 1.7% two or more races (2000); Density: 883.9 persons per square mile (2000); Age: 21.4% under 18, 34.2% over 64 (2000); Marriage status: 16.1% never married, 60.4% now married, 17.7% widowed, 5.8% divorced (2000); Foreign born: 0.4% (2000); Ancestry (includes multiple ancestries): 58.7% Norwegian, 19.0% German, 12.1% Swedish, 4.5% English, 3.2% French (except Basque) (2000).
Economy: Agricultural area: grain, sugar beets, beans, sunflowers; livestock; dairying. Manufacturing: poultry processing, dairy products. Single-family building permits issued: 0 (2001) / 1 (2000); Multi-family building permits issued: 0 (2001) / 0 (2000); Employment by occupation: 6.6% management, 19.8% professional, 21.3% services, 23.4% sales, 1.5% farming, 14.7% construction, 12.7% production (2000).
Income: Per capita income: $15,296 (2000); Median household income: $28,333 (2000); Poverty rate: 11.1% (2000).
Taxes: Total city taxes per capita: $132 (1997); City property taxes per capita: $130 (1997).
Education: High school graduation rate: 79.5% (2000); College graduation rate: 9.9% (2000).

School District(s)

Ashby (KG-12)
2000 Enrollment: 320 218-747-2257
Housing: Homeownership rate: 72.5% (2000); Median home value: $60,000 (2000); Median rent: $292 per month (2000); Median age of housing: 48 years (2000).
Transportation: Commute to work: 87.0% car, 0.0% public transportation, 9.3% walk, 3.6% work from home (2000); Travel time to work: 37.6% less than 15 minutes, 31.7% 15 to 30 minutes, 19.4% 30 to 45 minutes, 4.8% 45 to 60 minutes, 6.5% 60 minutes or more (2000)

BARRETT (city). Covers a land area of 2.061 square miles and a water area of 0.042 square miles. Located at 45.91° N. Lat.; 95.88° W. Long. Elevation is 1,166 feet.
Population: 355 (2000); Race: 99.2% White, 0.0% Black, 0.0% Asian, 0.8% American Indian and Alaska Native, 0.0% Hispanic of any race, 0.0% two or more races (2000); Density: 172.2 persons per square mile (2000); Age: 14.2% under 18, 45.0% over 64 (2000); Marriage status: 17.6% never married, 46.3% now married, 25.6% widowed, 10.5% divorced (2000); Foreign born: 0.3% (2000); Ancestry (includes multiple ancestries): 45.0% Norwegian, 40.3% German, 13.9% Swedish, 8.1% Irish, 5.8% English (2000).
Economy: Dairying; livestock; grain, sugar beets, sunflowers. Manufacturing: machinery, silk screening. Single-family building permits issued: 1 (2001) / 2 (2000); Multi-family building permits issued: 0 (2001) / 0 (2000); Employment by occupation: 14.9% management, 21.6% professional, 16.4% services, 12.7% sales, 3.0% farming, 10.4% construction, 20.9% production (2000).
Income: Per capita income: $13,954 (2000); Median household income: $28,750 (2000); Poverty rate: 8.8% (2000).
Taxes: Total city taxes per capita: $229 (1997); City property taxes per capita: $223 (1997).
Education: High school graduation rate: 73.7% (2000); College graduation rate: 16.3% (2000).

School District(s)

West Central Area (PK-12)
2000 Enrollment: 928 320-528-2650
Housing: Homeownership rate: 81.3% (2000); Median home value: $40,000 (2000); Median rent: $271 per month (2000); Median age of housing: 60+ years (2000).
Transportation: Commute to work: 88.1% car, 0.0% public transportation, 9.0% walk, 3.0% work from home (2000); Travel time to work: 53.1% less than 15 minutes, 20.0% 15 to 30 minutes, 18.5% 30 to 45 minutes, 4.6% 45 to 60 minutes, 3.8% 60 minutes or more (2000)

DELAWARE (township). Covers a land area of 35.455 square miles and a water area of 0.875 square miles. Located at 45.89° N. Lat.; 96.07° W. Long.
Population: 119 (2000); Race: 100.0% White, 0.0% Black, 0.0% Asian, 0.0% American Indian and Alaska Native, 0.0% Hispanic of any race, 0.0% two or more races (2000); Density: 3.4 persons per square mile (2000); Age: 26.5% under 18, 6.6% over 64 (2000); Marriage status: 17.6% never married, 76.9% now married, 2.8% widowed, 2.8% divorced (2000); Foreign born: 0.0% (2000); Ancestry (includes multiple ancestries): 50.0% Norwegian, 27.9% German, 19.9% Swedish, 11.8% English, 11.8% Irish (2000).
Economy: Employment by occupation: 41.9% management, 4.7% professional, 14.0% services, 18.6% sales, 0.0% farming, 4.7% construction, 16.3% production (2000).
Income: Per capita income: $19,196 (2000); Median household income: $46,875 (2000); Poverty rate: 9.6% (2000).
Taxes: Total city taxes per capita: $53 (1997); City property taxes per capita: $53 (1997).
Education: High school graduation rate: 87.6% (2000); College graduation rate: 33.7% (2000).
Housing: Homeownership rate: 70.6% (2000); Median home value: $80,000 (2000); Median rent: $192 per month (2000); Median age of housing: 51 years (2000).
Transportation: Commute to work: 61.0% car, 2.4% public transportation, 9.8% walk, 26.8% work from home (2000); Travel time to work: 38.3% less than 15 minutes, 46.7% 15 to 30 minutes, 11.7% 30 to 45 minutes, 0.0% 45 to 60 minutes, 3.3% 60 minutes or more (2000)

ELBOW LAKE (city). Covers a land area of 1.349 square miles and a water area of 0.370 square miles. Located at 45.99° N. Lat.; 95.97° W. Long. Elevation is 1,222 feet.
History: Elbow Lake was established as the seat of Grant County. When an election appeared to transfer this honor to a neighboring town, the citizens of Elbow Lake exposed the election fraud and made a night raid to recapture the official county records. Many of Elbow Lake's early residents were of Scandinavian heritage.
Population: 1,275 (2000); Race: 97.7% White, 0.2% Black, 0.4% Asian, 0.0% American Indian and Alaska Native, 2.3% Hispanic of any race, 0.0% two or more races (2000); Density: 944.9 persons per square mile (2000); Age: 24.7% under 18, 25.3% over 64 (2000); Marriage status: 18.1% never married, 61.4% now married, 12.3% widowed, 8.3% divorced (2000); Foreign born: 1.7% (2000); Ancestry (includes multiple ancestries): 42.6%

German, 40.0% Norwegian, 12.1% Swedish, 7.4% Irish, 6.1% English (2000).
Economy: Single-family building permits issued: 0 (2001) / 4 (2000); Multi-family building permits issued: 0 (2001) / 0 (2000); Employment by occupation: 12.4% management, 21.7% professional, 13.3% services, 24.9% sales, 0.4% farming, 12.4% construction, 15.1% production (2000).
Income: Per capita income: $16,429 (2000); Median household income: $30,441 (2000); Poverty rate: 7.7% (2000).
Taxes: Total city taxes per capita: $213 (1997); City property taxes per capita: $208 (1997).
Education: High school graduation rate: 84.8% (2000); College graduation rate: 17.4% (2000).
Housing: Homeownership rate: 72.9% (2000); Median home value: $52,100 (2000); Median rent: $326 per month (2000); Median age of housing: 47 years (2000).
Newspapers: Grant County Herald (1 x week)
Transportation: Commute to work: 88.9% car, 0.0% public transportation, 5.6% walk, 4.4% work from home (2000); Travel time to work: 60.7% less than 15 minutes, 20.3% 15 to 30 minutes, 12.1% 30 to 45 minutes, 4.0% 45 to 60 minutes, 2.8% 60 minutes or more (2000)

ELBOW LAKE (township). Covers a land area of 35.419 square miles and a water area of 0.322 square miles. Located at 45.97° N. Lat.; 96.07° W. Long. Elevation is 1,222 feet.
Population: 157 (2000); Race: 98.5% White, 0.0% Black, 0.0% Asian, 0.0% American Indian and Alaska Native, 0.0% Hispanic of any race, 1.5% two or more races (2000); Density: 4.4 persons per square mile (2000); Age: 21.8% under 18, 18.8% over 64 (2000); Marriage status: 25.0% never married, 69.4% now married, 3.7% widowed, 1.9% divorced (2000); Foreign born: 0.0% (2000); Ancestry (includes multiple ancestries): 55.6% Norwegian, 51.9% German, 7.5% Swedish, 4.5% French (except Basque), 3.8% Italian (2000).
Economy: Farm trading point: poultry, livestock; grain, sugar beets, beans, alfalfa; dairying. Manufacturing: automotive grease, fertilizer machining. Employment by occupation: 11.1% management, 9.9% professional, 19.8% services, 35.8% sales, 6.2% farming, 2.5% construction, 14.8% production (2000).
Income: Per capita income: $15,715 (2000); Median household income: $25,250 (2000); Poverty rate: 6.8% (2000).
Taxes: Total city taxes per capita: $110 (1997); City property taxes per capita: $110 (1997).
Education: High school graduation rate: 91.5% (2000); College graduation rate: 14.9% (2000).
Housing: Homeownership rate: 88.3% (2000); Median home value: $63,000 (2000); Median rent: $185 per month (2000); Median age of housing: 50 years (2000).
Transportation: Commute to work: 90.1% car, 0.0% public transportation, 0.0% walk, 9.9% work from home (2000); Travel time to work: 57.5% less than 15 minutes, 20.5% 15 to 30 minutes, 17.8% 30 to 45 minutes, 0.0% 45 to 60 minutes, 4.1% 60 minutes or more (2000)

ELK LAKE (township). Covers a land area of 32.173 square miles and a water area of 3.310 square miles. Located at 45.90° N. Lat.; 95.83° W. Long.
Population: 298 (2000); Race: 98.5% White, 0.0% Black, 0.0% Asian, 0.0% American Indian and Alaska Native, 3.0% Hispanic of any race, 0.8% two or more races (2000); Density: 9.3 persons per square mile (2000); Age: 26.5% under 18, 17.8% over 64 (2000); Marriage status: 14.2% never married, 81.4% now married, 1.0% widowed, 3.4% divorced (2000); Foreign born: 0.4% (2000); Ancestry (includes multiple ancestries): 53.0% Norwegian, 31.4% German, 17.8% Swedish, 8.7% Polish, 6.8% Irish (2000).
Economy: Employment by occupation: 16.7% management, 17.4% professional, 13.6% services, 14.4% sales, 2.3% farming, 14.4% construction, 21.2% production (2000).
Income: Per capita income: $16,365 (2000); Median household income: $47,125 (2000); Poverty rate: 6.8% (2000).
Taxes: Total city taxes per capita: $34 (1997); City property taxes per capita: $34 (1997).
Education: High school graduation rate: 82.9% (2000); College graduation rate: 16.6% (2000).
Housing: Homeownership rate: 90.4% (2000); Median home value: $114,100 (2000); Median age of housing: 34 years (2000).
Transportation: Commute to work: 88.5% car, 0.0% public transportation, 1.5% walk, 10.0% work from home (2000); Travel time to work: 36.8% less than 15 minutes, 39.3% 15 to 30 minutes, 13.7% 30 to 45 minutes, 3.4% 45 to 60 minutes, 6.8% 60 minutes or more (2000)

ERDAHL (township). Covers a land area of 33.868 square miles and a water area of 2.026 square miles. Located at 45.98° N. Lat.; 95.82° W. Long. Elevation is 1,265 feet.
Population: 343 (2000); Race: 99.4% White, 0.0% Black, 0.0% Asian, 0.6% American Indian and Alaska Native, 0.0% Hispanic of any race, 0.0% two or more races (2000); Density: 10.1 persons per square mile (2000); Age: 29.0% under 18, 13.9% over 64 (2000); Marriage status: 25.0% never married, 60.7% now married, 5.9% widowed, 8.5% divorced (2000); Foreign born: 0.0% (2000); Ancestry (includes multiple ancestries): 41.2% Norwegian, 31.9% German, 11.3% Swedish, 10.1% English, 6.4% French (except Basque) (2000).
Economy: Employment by occupation: 15.4% management, 14.8% professional, 19.8% services, 22.8% sales, 5.6% farming, 7.4% construction, 14.2% production (2000).
Income: Per capita income: $16,959 (2000); Median household income: $38,125 (2000); Poverty rate: 8.7% (2000).
Taxes: Total city taxes per capita: $83 (1997); City property taxes per capita: $83 (1997).
Education: High school graduation rate: 92.7% (2000); College graduation rate: 18.7% (2000).
Housing: Homeownership rate: 80.3% (2000); Median home value: $91,400 (2000); Median rent: $175 per month (2000); Median age of housing: 31 years (2000).
Transportation: Commute to work: 85.0% car, 0.0% public transportation, 3.8% walk, 10.0% work from home (2000); Travel time to work: 45.8% less than 15 minutes, 38.9% 15 to 30 minutes, 7.6% 30 to 45 minutes, 4.9% 45 to 60 minutes, 2.8% 60 minutes or more (2000)

GORTON (township). Covers a land area of 34.650 square miles and a water area of 0 square miles. Located at 45.88° N. Lat.; 96.20° W. Long.
Population: 64 (2000); Race: 96.6% White, 0.0% Black, 0.0% Asian, 0.0% American Indian and Alaska Native, 0.0% Hispanic of any race, 3.4% two or more races (2000); Density: 1.8 persons per square mile (2000); Age: 20.7% under 18, 24.1% over 64 (2000); Marriage status: 0.0% never married, 76.1% now married, 10.9% widowed, 13.0% divorced (2000); Foreign born: 0.0% (2000); Ancestry (includes multiple ancestries): 51.7% German, 24.1% Norwegian, 19.0% Swedish, 12.1% Irish, 3.4% English (2000).
Economy: Employment by occupation: 36.7% management, 10.0% professional, 13.3% services, 23.3% sales, 0.0% farming, 6.7% construction, 10.0% production (2000).
Income: Per capita income: $19,357 (2000); Median household income: $43,000 (2000); Poverty rate: 19.0% (2000).
Taxes: Total city taxes per capita: $213 (1997); City property taxes per capita: $213 (1997).
Education: High school graduation rate: 93.5% (2000); College graduation rate: 17.4% (2000).
Housing: Homeownership rate: 100.0% (2000); Median home value: $46,800 (2000); Median age of housing: 60+ years (2000).
Transportation: Commute to work: 86.7% car, 0.0% public transportation, 0.0% walk, 13.3% work from home (2000); Travel time to work: 38.5% less than 15 minutes, 30.8% 15 to 30 minutes, 30.8% 30 to 45 minutes, 0.0% 45 to 60 minutes, 0.0% 60 minutes or more (2000)

HERMAN (city). Covers a land area of 1.034 square miles and a water area of 0 square miles. Located at 45.80° N. Lat.; 96.14° W. Long. Elevation is 1,073 feet.
Population: 452 (2000); Race: 98.7% White, 0.0% Black, 1.3% Asian, 0.0% American Indian and Alaska Native, 0.0% Hispanic of any race, 0.0% two or more races (2000); Density: 437.2 persons per square mile (2000); Age: 20.4% under 18, 29.6% over 64 (2000); Marriage status: 20.5% never married, 57.3% now married, 12.4% widowed, 9.8% divorced (2000); Foreign born: 1.8% (2000); Ancestry (includes multiple ancestries): 46.1% German, 26.8% Norwegian, 11.8% Irish, 8.3% Swedish, 4.8% United States or American (2000).
Economy: Grain; livestock, poultry; dairying. Manufacturing: wire harnesses; light manufacturing. Single-family building permits issued: 1 (2001) / 0 (2000); Multi-family building permits issued: 0 (2001) / 0 (2000); Employment by occupation: 6.5% management, 27.0% professional, 12.0% services, 25.0% sales, 3.0% farming, 10.0% construction, 16.5% production (2000).
Income: Per capita income: $17,475 (2000); Median household income: $31,429 (2000); Poverty rate: 8.6% (2000).
Taxes: Total city taxes per capita: $86 (1997); City property taxes per capita: $86 (1997).

Education: High school graduation rate: 77.4% (2000); College graduation rate: 18.7% (2000).

School District(s)

Herman-Norcross (PK-12)
2000 Enrollment: 149 320-677-2291

Housing: Homeownership rate: 85.0% (2000); Median home value: $40,000 (2000); Median rent: $232 per month (2000); Median age of housing: 45 years (2000).

Newspapers: The Herman Review (1 x week)

Transportation: Commute to work: 87.4% car, 0.0% public transportation, 9.6% walk, 3.0% work from home (2000); Travel time to work: 39.6% less than 15 minutes, 27.1% 15 to 30 minutes, 20.3% 30 to 45 minutes, 8.3% 45 to 60 minutes, 4.7% 60 minutes or more (2000)

HOFFMAN (city). Covers a land area of 2.100 square miles and a water area of 0 square miles. Located at 45.83° N. Lat.; 95.78° W. Long. Elevation is 1,254 feet.

Population: 672 (2000); Race: 99.5% White, 0.0% Black, 0.0% Asian, 0.0% American Indian and Alaska Native, 0.2% Hispanic of any race, 0.5% two or more races (2000); Density: 319.9 persons per square mile (2000); Age: 18.7% under 18, 30.2% over 64 (2000); Marriage status: 20.0% never married, 53.5% now married, 20.4% widowed, 6.1% divorced (2000); Foreign born: 0.3% (2000); Ancestry (includes multiple ancestries): 34.7% German, 34.4% Norwegian, 21.8% Swedish, 8.3% Irish, 5.2% English (2000).

Economy: Agricultural area: grain, sunflowers, sugar beets; livestock, poultry; dairying. Manufacturing: aseptic food products. Single-family building permits issued: 1 (2001) / 3 (2000); Multi-family building permits issued: 0 (2001) / 0 (2000); Employment by occupation: 11.7% management, 14.4% professional, 18.4% services, 23.4% sales, 1.3% farming, 8.4% construction, 22.4% production (2000).

Income: Per capita income: $16,725 (2000); Median household income: $29,464 (2000); Poverty rate: 10.6% (2000).

Taxes: Total city taxes per capita: $55 (1997); City property taxes per capita: $54 (1997).

Education: High school graduation rate: 71.1% (2000); College graduation rate: 11.9% (2000).

Housing: Homeownership rate: 73.1% (2000); Median home value: $47,300 (2000); Median rent: $286 per month (2000); Median age of housing: 50 years (2000).

Newspapers: Hoffman Tribune (1 x week)

Transportation: Commute to work: 86.1% car, 0.0% public transportation, 9.8% walk, 3.4% work from home (2000); Travel time to work: 51.7% less than 15 minutes, 28.3% 15 to 30 minutes, 13.3% 30 to 45 minutes, 1.0% 45 to 60 minutes, 5.6% 60 minutes or more (2000)

LAND (township). Covers a land area of 33.559 square miles and a water area of 0.311 square miles. Located at 45.79° N. Lat.; 95.81° W. Long.

Population: 244 (2000); Race: 100.0% White, 0.0% Black, 0.0% Asian, 0.0% American Indian and Alaska Native, 0.0% Hispanic of any race, 0.0% two or more races (2000); Density: 7.3 persons per square mile (2000); Age: 34.1% under 18, 11.0% over 64 (2000); Marriage status: 26.1% never married, 68.1% now married, 1.1% widowed, 4.8% divorced (2000); Foreign born: 0.0% (2000); Ancestry (includes multiple ancestries): 48.5% German, 46.6% Norwegian, 22.3% Swedish, 6.1% Irish, 5.7% French (except Basque) (2000).

Economy: Employment by occupation: 18.4% management, 18.4% professional, 12.8% services, 16.0% sales, 5.6% farming, 8.0% construction, 20.8% production (2000).

Income: Per capita income: $14,788 (2000); Median household income: $43,750 (2000); Poverty rate: 7.6% (2000).

Taxes: Total city taxes per capita: $68 (1997); City property taxes per capita: $68 (1997).

Education: High school graduation rate: 91.2% (2000); College graduation rate: 17.6% (2000).

Housing: Homeownership rate: 91.1% (2000); Median home value: $98,300 (2000); Median rent: $275 per month (2000); Median age of housing: 40 years (2000).

Transportation: Commute to work: 83.7% car, 0.0% public transportation, 3.3% walk, 13.0% work from home (2000); Travel time to work: 42.1% less than 15 minutes, 34.6% 15 to 30 minutes, 13.1% 30 to 45 minutes, 3.7% 45 to 60 minutes, 6.5% 60 minutes or more (2000)

LAWRENCE (township). Covers a land area of 35.062 square miles and a water area of 0.775 square miles. Located at 46.05° N. Lat.; 96.21° W. Long.

Population: 96 (2000); Race: 89.3% White, 0.0% Black, 0.0% Asian, 0.0% American Indian and Alaska Native, 0.0% Hispanic of any race, 10.7% two or more races (2000); Density: 2.7 persons per square mile (2000); Age: 25.9% under 18, 14.3% over 64 (2000); Marriage status: 24.2% never married, 68.1% now married, 7.7% widowed, 0.0% divorced (2000); Foreign born: 0.0% (2000); Ancestry (includes multiple ancestries): 56.3% Norwegian, 52.7% German, 10.7% Other groups, 6.3% English, 4.5% Swedish (2000).

Economy: Single-family building permits issued: 0 (2001) / 0 (2000); Multi-family building permits issued: 0 (2001) / 0 (2000); Employment by occupation: 36.5% management, 3.2% professional, 3.2% services, 22.2% sales, 11.1% farming, 3.2% construction, 20.6% production (2000).

Income: Per capita income: $26,071 (2000); Median household income: $47,500 (2000); Poverty rate: 2.7% (2000).

Taxes: Total city taxes per capita: $156 (1997); City property taxes per capita: $156 (1997).

Education: High school graduation rate: 90.8% (2000); College graduation rate: 18.4% (2000).

Housing: Homeownership rate: 95.5% (2000); Median home value: $63,300 (2000); Median age of housing: 60 years (2000).

Transportation: Commute to work: 55.6% car, 1.6% public transportation, 19.0% walk, 23.8% work from home (2000); Travel time to work: 56.3% less than 15 minutes, 12.5% 15 to 30 minutes, 20.8% 30 to 45 minutes, 10.4% 45 to 60 minutes, 0.0% 60 minutes or more (2000)

LIEN (township). Covers a land area of 32.149 square miles and a water area of 2.200 square miles. Located at 45.90° N. Lat.; 95.92° W. Long.

Population: 117 (2000); Race: 100.0% White, 0.0% Black, 0.0% Asian, 0.0% American Indian and Alaska Native, 0.0% Hispanic of any race, 0.0% two or more races (2000); Density: 3.6 persons per square mile (2000); Age: 29.1% under 18, 10.6% over 64 (2000); Marriage status: 18.6% never married, 76.3% now married, 5.1% widowed, 0.0% divorced (2000); Foreign born: 0.0% (2000); Ancestry (includes multiple ancestries): 52.3% Norwegian, 34.4% German, 13.2% Swedish, 7.9% English, 6.0% Irish (2000).

Economy: Employment by occupation: 34.5% management, 3.4% professional, 10.3% services, 13.8% sales, 4.6% farming, 14.9% construction, 18.4% production (2000).

Income: Per capita income: $17,580 (2000); Median household income: $38,750 (2000); Poverty rate: 14.6% (2000).

Taxes: Total city taxes per capita: $61 (1997); City property taxes per capita: $61 (1997).

Education: High school graduation rate: 94.1% (2000); College graduation rate: 14.9% (2000).

Housing: Homeownership rate: 92.7% (2000); Median home value: $68,300 (2000); Median age of housing: 54 years (2000).

Transportation: Commute to work: 63.7% car, 0.0% public transportation, 5.0% walk, 26.3% work from home (2000); Travel time to work: 72.9% less than 15 minutes, 18.6% 15 to 30 minutes, 5.1% 30 to 45 minutes, 3.4% 45 to 60 minutes, 0.0% 60 minutes or more (2000)

LOGAN (township). Covers a land area of 34.791 square miles and a water area of 0.115 square miles. Located at 45.79° N. Lat.; 96.18° W. Long.

Population: 115 (2000); Race: 100.0% White, 0.0% Black, 0.0% Asian, 0.0% American Indian and Alaska Native, 0.0% Hispanic of any race, 0.0% two or more races (2000); Density: 3.3 persons per square mile (2000); Age: 21.2% under 18, 14.4% over 64 (2000); Marriage status: 24.1% never married, 59.8% now married, 11.5% widowed, 4.6% divorced (2000); Foreign born: 0.0% (2000); Ancestry (includes multiple ancestries): 59.6% German, 17.3% Norwegian, 13.5% Swedish, 10.6% United States or American, 9.6% Dutch (2000).

Economy: Employment by occupation: 17.5% management, 7.5% professional, 7.5% services, 40.0% sales, 12.5% farming, 5.0% construction, 10.0% production (2000).

Income: Per capita income: $16,284 (2000); Median household income: $27,083 (2000); Poverty rate: 6.7% (2000).

Taxes: Total city taxes per capita: $120 (1997); City property taxes per capita: $120 (1997).

Education: High school graduation rate: 97.1% (2000); College graduation rate: 4.3% (2000).

Housing: Homeownership rate: 86.0% (2000); Median home value: $43,300 (2000); Median rent: $275 per month (2000); Median age of housing: 59 years (2000).

Transportation: Commute to work: 50.0% car, 0.0% public transportation, 10.0% walk, 40.0% work from home (2000); Travel time to work: 58.3% less

than 15 minutes, 8.3% 15 to 30 minutes, 25.0% 30 to 45 minutes, 0.0% 45 to 60 minutes, 8.3% 60 minutes or more (2000)

MACSVILLE (township). Covers a land area of 32.353 square miles and a water area of 3.816 square miles. Located at 45.80° N. Lat.; 96.06° W. Long.
Population: 128 (2000); Race: 100.0% White, 0.0% Black, 0.0% Asian, 0.0% American Indian and Alaska Native, 0.0% Hispanic of any race, 0.0% two or more races (2000); Density: 4.0 persons per square mile (2000); Age: 30.7% under 18, 10.9% over 64 (2000); Marriage status: 21.9% never married, 64.8% now married, 5.7% widowed, 7.6% divorced (2000); Foreign born: 0.0% (2000); Ancestry (includes multiple ancestries): 53.3% German, 27.7% Norwegian, 16.1% Swedish, 7.3% Danish, 5.8% English (2000).
Economy: Employment by occupation: 25.3% management, 11.0% professional, 14.3% services, 24.2% sales, 8.8% farming, 5.5% construction, 11.0% production (2000).
Income: Per capita income: $16,781 (2000); Median household income: $30,833 (2000); Poverty rate: 1.5% (2000).
Taxes: Total city taxes per capita: $87 (1997); City property taxes per capita: $87 (1997).
Education: High school graduation rate: 93.5% (2000); College graduation rate: 14.1% (2000).
Housing: Homeownership rate: 88.5% (2000); Median home value: $38,800 (2000); Median age of housing: 60+ years (2000).
Transportation: Commute to work: 64.8% car, 0.0% public transportation, 2.2% walk, 30.8% work from home (2000); Travel time to work: 44.4% less than 15 minutes, 31.7% 15 to 30 minutes, 17.5% 30 to 45 minutes, 0.0% 45 to 60 minutes, 6.3% 60 minutes or more (2000)

NORCROSS (city). Covers a land area of 1.566 square miles and a water area of 0 square miles. Located at 45.86° N. Lat.; 96.19° W. Long. Elevation is 1,041 feet.
Population: 59 (2000); Race: 100.0% White, 0.0% Black, 0.0% Asian, 0.0% American Indian and Alaska Native, 0.0% Hispanic of any race, 0.0% two or more races (2000); Density: 37.7 persons per square mile (2000); Age: 17.2% under 18, 34.5% over 64 (2000); Marriage status: 14.0% never married, 52.0% now married, 16.0% widowed, 18.0% divorced (2000); Foreign born: 0.0% (2000); Ancestry (includes multiple ancestries): 53.4% Norwegian, 31.0% Swedish, 22.4% German, 10.3% French (except Basque), 5.2% Danish (2000).
Economy: Dairying; grain. Employment by occupation: 28.6% management, 9.5% professional, 33.3% services, 19.0% sales, 0.0% farming, 9.5% construction, 0.0% production (2000).
Income: Per capita income: $14,507 (2000); Median household income: $11,875 (2000); Poverty rate: 24.1% (2000).
Taxes: Total city taxes per capita: $181 (1997); City property taxes per capita: $181 (1997).
Education: High school graduation rate: 77.8% (2000); College graduation rate: 6.7% (2000).
Housing: Homeownership rate: 87.1% (2000); Median home value: $14,500 (2000); Median rent: $225 per month (2000); Median age of housing: 57 years (2000).
Transportation: Commute to work: 100.0% car, 0.0% public transportation, 0.0% walk, 0.0% work from home (2000); Travel time to work: 47.6% less than 15 minutes, 23.8% 15 to 30 minutes, 28.6% 30 to 45 minutes, 0.0% 45 to 60 minutes, 0.0% 60 minutes or more (2000)

NORTH OTTAWA (township). Covers a land area of 35.760 square miles and a water area of 0 square miles. Located at 45.97° N. Lat.; 96.21° W. Long.
Population: 69 (2000); Race: 100.0% White, 0.0% Black, 0.0% Asian, 0.0% American Indian and Alaska Native, 0.0% Hispanic of any race, 0.0% two or more races (2000); Density: 1.9 persons per square mile (2000); Age: 35.5% under 18, 5.3% over 64 (2000); Marriage status: 7.5% never married, 81.1% now married, 0.0% widowed, 11.3% divorced (2000); Foreign born: 2.6% (2000); Ancestry (includes multiple ancestries): 51.3% German, 32.9% Norwegian, 11.8% Yugoslavian, 11.8% Swedish, 6.6% Italian (2000).
Economy: Employment by occupation: 44.7% management, 5.3% professional, 7.9% services, 31.6% sales, 0.0% farming, 5.3% construction, 5.3% production (2000).
Income: Per capita income: $19,451 (2000); Median household income: $36,875 (2000); Poverty rate: 18.9% (2000).
Taxes: Total city taxes per capita: $209 (1997); City property taxes per capita: $209 (1997).
Education: High school graduation rate: 91.3% (2000); College graduation rate: 26.1% (2000).
Housing: Homeownership rate: 100.0% (2000); Median home value: $96,300 (2000); Median age of housing: 37 years (2000).
Transportation: Commute to work: 68.4% car, 0.0% public transportation, 0.0% walk, 31.6% work from home (2000); Travel time to work: 42.3% less than 15 minutes, 30.8% 15 to 30 minutes, 26.9% 30 to 45 minutes, 0.0% 45 to 60 minutes, 0.0% 60 minutes or more (2000)

PELICAN LAKE (township). Covers a land area of 27.163 square miles and a water area of 8.225 square miles. Located at 46.06° N. Lat.; 95.82° W. Long.
Population: 425 (2000); Race: 100.0% White, 0.0% Black, 0.0% Asian, 0.0% American Indian and Alaska Native, 0.0% Hispanic of any race, 0.0% two or more races (2000); Density: 15.6 persons per square mile (2000); Age: 20.3% under 18, 18.5% over 64 (2000); Marriage status: 15.8% never married, 70.8% now married, 4.1% widowed, 9.3% divorced (2000); Foreign born: 0.5% (2000); Ancestry (includes multiple ancestries): 56.1% Norwegian, 24.9% German, 11.8% Swedish, 6.0% Dutch, 5.1% Irish (2000).
Economy: Employment by occupation: 15.0% management, 10.9% professional, 15.9% services, 33.6% sales, 1.8% farming, 11.4% construction, 11.4% production (2000).
Income: Per capita income: $18,329 (2000); Median household income: $36,667 (2000); Poverty rate: 7.0% (2000).
Taxes: Total city taxes per capita: $105 (1997); City property taxes per capita: $105 (1997).
Education: High school graduation rate: 86.2% (2000); College graduation rate: 15.3% (2000).
Housing: Homeownership rate: 89.9% (2000); Median home value: $90,000 (2000); Median rent: $275 per month (2000); Median age of housing: 30 years (2000).
Transportation: Commute to work: 94.4% car, 0.0% public transportation, 3.3% walk, 2.3% work from home (2000); Travel time to work: 44.5% less than 15 minutes, 27.3% 15 to 30 minutes, 20.6% 30 to 45 minutes, 1.4% 45 to 60 minutes, 6.2% 60 minutes or more (2000)

POMME DE TERRE (township). Covers a land area of 34.076 square miles and a water area of 1.810 square miles. Located at 46.07° N. Lat.; 95.94° W. Long.
Population: 165 (2000); Race: 100.0% White, 0.0% Black, 0.0% Asian, 0.0% American Indian and Alaska Native, 0.0% Hispanic of any race, 0.0% two or more races (2000); Density: 4.8 persons per square mile (2000); Age: 28.3% under 18, 15.9% over 64 (2000); Marriage status: 22.7% never married, 72.7% now married, 3.6% widowed, 0.9% divorced (2000); Foreign born: 0.0% (2000); Ancestry (includes multiple ancestries): 53.1% Norwegian, 49.7% German, 9.0% Danish, 8.3% Swedish, 8.3% Irish (2000).
Economy: Employment by occupation: 28.6% management, 14.3% professional, 10.0% services, 22.9% sales, 7.1% farming, 17.1% construction, 0.0% production (2000).
Income: Per capita income: $20,792 (2000); Median household income: $39,063 (2000); Poverty rate: 11.7% (2000).
Taxes: Total city taxes per capita: $76 (1997); City property taxes per capita: $76 (1997).
Education: High school graduation rate: 87.6% (2000); College graduation rate: 13.4% (2000).
Housing: Homeownership rate: 94.4% (2000); Median home value: $85,000 (2000); Median age of housing: 45 years (2000).
Transportation: Commute to work: 77.1% car, 0.0% public transportation, 0.0% walk, 22.9% work from home (2000); Travel time to work: 63.0% less than 15 minutes, 22.2% 15 to 30 minutes, 7.4% 30 to 45 minutes, 3.7% 45 to 60 minutes, 3.7% 60 minutes or more (2000)

ROSEVILLE (township). Covers a land area of 35.254 square miles and a water area of 0.678 square miles. Located at 45.79° N. Lat.; 95.95° W. Long.
Population: 154 (2000); Race: 100.0% White, 0.0% Black, 0.0% Asian, 0.0% American Indian and Alaska Native, 0.0% Hispanic of any race, 0.0% two or more races (2000); Density: 4.4 persons per square mile (2000); Age: 29.0% under 18, 8.4% over 64 (2000); Marriage status: 18.3% never married, 68.3% now married, 2.5% widowed, 10.8% divorced (2000); Foreign born: 0.0% (2000); Ancestry (includes multiple ancestries): 63.2% German, 32.3% Norwegian, 14.2% English, 13.5% Swedish, 3.9% Polish (2000).
Economy: Unemployment rate: 2.4% (11/2002); Total civilian labor force: 21,981 (11/2002); Employment by occupation: 49.5% management, 9.9% professional, 6.6% services, 9.9% sales, 5.5% farming, 2.2% construction, 16.5% production (2000).
Income: Per capita income: $17,117 (2000); Median household income: $42,679 (2000); Poverty rate: 9.7% (2000).

Education: High school graduation rate: 91.2% (2000); College graduation rate: 14.7% (2000).
Housing: Homeownership rate: 92.6% (2000); Median home value: $70,000 (2000); Median rent: $175 per month (2000); Median age of housing: 60+ years (2000).
Transportation: Commute to work: 63.7% car, 0.0% public transportation, 2.2% walk, 34.1% work from home (2000); Travel time to work: 36.7% less than 15 minutes, 51.7% 15 to 30 minutes, 5.0% 30 to 45 minutes, 3.3% 45 to 60 minutes, 3.3% 60 minutes or more (2000)

SANFORD (township). Covers a land area of 32.132 square miles and a water area of 2.020 square miles. Located at 45.98° N. Lat.; 95.94° W. Long.
Population: 169 (2000); Race: 98.7% White, 0.0% Black, 0.0% Asian, 0.0% American Indian and Alaska Native, 1.3% Hispanic of any race, 0.0% two or more races (2000); Density: 5.3 persons per square mile (2000); Age: 22.4% under 18, 15.1% over 64 (2000); Marriage status: 20.8% never married, 77.7% now married, 1.5% widowed, 0.0% divorced (2000); Foreign born: 1.3% (2000); Ancestry (includes multiple ancestries): 49.3% Norwegian, 36.2% German, 19.1% Swedish, 4.6% Scotch-Irish, 3.9% Danish (2000).
Economy: Employment by occupation: 28.7% management, 11.9% professional, 16.8% services, 20.8% sales, 0.0% farming, 9.9% construction, 11.9% production (2000).
Income: Per capita income: $22,169 (2000); Median household income: $45,417 (2000); Poverty rate: 0.0% (2000).
Taxes: Total city taxes per capita: $103 (1997); City property taxes per capita: $103 (1997).
Education: High school graduation rate: 90.2% (2000); College graduation rate: 23.2% (2000).
Housing: Homeownership rate: 94.9% (2000); Median home value: $77,500 (2000); Median rent: $175 per month (2000); Median age of housing: 49 years (2000).
Transportation: Commute to work: 67.3% car, 0.0% public transportation, 2.0% walk, 30.7% work from home (2000); Travel time to work: 61.4% less than 15 minutes, 22.9% 15 to 30 minutes, 12.9% 30 to 45 minutes, 2.9% 45 to 60 minutes, 0.0% 60 minutes or more (2000)

STONY BROOK (township). Covers a land area of 32.844 square miles and a water area of 1.840 square miles. Located at 46.06° N. Lat.; 96.08° W. Long.
Population: 164 (2000); Race: 100.0% White, 0.0% Black, 0.0% Asian, 0.0% American Indian and Alaska Native, 0.0% Hispanic of any race, 0.0% two or more races (2000); Density: 5.0 persons per square mile (2000); Age: 31.1% under 18, 16.8% over 64 (2000); Marriage status: 23.2% never married, 64.0% now married, 2.4% widowed, 10.4% divorced (2000); Foreign born: 0.0% (2000); Ancestry (includes multiple ancestries): 60.2% Norwegian, 52.8% German, 8.7% Swedish, 4.3% Danish, 3.1% Czech (2000).
Economy: Employment by occupation: 22.7% management, 8.0% professional, 10.7% services, 29.3% sales, 5.3% farming, 12.0% construction, 12.0% production (2000).
Income: Per capita income: $23,490 (2000); Median household income: $42,500 (2000); Poverty rate: 6.8% (2000).
Taxes: Total city taxes per capita: $108 (1997); City property taxes per capita: $108 (1997).
Education: High school graduation rate: 84.1% (2000); College graduation rate: 11.2% (2000).
Housing: Homeownership rate: 91.7% (2000); Median home value: $80,000 (2000); Median rent: $288 per month (2000); Median age of housing: 60+ years (2000).
Transportation: Commute to work: 85.3% car, 0.0% public transportation, 2.7% walk, 12.0% work from home (2000); Travel time to work: 37.9% less than 15 minutes, 43.9% 15 to 30 minutes, 12.1% 30 to 45 minutes, 3.0% 45 to 60 minutes, 3.0% 60 minutes or more (2000)

WENDELL (city). Covers a land area of 1.052 square miles and a water area of 0 square miles. Located at 46.03° N. Lat.; 96.09° W. Long. Elevation is 1,148 feet.
Population: 177 (2000); Race: 100.0% White, 0.0% Black, 0.0% Asian, 0.0% American Indian and Alaska Native, 0.0% Hispanic of any race, 0.0% two or more races (2000); Density: 168.3 persons per square mile (2000); Age: 21.9% under 18, 24.0% over 64 (2000); Marriage status: 20.5% never married, 66.0% now married, 7.7% widowed, 5.8% divorced (2000); Foreign born: 0.0% (2000); Ancestry (includes multiple ancestries): 55.2% Norwegian, 22.9% German, 7.8% Scandinavian, 6.8% Irish, 4.2% Swedish (2000).
Economy: Grain; dairying; poultry. Single-family building permits issued: 0 (2001) / 1 (2000); Multi-family building permits issued: 0 (2001) / 0 (2000); Employment by occupation: 7.2% management, 11.3% professional, 12.4% services, 27.8% sales, 5.2% farming, 13.4% construction, 22.7% production (2000).
Income: Per capita income: $16,413 (2000); Median household income: $35,625 (2000); Poverty rate: 2.6% (2000).
Taxes: Total city taxes per capita: $183 (1997); City property taxes per capita: $183 (1997).
Education: High school graduation rate: 83.6% (2000); College graduation rate: 8.6% (2000).
Housing: Homeownership rate: 97.5% (2000); Median home value: $27,500 (2000); Median rent: $325 per month (2000); Median age of housing: 60+ years (2000).
Transportation: Commute to work: 95.9% car, 0.0% public transportation, 4.1% walk, 0.0% work from home (2000); Travel time to work: 46.4% less than 15 minutes, 37.1% 15 to 30 minutes, 4.1% 30 to 45 minutes, 6.2% 45 to 60 minutes, 6.2% 60 minutes or more (2000)

Hennepin County

Located in eastern Minnesota; bounded on the northeast by the Mississippi River, on the northwest by the Crow River, and on the southeast by the Minnesota River; includes Lake Minnetonka in the southwest. Covers a land area of 556.60 square miles, a water area of 49.80 square miles, and is located in the Central Time Zone. The county government was organized in 1852. County seat is Minneapolis.

Hennepin County is part of the Minneapolis-St. Paul, MN-WI MSA. The entire metro area includes: Anoka County, MN; Carver County, MN; Chisago County, MN; Dakota County, MN; Hennepin County, MN; Isanti County, MN; Ramsey County, MN; Scott County, MN; Sherburne County, MN; Washington County, MN; Wright County, MN; Pierce County, WI; St. Croix County, WI

Weather Station: Minneapolis-St Paul Int'l Arpt. Elevation: 833 feet

	Jan	Feb	Mar	Apr	May	Jun	Jul	Aug	Sep	Oct	Nov	Dec
High	21	28	40	57	70	79	83	80	71	58	40	27
Low	4	11	23	36	48	58	63	61	51	39	25	11
Precip	1.0	0.8	1.9	2.4	3.3	4.2	4.0	4.0	2.7	2.2	2.0	1.0
Snow	13.2	7.9	10.6	3.2	tr	tr	tr	tr	tr	0.6	9.9	9.7

High and Low temperatures in degrees Fahrenheit; Precipitation and Snow in inches

Population: 1,116,200 (2000); Race: 80.6% White, 8.8% Black, 4.8% Asian, 1.0% American Indian and Alaska Native, 4.1% Hispanic of any race, 2.8% two or more races (2000); Density: 2,005.3 persons per square mile (2000); Age: 23.9% under 18, 10.9% over 64 (2000).
Religion: Five largest groups: 23.3% Catholic Church, 13.6% Evangelical Lutheran Church in America, 2.8% Jewish estimate, 2.1% The United Methodist Church, 2.0% Lutheran Church—Missouri Synod (2000).
Economy: Unemployment rate: 3.5% (11/2002); Total civilian labor force: 690,077 (11/2002); Leading industries: 11.7% manufacturing; 10.7% health care and social assistance; 9.9% administration, support, waste management, remediation services (2000); Companies that employ more than 1,000 persons: 63 (2000); Companies that employ more than 100 persons: 1,529 (2000); Farms: 574 totaling 69,128 acres (1997); Minority business ownership rate: 5.4% (1997); Women business ownership rate: 27.8% (1997); Retail sales per capita: $13,856 (1997). Single-family building permits issued: 2,730 (2001) / 2,706 (2000); Multi-family building permits issued: 1,856 (2001) / 2,218 (2000).
Income: Per capita income: $28,789 (2000); Median household income: $51,711 (2000); Poverty rate: 8.3% (2000); Bankruptcy rate: 4.04% (2001).
Taxes: Total county taxes per capita: $377 (2000); County property taxes per capita: $373 (2000).
Education: High school graduation rate: 90.6% (2000); College graduation rate: 39.1% (2000).
Housing: Homeownership rate: 66.2% (2000); Median home value: $143,400 (2000); Median rent: $615 per month (2000); Median age of housing: 36 years (2000).
Health: Birth rate: 140.4 per 10,000 population (1998); Age adjusted death rate: 80.6 per 10,000 population (1999); Infant mortality rate: 6.4 per 1,000 live births (1998); Age adjusted cancer mortality rate: 204.5 deaths per 100,000 population (1999). Air Quality Index: 97% good, 3% moderate, 0% unhealthy (percent of days in 2000). Number of physicians: 39.0 per 10,000 population (1999); Number of hospital beds: 33.3 per 10,000 population (1999).

Elections: 2000 Presidential election results: 53.6% Gore, 39.3% Bush, 6.2% Nader, 0.4% Buchanan
National and State Parks: Fort Snelling State Park; Minnesota Valley National Wildlife Refuge; Schmidt State Wildlife Management Area
Additional Information Contacts
Hennepin County Government Offices 612-348-3000
American Israel Chamber of Commerce 763-593-8666
Bloomington Chamber of Commerce 952-888-8818
Bloomington Convention Bureau.................. 952-858-8500
Brooklyn Center Chamber of Commerce.................. 763-566-8650
Eden Prairie Chamber of Commerce 952-947-0236
Edina Chamber of Commerce 952-806-9060
Excelsior Chamber of Commerce 952-474-6461
Greater Minneapolis Convention & Visitors Bureau.................. 612-661-4700
Lake Minnetonka Area Chamber.................. 763-471-0768
Minneapolis Area Association of Realtors.................. 952-933-9020
Minneapolis Chamber of Commerce 612-338-7750
Minnesota Association of Realtors.................. 952-935-8313
Minnesota Commercial Association of Realtors 952-908-1780
Minnetonka Chamber of Commerce 763-540-0234
North Hennepin Chamber 763-424-6744
North Metro Minneapolis Convention & Visitors Bureau..... 763-566-7722
Northwest Suburban Chamber of Commerce 763-420-3242
Richfield Chamber of Commerce.................. 612-866-5100
Rogers Chamber of Commerce 763-428-2921
U.S. Chamber of Commerce 952-832-9151
Wayzata Chamber of Commerce 763-473-9595

Hennepin County Communities

BLOOMINGTON (city). Covers a land area of 35.481 square miles and a water area of 2.889 square miles. Located at 44.83° N. Lat.; 93.31° W. Long. Elevation is 835 feet.
History: Fort Snelling National Cemetery to northeast. Incorporated 1953.
Population: 85,172 (2000); Race: 87.6% White, 3.6% Black, 5.0% Asian, 0.5% American Indian and Alaska Native, 2.6% Hispanic of any race, 1.9% two or more races (2000); Density: 2,400.5 persons per square mile (2000); Age: 20.5% under 18, 15.8% over 64 (2000); Marriage status: 26.8% never married, 57.3% now married, 6.5% widowed, 9.4% divorced (2000); Foreign born: 7.7% (2000); Ancestry (includes multiple ancestries): 32.4% German, 18.3% Norwegian, 12.9% Irish, 12.2% Swedish, 11.7% Other groups (2000).
Vital Statistics: Birth rate: 100.9 per 10,000 population (1998)
Economy: Railroad junction. Manufacturing includes machinery, bakery and dairy products, signs, medical products, fiberglass tanks, computer software, electronic equipment, coin meters, fabricated metal products, trailer hitches, lawn and garden equipment. Bloomington Art Center and the Mall of America are here. Unemployment rate: 3.1% (11/2002); Total civilian labor force: 60,174 (11/2002); Single-family building permits issued: 2 (2001) / 13 (2000); Multi-family building permits issued: 2 (2001) / 41 (2000); Employment by occupation: 19.1% management, 21.9% professional, 10.1% services, 32.0% sales, 0.1% farming, 6.4% construction, 10.4% production (2000).
Income: Per capita income: $29,782 (2000); Median household income: $54,628 (2000); Poverty rate: 4.0% (2000).
Taxes: Total city taxes per capita: $618 (2000); City property taxes per capita: $493 (2000).
Education: High school graduation rate: 92.2% (2000); College graduation rate: 35.4% (2000).

School District(s)

Bloomington (PK-12)
2000 Enrollment: 10,833 952-885-8450
Metropolitan Learning Alliance (11-12)
2000 Enrollment: 73 952-858-9170

Four-year College(s)

Bethany College of Missions (Private, Not-for-profit, Interdenominational)
2001 Enrollment: n/a 612-944-2121
Northwestern Health Sciences University (Private, Not-for-profit)
2001 Enrollment: 825 612-888-4777
2001 Tuition: In-state $8,400; Out-of-state $8,400
Minnesota Institute Acupuncture and Herbal Studies (Private, Not-for-profit)
2001 Enrollment: n/a 612-885-5435
National American University (Private, For-profit)
2001 Enrollment: 290 605-721-5225
2001 Tuition: In-state $11,520; Out-of-state $11,520

Two-year College(s)

Medical Institute of Minnesota (Private, For-profit)
2001 Enrollment: 864 612-844-0064
2001 Tuition: In-state $11,623; Out-of-state $11,623
Normandale Community College (Public)
2001 Enrollment: 7,504 952-487-8400
2001 Tuition: In-state $2,513; Out-of-state $5,025
Krs Computer and Business School (Private, For-profit)
2001 Enrollment: 303 952-835-1410
Housing: Homeownership rate: 70.7% (2000); Median home value: $147,000 (2000); Median rent: $718 per month (2000); Median age of housing: 31 years (2000).
Safety: Violent crime rate: 23.8 per 10,000 population; Property crime rate: 524.8 per 10,000 population (2001).
Newspapers: West Saint Paul/Mendota Heights Sun-Current (1 x week); Bloomington Sun-Current (1 x week); Richfield Sun-Current (1 x week); Edina Sun-Current (1 x week)
Transportation: Commute to work: 91.4% car, 2.9% public transportation, 1.5% walk, 3.4% work from home (2000); Travel time to work: 30.9% less than 15 minutes, 46.5% 15 to 30 minutes, 17.5% 30 to 45 minutes, 3.2% 45 to 60 minutes, 1.8% 60 minutes or more (2000)
Additional Information Contacts
Bloomington Chamber of Commerce 952-888-8818
Bloomington Convention Bureau.................. 952-858-8500
U.S. Chamber of Commerce 952-832-9151

BROOKLYN CENTER (city). Covers a land area of 7.944 square miles and a water area of 0.398 square miles. Located at 45.06° N. Lat.; 93.31° W. Long. Elevation is 860 feet.
History: Incorporated 1911.
Population: 29,172 (2000); Race: 72.2% White, 13.8% Black, 9.0% Asian, 0.4% American Indian and Alaska Native, 3.4% Hispanic of any race, 3.2% two or more races (2000); Density: 3,672.0 persons per square mile (2000); Age: 24.9% under 18, 15.5% over 64 (2000); Marriage status: 30.3% never married, 52.8% now married, 7.4% widowed, 9.5% divorced (2000); Foreign born: 11.3% (2000); Ancestry (includes multiple ancestries): 27.6% German, 22.8% Other groups, 13.8% Norwegian, 10.1% Irish, 10.0% Swedish (2000).
Vital Statistics: Birth rate: 128.2 per 10,000 population (1998)
Economy: Area has been marked by suburban and economic growth since the 1970s. Manufacturing: grinding wheels, custom banners, electrical equipment, construction materials, laboratory equipment, batteries, apparel, printing, packaging. Unemployment rate: 4.0% (11/2002); Total civilian labor force: 17,263 (11/2002); Single-family building permits issued: 2 (2001) / 3 (2000); Multi-family building permits issued: 0 (2001) / 0 (2000); Employment by occupation: 11.5% management, 16.4% professional, 13.7% services, 30.8% sales, 0.3% farming, 8.9% construction, 18.4% production (2000).
Income: Per capita income: $19,695 (2000); Median household income: $44,570 (2000); Poverty rate: 7.4% (2000).
Taxes: Total city taxes per capita: $419 (2000); City property taxes per capita: $365 (2000).
Education: High school graduation rate: 86.9% (2000); College graduation rate: 16.7% (2000).

School District(s)

Brooklyn Center (PK-12)
2000 Enrollment: 1,682 763-561-2120

Two-year College(s)

Minnesota School of Business-Brooklyn Center (Private, For-profit)
2001 Enrollment: 372 612-566-7777
2001 Tuition: In-state $10,800; Out-of-state $10,800
High Tech Institute (Private, For-profit)
2001 Enrollment: 458 612-560-9700
Housing: Homeownership rate: 68.9% (2000); Median home value: $105,600 (2000); Median rent: $608 per month (2000); Median age of housing: 39 years (2000).
Safety: Violent crime rate: 45.8 per 10,000 population; Property crime rate: 698.3 per 10,000 population (2001).
Transportation: Commute to work: 88.5% car, 5.2% public transportation, 2.1% walk, 2.8% work from home (2000); Travel time to work: 21.9% less than 15 minutes, 50.9% 15 to 30 minutes, 19.5% 30 to 45 minutes, 4.8% 45 to 60 minutes, 2.9% 60 minutes or more (2000)
Additional Information Contacts
Brooklyn Center Chamber of Commerce.................. 763-566-8650
North Metro Minneapolis Convention & Visitors Bureau..... 763-566-7722

BROOKLYN PARK (city). Covers a land area of 26.058 square miles and a water area of 0.487 square miles. Located at 45.10° N. Lat.; 93.34° W. Long. Elevation is 870 feet.
History: Chartered as a city 1969.
Population: 67,388 (2000); Race: 72.0% White, 13.4% Black, 9.2% Asian, 0.7% American Indian and Alaska Native, 2.9% Hispanic of any race, 3.6% two or more races (2000); Density: 2,586.1 persons per square mile (2000); Age: 28.8% under 18, 5.4% over 64 (2000); Marriage status: 30.4% never married, 57.7% now married, 3.1% widowed, 8.8% divorced (2000); Foreign born: 13.3% (2000); Ancestry (includes multiple ancestries): 28.4% German, 21.7% Other groups, 14.4% Norwegian, 10.3% Irish, 9.5% Swedish (2000).
Vital Statistics: Birth rate: 167.1 per 10,000 population (1998)
Economy: Manufacturing includes machinery, wood products, bakers products, fabricated metal products, tools, feeders, medical supplies, pharmaceutical products, printing and publishing. Unemployment rate: 4.0% (11/2002); Total civilian labor force: 43,425 (11/2002); Single-family building permits issued: 272 (2001) / 293 (2000); Multi-family building permits issued: 0 (2001) / 28 (2000); Employment by occupation: 14.9% management, 19.4% professional, 12.4% services, 30.0% sales, 0.0% farming, 7.1% construction, 16.2% production (2000).
Income: Per capita income: $23,199 (2000); Median household income: $56,572 (2000); Poverty rate: 5.1% (2000).
Taxes: Total city taxes per capita: $379 (2000); City property taxes per capita: $349 (2000).
Education: High school graduation rate: 90.5% (2000); College graduation rate: 27.3% (2000).

School District(s)

Aurora Charter School (KG-01)
2000 Enrollment: 53 651-646-3221
Odyssey Charter School (KG-11)
2000 Enrollment: 199 763-971-8200

Two-year College(s)

Hennepin Technical College (Public)
2001 Enrollment: 6,262 612-550-2109
2001 Tuition: In-state $2,496; Out-of-state $4,992
North Hennepin Community College (Public)
2001 Enrollment: 5,544 763-424-0702
2001 Tuition: In-state $2,508; Out-of-state $4,643
Housing: Homeownership rate: 73.2% (2000); Median home value: $131,000 (2000); Median rent: $627 per month (2000); Median age of housing: 23 years (2000).
Safety: Violent crime rate: 43.2 per 10,000 population; Property crime rate: 454.4 per 10,000 population (2001).
Transportation: Commute to work: 91.0% car, 4.5% public transportation, 0.8% walk, 3.1% work from home (2000); Travel time to work: 19.9% less than 15 minutes, 46.4% 15 to 30 minutes, 25.4% 30 to 45 minutes, 5.5% 45 to 60 minutes, 2.8% 60 minutes or more (2000)
Additional Information Contacts
North Hennepin Chamber 763-424-6744

CHAMPLIN (city). Covers a land area of 8.178 square miles and a water area of 0.617 square miles. Located at 45.17° N. Lat.; 93.38° W. Long. Elevation is 860 feet.
Population: 22,193 (2000); Race: 95.1% White, 2.3% Black, 1.6% Asian, 0.1% American Indian and Alaska Native, 0.7% Hispanic of any race, 0.5% two or more races (2000); Density: 2,713.9 persons per square mile (2000); Age: 33.6% under 18, 3.5% over 64 (2000); Marriage status: 23.3% never married, 64.4% now married, 2.6% widowed, 9.7% divorced (2000); Foreign born: 2.6% (2000); Ancestry (includes multiple ancestries): 40.1% German, 19.0% Norwegian, 11.9% Irish, 11.0% Swedish, 7.1% English (2000).
Vital Statistics: Birth rate: 155.9 per 10,000 population (1998)
Economy: Light manufacturing. Single-family building permits issued: 120 (2001) / 147 (2000); Multi-family building permits issued: 28 (2001) / 34 (2000); Employment by occupation: 16.4% management, 19.8% professional, 11.0% services, 28.7% sales, 0.0% farming, 8.6% construction, 15.4% production (2000).
Income: Per capita income: $24,041 (2000); Median household income: $65,831 (2000); Poverty rate: 2.5% (2000).
Taxes: Total city taxes per capita: $166 (1997); City property taxes per capita: $153 (1997).
Education: High school graduation rate: 94.3% (2000); College graduation rate: 26.3% (2000).
Housing: Homeownership rate: 88.9% (2000); Median home value: $137,600 (2000); Median rent: $603 per month (2000); Median age of housing: 16 years (2000).
Safety: Violent crime rate: 8.9 per 10,000 population; Property crime rate: 224.7 per 10,000 population (2001).
Transportation: Commute to work: 92.0% car, 3.8% public transportation, 0.6% walk, 3.1% work from home (2000); Travel time to work: 15.8% less than 15 minutes, 36.3% 15 to 30 minutes, 32.3% 30 to 45 minutes, 10.8% 45 to 60 minutes, 4.8% 60 minutes or more (2000)

CORCORAN (city). Covers a land area of 35.770 square miles and a water area of 0.144 square miles. Located at 45.10° N. Lat.; 93.57° W. Long. Elevation is 978 feet.
Population: 5,630 (2000); Race: 97.3% White, 0.4% Black, 0.6% Asian, 0.3% American Indian and Alaska Native, 1.7% Hispanic of any race, 1.0% two or more races (2000); Density: 157.4 persons per square mile (2000); Age: 33.2% under 18, 4.4% over 64 (2000); Marriage status: 24.8% never married, 66.9% now married, 1.9% widowed, 6.5% divorced (2000); Foreign born: 1.6% (2000); Ancestry (includes multiple ancestries): 40.7% German, 18.9% Norwegian, 11.7% Irish, 11.2% Swedish, 6.9% French (except Basque) (2000).
Economy: Manufacturing: fabricated metal products. Agriculture: dairying; poultry; grain, nursery products. Single-family building permits issued: 32 (2001) / 24 (2000); Multi-family building permits issued: 0 (2001) / 0 (2000); Employment by occupation: 18.0% management, 17.7% professional, 9.9% services, 27.0% sales, 0.9% farming, 13.0% construction, 13.6% production (2000).
Income: Per capita income: $29,467 (2000); Median household income: $78,984 (2000); Poverty rate: 0.9% (2000).
Taxes: Total city taxes per capita: $165 (1997); City property taxes per capita: $150 (1997).
Education: High school graduation rate: 93.8% (2000); College graduation rate: 25.3% (2000).
Housing: Homeownership rate: 96.0% (2000); Median home value: $187,300 (2000); Median rent: $670 per month (2000); Median age of housing: 23 years (2000).
Safety: Violent crime rate: 0.0 per 10,000 population; Property crime rate: 68.5 per 10,000 population (2001).
Transportation: Commute to work: 91.5% car, 0.4% public transportation, 1.9% walk, 5.9% work from home (2000); Travel time to work: 19.3% less than 15 minutes, 37.2% 15 to 30 minutes, 29.8% 30 to 45 minutes, 8.6% 45 to 60 minutes, 5.1% 60 minutes or more (2000)

CRYSTAL (city). Covers a land area of 5.777 square miles and a water area of 0.093 square miles. Located at 45.03° N. Lat.; 93.36° W. Long. Elevation is 877 feet.
Population: 22,698 (2000); Race: 88.5% White, 3.6% Black, 3.2% Asian, 0.8% American Indian and Alaska Native, 2.7% Hispanic of any race, 2.8% two or more races (2000); Density: 3,929.3 persons per square mile (2000); Age: 22.3% under 18, 14.1% over 64 (2000); Marriage status: 28.0% never married, 54.7% now married, 5.8% widowed, 11.5% divorced (2000); Foreign born: 6.6% (2000); Ancestry (includes multiple ancestries): 34.6% German, 17.3% Norwegian, 12.0% Swedish, 11.9% Other groups, 11.2% Irish (2000).
Vital Statistics: Birth rate: 142.3 per 10,000 population (1998)
Economy: Railroad junction. Manufacturing: textiles, light manufacturing. Crystal Airport in North. Single-family building permits issued: 50 (2001) / 23 (2000); Multi-family building permits issued: 0 (2001) / 2 (2000); Employment by occupation: 13.3% management, 19.2% professional, 12.6% services, 29.2% sales, 0.0% farming, 8.5% construction, 17.1% production (2000).
Income: Per capita income: $23,163 (2000); Median household income: $48,736 (2000); Poverty rate: 4.4% (2000).
Taxes: Total city taxes per capita: $256 (2000); City property taxes per capita: $235 (2000).
Education: High school graduation rate: 90.2% (2000); College graduation rate: 22.4% (2000).
Housing: Homeownership rate: 77.4% (2000); Median home value: $112,900 (2000); Median rent: $630 per month (2000); Median age of housing: 42 years (2000).
Safety: Violent crime rate: 17.4 per 10,000 population; Property crime rate: 361.3 per 10,000 population (2001).
Transportation: Commute to work: 92.6% car, 3.6% public transportation, 1.2% walk, 2.1% work from home (2000); Travel time to work: 27.0% less than 15 minutes, 46.4% 15 to 30 minutes, 19.8% 30 to 45 minutes, 3.5% 45 to 60 minutes, 3.2% 60 minutes or more (2000)

DAYTON (city). Covers a land area of 23.451 square miles and a water area of 1.716 square miles. Located at 45.19° N. Lat.; 93.48° W. Long. Elevation is 912 feet.
Population: 4,699 (2000); Race: 94.8% White, 0.5% Black, 1.9% Asian, 0.5% American Indian and Alaska Native, 0.5% Hispanic of any race, 2.1% two or more races (2000); Density: 200.4 persons per square mile (2000); Age: 30.9% under 18, 4.7% over 64 (2000); Marriage status: 25.1% never married, 62.0% now married, 3.4% widowed, 9.6% divorced (2000); Foreign born: 1.6% (2000); Ancestry (includes multiple ancestries): 39.8% German, 16.6% Swedish, 13.5% Norwegian, 13.1% Irish, 8.0% French (except Basque) (2000).
Economy: Manufacturing: transportation equipment, food. Single-family building permits issued: 8 (2001) / 3 (2000); Multi-family building permits issued: 0 (2001) / 0 (2000); Employment by occupation: 14.5% management, 17.5% professional, 10.8% services, 30.8% sales, 0.3% farming, 12.1% construction, 13.9% production (2000).
Income: Per capita income: $27,756 (2000); Median household income: $66,875 (2000); Poverty rate: 2.7% (2000).
Taxes: Total city taxes per capita: $241 (1997); City property taxes per capita: $213 (1997).
Education: High school graduation rate: 91.1% (2000); College graduation rate: 21.0% (2000).
Housing: Homeownership rate: 96.4% (2000); Median home value: $144,000 (2000); Median rent: $445 per month (2000); Median age of housing: 24 years (2000).
Safety: Violent crime rate: 4.2 per 10,000 population; Property crime rate: 25.3 per 10,000 population (2001).
Transportation: Commute to work: 92.2% car, 3.1% public transportation, 1.2% walk, 2.9% work from home (2000); Travel time to work: 15.2% less than 15 minutes, 35.1% 15 to 30 minutes, 28.5% 30 to 45 minutes, 15.8% 45 to 60 minutes, 5.4% 60 minutes or more (2000)

DEEPHAVEN (city). Covers a land area of 2.340 square miles and a water area of 0.059 square miles. Located at 44.93° N. Lat.; 93.52° W. Long. Elevation is 938 feet.
Population: 3,853 (2000); Race: 97.2% White, 0.0% Black, 0.4% Asian, 0.2% American Indian and Alaska Native, 1.4% Hispanic of any race, 1.3% two or more races (2000); Density: 1,646.4 persons per square mile (2000); Age: 30.2% under 18, 10.9% over 64 (2000); Marriage status: 16.5% never married, 72.7% now married, 3.8% widowed, 7.0% divorced (2000); Foreign born: 3.5% (2000); Ancestry (includes multiple ancestries): 29.7% German, 16.6% English, 15.6% Irish, 15.2% Norwegian, 12.7% Swedish (2000).
Economy: Manufacturing: printing and publishing. Single-family building permits issued: 7 (2001) / 5 (2000); Multi-family building permits issued: 0 (2001) / 0 (2000); Employment by occupation: 30.4% management, 24.1% professional, 6.2% services, 30.5% sales, 0.5% farming, 3.3% construction, 5.0% production (2000).
Income: Per capita income: $58,544 (2000); Median household income: $101,278 (2000); Poverty rate: 2.6% (2000).
Taxes: Total city taxes per capita: $305 (1997); City property taxes per capita: $263 (1997).
Education: High school graduation rate: 98.1% (2000); College graduation rate: 67.4% (2000).
Housing: Homeownership rate: 97.2% (2000); Median home value: $290,800 (2000); Median rent: $646 per month (2000); Median age of housing: 43 years (2000).
Safety: Violent crime rate: 2.3 per 10,000 population; Property crime rate: 86.8 per 10,000 population (2001).
Transportation: Commute to work: 89.6% car, 2.0% public transportation, 0.3% walk, 7.6% work from home (2000); Travel time to work: 15.6% less than 15 minutes, 47.5% 15 to 30 minutes, 28.5% 30 to 45 minutes, 4.8% 45 to 60 minutes, 3.5% 60 minutes or more (2000)

EDEN PRAIRIE (city). Covers a land area of 32.389 square miles and a water area of 2.834 square miles. Located at 44.85° N. Lat.; 93.46° W. Long. Elevation is 875 feet.
Population: 54,901 (2000); Race: 90.6% White, 2.1% Black, 5.1% Asian, 0.3% American Indian and Alaska Native, 1.6% Hispanic of any race, 1.4% two or more races (2000); Density: 1,695.1 persons per square mile (2000); Age: 30.4% under 18, 4.7% over 64 (2000); Marriage status: 24.7% never married, 65.4% now married, 2.3% widowed, 7.6% divorced (2000); Foreign born: 8.9% (2000); Ancestry (includes multiple ancestries): 35.0% German, 16.7% Norwegian, 13.1% Irish, 10.4% Swedish, 9.8% Other groups (2000).
Vital Statistics: Birth rate: 142.1 per 10,000 population (1998)
Economy: Manufacturing includes computer accessories, metallic balloons, printing and publishing, software, hearing aids, medical equipment, chemicals, electronic sensors, workstations, seed cleaning equipment, envelopes, packaging machinery, laser printers,medical optical sensors, motion controls, heating equipment and power supplies. Unemployment rate: 3.3% (11/2002); Total civilian labor force: 33,757 (11/2002); Single-family building permits issued: 310 (2001) / 264 (2000); Multi-family building permits issued: 251 (2001) / 327 (2000); Employment by occupation: 27.1% management, 25.9% professional, 8.1% services, 29.0% sales, 0.0% farming, 3.5% construction, 6.4% production (2000).
Income: Per capita income: $38,854 (2000); Median household income: $78,328 (2000); Poverty rate: 3.5% (2000).
Taxes: Total city taxes per capita: $409 (2000); City property taxes per capita: $358 (2000).
Education: High school graduation rate: 97.2% (2000); College graduation rate: 57.1% (2000).

School District(s)

Eden Prairie (PK-12)
2000 Enrollment: 10,417 952-975-7000

Two-year College(s)

Northwest Technical Institute (Private, For-profit)
2001 Enrollment: 31 612-944-0080
2001 Tuition: In-state $11,760; Out-of-state $11,760
Housing: Homeownership rate: 78.4% (2000); Median home value: $198,300 (2000); Median rent: $842 per month (2000); Median age of housing: 14 years (2000).
Safety: Violent crime rate: 10.6 per 10,000 population; Property crime rate: 259.5 per 10,000 population (2001).
Newspapers: Eden Prairie Sun Current (1 x week); Eden Prairie News (1 x week)
Transportation: Commute to work: 90.7% car, 2.8% public transportation, 1.0% walk, 4.9% work from home (2000); Travel time to work: 29.2% less than 15 minutes, 46.1% 15 to 30 minutes, 18.6% 30 to 45 minutes, 4.6% 45 to 60 minutes, 1.6% 60 minutes or more (2000)
Additional Information Contacts
Eden Prairie Chamber of Commerce 952-947-0236

EDINA (city). Covers a land area of 15.748 square miles and a water area of 0.296 square miles. Located at 44.89° N. Lat.; 93.35° W. Long. Elevation is 900 feet.
History: Site of the Southdale Shopping Center, the first covered one in the U.S., designed by Victor Gruen in the 1950s.
Population: 47,425 (2000); Race: 94.1% White, 1.1% Black, 2.6% Asian, 0.4% American Indian and Alaska Native, 1.2% Hispanic of any race, 1.4% two or more races (2000); Density: 3,011.4 persons per square mile (2000); Age: 22.9% under 18, 22.7% over 64 (2000); Marriage status: 20.6% never married, 62.1% now married, 8.9% widowed, 8.5% divorced (2000); Foreign born: 6.0% (2000); Ancestry (includes multiple ancestries): 28.8% German, 16.7% Norwegian, 15.3% Irish, 12.7% English, 12.7% Swedish (2000).
Vital Statistics: Birth rate: 96.2 per 10,000 population (1998)
Economy: Manufacturing includes electronic insulators, leather gift items, signs, microwave foods, lighting controls, folding tables, feed supplements, printing and publishing. Site of the Southdale Shopping Center, one of the largest shopping centers in theU.S. Unemployment rate: 2.5% (11/2002); Total civilian labor force: 26,947 (11/2002); Single-family building permits issued: 22 (2001) / 28 (2000); Multi-family building permits issued: 172 (2001) / 0 (2000); Employment by occupation: 26.4% management, 28.8% professional, 7.7% services, 30.7% sales, 0.0% farming, 2.2% construction, 4.1% production (2000).
Income: Per capita income: $44,195 (2000); Median household income: $66,019 (2000); Poverty rate: 3.3% (2000).
Taxes: Total city taxes per capita: $515 (2000); City property taxes per capita: $464 (2000).
Education: High school graduation rate: 96.9% (2000); College graduation rate: 58.5% (2000).

School District(s)

Edina (PK-12)
2000 Enrollment: 7,025 612-928-2500
Housing: Homeownership rate: 76.4% (2000); Median home value: $248,500 (2000); Median rent: $832 per month (2000); Median age of housing: 35 years (2000).
Hospitals: Fairview Southdale Hospital (390 beds)
Safety: Violent crime rate: 8.1 per 10,000 population; Property crime rate: 259.3 per 10,000 population (2001).
Transportation: Commute to work: 87.5% car, 3.2% public transportation, 1.6% walk, 6.8% work from home (2000); Travel time to work: 34.1% less

than 15 minutes, 44.9% 15 to 30 minutes, 16.9% 30 to 45 minutes, 2.0% 45 to 60 minutes, 2.2% 60 minutes or more (2000)
Additional Information Contacts
Edina Chamber of Commerce 952-806-9060
Minnesota Association of Realtors. 952-935-8313
Minnesota Commercial Association of Realtors 952-908-1780

EXCELSIOR (city). Covers a land area of 0.626 square miles and a water area of 0.047 square miles. Located at 44.90° N. Lat.; 93.56° W. Long.
History: Excelsior was organized in 1858 by the Excelsior Pioneer Association of New York City.
Population: 2,393 (2000); Race: 94.3% White, 1.2% Black, 2.6% Asian, 0.7% American Indian and Alaska Native, 1.5% Hispanic of any race, 0.7% two or more races (2000); Density: 3,822.9 persons per square mile (2000); Age: 17.9% under 18, 15.1% over 64 (2000); Marriage status: 32.5% never married, 44.1% now married, 8.9% widowed, 14.5% divorced (2000); Foreign born: 6.0% (2000); Ancestry (includes multiple ancestries): 36.6% German, 16.0% Norwegian, 14.4% Irish, 11.8% English, 11.4% Swedish (2000).
Economy: Single-family building permits issued: 1 (2001) / 0 (2000); Multi-family building permits issued: 0 (2001) / 0 (2000); Employment by occupation: 13.2% management, 23.1% professional, 13.4% services, 32.2% sales, 0.0% farming, 10.8% construction, 7.3% production (2000).
Income: Per capita income: $29,127 (2000); Median household income: $43,598 (2000); Poverty rate: 5.7% (2000).
Taxes: Total city taxes per capita: $281 (1997); City property taxes per capita: $238 (1997).
Education: High school graduation rate: 92.4% (2000); College graduation rate: 37.2% (2000).

School District(s)

Minnetonka (PK-12)
2000 Enrollment: 7,689 952-401-5000
Housing: Homeownership rate: 40.0% (2000); Median home value: $185,800 (2000); Median rent: $575 per month (2000); Median age of housing: 38 years (2000).
Transportation: Commute to work: 93.5% car, 1.3% public transportation, 2.2% walk, 2.3% work from home (2000); Travel time to work: 29.0% less than 15 minutes, 41.8% 15 to 30 minutes, 19.8% 30 to 45 minutes, 5.9% 45 to 60 minutes, 3.6% 60 minutes or more (2000)
Additional Information Contacts
Excelsior Chamber of Commerce 952-474-6461

GOLDEN VALLEY (city). Covers a land area of 10.231 square miles and a water area of 0.288 square miles. Located at 44.99° N. Lat.; 93.35° W. Long. Elevation is 910 feet.
History: Incorporated 1886.
Population: 20,281 (2000); Race: 91.0% White, 2.8% Black, 3.5% Asian, 0.2% American Indian and Alaska Native, 1.8% Hispanic of any race, 2.0% two or more races (2000); Density: 1,982.3 persons per square mile (2000); Age: 20.7% under 18, 19.6% over 64 (2000); Marriage status: 22.4% never married, 60.5% now married, 8.0% widowed, 9.1% divorced (2000); Foreign born: 7.3% (2000); Ancestry (includes multiple ancestries): 30.1% German, 17.1% Norwegian, 12.4% Swedish, 10.8% Irish, 9.8% Other groups (2000).
Vital Statistics: Birth rate: 111.4 per 10,000 population (1998)
Economy: Railroad junction. Chiefly residential, with some industry: transportation equipment, meat products, machinery, marketing exhibits, cast metal products, consumer goods; printing and publishing; research activity. Single-family building permits issued: 106 (2001) / 55 (2000); Multi-family building permits issued: 55 (2001) / 88 (2000); Employment by occupation: 20.5% management, 29.9% professional, 9.6% services, 28.5% sales, 0.0% farming, 4.3% construction, 7.3% production (2000).
Income: Per capita income: $34,094 (2000); Median household income: $62,063 (2000); Poverty rate: 3.0% (2000).
Taxes: Total city taxes per capita: $697 (2000); City property taxes per capita: $641 (2000).
Education: High school graduation rate: 94.3% (2000); College graduation rate: 46.7% (2000).

School District(s)

Perpich Center Arts Education (07-12)
2000 Enrollment: 0 612-591-4700
Housing: Homeownership rate: 81.4% (2000); Median home value: $160,300 (2000); Median rent: $638 per month (2000); Median age of housing: 37 years (2000).
Safety: Violent crime rate: 25.4 per 10,000 population; Property crime rate: 313.7 per 10,000 population (2001).
Transportation: Commute to work: 89.2% car, 3.2% public transportation, 1.3% walk, 5.6% work from home (2000); Travel time to work: 28.5% less than 15 minutes, 53.4% 15 to 30 minutes, 14.7% 30 to 45 minutes, 2.0% 45 to 60 minutes, 1.5% 60 minutes or more (2000)

GREENFIELD (city). Covers a land area of 20.437 square miles and a water area of 1.045 square miles. Located at 45.09° N. Lat.; 93.68° W. Long. Elevation is 1,052 feet.
Population: 2,544 (2000); Race: 96.9% White, 0.4% Black, 1.1% Asian, 0.0% American Indian and Alaska Native, 1.3% Hispanic of any race, 1.6% two or more races (2000); Density: 124.5 persons per square mile (2000); Age: 34.1% under 18, 4.3% over 64 (2000); Marriage status: 23.2% never married, 66.8% now married, 2.5% widowed, 7.6% divorced (2000); Foreign born: 1.4% (2000); Ancestry (includes multiple ancestries): 40.3% German, 16.6% Norwegian, 9.7% Swedish, 6.5% Irish, 5.6% English (2000).
Economy: On West fringe of Minneapolis-St. Paul (Twin Cities) urban area. Agriculture: livestock; grain, nursery products. Single-family building permits issued: 29 (2001) / 42 (2000); Multi-family building permits issued: 0 (2001) / 0 (2000); Employment by occupation: 21.1% management, 19.5% professional, 11.4% services, 24.7% sales, 0.7% farming, 11.3% construction, 11.3% production (2000).
Income: Per capita income: $29,270 (2000); Median household income: $80,933 (2000); Poverty rate: 2.5% (2000).
Taxes: Total city taxes per capita: $237 (1997); City property taxes per capita: $193 (1997).
Education: High school graduation rate: 94.6% (2000); College graduation rate: 28.6% (2000).
Housing: Homeownership rate: 88.1% (2000); Median home value: $212,500 (2000); Median rent: $564 per month (2000); Median age of housing: 20 years (2000).
Transportation: Commute to work: 90.2% car, 0.6% public transportation, 1.6% walk, 6.5% work from home (2000); Travel time to work: 16.7% less than 15 minutes, 25.9% 15 to 30 minutes, 31.9% 30 to 45 minutes, 17.3% 45 to 60 minutes, 8.2% 60 minutes or more (2000)

GREENWOOD (city). Covers a land area of 0.347 square miles and a water area of 0.252 square miles. Located at 44.91° N. Lat.; 93.55° W. Long.
Population: 729 (2000); Race: 96.5% White, 1.6% Black, 0.0% Asian, 0.0% American Indian and Alaska Native, 3.2% Hispanic of any race, 0.9% two or more races (2000); Density: 2,098.2 persons per square mile (2000); Age: 30.6% under 18, 9.2% over 64 (2000); Marriage status: 16.6% never married, 72.4% now married, 1.2% widowed, 9.7% divorced (2000); Foreign born: 4.3% (2000); Ancestry (includes multiple ancestries): 34.2% German, 14.2% English, 13.9% Irish, 13.5% Norwegian, 9.3% Swedish (2000).
Economy: Single-family building permits issued: 12 (2001) / 15 (2000); Multi-family building permits issued: 0 (2001) / 0 (2000); Employment by occupation: 29.4% management, 23.8% professional, 6.4% services, 30.6% sales, 0.0% farming, 5.4% construction, 4.4% production (2000).
Income: Per capita income: $63,200 (2000); Median household income: $102,719 (2000); Poverty rate: 0.8% (2000).
Education: High school graduation rate: 99.2% (2000); College graduation rate: 60.6% (2000).
Housing: Homeownership rate: 89.7% (2000); Median home value: $379,200 (2000); Median rent: $808 per month (2000); Median age of housing: 38 years (2000).
Transportation: Commute to work: 91.0% car, 0.0% public transportation, 0.5% walk, 6.5% work from home (2000); Travel time to work: 22.5% less than 15 minutes, 41.8% 15 to 30 minutes, 23.6% 30 to 45 minutes, 9.9% 45 to 60 minutes, 2.1% 60 minutes or more (2000)

HAMEL (unincorporated postal area, zip code 55340). Covers a land area of 36.573 square miles and a water area of 0.493 square miles. Located at 45.07° N. Lat.; 93.56° W. Long.
Population: 5,836 (2000); Race: 98.4% White, 0.5% Black, 0.0% Asian, 0.3% American Indian and Alaska Native, 1.8% Hispanic of any race, 0.5% two or more races (2000); Density: 159.6 persons per square mile (2000); Age: 34.1% under 18, 4.0% over 64 (2000); Marriage status: 24.5% never married, 67.1% now married, 2.2% widowed, 6.2% divorced (2000); Foreign born: 1.1% (2000); Ancestry (includes multiple ancestries): 42.8% German, 17.4% Norwegian, 13.2% Swedish, 11.6% Irish, 6.9% French (except Basque) (2000).
Economy: Employment by occupation: 21.9% management, 17.6% professional, 10.4% services, 27.3% sales, 0.5% farming, 10.1% construction, 12.1% production (2000).
Income: Per capita income: $38,583 (2000); Median household income: $80,493 (2000); Poverty rate: 1.3% (2000).

Education: High school graduation rate: 95.0% (2000); College graduation rate: 33.0% (2000).
Housing: Homeownership rate: 92.9% (2000); Median home value: $208,900 (2000); Median rent: $663 per month (2000); Median age of housing: 22 years (2000).
Transportation: Commute to work: 91.3% car, 0.7% public transportation, 2.0% walk, 5.7% work from home (2000); Travel time to work: 26.0% less than 15 minutes, 33.4% 15 to 30 minutes, 29.0% 30 to 45 minutes, 8.6% 45 to 60 minutes, 3.0% 60 minutes or more (2000)
Additional Information Contacts
Northwest Suburban Chamber of Commerce 763-420-3242

HASSAN (township). Covers a land area of 20.397 square miles and a water area of 0.922 square miles. Located at 45.19° N. Lat.; 93.57° W. Long.
Population: 2,463 (2000); Race: 98.8% White, 0.0% Black, 1.0% Asian, 0.1% American Indian and Alaska Native, 0.3% Hispanic of any race, 0.1% two or more races (2000); Density: 120.8 persons per square mile (2000); Age: 33.2% under 18, 4.6% over 64 (2000); Marriage status: 17.4% never married, 77.8% now married, 1.2% widowed, 3.6% divorced (2000); Foreign born: 2.9% (2000); Ancestry (includes multiple ancestries): 42.2% German, 21.2% Norwegian, 15.1% Swedish, 11.6% Irish, 7.6% French (except Basque) (2000).
Economy: Single-family building permits issued: 7 (2001) / 20 (2000); Multi-family building permits issued: 0 (2001) / 0 (2000); Employment by occupation: 22.5% management, 21.3% professional, 9.4% services, 21.4% sales, 1.0% farming, 11.1% construction, 13.2% production (2000).
Income: Per capita income: $27,350 (2000); Median household income: $79,158 (2000); Poverty rate: 0.3% (2000).
Taxes: Total city taxes per capita: $203 (2000); City property taxes per capita: $190 (2000).
Education: High school graduation rate: 95.1% (2000); College graduation rate: 30.1% (2000).
Housing: Homeownership rate: 98.1% (2000); Median home value: $171,900 (2000); Median rent: $518 per month (2000); Median age of housing: 21 years (2000).
Transportation: Commute to work: 88.9% car, 0.9% public transportation, 0.2% walk, 9.6% work from home (2000); Travel time to work: 16.3% less than 15 minutes, 33.2% 15 to 30 minutes, 32.9% 30 to 45 minutes, 9.0% 45 to 60 minutes, 8.6% 60 minutes or more (2000)

HOPKINS (city). Covers a land area of 4.076 square miles and a water area of 0 square miles. Located at 44.92° N. Lat.; 93.40° W. Long. Elevation is 918 feet.
History: Incorporated as West Minneapolis 1893, name changed 1928.
Population: 17,145 (2000); Race: 83.2% White, 5.4% Black, 5.7% Asian, 1.1% American Indian and Alaska Native, 5.7% Hispanic of any race, 2.0% two or more races (2000); Density: 4,205.9 persons per square mile (2000); Age: 19.3% under 18, 14.5% over 64 (2000); Marriage status: 37.2% never married, 41.8% now married, 8.5% widowed, 12.4% divorced (2000); Foreign born: 14.0% (2000); Ancestry (includes multiple ancestries): 29.5% German, 17.7% Other groups, 15.6% Norwegian, 11.6% Irish, 10.0% Swedish (2000).
Vital Statistics: Birth rate: 137.7 per 10,000 population (1998)
Economy: Railroad junction. Manufacturing includes machinery, computer and electronic parts, printing and publishing, steel siding, wall murals, air pollution equipment, gun drilling, packaging, labels, ophthamalic lenses, tools, jellies and candy, lumber, bakery products and software. Single-family building permits issued: 14 (2001) / 62 (2000); Multi-family building permits issued: 37 (2001) / 0 (2000); Employment by occupation: 16.4% management, 23.6% professional, 14.1% services, 30.3% sales, 0.0% farming, 4.8% construction, 10.7% production (2000).
Income: Per capita income: $26,759 (2000); Median household income: $39,203 (2000); Poverty rate: 9.3% (2000).
Taxes: Total city taxes per capita: $411 (2000); City property taxes per capita: $384 (2000).
Education: High school graduation rate: 91.0% (2000); College graduation rate: 35.0% (2000).

School District(s)
Hopkins (PK-12)
2000 Enrollment: 8,404 952-988-4000

Four-year College(s)
Alfred Adler Graduate School (Private, Not-for-profit)
2001 Enrollment: 168 612-988-4170

Housing: Homeownership rate: 38.5% (2000); Median home value: $132,400 (2000); Median rent: $675 per month (2000); Median age of housing: 30 years (2000).
Safety: Violent crime rate: 26.5 per 10,000 population; Property crime rate: 260.3 per 10,000 population (2001).
Transportation: Commute to work: 87.0% car, 5.6% public transportation, 3.2% walk, 3.3% work from home (2000); Travel time to work: 36.5% less than 15 minutes, 42.4% 15 to 30 minutes, 14.9% 30 to 45 minutes, 3.0% 45 to 60 minutes, 3.2% 60 minutes or more (2000)

INDEPENDENCE (city). Aka Lake Sarah. Covers a land area of 32.583 square miles and a water area of 2.003 square miles. Located at 45.01° N. Lat.; 93.69° W. Long.
Population: 3,236 (2000); Race: 98.5% White, 0.0% Black, 1.4% Asian, 0.0% American Indian and Alaska Native, 0.4% Hispanic of any race, 0.1% two or more races (2000); Density: 99.3 persons per square mile (2000); Age: 31.6% under 18, 7.6% over 64 (2000); Marriage status: 21.2% never married, 73.6% now married, 1.2% widowed, 4.0% divorced (2000); Foreign born: 3.0% (2000); Ancestry (includes multiple ancestries): 44.9% German, 17.5% Norwegian, 12.8% Swedish, 10.5% Irish, 8.5% Polish (2000).
Economy: Single-family building permits issued: 32 (2001) / 53 (2000); Multi-family building permits issued: 0 (2001) / 0 (2000); Employment by occupation: 23.9% management, 16.0% professional, 12.6% services, 24.4% sales, 0.4% farming, 9.1% construction, 13.7% production (2000).
Income: Per capita income: $35,753 (2000); Median household income: $79,126 (2000); Poverty rate: 1.3% (2000).
Taxes: Total city taxes per capita: $320 (1997); City property taxes per capita: $291 (1997).
Education: High school graduation rate: 96.0% (2000); College graduation rate: 35.0% (2000).
Housing: Homeownership rate: 95.2% (2000); Median home value: $234,900 (2000); Median rent: $725 per month (2000); Median age of housing: 25 years (2000).
Transportation: Commute to work: 91.3% car, 1.0% public transportation, 1.3% walk, 6.2% work from home (2000); Travel time to work: 15.9% less than 15 minutes, 36.7% 15 to 30 minutes, 30.3% 30 to 45 minutes, 10.6% 45 to 60 minutes, 6.5% 60 minutes or more (2000)

LONG LAKE (city). Covers a land area of 0.846 square miles and a water area of 0.098 square miles. Located at 44.98° N. Lat.; 93.57° W. Long. Elevation is 981 feet.
Population: 1,842 (2000); Race: 97.2% White, 1.1% Black, 0.4% Asian, 0.4% American Indian and Alaska Native, 0.3% Hispanic of any race, 0.7% two or more races (2000); Density: 2,177.1 persons per square mile (2000); Age: 24.5% under 18, 11.6% over 64 (2000); Marriage status: 25.3% never married, 60.3% now married, 3.2% widowed, 11.2% divorced (2000); Foreign born: 3.6% (2000); Ancestry (includes multiple ancestries): 35.2% German, 15.8% Norwegian, 13.8% Swedish, 12.2% Irish, 8.4% English (2000).
Economy: Light manufacturing. Single-family building permits issued: 8 (2001) / 3 (2000); Multi-family building permits issued: 10 (2001) / 0 (2000); Employment by occupation: 16.9% management, 20.7% professional, 9.3% services, 35.3% sales, 0.0% farming, 9.3% construction, 8.5% production (2000).
Income: Per capita income: $28,385 (2000); Median household income: $55,139 (2000); Poverty rate: 6.8% (2000).
Taxes: Total city taxes per capita: $433 (1997); City property taxes per capita: $406 (1997).
Education: High school graduation rate: 92.8% (2000); College graduation rate: 36.3% (2000).

School District(s)
Orono (PK-12)
2000 Enrollment: 2,587 952-449-8300

Housing: Homeownership rate: 71.8% (2000); Median home value: $151,100 (2000); Median rent: $594 per month (2000); Median age of housing: 30 years (2000).
Transportation: Commute to work: 89.2% car, 2.5% public transportation, 2.3% walk, 5.1% work from home (2000); Travel time to work: 28.5% less than 15 minutes, 40.7% 15 to 30 minutes, 21.2% 30 to 45 minutes, 5.3% 45 to 60 minutes, 4.4% 60 minutes or more (2000)

LORETTO (city). Covers a land area of 0.293 square miles and a water area of 0 square miles. Located at 45.05° N. Lat.; 93.63° W. Long.
Population: 570 (2000); Race: 100.0% White, 0.0% Black, 0.0% Asian, 0.0% American Indian and Alaska Native, 0.0% Hispanic of any race, 0.0% two or more races (2000); Density: 1,948.7 persons per square mile (2000); Age: 29.0% under 18, 10.6% over 64 (2000); Marriage status: 17.0% never married, 64.9% now married, 5.7% widowed, 12.5% divorced (2000);

Foreign born: 0.5% (2000); Ancestry (includes multiple ancestries): 60.2% German, 15.2% Irish, 12.0% Polish, 10.5% English, 9.2% Norwegian (2000).
Economy: Manufacturing: wedding cakes, metal stampings. Single-family building permits issued: 2 (2001) / 22 (2000); Multi-family building permits issued: 0 (2001) / 0 (2000); Employment by occupation: 12.8% management, 16.2% professional, 14.7% services, 30.0% sales, 0.6% farming, 12.8% construction, 12.8% production (2000).
Income: Per capita income: $27,443 (2000); Median household income: $54,375 (2000); Poverty rate: 1.6% (2000).
Taxes: Total city taxes per capita: $203 (1997); City property taxes per capita: $174 (1997).
Education: High school graduation rate: 89.2% (2000); College graduation rate: 21.1% (2000).
Housing: Homeownership rate: 67.2% (2000); Median home value: $152,700 (2000); Median rent: $347 per month (2000); Median age of housing: 22 years (2000).
Transportation: Commute to work: 92.6% car, 0.9% public transportation, 2.8% walk, 3.7% work from home (2000); Travel time to work: 31.1% less than 15 minutes, 30.8% 15 to 30 minutes, 24.0% 30 to 45 minutes, 9.9% 45 to 60 minutes, 4.2% 60 minutes or more (2000)

MAPLE GROVE (city). Covers a land area of 32.870 square miles and a water area of 2.075 square miles. Located at 45.11° N. Lat.; 93.45° W. Long. Elevation is 939 feet.
Population: 50,365 (2000); Race: 94.5% White, 1.5% Black, 2.2% Asian, 0.2% American Indian and Alaska Native, 1.2% Hispanic of any race, 1.2% two or more races (2000); Density: 1,532.3 persons per square mile (2000); Age: 30.7% under 18, 4.0% over 64 (2000); Marriage status: 22.6% never married, 67.8% now married, 2.3% widowed, 7.3% divorced (2000); Foreign born: 4.3% (2000); Ancestry (includes multiple ancestries): 39.7% German, 17.8% Norwegian, 12.7% Swedish, 12.3% Irish, 8.0% English (2000).
Vital Statistics: Birth rate: 131.2 per 10,000 population (1998)
Economy: Manufacturing: machining, gun drilling, sheet metal fabricating; ink, furniture, concrete products, machinery, aerospace material, building materials, foam products, wood products, burglar alarms, tool and die products, transportation equipment, medical equipment. Unemployment rate: 3.1% (11/2002); Total civilian labor force: 32,786 (11/2002); Employment by occupation: 22.5% management, 24.1% professional, 9.4% services, 30.1% sales, 0.1% farming, 6.3% construction, 7.6% production (2000).
Income: Per capita income: $30,544 (2000); Median household income: $76,111 (2000); Poverty rate: 1.4% (2000).
Taxes: Total city taxes per capita: $371 (2000); City property taxes per capita: $298 (2000).
Education: High school graduation rate: 96.7% (2000); College graduation rate: 41.7% (2000).
Housing: Homeownership rate: 92.5% (2000); Median home value: $155,300 (2000); Median rent: $857 per month (2000); Median age of housing: 16 years (2000).
Safety: Violent crime rate: 11.2 per 10,000 population; Property crime rate: 230.4 per 10,000 population (2001).
Transportation: Commute to work: 92.4% car, 3.0% public transportation, 0.7% walk, 3.5% work from home (2000); Travel time to work: 19.6% less than 15 minutes, 38.6% 15 to 30 minutes, 30.4% 30 to 45 minutes, 8.3% 45 to 60 minutes, 3.1% 60 minutes or more (2000)

MAPLE PLAIN (city). Covers a land area of 1.113 square miles and a water area of 0 square miles. Located at 45.00° N. Lat.; 93.65° W. Long.
Population: 2,088 (2000); Race: 98.4% White, 0.0% Black, 0.8% Asian, 0.0% American Indian and Alaska Native, 0.8% Hispanic of any race, 0.8% two or more races (2000); Density: 1,875.4 persons per square mile (2000); Age: 26.5% under 18, 12.2% over 64 (2000); Marriage status: 25.8% never married, 57.2% now married, 7.9% widowed, 9.1% divorced (2000); Foreign born: 1.7% (2000); Ancestry (includes multiple ancestries): 38.3% German, 20.5% Norwegian, 12.6% Swedish, 10.7% Irish, 6.8% English (2000).
Economy: Dairying in area. Manufacturing: concrete products, industrial patterns, wood products, machinery, molding; machining. Single-family building permits issued: 0 (2001) / 0 (2000); Multi-family building permits issued: 0 (2001) / 0 (2000); Employment by occupation: 15.4% management, 17.0% professional, 14.2% services, 28.0% sales, 0.4% farming, 10.1% construction, 14.9% production (2000).
Income: Per capita income: $22,218 (2000); Median household income: $50,938 (2000); Poverty rate: 4.4% (2000).
Taxes: Total city taxes per capita: $297 (1997); City property taxes per capita: $287 (1997).
Education: High school graduation rate: 88.7% (2000); College graduation rate: 25.5% (2000).
Housing: Homeownership rate: 64.6% (2000); Median home value: $142,500 (2000); Median rent: $601 per month (2000); Median age of housing: 27 years (2000).
Transportation: Commute to work: 93.5% car, 0.4% public transportation, 2.3% walk, 3.3% work from home (2000); Travel time to work: 27.5% less than 15 minutes, 34.9% 15 to 30 minutes, 26.1% 30 to 45 minutes, 8.7% 45 to 60 minutes, 2.7% 60 minutes or more (2000)

MEDICINE LAKE (city). Covers a land area of 0.173 square miles and a water area of 0.151 square miles. Located at 44.99° N. Lat.; 93.41° W. Long. Elevation is 900 feet.
Population: 368 (2000); Race: 93.9% White, 1.4% Black, 3.1% Asian, 0.6% American Indian and Alaska Native, 0.8% Hispanic of any race, 1.1% two or more races (2000); Density: 2,133.1 persons per square mile (2000); Age: 22.3% under 18, 10.6% over 64 (2000); Marriage status: 21.6% never married, 65.1% now married, 6.8% widowed, 6.5% divorced (2000); Foreign born: 3.6% (2000); Ancestry (includes multiple ancestries): 27.6% German, 22.3% Norwegian, 16.4% Swedish, 8.1% Dutch, 8.1% English (2000).
Economy: Single-family building permits issued: 0 (2001) / 0 (2000); Multi-family building permits issued: 0 (2001) / 0 (2000); Employment by occupation: 23.2% management, 26.1% professional, 9.5% services, 26.6% sales, 0.8% farming, 3.3% construction, 10.4% production (2000).
Income: Per capita income: $45,942 (2000); Median household income: $70,750 (2000); Poverty rate: 1.1% (2000).
Taxes: Total city taxes per capita: $402 (1997); City property taxes per capita: $336 (1997).
Education: High school graduation rate: 92.7% (2000); College graduation rate: 44.1% (2000).
Housing: Homeownership rate: 77.1% (2000); Median home value: $300,000 (2000); Median rent: $544 per month (2000); Median age of housing: 43 years (2000).
Transportation: Commute to work: 87.0% car, 2.9% public transportation, 0.0% walk, 7.1% work from home (2000); Travel time to work: 27.1% less than 15 minutes, 54.8% 15 to 30 minutes, 12.2% 30 to 45 minutes, 2.7% 45 to 60 minutes, 3.2% 60 minutes or more (2000)

MEDINA (city). Covers a land area of 25.566 square miles and a water area of 1.332 square miles. Located at 45.04° N. Lat.; 93.57° W. Long.
Population: 4,005 (2000); Race: 97.6% White, 0.1% Black, 0.6% Asian, 0.0% American Indian and Alaska Native, 0.9% Hispanic of any race, 0.6% two or more races (2000); Density: 156.7 persons per square mile (2000); Age: 32.9% under 18, 6.9% over 64 (2000); Marriage status: 23.8% never married, 69.7% now married, 1.6% widowed, 4.9% divorced (2000); Foreign born: 2.0% (2000); Ancestry (includes multiple ancestries): 38.8% German, 17.0% Norwegian, 13.2% Irish, 13.0% Swedish, 9.4% English (2000).
Economy: Manufacturing at Hamel: motor vehicle parts, paper products, fabricated metal products, machining, building equipment. Single-family building permits issued: 21 (2001) / 37 (2000); Multi-family building permits issued: 0 (2001) / 6 (2000); Employment by occupation: 24.0% management, 18.7% professional, 9.8% services, 32.8% sales, 0.0% farming, 6.2% construction, 8.5% production (2000).
Income: Per capita income: $49,127 (2000); Median household income: $88,847 (2000); Poverty rate: 1.3% (2000).
Taxes: Total city taxes per capita: $352 (1997); City property taxes per capita: $318 (1997).
Education: High school graduation rate: 96.3% (2000); College graduation rate: 44.0% (2000).
Housing: Homeownership rate: 93.3% (2000); Median home value: $209,100 (2000); Median rent: $547 per month (2000); Median age of housing: 22 years (2000).
Safety: Violent crime rate: 7.4 per 10,000 population; Property crime rate: 133.4 per 10,000 population (2001).
Transportation: Commute to work: 92.2% car, 1.2% public transportation, 0.5% walk, 5.3% work from home (2000); Travel time to work: 26.2% less than 15 minutes, 33.3% 15 to 30 minutes, 29.7% 30 to 45 minutes, 7.8% 45 to 60 minutes, 3.0% 60 minutes or more (2000)

MINNEAPOLIS (city). Covers a land area of 54.892 square miles and a water area of 3.507 square miles. Located at 44.96° N. Lat.; 93.26° W. Long. Elevation is 812 feet.
History: Minneapolis traces its beginnings to the settlement of St. Anthony, begun on the east side of the falls of the Mississippi River. Franklin Steele, who had built a cabin here in 1838, added a sawmill and a dam in 1847, attracting colonists (many of them French, including the guide Bottineau) to the location. The west side of the river was a military reservation at this time, but by 1855 settlement was permitted and a town grew up on the claim of

Colonel John H. Stevens. Here was the first use of the name Minneapolis, combining the Sioux word for water, "minne," with the Greek suffix "polis." St. Anthony and Minneapolis both grew rapidly in the 1850's. Minneapollis was incorporated as a city in 1867, and in 1872 St. Anthony was united with it as one city. The water power provided by the falls made Minneapolis an industrial city with flour milling predominant by the 1880's.

Population: 382,618 (2000); Race: 65.2% White, 17.6% Black, 6.3% Asian, 2.0% American Indian and Alaska Native, 7.6% Hispanic of any race, 4.6% two or more races (2000); Density: 6,970.3 persons per square mile (2000); Age: 22.0% under 18, 9.1% over 64 (2000); Marriage status: 46.2% never married, 37.9% now married, 5.1% widowed, 10.7% divorced (2000); Foreign born: 14.5% (2000); Ancestry (includes multiple ancestries): 28.8% Other groups, 21.5% German, 11.0% Norwegian, 10.1% Irish, 8.0% Swedish (2000).

Vital Statistics: Birth rate: 165.6 per 10,000 population (1998)

Economy: Unemployment rate: 4.0% (11/2002); Total civilian labor force: 216,776 (11/2002); Single-family building permits issued: 226 (2001) / 95 (2000); Multi-family building permits issued: 519 (2001) / 252 (2000); Employment by occupation: 14.1% management, 27.0% professional, 16.2% services, 25.7% sales, 0.1% farming, 4.8% construction, 12.0% production (2000).

Income: Per capita income: $22,685 (2000); Median household income: $37,974 (2000); Poverty rate: 16.9% (2000).

Taxes: Total city taxes per capita: $613 (2000); City property taxes per capita: $466 (2000).

Education: High school graduation rate: 85.0% (2000); College graduation rate: 37.4% (2000).

School District(s)

Cedar Riverside Community School (KG-08)
2000 Enrollment: 101 612-339-5767
El Colegio Charter School (09-12)
2000 Enrollment: 80 612-728-5466
Four Directions Charter Schools (09-12)
2000 Enrollment: 67 612-522-4436
Frederick Douglass Math/Sci Tech (N -N)
2000 Enrollment: n/a 651-374-1532
Harvest Prep School/Seed Academy (KG-06)
2000 Enrollment: 323 612-381-9743
Heart of the Earth Charter (KG-12)
2000 Enrollment: 221 612-331-8862
Minneapolis (PK-12)
2000 Enrollment: 48,834 612-668-0200
Minneapolis Area Office (KG-12)
2000 Enrollment: 2,673 612-373-1000
Minnesota Transitions Charter Sch (KG-12)
2000 Enrollment: 317 612-728-8915
Native Arts Charter School (07-12)
2000 Enrollment: 29 612-721-6631
New Visions Charter School (PK-08)
2000 Enrollment: 172 612-789-1236
Right Step Incorp. (KG-12)
2000 Enrollment: 0 612-521-6000
Sojourner Truth Academy (KG-07)
2000 Enrollment: 219 612-588-3599

Four-year College(s)

Walden University (Private, For-profit)
2001 Enrollment: 2,082 800-444-6795
Academy Education Center Inc (Private, For-profit)
2001 Enrollment: 367 952-851-0066
2001 Tuition: In-state $13,224; Out-of-state $13,224
Augsburg College (Private, Not-for-profit, Evangelical Lutheran Church)
2001 Enrollment: 2,911 612-330-1000
2001 Tuition: In-state $17,070; Out-of-state $17,070
The Art Institutes International Minnesota (Private, For-profit)
2001 Enrollment: 947 612-332-3361
2001 Tuition: In-state $14,844; Out-of-state $14,844
University of Minnesota-Twin Cities (Public)
2001 Enrollment: 46,597 612-625-5000
2001 Tuition: In-state $4,852; Out-of-state $14,318
Minneapolis College of Art and Design (Private, Not-for-profit)
2001 Enrollment: 628 612-874-3770
2001 Tuition: In-state $20,190; Out-of-state $20,190
North Central University (Private, Not-for-profit, Assemblies of God Church)
2001 Enrollment: 1,230 612-332-3491
2001 Tuition: In-state $8,280; Out-of-state $8,280
Native American Educational Services-Twin Cities (Private, Not-for-profit)
2001 Enrollment: n/a 612-721-6631
Minnesota School of Professional Psychology (Private, For-profit)
2001 Enrollment: 355 952-921-9500
Capella University (Private, For-profit)
2001 Enrollment: 3,759 888-227-3552
2001 Tuition: In-state $8,100; Out-of-state $8,100

Two-year College(s)

Lakeland Medical and Dental Academy Inc (Private, For-profit)
2001 Enrollment: 321 612-827-5656
2001 Tuition: In-state $10,125; Out-of-state $10,125
Methodist Hospital School of Radiologic Technology (Private, Not-for-profit, United Methodist)
2001 Enrollment: n/a 612-932-5410
Minneapolis Community and Technical College (Public)
2001 Enrollment: 7,041 612-341-7000
2001 Tuition: In-state $2,482; Out-of-state $4,965
Herzing College-Minneapolis Drafting School Campus (Private, For-profit)
2001 Enrollment: 147 763-535-8843
2001 Tuition: In-state $7,360; Out-of-state $7,360
Newgate Education and Research Center Inc (Private, Not-for-profit)
2001 Enrollment: n/a 612-378-0177
Veterans Affairs Medical Center School of Rad Techn (Public)
2001 Enrollment: n/a 612-725-2038
Dunwoody Institute (Private, Not-for-profit)
2001 Enrollment: 1,155 612-374-5800
2001 Tuition: In-state $7,500; Out-of-state $7,500
Musicians Technical Training Center (Private, For-profit)
2001 Enrollment: 284 612-338-0175
2001 Tuition: In-state $13,440; Out-of-state $13,440

Housing: Homeownership rate: 51.4% (2000); Median home value: $113,500 (2000); Median rent: $536 per month (2000); Median age of housing: 60+ years (2000).

Hospitals: Abbott-Northwestern Hospital (958 beds); Fairview Riverside Medical Center (1,100 beds); Fairview University Medical Center (719 beds); Health System Minnesota (461 beds); Hennepin County Medical Center (910 beds); North Memorial Health Care (518 beds); Shriners Hospitals for Crippled Children Twin Cities (40 beds); Veterans Affairs Medical Center (410 beds)

Safety: Violent crime rate: 106.0 per 10,000 population; Property crime rate: 587.5 per 10,000 population (2001).

Newspapers: Metro Lutheran (1 x month); Finance & Commerce (5 x week); Star Tribune (7 x week); Skyway News (1 x week); The Whittier Globe (1 x month); Minnesota Spokesman-Recorder (1 x week); American Jewish World (1 x week); City Pages (1 x week); The Southwest Journal (2 x month); Saint Paul Recorder (1 x week); The Minnesota Daily (5 x week); Insight News (1 x week)

Transportation: Commute to work: 72.9% car, 14.6% public transportation, 6.6% walk, 3.4% work from home (2000); Travel time to work: 26.1% less than 15 minutes, 50.0% 15 to 30 minutes, 17.0% 30 to 45 minutes, 3.3% 45 to 60 minutes, 3.7% 60 minutes or more (2000)

Airports: Minneapolis-St Paul International/Wold-C (primary service/large hub); Anoka County-Blaine Airport(Janes Field) (primary service/large hub); Flying Cloud (primary service/large hub); Crystal (primary service/large hub); Airlake (primary service/large hub)

Additional Information Contacts

Greater Minneapolis Convention & Visitors Bureau 612-661-4700
Minneapolis Area Association of Realtors 952-933-9020
Minneapolis Chamber of Commerce 612-338-7750

MINNETONKA (city). Covers a land area of 27.143 square miles and a water area of 1.080 square miles. Located at 44.93° N. Lat.; 93.46° W. Long. Elevation is 902 feet.

History: Incorporated 1956.

Population: 51,301 (2000); Race: 94.9% White, 1.6% Black, 2.0% Asian, 0.2% American Indian and Alaska Native, 1.4% Hispanic of any race, 1.0% two or more races (2000); Density: 1,890.0 persons per square mile (2000); Age: 23.2% under 18, 13.9% over 64 (2000); Marriage status: 23.0% never married, 62.1% now married, 5.7% widowed, 9.2% divorced (2000); Foreign born: 5.7% (2000); Ancestry (includes multiple ancestries): 31.7% German, 16.5% Norwegian, 13.6% Irish, 11.8% English, 11.2% Swedish (2000).

Vital Statistics: Birth rate: 90.6 per 10,000 population (1998)

Economy: Diversified manufacturing. Its population has increased significantly since 1970 due to the influx of former central-city Minneapolis residents to the outlying suburbs. Glen Lake Sanitorium in South. Unemployment rate: 2.7% (11/2002); Total civilian labor force: 34,674

(11/2002); Single-family building permits issued: 108 (2001) / 83 (2000); Multi-family building permits issued: 60 (2001) / 10 (2000); Employment by occupation: 23.1% management, 27.5% professional, 8.3% services, 30.0% sales, 0.1% farming, 4.5% construction, 6.5% production (2000).
Income: Per capita income: $40,410 (2000); Median household income: $69,979 (2000); Poverty rate: 2.6% (2000).
Taxes: Total city taxes per capita: $369 (2000); City property taxes per capita: $317 (2000).
Education: High school graduation rate: 95.9% (2000); College graduation rate: 51.6% (2000).

Two-year College(s)

Rasmussen College-Minnetonka (Private, For-profit)
2001 Enrollment: 255 952-545-2000
2001 Tuition: In-state $16,200; Out-of-state $16,200

Housing: Homeownership rate: 75.7% (2000); Median home value: $190,100 (2000); Median rent: $873 per month (2000); Median age of housing: 23 years (2000).
Safety: Violent crime rate: 10.8 per 10,000 population; Property crime rate: 230.1 per 10,000 population (2001).
Newspapers: Plymouth Sun Sailor (1 x week); Wayzata/Long Lake Sun Sailor (1 x week); Minnetonka Sun Sailor (1 x week); Hopkins Sun Sailor (1 x week); Excelsior-Shorewood Sun Sailor (1 x week); Lakeshore Weekly News (1 x week)
Transportation: Commute to work: 90.4% car, 2.6% public transportation, 0.8% walk, 5.5% work from home (2000); Travel time to work: 27.8% less than 15 minutes, 47.4% 15 to 30 minutes, 19.3% 30 to 45 minutes, 3.4% 45 to 60 minutes, 2.1% 60 minutes or more (2000)

Additional Information Contacts

American Israel Chamber of Commerce 763-593-8666
Minnetonka Chamber of Commerce 763-540-0234

MINNETONKA BEACH (city). Covers a land area of 0.518 square miles and a water area of 0 square miles. Located at 44.93° N. Lat.; 93.59° W. Long.
Population: 614 (2000); Race: 98.6% White, 0.0% Black, 0.0% Asian, 0.5% American Indian and Alaska Native, 0.0% Hispanic of any race, 1.0% two or more races (2000); Density: 1,186.5 persons per square mile (2000); Age: 32.3% under 18, 6.7% over 64 (2000); Marriage status: 20.8% never married, 70.4% now married, 1.8% widowed, 7.1% divorced (2000); Foreign born: 2.4% (2000); Ancestry (includes multiple ancestries): 28.5% German, 18.2% Irish, 16.3% Norwegian, 11.2% English, 5.8% Swedish (2000).
Economy: Single-family building permits issued: 0 (2001) / 3 (2000); Multi-family building permits issued: 0 (2001) / 0 (2000); Employment by occupation: 34.8% management, 21.2% professional, 8.3% services, 31.5% sales, 0.0% farming, 3.6% construction, 0.7% production (2000).
Income: Per capita income: $91,844 (2000); Median household income: $150,912 (2000); Poverty rate: 2.7% (2000).
Taxes: Total city taxes per capita: $534 (1997); City property taxes per capita: $480 (1997).
Education: High school graduation rate: 98.3% (2000); College graduation rate: 71.2% (2000).
Housing: Homeownership rate: 90.0% (2000); Median home value: $583,300 (2000); Median rent: $1,042 per month (2000); Median age of housing: 42 years (2000).
Transportation: Commute to work: 93.5% car, 0.0% public transportation, 0.0% walk, 4.5% work from home (2000); Travel time to work: 25.4% less than 15 minutes, 37.3% 15 to 30 minutes, 29.7% 30 to 45 minutes, 6.5% 45 to 60 minutes, 1.1% 60 minutes or more (2000)

MINNETRISTA (city). Covers a land area of 26.109 square miles and a water area of 4.717 square miles. Located at 44.92° N. Lat.; 93.70° W. Long. Elevation is 1,012 feet.
Population: 4,358 (2000); Race: 96.4% White, 0.7% Black, 0.9% Asian, 0.2% American Indian and Alaska Native, 1.7% Hispanic of any race, 0.3% two or more races (2000); Density: 166.9 persons per square mile (2000); Age: 29.4% under 18, 7.2% over 64 (2000); Marriage status: 22.0% never married, 72.3% now married, 1.4% widowed, 4.3% divorced (2000); Foreign born: 5.0% (2000); Ancestry (includes multiple ancestries): 38.2% German, 18.4% Norwegian, 15.4% Swedish, 12.4% Irish, 12.0% English (2000).
Economy: Single-family building permits issued: 68 (2001) / 59 (2000); Multi-family building permits issued: 0 (2001) / 0 (2000); Employment by occupation: 24.2% management, 15.8% professional, 12.1% services, 33.0% sales, 0.4% farming, 8.7% construction, 5.8% production (2000).
Income: Per capita income: $40,217 (2000); Median household income: $90,347 (2000); Poverty rate: 2.8% (2000).
Taxes: Total city taxes per capita: $357 (1997); City property taxes per capita: $319 (1997).
Education: High school graduation rate: 96.8% (2000); College graduation rate: 44.5% (2000).
Housing: Homeownership rate: 95.8% (2000); Median home value: $278,500 (2000); Median rent: $833 per month (2000); Median age of housing: 23 years (2000).
Safety: Violent crime rate: 15.9 per 10,000 population; Property crime rate: 298.5 per 10,000 population (2001).
Transportation: Commute to work: 87.1% car, 1.1% public transportation, 2.0% walk, 9.1% work from home (2000); Travel time to work: 13.4% less than 15 minutes, 32.7% 15 to 30 minutes, 37.7% 30 to 45 minutes, 11.0% 45 to 60 minutes, 5.2% 60 minutes or more (2000)

MOUND (city). Covers a land area of 2.945 square miles and a water area of 1.971 square miles. Located at 44.93° N. Lat.; 93.65° W. Long. Elevation is 942 feet.
History: Settled 1854, incorporated 1912.
Population: 9,435 (2000); Race: 96.7% White, 0.5% Black, 1.0% Asian, 0.2% American Indian and Alaska Native, 0.7% Hispanic of any race, 1.5% two or more races (2000); Density: 3,203.8 persons per square mile (2000); Age: 24.0% under 18, 8.9% over 64 (2000); Marriage status: 25.6% never married, 58.7% now married, 5.2% widowed, 10.5% divorced (2000); Foreign born: 2.4% (2000); Ancestry (includes multiple ancestries): 38.8% German, 17.4% Irish, 16.5% Norwegian, 11.4% Swedish, 9.8% English (2000).
Economy: Diverse light manufacturing. Single-family building permits issued: 23 (2001) / 22 (2000); Multi-family building permits issued: 0 (2001) / 0 (2000); Employment by occupation: 15.8% management, 18.0% professional, 12.9% services, 29.1% sales, 0.1% farming, 10.5% construction, 13.6% production (2000).
Income: Per capita income: $30,309 (2000); Median household income: $60,671 (2000); Poverty rate: 2.7% (2000).
Taxes: Total city taxes per capita: $191 (1997); City property taxes per capita: $165 (1997).
Education: High school graduation rate: 94.9% (2000); College graduation rate: 30.3% (2000).

School District(s)

Westonka (PK-12)
2000 Enrollment: 2,314 952-491-8001

Housing: Homeownership rate: 80.6% (2000); Median home value: $140,300 (2000); Median rent: $541 per month (2000); Median age of housing: 30 years (2000).
Safety: Violent crime rate: 22.0 per 10,000 population; Property crime rate: 389.1 per 10,000 population (2001).
Newspapers: The Laker Pioneer (1 x week); The Pioneer (1 x week)
Transportation: Commute to work: 92.2% car, 1.5% public transportation, 0.9% walk, 4.0% work from home (2000); Travel time to work: 17.3% less than 15 minutes, 29.7% 15 to 30 minutes, 34.7% 30 to 45 minutes, 12.3% 45 to 60 minutes, 6.0% 60 minutes or more (2000)

NEW HOPE (city). Covers a land area of 5.093 square miles and a water area of 0.016 square miles. Located at 45.03° N. Lat.; 93.38° W. Long. Elevation is 914 feet.
Population: 20,873 (2000); Race: 86.9% White, 5.9% Black, 2.6% Asian, 0.6% American Indian and Alaska Native, 3.7% Hispanic of any race, 2.2% two or more races (2000); Density: 4,098.6 persons per square mile (2000); Age: 21.5% under 18, 17.8% over 64 (2000); Marriage status: 26.5% never married, 52.9% now married, 9.5% widowed, 11.2% divorced (2000); Foreign born: 7.9% (2000); Ancestry (includes multiple ancestries): 30.7% German, 14.5% Norwegian, 13.8% Other groups, 10.8% Irish, 9.9% Swedish (2000).
Vital Statistics: Birth rate: 120.3 per 10,000 population (1998)
Economy: Manufacturing: lithography, electronic equipment, printing. Single-family building permits issued: 3 (2001) / 1 (2000); Multi-family building permits issued: 0 (2001) / 8 (2000); Employment by occupation: 16.6% management, 20.6% professional, 12.2% services, 30.0% sales, 0.1% farming, 6.5% construction, 14.0% production (2000).
Income: Per capita income: $23,562 (2000); Median household income: $46,795 (2000); Poverty rate: 6.5% (2000).
Taxes: Total city taxes per capita: $275 (1997); City property taxes per capita: $263 (1997).
Education: High school graduation rate: 89.5% (2000); College graduation rate: 29.8% (2000).

School District(s)

Robbinsdale (PK-12)
2000 Enrollment: 13,706 763-504-8011

Housing: Homeownership rate: 56.1% (2000); Median home value: $136,600 (2000); Median rent: $657 per month (2000); Median age of housing: 33 years (2000).

Safety: Violent crime rate: 18.0 per 10,000 population; Property crime rate: 266.4 per 10,000 population (2001).

Transportation: Commute to work: 91.0% car, 2.7% public transportation, 2.6% walk, 2.9% work from home (2000); Travel time to work: 27.7% less than 15 minutes, 45.6% 15 to 30 minutes, 20.4% 30 to 45 minutes, 4.0% 45 to 60 minutes, 2.3% 60 minutes or more (2000)

ORONO (city). Covers a land area of 16.075 square miles and a water area of 8.940 square miles. Located at 44.96° N. Lat.; 93.59° W. Long. Elevation is 950 feet.

Population: 7,538 (2000); Race: 98.1% White, 0.8% Black, 0.3% Asian, 0.1% American Indian and Alaska Native, 0.8% Hispanic of any race, 0.5% two or more races (2000); Density: 468.9 persons per square mile (2000); Age: 27.4% under 18, 9.1% over 64 (2000); Marriage status: 22.2% never married, 67.2% now married, 3.7% widowed, 6.9% divorced (2000); Foreign born: 2.3% (2000); Ancestry (includes multiple ancestries): 33.5% German, 16.7% Irish, 14.8% English, 14.4% Norwegian, 13.5% Swedish (2000).

Economy: Single-family building permits issued: 36 (2001) / 39 (2000); Multi-family building permits issued: 0 (2001) / 0 (2000); Employment by occupation: 26.5% management, 24.2% professional, 9.2% services, 26.4% sales, 0.0% farming, 6.5% construction, 7.2% production (2000).

Income: Per capita income: $65,825 (2000); Median household income: $88,314 (2000); Poverty rate: 1.2% (2000).

Taxes: Total city taxes per capita: $307 (1997); City property taxes per capita: $279 (1997).

Education: High school graduation rate: 97.2% (2000); College graduation rate: 50.7% (2000).

Housing: Homeownership rate: 93.8% (2000); Median home value: $324,400 (2000); Median rent: $788 per month (2000); Median age of housing: 35 years (2000).

Safety: Violent crime rate: 5.1 per 10,000 population; Property crime rate: 223.0 per 10,000 population (2001).

Transportation: Commute to work: 90.6% car, 0.6% public transportation, 1.1% walk, 7.2% work from home (2000); Travel time to work: 22.9% less than 15 minutes, 38.0% 15 to 30 minutes, 29.2% 30 to 45 minutes, 6.6% 45 to 60 minutes, 3.3% 60 minutes or more (2000)

OSSEO (city). Covers a land area of 0.765 square miles and a water area of 0 square miles. Located at 45.11° N. Lat.; 93.39° W. Long. Elevation is 888 feet.

History: Osseo was laid out in 1856 on the Bottineau Prairie, where the guide Pierre Bottineau had a land claim in the 1850's. The town was named for Osseo, son of the evening star in Longfellow's "Song of Hiawatha."

Population: 2,434 (2000); Race: 97.3% White, 0.8% Black, 0.0% Asian, 0.2% American Indian and Alaska Native, 0.7% Hispanic of any race, 1.5% two or more races (2000); Density: 3,179.7 persons per square mile (2000); Age: 19.3% under 18, 21.6% over 64 (2000); Marriage status: 32.1% never married, 45.3% now married, 11.7% widowed, 10.8% divorced (2000); Foreign born: 1.1% (2000); Ancestry (includes multiple ancestries): 48.7% German, 18.6% Norwegian, 12.1% Irish, 9.9% Swedish, 5.3% English (2000).

Economy: Single-family building permits issued: 0 (2001) / 0 (2000); Multi-family building permits issued: 0 (2001) / 0 (2000); Employment by occupation: 6.4% management, 15.0% professional, 13.3% services, 33.2% sales, 0.0% farming, 9.0% construction, 23.1% production (2000).

Income: Per capita income: $23,507 (2000); Median household income: $42,685 (2000); Poverty rate: 2.6% (2000).

Taxes: Total city taxes per capita: $311 (1997); City property taxes per capita: $295 (1997).

Education: High school graduation rate: 85.9% (2000); College graduation rate: 15.7% (2000).

School District(s)

Osseo (PK-12)
2000 Enrollment: 22,017 763-391-7000

Housing: Homeownership rate: 56.7% (2000); Median home value: $115,600 (2000); Median rent: $580 per month (2000); Median age of housing: 41 years (2000).

Safety: Violent crime rate: 8.1 per 10,000 population; Property crime rate: 235.8 per 10,000 population (2001).

Newspapers: South Crow River News (1 x week); Osseo-Maple Grove Press (1 x week); North Crow River News (1 x week); Champlin-Dayton Press (1 x week); Rockford Area News Leader (1 x week)

Transportation: Commute to work: 92.5% car, 3.8% public transportation, 1.3% walk, 1.3% work from home (2000); Travel time to work: 34.4% less than 15 minutes, 35.3% 15 to 30 minutes, 19.0% 30 to 45 minutes, 6.1% 45 to 60 minutes, 5.2% 60 minutes or more (2000)

PLYMOUTH (city). Covers a land area of 32.915 square miles and a water area of 2.410 square miles. Located at 45.01° N. Lat.; 93.45° W. Long. Elevation is 1,008 feet.

History: Incorporated 1955.

Population: 65,894 (2000); Race: 91.3% White, 2.6% Black, 3.7% Asian, 0.4% American Indian and Alaska Native, 1.7% Hispanic of any race, 1.3% two or more races (2000); Density: 2,002.0 persons per square mile (2000); Age: 26.9% under 18, 7.6% over 64 (2000); Marriage status: 25.7% never married, 62.9% now married, 3.2% widowed, 8.3% divorced (2000); Foreign born: 7.4% (2000); Ancestry (includes multiple ancestries): 33.7% German, 16.0% Norwegian, 12.9% Irish, 11.0% Swedish, 9.3% Other groups (2000).

Vital Statistics: Birth rate: 128.4 per 10,000 population (1998)

Economy: Highly diversified manufacturing. Unemployment rate: 3.1% (11/2002); Total civilian labor force: 42,364 (11/2002); Single-family building permits issued: 222 (2001) / 286 (2000); Multi-family building permits issued: 397 (2001) / 0 (2000); Employment by occupation: 26.4% management, 25.0% professional, 8.2% services, 28.7% sales, 0.2% farming, 4.4% construction, 7.0% production (2000).

Income: Per capita income: $36,309 (2000); Median household income: $77,008 (2000); Poverty rate: 2.6% (2000).

Taxes: Total city taxes per capita: $236 (2000); City property taxes per capita: $198 (2000).

Education: High school graduation rate: 96.2% (2000); College graduation rate: 51.0% (2000).

School District(s)

Intermediate School District 287 (PK-12)
2000 Enrollment: 2,104 763-559-3535

Four-year College(s)

Central Baptist Theological Seminary (Private, Not-for-profit, Baptist)
2001 Enrollment: n/a 612-522-7339

Two-year College(s)

Association Free Lutheran Bible School (Private, Not-for-profit, American Lutheran)
2001 Enrollment: n/a 612-544-9501

Housing: Homeownership rate: 76.6% (2000); Median home value: $197,600 (2000); Median rent: $807 per month (2000); Median age of housing: 17 years (2000).

Safety: Violent crime rate: 12.0 per 10,000 population; Property crime rate: 234.2 per 10,000 population (2001).

Transportation: Commute to work: 91.3% car, 2.4% public transportation, 1.0% walk, 4.6% work from home (2000); Travel time to work: 26.1% less than 15 minutes, 43.0% 15 to 30 minutes, 23.3% 30 to 45 minutes, 4.8% 45 to 60 minutes, 2.8% 60 minutes or more (2000)

RICHFIELD (city). Covers a land area of 6.896 square miles and a water area of 0.178 square miles. Located at 44.87° N. Lat.; 93.28° W. Long. Elevation is 842 feet.

History: Fort Snelling State Park and National Cemetery to East. Settled c.1851; incorporated 1964.

Population: 34,439 (2000); Race: 81.1% White, 7.1% Black, 5.1% Asian, 0.6% American Indian and Alaska Native, 6.2% Hispanic of any race, 2.9% two or more races (2000); Density: 4,993.9 persons per square mile (2000); Age: 20.3% under 18, 16.3% over 64 (2000); Marriage status: 31.2% never married, 51.3% now married, 7.6% widowed, 10.0% divorced (2000); Foreign born: 11.4% (2000); Ancestry (includes multiple ancestries): 28.6% German, 18.4% Other groups, 17.5% Norwegian, 13.8% Swedish, 12.5% Irish (2000).

Vital Statistics: Birth rate: 134.4 per 10,000 population (1998)

Economy: Zinc electroplating, printing and publishing, cabinets, diverse light manufacturing. Minneapolis-St. Paul International Airport on East. Unemployment rate: 3.3% (11/2002); Total civilian labor force: 22,371 (11/2002); Single-family building permits issued: 16 (2001) / 34 (2000); Multi-family building permits issued: 0 (2001) / 239 (2000); Employment by occupation: 12.8% management, 19.7% professional, 15.5% services, 33.1% sales, 0.1% farming, 6.9% construction, 12.0% production (2000).

Income: Per capita income: $24,709 (2000); Median household income: $45,519 (2000); Poverty rate: 6.3% (2000).

Taxes: Total city taxes per capita: $356 (2000); City property taxes per capita: $315 (2000).
Education: High school graduation rate: 89.7% (2000); College graduation rate: 27.3% (2000).

School District(s)

Richfield (PK-12)
2000 Enrollment: 4,257 612-798-6000
West Metro Education District (KG-10)
2000 Enrollment: 868 612-866-8480

Two-year College(s)

Minnesota School of Business (Private, For-profit)
2001 Enrollment: 770 612-861-2000
2001 Tuition: In-state $11,475; Out-of-state $11,475
Housing: Homeownership rate: 67.5% (2000); Median home value: $128,500 (2000); Median rent: $611 per month (2000); Median age of housing: 44 years (2000).
Safety: Violent crime rate: 37.1 per 10,000 population; Property crime rate: 364.6 per 10,000 population (2001).
Transportation: Commute to work: 87.0% car, 6.4% public transportation, 2.7% walk, 2.7% work from home (2000); Travel time to work: 33.0% less than 15 minutes, 45.1% 15 to 30 minutes, 15.8% 30 to 45 minutes, 3.0% 45 to 60 minutes, 3.0% 60 minutes or more (2000)
Additional Information Contacts
Richfield Chamber of Commerce. 612-866-5100

ROBBINSDALE (city). Covers a land area of 2.782 square miles and a water area of 0.185 square miles. Located at 45.02° N. Lat.; 93.33° W. Long. Elevation is 879 feet.
History: Robbinsdale was platted in 1887 and named for Andrew B. Robbins, pioneer owner of the land on which the town was established. Robbinsdale developed as a suburb of Minneapolis.
Population: 14,123 (2000); Race: 87.8% White, 6.7% Black, 2.2% Asian, 0.3% American Indian and Alaska Native, 2.2% Hispanic of any race, 1.6% two or more races (2000); Density: 5,076.0 persons per square mile (2000); Age: 21.9% under 18, 17.3% over 64 (2000); Marriage status: 29.5% never married, 48.8% now married, 9.8% widowed, 11.9% divorced (2000); Foreign born: 4.7% (2000); Ancestry (includes multiple ancestries): 31.9% German, 18.5% Norwegian, 14.1% Swedish, 12.8% Irish, 10.1% Other groups (2000).
Vital Statistics: Birth rate: 143.0 per 10,000 population (1998)
Economy: Single-family building permits issued: 5 (2001) / 3 (2000); Multi-family building permits issued: 0 (2001) / 0 (2000); Employment by occupation: 14.4% management, 22.8% professional, 13.4% services, 28.9% sales, 0.0% farming, 8.3% construction, 12.2% production (2000).
Income: Per capita income: $23,912 (2000); Median household income: $48,271 (2000); Poverty rate: 4.7% (2000).
Taxes: Total city taxes per capita: $260 (1997); City property taxes per capita: $246 (1997).
Education: High school graduation rate: 88.4% (2000); College graduation rate: 27.3% (2000).

Two-year College(s)

North Memorial Medical Center School of X-ray Techn (Private, Not-for-profit)
2001 Enrollment: n/a 612-520-5337
Housing: Homeownership rate: 74.1% (2000); Median home value: $112,000 (2000); Median rent: $588 per month (2000); Median age of housing: 46 years (2000).
Safety: Violent crime rate: 29.4 per 10,000 population; Property crime rate: 417.5 per 10,000 population (2001).
Newspapers: South Saint Paul/Inver Grove Heights Sun-Current (1 x week); Crystal-Robbinsdale Sun Post (1 x week); Brooklyn Center Sun Post (1 x week); New Hope-Golden Valley Sun Post (1 x week); Brooklyn Park Sun Post (1 x week)
Transportation: Commute to work: 88.0% car, 5.4% public transportation, 2.1% walk, 3.6% work from home (2000); Travel time to work: 24.4% less than 15 minutes, 48.8% 15 to 30 minutes, 20.4% 30 to 45 minutes, 3.7% 45 to 60 minutes, 2.7% 60 minutes or more (2000)

ROGERS (city). Covers a land area of 5.018 square miles and a water area of 0 square miles. Located at 45.19° N. Lat.; 93.56° W. Long. Elevation is 930 feet.
Population: 3,588 (2000); Race: 97.3% White, 0.1% Black, 0.8% Asian, 1.2% American Indian and Alaska Native, 0.3% Hispanic of any race, 0.6% two or more races (2000); Density: 715.1 persons per square mile (2000); Age: 33.7% under 18, 5.0% over 64 (2000); Marriage status: 16.4% never married, 75.6% now married, 2.5% widowed, 5.4% divorced (2000); Foreign born: 1.8% (2000); Ancestry (includes multiple ancestries): 47.9% German, 17.2% Norwegian, 13.2% Irish, 12.5% Swedish, 6.9% Polish (2000).
Economy: Grain, nursery crops; livestock; dairying. Manufacturing: machine tooling, metal stampings, steel fabrication, plastic packaging, lumber. Crow Hassan Regional Park to West. Single-family building permits issued: 352 (2001) / 286 (2000); Multi-family building permits issued: 0 (2001) / 0 (2000); Employment by occupation: 21.6% management, 17.5% professional, 8.5% services, 32.3% sales, 0.1% farming, 7.9% construction, 12.0% production (2000).
Income: Per capita income: $25,845 (2000); Median household income: $73,143 (2000); Poverty rate: 1.8% (2000).
Taxes: Total city taxes per capita: $823 (1997); City property taxes per capita: $648 (1997).
Education: High school graduation rate: 93.3% (2000); College graduation rate: 33.2% (2000).
Housing: Homeownership rate: 93.3% (2000); Median home value: $186,600 (2000); Median rent: $475 per month (2000); Median age of housing: 3 years (2000).
Transportation: Commute to work: 94.6% car, 0.6% public transportation, 0.3% walk, 4.1% work from home (2000); Travel time to work: 16.0% less than 15 minutes, 33.6% 15 to 30 minutes, 34.8% 30 to 45 minutes, 12.4% 45 to 60 minutes, 3.3% 60 minutes or more (2000)
Additional Information Contacts
Rogers Chamber of Commerce 763-428-2921

SAINT ANTHONY (city). Covers a land area of 2.280 square miles and a water area of 0.091 square miles. Located at 45.02° N. Lat.; 93.22° W. Long. Elevation is 920 feet.
Population: 8,012 (2000); Race: 90.7% White, 2.2% Black, 4.0% Asian, 1.4% American Indian and Alaska Native, 1.8% Hispanic of any race, 1.2% two or more races (2000); Density: 3,513.8 persons per square mile (2000); Age: 17.7% under 18, 25.8% over 64 (2000); Marriage status: 26.9% never married, 53.0% now married, 12.7% widowed, 7.4% divorced (2000); Foreign born: 7.1% (2000); Ancestry (includes multiple ancestries): 25.6% German, 16.1% Norwegian, 14.6% Swedish, 9.4% Irish, 9.1% Polish (2000).
Economy: Single-family building permits issued: 0 (2001) / 4 (2000); Multi-family building permits issued: 0 (2001) / 2 (2000); Employment by occupation: 15.9% management, 28.8% professional, 9.3% services, 30.1% sales, 0.4% farming, 5.8% construction, 9.7% production (2000).
Income: Per capita income: $26,290 (2000); Median household income: $46,883 (2000); Poverty rate: 5.1% (2000).
Education: High school graduation rate: 89.0% (2000); College graduation rate: 34.4% (2000).

School District(s)

Saint Anthony-New Brighton (PK-12)
2000 Enrollment: 1,542 612-706-1000
Housing: Homeownership rate: 67.8% (2000); Median home value: $145,100 (2000); Median rent: $677 per month (2000); Median age of housing: 34 years (2000).
Safety: Violent crime rate: 14.8 per 10,000 population; Property crime rate: 296.4 per 10,000 population (2001).
Transportation: Commute to work: 85.2% car, 7.8% public transportation, 2.0% walk, 4.4% work from home (2000); Travel time to work: 31.5% less than 15 minutes, 46.7% 15 to 30 minutes, 16.4% 30 to 45 minutes, 3.3% 45 to 60 minutes, 2.1% 60 minutes or more (2000)

SAINT BONIFACIUS (city). Covers a land area of 1.066 square miles and a water area of 0.003 square miles. Located at 44.90° N. Lat.; 93.74° W. Long. Elevation is 970 feet.
Population: 1,873 (2000); Race: 95.4% White, 0.2% Black, 1.4% Asian, 0.4% American Indian and Alaska Native, 1.9% Hispanic of any race, 1.4% two or more races (2000); Density: 1,756.5 persons per square mile (2000); Age: 29.3% under 18, 6.7% over 64 (2000); Marriage status: 20.7% never married, 69.8% now married, 2.8% widowed, 6.7% divorced (2000); Foreign born: 3.3% (2000); Ancestry (includes multiple ancestries): 51.9% German, 11.9% Norwegian, 11.2% Irish, 6.4% Swedish, 6.0% Other groups (2000).
Economy: Single-family building permits issued: 53 (2001) / 31 (2000); Multi-family building permits issued: 18 (2001) / 30 (2000); Employment by occupation: 17.0% management, 20.3% professional, 11.2% services, 25.4% sales, 0.3% farming, 12.0% construction, 13.9% production (2000).
Income: Per capita income: $24,933 (2000); Median household income: $65,446 (2000); Poverty rate: 3.2% (2000).
Education: High school graduation rate: 90.0% (2000); College graduation rate: 27.5% (2000).

Four-year College(s)

Crown College (Private, Not-for-profit, Christ and Missionary Alliance Church)
2001 Enrollment: 877 612-446-4100
2001 Tuition: In-state $10,600; Out-of-state $10,600

Housing: Homeownership rate: 83.2% (2000); Median home value: $153,900 (2000); Median rent: $591 per month (2000); Median age of housing: 17 years (2000).

Transportation: Commute to work: 93.8% car, 0.4% public transportation, 1.2% walk, 4.3% work from home (2000); Travel time to work: 17.2% less than 15 minutes, 31.6% 15 to 30 minutes, 28.9% 30 to 45 minutes, 14.4% 45 to 60 minutes, 7.9% 60 minutes or more (2000)

SAINT LOUIS PARK (city). Covers a land area of 10.704 square miles and a water area of 0.209 square miles. Located at 44.94° N. Lat.; 93.36° W. Long. Elevation is 909 feet.

Population: 44,126 (2000); Race: 89.3% White, 4.6% Black, 2.9% Asian, 0.4% American Indian and Alaska Native, 2.8% Hispanic of any race, 1.5% two or more races (2000); Density: 4,122.5 persons per square mile (2000); Age: 18.8% under 18, 14.7% over 64 (2000); Marriage status: 34.8% never married, 48.4% now married, 6.6% widowed, 10.1% divorced (2000); Foreign born: 8.7% (2000); Ancestry (includes multiple ancestries): 27.3% German, 16.1% Norwegian, 12.5% Irish, 12.1% Other groups, 9.5% Swedish (2000).

Vital Statistics: Birth rate: 132.6 per 10,000 population (1998)

Economy: Unemployment rate: 3.1% (11/2002); Total civilian labor force: 29,769 (11/2002); Single-family building permits issued: 32 (2001) / 13 (2000); Multi-family building permits issued: 67 (2001) / 200 (2000); Employment by occupation: 19.6% management, 26.2% professional, 10.0% services, 30.9% sales, 0.1% farming, 4.3% construction, 8.9% production (2000).

Income: Per capita income: $28,970 (2000); Median household income: $49,260 (2000); Poverty rate: 5.2% (2000).

Education: High school graduation rate: 92.8% (2000); College graduation rate: 43.2% (2000).

School District(s)

Saint Louis Park (PK-12)
2000 Enrollment: 4,231 952-928-6003

Housing: Homeownership rate: 63.5% (2000); Median home value: $135,800 (2000); Median rent: $679 per month (2000); Median age of housing: 42 years (2000).

Safety: Violent crime rate: 14.8 per 10,000 population; Property crime rate: 340.8 per 10,000 population (2001).

Transportation: Commute to work: 87.1% car, 6.1% public transportation, 2.1% walk, 4.0% work from home (2000); Travel time to work: 29.0% less than 15 minutes, 53.4% 15 to 30 minutes, 13.3% 30 to 45 minutes, 2.6% 45 to 60 minutes, 1.7% 60 minutes or more (2000)

SHOREWOOD (city). Covers a land area of 5.310 square miles and a water area of 8.039 square miles. Located at 44.90° N. Lat.; 93.57° W. Long.

Population: 7,400 (2000); Race: 98.5% White, 0.4% Black, 0.5% Asian, 0.2% American Indian and Alaska Native, 0.8% Hispanic of any race, 0.2% two or more races (2000); Density: 1,393.5 persons per square mile (2000); Age: 31.8% under 18, 8.0% over 64 (2000); Marriage status: 18.0% never married, 71.1% now married, 2.7% widowed, 8.2% divorced (2000); Foreign born: 2.8% (2000); Ancestry (includes multiple ancestries): 35.3% German, 17.6% Irish, 16.3% Norwegian, 14.9% English, 13.6% Swedish (2000).

Economy: Single-family building permits issued: 34 (2001) / 62 (2000); Multi-family building permits issued: 0 (2001) / 8 (2000); Employment by occupation: 28.2% management, 24.9% professional, 7.4% services, 27.5% sales, 0.3% farming, 6.2% construction, 5.5% production (2000).

Income: Per capita income: $44,425 (2000); Median household income: $96,589 (2000); Poverty rate: 1.7% (2000).

Taxes: Total city taxes per capita: $283 (1997); City property taxes per capita: $253 (1997).

Education: High school graduation rate: 96.8% (2000); College graduation rate: 58.8% (2000).

Housing: Homeownership rate: 94.2% (2000); Median home value: $254,300 (2000); Median rent: $916 per month (2000); Median age of housing: 23 years (2000).

Transportation: Commute to work: 90.9% car, 1.0% public transportation, 0.6% walk, 7.3% work from home (2000); Travel time to work: 22.2% less than 15 minutes, 36.8% 15 to 30 minutes, 23.3% 30 to 45 minutes, 13.1% 45 to 60 minutes, 4.7% 60 minutes or more (2000)

SPRING PARK (city). Covers a land area of 0.363 square miles and a water area of 0.255 square miles. Located at 44.93° N. Lat.; 93.62° W. Long.

Population: 1,717 (2000); Race: 97.1% White, 0.2% Black, 0.5% Asian, 0.8% American Indian and Alaska Native, 0.8% Hispanic of any race, 1.4% two or more races (2000); Density: 4,724.3 persons per square mile (2000); Age: 8.9% under 18, 33.5% over 64 (2000); Marriage status: 28.8% never married, 41.9% now married, 17.1% widowed, 12.2% divorced (2000); Foreign born: 2.2% (2000); Ancestry (includes multiple ancestries): 33.0% German, 14.1% Swedish, 13.2% Norwegian, 9.4% Irish, 7.8% English (2000).

Economy: Manufacturing: custom bottling; foods. Single-family building permits issued: 0 (2001) / 1 (2000); Multi-family building permits issued: 0 (2001) / 0 (2000); Employment by occupation: 21.3% management, 19.6% professional, 14.1% services, 28.4% sales, 0.5% farming, 8.3% construction, 7.8% production (2000).

Income: Per capita income: $30,290 (2000); Median household income: $36,071 (2000); Poverty rate: 8.8% (2000).

Taxes: Total city taxes per capita: $505 (1997); City property taxes per capita: $453 (1997).

Education: High school graduation rate: 88.6% (2000); College graduation rate: 30.0% (2000).

Housing: Homeownership rate: 26.7% (2000); Median home value: $194,200 (2000); Median rent: $705 per month (2000); Median age of housing: 28 years (2000).

Transportation: Commute to work: 85.8% car, 2.5% public transportation, 3.2% walk, 6.5% work from home (2000); Travel time to work: 21.1% less than 15 minutes, 32.1% 15 to 30 minutes, 31.8% 30 to 45 minutes, 7.1% 45 to 60 minutes, 8.0% 60 minutes or more (2000)

TONKA BAY (city). Covers a land area of 0.954 square miles and a water area of 0.023 square miles. Located at 44.91° N. Lat.; 93.58° W. Long.

Population: 1,547 (2000); Race: 98.3% White, 0.1% Black, 1.3% Asian, 0.0% American Indian and Alaska Native, 1.0% Hispanic of any race, 0.2% two or more races (2000); Density: 1,622.0 persons per square mile (2000); Age: 24.6% under 18, 8.7% over 64 (2000); Marriage status: 20.5% never married, 67.2% now married, 3.3% widowed, 9.0% divorced (2000); Foreign born: 2.0% (2000); Ancestry (includes multiple ancestries): 36.2% German, 18.1% Norwegian, 16.2% Irish, 11.7% Swedish, 10.3% English (2000).

Economy: Manufacturing of plastic prototypes. Single-family building permits issued: 8 (2001) / 7 (2000); Multi-family building permits issued: 0 (2001) / 0 (2000); Employment by occupation: 27.4% management, 21.7% professional, 10.7% services, 30.0% sales, 0.0% farming, 5.3% construction, 4.8% production (2000).

Income: Per capita income: $50,825 (2000); Median household income: $84,879 (2000); Poverty rate: 2.2% (2000).

Taxes: Total city taxes per capita: $300 (1997); City property taxes per capita: $268 (1997).

Education: High school graduation rate: 97.4% (2000); College graduation rate: 53.1% (2000).

Housing: Homeownership rate: 91.7% (2000); Median home value: $310,400 (2000); Median rent: $775 per month (2000); Median age of housing: 38 years (2000).

Transportation: Commute to work: 91.9% car, 0.7% public transportation, 0.2% walk, 5.9% work from home (2000); Travel time to work: 18.7% less than 15 minutes, 38.6% 15 to 30 minutes, 33.0% 30 to 45 minutes, 7.0% 45 to 60 minutes, 2.8% 60 minutes or more (2000)

WAYZATA (city). Covers a land area of 3.182 square miles and a water area of 0.051 square miles. Located at 44.97° N. Lat.; 93.51° W. Long. Elevation is 936 feet.

Population: 4,113 (2000); Race: 98.9% White, 0.4% Black, 0.3% Asian, 0.0% American Indian and Alaska Native, 0.6% Hispanic of any race, 0.2% two or more races (2000); Density: 1,292.6 persons per square mile (2000); Age: 19.6% under 18, 20.7% over 64 (2000); Marriage status: 26.1% never married, 56.4% now married, 8.8% widowed, 8.8% divorced (2000); Foreign born: 3.3% (2000); Ancestry (includes multiple ancestries): 34.6% German, 17.7% Irish, 16.7% Norwegian, 14.3% Swedish, 14.0% English (2000).

Economy: Railroad junction. Manufacturing includes sheet lead and lead products, bolts and nuts, dairy products, wire harnesses, magnetic tape head, pay phones, nuclear shielding products, transformers, printing and publishing, bakery products. Single-family building permits issued: 6 (2001) / 2 (2000); Multi-family building permits issued: 0 (2001) / 6 (2000); Employment by occupation: 28.2% management, 20.3% professional, 8.8% services, 33.3% sales, 0.0% farming, 3.3% construction, 6.2% production (2000).

Income: Per capita income: $63,859 (2000); Median household income: $65,833 (2000); Poverty rate: 2.3% (2000).
Taxes: Total city taxes per capita: $911 (2000); City property taxes per capita: $854 (2000).
Education: High school graduation rate: 96.5% (2000); College graduation rate: 48.1% (2000).

School District(s)

Wayzata (PK-12)
2000 Enrollment: 9,317 612-745-5000

Housing: Homeownership rate: 60.4% (2000); Median home value: $281,700 (2000); Median rent: $719 per month (2000); Median age of housing: 34 years (2000).
Safety: Violent crime rate: 9.6 per 10,000 population; Property crime rate: 457.1 per 10,000 population (2001).
Transportation: Commute to work: 82.5% car, 3.7% public transportation, 4.7% walk, 8.6% work from home (2000); Travel time to work: 34.4% less than 15 minutes, 40.5% 15 to 30 minutes, 19.6% 30 to 45 minutes, 2.2% 45 to 60 minutes, 3.3% 60 minutes or more (2000)
Additional Information Contacts
Lake Minnetonka Area Chamber 763-471-0768
Wayzata Chamber of Commerce 763-473-9595

WOODLAND (city). Covers a land area of 0.571 square miles and a water area of 0.039 square miles. Located at 44.95° N. Lat.; 93.50° W. Long. Elevation is 950 feet.
Population: 480 (2000); Race: 100.0% White, 0.0% Black, 0.0% Asian, 0.0% American Indian and Alaska Native, 0.0% Hispanic of any race, 0.0% two or more races (2000); Density: 840.7 persons per square mile (2000); Age: 27.4% under 18, 12.0% over 64 (2000); Marriage status: 21.1% never married, 69.9% now married, 4.0% widowed, 4.9% divorced (2000); Foreign born: 0.0% (2000); Ancestry (includes multiple ancestries): 44.6% German, 28.0% English, 24.5% Irish, 15.8% Norwegian, 6.8% Swedish (2000).
Economy: Single-family building permits issued: 0 (2001) / 0 (2000); Multi-family building permits issued: 0 (2001) / 0 (2000); Employment by occupation: 24.1% management, 26.7% professional, 5.1% services, 42.1% sales, 0.0% farming, 1.0% construction, 1.0% production (2000).
Income: Per capita income: $95,495 (2000); Median household income: $153,881 (2000); Poverty rate: 4.6% (2000).
Taxes: Total city taxes per capita: $279 (1997); City property taxes per capita: $277 (1997).
Education: High school graduation rate: 99.3% (2000); College graduation rate: 73.2% (2000).
Housing: Homeownership rate: 97.6% (2000); Median home value: $500,000 (2000); Median rent: $625 per month (2000); Median age of housing: 43 years (2000).
Transportation: Commute to work: 80.6% car, 1.1% public transportation, 1.1% walk, 16.1% work from home (2000); Travel time to work: 27.2% less than 15 minutes, 28.5% 15 to 30 minutes, 33.1% 30 to 45 minutes, 6.0% 45 to 60 minutes, 5.3% 60 minutes or more (2000)

Houston County

Located in southeastern Minnesota; bounded on the east by the Mississippi River and the Wisconsin border, and on the south by Iowa; drained by the Root River. Covers a land area of 558.40 square miles, a water area of 10.50 square miles, and is located in the Central Time Zone. The county government was organized in 1854. County seat is Caledonia.

Houston County is part of the La Crosse, WI-MN MSA. The entire metro area includes: Houston County, MN; La Crosse County, WI

Weather Station: Caledonia — Elevation: 1,174 feet

	Jan	Feb	Mar	Apr	May	Jun	Jul	Aug	Sep	Oct	Nov	Dec
High	23	29	41	56	69	78	82	79	71	59	41	28
Low	4	10	22	34	46	56	60	58	48	37	24	11
Precip	0.9	0.8	2.0	3.8	3.8	4.4	4.7	4.7	3.7	2.5	2.4	1.3
Snow	10.6	8.0	7.9	3.3	tr	0.0	0.0	0.0	0.0	0.2	5.6	9.2

High and Low temperatures in degrees Fahrenheit; Precipitation and Snow in inches

Population: 19,718 (2000); Race: 98.5% White, 0.2% Black, 0.5% Asian, 0.1% American Indian and Alaska Native, 0.7% Hispanic of any race, 0.4% two or more races (2000); Density: 35.3 persons per square mile (2000); Age: 27.2% under 18, 16.0% over 64 (2000).
Religion: Five largest groups: 35.4% Catholic Church, 27.8% Evangelical Lutheran Church in America, 7.7% Wisconsin Evangelical Lutheran Synod, 4.5% The United Methodist Church, 2.4% United Church of Christ (2000).
Economy: Unemployment rate: 2.8% (11/2002); Total civilian labor force: 12,076 (11/2002); Leading industries: 22.4% health care and social assistance; 14.9% manufacturing; 12.6% retail trade (2000); Companies that employ more than 1,000 persons: 0 (2000); Companies that employ more than 100 persons: 7 (2000); Farms: 954 totaling 298,173 acres (1997); Minority business ownership rate: 0.0% (1997); Women business ownership rate: 17.0% (1997); Retail sales per capita: $3,970 (1997). Single-family building permits issued: 68 (2001) / 71 (2000); Multi-family building permits issued: 0 (2001) / 2 (2000).
Income: Per capita income: $18,826 (2000); Median household income: $40,680 (2000); Poverty rate: 6.5% (2000); Bankruptcy rate: 1.12% (2001).
Taxes: Total county taxes per capita: $200 (2000); County property taxes per capita: $198 (2000).
Education: High school graduation rate: 85.5% (2000); College graduation rate: 20.5% (2000).
Housing: Homeownership rate: 81.1% (2000); Median home value: $88,600 (2000); Median rent: $322 per month (2000); Median age of housing: 38 years (2000).
Health: Birth rate: 92.8 per 10,000 population (1998); Age adjusted death rate: 77.6 per 10,000 population (1999); Age adjusted cancer mortality rate: 172.3 deaths per 100,000 population (1999). Number of physicians: 9.6 per 10,000 population (1999); Number of hospital beds: 40.6 per 10,000 population (1999).
Elections: 2000 Presidential election results: 44.3% Gore, 49.9% Bush, 4.1% Nader, 1.2% Buchanan
National and State Parks: Beaver Creek Valley State Park
Additional Information Contacts
Houston County Government Offices 507-725-5680
Caledonia Chamber of Commerce 507-725-5477
La Crescent Chamber of Commerce 507-895-2800

Houston County Communities

BLACK HAMMER (township). Covers a land area of 35.714 square miles and a water area of 0 square miles. Located at 43.65° N. Lat.; 91.67° W. Long. Elevation is 1,179 feet.
Population: 326 (2000); Race: 100.0% White, 0.0% Black, 0.0% Asian, 0.0% American Indian and Alaska Native, 0.0% Hispanic of any race, 0.0% two or more races (2000); Density: 9.1 persons per square mile (2000); Age: 29.2% under 18, 10.2% over 64 (2000); Marriage status: 29.0% never married, 59.5% now married, 5.0% widowed, 6.6% divorced (2000); Foreign born: 6.9% (2000); Ancestry (includes multiple ancestries): 62.7% Norwegian, 32.2% German, 6.0% English, 4.2% Irish, 3.0% Dutch (2000).
Economy: Employment by occupation: 25.6% management, 20.5% professional, 4.5% services, 11.9% sales, 13.6% farming, 5.7% construction, 18.2% production (2000).
Income: Per capita income: $14,673 (2000); Median household income: $37,857 (2000); Poverty rate: 9.3% (2000).
Taxes: Total city taxes per capita: $112 (1997); City property taxes per capita: $112 (1997).
Education: High school graduation rate: 85.4% (2000); College graduation rate: 32.9% (2000).
Housing: Homeownership rate: 86.8% (2000); Median home value: $52,500 (2000); Median rent: $125 per month (2000); Median age of housing: 60+ years (2000).
Transportation: Commute to work: 57.6% car, 0.0% public transportation, 5.8% walk, 36.6% work from home (2000); Travel time to work: 32.1% less than 15 minutes, 37.6% 15 to 30 minutes, 10.1% 30 to 45 minutes, 12.8% 45 to 60 minutes, 7.3% 60 minutes or more (2000)

BROWNSVILLE (city). Covers a land area of 1.789 square miles and a water area of 0.153 square miles. Located at 43.69° N. Lat.; 91.28° W. Long. Elevation is 639 feet.
Population: 517 (2000); Race: 100.0% White, 0.0% Black, 0.0% Asian, 0.0% American Indian and Alaska Native, 1.0% Hispanic of any race, 0.0% two or more races (2000); Density: 288.9 persons per square mile (2000); Age: 21.8% under 18, 13.2% over 64 (2000); Marriage status: 21.8% never married, 63.5% now married, 6.4% widowed, 8.3% divorced (2000); Foreign born: 0.4% (2000); Ancestry (includes multiple ancestries): 54.1% German, 18.1% Irish, 17.9% Norwegian, 6.2% English, 5.1% French (except Basque) (2000).
Economy: Single-family building permits issued: 2 (2001) / 3 (2000); Multi-family building permits issued: 0 (2001) / 2 (2000); Employment by occupation: 9.3% management, 10.8% professional, 13.8% services, 28.6% sales, 0.7% farming, 11.5% construction, 25.3% production (2000).

Income: Per capita income: $20,442 (2000); Median household income: $46,250 (2000); Poverty rate: 3.5% (2000).
Taxes: Total city taxes per capita: $78 (1997); City property taxes per capita: $70 (1997).
Education: High school graduation rate: 87.1% (2000); College graduation rate: 13.2% (2000).
Housing: Homeownership rate: 83.9% (2000); Median home value: $72,500 (2000); Median rent: $405 per month (2000); Median age of housing: 42 years (2000).
Transportation: Commute to work: 95.8% car, 0.8% public transportation, 1.1% walk, 2.3% work from home (2000); Travel time to work: 13.6% less than 15 minutes, 39.9% 15 to 30 minutes, 38.0% 30 to 45 minutes, 1.6% 45 to 60 minutes, 7.0% 60 minutes or more (2000)

BROWNSVILLE (township). Covers a land area of 28.454 square miles and a water area of 1.111 square miles. Located at 43.69° N. Lat.; 91.30° W. Long. Elevation is 639 feet.
Population: 462 (2000); Race: 99.6% White, 0.0% Black, 0.0% Asian, 0.4% American Indian and Alaska Native, 0.6% Hispanic of any race, 0.0% two or more races (2000); Density: 16.2 persons per square mile (2000); Age: 28.6% under 18, 8.8% over 64 (2000); Marriage status: 27.9% never married, 62.7% now married, 4.7% widowed, 4.7% divorced (2000); Foreign born: 0.6% (2000); Ancestry (includes multiple ancestries): 58.8% German, 19.8% Norwegian, 19.4% Irish, 4.7% English, 3.7% Swedish (2000).
Economy: Corn, oats. Employment by occupation: 12.0% management, 22.3% professional, 11.7% services, 21.9% sales, 2.6% farming, 12.4% construction, 17.2% production (2000).
Income: Per capita income: $17,552 (2000); Median household income: $45,625 (2000); Poverty rate: 12.0% (2000).
Taxes: Total city taxes per capita: $71 (1997); City property taxes per capita: $71 (1997).
Education: High school graduation rate: 89.0% (2000); College graduation rate: 20.3% (2000).
Housing: Homeownership rate: 97.1% (2000); Median home value: $104,500 (2000); Median rent: $375 per month (2000); Median age of housing: 41 years (2000).
Transportation: Commute to work: 83.2% car, 0.0% public transportation, 1.5% walk, 15.4% work from home (2000); Travel time to work: 7.4% less than 15 minutes, 47.2% 15 to 30 minutes, 35.5% 30 to 45 minutes, 8.7% 45 to 60 minutes, 1.3% 60 minutes or more (2000)

CALEDONIA (city). Covers a land area of 2.859 square miles and a water area of 0 square miles. Located at 43.63° N. Lat.; 91.49° W. Long. Elevation is 1,174 feet.
History: Caledonia was founded and named in 1852 by Sam McPhail. Local residents blamed Jacob Webster, who came to Caledonia in 1854, for the abundance of dandelions in Minnesota. Webster, it is said, sent to New England for dandelion seed, which grew prolifically in the Minnesota soil.
Population: 2,965 (2000); Race: 98.1% White, 0.2% Black, 0.2% Asian, 0.1% American Indian and Alaska Native, 1.2% Hispanic of any race, 1.3% two or more races (2000); Density: 1,037.1 persons per square mile (2000); Age: 25.9% under 18, 21.5% over 64 (2000); Marriage status: 23.1% never married, 56.4% now married, 12.5% widowed, 8.1% divorced (2000); Foreign born: 0.8% (2000); Ancestry (includes multiple ancestries): 58.2% German, 31.7% Norwegian, 14.4% Irish, 5.7% English, 3.6% Other groups (2000).
Economy: Single-family building permits issued: 7 (2001) / 7 (2000); Multi-family building permits issued: 0 (2001) / 0 (2000); Employment by occupation: 7.6% management, 21.4% professional, 19.2% services, 20.1% sales, 0.8% farming, 11.4% construction, 19.4% production (2000).
Income: Per capita income: $16,953 (2000); Median household income: $32,455 (2000); Poverty rate: 8.7% (2000).
Taxes: Total city taxes per capita: $106 (1997); City property taxes per capita: $100 (1997).
Education: High school graduation rate: 80.2% (2000); College graduation rate: 15.7% (2000).

School District(s)

Caledonia (PK-12)
2000 Enrollment: 1,009 507-725-3316
Housing: Homeownership rate: 73.7% (2000); Median home value: $73,400 (2000); Median rent: $271 per month (2000); Median age of housing: 43 years (2000).
Safety: Violent crime rate: 23.4 per 10,000 population; Property crime rate: 246.9 per 10,000 population (2001).
Newspapers: The Caledonia Argus (1 x week)
Transportation: Commute to work: 79.0% car, 0.1% public transportation, 13.9% walk, 4.4% work from home (2000); Travel time to work: 58.7% less than 15 minutes, 12.3% 15 to 30 minutes, 21.7% 30 to 45 minutes, 4.0% 45 to 60 minutes, 3.3% 60 minutes or more (2000)
Additional Information Contacts
Caledonia Chamber of Commerce 507-725-5477

CALEDONIA (township). Covers a land area of 33.832 square miles and a water area of 0.009 square miles. Located at 43.63° N. Lat.; 91.54° W. Long. Elevation is 1,174 feet.
History: Settled c.1855.
Population: 625 (2000); Race: 99.2% White, 0.0% Black, 0.0% Asian, 0.2% American Indian and Alaska Native, 0.2% Hispanic of any race, 0.6% two or more races (2000); Density: 18.5 persons per square mile (2000); Age: 35.1% under 18, 10.3% over 64 (2000); Marriage status: 25.1% never married, 68.2% now married, 4.2% widowed, 2.5% divorced (2000); Foreign born: 2.1% (2000); Ancestry (includes multiple ancestries): 64.8% German, 27.6% Norwegian, 13.2% Irish, 6.4% English, 4.1% Swedish (2000).
Economy: Grain, soybeans; livestock, poultry; dairying. Manufacturing: tubing, frozen food, software, sandpaper; lumber. Employment by occupation: 25.3% management, 19.8% professional, 11.8% services, 16.4% sales, 9.5% farming, 7.8% construction, 9.5% production (2000).
Income: Per capita income: $18,372 (2000); Median household income: $53,056 (2000); Poverty rate: 7.6% (2000).
Taxes: Total city taxes per capita: $78 (1997); City property taxes per capita: $78 (1997).
Education: High school graduation rate: 92.8% (2000); College graduation rate: 23.8% (2000).
Housing: Homeownership rate: 92.5% (2000); Median home value: $104,800 (2000); Median rent: $325 per month (2000); Median age of housing: 43 years (2000).
Transportation: Commute to work: 79.7% car, 0.0% public transportation, 3.2% walk, 17.1% work from home (2000); Travel time to work: 43.7% less than 15 minutes, 23.8% 15 to 30 minutes, 20.6% 30 to 45 minutes, 6.6% 45 to 60 minutes, 5.2% 60 minutes or more (2000)

CROOKED CREEK (township). Covers a land area of 32.054 square miles and a water area of 1.756 square miles. Located at 43.60° N. Lat.; 91.31° W. Long.
Population: 323 (2000); Race: 97.1% White, 1.6% Black, 0.0% Asian, 0.0% American Indian and Alaska Native, 1.3% Hispanic of any race, 0.0% two or more races (2000); Density: 10.1 persons per square mile (2000); Age: 32.7% under 18, 11.8% over 64 (2000); Marriage status: 25.0% never married, 63.4% now married, 3.6% widowed, 8.0% divorced (2000); Foreign born: 0.7% (2000); Ancestry (includes multiple ancestries): 55.9% German, 21.6% Norwegian, 12.7% Irish, 4.2% United States or American, 2.9% Swedish (2000).
Economy: Employment by occupation: 12.8% management, 14.2% professional, 14.9% services, 15.6% sales, 2.1% farming, 15.6% construction, 24.8% production (2000).
Income: Per capita income: $14,493 (2000); Median household income: $38,929 (2000); Poverty rate: 5.9% (2000).
Taxes: Total city taxes per capita: $34 (1997); City property taxes per capita: $34 (1997).
Education: High school graduation rate: 85.7% (2000); College graduation rate: 16.9% (2000).
Housing: Homeownership rate: 82.0% (2000); Median home value: $86,700 (2000); Median rent: $317 per month (2000); Median age of housing: 60+ years (2000).
Transportation: Commute to work: 86.0% car, 1.5% public transportation, 1.5% walk, 9.6% work from home (2000); Travel time to work: 4.1% less than 15 minutes, 52.8% 15 to 30 minutes, 26.0% 30 to 45 minutes, 15.4% 45 to 60 minutes, 1.6% 60 minutes or more (2000)

EITZEN (city). Covers a land area of 0.581 square miles and a water area of 0 square miles. Located at 43.50° N. Lat.; 91.46° W. Long. Elevation is 1,155 feet.
Population: 229 (2000); Race: 100.0% White, 0.0% Black, 0.0% Asian, 0.0% American Indian and Alaska Native, 0.0% Hispanic of any race, 0.0% two or more races (2000); Density: 394.4 persons per square mile (2000); Age: 23.7% under 18, 26.5% over 64 (2000); Marriage status: 13.3% never married, 68.0% now married, 11.3% widowed, 7.4% divorced (2000); Foreign born: 0.0% (2000); Ancestry (includes multiple ancestries): 59.5% German, 19.1% Norwegian, 13.6% Irish, 5.8% English, 5.4% French (except Basque) (2000).

Economy: Manufacturing: feeds. Single-family building permits issued: 2 (2001) / 1 (2000); Multi-family building permits issued: 0 (2001) / 0 (2000); Employment by occupation: 4.7% management, 11.6% professional, 17.1% services, 25.6% sales, 1.6% farming, 15.5% construction, 24.0% production (2000).
Income: Per capita income: $16,440 (2000); Median household income: $29,688 (2000); Poverty rate: 3.5% (2000).
Taxes: Total city taxes per capita: $120 (1997); City property taxes per capita: $111 (1997).
Education: High school graduation rate: 83.7% (2000); College graduation rate: 6.3% (2000).
Housing: Homeownership rate: 94.7% (2000); Median home value: $50,500 (2000); Median rent: $288 per month (2000); Median age of housing: 50 years (2000).
Transportation: Commute to work: 76.6% car, 1.6% public transportation, 11.3% walk, 10.5% work from home (2000); Travel time to work: 44.1% less than 15 minutes, 26.1% 15 to 30 minutes, 6.3% 30 to 45 minutes, 18.9% 45 to 60 minutes, 4.5% 60 minutes or more (2000)

HOKAH (city). Covers a land area of 0.714 square miles and a water area of 0.014 square miles. Located at 43.75° N. Lat.; 91.35° W. Long. Elevation is 654 feet.
Population: 614 (2000); Race: 97.3% White, 2.3% Black, 0.0% Asian, 0.3% American Indian and Alaska Native, 0.7% Hispanic of any race, 0.0% two or more races (2000); Density: 860.1 persons per square mile (2000); Age: 30.3% under 18, 12.1% over 64 (2000); Marriage status: 33.5% never married, 45.6% now married, 5.9% widowed, 15.0% divorced (2000); Foreign born: 2.0% (2000); Ancestry (includes multiple ancestries): 51.8% German, 19.8% Norwegian, 15.9% Irish, 5.4% Czech, 4.5% French (except Basque) (2000).
Economy: Single-family building permits issued: 0 (2001) / 0 (2000); Multi-family building permits issued: 0 (2001) / 0 (2000); Employment by occupation: 3.0% management, 8.4% professional, 19.5% services, 28.6% sales, 0.7% farming, 17.8% construction, 21.9% production (2000).
Income: Per capita income: $15,630 (2000); Median household income: $26,838 (2000); Poverty rate: 15.5% (2000).
Taxes: Total city taxes per capita: $148 (1997); City property taxes per capita: $142 (1997).
Education: High school graduation rate: 81.9% (2000); College graduation rate: 8.1% (2000).
Housing: Homeownership rate: 65.5% (2000); Median home value: $71,100 (2000); Median rent: $293 per month (2000); Median age of housing: 54 years (2000).
Transportation: Commute to work: 92.1% car, 0.7% public transportation, 2.4% walk, 3.4% work from home (2000); Travel time to work: 24.1% less than 15 minutes, 60.6% 15 to 30 minutes, 9.9% 30 to 45 minutes, 0.7% 45 to 60 minutes, 4.6% 60 minutes or more (2000)

HOKAH (township). Covers a land area of 23.787 square miles and a water area of 1.650 square miles. Located at 43.75° N. Lat.; 91.34° W. Long. Elevation is 654 feet.
Population: 545 (2000); Race: 99.6% White, 0.0% Black, 0.0% Asian, 0.4% American Indian and Alaska Native, 0.6% Hispanic of any race, 0.0% two or more races (2000); Density: 22.9 persons per square mile (2000); Age: 31.4% under 18, 7.8% over 64 (2000); Marriage status: 19.2% never married, 66.9% now married, 4.3% widowed, 9.6% divorced (2000); Foreign born: 0.4% (2000); Ancestry (includes multiple ancestries): 57.7% German, 17.2% Norwegian, 12.2% Irish, 7.2% English, 6.7% Polish (2000).
Economy: Grain, soybeans; livestock, poultry; dairying; timber. Manufacturing: lumber. Employment by occupation: 15.1% management, 25.1% professional, 15.4% services, 18.4% sales, 1.3% farming, 13.7% construction, 11.0% production (2000).
Income: Per capita income: $20,752 (2000); Median household income: $53,375 (2000); Poverty rate: 3.9% (2000).
Taxes: Total city taxes per capita: $54 (1997); City property taxes per capita: $54 (1997).
Education: High school graduation rate: 92.3% (2000); College graduation rate: 18.6% (2000).
Housing: Homeownership rate: 89.7% (2000); Median home value: $119,400 (2000); Median rent: $408 per month (2000); Median age of housing: 26 years (2000).
Transportation: Commute to work: 91.2% car, 1.7% public transportation, 0.0% walk, 7.1% work from home (2000); Travel time to work: 17.9% less than 15 minutes, 54.4% 15 to 30 minutes, 21.5% 30 to 45 minutes, 4.0% 45 to 60 minutes, 2.2% 60 minutes or more (2000)

HOUSTON (city). Covers a land area of 0.942 square miles and a water area of 0 square miles. Located at 43.76° N. Lat.; 91.56° W. Long. Elevation is 684 feet.
History: Houston was settled by people attracted to the many springs in the area. Houston's location on the Root River made it a busy port in steamboat days. Later, it became a dairy and poultry center.
Population: 1,020 (2000); Race: 99.6% White, 0.3% Black, 0.0% Asian, 0.0% American Indian and Alaska Native, 0.2% Hispanic of any race, 0.1% two or more races (2000); Density: 1,083.2 persons per square mile (2000); Age: 23.1% under 18, 28.1% over 64 (2000); Marriage status: 22.0% never married, 52.4% now married, 14.3% widowed, 11.3% divorced (2000); Foreign born: 0.8% (2000); Ancestry (includes multiple ancestries): 43.0% Norwegian, 35.1% German, 12.8% Irish, 7.4% English, 5.4% Swedish (2000).
Economy: Single-family building permits issued: 2 (2001) / 1 (2000); Multi-family building permits issued: 0 (2001) / 0 (2000); Employment by occupation: 7.1% management, 16.5% professional, 12.5% services, 22.5% sales, 2.2% farming, 11.2% construction, 27.9% production (2000).
Income: Per capita income: $17,087 (2000); Median household income: $29,236 (2000); Poverty rate: 10.3% (2000).
Taxes: Total city taxes per capita: $133 (1997); City property taxes per capita: $132 (1997).
Education: High school graduation rate: 77.9% (2000); College graduation rate: 15.9% (2000).

School District(s)

Houston (PK-12)
2000 Enrollment: 477 507-896-3378
Housing: Homeownership rate: 67.4% (2000); Median home value: $62,200 (2000); Median rent: $327 per month (2000); Median age of housing: 49 years (2000).
Transportation: Commute to work: 84.0% car, 0.0% public transportation, 10.8% walk, 4.3% work from home (2000); Travel time to work: 37.4% less than 15 minutes, 23.1% 15 to 30 minutes, 22.6% 30 to 45 minutes, 7.3% 45 to 60 minutes, 9.6% 60 minutes or more (2000)

HOUSTON (township). Covers a land area of 33.279 square miles and a water area of 0.266 square miles. Located at 43.78° N. Lat.; 91.55° W. Long. Elevation is 684 feet.
Population: 438 (2000); Race: 98.6% White, 0.0% Black, 0.5% Asian, 0.5% American Indian and Alaska Native, 0.0% Hispanic of any race, 0.5% two or more races (2000); Density: 13.2 persons per square mile (2000); Age: 24.8% under 18, 13.0% over 64 (2000); Marriage status: 22.8% never married, 65.0% now married, 6.4% widowed, 5.8% divorced (2000); Foreign born: 0.7% (2000); Ancestry (includes multiple ancestries): 45.0% Norwegian, 44.3% German, 11.1% Irish, 6.8% Swedish, 3.3% European (2000).
Economy: Grain, soybeans; livestock, poultry; dairying. Manufacturing: button parts and button machines, feeds. Employment by occupation: 20.1% management, 14.5% professional, 14.1% services, 20.9% sales, 2.4% farming, 10.8% construction, 17.3% production (2000).
Income: Per capita income: $18,933 (2000); Median household income: $42,000 (2000); Poverty rate: 7.3% (2000).
Taxes: Total city taxes per capita: $125 (1997); City property taxes per capita: $125 (1997).
Education: High school graduation rate: 84.9% (2000); College graduation rate: 25.3% (2000).
Housing: Homeownership rate: 84.5% (2000); Median home value: $90,300 (2000); Median rent: $372 per month (2000); Median age of housing: 37 years (2000).
Transportation: Commute to work: 85.4% car, 0.0% public transportation, 1.2% walk, 11.7% work from home (2000); Travel time to work: 45.9% less than 15 minutes, 21.6% 15 to 30 minutes, 26.1% 30 to 45 minutes, 3.7% 45 to 60 minutes, 2.8% 60 minutes or more (2000)

JEFFERSON (township). Covers a land area of 32.011 square miles and a water area of 2.796 square miles. Located at 43.53° N. Lat.; 91.28° W. Long.
Population: 129 (2000); Race: 100.0% White, 0.0% Black, 0.0% Asian, 0.0% American Indian and Alaska Native, 0.0% Hispanic of any race, 0.0% two or more races (2000); Density: 4.0 persons per square mile (2000); Age: 32.1% under 18, 23.9% over 64 (2000); Marriage status: 14.4% never married, 74.2% now married, 8.2% widowed, 3.1% divorced (2000); Foreign born: 0.0% (2000); Ancestry (includes multiple ancestries): 60.4% German, 17.9% Irish, 11.9% Norwegian, 3.7% United States or American, 2.2% Other groups (2000).

Economy: Employment by occupation: 30.5% management, 8.5% professional, 6.8% services, 25.4% sales, 0.0% farming, 11.9% construction, 16.9% production (2000).
Income: Per capita income: $12,247 (2000); Median household income: $25,938 (2000); Poverty rate: 7.5% (2000).
Taxes: Total city taxes per capita: $85 (1997); City property taxes per capita: $85 (1997).
Education: High school graduation rate: 83.8% (2000); College graduation rate: 7.5% (2000).
Housing: Homeownership rate: 91.3% (2000); Median home value: $60,000 (2000); Median rent: $275 per month (2000); Median age of housing: 47 years (2000).
Transportation: Commute to work: 79.7% car, 0.0% public transportation, 0.0% walk, 20.3% work from home (2000); Travel time to work: 29.8% less than 15 minutes, 21.3% 15 to 30 minutes, 23.4% 30 to 45 minutes, 17.0% 45 to 60 minutes, 8.5% 60 minutes or more (2000)

LA CRESCENT (city). Covers a land area of 3.012 square miles and a water area of 0.333 square miles. Located at 43.82° N. Lat.; 91.30° W. Long.
History: La Crescent had its beginning in 1851, when fur trader Peter Cameron arrived and envisioned a project to drain the lowlands by digging a canal to the Mississippi River. Although Cameron's project was abandoned, the town grew. First called Manton, the name was changed to La Crescent by the residents, because of their rivalry with nearby La Crosse. Orchards in the La Crescent area produced apples and plums.
Population: 4,923 (2000); Race: 97.7% White, 0.2% Black, 0.9% Asian, 0.0% American Indian and Alaska Native, 0.9% Hispanic of any race, 0.3% two or more races (2000); Density: 1,634.4 persons per square mile (2000); Age: 26.9% under 18, 15.5% over 64 (2000); Marriage status: 20.1% never married, 63.0% now married, 9.6% widowed, 7.3% divorced (2000); Foreign born: 1.0% (2000); Ancestry (includes multiple ancestries): 53.0% German, 30.1% Norwegian, 16.6% Irish, 6.8% Polish, 6.4% English (2000).
Economy: Single-family building permits issued: 21 (2001) / 22 (2000); Multi-family building permits issued: 0 (2001) / 0 (2000); Employment by occupation: 14.8% management, 23.1% professional, 14.9% services, 27.7% sales, 0.5% farming, 6.5% construction, 12.4% production (2000).
Income: Per capita income: $21,361 (2000); Median household income: $45,433 (2000); Poverty rate: 3.9% (2000).
Taxes: Total city taxes per capita: $164 (1997); City property taxes per capita: $150 (1997).
Education: High school graduation rate: 88.6% (2000); College graduation rate: 28.9% (2000).

School District(s)

Lacrescent Montessori Academy (KG-06)
2000 Enrollment: 57 507-895-4054

Housing: Homeownership rate: 77.4% (2000); Median home value: $104,900 (2000); Median rent: $388 per month (2000); Median age of housing: 27 years (2000).
Newspapers: Houston County News (1 x week); Companion (2 x month)
Transportation: Commute to work: 91.9% car, 0.6% public transportation, 2.2% walk, 4.7% work from home (2000); Travel time to work: 45.3% less than 15 minutes, 43.4% 15 to 30 minutes, 4.8% 30 to 45 minutes, 2.5% 45 to 60 minutes, 4.0% 60 minutes or more (2000)

Additional Information Contacts

La Crescent Chamber of Commerce 507-895-2800

LA CRESCENT (township). Covers a land area of 21.274 square miles and a water area of 1.485 square miles. Located at 43.82° N. Lat.; 91.33° W. Long.
History: Richard J. Dorer Memorial Hardwood State Forest to South.
Population: 1,487 (2000); Race: 97.9% White, 0.0% Black, 1.8% Asian, 0.0% American Indian and Alaska Native, 0.4% Hispanic of any race, 0.1% two or more races (2000); Density: 69.9 persons per square mile (2000); Age: 30.4% under 18, 9.4% over 64 (2000); Marriage status: 19.5% never married, 71.3% now married, 3.2% widowed, 6.0% divorced (2000); Foreign born: 2.3% (2000); Ancestry (includes multiple ancestries): 55.8% German, 22.5% Norwegian, 16.9% Irish, 7.9% English, 3.6% French (except Basque) (2000).
Economy: Agricultural area: grain, soybeans; livestock, poultry; dairying. Manufacturing: burial vaults, septic tanks, concrete, wood trusses. Lock and Dam No. 7 to North. Employment by occupation: 14.7% management, 22.9% professional, 12.4% services, 24.8% sales, 1.3% farming, 10.7% construction, 13.2% production (2000).
Income: Per capita income: $22,298 (2000); Median household income: $58,603 (2000); Poverty rate: 2.7% (2000).
Taxes: Total city taxes per capita: $52 (1997); City property taxes per capita: $48 (1997).
Education: High school graduation rate: 91.9% (2000); College graduation rate: 32.9% (2000).
Housing: Homeownership rate: 96.6% (2000); Median home value: $135,000 (2000); Median rent: $413 per month (2000); Median age of housing: 23 years (2000).
Transportation: Commute to work: 92.4% car, 0.0% public transportation, 0.5% walk, 6.6% work from home (2000); Travel time to work: 36.0% less than 15 minutes, 56.0% 15 to 30 minutes, 6.2% 30 to 45 minutes, 0.9% 45 to 60 minutes, 0.9% 60 minutes or more (2000)

MAYVILLE (township). Covers a land area of 30.544 square miles and a water area of 0.074 square miles. Located at 43.62° N. Lat.; 91.45° W. Long.
Population: 427 (2000); Race: 100.0% White, 0.0% Black, 0.0% Asian, 0.0% American Indian and Alaska Native, 0.0% Hispanic of any race, 0.0% two or more races (2000); Density: 14.0 persons per square mile (2000); Age: 32.8% under 18, 10.6% over 64 (2000); Marriage status: 30.3% never married, 62.8% now married, 4.6% widowed, 2.3% divorced (2000); Foreign born: 0.0% (2000); Ancestry (includes multiple ancestries): 57.5% German, 23.5% Norwegian, 12.1% Irish, 7.9% Luxemburger, 5.7% English (2000).
Economy: Employment by occupation: 19.7% management, 17.0% professional, 12.8% services, 18.8% sales, 5.5% farming, 13.3% construction, 12.8% production (2000).
Income: Per capita income: $15,475 (2000); Median household income: $41,979 (2000); Poverty rate: 7.9% (2000).
Taxes: Total city taxes per capita: $91 (1997); City property taxes per capita: $91 (1997).
Education: High school graduation rate: 83.4% (2000); College graduation rate: 12.3% (2000).
Housing: Homeownership rate: 87.3% (2000); Median home value: $102,100 (2000); Median rent: $275 per month (2000); Median age of housing: 50 years (2000).
Transportation: Commute to work: 78.9% car, 0.0% public transportation, 1.8% walk, 18.3% work from home (2000); Travel time to work: 36.5% less than 15 minutes, 24.2% 15 to 30 minutes, 33.7% 30 to 45 minutes, 3.9% 45 to 60 minutes, 1.7% 60 minutes or more (2000)

MONEY CREEK (township). Covers a land area of 35.600 square miles and a water area of 0.163 square miles. Located at 43.80° N. Lat.; 91.63° W. Long. Elevation is 704 feet.
Population: 547 (2000); Race: 99.6% White, 0.0% Black, 0.0% Asian, 0.0% American Indian and Alaska Native, 0.0% Hispanic of any race, 0.4% two or more races (2000); Density: 15.4 persons per square mile (2000); Age: 27.7% under 18, 9.8% over 64 (2000); Marriage status: 18.4% never married, 72.9% now married, 1.7% widowed, 7.1% divorced (2000); Foreign born: 0.5% (2000); Ancestry (includes multiple ancestries): 49.5% German, 42.5% Norwegian, 14.3% Irish, 7.1% Dutch, 6.6% English (2000).
Economy: Employment by occupation: 18.3% management, 18.0% professional, 9.0% services, 18.0% sales, 1.4% farming, 14.5% construction, 20.8% production (2000).
Income: Per capita income: $15,632 (2000); Median household income: $37,625 (2000); Poverty rate: 8.6% (2000).
Taxes: Total city taxes per capita: $81 (1997); City property taxes per capita: $81 (1997).
Education: High school graduation rate: 85.2% (2000); College graduation rate: 13.2% (2000).
Housing: Homeownership rate: 92.9% (2000); Median home value: $82,700 (2000); Median rent: $375 per month (2000); Median age of housing: 48 years (2000).
Transportation: Commute to work: 87.8% car, 0.0% public transportation, 1.4% walk, 9.4% work from home (2000); Travel time to work: 26.9% less than 15 minutes, 20.8% 15 to 30 minutes, 37.7% 30 to 45 minutes, 6.5% 45 to 60 minutes, 8.1% 60 minutes or more (2000)

MOUND PRAIRIE (township). Covers a land area of 36.236 square miles and a water area of 0.514 square miles. Located at 43.77° N. Lat.; 91.43° W. Long.
Population: 661 (2000); Race: 99.2% White, 0.0% Black, 0.0% Asian, 0.6% American Indian and Alaska Native, 0.0% Hispanic of any race, 0.0% two or more races (2000); Density: 18.2 persons per square mile (2000); Age: 30.0% under 18, 10.1% over 64 (2000); Marriage status: 22.0% never married, 66.4% now married, 4.1% widowed, 7.5% divorced (2000); Foreign born: 0.3% (2000); Ancestry (includes multiple ancestries): 53.4% German, 26.6% Norwegian, 12.1% Irish, 6.5% United States or American, 5.4% English (2000).

Economy: Employment by occupation: 23.9% management, 11.0% professional, 14.8% services, 22.5% sales, 2.7% farming, 11.0% construction, 14.0% production (2000).
Income: Per capita income: $19,487 (2000); Median household income: $50,234 (2000); Poverty rate: 2.4% (2000).
Taxes: Total city taxes per capita: $80 (1997); City property taxes per capita: $80 (1997).
Education: High school graduation rate: 86.2% (2000); College graduation rate: 21.0% (2000).
Housing: Homeownership rate: 90.8% (2000); Median home value: $100,800 (2000); Median rent: $425 per month (2000); Median age of housing: 30 years (2000).
Transportation: Commute to work: 83.3% car, 0.0% public transportation, 4.7% walk, 11.4% work from home (2000); Travel time to work: 18.2% less than 15 minutes, 46.5% 15 to 30 minutes, 28.3% 30 to 45 minutes, 4.7% 45 to 60 minutes, 2.2% 60 minutes or more (2000)

SHELDON (township). Covers a land area of 29.761 square miles and a water area of 0 square miles. Located at 43.70° N. Lat.; 91.55° W. Long. Elevation is 1,412 feet.
Population: 289 (2000); Race: 97.2% White, 0.0% Black, 0.0% Asian, 0.0% American Indian and Alaska Native, 2.2% Hispanic of any race, 0.0% two or more races (2000); Density: 9.7 persons per square mile (2000); Age: 27.1% under 18, 16.6% over 64 (2000); Marriage status: 26.6% never married, 62.2% now married, 3.9% widowed, 7.3% divorced (2000); Foreign born: 0.6% (2000); Ancestry (includes multiple ancestries): 44.6% Norwegian, 41.8% German, 16.9% Swedish, 5.5% Irish, 5.2% United States or American (2000).
Economy: Employment by occupation: 31.6% management, 6.3% professional, 7.9% services, 24.7% sales, 4.7% farming, 10.5% construction, 14.2% production (2000).
Income: Per capita income: $16,918 (2000); Median household income: $40,625 (2000); Poverty rate: 12.2% (2000).
Taxes: Total city taxes per capita: $63 (1997); City property taxes per capita: $63 (1997).
Education: High school graduation rate: 86.9% (2000); College graduation rate: 6.6% (2000).
Housing: Homeownership rate: 93.9% (2000); Median home value: $82,500 (2000); Median rent: $325 per month (2000); Median age of housing: 60+ years (2000).
Transportation: Commute to work: 73.4% car, 0.0% public transportation, 6.4% walk, 20.2% work from home (2000); Travel time to work: 33.3% less than 15 minutes, 36.0% 15 to 30 minutes, 18.7% 30 to 45 minutes, 10.0% 45 to 60 minutes, 2.0% 60 minutes or more (2000)

SPRING GROVE (city). Covers a land area of 0.896 square miles and a water area of 0 square miles. Located at 43.56° N. Lat.; 91.63° W. Long. Elevation is 1,322 feet.
Population: 1,304 (2000); Race: 98.2% White, 0.0% Black, 0.3% Asian, 0.0% American Indian and Alaska Native, 0.6% Hispanic of any race, 1.5% two or more races (2000); Density: 1,455.8 persons per square mile (2000); Age: 21.9% under 18, 29.6% over 64 (2000); Marriage status: 23.1% never married, 56.2% now married, 13.4% widowed, 7.3% divorced (2000); Foreign born: 1.2% (2000); Ancestry (includes multiple ancestries): 64.5% Norwegian, 31.7% German, 6.3% Irish, 3.5% Other groups, 3.3% English (2000).
Economy: Single-family building permits issued: 3 (2001) / 3 (2000); Multi-family building permits issued: 0 (2001) / 0 (2000); Employment by occupation: 9.8% management, 13.6% professional, 20.7% services, 20.7% sales, 2.7% farming, 9.7% construction, 22.9% production (2000).
Income: Per capita income: $16,307 (2000); Median household income: $29,643 (2000); Poverty rate: 11.0% (2000).
Taxes: Total city taxes per capita: $144 (1997); City property taxes per capita: $140 (1997).
Education: High school graduation rate: 76.4% (2000); College graduation rate: 11.5% (2000).

School District(s)

Spring Grove (PK-12)
2000 Enrollment: 411 507-498-3221

Housing: Homeownership rate: 74.5% (2000); Median home value: $56,800 (2000); Median rent: $250 per month (2000); Median age of housing: 48 years (2000).
Hospitals: Tweeten Health Care Center (71 beds)
Newspapers: Spring Grove Herald (1 x week)
Transportation: Commute to work: 82.5% car, 0.0% public transportation, 12.2% walk, 3.3% work from home (2000); Travel time to work: 63.6% less than 15 minutes, 15.8% 15 to 30 minutes, 9.8% 30 to 45 minutes, 8.0% 45 to 60 minutes, 2.8% 60 minutes or more (2000)

SPRING GROVE (township). Covers a land area of 35.008 square miles and a water area of 0 square miles. Located at 43.55° N. Lat.; 91.68° W. Long. Elevation is 1,322 feet.
Population: 422 (2000); Race: 99.5% White, 0.0% Black, 0.5% Asian, 0.0% American Indian and Alaska Native, 0.5% Hispanic of any race, 0.0% two or more races (2000); Density: 12.1 persons per square mile (2000); Age: 22.0% under 18, 14.1% over 64 (2000); Marriage status: 28.7% never married, 59.2% now married, 5.7% widowed, 6.4% divorced (2000); Foreign born: 0.5% (2000); Ancestry (includes multiple ancestries): 65.5% Norwegian, 28.4% German, 8.0% United States or American, 4.5% English, 4.0% Scotch-Irish (2000).
Economy: Grain, soybeans; livestock, poultry; dairying. Manufacturing includes fertilizers, consumer goods, hardwood timber, crushed limestone. Employment by occupation: 20.5% management, 13.8% professional, 10.7% services, 14.7% sales, 8.9% farming, 17.0% construction, 14.3% production (2000).
Income: Per capita income: $21,505 (2000); Median household income: $37,639 (2000); Poverty rate: 5.3% (2000).
Taxes: Total city taxes per capita: $118 (1997); City property taxes per capita: $118 (1997).
Education: High school graduation rate: 88.2% (2000); College graduation rate: 15.5% (2000).
Housing: Homeownership rate: 86.1% (2000); Median home value: $61,500 (2000); Median rent: $138 per month (2000); Median age of housing: 60+ years (2000).
Transportation: Commute to work: 73.7% car, 0.0% public transportation, 6.7% walk, 19.2% work from home (2000); Travel time to work: 50.8% less than 15 minutes, 28.7% 15 to 30 minutes, 10.5% 30 to 45 minutes, 5.5% 45 to 60 minutes, 4.4% 60 minutes or more (2000)

UNION (township). Covers a land area of 26.239 square miles and a water area of 0.022 square miles. Located at 43.72° N. Lat.; 91.40° W. Long.
Population: 385 (2000); Race: 99.8% White, 0.0% Black, 0.0% Asian, 0.2% American Indian and Alaska Native, 0.0% Hispanic of any race, 0.0% two or more races (2000); Density: 14.7 persons per square mile (2000); Age: 27.1% under 18, 7.8% over 64 (2000); Marriage status: 26.1% never married, 64.1% now married, 2.5% widowed, 7.4% divorced (2000); Foreign born: 0.7% (2000); Ancestry (includes multiple ancestries): 60.7% German, 24.6% Norwegian, 15.1% Irish, 10.2% French (except Basque), 6.1% Polish (2000).
Economy: Employment by occupation: 9.5% management, 24.1% professional, 12.4% services, 20.7% sales, 0.0% farming, 14.9% construction, 18.3% production (2000).
Income: Per capita income: $19,573 (2000); Median household income: $51,250 (2000); Poverty rate: 0.7% (2000).
Taxes: Total city taxes per capita: $55 (1997); City property taxes per capita: $55 (1997).
Education: High school graduation rate: 92.0% (2000); College graduation rate: 22.2% (2000).
Housing: Homeownership rate: 87.3% (2000); Median home value: $110,000 (2000); Median rent: $145 per month (2000); Median age of housing: 29 years (2000).
Transportation: Commute to work: 95.4% car, 0.0% public transportation, 0.0% walk, 4.6% work from home (2000); Travel time to work: 15.5% less than 15 minutes, 49.6% 15 to 30 minutes, 30.1% 30 to 45 minutes, 1.8% 45 to 60 minutes, 3.1% 60 minutes or more (2000)

WILMINGTON (township). Covers a land area of 35.985 square miles and a water area of 0 square miles. Located at 43.55° N. Lat.; 91.53° W. Long.
Population: 472 (2000); Race: 100.0% White, 0.0% Black, 0.0% Asian, 0.0% American Indian and Alaska Native, 0.7% Hispanic of any race, 0.0% two or more races (2000); Density: 13.1 persons per square mile (2000); Age: 26.2% under 18, 15.0% over 64 (2000); Marriage status: 19.1% never married, 73.5% now married, 2.5% widowed, 4.9% divorced (2000); Foreign born: 0.7% (2000); Ancestry (includes multiple ancestries): 51.2% Norwegian, 44.7% German, 10.0% English, 6.9% Irish, 3.5% Greek (2000).
Economy: Employment by occupation: 25.8% management, 13.6% professional, 14.4% services, 16.7% sales, 4.9% farming, 9.8% construction, 14.8% production (2000).
Income: Per capita income: $20,072 (2000); Median household income: $38,214 (2000); Poverty rate: 3.5% (2000).
Taxes: Total city taxes per capita: $109 (1997); City property taxes per capita: $109 (1997).

Education: High school graduation rate: 84.3% (2000); College graduation rate: 17.2% (2000).
Housing: Homeownership rate: 86.6% (2000); Median home value: $65,000 (2000); Median rent: $200 per month (2000); Median age of housing: 60+ years (2000).
Transportation: Commute to work: 75.8% car, 0.0% public transportation, 4.2% walk, 19.3% work from home (2000); Travel time to work: 42.3% less than 15 minutes, 31.0% 15 to 30 minutes, 4.7% 30 to 45 minutes, 12.2% 45 to 60 minutes, 9.9% 60 minutes or more (2000)

WINNEBAGO (township). Covers a land area of 35.191 square miles and a water area of 0 square miles. Located at 43.53° N. Lat.; 91.43° W. Long.
Population: 257 (2000); Race: 100.0% White, 0.0% Black, 0.0% Asian, 0.0% American Indian and Alaska Native, 0.0% Hispanic of any race, 0.0% two or more races (2000); Density: 7.3 persons per square mile (2000); Age: 30.3% under 18, 10.3% over 64 (2000); Marriage status: 32.3% never married, 61.6% now married, 3.0% widowed, 3.0% divorced (2000); Foreign born: 0.0% (2000); Ancestry (includes multiple ancestries): 60.5% German, 28.4% Norwegian, 5.0% Irish, 3.4% Italian, 2.7% Latvian (2000).
Economy: Employment by occupation: 29.9% management, 9.5% professional, 7.5% services, 21.8% sales, 10.9% farming, 4.8% construction, 15.6% production (2000).
Income: Per capita income: $18,021 (2000); Median household income: $38,750 (2000); Poverty rate: 8.0% (2000).
Taxes: Total city taxes per capita: $131 (1997); City property taxes per capita: $131 (1997).
Education: High school graduation rate: 90.0% (2000); College graduation rate: 10.0% (2000).
Housing: Homeownership rate: 87.2% (2000); Median home value: $80,000 (2000); Median rent: $225 per month (2000); Median age of housing: 60+ years (2000).
Transportation: Commute to work: 71.4% car, 0.0% public transportation, 4.1% walk, 24.5% work from home (2000); Travel time to work: 28.8% less than 15 minutes, 42.3% 15 to 30 minutes, 11.7% 30 to 45 minutes, 9.9% 45 to 60 minutes, 7.2% 60 minutes or more (2000)

YUCATAN (township). Covers a land area of 42.772 square miles and a water area of 0.153 square miles. Located at 43.71° N. Lat.; 91.68° W. Long.
Population: 351 (2000); Race: 97.7% White, 0.0% Black, 1.7% Asian, 0.0% American Indian and Alaska Native, 0.0% Hispanic of any race, 0.7% two or more races (2000); Density: 8.2 persons per square mile (2000); Age: 26.2% under 18, 9.3% over 64 (2000); Marriage status: 18.4% never married, 65.7% now married, 5.9% widowed, 10.0% divorced (2000); Foreign born: 1.7% (2000); Ancestry (includes multiple ancestries): 41.5% Norwegian, 40.9% German, 11.6% Irish, 9.3% English, 7.3% Czech (2000).
Economy: Employment by occupation: 20.8% management, 22.6% professional, 6.9% services, 17.0% sales, 1.9% farming, 10.7% construction, 20.1% production (2000).
Income: Per capita income: $18,130 (2000); Median household income: $40,417 (2000); Poverty rate: 7.3% (2000).
Taxes: Total city taxes per capita: $129 (1997); City property taxes per capita: $129 (1997).
Education: High school graduation rate: 93.6% (2000); College graduation rate: 20.2% (2000).
Housing: Homeownership rate: 88.4% (2000); Median home value: $96,300 (2000); Median rent: $263 per month (2000); Median age of housing: 60+ years (2000).
Transportation: Commute to work: 82.7% car, 0.0% public transportation, 2.0% walk, 15.3% work from home (2000); Travel time to work: 31.5% less than 15 minutes, 27.6% 15 to 30 minutes, 17.3% 30 to 45 minutes, 19.7% 45 to 60 minutes, 3.9% 60 minutes or more (2000)

Hubbard County

Located in northwest central Minnesota; watered in the south by small lakes. Covers a land area of 922.50 square miles, a water area of 76.90 square miles, and is located in the Central Time Zone. The county government was organized in 1883. County seat is Park Rapids.

Weather Station: Park Rapids Municipal Airport Elevation: 1,433 feet

	Jan	Feb	Mar	Apr	May	Jun	Jul	Aug	Sep	Oct	Nov	Dec
High	16	25	37	54	69	77	81	79	68	55	34	21
Low	-6	2	15	29	42	52	56	54	45	33	18	2
Precip	0.7	0.5	1.2	1.9	2.8	4.2	4.0	3.7	2.8	2.7	1.1	0.6
Snow	11.9	6.7	10.1	3.4	0.2	0.0	tr	0.0	tr	1.3	7.1	8.2

High and Low temperatures in degrees Fahrenheit; Precipitation and Snow in inches

Population: 18,376 (2000); Race: 96.7% White, 0.2% Black, 0.4% Asian, 1.6% American Indian and Alaska Native, 0.5% Hispanic of any race, 1.0% two or more races (2000); Density: 19.9 persons per square mile (2000); Age: 24.6% under 18, 17.9% over 64 (2000).
Religion: Five largest groups: 13.2% Evangelical Lutheran Church in America, 13.0% Catholic Church, 9.5% Lutheran Church—Missouri Synod, 4.8% The United Methodist Church, 2.5% Conservative Baptist Association of America (2000).
Economy: Unemployment rate: 5.0% (11/2002); Total civilian labor force: 9,059 (11/2002); Leading industries: 22.0% manufacturing; 18.4% retail trade; 16.8% health care and social assistance (2000); Companies that employ more than 1,000 persons: 0 (2000); Companies that employ more than 100 persons: 8 (2000); Farms: 431 totaling 130,530 acres (1997); Minority business ownership rate: 0.0% (1997); Women business ownership rate: 20.5% (1997); Retail sales per capita: $7,512 (1997). Single-family building permits issued: 36 (2001) / 29 (2000); Multi-family building permits issued: 8 (2001) / 26 (2000).
Income: Per capita income: $18,115 (2000); Median household income: $35,321 (2000); Poverty rate: 9.7% (2000); Bankruptcy rate: 2.21% (2001).
Taxes: Total county taxes per capita: $293 (2000); County property taxes per capita: $285 (2000).
Education: High school graduation rate: 86.1% (2000); College graduation rate: 20.2% (2000).
Housing: Homeownership rate: 83.4% (2000); Median home value: $97,300 (2000); Median rent: $319 per month (2000); Median age of housing: 26 years (2000).
Health: Birth rate: 103.9 per 10,000 population (1998); Age adjusted death rate: 90.2 per 10,000 population (1999); Age adjusted cancer mortality rate: 169.6 deaths per 100,000 population (1999). Number of physicians: 12.0 per 10,000 population (1999); Number of hospital beds: 21.2 per 10,000 population (1999).
Elections: 2000 Presidential election results: 37.8% Gore, 55.2% Bush, 5.0% Nader, 1.4% Buchanan
National and State Parks: Badoura State Forest; Lowe State Wildlife Management Area; Paul Bunyan State Forest; Rockwood State Wildlife Management Areas; Wolf Lake State Wildlife Management Area
Additional Information Contacts
Hubbard County Government Offices 218-732-3196

Hubbard County Communities

AKELEY (city). Covers a land area of 1.483 square miles and a water area of 0.028 square miles. Located at 47.00° N. Lat.; 94.72° W. Long. Elevation is 1,430 feet.
Population: 412 (2000); Race: 97.1% White, 0.0% Black, 1.2% Asian, 1.0% American Indian and Alaska Native, 0.7% Hispanic of any race, 0.7% two or more races (2000); Density: 277.7 persons per square mile (2000); Age: 24.3% under 18, 13.5% over 64 (2000); Marriage status: 23.0% never married, 54.0% now married, 8.6% widowed, 14.4% divorced (2000); Foreign born: 2.0% (2000); Ancestry (includes multiple ancestries): 42.6% German, 13.5% Irish, 12.5% Norwegian, 8.1% Swedish, 6.9% French (except Basque) (2000).
Economy: Single-family building permits issued: 1 (2001) / 0 (2000); Multi-family building permits issued: 0 (2001) / 0 (2000); Employment by occupation: 7.4% management, 14.4% professional, 26.9% services, 20.8% sales, 0.9% farming, 12.5% construction, 17.1% production (2000).
Income: Per capita income: $13,749 (2000); Median household income: $26,719 (2000); Poverty rate: 17.5% (2000).
Taxes: Total city taxes per capita: $90 (1997); City property taxes per capita: $90 (1997).
Education: High school graduation rate: 80.4% (2000); College graduation rate: 5.3% (2000).
Housing: Homeownership rate: 84.0% (2000); Median home value: $35,000 (2000); Median rent: $303 per month (2000); Median age of housing: 40 years (2000).
Transportation: Commute to work: 89.2% car, 0.0% public transportation, 6.6% walk, 4.2% work from home (2000); Travel time to work: 31.9% less

than 15 minutes, 52.9% 15 to 30 minutes, 6.4% 30 to 45 minutes, 1.5% 45 to 60 minutes, 7.4% 60 minutes or more (2000)

AKELEY (township). Covers a land area of 31.361 square miles and a water area of 3.062 square miles. Located at 47.01° N. Lat.; 94.73° W. Long. Elevation is 1,430 feet.
Population: 481 (2000); Race: 98.9% White, 0.0% Black, 0.0% Asian, 0.0% American Indian and Alaska Native, 0.0% Hispanic of any race, 1.1% two or more races (2000); Density: 15.3 persons per square mile (2000); Age: 19.2% under 18, 17.7% over 64 (2000); Marriage status: 19.7% never married, 59.8% now married, 6.0% widowed, 14.4% divorced (2000); Foreign born: 1.3% (2000); Ancestry (includes multiple ancestries): 48.3% German, 18.1% Norwegian, 11.5% Swedish, 10.8% English, 9.9% Irish (2000).
Economy: Alfalfa, oats, barley, rye, beans; sheep. Manufactures fixtures, wood products. Single-family building permits issued: 6 (2001) / 3 (2000); Multi-family building permits issued: 0 (2001) / 0 (2000); Employment by occupation: 10.2% management, 18.8% professional, 24.7% services, 8.6% sales, 2.2% farming, 18.3% construction, 17.2% production (2000).
Income: Per capita income: $14,910 (2000); Median household income: $33,571 (2000); Poverty rate: 10.6% (2000).
Taxes: Total city taxes per capita: $124 (1997); City property taxes per capita: $121 (1997).
Education: High school graduation rate: 83.0% (2000); College graduation rate: 19.6% (2000).
Housing: Homeownership rate: 92.2% (2000); Median home value: $135,000 (2000); Median rent: $258 per month (2000); Median age of housing: 23 years (2000).
Transportation: Commute to work: 90.8% car, 0.0% public transportation, 1.6% walk, 7.6% work from home (2000); Travel time to work: 27.6% less than 15 minutes, 37.6% 15 to 30 minutes, 21.8% 30 to 45 minutes, 4.7% 45 to 60 minutes, 8.2% 60 minutes or more (2000)

ARAGO (township). Covers a land area of 30.949 square miles and a water area of 4.423 square miles. Located at 47.03° N. Lat.; 95.10° W. Long. Elevation is 1,501 feet.
Population: 586 (2000); Race: 98.1% White, 0.5% Black, 0.0% Asian, 1.4% American Indian and Alaska Native, 0.3% Hispanic of any race, 0.0% two or more races (2000); Density: 18.9 persons per square mile (2000); Age: 24.9% under 18, 17.9% over 64 (2000); Marriage status: 14.2% never married, 72.0% now married, 5.9% widowed, 7.9% divorced (2000); Foreign born: 0.7% (2000); Ancestry (includes multiple ancestries): 47.9% German, 21.8% Norwegian, 14.3% English, 12.1% Irish, 6.0% French (except Basque) (2000).
Economy: Employment by occupation: 6.5% management, 8.5% professional, 19.9% services, 29.7% sales, 2.8% farming, 17.1% construction, 15.4% production (2000).
Income: Per capita income: $17,562 (2000); Median household income: $40,865 (2000); Poverty rate: 12.9% (2000).
Taxes: Total city taxes per capita: $113 (2000); City property taxes per capita: $111 (2000).
Education: High school graduation rate: 89.1% (2000); College graduation rate: 19.9% (2000).
Housing: Homeownership rate: 95.4% (2000); Median home value: $135,000 (2000); Median rent: $263 per month (2000); Median age of housing: 28 years (2000).
Transportation: Commute to work: 93.2% car, 0.8% public transportation, 0.0% walk, 5.9% work from home (2000); Travel time to work: 43.5% less than 15 minutes, 37.7% 15 to 30 minutes, 5.4% 30 to 45 minutes, 4.9% 45 to 60 minutes, 8.5% 60 minutes or more (2000)

BADOURA (township). Covers a land area of 35.495 square miles and a water area of 0.997 square miles. Located at 46.85° N. Lat.; 94.72° W. Long.
Population: 101 (2000); Race: 97.5% White, 0.0% Black, 0.0% Asian, 0.0% American Indian and Alaska Native, 0.0% Hispanic of any race, 2.5% two or more races (2000); Density: 2.8 persons per square mile (2000); Age: 13.8% under 18, 26.3% over 64 (2000); Marriage status: 35.2% never married, 54.9% now married, 4.2% widowed, 5.6% divorced (2000); Foreign born: 0.0% (2000); Ancestry (includes multiple ancestries): 51.2% German, 23.8% Norwegian, 13.8% English, 13.8% Swedish, 3.8% Scotch-Irish (2000).
Economy: Single-family building permits issued: 0 (2001) / 0 (2000); Multi-family building permits issued: 0 (2001) / 0 (2000); Employment by occupation: 8.1% management, 10.8% professional, 8.1% services, 40.5% sales, 5.4% farming, 10.8% construction, 16.2% production (2000).
Income: Per capita income: $13,465 (2000); Median household income: $31,875 (2000); Poverty rate: 17.5% (2000).
Taxes: Total city taxes per capita: $229 (1997); City property taxes per capita: $229 (1997).
Education: High school graduation rate: 89.8% (2000); College graduation rate: 10.2% (2000).
Housing: Homeownership rate: 91.4% (2000); Median home value: $90,000 (2000); Median age of housing: 40 years (2000).
Transportation: Commute to work: 89.2% car, 0.0% public transportation, 5.4% walk, 5.4% work from home (2000); Travel time to work: 17.1% less than 15 minutes, 11.4% 15 to 30 minutes, 60.0% 30 to 45 minutes, 11.4% 45 to 60 minutes, 0.0% 60 minutes or more (2000)

CLAY (township). Covers a land area of 33.395 square miles and a water area of 2.728 square miles. Located at 47.08° N. Lat.; 94.95° W. Long.
Population: 49 (2000); Race: 94.6% White, 0.0% Black, 0.0% Asian, 5.4% American Indian and Alaska Native, 0.0% Hispanic of any race, 0.0% two or more races (2000); Density: 1.5 persons per square mile (2000); Age: 5.4% under 18, 21.6% over 64 (2000); Marriage status: 5.7% never married, 77.1% now married, 5.7% widowed, 11.4% divorced (2000); Foreign born: 0.0% (2000); Ancestry (includes multiple ancestries): 48.6% German, 24.3% Norwegian, 21.6% Irish, 16.2% Swedish, 10.8% English (2000).
Economy: Employment by occupation: 0.0% management, 25.0% professional, 10.0% services, 25.0% sales, 0.0% farming, 20.0% construction, 20.0% production (2000).
Income: Per capita income: $28,130 (2000); Median household income: $36,250 (2000); Poverty rate: 5.4% (2000).
Taxes: Total city taxes per capita: $127 (1997); City property taxes per capita: $127 (1997).
Education: High school graduation rate: 100.0% (2000); College graduation rate: 31.4% (2000).
Housing: Homeownership rate: 81.8% (2000); Median home value: $137,500 (2000); Median age of housing: 28 years (2000).
Transportation: Commute to work: 90.0% car, 0.0% public transportation, 0.0% walk, 10.0% work from home (2000); Travel time to work: 0.0% less than 15 minutes, 88.9% 15 to 30 minutes, 11.1% 30 to 45 minutes, 0.0% 45 to 60 minutes, 0.0% 60 minutes or more (2000)

CLOVER (township). Covers a land area of 33.791 square miles and a water area of 1.839 square miles. Located at 47.10° N. Lat.; 95.13° W. Long.
Population: 134 (2000); Race: 98.6% White, 0.0% Black, 0.0% Asian, 1.4% American Indian and Alaska Native, 0.0% Hispanic of any race, 0.0% two or more races (2000); Density: 4.0 persons per square mile (2000); Age: 13.8% under 18, 20.3% over 64 (2000); Marriage status: 14.3% never married, 68.1% now married, 6.7% widowed, 10.9% divorced (2000); Foreign born: 1.4% (2000); Ancestry (includes multiple ancestries): 60.1% German, 23.2% Norwegian, 10.9% Irish, 8.7% English, 5.8% Swedish (2000).
Economy: Employment by occupation: 11.8% management, 5.9% professional, 27.5% services, 17.6% sales, 3.9% farming, 21.6% construction, 11.8% production (2000).
Income: Per capita income: $17,723 (2000); Median household income: $32,500 (2000); Poverty rate: 5.8% (2000).
Taxes: Total city taxes per capita: $127 (1997); City property taxes per capita: $127 (1997).
Education: High school graduation rate: 87.0% (2000); College graduation rate: 21.3% (2000).
Housing: Homeownership rate: 96.9% (2000); Median home value: $114,100 (2000); Median age of housing: 16 years (2000).
Transportation: Commute to work: 76.5% car, 0.0% public transportation, 7.8% walk, 11.8% work from home (2000); Travel time to work: 28.9% less than 15 minutes, 37.8% 15 to 30 minutes, 26.7% 30 to 45 minutes, 0.0% 45 to 60 minutes, 6.7% 60 minutes or more (2000)

CROW WING LAKE (township). Covers a land area of 29.453 square miles and a water area of 5.833 square miles. Located at 46.85° N. Lat.; 94.87° W. Long.
Population: 266 (2000); Race: 98.9% White, 0.0% Black, 0.0% Asian, 1.1% American Indian and Alaska Native, 0.0% Hispanic of any race, 0.0% two or more races (2000); Density: 9.0 persons per square mile (2000); Age: 17.0% under 18, 31.2% over 64 (2000); Marriage status: 15.4% never married, 67.2% now married, 9.7% widowed, 7.7% divorced (2000); Foreign born: 0.7% (2000); Ancestry (includes multiple ancestries): 37.2% German, 17.4% English, 14.5% Irish, 14.5% Norwegian, 8.5% Swedish (2000).
Economy: Employment by occupation: 14.7% management, 12.0% professional, 9.3% services, 25.3% sales, 5.3% farming, 13.3% construction, 20.0% production (2000).
Income: Per capita income: $21,673 (2000); Median household income: $41,875 (2000); Poverty rate: 7.1% (2000).

Taxes: Total city taxes per capita: $216 (1997); City property taxes per capita: $216 (1997).
Education: High school graduation rate: 89.6% (2000); College graduation rate: 18.1% (2000).
Housing: Homeownership rate: 98.5% (2000); Median home value: $105,900 (2000); Median rent: $475 per month (2000); Median age of housing: 30 years (2000).
Transportation: Commute to work: 93.2% car, 0.0% public transportation, 0.0% walk, 5.5% work from home (2000); Travel time to work: 8.7% less than 15 minutes, 40.6% 15 to 30 minutes, 17.4% 30 to 45 minutes, 18.8% 45 to 60 minutes, 14.5% 60 minutes or more (2000)

FARDEN (township). Covers a land area of 33.664 square miles and a water area of 2.515 square miles. Located at 47.37° N. Lat.; 94.72° W. Long.
Population: 994 (2000); Race: 84.6% White, 1.0% Black, 1.9% Asian, 9.0% American Indian and Alaska Native, 0.3% Hispanic of any race, 3.4% two or more races (2000); Density: 29.5 persons per square mile (2000); Age: 31.2% under 18, 10.2% over 64 (2000); Marriage status: 25.9% never married, 59.6% now married, 5.5% widowed, 9.0% divorced (2000); Foreign born: 2.4% (2000); Ancestry (includes multiple ancestries): 30.4% German, 21.0% Norwegian, 14.0% Other groups, 13.0% Swedish, 9.4% Irish (2000).
Economy: Employment by occupation: 9.8% management, 21.3% professional, 11.1% services, 27.3% sales, 3.3% farming, 11.5% construction, 15.8% production (2000).
Income: Per capita income: $16,642 (2000); Median household income: $41,842 (2000); Poverty rate: 8.3% (2000).
Taxes: Total city taxes per capita: $141 (1997); City property taxes per capita: $141 (1997).
Education: High school graduation rate: 86.9% (2000); College graduation rate: 21.4% (2000).
Housing: Homeownership rate: 85.9% (2000); Median home value: $102,900 (2000); Median rent: $375 per month (2000); Median age of housing: 26 years (2000).
Transportation: Commute to work: 94.9% car, 0.4% public transportation, 0.7% walk, 2.7% work from home (2000); Travel time to work: 44.0% less than 15 minutes, 41.3% 15 to 30 minutes, 5.3% 30 to 45 minutes, 2.3% 45 to 60 minutes, 7.1% 60 minutes or more (2000)

FERN (township). Covers a land area of 35.483 square miles and a water area of 0.684 square miles. Located at 47.35° N. Lat.; 95.10° W. Long.
Population: 209 (2000); Race: 97.6% White, 0.0% Black, 0.0% Asian, 2.4% American Indian and Alaska Native, 0.0% Hispanic of any race, 0.0% two or more races (2000); Density: 5.9 persons per square mile (2000); Age: 24.5% under 18, 9.9% over 64 (2000); Marriage status: 24.6% never married, 49.7% now married, 6.9% widowed, 18.9% divorced (2000); Foreign born: 0.9% (2000); Ancestry (includes multiple ancestries): 41.5% Norwegian, 25.9% German, 7.1% Swedish, 6.6% European, 6.1% Other groups (2000).
Economy: Employment by occupation: 7.1% management, 13.3% professional, 20.4% services, 23.0% sales, 2.7% farming, 19.5% construction, 14.2% production (2000).
Income: Per capita income: $14,764 (2000); Median household income: $41,000 (2000); Poverty rate: 5.7% (2000).
Taxes: Total city taxes per capita: $70 (1997); City property taxes per capita: $70 (1997).
Education: High school graduation rate: 82.9% (2000); College graduation rate: 15.7% (2000).
Housing: Homeownership rate: 91.6% (2000); Median home value: $110,000 (2000); Median rent: $225 per month (2000); Median age of housing: 24 years (2000).
Transportation: Commute to work: 94.7% car, 0.0% public transportation, 0.0% walk, 3.5% work from home (2000); Travel time to work: 7.3% less than 15 minutes, 48.6% 15 to 30 minutes, 35.8% 30 to 45 minutes, 1.8% 45 to 60 minutes, 6.4% 60 minutes or more (2000)

GUTHRIE (township). Covers a land area of 34.845 square miles and a water area of 0.500 square miles. Located at 47.28° N. Lat.; 94.83° W. Long. Elevation is 1,426 feet.
Population: 436 (2000); Race: 97.3% White, 0.0% Black, 0.0% Asian, 1.4% American Indian and Alaska Native, 0.0% Hispanic of any race, 1.2% two or more races (2000); Density: 12.5 persons per square mile (2000); Age: 24.8% under 18, 10.6% over 64 (2000); Marriage status: 18.8% never married, 67.2% now married, 6.4% widowed, 7.6% divorced (2000); Foreign born: 0.7% (2000); Ancestry (includes multiple ancestries): 33.5% Norwegian, 32.3% German, 13.5% Swedish, 10.1% Irish, 9.6% English (2000).
Economy: Employment by occupation: 15.5% management, 18.6% professional, 14.4% services, 11.9% sales, 3.6% farming, 22.2% construction, 13.9% production (2000).
Income: Per capita income: $21,561 (2000); Median household income: $41,250 (2000); Poverty rate: 12.1% (2000).
Taxes: Total city taxes per capita: $45 (1997); City property taxes per capita: $45 (1997).
Education: High school graduation rate: 83.4% (2000); College graduation rate: 17.7% (2000).
Housing: Homeownership rate: 95.1% (2000); Median home value: $55,700 (2000); Median rent: $425 per month (2000); Median age of housing: 24 years (2000).
Transportation: Commute to work: 95.3% car, 0.0% public transportation, 2.6% walk, 2.1% work from home (2000); Travel time to work: 16.0% less than 15 minutes, 53.5% 15 to 30 minutes, 21.4% 30 to 45 minutes, 4.3% 45 to 60 minutes, 4.8% 60 minutes or more (2000)

HART LAKE (township). Covers a land area of 33.817 square miles and a water area of 1.696 square miles. Located at 47.28° N. Lat.; 94.71° W. Long.
Population: 466 (2000); Race: 86.7% White, 0.0% Black, 0.0% Asian, 12.8% American Indian and Alaska Native, 0.0% Hispanic of any race, 0.5% two or more races (2000); Density: 13.8 persons per square mile (2000); Age: 25.0% under 18, 10.2% over 64 (2000); Marriage status: 26.9% never married, 58.4% now married, 2.6% widowed, 12.0% divorced (2000); Foreign born: 0.5% (2000); Ancestry (includes multiple ancestries): 31.1% German, 21.7% Norwegian, 19.6% Other groups, 13.5% Irish, 7.1% Swedish (2000).
Economy: Employment by occupation: 11.0% management, 26.4% professional, 15.4% services, 22.5% sales, 1.1% farming, 15.9% construction, 7.7% production (2000).
Income: Per capita income: $17,156 (2000); Median household income: $38,750 (2000); Poverty rate: 18.9% (2000).
Taxes: Total city taxes per capita: $78 (1997); City property taxes per capita: $78 (1997).
Education: High school graduation rate: 90.3% (2000); College graduation rate: 14.7% (2000).
Housing: Homeownership rate: 82.4% (2000); Median home value: $64,200 (2000); Median rent: $192 per month (2000); Median age of housing: 25 years (2000).
Transportation: Commute to work: 94.4% car, 1.1% public transportation, 1.1% walk, 3.4% work from home (2000); Travel time to work: 12.8% less than 15 minutes, 42.4% 15 to 30 minutes, 32.0% 30 to 45 minutes, 2.9% 45 to 60 minutes, 9.9% 60 minutes or more (2000)

HELGA (township). Covers a land area of 33.178 square miles and a water area of 2.470 square miles. Located at 47.35° N. Lat.; 94.85° W. Long.
Population: 1,109 (2000); Race: 97.0% White, 0.0% Black, 0.3% Asian, 1.9% American Indian and Alaska Native, 0.7% Hispanic of any race, 0.8% two or more races (2000); Density: 33.4 persons per square mile (2000); Age: 30.4% under 18, 7.1% over 64 (2000); Marriage status: 19.2% never married, 72.8% now married, 2.6% widowed, 5.3% divorced (2000); Foreign born: 0.9% (2000); Ancestry (includes multiple ancestries): 25.5% Norwegian, 25.5% German, 10.7% Swedish, 9.6% Irish, 7.2% Other groups (2000).
Economy: Single-family building permits issued: 15 (2001) / 3 (2000); Multi-family building permits issued: 0 (2001) / 0 (2000); Employment by occupation: 8.1% management, 19.3% professional, 10.3% services, 28.6% sales, 3.2% farming, 14.0% construction, 16.6% production (2000).
Income: Per capita income: $19,410 (2000); Median household income: $46,645 (2000); Poverty rate: 5.4% (2000).
Taxes: Total city taxes per capita: $60 (1997); City property taxes per capita: $59 (1997).
Education: High school graduation rate: 92.0% (2000); College graduation rate: 22.6% (2000).
Housing: Homeownership rate: 96.9% (2000); Median home value: $97,000 (2000); Median age of housing: 18 years (2000).
Transportation: Commute to work: 89.2% car, 1.3% public transportation, 3.9% walk, 5.0% work from home (2000); Travel time to work: 26.5% less than 15 minutes, 59.8% 15 to 30 minutes, 8.8% 30 to 45 minutes, 0.4% 45 to 60 minutes, 4.4% 60 minutes or more (2000)

HENDRICKSON (township). Covers a land area of 35.013 square miles and a water area of 0.775 square miles. Located at 47.21° N. Lat.; 94.82° W. Long.
Population: 229 (2000); Race: 99.2% White, 0.8% Black, 0.0% Asian, 0.0% American Indian and Alaska Native, 0.0% Hispanic of any race, 0.0% two or

more races (2000); Density: 6.5 persons per square mile (2000); Age: 28.3% under 18, 10.8% over 64 (2000); Marriage status: 17.3% never married, 74.3% now married, 4.7% widowed, 3.7% divorced (2000); Foreign born: 0.0% (2000); Ancestry (includes multiple ancestries): 40.4% German, 20.8% Norwegian, 19.2% Swedish, 5.4% Irish, 4.2% Other groups (2000).
Economy: Employment by occupation: 8.5% management, 21.2% professional, 21.2% services, 15.3% sales, 3.4% farming, 21.2% construction, 9.3% production (2000).
Income: Per capita income: $15,309 (2000); Median household income: $40,000 (2000); Poverty rate: 5.0% (2000).
Taxes: Total city taxes per capita: $11 (1997); City property taxes per capita: $11 (1997).
Education: High school graduation rate: 86.3% (2000); College graduation rate: 13.0% (2000).
Housing: Homeownership rate: 98.0% (2000); Median home value: $68,000 (2000); Median age of housing: 21 years (2000).
Transportation: Commute to work: 91.1% car, 0.0% public transportation, 1.8% walk, 7.1% work from home (2000); Travel time to work: 19.2% less than 15 minutes, 30.8% 15 to 30 minutes, 44.2% 30 to 45 minutes, 5.8% 45 to 60 minutes, 0.0% 60 minutes or more (2000)

HENRIETTA (township). Covers a land area of 31.691 square miles and a water area of 3.402 square miles. Located at 46.93° N. Lat.; 94.96° W. Long.
Population: 1,582 (2000); Race: 96.4% White, 0.2% Black, 1.2% Asian, 0.8% American Indian and Alaska Native, 0.4% Hispanic of any race, 1.1% two or more races (2000); Density: 49.9 persons per square mile (2000); Age: 26.6% under 18, 14.6% over 64 (2000); Marriage status: 17.8% never married, 70.8% now married, 5.1% widowed, 6.3% divorced (2000); Foreign born: 1.0% (2000); Ancestry (includes multiple ancestries): 46.5% German, 20.5% Norwegian, 12.0% Irish, 8.8% English, 8.5% Swedish (2000).
Economy: Employment by occupation: 15.1% management, 22.5% professional, 17.8% services, 23.0% sales, 0.7% farming, 9.1% construction, 11.8% production (2000).
Income: Per capita income: $18,760 (2000); Median household income: $40,061 (2000); Poverty rate: 9.4% (2000).
Taxes: Total city taxes per capita: $96 (1997); City property taxes per capita: $96 (1997).
Education: High school graduation rate: 89.2% (2000); College graduation rate: 27.2% (2000).
Housing: Homeownership rate: 87.5% (2000); Median home value: $104,300 (2000); Median rent: $328 per month (2000); Median age of housing: 27 years (2000).
Transportation: Commute to work: 90.8% car, 0.1% public transportation, 0.9% walk, 7.9% work from home (2000); Travel time to work: 62.6% less than 15 minutes, 25.4% 15 to 30 minutes, 6.3% 30 to 45 minutes, 1.1% 45 to 60 minutes, 4.6% 60 minutes or more (2000)

HUBBARD (township). Covers a land area of 32.788 square miles and a water area of 3.216 square miles. Located at 46.84° N. Lat.; 94.99° W. Long. Elevation is 1,415 feet.
Population: 786 (2000); Race: 99.2% White, 0.0% Black, 0.3% Asian, 0.3% American Indian and Alaska Native, 0.0% Hispanic of any race, 0.3% two or more races (2000); Density: 24.0 persons per square mile (2000); Age: 22.6% under 18, 21.9% over 64 (2000); Marriage status: 19.3% never married, 69.2% now married, 4.9% widowed, 6.6% divorced (2000); Foreign born: 0.3% (2000); Ancestry (includes multiple ancestries): 41.0% German, 26.7% Norwegian, 12.1% Swedish, 8.4% Irish, 8.1% English (2000).
Economy: Employment by occupation: 11.7% management, 11.4% professional, 16.1% services, 27.8% sales, 3.2% farming, 18.1% construction, 11.7% production (2000).
Income: Per capita income: $20,979 (2000); Median household income: $33,679 (2000); Poverty rate: 8.1% (2000).
Taxes: Total city taxes per capita: $115 (1997); City property taxes per capita: $115 (1997).
Education: High school graduation rate: 84.1% (2000); College graduation rate: 19.4% (2000).
Housing: Homeownership rate: 93.8% (2000); Median home value: $133,200 (2000); Median rent: $375 per month (2000); Median age of housing: 25 years (2000).
Transportation: Commute to work: 90.7% car, 0.0% public transportation, 1.8% walk, 7.5% work from home (2000); Travel time to work: 52.3% less than 15 minutes, 34.4% 15 to 30 minutes, 5.8% 30 to 45 minutes, 2.3% 45 to 60 minutes, 5.2% 60 minutes or more (2000)

LAKE ALICE (township). Covers a land area of 33.893 square miles and a water area of 0.830 square miles. Located at 47.19° N. Lat.; 95.12° W. Long.
Population: 87 (2000); Race: 95.3% White, 0.0% Black, 2.3% Asian, 0.0% American Indian and Alaska Native, 0.0% Hispanic of any race, 2.3% two or more races (2000); Density: 2.6 persons per square mile (2000); Age: 9.3% under 18, 18.6% over 64 (2000); Marriage status: 12.8% never married, 57.7% now married, 21.8% widowed, 7.7% divorced (2000); Foreign born: 2.3% (2000); Ancestry (includes multiple ancestries): 51.2% German, 10.5% English, 7.0% Irish, 7.0% British, 4.7% Scandinavian (2000).
Economy: Employment by occupation: 0.0% management, 36.0% professional, 24.0% services, 20.0% sales, 0.0% farming, 0.0% construction, 20.0% production (2000).
Income: Per capita income: $13,736 (2000); Median household income: $25,625 (2000); Poverty rate: 16.3% (2000).
Taxes: Total city taxes per capita: $20 (1997); City property taxes per capita: $20 (1997).
Education: High school graduation rate: 60.6% (2000); College graduation rate: 12.7% (2000).
Housing: Homeownership rate: 85.4% (2000); Median home value: $52,500 (2000); Median rent: $275 per month (2000); Median age of housing: 29 years (2000).
Transportation: Commute to work: 92.0% car, 0.0% public transportation, 0.0% walk, 8.0% work from home (2000); Travel time to work: 0.0% less than 15 minutes, 39.1% 15 to 30 minutes, 26.1% 30 to 45 minutes, 21.7% 45 to 60 minutes, 13.0% 60 minutes or more (2000)

LAKE EMMA (township). Covers a land area of 27.332 square miles and a water area of 8.777 square miles. Located at 47.01° N. Lat.; 94.95° W. Long.
Population: 900 (2000); Race: 97.7% White, 0.3% Black, 0.2% Asian, 0.4% American Indian and Alaska Native, 0.4% Hispanic of any race, 0.9% two or more races (2000); Density: 32.9 persons per square mile (2000); Age: 19.6% under 18, 20.0% over 64 (2000); Marriage status: 15.6% never married, 72.5% now married, 4.8% widowed, 7.2% divorced (2000); Foreign born: 1.0% (2000); Ancestry (includes multiple ancestries): 42.7% German, 27.2% Norwegian, 14.0% Swedish, 11.5% Irish, 10.6% English (2000).
Economy: Employment by occupation: 16.2% management, 23.1% professional, 10.9% services, 27.3% sales, 2.3% farming, 9.5% construction, 10.6% production (2000).
Income: Per capita income: $25,380 (2000); Median household income: $45,563 (2000); Poverty rate: 5.3% (2000).
Taxes: Total city taxes per capita: $139 (2000); City property taxes per capita: $138 (2000).
Education: High school graduation rate: 91.6% (2000); College graduation rate: 25.3% (2000).
Housing: Homeownership rate: 95.5% (2000); Median home value: $167,600 (2000); Median rent: $325 per month (2000); Median age of housing: 23 years (2000).
Transportation: Commute to work: 90.5% car, 0.0% public transportation, 1.7% walk, 7.4% work from home (2000); Travel time to work: 20.1% less than 15 minutes, 62.7% 15 to 30 minutes, 6.4% 30 to 45 minutes, 3.6% 45 to 60 minutes, 7.2% 60 minutes or more (2000)

LAKE GEORGE (township). Covers a land area of 33.791 square miles and a water area of 2.386 square miles. Located at 47.20° N. Lat.; 94.98° W. Long. Elevation is 1,429 feet.
Population: 383 (2000); Race: 95.9% White, 0.0% Black, 0.0% Asian, 0.5% American Indian and Alaska Native, 2.2% Hispanic of any race, 3.6% two or more races (2000); Density: 11.3 persons per square mile (2000); Age: 22.1% under 18, 19.7% over 64 (2000); Marriage status: 15.6% never married, 68.1% now married, 7.3% widowed, 9.0% divorced (2000); Foreign born: 1.6% (2000); Ancestry (includes multiple ancestries): 50.5% German, 24.6% Norwegian, 10.4% Swedish, 9.3% Irish, 9.0% Other groups (2000).
Economy: Employment by occupation: 11.5% management, 23.0% professional, 14.9% services, 18.9% sales, 1.4% farming, 17.6% construction, 12.8% production (2000).
Income: Per capita income: $16,320 (2000); Median household income: $35,078 (2000); Poverty rate: 7.4% (2000).
Taxes: Total city taxes per capita: $46 (1997); City property taxes per capita: $46 (1997).
Education: High school graduation rate: 84.6% (2000); College graduation rate: 16.2% (2000).

Housing: Homeownership rate: 86.8% (2000); Median home value: $95,000 (2000); Median rent: $363 per month (2000); Median age of housing: 26 years (2000).
Transportation: Commute to work: 93.9% car, 1.4% public transportation, 0.0% walk, 4.7% work from home (2000); Travel time to work: 10.6% less than 15 minutes, 24.8% 15 to 30 minutes, 46.8% 30 to 45 minutes, 12.8% 45 to 60 minutes, 5.0% 60 minutes or more (2000)

LAKE HATTIE (township). Covers a land area of 33.442 square miles and a water area of 1.025 square miles. Located at 47.28° N. Lat.; 95.11° W. Long.
Population: 130 (2000); Race: 94.1% White, 0.0% Black, 0.0% Asian, 5.9% American Indian and Alaska Native, 0.0% Hispanic of any race, 0.0% two or more races (2000); Density: 3.9 persons per square mile (2000); Age: 29.4% under 18, 19.1% over 64 (2000); Marriage status: 16.0% never married, 69.0% now married, 6.0% widowed, 9.0% divorced (2000); Foreign born: 1.5% (2000); Ancestry (includes multiple ancestries): 41.2% German, 27.2% Norwegian, 14.7% English, 12.5% Irish, 10.3% Swedish (2000).
Economy: Employment by occupation: 12.5% management, 8.3% professional, 4.2% services, 29.2% sales, 0.0% farming, 20.8% construction, 25.0% production (2000).
Income: Per capita income: $15,679 (2000); Median household income: $26,563 (2000); Poverty rate: 14.7% (2000).
Taxes: Total city taxes per capita: $79 (1997); City property taxes per capita: $79 (1997).
Education: High school graduation rate: 83.0% (2000); College graduation rate: 12.8% (2000).
Housing: Homeownership rate: 90.6% (2000); Median home value: $71,700 (2000); Median rent: $225 per month (2000); Median age of housing: 23 years (2000).
Transportation: Commute to work: 100.0% car, 0.0% public transportation, 0.0% walk, 0.0% work from home (2000); Travel time to work: 0.0% less than 15 minutes, 13.0% 15 to 30 minutes, 56.5% 30 to 45 minutes, 26.1% 45 to 60 minutes, 4.3% 60 minutes or more (2000)

LAKEPORT (township). Covers a land area of 29.541 square miles and a water area of 5.831 square miles. Located at 47.17° N. Lat.; 94.72° W. Long.
Population: 744 (2000); Race: 95.4% White, 0.0% Black, 0.0% Asian, 1.5% American Indian and Alaska Native, 0.7% Hispanic of any race, 3.1% two or more races (2000); Density: 25.2 persons per square mile (2000); Age: 26.1% under 18, 15.5% over 64 (2000); Marriage status: 19.0% never married, 66.3% now married, 5.9% widowed, 8.8% divorced (2000); Foreign born: 0.5% (2000); Ancestry (includes multiple ancestries): 42.3% German, 22.6% Norwegian, 9.1% English, 8.2% Irish, 7.6% Swedish (2000).
Economy: Employment by occupation: 10.8% management, 24.9% professional, 19.5% services, 22.2% sales, 0.7% farming, 14.5% construction, 7.4% production (2000).
Income: Per capita income: $17,750 (2000); Median household income: $36,397 (2000); Poverty rate: 10.7% (2000).
Taxes: Total city taxes per capita: $85 (1997); City property taxes per capita: $85 (1997).
Education: High school graduation rate: 88.5% (2000); College graduation rate: 25.5% (2000).
Housing: Homeownership rate: 90.1% (2000); Median home value: $105,700 (2000); Median rent: $456 per month (2000); Median age of housing: 26 years (2000).
Transportation: Commute to work: 92.6% car, 0.0% public transportation, 1.8% walk, 5.7% work from home (2000); Travel time to work: 31.8% less than 15 minutes, 40.4% 15 to 30 minutes, 19.9% 30 to 45 minutes, 5.2% 45 to 60 minutes, 2.6% 60 minutes or more (2000)

LAPORTE (city). Covers a land area of 0.697 square miles and a water area of 0 square miles. Located at 47.21° N. Lat.; 94.75° W. Long. Elevation is 1,370 feet.
Population: 145 (2000); Race: 96.9% White, 0.0% Black, 0.0% Asian, 0.0% American Indian and Alaska Native, 1.2% Hispanic of any race, 1.9% two or more races (2000); Density: 208.1 persons per square mile (2000); Age: 30.4% under 18, 17.4% over 64 (2000); Marriage status: 23.6% never married, 50.4% now married, 14.2% widowed, 11.8% divorced (2000); Foreign born: 0.0% (2000); Ancestry (includes multiple ancestries): 18.6% German, 18.0% Norwegian, 14.9% Swedish, 9.9% English, 8.1% United States or American (2000).
Economy: Manufacturing: stained glass. Employment by occupation: 0.0% management, 30.0% professional, 15.0% services, 33.3% sales, 0.0% farming, 13.3% construction, 8.3% production (2000).
Income: Per capita income: $13,412 (2000); Median household income: $28,500 (2000); Poverty rate: 18.0% (2000).
Taxes: Total city taxes per capita: $82 (1997); City property taxes per capita: $55 (1997).
Education: High school graduation rate: 81.9% (2000); College graduation rate: 16.2% (2000).

School District(s)

Laporte (PK-12)
2000 Enrollment: 366 218-224-2288
Housing: Homeownership rate: 85.3% (2000); Median home value: $48,000 (2000); Median rent: $417 per month (2000); Median age of housing: 59 years (2000).
Transportation: Commute to work: 90.0% car, 0.0% public transportation, 10.0% walk, 0.0% work from home (2000); Travel time to work: 20.0% less than 15 minutes, 45.0% 15 to 30 minutes, 21.7% 30 to 45 minutes, 13.3% 45 to 60 minutes, 0.0% 60 minutes or more (2000)

MANTRAP (township). Covers a land area of 30.831 square miles and a water area of 4.995 square miles. Located at 47.01° N. Lat.; 94.85° W. Long.
Population: 454 (2000); Race: 99.4% White, 0.2% Black, 0.0% Asian, 0.0% American Indian and Alaska Native, 0.0% Hispanic of any race, 0.4% two or more races (2000); Density: 14.7 persons per square mile (2000); Age: 20.5% under 18, 18.7% over 64 (2000); Marriage status: 16.5% never married, 68.7% now married, 5.2% widowed, 9.6% divorced (2000); Foreign born: 1.0% (2000); Ancestry (includes multiple ancestries): 44.0% German, 26.3% Norwegian, 13.5% English, 11.8% Swedish, 8.6% Irish (2000).
Economy: Single-family building permits issued: 2 (2001) / 2 (2000); Multi-family building permits issued: 0 (2001) / 0 (2000); Employment by occupation: 15.5% management, 21.3% professional, 10.1% services, 22.2% sales, 0.0% farming, 21.7% construction, 9.2% production (2000).
Income: Per capita income: $22,730 (2000); Median household income: $39,583 (2000); Poverty rate: 10.3% (2000).
Taxes: Total city taxes per capita: $129 (1997); City property taxes per capita: $129 (1997).
Education: High school graduation rate: 89.9% (2000); College graduation rate: 28.5% (2000).
Housing: Homeownership rate: 95.5% (2000); Median home value: $167,200 (2000); Median age of housing: 16 years (2000).
Transportation: Commute to work: 93.0% car, 0.0% public transportation, 1.0% walk, 6.0% work from home (2000); Travel time to work: 28.0% less than 15 minutes, 46.0% 15 to 30 minutes, 9.0% 30 to 45 minutes, 3.7% 45 to 60 minutes, 13.2% 60 minutes or more (2000)

NEVIS (city). Covers a land area of 0.936 square miles and a water area of 0.083 square miles. Located at 46.96° N. Lat.; 94.84° W. Long. Elevation is 1,470 feet.
Population: 364 (2000); Race: 98.3% White, 0.0% Black, 0.0% Asian, 1.8% American Indian and Alaska Native, 0.0% Hispanic of any race, 0.0% two or more races (2000); Density: 388.9 persons per square mile (2000); Age: 29.3% under 18, 19.8% over 64 (2000); Marriage status: 15.1% never married, 62.8% now married, 11.5% widowed, 10.5% divorced (2000); Foreign born: 2.0% (2000); Ancestry (includes multiple ancestries): 36.3% German, 16.5% Norwegian, 7.8% English, 6.8% Swedish, 6.8% Irish (2000).
Economy: Employment by occupation: 10.8% management, 20.9% professional, 23.6% services, 19.6% sales, 0.0% farming, 13.5% construction, 11.5% production (2000).
Income: Per capita income: $14,259 (2000); Median household income: $26,771 (2000); Poverty rate: 14.0% (2000).
Taxes: Total city taxes per capita: $71 (1997); City property taxes per capita: $66 (1997).
Education: High school graduation rate: 84.4% (2000); College graduation rate: 19.3% (2000).

School District(s)

Nevis (PK-12)
2000 Enrollment: 531 218-652-3500
Housing: Homeownership rate: 76.6% (2000); Median home value: $57,500 (2000); Median rent: $341 per month (2000); Median age of housing: 51 years (2000).
Newspapers: Northwoods Press (1 x week)
Transportation: Commute to work: 91.4% car, 0.0% public transportation, 6.4% walk, 2.1% work from home (2000); Travel time to work: 32.8% less than 15 minutes, 37.2% 15 to 30 minutes, 21.9% 30 to 45 minutes, 3.6% 45 to 60 minutes, 4.4% 60 minutes or more (2000)

NEVIS (township). Covers a land area of 27.766 square miles and a water area of 5.722 square miles. Located at 46.94° N. Lat.; 94.85° W. Long. Elevation is 1,470 feet.
Population: 875 (2000); Race: 98.9% White, 0.7% Black, 0.1% Asian, 0.2% American Indian and Alaska Native, 0.2% Hispanic of any race, 0.0% two or more races (2000); Density: 31.5 persons per square mile (2000); Age: 20.1% under 18, 19.9% over 64 (2000); Marriage status: 18.5% never married, 65.1% now married, 7.7% widowed, 8.7% divorced (2000); Foreign born: 1.3% (2000); Ancestry (includes multiple ancestries): 40.3% German, 19.4% Norwegian, 12.1% Irish, 11.8% English, 8.9% Swedish (2000).
Economy: Agriculture: oats, barley, rye, beans, alfalfa; sheep. Manufacturing: wood products. Employment by occupation: 12.3% management, 16.9% professional, 19.0% services, 19.9% sales, 1.2% farming, 19.0% construction, 11.7% production (2000).
Income: Per capita income: $19,315 (2000); Median household income: $40,804 (2000); Poverty rate: 5.1% (2000).
Taxes: Total city taxes per capita: $182 (2000); City property taxes per capita: $181 (2000).
Education: High school graduation rate: 93.4% (2000); College graduation rate: 23.7% (2000).
Housing: Homeownership rate: 91.7% (2000); Median home value: $137,500 (2000); Median rent: $246 per month (2000); Median age of housing: 25 years (2000).
Transportation: Commute to work: 93.1% car, 0.0% public transportation, 2.5% walk, 4.4% work from home (2000); Travel time to work: 29.4% less than 15 minutes, 48.4% 15 to 30 minutes, 13.4% 30 to 45 minutes, 1.3% 45 to 60 minutes, 7.5% 60 minutes or more (2000)

PARK RAPIDS (city). Covers a land area of 5.984 square miles and a water area of 0.104 square miles. Located at 46.91° N. Lat.; 95.05° W. Long. Elevation is 1,445 feet.
History: Park Rapids was founded in 1880. Wheat was the leading crop in the latter decades of the 1800's, but later diversification brought dairy farming, lumbering, and lath making.
Population: 3,276 (2000); Race: 97.7% White, 0.0% Black, 0.1% Asian, 1.3% American Indian and Alaska Native, 0.9% Hispanic of any race, 0.8% two or more races (2000); Density: 547.5 persons per square mile (2000); Age: 23.2% under 18, 28.4% over 64 (2000); Marriage status: 19.8% never married, 53.4% now married, 13.0% widowed, 13.8% divorced (2000); Foreign born: 1.2% (2000); Ancestry (includes multiple ancestries): 41.5% German, 20.7% Norwegian, 10.6% English, 9.8% Irish, 5.8% French (except Basque) (2000).
Economy: Single-family building permits issued: 9 (2001) / 18 (2000); Multi-family building permits issued: 8 (2001) / 26 (2000); Employment by occupation: 11.2% management, 17.3% professional, 15.3% services, 25.1% sales, 0.3% farming, 10.1% construction, 20.7% production (2000).
Income: Per capita income: $16,416 (2000); Median household income: $23,628 (2000); Poverty rate: 12.2% (2000).
Taxes: Total city taxes per capita: $226 (1997); City property taxes per capita: $199 (1997).
Education: High school graduation rate: 78.3% (2000); College graduation rate: 16.0% (2000).

School District(s)

Park Rapids (PK-12)
2000 Enrollment: 1,912 218-237-6500

Housing: Homeownership rate: 52.3% (2000); Median home value: $66,700 (2000); Median rent: $308 per month (2000); Median age of housing: 30 years (2000).
Hospitals: Saint Joseph's Area Health Services (50 beds)
Safety: Violent crime rate: 33.2 per 10,000 population; Property crime rate: 1,029.9 per 10,000 population (2001).
Newspapers: Park Rapids Enterprise (2 x week)
Transportation: Commute to work: 82.5% car, 2.1% public transportation, 7.8% walk, 6.3% work from home (2000); Travel time to work: 80.1% less than 15 minutes, 11.1% 15 to 30 minutes, 4.9% 30 to 45 minutes, 1.0% 45 to 60 minutes, 2.8% 60 minutes or more (2000)
Airports: Park Rapids Municipal

ROCKWOOD (township). Covers a land area of 33.152 square miles and a water area of 2.869 square miles. Located at 47.36° N. Lat.; 94.98° W. Long.
Population: 469 (2000); Race: 98.0% White, 0.0% Black, 0.0% Asian, 2.0% American Indian and Alaska Native, 1.8% Hispanic of any race, 0.0% two or more races (2000); Density: 14.1 persons per square mile (2000); Age: 31.7% under 18, 8.8% over 64 (2000); Marriage status: 14.6% never married, 77.7% now married, 3.4% widowed, 4.3% divorced (2000); Foreign born: 3.1% (2000); Ancestry (includes multiple ancestries): 31.5% German, 24.2% Norwegian, 9.9% Irish, 9.3% Swedish, 8.6% Other groups (2000).
Economy: Employment by occupation: 14.4% management, 19.1% professional, 21.4% services, 19.1% sales, 0.9% farming, 8.4% construction, 16.7% production (2000).
Income: Per capita income: $15,305 (2000); Median household income: $46,563 (2000); Poverty rate: 8.6% (2000).
Taxes: Total city taxes per capita: $65 (1997); City property taxes per capita: $65 (1997).
Education: High school graduation rate: 91.5% (2000); College graduation rate: 27.2% (2000).
Housing: Homeownership rate: 96.0% (2000); Median home value: $127,100 (2000); Median age of housing: 29 years (2000).
Transportation: Commute to work: 94.4% car, 0.0% public transportation, 0.0% walk, 5.6% work from home (2000); Travel time to work: 15.3% less than 15 minutes, 66.5% 15 to 30 minutes, 8.9% 30 to 45 minutes, 1.0% 45 to 60 minutes, 8.4% 60 minutes or more (2000)

SCHOOLCRAFT (township). Covers a land area of 34.500 square miles and a water area of 0.818 square miles. Located at 47.28° N. Lat.; 94.97° W. Long.
Population: 106 (2000); Race: 98.3% White, 0.0% Black, 1.7% Asian, 0.0% American Indian and Alaska Native, 1.7% Hispanic of any race, 0.0% two or more races (2000); Density: 3.1 persons per square mile (2000); Age: 29.9% under 18, 3.4% over 64 (2000); Marriage status: 30.2% never married, 62.5% now married, 3.1% widowed, 4.2% divorced (2000); Foreign born: 0.0% (2000); Ancestry (includes multiple ancestries): 49.6% German, 17.9% Norwegian, 15.4% Swedish, 8.5% Scottish, 8.5% Other groups (2000).
Economy: Employment by occupation: 14.8% management, 22.2% professional, 16.7% services, 25.9% sales, 0.0% farming, 7.4% construction, 13.0% production (2000).
Income: Per capita income: $14,103 (2000); Median household income: $36,250 (2000); Poverty rate: 17.1% (2000).
Taxes: Total city taxes per capita: $85 (1997); City property taxes per capita: $85 (1997).
Education: High school graduation rate: 94.5% (2000); College graduation rate: 19.2% (2000).
Housing: Homeownership rate: 89.7% (2000); Median home value: $107,800 (2000); Median age of housing: 25 years (2000).
Transportation: Commute to work: 92.3% car, 0.0% public transportation, 3.8% walk, 3.8% work from home (2000); Travel time to work: 18.0% less than 15 minutes, 52.0% 15 to 30 minutes, 20.0% 30 to 45 minutes, 0.0% 45 to 60 minutes, 10.0% 60 minutes or more (2000)

STEAMBOAT RIVER (township). Covers a land area of 34.523 square miles and a water area of 1.455 square miles. Located at 47.13° N. Lat.; 94.69° W. Long.
Population: 123 (2000); Race: 95.2% White, 0.0% Black, 0.0% Asian, 1.6% American Indian and Alaska Native, 0.0% Hispanic of any race, 3.2% two or more races (2000); Density: 3.6 persons per square mile (2000); Age: 27.2% under 18, 28.8% over 64 (2000); Marriage status: 7.4% never married, 83.2% now married, 5.3% widowed, 4.2% divorced (2000); Foreign born: 1.6% (2000); Ancestry (includes multiple ancestries): 32.8% German, 24.8% English, 23.2% Irish, 14.4% Norwegian, 9.6% Swedish (2000).
Economy: Employment by occupation: 42.3% management, 26.9% professional, 13.5% services, 3.8% sales, 0.0% farming, 3.8% construction, 9.6% production (2000).
Income: Per capita income: $20,335 (2000); Median household income: $42,750 (2000); Poverty rate: 7.2% (2000).
Taxes: Total city taxes per capita: $82 (1997); City property taxes per capita: $82 (1997).
Education: High school graduation rate: 83.5% (2000); College graduation rate: 31.9% (2000).
Housing: Homeownership rate: 87.8% (2000); Median home value: $170,000 (2000); Median rent: $375 per month (2000); Median age of housing: 27 years (2000).
Transportation: Commute to work: 65.4% car, 0.0% public transportation, 11.5% walk, 23.1% work from home (2000); Travel time to work: 52.5% less than 15 minutes, 12.5% 15 to 30 minutes, 22.5% 30 to 45 minutes, 5.0% 45 to 60 minutes, 7.5% 60 minutes or more (2000)

STRAIGHT RIVER (township). Covers a land area of 34.285 square miles and a water area of 1.065 square miles. Located at 46.84° N. Lat.; 95.09° W. Long.

Population: 662 (2000); Race: 97.6% White, 0.0% Black, 0.0% Asian, 0.0% American Indian and Alaska Native, 2.5% Hispanic of any race, 0.4% two or more races (2000); Density: 19.3 persons per square mile (2000); Age: 27.3% under 18, 14.3% over 64 (2000); Marriage status: 19.4% never married, 70.6% now married, 2.5% widowed, 7.5% divorced (2000); Foreign born: 1.3% (2000); Ancestry (includes multiple ancestries): 38.7% German, 21.6% Norwegian, 10.2% Irish, 10.0% Swedish, 8.0% Finnish (2000).
Economy: Employment by occupation: 12.1% management, 9.2% professional, 17.8% services, 27.9% sales, 5.4% farming, 12.1% construction, 15.6% production (2000).
Income: Per capita income: $14,887 (2000); Median household income: $30,952 (2000); Poverty rate: 11.3% (2000).
Taxes: Total city taxes per capita: $128 (1997); City property taxes per capita: $128 (1997).
Education: High school graduation rate: 82.7% (2000); College graduation rate: 9.0% (2000).
Housing: Homeownership rate: 90.4% (2000); Median home value: $106,900 (2000); Median rent: $382 per month (2000); Median age of housing: 23 years (2000).
Transportation: Commute to work: 88.1% car, 0.0% public transportation, 0.6% walk, 9.4% work from home (2000); Travel time to work: 54.8% less than 15 minutes, 28.5% 15 to 30 minutes, 5.0% 30 to 45 minutes, 4.6% 45 to 60 minutes, 7.1% 60 minutes or more (2000)

THORPE (township). Covers a land area of 34.787 square miles and a water area of 1.238 square miles. Located at 47.10° N. Lat.; 94.85° W. Long.
Population: 37 (2000); Race: 100.0% White, 0.0% Black, 0.0% Asian, 0.0% American Indian and Alaska Native, 0.0% Hispanic of any race, 0.0% two or more races (2000); Density: 1.1 persons per square mile (2000); Age: 5.3% under 18, 36.8% over 64 (2000); Marriage status: 5.3% never married, 73.7% now married, 5.3% widowed, 15.8% divorced (2000); Foreign born: 5.3% (2000); Ancestry (includes multiple ancestries): 47.4% German, 21.1% Irish, 21.1% Swedish, 15.8% Norwegian, 10.5% Dutch (2000).
Economy: Single-family building permits issued: 3 (2001) / 3 (2000); Multi-family building permits issued: 0 (2001) / 0 (2000); Employment by occupation: 0.0% management, 33.3% professional, 0.0% services, 0.0% sales, 0.0% farming, 33.3% construction, 33.3% production (2000).
Income: Per capita income: $18,576 (2000); Median household income: $31,875 (2000); Poverty rate: 10.5% (2000).
Taxes: Total city taxes per capita: $114 (1997); City property taxes per capita: $114 (1997).
Education: High school graduation rate: 94.4% (2000); College graduation rate: 16.7% (2000).
Housing: Homeownership rate: 100.0% (2000); Median home value: $95,000 (2000); Median age of housing: 22 years (2000).
Transportation: Commute to work: 100.0% car, 0.0% public transportation, 0.0% walk, 0.0% work from home (2000); Travel time to work: 0.0% less than 15 minutes, 100.0% 15 to 30 minutes, 0.0% 30 to 45 minutes, 0.0% 45 to 60 minutes, 0.0% 60 minutes or more (2000)

TODD (township). Covers a land area of 26.191 square miles and a water area of 3.513 square miles. Located at 46.94° N. Lat.; 95.08° W. Long.
Population: 1,422 (2000); Race: 97.6% White, 0.0% Black, 0.6% Asian, 0.3% American Indian and Alaska Native, 0.0% Hispanic of any race, 1.4% two or more races (2000); Density: 54.3 persons per square mile (2000); Age: 24.7% under 18, 14.5% over 64 (2000); Marriage status: 19.9% never married, 66.1% now married, 4.7% widowed, 9.3% divorced (2000); Foreign born: 1.1% (2000); Ancestry (includes multiple ancestries): 39.9% German, 24.6% Norwegian, 11.1% Irish, 10.7% Swedish, 8.4% English (2000).
Economy: Employment by occupation: 13.6% management, 15.5% professional, 14.6% services, 25.0% sales, 3.3% farming, 10.0% construction, 18.1% production (2000).
Income: Per capita income: $20,754 (2000); Median household income: $38,458 (2000); Poverty rate: 7.1% (2000).
Taxes: Total city taxes per capita: $50 (1997); City property taxes per capita: $50 (1997).
Education: High school graduation rate: 89.8% (2000); College graduation rate: 23.5% (2000).
Housing: Homeownership rate: 90.9% (2000); Median home value: $105,000 (2000); Median rent: $290 per month (2000); Median age of housing: 20 years (2000).
Transportation: Commute to work: 90.0% car, 0.0% public transportation, 1.9% walk, 7.6% work from home (2000); Travel time to work: 63.8% less than 15 minutes, 26.0% 15 to 30 minutes, 4.8% 30 to 45 minutes, 2.2% 45 to 60 minutes, 3.2% 60 minutes or more (2000)

WHITE OAK (township). Covers a land area of 34.401 square miles and a water area of 2.056 square miles. Located at 46.94° N. Lat.; 94.73° W. Long.
Population: 359 (2000); Race: 100.0% White, 0.0% Black, 0.0% Asian, 0.0% American Indian and Alaska Native, 0.0% Hispanic of any race, 0.0% two or more races (2000); Density: 10.4 persons per square mile (2000); Age: 20.7% under 18, 23.4% over 64 (2000); Marriage status: 25.0% never married, 62.5% now married, 8.1% widowed, 4.4% divorced (2000); Foreign born: 0.0% (2000); Ancestry (includes multiple ancestries): 36.2% German, 19.5% Norwegian, 12.2% Irish, 11.2% English, 9.4% French (except Basque) (2000).
Economy: Employment by occupation: 7.7% management, 22.1% professional, 19.2% services, 14.4% sales, 0.0% farming, 21.2% construction, 15.4% production (2000).
Income: Per capita income: $15,221 (2000); Median household income: $27,396 (2000); Poverty rate: 6.8% (2000).
Taxes: Total city taxes per capita: $150 (1997); City property taxes per capita: $150 (1997).
Education: High school graduation rate: 81.4% (2000); College graduation rate: 18.6% (2000).
Housing: Homeownership rate: 94.7% (2000); Median home value: $102,500 (2000); Median rent: $275 per month (2000); Median age of housing: 18 years (2000).
Transportation: Commute to work: 93.3% car, 0.0% public transportation, 1.9% walk, 4.8% work from home (2000); Travel time to work: 19.2% less than 15 minutes, 51.5% 15 to 30 minutes, 12.1% 30 to 45 minutes, 11.1% 45 to 60 minutes, 6.1% 60 minutes or more (2000)

Isanti County

Located in eastern Minnesota; drained by the Rum River. Covers a land area of 439.10 square miles, a water area of 12.80 square miles, and is located in the Central Time Zone. The county government was organized in 1857. County seat is Cambridge.

Isanti County is part of the Minneapolis-St. Paul, MN-WI MSA. The entire metro area includes: Anoka County, MN; Carver County, MN; Chisago County, MN; Dakota County, MN; Hennepin County, MN; Isanti County, MN; Ramsey County, MN; Scott County, MN; Sherburne County, MN; Washington County, MN; Wright County, MN; Pierce County, WI; St. Croix County, WI

Weather Station: Cambridge State Hosp Elevation: 958 feet

	Jan	Feb	Mar	Apr	May	Jun	Jul	Aug	Sep	Oct	Nov	Dec
High	19	26	37	55	69	77	81	78	68	56	38	25
Low	-1	7	19	33	45	54	59	57	47	35	21	7
Precip	1.0	0.6	1.4	2.2	3.2	4.5	4.3	4.1	3.1	2.5	1.9	0.8
Snow	10.1	5.5	7.9	1.9	tr	0.0	0.0	0.0	0.0	0.4	6.5	7.1

High and Low temperatures in degrees Fahrenheit; Precipitation and Snow in inches

Population: 31,287 (2000); Race: 97.6% White, 0.4% Black, 0.3% Asian, 0.5% American Indian and Alaska Native, 0.9% Hispanic of any race, 0.9% two or more races (2000); Density: 71.3 persons per square mile (2000); Age: 28.6% under 18, 10.9% over 64 (2000).
Religion: Five largest groups: 20.9% Evangelical Lutheran Church in America, 9.0% Catholic Church, 6.8% Baptist General Conference, 5.6% Lutheran Church—Missouri Synod, 1.5% The United Methodist Church (2000).
Economy: Unemployment rate: 4.9% (11/2002); Total civilian labor force: 16,974 (11/2002); Leading industries: 21.1% health care and social assistance; 18.6% manufacturing; 18.4% retail trade (2000); Companies that employ more than 1,000 persons: 0 (2000); Companies that employ more than 100 persons: 9 (2000); Farms: 746 totaling 139,417 acres (1997); Minority business ownership rate: 0.0% (1997); Women business ownership rate: 24.4% (1997); Retail sales per capita: $6,562 (1997). Single-family building permits issued: 663 (2001) / 326 (2000); Multi-family building permits issued: 144 (2001) / 4 (2000).
Income: Per capita income: $20,348 (2000); Median household income: $50,127 (2000); Poverty rate: 5.7% (2000); Bankruptcy rate: 4.54% (2001).
Taxes: Total county taxes per capita: $257 (2000); County property taxes per capita: $244 (2000).
Education: High school graduation rate: 86.6% (2000); College graduation rate: 14.5% (2000).

Housing: Homeownership rate: 85.2% (2000); Median home value: $110,700 (2000); Median rent: $474 per month (2000); Median age of housing: 25 years (2000).
Health: Birth rate: 125.3 per 10,000 population (1998); Age adjusted death rate: 77.0 per 10,000 population (1999); Age adjusted cancer mortality rate: 213.4 deaths per 100,000 population (1999). Number of physicians: 13.1 per 10,000 population (1999); Number of hospital beds: 25.9 per 10,000 population (1999).
Elections: 2000 Presidential election results: 41.8% Gore, 51.4% Bush, 5.0% Nader, 1.2% Buchanan
National and State Parks: Athens State Wildlife Management Area; Crooked Road State Wildlife Management Area; German Lake State Game Refuge; Marget Lake State Wildlife Management Area
Additional Information Contacts
Isanti County Government Offices........................763-689-3859
Cambridge Chamber of Commerce........................763-689-2505

Isanti County Communities

ATHENS (township). Covers a land area of 31.360 square miles and a water area of 0.392 square miles. Located at 45.44° N. Lat.; 93.24° W. Long.
Population: 2,322 (2000); Race: 97.7% White, 0.0% Black, 0.4% Asian, 1.0% American Indian and Alaska Native, 0.7% Hispanic of any race, 0.4% two or more races (2000); Density: 74.0 persons per square mile (2000); Age: 29.0% under 18, 6.3% over 64 (2000); Marriage status: 27.4% never married, 62.3% now married, 3.3% widowed, 7.0% divorced (2000); Foreign born: 0.9% (2000); Ancestry (includes multiple ancestries): 35.0% German, 19.2% Swedish, 17.4% Norwegian, 10.9% Irish, 8.1% Polish (2000).
Economy: Employment by occupation: 8.1% management, 13.6% professional, 12.7% services, 24.5% sales, 0.5% farming, 17.9% construction, 22.7% production (2000).
Income: Per capita income: $22,005 (2000); Median household income: $53,807 (2000); Poverty rate: 3.6% (2000).
Taxes: Total city taxes per capita: $66 (1997); City property taxes per capita: $66 (1997).
Education: High school graduation rate: 83.6% (2000); College graduation rate: 9.2% (2000).
Housing: Homeownership rate: 96.1% (2000); Median home value: $118,400 (2000); Median rent: $413 per month (2000); Median age of housing: 23 years (2000).
Transportation: Commute to work: 94.0% car, 0.4% public transportation, 1.4% walk, 3.7% work from home (2000); Travel time to work: 12.2% less than 15 minutes, 24.5% 15 to 30 minutes, 29.5% 30 to 45 minutes, 17.4% 45 to 60 minutes, 16.5% 60 minutes or more (2000)

BRADFORD (township). Covers a land area of 34.461 square miles and a water area of 1.482 square miles. Located at 45.50° N. Lat.; 93.32° W. Long.
Population: 3,472 (2000); Race: 97.4% White, 0.3% Black, 0.4% Asian, 0.5% American Indian and Alaska Native, 1.3% Hispanic of any race, 0.8% two or more races (2000); Density: 100.8 persons per square mile (2000); Age: 30.6% under 18, 6.0% over 64 (2000); Marriage status: 25.7% never married, 64.1% now married, 2.1% widowed, 8.1% divorced (2000); Foreign born: 1.2% (2000); Ancestry (includes multiple ancestries): 39.8% German, 24.2% Swedish, 17.0% Norwegian, 8.0% Irish, 7.9% Polish (2000).
Economy: Employment by occupation: 8.6% management, 15.9% professional, 16.1% services, 22.1% sales, 1.3% farming, 15.7% construction, 20.2% production (2000).
Income: Per capita income: $19,888 (2000); Median household income: $55,515 (2000); Poverty rate: 3.3% (2000).
Taxes: Total city taxes per capita: $71 (2000); City property taxes per capita: $70 (2000).
Education: High school graduation rate: 89.0% (2000); College graduation rate: 11.2% (2000).
Housing: Homeownership rate: 94.3% (2000); Median home value: $116,900 (2000); Median rent: $416 per month (2000); Median age of housing: 23 years (2000).
Transportation: Commute to work: 93.5% car, 0.5% public transportation, 0.2% walk, 4.6% work from home (2000); Travel time to work: 20.6% less than 15 minutes, 21.7% 15 to 30 minutes, 24.1% 30 to 45 minutes, 17.2% 45 to 60 minutes, 16.5% 60 minutes or more (2000)

BRAHAM (city). Covers a land area of 1.262 square miles and a water area of 0 square miles. Located at 45.72° N. Lat.; 93.17° W. Long. Elevation is 960 feet.
Population: 1,276 (2000); Race: 98.5% White, 0.6% Black, 0.3% Asian, 0.0% American Indian and Alaska Native, 0.8% Hispanic of any race, 0.6% two or more races (2000); Density: 1,010.9 persons per square mile (2000); Age: 29.0% under 18, 14.1% over 64 (2000); Marriage status: 27.7% never married, 51.4% now married, 9.9% widowed, 11.1% divorced (2000); Foreign born: 3.0% (2000); Ancestry (includes multiple ancestries): 35.6% German, 25.1% Swedish, 14.2% Norwegian, 12.1% Irish, 4.4% Polish (2000).
Economy: Livestock, poultry; dairying; grain, soybeans. Manufacturing: machinery, consumer goods, construction materials, pontoon boats, molded rubber. Single-family building permits issued: 9 (2001) / 5 (2000); Multi-family building permits issued: 0 (2001) / 0 (2000); Employment by occupation: 7.0% management, 16.7% professional, 18.5% services, 22.5% sales, 0.0% farming, 14.0% construction, 21.2% production (2000).
Income: Per capita income: $16,693 (2000); Median household income: $34,830 (2000); Poverty rate: 14.0% (2000).
Taxes: Total city taxes per capita: $266 (1997); City property taxes per capita: $247 (1997).
Education: High school graduation rate: 84.0% (2000); College graduation rate: 10.7% (2000).

School District(s)

Braham (PK-12)
2000 Enrollment: 974..............................320-396-3313
Housing: Homeownership rate: 66.5% (2000); Median home value: $82,000 (2000); Median rent: $294 per month (2000); Median age of housing: 34 years (2000).
Transportation: Commute to work: 93.2% car, 0.3% public transportation, 4.7% walk, 1.4% work from home (2000); Travel time to work: 31.2% less than 15 minutes, 32.7% 15 to 30 minutes, 8.9% 30 to 45 minutes, 7.9% 45 to 60 minutes, 19.3% 60 minutes or more (2000)

CAMBRIDGE (city). Covers a land area of 6.174 square miles and a water area of 0.083 square miles. Located at 45.56° N. Lat.; 93.22° W. Long. Elevation is 962 feet.
Population: 5,520 (2000); Race: 97.1% White, 1.2% Black, 0.1% Asian, 0.0% American Indian and Alaska Native, 0.4% Hispanic of any race, 1.1% two or more races (2000); Density: 894.1 persons per square mile (2000); Age: 24.0% under 18, 23.9% over 64 (2000); Marriage status: 27.6% never married, 48.6% now married, 14.1% widowed, 9.6% divorced (2000); Foreign born: 1.5% (2000); Ancestry (includes multiple ancestries): 31.5% German, 27.4% Swedish, 20.4% Norwegian, 11.9% Irish, 7.9% English (2000).
Economy: Single-family building permits issued: 100 (2001) / 81 (2000); Multi-family building permits issued: 0 (2001) / 0 (2000); Employment by occupation: 12.1% management, 20.8% professional, 10.4% services, 27.2% sales, 0.0% farming, 8.6% construction, 20.9% production (2000).
Income: Per capita income: $20,697 (2000); Median household income: $35,313 (2000); Poverty rate: 10.5% (2000).
Taxes: Total city taxes per capita: $673 (2000); City property taxes per capita: $632 (2000).
Education: High school graduation rate: 82.9% (2000); College graduation rate: 18.5% (2000).

School District(s)

Cambridge-Isanti (PK-12)
2000 Enrollment: 4,677..............................763-689-4988
Oak Land Vocational Cntr (07-12)
2000 Enrollment: 336..............................763-689-6215

Two-year College(s)

Cambridge Community College-Campus of Anoka-Ramsey (Public)
2001 Enrollment: n/a..............................763-689-7000
2001 Tuition: In-state $2,362; Out-of-state $4,725
Housing: Homeownership rate: 63.0% (2000); Median home value: $100,200 (2000); Median rent: $518 per month (2000); Median age of housing: 23 years (2000).
Hospitals: Cambridge Medical Center (86 beds)
Safety: Violent crime rate: 23.3 per 10,000 population; Property crime rate: 695.5 per 10,000 population (2001).
Newspapers: Scotsman (Rum River Area) (1 x week); County News (1 x week); Cambridge Star (2 x week)
Transportation: Commute to work: 90.4% car, 1.2% public transportation, 4.8% walk, 2.1% work from home (2000); Travel time to work: 53.3% less than 15 minutes, 13.6% 15 to 30 minutes, 11.8% 30 to 45 minutes, 9.6% 45 to 60 minutes, 11.8% 60 minutes or more (2000)
Additional Information Contacts
Cambridge Chamber of Commerce........................763-689-2505

CAMBRIDGE (township). Covers a land area of 30.648 square miles and a water area of 1.361 square miles. Located at 45.59° N. Lat.; 93.19° W. Long. Elevation is 962 feet.

Population: 2,413 (2000); Race: 97.3% White, 0.0% Black, 0.3% Asian, 0.7% American Indian and Alaska Native, 1.4% Hispanic of any race, 1.3% two or more races (2000); Density: 78.7 persons per square mile (2000); Age: 28.7% under 18, 9.4% over 64 (2000); Marriage status: 21.3% never married, 67.1% now married, 3.0% widowed, 8.6% divorced (2000); Foreign born: 2.2% (2000); Ancestry (includes multiple ancestries): 33.0% German, 30.8% Swedish, 17.9% Norwegian, 9.7% Irish, 6.5% French (except Basque) (2000).

Economy: Agricultural area: dairying; poultry, livestock; grain, soybeans. Manufacturing: machinery and instruments, fabricated metal, prepared foods, chemicals, printing and publishing. Employment by occupation: 7.8% management, 22.0% professional, 14.1% services, 20.0% sales, 0.3% farming, 15.8% construction, 20.1% production (2000).

Income: Per capita income: $20,747 (2000); Median household income: $57,148 (2000); Poverty rate: 5.4% (2000).

Taxes: Total city taxes per capita: $63 (1997); City property taxes per capita: $63 (1997).

Education: High school graduation rate: 88.0% (2000); College graduation rate: 18.8% (2000).

Housing: Homeownership rate: 92.9% (2000); Median home value: $117,300 (2000); Median rent: $400 per month (2000); Median age of housing: 26 years (2000).

Transportation: Commute to work: 96.6% car, 0.5% public transportation, 0.8% walk, 1.5% work from home (2000); Travel time to work: 36.8% less than 15 minutes, 17.0% 15 to 30 minutes, 9.2% 30 to 45 minutes, 16.5% 45 to 60 minutes, 20.5% 60 minutes or more (2000)

DALBO (township). Covers a land area of 35.466 square miles and a water area of 0.766 square miles. Located at 45.67° N. Lat.; 93.45° W. Long. Elevation is 980 feet.

Population: 634 (2000); Race: 97.8% White, 0.0% Black, 0.0% Asian, 0.0% American Indian and Alaska Native, 2.2% Hispanic of any race, 0.0% two or more races (2000); Density: 17.9 persons per square mile (2000); Age: 28.5% under 18, 10.3% over 64 (2000); Marriage status: 21.2% never married, 61.4% now married, 8.0% widowed, 9.4% divorced (2000); Foreign born: 0.6% (2000); Ancestry (includes multiple ancestries): 32.6% German, 29.3% Swedish, 15.5% Norwegian, 8.8% Irish, 4.4% English (2000).

Economy: Employment by occupation: 10.7% management, 14.8% professional, 11.3% services, 17.5% sales, 3.3% farming, 12.8% construction, 29.7% production (2000).

Income: Per capita income: $18,133 (2000); Median household income: $47,330 (2000); Poverty rate: 7.4% (2000).

Taxes: Total city taxes per capita: $36 (1997); City property taxes per capita: $36 (1997).

Education: High school graduation rate: 86.2% (2000); College graduation rate: 10.2% (2000).

Housing: Homeownership rate: 91.7% (2000); Median home value: $101,100 (2000); Median rent: $263 per month (2000); Median age of housing: 37 years (2000).

Transportation: Commute to work: 91.9% car, 0.6% public transportation, 1.6% walk, 4.7% work from home (2000); Travel time to work: 6.8% less than 15 minutes, 41.4% 15 to 30 minutes, 14.7% 30 to 45 minutes, 11.7% 45 to 60 minutes, 25.4% 60 minutes or more (2000)

ISANTI (city). Covers a land area of 2.122 square miles and a water area of 0.005 square miles. Located at 45.49° N. Lat.; 93.25° W. Long. Elevation is 932 feet.

Population: 2,324 (2000); Race: 97.5% White, 0.9% Black, 0.4% Asian, 0.3% American Indian and Alaska Native, 0.3% Hispanic of any race, 0.9% two or more races (2000); Density: 1,095.3 persons per square mile (2000); Age: 36.1% under 18, 7.6% over 64 (2000); Marriage status: 28.8% never married, 52.8% now married, 5.2% widowed, 13.1% divorced (2000); Foreign born: 0.9% (2000); Ancestry (includes multiple ancestries): 36.2% German, 22.9% Swedish, 15.1% Norwegian, 8.4% Irish, 5.9% French (except Basque) (2000).

Economy: Single-family building permits issued: 353 (2001) / 63 (2000); Multi-family building permits issued: 144 (2001) / 4 (2000); Employment by occupation: 8.6% management, 12.4% professional, 13.7% services, 25.3% sales, 0.0% farming, 12.9% construction, 27.1% production (2000).

Income: Per capita income: $16,662 (2000); Median household income: $43,587 (2000); Poverty rate: 8.0% (2000).

Taxes: Total city taxes per capita: $186 (1997); City property taxes per capita: $150 (1997).

Education: High school graduation rate: 84.7% (2000); College graduation rate: 8.8% (2000).

Housing: Homeownership rate: 76.0% (2000); Median home value: $100,500 (2000); Median rent: $460 per month (2000); Median age of housing: 13 years (2000).

Transportation: Commute to work: 95.1% car, 0.2% public transportation, 2.1% walk, 1.8% work from home (2000); Travel time to work: 27.5% less than 15 minutes, 18.9% 15 to 30 minutes, 21.3% 30 to 45 minutes, 15.5% 45 to 60 minutes, 16.7% 60 minutes or more (2000)

ISANTI (township). Covers a land area of 30.614 square miles and a water area of 0.846 square miles. Located at 45.52° N. Lat.; 93.22° W. Long. Elevation is 932 feet.

Population: 2,364 (2000); Race: 98.3% White, 0.0% Black, 0.1% Asian, 1.4% American Indian and Alaska Native, 2.0% Hispanic of any race, 0.0% two or more races (2000); Density: 77.2 persons per square mile (2000); Age: 34.0% under 18, 6.0% over 64 (2000); Marriage status: 18.8% never married, 70.4% now married, 1.8% widowed, 9.0% divorced (2000); Foreign born: 0.7% (2000); Ancestry (includes multiple ancestries): 39.4% German, 28.4% Swedish, 15.0% Norwegian, 10.9% Irish, 7.0% English (2000).

Economy: Poultry; grain, soybeans; dairying. Manufacturing: machine products, food processing, metal fabrication, trusses, consumer goods. Employment by occupation: 12.2% management, 21.9% professional, 11.6% services, 23.0% sales, 0.1% farming, 11.7% construction, 19.5% production (2000).

Income: Per capita income: $20,635 (2000); Median household income: $56,336 (2000); Poverty rate: 2.9% (2000).

Taxes: Total city taxes per capita: $57 (1997); City property taxes per capita: $57 (1997).

Education: High school graduation rate: 92.3% (2000); College graduation rate: 20.9% (2000).

Housing: Homeownership rate: 92.3% (2000); Median home value: $127,600 (2000); Median rent: $542 per month (2000); Median age of housing: 24 years (2000).

Transportation: Commute to work: 94.4% car, 0.0% public transportation, 0.2% walk, 5.0% work from home (2000); Travel time to work: 33.7% less than 15 minutes, 21.2% 15 to 30 minutes, 14.0% 30 to 45 minutes, 17.2% 45 to 60 minutes, 13.9% 60 minutes or more (2000)

MAPLE RIDGE (township). Covers a land area of 35.024 square miles and a water area of 0.665 square miles. Located at 45.68° N. Lat.; 93.34° W. Long.

Population: 737 (2000); Race: 98.6% White, 0.0% Black, 0.0% Asian, 0.8% American Indian and Alaska Native, 0.0% Hispanic of any race, 0.4% two or more races (2000); Density: 21.0 persons per square mile (2000); Age: 24.4% under 18, 10.4% over 64 (2000); Marriage status: 24.3% never married, 59.8% now married, 6.8% widowed, 9.1% divorced (2000); Foreign born: 1.1% (2000); Ancestry (includes multiple ancestries): 35.9% Swedish, 31.6% German, 14.6% Norwegian, 9.1% Irish, 6.0% English (2000).

Economy: Employment by occupation: 10.1% management, 15.9% professional, 11.3% services, 17.1% sales, 3.4% farming, 21.2% construction, 21.2% production (2000).

Income: Per capita income: $18,468 (2000); Median household income: $39,688 (2000); Poverty rate: 4.5% (2000).

Taxes: Total city taxes per capita: $33 (1997); City property taxes per capita: $33 (1997).

Education: High school graduation rate: 83.3% (2000); College graduation rate: 15.5% (2000).

Housing: Homeownership rate: 83.6% (2000); Median home value: $96,400 (2000); Median rent: $556 per month (2000); Median age of housing: 47 years (2000).

Transportation: Commute to work: 92.1% car, 0.0% public transportation, 2.2% walk, 5.2% work from home (2000); Travel time to work: 12.2% less than 15 minutes, 32.6% 15 to 30 minutes, 14.2% 30 to 45 minutes, 13.2% 45 to 60 minutes, 27.7% 60 minutes or more (2000)

NORTH BRANCH (township). Covers a land area of 34.647 square miles and a water area of 0.341 square miles. Located at 45.51° N. Lat.; 93.08° W. Long.

Population: 1,654 (2000); Race: 97.9% White, 0.0% Black, 0.6% Asian, 0.1% American Indian and Alaska Native, 1.0% Hispanic of any race, 1.1% two or more races (2000); Density: 47.7 persons per square mile (2000); Age: 26.9% under 18, 8.8% over 64 (2000); Marriage status: 23.5% never married, 62.6% now married, 5.0% widowed, 9.0% divorced (2000); Foreign born:

2.2% (2000); Ancestry (includes multiple ancestries): 39.5% German, 20.6% Swedish, 12.5% Irish, 11.4% Norwegian, 5.7% English (2000).
Economy: Employment by occupation: 11.7% management, 14.7% professional, 12.6% services, 24.6% sales, 1.1% farming, 13.9% construction, 21.4% production (2000).
Income: Per capita income: $21,849 (2000); Median household income: $55,833 (2000); Poverty rate: 2.3% (2000).
Taxes: Total city taxes per capita: $71 (1997); City property taxes per capita: $71 (1997).
Education: High school graduation rate: 86.1% (2000); College graduation rate: 10.5% (2000).
Housing: Homeownership rate: 94.1% (2000); Median home value: $98,600 (2000); Median rent: $525 per month (2000); Median age of housing: 26 years (2000).
Transportation: Commute to work: 93.2% car, 0.3% public transportation, 0.2% walk, 5.3% work from home (2000); Travel time to work: 18.5% less than 15 minutes, 22.1% 15 to 30 minutes, 18.4% 30 to 45 minutes, 23.2% 45 to 60 minutes, 17.8% 60 minutes or more (2000)

OXFORD (township). Covers a land area of 22.567 square miles and a water area of 1.160 square miles. Located at 45.43° N. Lat.; 93.07° W. Long.
Population: 799 (2000); Race: 97.8% White, 0.0% Black, 0.2% Asian, 1.0% American Indian and Alaska Native, 0.7% Hispanic of any race, 1.0% two or more races (2000); Density: 35.4 persons per square mile (2000); Age: 27.8% under 18, 5.7% over 64 (2000); Marriage status: 21.8% never married, 67.3% now married, 2.2% widowed, 8.7% divorced (2000); Foreign born: 0.5% (2000); Ancestry (includes multiple ancestries): 35.9% German, 29.1% Swedish, 16.4% Norwegian, 7.0% Irish, 6.4% United States or American (2000).
Economy: Employment by occupation: 15.2% management, 15.0% professional, 13.2% services, 18.1% sales, 1.8% farming, 18.8% construction, 17.9% production (2000).
Income: Per capita income: $21,529 (2000); Median household income: $60,000 (2000); Poverty rate: 1.5% (2000).
Taxes: Total city taxes per capita: $94 (1997); City property taxes per capita: $94 (1997).
Education: High school graduation rate: 87.5% (2000); College graduation rate: 11.6% (2000).
Housing: Homeownership rate: 96.0% (2000); Median home value: $129,900 (2000); Median rent: $375 per month (2000); Median age of housing: 21 years (2000).
Transportation: Commute to work: 94.5% car, 0.5% public transportation, 0.9% walk, 4.1% work from home (2000); Travel time to work: 4.8% less than 15 minutes, 23.6% 15 to 30 minutes, 21.9% 30 to 45 minutes, 32.7% 45 to 60 minutes, 17.1% 60 minutes or more (2000)

SPENCER BROOK (township). Covers a land area of 34.345 square miles and a water area of 1.080 square miles. Located at 45.51° N. Lat.; 93.44° W. Long.
Population: 1,495 (2000); Race: 97.5% White, 0.2% Black, 0.3% Asian, 1.1% American Indian and Alaska Native, 0.8% Hispanic of any race, 0.7% two or more races (2000); Density: 43.5 persons per square mile (2000); Age: 26.9% under 18, 8.6% over 64 (2000); Marriage status: 22.0% never married, 67.6% now married, 3.9% widowed, 6.6% divorced (2000); Foreign born: 0.6% (2000); Ancestry (includes multiple ancestries): 40.2% German, 19.5% Swedish, 16.4% Norwegian, 9.4% Irish, 6.4% English (2000).
Economy: Employment by occupation: 8.9% management, 14.3% professional, 11.0% services, 22.3% sales, 1.7% farming, 16.5% construction, 25.2% production (2000).
Income: Per capita income: $21,615 (2000); Median household income: $55,500 (2000); Poverty rate: 3.7% (2000).
Taxes: Total city taxes per capita: $94 (1997); City property taxes per capita: $88 (1997).
Education: High school graduation rate: 87.8% (2000); College graduation rate: 14.6% (2000).
Housing: Homeownership rate: 96.7% (2000); Median home value: $122,100 (2000); Median rent: $438 per month (2000); Median age of housing: 24 years (2000).
Transportation: Commute to work: 93.3% car, 0.4% public transportation, 1.5% walk, 4.5% work from home (2000); Travel time to work: 14.2% less than 15 minutes, 27.9% 15 to 30 minutes, 17.8% 30 to 45 minutes, 17.5% 45 to 60 minutes, 22.5% 60 minutes or more (2000)

SPRINGVALE (township). Covers a land area of 34.847 square miles and a water area of 0.478 square miles. Located at 45.59° N. Lat.; 93.33° W. Long. Elevation is 935 feet.
Population: 1,384 (2000); Race: 98.4% White, 0.2% Black, 0.2% Asian, 0.0% American Indian and Alaska Native, 0.9% Hispanic of any race, 0.5% two or more races (2000); Density: 39.7 persons per square mile (2000); Age: 28.8% under 18, 7.8% over 64 (2000); Marriage status: 22.5% never married, 64.7% now married, 3.4% widowed, 9.4% divorced (2000); Foreign born: 0.7% (2000); Ancestry (includes multiple ancestries): 33.5% German, 31.9% Swedish, 20.1% Norwegian, 10.8% Irish, 6.8% English (2000).
Economy: Employment by occupation: 7.2% management, 20.6% professional, 14.6% services, 20.3% sales, 1.5% farming, 16.6% construction, 19.2% production (2000).
Income: Per capita income: $20,260 (2000); Median household income: $53,942 (2000); Poverty rate: 3.7% (2000).
Taxes: Total city taxes per capita: $72 (1997); City property taxes per capita: $72 (1997).
Education: High school graduation rate: 86.9% (2000); College graduation rate: 15.6% (2000).
Housing: Homeownership rate: 96.5% (2000); Median home value: $118,900 (2000); Median rent: $675 per month (2000); Median age of housing: 23 years (2000).
Transportation: Commute to work: 92.1% car, 0.0% public transportation, 2.4% walk, 5.3% work from home (2000); Travel time to work: 27.0% less than 15 minutes, 25.3% 15 to 30 minutes, 12.1% 30 to 45 minutes, 12.1% 45 to 60 minutes, 23.4% 60 minutes or more (2000)

STANCHFIELD (township). Covers a land area of 33.804 square miles and a water area of 0.814 square miles. Located at 45.68° N. Lat.; 93.19° W. Long.
Population: 1,120 (2000); Race: 99.4% White, 0.3% Black, 0.3% Asian, 0.0% American Indian and Alaska Native, 0.3% Hispanic of any race, 0.0% two or more races (2000); Density: 33.1 persons per square mile (2000); Age: 26.6% under 18, 9.1% over 64 (2000); Marriage status: 26.2% never married, 63.3% now married, 4.5% widowed, 6.1% divorced (2000); Foreign born: 2.2% (2000); Ancestry (includes multiple ancestries): 39.8% German, 26.6% Swedish, 13.2% Norwegian, 6.0% Irish, 4.4% English (2000).
Economy: Employment by occupation: 11.5% management, 12.9% professional, 10.4% services, 23.6% sales, 0.9% farming, 15.9% construction, 24.8% production (2000).
Income: Per capita income: $20,351 (2000); Median household income: $50,588 (2000); Poverty rate: 5.6% (2000).
Taxes: Total city taxes per capita: $32 (1997); City property taxes per capita: $32 (1997).
Education: High school graduation rate: 86.9% (2000); College graduation rate: 14.2% (2000).
Housing: Homeownership rate: 91.5% (2000); Median home value: $96,700 (2000); Median rent: $389 per month (2000); Median age of housing: 38 years (2000).
Transportation: Commute to work: 92.4% car, 0.3% public transportation, 1.9% walk, 5.4% work from home (2000); Travel time to work: 28.1% less than 15 minutes, 24.9% 15 to 30 minutes, 9.4% 30 to 45 minutes, 10.8% 45 to 60 minutes, 26.9% 60 minutes or more (2000)

STANFORD (township). Covers a land area of 38.581 square miles and a water area of 0.835 square miles. Located at 45.44° N. Lat.; 93.37° W. Long.
Population: 2,075 (2000); Race: 97.6% White, 0.0% Black, 0.2% Asian, 0.9% American Indian and Alaska Native, 0.8% Hispanic of any race, 1.2% two or more races (2000); Density: 53.8 persons per square mile (2000); Age: 28.6% under 18, 7.3% over 64 (2000); Marriage status: 25.2% never married, 64.4% now married, 3.5% widowed, 7.0% divorced (2000); Foreign born: 0.8% (2000); Ancestry (includes multiple ancestries): 37.9% German, 19.5% Swedish, 14.0% Norwegian, 9.1% Irish, 9.1% English (2000).
Economy: Employment by occupation: 12.1% management, 13.5% professional, 12.2% services, 23.7% sales, 0.3% farming, 14.0% construction, 24.3% production (2000).
Income: Per capita income: $20,958 (2000); Median household income: $56,384 (2000); Poverty rate: 3.7% (2000).
Taxes: Total city taxes per capita: $82 (2000); City property taxes per capita: $81 (2000).
Education: High school graduation rate: 89.1% (2000); College graduation rate: 13.9% (2000).
Housing: Homeownership rate: 97.1% (2000); Median home value: $121,400 (2000); Median rent: $1,275 per month (2000); Median age of housing: 24 years (2000).
Transportation: Commute to work: 90.9% car, 1.0% public transportation, 0.9% walk, 6.8% work from home (2000); Travel time to work: 15.8% less than 15 minutes, 18.9% 15 to 30 minutes, 27.5% 30 to 45 minutes, 21.1% 45 to 60 minutes, 16.7% 60 minutes or more (2000)

WYANETT (township). Covers a land area of 33.201 square miles and a water area of 2.496 square miles. Located at 45.59° N. Lat.; 93.44° W. Long. Elevation is 969 feet.

Population: 1,698 (2000); Race: 96.0% White, 0.5% Black, 0.2% Asian, 0.7% American Indian and Alaska Native, 1.5% Hispanic of any race, 2.3% two or more races (2000); Density: 51.1 persons per square mile (2000); Age: 26.3% under 18, 11.7% over 64 (2000); Marriage status: 18.6% never married, 70.3% now married, 4.3% widowed, 6.9% divorced (2000); Foreign born: 1.7% (2000); Ancestry (includes multiple ancestries): 35.9% German, 21.8% Swedish, 16.0% Norwegian, 11.4% Irish, 9.1% English (2000).
Economy: Employment by occupation: 13.6% management, 16.0% professional, 13.0% services, 25.3% sales, 1.7% farming, 13.6% construction, 16.9% production (2000).
Income: Per capita income: $22,481 (2000); Median household income: $53,309 (2000); Poverty rate: 4.9% (2000).
Taxes: Total city taxes per capita: $50 (1997); City property taxes per capita: $50 (1997).
Education: High school graduation rate: 89.2% (2000); College graduation rate: 16.1% (2000).
Housing: Homeownership rate: 91.1% (2000); Median home value: $125,600 (2000); Median rent: $538 per month (2000); Median age of housing: 28 years (2000).
Transportation: Commute to work: 93.1% car, 0.2% public transportation, 1.3% walk, 5.1% work from home (2000); Travel time to work: 19.3% less than 15 minutes, 30.5% 15 to 30 minutes, 14.0% 30 to 45 minutes, 10.9% 45 to 60 minutes, 25.3% 60 minutes or more (2000)

Itasca County

Located in northern Minnesota; crossed by the Mississippi River; includes Bowstring, Pokegama, and Winnibigoshish Lakes, and Chippewa National Forest. Covers a land area of 2,665.10 square miles, a water area of 262.70 square miles, and is located in the Central Time Zone. The county government was organized in 1850. County seat is Grand Rapids.

Weather Station: Grand Rapids Forestry Lab — Elevation: 1,309 feet

	Jan	Feb	Mar	Apr	May	Jun	Jul	Aug	Sep	Oct	Nov	Dec
High	17	26	37	54	68	76	80	78	67	54	35	22
Low	-5	2	15	29	41	51	55	53	44	34	19	3
Precip	1.0	0.6	1.2	1.8	2.8	4.6	4.6	3.6	3.1	2.8	1.5	0.9
Snow	14.4	7.5	9.0	3.4	0.5	0.0	0.0	0.0	tr	1.1	9.5	11.3

High and Low temperatures in degrees Fahrenheit; Precipitation and Snow in inches

Weather Station: Pokegama Dam — Elevation: 1,279 feet

	Jan	Feb	Mar	Apr	May	Jun	Jul	Aug	Sep	Oct	Nov	Dec
High	na	na	na	54	68	76	80	78	67	na	na	na
Low	na	na	na	29	42	52	56	54	45	na	na	na
Precip	0.9	0.6	1.2	1.7	2.8	4.5	4.7	3.7	3.2	2.7	1.4	0.9
Snow	11.7	6.8	9.0	2.2	0.1	0.0	0.0	0.0	tr	1.1	7.3	8.9

High and Low temperatures in degrees Fahrenheit; Precipitation and Snow in inches

Population: 43,992 (2000); Race: 94.8% White, 0.3% Black, 0.2% Asian, 3.3% American Indian and Alaska Native, 0.8% Hispanic of any race, 1.2% two or more races (2000); Density: 16.5 persons per square mile (2000); Age: 24.3% under 18, 16.8% over 64 (2000).
Religion: Five largest groups: 29.1% Catholic Church, 10.6% Evangelical Lutheran Church in America, 7.1% Lutheran Church—Missouri Synod, 3.7% Presbyterian Church (U.S.A.), 1.7% The United Methodist Church (2000).
Economy: Unemployment rate: 6.0% (11/2002); Total civilian labor force: 20,375 (11/2002); Leading industries: 18.3% retail trade; 18.0% manufacturing; 15.8% health care and social assistance (2000); Companies that employ more than 1,000 persons: 0 (2000); Companies that employ more than 100 persons: 21 (2000); Farms: 415 totaling 103,716 acres (1997); Minority business ownership rate: 4.8% (1997); Women business ownership rate: 31.6% (1997); Retail sales per capita: $8,285 (1997). Single-family building permits issued: 304 (2001) / 348 (2000); Multi-family building permits issued: 22 (2001) / 0 (2000).
Income: Per capita income: $17,717 (2000); Median household income: $36,234 (2000); Poverty rate: 10.6% (2000); Bankruptcy rate: 2.85% (2001).
Taxes: Total county taxes per capita: $459 (2000); County property taxes per capita: $458 (2000).
Education: High school graduation rate: 85.6% (2000); College graduation rate: 17.6% (2000).
Housing: Homeownership rate: 82.9% (2000); Median home value: $81,700 (2000); Median rent: $357 per month (2000); Median age of housing: 29 years (2000).
Health: Birth rate: 93.2 per 10,000 population (1998); Age adjusted death rate: 83.7 per 10,000 population (1999); Age adjusted cancer mortality rate: 230.7 deaths per 100,000 population (1999). Air Quality Index: 100% good, 0% moderate, 0% unhealthy (percent of days in 2000). Number of physicians: 11.6 per 10,000 population (1999); Number of hospital beds: 49.8 per 10,000 population (1999).
Elections: 2000 Presidential election results: 48.7% Gore, 44.0% Bush, 5.2% Nader, 1.4% Buchanan
National and State Parks: Big Fork State Forest; Chippewa National Forest; Cutfoot Sioux National Recreation Trail; George Washington State Forest; Golden Anniversary State Forest; Scenic State Park

Additional Information Contacts

Itasca County Government Offices 218-327-2847
Deep River Chamber of Commerce 218-246-8055
Grand Rapids Chamber of Commerce 218-326-6619
Grand Rapids Convention & Visitors Bureau 218-326-9607
Itasca County Board of Realtors 218-326-4533

Itasca County Communities

ALVWOOD (township). Covers a land area of 35.098 square miles and a water area of 0.396 square miles. Located at 47.71° N. Lat.; 94.24° W. Long. Elevation is 1,380 feet.
Population: 74 (2000); Race: 100.0% White, 0.0% Black, 0.0% Asian, 0.0% American Indian and Alaska Native, 0.0% Hispanic of any race, 0.0% two or more races (2000); Density: 2.1 persons per square mile (2000); Age: 22.4% under 18, 17.1% over 64 (2000); Marriage status: 21.9% never married, 51.6% now married, 7.8% widowed, 18.8% divorced (2000); Foreign born: 0.0% (2000); Ancestry (includes multiple ancestries): 35.5% German, 26.3% Norwegian, 13.2% Swedish, 9.2% Czechoslovakian, 9.2% Irish (2000).
Economy: Employment by occupation: 11.4% management, 5.7% professional, 31.4% services, 14.3% sales, 5.7% farming, 0.0% construction, 31.4% production (2000).
Income: Per capita income: $8,847 (2000); Median household income: $19,167 (2000); Poverty rate: 38.2% (2000).
Taxes: Total city taxes per capita: $145 (1997); City property taxes per capita: $145 (1997).
Education: High school graduation rate: 64.8% (2000); College graduation rate: 0.0% (2000).
Housing: Homeownership rate: 93.8% (2000); Median home value: $23,800 (2000); Median age of housing: 30 years (2000).
Transportation: Commute to work: 91.4% car, 0.0% public transportation, 0.0% walk, 8.6% work from home (2000); Travel time to work: 28.1% less than 15 minutes, 53.1% 15 to 30 minutes, 12.5% 30 to 45 minutes, 0.0% 45 to 60 minutes, 6.3% 60 minutes or more (2000)

ARBO (township). Covers a land area of 33.606 square miles and a water area of 3.211 square miles. Located at 47.31° N. Lat.; 93.53° W. Long.
Population: 898 (2000); Race: 98.4% White, 0.0% Black, 0.3% Asian, 0.3% American Indian and Alaska Native, 2.3% Hispanic of any race, 0.0% two or more races (2000); Density: 26.7 persons per square mile (2000); Age: 23.9% under 18, 12.6% over 64 (2000); Marriage status: 20.3% never married, 70.8% now married, 4.5% widowed, 4.4% divorced (2000); Foreign born: 2.2% (2000); Ancestry (includes multiple ancestries): 37.1% German, 16.5% Norwegian, 10.1% Swedish, 9.8% Irish, 8.7% English (2000).
Economy: Employment by occupation: 11.5% management, 18.6% professional, 11.7% services, 24.0% sales, 0.6% farming, 13.0% construction, 20.6% production (2000).
Income: Per capita income: $20,035 (2000); Median household income: $42,371 (2000); Poverty rate: 5.8% (2000).
Taxes: Total city taxes per capita: $43 (1997); City property taxes per capita: $43 (1997).
Education: High school graduation rate: 92.0% (2000); College graduation rate: 22.9% (2000).
Housing: Homeownership rate: 92.6% (2000); Median home value: $93,400 (2000); Median rent: $383 per month (2000); Median age of housing: 30 years (2000).
Transportation: Commute to work: 97.4% car, 0.0% public transportation, 0.2% walk, 2.0% work from home (2000); Travel time to work: 20.4% less than 15 minutes, 61.8% 15 to 30 minutes, 8.8% 30 to 45 minutes, 2.5% 45 to 60 minutes, 6.5% 60 minutes or more (2000)

ARDENHURST (township). Covers a land area of 29.446 square miles and a water area of 5.614 square miles. Located at 47.80° N. Lat.; 94.22° W. Long.
Population: 172 (2000); Race: 98.1% White, 0.0% Black, 0.0% Asian, 0.0% American Indian and Alaska Native, 0.0% Hispanic of any race, 1.9% two or more races (2000); Density: 5.8 persons per square mile (2000); Age: 28.5% under 18, 24.7% over 64 (2000); Marriage status: 17.6% never married, 72.0% now married, 6.4% widowed, 4.0% divorced (2000); Foreign born: 1.9% (2000); Ancestry (includes multiple ancestries): 28.5% German, 17.7% Norwegian, 8.9% English, 5.7% Irish, 5.1% French (except Basque) (2000).
Economy: Employment by occupation: 7.7% management, 15.4% professional, 9.6% services, 17.3% sales, 0.0% farming, 23.1% construction, 26.9% production (2000).
Income: Per capita income: $13,251 (2000); Median household income: $29,107 (2000); Poverty rate: 6.3% (2000).
Taxes: Total city taxes per capita: $65 (1997); City property taxes per capita: $65 (1997).
Education: High school graduation rate: 85.3% (2000); College graduation rate: 27.5% (2000).
Housing: Homeownership rate: 97.0% (2000); Median home value: $84,000 (2000); Median age of housing: 26 years (2000).
Transportation: Commute to work: 71.2% car, 0.0% public transportation, 7.7% walk, 19.2% work from home (2000); Travel time to work: 50.0% less than 15 minutes, 28.6% 15 to 30 minutes, 9.5% 30 to 45 minutes, 0.0% 45 to 60 minutes, 11.9% 60 minutes or more (2000)

BALSAM (township). Covers a land area of 72.634 square miles and a water area of 10.689 square miles. Located at 47.50° N. Lat.; 93.42° W. Long.
Population: 553 (2000); Race: 99.3% White, 0.0% Black, 0.0% Asian, 0.0% American Indian and Alaska Native, 0.3% Hispanic of any race, 0.7% two or more races (2000); Density: 7.6 persons per square mile (2000); Age: 23.5% under 18, 18.6% over 64 (2000); Marriage status: 17.0% never married, 76.4% now married, 3.4% widowed, 3.2% divorced (2000); Foreign born: 1.5% (2000); Ancestry (includes multiple ancestries): 28.6% German, 17.5% Norwegian, 14.8% Irish, 11.0% English, 10.8% Swedish (2000).
Economy: Employment by occupation: 9.7% management, 17.6% professional, 12.3% services, 19.4% sales, 6.2% farming, 20.3% construction, 14.5% production (2000).
Income: Per capita income: $21,488 (2000); Median household income: $42,813 (2000); Poverty rate: 3.9% (2000).
Taxes: Total city taxes per capita: $166 (2000); City property taxes per capita: $166 (2000).
Education: High school graduation rate: 85.3% (2000); College graduation rate: 12.1% (2000).
Housing: Homeownership rate: 95.7% (2000); Median home value: $104,400 (2000); Median age of housing: 33 years (2000).
Transportation: Commute to work: 88.8% car, 0.0% public transportation, 0.9% walk, 10.3% work from home (2000); Travel time to work: 17.5% less than 15 minutes, 18.0% 15 to 30 minutes, 43.0% 30 to 45 minutes, 15.5% 45 to 60 minutes, 6.0% 60 minutes or more (2000)

BEARVILLE (township). Covers a land area of 71.816 square miles and a water area of 1.133 square miles. Located at 47.70° N. Lat.; 93.08° W. Long.
Population: 202 (2000); Race: 100.0% White, 0.0% Black, 0.0% Asian, 0.0% American Indian and Alaska Native, 0.0% Hispanic of any race, 0.0% two or more races (2000); Density: 2.8 persons per square mile (2000); Age: 7.8% under 18, 26.8% over 64 (2000); Marriage status: 12.5% never married, 75.7% now married, 5.6% widowed, 6.3% divorced (2000); Foreign born: 0.0% (2000); Ancestry (includes multiple ancestries): 19.0% Italian, 19.0% Norwegian, 14.4% Irish, 9.2% Swedish, 8.5% German (2000).
Economy: Employment by occupation: 18.2% management, 18.2% professional, 7.6% services, 33.3% sales, 0.0% farming, 9.1% construction, 13.6% production (2000).
Income: Per capita income: $28,563 (2000); Median household income: $43,958 (2000); Poverty rate: 7.8% (2000).
Taxes: Total city taxes per capita: $128 (1997); City property taxes per capita: $128 (1997).
Education: High school graduation rate: 92.0% (2000); College graduation rate: 29.7% (2000).
Housing: Homeownership rate: 92.6% (2000); Median home value: $140,600 (2000); Median rent: $125 per month (2000); Median age of housing: 24 years (2000).
Transportation: Commute to work: 92.4% car, 0.0% public transportation, 3.0% walk, 4.5% work from home (2000); Travel time to work: 22.2% less than 15 minutes, 27.0% 15 to 30 minutes, 31.7% 30 to 45 minutes, 0.0% 45 to 60 minutes, 19.0% 60 minutes or more (2000)

BIGFORK (city). Covers a land area of 1.780 square miles and a water area of 0.032 square miles. Located at 47.74° N. Lat.; 93.65° W. Long. Elevation is 1,318 feet.
Population: 469 (2000); Race: 97.6% White, 0.0% Black, 0.0% Asian, 1.8% American Indian and Alaska Native, 0.0% Hispanic of any race, 0.6% two or more races (2000); Density: 263.5 persons per square mile (2000); Age: 19.4% under 18, 25.4% over 64 (2000); Marriage status: 27.4% never married, 49.2% now married, 11.7% widowed, 11.7% divorced (2000); Foreign born: 0.4% (2000); Ancestry (includes multiple ancestries): 29.6% German, 18.5% Norwegian, 15.7% Swedish, 6.5% Irish, 4.6% United States or American (2000).
Economy: Single-family building permits issued: 0 (2001) / 0 (2000); Multi-family building permits issued: 0 (2001) / 0 (2000); Employment by occupation: 11.4% management, 13.8% professional, 21.9% services, 27.1% sales, 3.3% farming, 10.0% construction, 12.4% production (2000).
Income: Per capita income: $14,455 (2000); Median household income: $24,167 (2000); Poverty rate: 12.3% (2000).
Taxes: Total city taxes per capita: $93 (1997); City property taxes per capita: $93 (1997).
Education: High school graduation rate: 80.3% (2000); College graduation rate: 20.8% (2000).
Housing: Homeownership rate: 64.4% (2000); Median home value: $71,800 (2000); Median rent: $350 per month (2000); Median age of housing: 26 years (2000).
Hospitals: Northern Itasca Hospital District (20 beds)
Transportation: Commute to work: 76.7% car, 0.0% public transportation, 16.2% walk, 3.8% work from home (2000); Travel time to work: 77.7% less than 15 minutes, 13.4% 15 to 30 minutes, 1.0% 30 to 45 minutes, 2.5% 45 to 60 minutes, 5.4% 60 minutes or more (2000)

BIGFORK (township). Covers a land area of 49.229 square miles and a water area of 0.403 square miles. Located at 47.76° N. Lat.; 93.66° W. Long. Elevation is 1,318 feet.
Population: 311 (2000); Race: 99.3% White, 0.0% Black, 0.0% Asian, 0.7% American Indian and Alaska Native, 0.0% Hispanic of any race, 0.0% two or more races (2000); Density: 6.3 persons per square mile (2000); Age: 18.1% under 18, 28.3% over 64 (2000); Marriage status: 12.0% never married, 74.8% now married, 6.0% widowed, 7.1% divorced (2000); Foreign born: 0.0% (2000); Ancestry (includes multiple ancestries): 29.9% German, 17.4% Norwegian, 12.5% Swedish, 8.9% United States or American, 6.6% French (except Basque) (2000).
Economy: Timber, lumber; alfalfa; cattle. Employment by occupation: 22.6% management, 14.8% professional, 16.5% services, 19.1% sales, 3.5% farming, 7.0% construction, 16.5% production (2000).
Income: Per capita income: $24,359 (2000); Median household income: $38,125 (2000); Poverty rate: 3.0% (2000).
Taxes: Total city taxes per capita: $60 (1997); City property taxes per capita: $60 (1997).
Education: High school graduation rate: 82.5% (2000); College graduation rate: 12.4% (2000).
Housing: Homeownership rate: 92.3% (2000); Median home value: $95,000 (2000); Median rent: $275 per month (2000); Median age of housing: 26 years (2000).
Transportation: Commute to work: 93.0% car, 0.0% public transportation, 1.7% walk, 5.2% work from home (2000); Travel time to work: 70.6% less than 15 minutes, 19.3% 15 to 30 minutes, 1.8% 30 to 45 minutes, 0.0% 45 to 60 minutes, 8.3% 60 minutes or more (2000)

BLACKBERRY (township). Covers a land area of 35.086 square miles and a water area of 1.029 square miles. Located at 47.17° N. Lat.; 93.40° W. Long. Elevation is 1,293 feet.
Population: 717 (2000); Race: 98.9% White, 0.0% Black, 0.6% Asian, 0.4% American Indian and Alaska Native, 0.0% Hispanic of any race, 0.1% two or more races (2000); Density: 20.4 persons per square mile (2000); Age: 28.4% under 18, 9.3% over 64 (2000); Marriage status: 18.2% never married, 72.8% now married, 2.6% widowed, 6.4% divorced (2000); Foreign born: 1.4% (2000); Ancestry (includes multiple ancestries): 37.1% German, 14.9% Norwegian, 14.1% Irish, 13.2% Swedish, 12.2% Finnish (2000).
Economy: Employment by occupation: 4.0% management, 14.0% professional, 12.4% services, 28.9% sales, 1.2% farming, 19.9% construction, 19.6% production (2000).

Income: Per capita income: $15,776 (2000); Median household income: $41,667 (2000); Poverty rate: 9.9% (2000).
Taxes: Total city taxes per capita: $114 (2000); City property taxes per capita: $114 (2000).
Education: High school graduation rate: 83.7% (2000); College graduation rate: 12.0% (2000).
Housing: Homeownership rate: 95.9% (2000); Median home value: $81,400 (2000); Median rent: $375 per month (2000); Median age of housing: 25 years (2000).
Transportation: Commute to work: 95.3% car, 0.3% public transportation, 0.6% walk, 3.7% work from home (2000); Travel time to work: 20.7% less than 15 minutes, 61.2% 15 to 30 minutes, 6.1% 30 to 45 minutes, 2.9% 45 to 60 minutes, 9.1% 60 minutes or more (2000)

BOVEY (city). Covers a land area of 2.283 square miles and a water area of 0.026 square miles. Located at 47.29° N. Lat.; 93.41° W. Long. Elevation is 1,350 feet.
History: Bovey developed as a mining town, incorporated in 1904.
Population: 662 (2000); Race: 94.2% White, 0.0% Black, 0.3% Asian, 3.7% American Indian and Alaska Native, 2.1% Hispanic of any race, 1.3% two or more races (2000); Density: 290.0 persons per square mile (2000); Age: 22.4% under 18, 18.7% over 64 (2000); Marriage status: 22.3% never married, 51.6% now married, 11.1% widowed, 15.0% divorced (2000); Foreign born: 2.2% (2000); Ancestry (includes multiple ancestries): 26.7% German, 10.9% Norwegian, 9.6% Finnish, 8.0% Irish, 7.8% Other groups (2000).
Economy: Single-family building permits issued: 3 (2001) / 1 (2000); Multi-family building permits issued: 0 (2001) / 0 (2000); Employment by occupation: 7.2% management, 11.9% professional, 26.7% services, 29.6% sales, 1.1% farming, 10.8% construction, 12.6% production (2000).
Income: Per capita income: $16,127 (2000); Median household income: $25,662 (2000); Poverty rate: 22.3% (2000).
Taxes: Total city taxes per capita: $172 (1997); City property taxes per capita: $169 (1997).
Education: High school graduation rate: 85.8% (2000); College graduation rate: 10.4% (2000).
Housing: Homeownership rate: 65.2% (2000); Median home value: $37,200 (2000); Median rent: $354 per month (2000); Median age of housing: 59 years (2000).
Newspapers: Scenic Range News (1 x week)
Transportation: Commute to work: 89.1% car, 0.0% public transportation, 7.7% walk, 1.8% work from home (2000); Travel time to work: 32.3% less than 15 minutes, 49.1% 15 to 30 minutes, 10.8% 30 to 45 minutes, 4.1% 45 to 60 minutes, 3.7% 60 minutes or more (2000)

BOWSTRING (township). Covers a land area of 26.556 square miles and a water area of 9.394 square miles. Located at 47.56° N. Lat.; 93.83° W. Long. Elevation is 1,314 feet.
Population: 242 (2000); Race: 94.5% White, 0.0% Black, 0.0% Asian, 3.7% American Indian and Alaska Native, 0.0% Hispanic of any race, 1.8% two or more races (2000); Density: 9.1 persons per square mile (2000); Age: 22.9% under 18, 20.2% over 64 (2000); Marriage status: 20.7% never married, 66.5% now married, 6.4% widowed, 6.4% divorced (2000); Foreign born: 0.0% (2000); Ancestry (includes multiple ancestries): 37.6% German, 27.5% Swedish, 22.0% Norwegian, 11.0% Finnish, 6.4% Irish (2000).
Economy: Employment by occupation: 3.3% management, 22.0% professional, 17.6% services, 19.8% sales, 4.4% farming, 14.3% construction, 18.7% production (2000).
Income: Per capita income: $18,006 (2000); Median household income: $31,000 (2000); Poverty rate: 24.3% (2000).
Taxes: Total city taxes per capita: $80 (1997); City property taxes per capita: $80 (1997).
Education: High school graduation rate: 76.3% (2000); College graduation rate: 22.4% (2000).
Housing: Homeownership rate: 90.9% (2000); Median home value: $111,100 (2000); Median age of housing: 24 years (2000).
Transportation: Commute to work: 87.6% car, 1.1% public transportation, 5.6% walk, 5.6% work from home (2000); Travel time to work: 27.4% less than 15 minutes, 32.1% 15 to 30 minutes, 15.5% 30 to 45 minutes, 14.3% 45 to 60 minutes, 10.7% 60 minutes or more (2000)

CALUMET (city). Covers a land area of 1.591 square miles and a water area of 0.011 square miles. Located at 47.32° N. Lat.; 93.27° W. Long. Elevation is 1,392 feet.
Population: 383 (2000); Race: 95.2% White, 0.0% Black, 0.0% Asian, 4.3% American Indian and Alaska Native, 0.5% Hispanic of any race, 0.5% two or more races (2000); Density: 240.7 persons per square mile (2000); Age: 27.7% under 18, 18.0% over 64 (2000); Marriage status: 27.9% never married, 51.5% now married, 9.8% widowed, 10.8% divorced (2000); Foreign born: 1.0% (2000); Ancestry (includes multiple ancestries): 21.6% German, 14.0% Swedish, 8.1% Norwegian, 8.1% Finnish, 8.1% Other groups (2000).
Economy: Iron-mining district. Single-family building permits issued: 2 (2001) / 0 (2000); Multi-family building permits issued: 0 (2001) / 0 (2000); Employment by occupation: 7.3% management, 8.1% professional, 18.5% services, 25.0% sales, 0.0% farming, 15.3% construction, 25.8% production (2000).
Income: Per capita income: $12,293 (2000); Median household income: $22,250 (2000); Poverty rate: 17.5% (2000).
Taxes: Total city taxes per capita: $111 (1997); City property taxes per capita: $106 (1997).
Education: High school graduation rate: 80.5% (2000); College graduation rate: 2.3% (2000).
Housing: Homeownership rate: 76.8% (2000); Median home value: $33,800 (2000); Median rent: $196 per month (2000); Median age of housing: 53 years (2000).
Transportation: Commute to work: 91.8% car, 4.1% public transportation, 4.1% walk, 0.0% work from home (2000); Travel time to work: 19.7% less than 15 minutes, 36.1% 15 to 30 minutes, 27.9% 30 to 45 minutes, 12.3% 45 to 60 minutes, 4.1% 60 minutes or more (2000)

CARPENTER (township). Covers a land area of 100.905 square miles and a water area of 5.188 square miles. Located at 47.84° N. Lat.; 93.29° W. Long.
Population: 208 (2000); Race: 100.0% White, 0.0% Black, 0.0% Asian, 0.0% American Indian and Alaska Native, 0.0% Hispanic of any race, 0.0% two or more races (2000); Density: 2.1 persons per square mile (2000); Age: 12.5% under 18, 25.4% over 64 (2000); Marriage status: 18.0% never married, 69.7% now married, 3.8% widowed, 8.5% divorced (2000); Foreign born: 0.0% (2000); Ancestry (includes multiple ancestries): 25.0% Norwegian, 24.1% German, 15.2% Irish, 7.6% French (except Basque), 6.7% Swedish (2000).
Economy: Employment by occupation: 7.6% management, 20.3% professional, 12.7% services, 10.1% sales, 13.9% farming, 13.9% construction, 21.5% production (2000).
Income: Per capita income: $17,860 (2000); Median household income: $30,000 (2000); Poverty rate: 11.6% (2000).
Taxes: Total city taxes per capita: $103 (1997); City property taxes per capita: $103 (1997).
Education: High school graduation rate: 73.7% (2000); College graduation rate: 5.3% (2000).
Housing: Homeownership rate: 94.5% (2000); Median home value: $81,300 (2000); Median rent: <$100 per month (2000); Median age of housing: 36 years (2000).
Transportation: Commute to work: 94.9% car, 0.0% public transportation, 2.5% walk, 2.5% work from home (2000); Travel time to work: 28.6% less than 15 minutes, 28.6% 15 to 30 minutes, 20.8% 30 to 45 minutes, 13.0% 45 to 60 minutes, 9.1% 60 minutes or more (2000)

COHASSET (city). Aka Bass Brook. Covers a land area of 26.496 square miles and a water area of 8.752 square miles. Located at 47.25° N. Lat.; 93.62° W. Long. Elevation is 1,285 feet.
Population: 2,481 (2000); Race: 96.9% White, 0.0% Black, 0.2% Asian, 0.7% American Indian and Alaska Native, 0.0% Hispanic of any race, 2.2% two or more races (2000); Density: 93.6 persons per square mile (2000); Age: 23.2% under 18, 15.2% over 64 (2000); Marriage status: 20.1% never married, 65.3% now married, 7.5% widowed, 7.1% divorced (2000); Foreign born: 0.9% (2000); Ancestry (includes multiple ancestries): 34.4% German, 17.3% Norwegian, 10.9% Swedish, 9.6% Irish, 9.6% English (2000).
Economy: Light manufacturing. Employment by occupation: 9.1% management, 12.0% professional, 16.3% services, 31.5% sales, 0.4% farming, 11.8% construction, 18.9% production (2000).
Income: Per capita income: $21,071 (2000); Median household income: $44,054 (2000); Poverty rate: 5.6% (2000).
Taxes: Total city taxes per capita: $830 (2000); City property taxes per capita: $821 (2000).
Education: High school graduation rate: 89.4% (2000); College graduation rate: 21.5% (2000).
Housing: Homeownership rate: 90.2% (2000); Median home value: $116,400 (2000); Median rent: $394 per month (2000); Median age of housing: 23 years (2000).

Transportation: Commute to work: 95.2% car, 0.4% public transportation, 1.3% walk, 2.7% work from home (2000); Travel time to work: 50.8% less than 15 minutes, 41.8% 15 to 30 minutes, 2.1% 30 to 45 minutes, 2.1% 45 to 60 minutes, 3.1% 60 minutes or more (2000)

COLERAINE (city). Covers a land area of 6.219 square miles and a water area of 0.160 square miles. Located at 47.29° N. Lat.; 93.43° W. Long. Elevation is 1,300 feet.

History: Coleraine was built by the Oliver Mining Company as a model village for its employees. The town became a trading center for the nearby agricultural area.

Population: 1,110 (2000); Race: 97.2% White, 0.0% Black, 0.0% Asian, 0.1% American Indian and Alaska Native, 2.6% Hispanic of any race, 1.9% two or more races (2000); Density: 178.5 persons per square mile (2000); Age: 27.4% under 18, 16.7% over 64 (2000); Marriage status: 24.7% never married, 61.4% now married, 6.8% widowed, 7.1% divorced (2000); Foreign born: 1.5% (2000); Ancestry (includes multiple ancestries): 27.1% German, 15.1% Swedish, 13.2% Irish, 12.8% Norwegian, 11.0% Finnish (2000).

Economy: Single-family building permits issued: 1 (2001) / 1 (2000); Multi-family building permits issued: 0 (2001) / 0 (2000); Employment by occupation: 7.5% management, 23.3% professional, 15.4% services, 26.1% sales, 0.0% farming, 10.1% construction, 17.6% production (2000).

Income: Per capita income: $16,514 (2000); Median household income: $38,681 (2000); Poverty rate: 9.8% (2000).

Taxes: Total city taxes per capita: $193 (1997); City property taxes per capita: $189 (1997).

Education: High school graduation rate: 88.3% (2000); College graduation rate: 23.5% (2000).

School District(s)

Greenway (PK-12)
2000 Enrollment: 1,408 218-245-1566

Housing: Homeownership rate: 80.9% (2000); Median home value: $66,500 (2000); Median rent: $333 per month (2000); Median age of housing: 58 years (2000).

Transportation: Commute to work: 93.5% car, 0.0% public transportation, 3.5% walk, 3.1% work from home (2000); Travel time to work: 52.1% less than 15 minutes, 35.7% 15 to 30 minutes, 6.1% 30 to 45 minutes, 1.7% 45 to 60 minutes, 4.4% 60 minutes or more (2000)

DEER RIVER (city). Covers a land area of 1.061 square miles and a water area of 0 square miles. Located at 47.33° N. Lat.; 93.79° W. Long. Elevation is 1,291 feet.

Population: 903 (2000); Race: 86.1% White, 0.2% Black, 0.0% Asian, 10.9% American Indian and Alaska Native, 0.0% Hispanic of any race, 2.5% two or more races (2000); Density: 850.9 persons per square mile (2000); Age: 24.1% under 18, 25.7% over 64 (2000); Marriage status: 18.8% never married, 59.5% now married, 12.5% widowed, 9.2% divorced (2000); Foreign born: 0.9% (2000); Ancestry (includes multiple ancestries): 23.3% German, 14.2% Norwegian, 12.5% Other groups, 11.4% Finnish, 9.3% Swedish (2000).

Economy: Single-family building permits issued: 1 (2001) / 2 (2000); Multi-family building permits issued: 20 (2001) / 0 (2000); Employment by occupation: 4.5% management, 9.1% professional, 24.5% services, 27.3% sales, 0.6% farming, 12.7% construction, 21.2% production (2000).

Income: Per capita income: $13,078 (2000); Median household income: $21,900 (2000); Poverty rate: 17.3% (2000).

Taxes: Total city taxes per capita: $227 (1997); City property taxes per capita: $216 (1997).

Education: High school graduation rate: 79.5% (2000); College graduation rate: 11.3% (2000).

School District(s)

Deer River (PK-12)
2000 Enrollment: 1,095 218-246-2420

Housing: Homeownership rate: 64.1% (2000); Median home value: $53,900 (2000); Median rent: $323 per month (2000); Median age of housing: 41 years (2000).

Hospitals: Deer River Healthcare Center (20 beds)

Newspapers: Deer Path Shopper (1 x week); The Western Itasca Review (1 x week)

Transportation: Commute to work: 87.0% car, 0.9% public transportation, 9.9% walk, 0.9% work from home (2000); Travel time to work: 50.2% less than 15 minutes, 25.2% 15 to 30 minutes, 15.0% 30 to 45 minutes, 0.3% 45 to 60 minutes, 9.3% 60 minutes or more (2000)

Additional Information Contacts

Deep River Chamber of Commerce 218-246-8055

DEER RIVER (township). Covers a land area of 33.104 square miles and a water area of 2.303 square miles. Located at 47.37° N. Lat.; 93.75° W. Long. Elevation is 1,291 feet.

Population: 691 (2000); Race: 90.5% White, 0.0% Black, 0.7% Asian, 4.7% American Indian and Alaska Native, 0.0% Hispanic of any race, 4.1% two or more races (2000); Density: 20.9 persons per square mile (2000); Age: 31.9% under 18, 12.7% over 64 (2000); Marriage status: 18.7% never married, 69.2% now married, 3.7% widowed, 8.5% divorced (2000); Foreign born: 0.4% (2000); Ancestry (includes multiple ancestries): 25.6% Norwegian, 20.1% German, 11.2% Irish, 10.8% Swedish, 8.6% Finnish (2000).

Economy: In region of lakes and forests; resort area; supply point in timber area. Manufacturing: lumber, pulpwood products. Chippewa National Forest to South, West, and North. Employment by occupation: 7.1% management, 21.4% professional, 13.9% services, 22.1% sales, 2.5% farming, 15.4% construction, 17.5% production (2000).

Income: Per capita income: $15,836 (2000); Median household income: $35,208 (2000); Poverty rate: 14.9% (2000).

Taxes: Total city taxes per capita: $44 (1997); City property taxes per capita: $44 (1997).

Education: High school graduation rate: 84.9% (2000); College graduation rate: 18.4% (2000).

Housing: Homeownership rate: 95.9% (2000); Median home value: $88,800 (2000); Median rent: $425 per month (2000); Median age of housing: 27 years (2000).

Transportation: Commute to work: 95.9% car, 0.0% public transportation, 0.0% walk, 4.1% work from home (2000); Travel time to work: 39.3% less than 15 minutes, 25.3% 15 to 30 minutes, 24.1% 30 to 45 minutes, 4.3% 45 to 60 minutes, 7.0% 60 minutes or more (2000)

EFFIE (city). Covers a land area of 3.989 square miles and a water area of 0 square miles. Located at 47.84° N. Lat.; 93.63° W. Long. Elevation is 1,381 feet.

Population: 91 (2000); Race: 91.7% White, 0.0% Black, 4.2% Asian, 0.0% American Indian and Alaska Native, 6.3% Hispanic of any race, 4.2% two or more races (2000); Density: 22.8 persons per square mile (2000); Age: 26.0% under 18, 28.1% over 64 (2000); Marriage status: 8.3% never married, 76.4% now married, 5.6% widowed, 9.7% divorced (2000); Foreign born: 8.3% (2000); Ancestry (includes multiple ancestries): 31.3% German, 27.1% Irish, 15.6% French Canadian, 15.6% Norwegian, 7.3% Swedish (2000).

Economy: Timber; cattle; alfalfa. Single-family building permits issued: 0 (2001) / 0 (2000); Multi-family building permits issued: 0 (2001) / 0 (2000); Employment by occupation: 0.0% management, 12.9% professional, 16.1% services, 16.1% sales, 16.1% farming, 6.5% construction, 32.3% production (2000).

Income: Per capita income: $14,606 (2000); Median household income: $31,250 (2000); Poverty rate: 5.2% (2000).

Taxes: Total city taxes per capita: $8 (1997); City property taxes per capita: $0 (1997).

Education: High school graduation rate: 66.2% (2000); College graduation rate: 3.1% (2000).

Housing: Homeownership rate: 90.2% (2000); Median home value: $34,300 (2000); Median rent: $225 per month (2000); Median age of housing: 56 years (2000).

Transportation: Commute to work: 100.0% car, 0.0% public transportation, 0.0% walk, 0.0% work from home (2000); Travel time to work: 48.4% less than 15 minutes, 32.3% 15 to 30 minutes, 0.0% 30 to 45 minutes, 6.5% 45 to 60 minutes, 12.9% 60 minutes or more (2000)

FEELEY (township). Covers a land area of 31.556 square miles and a water area of 1.124 square miles. Located at 47.13° N. Lat.; 93.27° W. Long.

Population: 327 (2000); Race: 99.4% White, 0.0% Black, 0.0% Asian, 0.0% American Indian and Alaska Native, 0.0% Hispanic of any race, 0.6% two or more races (2000); Density: 10.4 persons per square mile (2000); Age: 21.2% under 18, 25.6% over 64 (2000); Marriage status: 17.4% never married, 72.7% now married, 3.8% widowed, 6.1% divorced (2000); Foreign born: 0.6% (2000); Ancestry (includes multiple ancestries): 28.5% German, 16.1% Swedish, 12.0% Norwegian, 11.7% United States or American, 9.2% English (2000).

Economy: Employment by occupation: 6.9% management, 19.8% professional, 23.3% services, 21.6% sales, 0.0% farming, 12.9% construction, 15.5% production (2000).

Income: Per capita income: $17,469 (2000); Median household income: $40,625 (2000); Poverty rate: 10.4% (2000).

Taxes: Total city taxes per capita: $234 (1997); City property taxes per capita: $234 (1997).

Education: High school graduation rate: 82.0% (2000); College graduation rate: 24.9% (2000).
Housing: Homeownership rate: 95.3% (2000); Median home value: $87,900 (2000); Median rent: $275 per month (2000); Median age of housing: 27 years (2000).
Transportation: Commute to work: 97.4% car, 0.0% public transportation, 2.6% walk, 0.0% work from home (2000); Travel time to work: 19.0% less than 15 minutes, 57.8% 15 to 30 minutes, 13.8% 30 to 45 minutes, 3.4% 45 to 60 minutes, 6.0% 60 minutes or more (2000)

GOOD HOPE (township). Covers a land area of 30.829 square miles and a water area of 3.849 square miles. Located at 47.63° N. Lat.; 94.20° W. Long.
Population: 79 (2000); Race: 100.0% White, 0.0% Black, 0.0% Asian, 0.0% American Indian and Alaska Native, 0.0% Hispanic of any race, 0.0% two or more races (2000); Density: 2.6 persons per square mile (2000); Age: 21.1% under 18, 29.8% over 64 (2000); Marriage status: 0.0% never married, 82.2% now married, 13.3% widowed, 4.4% divorced (2000); Foreign born: 0.0% (2000); Ancestry (includes multiple ancestries): 50.9% German, 12.3% Danish, 8.8% Polish, 8.8% Irish, 8.8% Finnish (2000).
Economy: Employment by occupation: 25.0% management, 16.7% professional, 16.7% services, 0.0% sales, 16.7% farming, 25.0% construction, 0.0% production (2000).
Income: Per capita income: $12,623 (2000); Median household income: $25,000 (2000); Poverty rate: 15.8% (2000).
Taxes: Total city taxes per capita: $65 (1997); City property taxes per capita: $65 (1997).
Education: High school graduation rate: 75.6% (2000); College graduation rate: 0.0% (2000).
Housing: Homeownership rate: 100.0% (2000); Median home value: $53,000 (2000); Median age of housing: 41 years (2000).
Transportation: Commute to work: 100.0% car, 0.0% public transportation, 0.0% walk, 0.0% work from home (2000); Travel time to work: 0.0% less than 15 minutes, 58.3% 15 to 30 minutes, 16.7% 30 to 45 minutes, 0.0% 45 to 60 minutes, 25.0% 60 minutes or more (2000)

GOODLAND (township). Covers a land area of 69.147 square miles and a water area of 3.134 square miles. Located at 47.21° N. Lat.; 93.14° W. Long. Elevation is 1,416 feet.
Population: 496 (2000); Race: 99.1% White, 0.0% Black, 0.4% Asian, 0.4% American Indian and Alaska Native, 0.0% Hispanic of any race, 0.0% two or more races (2000); Density: 7.2 persons per square mile (2000); Age: 15.7% under 18, 18.8% over 64 (2000); Marriage status: 18.0% never married, 66.0% now married, 7.2% widowed, 8.8% divorced (2000); Foreign born: 1.8% (2000); Ancestry (includes multiple ancestries): 29.6% German, 12.3% Swedish, 11.7% Norwegian, 11.4% Finnish, 8.1% Irish (2000).
Economy: Employment by occupation: 6.8% management, 13.6% professional, 9.7% services, 26.2% sales, 2.9% farming, 16.5% construction, 24.3% production (2000).
Income: Per capita income: $19,694 (2000); Median household income: $39,375 (2000); Poverty rate: 6.8% (2000).
Taxes: Total city taxes per capita: $143 (1997); City property taxes per capita: $143 (1997).
Education: High school graduation rate: 88.9% (2000); College graduation rate: 12.9% (2000).
Housing: Homeownership rate: 93.5% (2000); Median home value: $72,900 (2000); Median age of housing: 31 years (2000).
Transportation: Commute to work: 93.1% car, 0.0% public transportation, 2.0% walk, 4.9% work from home (2000); Travel time to work: 9.8% less than 15 minutes, 33.7% 15 to 30 minutes, 44.6% 30 to 45 minutes, 7.3% 45 to 60 minutes, 4.7% 60 minutes or more (2000)

GRAND RAPIDS (city). Covers a land area of 7.340 square miles and a water area of 0.741 square miles. Located at 47.23° N. Lat.; 93.52° W. Long. Elevation is 1,290 feet.
History: Grand Rapids began as a service center for logging camps. Later, the Blandin Paper Company's manufacturing operations became a principal industry, along with iron mining and processing. Film star Judy Garland began her career at the age of two in her parents' vaudeville theater in Grand Rapids.
Population: 7,764 (2000); Race: 95.6% White, 0.6% Black, 0.3% Asian, 2.5% American Indian and Alaska Native, 0.9% Hispanic of any race, 0.9% two or more races (2000); Density: 1,057.8 persons per square mile (2000); Age: 21.7% under 18, 22.6% over 64 (2000); Marriage status: 24.6% never married, 50.1% now married, 12.3% widowed, 12.9% divorced (2000); Foreign born: 2.1% (2000); Ancestry (includes multiple ancestries): 28.7% German, 15.8% Norwegian, 12.3% Irish, 10.7% Swedish, 8.3% English (2000).
Economy: Single-family building permits issued: 17 (2001) / 10 (2000); Multi-family building permits issued: 2 (2001) / 0 (2000); Employment by occupation: 9.1% management, 19.4% professional, 17.2% services, 25.5% sales, 0.2% farming, 9.5% construction, 19.1% production (2000).
Income: Per capita income: $17,223 (2000); Median household income: $28,991 (2000); Poverty rate: 11.2% (2000).
Taxes: Total city taxes per capita: $335 (1997); City property taxes per capita: $321 (1997).
Education: High school graduation rate: 86.7% (2000); College graduation rate: 18.0% (2000).

School District(s)

Grand Rapids (PK-12)
2000 Enrollment: 4,383 218-327-5704

Two-year College(s)

Itasca Community College (Public)
2001 Enrollment: 1,120 218-327-4460
2001 Tuition: In-state $2,399; Out-of-state $4,798

Housing: Homeownership rate: 59.4% (2000); Median home value: $78,000 (2000); Median rent: $373 per month (2000); Median age of housing: 34 years (2000).
Hospitals: Itasca Medical Center (108 beds)
Safety: Violent crime rate: 12.7 per 10,000 population; Property crime rate: 66.3 per 10,000 population (2001).
Newspapers: Grand Rapids Herald-Review (2 x week)
Transportation: Commute to work: 87.4% car, 1.5% public transportation, 6.1% walk, 3.7% work from home (2000); Travel time to work: 76.2% less than 15 minutes, 14.9% 15 to 30 minutes, 4.0% 30 to 45 minutes, 0.7% 45 to 60 minutes, 4.2% 60 minutes or more (2000)

Additional Information Contacts

Grand Rapids Chamber of Commerce 218-326-6619
Grand Rapids Convention & Visitors Bureau 218-326-9607
Itasca County Board of Realtors 218-326-4533

GRAND RAPIDS (township). Covers a land area of 33.726 square miles and a water area of 2.305 square miles. Located at 47.23° N. Lat.; 93.52° W. Long. Elevation is 1,290 feet.
History: Forest History Center here.. Settled 1877, Incorporated 1891.
Population: 11,747 (2000); Race: 96.6% White, 0.4% Black, 0.2% Asian, 1.8% American Indian and Alaska Native, 0.8% Hispanic of any race, 0.8% two or more races (2000); Density: 348.3 persons per square mile (2000); Age: 23.6% under 18, 19.5% over 64 (2000); Marriage status: 23.5% never married, 54.1% now married, 10.0% widowed, 12.3% divorced (2000); Foreign born: 1.8% (2000); Ancestry (includes multiple ancestries): 29.2% German, 14.2% Norwegian, 11.7% Irish, 10.3% Swedish, 8.4% English (2000).
Economy: Cattle; alfalfa; timber. Manufacturing of coated papers, corn cribbing, packaging, concrete, furniture, strand board. Printing and publishing. Employment by occupation: 8.8% management, 17.9% professional, 16.0% services, 26.8% sales, 0.2% farming, 10.5% construction, 19.9% production (2000).
Income: Per capita income: $17,095 (2000); Median household income: $31,572 (2000); Poverty rate: 10.5% (2000).
Taxes: Total city taxes per capita: $48 (2000); City property taxes per capita: $48 (2000).
Education: High school graduation rate: 85.8% (2000); College graduation rate: 17.7% (2000).
Housing: Homeownership rate: 68.2% (2000); Median home value: $82,100 (2000); Median rent: $381 per month (2000); Median age of housing: 30 years (2000).
Transportation: Commute to work: 90.6% car, 1.0% public transportation, 4.1% walk, 3.4% work from home (2000); Travel time to work: 71.6% less than 15 minutes, 18.6% 15 to 30 minutes, 4.2% 30 to 45 minutes, 1.3% 45 to 60 minutes, 4.4% 60 minutes or more (2000)

GRATTAN (township). Covers a land area of 34.759 square miles and a water area of 0.873 square miles. Located at 47.81° N. Lat.; 94.10° W. Long.
Population: 44 (2000); Race: 100.0% White, 0.0% Black, 0.0% Asian, 0.0% American Indian and Alaska Native, 0.0% Hispanic of any race, 0.0% two or more races (2000); Density: 1.3 persons per square mile (2000); Age: 30.8% under 18, 19.2% over 64 (2000); Marriage status: 38.1% never married, 52.4% now married, 9.5% widowed, 0.0% divorced (2000); Foreign born: 0.0% (2000); Ancestry (includes multiple ancestries): 57.7% Norwegian, 44.2% Swedish, 13.5% United States or American, 13.5% Irish, 11.5% German (2000).

Economy: Employment by occupation: 0.0% management, 0.0% professional, 31.6% services, 10.5% sales, 47.4% farming, 10.5% construction, 0.0% production (2000).
Income: Per capita income: $21,404 (2000); Median household income: $36,250 (2000); Poverty rate: 13.5% (2000).
Taxes: Total city taxes per capita: $33 (1997); City property taxes per capita: $33 (1997).
Education: High school graduation rate: 86.2% (2000); College graduation rate: 3.4% (2000).
Housing: Homeownership rate: 72.2% (2000); Median home value: $85,000 (2000); Median age of housing: 29 years (2000).
Transportation: Commute to work: 63.2% car, 0.0% public transportation, 0.0% walk, 26.3% work from home (2000); Travel time to work: 0.0% less than 15 minutes, 35.7% 15 to 30 minutes, 50.0% 30 to 45 minutes, 0.0% 45 to 60 minutes, 14.3% 60 minutes or more (2000)

GREENWAY (township). Covers a land area of 33.463 square miles and a water area of 2.603 square miles. Located at 47.31° N. Lat.; 93.25° W. Long.
Population: 2,018 (2000); Race: 95.6% White, 0.0% Black, 0.1% Asian, 2.0% American Indian and Alaska Native, 0.5% Hispanic of any race, 1.9% two or more races (2000); Density: 60.3 persons per square mile (2000); Age: 23.9% under 18, 16.0% over 64 (2000); Marriage status: 22.9% never married, 61.4% now married, 7.5% widowed, 8.2% divorced (2000); Foreign born: 1.0% (2000); Ancestry (includes multiple ancestries): 22.7% German, 13.0% Norwegian, 11.4% Swedish, 8.8% Irish, 8.2% Finnish (2000).
Economy: Employment by occupation: 7.9% management, 16.3% professional, 14.9% services, 24.8% sales, 0.5% farming, 15.2% construction, 20.5% production (2000).
Income: Per capita income: $18,162 (2000); Median household income: $35,729 (2000); Poverty rate: 12.4% (2000).
Taxes: Total city taxes per capita: $55 (1997); City property taxes per capita: $55 (1997).
Education: High school graduation rate: 87.0% (2000); College graduation rate: 13.5% (2000).
Housing: Homeownership rate: 84.0% (2000); Median home value: $52,400 (2000); Median rent: $357 per month (2000); Median age of housing: 44 years (2000).
Transportation: Commute to work: 96.9% car, 0.8% public transportation, 1.2% walk, 0.8% work from home (2000); Travel time to work: 16.8% less than 15 minutes, 52.0% 15 to 30 minutes, 22.3% 30 to 45 minutes, 4.6% 45 to 60 minutes, 4.2% 60 minutes or more (2000)

HARRIS (township). Covers a land area of 31.903 square miles and a water area of 3.960 square miles. Located at 47.16° N. Lat.; 93.52° W. Long.
Population: 3,328 (2000); Race: 98.4% White, 0.8% Black, 0.3% Asian, 0.0% American Indian and Alaska Native, 0.7% Hispanic of any race, 0.1% two or more races (2000); Density: 104.3 persons per square mile (2000); Age: 22.4% under 18, 14.7% over 64 (2000); Marriage status: 20.3% never married, 65.8% now married, 5.7% widowed, 8.1% divorced (2000); Foreign born: 1.6% (2000); Ancestry (includes multiple ancestries): 34.8% German, 17.1% Norwegian, 9.4% Swedish, 7.9% Irish, 7.4% Finnish (2000).
Economy: Employment by occupation: 11.8% management, 21.1% professional, 14.3% services, 23.0% sales, 1.4% farming, 10.8% construction, 17.5% production (2000).
Income: Per capita income: $20,757 (2000); Median household income: $47,344 (2000); Poverty rate: 6.5% (2000).
Taxes: Total city taxes per capita: $105 (2000); City property taxes per capita: $105 (2000).
Education: High school graduation rate: 90.1% (2000); College graduation rate: 26.7% (2000).
Housing: Homeownership rate: 91.5% (2000); Median home value: $114,900 (2000); Median rent: $343 per month (2000); Median age of housing: 26 years (2000).
Transportation: Commute to work: 93.4% car, 0.4% public transportation, 0.8% walk, 4.6% work from home (2000); Travel time to work: 37.6% less than 15 minutes, 46.1% 15 to 30 minutes, 3.3% 30 to 45 minutes, 3.3% 45 to 60 minutes, 9.8% 60 minutes or more (2000)

IRON RANGE (township). Covers a land area of 27.179 square miles and a water area of 1.752 square miles. Located at 47.32° N. Lat.; 93.37° W. Long.
Population: 651 (2000); Race: 97.3% White, 0.0% Black, 0.0% Asian, 0.4% American Indian and Alaska Native, 0.0% Hispanic of any race, 1.9% two or more races (2000); Density: 24.0 persons per square mile (2000); Age: 25.1% under 18, 16.5% over 64 (2000); Marriage status: 27.7% never married, 54.4% now married, 8.4% widowed, 9.5% divorced (2000); Foreign born: 0.3% (2000); Ancestry (includes multiple ancestries): 23.8% German, 16.5% Norwegian, 10.0% Swedish, 9.2% Irish, 7.8% French (except Basque) (2000).
Economy: Employment by occupation: 3.2% management, 12.5% professional, 25.1% services, 23.8% sales, 0.6% farming, 13.2% construction, 21.5% production (2000).
Income: Per capita income: $16,384 (2000); Median household income: $35,000 (2000); Poverty rate: 15.0% (2000).
Taxes: Total city taxes per capita: $66 (1997); City property taxes per capita: $66 (1997).
Education: High school graduation rate: 86.5% (2000); College graduation rate: 7.1% (2000).
Housing: Homeownership rate: 85.5% (2000); Median home value: $62,000 (2000); Median rent: $288 per month (2000); Median age of housing: 40 years (2000).
Transportation: Commute to work: 93.6% car, 0.3% public transportation, 3.3% walk, 2.0% work from home (2000); Travel time to work: 14.0% less than 15 minutes, 53.2% 15 to 30 minutes, 23.2% 30 to 45 minutes, 5.5% 45 to 60 minutes, 4.1% 60 minutes or more (2000)

KEEWATIN (city). Covers a land area of 2.457 square miles and a water area of 0.425 square miles. Located at 47.39° N. Lat.; 93.07° W. Long. Elevation is 1,469 feet.
History: Large ore deposits were found here about 1904, but the village of Keewatin developed slowly until 1909, when mining became more active.
Population: 1,164 (2000); Race: 96.6% White, 1.5% Black, 0.0% Asian, 0.4% American Indian and Alaska Native, 0.2% Hispanic of any race, 1.3% two or more races (2000); Density: 473.7 persons per square mile (2000); Age: 25.4% under 18, 17.7% over 64 (2000); Marriage status: 25.9% never married, 51.7% now married, 10.3% widowed, 12.1% divorced (2000); Foreign born: 0.8% (2000); Ancestry (includes multiple ancestries): 17.7% German, 16.1% Norwegian, 10.5% Italian, 10.5% Finnish, 10.1% Swedish (2000).
Economy: Single-family building permits issued: 2 (2001) / 2 (2000); Multi-family building permits issued: 0 (2001) / 0 (2000); Employment by occupation: 7.8% management, 8.9% professional, 22.1% services, 20.7% sales, 0.4% farming, 12.6% construction, 27.5% production (2000).
Income: Per capita income: $15,066 (2000); Median household income: $28,795 (2000); Poverty rate: 13.7% (2000).
Taxes: Total city taxes per capita: $71 (1997); City property taxes per capita: $68 (1997).
Education: High school graduation rate: 83.8% (2000); College graduation rate: 8.4% (2000).
Housing: Homeownership rate: 80.6% (2000); Median home value: $40,900 (2000); Median rent: $229 per month (2000); Median age of housing: 55 years (2000).
Transportation: Commute to work: 90.9% car, 0.0% public transportation, 7.5% walk, 1.6% work from home (2000); Travel time to work: 40.0% less than 15 minutes, 43.9% 15 to 30 minutes, 8.2% 30 to 45 minutes, 3.1% 45 to 60 minutes, 4.7% 60 minutes or more (2000)

KINGHURST (township). Covers a land area of 33.208 square miles and a water area of 2.105 square miles. Located at 47.72° N. Lat.; 94.09° W. Long.
Population: 131 (2000); Race: 96.5% White, 0.0% Black, 0.0% Asian, 0.7% American Indian and Alaska Native, 0.0% Hispanic of any race, 0.0% two or more races (2000); Density: 3.9 persons per square mile (2000); Age: 22.0% under 18, 22.7% over 64 (2000); Marriage status: 17.6% never married, 70.6% now married, 7.6% widowed, 4.2% divorced (2000); Foreign born: 0.0% (2000); Ancestry (includes multiple ancestries): 44.0% German, 18.4% Norwegian, 16.3% Swedish, 11.3% Irish, 5.7% English (2000).
Economy: Employment by occupation: 6.3% management, 33.3% professional, 16.7% services, 14.6% sales, 0.0% farming, 20.8% construction, 8.3% production (2000).
Income: Per capita income: $12,691 (2000); Median household income: $25,938 (2000); Poverty rate: 7.1% (2000).
Taxes: Total city taxes per capita: $61 (1997); City property taxes per capita: $61 (1997).
Education: High school graduation rate: 75.0% (2000); College graduation rate: 14.8% (2000).
Housing: Homeownership rate: 93.0% (2000); Median home value: $80,000 (2000); Median age of housing: 27 years (2000).
Transportation: Commute to work: 81.4% car, 0.0% public transportation, 9.3% walk, 9.3% work from home (2000); Travel time to work: 28.2% less

than 15 minutes, 35.9% 15 to 30 minutes, 30.8% 30 to 45 minutes, 0.0% 45 to 60 minutes, 5.1% 60 minutes or more (2000)

LA PRAIRIE (city). Covers a land area of 1.137 square miles and a water area of 0.003 square miles. Located at 47.22° N. Lat.; 93.49° W. Long.
Population: 605 (2000); Race: 97.8% White, 0.0% Black, 0.0% Asian, 0.3% American Indian and Alaska Native, 1.4% Hispanic of any race, 1.9% two or more races (2000); Density: 532.0 persons per square mile (2000); Age: 28.7% under 18, 14.5% over 64 (2000); Marriage status: 24.4% never married, 55.9% now married, 6.9% widowed, 12.7% divorced (2000); Foreign born: 0.0% (2000); Ancestry (includes multiple ancestries): 25.1% German, 12.1% Finnish, 10.2% United States or American, 9.6% Norwegian, 8.7% Swedish (2000).
Economy: Agriculture: alfalfa; cattle; dairying; timber. Single-family building permits issued: 4 (2001) / 2 (2000); Multi-family building permits issued: 0 (2001) / 0 (2000); Employment by occupation: 9.0% management, 18.4% professional, 15.0% services, 27.8% sales, 0.0% farming, 10.5% construction, 19.2% production (2000).
Income: Per capita income: $18,632 (2000); Median household income: $39,375 (2000); Poverty rate: 10.0% (2000).
Taxes: Total city taxes per capita: $421 (1997); City property taxes per capita: $387 (1997).
Education: High school graduation rate: 87.3% (2000); College graduation rate: 14.2% (2000).
Housing: Homeownership rate: 81.8% (2000); Median home value: $88,600 (2000); Median rent: $385 per month (2000); Median age of housing: 27 years (2000).
Transportation: Commute to work: 94.3% car, 0.0% public transportation, 1.1% walk, 4.5% work from home (2000); Travel time to work: 72.7% less than 15 minutes, 16.2% 15 to 30 minutes, 5.5% 30 to 45 minutes, 2.0% 45 to 60 minutes, 3.6% 60 minutes or more (2000)

LAKE JESSIE (township). Covers a land area of 33.412 square miles and a water area of 3.264 square miles. Located at 47.63° N. Lat.; 93.81° W. Long.
Population: 335 (2000); Race: 98.5% White, 0.9% Black, 0.0% Asian, 0.0% American Indian and Alaska Native, 0.6% Hispanic of any race, 0.6% two or more races (2000); Density: 10.0 persons per square mile (2000); Age: 26.0% under 18, 19.6% over 64 (2000); Marriage status: 15.6% never married, 66.5% now married, 10.3% widowed, 7.6% divorced (2000); Foreign born: 0.3% (2000); Ancestry (includes multiple ancestries): 33.9% German, 25.1% Norwegian, 15.2% Irish, 12.9% Swedish, 9.4% English (2000).
Economy: Employment by occupation: 11.8% management, 14.5% professional, 13.6% services, 20.0% sales, 1.8% farming, 17.3% construction, 20.9% production (2000).
Income: Per capita income: $18,865 (2000); Median household income: $33,438 (2000); Poverty rate: 17.9% (2000).
Taxes: Total city taxes per capita: $80 (1997); City property taxes per capita: $80 (1997).
Education: High school graduation rate: 79.7% (2000); College graduation rate: 8.5% (2000).
Housing: Homeownership rate: 91.7% (2000); Median home value: $121,400 (2000); Median rent: $275 per month (2000); Median age of housing: 27 years (2000).
Transportation: Commute to work: 82.7% car, 0.0% public transportation, 4.5% walk, 11.8% work from home (2000); Travel time to work: 17.5% less than 15 minutes, 35.1% 15 to 30 minutes, 27.8% 30 to 45 minutes, 9.3% 45 to 60 minutes, 10.3% 60 minutes or more (2000)

LAWRENCE (township). Covers a land area of 33.736 square miles and a water area of 2.283 square miles. Located at 47.41° N. Lat.; 93.38° W. Long.
Population: 441 (2000); Race: 94.4% White, 0.0% Black, 0.0% Asian, 2.2% American Indian and Alaska Native, 0.2% Hispanic of any race, 3.3% two or more races (2000); Density: 13.1 persons per square mile (2000); Age: 23.2% under 18, 15.8% over 64 (2000); Marriage status: 25.2% never married, 60.1% now married, 4.8% widowed, 9.9% divorced (2000); Foreign born: 0.7% (2000); Ancestry (includes multiple ancestries): 28.9% German, 16.9% Norwegian, 10.2% Irish, 8.9% English, 7.2% French (except Basque) (2000).
Economy: Employment by occupation: 10.8% management, 10.8% professional, 17.6% services, 19.9% sales, 2.3% farming, 15.3% construction, 23.3% production (2000).
Income: Per capita income: $15,256 (2000); Median household income: $34,821 (2000); Poverty rate: 14.8% (2000).
Taxes: Total city taxes per capita: $43 (1997); City property taxes per capita: $43 (1997).
Education: High school graduation rate: 79.6% (2000); College graduation rate: 7.1% (2000).
Housing: Homeownership rate: 96.8% (2000); Median home value: $90,400 (2000); Median rent: $625 per month (2000); Median age of housing: 29 years (2000).
Transportation: Commute to work: 84.9% car, 0.0% public transportation, 7.0% walk, 8.1% work from home (2000); Travel time to work: 27.8% less than 15 minutes, 17.1% 15 to 30 minutes, 35.4% 30 to 45 minutes, 13.9% 45 to 60 minutes, 5.7% 60 minutes or more (2000)

LIBERTY (township). Covers a land area of 70.700 square miles and a water area of 1.702 square miles. Located at 47.71° N. Lat.; 93.82° W. Long.
Population: 91 (2000); Race: 94.7% White, 0.0% Black, 5.3% Asian, 0.0% American Indian and Alaska Native, 5.3% Hispanic of any race, 0.0% two or more races (2000); Density: 1.3 persons per square mile (2000); Age: 17.1% under 18, 23.7% over 64 (2000); Marriage status: 4.5% never married, 77.3% now married, 6.1% widowed, 12.1% divorced (2000); Foreign born: 7.9% (2000); Ancestry (includes multiple ancestries): 32.9% Norwegian, 15.8% German, 10.5% Other groups, 9.2% Irish, 9.2% United States or American (2000).
Economy: Employment by occupation: 30.3% management, 15.2% professional, 24.2% services, 24.2% sales, 0.0% farming, 0.0% construction, 6.1% production (2000).
Income: Per capita income: $22,462 (2000); Median household income: $25,938 (2000); Poverty rate: 3.9% (2000).
Taxes: Total city taxes per capita: $56 (1997); City property taxes per capita: $56 (1997).
Education: High school graduation rate: 68.3% (2000); College graduation rate: 20.6% (2000).
Housing: Homeownership rate: 94.1% (2000); Median home value: $81,000 (2000); Median age of housing: 29 years (2000).
Transportation: Commute to work: 57.6% car, 0.0% public transportation, 18.2% walk, 24.2% work from home (2000); Travel time to work: 28.0% less than 15 minutes, 52.0% 15 to 30 minutes, 20.0% 30 to 45 minutes, 0.0% 45 to 60 minutes, 0.0% 60 minutes or more (2000)

LONE PINE (township). Covers a land area of 32.817 square miles and a water area of 4.090 square miles. Located at 47.35° N. Lat.; 93.12° W. Long.
Population: 526 (2000); Race: 99.3% White, 0.0% Black, 0.0% Asian, 0.4% American Indian and Alaska Native, 0.5% Hispanic of any race, 0.4% two or more races (2000); Density: 16.0 persons per square mile (2000); Age: 20.7% under 18, 20.9% over 64 (2000); Marriage status: 14.4% never married, 69.0% now married, 8.7% widowed, 7.9% divorced (2000); Foreign born: 1.5% (2000); Ancestry (includes multiple ancestries): 21.8% German, 14.5% Finnish, 14.2% English, 14.0% Irish, 13.2% Swedish (2000).
Economy: Employment by occupation: 18.3% management, 23.4% professional, 4.6% services, 25.4% sales, 0.0% farming, 12.7% construction, 15.7% production (2000).
Income: Per capita income: $23,986 (2000); Median household income: $43,611 (2000); Poverty rate: 4.4% (2000).
Taxes: Total city taxes per capita: $27 (1997); City property taxes per capita: $27 (1997).
Education: High school graduation rate: 89.1% (2000); College graduation rate: 22.0% (2000).
Housing: Homeownership rate: 95.8% (2000); Median home value: $100,000 (2000); Median rent: $400 per month (2000); Median age of housing: 41 years (2000).
Transportation: Commute to work: 99.5% car, 0.0% public transportation, 0.5% walk, 0.0% work from home (2000); Travel time to work: 5.4% less than 15 minutes, 46.2% 15 to 30 minutes, 36.0% 30 to 45 minutes, 8.6% 45 to 60 minutes, 3.8% 60 minutes or more (2000)

MARBLE (city). Covers a land area of 4.309 square miles and a water area of 0.099 square miles. Located at 47.31° N. Lat.; 93.29° W. Long.
History: Marble began as a company town, established in 1909 by the Oliver Iron Mining Company for its employees at the Hill Mine.
Population: 695 (2000); Race: 94.7% White, 0.0% Black, 0.3% Asian, 1.2% American Indian and Alaska Native, 1.3% Hispanic of any race, 2.6% two or more races (2000); Density: 161.3 persons per square mile (2000); Age: 24.4% under 18, 15.4% over 64 (2000); Marriage status: 22.7% never married, 60.3% now married, 8.5% widowed, 8.5% divorced (2000); Foreign born: 1.8% (2000); Ancestry (includes multiple ancestries): 22.2% German, 14.8% Norwegian, 10.7% Swedish, 9.8% Other groups, 9.4% Irish (2000).
Economy: Employment by occupation: 5.2% management, 13.8% professional, 24.5% services, 21.2% sales, 0.0% farming, 16.4% construction, 19.0% production (2000).

Income: Per capita income: $14,620 (2000); Median household income: $27,361 (2000); Poverty rate: 15.8% (2000).
Taxes: Total city taxes per capita: $77 (1997); City property taxes per capita: $77 (1997).
Education: High school graduation rate: 86.7% (2000); College graduation rate: 9.4% (2000).
Housing: Homeownership rate: 75.4% (2000); Median home value: $44,300 (2000); Median rent: $355 per month (2000); Median age of housing: 55 years (2000).
Transportation: Commute to work: 93.9% car, 0.8% public transportation, 1.9% walk, 2.7% work from home (2000); Travel time to work: 19.5% less than 15 minutes, 48.4% 15 to 30 minutes, 21.9% 30 to 45 minutes, 4.3% 45 to 60 minutes, 5.9% 60 minutes or more (2000)

MARCELL (township). Covers a land area of 47.907 square miles and a water area of 9.265 square miles. Located at 47.59° N. Lat.; 93.67° W. Long. Elevation is 1,386 feet.
Population: 394 (2000); Race: 100.0% White, 0.0% Black, 0.0% Asian, 0.0% American Indian and Alaska Native, 0.0% Hispanic of any race, 0.0% two or more races (2000); Density: 8.2 persons per square mile (2000); Age: 14.5% under 18, 20.2% over 64 (2000); Marriage status: 14.6% never married, 71.4% now married, 4.0% widowed, 10.0% divorced (2000); Foreign born: 0.5% (2000); Ancestry (includes multiple ancestries): 28.7% German, 23.5% Norwegian, 14.2% Swedish, 11.2% Irish, 9.8% Finnish (2000).
Economy: Employment by occupation: 13.2% management, 23.7% professional, 11.2% services, 21.1% sales, 2.0% farming, 15.1% construction, 13.8% production (2000).
Income: Per capita income: $21,010 (2000); Median household income: $39,167 (2000); Poverty rate: 8.5% (2000).
Taxes: Total city taxes per capita: $169 (1997); City property taxes per capita: $169 (1997).
Education: High school graduation rate: 91.9% (2000); College graduation rate: 22.1% (2000).
Housing: Homeownership rate: 94.9% (2000); Median home value: $125,000 (2000); Median rent: $325 per month (2000); Median age of housing: 26 years (2000).
Transportation: Commute to work: 88.7% car, 0.0% public transportation, 4.0% walk, 7.3% work from home (2000); Travel time to work: 35.0% less than 15 minutes, 31.4% 15 to 30 minutes, 17.9% 30 to 45 minutes, 10.0% 45 to 60 minutes, 5.7% 60 minutes or more (2000)

MAX (township). Covers a land area of 28.712 square miles and a water area of 5.509 square miles. Located at 47.62° N. Lat.; 94.09° W. Long. Elevation is 1,373 feet.
Population: 156 (2000); Race: 72.4% White, 0.0% Black, 1.3% Asian, 10.9% American Indian and Alaska Native, 1.9% Hispanic of any race, 12.8% two or more races (2000); Density: 5.4 persons per square mile (2000); Age: 24.4% under 18, 13.5% over 64 (2000); Marriage status: 14.8% never married, 50.8% now married, 10.7% widowed, 23.8% divorced (2000); Foreign born: 3.2% (2000); Ancestry (includes multiple ancestries): 21.2% Other groups, 17.9% Irish, 12.2% German, 11.5% Norwegian, 10.9% Swedish (2000).
Economy: Employment by occupation: 0.0% management, 13.6% professional, 30.5% services, 13.6% sales, 0.0% farming, 23.7% construction, 18.6% production (2000).
Income: Per capita income: $13,889 (2000); Median household income: $21,500 (2000); Poverty rate: 20.5% (2000).
Education: High school graduation rate: 73.8% (2000); College graduation rate: 14.0% (2000).
Housing: Homeownership rate: 77.6% (2000); Median home value: $40,000 (2000); Median rent: $330 per month (2000); Median age of housing: 33 years (2000).
Transportation: Commute to work: 96.6% car, 3.4% public transportation, 0.0% walk, 0.0% work from home (2000); Travel time to work: 25.4% less than 15 minutes, 6.8% 15 to 30 minutes, 13.6% 30 to 45 minutes, 10.2% 45 to 60 minutes, 44.1% 60 minutes or more (2000)

MOOSE PARK (township). Covers a land area of 36.510 square miles and a water area of 0.048 square miles. Located at 47.70° N. Lat.; 94.36° W. Long.
Population: 80 (2000); Race: 100.0% White, 0.0% Black, 0.0% Asian, 0.0% American Indian and Alaska Native, 0.0% Hispanic of any race, 0.0% two or more races (2000); Density: 2.2 persons per square mile (2000); Age: 16.1% under 18, 30.6% over 64 (2000); Marriage status: 5.6% never married, 66.7% now married, 16.7% widowed, 11.1% divorced (2000); Foreign born: 0.0% (2000); Ancestry (includes multiple ancestries): 29.0% Norwegian, 27.4% German, 8.1% Swedish, 6.5% English, 6.5% Czechoslovakian (2000).
Economy: Employment by occupation: 8.3% management, 8.3% professional, 16.7% services, 33.3% sales, 20.8% farming, 0.0% construction, 12.5% production (2000).
Income: Per capita income: $15,434 (2000); Median household income: $28,750 (2000); Poverty rate: 16.1% (2000).
Taxes: Total city taxes per capita: $67 (1997); City property taxes per capita: $67 (1997).
Education: High school graduation rate: 72.9% (2000); College graduation rate: 2.1% (2000).
Housing: Homeownership rate: 93.8% (2000); Median home value: $106,300 (2000); Median age of housing: 33 years (2000).
Transportation: Commute to work: 100.0% car, 0.0% public transportation, 0.0% walk, 0.0% work from home (2000); Travel time to work: 0.0% less than 15 minutes, 66.7% 15 to 30 minutes, 8.3% 30 to 45 minutes, 8.3% 45 to 60 minutes, 16.7% 60 minutes or more (2000)

MORSE (township). Covers a land area of 36.374 square miles and a water area of 0.887 square miles. Located at 47.33° N. Lat.; 93.84° W. Long.
Population: 605 (2000); Race: 88.9% White, 0.0% Black, 0.0% Asian, 7.1% American Indian and Alaska Native, 0.2% Hispanic of any race, 4.1% two or more races (2000); Density: 16.6 persons per square mile (2000); Age: 31.9% under 18, 10.3% over 64 (2000); Marriage status: 19.7% never married, 70.6% now married, 5.2% widowed, 4.5% divorced (2000); Foreign born: 0.2% (2000); Ancestry (includes multiple ancestries): 37.2% German, 18.4% Norwegian, 18.2% Irish, 13.0% Other groups, 10.6% Finnish (2000).
Economy: Employment by occupation: 4.6% management, 15.1% professional, 16.2% services, 23.6% sales, 3.9% farming, 9.3% construction, 27.4% production (2000).
Income: Per capita income: $14,499 (2000); Median household income: $39,821 (2000); Poverty rate: 12.4% (2000).
Taxes: Total city taxes per capita: $157 (1997); City property taxes per capita: $157 (1997).
Education: High school graduation rate: 77.0% (2000); College graduation rate: 9.6% (2000).
Housing: Homeownership rate: 98.0% (2000); Median home value: $70,000 (2000); Median rent: $225 per month (2000); Median age of housing: 26 years (2000).
Transportation: Commute to work: 87.9% car, 1.6% public transportation, 0.0% walk, 10.5% work from home (2000); Travel time to work: 33.0% less than 15 minutes, 33.0% 15 to 30 minutes, 21.3% 30 to 45 minutes, 5.7% 45 to 60 minutes, 7.0% 60 minutes or more (2000)

NASHWAUK (city). Covers a land area of 5.638 square miles and a water area of 0.315 square miles. Located at 47.37° N. Lat.; 93.16° W. Long. Elevation is 1,486 feet.
History: Nashwauk was founded in the early 1900's when iron ore was discovered on a site that had been a logging camp. Nashwauk's first wealth came from the operations of the Hawkins, Crosby, and Larue mines.
Population: 935 (2000); Race: 97.5% White, 0.0% Black, 0.0% Asian, 1.1% American Indian and Alaska Native, 1.1% Hispanic of any race, 1.4% two or more races (2000); Density: 165.8 persons per square mile (2000); Age: 19.6% under 18, 26.0% over 64 (2000); Marriage status: 21.3% never married, 55.1% now married, 14.2% widowed, 9.4% divorced (2000); Foreign born: 1.6% (2000); Ancestry (includes multiple ancestries): 26.5% German, 12.7% Finnish, 12.7% Italian, 12.1% Norwegian, 11.0% Irish (2000).
Economy: Employment by occupation: 10.2% management, 10.9% professional, 17.4% services, 24.5% sales, 0.0% farming, 19.3% construction, 17.7% production (2000).
Income: Per capita income: $15,954 (2000); Median household income: $26,146 (2000); Poverty rate: 14.6% (2000).
Taxes: Total city taxes per capita: $91 (1997); City property taxes per capita: $88 (1997).
Education: High school graduation rate: 81.7% (2000); College graduation rate: 10.8% (2000).

School District(s)

Nashwauk-Keewatin (PK-12)
2000 Enrollment: 701 218-885-2705
Housing: Homeownership rate: 79.6% (2000); Median home value: $44,100 (2000); Median rent: $307 per month (2000); Median age of housing: 57 years (2000).
Newspapers: Eastern Itascan (1 x week)
Transportation: Commute to work: 89.1% car, 0.0% public transportation, 8.0% walk, 1.9% work from home (2000); Travel time to work: 42.7% less

than 15 minutes, 36.8% 15 to 30 minutes, 14.7% 30 to 45 minutes, 3.6% 45 to 60 minutes, 2.3% 60 minutes or more (2000)

NASHWAUK (township). Covers a land area of 65.926 square miles and a water area of 2.450 square miles. Located at 47.39° N. Lat.; 93.18° W. Long. Elevation is 1,486 feet.
History: Growth followed discovery of iron nearby in early 1900s.
Population: 1,666 (2000); Race: 97.9% White, 0.0% Black, 0.0% Asian, 0.6% American Indian and Alaska Native, 0.6% Hispanic of any race, 1.3% two or more races (2000); Density: 25.3 persons per square mile (2000); Age: 22.0% under 18, 21.1% over 64 (2000); Marriage status: 19.4% never married, 60.7% now married, 10.1% widowed, 9.8% divorced (2000); Foreign born: 1.0% (2000); Ancestry (includes multiple ancestries): 28.8% German, 13.7% Norwegian, 12.3% Finnish, 11.3% Italian, 9.5% Irish (2000).
Economy: Iron mining; timber. Manufacturing of pulpwood. Employment by occupation: 8.2% management, 11.1% professional, 16.8% services, 23.8% sales, 0.0% farming, 21.1% construction, 19.0% production (2000).
Income: Per capita income: $16,118 (2000); Median household income: $31,151 (2000); Poverty rate: 10.7% (2000).
Taxes: Total city taxes per capita: $39 (1997); City property taxes per capita: $39 (1997).
Education: High school graduation rate: 80.1% (2000); College graduation rate: 10.0% (2000).
Housing: Homeownership rate: 86.5% (2000); Median home value: $47,700 (2000); Median rent: $308 per month (2000); Median age of housing: 48 years (2000).
Transportation: Commute to work: 93.0% car, 0.3% public transportation, 4.0% walk, 1.6% work from home (2000); Travel time to work: 34.0% less than 15 minutes, 30.3% 15 to 30 minutes, 24.3% 30 to 45 minutes, 6.8% 45 to 60 minutes, 4.7% 60 minutes or more (2000)

NORE (township). Covers a land area of 36.297 square miles and a water area of 0.131 square miles. Located at 47.82° N. Lat.; 94.37° W. Long.
Population: 55 (2000); Race: 100.0% White, 0.0% Black, 0.0% Asian, 0.0% American Indian and Alaska Native, 0.0% Hispanic of any race, 0.0% two or more races (2000); Density: 1.5 persons per square mile (2000); Age: 22.0% under 18, 34.0% over 64 (2000); Marriage status: 12.2% never married, 75.6% now married, 7.3% widowed, 4.9% divorced (2000); Foreign born: 0.0% (2000); Ancestry (includes multiple ancestries): 50.0% Norwegian, 42.0% German, 22.0% Other groups, 6.0% United States or American, 6.0% Scotch-Irish (2000).
Economy: Employment by occupation: 0.0% management, 8.3% professional, 25.0% services, 0.0% sales, 0.0% farming, 0.0% construction, 66.7% production (2000).
Income: Per capita income: $10,398 (2000); Median household income: $28,125 (2000); Poverty rate: 20.0% (2000).
Taxes: Total city taxes per capita: $25 (1997); City property taxes per capita: $25 (1997).
Education: High school graduation rate: 53.8% (2000); College graduation rate: 10.3% (2000).
Housing: Homeownership rate: 89.5% (2000); Median home value: $27,500 (2000); Median rent: $275 per month (2000); Median age of housing: 42 years (2000).
Transportation: Commute to work: 75.0% car, 0.0% public transportation, 0.0% walk, 25.0% work from home (2000); Travel time to work: 44.4% less than 15 minutes, 33.3% 15 to 30 minutes, 0.0% 30 to 45 minutes, 0.0% 45 to 60 minutes, 22.2% 60 minutes or more (2000)

OTENEAGEN (township). Covers a land area of 36.115 square miles and a water area of 0.205 square miles. Located at 47.46° N. Lat.; 93.85° W. Long.
Population: 246 (2000); Race: 87.6% White, 0.0% Black, 1.2% Asian, 6.2% American Indian and Alaska Native, 2.9% Hispanic of any race, 3.7% two or more races (2000); Density: 6.8 persons per square mile (2000); Age: 35.5% under 18, 4.5% over 64 (2000); Marriage status: 28.9% never married, 61.7% now married, 1.0% widowed, 8.5% divorced (2000); Foreign born: 2.1% (2000); Ancestry (includes multiple ancestries): 27.3% Finnish, 20.2% German, 14.0% Other groups, 14.0% Swedish, 14.0% Norwegian (2000).
Economy: Employment by occupation: 7.3% management, 22.0% professional, 28.0% services, 17.1% sales, 2.4% farming, 8.5% construction, 14.6% production (2000).
Income: Per capita income: $13,527 (2000); Median household income: $30,313 (2000); Poverty rate: 28.9% (2000).
Taxes: Total city taxes per capita: $13 (1997); City property taxes per capita: $13 (1997).
Education: High school graduation rate: 83.2% (2000); College graduation rate: 18.1% (2000).
Housing: Homeownership rate: 92.1% (2000); Median home value: $50,000 (2000); Median age of housing: 24 years (2000).
Transportation: Commute to work: 82.9% car, 0.0% public transportation, 0.0% walk, 17.1% work from home (2000); Travel time to work: 16.2% less than 15 minutes, 38.2% 15 to 30 minutes, 33.8% 30 to 45 minutes, 8.8% 45 to 60 minutes, 2.9% 60 minutes or more (2000)

PENGILLY (unincorporated postal area, zip code 55775). Covers a land area of 19.091 square miles and a water area of 4.228 square miles. Located at 47.30° N. Lat.; 93.20° W. Long. Elevation is 1,355 feet.
Population: 1,351 (2000); Race: 97.3% White, 0.0% Black, 0.0% Asian, 1.3% American Indian and Alaska Native, 0.2% Hispanic of any race, 1.4% two or more races (2000); Density: 70.8 persons per square mile (2000); Age: 19.5% under 18, 20.7% over 64 (2000); Marriage status: 19.1% never married, 66.8% now married, 7.5% widowed, 6.6% divorced (2000); Foreign born: 0.6% (2000); Ancestry (includes multiple ancestries): 22.9% German, 14.3% Norwegian, 12.5% Irish, 12.5% Swedish, 10.8% Finnish (2000).
Economy: Iron mines nearby. Employment by occupation: 12.0% management, 19.7% professional, 8.2% services, 28.4% sales, 0.7% farming, 14.6% construction, 16.4% production (2000).
Income: Per capita income: $24,058 (2000); Median household income: $44,511 (2000); Poverty rate: 5.8% (2000).
Education: High school graduation rate: 88.3% (2000); College graduation rate: 19.1% (2000).
Housing: Homeownership rate: 94.3% (2000); Median home value: $82,400 (2000); Median rent: $406 per month (2000); Median age of housing: 39 years (2000).
Transportation: Commute to work: 99.3% car, 0.0% public transportation, 0.2% walk, 0.5% work from home (2000); Travel time to work: 10.4% less than 15 minutes, 53.1% 15 to 30 minutes, 28.1% 30 to 45 minutes, 5.8% 45 to 60 minutes, 2.7% 60 minutes or more (2000)

POMROY (township). Covers a land area of 36.755 square miles and a water area of 0.265 square miles. Located at 47.76° N. Lat.; 93.98° W. Long. Elevation is 1,372 feet.
Population: 33 (2000); Race: 95.1% White, 0.0% Black, 0.0% Asian, 4.9% American Indian and Alaska Native, 0.0% Hispanic of any race, 0.0% two or more races (2000); Density: 0.9 persons per square mile (2000); Age: 26.8% under 18, 14.6% over 64 (2000); Marriage status: 25.0% never married, 59.4% now married, 12.5% widowed, 3.1% divorced (2000); Foreign born: 0.0% (2000); Ancestry (includes multiple ancestries): 31.7% German, 19.5% Irish, 17.1% Italian, 9.8% Scandinavian, 4.9% Other groups (2000).
Economy: Employment by occupation: 30.8% management, 0.0% professional, 0.0% services, 15.4% sales, 0.0% farming, 30.8% construction, 23.1% production (2000).
Income: Per capita income: $11,412 (2000); Median household income: $32,500 (2000); Poverty rate: 0.0% (2000).
Taxes: Total city taxes per capita: $61 (1997); City property taxes per capita: $61 (1997).
Education: High school graduation rate: 85.7% (2000); College graduation rate: 7.1% (2000).
Housing: Homeownership rate: 57.1% (2000); Median home value: $45,000 (2000); Median age of housing: 28 years (2000).
Transportation: Commute to work: 81.8% car, 0.0% public transportation, 0.0% walk, 18.2% work from home (2000); Travel time to work: 0.0% less than 15 minutes, 44.4% 15 to 30 minutes, 0.0% 30 to 45 minutes, 0.0% 45 to 60 minutes, 55.6% 60 minutes or more (2000)

SAGO (township). Covers a land area of 33.812 square miles and a water area of 0.600 square miles. Located at 47.05° N. Lat.; 93.24° W. Long.
Population: 205 (2000); Race: 95.5% White, 0.0% Black, 0.0% Asian, 3.3% American Indian and Alaska Native, 0.0% Hispanic of any race, 1.2% two or more races (2000); Density: 6.1 persons per square mile (2000); Age: 33.7% under 18, 9.9% over 64 (2000); Marriage status: 19.6% never married, 71.7% now married, 1.1% widowed, 7.6% divorced (2000); Foreign born: 0.0% (2000); Ancestry (includes multiple ancestries): 41.2% German, 15.2% English, 14.8% Irish, 8.2% Polish, 7.8% United States or American (2000).
Economy: Employment by occupation: 8.4% management, 5.6% professional, 23.4% services, 29.0% sales, 0.0% farming, 7.5% construction, 26.2% production (2000).
Income: Per capita income: $14,205 (2000); Median household income: $40,179 (2000); Poverty rate: 5.8% (2000).
Taxes: Total city taxes per capita: $132 (2000); City property taxes per capita: $132 (2000).

Education: High school graduation rate: 82.7% (2000); College graduation rate: 9.6% (2000).
Housing: Homeownership rate: 92.3% (2000); Median home value: $61,700 (2000); Median rent: $250 per month (2000); Median age of housing: 27 years (2000).
Transportation: Commute to work: 93.1% car, 0.0% public transportation, 0.0% walk, 6.9% work from home (2000); Travel time to work: 20.2% less than 15 minutes, 43.6% 15 to 30 minutes, 21.3% 30 to 45 minutes, 6.4% 45 to 60 minutes, 8.5% 60 minutes or more (2000)

SAND LAKE (township). Covers a land area of 29.537 square miles and a water area of 8.033 square miles. Located at 47.61° N. Lat.; 93.98° W. Long.
Population: 128 (2000); Race: 87.2% White, 4.7% Black, 0.0% Asian, 2.7% American Indian and Alaska Native, 0.0% Hispanic of any race, 5.4% two or more races (2000); Density: 4.3 persons per square mile (2000); Age: 34.5% under 18, 15.5% over 64 (2000); Marriage status: 15.2% never married, 71.4% now married, 4.8% widowed, 8.6% divorced (2000); Foreign born: 2.0% (2000); Ancestry (includes multiple ancestries): 37.8% German, 14.9% Other groups, 14.2% Norwegian, 13.5% Irish, 8.8% Finnish (2000).
Economy: Employment by occupation: 23.4% management, 25.5% professional, 17.0% services, 12.8% sales, 10.6% farming, 4.3% construction, 6.4% production (2000).
Income: Per capita income: $11,320 (2000); Median household income: $21,429 (2000); Poverty rate: 35.1% (2000).
Taxes: Total city taxes per capita: $193 (1997); City property taxes per capita: $193 (1997).
Education: High school graduation rate: 79.8% (2000); College graduation rate: 20.2% (2000).
Housing: Homeownership rate: 96.6% (2000); Median home value: $108,300 (2000); Median age of housing: 25 years (2000).
Transportation: Commute to work: 88.9% car, 0.0% public transportation, 0.0% walk, 11.1% work from home (2000); Travel time to work: 7.5% less than 15 minutes, 17.5% 15 to 30 minutes, 42.5% 30 to 45 minutes, 10.0% 45 to 60 minutes, 22.5% 60 minutes or more (2000)

SPANG (township). Covers a land area of 52.221 square miles and a water area of 0.634 square miles. Located at 47.07° N. Lat.; 93.60° W. Long.
Population: 262 (2000); Race: 99.1% White, 0.9% Black, 0.0% Asian, 0.0% American Indian and Alaska Native, 0.0% Hispanic of any race, 0.0% two or more races (2000); Density: 5.0 persons per square mile (2000); Age: 32.2% under 18, 9.7% over 64 (2000); Marriage status: 17.0% never married, 70.8% now married, 8.8% widowed, 3.5% divorced (2000); Foreign born: 0.0% (2000); Ancestry (includes multiple ancestries): 23.3% German, 15.4% Norwegian, 12.8% United States or American, 12.3% Swedish, 9.7% Irish (2000).
Economy: Employment by occupation: 13.0% management, 20.0% professional, 10.0% services, 24.0% sales, 5.0% farming, 8.0% construction, 20.0% production (2000).
Income: Per capita income: $17,033 (2000); Median household income: $43,125 (2000); Poverty rate: 9.3% (2000).
Taxes: Total city taxes per capita: $116 (1997); City property taxes per capita: $116 (1997).
Education: High school graduation rate: 88.4% (2000); College graduation rate: 19.9% (2000).
Housing: Homeownership rate: 97.9% (2000); Median home value: $83,800 (2000); Median age of housing: 23 years (2000).
Transportation: Commute to work: 92.0% car, 0.0% public transportation, 0.0% walk, 8.0% work from home (2000); Travel time to work: 12.0% less than 15 minutes, 53.3% 15 to 30 minutes, 15.2% 30 to 45 minutes, 10.9% 45 to 60 minutes, 8.7% 60 minutes or more (2000)

SPLITHAND (township). Covers a land area of 32.595 square miles and a water area of 0.746 square miles. Located at 47.06° N. Lat.; 93.39° W. Long.
Population: 256 (2000); Race: 96.7% White, 0.0% Black, 0.0% Asian, 0.0% American Indian and Alaska Native, 0.0% Hispanic of any race, 1.5% two or more races (2000); Density: 7.9 persons per square mile (2000); Age: 26.1% under 18, 11.4% over 64 (2000); Marriage status: 15.3% never married, 74.9% now married, 1.4% widowed, 8.4% divorced (2000); Foreign born: 3.3% (2000); Ancestry (includes multiple ancestries): 34.6% German, 12.5% Norwegian, 10.3% Finnish, 8.1% Irish, 8.1% Swedish (2000).
Economy: Employment by occupation: 8.3% management, 13.2% professional, 11.1% services, 30.6% sales, 0.0% farming, 18.1% construction, 18.8% production (2000).
Income: Per capita income: $15,904 (2000); Median household income: $37,292 (2000); Poverty rate: 8.1% (2000).
Taxes: Total city taxes per capita: $31 (2000); City property taxes per capita: $31 (2000).
Education: High school graduation rate: 82.8% (2000); College graduation rate: 11.8% (2000).
Housing: Homeownership rate: 96.1% (2000); Median home value: $69,400 (2000); Median rent: $425 per month (2000); Median age of housing: 30 years (2000).
Transportation: Commute to work: 94.4% car, 0.0% public transportation, 0.0% walk, 4.2% work from home (2000); Travel time to work: 5.8% less than 15 minutes, 63.8% 15 to 30 minutes, 15.2% 30 to 45 minutes, 4.3% 45 to 60 minutes, 10.9% 60 minutes or more (2000)

SPRING LAKE (unincorporated postal area, zip code 56680). Covers a land area of 22.346 square miles and a water area of 1.867 square miles. Located at 47.66° N. Lat.; 93.94° W. Long. Elevation is 1,350 feet.
Population: 80 (2000); Race: 95.9% White, 2.1% Black, 0.0% Asian, 2.1% American Indian and Alaska Native, 0.0% Hispanic of any race, 0.0% two or more races (2000); Density: 3.6 persons per square mile (2000); Age: 24.7% under 18, 22.7% over 64 (2000); Marriage status: 16.0% never married, 65.4% now married, 6.2% widowed, 12.3% divorced (2000); Foreign born: 3.1% (2000); Ancestry (includes multiple ancestries): 42.3% German, 15.5% Swedish, 13.4% Norwegian, 13.4% Finnish, 12.4% Irish (2000).
Economy: Employment by occupation: 22.0% management, 17.1% professional, 36.6% services, 9.8% sales, 4.9% farming, 4.9% construction, 4.9% production (2000).
Income: Per capita income: $21,862 (2000); Median household income: $18,125 (2000); Poverty rate: 26.8% (2000).
Education: High school graduation rate: 72.9% (2000); College graduation rate: 10.0% (2000).
Housing: Homeownership rate: 95.5% (2000); Median home value: $91,700 (2000); Median age of housing: 20 years (2000).
Transportation: Commute to work: 95.1% car, 0.0% public transportation, 0.0% walk, 4.9% work from home (2000); Travel time to work: 0.0% less than 15 minutes, 20.5% 15 to 30 minutes, 56.4% 30 to 45 minutes, 5.1% 45 to 60 minutes, 17.9% 60 minutes or more (2000)

SQUAW LAKE (city). Covers a land area of 0.821 square miles and a water area of 0.031 square miles. Located at 47.62° N. Lat.; 94.13° W. Long. Elevation is 1,360 feet.
Population: 99 (2000); Race: 57.0% White, 0.0% Black, 1.1% Asian, 41.9% American Indian and Alaska Native, 0.0% Hispanic of any race, 0.0% two or more races (2000); Density: 120.7 persons per square mile (2000); Age: 26.9% under 18, 19.4% over 64 (2000); Marriage status: 37.0% never married, 30.1% now married, 30.1% widowed, 2.7% divorced (2000); Foreign born: 1.1% (2000); Ancestry (includes multiple ancestries): 39.8% Other groups, 20.4% Finnish, 16.1% Swedish, 11.8% Norwegian, 3.2% German (2000).
Economy: Cattle, sheep, poultry; oats, wild rice; timber. Also in Blackduck State Forest and part of Chippewa National Forest (boundaries overlap). Employment by occupation: 8.0% management, 12.0% professional, 36.0% services, 28.0% sales, 0.0% farming, 0.0% construction, 16.0% production (2000).
Income: Per capita income: $9,895 (2000); Median household income: $11,875 (2000); Poverty rate: 49.5% (2000).
Taxes: Total city taxes per capita: $53 (1997); City property taxes per capita: $33 (1997).
Education: High school graduation rate: 76.3% (2000); College graduation rate: 8.5% (2000).
Housing: Homeownership rate: 60.5% (2000); Median home value: $37,500 (2000); Median rent: $139 per month (2000); Median age of housing: 28 years (2000).
Transportation: Commute to work: 80.0% car, 0.0% public transportation, 20.0% walk, 0.0% work from home (2000); Travel time to work: 28.0% less than 15 minutes, 16.0% 15 to 30 minutes, 12.0% 30 to 45 minutes, 8.0% 45 to 60 minutes, 36.0% 60 minutes or more (2000)

STOKES (township). Covers a land area of 52.536 square miles and a water area of 4.808 square miles. Located at 47.68° N. Lat.; 93.70° W. Long.
Population: 259 (2000); Race: 98.0% White, 0.0% Black, 2.0% Asian, 0.0% American Indian and Alaska Native, 0.8% Hispanic of any race, 0.0% two or more races (2000); Density: 4.9 persons per square mile (2000); Age: 24.8% under 18, 26.8% over 64 (2000); Marriage status: 13.1% never married, 75.9% now married, 5.5% widowed, 5.5% divorced (2000); Foreign born:

2.0% (2000); Ancestry (includes multiple ancestries): 33.5% German, 13.0% Norwegian, 10.6% Irish, 7.9% Swedish, 6.3% English (2000).
Economy: Employment by occupation: 5.4% management, 20.4% professional, 16.1% services, 24.7% sales, 2.2% farming, 16.1% construction, 15.1% production (2000).
Income: Per capita income: $18,444 (2000); Median household income: $33,750 (2000); Poverty rate: 11.0% (2000).
Taxes: Total city taxes per capita: $53 (1997); City property taxes per capita: $53 (1997).
Education: High school graduation rate: 84.3% (2000); College graduation rate: 19.5% (2000).
Housing: Homeownership rate: 94.9% (2000); Median home value: $112,500 (2000); Median rent: $125 per month (2000); Median age of housing: 24 years (2000).
Transportation: Commute to work: 88.6% car, 0.0% public transportation, 2.3% walk, 6.8% work from home (2000); Travel time to work: 57.3% less than 15 minutes, 22.0% 15 to 30 minutes, 6.1% 30 to 45 minutes, 6.1% 45 to 60 minutes, 8.5% 60 minutes or more (2000)

SWAN RIVER (unincorporated postal area, zip code 55784). Covers a land area of 24.701 square miles and a water area of 0.007 square miles. Located at 47.06° N. Lat.; 93.20° W. Long. Elevation is 1,293 feet.
Population: 77 (2000); Race: 100.0% White, 0.0% Black, 0.0% Asian, 0.0% American Indian and Alaska Native, 0.0% Hispanic of any race, 0.0% two or more races (2000); Density: 3.1 persons per square mile (2000); Age: 18.2% under 18, 18.2% over 64 (2000); Marriage status: 14.6% never married, 69.7% now married, 0.0% widowed, 15.7% divorced (2000); Foreign born: 0.0% (2000); Ancestry (includes multiple ancestries): 32.3% German, 24.2% Swedish, 16.2% Finnish, 12.1% Polish, 7.1% English (2000).
Economy: Employment by occupation: 5.9% management, 14.7% professional, 23.5% services, 17.6% sales, 0.0% farming, 0.0% construction, 38.2% production (2000).
Income: Per capita income: $14,348 (2000); Median household income: $28,750 (2000); Poverty rate: 13.1% (2000).
Education: High school graduation rate: 81.5% (2000); College graduation rate: 0.0% (2000).
Housing: Homeownership rate: 100.0% (2000); Median home value: $67,500 (2000); Median age of housing: 27 years (2000).
Transportation: Commute to work: 94.1% car, 0.0% public transportation, 0.0% walk, 5.9% work from home (2000); Travel time to work: 34.4% less than 15 minutes, 18.8% 15 to 30 minutes, 18.8% 30 to 45 minutes, 9.4% 45 to 60 minutes, 18.8% 60 minutes or more (2000)

TACONITE (city). Covers a land area of 4.883 square miles and a water area of 0.364 square miles. Located at 47.31° N. Lat.; 93.36° W. Long.
Population: 315 (2000); Race: 95.2% White, 0.0% Black, 0.0% Asian, 0.9% American Indian and Alaska Native, 0.0% Hispanic of any race, 3.9% two or more races (2000); Density: 64.5 persons per square mile (2000); Age: 24.9% under 18, 18.6% over 64 (2000); Marriage status: 21.9% never married, 57.6% now married, 10.8% widowed, 9.7% divorced (2000); Foreign born: 0.0% (2000); Ancestry (includes multiple ancestries): 19.8% German, 14.4% Norwegian, 13.2% Irish, 11.1% Swedish, 10.5% Finnish (2000).
Economy: Iron mines in area; manufacturing of concrete. Employment by occupation: 1.9% management, 9.1% professional, 24.7% services, 27.9% sales, 0.0% farming, 11.0% construction, 25.3% production (2000).
Income: Per capita income: $16,357 (2000); Median household income: $30,250 (2000); Poverty rate: 17.1% (2000).
Taxes: Total city taxes per capita: $243 (1997); City property taxes per capita: $240 (1997).
Education: High school graduation rate: 92.6% (2000); College graduation rate: 5.5% (2000).
Housing: Homeownership rate: 76.1% (2000); Median home value: $40,400 (2000); Median rent: $275 per month (2000); Median age of housing: 58 years (2000).
Transportation: Commute to work: 89.1% car, 0.7% public transportation, 6.1% walk, 2.7% work from home (2000); Travel time to work: 20.3% less than 15 minutes, 59.4% 15 to 30 minutes, 16.8% 30 to 45 minutes, 1.4% 45 to 60 minutes, 2.1% 60 minutes or more (2000)

TALMOON (unincorporated postal area, zip code 56637). Covers a land area of 31.808 square miles and a water area of 0.613 square miles. Located at 47.61° N. Lat.; 93.83° W. Long. Elevation is 1,359 feet.
Population: 277 (2000); Race: 98.3% White, 1.0% Black, 0.0% Asian, 0.0% American Indian and Alaska Native, 0.7% Hispanic of any race, 0.7% two or more races (2000); Density: 8.7 persons per square mile (2000); Age: 29.8% under 18, 14.5% over 64 (2000); Marriage status: 14.6% never married, 67.9% now married, 9.0% widowed, 8.5% divorced (2000); Foreign born: 0.3% (2000); Ancestry (includes multiple ancestries): 33.9% German, 26.6% Norwegian, 12.8% Swedish, 12.5% Irish, 8.0% English (2000).
Economy: Employment by occupation: 12.6% management, 12.6% professional, 10.5% services, 27.4% sales, 4.2% farming, 14.7% construction, 17.9% production (2000).
Income: Per capita income: $14,133 (2000); Median household income: $37,500 (2000); Poverty rate: 13.6% (2000).
Education: High school graduation rate: 85.2% (2000); College graduation rate: 8.7% (2000).
Housing: Homeownership rate: 90.6% (2000); Median home value: $99,300 (2000); Median age of housing: 31 years (2000).
Transportation: Commute to work: 78.9% car, 0.0% public transportation, 7.4% walk, 13.7% work from home (2000); Travel time to work: 28.0% less than 15 minutes, 30.5% 15 to 30 minutes, 26.8% 30 to 45 minutes, 8.5% 45 to 60 minutes, 6.1% 60 minutes or more (2000)

THIRD RIVER (township). Covers a land area of 34.931 square miles and a water area of 1.420 square miles. Located at 47.62° N. Lat.; 94.31° W. Long.
Population: 65 (2000); Race: 91.3% White, 0.0% Black, 0.0% Asian, 8.8% American Indian and Alaska Native, 0.0% Hispanic of any race, 0.0% two or more races (2000); Density: 1.9 persons per square mile (2000); Age: 13.8% under 18, 11.3% over 64 (2000); Marriage status: 23.6% never married, 48.6% now married, 9.7% widowed, 18.1% divorced (2000); Foreign born: 0.0% (2000); Ancestry (includes multiple ancestries): 31.3% Swedish, 27.5% German, 27.5% English, 21.3% Norwegian, 16.3% Irish (2000).
Economy: Employment by occupation: 13.9% management, 25.0% professional, 5.6% services, 19.4% sales, 0.0% farming, 8.3% construction, 27.8% production (2000).
Income: Per capita income: $16,679 (2000); Median household income: $30,750 (2000); Poverty rate: 13.8% (2000).
Taxes: Total city taxes per capita: $66 (1997); City property taxes per capita: $66 (1997).
Education: High school graduation rate: 98.3% (2000); College graduation rate: 21.7% (2000).
Housing: Homeownership rate: 91.2% (2000); Median home value: $82,500 (2000); Median age of housing: 20 years (2000).
Transportation: Commute to work: 94.4% car, 0.0% public transportation, 0.0% walk, 5.6% work from home (2000); Travel time to work: 0.0% less than 15 minutes, 32.4% 15 to 30 minutes, 14.7% 30 to 45 minutes, 5.9% 45 to 60 minutes, 47.1% 60 minutes or more (2000)

TROUT LAKE (township). Covers a land area of 30.542 square miles and a water area of 4.130 square miles. Located at 47.23° N. Lat.; 93.37° W. Long.
Population: 951 (2000); Race: 98.9% White, 0.0% Black, 0.0% Asian, 0.4% American Indian and Alaska Native, 0.3% Hispanic of any race, 0.7% two or more races (2000); Density: 31.1 persons per square mile (2000); Age: 26.1% under 18, 8.3% over 64 (2000); Marriage status: 22.3% never married, 63.5% now married, 5.3% widowed, 8.9% divorced (2000); Foreign born: 1.1% (2000); Ancestry (includes multiple ancestries): 34.4% German, 18.5% Norwegian, 16.0% Swedish, 12.6% Finnish, 10.2% Irish (2000).
Economy: Employment by occupation: 7.6% management, 16.6% professional, 13.9% services, 23.5% sales, 0.2% farming, 20.5% construction, 17.7% production (2000).
Income: Per capita income: $19,046 (2000); Median household income: $43,750 (2000); Poverty rate: 6.8% (2000).
Taxes: Total city taxes per capita: $106 (1997); City property taxes per capita: $106 (1997).
Education: High school graduation rate: 89.3% (2000); College graduation rate: 14.5% (2000).
Housing: Homeownership rate: 94.9% (2000); Median home value: $91,600 (2000); Median rent: $375 per month (2000); Median age of housing: 22 years (2000).
Transportation: Commute to work: 95.3% car, 0.0% public transportation, 0.0% walk, 4.7% work from home (2000); Travel time to work: 24.3% less than 15 minutes, 53.6% 15 to 30 minutes, 12.0% 30 to 45 minutes, 1.6% 45 to 60 minutes, 8.5% 60 minutes or more (2000)

WABANA (township). Covers a land area of 29.104 square miles and a water area of 6.887 square miles. Located at 47.40° N. Lat.; 93.51° W. Long.
Population: 487 (2000); Race: 99.6% White, 0.0% Black, 0.0% Asian, 0.0% American Indian and Alaska Native, 0.0% Hispanic of any race, 0.4% two or more races (2000); Density: 16.7 persons per square mile (2000); Age: 24.6% under 18, 13.8% over 64 (2000); Marriage status: 12.7% never married,

75.5% now married, 2.8% widowed, 9.0% divorced (2000); Foreign born: 1.2% (2000); Ancestry (includes multiple ancestries): 37.4% German, 11.8% Norwegian, 10.0% English, 9.3% Irish, 8.9% Swedish (2000).
Economy: Employment by occupation: 13.6% management, 21.3% professional, 8.5% services, 24.7% sales, 0.0% farming, 14.0% construction, 17.9% production (2000).
Income: Per capita income: $27,789 (2000); Median household income: $51,563 (2000); Poverty rate: 3.9% (2000).
Taxes: Total city taxes per capita: $78 (1997); City property taxes per capita: $78 (1997).
Education: High school graduation rate: 93.3% (2000); College graduation rate: 34.8% (2000).
Housing: Homeownership rate: 95.3% (2000); Median home value: $134,400 (2000); Median rent: $475 per month (2000); Median age of housing: 27 years (2000).
Transportation: Commute to work: 96.6% car, 0.0% public transportation, 0.0% walk, 3.4% work from home (2000); Travel time to work: 6.2% less than 15 minutes, 65.6% 15 to 30 minutes, 19.8% 30 to 45 minutes, 4.4% 45 to 60 minutes, 4.0% 60 minutes or more (2000)

WARBA (city). Covers a land area of 3.193 square miles and a water area of 0.062 square miles. Located at 47.13° N. Lat.; 93.26° W. Long. Elevation is 1,280 feet.
Population: 183 (2000); Race: 99.0% White, 0.0% Black, 0.0% Asian, 0.0% American Indian and Alaska Native, 0.0% Hispanic of any race, 1.0% two or more races (2000); Density: 57.3 persons per square mile (2000); Age: 22.4% under 18, 12.8% over 64 (2000); Marriage status: 13.3% never married, 62.7% now married, 5.1% widowed, 19.0% divorced (2000); Foreign born: 0.0% (2000); Ancestry (includes multiple ancestries): 27.6% German, 24.0% Irish, 11.7% United States or American, 11.7% Swedish, 10.2% Polish (2000).
Economy: Agriculture: alfalfa; cattle. Employment by occupation: 3.5% management, 14.1% professional, 21.2% services, 17.6% sales, 0.0% farming, 25.9% construction, 17.6% production (2000).
Income: Per capita income: $11,772 (2000); Median household income: $27,500 (2000); Poverty rate: 19.6% (2000).
Taxes: Total city taxes per capita: $87 (1997); City property taxes per capita: $80 (1997).
Education: High school graduation rate: 86.2% (2000); College graduation rate: 8.3% (2000).
Housing: Homeownership rate: 79.1% (2000); Median home value: $60,000 (2000); Median rent: $322 per month (2000); Median age of housing: 32 years (2000).
Transportation: Commute to work: 92.6% car, 4.9% public transportation, 0.0% walk, 2.5% work from home (2000); Travel time to work: 7.6% less than 15 minutes, 41.8% 15 to 30 minutes, 27.8% 30 to 45 minutes, 11.4% 45 to 60 minutes, 11.4% 60 minutes or more (2000)

WAWINA (township). Covers a land area of 36.536 square miles and a water area of 0.015 square miles. Located at 47.06° N. Lat.; 93.11° W. Long. Elevation is 1,267 feet.
Population: 110 (2000); Race: 100.0% White, 0.0% Black, 0.0% Asian, 0.0% American Indian and Alaska Native, 0.0% Hispanic of any race, 0.0% two or more races (2000); Density: 3.0 persons per square mile (2000); Age: 29.8% under 18, 19.1% over 64 (2000); Marriage status: 25.7% never married, 63.5% now married, 8.1% widowed, 2.7% divorced (2000); Foreign born: 0.0% (2000); Ancestry (includes multiple ancestries): 22.3% United States or American, 19.1% Finnish, 16.0% German, 11.7% Irish, 11.7% Swedish (2000).
Economy: Employment by occupation: 3.1% management, 6.3% professional, 6.3% services, 9.4% sales, 15.6% farming, 21.9% construction, 37.5% production (2000).
Income: Per capita income: $10,860 (2000); Median household income: $19,167 (2000); Poverty rate: 7.4% (2000).
Taxes: Total city taxes per capita: $475 (1997); City property taxes per capita: $475 (1997).
Education: High school graduation rate: 73.7% (2000); College graduation rate: 5.3% (2000).
Housing: Homeownership rate: 94.3% (2000); Median home value: $75,000 (2000); Median age of housing: 32 years (2000).
Transportation: Commute to work: 87.5% car, 0.0% public transportation, 0.0% walk, 0.0% work from home (2000); Travel time to work: 46.9% less than 15 minutes, 15.6% 15 to 30 minutes, 25.0% 30 to 45 minutes, 6.3% 45 to 60 minutes, 6.3% 60 minutes or more (2000)

WILDWOOD (township). Covers a land area of 30.246 square miles and a water area of 3.159 square miles. Located at 47.06° N. Lat.; 93.50° W. Long.
Population: 193 (2000); Race: 96.6% White, 0.0% Black, 1.0% Asian, 0.0% American Indian and Alaska Native, 0.0% Hispanic of any race, 2.4% two or more races (2000); Density: 6.4 persons per square mile (2000); Age: 24.0% under 18, 11.5% over 64 (2000); Marriage status: 13.5% never married, 71.2% now married, 4.3% widowed, 11.0% divorced (2000); Foreign born: 2.9% (2000); Ancestry (includes multiple ancestries): 25.0% German, 10.1% Other groups, 9.1% French (except Basque), 8.2% Danish, 8.2% Swedish (2000).
Economy: Employment by occupation: 2.1% management, 22.3% professional, 19.1% services, 19.1% sales, 0.0% farming, 11.7% construction, 25.5% production (2000).
Income: Per capita income: $21,379 (2000); Median household income: $38,500 (2000); Poverty rate: 9.6% (2000).
Taxes: Total city taxes per capita: $127 (1997); City property taxes per capita: $127 (1997).
Education: High school graduation rate: 85.6% (2000); College graduation rate: 11.0% (2000).
Housing: Homeownership rate: 93.9% (2000); Median home value: $95,400 (2000); Median rent: $175 per month (2000); Median age of housing: 24 years (2000).
Transportation: Commute to work: 95.7% car, 0.0% public transportation, 2.2% walk, 2.2% work from home (2000); Travel time to work: 21.1% less than 15 minutes, 46.7% 15 to 30 minutes, 24.4% 30 to 45 minutes, 0.0% 45 to 60 minutes, 7.8% 60 minutes or more (2000)

WIRT (township). Covers a land area of 34.097 square miles and a water area of 2.066 square miles. Located at 47.74° N. Lat.; 93.95° W. Long. Elevation is 1,330 feet.
Population: 94 (2000); Race: 82.6% White, 3.7% Black, 1.8% Asian, 8.3% American Indian and Alaska Native, 0.0% Hispanic of any race, 0.0% two or more races (2000); Density: 2.8 persons per square mile (2000); Age: 30.3% under 18, 19.3% over 64 (2000); Marriage status: 20.5% never married, 65.1% now married, 3.6% widowed, 10.8% divorced (2000); Foreign born: 1.8% (2000); Ancestry (includes multiple ancestries): 26.6% Czech, 25.7% Norwegian, 20.2% Other groups, 18.3% German, 16.5% Swedish (2000).
Economy: Employment by occupation: 8.1% management, 8.1% professional, 10.8% services, 16.2% sales, 13.5% farming, 0.0% construction, 43.2% production (2000).
Income: Per capita income: $14,794 (2000); Median household income: $32,500 (2000); Poverty rate: 5.5% (2000).
Taxes: Total city taxes per capita: $121 (1997); City property taxes per capita: $121 (1997).
Education: High school graduation rate: 75.4% (2000); College graduation rate: 15.9% (2000).
Housing: Homeownership rate: 85.4% (2000); Median home value: $45,000 (2000); Median rent: $275 per month (2000); Median age of housing: 24 years (2000).
Transportation: Commute to work: 81.1% car, 0.0% public transportation, 0.0% walk, 8.1% work from home (2000); Travel time to work: 5.9% less than 15 minutes, 26.5% 15 to 30 minutes, 38.2% 30 to 45 minutes, 0.0% 45 to 60 minutes, 29.4% 60 minutes or more (2000)

ZEMPLE (city). Covers a land area of 0.668 square miles and a water area of 0 square miles. Located at 47.32° N. Lat.; 93.79° W. Long.
Population: 75 (2000); Race: 90.2% White, 0.0% Black, 0.0% Asian, 9.8% American Indian and Alaska Native, 0.0% Hispanic of any race, 0.0% two or more races (2000); Density: 112.2 persons per square mile (2000); Age: 29.5% under 18, 11.5% over 64 (2000); Marriage status: 27.1% never married, 56.3% now married, 8.3% widowed, 8.3% divorced (2000); Foreign born: 0.0% (2000); Ancestry (includes multiple ancestries): 27.9% German, 26.2% English, 26.2% Norwegian, 13.1% Finnish, 11.5% Irish (2000).
Economy: In Chippewa National Forest. Single-family building permits issued: 0 (2001) / 0 (2000); Multi-family building permits issued: 0 (2001) / 0 (2000); Employment by occupation: 0.0% management, 17.6% professional, 50.0% services, 0.0% sales, 0.0% farming, 8.8% construction, 23.5% production (2000).
Income: Per capita income: $10,615 (2000); Median household income: $25,750 (2000); Poverty rate: 19.7% (2000).
Taxes: Total city taxes per capita: $145 (1997); City property taxes per capita: $145 (1997).
Education: High school graduation rate: 87.2% (2000); College graduation rate: 5.1% (2000).

Housing: Homeownership rate: 84.6% (2000); Median home value: $41,000 (2000); Median rent: $125 per month (2000); Median age of housing: 24 years (2000).
Transportation: Commute to work: 88.2% car, 0.0% public transportation, 0.0% walk, 11.8% work from home (2000); Travel time to work: 40.0% less than 15 minutes, 23.3% 15 to 30 minutes, 6.7% 30 to 45 minutes, 6.7% 45 to 60 minutes, 23.3% 60 minutes or more (2000)

Jackson County

Located in southwestern Minnesota; bounded on the south by Iowa; watered by the Des Moines River; includes part of Coteau des Prairies, and Heron Lake. Covers a land area of 701.70 square miles, a water area of 17.80 square miles, and is located in the Central Time Zone. The county government was organized in 1857. County seat is Jackson.
Population: 11,268 (2000); Race: 97.4% White, 0.1% Black, 1.6% Asian, 0.1% American Indian and Alaska Native, 1.4% Hispanic of any race, 0.1% two or more races (2000); Density: 16.1 persons per square mile (2000); Age: 24.6% under 18, 20.5% over 64 (2000).
Religion: Five largest groups: 26.8% Evangelical Lutheran Church in America, 25.6% Lutheran Church—Missouri Synod, 19.2% Catholic Church, 6.2% The United Methodist Church, 2.8% Presbyterian Church (U.S.A.) (2000).
Economy: Unemployment rate: 2.2% (11/2002); Total civilian labor force: 6,382 (11/2002); Leading industries: 21.7% manufacturing; 20.7% health care and social assistance; 10.1% retail trade (2000); Companies that employ more than 1,000 persons: 0 (2000); Companies that employ more than 100 persons: 5 (2000); Farms: 963 totaling 383,631 acres (1997); Minority business ownership rate: 0.0% (1997); Women business ownership rate: 20.0% (1997); Retail sales per capita: $4,941 (1997). Single-family building permits issued: 21 (2001) / 26 (2000); Multi-family building permits issued: 2 (2001) / 0 (2000).
Income: Per capita income: $17,499 (2000); Median household income: $36,746 (2000); Poverty rate: 8.6% (2000); Bankruptcy rate: 1.67% (2001).
Taxes: Total county taxes per capita: $429 (2000); County property taxes per capita: $428 (2000).
Education: High school graduation rate: 84.1% (2000); College graduation rate: 14.2% (2000).
Housing: Homeownership rate: 79.1% (2000); Median home value: $56,800 (2000); Median rent: $273 per month (2000); Median age of housing: 51 years (2000).
Health: Birth rate: 101.2 per 10,000 population (1998); Age adjusted death rate: 70.7 per 10,000 population (1999); Age adjusted cancer mortality rate: 123.2 deaths per 100,000 population (1999). Number of physicians: 4.4 per 10,000 population (1999); Number of hospital beds: 36.4 per 10,000 population (1999).
Elections: 2000 Presidential election results: 43.5% Gore, 51.0% Bush, 3.6% Nader, 1.4% Buchanan
National and State Parks: Arzt State Wildlife Management Area; Bootleg State Wildlife Management Area; Caraway State Wildlife Management Area; Cotton-Jack State Wildlife Management Ar; Crosse State Wildlife Management Area; Husen State Wildlife Management Area; Killen Woods State Park; Laurs Lake State Wildlife Management Area; Little Sioux State Wildlife Management Area; Minnesota Slough State Wildlife Management A; Pavelko State Wildlife Management Area; Sangl State Wildlife Management Area; Summers State Wildlife Management Area; Winkler State Wildlife Management Area
Additional Information Contacts
Jackson County Government Offices.................... 507-847-2763
Jackson Chamber of Commerce.......................... 507-847-3867

Jackson County Communities

ALBA (township). Covers a land area of 35.274 square miles and a water area of 0.014 square miles. Located at 43.72° N. Lat.; 95.40° W. Long.
Population: 200 (2000); Race: 100.0% White, 0.0% Black, 0.0% Asian, 0.0% American Indian and Alaska Native, 1.2% Hispanic of any race, 0.0% two or more races (2000); Density: 5.7 persons per square mile (2000); Age: 22.6% under 18, 21.4% over 64 (2000); Marriage status: 26.9% never married, 59.0% now married, 11.2% widowed, 3.0% divorced (2000); Foreign born: 0.0% (2000); Ancestry (includes multiple ancestries): 75.0% German, 8.3% Norwegian, 6.0% Irish, 5.4% Danish, 4.2% Dutch (2000).
Economy: Employment by occupation: 17.6% management, 7.1% professional, 21.2% services, 22.4% sales, 3.5% farming, 9.4% construction, 18.8% production (2000).
Income: Per capita income: $13,699 (2000); Median household income: $25,179 (2000); Poverty rate: 10.7% (2000).
Taxes: Total city taxes per capita: $164 (1997); City property taxes per capita: $164 (1997).
Education: High school graduation rate: 90.2% (2000); College graduation rate: 4.9% (2000).
Housing: Homeownership rate: 85.7% (2000); Median home value: $66,700 (2000); Median rent: $275 per month (2000); Median age of housing: 60+ years (2000).
Transportation: Commute to work: 85.2% car, 0.0% public transportation, 3.7% walk, 11.1% work from home (2000); Travel time to work: 41.7% less than 15 minutes, 55.6% 15 to 30 minutes, 2.8% 30 to 45 minutes, 0.0% 45 to 60 minutes, 0.0% 60 minutes or more (2000)

ALPHA (city). Covers a land area of 0.177 square miles and a water area of 0 square miles. Located at 43.63° N. Lat.; 94.87° W. Long. Elevation is 1,387 feet.
Population: 126 (2000); Race: 100.0% White, 0.0% Black, 0.0% Asian, 0.0% American Indian and Alaska Native, 1.6% Hispanic of any race, 0.0% two or more races (2000); Density: 711.5 persons per square mile (2000); Age: 26.4% under 18, 16.8% over 64 (2000); Marriage status: 12.9% never married, 77.4% now married, 5.4% widowed, 4.3% divorced (2000); Foreign born: 0.0% (2000); Ancestry (includes multiple ancestries): 50.4% German, 16.8% Norwegian, 10.4% Irish, 6.4% Swedish, 5.6% Other groups (2000).
Economy: Agriculture area: grain, soybeans, alfalfa; livestock. Single-family building permits issued: 0 (2001) / 0 (2000); Multi-family building permits issued: 0 (2001) / 0 (2000); Employment by occupation: 10.6% management, 6.1% professional, 12.1% services, 21.2% sales, 3.0% farming, 9.1% construction, 37.9% production (2000).
Income: Per capita income: $18,769 (2000); Median household income: $41,750 (2000); Poverty rate: 2.4% (2000).
Taxes: Total city taxes per capita: $98 (1997); City property taxes per capita: $98 (1997).
Education: High school graduation rate: 86.9% (2000); College graduation rate: 2.4% (2000).
Housing: Homeownership rate: 80.4% (2000); Median home value: $25,800 (2000); Median rent: $250 per month (2000); Median age of housing: 47 years (2000).
Transportation: Commute to work: 83.3% car, 0.0% public transportation, 13.6% walk, 0.0% work from home (2000); Travel time to work: 57.6% less than 15 minutes, 36.4% 15 to 30 minutes, 4.5% 30 to 45 minutes, 1.5% 45 to 60 minutes, 0.0% 60 minutes or more (2000)

BELMONT (township). Covers a land area of 36.001 square miles and a water area of 0.240 square miles. Located at 43.71° N. Lat.; 95.03° W. Long.
Population: 223 (2000); Race: 100.0% White, 0.0% Black, 0.0% Asian, 0.0% American Indian and Alaska Native, 0.9% Hispanic of any race, 0.0% two or more races (2000); Density: 6.2 persons per square mile (2000); Age: 19.1% under 18, 22.3% over 64 (2000); Marriage status: 25.5% never married, 66.0% now married, 3.7% widowed, 4.8% divorced (2000); Foreign born: 0.0% (2000); Ancestry (includes multiple ancestries): 50.0% German, 40.5% Norwegian, 9.1% Irish, 7.7% United States or American, 6.8% Swedish (2000).
Economy: Employment by occupation: 41.1% management, 18.8% professional, 6.3% services, 3.6% sales, 3.6% farming, 3.6% construction, 23.2% production (2000).
Income: Per capita income: $23,215 (2000); Median household income: $47,813 (2000); Poverty rate: 6.4% (2000).
Taxes: Total city taxes per capita: $102 (1997); City property taxes per capita: $102 (1997).
Education: High school graduation rate: 80.6% (2000); College graduation rate: 18.8% (2000).
Housing: Homeownership rate: 91.2% (2000); Median home value: $58,800 (2000); Median rent: $225 per month (2000); Median age of housing: 48 years (2000).
Transportation: Commute to work: 68.8% car, 0.0% public transportation, 0.0% walk, 31.3% work from home (2000); Travel time to work: 36.4% less than 15 minutes, 37.7% 15 to 30 minutes, 18.2% 30 to 45 minutes, 5.2% 45 to 60 minutes, 2.6% 60 minutes or more (2000)

CHRISTIANIA (township). Covers a land area of 35.445 square miles and a water area of 0.787 square miles. Located at 43.80° N. Lat.; 95.04° W. Long.
Population: 331 (2000); Race: 100.0% White, 0.0% Black, 0.0% Asian, 0.0% American Indian and Alaska Native, 0.0% Hispanic of any race, 0.0% two or more races (2000); Density: 9.3 persons per square mile (2000); Age:

27.5% under 18, 14.3% over 64 (2000); Marriage status: 19.2% never married, 71.8% now married, 4.9% widowed, 4.2% divorced (2000); Foreign born: 0.8% (2000); Ancestry (includes multiple ancestries): 50.7% German, 40.9% Norwegian, 7.0% Swedish, 5.6% English, 5.0% Irish (2000).
Economy: Employment by occupation: 17.6% management, 18.1% professional, 12.1% services, 17.6% sales, 4.0% farming, 9.5% construction, 21.1% production (2000).
Income: Per capita income: $19,565 (2000); Median household income: $41,172 (2000); Poverty rate: 1.7% (2000).
Taxes: Total city taxes per capita: $102 (1997); City property taxes per capita: $102 (1997).
Education: High school graduation rate: 89.8% (2000); College graduation rate: 20.4% (2000).
Housing: Homeownership rate: 82.4% (2000); Median home value: $108,300 (2000); Median rent: $225 per month (2000); Median age of housing: 39 years (2000).
Transportation: Commute to work: 85.8% car, 0.0% public transportation, 4.6% walk, 9.6% work from home (2000); Travel time to work: 52.2% less than 15 minutes, 40.4% 15 to 30 minutes, 4.5% 30 to 45 minutes, 1.7% 45 to 60 minutes, 1.1% 60 minutes or more (2000)

DELAFIELD (township). Covers a land area of 34.654 square miles and a water area of 0.402 square miles. Located at 43.81° N. Lat.; 95.14° W. Long.
Population: 281 (2000); Race: 100.0% White, 0.0% Black, 0.0% Asian, 0.0% American Indian and Alaska Native, 0.0% Hispanic of any race, 0.0% two or more races (2000); Density: 8.1 persons per square mile (2000); Age: 24.5% under 18, 20.1% over 64 (2000); Marriage status: 15.2% never married, 80.5% now married, 3.3% widowed, 1.0% divorced (2000); Foreign born: 0.0% (2000); Ancestry (includes multiple ancestries): 58.4% German, 25.7% Norwegian, 10.0% English, 7.4% Irish, 7.1% Swedish (2000).
Economy: Employment by occupation: 16.8% management, 12.2% professional, 12.2% services, 30.5% sales, 0.0% farming, 6.9% construction, 21.4% production (2000).
Income: Per capita income: $18,258 (2000); Median household income: $37,750 (2000); Poverty rate: 15.2% (2000).
Taxes: Total city taxes per capita: $116 (1997); City property taxes per capita: $116 (1997).
Education: High school graduation rate: 83.2% (2000); College graduation rate: 15.7% (2000).
Housing: Homeownership rate: 85.2% (2000); Median home value: $76,900 (2000); Median rent: $275 per month (2000); Median age of housing: 60 years (2000).
Transportation: Commute to work: 85.5% car, 0.0% public transportation, 0.0% walk, 14.5% work from home (2000); Travel time to work: 58.9% less than 15 minutes, 29.5% 15 to 30 minutes, 8.9% 30 to 45 minutes, 0.0% 45 to 60 minutes, 2.7% 60 minutes or more (2000)

DES MOINES (township). Covers a land area of 31.743 square miles and a water area of 0.654 square miles. Located at 43.63° N. Lat.; 95.02° W. Long.
Population: 273 (2000); Race: 100.0% White, 0.0% Black, 0.0% Asian, 0.0% American Indian and Alaska Native, 0.0% Hispanic of any race, 0.0% two or more races (2000); Density: 8.6 persons per square mile (2000); Age: 25.7% under 18, 14.3% over 64 (2000); Marriage status: 19.4% never married, 69.0% now married, 4.2% widowed, 7.4% divorced (2000); Foreign born: 0.0% (2000); Ancestry (includes multiple ancestries): 32.7% German, 22.4% Norwegian, 12.1% United States or American, 9.6% Czech, 8.8% Swedish (2000).
Economy: Employment by occupation: 30.8% management, 3.8% professional, 11.3% services, 28.3% sales, 2.5% farming, 10.7% construction, 12.6% production (2000).
Income: Per capita income: $21,496 (2000); Median household income: $44,167 (2000); Poverty rate: 1.1% (2000).
Taxes: Total city taxes per capita: $242 (2000); City property taxes per capita: $242 (2000).
Education: High school graduation rate: 87.6% (2000); College graduation rate: 16.1% (2000).
Housing: Homeownership rate: 80.7% (2000); Median home value: $118,100 (2000); Median rent: $475 per month (2000); Median age of housing: 46 years (2000).
Transportation: Commute to work: 74.7% car, 0.0% public transportation, 6.3% walk, 19.0% work from home (2000); Travel time to work: 64.8% less than 15 minutes, 18.8% 15 to 30 minutes, 10.9% 30 to 45 minutes, 3.1% 45 to 60 minutes, 2.3% 60 minutes or more (2000)

ENTERPRISE (township). Covers a land area of 35.972 square miles and a water area of 0.051 square miles. Located at 43.72° N. Lat.; 94.92° W. Long.
Population: 204 (2000); Race: 100.0% White, 0.0% Black, 0.0% Asian, 0.0% American Indian and Alaska Native, 0.0% Hispanic of any race, 0.0% two or more races (2000); Density: 5.7 persons per square mile (2000); Age: 21.8% under 18, 26.6% over 64 (2000); Marriage status: 13.1% never married, 72.5% now married, 9.2% widowed, 5.2% divorced (2000); Foreign born: 0.5% (2000); Ancestry (includes multiple ancestries): 45.7% German, 19.7% Norwegian, 9.0% Irish, 7.4% Czech, 6.9% Swedish (2000).
Economy: Employment by occupation: 24.7% management, 15.5% professional, 22.7% services, 7.2% sales, 5.2% farming, 10.3% construction, 14.4% production (2000).
Income: Per capita income: $19,946 (2000); Median household income: $42,917 (2000); Poverty rate: 2.1% (2000).
Taxes: Total city taxes per capita: $158 (1997); City property taxes per capita: $158 (1997).
Education: High school graduation rate: 88.2% (2000); College graduation rate: 10.4% (2000).
Housing: Homeownership rate: 81.6% (2000); Median home value: $58,600 (2000); Median rent: $242 per month (2000); Median age of housing: 60+ years (2000).
Transportation: Commute to work: 72.9% car, 0.0% public transportation, 5.2% walk, 19.8% work from home (2000); Travel time to work: 39.0% less than 15 minutes, 48.1% 15 to 30 minutes, 11.7% 30 to 45 minutes, 0.0% 45 to 60 minutes, 1.3% 60 minutes or more (2000)

EWINGTON (township). Covers a land area of 35.740 square miles and a water area of 0 square miles. Located at 43.62° N. Lat.; 95.40° W. Long.
Population: 233 (2000); Race: 100.0% White, 0.0% Black, 0.0% Asian, 0.0% American Indian and Alaska Native, 0.0% Hispanic of any race, 0.0% two or more races (2000); Density: 6.5 persons per square mile (2000); Age: 19.2% under 18, 14.1% over 64 (2000); Marriage status: 19.3% never married, 69.0% now married, 3.6% widowed, 8.1% divorced (2000); Foreign born: 0.9% (2000); Ancestry (includes multiple ancestries): 66.2% German, 10.3% Dutch, 8.5% Irish, 4.7% Swedish, 3.8% United States or American (2000).
Economy: Employment by occupation: 26.1% management, 9.2% professional, 14.8% services, 21.8% sales, 4.9% farming, 5.6% construction, 17.6% production (2000).
Income: Per capita income: $19,371 (2000); Median household income: $41,458 (2000); Poverty rate: 3.9% (2000).
Taxes: Total city taxes per capita: $93 (1997); City property taxes per capita: $93 (1997).
Education: High school graduation rate: 89.0% (2000); College graduation rate: 9.9% (2000).
Housing: Homeownership rate: 74.0% (2000); Median home value: $66,000 (2000); Median rent: $363 per month (2000); Median age of housing: 60+ years (2000).
Transportation: Commute to work: 80.4% car, 0.0% public transportation, 3.6% walk, 15.9% work from home (2000); Travel time to work: 23.3% less than 15 minutes, 47.4% 15 to 30 minutes, 21.6% 30 to 45 minutes, 3.4% 45 to 60 minutes, 4.3% 60 minutes or more (2000)

HERON LAKE (city). Covers a land area of 1.062 square miles and a water area of 0 square miles. Located at 43.79° N. Lat.; 95.32° W. Long. Elevation is 1,420 feet.
History: The town of Heron Lake was settled in 1871 when the railroad arrived. In 1873, swarms of grasshoppers appeared, the beginning of a plague that lasted until 1877. The clouds of grasshoppers were so thick that they hid the sun, and devoured every leaf, making it impossible to raise crops during those years.
Population: 768 (2000); Race: 94.0% White, 0.0% Black, 0.0% Asian, 0.0% American Indian and Alaska Native, 9.4% Hispanic of any race, 0.9% two or more races (2000); Density: 723.4 persons per square mile (2000); Age: 26.6% under 18, 23.8% over 64 (2000); Marriage status: 25.3% never married, 54.5% now married, 12.7% widowed, 7.5% divorced (2000); Foreign born: 3.9% (2000); Ancestry (includes multiple ancestries): 54.4% German, 10.7% Irish, 10.5% Norwegian, 9.8% Other groups, 4.6% United States or American (2000).
Economy: Single-family building permits issued: 0 (2001) / 6 (2000); Multi-family building permits issued: 0 (2001) / 0 (2000); Employment by occupation: 10.0% management, 16.6% professional, 19.1% services, 20.0% sales, 3.7% farming, 12.0% construction, 18.6% production (2000).

Income: Per capita income: $15,657 (2000); Median household income: $32,222 (2000); Poverty rate: 13.1% (2000).
Taxes: Total city taxes per capita: $118 (1997); City property taxes per capita: $116 (1997).
Education: High school graduation rate: 76.9% (2000); College graduation rate: 13.9% (2000).

School District(s)

Heron Lake-Okabena (KG-12)
2000 Enrollment: 369 507-793-2307
Housing: Homeownership rate: 83.3% (2000); Median home value: $33,800 (2000); Median rent: $255 per month (2000); Median age of housing: 55 years (2000).
Newspapers: Tri County News (1 x week)
Transportation: Commute to work: 91.4% car, 0.0% public transportation, 4.3% walk, 3.4% work from home (2000); Travel time to work: 35.8% less than 15 minutes, 45.9% 15 to 30 minutes, 12.7% 30 to 45 minutes, 2.4% 45 to 60 minutes, 3.3% 60 minutes or more (2000)

HERON LAKE (township). Covers a land area of 38.757 square miles and a water area of 5.139 square miles. Located at 43.71° N. Lat.; 95.18° W. Long. Elevation is 1,420 feet.
Population: 401 (2000); Race: 99.5% White, 0.0% Black, 0.0% Asian, 0.0% American Indian and Alaska Native, 0.5% Hispanic of any race, 0.5% two or more races (2000); Density: 10.3 persons per square mile (2000); Age: 26.6% under 18, 16.5% over 64 (2000); Marriage status: 22.8% never married, 70.0% now married, 3.8% widowed, 3.4% divorced (2000); Foreign born: 0.0% (2000); Ancestry (includes multiple ancestries): 62.0% German, 7.9% Norwegian, 6.9% United States or American, 4.3% English, 3.6% Irish (2000).
Economy: Grain, soybeans; livestock. Employment by occupation: 21.0% management, 17.6% professional, 14.1% services, 20.5% sales, 1.0% farming, 12.2% construction, 13.7% production (2000).
Income: Per capita income: $14,380 (2000); Median household income: $40,714 (2000); Poverty rate: 9.8% (2000).
Taxes: Total city taxes per capita: $74 (1997); City property taxes per capita: $74 (1997).
Education: High school graduation rate: 86.6% (2000); College graduation rate: 12.3% (2000).
Housing: Homeownership rate: 86.0% (2000); Median home value: $86,700 (2000); Median rent: $188 per month (2000); Median age of housing: 55 years (2000).
Transportation: Commute to work: 77.5% car, 1.0% public transportation, 2.5% walk, 19.1% work from home (2000); Travel time to work: 33.9% less than 15 minutes, 46.7% 15 to 30 minutes, 12.7% 30 to 45 minutes, 2.4% 45 to 60 minutes, 4.2% 60 minutes or more (2000)

HUNTER (township). Covers a land area of 35.698 square miles and a water area of 0.063 square miles. Located at 43.62° N. Lat.; 95.14° W. Long.
Population: 258 (2000); Race: 98.8% White, 0.0% Black, 1.2% Asian, 0.0% American Indian and Alaska Native, 1.2% Hispanic of any race, 0.0% two or more races (2000); Density: 7.2 persons per square mile (2000); Age: 25.7% under 18, 24.1% over 64 (2000); Marriage status: 22.8% never married, 67.8% now married, 4.0% widowed, 5.4% divorced (2000); Foreign born: 1.2% (2000); Ancestry (includes multiple ancestries): 51.8% German, 15.0% Norwegian, 10.7% Czech, 5.1% Irish, 3.6% Dutch (2000).
Economy: Employment by occupation: 22.0% management, 16.7% professional, 12.1% services, 16.7% sales, 2.3% farming, 7.6% construction, 22.7% production (2000).
Income: Per capita income: $18,729 (2000); Median household income: $41,786 (2000); Poverty rate: 3.2% (2000).
Taxes: Total city taxes per capita: $144 (1997); City property taxes per capita: $144 (1997).
Education: High school graduation rate: 90.6% (2000); College graduation rate: 11.6% (2000).
Housing: Homeownership rate: 92.3% (2000); Median home value: $58,800 (2000); Median rent: $225 per month (2000); Median age of housing: 56 years (2000).
Transportation: Commute to work: 83.3% car, 0.0% public transportation, 3.0% walk, 13.6% work from home (2000); Travel time to work: 27.2% less than 15 minutes, 64.9% 15 to 30 minutes, 7.9% 30 to 45 minutes, 0.0% 45 to 60 minutes, 0.0% 60 minutes or more (2000)

JACKSON (city). Covers a land area of 3.798 square miles and a water area of 0.208 square miles. Located at 43.62° N. Lat.; 94.99° W. Long. Elevation is 1,485 feet.
History: The first tow mill in Minnesota opened in Jackson in 1861, producing tow rope made from flax grown in the surrounding area.
Population: 3,501 (2000); Race: 93.6% White, 0.4% Black, 5.1% Asian, 0.3% American Indian and Alaska Native, 0.7% Hispanic of any race, 0.0% two or more races (2000); Density: 921.7 persons per square mile (2000); Age: 23.5% under 18, 22.5% over 64 (2000); Marriage status: 22.4% never married, 56.3% now married, 12.5% widowed, 8.8% divorced (2000); Foreign born: 3.0% (2000); Ancestry (includes multiple ancestries): 40.5% German, 16.3% Norwegian, 7.8% English, 7.7% Other groups, 7.4% Czech (2000).
Economy: Single-family building permits issued: 2 (2001) / 1 (2000); Multi-family building permits issued: 2 (2001) / 0 (2000); Employment by occupation: 11.9% management, 11.9% professional, 18.4% services, 28.7% sales, 1.5% farming, 9.1% construction, 18.5% production (2000).
Income: Per capita income: $18,444 (2000); Median household income: $33,452 (2000); Poverty rate: 11.1% (2000).
Taxes: Total city taxes per capita: $194 (1997); City property taxes per capita: $187 (1997).
Education: High school graduation rate: 81.4% (2000); College graduation rate: 16.5% (2000).

School District(s)

Jackson County Central (PK-12)
2000 Enrollment: 1,343 507-847-3608
Jackson County Central (N -N)
2000 Enrollment: n/a 507-847-3608
Housing: Homeownership rate: 71.0% (2000); Median home value: $61,000 (2000); Median rent: $291 per month (2000); Median age of housing: 43 years (2000).
Hospitals: Jackson Medical Center (20 beds)
Safety: Violent crime rate: 31.1 per 10,000 population; Property crime rate: 375.8 per 10,000 population (2001).
Newspapers: Livewire (1 x week); Jackson County Pilot (1 x week)
Transportation: Commute to work: 93.2% car, 0.8% public transportation, 3.0% walk, 2.8% work from home (2000); Travel time to work: 78.6% less than 15 minutes, 11.1% 15 to 30 minutes, 7.1% 30 to 45 minutes, 1.4% 45 to 60 minutes, 1.8% 60 minutes or more (2000)
Additional Information Contacts
Jackson Chamber of Commerce 507-847-3867

KIMBALL (township). Covers a land area of 35.933 square miles and a water area of 0.039 square miles. Located at 43.80° N. Lat.; 94.91° W. Long.
Population: 158 (2000); Race: 98.6% White, 0.0% Black, 0.0% Asian, 1.4% American Indian and Alaska Native, 1.4% Hispanic of any race, 0.0% two or more races (2000); Density: 4.4 persons per square mile (2000); Age: 26.8% under 18, 21.1% over 64 (2000); Marriage status: 14.4% never married, 73.9% now married, 7.2% widowed, 4.5% divorced (2000); Foreign born: 0.0% (2000); Ancestry (includes multiple ancestries): 51.4% German, 27.5% Norwegian, 9.9% English, 9.2% Swedish, 9.2% Irish (2000).
Economy: Employment by occupation: 30.5% management, 16.9% professional, 8.5% services, 15.3% sales, 3.4% farming, 3.4% construction, 22.0% production (2000).
Income: Per capita income: $20,358 (2000); Median household income: $45,938 (2000); Poverty rate: 5.7% (2000).
Taxes: Total city taxes per capita: $197 (1997); City property taxes per capita: $197 (1997).
Education: High school graduation rate: 79.6% (2000); College graduation rate: 8.6% (2000).
Housing: Homeownership rate: 80.8% (2000); Median home value: $85,000 (2000); Median rent: $125 per month (2000); Median age of housing: 60+ years (2000).
Transportation: Commute to work: 64.9% car, 0.0% public transportation, 0.0% walk, 35.1% work from home (2000); Travel time to work: 16.2% less than 15 minutes, 73.0% 15 to 30 minutes, 8.1% 30 to 45 minutes, 0.0% 45 to 60 minutes, 2.7% 60 minutes or more (2000)

LA CROSSE (township). Covers a land area of 34.867 square miles and a water area of 0.074 square miles. Located at 43.79° N. Lat.; 95.39° W. Long.
Population: 180 (2000); Race: 100.0% White, 0.0% Black, 0.0% Asian, 0.0% American Indian and Alaska Native, 0.0% Hispanic of any race, 0.0% two or more races (2000); Density: 5.2 persons per square mile (2000); Age: 22.8% under 18, 18.3% over 64 (2000); Marriage status: 29.7% never married, 68.0% now married, 0.0% widowed, 2.3% divorced (2000); Foreign born: 0.0% (2000); Ancestry (includes multiple ancestries): 56.9% German, 11.4% Norwegian, 9.4% United States or American, 5.4% Irish, 4.5% Austrian (2000).

Economy: Employment by occupation: 38.9% management, 18.5% professional, 9.3% services, 16.7% sales, 3.7% farming, 3.7% construction, 9.3% production (2000).
Income: Per capita income: $15,851 (2000); Median household income: $40,000 (2000); Poverty rate: 6.4% (2000).
Taxes: Total city taxes per capita: $136 (1997); City property taxes per capita: $136 (1997).
Education: High school graduation rate: 93.1% (2000); College graduation rate: 7.7% (2000).
Housing: Homeownership rate: 83.6% (2000); Median home value: $82,500 (2000); Median rent: $213 per month (2000); Median age of housing: 59 years (2000).
Transportation: Commute to work: 69.4% car, 0.0% public transportation, 1.9% walk, 28.7% work from home (2000); Travel time to work: 50.6% less than 15 minutes, 27.3% 15 to 30 minutes, 22.1% 30 to 45 minutes, 0.0% 45 to 60 minutes, 0.0% 60 minutes or more (2000)

LAKEFIELD (city). Covers a land area of 1.068 square miles and a water area of 0 square miles. Located at 43.67° N. Lat.; 95.17° W. Long. Elevation is 1,476 feet.
History: Settled 1879; incorporated 1887.
Population: 1,721 (2000); Race: 99.6% White, 0.0% Black, 0.0% Asian, 0.2% American Indian and Alaska Native, 1.1% Hispanic of any race, 0.0% two or more races (2000); Density: 1,611.0 persons per square mile (2000); Age: 22.7% under 18, 26.3% over 64 (2000); Marriage status: 20.7% never married, 58.6% now married, 13.6% widowed, 7.1% divorced (2000); Foreign born: 0.5% (2000); Ancestry (includes multiple ancestries): 56.6% German, 16.5% Norwegian, 4.7% English, 4.6% Irish, 4.0% Swedish (2000).
Economy: Agriculture trading point: grain; livestock). Manufacturing: gas fireplaces. Single-family building permits issued: 5 (2001) / 0 (2000); Multi-family building permits issued: 0 (2001) / 0 (2000); Employment by occupation: 12.6% management, 16.8% professional, 15.6% services, 22.4% sales, 2.3% farming, 9.9% construction, 20.4% production (2000).
Income: Per capita income: $16,003 (2000); Median household income: $31,250 (2000); Poverty rate: 9.0% (2000).
Taxes: Total city taxes per capita: $133 (1997); City property taxes per capita: $128 (1997).
Education: High school graduation rate: 80.0% (2000); College graduation rate: 12.4% (2000).
Housing: Homeownership rate: 84.2% (2000); Median home value: $44,600 (2000); Median rent: $248 per month (2000); Median age of housing: 54 years (2000).
Safety: Violent crime rate: 5.8 per 10,000 population; Property crime rate: 34.5 per 10,000 population (2001).
Newspapers: Lakefield Standard (1 x week)
Transportation: Commute to work: 89.9% car, 0.0% public transportation, 5.2% walk, 2.5% work from home (2000); Travel time to work: 49.1% less than 15 minutes, 37.2% 15 to 30 minutes, 7.7% 30 to 45 minutes, 2.1% 45 to 60 minutes, 3.9% 60 minutes or more (2000)

MIDDLETOWN (township). Covers a land area of 35.747 square miles and a water area of 0.464 square miles. Located at 43.54° N. Lat.; 95.04° W. Long.
Population: 243 (2000); Race: 99.6% White, 0.0% Black, 0.0% Asian, 0.0% American Indian and Alaska Native, 1.3% Hispanic of any race, 0.0% two or more races (2000); Density: 6.8 persons per square mile (2000); Age: 16.1% under 18, 19.6% over 64 (2000); Marriage status: 23.6% never married, 66.0% now married, 6.9% widowed, 3.4% divorced (2000); Foreign born: 0.0% (2000); Ancestry (includes multiple ancestries): 50.4% German, 19.6% Czech, 11.6% Norwegian, 7.1% United States or American, 5.4% English (2000).
Economy: Employment by occupation: 33.1% management, 5.9% professional, 11.0% services, 24.3% sales, 5.9% farming, 12.5% construction, 7.4% production (2000).
Income: Per capita income: $20,394 (2000); Median household income: $39,219 (2000); Poverty rate: 9.8% (2000).
Taxes: Total city taxes per capita: $222 (1997); City property taxes per capita: $222 (1997).
Education: High school graduation rate: 88.6% (2000); College graduation rate: 8.4% (2000).
Housing: Homeownership rate: 79.2% (2000); Median home value: $67,500 (2000); Median rent: $284 per month (2000); Median age of housing: 51 years (2000).
Transportation: Commute to work: 72.2% car, 3.8% public transportation, 2.3% walk, 21.8% work from home (2000); Travel time to work: 45.2% less than 15 minutes, 44.2% 15 to 30 minutes, 6.7% 30 to 45 minutes, 0.0% 45 to 60 minutes, 3.8% 60 minutes or more (2000)

MINNEOTA (township). Covers a land area of 33.586 square miles and a water area of 2.639 square miles. Located at 43.53° N. Lat.; 95.14° W. Long.
Population: 285 (2000); Race: 100.0% White, 0.0% Black, 0.0% Asian, 0.0% American Indian and Alaska Native, 0.0% Hispanic of any race, 0.0% two or more races (2000); Density: 8.5 persons per square mile (2000); Age: 30.1% under 18, 10.0% over 64 (2000); Marriage status: 15.9% never married, 74.0% now married, 2.6% widowed, 7.5% divorced (2000); Foreign born: 0.0% (2000); Ancestry (includes multiple ancestries): 52.8% German, 9.4% Czech, 7.0% English, 6.7% Norwegian, 6.4% Dutch (2000).
Economy: Employment by occupation: 21.9% management, 9.9% professional, 12.6% services, 20.5% sales, 5.3% farming, 16.6% construction, 13.2% production (2000).
Income: Per capita income: $15,071 (2000); Median household income: $42,969 (2000); Poverty rate: 9.1% (2000).
Taxes: Total city taxes per capita: $93 (1997); City property taxes per capita: $93 (1997).
Education: High school graduation rate: 87.3% (2000); College graduation rate: 5.4% (2000).
Housing: Homeownership rate: 81.4% (2000); Median home value: $107,100 (2000); Median rent: $308 per month (2000); Median age of housing: 48 years (2000).
Transportation: Commute to work: 74.7% car, 0.0% public transportation, 0.0% walk, 25.3% work from home (2000); Travel time to work: 11.6% less than 15 minutes, 77.7% 15 to 30 minutes, 8.9% 30 to 45 minutes, 1.8% 45 to 60 minutes, 0.0% 60 minutes or more (2000)

OKABENA (city). Covers a land area of 0.207 square miles and a water area of 0 square miles. Located at 43.74° N. Lat.; 95.31° W. Long. Elevation is 1,424 feet.
Population: 185 (2000); Race: 100.0% White, 0.0% Black, 0.0% Asian, 0.0% American Indian and Alaska Native, 3.5% Hispanic of any race, 0.0% two or more races (2000); Density: 893.3 persons per square mile (2000); Age: 29.8% under 18, 17.2% over 64 (2000); Marriage status: 26.3% never married, 57.7% now married, 7.7% widowed, 8.3% divorced (2000); Foreign born: 3.5% (2000); Ancestry (includes multiple ancestries): 56.1% German, 9.1% Norwegian, 8.6% Irish, 6.1% English, 6.1% Welsh (2000).
Economy: Grain; livestock. Single-family building permits issued: 0 (2001) / 0 (2000); Multi-family building permits issued: 0 (2001) / 0 (2000); Employment by occupation: 15.1% management, 12.9% professional, 12.9% services, 20.4% sales, 2.2% farming, 11.8% construction, 24.7% production (2000).
Income: Per capita income: $14,332 (2000); Median household income: $32,188 (2000); Poverty rate: 1.5% (2000).
Taxes: Total city taxes per capita: $170 (1997); City property taxes per capita: $170 (1997).
Education: High school graduation rate: 87.7% (2000); College graduation rate: 10.7% (2000).
Housing: Homeownership rate: 97.4% (2000); Median home value: $27,300 (2000); Median age of housing: 60+ years (2000).
Transportation: Commute to work: 77.3% car, 0.0% public transportation, 18.2% walk, 2.3% work from home (2000); Travel time to work: 39.5% less than 15 minutes, 25.6% 15 to 30 minutes, 27.9% 30 to 45 minutes, 0.0% 45 to 60 minutes, 7.0% 60 minutes or more (2000)

PETERSBURG (township). Covers a land area of 36.088 square miles and a water area of 0.029 square miles. Located at 43.55° N. Lat.; 94.90° W. Long. Elevation is 1,300 feet.
Population: 269 (2000); Race: 99.3% White, 0.0% Black, 0.7% Asian, 0.0% American Indian and Alaska Native, 0.0% Hispanic of any race, 0.0% two or more races (2000); Density: 7.5 persons per square mile (2000); Age: 25.5% under 18, 14.6% over 64 (2000); Marriage status: 21.2% never married, 71.7% now married, 1.9% widowed, 5.2% divorced (2000); Foreign born: 0.7% (2000); Ancestry (includes multiple ancestries): 51.7% German, 16.5% Norwegian, 12.0% United States or American, 9.4% English, 8.6% Irish (2000).
Economy: Employment by occupation: 20.1% management, 9.7% professional, 6.9% services, 27.1% sales, 2.8% farming, 9.7% construction, 23.6% production (2000).
Income: Per capita income: $16,799 (2000); Median household income: $44,688 (2000); Poverty rate: 6.4% (2000).
Taxes: Total city taxes per capita: $117 (1997); City property taxes per capita: $117 (1997).

Education: High school graduation rate: 93.4% (2000); College graduation rate: 8.8% (2000).
Housing: Homeownership rate: 82.4% (2000); Median home value: $75,000 (2000); Median rent: $233 per month (2000); Median age of housing: 60+ years (2000).
Transportation: Commute to work: 87.5% car, 0.0% public transportation, 4.2% walk, 6.9% work from home (2000); Travel time to work: 38.8% less than 15 minutes, 53.7% 15 to 30 minutes, 1.5% 30 to 45 minutes, 3.0% 45 to 60 minutes, 3.0% 60 minutes or more (2000)

ROST (township). Covers a land area of 36.092 square miles and a water area of 0 square miles. Located at 43.61° N. Lat.; 95.28° W. Long. Elevation is 1,441 feet.
Population: 250 (2000); Race: 99.1% White, 0.0% Black, 0.9% Asian, 0.0% American Indian and Alaska Native, 0.0% Hispanic of any race, 0.0% two or more races (2000); Density: 6.9 persons per square mile (2000); Age: 25.3% under 18, 24.0% over 64 (2000); Marriage status: 9.4% never married, 87.1% now married, 2.4% widowed, 1.2% divorced (2000); Foreign born: 0.9% (2000); Ancestry (includes multiple ancestries): 60.2% German, 18.1% Norwegian, 5.0% Dutch, 4.1% English, 3.2% United States or American (2000).
Economy: Employment by occupation: 27.4% management, 20.4% professional, 16.8% services, 17.7% sales, 3.5% farming, 9.7% construction, 4.4% production (2000).
Income: Per capita income: $16,820 (2000); Median household income: $43,056 (2000); Poverty rate: 3.2% (2000).
Taxes: Total city taxes per capita: $161 (1997); City property taxes per capita: $161 (1997).
Education: High school graduation rate: 87.9% (2000); College graduation rate: 17.2% (2000).
Housing: Homeownership rate: 78.6% (2000); Median home value: $68,800 (2000); Median rent: $263 per month (2000); Median age of housing: 60+ years (2000).
Transportation: Commute to work: 78.0% car, 0.0% public transportation, 0.0% walk, 22.0% work from home (2000); Travel time to work: 35.3% less than 15 minutes, 40.0% 15 to 30 minutes, 24.7% 30 to 45 minutes, 0.0% 45 to 60 minutes, 0.0% 60 minutes or more (2000)

ROUND LAKE (township). Covers a land area of 33.795 square miles and a water area of 2.028 square miles. Located at 43.53° N. Lat.; 95.38° W. Long.
Population: 202 (2000); Race: 100.0% White, 0.0% Black, 0.0% Asian, 0.0% American Indian and Alaska Native, 0.0% Hispanic of any race, 0.0% two or more races (2000); Density: 6.0 persons per square mile (2000); Age: 30.3% under 18, 8.1% over 64 (2000); Marriage status: 10.9% never married, 83.3% now married, 1.9% widowed, 3.8% divorced (2000); Foreign born: 0.0% (2000); Ancestry (includes multiple ancestries): 68.7% German, 13.3% Norwegian, 6.2% English, 5.2% Irish, 3.8% Dutch (2000).
Economy: Employment by occupation: 32.8% management, 9.5% professional, 11.2% services, 18.1% sales, 0.0% farming, 10.3% construction, 18.1% production (2000).
Income: Per capita income: $18,982 (2000); Median household income: $33,438 (2000); Poverty rate: 11.8% (2000).
Taxes: Total city taxes per capita: $184 (1997); City property taxes per capita: $184 (1997).
Education: High school graduation rate: 89.4% (2000); College graduation rate: 12.0% (2000).
Housing: Homeownership rate: 72.8% (2000); Median home value: $99,200 (2000); Median rent: $117 per month (2000); Median age of housing: 57 years (2000).
Transportation: Commute to work: 71.6% car, 0.0% public transportation, 1.7% walk, 26.7% work from home (2000); Travel time to work: 37.6% less than 15 minutes, 28.2% 15 to 30 minutes, 29.4% 30 to 45 minutes, 4.7% 45 to 60 minutes, 0.0% 60 minutes or more (2000)

SIOUX VALLEY (township). Covers a land area of 35.684 square miles and a water area of 0.514 square miles. Located at 43.54° N. Lat.; 95.26° W. Long. Elevation is 1,474 feet.
Population: 270 (2000); Race: 100.0% White, 0.0% Black, 0.0% Asian, 0.0% American Indian and Alaska Native, 2.8% Hispanic of any race, 0.0% two or more races (2000); Density: 7.6 persons per square mile (2000); Age: 31.0% under 18, 13.4% over 64 (2000); Marriage status: 18.0% never married, 81.0% now married, 0.9% widowed, 0.0% divorced (2000); Foreign born: 0.0% (2000); Ancestry (includes multiple ancestries): 78.9% German, 10.9% Norwegian, 10.6% Irish, 5.3% Dutch, 4.6% Danish (2000).
Economy: Employment by occupation: 24.7% management, 17.3% professional, 4.7% services, 32.7% sales, 2.0% farming, 4.0% construction, 14.7% production (2000).
Income: Per capita income: $16,462 (2000); Median household income: $50,313 (2000); Poverty rate: 15.5% (2000).
Taxes: Total city taxes per capita: $97 (1997); City property taxes per capita: $97 (1997).
Education: High school graduation rate: 96.2% (2000); College graduation rate: 20.9% (2000).
Housing: Homeownership rate: 76.3% (2000); Median home value: $84,200 (2000); Median rent: $225 per month (2000); Median age of housing: 60+ years (2000).
Transportation: Commute to work: 76.7% car, 0.0% public transportation, 8.7% walk, 14.7% work from home (2000); Travel time to work: 25.0% less than 15 minutes, 54.7% 15 to 30 minutes, 14.1% 30 to 45 minutes, 3.9% 45 to 60 minutes, 2.3% 60 minutes or more (2000)

WEIMER (township). Covers a land area of 30.604 square miles and a water area of 4.305 square miles. Located at 43.80° N. Lat.; 95.28° W. Long.
Population: 172 (2000); Race: 100.0% White, 0.0% Black, 0.0% Asian, 0.0% American Indian and Alaska Native, 0.0% Hispanic of any race, 0.0% two or more races (2000); Density: 5.6 persons per square mile (2000); Age: 26.6% under 18, 15.6% over 64 (2000); Marriage status: 20.1% never married, 69.4% now married, 5.6% widowed, 4.9% divorced (2000); Foreign born: 0.0% (2000); Ancestry (includes multiple ancestries): 69.4% German, 30.6% Norwegian, 9.2% Irish, 5.2% Danish, 4.6% Other groups (2000).
Economy: Employment by occupation: 17.9% management, 15.4% professional, 7.7% services, 30.8% sales, 2.6% farming, 5.1% construction, 20.5% production (2000).
Income: Per capita income: $16,587 (2000); Median household income: $31,667 (2000); Poverty rate: 4.1% (2000).
Taxes: Total city taxes per capita: $152 (1997); City property taxes per capita: $152 (1997).
Education: High school graduation rate: 92.6% (2000); College graduation rate: 14.8% (2000).
Housing: Homeownership rate: 75.0% (2000); Median home value: $46,400 (2000); Median rent: $325 per month (2000); Median age of housing: 57 years (2000).
Transportation: Commute to work: 78.2% car, 0.0% public transportation, 0.0% walk, 17.9% work from home (2000); Travel time to work: 43.8% less than 15 minutes, 35.9% 15 to 30 minutes, 12.5% 30 to 45 minutes, 0.0% 45 to 60 minutes, 7.8% 60 minutes or more (2000)

WEST HERON LAKE (township). Covers a land area of 27.384 square miles and a water area of 0.109 square miles. Located at 43.72° N. Lat.; 95.28° W. Long.
Population: 202 (2000); Race: 100.0% White, 0.0% Black, 0.0% Asian, 0.0% American Indian and Alaska Native, 1.5% Hispanic of any race, 0.0% two or more races (2000); Density: 7.4 persons per square mile (2000); Age: 33.7% under 18, 10.9% over 64 (2000); Marriage status: 19.0% never married, 77.6% now married, 2.0% widowed, 1.4% divorced (2000); Foreign born: 1.0% (2000); Ancestry (includes multiple ancestries): 67.3% German, 14.4% Norwegian, 12.4% Swedish, 11.4% United States or American, 6.9% Irish (2000).
Economy: Employment by occupation: 30.8% management, 15.0% professional, 11.2% services, 22.4% sales, 3.7% farming, 8.4% construction, 8.4% production (2000).
Income: Per capita income: $14,897 (2000); Median household income: $41,250 (2000); Poverty rate: 0.0% (2000).
Taxes: Total city taxes per capita: $114 (2000); City property taxes per capita: $114 (2000).
Education: High school graduation rate: 92.6% (2000); College graduation rate: 23.1% (2000).
Housing: Homeownership rate: 80.6% (2000); Median home value: $80,800 (2000); Median age of housing: 60+ years (2000).
Transportation: Commute to work: 78.5% car, 0.0% public transportation, 0.0% walk, 21.5% work from home (2000); Travel time to work: 45.2% less than 15 minutes, 29.8% 15 to 30 minutes, 25.0% 30 to 45 minutes, 0.0% 45 to 60 minutes, 0.0% 60 minutes or more (2000)

WILDER (city). Covers a land area of 0.793 square miles and a water area of 0.007 square miles. Located at 43.82° N. Lat.; 95.19° W. Long. Elevation is 1,454 feet.
Population: 69 (2000); Race: 100.0% White, 0.0% Black, 0.0% Asian, 0.0% American Indian and Alaska Native, 0.0% Hispanic of any race, 0.0% two or more races (2000); Density: 87.0 persons per square mile (2000); Age: 20.4%

under 18, 6.5% over 64 (2000); Marriage status: 35.7% never married, 47.6% now married, 2.4% widowed, 14.3% divorced (2000); Foreign born: 0.0% (2000); Ancestry (includes multiple ancestries): 40.9% German, 25.8% Norwegian, 9.7% Swedish, 8.6% Irish, 8.6% United States or American (2000).
Economy: Grain; livestock area. Single-family building permits issued: 0 (2001) / 0 (2000); Multi-family building permits issued: 0 (2001) / 0 (2000); Employment by occupation: 8.8% management, 7.0% professional, 24.6% services, 21.1% sales, 5.3% farming, 10.5% construction, 22.8% production (2000).
Income: Per capita income: $14,222 (2000); Median household income: $41,875 (2000); Poverty rate: 11.8% (2000).
Taxes: Total city taxes per capita: $85 (1997); City property taxes per capita: $61 (1997).
Education: High school graduation rate: 82.5% (2000); College graduation rate: 3.5% (2000).
Housing: Homeownership rate: 100.0% (2000); Median home value: $36,300 (2000); Median age of housing: 60+ years (2000).
Transportation: Commute to work: 86.0% car, 0.0% public transportation, 0.0% walk, 5.3% work from home (2000); Travel time to work: 48.1% less than 15 minutes, 33.3% 15 to 30 minutes, 3.7% 30 to 45 minutes, 3.7% 45 to 60 minutes, 11.1% 60 minutes or more (2000)

WISCONSIN (township). Covers a land area of 35.526 square miles and a water area of 0 square miles. Located at 43.63° N. Lat.; 94.90° W. Long.
Population: 263 (2000); Race: 99.3% White, 0.0% Black, 0.0% Asian, 0.0% American Indian and Alaska Native, 1.4% Hispanic of any race, 0.7% two or more races (2000); Density: 7.4 persons per square mile (2000); Age: 27.1% under 18, 17.7% over 64 (2000); Marriage status: 13.2% never married, 78.3% now married, 0.0% widowed, 8.5% divorced (2000); Foreign born: 0.0% (2000); Ancestry (includes multiple ancestries): 45.8% German, 17.0% Norwegian, 10.5% English, 8.3% Danish, 7.6% Irish (2000).
Economy: Employment by occupation: 14.8% management, 22.5% professional, 14.8% services, 25.4% sales, 2.8% farming, 9.9% construction, 9.9% production (2000).
Income: Per capita income: $16,996 (2000); Median household income: $46,607 (2000); Poverty rate: 1.4% (2000).
Taxes: Total city taxes per capita: $102 (1997); City property taxes per capita: $102 (1997).
Education: High school graduation rate: 81.5% (2000); College graduation rate: 25.6% (2000).
Housing: Homeownership rate: 79.6% (2000); Median home value: $59,400 (2000); Median rent: $213 per month (2000); Median age of housing: 60+ years (2000).
Transportation: Commute to work: 90.1% car, 0.0% public transportation, 0.0% walk, 9.9% work from home (2000); Travel time to work: 57.5% less than 15 minutes, 24.4% 15 to 30 minutes, 15.7% 30 to 45 minutes, 0.8% 45 to 60 minutes, 1.6% 60 minutes or more (2000)

Kanabec County

Located in eastern Minnesota; drained by the Snake River. Covers a land area of 524.90 square miles, a water area of 8.50 square miles, and is located in the Central Time Zone. The county government was organized in 1858. County seat is Mora.

Weather Station: Mora — Elevation: 1,003 feet

	Jan	Feb	Mar	Apr	May	Jun	Jul	Aug	Sep	Oct	Nov	Dec
High	20	28	39	56	70	78	82	80	70	57	39	25
Low	-6	3	16	30	42	50	55	53	43	32	19	3
Precip	0.8	0.6	1.7	2.2	3.2	3.9	4.0	3.9	3.1	2.6	1.8	0.8
Snow	11.3	6.5	8.0	1.8	tr	0.0	0.0	0.0	0.0	0.3	7.2	8.1

High and Low temperatures in degrees Fahrenheit; Precipitation and Snow in inches

Population: 14,996 (2000); Race: 97.8% White, 0.1% Black, 0.3% Asian, 0.6% American Indian and Alaska Native, 0.8% Hispanic of any race, 1.0% two or more races (2000); Density: 28.6 persons per square mile (2000); Age: 27.5% under 18, 14.1% over 64 (2000).
Religion: Five largest groups: 18.0% Evangelical Lutheran Church in America, 10.6% Lutheran Church—Missouri Synod, 8.3% Catholic Church, 3.2% Baptist General Conference, 2.6% The United Methodist Church (2000).
Economy: Unemployment rate: 7.6% (11/2002); Total civilian labor force: 6,497 (11/2002); Leading industries: 20.8% manufacturing; 19.5% health care and social assistance; 18.9% retail trade (2000); Companies that employ more than 1,000 persons: 0 (2000); Companies that employ more than 100 persons: 7 (2000); Farms: 626 totaling 138,850 acres (1997); Minority business ownership rate: 0.0% (1997); Women business ownership rate: 28.7% (1997); Retail sales per capita: $8,156 (1997). Single-family building permits issued: 70 (2001) / 83 (2000); Multi-family building permits issued: 30 (2001) / 2 (2000).
Income: Per capita income: $17,741 (2000); Median household income: $38,520 (2000); Poverty rate: 9.5% (2000); Bankruptcy rate: 4.39% (2001).
Taxes: Total county taxes per capita: $290 (2000); County property taxes per capita: $287 (2000).
Education: High school graduation rate: 80.6% (2000); College graduation rate: 10.5% (2000).
Housing: Homeownership rate: 84.0% (2000); Median home value: $90,400 (2000); Median rent: $377 per month (2000); Median age of housing: 27 years (2000).
Health: Birth rate: 111.4 per 10,000 population (1998); Age adjusted death rate: 94.9 per 10,000 population (1999); Age adjusted cancer mortality rate: 229.4 deaths per 100,000 population (1999). Number of physicians: 8.7 per 10,000 population (1999); Number of hospital beds: 20.7 per 10,000 population (1999).
Elections: 2000 Presidential election results: 41.6% Gore, 51.1% Bush, 5.1% Nader, 1.6% Buchanan
National and State Parks: Ann Lake State Wildlife Management Area; Bean Dam State Wildlife Management Area; Hay-Snake State Wildlife Management Area; Lake Five State Wildlife Management Area; Rice Creek State Wildlife Management Area; Snake River State Forest; Tosher Creek State Wildlife Management Area; Whited State Wildlife Management Area
Additional Information Contacts
Kanabec County Government Offices 320-679-6440
Eastern Minnesota Association of Realtors 320-679-0392
Mora Area Chamber of Commerce 320-679-5792

Kanabec County Communities

ANN LAKE (township). Covers a land area of 31.572 square miles and a water area of 0.849 square miles. Located at 45.93° N. Lat.; 93.42° W. Long.
Population: 377 (2000); Race: 98.5% White, 0.0% Black, 0.0% Asian, 0.0% American Indian and Alaska Native, 0.0% Hispanic of any race, 1.5% two or more races (2000); Density: 11.9 persons per square mile (2000); Age: 26.8% under 18, 12.5% over 64 (2000); Marriage status: 24.6% never married, 58.5% now married, 6.8% widowed, 10.2% divorced (2000); Foreign born: 0.0% (2000); Ancestry (includes multiple ancestries): 44.1% German, 16.8% Norwegian, 12.0% Swedish, 10.5% Irish, 8.8% English (2000).
Economy: Employment by occupation: 4.7% management, 10.9% professional, 11.5% services, 22.4% sales, 2.6% farming, 19.8% construction, 28.1% production (2000).
Income: Per capita income: $18,318 (2000); Median household income: $45,313 (2000); Poverty rate: 8.4% (2000).
Taxes: Total city taxes per capita: $62 (1997); City property taxes per capita: $62 (1997).
Education: High school graduation rate: 79.0% (2000); College graduation rate: 6.6% (2000).
Housing: Homeownership rate: 94.0% (2000); Median home value: $90,800 (2000); Median rent: $350 per month (2000); Median age of housing: 27 years (2000).
Transportation: Commute to work: 92.6% car, 0.0% public transportation, 1.6% walk, 4.2% work from home (2000); Travel time to work: 19.2% less than 15 minutes, 31.9% 15 to 30 minutes, 13.7% 30 to 45 minutes, 4.9% 45 to 60 minutes, 30.2% 60 minutes or more (2000)

ARTHUR (township). Covers a land area of 30.311 square miles and a water area of 0.988 square miles. Located at 45.84° N. Lat.; 93.32° W. Long.
Population: 1,905 (2000); Race: 96.3% White, 0.5% Black, 0.3% Asian, 1.0% American Indian and Alaska Native, 0.6% Hispanic of any race, 1.5% two or more races (2000); Density: 62.8 persons per square mile (2000); Age: 30.9% under 18, 10.3% over 64 (2000); Marriage status: 23.8% never married, 62.1% now married, 3.9% widowed, 10.2% divorced (2000); Foreign born: 0.8% (2000); Ancestry (includes multiple ancestries): 34.0% German, 23.8% Swedish, 15.6% Norwegian, 8.0% Irish, 5.5% English (2000).
Economy: Single-family building permits issued: 14 (2001) / 16 (2000); Multi-family building permits issued: 0 (2001) / 0 (2000); Employment by occupation: 9.5% management, 17.1% professional, 13.1% services, 26.6% sales, 1.2% farming, 12.1% construction, 20.4% production (2000).
Income: Per capita income: $18,506 (2000); Median household income: $44,485 (2000); Poverty rate: 5.9% (2000).

Taxes: Total city taxes per capita: $40 (1997); City property taxes per capita: $31 (1997).
Education: High school graduation rate: 86.3% (2000); College graduation rate: 15.6% (2000).
Housing: Homeownership rate: 85.0% (2000); Median home value: $107,700 (2000); Median rent: $429 per month (2000); Median age of housing: 25 years (2000).
Transportation: Commute to work: 95.5% car, 0.0% public transportation, 1.9% walk, 2.1% work from home (2000); Travel time to work: 48.2% less than 15 minutes, 16.4% 15 to 30 minutes, 14.4% 30 to 45 minutes, 4.9% 45 to 60 minutes, 16.0% 60 minutes or more (2000)

BRUNSWICK (township). Covers a land area of 34.632 square miles and a water area of 0.741 square miles. Located at 45.77° N. Lat.; 93.31° W. Long. Elevation is 962 feet.
Population: 1,263 (2000); Race: 98.6% White, 0.1% Black, 0.3% Asian, 0.9% American Indian and Alaska Native, 1.7% Hispanic of any race, 0.1% two or more races (2000); Density: 36.5 persons per square mile (2000); Age: 30.6% under 18, 10.5% over 64 (2000); Marriage status: 21.1% never married, 68.1% now married, 3.0% widowed, 7.8% divorced (2000); Foreign born: 0.9% (2000); Ancestry (includes multiple ancestries): 35.9% German, 25.4% Swedish, 15.1% Norwegian, 11.7% Irish, 6.5% English (2000).
Economy: Single-family building permits issued: 7 (2001) / 9 (2000); Multi-family building permits issued: 0 (2001) / 0 (2000); Employment by occupation: 9.0% management, 16.2% professional, 14.4% services, 21.2% sales, 0.3% farming, 14.3% construction, 24.6% production (2000).
Income: Per capita income: $17,295 (2000); Median household income: $45,278 (2000); Poverty rate: 6.4% (2000).
Taxes: Total city taxes per capita: $28 (1997); City property taxes per capita: $28 (1997).
Education: High school graduation rate: 82.9% (2000); College graduation rate: 9.3% (2000).
Housing: Homeownership rate: 92.1% (2000); Median home value: $91,800 (2000); Median rent: $375 per month (2000); Median age of housing: 28 years (2000).
Transportation: Commute to work: 91.4% car, 0.3% public transportation, 1.0% walk, 6.9% work from home (2000); Travel time to work: 21.5% less than 15 minutes, 35.1% 15 to 30 minutes, 15.8% 30 to 45 minutes, 5.0% 45 to 60 minutes, 22.7% 60 minutes or more (2000)

COMFORT (township). Covers a land area of 35.511 square miles and a water area of 0.487 square miles. Located at 45.85° N. Lat.; 93.21° W. Long.
Population: 931 (2000); Race: 98.5% White, 0.3% Black, 0.2% Asian, 0.0% American Indian and Alaska Native, 1.8% Hispanic of any race, 1.0% two or more races (2000); Density: 26.2 persons per square mile (2000); Age: 29.5% under 18, 10.7% over 64 (2000); Marriage status: 22.8% never married, 65.5% now married, 4.1% widowed, 7.6% divorced (2000); Foreign born: 1.2% (2000); Ancestry (includes multiple ancestries): 41.0% German, 26.1% Swedish, 17.6% Norwegian, 9.4% Irish, 8.7% United States or American (2000).
Economy: Single-family building permits issued: 8 (2001) / 8 (2000); Multi-family building permits issued: 0 (2001) / 0 (2000); Employment by occupation: 12.3% management, 11.5% professional, 12.3% services, 26.8% sales, 0.0% farming, 13.7% construction, 23.5% production (2000).
Income: Per capita income: $20,268 (2000); Median household income: $36,750 (2000); Poverty rate: 10.6% (2000).
Taxes: Total city taxes per capita: $27 (1997); City property taxes per capita: $25 (1997).
Education: High school graduation rate: 86.1% (2000); College graduation rate: 14.2% (2000).
Housing: Homeownership rate: 88.1% (2000); Median home value: $98,600 (2000); Median rent: $384 per month (2000); Median age of housing: 25 years (2000).
Transportation: Commute to work: 87.3% car, 0.0% public transportation, 1.6% walk, 9.8% work from home (2000); Travel time to work: 38.8% less than 15 minutes, 33.6% 15 to 30 minutes, 11.6% 30 to 45 minutes, 3.9% 45 to 60 minutes, 12.2% 60 minutes or more (2000)

FORD (township). Covers a land area of 36.194 square miles and a water area of 0.095 square miles. Located at 46.12° N. Lat.; 93.23° W. Long.
Population: 177 (2000); Race: 91.7% White, 0.0% Black, 1.7% Asian, 0.0% American Indian and Alaska Native, 0.0% Hispanic of any race, 6.7% two or more races (2000); Density: 4.9 persons per square mile (2000); Age: 27.2% under 18, 13.3% over 64 (2000); Marriage status: 29.2% never married, 54.9% now married, 6.3% widowed, 9.7% divorced (2000); Foreign born: 1.7% (2000); Ancestry (includes multiple ancestries): 31.1% Swedish, 31.1% German, 15.0% Norwegian, 12.8% French (except Basque), 9.4% Other groups (2000).
Economy: Employment by occupation: 15.1% management, 3.5% professional, 10.5% services, 23.3% sales, 5.8% farming, 19.8% construction, 22.1% production (2000).
Income: Per capita income: $17,102 (2000); Median household income: $38,125 (2000); Poverty rate: 15.6% (2000).
Taxes: Total city taxes per capita: $65 (1997); City property taxes per capita: $65 (1997).
Education: High school graduation rate: 82.9% (2000); College graduation rate: 8.5% (2000).
Housing: Homeownership rate: 91.8% (2000); Median home value: $57,500 (2000); Median rent: $350 per month (2000); Median age of housing: 25 years (2000).
Transportation: Commute to work: 95.2% car, 0.0% public transportation, 1.2% walk, 3.6% work from home (2000); Travel time to work: 3.8% less than 15 minutes, 61.3% 15 to 30 minutes, 16.3% 30 to 45 minutes, 0.0% 45 to 60 minutes, 18.8% 60 minutes or more (2000)

GRASS LAKE (township). Covers a land area of 34.568 square miles and a water area of 0.268 square miles. Located at 45.76° N. Lat.; 93.18° W. Long.
Population: 928 (2000); Race: 98.1% White, 0.0% Black, 0.2% Asian, 0.6% American Indian and Alaska Native, 0.2% Hispanic of any race, 0.9% two or more races (2000); Density: 26.8 persons per square mile (2000); Age: 26.9% under 18, 11.2% over 64 (2000); Marriage status: 23.3% never married, 68.1% now married, 3.3% widowed, 5.2% divorced (2000); Foreign born: 0.4% (2000); Ancestry (includes multiple ancestries): 36.7% German, 29.8% Swedish, 18.2% Norwegian, 7.2% Irish, 5.0% English (2000).
Economy: Single-family building permits issued: 8 (2001) / 9 (2000); Multi-family building permits issued: 0 (2001) / 0 (2000); Employment by occupation: 9.2% management, 11.2% professional, 14.5% services, 21.9% sales, 1.0% farming, 15.1% construction, 27.1% production (2000).
Income: Per capita income: $17,110 (2000); Median household income: $39,083 (2000); Poverty rate: 5.7% (2000).
Taxes: Total city taxes per capita: $31 (1997); City property taxes per capita: $31 (1997).
Education: High school graduation rate: 80.8% (2000); College graduation rate: 7.7% (2000).
Housing: Homeownership rate: 93.5% (2000); Median home value: $98,400 (2000); Median rent: $320 per month (2000); Median age of housing: 28 years (2000).
Transportation: Commute to work: 90.7% car, 0.0% public transportation, 4.4% walk, 3.8% work from home (2000); Travel time to work: 26.8% less than 15 minutes, 33.1% 15 to 30 minutes, 14.0% 30 to 45 minutes, 6.9% 45 to 60 minutes, 19.1% 60 minutes or more (2000)

GRASSTON (city). Covers a land area of 0.950 square miles and a water area of 0 square miles. Located at 45.79° N. Lat.; 93.14° W. Long. Elevation is 966 feet.
Population: 105 (2000); Race: 97.0% White, 0.0% Black, 0.0% Asian, 3.0% American Indian and Alaska Native, 0.0% Hispanic of any race, 0.0% two or more races (2000); Density: 110.5 persons per square mile (2000); Age: 21.0% under 18, 7.0% over 64 (2000); Marriage status: 27.7% never married, 62.7% now married, 2.4% widowed, 7.2% divorced (2000); Foreign born: 0.0% (2000); Ancestry (includes multiple ancestries): 47.0% German, 28.0% Norwegian, 15.0% Swedish, 13.0% Irish, 9.0% Other groups (2000).
Economy: Dairying. Manufacturing: feeds. Single-family building permits issued: 0 (2001) / 0 (2000); Multi-family building permits issued: 0 (2001) / 0 (2000); Employment by occupation: 2.0% management, 30.6% professional, 8.2% services, 18.4% sales, 0.0% farming, 28.6% construction, 12.2% production (2000).
Income: Per capita income: $16,306 (2000); Median household income: $41,250 (2000); Poverty rate: 8.0% (2000).
Taxes: Total city taxes per capita: $74 (1997); City property taxes per capita: $74 (1997).
Education: High school graduation rate: 73.4% (2000); College graduation rate: 15.6% (2000).
Housing: Homeownership rate: 86.1% (2000); Median home value: $45,000 (2000); Median rent: $375 per month (2000); Median age of housing: 60+ years (2000).
Transportation: Commute to work: 95.7% car, 0.0% public transportation, 4.3% walk, 0.0% work from home (2000); Travel time to work: 17.0% less than 15 minutes, 29.8% 15 to 30 minutes, 8.5% 30 to 45 minutes, 23.4% 45 to 60 minutes, 21.3% 60 minutes or more (2000)

HAY BROOK (township). Covers a land area of 36.271 square miles and a water area of 0.169 square miles. Located at 46.11° N. Lat.; 93.35° W. Long.
Population: 218 (2000); Race: 98.7% White, 0.0% Black, 0.0% Asian, 0.0% American Indian and Alaska Native, 1.3% Hispanic of any race, 1.3% two or more races (2000); Density: 6.0 persons per square mile (2000); Age: 29.6% under 18, 9.0% over 64 (2000); Marriage status: 17.4% never married, 69.2% now married, 3.5% widowed, 9.9% divorced (2000); Foreign born: 0.0% (2000); Ancestry (includes multiple ancestries): 24.0% German, 16.7% Norwegian, 15.9% Swedish, 6.9% Irish, 6.4% English (2000).
Economy: Employment by occupation: 13.5% management, 10.6% professional, 17.3% services, 18.3% sales, 5.8% farming, 14.4% construction, 20.2% production (2000).
Income: Per capita income: $14,696 (2000); Median household income: $33,542 (2000); Poverty rate: 15.7% (2000).
Taxes: Total city taxes per capita: $47 (1997); City property taxes per capita: $47 (1997).
Education: High school graduation rate: 79.7% (2000); College graduation rate: 5.7% (2000).
Housing: Homeownership rate: 100.0% (2000); Median home value: $82,500 (2000); Median age of housing: 26 years (2000).
Transportation: Commute to work: 86.3% car, 0.0% public transportation, 0.0% walk, 13.7% work from home (2000); Travel time to work: 34.1% less than 15 minutes, 51.1% 15 to 30 minutes, 6.8% 30 to 45 minutes, 0.0% 45 to 60 minutes, 8.0% 60 minutes or more (2000)

HILLMAN (township). Covers a land area of 36.785 square miles and a water area of 0.154 square miles. Located at 46.01° N. Lat.; 93.37° W. Long.
Population: 384 (2000); Race: 93.2% White, 0.0% Black, 0.0% Asian, 3.3% American Indian and Alaska Native, 3.3% Hispanic of any race, 3.5% two or more races (2000); Density: 10.4 persons per square mile (2000); Age: 22.0% under 18, 18.5% over 64 (2000); Marriage status: 19.2% never married, 65.3% now married, 6.5% widowed, 9.0% divorced (2000); Foreign born: 0.5% (2000); Ancestry (includes multiple ancestries): 29.6% German, 20.5% Norwegian, 13.7% Swedish, 13.2% Other groups, 4.8% English (2000).
Economy: Employment by occupation: 7.7% management, 11.2% professional, 17.9% services, 20.4% sales, 1.5% farming, 15.3% construction, 26.0% production (2000).
Income: Per capita income: $16,715 (2000); Median household income: $39,375 (2000); Poverty rate: 12.9% (2000).
Taxes: Total city taxes per capita: $40 (1997); City property taxes per capita: $40 (1997).
Education: High school graduation rate: 74.8% (2000); College graduation rate: 9.3% (2000).
Housing: Homeownership rate: 91.9% (2000); Median home value: $64,400 (2000); Median rent: $425 per month (2000); Median age of housing: 23 years (2000).
Transportation: Commute to work: 86.6% car, 0.0% public transportation, 2.1% walk, 9.8% work from home (2000); Travel time to work: 13.7% less than 15 minutes, 51.4% 15 to 30 minutes, 9.7% 30 to 45 minutes, 5.7% 45 to 60 minutes, 19.4% 60 minutes or more (2000)

KANABEC (township). Covers a land area of 35.957 square miles and a water area of 0.361 square miles. Located at 45.85° N. Lat.; 93.45° W. Long.
Population: 853 (2000); Race: 98.7% White, 0.0% Black, 0.8% Asian, 0.0% American Indian and Alaska Native, 0.0% Hispanic of any race, 0.5% two or more races (2000); Density: 23.7 persons per square mile (2000); Age: 28.6% under 18, 8.2% over 64 (2000); Marriage status: 26.4% never married, 56.6% now married, 3.7% widowed, 13.3% divorced (2000); Foreign born: 1.1% (2000); Ancestry (includes multiple ancestries): 30.9% German, 15.1% Swedish, 9.1% Norwegian, 7.7% United States or American, 7.6% Dutch (2000).
Economy: Employment by occupation: 6.0% management, 6.9% professional, 19.4% services, 16.4% sales, 3.7% farming, 15.6% construction, 32.0% production (2000).
Income: Per capita income: $16,711 (2000); Median household income: $40,200 (2000); Poverty rate: 16.8% (2000).
Taxes: Total city taxes per capita: $98 (1997); City property taxes per capita: $98 (1997).
Education: High school graduation rate: 73.8% (2000); College graduation rate: 3.2% (2000).
Housing: Homeownership rate: 90.8% (2000); Median home value: $60,000 (2000); Median rent: $333 per month (2000); Median age of housing: 25 years (2000).
Transportation: Commute to work: 91.8% car, 0.8% public transportation, 0.0% walk, 7.4% work from home (2000); Travel time to work: 20.5% less than 15 minutes, 24.7% 15 to 30 minutes, 15.8% 30 to 45 minutes, 5.0% 45 to 60 minutes, 34.1% 60 minutes or more (2000)

KNIFE LAKE (township). Covers a land area of 30.671 square miles and a water area of 1.147 square miles. Located at 45.94° N. Lat.; 93.29° W. Long.
Population: 1,049 (2000); Race: 96.5% White, 0.0% Black, 1.0% Asian, 0.7% American Indian and Alaska Native, 0.7% Hispanic of any race, 1.8% two or more races (2000); Density: 34.2 persons per square mile (2000); Age: 27.1% under 18, 14.4% over 64 (2000); Marriage status: 19.3% never married, 65.6% now married, 5.8% widowed, 9.4% divorced (2000); Foreign born: 1.5% (2000); Ancestry (includes multiple ancestries): 35.3% German, 19.5% Swedish, 18.6% Norwegian, 8.5% Irish, 7.6% English (2000).
Economy: Single-family building permits issued: 3 (2001) / 11 (2000); Multi-family building permits issued: 0 (2001) / 0 (2000); Employment by occupation: 11.1% management, 14.9% professional, 22.4% services, 24.7% sales, 0.8% farming, 10.5% construction, 15.5% production (2000).
Income: Per capita income: $19,387 (2000); Median household income: $39,167 (2000); Poverty rate: 7.4% (2000).
Taxes: Total city taxes per capita: $40 (1997); City property taxes per capita: $38 (1997).
Education: High school graduation rate: 79.5% (2000); College graduation rate: 10.3% (2000).
Housing: Homeownership rate: 92.5% (2000); Median home value: $116,200 (2000); Median rent: $450 per month (2000); Median age of housing: 28 years (2000).
Transportation: Commute to work: 89.0% car, 1.3% public transportation, 1.1% walk, 8.0% work from home (2000); Travel time to work: 43.9% less than 15 minutes, 23.8% 15 to 30 minutes, 7.7% 30 to 45 minutes, 4.7% 45 to 60 minutes, 19.9% 60 minutes or more (2000)

KROSCHEL (township). Covers a land area of 34.876 square miles and a water area of 1.173 square miles. Located at 46.13° N. Lat.; 93.10° W. Long. Elevation is 1,110 feet.
Population: 218 (2000); Race: 99.1% White, 0.0% Black, 0.0% Asian, 0.0% American Indian and Alaska Native, 0.0% Hispanic of any race, 0.9% two or more races (2000); Density: 6.3 persons per square mile (2000); Age: 20.9% under 18, 19.1% over 64 (2000); Marriage status: 14.7% never married, 73.3% now married, 6.3% widowed, 5.8% divorced (2000); Foreign born: 2.1% (2000); Ancestry (includes multiple ancestries): 30.6% German, 22.6% Swedish, 19.1% Norwegian, 9.8% Irish, 6.0% United States or American (2000).
Economy: Single-family building permits issued: 0 (2001) / 0 (2000); Multi-family building permits issued: 0 (2001) / 0 (2000); Employment by occupation: 16.5% management, 9.7% professional, 17.5% services, 15.5% sales, 4.9% farming, 19.4% construction, 16.5% production (2000).
Income: Per capita income: $18,476 (2000); Median household income: $33,611 (2000); Poverty rate: 15.7% (2000).
Taxes: Total city taxes per capita: $72 (1997); City property taxes per capita: $72 (1997).
Education: High school graduation rate: 76.8% (2000); College graduation rate: 4.5% (2000).
Housing: Homeownership rate: 96.2% (2000); Median home value: $102,500 (2000); Median rent: $950 per month (2000); Median age of housing: 30 years (2000).
Transportation: Commute to work: 90.1% car, 0.0% public transportation, 5.0% walk, 5.0% work from home (2000); Travel time to work: 9.4% less than 15 minutes, 40.6% 15 to 30 minutes, 40.6% 30 to 45 minutes, 0.0% 45 to 60 minutes, 9.4% 60 minutes or more (2000)

MORA (city). Covers a land area of 4.087 square miles and a water area of 0.156 square miles. Located at 45.87° N. Lat.; 93.29° W. Long. Elevation is 1,010 feet.
History: Mora began as a lumber town. The town was platted in 1881 and named for Mora, Sweden. When lumbering declined, Mora turned to a cooperative creamery, a grist mill, and a machine shop which manufactured buttermilk driers.
Population: 3,193 (2000); Race: 98.8% White, 0.0% Black, 0.0% Asian, 0.3% American Indian and Alaska Native, 0.6% Hispanic of any race, 0.5% two or more races (2000); Density: 781.2 persons per square mile (2000); Age: 23.6% under 18, 23.3% over 64 (2000); Marriage status: 22.5% never married, 53.5% now married, 12.2% widowed, 11.9% divorced (2000); Foreign born: 1.0% (2000); Ancestry (includes multiple ancestries): 30.7%

German, 23.3% Swedish, 15.2% Norwegian, 8.4% Irish, 6.9% English (2000).
Economy: Single-family building permits issued: 12 (2001) / 15 (2000); Multi-family building permits issued: 30 (2001) / 2 (2000); Employment by occupation: 12.8% management, 15.1% professional, 16.9% services, 20.4% sales, 0.1% farming, 12.4% construction, 22.3% production (2000).
Income: Per capita income: $17,949 (2000); Median household income: $30,566 (2000); Poverty rate: 9.0% (2000).
Taxes: Total city taxes per capita: $90 (1997); City property taxes per capita: $78 (1997).
Education: High school graduation rate: 78.4% (2000); College graduation rate: 13.8% (2000).

School District(s)

Mora (PK-12)
2000 Enrollment: 1,991 320-679-6200

Housing: Homeownership rate: 64.6% (2000); Median home value: $84,500 (2000); Median rent: $375 per month (2000); Median age of housing: 36 years (2000).
Hospitals: Kanabec Hospital (49 beds)
Safety: Violent crime rate: 15.5 per 10,000 population; Property crime rate: 737.5 per 10,000 population (2001).
Newspapers: Mora Advertiser (1 x week); Kanabec County Times (1 x week)
Transportation: Commute to work: 91.0% car, 0.4% public transportation, 5.7% walk, 2.7% work from home (2000); Travel time to work: 55.8% less than 15 minutes, 10.5% 15 to 30 minutes, 17.1% 30 to 45 minutes, 4.8% 45 to 60 minutes, 11.8% 60 minutes or more (2000)
Airports: Mora Municipal
Additional Information Contacts
Eastern Minnesota Association of Realtors 320-679-0392
Mora Area Chamber of Commerce 320-679-5792

OGILVIE (city). Covers a land area of 0.935 square miles and a water area of 0 square miles. Located at 45.83° N. Lat.; 93.42° W. Long. Elevation is 1,047 feet.
Population: 474 (2000); Race: 94.3% White, 0.0% Black, 2.1% Asian, 2.6% American Indian and Alaska Native, 0.7% Hispanic of any race, 0.9% two or more races (2000); Density: 507.0 persons per square mile (2000); Age: 31.8% under 18, 14.2% over 64 (2000); Marriage status: 32.2% never married, 36.6% now married, 9.5% widowed, 21.8% divorced (2000); Foreign born: 0.9% (2000); Ancestry (includes multiple ancestries): 38.9% German, 15.6% Norwegian, 12.6% Other groups, 8.1% Dutch, 7.8% Swedish (2000).
Economy: Grain, potatoes; livestock, poultry; dairying; manufacturing. Single-family building permits issued: 2 (2001) / 1 (2000); Multi-family building permits issued: 0 (2001) / 0 (2000); Employment by occupation: 6.3% management, 12.6% professional, 31.4% services, 16.6% sales, 0.0% farming, 10.9% construction, 22.3% production (2000).
Income: Per capita income: $15,198 (2000); Median household income: $27,292 (2000); Poverty rate: 14.6% (2000).
Taxes: Total city taxes per capita: $87 (1997); City property taxes per capita: $84 (1997).
Education: High school graduation rate: 73.6% (2000); College graduation rate: 9.4% (2000).

School District(s)

Ogilvie (KG-12)
2000 Enrollment: 757 320-272-5070

Housing: Homeownership rate: 70.1% (2000); Median home value: $52,000 (2000); Median rent: $364 per month (2000); Median age of housing: 42 years (2000).
Transportation: Commute to work: 85.0% car, 0.0% public transportation, 8.1% walk, 5.2% work from home (2000); Travel time to work: 28.7% less than 15 minutes, 29.3% 15 to 30 minutes, 14.0% 30 to 45 minutes, 11.0% 45 to 60 minutes, 17.1% 60 minutes or more (2000)

PEACE (township). Covers a land area of 36.408 square miles and a water area of 1.562 square miles. Located at 46.01° N. Lat.; 93.25° W. Long.
Population: 963 (2000); Race: 96.8% White, 0.0% Black, 0.9% Asian, 1.3% American Indian and Alaska Native, 0.2% Hispanic of any race, 1.0% two or more races (2000); Density: 26.5 persons per square mile (2000); Age: 29.8% under 18, 14.3% over 64 (2000); Marriage status: 22.5% never married, 64.4% now married, 4.5% widowed, 8.7% divorced (2000); Foreign born: 1.1% (2000); Ancestry (includes multiple ancestries): 34.0% German, 21.6% Swedish, 12.9% Norwegian, 9.1% Irish, 7.1% English (2000).
Economy: Single-family building permits issued: 7 (2001) / 5 (2000); Multi-family building permits issued: 0 (2001) / 0 (2000); Employment by occupation: 8.7% management, 7.5% professional, 15.9% services, 23.4% sales, 2.3% farming, 13.4% construction, 28.8% production (2000).
Income: Per capita income: $14,546 (2000); Median household income: $33,929 (2000); Poverty rate: 15.9% (2000).
Taxes: Total city taxes per capita: $81 (1997); City property taxes per capita: $80 (1997).
Education: High school graduation rate: 83.2% (2000); College graduation rate: 6.4% (2000).
Housing: Homeownership rate: 92.0% (2000); Median home value: $85,800 (2000); Median rent: $388 per month (2000); Median age of housing: 23 years (2000).
Transportation: Commute to work: 95.3% car, 0.5% public transportation, 1.8% walk, 2.4% work from home (2000); Travel time to work: 18.8% less than 15 minutes, 35.5% 15 to 30 minutes, 11.8% 30 to 45 minutes, 8.3% 45 to 60 minutes, 25.5% 60 minutes or more (2000)

POMROY (township). Covers a land area of 37.600 square miles and a water area of 0.097 square miles. Located at 46.04° N. Lat.; 93.12° W. Long.
Population: 390 (2000); Race: 96.8% White, 0.0% Black, 0.0% Asian, 0.5% American Indian and Alaska Native, 1.6% Hispanic of any race, 2.7% two or more races (2000); Density: 10.4 persons per square mile (2000); Age: 21.9% under 18, 16.0% over 64 (2000); Marriage status: 20.7% never married, 71.1% now married, 3.3% widowed, 4.9% divorced (2000); Foreign born: 1.1% (2000); Ancestry (includes multiple ancestries): 41.7% German, 13.9% Swedish, 13.1% Norwegian, 7.2% English, 6.4% United States or American (2000).
Economy: Employment by occupation: 11.5% management, 12.6% professional, 17.6% services, 24.7% sales, 3.3% farming, 15.4% construction, 14.8% production (2000).
Income: Per capita income: $20,134 (2000); Median household income: $41,429 (2000); Poverty rate: 10.7% (2000).
Taxes: Total city taxes per capita: $39 (1997); City property taxes per capita: $39 (1997).
Education: High school graduation rate: 80.8% (2000); College graduation rate: 6.6% (2000).
Housing: Homeownership rate: 92.1% (2000); Median home value: $92,500 (2000); Median rent: $450 per month (2000); Median age of housing: 27 years (2000).
Transportation: Commute to work: 87.4% car, 0.0% public transportation, 1.1% walk, 10.4% work from home (2000); Travel time to work: 12.9% less than 15 minutes, 45.4% 15 to 30 minutes, 19.6% 30 to 45 minutes, 1.2% 45 to 60 minutes, 20.9% 60 minutes or more (2000)

QUAMBA (city). Covers a land area of 0.733 square miles and a water area of 0 square miles. Located at 45.91° N. Lat.; 93.17° W. Long.
Population: 98 (2000); Race: 100.0% White, 0.0% Black, 0.0% Asian, 0.0% American Indian and Alaska Native, 0.0% Hispanic of any race, 0.0% two or more races (2000); Density: 133.6 persons per square mile (2000); Age: 32.7% under 18, 6.1% over 64 (2000); Marriage status: 21.1% never married, 49.3% now married, 2.8% widowed, 26.8% divorced (2000); Foreign born: 2.0% (2000); Ancestry (includes multiple ancestries): 19.4% German, 17.3% Swedish, 14.3% Irish, 13.3% Polish, 10.2% Norwegian (2000).
Economy: Dairying; livestock; barley. Single-family building permits issued: 0 (2001) / 0 (2000); Multi-family building permits issued: 0 (2001) / 0 (2000); Employment by occupation: 7.5% management, 7.5% professional, 15.1% services, 32.1% sales, 0.0% farming, 17.0% construction, 20.8% production (2000).
Income: Per capita income: $15,923 (2000); Median household income: $38,125 (2000); Poverty rate: 7.4% (2000).
Taxes: Total city taxes per capita: $16 (1997); City property taxes per capita: $16 (1997).
Education: High school graduation rate: 75.8% (2000); College graduation rate: 12.9% (2000).
Housing: Homeownership rate: 96.8% (2000); Median home value: $48,300 (2000); Median rent: $625 per month (2000); Median age of housing: 55 years (2000).
Transportation: Commute to work: 80.4% car, 0.0% public transportation, 3.9% walk, 15.7% work from home (2000); Travel time to work: 30.2% less than 15 minutes, 37.2% 15 to 30 minutes, 4.7% 30 to 45 minutes, 7.0% 45 to 60 minutes, 20.9% 60 minutes or more (2000)

SOUTH FORK (township). Covers a land area of 36.344 square miles and a water area of 0.038 square miles. Located at 45.78° N. Lat.; 93.45° W. Long.
Population: 662 (2000); Race: 100.0% White, 0.0% Black, 0.0% Asian, 0.0% American Indian and Alaska Native, 1.3% Hispanic of any race, 0.0%

two or more races (2000); Density: 18.2 persons per square mile (2000); Age: 29.4% under 18, 8.4% over 64 (2000); Marriage status: 24.4% never married, 63.7% now married, 2.6% widowed, 9.4% divorced (2000); Foreign born: 1.0% (2000); Ancestry (includes multiple ancestries): 41.5% German, 19.6% Norwegian, 17.6% Swedish, 9.6% Irish, 6.4% United States or American (2000).
Economy: Single-family building permits issued: 4 (2001) / 4 (2000); Multi-family building permits issued: 0 (2001) / 0 (2000); Employment by occupation: 20.1% management, 5.5% professional, 12.5% services, 21.3% sales, 2.0% farming, 14.9% construction, 23.6% production (2000).
Income: Per capita income: $18,546 (2000); Median household income: $45,268 (2000); Poverty rate: 9.0% (2000).
Taxes: Total city taxes per capita: $15 (1997); City property taxes per capita: $13 (1997).
Education: High school graduation rate: 77.4% (2000); College graduation rate: 6.4% (2000).
Housing: Homeownership rate: 90.8% (2000); Median home value: $88,100 (2000); Median rent: $325 per month (2000); Median age of housing: 25 years (2000).
Transportation: Commute to work: 90.1% car, 0.0% public transportation, 0.9% walk, 9.0% work from home (2000); Travel time to work: 24.8% less than 15 minutes, 23.4% 15 to 30 minutes, 21.5% 30 to 45 minutes, 12.9% 45 to 60 minutes, 17.5% 60 minutes or more (2000)

WHITED (township). Covers a land area of 30.473 square miles and a water area of 0.166 square miles. Located at 45.93° N. Lat.; 93.19° W. Long.
Population: 808 (2000); Race: 98.8% White, 0.0% Black, 0.0% Asian, 0.2% American Indian and Alaska Native, 0.2% Hispanic of any race, 1.0% two or more races (2000); Density: 26.5 persons per square mile (2000); Age: 29.4% under 18, 9.6% over 64 (2000); Marriage status: 22.2% never married, 65.0% now married, 3.2% widowed, 9.6% divorced (2000); Foreign born: 0.0% (2000); Ancestry (includes multiple ancestries): 34.8% German, 20.8% Swedish, 18.8% Norwegian, 7.9% Irish, 6.9% United States or American (2000).
Economy: Single-family building permits issued: 5 (2001) / 5 (2000); Multi-family building permits issued: 0 (2001) / 0 (2000); Employment by occupation: 10.8% management, 11.0% professional, 17.0% services, 21.3% sales, 0.7% farming, 18.0% construction, 21.1% production (2000).
Income: Per capita income: $17,129 (2000); Median household income: $42,708 (2000); Poverty rate: 6.9% (2000).
Taxes: Total city taxes per capita: $26 (1997); City property taxes per capita: $24 (1997).
Education: High school graduation rate: 84.5% (2000); College graduation rate: 8.7% (2000).
Housing: Homeownership rate: 92.9% (2000); Median home value: $91,700 (2000); Median rent: $340 per month (2000); Median age of housing: 24 years (2000).
Transportation: Commute to work: 91.5% car, 0.0% public transportation, 1.0% walk, 7.5% work from home (2000); Travel time to work: 37.1% less than 15 minutes, 26.6% 15 to 30 minutes, 8.3% 30 to 45 minutes, 5.4% 45 to 60 minutes, 22.6% 60 minutes or more (2000)

Kandiyohi County

Located in southwest central Minnesota; watered by several lakes. Covers a land area of 796.10 square miles, a water area of 65.90 square miles, and is located in the Central Time Zone. The county government was organized in 1858. County seat is Willmar.

Weather Station: New London — Elevation: 1,240 feet

	Jan	Feb	Mar	Apr	May	Jun	Jul	Aug	Sep	Oct	Nov	Dec
High	21	28	40	58	72	80	84	81	72	58	39	25
Low	0	8	20	34	47	56	61	59	50	37	22	8
Precip	1.1	0.7	2.1	2.5	3.6	5.7	4.1	4.0	3.6	2.4	1.6	0.9
Snow	12.1	7.1	10.7	3.2	tr	0.0	0.0	0.0	tr	0.6	9.9	9.1

High and Low temperatures in degrees Fahrenheit; Precipitation and Snow in inches

Weather Station: Willmar State Hospital — Elevation: 1,125 feet

	Jan	Feb	Mar	Apr	May	Jun	Jul	Aug	Sep	Oct	Nov	Dec
High	20	26	38	56	70	79	82	80	72	58	38	25
Low	-0	7	20	34	47	57	61	58	48	36	22	7
Precip	0.8	0.6	1.5	2.2	3.2	5.2	3.8	3.8	2.9	2.2	1.5	0.6
Snow	11.6	7.2	9.5	2.3	tr	0.0	0.0	0.0	tr	0.4	8.3	7.9

High and Low temperatures in degrees Fahrenheit; Precipitation and Snow in inches

Population: 41,203 (2000); Race: 93.6% White, 0.7% Black, 0.3% Asian, 0.2% American Indian and Alaska Native, 7.9% Hispanic of any race, 1.2% two or more races (2000); Density: 51.8 persons per square mile (2000); Age: 26.6% under 18, 15.0% over 64 (2000).
Religion: Five largest groups: 38.1% Evangelical Lutheran Church in America, 13.7% Catholic Church, 4.1% Christian Reformed Church in North America, 3.4% Lutheran Church—Missouri Synod, 3.0% Presbyterian Church (U.S.A.) (2000).
Economy: Unemployment rate: 3.1% (11/2002); Total civilian labor force: 22,046 (11/2002); Leading industries: 21.9% health care and social assistance; 16.7% manufacturing; 14.4% retail trade (2000); Companies that employ more than 1,000 persons: 2 (2000); Companies that employ more than 100 persons: 30 (2000); Farms: 1,131 totaling 378,831 acres (1997); Minority business ownership rate: 0.0% (1997); Women business ownership rate: 20.0% (1997); Retail sales per capita: $10,924 (1997). Single-family building permits issued: 170 (2001) / 152 (2000); Multi-family building permits issued: 14 (2001) / 60 (2000).
Income: Per capita income: $19,627 (2000); Median household income: $39,772 (2000); Poverty rate: 9.2% (2000); Bankruptcy rate: 2.05% (2001).
Taxes: Total county taxes per capita: $316 (2000); County property taxes per capita: $297 (2000).
Education: High school graduation rate: 83.5% (2000); College graduation rate: 18.3% (2000).
Housing: Homeownership rate: 75.5% (2000); Median home value: $90,400 (2000); Median rent: $390 per month (2000); Median age of housing: 30 years (2000).
Health: Birth rate: 126.2 per 10,000 population (1998); Age adjusted death rate: 76.9 per 10,000 population (1999); Age adjusted cancer mortality rate: 199.6 deaths per 100,000 population (1999). Air Quality Index: 80% good, 20% moderate, 0% unhealthy (percent of days in 2000). Number of physicians: 24.5 per 10,000 population (1999); Number of hospital beds: 89.1 per 10,000 population (1999).
Elections: 2000 Presidential election results: 42.6% Gore, 52.0% Bush, 3.8% Nader, 1.2% Buchanan
National and State Parks: Burbank State Wildlife Management Area; Dietrich Lange State Wildlife Management Are; Eagle Lake State Wildlife Management Area; Follies State Wildlife Management Area; Gennesse State Wildlife Management Area; Kandi State Wildlife Management Area; Luce Line State Trail; Oleander State Wildlife Management Area; Roseville State Wildlife Management Area; Sibley State Park; Willmar State Wildlife Management Area; Yohi State Wildlife Management Area
Additional Information Contacts
Kandiyohi County Government Offices 320-231-6215
West Central Association of Realtors 320-235-6881
Willmar Chamber of Commerce 320-235-0300

Kandiyohi County Communities

ARCTANDER (township). Covers a land area of 34.453 square miles and a water area of 1.628 square miles. Located at 45.28° N. Lat.; 95.19° W. Long.
Population: 401 (2000); Race: 100.0% White, 0.0% Black, 0.0% Asian, 0.0% American Indian and Alaska Native, 0.0% Hispanic of any race, 0.0% two or more races (2000); Density: 11.6 persons per square mile (2000); Age: 26.1% under 18, 16.5% over 64 (2000); Marriage status: 16.0% never married, 76.1% now married, 5.2% widowed, 2.6% divorced (2000); Foreign born: 0.0% (2000); Ancestry (includes multiple ancestries): 50.0% Norwegian, 28.2% German, 19.0% Swedish, 12.8% Irish, 4.8% Dutch (2000).
Economy: Employment by occupation: 24.7% management, 19.3% professional, 16.6% services, 16.1% sales, 2.2% farming, 9.9% construction, 11.2% production (2000).
Income: Per capita income: $17,848 (2000); Median household income: $42,656 (2000); Poverty rate: 5.1% (2000).
Taxes: Total city taxes per capita: $28 (1997); City property taxes per capita: $28 (1997).
Education: High school graduation rate: 80.1% (2000); College graduation rate: 15.9% (2000).
Housing: Homeownership rate: 89.2% (2000); Median home value: $86,900 (2000); Median rent: $515 per month (2000); Median age of housing: 36 years (2000).
Transportation: Commute to work: 77.1% car, 0.0% public transportation, 1.8% walk, 18.4% work from home (2000); Travel time to work: 6.6% less than 15 minutes, 55.5% 15 to 30 minutes, 29.1% 30 to 45 minutes, 4.4% 45 to 60 minutes, 4.4% 60 minutes or more (2000)

ATWATER (city). Covers a land area of 1.024 square miles and a water area of 0.049 square miles. Located at 45.13° N. Lat.; 94.77° W. Long. Elevation is 1,215 feet.
Population: 1,079 (2000); Race: 99.3% White, 0.0% Black, 0.0% Asian, 0.3% American Indian and Alaska Native, 0.0% Hispanic of any race, 0.5% two or more races (2000); Density: 1,053.3 persons per square mile (2000); Age: 23.4% under 18, 18.3% over 64 (2000); Marriage status: 25.2% never married, 54.9% now married, 11.2% widowed, 8.7% divorced (2000); Foreign born: 0.2% (2000); Ancestry (includes multiple ancestries): 46.1% German, 25.7% Norwegian, 22.0% Swedish, 7.8% Irish, 5.0% English (2000).
Economy: Grain, sugar beets, peas, beans; livestock, poultry; dairying. Manufacturing: turkey feeds, agricultural equipment. Single-family building permits issued: 0 (2001) / 3 (2000); Multi-family building permits issued: 4 (2001) / 0 (2000); Employment by occupation: 9.3% management, 17.6% professional, 20.2% services, 20.2% sales, 2.2% farming, 8.5% construction, 22.0% production (2000).
Income: Per capita income: $21,112 (2000); Median household income: $39,265 (2000); Poverty rate: 5.5% (2000).
Taxes: Total city taxes per capita: $201 (1997); City property taxes per capita: $192 (1997).
Education: High school graduation rate: 84.0% (2000); College graduation rate: 13.6% (2000).

School District(s)

A.C.G.C. (PK-12)
2000 Enrollment: 989 320-857-2271

Housing: Homeownership rate: 78.4% (2000); Median home value: $66,900 (2000); Median rent: $345 per month (2000); Median age of housing: 43 years (2000).
Transportation: Commute to work: 92.2% car, 0.7% public transportation, 4.8% walk, 2.0% work from home (2000); Travel time to work: 28.1% less than 15 minutes, 53.6% 15 to 30 minutes, 11.2% 30 to 45 minutes, 2.3% 45 to 60 minutes, 4.8% 60 minutes or more (2000)

BLOMKEST (city). Covers a land area of 1.034 square miles and a water area of 0 square miles. Located at 44.94° N. Lat.; 95.02° W. Long.
Population: 186 (2000); Race: 92.0% White, 0.0% Black, 1.1% Asian, 0.0% American Indian and Alaska Native, 4.0% Hispanic of any race, 4.0% two or more races (2000); Density: 179.8 persons per square mile (2000); Age: 28.4% under 18, 13.6% over 64 (2000); Marriage status: 19.3% never married, 68.6% now married, 5.0% widowed, 7.1% divorced (2000); Foreign born: 3.4% (2000); Ancestry (includes multiple ancestries): 37.5% German, 23.9% Norwegian, 17.0% Swedish, 13.1% Dutch, 9.1% Other groups (2000).
Economy: Manufacturing: machinery. Agriculture: grains; livestock, poultry; dairying. Single-family building permits issued: 0 (2001) / 0 (2000); Multi-family building permits issued: 0 (2001) / 0 (2000); Employment by occupation: 4.8% management, 16.7% professional, 9.5% services, 32.1% sales, 3.6% farming, 13.1% construction, 20.2% production (2000).
Income: Per capita income: $16,072 (2000); Median household income: $34,583 (2000); Poverty rate: 4.0% (2000).
Taxes: Total city taxes per capita: $112 (1997); City property taxes per capita: $112 (1997).
Education: High school graduation rate: 75.2% (2000); College graduation rate: 12.0% (2000).
Housing: Homeownership rate: 92.3% (2000); Median home value: $63,100 (2000); Median age of housing: 44 years (2000).
Transportation: Commute to work: 92.9% car, 0.0% public transportation, 4.8% walk, 2.4% work from home (2000); Travel time to work: 31.7% less than 15 minutes, 37.8% 15 to 30 minutes, 13.4% 30 to 45 minutes, 8.5% 45 to 60 minutes, 8.5% 60 minutes or more (2000)

BURBANK (township). Covers a land area of 32.953 square miles and a water area of 2.753 square miles. Located at 45.35° N. Lat.; 94.95° W. Long.
Population: 510 (2000); Race: 99.6% White, 0.0% Black, 0.0% Asian, 0.0% American Indian and Alaska Native, 0.0% Hispanic of any race, 0.4% two or more races (2000); Density: 15.5 persons per square mile (2000); Age: 27.7% under 18, 5.4% over 64 (2000); Marriage status: 19.3% never married, 73.6% now married, 1.6% widowed, 5.4% divorced (2000); Foreign born: 1.4% (2000); Ancestry (includes multiple ancestries): 46.4% Norwegian, 41.8% German, 12.6% Swedish, 8.9% Irish, 5.6% English (2000).
Economy: Employment by occupation: 17.4% management, 12.3% professional, 10.5% services, 22.8% sales, 2.9% farming, 15.6% construction, 18.5% production (2000).
Income: Per capita income: $20,587 (2000); Median household income: $43,375 (2000); Poverty rate: 5.6% (2000).
Taxes: Total city taxes per capita: $48 (1997); City property taxes per capita: $48 (1997).
Education: High school graduation rate: 85.9% (2000); College graduation rate: 13.2% (2000).
Housing: Homeownership rate: 89.6% (2000); Median home value: $120,200 (2000); Median rent: $325 per month (2000); Median age of housing: 25 years (2000).
Transportation: Commute to work: 86.4% car, 0.0% public transportation, 2.2% walk, 11.4% work from home (2000); Travel time to work: 29.3% less than 15 minutes, 39.3% 15 to 30 minutes, 18.6% 30 to 45 minutes, 2.9% 45 to 60 minutes, 9.9% 60 minutes or more (2000)

COLFAX (township). Covers a land area of 32.771 square miles and a water area of 3.121 square miles. Located at 45.36° N. Lat.; 95.06° W. Long.
Population: 557 (2000); Race: 100.0% White, 0.0% Black, 0.0% Asian, 0.0% American Indian and Alaska Native, 0.0% Hispanic of any race, 0.0% two or more races (2000); Density: 17.0 persons per square mile (2000); Age: 25.6% under 18, 10.6% over 64 (2000); Marriage status: 27.5% never married, 66.6% now married, 1.8% widowed, 4.1% divorced (2000); Foreign born: 1.3% (2000); Ancestry (includes multiple ancestries): 43.3% Norwegian, 38.1% German, 17.4% Swedish, 7.1% Irish, 4.7% Dutch (2000).
Economy: Employment by occupation: 11.0% management, 13.6% professional, 12.5% services, 27.2% sales, 3.5% farming, 10.7% construction, 21.4% production (2000).
Income: Per capita income: $16,654 (2000); Median household income: $41,417 (2000); Poverty rate: 6.1% (2000).
Taxes: Total city taxes per capita: $56 (1997); City property taxes per capita: $56 (1997).
Education: High school graduation rate: 88.6% (2000); College graduation rate: 15.7% (2000).
Housing: Homeownership rate: 88.3% (2000); Median home value: $112,500 (2000); Median rent: $388 per month (2000); Median age of housing: 26 years (2000).
Transportation: Commute to work: 86.5% car, 0.0% public transportation, 1.2% walk, 9.7% work from home (2000); Travel time to work: 21.2% less than 15 minutes, 47.2% 15 to 30 minutes, 24.1% 30 to 45 minutes, 0.3% 45 to 60 minutes, 7.2% 60 minutes or more (2000)

DOVRE (township). Covers a land area of 27.185 square miles and a water area of 7.271 square miles. Located at 45.20° N. Lat.; 95.04° W. Long.
Population: 1,968 (2000); Race: 98.3% White, 0.2% Black, 0.1% Asian, 0.1% American Indian and Alaska Native, 1.6% Hispanic of any race, 0.7% two or more races (2000); Density: 72.4 persons per square mile (2000); Age: 27.5% under 18, 8.8% over 64 (2000); Marriage status: 18.7% never married, 74.4% now married, 2.6% widowed, 4.3% divorced (2000); Foreign born: 0.9% (2000); Ancestry (includes multiple ancestries): 42.3% German, 33.7% Norwegian, 16.1% Swedish, 6.9% Irish, 4.9% Dutch (2000).
Economy: Employment by occupation: 15.7% management, 26.4% professional, 8.9% services, 30.1% sales, 0.8% farming, 9.1% construction, 9.1% production (2000).
Income: Per capita income: $25,824 (2000); Median household income: $60,489 (2000); Poverty rate: 4.7% (2000).
Taxes: Total city taxes per capita: $76 (2000); City property taxes per capita: $72 (2000).
Education: High school graduation rate: 95.7% (2000); College graduation rate: 37.5% (2000).
Housing: Homeownership rate: 92.3% (2000); Median home value: $147,100 (2000); Median rent: $430 per month (2000); Median age of housing: 22 years (2000).
Transportation: Commute to work: 93.8% car, 0.2% public transportation, 0.5% walk, 5.5% work from home (2000); Travel time to work: 56.7% less than 15 minutes, 34.4% 15 to 30 minutes, 3.0% 30 to 45 minutes, 2.1% 45 to 60 minutes, 3.9% 60 minutes or more (2000)

EAST LAKE LILLIAN (township). Covers a land area of 33.618 square miles and a water area of 2.248 square miles. Located at 44.94° N. Lat.; 94.83° W. Long.
Population: 225 (2000); Race: 98.3% White, 1.7% Black, 0.0% Asian, 0.0% American Indian and Alaska Native, 0.0% Hispanic of any race, 0.0% two or more races (2000); Density: 6.7 persons per square mile (2000); Age: 26.2% under 18, 12.2% over 64 (2000); Marriage status: 20.2% never married, 62.8% now married, 6.6% widowed, 10.4% divorced (2000); Foreign born: 0.4% (2000); Ancestry (includes multiple ancestries): 50.6% German, 27.8% Norwegian, 15.6% Swedish, 3.8% United States or American, 3.8% French (except Basque) (2000).

Economy: Employment by occupation: 18.1% management, 10.7% professional, 12.8% services, 32.9% sales, 1.3% farming, 10.1% construction, 14.1% production (2000).
Income: Per capita income: $17,621 (2000); Median household income: $39,750 (2000); Poverty rate: 7.6% (2000).
Taxes: Total city taxes per capita: $75 (1997); City property taxes per capita: $75 (1997).
Education: High school graduation rate: 87.5% (2000); College graduation rate: 7.5% (2000).
Housing: Homeownership rate: 82.8% (2000); Median home value: $68,000 (2000); Median rent: $325 per month (2000); Median age of housing: 42 years (2000).
Transportation: Commute to work: 87.6% car, 0.0% public transportation, 0.0% walk, 12.4% work from home (2000); Travel time to work: 26.8% less than 15 minutes, 31.5% 15 to 30 minutes, 26.0% 30 to 45 minutes, 6.3% 45 to 60 minutes, 9.4% 60 minutes or more (2000)

EDWARDS (township). Covers a land area of 35.371 square miles and a water area of 0.373 square miles. Located at 45.02° N. Lat.; 95.20° W. Long.
Population: 304 (2000); Race: 95.0% White, 2.5% Black, 0.0% Asian, 0.0% American Indian and Alaska Native, 2.5% Hispanic of any race, 0.0% two or more races (2000); Density: 8.6 persons per square mile (2000); Age: 30.4% under 18, 10.7% over 64 (2000); Marriage status: 29.6% never married, 62.3% now married, 3.1% widowed, 4.9% divorced (2000); Foreign born: 0.0% (2000); Ancestry (includes multiple ancestries): 45.4% German, 27.5% Dutch, 15.7% Norwegian, 10.4% Swedish, 6.8% United States or American (2000).
Economy: Employment by occupation: 27.2% management, 6.8% professional, 12.2% services, 26.5% sales, 4.8% farming, 8.2% construction, 14.3% production (2000).
Income: Per capita income: $16,256 (2000); Median household income: $44,063 (2000); Poverty rate: 5.7% (2000).
Taxes: Total city taxes per capita: $48 (1997); City property taxes per capita: $48 (1997).
Education: High school graduation rate: 80.3% (2000); College graduation rate: 4.0% (2000).
Housing: Homeownership rate: 88.4% (2000); Median home value: $107,300 (2000); Median rent: $142 per month (2000); Median age of housing: 51 years (2000).
Transportation: Commute to work: 82.3% car, 0.0% public transportation, 4.1% walk, 13.6% work from home (2000); Travel time to work: 45.7% less than 15 minutes, 37.8% 15 to 30 minutes, 11.0% 30 to 45 minutes, 1.6% 45 to 60 minutes, 3.9% 60 minutes or more (2000)

FAHLUN (township). Covers a land area of 29.481 square miles and a water area of 6.538 square miles. Located at 45.02° N. Lat.; 94.93° W. Long.
Population: 412 (2000); Race: 100.0% White, 0.0% Black, 0.0% Asian, 0.0% American Indian and Alaska Native, 0.0% Hispanic of any race, 0.0% two or more races (2000); Density: 14.0 persons per square mile (2000); Age: 28.4% under 18, 13.0% over 64 (2000); Marriage status: 17.9% never married, 73.7% now married, 3.2% widowed, 5.1% divorced (2000); Foreign born: 0.0% (2000); Ancestry (includes multiple ancestries): 32.1% German, 27.5% Swedish, 27.2% Norwegian, 4.9% English, 4.7% European (2000).
Economy: Employment by occupation: 16.7% management, 12.5% professional, 14.4% services, 27.3% sales, 4.6% farming, 11.6% construction, 13.0% production (2000).
Income: Per capita income: $16,221 (2000); Median household income: $39,583 (2000); Poverty rate: 5.8% (2000).
Taxes: Total city taxes per capita: $86 (1997); City property taxes per capita: $86 (1997).
Education: High school graduation rate: 88.3% (2000); College graduation rate: 13.3% (2000).
Housing: Homeownership rate: 92.4% (2000); Median home value: $90,400 (2000); Median rent: $475 per month (2000); Median age of housing: 39 years (2000).
Transportation: Commute to work: 91.9% car, 0.0% public transportation, 0.5% walk, 7.6% work from home (2000); Travel time to work: 16.4% less than 15 minutes, 64.1% 15 to 30 minutes, 8.2% 30 to 45 minutes, 3.1% 45 to 60 minutes, 8.2% 60 minutes or more (2000)

GENNESSEE (township). Covers a land area of 32.385 square miles and a water area of 2.547 square miles. Located at 45.11° N. Lat.; 94.81° W. Long.
Population: 458 (2000); Race: 100.0% White, 0.0% Black, 0.0% Asian, 0.0% American Indian and Alaska Native, 3.3% Hispanic of any race, 0.0% two or more races (2000); Density: 14.1 persons per square mile (2000); Age: 24.5% under 18, 9.6% over 64 (2000); Marriage status: 24.3% never married, 65.2% now married, 2.2% widowed, 8.3% divorced (2000); Foreign born: 0.5% (2000); Ancestry (includes multiple ancestries): 39.8% German, 32.0% Norwegian, 31.5% Swedish, 8.9% English, 6.1% Irish (2000).
Economy: Employment by occupation: 13.2% management, 13.2% professional, 10.5% services, 24.1% sales, 1.9% farming, 14.8% construction, 22.2% production (2000).
Income: Per capita income: $20,088 (2000); Median household income: $50,982 (2000); Poverty rate: 3.8% (2000).
Taxes: Total city taxes per capita: $42 (1997); City property taxes per capita: $42 (1997).
Education: High school graduation rate: 90.6% (2000); College graduation rate: 12.8% (2000).
Housing: Homeownership rate: 93.8% (2000); Median home value: $89,500 (2000); Median rent: $325 per month (2000); Median age of housing: 27 years (2000).
Transportation: Commute to work: 87.9% car, 0.0% public transportation, 2.3% walk, 9.7% work from home (2000); Travel time to work: 25.4% less than 15 minutes, 57.3% 15 to 30 minutes, 12.1% 30 to 45 minutes, 3.9% 45 to 60 minutes, 1.3% 60 minutes or more (2000)

GREEN LAKE (township). Covers a land area of 30.440 square miles and a water area of 3.791 square miles. Located at 45.20° N. Lat.; 94.93° W. Long.
Population: 1,473 (2000); Race: 98.1% White, 0.4% Black, 0.2% Asian, 0.0% American Indian and Alaska Native, 0.9% Hispanic of any race, 0.3% two or more races (2000); Density: 48.4 persons per square mile (2000); Age: 26.5% under 18, 10.3% over 64 (2000); Marriage status: 19.3% never married, 71.9% now married, 3.3% widowed, 5.5% divorced (2000); Foreign born: 0.9% (2000); Ancestry (includes multiple ancestries): 40.0% German, 34.9% Norwegian, 17.6% Swedish, 10.0% Irish, 5.3% English (2000).
Economy: Employment by occupation: 15.3% management, 23.4% professional, 13.0% services, 25.0% sales, 1.4% farming, 9.7% construction, 12.1% production (2000).
Income: Per capita income: $25,535 (2000); Median household income: $51,688 (2000); Poverty rate: 2.2% (2000).
Taxes: Total city taxes per capita: $62 (1997); City property taxes per capita: $62 (1997).
Education: High school graduation rate: 93.4% (2000); College graduation rate: 28.6% (2000).
Housing: Homeownership rate: 94.3% (2000); Median home value: $156,000 (2000); Median rent: $371 per month (2000); Median age of housing: 25 years (2000).
Transportation: Commute to work: 93.3% car, 0.0% public transportation, 0.9% walk, 5.3% work from home (2000); Travel time to work: 35.8% less than 15 minutes, 50.4% 15 to 30 minutes, 4.9% 30 to 45 minutes, 3.5% 45 to 60 minutes, 5.4% 60 minutes or more (2000)

HARRISON (township). Covers a land area of 31.735 square miles and a water area of 3.526 square miles. Located at 45.20° N. Lat.; 94.81° W. Long.
Population: 665 (2000); Race: 99.3% White, 0.0% Black, 0.3% Asian, 0.0% American Indian and Alaska Native, 0.7% Hispanic of any race, 0.1% two or more races (2000); Density: 21.0 persons per square mile (2000); Age: 25.8% under 18, 14.7% over 64 (2000); Marriage status: 17.0% never married, 71.3% now married, 6.4% widowed, 5.3% divorced (2000); Foreign born: 0.3% (2000); Ancestry (includes multiple ancestries): 46.4% German, 22.8% Norwegian, 16.6% Swedish, 6.3% Dutch, 6.0% Irish (2000).
Economy: Employment by occupation: 20.0% management, 17.0% professional, 11.0% services, 23.3% sales, 1.9% farming, 12.3% construction, 14.5% production (2000).
Income: Per capita income: $18,166 (2000); Median household income: $41,429 (2000); Poverty rate: 5.0% (2000).
Taxes: Total city taxes per capita: $97 (1997); City property taxes per capita: $97 (1997).
Education: High school graduation rate: 86.8% (2000); College graduation rate: 16.1% (2000).
Housing: Homeownership rate: 95.1% (2000); Median home value: $108,200 (2000); Median rent: $300 per month (2000); Median age of housing: 37 years (2000).
Transportation: Commute to work: 88.2% car, 0.5% public transportation, 0.5% walk, 9.6% work from home (2000); Travel time to work: 20.4% less than 15 minutes, 56.8% 15 to 30 minutes, 10.3% 30 to 45 minutes, 3.6% 45 to 60 minutes, 8.8% 60 minutes or more (2000)

HAWICK (unincorporated postal area, zip code 56246). Covers a land area of 22.939 square miles and a water area of 0.151 square miles. Located at 45.34° N. Lat.; 94.83° W. Long. Elevation is 1,238 feet.
Population: 435 (2000); Race: 98.0% White, 0.0% Black, 0.0% Asian, 0.7% American Indian and Alaska Native, 1.1% Hispanic of any race, 0.4% two or more races (2000); Density: 19.0 persons per square mile (2000); Age: 36.6% under 18, 10.8% over 64 (2000); Marriage status: 29.8% never married, 62.9% now married, 2.8% widowed, 4.6% divorced (2000); Foreign born: 0.2% (2000); Ancestry (includes multiple ancestries): 48.6% German, 25.6% Norwegian, 9.5% Swedish, 8.6% Irish, 6.6% Dutch (2000).
Economy: Employment by occupation: 17.3% management, 9.1% professional, 21.6% services, 19.7% sales, 5.3% farming, 12.5% construction, 14.4% production (2000).
Income: Per capita income: $15,124 (2000); Median household income: $37,361 (2000); Poverty rate: 12.6% (2000).
Education: High school graduation rate: 86.7% (2000); College graduation rate: 7.5% (2000).
Housing: Homeownership rate: 84.7% (2000); Median home value: $73,300 (2000); Median rent: $300 per month (2000); Median age of housing: 32 years (2000).
Transportation: Commute to work: 84.5% car, 2.0% public transportation, 4.0% walk, 9.5% work from home (2000); Travel time to work: 39.2% less than 15 minutes, 39.2% 15 to 30 minutes, 15.5% 30 to 45 minutes, 3.9% 45 to 60 minutes, 2.2% 60 minutes or more (2000)

HOLLAND (township). Covers a land area of 35.348 square miles and a water area of 0.012 square miles. Located at 44.92° N. Lat.; 95.19° W. Long.
Population: 369 (2000); Race: 100.0% White, 0.0% Black, 0.0% Asian, 0.0% American Indian and Alaska Native, 0.0% Hispanic of any race, 0.0% two or more races (2000); Density: 10.4 persons per square mile (2000); Age: 34.1% under 18, 8.3% over 64 (2000); Marriage status: 24.6% never married, 71.0% now married, 0.3% widowed, 4.1% divorced (2000); Foreign born: 0.0% (2000); Ancestry (includes multiple ancestries): 52.6% Dutch, 42.4% German, 10.2% Swedish, 9.6% Norwegian, 6.3% Polish (2000).
Economy: Employment by occupation: 27.1% management, 19.0% professional, 12.4% services, 14.3% sales, 4.8% farming, 8.1% construction, 14.3% production (2000).
Income: Per capita income: $16,243 (2000); Median household income: $45,313 (2000); Poverty rate: 7.0% (2000).
Taxes: Total city taxes per capita: $85 (1997); City property taxes per capita: $85 (1997).
Education: High school graduation rate: 87.8% (2000); College graduation rate: 11.4% (2000).
Housing: Homeownership rate: 81.6% (2000); Median home value: $76,000 (2000); Median rent: $325 per month (2000); Median age of housing: 50 years (2000).
Transportation: Commute to work: 85.6% car, 0.0% public transportation, 0.0% walk, 14.4% work from home (2000); Travel time to work: 44.4% less than 15 minutes, 36.0% 15 to 30 minutes, 15.7% 30 to 45 minutes, 2.2% 45 to 60 minutes, 1.7% 60 minutes or more (2000)

IRVING (township). Covers a land area of 32.803 square miles and a water area of 3.325 square miles. Located at 45.26° N. Lat.; 94.83° W. Long.
Population: 787 (2000); Race: 98.5% White, 0.0% Black, 1.3% Asian, 0.0% American Indian and Alaska Native, 0.3% Hispanic of any race, 0.0% two or more races (2000); Density: 24.0 persons per square mile (2000); Age: 23.5% under 18, 17.7% over 64 (2000); Marriage status: 17.1% never married, 72.5% now married, 2.5% widowed, 7.8% divorced (2000); Foreign born: 1.5% (2000); Ancestry (includes multiple ancestries): 39.7% German, 33.6% Norwegian, 18.0% Swedish, 9.1% Irish, 5.9% English (2000).
Economy: Employment by occupation: 15.4% management, 19.4% professional, 14.4% services, 25.7% sales, 1.3% farming, 12.0% construction, 11.8% production (2000).
Income: Per capita income: $21,715 (2000); Median household income: $47,188 (2000); Poverty rate: 7.7% (2000).
Taxes: Total city taxes per capita: $203 (1997); City property taxes per capita: $203 (1997).
Education: High school graduation rate: 93.5% (2000); College graduation rate: 17.0% (2000).
Housing: Homeownership rate: 91.3% (2000); Median home value: $139,400 (2000); Median rent: $363 per month (2000); Median age of housing: 26 years (2000).
Transportation: Commute to work: 92.6% car, 0.0% public transportation, 0.0% walk, 7.4% work from home (2000); Travel time to work: 24.1% less than 15 minutes, 40.4% 15 to 30 minutes, 24.4% 30 to 45 minutes, 2.9% 45 to 60 minutes, 8.3% 60 minutes or more (2000)

KANDIYOHI (city). Covers a land area of 0.316 square miles and a water area of 0 square miles. Located at 45.13° N. Lat.; 94.93° W. Long. Elevation is 1,223 feet.
Population: 555 (2000); Race: 95.7% White, 1.3% Black, 0.0% Asian, 0.4% American Indian and Alaska Native, 1.5% Hispanic of any race, 1.1% two or more races (2000); Density: 1,754.2 persons per square mile (2000); Age: 30.3% under 18, 11.5% over 64 (2000); Marriage status: 28.5% never married, 61.0% now married, 4.4% widowed, 6.1% divorced (2000); Foreign born: 0.9% (2000); Ancestry (includes multiple ancestries): 48.4% German, 33.5% Norwegian, 22.0% Swedish, 7.9% Dutch, 5.0% English (2000).
Economy: Single-family building permits issued: 0 (2001) / 5 (2000); Multi-family building permits issued: 0 (2001) / 0 (2000); Employment by occupation: 8.6% management, 19.8% professional, 10.6% services, 28.4% sales, 0.3% farming, 15.8% construction, 16.5% production (2000).
Income: Per capita income: $15,897 (2000); Median household income: $36,364 (2000); Poverty rate: 5.2% (2000).
Taxes: Total city taxes per capita: $91 (1997); City property taxes per capita: $87 (1997).
Education: High school graduation rate: 90.3% (2000); College graduation rate: 14.4% (2000).
Housing: Homeownership rate: 68.7% (2000); Median home value: $76,700 (2000); Median rent: $343 per month (2000); Median age of housing: 28 years (2000).
Transportation: Commute to work: 95.7% car, 0.0% public transportation, 0.0% walk, 3.3% work from home (2000); Travel time to work: 47.4% less than 15 minutes, 44.0% 15 to 30 minutes, 2.1% 30 to 45 minutes, 0.7% 45 to 60 minutes, 5.8% 60 minutes or more (2000)

KANDIYOHI (township). Covers a land area of 33.313 square miles and a water area of 2.045 square miles. Located at 45.10° N. Lat.; 94.93° W. Long. Elevation is 1,223 feet.
Population: 600 (2000); Race: 97.7% White, 0.5% Black, 0.0% Asian, 0.0% American Indian and Alaska Native, 1.6% Hispanic of any race, 1.8% two or more races (2000); Density: 18.0 persons per square mile (2000); Age: 24.1% under 18, 13.4% over 64 (2000); Marriage status: 16.9% never married, 73.3% now married, 5.0% widowed, 4.8% divorced (2000); Foreign born: 0.3% (2000); Ancestry (includes multiple ancestries): 37.7% German, 30.6% Norwegian, 17.3% Swedish, 10.0% Irish, 6.8% Dutch (2000).
Economy: Livestock, poultry; grain, sugar beets, alfalfa; dairying. Employment by occupation: 21.2% management, 19.8% professional, 13.0% services, 24.9% sales, 0.3% farming, 9.3% construction, 11.6% production (2000).
Income: Per capita income: $22,399 (2000); Median household income: $50,781 (2000); Poverty rate: 5.2% (2000).
Taxes: Total city taxes per capita: $94 (1997); City property taxes per capita: $94 (1997).
Education: High school graduation rate: 90.9% (2000); College graduation rate: 19.1% (2000).
Housing: Homeownership rate: 95.2% (2000); Median home value: $99,800 (2000); Median rent: $250 per month (2000); Median age of housing: 28 years (2000).
Transportation: Commute to work: 90.6% car, 0.0% public transportation, 1.4% walk, 8.0% work from home (2000); Travel time to work: 56.0% less than 15 minutes, 33.4% 15 to 30 minutes, 5.6% 30 to 45 minutes, 2.2% 45 to 60 minutes, 2.8% 60 minutes or more (2000)

LAKE ANDREW (township). Covers a land area of 29.348 square miles and a water area of 6.587 square miles. Located at 45.27° N. Lat.; 95.07° W. Long.
Population: 1,051 (2000); Race: 99.4% White, 0.3% Black, 0.0% Asian, 0.0% American Indian and Alaska Native, 0.0% Hispanic of any race, 0.3% two or more races (2000); Density: 35.8 persons per square mile (2000); Age: 21.4% under 18, 18.3% over 64 (2000); Marriage status: 20.1% never married, 71.5% now married, 3.1% widowed, 5.3% divorced (2000); Foreign born: 0.6% (2000); Ancestry (includes multiple ancestries): 40.6% Norwegian, 38.2% German, 15.9% Swedish, 7.0% English, 6.5% Irish (2000).
Economy: Employment by occupation: 16.8% management, 20.7% professional, 10.1% services, 29.9% sales, 1.6% farming, 11.1% construction, 9.8% production (2000).
Income: Per capita income: $27,344 (2000); Median household income: $54,464 (2000); Poverty rate: 2.5% (2000).

Taxes: Total city taxes per capita: $99 (1997); City property taxes per capita: $99 (1997).
Education: High school graduation rate: 87.5% (2000); College graduation rate: 22.0% (2000).
Housing: Homeownership rate: 94.7% (2000); Median home value: $141,700 (2000); Median rent: $385 per month (2000); Median age of housing: 28 years (2000).
Transportation: Commute to work: 89.5% car, 0.2% public transportation, 0.4% walk, 8.9% work from home (2000); Travel time to work: 22.0% less than 15 minutes, 56.9% 15 to 30 minutes, 10.6% 30 to 45 minutes, 2.2% 45 to 60 minutes, 8.4% 60 minutes or more (2000)

LAKE ELIZABETH (township). Covers a land area of 34.444 square miles and a water area of 1.534 square miles. Located at 45.03° N. Lat.; 94.80° W. Long.
Population: 277 (2000); Race: 100.0% White, 0.0% Black, 0.0% Asian, 0.0% American Indian and Alaska Native, 0.0% Hispanic of any race, 0.0% two or more races (2000); Density: 8.0 persons per square mile (2000); Age: 32.0% under 18, 15.8% over 64 (2000); Marriage status: 35.2% never married, 60.6% now married, 3.2% widowed, 0.9% divorced (2000); Foreign born: 0.0% (2000); Ancestry (includes multiple ancestries): 46.7% German, 23.7% Norwegian, 21.3% Swedish, 5.5% English, 5.2% European (2000).
Economy: Employment by occupation: 21.3% management, 9.4% professional, 12.6% services, 19.7% sales, 9.4% farming, 10.2% construction, 17.3% production (2000).
Income: Per capita income: $15,365 (2000); Median household income: $37,813 (2000); Poverty rate: 9.3% (2000).
Taxes: Total city taxes per capita: $86 (1997); City property taxes per capita: $86 (1997).
Education: High school graduation rate: 76.6% (2000); College graduation rate: 11.4% (2000).
Housing: Homeownership rate: 92.0% (2000); Median home value: $68,300 (2000); Median rent: $475 per month (2000); Median age of housing: 46 years (2000).
Transportation: Commute to work: 82.0% car, 0.8% public transportation, 9.0% walk, 4.1% work from home (2000); Travel time to work: 33.3% less than 15 minutes, 38.5% 15 to 30 minutes, 17.9% 30 to 45 minutes, 6.8% 45 to 60 minutes, 3.4% 60 minutes or more (2000)

LAKE LILLIAN (city). Covers a land area of 0.460 square miles and a water area of 0 square miles. Located at 44.94° N. Lat.; 94.88° W. Long. Elevation is 1,107 feet.
Population: 257 (2000); Race: 98.8% White, 0.0% Black, 0.0% Asian, 0.0% American Indian and Alaska Native, 7.5% Hispanic of any race, 0.0% two or more races (2000); Density: 559.0 persons per square mile (2000); Age: 23.6% under 18, 24.8% over 64 (2000); Marriage status: 19.6% never married, 45.6% now married, 17.6% widowed, 17.2% divorced (2000); Foreign born: 2.0% (2000); Ancestry (includes multiple ancestries): 36.2% German, 22.8% Norwegian, 15.0% Swedish, 7.9% Other groups, 6.7% Irish (2000).
Economy: Single-family building permits issued: 0 (2001) / 0 (2000); Multi-family building permits issued: 0 (2001) / 0 (2000); Employment by occupation: 10.3% management, 8.6% professional, 8.6% services, 33.6% sales, 4.3% farming, 8.6% construction, 25.9% production (2000).
Income: Per capita income: $16,881 (2000); Median household income: $26,458 (2000); Poverty rate: 14.6% (2000).
Taxes: Total city taxes per capita: $120 (1997); City property taxes per capita: $116 (1997).
Education: High school graduation rate: 67.8% (2000); College graduation rate: 4.5% (2000).
Housing: Homeownership rate: 88.4% (2000); Median home value: $43,800 (2000); Median rent: $275 per month (2000); Median age of housing: 44 years (2000).
Transportation: Commute to work: 84.5% car, 0.0% public transportation, 12.1% walk, 1.7% work from home (2000); Travel time to work: 51.8% less than 15 minutes, 11.4% 15 to 30 minutes, 19.3% 30 to 45 minutes, 14.0% 45 to 60 minutes, 3.5% 60 minutes or more (2000)

LAKE LILLIAN (township). Covers a land area of 35.623 square miles and a water area of 0.567 square miles. Located at 44.92° N. Lat.; 94.93° W. Long. Elevation is 1,107 feet.
Population: 221 (2000); Race: 96.8% White, 0.0% Black, 0.0% Asian, 0.0% American Indian and Alaska Native, 3.2% Hispanic of any race, 0.5% two or more races (2000); Density: 6.2 persons per square mile (2000); Age: 22.7% under 18, 20.5% over 64 (2000); Marriage status: 13.9% never married, 73.3% now married, 10.6% widowed, 2.2% divorced (2000); Foreign born: 0.0% (2000); Ancestry (includes multiple ancestries): 44.5% German, 30.0% Swedish, 20.9% Norwegian, 8.2% Irish, 6.8% Dutch (2000).
Economy: Livestock; grain; dairying. Manufacturing: agricultural equipment. Employment by occupation: 26.1% management, 19.8% professional, 17.1% services, 18.0% sales, 1.8% farming, 9.0% construction, 8.1% production (2000).
Income: Per capita income: $18,203 (2000); Median household income: $40,000 (2000); Poverty rate: 2.7% (2000).
Taxes: Total city taxes per capita: $74 (1997); City property taxes per capita: $74 (1997).
Education: High school graduation rate: 81.0% (2000); College graduation rate: 15.8% (2000).
Housing: Homeownership rate: 86.4% (2000); Median home value: $98,600 (2000); Median rent: $338 per month (2000); Median age of housing: 38 years (2000).
Transportation: Commute to work: 78.0% car, 0.0% public transportation, 1.8% walk, 20.2% work from home (2000); Travel time to work: 27.6% less than 15 minutes, 52.9% 15 to 30 minutes, 17.2% 30 to 45 minutes, 0.0% 45 to 60 minutes, 2.3% 60 minutes or more (2000)

MAMRE (township). Covers a land area of 33.882 square miles and a water area of 1.700 square miles. Located at 45.19° N. Lat.; 95.17° W. Long.
Population: 384 (2000); Race: 98.4% White, 0.0% Black, 1.6% Asian, 0.0% American Indian and Alaska Native, 3.1% Hispanic of any race, 0.0% two or more races (2000); Density: 11.3 persons per square mile (2000); Age: 31.3% under 18, 9.4% over 64 (2000); Marriage status: 23.2% never married, 67.0% now married, 3.9% widowed, 6.0% divorced (2000); Foreign born: 2.3% (2000); Ancestry (includes multiple ancestries): 46.5% German, 25.8% Norwegian, 20.9% Swedish, 9.4% Dutch, 6.3% Irish (2000).
Economy: Employment by occupation: 19.7% management, 12.6% professional, 8.6% services, 22.2% sales, 5.1% farming, 10.6% construction, 21.2% production (2000).
Income: Per capita income: $16,668 (2000); Median household income: $46,250 (2000); Poverty rate: 12.0% (2000).
Taxes: Total city taxes per capita: $57 (1997); City property taxes per capita: $57 (1997).
Education: High school graduation rate: 83.8% (2000); College graduation rate: 14.5% (2000).
Housing: Homeownership rate: 82.8% (2000); Median home value: $115,600 (2000); Median rent: $375 per month (2000); Median age of housing: 60+ years (2000).
Transportation: Commute to work: 85.4% car, 0.0% public transportation, 7.1% walk, 7.6% work from home (2000); Travel time to work: 29.5% less than 15 minutes, 51.9% 15 to 30 minutes, 13.7% 30 to 45 minutes, 2.2% 45 to 60 minutes, 2.7% 60 minutes or more (2000)

NEW LONDON (city). Covers a land area of 0.966 square miles and a water area of 0.060 square miles. Located at 45.29° N. Lat.; 94.94° W. Long. Elevation is 1,215 feet.
Population: 1,066 (2000); Race: 98.2% White, 0.2% Black, 0.0% Asian, 0.0% American Indian and Alaska Native, 1.7% Hispanic of any race, 0.8% two or more races (2000); Density: 1,103.4 persons per square mile (2000); Age: 24.3% under 18, 27.6% over 64 (2000); Marriage status: 17.7% never married, 54.1% now married, 19.5% widowed, 8.6% divorced (2000); Foreign born: 2.2% (2000); Ancestry (includes multiple ancestries): 36.2% Norwegian, 31.6% German, 23.1% Swedish, 6.8% Irish, 4.8% English (2000).
Economy: Single-family building permits issued: 8 (2001) / 0 (2000); Multi-family building permits issued: 0 (2001) / 4 (2000); Employment by occupation: 8.6% management, 19.2% professional, 16.9% services, 25.7% sales, 0.2% farming, 12.2% construction, 17.2% production (2000).
Income: Per capita income: $16,216 (2000); Median household income: $34,018 (2000); Poverty rate: 6.8% (2000).
Taxes: Total city taxes per capita: $189 (1997); City property taxes per capita: $178 (1997).
Education: High school graduation rate: 79.7% (2000); College graduation rate: 14.9% (2000).

School District(s)

New London-Spicer (PK-12)
2000 Enrollment: 1,814 320-354-2252

Housing: Homeownership rate: 76.3% (2000); Median home value: $81,400 (2000); Median rent: $338 per month (2000); Median age of housing: 42 years (2000).
Transportation: Commute to work: 91.8% car, 0.0% public transportation, 3.7% walk, 4.1% work from home (2000); Travel time to work: 37.9% less

than 15 minutes, 41.9% 15 to 30 minutes, 13.1% 30 to 45 minutes, 3.1% 45 to 60 minutes, 4.0% 60 minutes or more (2000)

NEW LONDON (township). Covers a land area of 24.794 square miles and a water area of 9.926 square miles. Located at 45.28° N. Lat.; 94.94° W. Long. Elevation is 1,215 feet.
Population: 3,057 (2000); Race: 98.6% White, 0.1% Black, 0.1% Asian, 0.1% American Indian and Alaska Native, 0.1% Hispanic of any race, 1.0% two or more races (2000); Density: 123.3 persons per square mile (2000); Age: 26.7% under 18, 10.9% over 64 (2000); Marriage status: 22.2% never married, 65.2% now married, 4.7% widowed, 7.8% divorced (2000); Foreign born: 0.6% (2000); Ancestry (includes multiple ancestries): 37.3% German, 36.1% Norwegian, 15.8% Swedish, 10.5% Irish, 7.1% English (2000).
Economy: Manufacturing: machinery, concrete. Fish hatchery here. Employment by occupation: 10.3% management, 22.8% professional, 13.4% services, 24.4% sales, 1.1% farming, 11.5% construction, 16.6% production (2000).
Income: Per capita income: $24,336 (2000); Median household income: $51,394 (2000); Poverty rate: 4.8% (2000).
Taxes: Total city taxes per capita: $34 (1997); City property taxes per capita: $34 (1997).
Education: High school graduation rate: 91.6% (2000); College graduation rate: 25.6% (2000).
Housing: Homeownership rate: 91.1% (2000); Median home value: $128,800 (2000); Median rent: $420 per month (2000); Median age of housing: 26 years (2000).
Transportation: Commute to work: 93.5% car, 0.2% public transportation, 1.2% walk, 4.1% work from home (2000); Travel time to work: 30.6% less than 15 minutes, 48.6% 15 to 30 minutes, 10.5% 30 to 45 minutes, 2.6% 45 to 60 minutes, 7.7% 60 minutes or more (2000)

NORWAY LAKE (township). Covers a land area of 32.635 square miles and a water area of 2.771 square miles. Located at 45.36° N. Lat.; 95.18° W. Long.
Population: 284 (2000); Race: 100.0% White, 0.0% Black, 0.0% Asian, 0.0% American Indian and Alaska Native, 0.0% Hispanic of any race, 0.0% two or more races (2000); Density: 8.7 persons per square mile (2000); Age: 21.9% under 18, 14.7% over 64 (2000); Marriage status: 22.1% never married, 63.8% now married, 6.0% widowed, 8.1% divorced (2000); Foreign born: 0.0% (2000); Ancestry (includes multiple ancestries): 68.8% Norwegian, 26.2% German, 12.5% Swedish, 5.4% Irish, 4.7% Dutch (2000).
Economy: Employment by occupation: 23.8% management, 9.3% professional, 17.9% services, 17.2% sales, 0.7% farming, 14.6% construction, 16.6% production (2000).
Income: Per capita income: $16,803 (2000); Median household income: $36,042 (2000); Poverty rate: 4.0% (2000).
Taxes: Total city taxes per capita: $58 (1997); City property taxes per capita: $58 (1997).
Education: High school graduation rate: 87.8% (2000); College graduation rate: 8.8% (2000).
Housing: Homeownership rate: 97.2% (2000); Median home value: $82,500 (2000); Median age of housing: 43 years (2000).
Transportation: Commute to work: 82.9% car, 0.0% public transportation, 4.8% walk, 12.3% work from home (2000); Travel time to work: 11.7% less than 15 minutes, 44.5% 15 to 30 minutes, 35.2% 30 to 45 minutes, 5.5% 45 to 60 minutes, 3.1% 60 minutes or more (2000)

PENNOCK (city). Covers a land area of 0.987 square miles and a water area of 0 square miles. Located at 45.14° N. Lat.; 95.17° W. Long. Elevation is 1,131 feet.
Population: 504 (2000); Race: 92.3% White, 0.4% Black, 0.0% Asian, 0.0% American Indian and Alaska Native, 10.1% Hispanic of any race, 0.0% two or more races (2000); Density: 510.5 persons per square mile (2000); Age: 35.3% under 18, 7.7% over 64 (2000); Marriage status: 29.2% never married, 57.0% now married, 5.1% widowed, 8.7% divorced (2000); Foreign born: 2.2% (2000); Ancestry (includes multiple ancestries): 47.2% German, 32.5% Norwegian, 13.7% Swedish, 11.3% Irish, 8.7% Other groups (2000).
Economy: Dairying; poultry, livestock; grain, sugar beets. Single-family building permits issued: 1 (2001) / 5 (2000); Multi-family building permits issued: 0 (2001) / 0 (2000); Employment by occupation: 6.4% management, 11.7% professional, 10.9% services, 29.4% sales, 1.9% farming, 15.5% construction, 24.2% production (2000).
Income: Per capita income: $16,296 (2000); Median household income: $42,273 (2000); Poverty rate: 4.6% (2000).
Taxes: Total city taxes per capita: $72 (1997); City property taxes per capita: $70 (1997).
Education: High school graduation rate: 83.7% (2000); College graduation rate: 8.0% (2000).
Housing: Homeownership rate: 85.2% (2000); Median home value: $64,500 (2000); Median rent: $363 per month (2000); Median age of housing: 38 years (2000).
Transportation: Commute to work: 95.0% car, 0.0% public transportation, 3.5% walk, 1.6% work from home (2000); Travel time to work: 34.3% less than 15 minutes, 53.1% 15 to 30 minutes, 4.7% 30 to 45 minutes, 3.5% 45 to 60 minutes, 4.3% 60 minutes or more (2000)

PRINSBURG (city). Covers a land area of 1.055 square miles and a water area of 0 square miles. Located at 44.93° N. Lat.; 95.19° W. Long. Elevation is 1,104 feet.
Population: 458 (2000); Race: 100.0% White, 0.0% Black, 0.0% Asian, 0.0% American Indian and Alaska Native, 0.0% Hispanic of any race, 0.0% two or more races (2000); Density: 434.3 persons per square mile (2000); Age: 24.8% under 18, 28.4% over 64 (2000); Marriage status: 12.0% never married, 78.6% now married, 8.5% widowed, 0.9% divorced (2000); Foreign born: 2.0% (2000); Ancestry (includes multiple ancestries): 71.6% Dutch, 33.4% German, 3.4% Norwegian, 2.3% Polish, 2.3% Irish (2000).
Economy: Single-family building permits issued: 0 (2001) / 2 (2000); Multi-family building permits issued: 2 (2001) / 0 (2000); Employment by occupation: 13.5% management, 17.6% professional, 14.5% services, 28.0% sales, 1.0% farming, 13.0% construction, 12.4% production (2000).
Income: Per capita income: $21,545 (2000); Median household income: $38,125 (2000); Poverty rate: 2.3% (2000).
Taxes: Total city taxes per capita: $81 (1997); City property taxes per capita: $81 (1997).
Education: High school graduation rate: 70.3% (2000); College graduation rate: 13.4% (2000).

School District(s)

Prinsburg (UG-UG)
2000 Enrollment: 0 320-978-4721
Housing: Homeownership rate: 94.0% (2000); Median home value: $64,300 (2000); Median rent: $319 per month (2000); Median age of housing: 44 years (2000).
Transportation: Commute to work: 83.7% car, 0.0% public transportation, 9.5% walk, 6.8% work from home (2000); Travel time to work: 59.3% less than 15 minutes, 31.6% 15 to 30 minutes, 6.8% 30 to 45 minutes, 0.0% 45 to 60 minutes, 2.3% 60 minutes or more (2000)

RAYMOND (city). Covers a land area of 0.610 square miles and a water area of 0 square miles. Located at 45.01° N. Lat.; 95.23° W. Long. Elevation is 1,084 feet.
Population: 803 (2000); Race: 93.5% White, 0.5% Black, 0.0% Asian, 0.7% American Indian and Alaska Native, 7.4% Hispanic of any race, 1.7% two or more races (2000); Density: 1,316.3 persons per square mile (2000); Age: 31.1% under 18, 15.2% over 64 (2000); Marriage status: 18.2% never married, 65.5% now married, 7.6% widowed, 8.7% divorced (2000); Foreign born: 1.1% (2000); Ancestry (includes multiple ancestries): 56.6% German, 22.4% Norwegian, 19.7% Dutch, 8.6% Other groups, 7.9% Swedish (2000).
Economy: Grain, sugar beets; poultry, livestock; dairying. Light manufacturing. Single-family building permits issued: 1 (2001) / 0 (2000); Multi-family building permits issued: 0 (2001) / 0 (2000); Employment by occupation: 9.9% management, 13.6% professional, 16.9% services, 24.1% sales, 2.0% farming, 9.7% construction, 23.8% production (2000).
Income: Per capita income: $15,399 (2000); Median household income: $34,083 (2000); Poverty rate: 10.8% (2000).
Taxes: Total city taxes per capita: $51 (1997); City property taxes per capita: $48 (1997).
Education: High school graduation rate: 78.6% (2000); College graduation rate: 11.9% (2000).
Housing: Homeownership rate: 75.9% (2000); Median home value: $61,200 (2000); Median rent: $300 per month (2000); Median age of housing: 40 years (2000).
Newspapers: Raymond-Prinsburg News (1 x week)
Transportation: Commute to work: 90.5% car, 0.0% public transportation, 3.6% walk, 5.9% work from home (2000); Travel time to work: 31.8% less than 15 minutes, 56.8% 15 to 30 minutes, 7.6% 30 to 45 minutes, 1.4% 45 to 60 minutes, 2.4% 60 minutes or more (2000)

REGAL (city). Covers a land area of 0.504 square miles and a water area of 0 square miles. Located at 45.40° N. Lat.; 94.84° W. Long. Elevation is 1,219 feet.
Population: 40 (2000); Race: 100.0% White, 0.0% Black, 0.0% Asian, 0.0% American Indian and Alaska Native, 0.0% Hispanic of any race, 0.0% two or

more races (2000); Density: 79.4 persons per square mile (2000); Age: 0.0% under 18, 35.5% over 64 (2000); Marriage status: 38.7% never married, 45.2% now married, 16.1% widowed, 0.0% divorced (2000); Foreign born: 0.0% (2000); Ancestry (includes multiple ancestries): 77.4% German, 12.9% Swedish, 9.7% Polish, 6.5% Irish (2000).
Economy: Dairying. Employment by occupation: 16.7% management, 16.7% professional, 41.7% services, 0.0% sales, 0.0% farming, 16.7% construction, 8.3% production (2000).
Income: Per capita income: $26,710 (2000); Median household income: $39,167 (2000); Poverty rate: 0.0% (2000).
Taxes: Total city taxes per capita: $98 (1997); City property taxes per capita: $39 (1997).
Education: High school graduation rate: 80.0% (2000); College graduation rate: 24.0% (2000).
Housing: Homeownership rate: 83.3% (2000); Median home value: $34,400 (2000); Median rent: $263 per month (2000); Median age of housing: 30 years (2000).
Transportation: Commute to work: 75.0% car, 0.0% public transportation, 25.0% walk, 0.0% work from home (2000); Travel time to work: 41.7% less than 15 minutes, 41.7% 15 to 30 minutes, 16.7% 30 to 45 minutes, 0.0% 45 to 60 minutes, 0.0% 60 minutes or more (2000)

ROSELAND (township). Covers a land area of 35.134 square miles and a water area of 0.010 square miles. Located at 44.93° N. Lat.; 95.07° W. Long.
Population: 477 (2000); Race: 100.0% White, 0.0% Black, 0.0% Asian, 0.0% American Indian and Alaska Native, 2.1% Hispanic of any race, 0.0% two or more races (2000); Density: 13.6 persons per square mile (2000); Age: 35.5% under 18, 10.5% over 64 (2000); Marriage status: 17.7% never married, 73.2% now married, 3.8% widowed, 5.3% divorced (2000); Foreign born: 0.4% (2000); Ancestry (includes multiple ancestries): 38.6% German, 31.6% Dutch, 16.6% Swedish, 15.8% Norwegian, 6.6% Irish (2000).
Economy: Employment by occupation: 15.1% management, 18.1% professional, 14.2% services, 22.8% sales, 3.0% farming, 9.1% construction, 17.7% production (2000).
Income: Per capita income: $15,225 (2000); Median household income: $40,625 (2000); Poverty rate: 9.1% (2000).
Taxes: Total city taxes per capita: $50 (1997); City property taxes per capita: $50 (1997).
Education: High school graduation rate: 80.8% (2000); College graduation rate: 16.4% (2000).
Housing: Homeownership rate: 87.0% (2000); Median home value: $66,800 (2000); Median rent: $425 per month (2000); Median age of housing: 60 years (2000).
Transportation: Commute to work: 83.4% car, 0.0% public transportation, 5.2% walk, 9.2% work from home (2000); Travel time to work: 24.5% less than 15 minutes, 53.4% 15 to 30 minutes, 13.0% 30 to 45 minutes, 2.9% 45 to 60 minutes, 6.3% 60 minutes or more (2000)

ROSEVILLE (township). Covers a land area of 34.967 square miles and a water area of 0.435 square miles. Located at 45.36° N. Lat.; 94.83° W. Long.
Population: 570 (2000); Race: 98.5% White, 0.0% Black, 0.0% Asian, 0.5% American Indian and Alaska Native, 0.8% Hispanic of any race, 0.3% two or more races (2000); Density: 16.3 persons per square mile (2000); Age: 36.9% under 18, 9.5% over 64 (2000); Marriage status: 27.4% never married, 64.5% now married, 4.7% widowed, 3.3% divorced (2000); Foreign born: 0.2% (2000); Ancestry (includes multiple ancestries): 56.3% German, 19.5% Norwegian, 8.1% Irish, 5.1% Swedish, 5.1% Dutch (2000).
Economy: Unemployment rate: 2.4% (11/2002); Total civilian labor force: 21,981 (11/2002); Employment by occupation: 20.0% management, 6.3% professional, 18.9% services, 24.6% sales, 5.3% farming, 9.5% construction, 15.4% production (2000).
Income: Per capita income: $14,404 (2000); Median household income: $35,962 (2000); Poverty rate: 11.8% (2000).
Taxes: Total city taxes per capita: $77 (1997); City property taxes per capita: $77 (1997).
Education: High school graduation rate: 84.5% (2000); College graduation rate: 10.3% (2000).
Housing: Homeownership rate: 84.2% (2000); Median home value: $91,800 (2000); Median rent: $313 per month (2000); Median age of housing: 32 years (2000).
Transportation: Commute to work: 83.2% car, 1.4% public transportation, 3.6% walk, 11.8% work from home (2000); Travel time to work: 36.2% less than 15 minutes, 35.0% 15 to 30 minutes, 18.7% 30 to 45 minutes, 5.3% 45 to 60 minutes, 4.9% 60 minutes or more (2000)

SAINT JOHNS (township). Covers a land area of 34.686 square miles and a water area of 0.319 square miles. Located at 45.11° N. Lat.; 95.18° W. Long.
Population: 386 (2000); Race: 99.5% White, 0.0% Black, 0.0% Asian, 0.0% American Indian and Alaska Native, 2.1% Hispanic of any race, 0.3% two or more races (2000); Density: 11.1 persons per square mile (2000); Age: 23.1% under 18, 9.6% over 64 (2000); Marriage status: 21.2% never married, 70.6% now married, 4.7% widowed, 3.5% divorced (2000); Foreign born: 0.0% (2000); Ancestry (includes multiple ancestries): 46.1% German, 37.6% Norwegian, 20.2% Swedish, 17.4% Dutch, 7.3% Irish (2000).
Economy: Employment by occupation: 17.6% management, 18.4% professional, 11.5% services, 19.7% sales, 3.7% farming, 12.3% construction, 16.8% production (2000).
Income: Per capita income: $21,653 (2000); Median household income: $48,125 (2000); Poverty rate: 4.4% (2000).
Education: High school graduation rate: 91.8% (2000); College graduation rate: 13.8% (2000).
Housing: Homeownership rate: 82.1% (2000); Median home value: $111,600 (2000); Median rent: $258 per month (2000); Median age of housing: 36 years (2000).
Transportation: Commute to work: 92.1% car, 0.0% public transportation, 0.8% walk, 7.0% work from home (2000); Travel time to work: 38.2% less than 15 minutes, 51.1% 15 to 30 minutes, 7.1% 30 to 45 minutes, 2.2% 45 to 60 minutes, 1.3% 60 minutes or more (2000)

SPICER (city). Covers a land area of 1.084 square miles and a water area of 0.007 square miles. Located at 45.23° N. Lat.; 94.93° W. Long. Elevation is 1,171 feet.
Population: 1,126 (2000); Race: 98.3% White, 0.2% Black, 0.2% Asian, 0.2% American Indian and Alaska Native, 1.5% Hispanic of any race, 0.1% two or more races (2000); Density: 1,038.4 persons per square mile (2000); Age: 21.4% under 18, 20.9% over 64 (2000); Marriage status: 21.6% never married, 54.8% now married, 10.7% widowed, 12.9% divorced (2000); Foreign born: 0.8% (2000); Ancestry (includes multiple ancestries): 36.6% German, 31.8% Norwegian, 15.3% Swedish, 7.0% Irish, 6.2% English (2000).
Economy: Grain, sugar beets, beans; livestock, poultry; dairying; light manufacturing. Single-family building permits issued: 11 (2001) / 2 (2000); Multi-family building permits issued: 0 (2001) / 0 (2000); Employment by occupation: 15.1% management, 19.0% professional, 14.0% services, 26.6% sales, 0.0% farming, 10.6% construction, 14.7% production (2000).
Income: Per capita income: $21,103 (2000); Median household income: $33,913 (2000); Poverty rate: 8.7% (2000).
Taxes: Total city taxes per capita: $380 (1997); City property taxes per capita: $366 (1997).
Education: High school graduation rate: 83.1% (2000); College graduation rate: 21.4% (2000).
Housing: Homeownership rate: 64.1% (2000); Median home value: $96,700 (2000); Median rent: $363 per month (2000); Median age of housing: 24 years (2000).
Newspapers: Kandiyohi County Times (1 x week)
Transportation: Commute to work: 90.3% car, 1.8% public transportation, 3.3% walk, 4.2% work from home (2000); Travel time to work: 33.8% less than 15 minutes, 48.3% 15 to 30 minutes, 7.8% 30 to 45 minutes, 0.8% 45 to 60 minutes, 9.3% 60 minutes or more (2000)

SUNBURG (city). Covers a land area of 0.483 square miles and a water area of 0.021 square miles. Located at 45.34° N. Lat.; 95.24° W. Long. Elevation is 1,259 feet.
Population: 110 (2000); Race: 100.0% White, 0.0% Black, 0.0% Asian, 0.0% American Indian and Alaska Native, 0.0% Hispanic of any race, 0.0% two or more races (2000); Density: 227.9 persons per square mile (2000); Age: 15.9% under 18, 31.8% over 64 (2000); Marriage status: 36.5% never married, 49.0% now married, 9.4% widowed, 5.2% divorced (2000); Foreign born: 1.9% (2000); Ancestry (includes multiple ancestries): 67.3% Norwegian, 21.5% German, 15.9% Swedish, 5.6% Irish, 5.6% Dutch (2000).
Economy: Single-family building permits issued: 0 (2001) / 1 (2000); Multi-family building permits issued: 0 (2001) / 0 (2000); Employment by occupation: 13.6% management, 15.9% professional, 13.6% services, 22.7% sales, 0.0% farming, 13.6% construction, 20.5% production (2000).
Income: Per capita income: $11,654 (2000); Median household income: $22,500 (2000); Poverty rate: 17.8% (2000).
Taxes: Total city taxes per capita: $155 (1997); City property taxes per capita: $155 (1997).

Education: High school graduation rate: 60.0% (2000); College graduation rate: 1.3% (2000).
Housing: Homeownership rate: 86.8% (2000); Median home value: $32,500 (2000); Median rent: $225 per month (2000); Median age of housing: 60+ years (2000).
Transportation: Commute to work: 79.5% car, 0.0% public transportation, 18.2% walk, 2.3% work from home (2000); Travel time to work: 23.3% less than 15 minutes, 11.6% 15 to 30 minutes, 44.2% 30 to 45 minutes, 7.0% 45 to 60 minutes, 14.0% 60 minutes or more (2000)

WHITEFIELD (township). Covers a land area of 35.290 square miles and a water area of 0.938 square miles. Located at 45.02° N. Lat.; 95.07° W. Long.
Population: 571 (2000); Race: 97.1% White, 0.0% Black, 0.0% Asian, 0.3% American Indian and Alaska Native, 3.8% Hispanic of any race, 0.2% two or more races (2000); Density: 16.2 persons per square mile (2000); Age: 30.5% under 18, 11.7% over 64 (2000); Marriage status: 23.3% never married, 66.8% now married, 5.5% widowed, 4.3% divorced (2000); Foreign born: 4.1% (2000); Ancestry (includes multiple ancestries): 32.6% German, 20.4% Swedish, 19.2% Norwegian, 13.9% Dutch, 5.0% Other groups (2000).
Economy: Employment by occupation: 22.7% management, 15.3% professional, 14.0% services, 19.7% sales, 6.7% farming, 6.7% construction, 15.0% production (2000).
Income: Per capita income: $20,288 (2000); Median household income: $44,375 (2000); Poverty rate: 4.3% (2000).
Taxes: Total city taxes per capita: $65 (1997); City property taxes per capita: $65 (1997).
Education: High school graduation rate: 82.1% (2000); College graduation rate: 6.2% (2000).
Housing: Homeownership rate: 86.5% (2000); Median home value: $80,300 (2000); Median rent: $458 per month (2000); Median age of housing: 45 years (2000).
Transportation: Commute to work: 82.8% car, 0.0% public transportation, 6.4% walk, 10.8% work from home (2000); Travel time to work: 50.4% less than 15 minutes, 41.3% 15 to 30 minutes, 5.7% 30 to 45 minutes, 0.8% 45 to 60 minutes, 1.9% 60 minutes or more (2000)

WILLMAR (city). Covers a land area of 11.840 square miles and a water area of 1.759 square miles. Located at 45.12° N. Lat.; 95.04° W. Long. Elevation is 1,131 feet.
History: Willmar was founded in 1869 on land owned by the St. Paul & Pacific Railroad Company, though there had been settlers here as early as 1856. The town was named for Leon Willmar, a railroad agent. Willmar became a division point for the Great Northern Railway, and a shipping center for grain and livestock.
Population: 18,351 (2000); Race: 88.0% White, 1.3% Black, 0.4% Asian, 0.2% American Indian and Alaska Native, 15.4% Hispanic of any race, 2.1% two or more races (2000); Density: 1,549.9 persons per square mile (2000); Age: 26.2% under 18, 16.4% over 64 (2000); Marriage status: 28.7% never married, 53.3% now married, 8.7% widowed, 9.3% divorced (2000); Foreign born: 7.0% (2000); Ancestry (includes multiple ancestries): 34.0% German, 25.2% Norwegian, 16.3% Other groups, 13.5% Swedish, 6.4% Irish (2000).
Vital Statistics: Birth rate: 149.3 per 10,000 population (1998)
Economy: Single-family building permits issued: 38 (2001) / 16 (2000); Multi-family building permits issued: 8 (2001) / 56 (2000); Employment by occupation: 9.8% management, 17.7% professional, 16.8% services, 24.5% sales, 1.4% farming, 7.2% construction, 22.7% production (2000).
Income: Per capita income: $18,515 (2000); Median household income: $33,455 (2000); Poverty rate: 13.1% (2000).
Taxes: Total city taxes per capita: $238 (2000); City property taxes per capita: $147 (2000).
Education: High school graduation rate: 79.2% (2000); College graduation rate: 17.7% (2000).

School District(s)

Willmar (PK-12)
2000 Enrollment: 4,587 320-231-8500

Two-year College(s)

Rice Memorial Hospital School of X-ray Technology (Public)
2001 Enrollment: n/a 320-231-4530
2001 Tuition: In-state $600; Out-of-state $600
Ridgewater College (Public)
2001 Enrollment: 3,801 800-722-1151
2001 Tuition: In-state $2,433; Out-of-state $4,866

Housing: Homeownership rate: 62.7% (2000); Median home value: $83,700 (2000); Median rent: $400 per month (2000); Median age of housing: 30 years (2000).
Hospitals: Rice Memorial Hospital (136 beds); Willmar Regional Treatment Center (467 beds)
Safety: Violent crime rate: 31.8 per 10,000 population; Property crime rate: 362.3 per 10,000 population (2001).
Newspapers: West Central Tribune (6 x week); Sunday Reminder (1 x week)
Transportation: Commute to work: 89.7% car, 2.9% public transportation, 3.9% walk, 2.8% work from home (2000); Travel time to work: 72.4% less than 15 minutes, 16.0% 15 to 30 minutes, 6.1% 30 to 45 minutes, 2.2% 45 to 60 minutes, 3.3% 60 minutes or more (2000)

Additional Information Contacts

West Central Association of Realtors 320-235-6881
Willmar Chamber of Commerce 320-235-0300

WILLMAR (township). Covers a land area of 23.034 square miles and a water area of 0.055 square miles. Located at 45.11° N. Lat.; 95.08° W. Long. Elevation is 1,131 feet.
History: Settled 1856; Incorporated as a city 1901.
Population: 661 (2000); Race: 92.3% White, 0.0% Black, 1.4% Asian, 0.8% American Indian and Alaska Native, 10.9% Hispanic of any race, 2.1% two or more races (2000); Density: 28.7 persons per square mile (2000); Age: 32.5% under 18, 9.9% over 64 (2000); Marriage status: 38.0% never married, 54.1% now married, 2.7% widowed, 5.2% divorced (2000); Foreign born: 8.0% (2000); Ancestry (includes multiple ancestries): 38.2% German, 26.5% Norwegian, 12.5% Other groups, 10.6% Swedish, 7.6% English (2000).
Economy: Railroad junction. Shipping center for grain and livestock. Manufacturing includes consumer goods, beverages, fabricated metal products, building materials, machinery, wood products, turkey processing, printing and publishing. Employment by occupation: 9.6% management, 16.9% professional, 19.1% services, 18.0% sales, 5.1% farming, 10.3% construction, 21.0% production (2000).
Income: Per capita income: $15,732 (2000); Median household income: $44,688 (2000); Poverty rate: 12.2% (2000).
Taxes: Total city taxes per capita: $89 (1997); City property taxes per capita: $87 (1997).
Education: High school graduation rate: 80.3% (2000); College graduation rate: 15.0% (2000).
Housing: Homeownership rate: 72.8% (2000); Median home value: $121,300 (2000); Median rent: $386 per month (2000); Median age of housing: 26 years (2000).
Transportation: Commute to work: 90.7% car, 0.0% public transportation, 3.7% walk, 5.6% work from home (2000); Travel time to work: 70.2% less than 15 minutes, 22.7% 15 to 30 minutes, 1.6% 30 to 45 minutes, 1.6% 45 to 60 minutes, 3.9% 60 minutes or more (2000)

Kittson County

Located in northwestern Minnesota; bounded on the west by the Red River and the North Dakota border, and on the north by the Canadian province of Manitoba; drained by Two Rivers. Covers a land area of 1,097.10 square miles, a water area of 6.40 square miles, and is located in the Central Time Zone. The county government was organized in 1879. County seat is Hallock.
Population: 5,285 (2000); Race: 97.7% White, 0.4% Black, 0.3% Asian, 0.6% American Indian and Alaska Native, 1.3% Hispanic of any race, 0.9% two or more races (2000); Density: 4.8 persons per square mile (2000); Age: 25.1% under 18, 21.6% over 64 (2000).
Religion: Five largest groups: 53.6% Evangelical Lutheran Church in America, 15.6% Catholic Church, 4.4% The Evangelical Covenant Church, 3.9% Presbyterian Church (U.S.A.), 2.0% Assemblies of God (2000).
Economy: Unemployment rate: 4.8% (11/2002); Total civilian labor force: 2,195 (11/2002); Leading industries: Companies that employ more than 1,000 persons: 0 (2000); Companies that employ more than 100 persons: 1 (2000); Farms: 558 totaling 501,466 acres (1997); Minority business ownership rate: 0.0% (1997); Women business ownership rate: 0.0% (1997); Retail sales per capita: $7,096 (1997). Single-family building permits issued: 10 (2001) / 10 (2000); Multi-family building permits issued: 0 (2001) / 0 (2000).
Income: Per capita income: $16,525 (2000); Median household income: $32,515 (2000); Poverty rate: 10.2% (2000); Bankruptcy rate: 2.50% (2001).
Taxes: Total county taxes per capita: $434 (2000); County property taxes per capita: $423 (2000).
Education: High school graduation rate: 79.7% (2000); College graduation rate: 14.8% (2000).
Housing: Homeownership rate: 82.7% (2000); Median home value: $39,400 (2000); Median rent: $258 per month (2000); Median age of housing: 45 years (2000).

Health: Birth rate: 115.4 per 10,000 population (1998); Age adjusted death rate: 85.4 per 10,000 population (1999); Age adjusted cancer mortality rate: 185.2 (Unreliable figure as per CDC) deaths per 100,000 population (1999). Number of physicians: 11.4 per 10,000 population (1999); Number of hospital beds: 194.9 per 10,000 population (1999).
Elections: 2000 Presidential election results: 42.0% Gore, 51.3% Bush, 2.6% Nader, 3.3% Buchanan
National and State Parks: Beaches State Wildlife Management Area; Hazelton State Game Refuge; Joe River State Wildlife Area; Lake Bronson State Park; Skull Lake State Wildlife Management Area; Twin Lakes State Wildlife Management Area
Additional Information Contacts
Kittson County Government Offices 218-843-2655

Kittson County Communities

ARVESON (township). Covers a land area of 31.306 square miles and a water area of 3.295 square miles. Located at 48.58° N. Lat.; 96.47° W. Long.
Population: 100 (2000); Race: 100.0% White, 0.0% Black, 0.0% Asian, 0.0% American Indian and Alaska Native, 0.0% Hispanic of any race, 0.0% two or more races (2000); Density: 3.2 persons per square mile (2000); Age: 17.6% under 18, 23.1% over 64 (2000); Marriage status: 14.1% never married, 76.9% now married, 2.6% widowed, 6.4% divorced (2000); Foreign born: 3.3% (2000); Ancestry (includes multiple ancestries): 41.8% Norwegian, 36.3% German, 29.7% Swedish, 4.4% Danish, 3.3% Swiss (2000).
Economy: Employment by occupation: 12.5% management, 17.5% professional, 15.0% services, 20.0% sales, 0.0% farming, 10.0% construction, 25.0% production (2000).
Income: Per capita income: $12,535 (2000); Median household income: $27,188 (2000); Poverty rate: 25.3% (2000).
Taxes: Total city taxes per capita: $73 (1997); City property taxes per capita: $73 (1997).
Education: High school graduation rate: 76.4% (2000); College graduation rate: 8.3% (2000).
Housing: Homeownership rate: 100.0% (2000); Median home value: $38,800 (2000); Median age of housing: 46 years (2000).
Transportation: Commute to work: 95.0% car, 0.0% public transportation, 0.0% walk, 5.0% work from home (2000); Travel time to work: 78.9% less than 15 minutes, 10.5% 15 to 30 minutes, 5.3% 30 to 45 minutes, 0.0% 45 to 60 minutes, 5.3% 60 minutes or more (2000)

CANNON (township). Covers a land area of 35.743 square miles and a water area of 0 square miles. Located at 48.82° N. Lat.; 96.60° W. Long.
Population: 22 (2000); Race: 93.3% White, 0.0% Black, 0.0% Asian, 0.0% American Indian and Alaska Native, 0.0% Hispanic of any race, 6.7% two or more races (2000); Density: 0.6 persons per square mile (2000); Age: 16.7% under 18, 40.0% over 64 (2000); Marriage status: 25.0% never married, 67.9% now married, 7.1% widowed, 0.0% divorced (2000); Foreign born: 0.0% (2000); Ancestry (includes multiple ancestries): 60.0% Norwegian, 33.3% Swedish, 16.7% German, 16.7% United States or American, 13.3% Scotch-Irish (2000).
Economy: Employment by occupation: 18.2% management, 0.0% professional, 27.3% services, 18.2% sales, 36.4% farming, 0.0% construction, 0.0% production (2000).
Income: Per capita income: $15,140 (2000); Median household income: $36,250 (2000); Poverty rate: 13.3% (2000).
Taxes: Total city taxes per capita: $294 (1997); City property taxes per capita: $294 (1997).
Education: High school graduation rate: 92.0% (2000); College graduation rate: 16.0% (2000).
Housing: Homeownership rate: 86.7% (2000); Median home value: $45,000 (2000); Median age of housing: 52 years (2000).
Transportation: Commute to work: 81.8% car, 0.0% public transportation, 0.0% walk, 18.2% work from home (2000); Travel time to work: 22.2% less than 15 minutes, 22.2% 15 to 30 minutes, 55.6% 30 to 45 minutes, 0.0% 45 to 60 minutes, 0.0% 60 minutes or more (2000)

CARIBOU (township). Covers a land area of 44.193 square miles and a water area of 0.030 square miles. Located at 48.95° N. Lat.; 96.45° W. Long.
Population: 48 (2000); Race: 100.0% White, 0.0% Black, 0.0% Asian, 0.0% American Indian and Alaska Native, 0.0% Hispanic of any race, 0.0% two or more races (2000); Density: 1.1 persons per square mile (2000); Age: 14.0% under 18, 18.6% over 64 (2000); Marriage status: 34.2% never married, 60.5% now married, 5.3% widowed, 0.0% divorced (2000); Foreign born: 0.0% (2000); Ancestry (includes multiple ancestries): 32.6% German, 27.9% Norwegian, 9.3% Polish, 7.0% English, 4.7% Swedish (2000).
Economy: Employment by occupation: 22.7% management, 0.0% professional, 31.8% services, 0.0% sales, 13.6% farming, 0.0% construction, 31.8% production (2000).
Income: Per capita income: $8,835 (2000); Median household income: $30,625 (2000); Poverty rate: 16.3% (2000).
Taxes: Total city taxes per capita: $22 (1997); City property taxes per capita: $22 (1997).
Education: High school graduation rate: 80.0% (2000); College graduation rate: 0.0% (2000).
Housing: Homeownership rate: 100.0% (2000); Median age of housing: 37 years (2000).
Transportation: Commute to work: 77.3% car, 0.0% public transportation, 0.0% walk, 22.7% work from home (2000); Travel time to work: 0.0% less than 15 minutes, 17.6% 15 to 30 minutes, 17.6% 30 to 45 minutes, 11.8% 45 to 60 minutes, 52.9% 60 minutes or more (2000)

CLOW (township). Covers a land area of 45.504 square miles and a water area of 0.044 square miles. Located at 48.94° N. Lat.; 96.99° W. Long.
Population: 37 (2000); Race: 97.9% White, 0.0% Black, 0.0% Asian, 0.0% American Indian and Alaska Native, 0.0% Hispanic of any race, 2.1% two or more races (2000); Density: 0.8 persons per square mile (2000); Age: 31.3% under 18, 4.2% over 64 (2000); Marriage status: 11.4% never married, 82.9% now married, 5.7% widowed, 0.0% divorced (2000); Foreign born: 0.0% (2000); Ancestry (includes multiple ancestries): 37.5% German, 27.1% Swedish, 4.2% Irish, 4.2% English, 4.2% Polish (2000).
Economy: Employment by occupation: 14.3% management, 9.5% professional, 0.0% services, 14.3% sales, 0.0% farming, 14.3% construction, 47.6% production (2000).
Income: Per capita income: $15,044 (2000); Median household income: $32,083 (2000); Poverty rate: 4.2% (2000).
Taxes: Total city taxes per capita: $484 (1997); City property taxes per capita: $484 (1997).
Education: High school graduation rate: 100.0% (2000); College graduation rate: 9.1% (2000).
Housing: Homeownership rate: 76.5% (2000); Median home value: $17,500 (2000); Median rent: $225 per month (2000); Median age of housing: 55 years (2000).
Transportation: Commute to work: 47.6% car, 0.0% public transportation, 0.0% walk, 52.4% work from home (2000); Travel time to work: 40.0% less than 15 minutes, 40.0% 15 to 30 minutes, 0.0% 30 to 45 minutes, 0.0% 45 to 60 minutes, 20.0% 60 minutes or more (2000)

DAVIS (township). Covers a land area of 35.277 square miles and a water area of 0.043 square miles. Located at 48.59° N. Lat.; 96.85° W. Long.
Population: 48 (2000); Race: 100.0% White, 0.0% Black, 0.0% Asian, 0.0% American Indian and Alaska Native, 0.0% Hispanic of any race, 0.0% two or more races (2000); Density: 1.4 persons per square mile (2000); Age: 24.5% under 18, 22.6% over 64 (2000); Marriage status: 20.5% never married, 79.5% now married, 0.0% widowed, 0.0% divorced (2000); Foreign born: 0.0% (2000); Ancestry (includes multiple ancestries): 30.2% Swedish, 26.4% Polish, 24.5% German, 20.8% Norwegian, 18.9% French (except Basque) (2000).
Economy: Employment by occupation: 37.5% management, 25.0% professional, 8.3% services, 8.3% sales, 12.5% farming, 0.0% construction, 8.3% production (2000).
Income: Per capita income: $17,189 (2000); Median household income: $33,750 (2000); Poverty rate: 0.0% (2000).
Taxes: Total city taxes per capita: $298 (1997); City property taxes per capita: $298 (1997).
Education: High school graduation rate: 85.7% (2000); College graduation rate: 20.0% (2000).
Housing: Homeownership rate: 88.9% (2000); Median home value: $32,500 (2000); Median rent: $425 per month (2000); Median age of housing: 60+ years (2000).
Transportation: Commute to work: 83.3% car, 0.0% public transportation, 0.0% walk, 16.7% work from home (2000); Travel time to work: 60.0% less than 15 minutes, 20.0% 15 to 30 minutes, 10.0% 30 to 45 minutes, 10.0% 45 to 60 minutes, 0.0% 60 minutes or more (2000)

DEERWOOD (township). Covers a land area of 35.614 square miles and a water area of 0 square miles. Located at 48.59° N. Lat.; 96.59° W. Long. Elevation is 998 feet.
Population: 186 (2000); Race: 95.8% White, 0.0% Black, 4.2% Asian, 0.0% American Indian and Alaska Native, 1.6% Hispanic of any race, 0.0% two or

more races (2000); Density: 5.2 persons per square mile (2000); Age: 25.0% under 18, 18.2% over 64 (2000); Marriage status: 23.6% never married, 59.9% now married, 7.0% widowed, 9.6% divorced (2000); Foreign born: 4.2% (2000); Ancestry (includes multiple ancestries): 46.9% Norwegian, 24.5% Swedish, 18.8% German, 6.8% French (except Basque), 6.3% United States or American (2000).
Economy: Employment by occupation: 11.7% management, 25.5% professional, 6.4% services, 14.9% sales, 5.3% farming, 7.4% construction, 28.7% production (2000).
Income: Per capita income: $13,680 (2000); Median household income: $29,167 (2000); Poverty rate: 23.6% (2000).
Taxes: Total city taxes per capita: $57 (1997); City property taxes per capita: $57 (1997).
Education: High school graduation rate: 73.7% (2000); College graduation rate: 12.4% (2000).
Housing: Homeownership rate: 100.0% (2000); Median home value: $48,300 (2000); Median age of housing: 39 years (2000).
Transportation: Commute to work: 78.7% car, 0.0% public transportation, 18.1% walk, 3.2% work from home (2000); Travel time to work: 45.1% less than 15 minutes, 6.6% 15 to 30 minutes, 13.2% 30 to 45 minutes, 25.3% 45 to 60 minutes, 9.9% 60 minutes or more (2000)

DONALDSON (city). Covers a land area of 0.826 square miles and a water area of 0 square miles. Located at 48.57° N. Lat.; 96.89° W. Long. Elevation is 827 feet.
History: Donaldson was named for Captain Hugh Donaldson, a former Civil War officer who managed a very large farm in this area.
Population: 41 (2000); Race: 100.0% White, 0.0% Black, 0.0% Asian, 0.0% American Indian and Alaska Native, 0.0% Hispanic of any race, 0.0% two or more races (2000); Density: 49.6 persons per square mile (2000); Age: 36.5% under 18, 9.6% over 64 (2000); Marriage status: 27.3% never married, 33.3% now married, 6.1% widowed, 33.3% divorced (2000); Foreign born: 0.0% (2000); Ancestry (includes multiple ancestries): 28.8% Scandinavian, 28.8% Norwegian, 28.8% Swedish, 19.2% German, 11.5% Polish (2000).
Economy: Employment by occupation: 15.4% management, 0.0% professional, 15.4% services, 46.2% sales, 0.0% farming, 0.0% construction, 23.1% production (2000).
Income: Per capita income: $11,637 (2000); Median household income: $26,875 (2000); Poverty rate: 7.7% (2000).
Taxes: Total city taxes per capita: $173 (1997); City property taxes per capita: $135 (1997).
Education: High school graduation rate: 89.7% (2000); College graduation rate: 6.9% (2000).
Housing: Homeownership rate: 90.0% (2000); Median home value: $13,800 (2000); Median age of housing: 48 years (2000).
Transportation: Commute to work: 84.6% car, 0.0% public transportation, 15.4% walk, 0.0% work from home (2000); Travel time to work: 30.8% less than 15 minutes, 30.8% 15 to 30 minutes, 23.1% 30 to 45 minutes, 15.4% 45 to 60 minutes, 0.0% 60 minutes or more (2000)

GRANVILLE (township). Covers a land area of 34.507 square miles and a water area of 0.008 square miles. Located at 48.85° N. Lat.; 96.87° W. Long.
Population: 104 (2000); Race: 98.2% White, 0.0% Black, 0.0% Asian, 0.0% American Indian and Alaska Native, 0.9% Hispanic of any race, 1.8% two or more races (2000); Density: 3.0 persons per square mile (2000); Age: 27.3% under 18, 13.6% over 64 (2000); Marriage status: 14.0% never married, 73.3% now married, 8.1% widowed, 4.7% divorced (2000); Foreign born: 0.0% (2000); Ancestry (includes multiple ancestries): 55.5% Swedish, 20.0% German, 12.7% Norwegian, 12.7% Polish, 10.0% United States or American (2000).
Economy: Employment by occupation: 8.3% management, 15.0% professional, 25.0% services, 21.7% sales, 1.7% farming, 16.7% construction, 11.7% production (2000).
Income: Per capita income: $16,403 (2000); Median household income: $42,292 (2000); Poverty rate: 13.9% (2000).
Taxes: Total city taxes per capita: $286 (1997); City property taxes per capita: $286 (1997).
Education: High school graduation rate: 90.5% (2000); College graduation rate: 9.5% (2000).
Housing: Homeownership rate: 100.0% (2000); Median home value: $45,700 (2000); Median age of housing: 55 years (2000).
Transportation: Commute to work: 89.8% car, 0.0% public transportation, 0.0% walk, 10.2% work from home (2000); Travel time to work: 22.6% less than 15 minutes, 47.2% 15 to 30 minutes, 24.5% 30 to 45 minutes, 5.7% 45 to 60 minutes, 0.0% 60 minutes or more (2000)

HALLOCK (city). Covers a land area of 2.086 square miles and a water area of 0 square miles. Located at 48.77° N. Lat.; 96.94° W. Long. Elevation is 817 feet.
History: Hallock was named for Charles W. Hallock (1834-1917), a journalist and editor, founder of "Forest and Stream" magazine. The town was established in an area with an abundance of game, and Hallock was a great sportsman. The old Pembina Trail through the Hallock area was used for generations by pioneers, and perhaps even as early as the 1300's by a Norse-Gothic party which is thought to have visited this part of Minnesota.
Population: 1,196 (2000); Race: 98.3% White, 0.0% Black, 0.6% Asian, 0.3% American Indian and Alaska Native, 0.8% Hispanic of any race, 0.8% two or more races (2000); Density: 573.2 persons per square mile (2000); Age: 25.1% under 18, 27.6% over 64 (2000); Marriage status: 16.9% never married, 61.1% now married, 13.4% widowed, 8.7% divorced (2000); Foreign born: 2.3% (2000); Ancestry (includes multiple ancestries): 33.2% Swedish, 28.7% Norwegian, 19.2% German, 7.2% Polish, 6.9% Irish (2000).
Economy: Single-family building permits issued: 2 (2001) / 1 (2000); Multi-family building permits issued: 0 (2001) / 0 (2000); Employment by occupation: 15.2% management, 19.0% professional, 15.4% services, 29.7% sales, 1.7% farming, 9.5% construction, 9.5% production (2000).
Income: Per capita income: $18,156 (2000); Median household income: $37,063 (2000); Poverty rate: 4.8% (2000).
Taxes: Total city taxes per capita: $103 (1997); City property taxes per capita: $99 (1997).
Education: High school graduation rate: 82.1% (2000); College graduation rate: 18.6% (2000).

School District(s)

Kittson Central (PK-12)
2000 Enrollment: 472 218-843-3682

Housing: Homeownership rate: 81.6% (2000); Median home value: $49,000 (2000); Median rent: $350 per month (2000); Median age of housing: 43 years (2000).
Hospitals: Kittson Memorial Health Care Center (15 beds)
Newspapers: Kittson County Enterprise (1 x week)
Transportation: Commute to work: 85.4% car, 0.0% public transportation, 9.3% walk, 5.3% work from home (2000); Travel time to work: 70.0% less than 15 minutes, 16.8% 15 to 30 minutes, 7.2% 30 to 45 minutes, 3.1% 45 to 60 minutes, 2.9% 60 minutes or more (2000)

HALLOCK (township). Covers a land area of 33.931 square miles and a water area of 0 square miles. Located at 48.75° N. Lat.; 96.98° W. Long. Elevation is 817 feet.
History: Plotted 1879, incorporated 1887.
Population: 108 (2000); Race: 100.0% White, 0.0% Black, 0.0% Asian, 0.0% American Indian and Alaska Native, 0.0% Hispanic of any race, 0.0% two or more races (2000); Density: 3.2 persons per square mile (2000); Age: 37.1% under 18, 11.2% over 64 (2000); Marriage status: 18.8% never married, 78.1% now married, 3.1% widowed, 0.0% divorced (2000); Foreign born: 0.0% (2000); Ancestry (includes multiple ancestries): 57.3% Norwegian, 46.1% Swedish, 21.3% German, 6.7% Scottish, 6.7% Ukrainian (2000).
Economy: Grain, potatoes, sunflowers, flax, sheep, alfalfa, sugar beets; livestock. Manufacturing: concrete products. Hunting and fishing in vicinity. Employment by occupation: 33.3% management, 19.0% professional, 19.0% services, 16.7% sales, 0.0% farming, 0.0% construction, 11.9% production (2000).
Income: Per capita income: $20,834 (2000); Median household income: $45,000 (2000); Poverty rate: 0.0% (2000).
Taxes: Total city taxes per capita: $187 (1997); City property taxes per capita: $187 (1997).
Education: High school graduation rate: 96.2% (2000); College graduation rate: 19.2% (2000).
Housing: Homeownership rate: 100.0% (2000); Median home value: $75,000 (2000); Median age of housing: 50 years (2000).
Transportation: Commute to work: 69.0% car, 0.0% public transportation, 9.5% walk, 21.4% work from home (2000); Travel time to work: 87.9% less than 15 minutes, 12.1% 15 to 30 minutes, 0.0% 30 to 45 minutes, 0.0% 45 to 60 minutes, 0.0% 60 minutes or more (2000)

HALMA (city). Covers a land area of 0.929 square miles and a water area of 0.006 square miles. Located at 48.66° N. Lat.; 96.59° W. Long. Elevation is 1,001 feet.
Population: 78 (2000); Race: 96.6% White, 0.0% Black, 0.0% Asian, 0.0% American Indian and Alaska Native, 3.4% Hispanic of any race, 3.4% two or more races (2000); Density: 83.9 persons per square mile (2000); Age: 21.8%

under 18, 6.9% over 64 (2000); Marriage status: 27.6% never married, 60.5% now married, 0.0% widowed, 11.8% divorced (2000); Foreign born: 3.4% (2000); Ancestry (includes multiple ancestries): 55.2% Norwegian, 33.3% German, 25.3% Polish, 24.1% Swedish, 5.7% Ukrainian (2000).
Economy: Grain, sunflowers. Employment by occupation: 0.0% management, 5.0% professional, 7.5% services, 17.5% sales, 7.5% farming, 12.5% construction, 50.0% production (2000).
Income: Per capita income: $13,541 (2000); Median household income: $27,917 (2000); Poverty rate: 5.7% (2000).
Taxes: Total city taxes per capita: $62 (1997); City property taxes per capita: $46 (1997).
Education: High school graduation rate: 74.1% (2000); College graduation rate: 0.0% (2000).
Housing: Homeownership rate: 100.0% (2000); Median home value: $21,300 (2000); Median age of housing: 50 years (2000).
Transportation: Commute to work: 100.0% car, 0.0% public transportation, 0.0% walk, 0.0% work from home (2000); Travel time to work: 37.5% less than 15 minutes, 10.0% 15 to 30 minutes, 0.0% 30 to 45 minutes, 0.0% 45 to 60 minutes, 52.5% 60 minutes or more (2000)

HAMPDEN (township). Covers a land area of 35.983 square miles and a water area of 0 square miles. Located at 48.84° N. Lat.; 97.00° W. Long.
Population: 51 (2000); Race: 100.0% White, 0.0% Black, 0.0% Asian, 0.0% American Indian and Alaska Native, 0.0% Hispanic of any race, 0.0% two or more races (2000); Density: 1.4 persons per square mile (2000); Age: 18.8% under 18, 28.1% over 64 (2000); Marriage status: 0.0% never married, 80.8% now married, 19.2% widowed, 0.0% divorced (2000); Foreign born: 0.0% (2000); Ancestry (includes multiple ancestries): 50.0% German, 46.9% English, 28.1% Swedish, 25.0% Norwegian, 6.3% Scottish (2000).
Economy: Employment by occupation: 8.7% management, 21.7% professional, 0.0% services, 17.4% sales, 8.7% farming, 21.7% construction, 21.7% production (2000).
Income: Per capita income: $28,822 (2000); Median household income: $49,375 (2000); Poverty rate: 0.0% (2000).
Taxes: Total city taxes per capita: $434 (1997); City property taxes per capita: $434 (1997).
Education: High school graduation rate: 76.9% (2000); College graduation rate: 30.8% (2000).
Housing: Homeownership rate: 88.9% (2000); Median home value: $37,500 (2000); Median age of housing: 45 years (2000).
Transportation: Commute to work: 100.0% car, 0.0% public transportation, 0.0% walk, 0.0% work from home (2000); Travel time to work: 43.5% less than 15 minutes, 30.4% 15 to 30 minutes, 26.1% 30 to 45 minutes, 0.0% 45 to 60 minutes, 0.0% 60 minutes or more (2000)

HAZELTON (township). Covers a land area of 35.985 square miles and a water area of 0 square miles. Located at 48.76° N. Lat.; 96.72° W. Long.
Population: 99 (2000); Race: 100.0% White, 0.0% Black, 0.0% Asian, 0.0% American Indian and Alaska Native, 0.0% Hispanic of any race, 0.0% two or more races (2000); Density: 2.8 persons per square mile (2000); Age: 23.1% under 18, 8.8% over 64 (2000); Marriage status: 34.7% never married, 54.2% now married, 5.6% widowed, 5.6% divorced (2000); Foreign born: 0.0% (2000); Ancestry (includes multiple ancestries): 47.3% Swedish, 36.3% Norwegian, 22.0% German, 16.5% Polish, 6.6% French Canadian (2000).
Economy: Employment by occupation: 31.4% management, 3.9% professional, 15.7% services, 15.7% sales, 7.8% farming, 3.9% construction, 21.6% production (2000).
Income: Per capita income: $18,658 (2000); Median household income: $37,188 (2000); Poverty rate: 0.0% (2000).
Taxes: Total city taxes per capita: $189 (1997); City property taxes per capita: $189 (1997).
Education: High school graduation rate: 88.3% (2000); College graduation rate: 23.3% (2000).
Housing: Homeownership rate: 90.0% (2000); Median home value: $24,600 (2000); Median rent: $138 per month (2000); Median age of housing: 45 years (2000).
Transportation: Commute to work: 87.5% car, 0.0% public transportation, 0.0% walk, 12.5% work from home (2000); Travel time to work: 19.0% less than 15 minutes, 52.4% 15 to 30 minutes, 11.9% 30 to 45 minutes, 9.5% 45 to 60 minutes, 7.1% 60 minutes or more (2000)

HILL (township). Covers a land area of 31.986 square miles and a water area of 0.288 square miles. Located at 48.84° N. Lat.; 97.11° W. Long.
Population: 18 (2000); Race: 100.0% White, 0.0% Black, 0.0% Asian, 0.0% American Indian and Alaska Native, 0.0% Hispanic of any race, 0.0% two or more races (2000); Density: 0.6 persons per square mile (2000); Age: 18.2% under 18, 13.6% over 64 (2000); Marriage status: 16.7% never married, 83.3% now married, 0.0% widowed, 0.0% divorced (2000); Foreign born: 0.0% (2000); Ancestry (includes multiple ancestries): 40.9% Norwegian, 31.8% Scotch-Irish, 22.7% Swedish, 13.6% Polish, 9.1% German (2000).
Economy: Employment by occupation: 6.3% management, 31.3% professional, 12.5% services, 12.5% sales, 18.8% farming, 18.8% construction, 0.0% production (2000).
Income: Per capita income: $9,814 (2000); Median household income: $34,167 (2000); Poverty rate: 27.3% (2000).
Taxes: Total city taxes per capita: $400 (1997); City property taxes per capita: $400 (1997).
Education: High school graduation rate: 94.4% (2000); College graduation rate: 16.7% (2000).
Housing: Homeownership rate: 75.0% (2000); Median home value: $37,500 (2000); Median age of housing: 60+ years (2000).
Transportation: Commute to work: 81.3% car, 0.0% public transportation, 0.0% walk, 18.8% work from home (2000); Travel time to work: 7.7% less than 15 minutes, 69.2% 15 to 30 minutes, 0.0% 30 to 45 minutes, 0.0% 45 to 60 minutes, 23.1% 60 minutes or more (2000)

HUMBOLDT (city). Covers a land area of 0.105 square miles and a water area of 0 square miles. Located at 48.92° N. Lat.; 97.09° W. Long. Elevation is 793 feet.
History: Humboldt was founded by James J. Hill, the railroad builder, who owned the town site. Hill named the town for the German naturalist Baron Alexander von Humboldt, as a tribute to the many German people who had invested in Hill's railway bonds.
Population: 61 (2000); Race: 100.0% White, 0.0% Black, 0.0% Asian, 0.0% American Indian and Alaska Native, 0.0% Hispanic of any race, 0.0% two or more races (2000); Density: 579.7 persons per square mile (2000); Age: 28.3% under 18, 4.3% over 64 (2000); Marriage status: 20.0% never married, 68.6% now married, 5.7% widowed, 5.7% divorced (2000); Foreign born: 6.5% (2000); Ancestry (includes multiple ancestries): 37.0% German, 32.6% English, 26.1% Irish, 21.7% Norwegian, 10.9% Canadian (2000).
Economy: Employment by occupation: 6.9% management, 17.2% professional, 0.0% services, 13.8% sales, 0.0% farming, 17.2% construction, 44.8% production (2000).
Income: Per capita income: $18,511 (2000); Median household income: $53,125 (2000); Poverty rate: 0.0% (2000).
Taxes: Total city taxes per capita: $61 (1997); City property taxes per capita: $61 (1997).
Education: High school graduation rate: 100.0% (2000); College graduation rate: 21.2% (2000).
Housing: Homeownership rate: 90.5% (2000); Median home value: $17,900 (2000); Median age of housing: 60+ years (2000).
Transportation: Commute to work: 100.0% car, 0.0% public transportation, 0.0% walk, 0.0% work from home (2000); Travel time to work: 34.5% less than 15 minutes, 58.6% 15 to 30 minutes, 6.9% 30 to 45 minutes, 0.0% 45 to 60 minutes, 0.0% 60 minutes or more (2000)

JUPITER (township). Covers a land area of 35.721 square miles and a water area of 0 square miles. Located at 48.68° N. Lat.; 96.72° W. Long.
Population: 136 (2000); Race: 100.0% White, 0.0% Black, 0.0% Asian, 0.0% American Indian and Alaska Native, 0.0% Hispanic of any race, 0.0% two or more races (2000); Density: 3.8 persons per square mile (2000); Age: 22.2% under 18, 31.7% over 64 (2000); Marriage status: 12.0% never married, 81.0% now married, 4.0% widowed, 3.0% divorced (2000); Foreign born: 6.3% (2000); Ancestry (includes multiple ancestries): 49.2% Norwegian, 48.4% Swedish, 15.9% German, 5.6% Danish, 5.6% Polish (2000).
Economy: Employment by occupation: 41.3% management, 10.9% professional, 23.9% services, 4.3% sales, 4.3% farming, 2.2% construction, 13.0% production (2000).
Income: Per capita income: $18,712 (2000); Median household income: $43,542 (2000); Poverty rate: 3.2% (2000).
Taxes: Total city taxes per capita: $151 (1997); City property taxes per capita: $151 (1997).
Education: High school graduation rate: 75.5% (2000); College graduation rate: 17.3% (2000).
Housing: Homeownership rate: 95.8% (2000); Median home value: $60,000 (2000); Median rent: $175 per month (2000); Median age of housing: 42 years (2000).
Transportation: Commute to work: 69.0% car, 0.0% public transportation, 0.0% walk, 31.0% work from home (2000); Travel time to work: 27.6% less than 15 minutes, 44.8% 15 to 30 minutes, 6.9% 30 to 45 minutes, 6.9% 45 to 60 minutes, 13.8% 60 minutes or more (2000)

KARLSTAD (city). Covers a land area of 1.520 square miles and a water area of 0 square miles. Located at 48.57° N. Lat.; 96.51° W. Long. Elevation is 1,048 feet.
History: Karlstad was settled in 1883 by August Carlson and his family. The town grew after the Soo Line officials built their railroad here in 1904. An early industry in Karlstad was a cooperative creamery.
Population: 794 (2000); Race: 97.1% White, 0.0% Black, 0.0% Asian, 1.1% American Indian and Alaska Native, 0.7% Hispanic of any race, 1.7% two or more races (2000); Density: 522.3 persons per square mile (2000); Age: 24.0% under 18, 27.7% over 64 (2000); Marriage status: 19.8% never married, 55.7% now married, 15.9% widowed, 8.6% divorced (2000); Foreign born: 1.4% (2000); Ancestry (includes multiple ancestries): 52.8% Norwegian, 34.8% Swedish, 13.7% German, 5.8% Polish, 4.6% English (2000).
Economy: Single-family building permits issued: 2 (2001) / 2 (2000); Multi-family building permits issued: 0 (2001) / 0 (2000); Employment by occupation: 12.2% management, 15.2% professional, 20.7% services, 16.5% sales, 0.6% farming, 9.8% construction, 25.0% production (2000).
Income: Per capita income: $13,274 (2000); Median household income: $25,208 (2000); Poverty rate: 13.4% (2000).
Taxes: Total city taxes per capita: $258 (1997); City property taxes per capita: $257 (1997).
Education: High school graduation rate: 72.8% (2000); College graduation rate: 13.2% (2000).

School District(s)

Tri-County (PK-12)
2000 Enrollment: 335 218-436-2261
Housing: Homeownership rate: 66.3% (2000); Median home value: $47,300 (2000); Median rent: $224 per month (2000); Median age of housing: 33 years (2000).
Newspapers: North Star News (1 x week)
Transportation: Commute to work: 79.3% car, 4.0% public transportation, 11.8% walk, 5.0% work from home (2000); Travel time to work: 51.8% less than 15 minutes, 17.6% 15 to 30 minutes, 9.8% 30 to 45 minutes, 10.4% 45 to 60 minutes, 10.4% 60 minutes or more (2000)

KENNEDY (city). Covers a land area of 0.420 square miles and a water area of 0 square miles. Located at 48.64° N. Lat.; 96.90° W. Long. Elevation is 826 feet.
History: Kennedy was named for John Stewart Kennedy, who was connected with the James J. Hill railroad interests.
Population: 255 (2000); Race: 96.6% White, 0.0% Black, 0.0% Asian, 0.0% American Indian and Alaska Native, 9.7% Hispanic of any race, 0.0% two or more races (2000); Density: 607.9 persons per square mile (2000); Age: 22.0% under 18, 20.3% over 64 (2000); Marriage status: 15.5% never married, 69.1% now married, 8.8% widowed, 6.7% divorced (2000); Foreign born: 0.8% (2000); Ancestry (includes multiple ancestries): 37.7% Swedish, 37.7% Norwegian, 13.1% German, 6.8% Dutch, 6.4% Scandinavian (2000).
Economy: Single-family building permits issued: 0 (2001) / 1 (2000); Multi-family building permits issued: 0 (2001) / 0 (2000); Employment by occupation: 24.4% management, 21.8% professional, 15.1% services, 17.6% sales, 3.4% farming, 8.4% construction, 9.2% production (2000).
Income: Per capita income: $23,094 (2000); Median household income: $33,438 (2000); Poverty rate: 5.9% (2000).
Taxes: Total city taxes per capita: $152 (1997); City property taxes per capita: $148 (1997).
Education: High school graduation rate: 83.6% (2000); College graduation rate: 17.0% (2000).
Housing: Homeownership rate: 83.6% (2000); Median home value: $22,000 (2000); Median rent: $300 per month (2000); Median age of housing: 47 years (2000).
Transportation: Commute to work: 89.1% car, 0.0% public transportation, 9.2% walk, 1.7% work from home (2000); Travel time to work: 48.7% less than 15 minutes, 27.4% 15 to 30 minutes, 13.7% 30 to 45 minutes, 3.4% 45 to 60 minutes, 6.8% 60 minutes or more (2000)

LAKE BRONSON (city). Covers a land area of 0.600 square miles and a water area of 0 square miles. Located at 48.73° N. Lat.; 96.66° W. Long. Elevation is 945 feet.
Population: 246 (2000); Race: 91.9% White, 7.5% Black, 0.0% Asian, 0.0% American Indian and Alaska Native, 0.7% Hispanic of any race, 0.7% two or more races (2000); Density: 410.3 persons per square mile (2000); Age: 25.4% under 18, 20.7% over 64 (2000); Marriage status: 18.7% never married, 50.2% now married, 13.8% widowed, 17.3% divorced (2000); Foreign born: 0.0% (2000); Ancestry (includes multiple ancestries): 44.1% Swedish, 35.3% Norwegian, 13.2% German, 9.8% Irish, 8.8% Polish (2000).
Economy: Agricultural: grain, potatoes, sugar beets, beans, flax, sunflowers; livestock. Manufacturing: fertilizer. Single-family building permits issued: 0 (2001) / 0 (2000); Multi-family building permits issued: 0 (2001) / 0 (2000); Employment by occupation: 9.3% management, 8.3% professional, 13.9% services, 13.9% sales, 4.6% farming, 24.1% construction, 25.9% production (2000).
Income: Per capita income: $12,239 (2000); Median household income: $25,278 (2000); Poverty rate: 24.1% (2000).
Taxes: Total city taxes per capita: $68 (1997); City property taxes per capita: $56 (1997).
Education: High school graduation rate: 75.4% (2000); College graduation rate: 4.7% (2000).
Housing: Homeownership rate: 82.1% (2000); Median home value: $20,900 (2000); Median rent: $150 per month (2000); Median age of housing: 56 years (2000).
Transportation: Commute to work: 85.8% car, 0.0% public transportation, 8.5% walk, 5.7% work from home (2000); Travel time to work: 35.0% less than 15 minutes, 31.0% 15 to 30 minutes, 12.0% 30 to 45 minutes, 18.0% 45 to 60 minutes, 4.0% 60 minutes or more (2000)

LANCASTER (city). Covers a land area of 2.247 square miles and a water area of 0 square miles. Located at 48.85° N. Lat.; 96.80° W. Long. Elevation is 907 feet.
History: Lancaster was incorporated in 1905, and developed around the dairy industry.
Population: 363 (2000); Race: 97.7% White, 0.0% Black, 0.3% Asian, 0.9% American Indian and Alaska Native, 2.8% Hispanic of any race, 1.1% two or more races (2000); Density: 161.6 persons per square mile (2000); Age: 28.1% under 18, 21.0% over 64 (2000); Marriage status: 22.3% never married, 56.8% now married, 13.6% widowed, 7.2% divorced (2000); Foreign born: 1.1% (2000); Ancestry (includes multiple ancestries): 45.2% Swedish, 19.3% German, 18.5% Norwegian, 18.2% Polish, 7.1% Other groups (2000).
Economy: Single-family building permits issued: 1 (2001) / 1 (2000); Multi-family building permits issued: 0 (2001) / 0 (2000); Employment by occupation: 10.1% management, 18.2% professional, 15.5% services, 14.2% sales, 5.4% farming, 10.8% construction, 25.7% production (2000).
Income: Per capita income: $16,191 (2000); Median household income: $33,750 (2000); Poverty rate: 9.7% (2000).
Taxes: Total city taxes per capita: $53 (1997); City property taxes per capita: $50 (1997).
Education: High school graduation rate: 74.5% (2000); College graduation rate: 13.4% (2000).

School District(s)

Lancaster (PK-12)
2000 Enrollment: 233 218-762-5400
Housing: Homeownership rate: 78.7% (2000); Median home value: $32,500 (2000); Median rent: $256 per month (2000); Median age of housing: 41 years (2000).
Transportation: Commute to work: 91.1% car, 0.0% public transportation, 6.8% walk, 2.1% work from home (2000); Travel time to work: 39.2% less than 15 minutes, 34.3% 15 to 30 minutes, 23.1% 30 to 45 minutes, 0.0% 45 to 60 minutes, 3.5% 60 minutes or more (2000)

NORTH RED RIVER (township). Covers a land area of 23.384 square miles and a water area of 0.311 square miles. Located at 48.76° N. Lat.; 97.11° W. Long.
Population: 3 (2000); Race: 100.0% White, 0.0% Black, 0.0% Asian, 0.0% American Indian and Alaska Native, 0.0% Hispanic of any race, 0.0% two or more races (2000); Density: 0.1 persons per square mile (2000); Age: 0.0% under 18, 33.3% over 64 (2000); Marriage status: 66.7% never married, 0.0% now married, 33.3% widowed, 0.0% divorced (2000); Foreign born: 0.0% (2000); Ancestry (includes multiple ancestries): 66.7% Irish, 66.7% Swedish, 33.3% German (2000).
Economy: Employment by occupation: 50.0% management, 0.0% professional, 0.0% services, 50.0% sales, 0.0% farming, 0.0% construction, 0.0% production (2000).
Income: Per capita income: $8,983 (2000); Median household income: $13,750 (2000); Poverty rate: 33.3% (2000).
Taxes: Total city taxes per capita: $435 (1997); City property taxes per capita: $435 (1997).
Education: High school graduation rate: 100.0% (2000); College graduation rate: 0.0% (2000).

Housing: Homeownership rate: 50.0% (2000); Median age of housing: 60+ years (2000).
Transportation: Commute to work: 100.0% car, 0.0% public transportation, 0.0% walk, 0.0% work from home (2000); Travel time to work: 50.0% less than 15 minutes, 50.0% 15 to 30 minutes, 0.0% 30 to 45 minutes, 0.0% 45 to 60 minutes, 0.0% 60 minutes or more (2000)

NORWAY (township). Covers a land area of 35.055 square miles and a water area of 0.136 square miles. Located at 48.67° N. Lat.; 96.60° W. Long.
Population: 94 (2000); Race: 100.0% White, 0.0% Black, 0.0% Asian, 0.0% American Indian and Alaska Native, 0.0% Hispanic of any race, 0.0% two or more races (2000); Density: 2.7 persons per square mile (2000); Age: 22.2% under 18, 21.2% over 64 (2000); Marriage status: 20.3% never married, 55.7% now married, 21.5% widowed, 2.5% divorced (2000); Foreign born: 0.0% (2000); Ancestry (includes multiple ancestries): 39.4% Norwegian, 38.4% Swedish, 17.2% Polish, 9.1% German, 6.1% Other groups (2000).
Economy: Employment by occupation: 17.1% management, 7.3% professional, 12.2% services, 36.6% sales, 4.9% farming, 22.0% construction, 0.0% production (2000).
Income: Per capita income: $14,754 (2000); Median household income: $32,188 (2000); Poverty rate: 7.1% (2000).
Taxes: Total city taxes per capita: $159 (1997); City property taxes per capita: $159 (1997).
Education: High school graduation rate: 87.7% (2000); College graduation rate: 9.6% (2000).
Housing: Homeownership rate: 90.9% (2000); Median home value: $81,000 (2000); Median age of housing: 28 years (2000).
Transportation: Commute to work: 95.1% car, 0.0% public transportation, 0.0% walk, 4.9% work from home (2000); Travel time to work: 48.7% less than 15 minutes, 25.6% 15 to 30 minutes, 12.8% 30 to 45 minutes, 0.0% 45 to 60 minutes, 12.8% 60 minutes or more (2000)

PELAN (township). Covers a land area of 35.634 square miles and a water area of <.001 square miles. Located at 48.66° N. Lat.; 96.41° W. Long.
Population: 61 (2000); Race: 79.6% White, 0.0% Black, 0.0% Asian, 20.4% American Indian and Alaska Native, 0.0% Hispanic of any race, 0.0% two or more races (2000); Density: 1.7 persons per square mile (2000); Age: 24.5% under 18, 12.2% over 64 (2000); Marriage status: 18.9% never married, 75.7% now married, 5.4% widowed, 0.0% divorced (2000); Foreign born: 0.0% (2000); Ancestry (includes multiple ancestries): 49.0% Norwegian, 20.4% Other groups, 18.4% Swedish, 14.3% German, 6.1% French (except Basque) (2000).
Economy: Employment by occupation: 8.3% management, 8.3% professional, 8.3% services, 12.5% sales, 0.0% farming, 0.0% construction, 62.5% production (2000).
Income: Per capita income: $19,616 (2000); Median household income: $37,250 (2000); Poverty rate: 0.0% (2000).
Taxes: Total city taxes per capita: $74 (1997); City property taxes per capita: $74 (1997).
Education: High school graduation rate: 78.4% (2000); College graduation rate: 16.2% (2000).
Housing: Homeownership rate: 61.1% (2000); Median home value: $65,000 (2000); Median rent: $250 per month (2000); Median age of housing: 56 years (2000).
Transportation: Commute to work: 100.0% car, 0.0% public transportation, 0.0% walk, 0.0% work from home (2000); Travel time to work: 29.2% less than 15 minutes, 8.3% 15 to 30 minutes, 41.7% 30 to 45 minutes, 8.3% 45 to 60 minutes, 12.5% 60 minutes or more (2000)

PERCY (township). Covers a land area of 34.842 square miles and a water area of 0.475 square miles. Located at 48.73° N. Lat.; 96.63° W. Long.
Population: 48 (2000); Race: 100.0% White, 0.0% Black, 0.0% Asian, 0.0% American Indian and Alaska Native, 0.0% Hispanic of any race, 0.0% two or more races (2000); Density: 1.4 persons per square mile (2000); Age: 19.0% under 18, 19.0% over 64 (2000); Marriage status: 30.6% never married, 58.3% now married, 11.1% widowed, 0.0% divorced (2000); Foreign born: 0.0% (2000); Ancestry (includes multiple ancestries): 31.0% Swedish, 26.2% German, 23.8% Norwegian, 19.0% Ukrainian, 9.5% Irish (2000).
Economy: Employment by occupation: 12.5% management, 0.0% professional, 12.5% services, 25.0% sales, 8.3% farming, 12.5% construction, 29.2% production (2000).
Income: Per capita income: $17,981 (2000); Median household income: $25,000 (2000); Poverty rate: 4.8% (2000).
Taxes: Total city taxes per capita: $79 (1997); City property taxes per capita: $79 (1997).
Education: High school graduation rate: 86.2% (2000); College graduation rate: 0.0% (2000).
Housing: Homeownership rate: 81.0% (2000); Median home value: $22,500 (2000); Median age of housing: 42 years (2000).
Transportation: Commute to work: 87.5% car, 0.0% public transportation, 8.3% walk, 4.2% work from home (2000); Travel time to work: 34.8% less than 15 minutes, 21.7% 15 to 30 minutes, 0.0% 30 to 45 minutes, 21.7% 45 to 60 minutes, 21.7% 60 minutes or more (2000)

POPPLETON (township). Covers a land area of 35.042 square miles and a water area of 0.006 square miles. Located at 48.84° N. Lat.; 96.74° W. Long.
Population: 123 (2000); Race: 98.1% White, 0.0% Black, 0.0% Asian, 0.0% American Indian and Alaska Native, 3.8% Hispanic of any race, 1.9% two or more races (2000); Density: 3.5 persons per square mile (2000); Age: 17.3% under 18, 21.2% over 64 (2000); Marriage status: 21.6% never married, 72.7% now married, 2.3% widowed, 3.4% divorced (2000); Foreign born: 4.8% (2000); Ancestry (includes multiple ancestries): 26.9% Swedish, 25.0% Norwegian, 17.3% Polish, 16.3% German, 12.5% Ukrainian (2000).
Economy: Employment by occupation: 17.8% management, 35.6% professional, 8.9% services, 6.7% sales, 0.0% farming, 6.7% construction, 24.4% production (2000).
Income: Per capita income: $26,665 (2000); Median household income: $25,357 (2000); Poverty rate: 18.3% (2000).
Taxes: Total city taxes per capita: $50 (1997); City property taxes per capita: $50 (1997).
Education: High school graduation rate: 71.1% (2000); College graduation rate: 10.8% (2000).
Housing: Homeownership rate: 91.8% (2000); Median home value: $33,800 (2000); Median age of housing: 37 years (2000).
Transportation: Commute to work: 71.1% car, 0.0% public transportation, 4.4% walk, 24.4% work from home (2000); Travel time to work: 29.4% less than 15 minutes, 41.2% 15 to 30 minutes, 14.7% 30 to 45 minutes, 8.8% 45 to 60 minutes, 5.9% 60 minutes or more (2000)

RICHARDVILLE (township). Covers a land area of 45.235 square miles and a water area of 0.051 square miles. Located at 48.94° N. Lat.; 96.87° W. Long.
Population: 110 (2000); Race: 100.0% White, 0.0% Black, 0.0% Asian, 0.0% American Indian and Alaska Native, 0.0% Hispanic of any race, 0.0% two or more races (2000); Density: 2.4 persons per square mile (2000); Age: 28.4% under 18, 10.3% over 64 (2000); Marriage status: 20.9% never married, 71.4% now married, 7.7% widowed, 0.0% divorced (2000); Foreign born: 1.7% (2000); Ancestry (includes multiple ancestries): 37.9% Polish, 25.0% Swedish, 23.3% German, 19.0% Norwegian, 11.2% Irish (2000).
Economy: Employment by occupation: 20.0% management, 6.7% professional, 11.7% services, 28.3% sales, 13.3% farming, 3.3% construction, 16.7% production (2000).
Income: Per capita income: $13,892 (2000); Median household income: $37,813 (2000); Poverty rate: 5.3% (2000).
Taxes: Total city taxes per capita: $51 (1997); City property taxes per capita: $51 (1997).
Education: High school graduation rate: 77.8% (2000); College graduation rate: 9.7% (2000).
Housing: Homeownership rate: 82.9% (2000); Median home value: $72,500 (2000); Median age of housing: 39 years (2000).
Transportation: Commute to work: 96.7% car, 0.0% public transportation, 0.0% walk, 3.3% work from home (2000); Travel time to work: 27.6% less than 15 minutes, 43.1% 15 to 30 minutes, 22.4% 30 to 45 minutes, 3.4% 45 to 60 minutes, 3.4% 60 minutes or more (2000)

SAINT JOSEPH (township). Covers a land area of 44.781 square miles and a water area of 0.235 square miles. Located at 48.97° N. Lat.; 96.74° W. Long.
Population: 57 (2000); Race: 95.6% White, 0.0% Black, 0.0% Asian, 0.0% American Indian and Alaska Native, 0.0% Hispanic of any race, 4.4% two or more races (2000); Density: 1.3 persons per square mile (2000); Age: 11.1% under 18, 31.1% over 64 (2000); Marriage status: 17.8% never married, 64.4% now married, 8.9% widowed, 8.9% divorced (2000); Foreign born: 6.7% (2000); Ancestry (includes multiple ancestries): 48.9% Polish, 22.2% French (except Basque), 6.7% Swedish, 6.7% German, 4.4% Dutch (2000).
Economy: Employment by occupation: 8.0% management, 8.0% professional, 32.0% services, 36.0% sales, 0.0% farming, 0.0% construction, 16.0% production (2000).
Income: Per capita income: $15,153 (2000); Median household income: $21,667 (2000); Poverty rate: 4.4% (2000).

Education: High school graduation rate: 62.2% (2000); College graduation rate: 5.4% (2000).
Housing: Homeownership rate: 91.3% (2000); Median home value: $92,500 (2000); Median age of housing: 45 years (2000).
Transportation: Commute to work: 84.2% car, 0.0% public transportation, 0.0% walk, 15.8% work from home (2000); Travel time to work: 0.0% less than 15 minutes, 37.5% 15 to 30 minutes, 50.0% 30 to 45 minutes, 12.5% 45 to 60 minutes, 0.0% 60 minutes or more (2000)

SAINT VINCENT (city). Covers a land area of 1.083 square miles and a water area of 0.070 square miles. Located at 48.96° N. Lat.; 97.22° W. Long. Elevation is 788 feet.
History: St. Vincent began with a trading post established near here in the 1790's. The town was later named for St. Vincent de Paul, a 17th-century priest known for his work among the poor.
Population: 117 (2000); Race: 90.7% White, 0.0% Black, 0.0% Asian, 6.5% American Indian and Alaska Native, 0.0% Hispanic of any race, 2.8% two or more races (2000); Density: 108.0 persons per square mile (2000); Age: 30.8% under 18, 7.5% over 64 (2000); Marriage status: 25.0% never married, 56.6% now married, 18.4% widowed, 0.0% divorced (2000); Foreign born: 19.6% (2000); Ancestry (includes multiple ancestries): 33.6% English, 18.7% German, 17.8% Norwegian, 13.1% Irish, 13.1% Swedish (2000).
Economy: Single-family building permits issued: 0 (2001) / 0 (2000); Multi-family building permits issued: 0 (2001) / 0 (2000); Employment by occupation: 0.0% management, 10.4% professional, 16.7% services, 31.3% sales, 6.3% farming, 8.3% construction, 27.1% production (2000).
Income: Per capita income: $13,322 (2000); Median household income: $30,500 (2000); Poverty rate: 21.5% (2000).
Education: High school graduation rate: 85.5% (2000); College graduation rate: 3.2% (2000).
Housing: Homeownership rate: 86.0% (2000); Median home value: $24,200 (2000); Median rent: $250 per month (2000); Median age of housing: 60+ years (2000).
Transportation: Commute to work: 93.8% car, 0.0% public transportation, 0.0% walk, 6.3% work from home (2000); Travel time to work: 64.4% less than 15 minutes, 26.7% 15 to 30 minutes, 8.9% 30 to 45 minutes, 0.0% 45 to 60 minutes, 0.0% 60 minutes or more (2000)

SAINT VINCENT (township). Covers a land area of 54.164 square miles and a water area of 0.303 square miles. Located at 48.95° N. Lat.; 97.13° W. Long. Elevation is 788 feet.
Population: 74 (2000); Race: 100.0% White, 0.0% Black, 0.0% Asian, 0.0% American Indian and Alaska Native, 0.0% Hispanic of any race, 0.0% two or more races (2000); Density: 1.4 persons per square mile (2000); Age: 29.8% under 18, 19.1% over 64 (2000); Marriage status: 18.6% never married, 74.3% now married, 2.9% widowed, 4.3% divorced (2000); Foreign born: 2.1% (2000); Ancestry (includes multiple ancestries): 35.1% Norwegian, 35.1% German, 33.0% English, 17.0% Swedish, 11.7% Polish (2000).
Economy: Employment by occupation: 33.3% management, 12.1% professional, 3.0% services, 12.1% sales, 12.1% farming, 12.1% construction, 15.2% production (2000).
Income: Per capita income: $20,491 (2000); Median household income: $45,000 (2000); Poverty rate: 2.1% (2000).
Education: High school graduation rate: 83.9% (2000); College graduation rate: 43.5% (2000).
Housing: Homeownership rate: 79.4% (2000); Median home value: $45,000 (2000); Median rent: $200 per month (2000); Median age of housing: 60+ years (2000).
Transportation: Commute to work: 71.0% car, 0.0% public transportation, 6.5% walk, 22.6% work from home (2000); Travel time to work: 54.2% less than 15 minutes, 45.8% 15 to 30 minutes, 0.0% 30 to 45 minutes, 0.0% 45 to 60 minutes, 0.0% 60 minutes or more (2000)

SKANE (township). Covers a land area of 35.466 square miles and a water area of 0 square miles. Located at 48.67° N. Lat.; 96.98° W. Long.
Population: 65 (2000); Race: 100.0% White, 0.0% Black, 0.0% Asian, 0.0% American Indian and Alaska Native, 0.0% Hispanic of any race, 0.0% two or more races (2000); Density: 1.8 persons per square mile (2000); Age: 23.4% under 18, 6.4% over 64 (2000); Marriage status: 22.5% never married, 57.5% now married, 12.5% widowed, 7.5% divorced (2000); Foreign born: 0.0% (2000); Ancestry (includes multiple ancestries): 46.8% Swedish, 38.3% Norwegian, 31.9% German, 17.0% French (except Basque), 6.4% Scottish (2000).
Economy: Employment by occupation: 24.0% management, 12.0% professional, 8.0% services, 36.0% sales, 0.0% farming, 20.0% construction, 0.0% production (2000).
Income: Per capita income: $22,098 (2000); Median household income: $40,833 (2000); Poverty rate: 4.3% (2000).
Taxes: Total city taxes per capita: $171 (1997); City property taxes per capita: $171 (1997).
Education: High school graduation rate: 90.9% (2000); College graduation rate: 33.3% (2000).
Housing: Homeownership rate: 81.8% (2000); Median home value: $25,000 (2000); Median rent: $175 per month (2000); Median age of housing: 59 years (2000).
Transportation: Commute to work: 76.0% car, 0.0% public transportation, 0.0% walk, 24.0% work from home (2000); Travel time to work: 47.4% less than 15 minutes, 52.6% 15 to 30 minutes, 0.0% 30 to 45 minutes, 0.0% 45 to 60 minutes, 0.0% 60 minutes or more (2000)

SOUTH RED RIVER (township). Covers a land area of 17.561 square miles and a water area of 0.238 square miles. Located at 48.66° N. Lat.; 97.07° W. Long.
Population: 23 (2000); Race: 100.0% White, 0.0% Black, 0.0% Asian, 0.0% American Indian and Alaska Native, 0.0% Hispanic of any race, 0.0% two or more races (2000); Density: 1.3 persons per square mile (2000); Age: 0.0% under 18, 50.0% over 64 (2000); Marriage status: 16.7% never married, 66.7% now married, 16.7% widowed, 0.0% divorced (2000); Foreign born: 0.0% (2000); Ancestry (includes multiple ancestries): 83.3% Swedish, 16.7% Norwegian, 16.7% Danish (2000).
Economy: Employment by occupation: 0.0% management, 25.0% professional, 25.0% services, 25.0% sales, 0.0% farming, 0.0% construction, 25.0% production (2000).
Income: Per capita income: $27,633 (2000); Median household income: $41,875 (2000); Poverty rate: 0.0% (2000).
Taxes: Total city taxes per capita: $923 (1997); City property taxes per capita: $923 (1997).
Education: High school graduation rate: 83.3% (2000); College graduation rate: 16.7% (2000).
Housing: Homeownership rate: 100.0% (2000); Median age of housing: 60+ years (2000).
Transportation: Commute to work: 100.0% car, 0.0% public transportation, 0.0% walk, 0.0% work from home (2000); Travel time to work: 50.0% less than 15 minutes, 50.0% 15 to 30 minutes, 0.0% 30 to 45 minutes, 0.0% 45 to 60 minutes, 0.0% 60 minutes or more (2000)

SPRING BROOK (township). Covers a land area of 35.919 square miles and a water area of 0.007 square miles. Located at 48.59° N. Lat.; 96.72° W. Long.
Population: 74 (2000); Race: 100.0% White, 0.0% Black, 0.0% Asian, 0.0% American Indian and Alaska Native, 0.0% Hispanic of any race, 0.0% two or more races (2000); Density: 2.1 persons per square mile (2000); Age: 25.4% under 18, 16.4% over 64 (2000); Marriage status: 6.0% never married, 94.0% now married, 0.0% widowed, 0.0% divorced (2000); Foreign born: 0.0% (2000); Ancestry (includes multiple ancestries): 56.7% Norwegian, 22.4% Swedish, 14.9% United States or American, 13.4% German, 3.0% French (except Basque) (2000).
Economy: Employment by occupation: 27.6% management, 20.7% professional, 17.2% services, 13.8% sales, 0.0% farming, 6.9% construction, 13.8% production (2000).
Income: Per capita income: $13,637 (2000); Median household income: $36,875 (2000); Poverty rate: 7.5% (2000).
Taxes: Total city taxes per capita: $250 (1997); City property taxes per capita: $250 (1997).
Education: High school graduation rate: 96.0% (2000); College graduation rate: 30.0% (2000).
Housing: Homeownership rate: 80.8% (2000); Median home value: $70,000 (2000); Median age of housing: 41 years (2000).
Transportation: Commute to work: 72.4% car, 6.9% public transportation, 6.9% walk, 13.8% work from home (2000); Travel time to work: 36.0% less than 15 minutes, 48.0% 15 to 30 minutes, 16.0% 30 to 45 minutes, 0.0% 45 to 60 minutes, 0.0% 60 minutes or more (2000)

SVEA (township). Covers a land area of 35.836 square miles and a water area of 0 square miles. Located at 48.59° N. Lat.; 96.98° W. Long.
Population: 60 (2000); Race: 100.0% White, 0.0% Black, 0.0% Asian, 0.0% American Indian and Alaska Native, 0.0% Hispanic of any race, 0.0% two or more races (2000); Density: 1.7 persons per square mile (2000); Age: 37.3% under 18, 1.5% over 64 (2000); Marriage status: 21.4% never married, 71.4% now married, 7.1% widowed, 0.0% divorced (2000); Foreign born: 0.0% (2000); Ancestry (includes multiple ancestries): 35.8% Swedish, 31.3%

Norwegian, 22.4% German, 16.4% United States or American, 13.4% Irish (2000).
Economy: Employment by occupation: 69.6% management, 17.4% professional, 0.0% services, 8.7% sales, 0.0% farming, 0.0% construction, 4.3% production (2000).
Income: Per capita income: $25,079 (2000); Median household income: $36,563 (2000); Poverty rate: 9.0% (2000).
Taxes: Total city taxes per capita: $644 (1997); City property taxes per capita: $644 (1997).
Education: High school graduation rate: 100.0% (2000); College graduation rate: 10.8% (2000).
Housing: Homeownership rate: 100.0% (2000); Median home value: $67,500 (2000); Median age of housing: 45 years (2000).
Transportation: Commute to work: 82.6% car, 0.0% public transportation, 0.0% walk, 17.4% work from home (2000); Travel time to work: 52.6% less than 15 minutes, 42.1% 15 to 30 minutes, 5.3% 30 to 45 minutes, 0.0% 45 to 60 minutes, 0.0% 60 minutes or more (2000)

TEGNER (township). Covers a land area of 35.680 square miles and a water area of 0.020 square miles. Located at 48.66° N. Lat.; 96.85° W. Long.
Population: 67 (2000); Race: 100.0% White, 0.0% Black, 0.0% Asian, 0.0% American Indian and Alaska Native, 7.9% Hispanic of any race, 0.0% two or more races (2000); Density: 1.9 persons per square mile (2000); Age: 26.3% under 18, 13.2% over 64 (2000); Marriage status: 6.9% never married, 77.6% now married, 6.9% widowed, 8.6% divorced (2000); Foreign born: 2.6% (2000); Ancestry (includes multiple ancestries): 46.1% Swedish, 34.2% Norwegian, 15.8% United States or American, 13.2% German, 5.3% Polish (2000).
Economy: Employment by occupation: 23.7% management, 34.2% professional, 0.0% services, 18.4% sales, 0.0% farming, 5.3% construction, 18.4% production (2000).
Income: Per capita income: $14,021 (2000); Median household income: $31,250 (2000); Poverty rate: 19.4% (2000).
Taxes: Total city taxes per capita: $264 (1997); City property taxes per capita: $264 (1997).
Education: High school graduation rate: 79.6% (2000); College graduation rate: 27.8% (2000).
Housing: Homeownership rate: 85.7% (2000); Median home value: $43,000 (2000); Median rent: $125 per month (2000); Median age of housing: 55 years (2000).
Transportation: Commute to work: 78.9% car, 0.0% public transportation, 5.3% walk, 15.8% work from home (2000); Travel time to work: 56.3% less than 15 minutes, 28.1% 15 to 30 minutes, 9.4% 30 to 45 minutes, 0.0% 45 to 60 minutes, 6.3% 60 minutes or more (2000)

TEIEN (township). Covers a land area of 28.753 square miles and a water area of 0.492 square miles. Located at 48.57° N. Lat.; 97.09° W. Long.
Population: 85 (2000); Race: 100.0% White, 0.0% Black, 0.0% Asian, 0.0% American Indian and Alaska Native, 0.0% Hispanic of any race, 0.0% two or more races (2000); Density: 3.0 persons per square mile (2000); Age: 14.1% under 18, 32.3% over 64 (2000); Marriage status: 19.5% never married, 74.7% now married, 2.3% widowed, 3.4% divorced (2000); Foreign born: 2.0% (2000); Ancestry (includes multiple ancestries): 37.4% Norwegian, 20.2% Swedish, 7.1% German, 6.1% Irish, 3.0% Polish (2000).
Economy: Employment by occupation: 32.7% management, 20.4% professional, 14.3% services, 12.2% sales, 14.3% farming, 6.1% construction, 0.0% production (2000).
Income: Per capita income: $21,792 (2000); Median household income: $36,250 (2000); Poverty rate: 4.0% (2000).
Taxes: Total city taxes per capita: $295 (1997); City property taxes per capita: $295 (1997).
Education: High school graduation rate: 70.5% (2000); College graduation rate: 25.6% (2000).
Housing: Homeownership rate: 87.2% (2000); Median home value: $55,800 (2000); Median rent: $275 per month (2000); Median age of housing: 41 years (2000).
Transportation: Commute to work: 68.1% car, 0.0% public transportation, 8.5% walk, 23.4% work from home (2000); Travel time to work: 69.4% less than 15 minutes, 0.0% 15 to 30 minutes, 19.4% 30 to 45 minutes, 0.0% 45 to 60 minutes, 11.1% 60 minutes or more (2000)

THOMPSON (township). Covers a land area of 35.975 square miles and a water area of 0.005 square miles. Located at 48.76° N. Lat.; 96.87° W. Long.
Population: 178 (2000); Race: 100.0% White, 0.0% Black, 0.0% Asian, 0.0% American Indian and Alaska Native, 0.0% Hispanic of any race, 0.0% two or more races (2000); Density: 4.9 persons per square mile (2000); Age: 29.2% under 18, 18.4% over 64 (2000); Marriage status: 21.4% never married, 69.7% now married, 4.1% widowed, 4.8% divorced (2000); Foreign born: 0.5% (2000); Ancestry (includes multiple ancestries): 36.2% Norwegian, 29.7% Swedish, 16.8% German, 6.5% Irish, 5.9% French (except Basque) (2000).
Economy: Employment by occupation: 20.2% management, 3.6% professional, 28.6% services, 17.9% sales, 4.8% farming, 2.4% construction, 22.6% production (2000).
Income: Per capita income: $15,142 (2000); Median household income: $31,458 (2000); Poverty rate: 15.1% (2000).
Taxes: Total city taxes per capita: $126 (1997); City property taxes per capita: $126 (1997).
Education: High school graduation rate: 77.0% (2000); College graduation rate: 6.6% (2000).
Housing: Homeownership rate: 85.9% (2000); Median home value: $34,300 (2000); Median rent: $263 per month (2000); Median age of housing: 48 years (2000).
Transportation: Commute to work: 90.5% car, 0.0% public transportation, 0.0% walk, 9.5% work from home (2000); Travel time to work: 67.2% less than 15 minutes, 26.9% 15 to 30 minutes, 6.0% 30 to 45 minutes, 0.0% 45 to 60 minutes, 0.0% 60 minutes or more (2000)

Koochiching County

Located in northern Minnesota; bounded on the north by the Rainy River and the Canadian province of Ontario; drained by the Big Fork and Little Fork Rivers; includes part of Rainy Lake. Covers a land area of 3,102.40 square miles, a water area of 52.00 square miles, and is located in the Central Time Zone. The county government was organized in 1906. County seat is International Falls.

Weather Station: Big Falls — Elevation: 1,217 feet

	Jan	Feb	Mar	Apr	May	Jun	Jul	Aug	Sep	Oct	Nov	Dec
High	16	26	39	55	69	77	81	78	68	55	na	21
Low	-9	-0	13	27	40	49	53	51	42	na	na	na
Precip	0.9	0.6	1.1	1.7	2.8	4.2	3.7	3.3	3.3	2.4	1.4	0.9
Snow	12.4	8.7	9.5	4.3	0.3	0.0	0.0	tr	tr	1.4	10.0	11.6

High and Low temperatures in degrees Fahrenheit; Precipitation and Snow in inches

Weather Station: International Falls Int'l Arpt. — Elevation: 1,177 feet

	Jan	Feb	Mar	Apr	May	Jun	Jul	Aug	Sep	Oct	Nov	Dec
High	13	21	33	51	66	74	78	76	64	51	32	18
Low	-9	-1	12	28	40	50	54	52	42	32	17	-1
Precip	0.9	0.7	1.0	1.4	2.6	3.9	3.3	3.1	3.1	2.1	1.3	0.7
Snow	15.3	10.6	9.1	5.7	0.3	tr	tr	tr	0.1	2.5	13.6	13.8

High and Low temperatures in degrees Fahrenheit; Precipitation and Snow in inches

Population: 14,355 (2000); Race: 96.0% White, 0.3% Black, 0.2% Asian, 2.4% American Indian and Alaska Native, 0.5% Hispanic of any race, 1.0% two or more races (2000); Density: 4.6 persons per square mile (2000); Age: 23.9% under 18, 17.9% over 64 (2000).
Religion: Five largest groups: 31.8% Catholic Church, 19.8% Evangelical Lutheran Church in America, 2.7% The Evangelical Covenant Church, 2.5% The Association of Free Lutheran Congregations, 2.3% Lutheran Church—Missouri Synod (2000).
Economy: Unemployment rate: 7.0% (11/2002); Total civilian labor force: 6,103 (11/2002); Leading industries: 26.9% manufacturing; 16.6% retail trade; 14.3% health care and social assistance (2000); Companies that employ more than 1,000 persons: 1 (2000); Companies that employ more than 100 persons: 5 (2000); Farms: 213 totaling 76,635 acres (1997); Minority business ownership rate: 0.0% (1997); Women business ownership rate: 26.1% (1997); Retail sales per capita: $8,204 (1997). Single-family building permits issued: 71 (2001) / 48 (2000); Multi-family building permits issued: 2 (2001) / 2 (2000).
Income: Per capita income: $19,167 (2000); Median household income: $36,262 (2000); Poverty rate: 12.1% (2000); Bankruptcy rate: 2.39% (2001).
Taxes: Total county taxes per capita: $228 (1997); County property taxes per capita: $227 (1997).
Education: High school graduation rate: 81.9% (2000); College graduation rate: 15.1% (2000).
Housing: Homeownership rate: 80.4% (2000); Median home value: $65,400 (2000); Median rent: $296 per month (2000); Median age of housing: 36 years (2000).
Health: Birth rate: 119.1 per 10,000 population (1998); Age adjusted death rate: 98.8 per 10,000 population (1999); Age adjusted cancer mortality rate:

201.7 deaths per 100,000 population (1999). Number of physicians: 10.4 per 10,000 population (1999); Number of hospital beds: 25.1 per 10,000 population (1999).
Elections: 2000 Presidential election results: 42.2% Gore, 51.2% Bush, 4.4% Nader, 1.5% Buchanan
National and State Parks: Gold Portage State Wildlife Management Area; Grand Mound State Park; Koochiching State Forest; Pine Island State Forest; Smokey Bear State Forest
Additional Information Contacts
Koochiching County Government Offices 218-283-1152
Internatl Falls Chamber of Commerce 218-283-9400
Little Fork Chamber of Commerce 218-278-6617

Koochiching County Communities

BIG FALLS (city). Covers a land area of 6.037 square miles and a water area of 0 square miles. Located at 48.19° N. Lat.; 93.80° W. Long. Elevation is 1,210 feet.
Population: 264 (2000); Race: 96.4% White, 0.0% Black, 0.0% Asian, 0.4% American Indian and Alaska Native, 0.0% Hispanic of any race, 3.2% two or more races (2000); Density: 43.7 persons per square mile (2000); Age: 21.4% under 18, 16.3% over 64 (2000); Marriage status: 20.7% never married, 59.2% now married, 3.3% widowed, 16.9% divorced (2000); Foreign born: 1.2% (2000); Ancestry (includes multiple ancestries): 39.7% German, 27.0% Norwegian, 9.5% Irish, 9.1% Swedish, 6.7% English (2000).
Economy: Timber; pulpwood, lumber. Single-family building permits issued: 1 (2001) / 0 (2000); Multi-family building permits issued: 0 (2001) / 0 (2000); Employment by occupation: 1.7% management, 6.7% professional, 12.5% services, 15.0% sales, 9.2% farming, 12.5% construction, 42.5% production (2000).
Income: Per capita income: $14,528 (2000); Median household income: $26,458 (2000); Poverty rate: 14.7% (2000).
Taxes: Total city taxes per capita: $153 (1997); City property taxes per capita: $153 (1997).
Education: High school graduation rate: 81.5% (2000); College graduation rate: 6.9% (2000).
Housing: Homeownership rate: 65.9% (2000); Median home value: $31,900 (2000); Median rent: $264 per month (2000); Median age of housing: 33 years (2000).
Transportation: Commute to work: 88.1% car, 0.0% public transportation, 8.5% walk, 3.4% work from home (2000); Travel time to work: 66.7% less than 15 minutes, 12.3% 15 to 30 minutes, 7.9% 30 to 45 minutes, 7.0% 45 to 60 minutes, 6.1% 60 minutes or more (2000)

BIRCHDALE (unincorporated postal area, zip code 56629). Covers a land area of 66.125 square miles and a water area of 0.024 square miles. Located at 48.55° N. Lat.; 94.17° W. Long.
Population: 26 (2000); Race: 100.0% White, 0.0% Black, 0.0% Asian, 0.0% American Indian and Alaska Native, 0.0% Hispanic of any race, 0.0% two or more races (2000); Density: 0.4 persons per square mile (2000); Age: 14.3% under 18, 21.4% over 64 (2000); Marriage status: 0.0% never married, 75.0% now married, 25.0% widowed, 0.0% divorced (2000); Foreign born: 14.3% (2000); Ancestry (includes multiple ancestries): 28.6% Danish, 25.0% German, 14.3% Swedish, 7.1% Scottish, 7.1% United States or American (2000).
Economy: Employment by occupation: 27.3% management, 18.2% professional, 0.0% services, 18.2% sales, 18.2% farming, 0.0% construction, 18.2% production (2000).
Income: Per capita income: $15,129 (2000); Median household income: $21,667 (2000); Poverty rate: 28.6% (2000).
Education: High school graduation rate: 83.3% (2000); College graduation rate: 8.3% (2000).
Housing: Homeownership rate: 80.0% (2000); Median home value: $22,500 (2000); Median rent: <$100 per month (2000); Median age of housing: 17 years (2000).
Transportation: Commute to work: 100.0% car, 0.0% public transportation, 0.0% walk, 0.0% work from home (2000); Travel time to work: 45.5% less than 15 minutes, 0.0% 15 to 30 minutes, 18.2% 30 to 45 minutes, 18.2% 45 to 60 minutes, 18.2% 60 minutes or more (2000)

INTERNATIONAL FALLS (city). Covers a land area of 6.269 square miles and a water area of 0.125 square miles. Located at 48.59° N. Lat.; 93.40° W. Long. Elevation is 1,128 feet.
History: International Falls was the location in 1731 of a trading post called St. Pierre, built by a son and nephew of La Verendrye. The town that developed here became a port of entry to Ontario, Canada, and the headquarters of the Immigration and Customs Border Patrol. After 1900, the falls on the Rainy River (called Koochiching Falls) provided power for industries including a paper company and an insulite mill (producing wallboard and insulating materials from paper waste).
Population: 6,703 (2000); Race: 95.3% White, 0.2% Black, 0.0% Asian, 3.2% American Indian and Alaska Native, 0.5% Hispanic of any race, 1.2% two or more races (2000); Density: 1,069.3 persons per square mile (2000); Age: 22.5% under 18, 21.2% over 64 (2000); Marriage status: 24.6% never married, 53.5% now married, 10.3% widowed, 11.6% divorced (2000); Foreign born: 7.3% (2000); Ancestry (includes multiple ancestries): 23.0% Norwegian, 19.8% German, 15.0% Swedish, 11.3% Irish, 7.3% French (except Basque) (2000).
Economy: Single-family building permits issued: 6 (2001) / 7 (2000); Multi-family building permits issued: 2 (2001) / 0 (2000); Employment by occupation: 8.9% management, 14.8% professional, 19.2% services, 25.2% sales, 0.0% farming, 8.3% construction, 23.6% production (2000).
Income: Per capita income: $19,171 (2000); Median household income: $29,908 (2000); Poverty rate: 14.5% (2000).
Taxes: Total city taxes per capita: $241 (2000); City property taxes per capita: $221 (2000).
Education: High school graduation rate: 81.9% (2000); College graduation rate: 13.1% (2000).

School District(s)
International Falls (PK-12)
2000 Enrollment: 1,615 218-283-8468

Two-year College(s)
Rainy River Community College (Public)
2001 Enrollment: 536 218-285-7722
2001 Tuition: In-state $2,338; Out-of-state $2,338
Housing: Homeownership rate: 71.0% (2000); Median home value: $57,200 (2000); Median rent: $302 per month (2000); Median age of housing: 43 years (2000).
Hospitals: Falls Memorial Hospital (49 beds)
Safety: Violent crime rate: 28.0 per 10,000 population; Property crime rate: 327.7 per 10,000 population (2001).
Newspapers: The Daily Journal (5 x week); Border Shopper (1 x week)
Transportation: Commute to work: 86.8% car, 1.0% public transportation, 6.3% walk, 4.1% work from home (2000); Travel time to work: 82.6% less than 15 minutes, 12.3% 15 to 30 minutes, 3.1% 30 to 45 minutes, 1.1% 45 to 60 minutes, 0.9% 60 minutes or more (2000)
Airports: Falls International (primary service)
Additional Information Contacts
Internatl Falls Chamber of Commerce 218-283-9400

LITTLEFORK (city). Covers a land area of 1.178 square miles and a water area of 0 square miles. Located at 48.39° N. Lat.; 93.55° W. Long. Elevation is 1,085 feet.
History: Littlefork was settled about 1905 at a bend of the Littlefork River. Lumber and farming were early industries.
Population: 680 (2000); Race: 99.8% White, 0.0% Black, 0.2% Asian, 0.0% American Indian and Alaska Native, 0.0% Hispanic of any race, 0.0% two or more races (2000); Density: 577.1 persons per square mile (2000); Age: 26.7% under 18, 22.2% over 64 (2000); Marriage status: 19.9% never married, 57.9% now married, 14.8% widowed, 7.5% divorced (2000); Foreign born: 0.9% (2000); Ancestry (includes multiple ancestries): 31.4% German, 26.2% Norwegian, 15.1% Swedish, 11.2% Irish, 7.7% English (2000).
Economy: Single-family building permits issued: 1 (2001) / 0 (2000); Multi-family building permits issued: 0 (2001) / 2 (2000); Employment by occupation: 6.4% management, 16.0% professional, 11.4% services, 27.0% sales, 7.8% farming, 13.5% construction, 17.8% production (2000).
Income: Per capita income: $18,532 (2000); Median household income: $37,917 (2000); Poverty rate: 8.7% (2000).
Taxes: Total city taxes per capita: $111 (1997); City property taxes per capita: $107 (1997).
Education: High school graduation rate: 78.8% (2000); College graduation rate: 13.3% (2000).

School District(s)
Littlefork-Big Falls (PK-12)
2000 Enrollment: 349 218-278-6614
Housing: Homeownership rate: 79.9% (2000); Median home value: $61,300 (2000); Median rent: $263 per month (2000); Median age of housing: 35 years (2000).
Transportation: Commute to work: 88.9% car, 0.0% public transportation, 9.6% walk, 1.1% work from home (2000); Travel time to work: 48.9% less

than 15 minutes, 28.7% 15 to 30 minutes, 14.9% 30 to 45 minutes, 3.0% 45 to 60 minutes, 4.5% 60 minutes or more (2000)

Additional Information Contacts

Little Fork Chamber of Commerce 218-278-6617

LOMAN (unincorporated postal area, zip code 56654). Covers a land area of 105.562 square miles and a water area of 0.026 square miles. Located at 48.52° N. Lat.; 93.83° W. Long. Elevation is 1,100 feet.

Population: 130 (2000); Race: 100.0% White, 0.0% Black, 0.0% Asian, 0.0% American Indian and Alaska Native, 0.0% Hispanic of any race, 0.0% two or more races (2000); Density: 1.2 persons per square mile (2000); Age: 27.5% under 18, 23.5% over 64 (2000); Marriage status: 17.0% never married, 61.6% now married, 7.1% widowed, 14.3% divorced (2000); Foreign born: 12.1% (2000); Ancestry (includes multiple ancestries): 43.0% German, 22.1% Norwegian, 14.1% Swedish, 12.1% English, 6.7% Irish (2000).

Economy: Employment by occupation: 10.3% management, 15.5% professional, 13.8% services, 19.0% sales, 0.0% farming, 12.1% construction, 29.3% production (2000).

Income: Per capita income: $13,919 (2000); Median household income: $35,938 (2000); Poverty rate: 18.8% (2000).

Education: High school graduation rate: 74.7% (2000); College graduation rate: 8.1% (2000).

Housing: Homeownership rate: 93.0% (2000); Median home value: $62,500 (2000); Median rent: $200 per month (2000); Median age of housing: 34 years (2000).

Transportation: Commute to work: 96.6% car, 0.0% public transportation, 0.0% walk, 3.4% work from home (2000); Travel time to work: 12.5% less than 15 minutes, 21.4% 15 to 30 minutes, 55.4% 30 to 45 minutes, 3.6% 45 to 60 minutes, 7.1% 60 minutes or more (2000)

MIZPAH (city). Covers a land area of 3.030 square miles and a water area of 0 square miles. Located at 47.92° N. Lat.; 94.20° W. Long. Elevation is 1,385 feet.

Population: 78 (2000); Race: 78.6% White, 0.0% Black, 0.0% Asian, 21.4% American Indian and Alaska Native, 0.0% Hispanic of any race, 0.0% two or more races (2000); Density: 25.7 persons per square mile (2000); Age: 18.6% under 18, 11.4% over 64 (2000); Marriage status: 11.9% never married, 69.5% now married, 6.8% widowed, 11.9% divorced (2000); Foreign born: 0.0% (2000); Ancestry (includes multiple ancestries): 31.4% German, 25.7% Norwegian, 15.7% Other groups, 10.0% Swedish, 10.0% English (2000).

Economy: In forest area. Timber, alfalfa; cattle. Manufacturing of valve lifters. Employment by occupation: 37.1% management, 5.7% professional, 34.3% services, 0.0% sales, 11.4% farming, 11.4% construction, 0.0% production (2000).

Income: Per capita income: $18,519 (2000); Median household income: $34,375 (2000); Poverty rate: 25.7% (2000).

Taxes: Total city taxes per capita: $20 (1997); City property taxes per capita: $10 (1997).

Education: High school graduation rate: 73.5% (2000); College graduation rate: 8.2% (2000).

Housing: Homeownership rate: 66.7% (2000); Median home value: $12,500 (2000); Median rent: $250 per month (2000); Median age of housing: 56 years (2000).

Transportation: Commute to work: 62.9% car, 0.0% public transportation, 20.0% walk, 5.7% work from home (2000); Travel time to work: 66.7% less than 15 minutes, 12.1% 15 to 30 minutes, 15.2% 30 to 45 minutes, 6.1% 45 to 60 minutes, 0.0% 60 minutes or more (2000)

NORTHOME (city). Covers a land area of 1.520 square miles and a water area of 0.369 square miles. Located at 47.87° N. Lat.; 94.27° W. Long. Elevation is 1,429 feet.

Population: 230 (2000); Race: 96.9% White, 0.0% Black, 0.0% Asian, 1.3% American Indian and Alaska Native, 0.0% Hispanic of any race, 1.8% two or more races (2000); Density: 151.3 persons per square mile (2000); Age: 20.1% under 18, 40.6% over 64 (2000); Marriage status: 23.4% never married, 43.6% now married, 24.5% widowed, 8.5% divorced (2000); Foreign born: 1.8% (2000); Ancestry (includes multiple ancestries): 38.4% German, 22.3% Norwegian, 13.8% Irish, 10.3% Swedish, 5.4% French (except Basque) (2000).

Economy: Livestock; alfalfa; timber. Manufacturing: meat processing, printing. Logging. Chippewa National Forest to Southeast. Single-family building permits issued: 0 (2001) / 0 (2000); Multi-family building permits issued: 0 (2001) / 0 (2000); Employment by occupation: 10.6% management, 19.7% professional, 9.1% services, 33.3% sales, 0.0% farming, 19.7% construction, 7.6% production (2000).

Income: Per capita income: $14,758 (2000); Median household income: $25,417 (2000); Poverty rate: 24.2% (2000).

Taxes: Total city taxes per capita: $47 (1997); City property taxes per capita: $47 (1997).

Education: High school graduation rate: 67.3% (2000); College graduation rate: 9.9% (2000).

School District(s)

South Koochiching (PK-12)
2000 Enrollment: 396 218-897-5277

Housing: Homeownership rate: 66.7% (2000); Median home value: $32,500 (2000); Median rent: $229 per month (2000); Median age of housing: 41 years (2000).

Newspapers: Northome Record (1 x week)

Transportation: Commute to work: 77.3% car, 0.0% public transportation, 15.2% walk, 7.6% work from home (2000); Travel time to work: 45.9% less than 15 minutes, 19.7% 15 to 30 minutes, 13.1% 30 to 45 minutes, 4.9% 45 to 60 minutes, 16.4% 60 minutes or more (2000)

RANIER (city). Covers a land area of 0.148 square miles and a water area of 0.002 square miles. Located at 48.61° N. Lat.; 93.34° W. Long.

Population: 188 (2000); Race: 96.8% White, 0.0% Black, 0.0% Asian, 1.6% American Indian and Alaska Native, 0.0% Hispanic of any race, 1.6% two or more races (2000); Density: 1,268.1 persons per square mile (2000); Age: 21.6% under 18, 21.6% over 64 (2000); Marriage status: 23.9% never married, 59.4% now married, 9.0% widowed, 7.7% divorced (2000); Foreign born: 14.7% (2000); Ancestry (includes multiple ancestries): 35.3% German, 34.7% Norwegian, 13.2% English, 13.2% Polish, 9.5% Swedish (2000).

Economy: Port of entry. Manufacturing: fishing tackle. Voyageurs National Park to East. Single-family building permits issued: 1 (2001) / 0 (2000); Multi-family building permits issued: 0 (2001) / 0 (2000); Employment by occupation: 20.0% management, 9.5% professional, 26.3% services, 21.1% sales, 0.0% farming, 5.3% construction, 17.9% production (2000).

Income: Per capita income: $20,784 (2000); Median household income: $39,375 (2000); Poverty rate: 0.0% (2000).

Taxes: Total city taxes per capita: $32 (1997); City property taxes per capita: $32 (1997).

Education: High school graduation rate: 92.8% (2000); College graduation rate: 22.3% (2000).

Housing: Homeownership rate: 83.6% (2000); Median home value: $70,000 (2000); Median rent: $525 per month (2000); Median age of housing: 56 years (2000).

Transportation: Commute to work: 86.3% car, 0.0% public transportation, 10.5% walk, 0.0% work from home (2000); Travel time to work: 72.6% less than 15 minutes, 18.9% 15 to 30 minutes, 0.0% 30 to 45 minutes, 0.0% 45 to 60 minutes, 8.4% 60 minutes or more (2000)

RAY (unincorporated postal area, zip code 56669). Covers a land area of 153.692 square miles and a water area of 0.213 square miles. Located at 48.44° N. Lat.; 93.14° W. Long. Elevation is 1,180 feet.

Population: 402 (2000); Race: 100.0% White, 0.0% Black, 0.0% Asian, 0.0% American Indian and Alaska Native, 0.0% Hispanic of any race, 0.0% two or more races (2000); Density: 2.6 persons per square mile (2000); Age: 4.8% under 18, 16.2% over 64 (2000); Marriage status: 14.7% never married, 62.4% now married, 11.8% widowed, 11.1% divorced (2000); Foreign born: 3.2% (2000); Ancestry (includes multiple ancestries): 20.6% German, 19.7% Norwegian, 10.8% French (except Basque), 10.5% Swedish, 10.5% Finnish (2000).

Economy: Employment by occupation: 9.1% management, 7.4% professional, 18.2% services, 34.1% sales, 3.4% farming, 5.7% construction, 22.2% production (2000).

Income: Per capita income: $22,905 (2000); Median household income: $30,625 (2000); Poverty rate: 8.9% (2000).

Education: High school graduation rate: 76.2% (2000); College graduation rate: 10.6% (2000).

Housing: Homeownership rate: 95.2% (2000); Median home value: $120,000 (2000); Median age of housing: 38 years (2000).

Transportation: Commute to work: 92.6% car, 0.0% public transportation, 7.4% walk, 0.0% work from home (2000); Travel time to work: 27.2% less than 15 minutes, 38.3% 15 to 30 minutes, 28.4% 30 to 45 minutes, 2.5% 45 to 60 minutes, 3.7% 60 minutes or more (2000)

Lac qui Parle County

Located in southwestern Minnesota; bounded on the west by South Dakota, and on the north and east by the Minnesota River, flowing through Lac qui

Parle; drained by the Lac qui Parle River. Covers a land area of 764.90 square miles, a water area of 13.20 square miles, and is located in the Central Time Zone. The county government was organized in 1863. County seat is Madison.

Weather Station: Madison Sewage Plant Elevation: 1,079 feet

	Jan	Feb	Mar	Apr	May	Jun	Jul	Aug	Sep	Oct	Nov	Dec
High	23	30	41	59	73	82	86	84	75	63	42	29
Low	2	10	21	34	46	57	61	58	48	37	23	9
Precip	0.8	0.6	1.5	2.2	2.9	3.8	3.5	3.0	2.1	2.6	1.3	0.5
Snow	8.6	6.9	8.4	2.3	tr	0.0	0.0	0.0	tr	0.5	5.8	5.1

High and Low temperatures in degrees Fahrenheit; Precipitation and Snow in inches

Weather Station: Montevideo 1 SW Elevation: 984 feet

	Jan	Feb	Mar	Apr	May	Jun	Jul	Aug	Sep	Oct	Nov	Dec
High	21	28	40	58	72	81	84	82	74	61	40	27
Low	1	9	22	34	47	57	61	58	48	37	22	9
Precip	0.9	0.9	1.6	2.3	3.2	4.2	3.4	3.2	2.4	2.1	1.4	0.7
Snow	10.6	7.9	9.7	2.0	tr	0.0	0.0	0.0	tr	0.6	8.5	7.4

High and Low temperatures in degrees Fahrenheit; Precipitation and Snow in inches

Population: 8,067 (2000); Race: 98.9% White, 0.1% Black, 0.4% Asian, 0.2% American Indian and Alaska Native, 0.2% Hispanic of any race, 0.4% two or more races (2000); Density: 10.5 persons per square mile (2000); Age: 24.5% under 18, 23.3% over 64 (2000).
Religion: Five largest groups: 77.3% Evangelical Lutheran Church in America, 15.1% Catholic Church, 9.1% Lutheran Church—Missouri Synod, 2.2% United Church of Christ, 1.7% Presbyterian Church (U.S.A.) (2000).
Economy: Unemployment rate: 2.4% (11/2002); Total civilian labor force: 3,642 (11/2002); Leading industries: 21.6% health care and social assistance; 17.4% retail trade; 14.9% manufacturing (2000); Companies that employ more than 1,000 persons: 0 (2000); Companies that employ more than 100 persons: 3 (2000); Farms: 790 totaling 397,519 acres (1997); Minority business ownership rate: 0.0% (1997); Women business ownership rate: 0.0% (1997); Retail sales per capita: $6,170 (1997). Single-family building permits issued: 11 (2001) / 12 (2000); Multi-family building permits issued: 0 (2001) / 0 (2000).
Income: Per capita income: $17,399 (2000); Median household income: $32,626 (2000); Poverty rate: 8.5% (2000); Bankruptcy rate: 1.66% (2001).
Taxes: Total county taxes per capita: $251 (1997); County property taxes per capita: $251 (1997).
Education: High school graduation rate: 80.8% (2000); College graduation rate: 13.0% (2000).
Housing: Homeownership rate: 80.7% (2000); Median home value: $43,100 (2000); Median rent: $259 per month (2000); Median age of housing: 59 years (2000).
Health: Birth rate: 83.1 per 10,000 population (1998); Age adjusted death rate: 98.9 per 10,000 population (1999); Age adjusted cancer mortality rate: 319.0 deaths per 100,000 population (1999). Number of physicians: 6.2 per 10,000 population (1999); Number of hospital beds: 131.4 per 10,000 population (1999).
Elections: 2000 Presidential election results: 50.4% Gore, 43.6% Bush, 3.6% Nader, 2.0% Buchanan
National and State Parks: Acton Marsh State Wildlife Management Area; Baxter State Wildlife Management Area; Borchardt-Rosin State Wildlife Management A; Christopherson State Wildlife Management Are; Church State Wildlife Management Area; Dacotah State Wildlife Management Area; De vorak State Wildlife Management Area; Flinks State Wildlife Management Area; Hamlin State Wildlife Management Area; Haydenville State Wildlife Management Area; Kemen State Wildlife Management Area; Kibler State Wildlife Management Area; Kibler State Wildlife Management Area; Medicine Pipe State Wildlife Management Area; Plantation State Wildlife Management Area; Stony Run State Wildlife Management Area; Sweetwater State Wildlife Management Area; Ten-Well State Wildlife Management Area; Wild Wings State Wildlife Management Area
Additional Information Contacts
Lac qui Parle County Government Offices 320-598-7444
Dawson Chamber of Commerce 320-769-2981
Madison Chamber of Commerce 320-598-7373

Lac qui Parle County Communities

AGASSIZ (township). Covers a land area of 34.921 square miles and a water area of 2.407 square miles. Located at 45.19° N. Lat.; 96.29° W. Long.
Population: 104 (2000); Race: 100.0% White, 0.0% Black, 0.0% Asian, 0.0% American Indian and Alaska Native, 0.0% Hispanic of any race, 0.0% two or more races (2000); Density: 3.0 persons per square mile (2000); Age: 29.5% under 18, 19.2% over 64 (2000); Marriage status: 26.7% never married, 63.3% now married, 5.0% widowed, 5.0% divorced (2000); Foreign born: 0.0% (2000); Ancestry (includes multiple ancestries): 50.0% German, 16.7% United States or American, 16.7% Norwegian, 15.4% Danish, 10.3% Irish (2000).
Economy: Employment by occupation: 15.4% management, 20.5% professional, 10.3% services, 15.4% sales, 2.6% farming, 10.3% construction, 25.6% production (2000).
Income: Per capita income: $12,582 (2000); Median household income: $23,750 (2000); Poverty rate: 26.9% (2000).
Taxes: Total city taxes per capita: $51 (1997); City property taxes per capita: $51 (1997).
Education: High school graduation rate: 84.3% (2000); College graduation rate: 11.8% (2000).
Housing: Homeownership rate: 68.8% (2000); Median home value: $17,500 (2000); Median rent: $225 per month (2000); Median age of housing: 60+ years (2000).
Transportation: Commute to work: 100.0% car, 0.0% public transportation, 0.0% walk, 0.0% work from home (2000); Travel time to work: 30.8% less than 15 minutes, 35.9% 15 to 30 minutes, 15.4% 30 to 45 minutes, 12.8% 45 to 60 minutes, 5.1% 60 minutes or more (2000)

ARENA (township). Covers a land area of 36.699 square miles and a water area of 0.394 square miles. Located at 45.02° N. Lat.; 96.28° W. Long.
Population: 153 (2000); Race: 98.9% White, 1.1% Black, 0.0% Asian, 0.0% American Indian and Alaska Native, 0.0% Hispanic of any race, 0.0% two or more races (2000); Density: 4.2 persons per square mile (2000); Age: 35.1% under 18, 1.6% over 64 (2000); Marriage status: 21.9% never married, 73.0% now married, 0.0% widowed, 5.1% divorced (2000); Foreign born: 0.0% (2000); Ancestry (includes multiple ancestries): 43.2% German, 31.4% Norwegian, 11.9% Swedish, 6.5% Danish, 5.4% Dutch (2000).
Economy: Employment by occupation: 40.8% management, 8.7% professional, 10.7% services, 11.7% sales, 5.8% farming, 14.6% construction, 7.8% production (2000).
Income: Per capita income: $15,697 (2000); Median household income: $42,813 (2000); Poverty rate: 8.6% (2000).
Taxes: Total city taxes per capita: $107 (1997); City property taxes per capita: $107 (1997).
Education: High school graduation rate: 91.8% (2000); College graduation rate: 8.2% (2000).
Housing: Homeownership rate: 93.8% (2000); Median home value: $52,500 (2000); Median age of housing: 60+ years (2000).
Transportation: Commute to work: 51.5% car, 0.0% public transportation, 4.0% walk, 44.6% work from home (2000); Travel time to work: 69.6% less than 15 minutes, 8.9% 15 to 30 minutes, 14.3% 30 to 45 minutes, 0.0% 45 to 60 minutes, 7.1% 60 minutes or more (2000)

AUGUSTA (township). Covers a land area of 28.505 square miles and a water area of 0.154 square miles. Located at 45.02° N. Lat.; 96.40° W. Long.
Population: 119 (2000); Race: 100.0% White, 0.0% Black, 0.0% Asian, 0.0% American Indian and Alaska Native, 0.0% Hispanic of any race, 0.0% two or more races (2000); Density: 4.2 persons per square mile (2000); Age: 20.5% under 18, 26.2% over 64 (2000); Marriage status: 21.7% never married, 65.1% now married, 4.7% widowed, 8.5% divorced (2000); Foreign born: 0.0% (2000); Ancestry (includes multiple ancestries): 63.9% German, 39.3% Norwegian, 6.6% Swedish, 5.7% English, 4.9% Danish (2000).
Economy: Employment by occupation: 42.6% management, 13.1% professional, 3.3% services, 21.3% sales, 0.0% farming, 6.6% construction, 13.1% production (2000).
Income: Per capita income: $15,506 (2000); Median household income: $39,375 (2000); Poverty rate: 7.4% (2000).
Taxes: Total city taxes per capita: $77 (1997); City property taxes per capita: $77 (1997).
Education: High school graduation rate: 73.9% (2000); College graduation rate: 8.7% (2000).
Housing: Homeownership rate: 77.1% (2000); Median home value: $50,000 (2000); Median age of housing: 60+ years (2000).
Transportation: Commute to work: 67.2% car, 0.0% public transportation, 1.6% walk, 31.1% work from home (2000); Travel time to work: 26.2% less than 15 minutes, 50.0% 15 to 30 minutes, 9.5% 30 to 45 minutes, 0.0% 45 to 60 minutes, 14.3% 60 minutes or more (2000)

BAXTER (township). Covers a land area of 35.865 square miles and a water area of 0.081 square miles. Located at 44.92° N. Lat.; 95.90° W. Long.

Population: 209 (2000); Race: 100.0% White, 0.0% Black, 0.0% Asian, 0.0% American Indian and Alaska Native, 0.0% Hispanic of any race, 0.0% two or more races (2000); Density: 5.8 persons per square mile (2000); Age: 27.7% under 18, 16.4% over 64 (2000); Marriage status: 11.1% never married, 84.2% now married, 1.2% widowed, 3.5% divorced (2000); Foreign born: 0.0% (2000); Ancestry (includes multiple ancestries): 66.8% Norwegian, 36.8% German, 8.2% Swedish, 7.3% Irish, 2.7% Polish (2000).
Economy: Employment by occupation: 15.5% management, 9.5% professional, 16.4% services, 34.5% sales, 2.6% farming, 13.8% construction, 7.8% production (2000).
Income: Per capita income: $15,622 (2000); Median household income: $40,417 (2000); Poverty rate: 11.4% (2000).
Taxes: Total city taxes per capita: $88 (1997); City property taxes per capita: $88 (1997).
Education: High school graduation rate: 85.2% (2000); College graduation rate: 12.9% (2000).
Housing: Homeownership rate: 84.2% (2000); Median home value: $57,000 (2000); Median rent: $238 per month (2000); Median age of housing: 60+ years (2000).
Transportation: Commute to work: 80.7% car, 0.0% public transportation, 2.8% walk, 16.5% work from home (2000); Travel time to work: 36.3% less than 15 minutes, 53.8% 15 to 30 minutes, 0.0% 30 to 45 minutes, 3.3% 45 to 60 minutes, 6.6% 60 minutes or more (2000)

BELLINGHAM (city). Covers a land area of 0.400 square miles and a water area of 0 square miles. Located at 45.13° N. Lat.; 96.28° W. Long. Elevation is 1,050 feet.
Population: 205 (2000); Race: 100.0% White, 0.0% Black, 0.0% Asian, 0.0% American Indian and Alaska Native, 0.9% Hispanic of any race, 0.0% two or more races (2000); Density: 512.8 persons per square mile (2000); Age: 21.3% under 18, 33.8% over 64 (2000); Marriage status: 18.8% never married, 63.1% now married, 12.5% widowed, 5.7% divorced (2000); Foreign born: 0.0% (2000); Ancestry (includes multiple ancestries): 40.7% German, 25.0% Norwegian, 5.6% French (except Basque), 5.1% Polish, 3.2% English (2000).
Economy: Corn, soybeans, oats, wheat; hogs, cattle, sheep. Manufacturing: concrete, fertilizers. Single-family building permits issued: 0 (2001) / 0 (2000); Multi-family building permits issued: 0 (2001) / 0 (2000); Employment by occupation: 6.7% management, 21.1% professional, 12.2% services, 24.4% sales, 4.4% farming, 12.2% construction, 18.9% production (2000).
Income: Per capita income: $15,888 (2000); Median household income: $27,083 (2000); Poverty rate: 13.5% (2000).
Taxes: Total city taxes per capita: $58 (1997); City property taxes per capita: $58 (1997).
Education: High school graduation rate: 75.6% (2000); College graduation rate: 13.8% (2000).

School District(s)

Bellingham (KG-06)
2000 Enrollment: 75 320-568-2118
Housing: Homeownership rate: 82.0% (2000); Median home value: $19,400 (2000); Median rent: $150 per month (2000); Median age of housing: 60+ years (2000).
Transportation: Commute to work: 86.0% car, 0.0% public transportation, 11.8% walk, 2.2% work from home (2000); Travel time to work: 56.0% less than 15 minutes, 30.8% 15 to 30 minutes, 11.0% 30 to 45 minutes, 2.2% 45 to 60 minutes, 0.0% 60 minutes or more (2000)

BOYD (city). Covers a land area of 0.534 square miles and a water area of 0 square miles. Located at 44.85° N. Lat.; 95.90° W. Long. Elevation is 1,055 feet.
Population: 210 (2000); Race: 97.6% White, 0.0% Black, 1.4% Asian, 0.0% American Indian and Alaska Native, 0.0% Hispanic of any race, 1.0% two or more races (2000); Density: 393.5 persons per square mile (2000); Age: 18.8% under 18, 17.9% over 64 (2000); Marriage status: 20.3% never married, 54.2% now married, 14.1% widowed, 11.3% divorced (2000); Foreign born: 3.4% (2000); Ancestry (includes multiple ancestries): 38.6% Norwegian, 34.3% German, 8.2% Polish, 6.3% English, 4.8% Swedish (2000).
Economy: Livestock; poultry; grain; dairying. Manufacturing: fertilizers. Employment by occupation: 11.7% management, 2.7% professional, 9.9% services, 25.2% sales, 0.0% farming, 18.0% construction, 32.4% production (2000).
Income: Per capita income: $16,917 (2000); Median household income: $30,625 (2000); Poverty rate: 6.8% (2000).
Taxes: Total city taxes per capita: $224 (1997); City property taxes per capita: $224 (1997).
Education: High school graduation rate: 73.5% (2000); College graduation rate: 1.3% (2000).
Housing: Homeownership rate: 85.3% (2000); Median home value: $17,500 (2000); Median rent: $169 per month (2000); Median age of housing: 60+ years (2000).
Transportation: Commute to work: 82.9% car, 0.0% public transportation, 11.7% walk, 4.5% work from home (2000); Travel time to work: 25.5% less than 15 minutes, 50.9% 15 to 30 minutes, 21.7% 30 to 45 minutes, 0.0% 45 to 60 minutes, 1.9% 60 minutes or more (2000)

CAMP RELEASE (township). Covers a land area of 29.311 square miles and a water area of 0 square miles. Located at 44.92° N. Lat.; 95.80° W. Long.
Population: 293 (2000); Race: 96.6% White, 0.0% Black, 2.7% Asian, 0.7% American Indian and Alaska Native, 0.0% Hispanic of any race, 0.0% two or more races (2000); Density: 10.0 persons per square mile (2000); Age: 30.7% under 18, 13.7% over 64 (2000); Marriage status: 20.7% never married, 66.1% now married, 8.8% widowed, 4.4% divorced (2000); Foreign born: 1.4% (2000); Ancestry (includes multiple ancestries): 48.5% Norwegian, 41.3% German, 9.2% Dutch, 9.2% Swedish, 6.8% English (2000).
Economy: Employment by occupation: 30.4% management, 6.8% professional, 12.2% services, 24.3% sales, 0.7% farming, 10.1% construction, 15.5% production (2000).
Income: Per capita income: $20,174 (2000); Median household income: $34,286 (2000); Poverty rate: 6.1% (2000).
Taxes: Total city taxes per capita: $53 (1997); City property taxes per capita: $53 (1997).
Education: High school graduation rate: 89.8% (2000); College graduation rate: 14.4% (2000).
Housing: Homeownership rate: 91.4% (2000); Median home value: $125,000 (2000); Median rent: $250 per month (2000); Median age of housing: 40 years (2000).
Transportation: Commute to work: 78.8% car, 0.0% public transportation, 4.1% walk, 11.0% work from home (2000); Travel time to work: 70.0% less than 15 minutes, 17.7% 15 to 30 minutes, 5.4% 30 to 45 minutes, 1.5% 45 to 60 minutes, 5.4% 60 minutes or more (2000)

CERRO GORDO (township). Covers a land area of 35.777 square miles and a water area of 0.091 square miles. Located at 45.02° N. Lat.; 96.03° W. Long. Elevation is 1,040 feet.
Population: 256 (2000); Race: 95.9% White, 0.0% Black, 1.2% Asian, 2.0% American Indian and Alaska Native, 0.0% Hispanic of any race, 0.8% two or more races (2000); Density: 7.2 persons per square mile (2000); Age: 29.9% under 18, 9.0% over 64 (2000); Marriage status: 26.8% never married, 67.0% now married, 5.2% widowed, 1.0% divorced (2000); Foreign born: 1.2% (2000); Ancestry (includes multiple ancestries): 71.7% Norwegian, 28.7% German, 6.1% Other groups, 6.1% Swedish, 4.1% Irish (2000).
Economy: Employment by occupation: 26.0% management, 20.5% professional, 9.6% services, 17.8% sales, 1.4% farming, 9.6% construction, 15.1% production (2000).
Income: Per capita income: $16,486 (2000); Median household income: $52,500 (2000); Poverty rate: 1.6% (2000).
Taxes: Total city taxes per capita: $89 (1997); City property taxes per capita: $89 (1997).
Education: High school graduation rate: 91.0% (2000); College graduation rate: 19.4% (2000).
Housing: Homeownership rate: 82.4% (2000); Median home value: $45,000 (2000); Median rent: $275 per month (2000); Median age of housing: 60+ years (2000).
Transportation: Commute to work: 80.4% car, 0.0% public transportation, 5.6% walk, 14.0% work from home (2000); Travel time to work: 35.0% less than 15 minutes, 44.7% 15 to 30 minutes, 8.1% 30 to 45 minutes, 5.7% 45 to 60 minutes, 6.5% 60 minutes or more (2000)

DAWSON (city). Covers a land area of 1.475 square miles and a water area of 0 square miles. Located at 44.93° N. Lat.; 96.05° W. Long. Elevation is 1,058 feet.
History: Incorporated as village 1885, as city 1911.
Population: 1,539 (2000); Race: 98.0% White, 0.3% Black, 0.6% Asian, 0.0% American Indian and Alaska Native, 0.7% Hispanic of any race, 1.1% two or more races (2000); Density: 1,043.4 persons per square mile (2000); Age: 22.7% under 18, 28.7% over 64 (2000); Marriage status: 17.4% never married, 60.3% now married, 14.9% widowed, 7.4% divorced (2000);

Foreign born: 1.3% (2000); Ancestry (includes multiple ancestries): 54.0% Norwegian, 33.7% German, 13.4% Swedish, 4.5% Dutch, 4.0% Irish (2000).
Economy: Trade center and shipping point for agricultural area: grain, soybeans; livestock, poultry; dairying. Single-family building permits issued: 1 (2001) / 1 (2000); Multi-family building permits issued: 0 (2001) / 0 (2000); Employment by occupation: 9.7% management, 15.7% professional, 18.1% services, 26.8% sales, 1.0% farming, 6.9% construction, 21.9% production (2000).
Income: Per capita income: $19,084 (2000); Median household income: $31,442 (2000); Poverty rate: 7.4% (2000).
Taxes: Total city taxes per capita: $231 (1997); City property taxes per capita: $223 (1997).
Education: High school graduation rate: 76.8% (2000); College graduation rate: 13.3% (2000).

School District(s)

Dawson-Boyd (PK-12)
2000 Enrollment: 629 320-769-2955
Housing: Homeownership rate: 74.4% (2000); Median home value: $51,300 (2000); Median rent: $291 per month (2000); Median age of housing: 47 years (2000).
Hospitals: Johnson Memorial Health Services (94 beds)
Safety: Violent crime rate: 12.9 per 10,000 population; Property crime rate: 141.4 per 10,000 population (2001).
Newspapers: Dawson Sentinel (1 x week)
Transportation: Commute to work: 84.9% car, 1.7% public transportation, 8.9% walk, 3.9% work from home (2000); Travel time to work: 70.1% less than 15 minutes, 16.9% 15 to 30 minutes, 8.8% 30 to 45 minutes, 1.9% 45 to 60 minutes, 2.3% 60 minutes or more (2000)
Additional Information Contacts
Dawson Chamber of Commerce 320-769-2981

FREELAND (township). Covers a land area of 36.436 square miles and a water area of 0 square miles. Located at 44.85° N. Lat.; 96.26° W. Long.
Population: 127 (2000); Race: 100.0% White, 0.0% Black, 0.0% Asian, 0.0% American Indian and Alaska Native, 0.0% Hispanic of any race, 0.0% two or more races (2000); Density: 3.5 persons per square mile (2000); Age: 30.4% under 18, 12.3% over 64 (2000); Marriage status: 28.8% never married, 61.5% now married, 2.9% widowed, 6.7% divorced (2000); Foreign born: 0.0% (2000); Ancestry (includes multiple ancestries): 55.1% German, 29.7% Norwegian, 11.6% United States or American, 8.0% Other groups, 8.0% Swedish (2000).
Economy: Employment by occupation: 7.0% management, 12.3% professional, 19.3% services, 14.0% sales, 3.5% farming, 10.5% construction, 33.3% production (2000).
Income: Per capita income: $14,059 (2000); Median household income: $30,000 (2000); Poverty rate: 21.7% (2000).
Taxes: Total city taxes per capita: $94 (2000); City property taxes per capita: $94 (2000).
Education: High school graduation rate: 90.0% (2000); College graduation rate: 18.9% (2000).
Housing: Homeownership rate: 79.2% (2000); Median home value: $55,000 (2000); Median rent: $275 per month (2000); Median age of housing: 60+ years (2000).
Transportation: Commute to work: 93.0% car, 0.0% public transportation, 0.0% walk, 7.0% work from home (2000); Travel time to work: 22.6% less than 15 minutes, 64.2% 15 to 30 minutes, 5.7% 30 to 45 minutes, 0.0% 45 to 60 minutes, 7.5% 60 minutes or more (2000)

GARFIELD (township). Covers a land area of 37.189 square miles and a water area of 0.039 square miles. Located at 44.94° N. Lat.; 96.29° W. Long.
Population: 187 (2000); Race: 100.0% White, 0.0% Black, 0.0% Asian, 0.0% American Indian and Alaska Native, 0.0% Hispanic of any race, 0.0% two or more races (2000); Density: 5.0 persons per square mile (2000); Age: 36.0% under 18, 16.1% over 64 (2000); Marriage status: 14.7% never married, 77.5% now married, 3.9% widowed, 3.9% divorced (2000); Foreign born: 0.0% (2000); Ancestry (includes multiple ancestries): 61.8% Norwegian, 41.9% German, 8.1% Swedish, 3.8% Danish, 2.2% Scandinavian (2000).
Economy: Employment by occupation: 31.0% management, 28.2% professional, 5.6% services, 18.3% sales, 7.0% farming, 8.5% construction, 1.4% production (2000).
Income: Per capita income: $25,220 (2000); Median household income: $40,625 (2000); Poverty rate: 5.4% (2000).
Taxes: Total city taxes per capita: $122 (1997); City property taxes per capita: $122 (1997).
Education: High school graduation rate: 80.5% (2000); College graduation rate: 27.4% (2000).
Housing: Homeownership rate: 86.9% (2000); Median home value: $53,300 (2000); Median rent: $125 per month (2000); Median age of housing: 60+ years (2000).
Transportation: Commute to work: 76.1% car, 0.0% public transportation, 0.0% walk, 23.9% work from home (2000); Travel time to work: 20.4% less than 15 minutes, 59.3% 15 to 30 minutes, 7.4% 30 to 45 minutes, 5.6% 45 to 60 minutes, 7.4% 60 minutes or more (2000)

HAMLIN (township). Covers a land area of 35.881 square miles and a water area of 0.206 square miles. Located at 44.92° N. Lat.; 96.15° W. Long.
Population: 185 (2000); Race: 100.0% White, 0.0% Black, 0.0% Asian, 0.0% American Indian and Alaska Native, 0.0% Hispanic of any race, 0.0% two or more races (2000); Density: 5.2 persons per square mile (2000); Age: 29.4% under 18, 11.8% over 64 (2000); Marriage status: 16.7% never married, 76.2% now married, 1.6% widowed, 5.6% divorced (2000); Foreign born: 0.0% (2000); Ancestry (includes multiple ancestries): 51.2% Norwegian, 48.2% German, 8.2% Swedish, 7.1% Irish, 4.7% Italian (2000).
Economy: Employment by occupation: 29.8% management, 13.1% professional, 14.3% services, 14.3% sales, 4.8% farming, 13.1% construction, 10.7% production (2000).
Income: Per capita income: $15,948 (2000); Median household income: $30,833 (2000); Poverty rate: 8.8% (2000).
Taxes: Total city taxes per capita: $95 (1997); City property taxes per capita: $95 (1997).
Education: High school graduation rate: 84.2% (2000); College graduation rate: 5.3% (2000).
Housing: Homeownership rate: 93.9% (2000); Median home value: $61,300 (2000); Median age of housing: 60+ years (2000).
Transportation: Commute to work: 81.0% car, 0.0% public transportation, 2.4% walk, 16.7% work from home (2000); Travel time to work: 57.1% less than 15 minutes, 34.3% 15 to 30 minutes, 5.7% 30 to 45 minutes, 0.0% 45 to 60 minutes, 2.9% 60 minutes or more (2000)

HANTHO (township). Covers a land area of 30.134 square miles and a water area of 3.110 square miles. Located at 45.10° N. Lat.; 96.05° W. Long.
Population: 154 (2000); Race: 96.6% White, 0.0% Black, 0.0% Asian, 3.4% American Indian and Alaska Native, 0.0% Hispanic of any race, 0.0% two or more races (2000); Density: 5.1 persons per square mile (2000); Age: 42.9% under 18, 11.3% over 64 (2000); Marriage status: 27.4% never married, 65.0% now married, 3.4% widowed, 4.3% divorced (2000); Foreign born: 0.0% (2000); Ancestry (includes multiple ancestries): 66.7% Norwegian, 33.9% German, 6.2% Swedish, 3.4% Scandinavian, 3.4% Other groups (2000).
Economy: Employment by occupation: 34.8% management, 13.0% professional, 5.8% services, 18.8% sales, 1.4% farming, 10.1% construction, 15.9% production (2000).
Income: Per capita income: $12,854 (2000); Median household income: $37,083 (2000); Poverty rate: 2.3% (2000).
Taxes: Total city taxes per capita: $65 (1997); City property taxes per capita: $65 (1997).
Education: High school graduation rate: 93.6% (2000); College graduation rate: 33.0% (2000).
Housing: Homeownership rate: 85.5% (2000); Median home value: $19,500 (2000); Median rent: $263 per month (2000); Median age of housing: 60+ years (2000).
Transportation: Commute to work: 88.4% car, 0.0% public transportation, 0.0% walk, 11.6% work from home (2000); Travel time to work: 11.5% less than 15 minutes, 65.6% 15 to 30 minutes, 1.6% 30 to 45 minutes, 9.8% 45 to 60 minutes, 11.5% 60 minutes or more (2000)

LAC QUI PARLE (township). Covers a land area of 28.735 square miles and a water area of 2.766 square miles. Located at 45.01° N. Lat.; 95.91° W. Long.
Population: 183 (2000); Race: 100.0% White, 0.0% Black, 0.0% Asian, 0.0% American Indian and Alaska Native, 0.0% Hispanic of any race, 0.0% two or more races (2000); Density: 6.4 persons per square mile (2000); Age: 23.8% under 18, 13.1% over 64 (2000); Marriage status: 8.5% never married, 82.2% now married, 4.7% widowed, 4.7% divorced (2000); Foreign born: 0.0% (2000); Ancestry (includes multiple ancestries): 55.0% Norwegian, 30.0% German, 26.9% Swedish, 6.3% Danish, 4.4% English (2000).
Economy: Employment by occupation: 38.2% management, 19.1% professional, 6.7% services, 16.9% sales, 1.1% farming, 5.6% construction, 12.4% production (2000).

Income: Per capita income: $16,769 (2000); Median household income: $33,906 (2000); Poverty rate: 15.0% (2000).
Taxes: Total city taxes per capita: $80 (1997); City property taxes per capita: $80 (1997).
Education: High school graduation rate: 91.4% (2000); College graduation rate: 20.7% (2000).
Housing: Homeownership rate: 94.1% (2000); Median home value: $50,000 (2000); Median age of housing: 60+ years (2000).
Transportation: Commute to work: 71.1% car, 0.0% public transportation, 1.2% walk, 27.7% work from home (2000); Travel time to work: 28.3% less than 15 minutes, 53.3% 15 to 30 minutes, 10.0% 30 to 45 minutes, 6.7% 45 to 60 minutes, 1.7% 60 minutes or more (2000)

LAKE SHORE (township). Covers a land area of 51.661 square miles and a water area of 2.242 square miles. Located at 45.14° N. Lat.; 96.16° W. Long.
Population: 239 (2000); Race: 98.8% White, 0.0% Black, 0.0% Asian, 0.0% American Indian and Alaska Native, 0.0% Hispanic of any race, 1.2% two or more races (2000); Density: 4.6 persons per square mile (2000); Age: 28.5% under 18, 8.3% over 64 (2000); Marriage status: 23.2% never married, 71.2% now married, 2.5% widowed, 3.0% divorced (2000); Foreign born: 0.0% (2000); Ancestry (includes multiple ancestries): 53.8% German, 52.6% Norwegian, 11.5% Danish, 4.0% Swedish, 4.0% Scottish (2000).
Economy: Employment by occupation: 23.8% management, 13.8% professional, 18.5% services, 20.0% sales, 2.3% farming, 8.5% construction, 13.1% production (2000).
Income: Per capita income: $15,992 (2000); Median household income: $37,250 (2000); Poverty rate: 4.0% (2000).
Taxes: Total city taxes per capita: $78 (1997); City property taxes per capita: $78 (1997).
Education: High school graduation rate: 93.8% (2000); College graduation rate: 14.2% (2000).
Housing: Homeownership rate: 79.8% (2000); Median home value: $38,100 (2000); Median rent: $150 per month (2000); Median age of housing: 60+ years (2000).
Transportation: Commute to work: 85.4% car, 0.0% public transportation, 1.5% walk, 13.1% work from home (2000); Travel time to work: 46.0% less than 15 minutes, 41.6% 15 to 30 minutes, 6.2% 30 to 45 minutes, 4.4% 45 to 60 minutes, 1.8% 60 minutes or more (2000)

LOUISBURG (city). Covers a land area of 0.306 square miles and a water area of 0 square miles. Located at 45.16° N. Lat.; 96.17° W. Long. Elevation is 1,043 feet.
Population: 26 (2000); Race: 100.0% White, 0.0% Black, 0.0% Asian, 0.0% American Indian and Alaska Native, 0.0% Hispanic of any race, 0.0% two or more races (2000); Density: 85.0 persons per square mile (2000); Age: 19.2% under 18, 42.3% over 64 (2000); Marriage status: 33.3% never married, 66.7% now married, 0.0% widowed, 0.0% divorced (2000); Foreign born: 0.0% (2000); Ancestry (includes multiple ancestries): 50.0% Norwegian, 42.3% German, 34.6% Irish, 11.5% Danish (2000).
Economy: Grain; dairying; livestock. In Lac qui Parle Wildlife Area. Employment by occupation: 18.2% management, 0.0% professional, 0.0% services, 9.1% sales, 0.0% farming, 27.3% construction, 45.5% production (2000).
Income: Per capita income: $14,535 (2000); Median household income: $18,750 (2000); Poverty rate: 0.0% (2000).
Taxes: Total city taxes per capita: $211 (1997); City property taxes per capita: $211 (1997).
Education: High school graduation rate: 90.5% (2000); College graduation rate: 19.0% (2000).
Housing: Homeownership rate: 73.3% (2000); Median home value: <$10,000 (2000); Median rent: <$100 per month (2000); Median age of housing: 60+ years (2000).
Transportation: Commute to work: 45.5% car, 0.0% public transportation, 54.5% walk, 0.0% work from home (2000); Travel time to work: 54.5% less than 15 minutes, 45.5% 15 to 30 minutes, 0.0% 30 to 45 minutes, 0.0% 45 to 60 minutes, 0.0% 60 minutes or more (2000)

MADISON (city). Covers a land area of 1.017 square miles and a water area of 0 square miles. Located at 45.01° N. Lat.; 96.18° W. Long. Elevation is 1,100 feet.
History: Madison was founded by Jacob F. Jacobson, who led a group of settlers from Iowa to this location. The town developed around a cooperative creamery, a flour mill, grain elevators, and a livestock shipping association.
Population: 1,768 (2000); Race: 99.4% White, 0.1% Black, 0.0% Asian, 0.1% American Indian and Alaska Native, 0.0% Hispanic of any race, 0.4% two or more races (2000); Density: 1,737.6 persons per square mile (2000); Age: 18.7% under 18, 36.7% over 64 (2000); Marriage status: 19.2% never married, 53.8% now married, 19.3% widowed, 7.7% divorced (2000); Foreign born: 0.9% (2000); Ancestry (includes multiple ancestries): 46.8% Norwegian, 40.2% German, 8.6% Swedish, 5.2% Irish, 4.3% English (2000).
Economy: Single-family building permits issued: 4 (2001) / 0 (2000); Multi-family building permits issued: 0 (2001) / 0 (2000); Employment by occupation: 8.9% management, 14.6% professional, 18.5% services, 28.4% sales, 0.3% farming, 9.0% construction, 20.4% production (2000).
Income: Per capita income: $17,435 (2000); Median household income: $27,102 (2000); Poverty rate: 7.8% (2000).
Taxes: Total city taxes per capita: $138 (1997); City property taxes per capita: $129 (1997).
Education: High school graduation rate: 74.5% (2000); College graduation rate: 11.7% (2000).

School District(s)

Lac Qui Parle Valley (PK-12)
2000 Enrollment: 1,211 320-752-4205
Housing: Homeownership rate: 75.2% (2000); Median home value: $41,700 (2000); Median rent: $240 per month (2000); Median age of housing: 53 years (2000).
Hospitals: Madison Hospital (21 beds)
Safety: Violent crime rate: 0.0 per 10,000 population; Property crime rate: 251.8 per 10,000 population (2001).
Newspapers: The Western Guard (1 x week)
Transportation: Commute to work: 83.7% car, 0.8% public transportation, 9.6% walk, 4.7% work from home (2000); Travel time to work: 67.8% less than 15 minutes, 17.6% 15 to 30 minutes, 8.1% 30 to 45 minutes, 1.4% 45 to 60 minutes, 5.0% 60 minutes or more (2000)
Additional Information Contacts
Madison Chamber of Commerce 320-598-7373

MADISON (township). Covers a land area of 34.588 square miles and a water area of 0.368 square miles. Located at 45.02° N. Lat.; 96.17° W. Long. Elevation is 1,100 feet.
History: Settled c.1875, plotted 1884, incorporated as city 1902.
Population: 251 (2000); Race: 99.1% White, 0.0% Black, 0.9% Asian, 0.0% American Indian and Alaska Native, 0.0% Hispanic of any race, 0.0% two or more races (2000); Density: 7.3 persons per square mile (2000); Age: 23.1% under 18, 17.1% over 64 (2000); Marriage status: 20.1% never married, 71.1% now married, 2.6% widowed, 6.2% divorced (2000); Foreign born: 3.0% (2000); Ancestry (includes multiple ancestries): 60.7% German, 36.3% Norwegian, 9.0% English, 6.8% Swedish, 6.0% Irish (2000).
Economy: Railroad terminus. Agricultural trade center: grain, soybeans; livestock, poultry; dairying. Manufacturing: fertilizers, bakery products, fabricated metal products, feeds. Employment by occupation: 18.0% management, 2.3% professional, 26.6% services, 16.4% sales, 2.3% farming, 10.9% construction, 23.4% production (2000).
Income: Per capita income: $16,039 (2000); Median household income: $38,750 (2000); Poverty rate: 3.0% (2000).
Taxes: Total city taxes per capita: $48 (2000); City property taxes per capita: $48 (2000).
Education: High school graduation rate: 89.6% (2000); College graduation rate: 11.0% (2000).
Housing: Homeownership rate: 91.4% (2000); Median home value: $42,500 (2000); Median age of housing: 60+ years (2000).
Transportation: Commute to work: 90.3% car, 0.0% public transportation, 0.0% walk, 9.7% work from home (2000); Travel time to work: 59.8% less than 15 minutes, 26.8% 15 to 30 minutes, 4.5% 30 to 45 minutes, 1.8% 45 to 60 minutes, 7.1% 60 minutes or more (2000)

MANFRED (township). Covers a land area of 33.119 square miles and a water area of 0.301 square miles. Located at 44.85° N. Lat.; 96.40° W. Long.
Population: 111 (2000); Race: 100.0% White, 0.0% Black, 0.0% Asian, 0.0% American Indian and Alaska Native, 0.0% Hispanic of any race, 0.0% two or more races (2000); Density: 3.4 persons per square mile (2000); Age: 32.4% under 18, 22.9% over 64 (2000); Marriage status: 23.8% never married, 62.5% now married, 10.0% widowed, 3.8% divorced (2000); Foreign born: 0.0% (2000); Ancestry (includes multiple ancestries): 57.1% German, 30.5% Norwegian, 11.4% English, 7.6% Belgian, 7.6% Polish (2000).
Economy: Employment by occupation: 36.4% management, 15.2% professional, 24.2% services, 6.1% sales, 0.0% farming, 0.0% construction, 18.2% production (2000).
Income: Per capita income: $12,928 (2000); Median household income: $27,083 (2000); Poverty rate: 16.2% (2000).

Taxes: Total city taxes per capita: $107 (1997); City property taxes per capita: $107 (1997).
Education: High school graduation rate: 76.1% (2000); College graduation rate: 15.5% (2000).
Housing: Homeownership rate: 82.5% (2000); Median home value: <$10,000 (2000); Median rent: <$100 per month (2000); Median age of housing: 60+ years (2000).
Transportation: Commute to work: 80.0% car, 0.0% public transportation, 14.3% walk, 5.7% work from home (2000); Travel time to work: 39.4% less than 15 minutes, 39.4% 15 to 30 minutes, 18.2% 30 to 45 minutes, 3.0% 45 to 60 minutes, 0.0% 60 minutes or more (2000)

MARIETTA (city). Covers a land area of 0.391 square miles and a water area of 0 square miles. Located at 45.01° N. Lat.; 96.41° W. Long.
Population: 174 (2000); Race: 100.0% White, 0.0% Black, 0.0% Asian, 0.0% American Indian and Alaska Native, 0.0% Hispanic of any race, 0.0% two or more races (2000); Density: 445.2 persons per square mile (2000); Age: 16.2% under 18, 33.1% over 64 (2000); Marriage status: 27.3% never married, 49.2% now married, 9.8% widowed, 13.6% divorced (2000); Foreign born: 0.0% (2000); Ancestry (includes multiple ancestries): 60.1% German, 34.5% Norwegian, 11.5% English, 6.8% Irish, 5.4% Dutch (2000).
Economy: Grain; livestock; dairying. Single-family building permits issued: 0 (2001) / 0 (2000); Multi-family building permits issued: 0 (2001) / 0 (2000); Employment by occupation: 10.0% management, 3.3% professional, 21.7% services, 16.7% sales, 3.3% farming, 11.7% construction, 33.3% production (2000).
Income: Per capita income: $12,688 (2000); Median household income: $16,923 (2000); Poverty rate: 21.6% (2000).
Taxes: Total city taxes per capita: $64 (1997); City property taxes per capita: $53 (1997).
Education: High school graduation rate: 75.0% (2000); College graduation rate: 7.1% (2000).
Housing: Homeownership rate: 85.9% (2000); Median home value: $20,000 (2000); Median rent: $188 per month (2000); Median age of housing: 60 years (2000).
Transportation: Commute to work: 89.7% car, 0.0% public transportation, 6.9% walk, 0.0% work from home (2000); Travel time to work: 34.5% less than 15 minutes, 36.2% 15 to 30 minutes, 25.9% 30 to 45 minutes, 3.4% 45 to 60 minutes, 0.0% 60 minutes or more (2000)

MAXWELL (township). Covers a land area of 36.223 square miles and a water area of 0.066 square miles. Located at 44.85° N. Lat.; 96.04° W. Long.
Population: 206 (2000); Race: 100.0% White, 0.0% Black, 0.0% Asian, 0.0% American Indian and Alaska Native, 0.0% Hispanic of any race, 0.0% two or more races (2000); Density: 5.7 persons per square mile (2000); Age: 27.9% under 18, 12.3% over 64 (2000); Marriage status: 17.2% never married, 73.9% now married, 5.1% widowed, 3.8% divorced (2000); Foreign born: 0.0% (2000); Ancestry (includes multiple ancestries): 47.1% German, 35.8% Norwegian, 18.6% Swedish, 11.8% English, 3.4% Dutch (2000).
Economy: Employment by occupation: 24.3% management, 13.9% professional, 12.2% services, 17.4% sales, 3.5% farming, 6.1% construction, 22.6% production (2000).
Income: Per capita income: $16,161 (2000); Median household income: $36,250 (2000); Poverty rate: 7.4% (2000).
Taxes: Total city taxes per capita: $107 (1997); City property taxes per capita: $107 (1997).
Education: High school graduation rate: 80.0% (2000); College graduation rate: 19.3% (2000).
Housing: Homeownership rate: 79.5% (2000); Median home value: $36,300 (2000); Median rent: $213 per month (2000); Median age of housing: 60+ years (2000).
Transportation: Commute to work: 70.4% car, 0.0% public transportation, 2.6% walk, 25.2% work from home (2000); Travel time to work: 55.8% less than 15 minutes, 31.4% 15 to 30 minutes, 12.8% 30 to 45 minutes, 0.0% 45 to 60 minutes, 0.0% 60 minutes or more (2000)

MEHURIN (township). Covers a land area of 28.667 square miles and a water area of 0.378 square miles. Located at 44.92° N. Lat.; 96.40° W. Long.
Population: 103 (2000); Race: 100.0% White, 0.0% Black, 0.0% Asian, 0.0% American Indian and Alaska Native, 0.0% Hispanic of any race, 0.0% two or more races (2000); Density: 3.6 persons per square mile (2000); Age: 19.4% under 18, 14.3% over 64 (2000); Marriage status: 10.6% never married, 81.2% now married, 3.5% widowed, 4.7% divorced (2000); Foreign born: 0.0% (2000); Ancestry (includes multiple ancestries): 53.1% German, 36.7% Norwegian, 9.2% United States or American, 6.1% Irish, 4.1% Danish (2000).
Economy: Employment by occupation: 32.8% management, 0.0% professional, 19.0% services, 25.9% sales, 3.4% farming, 10.3% construction, 8.6% production (2000).
Income: Per capita income: $19,870 (2000); Median household income: $30,625 (2000); Poverty rate: 26.5% (2000).
Taxes: Total city taxes per capita: $146 (1997); City property taxes per capita: $146 (1997).
Education: High school graduation rate: 91.7% (2000); College graduation rate: 2.8% (2000).
Housing: Homeownership rate: 79.1% (2000); Median home value: $22,500 (2000); Median rent: $175 per month (2000); Median age of housing: 60+ years (2000).
Transportation: Commute to work: 65.5% car, 0.0% public transportation, 3.4% walk, 31.0% work from home (2000); Travel time to work: 25.0% less than 15 minutes, 40.0% 15 to 30 minutes, 15.0% 30 to 45 minutes, 7.5% 45 to 60 minutes, 12.5% 60 minutes or more (2000)

NASSAU (city). Covers a land area of 0.158 square miles and a water area of 0 square miles. Located at 45.06° N. Lat.; 96.44° W. Long. Elevation is 1,123 feet.
Population: 83 (2000); Race: 100.0% White, 0.0% Black, 0.0% Asian, 0.0% American Indian and Alaska Native, 0.0% Hispanic of any race, 0.0% two or more races (2000); Density: 524.8 persons per square mile (2000); Age: 21.7% under 18, 22.9% over 64 (2000); Marriage status: 12.3% never married, 66.2% now married, 12.3% widowed, 9.2% divorced (2000); Foreign born: 0.0% (2000); Ancestry (includes multiple ancestries): 36.1% German, 34.9% Norwegian, 7.2% United States or American, 6.0% Dutch, 2.4% Irish (2000).
Economy: Grain. Manufacturing of feeds, fertilizers. Employment by occupation: 13.9% management, 5.6% professional, 22.2% services, 16.7% sales, 5.6% farming, 11.1% construction, 25.0% production (2000).
Income: Per capita income: $12,748 (2000); Median household income: $27,500 (2000); Poverty rate: 12.0% (2000).
Taxes: Total city taxes per capita: $107 (1997); City property taxes per capita: $107 (1997).
Education: High school graduation rate: 69.8% (2000); College graduation rate: 0.0% (2000).
Housing: Homeownership rate: 84.6% (2000); Median home value: <$10,000 (2000); Median rent: $175 per month (2000); Median age of housing: 60+ years (2000).
Transportation: Commute to work: 88.9% car, 0.0% public transportation, 11.1% walk, 0.0% work from home (2000); Travel time to work: 27.8% less than 15 minutes, 55.6% 15 to 30 minutes, 11.1% 30 to 45 minutes, 0.0% 45 to 60 minutes, 5.6% 60 minutes or more (2000)

PERRY (township). Covers a land area of 36.861 square miles and a water area of 0.129 square miles. Located at 45.11° N. Lat.; 96.29° W. Long.
Population: 137 (2000); Race: 98.7% White, 0.0% Black, 0.0% Asian, 0.0% American Indian and Alaska Native, 1.3% Hispanic of any race, 0.0% two or more races (2000); Density: 3.7 persons per square mile (2000); Age: 30.8% under 18, 17.6% over 64 (2000); Marriage status: 12.7% never married, 74.6% now married, 1.7% widowed, 11.0% divorced (2000); Foreign born: 3.8% (2000); Ancestry (includes multiple ancestries): 59.1% German, 43.4% Norwegian, 11.9% Danish, 5.0% French (except Basque), 3.1% Swedish (2000).
Economy: Employment by occupation: 33.8% management, 16.9% professional, 9.2% services, 21.5% sales, 7.7% farming, 7.7% construction, 3.1% production (2000).
Income: Per capita income: $16,788 (2000); Median household income: $30,833 (2000); Poverty rate: 7.2% (2000).
Taxes: Total city taxes per capita: $99 (1997); City property taxes per capita: $99 (1997).
Education: High school graduation rate: 82.4% (2000); College graduation rate: 7.8% (2000).
Housing: Homeownership rate: 89.1% (2000); Median home value: $52,500 (2000); Median rent: $275 per month (2000); Median age of housing: 55 years (2000).
Transportation: Commute to work: 66.2% car, 0.0% public transportation, 3.1% walk, 30.8% work from home (2000); Travel time to work: 24.4% less than 15 minutes, 17.8% 15 to 30 minutes, 22.2% 30 to 45 minutes, 11.1% 45 to 60 minutes, 24.4% 60 minutes or more (2000)

PROVIDENCE (township). Covers a land area of 36.095 square miles and a water area of 0.009 square miles. Located at 44.84° N. Lat.; 96.16° W. Long. Elevation is 1,081 feet.

Population: 186 (2000); Race: 100.0% White, 0.0% Black, 0.0% Asian, 0.0% American Indian and Alaska Native, 0.0% Hispanic of any race, 0.0% two or more races (2000); Density: 5.2 persons per square mile (2000); Age: 17.5% under 18, 22.0% over 64 (2000); Marriage status: 21.2% never married, 73.2% now married, 1.1% widowed, 4.5% divorced (2000); Foreign born: 1.0% (2000); Ancestry (includes multiple ancestries): 47.5% Norwegian, 36.0% German, 26.5% Swedish, 6.5% English, 2.5% Danish (2000).
Economy: Employment by occupation: 19.8% management, 19.8% professional, 6.0% services, 17.2% sales, 6.9% farming, 6.0% construction, 24.1% production (2000).
Income: Per capita income: $19,254 (2000); Median household income: $45,313 (2000); Poverty rate: 10.5% (2000).
Taxes: Total city taxes per capita: $71 (1997); City property taxes per capita: $71 (1997).
Education: High school graduation rate: 89.3% (2000); College graduation rate: 16.8% (2000).
Housing: Homeownership rate: 75.9% (2000); Median home value: $64,000 (2000); Median rent: $225 per month (2000); Median age of housing: 58 years (2000).
Transportation: Commute to work: 78.4% car, 0.0% public transportation, 8.6% walk, 12.9% work from home (2000); Travel time to work: 31.7% less than 15 minutes, 58.4% 15 to 30 minutes, 5.0% 30 to 45 minutes, 0.0% 45 to 60 minutes, 5.0% 60 minutes or more (2000)

RIVERSIDE (township). Covers a land area of 34.427 square miles and a water area of 0.056 square miles. Located at 44.93° N. Lat.; 96.04° W. Long.
Population: 301 (2000); Race: 98.4% White, 0.0% Black, 1.6% Asian, 0.0% American Indian and Alaska Native, 0.0% Hispanic of any race, 0.0% two or more races (2000); Density: 8.7 persons per square mile (2000); Age: 28.8% under 18, 17.3% over 64 (2000); Marriage status: 23.4% never married, 70.5% now married, 1.6% widowed, 4.5% divorced (2000); Foreign born: 1.6% (2000); Ancestry (includes multiple ancestries): 68.6% Norwegian, 30.8% German, 14.7% Swedish, 7.1% English, 2.6% Belgian (2000).
Economy: Employment by occupation: 25.6% management, 15.4% professional, 13.5% services, 14.1% sales, 1.3% farming, 11.5% construction, 18.6% production (2000).
Income: Per capita income: $19,205 (2000); Median household income: $43,750 (2000); Poverty rate: 11.1% (2000).
Education: High school graduation rate: 86.7% (2000); College graduation rate: 15.2% (2000).
Housing: Homeownership rate: 88.0% (2000); Median home value: $81,700 (2000); Median rent: $225 per month (2000); Median age of housing: 28 years (2000).
Transportation: Commute to work: 87.4% car, 0.0% public transportation, 6.6% walk, 6.0% work from home (2000); Travel time to work: 66.2% less than 15 minutes, 26.1% 15 to 30 minutes, 7.0% 30 to 45 minutes, 0.0% 45 to 60 minutes, 0.7% 60 minutes or more (2000)

TEN MILE LAKE (township). Covers a land area of 35.248 square miles and a water area of 0.258 square miles. Located at 44.85° N. Lat.; 95.90° W. Long.
Population: 195 (2000); Race: 100.0% White, 0.0% Black, 0.0% Asian, 0.0% American Indian and Alaska Native, 0.0% Hispanic of any race, 0.0% two or more races (2000); Density: 5.5 persons per square mile (2000); Age: 29.7% under 18, 17.1% over 64 (2000); Marriage status: 21.5% never married, 75.4% now married, 2.3% widowed, 0.8% divorced (2000); Foreign born: 0.0% (2000); Ancestry (includes multiple ancestries): 66.9% Norwegian, 34.9% German, 8.6% Dutch, 3.4% Danish, 3.4% Swedish (2000).
Economy: Employment by occupation: 46.2% management, 6.4% professional, 7.7% services, 23.1% sales, 5.1% farming, 6.4% construction, 5.1% production (2000).
Income: Per capita income: $22,717 (2000); Median household income: $46,250 (2000); Poverty rate: 5.1% (2000).
Taxes: Total city taxes per capita: $159 (1997); City property taxes per capita: $159 (1997).
Education: High school graduation rate: 90.5% (2000); College graduation rate: 13.3% (2000).
Housing: Homeownership rate: 90.6% (2000); Median home value: $55,700 (2000); Median rent: $275 per month (2000); Median age of housing: 60+ years (2000).
Transportation: Commute to work: 67.1% car, 0.0% public transportation, 2.6% walk, 30.3% work from home (2000); Travel time to work: 28.3% less than 15 minutes, 41.5% 15 to 30 minutes, 5.7% 30 to 45 minutes, 15.1% 45 to 60 minutes, 9.4% 60 minutes or more (2000)

WALTER (township). Covers a land area of 29.025 square miles and a water area of 0 square miles. Located at 45.10° N. Lat.; 96.40° W. Long.
Population: 186 (2000); Race: 100.0% White, 0.0% Black, 0.0% Asian, 0.0% American Indian and Alaska Native, 0.0% Hispanic of any race, 0.0% two or more races (2000); Density: 6.4 persons per square mile (2000); Age: 29.1% under 18, 20.7% over 64 (2000); Marriage status: 16.8% never married, 77.4% now married, 5.8% widowed, 0.0% divorced (2000); Foreign born: 1.0% (2000); Ancestry (includes multiple ancestries): 76.8% German, 24.6% Norwegian, 3.4% French (except Basque), 3.0% Swedish, 3.0% Irish (2000).
Economy: Employment by occupation: 44.0% management, 9.5% professional, 9.5% services, 20.2% sales, 10.7% farming, 3.6% construction, 2.4% production (2000).
Income: Per capita income: $14,961 (2000); Median household income: $28,125 (2000); Poverty rate: 6.9% (2000).
Taxes: Total city taxes per capita: $41 (1997); City property taxes per capita: $41 (1997).
Education: High school graduation rate: 81.9% (2000); College graduation rate: 9.4% (2000).
Housing: Homeownership rate: 85.9% (2000); Median home value: $19,200 (2000); Median rent: $175 per month (2000); Median age of housing: 60+ years (2000).
Transportation: Commute to work: 72.6% car, 0.0% public transportation, 15.5% walk, 11.9% work from home (2000); Travel time to work: 44.6% less than 15 minutes, 33.8% 15 to 30 minutes, 16.2% 30 to 45 minutes, 0.0% 45 to 60 minutes, 5.4% 60 minutes or more (2000)

YELLOW BANK (township). Covers a land area of 35.216 square miles and a water area of 0.132 square miles. Located at 45.20° N. Lat.; 96.40° W. Long.
Population: 177 (2000); Race: 97.2% White, 0.0% Black, 0.0% Asian, 0.0% American Indian and Alaska Native, 2.8% Hispanic of any race, 0.0% two or more races (2000); Density: 5.0 persons per square mile (2000); Age: 20.8% under 18, 12.5% over 64 (2000); Marriage status: 24.8% never married, 64.5% now married, 10.7% widowed, 0.0% divorced (2000); Foreign born: 3.5% (2000); Ancestry (includes multiple ancestries): 65.3% German, 18.8% Norwegian, 14.6% Swedish, 4.9% Polish, 4.2% United States or American (2000).
Economy: Employment by occupation: 29.6% management, 8.6% professional, 24.7% services, 18.5% sales, 4.9% farming, 7.4% construction, 6.2% production (2000).
Income: Per capita income: $14,867 (2000); Median household income: $33,036 (2000); Poverty rate: 4.2% (2000).
Taxes: Total city taxes per capita: $54 (1997); City property taxes per capita: $54 (1997).
Education: High school graduation rate: 77.6% (2000); College graduation rate: 9.2% (2000).
Housing: Homeownership rate: 88.3% (2000); Median home value: $88,300 (2000); Median rent: $213 per month (2000); Median age of housing: 60+ years (2000).
Transportation: Commute to work: 81.5% car, 0.0% public transportation, 0.0% walk, 18.5% work from home (2000); Travel time to work: 36.4% less than 15 minutes, 51.5% 15 to 30 minutes, 12.1% 30 to 45 minutes, 0.0% 45 to 60 minutes, 0.0% 60 minutes or more (2000)

Lake County

Located in northeastern Minnesota; bounded on the south by Lake Superior, and on the north by a chain of lakes along the Ontario (province of Canada) border; includes many lakes, and Superior National Forest. Covers a land area of 2,099.20 square miles, a water area of 891.70 square miles, and is located in the Central Time Zone. The county government was organized in 1856. County seat is Two Harbors.

Weather Station: Baudette Int'l Airport — Elevation: 1,079 feet

	Jan	Feb	Mar	Apr	May	Jun	Jul	Aug	Sep	Oct	Nov	Dec
High	15	24	36	53	68	76	80	78	68	54	34	20
Low	-8	-1	12	28	42	51	56	53	44	33	18	1
Precip	0.6	0.4	0.7	1.2	2.7	3.6	3.4	3.2	2.7	2.2	1.0	0.6
Snow	9.5	6.3	5.2	2.8	tr	0.0	0.0	0.0	tr	1.0	9.6	8.8

High and Low temperatures in degrees Fahrenheit; Precipitation and Snow in inches

Weather Station: Two Harbors Elevation: 623 feet

	Jan	Feb	Mar	Apr	May	Jun	Jul	Aug	Sep	Oct	Nov	Dec
High	22	27	36	48	58	67	74	73	65	54	39	28
Low	5	10	20	31	39	45	53	56	48	37	26	12
Precip	1.0	0.7	1.6	2.2	3.0	4.0	4.3	3.9	4.1	2.6	2.1	1.1
Snow	na	na	7.7	2.5	tr	0.0	0.0	0.0	0.0	tr	na	na

High and Low temperatures in degrees Fahrenheit; Precipitation and Snow in inches

Weather Station: Winton Power Plant Elevation: 1,335 feet

	Jan	Feb	Mar	Apr	May	Jun	Jul	Aug	Sep	Oct	Nov	Dec
High	15	23	35	50	66	73	78	75	64	51	32	18
Low	-7	-1	12	27	41	51	56	54	45	34	18	0
Precip	1.0	0.7	1.2	1.7	2.9	4.2	3.7	3.9	3.7	2.6	1.7	1.0
Snow	na	7.2	na	2.5	0.3	0.0	0.0	0.0	tr	0.6	na	na

High and Low temperatures in degrees Fahrenheit; Precipitation and Snow in inches

Population: 11,058 (2000); Race: 97.9% White, 0.0% Black, 0.1% Asian, 1.2% American Indian and Alaska Native, 0.3% Hispanic of any race, 0.8% two or more races (2000); Density: 5.3 persons per square mile (2000); Age: 22.3% under 18, 20.1% over 64 (2000).
Religion: Five largest groups: 27.0% Evangelical Lutheran Church in America, 20.9% Catholic Church, 2.3% United Church of Christ, 1.9% Presbyterian Church (U.S.A.), 1.8% Assemblies of God (2000).
Economy: Unemployment rate: 3.5% (11/2002); Total civilian labor force: 5,886 (11/2002); Leading industries: 17.7% accommodation & food services; 16.7% health care and social assistance; 16.4% manufacturing (2000); Companies that employ more than 1,000 persons: 0 (2000); Companies that employ more than 100 persons: 4 (2000); Farms: 37 totaling 3,970 acres (1997); Minority business ownership rate: 0.0% (1997); Women business ownership rate: 24.5% (1997); Retail sales per capita: $11,379 (1997). Single-family building permits issued: 91 (2001) / 126 (2000); Multi-family building permits issued: 0 (2001) / 5 (2000).
Income: Per capita income: $19,761 (2000); Median household income: $40,402 (2000); Poverty rate: 7.4% (2000); Bankruptcy rate: 2.94% (2001).
Taxes: Total county taxes per capita: $548 (2000); County property taxes per capita: $546 (2000).
Education: High school graduation rate: 86.4% (2000); College graduation rate: 19.5% (2000).
Housing: Homeownership rate: 84.0% (2000); Median home value: $71,300 (2000); Median rent: $366 per month (2000); Median age of housing: 40 years (2000).
Health: Birth rate: 97.7 per 10,000 population (1998); Age adjusted death rate: 78.1 per 10,000 population (1999); Age adjusted cancer mortality rate: 187.4 deaths per 100,000 population (1999). Air Quality Index: 97% good, 3% moderate, 0% unhealthy (percent of days in 2000). Number of physicians: 16.3 per 10,000 population (1999); Number of hospital beds: 59.7 per 10,000 population (1999).
Elections: 2000 Presidential election results: 54.5% Gore, 37.6% Bush, 6.5% Nader, 0.9% Buchanan
National and State Parks: Baptism River State Park; Bear Island State Forest; Finland State Forest; George H Crosby Manitou State Park; Gooseberry Falls State Park; Isabella Lake State Forest; Lake Insula State Forest; Minnesota State Forest; Split Rock Lighthouse State Park; Superior National Forest; Tettegouche State Park
Additional Information Contacts
Lake County Government Offices 218-834-8300

Lake County Communities

BEAVER BAY (city). Covers a land area of 0.485 square miles and a water area of 0.540 square miles. Located at 47.25° N. Lat.; 91.30° W. Long. Elevation is 650 feet.
History: The town of Beaver Bay, at the mouth of the Beaver River, was platted in 1856, though a community was in existence here many years before that.
Population: 175 (2000); Race: 90.3% White, 1.2% Black, 0.0% Asian, 5.5% American Indian and Alaska Native, 0.0% Hispanic of any race, 3.0% two or more races (2000); Density: 360.5 persons per square mile (2000); Age: 15.2% under 18, 16.4% over 64 (2000); Marriage status: 24.3% never married, 52.9% now married, 7.1% widowed, 15.7% divorced (2000); Foreign born: 1.2% (2000); Ancestry (includes multiple ancestries): 30.3% Norwegian, 20.0% German, 10.9% Swedish, 7.9% English, 7.3% Finnish (2000).
Economy: Single-family building permits issued: 1 (2001) / 0 (2000); Multi-family building permits issued: 0 (2001) / 0 (2000); Employment by occupation: 10.0% management, 7.5% professional, 40.0% services, 15.0% sales, 0.0% farming, 16.3% construction, 11.3% production (2000).
Income: Per capita income: $18,415 (2000); Median household income: $30,000 (2000); Poverty rate: 21.2% (2000).
Taxes: Total city taxes per capita: $235 (1997); City property taxes per capita: $215 (1997).
Education: High school graduation rate: 89.6% (2000); College graduation rate: 13.0% (2000).
Housing: Homeownership rate: 58.4% (2000); Median home value: $60,000 (2000); Median rent: $377 per month (2000); Median age of housing: 42 years (2000).
Transportation: Commute to work: 81.3% car, 0.0% public transportation, 5.0% walk, 11.3% work from home (2000); Travel time to work: 49.3% less than 15 minutes, 14.1% 15 to 30 minutes, 7.0% 30 to 45 minutes, 12.7% 45 to 60 minutes, 16.9% 60 minutes or more (2000)

BEAVER BAY (township). Covers a land area of 138.557 square miles and a water area of 1.623 square miles. Located at 47.32° N. Lat.; 91.31° W. Long. Elevation is 650 feet.
Population: 582 (2000); Race: 96.8% White, 0.0% Black, 0.0% Asian, 0.3% American Indian and Alaska Native, 0.0% Hispanic of any race, 2.8% two or more races (2000); Density: 4.2 persons per square mile (2000); Age: 22.7% under 18, 21.3% over 64 (2000); Marriage status: 19.1% never married, 68.4% now married, 7.3% widowed, 5.1% divorced (2000); Foreign born: 2.3% (2000); Ancestry (includes multiple ancestries): 29.2% German, 22.0% Norwegian, 10.5% Finnish, 8.8% Swedish, 8.8% Irish (2000).
Economy: Resort area. Employment by occupation: 13.3% management, 22.4% professional, 23.7% services, 9.1% sales, 1.2% farming, 20.7% construction, 9.5% production (2000).
Income: Per capita income: $19,188 (2000); Median household income: $43,438 (2000); Poverty rate: 6.2% (2000).
Taxes: Total city taxes per capita: $44 (1997); City property taxes per capita: $44 (1997).
Education: High school graduation rate: 85.6% (2000); College graduation rate: 23.4% (2000).
Housing: Homeownership rate: 89.6% (2000); Median home value: $91,300 (2000); Median rent: $531 per month (2000); Median age of housing: 29 years (2000).
Transportation: Commute to work: 86.0% car, 0.0% public transportation, 4.7% walk, 6.8% work from home (2000); Travel time to work: 46.8% less than 15 minutes, 27.3% 15 to 30 minutes, 10.0% 30 to 45 minutes, 6.8% 45 to 60 minutes, 9.1% 60 minutes or more (2000)

CRYSTAL BAY (township). Covers a land area of 203.681 square miles and a water area of 6.560 square miles. Located at 47.57° N. Lat.; 91.21° W. Long.
Population: 607 (2000); Race: 98.4% White, 0.0% Black, 0.0% Asian, 0.0% American Indian and Alaska Native, 0.9% Hispanic of any race, 1.6% two or more races (2000); Density: 3.0 persons per square mile (2000); Age: 27.4% under 18, 10.8% over 64 (2000); Marriage status: 26.9% never married, 59.2% now married, 5.4% widowed, 8.5% divorced (2000); Foreign born: 3.6% (2000); Ancestry (includes multiple ancestries): 23.9% Norwegian, 22.9% German, 13.1% Swedish, 11.6% Finnish, 7.1% United States or American (2000).
Economy: Employment by occupation: 7.0% management, 17.7% professional, 28.8% services, 9.7% sales, 1.0% farming, 22.7% construction, 13.0% production (2000).
Income: Per capita income: $14,161 (2000); Median household income: $35,000 (2000); Poverty rate: 9.7% (2000).
Taxes: Total city taxes per capita: $51 (1997); City property taxes per capita: $51 (1997).
Education: High school graduation rate: 78.3% (2000); College graduation rate: 16.5% (2000).
Housing: Homeownership rate: 80.0% (2000); Median home value: $77,800 (2000); Median rent: $339 per month (2000); Median age of housing: 34 years (2000).
Transportation: Commute to work: 94.7% car, 0.0% public transportation, 1.1% walk, 4.2% work from home (2000); Travel time to work: 19.0% less than 15 minutes, 31.1% 15 to 30 minutes, 11.7% 30 to 45 minutes, 24.5% 45 to 60 minutes, 13.6% 60 minutes or more (2000)

FALL LAKE (township). Covers a land area of 456.803 square miles and a water area of 130.543 square miles. Located at 47.96° N. Lat.; 91.54° W. Long.
Population: 584 (2000); Race: 96.2% White, 0.0% Black, 0.0% Asian, 2.5% American Indian and Alaska Native, 0.4% Hispanic of any race, 1.3% two or

more races (2000); Density: 1.3 persons per square mile (2000); Age: 13.2% under 18, 16.8% over 64 (2000); Marriage status: 15.5% never married, 71.0% now married, 3.8% widowed, 9.7% divorced (2000); Foreign born: 1.1% (2000); Ancestry (includes multiple ancestries): 33.0% German, 14.2% English, 10.8% United States or American, 10.1% Finnish, 10.1% Irish (2000).
Economy: Employment by occupation: 22.6% management, 16.7% professional, 11.5% services, 23.3% sales, 0.7% farming, 15.0% construction, 10.1% production (2000).
Income: Per capita income: $24,114 (2000); Median household income: $48,036 (2000); Poverty rate: 6.8% (2000).
Taxes: Total city taxes per capita: $202 (1997); City property taxes per capita: $202 (1997).
Education: High school graduation rate: 92.1% (2000); College graduation rate: 33.3% (2000).
Housing: Homeownership rate: 86.4% (2000); Median home value: $128,100 (2000); Median rent: $375 per month (2000); Median age of housing: 28 years (2000).
Transportation: Commute to work: 80.4% car, 0.0% public transportation, 8.4% walk, 10.9% work from home (2000); Travel time to work: 46.1% less than 15 minutes, 37.0% 15 to 30 minutes, 7.9% 30 to 45 minutes, 5.1% 45 to 60 minutes, 3.9% 60 minutes or more (2000)

FINLAND (unincorporated postal area, zip code 55603). Covers a land area of 286.535 square miles and a water area of 4.742 square miles. Located at 47.50° N. Lat.; 91.20° W. Long. Elevation is 1,330 feet.
Population: 603 (2000); Race: 97.2% White, 0.0% Black, 0.0% Asian, 0.0% American Indian and Alaska Native, 1.1% Hispanic of any race, 2.8% two or more races (2000); Density: 2.1 persons per square mile (2000); Age: 26.2% under 18, 10.8% over 64 (2000); Marriage status: 25.0% never married, 61.8% now married, 7.2% widowed, 6.0% divorced (2000); Foreign born: 4.1% (2000); Ancestry (includes multiple ancestries): 23.6% German, 20.0% Norwegian, 14.5% Finnish, 10.6% Swedish, 7.3% Irish (2000).
Economy: Employment by occupation: 7.4% management, 18.7% professional, 26.8% services, 8.9% sales, 1.2% farming, 21.8% construction, 15.2% production (2000).
Income: Per capita income: $15,656 (2000); Median household income: $36,250 (2000); Poverty rate: 11.0% (2000).
Education: High school graduation rate: 81.3% (2000); College graduation rate: 12.7% (2000).
Housing: Homeownership rate: 81.8% (2000); Median home value: $74,600 (2000); Median rent: $357 per month (2000); Median age of housing: 32 years (2000).
Transportation: Commute to work: 92.2% car, 0.0% public transportation, 2.1% walk, 5.8% work from home (2000); Travel time to work: 21.0% less than 15 minutes, 32.3% 15 to 30 minutes, 14.8% 30 to 45 minutes, 21.0% 45 to 60 minutes, 10.9% 60 minutes or more (2000)

ISABELLA (unincorporated postal area, zip code 55607). Covers a land area of 117.655 square miles and a water area of 3.818 square miles. Located at 47.66° N. Lat.; 91.53° W. Long. Elevation is 1,927 feet.
Population: 126 (2000); Race: 90.2% White, 0.0% Black, 0.0% Asian, 5.5% American Indian and Alaska Native, 0.0% Hispanic of any race, 4.3% two or more races (2000); Density: 1.1 persons per square mile (2000); Age: 17.7% under 18, 7.9% over 64 (2000); Marriage status: 40.9% never married, 50.3% now married, 4.0% widowed, 4.7% divorced (2000); Foreign born: 0.0% (2000); Ancestry (includes multiple ancestries): 52.4% German, 11.6% Irish, 11.0% Finnish, 9.8% Other groups, 6.7% Swedish (2000).
Economy: Employment by occupation: 12.5% management, 17.0% professional, 19.3% services, 9.1% sales, 13.6% farming, 9.1% construction, 19.3% production (2000).
Income: Per capita income: $16,188 (2000); Median household income: $36,563 (2000); Poverty rate: 4.3% (2000).
Education: High school graduation rate: 83.0% (2000); College graduation rate: 22.6% (2000).
Housing: Homeownership rate: 98.5% (2000); Median home value: $86,000 (2000); Median age of housing: 27 years (2000).
Transportation: Commute to work: 73.3% car, 0.0% public transportation, 0.0% walk, 15.1% work from home (2000); Travel time to work: 17.8% less than 15 minutes, 20.5% 15 to 30 minutes, 35.6% 30 to 45 minutes, 13.7% 45 to 60 minutes, 12.3% 60 minutes or more (2000)

SILVER BAY (city). Covers a land area of 7.716 square miles and a water area of 0.449 square miles. Located at 47.29° N. Lat.; 91.27° W. Long. Elevation is 900 feet.
History: Split Rock Lighthouse to Southwest.
Population: 2,068 (2000); Race: 98.1% White, 0.0% Black, 0.0% Asian, 1.2% American Indian and Alaska Native, 0.4% Hispanic of any race, 0.7% two or more races (2000); Density: 268.0 persons per square mile (2000); Age: 25.1% under 18, 27.0% over 64 (2000); Marriage status: 16.4% never married, 63.5% now married, 9.4% widowed, 10.7% divorced (2000); Foreign born: 2.4% (2000); Ancestry (includes multiple ancestries): 27.1% German, 20.4% Norwegian, 16.0% Swedish, 9.1% English, 8.5% Irish (2000).
Economy: Terminus of Reserve Mining Company railroad from nearby Babbitt, in Mesabi Iron Range to North. Manufacturing of iron ore pellets. Superior National Forest to Northwest. Single-family building permits issued: 4 (2001) / 4 (2000); Multi-family building permits issued: 0 (2001) / 0 (2000); Employment by occupation: 9.6% management, 15.3% professional, 25.6% services, 20.0% sales, 0.2% farming, 14.7% construction, 14.7% production (2000).
Income: Per capita income: $16,958 (2000); Median household income: $36,524 (2000); Poverty rate: 6.8% (2000).
Taxes: Total city taxes per capita: $411 (1997); City property taxes per capita: $403 (1997).
Education: High school graduation rate: 85.6% (2000); College graduation rate: 15.7% (2000).
Housing: Homeownership rate: 89.3% (2000); Median home value: $47,500 (2000); Median rent: $391 per month (2000); Median age of housing: 43 years (2000).
Safety: Violent crime rate: 4.8 per 10,000 population; Property crime rate: 119.6 per 10,000 population (2001).
Transportation: Commute to work: 93.2% car, 0.0% public transportation, 3.3% walk, 2.0% work from home (2000); Travel time to work: 74.0% less than 15 minutes, 8.4% 15 to 30 minutes, 9.6% 30 to 45 minutes, 4.1% 45 to 60 minutes, 3.9% 60 minutes or more (2000)

SILVER CREEK (township). Covers a land area of 294.828 square miles and a water area of 1.818 square miles. Located at 47.26° N. Lat.; 91.57° W. Long.
Population: 1,178 (2000); Race: 98.9% White, 0.0% Black, 0.1% Asian, 0.5% American Indian and Alaska Native, 0.0% Hispanic of any race, 0.4% two or more races (2000); Density: 4.0 persons per square mile (2000); Age: 19.3% under 18, 14.4% over 64 (2000); Marriage status: 20.0% never married, 68.2% now married, 4.0% widowed, 7.8% divorced (2000); Foreign born: 0.7% (2000); Ancestry (includes multiple ancestries): 25.4% German, 24.5% Swedish, 23.3% Norwegian, 9.5% Irish, 5.9% Finnish (2000).
Economy: Employment by occupation: 6.8% management, 15.6% professional, 21.0% services, 22.1% sales, 2.7% farming, 10.6% construction, 21.3% production (2000).
Income: Per capita income: $20,522 (2000); Median household income: $45,662 (2000); Poverty rate: 3.0% (2000).
Taxes: Total city taxes per capita: $85 (1997); City property taxes per capita: $85 (1997).
Education: High school graduation rate: 92.0% (2000); College graduation rate: 16.0% (2000).
Housing: Homeownership rate: 90.8% (2000); Median home value: $113,100 (2000); Median rent: $450 per month (2000); Median age of housing: 34 years (2000).
Transportation: Commute to work: 94.4% car, 0.0% public transportation, 1.3% walk, 3.4% work from home (2000); Travel time to work: 39.7% less than 15 minutes, 30.7% 15 to 30 minutes, 12.4% 30 to 45 minutes, 12.4% 45 to 60 minutes, 4.8% 60 minutes or more (2000)

STONY RIVER (township). Covers a land area of 547.704 square miles and a water area of 31.164 square miles. Located at 47.68° N. Lat.; 91.52° W. Long.
Population: 179 (2000); Race: 88.9% White, 0.0% Black, 0.0% Asian, 4.5% American Indian and Alaska Native, 0.0% Hispanic of any race, 6.6% two or more races (2000); Density: 0.3 persons per square mile (2000); Age: 17.2% under 18, 9.6% over 64 (2000); Marriage status: 35.4% never married, 53.4% now married, 4.5% widowed, 6.7% divorced (2000); Foreign born: 0.5% (2000); Ancestry (includes multiple ancestries): 46.0% German, 12.6% Finnish, 11.1% Irish, 8.1% Other groups, 5.6% Swedish (2000).
Economy: Employment by occupation: 10.4% management, 14.2% professional, 17.0% services, 12.3% sales, 11.3% farming, 12.3% construction, 22.6% production (2000).
Income: Per capita income: $16,558 (2000); Median household income: $36,563 (2000); Poverty rate: 3.5% (2000).
Taxes: Total city taxes per capita: $34 (1997); City property taxes per capita: $34 (1997).

Education: High school graduation rate: 82.7% (2000); College graduation rate: 18.0% (2000).
Housing: Homeownership rate: 98.8% (2000); Median home value: $81,000 (2000); Median age of housing: 30 years (2000).
Transportation: Commute to work: 76.0% car, 0.0% public transportation, 0.0% walk, 14.4% work from home (2000); Travel time to work: 14.6% less than 15 minutes, 22.5% 15 to 30 minutes, 33.7% 30 to 45 minutes, 13.5% 45 to 60 minutes, 15.7% 60 minutes or more (2000)

TWO HARBORS (city). Covers a land area of 3.224 square miles and a water area of 0 square miles. Located at 47.02° N. Lat.; 91.67° W. Long. Elevation is 636 feet.
History: The first settlement here was called Agate Bay. Completion of the railroad and the ore docks in 1884 gave birth to a second city, Two Harbors, named for the two harbors of Agate Bay and Burlington Bay. Incorporated as a village in 1888, Two Harbors became a city in 1907. It served as the ore-shipping terminal of the Duluth Iron Range Railway, which later merged with the Duluth, Missabe & Northern.
Population: 3,613 (2000); Race: 97.3% White, 0.0% Black, 0.3% Asian, 2.0% American Indian and Alaska Native, 0.6% Hispanic of any race, 0.4% two or more races (2000); Density: 1,120.7 persons per square mile (2000); Age: 23.3% under 18, 21.5% over 64 (2000); Marriage status: 20.2% never married, 56.6% now married, 10.4% widowed, 12.7% divorced (2000); Foreign born: 1.5% (2000); Ancestry (includes multiple ancestries): 21.9% Swedish, 19.7% Norwegian, 15.6% German, 11.1% Irish, 10.0% Finnish (2000).
Economy: Single-family building permits issued: 9 (2001) / 7 (2000); Multi-family building permits issued: 0 (2001) / 5 (2000); Employment by occupation: 15.6% management, 18.5% professional, 15.8% services, 22.5% sales, 1.4% farming, 9.6% construction, 16.6% production (2000).
Income: Per capita income: $19,793 (2000); Median household income: $37,708 (2000); Poverty rate: 9.5% (2000).
Taxes: Total city taxes per capita: $153 (1997); City property taxes per capita: $135 (1997).
Education: High school graduation rate: 86.4% (2000); College graduation rate: 19.2% (2000).

School District(s)

Lake Superior (PK-12)
2000 Enrollment: 2,045 218-834-8216

Housing: Homeownership rate: 72.2% (2000); Median home value: $70,200 (2000); Median rent: $344 per month (2000); Median age of housing: 59 years (2000).
Hospitals: Lake View Memorial Hospital and C&NC (80 beds)
Safety: Violent crime rate: 13.7 per 10,000 population; Property crime rate: 65.7 per 10,000 population (2001).
Newspapers: Lake County News-Chronicle (1 x week)
Transportation: Commute to work: 83.5% car, 0.0% public transportation, 11.3% walk, 4.8% work from home (2000); Travel time to work: 67.6% less than 15 minutes, 5.6% 15 to 30 minutes, 18.2% 30 to 45 minutes, 6.4% 45 to 60 minutes, 2.2% 60 minutes or more (2000)
Airports: Richard B Helgeson

Lake of the Woods County

Located in northwestern Minnesota; bounded on the northeast by the Rainy River, and extending north between the Canadian provinces of Manitoba and Ontario; includes part of Lake of the Woods. Covers a land area of 1,296.70 square miles, a water area of 478.40 square miles, and is located in the Central Time Zone. The county government was organized in 1923. County seat is Baudette.

Weather Station: Baudette Int'l Airport — Elevation: 1,079 feet

	Jan	Feb	Mar	Apr	May	Jun	Jul	Aug	Sep	Oct	Nov	Dec
High	15	24	36	53	68	76	80	78	68	54	34	20
Low	-8	-1	12	28	42	51	56	53	44	33	18	1
Precip	0.6	0.4	0.7	1.2	2.7	3.6	3.4	3.2	2.7	2.2	1.0	0.6
Snow	9.5	6.3	5.2	2.8	tr	0.0	0.0	0.0	tr	1.0	9.6	8.8

High and Low temperatures in degrees Fahrenheit; Precipitation and Snow in inches

Population: 4,522 (2000); Race: 97.0% White, 0.2% Black, 0.2% Asian, 1.4% American Indian and Alaska Native, 0.4% Hispanic of any race, 0.9% two or more races (2000); Density: 3.5 persons per square mile (2000); Age: 24.5% under 18, 17.3% over 64 (2000).
Religion: Five largest groups: 35.2% Evangelical Lutheran Church in America, 14.9% Catholic Church, 5.3% United Church of Christ, 3.2% Lutheran Church—Missouri Synod, 1.5% Assemblies of God (2000).
Economy: Unemployment rate: 4.8% (11/2002); Total civilian labor force: 2,556 (11/2002); Leading industries: 22.4% manufacturing; 22.2% accommodation & food services; 17.4% retail trade (2000); Companies that employ more than 1,000 persons: 0 (2000); Companies that employ more than 100 persons: 2 (2000); Farms: 196 totaling 117,644 acres (1997); Minority business ownership rate: 0.0% (1997); Women business ownership rate: 45.0% (1997); Retail sales per capita: $5,798 (1997). Single-family building permits issued: 1 (2001) / 3 (2000); Multi-family building permits issued: 0 (2001) / 0 (2000).
Income: Per capita income: $16,976 (2000); Median household income: $32,861 (2000); Poverty rate: 9.8% (2000); Bankruptcy rate: 3.63% (2001).
Taxes: Total county taxes per capita: $400 (1997); County property taxes per capita: $392 (1997).
Education: High school graduation rate: 84.6% (2000); College graduation rate: 17.2% (2000).
Housing: Homeownership rate: 85.4% (2000); Median home value: $74,000 (2000); Median rent: $273 per month (2000); Median age of housing: 27 years (2000).
Health: Birth rate: 73.0 per 10,000 population (1998); Age adjusted death rate: 78.9 per 10,000 population (1999); Age adjusted cancer mortality rate: 188.4 (Unreliable figure as per CDC) deaths per 100,000 population (1999). Number of physicians: 8.8 per 10,000 population (1999); Number of hospital beds: 148.2 per 10,000 population (1999).
Elections: 2000 Presidential election results: 38.8% Gore, 55.6% Bush, 3.4% Nader, 1.5% Buchanan
National and State Parks: Northwest Angle State Forest; Zippel Bay State Park

Additional Information Contacts

Lake of the Woods County Government Offices........... 218-634-2836
Baudette Chamber of Commerce...................... 218-634-1351

Lake of the Woods County Communities

ANGLE (township). Covers a land area of 123.093 square miles and a water area of 473.250 square miles. Located at 49.25° N. Lat.; 95.06° W. Long.
Population: 152 (2000); Race: 100.0% White, 0.0% Black, 0.0% Asian, 0.0% American Indian and Alaska Native, 0.0% Hispanic of any race, 0.0% two or more races (2000); Density: 1.2 persons per square mile (2000); Age: 12.3% under 18, 0.0% over 64 (2000); Marriage status: 23.3% never married, 72.2% now married, 0.0% widowed, 4.5% divorced (2000); Foreign born: 0.0% (2000); Ancestry (includes multiple ancestries): 34.9% German, 29.5% Norwegian, 22.6% French (except Basque), 16.4% Irish, 15.1% Scandinavian (2000).
Economy: Employment by occupation: 33.9% management, 6.1% professional, 5.2% services, 0.0% sales, 6.1% farming, 29.6% construction, 19.1% production (2000).
Income: Per capita income: $13,932 (2000); Median household income: $28,500 (2000); Poverty rate: 12.3% (2000).
Education: High school graduation rate: 94.4% (2000); College graduation rate: 21.5% (2000).
Housing: Homeownership rate: 75.0% (2000); Median home value: $95,000 (2000); Median rent: $175 per month (2000); Median age of housing: 23 years (2000).
Transportation: Commute to work: 67.8% car, 0.0% public transportation, 18.3% walk, 13.9% work from home (2000); Travel time to work: 70.7% less than 15 minutes, 12.1% 15 to 30 minutes, 0.0% 30 to 45 minutes, 0.0% 45 to 60 minutes, 17.2% 60 minutes or more (2000)

ANGLE INLET (unincorporated postal area, zip code 56711). Covers a land area of 16.457 square miles and a water area of 0.020 square miles. Located at 49.34° N. Lat.; 95.03° W. Long. Elevation is 1,065 feet.
Population: 121 (2000); Race: 100.0% White, 0.0% Black, 0.0% Asian, 0.0% American Indian and Alaska Native, 0.0% Hispanic of any race, 0.0% two or more races (2000); Density: 7.4 persons per square mile (2000); Age: 14.9% under 18, 0.0% over 64 (2000); Marriage status: 28.7% never married, 65.7% now married, 0.0% widowed, 5.6% divorced (2000); Foreign born: 0.0% (2000); Ancestry (includes multiple ancestries): 37.2% German, 29.8% Norwegian, 27.3% French (except Basque), 18.2% Scandinavian, 14.9% English (2000).
Economy: Employment by occupation: 28.1% management, 0.0% professional, 6.3% services, 0.0% sales, 7.3% farming, 35.4% construction, 22.9% production (2000).
Income: Per capita income: $12,073 (2000); Median household income: $28,500 (2000); Poverty rate: 5.0% (2000).

Education: High school graduation rate: 92.7% (2000); College graduation rate: 19.5% (2000).
Housing: Homeownership rate: 66.7% (2000); Median rent: $175 per month (2000); Median age of housing: 22 years (2000).
Transportation: Commute to work: 74.0% car, 0.0% public transportation, 21.9% walk, 4.2% work from home (2000); Travel time to work: 76.1% less than 15 minutes, 5.4% 15 to 30 minutes, 0.0% 30 to 45 minutes, 0.0% 45 to 60 minutes, 18.5% 60 minutes or more (2000)

BAUDETTE (city). Covers a land area of 3.304 square miles and a water area of 0.419 square miles. Located at 48.71° N. Lat.; 94.59° W. Long. Elevation is 1,075 feet.
History: Baudette developed as a port of entry on the border with Manitoba, Canada, and as a gateway to the recreation area of the Lake of the Woods. It began as a trading center for a farm area that produced flax, alfalfa, clover, and potatoes.
Population: 1,104 (2000); Race: 94.2% White, 0.3% Black, 1.0% Asian, 3.2% American Indian and Alaska Native, 0.1% Hispanic of any race, 1.3% two or more races (2000); Density: 334.1 persons per square mile (2000); Age: 25.7% under 18, 25.0% over 64 (2000); Marriage status: 19.7% never married, 51.5% now married, 17.5% widowed, 11.2% divorced (2000); Foreign born: 4.6% (2000); Ancestry (includes multiple ancestries): 30.6% Norwegian, 25.4% German, 12.0% Swedish, 9.8% Irish, 6.8% English (2000).
Economy: Single-family building permits issued: 1 (2001) / 3 (2000); Multi-family building permits issued: 0 (2001) / 0 (2000); Employment by occupation: 10.1% management, 22.0% professional, 20.0% services, 20.9% sales, 0.7% farming, 6.6% construction, 19.6% production (2000).
Income: Per capita income: $16,653 (2000); Median household income: $31,281 (2000); Poverty rate: 9.1% (2000).
Taxes: Total city taxes per capita: $68 (1997); City property taxes per capita: $66 (1997).
Education: High school graduation rate: 80.0% (2000); College graduation rate: 21.8% (2000).

School District(s)

Lake of the Woods (PK-12)
2000 Enrollment: 786 218-634-2735
Housing: Homeownership rate: 65.1% (2000); Median home value: $55,500 (2000); Median rent: $300 per month (2000); Median age of housing: 39 years (2000).
Hospitals: Lakewood Health Center (18 beds)
Newspapers: The Baudette Region (1 x week)
Transportation: Commute to work: 73.3% car, 0.0% public transportation, 17.0% walk, 7.0% work from home (2000); Travel time to work: 86.3% less than 15 minutes, 7.6% 15 to 30 minutes, 2.4% 30 to 45 minutes, 3.1% 45 to 60 minutes, 0.7% 60 minutes or more (2000)
Airports: Baudette International
Additional Information Contacts
Baudette Chamber of Commerce 218-634-1351

BOONE (township). Covers a land area of 35.754 square miles and a water area of 0 square miles. Located at 48.61° N. Lat.; 94.65° W. Long.
Population: 58 (2000); Race: 93.4% White, 0.0% Black, 0.0% Asian, 0.0% American Indian and Alaska Native, 0.0% Hispanic of any race, 6.6% two or more races (2000); Density: 1.6 persons per square mile (2000); Age: 14.3% under 18, 22.0% over 64 (2000); Marriage status: 42.3% never married, 57.7% now married, 0.0% widowed, 0.0% divorced (2000); Foreign born: 0.0% (2000); Ancestry (includes multiple ancestries): 27.5% Norwegian, 22.0% Scandinavian, 22.0% Swedish, 22.0% French (except Basque), 17.6% English (2000).
Economy: Employment by occupation: 0.0% management, 8.6% professional, 12.1% services, 37.9% sales, 0.0% farming, 10.3% construction, 31.0% production (2000).
Income: Per capita income: $21,679 (2000); Median household income: $60,714 (2000); Poverty rate: 0.0% (2000).
Education: High school graduation rate: 100.0% (2000); College graduation rate: 7.0% (2000).
Housing: Homeownership rate: 100.0% (2000); Median age of housing: 56 years (2000).
Transportation: Commute to work: 100.0% car, 0.0% public transportation, 0.0% walk, 0.0% work from home (2000); Travel time to work: 12.1% less than 15 minutes, 70.7% 15 to 30 minutes, 0.0% 30 to 45 minutes, 17.2% 45 to 60 minutes, 0.0% 60 minutes or more (2000)

CHILGREN (township). Covers a land area of 35.941 square miles and a water area of 0.031 square miles. Located at 48.85° N. Lat.; 95.04° W. Long.
Population: 179 (2000); Race: 100.0% White, 0.0% Black, 0.0% Asian, 0.0% American Indian and Alaska Native, 0.0% Hispanic of any race, 0.0% two or more races (2000); Density: 5.0 persons per square mile (2000); Age: 34.5% under 18, 11.2% over 64 (2000); Marriage status: 9.2% never married, 77.6% now married, 0.0% widowed, 13.2% divorced (2000); Foreign born: 6.3% (2000); Ancestry (includes multiple ancestries): 37.7% Norwegian, 29.1% German, 14.3% Other groups, 8.5% Swedish, 8.1% Czechoslovakian (2000).
Economy: Employment by occupation: 0.0% management, 0.0% professional, 29.1% services, 41.8% sales, 0.0% farming, 14.5% construction, 14.5% production (2000).
Income: Per capita income: $10,239 (2000); Median household income: $25,000 (2000); Poverty rate: 29.1% (2000).
Education: High school graduation rate: 81.9% (2000); College graduation rate: 16.7% (2000).
Housing: Homeownership rate: 100.0% (2000); Median home value: $75,000 (2000); Median age of housing: 24 years (2000).
Transportation: Commute to work: 100.0% car, 0.0% public transportation, 0.0% walk, 0.0% work from home (2000); Travel time to work: 0.0% less than 15 minutes, 76.4% 15 to 30 minutes, 23.6% 30 to 45 minutes, 0.0% 45 to 60 minutes, 0.0% 60 minutes or more (2000)

FOREST AREA (township). Covers a land area of 502.781 square miles and a water area of 0.901 square miles. Located at 48.53° N. Lat.; 95.04° W. Long.
Population: 7 (2000); Race: 100.0% White, 0.0% Black, 0.0% Asian, 0.0% American Indian and Alaska Native, 0.0% Hispanic of any race, 0.0% two or more races (2000); Density: 0.0 persons per square mile (2000); Age: 0.0% under 18, 0.0% over 64 (2000); Marriage status: 100.0% never married, 0.0% now married, 0.0% widowed, 0.0% divorced (2000); Foreign born: 0.0% (2000); Ancestry (includes multiple ancestries): 100.0% German (2000).
Economy: Employment by occupation: 0.0% management, 100.0% professional, 0.0% services, 0.0% sales, 0.0% farming, 0.0% construction, 0.0% production (2000).
Income: Per capita income: $35,000 (2000); Median household income: $36,250 (2000); Poverty rate: 0.0% (2000).
Education: High school graduation rate: 100.0% (2000); College graduation rate: 0.0% (2000).
Housing: Homeownership rate: 100.0% (2000); Median age of housing: 53 years (2000).
Transportation: Commute to work: 0.0% car, 0.0% public transportation, 100.0% walk, 0.0% work from home (2000); Travel time to work: 100.0% less than 15 minutes, 0.0% 15 to 30 minutes, 0.0% 30 to 45 minutes, 0.0% 45 to 60 minutes, 0.0% 60 minutes or more (2000)

GUDRID (township). Covers a land area of 28.361 square miles and a water area of 0.761 square miles. Located at 48.68° N. Lat.; 94.49° W. Long.
Population: 235 (2000); Race: 99.1% White, 0.0% Black, 0.0% Asian, 0.0% American Indian and Alaska Native, 0.0% Hispanic of any race, 0.9% two or more races (2000); Density: 8.3 persons per square mile (2000); Age: 13.5% under 18, 12.2% over 64 (2000); Marriage status: 11.3% never married, 81.8% now married, 1.5% widowed, 5.4% divorced (2000); Foreign born: 0.9% (2000); Ancestry (includes multiple ancestries): 30.4% Norwegian, 26.5% German, 22.2% Swedish, 15.7% English, 8.7% Slovak (2000).
Economy: Employment by occupation: 12.3% management, 25.4% professional, 15.4% services, 13.8% sales, 5.4% farming, 13.1% construction, 14.6% production (2000).
Income: Per capita income: $22,074 (2000); Median household income: $47,955 (2000); Poverty rate: 1.3% (2000).
Education: High school graduation rate: 95.5% (2000); College graduation rate: 33.0% (2000).
Housing: Homeownership rate: 100.0% (2000); Median home value: $68,300 (2000); Median age of housing: 24 years (2000).
Transportation: Commute to work: 92.3% car, 0.0% public transportation, 0.0% walk, 7.7% work from home (2000); Travel time to work: 66.7% less than 15 minutes, 19.2% 15 to 30 minutes, 1.7% 30 to 45 minutes, 5.8% 45 to 60 minutes, 6.7% 60 minutes or more (2000)

LAKEWOOD (township). Covers a land area of 30.963 square miles and a water area of 0.074 square miles. Located at 48.93° N. Lat.; 95.04° W. Long.
Population: 116 (2000); Race: 100.0% White, 0.0% Black, 0.0% Asian, 0.0% American Indian and Alaska Native, 0.0% Hispanic of any race, 0.0% two or more races (2000); Density: 3.7 persons per square mile (2000); Age: 30.3% under 18, 22.6% over 64 (2000); Marriage status: 32.5% never married, 50.4% now married, 12.2% widowed, 4.9% divorced (2000);

Foreign born: 0.0% (2000); Ancestry (includes multiple ancestries): 43.2% Norwegian, 23.9% Swedish, 23.2% German, 3.9% French (except Basque), 3.9% Czech (2000).
Economy: Employment by occupation: 6.0% management, 7.2% professional, 30.1% services, 7.2% sales, 0.0% farming, 8.4% construction, 41.0% production (2000).
Income: Per capita income: $12,599 (2000); Median household income: $33,472 (2000); Poverty rate: 0.0% (2000).
Education: High school graduation rate: 80.4% (2000); College graduation rate: 14.7% (2000).
Housing: Homeownership rate: 91.2% (2000); Median home value: $90,600 (2000); Median age of housing: 31 years (2000).
Transportation: Commute to work: 86.7% car, 0.0% public transportation, 0.0% walk, 0.0% work from home (2000); Travel time to work: 56.6% less than 15 minutes, 36.1% 15 to 30 minutes, 7.2% 30 to 45 minutes, 0.0% 45 to 60 minutes, 0.0% 60 minutes or more (2000)

MCDOUGALD (township). Covers a land area of 35.298 square miles and a water area of 0 square miles. Located at 48.75° N. Lat.; 94.87° W. Long.
Population: 236 (2000); Race: 100.0% White, 0.0% Black, 0.0% Asian, 0.0% American Indian and Alaska Native, 0.0% Hispanic of any race, 0.0% two or more races (2000); Density: 6.7 persons per square mile (2000); Age: 19.0% under 18, 13.6% over 64 (2000); Marriage status: 10.2% never married, 72.2% now married, 5.4% widowed, 12.2% divorced (2000); Foreign born: 0.0% (2000); Ancestry (includes multiple ancestries): 43.8% German, 13.6% Swedish, 12.8% Irish, 8.7% Polish, 8.3% Norwegian (2000).
Economy: Employment by occupation: 0.0% management, 13.7% professional, 16.9% services, 16.1% sales, 0.0% farming, 7.3% construction, 46.0% production (2000).
Income: Per capita income: $13,468 (2000); Median household income: $29,688 (2000); Poverty rate: 3.3% (2000).
Education: High school graduation rate: 86.9% (2000); College graduation rate: 2.6% (2000).
Housing: Homeownership rate: 92.0% (2000); Median home value: $33,300 (2000); Median age of housing: 42 years (2000).
Transportation: Commute to work: 100.0% car, 0.0% public transportation, 0.0% walk, 0.0% work from home (2000); Travel time to work: 21.0% less than 15 minutes, 48.4% 15 to 30 minutes, 30.6% 30 to 45 minutes, 0.0% 45 to 60 minutes, 0.0% 60 minutes or more (2000)

MYHRE (township). Covers a land area of 35.691 square miles and a water area of 0.097 square miles. Located at 48.75° N. Lat.; 95.01° W. Long.
Population: 213 (2000); Race: 100.0% White, 0.0% Black, 0.0% Asian, 0.0% American Indian and Alaska Native, 0.0% Hispanic of any race, 0.0% two or more races (2000); Density: 6.0 persons per square mile (2000); Age: 28.6% under 18, 9.7% over 64 (2000); Marriage status: 31.9% never married, 48.6% now married, 1.4% widowed, 18.1% divorced (2000); Foreign born: 0.0% (2000); Ancestry (includes multiple ancestries): 26.9% United States or American, 21.7% German, 13.1% Swedish, 12.6% Norwegian, 5.1% French (except Basque) (2000).
Economy: Employment by occupation: 2.5% management, 8.8% professional, 21.3% services, 20.0% sales, 8.8% farming, 12.5% construction, 26.3% production (2000).
Income: Per capita income: $11,809 (2000); Median household income: $31,563 (2000); Poverty rate: 8.6% (2000).
Education: High school graduation rate: 74.3% (2000); College graduation rate: 8.6% (2000).
Housing: Homeownership rate: 81.4% (2000); Median home value: $102,500 (2000); Median rent: $238 per month (2000); Median age of housing: 30 years (2000).
Transportation: Commute to work: 92.5% car, 0.0% public transportation, 1.3% walk, 6.3% work from home (2000); Travel time to work: 12.0% less than 15 minutes, 56.0% 15 to 30 minutes, 21.3% 30 to 45 minutes, 0.0% 45 to 60 minutes, 10.7% 60 minutes or more (2000)

OAK ISLAND (unincorporated postal area, zip code 56741). Covers a land area of 4.719 square miles and a water area of 0 square miles. Located at 49.24° N. Lat.; 94.84° W. Long.
Population: 31 (2000); Race: 100.0% White, 0.0% Black, 0.0% Asian, 0.0% American Indian and Alaska Native, 0.0% Hispanic of any race, 0.0% two or more races (2000); Density: 6.6 persons per square mile (2000); Age: 0.0% under 18, 0.0% over 64 (2000); Marriage status: 0.0% never married, 100.0% now married, 0.0% widowed, 0.0% divorced (2000); Foreign born: 0.0% (2000); Ancestry (includes multiple ancestries): 48.0% Irish, 28.0% Norwegian, 24.0% German (2000).
Economy: Employment by occupation: 63.2% management, 36.8% professional, 0.0% services, 0.0% sales, 0.0% farming, 0.0% construction, 0.0% production (2000).
Income: Per capita income: $22,928 (2000); Median household income: $43,750 (2000); Poverty rate: 48.0% (2000).
Education: High school graduation rate: 100.0% (2000); College graduation rate: 28.0% (2000).
Housing: Homeownership rate: 100.0% (2000); Median home value: $95,000 (2000); Median age of housing: 23 years (2000).
Transportation: Commute to work: 36.8% car, 0.0% public transportation, 0.0% walk, 63.2% work from home (2000); Travel time to work: 0.0% less than 15 minutes, 100.0% 15 to 30 minutes, 0.0% 30 to 45 minutes, 0.0% 45 to 60 minutes, 0.0% 60 minutes or more (2000)

POTAMO (township). Covers a land area of 35.006 square miles and a water area of 0 square miles. Located at 48.66° N. Lat.; 94.89° W. Long.
Population: 109 (2000); Race: 100.0% White, 0.0% Black, 0.0% Asian, 0.0% American Indian and Alaska Native, 0.0% Hispanic of any race, 0.0% two or more races (2000); Density: 3.1 persons per square mile (2000); Age: 24.0% under 18, 0.0% over 64 (2000); Marriage status: 20.4% never married, 71.3% now married, 0.0% widowed, 8.3% divorced (2000); Foreign born: 0.0% (2000); Ancestry (includes multiple ancestries): 51.2% German, 17.1% Italian, 14.7% Dutch, 12.4% Scandinavian, 11.6% Swedish (2000).
Economy: Employment by occupation: 29.6% management, 13.6% professional, 0.0% services, 18.5% sales, 0.0% farming, 0.0% construction, 38.3% production (2000).
Income: Per capita income: $20,806 (2000); Median household income: $41,000 (2000); Poverty rate: 14.7% (2000).
Education: High school graduation rate: 93.3% (2000); College graduation rate: 20.2% (2000).
Housing: Homeownership rate: 75.0% (2000); Median age of housing: 30 years (2000).
Transportation: Commute to work: 73.6% car, 0.0% public transportation, 0.0% walk, 26.4% work from home (2000); Travel time to work: 0.0% less than 15 minutes, 43.4% 15 to 30 minutes, 18.9% 30 to 45 minutes, 20.8% 45 to 60 minutes, 17.0% 60 minutes or more (2000)

PROSPER (township). Covers a land area of 12.527 square miles and a water area of 0 square miles. Located at 48.95° N. Lat.; 94.93° W. Long.
Population: 155 (2000); Race: 90.8% White, 0.0% Black, 0.0% Asian, 0.0% American Indian and Alaska Native, 0.0% Hispanic of any race, 9.2% two or more races (2000); Density: 12.4 persons per square mile (2000); Age: 10.2% under 18, 19.4% over 64 (2000); Marriage status: 0.0% never married, 70.5% now married, 0.0% widowed, 29.5% divorced (2000); Foreign born: 0.0% (2000); Ancestry (includes multiple ancestries): 36.7% English, 35.7% Norwegian, 31.6% Irish, 18.4% German, 11.2% Scotch-Irish (2000).
Economy: Employment by occupation: 25.0% management, 0.0% professional, 0.0% services, 12.5% sales, 0.0% farming, 0.0% construction, 62.5% production (2000).
Income: Per capita income: $34,557 (2000); Median household income: $62,625 (2000); Poverty rate: 27.6% (2000).
Education: High school graduation rate: 79.5% (2000); College graduation rate: 30.7% (2000).
Housing: Homeownership rate: 100.0% (2000); Median home value: $93,300 (2000); Median age of housing: 22 years (2000).
Transportation: Commute to work: 71.4% car, 0.0% public transportation, 28.6% walk, 0.0% work from home (2000); Travel time to work: 28.6% less than 15 minutes, 0.0% 15 to 30 minutes, 71.4% 30 to 45 minutes, 0.0% 45 to 60 minutes, 0.0% 60 minutes or more (2000)

RAPID RIVER (township). Covers a land area of 36.489 square miles and a water area of 0 square miles. Located at 48.56° N. Lat.; 94.48° W. Long.
Population: 23 (2000); Race: 100.0% White, 0.0% Black, 0.0% Asian, 0.0% American Indian and Alaska Native, 0.0% Hispanic of any race, 0.0% two or more races (2000); Density: 0.6 persons per square mile (2000); Age: 0.0% under 18, 0.0% over 64 (2000); Marriage status: 0.0% never married, 100.0% now married, 0.0% widowed, 0.0% divorced (2000); Foreign born: 50.0% (2000); Ancestry (includes multiple ancestries): 50.0% German, 50.0% Italian, 50.0% Irish (2000).
Economy: Income: Per capita income: $5,921 (2000); Median household income: $11,250 (2000); Poverty rate: 0.0% (2000).
Education: High school graduation rate: 50.0% (2000); College graduation rate: 50.0% (2000).
Housing: Homeownership rate: 100.0% (2000); Median age of housing: 40 years (2000).

RULIEN (township). Covers a land area of 36.422 square miles and a water area of 0.026 square miles. Located at 48.58° N. Lat.; 94.74° W. Long.
Population: 3 (2000); Race: 100.0% White, 0.0% Black, 0.0% Asian, 0.0% American Indian and Alaska Native, 0.0% Hispanic of any race, 0.0% two or more races (2000); Density: 0.1 persons per square mile (2000); Age: 35.0% under 18, 0.0% over 64 (2000); Marriage status: 0.0% never married, 100.0% now married, 0.0% widowed, 0.0% divorced (2000); Foreign born: 0.0% (2000); Ancestry (includes multiple ancestries): 70.0% Norwegian, 65.0% German, 35.0% Swedish (2000).
Economy: Employment by occupation: 0.0% management, 0.0% professional, 0.0% services, 53.8% sales, 0.0% farming, 46.2% construction, 0.0% production (2000).
Income: Per capita income: $9,165 (2000); Median household income: $28,750 (2000); Poverty rate: 0.0% (2000).
Education: High school graduation rate: 100.0% (2000); College graduation rate: 0.0% (2000).
Housing: Homeownership rate: 100.0% (2000); Median age of housing: 5 years (2000).
Transportation: Commute to work: 53.8% car, 0.0% public transportation, 0.0% walk, 46.2% work from home (2000); Travel time to work: 0.0% less than 15 minutes, 0.0% 15 to 30 minutes, 0.0% 30 to 45 minutes, 100.0% 45 to 60 minutes, 0.0% 60 minutes or more (2000)

SPOONER (township). Covers a land area of 33.475 square miles and a water area of 0.068 square miles. Located at 48.68° N. Lat.; 94.63° W. Long.
Population: 281 (2000); Race: 88.9% White, 0.0% Black, 0.0% Asian, 10.4% American Indian and Alaska Native, 0.0% Hispanic of any race, 0.7% two or more races (2000); Density: 8.4 persons per square mile (2000); Age: 30.8% under 18, 12.5% over 64 (2000); Marriage status: 21.6% never married, 59.1% now married, 6.7% widowed, 12.5% divorced (2000); Foreign born: 18.6% (2000); Ancestry (includes multiple ancestries): 17.2% German, 17.2% Norwegian, 10.4% Other groups, 10.0% Swedish, 9.3% Czech (2000).
Economy: Employment by occupation: 2.7% management, 10.0% professional, 17.3% services, 22.7% sales, 0.0% farming, 18.7% construction, 28.7% production (2000).
Income: Per capita income: $21,978 (2000); Median household income: $36,389 (2000); Poverty rate: 21.1% (2000).
Education: High school graduation rate: 73.6% (2000); College graduation rate: 9.8% (2000).
Housing: Homeownership rate: 85.6% (2000); Median home value: $105,300 (2000); Median rent: $258 per month (2000); Median age of housing: 22 years (2000).
Transportation: Commute to work: 94.7% car, 0.0% public transportation, 3.0% walk, 2.3% work from home (2000); Travel time to work: 83.8% less than 15 minutes, 14.6% 15 to 30 minutes, 0.0% 30 to 45 minutes, 0.0% 45 to 60 minutes, 1.5% 60 minutes or more (2000)

SWIFTWATER (township). Covers a land area of 35.457 square miles and a water area of 0.022 square miles. Located at 48.50° N. Lat.; 94.61° W. Long.
Population: 77 (2000); Race: 100.0% White, 0.0% Black, 0.0% Asian, 0.0% American Indian and Alaska Native, 0.0% Hispanic of any race, 0.0% two or more races (2000); Density: 2.2 persons per square mile (2000); Age: 0.0% under 18, 14.1% over 64 (2000); Marriage status: 15.4% never married, 62.8% now married, 9.0% widowed, 12.8% divorced (2000); Foreign born: 0.0% (2000); Ancestry (includes multiple ancestries): 26.9% Norwegian, 23.1% German, 12.8% English, 12.8% Swedish (2000).
Economy: Employment by occupation: 25.6% management, 0.0% professional, 58.1% services, 0.0% sales, 0.0% farming, 0.0% construction, 16.3% production (2000).
Income: Per capita income: $15,937 (2000); Median household income: $28,750 (2000); Poverty rate: 9.0% (2000).
Education: High school graduation rate: 84.9% (2000); College graduation rate: 0.0% (2000).
Housing: Homeownership rate: 100.0% (2000); Median age of housing: 60+ years (2000).
Transportation: Commute to work: 74.4% car, 0.0% public transportation, 0.0% walk, 25.6% work from home (2000); Travel time to work: 0.0% less than 15 minutes, 100.0% 15 to 30 minutes, 0.0% 30 to 45 minutes, 0.0% 45 to 60 minutes, 0.0% 60 minutes or more (2000)

WABANICA (township). Covers a land area of 35.868 square miles and a water area of 0.215 square miles. Located at 48.76° N. Lat.; 94.72° W. Long.
Population: 291 (2000); Race: 97.8% White, 0.0% Black, 0.0% Asian, 0.0% American Indian and Alaska Native, 0.0% Hispanic of any race, 2.2% two or more races (2000); Density: 8.1 persons per square mile (2000); Age: 31.0% under 18, 20.6% over 64 (2000); Marriage status: 12.2% never married, 73.8% now married, 10.7% widowed, 3.3% divorced (2000); Foreign born: 1.6% (2000); Ancestry (includes multiple ancestries): 38.7% Norwegian, 25.0% German, 11.3% Swedish, 7.7% United States or American, 6.0% French (except Basque) (2000).
Economy: Employment by occupation: 27.2% management, 4.6% professional, 34.4% services, 12.6% sales, 0.0% farming, 6.0% construction, 15.2% production (2000).
Income: Per capita income: $12,429 (2000); Median household income: $29,318 (2000); Poverty rate: 8.0% (2000).
Education: High school graduation rate: 89.2% (2000); College graduation rate: 12.4% (2000).
Housing: Homeownership rate: 95.9% (2000); Median home value: $89,700 (2000); Median rent: $125 per month (2000); Median age of housing: 26 years (2000).
Transportation: Commute to work: 70.2% car, 0.0% public transportation, 0.0% walk, 29.8% work from home (2000); Travel time to work: 50.5% less than 15 minutes, 32.3% 15 to 30 minutes, 5.1% 30 to 45 minutes, 0.0% 45 to 60 minutes, 12.1% 60 minutes or more (2000)

WALHALLA (township). Covers a land area of 34.842 square miles and a water area of 0 square miles. Located at 48.67° N. Lat.; 94.74° W. Long.
Population: 156 (2000); Race: 100.0% White, 0.0% Black, 0.0% Asian, 0.0% American Indian and Alaska Native, 0.0% Hispanic of any race, 0.0% two or more races (2000); Density: 4.5 persons per square mile (2000); Age: 24.5% under 18, 11.9% over 64 (2000); Marriage status: 20.2% never married, 68.5% now married, 4.8% widowed, 6.5% divorced (2000); Foreign born: 0.0% (2000); Ancestry (includes multiple ancestries): 32.2% Swedish, 24.5% German, 14.7% Norwegian, 14.7% Irish, 14.7% United States or American (2000).
Economy: Employment by occupation: 17.8% management, 10.3% professional, 23.4% services, 18.7% sales, 0.0% farming, 10.3% construction, 19.6% production (2000).
Income: Per capita income: $19,990 (2000); Median household income: $37,955 (2000); Poverty rate: 4.9% (2000).
Education: High school graduation rate: 100.0% (2000); College graduation rate: 24.2% (2000).
Housing: Homeownership rate: 88.1% (2000); Median rent: $275 per month (2000); Median age of housing: 41 years (2000).
Transportation: Commute to work: 89.0% car, 0.0% public transportation, 0.0% walk, 11.0% work from home (2000); Travel time to work: 21.3% less than 15 minutes, 50.6% 15 to 30 minutes, 16.9% 30 to 45 minutes, 0.0% 45 to 60 minutes, 11.2% 60 minutes or more (2000)

WHEELER (township). Covers a land area of 18.890 square miles and a water area of 0.634 square miles. Located at 48.82° N. Lat.; 94.74° W. Long.
Population: 386 (2000); Race: 100.0% White, 0.0% Black, 0.0% Asian, 0.0% American Indian and Alaska Native, 0.0% Hispanic of any race, 0.0% two or more races (2000); Density: 20.4 persons per square mile (2000); Age: 39.3% under 18, 6.0% over 64 (2000); Marriage status: 23.1% never married, 66.2% now married, 3.8% widowed, 6.8% divorced (2000); Foreign born: 0.0% (2000); Ancestry (includes multiple ancestries): 54.7% German, 28.7% Norwegian, 13.0% Irish, 12.7% Swedish, 10.3% Czech (2000).
Economy: Employment by occupation: 24.0% management, 13.1% professional, 16.4% services, 14.8% sales, 0.0% farming, 8.7% construction, 23.0% production (2000).
Income: Per capita income: $17,055 (2000); Median household income: $37,321 (2000); Poverty rate: 3.6% (2000).
Education: High school graduation rate: 95.5% (2000); College graduation rate: 10.1% (2000).
Housing: Homeownership rate: 94.2% (2000); Median home value: $75,000 (2000); Median age of housing: 21 years (2000).
Transportation: Commute to work: 78.7% car, 0.0% public transportation, 4.9% walk, 16.4% work from home (2000); Travel time to work: 49.0% less than 15 minutes, 37.3% 15 to 30 minutes, 0.0% 30 to 45 minutes, 2.6% 45 to 60 minutes, 11.1% 60 minutes or more (2000)

WILLIAMS (city). Covers a land area of 0.978 square miles and a water area of 0 square miles. Located at 48.76° N. Lat.; 94.95° W. Long. Elevation is 1,147 feet.
Population: 210 (2000); Race: 93.6% White, 3.4% Black, 0.0% Asian, 0.0% American Indian and Alaska Native, 7.3% Hispanic of any race, 0.0% two or more races (2000); Density: 214.6 persons per square mile (2000); Age:

24.0% under 18, 23.6% over 64 (2000); Marriage status: 20.2% never married, 50.3% now married, 16.4% widowed, 13.1% divorced (2000); Foreign born: 0.4% (2000); Ancestry (includes multiple ancestries): 28.3% German, 17.6% Norwegian, 17.2% Swedish, 8.6% Irish, 8.6% Other groups (2000).
Economy: Agriculture includes potatoes, oats, barley, alfalfa, flax, wheat. Light manufacturing. Employment by occupation: 3.8% management, 0.9% professional, 14.2% services, 32.1% sales, 1.9% farming, 17.0% construction, 30.2% production (2000).
Income: Per capita income: $11,888 (2000); Median household income: $26,364 (2000); Poverty rate: 19.3% (2000).
Taxes: Total city taxes per capita: $129 (1997); City property taxes per capita: $129 (1997).
Education: High school graduation rate: 73.8% (2000); College graduation rate: 12.1% (2000).
Housing: Homeownership rate: 90.5% (2000); Median home value: $38,100 (2000); Median rent: $288 per month (2000); Median age of housing: 52 years (2000).
Newspapers: The Northern Light (1 x week)
Transportation: Commute to work: 91.5% car, 0.0% public transportation, 6.6% walk, 0.0% work from home (2000); Travel time to work: 17.9% less than 15 minutes, 38.7% 15 to 30 minutes, 37.7% 30 to 45 minutes, 0.0% 45 to 60 minutes, 5.7% 60 minutes or more (2000)

ZIPPEL (township). Covers a land area of 32.611 square miles and a water area of 0.662 square miles. Located at 48.83° N. Lat.; 94.90° W. Long.
Population: 140 (2000); Race: 100.0% White, 0.0% Black, 0.0% Asian, 0.0% American Indian and Alaska Native, 0.0% Hispanic of any race, 0.0% two or more races (2000); Density: 4.3 persons per square mile (2000); Age: 8.7% under 18, 23.3% over 64 (2000); Marriage status: 18.1% never married, 38.3% now married, 26.6% widowed, 17.0% divorced (2000); Foreign born: 0.0% (2000); Ancestry (includes multiple ancestries): 29.1% French (except Basque), 28.2% Norwegian, 13.6% German, 12.6% Irish, 9.7% Slovak (2000).
Economy: Employment by occupation: 54.3% management, 11.4% professional, 0.0% services, 22.9% sales, 0.0% farming, 0.0% construction, 11.4% production (2000).
Income: Per capita income: $22,272 (2000); Median household income: $20,750 (2000); Poverty rate: 24.3% (2000).
Education: High school graduation rate: 72.1% (2000); College graduation rate: 16.3% (2000).
Housing: Homeownership rate: 100.0% (2000); Median home value: $91,900 (2000); Median age of housing: 23 years (2000).
Transportation: Commute to work: 74.3% car, 0.0% public transportation, 0.0% walk, 25.7% work from home (2000); Travel time to work: 0.0% less than 15 minutes, 34.6% 15 to 30 minutes, 19.2% 30 to 45 minutes, 46.2% 45 to 60 minutes, 0.0% 60 minutes or more (2000)

Le Sueur County

Located in southern Minnesota; bounded on the west by the Minnesota River. Covers a land area of 448.50 square miles, a water area of 25.40 square miles, and is located in the Central Time Zone. The county government was organized in 1853. County seat is Le Center.
Population: 25,426 (2000); Race: 96.4% White, 0.2% Black, 0.3% Asian, 0.3% American Indian and Alaska Native, 3.7% Hispanic of any race, 0.7% two or more races (2000); Density: 56.7 persons per square mile (2000); Age: 27.4% under 18, 14.0% over 64 (2000).
Religion: Five largest groups: 39.0% Catholic Church, 17.1% Evangelical Lutheran Church in America, 5.0% Lutheran Church—Missouri Synod, 4.3% The United Methodist Church, 3.8% United Church of Christ (2000).
Economy: Unemployment rate: 3.6% (11/2002); Total civilian labor force: 15,560 (11/2002); Leading industries: 35.3% manufacturing; 11.3% retail trade; 9.0% accommodation & food services (2000); Companies that employ more than 1,000 persons: 0 (2000); Companies that employ more than 100 persons: 17 (2000); Farms: 877 totaling 214,652 acres (1997); Minority business ownership rate: 0.0% (1997); Women business ownership rate: 22.4% (1997); Retail sales per capita: $5,993 (1997). Single-family building permits issued: 152 (2001) / 159 (2000); Multi-family building permits issued: 80 (2001) / 45 (2000).
Income: Per capita income: $20,151 (2000); Median household income: $45,933 (2000); Poverty rate: 6.9% (2000); Bankruptcy rate: 2.96% (2001).
Taxes: Total county taxes per capita: $258 (2000); County property taxes per capita: $255 (2000).
Education: High school graduation rate: 84.6% (2000); College graduation rate: 16.9% (2000).
Housing: Homeownership rate: 82.9% (2000); Median home value: $105,600 (2000); Median rent: $373 per month (2000); Median age of housing: 37 years (2000).
Health: Birth rate: 119.2 per 10,000 population (1998); Age adjusted death rate: 72.7 per 10,000 population (1999); Age adjusted cancer mortality rate: 171.0 deaths per 100,000 population (1999). Number of physicians: 8.7 per 10,000 population (1999); Number of hospital beds: 40.1 per 10,000 population (1999).
Elections: 2000 Presidential election results: 43.5% Gore, 49.8% Bush, 4.9% Nader, 1.5% Buchanan
National and State Parks: Bardel State Wildlife Management Area; Chadderdon State Wildlife Management Area; Diamond Lake State Wildlife Management Ar; Factor State Wildlife Management Area; Murphy State Wildlife Management Area; Ottawa State Wildlife Management Area; Paddy Marsh State Wildlife Management Are; Saint Thomas State Wildlife Management Area; Sakatah State Park; Sautter State Wildlife Management Area; Shanghai Lake State Wildlife Management A; Sheas Lake State Wildlife Management Area
Additional Information Contacts
Le Sueur County Government Offices.................... 507-357-2251
Elysian Area Chamber of Commerce...................... 507-267-4040
Le Center Chamber of Commerce......................... 507-357-6737
Le Sueur Chamber of Commerce.......................... 507-665-2501
Waterville Chamber of Commerce........................ 507-362-4609

Le Sueur County Communities

CLEVELAND (city). Covers a land area of 0.598 square miles and a water area of 0 square miles. Located at 44.32° N. Lat.; 93.83° W. Long. Elevation is 1,051 feet.
Population: 673 (2000); Race: 100.0% White, 0.0% Black, 0.0% Asian, 0.0% American Indian and Alaska Native, 0.0% Hispanic of any race, 0.0% two or more races (2000); Density: 1,125.6 persons per square mile (2000); Age: 32.5% under 18, 9.3% over 64 (2000); Marriage status: 21.6% never married, 61.7% now married, 6.2% widowed, 10.4% divorced (2000); Foreign born: 0.5% (2000); Ancestry (includes multiple ancestries): 53.3% German, 16.1% Irish, 14.2% Norwegian, 9.6% Swedish, 3.9% United States or American (2000).
Economy: Single-family building permits issued: 6 (2001) / 1 (2000); Multi-family building permits issued: 2 (2001) / 0 (2000); Employment by occupation: 8.1% management, 22.6% professional, 11.6% services, 22.6% sales, 0.0% farming, 14.0% construction, 21.2% production (2000).
Income: Per capita income: $17,424 (2000); Median household income: $46,458 (2000); Poverty rate: 7.4% (2000).
Taxes: Total city taxes per capita: $70 (1997); City property taxes per capita: $63 (1997).
Education: High school graduation rate: 93.4% (2000); College graduation rate: 14.7% (2000).

School District(s)

Cleveland (PK-12)
2000 Enrollment: 452 507-931-5953
Housing: Homeownership rate: 81.5% (2000); Median home value: $89,000 (2000); Median rent: $332 per month (2000); Median age of housing: 32 years (2000).
Transportation: Commute to work: 93.2% car, 0.5% public transportation, 3.3% walk, 1.6% work from home (2000); Travel time to work: 40.4% less than 15 minutes, 45.2% 15 to 30 minutes, 9.7% 30 to 45 minutes, 1.4% 45 to 60 minutes, 3.3% 60 minutes or more (2000)

CLEVELAND (township). Covers a land area of 33.413 square miles and a water area of 3.739 square miles. Located at 44.31° N. Lat.; 93.82° W. Long. Elevation is 1,051 feet.
Population: 615 (2000); Race: 99.5% White, 0.0% Black, 0.5% Asian, 0.0% American Indian and Alaska Native, 0.8% Hispanic of any race, 0.0% two or more races (2000); Density: 18.4 persons per square mile (2000); Age: 23.6% under 18, 12.8% over 64 (2000); Marriage status: 26.5% never married, 62.2% now married, 4.7% widowed, 6.6% divorced (2000); Foreign born: 0.8% (2000); Ancestry (includes multiple ancestries): 61.6% German, 23.0% Irish, 8.8% English, 7.5% Swedish, 6.9% Czech (2000).
Economy: Employment by occupation: 19.1% management, 17.5% professional, 12.3% services, 18.6% sales, 1.6% farming, 10.7% construction, 20.2% production (2000).

Income: Per capita income: $21,314 (2000); Median household income: $50,972 (2000); Poverty rate: 1.6% (2000).
Taxes: Total city taxes per capita: $56 (1997); City property taxes per capita: $56 (1997).
Education: High school graduation rate: 93.4% (2000); College graduation rate: 13.0% (2000).
Housing: Homeownership rate: 94.5% (2000); Median home value: $130,400 (2000); Median rent: $508 per month (2000); Median age of housing: 27 years (2000).
Transportation: Commute to work: 85.0% car, 0.8% public transportation, 4.6% walk, 8.6% work from home (2000); Travel time to work: 27.3% less than 15 minutes, 44.0% 15 to 30 minutes, 20.5% 30 to 45 minutes, 2.3% 45 to 60 minutes, 5.9% 60 minutes or more (2000)

CORDOVA (township). Covers a land area of 34.743 square miles and a water area of 1.458 square miles. Located at 44.31° N. Lat.; 93.71° W. Long.
Population: 517 (2000); Race: 99.6% White, 0.4% Black, 0.0% Asian, 0.0% American Indian and Alaska Native, 0.0% Hispanic of any race, 0.0% two or more races (2000); Density: 14.9 persons per square mile (2000); Age: 30.7% under 18, 13.4% over 64 (2000); Marriage status: 22.2% never married, 65.8% now married, 5.5% widowed, 6.5% divorced (2000); Foreign born: 0.0% (2000); Ancestry (includes multiple ancestries): 65.8% German, 20.8% Irish, 8.3% Czech, 7.0% French (except Basque), 5.4% United States or American (2000).
Economy: Employment by occupation: 16.0% management, 14.4% professional, 10.6% services, 20.5% sales, 3.0% farming, 9.5% construction, 25.9% production (2000).
Income: Per capita income: $15,964 (2000); Median household income: $37,361 (2000); Poverty rate: 5.5% (2000).
Taxes: Total city taxes per capita: $72 (1997); City property taxes per capita: $72 (1997).
Education: High school graduation rate: 82.9% (2000); College graduation rate: 8.4% (2000).
Housing: Homeownership rate: 92.1% (2000); Median home value: $118,800 (2000); Median rent: $375 per month (2000); Median age of housing: 35 years (2000).
Transportation: Commute to work: 83.1% car, 0.0% public transportation, 1.9% walk, 13.5% work from home (2000); Travel time to work: 45.8% less than 15 minutes, 29.3% 15 to 30 minutes, 21.8% 30 to 45 minutes, 0.0% 45 to 60 minutes, 3.1% 60 minutes or more (2000)

DERRYNANE (township). Covers a land area of 35.800 square miles and a water area of 0.312 square miles. Located at 44.49° N. Lat.; 93.71° W. Long.
Population: 549 (2000); Race: 97.1% White, 0.0% Black, 1.3% Asian, 0.9% American Indian and Alaska Native, 0.0% Hispanic of any race, 0.7% two or more races (2000); Density: 15.3 persons per square mile (2000); Age: 30.9% under 18, 12.9% over 64 (2000); Marriage status: 26.8% never married, 64.5% now married, 4.3% widowed, 4.5% divorced (2000); Foreign born: 0.9% (2000); Ancestry (includes multiple ancestries): 49.5% German, 22.1% Irish, 11.8% Czech, 11.6% Polish, 5.3% United States or American (2000).
Economy: Employment by occupation: 14.2% management, 11.4% professional, 15.9% services, 17.3% sales, 1.7% farming, 17.3% construction, 22.1% production (2000).
Income: Per capita income: $19,485 (2000); Median household income: $53,333 (2000); Poverty rate: 7.8% (2000).
Taxes: Total city taxes per capita: $43 (1997); City property taxes per capita: $43 (1997).
Education: High school graduation rate: 86.6% (2000); College graduation rate: 6.6% (2000).
Housing: Homeownership rate: 85.6% (2000); Median home value: $150,000 (2000); Median rent: $438 per month (2000); Median age of housing: 47 years (2000).
Transportation: Commute to work: 85.9% car, 0.0% public transportation, 2.8% walk, 11.3% work from home (2000); Travel time to work: 23.1% less than 15 minutes, 33.9% 15 to 30 minutes, 23.1% 30 to 45 minutes, 10.8% 45 to 60 minutes, 9.2% 60 minutes or more (2000)

ELYSIAN (city). Covers a land area of 0.882 square miles and a water area of 0 square miles. Located at 44.20° N. Lat.; 93.67° W. Long.
Population: 486 (2000); Race: 100.0% White, 0.0% Black, 0.0% Asian, 0.0% American Indian and Alaska Native, 0.0% Hispanic of any race, 0.0% two or more races (2000); Density: 551.3 persons per square mile (2000); Age: 27.1% under 18, 12.5% over 64 (2000); Marriage status: 21.3% never married, 63.1% now married, 6.7% widowed, 9.0% divorced (2000); Foreign born: 0.4% (2000); Ancestry (includes multiple ancestries): 55.5% German, 17.8% Norwegian, 13.0% Irish, 3.8% English, 3.2% French (except Basque) (2000).
Economy: Single-family building permits issued: 11 (2001) / 11 (2000); Multi-family building permits issued: 0 (2001) / 0 (2000); Employment by occupation: 7.2% management, 12.5% professional, 9.8% services, 29.4% sales, 0.0% farming, 13.2% construction, 27.9% production (2000).
Income: Per capita income: $15,815 (2000); Median household income: $37,750 (2000); Poverty rate: 7.1% (2000).
Taxes: Total city taxes per capita: $283 (1997); City property taxes per capita: $261 (1997).
Education: High school graduation rate: 88.4% (2000); College graduation rate: 12.8% (2000).
Housing: Homeownership rate: 83.6% (2000); Median home value: $98,000 (2000); Median rent: $225 per month (2000); Median age of housing: 33 years (2000).
Newspapers: Elysian Enterprise (1 x week)
Transportation: Commute to work: 90.9% car, 0.0% public transportation, 4.9% walk, 4.2% work from home (2000); Travel time to work: 26.8% less than 15 minutes, 39.0% 15 to 30 minutes, 22.0% 30 to 45 minutes, 7.9% 45 to 60 minutes, 4.3% 60 minutes or more (2000)
Additional Information Contacts
Elysian Area Chamber of Commerce. 507-267-4040

ELYSIAN (township). Covers a land area of 30.313 square miles and a water area of 5.030 square miles. Located at 44.24° N. Lat.; 93.69° W. Long.
Population: 985 (2000); Race: 99.3% White, 0.0% Black, 0.1% Asian, 0.6% American Indian and Alaska Native, 0.5% Hispanic of any race, 0.0% two or more races (2000); Density: 32.5 persons per square mile (2000); Age: 22.2% under 18, 12.5% over 64 (2000); Marriage status: 20.3% never married, 67.4% now married, 4.3% widowed, 8.0% divorced (2000); Foreign born: 0.2% (2000); Ancestry (includes multiple ancestries): 60.9% German, 16.1% Irish, 14.6% Norwegian, 6.9% English, 4.2% Swedish (2000).
Economy: Grain, soybeans, peas; livestock, poultry; dairying. Manufacturing: plastic molding, light manufacturing. Employment by occupation: 14.1% management, 14.7% professional, 15.0% services, 23.7% sales, 2.3% farming, 12.4% construction, 17.9% production (2000).
Income: Per capita income: $22,265 (2000); Median household income: $51,176 (2000); Poverty rate: 3.8% (2000).
Taxes: Total city taxes per capita: $61 (1997); City property taxes per capita: $61 (1997).
Education: High school graduation rate: 89.8% (2000); College graduation rate: 19.4% (2000).
Housing: Homeownership rate: 86.9% (2000); Median home value: $124,200 (2000); Median rent: $300 per month (2000); Median age of housing: 31 years (2000).
Transportation: Commute to work: 87.9% car, 0.0% public transportation, 1.1% walk, 10.9% work from home (2000); Travel time to work: 15.0% less than 15 minutes, 44.7% 15 to 30 minutes, 29.9% 30 to 45 minutes, 4.7% 45 to 60 minutes, 5.7% 60 minutes or more (2000)

HEIDELBERG (city). Covers a land area of 0.518 square miles and a water area of 0 square miles. Located at 44.49° N. Lat.; 93.62° W. Long. Elevation is 1,045 feet.
Population: 72 (2000); Race: 100.0% White, 0.0% Black, 0.0% Asian, 0.0% American Indian and Alaska Native, 0.0% Hispanic of any race, 0.0% two or more races (2000); Density: 139.0 persons per square mile (2000); Age: 31.4% under 18, 5.7% over 64 (2000); Marriage status: 12.5% never married, 79.2% now married, 4.2% widowed, 4.2% divorced (2000); Foreign born: 0.0% (2000); Ancestry (includes multiple ancestries): 57.1% German, 17.1% Swedish, 17.1% Czech, 15.7% Czechoslovakian, 10.0% British (2000).
Economy: Grain; livestock, poultry; dairying. Single-family building permits issued: 2 (2001) / 5 (2000); Multi-family building permits issued: 0 (2001) / 0 (2000); Employment by occupation: 7.5% management, 12.5% professional, 17.5% services, 20.0% sales, 0.0% farming, 25.0% construction, 17.5% production (2000).
Income: Per capita income: $17,389 (2000); Median household income: $56,094 (2000); Poverty rate: 0.0% (2000).
Taxes: Total city taxes per capita: $125 (2000); City property taxes per capita: $56 (2000).
Education: High school graduation rate: 78.6% (2000); College graduation rate: 7.1% (2000).
Housing: Homeownership rate: 100.0% (2000); Median home value: $95,000 (2000); Median age of housing: 42 years (2000).
Transportation: Commute to work: 89.5% car, 0.0% public transportation, 5.3% walk, 5.3% work from home (2000); Travel time to work: 30.6% less

than 15 minutes, 11.1% 15 to 30 minutes, 33.3% 30 to 45 minutes, 16.7% 45 to 60 minutes, 8.3% 60 minutes or more (2000)

KASOTA (city). Covers a land area of 1.010 square miles and a water area of 0 square miles. Located at 44.29° N. Lat.; 93.96° W. Long.
Population: 680 (2000); Race: 89.1% White, 0.4% Black, 5.4% Asian, 2.1% American Indian and Alaska Native, 1.3% Hispanic of any race, 2.7% two or more races (2000); Density: 673.4 persons per square mile (2000); Age: 26.3% under 18, 10.0% over 64 (2000); Marriage status: 27.8% never married, 54.4% now married, 5.0% widowed, 12.7% divorced (2000); Foreign born: 3.2% (2000); Ancestry (includes multiple ancestries): 53.2% German, 13.0% Other groups, 8.8% Irish, 7.5% Norwegian, 6.9% Swedish (2000).
Economy: Single-family building permits issued: 2 (2001) / 3 (2000); Multi-family building permits issued: 0 (2001) / 0 (2000); Employment by occupation: 4.5% management, 9.0% professional, 25.8% services, 21.5% sales, 0.0% farming, 11.5% construction, 27.8% production (2000).
Income: Per capita income: $17,503 (2000); Median household income: $39,097 (2000); Poverty rate: 7.8% (2000).
Taxes: Total city taxes per capita: $71 (1997); City property taxes per capita: $55 (1997).
Education: High school graduation rate: 82.1% (2000); College graduation rate: 10.6% (2000).
Housing: Homeownership rate: 84.7% (2000); Median home value: $79,500 (2000); Median rent: $338 per month (2000); Median age of housing: 60+ years (2000).
Transportation: Commute to work: 95.5% car, 0.0% public transportation, 1.3% walk, 2.3% work from home (2000); Travel time to work: 42.2% less than 15 minutes, 47.6% 15 to 30 minutes, 4.3% 30 to 45 minutes, 3.3% 45 to 60 minutes, 2.6% 60 minutes or more (2000)

KASOTA (township). Covers a land area of 37.577 square miles and a water area of 1.658 square miles. Located at 44.29° N. Lat.; 93.94° W. Long.
Population: 1,487 (2000); Race: 98.2% White, 0.0% Black, 0.3% Asian, 0.0% American Indian and Alaska Native, 1.4% Hispanic of any race, 0.8% two or more races (2000); Density: 39.6 persons per square mile (2000); Age: 23.8% under 18, 11.8% over 64 (2000); Marriage status: 20.8% never married, 71.9% now married, 3.6% widowed, 3.7% divorced (2000); Foreign born: 1.2% (2000); Ancestry (includes multiple ancestries): 53.0% German, 13.2% Norwegian, 11.9% Irish, 8.6% Swedish, 5.8% English (2000).
Economy: Employment by occupation: 16.6% management, 18.1% professional, 11.5% services, 28.2% sales, 0.2% farming, 9.5% construction, 15.8% production (2000).
Income: Per capita income: $25,575 (2000); Median household income: $57,650 (2000); Poverty rate: 5.4% (2000).
Taxes: Total city taxes per capita: $71 (2000); City property taxes per capita: $71 (2000).
Education: High school graduation rate: 92.9% (2000); College graduation rate: 28.3% (2000).
Housing: Homeownership rate: 90.6% (2000); Median home value: $144,300 (2000); Median rent: $458 per month (2000); Median age of housing: 25 years (2000).
Transportation: Commute to work: 92.4% car, 0.3% public transportation, 0.9% walk, 5.8% work from home (2000); Travel time to work: 36.1% less than 15 minutes, 49.1% 15 to 30 minutes, 8.2% 30 to 45 minutes, 1.3% 45 to 60 minutes, 5.4% 60 minutes or more (2000)

KILKENNY (city). Covers a land area of 0.123 square miles and a water area of 0 square miles. Located at 44.31° N. Lat.; 93.57° W. Long. Elevation is 1,057 feet.
Population: 148 (2000); Race: 96.4% White, 0.0% Black, 1.2% Asian, 0.0% American Indian and Alaska Native, 0.0% Hispanic of any race, 2.4% two or more races (2000); Density: 1,205.8 persons per square mile (2000); Age: 25.7% under 18, 9.6% over 64 (2000); Marriage status: 21.5% never married, 62.2% now married, 8.9% widowed, 7.4% divorced (2000); Foreign born: 3.6% (2000); Ancestry (includes multiple ancestries): 54.5% German, 30.5% Irish, 18.6% Czech, 11.4% English, 4.2% French (except Basque) (2000).
Economy: Employment by occupation: 2.1% management, 4.3% professional, 12.8% services, 36.2% sales, 0.0% farming, 14.9% construction, 29.8% production (2000).
Income: Per capita income: $16,198 (2000); Median household income: $39,583 (2000); Poverty rate: 3.6% (2000).
Taxes: Total city taxes per capita: $49 (1997); City property taxes per capita: $43 (1997).
Education: High school graduation rate: 73.1% (2000); College graduation rate: 3.7% (2000).
Housing: Homeownership rate: 96.9% (2000); Median home value: $48,800 (2000); Median rent: $525 per month (2000); Median age of housing: 60+ years (2000).
Transportation: Commute to work: 95.7% car, 0.0% public transportation, 0.0% walk, 4.3% work from home (2000); Travel time to work: 13.6% less than 15 minutes, 37.5% 15 to 30 minutes, 23.9% 30 to 45 minutes, 14.8% 45 to 60 minutes, 10.2% 60 minutes or more (2000)

KILKENNY (township). Covers a land area of 33.837 square miles and a water area of 2.236 square miles. Located at 44.32° N. Lat.; 93.59° W. Long. Elevation is 1,057 feet.
Population: 393 (2000); Race: 100.0% White, 0.0% Black, 0.0% Asian, 0.0% American Indian and Alaska Native, 2.6% Hispanic of any race, 0.0% two or more races (2000); Density: 11.6 persons per square mile (2000); Age: 22.6% under 18, 16.3% over 64 (2000); Marriage status: 13.5% never married, 67.6% now married, 12.0% widowed, 6.9% divorced (2000); Foreign born: 0.0% (2000); Ancestry (includes multiple ancestries): 54.2% German, 13.8% Irish, 10.0% Czech, 6.6% French (except Basque), 4.6% English (2000).
Economy: Dairying. Employment by occupation: 17.6% management, 17.6% professional, 11.9% services, 12.6% sales, 2.5% farming, 17.0% construction, 20.8% production (2000).
Income: Per capita income: $21,346 (2000); Median household income: $45,625 (2000); Poverty rate: 10.0% (2000).
Taxes: Total city taxes per capita: $78 (1997); City property taxes per capita: $78 (1997).
Education: High school graduation rate: 84.1% (2000); College graduation rate: 8.8% (2000).
Housing: Homeownership rate: 89.6% (2000); Median home value: $115,200 (2000); Median age of housing: 45 years (2000).
Transportation: Commute to work: 83.0% car, 0.0% public transportation, 1.3% walk, 15.7% work from home (2000); Travel time to work: 19.4% less than 15 minutes, 38.8% 15 to 30 minutes, 25.4% 30 to 45 minutes, 5.2% 45 to 60 minutes, 11.2% 60 minutes or more (2000)

LANESBURGH (township). Covers a land area of 32.931 square miles and a water area of 1.518 square miles. Located at 44.49° N. Lat.; 93.58° W. Long.
Population: 2,074 (2000); Race: 99.2% White, 0.0% Black, 0.0% Asian, 0.2% American Indian and Alaska Native, 0.0% Hispanic of any race, 0.6% two or more races (2000); Density: 63.0 persons per square mile (2000); Age: 34.8% under 18, 6.5% over 64 (2000); Marriage status: 22.8% never married, 71.5% now married, 2.4% widowed, 3.3% divorced (2000); Foreign born: 0.2% (2000); Ancestry (includes multiple ancestries): 46.2% German, 25.6% Czech, 13.4% Norwegian, 10.0% Irish, 7.6% Czechoslovakian (2000).
Economy: Employment by occupation: 11.8% management, 14.6% professional, 14.7% services, 23.4% sales, 1.7% farming, 14.8% construction, 19.0% production (2000).
Income: Per capita income: $20,782 (2000); Median household income: $62,986 (2000); Poverty rate: 3.4% (2000).
Taxes: Total city taxes per capita: $40 (1997); City property taxes per capita: $39 (1997).
Education: High school graduation rate: 90.1% (2000); College graduation rate: 16.5% (2000).
Housing: Homeownership rate: 91.5% (2000); Median home value: $146,900 (2000); Median rent: $470 per month (2000); Median age of housing: 24 years (2000).
Transportation: Commute to work: 91.6% car, 0.4% public transportation, 1.2% walk, 6.7% work from home (2000); Travel time to work: 40.2% less than 15 minutes, 15.3% 15 to 30 minutes, 27.1% 30 to 45 minutes, 10.1% 45 to 60 minutes, 7.2% 60 minutes or more (2000)

LE CENTER (city). Covers a land area of 1.486 square miles and a water area of 0 square miles. Located at 44.38° N. Lat.; 93.73° W. Long. Elevation is 1,052 feet.
History: Le Center was orginally called Le Sueur Center. It became the county seat after a lengthy dispute with the village of Le Sueur. Ginseng, an herb abundant here in pioneer days, was a source of revenue to the early settlers.
Population: 2,240 (2000); Race: 92.3% White, 0.1% Black, 0.2% Asian, 0.2% American Indian and Alaska Native, 10.4% Hispanic of any race, 0.8% two or more races (2000); Density: 1,507.2 persons per square mile (2000); Age: 27.1% under 18, 18.1% over 64 (2000); Marriage status: 23.0% never married, 59.2% now married, 9.4% widowed, 8.4% divorced (2000); Foreign born: 5.7% (2000); Ancestry (includes multiple ancestries): 48.6% German, 19.1% Irish, 10.9% Other groups, 8.6% Czech, 6.5% Norwegian (2000).

Economy: Single-family building permits issued: 8 (2001) / 13 (2000); Multi-family building permits issued: 0 (2001) / 0 (2000); Employment by occupation: 7.1% management, 13.5% professional, 15.6% services, 22.1% sales, 0.6% farming, 8.9% construction, 32.2% production (2000).
Income: Per capita income: $17,225 (2000); Median household income: $38,690 (2000); Poverty rate: 7.6% (2000).
Taxes: Total city taxes per capita: $112 (1997); City property taxes per capita: $107 (1997).
Education: High school graduation rate: 75.5% (2000); College graduation rate: 12.3% (2000).

School District(s)

Lecenter (PK-12)
2000 Enrollment: 757 507-357-6802
Housing: Homeownership rate: 74.1% (2000); Median home value: $87,000 (2000); Median rent: $367 per month (2000); Median age of housing: 41 years (2000).
Newspapers: Le Center Leader (1 x week)
Transportation: Commute to work: 89.1% car, 0.0% public transportation, 7.6% walk, 2.9% work from home (2000); Travel time to work: 48.3% less than 15 minutes, 26.7% 15 to 30 minutes, 12.9% 30 to 45 minutes, 6.1% 45 to 60 minutes, 6.1% 60 minutes or more (2000)
Additional Information Contacts
Le Center Chamber of Commerce 507-357-6737

LE SUEUR (city). Covers a land area of 4.462 square miles and a water area of 0.187 square miles. Located at 44.46° N. Lat.; 93.90° W. Long. Elevation is 760 feet.
History: Le Sueur was named for Pierre Charles Le Sueur, the French explorer who visited the valley of the Minnesota River in the late 1600's. From 1858 to 1863, this was the home of Dr. W.W. Mayo, who later founded the Mayo Clinic in Rochester. Dr. Mayo's first son, William, was born here in 1861. The Green Giant Company, packers of peas and corn, was founded in Le Sueur.
Population: 3,922 (2000); Race: 92.9% White, 0.9% Black, 0.1% Asian, 0.3% American Indian and Alaska Native, 9.7% Hispanic of any race, 1.2% two or more races (2000); Density: 879.0 persons per square mile (2000); Age: 27.5% under 18, 17.5% over 64 (2000); Marriage status: 23.7% never married, 62.4% now married, 6.7% widowed, 7.2% divorced (2000); Foreign born: 3.3% (2000); Ancestry (includes multiple ancestries): 45.3% German, 13.7% Other groups, 11.5% Norwegian, 10.1% Irish, 7.5% Swedish (2000).
Economy: Single-family building permits issued: 10 (2001) / 8 (2000); Multi-family building permits issued: 64 (2001) / 34 (2000); Employment by occupation: 8.9% management, 17.1% professional, 14.6% services, 22.0% sales, 0.9% farming, 6.3% construction, 30.2% production (2000).
Income: Per capita income: $21,605 (2000); Median household income: $42,372 (2000); Poverty rate: 8.8% (2000).
Taxes: Total city taxes per capita: $210 (2000); City property taxes per capita: $200 (2000).
Education: High school graduation rate: 81.9% (2000); College graduation rate: 18.0% (2000).

School District(s)

Lesueur-Henderson (PK-12)
2000 Enrollment: 1,442 507-665-8828
Housing: Homeownership rate: 72.6% (2000); Median home value: $94,800 (2000); Median rent: $362 per month (2000); Median age of housing: 40 years (2000).
Hospitals: Minnesota Valley Memorial Hospital (109 beds)
Newspapers: Le Sueur News Herald (1 x week)
Transportation: Commute to work: 87.4% car, 1.0% public transportation, 5.6% walk, 4.0% work from home (2000); Travel time to work: 59.1% less than 15 minutes, 18.8% 15 to 30 minutes, 7.6% 30 to 45 minutes, 7.8% 45 to 60 minutes, 6.7% 60 minutes or more (2000)
Additional Information Contacts
Le Sueur Chamber of Commerce 507-665-2501

LEXINGTON (township). Covers a land area of 34.093 square miles and a water area of 0.677 square miles. Located at 44.41° N. Lat.; 93.70° W. Long.
Population: 763 (2000); Race: 99.4% White, 0.0% Black, 0.1% Asian, 0.2% American Indian and Alaska Native, 0.0% Hispanic of any race, 0.2% two or more races (2000); Density: 22.4 persons per square mile (2000); Age: 27.9% under 18, 13.0% over 64 (2000); Marriage status: 25.3% never married, 61.3% now married, 4.5% widowed, 8.9% divorced (2000); Foreign born: 0.6% (2000); Ancestry (includes multiple ancestries): 52.8% German, 22.0% Czech, 15.6% Irish, 11.3% Norwegian, 8.4% Polish (2000).
Economy: Employment by occupation: 11.2% management, 12.7% professional, 13.2% services, 18.8% sales, 4.1% farming, 14.4% construction, 25.6% production (2000).
Income: Per capita income: $18,968 (2000); Median household income: $47,125 (2000); Poverty rate: 8.6% (2000).
Taxes: Total city taxes per capita: $52 (1997); City property taxes per capita: $52 (1997).
Education: High school graduation rate: 83.7% (2000); College graduation rate: 10.2% (2000).
Housing: Homeownership rate: 91.5% (2000); Median home value: $131,300 (2000); Median rent: $325 per month (2000); Median age of housing: 43 years (2000).
Transportation: Commute to work: 91.5% car, 0.0% public transportation, 0.8% walk, 4.0% work from home (2000); Travel time to work: 42.4% less than 15 minutes, 23.0% 15 to 30 minutes, 12.3% 30 to 45 minutes, 7.3% 45 to 60 minutes, 14.9% 60 minutes or more (2000)

MONTGOMERY (city). Covers a land area of 1.560 square miles and a water area of 0 square miles. Located at 44.44° N. Lat.; 93.58° W. Long. Elevation is 1,065 feet.
Population: 2,794 (2000); Race: 93.1% White, 0.3% Black, 0.3% Asian, 0.1% American Indian and Alaska Native, 9.2% Hispanic of any race, 0.8% two or more races (2000); Density: 1,790.7 persons per square mile (2000); Age: 28.8% under 18, 14.6% over 64 (2000); Marriage status: 28.8% never married, 55.4% now married, 8.2% widowed, 7.6% divorced (2000); Foreign born: 3.7% (2000); Ancestry (includes multiple ancestries): 31.2% German, 26.7% Czech, 11.4% Norwegian, 10.7% Other groups, 9.4% Irish (2000).
Economy: Single-family building permits issued: 11 (2001) / 14 (2000); Multi-family building permits issued: 14 (2001) / 0 (2000); Employment by occupation: 7.6% management, 14.5% professional, 11.8% services, 21.5% sales, 1.3% farming, 11.3% construction, 32.0% production (2000).
Income: Per capita income: $16,128 (2000); Median household income: $34,145 (2000); Poverty rate: 11.6% (2000).
Taxes: Total city taxes per capita: $234 (1997); City property taxes per capita: $215 (1997).
Education: High school graduation rate: 77.0% (2000); College graduation rate: 14.9% (2000).

School District(s)

Montgomery-Lonsdale (PK-12)
2000 Enrollment: 1,157 507-364-8100
Housing: Homeownership rate: 76.9% (2000); Median home value: $89,800 (2000); Median rent: $389 per month (2000); Median age of housing: 48 years (2000).
Newspapers: Montgomery Messenger (1 x week)
Transportation: Commute to work: 89.0% car, 0.6% public transportation, 6.4% walk, 3.4% work from home (2000); Travel time to work: 43.8% less than 15 minutes, 19.2% 15 to 30 minutes, 18.7% 30 to 45 minutes, 12.0% 45 to 60 minutes, 6.3% 60 minutes or more (2000)

MONTGOMERY (township). Covers a land area of 33.677 square miles and a water area of 0.888 square miles. Located at 44.40° N. Lat.; 93.59° W. Long. Elevation is 1,065 feet.
History: Platted 1877, incorporated 1902.
Population: 745 (2000); Race: 100.0% White, 0.0% Black, 0.0% Asian, 0.0% American Indian and Alaska Native, 1.3% Hispanic of any race, 0.0% two or more races (2000); Density: 22.1 persons per square mile (2000); Age: 28.7% under 18, 12.4% over 64 (2000); Marriage status: 23.9% never married, 67.8% now married, 4.3% widowed, 4.0% divorced (2000); Foreign born: 0.3% (2000); Ancestry (includes multiple ancestries): 42.5% German, 29.1% Czech, 11.5% Czechoslovakian, 10.1% Irish, 9.3% Norwegian (2000).
Economy: Agricultural trade center: grain, peas, soybeans; livestock, poultry; dairying. Manufacturing: canned peas and corn, fireplaces, printing and publishing, hardware. Employment by occupation: 15.7% management, 18.4% professional, 12.4% services, 20.1% sales, 2.0% farming, 12.2% construction, 19.2% production (2000).
Income: Per capita income: $20,180 (2000); Median household income: $45,227 (2000); Poverty rate: 3.5% (2000).
Taxes: Total city taxes per capita: $57 (1997); City property taxes per capita: $57 (1997).
Education: High school graduation rate: 82.9% (2000); College graduation rate: 16.0% (2000).
Housing: Homeownership rate: 88.5% (2000); Median home value: $130,000 (2000); Median rent: $425 per month (2000); Median age of housing: 33 years (2000).
Transportation: Commute to work: 89.0% car, 0.0% public transportation, 3.3% walk, 7.8% work from home (2000); Travel time to work: 39.1% less

than 15 minutes, 25.8% 15 to 30 minutes, 16.3% 30 to 45 minutes, 8.4% 45 to 60 minutes, 10.3% 60 minutes or more (2000)

OTTAWA (township). Covers a land area of 15.113 square miles and a water area of 0.230 square miles. Located at 44.40° N. Lat.; 93.92° W. Long. Elevation is 796 feet.
Population: 290 (2000); Race: 99.6% White, 0.0% Black, 0.0% Asian, 0.4% American Indian and Alaska Native, 0.0% Hispanic of any race, 0.0% two or more races (2000); Density: 19.2 persons per square mile (2000); Age: 26.1% under 18, 14.1% over 64 (2000); Marriage status: 15.1% never married, 64.4% now married, 13.8% widowed, 6.7% divorced (2000); Foreign born: 0.0% (2000); Ancestry (includes multiple ancestries): 67.8% German, 10.1% Irish, 7.6% Norwegian, 6.2% Polish, 6.2% French (except Basque) (2000).
Economy: Employment by occupation: 22.4% management, 19.2% professional, 7.1% services, 18.6% sales, 1.3% farming, 19.2% construction, 12.2% production (2000).
Income: Per capita income: $22,908 (2000); Median household income: $48,750 (2000); Poverty rate: 3.3% (2000).
Taxes: Total city taxes per capita: $25 (1997); City property taxes per capita: $25 (1997).
Education: High school graduation rate: 90.4% (2000); College graduation rate: 21.7% (2000).
Housing: Homeownership rate: 82.4% (2000); Median home value: $105,800 (2000); Median rent: $350 per month (2000); Median age of housing: 49 years (2000).
Transportation: Commute to work: 86.8% car, 0.0% public transportation, 1.3% walk, 11.9% work from home (2000); Travel time to work: 37.6% less than 15 minutes, 36.8% 15 to 30 minutes, 10.5% 30 to 45 minutes, 11.3% 45 to 60 minutes, 3.8% 60 minutes or more (2000)

SHARON (township). Covers a land area of 35.746 square miles and a water area of 0.137 square miles. Located at 44.41° N. Lat.; 93.84° W. Long.
Population: 658 (2000); Race: 95.3% White, 0.0% Black, 0.0% Asian, 2.3% American Indian and Alaska Native, 0.4% Hispanic of any race, 2.2% two or more races (2000); Density: 18.4 persons per square mile (2000); Age: 30.0% under 18, 9.6% over 64 (2000); Marriage status: 26.9% never married, 67.6% now married, 1.1% widowed, 4.4% divorced (2000); Foreign born: 0.6% (2000); Ancestry (includes multiple ancestries): 63.4% German, 19.8% Irish, 12.2% Norwegian, 6.6% Swedish, 3.2% Polish (2000).
Economy: Employment by occupation: 18.8% management, 12.2% professional, 15.9% services, 15.9% sales, 2.7% farming, 8.8% construction, 25.7% production (2000).
Income: Per capita income: $21,314 (2000); Median household income: $52,841 (2000); Poverty rate: 6.6% (2000).
Taxes: Total city taxes per capita: $95 (1997); City property taxes per capita: $95 (1997).
Education: High school graduation rate: 89.7% (2000); College graduation rate: 21.3% (2000).
Housing: Homeownership rate: 91.8% (2000); Median home value: $145,300 (2000); Median rent: $188 per month (2000); Median age of housing: 43 years (2000).
Transportation: Commute to work: 87.7% car, 0.0% public transportation, 2.9% walk, 9.3% work from home (2000); Travel time to work: 53.4% less than 15 minutes, 32.0% 15 to 30 minutes, 5.4% 30 to 45 minutes, 3.5% 45 to 60 minutes, 5.7% 60 minutes or more (2000)

TYRONE (township). Covers a land area of 36.073 square miles and a water area of 0.122 square miles. Located at 44.49° N. Lat.; 93.84° W. Long.
Population: 564 (2000); Race: 98.7% White, 0.4% Black, 0.0% Asian, 0.4% American Indian and Alaska Native, 2.5% Hispanic of any race, 0.0% two or more races (2000); Density: 15.6 persons per square mile (2000); Age: 25.9% under 18, 13.0% over 64 (2000); Marriage status: 18.7% never married, 76.8% now married, 2.1% widowed, 2.3% divorced (2000); Foreign born: 0.8% (2000); Ancestry (includes multiple ancestries): 58.6% German, 20.2% Irish, 9.3% Swedish, 7.8% Norwegian, 6.6% Polish (2000).
Economy: Employment by occupation: 22.0% management, 14.8% professional, 8.6% services, 20.1% sales, 1.6% farming, 11.2% construction, 21.7% production (2000).
Income: Per capita income: $22,470 (2000); Median household income: $60,556 (2000); Poverty rate: 4.7% (2000).
Taxes: Total city taxes per capita: $77 (1997); City property taxes per capita: $77 (1997).
Education: High school graduation rate: 92.7% (2000); College graduation rate: 18.4% (2000).
Housing: Homeownership rate: 94.9% (2000); Median home value: $132,300 (2000); Median rent: $525 per month (2000); Median age of housing: 49 years (2000).
Transportation: Commute to work: 87.7% car, 0.0% public transportation, 0.3% walk, 11.9% work from home (2000); Travel time to work: 40.6% less than 15 minutes, 24.1% 15 to 30 minutes, 19.2% 30 to 45 minutes, 11.7% 45 to 60 minutes, 4.5% 60 minutes or more (2000)

WASHINGTON (township). Covers a land area of 12.031 square miles and a water area of 3.215 square miles. Located at 44.26° N. Lat.; 93.85° W. Long.
Population: 797 (2000); Race: 99.4% White, 0.0% Black, 0.4% Asian, 0.0% American Indian and Alaska Native, 0.0% Hispanic of any race, 0.0% two or more races (2000); Density: 66.2 persons per square mile (2000); Age: 23.0% under 18, 11.4% over 64 (2000); Marriage status: 17.9% never married, 72.8% now married, 3.5% widowed, 5.8% divorced (2000); Foreign born: 0.1% (2000); Ancestry (includes multiple ancestries): 56.5% German, 17.8% Irish, 14.7% Norwegian, 8.3% English, 4.5% French (except Basque) (2000).
Economy: Employment by occupation: 16.1% management, 27.7% professional, 6.0% services, 27.9% sales, 0.0% farming, 11.4% construction, 11.0% production (2000).
Income: Per capita income: $37,717 (2000); Median household income: $69,188 (2000); Poverty rate: 0.9% (2000).
Taxes: Total city taxes per capita: $58 (1997); City property taxes per capita: $58 (1997).
Education: High school graduation rate: 96.5% (2000); College graduation rate: 40.1% (2000).
Housing: Homeownership rate: 92.2% (2000); Median home value: $187,500 (2000); Median rent: $483 per month (2000); Median age of housing: 24 years (2000).
Transportation: Commute to work: 96.1% car, 0.0% public transportation, 0.0% walk, 3.5% work from home (2000); Travel time to work: 15.4% less than 15 minutes, 67.8% 15 to 30 minutes, 6.5% 30 to 45 minutes, 4.2% 45 to 60 minutes, 6.1% 60 minutes or more (2000)

WATERVILLE (city). Covers a land area of 1.683 square miles and a water area of 0.622 square miles. Located at 44.21° N. Lat.; 93.56° W. Long. Elevation is 1,007 feet.
Population: 1,833 (2000); Race: 97.6% White, 0.0% Black, 0.1% Asian, 0.8% American Indian and Alaska Native, 0.2% Hispanic of any race, 1.4% two or more races (2000); Density: 1,088.8 persons per square mile (2000); Age: 22.3% under 18, 21.1% over 64 (2000); Marriage status: 23.2% never married, 58.2% now married, 9.4% widowed, 9.2% divorced (2000); Foreign born: 0.6% (2000); Ancestry (includes multiple ancestries): 48.4% German, 12.9% Norwegian, 11.3% Irish, 5.1% Swedish, 4.7% Other groups (2000).
Economy: Single-family building permits issued: 7 (2001) / 6 (2000); Multi-family building permits issued: 0 (2001) / 11 (2000); Employment by occupation: 11.5% management, 15.2% professional, 17.2% services, 19.7% sales, 1.7% farming, 9.5% construction, 25.1% production (2000).
Income: Per capita income: $17,958 (2000); Median household income: $35,950 (2000); Poverty rate: 10.6% (2000).
Taxes: Total city taxes per capita: $209 (1997); City property taxes per capita: $198 (1997).
Education: High school graduation rate: 79.5% (2000); College graduation rate: 11.9% (2000).

School District(s)

Waterville-Elysian-Morristown (PK-12)
2000 Enrollment: 1,049 507-362-4432
Housing: Homeownership rate: 76.9% (2000); Median home value: $83,700 (2000); Median rent: $329 per month (2000); Median age of housing: 48 years (2000).
Newspapers: Lake Region Life (1 x week)
Transportation: Commute to work: 88.8% car, 1.1% public transportation, 5.3% walk, 4.1% work from home (2000); Travel time to work: 36.7% less than 15 minutes, 27.0% 15 to 30 minutes, 23.1% 30 to 45 minutes, 3.7% 45 to 60 minutes, 9.5% 60 minutes or more (2000)
Additional Information Contacts
Waterville Chamber of Commerce. 507-362-4609

WATERVILLE (township). Covers a land area of 30.380 square miles and a water area of 3.399 square miles. Located at 44.23° N. Lat.; 93.57° W. Long. Elevation is 1,007 feet.
History: Incorporated as village 1878, as city 1898.
Population: 742 (2000); Race: 98.7% White, 0.9% Black, 0.0% Asian, 0.3% American Indian and Alaska Native, 0.1% Hispanic of any race, 0.0% two or more races (2000); Density: 24.4 persons per square mile (2000); Age: 24.3%

under 18, 13.3% over 64 (2000); Marriage status: 22.6% never married, 70.9% now married, 3.4% widowed, 3.1% divorced (2000); Foreign born: 0.1% (2000); Ancestry (includes multiple ancestries): 58.6% German, 15.5% Norwegian, 10.6% Irish, 8.1% Swedish, 5.6% United States or American (2000).
Economy: Resort area. Agricultural trade center: grain, soybeans, peas; livestock, poultry; dairying. Manufacturing of communications equipment, plastic bags. Employment by occupation: 10.7% management, 23.2% professional, 15.3% services, 19.4% sales, 1.0% farming, 14.3% construction, 16.2% production (2000).
Income: Per capita income: $19,604 (2000); Median household income: $53,929 (2000); Poverty rate: 2.1% (2000).
Taxes: Total city taxes per capita: $90 (1997); City property taxes per capita: $90 (1997).
Education: High school graduation rate: 88.6% (2000); College graduation rate: 20.4% (2000).
Housing: Homeownership rate: 93.6% (2000); Median home value: $136,200 (2000); Median rent: $525 per month (2000); Median age of housing: 43 years (2000).
Transportation: Commute to work: 92.3% car, 0.0% public transportation, 3.7% walk, 3.2% work from home (2000); Travel time to work: 30.9% less than 15 minutes, 39.6% 15 to 30 minutes, 18.7% 30 to 45 minutes, 3.8% 45 to 60 minutes, 6.9% 60 minutes or more (2000)

Lincoln County

Located in southwestern Minnesota; bounded on the west by South Dakota; includes part of Coteau des Prairies. Covers a land area of 537.00 square miles, a water area of 11.40 square miles, and is located in the Central Time Zone. The county government was organized in 1873. County seat is Ivanhoe.
Population: 6,429 (2000); Race: 99.3% White, 0.0% Black, 0.3% Asian, 0.1% American Indian and Alaska Native, 0.5% Hispanic of any race, 0.0% two or more races (2000); Density: 12.0 persons per square mile (2000); Age: 23.7% under 18, 24.3% over 64 (2000).
Religion: Five largest groups: 46.5% Evangelical Lutheran Church in America, 28.3% Catholic Church, 7.8% Wisconsin Evangelical Lutheran Synod, 5.7% The United Methodist Church, 1.5% Hutterian Brethren (2000).
Economy: Unemployment rate: 2.2% (11/2002); Total civilian labor force: 2,898 (11/2002); Leading industries: Companies that employ more than 1,000 persons: 0 (2000); Companies that employ more than 100 persons: 3 (2000); Farms: 724 totaling 269,646 acres (1997); Minority business ownership rate: 0.0% (1997); Women business ownership rate: 20.4% (1997); Retail sales per capita: $5,438 (1997). Single-family building permits issued: 0 (2001) / 3 (2000); Multi-family building permits issued: 0 (2001) / 10 (2000).
Income: Per capita income: $16,009 (2000); Median household income: $31,607 (2000); Poverty rate: 9.7% (2000); Bankruptcy rate: 0.76% (2001).
Taxes: Total county taxes per capita: $336 (1997); County property taxes per capita: $335 (1997).
Education: High school graduation rate: 79.8% (2000); College graduation rate: 14.1% (2000).
Housing: Homeownership rate: 80.4% (2000); Median home value: $43,700 (2000); Median rent: $237 per month (2000); Median age of housing: 50 years (2000).
Health: Birth rate: 93.3 per 10,000 population (1998); Age adjusted death rate: 71.3 per 10,000 population (1999); Age adjusted cancer mortality rate: 123.6 (Unreliable figure as per CDC) deaths per 100,000 population (1999). Number of physicians: 4.7 per 10,000 population (1999); Number of hospital beds: 336.0 per 10,000 population (1999).
Elections: 2000 Presidential election results: 48.4% Gore, 46.1% Bush, 3.2% Nader, 1.6% Buchanan
National and State Parks: Ash Lake State Wildlife Management Area; Blue Wing State Wildlife Management Area; Chain-O-Sloughs State Wildlife Management; Chen-Bay State Wildlife Management Area; Christine State Wildlife Management Area; Collinson State Wildlife Management Area; Dorer State Wildlife Management Area; Dorer State Wildlife Management Area; Emerald State Wildlife Management Area; Expectation State Wildlife Management Areas; Hendricks State Wildlife Management Area; Horse State Wildlife Management Area; Iron Horse State Wildlife Management Area; Ivanhoe State Wildlife Management Area; Johnson State Wildlife Management Area; Kvermo State Wildlife Management Area; Little Twin State Wildlife Management Area; Minn-Kota State Wildlife Management Area; Muskrat Junction State Wildlife Management A; Platyrhynchos State Wildlife Management Area; Poposki State Wildlife Management Area; Prairie Dell State Wildlife Management Area; Shaokatan State Wildlife Management Area; Sioux Lookout State Wildlife Management Area; Sokota State Wildlife Management Area; Suhr State Wildlife Management Area; Two Sloughs State Wildlife Management Area
Additional Information Contacts
Lincoln County Government Offices 507-694-1529
Lake Benton Chamber of Commerce 507-368-9577
Tyler Chamber of Commerce 507-247-3905

Lincoln County Communities

ALTA VISTA (township). Covers a land area of 36.508 square miles and a water area of 0 square miles. Located at 44.58° N. Lat.; 96.14° W. Long.
Population: 212 (2000); Race: 100.0% White, 0.0% Black, 0.0% Asian, 0.0% American Indian and Alaska Native, 0.0% Hispanic of any race, 0.0% two or more races (2000); Density: 5.8 persons per square mile (2000); Age: 14.6% under 18, 28.1% over 64 (2000); Marriage status: 23.7% never married, 64.4% now married, 11.9% widowed, 0.0% divorced (2000); Foreign born: 3.1% (2000); Ancestry (includes multiple ancestries): 31.3% German, 21.4% Norwegian, 17.2% Belgian, 13.0% Polish, 5.7% Icelander (2000).
Economy: Employment by occupation: 26.0% management, 12.5% professional, 14.4% services, 15.4% sales, 4.8% farming, 8.7% construction, 18.3% production (2000).
Income: Per capita income: $22,063 (2000); Median household income: $58,125 (2000); Poverty rate: 10.9% (2000).
Taxes: Total city taxes per capita: $54 (1997); City property taxes per capita: $54 (1997).
Education: High school graduation rate: 77.9% (2000); College graduation rate: 6.9% (2000).
Housing: Homeownership rate: 92.4% (2000); Median home value: $73,800 (2000); Median rent: $225 per month (2000); Median age of housing: 60 years (2000).
Transportation: Commute to work: 71.2% car, 0.0% public transportation, 13.5% walk, 15.4% work from home (2000); Travel time to work: 30.7% less than 15 minutes, 47.7% 15 to 30 minutes, 18.2% 30 to 45 minutes, 3.4% 45 to 60 minutes, 0.0% 60 minutes or more (2000)

ARCO (city). Covers a land area of 0.647 square miles and a water area of 0.121 square miles. Located at 44.38° N. Lat.; 96.18° W. Long. Elevation is 1,700 feet.
Population: 100 (2000); Race: 100.0% White, 0.0% Black, 0.0% Asian, 0.0% American Indian and Alaska Native, 0.0% Hispanic of any race, 0.0% two or more races (2000); Density: 154.6 persons per square mile (2000); Age: 17.6% under 18, 28.4% over 64 (2000); Marriage status: 19.8% never married, 60.5% now married, 7.0% widowed, 12.8% divorced (2000); Foreign born: 0.0% (2000); Ancestry (includes multiple ancestries): 46.1% German, 11.8% Polish, 10.8% Norwegian, 6.9% Swedish, 3.9% Irish (2000).
Economy: Grain; livestock; dairying. Manufactures feeds. Single-family building permits issued: 0 (2001) / 0 (2000); Multi-family building permits issued: 0 (2001) / 0 (2000); Employment by occupation: 17.4% management, 10.9% professional, 28.3% services, 13.0% sales, 0.0% farming, 13.0% construction, 17.4% production (2000).
Income: Per capita income: $13,479 (2000); Median household income: $30,625 (2000); Poverty rate: 4.9% (2000).
Taxes: Total city taxes per capita: $91 (1997); City property taxes per capita: $71 (1997).
Education: High school graduation rate: 72.6% (2000); College graduation rate: 9.7% (2000).
Housing: Homeownership rate: 85.4% (2000); Median home value: $14,200 (2000); Median rent: $175 per month (2000); Median age of housing: 60+ years (2000).
Transportation: Commute to work: 84.1% car, 0.0% public transportation, 11.4% walk, 4.5% work from home (2000); Travel time to work: 38.1% less than 15 minutes, 40.5% 15 to 30 minutes, 21.4% 30 to 45 minutes, 0.0% 45 to 60 minutes, 0.0% 60 minutes or more (2000)

ASH LAKE (township). Covers a land area of 36.057 square miles and a water area of 0.596 square miles. Located at 44.42° N. Lat.; 96.25° W. Long.
Population: 177 (2000); Race: 100.0% White, 0.0% Black, 0.0% Asian, 0.0% American Indian and Alaska Native, 0.0% Hispanic of any race, 0.0% two or more races (2000); Density: 4.9 persons per square mile (2000); Age: 32.0% under 18, 16.6% over 64 (2000); Marriage status: 22.5% never married, 71.3% now married, 1.6% widowed, 4.7% divorced (2000); Foreign born: 0.0% (2000); Ancestry (includes multiple ancestries): 64.1% German, 21.5% Polish, 16.6% Irish, 13.8% Belgian, 8.8% Norwegian (2000).

Economy: Employment by occupation: 19.7% management, 26.3% professional, 10.5% services, 17.1% sales, 2.6% farming, 14.5% construction, 9.2% production (2000).
Income: Per capita income: $12,639 (2000); Median household income: $31,750 (2000); Poverty rate: 30.9% (2000).
Taxes: Total city taxes per capita: $19 (1997); City property taxes per capita: $19 (1997).
Education: High school graduation rate: 90.8% (2000); College graduation rate: 16.5% (2000).
Housing: Homeownership rate: 76.2% (2000); Median home value: $45,000 (2000); Median rent: $175 per month (2000); Median age of housing: 46 years (2000).
Transportation: Commute to work: 71.1% car, 0.0% public transportation, 0.0% walk, 28.9% work from home (2000); Travel time to work: 63.0% less than 15 minutes, 18.5% 15 to 30 minutes, 7.4% 30 to 45 minutes, 0.0% 45 to 60 minutes, 11.1% 60 minutes or more (2000)

DIAMOND LAKE (township). Covers a land area of 32.184 square miles and a water area of 2.823 square miles. Located at 44.32° N. Lat.; 96.25° W. Long.
Population: 231 (2000); Race: 100.0% White, 0.0% Black, 0.0% Asian, 0.0% American Indian and Alaska Native, 0.0% Hispanic of any race, 0.0% two or more races (2000); Density: 7.2 persons per square mile (2000); Age: 28.7% under 18, 19.0% over 64 (2000); Marriage status: 18.6% never married, 70.7% now married, 3.7% widowed, 6.9% divorced (2000); Foreign born: 0.8% (2000); Ancestry (includes multiple ancestries): 36.4% German, 14.6% Norwegian, 12.1% Dutch, 7.7% Danish, 7.3% Italian (2000).
Economy: Employment by occupation: 29.5% management, 14.3% professional, 16.2% services, 10.5% sales, 10.5% farming, 7.6% construction, 11.4% production (2000).
Income: Per capita income: $12,689 (2000); Median household income: $31,250 (2000); Poverty rate: 17.4% (2000).
Taxes: Total city taxes per capita: $29 (1997); City property taxes per capita: $29 (1997).
Education: High school graduation rate: 79.0% (2000); College graduation rate: 9.3% (2000).
Housing: Homeownership rate: 88.8% (2000); Median home value: $52,500 (2000); Median rent: $275 per month (2000); Median age of housing: 46 years (2000).
Transportation: Commute to work: 68.0% car, 1.9% public transportation, 8.7% walk, 21.4% work from home (2000); Travel time to work: 40.7% less than 15 minutes, 25.9% 15 to 30 minutes, 18.5% 30 to 45 minutes, 3.7% 45 to 60 minutes, 11.1% 60 minutes or more (2000)

DRAMMEN (township). Covers a land area of 38.632 square miles and a water area of 0.021 square miles. Located at 44.33° N. Lat.; 96.39° W. Long.
Population: 141 (2000); Race: 100.0% White, 0.0% Black, 0.0% Asian, 0.0% American Indian and Alaska Native, 0.0% Hispanic of any race, 0.0% two or more races (2000); Density: 3.6 persons per square mile (2000); Age: 26.2% under 18, 19.1% over 64 (2000); Marriage status: 18.6% never married, 76.1% now married, 0.0% widowed, 5.3% divorced (2000); Foreign born: 0.0% (2000); Ancestry (includes multiple ancestries): 63.8% German, 12.1% Irish, 11.3% Norwegian, 9.9% United States or American, 9.2% Polish (2000).
Economy: Employment by occupation: 14.8% management, 17.3% professional, 21.0% services, 11.1% sales, 13.6% farming, 4.9% construction, 17.3% production (2000).
Income: Per capita income: $13,056 (2000); Median household income: $35,000 (2000); Poverty rate: 4.3% (2000).
Taxes: Total city taxes per capita: $81 (1997); City property taxes per capita: $81 (1997).
Education: High school graduation rate: 83.9% (2000); College graduation rate: 5.7% (2000).
Housing: Homeownership rate: 77.6% (2000); Median home value: $25,000 (2000); Median rent: $188 per month (2000); Median age of housing: 60+ years (2000).
Transportation: Commute to work: 90.1% car, 0.0% public transportation, 2.5% walk, 7.4% work from home (2000); Travel time to work: 20.0% less than 15 minutes, 42.7% 15 to 30 minutes, 30.7% 30 to 45 minutes, 6.7% 45 to 60 minutes, 0.0% 60 minutes or more (2000)

HANSONVILLE (township). Covers a land area of 33.501 square miles and a water area of 0.278 square miles. Located at 44.59° N. Lat.; 96.38° W. Long.
Population: 122 (2000); Race: 100.0% White, 0.0% Black, 0.0% Asian, 0.0% American Indian and Alaska Native, 0.0% Hispanic of any race, 0.0% two or more races (2000); Density: 3.6 persons per square mile (2000); Age: 25.8% under 18, 23.6% over 64 (2000); Marriage status: 8.8% never married, 80.9% now married, 4.4% widowed, 5.9% divorced (2000); Foreign born: 0.0% (2000); Ancestry (includes multiple ancestries): 30.3% Norwegian, 22.5% Polish, 13.5% English, 10.1% Scandinavian, 9.0% German (2000).
Economy: Employment by occupation: 28.3% management, 19.6% professional, 15.2% services, 8.7% sales, 6.5% farming, 13.0% construction, 8.7% production (2000).
Income: Per capita income: $13,725 (2000); Median household income: $20,000 (2000); Poverty rate: 4.5% (2000).
Taxes: Total city taxes per capita: $28 (1997); City property taxes per capita: $28 (1997).
Education: High school graduation rate: 59.4% (2000); College graduation rate: 6.3% (2000).
Housing: Homeownership rate: 89.5% (2000); Median home value: $37,500 (2000); Median age of housing: 60+ years (2000).
Transportation: Commute to work: 63.0% car, 0.0% public transportation, 8.7% walk, 28.3% work from home (2000); Travel time to work: 63.6% less than 15 minutes, 30.3% 15 to 30 minutes, 6.1% 30 to 45 minutes, 0.0% 45 to 60 minutes, 0.0% 60 minutes or more (2000)

HENDRICKS (city). Covers a land area of 0.962 square miles and a water area of 0.011 square miles. Located at 44.50° N. Lat.; 96.42° W. Long. Elevation is 1,787 feet.
Population: 725 (2000); Race: 100.0% White, 0.0% Black, 0.0% Asian, 0.0% American Indian and Alaska Native, 0.0% Hispanic of any race, 0.0% two or more races (2000); Density: 753.5 persons per square mile (2000); Age: 22.5% under 18, 37.4% over 64 (2000); Marriage status: 18.0% never married, 55.1% now married, 20.5% widowed, 6.4% divorced (2000); Foreign born: 0.0% (2000); Ancestry (includes multiple ancestries): 47.8% Norwegian, 32.5% German, 6.5% Irish, 5.7% Polish, 5.0% Swedish (2000).
Economy: Single-family building permits issued: 0 (2001) / 0 (2000); Multi-family building permits issued: 0 (2001) / 0 (2000); Employment by occupation: 9.5% management, 17.0% professional, 25.8% services, 17.4% sales, 2.3% farming, 9.1% construction, 18.9% production (2000).
Income: Per capita income: $15,828 (2000); Median household income: $26,042 (2000); Poverty rate: 8.4% (2000).
Taxes: Total city taxes per capita: $91 (1997); City property taxes per capita: $89 (1997).
Education: High school graduation rate: 74.0% (2000); College graduation rate: 18.2% (2000).

School District(s)

Hendricks (PK-06)
2000 Enrollment: 226 507-275-3116
Lake Hendricks 05-4 (KG-12)
2000 Enrollment: 0 507-275-3116

Housing: Homeownership rate: 78.2% (2000); Median home value: $39,200 (2000); Median rent: $192 per month (2000); Median age of housing: 53 years (2000).
Hospitals: Hendricks Community Hospital (26 beds)
Newspapers: The Hendricks Pioneer (1 x week)
Transportation: Commute to work: 81.1% car, 0.8% public transportation, 9.3% walk, 4.2% work from home (2000); Travel time to work: 64.9% less than 15 minutes, 12.9% 15 to 30 minutes, 13.3% 30 to 45 minutes, 5.6% 45 to 60 minutes, 3.2% 60 minutes or more (2000)

HENDRICKS (township). Covers a land area of 35.152 square miles and a water area of 1.318 square miles. Located at 44.51° N. Lat.; 96.39° W. Long. Elevation is 1,787 feet.
Population: 220 (2000); Race: 100.0% White, 0.0% Black, 0.0% Asian, 0.0% American Indian and Alaska Native, 0.0% Hispanic of any race, 0.0% two or more races (2000); Density: 6.3 persons per square mile (2000); Age: 30.6% under 18, 17.5% over 64 (2000); Marriage status: 24.9% never married, 69.0% now married, 5.1% widowed, 1.0% divorced (2000); Foreign born: 0.0% (2000); Ancestry (includes multiple ancestries): 38.5% German, 30.2% Norwegian, 23.4% Polish, 9.9% Swedish, 5.6% English (2000).
Economy: Grain; poultry, livestock; dairying. Employment by occupation: 18.5% management, 15.6% professional, 17.0% services, 19.3% sales, 0.0% farming, 11.9% construction, 17.8% production (2000).
Income: Per capita income: $14,583 (2000); Median household income: $41,111 (2000); Poverty rate: 12.3% (2000).
Taxes: Total city taxes per capita: $131 (1997); City property taxes per capita: $131 (1997).
Education: High school graduation rate: 83.9% (2000); College graduation rate: 16.8% (2000).

Housing: Homeownership rate: 92.1% (2000); Median home value: $85,000 (2000); Median rent: $500 per month (2000); Median age of housing: 39 years (2000).
Transportation: Commute to work: 84.3% car, 0.0% public transportation, 0.0% walk, 14.2% work from home (2000); Travel time to work: 59.1% less than 15 minutes, 21.7% 15 to 30 minutes, 10.4% 30 to 45 minutes, 6.1% 45 to 60 minutes, 2.6% 60 minutes or more (2000)

HOPE (township). Covers a land area of 34.836 square miles and a water area of 0 square miles. Located at 44.23° N. Lat.; 96.14° W. Long.
Population: 292 (2000); Race: 100.0% White, 0.0% Black, 0.0% Asian, 0.0% American Indian and Alaska Native, 0.0% Hispanic of any race, 0.0% two or more races (2000); Density: 8.4 persons per square mile (2000); Age: 31.9% under 18, 9.8% over 64 (2000); Marriage status: 17.9% never married, 75.7% now married, 2.8% widowed, 3.6% divorced (2000); Foreign born: 0.0% (2000); Ancestry (includes multiple ancestries): 45.4% Danish, 32.2% German, 15.0% Dutch, 8.3% Norwegian, 6.7% English (2000).
Economy: Employment by occupation: 24.0% management, 16.2% professional, 19.6% services, 16.2% sales, 2.2% farming, 6.7% construction, 15.1% production (2000).
Income: Per capita income: $16,916 (2000); Median household income: $41,667 (2000); Poverty rate: 5.5% (2000).
Taxes: Total city taxes per capita: $22 (1997); City property taxes per capita: $22 (1997).
Education: High school graduation rate: 91.9% (2000); College graduation rate: 18.2% (2000).
Housing: Homeownership rate: 89.7% (2000); Median home value: $83,000 (2000); Median rent: $100 per month (2000); Median age of housing: 51 years (2000).
Transportation: Commute to work: 78.8% car, 0.0% public transportation, 2.2% walk, 19.0% work from home (2000); Travel time to work: 49.7% less than 15 minutes, 13.8% 15 to 30 minutes, 31.7% 30 to 45 minutes, 2.8% 45 to 60 minutes, 2.1% 60 minutes or more (2000)

IVANHOE (city). Covers a land area of 0.911 square miles and a water area of 0 square miles. Located at 44.46° N. Lat.; 96.24° W. Long. Elevation is 1,650 feet.
History: Ivanhoe was named for the hero of Sir Walter Scott's novel of that name. Some of the streets in the town were named for other characters in the book.
Population: 679 (2000); Race: 100.0% White, 0.0% Black, 0.0% Asian, 0.0% American Indian and Alaska Native, 0.0% Hispanic of any race, 0.0% two or more races (2000); Density: 745.2 persons per square mile (2000); Age: 17.9% under 18, 30.6% over 64 (2000); Marriage status: 20.4% never married, 51.9% now married, 21.1% widowed, 6.6% divorced (2000); Foreign born: 0.3% (2000); Ancestry (includes multiple ancestries): 46.1% German, 29.7% Polish, 15.7% Norwegian, 7.1% Irish, 6.1% Belgian (2000).
Economy: Single-family building permits issued: 0 (2001) / 0 (2000); Multi-family building permits issued: 0 (2001) / 0 (2000); Employment by occupation: 13.6% management, 15.4% professional, 14.5% services, 24.4% sales, 4.8% farming, 8.4% construction, 19.0% production (2000).
Income: Per capita income: $17,775 (2000); Median household income: $28,125 (2000); Poverty rate: 8.6% (2000).
Taxes: Total city taxes per capita: $82 (1997); City property taxes per capita: $81 (1997).
Education: High school graduation rate: 76.7% (2000); College graduation rate: 18.1% (2000).

School District(s)

Ivanhoe (07-12)
2000 Enrollment: 238 507-694-1540
Housing: Homeownership rate: 74.1% (2000); Median home value: $39,000 (2000); Median rent: $223 per month (2000); Median age of housing: 40 years (2000).
Hospitals: Divine Providence (18 beds)
Newspapers: The Ivanhoe Times (1 x week)
Transportation: Commute to work: 87.8% car, 0.6% public transportation, 6.7% walk, 4.3% work from home (2000); Travel time to work: 56.9% less than 15 minutes, 15.7% 15 to 30 minutes, 23.6% 30 to 45 minutes, 1.6% 45 to 60 minutes, 2.2% 60 minutes or more (2000)

LAKE BENTON (city). Covers a land area of 3.825 square miles and a water area of 0.824 square miles. Located at 44.26° N. Lat.; 96.28° W. Long. Elevation is 1,758 feet.
History: Lake Benton was founded on the southern shore of what was once a large lake. Both lake and town were named for Thomas H. Benton of Missouri by his son-in-law, John C. Fremont, who explored in this area in 1838.
Population: 703 (2000); Race: 98.7% White, 0.0% Black, 1.3% Asian, 0.0% American Indian and Alaska Native, 0.3% Hispanic of any race, 0.0% two or more races (2000); Density: 183.8 persons per square mile (2000); Age: 20.9% under 18, 28.8% over 64 (2000); Marriage status: 17.0% never married, 54.7% now married, 17.4% widowed, 10.9% divorced (2000); Foreign born: 1.3% (2000); Ancestry (includes multiple ancestries): 47.3% German, 13.6% Norwegian, 11.2% Danish, 6.9% Irish, 5.3% United States or American (2000).
Economy: Single-family building permits issued: 0 (2001) / 2 (2000); Multi-family building permits issued: 0 (2001) / 10 (2000); Employment by occupation: 8.2% management, 15.1% professional, 21.1% services, 20.8% sales, 3.5% farming, 10.7% construction, 20.8% production (2000).
Income: Per capita income: $15,922 (2000); Median household income: $29,583 (2000); Poverty rate: 5.7% (2000).
Taxes: Total city taxes per capita: $77 (1997); City property taxes per capita: $76 (1997).
Education: High school graduation rate: 78.1% (2000); College graduation rate: 12.2% (2000).

School District(s)

Lake Benton (PK-12)
2000 Enrollment: 218 507-368-4236
Housing: Homeownership rate: 73.7% (2000); Median home value: $39,300 (2000); Median rent: $223 per month (2000); Median age of housing: 46 years (2000).
Newspapers: Lake Benton Valley Journal (1 x week)
Transportation: Commute to work: 89.6% car, 0.0% public transportation, 7.9% walk, 2.5% work from home (2000); Travel time to work: 53.6% less than 15 minutes, 26.3% 15 to 30 minutes, 13.0% 30 to 45 minutes, 3.2% 45 to 60 minutes, 3.9% 60 minutes or more (2000)
Additional Information Contacts
Lake Benton Chamber of Commerce. 507-368-9577

LAKE BENTON (township). Covers a land area of 33.298 square miles and a water area of 0.499 square miles. Located at 44.25° N. Lat.; 96.25° W. Long. Elevation is 1,758 feet.
Population: 244 (2000); Race: 100.0% White, 0.0% Black, 0.0% Asian, 0.0% American Indian and Alaska Native, 0.0% Hispanic of any race, 0.0% two or more races (2000); Density: 7.3 persons per square mile (2000); Age: 29.0% under 18, 9.2% over 64 (2000); Marriage status: 19.8% never married, 63.6% now married, 6.0% widowed, 10.6% divorced (2000); Foreign born: 0.0% (2000); Ancestry (includes multiple ancestries): 47.7% German, 18.0% Danish, 14.5% Norwegian, 8.5% Swedish, 6.7% Dutch (2000).
Economy: Agriculture: grain, soybeans; poultry; dairying. Manufacturing: printing, animal feeds. Resort area. Employment by occupation: 25.5% management, 5.5% professional, 11.7% services, 17.2% sales, 5.5% farming, 16.6% construction, 17.9% production (2000).
Income: Per capita income: $13,870 (2000); Median household income: $35,625 (2000); Poverty rate: 8.8% (2000).
Taxes: Total city taxes per capita: $111 (1997); City property taxes per capita: $111 (1997).
Education: High school graduation rate: 86.0% (2000); College graduation rate: 9.0% (2000).
Housing: Homeownership rate: 84.7% (2000); Median home value: $75,500 (2000); Median rent: $125 per month (2000); Median age of housing: 43 years (2000).
Transportation: Commute to work: 78.6% car, 0.0% public transportation, 2.9% walk, 18.6% work from home (2000); Travel time to work: 45.6% less than 15 minutes, 16.7% 15 to 30 minutes, 19.3% 30 to 45 minutes, 11.4% 45 to 60 minutes, 7.0% 60 minutes or more (2000)

LAKE STAY (township). Covers a land area of 35.013 square miles and a water area of 0.611 square miles. Located at 44.41° N. Lat.; 96.15° W. Long.
Population: 143 (2000); Race: 100.0% White, 0.0% Black, 0.0% Asian, 0.0% American Indian and Alaska Native, 0.0% Hispanic of any race, 0.0% two or more races (2000); Density: 4.1 persons per square mile (2000); Age: 22.6% under 18, 15.1% over 64 (2000); Marriage status: 14.2% never married, 75.6% now married, 6.3% widowed, 3.9% divorced (2000); Foreign born: 1.3% (2000); Ancestry (includes multiple ancestries): 39.0% German, 15.7% Polish, 14.5% Danish, 14.5% Norwegian, 12.6% Irish (2000).
Economy: Employment by occupation: 26.2% management, 15.5% professional, 11.9% services, 25.0% sales, 2.4% farming, 11.9% construction, 7.1% production (2000).

Income: Per capita income: $26,657 (2000); Median household income: $39,688 (2000); Poverty rate: 8.8% (2000).
Taxes: Total city taxes per capita: $106 (1997); City property taxes per capita: $106 (1997).
Education: High school graduation rate: 80.5% (2000); College graduation rate: 11.9% (2000).
Housing: Homeownership rate: 90.6% (2000); Median home value: $37,500 (2000); Median age of housing: 60+ years (2000).
Transportation: Commute to work: 78.6% car, 0.0% public transportation, 2.4% walk, 19.0% work from home (2000); Travel time to work: 39.7% less than 15 minutes, 41.2% 15 to 30 minutes, 16.2% 30 to 45 minutes, 2.9% 45 to 60 minutes, 0.0% 60 minutes or more (2000)

LIMESTONE (township). Covers a land area of 34.266 square miles and a water area of 0.334 square miles. Located at 44.49° N. Lat.; 96.15° W. Long.
Population: 159 (2000); Race: 100.0% White, 0.0% Black, 0.0% Asian, 0.0% American Indian and Alaska Native, 0.0% Hispanic of any race, 0.0% two or more races (2000); Density: 4.6 persons per square mile (2000); Age: 20.0% under 18, 24.8% over 64 (2000); Marriage status: 24.0% never married, 66.4% now married, 7.2% widowed, 2.4% divorced (2000); Foreign born: 0.0% (2000); Ancestry (includes multiple ancestries): 33.8% German, 26.9% Polish, 20.7% Norwegian, 15.9% Belgian, 8.3% Icelander (2000).
Economy: Employment by occupation: 54.2% management, 10.8% professional, 6.0% services, 8.4% sales, 8.4% farming, 4.8% construction, 7.2% production (2000).
Income: Per capita income: $14,123 (2000); Median household income: $33,750 (2000); Poverty rate: 11.0% (2000).
Taxes: Total city taxes per capita: $101 (2000); City property taxes per capita: $101 (2000).
Education: High school graduation rate: 81.1% (2000); College graduation rate: 9.9% (2000).
Housing: Homeownership rate: 85.2% (2000); Median home value: $80,000 (2000); Median rent: $225 per month (2000); Median age of housing: 60+ years (2000).
Transportation: Commute to work: 42.2% car, 0.0% public transportation, 0.0% walk, 57.8% work from home (2000); Travel time to work: 22.9% less than 15 minutes, 51.4% 15 to 30 minutes, 20.0% 30 to 45 minutes, 0.0% 45 to 60 minutes, 5.7% 60 minutes or more (2000)

MARBLE (township). Covers a land area of 36.458 square miles and a water area of 0.079 square miles. Located at 44.58° N. Lat.; 96.28° W. Long.
Population: 195 (2000); Race: 94.4% White, 0.0% Black, 0.0% Asian, 0.0% American Indian and Alaska Native, 5.6% Hispanic of any race, 0.0% two or more races (2000); Density: 5.3 persons per square mile (2000); Age: 23.4% under 18, 16.2% over 64 (2000); Marriage status: 24.7% never married, 67.9% now married, 4.9% widowed, 2.5% divorced (2000); Foreign born: 3.0% (2000); Ancestry (includes multiple ancestries): 46.7% Polish, 25.9% German, 18.8% Norwegian, 9.1% Dutch, 7.6% Belgian (2000).
Economy: Employment by occupation: 22.3% management, 6.6% professional, 19.0% services, 17.4% sales, 1.7% farming, 5.0% construction, 28.1% production (2000).
Income: Per capita income: $14,089 (2000); Median household income: $35,208 (2000); Poverty rate: 9.1% (2000).
Taxes: Total city taxes per capita: $20 (1997); City property taxes per capita: $20 (1997).
Education: High school graduation rate: 77.8% (2000); College graduation rate: 5.2% (2000).
Housing: Homeownership rate: 81.6% (2000); Median home value: $45,000 (2000); Median rent: $400 per month (2000); Median age of housing: 60+ years (2000).
Transportation: Commute to work: 79.3% car, 0.0% public transportation, 4.3% walk, 16.4% work from home (2000); Travel time to work: 26.8% less than 15 minutes, 54.6% 15 to 30 minutes, 13.4% 30 to 45 minutes, 0.0% 45 to 60 minutes, 5.2% 60 minutes or more (2000)

MARSHFIELD (township). Covers a land area of 34.825 square miles and a water area of 1.159 square miles. Located at 44.33° N. Lat.; 96.15° W. Long.
Population: 231 (2000); Race: 100.0% White, 0.0% Black, 0.0% Asian, 0.0% American Indian and Alaska Native, 0.0% Hispanic of any race, 0.0% two or more races (2000); Density: 6.6 persons per square mile (2000); Age: 28.2% under 18, 14.9% over 64 (2000); Marriage status: 18.1% never married, 73.2% now married, 4.0% widowed, 4.7% divorced (2000); Foreign born: 0.0% (2000); Ancestry (includes multiple ancestries): 45.1% German, 26.2% Danish, 16.9% Norwegian, 8.2% Swedish, 7.7% United States or American (2000).
Economy: Employment by occupation: 24.3% management, 17.8% professional, 7.5% services, 32.7% sales, 0.9% farming, 7.5% construction, 9.3% production (2000).
Income: Per capita income: $18,092 (2000); Median household income: $35,625 (2000); Poverty rate: 10.8% (2000).
Taxes: Total city taxes per capita: $64 (1997); City property taxes per capita: $64 (1997).
Education: High school graduation rate: 90.6% (2000); College graduation rate: 15.9% (2000).
Housing: Homeownership rate: 82.9% (2000); Median home value: $88,800 (2000); Median rent: $200 per month (2000); Median age of housing: 57 years (2000).
Transportation: Commute to work: 86.0% car, 0.0% public transportation, 0.9% walk, 13.1% work from home (2000); Travel time to work: 40.9% less than 15 minutes, 20.4% 15 to 30 minutes, 30.1% 30 to 45 minutes, 2.2% 45 to 60 minutes, 6.5% 60 minutes or more (2000)

ROYAL (township). Covers a land area of 32.812 square miles and a water area of 1.097 square miles. Located at 44.50° N. Lat.; 96.25° W. Long.
Population: 205 (2000); Race: 100.0% White, 0.0% Black, 0.0% Asian, 0.0% American Indian and Alaska Native, 0.0% Hispanic of any race, 0.0% two or more races (2000); Density: 6.2 persons per square mile (2000); Age: 30.7% under 18, 14.2% over 64 (2000); Marriage status: 26.3% never married, 54.4% now married, 13.1% widowed, 6.3% divorced (2000); Foreign born: 1.8% (2000); Ancestry (includes multiple ancestries): 61.9% Polish, 39.9% German, 11.0% Norwegian, 6.9% Irish, 4.6% Danish (2000).
Economy: Employment by occupation: 43.6% management, 5.5% professional, 7.3% services, 20.0% sales, 5.5% farming, 8.2% construction, 10.0% production (2000).
Income: Per capita income: $12,068 (2000); Median household income: $28,333 (2000); Poverty rate: 22.2% (2000).
Taxes: Total city taxes per capita: $84 (1997); City property taxes per capita: $84 (1997).
Education: High school graduation rate: 78.6% (2000); College graduation rate: 12.9% (2000).
Housing: Homeownership rate: 88.2% (2000); Median home value: $55,000 (2000); Median age of housing: 46 years (2000).
Transportation: Commute to work: 65.7% car, 0.0% public transportation, 2.8% walk, 31.5% work from home (2000); Travel time to work: 48.6% less than 15 minutes, 23.0% 15 to 30 minutes, 17.6% 30 to 45 minutes, 5.4% 45 to 60 minutes, 5.4% 60 minutes or more (2000)

SHAOKATAN (township). Covers a land area of 36.659 square miles and a water area of 1.636 square miles. Located at 44.40° N. Lat.; 96.37° W. Long.
Population: 192 (2000); Race: 100.0% White, 0.0% Black, 0.0% Asian, 0.0% American Indian and Alaska Native, 0.0% Hispanic of any race, 0.0% two or more races (2000); Density: 5.2 persons per square mile (2000); Age: 29.9% under 18, 23.4% over 64 (2000); Marriage status: 21.5% never married, 77.2% now married, 1.3% widowed, 0.0% divorced (2000); Foreign born: 0.0% (2000); Ancestry (includes multiple ancestries): 55.8% German, 27.4% Norwegian, 13.7% Polish, 10.7% Irish, 9.1% Danish (2000).
Economy: Employment by occupation: 34.0% management, 7.4% professional, 6.4% services, 26.6% sales, 3.2% farming, 12.8% construction, 9.6% production (2000).
Income: Per capita income: $11,859 (2000); Median household income: $28,929 (2000); Poverty rate: 14.2% (2000).
Taxes: Total city taxes per capita: $72 (1997); City property taxes per capita: $72 (1997).
Education: High school graduation rate: 91.2% (2000); College graduation rate: 20.0% (2000).
Housing: Homeownership rate: 88.6% (2000); Median home value: $88,300 (2000); Median rent: <$100 per month (2000); Median age of housing: 52 years (2000).
Transportation: Commute to work: 73.4% car, 0.0% public transportation, 2.1% walk, 24.5% work from home (2000); Travel time to work: 36.6% less than 15 minutes, 16.9% 15 to 30 minutes, 35.2% 30 to 45 minutes, 11.3% 45 to 60 minutes, 0.0% 60 minutes or more (2000)

TYLER (city). Covers a land area of 1.925 square miles and a water area of 0 square miles. Located at 44.27° N. Lat.; 96.13° W. Long. Elevation is 1,733 feet.
History: Tyler was settled in the early 1870's by Danish immigrants who were followers of Nikolai Frederik Severin Grundtvig. The town was named

for C.B. Tyler, a pioneer settler of southwestern Minnesota. Grundtvig (1783-1872) was a Danish theologian and poet who believed strongly in patriotism. His followers were called Grundtvigians.
Population: 1,218 (2000); Race: 98.2% White, 0.0% Black, 0.7% Asian, 0.3% American Indian and Alaska Native, 1.6% Hispanic of any race, 0.0% two or more races (2000); Density: 632.8 persons per square mile (2000); Age: 20.6% under 18, 29.3% over 64 (2000); Marriage status: 16.4% never married, 64.6% now married, 13.1% widowed, 5.8% divorced (2000); Foreign born: 1.3% (2000); Ancestry (includes multiple ancestries): 42.6% German, 21.4% Danish, 14.3% Norwegian, 8.2% Irish, 6.0% Belgian (2000).
Economy: Single-family building permits issued: 0 (2001) / 1 (2000); Multi-family building permits issued: 0 (2001) / 0 (2000); Employment by occupation: 8.9% management, 17.5% professional, 20.3% services, 18.5% sales, 1.4% farming, 15.3% construction, 18.0% production (2000).
Income: Per capita income: $17,451 (2000); Median household income: $31,196 (2000); Poverty rate: 6.1% (2000).
Taxes: Total city taxes per capita: $100 (1997); City property taxes per capita: $96 (1997).
Education: High school graduation rate: 79.4% (2000); College graduation rate: 14.7% (2000).

School District(s)

Tyler (09-12)
2000 Enrollment: 234 507-247-5911
Housing: Homeownership rate: 76.8% (2000); Median home value: $47,500 (2000); Median rent: $325 per month (2000); Median age of housing: 48 years (2000).
Hospitals: Tyler Healthcare Center (20 beds)
Newspapers: Tyler Tribute (1 x week)
Transportation: Commute to work: 85.9% car, 0.2% public transportation, 8.5% walk, 5.0% work from home (2000); Travel time to work: 61.5% less than 15 minutes, 11.2% 15 to 30 minutes, 24.7% 30 to 45 minutes, 0.9% 45 to 60 minutes, 1.7% 60 minutes or more (2000)
Additional Information Contacts
Tyler Chamber of Commerce 507-247-3905

VERDI (township). Covers a land area of 38.559 square miles and a water area of 0 square miles. Located at 44.23° N. Lat.; 96.39° W. Long. Elevation is 1,771 feet.
Population: 240 (2000); Race: 99.1% White, 0.0% Black, 0.0% Asian, 0.9% American Indian and Alaska Native, 0.9% Hispanic of any race, 0.0% two or more races (2000); Density: 6.2 persons per square mile (2000); Age: 25.7% under 18, 14.8% over 64 (2000); Marriage status: 16.6% never married, 77.1% now married, 4.0% widowed, 2.3% divorced (2000); Foreign born: 0.0% (2000); Ancestry (includes multiple ancestries): 61.7% German, 13.9% Dutch, 10.0% Irish, 9.6% Norwegian, 5.7% United States or American (2000).
Economy: Employment by occupation: 24.6% management, 10.5% professional, 23.7% services, 18.4% sales, 2.6% farming, 7.0% construction, 13.2% production (2000).
Income: Per capita income: $13,068 (2000); Median household income: $31,786 (2000); Poverty rate: 14.6% (2000).
Taxes: Total city taxes per capita: $71 (1997); City property taxes per capita: $71 (1997).
Education: High school graduation rate: 78.4% (2000); College graduation rate: 15.5% (2000).
Housing: Homeownership rate: 82.6% (2000); Median home value: $35,800 (2000); Median rent: $225 per month (2000); Median age of housing: 60+ years (2000).
Transportation: Commute to work: 84.5% car, 0.0% public transportation, 1.8% walk, 13.6% work from home (2000); Travel time to work: 46.3% less than 15 minutes, 36.8% 15 to 30 minutes, 10.5% 30 to 45 minutes, 6.3% 45 to 60 minutes, 0.0% 60 minutes or more (2000)

Lyon County

Located in southwestern Minnesota; drained by the Yellow Medicine, Cottonwood, and Redwood Rivers. Covers a land area of 714.20 square miles, a water area of 7.30 square miles, and is located in the Central Time Zone. The county government was organized in 1871. County seat is Marshall.

Weather Station: Marshall — Elevation: 1,151 feet

	Jan	Feb	Mar	Apr	May	Jun	Jul	Aug	Sep	Oct	Nov	Dec
High	23	29	40	57	71	80	84	82	73	60	40	27
Low	3	10	22	35	47	57	62	59	49	37	23	10
Precip	0.8	0.6	1.8	2.4	3.1	3.7	3.5	3.2	2.4	2.1	1.6	0.8
Snow	9.5	5.7	8.4	1.8	tr	0.0	0.0	0.0	0.0	0.8	7.6	8.3

High and Low temperatures in degrees Fahrenheit; Precipitation and Snow in inches

Weather Station: Tracy — Elevation: 1,400 feet

	Jan	Feb	Mar	Apr	May	Jun	Jul	Aug	Sep	Oct	Nov	Dec
High	21	27	38	55	69	79	83	80	71	59	40	26
Low	3	9	22	34	47	57	62	59	49	36	23	9
Precip	0.7	0.5	2.0	2.8	3.3	4.0	3.2	3.1	2.9	2.1	1.7	0.7
Snow	8.4	4.8	10.3	3.8	tr	0.0	0.0	0.0	tr	1.0	8.2	7.6

High and Low temperatures in degrees Fahrenheit; Precipitation and Snow in inches

Population: 25,425 (2000); Race: 93.1% White, 1.3% Black, 1.8% Asian, 0.3% American Indian and Alaska Native, 4.0% Hispanic of any race, 1.1% two or more races (2000); Density: 35.6 persons per square mile (2000); Age: 26.1% under 18, 14.6% over 64 (2000).
Religion: Five largest groups: 34.4% Catholic Church, 18.0% Evangelical Lutheran Church in America, 4.8% The United Methodist Church, 3.8% Wisconsin Evangelical Lutheran Synod, 1.9% Presbyterian Church (U.S.A.) (2000).
Economy: Unemployment rate: 2.4% (11/2002); Total civilian labor force: 14,775 (11/2002); Leading industries: 16.4% manufacturing; 14.5% retail trade; 12.4% health care and social assistance (2000); Companies that employ more than 1,000 persons: 1 (2000); Companies that employ more than 100 persons: 22 (2000); Farms: 931 totaling 403,001 acres (1997); Minority business ownership rate: 0.0% (1997); Women business ownership rate: 19.5% (1997); Retail sales per capita: $11,884 (1997). Single-family building permits issued: 91 (2001) / 67 (2000); Multi-family building permits issued: 32 (2001) / 30 (2000).
Income: Per capita income: $18,013 (2000); Median household income: $38,996 (2000); Poverty rate: 10.1% (2000); Bankruptcy rate: 1.99% (2001).
Taxes: Total county taxes per capita: $248 (2000); County property taxes per capita: $248 (2000).
Education: High school graduation rate: 82.6% (2000); College graduation rate: 21.4% (2000).
Housing: Homeownership rate: 68.4% (2000); Median home value: $81,000 (2000); Median rent: $386 per month (2000); Median age of housing: 37 years (2000).
Health: Birth rate: 139.2 per 10,000 population (1998); Age adjusted death rate: 72.2 per 10,000 population (1999); Age adjusted cancer mortality rate: 170.4 deaths per 100,000 population (1999). Number of physicians: 10.2 per 10,000 population (1999); Number of hospital beds: 59.0 per 10,000 population (1999).
Elections: 2000 Presidential election results: 41.2% Gore, 53.0% Bush, 4.0% Nader, 1.3% Buchanan
National and State Parks: Camden State Park; Gadwall State Wildlife Management Area; Garvin State Wildlife Management Area; Grandview State Wildlife Management Area; Greenhead State Wildlife Management Area; Hope State Wildlife Management Area; Nyroca Flats State Wildlife Management Area; Shelburne State Wildlife Management Area; Vallers State Wildlife Management Area
Additional Information Contacts
Lyon County Government Offices 507-537-6980
Marshall Area Chamber of Commerce 507-532-4484
Marshall Convention Bureau 507-537-1865
Tracy Chamber of Commerce 507-629-4021

Lyon County Communities

AMIRET (township). Covers a land area of 36.303 square miles and a water area of 0 square miles. Located at 44.33° N. Lat.; 95.66° W. Long. Elevation is 1,283 feet.
Population: 230 (2000); Race: 100.0% White, 0.0% Black, 0.0% Asian, 0.0% American Indian and Alaska Native, 0.0% Hispanic of any race, 0.0% two or more races (2000); Density: 6.3 persons per square mile (2000); Age: 29.4% under 18, 14.9% over 64 (2000); Marriage status: 22.2% never married, 71.1% now married, 3.9% widowed, 2.8% divorced (2000); Foreign born: 0.0% (2000); Ancestry (includes multiple ancestries): 41.2% German, 19.7% Irish, 9.6% Belgian, 9.2% Norwegian, 8.8% French (except Basque) (2000).

Economy: Employment by occupation: 14.3% management, 14.3% professional, 18.1% services, 18.1% sales, 1.9% farming, 18.1% construction, 15.2% production (2000).
Income: Per capita income: $16,683 (2000); Median household income: $49,375 (2000); Poverty rate: 13.2% (2000).
Taxes: Total city taxes per capita: $96 (2000); City property taxes per capita: $91 (2000).
Education: High school graduation rate: 77.6% (2000); College graduation rate: 16.8% (2000).
Housing: Homeownership rate: 75.0% (2000); Median home value: $29,200 (2000); Median rent: $258 per month (2000); Median age of housing: 60+ years (2000).
Transportation: Commute to work: 85.7% car, 0.0% public transportation, 3.8% walk, 10.5% work from home (2000); Travel time to work: 22.3% less than 15 minutes, 67.0% 15 to 30 minutes, 8.5% 30 to 45 minutes, 0.0% 45 to 60 minutes, 2.1% 60 minutes or more (2000)

BALATON (city). Covers a land area of 1.358 square miles and a water area of 0.129 square miles. Located at 44.23° N. Lat.; 95.87° W. Long. Elevation is 1,523 feet.
Population: 637 (2000); Race: 100.0% White, 0.0% Black, 0.0% Asian, 0.0% American Indian and Alaska Native, 2.2% Hispanic of any race, 0.0% two or more races (2000); Density: 468.9 persons per square mile (2000); Age: 24.9% under 18, 20.8% over 64 (2000); Marriage status: 22.3% never married, 61.2% now married, 10.6% widowed, 6.0% divorced (2000); Foreign born: 0.0% (2000); Ancestry (includes multiple ancestries): 37.6% German, 23.5% Norwegian, 13.8% Swedish, 5.9% Irish, 4.8% Dutch (2000).
Economy: Grain; livestock; dairying. Manufacturing: fertilizers. Employment by occupation: 10.5% management, 17.0% professional, 14.4% services, 21.6% sales, 0.0% farming, 10.8% construction, 25.8% production (2000).
Income: Per capita income: $16,167 (2000); Median household income: $36,442 (2000); Poverty rate: 6.0% (2000).
Taxes: Total city taxes per capita: $265 (1997); City property taxes per capita: $265 (1997).
Education: High school graduation rate: 85.4% (2000); College graduation rate: 13.1% (2000).

School District(s)

Balaton (PK-08)
2000 Enrollment: 107 507-734-5601
Yankton Country Charter School (08-12)
2000 Enrollment: 20 507-734-5433

Housing: Homeownership rate: 80.2% (2000); Median home value: $40,900 (2000); Median rent: $313 per month (2000); Median age of housing: 52 years (2000).
Newspapers: Balaton Press-Tribune (1 x week)
Transportation: Commute to work: 93.6% car, 1.3% public transportation, 0.7% walk, 2.7% work from home (2000); Travel time to work: 27.0% less than 15 minutes, 50.9% 15 to 30 minutes, 18.7% 30 to 45 minutes, 0.0% 45 to 60 minutes, 3.5% 60 minutes or more (2000)

CLIFTON (township). Covers a land area of 36.080 square miles and a water area of 0.073 square miles. Located at 44.40° N. Lat.; 95.64° W. Long.
Population: 288 (2000); Race: 100.0% White, 0.0% Black, 0.0% Asian, 0.0% American Indian and Alaska Native, 0.0% Hispanic of any race, 0.0% two or more races (2000); Density: 8.0 persons per square mile (2000); Age: 37.9% under 18, 8.6% over 64 (2000); Marriage status: 13.4% never married, 75.3% now married, 3.2% widowed, 8.1% divorced (2000); Foreign born: 0.0% (2000); Ancestry (includes multiple ancestries): 40.0% German, 26.1% Belgian, 10.7% Dutch, 8.9% Norwegian, 5.4% Swedish (2000).
Economy: Employment by occupation: 24.6% management, 13.4% professional, 8.2% services, 25.4% sales, 0.7% farming, 14.2% construction, 13.4% production (2000).
Income: Per capita income: $19,237 (2000); Median household income: $48,750 (2000); Poverty rate: 6.8% (2000).
Taxes: Total city taxes per capita: $73 (1997); City property taxes per capita: $73 (1997).
Education: High school graduation rate: 90.9% (2000); College graduation rate: 15.2% (2000).
Housing: Homeownership rate: 77.4% (2000); Median home value: $83,300 (2000); Median rent: $288 per month (2000); Median age of housing: 55 years (2000).
Transportation: Commute to work: 80.6% car, 0.0% public transportation, 1.5% walk, 17.9% work from home (2000); Travel time to work: 27.3% less than 15 minutes, 54.5% 15 to 30 minutes, 7.3% 30 to 45 minutes, 0.0% 45 to 60 minutes, 10.9% 60 minutes or more (2000)

COON CREEK (township). Covers a land area of 35.904 square miles and a water area of 0.524 square miles. Located at 44.32° N. Lat.; 96.00° W. Long.
Population: 282 (2000); Race: 99.0% White, 0.0% Black, 0.6% Asian, 0.0% American Indian and Alaska Native, 0.0% Hispanic of any race, 0.3% two or more races (2000); Density: 7.9 persons per square mile (2000); Age: 32.3% under 18, 11.6% over 64 (2000); Marriage status: 26.3% never married, 64.0% now married, 5.1% widowed, 4.7% divorced (2000); Foreign born: 0.6% (2000); Ancestry (includes multiple ancestries): 45.5% German, 20.3% Norwegian, 12.6% Dutch, 11.3% French (except Basque), 10.3% Belgian (2000).
Economy: Employment by occupation: 25.9% management, 8.6% professional, 3.1% services, 29.0% sales, 1.2% farming, 11.7% construction, 20.4% production (2000).
Income: Per capita income: $14,150 (2000); Median household income: $42,083 (2000); Poverty rate: 6.1% (2000).
Taxes: Total city taxes per capita: $88 (1997); City property taxes per capita: $88 (1997).
Education: High school graduation rate: 92.6% (2000); College graduation rate: 14.4% (2000).
Housing: Homeownership rate: 89.0% (2000); Median home value: $67,500 (2000); Median rent: $425 per month (2000); Median age of housing: 48 years (2000).
Transportation: Commute to work: 76.6% car, 1.3% public transportation, 1.9% walk, 19.0% work from home (2000); Travel time to work: 31.3% less than 15 minutes, 43.8% 15 to 30 minutes, 14.1% 30 to 45 minutes, 1.6% 45 to 60 minutes, 9.4% 60 minutes or more (2000)

COTTONWOOD (city). Covers a land area of 0.857 square miles and a water area of 0 square miles. Located at 44.60° N. Lat.; 95.67° W. Long. Elevation is 936 feet.
Population: 1,148 (2000); Race: 95.5% White, 0.0% Black, 0.9% Asian, 0.0% American Indian and Alaska Native, 2.4% Hispanic of any race, 0.4% two or more races (2000); Density: 1,339.0 persons per square mile (2000); Age: 29.1% under 18, 15.3% over 64 (2000); Marriage status: 20.8% never married, 67.7% now married, 5.9% widowed, 5.6% divorced (2000); Foreign born: 2.7% (2000); Ancestry (includes multiple ancestries): 43.6% German, 28.9% Norwegian, 9.2% Belgian, 7.2% Swedish, 6.4% Irish (2000).
Economy: Agricultural area: dairying; livestock; grain, soybeans, alfalfa; light manufacturing (cabinets). Single-family building permits issued: 8 (2001) / 5 (2000); Multi-family building permits issued: 0 (2001) / 0 (2000); Employment by occupation: 13.8% management, 13.9% professional, 14.7% services, 28.2% sales, 0.6% farming, 7.9% construction, 20.7% production (2000).
Income: Per capita income: $19,847 (2000); Median household income: $39,792 (2000); Poverty rate: 4.5% (2000).
Taxes: Total city taxes per capita: $207 (1997); City property taxes per capita: $205 (1997).
Education: High school graduation rate: 84.4% (2000); College graduation rate: 19.4% (2000).

School District(s)

Lakeview (PK-12)
2000 Enrollment: 569 507-423-5164

Housing: Homeownership rate: 75.0% (2000); Median home value: $79,600 (2000); Median rent: $285 per month (2000); Median age of housing: 35 years (2000).
Newspapers: Tri-County News (1 x week)
Transportation: Commute to work: 87.7% car, 0.0% public transportation, 8.4% walk, 3.5% work from home (2000); Travel time to work: 48.9% less than 15 minutes, 44.8% 15 to 30 minutes, 3.6% 30 to 45 minutes, 1.0% 45 to 60 minutes, 1.7% 60 minutes or more (2000)

CUSTER (township). Covers a land area of 35.450 square miles and a water area of 0.445 square miles. Located at 44.23° N. Lat.; 95.78° W. Long.
Population: 220 (2000); Race: 99.0% White, 0.0% Black, 0.0% Asian, 0.0% American Indian and Alaska Native, 6.1% Hispanic of any race, 1.0% two or more races (2000); Density: 6.2 persons per square mile (2000); Age: 18.2% under 18, 19.7% over 64 (2000); Marriage status: 11.8% never married, 73.4% now married, 8.3% widowed, 6.5% divorced (2000); Foreign born: 0.0% (2000); Ancestry (includes multiple ancestries): 42.9% German, 27.3% Norwegian, 10.1% Irish, 10.1% Swedish, 8.1% Belgian (2000).
Economy: Employment by occupation: 29.6% management, 12.8% professional, 15.2% services, 23.2% sales, 3.2% farming, 4.8% construction, 11.2% production (2000).

Income: Per capita income: $19,334 (2000); Median household income: $41,250 (2000); Poverty rate: 11.1% (2000).
Taxes: Total city taxes per capita: $112 (1997); City property taxes per capita: $112 (1997).
Education: High school graduation rate: 82.5% (2000); College graduation rate: 9.1% (2000).
Housing: Homeownership rate: 85.2% (2000); Median home value: $112,500 (2000); Median rent: $208 per month (2000); Median age of housing: 60+ years (2000).
Transportation: Commute to work: 81.6% car, 0.0% public transportation, 3.2% walk, 15.2% work from home (2000); Travel time to work: 25.5% less than 15 minutes, 52.8% 15 to 30 minutes, 16.0% 30 to 45 minutes, 0.0% 45 to 60 minutes, 5.7% 60 minutes or more (2000)

EIDSVOLD (township). Covers a land area of 33.506 square miles and a water area of 0.069 square miles. Located at 44.59° N. Lat.; 96.02° W. Long.
Population: 223 (2000); Race: 100.0% White, 0.0% Black, 0.0% Asian, 0.0% American Indian and Alaska Native, 0.0% Hispanic of any race, 0.0% two or more races (2000); Density: 6.7 persons per square mile (2000); Age: 37.3% under 18, 16.9% over 64 (2000); Marriage status: 24.4% never married, 61.6% now married, 9.9% widowed, 4.1% divorced (2000); Foreign born: 0.0% (2000); Ancestry (includes multiple ancestries): 38.1% Belgian, 28.8% German, 15.3% Norwegian, 7.6% United States or American, 6.4% Polish (2000).
Economy: Employment by occupation: 22.6% management, 8.7% professional, 14.8% services, 26.1% sales, 6.1% farming, 7.8% construction, 13.9% production (2000).
Income: Per capita income: $13,896 (2000); Median household income: $43,125 (2000); Poverty rate: 12.3% (2000).
Taxes: Total city taxes per capita: $44 (1997); City property taxes per capita: $44 (1997).
Education: High school graduation rate: 83.6% (2000); College graduation rate: 9.4% (2000).
Housing: Homeownership rate: 92.9% (2000); Median home value: $68,800 (2000); Median rent: $225 per month (2000); Median age of housing: 60+ years (2000).
Transportation: Commute to work: 85.2% car, 0.0% public transportation, 7.0% walk, 7.8% work from home (2000); Travel time to work: 39.6% less than 15 minutes, 35.8% 15 to 30 minutes, 18.9% 30 to 45 minutes, 1.9% 45 to 60 minutes, 3.8% 60 minutes or more (2000)

FAIRVIEW (township). Covers a land area of 33.211 square miles and a water area of 0 square miles. Located at 44.50° N. Lat.; 95.76° W. Long.
Population: 485 (2000); Race: 99.6% White, 0.0% Black, 0.4% Asian, 0.0% American Indian and Alaska Native, 0.0% Hispanic of any race, 0.0% two or more races (2000); Density: 14.6 persons per square mile (2000); Age: 31.6% under 18, 9.8% over 64 (2000); Marriage status: 23.2% never married, 71.3% now married, 2.0% widowed, 3.4% divorced (2000); Foreign born: 0.4% (2000); Ancestry (includes multiple ancestries): 39.7% German, 21.4% Belgian, 11.1% Norwegian, 9.6% Irish, 8.9% French (except Basque) (2000).
Economy: Employment by occupation: 23.6% management, 9.1% professional, 11.4% services, 29.9% sales, 2.8% farming, 11.4% construction, 11.8% production (2000).
Income: Per capita income: $21,641 (2000); Median household income: $48,875 (2000); Poverty rate: 2.2% (2000).
Taxes: Total city taxes per capita: $31 (1997); City property taxes per capita: $31 (1997).
Education: High school graduation rate: 88.0% (2000); College graduation rate: 17.0% (2000).
Housing: Homeownership rate: 89.2% (2000); Median home value: $80,400 (2000); Median rent: $320 per month (2000); Median age of housing: 47 years (2000).
Transportation: Commute to work: 85.1% car, 0.8% public transportation, 4.0% walk, 10.1% work from home (2000); Travel time to work: 70.4% less than 15 minutes, 25.1% 15 to 30 minutes, 1.8% 30 to 45 minutes, 2.7% 45 to 60 minutes, 0.0% 60 minutes or more (2000)

FLORENCE (city). Covers a land area of 0.249 square miles and a water area of 0 square miles. Located at 44.23° N. Lat.; 96.05° W. Long.
Population: 61 (2000); Race: 100.0% White, 0.0% Black, 0.0% Asian, 0.0% American Indian and Alaska Native, 0.0% Hispanic of any race, 0.0% two or more races (2000); Density: 245.5 persons per square mile (2000); Age: 27.9% under 18, 14.0% over 64 (2000); Marriage status: 12.1% never married, 81.8% now married, 0.0% widowed, 6.1% divorced (2000); Foreign born: 0.0% (2000); Ancestry (includes multiple ancestries): 23.3% Dutch, 18.6% Norwegian, 18.6% Danish, 14.0% Swedish, 9.3% English (2000).
Economy: Railroad junction. Grain, soybeans; livestock; dairying. Employment by occupation: 19.0% management, 0.0% professional, 9.5% services, 38.1% sales, 0.0% farming, 33.3% construction, 0.0% production (2000).
Income: Per capita income: $16,312 (2000); Median household income: $43,125 (2000); Poverty rate: 0.0% (2000).
Taxes: Total city taxes per capita: $57 (1997); City property taxes per capita: $38 (1997).
Education: High school graduation rate: 67.7% (2000); College graduation rate: 6.5% (2000).
Housing: Homeownership rate: 100.0% (2000); Median home value: $33,800 (2000); Median age of housing: 60+ years (2000).
Transportation: Commute to work: 81.0% car, 0.0% public transportation, 19.0% walk, 0.0% work from home (2000); Travel time to work: 57.1% less than 15 minutes, 33.3% 15 to 30 minutes, 9.5% 30 to 45 minutes, 0.0% 45 to 60 minutes, 0.0% 60 minutes or more (2000)

GARVIN (city). Covers a land area of 0.269 square miles and a water area of 0.011 square miles. Located at 44.21° N. Lat.; 95.76° W. Long. Elevation is 1,560 feet.
Population: 159 (2000); Race: 95.7% White, 0.0% Black, 1.6% Asian, 0.0% American Indian and Alaska Native, 0.0% Hispanic of any race, 2.2% two or more races (2000); Density: 590.3 persons per square mile (2000); Age: 31.5% under 18, 7.1% over 64 (2000); Marriage status: 19.1% never married, 72.1% now married, 2.9% widowed, 5.9% divorced (2000); Foreign born: 1.6% (2000); Ancestry (includes multiple ancestries): 47.8% German, 24.5% Norwegian, 9.2% English, 8.7% Swedish, 8.2% Danish (2000).
Economy: Single-family building permits issued: 0 (2001) / 0 (2000); Multi-family building permits issued: 0 (2001) / 0 (2000); Employment by occupation: 4.3% management, 6.5% professional, 25.8% services, 19.4% sales, 0.0% farming, 23.7% construction, 20.4% production (2000).
Income: Per capita income: $13,108 (2000); Median household income: $38,750 (2000); Poverty rate: 8.2% (2000).
Taxes: Total city taxes per capita: $100 (1997); City property taxes per capita: $86 (1997).
Education: High school graduation rate: 86.8% (2000); College graduation rate: 9.6% (2000).
Housing: Homeownership rate: 82.5% (2000); Median home value: $25,300 (2000); Median rent: $365 per month (2000); Median age of housing: 60+ years (2000).
Transportation: Commute to work: 92.5% car, 0.0% public transportation, 3.2% walk, 0.0% work from home (2000); Travel time to work: 18.3% less than 15 minutes, 48.4% 15 to 30 minutes, 21.5% 30 to 45 minutes, 3.2% 45 to 60 minutes, 8.6% 60 minutes or more (2000)

GHENT (city). Covers a land area of 0.269 square miles and a water area of 0 square miles. Located at 44.51° N. Lat.; 95.89° W. Long. Elevation is 1,164 feet.
History: Early Belgian settlement.
Population: 315 (2000); Race: 98.4% White, 0.0% Black, 0.7% Asian, 0.3% American Indian and Alaska Native, 0.0% Hispanic of any race, 0.7% two or more races (2000); Density: 1,173.0 persons per square mile (2000); Age: 24.3% under 18, 6.9% over 64 (2000); Marriage status: 28.7% never married, 58.7% now married, 5.7% widowed, 6.9% divorced (2000); Foreign born: 0.7% (2000); Ancestry (includes multiple ancestries): 43.4% German, 27.6% Belgian, 17.4% Norwegian, 9.5% French (except Basque), 9.2% Irish (2000).
Economy: Grain; livestock, poultry; dairying. Manufacturing: feeds. Single-family building permits issued: 0 (2001) / 0 (2000); Multi-family building permits issued: 0 (2001) / 0 (2000); Employment by occupation: 9.5% management, 10.5% professional, 14.0% services, 30.5% sales, 0.0% farming, 14.0% construction, 21.5% production (2000).
Income: Per capita income: $17,313 (2000); Median household income: $43,125 (2000); Poverty rate: 7.6% (2000).
Taxes: Total city taxes per capita: $86 (1997); City property taxes per capita: $73 (1997).
Education: High school graduation rate: 89.4% (2000); College graduation rate: 11.2% (2000).
Housing: Homeownership rate: 82.8% (2000); Median home value: $60,800 (2000); Median rent: $163 per month (2000); Median age of housing: 38 years (2000).
Transportation: Commute to work: 90.2% car, 1.0% public transportation, 6.2% walk, 2.6% work from home (2000); Travel time to work: 73.0% less than 15 minutes, 21.2% 15 to 30 minutes, 2.1% 30 to 45 minutes, 2.6% 45 to 60 minutes, 1.1% 60 minutes or more (2000)

GRANDVIEW (township). Covers a land area of 35.166 square miles and a water area of 0.013 square miles. Located at 44.50° N. Lat.; 95.89° W. Long.
Population: 317 (2000); Race: 100.0% White, 0.0% Black, 0.0% Asian, 0.0% American Indian and Alaska Native, 0.6% Hispanic of any race, 0.0% two or more races (2000); Density: 9.0 persons per square mile (2000); Age: 32.8% under 18, 17.5% over 64 (2000); Marriage status: 26.0% never married, 62.1% now married, 4.1% widowed, 7.8% divorced (2000); Foreign born: 0.0% (2000); Ancestry (includes multiple ancestries): 47.4% Belgian, 33.8% German, 13.0% Norwegian, 12.0% Dutch, 11.0% Irish (2000).
Economy: Employment by occupation: 30.8% management, 15.0% professional, 14.3% services, 13.5% sales, 0.0% farming, 12.0% construction, 14.3% production (2000).
Income: Per capita income: $16,470 (2000); Median household income: $46,000 (2000); Poverty rate: 3.3% (2000).
Taxes: Total city taxes per capita: $41 (1997); City property taxes per capita: $41 (1997).
Education: High school graduation rate: 84.1% (2000); College graduation rate: 17.0% (2000).
Housing: Homeownership rate: 76.2% (2000); Median home value: $100,000 (2000); Median rent: $235 per month (2000); Median age of housing: 60+ years (2000).
Transportation: Commute to work: 78.9% car, 0.0% public transportation, 5.3% walk, 15.8% work from home (2000); Travel time to work: 58.0% less than 15 minutes, 34.8% 15 to 30 minutes, 1.8% 30 to 45 minutes, 0.0% 45 to 60 minutes, 5.4% 60 minutes or more (2000)

ISLAND LAKE (township). Covers a land area of 35.703 square miles and a water area of 0.491 square miles. Located at 44.42° N. Lat.; 96.02° W. Long.
Population: 208 (2000); Race: 97.2% White, 0.0% Black, 0.0% Asian, 2.8% American Indian and Alaska Native, 0.0% Hispanic of any race, 0.0% two or more races (2000); Density: 5.8 persons per square mile (2000); Age: 29.2% under 18, 10.2% over 64 (2000); Marriage status: 23.8% never married, 70.8% now married, 3.6% widowed, 1.8% divorced (2000); Foreign born: 0.0% (2000); Ancestry (includes multiple ancestries): 46.3% German, 25.0% Norwegian, 16.7% Belgian, 8.8% United States or American, 8.8% Danish (2000).
Economy: Employment by occupation: 31.5% management, 17.7% professional, 1.6% services, 21.8% sales, 4.0% farming, 13.7% construction, 9.7% production (2000).
Income: Per capita income: $18,522 (2000); Median household income: $44,688 (2000); Poverty rate: 12.0% (2000).
Taxes: Total city taxes per capita: $24 (1997); City property taxes per capita: $24 (1997).
Education: High school graduation rate: 85.7% (2000); College graduation rate: 10.7% (2000).
Housing: Homeownership rate: 93.2% (2000); Median home value: $78,600 (2000); Median rent: $475 per month (2000); Median age of housing: 52 years (2000).
Transportation: Commute to work: 71.4% car, 0.0% public transportation, 1.6% walk, 25.4% work from home (2000); Travel time to work: 17.0% less than 15 minutes, 76.6% 15 to 30 minutes, 6.4% 30 to 45 minutes, 0.0% 45 to 60 minutes, 0.0% 60 minutes or more (2000)

LAKE MARSHALL (township). Covers a land area of 29.582 square miles and a water area of 0.385 square miles. Located at 44.42° N. Lat.; 95.80° W. Long.
Population: 517 (2000); Race: 96.4% White, 0.4% Black, 2.1% Asian, 0.0% American Indian and Alaska Native, 0.6% Hispanic of any race, 1.1% two or more races (2000); Density: 17.5 persons per square mile (2000); Age: 30.8% under 18, 6.2% over 64 (2000); Marriage status: 21.5% never married, 70.3% now married, 5.5% widowed, 2.8% divorced (2000); Foreign born: 3.8% (2000); Ancestry (includes multiple ancestries): 44.5% German, 22.0% Belgian, 18.2% Norwegian, 6.8% French (except Basque), 6.2% Dutch (2000).
Economy: Employment by occupation: 16.4% management, 11.3% professional, 9.1% services, 32.4% sales, 0.6% farming, 9.1% construction, 21.1% production (2000).
Income: Per capita income: $21,461 (2000); Median household income: $56,607 (2000); Poverty rate: 4.1% (2000).
Taxes: Total city taxes per capita: $39 (1997); City property taxes per capita: $39 (1997).
Education: High school graduation rate: 88.3% (2000); College graduation rate: 24.0% (2000).
Housing: Homeownership rate: 83.8% (2000); Median home value: $123,100 (2000); Median rent: $475 per month (2000); Median age of housing: 30 years (2000).
Transportation: Commute to work: 92.4% car, 0.0% public transportation, 0.0% walk, 7.0% work from home (2000); Travel time to work: 78.6% less than 15 minutes, 17.0% 15 to 30 minutes, 2.0% 30 to 45 minutes, 0.7% 45 to 60 minutes, 1.7% 60 minutes or more (2000)

LUCAS (township). Covers a land area of 33.801 square miles and a water area of 1.848 square miles. Located at 44.59° N. Lat.; 95.67° W. Long.
Population: 260 (2000); Race: 95.3% White, 0.0% Black, 0.0% Asian, 0.0% American Indian and Alaska Native, 4.7% Hispanic of any race, 4.0% two or more races (2000); Density: 7.7 persons per square mile (2000); Age: 34.8% under 18, 4.3% over 64 (2000); Marriage status: 18.9% never married, 77.2% now married, 0.6% widowed, 3.3% divorced (2000); Foreign born: 0.0% (2000); Ancestry (includes multiple ancestries): 32.4% German, 22.5% Norwegian, 17.8% Belgian, 8.7% Irish, 8.3% Dutch (2000).
Economy: Employment by occupation: 19.4% management, 18.7% professional, 16.5% services, 18.7% sales, 2.2% farming, 7.2% construction, 17.3% production (2000).
Income: Per capita income: $24,564 (2000); Median household income: $55,313 (2000); Poverty rate: 0.0% (2000).
Taxes: Total city taxes per capita: $94 (1997); City property taxes per capita: $94 (1997).
Education: High school graduation rate: 98.0% (2000); College graduation rate: 22.9% (2000).
Housing: Homeownership rate: 78.8% (2000); Median home value: $108,300 (2000); Median rent: $213 per month (2000); Median age of housing: 60+ years (2000).
Transportation: Commute to work: 87.1% car, 0.0% public transportation, 3.6% walk, 9.4% work from home (2000); Travel time to work: 46.0% less than 15 minutes, 42.1% 15 to 30 minutes, 1.6% 30 to 45 minutes, 2.4% 45 to 60 minutes, 7.9% 60 minutes or more (2000)

LYND (city). Covers a land area of 0.419 square miles and a water area of 0 square miles. Located at 44.38° N. Lat.; 95.89° W. Long. Elevation is 1,320 feet.
Population: 346 (2000); Race: 82.3% White, 1.3% Black, 3.8% Asian, 0.0% American Indian and Alaska Native, 15.1% Hispanic of any race, 0.6% two or more races (2000); Density: 826.1 persons per square mile (2000); Age: 23.0% under 18, 11.0% over 64 (2000); Marriage status: 31.7% never married, 47.1% now married, 8.5% widowed, 12.7% divorced (2000); Foreign born: 10.7% (2000); Ancestry (includes multiple ancestries): 40.4% German, 20.2% Other groups, 10.4% Norwegian, 7.9% Irish, 6.9% Belgian (2000).
Economy: Single-family building permits issued: 1 (2001) / 0 (2000); Multi-family building permits issued: 0 (2001) / 0 (2000); Employment by occupation: 8.8% management, 5.3% professional, 16.4% services, 21.6% sales, 1.2% farming, 11.1% construction, 35.7% production (2000).
Income: Per capita income: $15,026 (2000); Median household income: $36,125 (2000); Poverty rate: 15.7% (2000).
Taxes: Total city taxes per capita: $115 (1997); City property taxes per capita: $105 (1997).
Education: High school graduation rate: 78.5% (2000); College graduation rate: 8.5% (2000).

School District(s)

Lynd (PK-08)
2000 Enrollment: 94 507-865-4404
Housing: Homeownership rate: 69.6% (2000); Median home value: $58,900 (2000); Median rent: $313 per month (2000); Median age of housing: 45 years (2000).
Transportation: Commute to work: 97.0% car, 0.0% public transportation, 2.4% walk, 0.6% work from home (2000); Travel time to work: 52.4% less than 15 minutes, 44.0% 15 to 30 minutes, 3.0% 30 to 45 minutes, 0.0% 45 to 60 minutes, 0.6% 60 minutes or more (2000)

LYND (township). Covers a land area of 35.880 square miles and a water area of 0.044 square miles. Located at 44.40° N. Lat.; 95.88° W. Long. Elevation is 1,320 feet.
Population: 471 (2000); Race: 98.8% White, 0.0% Black, 0.4% Asian, 0.0% American Indian and Alaska Native, 2.1% Hispanic of any race, 0.8% two or more races (2000); Density: 13.1 persons per square mile (2000); Age: 31.6% under 18, 8.9% over 64 (2000); Marriage status: 21.9% never married, 72.8% now married, 1.1% widowed, 4.3% divorced (2000); Foreign born: 1.4% (2000); Ancestry (includes multiple ancestries): 41.1% German, 18.6% Belgian, 16.7% Norwegian, 15.7% Swedish, 9.7% Irish (2000).

Economy: Agriculture: dairying; poultry, livestock; grain, soybeans. Employment by occupation: 22.9% management, 21.2% professional, 12.7% services, 20.9% sales, 1.0% farming, 6.5% construction, 14.7% production (2000).
Income: Per capita income: $21,921 (2000); Median household income: $57,083 (2000); Poverty rate: 0.8% (2000).
Taxes: Total city taxes per capita: $34 (1997); City property taxes per capita: $34 (1997).
Education: High school graduation rate: 94.7% (2000); College graduation rate: 28.1% (2000).
Housing: Homeownership rate: 88.0% (2000); Median home value: $114,700 (2000); Median rent: $106 per month (2000); Median age of housing: 30 years (2000).
Transportation: Commute to work: 87.8% car, 0.0% public transportation, 1.0% walk, 11.2% work from home (2000); Travel time to work: 59.8% less than 15 minutes, 35.0% 15 to 30 minutes, 3.1% 30 to 45 minutes, 2.0% 45 to 60 minutes, 0.0% 60 minutes or more (2000)

LYONS (township). Covers a land area of 35.184 square miles and a water area of 0.295 square miles. Located at 44.33° N. Lat.; 95.90° W. Long.
Population: 208 (2000); Race: 100.0% White, 0.0% Black, 0.0% Asian, 0.0% American Indian and Alaska Native, 0.0% Hispanic of any race, 0.0% two or more races (2000); Density: 5.9 persons per square mile (2000); Age: 29.2% under 18, 9.7% over 64 (2000); Marriage status: 17.6% never married, 73.3% now married, 1.8% widowed, 7.3% divorced (2000); Foreign born: 0.0% (2000); Ancestry (includes multiple ancestries): 35.6% German, 27.8% Norwegian, 11.6% Swedish, 10.6% Belgian, 10.2% Danish (2000).
Economy: Employment by occupation: 25.7% management, 7.6% professional, 17.1% services, 20.0% sales, 0.0% farming, 16.2% construction, 13.3% production (2000).
Income: Per capita income: $13,625 (2000); Median household income: $36,250 (2000); Poverty rate: 6.5% (2000).
Taxes: Total city taxes per capita: $105 (1997); City property taxes per capita: $105 (1997).
Education: High school graduation rate: 90.8% (2000); College graduation rate: 5.6% (2000).
Housing: Homeownership rate: 89.2% (2000); Median home value: $95,000 (2000); Median rent: $225 per month (2000); Median age of housing: 58 years (2000).
Transportation: Commute to work: 80.6% car, 1.9% public transportation, 0.0% walk, 15.5% work from home (2000); Travel time to work: 24.1% less than 15 minutes, 54.0% 15 to 30 minutes, 12.6% 30 to 45 minutes, 2.3% 45 to 60 minutes, 6.9% 60 minutes or more (2000)

MARSHALL (city). Covers a land area of 8.286 square miles and a water area of 0 square miles. Located at 44.44° N. Lat.; 95.78° W. Long. Elevation is 1,174 feet.
History: Marshall developed as the center of a prosperous farming area. Industries here included a roller mill, hatcheries, a creamery, and a wholesale fruit company.
Population: 12,735 (2000); Race: 90.5% White, 2.6% Black, 1.8% Asian, 0.4% American Indian and Alaska Native, 5.4% Hispanic of any race, 1.5% two or more races (2000); Density: 1,537.0 persons per square mile (2000); Age: 23.8% under 18, 12.4% over 64 (2000); Marriage status: 35.5% never married, 51.6% now married, 7.4% widowed, 5.5% divorced (2000); Foreign born: 6.6% (2000); Ancestry (includes multiple ancestries): 39.5% German, 17.7% Norwegian, 10.2% Other groups, 9.5% Irish, 8.2% Belgian (2000).
Vital Statistics: Birth rate: 151.6 per 10,000 population (1998)
Economy: Single-family building permits issued: 46 (2001) / 35 (2000); Multi-family building permits issued: 32 (2001) / 26 (2000); Employment by occupation: 14.9% management, 17.2% professional, 14.4% services, 28.0% sales, 0.4% farming, 6.8% construction, 18.2% production (2000).
Income: Per capita income: $18,588 (2000); Median household income: $37,950 (2000); Poverty rate: 12.4% (2000).
Taxes: Total city taxes per capita: $326 (2000); City property taxes per capita: $297 (2000).
Education: High school graduation rate: 82.7% (2000); College graduation rate: 28.6% (2000).

School District(s)

Marshall (PK-12)
2000 Enrollment: 2,439 507-537-6924

Four-year College(s)

Southwest State University (Public)
2001 Enrollment: 5,056 507-537-7021
2001 Tuition: In-state $3,067; Out-of-state $3,067

Housing: Homeownership rate: 56.7% (2000); Median home value: $92,700 (2000); Median rent: $422 per month (2000); Median age of housing: 29 years (2000).
Hospitals: Weiner Memorial Medical Center (49 beds)
Newspapers: Marshall Independent (6 x week); Country Spirit (1 x week)
Transportation: Commute to work: 87.4% car, 2.4% public transportation, 7.1% walk, 2.3% work from home (2000); Travel time to work: 83.6% less than 15 minutes, 11.4% 15 to 30 minutes, 2.6% 30 to 45 minutes, 1.0% 45 to 60 minutes, 1.3% 60 minutes or more (2000)

Additional Information Contacts

Marshall Area Chamber of Commerce 507-532-4484
Marshall Convention Bureau 507-537-1865

MINNEOTA (city). Aka Minnesota. Covers a land area of 1.450 square miles and a water area of 0 square miles. Located at 44.56° N. Lat.; 95.98° W. Long. Elevation is 1,168 feet.
History: Settled 1868, incorporated 1881.
Population: 1,449 (2000); Race: 97.9% White, 0.0% Black, 0.3% Asian, 0.0% American Indian and Alaska Native, 4.0% Hispanic of any race, 0.4% two or more races (2000); Density: 999.5 persons per square mile (2000); Age: 23.5% under 18, 26.2% over 64 (2000); Marriage status: 19.5% never married, 63.5% now married, 10.8% widowed, 6.2% divorced (2000); Foreign born: 2.5% (2000); Ancestry (includes multiple ancestries): 42.8% German, 23.6% Belgian, 18.5% Norwegian, 8.1% Polish, 5.0% Dutch (2000).
Economy: Grain; livestock, poultry; dairying. Manufacturing: fertilizers, transformers, trusses and rafters. Single-family building permits issued: 0 (2001) / 5 (2000); Multi-family building permits issued: 0 (2001) / 4 (2000); Employment by occupation: 16.1% management, 14.9% professional, 17.4% services, 19.2% sales, 2.4% farming, 10.8% construction, 19.1% production (2000).
Income: Per capita income: $17,390 (2000); Median household income: $36,375 (2000); Poverty rate: 8.3% (2000).
Taxes: Total city taxes per capita: $131 (1997); City property taxes per capita: $129 (1997).
Education: High school graduation rate: 72.8% (2000); College graduation rate: 15.1% (2000).

School District(s)

Minneota (PK-12)
2000 Enrollment: 526 507-872-6532

Housing: Homeownership rate: 76.6% (2000); Median home value: $65,800 (2000); Median rent: $320 per month (2000); Median age of housing: 44 years (2000).
Newspapers: Minneota Mascot (1 x week)
Transportation: Commute to work: 88.4% car, 0.0% public transportation, 7.6% walk, 3.7% work from home (2000); Travel time to work: 45.4% less than 15 minutes, 47.8% 15 to 30 minutes, 3.8% 30 to 45 minutes, 0.6% 45 to 60 minutes, 2.4% 60 minutes or more (2000)

MONROE (township). Covers a land area of 33.892 square miles and a water area of 0.295 square miles. Located at 44.23° N. Lat.; 95.64° W. Long.
Population: 242 (2000); Race: 100.0% White, 0.0% Black, 0.0% Asian, 0.0% American Indian and Alaska Native, 0.8% Hispanic of any race, 0.0% two or more races (2000); Density: 7.1 persons per square mile (2000); Age: 30.9% under 18, 13.1% over 64 (2000); Marriage status: 21.1% never married, 73.4% now married, 3.0% widowed, 2.5% divorced (2000); Foreign born: 0.0% (2000); Ancestry (includes multiple ancestries): 42.9% German, 22.4% Norwegian, 15.1% Belgian, 7.3% Swedish, 6.6% United States or American (2000).
Economy: Employment by occupation: 26.9% management, 13.1% professional, 10.0% services, 17.7% sales, 3.1% farming, 8.5% construction, 20.8% production (2000).
Income: Per capita income: $18,952 (2000); Median household income: $43,542 (2000); Poverty rate: 3.1% (2000).
Taxes: Total city taxes per capita: $117 (1997); City property taxes per capita: $117 (1997).
Education: High school graduation rate: 84.7% (2000); College graduation rate: 17.2% (2000).
Housing: Homeownership rate: 79.5% (2000); Median home value: $90,000 (2000); Median rent: $250 per month (2000); Median age of housing: 51 years (2000).
Transportation: Commute to work: 92.8% car, 0.0% public transportation, 1.6% walk, 5.6% work from home (2000); Travel time to work: 38.1% less than 15 minutes, 24.6% 15 to 30 minutes, 37.3% 30 to 45 minutes, 0.0% 45 to 60 minutes, 0.0% 60 minutes or more (2000)

NORDLAND (township). Covers a land area of 35.105 square miles and a water area of 0 square miles. Located at 44.50° N. Lat.; 96.01° W. Long.
Population: 251 (2000); Race: 100.0% White, 0.0% Black, 0.0% Asian, 0.0% American Indian and Alaska Native, 0.0% Hispanic of any race, 0.0% two or more races (2000); Density: 7.1 persons per square mile (2000); Age: 42.1% under 18, 4.3% over 64 (2000); Marriage status: 28.4% never married, 66.8% now married, 1.1% widowed, 3.7% divorced (2000); Foreign born: 0.0% (2000); Ancestry (includes multiple ancestries): 41.1% Norwegian, 31.4% Belgian, 26.8% German, 8.2% Dutch, 8.2% Irish (2000).
Economy: Employment by occupation: 30.6% management, 9.0% professional, 20.1% services, 12.5% sales, 4.2% farming, 6.9% construction, 16.7% production (2000).
Income: Per capita income: $14,435 (2000); Median household income: $41,071 (2000); Poverty rate: 10.7% (2000).
Taxes: Total city taxes per capita: $83 (1997); City property taxes per capita: $83 (1997).
Education: High school graduation rate: 92.4% (2000); College graduation rate: 14.6% (2000).
Housing: Homeownership rate: 91.7% (2000); Median home value: $78,800 (2000); Median rent: $200 per month (2000); Median age of housing: 60 years (2000).
Transportation: Commute to work: 78.9% car, 0.0% public transportation, 4.9% walk, 16.2% work from home (2000); Travel time to work: 47.9% less than 15 minutes, 36.1% 15 to 30 minutes, 9.2% 30 to 45 minutes, 1.7% 45 to 60 minutes, 5.0% 60 minutes or more (2000)

ROCK LAKE (township). Covers a land area of 33.122 square miles and a water area of 1.481 square miles. Located at 44.24° N. Lat.; 95.90° W. Long.
Population: 282 (2000); Race: 97.2% White, 1.1% Black, 0.0% Asian, 0.0% American Indian and Alaska Native, 0.0% Hispanic of any race, 1.8% two or more races (2000); Density: 8.5 persons per square mile (2000); Age: 21.5% under 18, 16.5% over 64 (2000); Marriage status: 22.8% never married, 66.2% now married, 5.9% widowed, 5.1% divorced (2000); Foreign born: 0.0% (2000); Ancestry (includes multiple ancestries): 45.8% German, 12.3% Norwegian, 12.3% Swedish, 11.3% United States or American, 9.5% Irish (2000).
Economy: Employment by occupation: 12.0% management, 12.0% professional, 14.4% services, 22.2% sales, 4.8% farming, 10.2% construction, 24.6% production (2000).
Income: Per capita income: $19,008 (2000); Median household income: $40,000 (2000); Poverty rate: 6.3% (2000).
Taxes: Total city taxes per capita: $112 (1997); City property taxes per capita: $112 (1997).
Education: High school graduation rate: 82.7% (2000); College graduation rate: 12.2% (2000).
Housing: Homeownership rate: 86.9% (2000); Median home value: $85,000 (2000); Median rent: $325 per month (2000); Median age of housing: 60+ years (2000).
Transportation: Commute to work: 85.0% car, 0.0% public transportation, 1.2% walk, 13.8% work from home (2000); Travel time to work: 25.7% less than 15 minutes, 43.1% 15 to 30 minutes, 25.0% 30 to 45 minutes, 3.5% 45 to 60 minutes, 2.8% 60 minutes or more (2000)

RUSSELL (city). Covers a land area of 0.894 square miles and a water area of 0.050 square miles. Located at 44.31° N. Lat.; 95.95° W. Long. Elevation is 1,527 feet.
Population: 371 (2000); Race: 98.9% White, 0.0% Black, 0.0% Asian, 0.0% American Indian and Alaska Native, 5.3% Hispanic of any race, 0.0% two or more races (2000); Density: 415.0 persons per square mile (2000); Age: 30.1% under 18, 17.7% over 64 (2000); Marriage status: 24.0% never married, 58.0% now married, 11.7% widowed, 6.4% divorced (2000); Foreign born: 2.4% (2000); Ancestry (includes multiple ancestries): 43.3% German, 11.3% Norwegian, 11.3% Polish, 9.2% Swedish, 8.7% English (2000).
Economy: Grain, soybeans, alfalfa; poultry, cattle, sheep, hogs; dairying. Single-family building permits issued: 0 (2001) / 0 (2000); Multi-family building permits issued: 0 (2001) / 0 (2000); Employment by occupation: 11.8% management, 8.4% professional, 12.9% services, 20.2% sales, 0.0% farming, 15.2% construction, 31.5% production (2000).
Income: Per capita income: $14,767 (2000); Median household income: $32,045 (2000); Poverty rate: 9.8% (2000).
Taxes: Total city taxes per capita: $104 (1997); City property taxes per capita: $104 (1997).
Education: High school graduation rate: 76.7% (2000); College graduation rate: 10.1% (2000).

School District(s)

Russell (06-08)
2000 Enrollment: 162 507-823-4371
Housing: Homeownership rate: 86.3% (2000); Median home value: $55,600 (2000); Median rent: $258 per month (2000); Median age of housing: 54 years (2000).
Transportation: Commute to work: 97.7% car, 1.1% public transportation, 1.1% walk, 0.0% work from home (2000); Travel time to work: 18.2% less than 15 minutes, 58.0% 15 to 30 minutes, 11.4% 30 to 45 minutes, 0.0% 45 to 60 minutes, 12.5% 60 minutes or more (2000)

SHELBURNE (township). Covers a land area of 34.886 square miles and a water area of 1.046 square miles. Located at 44.23° N. Lat.; 96.02° W. Long.
Population: 180 (2000); Race: 98.8% White, 0.0% Black, 0.0% Asian, 0.0% American Indian and Alaska Native, 0.0% Hispanic of any race, 1.2% two or more races (2000); Density: 5.2 persons per square mile (2000); Age: 19.8% under 18, 21.6% over 64 (2000); Marriage status: 16.4% never married, 70.0% now married, 6.4% widowed, 7.1% divorced (2000); Foreign born: 0.0% (2000); Ancestry (includes multiple ancestries): 39.5% German, 16.0% Danish, 14.8% Dutch, 13.0% Swedish, 10.5% Norwegian (2000).
Economy: Employment by occupation: 43.3% management, 12.2% professional, 6.7% services, 23.3% sales, 0.0% farming, 3.3% construction, 11.1% production (2000).
Income: Per capita income: $16,171 (2000); Median household income: $32,917 (2000); Poverty rate: 4.3% (2000).
Taxes: Total city taxes per capita: $31 (1997); City property taxes per capita: $31 (1997).
Education: High school graduation rate: 83.1% (2000); College graduation rate: 11.0% (2000).
Housing: Homeownership rate: 84.3% (2000); Median home value: $52,500 (2000); Median rent: $325 per month (2000); Median age of housing: 60+ years (2000).
Transportation: Commute to work: 70.0% car, 0.0% public transportation, 0.0% walk, 30.0% work from home (2000); Travel time to work: 33.3% less than 15 minutes, 31.7% 15 to 30 minutes, 28.6% 30 to 45 minutes, 0.0% 45 to 60 minutes, 6.3% 60 minutes or more (2000)

SODUS (township). Covers a land area of 36.327 square miles and a water area of 0.020 square miles. Located at 44.32° N. Lat.; 95.78° W. Long.
Population: 282 (2000); Race: 99.2% White, 0.0% Black, 0.0% Asian, 0.0% American Indian and Alaska Native, 0.0% Hispanic of any race, 0.8% two or more races (2000); Density: 7.8 persons per square mile (2000); Age: 25.2% under 18, 12.2% over 64 (2000); Marriage status: 12.6% never married, 78.3% now married, 4.8% widowed, 4.3% divorced (2000); Foreign born: 1.1% (2000); Ancestry (includes multiple ancestries): 43.9% German, 23.7% Belgian, 11.1% Norwegian, 9.5% French (except Basque), 6.9% Swedish (2000).
Economy: Employment by occupation: 28.6% management, 11.6% professional, 4.1% services, 23.8% sales, 4.1% farming, 12.2% construction, 15.6% production (2000).
Income: Per capita income: $17,986 (2000); Median household income: $44,063 (2000); Poverty rate: 6.1% (2000).
Taxes: Total city taxes per capita: $59 (1997); City property taxes per capita: $59 (1997).
Education: High school graduation rate: 84.2% (2000); College graduation rate: 12.1% (2000).
Housing: Homeownership rate: 91.3% (2000); Median home value: $133,300 (2000); Median rent: $175 per month (2000); Median age of housing: 55 years (2000).
Transportation: Commute to work: 75.9% car, 0.0% public transportation, 4.8% walk, 15.9% work from home (2000); Travel time to work: 32.0% less than 15 minutes, 54.1% 15 to 30 minutes, 10.7% 30 to 45 minutes, 0.0% 45 to 60 minutes, 3.3% 60 minutes or more (2000)

STANLEY (township). Covers a land area of 35.155 square miles and a water area of 0 square miles. Located at 44.49° N. Lat.; 95.64° W. Long.
Population: 254 (2000); Race: 98.9% White, 0.0% Black, 1.1% Asian, 0.0% American Indian and Alaska Native, 0.0% Hispanic of any race, 0.0% two or more races (2000); Density: 7.2 persons per square mile (2000); Age: 32.5% under 18, 11.2% over 64 (2000); Marriage status: 20.4% never married, 76.7% now married, 1.9% widowed, 1.0% divorced (2000); Foreign born: 2.2% (2000); Ancestry (includes multiple ancestries): 42.2% German, 28.2%

Belgian, 17.0% Norwegian, 7.9% French (except Basque), 7.6% English (2000).
Economy: Employment by occupation: 30.5% management, 10.6% professional, 11.3% services, 19.2% sales, 4.6% farming, 6.0% construction, 17.9% production (2000).
Income: Per capita income: $18,009 (2000); Median household income: $56,250 (2000); Poverty rate: 2.2% (2000).
Taxes: Total city taxes per capita: $48 (1997); City property taxes per capita: $48 (1997).
Education: High school graduation rate: 86.4% (2000); College graduation rate: 17.9% (2000).
Housing: Homeownership rate: 84.1% (2000); Median home value: $110,000 (2000); Median rent: $342 per month (2000); Median age of housing: 60+ years (2000).
Transportation: Commute to work: 79.1% car, 0.0% public transportation, 5.4% walk, 15.5% work from home (2000); Travel time to work: 50.4% less than 15 minutes, 44.0% 15 to 30 minutes, 5.6% 30 to 45 minutes, 0.0% 45 to 60 minutes, 0.0% 60 minutes or more (2000)

TAUNTON (city). Covers a land area of 1.002 square miles and a water area of 0 square miles. Located at 44.59° N. Lat.; 96.06° W. Long. Elevation is 1,175 feet.
Population: 207 (2000); Race: 100.0% White, 0.0% Black, 0.0% Asian, 0.0% American Indian and Alaska Native, 0.0% Hispanic of any race, 0.0% two or more races (2000); Density: 206.5 persons per square mile (2000); Age: 17.1% under 18, 41.7% over 64 (2000); Marriage status: 19.9% never married, 33.1% now married, 41.7% widowed, 5.3% divorced (2000); Foreign born: 2.9% (2000); Ancestry (includes multiple ancestries): 30.9% German, 19.4% Belgian, 18.3% Swedish, 16.6% Norwegian, 12.0% Irish (2000).
Economy: Agriculture: alfalfa; dairying; livestock. Manufacturing of feeds. Single-family building permits issued: 0 (2001) / 0 (2000); Multi-family building permits issued: 0 (2001) / 0 (2000); Employment by occupation: 15.0% management, 6.7% professional, 16.7% services, 15.0% sales, 0.0% farming, 18.3% construction, 28.3% production (2000).
Income: Per capita income: $14,658 (2000); Median household income: $23,125 (2000); Poverty rate: 25.0% (2000).
Taxes: Total city taxes per capita: $133 (1997); City property taxes per capita: $116 (1997).
Education: High school graduation rate: 70.6% (2000); College graduation rate: 5.9% (2000).
Housing: Homeownership rate: 88.1% (2000); Median home value: $29,200 (2000); Median rent: $263 per month (2000); Median age of housing: 59 years (2000).
Transportation: Commute to work: 86.7% car, 0.0% public transportation, 3.3% walk, 10.0% work from home (2000); Travel time to work: 29.6% less than 15 minutes, 51.9% 15 to 30 minutes, 13.0% 30 to 45 minutes, 5.6% 45 to 60 minutes, 0.0% 60 minutes or more (2000)

TRACY (city). Covers a land area of 2.170 square miles and a water area of 0.063 square miles. Located at 44.23° N. Lat.; 95.61° W. Long. Elevation is 1,398 feet.
History: Tracy was named for a president of the Chicago & North Western Railway. Its annual celebration of Box Car Day also commemorated its railroad heritage.
Population: 2,268 (2000); Race: 86.6% White, 0.4% Black, 7.6% Asian, 1.1% American Indian and Alaska Native, 4.8% Hispanic of any race, 0.8% two or more races (2000); Density: 1,045.2 persons per square mile (2000); Age: 27.5% under 18, 26.2% over 64 (2000); Marriage status: 20.0% never married, 56.3% now married, 15.2% widowed, 8.4% divorced (2000); Foreign born: 6.3% (2000); Ancestry (includes multiple ancestries): 33.3% German, 16.6% Norwegian, 12.9% Other groups, 8.2% Irish, 6.9% Swedish (2000).
Economy: Single-family building permits issued: 4 (2001) / 1 (2000); Multi-family building permits issued: 0 (2001) / 0 (2000); Employment by occupation: 9.3% management, 16.2% professional, 25.9% services, 20.5% sales, 0.4% farming, 7.6% construction, 20.0% production (2000).
Income: Per capita income: $15,574 (2000); Median household income: $31,356 (2000); Poverty rate: 13.6% (2000).
Taxes: Total city taxes per capita: $191 (2000); City property taxes per capita: $182 (2000).
Education: High school graduation rate: 76.2% (2000); College graduation rate: 14.5% (2000).

School District(s)

Tracy (PK-12)
2000 Enrollment: 856 507-629-5500

Housing: Homeownership rate: 75.7% (2000); Median home value: $46,800 (2000); Median rent: $248 per month (2000); Median age of housing: 48 years (2000).
Hospitals: Tracy Area Medical Services (37 beds)
Newspapers: Tracy Headlight-Herald (1 x week)
Transportation: Commute to work: 91.5% car, 0.0% public transportation, 5.0% walk, 3.2% work from home (2000); Travel time to work: 59.9% less than 15 minutes, 14.5% 15 to 30 minutes, 20.3% 30 to 45 minutes, 1.3% 45 to 60 minutes, 4.1% 60 minutes or more (2000)
Additional Information Contacts
Tracy Chamber of Commerce 507-629-4021

VALLERS (township). Covers a land area of 36.349 square miles and a water area of 0 square miles. Located at 44.57° N. Lat.; 95.78° W. Long.
Population: 243 (2000); Race: 99.2% White, 0.0% Black, 0.0% Asian, 0.0% American Indian and Alaska Native, 0.0% Hispanic of any race, 0.8% two or more races (2000); Density: 6.7 persons per square mile (2000); Age: 28.9% under 18, 7.2% over 64 (2000); Marriage status: 24.9% never married, 68.4% now married, 3.1% widowed, 3.6% divorced (2000); Foreign born: 0.0% (2000); Ancestry (includes multiple ancestries): 32.9% German, 29.3% Norwegian, 25.3% Belgian, 9.6% Dutch, 9.2% French (except Basque) (2000).
Economy: Employment by occupation: 19.6% management, 5.4% professional, 16.9% services, 31.8% sales, 3.4% farming, 15.5% construction, 7.4% production (2000).
Income: Per capita income: $17,218 (2000); Median household income: $46,250 (2000); Poverty rate: 4.0% (2000).
Taxes: Total city taxes per capita: $73 (1997); City property taxes per capita: $73 (1997).
Education: High school graduation rate: 90.2% (2000); College graduation rate: 7.0% (2000).
Housing: Homeownership rate: 71.8% (2000); Median home value: $88,800 (2000); Median rent: $288 per month (2000); Median age of housing: 60+ years (2000).
Transportation: Commute to work: 76.4% car, 0.0% public transportation, 4.7% walk, 17.6% work from home (2000); Travel time to work: 27.0% less than 15 minutes, 60.7% 15 to 30 minutes, 4.1% 30 to 45 minutes, 2.5% 45 to 60 minutes, 5.7% 60 minutes or more (2000)

WESTERHEIM (township). Covers a land area of 36.345 square miles and a water area of 0.006 square miles. Located at 44.59° N. Lat.; 95.90° W. Long.
Population: 286 (2000); Race: 96.2% White, 0.0% Black, 0.0% Asian, 0.0% American Indian and Alaska Native, 3.8% Hispanic of any race, 3.8% two or more races (2000); Density: 7.9 persons per square mile (2000); Age: 32.5% under 18, 9.2% over 64 (2000); Marriage status: 27.8% never married, 68.2% now married, 1.8% widowed, 2.2% divorced (2000); Foreign born: 1.4% (2000); Ancestry (includes multiple ancestries): 37.3% Belgian, 28.4% Norwegian, 21.9% German, 9.9% Swedish, 6.5% Polish (2000).
Economy: Employment by occupation: 30.1% management, 9.8% professional, 21.7% services, 15.4% sales, 2.8% farming, 2.8% construction, 17.5% production (2000).
Income: Per capita income: $15,288 (2000); Median household income: $48,393 (2000); Poverty rate: 9.0% (2000).
Taxes: Total city taxes per capita: $57 (1997); City property taxes per capita: $57 (1997).
Education: High school graduation rate: 90.4% (2000); College graduation rate: 12.9% (2000).
Housing: Homeownership rate: 73.7% (2000); Median home value: $56,700 (2000); Median rent: $308 per month (2000); Median age of housing: 55 years (2000).
Transportation: Commute to work: 71.3% car, 0.0% public transportation, 3.5% walk, 25.2% work from home (2000); Travel time to work: 47.7% less than 15 minutes, 42.1% 15 to 30 minutes, 6.5% 30 to 45 minutes, 0.0% 45 to 60 minutes, 3.7% 60 minutes or more (2000)

Mahnomen County

Located in northwestern Minnesota; drained by the Wild Rice River. Covers a land area of 556.10 square miles, a water area of 26.90 square miles, and is located in the Central Time Zone. The county government was organized in 1906. County seat is Mahnomen.

Weather Station: Mahnomen 1 W Elevation: 1,200 feet

	Jan	Feb	Mar	Apr	May	Jun	Jul	Aug	Sep	Oct	Nov	Dec
High	15	23	35	54	70	77	81	80	70	56	34	21
Low	-5	2	16	31	44	53	57	55	45	34	18	3
Precip	0.9	0.6	1.1	1.6	2.5	4.2	3.3	3.1	2.4	2.3	1.0	0.7
Snow	10.2	6.5	7.5	2.6	tr	0.0	0.0	0.0	tr	1.4	7.9	7.6

High and Low temperatures in degrees Fahrenheit; Precipitation and Snow in inches

Population: 5,190 (2000); Race: 63.1% White, 0.1% Black, 0.9% Asian, 26.6% American Indian and Alaska Native, 1.0% Hispanic of any race, 8.7% two or more races (2000); Density: 9.3 persons per square mile (2000); Age: 29.4% under 18, 16.9% over 64 (2000).
Religion: Five largest groups: 39.4% Catholic Church, 18.0% Evangelical Lutheran Church in America, 5.1% Episcopal Church, 1.3% Lutheran Church—Missouri Synod, 1.2% United Church of Christ (2000).
Economy: Unemployment rate: 5.0% (11/2002); Total civilian labor force: 2,423 (11/2002); Leading industries: Companies that employ more than 1,000 persons: 0 (2000); Companies that employ more than 100 persons: 1 (2000); Farms: 341 totaling 189,927 acres (1997); Minority business ownership rate: 0.0% (1997); Women business ownership rate: 0.0% (1997); Retail sales per capita: $5,640 (1997). Single-family building permits issued: 2 (2001) / 3 (2000); Multi-family building permits issued: 8 (2001) / 0 (2000).
Income: Per capita income: $13,438 (2000); Median household income: $30,053 (2000); Poverty rate: 16.7% (2000); Bankruptcy rate: 1.56% (2001).
Taxes: Total county taxes per capita: $550 (1997); County property taxes per capita: $549 (1997).
Education: High school graduation rate: 75.0% (2000); College graduation rate: 12.4% (2000).
Housing: Homeownership rate: 77.3% (2000); Median home value: $53,100 (2000); Median rent: $238 per month (2000); Median age of housing: 39 years (2000).
Health: Birth rate: 148.4 per 10,000 population (1998); Age adjusted death rate: 100.3 per 10,000 population (1999); Age adjusted cancer mortality rate: 258.3 (Unreliable figure as per CDC) deaths per 100,000 population (1999). Number of physicians: 7.7 per 10,000 population (1999); Number of hospital beds: 127.2 per 10,000 population (1999).
Elections: 2000 Presidential election results: 41.4% Gore, 50.5% Bush, 4.3% Nader, 3.2% Buchanan
National and State Parks: Beaulife State Wildlife Management Area; Bejou State Wildlife Management Area; Budde Meadow State Wildlife Managment Area; Dittmer State Wildlife Management Area; Foot State Wildlife Management Area; Gregory State Wildlife Management Area; Killian State Wildlife Management Area; Little Elbow Lake State Park; Loncrace State Wildlife Management Area; Mahgre State Wildlife Management Area; Rush Lake State Wildlife Management Area; Vanose State Wildlife Management Area; Wambach State Wildlife Management Area; Warren Lake State Wildlife Management Area; Waubun State Wildlife Management Area
Additional Information Contacts
Mahnomen County Government Offices 218-935-5669

Mahnomen County Communities

BEAULIEU (township). Covers a land area of 33.491 square miles and a water area of 2.135 square miles. Located at 47.39° N. Lat.; 95.74° W. Long. Elevation is 1,310 feet.
Population: 108 (2000); Race: 61.3% White, 0.0% Black, 0.0% Asian, 36.3% American Indian and Alaska Native, 2.4% Hispanic of any race, 2.4% two or more races (2000); Density: 3.2 persons per square mile (2000); Age: 24.2% under 18, 6.5% over 64 (2000); Marriage status: 35.2% never married, 53.3% now married, 1.9% widowed, 9.5% divorced (2000); Foreign born: 2.4% (2000); Ancestry (includes multiple ancestries): 43.5% Other groups, 34.7% German, 8.1% Norwegian, 4.8% Czech, 4.0% French (except Basque) (2000).
Economy: Employment by occupation: 33.9% management, 6.8% professional, 28.8% services, 11.9% sales, 6.8% farming, 8.5% construction, 3.4% production (2000).
Income: Per capita income: $19,659 (2000); Median household income: $37,500 (2000); Poverty rate: 14.5% (2000).
Taxes: Total city taxes per capita: $67 (1997); City property taxes per capita: $67 (1997).
Education: High school graduation rate: 71.2% (2000); College graduation rate: 2.7% (2000).
Housing: Homeownership rate: 76.2% (2000); Median home value: $24,400 (2000); Median rent: $200 per month (2000); Median age of housing: 52 years (2000).
Transportation: Commute to work: 54.2% car, 0.0% public transportation, 25.4% walk, 20.3% work from home (2000); Travel time to work: 21.3% less than 15 minutes, 51.1% 15 to 30 minutes, 12.8% 30 to 45 minutes, 0.0% 45 to 60 minutes, 14.9% 60 minutes or more (2000)

BEJOU (city). Covers a land area of 0.376 square miles and a water area of 0 square miles. Located at 47.44° N. Lat.; 95.97° W. Long. Elevation is 1,222 feet.
Population: 94 (2000); Race: 90.7% White, 0.0% Black, 2.8% Asian, 4.6% American Indian and Alaska Native, 0.0% Hispanic of any race, 1.9% two or more races (2000); Density: 250.1 persons per square mile (2000); Age: 40.7% under 18, 6.5% over 64 (2000); Marriage status: 39.5% never married, 54.3% now married, 6.2% widowed, 0.0% divorced (2000); Foreign born: 0.9% (2000); Ancestry (includes multiple ancestries): 53.7% Norwegian, 24.1% Dutch, 20.4% Other groups, 11.1% Irish, 7.4% German (2000).
Economy: Employment by occupation: 18.6% management, 7.0% professional, 18.6% services, 30.2% sales, 4.7% farming, 4.7% construction, 16.3% production (2000).
Income: Per capita income: $10,210 (2000); Median household income: $32,750 (2000); Poverty rate: 12.0% (2000).
Taxes: Total city taxes per capita: $38 (1997); City property taxes per capita: $19 (1997).
Education: High school graduation rate: 81.1% (2000); College graduation rate: 0.0% (2000).
Housing: Homeownership rate: 71.4% (2000); Median home value: $26,500 (2000); Median rent: $133 per month (2000); Median age of housing: 50 years (2000).
Transportation: Commute to work: 81.4% car, 7.0% public transportation, 11.6% walk, 0.0% work from home (2000); Travel time to work: 48.8% less than 15 minutes, 44.2% 15 to 30 minutes, 0.0% 30 to 45 minutes, 0.0% 45 to 60 minutes, 7.0% 60 minutes or more (2000)

BEJOU (township). Covers a land area of 37.333 square miles and a water area of 0.026 square miles. Located at 47.45° N. Lat.; 95.98° W. Long. Elevation is 1,222 feet.
Population: 98 (2000); Race: 81.0% White, 0.0% Black, 0.0% Asian, 4.8% American Indian and Alaska Native, 0.0% Hispanic of any race, 14.3% two or more races (2000); Density: 2.6 persons per square mile (2000); Age: 27.4% under 18, 6.0% over 64 (2000); Marriage status: 34.3% never married, 49.3% now married, 3.0% widowed, 13.4% divorced (2000); Foreign born: 0.0% (2000); Ancestry (includes multiple ancestries): 44.0% Norwegian, 28.6% German, 16.7% Dutch, 14.3% Irish, 10.7% Other groups (2000).
Economy: Grain, wild rice, alfalfa; livestock. Employment by occupation: 25.6% management, 17.9% professional, 20.5% services, 12.8% sales, 0.0% farming, 12.8% construction, 10.3% production (2000).
Income: Per capita income: $13,082 (2000); Median household income: $30,938 (2000); Poverty rate: 4.8% (2000).
Taxes: Total city taxes per capita: $58 (1997); City property taxes per capita: $58 (1997).
Education: High school graduation rate: 75.9% (2000); College graduation rate: 7.4% (2000).
Housing: Homeownership rate: 75.8% (2000); Median home value: $17,500 (2000); Median rent: $375 per month (2000); Median age of housing: 60+ years (2000).
Transportation: Commute to work: 94.7% car, 0.0% public transportation, 0.0% walk, 5.3% work from home (2000); Travel time to work: 30.6% less than 15 minutes, 44.4% 15 to 30 minutes, 13.9% 30 to 45 minutes, 5.6% 45 to 60 minutes, 5.6% 60 minutes or more (2000)

CHIEF (township). Covers a land area of 34.638 square miles and a water area of 1.513 square miles. Located at 47.34° N. Lat.; 95.84° W. Long.
Population: 132 (2000); Race: 94.5% White, 0.0% Black, 0.0% Asian, 5.5% American Indian and Alaska Native, 0.0% Hispanic of any race, 0.0% two or more races (2000); Density: 3.8 persons per square mile (2000); Age: 34.6% under 18, 15.0% over 64 (2000); Marriage status: 26.7% never married, 60.0% now married, 4.4% widowed, 8.9% divorced (2000); Foreign born: 0.0% (2000); Ancestry (includes multiple ancestries): 56.7% German, 21.3% Norwegian, 13.4% Irish, 6.3% Czech, 5.5% Other groups (2000).
Economy: Employment by occupation: 27.3% management, 14.5% professional, 21.8% services, 20.0% sales, 3.6% farming, 0.0% construction, 12.7% production (2000).
Income: Per capita income: $11,825 (2000); Median household income: $29,792 (2000); Poverty rate: 15.2% (2000).
Taxes: Total city taxes per capita: $43 (1997); City property taxes per capita: $43 (1997).

Education: High school graduation rate: 86.3% (2000); College graduation rate: 17.8% (2000).
Housing: Homeownership rate: 91.5% (2000); Median home value: $83,300 (2000); Median age of housing: 36 years (2000).
Transportation: Commute to work: 60.0% car, 0.0% public transportation, 3.6% walk, 36.4% work from home (2000); Travel time to work: 51.4% less than 15 minutes, 40.0% 15 to 30 minutes, 0.0% 30 to 45 minutes, 0.0% 45 to 60 minutes, 8.6% 60 minutes or more (2000)

CLOVER (township). Covers a land area of 34.723 square miles and a water area of 0.894 square miles. Located at 47.36° N. Lat.; 95.59° W. Long.
Population: 123 (2000); Race: 47.0% White, 0.0% Black, 0.0% Asian, 46.3% American Indian and Alaska Native, 0.0% Hispanic of any race, 6.7% two or more races (2000); Density: 3.5 persons per square mile (2000); Age: 28.9% under 18, 8.1% over 64 (2000); Marriage status: 35.4% never married, 48.7% now married, 6.2% widowed, 9.7% divorced (2000); Foreign born: 0.0% (2000); Ancestry (includes multiple ancestries): 56.4% Other groups, 16.8% English, 7.4% German, 3.4% Norwegian, 2.7% Portuguese (2000).
Economy: Employment by occupation: 3.6% management, 9.1% professional, 29.1% services, 5.5% sales, 12.7% farming, 18.2% construction, 21.8% production (2000).
Income: Per capita income: $13,523 (2000); Median household income: $21,750 (2000); Poverty rate: 21.5% (2000).
Taxes: Total city taxes per capita: $8 (1997); City property taxes per capita: $8 (1997).
Education: High school graduation rate: 71.6% (2000); College graduation rate: 7.4% (2000).
Housing: Homeownership rate: 83.6% (2000); Median home value: $45,000 (2000); Median rent: $325 per month (2000); Median age of housing: 26 years (2000).
Transportation: Commute to work: 77.8% car, 0.0% public transportation, 7.4% walk, 7.4% work from home (2000); Travel time to work: 12.0% less than 15 minutes, 34.0% 15 to 30 minutes, 34.0% 30 to 45 minutes, 4.0% 45 to 60 minutes, 16.0% 60 minutes or more (2000)

GREGORY (township). Covers a land area of 35.078 square miles and a water area of 1.084 square miles. Located at 47.45° N. Lat.; 95.84° W. Long.
Population: 97 (2000); Race: 93.5% White, 0.0% Black, 0.0% Asian, 2.8% American Indian and Alaska Native, 0.0% Hispanic of any race, 3.7% two or more races (2000); Density: 2.8 persons per square mile (2000); Age: 16.8% under 18, 22.4% over 64 (2000); Marriage status: 36.3% never married, 52.7% now married, 7.7% widowed, 3.3% divorced (2000); Foreign born: 0.0% (2000); Ancestry (includes multiple ancestries): 32.7% German, 28.0% Dutch, 15.9% Czech, 13.1% Norwegian, 13.1% Irish (2000).
Economy: Employment by occupation: 24.4% management, 6.7% professional, 42.2% services, 8.9% sales, 4.4% farming, 0.0% construction, 13.3% production (2000).
Income: Per capita income: $14,656 (2000); Median household income: $31,250 (2000); Poverty rate: 7.5% (2000).
Taxes: Total city taxes per capita: $84 (1997); City property taxes per capita: $84 (1997).
Education: High school graduation rate: 73.4% (2000); College graduation rate: 7.6% (2000).
Housing: Homeownership rate: 100.0% (2000); Median age of housing: 56 years (2000).
Transportation: Commute to work: 51.1% car, 0.0% public transportation, 0.0% walk, 48.9% work from home (2000); Travel time to work: 4.3% less than 15 minutes, 60.9% 15 to 30 minutes, 30.4% 30 to 45 minutes, 0.0% 45 to 60 minutes, 4.3% 60 minutes or more (2000)

HEIER (township). Covers a land area of 33.550 square miles and a water area of 2.622 square miles. Located at 47.44° N. Lat.; 95.75° W. Long.
Population: 154 (2000); Race: 78.4% White, 0.0% Black, 0.0% Asian, 6.4% American Indian and Alaska Native, 0.0% Hispanic of any race, 15.2% two or more races (2000); Density: 4.6 persons per square mile (2000); Age: 28.8% under 18, 10.4% over 64 (2000); Marriage status: 26.0% never married, 61.5% now married, 10.4% widowed, 2.1% divorced (2000); Foreign born: 0.0% (2000); Ancestry (includes multiple ancestries): 45.6% Norwegian, 38.4% German, 15.2% Other groups, 12.0% Danish, 10.4% Swedish (2000).
Economy: Employment by occupation: 15.9% management, 14.5% professional, 23.2% services, 10.1% sales, 0.0% farming, 23.2% construction, 13.0% production (2000).
Income: Per capita income: $15,290 (2000); Median household income: $34,167 (2000); Poverty rate: 7.3% (2000).
Taxes: Total city taxes per capita: $37 (1997); City property taxes per capita: $37 (1997).
Education: High school graduation rate: 69.8% (2000); College graduation rate: 9.3% (2000).
Housing: Homeownership rate: 85.5% (2000); Median home value: $45,000 (2000); Median rent: $125 per month (2000); Median age of housing: 50 years (2000).
Transportation: Commute to work: 89.6% car, 0.0% public transportation, 0.0% walk, 10.4% work from home (2000); Travel time to work: 26.7% less than 15 minutes, 20.0% 15 to 30 minutes, 30.0% 30 to 45 minutes, 3.3% 45 to 60 minutes, 20.0% 60 minutes or more (2000)

ISLAND LAKE (township). Covers a land area of 34.301 square miles and a water area of 2.323 square miles. Located at 47.45° N. Lat.; 95.65° W. Long.
Population: 218 (2000); Race: 71.8% White, 0.0% Black, 1.3% Asian, 21.1% American Indian and Alaska Native, 0.0% Hispanic of any race, 5.7% two or more races (2000); Density: 6.4 persons per square mile (2000); Age: 23.8% under 18, 28.6% over 64 (2000); Marriage status: 24.9% never married, 46.6% now married, 13.8% widowed, 14.8% divorced (2000); Foreign born: 2.6% (2000); Ancestry (includes multiple ancestries): 33.5% Norwegian, 32.2% Other groups, 26.0% German, 11.0% Irish, 10.6% Swedish (2000).
Economy: Employment by occupation: 28.6% management, 9.5% professional, 13.1% services, 16.7% sales, 0.0% farming, 15.5% construction, 16.7% production (2000).
Income: Per capita income: $14,162 (2000); Median household income: $25,673 (2000); Poverty rate: 18.0% (2000).
Taxes: Total city taxes per capita: $139 (1997); City property taxes per capita: $139 (1997).
Education: High school graduation rate: 75.0% (2000); College graduation rate: 12.2% (2000).
Housing: Homeownership rate: 85.3% (2000); Median home value: $55,000 (2000); Median rent: $367 per month (2000); Median age of housing: 32 years (2000).
Transportation: Commute to work: 76.2% car, 0.0% public transportation, 4.8% walk, 19.0% work from home (2000); Travel time to work: 13.2% less than 15 minutes, 47.1% 15 to 30 minutes, 17.6% 30 to 45 minutes, 7.4% 45 to 60 minutes, 14.7% 60 minutes or more (2000)

LA GARDE (township). Covers a land area of 33.600 square miles and a water area of 2.211 square miles. Located at 47.27° N. Lat.; 95.73° W. Long.
Population: 137 (2000); Race: 68.4% White, 0.0% Black, 0.0% Asian, 22.2% American Indian and Alaska Native, 10.3% Hispanic of any race, 8.5% two or more races (2000); Density: 4.1 persons per square mile (2000); Age: 35.0% under 18, 18.8% over 64 (2000); Marriage status: 24.7% never married, 56.5% now married, 10.6% widowed, 8.2% divorced (2000); Foreign born: 3.4% (2000); Ancestry (includes multiple ancestries): 46.2% German, 27.4% Other groups, 19.7% Norwegian, 5.1% Italian, 2.6% United States or American (2000).
Economy: Employment by occupation: 23.3% management, 20.9% professional, 18.6% services, 18.6% sales, 0.0% farming, 4.7% construction, 14.0% production (2000).
Income: Per capita income: $9,926 (2000); Median household income: $31,563 (2000); Poverty rate: 19.7% (2000).
Taxes: Total city taxes per capita: $49 (1997); City property taxes per capita: $49 (1997).
Education: High school graduation rate: 54.9% (2000); College graduation rate: 12.7% (2000).
Housing: Homeownership rate: 100.0% (2000); Median home value: $51,000 (2000); Median age of housing: 54 years (2000).
Transportation: Commute to work: 86.0% car, 0.0% public transportation, 4.7% walk, 9.3% work from home (2000); Travel time to work: 41.0% less than 15 minutes, 43.6% 15 to 30 minutes, 15.4% 30 to 45 minutes, 0.0% 45 to 60 minutes, 0.0% 60 minutes or more (2000)

LAKE GROVE (township). Covers a land area of 34.913 square miles and a water area of 1.432 square miles. Located at 47.20° N. Lat.; 95.85° W. Long.
Population: 203 (2000); Race: 89.4% White, 0.0% Black, 0.0% Asian, 1.5% American Indian and Alaska Native, 0.0% Hispanic of any race, 9.1% two or more races (2000); Density: 5.8 persons per square mile (2000); Age: 20.2% under 18, 21.2% over 64 (2000); Marriage status: 22.6% never married, 58.9% now married, 6.5% widowed, 11.9% divorced (2000); Foreign born: 1.0% (2000); Ancestry (includes multiple ancestries): 40.4% German, 23.7% Norwegian, 8.6% Czech, 7.1% Other groups, 4.5% Czechoslovakian (2000).

Economy: Employment by occupation: 17.5% management, 10.3% professional, 28.9% services, 20.6% sales, 2.1% farming, 7.2% construction, 13.4% production (2000).
Income: Per capita income: $14,439 (2000); Median household income: $30,417 (2000); Poverty rate: 11.3% (2000).
Taxes: Total city taxes per capita: $45 (1997); City property taxes per capita: $45 (1997).
Education: High school graduation rate: 53.3% (2000); College graduation rate: 10.0% (2000).
Housing: Homeownership rate: 100.0% (2000); Median home value: $50,000 (2000); Median age of housing: 40 years (2000).
Transportation: Commute to work: 83.5% car, 0.0% public transportation, 5.2% walk, 8.2% work from home (2000); Travel time to work: 27.0% less than 15 minutes, 55.1% 15 to 30 minutes, 3.4% 30 to 45 minutes, 0.0% 45 to 60 minutes, 14.6% 60 minutes or more (2000)

LITTLE ELBOW (township). Covers a land area of 31.308 square miles and a water area of 4.487 square miles. Located at 47.21° N. Lat.; 95.64° W. Long.
Population: 225 (2000); Race: 27.2% White, 0.0% Black, 2.6% Asian, 66.8% American Indian and Alaska Native, 0.0% Hispanic of any race, 1.3% two or more races (2000); Density: 7.2 persons per square mile (2000); Age: 28.4% under 18, 7.8% over 64 (2000); Marriage status: 33.9% never married, 55.4% now married, 2.2% widowed, 8.6% divorced (2000); Foreign born: 2.6% (2000); Ancestry (includes multiple ancestries): 72.0% Other groups, 9.9% Norwegian, 6.0% German, 3.0% Scandinavian, 1.7% Danish (2000).
Economy: Employment by occupation: 8.9% management, 18.8% professional, 38.6% services, 22.8% sales, 0.0% farming, 10.9% construction, 0.0% production (2000).
Income: Per capita income: $10,101 (2000); Median household income: $21,750 (2000); Poverty rate: 31.9% (2000).
Taxes: Total city taxes per capita: $144 (2000); City property taxes per capita: $144 (2000).
Education: High school graduation rate: 90.6% (2000); College graduation rate: 5.8% (2000).
Housing: Homeownership rate: 89.0% (2000); Median home value: $58,300 (2000); Median rent: $175 per month (2000); Median age of housing: 43 years (2000).
Transportation: Commute to work: 87.1% car, 2.0% public transportation, 0.0% walk, 6.9% work from home (2000); Travel time to work: 17.0% less than 15 minutes, 33.0% 15 to 30 minutes, 29.8% 30 to 45 minutes, 16.0% 45 to 60 minutes, 4.3% 60 minutes or more (2000)

MAHNOMEN (city). Covers a land area of 0.959 square miles and a water area of 0 square miles. Located at 47.31° N. Lat.; 95.96° W. Long. Elevation is 1,210 feet.
History: The name of Mahnomen is of Chippewa origin, meaning "wild rice." Mahnomen grew as the center of an agricultural area with cooperatives marketing livestock, poultry, and dairy products.
Population: 1,202 (2000); Race: 73.9% White, 0.0% Black, 1.4% Asian, 15.3% American Indian and Alaska Native, 0.9% Hispanic of any race, 9.4% two or more races (2000); Density: 1,252.9 persons per square mile (2000); Age: 23.7% under 18, 26.5% over 64 (2000); Marriage status: 21.1% never married, 50.3% now married, 20.9% widowed, 7.6% divorced (2000); Foreign born: 2.0% (2000); Ancestry (includes multiple ancestries): 48.2% German, 25.6% Other groups, 23.1% Norwegian, 6.6% Irish, 5.3% Swedish (2000).
Economy: Single-family building permits issued: 2 (2001) / 3 (2000); Multi-family building permits issued: 8 (2001) / 0 (2000); Employment by occupation: 9.7% management, 21.3% professional, 26.3% services, 25.4% sales, 0.6% farming, 9.9% construction, 6.9% production (2000).
Income: Per capita income: $14,538 (2000); Median household income: $26,000 (2000); Poverty rate: 14.0% (2000).
Taxes: Total city taxes per capita: $199 (1997); City property taxes per capita: $198 (1997).
Education: High school graduation rate: 71.6% (2000); College graduation rate: 16.8% (2000).

School District(s)

Mahnomen (PK-12)
2000 Enrollment: 708 218-935-2211

Two-year College(s)

White Earth Tribal and Community College (Public)
2001 Enrollment: 79 218-935-0417
2001 Tuition: In-state $2,040; Out-of-state $2,040

Housing: Homeownership rate: 68.2% (2000); Median home value: $48,100 (2000); Median rent: $301 per month (2000); Median age of housing: 50 years (2000).
Hospitals: Mahnomen Health Center (63 beds)
Newspapers: The Mahnomen Pioneer (1 x week)
Transportation: Commute to work: 82.2% car, 1.1% public transportation, 12.7% walk, 3.8% work from home (2000); Travel time to work: 76.0% less than 15 minutes, 13.2% 15 to 30 minutes, 5.9% 30 to 45 minutes, 2.0% 45 to 60 minutes, 2.9% 60 minutes or more (2000)

MARSH CREEK (township). Covers a land area of 37.649 square miles and a water area of 0.012 square miles. Located at 47.34° N. Lat.; 95.99° W. Long.
Population: 128 (2000); Race: 86.5% White, 0.0% Black, 0.0% Asian, 4.0% American Indian and Alaska Native, 4.0% Hispanic of any race, 5.6% two or more races (2000); Density: 3.4 persons per square mile (2000); Age: 32.5% under 18, 22.2% over 64 (2000); Marriage status: 10.2% never married, 67.0% now married, 10.2% widowed, 12.5% divorced (2000); Foreign born: 1.6% (2000); Ancestry (includes multiple ancestries): 44.4% German, 27.8% Norwegian, 21.4% Other groups, 17.5% Swedish, 11.9% Russian (2000).
Economy: Employment by occupation: 22.6% management, 11.3% professional, 22.6% services, 27.4% sales, 0.0% farming, 16.1% construction, 0.0% production (2000).
Income: Per capita income: $13,599 (2000); Median household income: $37,321 (2000); Poverty rate: 8.7% (2000).
Taxes: Total city taxes per capita: $60 (1997); City property taxes per capita: $60 (1997).
Education: High school graduation rate: 84.3% (2000); College graduation rate: 18.1% (2000).
Housing: Homeownership rate: 85.7% (2000); Median home value: $56,700 (2000); Median rent: $325 per month (2000); Median age of housing: 41 years (2000).
Transportation: Commute to work: 77.4% car, 0.0% public transportation, 0.0% walk, 22.6% work from home (2000); Travel time to work: 85.4% less than 15 minutes, 8.3% 15 to 30 minutes, 6.3% 30 to 45 minutes, 0.0% 45 to 60 minutes, 0.0% 60 minutes or more (2000)

NAYTAHWAUSH (CDP). Covers a land area of 19.453 square miles and a water area of 0.315 square miles. Located at 47.26° N. Lat.; 95.63° W. Long. Elevation is 1,516 feet.
Population: 583 (2000); Race: 6.8% White, 0.5% Black, 2.0% Asian, 86.1% American Indian and Alaska Native, 1.2% Hispanic of any race, 3.9% two or more races (2000); Density: 30.0 persons per square mile (2000); Age: 44.5% under 18, 5.3% over 64 (2000); Marriage status: 53.8% never married, 30.8% now married, 3.7% widowed, 11.7% divorced (2000); Foreign born: 1.4% (2000); Ancestry (includes multiple ancestries): 92.0% Other groups, 1.2% German, 1.1% United States or American, 1.1% Norwegian, 0.5% Scotch-Irish (2000).
Economy: Employment by occupation: 10.0% management, 11.9% professional, 33.8% services, 15.6% sales, 0.0% farming, 20.6% construction, 8.1% production (2000).
Income: Per capita income: $8,296 (2000); Median household income: $26,429 (2000); Poverty rate: 37.1% (2000).
Education: High school graduation rate: 72.7% (2000); College graduation rate: 5.0% (2000).
Housing: Homeownership rate: 44.8% (2000); Median home value: $44,400 (2000); Median rent: <$100 per month (2000); Median age of housing: 23 years (2000).
Transportation: Commute to work: 89.1% car, 0.0% public transportation, 0.0% walk, 3.8% work from home (2000); Travel time to work: 33.3% less than 15 minutes, 22.0% 15 to 30 minutes, 27.3% 30 to 45 minutes, 3.3% 45 to 60 minutes, 14.0% 60 minutes or more (2000)

OAKLAND (township). Covers a land area of 32.210 square miles and a water area of 3.221 square miles. Located at 47.17° N. Lat.; 95.74° W. Long.
Population: 260 (2000); Race: 73.8% White, 0.0% Black, 0.8% Asian, 18.5% American Indian and Alaska Native, 0.0% Hispanic of any race, 5.8% two or more races (2000); Density: 8.1 persons per square mile (2000); Age: 29.2% under 18, 8.8% over 64 (2000); Marriage status: 27.6% never married, 60.7% now married, 5.6% widowed, 6.1% divorced (2000); Foreign born: 0.4% (2000); Ancestry (includes multiple ancestries): 39.6% German, 29.6% Other groups, 29.6% Norwegian, 10.4% Czech, 6.5% Swedish (2000).
Economy: Employment by occupation: 19.1% management, 16.9% professional, 9.6% services, 15.4% sales, 5.1% farming, 16.2% construction, 17.6% production (2000).

Income: Per capita income: $16,193 (2000); Median household income: $43,333 (2000); Poverty rate: 8.9% (2000).
Taxes: Total city taxes per capita: $31 (1997); City property taxes per capita: $31 (1997).
Education: High school graduation rate: 74.5% (2000); College graduation rate: 6.4% (2000).
Housing: Homeownership rate: 88.0% (2000); Median home value: $65,800 (2000); Median rent: $350 per month (2000); Median age of housing: 32 years (2000).
Transportation: Commute to work: 91.7% car, 0.0% public transportation, 2.3% walk, 6.0% work from home (2000); Travel time to work: 14.4% less than 15 minutes, 42.4% 15 to 30 minutes, 22.4% 30 to 45 minutes, 7.2% 45 to 60 minutes, 13.6% 60 minutes or more (2000)

PEMBINA (township). Covers a land area of 36.493 square miles and a water area of 0.098 square miles. Located at 47.27° N. Lat.; 95.98° W. Long.
Population: 471 (2000); Race: 87.7% White, 0.0% Black, 0.0% Asian, 2.0% American Indian and Alaska Native, 0.5% Hispanic of any race, 10.2% two or more races (2000); Density: 12.9 persons per square mile (2000); Age: 22.7% under 18, 20.2% over 64 (2000); Marriage status: 14.2% never married, 79.2% now married, 3.6% widowed, 3.1% divorced (2000); Foreign born: 0.0% (2000); Ancestry (includes multiple ancestries): 53.0% German, 29.8% Norwegian, 13.4% Other groups, 13.0% Czech, 12.0% Irish (2000).
Economy: Employment by occupation: 14.1% management, 17.5% professional, 18.8% services, 23.1% sales, 3.8% farming, 9.4% construction, 13.2% production (2000).
Income: Per capita income: $15,976 (2000); Median household income: $39,722 (2000); Poverty rate: 2.7% (2000).
Taxes: Total city taxes per capita: $40 (1997); City property taxes per capita: $40 (1997).
Education: High school graduation rate: 81.8% (2000); College graduation rate: 14.1% (2000).
Housing: Homeownership rate: 91.6% (2000); Median home value: $81,300 (2000); Median rent: $288 per month (2000); Median age of housing: 32 years (2000).
Transportation: Commute to work: 81.0% car, 0.0% public transportation, 8.7% walk, 9.5% work from home (2000); Travel time to work: 83.3% less than 15 minutes, 5.7% 15 to 30 minutes, 4.8% 30 to 45 minutes, 3.3% 45 to 60 minutes, 2.9% 60 minutes or more (2000)

POPPLE GROVE (township). Covers a land area of 37.313 square miles and a water area of 0.135 square miles. Located at 47.19° N. Lat.; 95.98° W. Long.
Population: 154 (2000); Race: 74.5% White, 0.0% Black, 0.0% Asian, 15.3% American Indian and Alaska Native, 0.0% Hispanic of any race, 10.2% two or more races (2000); Density: 4.1 persons per square mile (2000); Age: 29.9% under 18, 17.5% over 64 (2000); Marriage status: 27.1% never married, 53.3% now married, 11.2% widowed, 8.4% divorced (2000); Foreign born: 0.0% (2000); Ancestry (includes multiple ancestries): 43.8% German, 21.2% United States or American, 19.0% Other groups, 18.2% Norwegian, 14.6% Czech (2000).
Economy: Employment by occupation: 32.3% management, 13.8% professional, 20.0% services, 12.3% sales, 10.8% farming, 1.5% construction, 9.2% production (2000).
Income: Per capita income: $15,011 (2000); Median household income: $37,500 (2000); Poverty rate: 2.9% (2000).
Taxes: Total city taxes per capita: $74 (1997); City property taxes per capita: $74 (1997).
Education: High school graduation rate: 65.1% (2000); College graduation rate: 12.8% (2000).
Housing: Homeownership rate: 92.3% (2000); Median home value: $45,000 (2000); Median age of housing: 52 years (2000).
Transportation: Commute to work: 61.5% car, 0.0% public transportation, 3.1% walk, 35.4% work from home (2000); Travel time to work: 54.8% less than 15 minutes, 26.2% 15 to 30 minutes, 16.7% 30 to 45 minutes, 2.4% 45 to 60 minutes, 0.0% 60 minutes or more (2000)

ROSEDALE (township). Covers a land area of 34.911 square miles and a water area of 1.427 square miles. Located at 47.27° N. Lat.; 95.87° W. Long.
Population: 136 (2000); Race: 80.9% White, 0.0% Black, 1.3% Asian, 1.3% American Indian and Alaska Native, 0.0% Hispanic of any race, 10.5% two or more races (2000); Density: 3.9 persons per square mile (2000); Age: 32.9% under 18, 15.1% over 64 (2000); Marriage status: 31.0% never married, 54.3% now married, 8.6% widowed, 6.0% divorced (2000); Foreign born: 1.3% (2000); Ancestry (includes multiple ancestries): 73.0% German, 37.5% Norwegian, 13.2% Other groups, 4.6% French (except Basque), 3.9% Danish (2000).
Economy: Employment by occupation: 26.7% management, 6.7% professional, 21.3% services, 13.3% sales, 22.7% farming, 4.0% construction, 5.3% production (2000).
Income: Per capita income: $13,134 (2000); Median household income: $36,250 (2000); Poverty rate: 15.8% (2000).
Taxes: Total city taxes per capita: $30 (1997); City property taxes per capita: $30 (1997).
Education: High school graduation rate: 80.7% (2000); College graduation rate: 7.2% (2000).
Housing: Homeownership rate: 81.5% (2000); Median home value: $57,500 (2000); Median rent: $425 per month (2000); Median age of housing: 48 years (2000).
Transportation: Commute to work: 66.7% car, 0.0% public transportation, 0.0% walk, 33.3% work from home (2000); Travel time to work: 34.0% less than 15 minutes, 60.0% 15 to 30 minutes, 0.0% 30 to 45 minutes, 6.0% 45 to 60 minutes, 0.0% 60 minutes or more (2000)

TWIN LAKES (township). Covers a land area of 32.780 square miles and a water area of 3.234 square miles. Located at 47.26° N. Lat.; 95.63° W. Long.
Population: 847 (2000); Race: 11.1% White, 0.4% Black, 1.3% Asian, 81.8% American Indian and Alaska Native, 1.9% Hispanic of any race, 4.3% two or more races (2000); Density: 25.8 persons per square mile (2000); Age: 44.3% under 18, 6.4% over 64 (2000); Marriage status: 48.1% never married, 38.8% now married, 3.0% widowed, 10.1% divorced (2000); Foreign born: 1.0% (2000); Ancestry (includes multiple ancestries): 87.1% Other groups, 3.9% Norwegian, 2.4% German, 1.0% Scotch-Irish, 0.7% United States or American (2000).
Economy: Employment by occupation: 9.0% management, 16.7% professional, 30.0% services, 17.2% sales, 1.7% farming, 16.3% construction, 9.0% production (2000).
Income: Per capita income: $8,914 (2000); Median household income: $26,250 (2000); Poverty rate: 37.1% (2000).
Taxes: Total city taxes per capita: $5 (1997); City property taxes per capita: $5 (1997).
Education: High school graduation rate: 76.6% (2000); College graduation rate: 8.2% (2000).
Housing: Homeownership rate: 53.6% (2000); Median home value: $49,400 (2000); Median rent: <$100 per month (2000); Median age of housing: 25 years (2000).
Transportation: Commute to work: 90.4% car, 0.0% public transportation, 0.9% walk, 3.9% work from home (2000); Travel time to work: 28.6% less than 15 minutes, 33.6% 15 to 30 minutes, 23.6% 30 to 45 minutes, 2.3% 45 to 60 minutes, 11.8% 60 minutes or more (2000)

WAUBUN (city). Covers a land area of 0.511 square miles and a water area of 0 square miles. Located at 47.18° N. Lat.; 95.94° W. Long. Elevation is 1,240 feet.
Population: 403 (2000); Race: 59.6% White, 0.0% Black, 1.2% Asian, 12.9% American Indian and Alaska Native, 0.7% Hispanic of any race, 26.3% two or more races (2000); Density: 788.2 persons per square mile (2000); Age: 28.9% under 18, 17.8% over 64 (2000); Marriage status: 20.6% never married, 49.1% now married, 15.3% widowed, 15.0% divorced (2000); Foreign born: 1.6% (2000); Ancestry (includes multiple ancestries): 44.8% German, 32.9% Other groups, 17.6% Norwegian, 9.6% French (except Basque), 8.9% Czech (2000).
Economy: Resort area. Agriculture includes grain, sunflowers, alfalfa, wild rice. Employment by occupation: 5.3% management, 28.4% professional, 16.3% services, 17.9% sales, 0.0% farming, 20.0% construction, 12.1% production (2000).
Income: Per capita income: $14,968 (2000); Median household income: $31,042 (2000); Poverty rate: 11.4% (2000).
Taxes: Total city taxes per capita: $154 (1997); City property taxes per capita: $149 (1997).
Education: High school graduation rate: 84.0% (2000); College graduation rate: 18.4% (2000).

School District(s)

Waubun (PK-12)
2000 Enrollment: 636 218-473-2171

Housing: Homeownership rate: 73.0% (2000); Median home value: $54,700 (2000); Median rent: $288 per month (2000); Median age of housing: 31 years (2000).
Transportation: Commute to work: 87.9% car, 0.0% public transportation, 4.7% walk, 5.8% work from home (2000); Travel time to work: 48.6% less

than 15 minutes, 27.4% 15 to 30 minutes, 15.1% 30 to 45 minutes, 1.1% 45 to 60 minutes, 7.8% 60 minutes or more (2000)

Marshall County

Located in northwestern Minnesota; bounded on the west by the Red River of the North and the North Dakota border; drained by the Snake, Thief, and Middle Rivers. Covers a land area of 1,772.20 square miles, a water area of 40.60 square miles, and is located in the Central Time Zone. The county government was organized in 1879. County seat is Warren.

Weather Station: Agassiz Refuge — Elevation: 1,141 feet

	Jan	Feb	Mar	Apr	May	Jun	Jul	Aug	Sep	Oct	Nov	Dec
High	14	22	35	53	69	76	80	79	68	55	33	19
Low	-7	0	13	29	43	52	57	54	44	33	17	1
Precip	0.6	0.5	0.7	1.3	2.8	3.5	3.6	3.0	2.6	1.7	1.1	0.5
Snow	9.3	5.4	6.0	2.1	tr	0.0	0.0	0.0	tr	1.1	7.9	7.7

High and Low temperatures in degrees Fahrenheit; Precipitation and Snow in inches

Weather Station: Argyle 4 E — Elevation: 869 feet

	Jan	Feb	Mar	Apr	May	Jun	Jul	Aug	Sep	Oct	Nov	Dec
High	12	20	32	52	69	77	81	80	69	55	34	19
Low	-9	-2	12	28	41	51	55	52	42	31	16	0
Precip	0.8	0.6	0.9	1.1	2.3	3.2	3.1	2.4	2.3	1.5	1.0	0.6
Snow	10.2	6.5	6.4	1.9	tr	0.0	0.0	0.0	tr	0.9	7.3	7.6

High and Low temperatures in degrees Fahrenheit; Precipitation and Snow in inches

Population: 10,155 (2000); Race: 96.6% White, 0.2% Black, 0.3% Asian, 0.3% American Indian and Alaska Native, 2.8% Hispanic of any race, 1.0% two or more races (2000); Density: 5.7 persons per square mile (2000); Age: 25.3% under 18, 18.6% over 64 (2000).
Religion: Five largest groups: 38.0% Evangelical Lutheran Church in America, 32.6% Catholic Church, 4.5% The Association of Free Lutheran Congregations, 3.8% Lutheran Church—Missouri Synod, 1.6% The United Methodist Church (2000).
Economy: Unemployment rate: 6.5% (11/2002); Total civilian labor force: 4,448 (11/2002); Leading industries: 15.7% health care and social assistance; 14.7% retail trade; 13.0% wholesale trade (2000); Companies that employ more than 1,000 persons: 0 (2000); Companies that employ more than 100 persons: 1 (2000); Farms: 1,144 totaling 774,342 acres (1997); Minority business ownership rate: 0.0% (1997); Women business ownership rate: 24.0% (1997); Retail sales per capita: $6,860 (1997). Single-family building permits issued: 9 (2001) / 6 (2000); Multi-family building permits issued: 4 (2001) / 0 (2000).
Income: Per capita income: $16,317 (2000); Median household income: $34,804 (2000); Poverty rate: 9.8% (2000); Bankruptcy rate: 2.96% (2001).
Taxes: Total county taxes per capita: $273 (2000); County property taxes per capita: $273 (2000).
Education: High school graduation rate: 79.1% (2000); College graduation rate: 12.0% (2000).
Housing: Homeownership rate: 83.8% (2000); Median home value: $50,500 (2000); Median rent: $246 per month (2000); Median age of housing: 39 years (2000).
Health: Birth rate: 112.3 per 10,000 population (1998); Age adjusted death rate: 67.0 per 10,000 population (1999); Age adjusted cancer mortality rate: 121.4 (Unreliable figure as per CDC) deaths per 100,000 population (1999). Number of physicians: 2.0 per 10,000 population (1999); Number of hospital beds: 20.7 per 10,000 population (1999).
Elections: 2000 Presidential election results: 36.7% Gore, 56.0% Bush, 3.1% Nader, 3.7% Buchanan
National and State Parks: Agassiz National Wildlife Refuge; Espelie State Wildlife Management Area; Florian State Wildlife Management Area; Grygla State Wildlife Management Area; Old Mill State Park; Old Mill State Park; Thief Lake State Wildlife Management Area
Additional Information Contacts
Marshall County Government Offices 218-745-4851

Marshall County Communities

AGDER (township). Covers a land area of 44.257 square miles and a water area of 0.009 square miles. Located at 48.21° N. Lat.; 96.04° W. Long.
Population: 108 (2000); Race: 100.0% White, 0.0% Black, 0.0% Asian, 0.0% American Indian and Alaska Native, 0.0% Hispanic of any race, 0.0% two or more races (2000); Density: 2.4 persons per square mile (2000); Age: 32.8% under 18, 6.9% over 64 (2000); Marriage status: 14.3% never married, 76.2% now married, 6.0% widowed, 3.6% divorced (2000); Foreign born: 0.0% (2000); Ancestry (includes multiple ancestries): 42.2% Norwegian, 22.4% German, 17.2% English, 12.1% Swedish, 7.8% French (except Basque) (2000).
Economy: Employment by occupation: 17.7% management, 11.3% professional, 19.4% services, 22.6% sales, 0.0% farming, 11.3% construction, 17.7% production (2000).
Income: Per capita income: $15,519 (2000); Median household income: $34,375 (2000); Poverty rate: 16.4% (2000).
Education: High school graduation rate: 88.0% (2000); College graduation rate: 2.7% (2000).
Housing: Homeownership rate: 90.5% (2000); Median home value: $51,700 (2000); Median rent: $500 per month (2000); Median age of housing: 38 years (2000).
Transportation: Commute to work: 77.4% car, 0.0% public transportation, 4.8% walk, 14.5% work from home (2000); Travel time to work: 26.4% less than 15 minutes, 56.6% 15 to 30 minutes, 5.7% 30 to 45 minutes, 0.0% 45 to 60 minutes, 11.3% 60 minutes or more (2000)

ALMA (township). Covers a land area of 36.405 square miles and a water area of 0.014 square miles. Located at 48.32° N. Lat.; 96.69° W. Long.
Population: 94 (2000); Race: 100.0% White, 0.0% Black, 0.0% Asian, 0.0% American Indian and Alaska Native, 0.0% Hispanic of any race, 0.0% two or more races (2000); Density: 2.6 persons per square mile (2000); Age: 27.7% under 18, 12.8% over 64 (2000); Marriage status: 29.6% never married, 56.8% now married, 2.5% widowed, 11.1% divorced (2000); Foreign born: 0.0% (2000); Ancestry (includes multiple ancestries): 43.6% Polish, 38.3% Norwegian, 21.3% German, 13.8% Swedish, 4.3% Finnish (2000).
Economy: Employment by occupation: 14.6% management, 16.7% professional, 12.5% services, 16.7% sales, 8.3% farming, 22.9% construction, 8.3% production (2000).
Income: Per capita income: $15,793 (2000); Median household income: $36,563 (2000); Poverty rate: 1.1% (2000).
Taxes: Total city taxes per capita: $101 (1997); City property taxes per capita: $101 (1997).
Education: High school graduation rate: 84.6% (2000); College graduation rate: 12.3% (2000).
Housing: Homeownership rate: 94.7% (2000); Median home value: $58,300 (2000); Median rent: $325 per month (2000); Median age of housing: 60+ years (2000).
Transportation: Commute to work: 90.9% car, 0.0% public transportation, 4.5% walk, 4.5% work from home (2000); Travel time to work: 35.7% less than 15 minutes, 52.4% 15 to 30 minutes, 0.0% 30 to 45 minutes, 9.5% 45 to 60 minutes, 2.4% 60 minutes or more (2000)

ALVARADO (city). Covers a land area of 0.213 square miles and a water area of 0 square miles. Located at 48.19° N. Lat.; 96.99° W. Long. Elevation is 812 feet.
Population: 371 (2000); Race: 95.6% White, 0.0% Black, 0.0% Asian, 0.0% American Indian and Alaska Native, 4.4% Hispanic of any race, 0.0% two or more races (2000); Density: 1,738.4 persons per square mile (2000); Age: 27.5% under 18, 14.3% over 64 (2000); Marriage status: 23.8% never married, 63.0% now married, 7.5% widowed, 5.7% divorced (2000); Foreign born: 3.5% (2000); Ancestry (includes multiple ancestries): 55.3% Norwegian, 32.5% Swedish, 18.7% German, 11.1% Irish, 4.7% Other groups (2000).
Economy: Grain, beans, sugar beets, sunflowers, flax; cattle, sheep. Manufacturing: dry-bean processing. Single-family building permits issued: 0 (2001) / 0 (2000); Multi-family building permits issued: 0 (2001) / 0 (2000); Employment by occupation: 9.1% management, 19.4% professional, 20.0% services, 21.7% sales, 1.7% farming, 13.7% construction, 14.3% production (2000).
Income: Per capita income: $16,015 (2000); Median household income: $40,625 (2000); Poverty rate: 4.7% (2000).
Taxes: Total city taxes per capita: $172 (1997); City property taxes per capita: $166 (1997).
Education: High school graduation rate: 79.9% (2000); College graduation rate: 15.4% (2000).
Housing: Homeownership rate: 82.7% (2000); Median home value: $61,300 (2000); Median rent: $245 per month (2000); Median age of housing: 30 years (2000).
Transportation: Commute to work: 88.2% car, 0.0% public transportation, 5.3% walk, 4.1% work from home (2000); Travel time to work: 27.0% less than 15 minutes, 39.3% 15 to 30 minutes, 25.2% 30 to 45 minutes, 5.5% 45 to 60 minutes, 3.1% 60 minutes or more (2000)

ARGYLE (city). Covers a land area of 1.544 square miles and a water area of 0 square miles. Located at 48.33° N. Lat.; 96.81° W. Long. Elevation is 847 feet.
History: Argyle was first known as Louisa, and later as Middle River. It was given its present name when a large number of Scottish immigrants settled in the town.
Population: 656 (2000); Race: 93.6% White, 0.0% Black, 1.8% Asian, 0.0% American Indian and Alaska Native, 3.5% Hispanic of any race, 1.7% two or more races (2000); Density: 424.9 persons per square mile (2000); Age: 30.7% under 18, 21.3% over 64 (2000); Marriage status: 19.4% never married, 68.2% now married, 7.5% widowed, 4.9% divorced (2000); Foreign born: 4.7% (2000); Ancestry (includes multiple ancestries): 34.0% Norwegian, 26.1% French (except Basque), 24.9% Polish, 14.0% German, 13.5% Swedish (2000).
Economy: Single-family building permits issued: 0 (2001) / 3 (2000); Multi-family building permits issued: 0 (2001) / 0 (2000); Employment by occupation: 15.6% management, 21.5% professional, 14.1% services, 22.7% sales, 4.3% farming, 10.2% construction, 11.7% production (2000).
Income: Per capita income: $15,974 (2000); Median household income: $36,154 (2000); Poverty rate: 15.2% (2000).
Taxes: Total city taxes per capita: $75 (1997); City property taxes per capita: $68 (1997).
Education: High school graduation rate: 74.1% (2000); College graduation rate: 18.1% (2000).
Housing: Homeownership rate: 84.8% (2000); Median home value: $46,500 (2000); Median rent: $323 per month (2000); Median age of housing: 45 years (2000).
Transportation: Commute to work: 88.2% car, 0.0% public transportation, 9.8% walk, 2.0% work from home (2000); Travel time to work: 55.8% less than 15 minutes, 22.1% 15 to 30 minutes, 12.0% 30 to 45 minutes, 4.0% 45 to 60 minutes, 6.0% 60 minutes or more (2000)

AUGSBURG (township). Covers a land area of 36.156 square miles and a water area of 0 square miles. Located at 48.51° N. Lat.; 96.72° W. Long.
Population: 98 (2000); Race: 84.6% White, 0.0% Black, 1.7% Asian, 7.7% American Indian and Alaska Native, 0.0% Hispanic of any race, 6.0% two or more races (2000); Density: 2.7 persons per square mile (2000); Age: 31.6% under 18, 19.7% over 64 (2000); Marriage status: 17.4% never married, 68.6% now married, 5.8% widowed, 8.1% divorced (2000); Foreign born: 1.7% (2000); Ancestry (includes multiple ancestries): 40.2% Norwegian, 31.6% Polish, 29.1% Swedish, 19.7% German, 8.5% Other groups (2000).
Economy: Employment by occupation: 25.6% management, 10.3% professional, 12.8% services, 23.1% sales, 7.7% farming, 0.0% construction, 20.5% production (2000).
Income: Per capita income: $11,206 (2000); Median household income: $38,125 (2000); Poverty rate: 17.1% (2000).
Taxes: Total city taxes per capita: $61 (1997); City property taxes per capita: $61 (1997).
Education: High school graduation rate: 69.0% (2000); College graduation rate: 16.9% (2000).
Housing: Homeownership rate: 77.8% (2000); Median home value: $28,300 (2000); Median rent: $525 per month (2000); Median age of housing: 59 years (2000).
Transportation: Commute to work: 66.7% car, 0.0% public transportation, 5.1% walk, 28.2% work from home (2000); Travel time to work: 14.3% less than 15 minutes, 32.1% 15 to 30 minutes, 17.9% 30 to 45 minutes, 14.3% 45 to 60 minutes, 21.4% 60 minutes or more (2000)

BIG WOODS (township). Covers a land area of 30.574 square miles and a water area of 0.380 square miles. Located at 48.31° N. Lat.; 97.07° W. Long. Elevation is 801 feet.
Population: 79 (2000); Race: 96.9% White, 0.0% Black, 0.0% Asian, 3.1% American Indian and Alaska Native, 0.0% Hispanic of any race, 0.0% two or more races (2000); Density: 2.6 persons per square mile (2000); Age: 30.2% under 18, 26.0% over 64 (2000); Marriage status: 14.5% never married, 75.4% now married, 5.8% widowed, 4.3% divorced (2000); Foreign born: 0.0% (2000); Ancestry (includes multiple ancestries): 77.1% Norwegian, 11.5% Swedish, 11.5% Polish, 10.4% French (except Basque), 8.3% Scottish (2000).
Economy: Employment by occupation: 42.9% management, 14.3% professional, 7.1% services, 14.3% sales, 0.0% farming, 3.6% construction, 17.9% production (2000).
Income: Per capita income: $16,392 (2000); Median household income: $38,125 (2000); Poverty rate: 0.0% (2000).
Taxes: Total city taxes per capita: $132 (1997); City property taxes per capita: $132 (1997).
Education: High school graduation rate: 82.1% (2000); College graduation rate: 13.4% (2000).
Housing: Homeownership rate: 85.3% (2000); Median home value: $48,300 (2000); Median age of housing: 60+ years (2000).
Transportation: Commute to work: 92.9% car, 0.0% public transportation, 0.0% walk, 7.1% work from home (2000); Travel time to work: 34.6% less than 15 minutes, 26.9% 15 to 30 minutes, 15.4% 30 to 45 minutes, 23.1% 45 to 60 minutes, 0.0% 60 minutes or more (2000)

BLOOMER (township). Covers a land area of 36.396 square miles and a water area of 0 square miles. Located at 48.33° N. Lat.; 96.94° W. Long.
Population: 92 (2000); Race: 100.0% White, 0.0% Black, 0.0% Asian, 0.0% American Indian and Alaska Native, 0.0% Hispanic of any race, 0.0% two or more races (2000); Density: 2.5 persons per square mile (2000); Age: 10.5% under 18, 13.2% over 64 (2000); Marriage status: 26.4% never married, 63.9% now married, 4.2% widowed, 5.6% divorced (2000); Foreign born: 2.6% (2000); Ancestry (includes multiple ancestries): 34.2% Norwegian, 32.9% Polish, 23.7% Swedish, 22.4% French (except Basque), 15.8% French Canadian (2000).
Economy: Employment by occupation: 32.5% management, 17.5% professional, 10.0% services, 2.5% sales, 0.0% farming, 5.0% construction, 32.5% production (2000).
Income: Per capita income: $15,853 (2000); Median household income: $33,438 (2000); Poverty rate: 6.6% (2000).
Taxes: Total city taxes per capita: $289 (1997); City property taxes per capita: $289 (1997).
Education: High school graduation rate: 84.2% (2000); College graduation rate: 5.3% (2000).
Housing: Homeownership rate: 100.0% (2000); Median home value: $54,500 (2000); Median age of housing: 60+ years (2000).
Transportation: Commute to work: 80.6% car, 0.0% public transportation, 0.0% walk, 19.4% work from home (2000); Travel time to work: 6.9% less than 15 minutes, 31.0% 15 to 30 minutes, 34.5% 30 to 45 minutes, 17.2% 45 to 60 minutes, 10.3% 60 minutes or more (2000)

BOXVILLE (township). Covers a land area of 8.383 square miles and a water area of 0 square miles. Located at 48.18° N. Lat.; 96.83° W. Long.
Population: 31 (2000); Race: 100.0% White, 0.0% Black, 0.0% Asian, 0.0% American Indian and Alaska Native, 0.0% Hispanic of any race, 0.0% two or more races (2000); Density: 3.7 persons per square mile (2000); Age: 0.0% under 18, 51.5% over 64 (2000); Marriage status: 3.0% never married, 84.8% now married, 12.1% widowed, 0.0% divorced (2000); Foreign born: 0.0% (2000); Ancestry (includes multiple ancestries): 39.4% Norwegian, 27.3% Swedish, 21.2% Scotch-Irish, 12.1% German, 6.1% Finnish (2000).
Economy: Employment by occupation: 23.1% management, 15.4% professional, 15.4% services, 15.4% sales, 0.0% farming, 15.4% construction, 15.4% production (2000).
Income: Per capita income: $31,503 (2000); Median household income: $46,875 (2000); Poverty rate: 0.0% (2000).
Taxes: Total city taxes per capita: $89 (1997); City property taxes per capita: $89 (1997).
Education: High school graduation rate: 100.0% (2000); College graduation rate: 9.1% (2000).
Housing: Homeownership rate: 100.0% (2000); Median home value: $61,700 (2000); Median age of housing: 57 years (2000).
Transportation: Commute to work: 76.9% car, 0.0% public transportation, 0.0% walk, 23.1% work from home (2000); Travel time to work: 80.0% less than 15 minutes, 0.0% 15 to 30 minutes, 0.0% 30 to 45 minutes, 20.0% 45 to 60 minutes, 0.0% 60 minutes or more (2000)

CEDAR (township). Covers a land area of 32.130 square miles and a water area of 4.142 square miles. Located at 48.41° N. Lat.; 96.04° W. Long.
Population: 94 (2000); Race: 100.0% White, 0.0% Black, 0.0% Asian, 0.0% American Indian and Alaska Native, 0.0% Hispanic of any race, 0.0% two or more races (2000); Density: 2.9 persons per square mile (2000); Age: 16.1% under 18, 23.2% over 64 (2000); Marriage status: 32.0% never married, 60.8% now married, 7.2% widowed, 0.0% divorced (2000); Foreign born: 1.8% (2000); Ancestry (includes multiple ancestries): 54.5% Norwegian, 23.2% German, 8.9% Finnish, 8.0% Scandinavian, 7.1% English (2000).
Economy: Employment by occupation: 26.9% management, 7.7% professional, 7.7% services, 7.7% sales, 5.8% farming, 17.3% construction, 26.9% production (2000).
Income: Per capita income: $15,739 (2000); Median household income: $36,250 (2000); Poverty rate: 1.8% (2000).

Taxes: Total city taxes per capita: $56 (1997); City property taxes per capita: $56 (1997).
Education: High school graduation rate: 66.3% (2000); College graduation rate: 3.6% (2000).
Housing: Homeownership rate: 87.5% (2000); Median home value: $60,000 (2000); Median rent: $125 per month (2000); Median age of housing: 34 years (2000).
Transportation: Commute to work: 86.5% car, 0.0% public transportation, 0.0% walk, 13.5% work from home (2000); Travel time to work: 0.0% less than 15 minutes, 17.8% 15 to 30 minutes, 46.7% 30 to 45 minutes, 17.8% 45 to 60 minutes, 17.8% 60 minutes or more (2000)

COMO (township). Covers a land area of 36.348 square miles and a water area of 0 square miles. Located at 48.50° N. Lat.; 96.04° W. Long.
Population: 52 (2000); Race: 100.0% White, 0.0% Black, 0.0% Asian, 0.0% American Indian and Alaska Native, 0.0% Hispanic of any race, 0.0% two or more races (2000); Density: 1.4 persons per square mile (2000); Age: 20.8% under 18, 0.0% over 64 (2000); Marriage status: 18.4% never married, 76.3% now married, 5.3% widowed, 0.0% divorced (2000); Foreign born: 0.0% (2000); Ancestry (includes multiple ancestries): 50.0% Norwegian, 45.8% German, 25.0% Swedish, 18.8% Irish, 8.3% English (2000).
Economy: Employment by occupation: 16.0% management, 8.0% professional, 0.0% services, 24.0% sales, 0.0% farming, 36.0% construction, 16.0% production (2000).
Income: Per capita income: $12,950 (2000); Median household income: $39,167 (2000); Poverty rate: 0.0% (2000).
Taxes: Total city taxes per capita: $88 (1997); City property taxes per capita: $88 (1997).
Education: High school graduation rate: 100.0% (2000); College graduation rate: 0.0% (2000).
Housing: Homeownership rate: 83.3% (2000); Median home value: $47,500 (2000); Median age of housing: 35 years (2000).
Transportation: Commute to work: 92.0% car, 0.0% public transportation, 0.0% walk, 8.0% work from home (2000); Travel time to work: 0.0% less than 15 minutes, 65.2% 15 to 30 minutes, 17.4% 30 to 45 minutes, 8.7% 45 to 60 minutes, 8.7% 60 minutes or more (2000)

COMSTOCK (township). Covers a land area of 45.268 square miles and a water area of 0 square miles. Located at 48.23° N. Lat.; 96.56° W. Long.
Population: 135 (2000); Race: 100.0% White, 0.0% Black, 0.0% Asian, 0.0% American Indian and Alaska Native, 0.0% Hispanic of any race, 0.0% two or more races (2000); Density: 3.0 persons per square mile (2000); Age: 30.7% under 18, 15.3% over 64 (2000); Marriage status: 19.0% never married, 62.9% now married, 6.7% widowed, 11.4% divorced (2000); Foreign born: 0.0% (2000); Ancestry (includes multiple ancestries): 51.8% German, 35.0% Swedish, 23.4% Norwegian, 10.2% Polish, 7.3% Irish (2000).
Economy: Employment by occupation: 18.6% management, 13.6% professional, 1.7% services, 15.3% sales, 6.8% farming, 25.4% construction, 18.6% production (2000).
Income: Per capita income: $13,890 (2000); Median household income: $33,125 (2000); Poverty rate: 13.9% (2000).
Taxes: Total city taxes per capita: $102 (1997); City property taxes per capita: $102 (1997).
Education: High school graduation rate: 65.5% (2000); College graduation rate: 16.1% (2000).
Housing: Homeownership rate: 87.0% (2000); Median home value: $51,300 (2000); Median age of housing: 46 years (2000).
Transportation: Commute to work: 79.7% car, 0.0% public transportation, 3.4% walk, 16.9% work from home (2000); Travel time to work: 8.2% less than 15 minutes, 46.9% 15 to 30 minutes, 16.3% 30 to 45 minutes, 14.3% 45 to 60 minutes, 14.3% 60 minutes or more (2000)

DONNELLY (township). Covers a land area of 36.108 square miles and a water area of 0 square miles. Located at 48.49° N. Lat.; 96.97° W. Long.
Population: 28 (2000); Race: 100.0% White, 0.0% Black, 0.0% Asian, 0.0% American Indian and Alaska Native, 0.0% Hispanic of any race, 0.0% two or more races (2000); Density: 0.8 persons per square mile (2000); Age: 0.0% under 18, 52.2% over 64 (2000); Marriage status: 21.7% never married, 78.3% now married, 0.0% widowed, 0.0% divorced (2000); Foreign born: 0.0% (2000); Ancestry (includes multiple ancestries): 52.2% Norwegian, 34.8% Swedish, 13.0% English, 13.0% French (except Basque), 13.0% German (2000).
Economy: Employment by occupation: 50.0% management, 0.0% professional, 12.5% services, 0.0% sales, 0.0% farming, 18.8% construction, 18.8% production (2000).
Income: Per capita income: $19,561 (2000); Median household income: $40,625 (2000); Poverty rate: 0.0% (2000).
Taxes: Total city taxes per capita: $1,086 (1997); City property taxes per capita: $1,086 (1997).
Education: High school graduation rate: 90.0% (2000); College graduation rate: 25.0% (2000).
Housing: Homeownership rate: 100.0% (2000); Median age of housing: 19 years (2000).
Transportation: Commute to work: 100.0% car, 0.0% public transportation, 0.0% walk, 0.0% work from home (2000); Travel time to work: 42.9% less than 15 minutes, 14.3% 15 to 30 minutes, 21.4% 30 to 45 minutes, 21.4% 45 to 60 minutes, 0.0% 60 minutes or more (2000)

EAGLE POINT (township). Covers a land area of 27.880 square miles and a water area of 0.427 square miles. Located at 48.50° N. Lat.; 97.09° W. Long.
Population: 33 (2000); Race: 100.0% White, 0.0% Black, 0.0% Asian, 0.0% American Indian and Alaska Native, 0.0% Hispanic of any race, 0.0% two or more races (2000); Density: 1.2 persons per square mile (2000); Age: 13.8% under 18, 24.1% over 64 (2000); Marriage status: 4.0% never married, 88.0% now married, 8.0% widowed, 0.0% divorced (2000); Foreign born: 0.0% (2000); Ancestry (includes multiple ancestries): 55.2% Swedish, 34.5% Norwegian, 13.8% Irish, 13.8% Ukrainian, 10.3% French Canadian (2000).
Economy: Employment by occupation: 35.3% management, 0.0% professional, 0.0% services, 23.5% sales, 0.0% farming, 17.6% construction, 23.5% production (2000).
Income: Per capita income: $16,069 (2000); Median household income: $40,000 (2000); Poverty rate: 20.7% (2000).
Taxes: Total city taxes per capita: $128 (1997); City property taxes per capita: $128 (1997).
Education: High school graduation rate: 79.2% (2000); College graduation rate: 0.0% (2000).
Housing: Homeownership rate: 100.0% (2000); Median home value: $55,000 (2000); Median age of housing: 60 years (2000).
Transportation: Commute to work: 86.7% car, 0.0% public transportation, 0.0% walk, 13.3% work from home (2000); Travel time to work: 61.5% less than 15 minutes, 23.1% 15 to 30 minutes, 15.4% 30 to 45 minutes, 0.0% 45 to 60 minutes, 0.0% 60 minutes or more (2000)

EAST PARK (township). Covers a land area of 33.776 square miles and a water area of 2.513 square miles. Located at 48.49° N. Lat.; 96.30° W. Long.
Population: 19 (2000); Race: 100.0% White, 0.0% Black, 0.0% Asian, 0.0% American Indian and Alaska Native, 10.0% Hispanic of any race, 0.0% two or more races (2000); Density: 0.6 persons per square mile (2000); Age: 30.0% under 18, 20.0% over 64 (2000); Marriage status: 14.3% never married, 85.7% now married, 0.0% widowed, 0.0% divorced (2000); Foreign born: 0.0% (2000); Ancestry (includes multiple ancestries): 55.0% Norwegian, 35.0% Polish, 25.0% Swedish, 10.0% German, 10.0% Other groups (2000).
Economy: Employment by occupation: 22.2% management, 0.0% professional, 0.0% services, 33.3% sales, 0.0% farming, 0.0% construction, 44.4% production (2000).
Income: Per capita income: $7,750 (2000); Median household income: $16,250 (2000); Poverty rate: 25.0% (2000).
Taxes: Total city taxes per capita: $133 (1997); City property taxes per capita: $133 (1997).
Education: High school graduation rate: 71.4% (2000); College graduation rate: 0.0% (2000).
Housing: Homeownership rate: 100.0% (2000); Median home value: $55,000 (2000); Median age of housing: 29 years (2000).
Transportation: Commute to work: 100.0% car, 0.0% public transportation, 0.0% walk, 0.0% work from home (2000); Travel time to work: 0.0% less than 15 minutes, 22.2% 15 to 30 minutes, 55.6% 30 to 45 minutes, 0.0% 45 to 60 minutes, 22.2% 60 minutes or more (2000)

EAST VALLEY (township). Covers a land area of 22.027 square miles and a water area of 12.869 square miles. Located at 48.33° N. Lat.; 96.04° W. Long.
Population: 45 (2000); Race: 100.0% White, 0.0% Black, 0.0% Asian, 0.0% American Indian and Alaska Native, 0.0% Hispanic of any race, 0.0% two or more races (2000); Density: 2.0 persons per square mile (2000); Age: 8.5% under 18, 12.8% over 64 (2000); Marriage status: 29.8% never married, 51.1% now married, 4.3% widowed, 14.9% divorced (2000); Foreign born: 4.3% (2000); Ancestry (includes multiple ancestries): 59.6% Norwegian, 14.9% German, 8.5% Greek, 6.4% Finnish, 4.3% Swedish (2000).

Economy: Employment by occupation: 14.8% management, 14.8% professional, 7.4% services, 40.7% sales, 0.0% farming, 11.1% construction, 11.1% production (2000).
Income: Per capita income: $17,760 (2000); Median household income: $26,250 (2000); Poverty rate: 17.0% (2000).
Taxes: Total city taxes per capita: $36 (1997); City property taxes per capita: $36 (1997).
Education: High school graduation rate: 76.5% (2000); College graduation rate: 5.9% (2000).
Housing: Homeownership rate: 81.8% (2000); Median rent: $325 per month (2000); Median age of housing: 38 years (2000).
Transportation: Commute to work: 74.1% car, 0.0% public transportation, 0.0% walk, 25.9% work from home (2000); Travel time to work: 0.0% less than 15 minutes, 90.0% 15 to 30 minutes, 10.0% 30 to 45 minutes, 0.0% 45 to 60 minutes, 0.0% 60 minutes or more (2000)

ECKVOLL (township). Covers a land area of 35.457 square miles and a water area of 0 square miles. Located at 48.32° N. Lat.; 95.76° W. Long.
Population: 104 (2000); Race: 100.0% White, 0.0% Black, 0.0% Asian, 0.0% American Indian and Alaska Native, 0.0% Hispanic of any race, 0.0% two or more races (2000); Density: 2.9 persons per square mile (2000); Age: 31.9% under 18, 31.9% over 64 (2000); Marriage status: 15.6% never married, 79.7% now married, 0.0% widowed, 4.7% divorced (2000); Foreign born: 0.0% (2000); Ancestry (includes multiple ancestries): 71.4% Norwegian, 17.6% German, 7.7% English, 6.6% United States or American, 4.4% Finnish (2000).
Economy: Employment by occupation: 44.4% management, 0.0% professional, 0.0% services, 18.5% sales, 0.0% farming, 0.0% construction, 37.0% production (2000).
Income: Per capita income: $20,180 (2000); Median household income: $31,250 (2000); Poverty rate: 6.6% (2000).
Education: High school graduation rate: 55.2% (2000); College graduation rate: 10.3% (2000).
Housing: Homeownership rate: 92.6% (2000); Median home value: $40,000 (2000); Median age of housing: 32 years (2000).
Transportation: Commute to work: 70.4% car, 0.0% public transportation, 0.0% walk, 18.5% work from home (2000); Travel time to work: 31.8% less than 15 minutes, 9.1% 15 to 30 minutes, 13.6% 30 to 45 minutes, 45.5% 45 to 60 minutes, 0.0% 60 minutes or more (2000)

ESPELIE (township). Covers a land area of 44.647 square miles and a water area of 0 square miles. Located at 48.22° N. Lat.; 95.67° W. Long. Elevation is 1,177 feet.
Population: 58 (2000); Race: 100.0% White, 0.0% Black, 0.0% Asian, 0.0% American Indian and Alaska Native, 0.0% Hispanic of any race, 0.0% two or more races (2000); Density: 1.3 persons per square mile (2000); Age: 39.4% under 18, 6.1% over 64 (2000); Marriage status: 23.9% never married, 73.9% now married, 0.0% widowed, 2.2% divorced (2000); Foreign born: 0.0% (2000); Ancestry (includes multiple ancestries): 83.3% Norwegian, 15.2% Swedish, 9.1% Finnish, 4.5% Danish, 4.5% Yugoslavian (2000).
Economy: Employment by occupation: 50.0% management, 11.8% professional, 8.8% services, 11.8% sales, 2.9% farming, 14.7% construction, 0.0% production (2000).
Income: Per capita income: $12,565 (2000); Median household income: $43,750 (2000); Poverty rate: 13.6% (2000).
Taxes: Total city taxes per capita: $122 (1997); City property taxes per capita: $122 (1997).
Education: High school graduation rate: 89.2% (2000); College graduation rate: 5.4% (2000).
Housing: Homeownership rate: 100.0% (2000); Median home value: $112,500 (2000); Median age of housing: 26 years (2000).
Transportation: Commute to work: 68.8% car, 0.0% public transportation, 0.0% walk, 31.3% work from home (2000); Travel time to work: 36.4% less than 15 minutes, 18.2% 15 to 30 minutes, 22.7% 30 to 45 minutes, 13.6% 45 to 60 minutes, 9.1% 60 minutes or more (2000)

EXCEL (township). Covers a land area of 46.809 square miles and a water area of 0 square miles. Located at 48.21° N. Lat.; 96.18° W. Long.
Population: 280 (2000); Race: 100.0% White, 0.0% Black, 0.0% Asian, 0.0% American Indian and Alaska Native, 0.0% Hispanic of any race, 0.0% two or more races (2000); Density: 6.0 persons per square mile (2000); Age: 28.6% under 18, 7.3% over 64 (2000); Marriage status: 22.6% never married, 74.9% now married, 1.7% widowed, 0.8% divorced (2000); Foreign born: 0.0% (2000); Ancestry (includes multiple ancestries): 58.5% Norwegian, 33.2% German, 8.0% Swedish, 5.6% Polish, 5.6% English (2000).
Economy: Employment by occupation: 21.7% management, 10.6% professional, 22.4% services, 16.8% sales, 0.0% farming, 14.3% construction, 14.3% production (2000).
Income: Per capita income: $15,511 (2000); Median household income: $47,813 (2000); Poverty rate: 5.6% (2000).
Taxes: Total city taxes per capita: $124 (1997); City property taxes per capita: $124 (1997).
Education: High school graduation rate: 87.9% (2000); College graduation rate: 17.2% (2000).
Housing: Homeownership rate: 95.3% (2000); Median home value: $93,300 (2000); Median age of housing: 29 years (2000).
Transportation: Commute to work: 89.9% car, 0.0% public transportation, 0.0% walk, 9.4% work from home (2000); Travel time to work: 27.8% less than 15 minutes, 59.0% 15 to 30 minutes, 6.3% 30 to 45 minutes, 2.8% 45 to 60 minutes, 4.2% 60 minutes or more (2000)

FOLDAHL (township). Covers a land area of 36.289 square miles and a water area of 0 square miles. Located at 48.32° N. Lat.; 96.57° W. Long. Elevation is 986 feet.
Population: 94 (2000); Race: 98.0% White, 0.0% Black, 0.0% Asian, 0.0% American Indian and Alaska Native, 0.0% Hispanic of any race, 2.0% two or more races (2000); Density: 2.6 persons per square mile (2000); Age: 26.0% under 18, 22.0% over 64 (2000); Marriage status: 27.9% never married, 68.6% now married, 3.5% widowed, 0.0% divorced (2000); Foreign born: 0.0% (2000); Ancestry (includes multiple ancestries): 53.0% Norwegian, 36.0% Swedish, 23.0% German, 13.0% Polish, 10.0% English (2000).
Economy: Employment by occupation: 7.5% management, 17.5% professional, 0.0% services, 5.0% sales, 5.0% farming, 25.0% construction, 40.0% production (2000).
Income: Per capita income: $14,870 (2000); Median household income: $34,286 (2000); Poverty rate: 2.0% (2000).
Taxes: Total city taxes per capita: $68 (1997); City property taxes per capita: $68 (1997).
Education: High school graduation rate: 70.4% (2000); College graduation rate: 12.7% (2000).
Housing: Homeownership rate: 94.7% (2000); Median home value: $65,000 (2000); Median age of housing: 36 years (2000).
Transportation: Commute to work: 95.0% car, 0.0% public transportation, 0.0% walk, 5.0% work from home (2000); Travel time to work: 7.9% less than 15 minutes, 50.0% 15 to 30 minutes, 10.5% 30 to 45 minutes, 7.9% 45 to 60 minutes, 23.7% 60 minutes or more (2000)

FORK (township). Covers a land area of 26.595 square miles and a water area of 0.496 square miles. Located at 48.40° N. Lat.; 97.09° W. Long.
Population: 14 (2000); Race: 100.0% White, 0.0% Black, 0.0% Asian, 0.0% American Indian and Alaska Native, 0.0% Hispanic of any race, 0.0% two or more races (2000); Density: 0.5 persons per square mile (2000); Age: 31.6% under 18, 0.0% over 64 (2000); Marriage status: 15.4% never married, 69.2% now married, 0.0% widowed, 15.4% divorced (2000); Foreign born: 0.0% (2000); Ancestry (includes multiple ancestries): 57.9% Polish, 52.6% Norwegian, 26.3% Swedish, 21.1% German, 15.8% Irish (2000).
Economy: Employment by occupation: 50.0% management, 10.0% professional, 20.0% services, 20.0% sales, 0.0% farming, 0.0% construction, 0.0% production (2000).
Income: Per capita income: $5,868 (2000); Median household income: $31,250 (2000); Poverty rate: 31.6% (2000).
Taxes: Total city taxes per capita: $517 (1997); City property taxes per capita: $517 (1997).
Education: High school graduation rate: 84.6% (2000); College graduation rate: 15.4% (2000).
Housing: Homeownership rate: 66.7% (2000); Median age of housing: 40 years (2000).
Transportation: Commute to work: 90.0% car, 0.0% public transportation, 0.0% walk, 10.0% work from home (2000); Travel time to work: 22.2% less than 15 minutes, 66.7% 15 to 30 minutes, 11.1% 30 to 45 minutes, 0.0% 45 to 60 minutes, 0.0% 60 minutes or more (2000)

GATZKE (unincorporated postal area, zip code 56724). Covers a land area of 118.747 square miles and a water area of 0.048 square miles. Located at 48.44° N. Lat.; 95.74° W. Long.
Population: 226 (2000); Race: 97.5% White, 2.5% Black, 0.0% Asian, 0.0% American Indian and Alaska Native, 0.0% Hispanic of any race, 0.0% two or more races (2000); Density: 1.9 persons per square mile (2000); Age: 12.4% under 18, 25.4% over 64 (2000); Marriage status: 16.5% never married, 74.4% now married, 2.8% widowed, 6.3% divorced (2000); Foreign born: 0.0% (2000); Ancestry (includes multiple ancestries): 65.7% Norwegian,

19.4% German, 16.9% Swedish, 4.5% French (except Basque), 4.5% Irish (2000).
Economy: Employment by occupation: 13.7% management, 10.5% professional, 11.6% services, 17.9% sales, 0.0% farming, 10.5% construction, 35.8% production (2000).
Income: Per capita income: $18,382 (2000); Median household income: $36,964 (2000); Poverty rate: 6.5% (2000).
Education: High school graduation rate: 79.3% (2000); College graduation rate: 11.2% (2000).
Housing: Homeownership rate: 90.4% (2000); Median home value: $73,800 (2000); Median rent: <$100 per month (2000); Median age of housing: 29 years (2000).
Transportation: Commute to work: 84.2% car, 0.0% public transportation, 0.0% walk, 14.7% work from home (2000); Travel time to work: 14.8% less than 15 minutes, 9.9% 15 to 30 minutes, 50.6% 30 to 45 minutes, 14.8% 45 to 60 minutes, 9.9% 60 minutes or more (2000)

GRAND PLAIN (township). Covers a land area of 44.878 square miles and a water area of 0.007 square miles. Located at 48.20° N. Lat.; 95.92° W. Long.
Population: 55 (2000); Race: 100.0% White, 0.0% Black, 0.0% Asian, 0.0% American Indian and Alaska Native, 0.0% Hispanic of any race, 0.0% two or more races (2000); Density: 1.2 persons per square mile (2000); Age: 21.6% under 18, 25.5% over 64 (2000); Marriage status: 19.0% never married, 66.7% now married, 2.4% widowed, 11.9% divorced (2000); Foreign born: 0.0% (2000); Ancestry (includes multiple ancestries): 43.1% Norwegian, 21.6% German, 11.8% Swedish, 11.8% Polish, 7.8% Danish (2000).
Economy: Single-family building permits issued: 0 (2001) / 0 (2000); Multi-family building permits issued: 0 (2001) / 0 (2000); Employment by occupation: 34.6% management, 0.0% professional, 0.0% services, 38.5% sales, 15.4% farming, 3.8% construction, 7.7% production (2000).
Income: Per capita income: $15,398 (2000); Median household income: $31,563 (2000); Poverty rate: 37.3% (2000).
Taxes: Total city taxes per capita: $153 (1997); City property taxes per capita: $153 (1997).
Education: High school graduation rate: 86.5% (2000); College graduation rate: 5.4% (2000).
Housing: Homeownership rate: 100.0% (2000); Median home value: $118,800 (2000); Median age of housing: 29 years (2000).
Transportation: Commute to work: 53.8% car, 0.0% public transportation, 0.0% walk, 46.2% work from home (2000); Travel time to work: 14.3% less than 15 minutes, 57.1% 15 to 30 minutes, 14.3% 30 to 45 minutes, 0.0% 45 to 60 minutes, 14.3% 60 minutes or more (2000)

GRYGLA (city). Covers a land area of 0.627 square miles and a water area of 0 square miles. Located at 48.30° N. Lat.; 95.62° W. Long. Elevation is 1,179 feet.
Population: 228 (2000); Race: 97.6% White, 0.0% Black, 2.4% Asian, 0.0% American Indian and Alaska Native, 0.0% Hispanic of any race, 0.0% two or more races (2000); Density: 363.8 persons per square mile (2000); Age: 24.0% under 18, 29.9% over 64 (2000); Marriage status: 33.0% never married, 41.1% now married, 9.6% widowed, 16.3% divorced (2000); Foreign born: 2.4% (2000); Ancestry (includes multiple ancestries): 56.3% Norwegian, 15.0% Swedish, 14.2% German, 4.3% Finnish, 4.3% English (2000).
Economy: Timber; cattle, sheep; grain. Manufacturing: wood milling. Agassiz National Wildlife Refuge to West. Single-family building permits issued: 2 (2001) / 0 (2000); Multi-family building permits issued: 4 (2001) / 0 (2000); Employment by occupation: 5.1% management, 21.2% professional, 15.2% services, 6.1% sales, 4.0% farming, 8.1% construction, 40.4% production (2000).
Income: Per capita income: $14,635 (2000); Median household income: $25,625 (2000); Poverty rate: 17.7% (2000).
Taxes: Total city taxes per capita: $115 (1997); City property taxes per capita: $101 (1997).
Education: High school graduation rate: 61.8% (2000); College graduation rate: 9.1% (2000).

School District(s)

Grygla (PK-12)
2000 Enrollment: 201 218-294-6155
Housing: Homeownership rate: 75.6% (2000); Median home value: $47,500 (2000); Median rent: $208 per month (2000); Median age of housing: 26 years (2000).
Newspapers: Grygla Eagle (1 x week)
Transportation: Commute to work: 64.6% car, 0.0% public transportation, 24.2% walk, 7.1% work from home (2000); Travel time to work: 60.9% less than 15 minutes, 6.5% 15 to 30 minutes, 7.6% 30 to 45 minutes, 17.4% 45 to 60 minutes, 7.6% 60 minutes or more (2000)

HOLT (city). Covers a land area of 1.009 square miles and a water area of 0 square miles. Located at 48.29° N. Lat.; 96.19° W. Long. Elevation is 1,155 feet.
Population: 89 (2000); Race: 92.5% White, 0.0% Black, 0.0% Asian, 1.3% American Indian and Alaska Native, 0.0% Hispanic of any race, 6.3% two or more races (2000); Density: 88.2 persons per square mile (2000); Age: 17.5% under 18, 5.0% over 64 (2000); Marriage status: 21.7% never married, 71.0% now married, 0.0% widowed, 7.2% divorced (2000); Foreign born: 0.0% (2000); Ancestry (includes multiple ancestries): 52.5% Norwegian, 30.0% German, 22.5% Swedish, 5.0% Other groups, 3.8% French (except Basque) (2000).
Economy: Employment by occupation: 5.1% management, 10.3% professional, 15.4% services, 41.0% sales, 0.0% farming, 12.8% construction, 15.4% production (2000).
Income: Per capita income: $14,796 (2000); Median household income: $32,500 (2000); Poverty rate: 8.8% (2000).
Taxes: Total city taxes per capita: $35 (1997); City property taxes per capita: $35 (1997).
Education: High school graduation rate: 65.3% (2000); College graduation rate: 12.2% (2000).
Housing: Homeownership rate: 97.1% (2000); Median home value: $27,500 (2000); Median age of housing: 59 years (2000).
Transportation: Commute to work: 89.7% car, 0.0% public transportation, 5.1% walk, 5.1% work from home (2000); Travel time to work: 10.8% less than 15 minutes, 67.6% 15 to 30 minutes, 10.8% 30 to 45 minutes, 5.4% 45 to 60 minutes, 5.4% 60 minutes or more (2000)

HOLT (township). Covers a land area of 33.697 square miles and a water area of 0 square miles. Located at 48.33° N. Lat.; 96.18° W. Long. Elevation is 1,155 feet.
Population: 147 (2000); Race: 100.0% White, 0.0% Black, 0.0% Asian, 0.0% American Indian and Alaska Native, 0.0% Hispanic of any race, 0.0% two or more races (2000); Density: 4.4 persons per square mile (2000); Age: 22.8% under 18, 22.8% over 64 (2000); Marriage status: 26.2% never married, 59.5% now married, 5.6% widowed, 8.7% divorced (2000); Foreign born: 0.0% (2000); Ancestry (includes multiple ancestries): 65.8% Norwegian, 26.8% German, 20.1% Swedish, 6.7% Northern European, 4.0% Lithuanian (2000).
Economy: Agricultural area: grain, beans, potatoes; livestock. Agassiz National Wildlife Refuge to East. Employment by occupation: 4.8% management, 16.1% professional, 14.5% services, 25.8% sales, 0.0% farming, 6.5% construction, 32.3% production (2000).
Income: Per capita income: $13,720 (2000); Median household income: $28,750 (2000); Poverty rate: 12.8% (2000).
Taxes: Total city taxes per capita: $51 (1997); City property taxes per capita: $51 (1997).
Education: High school graduation rate: 79.5% (2000); College graduation rate: 3.6% (2000).
Housing: Homeownership rate: 93.5% (2000); Median home value: $75,000 (2000); Median rent: $175 per month (2000); Median age of housing: 51 years (2000).
Transportation: Commute to work: 90.3% car, 0.0% public transportation, 0.0% walk, 9.7% work from home (2000); Travel time to work: 10.7% less than 15 minutes, 58.9% 15 to 30 minutes, 23.2% 30 to 45 minutes, 0.0% 45 to 60 minutes, 7.1% 60 minutes or more (2000)

HUNTLY (township). Covers a land area of 36.029 square miles and a water area of 0.567 square miles. Located at 48.50° N. Lat.; 96.18° W. Long.
Population: 68 (2000); Race: 97.3% White, 0.0% Black, 0.0% Asian, 0.0% American Indian and Alaska Native, 0.0% Hispanic of any race, 2.7% two or more races (2000); Density: 1.9 persons per square mile (2000); Age: 24.3% under 18, 12.2% over 64 (2000); Marriage status: 30.3% never married, 60.6% now married, 7.6% widowed, 1.5% divorced (2000); Foreign born: 0.0% (2000); Ancestry (includes multiple ancestries): 68.9% Norwegian, 23.0% German, 20.3% Swedish, 6.8% Irish, 4.1% English (2000).
Economy: Employment by occupation: 7.3% management, 7.3% professional, 7.3% services, 2.4% sales, 7.3% farming, 22.0% construction, 46.3% production (2000).
Income: Per capita income: $11,968 (2000); Median household income: $25,750 (2000); Poverty rate: 4.1% (2000).
Taxes: Total city taxes per capita: $12 (1997); City property taxes per capita: $12 (1997).

Education: High school graduation rate: 79.6% (2000); College graduation rate: 6.1% (2000).
Housing: Homeownership rate: 94.1% (2000); Median home value: $85,000 (2000); Median age of housing: 42 years (2000).
Transportation: Commute to work: 90.2% car, 0.0% public transportation, 4.9% walk, 4.9% work from home (2000); Travel time to work: 15.4% less than 15 minutes, 17.9% 15 to 30 minutes, 33.3% 30 to 45 minutes, 28.2% 45 to 60 minutes, 5.1% 60 minutes or more (2000)

LINCOLN (township). Covers a land area of 35.561 square miles and a water area of 0 square miles. Located at 48.49° N. Lat.; 96.45° W. Long.
Population: 124 (2000); Race: 100.0% White, 0.0% Black, 0.0% Asian, 0.0% American Indian and Alaska Native, 0.0% Hispanic of any race, 0.0% two or more races (2000); Density: 3.5 persons per square mile (2000); Age: 26.2% under 18, 16.7% over 64 (2000); Marriage status: 23.7% never married, 61.9% now married, 9.3% widowed, 5.2% divorced (2000); Foreign born: 0.0% (2000); Ancestry (includes multiple ancestries): 73.0% Norwegian, 42.9% Swedish, 12.7% German, 6.3% Danish, 5.6% Russian (2000).
Economy: Employment by occupation: 9.4% management, 5.7% professional, 13.2% services, 24.5% sales, 7.5% farming, 11.3% construction, 28.3% production (2000).
Income: Per capita income: $12,943 (2000); Median household income: $33,125 (2000); Poverty rate: 26.2% (2000).
Taxes: Total city taxes per capita: $73 (1997); City property taxes per capita: $73 (1997).
Education: High school graduation rate: 80.7% (2000); College graduation rate: 3.6% (2000).
Housing: Homeownership rate: 87.2% (2000); Median home value: $35,000 (2000); Median age of housing: 45 years (2000).
Transportation: Commute to work: 94.1% car, 0.0% public transportation, 0.0% walk, 5.9% work from home (2000); Travel time to work: 41.7% less than 15 minutes, 31.3% 15 to 30 minutes, 8.3% 30 to 45 minutes, 8.3% 45 to 60 minutes, 10.4% 60 minutes or more (2000)

LINSELL (township). Covers a land area of 35.834 square miles and a water area of 0 square miles. Located at 48.49° N. Lat.; 95.68° W. Long.
Population: 36 (2000); Race: 100.0% White, 0.0% Black, 0.0% Asian, 0.0% American Indian and Alaska Native, 0.0% Hispanic of any race, 0.0% two or more races (2000); Density: 1.0 persons per square mile (2000); Age: 18.5% under 18, 7.4% over 64 (2000); Marriage status: 31.8% never married, 59.1% now married, 9.1% widowed, 0.0% divorced (2000); Foreign born: 0.0% (2000); Ancestry (includes multiple ancestries): 66.7% Norwegian, 25.9% Swedish, 18.5% German, 7.4% Other groups, 7.4% French (except Basque) (2000).
Economy: Employment by occupation: 27.3% management, 0.0% professional, 18.2% services, 18.2% sales, 0.0% farming, 18.2% construction, 18.2% production (2000).
Income: Per capita income: $20,770 (2000); Median household income: $42,500 (2000); Poverty rate: 11.1% (2000).
Taxes: Total city taxes per capita: $116 (1997); City property taxes per capita: $116 (1997).
Education: High school graduation rate: 72.2% (2000); College graduation rate: 0.0% (2000).
Housing: Homeownership rate: 100.0% (2000); Median home value: $37,500 (2000); Median age of housing: 30 years (2000).
Transportation: Commute to work: 81.8% car, 0.0% public transportation, 0.0% walk, 18.2% work from home (2000); Travel time to work: 11.1% less than 15 minutes, 22.2% 15 to 30 minutes, 33.3% 30 to 45 minutes, 0.0% 45 to 60 minutes, 33.3% 60 minutes or more (2000)

MARSH GROVE (township). Covers a land area of 35.806 square miles and a water area of 0.002 square miles. Located at 48.33° N. Lat.; 96.44° W. Long.
Population: 145 (2000); Race: 100.0% White, 0.0% Black, 0.0% Asian, 0.0% American Indian and Alaska Native, 0.0% Hispanic of any race, 0.0% two or more races (2000); Density: 4.0 persons per square mile (2000); Age: 32.1% under 18, 20.6% over 64 (2000); Marriage status: 19.6% never married, 72.5% now married, 5.9% widowed, 2.0% divorced (2000); Foreign born: 0.0% (2000); Ancestry (includes multiple ancestries): 72.5% Norwegian, 14.5% Swedish, 10.7% German, 10.7% Polish, 7.6% Czech (2000).
Economy: Employment by occupation: 23.7% management, 15.3% professional, 15.3% services, 18.6% sales, 6.8% farming, 6.8% construction, 13.6% production (2000).
Income: Per capita income: $13,827 (2000); Median household income: $35,625 (2000); Poverty rate: 15.3% (2000).
Taxes: Total city taxes per capita: $87 (1997); City property taxes per capita: $87 (1997).
Education: High school graduation rate: 71.8% (2000); College graduation rate: 7.1% (2000).
Housing: Homeownership rate: 80.0% (2000); Median home value: $90,000 (2000); Median rent: $275 per month (2000); Median age of housing: 35 years (2000).
Transportation: Commute to work: 79.7% car, 0.0% public transportation, 0.0% walk, 20.3% work from home (2000); Travel time to work: 25.5% less than 15 minutes, 25.5% 15 to 30 minutes, 44.7% 30 to 45 minutes, 0.0% 45 to 60 minutes, 4.3% 60 minutes or more (2000)

MCCREA (township). Covers a land area of 44.977 square miles and a water area of 0 square miles. Located at 48.21° N. Lat.; 96.69° W. Long.
Population: 250 (2000); Race: 98.1% White, 0.0% Black, 0.0% Asian, 0.0% American Indian and Alaska Native, 1.9% Hispanic of any race, 0.0% two or more races (2000); Density: 5.6 persons per square mile (2000); Age: 18.7% under 18, 17.5% over 64 (2000); Marriage status: 8.1% never married, 83.8% now married, 5.7% widowed, 2.4% divorced (2000); Foreign born: 1.6% (2000); Ancestry (includes multiple ancestries): 31.9% Norwegian, 28.4% German, 27.2% Swedish, 12.5% Polish, 10.1% French (except Basque) (2000).
Economy: Employment by occupation: 20.7% management, 16.4% professional, 8.6% services, 26.4% sales, 7.1% farming, 10.7% construction, 10.0% production (2000).
Income: Per capita income: $23,676 (2000); Median household income: $52,500 (2000); Poverty rate: 4.3% (2000).
Taxes: Total city taxes per capita: $48 (1997); City property taxes per capita: $48 (1997).
Education: High school graduation rate: 88.7% (2000); College graduation rate: 17.2% (2000).
Housing: Homeownership rate: 89.7% (2000); Median home value: $70,500 (2000); Median rent: $375 per month (2000); Median age of housing: 32 years (2000).
Transportation: Commute to work: 84.8% car, 0.0% public transportation, 7.2% walk, 6.5% work from home (2000); Travel time to work: 72.9% less than 15 minutes, 10.1% 15 to 30 minutes, 3.9% 30 to 45 minutes, 7.8% 45 to 60 minutes, 5.4% 60 minutes or more (2000)

MIDDLE RIVER (city). Covers a land area of 0.498 square miles and a water area of 0 square miles. Located at 48.43° N. Lat.; 96.16° W. Long. Elevation is 1,141 feet.
Population: 319 (2000); Race: 95.0% White, 0.0% Black, 0.9% Asian, 0.0% American Indian and Alaska Native, 0.9% Hispanic of any race, 4.0% two or more races (2000); Density: 639.9 persons per square mile (2000); Age: 24.8% under 18, 14.0% over 64 (2000); Marriage status: 26.0% never married, 45.0% now married, 10.9% widowed, 18.2% divorced (2000); Foreign born: 0.9% (2000); Ancestry (includes multiple ancestries): 55.6% Norwegian, 11.2% Swedish, 9.9% Polish, 8.1% German, 6.2% Irish (2000).
Economy: Single-family building permits issued: 2 (2001) / 0 (2000); Multi-family building permits issued: 0 (2001) / 0 (2000); Employment by occupation: 7.0% management, 18.6% professional, 17.1% services, 21.7% sales, 0.0% farming, 11.6% construction, 24.0% production (2000).
Income: Per capita income: $14,059 (2000); Median household income: $23,929 (2000); Poverty rate: 10.6% (2000).
Taxes: Total city taxes per capita: $102 (1997); City property taxes per capita: $95 (1997).
Education: High school graduation rate: 84.6% (2000); College graduation rate: 13.1% (2000).
Housing: Homeownership rate: 72.3% (2000); Median home value: $29,400 (2000); Median rent: $189 per month (2000); Median age of housing: 34 years (2000).
Transportation: Commute to work: 87.6% car, 0.8% public transportation, 6.2% walk, 5.4% work from home (2000); Travel time to work: 33.6% less than 15 minutes, 23.8% 15 to 30 minutes, 23.0% 30 to 45 minutes, 15.6% 45 to 60 minutes, 4.1% 60 minutes or more (2000)

MIDDLE RIVER (township). Covers a land area of 34.811 square miles and a water area of 0 square miles. Located at 48.31° N. Lat.; 96.82° W. Long. Elevation is 1,141 feet.
Population: 102 (2000); Race: 100.0% White, 0.0% Black, 0.0% Asian, 0.0% American Indian and Alaska Native, 0.0% Hispanic of any race, 0.0% two or more races (2000); Density: 2.9 persons per square mile (2000); Age: 25.0% under 18, 10.4% over 64 (2000); Marriage status: 23.2% never

married, 67.1% now married, 4.9% widowed, 4.9% divorced (2000); Foreign born: 2.1% (2000); Ancestry (includes multiple ancestries): 35.4% Polish, 21.9% Norwegian, 21.9% French (except Basque), 20.8% German, 15.6% Irish (2000).
Economy: Falls. Wheat, sugar beets, potatoes, beans, sunflowers. Manufacturing: flour milling, transportation equipment. Agassiz National Wildlife Refuge to Southeast. Employment by occupation: 23.2% management, 23.2% professional, 14.3% services, 25.0% sales, 1.8% farming, 1.8% construction, 10.7% production (2000).
Income: Per capita income: $16,793 (2000); Median household income: $37,500 (2000); Poverty rate: 7.3% (2000).
Taxes: Total city taxes per capita: $180 (1997); City property taxes per capita: $180 (1997).
Education: High school graduation rate: 97.1% (2000); College graduation rate: 16.2% (2000).
Housing: Homeownership rate: 81.0% (2000); Median home value: $70,000 (2000); Median rent: $225 per month (2000); Median age of housing: 45 years (2000).
Transportation: Commute to work: 85.7% car, 0.0% public transportation, 0.0% walk, 14.3% work from home (2000); Travel time to work: 70.8% less than 15 minutes, 14.6% 15 to 30 minutes, 0.0% 30 to 45 minutes, 12.5% 45 to 60 minutes, 2.1% 60 minutes or more (2000)

MOOSE RIVER (township). Covers a land area of 33.640 square miles and a water area of 2.011 square miles. Located at 48.49° N. Lat.; 95.80° W. Long.
Population: 28 (2000); Race: 100.0% White, 0.0% Black, 0.0% Asian, 0.0% American Indian and Alaska Native, 0.0% Hispanic of any race, 0.0% two or more races (2000); Density: 0.8 persons per square mile (2000); Age: 0.0% under 18, 42.3% over 64 (2000); Marriage status: 0.0% never married, 92.3% now married, 0.0% widowed, 7.7% divorced (2000); Foreign born: 0.0% (2000); Ancestry (includes multiple ancestries): 46.2% Norwegian, 30.8% German, 15.4% Swedish (2000).
Economy: Employment by occupation: 0.0% management, 16.7% professional, 0.0% services, 0.0% sales, 0.0% farming, 33.3% construction, 50.0% production (2000).
Income: Per capita income: $24,138 (2000); Median household income: $41,250 (2000); Poverty rate: 0.0% (2000).
Taxes: Total city taxes per capita: $64 (1997); City property taxes per capita: $64 (1997).
Education: High school graduation rate: 80.8% (2000); College graduation rate: 7.7% (2000).
Housing: Homeownership rate: 100.0% (2000); Median home value: $22,500 (2000); Median age of housing: 35 years (2000).
Transportation: Commute to work: 100.0% car, 0.0% public transportation, 0.0% walk, 0.0% work from home (2000); Travel time to work: 0.0% less than 15 minutes, 25.0% 15 to 30 minutes, 75.0% 30 to 45 minutes, 0.0% 45 to 60 minutes, 0.0% 60 minutes or more (2000)

MOYLAN (township). Covers a land area of 45.117 square miles and a water area of 0.013 square miles. Located at 48.22° N. Lat.; 95.78° W. Long.
Population: 128 (2000); Race: 97.1% White, 0.0% Black, 1.9% Asian, 0.0% American Indian and Alaska Native, 1.0% Hispanic of any race, 0.0% two or more races (2000); Density: 2.8 persons per square mile (2000); Age: 25.0% under 18, 19.2% over 64 (2000); Marriage status: 16.3% never married, 67.5% now married, 6.3% widowed, 10.0% divorced (2000); Foreign born: 2.9% (2000); Ancestry (includes multiple ancestries): 50.0% Norwegian, 17.3% Swedish, 17.3% German, 10.6% Irish, 8.7% Polish (2000).
Economy: Employment by occupation: 26.1% management, 8.7% professional, 13.0% services, 21.7% sales, 0.0% farming, 4.3% construction, 26.1% production (2000).
Income: Per capita income: $14,990 (2000); Median household income: $25,833 (2000); Poverty rate: 32.7% (2000).
Taxes: Total city taxes per capita: $77 (1997); City property taxes per capita: $77 (1997).
Education: High school graduation rate: 80.3% (2000); College graduation rate: 5.3% (2000).
Housing: Homeownership rate: 77.8% (2000); Median home value: $65,000 (2000); Median rent: $175 per month (2000); Median age of housing: 41 years (2000).
Transportation: Commute to work: 68.2% car, 0.0% public transportation, 0.0% walk, 31.8% work from home (2000); Travel time to work: 20.0% less than 15 minutes, 33.3% 15 to 30 minutes, 20.0% 30 to 45 minutes, 10.0% 45 to 60 minutes, 16.7% 60 minutes or more (2000)

NELSON PARK (township). Covers a land area of 36.137 square miles and a water area of 0.050 square miles. Located at 48.49° N. Lat.; 96.56° W. Long.
Population: 158 (2000); Race: 100.0% White, 0.0% Black, 0.0% Asian, 0.0% American Indian and Alaska Native, 0.0% Hispanic of any race, 0.0% two or more races (2000); Density: 4.4 persons per square mile (2000); Age: 30.8% under 18, 16.8% over 64 (2000); Marriage status: 18.6% never married, 74.3% now married, 3.5% widowed, 3.5% divorced (2000); Foreign born: 0.0% (2000); Ancestry (includes multiple ancestries): 63.6% Polish, 21.7% Norwegian, 16.1% German, 14.7% Swedish, 3.5% English (2000).
Economy: Employment by occupation: 19.4% management, 20.9% professional, 14.9% services, 22.4% sales, 0.0% farming, 7.5% construction, 14.9% production (2000).
Income: Per capita income: $12,661 (2000); Median household income: $35,000 (2000); Poverty rate: 7.7% (2000).
Taxes: Total city taxes per capita: $64 (1997); City property taxes per capita: $64 (1997).
Education: High school graduation rate: 75.8% (2000); College graduation rate: 10.5% (2000).
Housing: Homeownership rate: 94.6% (2000); Median home value: $38,300 (2000); Median age of housing: 51 years (2000).
Transportation: Commute to work: 94.0% car, 0.0% public transportation, 1.5% walk, 4.5% work from home (2000); Travel time to work: 34.4% less than 15 minutes, 21.9% 15 to 30 minutes, 21.9% 30 to 45 minutes, 9.4% 45 to 60 minutes, 12.5% 60 minutes or more (2000)

NEW FOLDEN (township). Covers a land area of 35.024 square miles and a water area of 0 square miles. Located at 48.34° N. Lat.; 96.30° W. Long.
Population: 197 (2000); Race: 93.9% White, 0.0% Black, 0.0% Asian, 0.0% American Indian and Alaska Native, 0.0% Hispanic of any race, 6.1% two or more races (2000); Density: 5.6 persons per square mile (2000); Age: 27.0% under 18, 12.8% over 64 (2000); Marriage status: 24.7% never married, 58.0% now married, 10.0% widowed, 7.3% divorced (2000); Foreign born: 0.0% (2000); Ancestry (includes multiple ancestries): 77.6% Norwegian, 18.4% Swedish, 10.7% German, 7.1% Polish, 2.0% Czech (2000).
Economy: Employment by occupation: 17.7% management, 13.5% professional, 11.5% services, 19.8% sales, 2.1% farming, 13.5% construction, 21.9% production (2000).
Income: Per capita income: $15,905 (2000); Median household income: $35,625 (2000); Poverty rate: 5.1% (2000).
Taxes: Total city taxes per capita: $101 (1997); City property taxes per capita: $101 (1997).
Education: High school graduation rate: 74.6% (2000); College graduation rate: 7.5% (2000).
Housing: Homeownership rate: 93.7% (2000); Median home value: $70,000 (2000); Median rent: <$100 per month (2000); Median age of housing: 37 years (2000).
Transportation: Commute to work: 95.8% car, 0.0% public transportation, 0.0% walk, 4.2% work from home (2000); Travel time to work: 24.2% less than 15 minutes, 41.8% 15 to 30 minutes, 19.8% 30 to 45 minutes, 0.0% 45 to 60 minutes, 14.3% 60 minutes or more (2000)

NEW MAINE (township). Covers a land area of 36.877 square miles and a water area of 0 square miles. Located at 48.40° N. Lat.; 96.33° W. Long.
Population: 194 (2000); Race: 100.0% White, 0.0% Black, 0.0% Asian, 0.0% American Indian and Alaska Native, 0.0% Hispanic of any race, 0.0% two or more races (2000); Density: 5.3 persons per square mile (2000); Age: 23.6% under 18, 9.0% over 64 (2000); Marriage status: 25.9% never married, 68.7% now married, 1.8% widowed, 3.6% divorced (2000); Foreign born: 0.0% (2000); Ancestry (includes multiple ancestries): 55.3% Norwegian, 19.1% Swedish, 14.1% German, 10.1% Scandinavian, 4.5% Polish (2000).
Economy: Employment by occupation: 7.4% management, 7.4% professional, 11.7% services, 23.4% sales, 0.0% farming, 11.7% construction, 38.3% production (2000).
Income: Per capita income: $12,554 (2000); Median household income: $32,813 (2000); Poverty rate: 17.6% (2000).
Taxes: Total city taxes per capita: $34 (1997); City property taxes per capita: $34 (1997).
Education: High school graduation rate: 80.7% (2000); College graduation rate: 4.4% (2000).
Housing: Homeownership rate: 97.4% (2000); Median home value: $47,500 (2000); Median rent: $175 per month (2000); Median age of housing: 29 years (2000).

Transportation: Commute to work: 89.4% car, 0.0% public transportation, 0.0% walk, 10.6% work from home (2000); Travel time to work: 21.4% less than 15 minutes, 35.7% 15 to 30 minutes, 32.1% 30 to 45 minutes, 8.3% 45 to 60 minutes, 2.4% 60 minutes or more (2000)

NEW SOLUM (township). Covers a land area of 46.280 square miles and a water area of 0 square miles. Located at 48.22° N. Lat.; 96.29° W. Long.
Population: 313 (2000); Race: 97.4% White, 0.0% Black, 0.0% Asian, 0.0% American Indian and Alaska Native, 0.0% Hispanic of any race, 2.6% two or more races (2000); Density: 6.8 persons per square mile (2000); Age: 29.1% under 18, 2.9% over 64 (2000); Marriage status: 25.6% never married, 66.7% now married, 3.8% widowed, 3.8% divorced (2000); Foreign born: 0.0% (2000); Ancestry (includes multiple ancestries): 63.4% Norwegian, 21.0% German, 14.9% Swedish, 4.9% Danish, 4.2% Polish (2000).
Economy: Employment by occupation: 7.7% management, 15.4% professional, 11.2% services, 23.1% sales, 0.0% farming, 9.5% construction, 33.1% production (2000).
Income: Per capita income: $18,252 (2000); Median household income: $43,542 (2000); Poverty rate: 1.0% (2000).
Taxes: Total city taxes per capita: $68 (1997); City property taxes per capita: $68 (1997).
Education: High school graduation rate: 88.9% (2000); College graduation rate: 3.7% (2000).
Housing: Homeownership rate: 94.4% (2000); Median home value: $65,000 (2000); Median rent: $225 per month (2000); Median age of housing: 35 years (2000).
Transportation: Commute to work: 91.1% car, 0.0% public transportation, 0.6% walk, 8.3% work from home (2000); Travel time to work: 14.2% less than 15 minutes, 61.3% 15 to 30 minutes, 16.8% 30 to 45 minutes, 1.3% 45 to 60 minutes, 6.5% 60 minutes or more (2000)

NEWFOLDEN (city). Covers a land area of 0.894 square miles and a water area of 0 square miles. Located at 48.35° N. Lat.; 96.32° W. Long. Elevation is 1,093 feet.
History: Scandinavian settlers began to come to Newfolden in 1882, and named the town for a seaport in northern Norway.
Population: 362 (2000); Race: 100.0% White, 0.0% Black, 0.0% Asian, 0.0% American Indian and Alaska Native, 0.5% Hispanic of any race, 0.0% two or more races (2000); Density: 404.9 persons per square mile (2000); Age: 26.4% under 18, 23.4% over 64 (2000); Marriage status: 19.9% never married, 61.7% now married, 13.2% widowed, 5.2% divorced (2000); Foreign born: 0.0% (2000); Ancestry (includes multiple ancestries): 55.4% Norwegian, 21.7% Swedish, 15.8% German, 7.1% Polish, 4.6% French (except Basque) (2000).
Economy: Single-family building permits issued: 0 (2001) / 0 (2000); Multi-family building permits issued: 0 (2001) / 0 (2000); Employment by occupation: 10.1% management, 11.5% professional, 12.2% services, 21.6% sales, 1.4% farming, 7.4% construction, 35.8% production (2000).
Income: Per capita income: $14,195 (2000); Median household income: $26,818 (2000); Poverty rate: 12.0% (2000).
Taxes: Total city taxes per capita: $76 (1997); City property taxes per capita: $76 (1997).
Education: High school graduation rate: 75.1% (2000); College graduation rate: 8.3% (2000).

School District(s)

Marshall County Central Schools (PK-12)
2000 Enrollment: 376 218-874-8530
Housing: Homeownership rate: 71.4% (2000); Median home value: $37,900 (2000); Median rent: $250 per month (2000); Median age of housing: 45 years (2000).
Transportation: Commute to work: 87.2% car, 0.0% public transportation, 11.5% walk, 1.4% work from home (2000); Travel time to work: 35.6% less than 15 minutes, 34.9% 15 to 30 minutes, 22.6% 30 to 45 minutes, 0.0% 45 to 60 minutes, 6.8% 60 minutes or more (2000)

OAK PARK (township). Covers a land area of 38.895 square miles and a water area of 0.424 square miles. Located at 48.21° N. Lat.; 97.07° W. Long.
Population: 165 (2000); Race: 100.0% White, 0.0% Black, 0.0% Asian, 0.0% American Indian and Alaska Native, 0.0% Hispanic of any race, 0.0% two or more races (2000); Density: 4.2 persons per square mile (2000); Age: 25.6% under 18, 8.3% over 64 (2000); Marriage status: 21.0% never married, 66.9% now married, 3.2% widowed, 8.9% divorced (2000); Foreign born: 0.0% (2000); Ancestry (includes multiple ancestries): 71.8% Norwegian, 16.7% Swedish, 11.5% German, 9.0% French (except Basque), 5.8% Polish (2000).
Economy: Employment by occupation: 19.2% management, 15.4% professional, 10.3% services, 26.9% sales, 0.0% farming, 7.7% construction, 20.5% production (2000).
Income: Per capita income: $23,560 (2000); Median household income: $43,438 (2000); Poverty rate: 5.1% (2000).
Taxes: Total city taxes per capita: $164 (1997); City property taxes per capita: $164 (1997).
Education: High school graduation rate: 94.5% (2000); College graduation rate: 12.8% (2000).
Housing: Homeownership rate: 79.7% (2000); Median home value: $67,500 (2000); Median rent: $275 per month (2000); Median age of housing: 60+ years (2000).
Transportation: Commute to work: 93.6% car, 0.0% public transportation, 0.0% walk, 6.4% work from home (2000); Travel time to work: 20.5% less than 15 minutes, 30.1% 15 to 30 minutes, 46.6% 30 to 45 minutes, 0.0% 45 to 60 minutes, 2.7% 60 minutes or more (2000)

OSLO (city). Covers a land area of 0.357 square miles and a water area of 0.024 square miles. Located at 48.19° N. Lat.; 97.13° W. Long. Elevation is 810 feet.
Population: 347 (2000); Race: 80.4% White, 0.0% Black, 0.0% Asian, 0.0% American Indian and Alaska Native, 32.2% Hispanic of any race, 1.8% two or more races (2000); Density: 973.0 persons per square mile (2000); Age: 28.5% under 18, 18.6% over 64 (2000); Marriage status: 15.0% never married, 66.9% now married, 9.9% widowed, 8.2% divorced (2000); Foreign born: 10.1% (2000); Ancestry (includes multiple ancestries): 33.5% Norwegian, 29.5% Other groups, 12.1% Swedish, 11.3% Polish, 8.8% German (2000).
Economy: Agriculture: grain, potatoes, beans, sunflowers, sugar beets; livestock, poultry. Manufacturing of fertilizer. Employment by occupation: 9.9% management, 14.2% professional, 16.3% services, 24.8% sales, 1.4% farming, 16.3% construction, 17.0% production (2000).
Income: Per capita income: $15,290 (2000); Median household income: $34,375 (2000); Poverty rate: 14.8% (2000).
Taxes: Total city taxes per capita: $214 (1997); City property taxes per capita: $209 (1997).
Education: High school graduation rate: 71.1% (2000); College graduation rate: 12.6% (2000).
Housing: Homeownership rate: 90.3% (2000); Median home value: $46,000 (2000); Median rent: $213 per month (2000); Median age of housing: 35 years (2000).
Transportation: Commute to work: 92.1% car, 0.0% public transportation, 6.5% walk, 1.4% work from home (2000); Travel time to work: 21.2% less than 15 minutes, 20.4% 15 to 30 minutes, 38.7% 30 to 45 minutes, 9.5% 45 to 60 minutes, 10.2% 60 minutes or more (2000)

PARKER (township). Covers a land area of 35.868 square miles and a water area of 0 square miles. Located at 48.40° N. Lat.; 96.96° W. Long.
Population: 57 (2000); Race: 100.0% White, 0.0% Black, 0.0% Asian, 0.0% American Indian and Alaska Native, 0.0% Hispanic of any race, 0.0% two or more races (2000); Density: 1.6 persons per square mile (2000); Age: 40.5% under 18, 4.8% over 64 (2000); Marriage status: 33.3% never married, 66.7% now married, 0.0% widowed, 0.0% divorced (2000); Foreign born: 0.0% (2000); Ancestry (includes multiple ancestries): 42.9% French (except Basque), 26.2% Norwegian, 21.4% Swedish, 19.0% Polish, 9.5% German (2000).
Economy: Employment by occupation: 38.5% management, 30.8% professional, 15.4% services, 15.4% sales, 0.0% farming, 0.0% construction, 0.0% production (2000).
Income: Per capita income: $8,538 (2000); Median household income: $9,688 (2000); Poverty rate: 45.2% (2000).
Taxes: Total city taxes per capita: $614 (2000); City property taxes per capita: $614 (2000).
Education: High school graduation rate: 100.0% (2000); College graduation rate: 0.0% (2000).
Housing: Homeownership rate: 100.0% (2000); Median home value: $57,500 (2000); Median age of housing: 60+ years (2000).
Transportation: Commute to work: 100.0% car, 0.0% public transportation, 0.0% walk, 0.0% work from home (2000); Travel time to work: 53.8% less than 15 minutes, 30.8% 15 to 30 minutes, 0.0% 30 to 45 minutes, 0.0% 45 to 60 minutes, 15.4% 60 minutes or more (2000)

ROLLIS (township). Covers a land area of 35.978 square miles and a water area of 0 square miles. Located at 48.41° N. Lat.; 95.78° W. Long.
Population: 141 (2000); Race: 96.1% White, 3.9% Black, 0.0% Asian, 0.0% American Indian and Alaska Native, 0.0% Hispanic of any race, 0.0% two or

more races (2000); Density: 3.9 persons per square mile (2000); Age: 11.0% under 18, 22.8% over 64 (2000); Marriage status: 15.9% never married, 76.1% now married, 2.7% widowed, 5.3% divorced (2000); Foreign born: 0.0% (2000); Ancestry (includes multiple ancestries): 74.0% Norwegian, 18.1% German, 15.0% Swedish, 6.3% Polish, 5.5% French (except Basque) (2000).
Economy: Employment by occupation: 12.9% management, 12.9% professional, 14.5% services, 11.3% sales, 0.0% farming, 12.9% construction, 35.5% production (2000).
Income: Per capita income: $17,254 (2000); Median household income: $25,714 (2000); Poverty rate: 7.9% (2000).
Taxes: Total city taxes per capita: $40 (1997); City property taxes per capita: $40 (1997).
Education: High school graduation rate: 83.5% (2000); College graduation rate: 14.6% (2000).
Housing: Homeownership rate: 82.0% (2000); Median home value: $75,000 (2000); Median rent: <$100 per month (2000); Median age of housing: 29 years (2000).
Transportation: Commute to work: 90.3% car, 0.0% public transportation, 0.0% walk, 8.1% work from home (2000); Travel time to work: 12.3% less than 15 minutes, 5.3% 15 to 30 minutes, 43.9% 30 to 45 minutes, 29.8% 45 to 60 minutes, 8.8% 60 minutes or more (2000)

SINNOTT (township). Covers a land area of 36.157 square miles and a water area of 0 square miles. Located at 48.50° N. Lat.; 96.85° W. Long.
Population: 52 (2000); Race: 100.0% White, 0.0% Black, 0.0% Asian, 0.0% American Indian and Alaska Native, 0.0% Hispanic of any race, 0.0% two or more races (2000); Density: 1.4 persons per square mile (2000); Age: 14.8% under 18, 48.1% over 64 (2000); Marriage status: 22.9% never married, 64.6% now married, 12.5% widowed, 0.0% divorced (2000); Foreign born: 0.0% (2000); Ancestry (includes multiple ancestries): 46.3% Norwegian, 42.6% Swedish, 27.8% Polish, 24.1% German, 5.6% English (2000).
Economy: Employment by occupation: 47.1% management, 11.8% professional, 17.6% services, 0.0% sales, 0.0% farming, 0.0% construction, 23.5% production (2000).
Income: Per capita income: $19,459 (2000); Median household income: $26,875 (2000); Poverty rate: 14.8% (2000).
Taxes: Total city taxes per capita: $500 (1997); City property taxes per capita: $500 (1997).
Education: High school graduation rate: 75.0% (2000); College graduation rate: 4.5% (2000).
Housing: Homeownership rate: 84.0% (2000); Median home value: $34,200 (2000); Median rent: $225 per month (2000); Median age of housing: 60+ years (2000).
Transportation: Commute to work: 86.7% car, 0.0% public transportation, 0.0% walk, 13.3% work from home (2000); Travel time to work: 46.2% less than 15 minutes, 7.7% 15 to 30 minutes, 46.2% 30 to 45 minutes, 0.0% 45 to 60 minutes, 0.0% 60 minutes or more (2000)

SPRUCE VALLEY (township). Covers a land area of 36.313 square miles and a water area of 0.006 square miles. Located at 48.42° N. Lat.; 96.17° W. Long.
Population: 238 (2000); Race: 98.7% White, 0.0% Black, 1.3% Asian, 0.0% American Indian and Alaska Native, 0.0% Hispanic of any race, 0.0% two or more races (2000); Density: 6.6 persons per square mile (2000); Age: 19.3% under 18, 14.8% over 64 (2000); Marriage status: 13.9% never married, 75.8% now married, 5.2% widowed, 5.2% divorced (2000); Foreign born: 4.5% (2000); Ancestry (includes multiple ancestries): 57.8% Norwegian, 27.8% Swedish, 16.6% Polish, 14.8% German, 4.5% French (except Basque) (2000).
Economy: Employment by occupation: 17.9% management, 6.0% professional, 9.4% services, 28.2% sales, 0.0% farming, 3.4% construction, 35.0% production (2000).
Income: Per capita income: $22,198 (2000); Median household income: $41,364 (2000); Poverty rate: 2.7% (2000).
Taxes: Total city taxes per capita: $36 (1997); City property taxes per capita: $36 (1997).
Education: High school graduation rate: 84.8% (2000); College graduation rate: 8.8% (2000).
Housing: Homeownership rate: 95.8% (2000); Median home value: $38,300 (2000); Median age of housing: 44 years (2000).
Transportation: Commute to work: 85.5% car, 0.0% public transportation, 1.7% walk, 12.8% work from home (2000); Travel time to work: 19.6% less than 15 minutes, 16.7% 15 to 30 minutes, 38.2% 30 to 45 minutes, 14.7% 45 to 60 minutes, 10.8% 60 minutes or more (2000)

STEPHEN (city). Covers a land area of 0.819 square miles and a water area of 0 square miles. Located at 48.45° N. Lat.; 96.87° W. Long. Elevation is 828 feet.
History: Stephen was named for a farm owned by Lord Ramsey, which had been called Stephen Farm in honor of Lord Mount Stephen, an official of the Canadian Railway. As the southern terminus of the stage line, Stephen became a trading center when the railroad arrived.
Population: 708 (2000); Race: 90.6% White, 0.0% Black, 0.6% Asian, 0.0% American Indian and Alaska Native, 6.8% Hispanic of any race, 3.3% two or more races (2000); Density: 865.0 persons per square mile (2000); Age: 24.9% under 18, 19.3% over 64 (2000); Marriage status: 25.5% never married, 56.6% now married, 13.8% widowed, 4.1% divorced (2000); Foreign born: 5.3% (2000); Ancestry (includes multiple ancestries): 29.6% Polish, 29.4% Norwegian, 17.4% Swedish, 16.4% German, 10.2% French (except Basque) (2000).
Economy: Single-family building permits issued: 1 (2001) / 1 (2000); Multi-family building permits issued: 0 (2001) / 0 (2000); Employment by occupation: 15.3% management, 20.1% professional, 18.5% services, 17.2% sales, 3.5% farming, 8.0% construction, 17.5% production (2000).
Income: Per capita income: $17,152 (2000); Median household income: $33,207 (2000); Poverty rate: 6.2% (2000).
Taxes: Total city taxes per capita: $140 (1997); City property taxes per capita: $137 (1997).
Education: High school graduation rate: 78.2% (2000); College graduation rate: 16.1% (2000).

School District(s)

Stephen-Argyle Central Schools (PK-12)
2000 Enrollment: 447 218-478-3315
Housing: Homeownership rate: 79.7% (2000); Median home value: $41,900 (2000); Median rent: $217 per month (2000); Median age of housing: 35 years (2000).
Newspapers: The Messenger (1 x week)
Transportation: Commute to work: 84.2% car, 0.0% public transportation, 10.6% walk, 3.6% work from home (2000); Travel time to work: 55.1% less than 15 minutes, 19.2% 15 to 30 minutes, 14.7% 30 to 45 minutes, 3.4% 45 to 60 minutes, 7.5% 60 minutes or more (2000)

STRANDQUIST (city). Covers a land area of 0.262 square miles and a water area of 0 square miles. Located at 48.49° N. Lat.; 96.44° W. Long. Elevation is 1,062 feet.
History: Strandquist was named for a Swedish merchant, the first storekeeper and postmaster of the community.
Population: 88 (2000); Race: 95.3% White, 0.0% Black, 0.0% Asian, 2.4% American Indian and Alaska Native, 0.0% Hispanic of any race, 2.4% two or more races (2000); Density: 335.6 persons per square mile (2000); Age: 20.0% under 18, 22.4% over 64 (2000); Marriage status: 29.2% never married, 55.6% now married, 8.3% widowed, 6.9% divorced (2000); Foreign born: 0.0% (2000); Ancestry (includes multiple ancestries): 35.3% Norwegian, 23.5% Irish, 17.6% Swedish, 15.3% German, 12.9% Danish (2000).
Economy: Employment by occupation: 6.3% management, 15.6% professional, 31.3% services, 12.5% sales, 0.0% farming, 12.5% construction, 21.9% production (2000).
Income: Per capita income: $12,962 (2000); Median household income: $19,688 (2000); Poverty rate: 10.8% (2000).
Taxes: Total city taxes per capita: $53 (1997); City property taxes per capita: $32 (1997).
Education: High school graduation rate: 54.1% (2000); College graduation rate: 0.0% (2000).
Housing: Homeownership rate: 84.2% (2000); Median home value: $21,900 (2000); Median rent: $225 per month (2000); Median age of housing: 49 years (2000).
Transportation: Commute to work: 100.0% car, 0.0% public transportation, 0.0% walk, 0.0% work from home (2000); Travel time to work: 16.7% less than 15 minutes, 13.3% 15 to 30 minutes, 23.3% 30 to 45 minutes, 16.7% 45 to 60 minutes, 30.0% 60 minutes or more (2000)

TAMARAC (township). Covers a land area of 35.280 square miles and a water area of 0 square miles. Located at 48.41° N. Lat.; 96.86° W. Long.
Population: 94 (2000); Race: 100.0% White, 0.0% Black, 0.0% Asian, 0.0% American Indian and Alaska Native, 0.0% Hispanic of any race, 0.0% two or more races (2000); Density: 2.7 persons per square mile (2000); Age: 16.7% under 18, 8.3% over 64 (2000); Marriage status: 11.3% never married, 71.0% now married, 14.5% widowed, 3.2% divorced (2000); Foreign born: 0.0% (2000); Ancestry (includes multiple ancestries): 37.5% Norwegian, 29.2%

German, 26.4% Swedish, 15.3% Polish, 12.5% French (except Basque) (2000).
Economy: Employment by occupation: 14.7% management, 0.0% professional, 14.7% services, 38.2% sales, 0.0% farming, 8.8% construction, 23.5% production (2000).
Income: Per capita income: $21,411 (2000); Median household income: $55,000 (2000); Poverty rate: 6.9% (2000).
Taxes: Total city taxes per capita: $218 (1997); City property taxes per capita: $218 (1997).
Education: High school graduation rate: 89.7% (2000); College graduation rate: 5.2% (2000).
Housing: Homeownership rate: 100.0% (2000); Median home value: $52,500 (2000); Median age of housing: 30 years (2000).
Transportation: Commute to work: 88.2% car, 0.0% public transportation, 0.0% walk, 11.8% work from home (2000); Travel time to work: 56.7% less than 15 minutes, 23.3% 15 to 30 minutes, 20.0% 30 to 45 minutes, 0.0% 45 to 60 minutes, 0.0% 60 minutes or more (2000)

THIEF LAKE (township). Covers a land area of 27.626 square miles and a water area of 8.868 square miles. Located at 48.47° N. Lat.; 95.93° W. Long.
Population: 48 (2000); Race: 100.0% White, 0.0% Black, 0.0% Asian, 0.0% American Indian and Alaska Native, 0.0% Hispanic of any race, 0.0% two or more races (2000); Density: 1.7 persons per square mile (2000); Age: 32.0% under 18, 10.0% over 64 (2000); Marriage status: 0.0% never married, 85.3% now married, 2.9% widowed, 11.8% divorced (2000); Foreign born: 0.0% (2000); Ancestry (includes multiple ancestries): 40.0% Norwegian, 36.0% Swedish, 24.0% Czech, 22.0% Italian, 8.0% Czechoslovakian (2000).
Economy: Employment by occupation: 25.9% management, 7.4% professional, 7.4% services, 22.2% sales, 0.0% farming, 14.8% construction, 22.2% production (2000).
Income: Per capita income: $12,304 (2000); Median household income: $18,750 (2000); Poverty rate: 4.0% (2000).
Taxes: Total city taxes per capita: $31 (1997); City property taxes per capita: $31 (1997).
Education: High school graduation rate: 76.5% (2000); College graduation rate: 5.9% (2000).
Housing: Homeownership rate: 76.2% (2000); Median age of housing: 52 years (2000).
Transportation: Commute to work: 48.1% car, 0.0% public transportation, 14.8% walk, 37.0% work from home (2000); Travel time to work: 47.1% less than 15 minutes, 11.8% 15 to 30 minutes, 17.6% 30 to 45 minutes, 23.5% 45 to 60 minutes, 0.0% 60 minutes or more (2000)

VALLEY (township). Covers a land area of 33.935 square miles and a water area of 0 square miles. Located at 48.32° N. Lat.; 95.66° W. Long.
Population: 164 (2000); Race: 97.3% White, 2.7% Black, 0.0% Asian, 0.0% American Indian and Alaska Native, 2.7% Hispanic of any race, 0.0% two or more races (2000); Density: 4.8 persons per square mile (2000); Age: 26.7% under 18, 22.7% over 64 (2000); Marriage status: 12.9% never married, 81.9% now married, 4.3% widowed, 0.9% divorced (2000); Foreign born: 0.0% (2000); Ancestry (includes multiple ancestries): 60.7% Norwegian, 27.3% German, 8.0% French (except Basque), 7.3% Irish, 6.0% English (2000).
Economy: Employment by occupation: 17.7% management, 4.8% professional, 9.7% services, 17.7% sales, 0.0% farming, 6.5% construction, 43.5% production (2000).
Income: Per capita income: $14,634 (2000); Median household income: $33,125 (2000); Poverty rate: 4.0% (2000).
Taxes: Total city taxes per capita: $68 (1997); City property taxes per capita: $68 (1997).
Education: High school graduation rate: 87.6% (2000); College graduation rate: 7.2% (2000).
Housing: Homeownership rate: 92.9% (2000); Median home value: $29,600 (2000); Median rent: $125 per month (2000); Median age of housing: 27 years (2000).
Transportation: Commute to work: 82.8% car, 0.0% public transportation, 0.0% walk, 17.2% work from home (2000); Travel time to work: 27.1% less than 15 minutes, 18.8% 15 to 30 minutes, 0.0% 30 to 45 minutes, 37.5% 45 to 60 minutes, 16.7% 60 minutes or more (2000)

VEGA (township). Covers a land area of 44.948 square miles and a water area of 0 square miles. Located at 48.21° N. Lat.; 96.96° W. Long.
Population: 155 (2000); Race: 98.7% White, 0.0% Black, 0.0% Asian, 0.6% American Indian and Alaska Native, 0.6% Hispanic of any race, 0.6% two or more races (2000); Density: 3.4 persons per square mile (2000); Age: 33.5% under 18, 18.7% over 64 (2000); Marriage status: 23.2% never married, 65.2% now married, 8.0% widowed, 3.6% divorced (2000); Foreign born: 0.6% (2000); Ancestry (includes multiple ancestries): 36.1% Norwegian, 32.3% Swedish, 18.1% German, 16.1% Irish, 9.7% Polish (2000).
Economy: Employment by occupation: 22.4% management, 10.3% professional, 17.2% services, 24.1% sales, 0.0% farming, 13.8% construction, 12.1% production (2000).
Income: Per capita income: $18,212 (2000); Median household income: $51,875 (2000); Poverty rate: 0.6% (2000).
Taxes: Total city taxes per capita: $205 (1997); City property taxes per capita: $205 (1997).
Education: High school graduation rate: 91.8% (2000); College graduation rate: 17.3% (2000).
Housing: Homeownership rate: 96.2% (2000); Median home value: $72,500 (2000); Median age of housing: 60+ years (2000).
Transportation: Commute to work: 98.2% car, 0.0% public transportation, 0.0% walk, 1.8% work from home (2000); Travel time to work: 40.0% less than 15 minutes, 29.1% 15 to 30 minutes, 16.4% 30 to 45 minutes, 5.5% 45 to 60 minutes, 9.1% 60 minutes or more (2000)

VELDT (township). Covers a land area of 35.296 square miles and a water area of 0.091 square miles. Located at 48.41° N. Lat.; 95.66° W. Long.
Population: 56 (2000); Race: 100.0% White, 0.0% Black, 0.0% Asian, 0.0% American Indian and Alaska Native, 0.0% Hispanic of any race, 0.0% two or more races (2000); Density: 1.6 persons per square mile (2000); Age: 18.6% under 18, 28.8% over 64 (2000); Marriage status: 8.3% never married, 77.1% now married, 4.2% widowed, 10.4% divorced (2000); Foreign born: 0.0% (2000); Ancestry (includes multiple ancestries): 69.5% Norwegian, 13.6% German, 13.6% Swedish, 6.8% Irish (2000).
Economy: Employment by occupation: 29.0% management, 0.0% professional, 6.5% services, 25.8% sales, 0.0% farming, 0.0% construction, 38.7% production (2000).
Income: Per capita income: $19,908 (2000); Median household income: $35,000 (2000); Poverty rate: 3.4% (2000).
Taxes: Total city taxes per capita: $292 (1997); City property taxes per capita: $292 (1997).
Education: High school graduation rate: 66.7% (2000); College graduation rate: 4.2% (2000).
Housing: Homeownership rate: 91.7% (2000); Median home value: $87,500 (2000); Median age of housing: 28 years (2000).
Transportation: Commute to work: 77.4% car, 0.0% public transportation, 0.0% walk, 22.6% work from home (2000); Travel time to work: 33.3% less than 15 minutes, 16.7% 15 to 30 minutes, 41.7% 30 to 45 minutes, 8.3% 45 to 60 minutes, 0.0% 60 minutes or more (2000)

VIKING (city). Covers a land area of 0.510 square miles and a water area of 0 square miles. Located at 48.22° N. Lat.; 96.40° W. Long. Elevation is 1,065 feet.
Population: 92 (2000); Race: 100.0% White, 0.0% Black, 0.0% Asian, 0.0% American Indian and Alaska Native, 0.0% Hispanic of any race, 0.0% two or more races (2000); Density: 180.3 persons per square mile (2000); Age: 36.3% under 18, 20.9% over 64 (2000); Marriage status: 17.7% never married, 67.7% now married, 4.8% widowed, 9.7% divorced (2000); Foreign born: 0.0% (2000); Ancestry (includes multiple ancestries): 61.5% Norwegian, 33.0% Swedish, 13.2% Polish, 12.1% Scandinavian, 9.9% Ukrainian (2000).
Economy: Employment by occupation: 8.1% management, 10.8% professional, 27.0% services, 21.6% sales, 0.0% farming, 10.8% construction, 21.6% production (2000).
Income: Per capita income: $11,812 (2000); Median household income: $28,750 (2000); Poverty rate: 14.3% (2000).
Taxes: Total city taxes per capita: $40 (1997); City property taxes per capita: $40 (1997).
Education: High school graduation rate: 78.6% (2000); College graduation rate: 7.1% (2000).
Housing: Homeownership rate: 100.0% (2000); Median home value: $32,500 (2000); Median age of housing: 57 years (2000).
Transportation: Commute to work: 69.7% car, 0.0% public transportation, 6.1% walk, 24.2% work from home (2000); Travel time to work: 56.0% less than 15 minutes, 20.0% 15 to 30 minutes, 16.0% 30 to 45 minutes, 0.0% 45 to 60 minutes, 8.0% 60 minutes or more (2000)

VIKING (township). Covers a land area of 44.946 square miles and a water area of 0 square miles. Located at 48.22° N. Lat.; 96.43° W. Long. Elevation is 1,065 feet.

Population: 145 (2000); Race: 98.0% White, 0.0% Black, 0.0% Asian, 0.7% American Indian and Alaska Native, 0.0% Hispanic of any race, 1.3% two or more races (2000); Density: 3.2 persons per square mile (2000); Age: 20.7% under 18, 20.0% over 64 (2000); Marriage status: 19.7% never married, 73.0% now married, 5.7% widowed, 1.6% divorced (2000); Foreign born: 1.3% (2000); Ancestry (includes multiple ancestries): 56.0% Norwegian, 18.7% German, 16.7% Swedish, 11.3% Polish, 9.3% Irish (2000).
Economy: Grain area; sunflowers, flax, alfalfa; cattle, sheep. Employment by occupation: 24.6% management, 12.3% professional, 4.6% services, 32.3% sales, 3.1% farming, 6.2% construction, 16.9% production (2000).
Income: Per capita income: $17,015 (2000); Median household income: $33,542 (2000); Poverty rate: 4.0% (2000).
Taxes: Total city taxes per capita: $187 (1997); City property taxes per capita: $187 (1997).
Education: High school graduation rate: 78.3% (2000); College graduation rate: 4.7% (2000).
Housing: Homeownership rate: 90.9% (2000); Median home value: $65,000 (2000); Median rent: $250 per month (2000); Median age of housing: 26 years (2000).
Transportation: Commute to work: 88.9% car, 0.0% public transportation, 1.6% walk, 9.5% work from home (2000); Travel time to work: 12.3% less than 15 minutes, 56.1% 15 to 30 minutes, 15.8% 30 to 45 minutes, 3.5% 45 to 60 minutes, 12.3% 60 minutes or more (2000)

WANGER (township). Covers a land area of 36.009 square miles and a water area of 0.044 square miles. Located at 48.40° N. Lat.; 96.72° W. Long.
Population: 95 (2000); Race: 100.0% White, 0.0% Black, 0.0% Asian, 0.0% American Indian and Alaska Native, 0.0% Hispanic of any race, 0.0% two or more races (2000); Density: 2.6 persons per square mile (2000); Age: 26.5% under 18, 27.6% over 64 (2000); Marriage status: 19.0% never married, 67.1% now married, 13.9% widowed, 0.0% divorced (2000); Foreign born: 0.0% (2000); Ancestry (includes multiple ancestries): 50.0% Polish, 20.4% Norwegian, 19.4% German, 9.2% Russian, 8.2% Swedish (2000).
Economy: Employment by occupation: 22.7% management, 9.1% professional, 0.0% services, 13.6% sales, 9.1% farming, 27.3% construction, 18.2% production (2000).
Income: Per capita income: $14,143 (2000); Median household income: $28,750 (2000); Poverty rate: 17.3% (2000).
Taxes: Total city taxes per capita: $184 (1997); City property taxes per capita: $184 (1997).
Education: High school graduation rate: 61.8% (2000); College graduation rate: 17.6% (2000).
Housing: Homeownership rate: 92.1% (2000); Median home value: $32,500 (2000); Median age of housing: 57 years (2000).
Transportation: Commute to work: 36.4% car, 0.0% public transportation, 13.6% walk, 50.0% work from home (2000); Travel time to work: 27.3% less than 15 minutes, 36.4% 15 to 30 minutes, 0.0% 30 to 45 minutes, 18.2% 45 to 60 minutes, 18.2% 60 minutes or more (2000)

WARREN (city). Covers a land area of 1.429 square miles and a water area of 0 square miles. Located at 48.19° N. Lat.; 96.77° W. Long. Elevation is 854 feet.
History: Warren grew up in a prairie area of grain and alfalfa fields. Before an election established Warren as the seat of Marshall County, a battle went on for years between Warren and nearby Argyle. The county safe with its contents of legal papers was moved back and forth between the two towns, with residents feeling that whichever town had the safe also had the honor of the county seat.
Population: 1,678 (2000); Race: 98.0% White, 0.5% Black, 0.2% Asian, 0.0% American Indian and Alaska Native, 3.1% Hispanic of any race, 0.5% two or more races (2000); Density: 1,174.1 persons per square mile (2000); Age: 23.1% under 18, 25.1% over 64 (2000); Marriage status: 20.9% never married, 57.1% now married, 15.1% widowed, 6.9% divorced (2000); Foreign born: 1.9% (2000); Ancestry (includes multiple ancestries): 38.9% Norwegian, 20.6% German, 17.2% Swedish, 13.2% Polish, 7.7% French (except Basque) (2000).
Economy: Single-family building permits issued: 4 (2001) / 2 (2000); Multi-family building permits issued: 0 (2001) / 0 (2000); Employment by occupation: 15.1% management, 17.6% professional, 20.7% services, 21.4% sales, 3.0% farming, 9.3% construction, 12.8% production (2000).
Income: Per capita income: $17,547 (2000); Median household income: $36,250 (2000); Poverty rate: 10.2% (2000).
Taxes: Total city taxes per capita: $92 (1997); City property taxes per capita: $81 (1997).
Education: High school graduation rate: 78.6% (2000); College graduation rate: 16.9% (2000).

School District(s)

Warren-Alvarado-Oslo (PK-12)
2000 Enrollment: 646 218-745-5393
Housing: Homeownership rate: 68.7% (2000); Median home value: $53,400 (2000); Median rent: $270 per month (2000); Median age of housing: 40 years (2000).
Hospitals: North Valley Health Center (20 beds)
Newspapers: Warren Sheaf (1 x week)
Transportation: Commute to work: 90.8% car, 0.0% public transportation, 5.4% walk, 3.0% work from home (2000); Travel time to work: 66.3% less than 15 minutes, 8.1% 15 to 30 minutes, 16.5% 30 to 45 minutes, 7.5% 45 to 60 minutes, 1.6% 60 minutes or more (2000)

WARRENTON (township). Covers a land area of 35.460 square miles and a water area of 0 square miles. Located at 48.24° N. Lat.; 96.81° W. Long.
Population: 93 (2000); Race: 100.0% White, 0.0% Black, 0.0% Asian, 0.0% American Indian and Alaska Native, 0.0% Hispanic of any race, 0.0% two or more races (2000); Density: 2.6 persons per square mile (2000); Age: 34.4% under 18, 6.4% over 64 (2000); Marriage status: 9.5% never married, 85.7% now married, 2.4% widowed, 2.4% divorced (2000); Foreign born: 0.0% (2000); Ancestry (includes multiple ancestries): 38.4% German, 27.2% Norwegian, 20.0% Swedish, 17.6% United States or American, 10.4% Scottish (2000).
Economy: Employment by occupation: 22.6% management, 12.9% professional, 12.9% services, 24.2% sales, 0.0% farming, 25.8% construction, 1.6% production (2000).
Income: Per capita income: $15,356 (2000); Median household income: $42,083 (2000); Poverty rate: 0.0% (2000).
Taxes: Total city taxes per capita: $240 (1997); City property taxes per capita: $240 (1997).
Education: High school graduation rate: 95.0% (2000); College graduation rate: 13.8% (2000).
Housing: Homeownership rate: 92.3% (2000); Median home value: $65,000 (2000); Median rent: $325 per month (2000); Median age of housing: 36 years (2000).
Transportation: Commute to work: 90.3% car, 0.0% public transportation, 9.7% walk, 0.0% work from home (2000); Travel time to work: 62.9% less than 15 minutes, 9.7% 15 to 30 minutes, 17.7% 30 to 45 minutes, 3.2% 45 to 60 minutes, 6.5% 60 minutes or more (2000)

WEST VALLEY (township). Covers a land area of 36.388 square miles and a water area of 0 square miles. Located at 48.42° N. Lat.; 96.44° W. Long.
Population: 147 (2000); Race: 92.1% White, 0.0% Black, 0.0% Asian, 7.9% American Indian and Alaska Native, 0.0% Hispanic of any race, 0.0% two or more races (2000); Density: 4.0 persons per square mile (2000); Age: 28.6% under 18, 11.4% over 64 (2000); Marriage status: 33.3% never married, 46.8% now married, 10.8% widowed, 9.0% divorced (2000); Foreign born: 0.0% (2000); Ancestry (includes multiple ancestries): 64.3% Norwegian, 42.1% Swedish, 12.1% German, 7.9% Other groups, 7.1% Russian (2000).
Economy: Employment by occupation: 17.8% management, 15.1% professional, 2.7% services, 12.3% sales, 2.7% farming, 27.4% construction, 21.9% production (2000).
Income: Per capita income: $13,478 (2000); Median household income: $25,625 (2000); Poverty rate: 7.9% (2000).
Taxes: Total city taxes per capita: $115 (1997); City property taxes per capita: $115 (1997).
Education: High school graduation rate: 88.8% (2000); College graduation rate: 16.3% (2000).
Housing: Homeownership rate: 94.3% (2000); Median home value: $26,300 (2000); Median age of housing: 48 years (2000).
Transportation: Commute to work: 91.8% car, 0.0% public transportation, 0.0% walk, 8.2% work from home (2000); Travel time to work: 13.4% less than 15 minutes, 38.8% 15 to 30 minutes, 37.3% 30 to 45 minutes, 3.0% 45 to 60 minutes, 7.5% 60 minutes or more (2000)

WHITEFORD (township). Covers a land area of 33.499 square miles and a water area of 2.807 square miles. Located at 48.43° N. Lat.; 95.93° W. Long.
Population: 38 (2000); Race: 100.0% White, 0.0% Black, 0.0% Asian, 0.0% American Indian and Alaska Native, 0.0% Hispanic of any race, 0.0% two or more races (2000); Density: 1.1 persons per square mile (2000); Age: 31.1% under 18, 4.4% over 64 (2000); Marriage status: 0.0% never married, 93.5% now married, 6.5% widowed, 0.0% divorced (2000); Foreign born: 0.0%

(2000); Ancestry (includes multiple ancestries): 60.0% Swedish, 51.1% Norwegian, 11.1% German, 11.1% Polish, 4.4% Czech (2000).
Economy: Employment by occupation: 27.3% management, 9.1% professional, 18.2% services, 0.0% sales, 0.0% farming, 0.0% construction, 45.5% production (2000).
Income: Per capita income: $23,091 (2000); Median household income: $49,583 (2000); Poverty rate: 0.0% (2000).
Taxes: Total city taxes per capita: $85 (1997); City property taxes per capita: $85 (1997).
Education: High school graduation rate: 100.0% (2000); College graduation rate: 7.1% (2000).
Housing: Homeownership rate: 100.0% (2000); Median home value: $85,000 (2000); Median age of housing: 39 years (2000).
Transportation: Commute to work: 95.5% car, 0.0% public transportation, 0.0% walk, 4.5% work from home (2000); Travel time to work: 9.5% less than 15 minutes, 9.5% 15 to 30 minutes, 38.1% 30 to 45 minutes, 42.9% 45 to 60 minutes, 0.0% 60 minutes or more (2000)

WRIGHT (township). Covers a land area of 36.005 square miles and a water area of 0.100 square miles. Located at 48.41° N. Lat.; 96.58° W. Long.
Population: 126 (2000); Race: 100.0% White, 0.0% Black, 0.0% Asian, 0.0% American Indian and Alaska Native, 0.0% Hispanic of any race, 0.0% two or more races (2000); Density: 3.5 persons per square mile (2000); Age: 18.4% under 18, 19.1% over 64 (2000); Marriage status: 32.5% never married, 57.5% now married, 8.3% widowed, 1.7% divorced (2000); Foreign born: 0.0% (2000); Ancestry (includes multiple ancestries): 49.3% Polish, 25.7% Norwegian, 17.6% German, 13.2% French (except Basque), 9.6% Swedish (2000).
Economy: Employment by occupation: 12.7% management, 22.2% professional, 14.3% services, 15.9% sales, 6.3% farming, 3.2% construction, 25.4% production (2000).
Income: Per capita income: $15,138 (2000); Median household income: $38,125 (2000); Poverty rate: 12.5% (2000).
Taxes: Total city taxes per capita: $71 (1997); City property taxes per capita: $71 (1997).
Education: High school graduation rate: 68.5% (2000); College graduation rate: 2.2% (2000).
Housing: Homeownership rate: 85.2% (2000); Median home value: $23,800 (2000); Median rent: $175 per month (2000); Median age of housing: 56 years (2000).
Transportation: Commute to work: 93.7% car, 0.0% public transportation, 0.0% walk, 3.2% work from home (2000); Travel time to work: 13.1% less than 15 minutes, 70.5% 15 to 30 minutes, 13.1% 30 to 45 minutes, 0.0% 45 to 60 minutes, 3.3% 60 minutes or more (2000)

Martin County

Located in southern Minnesota; bounded on the south by Iowa; watered by Tuttle Lake and by the Middle Chain of Lakes. Covers a land area of 709.30 square miles, a water area of 20.20 square miles, and is located in the Central Time Zone. The county government was organized in 1857. County seat is Fairmont.

Weather Station: Fairmont — Elevation: 1,184 feet

	Jan	Feb	Mar	Apr	May	Jun	Jul	Aug	Sep	Oct	Nov	Dec
High	22	29	40	57	71	80	83	80	72	59	41	27
Low	4	11	23	36	49	58	62	60	51	39	24	11
Precip	0.8	0.7	2.0	3.2	3.9	4.4	4.2	4.2	2.7	2.4	2.0	1.0
Snow	9.5	6.2	8.3	3.2	tr	0.0	0.0	0.0	0.0	0.6	6.0	8.7

High and Low temperatures in degrees Fahrenheit; Precipitation and Snow in inches

Population: 21,802 (2000); Race: 97.6% White, 0.1% Black, 0.7% Asian, 0.3% American Indian and Alaska Native, 1.4% Hispanic of any race, 0.5% two or more races (2000); Density: 30.7 persons per square mile (2000); Age: 25.0% under 18, 19.8% over 64 (2000).
Religion: Five largest groups: 25.5% Lutheran Church—Missouri Synod, 20.9% Evangelical Lutheran Church in America, 15.9% Catholic Church, 7.9% United Church of Christ, 7.1% The United Methodist Church (2000).
Economy: Unemployment rate: 3.2% (11/2002); Total civilian labor force: 11,045 (11/2002); Leading industries: 25.7% manufacturing; 17.7% retail trade; 17.6% health care and social assistance (2000); Companies that employ more than 1,000 persons: 0 (2000); Companies that employ more than 100 persons: 15 (2000); Farms: 987 totaling 420,634 acres (1997); Minority business ownership rate: 0.0% (1997); Women business ownership rate: 23.7% (1997); Retail sales per capita: $11,289 (1997). Single-family building permits issued: 33 (2001) / 36 (2000); Multi-family building permits issued: 8 (2001) / 56 (2000).
Income: Per capita income: $18,529 (2000); Median household income: $34,810 (2000); Poverty rate: 10.5% (2000); Bankruptcy rate: 3.23% (2001).
Taxes: Total county taxes per capita: $201 (1997); County property taxes per capita: $200 (1997).
Education: High school graduation rate: 83.7% (2000); College graduation rate: 16.1% (2000).
Housing: Homeownership rate: 77.4% (2000); Median home value: $62,200 (2000); Median rent: $268 per month (2000); Median age of housing: 48 years (2000).
Health: Birth rate: 107.8 per 10,000 population (1998); Age adjusted death rate: 72.9 per 10,000 population (1999); Age adjusted cancer mortality rate: 135.6 deaths per 100,000 population (1999). Number of physicians: 13.3 per 10,000 population (1999); Number of hospital beds: 43.6 per 10,000 population (1999).
Elections: 2000 Presidential election results: 40.2% Gore, 54.8% Bush, 3.6% Nader, 0.9% Buchanan
National and State Parks: Ceylon State Wildlife Management Areas; East Chain State Wildlife Management Area; Luedtke State Wildlife Management Area; Perch Creek State Wildlife Management Area
Additional Information Contacts
Martin County Government Offices. 507-238-3126
Fairmont Area Chamber of Commerce 507-235-5547
Fairmont Convention & Visitors Bureau 507-235-8585
Sherburn Chamber of Commerce. 507-764-2607

Martin County Communities

CEDAR (township). Covers a land area of 34.526 square miles and a water area of 1.254 square miles. Located at 43.80° N. Lat.; 94.78° W. Long.
Population: 260 (2000); Race: 100.0% White, 0.0% Black, 0.0% Asian, 0.0% American Indian and Alaska Native, 0.0% Hispanic of any race, 0.0% two or more races (2000); Density: 7.5 persons per square mile (2000); Age: 28.2% under 18, 14.5% over 64 (2000); Marriage status: 26.2% never married, 65.1% now married, 5.1% widowed, 3.6% divorced (2000); Foreign born: 0.8% (2000); Ancestry (includes multiple ancestries): 50.4% German, 35.9% Swedish, 23.0% Norwegian, 6.5% Irish, 4.8% English (2000).
Economy: Employment by occupation: 18.5% management, 25.8% professional, 5.6% services, 15.3% sales, 5.6% farming, 4.8% construction, 24.2% production (2000).
Income: Per capita income: $20,390 (2000); Median household income: $45,000 (2000); Poverty rate: 1.2% (2000).
Taxes: Total city taxes per capita: $163 (1997); City property taxes per capita: $163 (1997).
Education: High school graduation rate: 91.1% (2000); College graduation rate: 17.8% (2000).
Housing: Homeownership rate: 80.0% (2000); Median home value: $84,000 (2000); Median rent: $213 per month (2000); Median age of housing: 60+ years (2000).
Transportation: Commute to work: 74.2% car, 0.0% public transportation, 10.8% walk, 15.0% work from home (2000); Travel time to work: 25.5% less than 15 minutes, 52.9% 15 to 30 minutes, 9.8% 30 to 45 minutes, 3.9% 45 to 60 minutes, 7.8% 60 minutes or more (2000)

CENTER CREEK (township). Covers a land area of 35.463 square miles and a water area of 0.026 square miles. Located at 43.70° N. Lat.; 94.31° W. Long.
Population: 269 (2000); Race: 99.3% White, 0.0% Black, 0.7% Asian, 0.0% American Indian and Alaska Native, 0.0% Hispanic of any race, 0.0% two or more races (2000); Density: 7.6 persons per square mile (2000); Age: 23.6% under 18, 12.7% over 64 (2000); Marriage status: 17.2% never married, 66.1% now married, 7.3% widowed, 9.4% divorced (2000); Foreign born: 1.1% (2000); Ancestry (includes multiple ancestries): 46.1% German, 15.1% Irish, 9.5% English, 7.7% Swedish, 6.0% United States or American (2000).
Economy: Employment by occupation: 20.5% management, 11.8% professional, 18.6% services, 23.0% sales, 3.1% farming, 8.1% construction, 14.9% production (2000).
Income: Per capita income: $16,689 (2000); Median household income: $40,859 (2000); Poverty rate: 3.6% (2000).
Taxes: Total city taxes per capita: $130 (1997); City property taxes per capita: $130 (1997).
Education: High school graduation rate: 87.8% (2000); College graduation rate: 7.3% (2000).

Housing: Homeownership rate: 78.4% (2000); Median home value: $49,400 (2000); Median rent: $219 per month (2000); Median age of housing: 57 years (2000).
Transportation: Commute to work: 88.5% car, 0.0% public transportation, 0.0% walk, 11.5% work from home (2000); Travel time to work: 33.1% less than 15 minutes, 63.3% 15 to 30 minutes, 0.7% 30 to 45 minutes, 1.4% 45 to 60 minutes, 1.4% 60 minutes or more (2000)

CEYLON (city). Covers a land area of 0.650 square miles and a water area of 0 square miles. Located at 43.53° N. Lat.; 94.63° W. Long. Elevation is 1,260 feet.
Population: 413 (2000); Race: 99.5% White, 0.0% Black, 0.0% Asian, 0.5% American Indian and Alaska Native, 0.5% Hispanic of any race, 0.0% two or more races (2000); Density: 635.8 persons per square mile (2000); Age: 18.4% under 18, 26.6% over 64 (2000); Marriage status: 15.2% never married, 70.5% now married, 7.0% widowed, 7.3% divorced (2000); Foreign born: 1.1% (2000); Ancestry (includes multiple ancestries): 61.2% German, 12.2% Norwegian, 7.3% Polish, 7.0% Irish, 6.8% Other groups (2000).
Economy: Grain, soybeans; livestock. Manufacturing: fertilizer, awnings. Single-family building permits issued: 0 (2001) / 0 (2000); Multi-family building permits issued: 0 (2001) / 0 (2000); Employment by occupation: 8.0% management, 14.2% professional, 12.3% services, 19.8% sales, 1.9% farming, 11.1% construction, 32.7% production (2000).
Income: Per capita income: $15,607 (2000); Median household income: $31,100 (2000); Poverty rate: 17.6% (2000).
Taxes: Total city taxes per capita: $178 (1997); City property taxes per capita: $171 (1997).
Education: High school graduation rate: 74.5% (2000); College graduation rate: 6.0% (2000).
Housing: Homeownership rate: 88.9% (2000); Median home value: $18,200 (2000); Median rent: $310 per month (2000); Median age of housing: 60+ years (2000).
Transportation: Commute to work: 88.8% car, 0.0% public transportation, 6.9% walk, 1.3% work from home (2000); Travel time to work: 33.5% less than 15 minutes, 43.0% 15 to 30 minutes, 17.7% 30 to 45 minutes, 3.8% 45 to 60 minutes, 1.9% 60 minutes or more (2000)

DUNNELL (city). Covers a land area of 0.378 square miles and a water area of 0 square miles. Located at 43.56° N. Lat.; 94.77° W. Long. Elevation is 1,312 feet.
Population: 197 (2000); Race: 100.0% White, 0.0% Black, 0.0% Asian, 0.0% American Indian and Alaska Native, 0.0% Hispanic of any race, 0.0% two or more races (2000); Density: 521.9 persons per square mile (2000); Age: 23.1% under 18, 18.1% over 64 (2000); Marriage status: 30.1% never married, 57.8% now married, 9.8% widowed, 2.3% divorced (2000); Foreign born: 0.0% (2000); Ancestry (includes multiple ancestries): 42.7% German, 19.6% Swedish, 18.1% Norwegian, 15.1% Danish, 8.5% Irish (2000).
Economy: Grain, soybeans; livestock. Single-family building permits issued: 0 (2001) / 0 (2000); Multi-family building permits issued: 0 (2001) / 0 (2000); Employment by occupation: 9.5% management, 9.5% professional, 14.3% services, 16.2% sales, 0.0% farming, 7.6% construction, 42.9% production (2000).
Income: Per capita income: $16,333 (2000); Median household income: $38,333 (2000); Poverty rate: 3.0% (2000).
Taxes: Total city taxes per capita: $263 (1997); City property taxes per capita: $257 (1997).
Education: High school graduation rate: 72.9% (2000); College graduation rate: 15.8% (2000).
Housing: Homeownership rate: 95.2% (2000); Median home value: $24,800 (2000); Median rent: $313 per month (2000); Median age of housing: 60+ years (2000).
Transportation: Commute to work: 90.3% car, 0.0% public transportation, 5.8% walk, 3.9% work from home (2000); Travel time to work: 47.5% less than 15 minutes, 36.4% 15 to 30 minutes, 10.1% 30 to 45 minutes, 0.0% 45 to 60 minutes, 6.1% 60 minutes or more (2000)

EAST CHAIN (township). Covers a land area of 35.246 square miles and a water area of 0.739 square miles. Located at 43.54° N. Lat.; 94.31° W. Long.
Population: 345 (2000); Race: 99.4% White, 0.0% Black, 0.6% Asian, 0.0% American Indian and Alaska Native, 0.0% Hispanic of any race, 0.0% two or more races (2000); Density: 9.8 persons per square mile (2000); Age: 29.1% under 18, 13.1% over 64 (2000); Marriage status: 20.1% never married, 73.6% now married, 5.9% widowed, 0.4% divorced (2000); Foreign born: 0.0% (2000); Ancestry (includes multiple ancestries): 29.1% German, 22.5% Swedish, 19.4% Norwegian, 9.4% English, 7.4% Irish (2000).
Economy: Employment by occupation: 28.4% management, 17.4% professional, 9.5% services, 18.9% sales, 4.7% farming, 2.6% construction, 18.4% production (2000).
Income: Per capita income: $20,762 (2000); Median household income: $43,750 (2000); Poverty rate: 6.3% (2000).
Taxes: Total city taxes per capita: $98 (1997); City property taxes per capita: $98 (1997).
Education: High school graduation rate: 94.2% (2000); College graduation rate: 21.7% (2000).
Housing: Homeownership rate: 69.0% (2000); Median home value: $53,900 (2000); Median rent: $204 per month (2000); Median age of housing: 60+ years (2000).
Transportation: Commute to work: 82.7% car, 0.0% public transportation, 3.8% walk, 10.8% work from home (2000); Travel time to work: 34.5% less than 15 minutes, 54.5% 15 to 30 minutes, 6.1% 30 to 45 minutes, 0.0% 45 to 60 minutes, 4.8% 60 minutes or more (2000)

ELM CREEK (township). Covers a land area of 34.888 square miles and a water area of 1.280 square miles. Located at 43.73° N. Lat.; 94.80° W. Long.
Population: 209 (2000); Race: 100.0% White, 0.0% Black, 0.0% Asian, 0.0% American Indian and Alaska Native, 0.0% Hispanic of any race, 0.0% two or more races (2000); Density: 6.0 persons per square mile (2000); Age: 28.2% under 18, 10.3% over 64 (2000); Marriage status: 20.1% never married, 72.0% now married, 5.5% widowed, 2.4% divorced (2000); Foreign born: 0.0% (2000); Ancestry (includes multiple ancestries): 45.1% German, 19.2% Swedish, 14.1% Norwegian, 8.9% Irish, 7.0% United States or American (2000).
Economy: Employment by occupation: 33.9% management, 21.0% professional, 6.5% services, 13.7% sales, 4.0% farming, 4.0% construction, 16.9% production (2000).
Income: Per capita income: $22,173 (2000); Median household income: $46,250 (2000); Poverty rate: 7.5% (2000).
Taxes: Total city taxes per capita: $197 (1997); City property taxes per capita: $197 (1997).
Education: High school graduation rate: 92.8% (2000); College graduation rate: 23.7% (2000).
Housing: Homeownership rate: 79.7% (2000); Median home value: $82,500 (2000); Median rent: $950 per month (2000); Median age of housing: 47 years (2000).
Transportation: Commute to work: 84.2% car, 0.0% public transportation, 3.3% walk, 12.5% work from home (2000); Travel time to work: 54.3% less than 15 minutes, 29.5% 15 to 30 minutes, 13.3% 30 to 45 minutes, 1.0% 45 to 60 minutes, 1.9% 60 minutes or more (2000)

FAIRMONT (city). Covers a land area of 14.567 square miles and a water area of 1.962 square miles. Located at 43.65° N. Lat.; 94.45° W. Long. Elevation is 1,195 feet.
History: Fairmont had its beginnings in the days of fur trading. The town was laid out in 1857 around the homes of early settlers E. Banks Hall and William H. Budd. In the 1870's a group of English farmers came to Fairmont at the instigation of a land promoter. This group became known as the "Fairmont Sportsmen," credited with introducing fox-hunting in Minnesota.
Population: 10,889 (2000); Race: 96.0% White, 0.2% Black, 1.2% Asian, 0.6% American Indian and Alaska Native, 2.4% Hispanic of any race, 0.6% two or more races (2000); Density: 747.5 persons per square mile (2000); Age: 24.8% under 18, 21.1% over 64 (2000); Marriage status: 21.2% never married, 57.6% now married, 10.8% widowed, 10.4% divorced (2000); Foreign born: 2.2% (2000); Ancestry (includes multiple ancestries): 51.2% German, 15.3% Norwegian, 8.2% Irish, 8.0% English, 5.8% Swedish (2000).
Vital Statistics: Birth rate: 113.0 per 10,000 population (1998)
Economy: Single-family building permits issued: 10 (2001) / 20 (2000); Multi-family building permits issued: 8 (2001) / 54 (2000); Employment by occupation: 9.3% management, 18.9% professional, 17.6% services, 24.1% sales, 1.8% farming, 8.2% construction, 20.1% production (2000).
Income: Per capita income: $18,658 (2000); Median household income: $33,709 (2000); Poverty rate: 12.7% (2000).
Taxes: Total city taxes per capita: $188 (2000); City property taxes per capita: $164 (2000).
Education: High school graduation rate: 83.4% (2000); College graduation rate: 18.1% (2000).

School District(s)

Fairmont Area Schools (KG-12)
2000 Enrollment: 1,960 507-238-4234
Southern Plains Ed. Coop. (PK-12)
2000 Enrollment: 225 507-238-1472

Housing: Homeownership rate: 73.8% (2000); Median home value: $69,800 (2000); Median rent: $274 per month (2000); Median age of housing: 45 years (2000).
Hospitals: Fairmont Medical Center (94 beds)
Safety: Violent crime rate: 21.8 per 10,000 population; Property crime rate: 413.4 per 10,000 population (2001).
Newspapers: The Sentinel (6 x week); Fairmont Photo Press (1 x week)
Transportation: Commute to work: 90.7% car, 1.2% public transportation, 3.8% walk, 3.1% work from home (2000); Travel time to work: 77.0% less than 15 minutes, 13.3% 15 to 30 minutes, 5.3% 30 to 45 minutes, 1.5% 45 to 60 minutes, 2.9% 60 minutes or more (2000)
Additional Information Contacts
Fairmont Area Chamber of Commerce 507-235-5547
Fairmont Convention & Visitors Bureau 507-235-8585

FAIRMONT (township). Covers a land area of 20.618 square miles and a water area of 1.276 square miles. Located at 43.61° N. Lat.; 94.39° W. Long. Elevation is 1,195 feet.
History: Courthouse has pioneer relics. Plotted 1857, Incorporated as village 1878, as city 1902.
Population: 298 (2000); Race: 97.1% White, 0.0% Black, 0.0% Asian, 0.0% American Indian and Alaska Native, 3.9% Hispanic of any race, 2.9% two or more races (2000); Density: 14.5 persons per square mile (2000); Age: 35.0% under 18, 8.5% over 64 (2000); Marriage status: 20.0% never married, 70.0% now married, 6.5% widowed, 3.5% divorced (2000); Foreign born: 0.0% (2000); Ancestry (includes multiple ancestries): 61.4% German, 12.4% Polish, 10.1% Swedish, 9.2% Norwegian, 6.2% English (2000).
Economy: Railroad junction and shipping point for agricultural area: grain, soybeans; livestock. Manufacturing includes lumber, electrical equipment, stained glass windows, prepared foods, machinery, asphalt, printing and publishing. Resorts. Employment by occupation: 18.5% management, 20.4% professional, 18.5% services, 18.5% sales, 3.2% farming, 7.6% construction, 13.4% production (2000).
Income: Per capita income: $19,656 (2000); Median household income: $51,250 (2000); Poverty rate: 5.2% (2000).
Taxes: Total city taxes per capita: $140 (1997); City property taxes per capita: $140 (1997).
Education: High school graduation rate: 97.4% (2000); College graduation rate: 24.1% (2000).
Housing: Homeownership rate: 85.6% (2000); Median home value: $118,200 (2000); Median rent: $508 per month (2000); Median age of housing: 36 years (2000).
Transportation: Commute to work: 89.0% car, 0.0% public transportation, 1.9% walk, 9.0% work from home (2000); Travel time to work: 73.8% less than 15 minutes, 16.3% 15 to 30 minutes, 7.8% 30 to 45 minutes, 0.7% 45 to 60 minutes, 1.4% 60 minutes or more (2000)

FOX LAKE (township). Covers a land area of 34.107 square miles and a water area of 1.502 square miles. Located at 43.71° N. Lat.; 94.67° W. Long.
Population: 289 (2000); Race: 100.0% White, 0.0% Black, 0.0% Asian, 0.0% American Indian and Alaska Native, 0.7% Hispanic of any race, 0.0% two or more races (2000); Density: 8.5 persons per square mile (2000); Age: 28.4% under 18, 13.8% over 64 (2000); Marriage status: 15.9% never married, 70.5% now married, 4.3% widowed, 9.2% divorced (2000); Foreign born: 0.0% (2000); Ancestry (includes multiple ancestries): 54.1% German, 13.1% Norwegian, 9.7% Irish, 9.3% Polish, 9.0% Swedish (2000).
Economy: Employment by occupation: 30.8% management, 10.5% professional, 14.7% services, 12.6% sales, 8.4% farming, 7.0% construction, 16.1% production (2000).
Income: Per capita income: $14,888 (2000); Median household income: $32,188 (2000); Poverty rate: 16.4% (2000).
Taxes: Total city taxes per capita: $132 (1997); City property taxes per capita: $132 (1997).
Education: High school graduation rate: 86.1% (2000); College graduation rate: 8.9% (2000).
Housing: Homeownership rate: 73.8% (2000); Median home value: $79,000 (2000); Median rent: $235 per month (2000); Median age of housing: 51 years (2000).
Transportation: Commute to work: 77.7% car, 0.0% public transportation, 0.0% walk, 20.9% work from home (2000); Travel time to work: 40.0% less than 15 minutes, 49.1% 15 to 30 minutes, 9.1% 30 to 45 minutes, 0.0% 45 to 60 minutes, 1.8% 60 minutes or more (2000)

FRASER (township). Covers a land area of 36.506 square miles and a water area of 0.251 square miles. Located at 43.71° N. Lat.; 94.55° W. Long.
Population: 316 (2000); Race: 100.0% White, 0.0% Black, 0.0% Asian, 0.0% American Indian and Alaska Native, 0.6% Hispanic of any race, 0.0% two or more races (2000); Density: 8.7 persons per square mile (2000); Age: 32.8% under 18, 11.1% over 64 (2000); Marriage status: 23.8% never married, 67.7% now married, 4.6% widowed, 3.8% divorced (2000); Foreign born: 0.8% (2000); Ancestry (includes multiple ancestries): 53.1% German, 13.3% Norwegian, 9.4% Irish, 4.2% Polish, 3.3% Swedish (2000).
Economy: Employment by occupation: 20.8% management, 7.1% professional, 16.4% services, 17.5% sales, 8.7% farming, 8.2% construction, 21.3% production (2000).
Income: Per capita income: $19,421 (2000); Median household income: $44,219 (2000); Poverty rate: 6.5% (2000).
Taxes: Total city taxes per capita: $129 (1997); City property taxes per capita: $129 (1997).
Education: High school graduation rate: 92.3% (2000); College graduation rate: 4.3% (2000).
Housing: Homeownership rate: 79.7% (2000); Median home value: $64,200 (2000); Median rent: $281 per month (2000); Median age of housing: 59 years (2000).
Transportation: Commute to work: 78.8% car, 1.1% public transportation, 1.7% walk, 16.2% work from home (2000); Travel time to work: 37.3% less than 15 minutes, 52.7% 15 to 30 minutes, 6.7% 30 to 45 minutes, 0.0% 45 to 60 minutes, 3.3% 60 minutes or more (2000)

GALENA (township). Covers a land area of 34.874 square miles and a water area of 0.507 square miles. Located at 43.79° N. Lat.; 94.68° W. Long.
Population: 237 (2000); Race: 96.5% White, 0.0% Black, 0.0% Asian, 3.5% American Indian and Alaska Native, 0.0% Hispanic of any race, 0.0% two or more races (2000); Density: 6.8 persons per square mile (2000); Age: 22.2% under 18, 16.1% over 64 (2000); Marriage status: 23.2% never married, 72.2% now married, 3.5% widowed, 1.0% divorced (2000); Foreign born: 0.0% (2000); Ancestry (includes multiple ancestries): 49.6% German, 27.4% Norwegian, 26.5% Swedish, 11.3% Irish, 4.8% English (2000).
Economy: Employment by occupation: 33.3% management, 20.8% professional, 4.9% services, 20.1% sales, 2.8% farming, 6.9% construction, 11.1% production (2000).
Income: Per capita income: $17,578 (2000); Median household income: $38,958 (2000); Poverty rate: 3.0% (2000).
Taxes: Total city taxes per capita: $208 (1997); City property taxes per capita: $208 (1997).
Education: High school graduation rate: 89.9% (2000); College graduation rate: 20.1% (2000).
Housing: Homeownership rate: 87.0% (2000); Median home value: $75,000 (2000); Median rent: $200 per month (2000); Median age of housing: 60+ years (2000).
Transportation: Commute to work: 77.3% car, 0.0% public transportation, 2.1% walk, 20.6% work from home (2000); Travel time to work: 37.5% less than 15 minutes, 42.0% 15 to 30 minutes, 18.8% 30 to 45 minutes, 1.8% 45 to 60 minutes, 0.0% 60 minutes or more (2000)

GRANADA (city). Covers a land area of 0.587 square miles and a water area of 0 square miles. Located at 43.69° N. Lat.; 94.34° W. Long. Elevation is 1,133 feet.
Population: 317 (2000); Race: 99.3% White, 0.0% Black, 0.7% Asian, 0.0% American Indian and Alaska Native, 1.4% Hispanic of any race, 0.0% two or more races (2000); Density: 539.9 persons per square mile (2000); Age: 25.3% under 18, 13.7% over 64 (2000); Marriage status: 22.0% never married, 58.1% now married, 8.1% widowed, 11.9% divorced (2000); Foreign born: 0.7% (2000); Ancestry (includes multiple ancestries): 59.7% German, 17.7% Irish, 13.7% Norwegian, 9.6% Swedish, 9.6% English (2000).
Economy: Grain, soybeans; livestock. Manufacturing: fertilizer. Single-family building permits issued: 1 (2001) / 1 (2000); Multi-family building permits issued: 0 (2001) / 0 (2000); Employment by occupation: 7.2% management, 17.6% professional, 15.0% services, 20.9% sales, 2.6% farming, 9.8% construction, 26.8% production (2000).
Income: Per capita income: $14,506 (2000); Median household income: $31,042 (2000); Poverty rate: 6.8% (2000).
Taxes: Total city taxes per capita: $66 (1997); City property taxes per capita: $63 (1997).
Education: High school graduation rate: 85.4% (2000); College graduation rate: 10.6% (2000).

School District(s)
Granada Huntley-East Chain (PK-12)
2000 Enrollment: 324 507-447-2211

Housing: Homeownership rate: 84.9% (2000); Median home value: $31,500 (2000); Median rent: $188 per month (2000); Median age of housing: 60+ years (2000).
Transportation: Commute to work: 94.1% car, 0.0% public transportation, 2.6% walk, 3.3% work from home (2000); Travel time to work: 36.5% less than 15 minutes, 49.3% 15 to 30 minutes, 6.8% 30 to 45 minutes, 2.0% 45 to 60 minutes, 5.4% 60 minutes or more (2000)

JAY (township). Covers a land area of 36.262 square miles and a water area of 0.007 square miles. Located at 43.63° N. Lat.; 94.80° W. Long.
Population: 269 (2000); Race: 100.0% White, 0.0% Black, 0.0% Asian, 0.0% American Indian and Alaska Native, 0.0% Hispanic of any race, 0.0% two or more races (2000); Density: 7.4 persons per square mile (2000); Age: 30.5% under 18, 16.9% over 64 (2000); Marriage status: 18.7% never married, 76.4% now married, 0.5% widowed, 4.4% divorced (2000); Foreign born: 0.0% (2000); Ancestry (includes multiple ancestries): 48.5% German, 12.5% Dutch, 11.4% Norwegian, 9.2% Irish, 8.5% Swedish (2000).
Economy: Employment by occupation: 22.1% management, 16.8% professional, 3.8% services, 19.8% sales, 1.5% farming, 8.4% construction, 27.5% production (2000).
Income: Per capita income: $16,381 (2000); Median household income: $37,500 (2000); Poverty rate: 8.2% (2000).
Education: High school graduation rate: 84.1% (2000); College graduation rate: 14.6% (2000).
Housing: Homeownership rate: 85.1% (2000); Median home value: $71,000 (2000); Median rent: $258 per month (2000); Median age of housing: 60+ years (2000).
Transportation: Commute to work: 85.5% car, 0.0% public transportation, 0.0% walk, 14.5% work from home (2000); Travel time to work: 57.1% less than 15 minutes, 30.4% 15 to 30 minutes, 8.9% 30 to 45 minutes, 3.6% 45 to 60 minutes, 0.0% 60 minutes or more (2000)

LAKE BELT (township). Covers a land area of 34.490 square miles and a water area of 0.985 square miles. Located at 43.54° N. Lat.; 94.66° W. Long.
Population: 237 (2000); Race: 100.0% White, 0.0% Black, 0.0% Asian, 0.0% American Indian and Alaska Native, 0.0% Hispanic of any race, 0.0% two or more races (2000); Density: 6.9 persons per square mile (2000); Age: 34.7% under 18, 13.5% over 64 (2000); Marriage status: 18.0% never married, 66.3% now married, 7.9% widowed, 7.9% divorced (2000); Foreign born: 0.4% (2000); Ancestry (includes multiple ancestries): 66.9% German, 30.3% Norwegian, 7.2% Irish, 4.8% Swedish, 3.6% Danish (2000).
Economy: Employment by occupation: 23.3% management, 13.2% professional, 12.4% services, 10.1% sales, 1.6% farming, 10.9% construction, 28.7% production (2000).
Income: Per capita income: $11,866 (2000); Median household income: $31,563 (2000); Poverty rate: 7.7% (2000).
Taxes: Total city taxes per capita: $106 (1997); City property taxes per capita: $106 (1997).
Education: High school graduation rate: 87.8% (2000); College graduation rate: 12.8% (2000).
Housing: Homeownership rate: 76.8% (2000); Median home value: $78,000 (2000); Median rent: $457 per month (2000); Median age of housing: 50 years (2000).
Transportation: Commute to work: 83.7% car, 0.0% public transportation, 4.7% walk, 11.6% work from home (2000); Travel time to work: 28.9% less than 15 minutes, 27.2% 15 to 30 minutes, 39.5% 30 to 45 minutes, 1.8% 45 to 60 minutes, 2.6% 60 minutes or more (2000)

LAKE FREMONT (township). Covers a land area of 35.969 square miles and a water area of 0 square miles. Located at 43.54° N. Lat.; 94.78° W. Long.
Population: 175 (2000); Race: 97.5% White, 0.0% Black, 2.5% Asian, 0.0% American Indian and Alaska Native, 0.0% Hispanic of any race, 0.0% two or more races (2000); Density: 4.9 persons per square mile (2000); Age: 25.5% under 18, 10.8% over 64 (2000); Marriage status: 14.4% never married, 77.5% now married, 5.0% widowed, 3.1% divorced (2000); Foreign born: 2.5% (2000); Ancestry (includes multiple ancestries): 60.8% German, 18.1% Swedish, 5.9% Norwegian, 5.9% Danish, 3.9% English (2000).
Economy: Employment by occupation: 22.3% management, 4.5% professional, 17.9% services, 18.8% sales, 8.0% farming, 15.2% construction, 13.4% production (2000).
Income: Per capita income: $20,036 (2000); Median household income: $35,938 (2000); Poverty rate: 1.5% (2000).
Taxes: Total city taxes per capita: $200 (1997); City property taxes per capita: $200 (1997).
Education: High school graduation rate: 92.9% (2000); College graduation rate: 16.4% (2000).
Housing: Homeownership rate: 81.6% (2000); Median home value: $63,000 (2000); Median rent: $238 per month (2000); Median age of housing: 60+ years (2000).
Transportation: Commute to work: 74.1% car, 1.8% public transportation, 5.4% walk, 18.8% work from home (2000); Travel time to work: 34.1% less than 15 minutes, 29.7% 15 to 30 minutes, 20.9% 30 to 45 minutes, 8.8% 45 to 60 minutes, 6.6% 60 minutes or more (2000)

MANYASKA (township). Covers a land area of 33.836 square miles and a water area of 0.563 square miles. Located at 43.64° N. Lat.; 94.68° W. Long.
Population: 337 (2000); Race: 99.5% White, 0.0% Black, 0.0% Asian, 0.0% American Indian and Alaska Native, 0.0% Hispanic of any race, 0.5% two or more races (2000); Density: 10.0 persons per square mile (2000); Age: 25.0% under 18, 14.0% over 64 (2000); Marriage status: 20.8% never married, 70.6% now married, 5.0% widowed, 3.6% divorced (2000); Foreign born: 0.0% (2000); Ancestry (includes multiple ancestries): 58.0% German, 14.3% Norwegian, 10.2% Swedish, 7.7% English, 6.0% Irish (2000).
Economy: Employment by occupation: 24.8% management, 16.3% professional, 12.9% services, 23.8% sales, 2.0% farming, 7.9% construction, 12.4% production (2000).
Income: Per capita income: $22,468 (2000); Median household income: $46,563 (2000); Poverty rate: 5.5% (2000).
Taxes: Total city taxes per capita: $117 (1997); City property taxes per capita: $117 (1997).
Education: High school graduation rate: 88.2% (2000); College graduation rate: 21.2% (2000).
Housing: Homeownership rate: 88.7% (2000); Median home value: $99,400 (2000); Median rent: $192 per month (2000); Median age of housing: 46 years (2000).
Transportation: Commute to work: 83.2% car, 1.0% public transportation, 2.6% walk, 13.3% work from home (2000); Travel time to work: 44.1% less than 15 minutes, 47.1% 15 to 30 minutes, 6.5% 30 to 45 minutes, 0.0% 45 to 60 minutes, 2.4% 60 minutes or more (2000)

NASHVILLE (township). Covers a land area of 36.456 square miles and a water area of 0 square miles. Located at 43.81° N. Lat.; 94.30° W. Long.
Population: 234 (2000); Race: 100.0% White, 0.0% Black, 0.0% Asian, 0.0% American Indian and Alaska Native, 0.0% Hispanic of any race, 0.0% two or more races (2000); Density: 6.4 persons per square mile (2000); Age: 19.8% under 18, 20.5% over 64 (2000); Marriage status: 19.3% never married, 70.9% now married, 5.4% widowed, 4.5% divorced (2000); Foreign born: 0.0% (2000); Ancestry (includes multiple ancestries): 43.8% German, 14.7% English, 9.7% United States or American, 7.4% Norwegian, 7.0% Irish (2000).
Economy: Employment by occupation: 19.1% management, 16.0% professional, 22.9% services, 19.1% sales, 1.5% farming, 7.6% construction, 13.7% production (2000).
Income: Per capita income: $25,088 (2000); Median household income: $39,750 (2000); Poverty rate: 3.5% (2000).
Taxes: Total city taxes per capita: $145 (1997); City property taxes per capita: $145 (1997).
Education: High school graduation rate: 89.1% (2000); College graduation rate: 13.5% (2000).
Housing: Homeownership rate: 80.4% (2000); Median home value: $83,000 (2000); Median rent: $125 per month (2000); Median age of housing: 60+ years (2000).
Transportation: Commute to work: 91.9% car, 0.0% public transportation, 0.0% walk, 8.1% work from home (2000); Travel time to work: 26.5% less than 15 minutes, 34.5% 15 to 30 minutes, 14.2% 30 to 45 minutes, 9.7% 45 to 60 minutes, 15.0% 60 minutes or more (2000)

NORTHROP (city). Covers a land area of 0.150 square miles and a water area of 0 square miles. Located at 43.73° N. Lat.; 94.43° W. Long. Elevation is 1,042 feet.
Population: 262 (2000); Race: 100.0% White, 0.0% Black, 0.0% Asian, 0.0% American Indian and Alaska Native, 0.0% Hispanic of any race, 0.0% two or more races (2000); Density: 1,747.4 persons per square mile (2000); Age: 18.0% under 18, 18.4% over 64 (2000); Marriage status: 10.1% never married, 75.4% now married, 5.0% widowed, 9.5% divorced (2000); Foreign born: 0.0% (2000); Ancestry (includes multiple ancestries): 63.6% German, 19.7% Norwegian, 10.5% Irish, 5.0% English, 3.8% Danish (2000).
Economy: Grain, soybeans; livestock. Single-family building permits issued: 0 (2001) / 0 (2000); Multi-family building permits issued: 0 (2001) / 0

(2000); Employment by occupation: 15.3% management, 10.4% professional, 24.3% services, 15.3% sales, 0.0% farming, 7.6% construction, 27.1% production (2000).
Income: Per capita income: $35,785 (2000); Median household income: $38,333 (2000); Poverty rate: 6.7% (2000).
Taxes: Total city taxes per capita: $128 (1997); City property taxes per capita: $117 (1997).
Education: High school graduation rate: 81.7% (2000); College graduation rate: 7.5% (2000).
Housing: Homeownership rate: 88.2% (2000); Median home value: $50,800 (2000); Median rent: $313 per month (2000); Median age of housing: 43 years (2000).
Transportation: Commute to work: 93.8% car, 0.0% public transportation, 0.0% walk, 4.9% work from home (2000); Travel time to work: 54.7% less than 15 minutes, 33.6% 15 to 30 minutes, 7.3% 30 to 45 minutes, 2.9% 45 to 60 minutes, 1.5% 60 minutes or more (2000)

PLEASANT PRAIRIE (township). Covers a land area of 35.776 square miles and a water area of 0.202 square miles. Located at 43.63° N. Lat.; 94.31° W. Long.
Population: 273 (2000); Race: 99.1% White, 0.0% Black, 0.0% Asian, 0.0% American Indian and Alaska Native, 0.0% Hispanic of any race, 0.9% two or more races (2000); Density: 7.6 persons per square mile (2000); Age: 19.7% under 18, 25.8% over 64 (2000); Marriage status: 18.5% never married, 68.2% now married, 10.8% widowed, 2.6% divorced (2000); Foreign born: 0.0% (2000); Ancestry (includes multiple ancestries): 58.8% German, 13.3% Irish, 8.6% Norwegian, 6.9% English, 5.6% Polish (2000).
Economy: Employment by occupation: 19.3% management, 12.3% professional, 7.9% services, 20.2% sales, 1.8% farming, 15.8% construction, 22.8% production (2000).
Income: Per capita income: $15,325 (2000); Median household income: $34,375 (2000); Poverty rate: 12.9% (2000).
Taxes: Total city taxes per capita: $78 (1997); City property taxes per capita: $78 (1997).
Education: High school graduation rate: 84.9% (2000); College graduation rate: 13.4% (2000).
Housing: Homeownership rate: 88.3% (2000); Median home value: $67,500 (2000); Median rent: $200 per month (2000); Median age of housing: 56 years (2000).
Transportation: Commute to work: 89.1% car, 0.9% public transportation, 3.6% walk, 6.4% work from home (2000); Travel time to work: 29.1% less than 15 minutes, 52.4% 15 to 30 minutes, 5.8% 30 to 45 minutes, 0.0% 45 to 60 minutes, 12.6% 60 minutes or more (2000)

ROLLING GREEN (township). Covers a land area of 34.914 square miles and a water area of 0.747 square miles. Located at 43.63° N. Lat.; 94.54° W. Long.
Population: 309 (2000); Race: 97.9% White, 0.0% Black, 2.1% Asian, 0.0% American Indian and Alaska Native, 0.0% Hispanic of any race, 0.0% two or more races (2000); Density: 8.9 persons per square mile (2000); Age: 24.8% under 18, 11.8% over 64 (2000); Marriage status: 20.6% never married, 72.3% now married, 1.1% widowed, 6.0% divorced (2000); Foreign born: 0.9% (2000); Ancestry (includes multiple ancestries): 61.0% German, 18.1% Irish, 9.4% English, 4.5% Danish, 4.5% Norwegian (2000).
Economy: Employment by occupation: 21.4% management, 9.3% professional, 9.3% services, 30.2% sales, 6.0% farming, 6.0% construction, 17.6% production (2000).
Income: Per capita income: $18,539 (2000); Median household income: $42,813 (2000); Poverty rate: 8.5% (2000).
Taxes: Total city taxes per capita: $143 (1997); City property taxes per capita: $143 (1997).
Education: High school graduation rate: 91.2% (2000); College graduation rate: 10.6% (2000).
Housing: Homeownership rate: 75.8% (2000); Median home value: $93,300 (2000); Median rent: $142 per month (2000); Median age of housing: 60+ years (2000).
Transportation: Commute to work: 80.2% car, 0.0% public transportation, 3.4% walk, 16.4% work from home (2000); Travel time to work: 61.5% less than 15 minutes, 30.4% 15 to 30 minutes, 6.8% 30 to 45 minutes, 0.0% 45 to 60 minutes, 1.4% 60 minutes or more (2000)

RUTLAND (township). Covers a land area of 35.535 square miles and a water area of 1.411 square miles. Located at 43.71° N. Lat.; 94.44° W. Long.
Population: 472 (2000); Race: 98.1% White, 0.0% Black, 0.0% Asian, 0.0% American Indian and Alaska Native, 0.6% Hispanic of any race, 1.5% two or more races (2000); Density: 13.3 persons per square mile (2000); Age: 25.4% under 18, 10.0% over 64 (2000); Marriage status: 24.0% never married, 70.2% now married, 1.3% widowed, 4.4% divorced (2000); Foreign born: 0.9% (2000); Ancestry (includes multiple ancestries): 60.3% German, 11.9% Norwegian, 8.7% United States or American, 8.1% Swedish, 6.4% Danish (2000).
Economy: Employment by occupation: 15.7% management, 14.6% professional, 17.5% services, 11.6% sales, 4.9% farming, 8.6% construction, 27.2% production (2000).
Income: Per capita income: $16,757 (2000); Median household income: $41,786 (2000); Poverty rate: 9.0% (2000).
Taxes: Total city taxes per capita: $80 (1997); City property taxes per capita: $80 (1997).
Education: High school graduation rate: 90.9% (2000); College graduation rate: 11.3% (2000).
Housing: Homeownership rate: 84.1% (2000); Median home value: $90,400 (2000); Median rent: $319 per month (2000); Median age of housing: 60 years (2000).
Transportation: Commute to work: 84.0% car, 0.0% public transportation, 0.7% walk, 14.2% work from home (2000); Travel time to work: 48.7% less than 15 minutes, 34.3% 15 to 30 minutes, 16.1% 30 to 45 minutes, 0.0% 45 to 60 minutes, 0.9% 60 minutes or more (2000)

SHERBURN (city). Aka Sherburne. Covers a land area of 0.886 square miles and a water area of 0 square miles. Located at 43.65° N. Lat.; 94.72° W. Long. Elevation is 1,295 feet.
History: Also spelled Sherburne.
Population: 1,082 (2000); Race: 98.6% White, 0.0% Black, 0.4% Asian, 0.3% American Indian and Alaska Native, 1.1% Hispanic of any race, 0.7% two or more races (2000); Density: 1,220.6 persons per square mile (2000); Age: 23.7% under 18, 22.0% over 64 (2000); Marriage status: 23.1% never married, 56.9% now married, 13.4% widowed, 6.5% divorced (2000); Foreign born: 0.7% (2000); Ancestry (includes multiple ancestries): 47.3% German, 11.8% Norwegian, 7.1% Swedish, 5.1% United States or American, 5.0% Danish (2000).
Economy: Grain, soybeans; livestock. Manufacturing of lawn equipment. Employment by occupation: 9.1% management, 15.0% professional, 18.2% services, 19.2% sales, 1.8% farming, 9.3% construction, 27.5% production (2000).
Income: Per capita income: $15,079 (2000); Median household income: $26,643 (2000); Poverty rate: 10.6% (2000).
Education: High school graduation rate: 79.3% (2000); College graduation rate: 13.4% (2000).

School District(s)

Martin County West (PK-12)
2000 Enrollment: 976 507-728-8276
Housing: Homeownership rate: 76.7% (2000); Median home value: $51,300 (2000); Median rent: $303 per month (2000); Median age of housing: 47 years (2000).
Newspapers: The West Martin Weekly News (1 x week)
Transportation: Commute to work: 94.1% car, 0.0% public transportation, 2.4% walk, 2.6% work from home (2000); Travel time to work: 45.3% less than 15 minutes, 36.6% 15 to 30 minutes, 8.5% 30 to 45 minutes, 2.0% 45 to 60 minutes, 7.5% 60 minutes or more (2000)
Additional Information Contacts
Sherburn Chamber of Commerce. 507-764-2607

SILVER LAKE (township). Covers a land area of 34.918 square miles and a water area of 2.369 square miles. Located at 43.54° N. Lat.; 94.43° W. Long.
Population: 494 (2000); Race: 99.4% White, 0.0% Black, 0.6% Asian, 0.0% American Indian and Alaska Native, 0.0% Hispanic of any race, 0.0% two or more races (2000); Density: 14.1 persons per square mile (2000); Age: 26.6% under 18, 15.2% over 64 (2000); Marriage status: 15.9% never married, 74.7% now married, 5.2% widowed, 4.2% divorced (2000); Foreign born: 0.8% (2000); Ancestry (includes multiple ancestries): 56.6% German, 18.7% Polish, 13.6% English, 11.2% Irish, 10.1% Swedish (2000).
Economy: Employment by occupation: 18.8% management, 19.4% professional, 9.0% services, 20.8% sales, 3.8% farming, 4.2% construction, 24.0% production (2000).
Income: Per capita income: $20,496 (2000); Median household income: $35,000 (2000); Poverty rate: 9.1% (2000).
Taxes: Total city taxes per capita: $85 (1997); City property taxes per capita: $85 (1997).
Education: High school graduation rate: 91.8% (2000); College graduation rate: 23.0% (2000).

Housing: Homeownership rate: 82.3% (2000); Median home value: $120,800 (2000); Median rent: $238 per month (2000); Median age of housing: 46 years (2000).
Transportation: Commute to work: 84.9% car, 0.0% public transportation, 3.2% walk, 10.9% work from home (2000); Travel time to work: 36.8% less than 15 minutes, 51.0% 15 to 30 minutes, 5.9% 30 to 45 minutes, 1.6% 45 to 60 minutes, 4.7% 60 minutes or more (2000)

TENHASSEN (township). Covers a land area of 32.025 square miles and a water area of 4.600 square miles. Located at 43.53° N. Lat.; 94.53° W. Long.
Population: 253 (2000); Race: 100.0% White, 0.0% Black, 0.0% Asian, 0.0% American Indian and Alaska Native, 0.0% Hispanic of any race, 0.0% two or more races (2000); Density: 7.9 persons per square mile (2000); Age: 17.2% under 18, 22.5% over 64 (2000); Marriage status: 21.1% never married, 65.1% now married, 7.3% widowed, 6.4% divorced (2000); Foreign born: 0.0% (2000); Ancestry (includes multiple ancestries): 56.1% German, 5.7% Norwegian, 4.5% Irish, 3.7% Danish, 3.7% Polish (2000).
Economy: Employment by occupation: 23.0% management, 14.1% professional, 11.9% services, 22.2% sales, 3.0% farming, 8.9% construction, 17.0% production (2000).
Income: Per capita income: $23,902 (2000); Median household income: $36,146 (2000); Poverty rate: 7.0% (2000).
Taxes: Total city taxes per capita: $95 (1997); City property taxes per capita: $95 (1997).
Education: High school graduation rate: 83.3% (2000); College graduation rate: 19.3% (2000).
Housing: Homeownership rate: 86.9% (2000); Median home value: $87,500 (2000); Median rent: $275 per month (2000); Median age of housing: 60+ years (2000).
Transportation: Commute to work: 82.2% car, 0.0% public transportation, 0.0% walk, 17.8% work from home (2000); Travel time to work: 12.6% less than 15 minutes, 64.0% 15 to 30 minutes, 12.6% 30 to 45 minutes, 7.2% 45 to 60 minutes, 3.6% 60 minutes or more (2000)

TRIMONT (city). Covers a land area of 0.769 square miles and a water area of 0 square miles. Located at 43.76° N. Lat.; 94.71° W. Long. Elevation is 1,236 feet.
History: Formed by merger of Monterey and Triumph in late 1950s.
Population: 754 (2000); Race: 98.3% White, 0.5% Black, 0.0% Asian, 0.3% American Indian and Alaska Native, 0.0% Hispanic of any race, 0.9% two or more races (2000); Density: 980.3 persons per square mile (2000); Age: 22.3% under 18, 29.2% over 64 (2000); Marriage status: 12.7% never married, 63.6% now married, 16.7% widowed, 6.9% divorced (2000); Foreign born: 0.8% (2000); Ancestry (includes multiple ancestries): 51.8% German, 19.2% Swedish, 17.6% Norwegian, 11.2% Irish, 5.2% English (2000).
Economy: In grain, livestock, and poultry area. Soybeans. Manufacturing: meat processing fertilizers, bin level indicator switches, mugs, and specialties. Single-family building permits issued: 1 (2001) / 2 (2000); Multi-family building permits issued: 0 (2001) / 0 (2000); Employment by occupation: 15.7% management, 12.7% professional, 14.0% services, 21.1% sales, 2.3% farming, 12.0% construction, 22.1% production (2000).
Income: Per capita income: $19,819 (2000); Median household income: $28,125 (2000); Poverty rate: 11.5% (2000).
Taxes: Total city taxes per capita: $152 (1997); City property taxes per capita: $151 (1997).
Education: High school graduation rate: 75.2% (2000); College graduation rate: 15.2% (2000).
Housing: Homeownership rate: 83.5% (2000); Median home value: $36,400 (2000); Median rent: $255 per month (2000); Median age of housing: 50 years (2000).
Transportation: Commute to work: 81.8% car, 1.0% public transportation, 9.8% walk, 6.1% work from home (2000); Travel time to work: 42.8% less than 15 minutes, 36.7% 15 to 30 minutes, 15.5% 30 to 45 minutes, 2.5% 45 to 60 minutes, 2.5% 60 minutes or more (2000)

TRUMAN (city). Covers a land area of 1.085 square miles and a water area of 0 square miles. Located at 43.82° N. Lat.; 94.43° W. Long. Elevation is 1,110 feet.
Population: 1,259 (2000); Race: 99.5% White, 0.2% Black, 0.0% Asian, 0.0% American Indian and Alaska Native, 0.2% Hispanic of any race, 0.3% two or more races (2000); Density: 1,160.1 persons per square mile (2000); Age: 22.9% under 18, 27.7% over 64 (2000); Marriage status: 19.2% never married, 61.6% now married, 14.1% widowed, 5.0% divorced (2000); Foreign born: 1.0% (2000); Ancestry (includes multiple ancestries): 59.8% German, 18.7% Norwegian, 7.4% Swedish, 6.8% English, 6.3% Irish (2000).
Economy: Agriculture includes soybeans, grain; livestock. Manufacturing of concrete, lumber. Single-family building permits issued: 2 (2001) / 0 (2000); Multi-family building permits issued: 0 (2001) / 2 (2000); Employment by occupation: 9.9% management, 16.2% professional, 19.0% services, 24.0% sales, 3.6% farming, 9.1% construction, 18.3% production (2000).
Income: Per capita income: $18,305 (2000); Median household income: $35,000 (2000); Poverty rate: 9.2% (2000).
Taxes: Total city taxes per capita: $110 (1997); City property taxes per capita: $103 (1997).
Education: High school graduation rate: 77.5% (2000); College graduation rate: 15.3% (2000).

School District(s)

Truman (PK-12)
2000 Enrollment: 414 507-776-2111

Housing: Homeownership rate: 72.5% (2000); Median home value: $52,700 (2000); Median rent: $246 per month (2000); Median age of housing: 47 years (2000).
Newspapers: The Truman Tribune (1 x week)
Transportation: Commute to work: 84.0% car, 0.4% public transportation, 11.7% walk, 3.1% work from home (2000); Travel time to work: 54.8% less than 15 minutes, 32.2% 15 to 30 minutes, 7.8% 30 to 45 minutes, 3.0% 45 to 60 minutes, 2.2% 60 minutes or more (2000)

WAVERLY (township). Covers a land area of 36.628 square miles and a water area of 0.162 square miles. Located at 43.80° N. Lat.; 94.55° W. Long.
Population: 245 (2000); Race: 100.0% White, 0.0% Black, 0.0% Asian, 0.0% American Indian and Alaska Native, 0.0% Hispanic of any race, 0.0% two or more races (2000); Density: 6.7 persons per square mile (2000); Age: 26.4% under 18, 10.4% over 64 (2000); Marriage status: 15.0% never married, 79.4% now married, 2.2% widowed, 3.3% divorced (2000); Foreign born: 0.0% (2000); Ancestry (includes multiple ancestries): 74.9% German, 33.8% Norwegian, 10.8% Swedish, 3.5% United States or American, 3.0% English (2000).
Economy: Employment by occupation: 27.1% management, 9.8% professional, 15.8% services, 14.3% sales, 8.3% farming, 6.0% construction, 18.8% production (2000).
Income: Per capita income: $16,161 (2000); Median household income: $46,875 (2000); Poverty rate: 13.9% (2000).
Taxes: Total city taxes per capita: $152 (1997); City property taxes per capita: $152 (1997).
Education: High school graduation rate: 86.3% (2000); College graduation rate: 5.2% (2000).
Housing: Homeownership rate: 86.7% (2000); Median home value: $96,300 (2000); Median rent: $200 per month (2000); Median age of housing: 60+ years (2000).
Transportation: Commute to work: 77.1% car, 0.0% public transportation, 2.3% walk, 20.6% work from home (2000); Travel time to work: 38.5% less than 15 minutes, 49.0% 15 to 30 minutes, 6.7% 30 to 45 minutes, 0.0% 45 to 60 minutes, 5.8% 60 minutes or more (2000)

WELCOME (city). Covers a land area of 0.910 square miles and a water area of 0 square miles. Located at 43.66° N. Lat.; 94.61° W. Long. Elevation is 1,235 feet.
Population: 721 (2000); Race: 99.3% White, 0.0% Black, 0.0% Asian, 0.0% American Indian and Alaska Native, 1.8% Hispanic of any race, 0.4% two or more races (2000); Density: 792.4 persons per square mile (2000); Age: 26.5% under 18, 22.4% over 64 (2000); Marriage status: 19.0% never married, 59.2% now married, 10.1% widowed, 11.7% divorced (2000); Foreign born: 0.8% (2000); Ancestry (includes multiple ancestries): 58.3% German, 9.5% Norwegian, 9.4% English, 6.7% Swedish, 5.1% Irish (2000).
Economy: Railroad junction. Agriculture: grain, soybeans; livestock. Manufacturing of air conditioners. Single-family building permits issued: 1 (2001) / 1 (2000); Multi-family building permits issued: 0 (2001) / 0 (2000); Employment by occupation: 6.8% management, 11.2% professional, 17.4% services, 24.7% sales, 4.4% farming, 5.9% construction, 29.7% production (2000).
Income: Per capita income: $16,539 (2000); Median household income: $32,125 (2000); Poverty rate: 6.9% (2000).
Taxes: Total city taxes per capita: $224 (1997); City property taxes per capita: $217 (1997).
Education: High school graduation rate: 77.2% (2000); College graduation rate: 7.1% (2000).

Housing: Homeownership rate: 82.8% (2000); Median home value: $46,700 (2000); Median rent: $257 per month (2000); Median age of housing: 54 years (2000).
Transportation: Commute to work: 94.0% car, 0.0% public transportation, 2.4% walk, 3.6% work from home (2000); Travel time to work: 41.1% less than 15 minutes, 45.5% 15 to 30 minutes, 8.7% 30 to 45 minutes, 1.6% 45 to 60 minutes, 3.1% 60 minutes or more (2000)

WESTFORD (township). Covers a land area of 36.230 square miles and a water area of 0.367 square miles. Located at 43.81° N. Lat.; 94.43° W. Long.
Population: 331 (2000); Race: 99.4% White, 0.0% Black, 0.0% Asian, 0.0% American Indian and Alaska Native, 0.6% Hispanic of any race, 0.0% two or more races (2000); Density: 9.1 persons per square mile (2000); Age: 32.7% under 18, 11.0% over 64 (2000); Marriage status: 26.1% never married, 64.4% now married, 5.3% widowed, 4.2% divorced (2000); Foreign born: 0.0% (2000); Ancestry (includes multiple ancestries): 74.4% German, 11.8% Swedish, 9.0% Norwegian, 8.2% Dutch, 7.9% English (2000).
Economy: Employment by occupation: 23.7% management, 9.2% professional, 25.6% services, 20.3% sales, 5.3% farming, 4.3% construction, 11.6% production (2000).
Income: Per capita income: $16,963 (2000); Median household income: $45,833 (2000); Poverty rate: 7.3% (2000).
Taxes: Total city taxes per capita: $142 (2000); City property taxes per capita: $142 (2000).
Education: High school graduation rate: 88.4% (2000); College graduation rate: 21.3% (2000).
Housing: Homeownership rate: 86.4% (2000); Median home value: $81,400 (2000); Median rent: $288 per month (2000); Median age of housing: 60+ years (2000).
Transportation: Commute to work: 81.8% car, 0.0% public transportation, 2.9% walk, 15.3% work from home (2000); Travel time to work: 48.0% less than 15 minutes, 37.3% 15 to 30 minutes, 2.8% 30 to 45 minutes, 0.0% 45 to 60 minutes, 11.9% 60 minutes or more (2000)

McLeod County

Located in south central Minnesota; watered by forks of the Crow River. Covers a land area of 491.90 square miles, a water area of 13.80 square miles, and is located in the Central Time Zone. The county government was organized in 1856. County seat is Glencoe.

Weather Station: Hutchinson 1 N — Elevation: 1,092 feet

	Jan	Feb	Mar	Apr	May	Jun	Jul	Aug	Sep	Oct	Nov	Dec
High	21	28	39	57	71	80	83	81	72	59	40	26
Low	1	8	21	35	47	57	61	59	49	37	23	8
Precip	0.8	0.5	1.6	2.2	3.1	4.5	3.7	4.1	2.4	2.0	1.7	0.7
Snow	9.6	5.1	7.9	2.3	tr	0.0	tr	0.0	tr	0.2	7.2	7.1

High and Low temperatures in degrees Fahrenheit; Precipitation and Snow in inches

Weather Station: Stewart — Elevation: 1,040 feet

	Jan	Feb	Mar	Apr	May	Jun	Jul	Aug	Sep	Oct	Nov	Dec
High	21	28	40	57	71	81	84	81	73	60	40	26
Low	1	9	22	35	47	57	61	59	49	37	23	9
Precip	0.9	0.6	1.8	2.6	3.1	4.3	4.0	4.4	2.7	2.1	1.9	0.7
Snow	11.3	7.4	9.6	3.0	tr	0.0	0.0	0.0	0.0	0.3	8.5	8.6

High and Low temperatures in degrees Fahrenheit; Precipitation and Snow in inches

Population: 34,898 (2000); Race: 96.9% White, 0.2% Black, 0.6% Asian, 0.2% American Indian and Alaska Native, 3.2% Hispanic of any race, 0.6% two or more races (2000); Density: 70.9 persons per square mile (2000); Age: 27.8% under 18, 13.9% over 64 (2000).
Religion: Five largest groups: 25.6% Catholic Church, 25.3% Lutheran Church—Missouri Synod, 20.2% Evangelical Lutheran Church in America, 4.7% United Church of Christ, 2.8% Wisconsin Evangelical Lutheran Synod (2000).
Economy: Unemployment rate: 3.7% (11/2002); Total civilian labor force: 18,674 (11/2002); Leading industries: 46.7% manufacturing; 13.5% retail trade; 12.6% health care and social assistance (2000); Companies that employ more than 1,000 persons: 2 (2000); Companies that employ more than 100 persons: 22 (2000); Farms: 1,008 totaling 250,244 acres (1997); Minority business ownership rate: 0.0% (1997); Women business ownership rate: 19.8% (1997); Retail sales per capita: $8,502 (1997). Single-family building permits issued: 222 (2001) / 166 (2000); Multi-family building permits issued: 16 (2001) / 24 (2000).
Income: Per capita income: $20,137 (2000); Median household income: $45,953 (2000); Poverty rate: 4.8% (2000); Bankruptcy rate: 2.79% (2001).
Taxes: Total county taxes per capita: $224 (2000); County property taxes per capita: $222 (2000).
Education: High school graduation rate: 84.7% (2000); College graduation rate: 15.4% (2000).
Housing: Homeownership rate: 78.5% (2000); Median home value: $104,800 (2000); Median rent: $421 per month (2000); Median age of housing: 31 years (2000).
Health: Birth rate: 126.1 per 10,000 population (1998); Age adjusted death rate: 82.8 per 10,000 population (1999); Age adjusted cancer mortality rate: 202.5 deaths per 100,000 population (1999). Number of physicians: 8.6 per 10,000 population (1999); Number of hospital beds: 95.1 per 10,000 population (1999).
Elections: 2000 Presidential election results: 36.4% Gore, 57.1% Bush, 4.4% Nader, 1.5% Buchanan
National and State Parks: Halva Marsh State Wildlife Management Area; Hutchinson State Wildlife Management Area; Kujas Lake State Wildlife Management Area; Penn State Wildlife Management Area; Prieve State Wildlife Management Area; Ras-Lynn State Wildlife Management Area; Spiering State Wildlife Management Area
Additional Information Contacts
McLeod County Government Offices 320-864-5551
Glencoe Chamber of Commerce 320-864-3650
Hutchinson Chamber of Commerce 320-587-5252

McLeod County Communities

ACOMA (township). Covers a land area of 31.457 square miles and a water area of 3.329 square miles. Located at 44.94° N. Lat.; 94.43° W. Long.
Population: 1,185 (2000); Race: 97.9% White, 0.0% Black, 0.8% Asian, 0.0% American Indian and Alaska Native, 0.5% Hispanic of any race, 0.6% two or more races (2000); Density: 37.7 persons per square mile (2000); Age: 32.5% under 18, 6.8% over 64 (2000); Marriage status: 20.5% never married, 73.5% now married, 2.7% widowed, 3.4% divorced (2000); Foreign born: 1.0% (2000); Ancestry (includes multiple ancestries): 67.8% German, 16.5% Norwegian, 7.4% Swedish, 6.4% Irish, 5.3% Polish (2000).
Economy: Employment by occupation: 16.4% management, 15.8% professional, 9.3% services, 24.4% sales, 0.6% farming, 9.0% construction, 24.6% production (2000).
Income: Per capita income: $23,302 (2000); Median household income: $67,292 (2000); Poverty rate: 4.1% (2000).
Taxes: Total city taxes per capita: $48 (1997); City property taxes per capita: $48 (1997).
Education: High school graduation rate: 89.6% (2000); College graduation rate: 21.7% (2000).
Housing: Homeownership rate: 93.3% (2000); Median home value: $172,700 (2000); Median rent: $325 per month (2000); Median age of housing: 23 years (2000).
Transportation: Commute to work: 89.9% car, 0.3% public transportation, 0.9% walk, 8.5% work from home (2000); Travel time to work: 50.9% less than 15 minutes, 35.9% 15 to 30 minutes, 3.8% 30 to 45 minutes, 1.6% 45 to 60 minutes, 7.9% 60 minutes or more (2000)

BERGEN (township). Covers a land area of 35.336 square miles and a water area of 0.057 square miles. Located at 44.85° N. Lat.; 94.05° W. Long.
Population: 881 (2000); Race: 96.2% White, 0.0% Black, 0.8% Asian, 0.0% American Indian and Alaska Native, 4.5% Hispanic of any race, 0.0% two or more races (2000); Density: 24.9 persons per square mile (2000); Age: 29.2% under 18, 9.8% over 64 (2000); Marriage status: 27.9% never married, 62.3% now married, 2.6% widowed, 7.2% divorced (2000); Foreign born: 2.9% (2000); Ancestry (includes multiple ancestries): 61.9% German, 12.9% Norwegian, 6.5% Czech, 5.2% English, 5.0% Other groups (2000).
Economy: Employment by occupation: 14.7% management, 10.6% professional, 7.5% services, 20.1% sales, 5.8% farming, 13.7% construction, 27.6% production (2000).
Income: Per capita income: $20,808 (2000); Median household income: $52,115 (2000); Poverty rate: 5.8% (2000).
Taxes: Total city taxes per capita: $61 (1997); City property taxes per capita: $59 (1997).
Education: High school graduation rate: 83.4% (2000); College graduation rate: 12.6% (2000).
Housing: Homeownership rate: 91.6% (2000); Median home value: $141,400 (2000); Median rent: $375 per month (2000); Median age of housing: 42 years (2000).

Transportation: Commute to work: 88.1% car, 0.0% public transportation, 2.7% walk, 7.5% work from home (2000); Travel time to work: 28.1% less than 15 minutes, 31.1% 15 to 30 minutes, 16.6% 30 to 45 minutes, 13.2% 45 to 60 minutes, 11.1% 60 minutes or more (2000)

BISCAY (city). Covers a land area of 0.069 square miles and a water area of 0 square miles. Located at 44.82° N. Lat.; 94.27° W. Long. Elevation is 1,020 feet.
Population: 114 (2000); Race: 89.0% White, 0.0% Black, 0.0% Asian, 0.0% American Indian and Alaska Native, 11.0% Hispanic of any race, 0.0% two or more races (2000); Density: 1,642.4 persons per square mile (2000); Age: 15.4% under 18, 8.8% over 64 (2000); Marriage status: 16.5% never married, 62.0% now married, 7.6% widowed, 13.9% divorced (2000); Foreign born: 6.6% (2000); Ancestry (includes multiple ancestries): 49.5% German, 11.0% Other groups, 8.8% United States or American, 8.8% French (except Basque), 4.4% Finnish (2000).
Economy: Dairying; livestock; grain. Single-family building permits issued: 0 (2001) / 0 (2000); Multi-family building permits issued: 0 (2001) / 0 (2000); Employment by occupation: 9.0% management, 6.0% professional, 13.4% services, 16.4% sales, 0.0% farming, 20.9% construction, 34.3% production (2000).
Income: Per capita income: $22,988 (2000); Median household income: $49,583 (2000); Poverty rate: 0.0% (2000).
Taxes: Total city taxes per capita: $67 (1997); City property taxes per capita: $67 (1997).
Education: High school graduation rate: 90.0% (2000); College graduation rate: 4.3% (2000).
Housing: Homeownership rate: 100.0% (2000); Median home value: $68,800 (2000); Median age of housing: 31 years (2000).
Transportation: Commute to work: 100.0% car, 0.0% public transportation, 0.0% walk, 0.0% work from home (2000); Travel time to work: 18.8% less than 15 minutes, 64.1% 15 to 30 minutes, 3.1% 30 to 45 minutes, 12.5% 45 to 60 minutes, 1.6% 60 minutes or more (2000)

BROWNTON (city). Covers a land area of 0.377 square miles and a water area of 0 square miles. Located at 44.73° N. Lat.; 94.35° W. Long. Elevation is 1,021 feet.
Population: 807 (2000); Race: 93.4% White, 0.0% Black, 3.1% Asian, 0.0% American Indian and Alaska Native, 3.3% Hispanic of any race, 0.9% two or more races (2000); Density: 2,139.1 persons per square mile (2000); Age: 28.9% under 18, 19.4% over 64 (2000); Marriage status: 22.4% never married, 59.9% now married, 11.0% widowed, 6.7% divorced (2000); Foreign born: 1.2% (2000); Ancestry (includes multiple ancestries): 58.3% German, 10.4% Norwegian, 9.3% Other groups, 7.7% Irish, 6.5% Swedish (2000).
Economy: Agricultural area: dairying; poultry; grain, peas, soybeans; light manufacturing. Single-family building permits issued: 1 (2001) / 2 (2000); Multi-family building permits issued: 4 (2001) / 0 (2000); Employment by occupation: 7.7% management, 12.3% professional, 11.8% services, 23.1% sales, 1.3% farming, 9.3% construction, 34.4% production (2000).
Income: Per capita income: $17,290 (2000); Median household income: $36,932 (2000); Poverty rate: 9.3% (2000).
Taxes: Total city taxes per capita: $194 (1997); City property taxes per capita: $185 (1997).
Education: High school graduation rate: 76.2% (2000); College graduation rate: 14.0% (2000).

School District(s)

Mcleod West Schools (KG-12)
2000 Enrollment: 536 320-328-5214
Housing: Homeownership rate: 84.6% (2000); Median home value: $73,900 (2000); Median rent: $350 per month (2000); Median age of housing: 50 years (2000).
Newspapers: Brownton/Stewart Bulletin (1 x week)
Transportation: Commute to work: 85.6% car, 0.0% public transportation, 6.7% walk, 7.2% work from home (2000); Travel time to work: 20.5% less than 15 minutes, 52.9% 15 to 30 minutes, 9.7% 30 to 45 minutes, 6.4% 45 to 60 minutes, 10.5% 60 minutes or more (2000)

COLLINS (township). Covers a land area of 34.101 square miles and a water area of 1.519 square miles. Located at 44.76° N. Lat.; 94.42° W. Long.
Population: 476 (2000); Race: 100.0% White, 0.0% Black, 0.0% Asian, 0.0% American Indian and Alaska Native, 0.0% Hispanic of any race, 0.0% two or more races (2000); Density: 14.0 persons per square mile (2000); Age: 23.5% under 18, 14.4% over 64 (2000); Marriage status: 23.4% never married, 67.0% now married, 6.2% widowed, 3.4% divorced (2000); Foreign born: 0.4% (2000); Ancestry (includes multiple ancestries): 66.7% German, 9.3% Swedish, 6.9% Czech, 6.7% Danish, 6.1% Norwegian (2000).
Economy: Employment by occupation: 12.5% management, 15.8% professional, 11.0% services, 18.4% sales, 4.0% farming, 8.5% construction, 29.8% production (2000).
Income: Per capita income: $24,267 (2000); Median household income: $55,278 (2000); Poverty rate: 1.0% (2000).
Taxes: Total city taxes per capita: $124 (1997); City property taxes per capita: $122 (1997).
Education: High school graduation rate: 81.3% (2000); College graduation rate: 17.2% (2000).
Housing: Homeownership rate: 95.1% (2000); Median home value: $112,500 (2000); Median rent: $275 per month (2000); Median age of housing: 44 years (2000).
Transportation: Commute to work: 96.7% car, 0.0% public transportation, 1.1% walk, 2.2% work from home (2000); Travel time to work: 19.4% less than 15 minutes, 55.9% 15 to 30 minutes, 9.5% 30 to 45 minutes, 8.0% 45 to 60 minutes, 7.2% 60 minutes or more (2000)

GLENCOE (city). Covers a land area of 2.666 square miles and a water area of 0 square miles. Located at 44.77° N. Lat.; 94.15° W. Long. Elevation is 999 feet.
Population: 5,453 (2000); Race: 93.2% White, 0.0% Black, 0.4% Asian, 0.3% American Indian and Alaska Native, 13.5% Hispanic of any race, 0.5% two or more races (2000); Density: 2,045.6 persons per square mile (2000); Age: 28.2% under 18, 17.0% over 64 (2000); Marriage status: 19.8% never married, 63.0% now married, 10.3% widowed, 6.8% divorced (2000); Foreign born: 6.0% (2000); Ancestry (includes multiple ancestries): 56.9% German, 11.4% Other groups, 6.4% Norwegian, 6.0% Irish, 5.8% Swedish (2000).
Economy: Single-family building permits issued: 18 (2001) / 18 (2000); Multi-family building permits issued: 0 (2001) / 0 (2000); Employment by occupation: 7.4% management, 16.3% professional, 9.7% services, 29.1% sales, 1.2% farming, 11.1% construction, 25.2% production (2000).
Income: Per capita income: $20,450 (2000); Median household income: $46,723 (2000); Poverty rate: 2.1% (2000).
Taxes: Total city taxes per capita: $290 (2000); City property taxes per capita: $271 (2000).
Education: High school graduation rate: 77.8% (2000); College graduation rate: 12.1% (2000).

School District(s)

Glencoe-Silver Lake (PK-12)
2000 Enrollment: 1,892 320-864-2498
Housing: Homeownership rate: 77.2% (2000); Median home value: $96,200 (2000); Median rent: $433 per month (2000); Median age of housing: 34 years (2000).
Hospitals: Glencoe Regional Health Services
Safety: Violent crime rate: 12.7 per 10,000 population; Property crime rate: 292.1 per 10,000 population (2001).
Newspapers: The McLeod County Chronicle (1 x week); The Glencoe Enterprise (1 x week); Glencoe Advertiser (1 x week)
Transportation: Commute to work: 93.3% car, 0.0% public transportation, 3.4% walk, 3.2% work from home (2000); Travel time to work: 48.3% less than 15 minutes, 23.1% 15 to 30 minutes, 10.6% 30 to 45 minutes, 10.5% 45 to 60 minutes, 7.5% 60 minutes or more (2000)
Additional Information Contacts
Glencoe Chamber of Commerce 320-864-3650

GLENCOE (township). Covers a land area of 33.734 square miles and a water area of 0.114 square miles. Located at 44.75° N. Lat.; 94.18° W. Long. Elevation is 999 feet.
History: Plotted 1855.
Population: 565 (2000); Race: 98.3% White, 0.5% Black, 0.0% Asian, 0.5% American Indian and Alaska Native, 0.0% Hispanic of any race, 0.7% two or more races (2000); Density: 16.7 persons per square mile (2000); Age: 24.7% under 18, 13.4% over 64 (2000); Marriage status: 18.9% never married, 73.1% now married, 2.9% widowed, 5.1% divorced (2000); Foreign born: 0.9% (2000); Ancestry (includes multiple ancestries): 72.2% German, 9.0% United States or American, 7.0% Norwegian, 5.0% Irish, 4.0% English (2000).
Economy: Trading point in agricultural area: grain, peas; poultry, livestock; dairying. Manufacturing: machinery, fabricated metal products, food. Employment by occupation: 18.6% management, 10.5% professional, 6.6% services, 26.6% sales, 1.8% farming, 13.5% construction, 22.5% production (2000).

Income: Per capita income: $21,445 (2000); Median household income: $55,089 (2000); Poverty rate: 4.7% (2000).
Taxes: Total city taxes per capita: $85 (1997); City property taxes per capita: $85 (1997).
Education: High school graduation rate: 80.2% (2000); College graduation rate: 14.5% (2000).
Housing: Homeownership rate: 92.5% (2000); Median home value: $134,800 (2000); Median rent: $292 per month (2000); Median age of housing: 54 years (2000).
Transportation: Commute to work: 84.6% car, 0.6% public transportation, 3.6% walk, 11.2% work from home (2000); Travel time to work: 47.3% less than 15 minutes, 28.2% 15 to 30 minutes, 12.2% 30 to 45 minutes, 4.8% 45 to 60 minutes, 7.5% 60 minutes or more (2000)

HALE (township). Covers a land area of 34.153 square miles and a water area of 1.352 square miles. Located at 44.93° N. Lat.; 94.20° W. Long.
Population: 957 (2000); Race: 99.3% White, 0.0% Black, 0.0% Asian, 0.0% American Indian and Alaska Native, 0.7% Hispanic of any race, 0.2% two or more races (2000); Density: 28.0 persons per square mile (2000); Age: 27.4% under 18, 12.5% over 64 (2000); Marriage status: 28.4% never married, 61.7% now married, 6.1% widowed, 3.8% divorced (2000); Foreign born: 0.7% (2000); Ancestry (includes multiple ancestries): 40.8% German, 28.2% Polish, 24.3% Czech, 6.9% Norwegian, 4.8% Swedish (2000).
Economy: Employment by occupation: 17.3% management, 8.4% professional, 9.9% services, 22.6% sales, 2.1% farming, 9.9% construction, 29.8% production (2000).
Income: Per capita income: $18,198 (2000); Median household income: $50,446 (2000); Poverty rate: 5.7% (2000).
Taxes: Total city taxes per capita: $45 (1997); City property taxes per capita: $44 (1997).
Education: High school graduation rate: 80.8% (2000); College graduation rate: 7.0% (2000).
Housing: Homeownership rate: 92.4% (2000); Median home value: $110,000 (2000); Median rent: $404 per month (2000); Median age of housing: 32 years (2000).
Transportation: Commute to work: 85.7% car, 0.0% public transportation, 4.0% walk, 9.5% work from home (2000); Travel time to work: 22.3% less than 15 minutes, 48.4% 15 to 30 minutes, 11.6% 30 to 45 minutes, 6.1% 45 to 60 minutes, 11.6% 60 minutes or more (2000)

HASSAN VALLEY (township). Covers a land area of 34.188 square miles and a water area of 0.038 square miles. Located at 44.84° N. Lat.; 94.30° W. Long.
Population: 832 (2000); Race: 99.3% White, 0.0% Black, 0.0% Asian, 0.0% American Indian and Alaska Native, 0.2% Hispanic of any race, 0.0% two or more races (2000); Density: 24.3 persons per square mile (2000); Age: 28.4% under 18, 15.3% over 64 (2000); Marriage status: 21.8% never married, 70.7% now married, 4.4% widowed, 3.1% divorced (2000); Foreign born: 1.3% (2000); Ancestry (includes multiple ancestries): 61.7% German, 11.8% Norwegian, 7.3% Swedish, 6.5% Irish, 4.9% English (2000).
Economy: Employment by occupation: 17.3% management, 13.7% professional, 8.9% services, 24.3% sales, 4.4% farming, 14.3% construction, 17.0% production (2000).
Income: Per capita income: $19,958 (2000); Median household income: $56,691 (2000); Poverty rate: 9.4% (2000).
Taxes: Total city taxes per capita: $62 (1997); City property taxes per capita: $61 (1997).
Education: High school graduation rate: 80.7% (2000); College graduation rate: 11.7% (2000).
Housing: Homeownership rate: 96.9% (2000); Median home value: $127,200 (2000); Median rent: $175 per month (2000); Median age of housing: 35 years (2000).
Transportation: Commute to work: 83.9% car, 0.4% public transportation, 0.4% walk, 14.2% work from home (2000); Travel time to work: 62.8% less than 15 minutes, 23.6% 15 to 30 minutes, 2.7% 30 to 45 minutes, 3.4% 45 to 60 minutes, 7.4% 60 minutes or more (2000)

HELEN (township). Covers a land area of 35.222 square miles and a water area of 0.006 square miles. Located at 44.76° N. Lat.; 94.06° W. Long.
Population: 835 (2000); Race: 99.2% White, 0.0% Black, 0.0% Asian, 0.6% American Indian and Alaska Native, 0.5% Hispanic of any race, 0.0% two or more races (2000); Density: 23.7 persons per square mile (2000); Age: 27.8% under 18, 10.9% over 64 (2000); Marriage status: 21.5% never married, 73.6% now married, 2.1% widowed, 2.8% divorced (2000); Foreign born: 1.0% (2000); Ancestry (includes multiple ancestries): 72.6% German, 11.4% Irish, 10.2% Norwegian, 5.9% Swedish, 4.0% English (2000).
Economy: Employment by occupation: 14.0% management, 15.6% professional, 8.3% services, 25.0% sales, 4.4% farming, 12.1% construction, 20.5% production (2000).
Income: Per capita income: $21,010 (2000); Median household income: $56,375 (2000); Poverty rate: 2.5% (2000).
Taxes: Total city taxes per capita: $54 (1997); City property taxes per capita: $53 (1997).
Education: High school graduation rate: 88.7% (2000); College graduation rate: 14.2% (2000).
Housing: Homeownership rate: 96.7% (2000); Median home value: $137,500 (2000); Median rent: $325 per month (2000); Median age of housing: 35 years (2000).
Transportation: Commute to work: 85.4% car, 0.4% public transportation, 1.9% walk, 12.3% work from home (2000); Travel time to work: 44.8% less than 15 minutes, 21.0% 15 to 30 minutes, 16.0% 30 to 45 minutes, 10.4% 45 to 60 minutes, 7.8% 60 minutes or more (2000)

HUTCHINSON (city). Covers a land area of 7.417 square miles and a water area of 0.401 square miles. Located at 44.88° N. Lat.; 94.37° W. Long. Elevation is 1,056 feet.
History: Hutchinson was founded in 1855 by the Hutchinson brothers, Asa, Judson, and John, who were members of a family of singers that gave concerts throughout the country from 1841 to 1865. The Hutchinsons were abolitionists, and their music was a political statement in support of abolition, temperance, and woman suffrage. The town was incorporated in 1881, with a charter permitting woman to vote on all local issues. Hutchinson also became a center for game conservation, with the Minnesota Game Protective League founded here.
Population: 13,080 (2000); Race: 97.0% White, 0.3% Black, 1.0% Asian, 0.2% American Indian and Alaska Native, 1.6% Hispanic of any race, 0.8% two or more races (2000); Density: 1,763.6 persons per square mile (2000); Age: 27.5% under 18, 13.8% over 64 (2000); Marriage status: 25.2% never married, 59.8% now married, 6.9% widowed, 8.2% divorced (2000); Foreign born: 2.1% (2000); Ancestry (includes multiple ancestries): 55.2% German, 15.7% Norwegian, 10.4% Swedish, 9.0% Irish, 5.3% English (2000).
Vital Statistics: Birth rate: 136.9 per 10,000 population (1998)
Economy: Single-family building permits issued: 75 (2001) / 53 (2000); Multi-family building permits issued: 8 (2001) / 8 (2000); Employment by occupation: 10.0% management, 20.3% professional, 13.1% services, 19.3% sales, 0.2% farming, 11.1% construction, 26.1% production (2000).
Income: Per capita income: $19,970 (2000); Median household income: $42,278 (2000); Poverty rate: 5.4% (2000).
Taxes: Total city taxes per capita: $312 (2000); City property taxes per capita: $275 (2000).
Education: High school graduation rate: 87.8% (2000); College graduation rate: 21.2% (2000).

School District(s)

Hutchinson (PK-12)
2000 Enrollment: 3,134 320-587-2860

Two-year College(s)

Ridgewater College (Public)
2001 Enrollment: n/a 320-587-3636
2001 Tuition: In-state $2,433; Out-of-state $4,866

Housing: Homeownership rate: 69.1% (2000); Median home value: $108,200 (2000); Median rent: $459 per month (2000); Median age of housing: 25 years (2000).
Hospitals: Hutchinson Area Health Care (67 beds)
Safety: Violent crime rate: 35.6 per 10,000 population; Property crime rate: 489.4 per 10,000 population (2001).
Newspapers: The Hutchinson Leader (3 x week)
Transportation: Commute to work: 90.6% car, 1.1% public transportation, 3.3% walk, 4.0% work from home (2000); Travel time to work: 72.5% less than 15 minutes, 13.3% 15 to 30 minutes, 5.7% 30 to 45 minutes, 2.1% 45 to 60 minutes, 6.4% 60 minutes or more (2000)

Additional Information Contacts

Hutchinson Chamber of Commerce 320-587-5252

HUTCHINSON (township). Covers a land area of 32.368 square miles and a water area of 2.206 square miles. Located at 44.92° N. Lat.; 94.31° W. Long. Elevation is 1,056 feet.
History: Part of settlement burned in Sioux uprising of 1862. Founded 1855, incorporated 1881.
Population: 1,120 (2000); Race: 98.6% White, 0.4% Black, 0.0% Asian, 0.4% American Indian and Alaska Native, 0.0% Hispanic of any race, 0.6% two or more races (2000); Density: 34.6 persons per square mile (2000); Age: 26.7% under 18, 9.0% over 64 (2000); Marriage status: 19.7% never married,

68.2% now married, 4.7% widowed, 7.3% divorced (2000); Foreign born: 1.0% (2000); Ancestry (includes multiple ancestries): 51.8% German, 14.5% Norwegian, 11.7% Swedish, 10.6% Czech, 8.7% Irish (2000).
Economy: Manufacturing: agricultural equipment, concrete blocks, wood furniture, fertilizer, sheet metal, dry yeast, wood boxes, magnetic tapes, machining. Agriculture: grain, soybeans, peas; livestock, poultry; dairying. Employment by occupation: 14.0% management, 17.2% professional, 11.1% services, 16.0% sales, 1.4% farming, 8.2% construction, 32.0% production (2000).
Income: Per capita income: $22,269 (2000); Median household income: $59,821 (2000); Poverty rate: 3.2% (2000).
Taxes: Total city taxes per capita: $58 (1997); City property taxes per capita: $58 (1997).
Education: High school graduation rate: 92.8% (2000); College graduation rate: 14.4% (2000).
Housing: Homeownership rate: 97.5% (2000); Median home value: $139,000 (2000); Median rent: $475 per month (2000); Median age of housing: 29 years (2000).
Transportation: Commute to work: 91.0% car, 0.0% public transportation, 0.6% walk, 8.4% work from home (2000); Travel time to work: 53.4% less than 15 minutes, 31.9% 15 to 30 minutes, 6.0% 30 to 45 minutes, 2.7% 45 to 60 minutes, 6.0% 60 minutes or more (2000)

LESTER PRAIRIE (city). Covers a land area of 0.721 square miles and a water area of 0 square miles. Located at 44.88° N. Lat.; 94.04° W. Long. Elevation is 1,004 feet.
Population: 1,377 (2000); Race: 97.4% White, 0.1% Black, 0.0% Asian, 0.0% American Indian and Alaska Native, 2.3% Hispanic of any race, 1.4% two or more races (2000); Density: 1,910.4 persons per square mile (2000); Age: 30.2% under 18, 13.1% over 64 (2000); Marriage status: 21.9% never married, 65.4% now married, 5.7% widowed, 6.9% divorced (2000); Foreign born: 2.4% (2000); Ancestry (includes multiple ancestries): 62.1% German, 10.0% Norwegian, 8.3% Swedish, 8.1% Polish, 5.5% Irish (2000).
Economy: Manufacturing: feeds, plastic products, construction materials. Single-family building permits issued: 9 (2001) / 3 (2000); Multi-family building permits issued: 0 (2001) / 0 (2000); Employment by occupation: 9.8% management, 14.8% professional, 15.6% services, 26.1% sales, 1.2% farming, 7.0% construction, 25.4% production (2000).
Income: Per capita income: $18,223 (2000); Median household income: $44,271 (2000); Poverty rate: 5.1% (2000).
Taxes: Total city taxes per capita: $218 (1997); City property taxes per capita: $193 (1997).
Education: High school graduation rate: 84.7% (2000); College graduation rate: 11.9% (2000).

School District(s)

Lester Prairie (PK-12)
2000 Enrollment: 525 320-395-2521
Housing: Homeownership rate: 80.6% (2000); Median home value: $92,300 (2000); Median rent: $382 per month (2000); Median age of housing: 39 years (2000).
Newspapers: Prairie Ad News (1 x week)
Transportation: Commute to work: 85.0% car, 0.3% public transportation, 8.9% walk, 4.1% work from home (2000); Travel time to work: 35.7% less than 15 minutes, 25.9% 15 to 30 minutes, 16.3% 30 to 45 minutes, 14.5% 45 to 60 minutes, 7.7% 60 minutes or more (2000)

LYNN (township). Covers a land area of 31.779 square miles and a water area of 1.363 square miles. Located at 44.86° N. Lat.; 94.42° W. Long.
Population: 604 (2000); Race: 99.4% White, 0.0% Black, 0.0% Asian, 0.0% American Indian and Alaska Native, 0.0% Hispanic of any race, 0.6% two or more races (2000); Density: 19.0 persons per square mile (2000); Age: 32.5% under 18, 10.0% over 64 (2000); Marriage status: 22.3% never married, 70.2% now married, 3.9% widowed, 3.6% divorced (2000); Foreign born: 0.2% (2000); Ancestry (includes multiple ancestries): 73.0% German, 8.5% Danish, 7.7% Irish, 3.9% Norwegian, 3.2% United States or American (2000).
Economy: Employment by occupation: 21.4% management, 12.9% professional, 8.8% services, 19.9% sales, 0.0% farming, 14.4% construction, 22.6% production (2000).
Income: Per capita income: $19,699 (2000); Median household income: $51,250 (2000); Poverty rate: 5.9% (2000).
Taxes: Total city taxes per capita: $75 (1997); City property taxes per capita: $74 (1997).
Education: High school graduation rate: 94.1% (2000); College graduation rate: 14.9% (2000).
Housing: Homeownership rate: 85.2% (2000); Median home value: $145,000 (2000); Median rent: $338 per month (2000); Median age of housing: 30 years (2000).
Transportation: Commute to work: 81.5% car, 0.0% public transportation, 1.8% walk, 16.1% work from home (2000); Travel time to work: 42.6% less than 15 minutes, 48.6% 15 to 30 minutes, 3.5% 30 to 45 minutes, 0.0% 45 to 60 minutes, 5.3% 60 minutes or more (2000)

PENN (township). Covers a land area of 35.164 square miles and a water area of 0.920 square miles. Located at 44.67° N. Lat.; 94.30° W. Long.
Population: 309 (2000); Race: 99.3% White, 0.7% Black, 0.0% Asian, 0.0% American Indian and Alaska Native, 0.0% Hispanic of any race, 0.0% two or more races (2000); Density: 8.8 persons per square mile (2000); Age: 25.9% under 18, 9.8% over 64 (2000); Marriage status: 31.2% never married, 60.2% now married, 3.0% widowed, 5.6% divorced (2000); Foreign born: 0.0% (2000); Ancestry (includes multiple ancestries): 79.0% German, 9.1% Norwegian, 8.4% Irish, 2.4% Swedish, 2.1% English (2000).
Economy: Employment by occupation: 27.1% management, 5.8% professional, 13.5% services, 14.2% sales, 3.9% farming, 12.3% construction, 23.2% production (2000).
Income: Per capita income: $19,019 (2000); Median household income: $41,528 (2000); Poverty rate: 4.5% (2000).
Taxes: Total city taxes per capita: $58 (1997); City property taxes per capita: $58 (1997).
Education: High school graduation rate: 83.9% (2000); College graduation rate: 6.3% (2000).
Housing: Homeownership rate: 85.8% (2000); Median home value: $77,500 (2000); Median rent: $288 per month (2000); Median age of housing: 60+ years (2000).
Transportation: Commute to work: 74.2% car, 0.0% public transportation, 1.3% walk, 24.5% work from home (2000); Travel time to work: 21.4% less than 15 minutes, 53.0% 15 to 30 minutes, 9.4% 30 to 45 minutes, 0.0% 45 to 60 minutes, 16.2% 60 minutes or more (2000)

PLATO (city). Covers a land area of 0.341 square miles and a water area of 0 square miles. Located at 44.77° N. Lat.; 94.03° W. Long.
Population: 336 (2000); Race: 97.8% White, 0.0% Black, 2.2% Asian, 0.0% American Indian and Alaska Native, 0.0% Hispanic of any race, 0.0% two or more races (2000); Density: 985.0 persons per square mile (2000); Age: 19.1% under 18, 13.0% over 64 (2000); Marriage status: 20.8% never married, 64.9% now married, 9.0% widowed, 5.4% divorced (2000); Foreign born: 1.5% (2000); Ancestry (includes multiple ancestries): 69.4% German, 9.0% Norwegian, 8.3% Irish, 6.2% Swedish, 2.8% French (except Basque) (2000).
Economy: Grain; dairying. Manufacturing of cabinets. Single-family building permits issued: 0 (2001) / 1 (2000); Multi-family building permits issued: 0 (2001) / 0 (2000); Employment by occupation: 4.2% management, 22.2% professional, 11.1% services, 27.5% sales, 0.0% farming, 12.7% construction, 22.2% production (2000).
Income: Per capita income: $24,434 (2000); Median household income: $55,179 (2000); Poverty rate: 2.8% (2000).
Taxes: Total city taxes per capita: $186 (1997); City property taxes per capita: $169 (1997).
Education: High school graduation rate: 87.8% (2000); College graduation rate: 12.2% (2000).
Housing: Homeownership rate: 90.3% (2000); Median home value: $89,700 (2000); Median rent: $375 per month (2000); Median age of housing: 44 years (2000).
Transportation: Commute to work: 94.1% car, 0.0% public transportation, 3.2% walk, 2.7% work from home (2000); Travel time to work: 32.4% less than 15 minutes, 26.9% 15 to 30 minutes, 20.3% 30 to 45 minutes, 10.4% 45 to 60 minutes, 9.9% 60 minutes or more (2000)

RICH VALLEY (township). Covers a land area of 36.089 square miles and a water area of 0.118 square miles. Located at 44.85° N. Lat.; 94.20° W. Long.
Population: 727 (2000); Race: 99.2% White, 0.0% Black, 0.4% Asian, 0.3% American Indian and Alaska Native, 0.0% Hispanic of any race, 0.1% two or more races (2000); Density: 20.1 persons per square mile (2000); Age: 28.6% under 18, 12.8% over 64 (2000); Marriage status: 19.9% never married, 69.3% now married, 5.4% widowed, 5.4% divorced (2000); Foreign born: 0.7% (2000); Ancestry (includes multiple ancestries): 52.6% German, 21.2% Czech, 15.5% Polish, 9.3% Irish, 6.5% Norwegian (2000).
Economy: Employment by occupation: 20.0% management, 6.8% professional, 10.5% services, 14.0% sales, 2.3% farming, 12.5% construction, 34.0% production (2000).

Income: Per capita income: $21,226 (2000); Median household income: $49,318 (2000); Poverty rate: 5.1% (2000).
Taxes: Total city taxes per capita: $53 (1997); City property taxes per capita: $53 (1997).
Education: High school graduation rate: 84.1% (2000); College graduation rate: 10.0% (2000).
Housing: Homeownership rate: 91.0% (2000); Median home value: $129,300 (2000); Median rent: $338 per month (2000); Median age of housing: 43 years (2000).
Transportation: Commute to work: 85.1% car, 0.0% public transportation, 2.6% walk, 11.6% work from home (2000); Travel time to work: 28.5% less than 15 minutes, 47.4% 15 to 30 minutes, 6.1% 30 to 45 minutes, 7.3% 45 to 60 minutes, 10.8% 60 minutes or more (2000)

ROUND GROVE (township). Covers a land area of 35.726 square miles and a water area of 0.445 square miles. Located at 44.67° N. Lat.; 94.42° W. Long.
Population: 276 (2000); Race: 100.0% White, 0.0% Black, 0.0% Asian, 0.0% American Indian and Alaska Native, 0.0% Hispanic of any race, 0.0% two or more races (2000); Density: 7.7 persons per square mile (2000); Age: 27.1% under 18, 15.4% over 64 (2000); Marriage status: 28.3% never married, 64.8% now married, 6.0% widowed, 0.9% divorced (2000); Foreign born: 0.0% (2000); Ancestry (includes multiple ancestries): 66.4% German, 6.5% Polish, 6.2% Swedish, 5.1% United States or American, 5.1% English (2000).
Economy: Employment by occupation: 10.8% management, 14.9% professional, 12.2% services, 25.7% sales, 2.7% farming, 10.8% construction, 23.0% production (2000).
Income: Per capita income: $20,216 (2000); Median household income: $50,500 (2000); Poverty rate: 4.8% (2000).
Taxes: Total city taxes per capita: $140 (1997); City property taxes per capita: $140 (1997).
Education: High school graduation rate: 84.2% (2000); College graduation rate: 8.7% (2000).
Housing: Homeownership rate: 87.4% (2000); Median home value: $90,000 (2000); Median rent: $325 per month (2000); Median age of housing: 60+ years (2000).
Transportation: Commute to work: 89.7% car, 0.0% public transportation, 1.4% walk, 8.9% work from home (2000); Travel time to work: 18.0% less than 15 minutes, 41.4% 15 to 30 minutes, 18.8% 30 to 45 minutes, 5.3% 45 to 60 minutes, 16.5% 60 minutes or more (2000)

SILVER LAKE (city). Covers a land area of 0.347 square miles and a water area of 0 square miles. Located at 44.90° N. Lat.; 94.19° W. Long. Elevation is 1,050 feet.
Population: 761 (2000); Race: 98.3% White, 0.0% Black, 0.0% Asian, 0.0% American Indian and Alaska Native, 2.0% Hispanic of any race, 0.0% two or more races (2000); Density: 2,191.4 persons per square mile (2000); Age: 26.2% under 18, 18.5% over 64 (2000); Marriage status: 19.8% never married, 59.8% now married, 11.4% widowed, 8.9% divorced (2000); Foreign born: 1.3% (2000); Ancestry (includes multiple ancestries): 41.4% German, 31.3% Polish, 18.6% Czech, 6.0% Norwegian, 4.6% Irish (2000).
Economy: Grain, peas; livestock, poultry; dairying. Single-family building permits issued: 4 (2001) / 6 (2000); Multi-family building permits issued: 0 (2001) / 0 (2000); Employment by occupation: 6.7% management, 11.3% professional, 11.5% services, 14.9% sales, 2.1% farming, 15.4% construction, 38.2% production (2000).
Income: Per capita income: $18,126 (2000); Median household income: $36,833 (2000); Poverty rate: 7.3% (2000).
Taxes: Total city taxes per capita: $111 (1997); City property taxes per capita: $101 (1997).
Education: High school graduation rate: 80.6% (2000); College graduation rate: 8.7% (2000).
Housing: Homeownership rate: 74.4% (2000); Median home value: $80,300 (2000); Median rent: $338 per month (2000); Median age of housing: 50 years (2000).
Newspapers: Silver Lake Leader (1 x week)
Transportation: Commute to work: 89.7% car, 0.0% public transportation, 4.4% walk, 5.9% work from home (2000); Travel time to work: 24.0% less than 15 minutes, 47.7% 15 to 30 minutes, 11.4% 30 to 45 minutes, 7.6% 45 to 60 minutes, 9.3% 60 minutes or more (2000)

STEWART (city). Covers a land area of 0.809 square miles and a water area of <.001 square miles. Located at 44.72° N. Lat.; 94.48° W. Long. Elevation is 1,062 feet.
Population: 564 (2000); Race: 96.5% White, 0.0% Black, 0.4% Asian, 0.0% American Indian and Alaska Native, 3.5% Hispanic of any race, 0.0% two or more races (2000); Density: 697.3 persons per square mile (2000); Age: 26.8% under 18, 16.3% over 64 (2000); Marriage status: 26.2% never married, 55.2% now married, 7.4% widowed, 11.2% divorced (2000); Foreign born: 1.2% (2000); Ancestry (includes multiple ancestries): 55.4% German, 11.9% Norwegian, 8.8% Swedish, 8.4% Irish, 4.4% Other groups (2000).
Economy: Agricultural area: poultry; grain, soybeans; dairying. Manufacturing: feeds; metal polishing. Single-family building permits issued: 0 (2001) / 0 (2000); Multi-family building permits issued: 4 (2001) / 0 (2000); Employment by occupation: 9.4% management, 11.1% professional, 8.3% services, 21.2% sales, 1.7% farming, 11.1% construction, 37.2% production (2000).
Income: Per capita income: $16,512 (2000); Median household income: $38,542 (2000); Poverty rate: 7.1% (2000).
Taxes: Total city taxes per capita: $156 (1997); City property taxes per capita: $152 (1997).
Education: High school graduation rate: 80.2% (2000); College graduation rate: 6.8% (2000).
Housing: Homeownership rate: 83.5% (2000); Median home value: $68,500 (2000); Median rent: $329 per month (2000); Median age of housing: 51 years (2000).
Transportation: Commute to work: 87.4% car, 0.0% public transportation, 8.7% walk, 1.7% work from home (2000); Travel time to work: 29.2% less than 15 minutes, 39.9% 15 to 30 minutes, 16.7% 30 to 45 minutes, 1.4% 45 to 60 minutes, 12.8% 60 minutes or more (2000)

SUMTER (township). Covers a land area of 34.986 square miles and a water area of 0.782 square miles. Located at 44.75° N. Lat.; 94.32° W. Long. Elevation is 1,030 feet.
Population: 558 (2000); Race: 98.7% White, 0.0% Black, 0.0% Asian, 0.4% American Indian and Alaska Native, 0.4% Hispanic of any race, 0.9% two or more races (2000); Density: 15.9 persons per square mile (2000); Age: 26.8% under 18, 8.7% over 64 (2000); Marriage status: 25.4% never married, 69.8% now married, 2.1% widowed, 2.6% divorced (2000); Foreign born: 0.4% (2000); Ancestry (includes multiple ancestries): 66.5% German, 8.7% Norwegian, 7.9% Irish, 7.2% Swedish, 3.4% Welsh (2000).
Economy: Employment by occupation: 16.5% management, 13.0% professional, 8.3% services, 21.6% sales, 1.0% farming, 16.2% construction, 23.5% production (2000).
Income: Per capita income: $21,013 (2000); Median household income: $52,813 (2000); Poverty rate: 0.4% (2000).
Taxes: Total city taxes per capita: $48 (1997); City property taxes per capita: $47 (1997).
Education: High school graduation rate: 86.1% (2000); College graduation rate: 7.8% (2000).
Housing: Homeownership rate: 88.0% (2000); Median home value: $120,200 (2000); Median rent: $363 per month (2000); Median age of housing: 39 years (2000).
Transportation: Commute to work: 90.0% car, 0.0% public transportation, 2.9% walk, 6.5% work from home (2000); Travel time to work: 34.3% less than 15 minutes, 44.3% 15 to 30 minutes, 10.0% 30 to 45 minutes, 2.4% 45 to 60 minutes, 9.0% 60 minutes or more (2000)

WINSTED (city). Covers a land area of 1.351 square miles and a water area of 0 square miles. Located at 44.96° N. Lat.; 94.04° W. Long. Elevation is 1,027 feet.
Population: 2,094 (2000); Race: 98.5% White, 0.0% Black, 0.2% Asian, 0.9% American Indian and Alaska Native, 0.5% Hispanic of any race, 0.4% two or more races (2000); Density: 1,549.9 persons per square mile (2000); Age: 27.0% under 18, 17.0% over 64 (2000); Marriage status: 24.7% never married, 56.3% now married, 9.1% widowed, 10.0% divorced (2000); Foreign born: 0.7% (2000); Ancestry (includes multiple ancestries): 59.5% German, 11.2% Irish, 9.8% Polish, 7.9% Norwegian, 4.7% Swedish (2000).
Economy: Single-family building permits issued: 43 (2001) / 19 (2000); Multi-family building permits issued: 0 (2001) / 16 (2000); Employment by occupation: 10.8% management, 12.6% professional, 17.4% services, 23.0% sales, 0.9% farming, 8.7% construction, 26.7% production (2000).
Income: Per capita income: $19,896 (2000); Median household income: $41,588 (2000); Poverty rate: 5.4% (2000).
Taxes: Total city taxes per capita: $206 (1997); City property taxes per capita: $185 (1997).
Education: High school graduation rate: 84.1% (2000); College graduation rate: 11.7% (2000).

Housing: Homeownership rate: 72.9% (2000); Median home value: $101,600 (2000); Median rent: $358 per month (2000); Median age of housing: 27 years (2000).
Newspapers: Winsted-Lester Prairie Journal (1 x week)
Transportation: Commute to work: 90.4% car, 0.0% public transportation, 6.1% walk, 2.9% work from home (2000); Travel time to work: 46.7% less than 15 minutes, 18.7% 15 to 30 minutes, 16.1% 30 to 45 minutes, 11.0% 45 to 60 minutes, 7.5% 60 minutes or more (2000)

WINSTED (township). Covers a land area of 33.508 square miles and a water area of 1.107 square miles. Located at 44.93° N. Lat.; 94.06° W. Long. Elevation is 1,027 feet.
Population: 987 (2000); Race: 98.3% White, 0.1% Black, 0.5% Asian, 0.0% American Indian and Alaska Native, 0.5% Hispanic of any race, 0.6% two or more races (2000); Density: 29.5 persons per square mile (2000); Age: 29.6% under 18, 10.6% over 64 (2000); Marriage status: 23.7% never married, 69.8% now married, 3.3% widowed, 3.1% divorced (2000); Foreign born: 1.0% (2000); Ancestry (includes multiple ancestries): 65.9% German, 14.8% Polish, 10.9% Irish, 7.6% Norwegian, 6.4% Swedish (2000).
Economy: Agriculture includes grain, soybeans; livestock; dairying. Manufacturing: lumber, dairy processing equipment, fabricated stainless steel. Employment by occupation: 16.8% management, 11.3% professional, 16.8% services, 19.3% sales, 1.1% farming, 11.1% construction, 23.8% production (2000).
Income: Per capita income: $19,060 (2000); Median household income: $52,778 (2000); Poverty rate: 6.7% (2000).
Taxes: Total city taxes per capita: $63 (1997); City property taxes per capita: $62 (1997).
Education: High school graduation rate: 83.5% (2000); College graduation rate: 6.2% (2000).
Housing: Homeownership rate: 92.7% (2000); Median home value: $133,200 (2000); Median rent: $338 per month (2000); Median age of housing: 32 years (2000).
Transportation: Commute to work: 85.0% car, 0.4% public transportation, 3.1% walk, 10.3% work from home (2000); Travel time to work: 37.0% less than 15 minutes, 28.8% 15 to 30 minutes, 12.1% 30 to 45 minutes, 12.1% 45 to 60 minutes, 10.1% 60 minutes or more (2000)

Meeker County

Located in south central Minnesota; drained by the Crow River. Covers a land area of 608.50 square miles, a water area of 36.50 square miles, and is located in the Central Time Zone. The county government was organized in 1856. County seat is Litchfield.

Weather Station: Litchfield — Elevation: 1,131 feet

	Jan	Feb	Mar	Apr	May	Jun	Jul	Aug	Sep	Oct	Nov	Dec
High	21	28	40	57	71	80	84	81	72	60	39	26
Low	1	9	21	34	47	57	61	59	49	37	23	9
Precip	0.8	0.6	1.5	2.4	3.4	5.0	4.1	3.7	2.9	2.3	1.5	0.7
Snow	10.3	6.2	8.3	2.3	tr	0.0	0.0	0.0	0.0	0.3	9.1	7.5

High and Low temperatures in degrees Fahrenheit; Precipitation and Snow in inches

Population: 22,644 (2000); Race: 97.4% White, 0.3% Black, 0.3% Asian, 0.5% American Indian and Alaska Native, 1.7% Hispanic of any race, 0.5% two or more races (2000); Density: 37.2 persons per square mile (2000); Age: 27.1% under 18, 16.3% over 64 (2000).
Religion: Five largest groups: 29.8% Evangelical Lutheran Church in America, 19.7% Catholic Church, 3.6% Wisconsin Evangelical Lutheran Synod, 2.8% Lutheran Church—Missouri Synod, 2.5% The United Methodist Church (2000).
Economy: Unemployment rate: 5.3% (11/2002); Total civilian labor force: 9,800 (11/2002); Leading industries: 29.2% manufacturing; 16.0% health care and social assistance; 14.3% retail trade (2000); Companies that employ more than 1,000 persons: 0 (2000); Companies that employ more than 100 persons: 8 (2000); Farms: 1,016 totaling 293,213 acres (1997); Minority business ownership rate: 0.0% (1997); Women business ownership rate: 22.0% (1997); Retail sales per capita: $5,957 (1997). Single-family building permits issued: 158 (2001) / 141 (2000); Multi-family building permits issued: 18 (2001) / 6 (2000).
Income: Per capita income: $18,628 (2000); Median household income: $40,908 (2000); Poverty rate: 7.1% (2000); Bankruptcy rate: 3.14% (2001).
Taxes: Total county taxes per capita: $206 (1997); County property taxes per capita: $201 (1997).
Education: High school graduation rate: 81.5% (2000); College graduation rate: 13.9% (2000).
Housing: Homeownership rate: 81.5% (2000); Median home value: $89,200 (2000); Median rent: $382 per month (2000); Median age of housing: 37 years (2000).
Health: Birth rate: 126.7 per 10,000 population (1998); Age adjusted death rate: 84.1 per 10,000 population (1999); Age adjusted cancer mortality rate: 221.3 deaths per 100,000 population (1999). Number of physicians: 6.2 per 10,000 population (1999); Number of hospital beds: 16.8 per 10,000 population (1999).
Elections: 2000 Presidential election results: 41.3% Gore, 51.7% Bush, 4.8% Nader, 1.6% Buchanan
National and State Parks: Acton State Wildlife Management Area; Greenleaf State Wildlife Management Area; Knapp State Wildlife Management Area; Madsen State Wildlife Management Area; Minnie-Man State Wildlife Management Area; Popular State Wildlife Management Area; Wieker State Wildlife Management Area
Additional Information Contacts
Meeker County Government Offices 320-693-5200
Litchfield Chamber of Commerce 320-693-8184

Meeker County Communities

ACTON (township). Covers a land area of 33.037 square miles and a water area of 2.375 square miles. Located at 45.12° N. Lat.; 94.68° W. Long.
Population: 381 (2000); Race: 98.0% White, 0.0% Black, 0.0% Asian, 0.5% American Indian and Alaska Native, 1.5% Hispanic of any race, 0.0% two or more races (2000); Density: 11.5 persons per square mile (2000); Age: 28.1% under 18, 10.4% over 64 (2000); Marriage status: 21.8% never married, 65.4% now married, 6.1% widowed, 6.7% divorced (2000); Foreign born: 0.5% (2000); Ancestry (includes multiple ancestries): 37.2% German, 32.7% Norwegian, 24.8% Swedish, 7.1% Irish, 7.1% English (2000).
Economy: Employment by occupation: 20.8% management, 16.8% professional, 12.4% services, 18.3% sales, 5.4% farming, 4.5% construction, 21.8% production (2000).
Income: Per capita income: $16,502 (2000); Median household income: $37,813 (2000); Poverty rate: 9.1% (2000).
Taxes: Total city taxes per capita: $64 (1997); City property taxes per capita: $64 (1997).
Education: High school graduation rate: 83.3% (2000); College graduation rate: 15.9% (2000).
Housing: Homeownership rate: 87.8% (2000); Median home value: $88,100 (2000); Median rent: $388 per month (2000); Median age of housing: 42 years (2000).
Transportation: Commute to work: 82.2% car, 0.0% public transportation, 0.0% walk, 17.8% work from home (2000); Travel time to work: 31.9% less than 15 minutes, 41.0% 15 to 30 minutes, 13.3% 30 to 45 minutes, 6.0% 45 to 60 minutes, 7.8% 60 minutes or more (2000)

CEDAR MILLS (city). Covers a land area of 0.435 square miles and a water area of 0 square miles. Located at 44.94° N. Lat.; 94.52° W. Long. Elevation is 1,091 feet.
Population: 53 (2000); Race: 100.0% White, 0.0% Black, 0.0% Asian, 0.0% American Indian and Alaska Native, 0.0% Hispanic of any race, 0.0% two or more races (2000); Density: 121.8 persons per square mile (2000); Age: 24.6% under 18, 22.8% over 64 (2000); Marriage status: 20.8% never married, 56.3% now married, 10.4% widowed, 12.5% divorced (2000); Foreign born: 0.0% (2000); Ancestry (includes multiple ancestries): 54.4% German, 31.6% Norwegian, 8.8% Swedish, 3.5% English, 3.5% United States or American (2000).
Economy: Single-family building permits issued: 1 (2001) / 0 (2000); Multi-family building permits issued: 0 (2001) / 0 (2000); Employment by occupation: 3.4% management, 3.4% professional, 13.8% services, 27.6% sales, 0.0% farming, 13.8% construction, 37.9% production (2000).
Income: Per capita income: $17,998 (2000); Median household income: $36,875 (2000); Poverty rate: 0.0% (2000).
Taxes: Total city taxes per capita: $34 (1997); City property taxes per capita: $7 (1997).
Education: High school graduation rate: 67.4% (2000); College graduation rate: 2.3% (2000).
Housing: Homeownership rate: 92.9% (2000); Median home value: $55,000 (2000); Median rent: $275 per month (2000); Median age of housing: 53 years (2000).
Transportation: Commute to work: 72.4% car, 0.0% public transportation, 13.8% walk, 6.9% work from home (2000); Travel time to work: 29.6% less than 15 minutes, 59.3% 15 to 30 minutes, 0.0% 30 to 45 minutes, 0.0% 45 to 60 minutes, 11.1% 60 minutes or more (2000)

CEDAR MILLS (township). Covers a land area of 38.477 square miles and a water area of 0.472 square miles. Located at 44.94° N. Lat.; 94.55° W. Long. Elevation is 1,091 feet.
Population: 499 (2000); Race: 100.0% White, 0.0% Black, 0.0% Asian, 0.0% American Indian and Alaska Native, 0.4% Hispanic of any race, 0.0% two or more races (2000); Density: 13.0 persons per square mile (2000); Age: 29.0% under 18, 13.2% over 64 (2000); Marriage status: 23.9% never married, 59.9% now married, 10.0% widowed, 6.2% divorced (2000); Foreign born: 0.0% (2000); Ancestry (includes multiple ancestries): 73.2% German, 12.2% Norwegian, 8.4% Irish, 5.6% Swedish, 5.6% Danish (2000).
Economy: Grain; livestock; dairying. Employment by occupation: 12.0% management, 5.4% professional, 9.4% services, 16.3% sales, 1.8% farming, 12.0% construction, 43.1% production (2000).
Income: Per capita income: $17,227 (2000); Median household income: $48,125 (2000); Poverty rate: 6.2% (2000).
Taxes: Total city taxes per capita: $143 (1997); City property taxes per capita: $143 (1997).
Education: High school graduation rate: 85.4% (2000); College graduation rate: 7.6% (2000).
Housing: Homeownership rate: 87.0% (2000); Median home value: $98,900 (2000); Median rent: $363 per month (2000); Median age of housing: 33 years (2000).
Transportation: Commute to work: 89.8% car, 0.0% public transportation, 1.5% walk, 7.7% work from home (2000); Travel time to work: 23.3% less than 15 minutes, 59.3% 15 to 30 minutes, 11.5% 30 to 45 minutes, 0.0% 45 to 60 minutes, 5.9% 60 minutes or more (2000)

COLLINWOOD (township). Covers a land area of 31.042 square miles and a water area of 5.018 square miles. Located at 45.01° N. Lat.; 94.32° W. Long.
Population: 1,037 (2000); Race: 99.7% White, 0.0% Black, 0.0% Asian, 0.0% American Indian and Alaska Native, 0.5% Hispanic of any race, 0.1% two or more races (2000); Density: 33.4 persons per square mile (2000); Age: 28.6% under 18, 12.0% over 64 (2000); Marriage status: 21.6% never married, 71.2% now married, 1.5% widowed, 5.7% divorced (2000); Foreign born: 0.2% (2000); Ancestry (includes multiple ancestries): 38.1% German, 26.0% Swedish, 18.1% Norwegian, 9.8% Irish, 5.1% Finnish (2000).
Economy: Employment by occupation: 11.7% management, 14.1% professional, 12.3% services, 20.8% sales, 2.0% farming, 10.9% construction, 28.3% production (2000).
Income: Per capita income: $22,065 (2000); Median household income: $56,786 (2000); Poverty rate: 6.2% (2000).
Taxes: Total city taxes per capita: $103 (1997); City property taxes per capita: $103 (1997).
Education: High school graduation rate: 87.2% (2000); College graduation rate: 15.7% (2000).
Housing: Homeownership rate: 94.8% (2000); Median home value: $133,800 (2000); Median rent: $275 per month (2000); Median age of housing: 30 years (2000).
Transportation: Commute to work: 91.7% car, 0.0% public transportation, 0.9% walk, 7.3% work from home (2000); Travel time to work: 20.6% less than 15 minutes, 52.0% 15 to 30 minutes, 9.7% 30 to 45 minutes, 7.1% 45 to 60 minutes, 10.5% 60 minutes or more (2000)

COSMOS (city). Covers a land area of 1.121 square miles and a water area of 0.018 square miles. Located at 44.93° N. Lat.; 94.69° W. Long.
Population: 582 (2000); Race: 99.3% White, 0.0% Black, 0.7% Asian, 0.0% American Indian and Alaska Native, 0.0% Hispanic of any race, 0.0% two or more races (2000); Density: 519.3 persons per square mile (2000); Age: 21.7% under 18, 22.9% over 64 (2000); Marriage status: 17.8% never married, 65.3% now married, 6.1% widowed, 10.8% divorced (2000); Foreign born: 0.7% (2000); Ancestry (includes multiple ancestries): 51.4% German, 15.0% Norwegian, 11.6% Swedish, 4.6% United States or American, 4.2% Irish (2000).
Economy: Single-family building permits issued: 0 (2001) / 2 (2000); Multi-family building permits issued: 0 (2001) / 4 (2000); Employment by occupation: 9.7% management, 15.5% professional, 18.5% services, 15.1% sales, 0.8% farming, 9.2% construction, 31.1% production (2000).
Income: Per capita income: $15,447 (2000); Median household income: $30,278 (2000); Poverty rate: 10.0% (2000).
Taxes: Total city taxes per capita: $70 (1997); City property taxes per capita: $65 (1997).
Education: High school graduation rate: 67.1% (2000); College graduation rate: 5.2% (2000).
Housing: Homeownership rate: 81.3% (2000); Median home value: $59,300 (2000); Median rent: $355 per month (2000); Median age of housing: 44 years (2000).
Transportation: Commute to work: 85.7% car, 0.0% public transportation, 11.7% walk, 1.7% work from home (2000); Travel time to work: 45.6% less than 15 minutes, 27.9% 15 to 30 minutes, 15.9% 30 to 45 minutes, 3.5% 45 to 60 minutes, 7.1% 60 minutes or more (2000)

COSMOS (township). Covers a land area of 34.757 square miles and a water area of 0.344 square miles. Located at 44.92° N. Lat.; 94.68° W. Long.
Population: 229 (2000); Race: 98.8% White, 0.0% Black, 1.2% Asian, 0.0% American Indian and Alaska Native, 0.0% Hispanic of any race, 0.0% two or more races (2000); Density: 6.6 persons per square mile (2000); Age: 26.6% under 18, 16.6% over 64 (2000); Marriage status: 22.8% never married, 67.4% now married, 6.2% widowed, 3.6% divorced (2000); Foreign born: 1.2% (2000); Ancestry (includes multiple ancestries): 57.7% German, 17.4% Norwegian, 15.8% Swedish, 7.5% Irish, 6.2% English (2000).
Economy: Agricultural area: poultry; grain, soybeans, beans, peas; dairying. Manufacturing: metalworking machining. Employment by occupation: 17.4% management, 9.1% professional, 12.1% services, 22.0% sales, 1.5% farming, 12.9% construction, 25.0% production (2000).
Income: Per capita income: $17,438 (2000); Median household income: $40,000 (2000); Poverty rate: 8.3% (2000).
Taxes: Total city taxes per capita: $99 (1997); City property taxes per capita: $99 (1997).
Education: High school graduation rate: 86.0% (2000); College graduation rate: 10.4% (2000).
Housing: Homeownership rate: 89.6% (2000); Median home value: $95,000 (2000); Median rent: $275 per month (2000); Median age of housing: 50 years (2000).
Transportation: Commute to work: 83.3% car, 0.0% public transportation, 1.5% walk, 15.2% work from home (2000); Travel time to work: 32.1% less than 15 minutes, 47.3% 15 to 30 minutes, 10.7% 30 to 45 minutes, 1.8% 45 to 60 minutes, 8.0% 60 minutes or more (2000)

DANIELSON (township). Covers a land area of 34.491 square miles and a water area of 1.406 square miles. Located at 45.03° N. Lat.; 94.69° W. Long.
Population: 327 (2000); Race: 98.5% White, 0.0% Black, 0.0% Asian, 0.9% American Indian and Alaska Native, 1.5% Hispanic of any race, 0.6% two or more races (2000); Density: 9.5 persons per square mile (2000); Age: 31.2% under 18, 12.5% over 64 (2000); Marriage status: 23.8% never married, 72.8% now married, 0.8% widowed, 2.7% divorced (2000); Foreign born: 1.2% (2000); Ancestry (includes multiple ancestries): 44.3% German, 24.2% Swedish, 20.4% Norwegian, 6.7% Irish, 6.1% Dutch (2000).
Economy: Employment by occupation: 24.4% management, 5.7% professional, 13.6% services, 19.9% sales, 1.1% farming, 13.6% construction, 21.6% production (2000).
Income: Per capita income: $17,234 (2000); Median household income: $42,500 (2000); Poverty rate: 4.7% (2000).
Taxes: Total city taxes per capita: $68 (1997); City property taxes per capita: $68 (1997).
Education: High school graduation rate: 84.2% (2000); College graduation rate: 13.8% (2000).
Housing: Homeownership rate: 87.3% (2000); Median home value: $64,400 (2000); Median rent: $325 per month (2000); Median age of housing: 60+ years (2000).
Transportation: Commute to work: 83.2% car, 0.0% public transportation, 2.3% walk, 14.5% work from home (2000); Travel time to work: 18.9% less than 15 minutes, 43.2% 15 to 30 minutes, 26.4% 30 to 45 minutes, 5.4% 45 to 60 minutes, 6.1% 60 minutes or more (2000)

DARWIN (city). Covers a land area of 0.749 square miles and a water area of 0.078 square miles. Located at 45.09° N. Lat.; 94.40° W. Long. Elevation is 1,132 feet.
Population: 276 (2000); Race: 91.4% White, 0.0% Black, 0.0% Asian, 0.7% American Indian and Alaska Native, 4.5% Hispanic of any race, 3.3% two or more races (2000); Density: 368.7 persons per square mile (2000); Age: 27.5% under 18, 17.5% over 64 (2000); Marriage status: 19.0% never married, 63.4% now married, 6.5% widowed, 11.1% divorced (2000); Foreign born: 1.1% (2000); Ancestry (includes multiple ancestries): 45.4% German, 19.0% Swedish, 13.8% Norwegian, 13.0% Irish, 6.7% English (2000).
Economy: Single-family building permits issued: 8 (2001) / 0 (2000); Multi-family building permits issued: 0 (2001) / 0 (2000); Employment by

occupation: 3.5% management, 13.9% professional, 11.3% services, 16.5% sales, 0.0% farming, 7.8% construction, 47.0% production (2000).
Income: Per capita income: $16,813 (2000); Median household income: $34,286 (2000); Poverty rate: 10.2% (2000).
Taxes: Total city taxes per capita: $20 (1997); City property taxes per capita: $12 (1997).
Education: High school graduation rate: 63.5% (2000); College graduation rate: 9.4% (2000).
Housing: Homeownership rate: 78.6% (2000); Median home value: $63,200 (2000); Median rent: $350 per month (2000); Median age of housing: 44 years (2000).
Transportation: Commute to work: 94.3% car, 0.0% public transportation, 5.7% walk, 0.0% work from home (2000); Travel time to work: 46.2% less than 15 minutes, 35.8% 15 to 30 minutes, 2.8% 30 to 45 minutes, 5.7% 45 to 60 minutes, 9.4% 60 minutes or more (2000)

DARWIN (township). Covers a land area of 32.404 square miles and a water area of 2.949 square miles. Located at 45.10° N. Lat.; 94.42° W. Long. Elevation is 1,132 feet.
Population: 713 (2000); Race: 99.3% White, 0.0% Black, 0.0% Asian, 0.0% American Indian and Alaska Native, 0.7% Hispanic of any race, 0.0% two or more races (2000); Density: 22.0 persons per square mile (2000); Age: 20.8% under 18, 19.3% over 64 (2000); Marriage status: 19.3% never married, 67.6% now married, 6.0% widowed, 7.0% divorced (2000); Foreign born: 0.7% (2000); Ancestry (includes multiple ancestries): 44.6% German, 22.3% Swedish, 17.3% Norwegian, 8.0% Irish, 5.2% English (2000).
Economy: Dairying; poultry, livestock; grain, soybeans, beans, peas. Manufacturing: concrete. Employment by occupation: 22.1% management, 13.0% professional, 11.6% services, 17.4% sales, 3.0% farming, 10.2% construction, 22.7% production (2000).
Income: Per capita income: $20,763 (2000); Median household income: $41,818 (2000); Poverty rate: 6.8% (2000).
Taxes: Total city taxes per capita: $208 (2000); City property taxes per capita: $208 (2000).
Education: High school graduation rate: 88.6% (2000); College graduation rate: 9.9% (2000).
Housing: Homeownership rate: 90.7% (2000); Median home value: $139,000 (2000); Median rent: $400 per month (2000); Median age of housing: 28 years (2000).
Transportation: Commute to work: 88.4% car, 0.0% public transportation, 3.6% walk, 6.6% work from home (2000); Travel time to work: 37.0% less than 15 minutes, 38.5% 15 to 30 minutes, 10.4% 30 to 45 minutes, 5.3% 45 to 60 minutes, 8.9% 60 minutes or more (2000)

DASSEL (city). Covers a land area of 1.481 square miles and a water area of 0.090 square miles. Located at 45.08° N. Lat.; 94.31° W. Long. Elevation is 1,091 feet.
Population: 1,233 (2000); Race: 97.8% White, 0.0% Black, 1.1% Asian, 0.0% American Indian and Alaska Native, 1.2% Hispanic of any race, 0.8% two or more races (2000); Density: 832.7 persons per square mile (2000); Age: 25.6% under 18, 22.2% over 64 (2000); Marriage status: 17.4% never married, 60.4% now married, 14.6% widowed, 7.5% divorced (2000); Foreign born: 1.4% (2000); Ancestry (includes multiple ancestries): 31.6% German, 27.7% Swedish, 16.4% Norwegian, 11.0% Irish, 8.6% Finnish (2000).
Economy: Single-family building permits issued: 4 (2001) / 6 (2000); Multi-family building permits issued: 4 (2001) / 0 (2000); Employment by occupation: 8.2% management, 19.4% professional, 12.1% services, 22.8% sales, 2.5% farming, 11.7% construction, 23.3% production (2000).
Income: Per capita income: $17,476 (2000); Median household income: $37,500 (2000); Poverty rate: 5.0% (2000).
Taxes: Total city taxes per capita: $209 (1997); City property taxes per capita: $207 (1997).
Education: High school graduation rate: 81.3% (2000); College graduation rate: 14.3% (2000).
Housing: Homeownership rate: 69.7% (2000); Median home value: $89,600 (2000); Median rent: $413 per month (2000); Median age of housing: 43 years (2000).
Newspapers: Enterprise Dispatch (1 x week)
Transportation: Commute to work: 84.7% car, 0.0% public transportation, 9.6% walk, 4.4% work from home (2000); Travel time to work: 50.3% less than 15 minutes, 30.5% 15 to 30 minutes, 8.0% 30 to 45 minutes, 3.5% 45 to 60 minutes, 7.6% 60 minutes or more (2000)

DASSEL (township). Covers a land area of 30.200 square miles and a water area of 4.072 square miles. Located at 45.10° N. Lat.; 94.31° W. Long. Elevation is 1,091 feet.
Population: 1,361 (2000); Race: 99.6% White, 0.0% Black, 0.0% Asian, 0.0% American Indian and Alaska Native, 0.2% Hispanic of any race, 0.1% two or more races (2000); Density: 45.1 persons per square mile (2000); Age: 30.8% under 18, 9.6% over 64 (2000); Marriage status: 20.9% never married, 73.2% now married, 1.9% widowed, 4.0% divorced (2000); Foreign born: 0.5% (2000); Ancestry (includes multiple ancestries): 38.3% German, 26.9% Swedish, 18.5% Finnish, 9.9% Norwegian, 6.3% Irish (2000).
Economy: Grain, soybeans, peas, beans; livestock, poultry; dairying; light manufacturing. Lake resort. Employment by occupation: 15.1% management, 21.2% professional, 12.7% services, 21.7% sales, 1.4% farming, 10.9% construction, 17.0% production (2000).
Income: Per capita income: $19,845 (2000); Median household income: $54,167 (2000); Poverty rate: 3.5% (2000).
Taxes: Total city taxes per capita: $98 (2000); City property taxes per capita: $98 (2000).
Education: High school graduation rate: 94.6% (2000); College graduation rate: 21.2% (2000).
Housing: Homeownership rate: 90.6% (2000); Median home value: $141,900 (2000); Median rent: $388 per month (2000); Median age of housing: 29 years (2000).
Transportation: Commute to work: 90.7% car, 0.4% public transportation, 0.6% walk, 7.7% work from home (2000); Travel time to work: 34.6% less than 15 minutes, 30.5% 15 to 30 minutes, 10.7% 30 to 45 minutes, 6.1% 45 to 60 minutes, 18.0% 60 minutes or more (2000)

EDEN VALLEY (city). Covers a land area of 1.284 square miles and a water area of <.001 square miles. Located at 45.32° N. Lat.; 94.54° W. Long. Elevation is 1,123 feet.
Population: 866 (2000); Race: 97.9% White, 0.5% Black, 0.0% Asian, 0.0% American Indian and Alaska Native, 1.6% Hispanic of any race, 0.0% two or more races (2000); Density: 674.6 persons per square mile (2000); Age: 24.2% under 18, 23.4% over 64 (2000); Marriage status: 34.0% never married, 46.7% now married, 11.2% widowed, 8.0% divorced (2000); Foreign born: 2.3% (2000); Ancestry (includes multiple ancestries): 62.4% German, 15.5% Irish, 7.4% Swedish, 5.5% Norwegian, 3.8% Other groups (2000).
Economy: Single-family building permits issued: 4 (2001) / 2 (2000); Multi-family building permits issued: 0 (2001) / 0 (2000); Employment by occupation: 4.8% management, 8.0% professional, 15.0% services, 33.7% sales, 1.6% farming, 12.8% construction, 24.1% production (2000).
Income: Per capita income: $13,501 (2000); Median household income: $25,781 (2000); Poverty rate: 14.8% (2000).
Taxes: Total city taxes per capita: $131 (1997); City property taxes per capita: $123 (1997).
Education: High school graduation rate: 77.8% (2000); College graduation rate: 8.1% (2000).

School District(s)

Eden Valley-Watkins (PK-12)
2000 Enrollment: 858 320-453-6310
Housing: Homeownership rate: 68.7% (2000); Median home value: $70,900 (2000); Median rent: $353 per month (2000); Median age of housing: 39 years (2000).
Newspapers: Journal Patriot (1 x week)
Transportation: Commute to work: 91.9% car, 0.0% public transportation, 5.1% walk, 2.4% work from home (2000); Travel time to work: 38.7% less than 15 minutes, 28.7% 15 to 30 minutes, 15.5% 30 to 45 minutes, 9.7% 45 to 60 minutes, 7.5% 60 minutes or more (2000)

ELLSWORTH (township). Covers a land area of 29.447 square miles and a water area of 6.860 square miles. Located at 45.01° N. Lat.; 94.42° W. Long.
Population: 854 (2000); Race: 100.0% White, 0.0% Black, 0.0% Asian, 0.0% American Indian and Alaska Native, 0.0% Hispanic of any race, 0.0% two or more races (2000); Density: 29.0 persons per square mile (2000); Age: 23.2% under 18, 11.6% over 64 (2000); Marriage status: 20.2% never married, 70.7% now married, 4.6% widowed, 4.5% divorced (2000); Foreign born: 0.2% (2000); Ancestry (includes multiple ancestries): 62.5% German, 20.1% Swedish, 13.1% Norwegian, 7.6% Irish, 4.0% Czech (2000).
Economy: Employment by occupation: 12.7% management, 12.4% professional, 14.7% services, 27.4% sales, 0.6% farming, 9.8% construction, 22.4% production (2000).

Income: Per capita income: $22,039 (2000); Median household income: $51,406 (2000); Poverty rate: 3.8% (2000).
Taxes: Total city taxes per capita: $105 (1997); City property taxes per capita: $105 (1997).
Education: High school graduation rate: 90.0% (2000); College graduation rate: 15.9% (2000).
Housing: Homeownership rate: 96.3% (2000); Median home value: $148,000 (2000); Median rent: $263 per month (2000); Median age of housing: 26 years (2000).
Transportation: Commute to work: 92.9% car, 0.0% public transportation, 1.5% walk, 5.6% work from home (2000); Travel time to work: 13.5% less than 15 minutes, 59.4% 15 to 30 minutes, 12.8% 30 to 45 minutes, 3.8% 45 to 60 minutes, 10.6% 60 minutes or more (2000)

FOREST CITY (township). Covers a land area of 34.349 square miles and a water area of 1.374 square miles. Located at 45.19° N. Lat.; 94.43° W. Long. Elevation is 1,074 feet.
Population: 666 (2000); Race: 98.2% White, 1.0% Black, 0.0% Asian, 0.7% American Indian and Alaska Native, 0.0% Hispanic of any race, 0.0% two or more races (2000); Density: 19.4 persons per square mile (2000); Age: 31.8% under 18, 8.4% over 64 (2000); Marriage status: 19.8% never married, 74.3% now married, 3.3% widowed, 2.5% divorced (2000); Foreign born: 0.0% (2000); Ancestry (includes multiple ancestries): 54.0% German, 20.4% Swedish, 11.6% Norwegian, 8.4% Irish, 3.1% Scandinavian (2000).
Economy: Employment by occupation: 17.4% management, 12.7% professional, 11.3% services, 22.3% sales, 1.7% farming, 10.2% construction, 24.5% production (2000).
Income: Per capita income: $17,590 (2000); Median household income: $49,083 (2000); Poverty rate: 4.5% (2000).
Taxes: Total city taxes per capita: $74 (1997); City property taxes per capita: $74 (1997).
Education: High school graduation rate: 90.0% (2000); College graduation rate: 8.8% (2000).
Housing: Homeownership rate: 87.1% (2000); Median home value: $95,000 (2000); Median rent: $283 per month (2000); Median age of housing: 43 years (2000).
Transportation: Commute to work: 86.3% car, 0.0% public transportation, 2.0% walk, 11.7% work from home (2000); Travel time to work: 33.5% less than 15 minutes, 32.6% 15 to 30 minutes, 13.6% 30 to 45 minutes, 7.9% 45 to 60 minutes, 12.3% 60 minutes or more (2000)

FOREST PRAIRIE (township). Covers a land area of 34.280 square miles and a water area of 1.106 square miles. Located at 45.27° N. Lat.; 94.45° W. Long.
Population: 869 (2000); Race: 99.9% White, 0.1% Black, 0.0% Asian, 0.0% American Indian and Alaska Native, 0.2% Hispanic of any race, 0.0% two or more races (2000); Density: 25.3 persons per square mile (2000); Age: 29.1% under 18, 11.8% over 64 (2000); Marriage status: 20.1% never married, 71.3% now married, 2.8% widowed, 5.8% divorced (2000); Foreign born: 0.1% (2000); Ancestry (includes multiple ancestries): 67.3% German, 8.9% Norwegian, 7.1% Swedish, 7.1% Irish, 6.4% United States or American (2000).
Economy: Employment by occupation: 14.4% management, 11.4% professional, 13.6% services, 19.6% sales, 4.6% farming, 11.2% construction, 25.1% production (2000).
Income: Per capita income: $17,340 (2000); Median household income: $46,375 (2000); Poverty rate: 7.6% (2000).
Taxes: Total city taxes per capita: $97 (1997); City property taxes per capita: $97 (1997).
Education: High school graduation rate: 76.1% (2000); College graduation rate: 9.1% (2000).
Housing: Homeownership rate: 92.9% (2000); Median home value: $92,200 (2000); Median rent: $363 per month (2000); Median age of housing: 29 years (2000).
Transportation: Commute to work: 86.3% car, 0.0% public transportation, 2.2% walk, 11.2% work from home (2000); Travel time to work: 27.5% less than 15 minutes, 30.9% 15 to 30 minutes, 13.6% 30 to 45 minutes, 10.2% 45 to 60 minutes, 17.9% 60 minutes or more (2000)

GREENLEAF (township). Covers a land area of 35.809 square miles and a water area of 3.166 square miles. Located at 45.02° N. Lat.; 94.55° W. Long.
Population: 726 (2000); Race: 100.0% White, 0.0% Black, 0.0% Asian, 0.0% American Indian and Alaska Native, 0.3% Hispanic of any race, 0.0% two or more races (2000); Density: 20.3 persons per square mile (2000); Age: 17.3% under 18, 17.3% over 64 (2000); Marriage status: 15.8% never married, 74.6% now married, 3.2% widowed, 6.4% divorced (2000); Foreign born: 1.0% (2000); Ancestry (includes multiple ancestries): 48.6% German, 19.8% Norwegian, 16.9% Swedish, 6.6% Danish, 5.8% English (2000).
Economy: Employment by occupation: 14.4% management, 18.5% professional, 13.1% services, 20.6% sales, 3.9% farming, 8.1% construction, 21.4% production (2000).
Income: Per capita income: $21,973 (2000); Median household income: $46,190 (2000); Poverty rate: 1.9% (2000).
Taxes: Total city taxes per capita: $145 (2000); City property taxes per capita: $145 (2000).
Education: High school graduation rate: 90.5% (2000); College graduation rate: 15.8% (2000).
Housing: Homeownership rate: 93.1% (2000); Median home value: $125,000 (2000); Median rent: $246 per month (2000); Median age of housing: 28 years (2000).
Transportation: Commute to work: 86.0% car, 0.5% public transportation, 3.2% walk, 9.8% work from home (2000); Travel time to work: 26.4% less than 15 minutes, 48.1% 15 to 30 minutes, 14.7% 30 to 45 minutes, 2.9% 45 to 60 minutes, 7.9% 60 minutes or more (2000)

GROVE CITY (city). Covers a land area of 0.639 square miles and a water area of 0.047 square miles. Located at 45.14° N. Lat.; 94.68° W. Long. Elevation is 1,192 feet.
Population: 608 (2000); Race: 96.8% White, 0.0% Black, 1.0% Asian, 0.0% American Indian and Alaska Native, 2.2% Hispanic of any race, 2.2% two or more races (2000); Density: 951.8 persons per square mile (2000); Age: 28.4% under 18, 16.4% over 64 (2000); Marriage status: 23.8% never married, 56.6% now married, 9.8% widowed, 9.8% divorced (2000); Foreign born: 1.6% (2000); Ancestry (includes multiple ancestries): 38.4% German, 26.2% Norwegian, 21.3% Swedish, 11.6% Irish, 5.0% French (except Basque) (2000).
Economy: Agriculture: poultry, livestock; grain, soybeans; dairying. Manufacturing: aircraft drills, snowmobile attachments, fiberglass boats. Single-family building permits issued: 2 (2001) / 1 (2000); Multi-family building permits issued: 6 (2001) / 0 (2000); Employment by occupation: 5.5% management, 15.6% professional, 9.7% services, 26.6% sales, 0.3% farming, 11.1% construction, 31.1% production (2000).
Income: Per capita income: $14,237 (2000); Median household income: $29,313 (2000); Poverty rate: 12.3% (2000).
Taxes: Total city taxes per capita: $84 (1997); City property taxes per capita: $80 (1997).
Education: High school graduation rate: 83.0% (2000); College graduation rate: 11.1% (2000).
Housing: Homeownership rate: 66.7% (2000); Median home value: $61,800 (2000); Median rent: $305 per month (2000); Median age of housing: 42 years (2000).
Transportation: Commute to work: 87.1% car, 0.0% public transportation, 5.6% walk, 2.8% work from home (2000); Travel time to work: 43.2% less than 15 minutes, 35.6% 15 to 30 minutes, 11.5% 30 to 45 minutes, 2.9% 45 to 60 minutes, 6.8% 60 minutes or more (2000)

HARVEY (township). Covers a land area of 38.551 square miles and a water area of 0.412 square miles. Located at 45.19° N. Lat.; 94.56° W. Long.
Population: 445 (2000); Race: 100.0% White, 0.0% Black, 0.0% Asian, 0.0% American Indian and Alaska Native, 0.0% Hispanic of any race, 0.0% two or more races (2000); Density: 11.5 persons per square mile (2000); Age: 33.7% under 18, 9.6% over 64 (2000); Marriage status: 21.0% never married, 72.3% now married, 1.7% widowed, 5.0% divorced (2000); Foreign born: 0.0% (2000); Ancestry (includes multiple ancestries): 55.7% German, 15.4% Norwegian, 14.2% Swedish, 7.2% United States or American, 5.5% Irish (2000).
Economy: Employment by occupation: 20.2% management, 11.9% professional, 10.6% services, 14.7% sales, 3.2% farming, 7.3% construction, 32.1% production (2000).
Income: Per capita income: $18,299 (2000); Median household income: $46,750 (2000); Poverty rate: 8.7% (2000).
Taxes: Total city taxes per capita: $102 (1997); City property taxes per capita: $102 (1997).
Education: High school graduation rate: 76.9% (2000); College graduation rate: 10.8% (2000).
Housing: Homeownership rate: 94.9% (2000); Median home value: $83,300 (2000); Median rent: $358 per month (2000); Median age of housing: 47 years (2000).
Transportation: Commute to work: 80.7% car, 0.0% public transportation, 1.8% walk, 15.6% work from home (2000); Travel time to work: 35.3% less

than 15 minutes, 36.4% 15 to 30 minutes, 18.5% 30 to 45 minutes, 8.7% 45 to 60 minutes, 1.1% 60 minutes or more (2000)

KINGSTON (city). Covers a land area of 0.492 square miles and a water area of 0 square miles. Located at 45.19° N. Lat.; 94.31° W. Long. Elevation is 1,027 feet.
Population: 120 (2000); Race: 100.0% White, 0.0% Black, 0.0% Asian, 0.0% American Indian and Alaska Native, 0.0% Hispanic of any race, 0.0% two or more races (2000); Density: 244.0 persons per square mile (2000); Age: 29.7% under 18, 7.6% over 64 (2000); Marriage status: 22.3% never married, 64.5% now married, 5.8% widowed, 7.4% divorced (2000); Foreign born: 1.3% (2000); Ancestry (includes multiple ancestries): 35.4% German, 32.3% Finnish, 25.3% Swedish, 10.8% Norwegian, 9.5% French (except Basque) (2000).
Economy: Single-family building permits issued: 0 (2001) / 1 (2000); Multi-family building permits issued: 0 (2001) / 0 (2000); Employment by occupation: 7.7% management, 13.2% professional, 26.4% services, 9.9% sales, 3.3% farming, 12.1% construction, 27.5% production (2000).
Income: Per capita income: $13,525 (2000); Median household income: $39,375 (2000); Poverty rate: 2.5% (2000).
Taxes: Total city taxes per capita: $54 (1997); City property taxes per capita: $46 (1997).
Education: High school graduation rate: 79.5% (2000); College graduation rate: 9.6% (2000).
Housing: Homeownership rate: 96.0% (2000); Median home value: $60,000 (2000); Median rent: $325 per month (2000); Median age of housing: 59 years (2000).
Transportation: Commute to work: 96.5% car, 0.0% public transportation, 0.0% walk, 3.5% work from home (2000); Travel time to work: 8.5% less than 15 minutes, 51.2% 15 to 30 minutes, 24.4% 30 to 45 minutes, 9.8% 45 to 60 minutes, 6.1% 60 minutes or more (2000)

KINGSTON (township). Covers a land area of 51.817 square miles and a water area of 1.796 square miles. Located at 45.20° N. Lat.; 94.31° W. Long. Elevation is 1,027 feet.
Population: 1,266 (2000); Race: 97.8% White, 0.0% Black, 0.2% Asian, 1.1% American Indian and Alaska Native, 0.0% Hispanic of any race, 1.0% two or more races (2000); Density: 24.4 persons per square mile (2000); Age: 33.0% under 18, 12.2% over 64 (2000); Marriage status: 23.4% never married, 65.3% now married, 3.8% widowed, 7.5% divorced (2000); Foreign born: 0.5% (2000); Ancestry (includes multiple ancestries): 42.1% German, 17.2% Finnish, 17.1% Swedish, 11.2% Irish, 10.3% Norwegian (2000).
Economy: Fish processing. Agriculture: grain, livestock, dairying. Employment by occupation: 13.7% management, 12.8% professional, 15.5% services, 16.1% sales, 3.1% farming, 19.2% construction, 19.6% production (2000).
Income: Per capita income: $15,662 (2000); Median household income: $41,012 (2000); Poverty rate: 7.6% (2000).
Taxes: Total city taxes per capita: $92 (2000); City property taxes per capita: $92 (2000).
Education: High school graduation rate: 85.3% (2000); College graduation rate: 13.1% (2000).
Housing: Homeownership rate: 88.9% (2000); Median home value: $110,200 (2000); Median rent: $345 per month (2000); Median age of housing: 37 years (2000).
Transportation: Commute to work: 92.3% car, 0.0% public transportation, 2.8% walk, 3.7% work from home (2000); Travel time to work: 18.5% less than 15 minutes, 32.9% 15 to 30 minutes, 24.5% 30 to 45 minutes, 6.2% 45 to 60 minutes, 17.9% 60 minutes or more (2000)

LITCHFIELD (city). Covers a land area of 3.753 square miles and a water area of 0.923 square miles. Located at 45.12° N. Lat.; 94.52° W. Long. Elevation is 1,129 feet.
History: Litchfield was platted in 1869 and named for the three Litchfield brothers connected with the St. Paul & Pacific Railroad, which was built to the site of the new town. Litchfield developed as an industrial and trading center with creameries, a powdered-buttermilk plant, and a woolen mill. It also became a center for the many resorts on the lakes that surround it.
Population: 6,562 (2000); Race: 93.6% White, 0.6% Black, 0.4% Asian, 1.2% American Indian and Alaska Native, 4.5% Hispanic of any race, 0.9% two or more races (2000); Density: 1,748.4 persons per square mile (2000); Age: 25.2% under 18, 20.8% over 64 (2000); Marriage status: 24.6% never married, 55.0% now married, 11.3% widowed, 9.1% divorced (2000); Foreign born: 1.4% (2000); Ancestry (includes multiple ancestries): 43.5% German, 15.4% Swedish, 13.8% Norwegian, 8.5% Other groups, 8.4% Irish (2000).
Economy: Single-family building permits issued: 36 (2001) / 26 (2000); Multi-family building permits issued: 4 (2001) / 2 (2000); Employment by occupation: 6.9% management, 19.7% professional, 14.6% services, 23.4% sales, 0.8% farming, 8.1% construction, 26.5% production (2000).
Income: Per capita income: $19,819 (2000); Median household income: $36,021 (2000); Poverty rate: 7.8% (2000).
Taxes: Total city taxes per capita: $131 (1997); City property taxes per capita: $121 (1997).
Education: High school graduation rate: 77.2% (2000); College graduation rate: 16.6% (2000).

School District(s)

Litchfield (PK-12)
2000 Enrollment: 2,062 320-693-2444
Housing: Homeownership rate: 71.5% (2000); Median home value: $84,200 (2000); Median rent: $418 per month (2000); Median age of housing: 42 years (2000).
Hospitals: Meeker County Memorial Hospital (38 beds)
Safety: Violent crime rate: 10.6 per 10,000 population; Property crime rate: 366.4 per 10,000 population (2001).
Newspapers: Independent Review (1 x week); Meeker County Advertiser (1 x week)
Transportation: Commute to work: 89.5% car, 0.6% public transportation, 5.2% walk, 2.7% work from home (2000); Travel time to work: 61.1% less than 15 minutes, 16.7% 15 to 30 minutes, 13.2% 30 to 45 minutes, 4.0% 45 to 60 minutes, 5.1% 60 minutes or more (2000)
Additional Information Contacts
Litchfield Chamber of Commerce 320-693-8184

LITCHFIELD (township). Covers a land area of 31.730 square miles and a water area of 2.201 square miles. Located at 45.11° N. Lat.; 94.55° W. Long. Elevation is 1,129 feet.
History: Settled 1856, plotted 1869, incorporated 1872.
Population: 808 (2000); Race: 99.0% White, 0.5% Black, 0.6% Asian, 0.0% American Indian and Alaska Native, 0.0% Hispanic of any race, 0.0% two or more races (2000); Density: 25.5 persons per square mile (2000); Age: 29.8% under 18, 9.0% over 64 (2000); Marriage status: 20.8% never married, 70.4% now married, 1.7% widowed, 7.2% divorced (2000); Foreign born: 0.6% (2000); Ancestry (includes multiple ancestries): 46.0% German, 17.6% Norwegian, 15.8% Swedish, 7.3% Other groups, 7.2% English (2000).
Economy: Trading point in agricultural area: grain, soybeans, peas, beans; livestock, poultry; dairying. Manufacturing: manufacturing equipment, leather products, food, wood products, machinery, apparel, textiles, transportation equipment. Employment by occupation: 16.4% management, 19.5% professional, 14.9% services, 15.3% sales, 4.8% farming, 7.4% construction, 21.6% production (2000).
Income: Per capita income: $22,203 (2000); Median household income: $57,885 (2000); Poverty rate: 2.7% (2000).
Taxes: Total city taxes per capita: $104 (1997); City property taxes per capita: $104 (1997).
Education: High school graduation rate: 88.0% (2000); College graduation rate: 22.0% (2000).
Housing: Homeownership rate: 92.1% (2000); Median home value: $119,300 (2000); Median rent: $408 per month (2000); Median age of housing: 28 years (2000).
Transportation: Commute to work: 91.5% car, 0.4% public transportation, 3.6% walk, 4.5% work from home (2000); Travel time to work: 56.8% less than 15 minutes, 20.6% 15 to 30 minutes, 13.0% 30 to 45 minutes, 4.7% 45 to 60 minutes, 4.9% 60 minutes or more (2000)

MANANNAH (township). Covers a land area of 38.466 square miles and a water area of 0.125 square miles. Located at 45.27° N. Lat.; 94.57° W. Long. Elevation is 1,151 feet.
Population: 610 (2000); Race: 100.0% White, 0.0% Black, 0.0% Asian, 0.0% American Indian and Alaska Native, 0.0% Hispanic of any race, 0.0% two or more races (2000); Density: 15.9 persons per square mile (2000); Age: 34.5% under 18, 9.0% over 64 (2000); Marriage status: 23.8% never married, 66.8% now married, 4.3% widowed, 5.1% divorced (2000); Foreign born: 0.0% (2000); Ancestry (includes multiple ancestries): 60.7% German, 11.1% Irish, 8.2% Swedish, 4.2% United States or American, 3.6% Norwegian (2000).
Economy: Employment by occupation: 20.0% management, 8.3% professional, 12.4% services, 20.6% sales, 1.9% farming, 9.5% construction, 27.3% production (2000).
Income: Per capita income: $14,077 (2000); Median household income: $39,813 (2000); Poverty rate: 8.2% (2000).

Taxes: Total city taxes per capita: $70 (2000); City property taxes per capita: $70 (2000).
Education: High school graduation rate: 78.6% (2000); College graduation rate: 5.7% (2000).
Housing: Homeownership rate: 88.7% (2000); Median home value: $85,700 (2000); Median rent: $450 per month (2000); Median age of housing: 56 years (2000).
Transportation: Commute to work: 80.6% car, 0.0% public transportation, 4.4% walk, 14.0% work from home (2000); Travel time to work: 25.1% less than 15 minutes, 41.7% 15 to 30 minutes, 12.2% 30 to 45 minutes, 11.1% 45 to 60 minutes, 10.0% 60 minutes or more (2000)

SWEDE GROVE (township). Covers a land area of 34.694 square miles and a water area of 0.879 square miles. Located at 45.19° N. Lat.; 94.68° W. Long.
Population: 414 (2000); Race: 99.0% White, 0.0% Black, 0.0% Asian, 1.0% American Indian and Alaska Native, 0.0% Hispanic of any race, 0.0% two or more races (2000); Density: 11.9 persons per square mile (2000); Age: 29.4% under 18, 15.7% over 64 (2000); Marriage status: 28.8% never married, 61.7% now married, 4.8% widowed, 4.8% divorced (2000); Foreign born: 0.0% (2000); Ancestry (includes multiple ancestries): 51.1% German, 17.5% Swedish, 16.2% Norwegian, 8.5% Irish, 6.5% United States or American (2000).
Economy: Employment by occupation: 21.6% management, 6.5% professional, 12.1% services, 19.6% sales, 4.0% farming, 12.6% construction, 23.6% production (2000).
Income: Per capita income: $15,395 (2000); Median household income: $39,750 (2000); Poverty rate: 18.8% (2000).
Taxes: Total city taxes per capita: $57 (1997); City property taxes per capita: $57 (1997).
Education: High school graduation rate: 82.0% (2000); College graduation rate: 8.0% (2000).
Housing: Homeownership rate: 89.7% (2000); Median home value: $69,200 (2000); Median rent: $225 per month (2000); Median age of housing: 60+ years (2000).
Transportation: Commute to work: 88.5% car, 0.0% public transportation, 1.6% walk, 9.9% work from home (2000); Travel time to work: 36.4% less than 15 minutes, 34.7% 15 to 30 minutes, 12.7% 30 to 45 minutes, 8.7% 45 to 60 minutes, 7.5% 60 minutes or more (2000)

UNION GROVE (township). Covers a land area of 35.147 square miles and a water area of 0.832 square miles. Located at 45.28° N. Lat.; 94.68° W. Long.
Population: 625 (2000); Race: 99.5% White, 0.0% Black, 0.0% Asian, 0.0% American Indian and Alaska Native, 0.5% Hispanic of any race, 0.0% two or more races (2000); Density: 17.8 persons per square mile (2000); Age: 28.3% under 18, 12.6% over 64 (2000); Marriage status: 23.4% never married, 68.9% now married, 3.5% widowed, 4.3% divorced (2000); Foreign born: 0.0% (2000); Ancestry (includes multiple ancestries): 52.1% German, 24.3% Norwegian, 12.6% Swedish, 5.7% Irish, 5.3% French (except Basque) (2000).
Economy: Employment by occupation: 19.9% management, 11.7% professional, 7.0% services, 24.6% sales, 1.5% farming, 10.9% construction, 24.3% production (2000).
Income: Per capita income: $21,157 (2000); Median household income: $44,732 (2000); Poverty rate: 3.6% (2000).
Taxes: Total city taxes per capita: $84 (1997); City property taxes per capita: $84 (1997).
Education: High school graduation rate: 85.5% (2000); College graduation rate: 15.9% (2000).
Housing: Homeownership rate: 87.2% (2000); Median home value: $97,900 (2000); Median rent: $368 per month (2000); Median age of housing: 31 years (2000).
Transportation: Commute to work: 86.1% car, 0.0% public transportation, 3.6% walk, 9.8% work from home (2000); Travel time to work: 27.0% less than 15 minutes, 39.8% 15 to 30 minutes, 14.1% 30 to 45 minutes, 6.3% 45 to 60 minutes, 12.8% 60 minutes or more (2000)

WATKINS (city). Covers a land area of 0.511 square miles and a water area of 0 square miles. Located at 45.31° N. Lat.; 94.41° W. Long. Elevation is 1,162 feet.
Population: 880 (2000); Race: 98.6% White, 0.3% Black, 0.3% Asian, 0.0% American Indian and Alaska Native, 0.8% Hispanic of any race, 0.0% two or more races (2000); Density: 1,722.7 persons per square mile (2000); Age: 24.7% under 18, 24.9% over 64 (2000); Marriage status: 27.8% never married, 50.6% now married, 13.5% widowed, 8.1% divorced (2000); Foreign born: 0.6% (2000); Ancestry (includes multiple ancestries): 58.6% German, 10.6% Irish, 8.0% Swedish, 7.9% Norwegian, 4.3% French (except Basque) (2000).
Economy: Agriculture includes grain, soybeans, peas; livestock, poultry; dairying; light manufacturing. Single-family building permits issued: 3 (2001) / 1 (2000); Multi-family building permits issued: 4 (2001) / 0 (2000); Employment by occupation: 6.3% management, 7.1% professional, 21.9% services, 25.4% sales, 0.3% farming, 13.1% construction, 26.0% production (2000).
Income: Per capita income: $15,950 (2000); Median household income: $32,188 (2000); Poverty rate: 12.2% (2000).
Taxes: Total city taxes per capita: $151 (1997); City property taxes per capita: $140 (1997).
Education: High school graduation rate: 63.5% (2000); College graduation rate: 4.6% (2000).
Housing: Homeownership rate: 74.8% (2000); Median home value: $68,100 (2000); Median rent: $209 per month (2000); Median age of housing: 40 years (2000).
Newspapers: The Eden Valley Journal-Watkins Patriot (1 x week)
Transportation: Commute to work: 86.2% car, 0.0% public transportation, 7.2% walk, 4.9% work from home (2000); Travel time to work: 34.4% less than 15 minutes, 22.1% 15 to 30 minutes, 19.6% 30 to 45 minutes, 9.4% 45 to 60 minutes, 14.5% 60 minutes or more (2000)

Mille Lacs County

Located in east central Minnesota; drained by the Rum River; includes part of Mille Lacs Lake. Covers a land area of 574.50 square miles, a water area of 107.30 square miles, and is located in the Central Time Zone. The county government was organized in 1857. County seat is Milaca.

Weather Station: Milaca 1 ENE — Elevation: 1,092 feet

	Jan	Feb	Mar	Apr	May	Jun	Jul	Aug	Sep	Oct	Nov	Dec
High	19	27	38	55	69	77	82	79	70	57	38	25
Low	-2	6	18	32	44	54	59	56	46	35	21	6
Precip	0.7	0.6	1.4	2.1	3.2	4.3	4.0	4.0	2.9	2.4	1.6	0.8
Snow	12.3	6.0	6.1	1.6	tr	0.0	0.0	0.0	0.0	0.3	6.0	7.9

High and Low temperatures in degrees Fahrenheit; Precipitation and Snow in inches

Population: 22,330 (2000); Race: 94.0% White, 0.2% Black, 0.3% Asian, 3.9% American Indian and Alaska Native, 1.2% Hispanic of any race, 1.3% two or more races (2000); Density: 38.9 persons per square mile (2000); Age: 27.0% under 18, 16.1% over 64 (2000).
Religion: Five largest groups: 20.7% Evangelical Lutheran Church in America, 17.5% Catholic Church, 4.7% Christian Reformed Church in North America, 4.2% Assemblies of God, 3.7% Lutheran Church—Missouri Synod (2000).
Economy: Unemployment rate: 6.9% (11/2002); Total civilian labor force: 9,625 (11/2002); Leading industries: 39.4% accommodation & food services; 13.7% health care and social assistance; 13.3% retail trade (2000); Companies that employ more than 1,000 persons: 2 (2000); Companies that employ more than 100 persons: 13 (2000); Farms: 711 totaling 134,622 acres (1997); Minority business ownership rate: 0.0% (1997); Women business ownership rate: 19.1% (1997); Retail sales per capita: $6,429 (1997). Single-family building permits issued: 208 (2001) / 187 (2000); Multi-family building permits issued: 25 (2001) / 6 (2000).
Income: Per capita income: $17,656 (2000); Median household income: $36,977 (2000); Poverty rate: 9.6% (2000); Bankruptcy rate: 6.03% (2001).
Taxes: Total county taxes per capita: $303 (1997); County property taxes per capita: $298 (1997).
Education: High school graduation rate: 81.3% (2000); College graduation rate: 12.2% (2000).
Housing: Homeownership rate: 79.8% (2000); Median home value: $91,000 (2000); Median rent: $355 per month (2000); Median age of housing: 28 years (2000).
Health: Birth rate: 132.6 per 10,000 population (1998); Age adjusted death rate: 88.6 per 10,000 population (1999); Age adjusted cancer mortality rate: 245.4 deaths per 100,000 population (1999). Air Quality Index: 84% good, 16% moderate, 0% unhealthy (percent of days in 2000). Number of physicians: 12.1 per 10,000 population (1999); Number of hospital beds: 66.7 per 10,000 population (1999).
Elections: 2000 Presidential election results: 42.7% Gore, 50.9% Bush, 4.4% Nader, 1.5% Buchanan
National and State Parks: Father Hennepin State Park; Kunkel State Wildlife Management Area; Mille Lacs Kathio State Park; Mille Lacs

National Wildlife Refuge; Mille Lacs State Wildlife Management Area; Rum River State Forest; Whitefish Lake State Wildlife Management
Additional Information Contacts
Mille Lacs County Government Offices 320-983-8218
Isle Chamber of Commerce 320-676-3939
Princeton Area Chamber of Commerce 763-389-1764

Mille Lacs County Communities

BOCK (city). Covers a land area of 0.131 square miles and a water area of 0 square miles. Located at 45.78° N. Lat.; 93.55° W. Long. Elevation is 1,105 feet.
Population: 106 (2000); Race: 97.9% White, 0.0% Black, 0.0% Asian, 0.0% American Indian and Alaska Native, 5.2% Hispanic of any race, 0.0% two or more races (2000); Density: 806.2 persons per square mile (2000); Age: 19.6% under 18, 23.7% over 64 (2000); Marriage status: 17.0% never married, 68.2% now married, 5.7% widowed, 9.1% divorced (2000); Foreign born: 0.0% (2000); Ancestry (includes multiple ancestries): 32.0% German, 22.7% Swedish, 22.7% Norwegian, 14.4% Irish, 8.2% Polish (2000).
Economy: Agricultural area: grain; livestock, poultry; dairying. Employment by occupation: 0.0% management, 4.9% professional, 19.5% services, 17.1% sales, 0.0% farming, 24.4% construction, 34.1% production (2000).
Income: Per capita income: $14,806 (2000); Median household income: $31,250 (2000); Poverty rate: 9.3% (2000).
Taxes: Total city taxes per capita: $44 (1997); City property taxes per capita: $9 (1997).
Education: High school graduation rate: 76.0% (2000); College graduation rate: 8.0% (2000).
Housing: Homeownership rate: 88.1% (2000); Median home value: $62,500 (2000); Median rent: $358 per month (2000); Median age of housing: 54 years (2000).
Transportation: Commute to work: 94.9% car, 0.0% public transportation, 0.0% walk, 5.1% work from home (2000); Travel time to work: 27.0% less than 15 minutes, 10.8% 15 to 30 minutes, 21.6% 30 to 45 minutes, 29.7% 45 to 60 minutes, 10.8% 60 minutes or more (2000)

BOGUS BROOK (township). Covers a land area of 36.201 square miles and a water area of 0.015 square miles. Located at 45.69° N. Lat.; 93.58° W. Long.
Population: 1,038 (2000); Race: 97.1% White, 0.5% Black, 0.2% Asian, 0.0% American Indian and Alaska Native, 1.2% Hispanic of any race, 2.2% two or more races (2000); Density: 28.7 persons per square mile (2000); Age: 34.4% under 18, 11.2% over 64 (2000); Marriage status: 17.8% never married, 73.6% now married, 2.7% widowed, 5.9% divorced (2000); Foreign born: 0.8% (2000); Ancestry (includes multiple ancestries): 36.0% German, 15.3% Norwegian, 15.0% Dutch, 10.1% Swedish, 7.5% Irish (2000).
Economy: Employment by occupation: 14.7% management, 12.7% professional, 12.3% services, 20.2% sales, 2.4% farming, 11.3% construction, 26.3% production (2000).
Income: Per capita income: $16,604 (2000); Median household income: $40,238 (2000); Poverty rate: 6.0% (2000).
Taxes: Total city taxes per capita: $7 (1997); City property taxes per capita: $7 (1997).
Education: High school graduation rate: 86.6% (2000); College graduation rate: 12.9% (2000).
Housing: Homeownership rate: 92.3% (2000); Median home value: $89,200 (2000); Median rent: $375 per month (2000); Median age of housing: 30 years (2000).
Transportation: Commute to work: 82.8% car, 0.0% public transportation, 3.9% walk, 12.3% work from home (2000); Travel time to work: 21.5% less than 15 minutes, 31.1% 15 to 30 minutes, 17.5% 30 to 45 minutes, 11.9% 45 to 60 minutes, 18.0% 60 minutes or more (2000)

BORGHOLM (township). Covers a land area of 34.967 square miles and a water area of 0 square miles. Located at 45.77° N. Lat.; 93.58° W. Long.
Population: 1,140 (2000); Race: 97.4% White, 0.0% Black, 0.6% Asian, 0.2% American Indian and Alaska Native, 0.7% Hispanic of any race, 1.1% two or more races (2000); Density: 32.6 persons per square mile (2000); Age: 30.9% under 18, 8.3% over 64 (2000); Marriage status: 20.4% never married, 64.7% now married, 4.3% widowed, 10.6% divorced (2000); Foreign born: 2.1% (2000); Ancestry (includes multiple ancestries): 40.1% German, 24.1% Swedish, 14.9% Norwegian, 7.6% Irish, 6.2% Polish (2000).
Economy: Employment by occupation: 14.1% management, 8.7% professional, 15.7% services, 22.8% sales, 0.6% farming, 13.8% construction, 24.2% production (2000).
Income: Per capita income: $15,778 (2000); Median household income: $43,393 (2000); Poverty rate: 10.4% (2000).
Taxes: Total city taxes per capita: $29 (1997); City property taxes per capita: $29 (1997).
Education: High school graduation rate: 84.0% (2000); College graduation rate: 10.8% (2000).
Housing: Homeownership rate: 95.3% (2000); Median home value: $105,700 (2000); Median rent: $418 per month (2000); Median age of housing: 27 years (2000).
Transportation: Commute to work: 89.9% car, 0.0% public transportation, 2.0% walk, 7.5% work from home (2000); Travel time to work: 35.7% less than 15 minutes, 20.9% 15 to 30 minutes, 13.7% 30 to 45 minutes, 14.4% 45 to 60 minutes, 15.3% 60 minutes or more (2000)

BRADBURY (township). Covers a land area of 36.671 square miles and a water area of 0.017 square miles. Located at 46.03° N. Lat.; 93.74° W. Long.
Population: 203 (2000); Race: 99.0% White, 0.0% Black, 0.0% Asian, 0.0% American Indian and Alaska Native, 0.0% Hispanic of any race, 1.0% two or more races (2000); Density: 5.5 persons per square mile (2000); Age: 25.1% under 18, 8.0% over 64 (2000); Marriage status: 24.4% never married, 64.4% now married, 3.1% widowed, 8.1% divorced (2000); Foreign born: 1.0% (2000); Ancestry (includes multiple ancestries): 34.7% German, 16.6% Swedish, 13.6% Polish, 12.6% Irish, 10.1% United States or American (2000).
Economy: Employment by occupation: 10.3% management, 29.9% professional, 15.9% services, 15.9% sales, 0.0% farming, 6.5% construction, 21.5% production (2000).
Income: Per capita income: $16,857 (2000); Median household income: $38,750 (2000); Poverty rate: 2.0% (2000).
Taxes: Total city taxes per capita: $57 (1997); City property taxes per capita: $57 (1997).
Education: High school graduation rate: 85.2% (2000); College graduation rate: 14.1% (2000).
Housing: Homeownership rate: 90.1% (2000); Median home value: $65,000 (2000); Median age of housing: 30 years (2000).
Transportation: Commute to work: 94.2% car, 0.0% public transportation, 1.9% walk, 3.9% work from home (2000); Travel time to work: 29.3% less than 15 minutes, 24.2% 15 to 30 minutes, 20.2% 30 to 45 minutes, 6.1% 45 to 60 minutes, 20.2% 60 minutes or more (2000)

DAILEY (township). Covers a land area of 31.004 square miles and a water area of 0 square miles. Located at 45.95° N. Lat.; 93.68° W. Long.
Population: 246 (2000); Race: 100.0% White, 0.0% Black, 0.0% Asian, 0.0% American Indian and Alaska Native, 2.8% Hispanic of any race, 0.0% two or more races (2000); Density: 7.9 persons per square mile (2000); Age: 31.9% under 18, 10.9% over 64 (2000); Marriage status: 18.6% never married, 73.9% now married, 2.1% widowed, 5.3% divorced (2000); Foreign born: 0.0% (2000); Ancestry (includes multiple ancestries): 46.4% German, 23.0% Norwegian, 13.3% Irish, 12.5% Swedish, 5.6% Dutch (2000).
Economy: Employment by occupation: 17.2% management, 4.7% professional, 14.1% services, 21.9% sales, 1.6% farming, 8.6% construction, 32.0% production (2000).
Income: Per capita income: $14,130 (2000); Median household income: $35,893 (2000); Poverty rate: 10.2% (2000).
Taxes: Total city taxes per capita: $42 (1997); City property taxes per capita: $42 (1997).
Education: High school graduation rate: 79.6% (2000); College graduation rate: 1.9% (2000).
Housing: Homeownership rate: 94.2% (2000); Median home value: $77,500 (2000); Median age of housing: 23 years (2000).
Transportation: Commute to work: 86.7% car, 0.0% public transportation, 2.3% walk, 10.9% work from home (2000); Travel time to work: 14.0% less than 15 minutes, 33.3% 15 to 30 minutes, 14.0% 30 to 45 minutes, 14.0% 45 to 60 minutes, 24.6% 60 minutes or more (2000)

EAST SIDE (township). Covers a land area of 21.397 square miles and a water area of 16.745 square miles. Located at 46.19° N. Lat.; 93.49° W. Long.
Population: 731 (2000); Race: 95.6% White, 0.7% Black, 0.7% Asian, 1.4% American Indian and Alaska Native, 2.3% Hispanic of any race, 1.2% two or more races (2000); Density: 34.2 persons per square mile (2000); Age: 16.5% under 18, 27.9% over 64 (2000); Marriage status: 13.4% never married, 71.7% now married, 6.4% widowed, 8.4% divorced (2000); Foreign born: 2.0% (2000); Ancestry (includes multiple ancestries): 28.7% German, 20.4% Norwegian, 19.8% Swedish, 12.6% English, 9.2% Irish (2000).

Economy: Employment by occupation: 9.2% management, 22.6% professional, 18.4% services, 16.3% sales, 2.1% farming, 11.7% construction, 19.8% production (2000).
Income: Per capita income: $18,937 (2000); Median household income: $36,875 (2000); Poverty rate: 9.2% (2000).
Taxes: Total city taxes per capita: $117 (1997); City property taxes per capita: $114 (1997).
Education: High school graduation rate: 85.6% (2000); College graduation rate: 11.8% (2000).
Housing: Homeownership rate: 94.4% (2000); Median home value: $111,100 (2000); Median rent: $419 per month (2000); Median age of housing: 33 years (2000).
Transportation: Commute to work: 92.7% car, 0.0% public transportation, 2.9% walk, 4.4% work from home (2000); Travel time to work: 39.5% less than 15 minutes, 19.5% 15 to 30 minutes, 15.3% 30 to 45 minutes, 5.0% 45 to 60 minutes, 20.7% 60 minutes or more (2000)

FORESTON (city). Covers a land area of 1.437 square miles and a water area of 0 square miles. Located at 45.73° N. Lat.; 93.70° W. Long. Elevation is 1,090 feet.
Population: 389 (2000); Race: 99.5% White, 0.0% Black, 0.0% Asian, 0.0% American Indian and Alaska Native, 1.0% Hispanic of any race, 0.0% two or more races (2000); Density: 270.7 persons per square mile (2000); Age: 30.1% under 18, 10.5% over 64 (2000); Marriage status: 29.1% never married, 57.1% now married, 6.2% widowed, 7.6% divorced (2000); Foreign born: 0.3% (2000); Ancestry (includes multiple ancestries): 46.8% German, 20.3% Swedish, 16.2% Norwegian, 10.0% Irish, 6.4% Polish (2000).
Economy: Poultry; grain; dairying; manufacturing: cabinet components. Employment by occupation: 13.8% management, 6.4% professional, 19.7% services, 15.3% sales, 0.0% farming, 13.8% construction, 31.0% production (2000).
Income: Per capita income: $16,666 (2000); Median household income: $37,500 (2000); Poverty rate: 5.7% (2000).
Taxes: Total city taxes per capita: $81 (1997); City property taxes per capita: $76 (1997).
Education: High school graduation rate: 82.8% (2000); College graduation rate: 9.7% (2000).
Housing: Homeownership rate: 81.1% (2000); Median home value: $76,300 (2000); Median rent: $427 per month (2000); Median age of housing: 36 years (2000).
Transportation: Commute to work: 86.2% car, 0.0% public transportation, 5.4% walk, 8.4% work from home (2000); Travel time to work: 43.0% less than 15 minutes, 15.6% 15 to 30 minutes, 18.8% 30 to 45 minutes, 9.7% 45 to 60 minutes, 12.9% 60 minutes or more (2000)

GREENBUSH (township). Covers a land area of 37.223 square miles and a water area of 0.090 square miles. Located at 45.60° N. Lat.; 93.68° W. Long.
Population: 1,135 (2000); Race: 96.8% White, 0.0% Black, 0.0% Asian, 0.4% American Indian and Alaska Native, 2.7% Hispanic of any race, 1.6% two or more races (2000); Density: 30.5 persons per square mile (2000); Age: 28.6% under 18, 8.3% over 64 (2000); Marriage status: 22.4% never married, 67.7% now married, 4.2% widowed, 5.8% divorced (2000); Foreign born: 1.3% (2000); Ancestry (includes multiple ancestries): 42.3% German, 17.3% Norwegian, 14.7% Irish, 13.4% Swedish, 7.3% French (except Basque) (2000).
Economy: Single-family building permits issued: 4 (2001) / 4 (2000); Multi-family building permits issued: 0 (2001) / 0 (2000); Employment by occupation: 12.8% management, 14.1% professional, 12.3% services, 19.9% sales, 0.8% farming, 14.3% construction, 25.8% production (2000).
Income: Per capita income: $21,843 (2000); Median household income: $52,452 (2000); Poverty rate: 7.1% (2000).
Taxes: Total city taxes per capita: $63 (1997); City property taxes per capita: $58 (1997).
Education: High school graduation rate: 85.1% (2000); College graduation rate: 11.4% (2000).
Housing: Homeownership rate: 93.3% (2000); Median home value: $109,800 (2000); Median rent: $356 per month (2000); Median age of housing: 30 years (2000).
Transportation: Commute to work: 92.4% car, 0.0% public transportation, 0.7% walk, 6.5% work from home (2000); Travel time to work: 25.0% less than 15 minutes, 27.6% 15 to 30 minutes, 18.3% 30 to 45 minutes, 14.0% 45 to 60 minutes, 15.1% 60 minutes or more (2000)

HAYLAND (township). Covers a land area of 35.903 square miles and a water area of 0.046 square miles. Located at 45.84° N. Lat.; 93.57° W. Long.
Population: 490 (2000); Race: 99.6% White, 0.0% Black, 0.0% Asian, 0.0% American Indian and Alaska Native, 0.0% Hispanic of any race, 0.4% two or more races (2000); Density: 13.6 persons per square mile (2000); Age: 31.7% under 18, 13.1% over 64 (2000); Marriage status: 20.4% never married, 66.7% now married, 4.5% widowed, 8.4% divorced (2000); Foreign born: 0.0% (2000); Ancestry (includes multiple ancestries): 43.1% German, 19.0% Swedish, 17.7% Norwegian, 7.0% Irish, 5.5% English (2000).
Economy: Employment by occupation: 11.8% management, 6.2% professional, 16.6% services, 23.2% sales, 0.0% farming, 13.3% construction, 28.9% production (2000).
Income: Per capita income: $16,836 (2000); Median household income: $35,446 (2000); Poverty rate: 13.1% (2000).
Taxes: Total city taxes per capita: $71 (1997); City property taxes per capita: $71 (1997).
Education: High school graduation rate: 81.0% (2000); College graduation rate: 5.1% (2000).
Housing: Homeownership rate: 97.1% (2000); Median home value: $88,000 (2000); Median age of housing: 24 years (2000).
Transportation: Commute to work: 82.4% car, 0.0% public transportation, 2.0% walk, 12.7% work from home (2000); Travel time to work: 23.5% less than 15 minutes, 28.5% 15 to 30 minutes, 22.9% 30 to 45 minutes, 12.8% 45 to 60 minutes, 12.3% 60 minutes or more (2000)

ISLE (city). Covers a land area of 2.104 square miles and a water area of 0.440 square miles. Located at 46.14° N. Lat.; 93.46° W. Long. Elevation is 1,260 feet.
Population: 707 (2000); Race: 91.8% White, 0.0% Black, 0.0% Asian, 6.5% American Indian and Alaska Native, 1.3% Hispanic of any race, 0.9% two or more races (2000); Density: 336.0 persons per square mile (2000); Age: 21.2% under 18, 25.0% over 64 (2000); Marriage status: 20.0% never married, 55.1% now married, 12.7% widowed, 12.2% divorced (2000); Foreign born: 1.0% (2000); Ancestry (includes multiple ancestries): 29.7% German, 23.0% Norwegian, 17.5% Swedish, 8.1% Irish, 6.6% Other groups (2000).
Economy: Grain; livestock, poultry; dairying. Manufacturing: fishing tackle, electroplating, printing and publishing; timber; sand and gravel. Granite quarries nearby. Single-family building permits issued: 6 (2001) / 16 (2000); Multi-family building permits issued: 0 (2001) / 0 (2000); Employment by occupation: 9.2% management, 24.2% professional, 15.4% services, 20.8% sales, 2.3% farming, 5.4% construction, 22.7% production (2000).
Income: Per capita income: $19,609 (2000); Median household income: $32,375 (2000); Poverty rate: 5.6% (2000).
Taxes: Total city taxes per capita: $367 (1997); City property taxes per capita: $365 (1997).
Education: High school graduation rate: 83.6% (2000); College graduation rate: 16.6% (2000).

School District(s)

Isle (PK-12)
2000 Enrollment: 571 320-676-3146
Housing: Homeownership rate: 70.2% (2000); Median home value: $74,800 (2000); Median rent: $284 per month (2000); Median age of housing: 30 years (2000).
Newspapers: Mille Lacs Messenger (1 x week); Bargain Hunter (1 x week)
Transportation: Commute to work: 84.4% car, 0.0% public transportation, 8.4% walk, 5.2% work from home (2000); Travel time to work: 60.3% less than 15 minutes, 15.2% 15 to 30 minutes, 11.8% 30 to 45 minutes, 4.6% 45 to 60 minutes, 8.0% 60 minutes or more (2000)
Additional Information Contacts
Isle Chamber of Commerce 320-676-3939

ISLE HARBOR (township). Covers a land area of 27.116 square miles and a water area of 5.037 square miles. Located at 46.12° N. Lat.; 93.50° W. Long.
Population: 590 (2000); Race: 96.5% White, 0.8% Black, 0.0% Asian, 1.5% American Indian and Alaska Native, 1.1% Hispanic of any race, 1.2% two or more races (2000); Density: 21.8 persons per square mile (2000); Age: 26.8% under 18, 16.1% over 64 (2000); Marriage status: 20.5% never married, 63.5% now married, 7.3% widowed, 8.7% divorced (2000); Foreign born: 0.8% (2000); Ancestry (includes multiple ancestries): 41.9% German, 21.3% Norwegian, 17.9% Swedish, 11.9% Irish, 7.1% English (2000).
Economy: Employment by occupation: 8.9% management, 9.9% professional, 17.7% services, 33.7% sales, 3.2% farming, 5.3% construction, 21.3% production (2000).
Income: Per capita income: $17,493 (2000); Median household income: $40,556 (2000); Poverty rate: 3.9% (2000).

Taxes: Total city taxes per capita: $61 (1997); City property taxes per capita: $61 (1997).
Education: High school graduation rate: 83.9% (2000); College graduation rate: 14.3% (2000).
Housing: Homeownership rate: 91.0% (2000); Median home value: $109,500 (2000); Median rent: $488 per month (2000); Median age of housing: 22 years (2000).
Transportation: Commute to work: 89.7% car, 0.7% public transportation, 1.1% walk, 8.5% work from home (2000); Travel time to work: 57.8% less than 15 minutes, 17.8% 15 to 30 minutes, 5.0% 30 to 45 minutes, 5.4% 45 to 60 minutes, 14.0% 60 minutes or more (2000)

KATHIO (township). Covers a land area of 42.408 square miles and a water area of 30.199 square miles. Located at 46.20° N. Lat.; 93.77° W. Long.
Population: 1,309 (2000); Race: 44.2% White, 0.5% Black, 0.7% Asian, 50.7% American Indian and Alaska Native, 1.0% Hispanic of any race, 2.7% two or more races (2000); Density: 30.9 persons per square mile (2000); Age: 30.7% under 18, 15.2% over 64 (2000); Marriage status: 34.5% never married, 47.7% now married, 6.5% widowed, 11.3% divorced (2000); Foreign born: 1.3% (2000); Ancestry (includes multiple ancestries): 47.8% Other groups, 16.3% German, 8.7% Norwegian, 5.6% Irish, 5.5% Swedish (2000).
Economy: Employment by occupation: 12.3% management, 16.1% professional, 31.4% services, 23.0% sales, 0.0% farming, 10.1% construction, 7.1% production (2000).
Income: Per capita income: $13,690 (2000); Median household income: $26,719 (2000); Poverty rate: 24.7% (2000).
Education: High school graduation rate: 78.9% (2000); College graduation rate: 9.1% (2000).
Housing: Homeownership rate: 77.5% (2000); Median home value: $89,800 (2000); Median rent: $169 per month (2000); Median age of housing: 20 years (2000).
Transportation: Commute to work: 93.6% car, 0.4% public transportation, 4.6% walk, 0.9% work from home (2000); Travel time to work: 64.3% less than 15 minutes, 17.0% 15 to 30 minutes, 9.6% 30 to 45 minutes, 3.8% 45 to 60 minutes, 5.4% 60 minutes or more (2000)

LEWIS (township). Covers a land area of 35.736 square miles and a water area of 0.245 square miles. Located at 46.03° N. Lat.; 93.48° W. Long.
Population: 51 (2000); Race: 92.1% White, 0.0% Black, 0.0% Asian, 0.0% American Indian and Alaska Native, 0.0% Hispanic of any race, 7.9% two or more races (2000); Density: 1.4 persons per square mile (2000); Age: 17.5% under 18, 14.3% over 64 (2000); Marriage status: 19.6% never married, 57.1% now married, 3.6% widowed, 19.6% divorced (2000); Foreign born: 0.0% (2000); Ancestry (includes multiple ancestries): 27.0% Swedish, 23.8% German, 19.0% Irish, 12.7% Other groups, 9.5% Polish (2000).
Economy: Employment by occupation: 18.4% management, 5.3% professional, 7.9% services, 10.5% sales, 0.0% farming, 10.5% construction, 47.4% production (2000).
Income: Per capita income: $20,360 (2000); Median household income: $33,750 (2000); Poverty rate: 25.4% (2000).
Taxes: Total city taxes per capita: $85 (1997); City property taxes per capita: $85 (1997).
Education: High school graduation rate: 82.7% (2000); College graduation rate: 3.8% (2000).
Housing: Homeownership rate: 93.8% (2000); Median home value: $85,000 (2000); Median age of housing: 19 years (2000).
Transportation: Commute to work: 81.6% car, 0.0% public transportation, 7.9% walk, 0.0% work from home (2000); Travel time to work: 50.0% less than 15 minutes, 18.4% 15 to 30 minutes, 0.0% 30 to 45 minutes, 0.0% 45 to 60 minutes, 31.6% 60 minutes or more (2000)

MILACA (city). Covers a land area of 3.192 square miles and a water area of 0 square miles. Located at 45.75° N. Lat.; 93.65° W. Long. Elevation is 1,079 feet.
History: The town of Milaca, whose name is a corruption of Mille Lacs, was started by a lumber company owned by James J. Hill. Dairying replaced lumbering as the principal industry.
Population: 2,580 (2000); Race: 97.5% White, 0.0% Black, 0.3% Asian, 0.5% American Indian and Alaska Native, 1.1% Hispanic of any race, 1.6% two or more races (2000); Density: 808.2 persons per square mile (2000); Age: 22.8% under 18, 25.5% over 64 (2000); Marriage status: 18.5% never married, 53.8% now married, 15.5% widowed, 12.2% divorced (2000); Foreign born: 0.9% (2000); Ancestry (includes multiple ancestries): 29.6% German, 21.6% Swedish, 19.9% Norwegian, 9.2% Dutch, 6.7% Irish (2000).
Economy: Single-family building permits issued: 6 (2001) / 8 (2000); Multi-family building permits issued: 22 (2001) / 6 (2000); Employment by occupation: 6.9% management, 24.1% professional, 15.6% services, 21.2% sales, 1.1% farming, 8.2% construction, 22.9% production (2000).
Income: Per capita income: $17,005 (2000); Median household income: $26,964 (2000); Poverty rate: 15.6% (2000).
Taxes: Total city taxes per capita: $183 (1997); City property taxes per capita: $176 (1997).
Education: High school graduation rate: 76.8% (2000); College graduation rate: 15.2% (2000).

School District(s)

Milaca (PK-12)
2000 Enrollment: 1,828 320-982-7210

Housing: Homeownership rate: 63.2% (2000); Median home value: $77,700 (2000); Median rent: $353 per month (2000); Median age of housing: 37 years (2000).
Newspapers: Mille Lacs County Times (1 x week)
Transportation: Commute to work: 89.4% car, 0.0% public transportation, 5.1% walk, 4.1% work from home (2000); Travel time to work: 50.1% less than 15 minutes, 21.6% 15 to 30 minutes, 16.1% 30 to 45 minutes, 6.2% 45 to 60 minutes, 6.0% 60 minutes or more (2000)

MILACA (township). Covers a land area of 32.904 square miles and a water area of 0 square miles. Located at 45.77° N. Lat.; 93.68° W. Long. Elevation is 1,079 feet.
History: Settled 1888; incorporated 1897.
Population: 1,189 (2000); Race: 99.7% White, 0.0% Black, 0.2% Asian, 0.0% American Indian and Alaska Native, 0.2% Hispanic of any race, 0.2% two or more races (2000); Density: 36.1 persons per square mile (2000); Age: 31.5% under 18, 10.7% over 64 (2000); Marriage status: 20.2% never married, 70.2% now married, 3.8% widowed, 5.7% divorced (2000); Foreign born: 0.8% (2000); Ancestry (includes multiple ancestries): 40.8% German, 23.3% Swedish, 13.9% Norwegian, 7.6% Irish, 5.8% Dutch (2000).
Economy: Trading point in agricultural area: grain; livestock, poultry; dairying. Manufacturing: concrete, coin and currency wrappers, medical instruments; printing and publishing. Employment by occupation: 10.0% management, 13.3% professional, 15.4% services, 24.6% sales, 1.4% farming, 11.7% construction, 23.6% production (2000).
Income: Per capita income: $17,403 (2000); Median household income: $45,313 (2000); Poverty rate: 4.5% (2000).
Taxes: Total city taxes per capita: $27 (1997); City property taxes per capita: $27 (1997).
Education: High school graduation rate: 86.2% (2000); College graduation rate: 11.8% (2000).
Housing: Homeownership rate: 92.9% (2000); Median home value: $111,200 (2000); Median rent: $450 per month (2000); Median age of housing: 24 years (2000).
Transportation: Commute to work: 91.5% car, 0.0% public transportation, 0.8% walk, 7.4% work from home (2000); Travel time to work: 40.2% less than 15 minutes, 18.8% 15 to 30 minutes, 13.6% 30 to 45 minutes, 11.0% 45 to 60 minutes, 16.4% 60 minutes or more (2000)

MILO (township). Covers a land area of 34.843 square miles and a water area of 0 square miles. Located at 45.68° N. Lat.; 93.68° W. Long.
Population: 1,076 (2000); Race: 98.4% White, 0.0% Black, 0.0% Asian, 0.5% American Indian and Alaska Native, 2.2% Hispanic of any race, 0.9% two or more races (2000); Density: 30.9 persons per square mile (2000); Age: 29.3% under 18, 9.8% over 64 (2000); Marriage status: 23.3% never married, 64.1% now married, 4.1% widowed, 8.5% divorced (2000); Foreign born: 0.3% (2000); Ancestry (includes multiple ancestries): 38.0% German, 23.1% Swedish, 18.7% Dutch, 12.9% Norwegian, 7.3% Irish (2000).
Economy: Employment by occupation: 16.0% management, 11.4% professional, 8.9% services, 19.8% sales, 0.9% farming, 13.3% construction, 29.8% production (2000).
Income: Per capita income: $18,327 (2000); Median household income: $44,868 (2000); Poverty rate: 8.7% (2000).
Taxes: Total city taxes per capita: $25 (1997); City property taxes per capita: $25 (1997).
Education: High school graduation rate: 81.0% (2000); College graduation rate: 11.0% (2000).
Housing: Homeownership rate: 93.8% (2000); Median home value: $97,100 (2000); Median rent: $333 per month (2000); Median age of housing: 35 years (2000).
Transportation: Commute to work: 86.4% car, 0.0% public transportation, 3.8% walk, 9.1% work from home (2000); Travel time to work: 41.4% less

than 15 minutes, 27.4% 15 to 30 minutes, 10.6% 30 to 45 minutes, 9.5% 45 to 60 minutes, 11.2% 60 minutes or more (2000)

MUDGETT (township). Covers a land area of 30.149 square miles and a water area of 0.088 square miles. Located at 45.95° N. Lat.; 93.58° W. Long.
Population: 85 (2000); Race: 97.8% White, 0.0% Black, 0.0% Asian, 0.0% American Indian and Alaska Native, 0.0% Hispanic of any race, 2.2% two or more races (2000); Density: 2.8 persons per square mile (2000); Age: 25.6% under 18, 5.6% over 64 (2000); Marriage status: 26.5% never married, 69.1% now married, 4.4% widowed, 0.0% divorced (2000); Foreign born: 0.0% (2000); Ancestry (includes multiple ancestries): 41.1% German, 16.7% Norwegian, 16.7% United States or American, 11.1% Irish, 10.0% English (2000).
Economy: Employment by occupation: 5.6% management, 20.4% professional, 18.5% services, 16.7% sales, 3.7% farming, 16.7% construction, 18.5% production (2000).
Income: Per capita income: $17,937 (2000); Median household income: $67,917 (2000); Poverty rate: 0.0% (2000).
Education: High school graduation rate: 83.9% (2000); College graduation rate: 22.6% (2000).
Housing: Homeownership rate: 92.9% (2000); Median home value: $225,000 (2000); Median age of housing: 26 years (2000).
Transportation: Commute to work: 75.9% car, 0.0% public transportation, 9.3% walk, 14.8% work from home (2000); Travel time to work: 26.1% less than 15 minutes, 28.3% 15 to 30 minutes, 26.1% 30 to 45 minutes, 13.0% 45 to 60 minutes, 6.5% 60 minutes or more (2000)

ONAMIA (city). Covers a land area of 0.903 square miles and a water area of <.001 square miles. Located at 46.07° N. Lat.; 93.66° W. Long. Elevation is 1,255 feet.
Population: 847 (2000); Race: 92.0% White, 0.8% Black, 0.0% Asian, 5.2% American Indian and Alaska Native, 0.0% Hispanic of any race, 1.9% two or more races (2000); Density: 938.3 persons per square mile (2000); Age: 28.3% under 18, 26.9% over 64 (2000); Marriage status: 28.2% never married, 52.2% now married, 10.6% widowed, 9.0% divorced (2000); Foreign born: 0.6% (2000); Ancestry (includes multiple ancestries): 29.0% German, 11.4% Irish, 9.5% Swedish, 8.2% Norwegian, 5.8% Other groups (2000).
Economy: Single-family building permits issued: 3 (2001) / 3 (2000); Multi-family building permits issued: 0 (2001) / 0 (2000); Employment by occupation: 2.7% management, 25.9% professional, 24.5% services, 21.4% sales, 0.3% farming, 5.1% construction, 20.1% production (2000).
Income: Per capita income: $12,857 (2000); Median household income: $21,250 (2000); Poverty rate: 14.6% (2000).
Taxes: Total city taxes per capita: $78 (1997); City property taxes per capita: $73 (1997).
Education: High school graduation rate: 71.4% (2000); College graduation rate: 17.4% (2000).

School District(s)

Onamia (PK-12)
2000 Enrollment: 846 320-532-4174

Housing: Homeownership rate: 52.9% (2000); Median home value: $62,900 (2000); Median rent: $273 per month (2000); Median age of housing: 32 years (2000).
Hospitals: Mille Lacs Health System (108 beds)
Transportation: Commute to work: 75.0% car, 0.0% public transportation, 20.9% walk, 3.4% work from home (2000); Travel time to work: 66.3% less than 15 minutes, 21.3% 15 to 30 minutes, 9.2% 30 to 45 minutes, 0.7% 45 to 60 minutes, 2.5% 60 minutes or more (2000)

ONAMIA (township). Covers a land area of 35.905 square miles and a water area of 0.191 square miles. Located at 46.01° N. Lat.; 93.64° W. Long. Elevation is 1,255 feet.
Population: 583 (2000); Race: 94.1% White, 0.3% Black, 0.2% Asian, 2.9% American Indian and Alaska Native, 0.8% Hispanic of any race, 2.1% two or more races (2000); Density: 16.2 persons per square mile (2000); Age: 29.8% under 18, 10.3% over 64 (2000); Marriage status: 23.5% never married, 60.2% now married, 6.1% widowed, 10.2% divorced (2000); Foreign born: 0.7% (2000); Ancestry (includes multiple ancestries): 44.7% German, 15.7% Norwegian, 14.7% Swedish, 8.2% Irish, 5.2% Other groups (2000).
Economy: Agriculture: grain; livestock, poultry; dairying. Manufacturing: lumber and wood chips, custom circuit hybrid manufacturing. Timber. Employment by occupation: 7.5% management, 11.4% professional, 27.8% services, 14.1% sales, 2.3% farming, 14.4% construction, 22.5% production (2000).
Income: Per capita income: $15,735 (2000); Median household income: $33,889 (2000); Poverty rate: 14.4% (2000).
Taxes: Total city taxes per capita: $119 (1997); City property taxes per capita: $119 (1997).
Education: High school graduation rate: 78.9% (2000); College graduation rate: 8.9% (2000).
Housing: Homeownership rate: 81.4% (2000); Median home value: $82,500 (2000); Median rent: $388 per month (2000); Median age of housing: 23 years (2000).
Transportation: Commute to work: 83.5% car, 0.0% public transportation, 5.4% walk, 9.1% work from home (2000); Travel time to work: 51.9% less than 15 minutes, 23.0% 15 to 30 minutes, 7.4% 30 to 45 minutes, 4.4% 45 to 60 minutes, 13.3% 60 minutes or more (2000)

PAGE (township). Covers a land area of 35.751 square miles and a water area of 0 square miles. Located at 45.85° N. Lat.; 93.69° W. Long. Elevation is 1,211 feet.
Population: 600 (2000); Race: 99.7% White, 0.0% Black, 0.0% Asian, 0.0% American Indian and Alaska Native, 0.0% Hispanic of any race, 0.3% two or more races (2000); Density: 16.8 persons per square mile (2000); Age: 31.0% under 18, 8.3% over 64 (2000); Marriage status: 21.1% never married, 67.4% now married, 3.8% widowed, 7.7% divorced (2000); Foreign born: 0.8% (2000); Ancestry (includes multiple ancestries): 39.3% German, 16.5% Norwegian, 15.1% Swedish, 7.7% Polish, 5.9% English (2000).
Economy: Employment by occupation: 5.7% management, 10.3% professional, 16.0% services, 22.4% sales, 1.2% farming, 15.7% construction, 28.7% production (2000).
Income: Per capita income: $17,050 (2000); Median household income: $45,556 (2000); Poverty rate: 3.0% (2000).
Taxes: Total city taxes per capita: $51 (1997); City property taxes per capita: $51 (1997).
Education: High school graduation rate: 84.7% (2000); College graduation rate: 8.2% (2000).
Housing: Homeownership rate: 95.9% (2000); Median home value: $96,000 (2000); Median rent: $300 per month (2000); Median age of housing: 20 years (2000).
Transportation: Commute to work: 86.4% car, 2.1% public transportation, 2.7% walk, 8.8% work from home (2000); Travel time to work: 17.5% less than 15 minutes, 30.5% 15 to 30 minutes, 22.2% 30 to 45 minutes, 12.6% 45 to 60 minutes, 17.2% 60 minutes or more (2000)

PEASE (city). Covers a land area of 0.433 square miles and a water area of 0 square miles. Located at 45.69° N. Lat.; 93.64° W. Long. Elevation is 1,028 feet.
Population: 163 (2000); Race: 100.0% White, 0.0% Black, 0.0% Asian, 0.0% American Indian and Alaska Native, 2.1% Hispanic of any race, 0.0% two or more races (2000); Density: 376.4 persons per square mile (2000); Age: 27.3% under 18, 12.8% over 64 (2000); Marriage status: 32.9% never married, 55.0% now married, 6.0% widowed, 6.0% divorced (2000); Foreign born: 0.0% (2000); Ancestry (includes multiple ancestries): 24.6% German, 22.5% Swedish, 21.4% Dutch, 16.0% Norwegian, 4.3% Czech (2000).
Economy: Dairying; grain; livestock. Employment by occupation: 4.6% management, 11.1% professional, 14.8% services, 20.4% sales, 2.8% farming, 13.0% construction, 33.3% production (2000).
Income: Per capita income: $17,344 (2000); Median household income: $35,833 (2000); Poverty rate: 10.2% (2000).
Taxes: Total city taxes per capita: $36 (1997); City property taxes per capita: $36 (1997).
Education: High school graduation rate: 88.2% (2000); College graduation rate: 9.2% (2000).
Housing: Homeownership rate: 82.4% (2000); Median home value: $75,800 (2000); Median rent: $471 per month (2000); Median age of housing: 54 years (2000).
Transportation: Commute to work: 92.5% car, 0.0% public transportation, 5.7% walk, 1.9% work from home (2000); Travel time to work: 35.6% less than 15 minutes, 23.1% 15 to 30 minutes, 18.3% 30 to 45 minutes, 3.8% 45 to 60 minutes, 19.2% 60 minutes or more (2000)

PRINCETON (city). Covers a land area of 4.431 square miles and a water area of 0.005 square miles. Located at 45.57° N. Lat.; 93.58° W. Long. Elevation is 983 feet.
History: Princeton developed as a shipping center for the surrounding farming area, with a creamery producing butter for export. For a time, Princeton served as the seat of Mille Lacs County.
Population: 3,933 (2000); Race: 97.0% White, 0.4% Black, 0.4% Asian, 1.1% American Indian and Alaska Native, 1.4% Hispanic of any race, 0.8%

two or more races (2000); Density: 887.7 persons per square mile (2000); Age: 24.6% under 18, 19.5% over 64 (2000); Marriage status: 25.6% never married, 50.4% now married, 12.1% widowed, 11.9% divorced (2000); Foreign born: 1.8% (2000); Ancestry (includes multiple ancestries): 39.0% German, 20.6% Norwegian, 19.2% Swedish, 10.6% Irish, 7.3% Other groups (2000).
Economy: Single-family building permits issued: 56 (2001) / 56 (2000); Multi-family building permits issued: 3 (2001) / 0 (2000); Employment by occupation: 5.1% management, 14.1% professional, 13.5% services, 26.4% sales, 0.7% farming, 9.7% construction, 30.5% production (2000).
Income: Per capita income: $18,381 (2000); Median household income: $35,216 (2000); Poverty rate: 6.7% (2000).
Taxes: Total city taxes per capita: $283 (1997); City property taxes per capita: $268 (1997).
Education: High school graduation rate: 76.8% (2000); College graduation rate: 11.6% (2000).

School District(s)

Princeton (PK-12)
2000 Enrollment: 3,095 763-389-2422
Housing: Homeownership rate: 64.9% (2000); Median home value: $88,400 (2000); Median rent: $394 per month (2000); Median age of housing: 28 years (2000).
Hospitals: Fairview Northland Regional Health Care (41 beds)
Safety: Violent crime rate: 25.2 per 10,000 population; Property crime rate: 505.7 per 10,000 population (2001).
Newspapers: Princeton Union-Eagle (1 x week); Town & Country Shopper (1 x week)
Transportation: Commute to work: 93.0% car, 0.0% public transportation, 4.1% walk, 2.0% work from home (2000); Travel time to work: 48.5% less than 15 minutes, 17.1% 15 to 30 minutes, 15.4% 30 to 45 minutes, 9.4% 45 to 60 minutes, 9.6% 60 minutes or more (2000)
Additional Information Contacts
Princeton Area Chamber of Commerce 763-389-1764

PRINCETON (township). Covers a land area of 32.575 square miles and a water area of 0.409 square miles. Located at 45.59° N. Lat.; 93.56° W. Long. Elevation is 983 feet.
History: Plotted 1856, incorporated 1877.
Population: 1,947 (2000); Race: 98.2% White, 0.1% Black, 0.4% Asian, 0.2% American Indian and Alaska Native, 1.9% Hispanic of any race, 0.9% two or more races (2000); Density: 59.8 persons per square mile (2000); Age: 28.5% under 18, 10.3% over 64 (2000); Marriage status: 24.1% never married, 64.8% now married, 3.7% widowed, 7.5% divorced (2000); Foreign born: 0.7% (2000); Ancestry (includes multiple ancestries): 41.8% German, 16.4% Swedish, 14.4% Norwegian, 6.9% Irish, 5.2% English (2000).
Economy: Shipping point in agricultural area; grain, soybeans; livestock, poultry; dairying. Manufacturing: fabricated metal products, wood products, transportation equipment, plastic products, printing and publishing. Sherburne National Wildlife Refuge to Southwest. Single-family building permits issued: 16 (2001) / 14 (2000); Multi-family building permits issued: 0 (2001) / 0 (2000); Employment by occupation: 10.8% management, 11.4% professional, 13.4% services, 27.1% sales, 0.5% farming, 14.6% construction, 22.3% production (2000).
Income: Per capita income: $20,736 (2000); Median household income: $52,083 (2000); Poverty rate: 4.7% (2000).
Taxes: Total city taxes per capita: $81 (2000); City property taxes per capita: $64 (2000).
Education: High school graduation rate: 87.2% (2000); College graduation rate: 12.9% (2000).
Housing: Homeownership rate: 94.7% (2000); Median home value: $112,400 (2000); Median rent: $389 per month (2000); Median age of housing: 27 years (2000).
Transportation: Commute to work: 89.2% car, 0.0% public transportation, 3.9% walk, 6.5% work from home (2000); Travel time to work: 41.2% less than 15 minutes, 16.9% 15 to 30 minutes, 13.0% 30 to 45 minutes, 11.9% 45 to 60 minutes, 17.1% 60 minutes or more (2000)

SOUTH HARBOR (township). Covers a land area of 21.308 square miles and a water area of 53.779 square miles. Located at 46.10° N. Lat.; 93.62° W. Long.
Population: 885 (2000); Race: 94.3% White, 0.0% Black, 0.8% Asian, 2.2% American Indian and Alaska Native, 0.5% Hispanic of any race, 2.8% two or more races (2000); Density: 41.5 persons per square mile (2000); Age: 25.3% under 18, 18.3% over 64 (2000); Marriage status: 18.0% never married, 69.1% now married, 3.5% widowed, 9.4% divorced (2000); Foreign born: 1.1% (2000); Ancestry (includes multiple ancestries): 35.7% German, 20.2% Swedish, 16.0% Norwegian, 8.0% Irish, 6.2% French (except Basque) (2000).
Economy: Employment by occupation: 14.5% management, 13.4% professional, 23.8% services, 18.6% sales, 1.0% farming, 13.7% construction, 15.0% production (2000).
Income: Per capita income: $19,742 (2000); Median household income: $36,058 (2000); Poverty rate: 10.6% (2000).
Taxes: Total city taxes per capita: $119 (1997); City property taxes per capita: $116 (1997).
Education: High school graduation rate: 84.1% (2000); College graduation rate: 16.2% (2000).
Housing: Homeownership rate: 81.9% (2000); Median home value: $128,000 (2000); Median rent: $336 per month (2000); Median age of housing: 33 years (2000).
Transportation: Commute to work: 88.3% car, 0.8% public transportation, 3.1% walk, 6.3% work from home (2000); Travel time to work: 56.3% less than 15 minutes, 17.3% 15 to 30 minutes, 8.6% 30 to 45 minutes, 3.9% 45 to 60 minutes, 13.9% 60 minutes or more (2000)

VINELAND (CDP). Covers a land area of 6.533 square miles and a water area of 0.119 square miles. Located at 46.18° N. Lat.; 93.75° W. Long. Elevation is 1,261 feet.
Population: 607 (2000); Race: 4.8% White, 0.0% Black, 0.4% Asian, 91.4% American Indian and Alaska Native, 1.5% Hispanic of any race, 1.9% two or more races (2000); Density: 92.9 persons per square mile (2000); Age: 43.8% under 18, 8.0% over 64 (2000); Marriage status: 58.5% never married, 24.0% now married, 5.6% widowed, 11.9% divorced (2000); Foreign born: 1.1% (2000); Ancestry (includes multiple ancestries): 80.3% Other groups, 2.2% German, 1.3% Norwegian, 0.9% Dutch, 0.7% Swedish (2000).
Economy: Employment by occupation: 9.5% management, 9.5% professional, 36.5% services, 30.4% sales, 0.0% farming, 7.4% construction, 6.8% production (2000).
Income: Per capita income: $7,738 (2000); Median household income: $20,208 (2000); Poverty rate: 40.6% (2000).
Education: High school graduation rate: 76.3% (2000); College graduation rate: 0.8% (2000).
Housing: Homeownership rate: 52.3% (2000); Median home value: $61,300 (2000); Median rent: $160 per month (2000); Median age of housing: 17 years (2000).
Transportation: Commute to work: 87.8% car, 0.0% public transportation, 10.8% walk, 0.0% work from home (2000); Travel time to work: 79.7% less than 15 minutes, 2.7% 15 to 30 minutes, 6.1% 30 to 45 minutes, 4.1% 45 to 60 minutes, 7.4% 60 minutes or more (2000)

WAHKON (city). Covers a land area of 0.979 square miles and a water area of <.001 square miles. Located at 46.12° N. Lat.; 93.52° W. Long. Elevation is 1,260 feet.
Population: 314 (2000); Race: 95.3% White, 0.0% Black, 0.0% Asian, 3.3% American Indian and Alaska Native, 0.7% Hispanic of any race, 1.5% two or more races (2000); Density: 320.7 persons per square mile (2000); Age: 16.4% under 18, 24.1% over 64 (2000); Marriage status: 16.1% never married, 48.8% now married, 16.1% widowed, 19.0% divorced (2000); Foreign born: 0.0% (2000); Ancestry (includes multiple ancestries): 28.8% German, 20.1% Norwegian, 16.8% Irish, 9.9% Swedish, 5.8% English (2000).
Economy: Agriculture includes grain; livestock, poultry; dairying. Manufacturing includes gears, log homes. Single-family building permits issued: 0 (2001) / 0 (2000); Multi-family building permits issued: 0 (2001) / 0 (2000); Employment by occupation: 4.4% management, 13.2% professional, 18.4% services, 21.9% sales, 0.0% farming, 15.8% construction, 26.3% production (2000).
Income: Per capita income: $16,088 (2000); Median household income: $22,321 (2000); Poverty rate: 22.6% (2000).
Taxes: Total city taxes per capita: $183 (1997); City property taxes per capita: $157 (1997).
Education: High school graduation rate: 83.6% (2000); College graduation rate: 7.9% (2000).
Housing: Homeownership rate: 78.3% (2000); Median home value: $74,100 (2000); Median rent: $321 per month (2000); Median age of housing: 33 years (2000).
Transportation: Commute to work: 93.0% car, 0.0% public transportation, 1.8% walk, 0.9% work from home (2000); Travel time to work: 43.4% less than 15 minutes, 18.6% 15 to 30 minutes, 14.2% 30 to 45 minutes, 8.8% 45 to 60 minutes, 15.0% 60 minutes or more (2000)

Morrison County

Located in central Minnesota; drained by the Mississippi River; includes Lake Alexander. Covers a land area of 1,124.50 square miles, a water area of 28.80 square miles, and is located in the Central Time Zone. The county government was organized in 1856. County seat is Little Falls.

Weather Station: Little Falls 1 N Elevation: 1,118 feet

	Jan	Feb	Mar	Apr	May	Jun	Jul	Aug	Sep	Oct	Nov	Dec
High	20	28	39	57	71	79	84	81	72	59	38	25
Low	-1	6	18	32	45	54	59	57	47	36	21	6
Precip	0.8	0.5	1.4	2.0	3.0	4.3	3.5	3.4	2.8	2.5	1.4	0.6
Snow	12.7	7.4	9.2	2.3	tr	0.0	0.0	0.0	tr	0.6	8.2	8.4

High and Low temperatures in degrees Fahrenheit; Precipitation and Snow in inches

Population: 31,712 (2000); Race: 98.6% White, 0.2% Black, 0.4% Asian, 0.2% American Indian and Alaska Native, 0.6% Hispanic of any race, 0.4% two or more races (2000); Density: 28.2 persons per square mile (2000); Age: 28.0% under 18, 15.6% over 64 (2000).
Religion: Five largest groups: 48.1% Catholic Church, 6.7% Lutheran Church—Missouri Synod, 5.5% Evangelical Lutheran Church in America, 1.5% The United Methodist Church, 1.4% The Christian and Missionary Alliance (2000).
Economy: Unemployment rate: 5.7% (11/2002); Total civilian labor force: 15,348 (11/2002); Leading industries: 23.2% manufacturing; 18.1% retail trade; 17.8% health care and social assistance (2000); Companies that employ more than 1,000 persons: 0 (2000); Companies that employ more than 100 persons: 12 (2000); Farms: 1,808 totaling 430,467 acres (1997); Minority business ownership rate: 0.0% (1997); Women business ownership rate: 20.8% (1997); Retail sales per capita: $8,134 (1997). Single-family building permits issued: 276 (2001) / 238 (2000); Multi-family building permits issued: 66 (2001) / 58 (2000).
Income: Per capita income: $16,566 (2000); Median household income: $37,047 (2000); Poverty rate: 11.1% (2000); Bankruptcy rate: 2.45% (2001).
Taxes: Total county taxes per capita: $275 (2000); County property taxes per capita: $272 (2000).
Education: High school graduation rate: 79.7% (2000); College graduation rate: 12.6% (2000).
Housing: Homeownership rate: 82.0% (2000); Median home value: $82,800 (2000); Median rent: $344 per month (2000); Median age of housing: 31 years (2000).
Health: Birth rate: 124.2 per 10,000 population (1998); Age adjusted death rate: 76.2 per 10,000 population (1999); Age adjusted cancer mortality rate: 186.3 deaths per 100,000 population (1999). Number of physicians: 10.1 per 10,000 population (1999); Number of hospital beds: 62.8 per 10,000 population (1999).
Elections: 2000 Presidential election results: 35.9% Gore, 55.9% Bush, 4.3% Nader, 3.4% Buchanan
National and State Parks: Charles A Lindbergh State Park; Coon Lake State Wildlife Management Area; Culdrum State Wildlife Management Area; Ereaua State Wildlife Management Area; Little Elk State Wildlife Management Area; Mud Lake State Wildlife Management Area; Popple Lake State Wildlife Management Area; Rice-Skunk Lake State Wildlife Management A; Sponsa State Wildlife Management Area; Wittiker State Wildlife Management Area
Additional Information Contacts
Morrison County Government Offices.................... 320-632-2941
Little Falls Chamber of Commerce...................... 320-632-5155
Upsala Chamber of Commerce............................ 320-573-4477

Morrison County Communities

AGRAM (township). Covers a land area of 19.675 square miles and a water area of 0.406 square miles. Located at 45.96° N. Lat.; 94.17° W. Long.
Population: 534 (2000); Race: 100.0% White, 0.0% Black, 0.0% Asian, 0.0% American Indian and Alaska Native, 0.0% Hispanic of any race, 0.0% two or more races (2000); Density: 27.1 persons per square mile (2000); Age: 32.2% under 18, 9.5% over 64 (2000); Marriage status: 23.4% never married, 68.5% now married, 3.0% widowed, 5.0% divorced (2000); Foreign born: 0.8% (2000); Ancestry (includes multiple ancestries): 58.7% German, 12.7% Norwegian, 11.6% Polish, 6.6% United States or American, 5.1% Swedish (2000).
Economy: Employment by occupation: 16.9% management, 19.8% professional, 16.2% services, 19.1% sales, 1.8% farming, 17.6% construction, 8.6% production (2000).
Income: Per capita income: $17,133 (2000); Median household income: $45,500 (2000); Poverty rate: 7.6% (2000).
Taxes: Total city taxes per capita: $73 (1997); City property taxes per capita: $73 (1997).
Education: High school graduation rate: 89.0% (2000); College graduation rate: 13.9% (2000).
Housing: Homeownership rate: 89.7% (2000); Median home value: $121,300 (2000); Median rent: $231 per month (2000); Median age of housing: 23 years (2000).
Transportation: Commute to work: 85.8% car, 0.0% public transportation, 2.9% walk, 11.3% work from home (2000); Travel time to work: 44.4% less than 15 minutes, 33.7% 15 to 30 minutes, 9.5% 30 to 45 minutes, 4.5% 45 to 60 minutes, 7.8% 60 minutes or more (2000)

BELLE PRAIRIE (township). Covers a land area of 44.486 square miles and a water area of 1.022 square miles. Located at 46.02° N. Lat.; 94.28° W. Long.
Population: 1,647 (2000); Race: 98.6% White, 0.9% Black, 0.4% Asian, 0.0% American Indian and Alaska Native, 0.8% Hispanic of any race, 0.1% two or more races (2000); Density: 37.0 persons per square mile (2000); Age: 29.7% under 18, 12.6% over 64 (2000); Marriage status: 18.9% never married, 70.2% now married, 5.1% widowed, 5.9% divorced (2000); Foreign born: 1.1% (2000); Ancestry (includes multiple ancestries): 53.0% German, 16.2% Polish, 11.9% Norwegian, 10.0% Swedish, 8.0% Irish (2000).
Economy: Employment by occupation: 14.6% management, 25.7% professional, 13.9% services, 23.3% sales, 1.3% farming, 8.5% construction, 12.7% production (2000).
Income: Per capita income: $21,809 (2000); Median household income: $50,156 (2000); Poverty rate: 4.7% (2000).
Taxes: Total city taxes per capita: $33 (1997); City property taxes per capita: $32 (1997).
Education: High school graduation rate: 86.3% (2000); College graduation rate: 26.2% (2000).
Housing: Homeownership rate: 90.7% (2000); Median home value: $102,600 (2000); Median rent: $425 per month (2000); Median age of housing: 26 years (2000).
Transportation: Commute to work: 92.0% car, 0.1% public transportation, 1.7% walk, 5.7% work from home (2000); Travel time to work: 50.7% less than 15 minutes, 29.0% 15 to 30 minutes, 8.6% 30 to 45 minutes, 6.4% 45 to 60 minutes, 5.4% 60 minutes or more (2000)

BELLEVUE (township). Covers a land area of 45.086 square miles and a water area of 0.656 square miles. Located at 45.87° N. Lat.; 94.28° W. Long.
Population: 1,115 (2000); Race: 98.2% White, 0.3% Black, 0.0% Asian, 0.4% American Indian and Alaska Native, 0.4% Hispanic of any race, 1.0% two or more races (2000); Density: 24.7 persons per square mile (2000); Age: 33.5% under 18, 7.8% over 64 (2000); Marriage status: 24.8% never married, 67.0% now married, 2.9% widowed, 5.3% divorced (2000); Foreign born: 0.2% (2000); Ancestry (includes multiple ancestries): 52.5% German, 25.9% Polish, 9.0% Norwegian, 7.3% Irish, 7.0% United States or American (2000).
Economy: Employment by occupation: 12.0% management, 13.5% professional, 12.6% services, 23.8% sales, 2.6% farming, 9.8% construction, 25.7% production (2000).
Income: Per capita income: $15,384 (2000); Median household income: $44,886 (2000); Poverty rate: 11.0% (2000).
Taxes: Total city taxes per capita: $93 (1997); City property taxes per capita: $93 (1997).
Education: High school graduation rate: 85.0% (2000); College graduation rate: 9.0% (2000).
Housing: Homeownership rate: 91.1% (2000); Median home value: $120,100 (2000); Median rent: $389 per month (2000); Median age of housing: 22 years (2000).
Transportation: Commute to work: 91.2% car, 0.0% public transportation, 0.4% walk, 6.8% work from home (2000); Travel time to work: 29.4% less than 15 minutes, 29.2% 15 to 30 minutes, 29.2% 30 to 45 minutes, 7.6% 45 to 60 minutes, 4.6% 60 minutes or more (2000)

BOWLUS (city). Covers a land area of 1.249 square miles and a water area of 0 square miles. Located at 45.82° N. Lat.; 94.40° W. Long. Elevation is 1,108 feet.
Population: 260 (2000); Race: 100.0% White, 0.0% Black, 0.0% Asian, 0.0% American Indian and Alaska Native, 0.0% Hispanic of any race, 0.0% two or more races (2000); Density: 208.2 persons per square mile (2000); Age: 27.2% under 18, 17.2% over 64 (2000); Marriage status: 20.6% never married, 64.5% now married, 11.0% widowed, 3.9% divorced (2000);

Foreign born: 0.0% (2000); Ancestry (includes multiple ancestries): 51.4% Polish, 41.4% German, 10.3% Norwegian, 2.8% Irish, 2.1% Finnish (2000).
Economy: Grain, potatoes, sunflowers; livestock, poultry; dairying. Manufacturing: feeds. Single-family building permits issued: 0 (2001) / 0 (2000); Multi-family building permits issued: 0 (2001) / 0 (2000); Employment by occupation: 7.2% management, 18.8% professional, 8.0% services, 15.2% sales, 0.0% farming, 9.4% construction, 41.3% production (2000).
Income: Per capita income: $13,868 (2000); Median household income: $32,222 (2000); Poverty rate: 10.3% (2000).
Taxes: Total city taxes per capita: $82 (1997); City property taxes per capita: $70 (1997).
Education: High school graduation rate: 69.8% (2000); College graduation rate: 8.5% (2000).
Housing: Homeownership rate: 85.1% (2000); Median home value: $70,000 (2000); Median rent: $314 per month (2000); Median age of housing: 55 years (2000).
Transportation: Commute to work: 93.4% car, 0.0% public transportation, 2.2% walk, 4.4% work from home (2000); Travel time to work: 16.9% less than 15 minutes, 32.3% 15 to 30 minutes, 40.8% 30 to 45 minutes, 5.4% 45 to 60 minutes, 4.6% 60 minutes or more (2000)

BUCKMAN (city). Covers a land area of 1.027 square miles and a water area of 0 square miles. Located at 45.89° N. Lat.; 94.09° W. Long. Elevation is 1,210 feet.
Population: 208 (2000); Race: 100.0% White, 0.0% Black, 0.0% Asian, 0.0% American Indian and Alaska Native, 0.0% Hispanic of any race, 0.0% two or more races (2000); Density: 202.5 persons per square mile (2000); Age: 32.4% under 18, 17.2% over 64 (2000); Marriage status: 26.4% never married, 61.5% now married, 5.4% widowed, 6.8% divorced (2000); Foreign born: 1.0% (2000); Ancestry (includes multiple ancestries): 65.2% German, 16.7% Polish, 5.4% United States or American, 3.9% French (except Basque), 3.9% Norwegian (2000).
Economy: Single-family building permits issued: 3 (2001) / 2 (2000); Multi-family building permits issued: 0 (2001) / 0 (2000); Employment by occupation: 9.5% management, 9.5% professional, 8.3% services, 23.8% sales, 6.0% farming, 22.6% construction, 20.2% production (2000).
Income: Per capita income: $13,700 (2000); Median household income: $32,500 (2000); Poverty rate: 6.9% (2000).
Taxes: Total city taxes per capita: $85 (1997); City property taxes per capita: $70 (1997).
Education: High school graduation rate: 85.3% (2000); College graduation rate: 5.5% (2000).
Housing: Homeownership rate: 87.0% (2000); Median home value: $66,300 (2000); Median rent: $363 per month (2000); Median age of housing: 43 years (2000).
Transportation: Commute to work: 88.9% car, 0.0% public transportation, 2.5% walk, 6.2% work from home (2000); Travel time to work: 42.1% less than 15 minutes, 30.3% 15 to 30 minutes, 14.5% 30 to 45 minutes, 10.5% 45 to 60 minutes, 2.6% 60 minutes or more (2000)

BUCKMAN (township). Covers a land area of 54.545 square miles and a water area of 0.052 square miles. Located at 45.86° N. Lat.; 94.10° W. Long. Elevation is 1,210 feet.
Population: 717 (2000); Race: 99.0% White, 0.0% Black, 0.7% Asian, 0.3% American Indian and Alaska Native, 0.0% Hispanic of any race, 0.0% two or more races (2000); Density: 13.1 persons per square mile (2000); Age: 33.7% under 18, 8.1% over 64 (2000); Marriage status: 30.6% never married, 64.2% now married, 2.4% widowed, 2.8% divorced (2000); Foreign born: 1.8% (2000); Ancestry (includes multiple ancestries): 66.3% German, 28.6% Polish, 5.7% United States or American, 3.7% Norwegian, 2.2% French (except Basque) (2000).
Economy: Agricultural area: dairying; poultry; potatoes, grain. Employment by occupation: 25.0% management, 7.9% professional, 12.8% services, 16.3% sales, 3.8% farming, 13.5% construction, 20.7% production (2000).
Income: Per capita income: $16,638 (2000); Median household income: $45,489 (2000); Poverty rate: 6.8% (2000).
Taxes: Total city taxes per capita: $35 (1997); City property taxes per capita: $35 (1997).
Education: High school graduation rate: 81.7% (2000); College graduation rate: 9.4% (2000).
Housing: Homeownership rate: 91.5% (2000); Median home value: $98,300 (2000); Median rent: $375 per month (2000); Median age of housing: 28 years (2000).
Transportation: Commute to work: 75.6% car, 0.0% public transportation, 2.1% walk, 21.3% work from home (2000); Travel time to work: 21.6% less than 15 minutes, 29.7% 15 to 30 minutes, 29.1% 30 to 45 minutes, 10.8% 45 to 60 minutes, 8.8% 60 minutes or more (2000)

BUH (township). Covers a land area of 35.816 square miles and a water area of 0.055 square miles. Located at 46.03° N. Lat.; 94.14° W. Long.
Population: 572 (2000); Race: 99.3% White, 0.0% Black, 0.0% Asian, 0.0% American Indian and Alaska Native, 3.4% Hispanic of any race, 0.0% two or more races (2000); Density: 16.0 persons per square mile (2000); Age: 30.1% under 18, 8.9% over 64 (2000); Marriage status: 32.4% never married, 61.3% now married, 3.2% widowed, 3.2% divorced (2000); Foreign born: 2.1% (2000); Ancestry (includes multiple ancestries): 71.3% German, 15.7% Polish, 5.9% United States or American, 5.5% Norwegian, 5.3% French (except Basque) (2000).
Economy: Employment by occupation: 30.9% management, 4.6% professional, 13.1% services, 21.6% sales, 8.5% farming, 8.9% construction, 12.4% production (2000).
Income: Per capita income: $13,168 (2000); Median household income: $33,036 (2000); Poverty rate: 14.1% (2000).
Education: High school graduation rate: 79.8% (2000); College graduation rate: 5.0% (2000).
Housing: Homeownership rate: 92.5% (2000); Median home value: $91,200 (2000); Median rent: $225 per month (2000); Median age of housing: 34 years (2000).
Transportation: Commute to work: 69.4% car, 0.0% public transportation, 11.4% walk, 18.5% work from home (2000); Travel time to work: 50.7% less than 15 minutes, 20.1% 15 to 30 minutes, 10.9% 30 to 45 minutes, 8.7% 45 to 60 minutes, 9.6% 60 minutes or more (2000)

CULDRUM (township). Covers a land area of 33.548 square miles and a water area of 0.231 square miles. Located at 45.96° N. Lat.; 94.59° W. Long.
Population: 505 (2000); Race: 99.2% White, 0.0% Black, 0.2% Asian, 0.0% American Indian and Alaska Native, 1.7% Hispanic of any race, 0.6% two or more races (2000); Density: 15.1 persons per square mile (2000); Age: 33.3% under 18, 15.1% over 64 (2000); Marriage status: 22.3% never married, 63.9% now married, 7.3% widowed, 6.5% divorced (2000); Foreign born: 1.2% (2000); Ancestry (includes multiple ancestries): 40.9% German, 24.4% Polish, 10.3% Swedish, 7.0% Norwegian, 4.8% United States or American (2000).
Economy: Employment by occupation: 25.4% management, 8.1% professional, 18.2% services, 14.4% sales, 5.7% farming, 12.0% construction, 16.3% production (2000).
Income: Per capita income: $14,174 (2000); Median household income: $34,712 (2000); Poverty rate: 3.5% (2000).
Taxes: Total city taxes per capita: $37 (1997); City property taxes per capita: $37 (1997).
Education: High school graduation rate: 79.0% (2000); College graduation rate: 6.8% (2000).
Housing: Homeownership rate: 88.2% (2000); Median home value: $86,700 (2000); Median rent: $100 per month (2000); Median age of housing: 33 years (2000).
Transportation: Commute to work: 72.4% car, 0.0% public transportation, 3.8% walk, 23.8% work from home (2000); Travel time to work: 26.9% less than 15 minutes, 45.6% 15 to 30 minutes, 11.3% 30 to 45 minutes, 10.6% 45 to 60 minutes, 5.6% 60 minutes or more (2000)

CUSHING (township). Covers a land area of 77.796 square miles and a water area of 2.126 square miles. Located at 46.14° N. Lat.; 94.46° W. Long. Elevation is 1,268 feet.
Population: 632 (2000); Race: 98.2% White, 1.5% Black, 0.0% Asian, 0.3% American Indian and Alaska Native, 0.0% Hispanic of any race, 0.0% two or more races (2000); Density: 8.1 persons per square mile (2000); Age: 30.9% under 18, 8.9% over 64 (2000); Marriage status: 24.6% never married, 66.9% now married, 3.8% widowed, 4.6% divorced (2000); Foreign born: 0.6% (2000); Ancestry (includes multiple ancestries): 47.8% German, 23.2% Polish, 17.5% Norwegian, 12.1% Irish, 7.4% Swedish (2000).
Economy: Employment by occupation: 12.5% management, 14.2% professional, 15.2% services, 18.3% sales, 1.7% farming, 11.1% construction, 27.0% production (2000).
Income: Per capita income: $16,470 (2000); Median household income: $41,591 (2000); Poverty rate: 12.1% (2000).
Taxes: Total city taxes per capita: $57 (1997); City property taxes per capita: $57 (1997).
Education: High school graduation rate: 80.3% (2000); College graduation rate: 7.2% (2000).

Housing: Homeownership rate: 94.6% (2000); Median home value: $66,700 (2000); Median rent: $375 per month (2000); Median age of housing: 27 years (2000).
Transportation: Commute to work: 91.3% car, 0.0% public transportation, 1.0% walk, 6.9% work from home (2000); Travel time to work: 12.3% less than 15 minutes, 46.8% 15 to 30 minutes, 16.7% 30 to 45 minutes, 8.9% 45 to 60 minutes, 15.2% 60 minutes or more (2000)

DARLING (township). Covers a land area of 33.942 square miles and a water area of 0.268 square miles. Located at 46.07° N. Lat.; 94.44° W. Long.
Population: 600 (2000); Race: 98.2% White, 0.8% Black, 1.0% Asian, 0.0% American Indian and Alaska Native, 0.0% Hispanic of any race, 0.0% two or more races (2000); Density: 17.7 persons per square mile (2000); Age: 29.0% under 18, 9.4% over 64 (2000); Marriage status: 26.9% never married, 64.3% now married, 3.6% widowed, 5.3% divorced (2000); Foreign born: 1.3% (2000); Ancestry (includes multiple ancestries): 50.9% German, 21.7% Polish, 9.4% Norwegian, 9.1% Swedish, 6.3% Irish (2000).
Economy: Employment by occupation: 12.6% management, 12.0% professional, 13.5% services, 19.3% sales, 4.6% farming, 16.0% construction, 22.1% production (2000).
Income: Per capita income: $17,415 (2000); Median household income: $46,875 (2000); Poverty rate: 6.5% (2000).
Taxes: Total city taxes per capita: $76 (1997); City property taxes per capita: $76 (1997).
Education: High school graduation rate: 91.5% (2000); College graduation rate: 11.6% (2000).
Housing: Homeownership rate: 93.3% (2000); Median home value: $97,200 (2000); Median rent: $363 per month (2000); Median age of housing: 30 years (2000).
Transportation: Commute to work: 87.1% car, 1.3% public transportation, 0.6% walk, 11.0% work from home (2000); Travel time to work: 39.2% less than 15 minutes, 35.3% 15 to 30 minutes, 10.6% 30 to 45 minutes, 11.0% 45 to 60 minutes, 3.9% 60 minutes or more (2000)

ELMDALE (city). Covers a land area of 3.413 square miles and a water area of 0 square miles. Located at 45.82° N. Lat.; 94.49° W. Long. Elevation is 1,169 feet.
Population: 107 (2000); Race: 100.0% White, 0.0% Black, 0.0% Asian, 0.0% American Indian and Alaska Native, 0.0% Hispanic of any race, 0.0% two or more races (2000); Density: 31.3 persons per square mile (2000); Age: 25.7% under 18, 16.8% over 64 (2000); Marriage status: 24.7% never married, 50.6% now married, 7.8% widowed, 16.9% divorced (2000); Foreign born: 0.0% (2000); Ancestry (includes multiple ancestries): 27.7% German, 23.8% Norwegian, 21.8% Polish, 6.9% Czech, 4.0% Swedish (2000).
Economy: Employment by occupation: 20.4% management, 14.3% professional, 8.2% services, 6.1% sales, 10.2% farming, 12.2% construction, 28.6% production (2000).
Income: Per capita income: $12,504 (2000); Median household income: $38,125 (2000); Poverty rate: 11.9% (2000).
Taxes: Total city taxes per capita: $67 (1997); City property taxes per capita: $60 (1997).
Education: High school graduation rate: 58.6% (2000); College graduation rate: 5.7% (2000).
Housing: Homeownership rate: 95.0% (2000); Median home value: $60,000 (2000); Median age of housing: 51 years (2000).
Transportation: Commute to work: 81.6% car, 0.0% public transportation, 0.0% walk, 18.4% work from home (2000); Travel time to work: 10.0% less than 15 minutes, 25.0% 15 to 30 minutes, 32.5% 30 to 45 minutes, 25.0% 45 to 60 minutes, 7.5% 60 minutes or more (2000)

ELMDALE (township). Covers a land area of 38.725 square miles and a water area of 0.981 square miles. Located at 45.82° N. Lat.; 94.56° W. Long. Elevation is 1,169 feet.
Population: 904 (2000); Race: 99.8% White, 0.0% Black, 0.0% Asian, 0.0% American Indian and Alaska Native, 0.2% Hispanic of any race, 0.0% two or more races (2000); Density: 23.3 persons per square mile (2000); Age: 33.3% under 18, 11.3% over 64 (2000); Marriage status: 25.0% never married, 66.9% now married, 3.7% widowed, 4.4% divorced (2000); Foreign born: 0.7% (2000); Ancestry (includes multiple ancestries): 57.0% German, 27.8% Polish, 11.6% Swedish, 6.7% Norwegian, 4.2% Irish (2000).
Economy: Employment by occupation: 18.6% management, 13.3% professional, 7.9% services, 19.5% sales, 3.6% farming, 11.0% construction, 26.2% production (2000).
Income: Per capita income: $19,406 (2000); Median household income: $41,696 (2000); Poverty rate: 7.4% (2000).
Taxes: Total city taxes per capita: $67 (2000); City property taxes per capita: $67 (2000).
Education: High school graduation rate: 83.1% (2000); College graduation rate: 13.3% (2000).
Housing: Homeownership rate: 92.8% (2000); Median home value: $98,800 (2000); Median rent: $350 per month (2000); Median age of housing: 37 years (2000).
Transportation: Commute to work: 82.8% car, 0.2% public transportation, 4.3% walk, 12.7% work from home (2000); Travel time to work: 26.0% less than 15 minutes, 27.9% 15 to 30 minutes, 25.2% 30 to 45 minutes, 13.2% 45 to 60 minutes, 7.7% 60 minutes or more (2000)

FLENSBURG (city). Covers a land area of 6.934 square miles and a water area of 0.081 square miles. Located at 45.94° N. Lat.; 94.53° W. Long. Elevation is 1,213 feet.
Population: 244 (2000); Race: 95.8% White, 0.0% Black, 1.5% Asian, 0.0% American Indian and Alaska Native, 0.0% Hispanic of any race, 2.7% two or more races (2000); Density: 35.2 persons per square mile (2000); Age: 30.5% under 18, 15.1% over 64 (2000); Marriage status: 24.6% never married, 64.1% now married, 9.7% widowed, 1.5% divorced (2000); Foreign born: 1.5% (2000); Ancestry (includes multiple ancestries): 48.6% German, 47.9% Polish, 8.9% Swedish, 6.6% French Canadian, 6.2% French (except Basque) (2000).
Economy: Grain, sunflowers, beans; livestock, poultry; dairying. Single-family building permits issued: 0 (2001) / 0 (2000); Multi-family building permits issued: 0 (2001) / 0 (2000); Employment by occupation: 19.7% management, 5.7% professional, 9.8% services, 27.0% sales, 1.6% farming, 10.7% construction, 25.4% production (2000).
Income: Per capita income: $15,652 (2000); Median household income: $34,107 (2000); Poverty rate: 8.2% (2000).
Taxes: Total city taxes per capita: $20 (1997); City property taxes per capita: $20 (1997).
Education: High school graduation rate: 82.3% (2000); College graduation rate: 10.4% (2000).
Housing: Homeownership rate: 86.7% (2000); Median home value: $40,800 (2000); Median rent: $450 per month (2000); Median age of housing: 50 years (2000).
Transportation: Commute to work: 76.7% car, 0.0% public transportation, 9.2% walk, 14.2% work from home (2000); Travel time to work: 22.3% less than 15 minutes, 42.7% 15 to 30 minutes, 17.5% 30 to 45 minutes, 8.7% 45 to 60 minutes, 8.7% 60 minutes or more (2000)

GENOLA (city). Covers a land area of 0.318 square miles and a water area of 0 square miles. Located at 45.96° N. Lat.; 94.11° W. Long. Elevation is 1,161 feet.
Population: 71 (2000); Race: 100.0% White, 0.0% Black, 0.0% Asian, 0.0% American Indian and Alaska Native, 0.0% Hispanic of any race, 0.0% two or more races (2000); Density: 223.2 persons per square mile (2000); Age: 31.4% under 18, 24.3% over 64 (2000); Marriage status: 25.9% never married, 51.9% now married, 11.1% widowed, 11.1% divorced (2000); Foreign born: 0.0% (2000); Ancestry (includes multiple ancestries): 70.0% German, 15.7% Czech, 8.6% Finnish, 2.9% Swedish, 2.9% Slovak (2000).
Economy: Agricultural area: grain; dairying. Single-family building permits issued: 1 (2001) / 1 (2000); Multi-family building permits issued: 0 (2001) / 0 (2000); Employment by occupation: 11.1% management, 11.1% professional, 18.5% services, 7.4% sales, 0.0% farming, 14.8% construction, 37.0% production (2000).
Income: Per capita income: $15,796 (2000); Median household income: $33,750 (2000); Poverty rate: 2.9% (2000).
Taxes: Total city taxes per capita: $152 (1997); City property taxes per capita: $89 (1997).
Education: High school graduation rate: 84.4% (2000); College graduation rate: 8.9% (2000).
Housing: Homeownership rate: 67.7% (2000); Median home value: $60,700 (2000); Median rent: $363 per month (2000); Median age of housing: 50 years (2000).
Transportation: Commute to work: 88.9% car, 0.0% public transportation, 0.0% walk, 11.1% work from home (2000); Travel time to work: 20.8% less than 15 minutes, 8.3% 15 to 30 minutes, 29.2% 30 to 45 minutes, 12.5% 45 to 60 minutes, 29.2% 60 minutes or more (2000)

GRANITE (township). Covers a land area of 36.123 square miles and a water area of 0.019 square miles. Located at 46.02° N. Lat.; 94.00° W. Long.
Population: 480 (2000); Race: 99.6% White, 0.0% Black, 0.0% Asian, 0.0% American Indian and Alaska Native, 0.4% Hispanic of any race, 0.4% two or more races (2000); Density: 13.3 persons per square mile (2000); Age: 33.8%

under 18, 3.4% over 64 (2000); Marriage status: 29.0% never married, 65.7% now married, 4.1% widowed, 1.2% divorced (2000); Foreign born: 0.0% (2000); Ancestry (includes multiple ancestries): 72.0% German, 20.7% Polish, 9.5% Norwegian, 4.5% Irish, 3.4% United States or American (2000).
Economy: Employment by occupation: 25.5% management, 11.1% professional, 16.9% services, 16.0% sales, 2.1% farming, 9.1% construction, 19.3% production (2000).
Income: Per capita income: $14,311 (2000); Median household income: $47,813 (2000); Poverty rate: 9.8% (2000).
Taxes: Total city taxes per capita: $46 (1997); City property taxes per capita: $46 (1997).
Education: High school graduation rate: 81.2% (2000); College graduation rate: 5.7% (2000).
Housing: Homeownership rate: 97.2% (2000); Median home value: $71,700 (2000); Median age of housing: 27 years (2000).
Transportation: Commute to work: 81.7% car, 0.0% public transportation, 2.5% walk, 15.8% work from home (2000); Travel time to work: 29.1% less than 15 minutes, 30.5% 15 to 30 minutes, 17.7% 30 to 45 minutes, 18.2% 45 to 60 minutes, 4.4% 60 minutes or more (2000)

GREEN PRAIRIE (township). Covers a land area of 16.039 square miles and a water area of 0.691 square miles. Located at 46.07° N. Lat.; 94.35° W. Long.
Population: 665 (2000); Race: 99.2% White, 0.0% Black, 0.0% Asian, 0.8% American Indian and Alaska Native, 0.0% Hispanic of any race, 0.0% two or more races (2000); Density: 41.5 persons per square mile (2000); Age: 28.6% under 18, 7.8% over 64 (2000); Marriage status: 19.7% never married, 68.0% now married, 4.1% widowed, 8.1% divorced (2000); Foreign born: 0.9% (2000); Ancestry (includes multiple ancestries): 52.8% German, 27.5% Polish, 13.0% Norwegian, 9.7% Swedish, 9.3% French (except Basque) (2000).
Economy: Employment by occupation: 8.9% management, 11.9% professional, 13.7% services, 19.6% sales, 2.1% farming, 13.7% construction, 30.1% production (2000).
Income: Per capita income: $17,013 (2000); Median household income: $39,444 (2000); Poverty rate: 5.2% (2000).
Taxes: Total city taxes per capita: $30 (1997); City property taxes per capita: $30 (1997).
Education: High school graduation rate: 85.6% (2000); College graduation rate: 12.9% (2000).
Housing: Homeownership rate: 95.0% (2000); Median home value: $99,500 (2000); Median rent: $250 per month (2000); Median age of housing: 28 years (2000).
Transportation: Commute to work: 91.9% car, 0.0% public transportation, 1.2% walk, 4.2% work from home (2000); Travel time to work: 56.1% less than 15 minutes, 26.6% 15 to 30 minutes, 9.1% 30 to 45 minutes, 4.1% 45 to 60 minutes, 4.1% 60 minutes or more (2000)

HARDING (city). Covers a land area of 3.263 square miles and a water area of 0 square miles. Located at 46.11° N. Lat.; 94.04° W. Long. Elevation is 1,265 feet.
History: Incorporated 1938.
Population: 105 (2000); Race: 100.0% White, 0.0% Black, 0.0% Asian, 0.0% American Indian and Alaska Native, 0.0% Hispanic of any race, 0.0% two or more races (2000); Density: 32.2 persons per square mile (2000); Age: 9.4% under 18, 22.2% over 64 (2000); Marriage status: 30.2% never married, 46.2% now married, 11.3% widowed, 12.3% divorced (2000); Foreign born: 0.0% (2000); Ancestry (includes multiple ancestries): 38.5% Polish, 32.5% German, 6.0% Irish, 5.1% Swedish, 4.3% Norwegian (2000).
Economy: Agricultural area: grain; livestock; dairying. Single-family building permits issued: 2 (2001) / 0 (2000); Multi-family building permits issued: 0 (2001) / 0 (2000); Employment by occupation: 7.8% management, 3.9% professional, 21.6% services, 13.7% sales, 0.0% farming, 29.4% construction, 23.5% production (2000).
Income: Per capita income: $18,060 (2000); Median household income: $35,000 (2000); Poverty rate: 26.5% (2000).
Taxes: Total city taxes per capita: $53 (1997); City property taxes per capita: $40 (1997).
Education: High school graduation rate: 71.6% (2000); College graduation rate: 5.3% (2000).
Housing: Homeownership rate: 82.6% (2000); Median home value: $45,000 (2000); Median rent: $275 per month (2000); Median age of housing: 29 years (2000).
Transportation: Commute to work: 94.1% car, 0.0% public transportation, 5.9% walk, 0.0% work from home (2000); Travel time to work: 13.7% less than 15 minutes, 29.4% 15 to 30 minutes, 19.6% 30 to 45 minutes, 15.7% 45 to 60 minutes, 21.6% 60 minutes or more (2000)

HILLMAN (city). Covers a land area of 0.539 square miles and a water area of 0 square miles. Located at 46.00° N. Lat.; 93.88° W. Long. Elevation is 1,315 feet.
Population: 29 (2000); Race: 100.0% White, 0.0% Black, 0.0% Asian, 0.0% American Indian and Alaska Native, 0.0% Hispanic of any race, 0.0% two or more races (2000); Density: 53.8 persons per square mile (2000); Age: 25.9% under 18, 0.0% over 64 (2000); Marriage status: 34.8% never married, 43.5% now married, 8.7% widowed, 13.0% divorced (2000); Foreign born: 0.0% (2000); Ancestry (includes multiple ancestries): 74.1% German, 37.0% Irish, 22.2% English, 7.4% French (except Basque) (2000).
Economy: Single-family building permits issued: 1 (2001) / 1 (2000); Multi-family building permits issued: 0 (2001) / 0 (2000); Employment by occupation: 0.0% management, 0.0% professional, 27.3% services, 27.3% sales, 0.0% farming, 18.2% construction, 27.3% production (2000).
Income: Per capita income: $11,126 (2000); Median household income: $26,250 (2000); Poverty rate: 7.4% (2000).
Taxes: Total city taxes per capita: $140 (1997); City property taxes per capita: $93 (1997).
Education: High school graduation rate: 66.7% (2000); College graduation rate: 0.0% (2000).
Housing: Homeownership rate: 100.0% (2000); Median home value: $61,700 (2000); Median age of housing: 60+ years (2000).
Transportation: Commute to work: 100.0% car, 0.0% public transportation, 0.0% walk, 0.0% work from home (2000); Travel time to work: 0.0% less than 15 minutes, 0.0% 15 to 30 minutes, 0.0% 30 to 45 minutes, 62.5% 45 to 60 minutes, 37.5% 60 minutes or more (2000)

HILLMAN (township). Covers a land area of 28.243 square miles and a water area of 0.013 square miles. Located at 45.96° N. Lat.; 93.96° W. Long. Elevation is 1,315 feet.
History: Incorporated 1938.
Population: 164 (2000); Race: 99.4% White, 0.0% Black, 0.0% Asian, 0.0% American Indian and Alaska Native, 10.1% Hispanic of any race, 0.6% two or more races (2000); Density: 5.8 persons per square mile (2000); Age: 34.3% under 18, 8.4% over 64 (2000); Marriage status: 24.0% never married, 68.8% now married, 2.4% widowed, 4.8% divorced (2000); Foreign born: 1.7% (2000); Ancestry (includes multiple ancestries): 65.7% German, 26.4% Polish, 12.9% Other groups, 2.8% Irish, 2.2% Jordanian (2000).
Economy: Dairying. Employment by occupation: 9.6% management, 10.8% professional, 12.0% services, 21.7% sales, 6.0% farming, 16.9% construction, 22.9% production (2000).
Income: Per capita income: $13,345 (2000); Median household income: $45,938 (2000); Poverty rate: 7.3% (2000).
Taxes: Total city taxes per capita: $52 (1997); City property taxes per capita: $52 (1997).
Education: High school graduation rate: 83.0% (2000); College graduation rate: 6.4% (2000).
Housing: Homeownership rate: 94.4% (2000); Median home value: $81,700 (2000); Median age of housing: 25 years (2000).
Transportation: Commute to work: 86.7% car, 0.0% public transportation, 2.4% walk, 10.8% work from home (2000); Travel time to work: 20.3% less than 15 minutes, 25.7% 15 to 30 minutes, 9.5% 30 to 45 minutes, 28.4% 45 to 60 minutes, 16.2% 60 minutes or more (2000)

LAKIN (township). Covers a land area of 35.821 square miles and a water area of 0 square miles. Located at 45.85° N. Lat.; 93.85° W. Long.
Population: 409 (2000); Race: 99.2% White, 0.0% Black, 0.0% Asian, 0.8% American Indian and Alaska Native, 0.0% Hispanic of any race, 0.0% two or more races (2000); Density: 11.4 persons per square mile (2000); Age: 31.5% under 18, 8.7% over 64 (2000); Marriage status: 31.6% never married, 57.4% now married, 3.9% widowed, 7.1% divorced (2000); Foreign born: 0.0% (2000); Ancestry (includes multiple ancestries): 59.3% German, 33.2% Polish, 11.8% Norwegian, 9.5% Irish, 8.4% Swedish (2000).
Economy: Employment by occupation: 20.1% management, 7.4% professional, 8.5% services, 13.8% sales, 7.4% farming, 13.2% construction, 29.6% production (2000).
Income: Per capita income: $14,415 (2000); Median household income: $38,500 (2000); Poverty rate: 13.9% (2000).
Taxes: Total city taxes per capita: $78 (1997); City property taxes per capita: $78 (1997).
Education: High school graduation rate: 73.3% (2000); College graduation rate: 3.8% (2000).

Housing: Homeownership rate: 92.4% (2000); Median home value: $120,000 (2000); Median age of housing: 33 years (2000).
Transportation: Commute to work: 71.4% car, 0.0% public transportation, 11.6% walk, 16.9% work from home (2000); Travel time to work: 18.5% less than 15 minutes, 30.6% 15 to 30 minutes, 23.6% 30 to 45 minutes, 14.6% 45 to 60 minutes, 12.7% 60 minutes or more (2000)

LASTRUP (city). Covers a land area of 0.444 square miles and a water area of 0.008 square miles. Located at 46.04° N. Lat.; 94.06° W. Long. Elevation is 1,239 feet.
Population: 99 (2000); Race: 100.0% White, 0.0% Black, 0.0% Asian, 0.0% American Indian and Alaska Native, 1.7% Hispanic of any race, 0.0% two or more races (2000); Density: 223.2 persons per square mile (2000); Age: 21.8% under 18, 11.8% over 64 (2000); Marriage status: 30.5% never married, 56.8% now married, 9.5% widowed, 3.2% divorced (2000); Foreign born: 0.0% (2000); Ancestry (includes multiple ancestries): 85.7% German, 21.0% Polish, 3.4% Italian, 3.4% Norwegian, 2.5% Irish (2000).
Economy: Dairying. Manufacturing: feeds. Single-family building permits issued: 0 (2001) / 0 (2000); Multi-family building permits issued: 0 (2001) / 0 (2000); Employment by occupation: 14.7% management, 7.4% professional, 0.0% services, 19.1% sales, 1.5% farming, 13.2% construction, 44.1% production (2000).
Income: Per capita income: $14,622 (2000); Median household income: $30,000 (2000); Poverty rate: 27.7% (2000).
Taxes: Total city taxes per capita: $85 (1997); City property taxes per capita: $66 (1997).
Education: High school graduation rate: 81.1% (2000); College graduation rate: 2.7% (2000).
Housing: Homeownership rate: 96.1% (2000); Median home value: $46,300 (2000); Median rent: $325 per month (2000); Median age of housing: 44 years (2000).
Transportation: Commute to work: 94.1% car, 0.0% public transportation, 5.9% walk, 0.0% work from home (2000); Travel time to work: 27.9% less than 15 minutes, 25.0% 15 to 30 minutes, 35.3% 30 to 45 minutes, 5.9% 45 to 60 minutes, 5.9% 60 minutes or more (2000)

LEIGH (township). Covers a land area of 35.961 square miles and a water area of 0.083 square miles. Located at 46.03° N. Lat.; 93.91° W. Long.
Population: 192 (2000); Race: 94.6% White, 0.0% Black, 0.0% Asian, 5.4% American Indian and Alaska Native, 0.0% Hispanic of any race, 0.0% two or more races (2000); Density: 5.3 persons per square mile (2000); Age: 30.7% under 18, 7.8% over 64 (2000); Marriage status: 26.0% never married, 50.4% now married, 12.6% widowed, 11.0% divorced (2000); Foreign born: 0.0% (2000); Ancestry (includes multiple ancestries): 59.0% German, 20.5% Polish, 9.6% Irish, 8.4% United States or American, 7.2% Dutch (2000).
Economy: Employment by occupation: 5.5% management, 8.8% professional, 29.7% services, 15.4% sales, 7.7% farming, 19.8% construction, 13.2% production (2000).
Income: Per capita income: $12,572 (2000); Median household income: $26,563 (2000); Poverty rate: 17.0% (2000).
Taxes: Total city taxes per capita: $33 (1997); City property taxes per capita: $33 (1997).
Education: High school graduation rate: 65.0% (2000); College graduation rate: 0.0% (2000).
Housing: Homeownership rate: 90.2% (2000); Median home value: $112,500 (2000); Median rent: <$100 per month (2000); Median age of housing: 23 years (2000).
Transportation: Commute to work: 85.1% car, 0.0% public transportation, 0.0% walk, 11.5% work from home (2000); Travel time to work: 5.2% less than 15 minutes, 37.7% 15 to 30 minutes, 14.3% 30 to 45 minutes, 16.9% 45 to 60 minutes, 26.0% 60 minutes or more (2000)

LITTLE FALLS (city). Covers a land area of 6.263 square miles and a water area of 0.501 square miles. Located at 45.97° N. Lat.; 94.36° W. Long. Elevation is 1,111 feet.
History: The rapids on the Mississippi River that gave Little Falls its name were called "Painted Rocks" by French explorers. A dam was built here in 1890, and lumber, flour, and paper mills grew up around it. Little Falls was the boyhood home of Charles A. Lindbergh, Jr., who made aviation history. The senior Lindbergh was a lawyer in Little Falls, and a representative in the U.S. congress from 1907 to 1917.
Population: 7,719 (2000); Race: 97.8% White, 0.4% Black, 0.9% Asian, 0.2% American Indian and Alaska Native, 0.8% Hispanic of any race, 0.6% two or more races (2000); Density: 1,232.5 persons per square mile (2000); Age: 25.2% under 18, 22.6% over 64 (2000); Marriage status: 26.3% never married, 51.0% now married, 11.3% widowed, 11.4% divorced (2000); Foreign born: 1.8% (2000); Ancestry (includes multiple ancestries): 42.9% German, 19.2% Polish, 10.7% Norwegian, 9.2% Swedish, 8.6% Irish (2000).
Economy: Single-family building permits issued: 28 (2001) / 26 (2000); Multi-family building permits issued: 50 (2001) / 42 (2000); Employment by occupation: 9.6% management, 21.3% professional, 13.6% services, 23.5% sales, 0.8% farming, 8.2% construction, 23.1% production (2000).
Income: Per capita income: $15,924 (2000); Median household income: $30,547 (2000); Poverty rate: 15.9% (2000).
Taxes: Total city taxes per capita: $190 (1997); City property taxes per capita: $172 (1997).
Education: High school graduation rate: 77.6% (2000); College graduation rate: 16.8% (2000).

School District(s)

Little Falls (PK-12)
2000 Enrollment: 3,457 320-632-2002

Housing: Homeownership rate: 64.8% (2000); Median home value: $72,100 (2000); Median rent: $362 per month (2000); Median age of housing: 41 years (2000).
Hospitals: Saint Gabriel's Hospital (49 beds)
Safety: Violent crime rate: 9.0 per 10,000 population; Property crime rate: 396.1 per 10,000 population (2001).
Newspapers: Morrison County Record (1 x week)
Transportation: Commute to work: 89.7% car, 0.2% public transportation, 5.8% walk, 2.9% work from home (2000); Travel time to work: 64.4% less than 15 minutes, 12.1% 15 to 30 minutes, 12.3% 30 to 45 minutes, 6.7% 45 to 60 minutes, 4.5% 60 minutes or more (2000)
Additional Information Contacts
Little Falls Chamber of Commerce 320-632-5155

LITTLE FALLS (township). Covers a land area of 34.683 square miles and a water area of 1.646 square miles. Located at 45.95° N. Lat.; 94.31° W. Long. Elevation is 1,111 feet.
History: Grew with establishment of mills that used falls in river as source of water power. Point of interest is Charles Lindbergh State Park to southwest, surrounding aviator's childhood home. Settled 1855, Incorporated as village 1879, as city 1889.
Population: 1,624 (2000); Race: 97.9% White, 0.0% Black, 0.5% Asian, 0.4% American Indian and Alaska Native, 0.2% Hispanic of any race, 0.8% two or more races (2000); Density: 46.8 persons per square mile (2000); Age: 29.3% under 18, 7.9% over 64 (2000); Marriage status: 23.1% never married, 71.0% now married, 2.9% widowed, 3.0% divorced (2000); Foreign born: 1.0% (2000); Ancestry (includes multiple ancestries): 52.9% German, 20.9% Polish, 11.0% Norwegian, 9.1% Irish, 8.4% Swedish (2000).
Economy: Resort and trade center for agricultural area: grain, sunflowers, potatoes, livestock, dairying. Manufacturing includes metal products, hardwood products, beverages, paper, concrete, transportation equipment, plastic products, printing and publishing. Granite quarry nearby. Employment by occupation: 15.7% management, 23.4% professional, 11.9% services, 23.4% sales, 0.7% farming, 10.8% construction, 14.1% production (2000).
Income: Per capita income: $22,083 (2000); Median household income: $56,196 (2000); Poverty rate: 2.5% (2000).
Taxes: Total city taxes per capita: $55 (1997); City property taxes per capita: $52 (1997).
Education: High school graduation rate: 90.1% (2000); College graduation rate: 26.9% (2000).
Housing: Homeownership rate: 95.3% (2000); Median home value: $123,500 (2000); Median rent: $363 per month (2000); Median age of housing: 22 years (2000).
Transportation: Commute to work: 92.8% car, 0.6% public transportation, 2.3% walk, 3.9% work from home (2000); Travel time to work: 51.5% less than 15 minutes, 20.5% 15 to 30 minutes, 16.3% 30 to 45 minutes, 7.7% 45 to 60 minutes, 3.9% 60 minutes or more (2000)

MORRILL (township). Covers a land area of 35.303 square miles and a water area of 0.011 square miles. Located at 45.86° N. Lat.; 93.97° W. Long. Elevation is 1,310 feet.
Population: 650 (2000); Race: 98.5% White, 0.0% Black, 1.2% Asian, 0.3% American Indian and Alaska Native, 0.6% Hispanic of any race, 0.0% two or more races (2000); Density: 18.4 persons per square mile (2000); Age: 29.7% under 18, 7.0% over 64 (2000); Marriage status: 31.9% never married, 60.5% now married, 2.6% widowed, 4.9% divorced (2000); Foreign born: 1.6% (2000); Ancestry (includes multiple ancestries): 59.3% German, 38.8% Polish, 4.5% Swedish, 4.3% United States or American, 4.2% Norwegian (2000).

Economy: Employment by occupation: 10.9% management, 9.9% professional, 13.9% services, 14.7% sales, 2.9% farming, 19.2% construction, 28.5% production (2000).
Income: Per capita income: $17,604 (2000); Median household income: $42,813 (2000); Poverty rate: 7.5% (2000).
Taxes: Total city taxes per capita: $43 (1997); City property taxes per capita: $36 (1997).
Education: High school graduation rate: 69.8% (2000); College graduation rate: 3.6% (2000).
Housing: Homeownership rate: 95.1% (2000); Median home value: $89,400 (2000); Median rent: $275 per month (2000); Median age of housing: 23 years (2000).
Transportation: Commute to work: 78.9% car, 0.5% public transportation, 4.9% walk, 14.3% work from home (2000); Travel time to work: 11.0% less than 15 minutes, 17.4% 15 to 30 minutes, 29.0% 30 to 45 minutes, 16.1% 45 to 60 minutes, 26.5% 60 minutes or more (2000)

MOTLEY (city). Covers a land area of 1.322 square miles and a water area of 0.068 square miles. Located at 46.33° N. Lat.; 94.64° W. Long. Elevation is 1,229 feet.
Population: 585 (2000); Race: 96.1% White, 0.0% Black, 0.6% Asian, 0.5% American Indian and Alaska Native, 4.0% Hispanic of any race, 1.3% two or more races (2000); Density: 442.7 persons per square mile (2000); Age: 27.2% under 18, 18.0% over 64 (2000); Marriage status: 20.1% never married, 56.0% now married, 12.0% widowed, 12.0% divorced (2000); Foreign born: 1.8% (2000); Ancestry (includes multiple ancestries): 34.3% German, 12.5% Norwegian, 8.9% Other groups, 7.8% Irish, 7.3% Polish (2000).
Economy: Single-family building permits issued: 6 (2001) / 4 (2000); Multi-family building permits issued: 16 (2001) / 0 (2000); Employment by occupation: 3.8% management, 15.9% professional, 23.1% services, 19.3% sales, 0.8% farming, 6.8% construction, 30.3% production (2000).
Income: Per capita income: $12,220 (2000); Median household income: $23,438 (2000); Poverty rate: 18.9% (2000).
Taxes: Total city taxes per capita: $198 (1997); City property taxes per capita: $182 (1997).
Education: High school graduation rate: 73.7% (2000); College graduation rate: 10.0% (2000).
Housing: Homeownership rate: 66.2% (2000); Median home value: $52,200 (2000); Median rent: $296 per month (2000); Median age of housing: 24 years (2000).
Transportation: Commute to work: 91.7% car, 0.0% public transportation, 4.3% walk, 1.6% work from home (2000); Travel time to work: 50.4% less than 15 minutes, 24.4% 15 to 30 minutes, 12.8% 30 to 45 minutes, 4.8% 45 to 60 minutes, 7.6% 60 minutes or more (2000)

MOTLEY (township). Covers a land area of 15.308 square miles and a water area of 0.581 square miles. Located at 46.30° N. Lat.; 94.59° W. Long. Elevation is 1,229 feet.
Population: 205 (2000); Race: 100.0% White, 0.0% Black, 0.0% Asian, 0.0% American Indian and Alaska Native, 0.0% Hispanic of any race, 0.0% two or more races (2000); Density: 13.4 persons per square mile (2000); Age: 24.2% under 18, 21.5% over 64 (2000); Marriage status: 15.4% never married, 74.5% now married, 4.7% widowed, 5.4% divorced (2000); Foreign born: 0.0% (2000); Ancestry (includes multiple ancestries): 31.7% German, 20.4% Norwegian, 18.8% Irish, 15.6% United States or American, 10.2% Swedish (2000).
Economy: Manufacturing: feeds, smoked fish, imitation seafood. Employment by occupation: 2.6% management, 12.8% professional, 14.1% services, 23.1% sales, 3.8% farming, 10.3% construction, 33.3% production (2000).
Income: Per capita income: $15,873 (2000); Median household income: $39,000 (2000); Poverty rate: 18.4% (2000).
Taxes: Total city taxes per capita: $43 (1997); City property taxes per capita: $43 (1997).
Education: High school graduation rate: 83.9% (2000); College graduation rate: 16.9% (2000).
Housing: Homeownership rate: 86.2% (2000); Median home value: $83,000 (2000); Median rent: $275 per month (2000); Median age of housing: 23 years (2000).
Transportation: Commute to work: 100.0% car, 0.0% public transportation, 0.0% walk, 0.0% work from home (2000); Travel time to work: 56.8% less than 15 minutes, 10.8% 15 to 30 minutes, 23.0% 30 to 45 minutes, 2.7% 45 to 60 minutes, 6.8% 60 minutes or more (2000)

MOUNT MORRIS (township). Covers a land area of 29.958 square miles and a water area of 0.011 square miles. Located at 45.95° N. Lat.; 93.84° W. Long.
Population: 90 (2000); Race: 100.0% White, 0.0% Black, 0.0% Asian, 0.0% American Indian and Alaska Native, 0.0% Hispanic of any race, 0.0% two or more races (2000); Density: 3.0 persons per square mile (2000); Age: 23.9% under 18, 12.7% over 64 (2000); Marriage status: 12.3% never married, 71.9% now married, 7.0% widowed, 8.8% divorced (2000); Foreign born: 0.0% (2000); Ancestry (includes multiple ancestries): 64.8% German, 21.1% Polish, 11.3% French (except Basque), 7.0% Swedish, 7.0% Norwegian (2000).
Economy: Employment by occupation: 40.0% management, 6.7% professional, 6.7% services, 13.3% sales, 3.3% farming, 6.7% construction, 23.3% production (2000).
Income: Per capita income: $9,483 (2000); Median household income: $19,375 (2000); Poverty rate: 26.8% (2000).
Taxes: Total city taxes per capita: $41 (1997); City property taxes per capita: $41 (1997).
Education: High school graduation rate: 63.5% (2000); College graduation rate: 1.9% (2000).
Housing: Homeownership rate: 92.3% (2000); Median age of housing: 26 years (2000).
Transportation: Commute to work: 63.3% car, 0.0% public transportation, 0.0% walk, 36.7% work from home (2000); Travel time to work: 31.6% less than 15 minutes, 42.1% 15 to 30 minutes, 15.8% 30 to 45 minutes, 10.5% 45 to 60 minutes, 0.0% 60 minutes or more (2000)

PARKER (township). Covers a land area of 38.428 square miles and a water area of 0 square miles. Located at 46.06° N. Lat.; 94.58° W. Long.
Population: 469 (2000); Race: 100.0% White, 0.0% Black, 0.0% Asian, 0.0% American Indian and Alaska Native, 0.0% Hispanic of any race, 0.0% two or more races (2000); Density: 12.2 persons per square mile (2000); Age: 34.7% under 18, 10.8% over 64 (2000); Marriage status: 25.0% never married, 67.2% now married, 2.5% widowed, 5.3% divorced (2000); Foreign born: 0.4% (2000); Ancestry (includes multiple ancestries): 54.1% German, 21.0% Polish, 8.8% Norwegian, 8.6% Swedish, 5.2% Irish (2000).
Economy: Employment by occupation: 25.1% management, 9.2% professional, 16.7% services, 12.7% sales, 0.8% farming, 10.0% construction, 25.5% production (2000).
Income: Per capita income: $14,805 (2000); Median household income: $38,250 (2000); Poverty rate: 8.8% (2000).
Taxes: Total city taxes per capita: $62 (2000); City property taxes per capita: $60 (2000).
Education: High school graduation rate: 81.0% (2000); College graduation rate: 4.8% (2000).
Housing: Homeownership rate: 91.8% (2000); Median home value: $81,900 (2000); Median rent: $475 per month (2000); Median age of housing: 30 years (2000).
Transportation: Commute to work: 74.0% car, 0.0% public transportation, 1.6% walk, 23.6% work from home (2000); Travel time to work: 25.7% less than 15 minutes, 39.8% 15 to 30 minutes, 17.8% 30 to 45 minutes, 7.3% 45 to 60 minutes, 9.4% 60 minutes or more (2000)

PIERZ (city). Covers a land area of 1.350 square miles and a water area of 0 square miles. Located at 45.97° N. Lat.; 94.10° W. Long. Elevation is 1,170 feet.
Population: 1,277 (2000); Race: 97.4% White, 0.4% Black, 0.0% Asian, 0.9% American Indian and Alaska Native, 0.0% Hispanic of any race, 1.3% two or more races (2000); Density: 945.8 persons per square mile (2000); Age: 25.0% under 18, 30.6% over 64 (2000); Marriage status: 22.8% never married, 54.1% now married, 16.5% widowed, 6.6% divorced (2000); Foreign born: 0.6% (2000); Ancestry (includes multiple ancestries): 57.6% German, 12.7% Polish, 4.9% Norwegian, 4.6% Irish, 4.6% United States or American (2000).
Economy: Single-family building permits issued: 4 (2001) / 3 (2000); Multi-family building permits issued: 0 (2001) / 16 (2000); Employment by occupation: 7.3% management, 12.0% professional, 24.8% services, 24.8% sales, 1.1% farming, 12.2% construction, 17.7% production (2000).
Income: Per capita income: $14,638 (2000); Median household income: $27,292 (2000); Poverty rate: 13.6% (2000).
Taxes: Total city taxes per capita: $101 (1997); City property taxes per capita: $86 (1997).
Education: High school graduation rate: 66.4% (2000); College graduation rate: 5.4% (2000).

School District(s)

Pierz (PK-12)
2000 Enrollment: 991 320-468-6458

Housing: Homeownership rate: 70.1% (2000); Median home value: $80,600 (2000); Median rent: $308 per month (2000); Median age of housing: 33 years (2000).

Transportation: Commute to work: 84.1% car, 1.0% public transportation, 9.5% walk, 5.4% work from home (2000); Travel time to work: 46.7% less than 15 minutes, 26.0% 15 to 30 minutes, 14.5% 30 to 45 minutes, 5.7% 45 to 60 minutes, 7.0% 60 minutes or more (2000)

PIERZ (township). Covers a land area of 28.161 square miles and a water area of 0 square miles. Located at 45.94° N. Lat.; 94.08° W. Long. Elevation is 1,170 feet.

Population: 513 (2000); Race: 100.0% White, 0.0% Black, 0.0% Asian, 0.0% American Indian and Alaska Native, 0.0% Hispanic of any race, 0.0% two or more races (2000); Density: 18.2 persons per square mile (2000); Age: 29.6% under 18, 9.3% over 64 (2000); Marriage status: 25.3% never married, 66.3% now married, 4.3% widowed, 4.0% divorced (2000); Foreign born: 0.0% (2000); Ancestry (includes multiple ancestries): 73.8% German, 18.3% Polish, 4.3% Irish, 3.7% Finnish, 3.7% French (except Basque) (2000).

Economy: In agricultural area; dairying; livestock; grain, potatoes, sunflowers. Manufacturing: redwood doors, concrete, feeds, fabricated metal products. Employment by occupation: 23.5% management, 11.6% professional, 15.5% services, 15.5% sales, 5.2% farming, 13.9% construction, 14.7% production (2000).

Income: Per capita income: $15,071 (2000); Median household income: $40,682 (2000); Poverty rate: 13.0% (2000).

Taxes: Total city taxes per capita: $45 (1997); City property taxes per capita: $45 (1997).

Education: High school graduation rate: 86.3% (2000); College graduation rate: 10.5% (2000).

Housing: Homeownership rate: 93.0% (2000); Median home value: $111,700 (2000); Median rent: $333 per month (2000); Median age of housing: 27 years (2000).

Transportation: Commute to work: 78.9% car, 0.0% public transportation, 1.6% walk, 19.5% work from home (2000); Travel time to work: 40.6% less than 15 minutes, 28.7% 15 to 30 minutes, 16.3% 30 to 45 minutes, 7.9% 45 to 60 minutes, 6.4% 60 minutes or more (2000)

PIKE CREEK (township). Covers a land area of 33.608 square miles and a water area of 0.173 square miles. Located at 45.97° N. Lat.; 94.42° W. Long.

Population: 932 (2000); Race: 99.7% White, 0.0% Black, 0.0% Asian, 0.1% American Indian and Alaska Native, 0.4% Hispanic of any race, 0.2% two or more races (2000); Density: 27.7 persons per square mile (2000); Age: 29.4% under 18, 13.1% over 64 (2000); Marriage status: 23.1% never married, 70.0% now married, 3.4% widowed, 3.4% divorced (2000); Foreign born: 0.4% (2000); Ancestry (includes multiple ancestries): 50.7% German, 40.0% Polish, 9.9% Swedish, 7.5% Norwegian, 4.7% Irish (2000).

Economy: Employment by occupation: 13.3% management, 13.8% professional, 16.4% services, 22.9% sales, 2.0% farming, 10.9% construction, 20.7% production (2000).

Income: Per capita income: $16,883 (2000); Median household income: $43,882 (2000); Poverty rate: 6.0% (2000).

Taxes: Total city taxes per capita: $75 (1997); City property taxes per capita: $75 (1997).

Education: High school graduation rate: 81.7% (2000); College graduation rate: 6.2% (2000).

Housing: Homeownership rate: 96.4% (2000); Median home value: $92,000 (2000); Median rent: $525 per month (2000); Median age of housing: 37 years (2000).

Transportation: Commute to work: 84.4% car, 0.0% public transportation, 3.3% walk, 11.8% work from home (2000); Travel time to work: 53.7% less than 15 minutes, 24.7% 15 to 30 minutes, 8.3% 30 to 45 minutes, 9.8% 45 to 60 minutes, 3.5% 60 minutes or more (2000)

PLATTE (township). Covers a land area of 35.761 square miles and a water area of 0.041 square miles. Located at 46.09° N. Lat.; 94.11° W. Long.

Population: 329 (2000); Race: 100.0% White, 0.0% Black, 0.0% Asian, 0.0% American Indian and Alaska Native, 0.0% Hispanic of any race, 0.0% two or more races (2000); Density: 9.2 persons per square mile (2000); Age: 29.0% under 18, 13.0% over 64 (2000); Marriage status: 24.4% never married, 58.8% now married, 8.0% widowed, 8.8% divorced (2000); Foreign born: 0.0% (2000); Ancestry (includes multiple ancestries): 54.4% German, 32.6% Polish, 8.5% Norwegian, 6.9% Irish, 4.8% French (except Basque) (2000).

Economy: Employment by occupation: 10.2% management, 8.8% professional, 18.4% services, 12.2% sales, 8.8% farming, 22.4% construction, 19.0% production (2000).

Income: Per capita income: $14,556 (2000); Median household income: $39,167 (2000); Poverty rate: 11.2% (2000).

Taxes: Total city taxes per capita: $26 (1997); City property taxes per capita: $26 (1997).

Education: High school graduation rate: 70.5% (2000); College graduation rate: 4.6% (2000).

Housing: Homeownership rate: 92.4% (2000); Median home value: $100,000 (2000); Median rent: $250 per month (2000); Median age of housing: 35 years (2000).

Transportation: Commute to work: 76.8% car, 0.0% public transportation, 4.2% walk, 19.0% work from home (2000); Travel time to work: 27.0% less than 15 minutes, 27.0% 15 to 30 minutes, 40.0% 30 to 45 minutes, 1.7% 45 to 60 minutes, 4.3% 60 minutes or more (2000)

PULASKI (township). Covers a land area of 30.967 square miles and a water area of 1.347 square miles. Located at 46.13° N. Lat.; 93.97° W. Long.

Population: 340 (2000); Race: 100.0% White, 0.0% Black, 0.0% Asian, 0.0% American Indian and Alaska Native, 0.0% Hispanic of any race, 0.0% two or more races (2000); Density: 11.0 persons per square mile (2000); Age: 23.1% under 18, 20.2% over 64 (2000); Marriage status: 21.3% never married, 68.0% now married, 7.7% widowed, 2.9% divorced (2000); Foreign born: 0.0% (2000); Ancestry (includes multiple ancestries): 47.8% German, 46.6% Polish, 5.9% English, 5.3% Irish, 5.0% French (except Basque) (2000).

Economy: Employment by occupation: 23.4% management, 5.0% professional, 13.5% services, 17.0% sales, 8.5% farming, 19.9% construction, 12.8% production (2000).

Income: Per capita income: $16,199 (2000); Median household income: $36,667 (2000); Poverty rate: 20.5% (2000).

Taxes: Total city taxes per capita: $91 (1997); City property taxes per capita: $91 (1997).

Education: High school graduation rate: 68.0% (2000); College graduation rate: 2.2% (2000).

Housing: Homeownership rate: 95.3% (2000); Median home value: $112,500 (2000); Median age of housing: 39 years (2000).

Transportation: Commute to work: 74.5% car, 0.0% public transportation, 2.8% walk, 22.7% work from home (2000); Travel time to work: 14.7% less than 15 minutes, 19.3% 15 to 30 minutes, 34.9% 30 to 45 minutes, 13.8% 45 to 60 minutes, 17.4% 60 minutes or more (2000)

RAIL PRAIRIE (township). Covers a land area of 39.389 square miles and a water area of 2.011 square miles. Located at 46.24° N. Lat.; 94.45° W. Long.

Population: 143 (2000); Race: 100.0% White, 0.0% Black, 0.0% Asian, 0.0% American Indian and Alaska Native, 0.0% Hispanic of any race, 0.0% two or more races (2000); Density: 3.6 persons per square mile (2000); Age: 17.0% under 18, 30.4% over 64 (2000); Marriage status: 12.7% never married, 64.4% now married, 9.3% widowed, 13.6% divorced (2000); Foreign born: 0.0% (2000); Ancestry (includes multiple ancestries): 42.2% German, 22.2% Swedish, 10.4% United States or American, 8.1% Norwegian, 7.4% Polish (2000).

Economy: Employment by occupation: 3.3% management, 16.7% professional, 15.0% services, 26.7% sales, 3.3% farming, 16.7% construction, 18.3% production (2000).

Income: Per capita income: $18,184 (2000); Median household income: $33,958 (2000); Poverty rate: 1.5% (2000).

Taxes: Total city taxes per capita: $135 (1997); City property taxes per capita: $135 (1997).

Education: High school graduation rate: 68.0% (2000); College graduation rate: 13.0% (2000).

Housing: Homeownership rate: 90.6% (2000); Median home value: $131,300 (2000); Median age of housing: 24 years (2000).

Transportation: Commute to work: 88.3% car, 0.0% public transportation, 3.3% walk, 3.3% work from home (2000); Travel time to work: 24.1% less than 15 minutes, 15.5% 15 to 30 minutes, 56.9% 30 to 45 minutes, 0.0% 45 to 60 minutes, 3.4% 60 minutes or more (2000)

RANDALL (city). Covers a land area of 2.082 square miles and a water area of 0 square miles. Located at 46.08° N. Lat.; 94.49° W. Long. Elevation is 1,182 feet.

History: Randall was incorporated in 1900 and named in honor of John H. Randall, a Northern Pacific Railway executive.
Population: 535 (2000); Race: 97.3% White, 0.0% Black, 0.0% Asian, 1.3% American Indian and Alaska Native, 0.6% Hispanic of any race, 1.3% two or more races (2000); Density: 256.9 persons per square mile (2000); Age: 26.1% under 18, 18.6% over 64 (2000); Marriage status: 25.5% never married, 55.3% now married, 8.7% widowed, 10.4% divorced (2000); Foreign born: 0.4% (2000); Ancestry (includes multiple ancestries): 46.4% German, 16.1% Polish, 14.0% Norwegian, 11.1% Swedish, 7.1% French (except Basque) (2000).
Economy: Single-family building permits issued: 26 (2001) / 2 (2000); Multi-family building permits issued: 0 (2001) / 0 (2000); Employment by occupation: 6.9% management, 12.1% professional, 19.8% services, 17.2% sales, 0.0% farming, 9.1% construction, 34.9% production (2000).
Income: Per capita income: $15,792 (2000); Median household income: $35,000 (2000); Poverty rate: 15.2% (2000).
Taxes: Total city taxes per capita: $61 (1997); City property taxes per capita: $60 (1997).
Education: High school graduation rate: 79.6% (2000); College graduation rate: 8.4% (2000).
Housing: Homeownership rate: 80.8% (2000); Median home value: $53,800 (2000); Median rent: $335 per month (2000); Median age of housing: 40 years (2000).
Transportation: Commute to work: 94.7% car, 0.0% public transportation, 2.2% walk, 3.1% work from home (2000); Travel time to work: 23.1% less than 15 minutes, 47.5% 15 to 30 minutes, 14.0% 30 to 45 minutes, 5.4% 45 to 60 minutes, 10.0% 60 minutes or more (2000)

RICHARDSON (township). Covers a land area of 34.145 square miles and a water area of 2.068 square miles. Located at 46.12° N. Lat.; 93.89° W. Long.
Population: 485 (2000); Race: 99.4% White, 0.0% Black, 0.0% Asian, 0.6% American Indian and Alaska Native, 0.0% Hispanic of any race, 0.0% two or more races (2000); Density: 14.2 persons per square mile (2000); Age: 23.4% under 18, 20.0% over 64 (2000); Marriage status: 11.7% never married, 73.0% now married, 8.1% widowed, 7.2% divorced (2000); Foreign born: 0.8% (2000); Ancestry (includes multiple ancestries): 50.1% German, 12.1% Norwegian, 11.7% Polish, 7.5% Irish, 6.7% Swedish (2000).
Economy: Employment by occupation: 11.6% management, 8.4% professional, 22.3% services, 18.3% sales, 0.0% farming, 17.5% construction, 21.9% production (2000).
Income: Per capita income: $16,531 (2000); Median household income: $33,438 (2000); Poverty rate: 8.3% (2000).
Taxes: Total city taxes per capita: $142 (1997); City property taxes per capita: $140 (1997).
Education: High school graduation rate: 74.8% (2000); College graduation rate: 3.4% (2000).
Housing: Homeownership rate: 93.1% (2000); Median home value: $99,500 (2000); Median rent: $238 per month (2000); Median age of housing: 30 years (2000).
Transportation: Commute to work: 88.4% car, 0.0% public transportation, 0.8% walk, 10.7% work from home (2000); Travel time to work: 13.4% less than 15 minutes, 31.9% 15 to 30 minutes, 19.4% 30 to 45 minutes, 18.1% 45 to 60 minutes, 17.1% 60 minutes or more (2000)

RIPLEY (township). Covers a land area of 47.693 square miles and a water area of 0.737 square miles. Located at 46.11° N. Lat.; 94.28° W. Long.
Population: 692 (2000); Race: 99.4% White, 0.0% Black, 0.0% Asian, 0.0% American Indian and Alaska Native, 0.6% Hispanic of any race, 0.6% two or more races (2000); Density: 14.5 persons per square mile (2000); Age: 31.5% under 18, 10.2% over 64 (2000); Marriage status: 23.5% never married, 67.2% now married, 2.3% widowed, 7.0% divorced (2000); Foreign born: 0.0% (2000); Ancestry (includes multiple ancestries): 46.0% German, 27.4% Polish, 8.4% French (except Basque), 6.8% Norwegian, 6.3% Irish (2000).
Economy: Employment by occupation: 14.6% management, 9.9% professional, 11.6% services, 23.9% sales, 3.9% farming, 12.2% construction, 23.9% production (2000).
Income: Per capita income: $14,881 (2000); Median household income: $38,875 (2000); Poverty rate: 14.1% (2000).
Taxes: Total city taxes per capita: $59 (1997); City property taxes per capita: $59 (1997).
Education: High school graduation rate: 78.7% (2000); College graduation rate: 10.1% (2000).
Housing: Homeownership rate: 96.1% (2000); Median home value: $93,800 (2000); Median rent: $625 per month (2000); Median age of housing: 25 years (2000).
Transportation: Commute to work: 84.2% car, 0.0% public transportation, 1.5% walk, 13.7% work from home (2000); Travel time to work: 17.6% less than 15 minutes, 45.0% 15 to 30 minutes, 21.5% 30 to 45 minutes, 5.9% 45 to 60 minutes, 10.0% 60 minutes or more (2000)

ROSING (township). Covers a land area of 18.148 square miles and a water area of 1.147 square miles. Located at 46.30° N. Lat.; 94.43° W. Long.
Population: 135 (2000); Race: 100.0% White, 0.0% Black, 0.0% Asian, 0.0% American Indian and Alaska Native, 0.0% Hispanic of any race, 0.0% two or more races (2000); Density: 7.4 persons per square mile (2000); Age: 22.1% under 18, 18.3% over 64 (2000); Marriage status: 13.3% never married, 76.2% now married, 5.7% widowed, 4.8% divorced (2000); Foreign born: 0.0% (2000); Ancestry (includes multiple ancestries): 40.5% German, 10.7% English, 9.2% Norwegian, 7.6% Swedish, 6.9% Polish (2000).
Economy: Employment by occupation: 10.0% management, 25.0% professional, 15.0% services, 21.7% sales, 0.0% farming, 15.0% construction, 13.3% production (2000).
Income: Per capita income: $19,955 (2000); Median household income: $43,500 (2000); Poverty rate: 5.3% (2000).
Taxes: Total city taxes per capita: $118 (1997); City property taxes per capita: $118 (1997).
Education: High school graduation rate: 87.9% (2000); College graduation rate: 13.1% (2000).
Housing: Homeownership rate: 94.6% (2000); Median home value: $119,400 (2000); Median age of housing: 15 years (2000).
Transportation: Commute to work: 100.0% car, 0.0% public transportation, 0.0% walk, 0.0% work from home (2000); Travel time to work: 13.8% less than 15 minutes, 65.5% 15 to 30 minutes, 17.2% 30 to 45 minutes, 0.0% 45 to 60 minutes, 3.4% 60 minutes or more (2000)

ROYALTON (city). Covers a land area of 1.723 square miles and a water area of 0 square miles. Located at 45.83° N. Lat.; 94.29° W. Long. Elevation is 1,083 feet.
Population: 816 (2000); Race: 99.8% White, 0.2% Black, 0.0% Asian, 0.0% American Indian and Alaska Native, 0.7% Hispanic of any race, 0.0% two or more races (2000); Density: 473.7 persons per square mile (2000); Age: 27.6% under 18, 12.8% over 64 (2000); Marriage status: 25.7% never married, 56.4% now married, 6.0% widowed, 11.9% divorced (2000); Foreign born: 0.4% (2000); Ancestry (includes multiple ancestries): 52.1% German, 28.6% Polish, 10.0% Norwegian, 5.6% French (except Basque), 5.6% Irish (2000).
Economy: Grain, potatoes; poultry; dairying. Manufacturing: dairy products, boat docks. Single-family building permits issued: 9 (2001) / 12 (2000); Multi-family building permits issued: 0 (2001) / 0 (2000); Employment by occupation: 6.5% management, 13.8% professional, 21.0% services, 16.5% sales, 1.8% farming, 12.9% construction, 27.5% production (2000).
Income: Per capita income: $15,926 (2000); Median household income: $33,173 (2000); Poverty rate: 9.0% (2000).
Taxes: Total city taxes per capita: $250 (1997); City property taxes per capita: $180 (1997).
Education: High school graduation rate: 79.9% (2000); College graduation rate: 9.6% (2000).

School District(s)

Royalton (KG-12)
2000 Enrollment: 729 320-584-5531

Housing: Homeownership rate: 73.1% (2000); Median home value: $83,400 (2000); Median rent: $363 per month (2000); Median age of housing: 34 years (2000).
Transportation: Commute to work: 88.8% car, 0.0% public transportation, 4.6% walk, 5.3% work from home (2000); Travel time to work: 25.7% less than 15 minutes, 42.1% 15 to 30 minutes, 25.7% 30 to 45 minutes, 4.6% 45 to 60 minutes, 1.9% 60 minutes or more (2000)

SCANDIA VALLEY (township). Covers a land area of 30.113 square miles and a water area of 8.612 square miles. Located at 46.22° N. Lat.; 94.59° W. Long.
Population: 1,074 (2000); Race: 99.1% White, 0.2% Black, 0.0% Asian, 0.0% American Indian and Alaska Native, 0.9% Hispanic of any race, 0.0% two or more races (2000); Density: 35.7 persons per square mile (2000); Age: 16.4% under 18, 24.6% over 64 (2000); Marriage status: 16.7% never married, 69.6% now married, 6.4% widowed, 7.3% divorced (2000); Foreign born: 1.3% (2000); Ancestry (includes multiple ancestries): 41.1% German, 14.1% Norwegian, 12.8% Swedish, 11.3% Irish, 7.9% Polish (2000).
Economy: Employment by occupation: 17.5% management, 11.4% professional, 13.6% services, 22.0% sales, 1.7% farming, 11.7% construction, 22.0% production (2000).

Income: Per capita income: $20,995 (2000); Median household income: $41,250 (2000); Poverty rate: 8.6% (2000).
Taxes: Total city taxes per capita: $264 (2000); City property taxes per capita: $264 (2000).
Education: High school graduation rate: 84.9% (2000); College graduation rate: 12.4% (2000).
Housing: Homeownership rate: 91.8% (2000); Median home value: $117,600 (2000); Median rent: $364 per month (2000); Median age of housing: 30 years (2000).
Transportation: Commute to work: 92.4% car, 0.0% public transportation, 2.0% walk, 5.2% work from home (2000); Travel time to work: 25.8% less than 15 minutes, 26.7% 15 to 30 minutes, 29.1% 30 to 45 minutes, 11.1% 45 to 60 minutes, 7.3% 60 minutes or more (2000)

SOBIESKI (city). Covers a land area of 4.184 square miles and a water area of 0 square miles. Located at 45.91° N. Lat.; 94.47° W. Long. Elevation is 1,133 feet.
Population: 196 (2000); Race: 100.0% White, 0.0% Black, 0.0% Asian, 0.0% American Indian and Alaska Native, 0.0% Hispanic of any race, 0.0% two or more races (2000); Density: 46.8 persons per square mile (2000); Age: 17.9% under 18, 20.3% over 64 (2000); Marriage status: 21.1% never married, 58.9% now married, 9.1% widowed, 10.9% divorced (2000); Foreign born: 0.0% (2000); Ancestry (includes multiple ancestries): 55.7% Polish, 41.5% German, 6.1% Norwegian, 3.8% Irish, 2.8% French (except Basque) (2000).
Economy: Grain, potatoes; livestock, poultry; dairying. Employment by occupation: 13.1% management, 7.5% professional, 18.7% services, 27.1% sales, 0.0% farming, 15.0% construction, 18.7% production (2000).
Income: Per capita income: $14,344 (2000); Median household income: $30,625 (2000); Poverty rate: 19.1% (2000).
Taxes: Total city taxes per capita: $49 (1997); City property taxes per capita: $29 (1997).
Education: High school graduation rate: 64.0% (2000); College graduation rate: 2.7% (2000).
Housing: Homeownership rate: 90.3% (2000); Median home value: $56,200 (2000); Median rent: $292 per month (2000); Median age of housing: 38 years (2000).
Transportation: Commute to work: 84.1% car, 0.0% public transportation, 3.7% walk, 12.1% work from home (2000); Travel time to work: 16.0% less than 15 minutes, 56.4% 15 to 30 minutes, 14.9% 30 to 45 minutes, 8.5% 45 to 60 minutes, 4.3% 60 minutes or more (2000)

SWAN RIVER (township). Covers a land area of 36.900 square miles and a water area of 0.855 square miles. Located at 45.88° N. Lat.; 94.42° W. Long.
Population: 755 (2000); Race: 99.7% White, 0.0% Black, 0.0% Asian, 0.0% American Indian and Alaska Native, 0.0% Hispanic of any race, 0.3% two or more races (2000); Density: 20.5 persons per square mile (2000); Age: 32.1% under 18, 8.2% over 64 (2000); Marriage status: 31.0% never married, 62.2% now married, 3.5% widowed, 3.2% divorced (2000); Foreign born: 0.0% (2000); Ancestry (includes multiple ancestries): 57.8% Polish, 46.6% German, 7.1% Norwegian, 6.1% Swedish, 4.7% Irish (2000).
Economy: Employment by occupation: 17.5% management, 17.0% professional, 10.9% services, 17.3% sales, 6.6% farming, 7.6% construction, 23.1% production (2000).
Income: Per capita income: $14,819 (2000); Median household income: $45,536 (2000); Poverty rate: 6.9% (2000).
Taxes: Total city taxes per capita: $32 (1997); City property taxes per capita: $32 (1997).
Education: High school graduation rate: 84.0% (2000); College graduation rate: 13.3% (2000).
Housing: Homeownership rate: 94.8% (2000); Median home value: $97,900 (2000); Median rent: $363 per month (2000); Median age of housing: 29 years (2000).
Transportation: Commute to work: 81.8% car, 0.0% public transportation, 4.9% walk, 12.8% work from home (2000); Travel time to work: 19.1% less than 15 minutes, 47.1% 15 to 30 minutes, 19.1% 30 to 45 minutes, 11.5% 45 to 60 minutes, 3.2% 60 minutes or more (2000)

SWANVILLE (city). Covers a land area of 0.506 square miles and a water area of 0 square miles. Located at 45.91° N. Lat.; 94.64° W. Long. Elevation is 1,183 feet.
Population: 351 (2000); Race: 99.4% White, 0.0% Black, 0.6% Asian, 0.0% American Indian and Alaska Native, 0.0% Hispanic of any race, 0.0% two or more races (2000); Density: 694.0 persons per square mile (2000); Age: 27.7% under 18, 20.9% over 64 (2000); Marriage status: 20.9% never married, 57.4% now married, 16.1% widowed, 5.6% divorced (2000); Foreign born: 0.0% (2000); Ancestry (includes multiple ancestries): 46.7% German, 17.4% Norwegian, 15.3% Polish, 12.1% Swedish, 4.4% Other groups (2000).
Economy: Single-family building permits issued: 2 (2001) / 3 (2000); Multi-family building permits issued: 0 (2001) / 0 (2000); Employment by occupation: 6.5% management, 16.1% professional, 15.5% services, 23.9% sales, 1.3% farming, 19.4% construction, 17.4% production (2000).
Income: Per capita income: $15,007 (2000); Median household income: $31,250 (2000); Poverty rate: 12.9% (2000).
Taxes: Total city taxes per capita: $62 (1997); City property taxes per capita: $55 (1997).
Education: High school graduation rate: 71.9% (2000); College graduation rate: 6.7% (2000).

School District(s)

Swanville (PK-12)
2000 Enrollment: 385 320-547-2431

Housing: Homeownership rate: 77.7% (2000); Median home value: $61,700 (2000); Median rent: $283 per month (2000); Median age of housing: 49 years (2000).
Transportation: Commute to work: 76.8% car, 0.0% public transportation, 18.1% walk, 5.2% work from home (2000); Travel time to work: 47.6% less than 15 minutes, 23.8% 15 to 30 minutes, 12.2% 30 to 45 minutes, 4.8% 45 to 60 minutes, 11.6% 60 minutes or more (2000)

SWANVILLE (township). Covers a land area of 35.341 square miles and a water area of 1.847 square miles. Located at 45.88° N. Lat.; 94.57° W. Long. Elevation is 1,183 feet.
Population: 534 (2000); Race: 100.0% White, 0.0% Black, 0.0% Asian, 0.0% American Indian and Alaska Native, 0.0% Hispanic of any race, 0.0% two or more races (2000); Density: 15.1 persons per square mile (2000); Age: 33.2% under 18, 12.7% over 64 (2000); Marriage status: 24.4% never married, 67.8% now married, 4.7% widowed, 3.0% divorced (2000); Foreign born: 0.4% (2000); Ancestry (includes multiple ancestries): 47.9% German, 25.5% Polish, 16.5% Swedish, 7.9% Norwegian, 4.2% Irish (2000).
Economy: Agriculture includes grain, sunflowers, potatoes; livestock; dairying. Manufacturing of concrete. Employment by occupation: 24.5% management, 14.2% professional, 6.0% services, 24.5% sales, 5.3% farming, 11.0% construction, 14.5% production (2000).
Income: Per capita income: $13,955 (2000); Median household income: $36,458 (2000); Poverty rate: 14.7% (2000).
Taxes: Total city taxes per capita: $67 (1997); City property taxes per capita: $67 (1997).
Education: High school graduation rate: 77.6% (2000); College graduation rate: 11.5% (2000).
Housing: Homeownership rate: 85.4% (2000); Median home value: $78,100 (2000); Median rent: $344 per month (2000); Median age of housing: 37 years (2000).
Transportation: Commute to work: 75.1% car, 0.0% public transportation, 6.1% walk, 18.1% work from home (2000); Travel time to work: 34.8% less than 15 minutes, 37.4% 15 to 30 minutes, 12.3% 30 to 45 minutes, 9.7% 45 to 60 minutes, 5.7% 60 minutes or more (2000)

TWO RIVERS (township). Covers a land area of 27.091 square miles and a water area of 0.484 square miles. Located at 45.80° N. Lat.; 94.38° W. Long.
Population: 582 (2000); Race: 99.6% White, 0.0% Black, 0.0% Asian, 0.4% American Indian and Alaska Native, 0.0% Hispanic of any race, 0.0% two or more races (2000); Density: 21.5 persons per square mile (2000); Age: 28.8% under 18, 8.1% over 64 (2000); Marriage status: 32.7% never married, 57.7% now married, 4.7% widowed, 4.9% divorced (2000); Foreign born: 0.0% (2000); Ancestry (includes multiple ancestries): 44.7% Polish, 41.3% German, 5.5% Swedish, 4.9% United States or American, 4.4% Irish (2000).
Economy: Employment by occupation: 14.1% management, 14.1% professional, 10.6% services, 16.3% sales, 3.8% farming, 15.6% construction, 25.6% production (2000).
Income: Per capita income: $19,067 (2000); Median household income: $47,656 (2000); Poverty rate: 5.5% (2000).
Taxes: Total city taxes per capita: $58 (1997); City property taxes per capita: $58 (1997).
Education: High school graduation rate: 86.6% (2000); College graduation rate: 12.5% (2000).
Housing: Homeownership rate: 87.0% (2000); Median home value: $95,000 (2000); Median rent: $267 per month (2000); Median age of housing: 28 years (2000).

Transportation: Commute to work: 79.4% car, 0.6% public transportation, 2.2% walk, 16.9% work from home (2000); Travel time to work: 17.7% less than 15 minutes, 31.6% 15 to 30 minutes, 33.5% 30 to 45 minutes, 7.9% 45 to 60 minutes, 9.4% 60 minutes or more (2000)

UPSALA (city). Covers a land area of 3.248 square miles and a water area of 0.002 square miles. Located at 45.80° N. Lat.; 94.56° W. Long.
Population: 424 (2000); Race: 100.0% White, 0.0% Black, 0.0% Asian, 0.0% American Indian and Alaska Native, 0.5% Hispanic of any race, 0.0% two or more races (2000); Density: 130.6 persons per square mile (2000); Age: 28.6% under 18, 20.7% over 64 (2000); Marriage status: 24.2% never married, 54.9% now married, 14.9% widowed, 6.0% divorced (2000); Foreign born: 0.7% (2000); Ancestry (includes multiple ancestries): 52.3% German, 25.5% Swedish, 12.5% Polish, 10.7% Norwegian, 5.2% Irish (2000).
Economy: Agriculture: grain, potatoes; dairying; livestock, poultry. Single-family building permits issued: 2 (2001) / 1 (2000); Multi-family building permits issued: 0 (2001) / 0 (2000); Employment by occupation: 11.4% management, 15.4% professional, 13.4% services, 24.4% sales, 2.0% farming, 13.9% construction, 19.4% production (2000).
Income: Per capita income: $16,382 (2000); Median household income: $30,000 (2000); Poverty rate: 13.7% (2000).
Taxes: Total city taxes per capita: $94 (1997); City property taxes per capita: $89 (1997).
Education: High school graduation rate: 79.4% (2000); College graduation rate: 16.6% (2000).

School District(s)

Upsala (PK-12)
2000 Enrollment: 424 320-573-2174
Housing: Homeownership rate: 69.9% (2000); Median home value: $63,200 (2000); Median rent: $364 per month (2000); Median age of housing: 49 years (2000).
Transportation: Commute to work: 83.8% car, 0.0% public transportation, 13.2% walk, 3.0% work from home (2000); Travel time to work: 59.2% less than 15 minutes, 7.9% 15 to 30 minutes, 17.3% 30 to 45 minutes, 8.9% 45 to 60 minutes, 6.8% 60 minutes or more (2000)
Additional Information Contacts
Upsala Chamber of Commerce 320-573-4477

Mower County

Located in southeastern Minnesota; bounded on the south by Iowa; drained by headwaters of the Cedar River. Covers a land area of 711.50 square miles, a water area of 0.20 square miles, and is located in the Central Time Zone. The county government was organized in 1855. County seat is Austin.

Weather Station: Austin 3 S — Elevation: 1,213 feet

	Jan	Feb	Mar	Apr	May	Jun	Jul	Aug	Sep	Oct	Nov	Dec
High	22	28	40	57	70	79	82	80	73	60	41	27
Low	4	10	24	36	47	57	61	58	49	38	25	10
Precip	0.9	0.5	1.6	3.1	4.0	3.9	4.5	4.4	3.5	2.5	1.9	0.9
Snow	na	6.5	5.9	2.8	tr	0.0	0.0	0.0	0.0	0.3	4.6	9.0

High and Low temperatures in degrees Fahrenheit; Precipitation and Snow in inches

Weather Station: Grand Meadow — Elevation: 1,348 feet

	Jan	Feb	Mar	Apr	May	Jun	Jul	Aug	Sep	Oct	Nov	Dec
High	20	27	38	54	68	78	81	79	71	58	40	26
Low	2	9	21	34	46	56	60	58	48	37	24	10
Precip	1.0	0.7	1.9	3.4	4.2	4.2	4.8	4.9	3.6	2.6	2.1	1.0
Snow	13.5	8.2	7.4	2.6	0.0	0.0	0.0	0.0	0.0	0.4	5.4	9.4

High and Low temperatures in degrees Fahrenheit; Precipitation and Snow in inches

Population: 38,603 (2000); Race: 95.0% White, 0.6% Black, 1.2% Asian, 0.3% American Indian and Alaska Native, 4.1% Hispanic of any race, 0.7% two or more races (2000); Density: 54.3 persons per square mile (2000); Age: 25.0% under 18, 19.5% over 64 (2000).
Religion: Five largest groups: 27.2% Evangelical Lutheran Church in America, 27.0% Catholic Church, 4.9% Lutheran Church—Missouri Synod, 4.7% The United Methodist Church, 2.0% Presbyterian Church (U.S.A.) (2000).
Economy: Unemployment rate: 3.0% (11/2002); Total civilian labor force: 20,343 (11/2002); Leading industries: 23.5% manufacturing; 19.1% health care and social assistance; 15.0% retail trade (2000); Companies that employ more than 1,000 persons: 1 (2000); Companies that employ more than 100 persons: 16 (2000); Farms: 1,123 totaling 404,238 acres (1997); Minority business ownership rate: 0.0% (1997); Women business ownership rate: 27.0% (1997); Retail sales per capita: $7,255 (1997). Single-family building permits issued: 82 (2001) / 107 (2000); Multi-family building permits issued: 160 (2001) / 13 (2000).
Income: Per capita income: $19,795 (2000); Median household income: $36,654 (2000); Poverty rate: 9.2% (2000); Bankruptcy rate: 3.41% (2001).
Taxes: Total county taxes per capita: $213 (2000); County property taxes per capita: $212 (2000).
Education: High school graduation rate: 82.3% (2000); College graduation rate: 14.7% (2000).
Housing: Homeownership rate: 78.3% (2000); Median home value: $71,400 (2000); Median rent: $329 per month (2000); Median age of housing: 48 years (2000).
Health: Birth rate: 121.0 per 10,000 population (1998); Age adjusted death rate: 83.7 per 10,000 population (1999); Age adjusted cancer mortality rate: 228.3 deaths per 100,000 population (1999). Number of physicians: 12.2 per 10,000 population (1999); Number of hospital beds: 20.2 per 10,000 population (1999).
Elections: 2000 Presidential election results: 57.9% Gore, 37.2% Bush, 3.7% Nader, 0.8% Buchanan
National and State Parks: Lake Louise State Park; Larson State Wildlife Management Area; Red Cedar State Wildlife Management Area; Rose State Wildlife Management Area
Additional Information Contacts
Mower County Government Offices 507-437-9493
Austin Board of Realtors 507-433-9204
Austin Chamber of Commerce 507-437-4561
Austin Convention Bureau 507-437-4563

Mower County Communities

ADAMS (city). Covers a land area of 1.011 square miles and a water area of 0 square miles. Located at 43.56° N. Lat.; 92.71° W. Long. Elevation is 1,286 feet.
Population: 800 (2000); Race: 99.4% White, 0.0% Black, 0.0% Asian, 0.0% American Indian and Alaska Native, 0.4% Hispanic of any race, 0.4% two or more races (2000); Density: 791.6 persons per square mile (2000); Age: 20.7% under 18, 36.8% over 64 (2000); Marriage status: 15.0% never married, 67.1% now married, 13.5% widowed, 4.4% divorced (2000); Foreign born: 0.2% (2000); Ancestry (includes multiple ancestries): 53.0% German, 25.0% Norwegian, 9.5% Irish, 4.4% United States or American, 4.4% English (2000).
Economy: Single-family building permits issued: 0 (2001) / 2 (2000); Multi-family building permits issued: 0 (2001) / 0 (2000); Employment by occupation: 13.3% management, 17.9% professional, 22.4% services, 17.9% sales, 2.7% farming, 10.3% construction, 15.5% production (2000).
Income: Per capita income: $16,550 (2000); Median household income: $31,289 (2000); Poverty rate: 6.3% (2000).
Taxes: Total city taxes per capita: $99 (1997); City property taxes per capita: $96 (1997).
Education: High school graduation rate: 72.4% (2000); College graduation rate: 10.9% (2000).

School District(s)

Southland (PK-12)
2000 Enrollment: 708 507-582-3283
Housing: Homeownership rate: 74.1% (2000); Median home value: $64,000 (2000); Median rent: $331 per month (2000); Median age of housing: 43 years (2000).
Transportation: Commute to work: 88.3% car, 1.8% public transportation, 5.8% walk, 4.0% work from home (2000); Travel time to work: 38.3% less than 15 minutes, 29.1% 15 to 30 minutes, 17.9% 30 to 45 minutes, 8.9% 45 to 60 minutes, 5.8% 60 minutes or more (2000)

ADAMS (township). Covers a land area of 34.938 square miles and a water area of 0 square miles. Located at 43.54° N. Lat.; 92.75° W. Long. Elevation is 1,286 feet.
Population: 475 (2000); Race: 100.0% White, 0.0% Black, 0.0% Asian, 0.0% American Indian and Alaska Native, 0.0% Hispanic of any race, 0.0% two or more races (2000); Density: 13.6 persons per square mile (2000); Age: 39.6% under 18, 7.4% over 64 (2000); Marriage status: 24.9% never married, 69.7% now married, 2.4% widowed, 3.0% divorced (2000); Foreign born: 0.0% (2000); Ancestry (includes multiple ancestries): 69.5% German, 21.0% Norwegian, 9.9% Irish, 7.6% English, 6.0% Dutch (2000).
Economy: Corn, oats, soybeans; cattle, sheep, hogs, poultry; dairying. Manufactures feeds and storage tanks. Printing and publishing industries. Employment by occupation: 23.5% management, 19.1% professional, 13.1%

services, 21.1% sales, 2.8% farming, 10.8% construction, 9.6% production (2000).
Income: Per capita income: $16,218 (2000); Median household income: $50,500 (2000); Poverty rate: 7.1% (2000).
Taxes: Total city taxes per capita: $136 (1997); City property taxes per capita: $136 (1997).
Education: High school graduation rate: 93.8% (2000); College graduation rate: 14.1% (2000).
Housing: Homeownership rate: 88.7% (2000); Median home value: $125,000 (2000); Median rent: $431 per month (2000); Median age of housing: 47 years (2000).
Transportation: Commute to work: 76.9% car, 0.8% public transportation, 3.6% walk, 18.6% work from home (2000); Travel time to work: 37.3% less than 15 minutes, 34.8% 15 to 30 minutes, 8.5% 30 to 45 minutes, 10.0% 45 to 60 minutes, 9.5% 60 minutes or more (2000)

AUSTIN (city). Covers a land area of 10.753 square miles and a water area of 0.092 square miles. Located at 43.66° N. Lat.; 92.97° W. Long. Elevation is 1,195 feet.
History: Austin was laid out in 1856 along the Cedar River. It was named for Austin R. Nicholas, the first to settle here. Though Austin won the county seat by election in 1857, two members of the county commission who lived in Austin had attempted earlier to wrest that honor in another way. Before a seat had been designated, county records were kept in a tin box. Figuring that wherever the box was, there was the county seat, the Austin commissioners made away with the box. Pursued by other commissioners, they bribed a bartender at a halfway station to hide the box in a snowbank before they were overcome and arrested.
Population: 23,314 (2000); Race: 92.9% White, 0.8% Black, 1.9% Asian, 0.3% American Indian and Alaska Native, 5.9% Hispanic of any race, 0.8% two or more races (2000); Density: 2,168.2 persons per square mile (2000); Age: 22.9% under 18, 22.1% over 64 (2000); Marriage status: 23.4% never married, 55.6% now married, 10.7% widowed, 10.2% divorced (2000); Foreign born: 5.3% (2000); Ancestry (includes multiple ancestries): 37.1% German, 24.0% Norwegian, 12.7% Irish, 9.8% Other groups, 7.2% English (2000).
Vital Statistics: Birth rate: 127.4 per 10,000 population (1998)
Economy: Single-family building permits issued: 34 (2001) / 40 (2000); Multi-family building permits issued: 160 (2001) / 13 (2000); Employment by occupation: 9.3% management, 16.1% professional, 17.4% services, 24.7% sales, 0.7% farming, 7.4% construction, 24.5% production (2000).
Income: Per capita income: $20,651 (2000); Median household income: $33,750 (2000); Poverty rate: 10.9% (2000).
Taxes: Total city taxes per capita: $144 (2000); City property taxes per capita: $121 (2000).
Education: High school graduation rate: 80.9% (2000); College graduation rate: 16.9% (2000).

School District(s)

Austin (PK-12)
2000 Enrollment: 4,259 507-433-0966

Two-year College(s)

Riverland Community College (Public)
2001 Enrollment: 3,478 507-433-0600
2001 Tuition: In-state $2,525; Out-of-state $5,056

Housing: Homeownership rate: 73.8% (2000); Median home value: $68,600 (2000); Median rent: $335 per month (2000); Median age of housing: 48 years (2000).
Hospitals: Austin Medical Center (138 beds)
Safety: Violent crime rate: 37.3 per 10,000 population; Property crime rate: 474.5 per 10,000 population (2001).
Newspapers: Austin Daily Herald (6 x week); Mower County Shopper (1 x week)
Transportation: Commute to work: 92.2% car, 1.5% public transportation, 3.4% walk, 1.7% work from home (2000); Travel time to work: 72.5% less than 15 minutes, 13.0% 15 to 30 minutes, 5.7% 30 to 45 minutes, 5.9% 45 to 60 minutes, 3.0% 60 minutes or more (2000)

Additional Information Contacts

Austin Board of Realtors 507-433-9204
Austin Chamber of Commerce 507-437-4561
Austin Convention Bureau 507-437-4563

AUSTIN (township). Covers a land area of 29.218 square miles and a water area of 0 square miles. Located at 43.63° N. Lat.; 93.00° W. Long. Elevation is 1,195 feet.
History: Incorporated 1868.
Population: 1,396 (2000); Race: 96.7% White, 0.0% Black, 0.8% Asian, 0.0% American Indian and Alaska Native, 2.6% Hispanic of any race, 0.3% two or more races (2000); Density: 47.8 persons per square mile (2000); Age: 30.2% under 18, 12.3% over 64 (2000); Marriage status: 23.1% never married, 67.0% now married, 4.7% widowed, 5.2% divorced (2000); Foreign born: 1.3% (2000); Ancestry (includes multiple ancestries): 49.3% German, 31.9% Norwegian, 7.5% Irish, 4.9% Other groups, 4.5% English (2000).
Economy: Railroad junction and industrial and commercial center of a rich farm region: corn; dairying; poultry, cattle, hogs, sheep. Manufacturing: foods, beverages, building materials, linens, furniture, cremation urns, paper products, compound containers; printing and publishing. Employment by occupation: 9.4% management, 19.6% professional, 15.8% services, 22.0% sales, 0.3% farming, 9.0% construction, 23.9% production (2000).
Income: Per capita income: $19,999 (2000); Median household income: $48,958 (2000); Poverty rate: 4.9% (2000).
Taxes: Total city taxes per capita: $49 (1997); City property taxes per capita: $49 (1997).
Education: High school graduation rate: 87.1% (2000); College graduation rate: 19.1% (2000).
Housing: Homeownership rate: 90.5% (2000); Median home value: $92,800 (2000); Median rent: $297 per month (2000); Median age of housing: 48 years (2000).
Transportation: Commute to work: 92.2% car, 0.0% public transportation, 0.7% walk, 6.4% work from home (2000); Travel time to work: 52.4% less than 15 minutes, 28.6% 15 to 30 minutes, 7.9% 30 to 45 minutes, 7.3% 45 to 60 minutes, 3.8% 60 minutes or more (2000)

BENNINGTON (township). Covers a land area of 36.144 square miles and a water area of 0 square miles. Located at 43.63° N. Lat.; 92.49° W. Long.
Population: 178 (2000); Race: 100.0% White, 0.0% Black, 0.0% Asian, 0.0% American Indian and Alaska Native, 0.0% Hispanic of any race, 0.0% two or more races (2000); Density: 4.9 persons per square mile (2000); Age: 25.3% under 18, 8.4% over 64 (2000); Marriage status: 22.5% never married, 67.5% now married, 1.3% widowed, 8.6% divorced (2000); Foreign born: 0.0% (2000); Ancestry (includes multiple ancestries): 56.3% German, 14.2% Norwegian, 9.5% Irish, 8.4% Danish, 7.9% United States or American (2000).
Economy: Employment by occupation: 27.1% management, 5.1% professional, 22.9% services, 13.6% sales, 2.5% farming, 21.2% construction, 7.6% production (2000).
Income: Per capita income: $24,386 (2000); Median household income: $50,833 (2000); Poverty rate: 8.4% (2000).
Taxes: Total city taxes per capita: $201 (1997); City property taxes per capita: $201 (1997).
Education: High school graduation rate: 95.9% (2000); College graduation rate: 7.3% (2000).
Housing: Homeownership rate: 90.9% (2000); Median home value: $87,500 (2000); Median rent: $275 per month (2000); Median age of housing: 60+ years (2000).
Transportation: Commute to work: 74.6% car, 3.4% public transportation, 1.7% walk, 20.3% work from home (2000); Travel time to work: 22.3% less than 15 minutes, 22.3% 15 to 30 minutes, 30.9% 30 to 45 minutes, 16.0% 45 to 60 minutes, 8.5% 60 minutes or more (2000)

BROWNSDALE (city). Covers a land area of 0.456 square miles and a water area of 0 square miles. Located at 43.74° N. Lat.; 92.86° W. Long. Elevation is 1,275 feet.
Population: 718 (2000); Race: 96.9% White, 0.0% Black, 0.0% Asian, 0.0% American Indian and Alaska Native, 2.6% Hispanic of any race, 1.2% two or more races (2000); Density: 1,574.4 persons per square mile (2000); Age: 25.7% under 18, 19.8% over 64 (2000); Marriage status: 24.5% never married, 60.1% now married, 6.7% widowed, 8.7% divorced (2000); Foreign born: 1.4% (2000); Ancestry (includes multiple ancestries): 43.7% German, 21.1% Norwegian, 9.9% Irish, 7.6% Other groups, 5.9% English (2000).
Economy: In agricultural area: dairying; poultry, livestock; corn, soybeans. Manufacturing: tunneling equipment, printing, feeds. Single-family building permits issued: 1 (2001) / 3 (2000); Multi-family building permits issued: 0 (2001) / 0 (2000); Employment by occupation: 8.7% management, 20.0% professional, 16.2% services, 22.3% sales, 1.2% farming, 12.8% construction, 18.8% production (2000).
Income: Per capita income: $15,778 (2000); Median household income: $32,857 (2000); Poverty rate: 7.4% (2000).
Taxes: Total city taxes per capita: $54 (1997); City property taxes per capita: $50 (1997).

Education: High school graduation rate: 82.1% (2000); College graduation rate: 9.1% (2000).
Housing: Homeownership rate: 83.2% (2000); Median home value: $70,400 (2000); Median rent: $285 per month (2000); Median age of housing: 44 years (2000).
Transportation: Commute to work: 87.1% car, 0.0% public transportation, 7.3% walk, 5.0% work from home (2000); Travel time to work: 28.3% less than 15 minutes, 46.2% 15 to 30 minutes, 6.2% 30 to 45 minutes, 12.9% 45 to 60 minutes, 6.5% 60 minutes or more (2000)

CLAYTON (township). Covers a land area of 36.222 square miles and a water area of 0 square miles. Located at 43.62° N. Lat.; 92.63° W. Long.
Population: 178 (2000); Race: 96.9% White, 0.0% Black, 1.6% Asian, 0.0% American Indian and Alaska Native, 1.6% Hispanic of any race, 0.0% two or more races (2000); Density: 4.9 persons per square mile (2000); Age: 33.9% under 18, 13.5% over 64 (2000); Marriage status: 31.3% never married, 63.9% now married, 4.8% widowed, 0.0% divorced (2000); Foreign born: 1.6% (2000); Ancestry (includes multiple ancestries): 43.2% German, 33.9% Norwegian, 11.5% Irish, 9.4% Other groups, 4.7% English (2000).
Economy: Employment by occupation: 23.3% management, 11.6% professional, 23.3% services, 15.1% sales, 8.1% farming, 9.3% construction, 9.3% production (2000).
Income: Per capita income: $32,453 (2000); Median household income: $75,739 (2000); Poverty rate: 5.2% (2000).
Taxes: Total city taxes per capita: $278 (1997); City property taxes per capita: $278 (1997).
Education: High school graduation rate: 70.8% (2000); College graduation rate: 13.3% (2000).
Housing: Homeownership rate: 89.8% (2000); Median home value: $106,300 (2000); Median age of housing: 60+ years (2000).
Transportation: Commute to work: 70.9% car, 4.7% public transportation, 4.7% walk, 19.8% work from home (2000); Travel time to work: 24.6% less than 15 minutes, 33.3% 15 to 30 minutes, 27.5% 30 to 45 minutes, 4.3% 45 to 60 minutes, 10.1% 60 minutes or more (2000)

DEXTER (city). Covers a land area of 1.449 square miles and a water area of 0 square miles. Located at 43.71° N. Lat.; 92.70° W. Long. Elevation is 1,416 feet.
Population: 333 (2000); Race: 96.0% White, 0.0% Black, 0.6% Asian, 0.0% American Indian and Alaska Native, 3.4% Hispanic of any race, 0.6% two or more races (2000); Density: 229.8 persons per square mile (2000); Age: 31.4% under 18, 16.2% over 64 (2000); Marriage status: 18.4% never married, 63.3% now married, 8.6% widowed, 9.8% divorced (2000); Foreign born: 4.0% (2000); Ancestry (includes multiple ancestries): 36.6% German, 28.7% Norwegian, 9.8% Irish, 7.0% English, 5.5% Other groups (2000).
Economy: Single-family building permits issued: 1 (2001) / 1 (2000); Multi-family building permits issued: 0 (2001) / 0 (2000); Employment by occupation: 4.2% management, 6.3% professional, 18.1% services, 30.6% sales, 5.6% farming, 11.8% construction, 23.6% production (2000).
Income: Per capita income: $14,199 (2000); Median household income: $31,875 (2000); Poverty rate: 10.4% (2000).
Taxes: Total city taxes per capita: $149 (1997); City property taxes per capita: $139 (1997).
Education: High school graduation rate: 79.4% (2000); College graduation rate: 1.4% (2000).
Housing: Homeownership rate: 83.6% (2000); Median home value: $60,600 (2000); Median rent: $175 per month (2000); Median age of housing: 48 years (2000).
Transportation: Commute to work: 89.9% car, 2.9% public transportation, 1.4% walk, 4.3% work from home (2000); Travel time to work: 28.0% less than 15 minutes, 25.0% 15 to 30 minutes, 38.6% 30 to 45 minutes, 3.8% 45 to 60 minutes, 4.5% 60 minutes or more (2000)

DEXTER (township). Covers a land area of 34.695 square miles and a water area of 0 square miles. Located at 43.71° N. Lat.; 92.76° W. Long. Elevation is 1,416 feet.
Population: 289 (2000); Race: 100.0% White, 0.0% Black, 0.0% Asian, 0.0% American Indian and Alaska Native, 0.0% Hispanic of any race, 0.0% two or more races (2000); Density: 8.3 persons per square mile (2000); Age: 31.0% under 18, 13.4% over 64 (2000); Marriage status: 14.3% never married, 71.4% now married, 4.6% widowed, 9.7% divorced (2000); Foreign born: 0.4% (2000); Ancestry (includes multiple ancestries): 56.7% German, 25.4% Norwegian, 12.3% English, 9.3% Irish, 4.5% Swedish (2000).
Economy: Dairying; corn, soybeans; cattle, sheep, hogs, poultry. Employment by occupation: 18.0% management, 17.2% professional, 10.7% services, 34.4% sales, 3.3% farming, 7.4% construction, 9.0% production (2000).
Income: Per capita income: $27,195 (2000); Median household income: $49,750 (2000); Poverty rate: 13.8% (2000).
Taxes: Total city taxes per capita: $149 (1997); City property taxes per capita: $149 (1997).
Education: High school graduation rate: 90.1% (2000); College graduation rate: 9.9% (2000).
Housing: Homeownership rate: 89.8% (2000); Median home value: $89,200 (2000); Median rent: $850 per month (2000); Median age of housing: 60+ years (2000).
Transportation: Commute to work: 77.5% car, 4.2% public transportation, 5.8% walk, 12.5% work from home (2000); Travel time to work: 16.2% less than 15 minutes, 30.5% 15 to 30 minutes, 35.2% 30 to 45 minutes, 16.2% 45 to 60 minutes, 1.9% 60 minutes or more (2000)

ELKTON (city). Covers a land area of 1.311 square miles and a water area of 0 square miles. Located at 43.66° N. Lat.; 92.70° W. Long. Elevation is 1,383 feet.
Population: 149 (2000); Race: 100.0% White, 0.0% Black, 0.0% Asian, 0.0% American Indian and Alaska Native, 5.1% Hispanic of any race, 0.0% two or more races (2000); Density: 113.7 persons per square mile (2000); Age: 35.0% under 18, 10.2% over 64 (2000); Marriage status: 21.0% never married, 65.0% now married, 8.0% widowed, 6.0% divorced (2000); Foreign born: 3.6% (2000); Ancestry (includes multiple ancestries): 50.4% German, 24.8% Irish, 16.1% Norwegian, 10.2% English, 8.0% Other groups (2000).
Economy: Corn, oats, soybeans; dairying. Single-family building permits issued: 0 (2001) / 3 (2000); Multi-family building permits issued: 0 (2001) / 0 (2000); Employment by occupation: 14.7% management, 20.6% professional, 17.6% services, 22.1% sales, 5.9% farming, 4.4% construction, 14.7% production (2000).
Income: Per capita income: $14,950 (2000); Median household income: $32,813 (2000); Poverty rate: 5.8% (2000).
Taxes: Total city taxes per capita: $74 (1997); City property taxes per capita: $74 (1997).
Education: High school graduation rate: 83.5% (2000); College graduation rate: 13.9% (2000).
Housing: Homeownership rate: 95.9% (2000); Median home value: $72,300 (2000); Median rent: $275 per month (2000); Median age of housing: 40 years (2000).
Transportation: Commute to work: 76.5% car, 7.4% public transportation, 11.8% walk, 1.5% work from home (2000); Travel time to work: 49.3% less than 15 minutes, 25.4% 15 to 30 minutes, 6.0% 30 to 45 minutes, 16.4% 45 to 60 minutes, 3.0% 60 minutes or more (2000)

FRANKFORD (township). Covers a land area of 29.980 square miles and a water area of 0.006 square miles. Located at 43.72° N. Lat.; 92.49° W. Long.
Population: 358 (2000); Race: 100.0% White, 0.0% Black, 0.0% Asian, 0.0% American Indian and Alaska Native, 0.0% Hispanic of any race, 0.0% two or more races (2000); Density: 11.9 persons per square mile (2000); Age: 31.8% under 18, 11.7% over 64 (2000); Marriage status: 21.1% never married, 68.5% now married, 3.0% widowed, 7.4% divorced (2000); Foreign born: 0.0% (2000); Ancestry (includes multiple ancestries): 58.7% German, 34.6% Norwegian, 18.7% Irish, 7.5% French (except Basque), 6.4% English (2000).
Economy: Employment by occupation: 14.2% management, 16.3% professional, 7.9% services, 21.6% sales, 6.3% farming, 14.7% construction, 18.9% production (2000).
Income: Per capita income: $21,845 (2000); Median household income: $56,250 (2000); Poverty rate: 5.6% (2000).
Taxes: Total city taxes per capita: $139 (1997); City property taxes per capita: $139 (1997).
Education: High school graduation rate: 83.5% (2000); College graduation rate: 13.0% (2000).
Housing: Homeownership rate: 86.1% (2000); Median home value: $108,300 (2000); Median rent: $375 per month (2000); Median age of housing: 55 years (2000).
Transportation: Commute to work: 86.1% car, 3.7% public transportation, 0.0% walk, 10.2% work from home (2000); Travel time to work: 24.4% less than 15 minutes, 26.2% 15 to 30 minutes, 31.0% 30 to 45 minutes, 14.3% 45 to 60 minutes, 4.2% 60 minutes or more (2000)

GRAND MEADOW (city). Covers a land area of 0.642 square miles and a water area of 0 square miles. Located at 43.70° N. Lat.; 92.57° W. Long. Elevation is 1,341 feet.

Population: 945 (2000); Race: 98.0% White, 0.0% Black, 0.0% Asian, 0.5% American Indian and Alaska Native, 1.2% Hispanic of any race, 0.6% two or more races (2000); Density: 1,470.9 persons per square mile (2000); Age: 24.5% under 18, 20.2% over 64 (2000); Marriage status: 20.2% never married, 61.1% now married, 9.8% widowed, 9.0% divorced (2000); Foreign born: 0.0% (2000); Ancestry (includes multiple ancestries): 40.9% German, 32.8% Norwegian, 7.8% English, 6.1% Irish, 5.8% Swedish (2000).
Economy: Employment by occupation: 10.4% management, 18.7% professional, 16.1% services, 28.5% sales, 2.4% farming, 9.4% construction, 14.5% production (2000).
Income: Per capita income: $18,509 (2000); Median household income: $38,188 (2000); Poverty rate: 4.8% (2000).
Taxes: Total city taxes per capita: $47 (1997); City property taxes per capita: $44 (1997).
Education: High school graduation rate: 82.1% (2000); College graduation rate: 11.8% (2000).

School District(s)

Grand Meadow (KG-12)
2000 Enrollment: 354 507-754-5318

Housing: Homeownership rate: 80.3% (2000); Median home value: $72,900 (2000); Median rent: $297 per month (2000); Median age of housing: 48 years (2000).
Newspapers: Meadow Area News (1 x week)
Transportation: Commute to work: 84.4% car, 3.4% public transportation, 7.1% walk, 4.5% work from home (2000); Travel time to work: 37.4% less than 15 minutes, 18.3% 15 to 30 minutes, 35.7% 30 to 45 minutes, 6.6% 45 to 60 minutes, 2.1% 60 minutes or more (2000)

GRAND MEADOW (township). Covers a land area of 35.704 square miles and a water area of 0 square miles. Located at 43.71° N. Lat.; 92.62° W. Long. Elevation is 1,341 feet.
Population: 344 (2000); Race: 98.0% White, 0.3% Black, 0.0% Asian, 0.0% American Indian and Alaska Native, 0.0% Hispanic of any race, 0.0% two or more races (2000); Density: 9.6 persons per square mile (2000); Age: 31.8% under 18, 14.1% over 64 (2000); Marriage status: 24.8% never married, 69.6% now married, 3.0% widowed, 2.6% divorced (2000); Foreign born: 0.7% (2000); Ancestry (includes multiple ancestries): 43.0% German, 28.2% Norwegian, 10.5% Irish, 9.5% English, 6.2% United States or American (2000).
Economy: Grain, corn, oats, soybeans, peas; cattle, hogs, sheep, poultry; dairying. Manufacturing: utility trailers, fertilizers; printing. Limestone quarry nearby. Employment by occupation: 21.7% management, 16.6% professional, 18.9% services, 12.0% sales, 4.6% farming, 9.1% construction, 17.1% production (2000).
Income: Per capita income: $19,984 (2000); Median household income: $52,344 (2000); Poverty rate: 2.0% (2000).
Taxes: Total city taxes per capita: $149 (1997); City property taxes per capita: $149 (1997).
Education: High school graduation rate: 89.4% (2000); College graduation rate: 15.4% (2000).
Housing: Homeownership rate: 84.6% (2000); Median home value: $114,300 (2000); Median rent: $408 per month (2000); Median age of housing: 60+ years (2000).
Transportation: Commute to work: 78.2% car, 2.9% public transportation, 3.4% walk, 14.9% work from home (2000); Travel time to work: 27.0% less than 15 minutes, 18.9% 15 to 30 minutes, 40.5% 30 to 45 minutes, 9.5% 45 to 60 minutes, 4.1% 60 minutes or more (2000)

LANSING (township). Covers a land area of 32.253 square miles and a water area of 0.086 square miles. Located at 43.71° N. Lat.; 92.98° W. Long. Elevation is 1,228 feet.
Population: 1,292 (2000); Race: 97.1% White, 0.8% Black, 0.1% Asian, 0.0% American Indian and Alaska Native, 3.0% Hispanic of any race, 0.1% two or more races (2000); Density: 40.1 persons per square mile (2000); Age: 27.1% under 18, 16.0% over 64 (2000); Marriage status: 22.4% never married, 64.5% now married, 5.7% widowed, 7.5% divorced (2000); Foreign born: 1.8% (2000); Ancestry (includes multiple ancestries): 41.9% German, 31.3% Norwegian, 11.3% Irish, 6.2% Danish, 4.8% English (2000).
Economy: Corn, soybeans; livestock; dairying. Manufacturing: feeds. Employment by occupation: 14.9% management, 11.6% professional, 16.2% services, 27.8% sales, 2.7% farming, 9.9% construction, 16.9% production (2000).
Income: Per capita income: $17,301 (2000); Median household income: $39,911 (2000); Poverty rate: 12.2% (2000).
Taxes: Total city taxes per capita: $104 (2000); City property taxes per capita: $104 (2000).
Education: High school graduation rate: 82.5% (2000); College graduation rate: 13.0% (2000).
Housing: Homeownership rate: 87.1% (2000); Median home value: $74,100 (2000); Median rent: $384 per month (2000); Median age of housing: 47 years (2000).
Transportation: Commute to work: 90.0% car, 0.3% public transportation, 1.5% walk, 7.6% work from home (2000); Travel time to work: 61.4% less than 15 minutes, 24.1% 15 to 30 minutes, 6.8% 30 to 45 minutes, 2.7% 45 to 60 minutes, 4.9% 60 minutes or more (2000)

LE ROY (city). Covers a land area of 0.635 square miles and a water area of 0 square miles. Located at 43.51° N. Lat.; 92.50° W. Long. Elevation is 1,285 feet.
Population: 925 (2000); Race: 98.1% White, 0.0% Black, 0.2% Asian, 0.3% American Indian and Alaska Native, 0.2% Hispanic of any race, 1.4% two or more races (2000); Density: 1,455.9 persons per square mile (2000); Age: 25.7% under 18, 18.8% over 64 (2000); Marriage status: 24.9% never married, 56.4% now married, 11.0% widowed, 7.7% divorced (2000); Foreign born: 0.3% (2000); Ancestry (includes multiple ancestries): 38.9% German, 31.1% Norwegian, 11.2% Irish, 9.9% United States or American, 7.9% English (2000).
Economy: Single-family building permits issued: 2 (2001) / 4 (2000); Multi-family building permits issued: 0 (2001) / 0 (2000); Employment by occupation: 6.2% management, 15.5% professional, 17.1% services, 18.3% sales, 1.8% farming, 12.2% construction, 28.9% production (2000).
Income: Per capita income: $17,446 (2000); Median household income: $34,286 (2000); Poverty rate: 6.7% (2000).
Education: High school graduation rate: 83.9% (2000); College graduation rate: 11.6% (2000).

School District(s)

Leroy (KG-12)
2000 Enrollment: 396 507-324-5743

Housing: Homeownership rate: 80.8% (2000); Median home value: $60,700 (2000); Median rent: $250 per month (2000); Median age of housing: 56 years (2000).
Newspapers: Le Roy Independent (1 x week)
Transportation: Commute to work: 80.9% car, 2.8% public transportation, 11.9% walk, 3.6% work from home (2000); Travel time to work: 46.6% less than 15 minutes, 11.9% 15 to 30 minutes, 9.8% 30 to 45 minutes, 21.3% 45 to 60 minutes, 10.4% 60 minutes or more (2000)

LE ROY (township). Covers a land area of 35.360 square miles and a water area of 0.026 square miles. Located at 43.54° N. Lat.; 92.52° W. Long. Elevation is 1,285 feet.
Population: 396 (2000); Race: 99.4% White, 0.0% Black, 0.0% Asian, 0.0% American Indian and Alaska Native, 0.0% Hispanic of any race, 0.6% two or more races (2000); Density: 11.2 persons per square mile (2000); Age: 21.6% under 18, 21.0% over 64 (2000); Marriage status: 20.0% never married, 71.9% now married, 3.5% widowed, 4.6% divorced (2000); Foreign born: 0.0% (2000); Ancestry (includes multiple ancestries): 40.3% Norwegian, 30.5% German, 7.5% United States or American, 6.9% Danish, 6.6% Irish (2000).
Economy: Corn, oats, soybeans, alfalfa, peas; cattle, sheep, hogs, poultry; dairying. Manufacturing: feeds, fertilizers, electrical equipment, furniture. Limestone deposits nearby. Employment by occupation: 20.5% management, 12.1% professional, 11.1% services, 20.0% sales, 4.7% farming, 12.6% construction, 18.9% production (2000).
Income: Per capita income: $24,077 (2000); Median household income: $37,857 (2000); Poverty rate: 3.2% (2000).
Taxes: Total city taxes per capita: $78 (1997); City property taxes per capita: $78 (1997).
Education: High school graduation rate: 79.8% (2000); College graduation rate: 11.1% (2000).
Housing: Homeownership rate: 89.6% (2000); Median home value: $78,200 (2000); Median rent: $275 per month (2000); Median age of housing: 58 years (2000).
Transportation: Commute to work: 80.0% car, 1.1% public transportation, 2.1% walk, 16.8% work from home (2000); Travel time to work: 48.1% less than 15 minutes, 14.6% 15 to 30 minutes, 12.0% 30 to 45 minutes, 15.8% 45 to 60 minutes, 9.5% 60 minutes or more (2000)

LODI (township). Covers a land area of 35.626 square miles and a water area of 0 square miles. Located at 43.55° N. Lat.; 92.61° W. Long.
Population: 249 (2000); Race: 100.0% White, 0.0% Black, 0.0% Asian, 0.0% American Indian and Alaska Native, 0.0% Hispanic of any race, 0.0% two or more races (2000); Density: 7.0 persons per square mile (2000); Age:

29.3% under 18, 14.1% over 64 (2000); Marriage status: 24.6% never married, 70.7% now married, 2.6% widowed, 2.1% divorced (2000); Foreign born: 0.0% (2000); Ancestry (includes multiple ancestries): 51.6% German, 27.0% Norwegian, 7.4% United States or American, 2.7% Danish, 1.6% Irish (2000).
Economy: Employment by occupation: 25.7% management, 8.8% professional, 12.5% services, 25.7% sales, 7.4% farming, 9.6% construction, 10.3% production (2000).
Income: Per capita income: $17,504 (2000); Median household income: $45,179 (2000); Poverty rate: 12.3% (2000).
Taxes: Total city taxes per capita: $222 (1997); City property taxes per capita: $222 (1997).
Education: High school graduation rate: 91.1% (2000); College graduation rate: 7.0% (2000).
Housing: Homeownership rate: 93.0% (2000); Median home value: $91,300 (2000); Median rent: $225 per month (2000); Median age of housing: 45 years (2000).
Transportation: Commute to work: 73.5% car, 3.7% public transportation, 2.2% walk, 20.6% work from home (2000); Travel time to work: 38.0% less than 15 minutes, 23.1% 15 to 30 minutes, 16.7% 30 to 45 minutes, 5.6% 45 to 60 minutes, 16.7% 60 minutes or more (2000)

LYLE (city). Covers a land area of 0.772 square miles and a water area of 0 square miles. Located at 43.50° N. Lat.; 92.94° W. Long. Elevation is 1,203 feet.
Population: 566 (2000); Race: 99.6% White, 0.0% Black, 0.0% Asian, 0.0% American Indian and Alaska Native, 0.4% Hispanic of any race, 0.4% two or more races (2000); Density: 733.2 persons per square mile (2000); Age: 32.1% under 18, 12.9% over 64 (2000); Marriage status: 28.4% never married, 59.4% now married, 4.0% widowed, 8.2% divorced (2000); Foreign born: 0.0% (2000); Ancestry (includes multiple ancestries): 36.2% German, 32.3% Norwegian, 11.7% Irish, 8.0% Danish, 6.9% United States or American (2000).
Economy: Single-family building permits issued: 2 (2001) / 4 (2000); Multi-family building permits issued: 0 (2001) / 0 (2000); Employment by occupation: 8.5% management, 12.6% professional, 18.4% services, 27.9% sales, 1.4% farming, 9.2% construction, 22.1% production (2000).
Income: Per capita income: $14,624 (2000); Median household income: $34,464 (2000); Poverty rate: 9.4% (2000).
Taxes: Total city taxes per capita: $194 (1997); City property taxes per capita: $190 (1997).
Education: High school graduation rate: 83.8% (2000); College graduation rate: 9.9% (2000).

School District(s)

Lyle (PK-12)
2000 Enrollment: 238 507-325-4146

Housing: Homeownership rate: 80.9% (2000); Median home value: $68,200 (2000); Median rent: $200 per month (2000); Median age of housing: 54 years (2000).
Transportation: Commute to work: 89.7% car, 0.0% public transportation, 8.5% walk, 1.1% work from home (2000); Travel time to work: 28.8% less than 15 minutes, 49.6% 15 to 30 minutes, 9.4% 30 to 45 minutes, 6.5% 45 to 60 minutes, 5.8% 60 minutes or more (2000)

LYLE (township). Covers a land area of 35.468 square miles and a water area of 0 square miles. Located at 43.54° N. Lat.; 92.99° W. Long. Elevation is 1,203 feet.
Population: 402 (2000); Race: 99.1% White, 0.0% Black, 0.0% Asian, 0.5% American Indian and Alaska Native, 0.0% Hispanic of any race, 0.5% two or more races (2000); Density: 11.3 persons per square mile (2000); Age: 22.1% under 18, 9.8% over 64 (2000); Marriage status: 27.7% never married, 54.5% now married, 3.7% widowed, 14.1% divorced (2000); Foreign born: 0.0% (2000); Ancestry (includes multiple ancestries): 42.1% German, 27.9% Norwegian, 15.3% Irish, 8.8% Danish, 7.9% English (2000).
Economy: Railroad junction. Alfalfa, soybeans, grain; dairying; poultry. Manufacturing: feeds, grain processing. Employment by occupation: 14.3% management, 10.2% professional, 14.7% services, 32.5% sales, 3.0% farming, 10.9% construction, 14.3% production (2000).
Income: Per capita income: $19,116 (2000); Median household income: $46,667 (2000); Poverty rate: 8.4% (2000).
Taxes: Total city taxes per capita: $116 (1997); City property taxes per capita: $116 (1997).
Education: High school graduation rate: 93.6% (2000); College graduation rate: 15.5% (2000).
Housing: Homeownership rate: 90.4% (2000); Median home value: $100,000 (2000); Median rent: $267 per month (2000); Median age of housing: 44 years (2000).
Transportation: Commute to work: 87.8% car, 0.0% public transportation, 0.0% walk, 12.2% work from home (2000); Travel time to work: 16.1% less than 15 minutes, 67.0% 15 to 30 minutes, 7.6% 30 to 45 minutes, 3.1% 45 to 60 minutes, 6.3% 60 minutes or more (2000)

MAPLEVIEW (city). Covers a land area of 0.187 square miles and a water area of 0 square miles. Located at 43.68° N. Lat.; 92.97° W. Long.
Population: 189 (2000); Race: 96.6% White, 0.0% Black, 3.4% Asian, 0.0% American Indian and Alaska Native, 6.1% Hispanic of any race, 0.0% two or more races (2000); Density: 1,010.9 persons per square mile (2000); Age: 11.5% under 18, 19.6% over 64 (2000); Marriage status: 27.8% never married, 46.5% now married, 11.8% widowed, 13.9% divorced (2000); Foreign born: 9.5% (2000); Ancestry (includes multiple ancestries): 42.6% German, 24.3% Norwegian, 9.5% Other groups, 8.8% Irish, 4.7% Dutch (2000).
Economy: Grain; dairying. Single-family building permits issued: 0 (2001) / 0 (2000); Multi-family building permits issued: 0 (2001) / 0 (2000); Employment by occupation: 0.0% management, 7.1% professional, 31.0% services, 17.9% sales, 1.2% farming, 10.7% construction, 32.1% production (2000).
Income: Per capita income: $16,884 (2000); Median household income: $30,909 (2000); Poverty rate: 12.8% (2000).
Taxes: Total city taxes per capita: $87 (1997); City property taxes per capita: $67 (1997).
Education: High school graduation rate: 71.5% (2000); College graduation rate: 1.6% (2000).
Housing: Homeownership rate: 81.8% (2000); Median home value: $30,600 (2000); Median rent: $325 per month (2000); Median age of housing: 60+ years (2000).
Transportation: Commute to work: 96.3% car, 0.0% public transportation, 1.3% walk, 0.0% work from home (2000); Travel time to work: 58.8% less than 15 minutes, 20.0% 15 to 30 minutes, 11.3% 30 to 45 minutes, 5.0% 45 to 60 minutes, 5.0% 60 minutes or more (2000)

MARSHALL (township). Covers a land area of 34.609 square miles and a water area of 0 square miles. Located at 43.63° N. Lat.; 92.75° W. Long.
Population: 382 (2000); Race: 100.0% White, 0.0% Black, 0.0% Asian, 0.0% American Indian and Alaska Native, 0.0% Hispanic of any race, 0.0% two or more races (2000); Density: 11.0 persons per square mile (2000); Age: 31.1% under 18, 10.4% over 64 (2000); Marriage status: 29.7% never married, 62.7% now married, 2.9% widowed, 4.7% divorced (2000); Foreign born: 0.5% (2000); Ancestry (includes multiple ancestries): 47.5% German, 28.7% Norwegian, 7.4% Irish, 4.4% English, 4.1% United States or American (2000).
Economy: Employment by occupation: 26.9% management, 15.5% professional, 10.9% services, 17.6% sales, 4.1% farming, 11.4% construction, 13.5% production (2000).
Income: Per capita income: $16,322 (2000); Median household income: $47,500 (2000); Poverty rate: 3.3% (2000).
Taxes: Total city taxes per capita: $151 (1997); City property taxes per capita: $151 (1997).
Education: High school graduation rate: 93.1% (2000); College graduation rate: 9.7% (2000).
Housing: Homeownership rate: 88.1% (2000); Median home value: $86,900 (2000); Median rent: $438 per month (2000); Median age of housing: 60+ years (2000).
Transportation: Commute to work: 77.2% car, 4.1% public transportation, 0.0% walk, 18.7% work from home (2000); Travel time to work: 21.7% less than 15 minutes, 44.6% 15 to 30 minutes, 23.6% 30 to 45 minutes, 8.3% 45 to 60 minutes, 1.9% 60 minutes or more (2000)

NEVADA (township). Covers a land area of 36.739 square miles and a water area of 0 square miles. Located at 43.54° N. Lat.; 92.87° W. Long.
Population: 353 (2000); Race: 99.1% White, 0.0% Black, 0.3% Asian, 0.0% American Indian and Alaska Native, 0.0% Hispanic of any race, 0.6% two or more races (2000); Density: 9.6 persons per square mile (2000); Age: 28.7% under 18, 16.8% over 64 (2000); Marriage status: 18.9% never married, 70.5% now married, 5.5% widowed, 5.1% divorced (2000); Foreign born: 0.3% (2000); Ancestry (includes multiple ancestries): 50.2% German, 29.1% Norwegian, 13.1% Irish, 12.5% French (except Basque), 5.5% English (2000).

Economy: Employment by occupation: 20.8% management, 8.2% professional, 13.2% services, 24.5% sales, 0.6% farming, 10.7% construction, 22.0% production (2000).
Income: Per capita income: $17,515 (2000); Median household income: $41,071 (2000); Poverty rate: 3.1% (2000).
Taxes: Total city taxes per capita: $229 (2000); City property taxes per capita: $229 (2000).
Education: High school graduation rate: 82.1% (2000); College graduation rate: 8.0% (2000).
Housing: Homeownership rate: 87.0% (2000); Median home value: $118,800 (2000); Median rent: $275 per month (2000); Median age of housing: 54 years (2000).
Transportation: Commute to work: 79.4% car, 1.3% public transportation, 1.9% walk, 17.4% work from home (2000); Travel time to work: 19.5% less than 15 minutes, 50.8% 15 to 30 minutes, 18.0% 30 to 45 minutes, 5.5% 45 to 60 minutes, 6.3% 60 minutes or more (2000)

PLEASANT VALLEY (township). Covers a land area of 30.113 square miles and a water area of 0 square miles. Located at 43.80° N. Lat.; 92.62° W. Long.
Population: 308 (2000); Race: 100.0% White, 0.0% Black, 0.0% Asian, 0.0% American Indian and Alaska Native, 0.0% Hispanic of any race, 0.0% two or more races (2000); Density: 10.2 persons per square mile (2000); Age: 44.5% under 18, 4.4% over 64 (2000); Marriage status: 31.2% never married, 62.4% now married, 3.8% widowed, 2.5% divorced (2000); Foreign born: 0.0% (2000); Ancestry (includes multiple ancestries): 69.9% German, 21.0% Norwegian, 14.9% Irish, 5.8% English, 5.2% Dutch (2000).
Economy: Employment by occupation: 16.7% management, 19.1% professional, 14.8% services, 19.8% sales, 2.5% farming, 18.5% construction, 8.6% production (2000).
Income: Per capita income: $14,242 (2000); Median household income: $46,250 (2000); Poverty rate: 3.0% (2000).
Taxes: Total city taxes per capita: $105 (1997); City property taxes per capita: $105 (1997).
Education: High school graduation rate: 91.6% (2000); College graduation rate: 12.8% (2000).
Housing: Homeownership rate: 98.1% (2000); Median home value: $119,800 (2000); Median age of housing: 52 years (2000).
Transportation: Commute to work: 80.5% car, 3.2% public transportation, 1.9% walk, 13.0% work from home (2000); Travel time to work: 12.7% less than 15 minutes, 35.8% 15 to 30 minutes, 39.6% 30 to 45 minutes, 3.0% 45 to 60 minutes, 9.0% 60 minutes or more (2000)

RACINE (city). Covers a land area of 0.441 square miles and a water area of 0 square miles. Located at 43.77° N. Lat.; 92.48° W. Long.
Population: 355 (2000); Race: 99.4% White, 0.0% Black, 0.0% Asian, 0.0% American Indian and Alaska Native, 0.0% Hispanic of any race, 0.6% two or more races (2000); Density: 804.4 persons per square mile (2000); Age: 28.5% under 18, 9.2% over 64 (2000); Marriage status: 23.7% never married, 66.9% now married, 5.7% widowed, 3.7% divorced (2000); Foreign born: 0.0% (2000); Ancestry (includes multiple ancestries): 59.8% German, 31.6% Norwegian, 12.3% Irish, 8.9% English, 5.8% Dutch (2000).
Economy: Single-family building permits issued: 7 (2001) / 3 (2000); Multi-family building permits issued: 0 (2001) / 0 (2000); Employment by occupation: 10.9% management, 22.3% professional, 17.1% services, 24.0% sales, 0.0% farming, 12.6% construction, 13.1% production (2000).
Income: Per capita income: $19,755 (2000); Median household income: $53,750 (2000); Poverty rate: 0.0% (2000).
Taxes: Total city taxes per capita: $124 (1997); City property taxes per capita: $118 (1997).
Education: High school graduation rate: 91.0% (2000); College graduation rate: 14.1% (2000).
Housing: Homeownership rate: 89.7% (2000); Median home value: $92,700 (2000); Median rent: $288 per month (2000); Median age of housing: 27 years (2000).
Transportation: Commute to work: 90.6% car, 7.0% public transportation, 2.3% walk, 0.0% work from home (2000); Travel time to work: 11.1% less than 15 minutes, 34.5% 15 to 30 minutes, 44.4% 30 to 45 minutes, 7.6% 45 to 60 minutes, 2.3% 60 minutes or more (2000)

RACINE (township). Covers a land area of 35.887 square miles and a water area of 0 square miles. Located at 43.78° N. Lat.; 92.51° W. Long.
Population: 445 (2000); Race: 97.6% White, 0.7% Black, 0.0% Asian, 0.0% American Indian and Alaska Native, 0.0% Hispanic of any race, 1.7% two or more races (2000); Density: 12.4 persons per square mile (2000); Age: 21.3% under 18, 14.0% over 64 (2000); Marriage status: 18.4% never married, 69.2% now married, 6.1% widowed, 6.3% divorced (2000); Foreign born: 1.9% (2000); Ancestry (includes multiple ancestries): 51.2% German, 30.3% Norwegian, 10.0% Irish, 6.2% English, 5.7% United States or American (2000).
Economy: Manufacturing: agricultural machinery. Agriculture: dairying; poultry; corn, soybeans, peas. Employment by occupation: 23.2% management, 12.2% professional, 11.0% services, 34.1% sales, 0.4% farming, 9.8% construction, 9.3% production (2000).
Income: Per capita income: $23,320 (2000); Median household income: $54,231 (2000); Poverty rate: 1.2% (2000).
Taxes: Total city taxes per capita: $158 (1997); City property taxes per capita: $158 (1997).
Education: High school graduation rate: 86.2% (2000); College graduation rate: 9.9% (2000).
Housing: Homeownership rate: 94.4% (2000); Median home value: $122,500 (2000); Median rent: $483 per month (2000); Median age of housing: 47 years (2000).
Transportation: Commute to work: 81.3% car, 0.8% public transportation, 4.1% walk, 13.0% work from home (2000); Travel time to work: 18.7% less than 15 minutes, 41.1% 15 to 30 minutes, 34.1% 30 to 45 minutes, 4.7% 45 to 60 minutes, 1.4% 60 minutes or more (2000)

RED ROCK (township). Covers a land area of 35.404 square miles and a water area of 0 square miles. Located at 43.72° N. Lat.; 92.87° W. Long.
Population: 715 (2000); Race: 100.0% White, 0.0% Black, 0.0% Asian, 0.0% American Indian and Alaska Native, 0.0% Hispanic of any race, 0.0% two or more races (2000); Density: 20.2 persons per square mile (2000); Age: 27.9% under 18, 11.5% over 64 (2000); Marriage status: 19.4% never married, 71.8% now married, 5.5% widowed, 3.3% divorced (2000); Foreign born: 0.7% (2000); Ancestry (includes multiple ancestries): 45.2% German, 30.5% Norwegian, 8.2% Irish, 6.8% English, 6.0% Swedish (2000).
Economy: Employment by occupation: 15.2% management, 16.8% professional, 14.9% services, 22.8% sales, 1.1% farming, 11.1% construction, 18.2% production (2000).
Income: Per capita income: $19,519 (2000); Median household income: $50,455 (2000); Poverty rate: 1.8% (2000).
Taxes: Total city taxes per capita: $79 (1997); City property taxes per capita: $79 (1997).
Education: High school graduation rate: 89.0% (2000); College graduation rate: 9.0% (2000).
Housing: Homeownership rate: 90.7% (2000); Median home value: $96,200 (2000); Median rent: $275 per month (2000); Median age of housing: 48 years (2000).
Transportation: Commute to work: 97.3% car, 0.0% public transportation, 1.1% walk, 1.6% work from home (2000); Travel time to work: 48.3% less than 15 minutes, 30.2% 15 to 30 minutes, 8.4% 30 to 45 minutes, 6.7% 45 to 60 minutes, 6.4% 60 minutes or more (2000)

ROSE CREEK (city). Covers a land area of 0.458 square miles and a water area of 0 square miles. Located at 43.60° N. Lat.; 92.83° W. Long. Elevation is 1,285 feet.
History: St. Croix National Scenic Riverway to East.
Population: 354 (2000); Race: 98.8% White, 0.6% Black, 0.0% Asian, 0.0% American Indian and Alaska Native, 2.3% Hispanic of any race, 0.6% two or more races (2000); Density: 773.4 persons per square mile (2000); Age: 25.2% under 18, 24.0% over 64 (2000); Marriage status: 20.2% never married, 65.0% now married, 9.1% widowed, 5.7% divorced (2000); Foreign born: 0.9% (2000); Ancestry (includes multiple ancestries): 55.4% German, 12.3% Norwegian, 12.0% Irish, 5.9% United States or American, 5.6% Danish (2000).
Economy: Grain, soybeans; livestock, poultry; dairying. Manufacturing: hunting feed. Single-family building permits issued: 1 (2001) / 1 (2000); Multi-family building permits issued: 0 (2001) / 0 (2000); Employment by occupation: 8.1% management, 11.8% professional, 20.5% services, 17.4% sales, 2.5% farming, 27.3% construction, 12.4% production (2000).
Income: Per capita income: $19,484 (2000); Median household income: $42,841 (2000); Poverty rate: 4.4% (2000).
Taxes: Total city taxes per capita: $27 (1997); City property taxes per capita: $24 (1997).
Education: High school graduation rate: 76.5% (2000); College graduation rate: 6.2% (2000).
Housing: Homeownership rate: 72.5% (2000); Median home value: $64,800 (2000); Median rent: $265 per month (2000); Median age of housing: 40 years (2000).
Transportation: Commute to work: 83.8% car, 3.8% public transportation, 8.8% walk, 3.8% work from home (2000); Travel time to work: 35.1% less

than 15 minutes, 42.9% 15 to 30 minutes, 11.7% 30 to 45 minutes, 7.8% 45 to 60 minutes, 2.6% 60 minutes or more (2000)

SARGEANT (city). Covers a land area of 0.834 square miles and a water area of 0 square miles. Located at 43.80° N. Lat.; 92.80° W. Long. Elevation is 1,382 feet.
Population: 76 (2000); Race: 93.5% White, 0.0% Black, 0.0% Asian, 2.2% American Indian and Alaska Native, 0.0% Hispanic of any race, 4.3% two or more races (2000); Density: 91.1 persons per square mile (2000); Age: 30.4% under 18, 26.1% over 64 (2000); Marriage status: 20.6% never married, 54.4% now married, 2.9% widowed, 22.1% divorced (2000); Foreign born: 0.0% (2000); Ancestry (includes multiple ancestries): 41.3% German, 29.3% Norwegian, 21.7% English, 9.8% French (except Basque), 8.7% Dutch (2000).
Economy: Employment by occupation: 6.5% management, 10.9% professional, 13.0% services, 37.0% sales, 0.0% farming, 15.2% construction, 17.4% production (2000).
Income: Per capita income: $14,485 (2000); Median household income: $38,333 (2000); Poverty rate: 15.4% (2000).
Taxes: Total city taxes per capita: $68 (1997); City property taxes per capita: $68 (1997).
Education: High school graduation rate: 93.0% (2000); College graduation rate: 14.0% (2000).
Housing: Homeownership rate: 94.1% (2000); Median home value: $55,000 (2000); Median age of housing: 60+ years (2000).
Transportation: Commute to work: 91.3% car, 0.0% public transportation, 0.0% walk, 8.7% work from home (2000); Travel time to work: 11.9% less than 15 minutes, 28.6% 15 to 30 minutes, 31.0% 30 to 45 minutes, 16.7% 45 to 60 minutes, 11.9% 60 minutes or more (2000)

SARGEANT (township). Covers a land area of 35.380 square miles and a water area of 0 square miles. Located at 43.79° N. Lat.; 92.73° W. Long. Elevation is 1,382 feet.
Population: 316 (2000); Race: 99.4% White, 0.0% Black, 0.6% Asian, 0.0% American Indian and Alaska Native, 0.0% Hispanic of any race, 0.0% two or more races (2000); Density: 8.9 persons per square mile (2000); Age: 29.3% under 18, 7.8% over 64 (2000); Marriage status: 13.3% never married, 80.6% now married, 2.8% widowed, 3.2% divorced (2000); Foreign born: 1.6% (2000); Ancestry (includes multiple ancestries): 45.5% German, 25.9% Norwegian, 8.7% Danish, 7.2% Irish, 6.2% English (2000).
Economy: Grain; livestock; dairying. Employment by occupation: 20.5% management, 19.2% professional, 11.0% services, 17.8% sales, 4.8% farming, 15.1% construction, 11.6% production (2000).
Income: Per capita income: $16,720 (2000); Median household income: $46,875 (2000); Poverty rate: 21.5% (2000).
Taxes: Total city taxes per capita: $128 (1997); City property taxes per capita: $128 (1997).
Education: High school graduation rate: 87.8% (2000); College graduation rate: 14.5% (2000).
Housing: Homeownership rate: 81.6% (2000); Median home value: $93,300 (2000); Median rent: $275 per month (2000); Median age of housing: 57 years (2000).
Transportation: Commute to work: 83.6% car, 0.0% public transportation, 8.2% walk, 8.2% work from home (2000); Travel time to work: 37.3% less than 15 minutes, 15.7% 15 to 30 minutes, 37.3% 30 to 45 minutes, 5.2% 45 to 60 minutes, 4.5% 60 minutes or more (2000)

TAOPI (city). Covers a land area of 0.392 square miles and a water area of 0 square miles. Located at 43.55° N. Lat.; 92.64° W. Long. Elevation is 1,242 feet.
Population: 93 (2000); Race: 100.0% White, 0.0% Black, 0.0% Asian, 0.0% American Indian and Alaska Native, 0.0% Hispanic of any race, 0.0% two or more races (2000); Density: 236.9 persons per square mile (2000); Age: 37.1% under 18, 4.8% over 64 (2000); Marriage status: 29.1% never married, 58.2% now married, 8.9% widowed, 3.8% divorced (2000); Foreign born: 0.0% (2000); Ancestry (includes multiple ancestries): 45.7% German, 28.6% Norwegian, 5.7% Swedish, 4.8% Irish, 1.9% Danish (2000).
Economy: Agriculture includes corn, oats, livestock, dairying, and poultry. Single-family building permits issued: 2 (2001) / 2 (2000); Multi-family building permits issued: 0 (2001) / 0 (2000); Employment by occupation: 22.2% management, 3.7% professional, 31.5% services, 14.8% sales, 0.0% farming, 7.4% construction, 20.4% production (2000).
Income: Per capita income: $11,250 (2000); Median household income: $33,750 (2000); Poverty rate: 4.8% (2000).
Taxes: Total city taxes per capita: $33 (1997); City property taxes per capita: $33 (1997).
Education: High school graduation rate: 92.9% (2000); College graduation rate: 3.6% (2000).
Housing: Homeownership rate: 100.0% (2000); Median home value: $35,000 (2000); Median age of housing: 29 years (2000).
Transportation: Commute to work: 90.7% car, 0.0% public transportation, 0.0% walk, 9.3% work from home (2000); Travel time to work: 26.5% less than 15 minutes, 38.8% 15 to 30 minutes, 8.2% 30 to 45 minutes, 16.3% 45 to 60 minutes, 10.2% 60 minutes or more (2000)

UDOLPHO (township). Covers a land area of 36.019 square miles and a water area of 0 square miles. Located at 43.80° N. Lat.; 92.98° W. Long.
Population: 458 (2000); Race: 97.8% White, 1.8% Black, 0.0% Asian, 0.0% American Indian and Alaska Native, 1.3% Hispanic of any race, 0.0% two or more races (2000); Density: 12.7 persons per square mile (2000); Age: 28.7% under 18, 18.5% over 64 (2000); Marriage status: 18.6% never married, 70.2% now married, 4.9% widowed, 6.3% divorced (2000); Foreign born: 0.7% (2000); Ancestry (includes multiple ancestries): 40.8% Norwegian, 34.5% German, 10.7% English, 10.7% Irish, 6.7% Czech (2000).
Economy: Employment by occupation: 15.7% management, 9.4% professional, 20.4% services, 14.0% sales, 5.5% farming, 15.7% construction, 19.1% production (2000).
Income: Per capita income: $19,140 (2000); Median household income: $40,179 (2000); Poverty rate: 8.9% (2000).
Taxes: Total city taxes per capita: $93 (1997); City property taxes per capita: $93 (1997).
Education: High school graduation rate: 86.7% (2000); College graduation rate: 5.8% (2000).
Housing: Homeownership rate: 86.4% (2000); Median home value: $102,900 (2000); Median rent: $313 per month (2000); Median age of housing: 60+ years (2000).
Transportation: Commute to work: 82.5% car, 0.9% public transportation, 3.1% walk, 13.5% work from home (2000); Travel time to work: 29.3% less than 15 minutes, 55.6% 15 to 30 minutes, 13.1% 30 to 45 minutes, 0.0% 45 to 60 minutes, 2.0% 60 minutes or more (2000)

WALTHAM (city). Covers a land area of 0.461 square miles and a water area of 0 square miles. Located at 43.82° N. Lat.; 92.87° W. Long. Elevation is 1,326 feet.
Population: 196 (2000); Race: 100.0% White, 0.0% Black, 0.0% Asian, 0.0% American Indian and Alaska Native, 5.7% Hispanic of any race, 0.0% two or more races (2000); Density: 425.0 persons per square mile (2000); Age: 27.6% under 18, 17.2% over 64 (2000); Marriage status: 26.1% never married, 58.0% now married, 10.1% widowed, 5.8% divorced (2000); Foreign born: 0.0% (2000); Ancestry (includes multiple ancestries): 58.6% German, 26.4% Norwegian, 11.5% Irish, 9.8% United States or American, 9.2% Polish (2000).
Economy: Single-family building permits issued: 0 (2001) / 0 (2000); Multi-family building permits issued: 0 (2001) / 0 (2000); Employment by occupation: 5.1% management, 5.1% professional, 24.4% services, 9.0% sales, 0.0% farming, 17.9% construction, 38.5% production (2000).
Income: Per capita income: $26,047 (2000); Median household income: $35,000 (2000); Poverty rate: 5.2% (2000).
Taxes: Total city taxes per capita: $93 (1997); City property taxes per capita: $81 (1997).
Education: High school graduation rate: 70.8% (2000); College graduation rate: 7.5% (2000).
Housing: Homeownership rate: 100.0% (2000); Median home value: $55,700 (2000); Median age of housing: 60+ years (2000).
Transportation: Commute to work: 94.9% car, 0.0% public transportation, 2.6% walk, 2.6% work from home (2000); Travel time to work: 32.9% less than 15 minutes, 44.7% 15 to 30 minutes, 11.8% 30 to 45 minutes, 9.2% 45 to 60 minutes, 1.3% 60 minutes or more (2000)

WALTHAM (township). Covers a land area of 35.901 square miles and a water area of 0 square miles. Located at 43.79° N. Lat.; 92.88° W. Long. Elevation is 1,326 feet.
Population: 416 (2000); Race: 95.4% White, 0.0% Black, 2.4% Asian, 2.2% American Indian and Alaska Native, 0.4% Hispanic of any race, 0.0% two or more races (2000); Density: 11.6 persons per square mile (2000); Age: 30.8% under 18, 10.6% over 64 (2000); Marriage status: 27.5% never married, 67.8% now married, 1.8% widowed, 2.9% divorced (2000); Foreign born: 1.1% (2000); Ancestry (includes multiple ancestries): 43.6% German, 23.9% Norwegian, 10.0% Irish, 8.0% Swedish, 7.3% English (2000).
Economy: Dairying; livestock; corn, soybeans. Employment by occupation: 17.0% management, 13.7% professional, 11.2% services, 23.2% sales, 2.9% farming, 10.4% construction, 21.6% production (2000).

Income: Per capita income: $16,228 (2000); Median household income: $47,500 (2000); Poverty rate: 6.0% (2000).
Taxes: Total city taxes per capita: $83 (1997); City property taxes per capita: $83 (1997).
Education: High school graduation rate: 88.1% (2000); College graduation rate: 8.3% (2000).
Housing: Homeownership rate: 90.5% (2000); Median home value: $86,500 (2000); Median rent: $288 per month (2000); Median age of housing: 60+ years (2000).
Transportation: Commute to work: 84.1% car, 0.0% public transportation, 2.1% walk, 13.8% work from home (2000); Travel time to work: 22.8% less than 15 minutes, 44.7% 15 to 30 minutes, 17.0% 30 to 45 minutes, 7.8% 45 to 60 minutes, 7.8% 60 minutes or more (2000)

WINDOM (township). Covers a land area of 36.035 square miles and a water area of 0 square miles. Located at 43.63° N. Lat.; 92.86° W. Long.
Population: 640 (2000); Race: 95.8% White, 0.3% Black, 0.3% Asian, 0.0% American Indian and Alaska Native, 3.9% Hispanic of any race, 1.4% two or more races (2000); Density: 17.8 persons per square mile (2000); Age: 31.7% under 18, 12.5% over 64 (2000); Marriage status: 23.1% never married, 68.2% now married, 3.1% widowed, 5.6% divorced (2000); Foreign born: 3.6% (2000); Ancestry (includes multiple ancestries): 42.8% German, 26.5% Norwegian, 11.1% Irish, 6.1% Other groups, 5.5% Swedish (2000).
Economy: Employment by occupation: 14.1% management, 11.7% professional, 14.7% services, 23.3% sales, 2.5% farming, 15.0% construction, 18.7% production (2000).
Income: Per capita income: $18,372 (2000); Median household income: $49,643 (2000); Poverty rate: 3.5% (2000).
Taxes: Total city taxes per capita: $55 (1997); City property taxes per capita: $55 (1997).
Education: High school graduation rate: 84.2% (2000); College graduation rate: 9.2% (2000).
Housing: Homeownership rate: 87.0% (2000); Median home value: $86,500 (2000); Median rent: $331 per month (2000); Median age of housing: 41 years (2000).
Transportation: Commute to work: 91.9% car, 0.3% public transportation, 0.6% walk, 7.1% work from home (2000); Travel time to work: 45.8% less than 15 minutes, 34.8% 15 to 30 minutes, 11.0% 30 to 45 minutes, 3.0% 45 to 60 minutes, 5.4% 60 minutes or more (2000)

Murray County

Located in southwestern Minnesota; drained by headwaters of the Des Moines River; includes Lake Shetek. Covers a land area of 704.40 square miles, a water area of 15.10 square miles, and is located in the Central Time Zone. The county government was organized in 1875. County seat is Slayton.

Weather Station: Lake Wilson Elevation: 1,646 feet

	Jan	Feb	Mar	Apr	May	Jun	Jul	Aug	Sep	Oct	Nov	Dec
High	23	29	41	57	71	80	83	80	73	60	40	27
Low	4	11	22	34	47	56	61	58	49	37	23	10
Precip	0.7	0.7	2.0	2.9	3.1	3.9	3.3	3.8	2.7	2.0	1.5	0.7
Snow	9.1	6.3	9.4	2.6	tr	0.0	0.0	0.0	tr	0.8	7.7	7.4

High and Low temperatures in degrees Fahrenheit; Precipitation and Snow in inches

Population: 9,165 (2000); Race: 98.3% White, 0.3% Black, 0.2% Asian, 0.3% American Indian and Alaska Native, 1.6% Hispanic of any race, 0.4% two or more races (2000); Density: 13.0 persons per square mile (2000); Age: 24.9% under 18, 21.3% over 64 (2000).
Religion: Five largest groups: 29.6% Catholic Church, 25.3% Evangelical Lutheran Church in America, 9.7% Lutheran Church—Missouri Synod, 6.0% Presbyterian Church (U.S.A.), 4.5% Reformed Church in America (2000).
Economy: Unemployment rate: 3.0% (11/2002); Total civilian labor force: 4,347 (11/2002); Leading industries: 18.7% health care and social assistance; 17.5% manufacturing; 14.6% retail trade (2000); Companies that employ more than 1,000 persons: 0 (2000); Companies that employ more than 100 persons: 1 (2000); Farms: 836 totaling 383,725 acres (1997); Minority business ownership rate: 0.0% (1997); Women business ownership rate: 0.0% (1997); Retail sales per capita: $5,652 (1997). Single-family building permits issued: 32 (2001) / 42 (2000); Multi-family building permits issued: 2 (2001) / 2 (2000).
Income: Per capita income: $17,936 (2000); Median household income: $34,966 (2000); Poverty rate: 8.3% (2000); Bankruptcy rate: 1.99% (2001).
Taxes: Total county taxes per capita: $346 (2000); County property taxes per capita: $344 (2000).
Education: High school graduation rate: 79.1% (2000); College graduation rate: 11.9% (2000).
Housing: Homeownership rate: 84.5% (2000); Median home value: $50,900 (2000); Median rent: $271 per month (2000); Median age of housing: 49 years (2000).
Health: Birth rate: 102.6 per 10,000 population (1998); Age adjusted death rate: 80.3 per 10,000 population (1999); Age adjusted cancer mortality rate: 188.1 deaths per 100,000 population (1999). Number of physicians: 5.5 per 10,000 population (1999); Number of hospital beds: 27.3 per 10,000 population (1999).
Elections: 2000 Presidential election results: 44.0% Gore, 50.6% Bush, 3.1% Nader, 1.5% Buchanan
National and State Parks: Avoca State Wildlife Management Area; Badger Lake State Wildlife Management Area; Bergman State Wildlife Management Area; Big Slough State Wildlife Management Area; Buffalo Lake State Wildlife Management Area; Chandler State Wildlife Management Area; County Line State Wildlife Management Are; Current Lake State Wildlife Management Area; Dovray State Wildlife Management Area; Great Oasis State Wildlife Management Area; Haberman State Wildlife Management Area; Hjermstad Lake State Wildlife Management Are; Irruption State Wildlife Management Area; Klinker State Wildlife Management Area; Lake Shetek State Park; Lange State Wildlife Management Area; Leeds State Wildlife Management Area; Lowville State Wildlife Management Areas; Mason State Wildlife Management Area; McCord-Laible State Wildlife Management; Nelson State Wildlife Management Area; Peters State Wildlife Management Area; Phelan State Wildlife Management Area; Reinhold State Wildlife Management Area; Rupp State Wildlife Management Area; Ruthton State Wildlife Management Area; Schoeberl State Wildlife Management Area; Shetek State Wildlife Management Area; Skandia State Wildlife Management Area; Sweetman State Wildlife Management Area; Tutt State Wildlife Management Area; Van Eck State Wildlife Management Area
Additional Information Contacts
Murray County Government Offices 507-836-6148
Slayton Chamber of Commerce 507-836-6902

Murray County Communities

AVOCA (city). Covers a land area of 1.087 square miles and a water area of 0.203 square miles. Located at 43.94° N. Lat.; 95.64° W. Long. Elevation is 1,540 feet.
Population: 146 (2000); Race: 93.9% White, 6.1% Black, 0.0% Asian, 0.0% American Indian and Alaska Native, 0.0% Hispanic of any race, 0.0% two or more races (2000); Density: 134.3 persons per square mile (2000); Age: 26.4% under 18, 10.8% over 64 (2000); Marriage status: 22.0% never married, 60.2% now married, 9.3% widowed, 8.5% divorced (2000); Foreign born: 0.0% (2000); Ancestry (includes multiple ancestries): 57.4% German, 14.9% Swedish, 14.9% Norwegian, 9.5% French (except Basque), 6.1% Irish (2000).
Economy: Corn, oats, soybeans, alfalfa; livestock, poultry; dairying. Employment by occupation: 6.7% management, 4.0% professional, 24.0% services, 17.3% sales, 0.0% farming, 22.7% construction, 25.3% production (2000).
Income: Per capita income: $13,184 (2000); Median household income: $29,375 (2000); Poverty rate: 12.6% (2000).
Taxes: Total city taxes per capita: $85 (1997); City property taxes per capita: $85 (1997).
Education: High school graduation rate: 84.3% (2000); College graduation rate: 2.9% (2000).
Housing: Homeownership rate: 82.1% (2000); Median home value: $18,900 (2000); Median rent: $238 per month (2000); Median age of housing: 60+ years (2000).
Transportation: Commute to work: 87.7% car, 0.0% public transportation, 2.7% walk, 6.8% work from home (2000); Travel time to work: 42.6% less than 15 minutes, 11.8% 15 to 30 minutes, 35.3% 30 to 45 minutes, 2.9% 45 to 60 minutes, 7.4% 60 minutes or more (2000)

BELFAST (township). Covers a land area of 35.910 square miles and a water area of 0.079 square miles. Located at 43.88° N. Lat.; 95.53° W. Long.
Population: 195 (2000); Race: 100.0% White, 0.0% Black, 0.0% Asian, 0.0% American Indian and Alaska Native, 0.0% Hispanic of any race, 0.0% two or more races (2000); Density: 5.4 persons per square mile (2000); Age: 29.2% under 18, 14.0% over 64 (2000); Marriage status: 26.6% never married, 61.2% now married, 5.8% widowed, 6.5% divorced (2000); Foreign born: 0.0% (2000); Ancestry (includes multiple ancestries): 77.5% German, 6.7% Dutch, 6.2% Danish, 6.2% Norwegian, 4.5% Irish (2000).

Economy: Employment by occupation: 25.0% management, 15.2% professional, 12.0% services, 14.1% sales, 2.2% farming, 9.8% construction, 21.7% production (2000).
Income: Per capita income: $14,856 (2000); Median household income: $34,375 (2000); Poverty rate: 4.6% (2000).
Taxes: Total city taxes per capita: $60 (1997); City property taxes per capita: $60 (1997).
Education: High school graduation rate: 80.8% (2000); College graduation rate: 16.7% (2000).
Housing: Homeownership rate: 85.7% (2000); Median home value: $65,000 (2000); Median rent: $275 per month (2000); Median age of housing: 59 years (2000).
Transportation: Commute to work: 76.1% car, 0.0% public transportation, 0.0% walk, 23.9% work from home (2000); Travel time to work: 34.3% less than 15 minutes, 30.0% 15 to 30 minutes, 22.9% 30 to 45 minutes, 5.7% 45 to 60 minutes, 7.1% 60 minutes or more (2000)

BONDIN (township). Covers a land area of 35.050 square miles and a water area of 0.206 square miles. Located at 43.88° N. Lat.; 95.63° W. Long.
Population: 335 (2000); Race: 97.5% White, 0.0% Black, 0.0% Asian, 0.0% American Indian and Alaska Native, 2.8% Hispanic of any race, 2.5% two or more races (2000); Density: 9.6 persons per square mile (2000); Age: 31.8% under 18, 13.1% over 64 (2000); Marriage status: 18.1% never married, 74.4% now married, 2.5% widowed, 5.0% divorced (2000); Foreign born: 0.0% (2000); Ancestry (includes multiple ancestries): 58.6% German, 10.9% Norwegian, 9.3% Dutch, 8.1% Irish, 3.1% English (2000).
Economy: Employment by occupation: 17.4% management, 16.3% professional, 15.1% services, 19.2% sales, 1.7% farming, 12.2% construction, 18.0% production (2000).
Income: Per capita income: $16,398 (2000); Median household income: $46,000 (2000); Poverty rate: 5.0% (2000).
Taxes: Total city taxes per capita: $132 (1997); City property taxes per capita: $132 (1997).
Education: High school graduation rate: 90.0% (2000); College graduation rate: 17.4% (2000).
Housing: Homeownership rate: 92.7% (2000); Median home value: $97,500 (2000); Median rent: $208 per month (2000); Median age of housing: 40 years (2000).
Transportation: Commute to work: 83.8% car, 0.0% public transportation, 0.0% walk, 14.4% work from home (2000); Travel time to work: 47.6% less than 15 minutes, 37.1% 15 to 30 minutes, 9.8% 30 to 45 minutes, 4.2% 45 to 60 minutes, 1.4% 60 minutes or more (2000)

CAMERON (township). Covers a land area of 35.880 square miles and a water area of 0.155 square miles. Located at 44.07° N. Lat.; 96.01° W. Long.
Population: 151 (2000); Race: 100.0% White, 0.0% Black, 0.0% Asian, 0.0% American Indian and Alaska Native, 0.0% Hispanic of any race, 0.0% two or more races (2000); Density: 4.2 persons per square mile (2000); Age: 30.5% under 18, 11.3% over 64 (2000); Marriage status: 26.0% never married, 65.4% now married, 3.8% widowed, 4.8% divorced (2000); Foreign born: 0.0% (2000); Ancestry (includes multiple ancestries): 44.7% German, 23.4% United States or American, 19.9% Norwegian, 17.7% Dutch, 10.6% Swedish (2000).
Economy: Employment by occupation: 30.8% management, 15.4% professional, 14.1% services, 21.8% sales, 2.6% farming, 5.1% construction, 10.3% production (2000).
Income: Per capita income: $12,991 (2000); Median household income: $25,833 (2000); Poverty rate: 17.0% (2000).
Taxes: Total city taxes per capita: $138 (1997); City property taxes per capita: $138 (1997).
Education: High school graduation rate: 80.7% (2000); College graduation rate: 7.2% (2000).
Housing: Homeownership rate: 87.3% (2000); Median home value: $93,300 (2000); Median rent: $175 per month (2000); Median age of housing: 54 years (2000).
Transportation: Commute to work: 79.5% car, 0.0% public transportation, 5.1% walk, 12.8% work from home (2000); Travel time to work: 27.9% less than 15 minutes, 60.3% 15 to 30 minutes, 11.8% 30 to 45 minutes, 0.0% 45 to 60 minutes, 0.0% 60 minutes or more (2000)

CHANARAMBIE (township). Covers a land area of 35.531 square miles and a water area of 0.004 square miles. Located at 43.98° N. Lat.; 95.99° W. Long.
Population: 223 (2000); Race: 100.0% White, 0.0% Black, 0.0% Asian, 0.0% American Indian and Alaska Native, 0.9% Hispanic of any race, 0.0% two or more races (2000); Density: 6.3 persons per square mile (2000); Age: 35.0% under 18, 13.6% over 64 (2000); Marriage status: 35.0% never married, 56.3% now married, 4.4% widowed, 4.4% divorced (2000); Foreign born: 0.5% (2000); Ancestry (includes multiple ancestries): 46.7% Dutch, 42.5% German, 10.7% United States or American, 8.4% Irish, 6.1% English (2000).
Economy: Employment by occupation: 44.7% management, 12.6% professional, 11.7% services, 5.8% sales, 1.9% farming, 2.9% construction, 20.4% production (2000).
Income: Per capita income: $11,696 (2000); Median household income: $31,875 (2000); Poverty rate: 11.2% (2000).
Taxes: Total city taxes per capita: $96 (1997); City property taxes per capita: $96 (1997).
Education: High school graduation rate: 77.7% (2000); College graduation rate: 14.9% (2000).
Housing: Homeownership rate: 89.5% (2000); Median home value: $67,500 (2000); Median rent: $325 per month (2000); Median age of housing: 50 years (2000).
Transportation: Commute to work: 62.3% car, 0.0% public transportation, 6.6% walk, 31.1% work from home (2000); Travel time to work: 39.7% less than 15 minutes, 46.6% 15 to 30 minutes, 8.2% 30 to 45 minutes, 0.0% 45 to 60 minutes, 5.5% 60 minutes or more (2000)

CHANDLER (city). Covers a land area of 0.805 square miles and a water area of 0 square miles. Located at 43.92° N. Lat.; 95.94° W. Long. Elevation is 1,651 feet.
Population: 276 (2000); Race: 92.6% White, 0.0% Black, 0.7% Asian, 1.5% American Indian and Alaska Native, 18.1% Hispanic of any race, 0.0% two or more races (2000); Density: 342.7 persons per square mile (2000); Age: 20.3% under 18, 31.7% over 64 (2000); Marriage status: 20.2% never married, 61.9% now married, 17.0% widowed, 0.9% divorced (2000); Foreign born: 15.5% (2000); Ancestry (includes multiple ancestries): 48.0% Dutch, 16.6% Other groups, 13.7% German, 3.7% English, 2.6% Swedish (2000).
Economy: Agriculture: corn, oats, soybeans; livestock, poultry; dairying. Manufacturing: fertilizer, meat processing, concrete products. Single-family building permits issued: 0 (2001) / 0 (2000); Multi-family building permits issued: 0 (2001) / 0 (2000); Employment by occupation: 16.0% management, 8.8% professional, 16.8% services, 21.6% sales, 4.0% farming, 4.8% construction, 28.0% production (2000).
Income: Per capita income: $16,134 (2000); Median household income: $26,875 (2000); Poverty rate: 15.1% (2000).
Taxes: Total city taxes per capita: $170 (1997); City property taxes per capita: $170 (1997).
Education: High school graduation rate: 51.9% (2000); College graduation rate: 5.9% (2000).
Housing: Homeownership rate: 72.2% (2000); Median home value: $55,500 (2000); Median rent: $255 per month (2000); Median age of housing: 37 years (2000).
Transportation: Commute to work: 64.0% car, 0.0% public transportation, 32.0% walk, 4.0% work from home (2000); Travel time to work: 76.7% less than 15 minutes, 19.2% 15 to 30 minutes, 2.5% 30 to 45 minutes, 0.0% 45 to 60 minutes, 1.7% 60 minutes or more (2000)

CURRIE (city). Covers a land area of 0.572 square miles and a water area of 0 square miles. Located at 44.07° N. Lat.; 95.66° W. Long. Elevation is 1,481 feet.
Population: 225 (2000); Race: 100.0% White, 0.0% Black, 0.0% Asian, 0.0% American Indian and Alaska Native, 0.0% Hispanic of any race, 0.0% two or more races (2000); Density: 393.0 persons per square mile (2000); Age: 8.9% under 18, 40.0% over 64 (2000); Marriage status: 18.2% never married, 57.6% now married, 10.9% widowed, 13.3% divorced (2000); Foreign born: 1.1% (2000); Ancestry (includes multiple ancestries): 46.1% German, 17.2% French (except Basque), 17.2% Irish, 8.9% Norwegian, 8.9% English (2000).
Economy: Grain, soybeans; livestock, poultry; dairying. Single-family building permits issued: 0 (2001) / 1 (2000); Multi-family building permits issued: 0 (2001) / 0 (2000); Employment by occupation: 1.3% management, 6.3% professional, 26.6% services, 19.0% sales, 3.8% farming, 19.0% construction, 24.1% production (2000).
Income: Per capita income: $15,767 (2000); Median household income: $22,857 (2000); Poverty rate: 12.2% (2000).
Taxes: Total city taxes per capita: $87 (1997); City property taxes per capita: $84 (1997).
Education: High school graduation rate: 74.1% (2000); College graduation rate: 1.9% (2000).

Housing: Homeownership rate: 87.7% (2000); Median home value: $22,500 (2000); Median rent: $125 per month (2000); Median age of housing: 60+ years (2000).
Transportation: Commute to work: 83.5% car, 0.0% public transportation, 8.9% walk, 0.0% work from home (2000); Travel time to work: 31.6% less than 15 minutes, 38.0% 15 to 30 minutes, 13.9% 30 to 45 minutes, 10.1% 45 to 60 minutes, 6.3% 60 minutes or more (2000)

DES MOINES RIVER (township). Covers a land area of 35.611 square miles and a water area of 0.410 square miles. Located at 43.97° N. Lat.; 95.53° W. Long.
Population: 182 (2000); Race: 99.1% White, 0.0% Black, 0.0% Asian, 0.9% American Indian and Alaska Native, 0.0% Hispanic of any race, 0.0% two or more races (2000); Density: 5.1 persons per square mile (2000); Age: 25.6% under 18, 21.0% over 64 (2000); Marriage status: 23.5% never married, 69.3% now married, 4.2% widowed, 3.0% divorced (2000); Foreign born: 0.0% (2000); Ancestry (includes multiple ancestries): 63.9% German, 21.5% Norwegian, 13.2% Dutch, 6.4% English, 4.6% United States or American (2000).
Economy: Employment by occupation: 25.2% management, 18.4% professional, 15.5% services, 10.7% sales, 1.0% farming, 5.8% construction, 23.3% production (2000).
Income: Per capita income: $15,966 (2000); Median household income: $35,500 (2000); Poverty rate: 7.3% (2000).
Taxes: Total city taxes per capita: $88 (1997); City property taxes per capita: $88 (1997).
Education: High school graduation rate: 76.0% (2000); College graduation rate: 21.2% (2000).
Housing: Homeownership rate: 72.4% (2000); Median home value: $27,500 (2000); Median rent: $125 per month (2000); Median age of housing: 60+ years (2000).
Transportation: Commute to work: 77.8% car, 0.0% public transportation, 0.0% walk, 22.2% work from home (2000); Travel time to work: 24.7% less than 15 minutes, 35.1% 15 to 30 minutes, 28.6% 30 to 45 minutes, 5.2% 45 to 60 minutes, 6.5% 60 minutes or more (2000)

DOVRAY (city). Covers a land area of 0.250 square miles and a water area of 0 square miles. Located at 44.05° N. Lat.; 95.54° W. Long.
Population: 67 (2000); Race: 100.0% White, 0.0% Black, 0.0% Asian, 0.0% American Indian and Alaska Native, 0.0% Hispanic of any race, 0.0% two or more races (2000); Density: 268.0 persons per square mile (2000); Age: 9.8% under 18, 27.9% over 64 (2000); Marriage status: 22.4% never married, 70.7% now married, 3.4% widowed, 3.4% divorced (2000); Foreign born: 0.0% (2000); Ancestry (includes multiple ancestries): 47.5% German, 37.7% Norwegian, 11.5% English, 9.8% Irish, 8.2% French (except Basque) (2000).
Economy: Single-family building permits issued: 0 (2001) / 0 (2000); Multi-family building permits issued: 0 (2001) / 0 (2000); Employment by occupation: 2.8% management, 0.0% professional, 41.7% services, 27.8% sales, 5.6% farming, 5.6% construction, 16.7% production (2000).
Income: Per capita income: $17,461 (2000); Median household income: $37,500 (2000); Poverty rate: 13.1% (2000).
Taxes: Total city taxes per capita: $109 (1997); City property taxes per capita: $91 (1997).
Education: High school graduation rate: 84.3% (2000); College graduation rate: 5.9% (2000).
Housing: Homeownership rate: 93.8% (2000); Median home value: $18,100 (2000); Median rent: $125 per month (2000); Median age of housing: 60+ years (2000).
Transportation: Commute to work: 80.6% car, 0.0% public transportation, 8.3% walk, 0.0% work from home (2000); Travel time to work: 55.6% less than 15 minutes, 25.0% 15 to 30 minutes, 5.6% 30 to 45 minutes, 8.3% 45 to 60 minutes, 5.6% 60 minutes or more (2000)

DOVRAY (township). Covers a land area of 35.320 square miles and a water area of 0.366 square miles. Located at 44.05° N. Lat.; 95.51° W. Long.
Population: 167 (2000); Race: 100.0% White, 0.0% Black, 0.0% Asian, 0.0% American Indian and Alaska Native, 0.0% Hispanic of any race, 0.0% two or more races (2000); Density: 4.7 persons per square mile (2000); Age: 23.1% under 18, 22.5% over 64 (2000); Marriage status: 17.1% never married, 70.0% now married, 5.0% widowed, 7.9% divorced (2000); Foreign born: 0.0% (2000); Ancestry (includes multiple ancestries): 51.5% German, 42.6% Norwegian, 6.5% United States or American, 5.3% Dutch, 4.7% Irish (2000).
Economy: Dairying; grain. Manufacturing: feeds. Employment by occupation: 20.2% management, 18.1% professional, 12.8% services, 17.0% sales, 0.0% farming, 16.0% construction, 16.0% production (2000).
Income: Per capita income: $20,242 (2000); Median household income: $35,694 (2000); Poverty rate: 1.2% (2000).
Taxes: Total city taxes per capita: $146 (1997); City property taxes per capita: $146 (1997).
Education: High school graduation rate: 74.8% (2000); College graduation rate: 12.2% (2000).
Housing: Homeownership rate: 97.2% (2000); Median home value: $31,900 (2000); Median age of housing: 60+ years (2000).
Transportation: Commute to work: 77.7% car, 0.0% public transportation, 0.0% walk, 22.3% work from home (2000); Travel time to work: 57.5% less than 15 minutes, 26.0% 15 to 30 minutes, 8.2% 30 to 45 minutes, 5.5% 45 to 60 minutes, 2.7% 60 minutes or more (2000)

ELLSBOROUGH (township). Covers a land area of 35.095 square miles and a water area of 0.718 square miles. Located at 44.15° N. Lat.; 95.99° W. Long.
Population: 198 (2000); Race: 97.3% White, 2.7% Black, 0.0% Asian, 0.0% American Indian and Alaska Native, 0.0% Hispanic of any race, 0.0% two or more races (2000); Density: 5.6 persons per square mile (2000); Age: 39.4% under 18, 6.6% over 64 (2000); Marriage status: 26.8% never married, 66.0% now married, 2.6% widowed, 4.6% divorced (2000); Foreign born: 0.0% (2000); Ancestry (includes multiple ancestries): 38.5% Norwegian, 27.4% Swedish, 22.6% German, 9.3% English, 8.4% Dutch (2000).
Economy: Employment by occupation: 26.5% management, 10.2% professional, 16.3% services, 14.3% sales, 2.0% farming, 9.2% construction, 21.4% production (2000).
Income: Per capita income: $10,551 (2000); Median household income: $34,688 (2000); Poverty rate: 12.4% (2000).
Taxes: Total city taxes per capita: $94 (1997); City property taxes per capita: $94 (1997).
Education: High school graduation rate: 92.2% (2000); College graduation rate: 6.1% (2000).
Housing: Homeownership rate: 80.0% (2000); Median home value: $48,300 (2000); Median age of housing: 60+ years (2000).
Transportation: Commute to work: 73.5% car, 0.0% public transportation, 8.2% walk, 18.4% work from home (2000); Travel time to work: 31.3% less than 15 minutes, 28.7% 15 to 30 minutes, 36.3% 30 to 45 minutes, 0.0% 45 to 60 minutes, 3.8% 60 minutes or more (2000)

FENTON (township). Covers a land area of 35.772 square miles and a water area of 0.064 square miles. Located at 43.89° N. Lat.; 95.89° W. Long.
Population: 209 (2000); Race: 100.0% White, 0.0% Black, 0.0% Asian, 0.0% American Indian and Alaska Native, 0.0% Hispanic of any race, 0.0% two or more races (2000); Density: 5.8 persons per square mile (2000); Age: 30.7% under 18, 8.4% over 64 (2000); Marriage status: 22.6% never married, 70.7% now married, 2.4% widowed, 4.3% divorced (2000); Foreign born: 0.0% (2000); Ancestry (includes multiple ancestries): 38.1% Dutch, 32.6% German, 13.5% United States or American, 6.5% Swedish, 3.7% Irish (2000).
Economy: Employment by occupation: 39.4% management, 9.2% professional, 11.9% services, 13.8% sales, 0.0% farming, 8.3% construction, 17.4% production (2000).
Income: Per capita income: $16,951 (2000); Median household income: $39,167 (2000); Poverty rate: 1.9% (2000).
Taxes: Total city taxes per capita: $45 (1997); City property taxes per capita: $45 (1997).
Education: High school graduation rate: 82.2% (2000); College graduation rate: 12.6% (2000).
Housing: Homeownership rate: 93.2% (2000); Median home value: $82,800 (2000); Median age of housing: 55 years (2000).
Transportation: Commute to work: 70.6% car, 0.0% public transportation, 2.8% walk, 26.6% work from home (2000); Travel time to work: 31.3% less than 15 minutes, 45.0% 15 to 30 minutes, 21.3% 30 to 45 minutes, 0.0% 45 to 60 minutes, 2.5% 60 minutes or more (2000)

FULDA (city). Covers a land area of 0.966 square miles and a water area of 0.073 square miles. Located at 43.87° N. Lat.; 95.60° W. Long. Elevation is 1,532 feet.
History: Fulda was established in the 1870's when the railroad arrived. Many of the early residents were of German ancestry, and named their town for the ancient city in central Europe.
Population: 1,283 (2000); Race: 96.3% White, 0.7% Black, 0.0% Asian, 0.8% American Indian and Alaska Native, 3.5% Hispanic of any race, 0.2% two or more races (2000); Density: 1,328.3 persons per square mile (2000); Age: 24.0% under 18, 29.6% over 64 (2000); Marriage status: 19.1% never married, 62.4% now married, 14.8% widowed, 3.7% divorced (2000);

Foreign born: 2.2% (2000); Ancestry (includes multiple ancestries): 58.9% German, 9.7% Irish, 7.0% Norwegian, 6.1% Dutch, 5.1% Swedish (2000).
Economy: Single-family building permits issued: 3 (2001) / 2 (2000); Multi-family building permits issued: 0 (2001) / 0 (2000); Employment by occupation: 9.1% management, 15.7% professional, 20.8% services, 18.2% sales, 0.9% farming, 10.2% construction, 25.1% production (2000).
Income: Per capita income: $15,184 (2000); Median household income: $30,000 (2000); Poverty rate: 6.1% (2000).
Taxes: Total city taxes per capita: $142 (1997); City property taxes per capita: $134 (1997).
Education: High school graduation rate: 70.6% (2000); College graduation rate: 12.1% (2000).

School District(s)

Fulda (PK-12)
2000 Enrollment: 582 507-425-2514
Housing: Homeownership rate: 82.4% (2000); Median home value: $48,100 (2000); Median rent: $316 per month (2000); Median age of housing: 49 years (2000).
Newspapers: Fulda Free Press (1 x week)
Transportation: Commute to work: 82.3% car, 2.0% public transportation, 9.2% walk, 3.7% work from home (2000); Travel time to work: 53.4% less than 15 minutes, 31.2% 15 to 30 minutes, 10.2% 30 to 45 minutes, 1.0% 45 to 60 minutes, 4.2% 60 minutes or more (2000)

HADLEY (city). Covers a land area of 0.277 square miles and a water area of 0.115 square miles. Located at 44.00° N. Lat.; 95.85° W. Long.
Population: 81 (2000); Race: 100.0% White, 0.0% Black, 0.0% Asian, 0.0% American Indian and Alaska Native, 0.0% Hispanic of any race, 0.0% two or more races (2000); Density: 292.7 persons per square mile (2000); Age: 13.8% under 18, 29.9% over 64 (2000); Marriage status: 16.7% never married, 79.5% now married, 0.0% widowed, 3.8% divorced (2000); Foreign born: 2.3% (2000); Ancestry (includes multiple ancestries): 42.5% German, 27.6% Norwegian, 16.1% United States or American, 9.2% Dutch, 9.2% Swedish (2000).
Economy: Dairying. Single-family building permits issued: 0 (2001) / 0 (2000); Multi-family building permits issued: 0 (2001) / 0 (2000); Employment by occupation: 4.5% management, 27.3% professional, 20.5% services, 15.9% sales, 4.5% farming, 4.5% construction, 22.7% production (2000).
Income: Per capita income: $22,518 (2000); Median household income: $31,406 (2000); Poverty rate: 0.0% (2000).
Taxes: Total city taxes per capita: $112 (1997); City property taxes per capita: $112 (1997).
Education: High school graduation rate: 75.0% (2000); College graduation rate: 10.3% (2000).
Housing: Homeownership rate: 94.6% (2000); Median home value: $32,500 (2000); Median age of housing: 49 years (2000).
Transportation: Commute to work: 95.5% car, 0.0% public transportation, 0.0% walk, 4.5% work from home (2000); Travel time to work: 64.3% less than 15 minutes, 21.4% 15 to 30 minutes, 7.1% 30 to 45 minutes, 0.0% 45 to 60 minutes, 7.1% 60 minutes or more (2000)

HOLLY (township). Covers a land area of 35.784 square miles and a water area of 0 square miles. Located at 44.16° N. Lat.; 95.52° W. Long.
Population: 172 (2000); Race: 98.9% White, 1.1% Black, 0.0% Asian, 0.0% American Indian and Alaska Native, 1.1% Hispanic of any race, 0.0% two or more races (2000); Density: 4.8 persons per square mile (2000); Age: 34.1% under 18, 16.8% over 64 (2000); Marriage status: 18.4% never married, 65.4% now married, 7.4% widowed, 8.8% divorced (2000); Foreign born: 1.1% (2000); Ancestry (includes multiple ancestries): 46.5% German, 34.1% Norwegian, 18.9% Irish, 14.6% English, 9.2% Belgian (2000).
Economy: Employment by occupation: 22.6% management, 4.8% professional, 22.6% services, 22.6% sales, 11.9% farming, 6.0% construction, 9.5% production (2000).
Income: Per capita income: $14,055 (2000); Median household income: $37,500 (2000); Poverty rate: 10.3% (2000).
Taxes: Total city taxes per capita: $181 (1997); City property taxes per capita: $181 (1997).
Education: High school graduation rate: 81.5% (2000); College graduation rate: 7.6% (2000).
Housing: Homeownership rate: 84.7% (2000); Median home value: $45,000 (2000); Median rent: $113 per month (2000); Median age of housing: 60+ years (2000).
Transportation: Commute to work: 73.8% car, 0.0% public transportation, 0.0% walk, 26.2% work from home (2000); Travel time to work: 30.6% less than 15 minutes, 32.3% 15 to 30 minutes, 4.8% 30 to 45 minutes, 24.2% 45 to 60 minutes, 8.1% 60 minutes or more (2000)

IONA (city). Aka Iona Lake. Covers a land area of 0.787 square miles and a water area of 0 square miles. Located at 43.91° N. Lat.; 95.78° W. Long. Elevation is 1,629 feet.
Population: 173 (2000); Race: 100.0% White, 0.0% Black, 0.0% Asian, 0.0% American Indian and Alaska Native, 0.0% Hispanic of any race, 0.0% two or more races (2000); Density: 219.9 persons per square mile (2000); Age: 22.3% under 18, 22.9% over 64 (2000); Marriage status: 25.5% never married, 53.2% now married, 14.9% widowed, 6.4% divorced (2000); Foreign born: 0.0% (2000); Ancestry (includes multiple ancestries): 39.2% German, 17.5% Norwegian, 11.4% Irish, 8.4% French (except Basque), 6.0% Dutch (2000).
Economy: Employment by occupation: 2.6% management, 19.7% professional, 19.7% services, 10.5% sales, 3.9% farming, 10.5% construction, 32.9% production (2000).
Income: Per capita income: $14,746 (2000); Median household income: $25,625 (2000); Poverty rate: 8.4% (2000).
Taxes: Total city taxes per capita: $150 (1997); City property taxes per capita: $144 (1997).
Education: High school graduation rate: 61.8% (2000); College graduation rate: 6.5% (2000).
Housing: Homeownership rate: 92.4% (2000); Median home value: $29,300 (2000); Median rent: $275 per month (2000); Median age of housing: 60+ years (2000).
Transportation: Commute to work: 98.6% car, 0.0% public transportation, 0.0% walk, 1.4% work from home (2000); Travel time to work: 34.2% less than 15 minutes, 19.2% 15 to 30 minutes, 21.9% 30 to 45 minutes, 12.3% 45 to 60 minutes, 12.3% 60 minutes or more (2000)

IONA (township). Aka Iona Lake. Covers a land area of 34.357 square miles and a water area of 0.916 square miles. Located at 43.88° N. Lat.; 95.75° W. Long. Elevation is 1,629 feet.
Population: 195 (2000); Race: 100.0% White, 0.0% Black, 0.0% Asian, 0.0% American Indian and Alaska Native, 4.6% Hispanic of any race, 0.0% two or more races (2000); Density: 5.7 persons per square mile (2000); Age: 34.4% under 18, 7.7% over 64 (2000); Marriage status: 20.7% never married, 75.2% now married, 2.8% widowed, 1.4% divorced (2000); Foreign born: 2.1% (2000); Ancestry (includes multiple ancestries): 59.5% German, 12.8% Irish, 12.3% Norwegian, 9.2% Dutch, 5.6% Danish (2000).
Economy: Grain; livestock; dairying. Employment by occupation: 28.7% management, 12.9% professional, 15.8% services, 20.8% sales, 7.9% farming, 9.9% construction, 4.0% production (2000).
Income: Per capita income: $11,157 (2000); Median household income: $33,125 (2000); Poverty rate: 15.4% (2000).
Taxes: Total city taxes per capita: $82 (1997); City property taxes per capita: $82 (1997).
Education: High school graduation rate: 81.5% (2000); College graduation rate: 5.9% (2000).
Housing: Homeownership rate: 92.1% (2000); Median home value: $62,500 (2000); Median rent: $325 per month (2000); Median age of housing: 60+ years (2000).
Transportation: Commute to work: 72.7% car, 0.0% public transportation, 3.0% walk, 24.2% work from home (2000); Travel time to work: 25.3% less than 15 minutes, 57.3% 15 to 30 minutes, 12.0% 30 to 45 minutes, 2.7% 45 to 60 minutes, 2.7% 60 minutes or more (2000)

LAKE SARAH (township). Covers a land area of 32.861 square miles and a water area of 3.366 square miles. Located at 44.14° N. Lat.; 95.75° W. Long.
Population: 348 (2000); Race: 99.4% White, 0.0% Black, 0.6% Asian, 0.0% American Indian and Alaska Native, 0.0% Hispanic of any race, 0.0% two or more races (2000); Density: 10.6 persons per square mile (2000); Age: 14.4% under 18, 18.6% over 64 (2000); Marriage status: 13.3% never married, 75.2% now married, 5.8% widowed, 5.8% divorced (2000); Foreign born: 1.2% (2000); Ancestry (includes multiple ancestries): 62.8% German, 23.4% Norwegian, 15.6% Swedish, 6.6% Irish, 4.8% Dutch (2000).
Economy: Employment by occupation: 19.7% management, 14.6% professional, 11.1% services, 24.7% sales, 2.0% farming, 7.6% construction, 20.2% production (2000).
Income: Per capita income: $23,143 (2000); Median household income: $43,125 (2000); Poverty rate: 3.0% (2000).
Taxes: Total city taxes per capita: $113 (1997); City property taxes per capita: $113 (1997).

Education: High school graduation rate: 85.6% (2000); College graduation rate: 20.0% (2000).
Housing: Homeownership rate: 89.5% (2000); Median home value: $112,500 (2000); Median rent: $263 per month (2000); Median age of housing: 23 years (2000).
Transportation: Commute to work: 86.4% car, 0.0% public transportation, 3.0% walk, 10.6% work from home (2000); Travel time to work: 16.9% less than 15 minutes, 45.2% 15 to 30 minutes, 22.6% 30 to 45 minutes, 9.6% 45 to 60 minutes, 5.6% 60 minutes or more (2000)

LAKE WILSON (city). Covers a land area of 0.415 square miles and a water area of 0.082 square miles. Located at 43.99° N. Lat.; 95.95° W. Long. Elevation is 1,670 feet.
Population: 270 (2000); Race: 99.3% White, 0.0% Black, 0.0% Asian, 0.0% American Indian and Alaska Native, 8.0% Hispanic of any race, 0.0% two or more races (2000); Density: 650.1 persons per square mile (2000); Age: 20.7% under 18, 23.6% over 64 (2000); Marriage status: 17.2% never married, 60.3% now married, 13.4% widowed, 9.1% divorced (2000); Foreign born: 3.3% (2000); Ancestry (includes multiple ancestries): 50.4% German, 25.0% Dutch, 19.2% Norwegian, 9.4% Other groups, 6.5% Swedish (2000).
Economy: Agriculture: grain; livestock, poultry; dairying. Manufacturing: feeds. Single-family building permits issued: 0 (2001) / 0 (2000); Multi-family building permits issued: 0 (2001) / 0 (2000); Employment by occupation: 7.9% management, 9.3% professional, 20.7% services, 20.7% sales, 0.0% farming, 12.1% construction, 29.3% production (2000).
Income: Per capita income: $16,573 (2000); Median household income: $28,375 (2000); Poverty rate: 16.3% (2000).
Taxes: Total city taxes per capita: $63 (1997); City property taxes per capita: $60 (1997).
Education: High school graduation rate: 76.7% (2000); College graduation rate: 5.4% (2000).
Housing: Homeownership rate: 95.3% (2000); Median home value: $22,200 (2000); Median rent: $225 per month (2000); Median age of housing: 52 years (2000).
Transportation: Commute to work: 87.7% car, 0.0% public transportation, 7.2% walk, 5.1% work from home (2000); Travel time to work: 46.6% less than 15 minutes, 35.1% 15 to 30 minutes, 7.6% 30 to 45 minutes, 3.1% 45 to 60 minutes, 7.6% 60 minutes or more (2000)

LEEDS (township). Covers a land area of 35.353 square miles and a water area of 0.275 square miles. Located at 43.98° N. Lat.; 95.89° W. Long.
Population: 238 (2000); Race: 96.9% White, 0.0% Black, 0.0% Asian, 2.2% American Indian and Alaska Native, 0.0% Hispanic of any race, 0.9% two or more races (2000); Density: 6.7 persons per square mile (2000); Age: 32.8% under 18, 11.4% over 64 (2000); Marriage status: 14.7% never married, 70.6% now married, 7.1% widowed, 7.6% divorced (2000); Foreign born: 0.0% (2000); Ancestry (includes multiple ancestries): 36.7% German, 24.9% Dutch, 17.5% Norwegian, 11.4% United States or American, 5.7% Other groups (2000).
Economy: Employment by occupation: 34.8% management, 17.0% professional, 6.3% services, 20.5% sales, 7.1% farming, 8.0% construction, 6.3% production (2000).
Income: Per capita income: $31,218 (2000); Median household income: $40,625 (2000); Poverty rate: 16.6% (2000).
Taxes: Total city taxes per capita: $79 (1997); City property taxes per capita: $79 (1997).
Education: High school graduation rate: 80.7% (2000); College graduation rate: 11.0% (2000).
Housing: Homeownership rate: 92.7% (2000); Median home value: $65,000 (2000); Median rent: <$100 per month (2000); Median age of housing: 60+ years (2000).
Transportation: Commute to work: 68.8% car, 0.0% public transportation, 8.0% walk, 23.2% work from home (2000); Travel time to work: 66.3% less than 15 minutes, 19.8% 15 to 30 minutes, 7.0% 30 to 45 minutes, 7.0% 45 to 60 minutes, 0.0% 60 minutes or more (2000)

LIME LAKE (township). Covers a land area of 34.469 square miles and a water area of 0.449 square miles. Located at 43.97° N. Lat.; 95.65° W. Long.
Population: 225 (2000); Race: 96.6% White, 0.0% Black, 1.0% Asian, 0.0% American Indian and Alaska Native, 1.0% Hispanic of any race, 2.4% two or more races (2000); Density: 6.5 persons per square mile (2000); Age: 34.1% under 18, 13.7% over 64 (2000); Marriage status: 29.5% never married, 63.7% now married, 2.1% widowed, 4.8% divorced (2000); Foreign born: 2.0% (2000); Ancestry (includes multiple ancestries): 42.4% German, 19.0% Dutch, 16.1% Norwegian, 8.8% Irish, 5.4% United States or American (2000).
Economy: Employment by occupation: 25.7% management, 14.3% professional, 17.1% services, 18.1% sales, 0.0% farming, 16.2% construction, 8.6% production (2000).
Income: Per capita income: $14,354 (2000); Median household income: $37,500 (2000); Poverty rate: 7.8% (2000).
Taxes: Total city taxes per capita: $137 (1997); City property taxes per capita: $137 (1997).
Education: High school graduation rate: 88.6% (2000); College graduation rate: 6.1% (2000).
Housing: Homeownership rate: 79.7% (2000); Median home value: $58,000 (2000); Median rent: $205 per month (2000); Median age of housing: 55 years (2000).
Transportation: Commute to work: 83.7% car, 0.0% public transportation, 2.9% walk, 13.5% work from home (2000); Travel time to work: 55.6% less than 15 minutes, 14.4% 15 to 30 minutes, 22.2% 30 to 45 minutes, 7.8% 45 to 60 minutes, 0.0% 60 minutes or more (2000)

LOWVILLE (township). Covers a land area of 35.843 square miles and a water area of 0.138 square miles. Located at 44.05° N. Lat.; 95.87° W. Long. Elevation is 1,650 feet.
Population: 175 (2000); Race: 98.4% White, 0.0% Black, 1.6% Asian, 0.0% American Indian and Alaska Native, 0.0% Hispanic of any race, 0.0% two or more races (2000); Density: 4.9 persons per square mile (2000); Age: 26.0% under 18, 6.8% over 64 (2000); Marriage status: 27.7% never married, 64.8% now married, 4.4% widowed, 3.1% divorced (2000); Foreign born: 1.6% (2000); Ancestry (includes multiple ancestries): 44.3% German, 20.8% Swedish, 20.3% Norwegian, 15.1% Dutch, 10.4% Irish (2000).
Economy: Employment by occupation: 22.8% management, 11.4% professional, 12.3% services, 21.9% sales, 6.1% farming, 13.2% construction, 12.3% production (2000).
Income: Per capita income: $15,699 (2000); Median household income: $39,688 (2000); Poverty rate: 5.3% (2000).
Taxes: Total city taxes per capita: $131 (1997); City property taxes per capita: $131 (1997).
Education: High school graduation rate: 89.3% (2000); College graduation rate: 12.4% (2000).
Housing: Homeownership rate: 79.5% (2000); Median home value: $47,500 (2000); Median rent: $195 per month (2000); Median age of housing: 60+ years (2000).
Transportation: Commute to work: 73.7% car, 0.0% public transportation, 4.4% walk, 20.2% work from home (2000); Travel time to work: 39.6% less than 15 minutes, 44.0% 15 to 30 minutes, 4.4% 30 to 45 minutes, 9.9% 45 to 60 minutes, 2.2% 60 minutes or more (2000)

MASON (township). Covers a land area of 34.650 square miles and a water area of 1.293 square miles. Located at 44.07° N. Lat.; 95.75° W. Long.
Population: 284 (2000); Race: 98.6% White, 1.4% Black, 0.0% Asian, 0.0% American Indian and Alaska Native, 0.0% Hispanic of any race, 0.0% two or more races (2000); Density: 8.2 persons per square mile (2000); Age: 27.8% under 18, 17.2% over 64 (2000); Marriage status: 9.5% never married, 78.4% now married, 4.1% widowed, 8.1% divorced (2000); Foreign born: 1.4% (2000); Ancestry (includes multiple ancestries): 41.9% German, 19.9% Norwegian, 12.0% Swedish, 11.0% Dutch, 6.9% United States or American (2000).
Economy: Employment by occupation: 27.3% management, 15.2% professional, 14.4% services, 22.7% sales, 3.8% farming, 12.1% construction, 4.5% production (2000).
Income: Per capita income: $19,186 (2000); Median household income: $40,250 (2000); Poverty rate: 7.6% (2000).
Taxes: Total city taxes per capita: $160 (1997); City property taxes per capita: $160 (1997).
Education: High school graduation rate: 90.6% (2000); College graduation rate: 19.2% (2000).
Housing: Homeownership rate: 91.7% (2000); Median home value: $82,500 (2000); Median rent: $338 per month (2000); Median age of housing: 28 years (2000).
Transportation: Commute to work: 69.7% car, 0.0% public transportation, 5.3% walk, 25.0% work from home (2000); Travel time to work: 54.5% less than 15 minutes, 25.3% 15 to 30 minutes, 11.1% 30 to 45 minutes, 7.1% 45 to 60 minutes, 2.0% 60 minutes or more (2000)

MOULTON (township). Covers a land area of 35.154 square miles and a water area of 0 square miles. Located at 43.90° N. Lat.; 96.01° W. Long.

Population: 242 (2000); Race: 100.0% White, 0.0% Black, 0.0% Asian, 0.0% American Indian and Alaska Native, 0.0% Hispanic of any race, 0.0% two or more races (2000); Density: 6.9 persons per square mile (2000); Age: 31.8% under 18, 9.0% over 64 (2000); Marriage status: 18.7% never married, 79.1% now married, 1.1% widowed, 1.1% divorced (2000); Foreign born: 0.0% (2000); Ancestry (includes multiple ancestries): 70.6% Dutch, 18.4% German, 6.3% United States or American, 4.7% English, 2.0% Polish (2000).
Economy: Employment by occupation: 24.5% management, 7.2% professional, 15.8% services, 16.5% sales, 5.8% farming, 9.4% construction, 20.9% production (2000).
Income: Per capita income: $12,395 (2000); Median household income: $35,729 (2000); Poverty rate: 8.6% (2000).
Taxes: Total city taxes per capita: $46 (1997); City property taxes per capita: $46 (1997).
Education: High school graduation rate: 79.1% (2000); College graduation rate: 13.1% (2000).
Housing: Homeownership rate: 74.1% (2000); Median home value: $33,300 (2000); Median rent: $256 per month (2000); Median age of housing: 60+ years (2000).
Transportation: Commute to work: 74.6% car, 0.0% public transportation, 4.5% walk, 20.9% work from home (2000); Travel time to work: 63.2% less than 15 minutes, 17.9% 15 to 30 minutes, 12.3% 30 to 45 minutes, 2.8% 45 to 60 minutes, 3.8% 60 minutes or more (2000)

MURRAY (township). Covers a land area of 34.562 square miles and a water area of 0.917 square miles. Located at 44.07° N. Lat.; 95.65° W. Long.
Population: 204 (2000); Race: 99.0% White, 0.0% Black, 0.0% Asian, 0.0% American Indian and Alaska Native, 0.0% Hispanic of any race, 1.0% two or more races (2000); Density: 5.9 persons per square mile (2000); Age: 18.6% under 18, 14.8% over 64 (2000); Marriage status: 18.6% never married, 69.4% now married, 3.3% widowed, 8.7% divorced (2000); Foreign born: 1.0% (2000); Ancestry (includes multiple ancestries): 39.5% German, 12.9% Dutch, 11.9% Irish, 9.5% Norwegian, 6.7% Swedish (2000).
Economy: Employment by occupation: 22.8% management, 17.1% professional, 9.8% services, 22.0% sales, 6.5% farming, 13.0% construction, 8.9% production (2000).
Income: Per capita income: $30,562 (2000); Median household income: $42,361 (2000); Poverty rate: 4.8% (2000).
Taxes: Total city taxes per capita: $130 (1997); City property taxes per capita: $130 (1997).
Education: High school graduation rate: 91.4% (2000); College graduation rate: 12.9% (2000).
Housing: Homeownership rate: 83.7% (2000); Median home value: $66,300 (2000); Median rent: $225 per month (2000); Median age of housing: 37 years (2000).
Transportation: Commute to work: 81.0% car, 0.0% public transportation, 7.4% walk, 11.6% work from home (2000); Travel time to work: 47.7% less than 15 minutes, 37.4% 15 to 30 minutes, 5.6% 30 to 45 minutes, 6.5% 45 to 60 minutes, 2.8% 60 minutes or more (2000)

SHETEK (township). Covers a land area of 31.066 square miles and a water area of 4.413 square miles. Located at 44.15° N. Lat.; 95.63° W. Long.
Population: 313 (2000); Race: 100.0% White, 0.0% Black, 0.0% Asian, 0.0% American Indian and Alaska Native, 0.6% Hispanic of any race, 0.0% two or more races (2000); Density: 10.1 persons per square mile (2000); Age: 20.8% under 18, 14.2% over 64 (2000); Marriage status: 21.2% never married, 70.3% now married, 5.5% widowed, 3.1% divorced (2000); Foreign born: 0.0% (2000); Ancestry (includes multiple ancestries): 55.3% German, 21.5% Norwegian, 11.8% English, 10.9% French (except Basque), 10.0% Swedish (2000).
Economy: Employment by occupation: 31.4% management, 18.4% professional, 8.6% services, 20.0% sales, 1.6% farming, 5.4% construction, 14.6% production (2000).
Income: Per capita income: $25,683 (2000); Median household income: $40,357 (2000); Poverty rate: 2.1% (2000).
Taxes: Total city taxes per capita: $172 (1997); City property taxes per capita: $172 (1997).
Education: High school graduation rate: 90.4% (2000); College graduation rate: 17.1% (2000).
Housing: Homeownership rate: 91.3% (2000); Median home value: $96,700 (2000); Median rent: $425 per month (2000); Median age of housing: 33 years (2000).
Transportation: Commute to work: 83.8% car, 0.0% public transportation, 4.3% walk, 11.9% work from home (2000); Travel time to work: 36.8% less than 15 minutes, 25.8% 15 to 30 minutes, 29.4% 30 to 45 minutes, 6.7% 45 to 60 minutes, 1.2% 60 minutes or more (2000)

SKANDIA (township). Covers a land area of 35.202 square miles and a water area of 0.574 square miles. Located at 44.16° N. Lat.; 95.89° W. Long.
Population: 173 (2000); Race: 93.9% White, 0.0% Black, 2.7% Asian, 0.0% American Indian and Alaska Native, 0.0% Hispanic of any race, 3.4% two or more races (2000); Density: 4.9 persons per square mile (2000); Age: 18.2% under 18, 23.0% over 64 (2000); Marriage status: 15.4% never married, 77.2% now married, 2.4% widowed, 4.9% divorced (2000); Foreign born: 4.1% (2000); Ancestry (includes multiple ancestries): 26.4% German, 26.4% Norwegian, 24.3% Swedish, 13.5% Dutch, 4.1% United States or American (2000).
Economy: Employment by occupation: 31.9% management, 22.0% professional, 22.0% services, 12.1% sales, 2.2% farming, 7.7% construction, 2.2% production (2000).
Income: Per capita income: $51,480 (2000); Median household income: $20,750 (2000); Poverty rate: 18.9% (2000).
Taxes: Total city taxes per capita: $124 (1997); City property taxes per capita: $124 (1997).
Education: High school graduation rate: 80.6% (2000); College graduation rate: 19.4% (2000).
Housing: Homeownership rate: 80.6% (2000); Median home value: $37,500 (2000); Median age of housing: 60+ years (2000).
Transportation: Commute to work: 60.7% car, 0.0% public transportation, 15.7% walk, 20.2% work from home (2000); Travel time to work: 56.3% less than 15 minutes, 21.1% 15 to 30 minutes, 15.5% 30 to 45 minutes, 0.0% 45 to 60 minutes, 7.0% 60 minutes or more (2000)

SLAYTON (city). Covers a land area of 1.781 square miles and a water area of 0 square miles. Located at 43.98° N. Lat.; 95.75° W. Long. Elevation is 1,608 feet.
Population: 2,072 (2000); Race: 98.7% White, 0.0% Black, 0.2% Asian, 0.1% American Indian and Alaska Native, 0.1% Hispanic of any race, 0.7% two or more races (2000); Density: 1,163.3 persons per square mile (2000); Age: 22.1% under 18, 29.3% over 64 (2000); Marriage status: 17.3% never married, 62.2% now married, 14.1% widowed, 6.3% divorced (2000); Foreign born: 0.6% (2000); Ancestry (includes multiple ancestries): 49.5% German, 20.5% Norwegian, 10.0% Irish, 8.2% Swedish, 7.3% Dutch (2000).
Economy: Single-family building permits issued: 6 (2001) / 5 (2000); Multi-family building permits issued: 2 (2001) / 2 (2000); Employment by occupation: 9.7% management, 13.8% professional, 16.8% services, 29.3% sales, 1.6% farming, 10.5% construction, 18.3% production (2000).
Income: Per capita income: $17,395 (2000); Median household income: $36,500 (2000); Poverty rate: 8.7% (2000).
Taxes: Total city taxes per capita: $89 (1997); City property taxes per capita: $87 (1997).
Education: High school graduation rate: 78.4% (2000); College graduation rate: 10.5% (2000).

School District(s)

Murray County Central (PK-12)
2000 Enrollment: 871 507-836-6183

Housing: Homeownership rate: 79.1% (2000); Median home value: $53,700 (2000); Median rent: $291 per month (2000); Median age of housing: 47 years (2000).
Hospitals: Murray County Memorial Hospital (30 beds)
Safety: Violent crime rate: 14.3 per 10,000 population; Property crime rate: 105.1 per 10,000 population (2001).
Newspapers: Murray County Wheel/Herald (1 x week); Murray County News (1 x week)
Transportation: Commute to work: 91.0% car, 2.4% public transportation, 4.6% walk, 1.1% work from home (2000); Travel time to work: 64.0% less than 15 minutes, 10.7% 15 to 30 minutes, 14.7% 30 to 45 minutes, 4.8% 45 to 60 minutes, 5.7% 60 minutes or more (2000)
Additional Information Contacts
Slayton Chamber of Commerce 507-836-6902

SLAYTON (township). Covers a land area of 34.021 square miles and a water area of 0.269 square miles. Located at 43.98° N. Lat.; 95.74° W. Long. Elevation is 1,608 feet.
History: Settled 1881.
Population: 343 (2000); Race: 100.0% White, 0.0% Black, 0.0% Asian, 0.0% American Indian and Alaska Native, 0.0% Hispanic of any race, 0.0% two or more races (2000); Density: 10.1 persons per square mile (2000); Age: 28.6% under 18, 14.4% over 64 (2000); Marriage status: 18.8% never married, 72.7% now married, 2.8% widowed, 5.7% divorced (2000); Foreign born: 0.8% (2000); Ancestry (includes multiple ancestries): 62.0% German,

15.3% Dutch, 12.2% Norwegian, 11.0% Irish, 5.1% French (except Basque) (2000).
Economy: Trade center in agricultural area: grain, soybeans; livestock, poultry; dairying. Manufacturing: consumer goods, gravel; printing and publishing. Employment by occupation: 18.7% management, 12.6% professional, 18.2% services, 26.3% sales, 2.0% farming, 9.6% construction, 12.6% production (2000).
Income: Per capita income: $21,026 (2000); Median household income: $48,333 (2000); Poverty rate: 4.5% (2000).
Taxes: Total city taxes per capita: $77 (1997); City property taxes per capita: $77 (1997).
Education: High school graduation rate: 83.5% (2000); College graduation rate: 17.0% (2000).
Housing: Homeownership rate: 91.1% (2000); Median home value: $82,900 (2000); Median rent: $325 per month (2000); Median age of housing: 44 years (2000).
Transportation: Commute to work: 88.6% car, 0.0% public transportation, 0.0% walk, 8.8% work from home (2000); Travel time to work: 65.3% less than 15 minutes, 14.2% 15 to 30 minutes, 11.9% 30 to 45 minutes, 4.0% 45 to 60 minutes, 4.5% 60 minutes or more (2000)

THE LAKES (CDP). Covers a land area of 35.796 square miles and a water area of 9.676 square miles. Located at 44.12° N. Lat.; 95.70° W. Long.
Population: 619 (2000); Race: 99.0% White, 0.7% Black, 0.3% Asian, 0.0% American Indian and Alaska Native, 0.0% Hispanic of any race, 0.0% two or more races (2000); Density: 17.3 persons per square mile (2000); Age: 16.3% under 18, 15.0% over 64 (2000); Marriage status: 15.8% never married, 73.0% now married, 4.4% widowed, 6.8% divorced (2000); Foreign born: 0.7% (2000); Ancestry (includes multiple ancestries): 55.7% German, 18.0% Norwegian, 9.5% Swedish, 7.7% English, 7.4% French (except Basque) (2000).
Economy: Employment by occupation: 23.1% management, 20.8% professional, 7.9% services, 25.6% sales, 2.5% farming, 4.5% construction, 15.5% production (2000).
Income: Per capita income: $23,980 (2000); Median household income: $43,250 (2000); Poverty rate: 0.8% (2000).
Education: High school graduation rate: 90.2% (2000); College graduation rate: 20.6% (2000).
Housing: Homeownership rate: 94.2% (2000); Median home value: $115,600 (2000); Median rent: $275 per month (2000); Median age of housing: 25 years (2000).
Transportation: Commute to work: 88.2% car, 0.0% public transportation, 3.9% walk, 7.9% work from home (2000); Travel time to work: 33.3% less than 15 minutes, 33.6% 15 to 30 minutes, 20.5% 30 to 45 minutes, 8.6% 45 to 60 minutes, 4.0% 60 minutes or more (2000)

Nicollet County

Located in southern Minnesota; bounded on the south and east by the Minnesota River. Covers a land area of 452.30 square miles, a water area of 14.70 square miles, and is located in the Central Time Zone. The county government was organized in 1853. County seat is St. Peter.

Weather Station: Saint Peter 2 SW — Elevation: 849 feet

	Jan	Feb	Mar	Apr	May	Jun	Jul	Aug	Sep	Oct	Nov	Dec
High	23	29	41	58	72	80	84	81	73	61	41	28
Low	3	9	22	35	47	57	61	59	49	37	24	10
Precip	0.9	0.5	1.9	2.4	3.4	4.8	3.9	4.0	2.9	2.3	1.7	0.9
Snow	8.9	3.8	5.9	1.4	tr	0.0	0.0	0.0	0.0	tr	4.1	6.6

High and Low temperatures in degrees Fahrenheit; Precipitation and Snow in inches

Population: 29,771 (2000); Race: 96.5% White, 1.0% Black, 1.4% Asian, 0.0% American Indian and Alaska Native, 1.7% Hispanic of any race, 0.4% two or more races (2000); Density: 65.8 persons per square mile (2000); Age: 24.7% under 18, 10.9% over 64 (2000).
Religion: Five largest groups: 21.3% Catholic Church, 17.9% Evangelical Lutheran Church in America, 9.3% Wisconsin Evangelical Lutheran Synod, 2.4% The United Methodist Church, 2.0% The Evangelical Covenant Church (2000).
Economy: Unemployment rate: 2.2% (11/2002); Total civilian labor force: 19,511 (11/2002); Leading industries: 40.1% manufacturing; 12.3% health care and social assistance; 7.5% retail trade (2000); Companies that employ more than 1,000 persons: 1 (2000); Companies that employ more than 100 persons: 21 (2000); Farms: 723 totaling 249,259 acres (1997); Minority business ownership rate: 0.0% (1997); Women business ownership rate: 21.6% (1997); Retail sales per capita: $4,078 (1997). Single-family building permits issued: 139 (2001) / 92 (2000); Multi-family building permits issued: 36 (2001) / 47 (2000).
Income: Per capita income: $20,517 (2000); Median household income: $46,170 (2000); Poverty rate: 7.5% (2000); Bankruptcy rate: 1.11% (2001).
Taxes: Total county taxes per capita: $240 (1997); County property taxes per capita: $235 (1997).
Education: High school graduation rate: 90.1% (2000); College graduation rate: 29.3% (2000).
Housing: Homeownership rate: 75.6% (2000); Median home value: $113,400 (2000); Median rent: $442 per month (2000); Median age of housing: 30 years (2000).
Health: Birth rate: 111.2 per 10,000 population (1998); Age adjusted death rate: 68.4 per 10,000 population (1999); Age adjusted cancer mortality rate: 216.6 deaths per 100,000 population (1999). Air Quality Index: 98% good, 2% moderate, 0% unhealthy (percent of days in 2000). Number of physicians: 14.4 per 10,000 population (1999); Number of hospital beds: 37.3 per 10,000 population (1999).
Elections: 2000 Presidential election results: 45.9% Gore, 47.1% Bush, 5.5% Nader, 1.1% Buchanan
National and State Parks: Fort Ridgely State Park
Additional Information Contacts
Nicollet County Government Offices. 507-931-6800
St. Peter Area Chamber of Commerce 507-934-3400
St. Peter Chamber of Commerce 507-934-3400

Nicollet County Communities

BELGRADE (township). Covers a land area of 35.132 square miles and a water area of 0.187 square miles. Located at 44.21° N. Lat.; 94.05° W. Long.
Population: 1,033 (2000); Race: 99.6% White, 0.0% Black, 0.0% Asian, 0.0% American Indian and Alaska Native, 0.4% Hispanic of any race, 0.4% two or more races (2000); Density: 29.4 persons per square mile (2000); Age: 27.5% under 18, 9.9% over 64 (2000); Marriage status: 21.8% never married, 71.2% now married, 3.5% widowed, 3.5% divorced (2000); Foreign born: 0.9% (2000); Ancestry (includes multiple ancestries): 59.7% German, 11.8% Norwegian, 7.7% Swedish, 7.1% Irish, 6.1% French (except Basque) (2000).
Economy: Employment by occupation: 16.7% management, 20.5% professional, 11.5% services, 26.7% sales, 1.3% farming, 7.6% construction, 15.6% production (2000).
Income: Per capita income: $23,762 (2000); Median household income: $61,827 (2000); Poverty rate: 2.3% (2000).
Taxes: Total city taxes per capita: $161 (2000); City property taxes per capita: $161 (2000).
Education: High school graduation rate: 93.5% (2000); College graduation rate: 26.6% (2000).
Housing: Homeownership rate: 93.6% (2000); Median home value: $135,600 (2000); Median rent: $400 per month (2000); Median age of housing: 22 years (2000).
Transportation: Commute to work: 88.8% car, 1.2% public transportation, 2.3% walk, 7.4% work from home (2000); Travel time to work: 46.3% less than 15 minutes, 43.7% 15 to 30 minutes, 5.3% 30 to 45 minutes, 0.7% 45 to 60 minutes, 3.9% 60 minutes or more (2000)

BERNADOTTE (township). Covers a land area of 35.945 square miles and a water area of 0 square miles. Located at 44.41° N. Lat.; 94.30° W. Long.
Population: 346 (2000); Race: 95.9% White, 0.0% Black, 4.1% Asian, 0.0% American Indian and Alaska Native, 0.0% Hispanic of any race, 0.0% two or more races (2000); Density: 9.6 persons per square mile (2000); Age: 36.7% under 18, 8.5% over 64 (2000); Marriage status: 21.9% never married, 70.9% now married, 3.0% widowed, 4.2% divorced (2000); Foreign born: 2.5% (2000); Ancestry (includes multiple ancestries): 60.0% German, 16.7% Swedish, 13.2% Norwegian, 6.3% United States or American, 4.7% Dutch (2000).
Economy: Employment by occupation: 25.3% management, 6.8% professional, 7.4% services, 13.2% sales, 4.7% farming, 8.9% construction, 33.7% production (2000).
Income: Per capita income: $15,233 (2000); Median household income: $43,333 (2000); Poverty rate: 6.0% (2000).
Taxes: Total city taxes per capita: $80 (1997); City property taxes per capita: $80 (1997).
Education: High school graduation rate: 90.8% (2000); College graduation rate: 7.8% (2000).

Housing: Homeownership rate: 82.1% (2000); Median home value: $100,000 (2000); Median rent: $375 per month (2000); Median age of housing: 58 years (2000).
Transportation: Commute to work: 83.5% car, 0.0% public transportation, 1.1% walk, 15.4% work from home (2000); Travel time to work: 17.0% less than 15 minutes, 59.1% 15 to 30 minutes, 15.7% 30 to 45 minutes, 5.0% 45 to 60 minutes, 3.1% 60 minutes or more (2000)

BRIGHTON (township). Covers a land area of 17.975 square miles and a water area of 1.088 square miles. Located at 44.33° N. Lat.; 94.30° W. Long.
Population: 169 (2000); Race: 100.0% White, 0.0% Black, 0.0% Asian, 0.0% American Indian and Alaska Native, 0.0% Hispanic of any race, 0.0% two or more races (2000); Density: 9.4 persons per square mile (2000); Age: 27.5% under 18, 19.2% over 64 (2000); Marriage status: 23.0% never married, 73.4% now married, 0.0% widowed, 3.6% divorced (2000); Foreign born: 0.0% (2000); Ancestry (includes multiple ancestries): 79.7% German, 13.7% Norwegian, 3.8% Swedish, 3.8% Irish, 3.3% United States or American (2000).
Economy: Employment by occupation: 38.5% management, 5.8% professional, 10.6% services, 13.5% sales, 6.7% farming, 12.5% construction, 12.5% production (2000).
Income: Per capita income: $14,437 (2000); Median household income: $40,000 (2000); Poverty rate: 9.9% (2000).
Taxes: Total city taxes per capita: $126 (1997); City property taxes per capita: $126 (1997).
Education: High school graduation rate: 75.2% (2000); College graduation rate: 3.4% (2000).
Housing: Homeownership rate: 82.4% (2000); Median home value: $85,000 (2000); Median rent: $350 per month (2000); Median age of housing: 53 years (2000).
Transportation: Commute to work: 64.4% car, 0.0% public transportation, 0.0% walk, 35.6% work from home (2000); Travel time to work: 14.9% less than 15 minutes, 68.7% 15 to 30 minutes, 16.4% 30 to 45 minutes, 0.0% 45 to 60 minutes, 0.0% 60 minutes or more (2000)

COURTLAND (city). Covers a land area of 2.656 square miles and a water area of 0 square miles. Located at 44.26° N. Lat.; 94.34° W. Long. Elevation is 936 feet.
Population: 538 (2000); Race: 99.1% White, 0.0% Black, 0.0% Asian, 0.0% American Indian and Alaska Native, 0.4% Hispanic of any race, 0.9% two or more races (2000); Density: 202.5 persons per square mile (2000); Age: 32.3% under 18, 7.1% over 64 (2000); Marriage status: 19.4% never married, 70.5% now married, 3.9% widowed, 6.2% divorced (2000); Foreign born: 2.8% (2000); Ancestry (includes multiple ancestries): 66.6% German, 14.5% Norwegian, 8.5% Swedish, 6.5% Irish, 4.6% Dutch (2000).
Economy: Single-family building permits issued: 5 (2001) / 2 (2000); Multi-family building permits issued: 0 (2001) / 0 (2000); Employment by occupation: 13.9% management, 19.3% professional, 9.5% services, 21.3% sales, 0.7% farming, 10.1% construction, 25.3% production (2000).
Income: Per capita income: $23,267 (2000); Median household income: $58,906 (2000); Poverty rate: 2.6% (2000).
Taxes: Total city taxes per capita: $199 (1997); City property taxes per capita: $190 (1997).
Education: High school graduation rate: 85.5% (2000); College graduation rate: 28.1% (2000).
Housing: Homeownership rate: 82.7% (2000); Median home value: $113,100 (2000); Median rent: $552 per month (2000); Median age of housing: 26 years (2000).
Transportation: Commute to work: 93.6% car, 0.0% public transportation, 2.7% walk, 3.0% work from home (2000); Travel time to work: 38.0% less than 15 minutes, 45.3% 15 to 30 minutes, 11.8% 30 to 45 minutes, 1.0% 45 to 60 minutes, 3.8% 60 minutes or more (2000)

COURTLAND (township). Covers a land area of 37.849 square miles and a water area of 4.212 square miles. Located at 44.28° N. Lat.; 94.35° W. Long. Elevation is 936 feet.
Population: 715 (2000); Race: 97.8% White, 0.0% Black, 0.0% Asian, 0.0% American Indian and Alaska Native, 2.3% Hispanic of any race, 0.1% two or more races (2000); Density: 18.9 persons per square mile (2000); Age: 30.1% under 18, 7.8% over 64 (2000); Marriage status: 25.3% never married, 65.2% now married, 4.3% widowed, 5.2% divorced (2000); Foreign born: 0.3% (2000); Ancestry (includes multiple ancestries): 69.2% German, 10.4% Norwegian, 4.5% English, 4.3% Irish, 3.6% French (except Basque) (2000).
Economy: Manufacturing: concrete products, lumber. Employment by occupation: 20.4% management, 12.6% professional, 10.1% services, 22.0% sales, 3.0% farming, 9.4% construction, 22.5% production (2000).
Income: Per capita income: $19,041 (2000); Median household income: $53,977 (2000); Poverty rate: 7.8% (2000).
Taxes: Total city taxes per capita: $57 (1997); City property taxes per capita: $57 (1997).
Education: High school graduation rate: 84.1% (2000); College graduation rate: 16.6% (2000).
Housing: Homeownership rate: 90.6% (2000); Median home value: $121,700 (2000); Median rent: $275 per month (2000); Median age of housing: 37 years (2000).
Transportation: Commute to work: 86.2% car, 0.7% public transportation, 1.0% walk, 11.6% work from home (2000); Travel time to work: 56.2% less than 15 minutes, 34.2% 15 to 30 minutes, 5.5% 30 to 45 minutes, 1.4% 45 to 60 minutes, 2.7% 60 minutes or more (2000)

GRANBY (township). Covers a land area of 27.547 square miles and a water area of 6.362 square miles. Located at 44.33° N. Lat.; 94.19° W. Long.
Population: 259 (2000); Race: 100.0% White, 0.0% Black, 0.0% Asian, 0.0% American Indian and Alaska Native, 0.0% Hispanic of any race, 0.0% two or more races (2000); Density: 9.4 persons per square mile (2000); Age: 24.9% under 18, 20.8% over 64 (2000); Marriage status: 24.9% never married, 61.9% now married, 5.6% widowed, 7.6% divorced (2000); Foreign born: 0.8% (2000); Ancestry (includes multiple ancestries): 64.5% German, 14.7% Norwegian, 13.5% Swedish, 6.5% United States or American, 4.5% English (2000).
Economy: Employment by occupation: 31.5% management, 10.8% professional, 7.7% services, 19.2% sales, 3.1% farming, 10.8% construction, 16.9% production (2000).
Income: Per capita income: $15,713 (2000); Median household income: $42,031 (2000); Poverty rate: 0.8% (2000).
Taxes: Total city taxes per capita: $94 (1997); City property taxes per capita: $94 (1997).
Education: High school graduation rate: 77.3% (2000); College graduation rate: 11.0% (2000).
Housing: Homeownership rate: 88.5% (2000); Median home value: $112,500 (2000); Median rent: $275 per month (2000); Median age of housing: 44 years (2000).
Transportation: Commute to work: 67.4% car, 0.8% public transportation, 3.9% walk, 27.9% work from home (2000); Travel time to work: 35.5% less than 15 minutes, 43.0% 15 to 30 minutes, 11.8% 30 to 45 minutes, 2.2% 45 to 60 minutes, 7.5% 60 minutes or more (2000)

LAFAYETTE (city). Covers a land area of 1.154 square miles and a water area of 0 square miles. Located at 44.44° N. Lat.; 94.39° W. Long. Elevation is 1,014 feet.
Population: 529 (2000); Race: 98.9% White, 0.0% Black, 0.4% Asian, 0.0% American Indian and Alaska Native, 1.1% Hispanic of any race, 0.0% two or more races (2000); Density: 458.4 persons per square mile (2000); Age: 27.4% under 18, 23.6% over 64 (2000); Marriage status: 17.2% never married, 63.7% now married, 12.7% widowed, 6.5% divorced (2000); Foreign born: 1.1% (2000); Ancestry (includes multiple ancestries): 54.1% German, 16.1% Swedish, 6.6% Irish, 6.4% Norwegian, 6.2% United States or American (2000).
Economy: Single-family building permits issued: 4 (2001) / 0 (2000); Multi-family building permits issued: 0 (2001) / 0 (2000); Employment by occupation: 7.0% management, 14.8% professional, 13.5% services, 26.6% sales, 4.4% farming, 10.0% construction, 23.6% production (2000).
Income: Per capita income: $15,347 (2000); Median household income: $36,719 (2000); Poverty rate: 2.9% (2000).
Taxes: Total city taxes per capita: $209 (1997); City property taxes per capita: $209 (1997).
Education: High school graduation rate: 78.9% (2000); College graduation rate: 5.9% (2000).

School District(s)

Lafayette Public Charter School (KG-06)
2000 Enrollment: 43 507-228-8943
Housing: Homeownership rate: 78.1% (2000); Median home value: $68,300 (2000); Median rent: $384 per month (2000); Median age of housing: 49 years (2000).
Newspapers: Lafayette Nicollet Ledger (1 x week)
Transportation: Commute to work: 83.8% car, 0.0% public transportation, 9.6% walk, 3.9% work from home (2000); Travel time to work: 34.1% less than 15 minutes, 43.6% 15 to 30 minutes, 12.3% 30 to 45 minutes, 5.0% 45 to 60 minutes, 5.0% 60 minutes or more (2000)

LAFAYETTE (township). Covers a land area of 50.389 square miles and a water area of 0.071 square miles. Located at 44.40° N. Lat.; 94.43° W. Long. Elevation is 1,014 feet.
Population: 724 (2000); Race: 99.7% White, 0.0% Black, 0.0% Asian, 0.0% American Indian and Alaska Native, 0.0% Hispanic of any race, 0.3% two or more races (2000); Density: 14.4 persons per square mile (2000); Age: 27.4% under 18, 9.6% over 64 (2000); Marriage status: 22.2% never married, 69.4% now married, 3.3% widowed, 5.1% divorced (2000); Foreign born: 0.3% (2000); Ancestry (includes multiple ancestries): 72.3% German, 12.9% Norwegian, 7.7% Swedish, 4.8% Irish, 2.7% United States or American (2000).
Economy: Agricultural area; grain, soybeans, peas; livestock, poultry; dairying. Manufacturing: feeds, fertilizers, meat processing. Employment by occupation: 23.9% management, 19.4% professional, 8.1% services, 16.9% sales, 4.0% farming, 10.3% construction, 17.4% production (2000).
Income: Per capita income: $23,397 (2000); Median household income: $51,319 (2000); Poverty rate: 7.1% (2000).
Taxes: Total city taxes per capita: $104 (1997); City property taxes per capita: $104 (1997).
Education: High school graduation rate: 88.0% (2000); College graduation rate: 21.4% (2000).
Housing: Homeownership rate: 85.3% (2000); Median home value: $136,100 (2000); Median rent: $219 per month (2000); Median age of housing: 47 years (2000).
Transportation: Commute to work: 81.7% car, 0.0% public transportation, 3.1% walk, 14.2% work from home (2000); Travel time to work: 55.9% less than 15 minutes, 29.4% 15 to 30 minutes, 11.1% 30 to 45 minutes, 1.5% 45 to 60 minutes, 2.1% 60 minutes or more (2000)

LAKE PRAIRIE (township). Covers a land area of 54.798 square miles and a water area of 0.454 square miles. Located at 44.40° N. Lat.; 94.03° W. Long.
Population: 652 (2000); Race: 100.0% White, 0.0% Black, 0.0% Asian, 0.0% American Indian and Alaska Native, 0.0% Hispanic of any race, 0.0% two or more races (2000); Density: 11.9 persons per square mile (2000); Age: 27.3% under 18, 10.9% over 64 (2000); Marriage status: 21.0% never married, 67.0% now married, 6.9% widowed, 5.1% divorced (2000); Foreign born: 0.6% (2000); Ancestry (includes multiple ancestries): 43.5% German, 19.8% Norwegian, 17.7% Swedish, 12.4% Irish, 4.7% United States or American (2000).
Economy: Employment by occupation: 20.5% management, 14.2% professional, 14.0% services, 17.1% sales, 3.4% farming, 6.7% construction, 24.1% production (2000).
Income: Per capita income: $21,500 (2000); Median household income: $52,614 (2000); Poverty rate: 2.9% (2000).
Taxes: Total city taxes per capita: $85 (1997); City property taxes per capita: $85 (1997).
Education: High school graduation rate: 86.7% (2000); College graduation rate: 24.1% (2000).
Housing: Homeownership rate: 83.3% (2000); Median home value: $122,000 (2000); Median rent: $300 per month (2000); Median age of housing: 48 years (2000).
Transportation: Commute to work: 88.0% car, 0.0% public transportation, 2.7% walk, 9.4% work from home (2000); Travel time to work: 35.1% less than 15 minutes, 34.5% 15 to 30 minutes, 20.4% 30 to 45 minutes, 3.5% 45 to 60 minutes, 6.5% 60 minutes or more (2000)

NEW SWEDEN (township). Covers a land area of 35.787 square miles and a water area of 0.168 square miles. Located at 44.40° N. Lat.; 94.19° W. Long.
Population: 326 (2000); Race: 98.5% White, 0.0% Black, 0.6% Asian, 0.0% American Indian and Alaska Native, 1.5% Hispanic of any race, 0.9% two or more races (2000); Density: 9.1 persons per square mile (2000); Age: 33.3% under 18, 13.6% over 64 (2000); Marriage status: 21.7% never married, 74.6% now married, 0.8% widowed, 2.9% divorced (2000); Foreign born: 0.6% (2000); Ancestry (includes multiple ancestries): 56.5% German, 37.0% Swedish, 28.1% Norwegian, 6.2% English, 3.1% Scandinavian (2000).
Economy: Employment by occupation: 34.5% management, 9.7% professional, 9.7% services, 13.3% sales, 11.5% farming, 7.3% construction, 13.9% production (2000).
Income: Per capita income: $18,042 (2000); Median household income: $45,000 (2000); Poverty rate: 9.0% (2000).
Taxes: Total city taxes per capita: $49 (1997); City property taxes per capita: $49 (1997).
Education: High school graduation rate: 88.9% (2000); College graduation rate: 18.8% (2000).
Housing: Homeownership rate: 81.5% (2000); Median home value: $88,500 (2000); Median rent: $506 per month (2000); Median age of housing: 60+ years (2000).
Transportation: Commute to work: 73.6% car, 0.0% public transportation, 0.6% walk, 25.8% work from home (2000); Travel time to work: 28.9% less than 15 minutes, 34.7% 15 to 30 minutes, 29.8% 30 to 45 minutes, 1.7% 45 to 60 minutes, 5.0% 60 minutes or more (2000)

NICOLLET (city). Covers a land area of 0.882 square miles and a water area of 0 square miles. Located at 44.27° N. Lat.; 94.18° W. Long. Elevation is 980 feet.
Population: 889 (2000); Race: 98.6% White, 0.0% Black, 0.6% Asian, 0.0% American Indian and Alaska Native, 1.0% Hispanic of any race, 0.1% two or more races (2000); Density: 1,008.2 persons per square mile (2000); Age: 27.0% under 18, 10.0% over 64 (2000); Marriage status: 25.7% never married, 62.1% now married, 6.7% widowed, 5.5% divorced (2000); Foreign born: 1.5% (2000); Ancestry (includes multiple ancestries): 64.5% German, 18.5% Norwegian, 7.7% Swedish, 7.2% Irish, 4.8% French (except Basque) (2000).
Economy: Single-family building permits issued: 11 (2001) / 7 (2000); Multi-family building permits issued: 0 (2001) / 0 (2000); Employment by occupation: 9.6% management, 18.7% professional, 16.6% services, 19.5% sales, 2.1% farming, 9.1% construction, 24.5% production (2000).
Income: Per capita income: $19,237 (2000); Median household income: $42,500 (2000); Poverty rate: 3.7% (2000).
Taxes: Total city taxes per capita: $97 (1997); City property taxes per capita: $88 (1997).
Education: High school graduation rate: 88.8% (2000); College graduation rate: 17.3% (2000).

School District(s)

Nicollet (KG-12)
2000 Enrollment: 358 507-232-3411
Housing: Homeownership rate: 78.9% (2000); Median home value: $93,500 (2000); Median rent: $320 per month (2000); Median age of housing: 31 years (2000).
Transportation: Commute to work: 86.8% car, 0.0% public transportation, 7.8% walk, 4.1% work from home (2000); Travel time to work: 38.4% less than 15 minutes, 53.3% 15 to 30 minutes, 5.5% 30 to 45 minutes, 1.0% 45 to 60 minutes, 1.8% 60 minutes or more (2000)

NICOLLET (township). Covers a land area of 33.114 square miles and a water area of 0.321 square miles. Located at 44.24° N. Lat.; 94.18° W. Long. Elevation is 980 feet.
Population: 511 (2000); Race: 99.2% White, 0.0% Black, 0.8% Asian, 0.0% American Indian and Alaska Native, 0.0% Hispanic of any race, 0.0% two or more races (2000); Density: 15.4 persons per square mile (2000); Age: 29.5% under 18, 12.2% over 64 (2000); Marriage status: 19.1% never married, 73.8% now married, 4.4% widowed, 2.7% divorced (2000); Foreign born: 1.1% (2000); Ancestry (includes multiple ancestries): 70.2% German, 14.8% Irish, 12.7% Swedish, 10.1% Norwegian, 4.2% United States or American (2000).
Economy: Dairying; livestock; grain, soybeans, beans. Manufacturing: boating equipment, wood products. Employment by occupation: 14.5% management, 18.2% professional, 13.2% services, 23.0% sales, 3.1% farming, 8.8% construction, 19.2% production (2000).
Income: Per capita income: $21,451 (2000); Median household income: $50,000 (2000); Poverty rate: 2.7% (2000).
Taxes: Total city taxes per capita: $70 (1997); City property taxes per capita: $70 (1997).
Education: High school graduation rate: 92.5% (2000); College graduation rate: 20.8% (2000).
Housing: Homeownership rate: 95.6% (2000); Median home value: $114,400 (2000); Median rent: $300 per month (2000); Median age of housing: 52 years (2000).
Transportation: Commute to work: 89.4% car, 0.0% public transportation, 2.9% walk, 6.8% work from home (2000); Travel time to work: 23.8% less than 15 minutes, 61.7% 15 to 30 minutes, 8.3% 30 to 45 minutes, 1.4% 45 to 60 minutes, 4.8% 60 minutes or more (2000)

NORTH MANKATO (city). Covers a land area of 4.715 square miles and a water area of 0.082 square miles. Located at 44.17° N. Lat.; 94.02° W. Long.
History: Incorporated 1922.

Population: 11,798 (2000); Race: 96.5% White, 0.9% Black, 1.7% Asian, 0.1% American Indian and Alaska Native, 1.4% Hispanic of any race, 0.3% two or more races (2000); Density: 2,502.5 persons per square mile (2000); Age: 26.3% under 18, 9.7% over 64 (2000); Marriage status: 29.1% never married, 58.7% now married, 4.6% widowed, 7.6% divorced (2000); Foreign born: 3.1% (2000); Ancestry (includes multiple ancestries): 54.6% German, 16.4% Norwegian, 10.5% Irish, 7.9% Swedish, 6.9% English (2000).
Vital Statistics: Birth rate: 126.3 per 10,000 population (1998)
Economy: Agriculture: grain, soybeans, peas; livestock, poultry; dairying. Manufacturing: awards, printers, electronics, trusses, food and beverage processing, lumber brake systems. Single-family building permits issued: 25 (2001) / 41 (2000); Multi-family building permits issued: 36 (2001) / 21 (2000); Employment by occupation: 14.7% management, 22.4% professional, 10.0% services, 28.9% sales, 0.1% farming, 5.9% construction, 17.9% production (2000).
Income: Per capita income: $23,916 (2000); Median household income: $48,816 (2000); Poverty rate: 7.0% (2000).
Taxes: Total city taxes per capita: $202 (2000); City property taxes per capita: $178 (2000).
Education: High school graduation rate: 93.1% (2000); College graduation rate: 36.9% (2000).

Two-year College(s)

South Central Technical College-Mankato (Public)
2001 Enrollment: 3,165 507-389-7200
2001 Tuition: In-state $2,250; Out-of-state $4,500

Housing: Homeownership rate: 73.2% (2000); Median home value: $120,600 (2000); Median rent: $463 per month (2000); Median age of housing: 26 years (2000).
Safety: Violent crime rate: 8.4 per 10,000 population; Property crime rate: 231.4 per 10,000 population (2001).
Transportation: Commute to work: 94.0% car, 0.3% public transportation, 2.6% walk, 2.9% work from home (2000); Travel time to work: 68.1% less than 15 minutes, 21.6% 15 to 30 minutes, 4.2% 30 to 45 minutes, 2.0% 45 to 60 minutes, 4.1% 60 minutes or more (2000)

OSHAWA (township). Covers a land area of 29.323 square miles and a water area of 0.303 square miles. Located at 44.29° N. Lat.; 94.03° W. Long.
Population: 525 (2000); Race: 98.0% White, 0.0% Black, 1.3% Asian, 0.0% American Indian and Alaska Native, 1.1% Hispanic of any race, 0.7% two or more races (2000); Density: 17.9 persons per square mile (2000); Age: 23.8% under 18, 13.3% over 64 (2000); Marriage status: 29.1% never married, 61.1% now married, 4.3% widowed, 5.5% divorced (2000); Foreign born: 0.4% (2000); Ancestry (includes multiple ancestries): 57.5% German, 16.6% Norwegian, 15.8% Swedish, 11.6% Irish, 6.6% French (except Basque) (2000).
Economy: Employment by occupation: 17.3% management, 28.4% professional, 16.0% services, 18.3% sales, 0.0% farming, 5.9% construction, 14.1% production (2000).
Income: Per capita income: $19,768 (2000); Median household income: $54,271 (2000); Poverty rate: 2.9% (2000).
Taxes: Total city taxes per capita: $104 (1997); City property taxes per capita: $104 (1997).
Education: High school graduation rate: 91.4% (2000); College graduation rate: 31.5% (2000).
Housing: Homeownership rate: 91.2% (2000); Median home value: $140,000 (2000); Median rent: $475 per month (2000); Median age of housing: 38 years (2000).
Transportation: Commute to work: 82.4% car, 0.7% public transportation, 7.0% walk, 8.0% work from home (2000); Travel time to work: 51.6% less than 15 minutes, 30.0% 15 to 30 minutes, 7.9% 30 to 45 minutes, 4.3% 45 to 60 minutes, 6.1% 60 minutes or more (2000)

RIDGELY (township). Covers a land area of 18.680 square miles and a water area of 0.081 square miles. Located at 44.43° N. Lat.; 94.65° W. Long.
Population: 126 (2000); Race: 100.0% White, 0.0% Black, 0.0% Asian, 0.0% American Indian and Alaska Native, 0.0% Hispanic of any race, 0.0% two or more races (2000); Density: 6.7 persons per square mile (2000); Age: 27.5% under 18, 9.2% over 64 (2000); Marriage status: 25.3% never married, 67.5% now married, 1.2% widowed, 6.0% divorced (2000); Foreign born: 0.0% (2000); Ancestry (includes multiple ancestries): 76.1% German, 19.3% Irish, 3.7% Norwegian, 3.7% Other groups, 3.7% Swedish (2000).
Economy: Employment by occupation: 33.3% management, 15.8% professional, 17.5% services, 14.0% sales, 3.5% farming, 10.5% construction, 5.3% production (2000).
Income: Per capita income: $17,339 (2000); Median household income: $41,875 (2000); Poverty rate: 7.6% (2000).
Taxes: Total city taxes per capita: $145 (1997); City property taxes per capita: $145 (1997).
Education: High school graduation rate: 88.2% (2000); College graduation rate: 13.2% (2000).
Housing: Homeownership rate: 78.6% (2000); Median home value: $75,000 (2000); Median rent: $200 per month (2000); Median age of housing: 59 years (2000).
Transportation: Commute to work: 71.9% car, 0.0% public transportation, 0.0% walk, 28.1% work from home (2000); Travel time to work: 41.5% less than 15 minutes, 56.1% 15 to 30 minutes, 0.0% 30 to 45 minutes, 0.0% 45 to 60 minutes, 2.4% 60 minutes or more (2000)

SAINT PETER (city). Covers a land area of 5.423 square miles and a water area of 0.141 square miles. Located at 44.32° N. Lat.; 93.96° W. Long. Elevation is 812 feet.
History: St. Peter was founded in 1853 by Captain W.B. Dodd, who built the first section of a military road into Minnesota. In 1857 the residents of St. Peter erected a capitol building, hoping that the territorial legislature would move the capital from St. Paul to St. Peter. Their plans were foiled by a committee chairman who hid the bill from the legislature until the time limit had passed.
Population: 9,747 (2000); Race: 94.3% White, 1.9% Black, 1.9% Asian, 0.0% American Indian and Alaska Native, 3.0% Hispanic of any race, 0.6% two or more races (2000); Density: 1,797.3 persons per square mile (2000); Age: 19.7% under 18, 11.8% over 64 (2000); Marriage status: 42.4% never married, 44.7% now married, 6.2% widowed, 6.8% divorced (2000); Foreign born: 3.7% (2000); Ancestry (includes multiple ancestries): 38.2% German, 17.4% Norwegian, 12.5% Swedish, 10.5% Irish, 5.8% Other groups (2000).
Economy: Single-family building permits issued: 66 (2001) / 17 (2000); Multi-family building permits issued: 0 (2001) / 26 (2000); Employment by occupation: 9.5% management, 24.4% professional, 21.0% services, 22.6% sales, 0.6% farming, 6.5% construction, 15.4% production (2000).
Income: Per capita income: $16,634 (2000); Median household income: $40,344 (2000); Poverty rate: 11.8% (2000).
Education: High school graduation rate: 88.4% (2000); College graduation rate: 28.2% (2000).

School District(s)

Minnesota Valley Ed. Dist. (PK-12)
2000 Enrollment: 79 507-931-5420
Saint Peter (PK-12)
2000 Enrollment: 1,993 507-931-5703

Four-year College(s)

Gustavus Adolphus College (Private, Not-for-profit, Evangelical Lutheran Church)
2001 Enrollment: 2,562 507-933-8000
2001 Tuition: In-state $18,940; Out-of-state $18,940

Housing: Homeownership rate: 69.2% (2000); Median home value: $106,300 (2000); Median rent: $398 per month (2000); Median age of housing: 33 years (2000).
Hospitals: Community Hospital & Health Care Center; Saint Peter Regional Treatment Center (508 beds)
Safety: Violent crime rate: 26.4 per 10,000 population; Property crime rate: 347.1 per 10,000 population (2001).
Newspapers: Saint Peter Herald (1 x week)
Transportation: Commute to work: 74.1% car, 0.2% public transportation, 21.7% walk, 2.4% work from home (2000); Travel time to work: 67.0% less than 15 minutes, 25.6% 15 to 30 minutes, 3.8% 30 to 45 minutes, 0.5% 45 to 60 minutes, 3.1% 60 minutes or more (2000)

Additional Information Contacts

St. Peter Area Chamber of Commerce 507-934-3400
St. Peter Chamber of Commerce 507-934-3400

TRAVERSE (township). Covers a land area of 23.014 square miles and a water area of 0.603 square miles. Located at 44.36° N. Lat.; 94.02° W. Long. Elevation is 994 feet.
Population: 367 (2000); Race: 98.5% White, 0.6% Black, 0.0% Asian, 0.0% American Indian and Alaska Native, 0.0% Hispanic of any race, 0.9% two or more races (2000); Density: 15.9 persons per square mile (2000); Age: 27.3% under 18, 10.5% over 64 (2000); Marriage status: 25.4% never married, 67.7% now married, 1.5% widowed, 5.4% divorced (2000); Foreign born: 0.0% (2000); Ancestry (includes multiple ancestries): 60.7% German, 15.0% Swedish, 14.4% Irish, 9.3% Norwegian, 5.7% French (except Basque) (2000).
Economy: Employment by occupation: 17.4% management, 12.0% professional, 13.6% services, 19.6% sales, 1.6% farming, 16.8% construction, 19.0% production (2000).

Income: Per capita income: $21,861 (2000); Median household income: $55,250 (2000); Poverty rate: 2.7% (2000).
Taxes: Total city taxes per capita: $24 (1997); City property taxes per capita: $24 (1997).
Education: High school graduation rate: 89.2% (2000); College graduation rate: 18.1% (2000).
Housing: Homeownership rate: 87.5% (2000); Median home value: $111,300 (2000); Median rent: $425 per month (2000); Median age of housing: 32 years (2000).
Transportation: Commute to work: 91.4% car, 0.0% public transportation, 2.2% walk, 5.9% work from home (2000); Travel time to work: 55.2% less than 15 minutes, 35.1% 15 to 30 minutes, 3.4% 30 to 45 minutes, 0.6% 45 to 60 minutes, 5.7% 60 minutes or more (2000)

WEST NEWTON (township). Covers a land area of 37.664 square miles and a water area of 0.559 square miles. Located at 44.42° N. Lat.; 94.55° W. Long.
Population: 517 (2000); Race: 99.2% White, 0.0% Black, 0.0% Asian, 0.0% American Indian and Alaska Native, 0.4% Hispanic of any race, 0.4% two or more races (2000); Density: 13.7 persons per square mile (2000); Age: 28.7% under 18, 10.0% over 64 (2000); Marriage status: 27.2% never married, 66.4% now married, 1.5% widowed, 4.9% divorced (2000); Foreign born: 0.0% (2000); Ancestry (includes multiple ancestries): 73.0% German, 7.9% Norwegian, 6.7% Irish, 6.5% United States or American, 3.8% Swedish (2000).
Economy: Employment by occupation: 27.1% management, 11.7% professional, 12.9% services, 22.4% sales, 2.8% farming, 7.3% construction, 15.8% production (2000).
Income: Per capita income: $20,533 (2000); Median household income: $50,313 (2000); Poverty rate: 4.6% (2000).
Taxes: Total city taxes per capita: $74 (1997); City property taxes per capita: $74 (1997).
Education: High school graduation rate: 85.2% (2000); College graduation rate: 16.0% (2000).
Housing: Homeownership rate: 89.9% (2000); Median home value: $105,200 (2000); Median rent: $375 per month (2000); Median age of housing: 60+ years (2000).
Transportation: Commute to work: 75.5% car, 0.0% public transportation, 3.5% walk, 21.0% work from home (2000); Travel time to work: 35.9% less than 15 minutes, 53.1% 15 to 30 minutes, 4.5% 30 to 45 minutes, 2.9% 45 to 60 minutes, 3.7% 60 minutes or more (2000)

Nobles County

Located in southwestern Minnesota; bounded on the south by Iowa; watered by headwaters of the Little Rock River; includes Ocheda Lake, and part of Coteau des Prairies. Covers a land area of 715.40 square miles, a water area of 6.90 square miles, and is located in the Central Time Zone. The county government was organized in 1857. County seat is Worthington.

Weather Station: Worthington 2 NNE — Elevation: 1,568 feet

	Jan	Feb	Mar	Apr	May	Jun	Jul	Aug	Sep	Oct	Nov	Dec
High	22	28	39	55	69	79	83	80	72	59	40	26
Low	3	9	21	33	45	56	60	57	47	35	22	9
Precip	0.7	0.6	2.0	2.8	3.4	4.6	3.6	3.6	2.6	1.9	1.6	0.7
Snow	8.2	5.6	7.5	3.2	tr	0.0	0.0	0.0	tr	1.0	6.4	7.1

High and Low temperatures in degrees Fahrenheit; Precipitation and Snow in inches

Population: 20,832 (2000); Race: 87.2% White, 1.4% Black, 3.7% Asian, 0.6% American Indian and Alaska Native, 10.7% Hispanic of any race, 1.6% two or more races (2000); Density: 29.1 persons per square mile (2000); Age: 26.6% under 18, 17.3% over 64 (2000).
Religion: Five largest groups: 31.3% Catholic Church, 16.3% Evangelical Lutheran Church in America, 9.3% Presbyterian Church (U.S.A.), 7.8% Lutheran Church—Missouri Synod, 5.6% Christian Reformed Church in North America (2000).
Economy: Unemployment rate: 2.2% (11/2002); Total civilian labor force: 9,891 (11/2002); Leading industries: 26.3% manufacturing; 19.1% retail trade; 15.6% health care and social assistance (2000); Companies that employ more than 1,000 persons: 1 (2000); Companies that employ more than 100 persons: 11 (2000); Farms: 1,021 totaling 390,286 acres (1997); Minority business ownership rate: 0.0% (1997); Women business ownership rate: 13.7% (1997); Retail sales per capita: $10,497 (1997). Single-family building permits issued: 27 (2001) / 14 (2000); Multi-family building permits issued: 16 (2001) / 10 (2000).
Income: Per capita income: $16,987 (2000); Median household income: $35,684 (2000); Poverty rate: 11.7% (2000); Bankruptcy rate: 2.22% (2001).
Taxes: Total county taxes per capita: $218 (2000); County property taxes per capita: $217 (2000).
Education: High school graduation rate: 75.8% (2000); College graduation rate: 13.5% (2000).
Housing: Homeownership rate: 75.1% (2000); Median home value: $61,400 (2000); Median rent: $322 per month (2000); Median age of housing: 45 years (2000).
Health: Birth rate: 147.4 per 10,000 population (1998); Age adjusted death rate: 85.8 per 10,000 population (1999); Age adjusted cancer mortality rate: 212.1 deaths per 100,000 population (1999). Number of physicians: 13.4 per 10,000 population (1999); Number of hospital beds: 55.7 per 10,000 population (1999).
Elections: 2000 Presidential election results: 42.4% Gore, 53.7% Bush, 2.7% Nader, 0.8% Buchanan
National and State Parks: Dewald State Wildlife Management Area; Fulda State Wildlife Management Area; Fury State Wildlife Management Area; Groth State Wildlife Management Area
Additional Information Contacts
Nobles County Government Offices 507-372-8241
Worthington Chamber of Commerce. 507-372-2919

Nobles County Communities

ADRIAN (city). Covers a land area of 1.110 square miles and a water area of 0 square miles. Located at 43.63° N. Lat.; 95.93° W. Long. Elevation is 1,541 feet.
Population: 1,234 (2000); Race: 94.7% White, 0.0% Black, 3.0% Asian, 0.0% American Indian and Alaska Native, 2.4% Hispanic of any race, 0.6% two or more races (2000); Density: 1,111.5 persons per square mile (2000); Age: 24.9% under 18, 22.5% over 64 (2000); Marriage status: 20.0% never married, 60.6% now married, 14.3% widowed, 5.1% divorced (2000); Foreign born: 2.9% (2000); Ancestry (includes multiple ancestries): 60.2% German, 9.8% Irish, 7.0% Norwegian, 6.8% Dutch, 6.3% Other groups (2000).
Economy: Corn, oats, soybeans; cattle, sheep, poultry; dairying. Manufactures machinery, plastics, concrete. Single-family building permits issued: 1 (2001) / 0 (2000); Multi-family building permits issued: 4 (2001) / 4 (2000); Employment by occupation: 11.8% management, 15.4% professional, 18.7% services, 24.1% sales, 0.8% farming, 10.8% construction, 18.4% production (2000).
Income: Per capita income: $16,925 (2000); Median household income: $35,927 (2000); Poverty rate: 7.2% (2000).
Taxes: Total city taxes per capita: $170 (1997); City property taxes per capita: $159 (1997).
Education: High school graduation rate: 75.5% (2000); College graduation rate: 9.3% (2000).

School District(s)

Adrian (PK-12)
2000 Enrollment: 682 507-483-2266
Housing: Homeownership rate: 87.1% (2000); Median home value: $57,900 (2000); Median rent: $278 per month (2000); Median age of housing: 50 years (2000).
Hospitals: Arnold Memorial Health Care Center (41 beds)
Newspapers: Nobles County Review (1 x week)
Transportation: Commute to work: 86.8% car, 0.0% public transportation, 7.1% walk, 5.1% work from home (2000); Travel time to work: 49.4% less than 15 minutes, 32.6% 15 to 30 minutes, 11.2% 30 to 45 minutes, 4.4% 45 to 60 minutes, 2.4% 60 minutes or more (2000)

BIGELOW (city). Covers a land area of 0.378 square miles and a water area of 0 square miles. Located at 43.50° N. Lat.; 95.69° W. Long. Elevation is 1,636 feet.
Population: 231 (2000); Race: 98.2% White, 0.0% Black, 0.0% Asian, 0.9% American Indian and Alaska Native, 0.9% Hispanic of any race, 0.9% two or more races (2000); Density: 610.7 persons per square mile (2000); Age: 26.6% under 18, 14.4% over 64 (2000); Marriage status: 18.5% never married, 70.8% now married, 5.1% widowed, 5.6% divorced (2000); Foreign born: 2.7% (2000); Ancestry (includes multiple ancestries): 61.3% German, 10.8% Dutch, 7.7% United States or American, 6.8% Irish, 6.8% Norwegian (2000).
Economy: Single-family building permits issued: 0 (2001) / 0 (2000); Multi-family building permits issued: 0 (2001) / 0 (2000); Employment by

occupation: 12.7% management, 5.5% professional, 10.9% services, 27.3% sales, 1.8% farming, 14.5% construction, 27.3% production (2000).
Income: Per capita income: $15,227 (2000); Median household income: $32,750 (2000); Poverty rate: 12.2% (2000).
Taxes: Total city taxes per capita: $47 (1997); City property taxes per capita: $42 (1997).
Education: High school graduation rate: 78.2% (2000); College graduation rate: 7.7% (2000).
Housing: Homeownership rate: 95.3% (2000); Median home value: $44,600 (2000); Median rent: $225 per month (2000); Median age of housing: 48 years (2000).
Transportation: Commute to work: 91.6% car, 0.0% public transportation, 4.7% walk, 1.9% work from home (2000); Travel time to work: 41.9% less than 15 minutes, 56.2% 15 to 30 minutes, 0.0% 30 to 45 minutes, 0.0% 45 to 60 minutes, 1.9% 60 minutes or more (2000)

BIGELOW (township). Covers a land area of 34.462 square miles and a water area of 1.776 square miles. Located at 43.55° N. Lat.; 95.64° W. Long. Elevation is 1,636 feet.
Population: 384 (2000); Race: 98.1% White, 0.0% Black, 0.0% Asian, 0.0% American Indian and Alaska Native, 1.9% Hispanic of any race, 0.0% two or more races (2000); Density: 11.1 persons per square mile (2000); Age: 28.2% under 18, 15.0% over 64 (2000); Marriage status: 19.7% never married, 75.3% now married, 3.3% widowed, 1.7% divorced (2000); Foreign born: 0.8% (2000); Ancestry (includes multiple ancestries): 54.7% German, 17.2% Swedish, 10.7% Dutch, 7.2% Norwegian, 6.2% English (2000).
Economy: Grain, corn, soybeans; livestock, poultry; dairying. Manufacturing: feeds. Employment by occupation: 20.2% management, 13.0% professional, 14.9% services, 26.0% sales, 7.2% farming, 7.7% construction, 11.1% production (2000).
Income: Per capita income: $16,373 (2000); Median household income: $42,083 (2000); Poverty rate: 5.4% (2000).
Taxes: Total city taxes per capita: $78 (2000); City property taxes per capita: $78 (2000).
Education: High school graduation rate: 89.8% (2000); College graduation rate: 14.7% (2000).
Housing: Homeownership rate: 93.9% (2000); Median home value: $82,000 (2000); Median rent: $275 per month (2000); Median age of housing: 60+ years (2000).
Transportation: Commute to work: 73.6% car, 0.0% public transportation, 0.0% walk, 26.4% work from home (2000); Travel time to work: 58.2% less than 15 minutes, 38.6% 15 to 30 minutes, 0.7% 30 to 45 minutes, 2.6% 45 to 60 minutes, 0.0% 60 minutes or more (2000)

BLOOM (township). Covers a land area of 35.789 square miles and a water area of 0.068 square miles. Located at 43.81° N. Lat.; 95.74° W. Long.
Population: 213 (2000); Race: 97.3% White, 0.0% Black, 0.0% Asian, 0.0% American Indian and Alaska Native, 2.7% Hispanic of any race, 1.8% two or more races (2000); Density: 6.0 persons per square mile (2000); Age: 32.1% under 18, 2.7% over 64 (2000); Marriage status: 34.1% never married, 65.9% now married, 0.0% widowed, 0.0% divorced (2000); Foreign born: 0.9% (2000); Ancestry (includes multiple ancestries): 71.0% German, 10.7% Irish, 6.3% Norwegian, 3.6% United States or American, 3.1% French (except Basque) (2000).
Economy: Employment by occupation: 33.1% management, 13.4% professional, 4.7% services, 21.3% sales, 4.7% farming, 5.5% construction, 17.3% production (2000).
Income: Per capita income: $15,171 (2000); Median household income: $50,536 (2000); Poverty rate: 1.3% (2000).
Taxes: Total city taxes per capita: $99 (1997); City property taxes per capita: $99 (1997).
Education: High school graduation rate: 91.9% (2000); College graduation rate: 7.3% (2000).
Housing: Homeownership rate: 76.2% (2000); Median home value: $104,200 (2000); Median rent: $195 per month (2000); Median age of housing: 60+ years (2000).
Transportation: Commute to work: 76.0% car, 0.0% public transportation, 9.3% walk, 14.7% work from home (2000); Travel time to work: 21.8% less than 15 minutes, 69.1% 15 to 30 minutes, 6.4% 30 to 45 minutes, 1.8% 45 to 60 minutes, 0.9% 60 minutes or more (2000)

BREWSTER (city). Covers a land area of 1.201 square miles and a water area of 0 square miles. Located at 43.69° N. Lat.; 95.46° W. Long. Elevation is 1,490 feet.
Population: 502 (2000); Race: 99.0% White, 0.0% Black, 0.0% Asian, 0.6% American Indian and Alaska Native, 1.8% Hispanic of any race, 0.4% two or more races (2000); Density: 417.9 persons per square mile (2000); Age: 26.4% under 18, 17.0% over 64 (2000); Marriage status: 19.5% never married, 62.1% now married, 10.1% widowed, 8.3% divorced (2000); Foreign born: 0.4% (2000); Ancestry (includes multiple ancestries): 58.0% German, 12.4% Norwegian, 11.6% Irish, 7.6% Dutch, 5.8% Other groups (2000).
Economy: Corn, oats, soybeans; cattle, sheep, hogs, poultry; dairying. Manufacturing: feeds. Single-family building permits issued: 1 (2001) / 0 (2000); Multi-family building permits issued: 0 (2001) / 0 (2000); Employment by occupation: 11.6% management, 11.9% professional, 23.9% services, 17.5% sales, 0.7% farming, 9.3% construction, 25.0% production (2000).
Income: Per capita income: $16,263 (2000); Median household income: $38,125 (2000); Poverty rate: 10.8% (2000).
Taxes: Total city taxes per capita: $146 (1997); City property taxes per capita: $142 (1997).
Education: High school graduation rate: 75.1% (2000); College graduation rate: 8.0% (2000).

School District(s)

Brewster (PK-06)
2000 Enrollment: 171 507-842-5951

Housing: Homeownership rate: 88.1% (2000); Median home value: $41,700 (2000); Median rent: $256 per month (2000); Median age of housing: 52 years (2000).
Transportation: Commute to work: 93.2% car, 0.0% public transportation, 5.7% walk, 1.1% work from home (2000); Travel time to work: 50.2% less than 15 minutes, 33.7% 15 to 30 minutes, 8.8% 30 to 45 minutes, 2.3% 45 to 60 minutes, 5.0% 60 minutes or more (2000)

DEWALD (township). Covers a land area of 36.027 square miles and a water area of 0 square miles. Located at 43.62° N. Lat.; 95.76° W. Long.
Population: 291 (2000); Race: 94.6% White, 0.8% Black, 1.2% Asian, 1.9% American Indian and Alaska Native, 1.9% Hispanic of any race, 0.8% two or more races (2000); Density: 8.1 persons per square mile (2000); Age: 24.9% under 18, 15.6% over 64 (2000); Marriage status: 20.5% never married, 69.5% now married, 3.3% widowed, 6.7% divorced (2000); Foreign born: 1.2% (2000); Ancestry (includes multiple ancestries): 57.2% German, 15.6% Dutch, 6.6% Norwegian, 5.8% Swedish, 5.8% English (2000).
Economy: Employment by occupation: 19.5% management, 12.5% professional, 25.0% services, 18.8% sales, 1.6% farming, 16.4% construction, 6.3% production (2000).
Income: Per capita income: $18,814 (2000); Median household income: $40,625 (2000); Poverty rate: 10.1% (2000).
Taxes: Total city taxes per capita: $90 (1997); City property taxes per capita: $90 (1997).
Education: High school graduation rate: 78.7% (2000); College graduation rate: 6.9% (2000).
Housing: Homeownership rate: 84.2% (2000); Median home value: $70,500 (2000); Median rent: $225 per month (2000); Median age of housing: 60+ years (2000).
Transportation: Commute to work: 74.6% car, 4.0% public transportation, 0.0% walk, 19.8% work from home (2000); Travel time to work: 32.7% less than 15 minutes, 59.4% 15 to 30 minutes, 4.0% 30 to 45 minutes, 0.0% 45 to 60 minutes, 4.0% 60 minutes or more (2000)

DUNDEE (city). Covers a land area of 0.294 square miles and a water area of 0 square miles. Located at 43.84° N. Lat.; 95.46° W. Long. Elevation is 1,450 feet.
Population: 102 (2000); Race: 96.7% White, 0.0% Black, 0.0% Asian, 0.0% American Indian and Alaska Native, 3.3% Hispanic of any race, 3.3% two or more races (2000); Density: 346.9 persons per square mile (2000); Age: 25.0% under 18, 24.2% over 64 (2000); Marriage status: 26.8% never married, 47.4% now married, 17.5% widowed, 8.2% divorced (2000); Foreign born: 0.0% (2000); Ancestry (includes multiple ancestries): 40.0% German, 13.3% Norwegian, 8.3% Dutch, 6.7% United States or American, 5.8% Other groups (2000).
Economy: Grain; livestock, poultry; dairying. Single-family building permits issued: 0 (2001) / 0 (2000); Multi-family building permits issued: 0 (2001) / 0 (2000); Employment by occupation: 7.9% management, 3.2% professional, 30.2% services, 7.9% sales, 0.0% farming, 22.2% construction, 28.6% production (2000).
Income: Per capita income: $12,171 (2000); Median household income: $21,979 (2000); Poverty rate: 21.2% (2000).
Taxes: Total city taxes per capita: $70 (1997); City property taxes per capita: $70 (1997).

Education: High school graduation rate: 81.0% (2000); College graduation rate: 0.0% (2000).
Housing: Homeownership rate: 85.2% (2000); Median home value: $19,200 (2000); Median rent: $275 per month (2000); Median age of housing: 58 years (2000).
Transportation: Commute to work: 93.0% car, 0.0% public transportation, 3.5% walk, 3.5% work from home (2000); Travel time to work: 34.5% less than 15 minutes, 47.3% 15 to 30 minutes, 3.6% 30 to 45 minutes, 7.3% 45 to 60 minutes, 7.3% 60 minutes or more (2000)

ELK (township). Covers a land area of 36.096 square miles and a water area of 0 square miles. Located at 43.71° N. Lat.; 95.64° W. Long.
Population: 284 (2000); Race: 98.7% White, 0.0% Black, 0.0% Asian, 0.0% American Indian and Alaska Native, 0.0% Hispanic of any race, 1.3% two or more races (2000); Density: 7.9 persons per square mile (2000); Age: 28.3% under 18, 12.8% over 64 (2000); Marriage status: 27.8% never married, 66.5% now married, 2.9% widowed, 2.9% divorced (2000); Foreign born: 0.0% (2000); Ancestry (includes multiple ancestries): 52.0% German, 28.3% Dutch, 11.8% Swedish, 6.3% Norwegian, 6.3% English (2000).
Economy: Employment by occupation: 26.6% management, 9.7% professional, 17.5% services, 16.9% sales, 7.8% farming, 7.8% construction, 13.6% production (2000).
Income: Per capita income: $16,785 (2000); Median household income: $39,464 (2000); Poverty rate: 8.6% (2000).
Education: High school graduation rate: 87.6% (2000); College graduation rate: 10.8% (2000).
Housing: Homeownership rate: 79.4% (2000); Median home value: $63,800 (2000); Median rent: $213 per month (2000); Median age of housing: 60+ years (2000).
Transportation: Commute to work: 80.5% car, 0.0% public transportation, 4.5% walk, 14.9% work from home (2000); Travel time to work: 51.9% less than 15 minutes, 38.9% 15 to 30 minutes, 2.3% 30 to 45 minutes, 0.8% 45 to 60 minutes, 6.1% 60 minutes or more (2000)

ELLSWORTH (city). Covers a land area of 0.641 square miles and a water area of 0 square miles. Located at 43.52° N. Lat.; 96.02° W. Long. Elevation is 1,445 feet.
Population: 540 (2000); Race: 98.8% White, 0.0% Black, 0.4% Asian, 0.0% American Indian and Alaska Native, 0.0% Hispanic of any race, 0.8% two or more races (2000); Density: 842.8 persons per square mile (2000); Age: 22.8% under 18, 25.7% over 64 (2000); Marriage status: 22.7% never married, 50.9% now married, 20.1% widowed, 6.3% divorced (2000); Foreign born: 1.4% (2000); Ancestry (includes multiple ancestries): 56.9% German, 9.3% Dutch, 7.5% United States or American, 6.6% Irish, 5.2% Norwegian (2000).
Economy: Grain, corn, soybeans; sheep, cattle, hogs; dairying. Manufacturing: feeds, sausages. Single-family building permits issued: 0 (2001) / 0 (2000); Multi-family building permits issued: 0 (2001) / 0 (2000); Employment by occupation: 12.0% management, 12.0% professional, 18.7% services, 18.3% sales, 0.8% farming, 10.4% construction, 27.8% production (2000).
Income: Per capita income: $16,098 (2000); Median household income: $28,417 (2000); Poverty rate: 6.1% (2000).
Taxes: Total city taxes per capita: $146 (2000); City property taxes per capita: $144 (2000).
Education: High school graduation rate: 70.2% (2000); College graduation rate: 9.9% (2000).

School District(s)

Ellsworth (PK-12)
2000 Enrollment: 208 507-967-2242
Housing: Homeownership rate: 85.3% (2000); Median home value: $30,700 (2000); Median rent: $198 per month (2000); Median age of housing: 48 years (2000).
Transportation: Commute to work: 89.7% car, 0.0% public transportation, 7.9% walk, 1.7% work from home (2000); Travel time to work: 34.5% less than 15 minutes, 32.8% 15 to 30 minutes, 19.7% 30 to 45 minutes, 8.0% 45 to 60 minutes, 5.0% 60 minutes or more (2000)

GRAHAM LAKES (township). Covers a land area of 32.995 square miles and a water area of 1.806 square miles. Located at 43.79° N. Lat.; 95.50° W. Long.
Population: 251 (2000); Race: 100.0% White, 0.0% Black, 0.0% Asian, 0.0% American Indian and Alaska Native, 0.0% Hispanic of any race, 0.0% two or more races (2000); Density: 7.6 persons per square mile (2000); Age: 34.3% under 18, 14.6% over 64 (2000); Marriage status: 21.3% never married, 68.0% now married, 6.2% widowed, 4.5% divorced (2000); Foreign born: 1.7% (2000); Ancestry (includes multiple ancestries): 64.9% German, 12.1% Irish, 8.8% Norwegian, 7.1% English, 5.9% United States or American (2000).
Economy: Employment by occupation: 18.5% management, 10.2% professional, 17.6% services, 22.2% sales, 2.8% farming, 20.4% construction, 8.3% production (2000).
Income: Per capita income: $16,233 (2000); Median household income: $36,750 (2000); Poverty rate: 24.3% (2000).
Taxes: Total city taxes per capita: $111 (1997); City property taxes per capita: $111 (1997).
Education: High school graduation rate: 84.9% (2000); College graduation rate: 9.9% (2000).
Housing: Homeownership rate: 83.5% (2000); Median home value: $75,700 (2000); Median rent: $200 per month (2000); Median age of housing: 54 years (2000).
Transportation: Commute to work: 84.3% car, 0.0% public transportation, 1.9% walk, 13.9% work from home (2000); Travel time to work: 34.4% less than 15 minutes, 53.8% 15 to 30 minutes, 7.5% 30 to 45 minutes, 0.0% 45 to 60 minutes, 4.3% 60 minutes or more (2000)

GRAND PRAIRIE (township). Covers a land area of 35.372 square miles and a water area of 0 square miles. Located at 43.55° N. Lat.; 96.00° W. Long.
Population: 227 (2000); Race: 99.6% White, 0.0% Black, 0.0% Asian, 0.0% American Indian and Alaska Native, 0.4% Hispanic of any race, 0.0% two or more races (2000); Density: 6.4 persons per square mile (2000); Age: 29.8% under 18, 15.4% over 64 (2000); Marriage status: 25.6% never married, 63.1% now married, 6.3% widowed, 5.1% divorced (2000); Foreign born: 0.4% (2000); Ancestry (includes multiple ancestries): 65.8% German, 17.5% Dutch, 8.3% Irish, 5.7% Other groups, 4.4% English (2000).
Economy: Employment by occupation: 28.5% management, 9.8% professional, 13.8% services, 22.8% sales, 1.6% farming, 12.2% construction, 11.4% production (2000).
Income: Per capita income: $16,192 (2000); Median household income: $34,500 (2000); Poverty rate: 6.8% (2000).
Taxes: Total city taxes per capita: $95 (1997); City property taxes per capita: $95 (1997).
Education: High school graduation rate: 90.2% (2000); College graduation rate: 9.1% (2000).
Housing: Homeownership rate: 88.4% (2000); Median home value: $52,500 (2000); Median rent: $175 per month (2000); Median age of housing: 60+ years (2000).
Transportation: Commute to work: 68.6% car, 0.0% public transportation, 5.8% walk, 24.0% work from home (2000); Travel time to work: 50.0% less than 15 minutes, 32.6% 15 to 30 minutes, 9.8% 30 to 45 minutes, 5.4% 45 to 60 minutes, 2.2% 60 minutes or more (2000)

HERSEY (township). Covers a land area of 35.101 square miles and a water area of 0 square miles. Located at 43.70° N. Lat.; 95.50° W. Long.
Population: 257 (2000); Race: 99.2% White, 0.0% Black, 0.0% Asian, 0.0% American Indian and Alaska Native, 0.0% Hispanic of any race, 0.8% two or more races (2000); Density: 7.3 persons per square mile (2000); Age: 27.5% under 18, 15.8% over 64 (2000); Marriage status: 26.0% never married, 69.9% now married, 1.0% widowed, 3.1% divorced (2000); Foreign born: 0.8% (2000); Ancestry (includes multiple ancestries): 57.9% German, 11.3% Dutch, 9.6% Polish, 6.7% United States or American, 6.7% Swedish (2000).
Economy: Employment by occupation: 21.8% management, 9.2% professional, 10.9% services, 31.9% sales, 3.4% farming, 16.0% construction, 6.7% production (2000).
Income: Per capita income: $14,843 (2000); Median household income: $39,500 (2000); Poverty rate: 10.0% (2000).
Taxes: Total city taxes per capita: $112 (1997); City property taxes per capita: $112 (1997).
Education: High school graduation rate: 83.1% (2000); College graduation rate: 6.9% (2000).
Housing: Homeownership rate: 79.5% (2000); Median home value: $90,000 (2000); Median rent: $220 per month (2000); Median age of housing: 55 years (2000).
Transportation: Commute to work: 94.9% car, 0.0% public transportation, 0.0% walk, 5.1% work from home (2000); Travel time to work: 54.1% less than 15 minutes, 35.1% 15 to 30 minutes, 0.0% 30 to 45 minutes, 6.3% 45 to 60 minutes, 4.5% 60 minutes or more (2000)

INDIAN LAKE (township). Covers a land area of 33.616 square miles and a water area of 1.308 square miles. Located at 43.53° N. Lat.; 95.50° W. Long.

Population: 259 (2000); Race: 99.3% White, 0.0% Black, 0.0% Asian, 0.0% American Indian and Alaska Native, 2.1% Hispanic of any race, 0.0% two or more races (2000); Density: 7.7 persons per square mile (2000); Age: 31.1% under 18, 7.7% over 64 (2000); Marriage status: 16.5% never married, 74.8% now married, 3.2% widowed, 5.5% divorced (2000); Foreign born: 0.0% (2000); Ancestry (includes multiple ancestries): 51.0% German, 16.8% Norwegian, 12.2% Irish, 9.8% Dutch, 8.7% Swedish (2000).
Economy: Employment by occupation: 29.0% management, 16.7% professional, 13.0% services, 21.0% sales, 1.2% farming, 11.1% construction, 8.0% production (2000).
Income: Per capita income: $17,542 (2000); Median household income: $48,542 (2000); Poverty rate: 3.1% (2000).
Taxes: Total city taxes per capita: $110 (1997); City property taxes per capita: $110 (1997).
Education: High school graduation rate: 87.4% (2000); College graduation rate: 17.6% (2000).
Housing: Homeownership rate: 80.8% (2000); Median home value: $75,000 (2000); Median rent: $315 per month (2000); Median age of housing: 57 years (2000).
Transportation: Commute to work: 78.7% car, 0.0% public transportation, 1.9% walk, 18.1% work from home (2000); Travel time to work: 47.2% less than 15 minutes, 37.8% 15 to 30 minutes, 7.1% 30 to 45 minutes, 2.4% 45 to 60 minutes, 5.5% 60 minutes or more (2000)

KINBRAE (city). Covers a land area of 0.828 square miles and a water area of 0.172 square miles. Located at 43.82° N. Lat.; 95.48° W. Long. Elevation is 1,464 feet.
Population: 21 (2000); Race: 100.0% White, 0.0% Black, 0.0% Asian, 0.0% American Indian and Alaska Native, 0.0% Hispanic of any race, 0.0% two or more races (2000); Density: 25.4 persons per square mile (2000); Age: 39.3% under 18, 0.0% over 64 (2000); Marriage status: 21.1% never married, 68.4% now married, 0.0% widowed, 10.5% divorced (2000); Foreign born: 0.0% (2000); Ancestry (includes multiple ancestries): 64.3% German, 28.6% Dutch, 14.3% Italian, 14.3% Swedish, 14.3% Norwegian (2000).
Economy: Grain; livestock; dairying. Employment by occupation: 23.5% management, 0.0% professional, 52.9% services, 0.0% sales, 0.0% farming, 11.8% construction, 11.8% production (2000).
Income: Per capita income: $17,839 (2000); Median household income: $31,250 (2000); Poverty rate: 0.0% (2000).
Taxes: Total city taxes per capita: $222 (1997); City property taxes per capita: $167 (1997).
Education: High school graduation rate: 73.3% (2000); College graduation rate: 13.3% (2000).
Housing: Homeownership rate: 100.0% (2000); Median home value: $23,800 (2000); Median age of housing: 50 years (2000).
Transportation: Commute to work: 100.0% car, 0.0% public transportation, 0.0% walk, 0.0% work from home (2000); Travel time to work: 17.6% less than 15 minutes, 58.8% 15 to 30 minutes, 11.8% 30 to 45 minutes, 0.0% 45 to 60 minutes, 11.8% 60 minutes or more (2000)

LARKIN (township). Covers a land area of 35.774 square miles and a water area of 0.032 square miles. Located at 43.71° N. Lat.; 95.86° W. Long.
Population: 218 (2000); Race: 100.0% White, 0.0% Black, 0.0% Asian, 0.0% American Indian and Alaska Native, 0.0% Hispanic of any race, 0.0% two or more races (2000); Density: 6.1 persons per square mile (2000); Age: 33.5% under 18, 19.5% over 64 (2000); Marriage status: 18.4% never married, 73.4% now married, 7.0% widowed, 1.3% divorced (2000); Foreign born: 0.0% (2000); Ancestry (includes multiple ancestries): 51.6% German, 21.7% United States or American, 10.4% English, 7.2% Irish, 5.4% Norwegian (2000).
Economy: Employment by occupation: 30.2% management, 12.3% professional, 14.2% services, 15.1% sales, 7.5% farming, 5.7% construction, 15.1% production (2000).
Income: Per capita income: $13,805 (2000); Median household income: $31,875 (2000); Poverty rate: 15.8% (2000).
Taxes: Total city taxes per capita: $102 (1997); City property taxes per capita: $102 (1997).
Education: High school graduation rate: 78.3% (2000); College graduation rate: 9.4% (2000).
Housing: Homeownership rate: 88.2% (2000); Median home value: $59,400 (2000); Median rent: $244 per month (2000); Median age of housing: 60+ years (2000).
Transportation: Commute to work: 59.4% car, 0.0% public transportation, 6.6% walk, 32.1% work from home (2000); Travel time to work: 25.0% less than 15 minutes, 30.6% 15 to 30 minutes, 41.7% 30 to 45 minutes, 0.0% 45 to 60 minutes, 2.8% 60 minutes or more (2000)

LEOTA (township). Covers a land area of 36.170 square miles and a water area of 0 square miles. Located at 43.81° N. Lat.; 95.99° W. Long. Elevation is 1,725 feet.
Population: 463 (2000); Race: 97.4% White, 0.0% Black, 0.9% Asian, 0.7% American Indian and Alaska Native, 0.0% Hispanic of any race, 1.1% two or more races (2000); Density: 12.8 persons per square mile (2000); Age: 20.4% under 18, 26.5% over 64 (2000); Marriage status: 16.4% never married, 74.4% now married, 8.2% widowed, 1.0% divorced (2000); Foreign born: 2.2% (2000); Ancestry (includes multiple ancestries): 79.8% Dutch, 15.4% German, 3.7% Other groups, 3.7% Norwegian, 2.2% Irish (2000).
Economy: Employment by occupation: 29.4% management, 6.9% professional, 13.3% services, 14.9% sales, 4.4% farming, 6.0% construction, 25.0% production (2000).
Income: Per capita income: $14,948 (2000); Median household income: $31,818 (2000); Poverty rate: 12.8% (2000).
Taxes: Total city taxes per capita: $39 (1997); City property taxes per capita: $39 (1997).
Education: High school graduation rate: 69.7% (2000); College graduation rate: 12.0% (2000).
Housing: Homeownership rate: 89.1% (2000); Median home value: $46,200 (2000); Median rent: $175 per month (2000); Median age of housing: 48 years (2000).
Transportation: Commute to work: 71.0% car, 0.0% public transportation, 9.7% walk, 18.5% work from home (2000); Travel time to work: 51.0% less than 15 minutes, 25.7% 15 to 30 minutes, 18.3% 30 to 45 minutes, 1.5% 45 to 60 minutes, 3.5% 60 minutes or more (2000)

LISMORE (city). Covers a land area of 0.341 square miles and a water area of 0 square miles. Located at 43.74° N. Lat.; 95.94° W. Long. Elevation is 1,689 feet.
Population: 238 (2000); Race: 98.8% White, 0.0% Black, 0.0% Asian, 0.0% American Indian and Alaska Native, 0.0% Hispanic of any race, 1.2% two or more races (2000); Density: 696.9 persons per square mile (2000); Age: 33.3% under 18, 17.1% over 64 (2000); Marriage status: 22.5% never married, 58.6% now married, 13.1% widowed, 5.8% divorced (2000); Foreign born: 0.0% (2000); Ancestry (includes multiple ancestries): 55.0% German, 12.4% Irish, 12.4% Dutch, 6.6% United States or American, 5.8% Norwegian (2000).
Economy: Single-family building permits issued: 0 (2001) / 0 (2000); Multi-family building permits issued: 0 (2001) / 0 (2000); Employment by occupation: 9.2% management, 6.4% professional, 15.6% services, 22.0% sales, 4.6% farming, 10.1% construction, 32.1% production (2000).
Income: Per capita income: $12,623 (2000); Median household income: $24,773 (2000); Poverty rate: 19.8% (2000).
Taxes: Total city taxes per capita: $86 (1997); City property taxes per capita: $86 (1997).
Education: High school graduation rate: 85.6% (2000); College graduation rate: 6.3% (2000).
Housing: Homeownership rate: 98.0% (2000); Median home value: $24,500 (2000); Median age of housing: 60+ years (2000).
Transportation: Commute to work: 84.8% car, 0.0% public transportation, 10.5% walk, 4.8% work from home (2000); Travel time to work: 30.0% less than 15 minutes, 31.0% 15 to 30 minutes, 26.0% 30 to 45 minutes, 4.0% 45 to 60 minutes, 9.0% 60 minutes or more (2000)

LISMORE (township). Covers a land area of 35.811 square miles and a water area of 0 square miles. Located at 43.72° N. Lat.; 96.00° W. Long. Elevation is 1,689 feet.
Population: 232 (2000); Race: 100.0% White, 0.0% Black, 0.0% Asian, 0.0% American Indian and Alaska Native, 0.0% Hispanic of any race, 0.0% two or more races (2000); Density: 6.5 persons per square mile (2000); Age: 35.5% under 18, 17.3% over 64 (2000); Marriage status: 13.2% never married, 79.2% now married, 4.2% widowed, 3.5% divorced (2000); Foreign born: 0.0% (2000); Ancestry (includes multiple ancestries): 69.6% German, 11.7% Dutch, 11.7% Norwegian, 5.6% French (except Basque), 3.7% Irish (2000).
Economy: Grain, soybeans; livestock; dairying. Employment by occupation: 26.1% management, 13.6% professional, 4.5% services, 17.0% sales, 0.0% farming, 21.6% construction, 17.0% production (2000).
Income: Per capita income: $11,805 (2000); Median household income: $33,125 (2000); Poverty rate: 24.3% (2000).
Taxes: Total city taxes per capita: $114 (1997); City property taxes per capita: $114 (1997).
Education: High school graduation rate: 90.3% (2000); College graduation rate: 7.5% (2000).

Housing: Homeownership rate: 88.9% (2000); Median home value: $69,200 (2000); Median rent: $175 per month (2000); Median age of housing: 53 years (2000).
Transportation: Commute to work: 84.1% car, 0.0% public transportation, 5.7% walk, 10.2% work from home (2000); Travel time to work: 31.6% less than 15 minutes, 39.2% 15 to 30 minutes, 19.0% 30 to 45 minutes, 8.9% 45 to 60 minutes, 1.3% 60 minutes or more (2000)

LITTLE ROCK (township). Covers a land area of 35.968 square miles and a water area of 0 square miles. Located at 43.53° N. Lat.; 95.86° W. Long.
Population: 260 (2000); Race: 100.0% White, 0.0% Black, 0.0% Asian, 0.0% American Indian and Alaska Native, 0.0% Hispanic of any race, 0.0% two or more races (2000); Density: 7.2 persons per square mile (2000); Age: 32.3% under 18, 21.1% over 64 (2000); Marriage status: 13.5% never married, 79.7% now married, 4.7% widowed, 2.1% divorced (2000); Foreign born: 0.0% (2000); Ancestry (includes multiple ancestries): 65.0% German, 19.5% Dutch, 5.6% Irish, 5.3% United States or American, 5.3% Norwegian (2000).
Economy: Employment by occupation: 31.3% management, 11.6% professional, 16.1% services, 13.4% sales, 11.6% farming, 4.5% construction, 11.6% production (2000).
Income: Per capita income: $14,970 (2000); Median household income: $35,125 (2000); Poverty rate: 15.8% (2000).
Taxes: Total city taxes per capita: $159 (1997); City property taxes per capita: $159 (1997).
Education: High school graduation rate: 66.3% (2000); College graduation rate: 9.8% (2000).
Housing: Homeownership rate: 69.6% (2000); Median home value: $60,000 (2000); Median rent: $194 per month (2000); Median age of housing: 57 years (2000).
Transportation: Commute to work: 70.2% car, 0.0% public transportation, 1.8% walk, 26.3% work from home (2000); Travel time to work: 21.4% less than 15 minutes, 33.3% 15 to 30 minutes, 35.7% 30 to 45 minutes, 0.0% 45 to 60 minutes, 9.5% 60 minutes or more (2000)

LORAIN (township). Covers a land area of 34.823 square miles and a water area of 0.286 square miles. Located at 43.64° N. Lat.; 95.51° W. Long.
Population: 278 (2000); Race: 100.0% White, 0.0% Black, 0.0% Asian, 0.0% American Indian and Alaska Native, 0.0% Hispanic of any race, 0.0% two or more races (2000); Density: 8.0 persons per square mile (2000); Age: 19.9% under 18, 16.6% over 64 (2000); Marriage status: 22.2% never married, 69.7% now married, 3.4% widowed, 4.7% divorced (2000); Foreign born: 0.0% (2000); Ancestry (includes multiple ancestries): 59.2% German, 17.0% Dutch, 16.2% Norwegian, 6.9% Irish, 5.1% United States or American (2000).
Economy: Employment by occupation: 17.3% management, 16.7% professional, 10.7% services, 22.0% sales, 0.0% farming, 11.9% construction, 21.4% production (2000).
Income: Per capita income: $17,109 (2000); Median household income: $39,821 (2000); Poverty rate: 7.2% (2000).
Taxes: Total city taxes per capita: $100 (1997); City property taxes per capita: $100 (1997).
Education: High school graduation rate: 82.2% (2000); College graduation rate: 14.2% (2000).
Housing: Homeownership rate: 88.0% (2000); Median home value: $90,000 (2000); Median rent: $213 per month (2000); Median age of housing: 50 years (2000).
Transportation: Commute to work: 82.3% car, 0.0% public transportation, 1.9% walk, 14.6% work from home (2000); Travel time to work: 57.0% less than 15 minutes, 32.6% 15 to 30 minutes, 7.4% 30 to 45 minutes, 1.5% 45 to 60 minutes, 1.5% 60 minutes or more (2000)

OLNEY (township). Covers a land area of 35.421 square miles and a water area of 0.032 square miles. Located at 43.63° N. Lat.; 95.86° W. Long.
Population: 232 (2000); Race: 99.5% White, 0.0% Black, 0.0% Asian, 0.0% American Indian and Alaska Native, 0.0% Hispanic of any race, 0.5% two or more races (2000); Density: 6.5 persons per square mile (2000); Age: 36.4% under 18, 13.2% over 64 (2000); Marriage status: 15.4% never married, 81.4% now married, 3.2% widowed, 0.0% divorced (2000); Foreign born: 0.9% (2000); Ancestry (includes multiple ancestries): 56.8% German, 10.9% United States or American, 10.5% Dutch, 9.5% Norwegian, 9.1% Swedish (2000).
Economy: Employment by occupation: 37.1% management, 9.3% professional, 17.5% services, 12.4% sales, 11.3% farming, 8.2% construction, 4.1% production (2000).
Income: Per capita income: $12,378 (2000); Median household income: $34,375 (2000); Poverty rate: 1.8% (2000).
Taxes: Total city taxes per capita: $142 (1997); City property taxes per capita: $142 (1997).
Education: High school graduation rate: 85.7% (2000); College graduation rate: 10.5% (2000).
Housing: Homeownership rate: 87.5% (2000); Median home value: $65,000 (2000); Median rent: $275 per month (2000); Median age of housing: 60 years (2000).
Transportation: Commute to work: 64.2% car, 0.0% public transportation, 3.2% walk, 32.6% work from home (2000); Travel time to work: 51.6% less than 15 minutes, 39.1% 15 to 30 minutes, 4.7% 30 to 45 minutes, 0.0% 45 to 60 minutes, 4.7% 60 minutes or more (2000)

RANSOM (township). Covers a land area of 36.373 square miles and a water area of 0 square miles. Located at 43.53° N. Lat.; 95.76° W. Long. Elevation is 1,624 feet.
Population: 271 (2000); Race: 99.3% White, 0.0% Black, 0.7% Asian, 0.0% American Indian and Alaska Native, 0.0% Hispanic of any race, 0.0% two or more races (2000); Density: 7.5 persons per square mile (2000); Age: 29.3% under 18, 18.9% over 64 (2000); Marriage status: 23.9% never married, 66.8% now married, 3.8% widowed, 5.5% divorced (2000); Foreign born: 1.3% (2000); Ancestry (includes multiple ancestries): 63.8% German, 21.2% Dutch, 11.7% Norwegian, 4.6% Swedish, 4.2% Irish (2000).
Economy: Employment by occupation: 26.4% management, 7.9% professional, 15.0% services, 31.4% sales, 3.6% farming, 12.1% construction, 3.6% production (2000).
Income: Per capita income: $13,801 (2000); Median household income: $39,250 (2000); Poverty rate: 10.1% (2000).
Taxes: Total city taxes per capita: $56 (1997); City property taxes per capita: $56 (1997).
Education: High school graduation rate: 76.4% (2000); College graduation rate: 10.5% (2000).
Housing: Homeownership rate: 71.7% (2000); Median home value: $47,800 (2000); Median rent: $267 per month (2000); Median age of housing: 57 years (2000).
Transportation: Commute to work: 76.1% car, 0.0% public transportation, 0.0% walk, 23.9% work from home (2000); Travel time to work: 24.8% less than 15 minutes, 69.5% 15 to 30 minutes, 1.0% 30 to 45 minutes, 0.0% 45 to 60 minutes, 4.8% 60 minutes or more (2000)

READING (unincorporated postal area, zip code 56165). Covers a land area of 42.157 square miles and a water area of 0 square miles. Located at 43.72° N. Lat.; 95.70° W. Long. Elevation is 1,722 feet.
Population: 419 (2000); Race: 96.9% White, 0.0% Black, 1.3% Asian, 0.0% American Indian and Alaska Native, 0.4% Hispanic of any race, 1.3% two or more races (2000); Density: 9.9 persons per square mile (2000); Age: 31.7% under 18, 9.5% over 64 (2000); Marriage status: 24.2% never married, 66.0% now married, 4.6% widowed, 5.2% divorced (2000); Foreign born: 1.3% (2000); Ancestry (includes multiple ancestries): 64.8% German, 13.7% Dutch, 10.6% Irish, 8.1% Swedish, 4.8% Norwegian (2000).
Economy: Employment by occupation: 21.3% management, 13.0% professional, 18.1% services, 20.5% sales, 4.3% farming, 5.5% construction, 17.3% production (2000).
Income: Per capita income: $15,111 (2000); Median household income: $37,708 (2000); Poverty rate: 8.8% (2000).
Education: High school graduation rate: 88.9% (2000); College graduation rate: 8.6% (2000).
Housing: Homeownership rate: 78.0% (2000); Median home value: $40,000 (2000); Median rent: $225 per month (2000); Median age of housing: 60+ years (2000).
Transportation: Commute to work: 78.1% car, 0.8% public transportation, 4.8% walk, 16.3% work from home (2000); Travel time to work: 36.7% less than 15 minutes, 54.3% 15 to 30 minutes, 4.3% 30 to 45 minutes, 1.0% 45 to 60 minutes, 3.8% 60 minutes or more (2000)

ROUND LAKE (city). Covers a land area of 1.037 square miles and a water area of 0 square miles. Located at 43.53° N. Lat.; 95.46° W. Long. Elevation is 1,552 feet.
History: Near several small natural lakes of glacial origin, including Round Lake to Northeast.
Population: 424 (2000); Race: 95.3% White, 0.0% Black, 0.0% Asian, 0.0% American Indian and Alaska Native, 1.5% Hispanic of any race, 3.7% two or more races (2000); Density: 408.8 persons per square mile (2000); Age: 23.9% under 18, 19.2% over 64 (2000); Marriage status: 28.2% never married, 52.3% now married, 12.0% widowed, 7.5% divorced (2000);

Foreign born: 2.7% (2000); Ancestry (includes multiple ancestries): 53.4% German, 20.4% Norwegian, 12.1% Dutch, 7.6% Other groups, 4.9% Irish (2000).
Economy: Corn, soybeans; hogs; dairying. Manufacturing of candy and nuts. Single-family building permits issued: 0 (2001) / 0 (2000); Multi-family building permits issued: 0 (2001) / 0 (2000); Employment by occupation: 7.5% management, 6.0% professional, 9.5% services, 34.2% sales, 1.5% farming, 9.5% construction, 31.7% production (2000).
Income: Per capita income: $15,476 (2000); Median household income: $25,938 (2000); Poverty rate: 11.3% (2000).
Taxes: Total city taxes per capita: $115 (1997); City property taxes per capita: $113 (1997).
Education: High school graduation rate: 77.4% (2000); College graduation rate: 3.9% (2000).

School District(s)

Round Lake (07-12)
2000 Enrollment: 189 507-945-8123
Housing: Homeownership rate: 80.2% (2000); Median home value: $37,900 (2000); Median rent: $183 per month (2000); Median age of housing: 50 years (2000).
Transportation: Commute to work: 77.8% car, 0.0% public transportation, 19.1% walk, 1.5% work from home (2000); Travel time to work: 40.8% less than 15 minutes, 41.4% 15 to 30 minutes, 9.9% 30 to 45 minutes, 3.7% 45 to 60 minutes, 4.2% 60 minutes or more (2000)

RUSHMORE (city). Covers a land area of 0.253 square miles and a water area of 0 square miles. Located at 43.62° N. Lat.; 95.79° W. Long.
Population: 376 (2000); Race: 96.2% White, 0.0% Black, 3.3% Asian, 0.5% American Indian and Alaska Native, 1.8% Hispanic of any race, 0.0% two or more races (2000); Density: 1,484.9 persons per square mile (2000); Age: 30.2% under 18, 13.9% over 64 (2000); Marriage status: 20.5% never married, 61.1% now married, 11.9% widowed, 6.6% divorced (2000); Foreign born: 3.3% (2000); Ancestry (includes multiple ancestries): 53.1% German, 9.1% Norwegian, 7.8% Other groups, 6.5% Irish, 4.3% United States or American (2000).
Economy: Soybeans, grain; livestock, poultry; dairying. Manufacturing of fertilizers. Single-family building permits issued: 2 (2001) / 1 (2000); Multi-family building permits issued: 0 (2001) / 0 (2000); Employment by occupation: 8.8% management, 12.7% professional, 13.7% services, 27.0% sales, 0.0% farming, 19.1% construction, 18.6% production (2000).
Income: Per capita income: $14,216 (2000); Median household income: $33,750 (2000); Poverty rate: 5.3% (2000).
Taxes: Total city taxes per capita: $138 (1997); City property taxes per capita: $138 (1997).
Education: High school graduation rate: 71.5% (2000); College graduation rate: 8.9% (2000).
Housing: Homeownership rate: 85.4% (2000); Median home value: $41,000 (2000); Median rent: $263 per month (2000); Median age of housing: 60+ years (2000).
Transportation: Commute to work: 84.7% car, 0.0% public transportation, 5.4% walk, 7.4% work from home (2000); Travel time to work: 36.9% less than 15 minutes, 49.2% 15 to 30 minutes, 9.1% 30 to 45 minutes, 2.7% 45 to 60 minutes, 2.1% 60 minutes or more (2000)

SEWARD (township). Covers a land area of 35.647 square miles and a water area of 0.092 square miles. Located at 43.81° N. Lat.; 95.62° W. Long.
Population: 259 (2000); Race: 100.0% White, 0.0% Black, 0.0% Asian, 0.0% American Indian and Alaska Native, 0.0% Hispanic of any race, 0.0% two or more races (2000); Density: 7.3 persons per square mile (2000); Age: 22.7% under 18, 13.7% over 64 (2000); Marriage status: 21.4% never married, 74.3% now married, 1.6% widowed, 2.7% divorced (2000); Foreign born: 0.0% (2000); Ancestry (includes multiple ancestries): 59.7% German, 13.3% Norwegian, 9.9% Dutch, 9.4% Swedish, 6.9% United States or American (2000).
Economy: Employment by occupation: 27.3% management, 6.6% professional, 13.2% services, 20.7% sales, 4.1% farming, 9.1% construction, 19.0% production (2000).
Income: Per capita income: $19,348 (2000); Median household income: $36,607 (2000); Poverty rate: 9.4% (2000).
Taxes: Total city taxes per capita: $128 (1997); City property taxes per capita: $128 (1997).
Education: High school graduation rate: 89.6% (2000); College graduation rate: 9.8% (2000).
Housing: Homeownership rate: 87.5% (2000); Median home value: $59,300 (2000); Median rent: $163 per month (2000); Median age of housing: 60+ years (2000).
Transportation: Commute to work: 75.9% car, 0.0% public transportation, 4.3% walk, 19.8% work from home (2000); Travel time to work: 22.6% less than 15 minutes, 61.3% 15 to 30 minutes, 10.8% 30 to 45 minutes, 3.2% 45 to 60 minutes, 2.2% 60 minutes or more (2000)

SUMMIT LAKE (township). Covers a land area of 36.148 square miles and a water area of 0 square miles. Located at 43.71° N. Lat.; 95.74° W. Long.
Population: 368 (2000); Race: 96.8% White, 0.0% Black, 1.6% Asian, 0.0% American Indian and Alaska Native, 0.5% Hispanic of any race, 1.1% two or more races (2000); Density: 10.2 persons per square mile (2000); Age: 34.7% under 18, 10.1% over 64 (2000); Marriage status: 17.6% never married, 68.7% now married, 6.9% widowed, 6.9% divorced (2000); Foreign born: 1.6% (2000); Ancestry (includes multiple ancestries): 66.9% German, 15.5% Irish, 8.8% Dutch, 6.4% Norwegian, 5.3% United States or American (2000).
Economy: Employment by occupation: 23.9% management, 12.7% professional, 16.1% services, 23.9% sales, 2.4% farming, 4.9% construction, 16.1% production (2000).
Income: Per capita income: $13,955 (2000); Median household income: $38,958 (2000); Poverty rate: 6.9% (2000).
Taxes: Total city taxes per capita: $65 (1997); City property taxes per capita: $65 (1997).
Education: High school graduation rate: 92.6% (2000); College graduation rate: 7.8% (2000).
Housing: Homeownership rate: 82.9% (2000); Median home value: $39,700 (2000); Median rent: $263 per month (2000); Median age of housing: 60+ years (2000).
Transportation: Commute to work: 74.3% car, 1.0% public transportation, 5.0% walk, 19.8% work from home (2000); Travel time to work: 38.3% less than 15 minutes, 50.6% 15 to 30 minutes, 6.2% 30 to 45 minutes, 1.2% 45 to 60 minutes, 3.7% 60 minutes or more (2000)

WESTSIDE (township). Covers a land area of 35.300 square miles and a water area of 0 square miles. Located at 43.62° N. Lat.; 95.98° W. Long.
Population: 258 (2000); Race: 99.2% White, 0.8% Black, 0.0% Asian, 0.0% American Indian and Alaska Native, 3.1% Hispanic of any race, 0.0% two or more races (2000); Density: 7.3 persons per square mile (2000); Age: 36.3% under 18, 3.1% over 64 (2000); Marriage status: 22.9% never married, 73.4% now married, 3.7% widowed, 0.0% divorced (2000); Foreign born: 3.1% (2000); Ancestry (includes multiple ancestries): 70.6% German, 17.9% Dutch, 10.3% Norwegian, 6.5% United States or American, 6.1% English (2000).
Economy: Employment by occupation: 30.5% management, 9.9% professional, 7.1% services, 28.4% sales, 2.1% farming, 10.6% construction, 11.3% production (2000).
Income: Per capita income: $15,518 (2000); Median household income: $47,500 (2000); Poverty rate: 16.8% (2000).
Taxes: Total city taxes per capita: $125 (1997); City property taxes per capita: $125 (1997).
Education: High school graduation rate: 90.1% (2000); College graduation rate: 24.5% (2000).
Housing: Homeownership rate: 81.7% (2000); Median home value: $81,700 (2000); Median rent: $200 per month (2000); Median age of housing: 58 years (2000).
Transportation: Commute to work: 77.3% car, 0.0% public transportation, 6.4% walk, 13.5% work from home (2000); Travel time to work: 57.4% less than 15 minutes, 31.1% 15 to 30 minutes, 5.7% 30 to 45 minutes, 5.7% 45 to 60 minutes, 0.0% 60 minutes or more (2000)

WILMONT (city). Covers a land area of 1.139 square miles and a water area of 0 square miles. Located at 43.76° N. Lat.; 95.82° W. Long. Elevation is 1,735 feet.
Population: 332 (2000); Race: 99.4% White, 0.0% Black, 0.0% Asian, 0.6% American Indian and Alaska Native, 0.0% Hispanic of any race, 0.0% two or more races (2000); Density: 291.4 persons per square mile (2000); Age: 22.5% under 18, 21.6% over 64 (2000); Marriage status: 25.7% never married, 54.5% now married, 11.3% widowed, 8.6% divorced (2000); Foreign born: 0.6% (2000); Ancestry (includes multiple ancestries): 66.7% German, 13.0% Irish, 5.4% United States or American, 3.5% Other groups, 2.9% Swedish (2000).
Economy: Single-family building permits issued: 0 (2001) / 2 (2000); Multi-family building permits issued: 0 (2001) / 0 (2000); Employment by occupation: 11.0% management, 6.1% professional, 9.8% services, 31.1% sales, 0.0% farming, 25.6% construction, 16.5% production (2000).
Income: Per capita income: $16,160 (2000); Median household income: $29,464 (2000); Poverty rate: 6.8% (2000).

Taxes: Total city taxes per capita: $55 (1997); City property taxes per capita: $55 (1997).
Education: High school graduation rate: 81.7% (2000); College graduation rate: 5.2% (2000).
Housing: Homeownership rate: 92.9% (2000); Median home value: $37,100 (2000); Median rent: $263 per month (2000); Median age of housing: 58 years (2000).
Transportation: Commute to work: 83.6% car, 0.0% public transportation, 10.1% walk, 1.3% work from home (2000); Travel time to work: 36.3% less than 15 minutes, 51.6% 15 to 30 minutes, 8.3% 30 to 45 minutes, 2.5% 45 to 60 minutes, 1.3% 60 minutes or more (2000)

WILMONT (township). Covers a land area of 35.521 square miles and a water area of 0 square miles. Located at 43.81° N. Lat.; 95.88° W. Long. Elevation is 1,735 feet.
Population: 228 (2000); Race: 100.0% White, 0.0% Black, 0.0% Asian, 0.0% American Indian and Alaska Native, 0.0% Hispanic of any race, 0.0% two or more races (2000); Density: 6.4 persons per square mile (2000); Age: 26.3% under 18, 15.2% over 64 (2000); Marriage status: 26.3% never married, 64.6% now married, 8.0% widowed, 1.1% divorced (2000); Foreign born: 0.0% (2000); Ancestry (includes multiple ancestries): 71.9% German, 6.7% Dutch, 6.3% Norwegian, 5.8% United States or American, 5.4% Irish (2000).
Economy: Grain; livestock, poultry; dairying. Employment by occupation: 31.5% management, 10.2% professional, 11.1% services, 15.7% sales, 3.7% farming, 11.1% construction, 16.7% production (2000).
Income: Per capita income: $12,613 (2000); Median household income: $31,528 (2000); Poverty rate: 12.9% (2000).
Taxes: Total city taxes per capita: $106 (1997); City property taxes per capita: $106 (1997).
Education: High school graduation rate: 87.0% (2000); College graduation rate: 12.3% (2000).
Housing: Homeownership rate: 81.5% (2000); Median home value: $62,500 (2000); Median rent: $188 per month (2000); Median age of housing: 60+ years (2000).
Transportation: Commute to work: 64.8% car, 0.0% public transportation, 7.4% walk, 27.8% work from home (2000); Travel time to work: 29.5% less than 15 minutes, 52.6% 15 to 30 minutes, 9.0% 30 to 45 minutes, 6.4% 45 to 60 minutes, 2.6% 60 minutes or more (2000)

WORTHINGTON (city). Covers a land area of 7.146 square miles and a water area of 1.367 square miles. Located at 43.62° N. Lat.; 95.59° W. Long. Elevation is 1,585 feet.
History: Worthington began in 1871 as Okabena, a prohibition colony where early property deeds forbade the sale of liquor. The town later developed as a trading center for local farmers, with creameries and produce companies.
Population: 11,283 (2000); Race: 78.0% White, 2.5% Black, 6.3% Asian, 1.0% American Indian and Alaska Native, 19.0% Hispanic of any race, 2.5% two or more races (2000); Density: 1,578.9 persons per square mile (2000); Age: 25.7% under 18, 17.5% over 64 (2000); Marriage status: 25.5% never married, 59.8% now married, 8.7% widowed, 6.1% divorced (2000); Foreign born: 15.6% (2000); Ancestry (includes multiple ancestries): 36.8% German, 25.2% Other groups, 11.6% Norwegian, 6.9% Dutch, 6.4% Irish (2000).
Economy: Single-family building permits issued: 11 (2001) / 3 (2000); Multi-family building permits issued: 12 (2001) / 6 (2000); Employment by occupation: 9.0% management, 11.8% professional, 17.3% services, 23.4% sales, 0.7% farming, 7.2% construction, 30.5% production (2000).
Income: Per capita income: $18,078 (2000); Median household income: $36,250 (2000); Poverty rate: 13.3% (2000).
Taxes: Total city taxes per capita: $223 (2000); City property taxes per capita: $207 (2000).
Education: High school graduation rate: 71.7% (2000); College graduation rate: 16.4% (2000).

School District(s)

Worthington (PK-12)
2000 Enrollment: 2,391 507-372-2172
Housing: Homeownership rate: 66.0% (2000); Median home value: $69,900 (2000); Median rent: $344 per month (2000); Median age of housing: 39 years (2000).
Hospitals: Worthington Regional Hospital (93 beds)
Safety: Violent crime rate: 30.7 per 10,000 population; Property crime rate: 344.6 per 10,000 population (2001).
Newspapers: Worthington Daily Globe (6 x week)
Transportation: Commute to work: 91.8% car, 1.7% public transportation, 3.5% walk, 2.7% work from home (2000); Travel time to work: 76.9% less than 15 minutes, 11.0% 15 to 30 minutes, 4.4% 30 to 45 minutes, 3.7% 45 to 60 minutes, 3.9% 60 minutes or more (2000)
Additional Information Contacts
Worthington Chamber of Commerce 507-372-2919

WORTHINGTON (township). Covers a land area of 28.604 square miles and a water area of 0 square miles. Located at 43.63° N. Lat.; 95.62° W. Long. Elevation is 1,585 feet.
History: Settled 1871.
Population: 316 (2000); Race: 100.0% White, 0.0% Black, 0.0% Asian, 0.0% American Indian and Alaska Native, 0.0% Hispanic of any race, 0.0% two or more races (2000); Density: 11.0 persons per square mile (2000); Age: 24.5% under 18, 18.3% over 64 (2000); Marriage status: 15.5% never married, 78.3% now married, 4.7% widowed, 1.6% divorced (2000); Foreign born: 0.0% (2000); Ancestry (includes multiple ancestries): 55.1% German, 13.3% Dutch, 8.0% Norwegian, 7.4% Swedish, 7.1% United States or American (2000).
Economy: Resort. Agricultural trade center. Soybeans, corn, oats, alfalfa, cattle, sheep, hogs, poultry and dairying. Manufacturing includes machinery, poultry processing, printing and publishing, feeds, mobile homes and hog processing. Railroad junction to southwest. Employment by occupation: 19.2% management, 14.0% professional, 15.7% services, 23.8% sales, 0.6% farming, 10.5% construction, 16.3% production (2000).
Income: Per capita income: $19,390 (2000); Median household income: $41,000 (2000); Poverty rate: 4.0% (2000).
Taxes: Total city taxes per capita: $82 (1997); City property taxes per capita: $82 (1997).
Education: High school graduation rate: 89.7% (2000); College graduation rate: 19.8% (2000).
Housing: Homeownership rate: 93.9% (2000); Median home value: $89,300 (2000); Median rent: $425 per month (2000); Median age of housing: 42 years (2000).
Transportation: Commute to work: 78.8% car, 0.0% public transportation, 4.1% walk, 15.9% work from home (2000); Travel time to work: 76.9% less than 15 minutes, 18.9% 15 to 30 minutes, 0.7% 30 to 45 minutes, 0.0% 45 to 60 minutes, 3.5% 60 minutes or more (2000)

Norman County

Located in northwestern Minnesota; bounded on the west by the Red River of the North and the North Dakota border; drained by the Wild Rice River. Covers a land area of 876.30 square miles, a water area of 0.50 square miles, and is located in the Central Time Zone. The county government was organized in 1881. County seat is Ada.

Weather Station: Ada — Elevation: 908 feet

	Jan	Feb	Mar	Apr	May	Jun	Jul	Aug	Sep	Oct	Nov	Dec
High	17	24	36	55	71	79	83	82	71	57	36	22
Low	-4	4	17	32	44	54	59	56	46	34	19	4
Precip	0.8	0.6	1.1	1.7	3.0	4.4	3.2	2.7	2.4	2.1	0.9	0.7
Snow	na	5.5	na	1.3	tr	0.0	0.0	0.0	0.0	0.7	na	8.2

High and Low temperatures in degrees Fahrenheit; Precipitation and Snow in inches

Population: 7,442 (2000); Race: 95.6% White, 0.2% Black, 0.2% Asian, 1.2% American Indian and Alaska Native, 2.7% Hispanic of any race, 1.9% two or more races (2000); Density: 8.5 persons per square mile (2000); Age: 25.6% under 18, 21.0% over 64 (2000).
Religion: Five largest groups: 67.0% Evangelical Lutheran Church in America, 12.6% Catholic Church, 11.9% Lutheran Church—Missouri Synod, 2.5% The United Methodist Church, 0.8% United Church of Christ (2000).
Economy: Unemployment rate: 3.5% (11/2002); Total civilian labor force: 3,151 (11/2002); Leading industries: 13.6% wholesale trade; except pub other services; Informatio 8.5% (2000); Companies that employ more than 1,000 persons: 0 (2000); Companies that employ more than 100 persons: 1 (2000); Farms: 670 totaling 483,041 acres (1997); Minority business ownership rate: 0.0% (1997); Women business ownership rate: 27.1% (1997); Retail sales per capita: $10,534 (1997). Single-family building permits issued: 12 (2001) / 12 (2000); Multi-family building permits issued: 0 (2001) / 0 (2000).
Income: Per capita income: $15,895 (2000); Median household income: $32,535 (2000); Poverty rate: 10.3% (2000); Bankruptcy rate: 2.65% (2001).
Taxes: Total county taxes per capita: $570 (2000); County property taxes per capita: $561 (2000).
Education: High school graduation rate: 80.0% (2000); College graduation rate: 13.1% (2000).

Housing: Homeownership rate: 81.1% (2000); Median home value: $43,600 (2000); Median rent: $293 per month (2000); Median age of housing: 48 years (2000).
Health: Birth rate: 87.3 per 10,000 population (1998); Age adjusted death rate: 68.1 per 10,000 population (1999); Age adjusted cancer mortality rate: 152.7 deaths per 100,000 population (1999). Number of physicians: 4.0 per 10,000 population (1999); Number of hospital beds: 10.7 per 10,000 population (1999).
Elections: 2000 Presidential election results: 43.3% Gore, 49.7% Bush, 3.4% Nader, 3.2% Buchanan
National and State Parks: Agassiz Number 1 State Wildlife Management Area; Agassiz Number 2 State Wildlife Management Area; Dalby State Wildlife Management Area; Faith State Wildlife Management Area; Home Lake State Wildlife Management Area; Moccasin State Wildlife Management Area; Neal State Wildlife Management Area; Syre State Wildlife Management Area; Twin Valley State Wildlife Management Are; Vangsness State Wildlife Management Area
Additional Information Contacts
Norman County Government Offices 218-784-5471

Norman County Communities

ADA (city). Covers a land area of 1.342 square miles and a water area of 0 square miles. Located at 47.29° N. Lat.; 96.51° W. Long. Elevation is 907 feet.
History: Ada grew up around a sawmill that began in 1897, processing lumber floated down the Wild Rice River from the forests to the east. When lumbering declined in the 1920's, Ada became a shipping center for the potatoes and dairy products raised in Norman County. The city was named for the daughter of a railway official.
Population: 1,657 (2000); Race: 98.2% White, 0.0% Black, 0.0% Asian, 0.0% American Indian and Alaska Native, 1.9% Hispanic of any race, 0.8% two or more races (2000); Density: 1,234.4 persons per square mile (2000); Age: 24.9% under 18, 24.6% over 64 (2000); Marriage status: 17.5% never married, 60.5% now married, 15.0% widowed, 7.0% divorced (2000); Foreign born: 1.9% (2000); Ancestry (includes multiple ancestries): 57.1% Norwegian, 38.8% German, 7.3% Swedish, 6.0% French (except Basque), 3.6% English (2000).
Economy: Single-family building permits issued: 3 (2001) / 4 (2000); Multi-family building permits issued: 0 (2001) / 0 (2000); Employment by occupation: 11.1% management, 24.9% professional, 15.9% services, 21.2% sales, 2.7% farming, 13.0% construction, 11.1% production (2000).
Income: Per capita income: $16,921 (2000); Median household income: $29,583 (2000); Poverty rate: 13.7% (2000).
Education: High school graduation rate: 80.1% (2000); College graduation rate: 19.1% (2000).

School District(s)

Ada-Borup (PK-12)
2000 Enrollment: 549 218-784-5310
Housing: Homeownership rate: 73.2% (2000); Median home value: $51,100 (2000); Median rent: $341 per month (2000); Median age of housing: 42 years (2000).
Hospitals: Bridges Medical Services (63 beds)
Newspapers: Norman County Index (1 x week)
Transportation: Commute to work: 87.5% car, 0.0% public transportation, 8.1% walk, 4.1% work from home (2000); Travel time to work: 74.4% less than 15 minutes, 10.1% 15 to 30 minutes, 7.9% 30 to 45 minutes, 3.5% 45 to 60 minutes, 4.1% 60 minutes or more (2000)

ANTHONY (township). Covers a land area of 36.029 square miles and a water area of 0 square miles. Located at 47.36° N. Lat.; 96.65° W. Long.
Population: 85 (2000); Race: 100.0% White, 0.0% Black, 0.0% Asian, 0.0% American Indian and Alaska Native, 0.0% Hispanic of any race, 0.0% two or more races (2000); Density: 2.4 persons per square mile (2000); Age: 29.5% under 18, 5.7% over 64 (2000); Marriage status: 23.9% never married, 67.6% now married, 4.2% widowed, 4.2% divorced (2000); Foreign born: 2.3% (2000); Ancestry (includes multiple ancestries): 55.7% Norwegian, 37.5% German, 13.6% Dutch, 10.2% Irish, 6.8% French Canadian (2000).
Economy: Employment by occupation: 16.0% management, 10.0% professional, 16.0% services, 24.0% sales, 4.0% farming, 14.0% construction, 16.0% production (2000).
Income: Per capita income: $19,788 (2000); Median household income: $42,292 (2000); Poverty rate: 0.0% (2000).
Taxes: Total city taxes per capita: $155 (1997); City property taxes per capita: $155 (1997).
Education: High school graduation rate: 82.1% (2000); College graduation rate: 8.9% (2000).
Housing: Homeownership rate: 76.7% (2000); Median home value: $55,000 (2000); Median rent: $338 per month (2000); Median age of housing: 60+ years (2000).
Transportation: Commute to work: 92.0% car, 0.0% public transportation, 0.0% walk, 8.0% work from home (2000); Travel time to work: 30.4% less than 15 minutes, 47.8% 15 to 30 minutes, 15.2% 30 to 45 minutes, 6.5% 45 to 60 minutes, 0.0% 60 minutes or more (2000)

BEAR PARK (township). Covers a land area of 36.204 square miles and a water area of 0.053 square miles. Located at 47.44° N. Lat.; 96.12° W. Long.
Population: 209 (2000); Race: 100.0% White, 0.0% Black, 0.0% Asian, 0.0% American Indian and Alaska Native, 0.0% Hispanic of any race, 0.0% two or more races (2000); Density: 5.8 persons per square mile (2000); Age: 20.7% under 18, 20.7% over 64 (2000); Marriage status: 15.4% never married, 72.4% now married, 6.4% widowed, 5.8% divorced (2000); Foreign born: 0.0% (2000); Ancestry (includes multiple ancestries): 75.0% Norwegian, 20.7% German, 10.9% French (except Basque), 7.1% English, 7.1% Irish (2000).
Economy: Employment by occupation: 27.4% management, 12.6% professional, 15.8% services, 18.9% sales, 3.2% farming, 10.5% construction, 11.6% production (2000).
Income: Per capita income: $15,431 (2000); Median household income: $30,000 (2000); Poverty rate: 17.9% (2000).
Taxes: Total city taxes per capita: $42 (1997); City property taxes per capita: $42 (1997).
Education: High school graduation rate: 81.1% (2000); College graduation rate: 12.6% (2000).
Housing: Homeownership rate: 85.2% (2000); Median home value: $47,500 (2000); Median rent: $125 per month (2000); Median age of housing: 60+ years (2000).
Transportation: Commute to work: 80.0% car, 0.0% public transportation, 4.2% walk, 13.7% work from home (2000); Travel time to work: 26.8% less than 15 minutes, 32.9% 15 to 30 minutes, 30.5% 30 to 45 minutes, 7.3% 45 to 60 minutes, 2.4% 60 minutes or more (2000)

BORUP (city). Covers a land area of 0.244 square miles and a water area of 0 square miles. Located at 47.18° N. Lat.; 96.50° W. Long. Elevation is 912 feet.
Population: 91 (2000); Race: 82.2% White, 0.0% Black, 2.2% Asian, 6.7% American Indian and Alaska Native, 0.0% Hispanic of any race, 8.9% two or more races (2000); Density: 372.7 persons per square mile (2000); Age: 24.4% under 18, 18.9% over 64 (2000); Marriage status: 7.4% never married, 73.5% now married, 13.2% widowed, 5.9% divorced (2000); Foreign born: 5.6% (2000); Ancestry (includes multiple ancestries): 63.3% Norwegian, 30.0% German, 11.1% Other groups, 7.8% French (except Basque), 5.6% Czech (2000).
Economy: Employment by occupation: 0.0% management, 11.1% professional, 27.8% services, 47.2% sales, 0.0% farming, 0.0% construction, 13.9% production (2000).
Income: Per capita income: $17,081 (2000); Median household income: $41,042 (2000); Poverty rate: 0.0% (2000).
Taxes: Total city taxes per capita: $77 (2000); City property taxes per capita: $66 (2000).
Education: High school graduation rate: 74.1% (2000); College graduation rate: 7.4% (2000).
Housing: Homeownership rate: 79.4% (2000); Median home value: $23,500 (2000); Median rent: $375 per month (2000); Median age of housing: 49 years (2000).
Transportation: Commute to work: 94.4% car, 0.0% public transportation, 5.6% walk, 0.0% work from home (2000); Travel time to work: 44.4% less than 15 minutes, 22.2% 15 to 30 minutes, 16.7% 30 to 45 minutes, 16.7% 45 to 60 minutes, 0.0% 60 minutes or more (2000)

FLOM (township). Covers a land area of 35.978 square miles and a water area of 0.128 square miles. Located at 47.19° N. Lat.; 96.14° W. Long. Elevation is 1,285 feet.
Population: 226 (2000); Race: 87.1% White, 0.0% Black, 0.0% Asian, 12.9% American Indian and Alaska Native, 0.0% Hispanic of any race, 0.0% two or more races (2000); Density: 6.3 persons per square mile (2000); Age: 27.1% under 18, 20.9% over 64 (2000); Marriage status: 37.7% never married, 46.1% now married, 7.3% widowed, 8.9% divorced (2000); Foreign born: 0.0% (2000); Ancestry (includes multiple ancestries): 42.7%

Norwegian, 28.4% German, 12.9% Swedish, 8.0% Polish, 7.6% Danish (2000).
Economy: Employment by occupation: 18.3% management, 11.9% professional, 27.8% services, 21.4% sales, 5.6% farming, 9.5% construction, 5.6% production (2000).
Income: Per capita income: $13,687 (2000); Median household income: $30,833 (2000); Poverty rate: 8.0% (2000).
Taxes: Total city taxes per capita: $83 (1997); City property taxes per capita: $83 (1997).
Education: High school graduation rate: 72.3% (2000); College graduation rate: 10.1% (2000).
Housing: Homeownership rate: 81.1% (2000); Median home value: $40,000 (2000); Median rent: $232 per month (2000); Median age of housing: 53 years (2000).
Transportation: Commute to work: 81.9% car, 3.4% public transportation, 6.9% walk, 7.8% work from home (2000); Travel time to work: 35.5% less than 15 minutes, 46.7% 15 to 30 minutes, 10.3% 30 to 45 minutes, 0.0% 45 to 60 minutes, 7.5% 60 minutes or more (2000)

FOSSUM (township). Covers a land area of 36.018 square miles and a water area of 0.015 square miles. Located at 47.29° N. Lat.; 96.12° W. Long.
Population: 187 (2000); Race: 98.8% White, 1.2% Black, 0.0% Asian, 0.0% American Indian and Alaska Native, 3.7% Hispanic of any race, 0.0% two or more races (2000); Density: 5.2 persons per square mile (2000); Age: 23.5% under 18, 11.7% over 64 (2000); Marriage status: 11.8% never married, 74.8% now married, 2.4% widowed, 11.0% divorced (2000); Foreign born: 1.2% (2000); Ancestry (includes multiple ancestries): 58.0% Norwegian, 23.5% German, 7.4% Swedish, 4.9% Czech, 4.9% Other groups (2000).
Economy: Employment by occupation: 16.3% management, 10.5% professional, 15.1% services, 29.1% sales, 10.5% farming, 8.1% construction, 10.5% production (2000).
Income: Per capita income: $16,214 (2000); Median household income: $42,500 (2000); Poverty rate: 3.7% (2000).
Taxes: Total city taxes per capita: $58 (1997); City property taxes per capita: $58 (1997).
Education: High school graduation rate: 83.2% (2000); College graduation rate: 12.4% (2000).
Housing: Homeownership rate: 88.9% (2000); Median home value: $68,800 (2000); Median rent: $125 per month (2000); Median age of housing: 43 years (2000).
Transportation: Commute to work: 77.4% car, 0.0% public transportation, 13.1% walk, 7.1% work from home (2000); Travel time to work: 38.5% less than 15 minutes, 37.2% 15 to 30 minutes, 9.0% 30 to 45 minutes, 9.0% 45 to 60 minutes, 6.4% 60 minutes or more (2000)

GARY (city). Covers a land area of 0.321 square miles and a water area of 0 square miles. Located at 47.37° N. Lat.; 96.26° W. Long. Elevation is 1,103 feet.
Population: 215 (2000); Race: 98.2% White, 0.0% Black, 0.0% Asian, 0.0% American Indian and Alaska Native, 0.4% Hispanic of any race, 1.8% two or more races (2000); Density: 669.0 persons per square mile (2000); Age: 29.1% under 18, 22.0% over 64 (2000); Marriage status: 24.4% never married, 57.6% now married, 12.8% widowed, 5.2% divorced (2000); Foreign born: 0.9% (2000); Ancestry (includes multiple ancestries): 68.2% Norwegian, 25.1% German, 8.1% Irish, 4.5% French (except Basque), 4.0% United States or American (2000).
Economy: Agricultural area: grain, sunflowers, potatoes, alfalfa. Manufacturing: feeds, fertilizers. Employment by occupation: 10.4% management, 15.6% professional, 19.8% services, 31.3% sales, 2.1% farming, 11.5% construction, 9.4% production (2000).
Income: Per capita income: $15,683 (2000); Median household income: $36,875 (2000); Poverty rate: 14.8% (2000).
Taxes: Total city taxes per capita: $119 (1997); City property taxes per capita: $113 (1997).
Education: High school graduation rate: 81.9% (2000); College graduation rate: 14.1% (2000).
Housing: Homeownership rate: 94.3% (2000); Median home value: $30,400 (2000); Median rent: $242 per month (2000); Median age of housing: 60+ years (2000).
Transportation: Commute to work: 78.1% car, 0.0% public transportation, 9.4% walk, 12.5% work from home (2000); Travel time to work: 48.8% less than 15 minutes, 29.8% 15 to 30 minutes, 9.5% 30 to 45 minutes, 2.4% 45 to 60 minutes, 9.5% 60 minutes or more (2000)

GOOD HOPE (township). Covers a land area of 36.105 square miles and a water area of 0 square miles. Located at 47.46° N. Lat.; 96.65° W. Long.
Population: 44 (2000); Race: 100.0% White, 0.0% Black, 0.0% Asian, 0.0% American Indian and Alaska Native, 0.0% Hispanic of any race, 0.0% two or more races (2000); Density: 1.2 persons per square mile (2000); Age: 14.3% under 18, 28.6% over 64 (2000); Marriage status: 13.9% never married, 80.6% now married, 5.6% widowed, 0.0% divorced (2000); Foreign born: 4.8% (2000); Ancestry (includes multiple ancestries): 76.2% Norwegian, 38.1% German, 9.5% English, 4.8% Swedish, 4.8% Scottish (2000).
Economy: Employment by occupation: 9.1% management, 18.2% professional, 13.6% services, 9.1% sales, 0.0% farming, 13.6% construction, 36.4% production (2000).
Income: Per capita income: $12,100 (2000); Median household income: $24,375 (2000); Poverty rate: 5.0% (2000).
Taxes: Total city taxes per capita: $186 (1997); City property taxes per capita: $186 (1997).
Education: High school graduation rate: 88.9% (2000); College graduation rate: 5.6% (2000).
Housing: Homeownership rate: 85.0% (2000); Median home value: $225,000 (2000); Median rent: <$100 per month (2000); Median age of housing: 60+ years (2000).
Transportation: Commute to work: 80.0% car, 0.0% public transportation, 10.0% walk, 10.0% work from home (2000); Travel time to work: 11.1% less than 15 minutes, 38.9% 15 to 30 minutes, 33.3% 30 to 45 minutes, 16.7% 45 to 60 minutes, 0.0% 60 minutes or more (2000)

GREEN MEADOW (township). Covers a land area of 36.612 square miles and a water area of 0 square miles. Located at 47.37° N. Lat.; 96.37° W. Long.
Population: 114 (2000); Race: 100.0% White, 0.0% Black, 0.0% Asian, 0.0% American Indian and Alaska Native, 0.0% Hispanic of any race, 0.0% two or more races (2000); Density: 3.1 persons per square mile (2000); Age: 28.3% under 18, 16.8% over 64 (2000); Marriage status: 26.3% never married, 68.4% now married, 4.2% widowed, 1.1% divorced (2000); Foreign born: 1.8% (2000); Ancestry (includes multiple ancestries): 73.5% German, 41.6% Norwegian, 9.7% Irish, 8.8% Swedish, 2.7% Russian (2000).
Economy: Employment by occupation: 21.2% management, 6.1% professional, 12.1% services, 16.7% sales, 0.0% farming, 16.7% construction, 27.3% production (2000).
Income: Per capita income: $13,135 (2000); Median household income: $33,750 (2000); Poverty rate: 5.3% (2000).
Taxes: Total city taxes per capita: $70 (1997); City property taxes per capita: $70 (1997).
Education: High school graduation rate: 83.8% (2000); College graduation rate: 10.8% (2000).
Housing: Homeownership rate: 94.7% (2000); Median home value: $70,000 (2000); Median age of housing: 60+ years (2000).
Transportation: Commute to work: 74.2% car, 0.0% public transportation, 3.0% walk, 22.7% work from home (2000); Travel time to work: 39.2% less than 15 minutes, 23.5% 15 to 30 minutes, 5.9% 30 to 45 minutes, 0.0% 45 to 60 minutes, 31.4% 60 minutes or more (2000)

HALSTAD (city). Covers a land area of 0.292 square miles and a water area of 0 square miles. Located at 47.35° N. Lat.; 96.82° W. Long. Elevation is 872 feet.
Population: 622 (2000); Race: 92.1% White, 1.5% Black, 0.0% Asian, 0.3% American Indian and Alaska Native, 8.7% Hispanic of any race, 1.8% two or more races (2000); Density: 2,131.3 persons per square mile (2000); Age: 22.0% under 18, 29.6% over 64 (2000); Marriage status: 11.3% never married, 65.4% now married, 14.6% widowed, 8.7% divorced (2000); Foreign born: 4.4% (2000); Ancestry (includes multiple ancestries): 56.2% Norwegian, 24.2% German, 9.4% Other groups, 5.0% Irish, 4.2% Swedish (2000).
Economy: Single-family building permits issued: 0 (2001) / 0 (2000); Multi-family building permits issued: 0 (2001) / 0 (2000); Employment by occupation: 6.5% management, 20.6% professional, 21.4% services, 25.0% sales, 4.0% farming, 12.1% construction, 10.5% production (2000).
Income: Per capita income: $15,918 (2000); Median household income: $31,875 (2000); Poverty rate: 11.1% (2000).
Taxes: Total city taxes per capita: $209 (1997); City property taxes per capita: $205 (1997).
Education: High school graduation rate: 71.8% (2000); College graduation rate: 12.7% (2000).

School District(s)

Norman County West (PK-12)
2000 Enrollment: 415 218-456-2152

Housing: Homeownership rate: 70.7% (2000); Median home value: $46,500 (2000); Median rent: $233 per month (2000); Median age of housing: 42 years (2000).
Transportation: Commute to work: 75.2% car, 0.0% public transportation, 20.3% walk, 2.8% work from home (2000); Travel time to work: 63.2% less than 15 minutes, 13.4% 15 to 30 minutes, 8.8% 30 to 45 minutes, 13.0% 45 to 60 minutes, 1.7% 60 minutes or more (2000)

HALSTAD (township). Covers a land area of 37.910 square miles and a water area of 0 square miles. Located at 47.37° N. Lat.; 96.78° W. Long. Elevation is 872 feet.
Population: 142 (2000); Race: 96.1% White, 0.0% Black, 1.6% Asian, 0.0% American Indian and Alaska Native, 5.5% Hispanic of any race, 0.0% two or more races (2000); Density: 3.7 persons per square mile (2000); Age: 29.1% under 18, 15.7% over 64 (2000); Marriage status: 24.2% never married, 66.7% now married, 6.1% widowed, 3.0% divorced (2000); Foreign born: 1.6% (2000); Ancestry (includes multiple ancestries): 69.3% Norwegian, 29.1% German, 25.2% Swedish, 7.1% Other groups, 5.5% French (except Basque) (2000).
Economy: Agricultural area: grain, potatoes, sunflowers, sugar beets. Manufacturing: printing. Employment by occupation: 30.6% management, 16.1% professional, 9.7% services, 17.7% sales, 8.1% farming, 17.7% construction, 0.0% production (2000).
Income: Per capita income: $21,871 (2000); Median household income: $37,083 (2000); Poverty rate: 3.1% (2000).
Taxes: Total city taxes per capita: $95 (1997); City property taxes per capita: $95 (1997).
Education: High school graduation rate: 86.3% (2000); College graduation rate: 17.5% (2000).
Housing: Homeownership rate: 95.5% (2000); Median home value: $50,000 (2000); Median rent: $325 per month (2000); Median age of housing: 60+ years (2000).
Transportation: Commute to work: 75.8% car, 0.0% public transportation, 4.8% walk, 19.4% work from home (2000); Travel time to work: 34.0% less than 15 minutes, 36.0% 15 to 30 minutes, 12.0% 30 to 45 minutes, 18.0% 45 to 60 minutes, 0.0% 60 minutes or more (2000)

HEGNE (township). Covers a land area of 35.548 square miles and a water area of 0 square miles. Located at 47.29° N. Lat.; 96.63° W. Long.
Population: 48 (2000); Race: 100.0% White, 0.0% Black, 0.0% Asian, 0.0% American Indian and Alaska Native, 0.0% Hispanic of any race, 0.0% two or more races (2000); Density: 1.4 persons per square mile (2000); Age: 14.3% under 18, 24.5% over 64 (2000); Marriage status: 27.7% never married, 59.6% now married, 12.8% widowed, 0.0% divorced (2000); Foreign born: 0.0% (2000); Ancestry (includes multiple ancestries): 67.3% Norwegian, 34.7% German, 12.2% Northern European, 10.2% Dutch, 8.2% Swedish (2000).
Economy: Employment by occupation: 20.0% management, 36.7% professional, 0.0% services, 13.3% sales, 6.7% farming, 0.0% construction, 23.3% production (2000).
Income: Per capita income: $17,776 (2000); Median household income: $31,875 (2000); Poverty rate: 8.2% (2000).
Taxes: Total city taxes per capita: $159 (1997); City property taxes per capita: $159 (1997).
Education: High school graduation rate: 95.2% (2000); College graduation rate: 23.8% (2000).
Housing: Homeownership rate: 58.3% (2000); Median home value: $58,300 (2000); Median rent: $225 per month (2000); Median age of housing: 60+ years (2000).
Transportation: Commute to work: 93.3% car, 0.0% public transportation, 0.0% walk, 6.7% work from home (2000); Travel time to work: 57.1% less than 15 minutes, 14.3% 15 to 30 minutes, 0.0% 30 to 45 minutes, 21.4% 45 to 60 minutes, 7.1% 60 minutes or more (2000)

HENDRUM (city). Covers a land area of 0.283 square miles and a water area of 0 square miles. Located at 47.26° N. Lat.; 96.81° W. Long. Elevation is 877 feet.
Population: 315 (2000); Race: 96.5% White, 0.0% Black, 0.0% Asian, 2.4% American Indian and Alaska Native, 6.2% Hispanic of any race, 0.0% two or more races (2000); Density: 1,112.3 persons per square mile (2000); Age: 34.1% under 18, 8.2% over 64 (2000); Marriage status: 26.5% never married, 61.2% now married, 6.9% widowed, 5.3% divorced (2000); Foreign born: 0.3% (2000); Ancestry (includes multiple ancestries): 65.6% Norwegian, 21.2% German, 7.9% Other groups, 5.3% Swedish, 4.1% Polish (2000).
Economy: Single-family building permits issued: 1 (2001) / 1 (2000); Multi-family building permits issued: 0 (2001) / 0 (2000); Employment by occupation: 11.8% management, 17.0% professional, 18.3% services, 25.5% sales, 0.0% farming, 7.8% construction, 19.6% production (2000).
Income: Per capita income: $14,530 (2000); Median household income: $35,000 (2000); Poverty rate: 9.7% (2000).
Taxes: Total city taxes per capita: $162 (1997); City property taxes per capita: $158 (1997).
Education: High school graduation rate: 85.9% (2000); College graduation rate: 15.0% (2000).
Housing: Homeownership rate: 82.5% (2000); Median home value: $37,700 (2000); Median rent: $333 per month (2000); Median age of housing: 43 years (2000).
Transportation: Commute to work: 85.6% car, 0.0% public transportation, 9.8% walk, 2.0% work from home (2000); Travel time to work: 48.7% less than 15 minutes, 14.7% 15 to 30 minutes, 19.3% 30 to 45 minutes, 10.0% 45 to 60 minutes, 7.3% 60 minutes or more (2000)

HENDRUM (township). Covers a land area of 41.920 square miles and a water area of 0.082 square miles. Located at 47.27° N. Lat.; 96.76° W. Long. Elevation is 877 feet.
Population: 118 (2000); Race: 95.8% White, 0.0% Black, 4.2% Asian, 0.0% American Indian and Alaska Native, 0.0% Hispanic of any race, 0.0% two or more races (2000); Density: 2.8 persons per square mile (2000); Age: 21.2% under 18, 25.4% over 64 (2000); Marriage status: 9.1% never married, 86.9% now married, 4.0% widowed, 0.0% divorced (2000); Foreign born: 0.0% (2000); Ancestry (includes multiple ancestries): 43.2% Norwegian, 23.7% German, 21.2% Irish, 14.4% English, 6.8% Swedish (2000).
Economy: Wheat, potatoes, sunflowers, sugar beets, soybeans. Employment by occupation: 26.1% management, 13.0% professional, 0.0% services, 43.5% sales, 0.0% farming, 17.4% construction, 0.0% production (2000).
Income: Per capita income: $17,238 (2000); Median household income: $36,071 (2000); Poverty rate: 0.0% (2000).
Taxes: Total city taxes per capita: $209 (1997); City property taxes per capita: $209 (1997).
Education: High school graduation rate: 86.4% (2000); College graduation rate: 21.6% (2000).
Housing: Homeownership rate: 95.9% (2000); Median home value: $86,100 (2000); Median rent: $325 per month (2000); Median age of housing: 41 years (2000).
Transportation: Commute to work: 80.4% car, 0.0% public transportation, 0.0% walk, 19.6% work from home (2000); Travel time to work: 24.3% less than 15 minutes, 10.8% 15 to 30 minutes, 16.2% 30 to 45 minutes, 43.2% 45 to 60 minutes, 5.4% 60 minutes or more (2000)

HOME LAKE (township). Covers a land area of 35.898 square miles and a water area of 0.152 square miles. Located at 47.19° N. Lat.; 96.27° W. Long.
Population: 184 (2000); Race: 84.9% White, 0.0% Black, 0.0% Asian, 2.7% American Indian and Alaska Native, 0.0% Hispanic of any race, 12.3% two or more races (2000); Density: 5.1 persons per square mile (2000); Age: 34.7% under 18, 8.2% over 64 (2000); Marriage status: 18.4% never married, 77.6% now married, 3.3% widowed, 0.7% divorced (2000); Foreign born: 0.0% (2000); Ancestry (includes multiple ancestries): 56.2% Norwegian, 27.9% German, 12.3% Other groups, 6.4% Irish, 5.0% Swedish (2000).
Economy: Employment by occupation: 12.4% management, 17.1% professional, 23.8% services, 22.9% sales, 2.9% farming, 11.4% construction, 9.5% production (2000).
Income: Per capita income: $15,358 (2000); Median household income: $40,417 (2000); Poverty rate: 9.6% (2000).
Taxes: Total city taxes per capita: $59 (1997); City property taxes per capita: $59 (1997).
Education: High school graduation rate: 82.1% (2000); College graduation rate: 11.4% (2000).
Housing: Homeownership rate: 86.6% (2000); Median home value: $28,800 (2000); Median rent: $275 per month (2000); Median age of housing: 39 years (2000).
Transportation: Commute to work: 84.5% car, 0.0% public transportation, 0.0% walk, 12.6% work from home (2000); Travel time to work: 25.6% less than 15 minutes, 33.3% 15 to 30 minutes, 14.4% 30 to 45 minutes, 8.9% 45 to 60 minutes, 17.8% 60 minutes or more (2000)

LAKE IDA (township). Covers a land area of 32.314 square miles and a water area of 0 square miles. Located at 47.27° N. Lat.; 96.37° W. Long.
Population: 164 (2000); Race: 99.0% White, 0.0% Black, 0.0% Asian, 1.0% American Indian and Alaska Native, 6.0% Hispanic of any race, 0.0% two or more races (2000); Density: 5.1 persons per square mile (2000); Age: 26.4% under 18, 11.9% over 64 (2000); Marriage status: 24.5% never married,

67.3% now married, 3.1% widowed, 5.0% divorced (2000); Foreign born: 1.0% (2000); Ancestry (includes multiple ancestries): 51.7% Norwegian, 43.8% German, 12.4% Swedish, 9.5% Other groups, 5.0% English (2000).
Economy: Employment by occupation: 7.0% management, 7.0% professional, 33.3% services, 16.7% sales, 9.6% farming, 12.3% construction, 14.0% production (2000).
Income: Per capita income: $18,469 (2000); Median household income: $46,563 (2000); Poverty rate: 0.0% (2000).
Taxes: Total city taxes per capita: $88 (1997); City property taxes per capita: $88 (1997).
Education: High school graduation rate: 78.6% (2000); College graduation rate: 6.8% (2000).
Housing: Homeownership rate: 87.1% (2000); Median home value: $54,400 (2000); Median rent: $192 per month (2000); Median age of housing: 57 years (2000).
Transportation: Commute to work: 72.3% car, 0.9% public transportation, 1.8% walk, 19.6% work from home (2000); Travel time to work: 30.0% less than 15 minutes, 43.3% 15 to 30 minutes, 7.8% 30 to 45 minutes, 15.6% 45 to 60 minutes, 3.3% 60 minutes or more (2000)

LEE (township). Covers a land area of 39.698 square miles and a water area of 0 square miles. Located at 47.18° N. Lat.; 96.76° W. Long.
Population: 159 (2000); Race: 98.8% White, 1.3% Black, 0.0% Asian, 0.0% American Indian and Alaska Native, 0.0% Hispanic of any race, 0.0% two or more races (2000); Density: 4.0 persons per square mile (2000); Age: 36.9% under 18, 7.5% over 64 (2000); Marriage status: 18.3% never married, 73.0% now married, 1.7% widowed, 7.0% divorced (2000); Foreign born: 1.9% (2000); Ancestry (includes multiple ancestries): 60.0% Norwegian, 25.0% German, 13.1% Swedish, 11.3% Irish, 8.8% Scottish (2000).
Economy: Employment by occupation: 28.6% management, 11.1% professional, 12.7% services, 22.2% sales, 0.0% farming, 3.2% construction, 22.2% production (2000).
Income: Per capita income: $19,519 (2000); Median household income: $49,375 (2000); Poverty rate: 0.0% (2000).
Education: High school graduation rate: 90.4% (2000); College graduation rate: 14.9% (2000).
Housing: Homeownership rate: 96.4% (2000); Median home value: $61,300 (2000); Median rent: $225 per month (2000); Median age of housing: 43 years (2000).
Transportation: Commute to work: 86.9% car, 0.0% public transportation, 0.0% walk, 13.1% work from home (2000); Travel time to work: 30.2% less than 15 minutes, 18.9% 15 to 30 minutes, 34.0% 30 to 45 minutes, 9.4% 45 to 60 minutes, 7.5% 60 minutes or more (2000)

LOCKHART (township). Covers a land area of 36.253 square miles and a water area of 0 square miles. Located at 47.44° N. Lat.; 96.52° W. Long. Elevation is 894 feet.
Population: 63 (2000); Race: 100.0% White, 0.0% Black, 0.0% Asian, 0.0% American Indian and Alaska Native, 0.0% Hispanic of any race, 0.0% two or more races (2000); Density: 1.7 persons per square mile (2000); Age: 23.8% under 18, 12.7% over 64 (2000); Marriage status: 32.7% never married, 59.6% now married, 3.8% widowed, 3.8% divorced (2000); Foreign born: 6.3% (2000); Ancestry (includes multiple ancestries): 46.0% German, 36.5% Norwegian, 11.1% United States or American, 9.5% Irish, 6.3% Dutch (2000).
Economy: Employment by occupation: 26.7% management, 13.3% professional, 16.7% services, 10.0% sales, 6.7% farming, 13.3% construction, 13.3% production (2000).
Income: Per capita income: $19,424 (2000); Median household income: $36,250 (2000); Poverty rate: 25.4% (2000).
Taxes: Total city taxes per capita: $160 (1997); City property taxes per capita: $160 (1997).
Education: High school graduation rate: 87.0% (2000); College graduation rate: 23.9% (2000).
Housing: Homeownership rate: 92.3% (2000); Median home value: $20,000 (2000); Median rent: $325 per month (2000); Median age of housing: 60+ years (2000).
Transportation: Commute to work: 66.7% car, 0.0% public transportation, 0.0% walk, 33.3% work from home (2000); Travel time to work: 25.0% less than 15 minutes, 70.0% 15 to 30 minutes, 5.0% 30 to 45 minutes, 0.0% 45 to 60 minutes, 0.0% 60 minutes or more (2000)

MARY (township). Covers a land area of 35.432 square miles and a water area of 0 square miles. Located at 47.19° N. Lat.; 96.63° W. Long.
Population: 102 (2000); Race: 93.1% White, 0.0% Black, 0.0% Asian, 0.0% American Indian and Alaska Native, 0.0% Hispanic of any race, 6.9% two or more races (2000); Density: 2.9 persons per square mile (2000); Age: 32.1% under 18, 16.0% over 64 (2000); Marriage status: 15.6% never married, 80.2% now married, 4.2% widowed, 0.0% divorced (2000); Foreign born: 0.0% (2000); Ancestry (includes multiple ancestries): 43.5% German, 43.5% Norwegian, 9.9% Irish, 5.3% French (except Basque), 3.8% Finnish (2000).
Economy: Employment by occupation: 18.6% management, 11.9% professional, 16.9% services, 39.0% sales, 0.0% farming, 13.6% construction, 0.0% production (2000).
Income: Per capita income: $16,836 (2000); Median household income: $43,214 (2000); Poverty rate: 9.9% (2000).
Taxes: Total city taxes per capita: $88 (2000); City property taxes per capita: $88 (2000).
Education: High school graduation rate: 88.2% (2000); College graduation rate: 8.2% (2000).
Housing: Homeownership rate: 93.5% (2000); Median home value: $60,000 (2000); Median age of housing: 60+ years (2000).
Transportation: Commute to work: 81.4% car, 0.0% public transportation, 0.0% walk, 18.6% work from home (2000); Travel time to work: 14.6% less than 15 minutes, 31.3% 15 to 30 minutes, 37.5% 30 to 45 minutes, 6.3% 45 to 60 minutes, 10.4% 60 minutes or more (2000)

MCDONALDSVILLE (township). Covers a land area of 34.814 square miles and a water area of 0 square miles. Located at 47.27° N. Lat.; 96.51° W. Long.
Population: 186 (2000); Race: 100.0% White, 0.0% Black, 0.0% Asian, 0.0% American Indian and Alaska Native, 0.0% Hispanic of any race, 0.0% two or more races (2000); Density: 5.3 persons per square mile (2000); Age: 23.7% under 18, 16.8% over 64 (2000); Marriage status: 20.4% never married, 72.8% now married, 4.3% widowed, 2.5% divorced (2000); Foreign born: 0.0% (2000); Ancestry (includes multiple ancestries): 60.5% Norwegian, 38.9% German, 3.7% Northern European, 2.1% Irish, 1.6% United States or American (2000).
Economy: Employment by occupation: 16.8% management, 17.8% professional, 12.9% services, 29.7% sales, 6.9% farming, 7.9% construction, 7.9% production (2000).
Income: Per capita income: $16,739 (2000); Median household income: $48,333 (2000); Poverty rate: 6.8% (2000).
Taxes: Total city taxes per capita: $63 (1997); City property taxes per capita: $63 (1997).
Education: High school graduation rate: 88.1% (2000); College graduation rate: 18.5% (2000).
Housing: Homeownership rate: 94.2% (2000); Median home value: $82,500 (2000); Median rent: $425 per month (2000); Median age of housing: 35 years (2000).
Transportation: Commute to work: 83.2% car, 0.0% public transportation, 5.9% walk, 10.9% work from home (2000); Travel time to work: 80.0% less than 15 minutes, 10.0% 15 to 30 minutes, 0.0% 30 to 45 minutes, 10.0% 45 to 60 minutes, 0.0% 60 minutes or more (2000)

PERLEY (city). Covers a land area of 0.241 square miles and a water area of 0 square miles. Located at 47.17° N. Lat.; 96.80° W. Long. Elevation is 879 feet.
Population: 121 (2000); Race: 87.8% White, 0.0% Black, 1.5% Asian, 10.7% American Indian and Alaska Native, 0.0% Hispanic of any race, 0.0% two or more races (2000); Density: 501.4 persons per square mile (2000); Age: 29.0% under 18, 11.5% over 64 (2000); Marriage status: 25.0% never married, 63.0% now married, 2.8% widowed, 9.3% divorced (2000); Foreign born: 1.5% (2000); Ancestry (includes multiple ancestries): 53.4% Norwegian, 32.8% German, 15.3% Other groups, 9.2% Swedish, 6.1% Finnish (2000).
Economy: Wheat, sugar beets, sunflowers, potatoes. Single-family building permits issued: 0 (2001) / 0 (2000); Multi-family building permits issued: 0 (2001) / 0 (2000); Employment by occupation: 8.3% management, 21.7% professional, 13.3% services, 20.0% sales, 0.0% farming, 23.3% construction, 13.3% production (2000).
Income: Per capita income: $13,998 (2000); Median household income: $31,250 (2000); Poverty rate: 12.2% (2000).
Taxes: Total city taxes per capita: $144 (1997); City property taxes per capita: $144 (1997).
Education: High school graduation rate: 91.5% (2000); College graduation rate: 7.3% (2000).
Housing: Homeownership rate: 96.0% (2000); Median home value: $55,000 (2000); Median age of housing: 49 years (2000).
Transportation: Commute to work: 79.0% car, 3.2% public transportation, 6.5% walk, 3.2% work from home (2000); Travel time to work: 13.3% less

than 15 minutes, 31.7% 15 to 30 minutes, 35.0% 30 to 45 minutes, 13.3% 45 to 60 minutes, 6.7% 60 minutes or more (2000)

PLEASANT VIEW (township). Covers a land area of 36.245 square miles and a water area of 0 square miles. Located at 47.35° N. Lat.; 96.53° W. Long.
Population: 140 (2000); Race: 95.7% White, 0.0% Black, 0.0% Asian, 0.0% American Indian and Alaska Native, 0.0% Hispanic of any race, 0.0% two or more races (2000); Density: 3.9 persons per square mile (2000); Age: 26.4% under 18, 17.1% over 64 (2000); Marriage status: 23.7% never married, 69.3% now married, 5.3% widowed, 1.8% divorced (2000); Foreign born: 1.4% (2000); Ancestry (includes multiple ancestries): 67.1% Norwegian, 27.1% German, 14.3% English, 6.4% Czech, 4.3% Irish (2000).
Economy: Employment by occupation: 21.6% management, 13.5% professional, 12.2% services, 28.4% sales, 8.1% farming, 10.8% construction, 5.4% production (2000).
Income: Per capita income: $15,630 (2000); Median household income: $37,500 (2000); Poverty rate: 2.9% (2000).
Taxes: Total city taxes per capita: $152 (1997); City property taxes per capita: $152 (1997).
Education: High school graduation rate: 76.8% (2000); College graduation rate: 2.1% (2000).
Housing: Homeownership rate: 72.0% (2000); Median home value: $43,300 (2000); Median rent: $175 per month (2000); Median age of housing: 58 years (2000).
Transportation: Commute to work: 85.1% car, 0.0% public transportation, 0.0% walk, 14.9% work from home (2000); Travel time to work: 34.9% less than 15 minutes, 27.0% 15 to 30 minutes, 20.6% 30 to 45 minutes, 6.3% 45 to 60 minutes, 11.1% 60 minutes or more (2000)

ROCKWELL (township). Covers a land area of 32.311 square miles and a water area of 0 square miles. Located at 47.19° N. Lat.; 96.39° W. Long.
Population: 78 (2000); Race: 96.9% White, 0.0% Black, 0.0% Asian, 0.0% American Indian and Alaska Native, 0.0% Hispanic of any race, 3.1% two or more races (2000); Density: 2.4 persons per square mile (2000); Age: 21.5% under 18, 10.8% over 64 (2000); Marriage status: 15.7% never married, 76.5% now married, 3.9% widowed, 3.9% divorced (2000); Foreign born: 0.0% (2000); Ancestry (includes multiple ancestries): 63.1% Norwegian, 50.8% German, 7.7% English, 6.2% French (except Basque), 3.1% Irish (2000).
Economy: Employment by occupation: 15.4% management, 23.1% professional, 0.0% services, 0.0% sales, 26.9% farming, 15.4% construction, 19.2% production (2000).
Income: Per capita income: $19,917 (2000); Median household income: $40,500 (2000); Poverty rate: 4.6% (2000).
Taxes: Total city taxes per capita: $78 (1997); City property taxes per capita: $78 (1997).
Education: High school graduation rate: 80.4% (2000); College graduation rate: 17.4% (2000).
Housing: Homeownership rate: 80.8% (2000); Median home value: $32,500 (2000); Median rent: $142 per month (2000); Median age of housing: 42 years (2000).
Transportation: Commute to work: 84.6% car, 0.0% public transportation, 0.0% walk, 15.4% work from home (2000); Travel time to work: 31.8% less than 15 minutes, 36.4% 15 to 30 minutes, 0.0% 30 to 45 minutes, 13.6% 45 to 60 minutes, 18.2% 60 minutes or more (2000)

SHELLY (city). Covers a land area of 0.209 square miles and a water area of 0 square miles. Located at 47.45° N. Lat.; 96.81° W. Long. Elevation is 865 feet.
Population: 266 (2000); Race: 85.6% White, 0.0% Black, 0.0% Asian, 3.9% American Indian and Alaska Native, 18.3% Hispanic of any race, 3.5% two or more races (2000); Density: 1,271.2 persons per square mile (2000); Age: 27.6% under 18, 17.1% over 64 (2000); Marriage status: 27.2% never married, 53.8% now married, 10.8% widowed, 8.2% divorced (2000); Foreign born: 11.7% (2000); Ancestry (includes multiple ancestries): 61.9% Norwegian, 23.7% Other groups, 10.1% German, 6.6% Swedish, 5.8% Danish (2000).
Economy: Single-family building permits issued: 0 (2001) / 5 (2000); Multi-family building permits issued: 0 (2001) / 0 (2000); Employment by occupation: 13.4% management, 12.4% professional, 15.5% services, 13.4% sales, 8.2% farming, 10.3% construction, 26.8% production (2000).
Income: Per capita income: $15,338 (2000); Median household income: $28,750 (2000); Poverty rate: 14.8% (2000).
Taxes: Total city taxes per capita: $89 (1997); City property taxes per capita: $85 (1997).
Education: High school graduation rate: 78.3% (2000); College graduation rate: 14.9% (2000).
Housing: Homeownership rate: 83.0% (2000); Median home value: $26,400 (2000); Median rent: $454 per month (2000); Median age of housing: 57 years (2000).
Transportation: Commute to work: 100.0% car, 0.0% public transportation, 0.0% walk, 0.0% work from home (2000); Travel time to work: 30.9% less than 15 minutes, 25.5% 15 to 30 minutes, 17.0% 30 to 45 minutes, 9.6% 45 to 60 minutes, 17.0% 60 minutes or more (2000)

SHELLY (township). Covers a land area of 42.180 square miles and a water area of 0 square miles. Located at 47.45° N. Lat.; 96.78° W. Long. Elevation is 865 feet.
Population: 129 (2000); Race: 100.0% White, 0.0% Black, 0.0% Asian, 0.0% American Indian and Alaska Native, 0.8% Hispanic of any race, 0.0% two or more races (2000); Density: 3.1 persons per square mile (2000); Age: 22.0% under 18, 21.3% over 64 (2000); Marriage status: 7.9% never married, 70.3% now married, 9.9% widowed, 11.9% divorced (2000); Foreign born: 0.0% (2000); Ancestry (includes multiple ancestries): 70.1% Norwegian, 29.9% German, 9.4% French (except Basque), 6.3% Irish, 5.5% English (2000).
Economy: Wheat, potatoes, sugar beets. Manufacturing of fertilizers. Employment by occupation: 19.7% management, 18.2% professional, 16.7% services, 21.2% sales, 0.0% farming, 7.6% construction, 16.7% production (2000).
Income: Per capita income: $18,230 (2000); Median household income: $33,750 (2000); Poverty rate: 9.6% (2000).
Taxes: Total city taxes per capita: $84 (1997); City property taxes per capita: $84 (1997).
Education: High school graduation rate: 94.7% (2000); College graduation rate: 12.6% (2000).
Housing: Homeownership rate: 88.5% (2000); Median home value: $61,700 (2000); Median rent: $163 per month (2000); Median age of housing: 60 years (2000).
Transportation: Commute to work: 77.8% car, 0.0% public transportation, 3.2% walk, 14.3% work from home (2000); Travel time to work: 25.9% less than 15 minutes, 33.3% 15 to 30 minutes, 20.4% 30 to 45 minutes, 13.0% 45 to 60 minutes, 7.4% 60 minutes or more (2000)

SPRING CREEK (township). Covers a land area of 35.967 square miles and a water area of 0.120 square miles. Located at 47.45° N. Lat.; 96.38° W. Long.
Population: 83 (2000); Race: 100.0% White, 0.0% Black, 0.0% Asian, 0.0% American Indian and Alaska Native, 0.0% Hispanic of any race, 0.0% two or more races (2000); Density: 2.3 persons per square mile (2000); Age: 31.4% under 18, 11.8% over 64 (2000); Marriage status: 5.4% never married, 56.8% now married, 5.4% widowed, 32.4% divorced (2000); Foreign born: 0.0% (2000); Ancestry (includes multiple ancestries): 56.9% Norwegian, 49.0% German, 21.6% Czech, 17.6% Dutch, 13.7% Swedish (2000).
Economy: Employment by occupation: 38.5% management, 15.4% professional, 0.0% services, 15.4% sales, 0.0% farming, 15.4% construction, 15.4% production (2000).
Income: Per capita income: $9,214 (2000); Median household income: $12,292 (2000); Poverty rate: 37.3% (2000).
Taxes: Total city taxes per capita: $88 (1997); City property taxes per capita: $88 (1997).
Education: High school graduation rate: 57.1% (2000); College graduation rate: 5.7% (2000).
Housing: Homeownership rate: 77.3% (2000); Median home value: $112,500 (2000); Median age of housing: 60+ years (2000).
Transportation: Commute to work: 36.4% car, 0.0% public transportation, 0.0% walk, 63.6% work from home (2000); Travel time to work: 0.0% less than 15 minutes, 50.0% 15 to 30 minutes, 0.0% 30 to 45 minutes, 0.0% 45 to 60 minutes, 50.0% 60 minutes or more (2000)

STRAND (township). Covers a land area of 35.948 square miles and a water area of 0 square miles. Located at 47.36° N. Lat.; 96.24° W. Long.
Population: 129 (2000); Race: 100.0% White, 0.0% Black, 0.0% Asian, 0.0% American Indian and Alaska Native, 4.8% Hispanic of any race, 0.0% two or more races (2000); Density: 3.6 persons per square mile (2000); Age: 20.2% under 18, 14.4% over 64 (2000); Marriage status: 18.6% never married, 65.1% now married, 7.0% widowed, 9.3% divorced (2000); Foreign born: 4.8% (2000); Ancestry (includes multiple ancestries): 61.5% Norwegian, 46.2% German, 5.8% Swedish, 2.9% Other groups, 1.9% Belgian (2000).

Economy: Employment by occupation: 16.4% management, 14.8% professional, 14.8% services, 13.1% sales, 14.8% farming, 23.0% construction, 3.3% production (2000).
Income: Per capita income: $15,214 (2000); Median household income: $34,583 (2000); Poverty rate: 14.4% (2000).
Taxes: Total city taxes per capita: $70 (1997); City property taxes per capita: $70 (1997).
Education: High school graduation rate: 79.7% (2000); College graduation rate: 16.5% (2000).
Housing: Homeownership rate: 81.8% (2000); Median home value: $36,300 (2000); Median rent: $150 per month (2000); Median age of housing: 60+ years (2000).
Transportation: Commute to work: 78.7% car, 0.0% public transportation, 14.8% walk, 6.6% work from home (2000); Travel time to work: 36.8% less than 15 minutes, 38.6% 15 to 30 minutes, 12.3% 30 to 45 minutes, 8.8% 45 to 60 minutes, 3.5% 60 minutes or more (2000)

SUNDAL (township). Aka Sundahl. Covers a land area of 35.679 square miles and a water area of 0 square miles. Located at 47.47° N. Lat.; 96.26° W. Long.
Population: 145 (2000); Race: 86.7% White, 0.0% Black, 0.0% Asian, 1.2% American Indian and Alaska Native, 0.0% Hispanic of any race, 12.0% two or more races (2000); Density: 4.1 persons per square mile (2000); Age: 37.3% under 18, 12.0% over 64 (2000); Marriage status: 22.3% never married, 73.6% now married, 4.1% widowed, 0.0% divorced (2000); Foreign born: 0.0% (2000); Ancestry (includes multiple ancestries): 68.7% Norwegian, 16.9% German, 13.3% Other groups, 3.0% Swedish, 1.8% United States or American (2000).
Economy: Employment by occupation: 9.5% management, 24.3% professional, 6.8% services, 28.4% sales, 0.0% farming, 12.2% construction, 18.9% production (2000).
Income: Per capita income: $14,578 (2000); Median household income: $48,750 (2000); Poverty rate: 9.6% (2000).
Taxes: Total city taxes per capita: $73 (1997); City property taxes per capita: $73 (1997).
Education: High school graduation rate: 84.2% (2000); College graduation rate: 14.9% (2000).
Housing: Homeownership rate: 96.2% (2000); Median home value: $32,500 (2000); Median age of housing: 60 years (2000).
Transportation: Commute to work: 78.4% car, 0.0% public transportation, 2.7% walk, 18.9% work from home (2000); Travel time to work: 28.3% less than 15 minutes, 30.0% 15 to 30 minutes, 20.0% 30 to 45 minutes, 10.0% 45 to 60 minutes, 11.7% 60 minutes or more (2000)

TWIN VALLEY (city). Covers a land area of 0.876 square miles and a water area of 0 square miles. Located at 47.26° N. Lat.; 96.25° W. Long. Elevation is 1,097 feet.
Population: 865 (2000); Race: 95.5% White, 0.0% Black, 0.2% Asian, 0.3% American Indian and Alaska Native, 0.2% Hispanic of any race, 3.9% two or more races (2000); Density: 987.0 persons per square mile (2000); Age: 21.1% under 18, 37.4% over 64 (2000); Marriage status: 18.3% never married, 55.5% now married, 16.7% widowed, 9.5% divorced (2000); Foreign born: 1.2% (2000); Ancestry (includes multiple ancestries): 64.6% Norwegian, 35.4% German, 6.0% Swedish, 5.2% Other groups, 2.6% Irish (2000).
Economy: Agriculture includes wheat, sunflowers, potatoes, sugar beets, alfalfa. Manufacturing of chemicals, food products. Single-family building permits issued: 2 (2001) / 0 (2000); Multi-family building permits issued: 0 (2001) / 0 (2000); Employment by occupation: 6.0% management, 11.6% professional, 27.7% services, 30.8% sales, 4.7% farming, 10.4% construction, 8.8% production (2000).
Income: Per capita income: $13,865 (2000); Median household income: $23,083 (2000); Poverty rate: 10.9% (2000).
Taxes: Total city taxes per capita: $200 (1997); City property taxes per capita: $167 (1997).
Education: High school graduation rate: 72.7% (2000); College graduation rate: 6.6% (2000).

School District(s)

Norman County East (PK-12)
2000 Enrollment: 410 218-584-5151
Housing: Homeownership rate: 78.6% (2000); Median home value: $30,000 (2000); Median rent: $234 per month (2000); Median age of housing: 48 years (2000).
Newspapers: The Twin Valley Times (1 x week)
Transportation: Commute to work: 85.9% car, 0.0% public transportation, 10.9% walk, 2.2% work from home (2000); Travel time to work: 52.9% less than 15 minutes, 26.8% 15 to 30 minutes, 5.6% 30 to 45 minutes, 2.6% 45 to 60 minutes, 12.1% 60 minutes or more (2000)

WAUKON (township). Covers a land area of 36.177 square miles and a water area of 0 square miles. Located at 47.37° N. Lat.; 96.12° W. Long. Elevation is 1,178 feet.
Population: 147 (2000); Race: 97.4% White, 0.0% Black, 0.0% Asian, 2.6% American Indian and Alaska Native, 0.0% Hispanic of any race, 0.0% two or more races (2000); Density: 4.1 persons per square mile (2000); Age: 19.5% under 18, 23.4% over 64 (2000); Marriage status: 23.8% never married, 64.6% now married, 9.2% widowed, 2.3% divorced (2000); Foreign born: 0.0% (2000); Ancestry (includes multiple ancestries): 66.2% Norwegian, 42.2% German, 13.6% Swedish, 6.5% Dutch, 4.5% Czech (2000).
Economy: Employment by occupation: 13.4% management, 10.4% professional, 26.9% services, 22.4% sales, 4.5% farming, 6.0% construction, 16.4% production (2000).
Income: Per capita income: $17,945 (2000); Median household income: $33,125 (2000); Poverty rate: 9.1% (2000).
Taxes: Total city taxes per capita: $55 (1997); City property taxes per capita: $55 (1997).
Education: High school graduation rate: 82.6% (2000); College graduation rate: 5.0% (2000).
Housing: Homeownership rate: 92.2% (2000); Median home value: $45,000 (2000); Median rent: $458 per month (2000); Median age of housing: 60+ years (2000).
Transportation: Commute to work: 82.1% car, 0.0% public transportation, 3.0% walk, 11.9% work from home (2000); Travel time to work: 22.0% less than 15 minutes, 42.4% 15 to 30 minutes, 8.5% 30 to 45 minutes, 3.4% 45 to 60 minutes, 23.7% 60 minutes or more (2000)

WILD RICE (township). Covers a land area of 35.273 square miles and a water area of 0 square miles. Located at 47.27° N. Lat.; 96.25° W. Long.
Population: 334 (2000); Race: 99.4% White, 0.0% Black, 0.0% Asian, 0.0% American Indian and Alaska Native, 2.4% Hispanic of any race, 0.6% two or more races (2000); Density: 9.5 persons per square mile (2000); Age: 27.5% under 18, 10.9% over 64 (2000); Marriage status: 25.2% never married, 67.3% now married, 3.4% widowed, 4.1% divorced (2000); Foreign born: 0.0% (2000); Ancestry (includes multiple ancestries): 52.3% Norwegian, 28.1% German, 5.1% Swedish, 3.6% Other groups, 3.6% French (except Basque) (2000).
Economy: Employment by occupation: 12.3% management, 13.4% professional, 20.7% services, 22.9% sales, 4.5% farming, 14.0% construction, 12.3% production (2000).
Income: Per capita income: $13,530 (2000); Median household income: $35,625 (2000); Poverty rate: 7.3% (2000).
Taxes: Total city taxes per capita: $31 (1997); City property taxes per capita: $31 (1997).
Education: High school graduation rate: 81.7% (2000); College graduation rate: 8.9% (2000).
Housing: Homeownership rate: 84.7% (2000); Median home value: $50,000 (2000); Median rent: $181 per month (2000); Median age of housing: 35 years (2000).
Transportation: Commute to work: 84.1% car, 1.1% public transportation, 4.5% walk, 8.0% work from home (2000); Travel time to work: 67.9% less than 15 minutes, 22.2% 15 to 30 minutes, 1.9% 30 to 45 minutes, 1.2% 45 to 60 minutes, 6.8% 60 minutes or more (2000)

WINCHESTER (township). Covers a land area of 35.946 square miles and a water area of 0 square miles. Located at 47.19° N. Lat.; 96.49° W. Long.
Population: 74 (2000); Race: 93.7% White, 0.0% Black, 0.0% Asian, 0.0% American Indian and Alaska Native, 6.3% Hispanic of any race, 0.0% two or more races (2000); Density: 2.1 persons per square mile (2000); Age: 9.5% under 18, 15.9% over 64 (2000); Marriage status: 19.3% never married, 61.4% now married, 7.0% widowed, 12.3% divorced (2000); Foreign born: 6.3% (2000); Ancestry (includes multiple ancestries): 49.2% German, 38.1% Norwegian, 6.3% United States or American, 6.3% Other groups, 4.8% Irish (2000).
Economy: Employment by occupation: 24.1% management, 0.0% professional, 20.7% services, 24.1% sales, 17.2% farming, 0.0% construction, 13.8% production (2000).
Income: Per capita income: $9,306 (2000); Median household income: $18,750 (2000); Poverty rate: 27.0% (2000).
Education: High school graduation rate: 84.9% (2000); College graduation rate: 5.7% (2000).

Housing: Homeownership rate: 76.7% (2000); Median home value: $22,500 (2000); Median rent: $400 per month (2000); Median age of housing: 60+ years (2000).
Transportation: Commute to work: 69.0% car, 0.0% public transportation, 0.0% walk, 31.0% work from home (2000); Travel time to work: 30.0% less than 15 minutes, 60.0% 15 to 30 minutes, 10.0% 30 to 45 minutes, 0.0% 45 to 60 minutes, 0.0% 60 minutes or more (2000)

Olmsted County

Located in southeastern Minnesota; drained by the Root River and branches of the Zumbro River. Covers a land area of 653.00 square miles, a water area of 1.50 square miles, and is located in the Central Time Zone. The county government was organized in 1855. County seat is Rochester.

Olmsted County is part of the Rochester, MN MSA. The entire metro area includes: Olmsted County

Weather Station: Rochester Municipal Airport Elevation: 1,295 feet

	Jan	Feb	Mar	Apr	May	Jun	Jul	Aug	Sep	Oct	Nov	Dec
High	20	27	39	55	68	78	81	79	70	58	40	26
Low	3	10	22	35	46	56	60	58	49	37	24	10
Precip	0.9	0.8	1.9	3.1	3.5	3.7	4.6	4.2	3.2	2.3	2.0	1.0
Snow	11.8	7.9	8.9	4.2	tr	tr	tr	tr	tr	0.9	7.1	10.4

High and Low temperatures in degrees Fahrenheit; Precipitation and Snow in inches

Population: 124,277 (2000); Race: 90.3% White, 2.5% Black, 4.3% Asian, 0.3% American Indian and Alaska Native, 2.0% Hispanic of any race, 1.7% two or more races (2000); Density: 190.3 persons per square mile (2000); Age: 27.0% under 18, 10.8% over 64 (2000).
Religion: Five largest groups: 21.9% Catholic Church, 14.4% Evangelical Lutheran Church in America, 5.4% Lutheran Church—Missouri Synod, 4.9% The United Methodist Church, 1.6% United Church of Christ (2000).
Economy: Unemployment rate: 3.1% (11/2002); Total civilian labor force: 79,973 (11/2002); Leading industries: 38.0% health care and social assistance; 14.2% manufacturing; 13.4% retail trade (2000); Companies that employ more than 1,000 persons: 5 (2000); Companies that employ more than 100 persons: 89 (2000); Farms: 1,317 totaling 303,665 acres (1997); Minority business ownership rate: 3.9% (1997); Women business ownership rate: 28.3% (1997); Retail sales per capita: $12,508 (1997). Single-family building permits issued: 1,120 (2001) / 892 (2000); Multi-family building permits issued: 483 (2001) / 660 (2000).
Income: Per capita income: $24,939 (2000); Median household income: $51,316 (2000); Poverty rate: 6.4% (2000); Bankruptcy rate: 1.87% (2001).
Taxes: Total county taxes per capita: $291 (2000); County property taxes per capita: $280 (2000).
Education: High school graduation rate: 91.1% (2000); College graduation rate: 34.7% (2000).
Housing: Homeownership rate: 76.0% (2000); Median home value: $117,000 (2000); Median rent: $515 per month (2000); Median age of housing: 27 years (2000).
Health: Birth rate: 142.6 per 10,000 population (1998); Age adjusted death rate: 73.4 per 10,000 population (1999); Age adjusted cancer mortality rate: 196.9 deaths per 100,000 population (1999). Number of physicians: 195.9 per 10,000 population (1999); Number of hospital beds: 96.2 per 10,000 population (1999).
Elections: 2000 Presidential election results: 43.5% Gore, 51.6% Bush, 3.7% Nader, 0.6% Buchanan
National and State Parks: Gordon W Yeager State Wildlife Management Area; Keller State Wildlife Management Area; Oronoco State Park; Schumann State Wildlife Management Area; Suess State Wildlife Management Area
Additional Information Contacts
Olmsted County Government Offices 507-285-8115
Rochester Chamber of Commerce 507-288-1122
Rochester Convention & Visitors Bureau 507-288-4331
Southeast Minnesota Association of Realtors 507-285-9833
Stewartville Chamber of Commerce 507-533-6006

Olmsted County Communities

BYRON (city). Covers a land area of 1.424 square miles and a water area of 0 square miles. Located at 44.03° N. Lat.; 92.64° W. Long. Elevation is 1,262 feet.
Population: 3,500 (2000); Race: 97.8% White, 0.3% Black, 1.4% Asian, 0.0% American Indian and Alaska Native, 0.6% Hispanic of any race, 0.3% two or more races (2000); Density: 2,457.6 persons per square mile (2000); Age: 35.1% under 18, 5.3% over 64 (2000); Marriage status: 22.8% never married, 68.1% now married, 2.7% widowed, 6.5% divorced (2000); Foreign born: 1.7% (2000); Ancestry (includes multiple ancestries): 45.7% German, 27.5% Norwegian, 13.5% Irish, 7.7% English, 3.8% United States or American (2000).
Economy: Grain, soybeans; livestock, poultry; dairying. Manufacturing: elevators, agricultural machinery; printing. Employment by occupation: 9.5% management, 29.0% professional, 13.6% services, 26.7% sales, 0.2% farming, 9.9% construction, 11.1% production (2000).
Income: Per capita income: $20,297 (2000); Median household income: $58,879 (2000); Poverty rate: 3.6% (2000).
Taxes: Total city taxes per capita: $263 (1997); City property taxes per capita: $258 (1997).
Education: High school graduation rate: 95.6% (2000); College graduation rate: 25.7% (2000).

School District(s)

Byron (PK-12)
2000 Enrollment: 1,458 507-775-2383
Zumbro Ed. Dist. (PK-12)
2000 Enrollment: 72 507-775-2037

Housing: Homeownership rate: 84.9% (2000); Median home value: $114,700 (2000); Median rent: $518 per month (2000); Median age of housing: 18 years (2000).
Newspapers: Byron Review (1 x week)
Transportation: Commute to work: 94.8% car, 1.0% public transportation, 1.3% walk, 2.9% work from home (2000); Travel time to work: 29.8% less than 15 minutes, 61.2% 15 to 30 minutes, 5.1% 30 to 45 minutes, 1.1% 45 to 60 minutes, 2.9% 60 minutes or more (2000)

CASCADE (township). Covers a land area of 17.400 square miles and a water area of 0.051 square miles. Located at 44.05° N. Lat.; 92.51° W. Long.
Population: 3,183 (2000); Race: 91.3% White, 1.3% Black, 6.8% Asian, 0.0% American Indian and Alaska Native, 0.7% Hispanic of any race, 0.4% two or more races (2000); Density: 182.9 persons per square mile (2000); Age: 33.9% under 18, 4.0% over 64 (2000); Marriage status: 19.9% never married, 71.6% now married, 2.1% widowed, 6.4% divorced (2000); Foreign born: 6.6% (2000); Ancestry (includes multiple ancestries): 44.3% German, 18.0% Norwegian, 11.0% Irish, 9.8% English, 9.5% Other groups (2000).
Economy: Single-family building permits issued: 26 (2001) / 11 (2000); Multi-family building permits issued: 0 (2001) / 0 (2000); Employment by occupation: 16.7% management, 39.5% professional, 8.4% services, 21.3% sales, 0.0% farming, 5.7% construction, 8.4% production (2000).
Income: Per capita income: $31,099 (2000); Median household income: $84,619 (2000); Poverty rate: 2.1% (2000).
Taxes: Total city taxes per capita: $97 (2000); City property taxes per capita: $97 (2000).
Education: High school graduation rate: 92.0% (2000); College graduation rate: 50.9% (2000).
Housing: Homeownership rate: 93.5% (2000); Median home value: $213,400 (2000); Median rent: $154 per month (2000); Median age of housing: 17 years (2000).
Transportation: Commute to work: 92.4% car, 0.0% public transportation, 0.0% walk, 7.6% work from home (2000); Travel time to work: 45.6% less than 15 minutes, 46.3% 15 to 30 minutes, 5.5% 30 to 45 minutes, 0.8% 45 to 60 minutes, 1.7% 60 minutes or more (2000)

DOVER (city). Covers a land area of 1.067 square miles and a water area of 0 square miles. Located at 43.97° N. Lat.; 92.13° W. Long.
Population: 438 (2000); Race: 93.0% White, 0.0% Black, 0.4% Asian, 0.0% American Indian and Alaska Native, 5.6% Hispanic of any race, 2.3% two or more races (2000); Density: 410.4 persons per square mile (2000); Age: 34.4% under 18, 8.9% over 64 (2000); Marriage status: 21.4% never married, 58.3% now married, 4.6% widowed, 15.7% divorced (2000); Foreign born: 5.8% (2000); Ancestry (includes multiple ancestries): 52.6% German, 22.2% Norwegian, 10.4% Other groups, 9.1% Irish, 8.3% United States or American (2000).
Economy: Single-family building permits issued: 11 (2001) / 4 (2000); Multi-family building permits issued: 0 (2001) / 0 (2000); Employment by occupation: 3.0% management, 13.8% professional, 16.8% services, 21.6% sales, 1.3% farming, 28.0% construction, 15.5% production (2000).
Income: Per capita income: $15,804 (2000); Median household income: $41,250 (2000); Poverty rate: 3.0% (2000).
Taxes: Total city taxes per capita: $98 (2000); City property taxes per capita: $75 (2000).

Education: High school graduation rate: 83.1% (2000); College graduation rate: 5.3% (2000).
Housing: Homeownership rate: 76.3% (2000); Median home value: $86,800 (2000); Median rent: $414 per month (2000); Median age of housing: 51 years (2000).
Transportation: Commute to work: 96.1% car, 0.0% public transportation, 3.1% walk, 0.9% work from home (2000); Travel time to work: 21.6% less than 15 minutes, 33.9% 15 to 30 minutes, 39.2% 30 to 45 minutes, 2.2% 45 to 60 minutes, 3.1% 60 minutes or more (2000)

DOVER (township). Covers a land area of 34.580 square miles and a water area of 0 square miles. Located at 43.97° N. Lat.; 92.13° W. Long.
Population: 440 (2000); Race: 98.7% White, 0.0% Black, 0.4% Asian, 0.0% American Indian and Alaska Native, 0.0% Hispanic of any race, 0.9% two or more races (2000); Density: 12.7 persons per square mile (2000); Age: 29.7% under 18, 9.3% over 64 (2000); Marriage status: 33.1% never married, 61.1% now married, 2.4% widowed, 3.4% divorced (2000); Foreign born: 1.1% (2000); Ancestry (includes multiple ancestries): 52.8% German, 10.8% United States or American, 9.5% English, 9.1% Norwegian, 8.8% Irish (2000).
Economy: Dairying; poultry, livestock; grain, soybeans. Manufacturing: concrete. Single-family building permits issued: 2 (2001) / 2 (2000); Multi-family building permits issued: 0 (2001) / 0 (2000); Employment by occupation: 18.1% management, 17.8% professional, 12.3% services, 19.9% sales, 5.4% farming, 14.5% construction, 12.0% production (2000).
Income: Per capita income: $22,116 (2000); Median household income: $43,393 (2000); Poverty rate: 6.0% (2000).
Taxes: Total city taxes per capita: $119 (1997); City property taxes per capita: $115 (1997).
Education: High school graduation rate: 88.5% (2000); College graduation rate: 14.9% (2000).
Housing: Homeownership rate: 89.6% (2000); Median home value: $168,800 (2000); Median rent: $488 per month (2000); Median age of housing: 38 years (2000).
Transportation: Commute to work: 75.4% car, 1.8% public transportation, 2.2% walk, 20.7% work from home (2000); Travel time to work: 29.2% less than 15 minutes, 37.4% 15 to 30 minutes, 24.2% 30 to 45 minutes, 5.5% 45 to 60 minutes, 3.7% 60 minutes or more (2000)

ELMIRA (township). Covers a land area of 35.002 square miles and a water area of 0 square miles. Located at 43.88° N. Lat.; 92.15° W. Long.
Population: 352 (2000); Race: 99.4% White, 0.0% Black, 0.0% Asian, 0.0% American Indian and Alaska Native, 0.0% Hispanic of any race, 0.6% two or more races (2000); Density: 10.1 persons per square mile (2000); Age: 28.1% under 18, 14.6% over 64 (2000); Marriage status: 27.0% never married, 64.2% now married, 3.9% widowed, 4.9% divorced (2000); Foreign born: 0.6% (2000); Ancestry (includes multiple ancestries): 47.2% German, 25.6% Irish, 22.8% Norwegian, 9.3% French (except Basque), 8.7% English (2000).
Economy: Single-family building permits issued: 2 (2001) / 3 (2000); Multi-family building permits issued: 0 (2001) / 0 (2000); Employment by occupation: 22.8% management, 8.7% professional, 15.0% services, 22.3% sales, 7.3% farming, 10.2% construction, 13.6% production (2000).
Income: Per capita income: $23,243 (2000); Median household income: $65,156 (2000); Poverty rate: 1.7% (2000).
Taxes: Total city taxes per capita: $136 (1997); City property taxes per capita: $136 (1997).
Education: High school graduation rate: 85.8% (2000); College graduation rate: 19.5% (2000).
Housing: Homeownership rate: 80.7% (2000); Median home value: $155,600 (2000); Median rent: $1,175 per month (2000); Median age of housing: 50 years (2000).
Transportation: Commute to work: 72.9% car, 3.0% public transportation, 5.0% walk, 17.6% work from home (2000); Travel time to work: 31.7% less than 15 minutes, 14.6% 15 to 30 minutes, 42.1% 30 to 45 minutes, 6.7% 45 to 60 minutes, 4.9% 60 minutes or more (2000)

EYOTA (city). Covers a land area of 1.553 square miles and a water area of 0 square miles. Located at 43.98° N. Lat.; 92.23° W. Long. Elevation is 1,241 feet.
Population: 1,644 (2000); Race: 97.9% White, 0.2% Black, 0.8% Asian, 0.1% American Indian and Alaska Native, 0.2% Hispanic of any race, 0.8% two or more races (2000); Density: 1,058.4 persons per square mile (2000); Age: 32.1% under 18, 9.0% over 64 (2000); Marriage status: 23.8% never married, 62.4% now married, 3.6% widowed, 10.1% divorced (2000); Foreign born: 0.9% (2000); Ancestry (includes multiple ancestries): 49.1% German, 20.5% Norwegian, 17.0% Irish, 8.3% English, 5.5% Polish (2000).
Economy: Employment by occupation: 7.7% management, 25.8% professional, 12.8% services, 25.4% sales, 0.8% farming, 12.2% construction, 15.3% production (2000).
Income: Per capita income: $18,471 (2000); Median household income: $47,500 (2000); Poverty rate: 3.2% (2000).
Taxes: Total city taxes per capita: $83 (1997); City property taxes per capita: $78 (1997).
Education: High school graduation rate: 90.6% (2000); College graduation rate: 16.0% (2000).

School District(s)

Dover-Eyota (PK-12)
2000 Enrollment: 1,065 507-545-2125

Housing: Homeownership rate: 82.9% (2000); Median home value: $95,600 (2000); Median rent: $405 per month (2000); Median age of housing: 26 years (2000).
Transportation: Commute to work: 92.6% car, 1.1% public transportation, 3.2% walk, 2.6% work from home (2000); Travel time to work: 16.2% less than 15 minutes, 60.6% 15 to 30 minutes, 17.8% 30 to 45 minutes, 2.2% 45 to 60 minutes, 3.1% 60 minutes or more (2000)

EYOTA (township). Covers a land area of 34.180 square miles and a water area of 0 square miles. Located at 43.97° N. Lat.; 92.26° W. Long. Elevation is 1,241 feet.
Population: 448 (2000); Race: 98.0% White, 0.0% Black, 0.5% Asian, 0.5% American Indian and Alaska Native, 1.8% Hispanic of any race, 1.0% two or more races (2000); Density: 13.1 persons per square mile (2000); Age: 22.4% under 18, 14.8% over 64 (2000); Marriage status: 25.7% never married, 65.4% now married, 4.5% widowed, 4.5% divorced (2000); Foreign born: 1.8% (2000); Ancestry (includes multiple ancestries): 41.8% German, 17.9% Norwegian, 9.9% United States or American, 9.7% Irish, 7.7% Other groups (2000).
Economy: Railroad junction to West. Poultry, livestock; grain, soybeans; dairying. Manufacturing: feeds. Part of Richard J. Dorer Memorial Hardwood State Forest to South. Employment by occupation: 16.0% management, 13.9% professional, 16.4% services, 22.3% sales, 3.4% farming, 15.1% construction, 13.0% production (2000).
Income: Per capita income: $22,016 (2000); Median household income: $48,750 (2000); Poverty rate: 0.8% (2000).
Taxes: Total city taxes per capita: $127 (1997); City property taxes per capita: $127 (1997).
Education: High school graduation rate: 88.7% (2000); College graduation rate: 21.5% (2000).
Housing: Homeownership rate: 77.6% (2000); Median home value: $128,600 (2000); Median rent: $413 per month (2000); Median age of housing: 50 years (2000).
Transportation: Commute to work: 85.8% car, 1.7% public transportation, 4.7% walk, 7.7% work from home (2000); Travel time to work: 21.4% less than 15 minutes, 55.3% 15 to 30 minutes, 18.6% 30 to 45 minutes, 1.9% 45 to 60 minutes, 2.8% 60 minutes or more (2000)

FARMINGTON (township). Covers a land area of 35.787 square miles and a water area of 0 square miles. Located at 44.15° N. Lat.; 92.37° W. Long.
Population: 516 (2000); Race: 98.4% White, 0.0% Black, 0.6% Asian, 0.0% American Indian and Alaska Native, 0.0% Hispanic of any race, 1.0% two or more races (2000); Density: 14.4 persons per square mile (2000); Age: 28.3% under 18, 14.5% over 64 (2000); Marriage status: 22.6% never married, 67.1% now married, 6.2% widowed, 4.1% divorced (2000); Foreign born: 0.4% (2000); Ancestry (includes multiple ancestries): 63.9% German, 12.9% Norwegian, 6.6% Irish, 6.0% English, 3.8% United States or American (2000).
Economy: Single-family building permits issued: 1 (2001) / 2 (2000); Multi-family building permits issued: 0 (2001) / 0 (2000); Employment by occupation: 24.1% management, 19.2% professional, 10.5% services, 19.9% sales, 2.1% farming, 7.0% construction, 17.1% production (2000).
Income: Per capita income: $22,618 (2000); Median household income: $52,750 (2000); Poverty rate: 5.0% (2000).
Taxes: Total city taxes per capita: $89 (1997); City property taxes per capita: $87 (1997).
Education: High school graduation rate: 86.2% (2000); College graduation rate: 15.3% (2000).
Housing: Homeownership rate: 81.4% (2000); Median home value: $106,300 (2000); Median rent: $725 per month (2000); Median age of housing: 40 years (2000).
Transportation: Commute to work: 75.5% car, 1.4% public transportation, 6.0% walk, 17.0% work from home (2000); Travel time to work: 23.1% less

than 15 minutes, 55.6% 15 to 30 minutes, 15.4% 30 to 45 minutes, 0.9% 45 to 60 minutes, 5.1% 60 minutes or more (2000)

HAVERHILL (township). Covers a land area of 33.263 square miles and a water area of 0 square miles. Located at 44.06° N. Lat.; 92.40° W. Long.
Population: 1,601 (2000); Race: 95.1% White, 1.4% Black, 1.0% Asian, 0.0% American Indian and Alaska Native, 0.7% Hispanic of any race, 2.1% two or more races (2000); Density: 48.1 persons per square mile (2000); Age: 26.7% under 18, 10.6% over 64 (2000); Marriage status: 19.9% never married, 76.1% now married, 1.9% widowed, 2.1% divorced (2000); Foreign born: 1.5% (2000); Ancestry (includes multiple ancestries): 41.6% German, 16.3% Irish, 15.2% Norwegian, 12.5% English, 7.9% Swedish (2000).
Economy: Single-family building permits issued: 1 (2001) / 6 (2000); Multi-family building permits issued: 0 (2001) / 0 (2000); Employment by occupation: 13.5% management, 37.2% professional, 11.0% services, 20.9% sales, 0.5% farming, 8.9% construction, 8.0% production (2000).
Income: Per capita income: $34,804 (2000); Median household income: $75,343 (2000); Poverty rate: 2.8% (2000).
Taxes: Total city taxes per capita: $58 (1997); City property taxes per capita: $58 (1997).
Education: High school graduation rate: 94.3% (2000); College graduation rate: 44.2% (2000).
Housing: Homeownership rate: 91.8% (2000); Median home value: $211,300 (2000); Median rent: $432 per month (2000); Median age of housing: 25 years (2000).
Transportation: Commute to work: 92.6% car, 0.8% public transportation, 0.6% walk, 5.5% work from home (2000); Travel time to work: 28.6% less than 15 minutes, 64.3% 15 to 30 minutes, 3.2% 30 to 45 minutes, 0.0% 45 to 60 minutes, 4.0% 60 minutes or more (2000)

HIGH FOREST (township). Covers a land area of 41.356 square miles and a water area of 0.076 square miles. Located at 43.86° N. Lat.; 92.53° W. Long.
Population: 1,085 (2000); Race: 99.5% White, 0.0% Black, 0.2% Asian, 0.0% American Indian and Alaska Native, 1.4% Hispanic of any race, 0.3% two or more races (2000); Density: 26.2 persons per square mile (2000); Age: 29.6% under 18, 9.5% over 64 (2000); Marriage status: 22.5% never married, 71.3% now married, 1.9% widowed, 4.4% divorced (2000); Foreign born: 1.1% (2000); Ancestry (includes multiple ancestries): 43.3% German, 20.2% Norwegian, 12.8% Irish, 7.8% English, 5.0% United States or American (2000).
Economy: Single-family building permits issued: 4 (2001) / 3 (2000); Multi-family building permits issued: 0 (2001) / 0 (2000); Employment by occupation: 13.4% management, 25.8% professional, 12.6% services, 25.2% sales, 1.2% farming, 13.6% construction, 8.2% production (2000).
Income: Per capita income: $22,524 (2000); Median household income: $56,818 (2000); Poverty rate: 5.2% (2000).
Taxes: Total city taxes per capita: $87 (1997); City property taxes per capita: $76 (1997).
Education: High school graduation rate: 92.5% (2000); College graduation rate: 19.9% (2000).
Housing: Homeownership rate: 89.4% (2000); Median home value: $153,900 (2000); Median rent: $500 per month (2000); Median age of housing: 35 years (2000).
Transportation: Commute to work: 90.2% car, 0.7% public transportation, 2.7% walk, 6.1% work from home (2000); Travel time to work: 23.7% less than 15 minutes, 54.8% 15 to 30 minutes, 17.7% 30 to 45 minutes, 0.2% 45 to 60 minutes, 3.6% 60 minutes or more (2000)

KALMAR (township). Covers a land area of 34.081 square miles and a water area of 0 square miles. Located at 44.06° N. Lat.; 92.62° W. Long.
Population: 1,196 (2000); Race: 98.0% White, 0.0% Black, 0.4% Asian, 0.0% American Indian and Alaska Native, 0.2% Hispanic of any race, 1.5% two or more races (2000); Density: 35.1 persons per square mile (2000); Age: 26.8% under 18, 6.7% over 64 (2000); Marriage status: 22.9% never married, 70.1% now married, 1.9% widowed, 5.1% divorced (2000); Foreign born: 0.7% (2000); Ancestry (includes multiple ancestries): 41.3% German, 25.4% Norwegian, 11.1% Irish, 9.8% English, 4.2% Swedish (2000).
Economy: Single-family building permits issued: 7 (2001) / 5 (2000); Multi-family building permits issued: 0 (2001) / 0 (2000); Employment by occupation: 15.0% management, 27.4% professional, 10.3% services, 24.9% sales, 1.4% farming, 8.1% construction, 13.0% production (2000).
Income: Per capita income: $24,860 (2000); Median household income: $64,792 (2000); Poverty rate: 4.5% (2000).
Taxes: Total city taxes per capita: $93 (2000); City property taxes per capita: $93 (2000).
Education: High school graduation rate: 92.1% (2000); College graduation rate: 24.0% (2000).
Housing: Homeownership rate: 88.8% (2000); Median home value: $145,500 (2000); Median rent: $534 per month (2000); Median age of housing: 30 years (2000).
Transportation: Commute to work: 92.6% car, 0.0% public transportation, 1.4% walk, 5.7% work from home (2000); Travel time to work: 34.3% less than 15 minutes, 57.7% 15 to 30 minutes, 4.9% 30 to 45 minutes, 0.6% 45 to 60 minutes, 2.6% 60 minutes or more (2000)

MARION (township). Covers a land area of 33.614 square miles and a water area of 0 square miles. Located at 43.97° N. Lat.; 92.38° W. Long.
Population: 6,159 (2000); Race: 93.4% White, 3.3% Black, 1.1% Asian, 0.2% American Indian and Alaska Native, 0.9% Hispanic of any race, 1.6% two or more races (2000); Density: 183.2 persons per square mile (2000); Age: 28.1% under 18, 6.5% over 64 (2000); Marriage status: 25.5% never married, 66.0% now married, 2.4% widowed, 6.1% divorced (2000); Foreign born: 5.4% (2000); Ancestry (includes multiple ancestries): 52.0% German, 17.4% Norwegian, 14.3% Irish, 5.5% English, 4.0% Other groups (2000).
Economy: Employment by occupation: 9.5% management, 24.3% professional, 16.6% services, 21.1% sales, 0.6% farming, 13.0% construction, 14.8% production (2000).
Income: Per capita income: $25,441 (2000); Median household income: $61,470 (2000); Poverty rate: 1.5% (2000).
Taxes: Total city taxes per capita: $59 (2000); City property taxes per capita: $59 (2000).
Education: High school graduation rate: 92.4% (2000); College graduation rate: 19.3% (2000).
Housing: Homeownership rate: 91.6% (2000); Median home value: $121,100 (2000); Median rent: $558 per month (2000); Median age of housing: 30 years (2000).
Transportation: Commute to work: 94.3% car, 1.1% public transportation, 0.5% walk, 3.8% work from home (2000); Travel time to work: 32.8% less than 15 minutes, 56.4% 15 to 30 minutes, 6.7% 30 to 45 minutes, 1.0% 45 to 60 minutes, 3.1% 60 minutes or more (2000)

NEW HAVEN (township). Covers a land area of 35.754 square miles and a water area of 0.023 square miles. Located at 44.13° N. Lat.; 92.61° W. Long.
Population: 1,205 (2000); Race: 99.1% White, 0.0% Black, 0.0% Asian, 0.2% American Indian and Alaska Native, 0.4% Hispanic of any race, 0.6% two or more races (2000); Density: 33.7 persons per square mile (2000); Age: 25.1% under 18, 14.0% over 64 (2000); Marriage status: 18.5% never married, 71.6% now married, 4.1% widowed, 5.8% divorced (2000); Foreign born: 0.6% (2000); Ancestry (includes multiple ancestries): 48.8% German, 17.5% Norwegian, 11.2% Irish, 10.6% English, 6.6% United States or American (2000).
Economy: Single-family building permits issued: 5 (2001) / 12 (2000); Multi-family building permits issued: 0 (2001) / 0 (2000); Employment by occupation: 11.8% management, 25.5% professional, 13.0% services, 23.7% sales, 0.9% farming, 13.0% construction, 12.1% production (2000).
Income: Per capita income: $23,518 (2000); Median household income: $58,583 (2000); Poverty rate: 2.3% (2000).
Taxes: Total city taxes per capita: $54 (1997); City property taxes per capita: $54 (1997).
Education: High school graduation rate: 88.7% (2000); College graduation rate: 20.9% (2000).
Housing: Homeownership rate: 94.8% (2000); Median home value: $123,800 (2000); Median rent: $425 per month (2000); Median age of housing: 31 years (2000).
Transportation: Commute to work: 90.6% car, 1.3% public transportation, 1.0% walk, 6.7% work from home (2000); Travel time to work: 19.5% less than 15 minutes, 56.6% 15 to 30 minutes, 13.3% 30 to 45 minutes, 3.5% 45 to 60 minutes, 7.1% 60 minutes or more (2000)

ORION (township). Covers a land area of 35.693 square miles and a water area of 0 square miles. Located at 43.89° N. Lat.; 92.24° W. Long.
Population: 614 (2000); Race: 98.5% White, 1.0% Black, 0.0% Asian, 0.0% American Indian and Alaska Native, 0.5% Hispanic of any race, 0.5% two or more races (2000); Density: 17.2 persons per square mile (2000); Age: 26.9% under 18, 13.2% over 64 (2000); Marriage status: 13.8% never married, 73.3% now married, 4.6% widowed, 8.3% divorced (2000); Foreign born: 1.0% (2000); Ancestry (includes multiple ancestries): 47.1% German, 17.7% Norwegian, 10.3% Irish, 6.1% English, 5.2% United States or American (2000).

Economy: Single-family building permits issued: 4 (2001) / 3 (2000); Multi-family building permits issued: 0 (2001) / 0 (2000); Employment by occupation: 18.8% management, 20.0% professional, 15.0% services, 22.2% sales, 1.6% farming, 15.6% construction, 6.9% production (2000).
Income: Per capita income: $24,533 (2000); Median household income: $52,321 (2000); Poverty rate: 4.3% (2000).
Taxes: Total city taxes per capita: $64 (1997); City property taxes per capita: $64 (1997).
Education: High school graduation rate: 90.0% (2000); College graduation rate: 16.5% (2000).
Housing: Homeownership rate: 83.1% (2000); Median home value: $119,800 (2000); Median rent: $378 per month (2000); Median age of housing: 32 years (2000).
Transportation: Commute to work: 82.9% car, 0.9% public transportation, 0.9% walk, 11.7% work from home (2000); Travel time to work: 19.4% less than 15 minutes, 50.2% 15 to 30 minutes, 26.5% 30 to 45 minutes, 1.4% 45 to 60 minutes, 2.5% 60 minutes or more (2000)

ORONOCO (city). Covers a land area of 1.829 square miles and a water area of 0.307 square miles. Located at 44.16° N. Lat.; 92.54° W. Long. Elevation is 1,041 feet.
Population: 883 (2000); Race: 96.8% White, 0.0% Black, 1.8% Asian, 0.0% American Indian and Alaska Native, 1.3% Hispanic of any race, 1.4% two or more races (2000); Density: 482.8 persons per square mile (2000); Age: 27.8% under 18, 6.3% over 64 (2000); Marriage status: 24.2% never married, 64.5% now married, 3.6% widowed, 7.7% divorced (2000); Foreign born: 2.6% (2000); Ancestry (includes multiple ancestries): 44.6% German, 17.5% Norwegian, 12.0% Irish, 11.2% English, 5.8% United States or American (2000).
Economy: Employment by occupation: 10.5% management, 30.5% professional, 14.9% services, 21.7% sales, 0.0% farming, 10.9% construction, 11.6% production (2000).
Income: Per capita income: $27,965 (2000); Median household income: $67,656 (2000); Poverty rate: 2.1% (2000).
Taxes: Total city taxes per capita: $47 (1997); City property taxes per capita: $47 (1997).
Education: High school graduation rate: 93.3% (2000); College graduation rate: 31.7% (2000).
Housing: Homeownership rate: 92.7% (2000); Median home value: $138,600 (2000); Median rent: $575 per month (2000); Median age of housing: 26 years (2000).
Transportation: Commute to work: 91.6% car, 0.0% public transportation, 3.3% walk, 4.7% work from home (2000); Travel time to work: 25.3% less than 15 minutes, 60.2% 15 to 30 minutes, 7.3% 30 to 45 minutes, 3.7% 45 to 60 minutes, 3.5% 60 minutes or more (2000)

ORONOCO (township). Covers a land area of 32.606 square miles and a water area of 0.829 square miles. Located at 44.15° N. Lat.; 92.51° W. Long. Elevation is 1,041 feet.
Population: 2,239 (2000); Race: 95.4% White, 0.9% Black, 1.7% Asian, 0.0% American Indian and Alaska Native, 0.0% Hispanic of any race, 1.5% two or more races (2000); Density: 68.7 persons per square mile (2000); Age: 29.4% under 18, 8.1% over 64 (2000); Marriage status: 21.5% never married, 62.8% now married, 3.8% widowed, 11.9% divorced (2000); Foreign born: 2.8% (2000); Ancestry (includes multiple ancestries): 44.5% German, 17.8% Norwegian, 14.1% Irish, 7.0% English, 4.8% French (except Basque) (2000).
Economy: In agricultural area: grain, soybeans; livestock, poultry; dairying. Manufacturing of signs. Employment by occupation: 11.3% management, 28.3% professional, 14.5% services, 24.7% sales, 1.0% farming, 9.4% construction, 10.7% production (2000).
Income: Per capita income: $27,482 (2000); Median household income: $50,950 (2000); Poverty rate: 6.3% (2000).
Taxes: Total city taxes per capita: $48 (1997); City property taxes per capita: $48 (1997).
Education: High school graduation rate: 92.1% (2000); College graduation rate: 30.3% (2000).
Housing: Homeownership rate: 91.8% (2000); Median home value: $175,800 (2000); Median rent: $414 per month (2000); Median age of housing: 23 years (2000).
Transportation: Commute to work: 94.4% car, 0.5% public transportation, 0.8% walk, 4.4% work from home (2000); Travel time to work: 19.6% less than 15 minutes, 70.0% 15 to 30 minutes, 6.9% 30 to 45 minutes, 0.7% 45 to 60 minutes, 2.7% 60 minutes or more (2000)

PLEASANT GROVE (township). Covers a land area of 35.740 square miles and a water area of 0 square miles. Located at 43.89° N. Lat.; 92.37° W. Long.
Population: 787 (2000); Race: 98.4% White, 0.0% Black, 1.0% Asian, 0.0% American Indian and Alaska Native, 1.5% Hispanic of any race, 0.5% two or more races (2000); Density: 22.0 persons per square mile (2000); Age: 23.9% under 18, 13.6% over 64 (2000); Marriage status: 17.6% never married, 66.3% now married, 4.3% widowed, 11.7% divorced (2000); Foreign born: 2.0% (2000); Ancestry (includes multiple ancestries): 39.4% German, 26.2% Irish, 23.5% Norwegian, 11.6% English, 6.8% United States or American (2000).
Economy: Single-family building permits issued: 5 (2001) / 1 (2000); Multi-family building permits issued: 0 (2001) / 0 (2000); Employment by occupation: 9.8% management, 26.0% professional, 17.7% services, 17.0% sales, 0.9% farming, 15.1% construction, 13.5% production (2000).
Income: Per capita income: $24,822 (2000); Median household income: $52,054 (2000); Poverty rate: 2.7% (2000).
Taxes: Total city taxes per capita: $48 (1997); City property taxes per capita: $48 (1997).
Education: High school graduation rate: 90.5% (2000); College graduation rate: 26.3% (2000).
Housing: Homeownership rate: 86.5% (2000); Median home value: $115,500 (2000); Median rent: $363 per month (2000); Median age of housing: 29 years (2000).
Transportation: Commute to work: 90.9% car, 0.4% public transportation, 2.9% walk, 5.8% work from home (2000); Travel time to work: 10.6% less than 15 minutes, 72.2% 15 to 30 minutes, 9.2% 30 to 45 minutes, 2.6% 45 to 60 minutes, 5.4% 60 minutes or more (2000)

QUINCY (township). Covers a land area of 35.656 square miles and a water area of 0 square miles. Located at 44.07° N. Lat.; 92.14° W. Long.
Population: 356 (2000); Race: 94.3% White, 0.0% Black, 2.3% Asian, 0.0% American Indian and Alaska Native, 1.4% Hispanic of any race, 2.0% two or more races (2000); Density: 10.0 persons per square mile (2000); Age: 27.6% under 18, 11.1% over 64 (2000); Marriage status: 31.5% never married, 57.3% now married, 3.9% widowed, 7.2% divorced (2000); Foreign born: 2.3% (2000); Ancestry (includes multiple ancestries): 45.7% German, 24.1% Irish, 16.5% Norwegian, 12.8% English, 6.0% Other groups (2000).
Economy: Employment by occupation: 18.0% management, 19.6% professional, 9.5% services, 24.3% sales, 2.6% farming, 12.7% construction, 13.2% production (2000).
Income: Per capita income: $19,492 (2000); Median household income: $45,000 (2000); Poverty rate: 3.7% (2000).
Taxes: Total city taxes per capita: $61 (1997); City property taxes per capita: $61 (1997).
Education: High school graduation rate: 85.4% (2000); College graduation rate: 21.5% (2000).
Housing: Homeownership rate: 77.0% (2000); Median home value: $137,500 (2000); Median rent: $263 per month (2000); Median age of housing: 51 years (2000).
Transportation: Commute to work: 82.5% car, 1.1% public transportation, 4.2% walk, 12.2% work from home (2000); Travel time to work: 24.7% less than 15 minutes, 33.1% 15 to 30 minutes, 32.5% 30 to 45 minutes, 1.8% 45 to 60 minutes, 7.8% 60 minutes or more (2000)

ROCHESTER (city). Covers a land area of 39.609 square miles and a water area of 0.137 square miles. Located at 44.02° N. Lat.; 92.47° W. Long. Elevation is 988 feet.
History: Rochester was founded in 1854 by George Head, who named it for his former home of Rochester, New York. The site was a crossroads campground where immigrant wagon trains passed. In 1863, Dr. William Worrall Mayo, an English chemist who received his medical degree in Indiana, moved to Rochester. His two sons, William James and Charles Horace, followed him in the medical profession. When the Sisters of the Convent of St. Francis wanted to build a hospital in Rochester in 1889, they asked Dr. Mayo and his sons to direct it, and thus the chain of hospitals that became known as the Mayo Clinic began. In 1915 the Doctors Mayo affiliated with the University of Minnesota and established the Mayo Foundation.
Population: 85,806 (2000); Race: 87.6% White, 3.2% Black, 5.6% Asian, 0.4% American Indian and Alaska Native, 2.6% Hispanic of any race, 2.0% two or more races (2000); Density: 2,166.3 persons per square mile (2000); Age: 25.9% under 18, 11.4% over 64 (2000); Marriage status: 27.6% never married, 58.8% now married, 5.1% widowed, 8.5% divorced (2000); Foreign

born: 10.1% (2000); Ancestry (includes multiple ancestries): 35.8% German, 17.3% Norwegian, 11.8% Other groups, 11.8% Irish, 8.3% English (2000).
Vital Statistics: Birth rate: 162.3 per 10,000 population (1998)
Economy: Unemployment rate: 3.4% (11/2002); Total civilian labor force: 54,489 (11/2002); Single-family building permits issued: 787 (2001) / 590 (2000); Multi-family building permits issued: 391 (2001) / 660 (2000); Employment by occupation: 9.8% management, 37.0% professional, 14.4% services, 23.1% sales, 0.1% farming, 6.1% construction, 9.5% production (2000).
Income: Per capita income: $24,811 (2000); Median household income: $49,090 (2000); Poverty rate: 7.8% (2000).
Taxes: Total city taxes per capita: $369 (2000); City property taxes per capita: $227 (2000).
Education: High school graduation rate: 91.0% (2000); College graduation rate: 38.1% (2000).

School District(s)

Rochester (PK-12)
2000 Enrollment: 15,929 507-285-8551
Rochester Off-Campus Charter High (09-12)
2000 Enrollment: 89 507-282-3325
Studio Academy Charter School (10-12)
2000 Enrollment: 99 507-529-1662

Four-year College(s)

Mayo Medical School (Private, Not-for-profit)
2001 Enrollment: 165 507-284-3671
Mayo School of Health Related Sciences (Private, Not-for-profit)
2001 Enrollment: n/a 507-284-3678
Minnesota Bible College (Private, Not-for-profit, Christian Churches and Churches of Christ)
2001 Enrollment: 109 507-288-4563
2001 Tuition: In-state $6,450; Out-of-state $6,450
Mayo Graduate School (Private, Not-for-profit)
2001 Enrollment: 255 507-284-4076

Two-year College(s)

Rochester Community and Technical College (Public)
2001 Enrollment: 5,057 507-285-7210
2001 Tuition: In-state $1,888; Out-of-state $3,775

Housing: Homeownership rate: 70.9% (2000); Median home value: $114,400 (2000); Median rent: $524 per month (2000); Median age of housing: 27 years (2000).
Hospitals: Mayo Clinic (1,951 beds); Olmsted Medical Center Hospital (61 beds); Rochester Methodist Hospital (794 beds)
Safety: Violent crime rate: 29.3 per 10,000 population; Property crime rate: 371.0 per 10,000 population (2001).
Newspapers: Post-Bulletin (6 x week); Rochester Shopper (1 x week)
Transportation: Commute to work: 86.9% car, 4.2% public transportation, 4.7% walk, 3.1% work from home (2000); Travel time to work: 61.1% less than 15 minutes, 31.0% 15 to 30 minutes, 3.9% 30 to 45 minutes, 1.5% 45 to 60 minutes, 2.5% 60 minutes or more (2000)
Airports: Rochester International (primary service)

Additional Information Contacts

Rochester Chamber of Commerce 507-288-1122
Rochester Convention & Visitors Bureau 507-288-4331
Southeast Minnesota Association of Realtors 507-285-9833

ROCHESTER (township). Covers a land area of 22.313 square miles and a water area of 0.024 square miles. Located at 43.98° N. Lat.; 92.49° W. Long. Elevation is 988 feet.
History: Famous as the home of the Mayo Clinic, a combination of hospitals and hotels, founded (1889) by Dr. W.W. Mayo with his sons Charles Horace Mayo and William James Mayo. Incorporated 1858.
Population: 2,916 (2000); Race: 96.7% White, 0.4% Black, 1.4% Asian, 0.2% American Indian and Alaska Native, 1.7% Hispanic of any race, 1.3% two or more races (2000); Density: 130.7 persons per square mile (2000); Age: 28.7% under 18, 13.8% over 64 (2000); Marriage status: 11.9% never married, 80.5% now married, 3.0% widowed, 4.5% divorced (2000); Foreign born: 5.9% (2000); Ancestry (includes multiple ancestries): 32.4% German, 21.8% Norwegian, 16.3% Irish, 11.5% English, 5.0% Other groups (2000).
Economy: Railroad junction. It is a farm trade center. Manufacturing includes printing and publishing, food products, machinery, fabricated metal products, computers, construction materials and electronic equipment. Single-family building permits issued: 25 (2001) / 31 (2000); Multi-family building permits issued: 0 (2001) / 0 (2000); Employment by occupation: 15.2% management, 37.6% professional, 11.1% services, 26.3% sales, 0.0% farming, 4.9% construction, 5.0% production (2000).
Income: Per capita income: $39,377 (2000); Median household income: $81,789 (2000); Poverty rate: 0.9% (2000).
Taxes: Total city taxes per capita: $131 (2000); City property taxes per capita: $131 (2000).
Education: High school graduation rate: 95.6% (2000); College graduation rate: 53.9% (2000).
Housing: Homeownership rate: 98.4% (2000); Median home value: $149,300 (2000); Median rent: $443 per month (2000); Median age of housing: 31 years (2000).
Transportation: Commute to work: 95.1% car, 1.1% public transportation, 0.1% walk, 3.7% work from home (2000); Travel time to work: 53.1% less than 15 minutes, 44.7% 15 to 30 minutes, 1.1% 30 to 45 minutes, 0.3% 45 to 60 minutes, 0.8% 60 minutes or more (2000)

ROCK DELL (township). Covers a land area of 36.019 square miles and a water area of 0 square miles. Located at 43.89° N. Lat.; 92.61° W. Long.
Population: 627 (2000); Race: 99.4% White, 0.0% Black, 0.3% Asian, 0.3% American Indian and Alaska Native, 0.0% Hispanic of any race, 0.0% two or more races (2000); Density: 17.4 persons per square mile (2000); Age: 25.5% under 18, 9.0% over 64 (2000); Marriage status: 22.1% never married, 71.3% now married, 2.2% widowed, 4.3% divorced (2000); Foreign born: 0.3% (2000); Ancestry (includes multiple ancestries): 47.0% German, 35.7% Norwegian, 11.1% Irish, 7.9% English, 5.3% Dutch (2000).
Economy: Single-family building permits issued: 7 (2001) / 1 (2000); Multi-family building permits issued: 0 (2001) / 0 (2000); Employment by occupation: 14.9% management, 19.1% professional, 14.1% services, 24.5% sales, 2.3% farming, 10.4% construction, 14.6% production (2000).
Income: Per capita income: $24,343 (2000); Median household income: $55,313 (2000); Poverty rate: 5.9% (2000).
Taxes: Total city taxes per capita: $69 (1997); City property taxes per capita: $66 (1997).
Education: High school graduation rate: 89.3% (2000); College graduation rate: 18.7% (2000).
Housing: Homeownership rate: 84.8% (2000); Median home value: $138,400 (2000); Median rent: $338 per month (2000); Median age of housing: 53 years (2000).
Transportation: Commute to work: 90.5% car, 0.0% public transportation, 1.6% walk, 6.8% work from home (2000); Travel time to work: 8.7% less than 15 minutes, 60.3% 15 to 30 minutes, 20.3% 30 to 45 minutes, 4.3% 45 to 60 minutes, 6.4% 60 minutes or more (2000)

SALEM (township). Covers a land area of 35.724 square miles and a water area of 0.002 square miles. Located at 43.97° N. Lat.; 92.61° W. Long.
Population: 1,061 (2000); Race: 98.6% White, 0.0% Black, 0.3% Asian, 0.0% American Indian and Alaska Native, 0.0% Hispanic of any race, 0.8% two or more races (2000); Density: 29.7 persons per square mile (2000); Age: 24.6% under 18, 10.7% over 64 (2000); Marriage status: 22.8% never married, 66.3% now married, 5.1% widowed, 5.8% divorced (2000); Foreign born: 1.0% (2000); Ancestry (includes multiple ancestries): 40.8% German, 30.1% Norwegian, 10.9% Irish, 7.6% English, 4.1% Danish (2000).
Economy: Single-family building permits issued: 10 (2001) / 4 (2000); Multi-family building permits issued: 0 (2001) / 0 (2000); Employment by occupation: 12.7% management, 24.7% professional, 11.9% services, 26.2% sales, 1.0% farming, 11.9% construction, 11.7% production (2000).
Income: Per capita income: $28,340 (2000); Median household income: $54,107 (2000); Poverty rate: 2.7% (2000).
Taxes: Total city taxes per capita: $60 (1997); City property taxes per capita: $60 (1997).
Education: High school graduation rate: 88.7% (2000); College graduation rate: 20.0% (2000).
Housing: Homeownership rate: 89.3% (2000); Median home value: $135,000 (2000); Median rent: $425 per month (2000); Median age of housing: 35 years (2000).
Transportation: Commute to work: 89.4% car, 0.0% public transportation, 3.1% walk, 7.5% work from home (2000); Travel time to work: 27.6% less than 15 minutes, 61.9% 15 to 30 minutes, 6.8% 30 to 45 minutes, 1.8% 45 to 60 minutes, 1.8% 60 minutes or more (2000)

STEWARTVILLE (city). Covers a land area of 2.098 square miles and a water area of 0.042 square miles. Located at 43.85° N. Lat.; 92.48° W. Long. Elevation is 1,240 feet.
History: Stewartville was named for Charles N. Stewart, who established a mill here in 1858 on the banks of the Root River.
Population: 5,411 (2000); Race: 97.5% White, 0.2% Black, 0.4% Asian, 0.1% American Indian and Alaska Native, 0.7% Hispanic of any race, 1.5% two or more races (2000); Density: 2,579.6 persons per square mile (2000);

Age: 29.9% under 18, 11.8% over 64 (2000); Marriage status: 20.9% never married, 61.0% now married, 6.0% widowed, 12.1% divorced (2000); Foreign born: 1.5% (2000); Ancestry (includes multiple ancestries): 41.9% German, 25.4% Norwegian, 14.5% Irish, 7.3% English, 4.3% United States or American (2000).
Economy: Employment by occupation: 9.3% management, 25.4% professional, 13.8% services, 27.5% sales, 0.8% farming, 9.3% construction, 13.9% production (2000).
Income: Per capita income: $18,780 (2000); Median household income: $44,135 (2000); Poverty rate: 5.4% (2000).
Taxes: Total city taxes per capita: $141 (1997); City property taxes per capita: $136 (1997).
Education: High school graduation rate: 86.6% (2000); College graduation rate: 17.2% (2000).

School District(s)

Stewartville (PK-12)
2000 Enrollment: 1,827 507-533-1438
Housing: Homeownership rate: 80.3% (2000); Median home value: $99,700 (2000); Median rent: $471 per month (2000); Median age of housing: 24 years (2000).
Safety: Violent crime rate: 5.5 per 10,000 population; Property crime rate: 171.9 per 10,000 population (2001).
Newspapers: Stewartville Star (1 x week)
Transportation: Commute to work: 92.7% car, 0.8% public transportation, 3.6% walk, 1.4% work from home (2000); Travel time to work: 28.1% less than 15 minutes, 56.2% 15 to 30 minutes, 12.2% 30 to 45 minutes, 1.4% 45 to 60 minutes, 2.2% 60 minutes or more (2000)
Additional Information Contacts
Stewartville Chamber of Commerce 507-533-6006

VIOLA (township). Covers a land area of 35.751 square miles and a water area of 0 square miles. Located at 44.06° N. Lat.; 92.26° W. Long. Elevation is 1,129 feet.
Population: 555 (2000); Race: 100.0% White, 0.0% Black, 0.0% Asian, 0.0% American Indian and Alaska Native, 0.0% Hispanic of any race, 0.0% two or more races (2000); Density: 15.5 persons per square mile (2000); Age: 26.7% under 18, 9.8% over 64 (2000); Marriage status: 23.8% never married, 69.3% now married, 2.9% widowed, 4.0% divorced (2000); Foreign born: 0.4% (2000); Ancestry (includes multiple ancestries): 58.5% German, 17.5% Irish, 17.5% Norwegian, 9.5% English, 6.1% Polish (2000).
Economy: Employment by occupation: 16.6% management, 25.7% professional, 16.0% services, 18.4% sales, 4.5% farming, 9.4% construction, 9.4% production (2000).
Income: Per capita income: $21,587 (2000); Median household income: $54,250 (2000); Poverty rate: 2.9% (2000).
Taxes: Total city taxes per capita: $73 (1997); City property taxes per capita: $73 (1997).
Education: High school graduation rate: 88.3% (2000); College graduation rate: 18.1% (2000).
Housing: Homeownership rate: 84.6% (2000); Median home value: $106,300 (2000); Median rent: $550 per month (2000); Median age of housing: 60+ years (2000).
Transportation: Commute to work: 83.0% car, 0.0% public transportation, 4.7% walk, 12.3% work from home (2000); Travel time to work: 18.0% less than 15 minutes, 62.6% 15 to 30 minutes, 15.5% 30 to 45 minutes, 0.7% 45 to 60 minutes, 3.2% 60 minutes or more (2000)

Otter Tail County

Located in western Minnesota; drained by the Pelican, Pomme de Terre, and Otter Tail Rivers and numerous lakes. Covers a land area of 1,979.70 square miles, a water area of 245.20 square miles, and is located in the Central Time Zone. The county government was organized in 1858. County seat is Fergus Falls.

Weather Station: Fergus Falls — Elevation: 1,250 feet

	Jan	Feb	Mar	Apr	May	Jun	Jul	Aug	Sep	Oct	Nov	Dec
High	16	23	35	53	68	76	81	79	69	56	36	22
Low	-3	4	17	32	46	55	60	57	47	35	20	5
Precip	1.0	0.6	1.5	1.5	2.7	3.8	3.3	3.2	2.2	2.1	1.1	0.5
Snow	13.3	5.8	8.0	1.7	tr	0.0	0.0	0.0	0.0	0.3	7.3	7.9

High and Low temperatures in degrees Fahrenheit; Precipitation and Snow in inches

Weather Station: Ottertail — Elevation: 977 feet

	Jan	Feb	Mar	Apr	May	Jun	Jul	Aug	Sep	Oct	Nov	Dec
High	18	25	37	55	70	78	82	80	70	57	37	23
Low	-3	4	17	32	46	56	60	58	48	36	21	5
Precip	0.9	0.6	1.4	2.1	3.1	4.6	3.9	3.3	2.5	2.5	1.1	0.5
Snow	14.0	8.8	10.5	4.0	tr	tr	0.0	0.0	tr	1.4	9.9	8.6

High and Low temperatures in degrees Fahrenheit; Precipitation and Snow in inches

Population: 57,159 (2000); Race: 97.3% White, 0.4% Black, 0.3% Asian, 0.5% American Indian and Alaska Native, 1.7% Hispanic of any race, 0.7% two or more races (2000); Density: 28.9 persons per square mile (2000); Age: 25.0% under 18, 18.9% over 64 (2000).
Religion: Five largest groups: 30.9% Evangelical Lutheran Church in America, 14.1% Catholic Church, 12.5% Lutheran Church—Missouri Synod, 2.8% The United Methodist Church, 1.6% The Association of Free Lutheran Congregations (2000).
Economy: Unemployment rate: 4.2% (11/2002); Total civilian labor force: 27,447 (11/2002); Leading industries: 21.2% manufacturing; 18.9% health care and social assistance; 17.4% retail trade (2000); Companies that employ more than 1,000 persons: 0 (2000); Companies that employ more than 100 persons: 27 (2000); Farms: 2,647 totaling 840,353 acres (1997); Minority business ownership rate: 0.0% (1997); Women business ownership rate: 28.2% (1997); Retail sales per capita: $8,736 (1997). Single-family building permits issued: 103 (2001) / 112 (2000); Multi-family building permits issued: 41 (2001) / 15 (2000).
Income: Per capita income: $18,014 (2000); Median household income: $35,395 (2000); Poverty rate: 10.1% (2000); Bankruptcy rate: 2.29% (2001).
Taxes: Total county taxes per capita: $240 (2000); County property taxes per capita: $232 (2000).
Education: High school graduation rate: 81.4% (2000); College graduation rate: 17.2% (2000).
Housing: Homeownership rate: 80.0% (2000); Median home value: $84,000 (2000); Median rent: $329 per month (2000); Median age of housing: 33 years (2000).
Health: Birth rate: 108.6 per 10,000 population (1998); Age adjusted death rate: 81.2 per 10,000 population (1999); Age adjusted cancer mortality rate: 207.6 deaths per 100,000 population (1999). Number of physicians: 12.4 per 10,000 population (1999); Number of hospital beds: 71.7 per 10,000 population (1999).
Elections: 2000 Presidential election results: 34.5% Gore, 59.5% Bush, 3.9% Nader, 1.6% Buchanan
National and State Parks: Aastad State Wildlife Management Area; Almora State Wildlife Management Area; Amor State Wildlife Management Area; Bluff Creek State Wildlife Management Area; Butler State Wildlife Management Area; Copeland State Wildlife Management Area; Davies State Wildlife Management Area; Dead Lake State Wildlife Management Area; Doran State Wildlife Management Area; Eagle Lake State Wildlife Management Area; Eastern Township State Wildlife Management; Elmo State Wildlife Management Area; Fergus Falls State Wildlife Management Area; Folden Woods State Wildlife Management Area; Haarstick State Wildlife Management Area; Hi-view State Wildlife Management Area; Inman State Wildlife Management Area; Inspiration State Wildlife Management Are; Lake Sixteen State Wildlife Management Area; Maplewood State Park; Orwell State Wildlife Management Area; Oscar State Wildlife Management Area; Perham State Wildlife Management Area; Sunnyside Township State Game Refuge; Valdine State Wildlife Management Area
Additional Information Contacts
Otter Tail County Government Offices 218-739-4560
Battle Lake Chamber of Commerce 218-864-5889
Fergus Falls Chamber of Commerce 218-736-6951
Lake Region Association of Realtors 218-739-0595
Perham Area Chamber of Commerce 218-346-7710

Otter Tail County Communities

AASTAD (township). Covers a land area of 34.541 square miles and a water area of 0.946 square miles. Located at 46.14° N. Lat.; 96.09° W. Long.
Population: 187 (2000); Race: 100.0% White, 0.0% Black, 0.0% Asian, 0.0% American Indian and Alaska Native, 0.0% Hispanic of any race, 0.0% two or more races (2000); Density: 5.4 persons per square mile (2000); Age: 25.8% under 18, 9.3% over 64 (2000); Marriage status: 24.5% never married, 63.9% now married, 6.5% widowed, 5.2% divorced (2000); Foreign born: 0.0% (2000); Ancestry (includes multiple ancestries): 51.5% Norwegian, 39.2% German, 6.7% Swedish, 6.2% English, 5.7% Scandinavian (2000).

Economy: Employment by occupation: 15.5% management, 16.5% professional, 26.2% services, 9.7% sales, 4.9% farming, 11.7% construction, 15.5% production (2000).
Income: Per capita income: $16,496 (2000); Median household income: $41,563 (2000); Poverty rate: 8.8% (2000).
Taxes: Total city taxes per capita: $112 (1997); City property taxes per capita: $112 (1997).
Education: High school graduation rate: 86.0% (2000); College graduation rate: 14.7% (2000).
Housing: Homeownership rate: 94.0% (2000); Median home value: $87,000 (2000); Median age of housing: 60+ years (2000).
Transportation: Commute to work: 91.2% car, 0.0% public transportation, 0.0% walk, 8.8% work from home (2000); Travel time to work: 7.2% less than 15 minutes, 71.1% 15 to 30 minutes, 6.0% 30 to 45 minutes, 8.4% 45 to 60 minutes, 7.2% 60 minutes or more (2000)

AMOR (township). Covers a land area of 23.194 square miles and a water area of 11.984 square miles. Located at 46.41° N. Lat.; 95.70° W. Long.
Population: 558 (2000); Race: 99.6% White, 0.0% Black, 0.0% Asian, 0.0% American Indian and Alaska Native, 1.1% Hispanic of any race, 0.4% two or more races (2000); Density: 24.1 persons per square mile (2000); Age: 15.4% under 18, 25.9% over 64 (2000); Marriage status: 18.7% never married, 67.5% now married, 11.8% widowed, 1.9% divorced (2000); Foreign born: 1.1% (2000); Ancestry (includes multiple ancestries): 37.7% German, 33.0% Norwegian, 15.2% Swedish, 8.0% Irish, 6.7% English (2000).
Economy: Employment by occupation: 11.6% management, 17.8% professional, 17.8% services, 23.6% sales, 0.8% farming, 12.4% construction, 16.1% production (2000).
Income: Per capita income: $20,480 (2000); Median household income: $38,833 (2000); Poverty rate: 1.7% (2000).
Taxes: Total city taxes per capita: $150 (1997); City property taxes per capita: $150 (1997).
Education: High school graduation rate: 79.9% (2000); College graduation rate: 22.0% (2000).
Housing: Homeownership rate: 89.9% (2000); Median home value: $101,400 (2000); Median rent: $515 per month (2000); Median age of housing: 43 years (2000).
Transportation: Commute to work: 84.1% car, 0.0% public transportation, 2.1% walk, 10.7% work from home (2000); Travel time to work: 29.8% less than 15 minutes, 36.5% 15 to 30 minutes, 22.6% 30 to 45 minutes, 4.8% 45 to 60 minutes, 6.3% 60 minutes or more (2000)

AURDAL (township). Covers a land area of 32.168 square miles and a water area of 3.020 square miles. Located at 46.31° N. Lat.; 95.95° W. Long.
Population: 1,362 (2000); Race: 99.1% White, 0.3% Black, 0.1% Asian, 0.1% American Indian and Alaska Native, 0.8% Hispanic of any race, 0.3% two or more races (2000); Density: 42.3 persons per square mile (2000); Age: 27.5% under 18, 11.4% over 64 (2000); Marriage status: 20.7% never married, 72.5% now married, 3.3% widowed, 3.4% divorced (2000); Foreign born: 0.4% (2000); Ancestry (includes multiple ancestries): 46.5% German, 39.9% Norwegian, 14.9% Swedish, 6.1% English, 5.3% Irish (2000).
Economy: Single-family building permits issued: 6 (2001) / 3 (2000); Multi-family building permits issued: 0 (2001) / 0 (2000); Employment by occupation: 15.7% management, 18.8% professional, 16.1% services, 23.3% sales, 0.8% farming, 10.3% construction, 15.0% production (2000).
Income: Per capita income: $19,747 (2000); Median household income: $50,750 (2000); Poverty rate: 1.8% (2000).
Taxes: Total city taxes per capita: $30 (1997); City property taxes per capita: $30 (1997).
Education: High school graduation rate: 89.7% (2000); College graduation rate: 23.8% (2000).
Housing: Homeownership rate: 96.6% (2000); Median home value: $104,400 (2000); Median rent: $375 per month (2000); Median age of housing: 25 years (2000).
Transportation: Commute to work: 91.7% car, 0.8% public transportation, 0.4% walk, 6.3% work from home (2000); Travel time to work: 41.2% less than 15 minutes, 46.6% 15 to 30 minutes, 5.9% 30 to 45 minutes, 3.0% 45 to 60 minutes, 3.3% 60 minutes or more (2000)

BATTLE LAKE (city). Covers a land area of 1.201 square miles and a water area of 0.005 square miles. Located at 46.28° N. Lat.; 95.71° W. Long. Elevation is 1,372 feet.
History: Battle here (1795) between Chippewa and Sioux Indians.
Population: 686 (2000); Race: 98.6% White, 0.6% Black, 0.0% Asian, 0.6% American Indian and Alaska Native, 0.0% Hispanic of any race, 0.0% two or more races (2000); Density: 571.3 persons per square mile (2000); Age: 22.8% under 18, 30.6% over 64 (2000); Marriage status: 15.8% never married, 59.4% now married, 15.4% widowed, 9.4% divorced (2000); Foreign born: 0.7% (2000); Ancestry (includes multiple ancestries): 37.5% Norwegian, 34.9% German, 10.7% Swedish, 6.0% English, 4.8% Irish (2000).
Economy: Grain, sugar beets, beans, sunflowers; livestock; dairying. Manufacturing: printing and publishing, furniture. Single-family building permits issued: 2 (2001) / 3 (2000); Multi-family building permits issued: 8 (2001) / 0 (2000); Employment by occupation: 4.9% management, 23.9% professional, 26.1% services, 21.8% sales, 0.7% farming, 10.6% construction, 12.0% production (2000).
Income: Per capita income: $17,269 (2000); Median household income: $25,000 (2000); Poverty rate: 13.3% (2000).
Taxes: Total city taxes per capita: $151 (1997); City property taxes per capita: $140 (1997).
Education: High school graduation rate: 81.2% (2000); College graduation rate: 19.2% (2000).

School District(s)

Battle Lake (KG-12)
2000 Enrollment: 532 218-864-5215

Housing: Homeownership rate: 78.7% (2000); Median home value: $72,600 (2000); Median rent: $278 per month (2000); Median age of housing: 40 years (2000).
Newspapers: Battle Lake Review (1 x week)
Transportation: Commute to work: 82.7% car, 0.0% public transportation, 9.5% walk, 7.0% work from home (2000); Travel time to work: 49.6% less than 15 minutes, 30.3% 15 to 30 minutes, 12.1% 30 to 45 minutes, 3.8% 45 to 60 minutes, 4.2% 60 minutes or more (2000)

Additional Information Contacts

Battle Lake Chamber of Commerce 218-864-5889

BLOWERS (township). Covers a land area of 35.653 square miles and a water area of 0 square miles. Located at 46.59° N. Lat.; 95.20° W. Long.
Population: 319 (2000); Race: 98.7% White, 0.0% Black, 0.7% Asian, 0.7% American Indian and Alaska Native, 0.0% Hispanic of any race, 0.0% two or more races (2000); Density: 8.9 persons per square mile (2000); Age: 26.1% under 18, 12.9% over 64 (2000); Marriage status: 24.8% never married, 57.7% now married, 7.7% widowed, 9.8% divorced (2000); Foreign born: 4.6% (2000); Ancestry (includes multiple ancestries): 38.9% German, 17.5% Finnish, 10.9% Irish, 5.9% Norwegian, 5.3% Swedish (2000).
Economy: Employment by occupation: 22.8% management, 9.7% professional, 22.1% services, 15.9% sales, 6.2% farming, 6.9% construction, 16.6% production (2000).
Income: Per capita income: $13,819 (2000); Median household income: $30,000 (2000); Poverty rate: 12.5% (2000).
Taxes: Total city taxes per capita: $33 (1997); City property taxes per capita: $33 (1997).
Education: High school graduation rate: 73.5% (2000); College graduation rate: 2.6% (2000).
Housing: Homeownership rate: 84.7% (2000); Median home value: $65,800 (2000); Median rent: $308 per month (2000); Median age of housing: 32 years (2000).
Transportation: Commute to work: 74.5% car, 2.8% public transportation, 8.3% walk, 14.5% work from home (2000); Travel time to work: 24.2% less than 15 minutes, 52.4% 15 to 30 minutes, 9.7% 30 to 45 minutes, 5.6% 45 to 60 minutes, 8.1% 60 minutes or more (2000)

BLUFFTON (city). Covers a land area of 2.769 square miles and a water area of 0 square miles. Located at 46.46° N. Lat.; 95.23° W. Long. Elevation is 1,324 feet.
Population: 210 (2000); Race: 100.0% White, 0.0% Black, 0.0% Asian, 0.0% American Indian and Alaska Native, 0.0% Hispanic of any race, 0.0% two or more races (2000); Density: 75.8 persons per square mile (2000); Age: 30.1% under 18, 23.9% over 64 (2000); Marriage status: 20.6% never married, 72.9% now married, 5.2% widowed, 1.3% divorced (2000); Foreign born: 0.0% (2000); Ancestry (includes multiple ancestries): 59.8% German, 15.8% Norwegian, 8.1% United States or American, 7.7% Irish, 7.2% Finnish (2000).
Economy: Single-family building permits issued: 0 (2001) / 1 (2000); Multi-family building permits issued: 0 (2001) / 0 (2000); Employment by occupation: 17.0% management, 7.4% professional, 17.0% services, 30.9% sales, 0.0% farming, 13.8% construction, 13.8% production (2000).
Income: Per capita income: $12,105 (2000); Median household income: $31,250 (2000); Poverty rate: 8.6% (2000).
Taxes: Total city taxes per capita: $79 (1997); City property taxes per capita: $68 (1997).

Education: High school graduation rate: 69.7% (2000); College graduation rate: 6.1% (2000).
Housing: Homeownership rate: 84.0% (2000); Median home value: $45,000 (2000); Median rent: $267 per month (2000); Median age of housing: 30 years (2000).
Transportation: Commute to work: 76.1% car, 0.0% public transportation, 4.3% walk, 19.6% work from home (2000); Travel time to work: 67.6% less than 15 minutes, 14.9% 15 to 30 minutes, 9.5% 30 to 45 minutes, 0.0% 45 to 60 minutes, 8.1% 60 minutes or more (2000)

BLUFFTON (township). Covers a land area of 32.956 square miles and a water area of 0.029 square miles. Located at 46.49° N. Lat.; 95.22° W. Long. Elevation is 1,324 feet.
Population: 474 (2000); Race: 98.6% White, 0.4% Black, 0.0% Asian, 0.6% American Indian and Alaska Native, 0.0% Hispanic of any race, 0.4% two or more races (2000); Density: 14.4 persons per square mile (2000); Age: 30.7% under 18, 8.3% over 64 (2000); Marriage status: 25.1% never married, 66.4% now married, 2.9% widowed, 5.6% divorced (2000); Foreign born: 0.4% (2000); Ancestry (includes multiple ancestries): 58.8% German, 10.9% Norwegian, 10.1% Finnish, 6.7% Polish, 4.8% Irish (2000).
Economy: In agricultural area; dairying; grain. Manufacturing: chemical fertilizers. Employment by occupation: 17.6% management, 12.1% professional, 9.0% services, 16.4% sales, 3.5% farming, 12.5% construction, 28.9% production (2000).
Income: Per capita income: $18,379 (2000); Median household income: $45,179 (2000); Poverty rate: 8.3% (2000).
Taxes: Total city taxes per capita: $38 (1997); City property taxes per capita: $38 (1997).
Education: High school graduation rate: 85.4% (2000); College graduation rate: 10.2% (2000).
Housing: Homeownership rate: 88.2% (2000); Median home value: $93,000 (2000); Median rent: $294 per month (2000); Median age of housing: 45 years (2000).
Transportation: Commute to work: 81.3% car, 0.0% public transportation, 1.6% walk, 17.2% work from home (2000); Travel time to work: 42.5% less than 15 minutes, 43.9% 15 to 30 minutes, 9.4% 30 to 45 minutes, 2.4% 45 to 60 minutes, 1.9% 60 minutes or more (2000)

BUSE (township). Covers a land area of 28.152 square miles and a water area of 2.388 square miles. Located at 46.25° N. Lat.; 96.06° W. Long.
Population: 690 (2000); Race: 99.1% White, 0.0% Black, 0.0% Asian, 0.9% American Indian and Alaska Native, 0.0% Hispanic of any race, 0.0% two or more races (2000); Density: 24.5 persons per square mile (2000); Age: 28.7% under 18, 12.2% over 64 (2000); Marriage status: 25.9% never married, 63.5% now married, 5.1% widowed, 5.5% divorced (2000); Foreign born: 1.7% (2000); Ancestry (includes multiple ancestries): 39.7% Norwegian, 35.2% German, 8.4% Swedish, 7.5% Irish, 5.8% French (except Basque) (2000).
Economy: Single-family building permits issued: 2 (2001) / 0 (2000); Multi-family building permits issued: 0 (2001) / 0 (2000); Employment by occupation: 15.3% management, 16.4% professional, 14.8% services, 27.2% sales, 0.8% farming, 6.6% construction, 19.0% production (2000).
Income: Per capita income: $18,207 (2000); Median household income: $41,964 (2000); Poverty rate: 6.9% (2000).
Taxes: Total city taxes per capita: $39 (1997); City property taxes per capita: $39 (1997).
Education: High school graduation rate: 85.9% (2000); College graduation rate: 20.1% (2000).
Housing: Homeownership rate: 89.9% (2000); Median home value: $95,900 (2000); Median rent: $360 per month (2000); Median age of housing: 27 years (2000).
Transportation: Commute to work: 89.1% car, 0.0% public transportation, 1.1% walk, 8.8% work from home (2000); Travel time to work: 52.9% less than 15 minutes, 36.5% 15 to 30 minutes, 7.3% 30 to 45 minutes, 0.0% 45 to 60 minutes, 3.2% 60 minutes or more (2000)

BUTLER (township). Covers a land area of 35.095 square miles and a water area of 0.781 square miles. Located at 46.66° N. Lat.; 95.37° W. Long. Elevation is 1,462 feet.
Population: 315 (2000); Race: 97.0% White, 0.0% Black, 0.0% Asian, 0.0% American Indian and Alaska Native, 3.0% Hispanic of any race, 2.3% two or more races (2000); Density: 9.0 persons per square mile (2000); Age: 35.2% under 18, 17.3% over 64 (2000); Marriage status: 20.1% never married, 74.0% now married, 4.6% widowed, 1.4% divorced (2000); Foreign born: 1.3% (2000); Ancestry (includes multiple ancestries): 64.1% German, 26.6% Dutch, 11.6% Norwegian, 11.3% Finnish, 8.0% Danish (2000).
Economy: Employment by occupation: 34.9% management, 6.2% professional, 14.0% services, 20.2% sales, 6.2% farming, 7.8% construction, 10.9% production (2000).
Income: Per capita income: $10,353 (2000); Median household income: $29,479 (2000); Poverty rate: 14.0% (2000).
Taxes: Total city taxes per capita: $42 (1997); City property taxes per capita: $42 (1997).
Education: High school graduation rate: 69.7% (2000); College graduation rate: 8.6% (2000).
Housing: Homeownership rate: 86.1% (2000); Median home value: $90,000 (2000); Median rent: $325 per month (2000); Median age of housing: 27 years (2000).
Transportation: Commute to work: 54.3% car, 0.0% public transportation, 5.4% walk, 40.3% work from home (2000); Travel time to work: 19.5% less than 15 minutes, 62.3% 15 to 30 minutes, 6.5% 30 to 45 minutes, 6.5% 45 to 60 minutes, 5.2% 60 minutes or more (2000)

CANDOR (township). Covers a land area of 30.555 square miles and a water area of 3.950 square miles. Located at 46.67° N. Lat.; 95.86° W. Long.
Population: 534 (2000); Race: 97.6% White, 0.0% Black, 0.4% Asian, 0.0% American Indian and Alaska Native, 0.0% Hispanic of any race, 2.0% two or more races (2000); Density: 17.5 persons per square mile (2000); Age: 22.8% under 18, 14.8% over 64 (2000); Marriage status: 22.5% never married, 68.5% now married, 2.8% widowed, 6.1% divorced (2000); Foreign born: 1.2% (2000); Ancestry (includes multiple ancestries): 42.7% German, 25.8% Norwegian, 6.9% French (except Basque), 6.5% United States or American, 5.9% Dutch (2000).
Economy: Employment by occupation: 12.1% management, 11.8% professional, 13.9% services, 23.2% sales, 4.3% farming, 18.2% construction, 16.4% production (2000).
Income: Per capita income: $23,413 (2000); Median household income: $39,318 (2000); Poverty rate: 4.0% (2000).
Taxes: Total city taxes per capita: $112 (1997); City property taxes per capita: $112 (1997).
Education: High school graduation rate: 88.1% (2000); College graduation rate: 14.4% (2000).
Housing: Homeownership rate: 92.3% (2000); Median home value: $98,500 (2000); Median rent: $363 per month (2000); Median age of housing: 31 years (2000).
Transportation: Commute to work: 83.3% car, 1.1% public transportation, 5.5% walk, 8.7% work from home (2000); Travel time to work: 16.3% less than 15 minutes, 47.8% 15 to 30 minutes, 17.5% 30 to 45 minutes, 5.2% 45 to 60 minutes, 13.1% 60 minutes or more (2000)

CARLISLE (township). Covers a land area of 34.830 square miles and a water area of 0.810 square miles. Located at 46.32° N. Lat.; 96.20° W. Long. Elevation is 1,227 feet.
Population: 219 (2000); Race: 100.0% White, 0.0% Black, 0.0% Asian, 0.0% American Indian and Alaska Native, 0.0% Hispanic of any race, 0.0% two or more races (2000); Density: 6.3 persons per square mile (2000); Age: 32.0% under 18, 15.0% over 64 (2000); Marriage status: 25.8% never married, 66.2% now married, 3.3% widowed, 4.6% divorced (2000); Foreign born: 0.0% (2000); Ancestry (includes multiple ancestries): 53.0% Norwegian, 45.5% German, 7.0% Irish, 5.0% Polish, 4.5% Swedish (2000).
Economy: Employment by occupation: 20.0% management, 17.0% professional, 10.0% services, 30.0% sales, 0.0% farming, 10.0% construction, 13.0% production (2000).
Income: Per capita income: $15,094 (2000); Median household income: $41,500 (2000); Poverty rate: 0.0% (2000).
Taxes: Total city taxes per capita: $60 (1997); City property taxes per capita: $60 (1997).
Education: High school graduation rate: 87.2% (2000); College graduation rate: 17.6% (2000).
Housing: Homeownership rate: 88.4% (2000); Median home value: $64,300 (2000); Median rent: $225 per month (2000); Median age of housing: 45 years (2000).
Transportation: Commute to work: 78.0% car, 2.0% public transportation, 2.0% walk, 18.0% work from home (2000); Travel time to work: 32.9% less than 15 minutes, 52.4% 15 to 30 minutes, 12.2% 30 to 45 minutes, 0.0% 45 to 60 minutes, 2.4% 60 minutes or more (2000)

CLITHERALL (city). Aka Clitheral. Covers a land area of 0.201 square miles and a water area of 0 square miles. Located at 46.27° N. Lat.; 95.63° W. Long. Elevation is 1,348 feet.
Population: 118 (2000); Race: 100.0% White, 0.0% Black, 0.0% Asian, 0.0% American Indian and Alaska Native, 0.0% Hispanic of any race, 0.0%

two or more races (2000); Density: 586.2 persons per square mile (2000); Age: 20.9% under 18, 20.0% over 64 (2000); Marriage status: 13.6% never married, 63.6% now married, 6.8% widowed, 15.9% divorced (2000); Foreign born: 0.0% (2000); Ancestry (includes multiple ancestries): 43.6% German, 20.9% Norwegian, 8.2% Irish, 7.3% French (except Basque), 7.3% Dutch (2000).
Economy: Single-family building permits issued: 0 (2001) / 0 (2000); Multi-family building permits issued: 0 (2001) / 0 (2000); Employment by occupation: 23.8% management, 14.3% professional, 11.9% services, 16.7% sales, 2.4% farming, 9.5% construction, 21.4% production (2000).
Income: Per capita income: $15,113 (2000); Median household income: $26,667 (2000); Poverty rate: 10.0% (2000).
Taxes: Total city taxes per capita: $9 (1997); City property taxes per capita: $9 (1997).
Education: High school graduation rate: 59.5% (2000); College graduation rate: 12.7% (2000).
Housing: Homeownership rate: 83.3% (2000); Median home value: $22,500 (2000); Median rent: $275 per month (2000); Median age of housing: 52 years (2000).
Transportation: Commute to work: 95.2% car, 0.0% public transportation, 4.8% walk, 0.0% work from home (2000); Travel time to work: 26.2% less than 15 minutes, 40.5% 15 to 30 minutes, 28.6% 30 to 45 minutes, 0.0% 45 to 60 minutes, 4.8% 60 minutes or more (2000)

CLITHERALL (township). Aka Clitheral. Covers a land area of 29.319 square miles and a water area of 6.341 square miles. Located at 46.24° N. Lat.; 95.70° W. Long. Elevation is 1,348 feet.
Population: 549 (2000); Race: 100.0% White, 0.0% Black, 0.0% Asian, 0.0% American Indian and Alaska Native, 0.0% Hispanic of any race, 0.0% two or more races (2000); Density: 18.7 persons per square mile (2000); Age: 21.3% under 18, 14.7% over 64 (2000); Marriage status: 16.1% never married, 68.8% now married, 9.0% widowed, 6.1% divorced (2000); Foreign born: 2.2% (2000); Ancestry (includes multiple ancestries): 46.9% Norwegian, 43.0% German, 8.7% Swedish, 6.5% Irish, 5.0% English (2000).
Economy: Grain; livestock; dairying. Single-family building permits issued: 2 (2001) / 1 (2000); Multi-family building permits issued: 0 (2001) / 0 (2000); Employment by occupation: 18.5% management, 12.2% professional, 15.9% services, 20.3% sales, 3.0% farming, 17.3% construction, 12.9% production (2000).
Income: Per capita income: $17,724 (2000); Median household income: $33,558 (2000); Poverty rate: 15.6% (2000).
Taxes: Total city taxes per capita: $62 (1997); City property taxes per capita: $62 (1997).
Education: High school graduation rate: 85.4% (2000); College graduation rate: 20.1% (2000).
Housing: Homeownership rate: 87.7% (2000); Median home value: $126,600 (2000); Median rent: $338 per month (2000); Median age of housing: 27 years (2000).
Transportation: Commute to work: 85.8% car, 0.0% public transportation, 6.4% walk, 7.9% work from home (2000); Travel time to work: 38.6% less than 15 minutes, 25.6% 15 to 30 minutes, 21.1% 30 to 45 minutes, 6.1% 45 to 60 minutes, 8.5% 60 minutes or more (2000)

COMPTON (township). Covers a land area of 35.696 square miles and a water area of 0 square miles. Located at 46.41° N. Lat.; 95.21° W. Long.
Population: 799 (2000); Race: 98.9% White, 0.0% Black, 0.0% Asian, 0.0% American Indian and Alaska Native, 0.7% Hispanic of any race, 0.4% two or more races (2000); Density: 22.4 persons per square mile (2000); Age: 36.2% under 18, 9.4% over 64 (2000); Marriage status: 23.5% never married, 64.4% now married, 2.6% widowed, 9.5% divorced (2000); Foreign born: 0.2% (2000); Ancestry (includes multiple ancestries): 49.3% German, 15.8% Norwegian, 11.8% Swedish, 4.2% Irish, 3.9% United States or American (2000).
Economy: Single-family building permits issued: 4 (2001) / 3 (2000); Multi-family building permits issued: 0 (2001) / 0 (2000); Employment by occupation: 17.0% management, 13.7% professional, 11.3% services, 26.9% sales, 3.6% farming, 9.9% construction, 17.6% production (2000).
Income: Per capita income: $13,342 (2000); Median household income: $32,656 (2000); Poverty rate: 26.5% (2000).
Taxes: Total city taxes per capita: $38 (1997); City property taxes per capita: $38 (1997).
Education: High school graduation rate: 79.6% (2000); College graduation rate: 12.1% (2000).
Housing: Homeownership rate: 89.1% (2000); Median home value: $66,700 (2000); Median rent: $272 per month (2000); Median age of housing: 29 years (2000).
Transportation: Commute to work: 89.1% car, 0.0% public transportation, 4.7% walk, 5.6% work from home (2000); Travel time to work: 59.3% less than 15 minutes, 23.9% 15 to 30 minutes, 9.1% 30 to 45 minutes, 2.4% 45 to 60 minutes, 5.3% 60 minutes or more (2000)

CORLISS (township). Covers a land area of 35.029 square miles and a water area of 1.847 square miles. Located at 46.66° N. Lat.; 95.47° W. Long.
Population: 462 (2000); Race: 97.7% White, 0.4% Black, 0.0% Asian, 0.4% American Indian and Alaska Native, 0.4% Hispanic of any race, 1.5% two or more races (2000); Density: 13.2 persons per square mile (2000); Age: 30.3% under 18, 12.1% over 64 (2000); Marriage status: 17.3% never married, 73.4% now married, 4.0% widowed, 5.4% divorced (2000); Foreign born: 0.6% (2000); Ancestry (includes multiple ancestries): 57.6% German, 13.6% Norwegian, 7.9% Polish, 6.5% Irish, 4.4% French (except Basque) (2000).
Economy: Employment by occupation: 18.3% management, 15.3% professional, 10.6% services, 17.0% sales, 8.1% farming, 11.1% construction, 19.6% production (2000).
Income: Per capita income: $14,936 (2000); Median household income: $37,000 (2000); Poverty rate: 8.8% (2000).
Taxes: Total city taxes per capita: $108 (1997); City property taxes per capita: $108 (1997).
Education: High school graduation rate: 87.2% (2000); College graduation rate: 10.9% (2000).
Housing: Homeownership rate: 91.3% (2000); Median home value: $112,500 (2000); Median rent: $425 per month (2000); Median age of housing: 41 years (2000).
Transportation: Commute to work: 86.1% car, 0.0% public transportation, 2.6% walk, 11.3% work from home (2000); Travel time to work: 37.1% less than 15 minutes, 44.9% 15 to 30 minutes, 11.2% 30 to 45 minutes, 1.0% 45 to 60 minutes, 5.9% 60 minutes or more (2000)

DALTON (city). Covers a land area of 0.239 square miles and a water area of 0 square miles. Located at 46.17° N. Lat.; 95.91° W. Long. Elevation is 1,360 feet.
Population: 258 (2000); Race: 98.6% White, 1.4% Black, 0.0% Asian, 0.0% American Indian and Alaska Native, 0.7% Hispanic of any race, 0.0% two or more races (2000); Density: 1,077.3 persons per square mile (2000); Age: 25.6% under 18, 21.3% over 64 (2000); Marriage status: 23.0% never married, 49.8% now married, 15.0% widowed, 12.2% divorced (2000); Foreign born: 0.0% (2000); Ancestry (includes multiple ancestries): 58.8% Norwegian, 24.9% German, 7.6% Irish, 6.1% Swedish, 4.7% Other groups (2000).
Economy: Dairying; poultry; grain, alfalfa, sunflowers; light manufacturing. Single-family building permits issued: 0 (2001) / 0 (2000); Multi-family building permits issued: 0 (2001) / 0 (2000); Employment by occupation: 6.3% management, 17.2% professional, 16.4% services, 36.7% sales, 0.0% farming, 14.8% construction, 8.6% production (2000).
Income: Per capita income: $13,990 (2000); Median household income: $29,750 (2000); Poverty rate: 8.2% (2000).
Taxes: Total city taxes per capita: $75 (1997); City property taxes per capita: $66 (1997).
Education: High school graduation rate: 74.1% (2000); College graduation rate: 7.8% (2000).
Housing: Homeownership rate: 76.7% (2000); Median home value: $41,700 (2000); Median rent: $318 per month (2000); Median age of housing: 49 years (2000).
Transportation: Commute to work: 84.1% car, 0.0% public transportation, 12.7% walk, 1.6% work from home (2000); Travel time to work: 36.3% less than 15 minutes, 48.4% 15 to 30 minutes, 5.6% 30 to 45 minutes, 7.3% 45 to 60 minutes, 2.4% 60 minutes or more (2000)

DANE PRAIRIE (township). Covers a land area of 31.239 square miles and a water area of 4.536 square miles. Located at 46.23° N. Lat.; 95.95° W. Long.
Population: 892 (2000); Race: 99.7% White, 0.2% Black, 0.0% Asian, 0.0% American Indian and Alaska Native, 0.4% Hispanic of any race, 0.1% two or more races (2000); Density: 28.6 persons per square mile (2000); Age: 24.0% under 18, 12.3% over 64 (2000); Marriage status: 18.8% never married, 71.8% now married, 3.8% widowed, 5.6% divorced (2000); Foreign born: 0.2% (2000); Ancestry (includes multiple ancestries): 50.2% Norwegian, 35.8% German, 8.5% Swedish, 5.7% Irish, 4.6% Polish (2000).
Economy: Employment by occupation: 14.7% management, 20.8% professional, 13.7% services, 24.4% sales, 2.4% farming, 11.7% construction, 12.3% production (2000).
Income: Per capita income: $22,630 (2000); Median household income: $47,232 (2000); Poverty rate: 3.2% (2000).

Taxes: Total city taxes per capita: $46 (2000); City property taxes per capita: $45 (2000).
Education: High school graduation rate: 89.1% (2000); College graduation rate: 18.9% (2000).
Housing: Homeownership rate: 94.9% (2000); Median home value: $113,600 (2000); Median rent: $563 per month (2000); Median age of housing: 30 years (2000).
Transportation: Commute to work: 93.3% car, 0.6% public transportation, 0.6% walk, 4.3% work from home (2000); Travel time to work: 32.8% less than 15 minutes, 54.2% 15 to 30 minutes, 3.8% 30 to 45 minutes, 4.2% 45 to 60 minutes, 4.9% 60 minutes or more (2000)

DEAD LAKE (township). Covers a land area of 24.681 square miles and a water area of 10.426 square miles. Located at 46.49° N. Lat.; 95.71° W. Long.
Population: 452 (2000); Race: 98.5% White, 0.0% Black, 0.0% Asian, 1.5% American Indian and Alaska Native, 0.0% Hispanic of any race, 0.0% two or more races (2000); Density: 18.3 persons per square mile (2000); Age: 17.9% under 18, 19.8% over 64 (2000); Marriage status: 18.6% never married, 64.3% now married, 10.1% widowed, 7.0% divorced (2000); Foreign born: 0.0% (2000); Ancestry (includes multiple ancestries): 44.2% German, 23.5% Norwegian, 8.2% Irish, 8.0% Swedish, 6.0% French (except Basque) (2000).
Economy: Employment by occupation: 11.6% management, 20.7% professional, 8.6% services, 22.2% sales, 5.1% farming, 15.7% construction, 16.2% production (2000).
Income: Per capita income: $15,840 (2000); Median household income: $31,786 (2000); Poverty rate: 11.2% (2000).
Taxes: Total city taxes per capita: $124 (1997); City property taxes per capita: $124 (1997).
Education: High school graduation rate: 84.3% (2000); College graduation rate: 17.1% (2000).
Housing: Homeownership rate: 95.1% (2000); Median home value: $110,000 (2000); Median rent: $350 per month (2000); Median age of housing: 28 years (2000).
Transportation: Commute to work: 85.1% car, 1.5% public transportation, 3.1% walk, 7.2% work from home (2000); Travel time to work: 18.3% less than 15 minutes, 34.4% 15 to 30 minutes, 18.9% 30 to 45 minutes, 24.4% 45 to 60 minutes, 3.9% 60 minutes or more (2000)

DEER CREEK (city). Covers a land area of 4.019 square miles and a water area of 0 square miles. Located at 46.39° N. Lat.; 95.32° W. Long. Elevation is 1,393 feet.
Population: 328 (2000); Race: 97.4% White, 0.0% Black, 1.9% Asian, 0.0% American Indian and Alaska Native, 0.0% Hispanic of any race, 0.6% two or more races (2000); Density: 81.6 persons per square mile (2000); Age: 26.5% under 18, 17.7% over 64 (2000); Marriage status: 16.5% never married, 60.6% now married, 10.6% widowed, 12.3% divorced (2000); Foreign born: 2.6% (2000); Ancestry (includes multiple ancestries): 37.4% German, 11.6% Norwegian, 9.0% Swedish, 8.1% Irish, 3.9% United States or American (2000).
Economy: Single-family building permits issued: 0 (2001) / 1 (2000); Multi-family building permits issued: 0 (2001) / 0 (2000); Employment by occupation: 12.2% management, 16.0% professional, 18.3% services, 16.8% sales, 0.0% farming, 10.7% construction, 26.0% production (2000).
Income: Per capita income: $14,097 (2000); Median household income: $28,558 (2000); Poverty rate: 8.7% (2000).
Taxes: Total city taxes per capita: $112 (1997); City property taxes per capita: $105 (1997).
Education: High school graduation rate: 73.7% (2000); College graduation rate: 8.8% (2000).
Housing: Homeownership rate: 75.9% (2000); Median home value: $37,800 (2000); Median rent: $195 per month (2000); Median age of housing: 40 years (2000).
Transportation: Commute to work: 89.3% car, 0.0% public transportation, 5.3% walk, 3.8% work from home (2000); Travel time to work: 30.2% less than 15 minutes, 52.4% 15 to 30 minutes, 6.3% 30 to 45 minutes, 4.0% 45 to 60 minutes, 7.1% 60 minutes or more (2000)

DEER CREEK (township). Covers a land area of 32.304 square miles and a water area of 0.187 square miles. Located at 46.40° N. Lat.; 95.35° W. Long. Elevation is 1,393 feet.
Population: 348 (2000); Race: 99.4% White, 0.0% Black, 0.0% Asian, 0.0% American Indian and Alaska Native, 0.0% Hispanic of any race, 0.6% two or more races (2000); Density: 10.8 persons per square mile (2000); Age: 31.1% under 18, 12.3% over 64 (2000); Marriage status: 24.2% never married, 68.7% now married, 6.4% widowed, 0.8% divorced (2000); Foreign born: 1.1% (2000); Ancestry (includes multiple ancestries): 42.2% German, 15.1% Irish, 11.7% Finnish, 10.3% Swedish, 10.0% Norwegian (2000).
Economy: Agricultural area: dairying; poultry, livestock; grain, sunflowers, sugar beets. Employment by occupation: 24.1% management, 9.0% professional, 12.0% services, 15.1% sales, 3.6% farming, 10.8% construction, 25.3% production (2000).
Income: Per capita income: $11,672 (2000); Median household income: $35,000 (2000); Poverty rate: 10.8% (2000).
Taxes: Total city taxes per capita: $36 (1997); City property taxes per capita: $36 (1997).
Education: High school graduation rate: 84.1% (2000); College graduation rate: 7.7% (2000).
Housing: Homeownership rate: 96.4% (2000); Median home value: $78,800 (2000); Median age of housing: 60+ years (2000).
Transportation: Commute to work: 90.2% car, 0.0% public transportation, 2.5% walk, 5.5% work from home (2000); Travel time to work: 27.9% less than 15 minutes, 59.1% 15 to 30 minutes, 7.8% 30 to 45 minutes, 0.0% 45 to 60 minutes, 5.2% 60 minutes or more (2000)

DENT (city). Covers a land area of 0.383 square miles and a water area of 0.001 square miles. Located at 46.55° N. Lat.; 95.71° W. Long. Elevation is 1,363 feet.
Population: 192 (2000); Race: 95.7% White, 0.0% Black, 0.0% Asian, 0.0% American Indian and Alaska Native, 0.0% Hispanic of any race, 4.3% two or more races (2000); Density: 501.0 persons per square mile (2000); Age: 31.3% under 18, 13.7% over 64 (2000); Marriage status: 17.8% never married, 68.4% now married, 7.2% widowed, 6.6% divorced (2000); Foreign born: 0.0% (2000); Ancestry (includes multiple ancestries): 55.0% German, 13.3% Norwegian, 11.4% Irish, 10.9% Swedish, 8.5% French (except Basque) (2000).
Economy: Dairying; light manufacturing. Single-family building permits issued: 0 (2001) / 0 (2000); Multi-family building permits issued: 0 (2001) / 0 (2000); Employment by occupation: 4.6% management, 6.9% professional, 24.1% services, 25.3% sales, 0.0% farming, 14.9% construction, 24.1% production (2000).
Income: Per capita income: $12,024 (2000); Median household income: $30,938 (2000); Poverty rate: 12.9% (2000).
Taxes: Total city taxes per capita: $54 (1997); City property taxes per capita: $29 (1997).
Education: High school graduation rate: 70.8% (2000); College graduation rate: 3.1% (2000).
Housing: Homeownership rate: 86.3% (2000); Median home value: $43,000 (2000); Median rent: $275 per month (2000); Median age of housing: 60+ years (2000).
Transportation: Commute to work: 87.1% car, 0.0% public transportation, 8.2% walk, 4.7% work from home (2000); Travel time to work: 46.9% less than 15 minutes, 45.7% 15 to 30 minutes, 7.4% 30 to 45 minutes, 0.0% 45 to 60 minutes, 0.0% 60 minutes or more (2000)

DORA (township). Covers a land area of 28.942 square miles and a water area of 6.897 square miles. Located at 46.59° N. Lat.; 95.83° W. Long.
Population: 726 (2000); Race: 99.6% White, 0.0% Black, 0.0% Asian, 0.4% American Indian and Alaska Native, 0.0% Hispanic of any race, 0.0% two or more races (2000); Density: 25.1 persons per square mile (2000); Age: 20.4% under 18, 22.4% over 64 (2000); Marriage status: 12.0% never married, 77.0% now married, 3.7% widowed, 7.4% divorced (2000); Foreign born: 0.0% (2000); Ancestry (includes multiple ancestries): 44.0% German, 28.1% Norwegian, 11.3% Irish, 9.7% Swedish, 9.3% English (2000).
Economy: Employment by occupation: 14.3% management, 12.5% professional, 15.0% services, 23.6% sales, 3.2% farming, 16.1% construction, 15.4% production (2000).
Income: Per capita income: $20,479 (2000); Median household income: $37,159 (2000); Poverty rate: 9.7% (2000).
Taxes: Total city taxes per capita: $173 (1997); City property taxes per capita: $173 (1997).
Education: High school graduation rate: 85.5% (2000); College graduation rate: 15.4% (2000).
Housing: Homeownership rate: 89.8% (2000); Median home value: $100,600 (2000); Median rent: $325 per month (2000); Median age of housing: 25 years (2000).
Transportation: Commute to work: 90.1% car, 0.7% public transportation, 0.7% walk, 8.5% work from home (2000); Travel time to work: 30.1% less than 15 minutes, 32.5% 15 to 30 minutes, 21.7% 30 to 45 minutes, 3.6% 45 to 60 minutes, 12.0% 60 minutes or more (2000)

DUNN (township). Covers a land area of 26.200 square miles and a water area of 10.440 square miles. Located at 46.68° N. Lat.; 95.98° W. Long.
Population: 855 (2000); Race: 99.0% White, 0.0% Black, 0.0% Asian, 0.0% American Indian and Alaska Native, 0.1% Hispanic of any race, 0.9% two or more races (2000); Density: 32.6 persons per square mile (2000); Age: 18.3% under 18, 22.0% over 64 (2000); Marriage status: 11.5% never married, 75.2% now married, 5.5% widowed, 7.8% divorced (2000); Foreign born: 0.6% (2000); Ancestry (includes multiple ancestries): 45.2% Norwegian, 32.4% German, 9.3% Irish, 8.8% Swedish, 6.6% English (2000).
Economy: Single-family building permits issued: 5 (2001) / 4 (2000); Multi-family building permits issued: 0 (2001) / 0 (2000); Employment by occupation: 21.6% management, 13.7% professional, 16.0% services, 24.7% sales, 0.0% farming, 13.1% construction, 10.8% production (2000).
Income: Per capita income: $25,247 (2000); Median household income: $41,618 (2000); Poverty rate: 7.9% (2000).
Taxes: Total city taxes per capita: $271 (1997); City property taxes per capita: $271 (1997).
Education: High school graduation rate: 84.3% (2000); College graduation rate: 26.4% (2000).
Housing: Homeownership rate: 93.8% (2000); Median home value: $163,100 (2000); Median rent: $350 per month (2000); Median age of housing: 35 years (2000).
Transportation: Commute to work: 89.0% car, 0.0% public transportation, 6.0% walk, 4.4% work from home (2000); Travel time to work: 24.0% less than 15 minutes, 35.8% 15 to 30 minutes, 7.1% 30 to 45 minutes, 19.4% 45 to 60 minutes, 13.7% 60 minutes or more (2000)

EAGLE LAKE (township). Covers a land area of 31.867 square miles and a water area of 4.162 square miles. Located at 46.15° N. Lat.; 95.69° W. Long.
Population: 367 (2000); Race: 99.4% White, 0.0% Black, 0.6% Asian, 0.0% American Indian and Alaska Native, 0.0% Hispanic of any race, 0.0% two or more races (2000); Density: 11.5 persons per square mile (2000); Age: 28.6% under 18, 15.7% over 64 (2000); Marriage status: 16.9% never married, 76.4% now married, 3.7% widowed, 3.0% divorced (2000); Foreign born: 0.6% (2000); Ancestry (includes multiple ancestries): 50.9% Norwegian, 25.7% German, 16.9% Swedish, 4.9% Scandinavian, 4.6% Dutch (2000).
Economy: Employment by occupation: 20.6% management, 18.9% professional, 12.6% services, 21.7% sales, 4.6% farming, 15.4% construction, 6.3% production (2000).
Income: Per capita income: $15,792 (2000); Median household income: $31,875 (2000); Poverty rate: 12.4% (2000).
Taxes: Total city taxes per capita: $152 (1997); City property taxes per capita: $152 (1997).
Education: High school graduation rate: 82.1% (2000); College graduation rate: 20.0% (2000).
Housing: Homeownership rate: 85.3% (2000); Median home value: $118,200 (2000); Median rent: $363 per month (2000); Median age of housing: 25 years (2000).
Transportation: Commute to work: 85.7% car, 0.0% public transportation, 2.3% walk, 12.0% work from home (2000); Travel time to work: 27.3% less than 15 minutes, 27.9% 15 to 30 minutes, 31.2% 30 to 45 minutes, 7.8% 45 to 60 minutes, 5.8% 60 minutes or more (2000)

EASTERN (township). Covers a land area of 35.319 square miles and a water area of 1.246 square miles. Located at 46.13° N. Lat.; 95.19° W. Long.
Population: 256 (2000); Race: 98.3% White, 0.0% Black, 0.0% Asian, 0.0% American Indian and Alaska Native, 0.0% Hispanic of any race, 1.7% two or more races (2000); Density: 7.2 persons per square mile (2000); Age: 25.5% under 18, 15.5% over 64 (2000); Marriage status: 17.0% never married, 74.5% now married, 1.1% widowed, 7.4% divorced (2000); Foreign born: 0.0% (2000); Ancestry (includes multiple ancestries): 54.8% German, 18.0% Swedish, 11.7% Norwegian, 7.5% Polish, 5.4% United States or American (2000).
Economy: Employment by occupation: 24.1% management, 11.3% professional, 11.3% services, 15.8% sales, 5.3% farming, 13.5% construction, 18.8% production (2000).
Income: Per capita income: $17,964 (2000); Median household income: $31,563 (2000); Poverty rate: 12.7% (2000).
Taxes: Total city taxes per capita: $81 (1997); City property taxes per capita: $81 (1997).
Education: High school graduation rate: 80.0% (2000); College graduation rate: 7.6% (2000).
Housing: Homeownership rate: 88.0% (2000); Median home value: $73,800 (2000); Median rent: $215 per month (2000); Median age of housing: 52 years (2000).
Transportation: Commute to work: 83.5% car, 0.0% public transportation, 6.8% walk, 9.8% work from home (2000); Travel time to work: 27.5% less than 15 minutes, 34.2% 15 to 30 minutes, 32.5% 30 to 45 minutes, 1.7% 45 to 60 minutes, 4.2% 60 minutes or more (2000)

EDNA (township). Covers a land area of 26.194 square miles and a water area of 8.508 square miles. Located at 46.58° N. Lat.; 95.72° W. Long.
Population: 921 (2000); Race: 98.8% White, 0.4% Black, 0.0% Asian, 0.4% American Indian and Alaska Native, 0.0% Hispanic of any race, 0.3% two or more races (2000); Density: 35.2 persons per square mile (2000); Age: 27.1% under 18, 17.4% over 64 (2000); Marriage status: 16.8% never married, 71.9% now married, 5.1% widowed, 6.2% divorced (2000); Foreign born: 0.7% (2000); Ancestry (includes multiple ancestries): 50.3% German, 24.7% Norwegian, 9.7% English, 9.6% Polish, 8.3% Irish (2000).
Economy: Employment by occupation: 10.6% management, 25.8% professional, 11.4% services, 22.8% sales, 0.5% farming, 7.3% construction, 21.5% production (2000).
Income: Per capita income: $19,847 (2000); Median household income: $40,625 (2000); Poverty rate: 7.2% (2000).
Taxes: Total city taxes per capita: $162 (2000); City property taxes per capita: $162 (2000).
Education: High school graduation rate: 90.7% (2000); College graduation rate: 23.4% (2000).
Housing: Homeownership rate: 93.8% (2000); Median home value: $129,800 (2000); Median rent: $538 per month (2000); Median age of housing: 19 years (2000).
Transportation: Commute to work: 88.0% car, 0.0% public transportation, 3.3% walk, 7.4% work from home (2000); Travel time to work: 34.7% less than 15 minutes, 38.6% 15 to 30 minutes, 12.4% 30 to 45 minutes, 2.2% 45 to 60 minutes, 12.1% 60 minutes or more (2000)

EFFINGTON (township). Covers a land area of 32.979 square miles and a water area of 2.039 square miles. Located at 46.15° N. Lat.; 95.46° W. Long.
Population: 297 (2000); Race: 99.1% White, 0.0% Black, 0.0% Asian, 0.0% American Indian and Alaska Native, 0.9% Hispanic of any race, 0.9% two or more races (2000); Density: 9.0 persons per square mile (2000); Age: 29.9% under 18, 15.9% over 64 (2000); Marriage status: 26.8% never married, 69.5% now married, 1.6% widowed, 2.0% divorced (2000); Foreign born: 0.0% (2000); Ancestry (includes multiple ancestries): 59.8% German, 17.7% Polish, 10.4% Norwegian, 7.3% Swedish, 4.0% French (except Basque) (2000).
Economy: Employment by occupation: 27.7% management, 16.3% professional, 10.8% services, 17.5% sales, 11.4% farming, 6.0% construction, 10.2% production (2000).
Income: Per capita income: $13,734 (2000); Median household income: $30,000 (2000); Poverty rate: 6.7% (2000).
Taxes: Total city taxes per capita: $99 (1997); City property taxes per capita: $99 (1997).
Education: High school graduation rate: 73.8% (2000); College graduation rate: 11.7% (2000).
Housing: Homeownership rate: 86.6% (2000); Median home value: $64,200 (2000); Median rent: $325 per month (2000); Median age of housing: 56 years (2000).
Transportation: Commute to work: 65.1% car, 0.0% public transportation, 7.8% walk, 25.3% work from home (2000); Travel time to work: 38.7% less than 15 minutes, 33.9% 15 to 30 minutes, 20.2% 30 to 45 minutes, 7.3% 45 to 60 minutes, 0.0% 60 minutes or more (2000)

ELIZABETH (city). Covers a land area of 0.363 square miles and a water area of 0 square miles. Located at 46.37° N. Lat.; 96.13° W. Long. Elevation is 1,258 feet.
Population: 172 (2000); Race: 97.7% White, 0.0% Black, 0.0% Asian, 2.3% American Indian and Alaska Native, 0.0% Hispanic of any race, 0.0% two or more races (2000); Density: 473.5 persons per square mile (2000); Age: 28.4% under 18, 11.9% over 64 (2000); Marriage status: 20.8% never married, 54.6% now married, 10.8% widowed, 13.8% divorced (2000); Foreign born: 0.0% (2000); Ancestry (includes multiple ancestries): 52.3% German, 46.6% Norwegian, 7.4% Irish, 4.0% Swedish, 4.0% United States or American (2000).
Economy: Employment by occupation: 9.2% management, 5.3% professional, 10.5% services, 14.5% sales, 3.9% farming, 25.0% construction, 31.6% production (2000).

Income: Per capita income: $13,841 (2000); Median household income: $33,438 (2000); Poverty rate: 8.0% (2000).
Taxes: Total city taxes per capita: $68 (1997); City property taxes per capita: $56 (1997).
Education: High school graduation rate: 79.8% (2000); College graduation rate: 1.8% (2000).
Housing: Homeownership rate: 93.2% (2000); Median home value: $40,000 (2000); Median rent: $188 per month (2000); Median age of housing: 46 years (2000).
Transportation: Commute to work: 89.5% car, 0.0% public transportation, 6.6% walk, 3.9% work from home (2000); Travel time to work: 49.3% less than 15 minutes, 42.5% 15 to 30 minutes, 0.0% 30 to 45 minutes, 2.7% 45 to 60 minutes, 5.5% 60 minutes or more (2000)

ELIZABETH (township). Covers a land area of 31.835 square miles and a water area of 3.770 square miles. Located at 46.41° N. Lat.; 96.08° W. Long. Elevation is 1,258 feet.
Population: 722 (2000); Race: 99.2% White, 0.0% Black, 0.0% Asian, 0.0% American Indian and Alaska Native, 0.4% Hispanic of any race, 0.5% two or more races (2000); Density: 22.7 persons per square mile (2000); Age: 26.2% under 18, 13.9% over 64 (2000); Marriage status: 21.2% never married, 68.9% now married, 5.0% widowed, 4.9% divorced (2000); Foreign born: 0.0% (2000); Ancestry (includes multiple ancestries): 44.5% Norwegian, 39.1% German, 12.3% Swedish, 7.2% Irish, 5.7% English (2000).
Economy: Employment by occupation: 20.2% management, 23.0% professional, 13.6% services, 16.1% sales, 3.1% farming, 13.8% construction, 10.2% production (2000).
Income: Per capita income: $21,960 (2000); Median household income: $46,719 (2000); Poverty rate: 9.0% (2000).
Taxes: Total city taxes per capita: $129 (1997); City property taxes per capita: $129 (1997).
Education: High school graduation rate: 87.7% (2000); College graduation rate: 21.9% (2000).
Housing: Homeownership rate: 93.4% (2000); Median home value: $129,300 (2000); Median rent: $363 per month (2000); Median age of housing: 37 years (2000).
Transportation: Commute to work: 84.2% car, 0.0% public transportation, 5.2% walk, 9.6% work from home (2000); Travel time to work: 21.4% less than 15 minutes, 68.3% 15 to 30 minutes, 6.3% 30 to 45 minutes, 1.1% 45 to 60 minutes, 2.9% 60 minutes or more (2000)

ELMO (township). Covers a land area of 36.327 square miles and a water area of 0.475 square miles. Located at 46.23° N. Lat.; 95.34° W. Long.
Population: 344 (2000); Race: 98.1% White, 0.0% Black, 0.0% Asian, 0.0% American Indian and Alaska Native, 0.5% Hispanic of any race, 1.4% two or more races (2000); Density: 9.5 persons per square mile (2000); Age: 27.0% under 18, 15.3% over 64 (2000); Marriage status: 23.3% never married, 64.8% now married, 6.3% widowed, 5.6% divorced (2000); Foreign born: 0.0% (2000); Ancestry (includes multiple ancestries): 41.8% German, 27.0% Norwegian, 13.7% Swedish, 9.3% United States or American, 9.0% Irish (2000).
Economy: Employment by occupation: 18.6% management, 8.7% professional, 15.8% services, 15.8% sales, 8.7% farming, 11.5% construction, 20.8% production (2000).
Income: Per capita income: $12,554 (2000); Median household income: $28,125 (2000); Poverty rate: 14.2% (2000).
Taxes: Total city taxes per capita: $76 (1997); City property taxes per capita: $76 (1997).
Education: High school graduation rate: 64.0% (2000); College graduation rate: 1.7% (2000).
Housing: Homeownership rate: 91.9% (2000); Median home value: $34,800 (2000); Median rent: $315 per month (2000); Median age of housing: 59 years (2000).
Transportation: Commute to work: 86.5% car, 0.0% public transportation, 6.2% walk, 7.3% work from home (2000); Travel time to work: 36.4% less than 15 minutes, 23.0% 15 to 30 minutes, 22.4% 30 to 45 minutes, 5.5% 45 to 60 minutes, 12.7% 60 minutes or more (2000)

ERHARD (city). Covers a land area of 0.543 square miles and a water area of 0.017 square miles. Located at 46.48° N. Lat.; 96.09° W. Long. Elevation is 1,280 feet.
Population: 150 (2000); Race: 98.6% White, 0.0% Black, 0.0% Asian, 0.0% American Indian and Alaska Native, 0.0% Hispanic of any race, 1.4% two or more races (2000); Density: 276.4 persons per square mile (2000); Age: 14.2% under 18, 10.8% over 64 (2000); Marriage status: 26.0% never married, 55.0% now married, 6.1% widowed, 13.0% divorced (2000); Foreign born: 0.0% (2000); Ancestry (includes multiple ancestries): 53.4% Norwegian, 23.6% German, 16.9% Swedish, 7.4% English, 6.1% Finnish (2000).
Economy: Grain; dairying. Employment by occupation: 6.7% management, 7.8% professional, 8.9% services, 31.1% sales, 2.2% farming, 8.9% construction, 34.4% production (2000).
Income: Per capita income: $16,189 (2000); Median household income: $35,417 (2000); Poverty rate: 11.5% (2000).
Taxes: Total city taxes per capita: $46 (1997); City property taxes per capita: $41 (1997).
Education: High school graduation rate: 69.7% (2000); College graduation rate: 14.8% (2000).
Housing: Homeownership rate: 91.7% (2000); Median home value: $43,000 (2000); Median rent: $325 per month (2000); Median age of housing: 35 years (2000).
Transportation: Commute to work: 92.9% car, 0.0% public transportation, 0.0% walk, 3.5% work from home (2000); Travel time to work: 34.1% less than 15 minutes, 32.9% 15 to 30 minutes, 23.2% 30 to 45 minutes, 1.2% 45 to 60 minutes, 8.5% 60 minutes or more (2000)

ERHARDS GROVE (township). Covers a land area of 33.293 square miles and a water area of 1.678 square miles. Located at 46.49° N. Lat.; 96.09° W. Long.
Population: 467 (2000); Race: 96.2% White, 1.3% Black, 0.0% Asian, 1.7% American Indian and Alaska Native, 0.6% Hispanic of any race, 0.8% two or more races (2000); Density: 14.0 persons per square mile (2000); Age: 26.7% under 18, 14.0% over 64 (2000); Marriage status: 18.0% never married, 74.9% now married, 3.3% widowed, 3.8% divorced (2000); Foreign born: 0.8% (2000); Ancestry (includes multiple ancestries): 41.1% German, 40.7% Norwegian, 17.8% Swedish, 8.3% Irish, 5.3% English (2000).
Economy: Employment by occupation: 10.6% management, 19.4% professional, 9.5% services, 19.0% sales, 4.2% farming, 18.3% construction, 19.0% production (2000).
Income: Per capita income: $18,409 (2000); Median household income: $39,375 (2000); Poverty rate: 11.9% (2000).
Taxes: Total city taxes per capita: $86 (1997); City property taxes per capita: $86 (1997).
Education: High school graduation rate: 84.5% (2000); College graduation rate: 17.3% (2000).
Housing: Homeownership rate: 87.9% (2000); Median home value: $90,000 (2000); Median rent: $200 per month (2000); Median age of housing: 34 years (2000).
Transportation: Commute to work: 86.6% car, 0.0% public transportation, 1.5% walk, 11.1% work from home (2000); Travel time to work: 37.1% less than 15 minutes, 31.5% 15 to 30 minutes, 19.4% 30 to 45 minutes, 5.2% 45 to 60 minutes, 6.9% 60 minutes or more (2000)

EVERTS (township). Covers a land area of 23.135 square miles and a water area of 11.252 square miles. Located at 46.32° N. Lat.; 95.73° W. Long.
Population: 774 (2000); Race: 99.5% White, 0.0% Black, 0.0% Asian, 0.0% American Indian and Alaska Native, 0.3% Hispanic of any race, 0.3% two or more races (2000); Density: 33.5 persons per square mile (2000); Age: 13.0% under 18, 32.1% over 64 (2000); Marriage status: 11.6% never married, 71.6% now married, 12.2% widowed, 4.7% divorced (2000); Foreign born: 1.3% (2000); Ancestry (includes multiple ancestries): 46.6% German, 33.4% Norwegian, 9.8% Irish, 7.4% Danish, 7.2% Swedish (2000).
Economy: Single-family building permits issued: 0 (2001) / 1 (2000); Multi-family building permits issued: 0 (2001) / 0 (2000); Employment by occupation: 13.8% management, 25.1% professional, 15.9% services, 25.4% sales, 2.1% farming, 8.9% construction, 8.9% production (2000).
Income: Per capita income: $27,823 (2000); Median household income: $44,917 (2000); Poverty rate: 3.6% (2000).
Taxes: Total city taxes per capita: $97 (1997); City property taxes per capita: $97 (1997).
Education: High school graduation rate: 85.3% (2000); College graduation rate: 27.5% (2000).
Housing: Homeownership rate: 95.7% (2000); Median home value: $120,500 (2000); Median rent: $488 per month (2000); Median age of housing: 27 years (2000).
Transportation: Commute to work: 92.5% car, 0.0% public transportation, 0.6% walk, 6.9% work from home (2000); Travel time to work: 33.8% less than 15 minutes, 25.3% 15 to 30 minutes, 24.7% 30 to 45 minutes, 4.1% 45 to 60 minutes, 12.2% 60 minutes or more (2000)

FERGUS FALLS (city). Covers a land area of 13.060 square miles and a water area of 1.050 square miles. Located at 46.28° N. Lat.; 96.07° W. Long. Elevation is 1,211 feet.
History: Fergus Falls was first laid out in 1857 by Joseph Whitford, blacksmith, engineer, and frontiersman, who led an expedition here. The town was named for James Fergus, a Scot who came to Minnesota in 1854 and who financed Whitford's expedition. Fergus Falls was incorporated as a village in 1872, and developed as an industrial center with power supplied by the Red River Falls.
Population: 13,471 (2000); Race: 96.7% White, 1.1% Black, 0.4% Asian, 1.1% American Indian and Alaska Native, 1.0% Hispanic of any race, 0.2% two or more races (2000); Density: 1,031.5 persons per square mile (2000); Age: 23.4% under 18, 21.9% over 64 (2000); Marriage status: 25.6% never married, 51.7% now married, 11.9% widowed, 10.8% divorced (2000); Foreign born: 1.4% (2000); Ancestry (includes multiple ancestries): 40.8% Norwegian, 33.6% German, 10.7% Swedish, 5.4% Irish, 5.0% English (2000).
Vital Statistics: Birth rate: 115.1 per 10,000 population (1998)
Economy: Single-family building permits issued: 37 (2001) / 51 (2000); Multi-family building permits issued: 0 (2001) / 0 (2000); Employment by occupation: 9.3% management, 20.8% professional, 17.6% services, 29.6% sales, 1.1% farming, 6.8% construction, 14.8% production (2000).
Income: Per capita income: $18,929 (2000); Median household income: $31,454 (2000); Poverty rate: 10.8% (2000).
Taxes: Total city taxes per capita: $251 (2000); City property taxes per capita: $237 (2000).
Education: High school graduation rate: 80.1% (2000); College graduation rate: 19.8% (2000).

School District(s)

Fergus Falls (KG-12)
2000 Enrollment: 3,113 218-998-0544
Fergus Falls Area Special Education Coop (PK-10)
2000 Enrollment: 70 218-736-7576
Region 4-Lakes Country Service Coop (09-12)
2000 Enrollment: 55 218-739-3273

Two-year College(s)

Fergus Falls Community College (Public)
2001 Enrollment: 2,283 218-739-7500
2001 Tuition: In-state $2,640; Out-of-state $5,280

Housing: Homeownership rate: 65.0% (2000); Median home value: $76,000 (2000); Median rent: $349 per month (2000); Median age of housing: 41 years (2000).
Hospitals: Fergus Falls Regional Treatment Center (430 beds); Lake Region Healthcare Corporation (108 beds)
Safety: Violent crime rate: 21.3 per 10,000 population; Property crime rate: 411.3 per 10,000 population (2001).
Newspapers: Daily Journal (6 x week)
Transportation: Commute to work: 91.7% car, 1.6% public transportation, 3.8% walk, 2.6% work from home (2000); Travel time to work: 77.4% less than 15 minutes, 12.7% 15 to 30 minutes, 3.0% 30 to 45 minutes, 1.8% 45 to 60 minutes, 5.0% 60 minutes or more (2000)
Additional Information Contacts
Fergus Falls Chamber of Commerce 218-736-6951
Lake Region Association of Realtors 218-739-0595

FERGUS FALLS (township). Covers a land area of 27.940 square miles and a water area of 0.622 square miles. Located at 46.32° N. Lat.; 96.10° W. Long. Elevation is 1,211 feet.
History: Incorporated 1872.
Population: 1,051 (2000); Race: 99.8% White, 0.2% Black, 0.0% Asian, 0.0% American Indian and Alaska Native, 0.0% Hispanic of any race, 0.0% two or more races (2000); Density: 37.6 persons per square mile (2000); Age: 27.6% under 18, 13.5% over 64 (2000); Marriage status: 19.3% never married, 74.3% now married, 2.5% widowed, 4.0% divorced (2000); Foreign born: 0.5% (2000); Ancestry (includes multiple ancestries): 47.3% German, 45.4% Norwegian, 11.3% Swedish, 4.8% Irish, 4.5% French (except Basque) (2000).
Economy: Railroad junction. Agriculture is central to the economy: poultry, livestock; grain, sunflowers, sugar beets; dairying. Manufacturing: furniture, food and beverages, printing, consumer goods. State hospital. Municipal airport to West. Single-family building permits issued: 4 (2001) / 5 (2000); Multi-family building permits issued: 0 (2001) / 0 (2000); Employment by occupation: 14.5% management, 25.6% professional, 12.0% services, 26.8% sales, 1.3% farming, 7.9% construction, 12.0% production (2000).
Income: Per capita income: $20,003 (2000); Median household income: $54,345 (2000); Poverty rate: 2.3% (2000).
Taxes: Total city taxes per capita: $64 (2000); City property taxes per capita: $63 (2000).
Education: High school graduation rate: 89.1% (2000); College graduation rate: 25.2% (2000).
Housing: Homeownership rate: 96.8% (2000); Median home value: $110,900 (2000); Median rent: $317 per month (2000); Median age of housing: 26 years (2000).
Transportation: Commute to work: 88.8% car, 0.9% public transportation, 1.5% walk, 8.5% work from home (2000); Travel time to work: 62.9% less than 15 minutes, 25.7% 15 to 30 minutes, 6.6% 30 to 45 minutes, 1.8% 45 to 60 minutes, 3.0% 60 minutes or more (2000)

FOLDEN (township). Covers a land area of 34.494 square miles and a water area of 1.092 square miles. Located at 46.23° N. Lat.; 95.47° W. Long.
Population: 265 (2000); Race: 100.0% White, 0.0% Black, 0.0% Asian, 0.0% American Indian and Alaska Native, 0.7% Hispanic of any race, 0.0% two or more races (2000); Density: 7.7 persons per square mile (2000); Age: 17.1% under 18, 15.3% over 64 (2000); Marriage status: 23.8% never married, 67.6% now married, 4.1% widowed, 4.5% divorced (2000); Foreign born: 1.1% (2000); Ancestry (includes multiple ancestries): 44.0% German, 41.5% Norwegian, 5.8% Irish, 4.7% Swedish, 4.0% Polish (2000).
Economy: Employment by occupation: 19.1% management, 17.6% professional, 10.3% services, 16.2% sales, 0.7% farming, 12.5% construction, 23.5% production (2000).
Income: Per capita income: $18,252 (2000); Median household income: $38,333 (2000); Poverty rate: 6.9% (2000).
Taxes: Total city taxes per capita: $83 (1997); City property taxes per capita: $83 (1997).
Education: High school graduation rate: 83.2% (2000); College graduation rate: 10.1% (2000).
Housing: Homeownership rate: 91.3% (2000); Median home value: $64,200 (2000); Median age of housing: 37 years (2000).
Transportation: Commute to work: 82.1% car, 0.0% public transportation, 0.0% walk, 14.9% work from home (2000); Travel time to work: 31.6% less than 15 minutes, 23.7% 15 to 30 minutes, 27.2% 30 to 45 minutes, 7.9% 45 to 60 minutes, 9.6% 60 minutes or more (2000)

FRIBERG (township). Covers a land area of 32.741 square miles and a water area of 3.008 square miles. Located at 46.42° N. Lat.; 95.96° W. Long.
Population: 774 (2000); Race: 97.9% White, 0.0% Black, 1.6% Asian, 0.0% American Indian and Alaska Native, 0.7% Hispanic of any race, 0.4% two or more races (2000); Density: 23.6 persons per square mile (2000); Age: 29.7% under 18, 14.0% over 64 (2000); Marriage status: 24.5% never married, 64.4% now married, 3.8% widowed, 7.4% divorced (2000); Foreign born: 1.1% (2000); Ancestry (includes multiple ancestries): 38.3% Norwegian, 35.8% German, 8.3% Swedish, 6.0% Irish, 5.0% English (2000).
Economy: Employment by occupation: 20.2% management, 15.8% professional, 17.8% services, 23.2% sales, 1.2% farming, 9.4% construction, 12.3% production (2000).
Income: Per capita income: $19,184 (2000); Median household income: $40,556 (2000); Poverty rate: 8.6% (2000).
Taxes: Total city taxes per capita: $39 (1997); City property taxes per capita: $39 (1997).
Education: High school graduation rate: 83.3% (2000); College graduation rate: 15.8% (2000).
Housing: Homeownership rate: 93.3% (2000); Median home value: $97,900 (2000); Median rent: $313 per month (2000); Median age of housing: 26 years (2000).
Transportation: Commute to work: 90.8% car, 0.0% public transportation, 1.0% walk, 8.2% work from home (2000); Travel time to work: 12.8% less than 15 minutes, 65.8% 15 to 30 minutes, 10.6% 30 to 45 minutes, 6.3% 45 to 60 minutes, 4.6% 60 minutes or more (2000)

GIRARD (township). Covers a land area of 25.727 square miles and a water area of 9.978 square miles. Located at 46.31° N. Lat.; 95.60° W. Long.
Population: 697 (2000); Race: 99.6% White, 0.0% Black, 0.0% Asian, 0.0% American Indian and Alaska Native, 0.4% Hispanic of any race, 0.4% two or more races (2000); Density: 27.1 persons per square mile (2000); Age: 20.6% under 18, 20.9% over 64 (2000); Marriage status: 15.1% never married, 79.3% now married, 3.1% widowed, 2.6% divorced (2000); Foreign born: 1.7% (2000); Ancestry (includes multiple ancestries): 36.5% German, 33.5% Norwegian, 17.3% Swedish, 7.1% English, 5.8% Irish (2000).
Economy: Single-family building permits issued: 3 (2001) / 3 (2000); Multi-family building permits issued: 0 (2001) / 0 (2000); Employment by

occupation: 19.9% management, 23.2% professional, 14.8% services, 21.0% sales, 0.0% farming, 8.1% construction, 12.9% production (2000).
Income: Per capita income: $19,295 (2000); Median household income: $41,500 (2000); Poverty rate: 8.8% (2000).
Taxes: Total city taxes per capita: $150 (1997); City property taxes per capita: $150 (1997).
Education: High school graduation rate: 90.3% (2000); College graduation rate: 28.2% (2000).
Housing: Homeownership rate: 95.9% (2000); Median home value: $149,400 (2000); Median rent: $500 per month (2000); Median age of housing: 30 years (2000).
Transportation: Commute to work: 89.1% car, 0.0% public transportation, 2.3% walk, 7.9% work from home (2000); Travel time to work: 24.6% less than 15 minutes, 32.4% 15 to 30 minutes, 29.5% 30 to 45 minutes, 10.2% 45 to 60 minutes, 3.3% 60 minutes or more (2000)

GORMAN (township). Covers a land area of 32.532 square miles and a water area of 3.236 square miles. Located at 46.68° N. Lat.; 95.61° W. Long.
Population: 398 (2000); Race: 97.0% White, 0.0% Black, 0.0% Asian, 0.0% American Indian and Alaska Native, 0.5% Hispanic of any race, 2.5% two or more races (2000); Density: 12.2 persons per square mile (2000); Age: 23.7% under 18, 11.7% over 64 (2000); Marriage status: 23.6% never married, 71.9% now married, 0.0% widowed, 4.4% divorced (2000); Foreign born: 0.5% (2000); Ancestry (includes multiple ancestries): 54.3% German, 16.1% Norwegian, 16.1% Polish, 9.7% Swedish, 8.5% Irish (2000).
Economy: Employment by occupation: 20.7% management, 11.0% professional, 13.1% services, 20.3% sales, 4.2% farming, 14.3% construction, 16.5% production (2000).
Income: Per capita income: $20,466 (2000); Median household income: $48,750 (2000); Poverty rate: 4.6% (2000).
Taxes: Total city taxes per capita: $118 (1997); City property taxes per capita: $118 (1997).
Education: High school graduation rate: 87.3% (2000); College graduation rate: 21.6% (2000).
Housing: Homeownership rate: 87.5% (2000); Median home value: $118,800 (2000); Median rent: $325 per month (2000); Median age of housing: 44 years (2000).
Transportation: Commute to work: 86.0% car, 0.0% public transportation, 3.8% walk, 8.9% work from home (2000); Travel time to work: 57.5% less than 15 minutes, 27.1% 15 to 30 minutes, 7.5% 30 to 45 minutes, 0.9% 45 to 60 minutes, 7.0% 60 minutes or more (2000)

HENNING (city). Covers a land area of 3.094 square miles and a water area of 0 square miles. Located at 46.32° N. Lat.; 95.44° W. Long. Elevation is 1,439 feet.
Population: 719 (2000); Race: 100.0% White, 0.0% Black, 0.0% Asian, 0.0% American Indian and Alaska Native, 0.0% Hispanic of any race, 0.0% two or more races (2000); Density: 232.4 persons per square mile (2000); Age: 19.0% under 18, 34.7% over 64 (2000); Marriage status: 19.4% never married, 53.9% now married, 19.0% widowed, 7.7% divorced (2000); Foreign born: 0.8% (2000); Ancestry (includes multiple ancestries): 39.2% Norwegian, 38.2% German, 8.3% Swedish, 6.7% English, 5.3% Irish (2000).
Economy: Single-family building permits issued: 2 (2001) / 0 (2000); Multi-family building permits issued: 0 (2001) / 0 (2000); Employment by occupation: 11.2% management, 22.4% professional, 20.5% services, 17.9% sales, 2.6% farming, 8.6% construction, 16.8% production (2000).
Income: Per capita income: $15,450 (2000); Median household income: $21,944 (2000); Poverty rate: 19.0% (2000).
Taxes: Total city taxes per capita: $179 (1997); City property taxes per capita: $177 (1997).
Education: High school graduation rate: 72.2% (2000); College graduation rate: 10.0% (2000).

School District(s)

Henning (PK-12)
2000 Enrollment: 382 218-583-2927
Housing: Homeownership rate: 66.5% (2000); Median home value: $50,400 (2000); Median rent: $236 per month (2000); Median age of housing: 51 years (2000).
Newspapers: The Henning Advocate (1 x week)
Transportation: Commute to work: 81.2% car, 0.0% public transportation, 15.3% walk, 3.4% work from home (2000); Travel time to work: 59.5% less than 15 minutes, 16.3% 15 to 30 minutes, 11.1% 30 to 45 minutes, 7.9% 45 to 60 minutes, 5.2% 60 minutes or more (2000)

HENNING (township). Covers a land area of 32.586 square miles and a water area of 0.281 square miles. Located at 46.31° N. Lat.; 95.48° W. Long. Elevation is 1,439 feet.
Population: 426 (2000); Race: 100.0% White, 0.0% Black, 0.0% Asian, 0.0% American Indian and Alaska Native, 0.0% Hispanic of any race, 0.0% two or more races (2000); Density: 13.1 persons per square mile (2000); Age: 19.6% under 18, 30.3% over 64 (2000); Marriage status: 19.0% never married, 63.6% now married, 11.5% widowed, 5.9% divorced (2000); Foreign born: 1.4% (2000); Ancestry (includes multiple ancestries): 52.0% German, 33.0% Norwegian, 7.2% Irish, 6.5% Swedish, 5.1% Scandinavian (2000).
Economy: Grain, sunflowers; livestock, poultry; dairying. Resort area. Single-family building permits issued: 2 (2001) / 2 (2000); Multi-family building permits issued: 0 (2001) / 0 (2000); Employment by occupation: 20.3% management, 8.8% professional, 20.3% services, 22.0% sales, 1.6% farming, 11.5% construction, 15.4% production (2000).
Income: Per capita income: $13,215 (2000); Median household income: $31,875 (2000); Poverty rate: 9.3% (2000).
Taxes: Total city taxes per capita: $81 (1997); City property taxes per capita: $81 (1997).
Education: High school graduation rate: 78.4% (2000); College graduation rate: 5.6% (2000).
Housing: Homeownership rate: 88.7% (2000); Median home value: $77,500 (2000); Median rent: $225 per month (2000); Median age of housing: 38 years (2000).
Transportation: Commute to work: 80.0% car, 0.0% public transportation, 3.9% walk, 15.6% work from home (2000); Travel time to work: 50.7% less than 15 minutes, 19.1% 15 to 30 minutes, 16.4% 30 to 45 minutes, 6.6% 45 to 60 minutes, 7.2% 60 minutes or more (2000)

HOBART (township). Covers a land area of 28.771 square miles and a water area of 7.200 square miles. Located at 46.66° N. Lat.; 95.72° W. Long.
Population: 733 (2000); Race: 99.1% White, 0.6% Black, 0.0% Asian, 0.0% American Indian and Alaska Native, 0.3% Hispanic of any race, 0.3% two or more races (2000); Density: 25.5 persons per square mile (2000); Age: 21.0% under 18, 17.4% over 64 (2000); Marriage status: 19.2% never married, 69.6% now married, 4.3% widowed, 6.9% divorced (2000); Foreign born: 0.7% (2000); Ancestry (includes multiple ancestries): 52.3% German, 32.1% Norwegian, 9.7% English, 9.2% Swedish, 6.6% Irish (2000).
Economy: Employment by occupation: 17.3% management, 14.6% professional, 10.7% services, 26.0% sales, 3.3% farming, 9.9% construction, 18.2% production (2000).
Income: Per capita income: $18,614 (2000); Median household income: $42,115 (2000); Poverty rate: 6.9% (2000).
Education: High school graduation rate: 86.1% (2000); College graduation rate: 21.1% (2000).
Housing: Homeownership rate: 88.0% (2000); Median home value: $119,300 (2000); Median rent: $375 per month (2000); Median age of housing: 29 years (2000).
Transportation: Commute to work: 93.1% car, 0.6% public transportation, 1.2% walk, 3.9% work from home (2000); Travel time to work: 33.0% less than 15 minutes, 48.1% 15 to 30 minutes, 4.1% 30 to 45 minutes, 2.8% 45 to 60 minutes, 11.9% 60 minutes or more (2000)

HOMESTEAD (township). Covers a land area of 36.394 square miles and a water area of 0.155 square miles. Located at 46.58° N. Lat.; 95.34° W. Long.
Population: 371 (2000); Race: 98.1% White, 0.0% Black, 0.0% Asian, 0.2% American Indian and Alaska Native, 0.0% Hispanic of any race, 1.7% two or more races (2000); Density: 10.2 persons per square mile (2000); Age: 31.1% under 18, 8.9% over 64 (2000); Marriage status: 21.4% never married, 72.8% now married, 1.9% widowed, 3.8% divorced (2000); Foreign born: 1.2% (2000); Ancestry (includes multiple ancestries): 58.8% German, 19.0% Finnish, 16.4% Norwegian, 11.1% Irish, 6.7% Swedish (2000).
Economy: Employment by occupation: 18.6% management, 17.7% professional, 12.1% services, 17.2% sales, 3.3% farming, 2.8% construction, 28.4% production (2000).
Income: Per capita income: $14,596 (2000); Median household income: $38,036 (2000); Poverty rate: 11.8% (2000).
Taxes: Total city taxes per capita: $32 (1997); City property taxes per capita: $32 (1997).
Education: High school graduation rate: 86.6% (2000); College graduation rate: 11.5% (2000).

Housing: Homeownership rate: 90.5% (2000); Median home value: $88,800 (2000); Median rent: $225 per month (2000); Median age of housing: 49 years (2000).
Transportation: Commute to work: 88.5% car, 0.0% public transportation, 2.9% walk, 8.6% work from home (2000); Travel time to work: 34.6% less than 15 minutes, 43.5% 15 to 30 minutes, 8.4% 30 to 45 minutes, 6.8% 45 to 60 minutes, 6.8% 60 minutes or more (2000)

INMAN (township). Covers a land area of 36.563 square miles and a water area of 0 square miles. Located at 46.31° N. Lat.; 95.32° W. Long.
Population: 352 (2000); Race: 97.6% White, 2.4% Black, 0.0% Asian, 0.0% American Indian and Alaska Native, 0.0% Hispanic of any race, 0.0% two or more races (2000); Density: 9.6 persons per square mile (2000); Age: 33.1% under 18, 18.4% over 64 (2000); Marriage status: 15.2% never married, 66.7% now married, 9.5% widowed, 8.6% divorced (2000); Foreign born: 0.0% (2000); Ancestry (includes multiple ancestries): 38.6% German, 27.1% Norwegian, 7.8% English, 7.2% Polish, 6.9% Other groups (2000).
Economy: Employment by occupation: 17.9% management, 15.2% professional, 13.1% services, 17.2% sales, 12.4% farming, 4.8% construction, 19.3% production (2000).
Income: Per capita income: $12,351 (2000); Median household income: $26,250 (2000); Poverty rate: 20.0% (2000).
Taxes: Total city taxes per capita: $31 (1997); City property taxes per capita: $31 (1997).
Education: High school graduation rate: 74.3% (2000); College graduation rate: 4.3% (2000).
Housing: Homeownership rate: 87.9% (2000); Median home value: $67,500 (2000); Median rent: $275 per month (2000); Median age of housing: 47 years (2000).
Transportation: Commute to work: 76.2% car, 0.0% public transportation, 4.2% walk, 18.9% work from home (2000); Travel time to work: 45.7% less than 15 minutes, 31.0% 15 to 30 minutes, 6.0% 30 to 45 minutes, 6.0% 45 to 60 minutes, 11.2% 60 minutes or more (2000)

LEAF LAKE (township). Covers a land area of 32.807 square miles and a water area of 2.814 square miles. Located at 46.41° N. Lat.; 95.47° W. Long.
Population: 467 (2000); Race: 100.0% White, 0.0% Black, 0.0% Asian, 0.0% American Indian and Alaska Native, 1.0% Hispanic of any race, 0.0% two or more races (2000); Density: 14.2 persons per square mile (2000); Age: 26.5% under 18, 15.7% over 64 (2000); Marriage status: 20.9% never married, 70.7% now married, 2.5% widowed, 5.9% divorced (2000); Foreign born: 1.4% (2000); Ancestry (includes multiple ancestries): 46.0% German, 18.5% Finnish, 14.3% Norwegian, 6.6% Irish, 5.0% Other groups (2000).
Economy: Employment by occupation: 20.0% management, 19.5% professional, 13.2% services, 15.9% sales, 2.3% farming, 14.1% construction, 15.0% production (2000).
Income: Per capita income: $14,634 (2000); Median household income: $32,768 (2000); Poverty rate: 16.5% (2000).
Taxes: Total city taxes per capita: $80 (1997); City property taxes per capita: $80 (1997).
Education: High school graduation rate: 83.8% (2000); College graduation rate: 15.6% (2000).
Housing: Homeownership rate: 91.0% (2000); Median home value: $81,000 (2000); Median rent: $275 per month (2000); Median age of housing: 32 years (2000).
Transportation: Commute to work: 86.8% car, 0.0% public transportation, 0.9% walk, 11.4% work from home (2000); Travel time to work: 32.0% less than 15 minutes, 42.3% 15 to 30 minutes, 10.3% 30 to 45 minutes, 6.2% 45 to 60 minutes, 9.3% 60 minutes or more (2000)

LEAF MOUNTAIN (township). Covers a land area of 31.863 square miles and a water area of 4.081 square miles. Located at 46.15° N. Lat.; 95.59° W. Long.
Population: 309 (2000); Race: 99.1% White, 0.0% Black, 0.9% Asian, 0.0% American Indian and Alaska Native, 0.0% Hispanic of any race, 0.0% two or more races (2000); Density: 9.7 persons per square mile (2000); Age: 25.9% under 18, 15.4% over 64 (2000); Marriage status: 23.8% never married, 69.1% now married, 2.6% widowed, 4.5% divorced (2000); Foreign born: 1.5% (2000); Ancestry (includes multiple ancestries): 55.9% German, 16.0% Norwegian, 13.0% Polish, 11.1% Swedish, 9.9% Irish (2000).
Economy: Employment by occupation: 20.8% management, 21.5% professional, 14.8% services, 12.8% sales, 5.4% farming, 11.4% construction, 13.4% production (2000).
Income: Per capita income: $20,045 (2000); Median household income: $31,429 (2000); Poverty rate: 16.0% (2000).
Taxes: Total city taxes per capita: $87 (1997); City property taxes per capita: $87 (1997).
Education: High school graduation rate: 75.7% (2000); College graduation rate: 10.1% (2000).
Housing: Homeownership rate: 87.1% (2000); Median home value: $102,100 (2000); Median rent: $275 per month (2000); Median age of housing: 31 years (2000).
Transportation: Commute to work: 74.1% car, 0.0% public transportation, 8.2% walk, 16.3% work from home (2000); Travel time to work: 27.6% less than 15 minutes, 26.0% 15 to 30 minutes, 35.8% 30 to 45 minutes, 5.7% 45 to 60 minutes, 4.9% 60 minutes or more (2000)

LIDA (township). Covers a land area of 20.608 square miles and a water area of 15.013 square miles. Located at 46.60° N. Lat.; 95.96° W. Long.
Population: 697 (2000); Race: 99.5% White, 0.0% Black, 0.0% Asian, 0.3% American Indian and Alaska Native, 0.3% Hispanic of any race, 0.3% two or more races (2000); Density: 33.8 persons per square mile (2000); Age: 20.2% under 18, 18.6% over 64 (2000); Marriage status: 16.3% never married, 73.2% now married, 5.6% widowed, 4.9% divorced (2000); Foreign born: 0.7% (2000); Ancestry (includes multiple ancestries): 46.7% Norwegian, 39.9% German, 14.7% Swedish, 13.0% Irish, 5.5% French (except Basque) (2000).
Economy: Employment by occupation: 26.3% management, 13.9% professional, 8.5% services, 26.1% sales, 3.7% farming, 9.6% construction, 11.9% production (2000).
Income: Per capita income: $22,291 (2000); Median household income: $42,222 (2000); Poverty rate: 7.1% (2000).
Taxes: Total city taxes per capita: $155 (2000); City property taxes per capita: $155 (2000).
Education: High school graduation rate: 87.7% (2000); College graduation rate: 18.2% (2000).
Housing: Homeownership rate: 94.3% (2000); Median home value: $139,800 (2000); Median rent: $329 per month (2000); Median age of housing: 32 years (2000).
Transportation: Commute to work: 86.2% car, 1.1% public transportation, 2.3% walk, 10.3% work from home (2000); Travel time to work: 30.4% less than 15 minutes, 31.3% 15 to 30 minutes, 13.7% 30 to 45 minutes, 7.0% 45 to 60 minutes, 17.6% 60 minutes or more (2000)

MAINE (township). Covers a land area of 30.113 square miles and a water area of 5.841 square miles. Located at 46.40° N. Lat.; 95.85° W. Long.
Population: 686 (2000); Race: 99.0% White, 0.0% Black, 0.0% Asian, 0.7% American Indian and Alaska Native, 1.8% Hispanic of any race, 0.0% two or more races (2000); Density: 22.8 persons per square mile (2000); Age: 25.4% under 18, 15.7% over 64 (2000); Marriage status: 19.2% never married, 67.2% now married, 6.2% widowed, 7.5% divorced (2000); Foreign born: 0.9% (2000); Ancestry (includes multiple ancestries): 40.1% German, 36.5% Norwegian, 9.6% Irish, 9.3% Swedish, 4.9% French (except Basque) (2000).
Economy: Employment by occupation: 15.9% management, 17.8% professional, 17.2% services, 16.5% sales, 2.6% farming, 17.5% construction, 12.6% production (2000).
Income: Per capita income: $18,744 (2000); Median household income: $36,875 (2000); Poverty rate: 7.7% (2000).
Taxes: Total city taxes per capita: $82 (1997); City property taxes per capita: $82 (1997).
Education: High school graduation rate: 86.1% (2000); College graduation rate: 18.5% (2000).
Housing: Homeownership rate: 88.4% (2000); Median home value: $135,900 (2000); Median rent: $231 per month (2000); Median age of housing: 23 years (2000).
Transportation: Commute to work: 90.9% car, 0.0% public transportation, 3.3% walk, 5.9% work from home (2000); Travel time to work: 8.7% less than 15 minutes, 44.3% 15 to 30 minutes, 31.1% 30 to 45 minutes, 5.5% 45 to 60 minutes, 10.4% 60 minutes or more (2000)

MAPLEWOOD (township). Covers a land area of 31.974 square miles and a water area of 3.617 square miles. Located at 46.49° N. Lat.; 95.97° W. Long.
Population: 333 (2000); Race: 95.5% White, 0.0% Black, 0.0% Asian, 4.5% American Indian and Alaska Native, 0.0% Hispanic of any race, 0.0% two or more races (2000); Density: 10.4 persons per square mile (2000); Age: 25.0% under 18, 14.5% over 64 (2000); Marriage status: 23.7% never married, 66.8% now married, 3.3% widowed, 6.2% divorced (2000); Foreign born: 0.0% (2000); Ancestry (includes multiple ancestries): 43.1% German, 39.2% Norwegian, 12.0% Swedish, 3.6% Irish, 3.0% Other groups (2000).

Economy: Unemployment rate: 2.9% (11/2002); Total civilian labor force: 21,163 (11/2002); Employment by occupation: 19.9% management, 17.5% professional, 16.3% services, 15.1% sales, 2.4% farming, 13.3% construction, 15.7% production (2000).
Income: Per capita income: $23,181 (2000); Median household income: $45,250 (2000); Poverty rate: 3.3% (2000).
Taxes: Total city taxes per capita: $94 (1997); City property taxes per capita: $94 (1997).
Education: High school graduation rate: 76.3% (2000); College graduation rate: 21.6% (2000).
Housing: Homeownership rate: 93.7% (2000); Median home value: $95,000 (2000); Median rent: $392 per month (2000); Median age of housing: 28 years (2000).
Transportation: Commute to work: 88.0% car, 0.0% public transportation, 2.4% walk, 8.4% work from home (2000); Travel time to work: 26.3% less than 15 minutes, 34.9% 15 to 30 minutes, 24.3% 30 to 45 minutes, 11.8% 45 to 60 minutes, 2.6% 60 minutes or more (2000)

NEW YORK MILLS (city). Covers a land area of 1.250 square miles and a water area of 0 square miles. Located at 46.51° N. Lat.; 95.37° W. Long. Elevation is 1,413 feet.
History: New York Mills was settled by people of Finnish ancestry.
Population: 1,158 (2000); Race: 98.3% White, 0.0% Black, 0.0% Asian, 0.0% American Indian and Alaska Native, 2.2% Hispanic of any race, 1.4% two or more races (2000); Density: 926.7 persons per square mile (2000); Age: 22.3% under 18, 31.4% over 64 (2000); Marriage status: 21.9% never married, 51.8% now married, 17.4% widowed, 8.9% divorced (2000); Foreign born: 0.3% (2000); Ancestry (includes multiple ancestries): 33.4% German, 23.5% Finnish, 14.3% Norwegian, 7.0% Swedish, 5.8% English (2000).
Economy: Single-family building permits issued: 6 (2001) / 3 (2000); Multi-family building permits issued: 0 (2001) / 0 (2000); Employment by occupation: 7.5% management, 20.4% professional, 21.9% services, 17.6% sales, 1.3% farming, 10.8% construction, 20.4% production (2000).
Income: Per capita income: $15,949 (2000); Median household income: $27,596 (2000); Poverty rate: 17.1% (2000).
Taxes: Total city taxes per capita: $32 (1997); City property taxes per capita: $27 (1997).
Education: High school graduation rate: 75.8% (2000); College graduation rate: 19.4% (2000).

School District(s)

New York Mills (PK-12)
2000 Enrollment: 746 218-385-4200

Housing: Homeownership rate: 59.7% (2000); Median home value: $61,500 (2000); Median rent: $304 per month (2000); Median age of housing: 30 years (2000).
Newspapers: New York Mills Herald (1 x week)
Transportation: Commute to work: 85.1% car, 0.0% public transportation, 9.5% walk, 5.4% work from home (2000); Travel time to work: 69.3% less than 15 minutes, 21.7% 15 to 30 minutes, 4.3% 30 to 45 minutes, 2.1% 45 to 60 minutes, 2.5% 60 minutes or more (2000)

NEWTON (township). Covers a land area of 34.968 square miles and a water area of 0.254 square miles. Located at 46.49° N. Lat.; 95.35° W. Long.
Population: 751 (2000); Race: 97.6% White, 0.0% Black, 0.7% Asian, 0.8% American Indian and Alaska Native, 0.0% Hispanic of any race, 0.8% two or more races (2000); Density: 21.5 persons per square mile (2000); Age: 29.9% under 18, 11.3% over 64 (2000); Marriage status: 22.1% never married, 71.0% now married, 2.0% widowed, 4.9% divorced (2000); Foreign born: 1.1% (2000); Ancestry (includes multiple ancestries): 47.6% German, 30.0% Finnish, 11.0% Norwegian, 5.2% Irish, 4.9% Dutch (2000).
Economy: Employment by occupation: 12.5% management, 13.6% professional, 11.2% services, 22.9% sales, 3.0% farming, 10.4% construction, 26.4% production (2000).
Income: Per capita income: $15,925 (2000); Median household income: $39,196 (2000); Poverty rate: 8.5% (2000).
Taxes: Total city taxes per capita: $38 (1997); City property taxes per capita: $38 (1997).
Education: High school graduation rate: 88.2% (2000); College graduation rate: 10.1% (2000).
Housing: Homeownership rate: 88.1% (2000); Median home value: $67,800 (2000); Median rent: $300 per month (2000); Median age of housing: 31 years (2000).
Transportation: Commute to work: 83.6% car, 0.0% public transportation, 5.5% walk, 9.6% work from home (2000); Travel time to work: 56.2% less than 15 minutes, 35.3% 15 to 30 minutes, 6.0% 30 to 45 minutes, 1.2% 45 to 60 minutes, 1.2% 60 minutes or more (2000)

NIDAROS (township). Covers a land area of 30.876 square miles and a water area of 3.579 square miles. Located at 46.25° N. Lat.; 95.58° W. Long.
Population: 317 (2000); Race: 100.0% White, 0.0% Black, 0.0% Asian, 0.0% American Indian and Alaska Native, 0.0% Hispanic of any race, 0.0% two or more races (2000); Density: 10.3 persons per square mile (2000); Age: 23.1% under 18, 26.9% over 64 (2000); Marriage status: 19.4% never married, 68.5% now married, 8.5% widowed, 3.6% divorced (2000); Foreign born: 0.0% (2000); Ancestry (includes multiple ancestries): 41.9% German, 35.1% Norwegian, 22.7% Swedish, 7.5% Irish, 6.5% English (2000).
Economy: Single-family building permits issued: 0 (2001) / 0 (2000); Multi-family building permits issued: 0 (2001) / 0 (2000); Employment by occupation: 19.2% management, 15.0% professional, 10.0% services, 22.5% sales, 1.7% farming, 22.5% construction, 9.2% production (2000).
Income: Per capita income: $16,234 (2000); Median household income: $30,000 (2000); Poverty rate: 3.9% (2000).
Taxes: Total city taxes per capita: $268 (1997); City property taxes per capita: $268 (1997).
Education: High school graduation rate: 81.9% (2000); College graduation rate: 15.8% (2000).
Housing: Homeownership rate: 92.7% (2000); Median home value: $109,400 (2000); Median rent: $125 per month (2000); Median age of housing: 34 years (2000).
Transportation: Commute to work: 76.7% car, 0.0% public transportation, 5.2% walk, 18.1% work from home (2000); Travel time to work: 35.8% less than 15 minutes, 14.7% 15 to 30 minutes, 35.8% 30 to 45 minutes, 6.3% 45 to 60 minutes, 7.4% 60 minutes or more (2000)

NORWEGIAN GROVE (township). Covers a land area of 33.585 square miles and a water area of 2.062 square miles. Located at 46.59° N. Lat.; 96.23° W. Long. Elevation is 1,347 feet.
Population: 349 (2000); Race: 98.8% White, 0.0% Black, 0.0% Asian, 0.6% American Indian and Alaska Native, 0.0% Hispanic of any race, 0.6% two or more races (2000); Density: 10.4 persons per square mile (2000); Age: 26.2% under 18, 19.0% over 64 (2000); Marriage status: 24.8% never married, 62.0% now married, 6.9% widowed, 6.2% divorced (2000); Foreign born: 0.0% (2000); Ancestry (includes multiple ancestries): 63.7% Norwegian, 35.7% German, 6.0% Swedish, 4.2% Irish, 3.9% English (2000).
Economy: Employment by occupation: 15.6% management, 15.6% professional, 16.3% services, 22.4% sales, 2.7% farming, 13.6% construction, 13.6% production (2000).
Income: Per capita income: $12,029 (2000); Median household income: $28,571 (2000); Poverty rate: 23.8% (2000).
Taxes: Total city taxes per capita: $83 (1997); City property taxes per capita: $83 (1997).
Education: High school graduation rate: 76.0% (2000); College graduation rate: 9.3% (2000).
Housing: Homeownership rate: 92.0% (2000); Median home value: $66,100 (2000); Median rent: $325 per month (2000); Median age of housing: 34 years (2000).
Transportation: Commute to work: 84.4% car, 0.0% public transportation, 1.4% walk, 14.3% work from home (2000); Travel time to work: 34.9% less than 15 minutes, 39.7% 15 to 30 minutes, 12.7% 30 to 45 minutes, 10.3% 45 to 60 minutes, 2.4% 60 minutes or more (2000)

OAK VALLEY (township). Covers a land area of 35.699 square miles and a water area of 0 square miles. Located at 46.32° N. Lat.; 95.22° W. Long.
Population: 362 (2000); Race: 100.0% White, 0.0% Black, 0.0% Asian, 0.0% American Indian and Alaska Native, 0.0% Hispanic of any race, 0.0% two or more races (2000); Density: 10.1 persons per square mile (2000); Age: 26.0% under 18, 11.7% over 64 (2000); Marriage status: 24.2% never married, 65.1% now married, 4.0% widowed, 6.7% divorced (2000); Foreign born: 1.1% (2000); Ancestry (includes multiple ancestries): 56.0% German, 17.5% Norwegian, 9.6% Swedish, 8.2% English, 6.3% Irish (2000).
Economy: Employment by occupation: 25.7% management, 5.3% professional, 11.1% services, 18.7% sales, 5.3% farming, 6.4% construction, 27.5% production (2000).
Income: Per capita income: $10,439 (2000); Median household income: $23,500 (2000); Poverty rate: 22.2% (2000).
Taxes: Total city taxes per capita: $26 (1997); City property taxes per capita: $26 (1997).
Education: High school graduation rate: 70.4% (2000); College graduation rate: 5.6% (2000).

Housing: Homeownership rate: 92.7% (2000); Median home value: $66,700 (2000); Median rent: $175 per month (2000); Median age of housing: 52 years (2000).
Transportation: Commute to work: 69.0% car, 0.0% public transportation, 7.0% walk, 21.6% work from home (2000); Travel time to work: 32.8% less than 15 minutes, 44.0% 15 to 30 minutes, 13.4% 30 to 45 minutes, 2.2% 45 to 60 minutes, 7.5% 60 minutes or more (2000)

ORWELL (township). Covers a land area of 33.372 square miles and a water area of 1.547 square miles. Located at 46.23° N. Lat.; 96.19° W. Long.
Population: 173 (2000); Race: 100.0% White, 0.0% Black, 0.0% Asian, 0.0% American Indian and Alaska Native, 0.0% Hispanic of any race, 0.0% two or more races (2000); Density: 5.2 persons per square mile (2000); Age: 31.6% under 18, 15.8% over 64 (2000); Marriage status: 35.0% never married, 55.6% now married, 6.8% widowed, 2.6% divorced (2000); Foreign born: 0.0% (2000); Ancestry (includes multiple ancestries): 59.2% Norwegian, 40.8% German, 7.9% Swedish, 7.9% United States or American, 3.3% Dutch (2000).
Economy: Employment by occupation: 16.4% management, 21.9% professional, 24.7% services, 15.1% sales, 2.7% farming, 8.2% construction, 11.0% production (2000).
Income: Per capita income: $13,757 (2000); Median household income: $29,375 (2000); Poverty rate: 10.5% (2000).
Taxes: Total city taxes per capita: $65 (1997); City property taxes per capita: $65 (1997).
Education: High school graduation rate: 83.2% (2000); College graduation rate: 16.8% (2000).
Housing: Homeownership rate: 85.0% (2000); Median home value: $78,000 (2000); Median rent: <$100 per month (2000); Median age of housing: 48 years (2000).
Transportation: Commute to work: 79.5% car, 0.0% public transportation, 5.5% walk, 15.1% work from home (2000); Travel time to work: 40.3% less than 15 minutes, 35.5% 15 to 30 minutes, 12.9% 30 to 45 minutes, 6.5% 45 to 60 minutes, 4.8% 60 minutes or more (2000)

OSCAR (township). Covers a land area of 34.642 square miles and a water area of 1.406 square miles. Located at 46.40° N. Lat.; 96.20° W. Long.
Population: 218 (2000); Race: 92.1% White, 0.0% Black, 0.0% Asian, 1.3% American Indian and Alaska Native, 7.9% Hispanic of any race, 0.0% two or more races (2000); Density: 6.3 persons per square mile (2000); Age: 26.2% under 18, 11.8% over 64 (2000); Marriage status: 24.2% never married, 70.4% now married, 2.2% widowed, 3.2% divorced (2000); Foreign born: 7.9% (2000); Ancestry (includes multiple ancestries): 54.6% Norwegian, 32.3% German, 13.1% Swedish, 7.9% Irish, 7.0% English (2000).
Economy: Employment by occupation: 19.8% management, 17.5% professional, 1.6% services, 24.6% sales, 1.6% farming, 13.5% construction, 21.4% production (2000).
Income: Per capita income: $17,825 (2000); Median household income: $43,750 (2000); Poverty rate: 0.0% (2000).
Taxes: Total city taxes per capita: $96 (1997); City property taxes per capita: $96 (1997).
Education: High school graduation rate: 88.7% (2000); College graduation rate: 23.3% (2000).
Housing: Homeownership rate: 92.3% (2000); Median home value: $77,500 (2000); Median rent: $188 per month (2000); Median age of housing: 56 years (2000).
Transportation: Commute to work: 89.1% car, 0.0% public transportation, 0.0% walk, 10.9% work from home (2000); Travel time to work: 24.3% less than 15 minutes, 55.7% 15 to 30 minutes, 8.7% 30 to 45 minutes, 1.7% 45 to 60 minutes, 9.6% 60 minutes or more (2000)

OTTER TAIL (township). Covers a land area of 16.355 square miles and a water area of 14.067 square miles. Located at 46.39° N. Lat.; 95.60° W. Long.
Population: 556 (2000); Race: 99.6% White, 0.0% Black, 0.0% Asian, 0.0% American Indian and Alaska Native, 1.3% Hispanic of any race, 0.4% two or more races (2000); Density: 34.0 persons per square mile (2000); Age: 18.2% under 18, 25.4% over 64 (2000); Marriage status: 15.4% never married, 71.5% now married, 5.3% widowed, 7.8% divorced (2000); Foreign born: 0.0% (2000); Ancestry (includes multiple ancestries): 49.2% German, 32.6% Norwegian, 7.9% English, 7.3% Irish, 5.9% Swedish (2000).
Economy: Employment by occupation: 23.5% management, 16.5% professional, 11.8% services, 26.3% sales, 2.4% farming, 7.5% construction, 12.2% production (2000).
Income: Per capita income: $21,931 (2000); Median household income: $37,000 (2000); Poverty rate: 9.1% (2000).
Taxes: Total city taxes per capita: $147 (1997); City property taxes per capita: $147 (1997).
Education: High school graduation rate: 88.6% (2000); College graduation rate: 22.4% (2000).
Housing: Homeownership rate: 90.0% (2000); Median home value: $159,800 (2000); Median rent: $308 per month (2000); Median age of housing: 24 years (2000).
Transportation: Commute to work: 88.0% car, 0.0% public transportation, 1.2% walk, 10.8% work from home (2000); Travel time to work: 22.9% less than 15 minutes, 36.8% 15 to 30 minutes, 20.6% 30 to 45 minutes, 5.8% 45 to 60 minutes, 13.9% 60 minutes or more (2000)

OTTERTAIL (city). Aka Otter Tail. Covers a land area of 4.390 square miles and a water area of 0.751 square miles. Located at 46.42° N. Lat.; 95.56° W. Long. Elevation is 1,355 feet.
History: Sometimes Otter Tail.
Population: 451 (2000); Race: 99.5% White, 0.0% Black, 0.0% Asian, 0.5% American Indian and Alaska Native, 0.0% Hispanic of any race, 0.0% two or more races (2000); Density: 102.7 persons per square mile (2000); Age: 22.9% under 18, 11.1% over 64 (2000); Marriage status: 26.8% never married, 58.0% now married, 5.5% widowed, 9.7% divorced (2000); Foreign born: 0.0% (2000); Ancestry (includes multiple ancestries): 46.7% German, 28.1% Norwegian, 12.7% Swedish, 9.1% Irish, 6.6% English (2000).
Economy: Dairying; poultry; grain. Manufacturing: fur processing; concrete. Single-family building permits issued: 4 (2001) / 10 (2000); Multi-family building permits issued: 0 (2001) / 0 (2000); Employment by occupation: 14.8% management, 7.4% professional, 26.9% services, 21.3% sales, 0.9% farming, 13.0% construction, 15.7% production (2000).
Income: Per capita income: $18,612 (2000); Median household income: $32,188 (2000); Poverty rate: 12.7% (2000).
Taxes: Total city taxes per capita: $194 (1997); City property taxes per capita: $180 (1997).
Education: High school graduation rate: 86.7% (2000); College graduation rate: 11.2% (2000).
Housing: Homeownership rate: 82.0% (2000); Median home value: $90,000 (2000); Median rent: $306 per month (2000); Median age of housing: 19 years (2000).
Transportation: Commute to work: 90.6% car, 0.0% public transportation, 5.6% walk, 2.8% work from home (2000); Travel time to work: 40.1% less than 15 minutes, 36.2% 15 to 30 minutes, 11.1% 30 to 45 minutes, 3.4% 45 to 60 minutes, 9.2% 60 minutes or more (2000)

OTTO (township). Covers a land area of 31.245 square miles and a water area of 4.383 square miles. Located at 46.50° N. Lat.; 95.48° W. Long.
Population: 526 (2000); Race: 100.0% White, 0.0% Black, 0.0% Asian, 0.0% American Indian and Alaska Native, 0.0% Hispanic of any race, 0.0% two or more races (2000); Density: 16.8 persons per square mile (2000); Age: 29.3% under 18, 14.9% over 64 (2000); Marriage status: 22.4% never married, 67.8% now married, 4.9% widowed, 4.9% divorced (2000); Foreign born: 1.8% (2000); Ancestry (includes multiple ancestries): 46.0% German, 26.7% Finnish, 15.9% Norwegian, 9.0% English, 7.0% Swedish (2000).
Economy: Employment by occupation: 15.3% management, 14.5% professional, 14.1% services, 22.9% sales, 2.8% farming, 13.7% construction, 16.9% production (2000).
Income: Per capita income: $17,337 (2000); Median household income: $40,833 (2000); Poverty rate: 8.6% (2000).
Taxes: Total city taxes per capita: $72 (1997); City property taxes per capita: $72 (1997).
Education: High school graduation rate: 85.0% (2000); College graduation rate: 18.0% (2000).
Housing: Homeownership rate: 92.7% (2000); Median home value: $93,500 (2000); Median rent: $375 per month (2000); Median age of housing: 24 years (2000).
Transportation: Commute to work: 86.0% car, 0.0% public transportation, 1.2% walk, 12.8% work from home (2000); Travel time to work: 36.5% less than 15 minutes, 41.7% 15 to 30 minutes, 14.7% 30 to 45 minutes, 3.3% 45 to 60 minutes, 3.8% 60 minutes or more (2000)

PADDOCK (township). Aka Hillview. Covers a land area of 35.697 square miles and a water area of 0.056 square miles. Located at 46.66° N. Lat.; 95.21° W. Long.
Population: 323 (2000); Race: 100.0% White, 0.0% Black, 0.0% Asian, 0.0% American Indian and Alaska Native, 0.0% Hispanic of any race, 0.0% two or more races (2000); Density: 9.0 persons per square mile (2000); Age: 29.4% under 18, 5.8% over 64 (2000); Marriage status: 29.8% never married, 62.4% now married, 1.2% widowed, 6.6% divorced (2000); Foreign born:

1.3% (2000); Ancestry (includes multiple ancestries): 49.0% Finnish, 28.4% German, 14.8% Norwegian, 10.3% Swedish, 8.4% French (except Basque) (2000).
Economy: Employment by occupation: 21.7% management, 8.4% professional, 10.8% services, 14.5% sales, 7.2% farming, 13.3% construction, 24.1% production (2000).
Income: Per capita income: $14,081 (2000); Median household income: $33,542 (2000); Poverty rate: 11.8% (2000).
Education: High school graduation rate: 77.0% (2000); College graduation rate: 9.3% (2000).
Housing: Homeownership rate: 89.8% (2000); Median home value: $43,800 (2000); Median rent: $225 per month (2000); Median age of housing: 60+ years (2000).
Transportation: Commute to work: 76.1% car, 0.0% public transportation, 3.7% walk, 19.0% work from home (2000); Travel time to work: 20.5% less than 15 minutes, 43.2% 15 to 30 minutes, 28.0% 30 to 45 minutes, 0.0% 45 to 60 minutes, 8.3% 60 minutes or more (2000)

PARKERS PRAIRIE (city). Covers a land area of 1.177 square miles and a water area of 0 square miles. Located at 46.15° N. Lat.; 95.33° W. Long. Elevation is 1,464 feet.
Population: 991 (2000); Race: 98.4% White, 0.0% Black, 0.6% Asian, 0.0% American Indian and Alaska Native, 1.5% Hispanic of any race, 0.4% two or more races (2000); Density: 841.8 persons per square mile (2000); Age: 21.9% under 18, 31.1% over 64 (2000); Marriage status: 19.0% never married, 55.0% now married, 18.9% widowed, 7.1% divorced (2000); Foreign born: 2.4% (2000); Ancestry (includes multiple ancestries): 50.3% German, 16.5% Norwegian, 15.7% Swedish, 8.3% Irish, 6.4% English (2000).
Economy: Single-family building permits issued: 2 (2001) / 7 (2000); Multi-family building permits issued: 0 (2001) / 0 (2000); Employment by occupation: 10.6% management, 14.1% professional, 17.2% services, 25.6% sales, 0.3% farming, 9.2% construction, 23.0% production (2000).
Income: Per capita income: $16,748 (2000); Median household income: $28,618 (2000); Poverty rate: 12.2% (2000).
Taxes: Total city taxes per capita: $124 (1997); City property taxes per capita: $120 (1997).
Education: High school graduation rate: 69.5% (2000); College graduation rate: 8.7% (2000).

School District(s)

Parkers Prairie (PK-12)
2000 Enrollment: 642 218-338-6011
Housing: Homeownership rate: 83.0% (2000); Median home value: $55,700 (2000); Median rent: $291 per month (2000); Median age of housing: 47 years (2000).
Newspapers: Independent (1 x week)
Transportation: Commute to work: 85.8% car, 0.0% public transportation, 12.1% walk, 1.4% work from home (2000); Travel time to work: 50.4% less than 15 minutes, 12.3% 15 to 30 minutes, 31.1% 30 to 45 minutes, 0.9% 45 to 60 minutes, 5.3% 60 minutes or more (2000)

PARKERS PRAIRIE (township). Covers a land area of 32.646 square miles and a water area of 2.440 square miles. Located at 46.14° N. Lat.; 95.33° W. Long. Elevation is 1,464 feet.
Population: 345 (2000); Race: 100.0% White, 0.0% Black, 0.0% Asian, 0.0% American Indian and Alaska Native, 0.0% Hispanic of any race, 0.0% two or more races (2000); Density: 10.6 persons per square mile (2000); Age: 28.5% under 18, 7.2% over 64 (2000); Marriage status: 21.5% never married, 63.0% now married, 6.7% widowed, 8.9% divorced (2000); Foreign born: 1.7% (2000); Ancestry (includes multiple ancestries): 70.0% German, 18.7% Swedish, 11.8% Norwegian, 8.1% United States or American, 6.6% Polish (2000).
Economy: Manufacturing: food-processing equipment, seeds, animal feeds. Grain; livestock; dairying. Employment by occupation: 12.6% management, 19.2% professional, 8.2% services, 24.2% sales, 8.8% farming, 17.6% construction, 9.3% production (2000).
Income: Per capita income: $15,018 (2000); Median household income: $37,159 (2000); Poverty rate: 9.9% (2000).
Taxes: Total city taxes per capita: $89 (1997); City property taxes per capita: $89 (1997).
Education: High school graduation rate: 91.6% (2000); College graduation rate: 9.8% (2000).
Housing: Homeownership rate: 83.3% (2000); Median home value: $82,000 (2000); Median rent: $358 per month (2000); Median age of housing: 46 years (2000).
Transportation: Commute to work: 83.0% car, 0.0% public transportation, 2.8% walk, 14.2% work from home (2000); Travel time to work: 58.9% less than 15 minutes, 19.2% 15 to 30 minutes, 15.9% 30 to 45 minutes, 1.3% 45 to 60 minutes, 4.6% 60 minutes or more (2000)

PELICAN (township). Covers a land area of 31.216 square miles and a water area of 1.947 square miles. Located at 46.58° N. Lat.; 96.08° W. Long.
History: "Minnesota man," human skeleton believed to be prehistoric, was found nearby in 1932. Incorporated 1882.
Population: 831 (2000); Race: 85.4% White, 0.0% Black, 0.0% Asian, 1.0% American Indian and Alaska Native, 11.9% Hispanic of any race, 4.8% two or more races (2000); Density: 26.6 persons per square mile (2000); Age: 34.7% under 18, 10.0% over 64 (2000); Marriage status: 23.5% never married, 70.4% now married, 3.4% widowed, 2.6% divorced (2000); Foreign born: 10.8% (2000); Ancestry (includes multiple ancestries): 42.0% Norwegian, 24.3% German, 12.7% Other groups, 11.4% Swedish, 7.0% Yugoslavian (2000).
Economy: Trade center and shipping point for grain and livestock. Agriculture: dairying; livestock; grain, alfalfa, sunflowers. Manufacturing: lumber, feeds, turkey products. Single-family building permits issued: 4 (2001) / 0 (2000); Multi-family building permits issued: 0 (2001) / 0 (2000); Employment by occupation: 9.4% management, 20.6% professional, 10.7% services, 23.0% sales, 1.8% farming, 15.7% construction, 18.8% production (2000).
Income: Per capita income: $15,649 (2000); Median household income: $46,058 (2000); Poverty rate: 11.6% (2000).
Taxes: Total city taxes per capita: $83 (1997); City property taxes per capita: $83 (1997).
Education: High school graduation rate: 82.5% (2000); College graduation rate: 21.1% (2000).
Housing: Homeownership rate: 91.5% (2000); Median home value: $94,700 (2000); Median rent: $325 per month (2000); Median age of housing: 28 years (2000).
Transportation: Commute to work: 90.1% car, 0.0% public transportation, 4.4% walk, 5.0% work from home (2000); Travel time to work: 58.8% less than 15 minutes, 20.9% 15 to 30 minutes, 7.4% 30 to 45 minutes, 4.4% 45 to 60 minutes, 8.5% 60 minutes or more (2000)

PELICAN RAPIDS (city). Covers a land area of 2.621 square miles and a water area of 0.053 square miles. Located at 46.56° N. Lat.; 96.08° W. Long. Elevation is 1,305 feet.
Population: 2,374 (2000); Race: 81.4% White, 0.3% Black, 1.5% Asian, 0.2% American Indian and Alaska Native, 20.7% Hispanic of any race, 6.9% two or more races (2000); Density: 905.8 persons per square mile (2000); Age: 27.6% under 18, 21.2% over 64 (2000); Marriage status: 21.5% never married, 58.1% now married, 12.8% widowed, 7.6% divorced (2000); Foreign born: 20.5% (2000); Ancestry (includes multiple ancestries): 34.0% Norwegian, 24.1% German, 22.6% Other groups, 7.9% Swedish, 4.4% English (2000).
Economy: Single-family building permits issued: 2 (2001) / 1 (2000); Multi-family building permits issued: 20 (2001) / 0 (2000); Employment by occupation: 4.6% management, 19.7% professional, 17.3% services, 15.3% sales, 1.3% farming, 6.7% construction, 35.1% production (2000).
Income: Per capita income: $13,699 (2000); Median household income: $27,232 (2000); Poverty rate: 15.8% (2000).
Taxes: Total city taxes per capita: $178 (1997); City property taxes per capita: $173 (1997).
Education: High school graduation rate: 66.7% (2000); College graduation rate: 18.0% (2000).

School District(s)

Pelican Rapids (PK-12)
2000 Enrollment: 1,311 218-863-5910
Housing: Homeownership rate: 62.3% (2000); Median home value: $69,700 (2000); Median rent: $319 per month (2000); Median age of housing: 39 years (2000).
Newspapers: Pelican Rapids Press (1 x week)
Transportation: Commute to work: 73.0% car, 0.0% public transportation, 21.4% walk, 4.3% work from home (2000); Travel time to work: 77.5% less than 15 minutes, 7.3% 15 to 30 minutes, 7.3% 30 to 45 minutes, 4.4% 45 to 60 minutes, 3.5% 60 minutes or more (2000)

PERHAM (city). Covers a land area of 2.621 square miles and a water area of 0 square miles. Located at 46.59° N. Lat.; 95.57° W. Long. Elevation is 1,370 feet.
Population: 2,559 (2000); Race: 97.2% White, 0.3% Black, 0.8% Asian, 0.4% American Indian and Alaska Native, 1.7% Hispanic of any race, 0.4%

two or more races (2000); Density: 976.2 persons per square mile (2000); Age: 25.0% under 18, 24.5% over 64 (2000); Marriage status: 19.8% never married, 52.4% now married, 18.2% widowed, 9.6% divorced (2000); Foreign born: 2.1% (2000); Ancestry (includes multiple ancestries): 55.3% German, 17.0% Norwegian, 8.0% Irish, 6.5% English, 6.0% Polish (2000).
Economy: Single-family building permits issued: 8 (2001) / 9 (2000); Multi-family building permits issued: 13 (2001) / 15 (2000); Employment by occupation: 9.1% management, 16.1% professional, 21.1% services, 18.9% sales, 0.7% farming, 8.9% construction, 25.3% production (2000).
Income: Per capita income: $16,444 (2000); Median household income: $28,397 (2000); Poverty rate: 13.2% (2000).
Taxes: Total city taxes per capita: $253 (1997); City property taxes per capita: $249 (1997).
Education: High school graduation rate: 77.2% (2000); College graduation rate: 15.4% (2000).

School District(s)

Perham (PK-12)
2000 Enrollment: 1,740 218-346-4501
Housing: Homeownership rate: 59.2% (2000); Median home value: $69,300 (2000); Median rent: $339 per month (2000); Median age of housing: 32 years (2000).
Hospitals: Perham Memorial Hospital and Home (131 beds)
Newspapers: Enterprise Bulletin (1 x week)
Transportation: Commute to work: 85.1% car, 0.0% public transportation, 8.6% walk, 4.4% work from home (2000); Travel time to work: 74.2% less than 15 minutes, 15.2% 15 to 30 minutes, 6.7% 30 to 45 minutes, 1.4% 45 to 60 minutes, 2.5% 60 minutes or more (2000)
Additional Information Contacts
Perham Area Chamber of Commerce 218-346-7710

PERHAM (township). Covers a land area of 31.510 square miles and a water area of 1.824 square miles. Located at 46.60° N. Lat.; 95.58° W. Long. Elevation is 1,370 feet.
Population: 931 (2000); Race: 98.7% White, 0.0% Black, 0.4% Asian, 0.7% American Indian and Alaska Native, 3.3% Hispanic of any race, 0.0% two or more races (2000); Density: 29.5 persons per square mile (2000); Age: 32.3% under 18, 8.6% over 64 (2000); Marriage status: 24.4% never married, 63.0% now married, 3.0% widowed, 9.6% divorced (2000); Foreign born: 4.1% (2000); Ancestry (includes multiple ancestries): 57.5% German, 15.0% Norwegian, 11.4% Polish, 9.0% Finnish, 8.8% Dutch (2000).
Economy: Grain, potatoes; livestock, poultry. Manufacturing: tortillas, licorice, cheese; fertilizer, concrete. Municipal Airport to Northwest. Single-family building permits issued: 3 (2001) / 3 (2000); Multi-family building permits issued: 0 (2001) / 0 (2000); Employment by occupation: 14.1% management, 12.6% professional, 16.5% services, 24.0% sales, 3.0% farming, 9.5% construction, 20.3% production (2000).
Income: Per capita income: $20,639 (2000); Median household income: $45,500 (2000); Poverty rate: 5.2% (2000).
Taxes: Total city taxes per capita: $48 (1997); City property taxes per capita: $46 (1997).
Education: High school graduation rate: 86.8% (2000); College graduation rate: 13.9% (2000).
Housing: Homeownership rate: 88.7% (2000); Median home value: $119,400 (2000); Median rent: $363 per month (2000); Median age of housing: 25 years (2000).
Transportation: Commute to work: 92.5% car, 0.0% public transportation, 0.9% walk, 6.0% work from home (2000); Travel time to work: 69.8% less than 15 minutes, 14.6% 15 to 30 minutes, 6.1% 30 to 45 minutes, 3.1% 45 to 60 minutes, 6.4% 60 minutes or more (2000)

PINE LAKE (township). Covers a land area of 29.168 square miles and a water area of 6.571 square miles. Located at 46.59° N. Lat.; 95.47° W. Long.
Population: 656 (2000); Race: 99.4% White, 0.0% Black, 0.0% Asian, 0.0% American Indian and Alaska Native, 0.6% Hispanic of any race, 0.6% two or more races (2000); Density: 22.5 persons per square mile (2000); Age: 25.0% under 18, 12.7% over 64 (2000); Marriage status: 22.0% never married, 65.2% now married, 5.4% widowed, 7.4% divorced (2000); Foreign born: 0.6% (2000); Ancestry (includes multiple ancestries): 54.7% German, 19.5% Norwegian, 7.5% Swedish, 7.4% Finnish, 6.0% Polish (2000).
Economy: Employment by occupation: 14.6% management, 14.4% professional, 9.3% services, 26.5% sales, 2.5% farming, 13.0% construction, 19.7% production (2000).
Income: Per capita income: $19,878 (2000); Median household income: $43,056 (2000); Poverty rate: 6.8% (2000).
Taxes: Total city taxes per capita: $63 (1997); City property taxes per capita: $63 (1997).
Education: High school graduation rate: 85.7% (2000); College graduation rate: 17.7% (2000).
Housing: Homeownership rate: 88.8% (2000); Median home value: $110,800 (2000); Median rent: $385 per month (2000); Median age of housing: 21 years (2000).
Transportation: Commute to work: 87.0% car, 0.0% public transportation, 1.4% walk, 10.5% work from home (2000); Travel time to work: 53.2% less than 15 minutes, 35.1% 15 to 30 minutes, 6.6% 30 to 45 minutes, 3.5% 45 to 60 minutes, 1.6% 60 minutes or more (2000)

RICHVILLE (city). Covers a land area of 1.003 square miles and a water area of 0 square miles. Located at 46.50° N. Lat.; 95.62° W. Long. Elevation is 1,352 feet.
Population: 124 (2000); Race: 100.0% White, 0.0% Black, 0.0% Asian, 0.0% American Indian and Alaska Native, 0.0% Hispanic of any race, 0.0% two or more races (2000); Density: 123.7 persons per square mile (2000); Age: 25.2% under 18, 20.5% over 64 (2000); Marriage status: 17.3% never married, 55.1% now married, 12.2% widowed, 15.3% divorced (2000); Foreign born: 0.0% (2000); Ancestry (includes multiple ancestries): 55.1% German, 34.6% Norwegian, 10.2% Polish, 7.9% French Canadian, 7.1% Irish (2000).
Economy: Grain, potatoes; dairying. Employment by occupation: 7.5% management, 14.9% professional, 9.0% services, 14.9% sales, 7.5% farming, 7.5% construction, 38.8% production (2000).
Income: Per capita income: $16,290 (2000); Median household income: $33,750 (2000); Poverty rate: 12.6% (2000).
Taxes: Total city taxes per capita: $61 (1997); City property taxes per capita: $61 (1997).
Education: High school graduation rate: 77.0% (2000); College graduation rate: 4.6% (2000).
Housing: Homeownership rate: 81.1% (2000); Median home value: $45,000 (2000); Median rent: $300 per month (2000); Median age of housing: 35 years (2000).
Transportation: Commute to work: 89.6% car, 0.0% public transportation, 3.0% walk, 4.5% work from home (2000); Travel time to work: 31.3% less than 15 minutes, 32.8% 15 to 30 minutes, 12.5% 30 to 45 minutes, 14.1% 45 to 60 minutes, 9.4% 60 minutes or more (2000)

RUSH LAKE (township). Covers a land area of 26.789 square miles and a water area of 7.906 square miles. Located at 46.49° N. Lat.; 95.58° W. Long.
Population: 966 (2000); Race: 99.6% White, 0.0% Black, 0.0% Asian, 0.0% American Indian and Alaska Native, 0.0% Hispanic of any race, 0.4% two or more races (2000); Density: 36.1 persons per square mile (2000); Age: 27.1% under 18, 18.3% over 64 (2000); Marriage status: 19.0% never married, 71.8% now married, 5.6% widowed, 3.6% divorced (2000); Foreign born: 0.6% (2000); Ancestry (includes multiple ancestries): 48.7% German, 15.7% Norwegian, 7.8% Polish, 7.4% Irish, 7.0% Swedish (2000).
Economy: Employment by occupation: 12.1% management, 14.6% professional, 12.5% services, 26.5% sales, 3.1% farming, 13.4% construction, 17.7% production (2000).
Income: Per capita income: $19,800 (2000); Median household income: $40,000 (2000); Poverty rate: 9.5% (2000).
Taxes: Total city taxes per capita: $83 (1997); City property taxes per capita: $83 (1997).
Education: High school graduation rate: 85.3% (2000); College graduation rate: 17.4% (2000).
Housing: Homeownership rate: 92.3% (2000); Median home value: $109,500 (2000); Median rent: $419 per month (2000); Median age of housing: 25 years (2000).
Transportation: Commute to work: 91.5% car, 0.0% public transportation, 1.7% walk, 6.8% work from home (2000); Travel time to work: 44.6% less than 15 minutes, 35.5% 15 to 30 minutes, 9.6% 30 to 45 minutes, 6.2% 45 to 60 minutes, 4.1% 60 minutes or more (2000)

SAINT OLAF (township). Covers a land area of 32.294 square miles and a water area of 3.764 square miles. Located at 46.15° N. Lat.; 95.82° W. Long.
Population: 332 (2000); Race: 97.6% White, 0.0% Black, 0.0% Asian, 2.4% American Indian and Alaska Native, 0.0% Hispanic of any race, 0.0% two or more races (2000); Density: 10.3 persons per square mile (2000); Age: 22.8% under 18, 13.4% over 64 (2000); Marriage status: 18.6% never married, 72.8% now married, 5.7% widowed, 2.9% divorced (2000); Foreign born: 1.5% (2000); Ancestry (includes multiple ancestries): 57.0% Norwegian, 29.1% German, 8.3% Swedish, 3.9% English, 3.0% Irish (2000).

Economy: Employment by occupation: 18.3% management, 16.1% professional, 17.2% services, 16.7% sales, 2.2% farming, 15.6% construction, 14.0% production (2000).
Income: Per capita income: $17,878 (2000); Median household income: $40,865 (2000); Poverty rate: 6.8% (2000).
Education: High school graduation rate: 91.8% (2000); College graduation rate: 7.3% (2000).
Housing: Homeownership rate: 91.9% (2000); Median home value: $77,500 (2000); Median rent: $188 per month (2000); Median age of housing: 50 years (2000).
Transportation: Commute to work: 82.8% car, 0.0% public transportation, 2.2% walk, 15.1% work from home (2000); Travel time to work: 29.1% less than 15 minutes, 38.0% 15 to 30 minutes, 20.3% 30 to 45 minutes, 3.8% 45 to 60 minutes, 8.9% 60 minutes or more (2000)

SCAMBLER (township). Covers a land area of 32.120 square miles and a water area of 4.152 square miles. Located at 46.68° N. Lat.; 96.11° W. Long.
Population: 504 (2000); Race: 96.4% White, 0.0% Black, 0.0% Asian, 2.6% American Indian and Alaska Native, 0.4% Hispanic of any race, 1.0% two or more races (2000); Density: 15.7 persons per square mile (2000); Age: 21.6% under 18, 17.3% over 64 (2000); Marriage status: 18.9% never married, 66.2% now married, 8.4% widowed, 6.5% divorced (2000); Foreign born: 0.4% (2000); Ancestry (includes multiple ancestries): 53.8% Norwegian, 39.3% German, 8.9% Swedish, 7.7% English, 4.4% Irish (2000).
Economy: Single-family building permits issued: 2 (2001) / 0 (2000); Multi-family building permits issued: 0 (2001) / 0 (2000); Employment by occupation: 14.9% management, 14.9% professional, 15.7% services, 20.6% sales, 0.8% farming, 12.9% construction, 20.2% production (2000).
Income: Per capita income: $19,550 (2000); Median household income: $40,625 (2000); Poverty rate: 3.2% (2000).
Taxes: Total city taxes per capita: $173 (1997); City property taxes per capita: $173 (1997).
Education: High school graduation rate: 91.6% (2000); College graduation rate: 22.3% (2000).
Housing: Homeownership rate: 93.3% (2000); Median home value: $142,500 (2000); Median rent: $425 per month (2000); Median age of housing: 36 years (2000).
Transportation: Commute to work: 89.3% car, 0.0% public transportation, 0.0% walk, 9.8% work from home (2000); Travel time to work: 21.4% less than 15 minutes, 38.2% 15 to 30 minutes, 17.7% 30 to 45 minutes, 20.9% 45 to 60 minutes, 1.8% 60 minutes or more (2000)

STAR LAKE (township). Covers a land area of 25.023 square miles and a water area of 10.749 square miles. Located at 46.50° N. Lat.; 95.83° W. Long.
Population: 410 (2000); Race: 100.0% White, 0.0% Black, 0.0% Asian, 0.0% American Indian and Alaska Native, 0.0% Hispanic of any race, 0.0% two or more races (2000); Density: 16.4 persons per square mile (2000); Age: 18.7% under 18, 19.8% over 64 (2000); Marriage status: 16.7% never married, 64.9% now married, 5.2% widowed, 13.2% divorced (2000); Foreign born: 1.1% (2000); Ancestry (includes multiple ancestries): 46.3% German, 25.6% Norwegian, 10.9% Swedish, 8.9% Irish, 8.0% English (2000).
Economy: Employment by occupation: 16.9% management, 6.3% professional, 7.7% services, 21.1% sales, 6.3% farming, 17.6% construction, 23.9% production (2000).
Income: Per capita income: $20,736 (2000); Median household income: $29,500 (2000); Poverty rate: 9.0% (2000).
Taxes: Total city taxes per capita: $129 (1997); City property taxes per capita: $129 (1997).
Education: High school graduation rate: 81.7% (2000); College graduation rate: 14.9% (2000).
Housing: Homeownership rate: 93.7% (2000); Median home value: $100,000 (2000); Median rent: $275 per month (2000); Median age of housing: 35 years (2000).
Transportation: Commute to work: 88.0% car, 0.0% public transportation, 4.2% walk, 7.7% work from home (2000); Travel time to work: 12.2% less than 15 minutes, 27.5% 15 to 30 minutes, 30.5% 30 to 45 minutes, 9.2% 45 to 60 minutes, 20.6% 60 minutes or more (2000)

SVERDRUP (township). Covers a land area of 28.442 square miles and a water area of 7.216 square miles. Located at 46.33° N. Lat.; 95.84° W. Long.
Population: 577 (2000); Race: 98.7% White, 0.0% Black, 0.9% Asian, 0.0% American Indian and Alaska Native, 0.4% Hispanic of any race, 0.0% two or more races (2000); Density: 20.3 persons per square mile (2000); Age: 21.9% under 18, 16.8% over 64 (2000); Marriage status: 18.9% never married, 68.4% now married, 5.4% widowed, 7.3% divorced (2000); Foreign born: 0.7% (2000); Ancestry (includes multiple ancestries): 44.3% Norwegian, 29.0% German, 7.2% Irish, 6.6% Swedish, 5.0% United States or American (2000).
Economy: Single-family building permits issued: 0 (2001) / 1 (2000); Multi-family building permits issued: 0 (2001) / 0 (2000); Employment by occupation: 24.5% management, 18.4% professional, 11.6% services, 18.4% sales, 4.1% farming, 10.9% construction, 12.2% production (2000).
Income: Per capita income: $20,962 (2000); Median household income: $47,431 (2000); Poverty rate: 5.6% (2000).
Taxes: Total city taxes per capita: $65 (1997); City property taxes per capita: $65 (1997).
Education: High school graduation rate: 87.2% (2000); College graduation rate: 20.7% (2000).
Housing: Homeownership rate: 85.2% (2000); Median home value: $88,200 (2000); Median rent: $375 per month (2000); Median age of housing: 26 years (2000).
Transportation: Commute to work: 90.4% car, 0.0% public transportation, 1.0% walk, 7.9% work from home (2000); Travel time to work: 25.0% less than 15 minutes, 53.4% 15 to 30 minutes, 10.8% 30 to 45 minutes, 4.9% 45 to 60 minutes, 6.0% 60 minutes or more (2000)

TORDENSKJOLD (township). Covers a land area of 30.451 square miles and a water area of 5.560 square miles. Located at 46.23° N. Lat.; 95.84° W. Long.
Population: 550 (2000); Race: 99.5% White, 0.0% Black, 0.0% Asian, 0.3% American Indian and Alaska Native, 0.7% Hispanic of any race, 0.2% two or more races (2000); Density: 18.1 persons per square mile (2000); Age: 25.2% under 18, 19.1% over 64 (2000); Marriage status: 18.6% never married, 70.7% now married, 3.7% widowed, 7.0% divorced (2000); Foreign born: 0.9% (2000); Ancestry (includes multiple ancestries): 41.8% Norwegian, 38.5% German, 11.0% Swedish, 4.7% Dutch, 4.5% Irish (2000).
Economy: Employment by occupation: 17.5% management, 14.2% professional, 17.8% services, 16.0% sales, 4.4% farming, 16.7% construction, 13.5% production (2000).
Income: Per capita income: $18,229 (2000); Median household income: $37,981 (2000); Poverty rate: 5.1% (2000).
Taxes: Total city taxes per capita: $52 (1997); City property taxes per capita: $52 (1997).
Education: High school graduation rate: 85.3% (2000); College graduation rate: 8.4% (2000).
Housing: Homeownership rate: 88.8% (2000); Median home value: $88,300 (2000); Median rent: $363 per month (2000); Median age of housing: 30 years (2000).
Transportation: Commute to work: 82.1% car, 0.0% public transportation, 1.1% walk, 15.0% work from home (2000); Travel time to work: 26.7% less than 15 minutes, 48.3% 15 to 30 minutes, 16.8% 30 to 45 minutes, 2.2% 45 to 60 minutes, 6.0% 60 minutes or more (2000)

TRONDHJEM (township). Covers a land area of 33.067 square miles and a water area of 0.845 square miles. Located at 46.49° N. Lat.; 96.20° W. Long.
Population: 171 (2000); Race: 98.7% White, 0.0% Black, 1.3% Asian, 0.0% American Indian and Alaska Native, 4.5% Hispanic of any race, 0.0% two or more races (2000); Density: 5.2 persons per square mile (2000); Age: 23.7% under 18, 12.2% over 64 (2000); Marriage status: 21.0% never married, 74.2% now married, 1.6% widowed, 3.2% divorced (2000); Foreign born: 4.5% (2000); Ancestry (includes multiple ancestries): 57.1% Norwegian, 38.5% German, 12.2% Swedish, 9.0% Polish, 5.8% Other groups (2000).
Economy: Employment by occupation: 16.9% management, 9.1% professional, 16.9% services, 18.2% sales, 11.7% farming, 5.2% construction, 22.1% production (2000).
Income: Per capita income: $18,710 (2000); Median household income: $26,750 (2000); Poverty rate: 1.9% (2000).
Taxes: Total city taxes per capita: $93 (1997); City property taxes per capita: $93 (1997).
Education: High school graduation rate: 79.8% (2000); College graduation rate: 22.1% (2000).
Housing: Homeownership rate: 86.0% (2000); Median home value: $68,300 (2000); Median rent: $319 per month (2000); Median age of housing: 60+ years (2000).
Transportation: Commute to work: 74.0% car, 0.0% public transportation, 12.3% walk, 11.0% work from home (2000); Travel time to work: 49.2% less than 15 minutes, 21.5% 15 to 30 minutes, 16.9% 30 to 45 minutes, 12.3% 45 to 60 minutes, 0.0% 60 minutes or more (2000)

TUMULI (township). Covers a land area of 28.391 square miles and a water area of 7.121 square miles. Located at 46.15° N. Lat.; 95.94° W. Long.
Population: 434 (2000); Race: 99.3% White, 0.0% Black, 0.5% Asian, 0.0% American Indian and Alaska Native, 1.2% Hispanic of any race, 0.2% two or more races (2000); Density: 15.3 persons per square mile (2000); Age: 26.0% under 18, 12.4% over 64 (2000); Marriage status: 18.6% never married, 70.9% now married, 5.1% widowed, 5.4% divorced (2000); Foreign born: 0.5% (2000); Ancestry (includes multiple ancestries): 56.9% Norwegian, 32.4% German, 10.9% Swedish, 4.9% Irish, 3.4% English (2000).
Economy: Employment by occupation: 13.0% management, 14.0% professional, 25.4% services, 15.0% sales, 0.0% farming, 14.0% construction, 18.7% production (2000).
Income: Per capita income: $22,008 (2000); Median household income: $43,438 (2000); Poverty rate: 6.1% (2000).
Taxes: Total city taxes per capita: $86 (1997); City property taxes per capita: $86 (1997).
Education: High school graduation rate: 83.8% (2000); College graduation rate: 15.9% (2000).
Housing: Homeownership rate: 92.7% (2000); Median home value: $97,900 (2000); Median rent: $275 per month (2000); Median age of housing: 30 years (2000).
Transportation: Commute to work: 91.8% car, 0.0% public transportation, 0.0% walk, 8.2% work from home (2000); Travel time to work: 22.5% less than 15 minutes, 59.2% 15 to 30 minutes, 15.4% 30 to 45 minutes, 1.8% 45 to 60 minutes, 1.2% 60 minutes or more (2000)

UNDERWOOD (city). Covers a land area of 0.424 square miles and a water area of 0 square miles. Located at 46.28° N. Lat.; 95.87° W. Long.
Population: 319 (2000); Race: 97.2% White, 0.0% Black, 0.3% Asian, 0.0% American Indian and Alaska Native, 0.0% Hispanic of any race, 2.5% two or more races (2000); Density: 752.3 persons per square mile (2000); Age: 24.1% under 18, 29.7% over 64 (2000); Marriage status: 15.6% never married, 66.0% now married, 11.2% widowed, 7.2% divorced (2000); Foreign born: 0.0% (2000); Ancestry (includes multiple ancestries): 45.2% Norwegian, 30.0% German, 6.8% Irish, 4.6% Scandinavian, 4.6% English (2000).
Economy: Livestock, poultry; grain; dairying; light manufacturing. Single-family building permits issued: 3 (2001) / 0 (2000); Multi-family building permits issued: 0 (2001) / 0 (2000); Employment by occupation: 7.0% management, 17.8% professional, 24.0% services, 20.2% sales, 0.0% farming, 19.4% construction, 11.6% production (2000).
Income: Per capita income: $19,465 (2000); Median household income: $29,000 (2000); Poverty rate: 14.2% (2000).
Taxes: Total city taxes per capita: $113 (1997); City property taxes per capita: $107 (1997).
Education: High school graduation rate: 70.9% (2000); College graduation rate: 8.9% (2000).

School District(s)

Underwood (PK-12)
2000 Enrollment: 446 218-826-6101
Housing: Homeownership rate: 74.6% (2000); Median home value: $51,300 (2000); Median rent: $175 per month (2000); Median age of housing: 60+ years (2000).
Transportation: Commute to work: 72.0% car, 0.0% public transportation, 17.6% walk, 8.8% work from home (2000); Travel time to work: 39.5% less than 15 minutes, 50.0% 15 to 30 minutes, 1.8% 30 to 45 minutes, 2.6% 45 to 60 minutes, 6.1% 60 minutes or more (2000)

URBANK (city). Covers a land area of 0.731 square miles and a water area of 0 square miles. Located at 46.12° N. Lat.; 95.51° W. Long. Elevation is 1,477 feet.
Population: 59 (2000); Race: 100.0% White, 0.0% Black, 0.0% Asian, 0.0% American Indian and Alaska Native, 0.0% Hispanic of any race, 0.0% two or more races (2000); Density: 80.7 persons per square mile (2000); Age: 25.5% under 18, 18.2% over 64 (2000); Marriage status: 16.3% never married, 62.8% now married, 11.6% widowed, 9.3% divorced (2000); Foreign born: 0.0% (2000); Ancestry (includes multiple ancestries): 61.8% German, 23.6% Polish, 14.5% Norwegian, 12.7% Irish, 9.1% Swedish (2000).
Economy: Employment by occupation: 6.9% management, 13.8% professional, 6.9% services, 10.3% sales, 6.9% farming, 10.3% construction, 44.8% production (2000).
Income: Per capita income: $15,105 (2000); Median household income: $40,625 (2000); Poverty rate: 7.3% (2000).
Taxes: Total city taxes per capita: $52 (1997); City property taxes per capita: $26 (1997).
Education: High school graduation rate: 64.1% (2000); College graduation rate: 5.1% (2000).
Housing: Homeownership rate: 93.3% (2000); Median home value: $28,800 (2000); Median age of housing: 55 years (2000).
Transportation: Commute to work: 79.3% car, 0.0% public transportation, 13.8% walk, 0.0% work from home (2000); Travel time to work: 27.6% less than 15 minutes, 37.9% 15 to 30 minutes, 24.1% 30 to 45 minutes, 0.0% 45 to 60 minutes, 10.3% 60 minutes or more (2000)

VERGAS (city). Covers a land area of 1.454 square miles and a water area of 0.034 square miles. Located at 46.65° N. Lat.; 95.80° W. Long. Elevation is 1,400 feet.
Population: 311 (2000); Race: 98.3% White, 0.0% Black, 0.0% Asian, 0.0% American Indian and Alaska Native, 0.0% Hispanic of any race, 1.7% two or more races (2000); Density: 213.9 persons per square mile (2000); Age: 25.5% under 18, 21.1% over 64 (2000); Marriage status: 29.8% never married, 53.1% now married, 5.5% widowed, 11.6% divorced (2000); Foreign born: 0.6% (2000); Ancestry (includes multiple ancestries): 47.4% German, 21.1% Norwegian, 13.9% Swedish, 6.1% Irish, 5.8% English (2000).
Economy: Agriculture: dairying; poultry; grain, sugar beets. Manufacturing of cellulose insulation. Single-family building permits issued: 0 (2001) / 0 (2000); Multi-family building permits issued: 0 (2001) / 0 (2000); Employment by occupation: 11.7% management, 8.6% professional, 16.7% services, 27.8% sales, 1.9% farming, 14.2% construction, 19.1% production (2000).
Income: Per capita income: $14,461 (2000); Median household income: $27,344 (2000); Poverty rate: 7.9% (2000).
Taxes: Total city taxes per capita: $66 (1997); City property taxes per capita: $63 (1997).
Education: High school graduation rate: 75.6% (2000); College graduation rate: 13.9% (2000).
Housing: Homeownership rate: 73.0% (2000); Median home value: $66,900 (2000); Median rent: $365 per month (2000); Median age of housing: 52 years (2000).
Transportation: Commute to work: 85.0% car, 0.0% public transportation, 10.6% walk, 4.4% work from home (2000); Travel time to work: 39.2% less than 15 minutes, 41.8% 15 to 30 minutes, 15.7% 30 to 45 minutes, 2.0% 45 to 60 minutes, 1.3% 60 minutes or more (2000)

VINING (city). Covers a land area of 1.269 square miles and a water area of 0.041 square miles. Located at 46.26° N. Lat.; 95.53° W. Long. Elevation is 1,387 feet.
Population: 68 (2000); Race: 100.0% White, 0.0% Black, 0.0% Asian, 0.0% American Indian and Alaska Native, 0.0% Hispanic of any race, 0.0% two or more races (2000); Density: 53.6 persons per square mile (2000); Age: 6.3% under 18, 53.1% over 64 (2000); Marriage status: 22.6% never married, 61.3% now married, 9.7% widowed, 6.5% divorced (2000); Foreign born: 0.0% (2000); Ancestry (includes multiple ancestries): 62.5% Norwegian, 17.2% German, 15.6% Swedish, 10.9% United States or American, 6.3% Irish (2000).
Economy: Dairying; grain. Employment by occupation: 8.0% management, 8.0% professional, 16.0% services, 48.0% sales, 0.0% farming, 8.0% construction, 12.0% production (2000).
Income: Per capita income: $17,866 (2000); Median household income: $21,250 (2000); Poverty rate: 9.4% (2000).
Taxes: Total city taxes per capita: $91 (1997); City property taxes per capita: $57 (1997).
Education: High school graduation rate: 75.9% (2000); College graduation rate: 12.1% (2000).
Housing: Homeownership rate: 94.4% (2000); Median home value: $30,400 (2000); Median age of housing: 60+ years (2000).
Transportation: Commute to work: 84.0% car, 0.0% public transportation, 8.0% walk, 8.0% work from home (2000); Travel time to work: 8.7% less than 15 minutes, 13.0% 15 to 30 minutes, 60.9% 30 to 45 minutes, 17.4% 45 to 60 minutes, 0.0% 60 minutes or more (2000)

WESTERN (township). Covers a land area of 34.451 square miles and a water area of 1.153 square miles. Located at 46.15° N. Lat.; 96.21° W. Long. Elevation is 1,109 feet.
Population: 142 (2000); Race: 96.6% White, 0.0% Black, 3.4% Asian, 0.0% American Indian and Alaska Native, 0.0% Hispanic of any race, 0.0% two or more races (2000); Density: 4.1 persons per square mile (2000); Age: 28.6% under 18, 12.9% over 64 (2000); Marriage status: 23.7% never married, 72.8% now married, 0.0% widowed, 3.5% divorced (2000); Foreign born:

2.0% (2000); Ancestry (includes multiple ancestries): 38.1% German, 19.0% Norwegian, 10.2% Irish, 5.4% Scandinavian, 3.4% Swedish (2000).
Economy: Single-family building permits issued: 0 (2001) / 0 (2000); Multi-family building permits issued: 0 (2001) / 0 (2000); Employment by occupation: 23.8% management, 6.3% professional, 9.5% services, 27.0% sales, 4.8% farming, 3.2% construction, 25.4% production (2000).
Income: Per capita income: $16,961 (2000); Median household income: $43,000 (2000); Poverty rate: 5.4% (2000).
Taxes: Total city taxes per capita: $127 (1997); City property taxes per capita: $127 (1997).
Education: High school graduation rate: 78.3% (2000); College graduation rate: 9.8% (2000).
Housing: Homeownership rate: 83.0% (2000); Median home value: $82,500 (2000); Median rent: $450 per month (2000); Median age of housing: 60+ years (2000).
Transportation: Commute to work: 70.5% car, 0.0% public transportation, 9.8% walk, 16.4% work from home (2000); Travel time to work: 19.6% less than 15 minutes, 51.0% 15 to 30 minutes, 21.6% 30 to 45 minutes, 0.0% 45 to 60 minutes, 7.8% 60 minutes or more (2000)

WOODSIDE (township). Covers a land area of 36.226 square miles and a water area of 0 square miles. Located at 46.24° N. Lat.; 95.21° W. Long.
Population: 293 (2000); Race: 97.0% White, 0.0% Black, 1.4% Asian, 0.0% American Indian and Alaska Native, 0.0% Hispanic of any race, 1.7% two or more races (2000); Density: 8.1 persons per square mile (2000); Age: 36.8% under 18, 9.1% over 64 (2000); Marriage status: 29.9% never married, 59.3% now married, 3.7% widowed, 7.0% divorced (2000); Foreign born: 0.0% (2000); Ancestry (includes multiple ancestries): 39.2% German, 16.6% United States or American, 14.9% Irish, 8.4% Norwegian, 5.1% English (2000).
Economy: Employment by occupation: 20.2% management, 13.2% professional, 24.6% services, 7.0% sales, 2.6% farming, 13.2% construction, 19.3% production (2000).
Income: Per capita income: $9,716 (2000); Median household income: $24,125 (2000); Poverty rate: 19.6% (2000).
Taxes: Total city taxes per capita: $38 (1997); City property taxes per capita: $38 (1997).
Education: High school graduation rate: 87.0% (2000); College graduation rate: 8.1% (2000).
Housing: Homeownership rate: 93.7% (2000); Median home value: $101,800 (2000); Median rent: $275 per month (2000); Median age of housing: 48 years (2000).
Transportation: Commute to work: 69.4% car, 0.0% public transportation, 5.6% walk, 25.0% work from home (2000); Travel time to work: 22.2% less than 15 minutes, 37.0% 15 to 30 minutes, 22.2% 30 to 45 minutes, 7.4% 45 to 60 minutes, 11.1% 60 minutes or more (2000)

Pennington County

Located in northwestern Minnesota; drained by the Red Lake and Thief Rivers. Covers a land area of 616.50 square miles, a water area of 1.80 square miles, and is located in the Central Time Zone. The county government was organized in 1910. County seat is Thief River Falls.
Population: 13,584 (2000); Race: 97.5% White, 0.3% Black, 0.7% Asian, 0.9% American Indian and Alaska Native, 0.7% Hispanic of any race, 0.4% two or more races (2000); Density: 22.0 persons per square mile (2000); Age: 24.3% under 18, 15.9% over 64 (2000).
Religion: Five largest groups: 41.9% Evangelical Lutheran Church in America, 22.1% Catholic Church, 3.9% The Association of Free Lutheran Congregations, 2.3% The United Methodist Church, 2.0% The Evangelical Free Church of America (2000).
Economy: Unemployment rate: 2.8% (11/2002); Total civilian labor force: 8,390 (11/2002); Leading industries: 21.8% manufacturing; 19.4% wholesale trade; 16.6% health care and social assistance (2000); Companies that employ more than 1,000 persons: 0 (2000); Companies that employ more than 100 persons: 8 (2000); Farms: 528 totaling 312,752 acres (1997); Minority business ownership rate: 0.0% (1997); Women business ownership rate: 16.4% (1997); Retail sales per capita: $10,966 (1997). Single-family building permits issued: 25 (2001) / 22 (2000); Multi-family building permits issued: 19 (2001) / 18 (2000).
Income: Per capita income: $17,346 (2000); Median household income: $34,216 (2000); Poverty rate: 11.1% (2000); Bankruptcy rate: 3.49% (2001).
Taxes: Total county taxes per capita: $266 (2000); County property taxes per capita: $266 (2000).
Education: High school graduation rate: 81.3% (2000); College graduation rate: 14.9% (2000).
Housing: Homeownership rate: 74.6% (2000); Median home value: $63,300 (2000); Median rent: $301 per month (2000); Median age of housing: 34 years (2000).
Health: Birth rate: 125.2 per 10,000 population (1998); Age adjusted death rate: 85.1 per 10,000 population (1999); Age adjusted cancer mortality rate: 189.2 deaths per 100,000 population (1999). Number of physicians: 13.3 per 10,000 population (1999); Number of hospital beds: 116.3 per 10,000 population (1999).
Elections: 2000 Presidential election results: 38.9% Gore, 53.5% Bush, 4.0% Nader, 3.1% Buchanan
National and State Parks: Higinbotham State Wildlife Management Area
Additional Information Contacts
Pennington County Government Offices 218-683-7000
Thief River Fls Chamber of Commerce 218-681-3720

Pennington County Communities

BLACK RIVER (township). Covers a land area of 23.991 square miles and a water area of 0 square miles. Located at 48.00° N. Lat.; 96.30° W. Long.
Population: 98 (2000); Race: 96.0% White, 0.0% Black, 4.0% Asian, 0.0% American Indian and Alaska Native, 0.0% Hispanic of any race, 0.0% two or more races (2000); Density: 4.1 persons per square mile (2000); Age: 36.6% under 18, 0.0% over 64 (2000); Marriage status: 23.5% never married, 73.5% now married, 0.0% widowed, 2.9% divorced (2000); Foreign born: 4.0% (2000); Ancestry (includes multiple ancestries): 62.4% Norwegian, 37.6% German, 21.8% Swedish, 10.9% Irish, 4.0% Other groups (2000).
Economy: Employment by occupation: 13.1% management, 18.0% professional, 6.6% services, 27.9% sales, 0.0% farming, 9.8% construction, 24.6% production (2000).
Income: Per capita income: $14,156 (2000); Median household income: $53,750 (2000); Poverty rate: 2.0% (2000).
Taxes: Total city taxes per capita: $45 (1997); City property taxes per capita: $45 (1997).
Education: High school graduation rate: 93.4% (2000); College graduation rate: 24.6% (2000).
Housing: Homeownership rate: 100.0% (2000); Median home value: $57,500 (2000); Median age of housing: 53 years (2000).
Transportation: Commute to work: 86.9% car, 0.0% public transportation, 6.6% walk, 0.0% work from home (2000); Travel time to work: 31.1% less than 15 minutes, 49.2% 15 to 30 minutes, 6.6% 30 to 45 minutes, 0.0% 45 to 60 minutes, 13.1% 60 minutes or more (2000)

BRAY (township). Covers a land area of 35.891 square miles and a water area of 0.191 square miles. Located at 48.06° N. Lat.; 96.42° W. Long.
Population: 73 (2000); Race: 100.0% White, 0.0% Black, 0.0% Asian, 0.0% American Indian and Alaska Native, 0.0% Hispanic of any race, 0.0% two or more races (2000); Density: 2.0 persons per square mile (2000); Age: 16.9% under 18, 3.4% over 64 (2000); Marriage status: 25.5% never married, 68.6% now married, 0.0% widowed, 5.9% divorced (2000); Foreign born: 0.0% (2000); Ancestry (includes multiple ancestries): 52.5% Norwegian, 27.1% German, 11.9% Danish, 11.9% Swedish, 6.8% Czech (2000).
Economy: Employment by occupation: 17.2% management, 6.9% professional, 13.8% services, 41.4% sales, 0.0% farming, 6.9% construction, 13.8% production (2000).
Income: Per capita income: $18,176 (2000); Median household income: $41,563 (2000); Poverty rate: 13.6% (2000).
Taxes: Total city taxes per capita: $63 (1997); City property taxes per capita: $63 (1997).
Education: High school graduation rate: 69.4% (2000); College graduation rate: 0.0% (2000).
Housing: Homeownership rate: 90.0% (2000); Median home value: $85,000 (2000); Median rent: $175 per month (2000); Median age of housing: 60+ years (2000).
Transportation: Commute to work: 86.2% car, 0.0% public transportation, 0.0% walk, 13.8% work from home (2000); Travel time to work: 8.0% less than 15 minutes, 48.0% 15 to 30 minutes, 44.0% 30 to 45 minutes, 0.0% 45 to 60 minutes, 0.0% 60 minutes or more (2000)

CLOVER LEAF (township). Covers a land area of 26.856 square miles and a water area of 0.013 square miles. Located at 48.14° N. Lat.; 95.92° W. Long.

Population: 70 (2000); Race: 100.0% White, 0.0% Black, 0.0% Asian, 0.0% American Indian and Alaska Native, 0.0% Hispanic of any race, 0.0% two or more races (2000); Density: 2.6 persons per square mile (2000); Age: 17.1% under 18, 14.3% over 64 (2000); Marriage status: 27.3% never married, 68.2% now married, 4.5% widowed, 0.0% divorced (2000); Foreign born: 0.0% (2000); Ancestry (includes multiple ancestries): 67.1% Norwegian, 22.9% Swedish, 18.6% Polish, 11.4% German, 8.6% English (2000).
Economy: Employment by occupation: 3.3% management, 16.7% professional, 0.0% services, 36.7% sales, 0.0% farming, 0.0% construction, 43.3% production (2000).
Income: Per capita income: $14,026 (2000); Median household income: $31,667 (2000); Poverty rate: 1.4% (2000).
Taxes: Total city taxes per capita: $87 (1997); City property taxes per capita: $87 (1997).
Education: High school graduation rate: 72.0% (2000); College graduation rate: 4.0% (2000).
Housing: Homeownership rate: 92.3% (2000); Median home value: $55,000 (2000); Median rent: <$100 per month (2000); Median age of housing: 37 years (2000).
Transportation: Commute to work: 96.4% car, 0.0% public transportation, 0.0% walk, 3.6% work from home (2000); Travel time to work: 14.8% less than 15 minutes, 59.3% 15 to 30 minutes, 0.0% 30 to 45 minutes, 7.4% 45 to 60 minutes, 18.5% 60 minutes or more (2000)

DEER PARK (township). Covers a land area of 23.038 square miles and a water area of 0 square miles. Located at 47.98° N. Lat.; 95.78° W. Long.
Population: 130 (2000); Race: 100.0% White, 0.0% Black, 0.0% Asian, 0.0% American Indian and Alaska Native, 0.0% Hispanic of any race, 0.0% two or more races (2000); Density: 5.6 persons per square mile (2000); Age: 34.4% under 18, 10.9% over 64 (2000); Marriage status: 26.6% never married, 63.8% now married, 9.6% widowed, 0.0% divorced (2000); Foreign born: 0.0% (2000); Ancestry (includes multiple ancestries): 64.1% Norwegian, 32.0% German, 22.7% Swedish, 9.4% French (except Basque), 3.9% Danish (2000).
Economy: Employment by occupation: 42.9% management, 11.1% professional, 3.2% services, 14.3% sales, 7.9% farming, 3.2% construction, 17.5% production (2000).
Income: Per capita income: $13,216 (2000); Median household income: $38,750 (2000); Poverty rate: 3.1% (2000).
Taxes: Total city taxes per capita: $28 (1997); City property taxes per capita: $28 (1997).
Education: High school graduation rate: 92.5% (2000); College graduation rate: 13.8% (2000).
Housing: Homeownership rate: 90.2% (2000); Median home value: $28,800 (2000); Median age of housing: 29 years (2000).
Transportation: Commute to work: 72.1% car, 0.0% public transportation, 4.9% walk, 23.0% work from home (2000); Travel time to work: 19.1% less than 15 minutes, 17.0% 15 to 30 minutes, 53.2% 30 to 45 minutes, 0.0% 45 to 60 minutes, 10.6% 60 minutes or more (2000)

GOODRIDGE (city). Covers a land area of 0.187 square miles and a water area of 0 square miles. Located at 48.14° N. Lat.; 95.80° W. Long. Elevation is 1,170 feet.
Population: 98 (2000); Race: 100.0% White, 0.0% Black, 0.0% Asian, 0.0% American Indian and Alaska Native, 2.4% Hispanic of any race, 0.0% two or more races (2000); Density: 523.1 persons per square mile (2000); Age: 27.4% under 18, 9.5% over 64 (2000); Marriage status: 25.0% never married, 41.2% now married, 7.4% widowed, 26.5% divorced (2000); Foreign born: 0.0% (2000); Ancestry (includes multiple ancestries): 50.0% Norwegian, 31.0% German, 11.9% Swedish, 10.7% Czech, 9.5% English (2000).
Economy: Employment by occupation: 5.1% management, 23.1% professional, 38.5% services, 10.3% sales, 2.6% farming, 5.1% construction, 15.4% production (2000).
Income: Per capita income: $12,636 (2000); Median household income: $17,292 (2000); Poverty rate: 23.8% (2000).
Taxes: Total city taxes per capita: $44 (1997); City property taxes per capita: $44 (1997).
Education: High school graduation rate: 81.8% (2000); College graduation rate: 10.9% (2000).

School District(s)

Goodridge (KG-12)
2000 Enrollment: 193 218-378-4133
Housing: Homeownership rate: 62.2% (2000); Median home value: $11,300 (2000); Median rent: $206 per month (2000); Median age of housing: 30 years (2000).
Transportation: Commute to work: 74.4% car, 0.0% public transportation, 20.5% walk, 0.0% work from home (2000); Travel time to work: 38.5% less than 15 minutes, 33.3% 15 to 30 minutes, 23.1% 30 to 45 minutes, 0.0% 45 to 60 minutes, 5.1% 60 minutes or more (2000)

GOODRIDGE (township). Covers a land area of 26.808 square miles and a water area of 0 square miles. Located at 48.14° N. Lat.; 95.79° W. Long. Elevation is 1,170 feet.
Population: 54 (2000); Race: 100.0% White, 0.0% Black, 0.0% Asian, 0.0% American Indian and Alaska Native, 0.0% Hispanic of any race, 0.0% two or more races (2000); Density: 2.0 persons per square mile (2000); Age: 21.6% under 18, 15.7% over 64 (2000); Marriage status: 13.6% never married, 72.7% now married, 4.5% widowed, 9.1% divorced (2000); Foreign born: 3.9% (2000); Ancestry (includes multiple ancestries): 78.4% Norwegian, 11.8% German, 9.8% English, 7.8% Swedish, 3.9% Czech (2000).
Economy: Grain, sunflowers; sheep. Manufacturing: industrial controls. Employment by occupation: 15.8% management, 21.1% professional, 10.5% services, 36.8% sales, 0.0% farming, 15.8% construction, 0.0% production (2000).
Income: Per capita income: $13,643 (2000); Median household income: $21,875 (2000); Poverty rate: 45.1% (2000).
Taxes: Total city taxes per capita: $129 (1997); City property taxes per capita: $129 (1997).
Education: High school graduation rate: 78.9% (2000); College graduation rate: 5.3% (2000).
Housing: Homeownership rate: 100.0% (2000); Median age of housing: 60 years (2000).
Transportation: Commute to work: 84.2% car, 0.0% public transportation, 0.0% walk, 15.8% work from home (2000); Travel time to work: 25.0% less than 15 minutes, 25.0% 15 to 30 minutes, 18.8% 30 to 45 minutes, 0.0% 45 to 60 minutes, 31.3% 60 minutes or more (2000)

HICKORY (township). Covers a land area of 35.070 square miles and a water area of 0.002 square miles. Located at 47.97° N. Lat.; 95.65° W. Long.
Population: 83 (2000); Race: 95.6% White, 0.0% Black, 0.0% Asian, 2.2% American Indian and Alaska Native, 0.0% Hispanic of any race, 2.2% two or more races (2000); Density: 2.4 persons per square mile (2000); Age: 15.4% under 18, 18.7% over 64 (2000); Marriage status: 30.4% never married, 60.8% now married, 2.5% widowed, 6.3% divorced (2000); Foreign born: 0.0% (2000); Ancestry (includes multiple ancestries): 69.2% Norwegian, 7.7% Irish, 6.6% Swedish, 4.4% German, 4.4% Czech (2000).
Economy: Employment by occupation: 25.0% management, 3.8% professional, 13.5% services, 25.0% sales, 5.8% farming, 5.8% construction, 21.2% production (2000).
Income: Per capita income: $18,203 (2000); Median household income: $36,563 (2000); Poverty rate: 5.5% (2000).
Taxes: Total city taxes per capita: $49 (1997); City property taxes per capita: $49 (1997).
Education: High school graduation rate: 71.4% (2000); College graduation rate: 4.8% (2000).
Housing: Homeownership rate: 84.4% (2000); Median home value: $37,500 (2000); Median rent: $225 per month (2000); Median age of housing: 42 years (2000).
Transportation: Commute to work: 75.0% car, 0.0% public transportation, 0.0% walk, 25.0% work from home (2000); Travel time to work: 0.0% less than 15 minutes, 15.4% 15 to 30 minutes, 43.6% 30 to 45 minutes, 38.5% 45 to 60 minutes, 2.6% 60 minutes or more (2000)

HIGHLANDING (township). Covers a land area of 36.143 square miles and a water area of 0.037 square miles. Located at 48.05° N. Lat.; 95.78° W. Long.
Population: 192 (2000); Race: 100.0% White, 0.0% Black, 0.0% Asian, 0.0% American Indian and Alaska Native, 0.0% Hispanic of any race, 0.0% two or more races (2000); Density: 5.3 persons per square mile (2000); Age: 31.4% under 18, 11.9% over 64 (2000); Marriage status: 27.6% never married, 58.6% now married, 10.3% widowed, 3.4% divorced (2000); Foreign born: 3.1% (2000); Ancestry (includes multiple ancestries): 50.5% Norwegian, 25.8% Swedish, 12.9% German, 6.7% Polish, 6.7% Danish (2000).
Economy: Employment by occupation: 33.7% management, 9.9% professional, 12.9% services, 13.9% sales, 5.9% farming, 14.9% construction, 8.9% production (2000).
Income: Per capita income: $21,464 (2000); Median household income: $34,688 (2000); Poverty rate: 2.6% (2000).
Taxes: Total city taxes per capita: $33 (1997); City property taxes per capita: $27 (1997).

Education: High school graduation rate: 87.4% (2000); College graduation rate: 16.2% (2000).
Housing: Homeownership rate: 88.4% (2000); Median home value: $37,500 (2000); Median rent: $125 per month (2000); Median age of housing: 30 years (2000).
Transportation: Commute to work: 76.8% car, 0.0% public transportation, 0.0% walk, 23.2% work from home (2000); Travel time to work: 19.7% less than 15 minutes, 19.7% 15 to 30 minutes, 40.8% 30 to 45 minutes, 7.9% 45 to 60 minutes, 11.8% 60 minutes or more (2000)

KRATKA (township). Covers a land area of 36.066 square miles and a water area of 0.037 square miles. Located at 48.05° N. Lat.; 95.92° W. Long.
Population: 139 (2000); Race: 100.0% White, 0.0% Black, 0.0% Asian, 0.0% American Indian and Alaska Native, 0.0% Hispanic of any race, 0.0% two or more races (2000); Density: 3.9 persons per square mile (2000); Age: 24.0% under 18, 10.9% over 64 (2000); Marriage status: 31.4% never married, 66.7% now married, 2.0% widowed, 0.0% divorced (2000); Foreign born: 0.0% (2000); Ancestry (includes multiple ancestries): 68.2% Norwegian, 14.0% Polish, 10.9% German, 6.2% Swedish, 4.7% English (2000).
Economy: Employment by occupation: 19.0% management, 17.5% professional, 4.8% services, 28.6% sales, 6.3% farming, 12.7% construction, 11.1% production (2000).
Income: Per capita income: $17,326 (2000); Median household income: $46,250 (2000); Poverty rate: 0.0% (2000).
Taxes: Total city taxes per capita: $63 (1997); City property taxes per capita: $63 (1997).
Education: High school graduation rate: 83.1% (2000); College graduation rate: 16.9% (2000).
Housing: Homeownership rate: 92.7% (2000); Median home value: $65,000 (2000); Median age of housing: 55 years (2000).
Transportation: Commute to work: 84.1% car, 0.0% public transportation, 0.0% walk, 15.9% work from home (2000); Travel time to work: 7.5% less than 15 minutes, 50.9% 15 to 30 minutes, 35.8% 30 to 45 minutes, 0.0% 45 to 60 minutes, 5.7% 60 minutes or more (2000)

MAYFIELD (township). Covers a land area of 22.825 square miles and a water area of 0 square miles. Located at 48.00° N. Lat.; 95.89° W. Long.
Population: 76 (2000); Race: 100.0% White, 0.0% Black, 0.0% Asian, 0.0% American Indian and Alaska Native, 0.0% Hispanic of any race, 0.0% two or more races (2000); Density: 3.3 persons per square mile (2000); Age: 22.2% under 18, 11.1% over 64 (2000); Marriage status: 41.4% never married, 48.3% now married, 8.6% widowed, 1.7% divorced (2000); Foreign born: 0.0% (2000); Ancestry (includes multiple ancestries): 50.8% Norwegian, 17.5% French (except Basque), 15.9% Swedish, 9.5% English, 9.5% German (2000).
Economy: Employment by occupation: 6.9% management, 6.9% professional, 20.7% services, 13.8% sales, 13.8% farming, 13.8% construction, 24.1% production (2000).
Income: Per capita income: $11,743 (2000); Median household income: $36,250 (2000); Poverty rate: 20.6% (2000).
Taxes: Total city taxes per capita: $198 (1997); City property taxes per capita: $198 (1997).
Education: High school graduation rate: 71.9% (2000); College graduation rate: 0.0% (2000).
Housing: Homeownership rate: 84.0% (2000); Median age of housing: 36 years (2000).
Transportation: Commute to work: 79.3% car, 0.0% public transportation, 0.0% walk, 20.7% work from home (2000); Travel time to work: 0.0% less than 15 minutes, 39.1% 15 to 30 minutes, 34.8% 30 to 45 minutes, 0.0% 45 to 60 minutes, 26.1% 60 minutes or more (2000)

NORDEN (township). Covers a land area of 27.598 square miles and a water area of 0 square miles. Located at 48.13° N. Lat.; 96.30° W. Long.
Population: 385 (2000); Race: 97.4% White, 0.0% Black, 1.1% Asian, 0.5% American Indian and Alaska Native, 1.1% Hispanic of any race, 1.1% two or more races (2000); Density: 14.0 persons per square mile (2000); Age: 30.2% under 18, 9.0% over 64 (2000); Marriage status: 26.1% never married, 62.0% now married, 6.8% widowed, 5.1% divorced (2000); Foreign born: 1.6% (2000); Ancestry (includes multiple ancestries): 52.6% Norwegian, 22.5% German, 10.8% Swedish, 6.1% French (except Basque), 6.1% Irish (2000).
Economy: Single-family building permits issued: 1 (2001) / 0 (2000); Multi-family building permits issued: 0 (2001) / 0 (2000); Employment by occupation: 12.7% management, 12.2% professional, 11.3% services, 31.2% sales, 2.7% farming, 6.3% construction, 23.5% production (2000).
Income: Per capita income: $17,951 (2000); Median household income: $50,500 (2000); Poverty rate: 7.4% (2000).
Taxes: Total city taxes per capita: $40 (1997); City property taxes per capita: $40 (1997).
Education: High school graduation rate: 84.3% (2000); College graduation rate: 12.7% (2000).
Housing: Homeownership rate: 96.2% (2000); Median home value: $90,000 (2000); Median age of housing: 24 years (2000).
Transportation: Commute to work: 97.3% car, 0.0% public transportation, 0.0% walk, 2.7% work from home (2000); Travel time to work: 45.1% less than 15 minutes, 42.3% 15 to 30 minutes, 6.1% 30 to 45 minutes, 2.3% 45 to 60 minutes, 4.2% 60 minutes or more (2000)

NORTH (township). Covers a land area of 22.974 square miles and a water area of 0.429 square miles. Located at 48.14° N. Lat.; 96.18° W. Long.
Population: 726 (2000); Race: 99.5% White, 0.0% Black, 0.0% Asian, 0.5% American Indian and Alaska Native, 0.0% Hispanic of any race, 0.0% two or more races (2000); Density: 31.6 persons per square mile (2000); Age: 30.2% under 18, 13.1% over 64 (2000); Marriage status: 19.2% never married, 70.1% now married, 3.2% widowed, 7.5% divorced (2000); Foreign born: 0.5% (2000); Ancestry (includes multiple ancestries): 53.7% Norwegian, 19.0% German, 15.1% Swedish, 6.9% Polish, 6.7% English (2000).
Economy: Single-family building permits issued: 3 (2001) / 0 (2000); Multi-family building permits issued: 0 (2001) / 0 (2000); Employment by occupation: 16.2% management, 19.5% professional, 12.2% services, 24.4% sales, 3.0% farming, 8.2% construction, 16.5% production (2000).
Income: Per capita income: $17,361 (2000); Median household income: $46,406 (2000); Poverty rate: 2.6% (2000).
Taxes: Total city taxes per capita: $58 (2000); City property taxes per capita: $56 (2000).
Education: High school graduation rate: 89.5% (2000); College graduation rate: 24.4% (2000).
Housing: Homeownership rate: 94.7% (2000); Median home value: $84,000 (2000); Median rent: $319 per month (2000); Median age of housing: 29 years (2000).
Transportation: Commute to work: 91.9% car, 1.0% public transportation, 1.0% walk, 6.1% work from home (2000); Travel time to work: 73.4% less than 15 minutes, 19.4% 15 to 30 minutes, 2.7% 30 to 45 minutes, 1.6% 45 to 60 minutes, 3.0% 60 minutes or more (2000)

NUMEDAL (township). Covers a land area of 27.797 square miles and a water area of 0 square miles. Located at 48.14° N. Lat.; 96.42° W. Long.
Population: 91 (2000); Race: 100.0% White, 0.0% Black, 0.0% Asian, 0.0% American Indian and Alaska Native, 0.0% Hispanic of any race, 0.0% two or more races (2000); Density: 3.3 persons per square mile (2000); Age: 30.0% under 18, 10.0% over 64 (2000); Marriage status: 18.9% never married, 68.9% now married, 6.8% widowed, 5.4% divorced (2000); Foreign born: 0.0% (2000); Ancestry (includes multiple ancestries): 55.0% Norwegian, 22.0% German, 11.0% Swedish, 10.0% Irish, 6.0% United States or American (2000).
Economy: Single-family building permits issued: 0 (2001) / 0 (2000); Multi-family building permits issued: 0 (2001) / 0 (2000); Employment by occupation: 18.4% management, 18.4% professional, 8.2% services, 20.4% sales, 0.0% farming, 14.3% construction, 20.4% production (2000).
Income: Per capita income: $16,068 (2000); Median household income: $41,250 (2000); Poverty rate: 6.0% (2000).
Taxes: Total city taxes per capita: $78 (1997); City property taxes per capita: $78 (1997).
Education: High school graduation rate: 92.4% (2000); College graduation rate: 7.6% (2000).
Housing: Homeownership rate: 100.0% (2000); Median home value: $60,000 (2000); Median age of housing: 27 years (2000).
Transportation: Commute to work: 95.9% car, 0.0% public transportation, 0.0% walk, 4.1% work from home (2000); Travel time to work: 19.1% less than 15 minutes, 59.6% 15 to 30 minutes, 12.8% 30 to 45 minutes, 0.0% 45 to 60 minutes, 8.5% 60 minutes or more (2000)

POLK CENTRE (township). Covers a land area of 24.105 square miles and a water area of 0.007 square miles. Located at 48.00° N. Lat.; 96.40° W. Long.
Population: 79 (2000); Race: 100.0% White, 0.0% Black, 0.0% Asian, 0.0% American Indian and Alaska Native, 0.0% Hispanic of any race, 0.0% two or more races (2000); Density: 3.3 persons per square mile (2000); Age: 26.0% under 18, 20.5% over 64 (2000); Marriage status: 20.0% never married, 63.6% now married, 5.5% widowed, 10.9% divorced (2000); Foreign born: 0.0% (2000); Ancestry (includes multiple ancestries): 45.2% German, 24.7%

Swedish, 21.9% Norwegian, 17.8% French Canadian, 13.7% French (except Basque) (2000).
Economy: Employment by occupation: 6.5% management, 16.1% professional, 25.8% services, 19.4% sales, 0.0% farming, 6.5% construction, 25.8% production (2000).
Income: Per capita income: $13,136 (2000); Median household income: $31,250 (2000); Poverty rate: 8.2% (2000).
Taxes: Total city taxes per capita: $67 (1997); City property taxes per capita: $67 (1997).
Education: High school graduation rate: 88.0% (2000); College graduation rate: 12.0% (2000).
Housing: Homeownership rate: 86.7% (2000); Median home value: $80,000 (2000); Median age of housing: 60 years (2000).
Transportation: Commute to work: 87.1% car, 0.0% public transportation, 6.5% walk, 6.5% work from home (2000); Travel time to work: 13.8% less than 15 minutes, 69.0% 15 to 30 minutes, 10.3% 30 to 45 minutes, 6.9% 45 to 60 minutes, 0.0% 60 minutes or more (2000)

REINER (township). Covers a land area of 26.963 square miles and a water area of 0 square miles. Located at 48.14° N. Lat.; 95.67° W. Long.
Population: 94 (2000); Race: 100.0% White, 0.0% Black, 0.0% Asian, 0.0% American Indian and Alaska Native, 0.0% Hispanic of any race, 0.0% two or more races (2000); Density: 3.5 persons per square mile (2000); Age: 18.8% under 18, 17.7% over 64 (2000); Marriage status: 17.5% never married, 72.5% now married, 2.5% widowed, 7.5% divorced (2000); Foreign born: 0.0% (2000); Ancestry (includes multiple ancestries): 72.9% Norwegian, 11.5% German, 9.4% Irish, 9.4% French (except Basque), 6.3% United States or American (2000).
Economy: Employment by occupation: 18.2% management, 13.6% professional, 13.6% services, 25.0% sales, 0.0% farming, 4.5% construction, 25.0% production (2000).
Income: Per capita income: $18,003 (2000); Median household income: $31,563 (2000); Poverty rate: 0.0% (2000).
Taxes: Total city taxes per capita: $103 (1997); City property taxes per capita: $103 (1997).
Education: High school graduation rate: 75.4% (2000); College graduation rate: 7.2% (2000).
Housing: Homeownership rate: 85.7% (2000); Median home value: $75,000 (2000); Median rent: <$100 per month (2000); Median age of housing: 27 years (2000).
Transportation: Commute to work: 80.5% car, 0.0% public transportation, 0.0% walk, 14.6% work from home (2000); Travel time to work: 25.7% less than 15 minutes, 5.7% 15 to 30 minutes, 14.3% 30 to 45 minutes, 31.4% 45 to 60 minutes, 22.9% 60 minutes or more (2000)

RIVER FALLS (township). Covers a land area of 22.676 square miles and a water area of 0.039 square miles. Located at 47.99° N. Lat.; 96.16° W. Long.
Population: 194 (2000); Race: 100.0% White, 0.0% Black, 0.0% Asian, 0.0% American Indian and Alaska Native, 0.0% Hispanic of any race, 0.0% two or more races (2000); Density: 8.6 persons per square mile (2000); Age: 31.1% under 18, 3.1% over 64 (2000); Marriage status: 22.3% never married, 73.6% now married, 1.4% widowed, 2.7% divorced (2000); Foreign born: 1.0% (2000); Ancestry (includes multiple ancestries): 40.8% Norwegian, 28.6% German, 14.3% Swedish, 9.7% Scandinavian, 9.2% Czech (2000).
Economy: Employment by occupation: 11.8% management, 23.6% professional, 14.5% services, 21.8% sales, 1.8% farming, 11.8% construction, 14.5% production (2000).
Income: Per capita income: $17,186 (2000); Median household income: $43,750 (2000); Poverty rate: 5.1% (2000).
Taxes: Total city taxes per capita: $50 (1997); City property taxes per capita: $50 (1997).
Education: High school graduation rate: 89.3% (2000); College graduation rate: 13.2% (2000).
Housing: Homeownership rate: 97.0% (2000); Median home value: $71,700 (2000); Median rent: $525 per month (2000); Median age of housing: 32 years (2000).
Transportation: Commute to work: 94.4% car, 0.0% public transportation, 0.0% walk, 5.6% work from home (2000); Travel time to work: 21.8% less than 15 minutes, 65.3% 15 to 30 minutes, 3.0% 30 to 45 minutes, 0.0% 45 to 60 minutes, 9.9% 60 minutes or more (2000)

ROCKSBURY (township). Covers a land area of 34.305 square miles and a water area of 0.542 square miles. Located at 48.07° N. Lat.; 96.18° W. Long.
Population: 1,077 (2000); Race: 95.2% White, 0.0% Black, 0.0% Asian, 3.1% American Indian and Alaska Native, 1.9% Hispanic of any race, 0.5% two or more races (2000); Density: 31.4 persons per square mile (2000); Age: 30.5% under 18, 11.2% over 64 (2000); Marriage status: 24.3% never married, 64.7% now married, 4.3% widowed, 6.7% divorced (2000); Foreign born: 0.6% (2000); Ancestry (includes multiple ancestries): 46.9% Norwegian, 24.4% German, 15.7% Swedish, 9.3% Irish, 7.5% French (except Basque) (2000).
Economy: Single-family building permits issued: 3 (2001) / 3 (2000); Multi-family building permits issued: 0 (2001) / 0 (2000); Employment by occupation: 14.0% management, 11.6% professional, 15.9% services, 26.8% sales, 0.4% farming, 6.8% construction, 24.5% production (2000).
Income: Per capita income: $19,491 (2000); Median household income: $50,547 (2000); Poverty rate: 10.1% (2000).
Taxes: Total city taxes per capita: $78 (2000); City property taxes per capita: $77 (2000).
Education: High school graduation rate: 83.4% (2000); College graduation rate: 15.2% (2000).
Housing: Homeownership rate: 92.2% (2000); Median home value: $104,300 (2000); Median rent: $310 per month (2000); Median age of housing: 26 years (2000).
Transportation: Commute to work: 86.8% car, 3.2% public transportation, 0.9% walk, 8.4% work from home (2000); Travel time to work: 70.3% less than 15 minutes, 21.5% 15 to 30 minutes, 3.3% 30 to 45 minutes, 0.8% 45 to 60 minutes, 4.2% 60 minutes or more (2000)

SAINT HILAIRE (city). Covers a land area of 0.768 square miles and a water area of 0.068 square miles. Located at 48.01° N. Lat.; 96.21° W. Long. Elevation is 1,089 feet.
Population: 272 (2000); Race: 99.2% White, 0.0% Black, 0.0% Asian, 0.8% American Indian and Alaska Native, 0.0% Hispanic of any race, 0.0% two or more races (2000); Density: 354.0 persons per square mile (2000); Age: 25.3% under 18, 5.7% over 64 (2000); Marriage status: 29.7% never married, 45.5% now married, 6.7% widowed, 18.2% divorced (2000); Foreign born: 1.1% (2000); Ancestry (includes multiple ancestries): 50.2% German, 42.3% Norwegian, 14.0% French (except Basque), 9.1% Irish, 4.9% Swedish (2000).
Economy: Single-family building permits issued: 0 (2001) / 0 (2000); Multi-family building permits issued: 0 (2001) / 0 (2000); Employment by occupation: 5.0% management, 6.5% professional, 21.6% services, 28.8% sales, 2.9% farming, 7.9% construction, 27.3% production (2000).
Income: Per capita income: $13,317 (2000); Median household income: $26,250 (2000); Poverty rate: 14.1% (2000).
Education: High school graduation rate: 81.3% (2000); College graduation rate: 7.5% (2000).
Housing: Homeownership rate: 78.2% (2000); Median home value: $42,300 (2000); Median rent: $372 per month (2000); Median age of housing: 36 years (2000).
Transportation: Commute to work: 94.2% car, 0.0% public transportation, 4.3% walk, 1.4% work from home (2000); Travel time to work: 56.2% less than 15 minutes, 36.5% 15 to 30 minutes, 4.4% 30 to 45 minutes, 1.5% 45 to 60 minutes, 1.5% 60 minutes or more (2000)

SANDERS (township). Covers a land area of 36.164 square miles and a water area of 0 square miles. Located at 48.07° N. Lat.; 96.29° W. Long.
Population: 285 (2000); Race: 100.0% White, 0.0% Black, 0.0% Asian, 0.0% American Indian and Alaska Native, 1.4% Hispanic of any race, 0.0% two or more races (2000); Density: 7.9 persons per square mile (2000); Age: 26.2% under 18, 12.8% over 64 (2000); Marriage status: 22.1% never married, 64.9% now married, 7.7% widowed, 5.4% divorced (2000); Foreign born: 0.7% (2000); Ancestry (includes multiple ancestries): 39.7% Norwegian, 25.2% German, 12.8% Swedish, 11.7% Irish, 8.2% United States or American (2000).
Economy: Single-family building permits issued: 0 (2001) / 1 (2000); Multi-family building permits issued: 0 (2001) / 0 (2000); Employment by occupation: 14.5% management, 20.0% professional, 7.6% services, 26.2% sales, 2.8% farming, 3.4% construction, 25.5% production (2000).
Income: Per capita income: $14,376 (2000); Median household income: $36,250 (2000); Poverty rate: 18.8% (2000).
Taxes: Total city taxes per capita: $16 (1997); City property taxes per capita: $16 (1997).
Education: High school graduation rate: 82.9% (2000); College graduation rate: 12.4% (2000).
Housing: Homeownership rate: 88.5% (2000); Median home value: $48,900 (2000); Median rent: $220 per month (2000); Median age of housing: 29 years (2000).

Transportation: Commute to work: 95.1% car, 0.0% public transportation, 0.0% walk, 4.9% work from home (2000); Travel time to work: 35.6% less than 15 minutes, 55.6% 15 to 30 minutes, 5.9% 30 to 45 minutes, 1.5% 45 to 60 minutes, 1.5% 60 minutes or more (2000)

SILVERTON (township). Covers a land area of 26.633 square miles and a water area of 0 square miles. Located at 48.14° N. Lat.; 96.05° W. Long.
Population: 182 (2000); Race: 100.0% White, 0.0% Black, 0.0% Asian, 0.0% American Indian and Alaska Native, 0.0% Hispanic of any race, 0.0% two or more races (2000); Density: 6.8 persons per square mile (2000); Age: 32.4% under 18, 7.8% over 64 (2000); Marriage status: 34.4% never married, 58.8% now married, 1.3% widowed, 5.6% divorced (2000); Foreign born: 0.0% (2000); Ancestry (includes multiple ancestries): 67.6% Norwegian, 27.5% German, 9.8% Swedish, 8.3% Czech, 6.4% Czechoslovakian (2000).
Economy: Employment by occupation: 18.3% management, 15.6% professional, 14.7% services, 25.7% sales, 0.0% farming, 10.1% construction, 15.6% production (2000).
Income: Per capita income: $15,265 (2000); Median household income: $42,917 (2000); Poverty rate: 5.4% (2000).
Taxes: Total city taxes per capita: $57 (1997); City property taxes per capita: $57 (1997).
Education: High school graduation rate: 93.2% (2000); College graduation rate: 7.7% (2000).
Housing: Homeownership rate: 84.5% (2000); Median home value: $84,000 (2000); Median rent: $325 per month (2000); Median age of housing: 27 years (2000).
Transportation: Commute to work: 98.2% car, 0.0% public transportation, 0.0% walk, 1.8% work from home (2000); Travel time to work: 28.0% less than 15 minutes, 57.9% 15 to 30 minutes, 9.3% 30 to 45 minutes, 2.8% 45 to 60 minutes, 1.9% 60 minutes or more (2000)

SMILEY (township). Covers a land area of 36.014 square miles and a water area of 0.220 square miles. Located at 48.07° N. Lat.; 96.05° W. Long.
Population: 528 (2000); Race: 97.3% White, 0.0% Black, 0.0% Asian, 1.5% American Indian and Alaska Native, 0.0% Hispanic of any race, 1.3% two or more races (2000); Density: 14.7 persons per square mile (2000); Age: 30.2% under 18, 5.9% over 64 (2000); Marriage status: 29.7% never married, 56.8% now married, 2.6% widowed, 10.9% divorced (2000); Foreign born: 0.9% (2000); Ancestry (includes multiple ancestries): 45.7% Norwegian, 24.9% German, 10.2% Swedish, 9.1% Irish, 8.4% French (except Basque) (2000).
Economy: Employment by occupation: 15.3% management, 15.6% professional, 15.6% services, 21.8% sales, 1.0% farming, 8.4% construction, 22.4% production (2000).
Income: Per capita income: $17,431 (2000); Median household income: $47,386 (2000); Poverty rate: 12.0% (2000).
Taxes: Total city taxes per capita: $45 (1997); City property taxes per capita: $45 (1997).
Education: High school graduation rate: 89.4% (2000); College graduation rate: 9.6% (2000).
Housing: Homeownership rate: 89.5% (2000); Median home value: $84,300 (2000); Median rent: $300 per month (2000); Median age of housing: 25 years (2000).
Transportation: Commute to work: 94.4% car, 0.0% public transportation, 0.3% walk, 5.2% work from home (2000); Travel time to work: 37.2% less than 15 minutes, 52.4% 15 to 30 minutes, 2.8% 30 to 45 minutes, 3.8% 45 to 60 minutes, 3.8% 60 minutes or more (2000)

STAR (township). Covers a land area of 36.265 square miles and a water area of 0.003 square miles. Located at 48.07° N. Lat.; 95.66° W. Long.
Population: 147 (2000); Race: 90.6% White, 0.0% Black, 9.4% Asian, 0.0% American Indian and Alaska Native, 0.0% Hispanic of any race, 0.0% two or more races (2000); Density: 4.1 persons per square mile (2000); Age: 24.4% under 18, 29.1% over 64 (2000); Marriage status: 18.4% never married, 67.0% now married, 12.6% widowed, 1.9% divorced (2000); Foreign born: 3.9% (2000); Ancestry (includes multiple ancestries): 69.3% Norwegian, 16.5% German, 10.2% Czech, 9.4% Other groups, 6.3% Swedish (2000).
Economy: Employment by occupation: 16.7% management, 10.4% professional, 14.6% services, 22.9% sales, 10.4% farming, 4.2% construction, 20.8% production (2000).
Income: Per capita income: $12,443 (2000); Median household income: $21,250 (2000); Poverty rate: 32.3% (2000).
Taxes: Total city taxes per capita: $22 (1997); City property taxes per capita: $22 (1997).
Education: High school graduation rate: 73.1% (2000); College graduation rate: 4.3% (2000).
Housing: Homeownership rate: 84.3% (2000); Median home value: $130,000 (2000); Median rent: $275 per month (2000); Median age of housing: 42 years (2000).
Transportation: Commute to work: 72.9% car, 0.0% public transportation, 0.0% walk, 27.1% work from home (2000); Travel time to work: 22.9% less than 15 minutes, 37.1% 15 to 30 minutes, 28.6% 30 to 45 minutes, 0.0% 45 to 60 minutes, 11.4% 60 minutes or more (2000)

THIEF RIVER FALLS (city). Covers a land area of 4.778 square miles and a water area of 0.213 square miles. Located at 48.11° N. Lat.; 96.17° W. Long. Elevation is 1,133 feet.
History: The town at Thief River Falls was formerly called Rockstad, but was later named for the river. The Chippewa called it the Secret Earth River, but French and English fur traders mispronounced it as Stealing Earth River, from which it became Thief Lake, and finally Thief River Falls. The town developed as the center of an area drained for agriculture, and producing hay and forage for market.
Population: 8,410 (2000); Race: 97.2% White, 0.4% Black, 0.9% Asian, 0.9% American Indian and Alaska Native, 0.8% Hispanic of any race, 0.5% two or more races (2000); Density: 1,760.0 persons per square mile (2000); Age: 21.6% under 18, 19.0% over 64 (2000); Marriage status: 27.7% never married, 52.2% now married, 10.1% widowed, 9.9% divorced (2000); Foreign born: 2.1% (2000); Ancestry (includes multiple ancestries): 50.0% Norwegian, 21.2% German, 15.1% Swedish, 7.2% French (except Basque), 5.9% Irish (2000).
Economy: Single-family building permits issued: 18 (2001) / 18 (2000); Multi-family building permits issued: 19 (2001) / 18 (2000); Employment by occupation: 9.8% management, 17.8% professional, 17.6% services, 25.8% sales, 0.9% farming, 8.5% construction, 19.6% production (2000).
Income: Per capita income: $17,489 (2000); Median household income: $30,759 (2000); Poverty rate: 12.4% (2000).
Taxes: Total city taxes per capita: $135 (1997); City property taxes per capita: $125 (1997).
Education: High school graduation rate: 79.1% (2000); College graduation rate: 15.7% (2000).

School District(s)

Thief River Falls (PK-12)
2000 Enrollment: 2,164 218-681-8711

Two-year College(s)

Northland Community and Technical College (Public)
2001 Enrollment: 2,154 218-681-0701
2001 Tuition: In-state $2,656; Out-of-state $5,312

Housing: Homeownership rate: 66.3% (2000); Median home value: $59,800 (2000); Median rent: $302 per month (2000); Median age of housing: 37 years (2000).
Hospitals: Northwest Medical Center (99 beds)
Safety: Violent crime rate: 11.8 per 10,000 population; Property crime rate: 381.2 per 10,000 population (2001).
Newspapers: Northern Watch (1 x week); Thief River Falls Times (1 x week)
Transportation: Commute to work: 91.3% car, 1.7% public transportation, 3.7% walk, 2.5% work from home (2000); Travel time to work: 80.5% less than 15 minutes, 13.2% 15 to 30 minutes, 1.8% 30 to 45 minutes, 1.0% 45 to 60 minutes, 3.5% 60 minutes or more (2000)
Airports: Thief River Falls Regional (commercial service)
Additional Information Contacts
Thief River Fls Chamber of Commerce 218-681-3720

WYANDOTTE (township). Covers a land area of 22.627 square miles and a water area of 0 square miles. Located at 47.98° N. Lat.; 96.03° W. Long.
Population: 101 (2000); Race: 97.0% White, 0.0% Black, 3.0% Asian, 0.0% American Indian and Alaska Native, 0.0% Hispanic of any race, 0.0% two or more races (2000); Density: 4.5 persons per square mile (2000); Age: 21.8% under 18, 14.9% over 64 (2000); Marriage status: 25.3% never married, 62.7% now married, 4.8% widowed, 7.2% divorced (2000); Foreign born: 3.0% (2000); Ancestry (includes multiple ancestries): 54.5% Norwegian, 25.7% German, 16.8% Swedish, 14.9% Polish, 5.9% English (2000).
Economy: Employment by occupation: 4.2% management, 16.7% professional, 12.5% services, 37.5% sales, 0.0% farming, 10.4% construction, 18.8% production (2000).
Income: Per capita income: $23,144 (2000); Median household income: $39,583 (2000); Poverty rate: 4.0% (2000).
Taxes: Total city taxes per capita: $26 (1997); City property taxes per capita: $26 (1997).

Education: High school graduation rate: 80.3% (2000); College graduation rate: 11.3% (2000).
Housing: Homeownership rate: 95.2% (2000); Median home value: $105,000 (2000); Median age of housing: 36 years (2000).
Transportation: Commute to work: 95.8% car, 0.0% public transportation, 0.0% walk, 4.2% work from home (2000); Travel time to work: 13.0% less than 15 minutes, 69.6% 15 to 30 minutes, 13.0% 30 to 45 minutes, 4.3% 45 to 60 minutes, 0.0% 60 minutes or more (2000)

Pine County

Located in eastern Minnesota; bounded on the east by the St. Croix River and the Wisconsin border; drained by the Kettle River. Covers a land area of 1,411.00 square miles, a water area of 23.50 square miles, and is located in the Central Time Zone. The county government was organized in 1856. County seat is Pine City.
Population: 26,530 (2000); Race: 94.1% White, 1.3% Black, 0.3% Asian, 2.9% American Indian and Alaska Native, 1.8% Hispanic of any race, 1.1% two or more races (2000); Density: 18.8 persons per square mile (2000); Age: 25.5% under 18, 15.1% over 64 (2000).
Religion: Five largest groups: 17.0% Catholic Church, 13.8% Evangelical Lutheran Church in America, 6.0% Lutheran Church—Missouri Synod, 1.5% The Evangelical Free Church of America, 1.3% Baptist General Conference (2000).
Economy: Unemployment rate: 5.5% (11/2002); Total civilian labor force: 11,814 (11/2002); Leading industries: 21.3% retail trade; 18.2% health care and social assistance; 18.0% accommodation & food services (2000); Companies that employ more than 1,000 persons: 0 (2000); Companies that employ more than 100 persons: 4 (2000); Farms: 950 totaling 246,804 acres (1997); Minority business ownership rate: 0.0% (1997); Women business ownership rate: 26.2% (1997); Retail sales per capita: $6,477 (1997). Single-family building permits issued: 93 (2001) / 72 (2000); Multi-family building permits issued: 30 (2001) / 10 (2000).
Income: Per capita income: $17,445 (2000); Median household income: $37,379 (2000); Poverty rate: 11.3% (2000); Bankruptcy rate: 4.77% (2001).
Taxes: Total county taxes per capita: $270 (2000); County property taxes per capita: $268 (2000).
Education: High school graduation rate: 79.0% (2000); College graduation rate: 10.3% (2000).
Housing: Homeownership rate: 83.7% (2000); Median home value: $89,700 (2000); Median rent: $376 per month (2000); Median age of housing: 26 years (2000).
Health: Birth rate: 100.3 per 10,000 population (1998); Age adjusted death rate: 83.9 per 10,000 population (1999); Age adjusted cancer mortality rate: 225.9 deaths per 100,000 population (1999). Air Quality Index: 100% good, 0% moderate, 0% unhealthy (percent of days in 2000). Number of physicians: 4.5 per 10,000 population (1999); Number of hospital beds: 40.0 per 10,000 population (1999).
Elections: 2000 Presidential election results: 47.1% Gore, 44.8% Bush, 5.6% Nader, 2.0% Buchanan
National and State Parks: Banning State Park; Chengwatana State Forest; D A R Memorial State Forest; General C C Andrews State Forest; Kettle River State Wildlife Management Area; Mark State Wildlife Management Area; McGowan State Wildlife Management Area; Minnesota-Wisconsin Boundary State Trail; Nemadji State Forest; Pine County State Game Refuge; Rock Marsh State Wildlife Management Area; Saint Croix State Forest; Saint Croix State Park; Sandstone National Wildlife Refuge; Sandstone State Wildlife Management Area
Additional Information Contacts
Pine County Government Offices 320-629-5600
Hinckley Chamber of Commerce. 320-384-7837
Pine City Chamber of Commerce 320-629-3861
Sandstone Chamber of Commerce. 320-245-2271

Pine County Communities

ARLONE (township). Covers a land area of 36.595 square miles and a water area of 0.092 square miles. Located at 46.01° N. Lat.; 92.72° W. Long.
Population: 345 (2000); Race: 91.1% White, 2.0% Black, 0.6% Asian, 2.8% American Indian and Alaska Native, 1.7% Hispanic of any race, 3.1% two or more races (2000); Density: 9.4 persons per square mile (2000); Age: 30.2% under 18, 10.1% over 64 (2000); Marriage status: 28.1% never married, 63.5% now married, 1.8% widowed, 6.7% divorced (2000); Foreign born: 1.1% (2000); Ancestry (includes multiple ancestries): 38.0% German, 18.4% Norwegian, 12.8% Swedish, 9.2% Other groups, 8.7% Czech (2000).
Economy: Employment by occupation: 13.1% management, 12.6% professional, 28.0% services, 20.0% sales, 1.1% farming, 12.6% construction, 12.6% production (2000).
Income: Per capita income: $14,867 (2000); Median household income: $32,361 (2000); Poverty rate: 6.7% (2000).
Taxes: Total city taxes per capita: $46 (1997); City property taxes per capita: $46 (1997).
Education: High school graduation rate: 89.1% (2000); College graduation rate: 6.1% (2000).
Housing: Homeownership rate: 97.0% (2000); Median home value: $72,500 (2000); Median age of housing: 17 years (2000).
Transportation: Commute to work: 91.2% car, 0.0% public transportation, 2.9% walk, 5.9% work from home (2000); Travel time to work: 26.3% less than 15 minutes, 45.0% 15 to 30 minutes, 15.0% 30 to 45 minutes, 2.5% 45 to 60 minutes, 11.3% 60 minutes or more (2000)

ARNA (township). Covers a land area of 37.647 square miles and a water area of 0.174 square miles. Located at 46.10° N. Lat.; 92.35° W. Long.
Population: 86 (2000); Race: 89.7% White, 0.0% Black, 4.1% Asian, 6.2% American Indian and Alaska Native, 0.0% Hispanic of any race, 0.0% two or more races (2000); Density: 2.3 persons per square mile (2000); Age: 12.4% under 18, 10.3% over 64 (2000); Marriage status: 15.1% never married, 58.1% now married, 7.0% widowed, 19.8% divorced (2000); Foreign born: 4.1% (2000); Ancestry (includes multiple ancestries): 27.8% German, 26.8% Swedish, 20.6% English, 15.5% Irish, 11.3% Norwegian (2000).
Economy: Single-family building permits issued: 4 (2001) / 2 (2000); Multi-family building permits issued: 0 (2001) / 0 (2000); Employment by occupation: 5.4% management, 33.9% professional, 8.9% services, 1.8% sales, 0.0% farming, 30.4% construction, 19.6% production (2000).
Income: Per capita income: $19,521 (2000); Median household income: $30,875 (2000); Poverty rate: 10.3% (2000).
Taxes: Total city taxes per capita: $245 (1997); City property taxes per capita: $245 (1997).
Education: High school graduation rate: 91.0% (2000); College graduation rate: 12.8% (2000).
Housing: Homeownership rate: 95.7% (2000); Median home value: $48,300 (2000); Median rent: $225 per month (2000); Median age of housing: 33 years (2000).
Transportation: Commute to work: 83.9% car, 0.0% public transportation, 0.0% walk, 12.5% work from home (2000); Travel time to work: 6.1% less than 15 minutes, 36.7% 15 to 30 minutes, 32.7% 30 to 45 minutes, 8.2% 45 to 60 minutes, 16.3% 60 minutes or more (2000)

ASKOV (city). Covers a land area of 1.276 square miles and a water area of 0 square miles. Located at 46.18° N. Lat.; 92.78° W. Long. Elevation is 1,140 feet.
History: Askov was founded in 1905 by the Danish People's Society, which purchased cut-over and burned-over land and laid out a cooperative community. Rutabagas became a leading crop.
Population: 368 (2000); Race: 93.6% White, 0.0% Black, 0.5% Asian, 3.8% American Indian and Alaska Native, 3.3% Hispanic of any race, 0.0% two or more races (2000); Density: 288.3 persons per square mile (2000); Age: 25.1% under 18, 16.9% over 64 (2000); Marriage status: 27.8% never married, 53.7% now married, 8.0% widowed, 10.5% divorced (2000); Foreign born: 0.5% (2000); Ancestry (includes multiple ancestries): 30.4% German, 18.2% Danish, 16.4% Norwegian, 13.0% Irish, 10.7% Swedish (2000).
Economy: Single-family building permits issued: 0 (2001) / 2 (2000); Multi-family building permits issued: 0 (2001) / 0 (2000); Employment by occupation: 6.1% management, 20.3% professional, 23.9% services, 21.8% sales, 0.0% farming, 11.7% construction, 16.2% production (2000).
Income: Per capita income: $14,583 (2000); Median household income: $28,472 (2000); Poverty rate: 9.2% (2000).
Taxes: Total city taxes per capita: $89 (1997); City property taxes per capita: $81 (1997).
Education: High school graduation rate: 83.3% (2000); College graduation rate: 16.3% (2000).
Housing: Homeownership rate: 65.3% (2000); Median home value: $62,000 (2000); Median rent: $221 per month (2000); Median age of housing: 51 years (2000).
Newspapers: Askov American (1 x week)
Transportation: Commute to work: 91.6% car, 0.0% public transportation, 5.2% walk, 3.1% work from home (2000); Travel time to work: 45.4% less than 15 minutes, 29.2% 15 to 30 minutes, 13.0% 30 to 45 minutes, 2.2% 45 to 60 minutes, 10.3% 60 minutes or more (2000)

BARRY (township). Covers a land area of 35.175 square miles and a water area of 0.288 square miles. Located at 46.02° N. Lat.; 92.87° W. Long.
Population: 587 (2000); Race: 83.5% White, 0.0% Black, 0.3% Asian, 15.0% American Indian and Alaska Native, 1.0% Hispanic of any race, 1.2% two or more races (2000); Density: 16.7 persons per square mile (2000); Age: 33.2% under 18, 11.1% over 64 (2000); Marriage status: 22.4% never married, 62.8% now married, 3.2% widowed, 11.5% divorced (2000); Foreign born: 0.8% (2000); Ancestry (includes multiple ancestries): 29.2% German, 17.0% Other groups, 10.8% Norwegian, 9.4% Swedish, 8.9% United States or American (2000).
Economy: Employment by occupation: 9.0% management, 17.6% professional, 28.2% services, 14.1% sales, 3.1% farming, 16.9% construction, 11.0% production (2000).
Income: Per capita income: $14,740 (2000); Median household income: $35,227 (2000); Poverty rate: 17.7% (2000).
Taxes: Total city taxes per capita: $46 (1997); City property taxes per capita: $46 (1997).
Education: High school graduation rate: 73.2% (2000); College graduation rate: 9.5% (2000).
Housing: Homeownership rate: 81.3% (2000); Median home value: $104,900 (2000); Median rent: $275 per month (2000); Median age of housing: 22 years (2000).
Transportation: Commute to work: 89.2% car, 0.0% public transportation, 6.0% walk, 4.8% work from home (2000); Travel time to work: 39.2% less than 15 minutes, 16.0% 15 to 30 minutes, 27.4% 30 to 45 minutes, 2.5% 45 to 60 minutes, 14.8% 60 minutes or more (2000)

BIRCH CREEK (township). Covers a land area of 35.058 square miles and a water area of 0.023 square miles. Located at 46.37° N. Lat.; 92.98° W. Long.
Population: 217 (2000); Race: 98.7% White, 0.0% Black, 0.0% Asian, 0.9% American Indian and Alaska Native, 0.9% Hispanic of any race, 0.4% two or more races (2000); Density: 6.2 persons per square mile (2000); Age: 20.5% under 18, 21.4% over 64 (2000); Marriage status: 27.8% never married, 59.6% now married, 3.5% widowed, 9.1% divorced (2000); Foreign born: 0.0% (2000); Ancestry (includes multiple ancestries): 25.6% German, 21.8% Norwegian, 19.7% Swedish, 10.3% Polish, 9.0% Finnish (2000).
Economy: Employment by occupation: 20.4% management, 10.8% professional, 19.4% services, 18.3% sales, 2.2% farming, 18.3% construction, 10.8% production (2000).
Income: Per capita income: $15,839 (2000); Median household income: $37,344 (2000); Poverty rate: 10.7% (2000).
Taxes: Total city taxes per capita: $69 (1997); City property taxes per capita: $69 (1997).
Education: High school graduation rate: 80.4% (2000); College graduation rate: 5.5% (2000).
Housing: Homeownership rate: 95.7% (2000); Median home value: $75,000 (2000); Median age of housing: 41 years (2000).
Transportation: Commute to work: 82.2% car, 0.0% public transportation, 0.0% walk, 17.8% work from home (2000); Travel time to work: 0.0% less than 15 minutes, 37.8% 15 to 30 minutes, 23.0% 30 to 45 minutes, 10.8% 45 to 60 minutes, 28.4% 60 minutes or more (2000)

BREMEN (township). Covers a land area of 35.975 square miles and a water area of 0.218 square miles. Located at 46.28° N. Lat.; 93.00° W. Long.
Population: 246 (2000); Race: 97.3% White, 0.0% Black, 0.0% Asian, 0.0% American Indian and Alaska Native, 0.0% Hispanic of any race, 1.4% two or more races (2000); Density: 6.8 persons per square mile (2000); Age: 28.2% under 18, 11.4% over 64 (2000); Marriage status: 25.6% never married, 52.9% now married, 3.5% widowed, 18.0% divorced (2000); Foreign born: 0.0% (2000); Ancestry (includes multiple ancestries): 35.5% German, 16.8% Norwegian, 15.9% Swedish, 10.5% Irish, 7.3% Polish (2000).
Economy: Single-family building permits issued: 5 (2001) / 2 (2000); Multi-family building permits issued: 0 (2001) / 0 (2000); Employment by occupation: 17.9% management, 14.7% professional, 27.4% services, 12.6% sales, 3.2% farming, 15.8% construction, 8.4% production (2000).
Income: Per capita income: $12,504 (2000); Median household income: $30,278 (2000); Poverty rate: 5.9% (2000).
Taxes: Total city taxes per capita: $208 (1997); City property taxes per capita: $201 (1997).
Education: High school graduation rate: 81.0% (2000); College graduation rate: 5.9% (2000).
Housing: Homeownership rate: 96.3% (2000); Median home value: $40,000 (2000); Median age of housing: 24 years (2000).
Transportation: Commute to work: 94.6% car, 0.0% public transportation, 0.0% walk, 5.4% work from home (2000); Travel time to work: 6.9% less than 15 minutes, 36.8% 15 to 30 minutes, 29.9% 30 to 45 minutes, 8.0% 45 to 60 minutes, 18.4% 60 minutes or more (2000)

BROOK PARK (city). Covers a land area of 1.023 square miles and a water area of 0 square miles. Located at 45.95° N. Lat.; 93.07° W. Long. Elevation is 1,020 feet.
Population: 156 (2000); Race: 100.0% White, 0.0% Black, 0.0% Asian, 0.0% American Indian and Alaska Native, 0.0% Hispanic of any race, 0.0% two or more races (2000); Density: 152.5 persons per square mile (2000); Age: 28.9% under 18, 5.4% over 64 (2000); Marriage status: 36.7% never married, 41.7% now married, 6.7% widowed, 15.0% divorced (2000); Foreign born: 0.0% (2000); Ancestry (includes multiple ancestries): 19.5% German, 14.8% Swedish, 14.8% United States or American, 10.1% Norwegian, 6.7% Czech (2000).
Economy: Single-family building permits issued: 0 (2001) / 0 (2000); Multi-family building permits issued: 0 (2001) / 0 (2000); Employment by occupation: 6.5% management, 6.5% professional, 27.4% services, 32.3% sales, 0.0% farming, 9.7% construction, 17.7% production (2000).
Income: Per capita income: $14,353 (2000); Median household income: $43,750 (2000); Poverty rate: 13.5% (2000).
Taxes: Total city taxes per capita: $68 (1997); City property taxes per capita: $45 (1997).
Education: High school graduation rate: 62.4% (2000); College graduation rate: 0.0% (2000).
Housing: Homeownership rate: 87.5% (2000); Median home value: $47,000 (2000); Median rent: $400 per month (2000); Median age of housing: 47 years (2000).
Transportation: Commute to work: 93.5% car, 0.0% public transportation, 0.0% walk, 6.5% work from home (2000); Travel time to work: 3.4% less than 15 minutes, 51.7% 15 to 30 minutes, 5.2% 30 to 45 minutes, 13.8% 45 to 60 minutes, 25.9% 60 minutes or more (2000)

BROOK PARK (township). Covers a land area of 30.134 square miles and a water area of 0 square miles. Located at 45.94° N. Lat.; 93.08° W. Long. Elevation is 1,020 feet.
Population: 495 (2000); Race: 94.6% White, 1.0% Black, 0.0% Asian, 2.3% American Indian and Alaska Native, 0.6% Hispanic of any race, 1.5% two or more races (2000); Density: 16.4 persons per square mile (2000); Age: 29.5% under 18, 9.8% over 64 (2000); Marriage status: 22.2% never married, 60.9% now married, 3.0% widowed, 13.9% divorced (2000); Foreign born: 1.5% (2000); Ancestry (includes multiple ancestries): 36.8% German, 12.6% Norwegian, 10.9% Swedish, 9.4% Irish, 7.3% Other groups (2000).
Economy: Employment by occupation: 5.8% management, 8.4% professional, 17.8% services, 24.9% sales, 0.0% farming, 12.4% construction, 30.7% production (2000).
Income: Per capita income: $15,128 (2000); Median household income: $41,818 (2000); Poverty rate: 12.4% (2000).
Taxes: Total city taxes per capita: $58 (1997); City property taxes per capita: $58 (1997).
Education: High school graduation rate: 79.5% (2000); College graduation rate: 7.9% (2000).
Housing: Homeownership rate: 83.8% (2000); Median home value: $92,500 (2000); Median rent: $445 per month (2000); Median age of housing: 25 years (2000).
Transportation: Commute to work: 97.1% car, 1.9% public transportation, 0.0% walk, 1.0% work from home (2000); Travel time to work: 8.7% less than 15 minutes, 51.9% 15 to 30 minutes, 14.6% 30 to 45 minutes, 4.4% 45 to 60 minutes, 20.4% 60 minutes or more (2000)

BRUNO (city). Covers a land area of 1.000 square miles and a water area of 0 square miles. Located at 46.27° N. Lat.; 92.66° W. Long. Elevation is 1,151 feet.
Population: 102 (2000); Race: 94.9% White, 0.0% Black, 0.0% Asian, 5.1% American Indian and Alaska Native, 0.0% Hispanic of any race, 0.0% two or more races (2000); Density: 102.0 persons per square mile (2000); Age: 7.6% under 18, 15.2% over 64 (2000); Marriage status: 13.7% never married, 57.5% now married, 13.7% widowed, 15.1% divorced (2000); Foreign born: 0.0% (2000); Ancestry (includes multiple ancestries): 30.4% Norwegian, 25.3% German, 10.1% Other groups, 8.9% Irish, 5.1% Polish (2000).
Economy: Single-family building permits issued: 0 (2001) / 0 (2000); Multi-family building permits issued: 0 (2001) / 0 (2000); Employment by occupation: 0.0% management, 15.8% professional, 26.3% services, 31.6% sales, 0.0% farming, 15.8% construction, 10.5% production (2000).

Income: Per capita income: $15,439 (2000); Median household income: $28,125 (2000); Poverty rate: 19.0% (2000).
Taxes: Total city taxes per capita: $42 (1997); City property taxes per capita: $21 (1997).
Education: High school graduation rate: 62.5% (2000); College graduation rate: 0.0% (2000).
Housing: Homeownership rate: 76.7% (2000); Median home value: $38,400 (2000); Median rent: $242 per month (2000); Median age of housing: 60+ years (2000).
Transportation: Commute to work: 94.7% car, 0.0% public transportation, 0.0% walk, 0.0% work from home (2000); Travel time to work: 15.8% less than 15 minutes, 36.8% 15 to 30 minutes, 26.3% 30 to 45 minutes, 0.0% 45 to 60 minutes, 21.1% 60 minutes or more (2000)

BRUNO (township). Covers a land area of 34.921 square miles and a water area of 0.032 square miles. Located at 46.29° N. Lat.; 92.62° W. Long. Elevation is 1,151 feet.
Population: 179 (2000); Race: 100.0% White, 0.0% Black, 0.0% Asian, 0.0% American Indian and Alaska Native, 0.0% Hispanic of any race, 0.0% two or more races (2000); Density: 5.1 persons per square mile (2000); Age: 20.3% under 18, 18.8% over 64 (2000); Marriage status: 19.1% never married, 53.6% now married, 10.0% widowed, 17.3% divorced (2000); Foreign born: 0.0% (2000); Ancestry (includes multiple ancestries): 24.1% German, 21.1% Norwegian, 20.3% Polish, 19.5% Swedish, 9.8% Irish (2000).
Economy: Agricultural area (dairying). Employment by occupation: 17.0% management, 12.8% professional, 27.7% services, 4.3% sales, 0.0% farming, 25.5% construction, 12.8% production (2000).
Income: Per capita income: $13,490 (2000); Median household income: $28,750 (2000); Poverty rate: 33.3% (2000).
Taxes: Total city taxes per capita: $68 (1997); City property taxes per capita: $68 (1997).
Education: High school graduation rate: 81.4% (2000); College graduation rate: 8.8% (2000).
Housing: Homeownership rate: 89.8% (2000); Median home value: $95,000 (2000); Median rent: $125 per month (2000); Median age of housing: 22 years (2000).
Transportation: Commute to work: 80.9% car, 0.0% public transportation, 6.4% walk, 12.8% work from home (2000); Travel time to work: 34.1% less than 15 minutes, 19.5% 15 to 30 minutes, 19.5% 30 to 45 minutes, 4.9% 45 to 60 minutes, 22.0% 60 minutes or more (2000)

CHENGWATANA (township). Covers a land area of 45.753 square miles and a water area of 1.511 square miles. Located at 45.86° N. Lat.; 92.86° W. Long.
Population: 809 (2000); Race: 97.4% White, 0.2% Black, 0.5% Asian, 0.5% American Indian and Alaska Native, 0.6% Hispanic of any race, 1.4% two or more races (2000); Density: 17.7 persons per square mile (2000); Age: 25.9% under 18, 10.6% over 64 (2000); Marriage status: 27.4% never married, 55.0% now married, 4.4% widowed, 13.2% divorced (2000); Foreign born: 1.2% (2000); Ancestry (includes multiple ancestries): 41.2% German, 16.5% Swedish, 14.0% Norwegian, 11.1% United States or American, 7.4% Czech (2000).
Economy: Single-family building permits issued: 9 (2001) / 3 (2000); Multi-family building permits issued: 0 (2001) / 0 (2000); Employment by occupation: 15.4% management, 12.3% professional, 21.6% services, 16.5% sales, 3.2% farming, 10.2% construction, 20.8% production (2000).
Income: Per capita income: $16,974 (2000); Median household income: $41,429 (2000); Poverty rate: 12.6% (2000).
Taxes: Total city taxes per capita: $98 (1997); City property taxes per capita: $91 (1997).
Education: High school graduation rate: 83.5% (2000); College graduation rate: 10.1% (2000).
Housing: Homeownership rate: 88.3% (2000); Median home value: $118,000 (2000); Median rent: $475 per month (2000); Median age of housing: 25 years (2000).
Transportation: Commute to work: 87.4% car, 0.5% public transportation, 0.0% walk, 10.6% work from home (2000); Travel time to work: 22.2% less than 15 minutes, 29.5% 15 to 30 minutes, 13.6% 30 to 45 minutes, 5.6% 45 to 60 minutes, 29.0% 60 minutes or more (2000)

CLOVER (township). Covers a land area of 35.943 square miles and a water area of 0.198 square miles. Located at 46.01° N. Lat.; 92.62° W. Long.
Population: 316 (2000); Race: 91.8% White, 1.8% Black, 0.0% Asian, 0.6% American Indian and Alaska Native, 3.5% Hispanic of any race, 2.4% two or more races (2000); Density: 8.8 persons per square mile (2000); Age: 26.8% under 18, 10.0% over 64 (2000); Marriage status: 15.2% never married, 71.7% now married, 3.7% widowed, 9.3% divorced (2000); Foreign born: 2.6% (2000); Ancestry (includes multiple ancestries): 42.6% German, 20.6% Swedish, 7.9% Norwegian, 7.6% Dutch, 7.1% English (2000).
Economy: Single-family building permits issued: 2 (2001) / 0 (2000); Multi-family building permits issued: 0 (2001) / 0 (2000); Employment by occupation: 8.3% management, 19.5% professional, 23.7% services, 11.2% sales, 11.8% farming, 7.7% construction, 17.8% production (2000).
Income: Per capita income: $22,043 (2000); Median household income: $56,250 (2000); Poverty rate: 9.1% (2000).
Taxes: Total city taxes per capita: $68 (1997); City property taxes per capita: $68 (1997).
Education: High school graduation rate: 90.1% (2000); College graduation rate: 9.5% (2000).
Housing: Homeownership rate: 94.8% (2000); Median home value: $126,800 (2000); Median rent: $900 per month (2000); Median age of housing: 8 years (2000).
Transportation: Commute to work: 90.3% car, 1.8% public transportation, 0.0% walk, 7.9% work from home (2000); Travel time to work: 19.7% less than 15 minutes, 41.4% 15 to 30 minutes, 10.5% 30 to 45 minutes, 3.3% 45 to 60 minutes, 25.0% 60 minutes or more (2000)

CROSBY (township). Covers a land area of 43.503 square miles and a water area of 0.809 square miles. Located at 45.93° N. Lat.; 92.63° W. Long.
Population: 97 (2000); Race: 97.7% White, 0.0% Black, 0.0% Asian, 2.3% American Indian and Alaska Native, 0.0% Hispanic of any race, 0.0% two or more races (2000); Density: 2.2 persons per square mile (2000); Age: 25.3% under 18, 14.9% over 64 (2000); Marriage status: 26.5% never married, 52.9% now married, 7.4% widowed, 13.2% divorced (2000); Foreign born: 0.0% (2000); Ancestry (includes multiple ancestries): 47.1% German, 24.1% Norwegian, 20.7% Swedish, 9.2% Czech, 6.9% English (2000).
Economy: Single-family building permits issued: 0 (2001) / 0 (2000); Multi-family building permits issued: 0 (2001) / 0 (2000); Employment by occupation: 18.9% management, 18.9% professional, 0.0% services, 21.6% sales, 13.5% farming, 16.2% construction, 10.8% production (2000).
Income: Per capita income: $22,159 (2000); Median household income: $50,313 (2000); Poverty rate: 6.9% (2000).
Taxes: Total city taxes per capita: $66 (1997); City property taxes per capita: $66 (1997).
Education: High school graduation rate: 76.8% (2000); College graduation rate: 14.3% (2000).
Housing: Homeownership rate: 83.8% (2000); Median home value: $141,700 (2000); Median rent: $125 per month (2000); Median age of housing: 27 years (2000).
Transportation: Commute to work: 86.5% car, 0.0% public transportation, 0.0% walk, 13.5% work from home (2000); Travel time to work: 21.9% less than 15 minutes, 28.1% 15 to 30 minutes, 25.0% 30 to 45 minutes, 0.0% 45 to 60 minutes, 25.0% 60 minutes or more (2000)

DANFORTH (township). Covers a land area of 36.283 square miles and a water area of 0.028 square miles. Located at 46.11° N. Lat.; 92.62° W. Long.
Population: 84 (2000); Race: 100.0% White, 0.0% Black, 0.0% Asian, 0.0% American Indian and Alaska Native, 0.0% Hispanic of any race, 0.0% two or more races (2000); Density: 2.3 persons per square mile (2000); Age: 27.4% under 18, 6.5% over 64 (2000); Marriage status: 26.7% never married, 60.0% now married, 13.3% widowed, 0.0% divorced (2000); Foreign born: 0.0% (2000); Ancestry (includes multiple ancestries): 32.3% German, 22.6% Swedish, 12.9% Norwegian, 6.5% French Canadian, 6.5% Irish (2000).
Economy: Single-family building permits issued: 0 (2001) / 0 (2000); Multi-family building permits issued: 0 (2001) / 0 (2000); Employment by occupation: 11.8% management, 17.6% professional, 0.0% services, 14.7% sales, 0.0% farming, 47.1% construction, 8.8% production (2000).
Income: Per capita income: $22,171 (2000); Median household income: $49,375 (2000); Poverty rate: 40.3% (2000).
Taxes: Total city taxes per capita: $66 (1997); City property taxes per capita: $66 (1997).
Education: High school graduation rate: 91.1% (2000); College graduation rate: 13.3% (2000).
Housing: Homeownership rate: 100.0% (2000); Median age of housing: 31 years (2000).
Transportation: Commute to work: 82.4% car, 0.0% public transportation, 0.0% walk, 17.6% work from home (2000); Travel time to work: 14.3% less than 15 minutes, 7.1% 15 to 30 minutes, 10.7% 30 to 45 minutes, 0.0% 45 to 60 minutes, 67.9% 60 minutes or more (2000)

DELL GROVE (township). Covers a land area of 41.265 square miles and a water area of 1.119 square miles. Located at 46.11° N. Lat.; 93.00° W. Long.
Population: 699 (2000); Race: 95.5% White, 0.0% Black, 0.7% Asian, 2.2% American Indian and Alaska Native, 1.5% Hispanic of any race, 1.5% two or more races (2000); Density: 16.9 persons per square mile (2000); Age: 23.6% under 18, 16.2% over 64 (2000); Marriage status: 22.6% never married, 62.5% now married, 7.2% widowed, 7.8% divorced (2000); Foreign born: 1.8% (2000); Ancestry (includes multiple ancestries): 37.8% German, 18.5% Swedish, 11.3% Norwegian, 10.2% Irish, 9.2% English (2000).
Economy: Single-family building permits issued: 0 (2001) / 0 (2000); Multi-family building permits issued: 0 (2001) / 0 (2000); Employment by occupation: 12.0% management, 25.1% professional, 24.8% services, 10.0% sales, 1.1% farming, 7.1% construction, 19.9% production (2000).
Income: Per capita income: $18,399 (2000); Median household income: $41,838 (2000); Poverty rate: 9.5% (2000).
Taxes: Total city taxes per capita: $66 (1997); City property taxes per capita: $64 (1997).
Education: High school graduation rate: 84.1% (2000); College graduation rate: 15.1% (2000).
Housing: Homeownership rate: 91.3% (2000); Median home value: $88,300 (2000); Median rent: $467 per month (2000); Median age of housing: 31 years (2000).
Transportation: Commute to work: 85.4% car, 0.6% public transportation, 2.6% walk, 9.0% work from home (2000); Travel time to work: 31.4% less than 15 minutes, 32.4% 15 to 30 minutes, 15.4% 30 to 45 minutes, 6.4% 45 to 60 minutes, 14.4% 60 minutes or more (2000)

DENHAM (city). Covers a land area of 1.321 square miles and a water area of 0 square miles. Located at 46.36° N. Lat.; 92.94° W. Long. Elevation is 1,203 feet.
Population: 40 (2000); Race: 100.0% White, 0.0% Black, 0.0% Asian, 0.0% American Indian and Alaska Native, 0.0% Hispanic of any race, 0.0% two or more races (2000); Density: 30.3 persons per square mile (2000); Age: 39.2% under 18, 19.6% over 64 (2000); Marriage status: 25.8% never married, 48.4% now married, 19.4% widowed, 6.5% divorced (2000); Foreign born: 0.0% (2000); Ancestry (includes multiple ancestries): 47.1% Polish, 35.3% Czech, 25.5% Swedish, 11.8% German, 9.8% Norwegian (2000).
Economy: Single-family building permits issued: 0 (2001) / 0 (2000); Multi-family building permits issued: 0 (2001) / 0 (2000); Employment by occupation: 0.0% management, 0.0% professional, 0.0% services, 100.0% sales, 0.0% farming, 0.0% construction, 0.0% production (2000).
Income: Per capita income: $10,106 (2000); Median household income: $16,250 (2000); Poverty rate: 17.6% (2000).
Taxes: Total city taxes per capita: $128 (1997); City property taxes per capita: $103 (1997).
Education: High school graduation rate: 65.5% (2000); College graduation rate: 0.0% (2000).
Housing: Homeownership rate: 100.0% (2000); Median home value: $71,700 (2000); Median age of housing: 34 years (2000).
Transportation: Commute to work: 100.0% car, 0.0% public transportation, 0.0% walk, 0.0% work from home (2000); Travel time to work: 0.0% less than 15 minutes, 100.0% 15 to 30 minutes, 0.0% 30 to 45 minutes, 0.0% 45 to 60 minutes, 0.0% 60 minutes or more (2000)

FINLAYSON (city). Covers a land area of 2.752 square miles and a water area of 0.172 square miles. Located at 46.20° N. Lat.; 92.91° W. Long. Elevation is 1,114 feet.
Population: 314 (2000); Race: 98.9% White, 0.0% Black, 0.0% Asian, 0.0% American Indian and Alaska Native, 1.1% Hispanic of any race, 0.0% two or more races (2000); Density: 114.1 persons per square mile (2000); Age: 32.0% under 18, 12.5% over 64 (2000); Marriage status: 21.4% never married, 60.9% now married, 9.6% widowed, 8.1% divorced (2000); Foreign born: 0.0% (2000); Ancestry (includes multiple ancestries): 43.6% German, 25.2% Irish, 9.3% Norwegian, 9.1% Swedish, 7.6% Finnish (2000).
Economy: Single-family building permits issued: 0 (2001) / 0 (2000); Multi-family building permits issued: 0 (2001) / 0 (2000); Employment by occupation: 16.2% management, 11.0% professional, 18.8% services, 21.4% sales, 0.0% farming, 17.5% construction, 14.9% production (2000).
Income: Per capita income: $16,818 (2000); Median household income: $36,250 (2000); Poverty rate: 8.2% (2000).
Taxes: Total city taxes per capita: $128 (1997); City property taxes per capita: $128 (1997).
Education: High school graduation rate: 74.6% (2000); College graduation rate: 8.3% (2000).
Housing: Homeownership rate: 84.4% (2000); Median home value: $81,000 (2000); Median rent: $275 per month (2000); Median age of housing: 33 years (2000).
Transportation: Commute to work: 70.4% car, 0.0% public transportation, 19.1% walk, 10.5% work from home (2000); Travel time to work: 44.1% less than 15 minutes, 24.3% 15 to 30 minutes, 14.7% 30 to 45 minutes, 5.9% 45 to 60 minutes, 11.0% 60 minutes or more (2000)

FINLAYSON (township). Covers a land area of 33.740 square miles and a water area of 0.320 square miles. Located at 46.20° N. Lat.; 92.87° W. Long. Elevation is 1,114 feet.
Population: 506 (2000); Race: 96.3% White, 0.4% Black, 0.8% Asian, 1.7% American Indian and Alaska Native, 0.4% Hispanic of any race, 0.8% two or more races (2000); Density: 15.0 persons per square mile (2000); Age: 23.3% under 18, 12.0% over 64 (2000); Marriage status: 26.3% never married, 59.3% now married, 2.3% widowed, 12.0% divorced (2000); Foreign born: 3.1% (2000); Ancestry (includes multiple ancestries): 33.3% German, 13.4% Swedish, 9.5% English, 9.5% Norwegian, 8.9% Finnish (2000).
Economy: Cattle, sheep, poultry; oats, alfalfa; dairying. Manufacturing: plastic products. Employment by occupation: 12.7% management, 9.4% professional, 25.3% services, 22.4% sales, 2.4% farming, 13.9% construction, 13.9% production (2000).
Income: Per capita income: $15,070 (2000); Median household income: $30,357 (2000); Poverty rate: 12.4% (2000).
Taxes: Total city taxes per capita: $56 (1997); City property taxes per capita: $56 (1997).
Education: High school graduation rate: 76.6% (2000); College graduation rate: 3.0% (2000).
Housing: Homeownership rate: 89.7% (2000); Median home value: $80,700 (2000); Median rent: $345 per month (2000); Median age of housing: 29 years (2000).
Transportation: Commute to work: 77.1% car, 1.6% public transportation, 3.7% walk, 13.5% work from home (2000); Travel time to work: 33.5% less than 15 minutes, 31.6% 15 to 30 minutes, 18.4% 30 to 45 minutes, 0.9% 45 to 60 minutes, 15.6% 60 minutes or more (2000)

FLEMING (township). Covers a land area of 36.131 square miles and a water area of 0.031 square miles. Located at 46.21° N. Lat.; 92.64° W. Long.
Population: 115 (2000); Race: 94.6% White, 0.0% Black, 0.0% Asian, 2.2% American Indian and Alaska Native, 3.3% Hispanic of any race, 0.0% two or more races (2000); Density: 3.2 persons per square mile (2000); Age: 28.3% under 18, 21.7% over 64 (2000); Marriage status: 16.9% never married, 63.4% now married, 14.1% widowed, 5.6% divorced (2000); Foreign born: 0.0% (2000); Ancestry (includes multiple ancestries): 32.6% German, 17.4% Polish, 15.2% Norwegian, 14.1% Irish, 8.7% French (except Basque) (2000).
Economy: Employment by occupation: 10.5% management, 5.3% professional, 21.1% services, 28.9% sales, 10.5% farming, 2.6% construction, 21.1% production (2000).
Income: Per capita income: $15,441 (2000); Median household income: $26,875 (2000); Poverty rate: 4.3% (2000).
Taxes: Total city taxes per capita: $112 (1997); City property taxes per capita: $112 (1997).
Education: High school graduation rate: 63.9% (2000); College graduation rate: 6.6% (2000).
Housing: Homeownership rate: 100.0% (2000); Median home value: $71,700 (2000); Median age of housing: 36 years (2000).
Transportation: Commute to work: 75.0% car, 0.0% public transportation, 0.0% walk, 19.4% work from home (2000); Travel time to work: 17.2% less than 15 minutes, 20.7% 15 to 30 minutes, 34.5% 30 to 45 minutes, 0.0% 45 to 60 minutes, 27.6% 60 minutes or more (2000)

HENRIETTE (city). Covers a land area of 0.253 square miles and a water area of 0 square miles. Located at 45.87° N. Lat.; 93.12° W. Long. Elevation is 996 feet.
Population: 101 (2000); Race: 100.0% White, 0.0% Black, 0.0% Asian, 0.0% American Indian and Alaska Native, 0.0% Hispanic of any race, 0.0% two or more races (2000); Density: 398.8 persons per square mile (2000); Age: 35.8% under 18, 6.3% over 64 (2000); Marriage status: 30.1% never married, 47.9% now married, 8.2% widowed, 13.7% divorced (2000); Foreign born: 2.1% (2000); Ancestry (includes multiple ancestries): 27.4% Swedish, 23.2% German, 14.7% Norwegian, 13.7% French (except Basque), 11.6% Irish (2000).
Economy: Grain; livestock; dairying. Employment by occupation: 0.0% management, 13.0% professional, 8.7% services, 32.6% sales, 0.0% farming, 17.4% construction, 28.3% production (2000).

Income: Per capita income: $13,312 (2000); Median household income: $28,542 (2000); Poverty rate: 12.6% (2000).
Taxes: Total city taxes per capita: $35 (1997); City property taxes per capita: $23 (1997).
Education: High school graduation rate: 78.2% (2000); College graduation rate: 3.6% (2000).
Housing: Homeownership rate: 90.9% (2000); Median home value: $65,000 (2000); Median rent: $275 per month (2000); Median age of housing: 28 years (2000).
Transportation: Commute to work: 97.7% car, 0.0% public transportation, 0.0% walk, 2.3% work from home (2000); Travel time to work: 19.0% less than 15 minutes, 38.1% 15 to 30 minutes, 28.6% 30 to 45 minutes, 0.0% 45 to 60 minutes, 14.3% 60 minutes or more (2000)

HINCKLEY (city). Covers a land area of 2.842 square miles and a water area of 0.047 square miles. Located at 46.01° N. Lat.; 92.93° W. Long. Elevation is 1,031 feet.
History: A forst fire in 1894, centered in Hinckley, gave rise to the heroism of railway engineer Jim Root, who backed his train through a wall of flames and over a burning bridge, taking 350 people to safety.
Population: 1,291 (2000); Race: 91.0% White, 0.4% Black, 0.8% Asian, 6.3% American Indian and Alaska Native, 0.9% Hispanic of any race, 1.5% two or more races (2000); Density: 454.3 persons per square mile (2000); Age: 28.2% under 18, 13.2% over 64 (2000); Marriage status: 26.9% never married, 48.7% now married, 9.7% widowed, 14.7% divorced (2000); Foreign born: 1.9% (2000); Ancestry (includes multiple ancestries): 37.6% German, 15.1% Norwegian, 11.5% Swedish, 10.3% Irish, 9.8% Other groups (2000).
Economy: Single-family building permits issued: 4 (2001) / 5 (2000); Multi-family building permits issued: 0 (2001) / 0 (2000); Employment by occupation: 6.9% management, 18.3% professional, 28.3% services, 26.9% sales, 1.1% farming, 5.3% construction, 13.2% production (2000).
Income: Per capita income: $15,537 (2000); Median household income: $29,338 (2000); Poverty rate: 12.4% (2000).
Taxes: Total city taxes per capita: $503 (1997); City property taxes per capita: $479 (1997).
Education: High school graduation rate: 79.2% (2000); College graduation rate: 16.9% (2000).

School District(s)

Hinckley-Finlayson (PK-12)
2000 Enrollment: 1,168 320-384-6277
Housing: Homeownership rate: 59.2% (2000); Median home value: $79,500 (2000); Median rent: $344 per month (2000); Median age of housing: 34 years (2000).
Newspapers: The Hinckley News (1 x week)
Transportation: Commute to work: 88.1% car, 0.0% public transportation, 8.1% walk, 2.8% work from home (2000); Travel time to work: 62.6% less than 15 minutes, 16.0% 15 to 30 minutes, 6.6% 30 to 45 minutes, 3.8% 45 to 60 minutes, 11.0% 60 minutes or more (2000)
Additional Information Contacts
Hinckley Chamber of Commerce. 320-384-7837

HINCKLEY (township). Covers a land area of 35.826 square miles and a water area of 0.001 square miles. Located at 46.01° N. Lat.; 92.98° W. Long. Elevation is 1,031 feet.
History: Nearly destroyed in Great Fire of 1894, later rebuilt and became center for lumbering.
Population: 820 (2000); Race: 94.5% White, 0.2% Black, 0.5% Asian, 1.8% American Indian and Alaska Native, 2.0% Hispanic of any race, 1.4% two or more races (2000); Density: 22.9 persons per square mile (2000); Age: 30.3% under 18, 10.0% over 64 (2000); Marriage status: 21.0% never married, 63.9% now married, 3.0% widowed, 12.2% divorced (2000); Foreign born: 0.7% (2000); Ancestry (includes multiple ancestries): 41.9% German, 17.9% Swedish, 11.5% Norwegian, 7.9% French (except Basque), 7.5% Irish (2000).
Economy: Railroad junction. Oats; cattle, sheep, poultry; dairying. Manufacturing: machinery; meat processing; timber. Sandstone National Wildlife Refuge to Northeast. Employment by occupation: 13.6% management, 9.7% professional, 25.1% services, 22.1% sales, 1.7% farming, 10.2% construction, 17.6% production (2000).
Income: Per capita income: $15,118 (2000); Median household income: $38,500 (2000); Poverty rate: 12.9% (2000).
Taxes: Total city taxes per capita: $60 (1997); City property taxes per capita: $60 (1997).
Education: High school graduation rate: 82.5% (2000); College graduation rate: 9.3% (2000).
Housing: Homeownership rate: 87.5% (2000); Median home value: $95,500 (2000); Median rent: $378 per month (2000); Median age of housing: 28 years (2000).
Transportation: Commute to work: 88.9% car, 0.0% public transportation, 1.8% walk, 8.9% work from home (2000); Travel time to work: 46.4% less than 15 minutes, 28.9% 15 to 30 minutes, 6.4% 30 to 45 minutes, 0.3% 45 to 60 minutes, 18.1% 60 minutes or more (2000)

KERRICK (city). Covers a land area of 0.999 square miles and a water area of 0.003 square miles. Located at 46.34° N. Lat.; 92.58° W. Long. Elevation is 1,155 feet.
Population: 71 (2000); Race: 100.0% White, 0.0% Black, 0.0% Asian, 0.0% American Indian and Alaska Native, 0.0% Hispanic of any race, 0.0% two or more races (2000); Density: 71.0 persons per square mile (2000); Age: 20.3% under 18, 24.3% over 64 (2000); Marriage status: 32.2% never married, 45.8% now married, 13.6% widowed, 8.5% divorced (2000); Foreign born: 0.0% (2000); Ancestry (includes multiple ancestries): 35.1% German, 24.3% Norwegian, 16.2% Swedish, 12.2% English, 12.2% Danish (2000).
Economy: Employment by occupation: 22.6% management, 6.5% professional, 19.4% services, 22.6% sales, 0.0% farming, 16.1% construction, 12.9% production (2000).
Income: Per capita income: $14,324 (2000); Median household income: $38,750 (2000); Poverty rate: 2.7% (2000).
Taxes: Total city taxes per capita: $138 (1997); City property taxes per capita: $121 (1997).
Education: High school graduation rate: 83.0% (2000); College graduation rate: 7.5% (2000).
Housing: Homeownership rate: 100.0% (2000); Median home value: $56,000 (2000); Median age of housing: 36 years (2000).
Transportation: Commute to work: 100.0% car, 0.0% public transportation, 0.0% walk, 0.0% work from home (2000); Travel time to work: 12.9% less than 15 minutes, 9.7% 15 to 30 minutes, 25.8% 30 to 45 minutes, 0.0% 45 to 60 minutes, 51.6% 60 minutes or more (2000)

KERRICK (township). Covers a land area of 33.930 square miles and a water area of 0.936 square miles. Located at 46.37° N. Lat.; 92.61° W. Long. Elevation is 1,155 feet.
Population: 272 (2000); Race: 94.9% White, 0.0% Black, 0.0% Asian, 0.9% American Indian and Alaska Native, 0.0% Hispanic of any race, 1.2% two or more races (2000); Density: 8.0 persons per square mile (2000); Age: 23.8% under 18, 17.5% over 64 (2000); Marriage status: 29.6% never married, 59.2% now married, 4.9% widowed, 6.3% divorced (2000); Foreign born: 2.1% (2000); Ancestry (includes multiple ancestries): 27.7% German, 13.9% Norwegian, 12.3% Swedish, 9.6% Finnish, 8.4% Polish (2000).
Economy: Dairying. Single-family building permits issued: 2 (2001) / 3 (2000); Multi-family building permits issued: 0 (2001) / 0 (2000); Employment by occupation: 10.6% management, 20.6% professional, 12.5% services, 35.6% sales, 5.0% farming, 10.6% construction, 5.0% production (2000).
Income: Per capita income: $18,478 (2000); Median household income: $36,563 (2000); Poverty rate: 13.6% (2000).
Taxes: Total city taxes per capita: $43 (1997); City property taxes per capita: $43 (1997).
Education: High school graduation rate: 77.6% (2000); College graduation rate: 17.9% (2000).
Housing: Homeownership rate: 94.7% (2000); Median home value: $68,100 (2000); Median rent: $225 per month (2000); Median age of housing: 26 years (2000).
Transportation: Commute to work: 93.1% car, 0.0% public transportation, 2.5% walk, 4.4% work from home (2000); Travel time to work: 16.3% less than 15 minutes, 52.9% 15 to 30 minutes, 13.7% 30 to 45 minutes, 9.8% 45 to 60 minutes, 7.2% 60 minutes or more (2000)

KETTLE RIVER (township). Covers a land area of 30.221 square miles and a water area of 0.828 square miles. Located at 46.29° N. Lat.; 92.86° W. Long.
Population: 491 (2000); Race: 95.4% White, 0.0% Black, 0.0% Asian, 1.7% American Indian and Alaska Native, 1.9% Hispanic of any race, 1.5% two or more races (2000); Density: 16.2 persons per square mile (2000); Age: 27.0% under 18, 13.3% over 64 (2000); Marriage status: 18.3% never married, 68.1% now married, 5.0% widowed, 8.6% divorced (2000); Foreign born: 0.0% (2000); Ancestry (includes multiple ancestries): 31.1% German, 13.1% Polish, 11.0% Swedish, 11.0% United States or American, 7.5% Irish (2000).
Economy: Single-family building permits issued: 6 (2001) / 2 (2000); Multi-family building permits issued: 0 (2001) / 0 (2000); Employment by

occupation: 12.9% management, 9.3% professional, 20.1% services, 20.6% sales, 2.1% farming, 14.4% construction, 20.6% production (2000).
Income: Per capita income: $16,370 (2000); Median household income: $33,333 (2000); Poverty rate: 15.9% (2000).
Taxes: Total city taxes per capita: $141 (2000); City property taxes per capita: $136 (2000).
Education: High school graduation rate: 75.7% (2000); College graduation rate: 9.4% (2000).
Housing: Homeownership rate: 90.8% (2000); Median home value: $108,700 (2000); Median rent: $288 per month (2000); Median age of housing: 25 years (2000).
Transportation: Commute to work: 89.2% car, 0.0% public transportation, 3.2% walk, 6.5% work from home (2000); Travel time to work: 27.7% less than 15 minutes, 30.6% 15 to 30 minutes, 22.0% 30 to 45 minutes, 5.2% 45 to 60 minutes, 14.5% 60 minutes or more (2000)

MISSION CREEK (township). Covers a land area of 31.674 square miles and a water area of 0.115 square miles. Located at 45.93° N. Lat.; 92.96° W. Long.
Population: 590 (2000); Race: 98.5% White, 0.0% Black, 0.0% Asian, 1.2% American Indian and Alaska Native, 1.0% Hispanic of any race, 0.0% two or more races (2000); Density: 18.6 persons per square mile (2000); Age: 29.7% under 18, 12.4% over 64 (2000); Marriage status: 19.8% never married, 64.8% now married, 4.6% widowed, 10.9% divorced (2000); Foreign born: 1.2% (2000); Ancestry (includes multiple ancestries): 31.1% German, 12.4% Swedish, 11.7% Czech, 8.3% Irish, 6.8% United States or American (2000).
Economy: Employment by occupation: 9.9% management, 12.9% professional, 16.9% services, 14.7% sales, 3.3% farming, 13.2% construction, 29.0% production (2000).
Income: Per capita income: $16,448 (2000); Median household income: $38,194 (2000); Poverty rate: 10.6% (2000).
Taxes: Total city taxes per capita: $30 (1997); City property taxes per capita: $30 (1997).
Education: High school graduation rate: 77.9% (2000); College graduation rate: 7.4% (2000).
Housing: Homeownership rate: 89.6% (2000); Median home value: $94,500 (2000); Median rent: $558 per month (2000); Median age of housing: 28 years (2000).
Transportation: Commute to work: 90.7% car, 0.7% public transportation, 0.0% walk, 8.6% work from home (2000); Travel time to work: 27.8% less than 15 minutes, 31.8% 15 to 30 minutes, 13.9% 30 to 45 minutes, 8.2% 45 to 60 minutes, 18.4% 60 minutes or more (2000)

MUNCH (township). Covers a land area of 35.486 square miles and a water area of 0.569 square miles. Located at 45.95° N. Lat.; 92.84° W. Long.
Population: 222 (2000); Race: 96.0% White, 0.0% Black, 0.0% Asian, 2.2% American Indian and Alaska Native, 0.0% Hispanic of any race, 1.8% two or more races (2000); Density: 6.3 persons per square mile (2000); Age: 23.3% under 18, 11.2% over 64 (2000); Marriage status: 20.0% never married, 65.4% now married, 6.5% widowed, 8.1% divorced (2000); Foreign born: 1.3% (2000); Ancestry (includes multiple ancestries): 47.5% German, 19.7% Swedish, 16.6% Irish, 11.2% Norwegian, 7.6% Polish (2000).
Economy: Single-family building permits issued: 10 (2001) / 0 (2000); Multi-family building permits issued: 0 (2001) / 0 (2000); Employment by occupation: 16.4% management, 20.0% professional, 19.1% services, 20.0% sales, 0.0% farming, 3.6% construction, 20.9% production (2000).
Income: Per capita income: $19,588 (2000); Median household income: $34,375 (2000); Poverty rate: 6.7% (2000).
Taxes: Total city taxes per capita: $102 (1997); City property taxes per capita: $97 (1997).
Education: High school graduation rate: 84.0% (2000); College graduation rate: 6.2% (2000).
Housing: Homeownership rate: 93.7% (2000); Median home value: $82,500 (2000); Median rent: $425 per month (2000); Median age of housing: 20 years (2000).
Transportation: Commute to work: 97.2% car, 0.0% public transportation, 0.0% walk, 2.8% work from home (2000); Travel time to work: 16.3% less than 15 minutes, 38.5% 15 to 30 minutes, 13.5% 30 to 45 minutes, 10.6% 45 to 60 minutes, 21.2% 60 minutes or more (2000)

NEW DOSEY (township). Covers a land area of 112.829 square miles and a water area of 0.082 square miles. Located at 46.21° N. Lat.; 92.36° W. Long.
Population: 74 (2000); Race: 85.7% White, 0.0% Black, 0.0% Asian, 7.1% American Indian and Alaska Native, 0.0% Hispanic of any race, 7.1% two or more races (2000); Density: 0.7 persons per square mile (2000); Age: 7.1% under 18, 19.0% over 64 (2000); Marriage status: 5.1% never married, 69.2% now married, 12.8% widowed, 12.8% divorced (2000); Foreign born: 0.0% (2000); Ancestry (includes multiple ancestries): 35.7% English, 23.8% German, 21.4% Norwegian, 19.0% Irish, 16.7% Swedish (2000).
Economy: Employment by occupation: 28.6% management, 23.8% professional, 14.3% services, 23.8% sales, 0.0% farming, 0.0% construction, 9.5% production (2000).
Income: Per capita income: $24,298 (2000); Median household income: $24,500 (2000); Poverty rate: 7.1% (2000).
Taxes: Total city taxes per capita: $263 (1997); City property taxes per capita: $263 (1997).
Education: High school graduation rate: 92.3% (2000); College graduation rate: 25.6% (2000).
Housing: Homeownership rate: 80.0% (2000); Median home value: $85,000 (2000); Median age of housing: 31 years (2000).
Transportation: Commute to work: 90.5% car, 0.0% public transportation, 0.0% walk, 9.5% work from home (2000); Travel time to work: 0.0% less than 15 minutes, 52.6% 15 to 30 minutes, 26.3% 30 to 45 minutes, 10.5% 45 to 60 minutes, 10.5% 60 minutes or more (2000)

NICKERSON (township). Covers a land area of 73.884 square miles and a water area of 0.578 square miles. Located at 46.40° N. Lat.; 92.50° W. Long. Elevation is 1,156 feet.
Population: 154 (2000); Race: 100.0% White, 0.0% Black, 0.0% Asian, 0.0% American Indian and Alaska Native, 0.0% Hispanic of any race, 0.0% two or more races (2000); Density: 2.1 persons per square mile (2000); Age: 30.9% under 18, 12.9% over 64 (2000); Marriage status: 26.8% never married, 49.1% now married, 9.8% widowed, 14.3% divorced (2000); Foreign born: 0.0% (2000); Ancestry (includes multiple ancestries): 41.0% German, 20.1% Norwegian, 15.1% Polish, 13.7% United States or American, 9.4% Swedish (2000).
Economy: Single-family building permits issued: 0 (2001) / 0 (2000); Multi-family building permits issued: 0 (2001) / 0 (2000); Employment by occupation: 7.7% management, 3.8% professional, 13.5% services, 26.9% sales, 15.4% farming, 21.2% construction, 11.5% production (2000).
Income: Per capita income: $16,350 (2000); Median household income: $44,375 (2000); Poverty rate: 8.6% (2000).
Taxes: Total city taxes per capita: $92 (1997); City property taxes per capita: $92 (1997).
Education: High school graduation rate: 84.8% (2000); College graduation rate: 8.7% (2000).
Housing: Homeownership rate: 96.2% (2000); Median home value: $75,000 (2000); Median age of housing: 30 years (2000).
Transportation: Commute to work: 100.0% car, 0.0% public transportation, 0.0% walk, 0.0% work from home (2000); Travel time to work: 10.0% less than 15 minutes, 20.0% 15 to 30 minutes, 46.0% 30 to 45 minutes, 6.0% 45 to 60 minutes, 18.0% 60 minutes or more (2000)

NORMAN (township). Covers a land area of 35.692 square miles and a water area of 0.200 square miles. Located at 46.30° N. Lat.; 92.74° W. Long.
Population: 247 (2000); Race: 98.0% White, 0.0% Black, 0.0% Asian, 2.0% American Indian and Alaska Native, 0.0% Hispanic of any race, 0.0% two or more races (2000); Density: 6.9 persons per square mile (2000); Age: 18.7% under 18, 16.7% over 64 (2000); Marriage status: 20.4% never married, 63.9% now married, 6.0% widowed, 9.7% divorced (2000); Foreign born: 3.6% (2000); Ancestry (includes multiple ancestries): 24.7% German, 13.5% Swedish, 13.1% Norwegian, 8.4% United States or American, 8.0% Polish (2000).
Economy: Single-family building permits issued: 0 (2001) / 0 (2000); Multi-family building permits issued: 0 (2001) / 0 (2000); Employment by occupation: 13.4% management, 10.7% professional, 25.9% services, 19.6% sales, 3.6% farming, 8.9% construction, 17.9% production (2000).
Income: Per capita income: $16,698 (2000); Median household income: $29,583 (2000); Poverty rate: 12.0% (2000).
Taxes: Total city taxes per capita: $223 (1997); City property taxes per capita: $223 (1997).
Education: High school graduation rate: 74.3% (2000); College graduation rate: 7.0% (2000).
Housing: Homeownership rate: 90.8% (2000); Median home value: $125,000 (2000); Median rent: $225 per month (2000); Median age of housing: 23 years (2000).
Transportation: Commute to work: 88.2% car, 0.0% public transportation, 2.7% walk, 9.1% work from home (2000); Travel time to work: 10.0% less than 15 minutes, 51.0% 15 to 30 minutes, 21.0% 30 to 45 minutes, 3.0% 45 to 60 minutes, 15.0% 60 minutes or more (2000)

OGEMA (township). Covers a land area of 46.826 square miles and a water area of 1.223 square miles. Located at 46.04° N. Lat.; 92.46° W. Long.
Population: 298 (2000); Race: 46.7% White, 1.0% Black, 2.9% Asian, 41.3% American Indian and Alaska Native, 0.0% Hispanic of any race, 8.3% two or more races (2000); Density: 6.4 persons per square mile (2000); Age: 23.8% under 18, 5.7% over 64 (2000); Marriage status: 36.3% never married, 39.9% now married, 7.7% widowed, 16.1% divorced (2000); Foreign born: 7.6% (2000); Ancestry (includes multiple ancestries): 43.2% Other groups, 9.5% German, 8.6% Irish, 8.3% Swedish, 6.7% Norwegian (2000).
Economy: Employment by occupation: 9.8% management, 8.4% professional, 25.2% services, 18.2% sales, 0.0% farming, 28.7% construction, 9.8% production (2000).
Income: Per capita income: $13,042 (2000); Median household income: $28,750 (2000); Poverty rate: 34.0% (2000).
Taxes: Total city taxes per capita: $57 (1997); City property taxes per capita: $57 (1997).
Education: High school graduation rate: 75.9% (2000); College graduation rate: 10.5% (2000).
Housing: Homeownership rate: 72.6% (2000); Median home value: $77,000 (2000); Median rent: $200 per month (2000); Median age of housing: 15 years (2000).
Transportation: Commute to work: 88.2% car, 1.5% public transportation, 2.2% walk, 5.9% work from home (2000); Travel time to work: 30.5% less than 15 minutes, 21.9% 15 to 30 minutes, 27.3% 30 to 45 minutes, 9.4% 45 to 60 minutes, 10.9% 60 minutes or more (2000)

PARK (township). Covers a land area of 36.628 square miles and a water area of 0.136 square miles. Located at 46.28° N. Lat.; 92.52° W. Long.
Population: 37 (2000); Race: 100.0% White, 0.0% Black, 0.0% Asian, 0.0% American Indian and Alaska Native, 0.0% Hispanic of any race, 0.0% two or more races (2000); Density: 1.0 persons per square mile (2000); Age: 13.2% under 18, 17.0% over 64 (2000); Marriage status: 18.4% never married, 57.1% now married, 18.4% widowed, 6.1% divorced (2000); Foreign born: 0.0% (2000); Ancestry (includes multiple ancestries): 35.8% Swedish, 34.0% German, 9.4% Other groups, 7.5% Scottish, 7.5% Danish (2000).
Economy: Railroad junction. Agriculture: dairying; livestock; oats. Single-family building permits issued: 0 (2001) / 1 (2000); Multi-family building permits issued: 0 (2001) / 0 (2000); Employment by occupation: 6.3% management, 25.0% professional, 50.0% services, 6.3% sales, 0.0% farming, 12.5% construction, 0.0% production (2000).
Income: Per capita income: $17,398 (2000); Median household income: $42,000 (2000); Poverty rate: 0.0% (2000).
Taxes: Total city taxes per capita: $171 (1997); City property taxes per capita: $171 (1997).
Education: High school graduation rate: 67.4% (2000); College graduation rate: 9.3% (2000).
Housing: Homeownership rate: 100.0% (2000); Median age of housing: 34 years (2000).
Transportation: Commute to work: 100.0% car, 0.0% public transportation, 0.0% walk, 0.0% work from home (2000); Travel time to work: 9.4% less than 15 minutes, 6.3% 15 to 30 minutes, 31.3% 30 to 45 minutes, 34.4% 45 to 60 minutes, 18.8% 60 minutes or more (2000)

PARTRIDGE (township). Covers a land area of 34.875 square miles and a water area of 0.020 square miles. Located at 46.20° N. Lat.; 92.73° W. Long.
Population: 518 (2000); Race: 99.6% White, 0.0% Black, 0.0% Asian, 0.4% American Indian and Alaska Native, 0.6% Hispanic of any race, 0.0% two or more races (2000); Density: 14.9 persons per square mile (2000); Age: 26.8% under 18, 17.1% over 64 (2000); Marriage status: 19.8% never married, 67.5% now married, 5.3% widowed, 7.5% divorced (2000); Foreign born: 1.1% (2000); Ancestry (includes multiple ancestries): 30.5% German, 23.6% Danish, 16.2% Swedish, 13.0% Norwegian, 8.4% Irish (2000).
Economy: Employment by occupation: 14.0% management, 13.1% professional, 26.2% services, 20.8% sales, 2.3% farming, 7.7% construction, 15.8% production (2000).
Income: Per capita income: $23,262 (2000); Median household income: $34,722 (2000); Poverty rate: 4.7% (2000).
Taxes: Total city taxes per capita: $58 (1997); City property taxes per capita: $58 (1997).
Education: High school graduation rate: 84.1% (2000); College graduation rate: 9.1% (2000).
Housing: Homeownership rate: 91.0% (2000); Median home value: $97,500 (2000); Median rent: $425 per month (2000); Median age of housing: 30 years (2000).
Transportation: Commute to work: 89.0% car, 1.4% public transportation, 1.8% walk, 7.8% work from home (2000); Travel time to work: 24.4% less than 15 minutes, 39.3% 15 to 30 minutes, 19.4% 30 to 45 minutes, 3.5% 45 to 60 minutes, 13.4% 60 minutes or more (2000)

PINE CITY (city). Covers a land area of 2.827 square miles and a water area of 0.406 square miles. Located at 45.82° N. Lat.; 92.97° W. Long. Elevation is 950 feet.
History: The name of Pine City came from a translation of the Indian term "Chengwatana," which was used to refer to the place where the Snake River flows out of Cross Lake. Pine City was established on the river.
Population: 3,043 (2000); Race: 95.7% White, 0.0% Black, 0.0% Asian, 2.3% American Indian and Alaska Native, 1.8% Hispanic of any race, 2.0% two or more races (2000); Density: 1,076.3 persons per square mile (2000); Age: 25.6% under 18, 21.5% over 64 (2000); Marriage status: 28.1% never married, 46.4% now married, 13.9% widowed, 11.6% divorced (2000); Foreign born: 1.1% (2000); Ancestry (includes multiple ancestries): 35.3% German, 17.3% Norwegian, 14.7% Swedish, 7.7% Czech, 6.1% Irish (2000).
Economy: Single-family building permits issued: 5 (2001) / 2 (2000); Multi-family building permits issued: 30 (2001) / 10 (2000); Employment by occupation: 7.5% management, 14.2% professional, 20.0% services, 22.7% sales, 0.2% farming, 11.3% construction, 24.1% production (2000).
Income: Per capita income: $16,802 (2000); Median household income: $29,118 (2000); Poverty rate: 15.0% (2000).
Taxes: Total city taxes per capita: $186 (1997); City property taxes per capita: $168 (1997).
Education: High school graduation rate: 72.3% (2000); College graduation rate: 11.6% (2000).

School District(s)

Pine City (PK-12)
2000 Enrollment: 1,785 320-629-4000

Two-year College(s)

Pine Technical College (Public)
2001 Enrollment: 1,110 320-629-5100
2001 Tuition: In-state $2,560; Out-of-state $5,120

Housing: Homeownership rate: 66.9% (2000); Median home value: $84,400 (2000); Median rent: $398 per month (2000); Median age of housing: 36 years (2000).
Newspapers: Pine City Pioneer (1 x week)
Transportation: Commute to work: 88.8% car, 0.7% public transportation, 5.0% walk, 2.9% work from home (2000); Travel time to work: 42.4% less than 15 minutes, 27.7% 15 to 30 minutes, 9.4% 30 to 45 minutes, 4.3% 45 to 60 minutes, 16.2% 60 minutes or more (2000)
Additional Information Contacts
Pine City Chamber of Commerce 320-629-3861

PINE CITY (township). Covers a land area of 35.729 square miles and a water area of 0.879 square miles. Located at 45.82° N. Lat.; 92.91° W. Long. Elevation is 950 feet.
History: North West Company Fur Post State Historical Site to West. Platted 1869, incorporated 1881.
Population: 1,249 (2000); Race: 97.4% White, 0.3% Black, 0.8% Asian, 1.0% American Indian and Alaska Native, 0.0% Hispanic of any race, 0.4% two or more races (2000); Density: 35.0 persons per square mile (2000); Age: 25.6% under 18, 12.2% over 64 (2000); Marriage status: 24.7% never married, 64.8% now married, 5.0% widowed, 5.6% divorced (2000); Foreign born: 0.8% (2000); Ancestry (includes multiple ancestries): 35.9% German, 21.3% Swedish, 14.9% Norwegian, 11.8% Irish, 11.0% Czech (2000).
Economy: Manufacturing: fabricated metal products, electronic equipment, food products; oats, alfalfa, dairying, poultry, livestock. St. Croix National Scenic Riverway to East. Employment by occupation: 9.5% management, 13.0% professional, 19.7% services, 22.1% sales, 1.5% farming, 14.8% construction, 19.2% production (2000).
Income: Per capita income: $20,074 (2000); Median household income: $47,500 (2000); Poverty rate: 4.0% (2000).
Taxes: Total city taxes per capita: $96 (1997); City property taxes per capita: $95 (1997).
Education: High school graduation rate: 85.1% (2000); College graduation rate: 8.6% (2000).
Housing: Homeownership rate: 91.5% (2000); Median home value: $114,400 (2000); Median rent: $330 per month (2000); Median age of housing: 27 years (2000).
Transportation: Commute to work: 90.3% car, 0.3% public transportation, 1.2% walk, 6.6% work from home (2000); Travel time to work: 32.4% less than 15 minutes, 24.5% 15 to 30 minutes, 9.3% 30 to 45 minutes, 7.3% 45 to 60 minutes, 26.6% 60 minutes or more (2000)

PINE LAKE (township). Covers a land area of 33.105 square miles and a water area of 1.957 square miles. Located at 46.20° N. Lat.; 92.99° W. Long.
Population: 576 (2000); Race: 96.2% White, 0.0% Black, 0.0% Asian, 1.0% American Indian and Alaska Native, 0.5% Hispanic of any race, 2.3% two or more races (2000); Density: 17.4 persons per square mile (2000); Age: 26.1% under 18, 19.2% over 64 (2000); Marriage status: 18.4% never married, 68.7% now married, 5.1% widowed, 7.8% divorced (2000); Foreign born: 0.5% (2000); Ancestry (includes multiple ancestries): 39.0% German, 12.4% English, 11.5% Swedish, 11.5% Finnish, 11.1% Irish (2000).
Economy: Single-family building permits issued: 0 (2001) / 0 (2000); Multi-family building permits issued: 0 (2001) / 0 (2000); Employment by occupation: 13.4% management, 10.2% professional, 22.8% services, 19.9% sales, 3.7% farming, 11.8% construction, 18.3% production (2000).
Income: Per capita income: $16,903 (2000); Median household income: $41,094 (2000); Poverty rate: 12.4% (2000).
Taxes: Total city taxes per capita: $118 (1997); City property taxes per capita: $108 (1997).
Education: High school graduation rate: 85.7% (2000); College graduation rate: 11.3% (2000).
Housing: Homeownership rate: 87.4% (2000); Median home value: $105,000 (2000); Median rent: $425 per month (2000); Median age of housing: 30 years (2000).
Transportation: Commute to work: 83.5% car, 0.8% public transportation, 6.2% walk, 9.5% work from home (2000); Travel time to work: 28.3% less than 15 minutes, 20.1% 15 to 30 minutes, 18.7% 30 to 45 minutes, 8.2% 45 to 60 minutes, 24.7% 60 minutes or more (2000)

POKEGAMA (township). Covers a land area of 51.616 square miles and a water area of 3.411 square miles. Located at 45.85° N. Lat.; 93.04° W. Long.
Population: 2,570 (2000); Race: 99.0% White, 0.0% Black, 0.0% Asian, 1.0% American Indian and Alaska Native, 0.5% Hispanic of any race, 0.0% two or more races (2000); Density: 49.8 persons per square mile (2000); Age: 23.6% under 18, 15.8% over 64 (2000); Marriage status: 17.9% never married, 68.0% now married, 5.7% widowed, 8.4% divorced (2000); Foreign born: 0.2% (2000); Ancestry (includes multiple ancestries): 42.3% German, 13.1% Norwegian, 13.0% Swedish, 7.5% Polish, 7.3% Irish (2000).
Economy: Employment by occupation: 8.7% management, 12.5% professional, 19.6% services, 20.7% sales, 0.3% farming, 12.6% construction, 25.6% production (2000).
Income: Per capita income: $19,027 (2000); Median household income: $41,604 (2000); Poverty rate: 7.3% (2000).
Taxes: Total city taxes per capita: $76 (2000); City property taxes per capita: $75 (2000).
Education: High school graduation rate: 83.5% (2000); College graduation rate: 7.7% (2000).
Housing: Homeownership rate: 93.7% (2000); Median home value: $119,800 (2000); Median rent: $417 per month (2000); Median age of housing: 24 years (2000).
Transportation: Commute to work: 93.5% car, 0.0% public transportation, 0.8% walk, 5.7% work from home (2000); Travel time to work: 29.2% less than 15 minutes, 32.8% 15 to 30 minutes, 8.7% 30 to 45 minutes, 5.5% 45 to 60 minutes, 23.7% 60 minutes or more (2000)

ROCK CREEK (city). Covers a land area of 42.975 square miles and a water area of 0.335 square miles. Located at 45.75° N. Lat.; 92.92° W. Long. Elevation is 938 feet.
Population: 1,119 (2000); Race: 97.5% White, 0.6% Black, 0.4% Asian, 1.3% American Indian and Alaska Native, 0.6% Hispanic of any race, 0.0% two or more races (2000); Density: 26.0 persons per square mile (2000); Age: 31.2% under 18, 10.4% over 64 (2000); Marriage status: 21.6% never married, 62.1% now married, 5.8% widowed, 10.5% divorced (2000); Foreign born: 1.7% (2000); Ancestry (includes multiple ancestries): 40.2% German, 24.8% Swedish, 13.4% Norwegian, 9.7% Irish, 7.3% English (2000).
Economy: Some manufacturing. Agriculture: dairying; poultry, cattle, sheep; oats, alfalfa. Timber. St. Croix National Scenic Riverway to East and Northeast. Single-family building permits issued: 10 (2001) / 11 (2000); Multi-family building permits issued: 0 (2001) / 0 (2000); Employment by occupation: 13.6% management, 10.7% professional, 18.0% services, 24.8% sales, 0.5% farming, 11.4% construction, 20.9% production (2000).
Income: Per capita income: $17,281 (2000); Median household income: $45,000 (2000); Poverty rate: 11.5% (2000).
Taxes: Total city taxes per capita: $69 (1997); City property taxes per capita: $53 (1997).
Education: High school graduation rate: 82.5% (2000); College graduation rate: 8.2% (2000).
Housing: Homeownership rate: 91.8% (2000); Median home value: $91,400 (2000); Median rent: $463 per month (2000); Median age of housing: 29 years (2000).
Transportation: Commute to work: 85.7% car, 0.0% public transportation, 2.4% walk, 10.5% work from home (2000); Travel time to work: 30.7% less than 15 minutes, 23.4% 15 to 30 minutes, 15.2% 30 to 45 minutes, 12.3% 45 to 60 minutes, 18.4% 60 minutes or more (2000)

ROYALTON (township). Covers a land area of 34.345 square miles and a water area of 0.446 square miles. Located at 45.77° N. Lat.; 93.08° W. Long.
Population: 976 (2000); Race: 98.2% White, 1.3% Black, 0.0% Asian, 0.4% American Indian and Alaska Native, 0.2% Hispanic of any race, 0.0% two or more races (2000); Density: 28.4 persons per square mile (2000); Age: 28.9% under 18, 12.5% over 64 (2000); Marriage status: 24.3% never married, 61.3% now married, 5.1% widowed, 9.3% divorced (2000); Foreign born: 0.2% (2000); Ancestry (includes multiple ancestries): 40.2% German, 25.2% Swedish, 8.2% Norwegian, 5.6% Irish, 4.6% French (except Basque) (2000).
Economy: Single-family building permits issued: 10 (2001) / 10 (2000); Multi-family building permits issued: 0 (2001) / 0 (2000); Employment by occupation: 11.0% management, 14.9% professional, 12.4% services, 16.9% sales, 2.4% farming, 21.8% construction, 20.6% production (2000).
Income: Per capita income: $18,729 (2000); Median household income: $43,000 (2000); Poverty rate: 4.6% (2000).
Taxes: Total city taxes per capita: $35 (1997); City property taxes per capita: $33 (1997).
Education: High school graduation rate: 82.4% (2000); College graduation rate: 10.8% (2000).
Housing: Homeownership rate: 92.6% (2000); Median home value: $81,400 (2000); Median rent: $163 per month (2000); Median age of housing: 26 years (2000).
Transportation: Commute to work: 90.9% car, 0.0% public transportation, 2.2% walk, 6.0% work from home (2000); Travel time to work: 17.8% less than 15 minutes, 33.7% 15 to 30 minutes, 17.0% 30 to 45 minutes, 9.0% 45 to 60 minutes, 22.5% 60 minutes or more (2000)

RUTLEDGE (city). Covers a land area of 2.949 square miles and a water area of 0.073 square miles. Located at 46.25° N. Lat.; 92.86° W. Long. Elevation is 1,032 feet.
Population: 196 (2000); Race: 96.4% White, 0.0% Black, 0.0% Asian, 3.6% American Indian and Alaska Native, 0.0% Hispanic of any race, 0.0% two or more races (2000); Density: 66.5 persons per square mile (2000); Age: 20.6% under 18, 9.3% over 64 (2000); Marriage status: 24.8% never married, 68.2% now married, 0.0% widowed, 7.0% divorced (2000); Foreign born: 0.0% (2000); Ancestry (includes multiple ancestries): 21.6% Norwegian, 17.0% German, 12.4% Swedish, 5.7% United States or American, 5.7% Finnish (2000).
Economy: Oats; livestock, poultry; dairying. Employment by occupation: 6.7% management, 9.6% professional, 32.7% services, 20.2% sales, 3.8% farming, 18.3% construction, 8.7% production (2000).
Income: Per capita income: $19,040 (2000); Median household income: $33,750 (2000); Poverty rate: 19.6% (2000).
Taxes: Total city taxes per capita: $74 (1997); City property taxes per capita: $61 (1997).
Education: High school graduation rate: 66.2% (2000); College graduation rate: 2.2% (2000).
Housing: Homeownership rate: 93.7% (2000); Median home value: $37,900 (2000); Median rent: $138 per month (2000); Median age of housing: 29 years (2000).
Transportation: Commute to work: 88.1% car, 0.0% public transportation, 2.0% walk, 4.0% work from home (2000); Travel time to work: 22.7% less than 15 minutes, 46.4% 15 to 30 minutes, 2.1% 30 to 45 minutes, 3.1% 45 to 60 minutes, 25.8% 60 minutes or more (2000)

SANDSTONE (city). Covers a land area of 5.296 square miles and a water area of 0.140 square miles. Located at 46.13° N. Lat.; 92.86° W. Long. Elevation is 1,070 feet.
History: Sandstone was settled in 1885 when quarries began operation along the Kettle River. The stone, which varied from pink to dark red, was used in buildings throughout the midwest. Later, the town turned to agriculture and dairying.
Population: 1,549 (2000); Race: 92.8% White, 0.4% Black, 0.2% Asian, 5.8% American Indian and Alaska Native, 1.2% Hispanic of any race, 0.5% two or more races (2000); Density: 292.5 persons per square mile (2000);

Age: 22.4% under 18, 26.3% over 64 (2000); Marriage status: 19.6% never married, 57.1% now married, 12.9% widowed, 10.4% divorced (2000); Foreign born: 0.8% (2000); Ancestry (includes multiple ancestries): 29.7% German, 12.6% Swedish, 10.4% Norwegian, 9.4% Irish, 6.7% English (2000).
Economy: Single-family building permits issued: 2 (2001) / 2 (2000); Multi-family building permits issued: 0 (2001) / 0 (2000); Employment by occupation: 8.4% management, 18.6% professional, 33.4% services, 17.6% sales, 0.5% farming, 5.8% construction, 15.8% production (2000).
Income: Per capita income: $18,053 (2000); Median household income: $40,265 (2000); Poverty rate: 16.7% (2000).
Taxes: Total city taxes per capita: $131 (1997); City property taxes per capita: $124 (1997).
Education: High school graduation rate: 67.2% (2000); College graduation rate: 13.9% (2000).

School District(s)

East Central (PK-12)
2000 Enrollment: 1,059 320-245-2289
Housing: Homeownership rate: 57.1% (2000); Median home value: $64,800 (2000); Median rent: $462 per month (2000); Median age of housing: 42 years (2000).
Hospitals: Pine Medical Center (30 beds)
Newspapers: Pine County Courier (1 x week)
Transportation: Commute to work: 85.8% car, 0.0% public transportation, 7.4% walk, 5.8% work from home (2000); Travel time to work: 50.9% less than 15 minutes, 23.7% 15 to 30 minutes, 9.1% 30 to 45 minutes, 4.8% 45 to 60 minutes, 11.5% 60 minutes or more (2000)
Additional Information Contacts
Sandstone Chamber of Commerce........................ 320-245-2271

SANDSTONE (township). Covers a land area of 60.698 square miles and a water area of 0.164 square miles. Located at 46.10° N. Lat.; 92.80° W. Long. Elevation is 1,070 feet.
History: Settled 1885, when quarries were opened.
Population: 1,614 (2000); Race: 77.3% White, 15.6% Black, 0.1% Asian, 4.9% American Indian and Alaska Native, 17.2% Hispanic of any race, 1.4% two or more races (2000); Density: 26.6 persons per square mile (2000); Age: 14.6% under 18, 6.0% over 64 (2000); Marriage status: 20.1% never married, 68.7% now married, 3.0% widowed, 8.3% divorced (2000); Foreign born: 1.7% (2000); Ancestry (includes multiple ancestries): 17.4% German, 8.5% Swedish, 5.5% Norwegian, 4.3% Other groups, 3.9% Irish (2000).
Economy: Agriculture: livestock, poultry; dairying; oats, alfalfa. Manufacturing: construction supplies, government printing. Sandstone quarries nearby. Sandstone National Wildlife Refuge to Southeast. Employment by occupation: 9.4% management, 14.1% professional, 28.0% services, 17.7% sales, 2.8% farming, 12.7% construction, 15.2% production (2000).
Income: Per capita income: $18,193 (2000); Median household income: $45,250 (2000); Poverty rate: 7.7% (2000).
Taxes: Total city taxes per capita: $34 (1997); City property taxes per capita: $34 (1997).
Education: High school graduation rate: 76.6% (2000); College graduation rate: 8.5% (2000).
Housing: Homeownership rate: 94.7% (2000); Median home value: $83,100 (2000); Median rent: $338 per month (2000); Median age of housing: 26 years (2000).
Transportation: Commute to work: 89.5% car, 0.0% public transportation, 0.6% walk, 7.6% work from home (2000); Travel time to work: 40.8% less than 15 minutes, 33.7% 15 to 30 minutes, 11.7% 30 to 45 minutes, 0.6% 45 to 60 minutes, 13.2% 60 minutes or more (2000)

STURGEON LAKE (city). Covers a land area of 3.476 square miles and a water area of 0.036 square miles. Located at 46.38° N. Lat.; 92.82° W. Long. Elevation is 1,074 feet.
Population: 347 (2000); Race: 100.0% White, 0.0% Black, 0.0% Asian, 0.0% American Indian and Alaska Native, 0.5% Hispanic of any race, 0.0% two or more races (2000); Density: 99.8 persons per square mile (2000); Age: 31.0% under 18, 6.3% over 64 (2000); Marriage status: 27.6% never married, 58.4% now married, 4.7% widowed, 9.3% divorced (2000); Foreign born: 0.8% (2000); Ancestry (includes multiple ancestries): 40.3% German, 18.1% Swedish, 14.2% Polish, 14.2% Norwegian, 12.1% Irish (2000).
Economy: Employment by occupation: 4.5% management, 14.8% professional, 35.2% services, 16.5% sales, 5.7% farming, 10.8% construction, 12.5% production (2000).
Income: Per capita income: $15,501 (2000); Median household income: $36,875 (2000); Poverty rate: 15.3% (2000).
Taxes: Total city taxes per capita: $150 (1997); City property taxes per capita: $136 (1997).
Education: High school graduation rate: 78.0% (2000); College graduation rate: 13.5% (2000).
Housing: Homeownership rate: 85.1% (2000); Median home value: $80,000 (2000); Median rent: $338 per month (2000); Median age of housing: 23 years (2000).
Transportation: Commute to work: 94.1% car, 1.8% public transportation, 2.9% walk, 0.0% work from home (2000); Travel time to work: 36.5% less than 15 minutes, 19.4% 15 to 30 minutes, 28.2% 30 to 45 minutes, 5.9% 45 to 60 minutes, 10.0% 60 minutes or more (2000)

STURGEON LAKE (township). Covers a land area of 32.144 square miles and a water area of 0.077 square miles. Located at 46.36° N. Lat.; 92.84° W. Long. Elevation is 1,074 feet.
Population: 409 (2000); Race: 83.0% White, 10.8% Black, 0.5% Asian, 0.5% American Indian and Alaska Native, 4.4% Hispanic of any race, 0.7% two or more races (2000); Density: 12.7 persons per square mile (2000); Age: 23.8% under 18, 10.6% over 64 (2000); Marriage status: 20.3% never married, 71.2% now married, 3.9% widowed, 4.5% divorced (2000); Foreign born: 0.5% (2000); Ancestry (includes multiple ancestries): 26.8% German, 16.2% Polish, 11.5% Swedish, 10.8% Other groups, 8.8% Irish (2000).
Economy: Oats, alfalfa; cattle, poultry; dairying. Manufacturing of chemicals. Single-family building permits issued: 9 (2001) / 9 (2000); Multi-family building permits issued: 0 (2001) / 0 (2000); Employment by occupation: 7.0% management, 7.0% professional, 20.2% services, 17.5% sales, 1.8% farming, 27.2% construction, 19.3% production (2000).
Income: Per capita income: $13,563 (2000); Median household income: $40,250 (2000); Poverty rate: 4.3% (2000).
Taxes: Total city taxes per capita: $68 (1997); City property taxes per capita: $68 (1997).
Education: High school graduation rate: 70.6% (2000); College graduation rate: 2.4% (2000).
Housing: Homeownership rate: 96.6% (2000); Median home value: $73,200 (2000); Median rent: $300 per month (2000); Median age of housing: 27 years (2000).
Transportation: Commute to work: 86.4% car, 0.0% public transportation, 4.5% walk, 7.3% work from home (2000); Travel time to work: 27.5% less than 15 minutes, 38.2% 15 to 30 minutes, 13.7% 30 to 45 minutes, 0.0% 45 to 60 minutes, 20.6% 60 minutes or more (2000)

WILLOW RIVER (city). Covers a land area of 1.571 square miles and a water area of 0.152 square miles. Located at 46.32° N. Lat.; 92.83° W. Long. Elevation is 1,038 feet.
Population: 309 (2000); Race: 91.5% White, 0.0% Black, 0.0% Asian, 7.1% American Indian and Alaska Native, 0.0% Hispanic of any race, 1.4% two or more races (2000); Density: 196.7 persons per square mile (2000); Age: 27.1% under 18, 20.0% over 64 (2000); Marriage status: 33.2% never married, 41.3% now married, 11.1% widowed, 14.5% divorced (2000); Foreign born: 0.0% (2000); Ancestry (includes multiple ancestries): 32.2% German, 18.3% Norwegian, 18.3% Polish, 10.2% Irish, 9.8% Swedish (2000).
Economy: Dairying; poultry, livestock; alfalfa, oats; timber; manufacturing of lumber. Single-family building permits issued: 1 (2001) / 1 (2000); Multi-family building permits issued: 0 (2001) / 0 (2000); Employment by occupation: 6.7% management, 14.2% professional, 27.5% services, 21.7% sales, 0.0% farming, 17.5% construction, 12.5% production (2000).
Income: Per capita income: $16,620 (2000); Median household income: $25,938 (2000); Poverty rate: 16.9% (2000).
Taxes: Total city taxes per capita: $54 (1997); City property taxes per capita: $45 (1997).
Education: High school graduation rate: 80.3% (2000); College graduation rate: 10.9% (2000).

School District(s)

Willow River (PK-12)
2000 Enrollment: 488 218-372-3131
Housing: Homeownership rate: 67.1% (2000); Median home value: $61,300 (2000); Median rent: $268 per month (2000); Median age of housing: 50 years (2000).
Transportation: Commute to work: 89.9% car, 0.0% public transportation, 3.4% walk, 6.7% work from home (2000); Travel time to work: 38.7% less than 15 minutes, 31.5% 15 to 30 minutes, 18.0% 30 to 45 minutes, 3.6% 45 to 60 minutes, 8.1% 60 minutes or more (2000)

WILMA (township). Covers a land area of 36.340 square miles and a water area of 0.447 square miles. Located at 46.09° N. Lat.; 92.49° W. Long.

Population: 137 (2000); Race: 76.2% White, 4.3% Black, 3.7% Asian, 0.0% American Indian and Alaska Native, 0.0% Hispanic of any race, 15.9% two or more races (2000); Density: 3.8 persons per square mile (2000); Age: 60.4% under 18, 10.4% over 64 (2000); Marriage status: 58.8% never married, 30.9% now married, 3.7% widowed, 6.6% divorced (2000); Foreign born: 3.7% (2000); Ancestry (includes multiple ancestries): 40.9% Other groups, 16.5% German, 8.5% Norwegian, 7.3% Irish, 6.7% Croatian (2000).
Economy: Employment by occupation: 19.0% management, 9.5% professional, 33.3% services, 11.9% sales, 0.0% farming, 16.7% construction, 9.5% production (2000).
Income: Per capita income: $7,193 (2000); Median household income: $32,917 (2000); Poverty rate: 22.5% (2000).
Taxes: Total city taxes per capita: $78 (1997); City property taxes per capita: $78 (1997).
Education: High school graduation rate: 72.6% (2000); College graduation rate: 3.2% (2000).
Housing: Homeownership rate: 94.1% (2000); Median home value: $65,000 (2000); Median age of housing: 26 years (2000).
Transportation: Commute to work: 90.5% car, 0.0% public transportation, 0.0% walk, 9.5% work from home (2000); Travel time to work: 15.8% less than 15 minutes, 15.8% 15 to 30 minutes, 34.2% 30 to 45 minutes, 0.0% 45 to 60 minutes, 34.2% 60 minutes or more (2000)

WINDEMERE (township). Covers a land area of 30.511 square miles and a water area of 5.245 square miles. Located at 46.38° N. Lat.; 92.76° W. Long.
Population: 1,489 (2000); Race: 99.1% White, 0.0% Black, 0.0% Asian, 0.1% American Indian and Alaska Native, 0.8% Hispanic of any race, 0.7% two or more races (2000); Density: 48.8 persons per square mile (2000); Age: 20.9% under 18, 22.0% over 64 (2000); Marriage status: 15.6% never married, 66.3% now married, 6.8% widowed, 11.3% divorced (2000); Foreign born: 0.7% (2000); Ancestry (includes multiple ancestries): 31.7% German, 17.7% Swedish, 14.9% Norwegian, 11.2% Irish, 8.6% Polish (2000).
Economy: Single-family building permits issued: 11 (2001) / 11 (2000); Multi-family building permits issued: 0 (2001) / 0 (2000); Employment by occupation: 11.5% management, 16.4% professional, 23.0% services, 23.9% sales, 0.9% farming, 9.8% construction, 14.4% production (2000).
Income: Per capita income: $21,346 (2000); Median household income: $43,625 (2000); Poverty rate: 7.7% (2000).
Taxes: Total city taxes per capita: $100 (2000); City property taxes per capita: $93 (2000).
Education: High school graduation rate: 84.5% (2000); College graduation rate: 15.5% (2000).
Housing: Homeownership rate: 95.7% (2000); Median home value: $124,800 (2000); Median rent: $329 per month (2000); Median age of housing: 22 years (2000).
Transportation: Commute to work: 93.2% car, 0.0% public transportation, 2.4% walk, 4.4% work from home (2000); Travel time to work: 36.2% less than 15 minutes, 25.0% 15 to 30 minutes, 17.8% 30 to 45 minutes, 9.9% 45 to 60 minutes, 11.0% 60 minutes or more (2000)

Pipestone County

Located in southwestern Minnesota; bounded on the west by South Dakota; drained by headwaters of the Rock River. Covers a land area of 465.90 square miles, a water area of 0.30 squâre miles, and is located in the Central Time Zone. The county government was organized in 1857. County seat is Pipestone.

Weather Station: Pipestone — Elevation: 1,702 feet

	Jan	Feb	Mar	Apr	May	Jun	Jul	Aug	Sep	Oct	Nov	Dec
High	21	28	40	57	71	80	84	82	73	60	40	27
Low	0	7	20	32	45	54	58	56	45	33	19	6
Precip	0.5	0.5	1.8	2.4	3.2	4.0	3.4	3.1	2.8	2.3	1.5	0.6
Snow	5.9	5.0	6.5	3.4	tr	0.0	0.0	0.0	tr	0.8	6.3	6.1

High and Low temperatures in degrees Fahrenheit; Precipitation and Snow in inches

Population: 9,895 (2000); Race: 96.7% White, 0.1% Black, 0.9% Asian, 1.1% American Indian and Alaska Native, 0.5% Hispanic of any race, 0.9% two or more races (2000); Density: 21.2 persons per square mile (2000); Age: 25.7% under 18, 21.4% over 64 (2000).
Religion: Five largest groups: 19.0% Evangelical Lutheran Church in America, 18.0% Christian Reformed Church in North America, 16.5% Lutheran Church—Missouri Synod, 15.8% Catholic Church, 8.2% Reformed Church in America (2000).
Economy: Unemployment rate: 1.8% (11/2002); Total civilian labor force: 5,339 (11/2002); Leading industries: 17.3% manufacturing; 16.1% health care and social assistance; 14.2% wholesale trade (2000); Companies that employ more than 1,000 persons: 0 (2000); Companies that employ more than 100 persons: 8 (2000); Farms: 690 totaling 243,525 acres (1997); Minority business ownership rate: 0.0% (1997); Women business ownership rate: 11.7% (1997); Retail sales per capita: $9,329 (1997). Single-family building permits issued: 13 (2001) / 30 (2000); Multi-family building permits issued: 2 (2001) / 4 (2000).
Income: Per capita income: $16,450 (2000); Median household income: $31,909 (2000); Poverty rate: 9.5% (2000); Bankruptcy rate: 3.17% (2001).
Taxes: Total county taxes per capita: $304 (1997); County property taxes per capita: $304 (1997).
Education: High school graduation rate: 77.6% (2000); College graduation rate: 13.9% (2000).
Housing: Homeownership rate: 77.5% (2000); Median home value: $49,000 (2000); Median rent: $282 per month (2000); Median age of housing: 49 years (2000).
Health: Birth rate: 121.3 per 10,000 population (1998); Age adjusted death rate: 81.8 per 10,000 population (1999); Age adjusted cancer mortality rate: 181.6 deaths per 100,000 population (1999). Number of physicians: 6.1 per 10,000 population (1999); Number of hospital beds: 87.9 per 10,000 population (1999).
Elections: 2000 Presidential election results: 40.3% Gore, 55.0% Bush, 2.9% Nader, 1.3% Buchanan
National and State Parks: Altona State Wildlife Management Area; Burke State Wildlife Management Area; Holland State Wildlife Management Area; Pheasant Terrace State Wildlife Management A; Pipestone Indian State Wildlife Management A; Pipestone National Monument; Split Rock Creek State Park; Troy State Wildlife Management Area; Van Beek State Wildlife Management Area; Woodstock State Wildlife Management Area
Additional Information Contacts
Pipestone County Government Offices 507-825-6740
Pipestone Chamber of Commerce 507-825-3316

Pipestone County Communities

AETNA (township). Covers a land area of 35.226 square miles and a water area of 0.014 square miles. Located at 44.16° N. Lat.; 96.11° W. Long.
Population: 201 (2000); Race: 99.5% White, 0.0% Black, 0.0% Asian, 0.0% American Indian and Alaska Native, 0.0% Hispanic of any race, 0.5% two or more races (2000); Density: 5.7 persons per square mile (2000); Age: 25.2% under 18, 16.7% over 64 (2000); Marriage status: 20.5% never married, 72.9% now married, 6.6% widowed, 0.0% divorced (2000); Foreign born: 0.0% (2000); Ancestry (includes multiple ancestries): 47.1% German, 23.8% Norwegian, 19.5% Dutch, 12.4% French (except Basque), 8.6% Swedish (2000).
Economy: Employment by occupation: 25.5% management, 15.5% professional, 14.5% services, 21.8% sales, 8.2% farming, 7.3% construction, 7.3% production (2000).
Income: Per capita income: $13,623 (2000); Median household income: $32,292 (2000); Poverty rate: 14.3% (2000).
Taxes: Total city taxes per capita: $87 (1997); City property taxes per capita: $87 (1997).
Education: High school graduation rate: 87.0% (2000); College graduation rate: 9.6% (2000).
Housing: Homeownership rate: 90.8% (2000); Median home value: $75,000 (2000); Median rent: $225 per month (2000); Median age of housing: 60+ years (2000).
Transportation: Commute to work: 65.7% car, 0.0% public transportation, 8.6% walk, 25.7% work from home (2000); Travel time to work: 43.6% less than 15 minutes, 39.7% 15 to 30 minutes, 14.1% 30 to 45 minutes, 0.0% 45 to 60 minutes, 2.6% 60 minutes or more (2000)

ALTONA (township). Covers a land area of 43.054 square miles and a water area of 0 square miles. Located at 44.15° N. Lat.; 96.38° W. Long.
Population: 192 (2000); Race: 100.0% White, 0.0% Black, 0.0% Asian, 0.0% American Indian and Alaska Native, 0.0% Hispanic of any race, 0.0% two or more races (2000); Density: 4.5 persons per square mile (2000); Age: 36.4% under 18, 11.4% over 64 (2000); Marriage status: 22.0% never married, 71.2% now married, 3.8% widowed, 3.0% divorced (2000); Foreign born: 0.0% (2000); Ancestry (includes multiple ancestries): 28.8% German, 10.3% Dutch, 7.6% Norwegian, 7.1% United States or American, 6.5% Irish (2000).

Economy: Employment by occupation: 32.1% management, 4.8% professional, 23.8% services, 13.1% sales, 1.2% farming, 4.8% construction, 20.2% production (2000).
Income: Per capita income: $12,140 (2000); Median household income: $26,250 (2000); Poverty rate: 13.6% (2000).
Taxes: Total city taxes per capita: $53 (1997); City property taxes per capita: $53 (1997).
Education: High school graduation rate: 76.7% (2000); College graduation rate: 5.8% (2000).
Housing: Homeownership rate: 82.8% (2000); Median home value: $55,000 (2000); Median rent: $225 per month (2000); Median age of housing: 60 years (2000).
Transportation: Commute to work: 63.1% car, 0.0% public transportation, 0.0% walk, 36.9% work from home (2000); Travel time to work: 13.2% less than 15 minutes, 49.1% 15 to 30 minutes, 22.6% 30 to 45 minutes, 15.1% 45 to 60 minutes, 0.0% 60 minutes or more (2000)

BURKE (township). Covers a land area of 34.566 square miles and a water area of 0 square miles. Located at 43.98° N. Lat.; 96.13° W. Long.
Population: 246 (2000); Race: 100.0% White, 0.0% Black, 0.0% Asian, 0.0% American Indian and Alaska Native, 0.0% Hispanic of any race, 0.0% two or more races (2000); Density: 7.1 persons per square mile (2000); Age: 29.6% under 18, 6.6% over 64 (2000); Marriage status: 26.4% never married, 69.7% now married, 1.0% widowed, 3.0% divorced (2000); Foreign born: 0.0% (2000); Ancestry (includes multiple ancestries): 56.8% Dutch, 37.9% German, 4.5% Irish, 3.7% Danish, 3.3% Norwegian (2000).
Economy: Employment by occupation: 26.9% management, 2.8% professional, 22.1% services, 21.4% sales, 8.3% farming, 3.4% construction, 15.2% production (2000).
Income: Per capita income: $12,992 (2000); Median household income: $35,903 (2000); Poverty rate: 14.0% (2000).
Taxes: Total city taxes per capita: $45 (1997); City property taxes per capita: $45 (1997).
Education: High school graduation rate: 78.7% (2000); College graduation rate: 5.8% (2000).
Housing: Homeownership rate: 89.7% (2000); Median home value: $74,200 (2000); Median age of housing: 60+ years (2000).
Transportation: Commute to work: 75.9% car, 0.0% public transportation, 10.3% walk, 13.8% work from home (2000); Travel time to work: 42.4% less than 15 minutes, 47.2% 15 to 30 minutes, 3.2% 30 to 45 minutes, 7.2% 45 to 60 minutes, 0.0% 60 minutes or more (2000)

EDEN (township). Covers a land area of 42.867 square miles and a water area of 0.145 square miles. Located at 43.89° N. Lat.; 96.38° W. Long.
Population: 294 (2000); Race: 96.5% White, 0.0% Black, 0.0% Asian, 0.0% American Indian and Alaska Native, 0.0% Hispanic of any race, 3.5% two or more races (2000); Density: 6.9 persons per square mile (2000); Age: 36.5% under 18, 12.9% over 64 (2000); Marriage status: 18.8% never married, 74.0% now married, 2.7% widowed, 4.5% divorced (2000); Foreign born: 0.0% (2000); Ancestry (includes multiple ancestries): 48.4% German, 33.6% Norwegian, 15.4% Dutch, 5.7% Other groups, 4.7% Swedish (2000).
Economy: Employment by occupation: 31.0% management, 14.3% professional, 17.3% services, 14.9% sales, 7.1% farming, 8.9% construction, 6.5% production (2000).
Income: Per capita income: $13,603 (2000); Median household income: $42,813 (2000); Poverty rate: 6.0% (2000).
Taxes: Total city taxes per capita: $126 (1997); City property taxes per capita: $126 (1997).
Education: High school graduation rate: 89.9% (2000); College graduation rate: 10.6% (2000).
Housing: Homeownership rate: 86.4% (2000); Median home value: $70,000 (2000); Median rent: $225 per month (2000); Median age of housing: 59 years (2000).
Transportation: Commute to work: 74.7% car, 0.0% public transportation, 3.6% walk, 21.7% work from home (2000); Travel time to work: 50.8% less than 15 minutes, 26.9% 15 to 30 minutes, 6.9% 30 to 45 minutes, 6.9% 45 to 60 minutes, 8.5% 60 minutes or more (2000)

EDGERTON (city). Covers a land area of 1.160 square miles and a water area of 0 square miles. Located at 43.87° N. Lat.; 96.13° W. Long. Elevation is 1,573 feet.
Population: 1,033 (2000); Race: 98.5% White, 0.0% Black, 1.3% Asian, 0.0% American Indian and Alaska Native, 0.0% Hispanic of any race, 0.2% two or more races (2000); Density: 890.2 persons per square mile (2000); Age: 21.9% under 18, 34.0% over 64 (2000); Marriage status: 15.1% never married, 64.9% now married, 17.4% widowed, 2.6% divorced (2000); Foreign born: 2.5% (2000); Ancestry (includes multiple ancestries): 66.5% Dutch, 17.4% German, 5.1% Norwegian, 3.8% United States or American, 1.6% Other groups (2000).
Economy: Soybeans, grain; livestock, poultry; dairying. Manufacturing: printing, feeds, filters. Single-family building permits issued: 2 (2001) / 0 (2000); Multi-family building permits issued: 0 (2001) / 0 (2000); Employment by occupation: 9.6% management, 17.5% professional, 18.5% services, 20.5% sales, 5.7% farming, 6.5% construction, 21.7% production (2000).
Income: Per capita income: $15,517 (2000); Median household income: $30,104 (2000); Poverty rate: 4.9% (2000).
Taxes: Total city taxes per capita: $173 (1997); City property taxes per capita: $169 (1997).
Education: High school graduation rate: 65.3% (2000); College graduation rate: 12.7% (2000).

School District(s)

Edgerton (PK-12)
2000 Enrollment: 295 507-442-7881
Housing: Homeownership rate: 88.3% (2000); Median home value: $58,600 (2000); Median rent: $350 per month (2000); Median age of housing: 45 years (2000).
Newspapers: Edgerton Enterprise (1 x week)
Transportation: Commute to work: 82.5% car, 0.0% public transportation, 12.6% walk, 3.1% work from home (2000); Travel time to work: 74.7% less than 15 minutes, 16.2% 15 to 30 minutes, 5.5% 30 to 45 minutes, 0.0% 45 to 60 minutes, 3.6% 60 minutes or more (2000)

ELMER (township). Covers a land area of 35.237 square miles and a water area of 0 square miles. Located at 43.88° N. Lat.; 96.24° W. Long.
Population: 275 (2000); Race: 100.0% White, 0.0% Black, 0.0% Asian, 0.0% American Indian and Alaska Native, 0.0% Hispanic of any race, 0.0% two or more races (2000); Density: 7.8 persons per square mile (2000); Age: 37.3% under 18, 14.5% over 64 (2000); Marriage status: 14.2% never married, 79.6% now married, 3.3% widowed, 2.8% divorced (2000); Foreign born: 0.0% (2000); Ancestry (includes multiple ancestries): 48.2% Dutch, 35.0% German, 11.9% Norwegian, 5.8% Danish, 4.2% English (2000).
Economy: Employment by occupation: 31.5% management, 15.1% professional, 11.6% services, 10.3% sales, 6.8% farming, 4.8% construction, 19.9% production (2000).
Income: Per capita income: $15,772 (2000); Median household income: $44,250 (2000); Poverty rate: 0.6% (2000).
Taxes: Total city taxes per capita: $51 (1997); City property taxes per capita: $51 (1997).
Education: High school graduation rate: 83.0% (2000); College graduation rate: 11.5% (2000).
Housing: Homeownership rate: 80.6% (2000); Median home value: $75,000 (2000); Median rent: $229 per month (2000); Median age of housing: 60+ years (2000).
Transportation: Commute to work: 78.1% car, 0.0% public transportation, 0.0% walk, 19.9% work from home (2000); Travel time to work: 63.2% less than 15 minutes, 17.1% 15 to 30 minutes, 3.4% 30 to 45 minutes, 8.5% 45 to 60 minutes, 7.7% 60 minutes or more (2000)

FOUNTAIN PRAIRIE (township). Covers a land area of 37.176 square miles and a water area of 0 square miles. Located at 44.15° N. Lat.; 96.24° W. Long.
Population: 199 (2000); Race: 100.0% White, 0.0% Black, 0.0% Asian, 0.0% American Indian and Alaska Native, 0.0% Hispanic of any race, 0.0% two or more races (2000); Density: 5.4 persons per square mile (2000); Age: 33.5% under 18, 10.2% over 64 (2000); Marriage status: 14.6% never married, 85.4% now married, 0.0% widowed, 0.0% divorced (2000); Foreign born: 0.0% (2000); Ancestry (includes multiple ancestries): 64.2% German, 23.3% Dutch, 18.8% Norwegian, 10.2% Swedish, 8.0% Irish (2000).
Economy: Employment by occupation: 25.6% management, 15.6% professional, 6.7% services, 18.9% sales, 6.7% farming, 14.4% construction, 12.2% production (2000).
Income: Per capita income: $11,669 (2000); Median household income: $29,375 (2000); Poverty rate: 16.5% (2000).
Taxes: Total city taxes per capita: $116 (1997); City property taxes per capita: $116 (1997).
Education: High school graduation rate: 95.4% (2000); College graduation rate: 15.6% (2000).
Housing: Homeownership rate: 78.1% (2000); Median home value: $75,000 (2000); Median rent: $175 per month (2000); Median age of housing: 54 years (2000).

Transportation: Commute to work: 72.2% car, 0.0% public transportation, 6.7% walk, 21.1% work from home (2000); Travel time to work: 19.7% less than 15 minutes, 40.8% 15 to 30 minutes, 22.5% 30 to 45 minutes, 2.8% 45 to 60 minutes, 14.1% 60 minutes or more (2000)

GRANGE (township). Covers a land area of 36.132 square miles and a water area of 0 square miles. Located at 44.06° N. Lat.; 96.23° W. Long.
Population: 244 (2000); Race: 95.6% White, 0.0% Black, 0.0% Asian, 4.4% American Indian and Alaska Native, 0.0% Hispanic of any race, 0.0% two or more races (2000); Density: 6.8 persons per square mile (2000); Age: 28.3% under 18, 15.1% over 64 (2000); Marriage status: 25.6% never married, 66.8% now married, 5.5% widowed, 2.0% divorced (2000); Foreign born: 0.0% (2000); Ancestry (includes multiple ancestries): 41.0% German, 22.3% Dutch, 21.5% Norwegian, 9.2% United States or American, 7.6% Irish (2000).
Economy: Employment by occupation: 30.3% management, 16.0% professional, 9.2% services, 21.8% sales, 5.0% farming, 7.6% construction, 10.1% production (2000).
Income: Per capita income: $15,455 (2000); Median household income: $40,000 (2000); Poverty rate: 8.4% (2000).
Taxes: Total city taxes per capita: $89 (1997); City property taxes per capita: $89 (1997).
Education: High school graduation rate: 82.1% (2000); College graduation rate: 13.7% (2000).
Housing: Homeownership rate: 78.2% (2000); Median home value: $51,700 (2000); Median rent: $350 per month (2000); Median age of housing: 54 years (2000).
Transportation: Commute to work: 81.6% car, 0.0% public transportation, 1.8% walk, 16.7% work from home (2000); Travel time to work: 55.8% less than 15 minutes, 22.1% 15 to 30 minutes, 10.5% 30 to 45 minutes, 6.3% 45 to 60 minutes, 5.3% 60 minutes or more (2000)

GRAY (township). Covers a land area of 33.494 square miles and a water area of 0 square miles. Located at 43.97° N. Lat.; 96.25° W. Long.
Population: 234 (2000); Race: 100.0% White, 0.0% Black, 0.0% Asian, 0.0% American Indian and Alaska Native, 0.0% Hispanic of any race, 0.0% two or more races (2000); Density: 7.0 persons per square mile (2000); Age: 24.4% under 18, 14.5% over 64 (2000); Marriage status: 14.9% never married, 79.9% now married, 0.0% widowed, 5.2% divorced (2000); Foreign born: 0.0% (2000); Ancestry (includes multiple ancestries): 46.2% German, 22.2% Norwegian, 19.0% Dutch, 5.0% Irish, 4.5% Swedish (2000).
Economy: Employment by occupation: 33.3% management, 10.9% professional, 9.3% services, 30.2% sales, 0.0% farming, 9.3% construction, 7.0% production (2000).
Income: Per capita income: $28,770 (2000); Median household income: $46,875 (2000); Poverty rate: 3.2% (2000).
Taxes: Total city taxes per capita: $74 (1997); City property taxes per capita: $74 (1997).
Education: High school graduation rate: 92.3% (2000); College graduation rate: 20.6% (2000).
Housing: Homeownership rate: 95.2% (2000); Median home value: $90,000 (2000); Median rent: $225 per month (2000); Median age of housing: 40 years (2000).
Transportation: Commute to work: 87.1% car, 0.0% public transportation, 0.0% walk, 12.9% work from home (2000); Travel time to work: 79.6% less than 15 minutes, 12.0% 15 to 30 minutes, 5.6% 30 to 45 minutes, 0.0% 45 to 60 minutes, 2.8% 60 minutes or more (2000)

HATFIELD (city). Covers a land area of 2.760 square miles and a water area of 0 square miles. Located at 43.95° N. Lat.; 96.19° W. Long. Elevation is 1,685 feet.
Population: 47 (2000); Race: 100.0% White, 0.0% Black, 0.0% Asian, 0.0% American Indian and Alaska Native, 0.0% Hispanic of any race, 0.0% two or more races (2000); Density: 17.0 persons per square mile (2000); Age: 32.7% under 18, 6.1% over 64 (2000); Marriage status: 15.2% never married, 60.6% now married, 18.2% widowed, 6.1% divorced (2000); Foreign born: 0.0% (2000); Ancestry (includes multiple ancestries): 44.9% German, 24.5% Irish, 6.1% Other groups, 4.1% Danish, 4.1% Norwegian (2000).
Economy: Grain; livestock; dairying. Single-family building permits issued: 0 (2001) / 0 (2000); Multi-family building permits issued: 0 (2001) / 0 (2000); Employment by occupation: 5.0% management, 0.0% professional, 30.0% services, 45.0% sales, 0.0% farming, 20.0% construction, 0.0% production (2000).
Income: Per capita income: $11,796 (2000); Median household income: $25,938 (2000); Poverty rate: 26.5% (2000).
Taxes: Total city taxes per capita: $133 (1997); City property taxes per capita: $117 (1997).
Education: High school graduation rate: 82.1% (2000); College graduation rate: 7.1% (2000).
Housing: Homeownership rate: 66.7% (2000); Median home value: $20,000 (2000); Median rent: $315 per month (2000); Median age of housing: 60+ years (2000).
Transportation: Commute to work: 90.0% car, 0.0% public transportation, 0.0% walk, 10.0% work from home (2000); Travel time to work: 38.9% less than 15 minutes, 38.9% 15 to 30 minutes, 11.1% 30 to 45 minutes, 0.0% 45 to 60 minutes, 11.1% 60 minutes or more (2000)

HOLLAND (city). Covers a land area of 0.919 square miles and a water area of 0 square miles. Located at 44.08° N. Lat.; 96.19° W. Long. Elevation is 1,780 feet.
Population: 215 (2000); Race: 95.3% White, 3.3% Black, 0.0% Asian, 1.4% American Indian and Alaska Native, 1.9% Hispanic of any race, 0.0% two or more races (2000); Density: 233.9 persons per square mile (2000); Age: 20.8% under 18, 32.1% over 64 (2000); Marriage status: 19.0% never married, 61.5% now married, 10.3% widowed, 9.2% divorced (2000); Foreign born: 0.9% (2000); Ancestry (includes multiple ancestries): 48.1% German, 14.6% Dutch, 9.9% Other groups, 5.2% United States or American, 5.2% Irish (2000).
Economy: Agricultural area: grain, soybeans, peas, potatoes; poultry, livestock; dairying. Single-family building permits issued: 0 (2001) / 0 (2000); Multi-family building permits issued: 0 (2001) / 0 (2000); Employment by occupation: 7.7% management, 11.5% professional, 34.6% services, 9.0% sales, 7.7% farming, 7.7% construction, 21.8% production (2000).
Income: Per capita income: $12,982 (2000); Median household income: $21,058 (2000); Poverty rate: 18.4% (2000).
Taxes: Total city taxes per capita: $88 (1997); City property taxes per capita: $83 (1997).
Education: High school graduation rate: 65.6% (2000); College graduation rate: 8.0% (2000).
Housing: Homeownership rate: 81.9% (2000); Median home value: $33,800 (2000); Median rent: $225 per month (2000); Median age of housing: 60 years (2000).
Transportation: Commute to work: 87.2% car, 0.0% public transportation, 3.8% walk, 9.0% work from home (2000); Travel time to work: 40.8% less than 15 minutes, 42.3% 15 to 30 minutes, 8.5% 30 to 45 minutes, 2.8% 45 to 60 minutes, 5.6% 60 minutes or more (2000)

IHLEN (city). Covers a land area of 0.387 square miles and a water area of 0 square miles. Located at 43.90° N. Lat.; 96.36° W. Long. Elevation is 1,648 feet.
Population: 107 (2000); Race: 100.0% White, 0.0% Black, 0.0% Asian, 0.0% American Indian and Alaska Native, 0.0% Hispanic of any race, 0.0% two or more races (2000); Density: 276.1 persons per square mile (2000); Age: 25.5% under 18, 20.9% over 64 (2000); Marriage status: 18.6% never married, 68.6% now married, 2.3% widowed, 10.5% divorced (2000); Foreign born: 4.5% (2000); Ancestry (includes multiple ancestries): 62.7% German, 21.8% Norwegian, 19.1% English, 10.9% Swedish, 9.1% Dutch (2000).
Economy: Grain; livestock. Employment by occupation: 8.5% management, 16.9% professional, 22.0% services, 28.8% sales, 3.4% farming, 3.4% construction, 16.9% production (2000).
Income: Per capita income: $14,569 (2000); Median household income: $31,250 (2000); Poverty rate: 0.9% (2000).
Taxes: Total city taxes per capita: $63 (1997); City property taxes per capita: $53 (1997).
Education: High school graduation rate: 84.9% (2000); College graduation rate: 2.7% (2000).
Housing: Homeownership rate: 86.0% (2000); Median home value: $35,000 (2000); Median rent: $225 per month (2000); Median age of housing: 54 years (2000).
Transportation: Commute to work: 100.0% car, 0.0% public transportation, 0.0% walk, 0.0% work from home (2000); Travel time to work: 47.5% less than 15 minutes, 32.2% 15 to 30 minutes, 0.0% 30 to 45 minutes, 10.2% 45 to 60 minutes, 10.2% 60 minutes or more (2000)

JASPER (city). Covers a land area of 0.880 square miles and a water area of 0 square miles. Located at 43.85° N. Lat.; 96.40° W. Long. Elevation is 1,560 feet.
Population: 597 (2000); Race: 98.0% White, 0.0% Black, 0.0% Asian, 0.9% American Indian and Alaska Native, 0.0% Hispanic of any race, 1.1% two or

more races (2000); Density: 678.2 persons per square mile (2000); Age: 19.4% under 18, 30.8% over 64 (2000); Marriage status: 13.6% never married, 62.1% now married, 17.5% widowed, 6.9% divorced (2000); Foreign born: 0.4% (2000); Ancestry (includes multiple ancestries): 44.0% German, 37.4% Norwegian, 9.5% Dutch, 8.4% Irish, 6.1% Swedish (2000).
Economy: Single-family building permits issued: 1 (2001) / 0 (2000); Multi-family building permits issued: 0 (2001) / 4 (2000); Employment by occupation: 7.6% management, 8.8% professional, 25.2% services, 18.3% sales, 5.7% farming, 15.3% construction, 19.1% production (2000).
Income: Per capita income: $18,019 (2000); Median household income: $25,521 (2000); Poverty rate: 9.7% (2000).
Taxes: Total city taxes per capita: $91 (1997); City property taxes per capita: $84 (1997).
Education: High school graduation rate: 77.9% (2000); College graduation rate: 12.0% (2000).
Housing: Homeownership rate: 78.6% (2000); Median home value: $34,300 (2000); Median rent: $247 per month (2000); Median age of housing: 55 years (2000).
Newspapers: The Jasper Journal (1 x week)
Transportation: Commute to work: 91.7% car, 0.0% public transportation, 4.9% walk, 3.4% work from home (2000); Travel time to work: 35.7% less than 15 minutes, 38.0% 15 to 30 minutes, 14.1% 30 to 45 minutes, 9.4% 45 to 60 minutes, 2.7% 60 minutes or more (2000)

OSBORNE (township). Covers a land area of 34.888 square miles and a water area of 0 square miles. Located at 43.89° N. Lat.; 96.12° W. Long.
Population: 324 (2000); Race: 100.0% White, 0.0% Black, 0.0% Asian, 0.0% American Indian and Alaska Native, 0.0% Hispanic of any race, 0.0% two or more races (2000); Density: 9.3 persons per square mile (2000); Age: 27.1% under 18, 7.6% over 64 (2000); Marriage status: 16.7% never married, 80.8% now married, 2.4% widowed, 0.0% divorced (2000); Foreign born: 0.6% (2000); Ancestry (includes multiple ancestries): 76.1% Dutch, 17.8% German, 5.4% Norwegian, 2.5% Swedish, 1.6% Scottish (2000).
Economy: Employment by occupation: 27.7% management, 7.9% professional, 15.8% services, 23.2% sales, 5.6% farming, 4.5% construction, 15.3% production (2000).
Income: Per capita income: $15,959 (2000); Median household income: $37,083 (2000); Poverty rate: 9.6% (2000).
Taxes: Total city taxes per capita: $48 (1997); City property taxes per capita: $48 (1997).
Education: High school graduation rate: 83.7% (2000); College graduation rate: 18.1% (2000).
Housing: Homeownership rate: 83.9% (2000); Median home value: $88,800 (2000); Median rent: $286 per month (2000); Median age of housing: 51 years (2000).
Transportation: Commute to work: 66.1% car, 0.0% public transportation, 5.6% walk, 28.2% work from home (2000); Travel time to work: 70.9% less than 15 minutes, 18.1% 15 to 30 minutes, 5.5% 30 to 45 minutes, 2.4% 45 to 60 minutes, 3.1% 60 minutes or more (2000)

PIPESTONE (city). Covers a land area of 3.924 square miles and a water area of 0 square miles. Located at 43.99° N. Lat.; 96.31° W. Long. Elevation is 1,738 feet.
History: Pipestone was known very early for the red granite quarried here. American artist George Caitlin described this area, where Indians from many tribes came to get the stone which they carved into ceremonial pipes. Petroglyphs found here indicate a prehistoric mound building culture in the area.
Population: 4,280 (2000); Race: 94.2% White, 0.1% Black, 1.8% Asian, 1.9% American Indian and Alaska Native, 0.7% Hispanic of any race, 1.6% two or more races (2000); Density: 1,090.8 persons per square mile (2000); Age: 24.6% under 18, 21.6% over 64 (2000); Marriage status: 22.4% never married, 56.1% now married, 11.8% widowed, 9.7% divorced (2000); Foreign born: 2.2% (2000); Ancestry (includes multiple ancestries): 38.6% German, 19.2% Norwegian, 13.9% Dutch, 8.3% Irish, 5.8% Other groups (2000).
Economy: Single-family building permits issued: 3 (2001) / 22 (2000); Multi-family building permits issued: 2 (2001) / 0 (2000); Employment by occupation: 9.3% management, 19.0% professional, 20.0% services, 20.3% sales, 2.6% farming, 9.3% construction, 19.7% production (2000).
Income: Per capita income: $17,253 (2000); Median household income: $30,412 (2000); Poverty rate: 9.7% (2000).
Taxes: Total city taxes per capita: $206 (1997); City property taxes per capita: $188 (1997).
Education: High school graduation rate: 77.7% (2000); College graduation rate: 17.4% (2000).

School District(s)

Pipestone-Jasper (PK-12)
2000 Enrollment: 1,464 507-825-5861
Housing: Homeownership rate: 68.9% (2000); Median home value: $51,500 (2000); Median rent: $283 per month (2000); Median age of housing: 46 years (2000).
Hospitals: Pipestone County Medical Center (84 beds)
Newspapers: Pipestone County Star (1 x week); The Free Star (1 x week)
Transportation: Commute to work: 89.6% car, 0.0% public transportation, 7.2% walk, 1.5% work from home (2000); Travel time to work: 76.9% less than 15 minutes, 10.4% 15 to 30 minutes, 2.5% 30 to 45 minutes, 6.8% 45 to 60 minutes, 3.3% 60 minutes or more (2000)
Additional Information Contacts
Pipestone Chamber of Commerce 507-825-3316

ROCK (township). Covers a land area of 35.769 square miles and a water area of 0.090 square miles. Located at 44.07° N. Lat.; 96.13° W. Long.
Population: 184 (2000); Race: 98.4% White, 0.0% Black, 0.0% Asian, 1.6% American Indian and Alaska Native, 1.6% Hispanic of any race, 0.0% two or more races (2000); Density: 5.1 persons per square mile (2000); Age: 26.9% under 18, 13.0% over 64 (2000); Marriage status: 18.1% never married, 68.8% now married, 4.2% widowed, 9.0% divorced (2000); Foreign born: 1.0% (2000); Ancestry (includes multiple ancestries): 54.4% German, 40.9% Dutch, 7.3% Norwegian, 6.2% Danish, 4.1% Other groups (2000).
Economy: Employment by occupation: 30.0% management, 9.0% professional, 13.0% services, 11.0% sales, 4.0% farming, 10.0% construction, 23.0% production (2000).
Income: Per capita income: $16,874 (2000); Median household income: $39,643 (2000); Poverty rate: 15.5% (2000).
Taxes: Total city taxes per capita: $83 (1997); City property taxes per capita: $83 (1997).
Education: High school graduation rate: 76.3% (2000); College graduation rate: 9.2% (2000).
Housing: Homeownership rate: 73.3% (2000); Median home value: $84,300 (2000); Median rent: $125 per month (2000); Median age of housing: 60+ years (2000).
Transportation: Commute to work: 77.6% car, 0.0% public transportation, 0.0% walk, 22.4% work from home (2000); Travel time to work: 34.2% less than 15 minutes, 40.8% 15 to 30 minutes, 17.1% 30 to 45 minutes, 7.9% 45 to 60 minutes, 0.0% 60 minutes or more (2000)

RUTHTON (city). Covers a land area of 0.676 square miles and a water area of 0 square miles. Located at 44.17° N. Lat.; 96.10° W. Long. Elevation is 1,732 feet.
Population: 284 (2000); Race: 99.3% White, 0.0% Black, 0.0% Asian, 0.0% American Indian and Alaska Native, 0.0% Hispanic of any race, 0.7% two or more races (2000); Density: 419.8 persons per square mile (2000); Age: 24.8% under 18, 18.0% over 64 (2000); Marriage status: 16.2% never married, 68.5% now married, 10.0% widowed, 5.4% divorced (2000); Foreign born: 0.0% (2000); Ancestry (includes multiple ancestries): 44.1% German, 24.2% Norwegian, 23.5% Dutch, 14.7% Danish, 9.5% Belgian (2000).
Economy: Grain, soybeans; poultry; dairying. Single-family building permits issued: 0 (2001) / 0 (2000); Multi-family building permits issued: 0 (2001) / 0 (2000); Employment by occupation: 4.1% management, 8.8% professional, 23.0% services, 21.6% sales, 2.0% farming, 10.8% construction, 29.7% production (2000).
Income: Per capita income: $13,016 (2000); Median household income: $26,250 (2000); Poverty rate: 15.0% (2000).
Taxes: Total city taxes per capita: $96 (1997); City property taxes per capita: $86 (1997).
Education: High school graduation rate: 78.8% (2000); College graduation rate: 6.4% (2000).

School District(s)

Ruthton (PK-05)
2000 Enrollment: 284 507-658-3301
Housing: Homeownership rate: 86.2% (2000); Median home value: $27,500 (2000); Median rent: $278 per month (2000); Median age of housing: 60 years (2000).
Newspapers: Buffalo Ridge Gazette (1 x week)
Transportation: Commute to work: 90.2% car, 0.0% public transportation, 5.6% walk, 4.2% work from home (2000); Travel time to work: 30.7% less than 15 minutes, 36.5% 15 to 30 minutes, 25.5% 30 to 45 minutes, 0.0% 45 to 60 minutes, 7.3% 60 minutes or more (2000)

SWEET (township). Covers a land area of 41.302 square miles and a water area of 0.010 square miles. Located at 43.98° N. Lat.; 96.37° W. Long.
Population: 448 (2000); Race: 96.9% White, 0.0% Black, 0.0% Asian, 1.6% American Indian and Alaska Native, 2.9% Hispanic of any race, 0.0% two or more races (2000); Density: 10.8 persons per square mile (2000); Age: 23.5% under 18, 32.1% over 64 (2000); Marriage status: 20.1% never married, 47.5% now married, 26.9% widowed, 5.5% divorced (2000); Foreign born: 0.0% (2000); Ancestry (includes multiple ancestries): 49.6% German, 14.6% English, 14.6% Norwegian, 8.5% Dutch, 4.5% Other groups (2000).
Economy: Employment by occupation: 14.6% management, 20.0% professional, 10.3% services, 33.0% sales, 1.1% farming, 7.0% construction, 14.1% production (2000).
Income: Per capita income: $18,385 (2000); Median household income: $45,208 (2000); Poverty rate: 11.9% (2000).
Taxes: Total city taxes per capita: $56 (1997); City property taxes per capita: $56 (1997).
Education: High school graduation rate: 74.7% (2000); College graduation rate: 13.1% (2000).
Housing: Homeownership rate: 84.8% (2000); Median home value: $85,800 (2000); Median rent: $338 per month (2000); Median age of housing: 46 years (2000).
Transportation: Commute to work: 84.3% car, 0.0% public transportation, 8.1% walk, 7.6% work from home (2000); Travel time to work: 79.5% less than 15 minutes, 13.5% 15 to 30 minutes, 2.9% 30 to 45 minutes, 2.9% 45 to 60 minutes, 1.2% 60 minutes or more (2000)

TROSKY (city). Covers a land area of 1.661 square miles and a water area of 0 square miles. Located at 43.88° N. Lat.; 96.25° W. Long.
Population: 116 (2000); Race: 100.0% White, 0.0% Black, 0.0% Asian, 0.0% American Indian and Alaska Native, 0.0% Hispanic of any race, 0.0% two or more races (2000); Density: 69.8 persons per square mile (2000); Age: 23.3% under 18, 20.0% over 64 (2000); Marriage status: 19.5% never married, 62.3% now married, 6.5% widowed, 11.7% divorced (2000); Foreign born: 0.0% (2000); Ancestry (includes multiple ancestries): 36.7% German, 32.2% Dutch, 13.3% Norwegian, 7.8% English, 6.7% United States or American (2000).
Economy: Agriculture: corn, soybeans; livestock. Single-family building permits issued: 0 (2001) / 0 (2000); Multi-family building permits issued: 0 (2001) / 0 (2000); Employment by occupation: 6.7% management, 0.0% professional, 31.1% services, 17.8% sales, 0.0% farming, 8.9% construction, 35.6% production (2000).
Income: Per capita income: $16,741 (2000); Median household income: $36,250 (2000); Poverty rate: 0.0% (2000).
Taxes: Total city taxes per capita: $70 (1997); City property taxes per capita: $52 (1997).
Education: High school graduation rate: 67.2% (2000); College graduation rate: 0.0% (2000).
Housing: Homeownership rate: 100.0% (2000); Median home value: $15,000 (2000); Median age of housing: 60 years (2000).
Transportation: Commute to work: 91.1% car, 0.0% public transportation, 4.4% walk, 4.4% work from home (2000); Travel time to work: 51.2% less than 15 minutes, 32.6% 15 to 30 minutes, 0.0% 30 to 45 minutes, 0.0% 45 to 60 minutes, 16.3% 60 minutes or more (2000)

TROY (township). Covers a land area of 43.622 square miles and a water area of 0 square miles. Located at 44.06° N. Lat.; 96.37° W. Long.
Population: 318 (2000); Race: 100.0% White, 0.0% Black, 0.0% Asian, 0.0% American Indian and Alaska Native, 0.0% Hispanic of any race, 0.0% two or more races (2000); Density: 7.3 persons per square mile (2000); Age: 31.9% under 18, 10.1% over 64 (2000); Marriage status: 20.8% never married, 74.9% now married, 1.7% widowed, 2.6% divorced (2000); Foreign born: 1.3% (2000); Ancestry (includes multiple ancestries): 62.9% German, 21.5% Norwegian, 12.7% Dutch, 6.2% Irish, 4.2% United States or American (2000).
Economy: Employment by occupation: 26.3% management, 11.7% professional, 1.2% services, 25.1% sales, 5.3% farming, 8.8% construction, 21.6% production (2000).
Income: Per capita income: $16,518 (2000); Median household income: $35,357 (2000); Poverty rate: 13.4% (2000).
Taxes: Total city taxes per capita: $46 (1997); City property taxes per capita: $46 (1997).
Education: High school graduation rate: 86.8% (2000); College graduation rate: 11.0% (2000).
Housing: Homeownership rate: 81.6% (2000); Median home value: $58,100 (2000); Median rent: $363 per month (2000); Median age of housing: 60+ years (2000).
Transportation: Commute to work: 78.4% car, 0.6% public transportation, 1.2% walk, 19.8% work from home (2000); Travel time to work: 54.6% less than 15 minutes, 33.8% 15 to 30 minutes, 1.5% 30 to 45 minutes, 8.5% 45 to 60 minutes, 1.5% 60 minutes or more (2000)

WOODSTOCK (city). Covers a land area of 0.554 square miles and a water area of 0 square miles. Located at 44.00° N. Lat.; 96.10° W. Long.
Population: 132 (2000); Race: 100.0% White, 0.0% Black, 0.0% Asian, 0.0% American Indian and Alaska Native, 0.0% Hispanic of any race, 0.0% two or more races (2000); Density: 238.3 persons per square mile (2000); Age: 22.8% under 18, 34.6% over 64 (2000); Marriage status: 21.7% never married, 56.6% now married, 19.8% widowed, 1.9% divorced (2000); Foreign born: 0.0% (2000); Ancestry (includes multiple ancestries): 47.2% Dutch, 37.8% German, 12.6% Luxemburger, 11.8% Irish, 2.4% English (2000).
Economy: Agriculture includes corn, oats, soybeans; livestock; dairying. Manufacturing of feeds. Employment by occupation: 0.0% management, 1.9% professional, 29.6% services, 14.8% sales, 3.7% farming, 11.1% construction, 38.9% production (2000).
Income: Per capita income: $13,269 (2000); Median household income: $17,500 (2000); Poverty rate: 5.5% (2000).
Taxes: Total city taxes per capita: $101 (1997); City property taxes per capita: $101 (1997).
Education: High school graduation rate: 63.5% (2000); College graduation rate: 4.2% (2000).
Housing: Homeownership rate: 100.0% (2000); Median home value: $21,700 (2000); Median age of housing: 60+ years (2000).
Transportation: Commute to work: 83.3% car, 0.0% public transportation, 16.7% walk, 0.0% work from home (2000); Travel time to work: 42.6% less than 15 minutes, 42.6% 15 to 30 minutes, 3.7% 30 to 45 minutes, 5.6% 45 to 60 minutes, 5.6% 60 minutes or more (2000)

Polk County

Located in northwestern Minnesota; bounded on the west by the Red River of the North and the North Dakota border; drained by the Poplar, Sandhill, and Red Lake Rivers. Covers a land area of 1,970.40 square miles, a water area of 27.40 square miles, and is located in the Central Time Zone. The county government was organized in 1858. County seat is Crookston.

Polk County is part of the Grand Forks, ND-MN MSA. The entire metro area includes: Polk County, MN; Grand Forks County, ND

Weather Station: Crookston NW Exp. Station — Elevation: 885 feet

	Jan	Feb	Mar	Apr	May	Jun	Jul	Aug	Sep	Oct	Nov	Dec
High	14	21	33	53	69	77	81	80	69	55	34	20
Low	-6	2	15	31	44	54	58	55	45	33	18	2
Precip	0.5	0.5	0.8	1.3	2.6	3.4	3.0	2.9	2.3	1.8	0.9	0.5
Snow	9.8	6.5	6.4	1.7	0.1	0.0	0.0	0.0	0.0	0.5	6.6	7.3

High and Low temperatures in degrees Fahrenheit; Precipitation and Snow in inches

Weather Station: Fosston 1 E — Elevation: 1,309 feet

	Jan	Feb	Mar	Apr	May	Jun	Jul	Aug	Sep	Oct	Nov	Dec
High	14	22	34	52	68	76	80	78	68	54	34	20
Low	-8	-0	14	29	42	51	55	53	43	32	17	1
Precip	0.6	0.5	0.9	1.5	2.6	4.3	4.0	3.5	2.8	2.5	0.9	0.6
Snow	9.6	5.9	7.3	2.2	0.2	0.0	0.0	0.0	tr	1.1	8.0	7.3

High and Low temperatures in degrees Fahrenheit; Precipitation and Snow in inches

Population: 31,369 (2000); Race: 94.3% White, 0.5% Black, 0.5% Asian, 1.0% American Indian and Alaska Native, 4.6% Hispanic of any race, 1.2% two or more races (2000); Density: 15.9 persons per square mile (2000); Age: 25.9% under 18, 17.3% over 64 (2000).
Religion: Five largest groups: 31.5% Evangelical Lutheran Church in America, 26.7% Catholic Church, 5.0% Lutheran Church—Missouri Synod, 3.1% The Association of Free Lutheran Congregations, 2.5% Presbyterian Church (U.S.A.) (2000).
Economy: Unemployment rate: 3.3% (11/2002); Total civilian labor force: 17,546 (11/2002); Leading industries: 21.7% health care and social assistance; 17.6% retail trade; 15.6% manufacturing (2000); Companies that employ more than 1,000 persons: 0 (2000); Companies that employ more than 100 persons: 13 (2000); Farms: 1,366 totaling 1,051,813 acres (1997); Minority business ownership rate: 0.0% (1997); Women business ownership

rate: 15.8% (1997); Retail sales per capita: $6,626 (1997). Single-family building permits issued: 87 (2001) / 90 (2000); Multi-family building permits issued: 0 (2001) / 2 (2000).
Income: Per capita income: $17,279 (2000); Median household income: $35,105 (2000); Poverty rate: 10.9% (2000); Bankruptcy rate: 2.42% (2001).
Taxes: Total county taxes per capita: $322 (2000); County property taxes per capita: $321 (2000).
Education: High school graduation rate: 82.0% (2000); College graduation rate: 17.6% (2000).
Housing: Homeownership rate: 74.0% (2000); Median home value: $75,000 (2000); Median rent: $344 per month (2000); Median age of housing: 39 years (2000).
Health: Birth rate: 121.1 per 10,000 population (1998); Age adjusted death rate: 91.6 per 10,000 population (1999); Age adjusted cancer mortality rate: 241.2 deaths per 100,000 population (1999). Number of physicians: 5.7 per 10,000 population (1999); Number of hospital beds: 97.5 per 10,000 population (1999).
Elections: 2000 Presidential election results: 40.8% Gore, 53.8% Bush, 2.6% Nader, 2.4% Buchanan
National and State Parks: Bee Lake State Wildlife Management Area; Belgium State Wildlife Management Area; Brandsvold State Wildlife Management Area; Castor State Wildlife Management Areas; Dorr State Wildlife Management Area; Enerson State Wildlife Management Area; Erskine State Wildlife Management Area; Gully State Wildlife Management Area; Hangaard State Wildlife Management Area; Hasselton State Wildlife Management Area; Hill River State Wildlife Management Area; Hovland State Wildlife Management Area; Kakaik State Wildlife Management Area; Kroening State Wildlife Management Area; Lavoi State Wildlife Management Area; Lengby State Wildlife Management Area; Lessor State Wildlife Management Area; Pembina State Wildlife Management Area; Polk State Wildlife Management Areas; Rindahl State Wildlife Management Area; Sagaiigan State Wildlife Management Area; Shypoke State Wildlife Management Area; Stipa State Wildlife Management Area; Tilden State Wildlife Management Area
Additional Information Contacts
Polk County Government Offices 218-281-5408
Crookston Chamber of Commerce. 218-281-4320
East Grand Forks Chamber of Commerce 218-773-7481

Polk County Communities

ANDOVER (township). Covers a land area of 35.468 square miles and a water area of 0 square miles. Located at 47.72° N. Lat.; 96.66° W. Long.
Population: 154 (2000); Race: 100.0% White, 0.0% Black, 0.0% Asian, 0.0% American Indian and Alaska Native, 1.3% Hispanic of any race, 0.0% two or more races (2000); Density: 4.3 persons per square mile (2000); Age: 31.4% under 18, 13.8% over 64 (2000); Marriage status: 20.3% never married, 73.7% now married, 5.9% widowed, 0.0% divorced (2000); Foreign born: 0.0% (2000); Ancestry (includes multiple ancestries): 29.6% French (except Basque), 24.5% Norwegian, 22.0% German, 11.9% French Canadian, 10.1% Swedish (2000).
Economy: Employment by occupation: 26.2% management, 13.1% professional, 13.1% services, 26.2% sales, 6.6% farming, 6.6% construction, 8.2% production (2000).
Income: Per capita income: $21,486 (2000); Median household income: $53,750 (2000); Poverty rate: 0.0% (2000).
Taxes: Total city taxes per capita: $253 (1997); City property taxes per capita: $253 (1997).
Education: High school graduation rate: 86.6% (2000); College graduation rate: 7.2% (2000).
Housing: Homeownership rate: 81.0% (2000); Median home value: $88,300 (2000); Median rent: $318 per month (2000); Median age of housing: 43 years (2000).
Transportation: Commute to work: 81.0% car, 0.0% public transportation, 10.3% walk, 8.6% work from home (2000); Travel time to work: 83.0% less than 15 minutes, 13.2% 15 to 30 minutes, 3.8% 30 to 45 minutes, 0.0% 45 to 60 minutes, 0.0% 60 minutes or more (2000)

ANGUS (township). Covers a land area of 36.013 square miles and a water area of 0 square miles. Located at 48.06° N. Lat.; 96.70° W. Long. Elevation is 871 feet.
Population: 112 (2000); Race: 90.6% White, 0.0% Black, 0.0% Asian, 0.0% American Indian and Alaska Native, 0.0% Hispanic of any race, 9.4% two or more races (2000); Density: 3.1 persons per square mile (2000); Age: 22.6% under 18, 15.1% over 64 (2000); Marriage status: 17.4% never married, 76.7% now married, 5.8% widowed, 0.0% divorced (2000); Foreign born: 9.4% (2000); Ancestry (includes multiple ancestries): 23.6% Norwegian, 21.7% German, 20.8% Swedish, 20.8% Irish, 8.5% Czech (2000).
Economy: Employment by occupation: 32.7% management, 19.2% professional, 3.8% services, 19.2% sales, 1.9% farming, 0.0% construction, 23.1% production (2000).
Income: Per capita income: $22,543 (2000); Median household income: $58,125 (2000); Poverty rate: 4.7% (2000).
Taxes: Total city taxes per capita: $176 (1997); City property taxes per capita: $176 (1997).
Education: High school graduation rate: 97.3% (2000); College graduation rate: 33.3% (2000).
Housing: Homeownership rate: 90.0% (2000); Median home value: $64,300 (2000); Median rent: $125 per month (2000); Median age of housing: 30 years (2000).
Transportation: Commute to work: 88.5% car, 0.0% public transportation, 5.8% walk, 5.8% work from home (2000); Travel time to work: 36.7% less than 15 minutes, 28.6% 15 to 30 minutes, 28.6% 30 to 45 minutes, 4.1% 45 to 60 minutes, 2.0% 60 minutes or more (2000)

BADGER (township). Covers a land area of 35.672 square miles and a water area of 0.482 square miles. Located at 47.70° N. Lat.; 96.02° W. Long.
Population: 166 (2000); Race: 93.7% White, 0.0% Black, 1.9% Asian, 4.4% American Indian and Alaska Native, 0.0% Hispanic of any race, 0.0% two or more races (2000); Density: 4.7 persons per square mile (2000); Age: 15.8% under 18, 51.9% over 64 (2000); Marriage status: 27.0% never married, 38.3% now married, 27.7% widowed, 7.1% divorced (2000); Foreign born: 1.9% (2000); Ancestry (includes multiple ancestries): 44.9% Norwegian, 31.6% German, 7.6% Irish, 7.6% Czech, 3.8% Polish (2000).
Economy: Employment by occupation: 5.4% management, 13.5% professional, 21.6% services, 27.0% sales, 5.4% farming, 5.4% construction, 21.6% production (2000).
Income: Per capita income: $16,999 (2000); Median household income: $25,625 (2000); Poverty rate: 8.9% (2000).
Taxes: Total city taxes per capita: $87 (1997); City property taxes per capita: $87 (1997).
Education: High school graduation rate: 63.3% (2000); College graduation rate: 10.2% (2000).
Housing: Homeownership rate: 88.4% (2000); Median home value: $57,500 (2000); Median rent: $375 per month (2000); Median age of housing: 57 years (2000).
Transportation: Commute to work: 94.6% car, 0.0% public transportation, 0.0% walk, 5.4% work from home (2000); Travel time to work: 5.7% less than 15 minutes, 22.9% 15 to 30 minutes, 48.6% 30 to 45 minutes, 0.0% 45 to 60 minutes, 22.9% 60 minutes or more (2000)

BELGIUM (township). Covers a land area of 36.435 square miles and a water area of 0.017 square miles. Located at 47.97° N. Lat.; 96.57° W. Long.
Population: 111 (2000); Race: 100.0% White, 0.0% Black, 0.0% Asian, 0.0% American Indian and Alaska Native, 0.0% Hispanic of any race, 0.0% two or more races (2000); Density: 3.0 persons per square mile (2000); Age: 32.3% under 18, 3.2% over 64 (2000); Marriage status: 17.1% never married, 82.9% now married, 0.0% widowed, 0.0% divorced (2000); Foreign born: 0.0% (2000); Ancestry (includes multiple ancestries): 49.5% German, 48.4% Norwegian, 19.4% Irish, 14.0% French (except Basque), 12.9% Swedish (2000).
Economy: Employment by occupation: 10.9% management, 4.3% professional, 26.1% services, 17.4% sales, 0.0% farming, 8.7% construction, 32.6% production (2000).
Income: Per capita income: $10,385 (2000); Median household income: $38,750 (2000); Poverty rate: 21.5% (2000).
Taxes: Total city taxes per capita: $190 (1997); City property taxes per capita: $190 (1997).
Education: High school graduation rate: 78.3% (2000); College graduation rate: 11.7% (2000).
Housing: Homeownership rate: 86.2% (2000); Median home value: $85,000 (2000); Median rent: $125 per month (2000); Median age of housing: 29 years (2000).
Transportation: Commute to work: 83.7% car, 0.0% public transportation, 7.0% walk, 9.3% work from home (2000); Travel time to work: 12.8% less than 15 minutes, 25.6% 15 to 30 minutes, 53.8% 30 to 45 minutes, 0.0% 45 to 60 minutes, 7.7% 60 minutes or more (2000)

BELTRAMI (city). Covers a land area of 2.012 square miles and a water area of 0 square miles. Located at 47.54° N. Lat.; 96.53° W. Long. Elevation is 903 feet.

Population: 101 (2000); Race: 100.0% White, 0.0% Black, 0.0% Asian, 0.0% American Indian and Alaska Native, 0.0% Hispanic of any race, 0.0% two or more races (2000); Density: 50.2 persons per square mile (2000); Age: 22.7% under 18, 27.3% over 64 (2000); Marriage status: 18.9% never married, 71.6% now married, 6.8% widowed, 2.7% divorced (2000); Foreign born: 0.0% (2000); Ancestry (includes multiple ancestries): 58.0% Norwegian, 43.2% German, 12.5% English, 5.7% Irish, 5.7% Swedish (2000).
Economy: Grain, potatoes; dairying. Manufacturing: fertilizers. Single-family building permits issued: 0 (2001) / 0 (2000); Multi-family building permits issued: 0 (2001) / 0 (2000); Employment by occupation: 0.0% management, 17.1% professional, 34.3% services, 17.1% sales, 0.0% farming, 8.6% construction, 22.9% production (2000).
Income: Per capita income: $14,928 (2000); Median household income: $30,833 (2000); Poverty rate: 10.2% (2000).
Taxes: Total city taxes per capita: $163 (1997); City property taxes per capita: $163 (1997).
Education: High school graduation rate: 70.8% (2000); College graduation rate: 12.3% (2000).
Housing: Homeownership rate: 97.5% (2000); Median home value: $19,400 (2000); Median age of housing: 60+ years (2000).
Transportation: Commute to work: 82.9% car, 0.0% public transportation, 11.4% walk, 5.7% work from home (2000); Travel time to work: 21.2% less than 15 minutes, 33.3% 15 to 30 minutes, 27.3% 30 to 45 minutes, 6.1% 45 to 60 minutes, 12.1% 60 minutes or more (2000)

BRANDSVOLD (township). Covers a land area of 34.460 square miles and a water area of 0.924 square miles. Located at 47.62° N. Lat.; 95.74° W. Long.
Population: 241 (2000); Race: 97.4% White, 0.0% Black, 0.9% Asian, 0.0% American Indian and Alaska Native, 0.0% Hispanic of any race, 1.7% two or more races (2000); Density: 7.0 persons per square mile (2000); Age: 26.8% under 18, 15.3% over 64 (2000); Marriage status: 19.4% never married, 75.8% now married, 3.8% widowed, 1.1% divorced (2000); Foreign born: 1.7% (2000); Ancestry (includes multiple ancestries): 63.4% Norwegian, 14.5% German, 14.0% Swedish, 6.4% Czech, 5.5% English (2000).
Economy: Employment by occupation: 18.6% management, 19.5% professional, 16.8% services, 25.7% sales, 1.8% farming, 9.7% construction, 8.0% production (2000).
Income: Per capita income: $15,094 (2000); Median household income: $39,000 (2000); Poverty rate: 9.8% (2000).
Taxes: Total city taxes per capita: $46 (1997); City property taxes per capita: $46 (1997).
Education: High school graduation rate: 81.6% (2000); College graduation rate: 15.8% (2000).
Housing: Homeownership rate: 87.6% (2000); Median home value: $66,700 (2000); Median rent: $200 per month (2000); Median age of housing: 60+ years (2000).
Transportation: Commute to work: 85.0% car, 0.0% public transportation, 0.0% walk, 15.0% work from home (2000); Travel time to work: 55.2% less than 15 minutes, 29.2% 15 to 30 minutes, 3.1% 30 to 45 minutes, 5.2% 45 to 60 minutes, 7.3% 60 minutes or more (2000)

BRANDT (township). Covers a land area of 36.035 square miles and a water area of 0 square miles. Located at 48.06° N. Lat.; 96.59° W. Long.
Population: 62 (2000); Race: 82.8% White, 0.0% Black, 7.8% Asian, 0.0% American Indian and Alaska Native, 9.4% Hispanic of any race, 0.0% two or more races (2000); Density: 1.7 persons per square mile (2000); Age: 25.0% under 18, 15.6% over 64 (2000); Marriage status: 9.4% never married, 79.2% now married, 11.3% widowed, 0.0% divorced (2000); Foreign born: 9.4% (2000); Ancestry (includes multiple ancestries): 31.3% German, 17.2% Other groups, 15.6% Irish, 15.6% Norwegian, 14.1% French (except Basque) (2000).
Economy: Employment by occupation: 25.9% management, 14.8% professional, 11.1% services, 22.2% sales, 0.0% farming, 0.0% construction, 25.9% production (2000).
Income: Per capita income: $13,030 (2000); Median household income: $29,583 (2000); Poverty rate: 26.6% (2000).
Taxes: Total city taxes per capita: $138 (1997); City property taxes per capita: $138 (1997).
Education: High school graduation rate: 79.1% (2000); College graduation rate: 4.7% (2000).
Housing: Homeownership rate: 78.3% (2000); Median home value: $62,000 (2000); Median rent: $125 per month (2000); Median age of housing: 38 years (2000).
Transportation: Commute to work: 88.0% car, 0.0% public transportation, 0.0% walk, 12.0% work from home (2000); Travel time to work: 9.1% less than 15 minutes, 50.0% 15 to 30 minutes, 22.7% 30 to 45 minutes, 18.2% 45 to 60 minutes, 0.0% 60 minutes or more (2000)

BRISLET (township). Covers a land area of 26.970 square miles and a water area of 0 square miles. Located at 48.14° N. Lat.; 96.70° W. Long.
Population: 52 (2000); Race: 100.0% White, 0.0% Black, 0.0% Asian, 0.0% American Indian and Alaska Native, 0.0% Hispanic of any race, 0.0% two or more races (2000); Density: 1.9 persons per square mile (2000); Age: 28.3% under 18, 30.2% over 64 (2000); Marriage status: 25.6% never married, 69.8% now married, 0.0% widowed, 4.7% divorced (2000); Foreign born: 0.0% (2000); Ancestry (includes multiple ancestries): 45.3% German, 37.7% Norwegian, 26.4% Swedish, 24.5% Czech, 13.2% Polish (2000).
Economy: Employment by occupation: 57.1% management, 9.5% professional, 0.0% services, 33.3% sales, 0.0% farming, 0.0% construction, 0.0% production (2000).
Income: Per capita income: $18,949 (2000); Median household income: $39,375 (2000); Poverty rate: 0.0% (2000).
Taxes: Total city taxes per capita: $79 (1997); City property taxes per capita: $79 (1997).
Education: High school graduation rate: 83.3% (2000); College graduation rate: 13.9% (2000).
Housing: Homeownership rate: 100.0% (2000); Median home value: $47,500 (2000); Median age of housing: 55 years (2000).
Transportation: Commute to work: 76.2% car, 0.0% public transportation, 14.3% walk, 9.5% work from home (2000); Travel time to work: 47.4% less than 15 minutes, 15.8% 15 to 30 minutes, 26.3% 30 to 45 minutes, 10.5% 45 to 60 minutes, 0.0% 60 minutes or more (2000)

BYGLAND (township). Covers a land area of 28.164 square miles and a water area of 0 square miles. Located at 47.81° N. Lat.; 96.93° W. Long.
Population: 297 (2000); Race: 95.8% White, 0.0% Black, 0.0% Asian, 1.4% American Indian and Alaska Native, 1.7% Hispanic of any race, 2.8% two or more races (2000); Density: 10.5 persons per square mile (2000); Age: 23.3% under 18, 9.0% over 64 (2000); Marriage status: 27.6% never married, 60.1% now married, 3.7% widowed, 8.6% divorced (2000); Foreign born: 0.0% (2000); Ancestry (includes multiple ancestries): 60.1% Norwegian, 34.4% German, 8.0% Swedish, 6.9% French (except Basque), 4.9% Other groups (2000).
Economy: Employment by occupation: 19.6% management, 23.8% professional, 9.8% services, 16.8% sales, 4.2% farming, 14.0% construction, 11.9% production (2000).
Income: Per capita income: $18,260 (2000); Median household income: $47,500 (2000); Poverty rate: 11.0% (2000).
Taxes: Total city taxes per capita: $54 (1997); City property taxes per capita: $54 (1997).
Education: High school graduation rate: 88.0% (2000); College graduation rate: 15.0% (2000).
Housing: Homeownership rate: 94.2% (2000); Median home value: $87,500 (2000); Median rent: $325 per month (2000); Median age of housing: 52 years (2000).
Transportation: Commute to work: 82.9% car, 0.0% public transportation, 6.4% walk, 10.7% work from home (2000); Travel time to work: 16.8% less than 15 minutes, 56.8% 15 to 30 minutes, 14.4% 30 to 45 minutes, 1.6% 45 to 60 minutes, 10.4% 60 minutes or more (2000)

CHESTER (township). Covers a land area of 35.915 square miles and a water area of 0.029 square miles. Located at 47.81° N. Lat.; 95.77° W. Long.
Population: 79 (2000); Race: 94.8% White, 0.0% Black, 0.0% Asian, 0.0% American Indian and Alaska Native, 0.0% Hispanic of any race, 5.2% two or more races (2000); Density: 2.2 persons per square mile (2000); Age: 35.1% under 18, 22.7% over 64 (2000); Marriage status: 18.8% never married, 68.1% now married, 2.9% widowed, 10.1% divorced (2000); Foreign born: 2.1% (2000); Ancestry (includes multiple ancestries): 68.0% Norwegian, 24.7% Swedish, 14.4% Irish, 12.4% Ukrainian, 6.2% French (except Basque) (2000).
Economy: Employment by occupation: 15.4% management, 7.7% professional, 15.4% services, 33.3% sales, 0.0% farming, 20.5% construction, 7.7% production (2000).
Income: Per capita income: $16,830 (2000); Median household income: $53,125 (2000); Poverty rate: 14.1% (2000).
Taxes: Total city taxes per capita: $179 (1997); City property taxes per capita: $179 (1997).
Education: High school graduation rate: 86.2% (2000); College graduation rate: 6.9% (2000).

Housing: Homeownership rate: 100.0% (2000); Median home value: $22,500 (2000); Median age of housing: 35 years (2000).
Transportation: Commute to work: 64.1% car, 0.0% public transportation, 12.8% walk, 23.1% work from home (2000); Travel time to work: 23.3% less than 15 minutes, 36.7% 15 to 30 minutes, 30.0% 30 to 45 minutes, 0.0% 45 to 60 minutes, 10.0% 60 minutes or more (2000)

CLIMAX (city). Covers a land area of 1.145 square miles and a water area of 0 square miles. Located at 47.60° N. Lat.; 96.81° W. Long. Elevation is 865 feet.
Population: 243 (2000); Race: 95.1% White, 0.0% Black, 0.0% Asian, 0.0% American Indian and Alaska Native, 4.1% Hispanic of any race, 0.8% two or more races (2000); Density: 212.2 persons per square mile (2000); Age: 26.5% under 18, 24.1% over 64 (2000); Marriage status: 24.6% never married, 56.9% now married, 11.3% widowed, 7.2% divorced (2000); Foreign born: 4.9% (2000); Ancestry (includes multiple ancestries): 62.9% Norwegian, 21.2% German, 8.6% Irish, 4.9% Other groups, 4.1% Lebanese (2000).
Economy: Grain; livestock; dairying. Manufacturing: fertilizer blending. Employment by occupation: 0.0% management, 18.6% professional, 25.6% services, 20.9% sales, 2.3% farming, 12.8% construction, 19.8% production (2000).
Income: Per capita income: $14,320 (2000); Median household income: $24,688 (2000); Poverty rate: 11.8% (2000).
Taxes: Total city taxes per capita: $168 (1997); City property taxes per capita: $168 (1997).
Education: High school graduation rate: 75.6% (2000); College graduation rate: 12.2% (2000).

School District(s)

Climax (PK-12)
2000 Enrollment: 168 218-857-2385
Housing: Homeownership rate: 74.8% (2000); Median home value: $52,000 (2000); Median rent: $250 per month (2000); Median age of housing: 39 years (2000).
Transportation: Commute to work: 89.5% car, 0.0% public transportation, 10.5% walk, 0.0% work from home (2000); Travel time to work: 38.4% less than 15 minutes, 23.3% 15 to 30 minutes, 23.3% 30 to 45 minutes, 5.8% 45 to 60 minutes, 9.3% 60 minutes or more (2000)

COLUMBIA (township). Covers a land area of 34.494 square miles and a water area of 1.251 square miles. Located at 47.52° N. Lat.; 95.63° W. Long.
Population: 429 (2000); Race: 98.1% White, 0.0% Black, 0.0% Asian, 1.2% American Indian and Alaska Native, 0.0% Hispanic of any race, 0.7% two or more races (2000); Density: 12.4 persons per square mile (2000); Age: 31.1% under 18, 16.7% over 64 (2000); Marriage status: 19.0% never married, 69.0% now married, 5.2% widowed, 6.9% divorced (2000); Foreign born: 0.0% (2000); Ancestry (includes multiple ancestries): 43.9% Norwegian, 25.2% German, 10.0% Swedish, 8.7% English, 5.8% Irish (2000).
Economy: Employment by occupation: 5.9% management, 20.4% professional, 22.4% services, 19.7% sales, 2.0% farming, 10.5% construction, 19.1% production (2000).
Income: Per capita income: $12,870 (2000); Median household income: $26,827 (2000); Poverty rate: 6.3% (2000).
Taxes: Total city taxes per capita: $53 (1997); City property taxes per capita: $53 (1997).
Education: High school graduation rate: 76.8% (2000); College graduation rate: 16.3% (2000).
Housing: Homeownership rate: 83.4% (2000); Median home value: $71,700 (2000); Median rent: $275 per month (2000); Median age of housing: 41 years (2000).
Transportation: Commute to work: 91.3% car, 0.0% public transportation, 1.3% walk, 6.7% work from home (2000); Travel time to work: 59.7% less than 15 minutes, 31.7% 15 to 30 minutes, 6.5% 30 to 45 minutes, 1.4% 45 to 60 minutes, 0.7% 60 minutes or more (2000)

CROOKSTON (city). Covers a land area of 4.939 square miles and a water area of 0 square miles. Located at 47.77° N. Lat.; 96.60° W. Long. Elevation is 864 feet.
History: Crookston was settled in 1872 and named for Colonel William Crooks, chief engineer of the first railroad that came to this area. Incorporated as a city in 1879, Crookstone became a major trading center in northern Minnesota.
Population: 8,192 (2000); Race: 92.0% White, 1.0% Black, 1.0% Asian, 0.3% American Indian and Alaska Native, 8.2% Hispanic of any race, 1.2% two or more races (2000); Density: 1,658.8 persons per square mile (2000); Age: 23.8% under 18, 18.0% over 64 (2000); Marriage status: 32.9% never married, 49.9% now married, 8.9% widowed, 8.3% divorced (2000); Foreign born: 4.3% (2000); Ancestry (includes multiple ancestries): 33.7% German, 33.3% Norwegian, 11.5% Other groups, 11.3% French (except Basque), 8.4% Irish (2000).
Economy: Single-family building permits issued: 8 (2001) / 9 (2000); Multi-family building permits issued: 0 (2001) / 2 (2000); Employment by occupation: 9.8% management, 21.7% professional, 21.4% services, 23.1% sales, 1.5% farming, 8.7% construction, 13.7% production (2000).
Income: Per capita income: $17,219 (2000); Median household income: $34,609 (2000); Poverty rate: 12.5% (2000).
Taxes: Total city taxes per capita: $202 (1997); City property taxes per capita: $137 (1997).
Education: High school graduation rate: 82.1% (2000); College graduation rate: 20.8% (2000).

School District(s)

Crookston (PK-12)
2000 Enrollment: 1,699 218-281-5313

Four-year College(s)

University of Minnesota-Crookston (Public)
2001 Enrollment: 2,529 218-281-8343
2001 Tuition: In-state $4,187; Out-of-state $4,187
Housing: Homeownership rate: 63.4% (2000); Median home value: $62,400 (2000); Median rent: $341 per month (2000); Median age of housing: 47 years (2000).
Hospitals: Riverview Healthcare Association (49 beds)
Safety: Violent crime rate: 29.0 per 10,000 population; Property crime rate: 177.5 per 10,000 population (2001).
Newspapers: Crookston Daily Times (5 x week); Our Northland Diocese (22 x month)
Transportation: Commute to work: 87.7% car, 0.0% public transportation, 9.4% walk, 1.9% work from home (2000); Travel time to work: 77.3% less than 15 minutes, 11.4% 15 to 30 minutes, 6.7% 30 to 45 minutes, 3.3% 45 to 60 minutes, 1.3% 60 minutes or more (2000)
Additional Information Contacts
Crookston Chamber of Commerce........................ 218-281-4320

CROOKSTON (township). Covers a land area of 37.577 square miles and a water area of 0.028 square miles. Located at 47.79° N. Lat.; 96.53° W. Long. Elevation is 864 feet.
History: University of Minnesota— Crookston Campus. Settled 1872, incorporated 1879.
Population: 554 (2000); Race: 99.2% White, 0.0% Black, 0.4% Asian, 0.0% American Indian and Alaska Native, 0.0% Hispanic of any race, 0.4% two or more races (2000); Density: 14.7 persons per square mile (2000); Age: 27.5% under 18, 11.3% over 64 (2000); Marriage status: 24.4% never married, 61.9% now married, 8.2% widowed, 5.5% divorced (2000); Foreign born: 0.0% (2000); Ancestry (includes multiple ancestries): 38.0% Norwegian, 30.0% German, 13.1% French (except Basque), 7.4% Swedish, 7.0% Other groups (2000).
Economy: Railroad junction, trade center and shipping point in agricultural area: grain, sugar beets, potatoes, sunflowers; livestock; dairying. Manufacturing: food processing, concrete pipe, machinery, printing and publishing. Stock and produce show takes place annually. Employment by occupation: 12.7% management, 17.6% professional, 19.3% services, 23.8% sales, 0.0% farming, 10.2% construction, 16.4% production (2000).
Income: Per capita income: $19,664 (2000); Median household income: $54,688 (2000); Poverty rate: 6.7% (2000).
Taxes: Total city taxes per capita: $64 (1997); City property taxes per capita: $64 (1997).
Education: High school graduation rate: 93.5% (2000); College graduation rate: 28.7% (2000).
Housing: Homeownership rate: 91.8% (2000); Median home value: $107,600 (2000); Median rent: $350 per month (2000); Median age of housing: 32 years (2000).
Transportation: Commute to work: 92.6% car, 0.0% public transportation, 1.2% walk, 6.2% work from home (2000); Travel time to work: 48.5% less than 15 minutes, 33.5% 15 to 30 minutes, 7.9% 30 to 45 minutes, 9.3% 45 to 60 minutes, 0.9% 60 minutes or more (2000)

EAST GRAND FORKS (city). Covers a land area of 4.996 square miles and a water area of 0 square miles. Located at 47.93° N. Lat.; 97.01° W. Long. Elevation is 832 feet.
History: East Grand Forks was settled about 1880, on a site at the confluence of the Red River and the Red Lake River where a trading post had existed sometime in the 1700's. One of the early industries in East Grand Forks was a sugar beet factory, processing beets grown in the surrounding farm lands.

Population: 7,501 (2000); Race: 90.1% White, 0.7% Black, 0.4% Asian, 1.9% American Indian and Alaska Native, 7.9% Hispanic of any race, 2.1% two or more races (2000); Density: 1,501.5 persons per square mile (2000); Age: 28.9% under 18, 11.4% over 64 (2000); Marriage status: 28.6% never married, 55.6% now married, 7.1% widowed, 8.7% divorced (2000); Foreign born: 2.1% (2000); Ancestry (includes multiple ancestries): 36.1% Norwegian, 29.1% German, 13.2% Other groups, 9.1% Irish, 8.8% French (except Basque) (2000).

Economy: Single-family building permits issued: 34 (2001) / 34 (2000); Multi-family building permits issued: 0 (2001) / 0 (2000); Employment by occupation: 7.1% management, 18.1% professional, 15.5% services, 29.2% sales, 1.6% farming, 13.4% construction, 15.2% production (2000).

Income: Per capita income: $16,599 (2000); Median household income: $35,866 (2000); Poverty rate: 12.4% (2000).

Taxes: Total city taxes per capita: $159 (1997); City property taxes per capita: $136 (1997).

Education: High school graduation rate: 84.0% (2000); College graduation rate: 20.1% (2000).

School District(s)

East Grand Forks (PK-12)
2000 Enrollment: 1,905 218-773-3494

Two-year College(s)

Northwest Technical College-East Grand Forks (Public)
2001 Enrollment: n/a 218-773-3441

Housing: Homeownership rate: 66.9% (2000); Median home value: $96,100 (2000); Median rent: $410 per month (2000); Median age of housing: 28 years (2000).

Safety: Violent crime rate: 21.1 per 10,000 population; Property crime rate: 451.1 per 10,000 population (2001).

Newspapers: The Exponent (1 x week)

Transportation: Commute to work: 93.5% car, 0.8% public transportation, 2.0% walk, 2.8% work from home (2000); Travel time to work: 57.3% less than 15 minutes, 34.1% 15 to 30 minutes, 5.1% 30 to 45 minutes, 1.5% 45 to 60 minutes, 2.1% 60 minutes or more (2000)

Additional Information Contacts

East Grand Forks Chamber of Commerce 218-773-7481

EDEN (township). Covers a land area of 35.145 square miles and a water area of 1.105 square miles. Located at 47.71° N. Lat.; 95.65° W. Long.

Population: 215 (2000); Race: 98.9% White, 0.0% Black, 0.0% Asian, 1.1% American Indian and Alaska Native, 0.0% Hispanic of any race, 0.0% two or more races (2000); Density: 6.1 persons per square mile (2000); Age: 26.5% under 18, 14.8% over 64 (2000); Marriage status: 21.5% never married, 74.5% now married, 2.7% widowed, 1.3% divorced (2000); Foreign born: 1.1% (2000); Ancestry (includes multiple ancestries): 58.2% Norwegian, 40.2% German, 12.2% Swedish, 7.4% Scandinavian, 5.3% English (2000).

Economy: Employment by occupation: 27.3% management, 6.8% professional, 14.8% services, 30.7% sales, 5.7% farming, 2.3% construction, 12.5% production (2000).

Income: Per capita income: $11,713 (2000); Median household income: $29,375 (2000); Poverty rate: 15.9% (2000).

Taxes: Total city taxes per capita: $89 (1997); City property taxes per capita: $89 (1997).

Education: High school graduation rate: 84.0% (2000); College graduation rate: 8.8% (2000).

Housing: Homeownership rate: 86.3% (2000); Median home value: $30,800 (2000); Median age of housing: 60+ years (2000).

Transportation: Commute to work: 65.1% car, 0.0% public transportation, 7.0% walk, 27.9% work from home (2000); Travel time to work: 33.9% less than 15 minutes, 32.3% 15 to 30 minutes, 6.5% 30 to 45 minutes, 0.0% 45 to 60 minutes, 27.4% 60 minutes or more (2000)

ERSKINE (city). Covers a land area of 0.741 square miles and a water area of 0.273 square miles. Located at 47.66° N. Lat.; 96.01° W. Long. Elevation is 1,193 feet.

Population: 437 (2000); Race: 93.8% White, 0.0% Black, 0.0% Asian, 5.0% American Indian and Alaska Native, 0.7% Hispanic of any race, 0.9% two or more races (2000); Density: 590.0 persons per square mile (2000); Age: 28.9% under 18, 25.8% over 64 (2000); Marriage status: 23.4% never married, 49.2% now married, 15.9% widowed, 11.5% divorced (2000); Foreign born: 0.7% (2000); Ancestry (includes multiple ancestries): 53.8% Norwegian, 14.2% German, 14.0% Swedish, 8.3% Other groups, 4.0% Irish (2000).

Economy: Railroad junction. Agriculture: wheat, potatoes, sunflowers; dairying. Manufacturing: drill hitches, pallets. Single-family building permits issued: 0 (2001) / 0 (2000); Multi-family building permits issued: 0 (2001) / 0 (2000); Employment by occupation: 7.8% management, 12.6% professional, 28.7% services, 16.8% sales, 1.2% farming, 9.6% construction, 23.4% production (2000).

Income: Per capita income: $18,122 (2000); Median household income: $26,771 (2000); Poverty rate: 18.1% (2000).

Taxes: Total city taxes per capita: $257 (1997); City property taxes per capita: $249 (1997).

Education: High school graduation rate: 77.0% (2000); College graduation rate: 7.2% (2000).

School District(s)

Win-E-Mac (PK-12)
2000 Enrollment: 499 218-687-2236

Housing: Homeownership rate: 60.3% (2000); Median home value: $28,800 (2000); Median rent: $272 per month (2000); Median age of housing: 45 years (2000).

Newspapers: The Erskine Echo (1 x week)

Transportation: Commute to work: 90.4% car, 0.0% public transportation, 5.4% walk, 4.2% work from home (2000); Travel time to work: 62.5% less than 15 minutes, 11.9% 15 to 30 minutes, 13.1% 30 to 45 minutes, 4.4% 45 to 60 minutes, 8.1% 60 minutes or more (2000)

ESTHER (township). Covers a land area of 19.137 square miles and a water area of 0.243 square miles. Located at 48.05° N. Lat.; 97.05° W. Long.

Population: 158 (2000); Race: 98.0% White, 2.0% Black, 0.0% Asian, 0.0% American Indian and Alaska Native, 0.0% Hispanic of any race, 0.0% two or more races (2000); Density: 8.3 persons per square mile (2000); Age: 19.7% under 18, 17.8% over 64 (2000); Marriage status: 19.4% never married, 72.1% now married, 1.6% widowed, 7.0% divorced (2000); Foreign born: 1.3% (2000); Ancestry (includes multiple ancestries): 44.7% Norwegian, 23.0% German, 11.8% Swedish, 10.5% French (except Basque), 7.9% United States or American (2000).

Economy: Employment by occupation: 6.9% management, 23.0% professional, 12.6% services, 21.8% sales, 0.0% farming, 11.5% construction, 24.1% production (2000).

Income: Per capita income: $20,997 (2000); Median household income: $46,563 (2000); Poverty rate: 8.6% (2000).

Taxes: Total city taxes per capita: $63 (1997); City property taxes per capita: $63 (1997).

Education: High school graduation rate: 86.8% (2000); College graduation rate: 15.8% (2000).

Housing: Homeownership rate: 75.8% (2000); Median home value: $77,700 (2000); Median rent: $233 per month (2000); Median age of housing: 38 years (2000).

Transportation: Commute to work: 88.5% car, 0.0% public transportation, 4.6% walk, 6.9% work from home (2000); Travel time to work: 14.8% less than 15 minutes, 37.0% 15 to 30 minutes, 44.4% 30 to 45 minutes, 1.2% 45 to 60 minutes, 2.5% 60 minutes or more (2000)

EUCLID (township). Covers a land area of 35.559 square miles and a water area of 0 square miles. Located at 47.97° N. Lat.; 96.66° W. Long. Elevation is 891 feet.

Population: 149 (2000); Race: 100.0% White, 0.0% Black, 0.0% Asian, 0.0% American Indian and Alaska Native, 0.0% Hispanic of any race, 0.0% two or more races (2000); Density: 4.2 persons per square mile (2000); Age: 15.8% under 18, 22.0% over 64 (2000); Marriage status: 30.8% never married, 59.6% now married, 5.1% widowed, 4.5% divorced (2000); Foreign born: 0.0% (2000); Ancestry (includes multiple ancestries): 41.8% German, 26.0% Norwegian, 18.1% Irish, 15.8% French (except Basque), 8.5% Czech (2000).

Economy: Employment by occupation: 14.1% management, 25.0% professional, 10.9% services, 16.3% sales, 6.5% farming, 9.8% construction, 17.4% production (2000).

Income: Per capita income: $19,901 (2000); Median household income: $48,438 (2000); Poverty rate: 4.0% (2000).

Taxes: Total city taxes per capita: $164 (1997); City property taxes per capita: $164 (1997).

Education: High school graduation rate: 80.4% (2000); College graduation rate: 8.0% (2000).

Housing: Homeownership rate: 92.2% (2000); Median home value: $39,400 (2000); Median rent: $175 per month (2000); Median age of housing: 37 years (2000).

Transportation: Commute to work: 94.4% car, 0.0% public transportation, 0.0% walk, 5.6% work from home (2000); Travel time to work: 9.4% less than 15 minutes, 62.4% 15 to 30 minutes, 21.2% 30 to 45 minutes, 2.4% 45 to 60 minutes, 4.7% 60 minutes or more (2000)

FAIRFAX (township). Covers a land area of 35.976 square miles and a water area of 0 square miles. Located at 47.72° N. Lat.; 96.56° W. Long.
Population: 213 (2000); Race: 97.0% White, 0.0% Black, 0.0% Asian, 3.0% American Indian and Alaska Native, 0.0% Hispanic of any race, 0.0% two or more races (2000); Density: 5.9 persons per square mile (2000); Age: 28.6% under 18, 25.1% over 64 (2000); Marriage status: 26.6% never married, 65.8% now married, 3.8% widowed, 3.8% divorced (2000); Foreign born: 0.0% (2000); Ancestry (includes multiple ancestries): 36.9% German, 26.1% Norwegian, 16.7% French (except Basque), 8.9% Swedish, 6.9% French Canadian (2000).
Economy: Employment by occupation: 17.4% management, 9.3% professional, 12.8% services, 26.7% sales, 2.3% farming, 14.0% construction, 17.4% production (2000).
Income: Per capita income: $15,402 (2000); Median household income: $43,214 (2000); Poverty rate: 22.2% (2000).
Taxes: Total city taxes per capita: $132 (1997); City property taxes per capita: $132 (1997).
Education: High school graduation rate: 89.8% (2000); College graduation rate: 19.0% (2000).
Housing: Homeownership rate: 87.9% (2000); Median home value: $95,000 (2000); Median rent: $350 per month (2000); Median age of housing: 42 years (2000).
Transportation: Commute to work: 92.9% car, 0.0% public transportation, 0.0% walk, 7.1% work from home (2000); Travel time to work: 65.8% less than 15 minutes, 34.2% 15 to 30 minutes, 0.0% 30 to 45 minutes, 0.0% 45 to 60 minutes, 0.0% 60 minutes or more (2000)

FANNY (township). Covers a land area of 35.737 square miles and a water area of 0 square miles. Located at 47.89° N. Lat.; 96.67° W. Long.
Population: 105 (2000); Race: 100.0% White, 0.0% Black, 0.0% Asian, 0.0% American Indian and Alaska Native, 0.0% Hispanic of any race, 0.0% two or more races (2000); Density: 2.9 persons per square mile (2000); Age: 40.2% under 18, 6.9% over 64 (2000); Marriage status: 21.4% never married, 70.0% now married, 8.6% widowed, 0.0% divorced (2000); Foreign born: 0.0% (2000); Ancestry (includes multiple ancestries): 53.9% German, 23.5% Norwegian, 20.6% Irish, 8.8% Polish, 6.9% Czech (2000).
Economy: Employment by occupation: 28.0% management, 26.0% professional, 8.0% services, 22.0% sales, 0.0% farming, 12.0% construction, 4.0% production (2000).
Income: Per capita income: $27,809 (2000); Median household income: $59,063 (2000); Poverty rate: 0.0% (2000).
Taxes: Total city taxes per capita: $190 (1997); City property taxes per capita: $190 (1997).
Education: High school graduation rate: 91.2% (2000); College graduation rate: 38.6% (2000).
Housing: Homeownership rate: 87.1% (2000); Median home value: $152,500 (2000); Median rent: $275 per month (2000); Median age of housing: 35 years (2000).
Transportation: Commute to work: 88.0% car, 0.0% public transportation, 4.0% walk, 8.0% work from home (2000); Travel time to work: 15.2% less than 15 minutes, 39.1% 15 to 30 minutes, 45.7% 30 to 45 minutes, 0.0% 45 to 60 minutes, 0.0% 60 minutes or more (2000)

FARLEY (township). Covers a land area of 27.075 square miles and a water area of 0 square miles. Located at 48.14° N. Lat.; 96.81° W. Long.
Population: 50 (2000); Race: 100.0% White, 0.0% Black, 0.0% Asian, 0.0% American Indian and Alaska Native, 0.0% Hispanic of any race, 0.0% two or more races (2000); Density: 1.8 persons per square mile (2000); Age: 18.9% under 18, 21.6% over 64 (2000); Marriage status: 18.8% never married, 71.9% now married, 6.3% widowed, 3.1% divorced (2000); Foreign born: 0.0% (2000); Ancestry (includes multiple ancestries): 40.5% Norwegian, 16.2% German, 10.8% Swedish, 10.8% United States or American, 10.8% Slovak (2000).
Economy: Employment by occupation: 16.7% management, 22.2% professional, 27.8% services, 16.7% sales, 0.0% farming, 16.7% construction, 0.0% production (2000).
Income: Per capita income: $18,032 (2000); Median household income: $43,125 (2000); Poverty rate: 10.8% (2000).
Taxes: Total city taxes per capita: $379 (1997); City property taxes per capita: $379 (1997).
Education: High school graduation rate: 93.3% (2000); College graduation rate: 30.0% (2000).
Housing: Homeownership rate: 100.0% (2000); Median home value: $50,000 (2000); Median age of housing: 60+ years (2000).
Transportation: Commute to work: 88.9% car, 0.0% public transportation, 0.0% walk, 11.1% work from home (2000); Travel time to work: 68.8% less than 15 minutes, 12.5% 15 to 30 minutes, 6.3% 30 to 45 minutes, 12.5% 45 to 60 minutes, 0.0% 60 minutes or more (2000)

FERTILE (city). Covers a land area of 1.893 square miles and a water area of 0 square miles. Located at 47.53° N. Lat.; 96.28° W. Long. Elevation is 1,144 feet.
Population: 893 (2000); Race: 97.3% White, 0.0% Black, 1.2% Asian, 0.2% American Indian and Alaska Native, 0.0% Hispanic of any race, 1.2% two or more races (2000); Density: 471.9 persons per square mile (2000); Age: 20.4% under 18, 38.3% over 64 (2000); Marriage status: 20.5% never married, 50.7% now married, 21.0% widowed, 7.8% divorced (2000); Foreign born: 1.2% (2000); Ancestry (includes multiple ancestries): 69.7% Norwegian, 17.9% German, 10.0% Swedish, 5.0% Other groups, 3.7% French (except Basque) (2000).
Economy: Railroad terminus. Diversified farming area: grain, sunflowers, potatoes; dairying; poultry, livestock. Single-family building permits issued: 1 (2001) / 5 (2000); Multi-family building permits issued: 0 (2001) / 0 (2000); Employment by occupation: 8.3% management, 17.9% professional, 19.2% services, 21.5% sales, 5.3% farming, 8.9% construction, 18.9% production (2000).
Income: Per capita income: $14,866 (2000); Median household income: $23,021 (2000); Poverty rate: 17.0% (2000).
Taxes: Total city taxes per capita: $148 (1997); City property taxes per capita: $142 (1997).
Education: High school graduation rate: 69.0% (2000); College graduation rate: 13.1% (2000).

School District(s)

Fertile-Beltrami (PK-12)
2000 Enrollment: 592 218-945-6933
Housing: Homeownership rate: 72.7% (2000); Median home value: $49,400 (2000); Median rent: $273 per month (2000); Median age of housing: 44 years (2000).
Newspapers: The Fertile Journal (1 x week)
Transportation: Commute to work: 83.6% car, 0.7% public transportation, 8.4% walk, 6.0% work from home (2000); Travel time to work: 51.4% less than 15 minutes, 13.9% 15 to 30 minutes, 25.0% 30 to 45 minutes, 3.2% 45 to 60 minutes, 6.4% 60 minutes or more (2000)

FISHER (city). Covers a land area of 0.398 square miles and a water area of 0 square miles. Located at 47.80° N. Lat.; 96.80° W. Long. Elevation is 853 feet.
Population: 435 (2000); Race: 98.3% White, 0.0% Black, 0.0% Asian, 0.0% American Indian and Alaska Native, 2.2% Hispanic of any race, 1.0% two or more races (2000); Density: 1,092.3 persons per square mile (2000); Age: 26.6% under 18, 15.2% over 64 (2000); Marriage status: 21.6% never married, 61.8% now married, 10.0% widowed, 6.6% divorced (2000); Foreign born: 1.5% (2000); Ancestry (includes multiple ancestries): 52.5% Norwegian, 28.9% German, 7.5% Irish, 6.5% Swedish, 5.7% English (2000).
Economy: Single-family building permits issued: 0 (2001) / 0 (2000); Multi-family building permits issued: 0 (2001) / 0 (2000); Employment by occupation: 10.5% management, 21.1% professional, 11.1% services, 26.8% sales, 0.0% farming, 15.3% construction, 15.3% production (2000).
Income: Per capita income: $19,083 (2000); Median household income: $38,750 (2000); Poverty rate: 6.8% (2000).
Taxes: Total city taxes per capita: $85 (1997); City property taxes per capita: $83 (1997).
Education: High school graduation rate: 88.3% (2000); College graduation rate: 16.7% (2000).

School District(s)

Fisher (PK-12)
2000 Enrollment: 282 218-891-4105
Housing: Homeownership rate: 69.7% (2000); Median home value: $64,600 (2000); Median rent: $329 per month (2000); Median age of housing: 33 years (2000).
Transportation: Commute to work: 84.9% car, 0.5% public transportation, 10.2% walk, 3.8% work from home (2000); Travel time to work: 35.8% less than 15 minutes, 34.1% 15 to 30 minutes, 24.6% 30 to 45 minutes, 3.9% 45 to 60 minutes, 1.7% 60 minutes or more (2000)

FISHER (township). Covers a land area of 35.562 square miles and a water area of 0 square miles. Located at 47.80° N. Lat.; 96.80° W. Long. Elevation is 853 feet.
Population: 219 (2000); Race: 96.8% White, 0.0% Black, 0.0% Asian, 0.0% American Indian and Alaska Native, 3.2% Hispanic of any race, 0.0% two or

more races (2000); Density: 6.2 persons per square mile (2000); Age: 35.3% under 18, 8.1% over 64 (2000); Marriage status: 26.3% never married, 64.7% now married, 5.8% widowed, 3.2% divorced (2000); Foreign born: 2.7% (2000); Ancestry (includes multiple ancestries): 57.0% German, 44.8% Norwegian, 14.5% French (except Basque), 8.1% English, 5.0% Irish (2000).
Economy: Grain, potatoes, sunflowers; livestock; dairying. Employment by occupation: 32.7% management, 21.8% professional, 5.0% services, 16.8% sales, 9.9% farming, 5.0% construction, 8.9% production (2000).
Income: Per capita income: $21,074 (2000); Median household income: $65,000 (2000); Poverty rate: 0.5% (2000).
Taxes: Total city taxes per capita: $123 (1997); City property taxes per capita: $123 (1997).
Education: High school graduation rate: 92.1% (2000); College graduation rate: 11.8% (2000).
Housing: Homeownership rate: 85.7% (2000); Median home value: $89,200 (2000); Median rent: $308 per month (2000); Median age of housing: 51 years (2000).
Transportation: Commute to work: 83.5% car, 0.0% public transportation, 2.1% walk, 14.4% work from home (2000); Travel time to work: 47.0% less than 15 minutes, 42.2% 15 to 30 minutes, 9.6% 30 to 45 minutes, 1.2% 45 to 60 minutes, 0.0% 60 minutes or more (2000)

FOSSTON (city). Covers a land area of 1.625 square miles and a water area of 0.020 square miles. Located at 47.57° N. Lat.; 95.74° W. Long. Elevation is 1,298 feet.
History: Fosston was settled in the early 1880's. The early economy depended on potatoes, with some flax also grown on the drained marsh land.
Population: 1,575 (2000); Race: 96.9% White, 0.2% Black, 0.9% Asian, 0.9% American Indian and Alaska Native, 0.8% Hispanic of any race, 1.0% two or more races (2000); Density: 969.1 persons per square mile (2000); Age: 22.9% under 18, 28.0% over 64 (2000); Marriage status: 27.0% never married, 45.9% now married, 15.6% widowed, 11.5% divorced (2000); Foreign born: 1.6% (2000); Ancestry (includes multiple ancestries): 50.4% Norwegian, 18.7% German, 14.1% Swedish, 6.5% Irish, 3.8% English (2000).
Economy: Single-family building permits issued: 1 (2001) / 3 (2000); Multi-family building permits issued: 0 (2001) / 0 (2000); Employment by occupation: 11.6% management, 21.0% professional, 18.2% services, 22.1% sales, 1.5% farming, 10.4% construction, 15.1% production (2000).
Income: Per capita income: $17,064 (2000); Median household income: $27,634 (2000); Poverty rate: 14.9% (2000).
Taxes: Total city taxes per capita: $127 (1997); City property taxes per capita: $125 (1997).
Education: High school graduation rate: 74.7% (2000); College graduation rate: 14.1% (2000).

School District(s)

Fosston (PK-12)
2000 Enrollment: 682 218-435-6335
Housing: Homeownership rate: 66.6% (2000); Median home value: $54,500 (2000); Median rent: $319 per month (2000); Median age of housing: 43 years (2000).
Hospitals: First Care Medical Services (43 beds)
Newspapers: The Thirteen Towns (1 x week)
Transportation: Commute to work: 81.5% car, 3.3% public transportation, 9.6% walk, 4.8% work from home (2000); Travel time to work: 72.7% less than 15 minutes, 14.6% 15 to 30 minutes, 5.7% 30 to 45 minutes, 2.1% 45 to 60 minutes, 4.9% 60 minutes or more (2000)

GARDEN (township). Covers a land area of 33.792 square miles and a water area of 1.837 square miles. Located at 47.54° N. Lat.; 96.12° W. Long.
Population: 227 (2000); Race: 100.0% White, 0.0% Black, 0.0% Asian, 0.0% American Indian and Alaska Native, 0.0% Hispanic of any race, 0.0% two or more races (2000); Density: 6.7 persons per square mile (2000); Age: 24.3% under 18, 13.3% over 64 (2000); Marriage status: 19.0% never married, 71.8% now married, 3.4% widowed, 5.7% divorced (2000); Foreign born: 0.0% (2000); Ancestry (includes multiple ancestries): 66.5% Norwegian, 20.6% German, 18.8% Swedish, 5.0% Irish, 2.8% French Canadian (2000).
Economy: Employment by occupation: 17.6% management, 9.3% professional, 16.7% services, 18.5% sales, 1.9% farming, 13.0% construction, 23.1% production (2000).
Income: Per capita income: $16,056 (2000); Median household income: $39,583 (2000); Poverty rate: 7.8% (2000).
Taxes: Total city taxes per capita: $151 (1997); City property taxes per capita: $151 (1997).
Education: High school graduation rate: 80.8% (2000); College graduation rate: 14.1% (2000).
Housing: Homeownership rate: 91.8% (2000); Median home value: $52,500 (2000); Median rent: $175 per month (2000); Median age of housing: 60+ years (2000).
Transportation: Commute to work: 79.6% car, 0.0% public transportation, 0.0% walk, 20.4% work from home (2000); Travel time to work: 26.7% less than 15 minutes, 33.7% 15 to 30 minutes, 12.8% 30 to 45 minutes, 17.4% 45 to 60 minutes, 9.3% 60 minutes or more (2000)

GARFIELD (township). Covers a land area of 33.117 square miles and a water area of 0.756 square miles. Located at 47.54° N. Lat.; 96.26° W. Long.
Population: 391 (2000); Race: 95.4% White, 0.0% Black, 2.3% Asian, 1.8% American Indian and Alaska Native, 0.0% Hispanic of any race, 0.5% two or more races (2000); Density: 11.8 persons per square mile (2000); Age: 27.0% under 18, 15.3% over 64 (2000); Marriage status: 17.5% never married, 76.5% now married, 2.0% widowed, 4.0% divorced (2000); Foreign born: 2.3% (2000); Ancestry (includes multiple ancestries): 69.7% Norwegian, 21.1% German, 8.7% French (except Basque), 7.4% Irish, 5.3% Swedish (2000).
Economy: Employment by occupation: 13.1% management, 18.0% professional, 15.3% services, 22.4% sales, 4.4% farming, 18.6% construction, 8.2% production (2000).
Income: Per capita income: $15,760 (2000); Median household income: $32,292 (2000); Poverty rate: 9.7% (2000).
Taxes: Total city taxes per capita: $87 (2000); City property taxes per capita: $87 (2000).
Education: High school graduation rate: 89.6% (2000); College graduation rate: 17.2% (2000).
Housing: Homeownership rate: 92.5% (2000); Median home value: $76,700 (2000); Median rent: $358 per month (2000); Median age of housing: 31 years (2000).
Transportation: Commute to work: 84.5% car, 0.0% public transportation, 2.9% walk, 12.6% work from home (2000); Travel time to work: 34.2% less than 15 minutes, 19.1% 15 to 30 minutes, 36.2% 30 to 45 minutes, 5.3% 45 to 60 minutes, 5.3% 60 minutes or more (2000)

GENTILLY (township). Covers a land area of 32.024 square miles and a water area of 0 square miles. Located at 47.79° N. Lat.; 96.40° W. Long.
Population: 319 (2000); Race: 97.0% White, 0.0% Black, 0.0% Asian, 1.8% American Indian and Alaska Native, 2.1% Hispanic of any race, 0.0% two or more races (2000); Density: 10.0 persons per square mile (2000); Age: 31.6% under 18, 9.4% over 64 (2000); Marriage status: 22.3% never married, 70.0% now married, 5.3% widowed, 2.4% divorced (2000); Foreign born: 0.6% (2000); Ancestry (includes multiple ancestries): 26.7% French (except Basque), 26.1% Norwegian, 20.7% German, 19.5% French Canadian, 10.0% Irish (2000).
Economy: Employment by occupation: 5.5% management, 12.1% professional, 18.8% services, 26.1% sales, 1.2% farming, 15.8% construction, 20.6% production (2000).
Income: Per capita income: $15,313 (2000); Median household income: $34,583 (2000); Poverty rate: 7.3% (2000).
Taxes: Total city taxes per capita: $44 (1997); City property taxes per capita: $44 (1997).
Education: High school graduation rate: 91.6% (2000); College graduation rate: 9.4% (2000).
Housing: Homeownership rate: 91.5% (2000); Median home value: $60,000 (2000); Median rent: $263 per month (2000); Median age of housing: 49 years (2000).
Transportation: Commute to work: 86.7% car, 0.0% public transportation, 3.6% walk, 8.5% work from home (2000); Travel time to work: 29.8% less than 15 minutes, 58.9% 15 to 30 minutes, 3.3% 30 to 45 minutes, 2.0% 45 to 60 minutes, 6.0% 60 minutes or more (2000)

GODFREY (township). Covers a land area of 34.464 square miles and a water area of 1.479 square miles. Located at 47.63° N. Lat.; 96.22° W. Long.
Population: 327 (2000); Race: 99.0% White, 0.0% Black, 0.0% Asian, 0.0% American Indian and Alaska Native, 0.0% Hispanic of any race, 1.0% two or more races (2000); Density: 9.5 persons per square mile (2000); Age: 23.2% under 18, 15.3% over 64 (2000); Marriage status: 19.9% never married, 67.8% now married, 9.2% widowed, 3.1% divorced (2000); Foreign born: 0.0% (2000); Ancestry (includes multiple ancestries): 69.4% Norwegian, 23.9% German, 14.3% Swedish, 8.0% French (except Basque), 4.8% Czech (2000).

Economy: Employment by occupation: 16.8% management, 16.8% professional, 13.9% services, 16.8% sales, 6.4% farming, 11.0% construction, 18.5% production (2000).
Income: Per capita income: $25,283 (2000); Median household income: $42,273 (2000); Poverty rate: 1.9% (2000).
Taxes: Total city taxes per capita: $76 (1997); City property taxes per capita: $76 (1997).
Education: High school graduation rate: 88.0% (2000); College graduation rate: 18.9% (2000).
Housing: Homeownership rate: 80.2% (2000); Median home value: $117,700 (2000); Median rent: $375 per month (2000); Median age of housing: 36 years (2000).
Transportation: Commute to work: 83.8% car, 0.0% public transportation, 1.2% walk, 13.8% work from home (2000); Travel time to work: 29.2% less than 15 minutes, 36.8% 15 to 30 minutes, 21.5% 30 to 45 minutes, 4.2% 45 to 60 minutes, 8.3% 60 minutes or more (2000)

GRAND FORKS (township). Covers a land area of 14.182 square miles and a water area of 0.121 square miles. Located at 47.98° N. Lat.; 97.03° W. Long.
Population: 231 (2000); Race: 99.0% White, 0.0% Black, 0.0% Asian, 0.0% American Indian and Alaska Native, 1.0% Hispanic of any race, 1.0% two or more races (2000); Density: 16.3 persons per square mile (2000); Age: 27.7% under 18, 23.3% over 64 (2000); Marriage status: 17.0% never married, 68.0% now married, 7.8% widowed, 7.2% divorced (2000); Foreign born: 0.0% (2000); Ancestry (includes multiple ancestries): 55.4% Norwegian, 19.8% German, 12.4% French (except Basque), 10.9% Swedish, 6.9% Irish (2000).
Economy: Employment by occupation: 17.8% management, 17.8% professional, 11.1% services, 20.0% sales, 0.0% farming, 24.4% construction, 8.9% production (2000).
Income: Per capita income: $22,214 (2000); Median household income: $51,667 (2000); Poverty rate: 4.0% (2000).
Taxes: Total city taxes per capita: $45 (1997); City property taxes per capita: $45 (1997).
Education: High school graduation rate: 74.3% (2000); College graduation rate: 22.1% (2000).
Housing: Homeownership rate: 100.0% (2000); Median home value: $103,800 (2000); Median age of housing: 33 years (2000).
Transportation: Commute to work: 81.1% car, 0.0% public transportation, 5.6% walk, 13.3% work from home (2000); Travel time to work: 43.6% less than 15 minutes, 41.0% 15 to 30 minutes, 11.5% 30 to 45 minutes, 0.0% 45 to 60 minutes, 3.8% 60 minutes or more (2000)

GROVE PARK-TILDEN (township). Covers a land area of 69.293 square miles and a water area of 0.778 square miles. Located at 47.70° N. Lat.; 96.19° W. Long.
Population: 311 (2000); Race: 99.7% White, 0.0% Black, 0.0% Asian, 0.0% American Indian and Alaska Native, 0.0% Hispanic of any race, 0.3% two or more races (2000); Density: 4.5 persons per square mile (2000); Age: 25.6% under 18, 22.5% over 64 (2000); Marriage status: 18.8% never married, 67.6% now married, 9.8% widowed, 3.9% divorced (2000); Foreign born: 1.6% (2000); Ancestry (includes multiple ancestries): 47.5% Norwegian, 37.8% German, 13.8% French (except Basque), 9.7% Swedish, 5.9% French Canadian (2000).
Economy: Employment by occupation: 12.2% management, 7.6% professional, 12.2% services, 29.8% sales, 4.6% farming, 12.2% construction, 21.4% production (2000).
Income: Per capita income: $16,342 (2000); Median household income: $39,375 (2000); Poverty rate: 0.6% (2000).
Taxes: Total city taxes per capita: $135 (1997); City property taxes per capita: $135 (1997).
Education: High school graduation rate: 73.3% (2000); College graduation rate: 18.6% (2000).
Housing: Homeownership rate: 91.1% (2000); Median home value: $94,000 (2000); Median age of housing: 33 years (2000).
Transportation: Commute to work: 96.0% car, 0.0% public transportation, 0.0% walk, 4.0% work from home (2000); Travel time to work: 33.9% less than 15 minutes, 22.3% 15 to 30 minutes, 35.5% 30 to 45 minutes, 0.0% 45 to 60 minutes, 8.3% 60 minutes or more (2000)

GULLY (city). Covers a land area of 2.010 square miles and a water area of 0.009 square miles. Located at 47.76° N. Lat.; 95.62° W. Long.
Population: 106 (2000); Race: 96.8% White, 0.0% Black, 0.0% Asian, 0.0% American Indian and Alaska Native, 0.0% Hispanic of any race, 3.2% two or more races (2000); Density: 52.7 persons per square mile (2000); Age: 17.9% under 18, 30.5% over 64 (2000); Marriage status: 11.5% never married, 61.5% now married, 9.0% widowed, 17.9% divorced (2000); Foreign born: 2.1% (2000); Ancestry (includes multiple ancestries): 62.1% Norwegian, 24.2% Swedish, 8.4% Irish, 6.3% German, 4.2% Czech (2000).
Economy: Employment by occupation: 19.4% management, 0.0% professional, 6.5% services, 25.8% sales, 22.6% farming, 19.4% construction, 6.5% production (2000).
Income: Per capita income: $11,644 (2000); Median household income: $17,500 (2000); Poverty rate: 16.8% (2000).
Taxes: Total city taxes per capita: $87 (1997); City property taxes per capita: $71 (1997).
Education: High school graduation rate: 58.7% (2000); College graduation rate: 8.0% (2000).
Housing: Homeownership rate: 92.5% (2000); Median home value: $18,200 (2000); Median rent: $225 per month (2000); Median age of housing: 50 years (2000).
Transportation: Commute to work: 100.0% car, 0.0% public transportation, 0.0% walk, 0.0% work from home (2000); Travel time to work: 64.5% less than 15 minutes, 6.5% 15 to 30 minutes, 9.7% 30 to 45 minutes, 12.9% 45 to 60 minutes, 6.5% 60 minutes or more (2000)

GULLY (township). Covers a land area of 32.845 square miles and a water area of 0 square miles. Located at 47.79° N. Lat.; 95.66° W. Long.
Population: 99 (2000); Race: 99.1% White, 0.0% Black, 0.0% Asian, 0.9% American Indian and Alaska Native, 0.0% Hispanic of any race, 0.0% two or more races (2000); Density: 3.0 persons per square mile (2000); Age: 19.8% under 18, 7.5% over 64 (2000); Marriage status: 23.6% never married, 74.2% now married, 0.0% widowed, 2.2% divorced (2000); Foreign born: 0.0% (2000); Ancestry (includes multiple ancestries): 61.3% Norwegian, 17.9% German, 6.6% Irish, 5.7% English, 1.9% Other groups (2000).
Economy: Grain, sunflowers; dairying. Manufacturing: fertilizers. Employment by occupation: 30.8% management, 15.4% professional, 13.5% services, 17.3% sales, 13.5% farming, 0.0% construction, 9.6% production (2000).
Income: Per capita income: $13,039 (2000); Median household income: $23,750 (2000); Poverty rate: 4.7% (2000).
Taxes: Total city taxes per capita: $301 (1997); City property taxes per capita: $301 (1997).
Education: High school graduation rate: 90.1% (2000); College graduation rate: 15.5% (2000).
Housing: Homeownership rate: 92.3% (2000); Median home value: $42,500 (2000); Median age of housing: 34 years (2000).
Transportation: Commute to work: 59.6% car, 0.0% public transportation, 3.8% walk, 36.5% work from home (2000); Travel time to work: 39.4% less than 15 minutes, 18.2% 15 to 30 minutes, 33.3% 30 to 45 minutes, 9.1% 45 to 60 minutes, 0.0% 60 minutes or more (2000)

HAMMOND (township). Covers a land area of 36.326 square miles and a water area of 0 square miles. Located at 47.63° N. Lat.; 96.63° W. Long.
Population: 57 (2000); Race: 100.0% White, 0.0% Black, 0.0% Asian, 0.0% American Indian and Alaska Native, 0.0% Hispanic of any race, 0.0% two or more races (2000); Density: 1.6 persons per square mile (2000); Age: 22.2% under 18, 27.8% over 64 (2000); Marriage status: 33.3% never married, 56.9% now married, 9.8% widowed, 0.0% divorced (2000); Foreign born: 0.0% (2000); Ancestry (includes multiple ancestries): 64.8% Norwegian, 50.0% German, 11.1% Irish, 11.1% Swedish, 9.3% Scottish (2000).
Economy: Employment by occupation: 30.0% management, 45.0% professional, 20.0% services, 0.0% sales, 0.0% farming, 5.0% construction, 0.0% production (2000).
Income: Per capita income: $24,863 (2000); Median household income: $48,125 (2000); Poverty rate: 0.0% (2000).
Taxes: Total city taxes per capita: $828 (1997); City property taxes per capita: $828 (1997).
Education: High school graduation rate: 75.7% (2000); College graduation rate: 16.2% (2000).
Housing: Homeownership rate: 75.0% (2000); Median home value: $90,000 (2000); Median rent: $342 per month (2000); Median age of housing: 46 years (2000).
Transportation: Commute to work: 90.0% car, 0.0% public transportation, 0.0% walk, 10.0% work from home (2000); Travel time to work: 11.1% less than 15 minutes, 55.6% 15 to 30 minutes, 27.8% 30 to 45 minutes, 0.0% 45 to 60 minutes, 5.6% 60 minutes or more (2000)

HELGELAND (township). Covers a land area of 27.068 square miles and a water area of 0 square miles. Located at 48.14° N. Lat.; 96.58° W. Long.

Population: 52 (2000); Race: 100.0% White, 0.0% Black, 0.0% Asian, 0.0% American Indian and Alaska Native, 0.0% Hispanic of any race, 0.0% two or more races (2000); Density: 1.9 persons per square mile (2000); Age: 27.5% under 18, 25.0% over 64 (2000); Marriage status: 19.4% never married, 74.2% now married, 6.5% widowed, 0.0% divorced (2000); Foreign born: 0.0% (2000); Ancestry (includes multiple ancestries): 57.5% Norwegian, 52.5% German, 15.0% Swedish, 5.0% Czech (2000).
Economy: Employment by occupation: 26.7% management, 13.3% professional, 33.3% services, 13.3% sales, 13.3% farming, 0.0% construction, 0.0% production (2000).
Income: Per capita income: $14,768 (2000); Median household income: $43,750 (2000); Poverty rate: 0.0% (2000).
Taxes: Total city taxes per capita: $136 (1997); City property taxes per capita: $136 (1997).
Education: High school graduation rate: 63.0% (2000); College graduation rate: 25.9% (2000).
Housing: Homeownership rate: 100.0% (2000); Median home value: $112,500 (2000); Median age of housing: 32 years (2000).
Transportation: Commute to work: 100.0% car, 0.0% public transportation, 0.0% walk, 0.0% work from home (2000); Travel time to work: 26.7% less than 15 minutes, 40.0% 15 to 30 minutes, 33.3% 30 to 45 minutes, 0.0% 45 to 60 minutes, 0.0% 60 minutes or more (2000)

HIGDEM (township). Covers a land area of 23.237 square miles and a water area of 0.157 square miles. Located at 48.14° N. Lat.; 97.07° W. Long.
Population: 99 (2000); Race: 100.0% White, 0.0% Black, 0.0% Asian, 0.0% American Indian and Alaska Native, 0.0% Hispanic of any race, 0.0% two or more races (2000); Density: 4.3 persons per square mile (2000); Age: 20.6% under 18, 7.2% over 64 (2000); Marriage status: 16.3% never married, 77.5% now married, 0.0% widowed, 6.3% divorced (2000); Foreign born: 0.0% (2000); Ancestry (includes multiple ancestries): 67.0% Norwegian, 25.8% German, 22.7% Swedish, 8.2% Czech, 6.2% Irish (2000).
Economy: Employment by occupation: 14.8% management, 22.2% professional, 3.7% services, 27.8% sales, 13.0% farming, 13.0% construction, 5.6% production (2000).
Income: Per capita income: $18,333 (2000); Median household income: $46,563 (2000); Poverty rate: 10.3% (2000).
Taxes: Total city taxes per capita: $260 (1997); City property taxes per capita: $260 (1997).
Education: High school graduation rate: 94.1% (2000); College graduation rate: 14.7% (2000).
Housing: Homeownership rate: 74.4% (2000); Median home value: $72,500 (2000); Median rent: $358 per month (2000); Median age of housing: 46 years (2000).
Transportation: Commute to work: 77.8% car, 0.0% public transportation, 3.7% walk, 18.5% work from home (2000); Travel time to work: 38.6% less than 15 minutes, 18.2% 15 to 30 minutes, 29.5% 30 to 45 minutes, 9.1% 45 to 60 minutes, 4.5% 60 minutes or more (2000)

HILL RIVER (township). Covers a land area of 34.934 square miles and a water area of 1.333 square miles. Located at 47.71° N. Lat.; 95.77° W. Long.
Population: 162 (2000); Race: 99.0% White, 0.0% Black, 0.0% Asian, 0.0% American Indian and Alaska Native, 0.0% Hispanic of any race, 1.0% two or more races (2000); Density: 4.6 persons per square mile (2000); Age: 19.1% under 18, 13.9% over 64 (2000); Marriage status: 25.0% never married, 69.0% now married, 4.2% widowed, 1.8% divorced (2000); Foreign born: 0.0% (2000); Ancestry (includes multiple ancestries): 82.5% Norwegian, 14.4% Swedish, 12.4% German, 5.7% French Canadian, 4.6% Russian (2000).
Economy: Employment by occupation: 29.6% management, 5.1% professional, 5.1% services, 18.4% sales, 5.1% farming, 13.3% construction, 23.5% production (2000).
Income: Per capita income: $18,044 (2000); Median household income: $32,917 (2000); Poverty rate: 6.2% (2000).
Taxes: Total city taxes per capita: $58 (1997); City property taxes per capita: $58 (1997).
Education: High school graduation rate: 77.6% (2000); College graduation rate: 7.0% (2000).
Housing: Homeownership rate: 85.1% (2000); Median home value: $33,300 (2000); Median rent: $225 per month (2000); Median age of housing: 60+ years (2000).
Transportation: Commute to work: 74.0% car, 0.0% public transportation, 4.2% walk, 21.9% work from home (2000); Travel time to work: 28.0% less than 15 minutes, 57.3% 15 to 30 minutes, 4.0% 30 to 45 minutes, 5.3% 45 to 60 minutes, 5.3% 60 minutes or more (2000)

HUBBARD (township). Covers a land area of 41.347 square miles and a water area of 0.038 square miles. Located at 47.53° N. Lat.; 96.78° W. Long.
Population: 83 (2000); Race: 100.0% White, 0.0% Black, 0.0% Asian, 0.0% American Indian and Alaska Native, 0.0% Hispanic of any race, 0.0% two or more races (2000); Density: 2.0 persons per square mile (2000); Age: 21.7% under 18, 26.1% over 64 (2000); Marriage status: 25.3% never married, 56.0% now married, 13.3% widowed, 5.3% divorced (2000); Foreign born: 0.0% (2000); Ancestry (includes multiple ancestries): 75.0% Norwegian, 20.7% German, 5.4% Swedish, 2.2% Irish, 2.2% French (except Basque) (2000).
Economy: Employment by occupation: 23.5% management, 23.5% professional, 5.9% services, 17.6% sales, 5.9% farming, 17.6% construction, 5.9% production (2000).
Income: Per capita income: $20,561 (2000); Median household income: $43,438 (2000); Poverty rate: 3.3% (2000).
Taxes: Total city taxes per capita: $179 (1997); City property taxes per capita: $179 (1997).
Education: High school graduation rate: 83.1% (2000); College graduation rate: 9.9% (2000).
Housing: Homeownership rate: 84.6% (2000); Median home value: $109,400 (2000); Median age of housing: 60+ years (2000).
Transportation: Commute to work: 79.4% car, 0.0% public transportation, 0.0% walk, 14.7% work from home (2000); Travel time to work: 72.4% less than 15 minutes, 0.0% 15 to 30 minutes, 10.3% 30 to 45 minutes, 6.9% 45 to 60 minutes, 10.3% 60 minutes or more (2000)

HUNTSVILLE (township). Covers a land area of 35.541 square miles and a water area of 0.192 square miles. Located at 47.88° N. Lat.; 96.93° W. Long.
Population: 586 (2000); Race: 95.5% White, 0.0% Black, 0.0% Asian, 1.0% American Indian and Alaska Native, 3.2% Hispanic of any race, 0.3% two or more races (2000); Density: 16.5 persons per square mile (2000); Age: 36.5% under 18, 6.6% over 64 (2000); Marriage status: 25.7% never married, 65.9% now married, 5.3% widowed, 3.1% divorced (2000); Foreign born: 1.6% (2000); Ancestry (includes multiple ancestries): 35.7% Norwegian, 33.1% German, 21.5% French (except Basque), 12.7% Irish, 8.0% Czech (2000).
Economy: Employment by occupation: 12.1% management, 18.8% professional, 12.5% services, 21.7% sales, 1.3% farming, 15.7% construction, 17.9% production (2000).
Income: Per capita income: $16,115 (2000); Median household income: $53,929 (2000); Poverty rate: 6.6% (2000).
Taxes: Total city taxes per capita: $92 (1997); City property taxes per capita: $92 (1997).
Education: High school graduation rate: 90.1% (2000); College graduation rate: 14.2% (2000).
Housing: Homeownership rate: 94.0% (2000); Median home value: $105,100 (2000); Median rent: $400 per month (2000); Median age of housing: 28 years (2000).
Transportation: Commute to work: 94.6% car, 0.3% public transportation, 0.0% walk, 4.5% work from home (2000); Travel time to work: 33.4% less than 15 minutes, 56.9% 15 to 30 minutes, 7.7% 30 to 45 minutes, 0.7% 45 to 60 minutes, 1.3% 60 minutes or more (2000)

JOHNSON (township). Covers a land area of 35.679 square miles and a water area of 0 square miles. Located at 47.88° N. Lat.; 95.65° W. Long.
Population: 62 (2000); Race: 100.0% White, 0.0% Black, 0.0% Asian, 0.0% American Indian and Alaska Native, 0.0% Hispanic of any race, 0.0% two or more races (2000); Density: 1.7 persons per square mile (2000); Age: 6.3% under 18, 29.2% over 64 (2000); Marriage status: 30.4% never married, 56.5% now married, 13.0% widowed, 0.0% divorced (2000); Foreign born: 0.0% (2000); Ancestry (includes multiple ancestries): 64.6% Norwegian, 18.8% German, 16.7% Swedish, 10.4% Welsh, 10.4% Other groups (2000).
Economy: Employment by occupation: 59.1% management, 9.1% professional, 0.0% services, 9.1% sales, 13.6% farming, 0.0% construction, 9.1% production (2000).
Income: Per capita income: $11,073 (2000); Median household income: $20,313 (2000); Poverty rate: 12.5% (2000).
Taxes: Total city taxes per capita: $277 (1997); City property taxes per capita: $277 (1997).
Education: High school graduation rate: 65.1% (2000); College graduation rate: 9.3% (2000).
Housing: Homeownership rate: 88.5% (2000); Median age of housing: 60+ years (2000).
Transportation: Commute to work: 54.5% car, 0.0% public transportation, 0.0% walk, 45.5% work from home (2000); Travel time to work: 16.7% less

than 15 minutes, 66.7% 15 to 30 minutes, 0.0% 30 to 45 minutes, 16.7% 45 to 60 minutes, 0.0% 60 minutes or more (2000)

KERTSONVILLE (township). Covers a land area of 36.540 square miles and a water area of 0 square miles. Located at 47.70° N. Lat.; 96.41° W. Long.
Population: 105 (2000); Race: 100.0% White, 0.0% Black, 0.0% Asian, 0.0% American Indian and Alaska Native, 0.0% Hispanic of any race, 0.0% two or more races (2000); Density: 2.9 persons per square mile (2000); Age: 21.6% under 18, 17.6% over 64 (2000); Marriage status: 19.1% never married, 70.8% now married, 7.9% widowed, 2.2% divorced (2000); Foreign born: 0.0% (2000); Ancestry (includes multiple ancestries): 37.3% German, 26.5% Norwegian, 23.5% French Canadian, 22.5% French (except Basque), 13.7% English (2000).
Economy: Employment by occupation: 14.9% management, 21.3% professional, 23.4% services, 14.9% sales, 0.0% farming, 12.8% construction, 12.8% production (2000).
Income: Per capita income: $24,474 (2000); Median household income: $64,000 (2000); Poverty rate: 3.9% (2000).
Taxes: Total city taxes per capita: $81 (1997); City property taxes per capita: $81 (1997).
Education: High school graduation rate: 82.2% (2000); College graduation rate: 27.4% (2000).
Housing: Homeownership rate: 100.0% (2000); Median home value: $75,000 (2000); Median age of housing: 32 years (2000).
Transportation: Commute to work: 93.6% car, 0.0% public transportation, 6.4% walk, 0.0% work from home (2000); Travel time to work: 21.3% less than 15 minutes, 61.7% 15 to 30 minutes, 0.0% 30 to 45 minutes, 17.0% 45 to 60 minutes, 0.0% 60 minutes or more (2000)

KEYSTONE (township). Covers a land area of 35.635 square miles and a water area of 0 square miles. Located at 47.97° N. Lat.; 96.79° W. Long.
Population: 100 (2000); Race: 100.0% White, 0.0% Black, 0.0% Asian, 0.0% American Indian and Alaska Native, 0.0% Hispanic of any race, 0.0% two or more races (2000); Density: 2.8 persons per square mile (2000); Age: 26.5% under 18, 16.3% over 64 (2000); Marriage status: 10.7% never married, 77.3% now married, 4.0% widowed, 8.0% divorced (2000); Foreign born: 0.0% (2000); Ancestry (includes multiple ancestries): 39.8% German, 37.8% Norwegian, 18.4% Polish, 18.4% Czech, 8.2% Irish (2000).
Economy: Employment by occupation: 17.8% management, 0.0% professional, 17.8% services, 35.6% sales, 20.0% farming, 0.0% construction, 8.9% production (2000).
Income: Per capita income: $15,645 (2000); Median household income: $33,438 (2000); Poverty rate: 6.1% (2000).
Taxes: Total city taxes per capita: $287 (1997); City property taxes per capita: $287 (1997).
Education: High school graduation rate: 91.4% (2000); College graduation rate: 12.9% (2000).
Housing: Homeownership rate: 89.7% (2000); Median home value: $88,000 (2000); Median age of housing: 49 years (2000).
Transportation: Commute to work: 86.7% car, 0.0% public transportation, 0.0% walk, 13.3% work from home (2000); Travel time to work: 10.3% less than 15 minutes, 59.0% 15 to 30 minutes, 20.5% 30 to 45 minutes, 5.1% 45 to 60 minutes, 5.1% 60 minutes or more (2000)

KING (township). Covers a land area of 34.946 square miles and a water area of 0.342 square miles. Located at 47.62° N. Lat.; 95.87° W. Long.
Population: 195 (2000); Race: 96.5% White, 0.0% Black, 0.0% Asian, 3.5% American Indian and Alaska Native, 1.0% Hispanic of any race, 0.0% two or more races (2000); Density: 5.6 persons per square mile (2000); Age: 18.6% under 18, 19.6% over 64 (2000); Marriage status: 30.4% never married, 54.4% now married, 12.9% widowed, 2.3% divorced (2000); Foreign born: 2.5% (2000); Ancestry (includes multiple ancestries): 64.3% Norwegian, 29.1% German, 5.0% Other groups, 4.5% Irish, 2.5% English (2000).
Economy: Employment by occupation: 16.2% management, 11.4% professional, 9.5% services, 29.5% sales, 15.2% farming, 7.6% construction, 10.5% production (2000).
Income: Per capita income: $21,211 (2000); Median household income: $40,833 (2000); Poverty rate: 4.6% (2000).
Taxes: Total city taxes per capita: $76 (1997); City property taxes per capita: $76 (1997).
Education: High school graduation rate: 81.8% (2000); College graduation rate: 16.1% (2000).
Housing: Homeownership rate: 84.8% (2000); Median home value: $81,700 (2000); Median age of housing: 60+ years (2000).
Transportation: Commute to work: 82.9% car, 0.0% public transportation, 15.2% walk, 1.9% work from home (2000); Travel time to work: 70.9% less than 15 minutes, 18.4% 15 to 30 minutes, 7.8% 30 to 45 minutes, 0.0% 45 to 60 minutes, 2.9% 60 minutes or more (2000)

KNUTE (township). Covers a land area of 31.536 square miles and a water area of 3.317 square miles. Located at 47.63° N. Lat.; 96.00° W. Long.
Population: 496 (2000); Race: 98.5% White, 0.0% Black, 0.0% Asian, 0.4% American Indian and Alaska Native, 2.1% Hispanic of any race, 1.2% two or more races (2000); Density: 15.7 persons per square mile (2000); Age: 20.6% under 18, 28.5% over 64 (2000); Marriage status: 11.7% never married, 60.5% now married, 18.2% widowed, 9.7% divorced (2000); Foreign born: 1.0% (2000); Ancestry (includes multiple ancestries): 54.8% Norwegian, 20.0% German, 11.2% Swedish, 6.3% Irish, 4.0% French (except Basque) (2000).
Economy: Employment by occupation: 16.5% management, 16.0% professional, 14.9% services, 18.6% sales, 1.1% farming, 12.2% construction, 20.7% production (2000).
Income: Per capita income: $16,795 (2000); Median household income: $41,750 (2000); Poverty rate: 7.4% (2000).
Taxes: Total city taxes per capita: $21 (1997); City property taxes per capita: $21 (1997).
Education: High school graduation rate: 77.8% (2000); College graduation rate: 16.0% (2000).
Housing: Homeownership rate: 93.1% (2000); Median home value: $98,300 (2000); Median rent: $275 per month (2000); Median age of housing: 31 years (2000).
Transportation: Commute to work: 84.6% car, 0.0% public transportation, 9.6% walk, 5.9% work from home (2000); Travel time to work: 65.5% less than 15 minutes, 12.4% 15 to 30 minutes, 5.6% 30 to 45 minutes, 11.9% 45 to 60 minutes, 4.5% 60 minutes or more (2000)

LENGBY (city). Covers a land area of 0.238 square miles and a water area of 0.053 square miles. Located at 47.51° N. Lat.; 95.63° W. Long. Elevation is 1,386 feet.
Population: 79 (2000); Race: 100.0% White, 0.0% Black, 0.0% Asian, 0.0% American Indian and Alaska Native, 0.0% Hispanic of any race, 0.0% two or more races (2000); Density: 331.4 persons per square mile (2000); Age: 17.0% under 18, 21.6% over 64 (2000); Marriage status: 10.1% never married, 55.7% now married, 15.2% widowed, 19.0% divorced (2000); Foreign born: 5.7% (2000); Ancestry (includes multiple ancestries): 51.1% Norwegian, 20.5% German, 18.2% Swedish, 12.5% Ukrainian, 5.7% French (except Basque) (2000).
Economy: Employment by occupation: 14.6% management, 26.8% professional, 36.6% services, 4.9% sales, 0.0% farming, 9.8% construction, 7.3% production (2000).
Income: Per capita income: $15,864 (2000); Median household income: $24,583 (2000); Poverty rate: 9.1% (2000).
Taxes: Total city taxes per capita: $74 (1997); City property taxes per capita: $56 (1997).
Education: High school graduation rate: 87.0% (2000); College graduation rate: 0.0% (2000).
Housing: Homeownership rate: 84.1% (2000); Median home value: $30,400 (2000); Median rent: $185 per month (2000); Median age of housing: 60+ years (2000).
Transportation: Commute to work: 92.1% car, 0.0% public transportation, 7.9% walk, 0.0% work from home (2000); Travel time to work: 55.3% less than 15 minutes, 26.3% 15 to 30 minutes, 7.9% 30 to 45 minutes, 0.0% 45 to 60 minutes, 10.5% 60 minutes or more (2000)

LESSOR (township). Covers a land area of 35.604 square miles and a water area of 0.808 square miles. Located at 47.70° N. Lat.; 95.90° W. Long.
Population: 197 (2000); Race: 100.0% White, 0.0% Black, 0.0% Asian, 0.0% American Indian and Alaska Native, 0.0% Hispanic of any race, 0.0% two or more races (2000); Density: 5.5 persons per square mile (2000); Age: 29.3% under 18, 16.0% over 64 (2000); Marriage status: 25.4% never married, 65.5% now married, 6.2% widowed, 2.8% divorced (2000); Foreign born: 0.0% (2000); Ancestry (includes multiple ancestries): 58.7% Norwegian, 28.9% German, 12.4% French (except Basque), 10.2% Swedish, 4.0% Czech (2000).
Economy: Employment by occupation: 5.2% management, 16.7% professional, 21.9% services, 27.1% sales, 0.0% farming, 4.2% construction, 25.0% production (2000).
Income: Per capita income: $19,808 (2000); Median household income: $35,417 (2000); Poverty rate: 14.7% (2000).

Taxes: Total city taxes per capita: $49 (1997); City property taxes per capita: $49 (1997).
Education: High school graduation rate: 86.9% (2000); College graduation rate: 22.8% (2000).
Housing: Homeownership rate: 79.5% (2000); Median home value: $73,800 (2000); Median rent: $175 per month (2000); Median age of housing: 60+ years (2000).
Transportation: Commute to work: 86.5% car, 0.0% public transportation, 0.0% walk, 8.3% work from home (2000); Travel time to work: 38.6% less than 15 minutes, 36.4% 15 to 30 minutes, 6.8% 30 to 45 minutes, 12.5% 45 to 60 minutes, 5.7% 60 minutes or more (2000)

LIBERTY (township). Covers a land area of 36.066 square miles and a water area of 0.026 square miles. Located at 47.53° N. Lat.; 96.38° W. Long.
Population: 144 (2000); Race: 98.8% White, 0.0% Black, 0.0% Asian, 0.0% American Indian and Alaska Native, 3.0% Hispanic of any race, 1.2% two or more races (2000); Density: 4.0 persons per square mile (2000); Age: 30.3% under 18, 26.7% over 64 (2000); Marriage status: 10.7% never married, 81.0% now married, 5.0% widowed, 3.3% divorced (2000); Foreign born: 0.0% (2000); Ancestry (includes multiple ancestries): 67.9% Norwegian, 37.0% German, 11.5% Swedish, 9.1% French (except Basque), 4.8% Danish (2000).
Economy: Employment by occupation: 29.0% management, 15.9% professional, 20.3% services, 17.4% sales, 2.9% farming, 8.7% construction, 5.8% production (2000).
Income: Per capita income: $28,938 (2000); Median household income: $31,250 (2000); Poverty rate: 9.1% (2000).
Taxes: Total city taxes per capita: $113 (1997); City property taxes per capita: $113 (1997).
Education: High school graduation rate: 74.8% (2000); College graduation rate: 7.5% (2000).
Housing: Homeownership rate: 96.3% (2000); Median home value: $78,300 (2000); Median age of housing: 45 years (2000).
Transportation: Commute to work: 79.7% car, 0.0% public transportation, 8.7% walk, 11.6% work from home (2000); Travel time to work: 54.1% less than 15 minutes, 19.7% 15 to 30 minutes, 19.7% 30 to 45 minutes, 3.3% 45 to 60 minutes, 3.3% 60 minutes or more (2000)

LOWELL (township). Covers a land area of 34.589 square miles and a water area of 0 square miles. Located at 47.81° N. Lat.; 96.66° W. Long.
Population: 183 (2000); Race: 96.4% White, 0.0% Black, 0.0% Asian, 0.0% American Indian and Alaska Native, 3.6% Hispanic of any race, 0.0% two or more races (2000); Density: 5.3 persons per square mile (2000); Age: 34.5% under 18, 11.8% over 64 (2000); Marriage status: 15.0% never married, 73.2% now married, 5.2% widowed, 6.5% divorced (2000); Foreign born: 3.2% (2000); Ancestry (includes multiple ancestries): 65.5% German, 38.6% Norwegian, 9.1% French (except Basque), 5.9% Russian, 5.9% Swedish (2000).
Economy: Employment by occupation: 41.6% management, 10.1% professional, 12.4% services, 13.5% sales, 3.4% farming, 10.1% construction, 9.0% production (2000).
Income: Per capita income: $17,146 (2000); Median household income: $48,125 (2000); Poverty rate: 15.2% (2000).
Taxes: Total city taxes per capita: $257 (2000); City property taxes per capita: $257 (2000).
Education: High school graduation rate: 95.6% (2000); College graduation rate: 19.1% (2000).
Housing: Homeownership rate: 89.2% (2000); Median home value: $90,000 (2000); Median rent: $275 per month (2000); Median age of housing: 44 years (2000).
Transportation: Commute to work: 78.9% car, 0.0% public transportation, 4.4% walk, 16.7% work from home (2000); Travel time to work: 56.0% less than 15 minutes, 22.7% 15 to 30 minutes, 18.7% 30 to 45 minutes, 2.7% 45 to 60 minutes, 0.0% 60 minutes or more (2000)

MCINTOSH (city). Covers a land area of 0.994 square miles and a water area of 0.008 square miles. Located at 47.63° N. Lat.; 95.88° W. Long. Elevation is 1,223 feet.
Population: 638 (2000); Race: 98.1% White, 0.0% Black, 0.0% Asian, 1.1% American Indian and Alaska Native, 2.7% Hispanic of any race, 0.8% two or more races (2000); Density: 642.0 persons per square mile (2000); Age: 17.2% under 18, 32.5% over 64 (2000); Marriage status: 21.4% never married, 57.0% now married, 12.0% widowed, 9.6% divorced (2000); Foreign born: 0.9% (2000); Ancestry (includes multiple ancestries): 55.5% Norwegian, 24.8% German, 9.8% Swedish, 5.8% French (except Basque), 4.4% Irish (2000).
Economy: Grain, sunflowers; livestock; dairying. Single-family building permits issued: 2 (2001) / 1 (2000); Multi-family building permits issued: 0 (2001) / 0 (2000); Employment by occupation: 13.1% management, 22.0% professional, 23.2% services, 17.0% sales, 1.2% farming, 10.8% construction, 12.7% production (2000).
Income: Per capita income: $20,676 (2000); Median household income: $31,328 (2000); Poverty rate: 7.6% (2000).
Taxes: Total city taxes per capita: $86 (1997); City property taxes per capita: $82 (1997).
Education: High school graduation rate: 75.5% (2000); College graduation rate: 13.9% (2000).
Housing: Homeownership rate: 74.7% (2000); Median home value: $45,200 (2000); Median rent: $212 per month (2000); Median age of housing: 52 years (2000).
Transportation: Commute to work: 81.9% car, 0.0% public transportation, 14.7% walk, 3.5% work from home (2000); Travel time to work: 65.2% less than 15 minutes, 15.6% 15 to 30 minutes, 7.2% 30 to 45 minutes, 5.2% 45 to 60 minutes, 6.8% 60 minutes or more (2000)

MENTOR (city). Covers a land area of 1.891 square miles and a water area of 0 square miles. Located at 47.69° N. Lat.; 96.14° W. Long. Elevation is 1,168 feet.
Population: 150 (2000); Race: 100.0% White, 0.0% Black, 0.0% Asian, 0.0% American Indian and Alaska Native, 0.0% Hispanic of any race, 0.0% two or more races (2000); Density: 79.3 persons per square mile (2000); Age: 16.0% under 18, 21.8% over 64 (2000); Marriage status: 14.8% never married, 62.2% now married, 11.1% widowed, 11.9% divorced (2000); Foreign born: 0.0% (2000); Ancestry (includes multiple ancestries): 51.3% Norwegian, 22.4% German, 7.7% French (except Basque), 7.7% Other groups, 6.4% Irish (2000).
Economy: Grain; dairying. Single-family building permits issued: 0 (2001) / 0 (2000); Multi-family building permits issued: 0 (2001) / 0 (2000); Employment by occupation: 0.0% management, 8.6% professional, 34.3% services, 24.3% sales, 0.0% farming, 11.4% construction, 21.4% production (2000).
Income: Per capita income: $12,972 (2000); Median household income: $21,705 (2000); Poverty rate: 13.5% (2000).
Taxes: Total city taxes per capita: $132 (1997); City property taxes per capita: $132 (1997).
Education: High school graduation rate: 66.1% (2000); College graduation rate: 4.0% (2000).

School District(s)

Mentor (N -N)
2000 Enrollment: n/a 218-637-2015

Housing: Homeownership rate: 82.1% (2000); Median home value: $26,300 (2000); Median rent: $189 per month (2000); Median age of housing: 38 years (2000).
Transportation: Commute to work: 97.1% car, 0.0% public transportation, 0.0% walk, 2.9% work from home (2000); Travel time to work: 25.0% less than 15 minutes, 23.5% 15 to 30 minutes, 33.8% 30 to 45 minutes, 11.8% 45 to 60 minutes, 5.9% 60 minutes or more (2000)

NESBIT (township). Covers a land area of 35.985 square miles and a water area of 0 square miles. Located at 47.88° N. Lat.; 96.81° W. Long.
Population: 130 (2000); Race: 95.9% White, 0.0% Black, 0.0% Asian, 4.1% American Indian and Alaska Native, 1.6% Hispanic of any race, 0.0% two or more races (2000); Density: 3.6 persons per square mile (2000); Age: 27.6% under 18, 14.6% over 64 (2000); Marriage status: 30.9% never married, 61.7% now married, 0.0% widowed, 7.4% divorced (2000); Foreign born: 0.0% (2000); Ancestry (includes multiple ancestries): 42.3% German, 29.3% Norwegian, 12.2% Scotch-Irish, 8.9% French (except Basque), 6.5% Swedish (2000).
Economy: Employment by occupation: 23.9% management, 6.0% professional, 6.0% services, 35.8% sales, 0.0% farming, 14.9% construction, 13.4% production (2000).
Income: Per capita income: $18,744 (2000); Median household income: $42,083 (2000); Poverty rate: 5.9% (2000).
Taxes: Total city taxes per capita: $41 (1997); City property taxes per capita: $41 (1997).
Education: High school graduation rate: 88.2% (2000); College graduation rate: 22.4% (2000).
Housing: Homeownership rate: 73.9% (2000); Median home value: $85,000 (2000); Median rent: $325 per month (2000); Median age of housing: 55 years (2000).
Transportation: Commute to work: 86.6% car, 0.0% public transportation, 7.5% walk, 6.0% work from home (2000); Travel time to work: 36.5% less

than 15 minutes, 34.9% 15 to 30 minutes, 23.8% 30 to 45 minutes, 4.8% 45 to 60 minutes, 0.0% 60 minutes or more (2000)

NIELSVILLE (city). Covers a land area of 0.276 square miles and a water area of 0 square miles. Located at 47.52° N. Lat.; 96.81° W. Long. Elevation is 865 feet.
Population: 91 (2000); Race: 100.0% White, 0.0% Black, 0.0% Asian, 0.0% American Indian and Alaska Native, 18.0% Hispanic of any race, 0.0% two or more races (2000); Density: 329.9 persons per square mile (2000); Age: 24.7% under 18, 13.5% over 64 (2000); Marriage status: 23.2% never married, 59.4% now married, 2.9% widowed, 14.5% divorced (2000); Foreign born: 6.7% (2000); Ancestry (includes multiple ancestries): 57.3% Norwegian, 23.6% German, 20.2% Other groups, 5.6% French (except Basque), 5.6% Danish (2000).
Economy: Grain. Single-family building permits issued: 0 (2001) / 0 (2000); Multi-family building permits issued: 0 (2001) / 0 (2000); Employment by occupation: 4.5% management, 2.3% professional, 22.7% services, 13.6% sales, 25.0% farming, 9.1% construction, 22.7% production (2000).
Income: Per capita income: $14,921 (2000); Median household income: $27,750 (2000); Poverty rate: 0.0% (2000).
Taxes: Total city taxes per capita: $83 (1997); City property taxes per capita: $83 (1997).
Education: High school graduation rate: 63.6% (2000); College graduation rate: 3.6% (2000).
Housing: Homeownership rate: 76.3% (2000); Median home value: $14,700 (2000); Median rent: $375 per month (2000); Median age of housing: 60+ years (2000).
Transportation: Commute to work: 90.9% car, 0.0% public transportation, 9.1% walk, 0.0% work from home (2000); Travel time to work: 40.9% less than 15 minutes, 27.3% 15 to 30 minutes, 15.9% 30 to 45 minutes, 2.3% 45 to 60 minutes, 13.6% 60 minutes or more (2000)

NORTHLAND (township). Covers a land area of 36.154 square miles and a water area of 0 square miles. Located at 48.06° N. Lat.; 96.96° W. Long.
Population: 196 (2000); Race: 100.0% White, 0.0% Black, 0.0% Asian, 0.0% American Indian and Alaska Native, 0.0% Hispanic of any race, 0.0% two or more races (2000); Density: 5.4 persons per square mile (2000); Age: 30.3% under 18, 14.6% over 64 (2000); Marriage status: 29.0% never married, 62.3% now married, 4.3% widowed, 4.3% divorced (2000); Foreign born: 0.0% (2000); Ancestry (includes multiple ancestries): 29.2% Norwegian, 26.5% German, 16.8% Czech, 16.2% Swedish, 11.4% Irish (2000).
Economy: Employment by occupation: 13.2% management, 26.4% professional, 9.9% services, 15.4% sales, 0.0% farming, 15.4% construction, 19.8% production (2000).
Income: Per capita income: $18,614 (2000); Median household income: $38,333 (2000); Poverty rate: 10.8% (2000).
Taxes: Total city taxes per capita: $138 (1997); City property taxes per capita: $138 (1997).
Education: High school graduation rate: 83.9% (2000); College graduation rate: 22.3% (2000).
Housing: Homeownership rate: 88.7% (2000); Median home value: $125,000 (2000); Median rent: $325 per month (2000); Median age of housing: 45 years (2000).
Transportation: Commute to work: 89.9% car, 0.0% public transportation, 0.0% walk, 10.1% work from home (2000); Travel time to work: 26.3% less than 15 minutes, 63.7% 15 to 30 minutes, 8.8% 30 to 45 minutes, 0.0% 45 to 60 minutes, 1.3% 60 minutes or more (2000)

ONSTAD (township). Covers a land area of 35.562 square miles and a water area of 0.111 square miles. Located at 47.63° N. Lat.; 96.37° W. Long.
Population: 70 (2000); Race: 100.0% White, 0.0% Black, 0.0% Asian, 0.0% American Indian and Alaska Native, 0.0% Hispanic of any race, 0.0% two or more races (2000); Density: 2.0 persons per square mile (2000); Age: 42.4% under 18, 5.1% over 64 (2000); Marriage status: 22.0% never married, 70.7% now married, 0.0% widowed, 7.3% divorced (2000); Foreign born: 3.4% (2000); Ancestry (includes multiple ancestries): 79.7% Norwegian, 28.8% French (except Basque), 18.6% German, 11.9% Swedish, 3.4% French Canadian (2000).
Economy: Employment by occupation: 22.7% management, 27.3% professional, 9.1% services, 22.7% sales, 0.0% farming, 9.1% construction, 9.1% production (2000).
Income: Per capita income: $12,807 (2000); Median household income: $43,125 (2000); Poverty rate: 0.0% (2000).
Taxes: Total city taxes per capita: $64 (1997); City property taxes per capita: $64 (1997).
Education: High school graduation rate: 84.4% (2000); College graduation rate: 6.3% (2000).
Housing: Homeownership rate: 100.0% (2000); Median home value: $22,500 (2000); Median age of housing: 60+ years (2000).
Transportation: Commute to work: 90.9% car, 0.0% public transportation, 0.0% walk, 9.1% work from home (2000); Travel time to work: 0.0% less than 15 minutes, 80.0% 15 to 30 minutes, 10.0% 30 to 45 minutes, 0.0% 45 to 60 minutes, 10.0% 60 minutes or more (2000)

PARNELL (township). Covers a land area of 36.280 square miles and a water area of 0 square miles. Located at 47.88° N. Lat.; 96.53° W. Long.
Population: 87 (2000); Race: 100.0% White, 0.0% Black, 0.0% Asian, 0.0% American Indian and Alaska Native, 4.0% Hispanic of any race, 0.0% two or more races (2000); Density: 2.4 persons per square mile (2000); Age: 22.7% under 18, 18.7% over 64 (2000); Marriage status: 21.9% never married, 73.4% now married, 4.7% widowed, 0.0% divorced (2000); Foreign born: 0.0% (2000); Ancestry (includes multiple ancestries): 36.0% Norwegian, 33.3% French (except Basque), 32.0% German, 12.0% Dutch, 8.0% English (2000).
Economy: Employment by occupation: 9.1% management, 6.8% professional, 0.0% services, 34.1% sales, 0.0% farming, 15.9% construction, 34.1% production (2000).
Income: Per capita income: $22,360 (2000); Median household income: $45,000 (2000); Poverty rate: 4.0% (2000).
Taxes: Total city taxes per capita: $375 (1997); City property taxes per capita: $375 (1997).
Education: High school graduation rate: 89.4% (2000); College graduation rate: 8.5% (2000).
Housing: Homeownership rate: 83.9% (2000); Median home value: $53,000 (2000); Median rent: $242 per month (2000); Median age of housing: 36 years (2000).
Transportation: Commute to work: 90.9% car, 0.0% public transportation, 0.0% walk, 9.1% work from home (2000); Travel time to work: 0.0% less than 15 minutes, 70.0% 15 to 30 minutes, 17.5% 30 to 45 minutes, 0.0% 45 to 60 minutes, 12.5% 60 minutes or more (2000)

QUEEN (township). Covers a land area of 32.726 square miles and a water area of 3.880 square miles. Located at 47.64° N. Lat.; 95.62° W. Long.
Population: 198 (2000); Race: 100.0% White, 0.0% Black, 0.0% Asian, 0.0% American Indian and Alaska Native, 0.0% Hispanic of any race, 0.0% two or more races (2000); Density: 6.1 persons per square mile (2000); Age: 17.4% under 18, 25.3% over 64 (2000); Marriage status: 17.3% never married, 65.3% now married, 14.0% widowed, 3.3% divorced (2000); Foreign born: 0.0% (2000); Ancestry (includes multiple ancestries): 59.0% Norwegian, 21.9% Swedish, 11.2% German, 3.9% English, 2.8% Irish (2000).
Economy: Employment by occupation: 17.8% management, 19.2% professional, 12.3% services, 19.2% sales, 4.1% farming, 12.3% construction, 15.1% production (2000).
Income: Per capita income: $18,046 (2000); Median household income: $31,071 (2000); Poverty rate: 9.6% (2000).
Taxes: Total city taxes per capita: $71 (1997); City property taxes per capita: $71 (1997).
Education: High school graduation rate: 75.0% (2000); College graduation rate: 10.0% (2000).
Housing: Homeownership rate: 94.3% (2000); Median home value: $93,300 (2000); Median age of housing: 50 years (2000).
Transportation: Commute to work: 94.4% car, 0.0% public transportation, 0.0% walk, 5.6% work from home (2000); Travel time to work: 35.8% less than 15 minutes, 53.7% 15 to 30 minutes, 10.4% 30 to 45 minutes, 0.0% 45 to 60 minutes, 0.0% 60 minutes or more (2000)

REIS (township). Covers a land area of 34.019 square miles and a water area of 0 square miles. Located at 47.56° N. Lat.; 96.52° W. Long.
Population: 74 (2000); Race: 100.0% White, 0.0% Black, 0.0% Asian, 0.0% American Indian and Alaska Native, 0.0% Hispanic of any race, 0.0% two or more races (2000); Density: 2.2 persons per square mile (2000); Age: 12.5% under 18, 17.5% over 64 (2000); Marriage status: 17.8% never married, 61.6% now married, 5.5% widowed, 15.1% divorced (2000); Foreign born: 0.0% (2000); Ancestry (includes multiple ancestries): 66.3% Norwegian, 38.8% German, 12.5% Swedish, 2.5% Dutch, 2.5% French (except Basque) (2000).

Economy: Employment by occupation: 5.7% management, 17.1% professional, 45.7% services, 5.7% sales, 5.7% farming, 2.9% construction, 17.1% production (2000).
Income: Per capita income: $18,261 (2000); Median household income: $33,125 (2000); Poverty rate: 5.0% (2000).
Taxes: Total city taxes per capita: $215 (1997); City property taxes per capita: $215 (1997).
Education: High school graduation rate: 86.7% (2000); College graduation rate: 3.3% (2000).
Housing: Homeownership rate: 89.2% (2000); Median home value: $45,000 (2000); Median rent: $125 per month (2000); Median age of housing: 47 years (2000).
Transportation: Commute to work: 100.0% car, 0.0% public transportation, 0.0% walk, 0.0% work from home (2000); Travel time to work: 27.3% less than 15 minutes, 51.5% 15 to 30 minutes, 6.1% 30 to 45 minutes, 6.1% 45 to 60 minutes, 9.1% 60 minutes or more (2000)

RHINEHART (township). Covers a land area of 2.855 square miles and a water area of 0 square miles. Located at 47.87° N. Lat.; 97.00° W. Long.
Population: 91 (2000); Race: 100.0% White, 0.0% Black, 0.0% Asian, 0.0% American Indian and Alaska Native, 0.0% Hispanic of any race, 0.0% two or more races (2000); Density: 31.9 persons per square mile (2000); Age: 39.3% under 18, 11.2% over 64 (2000); Marriage status: 21.2% never married, 71.2% now married, 0.0% widowed, 7.6% divorced (2000); Foreign born: 0.0% (2000); Ancestry (includes multiple ancestries): 30.3% Norwegian, 23.6% German, 16.9% Swedish, 16.9% Irish, 14.6% French (except Basque) (2000).
Economy: Employment by occupation: 19.5% management, 12.2% professional, 34.1% services, 14.6% sales, 4.9% farming, 14.6% construction, 0.0% production (2000).
Income: Per capita income: $24,876 (2000); Median household income: $63,500 (2000); Poverty rate: 2.2% (2000).
Taxes: Total city taxes per capita: $61 (1997); City property taxes per capita: $61 (1997).
Education: High school graduation rate: 100.0% (2000); College graduation rate: 9.6% (2000).
Housing: Homeownership rate: 100.0% (2000); Median home value: $112,500 (2000); Median age of housing: 32 years (2000).
Transportation: Commute to work: 90.2% car, 0.0% public transportation, 0.0% walk, 0.0% work from home (2000); Travel time to work: 43.9% less than 15 minutes, 51.2% 15 to 30 minutes, 4.9% 30 to 45 minutes, 0.0% 45 to 60 minutes, 0.0% 60 minutes or more (2000)

ROOME (township). Covers a land area of 36.070 square miles and a water area of 0 square miles. Located at 47.71° N. Lat.; 96.79° W. Long.
Population: 185 (2000); Race: 100.0% White, 0.0% Black, 0.0% Asian, 0.0% American Indian and Alaska Native, 0.0% Hispanic of any race, 0.0% two or more races (2000); Density: 5.1 persons per square mile (2000); Age: 26.7% under 18, 14.8% over 64 (2000); Marriage status: 17.5% never married, 72.0% now married, 2.8% widowed, 7.7% divorced (2000); Foreign born: 1.1% (2000); Ancestry (includes multiple ancestries): 73.9% Norwegian, 15.9% German, 11.4% Swedish, 8.0% English, 7.4% Scottish (2000).
Economy: Employment by occupation: 22.2% management, 15.6% professional, 13.3% services, 20.0% sales, 3.3% farming, 8.9% construction, 16.7% production (2000).
Income: Per capita income: $19,929 (2000); Median household income: $48,125 (2000); Poverty rate: 1.1% (2000).
Taxes: Total city taxes per capita: $105 (1997); City property taxes per capita: $105 (1997).
Education: High school graduation rate: 87.4% (2000); College graduation rate: 17.6% (2000).
Housing: Homeownership rate: 90.8% (2000); Median home value: $71,300 (2000); Median rent: $525 per month (2000); Median age of housing: 51 years (2000).
Transportation: Commute to work: 77.8% car, 0.0% public transportation, 6.7% walk, 15.6% work from home (2000); Travel time to work: 40.8% less than 15 minutes, 36.8% 15 to 30 minutes, 19.7% 30 to 45 minutes, 2.6% 45 to 60 minutes, 0.0% 60 minutes or more (2000)

ROSEBUD (township). Covers a land area of 32.923 square miles and a water area of 2.119 square miles. Located at 47.55° N. Lat.; 95.73° W. Long.
Population: 343 (2000); Race: 93.2% White, 0.0% Black, 0.0% Asian, 2.2% American Indian and Alaska Native, 1.6% Hispanic of any race, 3.8% two or more races (2000); Density: 10.4 persons per square mile (2000); Age: 31.6% under 18, 14.6% over 64 (2000); Marriage status: 21.2% never married, 69.2% now married, 5.5% widowed, 4.0% divorced (2000); Foreign born: 2.4% (2000); Ancestry (includes multiple ancestries): 51.9% Norwegian, 19.7% German, 10.5% Swedish, 6.8% French Canadian, 5.7% English (2000).
Economy: Employment by occupation: 12.2% management, 20.9% professional, 14.5% services, 28.5% sales, 4.7% farming, 8.1% construction, 11.0% production (2000).
Income: Per capita income: $13,677 (2000); Median household income: $28,281 (2000); Poverty rate: 11.6% (2000).
Taxes: Total city taxes per capita: $67 (1997); City property taxes per capita: $67 (1997).
Education: High school graduation rate: 81.0% (2000); College graduation rate: 20.8% (2000).
Housing: Homeownership rate: 80.7% (2000); Median home value: $78,000 (2000); Median rent: $317 per month (2000); Median age of housing: 39 years (2000).
Transportation: Commute to work: 84.5% car, 0.0% public transportation, 2.4% walk, 11.3% work from home (2000); Travel time to work: 63.1% less than 15 minutes, 14.8% 15 to 30 minutes, 11.4% 30 to 45 minutes, 1.3% 45 to 60 minutes, 9.4% 60 minutes or more (2000)

RUSSIA (township). Covers a land area of 36.142 square miles and a water area of 0 square miles. Located at 47.62° N. Lat.; 96.52° W. Long.
Population: 33 (2000); Race: 100.0% White, 0.0% Black, 0.0% Asian, 0.0% American Indian and Alaska Native, 0.0% Hispanic of any race, 0.0% two or more races (2000); Density: 0.9 persons per square mile (2000); Age: 27.3% under 18, 15.2% over 64 (2000); Marriage status: 25.0% never married, 37.5% now married, 20.8% widowed, 16.7% divorced (2000); Foreign born: 6.1% (2000); Ancestry (includes multiple ancestries): 39.4% German, 33.3% Norwegian, 18.2% Irish, 15.2% Swedish, 9.1% Italian (2000).
Economy: Employment by occupation: 13.3% management, 0.0% professional, 0.0% services, 20.0% sales, 0.0% farming, 13.3% construction, 53.3% production (2000).
Income: Per capita income: $21,970 (2000); Median household income: $43,125 (2000); Poverty rate: 21.2% (2000).
Taxes: Total city taxes per capita: $429 (1997); City property taxes per capita: $429 (1997).
Education: High school graduation rate: 90.9% (2000); College graduation rate: 9.1% (2000).
Housing: Homeownership rate: 100.0% (2000); Median home value: $65,000 (2000); Median age of housing: 49 years (2000).
Transportation: Commute to work: 86.7% car, 0.0% public transportation, 0.0% walk, 13.3% work from home (2000); Travel time to work: 0.0% less than 15 minutes, 100.0% 15 to 30 minutes, 0.0% 30 to 45 minutes, 0.0% 45 to 60 minutes, 0.0% 60 minutes or more (2000)

SANDSVILLE (township). Covers a land area of 26.989 square miles and a water area of 0 square miles. Located at 48.13° N. Lat.; 96.96° W. Long.
Population: 58 (2000); Race: 100.0% White, 0.0% Black, 0.0% Asian, 0.0% American Indian and Alaska Native, 0.0% Hispanic of any race, 0.0% two or more races (2000); Density: 2.1 persons per square mile (2000); Age: 22.4% under 18, 14.9% over 64 (2000); Marriage status: 21.8% never married, 74.5% now married, 3.6% widowed, 0.0% divorced (2000); Foreign born: 0.0% (2000); Ancestry (includes multiple ancestries): 49.3% Norwegian, 26.9% German, 22.4% Czech, 10.4% Scottish, 9.0% Polish (2000).
Economy: Employment by occupation: 20.0% management, 11.4% professional, 5.7% services, 22.9% sales, 5.7% farming, 25.7% construction, 8.6% production (2000).
Income: Per capita income: $22,240 (2000); Median household income: $59,375 (2000); Poverty rate: 0.0% (2000).
Taxes: Total city taxes per capita: $348 (1997); City property taxes per capita: $348 (1997).
Education: High school graduation rate: 86.0% (2000); College graduation rate: 8.0% (2000).
Housing: Homeownership rate: 92.3% (2000); Median home value: $85,000 (2000); Median rent: <$100 per month (2000); Median age of housing: 42 years (2000).
Transportation: Commute to work: 78.8% car, 0.0% public transportation, 0.0% walk, 21.2% work from home (2000); Travel time to work: 42.3% less than 15 minutes, 23.1% 15 to 30 minutes, 26.9% 30 to 45 minutes, 7.7% 45 to 60 minutes, 0.0% 60 minutes or more (2000)

SCANDIA (township). Covers a land area of 36.062 square miles and a water area of 0 square miles. Located at 47.55° N. Lat.; 96.64° W. Long.

Population: 86 (2000); Race: 97.8% White, 0.0% Black, 0.0% Asian, 0.0% American Indian and Alaska Native, 2.2% Hispanic of any race, 0.0% two or more races (2000); Density: 2.4 persons per square mile (2000); Age: 45.2% under 18, 6.5% over 64 (2000); Marriage status: 5.6% never married, 94.4% now married, 0.0% widowed, 0.0% divorced (2000); Foreign born: 0.0% (2000); Ancestry (includes multiple ancestries): 73.1% Norwegian, 26.9% German, 11.8% Ukrainian, 8.6% Dutch, 7.5% Swedish (2000).
Economy: Employment by occupation: 42.2% management, 15.6% professional, 8.9% services, 11.1% sales, 8.9% farming, 6.7% construction, 6.7% production (2000).
Income: Per capita income: $16,253 (2000); Median household income: $47,083 (2000); Poverty rate: 3.2% (2000).
Taxes: Total city taxes per capita: $186 (1997); City property taxes per capita: $186 (1997).
Education: High school graduation rate: 91.8% (2000); College graduation rate: 28.6% (2000).
Housing: Homeownership rate: 91.3% (2000); Median home value: $66,700 (2000); Median age of housing: 42 years (2000).
Transportation: Commute to work: 62.2% car, 0.0% public transportation, 4.4% walk, 33.3% work from home (2000); Travel time to work: 50.0% less than 15 minutes, 30.0% 15 to 30 minutes, 10.0% 30 to 45 minutes, 0.0% 45 to 60 minutes, 10.0% 60 minutes or more (2000)

SLETTEN (township). Covers a land area of 35.988 square miles and a water area of 0.124 square miles. Located at 47.55° N. Lat.; 95.86° W. Long.
Population: 140 (2000); Race: 100.0% White, 0.0% Black, 0.0% Asian, 0.0% American Indian and Alaska Native, 0.0% Hispanic of any race, 0.0% two or more races (2000); Density: 3.9 persons per square mile (2000); Age: 21.4% under 18, 10.7% over 64 (2000); Marriage status: 14.9% never married, 78.7% now married, 4.3% widowed, 2.1% divorced (2000); Foreign born: 8.0% (2000); Ancestry (includes multiple ancestries): 53.6% Norwegian, 24.1% German, 19.6% Swedish, 12.5% French (except Basque), 11.6% Irish (2000).
Economy: Employment by occupation: 31.8% management, 11.4% professional, 9.1% services, 20.5% sales, 9.1% farming, 4.5% construction, 13.6% production (2000).
Income: Per capita income: $29,178 (2000); Median household income: $35,313 (2000); Poverty rate: 8.0% (2000).
Taxes: Total city taxes per capita: $153 (1997); City property taxes per capita: $153 (1997).
Education: High school graduation rate: 76.8% (2000); College graduation rate: 17.1% (2000).
Housing: Homeownership rate: 86.0% (2000); Median home value: $36,300 (2000); Median rent: <$100 per month (2000); Median age of housing: 60+ years (2000).
Transportation: Commute to work: 75.0% car, 0.0% public transportation, 11.4% walk, 13.6% work from home (2000); Travel time to work: 50.0% less than 15 minutes, 18.4% 15 to 30 minutes, 15.8% 30 to 45 minutes, 10.5% 45 to 60 minutes, 5.3% 60 minutes or more (2000)

SULLIVAN (township). Covers a land area of 35.645 square miles and a water area of 0.086 square miles. Located at 47.97° N. Lat.; 96.94° W. Long.
Population: 174 (2000); Race: 100.0% White, 0.0% Black, 0.0% Asian, 0.0% American Indian and Alaska Native, 0.0% Hispanic of any race, 0.0% two or more races (2000); Density: 4.9 persons per square mile (2000); Age: 30.3% under 18, 10.7% over 64 (2000); Marriage status: 25.4% never married, 71.5% now married, 3.1% widowed, 0.0% divorced (2000); Foreign born: 2.2% (2000); Ancestry (includes multiple ancestries): 47.2% Norwegian, 19.1% Czech, 18.5% German, 12.4% Swedish, 9.0% Irish (2000).
Economy: Employment by occupation: 17.6% management, 12.1% professional, 15.4% services, 23.1% sales, 4.4% farming, 9.9% construction, 17.6% production (2000).
Income: Per capita income: $16,360 (2000); Median household income: $45,250 (2000); Poverty rate: 2.2% (2000).
Taxes: Total city taxes per capita: $138 (1997); City property taxes per capita: $138 (1997).
Education: High school graduation rate: 84.7% (2000); College graduation rate: 10.8% (2000).
Housing: Homeownership rate: 92.2% (2000); Median home value: $77,100 (2000); Median rent: $1,625 per month (2000); Median age of housing: 45 years (2000).
Transportation: Commute to work: 89.9% car, 0.0% public transportation, 0.0% walk, 6.7% work from home (2000); Travel time to work: 45.8% less than 15 minutes, 42.2% 15 to 30 minutes, 9.6% 30 to 45 minutes, 2.4% 45 to 60 minutes, 0.0% 60 minutes or more (2000)

TABOR (township). Covers a land area of 36.242 square miles and a water area of 0 square miles. Located at 48.05° N. Lat.; 96.82° W. Long. Elevation is 843 feet.
Population: 122 (2000); Race: 96.9% White, 1.2% Black, 0.0% Asian, 0.0% American Indian and Alaska Native, 1.8% Hispanic of any race, 0.0% two or more races (2000); Density: 3.4 persons per square mile (2000); Age: 27.0% under 18, 16.6% over 64 (2000); Marriage status: 29.9% never married, 64.2% now married, 6.0% widowed, 0.0% divorced (2000); Foreign born: 0.0% (2000); Ancestry (includes multiple ancestries): 34.4% Norwegian, 31.9% Czech, 23.3% German, 8.0% Swedish, 7.4% Irish (2000).
Economy: Employment by occupation: 23.9% management, 21.1% professional, 4.2% services, 15.5% sales, 5.6% farming, 11.3% construction, 18.3% production (2000).
Income: Per capita income: $19,429 (2000); Median household income: $51,875 (2000); Poverty rate: 0.0% (2000).
Taxes: Total city taxes per capita: $148 (1997); City property taxes per capita: $148 (1997).
Education: High school graduation rate: 97.3% (2000); College graduation rate: 20.9% (2000).
Housing: Homeownership rate: 92.7% (2000); Median home value: $70,000 (2000); Median age of housing: 50 years (2000).
Transportation: Commute to work: 75.4% car, 0.0% public transportation, 10.1% walk, 11.6% work from home (2000); Travel time to work: 36.1% less than 15 minutes, 27.9% 15 to 30 minutes, 23.0% 30 to 45 minutes, 13.1% 45 to 60 minutes, 0.0% 60 minutes or more (2000)

TRAIL (city). Covers a land area of 0.993 square miles and a water area of 0 square miles. Located at 47.78° N. Lat.; 95.69° W. Long. Elevation is 1,224 feet.
Population: 62 (2000); Race: 94.4% White, 0.0% Black, 0.0% Asian, 5.6% American Indian and Alaska Native, 0.0% Hispanic of any race, 0.0% two or more races (2000); Density: 62.4 persons per square mile (2000); Age: 24.1% under 18, 16.7% over 64 (2000); Marriage status: 28.3% never married, 32.6% now married, 15.2% widowed, 23.9% divorced (2000); Foreign born: 0.0% (2000); Ancestry (includes multiple ancestries): 75.9% Norwegian, 14.8% French (except Basque), 9.3% German, 9.3% Irish, 9.3% Swedish (2000).
Economy: Employment by occupation: 17.6% management, 0.0% professional, 23.5% services, 0.0% sales, 0.0% farming, 23.5% construction, 35.3% production (2000).
Income: Per capita income: $16,211 (2000); Median household income: $30,000 (2000); Poverty rate: 22.2% (2000).
Taxes: Total city taxes per capita: $118 (1997); City property taxes per capita: $88 (1997).
Education: High school graduation rate: 61.0% (2000); College graduation rate: 0.0% (2000).
Housing: Homeownership rate: 92.9% (2000); Median home value: $10,000 (2000); Median rent: $175 per month (2000); Median age of housing: 44 years (2000).
Transportation: Commute to work: 88.2% car, 0.0% public transportation, 11.8% walk, 0.0% work from home (2000); Travel time to work: 41.2% less than 15 minutes, 35.3% 15 to 30 minutes, 0.0% 30 to 45 minutes, 0.0% 45 to 60 minutes, 23.5% 60 minutes or more (2000)

TYNSID (township). Covers a land area of 14.280 square miles and a water area of 0 square miles. Located at 47.71° N. Lat.; 96.88° W. Long.
Population: 58 (2000); Race: 100.0% White, 0.0% Black, 0.0% Asian, 0.0% American Indian and Alaska Native, 0.0% Hispanic of any race, 0.0% two or more races (2000); Density: 4.1 persons per square mile (2000); Age: 19.0% under 18, 3.2% over 64 (2000); Marriage status: 15.1% never married, 81.1% now married, 3.8% widowed, 0.0% divorced (2000); Foreign born: 1.6% (2000); Ancestry (includes multiple ancestries): 60.3% Norwegian, 27.0% German, 15.9% French (except Basque), 7.9% French Canadian, 7.9% Irish (2000).
Economy: Employment by occupation: 42.2% management, 11.1% professional, 2.2% services, 33.3% sales, 0.0% farming, 6.7% construction, 4.4% production (2000).
Income: Per capita income: $21,038 (2000); Median household income: $48,000 (2000); Poverty rate: 0.0% (2000).
Taxes: Total city taxes per capita: $127 (1997); City property taxes per capita: $127 (1997).
Education: High school graduation rate: 84.0% (2000); College graduation rate: 12.0% (2000).
Housing: Homeownership rate: 92.9% (2000); Median home value: $82,500 (2000); Median age of housing: 50 years (2000).

Transportation: Commute to work: 82.2% car, 0.0% public transportation, 4.4% walk, 13.3% work from home (2000); Travel time to work: 25.6% less than 15 minutes, 35.9% 15 to 30 minutes, 38.5% 30 to 45 minutes, 0.0% 45 to 60 minutes, 0.0% 60 minutes or more (2000)

VINELAND (township). Covers a land area of 45.820 square miles and a water area of 0 square miles. Located at 47.63° N. Lat.; 96.80° W. Long.

Population: 133 (2000); Race: 97.8% White, 0.0% Black, 0.0% Asian, 2.2% American Indian and Alaska Native, 4.5% Hispanic of any race, 0.0% two or more races (2000); Density: 2.9 persons per square mile (2000); Age: 30.6% under 18, 17.2% over 64 (2000); Marriage status: 22.9% never married, 63.5% now married, 6.3% widowed, 7.3% divorced (2000); Foreign born: 1.5% (2000); Ancestry (includes multiple ancestries): 61.9% Norwegian, 19.4% German, 9.0% Danish, 5.2% Irish, 4.5% French (except Basque) (2000).

Economy: Employment by occupation: 39.2% management, 0.0% professional, 9.8% services, 19.6% sales, 0.0% farming, 9.8% construction, 21.6% production (2000).

Income: Per capita income: $11,180 (2000); Median household income: $27,500 (2000); Poverty rate: 22.1% (2000).

Taxes: Total city taxes per capita: $191 (1997); City property taxes per capita: $191 (1997).

Education: High school graduation rate: 85.2% (2000); College graduation rate: 1.2% (2000).

Housing: Homeownership rate: 95.5% (2000); Median home value: $50,000 (2000); Median age of housing: 60+ years (2000).

Transportation: Commute to work: 80.4% car, 0.0% public transportation, 0.0% walk, 19.6% work from home (2000); Travel time to work: 46.3% less than 15 minutes, 26.8% 15 to 30 minutes, 26.8% 30 to 45 minutes, 0.0% 45 to 60 minutes, 0.0% 60 minutes or more (2000)

WINGER (city). Covers a land area of 0.350 square miles and a water area of 0 square miles. Located at 47.53° N. Lat.; 95.98° W. Long. Elevation is 1,232 feet.

Population: 205 (2000); Race: 95.2% White, 0.0% Black, 0.0% Asian, 3.4% American Indian and Alaska Native, 0.0% Hispanic of any race, 1.4% two or more races (2000); Density: 586.4 persons per square mile (2000); Age: 28.0% under 18, 19.8% over 64 (2000); Marriage status: 26.5% never married, 56.8% now married, 11.6% widowed, 5.2% divorced (2000); Foreign born: 0.0% (2000); Ancestry (includes multiple ancestries): 50.7% Norwegian, 29.0% German, 12.6% Swedish, 8.2% Irish, 7.2% Czech (2000).

Economy: Employment by occupation: 3.3% management, 17.6% professional, 33.0% services, 23.1% sales, 5.5% farming, 11.0% construction, 6.6% production (2000).

Income: Per capita income: $11,707 (2000); Median household income: $21,146 (2000); Poverty rate: 14.5% (2000).

Taxes: Total city taxes per capita: $101 (1997); City property taxes per capita: $75 (1997).

Education: High school graduation rate: 76.3% (2000); College graduation rate: 8.9% (2000).

Housing: Homeownership rate: 68.1% (2000); Median home value: $25,000 (2000); Median rent: $200 per month (2000); Median age of housing: 50 years (2000).

Transportation: Commute to work: 84.3% car, 0.0% public transportation, 6.7% walk, 9.0% work from home (2000); Travel time to work: 29.6% less than 15 minutes, 48.1% 15 to 30 minutes, 12.3% 30 to 45 minutes, 2.5% 45 to 60 minutes, 7.4% 60 minutes or more (2000)

WINGER (township). Covers a land area of 35.134 square miles and a water area of 0.490 square miles. Located at 47.55° N. Lat.; 96.00° W. Long. Elevation is 1,232 feet.

Population: 177 (2000); Race: 93.3% White, 0.0% Black, 0.0% Asian, 6.7% American Indian and Alaska Native, 0.0% Hispanic of any race, 0.0% two or more races (2000); Density: 5.0 persons per square mile (2000); Age: 35.6% under 18, 18.4% over 64 (2000); Marriage status: 24.3% never married, 56.8% now married, 5.4% widowed, 13.5% divorced (2000); Foreign born: 2.5% (2000); Ancestry (includes multiple ancestries): 70.6% Norwegian, 20.9% German, 9.8% Other groups, 3.7% Irish, 2.5% French (except Basque) (2000).

Economy: Agriculture includes grain, sunflowers, potatoes; poultry; dairying. Employment by occupation: 9.8% management, 21.6% professional, 25.5% services, 11.8% sales, 3.9% farming, 15.7% construction, 11.8% production (2000).

Income: Per capita income: $13,028 (2000); Median household income: $34,583 (2000); Poverty rate: 11.6% (2000).

Taxes: Total city taxes per capita: $126 (1997); City property taxes per capita: $126 (1997).

Education: High school graduation rate: 68.0% (2000); College graduation rate: 9.3% (2000).

Housing: Homeownership rate: 85.9% (2000); Median home value: $33,800 (2000); Median rent: $258 per month (2000); Median age of housing: 48 years (2000).

Transportation: Commute to work: 87.5% car, 0.0% public transportation, 4.2% walk, 4.2% work from home (2000); Travel time to work: 32.6% less than 15 minutes, 37.0% 15 to 30 minutes, 10.9% 30 to 45 minutes, 15.2% 45 to 60 minutes, 4.3% 60 minutes or more (2000)

WOODSIDE (township). Covers a land area of 30.837 square miles and a water area of 5.004 square miles. Located at 47.63° N. Lat.; 96.12° W. Long.

Population: 514 (2000); Race: 98.7% White, 0.0% Black, 0.0% Asian, 0.0% American Indian and Alaska Native, 0.0% Hispanic of any race, 1.3% two or more races (2000); Density: 16.7 persons per square mile (2000); Age: 23.5% under 18, 13.5% over 64 (2000); Marriage status: 14.0% never married, 75.3% now married, 3.6% widowed, 7.0% divorced (2000); Foreign born: 0.0% (2000); Ancestry (includes multiple ancestries): 51.9% Norwegian, 22.7% German, 12.1% French (except Basque), 10.0% Swedish, 7.9% Irish (2000).

Economy: Employment by occupation: 21.4% management, 16.3% professional, 15.1% services, 26.2% sales, 3.6% farming, 11.5% construction, 6.0% production (2000).

Income: Per capita income: $20,433 (2000); Median household income: $39,750 (2000); Poverty rate: 10.6% (2000).

Taxes: Total city taxes per capita: $332 (1997); City property taxes per capita: $332 (1997).

Education: High school graduation rate: 89.5% (2000); College graduation rate: 24.7% (2000).

Housing: Homeownership rate: 92.2% (2000); Median home value: $157,900 (2000); Median rent: $290 per month (2000); Median age of housing: 31 years (2000).

Transportation: Commute to work: 91.3% car, 0.0% public transportation, 1.2% walk, 6.0% work from home (2000); Travel time to work: 21.9% less than 15 minutes, 25.7% 15 to 30 minutes, 37.6% 30 to 45 minutes, 0.0% 45 to 60 minutes, 14.8% 60 minutes or more (2000)

Pope County

Located in western Minnesota; drained by the Chippewa River, and watered by Lake Minnewaska. Covers a land area of 670.10 square miles, a water area of 47.20 square miles, and is located in the Central Time Zone. The county government was organized in 1862. County seat is Glenwood.

Weather Station: Glenwood 2 WNW — Elevation: 1,197 feet

	Jan	Feb	Mar	Apr	May	Jun	Jul	Aug	Sep	Oct	Nov	Dec
High	20	27	38	57	70	79	83	80	71	59	39	25
Low	1	8	19	33	45	54	59	57	46	35	21	7
Precip	0.6	0.5	1.3	1.8	3.3	4.1	3.3	3.4	2.3	2.6	1.2	0.4
Snow	9.4	5.4	7.3	2.2	tr	0.0	0.0	0.0	0.0	0.4	5.6	5.8

High and Low temperatures in degrees Fahrenheit; Precipitation and Snow in inches

Population: 11,236 (2000); Race: 99.1% White, 0.2% Black, 0.2% Asian, 0.1% American Indian and Alaska Native, 0.3% Hispanic of any race, 0.4% two or more races (2000); Density: 16.8 persons per square mile (2000); Age: 24.8% under 18, 21.6% over 64 (2000).

Religion: Five largest groups: 46.5% Evangelical Lutheran Church in America, 16.4% Catholic Church, 4.3% Lutheran Church—Missouri Synod, 2.8% The Association of Free Lutheran Congregations, 2.5% The United Methodist Church (2000).

Economy: Unemployment rate: 2.9% (11/2002); Total civilian labor force: 5,448 (11/2002); Leading industries: 21.1% health care and social assistance; 16.6% manufacturing; 12.9% wholesale trade (2000); Companies that employ more than 1,000 persons: 0 (2000); Companies that employ more than 100 persons: 7 (2000); Farms: 825 totaling 324,730 acres (1997); Minority business ownership rate: 0.0% (1997); Women business ownership rate: 27.6% (1997); Retail sales per capita: $5,360 (1997). Single-family building permits issued: 180 (2001) / 125 (2000); Multi-family building permits issued: 5 (2001) / 140 (2000).

Income: Per capita income: $19,032 (2000); Median household income: $35,633 (2000); Poverty rate: 8.8% (2000); Bankruptcy rate: 1.46% (2001).

Taxes: Total county taxes per capita: $270 (2000); County property taxes per capita: $270 (2000).

Education: High school graduation rate: 81.8% (2000); College graduation rate: 14.7% (2000).
Housing: Homeownership rate: 80.8% (2000); Median home value: $74,100 (2000); Median rent: $302 per month (2000); Median age of housing: 42 years (2000).
Health: Birth rate: 81.0 per 10,000 population (1998); Age adjusted death rate: 78.2 per 10,000 population (1999); Age adjusted cancer mortality rate: 163.4 deaths per 100,000 population (1999). Number of physicians: 6.2 per 10,000 population (1999); Number of hospital beds: 33.8 per 10,000 population (1999).
Elections: 2000 Presidential election results: 46.3% Gore, 46.9% Bush, 4.4% Nader, 2.1% Buchanan
National and State Parks: Bangor State Wildlife Management Area; Farwell State Wildlife Management Area; Glacial Lakes State Park; Heinks State Wildlife Management Area; Little Jo State Wildlife Management Area; Lowry State Wildlife Management Area; New Prairie State Wildlife Management Are; Noordmans State Wildlife Management Area; Nora State Wildlife Management Area; Reno State Wildlife Management Area; Sedan State Wildlife Management Areas; Skarpness State Wildlife Management Area; Star Lake State Wildlife Management Area; Van Luik State Wildlife Management Area; Volkmann State Wildlife Management Area; Wade State Wildlife Management Area; White Bear State Wildlife Management Area
Additional Information Contacts
Pope County Government Offices 320-634-5727
Glenwood Chamber of Commerce. 320-634-3636
Starbuck Chamber of Commerce 320-239-4220

Pope County Communities

BANGOR (township). Covers a land area of 35.047 square miles and a water area of 0.056 square miles. Located at 45.54° N. Lat.; 95.18° W. Long.
Population: 217 (2000); Race: 99.1% White, 0.0% Black, 0.0% Asian, 0.9% American Indian and Alaska Native, 1.7% Hispanic of any race, 0.0% two or more races (2000); Density: 6.2 persons per square mile (2000); Age: 36.8% under 18, 11.7% over 64 (2000); Marriage status: 23.2% never married, 55.5% now married, 9.8% widowed, 11.6% divorced (2000); Foreign born: 0.0% (2000); Ancestry (includes multiple ancestries): 48.1% German, 15.6% Norwegian, 11.7% French (except Basque), 10.8% Swedish, 9.5% United States or American (2000).
Economy: Employment by occupation: 25.2% management, 5.2% professional, 14.8% services, 15.7% sales, 9.6% farming, 5.2% construction, 24.3% production (2000).
Income: Per capita income: $12,600 (2000); Median household income: $38,125 (2000); Poverty rate: 17.2% (2000).
Taxes: Total city taxes per capita: $39 (1997); City property taxes per capita: $39 (1997).
Education: High school graduation rate: 83.6% (2000); College graduation rate: 7.0% (2000).
Housing: Homeownership rate: 82.1% (2000); Median home value: $28,900 (2000); Median rent: $188 per month (2000); Median age of housing: 54 years (2000).
Transportation: Commute to work: 75.7% car, 0.0% public transportation, 0.0% walk, 24.3% work from home (2000); Travel time to work: 40.2% less than 15 minutes, 26.4% 15 to 30 minutes, 17.2% 30 to 45 minutes, 5.7% 45 to 60 minutes, 10.3% 60 minutes or more (2000)

BARSNESS (township). Covers a land area of 33.095 square miles and a water area of 2.193 square miles. Located at 45.54° N. Lat.; 95.42° W. Long.
Population: 138 (2000); Race: 100.0% White, 0.0% Black, 0.0% Asian, 0.0% American Indian and Alaska Native, 0.0% Hispanic of any race, 0.0% two or more races (2000); Density: 4.2 persons per square mile (2000); Age: 24.6% under 18, 5.9% over 64 (2000); Marriage status: 24.2% never married, 71.7% now married, 2.0% widowed, 2.0% divorced (2000); Foreign born: 0.0% (2000); Ancestry (includes multiple ancestries): 35.6% German, 31.4% Norwegian, 17.8% United States or American, 11.9% Dutch, 5.9% Irish (2000).
Economy: Employment by occupation: 22.8% management, 15.2% professional, 15.2% services, 21.5% sales, 2.5% farming, 7.6% construction, 15.2% production (2000).
Income: Per capita income: $19,867 (2000); Median household income: $33,125 (2000); Poverty rate: 5.1% (2000).
Taxes: Total city taxes per capita: $75 (1997); City property taxes per capita: $75 (1997).
Education: High school graduation rate: 94.9% (2000); College graduation rate: 15.2% (2000).
Housing: Homeownership rate: 90.2% (2000); Median home value: $55,000 (2000); Median age of housing: 60+ years (2000).
Transportation: Commute to work: 78.5% car, 0.0% public transportation, 5.1% walk, 16.5% work from home (2000); Travel time to work: 28.8% less than 15 minutes, 33.3% 15 to 30 minutes, 18.2% 30 to 45 minutes, 13.6% 45 to 60 minutes, 6.1% 60 minutes or more (2000)

BEN WADE (township). Covers a land area of 34.005 square miles and a water area of 1.402 square miles. Located at 45.70° N. Lat.; 95.58° W. Long.
Population: 252 (2000); Race: 98.2% White, 0.0% Black, 1.4% Asian, 0.0% American Indian and Alaska Native, 0.0% Hispanic of any race, 0.4% two or more races (2000); Density: 7.4 persons per square mile (2000); Age: 31.5% under 18, 9.7% over 64 (2000); Marriage status: 24.5% never married, 69.7% now married, 3.4% widowed, 2.4% divorced (2000); Foreign born: 1.4% (2000); Ancestry (includes multiple ancestries): 47.3% Norwegian, 33.3% German, 23.7% Czech, 8.2% Swedish, 5.0% Irish (2000).
Economy: Employment by occupation: 30.4% management, 14.9% professional, 8.1% services, 17.6% sales, 6.8% farming, 8.8% construction, 13.5% production (2000).
Income: Per capita income: $14,500 (2000); Median household income: $36,458 (2000); Poverty rate: 12.5% (2000).
Taxes: Total city taxes per capita: $57 (1997); City property taxes per capita: $57 (1997).
Education: High school graduation rate: 85.0% (2000); College graduation rate: 15.0% (2000).
Housing: Homeownership rate: 82.8% (2000); Median home value: $81,000 (2000); Median rent: $300 per month (2000); Median age of housing: 50 years (2000).
Transportation: Commute to work: 68.9% car, 0.0% public transportation, 6.8% walk, 24.3% work from home (2000); Travel time to work: 34.8% less than 15 minutes, 44.6% 15 to 30 minutes, 14.3% 30 to 45 minutes, 1.8% 45 to 60 minutes, 4.5% 60 minutes or more (2000)

BLUE MOUNDS (township). Covers a land area of 34.858 square miles and a water area of 1.116 square miles. Located at 45.54° N. Lat.; 95.56° W. Long.
Population: 207 (2000); Race: 100.0% White, 0.0% Black, 0.0% Asian, 0.0% American Indian and Alaska Native, 0.0% Hispanic of any race, 0.0% two or more races (2000); Density: 5.9 persons per square mile (2000); Age: 20.1% under 18, 9.8% over 64 (2000); Marriage status: 14.6% never married, 69.5% now married, 4.9% widowed, 11.0% divorced (2000); Foreign born: 2.1% (2000); Ancestry (includes multiple ancestries): 52.6% Norwegian, 28.9% German, 13.9% United States or American, 7.7% Swedish, 5.7% English (2000).
Economy: Employment by occupation: 33.6% management, 7.8% professional, 11.2% services, 15.5% sales, 6.0% farming, 6.0% construction, 19.8% production (2000).
Income: Per capita income: $23,466 (2000); Median household income: $37,708 (2000); Poverty rate: 9.3% (2000).
Taxes: Total city taxes per capita: $86 (1997); City property taxes per capita: $86 (1997).
Education: High school graduation rate: 80.7% (2000); College graduation rate: 16.6% (2000).
Housing: Homeownership rate: 90.8% (2000); Median home value: $60,000 (2000); Median age of housing: 60+ years (2000).
Transportation: Commute to work: 69.8% car, 0.0% public transportation, 4.3% walk, 25.9% work from home (2000); Travel time to work: 43.0% less than 15 minutes, 44.2% 15 to 30 minutes, 8.1% 30 to 45 minutes, 2.3% 45 to 60 minutes, 2.3% 60 minutes or more (2000)

CHIPPEWA FALLS (township). Covers a land area of 34.235 square miles and a water area of 1.116 square miles. Located at 45.52° N. Lat.; 95.30° W. Long.
Population: 231 (2000); Race: 100.0% White, 0.0% Black, 0.0% Asian, 0.0% American Indian and Alaska Native, 0.0% Hispanic of any race, 0.0% two or more races (2000); Density: 6.7 persons per square mile (2000); Age: 21.0% under 18, 13.6% over 64 (2000); Marriage status: 20.3% never married, 66.8% now married, 4.1% widowed, 8.8% divorced (2000); Foreign born: 0.0% (2000); Ancestry (includes multiple ancestries): 50.2% Norwegian, 40.5% German, 7.8% Swedish, 7.0% Danish, 5.4% English (2000).
Economy: Employment by occupation: 17.9% management, 12.6% professional, 4.0% services, 26.5% sales, 5.3% farming, 13.2% construction, 20.5% production (2000).
Income: Per capita income: $19,653 (2000); Median household income: $36,071 (2000); Poverty rate: 3.5% (2000).

Taxes: Total city taxes per capita: $38 (1997); City property taxes per capita: $38 (1997).
Education: High school graduation rate: 87.8% (2000); College graduation rate: 20.7% (2000).
Housing: Homeownership rate: 85.3% (2000); Median home value: $73,000 (2000); Median rent: $225 per month (2000); Median age of housing: 60+ years (2000).
Transportation: Commute to work: 78.2% car, 0.0% public transportation, 1.4% walk, 19.0% work from home (2000); Travel time to work: 19.3% less than 15 minutes, 52.9% 15 to 30 minutes, 19.3% 30 to 45 minutes, 5.0% 45 to 60 minutes, 3.4% 60 minutes or more (2000)

CYRUS (city). Covers a land area of 0.288 square miles and a water area of 0 square miles. Located at 45.61° N. Lat.; 95.73° W. Long. Elevation is 1,138 feet.
Population: 303 (2000); Race: 100.0% White, 0.0% Black, 0.0% Asian, 0.0% American Indian and Alaska Native, 0.0% Hispanic of any race, 0.0% two or more races (2000); Density: 1,050.6 persons per square mile (2000); Age: 19.4% under 18, 26.5% over 64 (2000); Marriage status: 23.4% never married, 57.4% now married, 11.9% widowed, 7.4% divorced (2000); Foreign born: 0.0% (2000); Ancestry (includes multiple ancestries): 45.6% German, 35.4% Norwegian, 4.4% Swedish, 4.1% United States or American, 3.1% French (except Basque) (2000).
Economy: Grain, soybeans, beans; dairying; poultry. Manufacturing: feeds. Single-family building permits issued: 0 (2001) / 0 (2000); Multi-family building permits issued: 0 (2001) / 0 (2000); Employment by occupation: 11.3% management, 15.8% professional, 21.8% services, 20.3% sales, 3.0% farming, 12.0% construction, 15.8% production (2000).
Income: Per capita income: $19,836 (2000); Median household income: $26,875 (2000); Poverty rate: 12.6% (2000).
Taxes: Total city taxes per capita: $91 (1997); City property taxes per capita: $85 (1997).
Education: High school graduation rate: 76.7% (2000); College graduation rate: 7.4% (2000).

School District(s)

Cyrus (PK-06)
2000 Enrollment: 82 320-795-2216
Housing: Homeownership rate: 75.0% (2000); Median home value: $39,700 (2000); Median rent: $260 per month (2000); Median age of housing: 50 years (2000).
Transportation: Commute to work: 92.2% car, 0.0% public transportation, 6.3% walk, 0.0% work from home (2000); Travel time to work: 48.4% less than 15 minutes, 35.9% 15 to 30 minutes, 7.0% 30 to 45 minutes, 1.6% 45 to 60 minutes, 7.0% 60 minutes or more (2000)

FARWELL (city). Covers a land area of 0.287 square miles and a water area of 0 square miles. Located at 45.75° N. Lat.; 95.61° W. Long. Elevation is 1,339 feet.
Population: 57 (2000); Race: 100.0% White, 0.0% Black, 0.0% Asian, 0.0% American Indian and Alaska Native, 0.0% Hispanic of any race, 0.0% two or more races (2000); Density: 198.3 persons per square mile (2000); Age: 10.4% under 18, 25.0% over 64 (2000); Marriage status: 47.7% never married, 31.8% now married, 13.6% widowed, 6.8% divorced (2000); Foreign born: 0.0% (2000); Ancestry (includes multiple ancestries): 58.3% Norwegian, 52.1% German, 25.0% Swedish, 16.7% Irish, 8.3% English (2000).
Economy: Grain; dairying. Single-family building permits issued: 0 (2001) / 0 (2000); Multi-family building permits issued: 0 (2001) / 0 (2000); Employment by occupation: 6.9% management, 13.8% professional, 6.9% services, 48.3% sales, 6.9% farming, 6.9% construction, 10.3% production (2000).
Income: Per capita income: $19,917 (2000); Median household income: $28,125 (2000); Poverty rate: 0.0% (2000).
Taxes: Total city taxes per capita: $41 (1997); City property taxes per capita: $41 (1997).
Education: High school graduation rate: 80.6% (2000); College graduation rate: 3.2% (2000).
Housing: Homeownership rate: 91.7% (2000); Median home value: $23,000 (2000); Median rent: $325 per month (2000); Median age of housing: 60+ years (2000).
Transportation: Commute to work: 82.8% car, 0.0% public transportation, 10.3% walk, 6.9% work from home (2000); Travel time to work: 25.9% less than 15 minutes, 48.1% 15 to 30 minutes, 18.5% 30 to 45 minutes, 7.4% 45 to 60 minutes, 0.0% 60 minutes or more (2000)

GILCHRIST (township). Covers a land area of 32.085 square miles and a water area of 3.455 square miles. Located at 45.44° N. Lat.; 95.34° W. Long.
Population: 239 (2000); Race: 99.1% White, 0.0% Black, 0.0% Asian, 0.0% American Indian and Alaska Native, 0.0% Hispanic of any race, 0.0% two or more races (2000); Density: 7.4 persons per square mile (2000); Age: 22.3% under 18, 25.1% over 64 (2000); Marriage status: 14.2% never married, 77.5% now married, 5.9% widowed, 2.4% divorced (2000); Foreign born: 1.4% (2000); Ancestry (includes multiple ancestries): 57.3% Norwegian, 19.9% German, 17.1% Swedish, 10.9% Irish, 4.7% French (except Basque) (2000).
Economy: Single-family building permits issued: 0 (2001) / 0 (2000); Multi-family building permits issued: 0 (2001) / 0 (2000); Employment by occupation: 25.0% management, 9.1% professional, 6.8% services, 22.7% sales, 4.5% farming, 4.5% construction, 27.3% production (2000).
Income: Per capita income: $17,520 (2000); Median household income: $38,125 (2000); Poverty rate: 7.2% (2000).
Taxes: Total city taxes per capita: $145 (1997); City property taxes per capita: $145 (1997).
Education: High school graduation rate: 77.1% (2000); College graduation rate: 22.3% (2000).
Housing: Homeownership rate: 93.5% (2000); Median home value: $87,500 (2000); Median age of housing: 47 years (2000).
Transportation: Commute to work: 94.3% car, 0.0% public transportation, 2.3% walk, 3.4% work from home (2000); Travel time to work: 23.5% less than 15 minutes, 41.2% 15 to 30 minutes, 24.7% 30 to 45 minutes, 10.6% 45 to 60 minutes, 0.0% 60 minutes or more (2000)

GLENWOOD (city). Covers a land area of 5.566 square miles and a water area of 0 square miles. Located at 45.65° N. Lat.; 95.38° W. Long. Elevation is 1,403 feet.
History: Glenwood grew up on the shores of Lake Minnewaska, in an area of ancient burial mounds. The grave of Princess Minnewaska, for whom the lake was named, is here. Early Glenwood residents of Norwegian descent formed musical groups that gave the town a reputation for cultural performances.
Population: 2,594 (2000); Race: 99.0% White, 0.1% Black, 0.5% Asian, 0.0% American Indian and Alaska Native, 0.7% Hispanic of any race, 0.2% two or more races (2000); Density: 466.0 persons per square mile (2000); Age: 20.9% under 18, 31.4% over 64 (2000); Marriage status: 18.8% never married, 55.8% now married, 17.2% widowed, 8.3% divorced (2000); Foreign born: 1.4% (2000); Ancestry (includes multiple ancestries): 37.0% German, 35.0% Norwegian, 11.7% Irish, 9.1% Swedish, 5.3% English (2000).
Economy: Single-family building permits issued: 8 (2001) / 10 (2000); Multi-family building permits issued: 5 (2001) / 0 (2000); Employment by occupation: 3.9% management, 22.4% professional, 21.7% services, 25.9% sales, 1.2% farming, 7.1% construction, 17.7% production (2000).
Income: Per capita income: $21,758 (2000); Median household income: $30,083 (2000); Poverty rate: 7.9% (2000).
Taxes: Total city taxes per capita: $269 (1997); City property taxes per capita: $255 (1997).
Education: High school graduation rate: 78.0% (2000); College graduation rate: 13.8% (2000).

School District(s)

Minnewaska (PK-12)
2000 Enrollment: 1,626 320-239-4820
Housing: Homeownership rate: 64.6% (2000); Median home value: $66,200 (2000); Median rent: $319 per month (2000); Median age of housing: 45 years (2000).
Hospitals: Glacial Ridge Hospital and Health Care Services (34 beds)
Safety: Violent crime rate: 0.0 per 10,000 population; Property crime rate: 125.9 per 10,000 population (2001).
Newspapers: Pope County Tribune (1 x week)
Transportation: Commute to work: 88.9% car, 0.0% public transportation, 5.6% walk, 4.3% work from home (2000); Travel time to work: 65.3% less than 15 minutes, 21.8% 15 to 30 minutes, 7.5% 30 to 45 minutes, 2.5% 45 to 60 minutes, 2.9% 60 minutes or more (2000)
Additional Information Contacts
Glenwood Chamber of Commerce 320-634-3636

GLENWOOD (township). Covers a land area of 40.088 square miles and a water area of 1.459 square miles. Located at 45.62° N. Lat.; 95.34° W. Long. Elevation is 1,403 feet.
History: Plotted 1866, incorporated as village 1881, incorporated as city 1912.

Population: 1,004 (2000); Race: 98.6% White, 0.0% Black, 0.5% Asian, 0.2% American Indian and Alaska Native, 0.2% Hispanic of any race, 0.6% two or more races (2000); Density: 25.0 persons per square mile (2000); Age: 25.2% under 18, 17.8% over 64 (2000); Marriage status: 18.7% never married, 66.1% now married, 8.0% widowed, 7.2% divorced (2000); Foreign born: 2.0% (2000); Ancestry (includes multiple ancestries): 43.3% German, 35.0% Norwegian, 11.5% Swedish, 8.6% Irish, 5.1% English (2000).
Economy: Railroad junction. Resort in agricultural area: poultry, livestock; grain, soybeans, beans; dairying. Light manufacturing. Municipal airport to East. Single-family building permits issued: 2 (2001) / 3 (2000); Multi-family building permits issued: 0 (2001) / 0 (2000); Employment by occupation: 19.1% management, 20.7% professional, 13.0% services, 22.2% sales, 2.0% farming, 9.8% construction, 13.2% production (2000).
Income: Per capita income: $26,117 (2000); Median household income: $41,481 (2000); Poverty rate: 9.6% (2000).
Taxes: Total city taxes per capita: $70 (1997); City property taxes per capita: $69 (1997).
Education: High school graduation rate: 89.6% (2000); College graduation rate: 24.5% (2000).
Housing: Homeownership rate: 90.2% (2000); Median home value: $107,400 (2000); Median rent: $380 per month (2000); Median age of housing: 30 years (2000).
Transportation: Commute to work: 86.5% car, 0.4% public transportation, 2.5% walk, 10.6% work from home (2000); Travel time to work: 57.7% less than 15 minutes, 23.7% 15 to 30 minutes, 14.7% 30 to 45 minutes, 1.4% 45 to 60 minutes, 2.6% 60 minutes or more (2000)

GROVE LAKE (township). Covers a land area of 32.004 square miles and a water area of 1.720 square miles. Located at 45.62° N. Lat.; 95.20° W. Long. Elevation is 1,353 feet.
Population: 268 (2000); Race: 99.0% White, 1.0% Black, 0.0% Asian, 0.0% American Indian and Alaska Native, 0.0% Hispanic of any race, 0.0% two or more races (2000); Density: 8.4 persons per square mile (2000); Age: 21.9% under 18, 19.9% over 64 (2000); Marriage status: 19.4% never married, 69.4% now married, 8.2% widowed, 2.9% divorced (2000); Foreign born: 1.5% (2000); Ancestry (includes multiple ancestries): 51.7% German, 20.9% Norwegian, 6.5% Irish, 5.5% French (except Basque), 5.5% United States or American (2000).
Economy: Employment by occupation: 24.0% management, 14.0% professional, 8.0% services, 15.0% sales, 2.0% farming, 12.0% construction, 25.0% production (2000).
Income: Per capita income: $16,170 (2000); Median household income: $36,250 (2000); Poverty rate: 9.5% (2000).
Taxes: Total city taxes per capita: $82 (1997); City property taxes per capita: $82 (1997).
Education: High school graduation rate: 71.1% (2000); College graduation rate: 0.0% (2000).
Housing: Homeownership rate: 94.3% (2000); Median home value: $67,500 (2000); Median rent: $275 per month (2000); Median age of housing: 36 years (2000).
Transportation: Commute to work: 91.8% car, 0.0% public transportation, 0.0% walk, 8.2% work from home (2000); Travel time to work: 15.6% less than 15 minutes, 56.7% 15 to 30 minutes, 16.7% 30 to 45 minutes, 1.1% 45 to 60 minutes, 10.0% 60 minutes or more (2000)

HOFF (township). Covers a land area of 35.965 square miles and a water area of 0.011 square miles. Located at 45.45° N. Lat.; 95.69° W. Long.
Population: 195 (2000); Race: 98.9% White, 0.0% Black, 0.0% Asian, 0.0% American Indian and Alaska Native, 0.0% Hispanic of any race, 1.1% two or more races (2000); Density: 5.4 persons per square mile (2000); Age: 32.6% under 18, 12.7% over 64 (2000); Marriage status: 25.7% never married, 66.2% now married, 2.9% widowed, 5.1% divorced (2000); Foreign born: 0.0% (2000); Ancestry (includes multiple ancestries): 38.1% Norwegian, 32.0% German, 14.9% Swedish, 11.6% Swiss, 11.0% Irish (2000).
Economy: Employment by occupation: 20.7% management, 18.4% professional, 8.0% services, 13.8% sales, 10.3% farming, 11.5% construction, 17.2% production (2000).
Income: Per capita income: $15,496 (2000); Median household income: $41,667 (2000); Poverty rate: 7.7% (2000).
Taxes: Total city taxes per capita: $57 (1997); City property taxes per capita: $57 (1997).
Education: High school graduation rate: 85.3% (2000); College graduation rate: 11.8% (2000).
Housing: Homeownership rate: 88.7% (2000); Median home value: $47,900 (2000); Median rent: $375 per month (2000); Median age of housing: 44 years (2000).
Transportation: Commute to work: 85.1% car, 0.0% public transportation, 0.0% walk, 14.9% work from home (2000); Travel time to work: 29.7% less than 15 minutes, 52.7% 15 to 30 minutes, 12.2% 30 to 45 minutes, 2.7% 45 to 60 minutes, 2.7% 60 minutes or more (2000)

LAKE JOHANNA (township). Covers a land area of 33.159 square miles and a water area of 2.693 square miles. Located at 45.44° N. Lat.; 95.20° W. Long.
Population: 151 (2000); Race: 98.5% White, 1.5% Black, 0.0% Asian, 0.0% American Indian and Alaska Native, 0.0% Hispanic of any race, 0.0% two or more races (2000); Density: 4.6 persons per square mile (2000); Age: 17.0% under 18, 22.2% over 64 (2000); Marriage status: 22.2% never married, 66.7% now married, 7.9% widowed, 3.2% divorced (2000); Foreign born: 0.0% (2000); Ancestry (includes multiple ancestries): 51.1% Norwegian, 14.1% German, 11.9% Irish, 8.1% English, 6.7% Swedish (2000).
Economy: Employment by occupation: 15.1% management, 17.8% professional, 9.6% services, 15.1% sales, 0.0% farming, 21.9% construction, 20.5% production (2000).
Income: Per capita income: $17,270 (2000); Median household income: $32,813 (2000); Poverty rate: 11.9% (2000).
Taxes: Total city taxes per capita: $69 (1997); City property taxes per capita: $69 (1997).
Education: High school graduation rate: 75.0% (2000); College graduation rate: 8.3% (2000).
Housing: Homeownership rate: 90.2% (2000); Median home value: $75,000 (2000); Median rent: $275 per month (2000); Median age of housing: 46 years (2000).
Transportation: Commute to work: 78.1% car, 0.0% public transportation, 0.0% walk, 21.9% work from home (2000); Travel time to work: 17.5% less than 15 minutes, 21.1% 15 to 30 minutes, 31.6% 30 to 45 minutes, 26.3% 45 to 60 minutes, 3.5% 60 minutes or more (2000)

LANGHEI (township). Covers a land area of 35.344 square miles and a water area of 0.579 square miles. Located at 45.46° N. Lat.; 95.57° W. Long.
Population: 217 (2000); Race: 100.0% White, 0.0% Black, 0.0% Asian, 0.0% American Indian and Alaska Native, 0.0% Hispanic of any race, 0.0% two or more races (2000); Density: 6.1 persons per square mile (2000); Age: 39.2% under 18, 19.8% over 64 (2000); Marriage status: 32.5% never married, 63.7% now married, 3.2% widowed, 0.6% divorced (2000); Foreign born: 0.0% (2000); Ancestry (includes multiple ancestries): 63.6% Norwegian, 30.0% German, 7.4% Swedish, 5.1% Danish, 4.6% French (except Basque) (2000).
Economy: Employment by occupation: 26.3% management, 13.1% professional, 5.1% services, 19.2% sales, 14.1% farming, 4.0% construction, 18.2% production (2000).
Income: Per capita income: $16,829 (2000); Median household income: $43,929 (2000); Poverty rate: 0.0% (2000).
Taxes: Total city taxes per capita: $72 (1997); City property taxes per capita: $72 (1997).
Education: High school graduation rate: 81.5% (2000); College graduation rate: 17.7% (2000).
Housing: Homeownership rate: 94.4% (2000); Median home value: $81,700 (2000); Median age of housing: 60 years (2000).
Transportation: Commute to work: 72.7% car, 0.0% public transportation, 7.1% walk, 20.2% work from home (2000); Travel time to work: 39.2% less than 15 minutes, 43.0% 15 to 30 minutes, 8.9% 30 to 45 minutes, 2.5% 45 to 60 minutes, 6.3% 60 minutes or more (2000)

LEVEN (township). Covers a land area of 32.724 square miles and a water area of 2.733 square miles. Located at 45.72° N. Lat.; 95.33° W. Long.
Population: 528 (2000); Race: 99.1% White, 0.0% Black, 0.0% Asian, 0.9% American Indian and Alaska Native, 0.0% Hispanic of any race, 0.0% two or more races (2000); Density: 16.1 persons per square mile (2000); Age: 28.7% under 18, 16.9% over 64 (2000); Marriage status: 18.6% never married, 71.1% now married, 6.7% widowed, 3.6% divorced (2000); Foreign born: 0.4% (2000); Ancestry (includes multiple ancestries): 57.3% German, 28.0% Norwegian, 9.2% Irish, 8.5% Czech, 6.4% Swedish (2000).
Economy: Single-family building permits issued: 1 (2001) / 13 (2000); Multi-family building permits issued: 0 (2001) / 0 (2000); Employment by occupation: 17.4% management, 24.3% professional, 10.8% services, 18.1% sales, 0.8% farming, 15.4% construction, 13.1% production (2000).
Income: Per capita income: $17,197 (2000); Median household income: $41,705 (2000); Poverty rate: 4.4% (2000).
Taxes: Total city taxes per capita: $92 (1997); City property taxes per capita: $92 (1997).

Education: High school graduation rate: 88.2% (2000); College graduation rate: 14.6% (2000).
Housing: Homeownership rate: 90.0% (2000); Median home value: $96,300 (2000); Median rent: $513 per month (2000); Median age of housing: 38 years (2000).
Transportation: Commute to work: 84.3% car, 0.4% public transportation, 0.8% walk, 14.6% work from home (2000); Travel time to work: 48.4% less than 15 minutes, 39.2% 15 to 30 minutes, 8.8% 30 to 45 minutes, 1.8% 45 to 60 minutes, 1.8% 60 minutes or more (2000)

LONG BEACH (city). Covers a land area of 1.503 square miles and a water area of 0.116 square miles. Located at 45.64° N. Lat.; 95.43° W. Long.
Population: 271 (2000); Race: 100.0% White, 0.0% Black, 0.0% Asian, 0.0% American Indian and Alaska Native, 1.5% Hispanic of any race, 0.0% two or more races (2000); Density: 180.3 persons per square mile (2000); Age: 24.7% under 18, 21.5% over 64 (2000); Marriage status: 11.9% never married, 75.2% now married, 7.3% widowed, 5.5% divorced (2000); Foreign born: 0.4% (2000); Ancestry (includes multiple ancestries): 43.6% Norwegian, 43.6% German, 12.7% Swedish, 7.6% Irish, 6.9% English (2000).
Economy: Single-family building permits issued: 6 (2001) / 1 (2000); Multi-family building permits issued: 0 (2001) / 0 (2000); Employment by occupation: 17.5% management, 29.2% professional, 5.0% services, 35.0% sales, 0.0% farming, 1.7% construction, 11.7% production (2000).
Income: Per capita income: $30,207 (2000); Median household income: $55,000 (2000); Poverty rate: 4.0% (2000).
Taxes: Total city taxes per capita: $46 (1997); City property taxes per capita: $8 (1997).
Education: High school graduation rate: 88.4% (2000); College graduation rate: 27.6% (2000).
Housing: Homeownership rate: 88.3% (2000); Median home value: $124,100 (2000); Median rent: $292 per month (2000); Median age of housing: 37 years (2000).
Transportation: Commute to work: 90.8% car, 3.3% public transportation, 0.0% walk, 5.8% work from home (2000); Travel time to work: 54.0% less than 15 minutes, 24.8% 15 to 30 minutes, 8.8% 30 to 45 minutes, 6.2% 45 to 60 minutes, 6.2% 60 minutes or more (2000)

LOWRY (city). Covers a land area of 0.371 square miles and a water area of 0 square miles. Located at 45.70° N. Lat.; 95.51° W. Long. Elevation is 1,368 feet.
Population: 271 (2000); Race: 96.0% White, 4.0% Black, 0.0% Asian, 0.0% American Indian and Alaska Native, 0.0% Hispanic of any race, 0.0% two or more races (2000); Density: 729.7 persons per square mile (2000); Age: 23.8% under 18, 19.8% over 64 (2000); Marriage status: 28.8% never married, 55.6% now married, 11.2% widowed, 4.4% divorced (2000); Foreign born: 0.0% (2000); Ancestry (includes multiple ancestries): 23.4% Norwegian, 18.5% German, 16.1% Czech, 14.1% Swedish, 11.7% United States or American (2000).
Economy: Livestock; grain; dairying. Manufacturing: printing and publishing. Single-family building permits issued: 2 (2001) / 0 (2000); Multi-family building permits issued: 0 (2001) / 0 (2000); Employment by occupation: 9.2% management, 6.1% professional, 16.8% services, 28.2% sales, 0.0% farming, 13.0% construction, 26.7% production (2000).
Income: Per capita income: $16,234 (2000); Median household income: $31,591 (2000); Poverty rate: 3.6% (2000).
Taxes: Total city taxes per capita: $150 (1997); City property taxes per capita: $137 (1997).
Education: High school graduation rate: 71.0% (2000); College graduation rate: 2.5% (2000).
Housing: Homeownership rate: 83.5% (2000); Median home value: $66,200 (2000); Median rent: $553 per month (2000); Median age of housing: 50 years (2000).
Transportation: Commute to work: 86.9% car, 0.0% public transportation, 11.5% walk, 1.5% work from home (2000); Travel time to work: 36.7% less than 15 minutes, 45.3% 15 to 30 minutes, 10.2% 30 to 45 minutes, 0.0% 45 to 60 minutes, 7.8% 60 minutes or more (2000)

MINNEWASKA (township). Covers a land area of 12.814 square miles and a water area of 12.603 square miles. Located at 45.65° N. Lat.; 95.46° W. Long.
Population: 504 (2000); Race: 99.0% White, 0.0% Black, 0.4% Asian, 0.0% American Indian and Alaska Native, 0.6% Hispanic of any race, 0.6% two or more races (2000); Density: 39.3 persons per square mile (2000); Age: 19.8% under 18, 19.4% over 64 (2000); Marriage status: 18.6% never married, 72.3% now married, 4.1% widowed, 5.0% divorced (2000); Foreign born: 1.2% (2000); Ancestry (includes multiple ancestries): 39.3% Norwegian, 35.2% German, 11.4% Swedish, 7.1% Irish, 5.7% English (2000).
Economy: Single-family building permits issued: 0 (2001) / 0 (2000); Multi-family building permits issued: 0 (2001) / 0 (2000); Employment by occupation: 22.0% management, 11.8% professional, 13.6% services, 31.0% sales, 0.7% farming, 6.3% construction, 14.6% production (2000).
Income: Per capita income: $19,838 (2000); Median household income: $38,000 (2000); Poverty rate: 7.1% (2000).
Taxes: Total city taxes per capita: $86 (1997); City property taxes per capita: $86 (1997).
Education: High school graduation rate: 94.2% (2000); College graduation rate: 21.1% (2000).
Housing: Homeownership rate: 93.3% (2000); Median home value: $108,700 (2000); Median rent: $550 per month (2000); Median age of housing: 36 years (2000).
Transportation: Commute to work: 92.6% car, 0.7% public transportation, 2.8% walk, 2.8% work from home (2000); Travel time to work: 65.9% less than 15 minutes, 17.8% 15 to 30 minutes, 12.3% 30 to 45 minutes, 2.9% 45 to 60 minutes, 1.1% 60 minutes or more (2000)

NEW PRAIRIE (township). Covers a land area of 35.166 square miles and a water area of 0.672 square miles. Located at 45.63° N. Lat.; 95.68° W. Long.
Population: 252 (2000); Race: 100.0% White, 0.0% Black, 0.0% Asian, 0.0% American Indian and Alaska Native, 0.0% Hispanic of any race, 0.0% two or more races (2000); Density: 7.2 persons per square mile (2000); Age: 29.5% under 18, 18.5% over 64 (2000); Marriage status: 26.6% never married, 67.0% now married, 5.5% widowed, 0.9% divorced (2000); Foreign born: 1.1% (2000); Ancestry (includes multiple ancestries): 42.2% German, 34.5% Norwegian, 8.0% Irish, 5.1% Swedish, 3.6% Danish (2000).
Economy: Single-family building permits issued: 0 (2001) / 0 (2000); Multi-family building permits issued: 0 (2001) / 0 (2000); Employment by occupation: 29.5% management, 3.8% professional, 15.2% services, 20.5% sales, 0.8% farming, 8.3% construction, 22.0% production (2000).
Income: Per capita income: $17,136 (2000); Median household income: $41,875 (2000); Poverty rate: 8.4% (2000).
Taxes: Total city taxes per capita: $95 (1997); City property taxes per capita: $91 (1997).
Education: High school graduation rate: 80.8% (2000); College graduation rate: 7.7% (2000).
Housing: Homeownership rate: 97.9% (2000); Median home value: $66,700 (2000); Median rent: <$100 per month (2000); Median age of housing: 44 years (2000).
Transportation: Commute to work: 79.5% car, 0.0% public transportation, 0.0% walk, 20.5% work from home (2000); Travel time to work: 24.8% less than 15 minutes, 61.0% 15 to 30 minutes, 3.8% 30 to 45 minutes, 0.0% 45 to 60 minutes, 10.5% 60 minutes or more (2000)

NORA (township). Covers a land area of 33.800 square miles and a water area of 2.394 square miles. Located at 45.70° N. Lat.; 95.69° W. Long.
Population: 207 (2000); Race: 100.0% White, 0.0% Black, 0.0% Asian, 0.0% American Indian and Alaska Native, 0.0% Hispanic of any race, 0.0% two or more races (2000); Density: 6.1 persons per square mile (2000); Age: 20.3% under 18, 12.6% over 64 (2000); Marriage status: 19.5% never married, 71.1% now married, 3.4% widowed, 6.0% divorced (2000); Foreign born: 1.1% (2000); Ancestry (includes multiple ancestries): 54.9% Norwegian, 36.3% German, 19.2% Swedish, 5.5% English, 3.3% United States or American (2000).
Economy: Employment by occupation: 51.9% management, 6.7% professional, 8.7% services, 17.3% sales, 1.9% farming, 6.7% construction, 6.7% production (2000).
Income: Per capita income: $16,833 (2000); Median household income: $33,250 (2000); Poverty rate: 7.7% (2000).
Taxes: Total city taxes per capita: $78 (1997); City property taxes per capita: $78 (1997).
Education: High school graduation rate: 88.1% (2000); College graduation rate: 9.7% (2000).
Housing: Homeownership rate: 78.0% (2000); Median home value: $80,800 (2000); Median rent: $175 per month (2000); Median age of housing: 60+ years (2000).
Transportation: Commute to work: 56.9% car, 0.0% public transportation, 5.9% walk, 33.3% work from home (2000); Travel time to work: 22.1% less than 15 minutes, 39.7% 15 to 30 minutes, 33.8% 30 to 45 minutes, 0.0% 45 to 60 minutes, 4.4% 60 minutes or more (2000)

RENO (township). Covers a land area of 29.780 square miles and a water area of 6.092 square miles. Located at 45.70° N. Lat.; 95.45° W. Long.
Population: 355 (2000); Race: 98.6% White, 0.0% Black, 0.0% Asian, 0.0% American Indian and Alaska Native, 0.0% Hispanic of any race, 1.4% two or more races (2000); Density: 11.9 persons per square mile (2000); Age: 30.9% under 18, 12.0% over 64 (2000); Marriage status: 17.6% never married, 72.9% now married, 5.3% widowed, 4.2% divorced (2000); Foreign born: 0.9% (2000); Ancestry (includes multiple ancestries): 38.4% German, 35.5% Norwegian, 15.8% Czech, 12.3% Swedish, 5.7% English (2000).
Economy: Employment by occupation: 28.4% management, 12.0% professional, 14.2% services, 15.8% sales, 7.1% farming, 9.3% construction, 13.1% production (2000).
Income: Per capita income: $15,518 (2000); Median household income: $48,000 (2000); Poverty rate: 10.6% (2000).
Taxes: Total city taxes per capita: $55 (1997); City property taxes per capita: $55 (1997).
Education: High school graduation rate: 85.6% (2000); College graduation rate: 12.5% (2000).
Housing: Homeownership rate: 87.0% (2000); Median home value: $128,100 (2000); Median rent: $125 per month (2000); Median age of housing: 26 years (2000).
Transportation: Commute to work: 74.9% car, 0.0% public transportation, 1.6% walk, 23.5% work from home (2000); Travel time to work: 44.3% less than 15 minutes, 42.9% 15 to 30 minutes, 7.9% 30 to 45 minutes, 5.0% 45 to 60 minutes, 0.0% 60 minutes or more (2000)

ROLLING FORKS (township). Covers a land area of 34.642 square miles and a water area of 1.245 square miles. Located at 45.44° N. Lat.; 95.43° W. Long.
Population: 160 (2000); Race: 100.0% White, 0.0% Black, 0.0% Asian, 0.0% American Indian and Alaska Native, 0.0% Hispanic of any race, 0.0% two or more races (2000); Density: 4.6 persons per square mile (2000); Age: 33.9% under 18, 18.5% over 64 (2000); Marriage status: 27.0% never married, 64.3% now married, 7.1% widowed, 1.6% divorced (2000); Foreign born: 1.2% (2000); Ancestry (includes multiple ancestries): 72.6% Norwegian, 23.8% German, 8.9% Czech, 7.7% Irish, 4.8% English (2000).
Economy: Single-family building permits issued: 0 (2001) / 0 (2000); Multi-family building permits issued: 0 (2001) / 0 (2000); Employment by occupation: 18.2% management, 16.9% professional, 16.9% services, 23.4% sales, 3.9% farming, 3.9% construction, 16.9% production (2000).
Income: Per capita income: $13,293 (2000); Median household income: $38,750 (2000); Poverty rate: 2.4% (2000).
Taxes: Total city taxes per capita: $79 (1997); City property taxes per capita: $79 (1997).
Education: High school graduation rate: 77.7% (2000); College graduation rate: 11.7% (2000).
Housing: Homeownership rate: 87.5% (2000); Median home value: $45,000 (2000); Median rent: $125 per month (2000); Median age of housing: 60+ years (2000).
Transportation: Commute to work: 80.5% car, 0.0% public transportation, 3.9% walk, 15.6% work from home (2000); Travel time to work: 21.5% less than 15 minutes, 49.2% 15 to 30 minutes, 29.2% 30 to 45 minutes, 0.0% 45 to 60 minutes, 0.0% 60 minutes or more (2000)

SEDAN (city). Covers a land area of 0.507 square miles and a water area of 0 square miles. Located at 45.57° N. Lat.; 95.24° W. Long. Elevation is 1,350 feet.
Population: 65 (2000); Race: 100.0% White, 0.0% Black, 0.0% Asian, 0.0% American Indian and Alaska Native, 0.0% Hispanic of any race, 0.0% two or more races (2000); Density: 128.2 persons per square mile (2000); Age: 21.1% under 18, 8.5% over 64 (2000); Marriage status: 33.3% never married, 47.6% now married, 3.2% widowed, 15.9% divorced (2000); Foreign born: 0.0% (2000); Ancestry (includes multiple ancestries): 62.0% German, 40.8% Norwegian, 7.0% Polish, 2.8% Pennsylvania German, 2.8% Irish (2000).
Economy: Dairying; light manufacturing. Employment by occupation: 5.7% management, 8.6% professional, 34.3% services, 11.4% sales, 0.0% farming, 20.0% construction, 20.0% production (2000).
Income: Per capita income: $16,355 (2000); Median household income: $29,375 (2000); Poverty rate: 15.5% (2000).
Taxes: Total city taxes per capita: $81 (1997); City property taxes per capita: $48 (1997).
Education: High school graduation rate: 86.4% (2000); College graduation rate: 20.5% (2000).
Housing: Homeownership rate: 81.8% (2000); Median home value: $30,000 (2000); Median rent: $200 per month (2000); Median age of housing: 44 years (2000).
Transportation: Commute to work: 85.7% car, 0.0% public transportation, 0.0% walk, 14.3% work from home (2000); Travel time to work: 36.7% less than 15 minutes, 56.7% 15 to 30 minutes, 6.7% 30 to 45 minutes, 0.0% 45 to 60 minutes, 0.0% 60 minutes or more (2000)

STARBUCK (city). Covers a land area of 1.575 square miles and a water area of 0 square miles. Located at 45.61° N. Lat.; 95.53° W. Long. Elevation is 1,162 feet.
Population: 1,314 (2000); Race: 99.2% White, 0.0% Black, 0.2% Asian, 0.0% American Indian and Alaska Native, 0.2% Hispanic of any race, 0.5% two or more races (2000); Density: 834.0 persons per square mile (2000); Age: 21.6% under 18, 32.0% over 64 (2000); Marriage status: 18.4% never married, 56.1% now married, 19.0% widowed, 6.5% divorced (2000); Foreign born: 0.7% (2000); Ancestry (includes multiple ancestries): 55.8% Norwegian, 31.0% German, 10.3% Swedish, 6.6% Irish, 5.0% English (2000).
Economy: Poultry, livetock; grain, soybeans, beans; dairying. Manufacturing: fabricated metal products, fertilizers, feeds. Single-family building permits issued: 7 (2001) / 9 (2000); Multi-family building permits issued: 0 (2001) / 6 (2000); Employment by occupation: 9.2% management, 19.4% professional, 22.8% services, 20.8% sales, 0.7% farming, 10.3% construction, 16.7% production (2000).
Income: Per capita income: $15,030 (2000); Median household income: $28,235 (2000); Poverty rate: 13.1% (2000).
Taxes: Total city taxes per capita: $179 (1997); City property taxes per capita: $168 (1997).
Education: High school graduation rate: 73.0% (2000); College graduation rate: 12.3% (2000).
Housing: Homeownership rate: 75.7% (2000); Median home value: $63,400 (2000); Median rent: $283 per month (2000); Median age of housing: 44 years (2000).
Hospitals: Minnewaska District Hospital (19 beds)
Newspapers: The Starbuck Times (1 x week)
Transportation: Commute to work: 85.9% car, 0.0% public transportation, 9.1% walk, 4.2% work from home (2000); Travel time to work: 62.5% less than 15 minutes, 19.2% 15 to 30 minutes, 9.7% 30 to 45 minutes, 2.9% 45 to 60 minutes, 5.7% 60 minutes or more (2000)
Additional Information Contacts
Starbuck Chamber of Commerce 320-239-4220

VILLARD (city). Covers a land area of 0.791 square miles and a water area of 0.004 square miles. Located at 45.71° N. Lat.; 95.27° W. Long. Elevation is 1,360 feet.
Population: 244 (2000); Race: 99.6% White, 0.0% Black, 0.0% Asian, 0.0% American Indian and Alaska Native, 0.0% Hispanic of any race, 0.4% two or more races (2000); Density: 308.5 persons per square mile (2000); Age: 25.6% under 18, 20.3% over 64 (2000); Marriage status: 18.4% never married, 61.7% now married, 10.7% widowed, 9.2% divorced (2000); Foreign born: 0.4% (2000); Ancestry (includes multiple ancestries): 58.9% German, 24.8% Norwegian, 9.3% French (except Basque), 6.1% Swedish, 5.7% Irish (2000).
Economy: Livestock and poultry area; dairy products; grain, soybeans, beans. Manufacturing: machinery. Single-family building permits issued: 1 (2001) / 1 (2000); Multi-family building permits issued: 0 (2001) / 0 (2000); Employment by occupation: 4.3% management, 7.8% professional, 35.7% services, 24.3% sales, 1.7% farming, 4.3% construction, 21.7% production (2000).
Income: Per capita income: $14,154 (2000); Median household income: $24,688 (2000); Poverty rate: 18.3% (2000).
Taxes: Total city taxes per capita: $124 (1997); City property taxes per capita: $112 (1997).
Education: High school graduation rate: 80.5% (2000); College graduation rate: 3.6% (2000).
Housing: Homeownership rate: 86.5% (2000); Median home value: $47,700 (2000); Median rent: $325 per month (2000); Median age of housing: 51 years (2000).
Transportation: Commute to work: 86.1% car, 0.0% public transportation, 1.7% walk, 6.1% work from home (2000); Travel time to work: 32.4% less than 15 minutes, 50.0% 15 to 30 minutes, 12.0% 30 to 45 minutes, 0.0% 45 to 60 minutes, 5.6% 60 minutes or more (2000)

WALDEN (township). Covers a land area of 32.858 square miles and a water area of 2.757 square miles. Located at 45.53° N. Lat.; 95.69° W. Long.

Population: 201 (2000); Race: 100.0% White, 0.0% Black, 0.0% Asian, 0.0% American Indian and Alaska Native, 0.0% Hispanic of any race, 0.0% two or more races (2000); Density: 6.1 persons per square mile (2000); Age: 28.8% under 18, 11.6% over 64 (2000); Marriage status: 16.0% never married, 77.1% now married, 4.9% widowed, 2.1% divorced (2000); Foreign born: 1.0% (2000); Ancestry (includes multiple ancestries): 42.9% Norwegian, 37.9% German, 12.6% Swedish, 9.1% Polish, 8.6% Dutch (2000).
Economy: Single-family building permits issued: 0 (2001) / 0 (2000); Multi-family building permits issued: 0 (2001) / 0 (2000); Employment by occupation: 29.7% management, 9.9% professional, 6.9% services, 23.8% sales, 6.9% farming, 6.9% construction, 15.8% production (2000).
Income: Per capita income: $15,066 (2000); Median household income: $37,000 (2000); Poverty rate: 8.6% (2000).
Taxes: Total city taxes per capita: $75 (1997); City property taxes per capita: $75 (1997).
Education: High school graduation rate: 77.9% (2000); College graduation rate: 16.4% (2000).
Housing: Homeownership rate: 76.9% (2000); Median home value: $73,000 (2000); Median rent: $163 per month (2000); Median age of housing: 60+ years (2000).
Transportation: Commute to work: 77.2% car, 0.0% public transportation, 7.9% walk, 14.9% work from home (2000); Travel time to work: 31.4% less than 15 minutes, 45.3% 15 to 30 minutes, 14.0% 30 to 45 minutes, 4.7% 45 to 60 minutes, 4.7% 60 minutes or more (2000)

WESTPORT (city). Covers a land area of 0.280 square miles and a water area of 0 square miles. Located at 45.71° N. Lat.; 95.16° W. Long. Elevation is 1,334 feet.
Population: 72 (2000); Race: 100.0% White, 0.0% Black, 0.0% Asian, 0.0% American Indian and Alaska Native, 0.0% Hispanic of any race, 0.0% two or more races (2000); Density: 257.4 persons per square mile (2000); Age: 35.6% under 18, 4.1% over 64 (2000); Marriage status: 32.0% never married, 44.0% now married, 10.0% widowed, 14.0% divorced (2000); Foreign born: 0.0% (2000); Ancestry (includes multiple ancestries): 63.0% German, 31.5% Norwegian, 11.0% Irish, 5.5% French Canadian, 4.1% Scottish (2000).
Economy: Employment by occupation: 12.8% management, 0.0% professional, 7.7% services, 38.5% sales, 5.1% farming, 5.1% construction, 30.8% production (2000).
Income: Per capita income: $14,501 (2000); Median household income: $38,438 (2000); Poverty rate: 4.3% (2000).
Taxes: Total city taxes per capita: $42 (1997); City property taxes per capita: $21 (1997).
Education: High school graduation rate: 92.1% (2000); College graduation rate: 5.3% (2000).
Housing: Homeownership rate: 87.5% (2000); Median home value: $41,700 (2000); Median rent: $513 per month (2000); Median age of housing: 50 years (2000).
Transportation: Commute to work: 100.0% car, 0.0% public transportation, 0.0% walk, 0.0% work from home (2000); Travel time to work: 23.1% less than 15 minutes, 61.5% 15 to 30 minutes, 0.0% 30 to 45 minutes, 5.1% 45 to 60 minutes, 10.3% 60 minutes or more (2000)

WESTPORT (township). Covers a land area of 34.549 square miles and a water area of 0.879 square miles. Located at 45.72° N. Lat.; 95.20° W. Long. Elevation is 1,334 feet.
Population: 279 (2000); Race: 99.0% White, 0.0% Black, 0.0% Asian, 0.0% American Indian and Alaska Native, 0.0% Hispanic of any race, 1.0% two or more races (2000); Density: 8.1 persons per square mile (2000); Age: 35.7% under 18, 8.4% over 64 (2000); Marriage status: 26.5% never married, 70.4% now married, 0.4% widowed, 2.7% divorced (2000); Foreign born: 0.6% (2000); Ancestry (includes multiple ancestries): 39.9% German, 16.1% Norwegian, 10.3% United States or American, 8.4% Irish, 6.8% Swedish (2000).
Economy: In grain area; manufacturing of fabricated metal products. Single-family building permits issued: 0 (2001) / 0 (2000); Multi-family building permits issued: 0 (2001) / 0 (2000); Employment by occupation: 38.1% management, 8.8% professional, 11.3% services, 16.9% sales, 11.3% farming, 6.3% construction, 7.5% production (2000).
Income: Per capita income: $14,185 (2000); Median household income: $42,188 (2000); Poverty rate: 13.2% (2000).
Taxes: Total city taxes per capita: $57 (1997); City property taxes per capita: $57 (1997).
Education: High school graduation rate: 89.7% (2000); College graduation rate: 10.3% (2000).
Housing: Homeownership rate: 89.0% (2000); Median home value: $96,700 (2000); Median rent: $150 per month (2000); Median age of housing: 43 years (2000).
Transportation: Commute to work: 54.1% car, 0.0% public transportation, 8.3% walk, 37.6% work from home (2000); Travel time to work: 43.9% less than 15 minutes, 23.5% 15 to 30 minutes, 23.5% 30 to 45 minutes, 7.1% 45 to 60 minutes, 2.0% 60 minutes or more (2000)

WHITE BEAR LAKE (township). Covers a land area of 32.735 square miles and a water area of 1.857 square miles. Located at 45.63° N. Lat.; 95.57° W. Long.
Population: 440 (2000); Race: 98.8% White, 0.0% Black, 0.0% Asian, 0.0% American Indian and Alaska Native, 0.2% Hispanic of any race, 1.2% two or more races (2000); Density: 13.4 persons per square mile (2000); Age: 29.7% under 18, 12.9% over 64 (2000); Marriage status: 17.6% never married, 76.6% now married, 3.2% widowed, 2.7% divorced (2000); Foreign born: 0.0% (2000); Ancestry (includes multiple ancestries): 47.7% Norwegian, 39.6% German, 11.5% Swedish, 9.9% Irish, 6.9% English (2000).
Economy: Single-family building permits issued: 108 (2001) / 43 (2000); Multi-family building permits issued: 0 (2001) / 134 (2000); Employment by occupation: 20.2% management, 21.7% professional, 14.7% services, 20.9% sales, 3.1% farming, 6.6% construction, 12.8% production (2000).
Income: Per capita income: $18,864 (2000); Median household income: $46,250 (2000); Poverty rate: 6.3% (2000).
Taxes: Total city taxes per capita: $42 (1997); City property taxes per capita: $42 (1997).
Education: High school graduation rate: 88.4% (2000); College graduation rate: 21.9% (2000).
Housing: Homeownership rate: 92.3% (2000); Median home value: $97,900 (2000); Median rent: $525 per month (2000); Median age of housing: 44 years (2000).
Transportation: Commute to work: 86.2% car, 0.0% public transportation, 0.0% walk, 11.4% work from home (2000); Travel time to work: 53.3% less than 15 minutes, 28.4% 15 to 30 minutes, 14.2% 30 to 45 minutes, 3.1% 45 to 60 minutes, 0.9% 60 minutes or more (2000)

Ramsey County

Located in eastern Minnesota; crossed in the south by the Mississippi River; includes several lakes. Covers a land area of 155.80 square miles, a water area of 14.40 square miles, and is located in the Central Time Zone. The county government was organized in 1849. County seat is St. Paul.

Ramsey County is part of the Minneapolis-St. Paul, MN-WI MSA. The entire metro area includes: Anoka County, MN; Carver County, MN; Chisago County, MN; Dakota County, MN; Hennepin County, MN; Isanti County, MN; Ramsey County, MN; Scott County, MN; Sherburne County, MN; Washington County, MN; Wright County, MN; Pierce County, WI; St. Croix County, WI

Weather Station: Saint Paul — Elevation: 898 feet

	Jan	Feb	Mar	Apr	May	Jun	Jul	Aug	Sep	Oct	Nov	Dec
High	22	29	41	58	71	79	83	81	72	59	40	27
Low	5	12	23	36	48	58	63	61	51	40	25	12
Precip	1.0	0.7	2.0	2.6	3.7	4.9	4.4	4.4	3.2	2.6	2.1	1.0
Snow	12.1	7.4	9.9	3.0	tr	0.0	0.0	0.0	tr	0.4	9.2	9.8

High and Low temperatures in degrees Fahrenheit; Precipitation and Snow in inches

Population: 511,035 (2000); Race: 77.4% White, 7.3% Black, 8.6% Asian, 0.9% American Indian and Alaska Native, 5.3% Hispanic of any race, 3.2% two or more races (2000); Density: 3,280.6 persons per square mile (2000); Age: 25.6% under 18, 11.7% over 64 (2000).
Religion: Five largest groups: 31.1% Catholic Church, 12.1% Evangelical Lutheran Church in America, 2.1% Baptist General Conference, 1.7% Lutheran Church—Missouri Synod, 1.6% Jewish estimate (2000).
Economy: Unemployment rate: 3.5% (11/2002); Total civilian labor force: 295,839 (11/2002); Leading industries: 13.4% health care and social assistance; 11.5% manufacturing; 10.9% retail trade (2000); Companies that employ more than 1,000 persons: 21 (2000); Companies that employ more than 100 persons: 510 (2000); Farms: 59 (1997); Minority business ownership rate: 7.0% (1997); Women business ownership rate: 29.7% (1997); Retail sales per capita: $11,355 (1997). Single-family building permits issued: 566 (2001) / 517 (2000); Multi-family building permits issued: 865 (2001) / 588 (2000).
Income: Per capita income: $23,536 (2000); Median household income: $45,722 (2000); Poverty rate: 10.6% (2000); Bankruptcy rate: 4.24% (2001).

Taxes: Total county taxes per capita: $341 (2000); County property taxes per capita: $339 (2000).
Education: High school graduation rate: 87.6% (2000); College graduation rate: 34.3% (2000).
Housing: Homeownership rate: 63.5% (2000); Median home value: $126,400 (2000); Median rent: $565 per month (2000); Median age of housing: 41 years (2000).
Health: Birth rate: 146.2 per 10,000 population (1998); Age adjusted death rate: 80.0 per 10,000 population (1999); Infant mortality rate: 9.1 per 1,000 live births (1998); Age adjusted cancer mortality rate: 206.1 deaths per 100,000 population (1999). Air Quality Index: 93% good, 7% moderate, 0% unhealthy (percent of days in 2000). Number of physicians: 33.3 per 10,000 population (1999); Number of hospital beds: 32.0 per 10,000 population (1999).
Elections: 2000 Presidential election results: 56.7% Gore, 35.9% Bush, 6.4% Nader, 0.6% Buchanan

Additional Information Contacts

Ramsey County Government Offices	651-266-8350
Minnesota Chamber of Commerce	888-292-4667
New Brighton Moundsview Chambe	651-631-1906
St. Paul Area Association of Realtors	651-774-5206
St. Paul Chamber of Commerce	651-646-2636
Suburban Chamber of Commerce	651-483-1313
Western Wisconsin Realtors Association	888-666-6566
White Bear Lake Chamber of Commerce	651-429-8593

Ramsey County Communities

ARDEN HILLS (city). Covers a land area of 8.877 square miles and a water area of 0.727 square miles. Located at 45.05° N. Lat.; 93.16° W. Long. Elevation is 880 feet.
Population: 9,652 (2000); Race: 93.2% White, 1.4% Black, 3.5% Asian, 0.3% American Indian and Alaska Native, 1.3% Hispanic of any race, 1.3% two or more races (2000); Density: 1,087.3 persons per square mile (2000); Age: 21.4% under 18, 13.2% over 64 (2000); Marriage status: 34.0% never married, 52.4% now married, 7.2% widowed, 6.4% divorced (2000); Foreign born: 5.4% (2000); Ancestry (includes multiple ancestries): 34.4% German, 16.5% Norwegian, 14.8% Swedish, 10.9% Irish, 9.4% English (2000).
Economy: Manufacturing: feeds, printing ink, furniture, electronic and medical equipment. Single-family building permits issued: 5 (2001) / 10 (2000); Multi-family building permits issued: 0 (2001) / 0 (2000); Employment by occupation: 17.5% management, 29.0% professional, 13.2% services, 29.7% sales, 0.0% farming, 3.8% construction, 6.8% production (2000).
Income: Per capita income: $29,609 (2000); Median household income: $64,773 (2000); Poverty rate: 3.9% (2000).
Taxes: Total city taxes per capita: $248 (1997); City property taxes per capita: $216 (1997).
Education: High school graduation rate: 91.9% (2000); College graduation rate: 51.1% (2000).
Housing: Homeownership rate: 87.0% (2000); Median home value: $171,800 (2000); Median rent: $660 per month (2000); Median age of housing: 26 years (2000).
Safety: Violent crime rate: 12.3 per 10,000 population; Property crime rate: 225.5 per 10,000 population (2001).
Transportation: Commute to work: 84.6% car, 0.8% public transportation, 8.7% walk, 5.2% work from home (2000); Travel time to work: 39.7% less than 15 minutes, 40.8% 15 to 30 minutes, 16.5% 30 to 45 minutes, 1.3% 45 to 60 minutes, 1.8% 60 minutes or more (2000)

FALCON HEIGHTS (city). Covers a land area of 2.240 square miles and a water area of 0 square miles. Located at 44.98° N. Lat.; 93.17° W. Long. Elevation is 970 feet.
History: University of Minnesota Agricultural College here.
Population: 5,572 (2000); Race: 77.3% White, 3.1% Black, 15.6% Asian, 1.0% American Indian and Alaska Native, 2.8% Hispanic of any race, 1.5% two or more races (2000); Density: 2,487.9 persons per square mile (2000); Age: 21.4% under 18, 11.6% over 64 (2000); Marriage status: 33.4% never married, 57.7% now married, 2.8% widowed, 6.0% divorced (2000); Foreign born: 19.3% (2000); Ancestry (includes multiple ancestries): 27.7% German, 22.2% Other groups, 12.6% Irish, 12.0% Norwegian, 8.9% Swedish (2000).
Economy: Minnesota State Fairgrounds. Single-family building permits issued: 0 (2001) / 2 (2000); Multi-family building permits issued: 0 (2001) / 2 (2000); Employment by occupation: 11.2% management, 48.9% professional, 11.9% services, 18.3% sales, 0.0% farming, 3.7% construction, 6.2% production (2000).
Income: Per capita income: $25,370 (2000); Median household income: $51,382 (2000); Poverty rate: 9.6% (2000).
Taxes: Total city taxes per capita: $111 (1997); City property taxes per capita: $104 (1997).
Education: High school graduation rate: 95.6% (2000); College graduation rate: 70.3% (2000).
Housing: Homeownership rate: 58.3% (2000); Median home value: $161,400 (2000); Median rent: $482 per month (2000); Median age of housing: 44 years (2000).
Safety: Violent crime rate: 8.9 per 10,000 population; Property crime rate: 188.2 per 10,000 population (2001).
Transportation: Commute to work: 67.3% car, 16.1% public transportation, 10.4% walk, 3.8% work from home (2000); Travel time to work: 34.2% less than 15 minutes, 45.1% 15 to 30 minutes, 15.7% 30 to 45 minutes, 1.8% 45 to 60 minutes, 3.3% 60 minutes or more (2000)

GEM LAKE (city). Covers a land area of 1.106 square miles and a water area of 0.030 square miles. Located at 45.05° N. Lat.; 93.04° W. Long. Elevation is 954 feet.
Population: 419 (2000); Race: 94.8% White, 1.7% Black, 1.0% Asian, 1.0% American Indian and Alaska Native, 1.2% Hispanic of any race, 0.7% two or more races (2000); Density: 378.7 persons per square mile (2000); Age: 25.5% under 18, 15.0% over 64 (2000); Marriage status: 23.9% never married, 57.8% now married, 5.5% widowed, 12.8% divorced (2000); Foreign born: 1.2% (2000); Ancestry (includes multiple ancestries): 39.3% German, 24.0% Swedish, 19.8% Norwegian, 16.0% Irish, 8.3% French Canadian (2000).
Economy: Single-family building permits issued: 3 (2001) / 0 (2000); Multi-family building permits issued: 0 (2001) / 0 (2000); Employment by occupation: 14.0% management, 20.2% professional, 14.9% services, 21.5% sales, 0.0% farming, 11.0% construction, 18.4% production (2000).
Income: Per capita income: $28,750 (2000); Median household income: $64,167 (2000); Poverty rate: 5.9% (2000).
Taxes: Total city taxes per capita: $216 (1997); City property taxes per capita: $189 (1997).
Education: High school graduation rate: 92.4% (2000); College graduation rate: 26.1% (2000).
Housing: Homeownership rate: 92.0% (2000); Median home value: $159,600 (2000); Median rent: $706 per month (2000); Median age of housing: 29 years (2000).
Transportation: Commute to work: 94.5% car, 0.9% public transportation, 2.7% walk, 1.8% work from home (2000); Travel time to work: 32.6% less than 15 minutes, 47.4% 15 to 30 minutes, 12.6% 30 to 45 minutes, 6.5% 45 to 60 minutes, 0.9% 60 minutes or more (2000)

LAUDERDALE (city). Covers a land area of 0.422 square miles and a water area of 0 square miles. Located at 44.99° N. Lat.; 93.20° W. Long. Elevation is 980 feet.
Population: 2,364 (2000); Race: 80.5% White, 3.1% Black, 11.4% Asian, 1.4% American Indian and Alaska Native, 6.5% Hispanic of any race, 2.7% two or more races (2000); Density: 5,597.2 persons per square mile (2000); Age: 16.8% under 18, 8.8% over 64 (2000); Marriage status: 42.0% never married, 47.3% now married, 3.8% widowed, 6.9% divorced (2000); Foreign born: 18.8% (2000); Ancestry (includes multiple ancestries): 25.6% German, 22.3% Other groups, 17.1% Norwegian, 12.7% Swedish, 8.3% Irish (2000).
Economy: Single-family building permits issued: 0 (2001) / 1 (2000); Multi-family building permits issued: 0 (2001) / 0 (2000); Employment by occupation: 10.7% management, 40.6% professional, 10.2% services, 23.1% sales, 0.0% farming, 4.8% construction, 10.6% production (2000).
Income: Per capita income: $23,293 (2000); Median household income: $39,063 (2000); Poverty rate: 9.3% (2000).
Taxes: Total city taxes per capita: $246 (1997); City property taxes per capita: $234 (1997).
Education: High school graduation rate: 96.1% (2000); College graduation rate: 56.9% (2000).
Housing: Homeownership rate: 50.5% (2000); Median home value: $113,300 (2000); Median rent: $550 per month (2000); Median age of housing: 37 years (2000).
Safety: Violent crime rate: 25.1 per 10,000 population; Property crime rate: 293.0 per 10,000 population (2001).
Transportation: Commute to work: 80.9% car, 8.8% public transportation, 5.9% walk, 1.3% work from home (2000); Travel time to work: 37.5% less than 15 minutes, 41.3% 15 to 30 minutes, 15.6% 30 to 45 minutes, 3.0% 45 to 60 minutes, 2.6% 60 minutes or more (2000)

LITTLE CANADA (city). Covers a land area of 3.995 square miles and a water area of 0.472 square miles. Located at 45.02° N. Lat.; 93.08° W. Long. Elevation is 905 feet.
Population: 9,771 (2000); Race: 85.2% White, 4.9% Black, 5.0% Asian, 1.1% American Indian and Alaska Native, 1.2% Hispanic of any race, 3.6% two or more races (2000); Density: 2,445.8 persons per square mile (2000); Age: 22.1% under 18, 13.0% over 64 (2000); Marriage status: 32.0% never married, 49.2% now married, 7.0% widowed, 11.7% divorced (2000); Foreign born: 8.6% (2000); Ancestry (includes multiple ancestries): 34.1% German, 13.6% Irish, 12.8% Other groups, 10.9% Norwegian, 7.9% Swedish (2000).
Economy: Railroad junction. Manufacturing: plastic products, store fixtures, printing, medical supplies. Single-family building permits issued: 5 (2001) / 28 (2000); Multi-family building permits issued: 2 (2001) / 12 (2000); Employment by occupation: 13.9% management, 23.9% professional, 12.0% services, 29.9% sales, 0.1% farming, 8.1% construction, 12.1% production (2000).
Income: Per capita income: $25,624 (2000); Median household income: $46,609 (2000); Poverty rate: 5.5% (2000).
Taxes: Total city taxes per capita: $224 (1997); City property taxes per capita: $202 (1997).
Education: High school graduation rate: 90.9% (2000); College graduation rate: 28.0% (2000).
Housing: Homeownership rate: 63.2% (2000); Median home value: $150,900 (2000); Median rent: $662 per month (2000); Median age of housing: 24 years (2000).
Safety: Violent crime rate: 18.2 per 10,000 population; Property crime rate: 389.8 per 10,000 population (2001).
Transportation: Commute to work: 93.7% car, 2.3% public transportation, 0.3% walk, 2.3% work from home (2000); Travel time to work: 29.3% less than 15 minutes, 47.7% 15 to 30 minutes, 17.2% 30 to 45 minutes, 2.8% 45 to 60 minutes, 3.0% 60 minutes or more (2000)

MAPLEWOOD (city). Covers a land area of 17.322 square miles and a water area of 0.667 square miles. Located at 44.99° N. Lat.; 93.02° W. Long. Elevation is 1,362 feet.
History: Incorporated 1957.
Population: 34,947 (2000); Race: 88.4% White, 2.8% Black, 3.9% Asian, 0.6% American Indian and Alaska Native, 2.9% Hispanic of any race, 3.1% two or more races (2000); Density: 2,017.5 persons per square mile (2000); Age: 24.8% under 18, 15.1% over 64 (2000); Marriage status: 25.9% never married, 56.5% now married, 7.4% widowed, 10.2% divorced (2000); Foreign born: 4.6% (2000); Ancestry (includes multiple ancestries): 38.7% German, 15.7% Irish, 12.5% Norwegian, 11.7% Swedish, 10.9% Other groups (2000).
Vital Statistics: Birth rate: 129.6 per 10,000 population (1998)
Economy: Manufacturing: dairy products, signs. Unemployment rate: 2.9% (11/2002); Total civilian labor force: 21,163 (11/2002); Single-family building permits issued: 166 (2001) / 64 (2000); Multi-family building permits issued: 116 (2001) / 65 (2000); Employment by occupation: 12.9% management, 21.6% professional, 14.2% services, 29.9% sales, 0.1% farming, 8.0% construction, 13.4% production (2000).
Income: Per capita income: $24,387 (2000); Median household income: $51,596 (2000); Poverty rate: 4.8% (2000).
Taxes: Total city taxes per capita: $259 (2000); City property taxes per capita: $229 (2000).
Education: High school graduation rate: 90.1% (2000); College graduation rate: 25.6% (2000).

School District(s)

East Metro Integration Dst 6067 (KG-08)
2000 Enrollment: 499 651-487-5450
North Saint Paul-Maplewood (PK-12)
2000 Enrollment: 11,554 651-748-7410

Housing: Homeownership rate: 75.6% (2000); Median home value: $132,200 (2000); Median rent: $654 per month (2000); Median age of housing: 26 years (2000).
Hospitals: Saint John's Hospital (178 beds)
Transportation: Commute to work: 93.1% car, 3.1% public transportation, 0.8% walk, 2.6% work from home (2000); Travel time to work: 27.1% less than 15 minutes, 48.3% 15 to 30 minutes, 17.1% 30 to 45 minutes, 3.8% 45 to 60 minutes, 3.7% 60 minutes or more (2000)

MOUNDS VIEW (city). Covers a land area of 4.114 square miles and a water area of 0.021 square miles. Located at 45.10° N. Lat.; 93.20° W. Long. Elevation is 899 feet.
Population: 12,738 (2000); Race: 90.7% White, 2.2% Black, 1.9% Asian, 1.5% American Indian and Alaska Native, 2.2% Hispanic of any race, 2.5% two or more races (2000); Density: 3,096.6 persons per square mile (2000); Age: 25.0% under 18, 9.1% over 64 (2000); Marriage status: 28.8% never married, 54.8% now married, 5.0% widowed, 11.3% divorced (2000); Foreign born: 5.0% (2000); Ancestry (includes multiple ancestries): 36.4% German, 15.2% Norwegian, 12.7% Swedish, 12.4% Irish, 9.2% Other groups (2000).
Vital Statistics: Birth rate: 131.1 per 10,000 population (1998)
Economy: Manufacturing: tools, skates, gaskets, data communications equipment, business checks. Single-family building permits issued: 3 (2001) / 7 (2000); Multi-family building permits issued: 2 (2001) / 2 (2000); Employment by occupation: 12.3% management, 18.3% professional, 12.1% services, 30.4% sales, 0.2% farming, 8.7% construction, 18.1% production (2000).
Income: Per capita income: $24,271 (2000); Median household income: $51,974 (2000); Poverty rate: 5.9% (2000).
Taxes: Total city taxes per capita: $336 (1997); City property taxes per capita: $300 (1997).
Education: High school graduation rate: 89.6% (2000); College graduation rate: 24.0% (2000).
Housing: Homeownership rate: 71.0% (2000); Median home value: $126,500 (2000); Median rent: $607 per month (2000); Median age of housing: 28 years (2000).
Safety: Violent crime rate: 31.1 per 10,000 population; Property crime rate: 428.7 per 10,000 population (2001).
Transportation: Commute to work: 93.3% car, 3.1% public transportation, 1.6% walk, 1.3% work from home (2000); Travel time to work: 27.3% less than 15 minutes, 42.1% 15 to 30 minutes, 21.8% 30 to 45 minutes, 5.8% 45 to 60 minutes, 2.9% 60 minutes or more (2000)

NEW BRIGHTON (city). Covers a land area of 6.641 square miles and a water area of 0.454 square miles. Located at 45.06° N. Lat.; 93.20° W. Long. Elevation is 920 feet.
History: A theological seminary is in New Brighton. Incorporated 1891.
Population: 22,206 (2000); Race: 89.4% White, 3.0% Black, 4.1% Asian, 0.6% American Indian and Alaska Native, 2.1% Hispanic of any race, 2.4% two or more races (2000); Density: 3,343.9 persons per square mile (2000); Age: 22.2% under 18, 12.4% over 64 (2000); Marriage status: 29.0% never married, 56.1% now married, 6.2% widowed, 8.7% divorced (2000); Foreign born: 6.8% (2000); Ancestry (includes multiple ancestries): 33.5% German, 14.8% Norwegian, 13.7% Irish, 12.5% Swedish, 9.4% Other groups (2000).
Vital Statistics: Birth rate: 114.8 per 10,000 population (1998)
Economy: Railroad junction. Manufacturing: metal products, machinery, leather, primary metals, printing and publishing, machining. Single-family building permits issued: 8 (2001) / 4 (2000); Multi-family building permits issued: 0 (2001) / 0 (2000); Employment by occupation: 16.1% management, 27.4% professional, 11.6% services, 29.1% sales, 0.0% farming, 5.2% construction, 10.6% production (2000).
Income: Per capita income: $27,574 (2000); Median household income: $52,856 (2000); Poverty rate: 4.7% (2000).
Taxes: Total city taxes per capita: $284 (2000); City property taxes per capita: $252 (2000).
Education: High school graduation rate: 92.9% (2000); College graduation rate: 40.6% (2000).

Four-year College(s)

United Theological Seminary (Private, Not-for-profit, United Church of Christ)
2001 Enrollment: 213 651-633-4311

Housing: Homeownership rate: 67.1% (2000); Median home value: $144,200 (2000); Median rent: $628 per month (2000); Median age of housing: 30 years (2000).
Safety: Violent crime rate: 9.4 per 10,000 population; Property crime rate: 295.0 per 10,000 population (2001).
Transportation: Commute to work: 91.1% car, 3.8% public transportation, 1.7% walk, 2.7% work from home (2000); Travel time to work: 31.8% less than 15 minutes, 44.6% 15 to 30 minutes, 17.5% 30 to 45 minutes, 4.7% 45 to 60 minutes, 1.4% 60 minutes or more (2000)

Additional Information Contacts

New Brighton Moundsview Chambe 651-631-1906

NORTH OAKS (city). Covers a land area of 7.313 square miles and a water area of 1.347 square miles. Located at 45.09° N. Lat.; 93.09° W. Long. Elevation is 955 feet.
Population: 3,883 (2000); Race: 92.1% White, 0.9% Black, 5.2% Asian, 0.0% American Indian and Alaska Native, 0.5% Hispanic of any race, 1.2%

two or more races (2000); Density: 531.0 persons per square mile (2000); Age: 28.0% under 18, 11.6% over 64 (2000); Marriage status: 18.9% never married, 77.3% now married, 1.7% widowed, 2.1% divorced (2000); Foreign born: 7.1% (2000); Ancestry (includes multiple ancestries): 31.1% German, 17.2% Irish, 14.2% Norwegian, 12.7% Swedish, 10.5% English (2000).
Economy: Single-family building permits issued: 42 (2001) / 55 (2000); Multi-family building permits issued: 0 (2001) / 0 (2000); Employment by occupation: 31.7% management, 40.5% professional, 2.0% services, 22.7% sales, 0.0% farming, 0.6% construction, 2.5% production (2000).
Income: Per capita income: $72,686 (2000); Median household income: $149,158 (2000); Poverty rate: 1.9% (2000).
Taxes: Total city taxes per capita: $219 (1997); City property taxes per capita: $157 (1997).
Education: High school graduation rate: 98.1% (2000); College graduation rate: 76.2% (2000).
Housing: Homeownership rate: 99.1% (2000); Median home value: $413,400 (2000); Median rent: $775 per month (2000); Median age of housing: 24 years (2000).
Safety: Violent crime rate: 5.1 per 10,000 population; Property crime rate: 152.9 per 10,000 population (2001).
Transportation: Commute to work: 90.2% car, 1.0% public transportation, 0.7% walk, 7.5% work from home (2000); Travel time to work: 15.7% less than 15 minutes, 53.7% 15 to 30 minutes, 23.4% 30 to 45 minutes, 4.1% 45 to 60 minutes, 3.2% 60 minutes or more (2000)

NORTH SAINT PAUL (city). Covers a land area of 2.887 square miles and a water area of 0.113 square miles. Located at 45.01° N. Lat.; 92.99° W. Long. Elevation is 984 feet.
Population: 11,929 (2000); Race: 93.8% White, 2.1% Black, 2.7% Asian, 0.3% American Indian and Alaska Native, 2.5% Hispanic of any race, 0.8% two or more races (2000); Density: 4,132.4 persons per square mile (2000); Age: 26.4% under 18, 11.5% over 64 (2000); Marriage status: 26.0% never married, 57.8% now married, 6.0% widowed, 10.2% divorced (2000); Foreign born: 4.5% (2000); Ancestry (includes multiple ancestries): 39.9% German, 15.5% Irish, 12.2% Norwegian, 10.9% Swedish, 7.7% Other groups (2000).
Vital Statistics: Birth rate: 137.5 per 10,000 population (1998)
Economy: Single-family building permits issued: 10 (2001) / 12 (2000); Multi-family building permits issued: 0 (2001) / 0 (2000); Employment by occupation: 10.4% management, 18.9% professional, 13.4% services, 31.2% sales, 0.1% farming, 10.1% construction, 15.9% production (2000).
Income: Per capita income: $22,411 (2000); Median household income: $50,923 (2000); Poverty rate: 4.2% (2000).
Taxes: Total city taxes per capita: $108 (1997); City property taxes per capita: $97 (1997).
Education: High school graduation rate: 89.7% (2000); College graduation rate: 20.0% (2000).
Housing: Homeownership rate: 72.4% (2000); Median home value: $118,700 (2000); Median rent: $574 per month (2000); Median age of housing: 35 years (2000).
Safety: Violent crime rate: 14.1 per 10,000 population; Property crime rate: 344.2 per 10,000 population (2001).
Newspapers: New Brighton Bulletin (1 x week); Saint Anthony Bulletin (1 x week); Roseville Review (1 x week); Ramsey County Review (1 x week); Oakdale-Lake Elmo Review (1 x week); Maplewood Review (1 x week); East Side Review (1 x week); Lillie Suburban Shopping Review (1 x week); Shoreview Arden Hills Bulletin (1 x week); Woodbury - South Maplewood Review (1 x week); South-West Review (1 x week)
Transportation: Commute to work: 90.7% car, 3.5% public transportation, 0.9% walk, 4.2% work from home (2000); Travel time to work: 28.7% less than 15 minutes, 45.3% 15 to 30 minutes, 18.4% 30 to 45 minutes, 5.5% 45 to 60 minutes, 2.0% 60 minutes or more (2000)

ROSEVILLE (city). Covers a land area of 13.243 square miles and a water area of 0.593 square miles. Located at 45.01° N. Lat.; 93.15° W. Long. Elevation is 950 feet.
History: Incorporated 1948.
Population: 33,690 (2000); Race: 90.1% White, 2.4% Black, 4.8% Asian, 0.5% American Indian and Alaska Native, 1.8% Hispanic of any race, 1.5% two or more races (2000); Density: 2,543.9 persons per square mile (2000); Age: 18.3% under 18, 20.2% over 64 (2000); Marriage status: 28.4% never married, 54.7% now married, 8.7% widowed, 8.2% divorced (2000); Foreign born: 6.5% (2000); Ancestry (includes multiple ancestries): 37.5% German, 14.9% Norwegian, 13.2% Irish, 12.0% Swedish, 10.3% Other groups (2000).
Vital Statistics: Birth rate: 93.5 per 10,000 population (1998)
Economy: Manufacturing: plastic flower pots, metal fabrication, thermal remediation equipment, graphics boards, metal finishing, school emblems, printing, bakery products, computer systems. Unemployment rate: 2.4% (11/2002); Total civilian labor force: 21,981 (11/2002); Single-family building permits issued: 18 (2001) / 27 (2000); Multi-family building permits issued: 0 (2001) / 30 (2000); Employment by occupation: 17.4% management, 31.1% professional, 10.3% services, 27.2% sales, 0.1% farming, 4.8% construction, 9.2% production (2000).
Income: Per capita income: $27,755 (2000); Median household income: $51,056 (2000); Poverty rate: 4.2% (2000).
Taxes: Total city taxes per capita: $436 (2000); City property taxes per capita: $378 (2000).
Education: High school graduation rate: 91.4% (2000); College graduation rate: 42.3% (2000).

School District(s)

Family Academy Charter School (KG-08)
2000 Enrollment: 105 651-633-1037
Mounds View (PK-12)
2000 Enrollment: 11,736 651-639-6212
Roseville (PK-12)
2000 Enrollment: 6,633 651-635-1600

Four-year College(s)

National American University (Private, For-profit)
2001 Enrollment: 235 605-394-4800
2001 Tuition: In-state $11,520; Out-of-state $11,520

Two-year College(s)

Minneapolis Business College Inc (Private, For-profit)
2001 Enrollment: 365 612-636-7406
2001 Tuition: In-state $9,220; Out-of-state $9,220

Housing: Homeownership rate: 67.4% (2000); Median home value: $143,400 (2000); Median rent: $656 per month (2000); Median age of housing: 35 years (2000).
Safety: Violent crime rate: 15.9 per 10,000 population; Property crime rate: 567.7 per 10,000 population (2001).
Transportation: Commute to work: 90.4% car, 2.6% public transportation, 3.0% walk, 3.3% work from home (2000); Travel time to work: 30.2% less than 15 minutes, 48.4% 15 to 30 minutes, 16.2% 30 to 45 minutes, 2.8% 45 to 60 minutes, 2.5% 60 minutes or more (2000)

SAINT PAUL (city). Covers a land area of 52.768 square miles and a water area of 3.406 square miles. Located at 44.95° N. Lat.; 93.11° W. Long. Elevation is 703 feet.
History: About 1840, some French-speaking Swiss colonists settled at a river landing along the Mississippi, around the cabin of Pierre Parrant, a French Canadian nicknamed Pig's Eye by soldiers and traders. First known as Pig's Eye, the community that grew up was soon renamed St. Paul by Father Lucian Galtier, who erected a log chapel at the landing in 1841. These first settlers were farmers who at first did not realize the importance in trade and commerce that their location at the head of navigation on the Mississippi River would give their city. St. Paul was platted in 1847, and soon became the terminus for steamboats plying the river. When the new Territory was formed in 1849, St. Paul became the capital, and was incorporated as a city in 1854. Though St. Paul had gotten off to an earlier start than its twin city, Minneapolis, their relatively equal development led to rivalry on many fronts.
Population: 287,151 (2000); Race: 67.0% White, 11.3% Black, 12.3% Asian, 1.2% American Indian and Alaska Native, 7.9% Hispanic of any race, 4.3% two or more races (2000); Density: 5,441.7 persons per square mile (2000); Age: 27.1% under 18, 10.4% over 64 (2000); Marriage status: 39.7% never married, 43.9% now married, 5.8% widowed, 10.6% divorced (2000); Foreign born: 14.3% (2000); Ancestry (includes multiple ancestries): 29.1% Other groups, 25.5% German, 12.8% Irish, 8.4% Norwegian, 6.4% Swedish (2000).
Vital Statistics: Birth rate: 173.2 per 10,000 population (1998)
Economy: Unemployment rate: 4.2% (11/2002); Total civilian labor force: 147,594 (11/2002); Single-family building permits issued: 116 (2001) / 130 (2000); Multi-family building permits issued: 477 (2001) / 229 (2000); Employment by occupation: 12.6% management, 25.2% professional, 15.7% services, 26.3% sales, 0.2% farming, 6.0% construction, 14.0% production (2000).
Income: Per capita income: $20,216 (2000); Median household income: $38,774 (2000); Poverty rate: 15.6% (2000).
Education: High school graduation rate: 83.8% (2000); College graduation rate: 32.0% (2000).

School District(s)

Acorn Dual Language Comm. Academy (KG-06)
2000 Enrollment: 270 651-738-4875

City Academy (09-12)
2000 Enrollment: 122 651-298-4624
Community of Peace Academy (KG-10)
2000 Enrollment: 421 651-776-5151
Concordia Creative Learning Academy (KG-06)
2000 Enrollment: 116 651-645-0200
Cyber Village Academy (04-08)
2000 Enrollment: 198 651-523-7170
Face To Face Academy (09-12)
2000 Enrollment: 43 651-772-5555
High School for Recording Arts (09-12)
2000 Enrollment: 135 651-917-6960
Higher Ground Academy (KG-10)
2000 Enrollment: 411 651-645-1000
Hope Academy Charter (KG-03)
2000 Enrollment: 387 651-225-9406
Learning Adventures Charter School (06-08)
2000 Enrollment: 44 651-649-5404
Metro Deaf Charter School (PK-08)
2000 Enrollment: 75 651-224-3995
Mexica Multicultural Education Charter (09-12)
2000 Enrollment: 53 651-453-0115
Minnesota Business Academy Charter (09-12)
2000 Enrollment: 236 651-726-2100
Minnesota Technology Charter School (09-12)
2000 Enrollment: 87 651-649-5403
Mn Institute of Technology Charter (KG-05)
2000 Enrollment: 281 612-381-9743
New Spirit School (KG-07)
2000 Enrollment: 297 651-225-9177
Opportunities for Learning (09-12)
2000 Enrollment: 109 651-649-5911
Saint Paul (PK-12)
2000 Enrollment: 45,115 651-293-5100
Saint Paul Family Learning Center (KG-06)
2000 Enrollment: 126 651-649-5402
Skills for Tomorrow Charter School (10-12)
2000 Enrollment: 80 651-647-6000
Skills for Tomorrow Junior High (07-09)
2000 Enrollment: 53 651-647-6000
Success Academy (N -N)
2000 Enrollment: n/a 651-917-8185
Twin Cities Academy (06-08)
2000 Enrollment: 177 651-205-4797

Four-year College(s)

Apostolic Bible Institute Inc (Private, Not-for-profit, International United Pentecostal Church)
2001 Enrollment: 54 651-739-7686
2001 Tuition: In-state $2,400; Out-of-state $2,400
Bethel College (Private, Not-for-profit, Baptist)
2001 Enrollment: 2,991 651-638-6400
2001 Tuition: In-state $16,780; Out-of-state $16,780
Bethel Theological Seminary (Private, Not-for-profit, Baptist)
2001 Enrollment: 887 651-638-6180
Concordia University (Private, Not-for-profit, Lutheran Church - Missouri Synod)
2001 Enrollment: 1,773 612-641-8278
2001 Tuition: In-state $15,786; Out-of-state $15,786
Hamline University (Private, Not-for-profit, United Methodist)
2001 Enrollment: 4,123 651-523-2800
2001 Tuition: In-state $17,038; Out-of-state $17,038
Luther Seminary (Private, Not-for-profit, American Evangelical Lutheran Church)
2001 Enrollment: 713 651-641-3456
MacAlester College (Private, Not-for-profit, Presbyterian Church (USA))
2001 Enrollment: 1,822 651-696-6000
2001 Tuition: In-state $22,480; Out-of-state $22,480
Metropolitan State University (Public)
2001 Enrollment: 6,010 651-772-7777
2001 Tuition: In-state $2,919; Out-of-state $6,642
Northwestern College (Private, Not-for-profit, Other Protestant)
2001 Enrollment: 2,277 651-631-5100
2001 Tuition: In-state $15,600; Out-of-state $15,600
University of Saint Thomas (Private, Not-for-profit, Roman Catholic)
2001 Enrollment: 11,473 651-962-5000
2001 Tuition: In-state $18,096; Out-of-state $18,096
College of Visual Arts (Private, Not-for-profit)
2001 Enrollment: 269 651-224-3416
2001 Tuition: In-state $12,998; Out-of-state $12,998
College of Saint Catherine-Saint Paul Campus (Private, Not-for-profit, Roman Catholic)
2001 Enrollment: 4,622 651-690-6000
2001 Tuition: In-state $13,604; Out-of-state $13,604
William Mitchell College of Law (Private, Not-for-profit)
2001 Enrollment: 1,015 612-227-9171
Regions Hospital Dietetic Internship (Private, Not-for-profit)
2001 Enrollment: 14 651-254-2712

Two-year College(s)

Regions Hospital School of Ophthalmic Med Techn (Private, Not-for-profit)
2001 Enrollment: 11 651-254-3000
2001 Tuition: In-state $4,100; Out-of-state $4,100
Saint Paul Technical College (Public)
2001 Enrollment: 5,359 651-221-1300
2001 Tuition: In-state $2,325; Out-of-state $4,650

Housing: Homeownership rate: 54.8% (2000); Median home value: $105,400 (2000); Median rent: $524 per month (2000); Median age of housing: 55 years (2000).
Hospitals: Children's Health Care - Saint Paul (116 beds); Bethesda Rehabilitation Hospital (264 beds); Gillette Children's Specialty Health Care (60 beds); Regions Hospital (435 beds); Saint Joseph's Hospital (401 beds); United Hospital (572 beds)
Safety: Violent crime rate: 77.0 per 10,000 population; Property crime rate: 579.2 per 10,000 population (2001).
Newspapers: Asian Pages (2 x month); Saint Paul Pioneer Press (7 x week); Saint Paul Legal Ledger (5 x week); The Catholic Spirit (1 x week); The Wanderer (1 x week); Villager (2 x month); Grand Gazette (1 x month); Minnesota Women's Press (2 x month); Park Bugle (1 x month); La Prensa de Minnesota (1 x week)
Transportation: Commute to work: 81.6% car, 8.7% public transportation, 5.4% walk, 3.0% work from home (2000); Travel time to work: 30.0% less than 15 minutes, 46.8% 15 to 30 minutes, 16.0% 30 to 45 minutes, 3.9% 45 to 60 minutes, 3.2% 60 minutes or more (2000); Amtrak: Service available.
Airports: St Paul Downtown Holman Field
Additional Information Contacts
Minnesota Chamber of Commerce. 888-292-4667
St. Paul Area Association of Realtors 651-774-5206
St. Paul Chamber of Commerce 651-646-2636
Suburban Chamber of Commerce 651-483-1313
Western Wisconsin Realtors Association. 888-666-6566

SHOREVIEW (city). Covers a land area of 11.194 square miles and a water area of 1.546 square miles. Located at 45.08° N. Lat.; 93.13° W. Long. Elevation is 950 feet.
History: Developed around seven natural lakes, includes Turtle Lake in North. Population more than doubled between 1970 and 1990. Settled 1850, set off from Mounds View and incorporated 1957.
Population: 25,924 (2000); Race: 93.3% White, 1.2% Black, 3.0% Asian, 0.2% American Indian and Alaska Native, 1.9% Hispanic of any race, 1.6% two or more races (2000); Density: 2,315.9 persons per square mile (2000); Age: 26.1% under 18, 9.7% over 64 (2000); Marriage status: 24.0% never married, 62.4% now married, 4.4% widowed, 9.2% divorced (2000); Foreign born: 5.5% (2000); Ancestry (includes multiple ancestries): 38.3% German, 15.9% Norwegian, 13.9% Swedish, 13.8% Irish, 8.3% English (2000).
Vital Statistics: Birth rate: 106.1 per 10,000 population (1998)
Economy: Manufacturing: furniture, machinery, metal products, light manufacturing. Unemployment rate: 2.6% (11/2002); Total civilian labor force: 17,841 (11/2002); Single-family building permits issued: 19 (2001) / 19 (2000); Multi-family building permits issued: 184 (2001) / 228 (2000); Employment by occupation: 21.8% management, 30.2% professional, 8.7% services, 25.9% sales, 0.1% farming, 4.9% construction, 8.5% production (2000).
Income: Per capita income: $32,399 (2000); Median household income: $69,719 (2000); Poverty rate: 2.1% (2000).
Taxes: Total city taxes per capita: $245 (2000); City property taxes per capita: $212 (2000).
Education: High school graduation rate: 96.0% (2000); College graduation rate: 46.9% (2000).
Housing: Homeownership rate: 87.3% (2000); Median home value: $157,400 (2000); Median rent: $688 per month (2000); Median age of housing: 22 years (2000).
Safety: Violent crime rate: 7.3 per 10,000 population; Property crime rate: 173.3 per 10,000 population (2001).

Transportation: Commute to work: 93.7% car, 1.8% public transportation, 0.8% walk, 3.2% work from home (2000); Travel time to work: 25.8% less than 15 minutes, 47.1% 15 to 30 minutes, 20.1% 30 to 45 minutes, 4.7% 45 to 60 minutes, 2.4% 60 minutes or more (2000)

VADNAIS HEIGHTS (city). Covers a land area of 7.287 square miles and a water area of 1.004 square miles. Located at 45.05° N. Lat.; 93.07° W. Long. Elevation is 900 feet.
Population: 13,069 (2000); Race: 91.4% White, 1.7% Black, 4.3% Asian, 0.4% American Indian and Alaska Native, 1.8% Hispanic of any race, 1.3% two or more races (2000); Density: 1,793.4 persons per square mile (2000); Age: 27.2% under 18, 7.7% over 64 (2000); Marriage status: 28.2% never married, 58.3% now married, 3.2% widowed, 10.2% divorced (2000); Foreign born: 5.1% (2000); Ancestry (includes multiple ancestries): 39.8% German, 14.7% Swedish, 14.5% Irish, 14.2% Norwegian, 7.8% Other groups (2000).
Vital Statistics: Birth rate: 133.9 per 10,000 population (1998)
Economy: Manufacturing: printed circuit boards, labels and nameplates, plastic molds, hearing aids. Single-family building permits issued: 45 (2001) / 40 (2000); Multi-family building permits issued: 0 (2001) / 6 (2000); Employment by occupation: 18.7% management, 21.7% professional, 10.3% services, 30.1% sales, 0.1% farming, 6.8% construction, 12.3% production (2000).
Income: Per capita income: $30,891 (2000); Median household income: $60,804 (2000); Poverty rate: 3.2% (2000).
Taxes: Total city taxes per capita: $237 (1997); City property taxes per capita: $209 (1997).
Education: High school graduation rate: 93.4% (2000); College graduation rate: 37.0% (2000).
Housing: Homeownership rate: 85.0% (2000); Median home value: $143,800 (2000); Median rent: $684 per month (2000); Median age of housing: 16 years (2000).
Safety: Violent crime rate: 15.1 per 10,000 population; Property crime rate: 250.6 per 10,000 population (2001).
Transportation: Commute to work: 92.9% car, 2.2% public transportation, 0.5% walk, 4.1% work from home (2000); Travel time to work: 23.8% less than 15 minutes, 46.8% 15 to 30 minutes, 21.4% 30 to 45 minutes, 5.7% 45 to 60 minutes, 2.3% 60 minutes or more (2000)

WHITE BEAR (township). Covers a land area of 7.461 square miles and a water area of 3.371 square miles. Located at 45.09° N. Lat.; 93.02° W. Long.
History: Incorporated 1922.
Population: 11,293 (2000); Race: 98.2% White, 0.3% Black, 1.0% Asian, 0.0% American Indian and Alaska Native, 1.1% Hispanic of any race, 0.2% two or more races (2000); Density: 1,513.7 persons per square mile (2000); Age: 28.1% under 18, 8.0% over 64 (2000); Marriage status: 23.0% never married, 66.0% now married, 4.0% widowed, 6.9% divorced (2000); Foreign born: 3.2% (2000); Ancestry (includes multiple ancestries): 39.9% German, 15.7% Irish, 14.2% Norwegian, 11.8% Swedish, 8.6% French (except Basque) (2000).
Economy: Manufacturing includes chemicals, medical supplies, electrical products, foods, consumer goods; machining, printing and publishing, steel fabricating, wood treating. Single-family building permits issued: 107 (2001) / 56 (2000); Multi-family building permits issued: 2 (2001) / 14 (2000); Employment by occupation: 16.1% management, 27.2% professional, 10.2% services, 28.1% sales, 0.0% farming, 6.6% construction, 11.7% production (2000).
Income: Per capita income: $28,847 (2000); Median household income: $70,000 (2000); Poverty rate: 2.8% (2000).
Taxes: Total city taxes per capita: $240 (2000); City property taxes per capita: $209 (2000).
Education: High school graduation rate: 93.1% (2000); College graduation rate: 39.0% (2000).
Housing: Homeownership rate: 93.1% (2000); Median home value: $158,400 (2000); Median rent: $715 per month (2000); Median age of housing: 19 years (2000).
Transportation: Commute to work: 93.3% car, 1.3% public transportation, 0.4% walk, 4.0% work from home (2000); Travel time to work: 23.2% less than 15 minutes, 40.7% 15 to 30 minutes, 28.7% 30 to 45 minutes, 4.2% 45 to 60 minutes, 3.3% 60 minutes or more (2000)

WHITE BEAR LAKE (city). Covers a land area of 8.178 square miles and a water area of 0.513 square miles. Located at 45.07° N. Lat.; 93.01° W. Long. Elevation is 950 feet.
Population: 24,325 (2000); Race: 94.6% White, 1.6% Black, 2.3% Asian, 0.2% American Indian and Alaska Native, 1.5% Hispanic of any race, 1.0% two or more races (2000); Density: 2,974.3 persons per square mile (2000); Age: 25.1% under 18, 14.7% over 64 (2000); Marriage status: 25.5% never married, 59.2% now married, 6.2% widowed, 9.1% divorced (2000); Foreign born: 3.3% (2000); Ancestry (includes multiple ancestries): 37.7% German, 14.5% Norwegian, 14.3% Irish, 11.9% Swedish, 7.3% French (except Basque) (2000).
Vital Statistics: Birth rate: 146.8 per 10,000 population (1998)
Economy: Unemployment rate: 3.5% (11/2002); Total civilian labor force: 16,824 (11/2002); Single-family building permits issued: 19 (2001) / 62 (2000); Multi-family building permits issued: 82 (2001) / 0 (2000); Employment by occupation: 14.7% management, 22.2% professional, 11.5% services, 29.6% sales, 0.1% farming, 8.7% construction, 13.2% production (2000).
Income: Per capita income: $24,338 (2000); Median household income: $52,934 (2000); Poverty rate: 4.4% (2000).
Taxes: Total city taxes per capita: $182 (2000); City property taxes per capita: $156 (2000).
Education: High school graduation rate: 91.7% (2000); College graduation rate: 30.2% (2000).

School District(s)

N.E. Metro Intermediate Dist. 916 (01-12)
2000 Enrollment: 548 651-415-5500
White Bear Lake (PK-12)
2000 Enrollment: 9,405 651-407-7500

Two-year College(s)

Century Community and Technical College (Public)
2001 Enrollment: 7,396 651-770-3300
2001 Tuition: In-state $2,294; Out-of-state $4,587

Housing: Homeownership rate: 74.7% (2000); Median home value: $130,400 (2000); Median rent: $680 per month (2000); Median age of housing: 34 years (2000).
Safety: Violent crime rate: 9.4 per 10,000 population; Property crime rate: 321.7 per 10,000 population (2001).
Newspapers: The White Bear Press (1 x week); Saint Croix Valley Press (1 x week); Quad Community Press (1 x week); Vadnais Heights Press (1 x week); Shoreview Press (1 x week); Forest Lake Press (1 x week)
Transportation: Commute to work: 93.2% car, 1.5% public transportation, 1.7% walk, 3.2% work from home (2000); Travel time to work: 29.0% less than 15 minutes, 42.0% 15 to 30 minutes, 21.0% 30 to 45 minutes, 5.5% 45 to 60 minutes, 2.6% 60 minutes or more (2000)
Additional Information Contacts
White Bear Lake Chamber of Commerce 651-429-8593

Red Lake County

Located in northwestern Minnesota; drained by the Red Lake River. Covers a land area of 432.40 square miles, a water area of 0.10 square miles, and is located in the Central Time Zone. The county government was organized in 1896. County seat is Red Lake Falls.

Weather Station: Red Lake Falls — Elevation: 1,072 feet

	Jan	Feb	Mar	Apr	May	Jun	Jul	Aug	Sep	Oct	Nov	Dec
High	14	21	35	54	69	77	82	80	69	55	34	20
Low	-6	1	16	31	44	53	57	54	45	33	18	2
Precip	0.7	0.5	1.0	1.4	2.6	3.7	3.4	3.7	2.6	1.8	1.0	0.5
Snow	11.5	8.0	8.4	2.2	tr	0.0	0.0	0.0	tr	0.9	9.5	8.7

High and Low temperatures in degrees Fahrenheit; Precipitation and Snow in inches

Population: 4,299 (2000); Race: 96.8% White, 0.0% Black, 0.3% Asian, 2.4% American Indian and Alaska Native, 0.5% Hispanic of any race, 0.6% two or more races (2000); Density: 9.9 persons per square mile (2000); Age: 25.4% under 18, 19.0% over 64 (2000).
Religion: Four largest groups: 56.6% Catholic Church, 23.7% Evangelical Lutheran Church in America, 8.4% Lutheran Church—Missouri Synod, 1.6% Presbyterian Church (U.S.A.) (2000).
Economy: Unemployment rate: 6.6% (11/2002); Total civilian labor force: 1,858 (11/2002); Leading industries: 31.5% manufacturing; 10.1% wholesale trade; 7.9% retail trade (2000); Companies that employ more than 1,000 persons: 0 (2000); Companies that employ more than 100 persons: 3 (2000); Farms: 376 totaling 204,977 acres (1997); Minority business ownership rate: 0.0% (1997); Women business ownership rate: 0.0% (1997); Retail sales per capita: $7,501 (1997). Single-family building permits issued: 5 (2001) / 2 (2000); Multi-family building permits issued: 0 (2001) / 2 (2000).

Income: Per capita income: $15,372 (2000); Median household income: $32,052 (2000); Poverty rate: 10.8% (2000); Bankruptcy rate: 2.85% (2001).
Taxes: Total county taxes per capita: $238 (1997); County property taxes per capita: $233 (1997).
Education: High school graduation rate: 78.8% (2000); College graduation rate: 10.7% (2000).
Housing: Homeownership rate: 79.4% (2000); Median home value: $43,200 (2000); Median rent: $243 per month (2000); Median age of housing: 43 years (2000).
Health: Birth rate: 111.7 per 10,000 population (1998); Age adjusted death rate: 89.5 per 10,000 population (1999); Age adjusted cancer mortality rate: 217.2 (Unreliable figure as per CDC) deaths per 100,000 population (1999). Number of physicians: 2.3 per 10,000 population (1999); Number of hospital beds: n/a (1999).
Elections: 2000 Presidential election results: 39.7% Gore, 52.2% Bush, 3.3% Nader, 4.2% Buchanan
National and State Parks: Moran State Wildlife Management Area
Additional Information Contacts
Red Lake County Government Offices 218-253-2598

Red Lake County Communities

BROOKS (city). Covers a land area of 1.163 square miles and a water area of 0 square miles. Located at 47.81° N. Lat.; 96.00° W. Long. Elevation is 1,125 feet.
Population: 141 (2000); Race: 100.0% White, 0.0% Black, 0.0% Asian, 0.0% American Indian and Alaska Native, 0.0% Hispanic of any race, 0.0% two or more races (2000); Density: 121.3 persons per square mile (2000); Age: 23.6% under 18, 23.6% over 64 (2000); Marriage status: 27.4% never married, 57.5% now married, 6.2% widowed, 8.8% divorced (2000); Foreign born: 0.7% (2000); Ancestry (includes multiple ancestries): 29.2% French (except Basque), 21.5% Norwegian, 20.1% German, 13.2% French Canadian, 9.0% Irish (2000).
Economy: Employment by occupation: 18.3% management, 10.0% professional, 31.7% services, 23.3% sales, 1.7% farming, 3.3% construction, 11.7% production (2000).
Income: Per capita income: $13,947 (2000); Median household income: $25,417 (2000); Poverty rate: 2.8% (2000).
Taxes: Total city taxes per capita: $106 (1997); City property taxes per capita: $86 (1997).
Education: High school graduation rate: 78.2% (2000); College graduation rate: 9.2% (2000).
Housing: Homeownership rate: 60.0% (2000); Median home value: $32,500 (2000); Median rent: $217 per month (2000); Median age of housing: 41 years (2000).
Transportation: Commute to work: 80.0% car, 0.0% public transportation, 6.7% walk, 13.3% work from home (2000); Travel time to work: 46.2% less than 15 minutes, 30.8% 15 to 30 minutes, 17.3% 30 to 45 minutes, 5.8% 45 to 60 minutes, 0.0% 60 minutes or more (2000)

BROWNS CREEK (township). Covers a land area of 12.071 square miles and a water area of 0 square miles. Located at 47.94° N. Lat.; 96.25° W. Long.
Population: 58 (2000); Race: 100.0% White, 0.0% Black, 0.0% Asian, 0.0% American Indian and Alaska Native, 8.5% Hispanic of any race, 0.0% two or more races (2000); Density: 4.8 persons per square mile (2000); Age: 33.8% under 18, 9.9% over 64 (2000); Marriage status: 28.1% never married, 66.7% now married, 5.3% widowed, 0.0% divorced (2000); Foreign born: 0.0% (2000); Ancestry (includes multiple ancestries): 63.4% German, 39.4% French (except Basque), 12.7% Norwegian, 11.3% Irish, 8.5% Swedish (2000).
Economy: Employment by occupation: 25.7% management, 17.1% professional, 22.9% services, 11.4% sales, 0.0% farming, 5.7% construction, 17.1% production (2000).
Income: Per capita income: $11,834 (2000); Median household income: $43,125 (2000); Poverty rate: 23.9% (2000).
Taxes: Total city taxes per capita: $97 (1997); City property taxes per capita: $97 (1997).
Education: High school graduation rate: 81.6% (2000); College graduation rate: 18.4% (2000).
Housing: Homeownership rate: 81.0% (2000); Median home value: $65,000 (2000); Median age of housing: 60+ years (2000).
Transportation: Commute to work: 91.4% car, 0.0% public transportation, 8.6% walk, 0.0% work from home (2000); Travel time to work: 31.4% less than 15 minutes, 45.7% 15 to 30 minutes, 22.9% 30 to 45 minutes, 0.0% 45 to 60 minutes, 0.0% 60 minutes or more (2000)

EMARDVILLE (township). Covers a land area of 45.630 square miles and a water area of 0 square miles. Located at 47.89° N. Lat.; 96.03° W. Long.
Population: 217 (2000); Race: 100.0% White, 0.0% Black, 0.0% Asian, 0.0% American Indian and Alaska Native, 0.0% Hispanic of any race, 0.0% two or more races (2000); Density: 4.8 persons per square mile (2000); Age: 28.9% under 18, 15.6% over 64 (2000); Marriage status: 21.5% never married, 65.0% now married, 5.1% widowed, 8.5% divorced (2000); Foreign born: 2.2% (2000); Ancestry (includes multiple ancestries): 44.9% German, 28.0% Norwegian, 18.2% French (except Basque), 8.0% Swedish, 6.7% Irish (2000).
Economy: Employment by occupation: 25.5% management, 15.1% professional, 8.5% services, 17.0% sales, 8.5% farming, 4.7% construction, 20.8% production (2000).
Income: Per capita income: $11,943 (2000); Median household income: $26,875 (2000); Poverty rate: 18.7% (2000).
Taxes: Total city taxes per capita: $101 (1997); City property taxes per capita: $101 (1997).
Education: High school graduation rate: 79.1% (2000); College graduation rate: 6.8% (2000).
Housing: Homeownership rate: 81.3% (2000); Median home value: $87,500 (2000); Median age of housing: 48 years (2000).
Transportation: Commute to work: 83.5% car, 0.0% public transportation, 0.0% walk, 16.5% work from home (2000); Travel time to work: 25.6% less than 15 minutes, 38.4% 15 to 30 minutes, 30.2% 30 to 45 minutes, 3.5% 45 to 60 minutes, 2.3% 60 minutes or more (2000)

EQUALITY (township). Covers a land area of 47.710 square miles and a water area of 0.024 square miles. Located at 47.91° N. Lat.; 95.76° W. Long.
Population: 123 (2000); Race: 100.0% White, 0.0% Black, 0.0% Asian, 0.0% American Indian and Alaska Native, 0.0% Hispanic of any race, 0.0% two or more races (2000); Density: 2.6 persons per square mile (2000); Age: 22.3% under 18, 25.0% over 64 (2000); Marriage status: 20.7% never married, 59.8% now married, 8.0% widowed, 11.5% divorced (2000); Foreign born: 0.0% (2000); Ancestry (includes multiple ancestries): 64.3% Norwegian, 30.4% German, 20.5% Irish, 10.7% French (except Basque), 6.3% Swedish (2000).
Economy: Employment by occupation: 21.6% management, 3.9% professional, 19.6% services, 17.6% sales, 0.0% farming, 0.0% construction, 37.3% production (2000).
Income: Per capita income: $19,046 (2000); Median household income: $31,250 (2000); Poverty rate: 9.8% (2000).
Taxes: Total city taxes per capita: $205 (1997); City property taxes per capita: $205 (1997).
Education: High school graduation rate: 71.6% (2000); College graduation rate: 4.9% (2000).
Housing: Homeownership rate: 80.8% (2000); Median home value: $42,500 (2000); Median rent: $125 per month (2000); Median age of housing: 47 years (2000).
Transportation: Commute to work: 74.5% car, 0.0% public transportation, 3.9% walk, 17.6% work from home (2000); Travel time to work: 9.5% less than 15 minutes, 42.9% 15 to 30 minutes, 47.6% 30 to 45 minutes, 0.0% 45 to 60 minutes, 0.0% 60 minutes or more (2000)

GARNES (township). Covers a land area of 48.306 square miles and a water area of 0 square miles. Located at 47.91° N. Lat.; 95.91° W. Long. Elevation is 1,156 feet.
Population: 174 (2000); Race: 100.0% White, 0.0% Black, 0.0% Asian, 0.0% American Indian and Alaska Native, 0.0% Hispanic of any race, 0.0% two or more races (2000); Density: 3.6 persons per square mile (2000); Age: 26.1% under 18, 4.0% over 64 (2000); Marriage status: 27.2% never married, 64.2% now married, 3.7% widowed, 4.9% divorced (2000); Foreign born: 1.0% (2000); Ancestry (includes multiple ancestries): 65.8% Norwegian, 18.6% Swedish, 12.6% French Canadian, 10.6% German, 8.5% French (except Basque) (2000).
Economy: Employment by occupation: 26.9% management, 11.1% professional, 12.0% services, 23.1% sales, 1.9% farming, 4.6% construction, 20.4% production (2000).
Income: Per capita income: $16,725 (2000); Median household income: $40,625 (2000); Poverty rate: 11.2% (2000).
Taxes: Total city taxes per capita: $20 (1997); City property taxes per capita: $20 (1997).

Education: High school graduation rate: 88.3% (2000); College graduation rate: 11.7% (2000).
Housing: Homeownership rate: 84.9% (2000); Median home value: $47,500 (2000); Median rent: $206 per month (2000); Median age of housing: 38 years (2000).
Transportation: Commute to work: 84.6% car, 0.0% public transportation, 0.0% walk, 15.4% work from home (2000); Travel time to work: 31.8% less than 15 minutes, 21.6% 15 to 30 minutes, 33.0% 30 to 45 minutes, 10.2% 45 to 60 minutes, 3.4% 60 minutes or more (2000)

GERVAIS (township). Covers a land area of 35.584 square miles and a water area of 0 square miles. Located at 47.90° N. Lat.; 96.15° W. Long.
Population: 250 (2000); Race: 95.6% White, 0.0% Black, 0.0% Asian, 1.3% American Indian and Alaska Native, 3.1% Hispanic of any race, 2.6% two or more races (2000); Density: 7.0 persons per square mile (2000); Age: 23.6% under 18, 10.9% over 64 (2000); Marriage status: 18.4% never married, 68.4% now married, 5.3% widowed, 7.9% divorced (2000); Foreign born: 0.9% (2000); Ancestry (includes multiple ancestries): 34.5% German, 29.3% Norwegian, 19.7% French (except Basque), 9.2% Swedish, 8.3% French Canadian (2000).
Economy: Employment by occupation: 19.3% management, 17.6% professional, 10.1% services, 22.7% sales, 3.4% farming, 10.9% construction, 16.0% production (2000).
Income: Per capita income: $18,022 (2000); Median household income: $42,188 (2000); Poverty rate: 12.9% (2000).
Taxes: Total city taxes per capita: $104 (1997); City property taxes per capita: $104 (1997).
Education: High school graduation rate: 81.4% (2000); College graduation rate: 12.8% (2000).
Housing: Homeownership rate: 92.6% (2000); Median home value: $70,000 (2000); Median rent: $288 per month (2000); Median age of housing: 35 years (2000).
Transportation: Commute to work: 83.1% car, 0.0% public transportation, 3.4% walk, 13.6% work from home (2000); Travel time to work: 20.6% less than 15 minutes, 48.0% 15 to 30 minutes, 21.6% 30 to 45 minutes, 2.9% 45 to 60 minutes, 6.9% 60 minutes or more (2000)

LAKE PLEASANT (township). Covers a land area of 35.907 square miles and a water area of 0 square miles. Located at 47.81° N. Lat.; 96.28° W. Long.
Population: 126 (2000); Race: 100.0% White, 0.0% Black, 0.0% Asian, 0.0% American Indian and Alaska Native, 1.5% Hispanic of any race, 0.0% two or more races (2000); Density: 3.5 persons per square mile (2000); Age: 31.8% under 18, 16.7% over 64 (2000); Marriage status: 29.0% never married, 67.0% now married, 4.0% widowed, 0.0% divorced (2000); Foreign born: 1.5% (2000); Ancestry (includes multiple ancestries): 60.6% German, 27.3% Norwegian, 21.2% French (except Basque), 13.6% English, 8.3% French Canadian (2000).
Economy: Employment by occupation: 27.4% management, 9.7% professional, 6.5% services, 27.4% sales, 4.8% farming, 6.5% construction, 17.7% production (2000).
Income: Per capita income: $13,242 (2000); Median household income: $41,875 (2000); Poverty rate: 13.6% (2000).
Taxes: Total city taxes per capita: $65 (1997); City property taxes per capita: $65 (1997).
Education: High school graduation rate: 82.7% (2000); College graduation rate: 9.9% (2000).
Housing: Homeownership rate: 81.8% (2000); Median home value: $88,000 (2000); Median rent: $525 per month (2000); Median age of housing: 60+ years (2000).
Transportation: Commute to work: 69.4% car, 0.0% public transportation, 6.5% walk, 24.2% work from home (2000); Travel time to work: 48.9% less than 15 minutes, 34.0% 15 to 30 minutes, 8.5% 30 to 45 minutes, 0.0% 45 to 60 minutes, 8.5% 60 minutes or more (2000)

LAMBERT (township). Covers a land area of 35.692 square miles and a water area of 0 square miles. Located at 47.81° N. Lat.; 95.89° W. Long.
Population: 154 (2000); Race: 100.0% White, 0.0% Black, 0.0% Asian, 0.0% American Indian and Alaska Native, 0.0% Hispanic of any race, 0.0% two or more races (2000); Density: 4.3 persons per square mile (2000); Age: 20.4% under 18, 15.6% over 64 (2000); Marriage status: 24.2% never married, 59.4% now married, 6.3% widowed, 10.2% divorced (2000); Foreign born: 0.0% (2000); Ancestry (includes multiple ancestries): 29.3% Norwegian, 27.9% French (except Basque), 24.5% German, 8.8% French Canadian, 6.1% Irish (2000).
Economy: Employment by occupation: 15.0% management, 6.7% professional, 21.7% services, 21.7% sales, 0.0% farming, 15.0% construction, 20.0% production (2000).
Income: Per capita income: $15,888 (2000); Median household income: $33,750 (2000); Poverty rate: 1.4% (2000).
Taxes: Total city taxes per capita: $51 (1997); City property taxes per capita: $51 (1997).
Education: High school graduation rate: 79.4% (2000); College graduation rate: 1.9% (2000).
Housing: Homeownership rate: 80.0% (2000); Median home value: $32,500 (2000); Median rent: $310 per month (2000); Median age of housing: 54 years (2000).
Transportation: Commute to work: 83.3% car, 0.0% public transportation, 0.0% walk, 16.7% work from home (2000); Travel time to work: 34.0% less than 15 minutes, 38.0% 15 to 30 minutes, 4.0% 30 to 45 minutes, 12.0% 45 to 60 minutes, 12.0% 60 minutes or more (2000)

LOUISVILLE (township). Covers a land area of 36.049 square miles and a water area of 0.025 square miles. Located at 47.89° N. Lat.; 96.42° W. Long.
Population: 192 (2000); Race: 100.0% White, 0.0% Black, 0.0% Asian, 0.0% American Indian and Alaska Native, 1.0% Hispanic of any race, 0.0% two or more races (2000); Density: 5.3 persons per square mile (2000); Age: 33.5% under 18, 8.5% over 64 (2000); Marriage status: 24.0% never married, 67.1% now married, 2.7% widowed, 6.2% divorced (2000); Foreign born: 0.0% (2000); Ancestry (includes multiple ancestries): 31.0% French (except Basque), 30.0% German, 21.5% Norwegian, 14.0% French Canadian, 9.5% Irish (2000).
Economy: Employment by occupation: 23.0% management, 14.9% professional, 13.8% services, 20.7% sales, 1.1% farming, 8.0% construction, 18.4% production (2000).
Income: Per capita income: $16,805 (2000); Median household income: $41,071 (2000); Poverty rate: 2.0% (2000).
Taxes: Total city taxes per capita: $87 (1997); City property taxes per capita: $87 (1997).
Education: High school graduation rate: 91.5% (2000); College graduation rate: 14.5% (2000).
Housing: Homeownership rate: 89.9% (2000); Median home value: $45,000 (2000); Median rent: $475 per month (2000); Median age of housing: 46 years (2000).
Transportation: Commute to work: 88.5% car, 0.0% public transportation, 2.3% walk, 5.7% work from home (2000); Travel time to work: 19.5% less than 15 minutes, 45.1% 15 to 30 minutes, 14.6% 30 to 45 minutes, 18.3% 45 to 60 minutes, 2.4% 60 minutes or more (2000)

OKLEE (city). Covers a land area of 0.656 square miles and a water area of 0 square miles. Located at 47.83° N. Lat.; 95.85° W. Long. Elevation is 1,143 feet.
Population: 396 (2000); Race: 100.0% White, 0.0% Black, 0.0% Asian, 0.0% American Indian and Alaska Native, 0.8% Hispanic of any race, 0.0% two or more races (2000); Density: 603.7 persons per square mile (2000); Age: 23.5% under 18, 25.6% over 64 (2000); Marriage status: 20.8% never married, 60.4% now married, 11.5% widowed, 7.3% divorced (2000); Foreign born: 0.8% (2000); Ancestry (includes multiple ancestries): 55.3% Norwegian, 23.8% French (except Basque), 16.5% German, 15.8% Swedish, 10.9% Irish (2000).
Economy: Falls. Grain, sugar beets, sunflowers, potatoes; cattle. Manufacturing: fertilizers, feeds. Single-family building permits issued: 0 (2001) / 0 (2000); Multi-family building permits issued: 0 (2001) / 0 (2000); Employment by occupation: 13.6% management, 14.2% professional, 16.0% services, 19.8% sales, 5.6% farming, 11.7% construction, 19.1% production (2000).
Income: Per capita income: $14,342 (2000); Median household income: $23,214 (2000); Poverty rate: 14.7% (2000).
Taxes: Total city taxes per capita: $79 (1997); City property taxes per capita: $77 (1997).
Education: High school graduation rate: 72.9% (2000); College graduation rate: 8.6% (2000).

School District(s)

Oklee (KG-12)
2000 Enrollment: 215 218-796-5136

Housing: Homeownership rate: 83.9% (2000); Median home value: $27,100 (2000); Median rent: $194 per month (2000); Median age of housing: 48 years (2000).
Newspapers: Oklee Herald (1 x week)

Transportation: Commute to work: 83.3% car, 0.0% public transportation, 11.7% walk, 4.9% work from home (2000); Travel time to work: 42.9% less than 15 minutes, 22.7% 15 to 30 minutes, 20.8% 30 to 45 minutes, 6.5% 45 to 60 minutes, 7.1% 60 minutes or more (2000)

PLUMMER (city). Covers a land area of 2.833 square miles and a water area of 0 square miles. Located at 47.91° N. Lat.; 96.04° W. Long. Elevation is 1,125 feet.
Population: 270 (2000); Race: 95.8% White, 0.0% Black, 4.2% Asian, 0.0% American Indian and Alaska Native, 0.0% Hispanic of any race, 0.0% two or more races (2000); Density: 95.3 persons per square mile (2000); Age: 24.2% under 18, 26.2% over 64 (2000); Marriage status: 19.4% never married, 54.0% now married, 12.8% widowed, 13.7% divorced (2000); Foreign born: 1.9% (2000); Ancestry (includes multiple ancestries): 38.5% Norwegian, 29.6% German, 10.8% French (except Basque), 10.0% Irish, 7.7% Swedish (2000).
Economy: Railroad junction. Grain, sugar beets, sunflowers, potatoes; cattle. Single-family building permits issued: 1 (2001) / 1 (2000); Multi-family building permits issued: 0 (2001) / 0 (2000); Employment by occupation: 9.7% management, 16.1% professional, 25.8% services, 18.3% sales, 0.0% farming, 0.0% construction, 30.1% production (2000).
Income: Per capita income: $17,506 (2000); Median household income: $29,286 (2000); Poverty rate: 8.5% (2000).
Taxes: Total city taxes per capita: $284 (1997); City property taxes per capita: $284 (1997).
Education: High school graduation rate: 77.2% (2000); College graduation rate: 7.2% (2000).

School District(s)

Plummer (PK-12)
2000 Enrollment: 168 218-465-4222

Housing: Homeownership rate: 74.8% (2000); Median home value: $31,300 (2000); Median rent: $235 per month (2000); Median age of housing: 32 years (2000).
Transportation: Commute to work: 83.9% car, 0.0% public transportation, 12.6% walk, 3.4% work from home (2000); Travel time to work: 35.7% less than 15 minutes, 46.4% 15 to 30 minutes, 9.5% 30 to 45 minutes, 3.6% 45 to 60 minutes, 4.8% 60 minutes or more (2000)

POPLAR RIVER (township). Covers a land area of 34.934 square miles and a water area of 0 square miles. Located at 47.81° N. Lat.; 96.02° W. Long.
Population: 125 (2000); Race: 100.0% White, 0.0% Black, 0.0% Asian, 0.0% American Indian and Alaska Native, 0.0% Hispanic of any race, 0.0% two or more races (2000); Density: 3.6 persons per square mile (2000); Age: 20.9% under 18, 17.1% over 64 (2000); Marriage status: 24.5% never married, 69.1% now married, 0.0% widowed, 6.4% divorced (2000); Foreign born: 4.7% (2000); Ancestry (includes multiple ancestries): 35.7% German, 26.4% French (except Basque), 20.2% Norwegian, 8.5% French Canadian, 7.8% Danish (2000).
Economy: Employment by occupation: 16.4% management, 16.4% professional, 18.0% services, 18.0% sales, 3.3% farming, 6.6% construction, 21.3% production (2000).
Income: Per capita income: $17,900 (2000); Median household income: $36,250 (2000); Poverty rate: 7.8% (2000).
Taxes: Total city taxes per capita: $71 (1997); City property taxes per capita: $71 (1997).
Education: High school graduation rate: 73.1% (2000); College graduation rate: 16.1% (2000).
Housing: Homeownership rate: 93.8% (2000); Median home value: $27,500 (2000); Median age of housing: 60+ years (2000).
Transportation: Commute to work: 85.2% car, 0.0% public transportation, 0.0% walk, 14.8% work from home (2000); Travel time to work: 17.3% less than 15 minutes, 48.1% 15 to 30 minutes, 21.2% 30 to 45 minutes, 9.6% 45 to 60 minutes, 3.8% 60 minutes or more (2000)

RED LAKE FALLS (city). Covers a land area of 2.121 square miles and a water area of 0 square miles. Located at 47.88° N. Lat.; 96.27° W. Long. Elevation is 1,037 feet.
History: A Northwest Company trading post was established in 1798 at Red Lake Falls by Jean Baptiste Cadotte. French settlers came in large numbers, hoping for a fortune in furs. When fur trading declined, the settlers turned to dairying.
Population: 1,590 (2000); Race: 92.6% White, 0.0% Black, 0.0% Asian, 6.2% American Indian and Alaska Native, 0.0% Hispanic of any race, 1.1% two or more races (2000); Density: 749.7 persons per square mile (2000); Age: 24.7% under 18, 21.6% over 64 (2000); Marriage status: 28.9% never married, 50.7% now married, 11.6% widowed, 8.8% divorced (2000); Foreign born: 1.2% (2000); Ancestry (includes multiple ancestries): 33.9% German, 31.1% Norwegian, 22.0% French (except Basque), 6.5% Irish, 5.7% Other groups (2000).
Economy: Single-family building permits issued: 4 (2001) / 1 (2000); Multi-family building permits issued: 0 (2001) / 2 (2000); Employment by occupation: 9.6% management, 18.5% professional, 15.7% services, 24.8% sales, 0.8% farming, 12.0% construction, 18.6% production (2000).
Income: Per capita income: $15,177 (2000); Median household income: $30,536 (2000); Poverty rate: 11.4% (2000).
Taxes: Total city taxes per capita: $118 (1997); City property taxes per capita: $114 (1997).
Education: High school graduation rate: 78.1% (2000); College graduation rate: 14.2% (2000).

School District(s)

Red Lake Falls (PK-12)
2000 Enrollment: 421 218-253-2139

Housing: Homeownership rate: 74.0% (2000); Median home value: $47,400 (2000); Median rent: $263 per month (2000); Median age of housing: 38 years (2000).
Newspapers: The Gazette (1 x week)
Transportation: Commute to work: 87.7% car, 0.4% public transportation, 9.3% walk, 2.4% work from home (2000); Travel time to work: 56.2% less than 15 minutes, 22.1% 15 to 30 minutes, 14.2% 30 to 45 minutes, 3.9% 45 to 60 minutes, 3.6% 60 minutes or more (2000)

RED LAKE FALLS (township). Covers a land area of 33.951 square miles and a water area of 0.033 square miles. Located at 47.89° N. Lat.; 96.27° W. Long. Elevation is 1,037 feet.
History: Established as fur-trading post before 1800. Incorporated as village 1881; as city 1898.
Population: 206 (2000); Race: 100.0% White, 0.0% Black, 0.0% Asian, 0.0% American Indian and Alaska Native, 0.0% Hispanic of any race, 0.0% two or more races (2000); Density: 6.1 persons per square mile (2000); Age: 16.9% under 18, 23.3% over 64 (2000); Marriage status: 22.0% never married, 68.3% now married, 4.3% widowed, 5.5% divorced (2000); Foreign born: 1.1% (2000); Ancestry (includes multiple ancestries): 51.3% German, 27.0% French (except Basque), 18.5% Norwegian, 7.4% English, 6.9% French Canadian (2000).
Economy: Terminus of Railroad spur from Dugdale (South). Resort. Agricultural trading point; grain, sugar beets, sunflowers, potatoes; cattle. Manufacturing: manufactured homes. Employment by occupation: 15.5% management, 4.8% professional, 4.8% services, 27.4% sales, 1.2% farming, 23.8% construction, 22.6% production (2000).
Income: Per capita income: $16,833 (2000); Median household income: $36,250 (2000); Poverty rate: 8.5% (2000).
Taxes: Total city taxes per capita: $71 (1997); City property taxes per capita: $67 (1997).
Education: High school graduation rate: 84.1% (2000); College graduation rate: 6.9% (2000).
Housing: Homeownership rate: 76.5% (2000); Median home value: $45,000 (2000); Median rent: $281 per month (2000); Median age of housing: 30 years (2000).
Transportation: Commute to work: 83.3% car, 0.0% public transportation, 0.0% walk, 16.7% work from home (2000); Travel time to work: 40.0% less than 15 minutes, 27.1% 15 to 30 minutes, 24.3% 30 to 45 minutes, 4.3% 45 to 60 minutes, 4.3% 60 minutes or more (2000)

RIVER (township). Covers a land area of 11.756 square miles and a water area of 0 square miles. Located at 47.94° N. Lat.; 96.16° W. Long.
Population: 65 (2000); Race: 100.0% White, 0.0% Black, 0.0% Asian, 0.0% American Indian and Alaska Native, 0.0% Hispanic of any race, 0.0% two or more races (2000); Density: 5.5 persons per square mile (2000); Age: 43.2% under 18, 2.5% over 64 (2000); Marriage status: 8.3% never married, 83.3% now married, 4.2% widowed, 4.2% divorced (2000); Foreign born: 0.0% (2000); Ancestry (includes multiple ancestries): 53.1% Norwegian, 40.7% German, 11.1% Swedish, 11.1% United States or American, 6.2% Scottish (2000).
Economy: Employment by occupation: 0.0% management, 10.3% professional, 12.8% services, 28.2% sales, 5.1% farming, 15.4% construction, 28.2% production (2000).
Income: Per capita income: $12,335 (2000); Median household income: $41,250 (2000); Poverty rate: 11.1% (2000).
Taxes: Total city taxes per capita: $44 (1997); City property taxes per capita: $44 (1997).

Education: High school graduation rate: 93.5% (2000); College graduation rate: 0.0% (2000).
Housing: Homeownership rate: 92.3% (2000); Median home value: $48,300 (2000); Median age of housing: 60 years (2000).
Transportation: Commute to work: 89.7% car, 0.0% public transportation, 0.0% walk, 10.3% work from home (2000); Travel time to work: 17.1% less than 15 minutes, 68.6% 15 to 30 minutes, 14.3% 30 to 45 minutes, 0.0% 45 to 60 minutes, 0.0% 60 minutes or more (2000)

TERREBONNE (township). Covers a land area of 35.995 square miles and a water area of 0 square miles. Located at 47.80° N. Lat.; 96.15° W. Long. Elevation is 1,091 feet.
Population: 140 (2000); Race: 100.0% White, 0.0% Black, 0.0% Asian, 0.0% American Indian and Alaska Native, 0.0% Hispanic of any race, 0.0% two or more races (2000); Density: 3.9 persons per square mile (2000); Age: 27.3% under 18, 21.1% over 64 (2000); Marriage status: 31.4% never married, 46.1% now married, 10.8% widowed, 11.8% divorced (2000); Foreign born: 0.0% (2000); Ancestry (includes multiple ancestries): 43.0% German, 33.6% French (except Basque), 32.0% Norwegian, 9.4% Swedish, 7.0% English (2000).
Economy: Employment by occupation: 21.2% management, 15.4% professional, 7.7% services, 9.6% sales, 9.6% farming, 15.4% construction, 21.2% production (2000).
Income: Per capita income: $13,924 (2000); Median household income: $34,375 (2000); Poverty rate: 8.6% (2000).
Taxes: Total city taxes per capita: $162 (1997); City property taxes per capita: $162 (1997).
Education: High school graduation rate: 76.8% (2000); College graduation rate: 4.9% (2000).
Housing: Homeownership rate: 87.0% (2000); Median home value: $34,200 (2000); Median rent: $275 per month (2000); Median age of housing: 60+ years (2000).
Transportation: Commute to work: 94.2% car, 0.0% public transportation, 0.0% walk, 5.8% work from home (2000); Travel time to work: 28.6% less than 15 minutes, 26.5% 15 to 30 minutes, 34.7% 30 to 45 minutes, 10.2% 45 to 60 minutes, 0.0% 60 minutes or more (2000)

WYLIE (township). Covers a land area of 12.074 square miles and a water area of 0 square miles. Located at 47.94° N. Lat.; 96.42° W. Long.
Population: 72 (2000); Race: 100.0% White, 0.0% Black, 0.0% Asian, 0.0% American Indian and Alaska Native, 0.0% Hispanic of any race, 0.0% two or more races (2000); Density: 6.0 persons per square mile (2000); Age: 32.8% under 18, 15.6% over 64 (2000); Marriage status: 27.5% never married, 52.9% now married, 3.9% widowed, 15.7% divorced (2000); Foreign born: 0.0% (2000); Ancestry (includes multiple ancestries): 51.6% German, 17.2% French (except Basque), 14.1% English, 12.5% French Canadian, 7.8% Norwegian (2000).
Economy: Employment by occupation: 28.0% management, 0.0% professional, 32.0% services, 12.0% sales, 0.0% farming, 0.0% construction, 28.0% production (2000).
Income: Per capita income: $12,959 (2000); Median household income: $36,250 (2000); Poverty rate: 10.9% (2000).
Taxes: Total city taxes per capita: $48 (1997); City property taxes per capita: $48 (1997).
Education: High school graduation rate: 53.7% (2000); College graduation rate: 0.0% (2000).
Housing: Homeownership rate: 91.3% (2000); Median home value: $45,000 (2000); Median age of housing: 37 years (2000).
Transportation: Commute to work: 80.0% car, 0.0% public transportation, 0.0% walk, 20.0% work from home (2000); Travel time to work: 15.0% less than 15 minutes, 35.0% 15 to 30 minutes, 50.0% 30 to 45 minutes, 0.0% 45 to 60 minutes, 0.0% 60 minutes or more (2000)

Redwood County

Located in southwestern Minnesota; bounded on the north by the Minnesota River; drained by the Redwood and Cottonwood Rivers. Covers a land area of 879.70 square miles, a water area of 1.50 square miles, and is located in the Central Time Zone. The county government was organized in 1862. County seat is Redwood Falls.

Weather Station: Lamberton SW Exp. Station — Elevation: 1,141 feet

	Jan	Feb	Mar	Apr	May	Jun	Jul	Aug	Sep	Oct	Nov	Dec
High	22	28	39	56	71	80	83	81	73	60	41	27
Low	2	9	21	34	46	57	60	57	47	35	22	8
Precip	0.7	0.5	1.8	2.8	3.1	3.9	3.6	3.3	2.7	2.0	1.4	0.6
Snow	9.7	6.0	8.6	2.8	0.0	0.0	0.0	0.0	0.0	0.3	7.1	7.2

High and Low temperatures in degrees Fahrenheit; Precipitation and Snow in inches

Weather Station: Redwood Falls Muni Airport — Elevation: 1,023 feet

	Jan	Feb	Mar	Apr	May	Jun	Jul	Aug	Sep	Oct	Nov	Dec
High	22	28	40	57	72	81	85	82	73	60	40	27
Low	4	11	24	37	49	59	62	60	50	38	24	10
Precip	0.7	0.6	1.7	2.6	3.1	4.0	3.8	3.6	2.6	2.0	1.6	0.6
Snow	6.8	4.9	7.8	2.0	tr	tr	0.0	0.0	tr	0.4	6.6	6.2

High and Low temperatures in degrees Fahrenheit; Precipitation and Snow in inches

Population: 16,815 (2000); Race: 95.2% White, 0.0% Black, 0.4% Asian, 3.5% American Indian and Alaska Native, 0.8% Hispanic of any race, 0.7% two or more races (2000); Density: 19.1 persons per square mile (2000); Age: 26.5% under 18, 19.3% over 64 (2000).
Religion: Five largest groups: 32.2% Catholic Church, 28.3% Evangelical Lutheran Church in America, 12.4% Wisconsin Evangelical Lutheran Synod, 7.6% The United Methodist Church, 2.4% Presbyterian Church (U.S.A.) (2000).
Economy: Unemployment rate: 2.7% (11/2002); Total civilian labor force: 8,686 (11/2002); Leading industries: 19.7% manufacturing; 17.0% health care and social assistance; 16.8% retail trade (2000); Companies that employ more than 1,000 persons: 0 (2000); Companies that employ more than 100 persons: 9 (2000); Farms: 1,168 totaling 508,129 acres (1997); Minority business ownership rate: 0.0% (1997); Women business ownership rate: 14.4% (1997); Retail sales per capita: $7,632 (1997). Single-family building permits issued: 31 (2001) / 34 (2000); Multi-family building permits issued: 16 (2001) / 2 (2000).
Income: Per capita income: $18,903 (2000); Median household income: $37,352 (2000); Poverty rate: 7.7% (2000); Bankruptcy rate: 1.09% (2001).
Taxes: Total county taxes per capita: $346 (2000); County property taxes per capita: $339 (2000).
Education: High school graduation rate: 80.2% (2000); College graduation rate: 13.4% (2000).
Housing: Homeownership rate: 80.0% (2000); Median home value: $57,900 (2000); Median rent: $314 per month (2000); Median age of housing: 47 years (2000).
Health: Birth rate: 111.8 per 10,000 population (1998); Age adjusted death rate: 86.2 per 10,000 population (1999); Age adjusted cancer mortality rate: 200.7 deaths per 100,000 population (1999). Number of physicians: 4.8 per 10,000 population (1999); Number of hospital beds: 17.8 per 10,000 population (1999).
Elections: 2000 Presidential election results: 34.6% Gore, 59.2% Bush, 4.1% Nader, 1.6% Buchanan
National and State Parks: Alexander Ramsey State Park; Daubs Lake State Wildlife Management Area; Delhi State Wildlife Management Area; Gales State Wildlife Management Area; Honner State Wildlife Management Area; Klabunde State Wildlife Management Area; Lamberton State Wildlife Management Area; Luescher-Barnum State Wildlife Management A; Mammenga State Wildlife Management Area; Paul State Wildlife Management Area; Rohlik State Wildlife Management Area; Waterbury State Wildlife Management Area; Westline State Wildlife Management Area; Willow Lake State Wildlife Management Area
Additional Information Contacts
Redwood County Government Offices 507-637-4016
Redwood Falls Chamber of Commerce 507-637-2828

Redwood County Communities

BELVIEW (city). Covers a land area of 0.945 square miles and a water area of 0 square miles. Located at 44.60° N. Lat.; 95.32° W. Long. Elevation is 1,076 feet.
Population: 412 (2000); Race: 99.8% White, 0.0% Black, 0.0% Asian, 0.0% American Indian and Alaska Native, 0.0% Hispanic of any race, 0.2% two or more races (2000); Density: 436.1 persons per square mile (2000); Age: 22.1% under 18, 35.0% over 64 (2000); Marriage status: 19.1% never married, 59.7% now married, 14.3% widowed, 6.9% divorced (2000); Foreign born: 0.0% (2000); Ancestry (includes multiple ancestries): 49.1% German, 48.6% Norwegian, 4.7% Swedish, 4.0% Belgian, 3.5% Irish (2000).
Economy: Livestock, poultry; grain, soybeans; dairying; granite.
Single-family building permits issued: 0 (2001) / 0 (2000); Multi-family

building permits issued: 0 (2001) / 0 (2000); Employment by occupation: 13.2% management, 10.8% professional, 17.4% services, 17.4% sales, 0.6% farming, 10.2% construction, 30.5% production (2000).
Income: Per capita income: $16,105 (2000); Median household income: $32,500 (2000); Poverty rate: 3.1% (2000).
Taxes: Total city taxes per capita: $114 (1997); City property taxes per capita: $114 (1997).
Education: High school graduation rate: 65.6% (2000); College graduation rate: 9.2% (2000).

School District(s)

Belview (KG-03)
2000 Enrollment: 0 507-644-3531
Housing: Homeownership rate: 81.2% (2000); Median home value: $41,500 (2000); Median rent: $603 per month (2000); Median age of housing: 47 years (2000).
Transportation: Commute to work: 83.2% car, 0.0% public transportation, 10.8% walk, 3.6% work from home (2000); Travel time to work: 37.9% less than 15 minutes, 44.7% 15 to 30 minutes, 13.0% 30 to 45 minutes, 3.1% 45 to 60 minutes, 1.2% 60 minutes or more (2000)

BROOKVILLE (township). Covers a land area of 35.832 square miles and a water area of 0 square miles. Located at 44.32° N. Lat.; 94.92° W. Long.
Population: 258 (2000); Race: 96.4% White, 0.0% Black, 0.0% Asian, 0.0% American Indian and Alaska Native, 2.9% Hispanic of any race, 3.6% two or more races (2000); Density: 7.2 persons per square mile (2000); Age: 29.7% under 18, 12.7% over 64 (2000); Marriage status: 16.0% never married, 75.0% now married, 3.3% widowed, 5.7% divorced (2000); Foreign born: 0.0% (2000); Ancestry (includes multiple ancestries): 68.1% German, 11.2% Danish, 10.9% Norwegian, 4.3% United States or American, 3.6% Italian (2000).
Economy: Employment by occupation: 40.0% management, 3.7% professional, 12.6% services, 11.1% sales, 11.1% farming, 1.5% construction, 20.0% production (2000).
Income: Per capita income: $14,802 (2000); Median household income: $33,875 (2000); Poverty rate: 6.5% (2000).
Taxes: Total city taxes per capita: $102 (1997); City property taxes per capita: $102 (1997).
Education: High school graduation rate: 81.1% (2000); College graduation rate: 12.8% (2000).
Housing: Homeownership rate: 88.0% (2000); Median home value: $70,500 (2000); Median rent: $275 per month (2000); Median age of housing: 60+ years (2000).
Transportation: Commute to work: 65.4% car, 0.0% public transportation, 3.0% walk, 30.1% work from home (2000); Travel time to work: 32.3% less than 15 minutes, 58.1% 15 to 30 minutes, 7.5% 30 to 45 minutes, 0.0% 45 to 60 minutes, 2.2% 60 minutes or more (2000)

CHARLESTOWN (township). Covers a land area of 33.833 square miles and a water area of 0.009 square miles. Located at 44.24° N. Lat.; 95.15° W. Long.
Population: 217 (2000); Race: 100.0% White, 0.0% Black, 0.0% Asian, 0.0% American Indian and Alaska Native, 0.0% Hispanic of any race, 0.0% two or more races (2000); Density: 6.4 persons per square mile (2000); Age: 28.2% under 18, 10.7% over 64 (2000); Marriage status: 19.4% never married, 74.4% now married, 1.1% widowed, 5.0% divorced (2000); Foreign born: 0.0% (2000); Ancestry (includes multiple ancestries): 70.5% German, 23.9% Norwegian, 6.8% French (except Basque), 5.6% Czech, 3.4% Swedish (2000).
Economy: Employment by occupation: 25.0% management, 14.7% professional, 16.2% services, 18.4% sales, 2.9% farming, 9.6% construction, 13.2% production (2000).
Income: Per capita income: $20,984 (2000); Median household income: $44,688 (2000); Poverty rate: 6.8% (2000).
Taxes: Total city taxes per capita: $92 (1997); City property taxes per capita: $92 (1997).
Education: High school graduation rate: 85.8% (2000); College graduation rate: 13.6% (2000).
Housing: Homeownership rate: 81.1% (2000); Median home value: $72,500 (2000); Median rent: $175 per month (2000); Median age of housing: 52 years (2000).
Transportation: Commute to work: 68.2% car, 0.0% public transportation, 16.7% walk, 15.2% work from home (2000); Travel time to work: 62.5% less than 15 minutes, 22.3% 15 to 30 minutes, 6.3% 30 to 45 minutes, 5.4% 45 to 60 minutes, 3.6% 60 minutes or more (2000)

CLEMENTS (city). Covers a land area of 0.385 square miles and a water area of 0 square miles. Located at 44.38° N. Lat.; 95.05° W. Long. Elevation is 1,050 feet.
Population: 191 (2000); Race: 99.0% White, 0.0% Black, 1.0% Asian, 0.0% American Indian and Alaska Native, 2.4% Hispanic of any race, 0.0% two or more races (2000); Density: 496.3 persons per square mile (2000); Age: 32.2% under 18, 16.6% over 64 (2000); Marriage status: 21.6% never married, 54.7% now married, 12.8% widowed, 10.8% divorced (2000); Foreign born: 2.4% (2000); Ancestry (includes multiple ancestries): 56.6% German, 14.1% Norwegian, 7.8% Swedish, 5.4% Other groups, 3.9% English (2000).
Economy: Corn, oats, soybeans; livestock. Manufacturing: fertilizers, plastic molds. Single-family building permits issued: 0 (2001) / 0 (2000); Multi-family building permits issued: 0 (2001) / 0 (2000); Employment by occupation: 21.9% management, 11.5% professional, 12.5% services, 15.6% sales, 1.0% farming, 16.7% construction, 20.8% production (2000).
Income: Per capita income: $15,204 (2000); Median household income: $35,000 (2000); Poverty rate: 3.5% (2000).
Taxes: Total city taxes per capita: $109 (1997); City property taxes per capita: $109 (1997).
Education: High school graduation rate: 81.3% (2000); College graduation rate: 7.0% (2000).
Housing: Homeownership rate: 97.6% (2000); Median home value: $24,600 (2000); Median age of housing: 52 years (2000).
Transportation: Commute to work: 74.5% car, 0.0% public transportation, 16.0% walk, 9.6% work from home (2000); Travel time to work: 30.6% less than 15 minutes, 56.5% 15 to 30 minutes, 7.1% 30 to 45 minutes, 2.4% 45 to 60 minutes, 3.5% 60 minutes or more (2000)

DELHI (city). Covers a land area of 0.768 square miles and a water area of 0 square miles. Located at 44.59° N. Lat.; 95.21° W. Long. Elevation is 1,030 feet.
Population: 69 (2000); Race: 100.0% White, 0.0% Black, 0.0% Asian, 0.0% American Indian and Alaska Native, 0.0% Hispanic of any race, 0.0% two or more races (2000); Density: 89.9 persons per square mile (2000); Age: 44.0% under 18, 4.4% over 64 (2000); Marriage status: 17.6% never married, 62.7% now married, 7.8% widowed, 11.8% divorced (2000); Foreign born: 2.2% (2000); Ancestry (includes multiple ancestries): 45.1% German, 28.6% Norwegian, 6.6% Swedish, 4.4% Irish, 2.2% French (except Basque) (2000).
Economy: Single-family building permits issued: 0 (2001) / 0 (2000); Multi-family building permits issued: 0 (2001) / 0 (2000); Employment by occupation: 0.0% management, 15.4% professional, 25.6% services, 15.4% sales, 0.0% farming, 20.5% construction, 23.1% production (2000).
Income: Per capita income: $9,829 (2000); Median household income: $31,875 (2000); Poverty rate: 2.2% (2000).
Taxes: Total city taxes per capita: $149 (1997); City property taxes per capita: $119 (1997).
Education: High school graduation rate: 87.8% (2000); College graduation rate: 12.2% (2000).
Housing: Homeownership rate: 93.5% (2000); Median home value: $23,800 (2000); Median rent: $225 per month (2000); Median age of housing: 60+ years (2000).
Transportation: Commute to work: 94.9% car, 0.0% public transportation, 0.0% walk, 5.1% work from home (2000); Travel time to work: 16.2% less than 15 minutes, 62.2% 15 to 30 minutes, 5.4% 30 to 45 minutes, 10.8% 45 to 60 minutes, 5.4% 60 minutes or more (2000)

DELHI (township). Covers a land area of 33.107 square miles and a water area of 0.085 square miles. Located at 44.58° N. Lat.; 95.19° W. Long. Elevation is 1,030 feet.
Population: 298 (2000); Race: 91.7% White, 0.0% Black, 0.0% Asian, 8.3% American Indian and Alaska Native, 1.0% Hispanic of any race, 0.0% two or more races (2000); Density: 9.0 persons per square mile (2000); Age: 29.8% under 18, 14.9% over 64 (2000); Marriage status: 17.9% never married, 69.6% now married, 4.2% widowed, 8.3% divorced (2000); Foreign born: 0.0% (2000); Ancestry (includes multiple ancestries): 45.4% German, 24.4% Norwegian, 9.2% Other groups, 8.3% English, 6.7% Czech (2000).
Economy: Grain. Employment by occupation: 19.9% management, 15.1% professional, 12.0% services, 28.9% sales, 3.0% farming, 4.8% construction, 16.3% production (2000).
Income: Per capita income: $18,748 (2000); Median household income: $55,833 (2000); Poverty rate: 5.4% (2000).
Taxes: Total city taxes per capita: $92 (1997); City property taxes per capita: $92 (1997).

Education: High school graduation rate: 88.0% (2000); College graduation rate: 12.0% (2000).
Housing: Homeownership rate: 93.1% (2000); Median home value: $115,300 (2000); Median rent: $325 per month (2000); Median age of housing: 56 years (2000).
Transportation: Commute to work: 86.7% car, 1.8% public transportation, 1.2% walk, 9.0% work from home (2000); Travel time to work: 52.3% less than 15 minutes, 38.4% 15 to 30 minutes, 7.9% 30 to 45 minutes, 0.0% 45 to 60 minutes, 1.3% 60 minutes or more (2000)

GALES (township). Covers a land area of 36.056 square miles and a water area of 0.131 square miles. Located at 44.33° N. Lat.; 95.53° W. Long.
Population: 144 (2000); Race: 100.0% White, 0.0% Black, 0.0% Asian, 0.0% American Indian and Alaska Native, 0.0% Hispanic of any race, 0.0% two or more races (2000); Density: 4.0 persons per square mile (2000); Age: 33.3% under 18, 9.9% over 64 (2000); Marriage status: 23.6% never married, 68.5% now married, 3.1% widowed, 4.7% divorced (2000); Foreign born: 0.0% (2000); Ancestry (includes multiple ancestries): 63.7% German, 22.8% Norwegian, 14.0% Belgian, 11.1% Swedish, 6.4% Polish (2000).
Economy: Employment by occupation: 29.4% management, 7.1% professional, 7.1% services, 22.4% sales, 5.9% farming, 9.4% construction, 18.8% production (2000).
Income: Per capita income: $16,554 (2000); Median household income: $47,500 (2000); Poverty rate: 14.6% (2000).
Taxes: Total city taxes per capita: $278 (2000); City property taxes per capita: $278 (2000).
Education: High school graduation rate: 90.8% (2000); College graduation rate: 16.3% (2000).
Housing: Homeownership rate: 80.4% (2000); Median home value: $82,500 (2000); Median rent: $125 per month (2000); Median age of housing: 60+ years (2000).
Transportation: Commute to work: 70.0% car, 0.0% public transportation, 2.5% walk, 27.5% work from home (2000); Travel time to work: 25.9% less than 15 minutes, 37.9% 15 to 30 minutes, 36.2% 30 to 45 minutes, 0.0% 45 to 60 minutes, 0.0% 60 minutes or more (2000)

GRANITE ROCK (township). Covers a land area of 36.316 square miles and a water area of 0.021 square miles. Located at 44.42° N. Lat.; 95.42° W. Long.
Population: 241 (2000); Race: 98.2% White, 0.0% Black, 0.0% Asian, 1.8% American Indian and Alaska Native, 1.1% Hispanic of any race, 0.0% two or more races (2000); Density: 6.6 persons per square mile (2000); Age: 38.5% under 18, 11.0% over 64 (2000); Marriage status: 29.5% never married, 60.5% now married, 3.3% widowed, 6.7% divorced (2000); Foreign born: 0.0% (2000); Ancestry (includes multiple ancestries): 50.2% German, 13.1% Czech, 12.7% Norwegian, 7.4% United States or American, 5.7% Danish (2000).
Economy: Employment by occupation: 36.6% management, 8.2% professional, 8.2% services, 25.4% sales, 6.7% farming, 6.0% construction, 9.0% production (2000).
Income: Per capita income: $12,631 (2000); Median household income: $35,000 (2000); Poverty rate: 12.1% (2000).
Taxes: Total city taxes per capita: $74 (1997); City property taxes per capita: $74 (1997).
Education: High school graduation rate: 94.2% (2000); College graduation rate: 2.6% (2000).
Housing: Homeownership rate: 70.8% (2000); Median home value: $75,000 (2000); Median rent: $213 per month (2000); Median age of housing: 60+ years (2000).
Transportation: Commute to work: 62.1% car, 0.0% public transportation, 2.3% walk, 35.6% work from home (2000); Travel time to work: 40.0% less than 15 minutes, 12.9% 15 to 30 minutes, 42.4% 30 to 45 minutes, 2.4% 45 to 60 minutes, 2.4% 60 minutes or more (2000)

HONNER (township). Covers a land area of 4.066 square miles and a water area of 0.084 square miles. Located at 44.55° N. Lat.; 95.08° W. Long.
Population: 86 (2000); Race: 100.0% White, 0.0% Black, 0.0% Asian, 0.0% American Indian and Alaska Native, 0.0% Hispanic of any race, 0.0% two or more races (2000); Density: 21.2 persons per square mile (2000); Age: 24.5% under 18, 4.1% over 64 (2000); Marriage status: 29.5% never married, 64.1% now married, 0.0% widowed, 6.4% divorced (2000); Foreign born: 0.0% (2000); Ancestry (includes multiple ancestries): 44.9% German, 29.6% Norwegian, 12.2% Danish, 10.2% Irish, 7.1% Swiss (2000).
Economy: Employment by occupation: 14.8% management, 9.8% professional, 29.5% services, 31.1% sales, 0.0% farming, 0.0% construction, 14.8% production (2000).
Income: Per capita income: $21,988 (2000); Median household income: $51,250 (2000); Poverty rate: 11.2% (2000).
Taxes: Total city taxes per capita: $113 (1997); City property taxes per capita: $113 (1997).
Education: High school graduation rate: 79.4% (2000); College graduation rate: 29.4% (2000).
Housing: Homeownership rate: 100.0% (2000); Median home value: $181,300 (2000); Median age of housing: 21 years (2000).
Transportation: Commute to work: 75.4% car, 0.0% public transportation, 0.0% walk, 3.3% work from home (2000); Travel time to work: 59.3% less than 15 minutes, 15.3% 15 to 30 minutes, 18.6% 30 to 45 minutes, 3.4% 45 to 60 minutes, 3.4% 60 minutes or more (2000)

JOHNSONVILLE (township). Covers a land area of 36.516 square miles and a water area of 0.046 square miles. Located at 44.33° N. Lat.; 95.42° W. Long.
Population: 166 (2000); Race: 100.0% White, 0.0% Black, 0.0% Asian, 0.0% American Indian and Alaska Native, 0.0% Hispanic of any race, 0.0% two or more races (2000); Density: 4.5 persons per square mile (2000); Age: 26.8% under 18, 14.8% over 64 (2000); Marriage status: 21.4% never married, 75.0% now married, 1.8% widowed, 1.8% divorced (2000); Foreign born: 2.8% (2000); Ancestry (includes multiple ancestries): 58.5% German, 10.6% Belgian, 7.7% Swedish, 7.0% European, 5.6% Norwegian (2000).
Economy: Employment by occupation: 31.4% management, 8.6% professional, 24.3% services, 15.7% sales, 0.0% farming, 7.1% construction, 12.9% production (2000).
Income: Per capita income: $16,611 (2000); Median household income: $44,167 (2000); Poverty rate: 4.9% (2000).
Taxes: Total city taxes per capita: $74 (1997); City property taxes per capita: $74 (1997).
Education: High school graduation rate: 87.2% (2000); College graduation rate: 19.1% (2000).
Housing: Homeownership rate: 84.6% (2000); Median home value: $63,300 (2000); Median rent: $275 per month (2000); Median age of housing: 60+ years (2000).
Transportation: Commute to work: 74.3% car, 0.0% public transportation, 2.9% walk, 22.9% work from home (2000); Travel time to work: 14.8% less than 15 minutes, 31.5% 15 to 30 minutes, 40.7% 30 to 45 minutes, 9.3% 45 to 60 minutes, 3.7% 60 minutes or more (2000)

KINTIRE (township). Covers a land area of 35.264 square miles and a water area of 0 square miles. Located at 44.58° N. Lat.; 95.29° W. Long.
Population: 214 (2000); Race: 98.2% White, 0.0% Black, 0.9% Asian, 0.0% American Indian and Alaska Native, 0.0% Hispanic of any race, 0.9% two or more races (2000); Density: 6.1 persons per square mile (2000); Age: 28.5% under 18, 19.0% over 64 (2000); Marriage status: 24.1% never married, 65.5% now married, 3.4% widowed, 6.9% divorced (2000); Foreign born: 0.9% (2000); Ancestry (includes multiple ancestries): 48.9% German, 33.9% Norwegian, 15.4% Swedish, 6.3% Irish, 5.9% Polish (2000).
Economy: Employment by occupation: 18.2% management, 2.5% professional, 25.6% services, 13.2% sales, 1.7% farming, 9.1% construction, 29.8% production (2000).
Income: Per capita income: $16,889 (2000); Median household income: $38,375 (2000); Poverty rate: 8.8% (2000).
Taxes: Total city taxes per capita: $94 (1997); City property taxes per capita: $94 (1997).
Education: High school graduation rate: 86.0% (2000); College graduation rate: 2.7% (2000).
Housing: Homeownership rate: 75.0% (2000); Median home value: $72,500 (2000); Median rent: $250 per month (2000); Median age of housing: 60+ years (2000).
Transportation: Commute to work: 79.0% car, 0.0% public transportation, 2.5% walk, 16.0% work from home (2000); Travel time to work: 45.0% less than 15 minutes, 39.0% 15 to 30 minutes, 11.0% 30 to 45 minutes, 0.0% 45 to 60 minutes, 5.0% 60 minutes or more (2000)

LAMBERTON (city). Covers a land area of 0.626 square miles and a water area of 0 square miles. Located at 44.22° N. Lat.; 95.26° W. Long. Elevation is 1,151 feet.
Population: 859 (2000); Race: 99.8% White, 0.0% Black, 0.0% Asian, 0.0% American Indian and Alaska Native, 0.0% Hispanic of any race, 0.2% two or more races (2000); Density: 1,371.6 persons per square mile (2000); Age: 20.7% under 18, 36.2% over 64 (2000); Marriage status: 17.6% never married, 57.1% now married, 19.7% widowed, 5.7% divorced (2000); Foreign born: 0.1% (2000); Ancestry (includes multiple ancestries): 55.2% German, 23.3% Norwegian, 7.0% Irish, 4.0% Swedish, 3.7% Danish (2000).

Economy: Single-family building permits issued: 0 (2001) / 0 (2000); Multi-family building permits issued: 0 (2001) / 0 (2000); Employment by occupation: 10.7% management, 11.9% professional, 12.8% services, 25.6% sales, 4.3% farming, 13.7% construction, 21.0% production (2000).
Income: Per capita income: $16,721 (2000); Median household income: $28,603 (2000); Poverty rate: 14.0% (2000).
Taxes: Total city taxes per capita: $134 (1997); City property taxes per capita: $131 (1997).
Education: High school graduation rate: 70.9% (2000); College graduation rate: 12.8% (2000).

School District(s)

Red Rock Central (PK-12)
2000 Enrollment: 577 507-752-7361
Housing: Homeownership rate: 78.4% (2000); Median home value: $34,000 (2000); Median rent: $233 per month (2000); Median age of housing: 49 years (2000).
Newspapers: Lamberton News (1 x week)
Transportation: Commute to work: 87.5% car, 0.0% public transportation, 5.3% walk, 4.7% work from home (2000); Travel time to work: 52.0% less than 15 minutes, 24.7% 15 to 30 minutes, 17.1% 30 to 45 minutes, 6.3% 45 to 60 minutes, 0.0% 60 minutes or more (2000)

LAMBERTON (township). Covers a land area of 35.389 square miles and a water area of 0.017 square miles. Located at 44.23° N. Lat.; 95.28° W. Long. Elevation is 1,151 feet.
Population: 235 (2000); Race: 100.0% White, 0.0% Black, 0.0% Asian, 0.0% American Indian and Alaska Native, 0.0% Hispanic of any race, 0.0% two or more races (2000); Density: 6.6 persons per square mile (2000); Age: 29.4% under 18, 17.9% over 64 (2000); Marriage status: 23.6% never married, 71.9% now married, 0.0% widowed, 4.5% divorced (2000); Foreign born: 0.0% (2000); Ancestry (includes multiple ancestries): 71.9% German, 19.6% Norwegian, 5.5% English, 4.3% Finnish, 3.4% Dutch (2000).
Economy: Grain, soybeans; livestock; dairying. Employment by occupation: 21.2% management, 14.4% professional, 12.5% services, 17.3% sales, 3.8% farming, 7.7% construction, 23.1% production (2000).
Income: Per capita income: $15,914 (2000); Median household income: $34,286 (2000); Poverty rate: 7.3% (2000).
Taxes: Total city taxes per capita: $65 (1997); City property taxes per capita: $65 (1997).
Education: High school graduation rate: 80.7% (2000); College graduation rate: 14.9% (2000).
Housing: Homeownership rate: 84.1% (2000); Median home value: $67,500 (2000); Median rent: $175 per month (2000); Median age of housing: 60+ years (2000).
Transportation: Commute to work: 82.4% car, 0.0% public transportation, 0.0% walk, 17.6% work from home (2000); Travel time to work: 57.1% less than 15 minutes, 22.6% 15 to 30 minutes, 8.3% 30 to 45 minutes, 8.3% 45 to 60 minutes, 3.6% 60 minutes or more (2000)

LUCAN (city). Covers a land area of 0.376 square miles and a water area of 0.004 square miles. Located at 44.40° N. Lat.; 95.41° W. Long.
Population: 226 (2000); Race: 95.5% White, 0.0% Black, 0.0% Asian, 0.0% American Indian and Alaska Native, 0.0% Hispanic of any race, 3.6% two or more races (2000); Density: 600.5 persons per square mile (2000); Age: 19.6% under 18, 26.3% over 64 (2000); Marriage status: 28.6% never married, 54.5% now married, 7.4% widowed, 9.5% divorced (2000); Foreign born: 0.9% (2000); Ancestry (includes multiple ancestries): 52.2% German, 14.3% Norwegian, 7.6% Irish, 4.0% Czech, 4.0% United States or American (2000).
Economy: Corn, oats, soybeans; livestock; dairying. Manufacturing: chassis liners, millwork. Single-family building permits issued: 0 (2001) / 0 (2000); Multi-family building permits issued: 0 (2001) / 0 (2000); Employment by occupation: 13.2% management, 14.0% professional, 14.0% services, 24.8% sales, 1.7% farming, 6.6% construction, 25.6% production (2000).
Income: Per capita income: $19,838 (2000); Median household income: $33,125 (2000); Poverty rate: 2.7% (2000).
Taxes: Total city taxes per capita: $122 (1997); City property taxes per capita: $118 (1997).
Education: High school graduation rate: 75.8% (2000); College graduation rate: 15.9% (2000).
Housing: Homeownership rate: 73.5% (2000); Median home value: $38,200 (2000); Median rent: $221 per month (2000); Median age of housing: 52 years (2000).
Transportation: Commute to work: 66.1% car, 0.0% public transportation, 22.3% walk, 9.9% work from home (2000); Travel time to work: 51.4% less than 15 minutes, 22.9% 15 to 30 minutes, 22.0% 30 to 45 minutes, 1.8% 45 to 60 minutes, 1.8% 60 minutes or more (2000)

MILROY (city). Covers a land area of 0.254 square miles and a water area of 0 square miles. Located at 44.41° N. Lat.; 95.55° W. Long. Elevation is 1,107 feet.
Population: 271 (2000); Race: 99.2% White, 0.0% Black, 0.8% Asian, 0.0% American Indian and Alaska Native, 0.0% Hispanic of any race, 0.0% two or more races (2000); Density: 1,066.0 persons per square mile (2000); Age: 25.9% under 18, 13.9% over 64 (2000); Marriage status: 26.7% never married, 53.9% now married, 8.7% widowed, 10.7% divorced (2000); Foreign born: 1.5% (2000); Ancestry (includes multiple ancestries): 38.2% German, 12.7% Norwegian, 10.0% Belgian, 7.7% Irish, 6.2% Danish (2000).
Economy: Grain, soybeans; livestock; dairying. Manufacturing: feeds. Single-family building permits issued: 0 (2001) / 1 (2000); Multi-family building permits issued: 0 (2001) / 0 (2000); Employment by occupation: 6.3% management, 8.7% professional, 21.3% services, 20.5% sales, 1.6% farming, 16.5% construction, 25.2% production (2000).
Income: Per capita income: $16,866 (2000); Median household income: $33,625 (2000); Poverty rate: 9.3% (2000).
Taxes: Total city taxes per capita: $228 (1997); City property taxes per capita: $221 (1997).
Education: High school graduation rate: 79.4% (2000); College graduation rate: 12.0% (2000).

School District(s)

Milroy (KG-08)
2000 Enrollment: 114 507-336-2563
Housing: Homeownership rate: 80.5% (2000); Median home value: $47,800 (2000); Median rent: $250 per month (2000); Median age of housing: 45 years (2000).
Transportation: Commute to work: 85.7% car, 0.0% public transportation, 4.0% walk, 10.3% work from home (2000); Travel time to work: 7.1% less than 15 minutes, 78.8% 15 to 30 minutes, 6.2% 30 to 45 minutes, 0.0% 45 to 60 minutes, 8.0% 60 minutes or more (2000)

MORGAN (city). Covers a land area of 0.549 square miles and a water area of 0 square miles. Located at 44.41° N. Lat.; 94.92° W. Long. Elevation is 1,050 feet.
Population: 903 (2000); Race: 97.0% White, 0.2% Black, 0.0% Asian, 1.1% American Indian and Alaska Native, 3.3% Hispanic of any race, 1.7% two or more races (2000); Density: 1,644.3 persons per square mile (2000); Age: 24.8% under 18, 30.5% over 64 (2000); Marriage status: 21.3% never married, 60.7% now married, 10.6% widowed, 7.4% divorced (2000); Foreign born: 0.9% (2000); Ancestry (includes multiple ancestries): 60.9% German, 11.0% Norwegian, 5.7% Irish, 5.2% United States or American, 5.1% Other groups (2000).
Economy: Single-family building permits issued: 1 (2001) / 0 (2000); Multi-family building permits issued: 0 (2001) / 0 (2000); Employment by occupation: 11.1% management, 14.3% professional, 20.5% services, 23.0% sales, 0.0% farming, 11.4% construction, 19.7% production (2000).
Income: Per capita income: $16,454 (2000); Median household income: $30,673 (2000); Poverty rate: 5.8% (2000).
Taxes: Total city taxes per capita: $160 (1997); City property taxes per capita: $156 (1997).
Education: High school graduation rate: 70.3% (2000); College graduation rate: 9.6% (2000).

School District(s)

Cedar Mountain (PK-12)
2000 Enrollment: 454 507-249-5990
Housing: Homeownership rate: 83.9% (2000); Median home value: $47,400 (2000); Median rent: $213 per month (2000); Median age of housing: 51 years (2000).
Newspapers: Morgan Messenger (1 x week)
Transportation: Commute to work: 87.7% car, 0.0% public transportation, 6.3% walk, 2.5% work from home (2000); Travel time to work: 49.2% less than 15 minutes, 42.7% 15 to 30 minutes, 3.1% 30 to 45 minutes, 1.1% 45 to 60 minutes, 3.9% 60 minutes or more (2000)

MORGAN (township). Covers a land area of 35.495 square miles and a water area of 0 square miles. Located at 44.40° N. Lat.; 94.92° W. Long. Elevation is 1,050 feet.
Population: 305 (2000); Race: 99.3% White, 0.7% Black, 0.0% Asian, 0.0% American Indian and Alaska Native, 0.0% Hispanic of any race, 0.0% two or more races (2000); Density: 8.6 persons per square mile (2000); Age: 28.3% under 18, 14.0% over 64 (2000); Marriage status: 19.0% never married, 74.3% now married, 3.1% widowed, 3.5% divorced (2000); Foreign born:

0.7% (2000); Ancestry (includes multiple ancestries): 70.7% German, 12.3% Norwegian, 11.3% Danish, 5.0% Other groups, 3.3% Irish (2000).
Economy: Grain, soybeans, sugar beets, alfalfa; livestock, poultry; dairying. Manufacturing: electrical components, feeds, fertilizer. Employment by occupation: 31.5% management, 16.1% professional, 11.2% services, 19.6% sales, 0.7% farming, 11.2% construction, 9.8% production (2000).
Income: Per capita income: $15,950 (2000); Median household income: $32,344 (2000); Poverty rate: 0.7% (2000).
Taxes: Total city taxes per capita: $73 (1997); City property taxes per capita: $73 (1997).
Education: High school graduation rate: 86.6% (2000); College graduation rate: 9.8% (2000).
Housing: Homeownership rate: 85.2% (2000); Median home value: $103,600 (2000); Median rent: $238 per month (2000); Median age of housing: 60+ years (2000).
Transportation: Commute to work: 74.1% car, 0.0% public transportation, 6.3% walk, 19.6% work from home (2000); Travel time to work: 49.6% less than 15 minutes, 40.9% 15 to 30 minutes, 7.8% 30 to 45 minutes, 0.0% 45 to 60 minutes, 1.7% 60 minutes or more (2000)

NEW AVON (township). Covers a land area of 36.003 square miles and a water area of 0 square miles. Located at 44.41° N. Lat.; 95.15° W. Long.
Population: 242 (2000); Race: 100.0% White, 0.0% Black, 0.0% Asian, 0.0% American Indian and Alaska Native, 0.0% Hispanic of any race, 0.0% two or more races (2000); Density: 6.7 persons per square mile (2000); Age: 29.0% under 18, 11.0% over 64 (2000); Marriage status: 24.1% never married, 72.2% now married, 0.0% widowed, 3.7% divorced (2000); Foreign born: 1.1% (2000); Ancestry (includes multiple ancestries): 61.8% German, 14.3% Norwegian, 11.4% United States or American, 11.4% Danish, 5.5% Irish (2000).
Economy: Employment by occupation: 26.8% management, 13.4% professional, 9.9% services, 17.6% sales, 4.2% farming, 16.2% construction, 12.0% production (2000).
Income: Per capita income: $17,437 (2000); Median household income: $45,250 (2000); Poverty rate: 5.5% (2000).
Taxes: Total city taxes per capita: $118 (1997); City property taxes per capita: $118 (1997).
Education: High school graduation rate: 86.8% (2000); College graduation rate: 14.3% (2000).
Housing: Homeownership rate: 83.8% (2000); Median home value: $72,500 (2000); Median rent: $250 per month (2000); Median age of housing: 55 years (2000).
Transportation: Commute to work: 80.6% car, 1.4% public transportation, 2.2% walk, 15.8% work from home (2000); Travel time to work: 34.2% less than 15 minutes, 36.8% 15 to 30 minutes, 18.8% 30 to 45 minutes, 4.3% 45 to 60 minutes, 6.0% 60 minutes or more (2000)

NORTH HERO (township). Covers a land area of 35.187 square miles and a water area of 0 square miles. Located at 44.23° N. Lat.; 95.40° W. Long.
Population: 172 (2000); Race: 100.0% White, 0.0% Black, 0.0% Asian, 0.0% American Indian and Alaska Native, 0.0% Hispanic of any race, 0.0% two or more races (2000); Density: 4.9 persons per square mile (2000); Age: 25.6% under 18, 9.7% over 64 (2000); Marriage status: 24.7% never married, 70.7% now married, 4.0% widowed, 0.7% divorced (2000); Foreign born: 0.0% (2000); Ancestry (includes multiple ancestries): 58.5% German, 18.2% Norwegian, 6.8% English, 6.8% Swedish, 5.1% Belgian (2000).
Economy: Employment by occupation: 34.0% management, 11.3% professional, 5.2% services, 16.5% sales, 10.3% farming, 9.3% construction, 13.4% production (2000).
Income: Per capita income: $13,857 (2000); Median household income: $29,125 (2000); Poverty rate: 14.8% (2000).
Taxes: Total city taxes per capita: $140 (1997); City property taxes per capita: $140 (1997).
Education: High school graduation rate: 85.2% (2000); College graduation rate: 23.0% (2000).
Housing: Homeownership rate: 75.3% (2000); Median home value: $58,300 (2000); Median rent: <$100 per month (2000); Median age of housing: 60+ years (2000).
Transportation: Commute to work: 65.3% car, 0.0% public transportation, 3.2% walk, 31.6% work from home (2000); Travel time to work: 43.1% less than 15 minutes, 35.4% 15 to 30 minutes, 18.5% 30 to 45 minutes, 3.1% 45 to 60 minutes, 0.0% 60 minutes or more (2000)

PAXTON (township). Covers a land area of 36.958 square miles and a water area of 0.018 square miles. Located at 44.50° N. Lat.; 95.03° W. Long.
Population: 577 (2000); Race: 61.5% White, 0.0% Black, 0.0% Asian, 30.1% American Indian and Alaska Native, 0.9% Hispanic of any race, 7.6% two or more races (2000); Density: 15.6 persons per square mile (2000); Age: 31.6% under 18, 7.0% over 64 (2000); Marriage status: 31.1% never married, 55.5% now married, 5.2% widowed, 8.2% divorced (2000); Foreign born: 0.0% (2000); Ancestry (includes multiple ancestries): 34.8% Other groups, 33.7% German, 8.1% Norwegian, 7.4% Irish, 5.4% Danish (2000).
Economy: Employment by occupation: 15.8% management, 18.0% professional, 16.2% services, 23.7% sales, 4.1% farming, 7.9% construction, 14.3% production (2000).
Income: Per capita income: $22,287 (2000); Median household income: $57,813 (2000); Poverty rate: 7.1% (2000).
Taxes: Total city taxes per capita: $43 (1997); City property taxes per capita: $43 (1997).
Education: High school graduation rate: 87.4% (2000); College graduation rate: 18.9% (2000).
Housing: Homeownership rate: 85.4% (2000); Median home value: $89,500 (2000); Median rent: $233 per month (2000); Median age of housing: 38 years (2000).
Transportation: Commute to work: 83.2% car, 0.0% public transportation, 1.1% walk, 14.9% work from home (2000); Travel time to work: 83.0% less than 15 minutes, 10.3% 15 to 30 minutes, 1.3% 30 to 45 minutes, 1.8% 45 to 60 minutes, 3.6% 60 minutes or more (2000)

REDWOOD FALLS (city). Covers a land area of 4.677 square miles and a water area of 0.100 square miles. Located at 44.54° N. Lat.; 95.10° W. Long. Elevation is 1,044 feet.
History: Plotted 1865; Incorporated as village 1875, as city 1891.
Population: 5,459 (2000); Race: 93.9% White, 0.0% Black, 0.7% Asian, 4.8% American Indian and Alaska Native, 1.1% Hispanic of any race, 0.5% two or more races (2000); Density: 1,167.1 persons per square mile (2000); Age: 25.0% under 18, 19.4% over 64 (2000); Marriage status: 22.4% never married, 56.3% now married, 10.3% widowed, 11.0% divorced (2000); Foreign born: 0.8% (2000); Ancestry (includes multiple ancestries): 55.7% German, 17.6% Norwegian, 7.1% Irish, 7.1% Other groups, 6.0% English (2000).
Economy: Agricultural area: soybeans, sugar beets, livestock, poultry and dairying. Manufacturing includes emergency rescue boards, hospital equipment, tallow and hides, commercial apartments, mobile homes, farm trailers and equipment and computer components. Shipping point for farm produce and granite from nearby quarries. Single-family building permits issued: 11 (2001) / 11 (2000); Multi-family building permits issued: 16 (2001) / 2 (2000); Employment by occupation: 12.7% management, 12.2% professional, 16.1% services, 29.0% sales, 0.4% farming, 10.3% construction, 19.4% production (2000).
Income: Per capita income: $22,279 (2000); Median household income: $38,812 (2000); Poverty rate: 7.5% (2000).
Taxes: Total city taxes per capita: $239 (2000); City property taxes per capita: $209 (2000).
Education: High school graduation rate: 81.1% (2000); College graduation rate: 16.0% (2000).

School District(s)

Redwood Falls (PK-12)
2000 Enrollment: 1,543 507-644-3531
Housing: Homeownership rate: 73.5% (2000); Median home value: $76,100 (2000); Median rent: $353 per month (2000); Median age of housing: 36 years (2000).
Hospitals: Redwood Falls Municipal Hospital (43 beds)
Safety: Violent crime rate: 47.1 per 10,000 population; Property crime rate: 375.1 per 10,000 population (2001).
Newspapers: The Redwood Gazette (2 x week); Redwood Livewire (1 x week)
Transportation: Commute to work: 89.2% car, 2.8% public transportation, 4.8% walk, 2.2% work from home (2000); Travel time to work: 80.1% less than 15 minutes, 11.9% 15 to 30 minutes, 2.9% 30 to 45 minutes, 2.6% 45 to 60 minutes, 2.5% 60 minutes or more (2000)
Additional Information Contacts
Redwood Falls Chamber of Commerce 507-637-2828

REDWOOD FALLS (township). Covers a land area of 34.282 square miles and a water area of 0.088 square miles. Located at 44.50° N. Lat.; 95.15° W. Long. Elevation is 1,044 feet.
Population: 256 (2000); Race: 98.4% White, 0.0% Black, 0.0% Asian, 1.6% American Indian and Alaska Native, 0.0% Hispanic of any race, 0.0% two or more races (2000); Density: 7.5 persons per square mile (2000); Age: 29.6% under 18, 16.6% over 64 (2000); Marriage status: 24.4% never married,

67.5% now married, 7.1% widowed, 1.0% divorced (2000); Foreign born: 1.6% (2000); Ancestry (includes multiple ancestries): 59.7% German, 11.5% Norwegian, 10.3% Swedish, 8.7% Irish, 8.3% English (2000).
Economy: Employment by occupation: 17.9% management, 18.6% professional, 12.9% services, 20.0% sales, 1.4% farming, 20.7% construction, 8.6% production (2000).
Income: Per capita income: $20,223 (2000); Median household income: $52,500 (2000); Poverty rate: 4.3% (2000).
Taxes: Total city taxes per capita: $63 (1997); City property taxes per capita: $63 (1997).
Education: High school graduation rate: 89.1% (2000); College graduation rate: 15.4% (2000).
Housing: Homeownership rate: 83.3% (2000); Median home value: $75,000 (2000); Median rent: $338 per month (2000); Median age of housing: 60+ years (2000).
Transportation: Commute to work: 84.8% car, 0.0% public transportation, 5.1% walk, 10.1% work from home (2000); Travel time to work: 71.0% less than 15 minutes, 19.4% 15 to 30 minutes, 2.4% 30 to 45 minutes, 0.0% 45 to 60 minutes, 7.3% 60 minutes or more (2000)

REVERE (city). Covers a land area of 0.575 square miles and a water area of 0 square miles. Located at 44.22° N. Lat.; 95.36° W. Long. Elevation is 1,151 feet.
Population: 100 (2000); Race: 100.0% White, 0.0% Black, 0.0% Asian, 0.0% American Indian and Alaska Native, 0.0% Hispanic of any race, 0.0% two or more races (2000); Density: 174.0 persons per square mile (2000); Age: 20.0% under 18, 28.4% over 64 (2000); Marriage status: 12.7% never married, 55.7% now married, 12.7% widowed, 19.0% divorced (2000); Foreign born: 0.0% (2000); Ancestry (includes multiple ancestries): 34.7% German, 28.4% Norwegian, 11.6% Irish, 8.4% English, 6.3% Polish (2000).
Economy: Grain; livestock; dairying; feeds. Single-family building permits issued: 0 (2001) / 0 (2000); Multi-family building permits issued: 0 (2001) / 0 (2000); Employment by occupation: 6.7% management, 36.7% professional, 20.0% services, 10.0% sales, 0.0% farming, 13.3% construction, 13.3% production (2000).
Income: Per capita income: $14,519 (2000); Median household income: $14,643 (2000); Poverty rate: 34.7% (2000).
Taxes: Total city taxes per capita: $80 (1997); City property taxes per capita: $63 (1997).
Education: High school graduation rate: 60.8% (2000); College graduation rate: 18.9% (2000).
Housing: Homeownership rate: 89.5% (2000); Median home value: $17,500 (2000); Median rent: $150 per month (2000); Median age of housing: 56 years (2000).
Transportation: Commute to work: 71.4% car, 0.0% public transportation, 7.1% walk, 21.4% work from home (2000); Travel time to work: 63.6% less than 15 minutes, 9.1% 15 to 30 minutes, 9.1% 30 to 45 minutes, 0.0% 45 to 60 minutes, 18.2% 60 minutes or more (2000)

SANBORN (city). Covers a land area of 2.130 square miles and a water area of 0 square miles. Located at 44.20° N. Lat.; 95.12° W. Long. Elevation is 1,089 feet.
Population: 434 (2000); Race: 99.8% White, 0.0% Black, 0.0% Asian, 0.0% American Indian and Alaska Native, 0.0% Hispanic of any race, 0.2% two or more races (2000); Density: 203.8 persons per square mile (2000); Age: 23.0% under 18, 23.9% over 64 (2000); Marriage status: 24.8% never married, 63.8% now married, 6.0% widowed, 5.4% divorced (2000); Foreign born: 0.0% (2000); Ancestry (includes multiple ancestries): 65.5% German, 9.4% Norwegian, 9.2% Irish, 6.7% Swedish, 6.4% Danish (2000).
Economy: Agriculture includes grain, soybeans, alfalfa; livestock, poultry; dairying. Manufacturing: meat processing, light manufacturing. Railroad junction to East. Single-family building permits issued: 0 (2001) / 0 (2000); Multi-family building permits issued: 0 (2001) / 0 (2000); Employment by occupation: 7.3% management, 6.3% professional, 15.5% services, 32.0% sales, 0.0% farming, 19.4% construction, 19.4% production (2000).
Income: Per capita income: $19,809 (2000); Median household income: $36,375 (2000); Poverty rate: 6.5% (2000).
Taxes: Total city taxes per capita: $138 (1997); City property taxes per capita: $124 (1997).
Education: High school graduation rate: 74.7% (2000); College graduation rate: 7.6% (2000).
Housing: Homeownership rate: 86.0% (2000); Median home value: $30,000 (2000); Median rent: $238 per month (2000); Median age of housing: 58 years (2000).
Newspapers: Sanborn Sentinel (1 x week)

Transportation: Commute to work: 88.6% car, 0.0% public transportation, 5.0% walk, 5.0% work from home (2000); Travel time to work: 36.5% less than 15 minutes, 37.0% 15 to 30 minutes, 17.2% 30 to 45 minutes, 3.6% 45 to 60 minutes, 5.7% 60 minutes or more (2000)

SEAFORTH (city). Covers a land area of 1.009 square miles and a water area of 0.002 square miles. Located at 44.47° N. Lat.; 95.32° W. Long. Elevation is 1,070 feet.
Population: 77 (2000); Race: 100.0% White, 0.0% Black, 0.0% Asian, 0.0% American Indian and Alaska Native, 0.0% Hispanic of any race, 0.0% two or more races (2000); Density: 76.3 persons per square mile (2000); Age: 12.1% under 18, 33.3% over 64 (2000); Marriage status: 15.5% never married, 55.2% now married, 6.9% widowed, 22.4% divorced (2000); Foreign born: 0.0% (2000); Ancestry (includes multiple ancestries): 63.6% German, 25.8% Norwegian, 16.7% Czech, 10.6% Irish, 6.1% English (2000).
Economy: Grain area. Employment by occupation: 13.8% management, 0.0% professional, 17.2% services, 31.0% sales, 0.0% farming, 27.6% construction, 10.3% production (2000).
Income: Per capita income: $15,089 (2000); Median household income: $27,143 (2000); Poverty rate: 9.4% (2000).
Taxes: Total city taxes per capita: $96 (1997); City property taxes per capita: $84 (1997).
Education: High school graduation rate: 84.2% (2000); College graduation rate: 5.3% (2000).
Housing: Homeownership rate: 77.8% (2000); Median home value: $13,900 (2000); Median rent: $275 per month (2000); Median age of housing: 60+ years (2000).
Transportation: Commute to work: 89.7% car, 0.0% public transportation, 10.3% walk, 0.0% work from home (2000); Travel time to work: 44.8% less than 15 minutes, 37.9% 15 to 30 minutes, 6.9% 30 to 45 minutes, 0.0% 45 to 60 minutes, 10.3% 60 minutes or more (2000)

SHERIDAN (township). Covers a land area of 33.953 square miles and a water area of 0.032 square miles. Located at 44.50° N. Lat.; 95.28° W. Long.
Population: 253 (2000); Race: 97.5% White, 0.0% Black, 1.1% Asian, 0.0% American Indian and Alaska Native, 0.0% Hispanic of any race, 1.5% two or more races (2000); Density: 7.5 persons per square mile (2000); Age: 34.2% under 18, 11.3% over 64 (2000); Marriage status: 28.2% never married, 65.1% now married, 3.8% widowed, 2.9% divorced (2000); Foreign born: 1.1% (2000); Ancestry (includes multiple ancestries): 65.1% German, 12.0% Norwegian, 9.8% Belgian, 8.0% Irish, 7.6% Czech (2000).
Economy: Employment by occupation: 23.0% management, 4.4% professional, 16.3% services, 17.0% sales, 4.4% farming, 17.8% construction, 17.0% production (2000).
Income: Per capita income: $19,099 (2000); Median household income: $48,594 (2000); Poverty rate: 9.3% (2000).
Taxes: Total city taxes per capita: $121 (1997); City property taxes per capita: $121 (1997).
Education: High school graduation rate: 82.0% (2000); College graduation rate: 3.6% (2000).
Housing: Homeownership rate: 80.2% (2000); Median home value: $55,000 (2000); Median rent: $125 per month (2000); Median age of housing: 60+ years (2000).
Transportation: Commute to work: 82.4% car, 0.0% public transportation, 1.5% walk, 16.0% work from home (2000); Travel time to work: 25.5% less than 15 minutes, 62.7% 15 to 30 minutes, 6.4% 30 to 45 minutes, 1.8% 45 to 60 minutes, 3.6% 60 minutes or more (2000)

SHERMAN (township). Covers a land area of 27.526 square miles and a water area of 0.015 square miles. Located at 44.49° N. Lat.; 94.93° W. Long.
Population: 301 (2000); Race: 58.4% White, 0.7% Black, 2.0% Asian, 38.3% American Indian and Alaska Native, 0.0% Hispanic of any race, 0.7% two or more races (2000); Density: 10.9 persons per square mile (2000); Age: 30.4% under 18, 11.6% over 64 (2000); Marriage status: 29.8% never married, 55.3% now married, 2.6% widowed, 12.3% divorced (2000); Foreign born: 2.0% (2000); Ancestry (includes multiple ancestries): 38.6% Other groups, 38.3% German, 5.6% Irish, 4.0% English, 3.6% Dutch (2000).
Economy: Employment by occupation: 21.8% management, 6.5% professional, 27.4% services, 18.5% sales, 5.6% farming, 5.6% construction, 14.5% production (2000).
Income: Per capita income: $23,549 (2000); Median household income: $60,625 (2000); Poverty rate: 9.6% (2000).
Taxes: Total city taxes per capita: $87 (1997); City property taxes per capita: $87 (1997).
Education: High school graduation rate: 79.7% (2000); College graduation rate: 3.7% (2000).

Housing: Homeownership rate: 88.7% (2000); Median home value: $83,900 (2000); Median rent: $225 per month (2000); Median age of housing: 31 years (2000).
Transportation: Commute to work: 81.0% car, 0.0% public transportation, 5.8% walk, 9.9% work from home (2000); Travel time to work: 69.7% less than 15 minutes, 21.1% 15 to 30 minutes, 0.9% 30 to 45 minutes, 0.0% 45 to 60 minutes, 8.3% 60 minutes or more (2000)

SPRINGDALE (township). Covers a land area of 35.810 square miles and a water area of 0.052 square miles. Located at 44.23° N. Lat.; 95.52° W. Long.
Population: 215 (2000); Race: 100.0% White, 0.0% Black, 0.0% Asian, 0.0% American Indian and Alaska Native, 0.0% Hispanic of any race, 0.0% two or more races (2000); Density: 6.0 persons per square mile (2000); Age: 25.3% under 18, 17.0% over 64 (2000); Marriage status: 17.9% never married, 72.4% now married, 5.1% widowed, 4.5% divorced (2000); Foreign born: 0.0% (2000); Ancestry (includes multiple ancestries): 47.4% German, 16.5% Swedish, 9.8% Norwegian, 7.7% English, 7.2% Belgian (2000).
Economy: Employment by occupation: 30.6% management, 19.4% professional, 12.2% services, 20.4% sales, 0.0% farming, 10.2% construction, 7.1% production (2000).
Income: Per capita income: $19,001 (2000); Median household income: $38,958 (2000); Poverty rate: 0.5% (2000).
Taxes: Total city taxes per capita: $132 (1997); City property taxes per capita: $132 (1997).
Education: High school graduation rate: 90.5% (2000); College graduation rate: 20.4% (2000).
Housing: Homeownership rate: 79.5% (2000); Median home value: $48,300 (2000); Median rent: $144 per month (2000); Median age of housing: 60+ years (2000).
Transportation: Commute to work: 65.3% car, 0.0% public transportation, 4.1% walk, 27.6% work from home (2000); Travel time to work: 67.6% less than 15 minutes, 11.3% 15 to 30 minutes, 19.7% 30 to 45 minutes, 1.4% 45 to 60 minutes, 0.0% 60 minutes or more (2000)

SUNDOWN (township). Covers a land area of 35.860 square miles and a water area of 0 square miles. Located at 44.32° N. Lat.; 95.05° W. Long.
Population: 242 (2000); Race: 99.1% White, 0.0% Black, 0.9% Asian, 0.0% American Indian and Alaska Native, 0.0% Hispanic of any race, 0.0% two or more races (2000); Density: 6.7 persons per square mile (2000); Age: 26.2% under 18, 17.9% over 64 (2000); Marriage status: 25.0% never married, 71.4% now married, 2.6% widowed, 1.0% divorced (2000); Foreign born: 0.9% (2000); Ancestry (includes multiple ancestries): 59.4% German, 10.9% Norwegian, 5.2% Polish, 5.2% Irish, 4.8% Other groups (2000).
Economy: Employment by occupation: 26.7% management, 6.9% professional, 12.1% services, 23.3% sales, 4.3% farming, 12.1% construction, 14.7% production (2000).
Income: Per capita income: $19,270 (2000); Median household income: $52,708 (2000); Poverty rate: 8.3% (2000).
Taxes: Total city taxes per capita: $78 (1997); City property taxes per capita: $78 (1997).
Education: High school graduation rate: 77.1% (2000); College graduation rate: 7.6% (2000).
Housing: Homeownership rate: 85.5% (2000); Median home value: $88,800 (2000); Median rent: $200 per month (2000); Median age of housing: 60+ years (2000).
Transportation: Commute to work: 71.9% car, 0.0% public transportation, 1.8% walk, 26.3% work from home (2000); Travel time to work: 32.1% less than 15 minutes, 41.7% 15 to 30 minutes, 10.7% 30 to 45 minutes, 0.0% 45 to 60 minutes, 15.5% 60 minutes or more (2000)

SWEDES FOREST (township). Covers a land area of 19.418 square miles and a water area of 0.143 square miles. Located at 44.64° N. Lat.; 95.31° W. Long.
Population: 121 (2000); Race: 100.0% White, 0.0% Black, 0.0% Asian, 0.0% American Indian and Alaska Native, 0.0% Hispanic of any race, 0.0% two or more races (2000); Density: 6.2 persons per square mile (2000); Age: 24.8% under 18, 14.3% over 64 (2000); Marriage status: 23.3% never married, 69.8% now married, 4.7% widowed, 2.3% divorced (2000); Foreign born: 0.0% (2000); Ancestry (includes multiple ancestries): 64.8% Norwegian, 35.2% German, 13.3% Swedish, 6.7% Dutch, 5.7% Danish (2000).
Economy: Employment by occupation: 30.5% management, 15.3% professional, 23.7% services, 3.4% sales, 3.4% farming, 13.6% construction, 10.2% production (2000).
Income: Per capita income: $18,718 (2000); Median household income: $44,167 (2000); Poverty rate: 1.9% (2000).
Taxes: Total city taxes per capita: $187 (1997); City property taxes per capita: $187 (1997).
Education: High school graduation rate: 94.9% (2000); College graduation rate: 19.0% (2000).
Housing: Homeownership rate: 77.3% (2000); Median home value: $60,000 (2000); Median rent: <$100 per month (2000); Median age of housing: 59 years (2000).
Transportation: Commute to work: 83.1% car, 0.0% public transportation, 0.0% walk, 16.9% work from home (2000); Travel time to work: 44.9% less than 15 minutes, 34.7% 15 to 30 minutes, 16.3% 30 to 45 minutes, 0.0% 45 to 60 minutes, 4.1% 60 minutes or more (2000)

THREE LAKES (township). Covers a land area of 35.405 square miles and a water area of 0 square miles. Located at 44.42° N. Lat.; 95.04° W. Long.
Population: 185 (2000); Race: 100.0% White, 0.0% Black, 0.0% Asian, 0.0% American Indian and Alaska Native, 0.0% Hispanic of any race, 0.0% two or more races (2000); Density: 5.2 persons per square mile (2000); Age: 26.3% under 18, 7.8% over 64 (2000); Marriage status: 38.9% never married, 54.2% now married, 3.8% widowed, 3.1% divorced (2000); Foreign born: 0.0% (2000); Ancestry (includes multiple ancestries): 58.7% German, 10.8% Norwegian, 8.4% Danish, 6.6% United States or American, 6.0% Irish (2000).
Economy: Employment by occupation: 28.4% management, 7.4% professional, 12.6% services, 26.3% sales, 3.2% farming, 7.4% construction, 14.7% production (2000).
Income: Per capita income: $14,896 (2000); Median household income: $34,219 (2000); Poverty rate: 6.0% (2000).
Taxes: Total city taxes per capita: $105 (1997); City property taxes per capita: $105 (1997).
Education: High school graduation rate: 92.9% (2000); College graduation rate: 5.1% (2000).
Housing: Homeownership rate: 75.8% (2000); Median home value: $55,000 (2000); Median rent: $315 per month (2000); Median age of housing: 60 years (2000).
Transportation: Commute to work: 81.7% car, 0.0% public transportation, 4.3% walk, 14.0% work from home (2000); Travel time to work: 46.3% less than 15 minutes, 50.0% 15 to 30 minutes, 3.8% 30 to 45 minutes, 0.0% 45 to 60 minutes, 0.0% 60 minutes or more (2000)

UNDERWOOD (township). Covers a land area of 34.978 square miles and a water area of 0.023 square miles. Located at 44.50° N. Lat.; 95.52° W. Long.
Population: 215 (2000); Race: 100.0% White, 0.0% Black, 0.0% Asian, 0.0% American Indian and Alaska Native, 0.0% Hispanic of any race, 0.0% two or more races (2000); Density: 6.1 persons per square mile (2000); Age: 35.7% under 18, 8.0% over 64 (2000); Marriage status: 24.0% never married, 62.7% now married, 4.0% widowed, 9.3% divorced (2000); Foreign born: 0.0% (2000); Ancestry (includes multiple ancestries): 43.2% German, 13.6% Norwegian, 10.8% Belgian, 4.7% Irish, 3.8% Northern European (2000).
Economy: Employment by occupation: 29.4% management, 17.5% professional, 12.7% services, 16.7% sales, 2.4% farming, 4.0% construction, 17.5% production (2000).
Income: Per capita income: $18,794 (2000); Median household income: $47,083 (2000); Poverty rate: 0.0% (2000).
Taxes: Total city taxes per capita: $100 (1997); City property taxes per capita: $100 (1997).
Education: High school graduation rate: 92.4% (2000); College graduation rate: 12.6% (2000).
Housing: Homeownership rate: 72.0% (2000); Median home value: $65,000 (2000); Median rent: $235 per month (2000); Median age of housing: 60+ years (2000).
Transportation: Commute to work: 81.0% car, 0.0% public transportation, 7.9% walk, 11.1% work from home (2000); Travel time to work: 28.6% less than 15 minutes, 38.4% 15 to 30 minutes, 30.4% 30 to 45 minutes, 2.7% 45 to 60 minutes, 0.0% 60 minutes or more (2000)

VAIL (township). Covers a land area of 35.053 square miles and a water area of 0.162 square miles. Located at 44.40° N. Lat.; 95.30° W. Long.
Population: 310 (2000); Race: 100.0% White, 0.0% Black, 0.0% Asian, 0.0% American Indian and Alaska Native, 0.0% Hispanic of any race, 0.0% two or more races (2000); Density: 8.8 persons per square mile (2000); Age: 28.2% under 18, 23.0% over 64 (2000); Marriage status: 19.5% never married, 69.3% now married, 10.4% widowed, 0.9% divorced (2000);

Foreign born: 0.0% (2000); Ancestry (includes multiple ancestries): 74.9% German, 6.2% Czech, 4.8% Irish, 3.8% Swiss, 3.1% Norwegian (2000).
Economy: Employment by occupation: 24.8% management, 11.0% professional, 10.3% services, 13.8% sales, 5.5% farming, 22.1% construction, 12.4% production (2000).
Income: Per capita income: $12,633 (2000); Median household income: $37,500 (2000); Poverty rate: 0.8% (2000).
Taxes: Total city taxes per capita: $104 (1997); City property taxes per capita: $104 (1997).
Education: High school graduation rate: 69.5% (2000); College graduation rate: 7.0% (2000).
Housing: Homeownership rate: 84.9% (2000); Median home value: $75,000 (2000); Median rent: $163 per month (2000); Median age of housing: 51 years (2000).
Transportation: Commute to work: 70.4% car, 0.0% public transportation, 4.2% walk, 23.9% work from home (2000); Travel time to work: 57.4% less than 15 minutes, 10.2% 15 to 30 minutes, 30.6% 30 to 45 minutes, 0.0% 45 to 60 minutes, 1.9% 60 minutes or more (2000)

VESTA (city). Covers a land area of 0.397 square miles and a water area of 0 square miles. Located at 44.50° N. Lat.; 95.41° W. Long. Elevation is 1,060 feet.
Population: 339 (2000); Race: 100.0% White, 0.0% Black, 0.0% Asian, 0.0% American Indian and Alaska Native, 1.9% Hispanic of any race, 0.0% two or more races (2000); Density: 853.2 persons per square mile (2000); Age: 29.5% under 18, 20.2% over 64 (2000); Marriage status: 17.1% never married, 64.6% now married, 13.3% widowed, 5.0% divorced (2000); Foreign born: 4.7% (2000); Ancestry (includes multiple ancestries): 46.0% German, 15.5% Polish, 13.0% English, 5.6% Irish, 5.6% Norwegian (2000).
Economy: Single-family building permits issued: 0 (2001) / 1 (2000); Multi-family building permits issued: 0 (2001) / 0 (2000); Employment by occupation: 16.2% management, 5.4% professional, 12.3% services, 25.4% sales, 4.6% farming, 7.7% construction, 28.5% production (2000).
Income: Per capita income: $12,302 (2000); Median household income: $25,536 (2000); Poverty rate: 14.3% (2000).
Taxes: Total city taxes per capita: $125 (1997); City property taxes per capita: $125 (1997).
Education: High school graduation rate: 74.3% (2000); College graduation rate: 9.6% (2000).
Housing: Homeownership rate: 92.9% (2000); Median home value: $31,300 (2000); Median rent: $658 per month (2000); Median age of housing: 51 years (2000).
Transportation: Commute to work: 89.2% car, 0.0% public transportation, 8.5% walk, 2.3% work from home (2000); Travel time to work: 44.1% less than 15 minutes, 34.6% 15 to 30 minutes, 13.4% 30 to 45 minutes, 3.9% 45 to 60 minutes, 3.9% 60 minutes or more (2000)

VESTA (township). Covers a land area of 34.816 square miles and a water area of 0.079 square miles. Located at 44.51° N. Lat.; 95.40° W. Long. Elevation is 1,060 feet.
Population: 206 (2000); Race: 100.0% White, 0.0% Black, 0.0% Asian, 0.0% American Indian and Alaska Native, 0.0% Hispanic of any race, 0.0% two or more races (2000); Density: 5.9 persons per square mile (2000); Age: 32.2% under 18, 18.6% over 64 (2000); Marriage status: 20.9% never married, 74.3% now married, 1.4% widowed, 3.4% divorced (2000); Foreign born: 0.0% (2000); Ancestry (includes multiple ancestries): 70.9% German, 12.1% Norwegian, 12.1% Czech, 11.1% Belgian, 8.0% Danish (2000).
Economy: Agriculture: grain, soybeans; livestock, poultry; dairying. Manufacturing: Western tack, feeds. Employment by occupation: 42.5% management, 10.0% professional, 13.8% services, 13.8% sales, 2.5% farming, 10.0% construction, 7.5% production (2000).
Income: Per capita income: $18,247 (2000); Median household income: $44,583 (2000); Poverty rate: 4.6% (2000).
Taxes: Total city taxes per capita: $194 (1997); City property taxes per capita: $194 (1997).
Education: High school graduation rate: 83.5% (2000); College graduation rate: 15.7% (2000).
Housing: Homeownership rate: 88.2% (2000); Median home value: $76,300 (2000); Median rent: $410 per month (2000); Median age of housing: 60+ years (2000).
Transportation: Commute to work: 82.1% car, 0.0% public transportation, 2.6% walk, 15.4% work from home (2000); Travel time to work: 24.2% less than 15 minutes, 57.6% 15 to 30 minutes, 7.6% 30 to 45 minutes, 6.1% 45 to 60 minutes, 4.5% 60 minutes or more (2000)

WABASSO (city). Covers a land area of 0.789 square miles and a water area of 0 square miles. Located at 44.40° N. Lat.; 95.25° W. Long. Elevation is 1,070 feet.
Population: 643 (2000); Race: 99.1% White, 0.3% Black, 0.2% Asian, 0.0% American Indian and Alaska Native, 0.0% Hispanic of any race, 0.5% two or more races (2000); Density: 815.1 persons per square mile (2000); Age: 29.0% under 18, 18.9% over 64 (2000); Marriage status: 23.2% never married, 60.9% now married, 9.9% widowed, 6.0% divorced (2000); Foreign born: 0.5% (2000); Ancestry (includes multiple ancestries): 60.7% German, 15.6% Norwegian, 6.7% Irish, 5.8% United States or American, 3.9% Czech (2000).
Economy: Agriculture: grain, soybeans, alfalfa; livestock, poultry; dairying. Manufacturing of wood products. Single-family building permits issued: 2 (2001) / 4 (2000); Multi-family building permits issued: 0 (2001) / 0 (2000); Employment by occupation: 13.7% management, 19.2% professional, 15.3% services, 24.3% sales, 0.6% farming, 9.3% construction, 17.6% production (2000).
Income: Per capita income: $20,013 (2000); Median household income: $35,972 (2000); Poverty rate: 8.0% (2000).
Taxes: Total city taxes per capita: $122 (1997); City property taxes per capita: $117 (1997).
Education: High school graduation rate: 79.6% (2000); College graduation rate: 20.6% (2000).

School District(s)

Wabasso (PK-12)
2000 Enrollment: 578 507-342-5114
Housing: Homeownership rate: 82.4% (2000); Median home value: $50,000 (2000); Median rent: $297 per month (2000); Median age of housing: 42 years (2000).
Newspapers: Wabasso Standard (1 x week)
Transportation: Commute to work: 76.5% car, 3.3% public transportation, 16.3% walk, 2.9% work from home (2000); Travel time to work: 60.4% less than 15 minutes, 24.8% 15 to 30 minutes, 8.4% 30 to 45 minutes, 0.7% 45 to 60 minutes, 5.7% 60 minutes or more (2000)

WALNUT GROVE (city). Covers a land area of 1.037 square miles and a water area of 0 square miles. Located at 44.22° N. Lat.; 95.46° W. Long. Elevation is 1,212 feet.
Population: 599 (2000); Race: 98.3% White, 0.0% Black, 0.0% Asian, 0.0% American Indian and Alaska Native, 1.2% Hispanic of any race, 1.3% two or more races (2000); Density: 577.7 persons per square mile (2000); Age: 19.2% under 18, 30.1% over 64 (2000); Marriage status: 12.9% never married, 67.7% now married, 12.3% widowed, 7.1% divorced (2000); Foreign born: 0.0% (2000); Ancestry (includes multiple ancestries): 37.6% German, 26.4% Norwegian, 8.9% Swedish, 8.2% English, 7.4% United States or American (2000).
Economy: In grain, livestock, and poultry area; dairy products; soybeans, alfalfa. Manufacturing of mining equipment. Single-family building permits issued: 0 (2001) / 0 (2000); Multi-family building permits issued: 0 (2001) / 0 (2000); Employment by occupation: 10.0% management, 11.5% professional, 27.4% services, 18.9% sales, 0.7% farming, 8.5% construction, 23.0% production (2000).
Income: Per capita income: $15,637 (2000); Median household income: $24,013 (2000); Poverty rate: 9.6% (2000).
Taxes: Total city taxes per capita: $91 (1997); City property taxes per capita: $91 (1997).
Education: High school graduation rate: 70.2% (2000); College graduation rate: 10.7% (2000).

School District(s)

Walnut Grove (PK-08)
2000 Enrollment: 201 507-859-2141
Housing: Homeownership rate: 85.0% (2000); Median home value: $28,300 (2000); Median rent: $238 per month (2000); Median age of housing: 48 years (2000).
Transportation: Commute to work: 83.6% car, 0.0% public transportation, 8.2% walk, 6.0% work from home (2000); Travel time to work: 52.0% less than 15 minutes, 16.7% 15 to 30 minutes, 23.8% 30 to 45 minutes, 3.2% 45 to 60 minutes, 4.4% 60 minutes or more (2000)

WANDA (city). Covers a land area of 0.251 square miles and a water area of 0.003 square miles. Located at 44.31° N. Lat.; 95.21° W. Long. Elevation is 1,100 feet.
Population: 103 (2000); Race: 100.0% White, 0.0% Black, 0.0% Asian, 0.0% American Indian and Alaska Native, 2.7% Hispanic of any race, 0.0% two or more races (2000); Density: 410.6 persons per square mile (2000);

Age: 21.4% under 18, 22.3% over 64 (2000); Marriage status: 27.6% never married, 55.1% now married, 17.3% widowed, 0.0% divorced (2000); Foreign born: 2.7% (2000); Ancestry (includes multiple ancestries): 68.8% German, 8.0% Irish, 5.4% Other groups, 3.6% French (except Basque), 1.8% Swiss (2000).
Economy: Agriculture: oats; livestock; dairying. Employment by occupation: 14.3% management, 14.3% professional, 25.4% services, 11.1% sales, 0.0% farming, 28.6% construction, 6.3% production (2000).
Income: Per capita income: $16,213 (2000); Median household income: $36,250 (2000); Poverty rate: 3.6% (2000).
Taxes: Total city taxes per capita: $194 (1997); City property taxes per capita: $153 (1997).
Education: High school graduation rate: 84.0% (2000); College graduation rate: 14.7% (2000).
Housing: Homeownership rate: 91.7% (2000); Median home value: $25,800 (2000); Median rent: $175 per month (2000); Median age of housing: 60+ years (2000).
Transportation: Commute to work: 73.3% car, 0.0% public transportation, 18.3% walk, 5.0% work from home (2000); Travel time to work: 56.1% less than 15 minutes, 15.8% 15 to 30 minutes, 15.8% 30 to 45 minutes, 12.3% 45 to 60 minutes, 0.0% 60 minutes or more (2000)

WATERBURY (township). Covers a land area of 36.184 square miles and a water area of 0.053 square miles. Located at 44.33° N. Lat.; 95.29° W. Long.
Population: 221 (2000); Race: 93.7% White, 0.0% Black, 6.3% Asian, 0.0% American Indian and Alaska Native, 0.0% Hispanic of any race, 0.0% two or more races (2000); Density: 6.1 persons per square mile (2000); Age: 19.4% under 18, 14.7% over 64 (2000); Marriage status: 24.7% never married, 63.3% now married, 6.0% widowed, 6.0% divorced (2000); Foreign born: 2.1% (2000); Ancestry (includes multiple ancestries): 49.2% German, 15.2% Norwegian, 9.9% Other groups, 5.2% Irish, 3.7% Swedish (2000).
Economy: Employment by occupation: 28.4% management, 11.1% professional, 11.1% services, 21.0% sales, 4.9% farming, 2.5% construction, 21.0% production (2000).
Income: Per capita income: $15,919 (2000); Median household income: $32,188 (2000); Poverty rate: 10.5% (2000).
Taxes: Total city taxes per capita: $105 (1997); City property taxes per capita: $105 (1997).
Education: High school graduation rate: 82.6% (2000); College graduation rate: 10.9% (2000).
Housing: Homeownership rate: 84.2% (2000); Median home value: $38,800 (2000); Median rent: <$100 per month (2000); Median age of housing: 60+ years (2000).
Transportation: Commute to work: 59.5% car, 0.0% public transportation, 2.5% walk, 38.0% work from home (2000); Travel time to work: 22.4% less than 15 minutes, 22.4% 15 to 30 minutes, 28.6% 30 to 45 minutes, 22.4% 45 to 60 minutes, 4.1% 60 minutes or more (2000)

WESTLINE (township). Covers a land area of 35.785 square miles and a water area of 0.162 square miles. Located at 44.40° N. Lat.; 95.52° W. Long.
Population: 203 (2000); Race: 100.0% White, 0.0% Black, 0.0% Asian, 0.0% American Indian and Alaska Native, 0.0% Hispanic of any race, 0.0% two or more races (2000); Density: 5.7 persons per square mile (2000); Age: 26.5% under 18, 13.0% over 64 (2000); Marriage status: 15.3% never married, 80.0% now married, 2.4% widowed, 2.4% divorced (2000); Foreign born: 0.0% (2000); Ancestry (includes multiple ancestries): 41.4% German, 16.7% Belgian, 14.4% Norwegian, 10.7% United States or American, 7.0% English (2000).
Economy: Employment by occupation: 27.8% management, 12.2% professional, 18.3% services, 17.4% sales, 0.0% farming, 11.3% construction, 13.0% production (2000).
Income: Per capita income: $16,764 (2000); Median household income: $41,250 (2000); Poverty rate: 11.2% (2000).
Taxes: Total city taxes per capita: $137 (1997); City property taxes per capita: $137 (1997).
Education: High school graduation rate: 89.8% (2000); College graduation rate: 12.9% (2000).
Housing: Homeownership rate: 84.8% (2000); Median home value: $82,500 (2000); Median rent: $208 per month (2000); Median age of housing: 55 years (2000).
Transportation: Commute to work: 79.1% car, 0.0% public transportation, 2.7% walk, 16.4% work from home (2000); Travel time to work: 31.5% less than 15 minutes, 48.9% 15 to 30 minutes, 19.6% 30 to 45 minutes, 0.0% 45 to 60 minutes, 0.0% 60 minutes or more (2000)

WILLOW LAKE (township). Covers a land area of 35.876 square miles and a water area of 0.184 square miles. Located at 44.32° N. Lat.; 95.16° W. Long.
Population: 247 (2000); Race: 98.4% White, 0.0% Black, 0.0% Asian, 1.6% American Indian and Alaska Native, 1.2% Hispanic of any race, 0.0% two or more races (2000); Density: 6.9 persons per square mile (2000); Age: 36.8% under 18, 5.4% over 64 (2000); Marriage status: 25.9% never married, 69.7% now married, 2.2% widowed, 2.2% divorced (2000); Foreign born: 0.0% (2000); Ancestry (includes multiple ancestries): 58.5% German, 9.7% United States or American, 7.4% Irish, 4.3% Norwegian, 2.7% Other groups (2000).
Economy: Employment by occupation: 23.6% management, 13.8% professional, 22.8% services, 12.2% sales, 3.3% farming, 5.7% construction, 18.7% production (2000).
Income: Per capita income: $14,050 (2000); Median household income: $45,000 (2000); Poverty rate: 14.0% (2000).
Taxes: Total city taxes per capita: $80 (1997); City property taxes per capita: $80 (1997).
Education: High school graduation rate: 93.1% (2000); College graduation rate: 12.4% (2000).
Housing: Homeownership rate: 81.9% (2000); Median home value: $76,700 (2000); Median rent: $300 per month (2000); Median age of housing: 60+ years (2000).
Transportation: Commute to work: 69.1% car, 0.0% public transportation, 13.0% walk, 13.8% work from home (2000); Travel time to work: 35.8% less than 15 minutes, 43.4% 15 to 30 minutes, 15.1% 30 to 45 minutes, 1.9% 45 to 60 minutes, 3.8% 60 minutes or more (2000)

Renville County

Located in southern Minnesota; bounded on the south by the Minnesota River. Covers a land area of 982.90 square miles, a water area of 4.30 square miles, and is located in the Central Time Zone. The county government was organized in 1855. County seat is Olivia.
Population: 17,154 (2000); Race: 95.8% White, 0.1% Black, 0.2% Asian, 0.4% American Indian and Alaska Native, 5.1% Hispanic of any race, 0.8% two or more races (2000); Density: 17.5 persons per square mile (2000); Age: 26.6% under 18, 19.8% over 64 (2000).
Religion: Five largest groups: 33.3% Evangelical Lutheran Church in America, 27.2% Catholic Church, 10.7% The United Methodist Church, 10.1% Wisconsin Evangelical Lutheran Synod, 1.6% Episcopal Church (2000).
Economy: Unemployment rate: 4.3% (11/2002); Total civilian labor force: 8,002 (11/2002); Leading industries: 20.6% manufacturing; 17.7% accommodation & food services; 14.2% health care and social assistance (2000); Companies that employ more than 1,000 persons: 0 (2000); Companies that employ more than 100 persons: 7 (2000); Farms: 1,114 totaling 601,103 acres (1997); Minority business ownership rate: 0.0% (1997); Women business ownership rate: 12.3% (1997); Retail sales per capita: $6,555 (1997). Single-family building permits issued: 28 (2001) / 29 (2000); Multi-family building permits issued: 4 (2001) / 0 (2000).
Income: Per capita income: $17,770 (2000); Median household income: $37,652 (2000); Poverty rate: 8.8% (2000); Bankruptcy rate: 2.37% (2001).
Taxes: Total county taxes per capita: $297 (2000); County property taxes per capita: $297 (2000).
Education: High school graduation rate: 80.9% (2000); College graduation rate: 12.6% (2000).
Housing: Homeownership rate: 81.0% (2000); Median home value: $57,700 (2000); Median rent: $308 per month (2000); Median age of housing: 49 years (2000).
Health: Birth rate: 116.6 per 10,000 population (1998); Age adjusted death rate: 77.2 per 10,000 population (1999); Age adjusted cancer mortality rate: 154.0 deaths per 100,000 population (1999). Number of physicians: 3.5 per 10,000 population (1999); Number of hospital beds: 14.6 per 10,000 population (1999).
Elections: 2000 Presidential election results: 43.5% Gore, 49.7% Bush, 4.4% Nader, 2.1% Buchanan
National and State Parks: Birch Coulee Battlefield State Historic Site; Dysband State Wildlife Managaement Area
Additional Information Contacts
Renville County Government Offices 320-523-3710
Olivia Chamber of Commerce 320-523-1350

Renville County Communities

BANDON (township). Covers a land area of 36.576 square miles and a water area of 0 square miles. Located at 44.59° N. Lat.; 94.80° W. Long.
Population: 202 (2000); Race: 93.0% White, 0.0% Black, 0.0% Asian, 0.0% American Indian and Alaska Native, 7.0% Hispanic of any race, 0.9% two or more races (2000); Density: 5.5 persons per square mile (2000); Age: 29.3% under 18, 9.3% over 64 (2000); Marriage status: 20.3% never married, 70.9% now married, 1.3% widowed, 7.6% divorced (2000); Foreign born: 0.9% (2000); Ancestry (includes multiple ancestries): 51.2% German, 31.2% Norwegian, 10.7% Swedish, 7.9% Other groups, 7.0% United States or American (2000).
Economy: Employment by occupation: 27.1% management, 11.9% professional, 7.6% services, 15.3% sales, 0.0% farming, 12.7% construction, 25.4% production (2000).
Income: Per capita income: $16,730 (2000); Median household income: $47,917 (2000); Poverty rate: 1.9% (2000).
Taxes: Total city taxes per capita: $154 (1997); City property taxes per capita: $154 (1997).
Education: High school graduation rate: 93.9% (2000); College graduation rate: 16.8% (2000).
Housing: Homeownership rate: 61.8% (2000); Median home value: $52,000 (2000); Median rent: $188 per month (2000); Median age of housing: 60+ years (2000).
Transportation: Commute to work: 88.1% car, 0.0% public transportation, 0.0% walk, 11.9% work from home (2000); Travel time to work: 28.8% less than 15 minutes, 48.1% 15 to 30 minutes, 12.5% 30 to 45 minutes, 1.9% 45 to 60 minutes, 8.7% 60 minutes or more (2000)

BEAVER FALLS (township). Covers a land area of 27.069 square miles and a water area of 0.067 square miles. Located at 44.59° N. Lat.; 95.04° W. Long.
Population: 331 (2000); Race: 82.7% White, 0.6% Black, 2.6% Asian, 7.3% American Indian and Alaska Native, 14.1% Hispanic of any race, 1.3% two or more races (2000); Density: 12.2 persons per square mile (2000); Age: 35.5% under 18, 6.1% over 64 (2000); Marriage status: 24.9% never married, 63.8% now married, 3.1% widowed, 8.3% divorced (2000); Foreign born: 2.9% (2000); Ancestry (includes multiple ancestries): 49.2% German, 21.1% Other groups, 12.5% Czech, 9.9% Norwegian, 9.3% Irish (2000).
Economy: Employment by occupation: 9.1% management, 12.8% professional, 14.0% services, 25.0% sales, 3.7% farming, 11.6% construction, 23.8% production (2000).
Income: Per capita income: $14,430 (2000); Median household income: $35,000 (2000); Poverty rate: 10.2% (2000).
Taxes: Total city taxes per capita: $70 (1997); City property taxes per capita: $70 (1997).
Education: High school graduation rate: 86.9% (2000); College graduation rate: 6.0% (2000).
Housing: Homeownership rate: 69.3% (2000); Median home value: $105,000 (2000); Median rent: $163 per month (2000); Median age of housing: 29 years (2000).
Transportation: Commute to work: 83.8% car, 0.0% public transportation, 5.0% walk, 10.6% work from home (2000); Travel time to work: 49.7% less than 15 minutes, 39.2% 15 to 30 minutes, 3.5% 30 to 45 minutes, 3.5% 45 to 60 minutes, 4.2% 60 minutes or more (2000)

BIRCH COOLEY (township). Covers a land area of 41.472 square miles and a water area of 0.011 square miles. Located at 44.57° N. Lat.; 94.92° W. Long.
Population: 257 (2000); Race: 89.1% White, 0.0% Black, 0.4% Asian, 0.7% American Indian and Alaska Native, 6.7% Hispanic of any race, 3.0% two or more races (2000); Density: 6.2 persons per square mile (2000); Age: 36.3% under 18, 10.5% over 64 (2000); Marriage status: 16.6% never married, 74.0% now married, 8.3% widowed, 1.1% divorced (2000); Foreign born: 2.6% (2000); Ancestry (includes multiple ancestries): 64.8% German, 15.4% Norwegian, 13.9% Other groups, 10.5% Irish, 4.5% Czech (2000).
Economy: Employment by occupation: 15.6% management, 22.7% professional, 14.8% services, 16.4% sales, 3.9% farming, 8.6% construction, 18.0% production (2000).
Income: Per capita income: $15,827 (2000); Median household income: $46,111 (2000); Poverty rate: 10.9% (2000).
Taxes: Total city taxes per capita: $136 (1997); City property taxes per capita: $136 (1997).
Education: High school graduation rate: 91.5% (2000); College graduation rate: 12.7% (2000).
Housing: Homeownership rate: 86.3% (2000); Median home value: $61,300 (2000); Median rent: $231 per month (2000); Median age of housing: 60+ years (2000).
Transportation: Commute to work: 86.7% car, 0.0% public transportation, 0.0% walk, 13.3% work from home (2000); Travel time to work: 45.9% less than 15 minutes, 40.5% 15 to 30 minutes, 7.2% 30 to 45 minutes, 1.8% 45 to 60 minutes, 4.5% 60 minutes or more (2000)

BIRD ISLAND (city). Covers a land area of 1.545 square miles and a water area of 0 square miles. Located at 44.76° N. Lat.; 94.89° W. Long. Elevation is 1,081 feet.
History: Bird Island was named for an isolated grove of trees that provided shelter for numerous birds. This was a favorite camping spot for early inhabitants and passing traders.
Population: 1,195 (2000); Race: 97.4% White, 0.2% Black, 0.0% Asian, 0.0% American Indian and Alaska Native, 1.6% Hispanic of any race, 1.5% two or more races (2000); Density: 773.6 persons per square mile (2000); Age: 25.0% under 18, 24.1% over 64 (2000); Marriage status: 26.8% never married, 55.3% now married, 11.6% widowed, 6.3% divorced (2000); Foreign born: 0.7% (2000); Ancestry (includes multiple ancestries): 55.4% German, 14.8% Norwegian, 9.9% Irish, 9.1% Swedish, 5.6% Czech (2000).
Economy: Single-family building permits issued: 2 (2001) / 3 (2000); Multi-family building permits issued: 4 (2001) / 0 (2000); Employment by occupation: 9.2% management, 18.6% professional, 17.2% services, 23.4% sales, 1.1% farming, 11.0% construction, 19.6% production (2000).
Income: Per capita income: $18,700 (2000); Median household income: $38,092 (2000); Poverty rate: 8.1% (2000).
Taxes: Total city taxes per capita: $149 (1997); City property taxes per capita: $142 (1997).
Education: High school graduation rate: 75.7% (2000); College graduation rate: 13.0% (2000).
Housing: Homeownership rate: 85.5% (2000); Median home value: $54,000 (2000); Median rent: $197 per month (2000); Median age of housing: 45 years (2000).
Newspapers: Bird Island Union (1 x week)
Transportation: Commute to work: 85.5% car, 4.4% public transportation, 5.7% walk, 4.0% work from home (2000); Travel time to work: 62.8% less than 15 minutes, 16.2% 15 to 30 minutes, 8.8% 30 to 45 minutes, 5.5% 45 to 60 minutes, 6.7% 60 minutes or more (2000)

BIRD ISLAND (township). Covers a land area of 32.985 square miles and a water area of 0 square miles. Located at 44.77° N. Lat.; 94.94° W. Long. Elevation is 1,081 feet.
Population: 269 (2000); Race: 97.0% White, 0.0% Black, 0.0% Asian, 0.0% American Indian and Alaska Native, 3.9% Hispanic of any race, 3.0% two or more races (2000); Density: 8.2 persons per square mile (2000); Age: 31.8% under 18, 12.0% over 64 (2000); Marriage status: 19.5% never married, 58.0% now married, 11.5% widowed, 10.9% divorced (2000); Foreign born: 2.1% (2000); Ancestry (includes multiple ancestries): 60.5% German, 16.7% Czech, 6.4% Norwegian, 6.4% Irish, 6.0% Dutch (2000).
Economy: Agricultural area. Manufacturing: fertilizers. Employment by occupation: 19.3% management, 20.2% professional, 7.3% services, 11.9% sales, 5.5% farming, 15.6% construction, 20.2% production (2000).
Income: Per capita income: $23,826 (2000); Median household income: $42,083 (2000); Poverty rate: 0.9% (2000).
Taxes: Total city taxes per capita: $122 (1997); City property taxes per capita: $122 (1997).
Education: High school graduation rate: 84.8% (2000); College graduation rate: 12.4% (2000).
Housing: Homeownership rate: 88.6% (2000); Median home value: $73,800 (2000); Median rent: $100 per month (2000); Median age of housing: 53 years (2000).
Transportation: Commute to work: 82.6% car, 0.0% public transportation, 1.8% walk, 15.6% work from home (2000); Travel time to work: 57.6% less than 15 minutes, 27.2% 15 to 30 minutes, 7.6% 30 to 45 minutes, 1.1% 45 to 60 minutes, 6.5% 60 minutes or more (2000)

BOON LAKE (township). Covers a land area of 37.276 square miles and a water area of 1.901 square miles. Located at 44.83° N. Lat.; 94.55° W. Long.
Population: 400 (2000); Race: 99.5% White, 0.0% Black, 0.0% Asian, 0.5% American Indian and Alaska Native, 0.0% Hispanic of any race, 0.0% two or more races (2000); Density: 10.7 persons per square mile (2000); Age: 23.7% under 18, 16.3% over 64 (2000); Marriage status: 26.7% never married, 65.5% now married, 2.6% widowed, 5.2% divorced (2000); Foreign born: 1.1% (2000); Ancestry (includes multiple ancestries): 65.8% German, 12.9%

Swedish, 10.8% Norwegian, 4.7% United States or American, 4.7% Irish (2000).
Economy: Employment by occupation: 24.1% management, 12.0% professional, 6.9% services, 25.9% sales, 3.2% farming, 8.8% construction, 19.0% production (2000).
Income: Per capita income: $20,541 (2000); Median household income: $44,792 (2000); Poverty rate: 6.1% (2000).
Taxes: Total city taxes per capita: $58 (1997); City property taxes per capita: $58 (1997).
Education: High school graduation rate: 89.5% (2000); College graduation rate: 12.8% (2000).
Housing: Homeownership rate: 89.0% (2000); Median home value: $137,500 (2000); Median rent: $269 per month (2000); Median age of housing: 34 years (2000).
Transportation: Commute to work: 79.8% car, 0.0% public transportation, 4.7% walk, 15.5% work from home (2000); Travel time to work: 27.2% less than 15 minutes, 55.6% 15 to 30 minutes, 10.0% 30 to 45 minutes, 0.0% 45 to 60 minutes, 7.2% 60 minutes or more (2000)

BROOKFIELD (township). Covers a land area of 36.151 square miles and a water area of 0.007 square miles. Located at 44.83° N. Lat.; 94.69° W. Long.
Population: 163 (2000); Race: 100.0% White, 0.0% Black, 0.0% Asian, 0.0% American Indian and Alaska Native, 0.0% Hispanic of any race, 0.0% two or more races (2000); Density: 4.5 persons per square mile (2000); Age: 22.7% under 18, 12.5% over 64 (2000); Marriage status: 17.9% never married, 75.2% now married, 4.1% widowed, 2.8% divorced (2000); Foreign born: 0.0% (2000); Ancestry (includes multiple ancestries): 64.2% German, 17.0% Norwegian, 14.8% Danish, 5.7% Swedish, 3.4% English (2000).
Economy: Employment by occupation: 21.2% management, 22.4% professional, 7.1% services, 17.6% sales, 7.1% farming, 7.1% construction, 17.6% production (2000).
Income: Per capita income: $16,628 (2000); Median household income: $39,444 (2000); Poverty rate: 17.6% (2000).
Taxes: Total city taxes per capita: $127 (1997); City property taxes per capita: $127 (1997).
Education: High school graduation rate: 91.6% (2000); College graduation rate: 11.8% (2000).
Housing: Homeownership rate: 79.7% (2000); Median home value: $78,800 (2000); Median rent: $175 per month (2000); Median age of housing: 44 years (2000).
Transportation: Commute to work: 68.2% car, 0.0% public transportation, 0.0% walk, 31.8% work from home (2000); Travel time to work: 24.1% less than 15 minutes, 48.3% 15 to 30 minutes, 17.2% 30 to 45 minutes, 3.4% 45 to 60 minutes, 6.9% 60 minutes or more (2000)

BUFFALO LAKE (city). Covers a land area of 0.622 square miles and a water area of 0 square miles. Located at 44.73° N. Lat.; 94.61° W. Long. Elevation is 1,074 feet.
Population: 768 (2000); Race: 93.9% White, 0.0% Black, 0.0% Asian, 0.3% American Indian and Alaska Native, 13.7% Hispanic of any race, 0.0% two or more races (2000); Density: 1,235.0 persons per square mile (2000); Age: 25.4% under 18, 25.5% over 64 (2000); Marriage status: 22.7% never married, 57.8% now married, 13.2% widowed, 6.3% divorced (2000); Foreign born: 10.3% (2000); Ancestry (includes multiple ancestries): 60.1% German, 14.3% Other groups, 13.4% Norwegian, 10.5% Swedish, 4.9% Irish (2000).
Economy: Agricultural area: dairying; poultry, livestock; grain, sugar beets, soybeans. Manufacturing: feeds, nylon ropes, beef processing. Single-family building permits issued: 2 (2001) / 1 (2000); Multi-family building permits issued: 0 (2001) / 0 (2000); Employment by occupation: 7.9% management, 7.3% professional, 21.7% services, 16.3% sales, 1.1% farming, 9.3% construction, 36.3% production (2000).
Income: Per capita income: $17,669 (2000); Median household income: $40,000 (2000); Poverty rate: 10.8% (2000).
Taxes: Total city taxes per capita: $446 (1997); City property taxes per capita: $446 (1997).
Education: High school graduation rate: 74.1% (2000); College graduation rate: 6.0% (2000).
Housing: Homeownership rate: 84.9% (2000); Median home value: $54,100 (2000); Median rent: $405 per month (2000); Median age of housing: 49 years (2000).
Transportation: Commute to work: 82.5% car, 0.0% public transportation, 11.3% walk, 4.5% work from home (2000); Travel time to work: 66.9% less than 15 minutes, 8.3% 15 to 30 minutes, 17.8% 30 to 45 minutes, 2.4% 45 to 60 minutes, 4.7% 60 minutes or more (2000)

CAIRO (township). Covers a land area of 33.941 square miles and a water area of 0.219 square miles. Located at 44.50° N. Lat.; 94.67° W. Long.
Population: 271 (2000); Race: 97.0% White, 0.0% Black, 0.0% Asian, 0.0% American Indian and Alaska Native, 0.8% Hispanic of any race, 3.0% two or more races (2000); Density: 8.0 persons per square mile (2000); Age: 29.4% under 18, 10.2% over 64 (2000); Marriage status: 25.6% never married, 65.7% now married, 1.9% widowed, 6.8% divorced (2000); Foreign born: 3.0% (2000); Ancestry (includes multiple ancestries): 67.9% German, 11.3% Norwegian, 6.0% Swedish, 4.2% Czech, 3.4% Dutch (2000).
Economy: Employment by occupation: 37.8% management, 11.2% professional, 14.0% services, 16.8% sales, 2.8% farming, 7.7% construction, 9.8% production (2000).
Income: Per capita income: $17,310 (2000); Median household income: $38,750 (2000); Poverty rate: 13.3% (2000).
Taxes: Total city taxes per capita: $115 (1997); City property taxes per capita: $115 (1997).
Education: High school graduation rate: 87.4% (2000); College graduation rate: 10.2% (2000).
Housing: Homeownership rate: 77.3% (2000); Median home value: $80,000 (2000); Median rent: $175 per month (2000); Median age of housing: 60+ years (2000).
Transportation: Commute to work: 71.1% car, 0.0% public transportation, 1.5% walk, 27.4% work from home (2000); Travel time to work: 53.1% less than 15 minutes, 26.5% 15 to 30 minutes, 12.2% 30 to 45 minutes, 4.1% 45 to 60 minutes, 4.1% 60 minutes or more (2000)

CAMP (township). Covers a land area of 28.489 square miles and a water area of 0.039 square miles. Located at 44.50° N. Lat.; 94.79° W. Long.
Population: 207 (2000); Race: 99.0% White, 0.0% Black, 0.0% Asian, 0.0% American Indian and Alaska Native, 0.0% Hispanic of any race, 1.0% two or more races (2000); Density: 7.3 persons per square mile (2000); Age: 27.0% under 18, 15.2% over 64 (2000); Marriage status: 31.2% never married, 51.9% now married, 11.0% widowed, 5.8% divorced (2000); Foreign born: 0.0% (2000); Ancestry (includes multiple ancestries): 50.5% German, 26.5% Norwegian, 8.3% Irish, 7.8% United States or American, 6.9% Swedish (2000).
Economy: Employment by occupation: 19.3% management, 10.8% professional, 18.1% services, 14.5% sales, 8.4% farming, 15.7% construction, 13.3% production (2000).
Income: Per capita income: $15,422 (2000); Median household income: $32,500 (2000); Poverty rate: 3.4% (2000).
Taxes: Total city taxes per capita: $119 (1997); City property taxes per capita: $119 (1997).
Education: High school graduation rate: 82.2% (2000); College graduation rate: 5.9% (2000).
Housing: Homeownership rate: 67.9% (2000); Median home value: $81,100 (2000); Median rent: $225 per month (2000); Median age of housing: 60+ years (2000).
Transportation: Commute to work: 88.0% car, 0.0% public transportation, 1.2% walk, 10.8% work from home (2000); Travel time to work: 29.7% less than 15 minutes, 31.1% 15 to 30 minutes, 20.3% 30 to 45 minutes, 4.1% 45 to 60 minutes, 14.9% 60 minutes or more (2000)

CROOKS (township). Covers a land area of 36.087 square miles and a water area of 0 square miles. Located at 44.84° N. Lat.; 95.17° W. Long.
Population: 213 (2000); Race: 100.0% White, 0.0% Black, 0.0% Asian, 0.0% American Indian and Alaska Native, 0.0% Hispanic of any race, 0.0% two or more races (2000); Density: 5.9 persons per square mile (2000); Age: 32.1% under 18, 15.8% over 64 (2000); Marriage status: 10.9% never married, 83.3% now married, 2.6% widowed, 3.2% divorced (2000); Foreign born: 0.0% (2000); Ancestry (includes multiple ancestries): 63.8% German, 16.7% Norwegian, 15.4% Dutch, 6.8% English, 5.4% Scandinavian (2000).
Economy: Employment by occupation: 25.0% management, 18.5% professional, 9.3% services, 26.9% sales, 0.0% farming, 6.5% construction, 13.9% production (2000).
Income: Per capita income: $18,019 (2000); Median household income: $46,250 (2000); Poverty rate: 4.5% (2000).
Taxes: Total city taxes per capita: $158 (1997); City property taxes per capita: $158 (1997).
Education: High school graduation rate: 91.6% (2000); College graduation rate: 14.0% (2000).
Housing: Homeownership rate: 85.3% (2000); Median home value: $73,300 (2000); Median rent: $375 per month (2000); Median age of housing: 51 years (2000).

Transportation: Commute to work: 72.2% car, 0.0% public transportation, 5.6% walk, 22.2% work from home (2000); Travel time to work: 51.2% less than 15 minutes, 35.7% 15 to 30 minutes, 10.7% 30 to 45 minutes, 0.0% 45 to 60 minutes, 2.4% 60 minutes or more (2000)

DANUBE (city). Covers a land area of 0.483 square miles and a water area of 0 square miles. Located at 44.79° N. Lat.; 95.10° W. Long.
Population: 529 (2000); Race: 96.8% White, 0.0% Black, 0.0% Asian, 0.0% American Indian and Alaska Native, 6.3% Hispanic of any race, 0.0% two or more races (2000); Density: 1,094.1 persons per square mile (2000); Age: 24.8% under 18, 20.0% over 64 (2000); Marriage status: 19.7% never married, 68.9% now married, 7.3% widowed, 4.1% divorced (2000); Foreign born: 2.2% (2000); Ancestry (includes multiple ancestries): 59.7% German, 18.8% Norwegian, 8.4% Swedish, 6.5% Other groups, 6.2% United States or American (2000).
Economy: Dairying; poultry, livestock; grain, soybeans; sand and gravel. Single-family building permits issued: 0 (2001) / 0 (2000); Multi-family building permits issued: 0 (2001) / 0 (2000); Employment by occupation: 14.4% management, 18.8% professional, 19.9% services, 20.3% sales, 3.3% farming, 7.7% construction, 15.5% production (2000).
Income: Per capita income: $18,807 (2000); Median household income: $40,000 (2000); Poverty rate: 5.6% (2000).
Taxes: Total city taxes per capita: $149 (1997); City property taxes per capita: $141 (1997).
Education: High school graduation rate: 80.2% (2000); College graduation rate: 10.9% (2000).
Housing: Homeownership rate: 87.9% (2000); Median home value: $50,700 (2000); Median rent: $325 per month (2000); Median age of housing: 50 years (2000).
Transportation: Commute to work: 86.8% car, 0.0% public transportation, 11.3% walk, 1.9% work from home (2000); Travel time to work: 70.4% less than 15 minutes, 15.4% 15 to 30 minutes, 10.4% 30 to 45 minutes, 1.2% 45 to 60 minutes, 2.7% 60 minutes or more (2000)

EMMET (township). Covers a land area of 34.761 square miles and a water area of 0 square miles. Located at 44.76° N. Lat.; 95.17° W. Long.
Population: 259 (2000); Race: 96.3% White, 0.0% Black, 0.0% Asian, 0.0% American Indian and Alaska Native, 0.7% Hispanic of any race, 3.7% two or more races (2000); Density: 7.5 persons per square mile (2000); Age: 26.3% under 18, 17.0% over 64 (2000); Marriage status: 20.3% never married, 71.2% now married, 5.2% widowed, 3.3% divorced (2000); Foreign born: 0.0% (2000); Ancestry (includes multiple ancestries): 50.7% German, 17.8% Norwegian, 11.1% Czech, 7.4% Swedish, 6.3% Irish (2000).
Economy: Employment by occupation: 16.2% management, 7.7% professional, 10.6% services, 24.6% sales, 2.8% farming, 9.9% construction, 28.2% production (2000).
Income: Per capita income: $16,276 (2000); Median household income: $37,500 (2000); Poverty rate: 11.5% (2000).
Taxes: Total city taxes per capita: $125 (1997); City property taxes per capita: $125 (1997).
Education: High school graduation rate: 84.9% (2000); College graduation rate: 8.9% (2000).
Housing: Homeownership rate: 87.9% (2000); Median home value: $71,000 (2000); Median rent: $335 per month (2000); Median age of housing: 60+ years (2000).
Transportation: Commute to work: 85.9% car, 0.0% public transportation, 0.0% walk, 14.1% work from home (2000); Travel time to work: 52.5% less than 15 minutes, 34.4% 15 to 30 minutes, 10.7% 30 to 45 minutes, 0.0% 45 to 60 minutes, 2.5% 60 minutes or more (2000)

ERICSON (township). Covers a land area of 36.307 square miles and a water area of 0.029 square miles. Located at 44.84° N. Lat.; 95.29° W. Long.
Population: 253 (2000); Race: 98.8% White, 0.0% Black, 1.2% Asian, 0.0% American Indian and Alaska Native, 0.0% Hispanic of any race, 0.0% two or more races (2000); Density: 7.0 persons per square mile (2000); Age: 22.4% under 18, 13.5% over 64 (2000); Marriage status: 23.6% never married, 65.0% now married, 7.4% widowed, 3.9% divorced (2000); Foreign born: 2.9% (2000); Ancestry (includes multiple ancestries): 45.7% German, 32.2% Norwegian, 13.9% Dutch, 11.0% Swedish, 4.5% Other groups (2000).
Economy: Employment by occupation: 34.3% management, 16.1% professional, 17.5% services, 16.1% sales, 1.4% farming, 3.5% construction, 11.2% production (2000).
Income: Per capita income: $21,454 (2000); Median household income: $51,250 (2000); Poverty rate: 4.1% (2000).
Taxes: Total city taxes per capita: $129 (1997); City property taxes per capita: $129 (1997).

Education: High school graduation rate: 95.0% (2000); College graduation rate: 17.4% (2000).
Housing: Homeownership rate: 88.2% (2000); Median home value: $84,000 (2000); Median rent: $225 per month (2000); Median age of housing: 48 years (2000).
Transportation: Commute to work: 74.1% car, 0.0% public transportation, 5.8% walk, 20.1% work from home (2000); Travel time to work: 28.8% less than 15 minutes, 52.3% 15 to 30 minutes, 13.5% 30 to 45 minutes, 3.6% 45 to 60 minutes, 1.8% 60 minutes or more (2000)

FAIRFAX (city). Covers a land area of 1.287 square miles and a water area of 0 square miles. Located at 44.52° N. Lat.; 94.72° W. Long. Elevation is 1,041 feet.
Population: 1,295 (2000); Race: 93.0% White, 0.0% Black, 0.0% Asian, 0.8% American Indian and Alaska Native, 8.4% Hispanic of any race, 1.2% two or more races (2000); Density: 1,006.6 persons per square mile (2000); Age: 24.9% under 18, 29.7% over 64 (2000); Marriage status: 21.5% never married, 59.2% now married, 14.5% widowed, 4.8% divorced (2000); Foreign born: 2.5% (2000); Ancestry (includes multiple ancestries): 56.6% German, 17.1% Norwegian, 9.8% Other groups, 8.1% Irish, 3.9% Swedish (2000).
Economy: Agriculture: grain; livestock, poultry. Manufacturing: beach cleaning machines, toys. Single-family building permits issued: 9 (2001) / 3 (2000); Multi-family building permits issued: 0 (2001) / 0 (2000); Employment by occupation: 9.6% management, 11.2% professional, 20.6% services, 17.8% sales, 1.9% farming, 14.1% construction, 24.8% production (2000).
Income: Per capita income: $18,297 (2000); Median household income: $33,700 (2000); Poverty rate: 9.2% (2000).
Taxes: Total city taxes per capita: $173 (2000); City property taxes per capita: $161 (2000).
Education: High school graduation rate: 74.0% (2000); College graduation rate: 10.8% (2000).
Housing: Homeownership rate: 80.9% (2000); Median home value: $49,900 (2000); Median rent: $306 per month (2000); Median age of housing: 47 years (2000).
Newspapers: Fairfax Standard (1 x week)
Transportation: Commute to work: 90.2% car, 0.0% public transportation, 5.4% walk, 4.0% work from home (2000); Travel time to work: 50.7% less than 15 minutes, 23.8% 15 to 30 minutes, 16.5% 30 to 45 minutes, 3.1% 45 to 60 minutes, 5.9% 60 minutes or more (2000)

FLORA (township). Covers a land area of 37.765 square miles and a water area of 0.105 square miles. Located at 44.65° N. Lat.; 95.17° W. Long.
Population: 245 (2000); Race: 98.3% White, 0.0% Black, 1.7% Asian, 0.0% American Indian and Alaska Native, 0.0% Hispanic of any race, 0.0% two or more races (2000); Density: 6.5 persons per square mile (2000); Age: 33.3% under 18, 8.5% over 64 (2000); Marriage status: 20.3% never married, 74.2% now married, 0.9% widowed, 4.6% divorced (2000); Foreign born: 1.7% (2000); Ancestry (includes multiple ancestries): 68.7% German, 19.7% Norwegian, 6.5% Irish, 5.8% Czech, 4.4% Swedish (2000).
Economy: Employment by occupation: 18.2% management, 14.7% professional, 17.5% services, 12.6% sales, 0.7% farming, 13.3% construction, 23.1% production (2000).
Income: Per capita income: $13,065 (2000); Median household income: $40,625 (2000); Poverty rate: 5.8% (2000).
Taxes: Total city taxes per capita: $112 (1997); City property taxes per capita: $112 (1997).
Education: High school graduation rate: 91.7% (2000); College graduation rate: 14.4% (2000).
Housing: Homeownership rate: 80.0% (2000); Median home value: $51,000 (2000); Median rent: $350 per month (2000); Median age of housing: 60+ years (2000).
Transportation: Commute to work: 80.9% car, 0.0% public transportation, 2.8% walk, 16.3% work from home (2000); Travel time to work: 19.5% less than 15 minutes, 61.9% 15 to 30 minutes, 12.7% 30 to 45 minutes, 4.2% 45 to 60 minutes, 1.7% 60 minutes or more (2000)

FRANKLIN (city). Covers a land area of 1.086 square miles and a water area of 0 square miles. Located at 44.52° N. Lat.; 94.88° W. Long.
Population: 498 (2000); Race: 97.4% White, 0.0% Black, 0.0% Asian, 0.0% American Indian and Alaska Native, 0.0% Hispanic of any race, 2.6% two or more races (2000); Density: 458.6 persons per square mile (2000); Age: 26.2% under 18, 26.0% over 64 (2000); Marriage status: 23.8% never married, 59.4% now married, 6.7% widowed, 10.1% divorced (2000);

Foreign born: 0.6% (2000); Ancestry (includes multiple ancestries): 52.3% German, 23.9% Norwegian, 8.0% Irish, 5.2% English, 5.0% Danish (2000).
Economy: Grain, sugar beets; livestock, poultry; dairying. Single-family building permits issued: 1 (2001) / 3 (2000); Multi-family building permits issued: 0 (2001) / 0 (2000); Employment by occupation: 12.7% management, 22.3% professional, 17.5% services, 11.4% sales, 2.2% farming, 12.2% construction, 21.8% production (2000).
Income: Per capita income: $16,212 (2000); Median household income: $37,583 (2000); Poverty rate: 9.0% (2000).
Taxes: Total city taxes per capita: $194 (1997); City property taxes per capita: $186 (1997).
Education: High school graduation rate: 70.3% (2000); College graduation rate: 12.6% (2000).
Housing: Homeownership rate: 80.8% (2000); Median home value: $38,800 (2000); Median rent: $294 per month (2000); Median age of housing: 51 years (2000).
Transportation: Commute to work: 87.7% car, 0.0% public transportation, 8.8% walk, 3.5% work from home (2000); Travel time to work: 34.2% less than 15 minutes, 36.5% 15 to 30 minutes, 10.0% 30 to 45 minutes, 5.9% 45 to 60 minutes, 13.2% 60 minutes or more (2000)

HAWK CREEK (township). Covers a land area of 30.514 square miles and a water area of 0.060 square miles. Located at 44.77° N. Lat.; 95.43° W. Long.
Population: 227 (2000); Race: 95.9% White, 0.0% Black, 2.1% Asian, 0.0% American Indian and Alaska Native, 0.0% Hispanic of any race, 2.1% two or more races (2000); Density: 7.4 persons per square mile (2000); Age: 24.6% under 18, 12.8% over 64 (2000); Marriage status: 23.4% never married, 68.8% now married, 2.6% widowed, 5.2% divorced (2000); Foreign born: 4.1% (2000); Ancestry (includes multiple ancestries): 63.1% Norwegian, 31.8% German, 23.6% Swedish, 8.7% Irish, 4.1% Other groups (2000).
Economy: Employment by occupation: 32.0% management, 10.7% professional, 16.5% services, 9.7% sales, 0.0% farming, 9.7% construction, 21.4% production (2000).
Income: Per capita income: $18,256 (2000); Median household income: $49,250 (2000); Poverty rate: 6.7% (2000).
Taxes: Total city taxes per capita: $146 (1997); City property taxes per capita: $146 (1997).
Education: High school graduation rate: 92.9% (2000); College graduation rate: 17.3% (2000).
Housing: Homeownership rate: 81.6% (2000); Median home value: $69,200 (2000); Median rent: $175 per month (2000); Median age of housing: 60+ years (2000).
Transportation: Commute to work: 90.1% car, 0.0% public transportation, 3.0% walk, 6.9% work from home (2000); Travel time to work: 50.0% less than 15 minutes, 37.2% 15 to 30 minutes, 8.5% 30 to 45 minutes, 0.0% 45 to 60 minutes, 4.3% 60 minutes or more (2000)

HECTOR (city). Covers a land area of 1.543 square miles and a water area of 0 square miles. Located at 44.74° N. Lat.; 94.71° W. Long. Elevation is 1,078 feet.
Population: 1,166 (2000); Race: 94.4% White, 0.0% Black, 0.4% Asian, 0.0% American Indian and Alaska Native, 6.8% Hispanic of any race, 1.1% two or more races (2000); Density: 755.7 persons per square mile (2000); Age: 25.2% under 18, 21.6% over 64 (2000); Marriage status: 22.4% never married, 56.4% now married, 12.1% widowed, 9.0% divorced (2000); Foreign born: 4.2% (2000); Ancestry (includes multiple ancestries): 52.9% German, 14.3% Norwegian, 12.7% Swedish, 7.6% Other groups, 6.0% Irish (2000).
Economy: Single-family building permits issued: 1 (2001) / 2 (2000); Multi-family building permits issued: 0 (2001) / 0 (2000); Employment by occupation: 12.3% management, 10.0% professional, 15.3% services, 20.0% sales, 1.4% farming, 9.6% construction, 31.4% production (2000).
Income: Per capita income: $18,406 (2000); Median household income: $33,000 (2000); Poverty rate: 8.4% (2000).
Taxes: Total city taxes per capita: $392 (1997); City property taxes per capita: $389 (1997).
Education: High school graduation rate: 78.1% (2000); College graduation rate: 13.1% (2000).

School District(s)

Buffalo Lake-Hector (PK-12)
2000 Enrollment: 628 320-848-2232
Housing: Homeownership rate: 85.9% (2000); Median home value: $56,200 (2000); Median rent: $309 per month (2000); Median age of housing: 45 years (2000).
Newspapers: News Mirror (1 x week)
Transportation: Commute to work: 89.0% car, 0.0% public transportation, 5.4% walk, 4.3% work from home (2000); Travel time to work: 67.6% less than 15 minutes, 10.9% 15 to 30 minutes, 13.7% 30 to 45 minutes, 2.6% 45 to 60 minutes, 5.1% 60 minutes or more (2000)

HECTOR (township). Covers a land area of 34.739 square miles and a water area of 0 square miles. Located at 44.75° N. Lat.; 94.69° W. Long. Elevation is 1,078 feet.
Population: 248 (2000); Race: 100.0% White, 0.0% Black, 0.0% Asian, 0.0% American Indian and Alaska Native, 0.0% Hispanic of any race, 0.0% two or more races (2000); Density: 7.1 persons per square mile (2000); Age: 24.6% under 18, 17.0% over 64 (2000); Marriage status: 22.4% never married, 65.9% now married, 2.9% widowed, 8.8% divorced (2000); Foreign born: 0.0% (2000); Ancestry (includes multiple ancestries): 65.5% German, 22.3% Swedish, 13.3% Norwegian, 8.0% Irish, 4.5% Polish (2000).
Economy: Grain, sugar beets, soybeans, beans; livestock, poultry; dairying. Manufacturing: electrical equipment, tools, consumer goods; meat processing. Employment by occupation: 14.7% management, 18.2% professional, 8.4% services, 16.8% sales, 6.3% farming, 8.4% construction, 27.3% production (2000).
Income: Per capita income: $17,645 (2000); Median household income: $45,313 (2000); Poverty rate: 2.7% (2000).
Taxes: Total city taxes per capita: $61 (1997); City property taxes per capita: $61 (1997).
Education: High school graduation rate: 87.6% (2000); College graduation rate: 11.4% (2000).
Housing: Homeownership rate: 93.0% (2000); Median home value: $71,700 (2000); Median rent: $275 per month (2000); Median age of housing: 48 years (2000).
Transportation: Commute to work: 72.1% car, 0.0% public transportation, 8.6% walk, 19.3% work from home (2000); Travel time to work: 57.5% less than 15 minutes, 15.0% 15 to 30 minutes, 23.0% 30 to 45 minutes, 2.7% 45 to 60 minutes, 1.8% 60 minutes or more (2000)

HENRYVILLE (township). Covers a land area of 36.271 square miles and a water area of 0 square miles. Located at 44.67° N. Lat.; 95.04° W. Long.
Population: 236 (2000); Race: 100.0% White, 0.0% Black, 0.0% Asian, 0.0% American Indian and Alaska Native, 0.0% Hispanic of any race, 0.0% two or more races (2000); Density: 6.5 persons per square mile (2000); Age: 19.2% under 18, 26.4% over 64 (2000); Marriage status: 23.2% never married, 66.1% now married, 4.5% widowed, 6.2% divorced (2000); Foreign born: 0.0% (2000); Ancestry (includes multiple ancestries): 47.6% German, 38.9% Czech, 10.1% Czechoslovakian, 9.1% Norwegian, 8.2% Irish (2000).
Economy: Employment by occupation: 37.6% management, 6.0% professional, 13.7% services, 18.8% sales, 0.0% farming, 7.7% construction, 16.2% production (2000).
Income: Per capita income: $21,623 (2000); Median household income: $43,333 (2000); Poverty rate: 2.4% (2000).
Taxes: Total city taxes per capita: $105 (1997); City property taxes per capita: $105 (1997).
Education: High school graduation rate: 76.8% (2000); College graduation rate: 7.7% (2000).
Housing: Homeownership rate: 85.7% (2000); Median home value: $59,000 (2000); Median rent: $325 per month (2000); Median age of housing: 60+ years (2000).
Transportation: Commute to work: 69.2% car, 1.7% public transportation, 11.1% walk, 17.9% work from home (2000); Travel time to work: 39.6% less than 15 minutes, 47.9% 15 to 30 minutes, 2.1% 30 to 45 minutes, 5.2% 45 to 60 minutes, 5.2% 60 minutes or more (2000)

KINGMAN (township). Covers a land area of 36.422 square miles and a water area of 0 square miles. Located at 44.84° N. Lat.; 94.93° W. Long.
Population: 252 (2000); Race: 100.0% White, 0.0% Black, 0.0% Asian, 0.0% American Indian and Alaska Native, 0.0% Hispanic of any race, 0.0% two or more races (2000); Density: 6.9 persons per square mile (2000); Age: 25.9% under 18, 10.3% over 64 (2000); Marriage status: 26.8% never married, 70.2% now married, 3.0% widowed, 0.0% divorced (2000); Foreign born: 0.0% (2000); Ancestry (includes multiple ancestries): 57.6% German, 17.3% Norwegian, 16.9% Swedish, 15.6% Czech, 10.7% Irish (2000).
Economy: Employment by occupation: 13.3% management, 10.2% professional, 8.6% services, 19.5% sales, 5.5% farming, 14.1% construction, 28.9% production (2000).
Income: Per capita income: $19,667 (2000); Median household income: $46,750 (2000); Poverty rate: 2.9% (2000).

Taxes: Total city taxes per capita: $140 (1997); City property taxes per capita: $140 (1997).
Education: High school graduation rate: 88.9% (2000); College graduation rate: 8.6% (2000).
Housing: Homeownership rate: 76.5% (2000); Median home value: $56,400 (2000); Median rent: $119 per month (2000); Median age of housing: 50 years (2000).
Transportation: Commute to work: 85.4% car, 0.0% public transportation, 3.3% walk, 11.4% work from home (2000); Travel time to work: 57.8% less than 15 minutes, 29.4% 15 to 30 minutes, 11.0% 30 to 45 minutes, 1.8% 45 to 60 minutes, 0.0% 60 minutes or more (2000)

MARTINSBURG (township). Covers a land area of 36.464 square miles and a water area of 0 square miles. Located at 44.67° N. Lat.; 94.69° W. Long.
Population: 215 (2000); Race: 97.9% White, 0.0% Black, 0.0% Asian, 2.1% American Indian and Alaska Native, 0.4% Hispanic of any race, 0.0% two or more races (2000); Density: 5.9 persons per square mile (2000); Age: 36.1% under 18, 10.4% over 64 (2000); Marriage status: 27.5% never married, 68.4% now married, 2.3% widowed, 1.8% divorced (2000); Foreign born: 0.0% (2000); Ancestry (includes multiple ancestries): 56.4% German, 19.1% Swedish, 12.4% Norwegian, 7.1% Other groups, 6.6% United States or American (2000).
Economy: Employment by occupation: 29.8% management, 11.3% professional, 8.9% services, 15.3% sales, 0.8% farming, 12.9% construction, 21.0% production (2000).
Income: Per capita income: $17,619 (2000); Median household income: $43,750 (2000); Poverty rate: 11.2% (2000).
Taxes: Total city taxes per capita: $86 (1997); City property taxes per capita: $86 (1997).
Education: High school graduation rate: 90.4% (2000); College graduation rate: 7.5% (2000).
Housing: Homeownership rate: 87.8% (2000); Median home value: $72,000 (2000); Median rent: $225 per month (2000); Median age of housing: 59 years (2000).
Transportation: Commute to work: 71.9% car, 0.0% public transportation, 8.3% walk, 19.8% work from home (2000); Travel time to work: 48.5% less than 15 minutes, 30.9% 15 to 30 minutes, 16.5% 30 to 45 minutes, 3.1% 45 to 60 minutes, 1.0% 60 minutes or more (2000)

MELVILLE (township). Covers a land area of 36.328 square miles and a water area of 0 square miles. Located at 44.75° N. Lat.; 94.80° W. Long.
Population: 242 (2000); Race: 100.0% White, 0.0% Black, 0.0% Asian, 0.0% American Indian and Alaska Native, 0.0% Hispanic of any race, 0.0% two or more races (2000); Density: 6.7 persons per square mile (2000); Age: 32.4% under 18, 13.0% over 64 (2000); Marriage status: 17.4% never married, 72.6% now married, 8.9% widowed, 1.1% divorced (2000); Foreign born: 0.0% (2000); Ancestry (includes multiple ancestries): 52.3% German, 19.8% Norwegian, 9.9% Irish, 6.9% Swedish, 3.4% Dutch (2000).
Economy: Employment by occupation: 29.0% management, 13.7% professional, 10.7% services, 24.4% sales, 3.1% farming, 6.1% construction, 13.0% production (2000).
Income: Per capita income: $18,676 (2000); Median household income: $40,893 (2000); Poverty rate: 5.7% (2000).
Taxes: Total city taxes per capita: $139 (1997); City property taxes per capita: $139 (1997).
Education: High school graduation rate: 91.2% (2000); College graduation rate: 15.3% (2000).
Housing: Homeownership rate: 91.7% (2000); Median home value: $85,800 (2000); Median age of housing: 57 years (2000).
Transportation: Commute to work: 74.0% car, 0.0% public transportation, 7.1% walk, 18.9% work from home (2000); Travel time to work: 60.2% less than 15 minutes, 17.5% 15 to 30 minutes, 22.3% 30 to 45 minutes, 0.0% 45 to 60 minutes, 0.0% 60 minutes or more (2000)

MORTON (city). Covers a land area of 1.214 square miles and a water area of 0.016 square miles. Located at 44.55° N. Lat.; 94.98° W. Long. Elevation is 845 feet.
History: Birch Coulee Battlefield Historic Site, set aside in commemoration of battle between Sioux Indians and U.S. Cavalry in 1862.
Population: 442 (2000); Race: 89.3% White, 0.0% Black, 2.0% Asian, 3.9% American Indian and Alaska Native, 4.8% Hispanic of any race, 4.8% two or more races (2000); Density: 364.0 persons per square mile (2000); Age: 22.9% under 18, 21.1% over 64 (2000); Marriage status: 27.6% never married, 52.1% now married, 10.3% widowed, 10.0% divorced (2000); Foreign born: 4.5% (2000); Ancestry (includes multiple ancestries): 44.9% German, 21.3% Norwegian, 15.4% Other groups, 10.0% Irish, 3.4% English (2000).
Economy: Grain, soybeans, peas, sugar beets; livestock, poultry; dairying. Manufacturing: rubber products. Single-family building permits issued: 0 (2001) / 1 (2000); Multi-family building permits issued: 0 (2001) / 0 (2000); Employment by occupation: 2.5% management, 5.0% professional, 23.5% services, 24.0% sales, 1.0% farming, 5.5% construction, 38.5% production (2000).
Income: Per capita income: $16,899 (2000); Median household income: $35,298 (2000); Poverty rate: 8.8% (2000).
Taxes: Total city taxes per capita: $291 (1997); City property taxes per capita: $287 (1997).
Education: High school graduation rate: 85.3% (2000); College graduation rate: 10.4% (2000).

School District(s)

Eci' Nompa Woonspe (05-12)
2000 Enrollment: 46 507-697-9055

Housing: Homeownership rate: 79.3% (2000); Median home value: $35,800 (2000); Median rent: $339 per month (2000); Median age of housing: 60+ years (2000).
Transportation: Commute to work: 91.4% car, 0.0% public transportation, 7.1% walk, 1.0% work from home (2000); Travel time to work: 60.7% less than 15 minutes, 25.0% 15 to 30 minutes, 6.1% 30 to 45 minutes, 0.5% 45 to 60 minutes, 7.7% 60 minutes or more (2000)

NORFOLK (township). Covers a land area of 35.698 square miles and a water area of 0 square miles. Located at 44.66° N. Lat.; 94.94° W. Long.
Population: 207 (2000); Race: 100.0% White, 0.0% Black, 0.0% Asian, 0.0% American Indian and Alaska Native, 0.0% Hispanic of any race, 0.0% two or more races (2000); Density: 5.8 persons per square mile (2000); Age: 34.8% under 18, 11.0% over 64 (2000); Marriage status: 22.1% never married, 67.5% now married, 3.2% widowed, 7.1% divorced (2000); Foreign born: 0.0% (2000); Ancestry (includes multiple ancestries): 65.2% German, 21.6% Czech, 16.7% Norwegian, 13.2% Irish, 4.0% French (except Basque) (2000).
Economy: Employment by occupation: 28.7% management, 17.6% professional, 6.5% services, 24.1% sales, 1.9% farming, 4.6% construction, 16.7% production (2000).
Income: Per capita income: $15,337 (2000); Median household income: $36,806 (2000); Poverty rate: 8.8% (2000).
Taxes: Total city taxes per capita: $92 (1997); City property taxes per capita: $92 (1997).
Education: High school graduation rate: 90.7% (2000); College graduation rate: 16.3% (2000).
Housing: Homeownership rate: 75.3% (2000); Median home value: $93,800 (2000); Median rent: $200 per month (2000); Median age of housing: 60+ years (2000).
Transportation: Commute to work: 83.0% car, 0.0% public transportation, 5.7% walk, 11.3% work from home (2000); Travel time to work: 61.7% less than 15 minutes, 23.4% 15 to 30 minutes, 4.3% 30 to 45 minutes, 10.6% 45 to 60 minutes, 0.0% 60 minutes or more (2000)

OLIVIA (city). Covers a land area of 2.331 square miles and a water area of 0 square miles. Located at 44.77° N. Lat.; 94.99° W. Long. Elevation is 1,074 feet.
History: Olivia was named by a railroad official for one of his friends.
Population: 2,570 (2000); Race: 96.9% White, 0.2% Black, 0.0% Asian, 0.0% American Indian and Alaska Native, 8.3% Hispanic of any race, 0.1% two or more races (2000); Density: 1,102.7 persons per square mile (2000); Age: 24.8% under 18, 21.7% over 64 (2000); Marriage status: 20.4% never married, 61.9% now married, 10.5% widowed, 7.2% divorced (2000); Foreign born: 1.3% (2000); Ancestry (includes multiple ancestries): 48.8% German, 16.5% Norwegian, 9.9% Irish, 8.8% Other groups, 8.2% Czech (2000).
Economy: Single-family building permits issued: 2 (2001) / 4 (2000); Multi-family building permits issued: 0 (2001) / 0 (2000); Employment by occupation: 13.5% management, 18.5% professional, 12.9% services, 24.7% sales, 2.6% farming, 6.9% construction, 20.9% production (2000).
Income: Per capita income: $17,889 (2000); Median household income: $35,060 (2000); Poverty rate: 11.3% (2000).
Taxes: Total city taxes per capita: $224 (2000); City property taxes per capita: $201 (2000).
Education: High school graduation rate: 77.1% (2000); College graduation rate: 19.7% (2000).

School District(s)
Bird Island-Olivia-Lake Lillian (PK-12)
2000 Enrollment: 1,034 320-365-4060
Housing: Homeownership rate: 75.7% (2000); Median home value: $67,900 (2000); Median rent: $343 per month (2000); Median age of housing: 42 years (2000).
Hospitals: Renville County Hospital (35 beds)
Safety: Violent crime rate: 30.8 per 10,000 population; Property crime rate: 411.9 per 10,000 population (2001).
Newspapers: Olivia Times Journal (1 x week)
Transportation: Commute to work: 90.6% car, 1.1% public transportation, 3.1% walk, 3.6% work from home (2000); Travel time to work: 63.8% less than 15 minutes, 14.3% 15 to 30 minutes, 13.8% 30 to 45 minutes, 4.6% 45 to 60 minutes, 3.5% 60 minutes or more (2000)
Additional Information Contacts
Olivia Chamber of Commerce 320-523-1350

OSCEOLA (township). Covers a land area of 36.297 square miles and a water area of 0 square miles. Located at 44.84° N. Lat.; 94.81° W. Long.
Population: 219 (2000); Race: 97.9% White, 0.0% Black, 0.0% Asian, 0.0% American Indian and Alaska Native, 1.5% Hispanic of any race, 1.0% two or more races (2000); Density: 6.0 persons per square mile (2000); Age: 32.8% under 18, 16.9% over 64 (2000); Marriage status: 25.3% never married, 60.3% now married, 8.2% widowed, 6.2% divorced (2000); Foreign born: 0.0% (2000); Ancestry (includes multiple ancestries): 45.1% German, 11.8% Norwegian, 8.7% Swedish, 8.7% Irish, 7.2% United States or American (2000).
Economy: Employment by occupation: 29.9% management, 9.2% professional, 14.9% services, 18.4% sales, 3.4% farming, 5.7% construction, 18.4% production (2000).
Income: Per capita income: $18,687 (2000); Median household income: $47,917 (2000); Poverty rate: 17.9% (2000).
Taxes: Total city taxes per capita: $136 (1997); City property taxes per capita: $136 (1997).
Education: High school graduation rate: 78.8% (2000); College graduation rate: 6.8% (2000).
Housing: Homeownership rate: 87.1% (2000); Median home value: $62,000 (2000); Median rent: $150 per month (2000); Median age of housing: 46 years (2000).
Transportation: Commute to work: 82.4% car, 0.0% public transportation, 0.0% walk, 17.6% work from home (2000); Travel time to work: 32.9% less than 15 minutes, 38.6% 15 to 30 minutes, 17.1% 30 to 45 minutes, 11.4% 45 to 60 minutes, 0.0% 60 minutes or more (2000)

PALMYRA (township). Covers a land area of 36.309 square miles and a water area of 0 square miles. Located at 44.68° N. Lat.; 94.80° W. Long.
Population: 215 (2000); Race: 98.1% White, 0.0% Black, 0.0% Asian, 0.0% American Indian and Alaska Native, 1.9% Hispanic of any race, 0.0% two or more races (2000); Density: 5.9 persons per square mile (2000); Age: 27.2% under 18, 13.1% over 64 (2000); Marriage status: 25.0% never married, 62.8% now married, 7.9% widowed, 4.3% divorced (2000); Foreign born: 1.0% (2000); Ancestry (includes multiple ancestries): 47.1% German, 41.7% Swedish, 11.2% United States or American, 11.2% English, 6.3% Norwegian (2000).
Economy: Employment by occupation: 26.1% management, 14.1% professional, 20.7% services, 17.4% sales, 0.0% farming, 7.6% construction, 14.1% production (2000).
Income: Per capita income: $18,838 (2000); Median household income: $38,125 (2000); Poverty rate: 5.9% (2000).
Taxes: Total city taxes per capita: $134 (1997); City property taxes per capita: $134 (1997).
Education: High school graduation rate: 89.5% (2000); College graduation rate: 12.6% (2000).
Housing: Homeownership rate: 73.2% (2000); Median home value: $70,000 (2000); Median rent: $150 per month (2000); Median age of housing: 50 years (2000).
Transportation: Commute to work: 83.7% car, 2.2% public transportation, 5.4% walk, 8.7% work from home (2000); Travel time to work: 23.8% less than 15 minutes, 52.4% 15 to 30 minutes, 9.5% 30 to 45 minutes, 1.2% 45 to 60 minutes, 13.1% 60 minutes or more (2000)

PRESTON LAKE (township). Covers a land area of 37.383 square miles and a water area of 1.516 square miles. Located at 44.75° N. Lat.; 94.56° W. Long.
Population: 293 (2000); Race: 99.0% White, 1.0% Black, 0.0% Asian, 0.0% American Indian and Alaska Native, 0.0% Hispanic of any race, 0.0% two or more races (2000); Density: 7.8 persons per square mile (2000); Age: 22.8% under 18, 22.5% over 64 (2000); Marriage status: 21.0% never married, 66.1% now married, 7.7% widowed, 5.2% divorced (2000); Foreign born: 0.0% (2000); Ancestry (includes multiple ancestries): 65.1% German, 13.4% Norwegian, 8.7% Irish, 6.7% Swedish, 5.0% English (2000).
Economy: Employment by occupation: 33.3% management, 11.3% professional, 18.9% services, 11.3% sales, 3.1% farming, 8.2% construction, 13.8% production (2000).
Income: Per capita income: $17,690 (2000); Median household income: $41,944 (2000); Poverty rate: 6.0% (2000).
Taxes: Total city taxes per capita: $125 (1997); City property taxes per capita: $125 (1997).
Education: High school graduation rate: 85.3% (2000); College graduation rate: 12.4% (2000).
Housing: Homeownership rate: 84.6% (2000); Median home value: $89,000 (2000); Median rent: $175 per month (2000); Median age of housing: 60+ years (2000).
Transportation: Commute to work: 66.9% car, 0.0% public transportation, 3.9% walk, 29.2% work from home (2000); Travel time to work: 25.7% less than 15 minutes, 41.3% 15 to 30 minutes, 20.2% 30 to 45 minutes, 5.5% 45 to 60 minutes, 7.3% 60 minutes or more (2000)

RENVILLE (city). Covers a land area of 1.394 square miles and a water area of 0 square miles. Located at 44.79° N. Lat.; 95.21° W. Long. Elevation is 1,069 feet.
History: Settled c.1863.
Population: 1,323 (2000); Race: 90.2% White, 0.3% Black, 0.0% Asian, 0.0% American Indian and Alaska Native, 11.4% Hispanic of any race, 0.1% two or more races (2000); Density: 948.9 persons per square mile (2000); Age: 26.5% under 18, 25.5% over 64 (2000); Marriage status: 18.8% never married, 65.7% now married, 11.0% widowed, 4.5% divorced (2000); Foreign born: 2.7% (2000); Ancestry (includes multiple ancestries): 43.1% German, 26.9% Norwegian, 12.5% Other groups, 9.2% Swedish, 8.5% Dutch (2000).
Economy: Grain, sugar beets, soybeans, beans; livestock, poultry; dairying. Manufacturing: feeds and fertilizers, beet sugar, tractor seats. Single-family building permits issued: 0 (2001) / 1 (2000); Multi-family building permits issued: 0 (2001) / 0 (2000); Employment by occupation: 10.2% management, 14.7% professional, 17.1% services, 20.9% sales, 3.5% farming, 12.1% construction, 21.6% production (2000).
Income: Per capita income: $16,139 (2000); Median household income: $37,206 (2000); Poverty rate: 10.0% (2000).
Taxes: Total city taxes per capita: $339 (1997); City property taxes per capita: $338 (1997).
Education: High school graduation rate: 75.2% (2000); College graduation rate: 12.8% (2000).

School District(s)
Renville County West (KG-12)
2000 Enrollment: 943 320-329-8362
Housing: Homeownership rate: 74.7% (2000); Median home value: $52,900 (2000); Median rent: $318 per month (2000); Median age of housing: 47 years (2000).
Newspapers: Renville County Star Farmer News (1 x week)
Transportation: Commute to work: 86.4% car, 0.0% public transportation, 7.7% walk, 4.9% work from home (2000); Travel time to work: 69.5% less than 15 minutes, 15.8% 15 to 30 minutes, 9.9% 30 to 45 minutes, 0.6% 45 to 60 minutes, 4.2% 60 minutes or more (2000)

SACRED HEART (city). Covers a land area of 0.992 square miles and a water area of 0 square miles. Located at 44.78° N. Lat.; 95.35° W. Long.
Population: 549 (2000); Race: 95.6% White, 0.0% Black, 0.4% Asian, 0.0% American Indian and Alaska Native, 4.8% Hispanic of any race, 0.4% two or more races (2000); Density: 553.2 persons per square mile (2000); Age: 23.8% under 18, 23.8% over 64 (2000); Marriage status: 28.1% never married, 56.9% now married, 8.7% widowed, 6.3% divorced (2000); Foreign born: 1.3% (2000); Ancestry (includes multiple ancestries): 46.0% Norwegian, 40.5% German, 11.2% Swedish, 5.3% Other groups, 5.1% English (2000).
Economy: Single-family building permits issued: 0 (2001) / 0 (2000); Multi-family building permits issued: 0 (2001) / 0 (2000); Employment by occupation: 9.2% management, 12.6% professional, 23.3% services, 17.6% sales, 2.3% farming, 8.4% construction, 26.7% production (2000).
Income: Per capita income: $18,089 (2000); Median household income: $32,333 (2000); Poverty rate: 10.9% (2000).
Taxes: Total city taxes per capita: $122 (1997); City property taxes per capita: $119 (1997).

Education: High school graduation rate: 79.2% (2000); College graduation rate: 8.0% (2000).
Housing: Homeownership rate: 77.7% (2000); Median home value: $33,900 (2000); Median rent: $307 per month (2000); Median age of housing: 60+ years (2000).
Transportation: Commute to work: 84.2% car, 1.9% public transportation, 8.1% walk, 2.7% work from home (2000); Travel time to work: 47.4% less than 15 minutes, 32.4% 15 to 30 minutes, 10.7% 30 to 45 minutes, 5.9% 45 to 60 minutes, 3.6% 60 minutes or more (2000)

SACRED HEART (township). Covers a land area of 51.489 square miles and a water area of 0.026 square miles. Located at 44.74° N. Lat.; 95.29° W. Long.
Population: 277 (2000); Race: 100.0% White, 0.0% Black, 0.0% Asian, 0.0% American Indian and Alaska Native, 1.6% Hispanic of any race, 0.0% two or more races (2000); Density: 5.4 persons per square mile (2000); Age: 31.1% under 18, 15.4% over 64 (2000); Marriage status: 18.9% never married, 73.2% now married, 2.6% widowed, 5.3% divorced (2000); Foreign born: 0.0% (2000); Ancestry (includes multiple ancestries): 47.2% Norwegian, 34.8% German, 6.9% Swedish, 3.9% Irish, 2.6% Dutch (2000).
Economy: Grain, sugar beets, soybeans; livestock; dairying; light manufacturing. Employment by occupation: 13.8% management, 16.7% professional, 10.9% services, 23.9% sales, 7.2% farming, 8.7% construction, 18.8% production (2000).
Income: Per capita income: $16,963 (2000); Median household income: $44,375 (2000); Poverty rate: 12.1% (2000).
Taxes: Total city taxes per capita: $184 (1997); City property taxes per capita: $184 (1997).
Education: High school graduation rate: 90.9% (2000); College graduation rate: 13.7% (2000).
Housing: Homeownership rate: 83.2% (2000); Median home value: $60,000 (2000); Median rent: $175 per month (2000); Median age of housing: 60+ years (2000).
Transportation: Commute to work: 88.4% car, 0.0% public transportation, 1.4% walk, 10.1% work from home (2000); Travel time to work: 53.2% less than 15 minutes, 26.6% 15 to 30 minutes, 8.9% 30 to 45 minutes, 3.2% 45 to 60 minutes, 8.1% 60 minutes or more (2000)

TROY (township). Covers a land area of 34.803 square miles and a water area of 0.030 square miles. Located at 44.76° N. Lat.; 95.06° W. Long.
Population: 325 (2000); Race: 100.0% White, 0.0% Black, 0.0% Asian, 0.0% American Indian and Alaska Native, 0.0% Hispanic of any race, 0.0% two or more races (2000); Density: 9.3 persons per square mile (2000); Age: 32.5% under 18, 13.2% over 64 (2000); Marriage status: 20.7% never married, 68.5% now married, 6.0% widowed, 4.7% divorced (2000); Foreign born: 0.0% (2000); Ancestry (includes multiple ancestries): 55.2% German, 13.9% Norwegian, 9.8% Irish, 7.9% Czech, 5.4% Swedish (2000).
Economy: Employment by occupation: 20.9% management, 20.9% professional, 11.0% services, 14.7% sales, 3.7% farming, 5.5% construction, 23.3% production (2000).
Income: Per capita income: $23,803 (2000); Median household income: $47,083 (2000); Poverty rate: 7.6% (2000).
Taxes: Total city taxes per capita: $97 (1997); City property taxes per capita: $97 (1997).
Education: High school graduation rate: 80.0% (2000); College graduation rate: 8.7% (2000).
Housing: Homeownership rate: 74.3% (2000); Median home value: $96,300 (2000); Median rent: $517 per month (2000); Median age of housing: 47 years (2000).
Transportation: Commute to work: 83.2% car, 1.2% public transportation, 3.7% walk, 10.6% work from home (2000); Travel time to work: 63.9% less than 15 minutes, 23.6% 15 to 30 minutes, 9.7% 30 to 45 minutes, 0.0% 45 to 60 minutes, 2.8% 60 minutes or more (2000)

WANG (township). Covers a land area of 36.199 square miles and a water area of 0 square miles. Located at 44.85° N. Lat.; 95.42° W. Long.
Population: 299 (2000); Race: 94.9% White, 0.0% Black, 0.0% Asian, 0.0% American Indian and Alaska Native, 6.0% Hispanic of any race, 0.0% two or more races (2000); Density: 8.3 persons per square mile (2000); Age: 30.1% under 18, 12.7% over 64 (2000); Marriage status: 23.4% never married, 69.4% now married, 2.0% widowed, 5.2% divorced (2000); Foreign born: 2.5% (2000); Ancestry (includes multiple ancestries): 53.8% Norwegian, 39.9% German, 12.7% Swedish, 6.0% Other groups, 5.1% Irish (2000).
Economy: Employment by occupation: 23.0% management, 19.3% professional, 10.4% services, 17.8% sales, 3.0% farming, 3.0% construction, 23.7% production (2000).
Income: Per capita income: $14,043 (2000); Median household income: $41,023 (2000); Poverty rate: 7.9% (2000).
Taxes: Total city taxes per capita: $168 (1997); City property taxes per capita: $168 (1997).
Education: High school graduation rate: 84.2% (2000); College graduation rate: 8.9% (2000).
Housing: Homeownership rate: 82.6% (2000); Median home value: $71,300 (2000); Median rent: $225 per month (2000); Median age of housing: 47 years (2000).
Transportation: Commute to work: 84.6% car, 0.0% public transportation, 0.0% walk, 13.8% work from home (2000); Travel time to work: 45.5% less than 15 minutes, 33.9% 15 to 30 minutes, 14.3% 30 to 45 minutes, 0.0% 45 to 60 minutes, 6.3% 60 minutes or more (2000)

WELLINGTON (township). Covers a land area of 36.100 square miles and a water area of 0.221 square miles. Located at 44.59° N. Lat.; 94.69° W. Long.
Population: 242 (2000); Race: 99.5% White, 0.0% Black, 0.0% Asian, 0.0% American Indian and Alaska Native, 1.4% Hispanic of any race, 0.0% two or more races (2000); Density: 6.7 persons per square mile (2000); Age: 25.7% under 18, 9.8% over 64 (2000); Marriage status: 30.9% never married, 63.0% now married, 2.2% widowed, 3.9% divorced (2000); Foreign born: 0.9% (2000); Ancestry (includes multiple ancestries): 67.8% German, 8.9% English, 6.5% Norwegian, 5.6% Swedish, 5.1% Irish (2000).
Economy: Employment by occupation: 15.5% management, 18.6% professional, 14.4% services, 15.5% sales, 1.0% farming, 12.4% construction, 22.7% production (2000).
Income: Per capita income: $15,746 (2000); Median household income: $38,281 (2000); Poverty rate: 8.9% (2000).
Taxes: Total city taxes per capita: $113 (1997); City property taxes per capita: $113 (1997).
Education: High school graduation rate: 84.6% (2000); College graduation rate: 9.1% (2000).
Housing: Homeownership rate: 88.9% (2000); Median home value: $78,600 (2000); Median rent: $188 per month (2000); Median age of housing: 60+ years (2000).
Transportation: Commute to work: 73.2% car, 0.0% public transportation, 7.2% walk, 17.5% work from home (2000); Travel time to work: 53.8% less than 15 minutes, 23.8% 15 to 30 minutes, 15.0% 30 to 45 minutes, 2.5% 45 to 60 minutes, 5.0% 60 minutes or more (2000)

WINFIELD (township). Covers a land area of 36.515 square miles and a water area of 0.053 square miles. Located at 44.85° N. Lat.; 95.06° W. Long.
Population: 252 (2000); Race: 100.0% White, 0.0% Black, 0.0% Asian, 0.0% American Indian and Alaska Native, 0.0% Hispanic of any race, 0.0% two or more races (2000); Density: 6.9 persons per square mile (2000); Age: 29.5% under 18, 11.6% over 64 (2000); Marriage status: 24.0% never married, 66.0% now married, 3.5% widowed, 6.5% divorced (2000); Foreign born: 1.6% (2000); Ancestry (includes multiple ancestries): 62.9% German, 19.5% Norwegian, 15.9% Irish, 9.6% Swedish, 9.6% Dutch (2000).
Economy: Employment by occupation: 30.4% management, 15.6% professional, 10.4% services, 18.5% sales, 3.0% farming, 3.0% construction, 19.3% production (2000).
Income: Per capita income: $15,181 (2000); Median household income: $35,893 (2000); Poverty rate: 7.6% (2000).
Taxes: Total city taxes per capita: $70 (1997); City property taxes per capita: $70 (1997).
Education: High school graduation rate: 91.5% (2000); College graduation rate: 11.0% (2000).
Housing: Homeownership rate: 87.9% (2000); Median home value: $67,500 (2000); Median rent: $142 per month (2000); Median age of housing: 60+ years (2000).
Transportation: Commute to work: 75.6% car, 0.0% public transportation, 3.7% walk, 20.7% work from home (2000); Travel time to work: 52.3% less than 15 minutes, 26.2% 15 to 30 minutes, 19.6% 30 to 45 minutes, 0.0% 45 to 60 minutes, 1.9% 60 minutes or more (2000)

Rice County

Located in southeastern Minnesota; drained by the Cannon and Straight Rivers; watered by several lakes. Covers a land area of 497.60 square miles, a water area of 18.60 square miles, and is located in the Central Time Zone. The county government was organized in 1853. County seat is Faribault.

Weather Station: Faribault Elevation: 938 feet

	Jan	Feb	Mar	Apr	May	Jun	Jul	Aug	Sep	Oct	Nov	Dec
High	22	28	40	57	70	79	83	80	72	60	41	27
Low	2	8	21	34	46	56	60	58	49	37	23	9
Precip	1.0	0.7	1.9	2.9	3.7	4.0	4.3	4.4	3.4	2.4	2.1	1.0
Snow	10.7	6.5	8.2	3.0	0.0	0.0	0.0	0.0	0.0	tr	5.8	8.6

High and Low temperatures in degrees Fahrenheit; Precipitation and Snow in inches

Population: 56,665 (2000); Race: 93.3% White, 1.3% Black, 1.6% Asian, 0.6% American Indian and Alaska Native, 5.4% Hispanic of any race, 1.4% two or more races (2000); Density: 113.9 persons per square mile (2000); Age: 25.2% under 18, 11.3% over 64 (2000).
Religion: Five largest groups: 29.1% Catholic Church, 16.9% Evangelical Lutheran Church in America, 7.8% Lutheran Church—Missouri Synod, 3.6% The United Methodist Church, 2.6% United Church of Christ (2000).
Economy: Unemployment rate: 3.5% (11/2002); Total civilian labor force: 29,922 (11/2002); Leading industries: 22.9% manufacturing; 14.9% health care and social assistance; 13.6% educational services (2000); Companies that employ more than 1,000 persons: 1 (2000); Companies that employ more than 100 persons: 38 (2000); Farms: 1,191 totaling 251,031 acres (1997); Minority business ownership rate: 2.4% (1997); Women business ownership rate: 26.5% (1997); Retail sales per capita: $7,779 (1997). Single-family building permits issued: 418 (2001) / 363 (2000); Multi-family building permits issued: 29 (2001) / 64 (2000).
Income: Per capita income: $19,695 (2000); Median household income: $48,651 (2000); Poverty rate: 6.9% (2000); Bankruptcy rate: 2.75% (2001).
Taxes: Total county taxes per capita: $185 (2000); County property taxes per capita: $180 (2000).
Education: High school graduation rate: 85.2% (2000); College graduation rate: 22.4% (2000).
Housing: Homeownership rate: 77.9% (2000); Median home value: $123,600 (2000); Median rent: $467 per month (2000); Median age of housing: 31 years (2000).
Health: Birth rate: 118.2 per 10,000 population (1998); Age adjusted death rate: 73.4 per 10,000 population (1999); Age adjusted cancer mortality rate: 178.9 deaths per 100,000 population (1999). Number of physicians: 12.9 per 10,000 population (1999); Number of hospital beds: 21.2 per 10,000 population (1999).
Elections: 2000 Presidential election results: 50.5% Gore, 41.8% Bush, 6.3% Nader, 0.9% Buchanan
National and State Parks: Nerstrand Big Woods State Park
Additional Information Contacts
Rice County Government Offices 507-332-6100
Faribault Chamber of Commerce. 507-334-4381
Northfield Chamber of Commerce. 507-645-5604

Rice County Communities

BRIDGEWATER (township). Covers a land area of 36.274 square miles and a water area of 0.109 square miles. Located at 44.41° N. Lat.; 93.21° W. Long.
Population: 1,898 (2000); Race: 97.0% White, 1.1% Black, 0.5% Asian, 0.3% American Indian and Alaska Native, 2.8% Hispanic of any race, 0.9% two or more races (2000); Density: 52.3 persons per square mile (2000); Age: 31.1% under 18, 7.9% over 64 (2000); Marriage status: 21.2% never married, 71.8% now married, 2.0% widowed, 5.1% divorced (2000); Foreign born: 2.5% (2000); Ancestry (includes multiple ancestries): 43.2% German, 21.4% Norwegian, 13.9% Irish, 11.4% English, 8.9% Swedish (2000).
Economy: Employment by occupation: 16.1% management, 20.7% professional, 10.0% services, 23.7% sales, 0.9% farming, 11.4% construction, 17.1% production (2000).
Income: Per capita income: $28,695 (2000); Median household income: $68,819 (2000); Poverty rate: 2.9% (2000).
Taxes: Total city taxes per capita: $70 (2000); City property taxes per capita: $70 (2000).
Education: High school graduation rate: 93.5% (2000); College graduation rate: 38.9% (2000).
Housing: Homeownership rate: 94.1% (2000); Median home value: $190,500 (2000); Median rent: $525 per month (2000); Median age of housing: 26 years (2000).
Transportation: Commute to work: 90.5% car, 0.2% public transportation, 2.0% walk, 7.3% work from home (2000); Travel time to work: 52.5% less than 15 minutes, 19.4% 15 to 30 minutes, 12.6% 30 to 45 minutes, 8.5% 45 to 60 minutes, 7.0% 60 minutes or more (2000)

CANNON CITY (township). Covers a land area of 30.648 square miles and a water area of 0.174 square miles. Located at 44.32° N. Lat.; 93.23° W. Long.
Population: 1,212 (2000); Race: 98.9% White, 0.0% Black, 0.6% Asian, 0.1% American Indian and Alaska Native, 0.0% Hispanic of any race, 0.4% two or more races (2000); Density: 39.5 persons per square mile (2000); Age: 30.8% under 18, 9.1% over 64 (2000); Marriage status: 22.3% never married, 67.3% now married, 4.2% widowed, 6.3% divorced (2000); Foreign born: 0.9% (2000); Ancestry (includes multiple ancestries): 46.1% German, 19.7% Norwegian, 16.2% Irish, 8.5% French (except Basque), 7.3% English (2000).
Economy: Employment by occupation: 15.8% management, 13.0% professional, 13.3% services, 22.0% sales, 1.2% farming, 16.0% construction, 18.6% production (2000).
Income: Per capita income: $20,756 (2000); Median household income: $55,682 (2000); Poverty rate: 3.3% (2000).
Taxes: Total city taxes per capita: $38 (1997); City property taxes per capita: $38 (1997).
Education: High school graduation rate: 90.1% (2000); College graduation rate: 15.6% (2000).
Housing: Homeownership rate: 89.4% (2000); Median home value: $126,700 (2000); Median rent: $413 per month (2000); Median age of housing: 33 years (2000).
Transportation: Commute to work: 87.1% car, 0.0% public transportation, 2.7% walk, 9.7% work from home (2000); Travel time to work: 41.7% less than 15 minutes, 30.6% 15 to 30 minutes, 9.0% 30 to 45 minutes, 6.3% 45 to 60 minutes, 12.5% 60 minutes or more (2000)

DUNDAS (city). Covers a land area of 1.535 square miles and a water area of 0 square miles. Located at 44.42° N. Lat.; 93.20° W. Long. Elevation is 958 feet.
History: Dundas was the location of the flour mills of the Archibald brothers, who were the first to use a new method for making flour that had been developed by a French family named La Croix.
Population: 547 (2000); Race: 97.9% White, 2.1% Black, 0.0% Asian, 0.0% American Indian and Alaska Native, 0.6% Hispanic of any race, 0.0% two or more races (2000); Density: 356.4 persons per square mile (2000); Age: 23.6% under 18, 9.1% over 64 (2000); Marriage status: 25.5% never married, 58.6% now married, 5.1% widowed, 10.7% divorced (2000); Foreign born: 0.6% (2000); Ancestry (includes multiple ancestries): 35.8% German, 19.2% Norwegian, 17.0% Irish, 11.1% Czech, 9.8% Swedish (2000).
Economy: Single-family building permits issued: 15 (2001) / 9 (2000); Multi-family building permits issued: 0 (2001) / 18 (2000); Employment by occupation: 10.2% management, 11.7% professional, 21.3% services, 22.2% sales, 2.1% farming, 15.9% construction, 16.5% production (2000).
Income: Per capita income: $20,316 (2000); Median household income: $51,429 (2000); Poverty rate: 7.8% (2000).
Taxes: Total city taxes per capita: $499 (1997); City property taxes per capita: $476 (1997).
Education: High school graduation rate: 87.8% (2000); College graduation rate: 14.1% (2000).

School District(s)

Peaks-Faribault (09-12)
2000 Enrollment: 31 507-645-0994
Housing: Homeownership rate: 88.5% (2000); Median home value: $112,300 (2000); Median rent: $511 per month (2000); Median age of housing: 38 years (2000).
Transportation: Commute to work: 97.9% car, 0.0% public transportation, 0.6% walk, 0.0% work from home (2000); Travel time to work: 58.3% less than 15 minutes, 19.3% 15 to 30 minutes, 16.0% 30 to 45 minutes, 3.0% 45 to 60 minutes, 3.3% 60 minutes or more (2000)

ERIN (township). Covers a land area of 34.796 square miles and a water area of 1.369 square miles. Located at 44.42° N. Lat.; 93.46° W. Long.
Population: 797 (2000); Race: 97.5% White, 0.0% Black, 0.5% Asian, 0.5% American Indian and Alaska Native, 0.0% Hispanic of any race, 1.5% two or more races (2000); Density: 22.9 persons per square mile (2000); Age: 27.0% under 18, 12.9% over 64 (2000); Marriage status: 27.5% never married, 63.4% now married, 2.0% widowed, 7.1% divorced (2000); Foreign born: 0.9% (2000); Ancestry (includes multiple ancestries): 39.8% German, 21.1% Czech, 11.6% Irish, 9.0% Czechoslovakian, 8.1% Swedish (2000).
Economy: Employment by occupation: 21.0% management, 12.3% professional, 6.0% services, 21.4% sales, 1.9% farming, 12.3% construction, 25.1% production (2000).
Income: Per capita income: $23,495 (2000); Median household income: $60,625 (2000); Poverty rate: 4.1% (2000).

Taxes: Total city taxes per capita: $54 (1997); City property taxes per capita: $54 (1997).
Education: High school graduation rate: 82.1% (2000); College graduation rate: 16.8% (2000).
Housing: Homeownership rate: 93.5% (2000); Median home value: $175,000 (2000); Median rent: $425 per month (2000); Median age of housing: 30 years (2000).
Transportation: Commute to work: 86.8% car, 0.0% public transportation, 1.1% walk, 11.5% work from home (2000); Travel time to work: 14.5% less than 15 minutes, 38.2% 15 to 30 minutes, 23.3% 30 to 45 minutes, 13.7% 45 to 60 minutes, 10.3% 60 minutes or more (2000)

FARIBAULT (city). Covers a land area of 12.657 square miles and a water area of 0.204 square miles. Located at 44.29° N. Lat.; 93.27° W. Long. Elevation is 971 feet.
History: Faribault was named for Alexander Faribault (1806-1882), who established one of his six trading posts here in 1826. French-Canadian trappers and traders joined Faribault at the post, followed by New Englanders who settled here. Episcopal clergyman Henry Benjamin Whipple came to Faribault in 1860 and established a mission and church. Faribault called itself the "Nation's Peony Capital" for the peonies grown here.
Population: 20,818 (2000); Race: 89.8% White, 2.5% Black, 1.9% Asian, 0.6% American Indian and Alaska Native, 8.6% Hispanic of any race, 2.0% two or more races (2000); Density: 1,644.8 persons per square mile (2000); Age: 26.0% under 18, 13.4% over 64 (2000); Marriage status: 29.4% never married, 52.5% now married, 7.2% widowed, 10.9% divorced (2000); Foreign born: 7.0% (2000); Ancestry (includes multiple ancestries): 35.4% German, 14.8% Norwegian, 12.7% Other groups, 11.4% Irish, 6.1% French (except Basque) (2000).
Vital Statistics: Birth rate: 137.4 per 10,000 population (1998)
Economy: Single-family building permits issued: 95 (2001) / 79 (2000); Multi-family building permits issued: 23 (2001) / 40 (2000); Employment by occupation: 9.6% management, 15.2% professional, 18.7% services, 21.6% sales, 0.8% farming, 9.7% construction, 24.3% production (2000).
Income: Per capita income: $18,610 (2000); Median household income: $40,865 (2000); Poverty rate: 9.0% (2000).
Taxes: Total city taxes per capita: $146 (2000); City property taxes per capita: $125 (2000).
Education: High school graduation rate: 81.3% (2000); College graduation rate: 14.3% (2000).

School District(s)

Academy for the Blind (N -N)
2000 Enrollment: n/a 507-332-3226
Academy for the Deaf (N -N)
2000 Enrollment: n/a 507-332-3363
Faribault (PK-12)
2000 Enrollment: 4,078 507-333-6000
Minnesota State Academies (PK-12)
2000 Enrollment: 198

Two-year College(s)

South Central Technical College-Faribault (Public)
2001 Enrollment: n/a 507-334-3965
2001 Tuition: In-state $2,250; Out-of-state $4,500

Housing: Homeownership rate: 73.1% (2000); Median home value: $105,600 (2000); Median rent: $444 per month (2000); Median age of housing: 38 years (2000).
Hospitals: District One Hospital (99 beds)
Newspapers: Faribault Daily News (6 x week)
Transportation: Commute to work: 92.0% car, 1.1% public transportation, 2.9% walk, 2.0% work from home (2000); Travel time to work: 59.2% less than 15 minutes, 20.4% 15 to 30 minutes, 8.6% 30 to 45 minutes, 6.3% 45 to 60 minutes, 5.6% 60 minutes or more (2000)
Airports: Faribault Municipal
Additional Information Contacts
Faribault Chamber of Commerce 507-334-4381

FOREST (township). Covers a land area of 32.717 square miles and a water area of 3.001 square miles. Located at 44.41° N. Lat.; 93.34° W. Long.
Population: 1,136 (2000); Race: 99.3% White, 0.0% Black, 0.0% Asian, 0.4% American Indian and Alaska Native, 2.8% Hispanic of any race, 0.3% two or more races (2000); Density: 34.7 persons per square mile (2000); Age: 28.7% under 18, 7.6% over 64 (2000); Marriage status: 19.5% never married, 69.7% now married, 2.6% widowed, 8.2% divorced (2000); Foreign born: 1.2% (2000); Ancestry (includes multiple ancestries): 38.6% German, 17.4% Norwegian, 15.5% Irish, 10.4% Swedish, 8.8% Czech (2000).
Economy: Employment by occupation: 18.0% management, 14.8% professional, 12.9% services, 23.5% sales, 1.8% farming, 11.4% construction, 17.6% production (2000).
Income: Per capita income: $24,401 (2000); Median household income: $62,443 (2000); Poverty rate: 2.2% (2000).
Taxes: Total city taxes per capita: $53 (1997); City property taxes per capita: $53 (1997).
Education: High school graduation rate: 92.5% (2000); College graduation rate: 21.3% (2000).
Housing: Homeownership rate: 91.9% (2000); Median home value: $183,600 (2000); Median rent: $375 per month (2000); Median age of housing: 27 years (2000).
Transportation: Commute to work: 90.1% car, 0.0% public transportation, 2.9% walk, 7.0% work from home (2000); Travel time to work: 15.4% less than 15 minutes, 36.6% 15 to 30 minutes, 26.1% 30 to 45 minutes, 14.6% 45 to 60 minutes, 7.2% 60 minutes or more (2000)

LONSDALE (city). Covers a land area of 1.323 square miles and a water area of 0.012 square miles. Located at 44.48° N. Lat.; 93.43° W. Long. Elevation is 1,094 feet.
Population: 1,491 (2000); Race: 98.9% White, 0.4% Black, 0.0% Asian, 0.1% American Indian and Alaska Native, 0.4% Hispanic of any race, 0.6% two or more races (2000); Density: 1,127.3 persons per square mile (2000); Age: 27.7% under 18, 11.6% over 64 (2000); Marriage status: 25.8% never married, 60.8% now married, 5.9% widowed, 7.4% divorced (2000); Foreign born: 0.4% (2000); Ancestry (includes multiple ancestries): 32.9% German, 29.9% Czech, 11.8% Norwegian, 10.5% Irish, 9.0% Czechoslovakian (2000).
Economy: Grain; livestock; dairying. Manufacturing: die-cutting and laminating, light manufacturing. Single-family building permits issued: 59 (2001) / 34 (2000); Multi-family building permits issued: 6 (2001) / 2 (2000); Employment by occupation: 8.9% management, 13.3% professional, 12.7% services, 24.0% sales, 0.4% farming, 17.3% construction, 23.4% production (2000).
Income: Per capita income: $20,368 (2000); Median household income: $50,054 (2000); Poverty rate: 6.1% (2000).
Taxes: Total city taxes per capita: $104 (1997); City property taxes per capita: $92 (1997).
Education: High school graduation rate: 86.1% (2000); College graduation rate: 9.8% (2000).
Housing: Homeownership rate: 86.1% (2000); Median home value: $113,100 (2000); Median rent: $375 per month (2000); Median age of housing: 27 years (2000).
Transportation: Commute to work: 93.7% car, 0.0% public transportation, 2.8% walk, 3.2% work from home (2000); Travel time to work: 20.9% less than 15 minutes, 33.2% 15 to 30 minutes, 22.7% 30 to 45 minutes, 15.8% 45 to 60 minutes, 7.4% 60 minutes or more (2000)

MORRISTOWN (city). Covers a land area of 0.868 square miles and a water area of 0.045 square miles. Located at 44.22° N. Lat.; 93.44° W. Long. Elevation is 996 feet.
Population: 981 (2000); Race: 96.3% White, 0.0% Black, 0.2% Asian, 0.4% American Indian and Alaska Native, 9.4% Hispanic of any race, 0.6% two or more races (2000); Density: 1,130.4 persons per square mile (2000); Age: 30.2% under 18, 13.4% over 64 (2000); Marriage status: 24.7% never married, 56.6% now married, 8.8% widowed, 9.8% divorced (2000); Foreign born: 2.6% (2000); Ancestry (includes multiple ancestries): 44.4% German, 14.4% Norwegian, 12.5% Other groups, 7.6% English, 6.9% Irish (2000).
Economy: Single-family building permits issued: 2 (2001) / 6 (2000); Multi-family building permits issued: 0 (2001) / 0 (2000); Employment by occupation: 10.6% management, 11.5% professional, 14.7% services, 22.9% sales, 0.5% farming, 12.4% construction, 27.4% production (2000).
Income: Per capita income: $15,762 (2000); Median household income: $36,538 (2000); Poverty rate: 10.8% (2000).
Taxes: Total city taxes per capita: $90 (1997); City property taxes per capita: $80 (1997).
Education: High school graduation rate: 76.0% (2000); College graduation rate: 11.1% (2000).
Housing: Homeownership rate: 85.2% (2000); Median home value: $81,600 (2000); Median rent: $444 per month (2000); Median age of housing: 36 years (2000).
Transportation: Commute to work: 91.7% car, 0.0% public transportation, 3.7% walk, 3.2% work from home (2000); Travel time to work: 22.0% less than 15 minutes, 51.4% 15 to 30 minutes, 13.3% 30 to 45 minutes, 5.7% 45 to 60 minutes, 7.6% 60 minutes or more (2000)

MORRISTOWN (township). Covers a land area of 33.527 square miles and a water area of 1.581 square miles. Located at 44.24° N. Lat.; 93.47° W. Long. Elevation is 996 feet.
Population: 665 (2000); Race: 100.0% White, 0.0% Black, 0.0% Asian, 0.0% American Indian and Alaska Native, 0.9% Hispanic of any race, 0.0% two or more races (2000); Density: 19.8 persons per square mile (2000); Age: 28.9% under 18, 15.3% over 64 (2000); Marriage status: 18.2% never married, 72.4% now married, 5.3% widowed, 4.1% divorced (2000); Foreign born: 0.0% (2000); Ancestry (includes multiple ancestries): 66.8% German, 14.7% Norwegian, 7.7% Irish, 6.8% French (except Basque), 3.6% English (2000).
Economy: Grain, soybeans; livestock; dairying. Employment by occupation: 15.3% management, 18.0% professional, 11.5% services, 20.8% sales, 3.6% farming, 12.3% construction, 18.6% production (2000).
Income: Per capita income: $20,340 (2000); Median household income: $51,932 (2000); Poverty rate: 4.9% (2000).
Taxes: Total city taxes per capita: $64 (1997); City property taxes per capita: $64 (1997).
Education: High school graduation rate: 87.1% (2000); College graduation rate: 18.3% (2000).
Housing: Homeownership rate: 89.5% (2000); Median home value: $129,800 (2000); Median rent: $467 per month (2000); Median age of housing: 43 years (2000).
Transportation: Commute to work: 85.0% car, 0.6% public transportation, 3.0% walk, 11.1% work from home (2000); Travel time to work: 22.1% less than 15 minutes, 48.9% 15 to 30 minutes, 15.6% 30 to 45 minutes, 2.5% 45 to 60 minutes, 10.9% 60 minutes or more (2000)

NERSTRAND (city). Covers a land area of 1.418 square miles and a water area of 0 square miles. Located at 44.34° N. Lat.; 93.06° W. Long. Elevation is 1,183 feet.
History: Holds annual "Ring Bologna Days."
Population: 233 (2000); Race: 99.2% White, 0.0% Black, 0.8% Asian, 0.0% American Indian and Alaska Native, 3.0% Hispanic of any race, 0.0% two or more races (2000); Density: 164.3 persons per square mile (2000); Age: 32.2% under 18, 17.4% over 64 (2000); Marriage status: 12.7% never married, 77.1% now married, 3.6% widowed, 6.6% divorced (2000); Foreign born: 0.8% (2000); Ancestry (includes multiple ancestries): 47.0% German, 27.5% Norwegian, 16.9% Swedish, 16.5% Irish, 4.2% Scandinavian (2000).
Economy: Dairying; poultry; grain, soybeans; light manufacturing. Single-family building permits issued: 0 (2001) / 0 (2000); Multi-family building permits issued: 0 (2001) / 0 (2000); Employment by occupation: 8.7% management, 15.4% professional, 10.6% services, 25.0% sales, 0.0% farming, 14.4% construction, 26.0% production (2000).
Income: Per capita income: $15,362 (2000); Median household income: $41,500 (2000); Poverty rate: 0.4% (2000).
Taxes: Total city taxes per capita: $119 (1997); City property taxes per capita: $119 (1997).
Education: High school graduation rate: 87.2% (2000); College graduation rate: 20.3% (2000).

School District(s)

Nerstrand Charter School (KG-05)
2000 Enrollment: 152 507-333-6850
Housing: Homeownership rate: 92.3% (2000); Median home value: $98,500 (2000); Median rent: $538 per month (2000); Median age of housing: 60+ years (2000).
Transportation: Commute to work: 90.4% car, 0.0% public transportation, 4.8% walk, 4.8% work from home (2000); Travel time to work: 13.1% less than 15 minutes, 58.6% 15 to 30 minutes, 15.2% 30 to 45 minutes, 6.1% 45 to 60 minutes, 7.1% 60 minutes or more (2000)

NORTHFIELD (city). Covers a land area of 6.993 square miles and a water area of 0.029 square miles. Located at 44.45° N. Lat.; 93.16° W. Long. Elevation is 915 feet.
History: Northfield was known as the Holstein Capital of America in the early 1900's, when the first Holstein breeders' club in the country was organized here in 1903. This was the location of the Schilling and Miller farms, which produced Spring Brooke Bess Burke, several times national butterfat champion. In 1876, outlaw Jesse James and his gang attempted to hold up the First National Bank in Northfield. Though several members of the gang were shot or apprehended, the James brothers escaped.
Population: 17,147 (2000); Race: 91.9% White, 0.9% Black, 2.7% Asian, 0.9% American Indian and Alaska Native, 5.6% Hispanic of any race, 1.7% two or more races (2000); Density: 2,452.2 persons per square mile (2000); Age: 20.0% under 18, 10.5% over 64 (2000); Marriage status: 39.5% never married, 49.4% now married, 4.9% widowed, 6.2% divorced (2000); Foreign born: 6.2% (2000); Ancestry (includes multiple ancestries): 32.4% German, 20.0% Norwegian, 10.7% Irish, 10.5% English, 10.5% Other groups (2000).
Vital Statistics: Birth rate: 112.6 per 10,000 population (1998)
Economy: Single-family building permits issued: 142 (2001) / 133 (2000); Multi-family building permits issued: 0 (2001) / 4 (2000); Employment by occupation: 10.4% management, 28.2% professional, 14.6% services, 27.5% sales, 0.7% farming, 6.0% construction, 12.6% production (2000).
Income: Per capita income: $18,619 (2000); Median household income: $49,972 (2000); Poverty rate: 7.2% (2000).
Taxes: Total city taxes per capita: $221 (2000); City property taxes per capita: $187 (2000).
Education: High school graduation rate: 87.4% (2000); College graduation rate: 43.0% (2000).

School District(s)

Northfield (PK-12)
2000 Enrollment: 3,861 507-663-0629
Village School of Northfield (KG-11)
2000 Enrollment: 67 507-663-8990

Four-year College(s)

Carleton College (Private, Not-for-profit)
2001 Enrollment: 1,948 507-646-4000
2001 Tuition: In-state $25,371; Out-of-state $25,371
Saint Olaf College (Private, Not-for-profit, Evangelical Lutheran Church)
2001 Enrollment: 3,011 507-646-2222
2001 Tuition: In-state $21,280; Out-of-state $21,280
Housing: Homeownership rate: 68.8% (2000); Median home value: $142,900 (2000); Median rent: $502 per month (2000); Median age of housing: 25 years (2000).
Hospitals: Northfield Hospital (37 beds)
Safety: Violent crime rate: 11.5 per 10,000 population; Property crime rate: 305.8 per 10,000 population (2001).
Newspapers: Northfield News (2 x week); Northfield Shopper (1 x week)
Transportation: Commute to work: 65.4% car, 0.8% public transportation, 26.3% walk, 5.5% work from home (2000); Travel time to work: 66.2% less than 15 minutes, 15.3% 15 to 30 minutes, 7.9% 30 to 45 minutes, 6.3% 45 to 60 minutes, 4.3% 60 minutes or more (2000)
Additional Information Contacts
Northfield Chamber of Commerce.............................. 507-645-5604

NORTHFIELD (township). Covers a land area of 38.910 square miles and a water area of 0 square miles. Located at 44.41° N. Lat.; 93.09° W. Long. Elevation is 915 feet.
History: On Sept. 7, 1876, Jesse and Frank James and their bandit gang attempted a bank robbery here, which failed and resulted in the deaths of two Northfield citizens. Each September, Northfield holds a festival that reenacts the robbery attempt. Carleton College and St. Olaf College are in the city. Historical Society Museum to southeast. Incorporated 1875.
Population: 780 (2000); Race: 98.4% White, 0.0% Black, 1.0% Asian, 0.6% American Indian and Alaska Native, 0.6% Hispanic of any race, 0.0% two or more races (2000); Density: 20.0 persons per square mile (2000); Age: 31.8% under 18, 8.1% over 64 (2000); Marriage status: 21.8% never married, 71.1% now married, 3.4% widowed, 3.6% divorced (2000); Foreign born: 1.4% (2000); Ancestry (includes multiple ancestries): 37.7% German, 33.6% Norwegian, 9.7% Irish, 9.2% Swedish, 8.7% English (2000).
Economy: Railroad junction and trade center for farming region: corn, oats, soybeans, livestock, poultry and dairying. Manufacturing includes printed circuit boards, toys, feeds and seeds and cereals. Carleton College, St. Olaf College and the Laura Baker School for mentally challenged children are in the city. Employment by occupation: 14.5% management, 19.2% professional, 13.6% services, 22.9% sales, 1.6% farming, 12.2% construction, 16.1% production (2000).
Income: Per capita income: $23,650 (2000); Median household income: $62,500 (2000); Poverty rate: 2.5% (2000).
Taxes: Total city taxes per capita: $171 (2000); City property taxes per capita: $171 (2000).
Education: High school graduation rate: 93.9% (2000); College graduation rate: 31.8% (2000).
Housing: Homeownership rate: 87.4% (2000); Median home value: $162,500 (2000); Median rent: $525 per month (2000); Median age of housing: 30 years (2000).
Transportation: Commute to work: 90.3% car, 0.0% public transportation, 1.2% walk, 7.9% work from home (2000); Travel time to work: 47.6% less than 15 minutes, 30.1% 15 to 30 minutes, 7.5% 30 to 45 minutes, 8.3% 45 to 60 minutes, 6.5% 60 minutes or more (2000)

RICHLAND (township). Covers a land area of 36.071 square miles and a water area of 0 square miles. Located at 44.24° N. Lat.; 93.09° W. Long.
Population: 471 (2000); Race: 99.4% White, 0.0% Black, 0.0% Asian, 0.0% American Indian and Alaska Native, 0.4% Hispanic of any race, 0.0% two or more races (2000); Density: 13.1 persons per square mile (2000); Age: 32.4% under 18, 10.4% over 64 (2000); Marriage status: 25.3% never married, 66.9% now married, 4.1% widowed, 3.6% divorced (2000); Foreign born: 0.8% (2000); Ancestry (includes multiple ancestries): 43.2% German, 21.6% Norwegian, 11.2% Irish, 8.9% English, 5.8% United States or American (2000).
Economy: Employment by occupation: 23.7% management, 11.8% professional, 16.0% services, 19.1% sales, 3.1% farming, 8.8% construction, 17.6% production (2000).
Income: Per capita income: $18,956 (2000); Median household income: $59,911 (2000); Poverty rate: 2.7% (2000).
Taxes: Total city taxes per capita: $72 (1997); City property taxes per capita: $72 (1997).
Education: High school graduation rate: 89.7% (2000); College graduation rate: 16.6% (2000).
Housing: Homeownership rate: 89.4% (2000); Median home value: $123,600 (2000); Median rent: $363 per month (2000); Median age of housing: 47 years (2000).
Transportation: Commute to work: 82.4% car, 0.4% public transportation, 0.0% walk, 15.3% work from home (2000); Travel time to work: 15.8% less than 15 minutes, 58.8% 15 to 30 minutes, 10.9% 30 to 45 minutes, 2.3% 45 to 60 minutes, 12.2% 60 minutes or more (2000)

SHIELDSVILLE (township). Covers a land area of 32.493 square miles and a water area of 4.052 square miles. Located at 44.32° N. Lat.; 93.45° W. Long.
Population: 1,153 (2000); Race: 98.9% White, 0.9% Black, 0.0% Asian, 0.2% American Indian and Alaska Native, 0.0% Hispanic of any race, 0.0% two or more races (2000); Density: 35.5 persons per square mile (2000); Age: 23.1% under 18, 11.9% over 64 (2000); Marriage status: 22.1% never married, 66.3% now married, 4.0% widowed, 7.5% divorced (2000); Foreign born: 0.4% (2000); Ancestry (includes multiple ancestries): 40.5% German, 14.1% Irish, 13.1% Norwegian, 9.2% French (except Basque), 8.3% Czech (2000).
Economy: Employment by occupation: 15.6% management, 12.8% professional, 14.3% services, 21.5% sales, 2.6% farming, 14.5% construction, 18.8% production (2000).
Income: Per capita income: $21,908 (2000); Median household income: $56,250 (2000); Poverty rate: 6.8% (2000).
Taxes: Total city taxes per capita: $52 (1997); City property taxes per capita: $52 (1997).
Education: High school graduation rate: 89.5% (2000); College graduation rate: 13.3% (2000).
Housing: Homeownership rate: 91.9% (2000); Median home value: $156,100 (2000); Median rent: $327 per month (2000); Median age of housing: 25 years (2000).
Transportation: Commute to work: 93.7% car, 0.0% public transportation, 1.1% walk, 4.3% work from home (2000); Travel time to work: 11.9% less than 15 minutes, 48.3% 15 to 30 minutes, 17.0% 30 to 45 minutes, 12.9% 45 to 60 minutes, 9.9% 60 minutes or more (2000)

WALCOTT (township). Covers a land area of 33.680 square miles and a water area of 0.022 square miles. Located at 44.23° N. Lat.; 93.24° W. Long. Elevation is 1,190 feet.
Population: 984 (2000); Race: 98.2% White, 0.0% Black, 0.7% Asian, 0.0% American Indian and Alaska Native, 1.1% Hispanic of any race, 0.4% two or more races (2000); Density: 29.2 persons per square mile (2000); Age: 29.1% under 18, 11.0% over 64 (2000); Marriage status: 23.7% never married, 68.4% now married, 3.6% widowed, 4.3% divorced (2000); Foreign born: 1.7% (2000); Ancestry (includes multiple ancestries): 49.2% German, 15.9% Irish, 14.1% Norwegian, 10.8% French (except Basque), 8.3% Dutch (2000).
Economy: Employment by occupation: 15.8% management, 18.1% professional, 13.8% services, 17.2% sales, 1.3% farming, 11.8% construction, 22.0% production (2000).
Income: Per capita income: $20,274 (2000); Median household income: $58,594 (2000); Poverty rate: 4.0% (2000).
Taxes: Total city taxes per capita: $44 (1997); City property taxes per capita: $44 (1997).
Education: High school graduation rate: 83.8% (2000); College graduation rate: 15.1% (2000).
Housing: Homeownership rate: 91.9% (2000); Median home value: $130,700 (2000); Median rent: $383 per month (2000); Median age of housing: 36 years (2000).
Transportation: Commute to work: 89.0% car, 0.0% public transportation, 1.1% walk, 9.7% work from home (2000); Travel time to work: 26.2% less than 15 minutes, 47.4% 15 to 30 minutes, 9.8% 30 to 45 minutes, 7.1% 45 to 60 minutes, 9.6% 60 minutes or more (2000)

WARSAW (township). Covers a land area of 32.451 square miles and a water area of 2.566 square miles. Located at 44.24° N. Lat.; 93.35° W. Long.
Population: 1,433 (2000); Race: 99.3% White, 0.0% Black, 0.0% Asian, 0.3% American Indian and Alaska Native, 1.3% Hispanic of any race, 0.0% two or more races (2000); Density: 44.2 persons per square mile (2000); Age: 27.7% under 18, 10.1% over 64 (2000); Marriage status: 23.8% never married, 66.0% now married, 4.0% widowed, 6.2% divorced (2000); Foreign born: 0.8% (2000); Ancestry (includes multiple ancestries): 55.0% German, 16.9% Irish, 14.5% Norwegian, 7.1% French (except Basque), 4.8% Swedish (2000).
Economy: Employment by occupation: 14.7% management, 15.1% professional, 13.2% services, 22.8% sales, 0.7% farming, 11.0% construction, 22.5% production (2000).
Income: Per capita income: $22,119 (2000); Median household income: $60,185 (2000); Poverty rate: 4.3% (2000).
Taxes: Total city taxes per capita: $48 (1997); City property taxes per capita: $48 (1997).
Education: High school graduation rate: 89.3% (2000); College graduation rate: 14.7% (2000).
Housing: Homeownership rate: 92.4% (2000); Median home value: $133,800 (2000); Median rent: $460 per month (2000); Median age of housing: 31 years (2000).
Transportation: Commute to work: 91.6% car, 0.0% public transportation, 1.4% walk, 6.1% work from home (2000); Travel time to work: 34.4% less than 15 minutes, 38.6% 15 to 30 minutes, 14.5% 30 to 45 minutes, 7.5% 45 to 60 minutes, 5.0% 60 minutes or more (2000)

WEBSTER (township). Covers a land area of 35.142 square miles and a water area of 0.571 square miles. Located at 44.51° N. Lat.; 93.33° W. Long.
Population: 1,825 (2000); Race: 99.0% White, 0.0% Black, 0.2% Asian, 0.2% American Indian and Alaska Native, 1.1% Hispanic of any race, 0.5% two or more races (2000); Density: 51.9 persons per square mile (2000); Age: 30.0% under 18, 6.5% over 64 (2000); Marriage status: 21.6% never married, 69.9% now married, 3.1% widowed, 5.4% divorced (2000); Foreign born: 1.3% (2000); Ancestry (includes multiple ancestries): 32.8% German, 20.4% Norwegian, 11.7% Czech, 9.4% Irish, 8.6% Swedish (2000).
Economy: Employment by occupation: 14.0% management, 13.1% professional, 13.8% services, 22.6% sales, 1.2% farming, 18.8% construction, 16.5% production (2000).
Income: Per capita income: $23,040 (2000); Median household income: $62,961 (2000); Poverty rate: 3.3% (2000).
Taxes: Total city taxes per capita: $118 (2000); City property taxes per capita: $117 (2000).
Education: High school graduation rate: 89.8% (2000); College graduation rate: 21.8% (2000).
Housing: Homeownership rate: 94.0% (2000); Median home value: $177,600 (2000); Median rent: $408 per month (2000); Median age of housing: 23 years (2000).
Transportation: Commute to work: 90.6% car, 1.4% public transportation, 1.9% walk, 5.5% work from home (2000); Travel time to work: 15.1% less than 15 minutes, 41.4% 15 to 30 minutes, 29.5% 30 to 45 minutes, 8.6% 45 to 60 minutes, 5.4% 60 minutes or more (2000)

WELLS (township). Covers a land area of 28.035 square miles and a water area of 3.950 square miles. Located at 44.32° N. Lat.; 93.33° W. Long.
Population: 1,743 (2000); Race: 98.4% White, 0.0% Black, 0.0% Asian, 0.4% American Indian and Alaska Native, 2.6% Hispanic of any race, 0.4% two or more races (2000); Density: 62.2 persons per square mile (2000); Age: 23.9% under 18, 11.2% over 64 (2000); Marriage status: 21.5% never married, 67.8% now married, 4.5% widowed, 6.1% divorced (2000); Foreign born: 0.9% (2000); Ancestry (includes multiple ancestries): 47.4% German, 15.0% Irish, 13.8% Norwegian, 10.9% French (except Basque), 8.9% Czech (2000).
Economy: Employment by occupation: 12.9% management, 16.2% professional, 12.7% services, 24.2% sales, 1.1% farming, 14.1% construction, 18.9% production (2000).
Income: Per capita income: $24,714 (2000); Median household income: $52,155 (2000); Poverty rate: 4.6% (2000).

Taxes: Total city taxes per capita: $65 (1997); City property taxes per capita: $65 (1997).
Education: High school graduation rate: 86.8% (2000); College graduation rate: 14.1% (2000).
Housing: Homeownership rate: 89.0% (2000); Median home value: $145,200 (2000); Median rent: $494 per month (2000); Median age of housing: 32 years (2000).
Transportation: Commute to work: 93.4% car, 0.0% public transportation, 1.6% walk, 3.8% work from home (2000); Travel time to work: 36.7% less than 15 minutes, 36.0% 15 to 30 minutes, 13.5% 30 to 45 minutes, 6.8% 45 to 60 minutes, 7.0% 60 minutes or more (2000)

WHEATLAND (township). Covers a land area of 33.782 square miles and a water area of 0.871 square miles. Located at 44.48° N. Lat.; 93.45° W. Long.
Population: 1,358 (2000); Race: 97.7% White, 0.0% Black, 0.3% Asian, 0.4% American Indian and Alaska Native, 0.7% Hispanic of any race, 1.6% two or more races (2000); Density: 40.2 persons per square mile (2000); Age: 33.9% under 18, 8.3% over 64 (2000); Marriage status: 24.5% never married, 66.4% now married, 3.1% widowed, 6.0% divorced (2000); Foreign born: 0.8% (2000); Ancestry (includes multiple ancestries): 41.4% German, 28.8% Czech, 10.4% Norwegian, 8.8% Czechoslovakian, 8.4% Irish (2000).
Economy: Employment by occupation: 17.0% management, 8.7% professional, 9.3% services, 23.5% sales, 2.1% farming, 17.0% construction, 22.5% production (2000).
Income: Per capita income: $20,402 (2000); Median household income: $54,286 (2000); Poverty rate: 3.6% (2000).
Taxes: Total city taxes per capita: $44 (1997); City property taxes per capita: $44 (1997).
Education: High school graduation rate: 87.8% (2000); College graduation rate: 12.3% (2000).
Housing: Homeownership rate: 93.9% (2000); Median home value: $136,200 (2000); Median rent: $600 per month (2000); Median age of housing: 29 years (2000).
Transportation: Commute to work: 84.8% car, 0.0% public transportation, 1.7% walk, 12.1% work from home (2000); Travel time to work: 21.7% less than 15 minutes, 29.9% 15 to 30 minutes, 30.1% 30 to 45 minutes, 13.1% 45 to 60 minutes, 5.2% 60 minutes or more (2000)

WHEELING (township). Covers a land area of 34.619 square miles and a water area of 0 square miles. Located at 44.32° N. Lat.; 93.09° W. Long.
Population: 541 (2000); Race: 99.4% White, 0.0% Black, 0.0% Asian, 0.0% American Indian and Alaska Native, 0.0% Hispanic of any race, 0.6% two or more races (2000); Density: 15.6 persons per square mile (2000); Age: 32.3% under 18, 6.6% over 64 (2000); Marriage status: 24.9% never married, 67.0% now married, 4.7% widowed, 3.4% divorced (2000); Foreign born: 0.6% (2000); Ancestry (includes multiple ancestries): 53.7% German, 29.0% Norwegian, 7.6% Czech, 7.6% Irish, 6.8% French (except Basque) (2000).
Economy: Employment by occupation: 18.6% management, 19.9% professional, 12.6% services, 18.9% sales, 3.3% farming, 10.3% construction, 16.3% production (2000).
Income: Per capita income: $17,944 (2000); Median household income: $48,056 (2000); Poverty rate: 5.7% (2000).
Taxes: Total city taxes per capita: $132 (1997); City property taxes per capita: $132 (1997).
Education: High school graduation rate: 90.9% (2000); College graduation rate: 22.6% (2000).
Housing: Homeownership rate: 86.9% (2000); Median home value: $144,400 (2000); Median rent: $610 per month (2000); Median age of housing: 60+ years (2000).
Transportation: Commute to work: 85.8% car, 0.0% public transportation, 0.3% walk, 10.5% work from home (2000); Travel time to work: 22.3% less than 15 minutes, 55.5% 15 to 30 minutes, 10.2% 30 to 45 minutes, 3.8% 45 to 60 minutes, 8.3% 60 minutes or more (2000)

Rock County

Located in southwestern Minnesota; bounded on the west by South Dakota, and on the south by Iowa; drained by the Rock River. Covers a land area of 482.60 square miles, a water area of 0.20 square miles, and is located in the Central Time Zone. The county government was organized in 1857. County seat is Luverne.

Weather Station: Luverne — Elevation: 1,499 feet

	Jan	Feb	Mar	Apr	May	Jun	Jul	Aug	Sep	Oct	Nov	Dec
High	24	31	43	59	72	81	85	83	75	62	41	28
Low	4	11	23	34	46	57	61	58	49	36	22	10
Precip	0.6	0.7	2.2	2.6	3.3	4.3	3.6	3.3	2.7	2.3	1.7	0.8
Snow	10.0	6.7	9.5	2.0	tr	0.0	0.0	0.0	tr	0.9	7.5	8.1

High and Low temperatures in degrees Fahrenheit; Precipitation and Snow in inches

Population: 9,721 (2000); Race: 97.1% White, 1.3% Black, 0.4% Asian, 0.4% American Indian and Alaska Native, 0.7% Hispanic of any race, 0.5% two or more races (2000); Density: 20.1 persons per square mile (2000); Age: 26.3% under 18, 20.5% over 64 (2000).
Religion: Five largest groups: 19.7% Evangelical Lutheran Church in America, 14.4% Catholic Church, 12.4% Reformed Church in America, 10.6% Lutheran Church—Missouri Synod, 8.8% Presbyterian Church (U.S.A.) (2000).
Economy: Unemployment rate: 1.9% (11/2002); Total civilian labor force: 4,564 (11/2002); Leading industries: 17.2% retail trade; 15.8% health care and social assistance; 14.7% finance & insurance (2000); Companies that employ more than 1,000 persons: 0 (2000); Companies that employ more than 100 persons: 6 (2000); Farms: 704 totaling 280,715 acres (1997); Minority business ownership rate: 0.0% (1997); Women business ownership rate: 47.5% (1997); Retail sales per capita: $8,667 (1997). Single-family building permits issued: 15 (2001) / 14 (2000); Multi-family building permits issued: 4 (2001) / 16 (2000).
Income: Per capita income: $17,411 (2000); Median household income: $38,102 (2000); Poverty rate: 8.0% (2000); Bankruptcy rate: 1.65% (2001).
Taxes: Total county taxes per capita: $238 (1997); County property taxes per capita: $238 (1997).
Education: High school graduation rate: 81.5% (2000); College graduation rate: 15.4% (2000).
Housing: Homeownership rate: 78.0% (2000); Median home value: $68,500 (2000); Median rent: $308 per month (2000); Median age of housing: 48 years (2000).
Health: Birth rate: 116.2 per 10,000 population (1998); Age adjusted death rate: 77.0 per 10,000 population (1999); Age adjusted cancer mortality rate: 135.2 (Unreliable figure as per CDC) deaths per 100,000 population (1999). Number of physicians: 13.4 per 10,000 population (1999); Number of hospital beds: 29.8 per 10,000 population (1999).
Elections: 2000 Presidential election results: 41.5% Gore, 55.3% Bush, 2.3% Nader, 0.4% Buchanan
National and State Parks: Blue Mounds State Park
Additional Information Contacts
Rock County Government Offices 507-283-5060
Luverne Chamber of Commerce 507-283-4061

Rock County Communities

BATTLE PLAIN (township). Covers a land area of 36.318 square miles and a water area of 0.015 square miles. Located at 43.80° N. Lat.; 96.11° W. Long.
Population: 233 (2000); Race: 100.0% White, 0.0% Black, 0.0% Asian, 0.0% American Indian and Alaska Native, 0.0% Hispanic of any race, 0.0% two or more races (2000); Density: 6.4 persons per square mile (2000); Age: 32.9% under 18, 5.7% over 64 (2000); Marriage status: 25.0% never married, 72.9% now married, 1.1% widowed, 1.1% divorced (2000); Foreign born: 0.0% (2000); Ancestry (includes multiple ancestries): 48.8% Dutch, 27.2% German, 12.2% Norwegian, 4.5% Irish, 4.1% French (except Basque) (2000).
Economy: Employment by occupation: 25.0% management, 10.0% professional, 22.1% services, 17.1% sales, 3.6% farming, 4.3% construction, 17.9% production (2000).
Income: Per capita income: $13,693 (2000); Median household income: $38,500 (2000); Poverty rate: 8.9% (2000).
Taxes: Total city taxes per capita: $86 (1997); City property taxes per capita: $86 (1997).
Education: High school graduation rate: 89.3% (2000); College graduation rate: 9.4% (2000).
Housing: Homeownership rate: 83.1% (2000); Median home value: $82,500 (2000); Median rent: $288 per month (2000); Median age of housing: 59 years (2000).
Transportation: Commute to work: 79.3% car, 0.0% public transportation, 0.0% walk, 20.7% work from home (2000); Travel time to work: 26.1% less than 15 minutes, 43.2% 15 to 30 minutes, 12.6% 30 to 45 minutes, 5.4% 45 to 60 minutes, 12.6% 60 minutes or more (2000)

BEAVER CREEK (city). Covers a land area of 0.495 square miles and a water area of 0 square miles. Located at 43.61° N. Lat.; 96.36° W. Long. Elevation is 1,460 feet.
Population: 250 (2000); Race: 94.7% White, 0.0% Black, 0.0% Asian, 0.0% American Indian and Alaska Native, 5.3% Hispanic of any race, 0.0% two or more races (2000); Density: 505.5 persons per square mile (2000); Age: 16.5% under 18, 20.2% over 64 (2000); Marriage status: 21.9% never married, 61.9% now married, 10.2% widowed, 6.0% divorced (2000); Foreign born: 4.5% (2000); Ancestry (includes multiple ancestries): 44.0% German, 21.8% Norwegian, 14.8% Dutch, 7.8% Swedish, 4.5% Other groups (2000).
Economy: Single-family building permits issued: 1 (2001) / 4 (2000); Multi-family building permits issued: 0 (2001) / 0 (2000); Employment by occupation: 13.5% management, 12.8% professional, 17.3% services, 21.8% sales, 0.8% farming, 10.5% construction, 23.3% production (2000).
Income: Per capita income: $14,924 (2000); Median household income: $34,167 (2000); Poverty rate: 7.8% (2000).
Taxes: Total city taxes per capita: $131 (1997); City property taxes per capita: $131 (1997).
Education: High school graduation rate: 81.2% (2000); College graduation rate: 10.6% (2000).
Housing: Homeownership rate: 83.0% (2000); Median home value: $52,400 (2000); Median rent: $180 per month (2000); Median age of housing: 49 years (2000).
Transportation: Commute to work: 93.9% car, 0.0% public transportation, 3.1% walk, 3.1% work from home (2000); Travel time to work: 25.2% less than 15 minutes, 35.4% 15 to 30 minutes, 36.2% 30 to 45 minutes, 3.1% 45 to 60 minutes, 0.0% 60 minutes or more (2000)

BEAVER CREEK (township). Covers a land area of 48.205 square miles and a water area of 0.006 square miles. Located at 43.63° N. Lat.; 96.36° W. Long. Elevation is 1,460 feet.
Population: 391 (2000); Race: 99.5% White, 0.0% Black, 0.0% Asian, 0.0% American Indian and Alaska Native, 0.5% Hispanic of any race, 0.5% two or more races (2000); Density: 8.1 persons per square mile (2000); Age: 25.9% under 18, 14.9% over 64 (2000); Marriage status: 21.8% never married, 66.0% now married, 7.1% widowed, 5.1% divorced (2000); Foreign born: 0.5% (2000); Ancestry (includes multiple ancestries): 49.5% German, 32.2% Norwegian, 27.8% Dutch, 6.5% Swedish, 5.7% Irish (2000).
Economy: Corn, oats, soybeans; hogs, cattle, poultry; dairying. Manufacturing: motor vehicle parts. Employment by occupation: 25.3% management, 16.2% professional, 15.7% services, 16.2% sales, 2.0% farming, 12.1% construction, 12.6% production (2000).
Income: Per capita income: $18,384 (2000); Median household income: $43,750 (2000); Poverty rate: 6.0% (2000).
Taxes: Total city taxes per capita: $261 (2000); City property taxes per capita: $258 (2000).
Education: High school graduation rate: 86.3% (2000); College graduation rate: 11.6% (2000).
Housing: Homeownership rate: 86.1% (2000); Median home value: $90,000 (2000); Median rent: $175 per month (2000); Median age of housing: 60+ years (2000).
Transportation: Commute to work: 78.1% car, 0.0% public transportation, 5.1% walk, 16.8% work from home (2000); Travel time to work: 42.3% less than 15 minutes, 28.8% 15 to 30 minutes, 24.5% 30 to 45 minutes, 3.1% 45 to 60 minutes, 1.2% 60 minutes or more (2000)

CLINTON (township). Covers a land area of 35.583 square miles and a water area of 0 square miles. Located at 43.53° N. Lat.; 96.24° W. Long.
Population: 292 (2000); Race: 100.0% White, 0.0% Black, 0.0% Asian, 0.0% American Indian and Alaska Native, 1.1% Hispanic of any race, 0.0% two or more races (2000); Density: 8.2 persons per square mile (2000); Age: 24.0% under 18, 17.9% over 64 (2000); Marriage status: 17.5% never married, 73.3% now married, 6.0% widowed, 3.2% divorced (2000); Foreign born: 1.1% (2000); Ancestry (includes multiple ancestries): 48.5% German, 42.7% Dutch, 13.4% Norwegian, 3.1% Danish, 2.7% United States or American (2000).
Economy: Employment by occupation: 33.6% management, 8.8% professional, 19.0% services, 13.9% sales, 4.4% farming, 4.4% construction, 16.1% production (2000).
Income: Per capita income: $16,251 (2000); Median household income: $42,500 (2000); Poverty rate: 4.2% (2000).
Education: High school graduation rate: 75.0% (2000); College graduation rate: 7.8% (2000).
Housing: Homeownership rate: 86.4% (2000); Median home value: $86,700 (2000); Median rent: $150 per month (2000); Median age of housing: 60+ years (2000).
Transportation: Commute to work: 63.7% car, 0.0% public transportation, 3.0% walk, 33.3% work from home (2000); Travel time to work: 34.4% less than 15 minutes, 37.8% 15 to 30 minutes, 20.0% 30 to 45 minutes, 5.6% 45 to 60 minutes, 2.2% 60 minutes or more (2000)

DENVER (township). Covers a land area of 34.177 square miles and a water area of 0 square miles. Located at 43.81° N. Lat.; 96.22° W. Long.
Population: 212 (2000); Race: 95.3% White, 0.0% Black, 0.0% Asian, 1.9% American Indian and Alaska Native, 4.3% Hispanic of any race, 2.8% two or more races (2000); Density: 6.2 persons per square mile (2000); Age: 33.6% under 18, 17.5% over 64 (2000); Marriage status: 18.2% never married, 80.4% now married, 0.0% widowed, 1.4% divorced (2000); Foreign born: 0.0% (2000); Ancestry (includes multiple ancestries): 33.6% German, 29.9% Dutch, 12.8% Norwegian, 5.7% Other groups, 4.3% English (2000).
Economy: Employment by occupation: 27.3% management, 13.6% professional, 18.2% services, 13.6% sales, 3.4% farming, 8.0% construction, 15.9% production (2000).
Income: Per capita income: $11,803 (2000); Median household income: $36,719 (2000); Poverty rate: 6.6% (2000).
Taxes: Total city taxes per capita: $104 (1997); City property taxes per capita: $104 (1997).
Education: High school graduation rate: 77.3% (2000); College graduation rate: 9.4% (2000).
Housing: Homeownership rate: 80.3% (2000); Median home value: $70,800 (2000); Median rent: $250 per month (2000); Median age of housing: 60+ years (2000).
Transportation: Commute to work: 76.1% car, 0.0% public transportation, 3.4% walk, 18.2% work from home (2000); Travel time to work: 29.2% less than 15 minutes, 36.1% 15 to 30 minutes, 5.6% 30 to 45 minutes, 26.4% 45 to 60 minutes, 2.8% 60 minutes or more (2000)

HARDWICK (city). Covers a land area of 1.740 square miles and a water area of 0 square miles. Located at 43.77° N. Lat.; 96.19° W. Long. Elevation is 607 feet.
Population: 222 (2000); Race: 94.4% White, 2.1% Black, 0.0% Asian, 3.4% American Indian and Alaska Native, 1.3% Hispanic of any race, 0.0% two or more races (2000); Density: 127.6 persons per square mile (2000); Age: 29.9% under 18, 21.8% over 64 (2000); Marriage status: 17.3% never married, 65.9% now married, 10.1% widowed, 6.7% divorced (2000); Foreign born: 0.0% (2000); Ancestry (includes multiple ancestries): 38.5% German, 18.8% Dutch, 16.7% Norwegian, 7.7% Other groups, 6.4% Irish (2000).
Economy: Corn, soybeans, oats; livestock; poultry; dairying. Single-family building permits issued: 0 (2001) / 0 (2000); Multi-family building permits issued: 0 (2001) / 0 (2000); Employment by occupation: 12.0% management, 7.6% professional, 21.7% services, 17.4% sales, 4.3% farming, 17.4% construction, 19.6% production (2000).
Income: Per capita income: $13,822 (2000); Median household income: $29,583 (2000); Poverty rate: 12.8% (2000).
Taxes: Total city taxes per capita: $71 (1997); City property taxes per capita: $62 (1997).
Education: High school graduation rate: 75.6% (2000); College graduation rate: 5.1% (2000).
Housing: Homeownership rate: 83.3% (2000); Median home value: $31,800 (2000); Median rent: $263 per month (2000); Median age of housing: 56 years (2000).
Transportation: Commute to work: 77.8% car, 0.0% public transportation, 22.2% walk, 0.0% work from home (2000); Travel time to work: 37.8% less than 15 minutes, 35.6% 15 to 30 minutes, 12.2% 30 to 45 minutes, 12.2% 45 to 60 minutes, 2.2% 60 minutes or more (2000)

HILLS (city). Covers a land area of 0.487 square miles and a water area of 0.009 square miles. Located at 43.52° N. Lat.; 96.35° W. Long. Elevation is 1,451 feet.
Population: 565 (2000); Race: 99.0% White, 1.0% Black, 0.0% Asian, 0.0% American Indian and Alaska Native, 0.0% Hispanic of any race, 0.0% two or more races (2000); Density: 1,160.7 persons per square mile (2000); Age: 22.7% under 18, 27.9% over 64 (2000); Marriage status: 17.8% never married, 62.8% now married, 13.3% widowed, 6.0% divorced (2000); Foreign born: 0.5% (2000); Ancestry (includes multiple ancestries): 32.6% German, 27.2% Dutch, 20.4% Norwegian, 5.2% Swedish, 3.8% Irish (2000).
Economy: Corn, oats, soybeans; hogs, cattle; dairying. Manufacturing: fertilizer. Railroad junction to West. Single-family building permits issued: 1

(2001) / 4 (2000); Multi-family building permits issued: 0 (2001) / 12 (2000); Employment by occupation: 13.4% management, 8.2% professional, 17.2% services, 24.6% sales, 0.7% farming, 18.3% construction, 17.5% production (2000).
Income: Per capita income: $15,824 (2000); Median household income: $33,125 (2000); Poverty rate: 5.6% (2000).
Taxes: Total city taxes per capita: $94 (1997); City property taxes per capita: $90 (1997).
Education: High school graduation rate: 77.4% (2000); College graduation rate: 15.1% (2000).

School District(s)

Hills-Beaver Creek (PK-12)
2000 Enrollment: 308 507-962-3240
Housing: Homeownership rate: 81.7% (2000); Median home value: $63,100 (2000); Median rent: $425 per month (2000); Median age of housing: 44 years (2000).
Transportation: Commute to work: 85.8% car, 1.1% public transportation, 7.5% walk, 4.9% work from home (2000); Travel time to work: 27.6% less than 15 minutes, 39.4% 15 to 30 minutes, 25.2% 30 to 45 minutes, 4.3% 45 to 60 minutes, 3.5% 60 minutes or more (2000)

KANARANZI (township). Covers a land area of 36.030 square miles and a water area of 0 square miles. Located at 43.55° N. Lat.; 96.10° W. Long. Elevation is 1,505 feet.
Population: 286 (2000); Race: 99.4% White, 0.6% Black, 0.0% Asian, 0.0% American Indian and Alaska Native, 0.0% Hispanic of any race, 0.0% two or more races (2000); Density: 7.9 persons per square mile (2000); Age: 23.1% under 18, 10.7% over 64 (2000); Marriage status: 24.7% never married, 72.5% now married, 0.8% widowed, 2.0% divorced (2000); Foreign born: 2.3% (2000); Ancestry (includes multiple ancestries): 53.2% German, 25.6% Dutch, 22.7% Norwegian, 5.8% Irish, 5.5% Swiss (2000).
Economy: Employment by occupation: 28.5% management, 7.3% professional, 9.3% services, 25.4% sales, 2.1% farming, 14.0% construction, 13.5% production (2000).
Income: Per capita income: $21,231 (2000); Median household income: $42,500 (2000); Poverty rate: 11.4% (2000).
Taxes: Total city taxes per capita: $108 (1997); City property taxes per capita: $108 (1997).
Education: High school graduation rate: 85.0% (2000); College graduation rate: 7.0% (2000).
Housing: Homeownership rate: 86.8% (2000); Median home value: $57,500 (2000); Median rent: $138 per month (2000); Median age of housing: 59 years (2000).
Transportation: Commute to work: 74.0% car, 1.6% public transportation, 2.6% walk, 20.8% work from home (2000); Travel time to work: 31.6% less than 15 minutes, 42.1% 15 to 30 minutes, 15.8% 30 to 45 minutes, 7.2% 45 to 60 minutes, 3.3% 60 minutes or more (2000)

KENNETH (city). Covers a land area of 1.055 square miles and a water area of 0 square miles. Located at 43.75° N. Lat.; 96.07° W. Long.
Population: 61 (2000); Race: 88.3% White, 0.0% Black, 0.0% Asian, 11.7% American Indian and Alaska Native, 0.0% Hispanic of any race, 0.0% two or more races (2000); Density: 57.8 persons per square mile (2000); Age: 18.3% under 18, 6.7% over 64 (2000); Marriage status: 32.7% never married, 59.2% now married, 8.2% widowed, 0.0% divorced (2000); Foreign born: 1.7% (2000); Ancestry (includes multiple ancestries): 38.3% Norwegian, 25.0% German, 11.7% Dutch, 11.7% Swedish, 3.3% Irish (2000).
Economy: Grain; livestock; dairying. Employment by occupation: 19.0% management, 9.5% professional, 21.4% services, 11.9% sales, 0.0% farming, 23.8% construction, 14.3% production (2000).
Income: Per capita income: $19,078 (2000); Median household income: $38,125 (2000); Poverty rate: 6.9% (2000).
Taxes: Total city taxes per capita: $96 (1997); City property taxes per capita: $84 (1997).
Education: High school graduation rate: 100.0% (2000); College graduation rate: 5.3% (2000).
Housing: Homeownership rate: 90.0% (2000); Median home value: $21,100 (2000); Median rent: $188 per month (2000); Median age of housing: 59 years (2000).
Transportation: Commute to work: 92.9% car, 0.0% public transportation, 7.1% walk, 0.0% work from home (2000); Travel time to work: 33.3% less than 15 minutes, 50.0% 15 to 30 minutes, 11.9% 30 to 45 minutes, 4.8% 45 to 60 minutes, 0.0% 60 minutes or more (2000)

LUVERNE (city). Covers a land area of 3.405 square miles and a water area of 0.012 square miles. Located at 43.65° N. Lat.; 96.21° W. Long. Elevation is 1,452 feet.
History: Joseph N. Nicollet visited this area in 1839, but it was in the 1870's that a settlement grew up at Luverne. Plagued at first by grasshoppers and forest fires, the town later became a prosperous livestock and grain raising area, with cooperatives and a creamery. The red granite for the Rock County courthouse was quarried in Luverne.
Population: 4,617 (2000); Race: 96.3% White, 2.4% Black, 0.3% Asian, 0.3% American Indian and Alaska Native, 0.4% Hispanic of any race, 0.6% two or more races (2000); Density: 1,356.1 persons per square mile (2000); Age: 24.2% under 18, 25.9% over 64 (2000); Marriage status: 20.7% never married, 63.5% now married, 11.7% widowed, 4.1% divorced (2000); Foreign born: 0.8% (2000); Ancestry (includes multiple ancestries): 48.0% German, 19.7% Dutch, 18.5% Norwegian, 6.6% Irish, 5.3% English (2000).
Economy: Single-family building permits issued: 3 (2001) / 2 (2000); Multi-family building permits issued: 4 (2001) / 4 (2000); Employment by occupation: 10.7% management, 20.9% professional, 18.9% services, 25.7% sales, 1.9% farming, 8.5% construction, 13.6% production (2000).
Income: Per capita income: $18,692 (2000); Median household income: $36,271 (2000); Poverty rate: 8.8% (2000).
Taxes: Total city taxes per capita: $126 (1997); City property taxes per capita: $114 (1997).
Education: High school graduation rate: 81.1% (2000); College graduation rate: 19.6% (2000).

School District(s)

Luverne (PK-12)
2000 Enrollment: 1,365 507-283-8088
Housing: Homeownership rate: 71.9% (2000); Median home value: $72,600 (2000); Median rent: $317 per month (2000); Median age of housing: 43 years (2000).
Hospitals: Luverne Community Hospital (28 beds)
Newspapers: Crescent (1 x week); The Rock County Star Herald (1 x week)
Transportation: Commute to work: 88.4% car, 0.2% public transportation, 7.2% walk, 2.9% work from home (2000); Travel time to work: 65.9% less than 15 minutes, 11.1% 15 to 30 minutes, 14.7% 30 to 45 minutes, 6.2% 45 to 60 minutes, 2.1% 60 minutes or more (2000)
Additional Information Contacts
Luverne Chamber of Commerce 507-283-4061

LUVERNE (township). Covers a land area of 32.624 square miles and a water area of 0.052 square miles. Located at 43.63° N. Lat.; 96.22° W. Long. Elevation is 1,452 feet.
History: Settled 1867, plotted 1870, incorporated as village 1877, as city 1904.
Population: 493 (2000); Race: 99.8% White, 0.0% Black, 0.0% Asian, 0.0% American Indian and Alaska Native, 0.4% Hispanic of any race, 0.2% two or more races (2000); Density: 15.1 persons per square mile (2000); Age: 28.9% under 18, 11.3% over 64 (2000); Marriage status: 24.2% never married, 71.9% now married, 1.4% widowed, 2.4% divorced (2000); Foreign born: 0.2% (2000); Ancestry (includes multiple ancestries): 57.5% German, 22.4% Norwegian, 18.6% Dutch, 10.0% Irish, 6.9% Swedish (2000).
Economy: Trading point in agricultural area: grain, milk, soybeans; livestock, poultry; dairying. Manufacturing: water tanks, truck mounts, and farm equipment, printing; granite quarries. Employment by occupation: 21.0% management, 8.3% professional, 15.2% services, 30.8% sales, 1.3% farming, 12.7% construction, 10.8% production (2000).
Income: Per capita income: $16,270 (2000); Median household income: $45,000 (2000); Poverty rate: 6.3% (2000).
Taxes: Total city taxes per capita: $58 (1997); City property taxes per capita: $58 (1997).
Education: High school graduation rate: 83.5% (2000); College graduation rate: 14.6% (2000).
Housing: Homeownership rate: 89.5% (2000); Median home value: $99,400 (2000); Median rent: $275 per month (2000); Median age of housing: 55 years (2000).
Transportation: Commute to work: 80.3% car, 0.0% public transportation, 3.2% walk, 16.6% work from home (2000); Travel time to work: 75.6% less than 15 minutes, 11.1% 15 to 30 minutes, 9.9% 30 to 45 minutes, 1.1% 45 to 60 minutes, 2.3% 60 minutes or more (2000)

MAGNOLIA (city). Covers a land area of 1.025 square miles and a water area of 0 square miles. Located at 43.64° N. Lat.; 96.07° W. Long.
Population: 221 (2000); Race: 79.2% White, 2.8% Black, 10.2% Asian, 1.9% American Indian and Alaska Native, 7.9% Hispanic of any race, 5.1%

two or more races (2000); Density: 215.6 persons per square mile (2000); Age: 33.8% under 18, 18.5% over 64 (2000); Marriage status: 17.6% never married, 68.6% now married, 7.8% widowed, 5.9% divorced (2000); Foreign born: 11.1% (2000); Ancestry (includes multiple ancestries): 48.1% German, 18.5% Norwegian, 14.8% Other groups, 12.5% Dutch, 5.1% Irish (2000).
Economy: Employment by occupation: 8.0% management, 4.5% professional, 25.0% services, 10.2% sales, 2.3% farming, 13.6% construction, 36.4% production (2000).
Income: Per capita income: $13,427 (2000); Median household income: $36,000 (2000); Poverty rate: 6.1% (2000).
Taxes: Total city taxes per capita: $87 (1997); City property taxes per capita: $87 (1997).
Education: High school graduation rate: 66.1% (2000); College graduation rate: 3.1% (2000).
Housing: Homeownership rate: 88.2% (2000); Median home value: $48,300 (2000); Median rent: $313 per month (2000); Median age of housing: 58 years (2000).
Transportation: Commute to work: 92.9% car, 0.0% public transportation, 0.0% walk, 7.1% work from home (2000); Travel time to work: 45.6% less than 15 minutes, 20.3% 15 to 30 minutes, 26.6% 30 to 45 minutes, 3.8% 45 to 60 minutes, 3.8% 60 minutes or more (2000)

MAGNOLIA (township). Covers a land area of 35.068 square miles and a water area of 0 square miles. Located at 43.63° N. Lat.; 96.10° W. Long.
Population: 250 (2000); Race: 98.8% White, 0.0% Black, 1.2% Asian, 0.0% American Indian and Alaska Native, 0.0% Hispanic of any race, 0.0% two or more races (2000); Density: 7.1 persons per square mile (2000); Age: 34.4% under 18, 7.9% over 64 (2000); Marriage status: 29.9% never married, 60.4% now married, 4.8% widowed, 4.8% divorced (2000); Foreign born: 2.0% (2000); Ancestry (includes multiple ancestries): 43.5% German, 28.9% Norwegian, 27.7% Dutch, 7.5% Irish, 6.7% United States or American (2000).
Economy: Grain; livestock; dairying. Manufacturing: feeds, protein blending. Employment by occupation: 28.5% management, 7.3% professional, 7.3% services, 30.7% sales, 4.4% farming, 8.8% construction, 13.1% production (2000).
Income: Per capita income: $16,452 (2000); Median household income: $43,250 (2000); Poverty rate: 5.5% (2000).
Taxes: Total city taxes per capita: $134 (1997); City property taxes per capita: $134 (1997).
Education: High school graduation rate: 94.4% (2000); College graduation rate: 6.3% (2000).
Housing: Homeownership rate: 75.0% (2000); Median home value: $90,800 (2000); Median rent: $175 per month (2000); Median age of housing: 40 years (2000).
Transportation: Commute to work: 80.9% car, 0.0% public transportation, 3.7% walk, 15.4% work from home (2000); Travel time to work: 40.0% less than 15 minutes, 17.4% 15 to 30 minutes, 18.3% 30 to 45 minutes, 15.7% 45 to 60 minutes, 8.7% 60 minutes or more (2000)

MARTIN (township). Covers a land area of 48.017 square miles and a water area of 0.007 square miles. Located at 43.54° N. Lat.; 96.37° W. Long.
Population: 451 (2000); Race: 99.6% White, 0.0% Black, 0.0% Asian, 0.4% American Indian and Alaska Native, 0.0% Hispanic of any race, 0.0% two or more races (2000); Density: 9.4 persons per square mile (2000); Age: 34.9% under 18, 7.5% over 64 (2000); Marriage status: 24.0% never married, 70.7% now married, 3.7% widowed, 1.6% divorced (2000); Foreign born: 0.9% (2000); Ancestry (includes multiple ancestries): 41.2% Dutch, 40.8% German, 16.0% Norwegian, 7.2% English, 6.1% Swedish (2000).
Economy: Employment by occupation: 27.5% management, 14.0% professional, 17.0% services, 15.8% sales, 6.4% farming, 10.6% construction, 8.7% production (2000).
Income: Per capita income: $15,635 (2000); Median household income: $46,964 (2000); Poverty rate: 6.1% (2000).
Taxes: Total city taxes per capita: $142 (1997); City property taxes per capita: $142 (1997).
Education: High school graduation rate: 88.0% (2000); College graduation rate: 15.1% (2000).
Housing: Homeownership rate: 85.7% (2000); Median home value: $67,100 (2000); Median rent: $175 per month (2000); Median age of housing: 60+ years (2000).
Transportation: Commute to work: 70.3% car, 0.8% public transportation, 3.4% walk, 25.5% work from home (2000); Travel time to work: 46.9% less than 15 minutes, 31.1% 15 to 30 minutes, 20.4% 30 to 45 minutes, 0.0% 45 to 60 minutes, 1.5% 60 minutes or more (2000)

MOUND (township). Covers a land area of 35.724 square miles and a water area of 0.116 square miles. Located at 43.71° N. Lat.; 96.24° W. Long.
Population: 257 (2000); Race: 100.0% White, 0.0% Black, 0.0% Asian, 0.0% American Indian and Alaska Native, 0.0% Hispanic of any race, 0.0% two or more races (2000); Density: 7.2 persons per square mile (2000); Age: 27.3% under 18, 12.0% over 64 (2000); Marriage status: 22.4% never married, 75.7% now married, 0.0% widowed, 1.9% divorced (2000); Foreign born: 1.5% (2000); Ancestry (includes multiple ancestries): 49.4% German, 29.2% Dutch, 19.5% Norwegian, 9.0% English, 6.4% Swedish (2000).
Economy: Employment by occupation: 29.9% management, 22.4% professional, 5.4% services, 19.7% sales, 3.4% farming, 9.5% construction, 9.5% production (2000).
Income: Per capita income: $22,343 (2000); Median household income: $44,688 (2000); Poverty rate: 6.7% (2000).
Taxes: Total city taxes per capita: $72 (1997); City property taxes per capita: $72 (1997).
Education: High school graduation rate: 89.2% (2000); College graduation rate: 19.9% (2000).
Housing: Homeownership rate: 74.7% (2000); Median home value: $85,800 (2000); Median rent: $410 per month (2000); Median age of housing: 34 years (2000).
Transportation: Commute to work: 87.9% car, 1.3% public transportation, 0.0% walk, 9.4% work from home (2000); Travel time to work: 54.1% less than 15 minutes, 26.7% 15 to 30 minutes, 11.9% 30 to 45 minutes, 1.5% 45 to 60 minutes, 5.9% 60 minutes or more (2000)

ROSE DELL (township). Covers a land area of 48.249 square miles and a water area of 0.016 square miles. Located at 43.80° N. Lat.; 96.38° W. Long.
Population: 214 (2000); Race: 100.0% White, 0.0% Black, 0.0% Asian, 0.0% American Indian and Alaska Native, 0.0% Hispanic of any race, 0.0% two or more races (2000); Density: 4.4 persons per square mile (2000); Age: 28.8% under 18, 25.5% over 64 (2000); Marriage status: 12.5% never married, 80.0% now married, 6.3% widowed, 1.3% divorced (2000); Foreign born: 0.0% (2000); Ancestry (includes multiple ancestries): 45.7% German, 36.1% Dutch, 13.0% Norwegian, 11.5% English, 10.6% Belgian (2000).
Economy: Employment by occupation: 27.6% management, 14.9% professional, 12.6% services, 10.3% sales, 8.0% farming, 9.2% construction, 17.2% production (2000).
Income: Per capita income: $16,567 (2000); Median household income: $37,250 (2000); Poverty rate: 6.3% (2000).
Taxes: Total city taxes per capita: $110 (1997); City property taxes per capita: $110 (1997).
Education: High school graduation rate: 75.0% (2000); College graduation rate: 7.6% (2000).
Housing: Homeownership rate: 95.0% (2000); Median home value: $45,000 (2000); Median rent: <$100 per month (2000); Median age of housing: 60+ years (2000).
Transportation: Commute to work: 75.3% car, 0.0% public transportation, 4.7% walk, 20.0% work from home (2000); Travel time to work: 11.8% less than 15 minutes, 42.6% 15 to 30 minutes, 29.4% 30 to 45 minutes, 16.2% 45 to 60 minutes, 0.0% 60 minutes or more (2000)

SPRINGWATER (township). Covers a land area of 48.657 square miles and a water area of 0 square miles. Located at 43.72° N. Lat.; 96.38° W. Long.
Population: 266 (2000); Race: 98.6% White, 0.0% Black, 0.0% Asian, 0.0% American Indian and Alaska Native, 0.0% Hispanic of any race, 1.4% two or more races (2000); Density: 5.5 persons per square mile (2000); Age: 35.8% under 18, 11.3% over 64 (2000); Marriage status: 8.6% never married, 87.4% now married, 0.0% widowed, 4.0% divorced (2000); Foreign born: 0.0% (2000); Ancestry (includes multiple ancestries): 52.6% German, 31.7% Norwegian, 25.6% Dutch, 2.4% Irish, 2.0% Belgian (2000).
Economy: Employment by occupation: 32.3% management, 13.7% professional, 11.8% services, 17.4% sales, 5.6% farming, 7.5% construction, 11.8% production (2000).
Income: Per capita income: $14,610 (2000); Median household income: $37,500 (2000); Poverty rate: 5.8% (2000).
Taxes: Total city taxes per capita: $124 (1997); City property taxes per capita: $124 (1997).
Education: High school graduation rate: 88.7% (2000); College graduation rate: 9.6% (2000).
Housing: Homeownership rate: 85.0% (2000); Median home value: $77,500 (2000); Median rent: $275 per month (2000); Median age of housing: 57 years (2000).

Transportation: Commute to work: 73.3% car, 0.0% public transportation, 0.0% walk, 26.7% work from home (2000); Travel time to work: 16.1% less than 15 minutes, 48.3% 15 to 30 minutes, 32.2% 30 to 45 minutes, 1.7% 45 to 60 minutes, 1.7% 60 minutes or more (2000)

STEEN (city). Covers a land area of 0.424 square miles and a water area of 0 square miles. Located at 43.51° N. Lat.; 96.26° W. Long. Elevation is 1,485 feet.
Population: 182 (2000); Race: 98.8% White, 1.2% Black, 0.0% Asian, 0.0% American Indian and Alaska Native, 0.0% Hispanic of any race, 0.0% two or more races (2000); Density: 429.5 persons per square mile (2000); Age: 26.2% under 18, 20.2% over 64 (2000); Marriage status: 17.3% never married, 66.1% now married, 10.2% widowed, 6.3% divorced (2000); Foreign born: 3.6% (2000); Ancestry (includes multiple ancestries): 48.8% Dutch, 28.0% German, 20.2% Norwegian, 11.3% Irish, 3.0% Other groups (2000).
Economy: Grain; livestock, poultry; dairying. Single-family building permits issued: 1 (2001) / 0 (2000); Multi-family building permits issued: 0 (2001) / 0 (2000); Employment by occupation: 3.3% management, 17.8% professional, 23.3% services, 15.6% sales, 0.0% farming, 6.7% construction, 33.3% production (2000).
Income: Per capita income: $15,531 (2000); Median household income: $36,875 (2000); Poverty rate: 2.4% (2000).
Taxes: Total city taxes per capita: $73 (1997); City property taxes per capita: $73 (1997).
Education: High school graduation rate: 69.4% (2000); College graduation rate: 12.6% (2000).
Housing: Homeownership rate: 89.9% (2000); Median home value: $52,800 (2000); Median rent: $275 per month (2000); Median age of housing: 60+ years (2000).
Transportation: Commute to work: 86.2% car, 0.0% public transportation, 11.5% walk, 2.3% work from home (2000); Travel time to work: 23.5% less than 15 minutes, 42.4% 15 to 30 minutes, 21.2% 30 to 45 minutes, 2.4% 45 to 60 minutes, 10.6% 60 minutes or more (2000)

VIENNA (township). Covers a land area of 34.957 square miles and a water area of 0 square miles. Located at 43.71° N. Lat.; 96.10° W. Long.
Population: 183 (2000); Race: 100.0% White, 0.0% Black, 0.0% Asian, 0.0% American Indian and Alaska Native, 0.0% Hispanic of any race, 0.0% two or more races (2000); Density: 5.2 persons per square mile (2000); Age: 26.7% under 18, 12.4% over 64 (2000); Marriage status: 22.0% never married, 64.6% now married, 7.1% widowed, 6.3% divorced (2000); Foreign born: 0.0% (2000); Ancestry (includes multiple ancestries): 52.8% German, 34.2% Norwegian, 26.1% Dutch, 6.2% Irish, 5.0% Scotch-Irish (2000).
Economy: Employment by occupation: 30.2% management, 15.1% professional, 9.3% services, 27.9% sales, 4.7% farming, 8.1% construction, 4.7% production (2000).
Income: Per capita income: $17,078 (2000); Median household income: $30,714 (2000); Poverty rate: 19.9% (2000).
Taxes: Total city taxes per capita: $120 (2000); City property taxes per capita: $120 (2000).
Education: High school graduation rate: 81.9% (2000); College graduation rate: 12.4% (2000).
Housing: Homeownership rate: 85.5% (2000); Median home value: $55,000 (2000); Median rent: $275 per month (2000); Median age of housing: 60+ years (2000).
Transportation: Commute to work: 75.6% car, 1.2% public transportation, 4.7% walk, 15.1% work from home (2000); Travel time to work: 42.5% less than 15 minutes, 30.1% 15 to 30 minutes, 12.3% 30 to 45 minutes, 8.2% 45 to 60 minutes, 6.8% 60 minutes or more (2000)

Roseau County

Located in northwestern Minnesota; bounded on the northeast by Lake of the Woods, and on the north by the Canadian province of Manitoba; drained by the Roseau River. Covers a land area of 1,662.50 square miles, a water area of 15.80 square miles, and is located in the Central Time Zone. The county government was organized in 1894. County seat is Roseau.

Weather Station: Warroad Elevation: 1,066 feet

	Jan	Feb	Mar	Apr	May	Jun	Jul	Aug	Sep	Oct	Nov	Dec
High	13	21	33	50	65	74	79	77	66	53	33	18
Low	-9	-2	11	27	42	52	56	54	44	33	16	-1
Precip	0.6	0.5	0.7	1.2	2.5	3.7	3.7	2.7	2.7	1.8	1.1	0.6
Snow	7.9	4.8	na	2.7	tr	0.0	0.0	0.0	tr	0.6	na	na

High and Low temperatures in degrees Fahrenheit; Precipitation and Snow in inches

Population: 16,338 (2000); Race: 95.6% White, 0.2% Black, 2.1% Asian, 1.4% American Indian and Alaska Native, 0.4% Hispanic of any race, 0.7% two or more races (2000); Density: 9.8 persons per square mile (2000); Age: 29.8% under 18, 12.6% over 64 (2000).
Religion: Five largest groups: 29.3% Evangelical Lutheran Church in America, 20.4% Catholic Church, 8.2% The Association of Free Lutheran Congregations, 2.9% Assemblies of God, 2.1% Baptist General Conference (2000).
Economy: Unemployment rate: 3.3% (11/2002); Total civilian labor force: 9,003 (11/2002); Leading industries: 9.5% retail trade; 9.0% health care and social assistance; 8.0% accommodation & food services (2000); Companies that employ more than 1,000 persons: 2 (2000); Companies that employ more than 100 persons: 4 (2000); Farms: 1,051 totaling 577,455 acres (1997); Minority business ownership rate: 0.0% (1997); Women business ownership rate: 24.6% (1997); Retail sales per capita: $7,354 (1997). Single-family building permits issued: 34 (2001) / 20 (2000); Multi-family building permits issued: 4 (2001) / 4 (2000).
Income: Per capita income: $17,053 (2000); Median household income: $39,852 (2000); Poverty rate: 6.6% (2000); Bankruptcy rate: 2.44% (2001).
Taxes: Total county taxes per capita: $158 (2000); County property taxes per capita: $158 (2000).
Education: High school graduation rate: 82.5% (2000); College graduation rate: 14.9% (2000).
Housing: Homeownership rate: 84.1% (2000); Median home value: $76,300 (2000); Median rent: $380 per month (2000); Median age of housing: 26 years (2000).
Health: Birth rate: 139.6 per 10,000 population (1998); Age adjusted death rate: 84.1 per 10,000 population (1999); Age adjusted cancer mortality rate: 202.4 deaths per 100,000 population (1999). Number of physicians: 6.1 per 10,000 population (1999); Number of hospital beds: 98.5 per 10,000 population (1999).
Elections: 2000 Presidential election results: 29.7% Gore, 65.5% Bush, 2.5% Nader, 1.8% Buchanan
National and State Parks: Hayes Lake State Park; Roseau River State Wildlife Management Area
Additional Information Contacts
Roseau County Government Offices 218-463-1282
Warroad Chamber of Commerce 218-386-3543

Roseau County Communities

BADGER (city). Covers a land area of 1.332 square miles and a water area of 0 square miles. Located at 48.78° N. Lat.; 96.01° W. Long. Elevation is 1,082 feet.
Population: 470 (2000); Race: 100.0% White, 0.0% Black, 0.0% Asian, 0.0% American Indian and Alaska Native, 0.0% Hispanic of any race, 0.0% two or more races (2000); Density: 352.9 persons per square mile (2000); Age: 30.6% under 18, 12.1% over 64 (2000); Marriage status: 27.2% never married, 49.5% now married, 9.1% widowed, 14.2% divorced (2000); Foreign born: 0.4% (2000); Ancestry (includes multiple ancestries): 54.8% Norwegian, 19.0% German, 9.1% Swedish, 7.3% Irish, 6.2% Czech (2000).
Economy: Grain, flax, alfalfa, sunflowers; dairying; livestock. Manufacturing: alfalfa pellets. Single-family building permits issued: 1 (2001) / 3 (2000); Multi-family building permits issued: 0 (2001) / 0 (2000); Employment by occupation: 8.8% management, 10.7% professional, 8.4% services, 21.1% sales, 1.1% farming, 2.7% construction, 47.1% production (2000).
Income: Per capita income: $15,727 (2000); Median household income: $30,234 (2000); Poverty rate: 9.9% (2000).
Taxes: Total city taxes per capita: $79 (1997); City property taxes per capita: $72 (1997).
Education: High school graduation rate: 82.4% (2000); College graduation rate: 11.2% (2000).

School District(s)

Badger (KG-12)
2000 Enrollment: 238 218-528-3201

Housing: Homeownership rate: 72.6% (2000); Median home value: $63,300 (2000); Median rent: $370 per month (2000); Median age of housing: 29 years (2000).
Transportation: Commute to work: 93.9% car, 0.0% public transportation, 3.1% walk, 2.3% work from home (2000); Travel time to work: 28.2% less than 15 minutes, 56.5% 15 to 30 minutes, 5.1% 30 to 45 minutes, 7.1% 45 to 60 minutes, 3.1% 60 minutes or more (2000)

BARNETT (township). Covers a land area of 37.043 square miles and a water area of 0 square miles. Located at 48.68° N. Lat.; 96.04° W. Long.
Population: 169 (2000); Race: 100.0% White, 0.0% Black, 0.0% Asian, 0.0% American Indian and Alaska Native, 1.9% Hispanic of any race, 0.0% two or more races (2000); Density: 4.6 persons per square mile (2000); Age: 33.3% under 18, 12.8% over 64 (2000); Marriage status: 27.4% never married, 63.7% now married, 7.1% widowed, 1.8% divorced (2000); Foreign born: 1.3% (2000); Ancestry (includes multiple ancestries): 46.8% German, 35.3% Norwegian, 11.5% Swedish, 7.1% Polish, 7.1% Scandinavian (2000).
Economy: Employment by occupation: 24.4% management, 11.0% professional, 2.4% services, 14.6% sales, 6.1% farming, 8.5% construction, 32.9% production (2000).
Income: Per capita income: $13,255 (2000); Median household income: $31,667 (2000); Poverty rate: 24.4% (2000).
Taxes: Total city taxes per capita: $47 (1997); City property taxes per capita: $47 (1997).
Education: High school graduation rate: 75.3% (2000); College graduation rate: 10.3% (2000).
Housing: Homeownership rate: 100.0% (2000); Median home value: $40,000 (2000); Median age of housing: 30 years (2000).
Transportation: Commute to work: 79.7% car, 0.0% public transportation, 0.0% walk, 20.3% work from home (2000); Travel time to work: 15.9% less than 15 minutes, 36.5% 15 to 30 minutes, 22.2% 30 to 45 minutes, 9.5% 45 to 60 minutes, 15.9% 60 minutes or more (2000)

BARTO (township). Covers a land area of 36.870 square miles and a water area of 0 square miles. Located at 48.75° N. Lat.; 96.19° W. Long.
Population: 142 (2000); Race: 100.0% White, 0.0% Black, 0.0% Asian, 0.0% American Indian and Alaska Native, 0.0% Hispanic of any race, 0.0% two or more races (2000); Density: 3.9 persons per square mile (2000); Age: 25.4% under 18, 17.4% over 64 (2000); Marriage status: 17.0% never married, 76.8% now married, 6.3% widowed, 0.0% divorced (2000); Foreign born: 0.7% (2000); Ancestry (includes multiple ancestries): 47.8% Polish, 29.7% Norwegian, 20.3% German, 7.2% Irish, 7.2% United States or American (2000).
Economy: Employment by occupation: 38.0% management, 2.8% professional, 7.0% services, 22.5% sales, 2.8% farming, 5.6% construction, 21.1% production (2000).
Income: Per capita income: $20,125 (2000); Median household income: $46,875 (2000); Poverty rate: 0.0% (2000).
Taxes: Total city taxes per capita: $128 (1997); City property taxes per capita: $128 (1997).
Education: High school graduation rate: 92.6% (2000); College graduation rate: 7.4% (2000).
Housing: Homeownership rate: 100.0% (2000); Median home value: $73,800 (2000); Median age of housing: 25 years (2000).
Transportation: Commute to work: 79.7% car, 0.0% public transportation, 5.8% walk, 14.5% work from home (2000); Travel time to work: 44.1% less than 15 minutes, 37.3% 15 to 30 minutes, 11.9% 30 to 45 minutes, 3.4% 45 to 60 minutes, 3.4% 60 minutes or more (2000)

BEAVER (township). Covers a land area of 35.430 square miles and a water area of 0.218 square miles. Located at 48.64° N. Lat.; 95.54° W. Long.
Population: 103 (2000); Race: 100.0% White, 0.0% Black, 0.0% Asian, 0.0% American Indian and Alaska Native, 0.0% Hispanic of any race, 0.0% two or more races (2000); Density: 2.9 persons per square mile (2000); Age: 22.0% under 18, 15.0% over 64 (2000); Marriage status: 31.5% never married, 52.3% now married, 10.8% widowed, 5.4% divorced (2000); Foreign born: 0.0% (2000); Ancestry (includes multiple ancestries): 47.2% Norwegian, 22.8% Swedish, 11.0% Polish, 11.0% German, 7.9% Irish (2000).
Economy: Employment by occupation: 8.6% management, 6.9% professional, 10.3% services, 25.9% sales, 0.0% farming, 1.7% construction, 46.6% production (2000).
Income: Per capita income: $17,265 (2000); Median household income: $46,250 (2000); Poverty rate: 4.8% (2000).
Taxes: Total city taxes per capita: $11 (1997); City property taxes per capita: $11 (1997).
Education: High school graduation rate: 71.3% (2000); College graduation rate: 13.8% (2000).
Housing: Homeownership rate: 92.2% (2000); Median home value: $45,700 (2000); Median age of housing: 28 years (2000).
Transportation: Commute to work: 91.4% car, 0.0% public transportation, 5.2% walk, 3.4% work from home (2000); Travel time to work: 16.1% less than 15 minutes, 42.9% 15 to 30 minutes, 28.6% 30 to 45 minutes, 12.5% 45 to 60 minutes, 0.0% 60 minutes or more (2000)

CEDARBEND (township). Covers a land area of 36.016 square miles and a water area of 0 square miles. Located at 48.84° N. Lat.; 95.40° W. Long.
Population: 230 (2000); Race: 99.0% White, 0.0% Black, 0.0% Asian, 0.0% American Indian and Alaska Native, 0.0% Hispanic of any race, 1.0% two or more races (2000); Density: 6.4 persons per square mile (2000); Age: 29.1% under 18, 8.2% over 64 (2000); Marriage status: 28.3% never married, 54.5% now married, 1.4% widowed, 15.9% divorced (2000); Foreign born: 3.6% (2000); Ancestry (includes multiple ancestries): 32.7% German, 31.1% Norwegian, 17.9% Swedish, 7.7% English, 4.1% Irish (2000).
Economy: Employment by occupation: 3.8% management, 13.5% professional, 10.6% services, 17.3% sales, 3.8% farming, 12.5% construction, 38.5% production (2000).
Income: Per capita income: $15,654 (2000); Median household income: $34,643 (2000); Poverty rate: 4.1% (2000).
Taxes: Total city taxes per capita: $220 (1997); City property taxes per capita: $220 (1997).
Education: High school graduation rate: 83.8% (2000); College graduation rate: 2.7% (2000).
Housing: Homeownership rate: 91.0% (2000); Median home value: $70,000 (2000); Median rent: $342 per month (2000); Median age of housing: 21 years (2000).
Transportation: Commute to work: 97.1% car, 0.0% public transportation, 0.0% walk, 2.9% work from home (2000); Travel time to work: 40.4% less than 15 minutes, 53.5% 15 to 30 minutes, 6.1% 30 to 45 minutes, 0.0% 45 to 60 minutes, 0.0% 60 minutes or more (2000)

DEER (township). Covers a land area of 36.149 square miles and a water area of 0 square miles. Located at 48.58° N. Lat.; 96.18° W. Long.
Population: 92 (2000); Race: 100.0% White, 0.0% Black, 0.0% Asian, 0.0% American Indian and Alaska Native, 0.0% Hispanic of any race, 0.0% two or more races (2000); Density: 2.5 persons per square mile (2000); Age: 20.3% under 18, 13.9% over 64 (2000); Marriage status: 23.9% never married, 70.1% now married, 6.0% widowed, 0.0% divorced (2000); Foreign born: 0.0% (2000); Ancestry (includes multiple ancestries): 69.6% Norwegian, 25.3% Swedish, 8.9% German, 7.6% Czechoslovakian, 6.3% Polish (2000).
Economy: Employment by occupation: 18.8% management, 12.5% professional, 6.3% services, 12.5% sales, 0.0% farming, 6.3% construction, 43.8% production (2000).
Income: Per capita income: $14,301 (2000); Median household income: $36,875 (2000); Poverty rate: 2.5% (2000).
Taxes: Total city taxes per capita: $75 (1997); City property taxes per capita: $75 (1997).
Education: High school graduation rate: 71.4% (2000); College graduation rate: 7.1% (2000).
Housing: Homeownership rate: 75.0% (2000); Median home value: $65,000 (2000); Median age of housing: 42 years (2000).
Transportation: Commute to work: 81.3% car, 0.0% public transportation, 0.0% walk, 18.8% work from home (2000); Travel time to work: 17.9% less than 15 minutes, 23.1% 15 to 30 minutes, 25.6% 30 to 45 minutes, 33.3% 45 to 60 minutes, 0.0% 60 minutes or more (2000)

DEWEY (township). Covers a land area of 34.764 square miles and a water area of 0 square miles. Located at 48.67° N. Lat.; 96.33° W. Long.
Population: 114 (2000); Race: 100.0% White, 0.0% Black, 0.0% Asian, 0.0% American Indian and Alaska Native, 0.0% Hispanic of any race, 0.0% two or more races (2000); Density: 3.3 persons per square mile (2000); Age: 26.7% under 18, 11.7% over 64 (2000); Marriage status: 25.5% never married, 64.3% now married, 5.1% widowed, 5.1% divorced (2000); Foreign born: 0.0% (2000); Ancestry (includes multiple ancestries): 51.7% Norwegian, 18.3% German, 16.7% Polish, 14.2% Swedish, 7.5% English (2000).
Economy: Employment by occupation: 36.8% management, 20.6% professional, 5.9% services, 11.8% sales, 0.0% farming, 5.9% construction, 19.1% production (2000).
Income: Per capita income: $28,404 (2000); Median household income: $35,179 (2000); Poverty rate: 9.2% (2000).
Taxes: Total city taxes per capita: $237 (1997); City property taxes per capita: $237 (1997).
Education: High school graduation rate: 92.6% (2000); College graduation rate: 13.6% (2000).
Housing: Homeownership rate: 90.0% (2000); Median home value: $27,500 (2000); Median age of housing: 25 years (2000).

Transportation: Commute to work: 64.7% car, 0.0% public transportation, 4.4% walk, 30.9% work from home (2000); Travel time to work: 40.4% less than 15 minutes, 17.0% 15 to 30 minutes, 12.8% 30 to 45 minutes, 25.5% 45 to 60 minutes, 4.3% 60 minutes or more (2000)

DIETER (township). Covers a land area of 44.398 square miles and a water area of 0 square miles. Located at 48.95° N. Lat.; 95.95° W. Long.
Population: 162 (2000); Race: 100.0% White, 0.0% Black, 0.0% Asian, 0.0% American Indian and Alaska Native, 0.0% Hispanic of any race, 0.0% two or more races (2000); Density: 3.6 persons per square mile (2000); Age: 23.7% under 18, 18.4% over 64 (2000); Marriage status: 27.6% never married, 57.7% now married, 5.7% widowed, 8.9% divorced (2000); Foreign born: 2.0% (2000); Ancestry (includes multiple ancestries): 73.0% Norwegian, 20.4% German, 14.5% Swedish, 6.6% Czech, 6.6% Irish (2000).
Economy: Employment by occupation: 19.4% management, 11.1% professional, 15.3% services, 6.9% sales, 0.0% farming, 5.6% construction, 41.7% production (2000).
Income: Per capita income: $18,128 (2000); Median household income: $45,875 (2000); Poverty rate: 5.9% (2000).
Taxes: Total city taxes per capita: $71 (1997); City property taxes per capita: $71 (1997).
Education: High school graduation rate: 73.4% (2000); College graduation rate: 8.3% (2000).
Housing: Homeownership rate: 91.7% (2000); Median home value: $56,700 (2000); Median age of housing: 31 years (2000).
Transportation: Commute to work: 82.9% car, 0.0% public transportation, 5.7% walk, 8.6% work from home (2000); Travel time to work: 26.6% less than 15 minutes, 53.1% 15 to 30 minutes, 3.1% 30 to 45 minutes, 14.1% 45 to 60 minutes, 3.1% 60 minutes or more (2000)

ENSTROM (township). Covers a land area of 35.977 square miles and a water area of 0.007 square miles. Located at 48.86° N. Lat.; 95.53° W. Long.
Population: 580 (2000); Race: 98.1% White, 0.0% Black, 0.0% Asian, 0.5% American Indian and Alaska Native, 1.5% Hispanic of any race, 1.2% two or more races (2000); Density: 16.1 persons per square mile (2000); Age: 34.2% under 18, 5.5% over 64 (2000); Marriage status: 26.8% never married, 59.6% now married, 6.1% widowed, 7.5% divorced (2000); Foreign born: 0.0% (2000); Ancestry (includes multiple ancestries): 57.0% Norwegian, 20.5% Swedish, 19.9% German, 5.0% Irish, 4.6% Polish (2000).
Economy: Employment by occupation: 5.2% management, 9.2% professional, 19.4% services, 14.2% sales, 0.0% farming, 8.9% construction, 43.1% production (2000).
Income: Per capita income: $15,544 (2000); Median household income: $45,972 (2000); Poverty rate: 8.1% (2000).
Taxes: Total city taxes per capita: $26 (1997); City property taxes per capita: $26 (1997).
Education: High school graduation rate: 89.7% (2000); College graduation rate: 7.9% (2000).
Housing: Homeownership rate: 90.2% (2000); Median home value: $86,700 (2000); Median rent: $263 per month (2000); Median age of housing: 23 years (2000).
Transportation: Commute to work: 95.3% car, 0.6% public transportation, 1.6% walk, 1.3% work from home (2000); Travel time to work: 18.4% less than 15 minutes, 66.0% 15 to 30 minutes, 7.6% 30 to 45 minutes, 2.5% 45 to 60 minutes, 5.4% 60 minutes or more (2000)

FALUN (township). Covers a land area of 35.584 square miles and a water area of 0 square miles. Located at 48.75° N. Lat.; 95.56° W. Long.
Population: 226 (2000); Race: 100.0% White, 0.0% Black, 0.0% Asian, 0.0% American Indian and Alaska Native, 0.0% Hispanic of any race, 0.0% two or more races (2000); Density: 6.4 persons per square mile (2000); Age: 26.0% under 18, 20.0% over 64 (2000); Marriage status: 22.5% never married, 68.1% now married, 4.9% widowed, 4.4% divorced (2000); Foreign born: 0.4% (2000); Ancestry (includes multiple ancestries): 41.6% Swedish, 40.4% Norwegian, 30.4% German, 7.6% Polish, 4.0% English (2000).
Economy: Employment by occupation: 15.2% management, 17.4% professional, 8.3% services, 15.2% sales, 7.6% farming, 9.8% construction, 26.5% production (2000).
Income: Per capita income: $16,702 (2000); Median household income: $34,444 (2000); Poverty rate: 8.4% (2000).
Taxes: Total city taxes per capita: $53 (1997); City property taxes per capita: $53 (1997).
Education: High school graduation rate: 76.8% (2000); College graduation rate: 16.1% (2000).
Housing: Homeownership rate: 90.4% (2000); Median home value: $56,700 (2000); Median rent: $275 per month (2000); Median age of housing: 40 years (2000).
Transportation: Commute to work: 95.4% car, 0.0% public transportation, 1.5% walk, 3.1% work from home (2000); Travel time to work: 7.1% less than 15 minutes, 67.5% 15 to 30 minutes, 18.3% 30 to 45 minutes, 2.4% 45 to 60 minutes, 4.8% 60 minutes or more (2000)

GOLDEN VALLEY (township). Covers a land area of 36.197 square miles and a water area of 0 square miles. Located at 48.56° N. Lat.; 95.67° W. Long.
Population: 190 (2000); Race: 99.5% White, 0.0% Black, 0.0% Asian, 0.0% American Indian and Alaska Native, 0.5% Hispanic of any race, 0.0% two or more races (2000); Density: 5.2 persons per square mile (2000); Age: 32.1% under 18, 9.5% over 64 (2000); Marriage status: 22.4% never married, 65.0% now married, 4.2% widowed, 8.4% divorced (2000); Foreign born: 0.0% (2000); Ancestry (includes multiple ancestries): 54.2% Norwegian, 27.9% German, 25.8% Swedish, 7.9% English, 2.6% French (except Basque) (2000).
Economy: Employment by occupation: 6.1% management, 7.1% professional, 10.2% services, 14.3% sales, 2.0% farming, 7.1% construction, 53.1% production (2000).
Income: Per capita income: $15,513 (2000); Median household income: $44,375 (2000); Poverty rate: 9.1% (2000).
Education: High school graduation rate: 78.2% (2000); College graduation rate: 1.7% (2000).
Housing: Homeownership rate: 94.7% (2000); Median home value: $72,500 (2000); Median rent: $225 per month (2000); Median age of housing: 25 years (2000).
Transportation: Commute to work: 87.8% car, 0.0% public transportation, 0.0% walk, 10.2% work from home (2000); Travel time to work: 15.9% less than 15 minutes, 35.2% 15 to 30 minutes, 30.7% 30 to 45 minutes, 11.4% 45 to 60 minutes, 6.8% 60 minutes or more (2000)

GREENBUSH (city). Covers a land area of 1.466 square miles and a water area of 0 square miles. Located at 48.69° N. Lat.; 96.18° W. Long. Elevation is 1,075 feet.
History: Greenbush came into existence in 1904 when the Great Northern Railway arrived, and the town was incorporated a year later. The town site was purchased from Ole O. Hereim, for whom the township was named. The name of Greenbush came from the heavy stand of evergreens nearby.
Population: 784 (2000); Race: 98.1% White, 0.0% Black, 0.4% Asian, 0.5% American Indian and Alaska Native, 0.3% Hispanic of any race, 0.8% two or more races (2000); Density: 534.6 persons per square mile (2000); Age: 21.9% under 18, 25.1% over 64 (2000); Marriage status: 14.8% never married, 63.0% now married, 14.1% widowed, 8.1% divorced (2000); Foreign born: 1.6% (2000); Ancestry (includes multiple ancestries): 50.2% Norwegian, 20.6% German, 14.8% Polish, 10.8% Swedish, 4.5% Czech (2000).
Economy: Single-family building permits issued: 1 (2001) / 1 (2000); Multi-family building permits issued: 0 (2001) / 0 (2000); Employment by occupation: 8.7% management, 14.4% professional, 13.3% services, 20.1% sales, 0.5% farming, 7.0% construction, 36.0% production (2000).
Income: Per capita income: $18,565 (2000); Median household income: $33,750 (2000); Poverty rate: 6.6% (2000).
Taxes: Total city taxes per capita: $113 (1997); City property taxes per capita: $111 (1997).
Education: High school graduation rate: 71.4% (2000); College graduation rate: 12.6% (2000).

School District(s)

Greenbush-Middle River (PK-12)
2000 Enrollment: 479 218-782-2231

Housing: Homeownership rate: 78.8% (2000); Median home value: $57,100 (2000); Median rent: $288 per month (2000); Median age of housing: 38 years (2000).
Hospitals: Greenbush Community Nursing Home & Community Clinic (60 beds)
Newspapers: New River Record (1 x week); The Tribune (1 x week)
Transportation: Commute to work: 90.7% car, 0.0% public transportation, 7.1% walk, 2.2% work from home (2000); Travel time to work: 40.3% less than 15 minutes, 17.1% 15 to 30 minutes, 24.6% 30 to 45 minutes, 12.0% 45 to 60 minutes, 5.9% 60 minutes or more (2000)

GRIMSTAD (township). Covers a land area of 37.074 square miles and a water area of 0 square miles. Located at 48.66° N. Lat.; 95.78° W. Long.

Population: 190 (2000); Race: 100.0% White, 0.0% Black, 0.0% Asian, 0.0% American Indian and Alaska Native, 0.0% Hispanic of any race, 0.0% two or more races (2000); Density: 5.1 persons per square mile (2000); Age: 25.1% under 18, 23.0% over 64 (2000); Marriage status: 12.5% never married, 77.6% now married, 5.9% widowed, 3.9% divorced (2000); Foreign born: 1.0% (2000); Ancestry (includes multiple ancestries): 52.9% Norwegian, 25.7% Swedish, 22.0% German, 7.9% English, 7.3% Irish (2000).
Economy: Employment by occupation: 9.6% management, 26.6% professional, 7.4% services, 10.6% sales, 0.0% farming, 9.6% construction, 36.2% production (2000).
Income: Per capita income: $15,762 (2000); Median household income: $42,500 (2000); Poverty rate: 5.2% (2000).
Taxes: Total city taxes per capita: $46 (1997); City property taxes per capita: $46 (1997).
Education: High school graduation rate: 80.0% (2000); College graduation rate: 5.2% (2000).
Housing: Homeownership rate: 92.1% (2000); Median home value: $60,000 (2000); Median rent: $275 per month (2000); Median age of housing: 29 years (2000).
Transportation: Commute to work: 85.1% car, 3.2% public transportation, 5.3% walk, 6.4% work from home (2000); Travel time to work: 20.5% less than 15 minutes, 64.8% 15 to 30 minutes, 8.0% 30 to 45 minutes, 6.8% 45 to 60 minutes, 0.0% 60 minutes or more (2000)

HEREIM (township). Covers a land area of 33.181 square miles and a water area of 0 square miles. Located at 48.69° N. Lat.; 96.19° W. Long.
Population: 248 (2000); Race: 94.7% White, 0.0% Black, 0.0% Asian, 1.5% American Indian and Alaska Native, 0.0% Hispanic of any race, 3.8% two or more races (2000); Density: 7.5 persons per square mile (2000); Age: 30.5% under 18, 8.0% over 64 (2000); Marriage status: 19.0% never married, 72.8% now married, 6.2% widowed, 2.1% divorced (2000); Foreign born: 1.5% (2000); Ancestry (includes multiple ancestries): 56.5% Norwegian, 20.6% German, 14.5% Polish, 13.4% Swedish, 6.9% French (except Basque) (2000).
Economy: Employment by occupation: 17.9% management, 9.3% professional, 15.0% services, 19.3% sales, 0.0% farming, 5.7% construction, 32.9% production (2000).
Income: Per capita income: $13,977 (2000); Median household income: $38,750 (2000); Poverty rate: 9.9% (2000).
Taxes: Total city taxes per capita: $35 (1997); City property taxes per capita: $35 (1997).
Education: High school graduation rate: 86.3% (2000); College graduation rate: 8.9% (2000).
Housing: Homeownership rate: 99.0% (2000); Median home value: $31,700 (2000); Median rent: $275 per month (2000); Median age of housing: 28 years (2000).
Transportation: Commute to work: 81.4% car, 0.0% public transportation, 0.0% walk, 18.6% work from home (2000); Travel time to work: 39.5% less than 15 minutes, 25.4% 15 to 30 minutes, 17.5% 30 to 45 minutes, 9.6% 45 to 60 minutes, 7.9% 60 minutes or more (2000)

HUSS (township). Covers a land area of 36.433 square miles and a water area of 0.007 square miles. Located at 48.58° N. Lat.; 96.07° W. Long.
Population: 145 (2000); Race: 100.0% White, 0.0% Black, 0.0% Asian, 0.0% American Indian and Alaska Native, 0.0% Hispanic of any race, 0.0% two or more races (2000); Density: 4.0 persons per square mile (2000); Age: 33.3% under 18, 19.1% over 64 (2000); Marriage status: 28.6% never married, 57.1% now married, 14.3% widowed, 0.0% divorced (2000); Foreign born: 0.0% (2000); Ancestry (includes multiple ancestries): 51.8% Norwegian, 19.1% Swedish, 9.2% German, 7.8% Scandinavian, 7.1% Czech (2000).
Economy: Employment by occupation: 45.0% management, 15.0% professional, 6.7% services, 1.7% sales, 0.0% farming, 1.7% construction, 30.0% production (2000).
Income: Per capita income: $12,248 (2000); Median household income: $21,458 (2000); Poverty rate: 19.1% (2000).
Taxes: Total city taxes per capita: $47 (1997); City property taxes per capita: $47 (1997).
Education: High school graduation rate: 70.8% (2000); College graduation rate: 6.7% (2000).
Housing: Homeownership rate: 88.9% (2000); Median home value: $129,200 (2000); Median rent: $225 per month (2000); Median age of housing: 36 years (2000).
Transportation: Commute to work: 60.0% car, 3.3% public transportation, 3.3% walk, 28.3% work from home (2000); Travel time to work: 18.6% less than 15 minutes, 27.9% 15 to 30 minutes, 27.9% 30 to 45 minutes, 20.9% 45 to 60 minutes, 4.7% 60 minutes or more (2000)

JADIS (township). Covers a land area of 49.641 square miles and a water area of 0 square miles. Located at 48.87° N. Lat.; 95.79° W. Long.
Population: 564 (2000); Race: 100.0% White, 0.0% Black, 0.0% Asian, 0.0% American Indian and Alaska Native, 0.0% Hispanic of any race, 0.0% two or more races (2000); Density: 11.4 persons per square mile (2000); Age: 29.0% under 18, 12.2% over 64 (2000); Marriage status: 21.0% never married, 66.4% now married, 3.3% widowed, 9.3% divorced (2000); Foreign born: 1.1% (2000); Ancestry (includes multiple ancestries): 49.5% Norwegian, 27.0% Swedish, 25.2% German, 4.7% Irish, 4.2% Scandinavian (2000).
Economy: Employment by occupation: 8.8% management, 17.6% professional, 11.1% services, 21.2% sales, 0.3% farming, 8.5% construction, 32.4% production (2000).
Income: Per capita income: $19,434 (2000); Median household income: $49,000 (2000); Poverty rate: 1.1% (2000).
Taxes: Total city taxes per capita: $30 (1997); City property taxes per capita: $28 (1997).
Education: High school graduation rate: 85.0% (2000); College graduation rate: 13.9% (2000).
Housing: Homeownership rate: 92.4% (2000); Median home value: $86,300 (2000); Median rent: $325 per month (2000); Median age of housing: 25 years (2000).
Transportation: Commute to work: 89.3% car, 0.0% public transportation, 1.3% walk, 9.4% work from home (2000); Travel time to work: 74.5% less than 15 minutes, 13.7% 15 to 30 minutes, 5.9% 30 to 45 minutes, 0.0% 45 to 60 minutes, 5.9% 60 minutes or more (2000)

LAKE (township). Covers a land area of 57.765 square miles and a water area of 0.391 square miles. Located at 48.92° N. Lat.; 95.36° W. Long.
Population: 2,087 (2000); Race: 92.2% White, 0.0% Black, 4.3% Asian, 2.1% American Indian and Alaska Native, 0.2% Hispanic of any race, 1.3% two or more races (2000); Density: 36.1 persons per square mile (2000); Age: 33.9% under 18, 6.1% over 64 (2000); Marriage status: 23.2% never married, 64.8% now married, 2.8% widowed, 9.3% divorced (2000); Foreign born: 4.4% (2000); Ancestry (includes multiple ancestries): 33.2% Norwegian, 30.1% German, 14.2% Swedish, 8.6% Other groups, 6.9% Irish (2000).
Economy: Single-family building permits issued: 9 (2001) / 9 (2000); Multi-family building permits issued: 4 (2001) / 4 (2000); Employment by occupation: 9.8% management, 10.4% professional, 9.8% services, 19.0% sales, 1.2% farming, 7.8% construction, 42.0% production (2000).
Income: Per capita income: $16,549 (2000); Median household income: $44,034 (2000); Poverty rate: 4.5% (2000).
Taxes: Total city taxes per capita: $70 (2000); City property taxes per capita: $69 (2000).
Education: High school graduation rate: 86.1% (2000); College graduation rate: 14.2% (2000).
Housing: Homeownership rate: 89.9% (2000); Median home value: $85,000 (2000); Median rent: $400 per month (2000); Median age of housing: 21 years (2000).
Transportation: Commute to work: 95.0% car, 0.7% public transportation, 0.6% walk, 3.3% work from home (2000); Travel time to work: 74.0% less than 15 minutes, 19.5% 15 to 30 minutes, 3.9% 30 to 45 minutes, 0.4% 45 to 60 minutes, 2.2% 60 minutes or more (2000)

LAONA (township). Covers a land area of 38.067 square miles and a water area of 0.014 square miles. Located at 48.85° N. Lat.; 95.15° W. Long.
Population: 578 (2000); Race: 95.3% White, 0.5% Black, 0.0% Asian, 3.5% American Indian and Alaska Native, 0.0% Hispanic of any race, 0.7% two or more races (2000); Density: 15.2 persons per square mile (2000); Age: 30.6% under 18, 8.8% over 64 (2000); Marriage status: 23.3% never married, 61.2% now married, 6.0% widowed, 9.6% divorced (2000); Foreign born: 2.6% (2000); Ancestry (includes multiple ancestries): 34.3% German, 25.6% Norwegian, 11.6% Swedish, 7.4% Irish, 6.8% Other groups (2000).
Economy: Employment by occupation: 10.0% management, 5.3% professional, 11.0% services, 16.3% sales, 0.7% farming, 10.3% construction, 46.3% production (2000).
Income: Per capita income: $15,112 (2000); Median household income: $37,250 (2000); Poverty rate: 7.1% (2000).
Taxes: Total city taxes per capita: $24 (1997); City property taxes per capita: $24 (1997).
Education: High school graduation rate: 78.3% (2000); College graduation rate: 7.8% (2000).

Housing: Homeownership rate: 95.0% (2000); Median home value: $64,300 (2000); Median rent: $325 per month (2000); Median age of housing: 21 years (2000).
Transportation: Commute to work: 98.0% car, 0.0% public transportation, 0.0% walk, 2.0% work from home (2000); Travel time to work: 30.2% less than 15 minutes, 54.6% 15 to 30 minutes, 7.9% 30 to 45 minutes, 3.8% 45 to 60 minutes, 3.4% 60 minutes or more (2000)

LIND (township). Covers a land area of 36.134 square miles and a water area of 0 square miles. Located at 48.57° N. Lat.; 96.31° W. Long.
Population: 58 (2000); Race: 100.0% White, 0.0% Black, 0.0% Asian, 0.0% American Indian and Alaska Native, 0.0% Hispanic of any race, 0.0% two or more races (2000); Density: 1.6 persons per square mile (2000); Age: 27.6% under 18, 32.8% over 64 (2000); Marriage status: 11.4% never married, 84.1% now married, 4.5% widowed, 0.0% divorced (2000); Foreign born: 0.0% (2000); Ancestry (includes multiple ancestries): 67.2% Norwegian, 37.9% German, 15.5% Swedish, 6.9% Dutch, 5.2% Danish (2000).
Economy: Employment by occupation: 58.6% management, 13.8% professional, 0.0% services, 0.0% sales, 6.9% farming, 13.8% construction, 6.9% production (2000).
Income: Per capita income: $11,005 (2000); Median household income: $26,250 (2000); Poverty rate: 0.0% (2000).
Taxes: Total city taxes per capita: $62 (1997); City property taxes per capita: $62 (1997).
Education: High school graduation rate: 70.3% (2000); College graduation rate: 5.4% (2000).
Housing: Homeownership rate: 100.0% (2000); Median home value: $104,200 (2000); Median age of housing: 37 years (2000).
Transportation: Commute to work: 37.9% car, 0.0% public transportation, 27.6% walk, 34.5% work from home (2000); Travel time to work: 68.4% less than 15 minutes, 21.1% 15 to 30 minutes, 10.5% 30 to 45 minutes, 0.0% 45 to 60 minutes, 0.0% 60 minutes or more (2000)

MALUNG (township). Covers a land area of 35.830 square miles and a water area of 0 square miles. Located at 48.76° N. Lat.; 95.68° W. Long.
Population: 427 (2000); Race: 98.9% White, 0.0% Black, 0.0% Asian, 0.4% American Indian and Alaska Native, 0.0% Hispanic of any race, 0.6% two or more races (2000); Density: 11.9 persons per square mile (2000); Age: 30.6% under 18, 9.5% over 64 (2000); Marriage status: 17.2% never married, 71.0% now married, 5.7% widowed, 6.0% divorced (2000); Foreign born: 1.3% (2000); Ancestry (includes multiple ancestries): 43.3% Norwegian, 26.3% Swedish, 24.6% German, 7.8% Irish, 5.0% French (except Basque) (2000).
Economy: Employment by occupation: 4.3% management, 25.2% professional, 6.2% services, 17.8% sales, 1.9% farming, 12.4% construction, 32.2% production (2000).
Income: Per capita income: $18,787 (2000); Median household income: $49,250 (2000); Poverty rate: 5.0% (2000).
Taxes: Total city taxes per capita: $27 (1997); City property taxes per capita: $27 (1997).
Education: High school graduation rate: 86.1% (2000); College graduation rate: 20.6% (2000).
Housing: Homeownership rate: 91.1% (2000); Median home value: $86,300 (2000); Median rent: $288 per month (2000); Median age of housing: 28 years (2000).
Transportation: Commute to work: 95.7% car, 0.0% public transportation, 2.0% walk, 1.6% work from home (2000); Travel time to work: 30.4% less than 15 minutes, 50.4% 15 to 30 minutes, 9.2% 30 to 45 minutes, 0.0% 45 to 60 minutes, 10.0% 60 minutes or more (2000)

MICKINOCK (township). Covers a land area of 37.690 square miles and a water area of 0 square miles. Located at 48.67° N. Lat.; 95.68° W. Long.
Population: 302 (2000); Race: 99.3% White, 0.0% Black, 0.0% Asian, 0.0% American Indian and Alaska Native, 0.0% Hispanic of any race, 0.7% two or more races (2000); Density: 8.0 persons per square mile (2000); Age: 25.8% under 18, 13.9% over 64 (2000); Marriage status: 24.1% never married, 66.0% now married, 7.5% widowed, 2.5% divorced (2000); Foreign born: 0.3% (2000); Ancestry (includes multiple ancestries): 51.9% Norwegian, 22.7% Swedish, 20.0% German, 5.4% Irish, 3.4% Polish (2000).
Economy: Employment by occupation: 15.6% management, 12.0% professional, 3.0% services, 16.8% sales, 3.6% farming, 7.2% construction, 41.9% production (2000).
Income: Per capita income: $17,697 (2000); Median household income: $48,281 (2000); Poverty rate: 7.5% (2000).
Taxes: Total city taxes per capita: $33 (1997); City property taxes per capita: $33 (1997).
Education: High school graduation rate: 81.9% (2000); College graduation rate: 9.0% (2000).
Housing: Homeownership rate: 95.3% (2000); Median home value: $69,000 (2000); Median rent: $225 per month (2000); Median age of housing: 35 years (2000).
Transportation: Commute to work: 91.5% car, 0.6% public transportation, 1.2% walk, 6.1% work from home (2000); Travel time to work: 14.2% less than 15 minutes, 52.3% 15 to 30 minutes, 21.3% 30 to 45 minutes, 5.8% 45 to 60 minutes, 6.5% 60 minutes or more (2000)

MOOSE (township). Covers a land area of 36.439 square miles and a water area of 0.004 square miles. Located at 48.84° N. Lat.; 96.08° W. Long.
Population: 134 (2000); Race: 99.2% White, 0.0% Black, 0.0% Asian, 0.0% American Indian and Alaska Native, 1.7% Hispanic of any race, 0.8% two or more races (2000); Density: 3.7 persons per square mile (2000); Age: 32.8% under 18, 14.3% over 64 (2000); Marriage status: 22.6% never married, 69.0% now married, 6.0% widowed, 2.4% divorced (2000); Foreign born: 1.7% (2000); Ancestry (includes multiple ancestries): 62.2% Norwegian, 23.5% German, 12.6% Swedish, 6.7% Polish, 4.2% United States or American (2000).
Economy: Employment by occupation: 20.0% management, 8.0% professional, 10.0% services, 36.0% sales, 0.0% farming, 2.0% construction, 24.0% production (2000).
Income: Per capita income: $13,419 (2000); Median household income: $28,750 (2000); Poverty rate: 18.5% (2000).
Taxes: Total city taxes per capita: $48 (1997); City property taxes per capita: $48 (1997).
Education: High school graduation rate: 77.6% (2000); College graduation rate: 10.5% (2000).
Housing: Homeownership rate: 93.8% (2000); Median home value: $60,000 (2000); Median rent: $325 per month (2000); Median age of housing: 41 years (2000).
Transportation: Commute to work: 84.0% car, 0.0% public transportation, 0.0% walk, 16.0% work from home (2000); Travel time to work: 21.4% less than 15 minutes, 40.5% 15 to 30 minutes, 31.0% 30 to 45 minutes, 0.0% 45 to 60 minutes, 7.1% 60 minutes or more (2000)

MORANVILLE (township). Covers a land area of 35.501 square miles and a water area of 0 square miles. Located at 48.85° N. Lat.; 95.28° W. Long.
Population: 940 (2000); Race: 97.8% White, 0.0% Black, 0.0% Asian, 1.6% American Indian and Alaska Native, 0.0% Hispanic of any race, 0.6% two or more races (2000); Density: 26.5 persons per square mile (2000); Age: 36.1% under 18, 6.9% over 64 (2000); Marriage status: 21.3% never married, 67.4% now married, 2.4% widowed, 9.0% divorced (2000); Foreign born: 1.5% (2000); Ancestry (includes multiple ancestries): 37.6% Norwegian, 31.2% German, 17.8% Swedish, 5.8% Irish, 4.8% Polish (2000).
Economy: Single-family building permits issued: 0 (2001) / 0 (2000); Multi-family building permits issued: 0 (2001) / 0 (2000); Employment by occupation: 9.6% management, 17.6% professional, 10.2% services, 17.6% sales, 1.6% farming, 10.0% construction, 33.2% production (2000).
Income: Per capita income: $14,975 (2000); Median household income: $41,094 (2000); Poverty rate: 7.8% (2000).
Taxes: Total city taxes per capita: $20 (1997); City property taxes per capita: $18 (1997).
Education: High school graduation rate: 86.4% (2000); College graduation rate: 14.9% (2000).
Housing: Homeownership rate: 97.1% (2000); Median home value: $90,800 (2000); Median rent: $225 per month (2000); Median age of housing: 18 years (2000).
Transportation: Commute to work: 96.1% car, 0.2% public transportation, 0.0% walk, 3.7% work from home (2000); Travel time to work: 56.7% less than 15 minutes, 27.2% 15 to 30 minutes, 10.1% 30 to 45 minutes, 2.4% 45 to 60 minutes, 3.6% 60 minutes or more (2000)

NERESON (township). Covers a land area of 36.265 square miles and a water area of 0 square miles. Located at 48.68° N. Lat.; 95.94° W. Long.
Population: 69 (2000); Race: 100.0% White, 0.0% Black, 0.0% Asian, 0.0% American Indian and Alaska Native, 0.0% Hispanic of any race, 0.0% two or more races (2000); Density: 1.9 persons per square mile (2000); Age: 29.5% under 18, 14.8% over 64 (2000); Marriage status: 32.9% never married, 56.6% now married, 6.6% widowed, 3.9% divorced (2000); Foreign born: 0.0% (2000); Ancestry (includes multiple ancestries): 72.7% Norwegian, 26.1% German, 5.7% Swedish, 5.7% Czech, 2.3% French Canadian (2000).

Economy: Employment by occupation: 24.5% management, 7.5% professional, 20.8% services, 11.3% sales, 3.8% farming, 0.0% construction, 32.1% production (2000).
Income: Per capita income: $13,899 (2000); Median household income: $29,375 (2000); Poverty rate: 2.3% (2000).
Taxes: Total city taxes per capita: $74 (1997); City property taxes per capita: $74 (1997).
Education: High school graduation rate: 72.4% (2000); College graduation rate: 10.3% (2000).
Housing: Homeownership rate: 100.0% (2000); Median home value: $33,800 (2000); Median age of housing: 43 years (2000).
Transportation: Commute to work: 86.8% car, 0.0% public transportation, 0.0% walk, 13.2% work from home (2000); Travel time to work: 10.9% less than 15 minutes, 39.1% 15 to 30 minutes, 19.6% 30 to 45 minutes, 21.7% 45 to 60 minutes, 8.7% 60 minutes or more (2000)

PALMVILLE (township). Covers a land area of 35.785 square miles and a water area of 0.035 square miles. Located at 48.58° N. Lat.; 95.78° W. Long.
Population: 55 (2000); Race: 100.0% White, 0.0% Black, 0.0% Asian, 0.0% American Indian and Alaska Native, 0.0% Hispanic of any race, 0.0% two or more races (2000); Density: 1.5 persons per square mile (2000); Age: 25.0% under 18, 14.6% over 64 (2000); Marriage status: 19.0% never married, 61.9% now married, 4.8% widowed, 14.3% divorced (2000); Foreign born: 0.0% (2000); Ancestry (includes multiple ancestries): 62.5% Norwegian, 29.2% Swedish, 12.5% Polish, 10.4% Other groups, 6.3% German (2000).
Economy: Employment by occupation: 29.2% management, 25.0% professional, 8.3% services, 16.7% sales, 0.0% farming, 8.3% construction, 12.5% production (2000).
Income: Per capita income: $17,408 (2000); Median household income: $40,000 (2000); Poverty rate: 10.4% (2000).
Taxes: Total city taxes per capita: $55 (1997); City property taxes per capita: $55 (1997).
Education: High school graduation rate: 85.3% (2000); College graduation rate: 26.5% (2000).
Housing: Homeownership rate: 100.0% (2000); Median age of housing: 25 years (2000).
Transportation: Commute to work: 79.2% car, 0.0% public transportation, 4.2% walk, 16.7% work from home (2000); Travel time to work: 10.0% less than 15 minutes, 40.0% 15 to 30 minutes, 30.0% 30 to 45 minutes, 0.0% 45 to 60 minutes, 20.0% 60 minutes or more (2000)

POHLITZ (township). Covers a land area of 42.420 square miles and a water area of 2.847 square miles. Located at 48.92° N. Lat.; 96.06° W. Long.
Population: 36 (2000); Race: 100.0% White, 0.0% Black, 0.0% Asian, 0.0% American Indian and Alaska Native, 0.0% Hispanic of any race, 0.0% two or more races (2000); Density: 0.8 persons per square mile (2000); Age: 27.1% under 18, 0.0% over 64 (2000); Marriage status: 5.7% never married, 80.0% now married, 5.7% widowed, 8.6% divorced (2000); Foreign born: 0.0% (2000); Ancestry (includes multiple ancestries): 70.8% Norwegian, 20.8% German, 6.3% Swedish, 4.2% United States or American, 4.2% Czech (2000).
Economy: Employment by occupation: 27.3% management, 12.1% professional, 6.1% services, 18.2% sales, 0.0% farming, 9.1% construction, 27.3% production (2000).
Income: Per capita income: $19,144 (2000); Median household income: $42,500 (2000); Poverty rate: 0.0% (2000).
Taxes: Total city taxes per capita: $93 (1997); City property taxes per capita: $93 (1997).
Education: High school graduation rate: 93.9% (2000); College graduation rate: 18.2% (2000).
Housing: Homeownership rate: 78.9% (2000); Median home value: $55,000 (2000); Median age of housing: 32 years (2000).
Transportation: Commute to work: 87.9% car, 0.0% public transportation, 6.1% walk, 6.1% work from home (2000); Travel time to work: 25.8% less than 15 minutes, 48.4% 15 to 30 minutes, 19.4% 30 to 45 minutes, 0.0% 45 to 60 minutes, 6.5% 60 minutes or more (2000)

POLONIA (township). Covers a land area of 36.688 square miles and a water area of 0.031 square miles. Located at 48.76° N. Lat.; 96.32° W. Long.
Population: 38 (2000); Race: 100.0% White, 0.0% Black, 0.0% Asian, 0.0% American Indian and Alaska Native, 0.0% Hispanic of any race, 0.0% two or more races (2000); Density: 1.0 persons per square mile (2000); Age: 19.4% under 18, 38.7% over 64 (2000); Marriage status: 16.0% never married, 72.0% now married, 12.0% widowed, 0.0% divorced (2000); Foreign born: 0.0% (2000); Ancestry (includes multiple ancestries): 45.2% Norwegian, 38.7% Polish, 32.3% German, 9.7% Czechoslovakian, 9.7% Scandinavian (2000).
Economy: Employment by occupation: 23.1% management, 38.5% professional, 0.0% services, 38.5% sales, 0.0% farming, 0.0% construction, 0.0% production (2000).
Income: Per capita income: $18,090 (2000); Median household income: $35,000 (2000); Poverty rate: 0.0% (2000).
Taxes: Total city taxes per capita: $172 (1997); City property taxes per capita: $172 (1997).
Education: High school graduation rate: 69.6% (2000); College graduation rate: 8.7% (2000).
Housing: Homeownership rate: 100.0% (2000); Median home value: $137,500 (2000); Median age of housing: 33 years (2000).
Transportation: Commute to work: 76.9% car, 0.0% public transportation, 0.0% walk, 23.1% work from home (2000); Travel time to work: 60.0% less than 15 minutes, 20.0% 15 to 30 minutes, 20.0% 30 to 45 minutes, 0.0% 45 to 60 minutes, 0.0% 60 minutes or more (2000)

POPLAR GROVE (township). Covers a land area of 35.958 square miles and a water area of 0.021 square miles. Located at 48.58° N. Lat.; 95.93° W. Long.
Population: 80 (2000); Race: 100.0% White, 0.0% Black, 0.0% Asian, 0.0% American Indian and Alaska Native, 0.0% Hispanic of any race, 0.0% two or more races (2000); Density: 2.2 persons per square mile (2000); Age: 18.8% under 18, 13.8% over 64 (2000); Marriage status: 22.4% never married, 67.2% now married, 4.5% widowed, 6.0% divorced (2000); Foreign born: 0.0% (2000); Ancestry (includes multiple ancestries): 36.3% Norwegian, 30.0% German, 25.0% Czech, 22.5% Swedish, 15.0% Polish (2000).
Economy: Employment by occupation: 30.4% management, 14.3% professional, 5.4% services, 3.6% sales, 8.9% farming, 3.6% construction, 33.9% production (2000).
Income: Per capita income: $15,665 (2000); Median household income: $36,875 (2000); Poverty rate: 3.8% (2000).
Taxes: Total city taxes per capita: $47 (1997); City property taxes per capita: $47 (1997).
Education: High school graduation rate: 87.3% (2000); College graduation rate: 3.6% (2000).
Housing: Homeownership rate: 81.3% (2000); Median home value: $75,000 (2000); Median rent: $375 per month (2000); Median age of housing: 32 years (2000).
Transportation: Commute to work: 60.7% car, 0.0% public transportation, 16.1% walk, 23.2% work from home (2000); Travel time to work: 25.6% less than 15 minutes, 4.7% 15 to 30 minutes, 46.5% 30 to 45 minutes, 20.9% 45 to 60 minutes, 2.3% 60 minutes or more (2000)

REINE (township). Covers a land area of 36.104 square miles and a water area of 0.077 square miles. Located at 48.56° N. Lat.; 95.52° W. Long.
Population: 115 (2000); Race: 100.0% White, 0.0% Black, 0.0% Asian, 0.0% American Indian and Alaska Native, 0.0% Hispanic of any race, 0.0% two or more races (2000); Density: 3.2 persons per square mile (2000); Age: 22.2% under 18, 15.2% over 64 (2000); Marriage status: 17.7% never married, 70.9% now married, 6.3% widowed, 5.1% divorced (2000); Foreign born: 0.0% (2000); Ancestry (includes multiple ancestries): 52.5% Norwegian, 30.3% Swedish, 28.3% German, 9.1% French (except Basque), 3.0% Irish (2000).
Economy: Employment by occupation: 17.5% management, 5.3% professional, 3.5% services, 40.4% sales, 0.0% farming, 8.8% construction, 24.6% production (2000).
Income: Per capita income: $17,283 (2000); Median household income: $47,188 (2000); Poverty rate: 5.1% (2000).
Taxes: Total city taxes per capita: $74 (1997); City property taxes per capita: $74 (1997).
Education: High school graduation rate: 84.5% (2000); College graduation rate: 5.6% (2000).
Housing: Homeownership rate: 95.0% (2000); Median home value: $68,800 (2000); Median rent: $275 per month (2000); Median age of housing: 31 years (2000).
Transportation: Commute to work: 96.5% car, 0.0% public transportation, 0.0% walk, 3.5% work from home (2000); Travel time to work: 0.0% less than 15 minutes, 3.6% 15 to 30 minutes, 56.4% 30 to 45 minutes, 34.5% 45 to 60 minutes, 5.5% 60 minutes or more (2000)

ROOSEVELT (city). Covers a land area of 1.033 square miles and a water area of 0 square miles. Located at 48.80° N. Lat.; 95.09° W. Long. Elevation is 1,163 feet.

Population: 166 (2000); Race: 100.0% White, 0.0% Black, 0.0% Asian, 0.0% American Indian and Alaska Native, 0.0% Hispanic of any race, 0.0% two or more races (2000); Density: 160.7 persons per square mile (2000); Age: 23.0% under 18, 9.9% over 64 (2000); Marriage status: 24.0% never married, 60.0% now married, 1.6% widowed, 14.4% divorced (2000); Foreign born: 0.0% (2000); Ancestry (includes multiple ancestries): 40.8% Norwegian, 30.9% German, 15.1% Swedish, 7.9% United States or American, 7.2% French (except Basque) (2000).
Economy: Agriculture: potatoes, grain, flax, sunflowers, alfalfa. Manufacturing of custom boat tops. Employment by occupation: 5.8% management, 5.8% professional, 17.4% services, 16.3% sales, 0.0% farming, 8.1% construction, 46.5% production (2000).
Income: Per capita income: $15,656 (2000); Median household income: $31,875 (2000); Poverty rate: 12.5% (2000).
Taxes: Total city taxes per capita: $22 (1997); City property taxes per capita: $16 (1997).
Education: High school graduation rate: 84.5% (2000); College graduation rate: 3.9% (2000).
Housing: Homeownership rate: 96.8% (2000); Median home value: $49,400 (2000); Median age of housing: 29 years (2000).
Transportation: Commute to work: 100.0% car, 0.0% public transportation, 0.0% walk, 0.0% work from home (2000); Travel time to work: 15.2% less than 15 minutes, 68.4% 15 to 30 minutes, 12.7% 30 to 45 minutes, 3.8% 45 to 60 minutes, 0.0% 60 minutes or more (2000)

ROSEAU (city). Covers a land area of 2.389 square miles and a water area of 0 square miles. Located at 48.84° N. Lat.; 95.76° W. Long. Elevation is 1,048 feet.
History: The name of Roseau came from the French "Riviere aux Roseaux," meaning "river of the rushes." Roseau developed as a trading and shipping center for the surrounding area. A round stone with incised figures within a circle, found near Roseau, may be prehistoric in origin.
Population: 2,756 (2000); Race: 96.3% White, 0.0% Black, 3.0% Asian, 0.2% American Indian and Alaska Native, 0.3% Hispanic of any race, 0.5% two or more races (2000); Density: 1,153.6 persons per square mile (2000); Age: 26.2% under 18, 18.8% over 64 (2000); Marriage status: 20.0% never married, 60.5% now married, 9.2% widowed, 10.3% divorced (2000); Foreign born: 4.4% (2000); Ancestry (includes multiple ancestries): 42.6% Norwegian, 23.0% German, 22.7% Swedish, 7.3% Irish, 4.7% Polish (2000).
Economy: Single-family building permits issued: 20 (2001) / 5 (2000); Multi-family building permits issued: 0 (2001) / 0 (2000); Employment by occupation: 8.8% management, 24.7% professional, 11.6% services, 20.0% sales, 0.2% farming, 4.1% construction, 30.6% production (2000).
Income: Per capita income: $18,371 (2000); Median household income: $35,096 (2000); Poverty rate: 6.1% (2000).
Taxes: Total city taxes per capita: $290 (2000); City property taxes per capita: $270 (2000).
Education: High school graduation rate: 81.2% (2000); College graduation rate: 22.8% (2000).

School District(s)

Roseau (PK-12)
2000 Enrollment: 1,516 218-463-1471
Housing: Homeownership rate: 71.0% (2000); Median home value: $78,000 (2000); Median rent: $408 per month (2000); Median age of housing: 33 years (2000).
Hospitals: Roseau Area Hospital & Homes (25 beds)
Safety: Violent crime rate: 0.0 per 10,000 population; Property crime rate: 344.6 per 10,000 population (2001).
Newspapers: Roseau Times-Region (1 x week)
Transportation: Commute to work: 84.1% car, 0.4% public transportation, 10.5% walk, 2.4% work from home (2000); Travel time to work: 82.8% less than 15 minutes, 9.9% 15 to 30 minutes, 4.9% 30 to 45 minutes, 0.0% 45 to 60 minutes, 2.3% 60 minutes or more (2000)

ROSS (township). Covers a land area of 35.784 square miles and a water area of 0 square miles. Located at 48.83° N. Lat.; 95.93° W. Long. Elevation is 1,035 feet.
Population: 454 (2000); Race: 99.8% White, 0.0% Black, 0.0% Asian, 0.0% American Indian and Alaska Native, 2.3% Hispanic of any race, 0.2% two or more races (2000); Density: 12.7 persons per square mile (2000); Age: 33.4% under 18, 9.6% over 64 (2000); Marriage status: 22.3% never married, 71.0% now married, 3.2% widowed, 3.5% divorced (2000); Foreign born: 1.5% (2000); Ancestry (includes multiple ancestries): 42.2% Norwegian, 27.1% German, 11.7% Swedish, 6.7% Polish, 5.0% English (2000).
Economy: Employment by occupation: 6.3% management, 18.4% professional, 14.5% services, 16.9% sales, 2.0% farming, 7.1% construction, 34.9% production (2000).
Income: Per capita income: $15,746 (2000); Median household income: $43,438 (2000); Poverty rate: 3.1% (2000).
Taxes: Total city taxes per capita: $31 (1997); City property taxes per capita: $31 (1997).
Education: High school graduation rate: 81.6% (2000); College graduation rate: 11.7% (2000).
Housing: Homeownership rate: 100.0% (2000); Median home value: $76,000 (2000); Median age of housing: 24 years (2000).
Transportation: Commute to work: 97.2% car, 0.0% public transportation, 0.0% walk, 2.8% work from home (2000); Travel time to work: 49.0% less than 15 minutes, 34.2% 15 to 30 minutes, 12.3% 30 to 45 minutes, 2.5% 45 to 60 minutes, 2.1% 60 minutes or more (2000)

SALOL (unincorporated postal area, zip code 56756). Covers a land area of 79.318 square miles and a water area of 0.007 square miles. Located at 48.86° N. Lat.; 95.51° W. Long. Elevation is 1,070 feet.
Population: 878 (2000); Race: 97.2% White, 0.0% Black, 1.3% Asian, 0.3% American Indian and Alaska Native, 1.0% Hispanic of any race, 1.0% two or more races (2000); Density: 11.1 persons per square mile (2000); Age: 34.1% under 18, 3.6% over 64 (2000); Marriage status: 27.2% never married, 59.2% now married, 3.8% widowed, 9.8% divorced (2000); Foreign born: 1.5% (2000); Ancestry (includes multiple ancestries): 53.0% Norwegian, 22.7% German, 21.3% Swedish, 4.0% French (except Basque), 3.7% Polish (2000).
Economy: Employment by occupation: 4.2% management, 11.4% professional, 18.4% services, 17.8% sales, 1.0% farming, 9.6% construction, 37.6% production (2000).
Income: Per capita income: $15,418 (2000); Median household income: $43,563 (2000); Poverty rate: 8.2% (2000).
Education: High school graduation rate: 92.4% (2000); College graduation rate: 8.8% (2000).
Housing: Homeownership rate: 90.7% (2000); Median home value: $85,400 (2000); Median rent: $281 per month (2000); Median age of housing: 21 years (2000).
Transportation: Commute to work: 92.1% car, 0.4% public transportation, 2.4% walk, 4.3% work from home (2000); Travel time to work: 27.3% less than 15 minutes, 61.1% 15 to 30 minutes, 5.9% 30 to 45 minutes, 1.7% 45 to 60 minutes, 4.0% 60 minutes or more (2000)

SKAGEN (township). Covers a land area of 35.073 square miles and a water area of 0.008 square miles. Located at 48.76° N. Lat.; 96.06° W. Long.
Population: 235 (2000); Race: 99.1% White, 0.0% Black, 0.0% Asian, 0.9% American Indian and Alaska Native, 0.0% Hispanic of any race, 0.0% two or more races (2000); Density: 6.7 persons per square mile (2000); Age: 24.9% under 18, 8.0% over 64 (2000); Marriage status: 12.6% never married, 79.9% now married, 4.6% widowed, 2.9% divorced (2000); Foreign born: 0.0% (2000); Ancestry (includes multiple ancestries): 54.7% Norwegian, 19.1% German, 18.7% Swedish, 12.4% Polish, 5.3% United States or American (2000).
Economy: Employment by occupation: 14.2% management, 11.2% professional, 15.7% services, 11.9% sales, 0.0% farming, 13.4% construction, 33.6% production (2000).
Income: Per capita income: $16,456 (2000); Median household income: $37,188 (2000); Poverty rate: 9.4% (2000).
Taxes: Total city taxes per capita: $39 (1997); City property taxes per capita: $39 (1997).
Education: High school graduation rate: 89.4% (2000); College graduation rate: 8.8% (2000).
Housing: Homeownership rate: 88.5% (2000); Median home value: $80,800 (2000); Median rent: $300 per month (2000); Median age of housing: 30 years (2000).
Transportation: Commute to work: 86.5% car, 0.0% public transportation, 0.0% walk, 13.5% work from home (2000); Travel time to work: 29.4% less than 15 minutes, 45.0% 15 to 30 minutes, 15.6% 30 to 45 minutes, 8.3% 45 to 60 minutes, 1.8% 60 minutes or more (2000)

SOLER (township). Covers a land area of 36.424 square miles and a water area of 0 square miles. Located at 48.83° N. Lat.; 96.20° W. Long.
Population: 104 (2000); Race: 100.0% White, 0.0% Black, 0.0% Asian, 0.0% American Indian and Alaska Native, 0.0% Hispanic of any race, 0.0% two or more races (2000); Density: 2.9 persons per square mile (2000); Age: 27.4% under 18, 13.7% over 64 (2000); Marriage status: 35.0% never married, 63.1% now married, 0.0% widowed, 1.9% divorced (2000); Foreign born: 0.0% (2000); Ancestry (includes multiple ancestries): 76.9%

Norwegian, 22.2% German, 7.7% Czechoslovakian, 6.8% Polish, 6.0% Swedish (2000).
Economy: Employment by occupation: 18.0% management, 18.0% professional, 9.8% services, 8.2% sales, 3.3% farming, 3.3% construction, 39.3% production (2000).
Income: Per capita income: $16,078 (2000); Median household income: $42,000 (2000); Poverty rate: 5.1% (2000).
Taxes: Total city taxes per capita: $68 (1997); City property taxes per capita: $68 (1997).
Education: High school graduation rate: 81.1% (2000); College graduation rate: 13.5% (2000).
Housing: Homeownership rate: 86.7% (2000); Median home value: $80,000 (2000); Median rent: $225 per month (2000); Median age of housing: 23 years (2000).
Transportation: Commute to work: 81.0% car, 0.0% public transportation, 0.0% walk, 19.0% work from home (2000); Travel time to work: 8.5% less than 15 minutes, 34.0% 15 to 30 minutes, 34.0% 30 to 45 minutes, 0.0% 45 to 60 minutes, 23.4% 60 minutes or more (2000)

SPRUCE (township). Covers a land area of 35.480 square miles and a water area of 0.053 square miles. Located at 48.84° N. Lat.; 95.69° W. Long.
Population: 614 (2000); Race: 96.6% White, 0.0% Black, 1.3% Asian, 0.0% American Indian and Alaska Native, 0.0% Hispanic of any race, 2.1% two or more races (2000); Density: 17.3 persons per square mile (2000); Age: 33.8% under 18, 10.8% over 64 (2000); Marriage status: 21.4% never married, 70.3% now married, 5.0% widowed, 3.3% divorced (2000); Foreign born: 3.1% (2000); Ancestry (includes multiple ancestries): 41.8% Norwegian, 25.6% Swedish, 21.8% German, 6.6% Irish, 4.8% English (2000).
Economy: Employment by occupation: 7.0% management, 13.0% professional, 14.6% services, 31.0% sales, 0.0% farming, 8.5% construction, 25.9% production (2000).
Income: Per capita income: $19,985 (2000); Median household income: $46,875 (2000); Poverty rate: 3.4% (2000).
Taxes: Total city taxes per capita: $29 (1997); City property taxes per capita: $29 (1997).
Education: High school graduation rate: 87.1% (2000); College graduation rate: 18.9% (2000).
Housing: Homeownership rate: 96.8% (2000); Median home value: $109,800 (2000); Median rent: <$100 per month (2000); Median age of housing: 23 years (2000).
Transportation: Commute to work: 94.2% car, 0.0% public transportation, 0.6% walk, 4.9% work from home (2000); Travel time to work: 57.5% less than 15 minutes, 27.9% 15 to 30 minutes, 11.6% 30 to 45 minutes, 1.7% 45 to 60 minutes, 1.4% 60 minutes or more (2000)

STAFFORD (township). Covers a land area of 36.052 square miles and a water area of 0 square miles. Located at 48.75° N. Lat.; 95.79° W. Long.
Population: 297 (2000); Race: 100.0% White, 0.0% Black, 0.0% Asian, 0.0% American Indian and Alaska Native, 0.0% Hispanic of any race, 0.0% two or more races (2000); Density: 8.2 persons per square mile (2000); Age: 33.3% under 18, 12.6% over 64 (2000); Marriage status: 20.6% never married, 69.1% now married, 3.9% widowed, 6.4% divorced (2000); Foreign born: 0.7% (2000); Ancestry (includes multiple ancestries): 40.4% Norwegian, 27.4% Swedish, 26.7% German, 5.6% Polish, 4.9% English (2000).
Economy: Employment by occupation: 13.2% management, 20.4% professional, 9.2% services, 10.5% sales, 1.3% farming, 12.5% construction, 32.9% production (2000).
Income: Per capita income: $19,200 (2000); Median household income: $51,071 (2000); Poverty rate: 7.4% (2000).
Taxes: Total city taxes per capita: $26 (1997); City property taxes per capita: $26 (1997).
Education: High school graduation rate: 84.9% (2000); College graduation rate: 20.7% (2000).
Housing: Homeownership rate: 94.4% (2000); Median home value: $81,700 (2000); Median age of housing: 25 years (2000).
Transportation: Commute to work: 92.7% car, 0.0% public transportation, 2.7% walk, 4.7% work from home (2000); Travel time to work: 57.3% less than 15 minutes, 30.1% 15 to 30 minutes, 7.0% 30 to 45 minutes, 2.8% 45 to 60 minutes, 2.8% 60 minutes or more (2000)

STOKES (township). Covers a land area of 36.025 square miles and a water area of 0 square miles. Located at 48.76° N. Lat.; 95.95° W. Long.
Population: 229 (2000); Race: 100.0% White, 0.0% Black, 0.0% Asian, 0.0% American Indian and Alaska Native, 0.0% Hispanic of any race, 0.0% two or more races (2000); Density: 6.4 persons per square mile (2000); Age: 25.8% under 18, 11.3% over 64 (2000); Marriage status: 26.3% never married, 71.9% now married, 1.2% widowed, 0.6% divorced (2000); Foreign born: 1.4% (2000); Ancestry (includes multiple ancestries): 50.7% Norwegian, 22.5% German, 12.7% Swedish, 4.7% Czech, 4.7% English (2000).
Economy: Employment by occupation: 5.2% management, 7.0% professional, 9.6% services, 19.1% sales, 7.0% farming, 13.0% construction, 39.1% production (2000).
Income: Per capita income: $17,653 (2000); Median household income: $39,531 (2000); Poverty rate: 9.6% (2000).
Taxes: Total city taxes per capita: $39 (1997); City property taxes per capita: $39 (1997).
Education: High school graduation rate: 75.4% (2000); College graduation rate: 2.8% (2000).
Housing: Homeownership rate: 92.7% (2000); Median home value: $65,000 (2000); Median rent: $125 per month (2000); Median age of housing: 26 years (2000).
Transportation: Commute to work: 89.2% car, 0.0% public transportation, 0.0% walk, 10.8% work from home (2000); Travel time to work: 19.2% less than 15 minutes, 50.5% 15 to 30 minutes, 12.1% 30 to 45 minutes, 7.1% 45 to 60 minutes, 11.1% 60 minutes or more (2000)

STRATHCONA (city). Covers a land area of 0.488 square miles and a water area of 0 square miles. Located at 48.55° N. Lat.; 96.16° W. Long. Elevation is 1,124 feet.
Population: 29 (2000); Race: 100.0% White, 0.0% Black, 0.0% Asian, 0.0% American Indian and Alaska Native, 0.0% Hispanic of any race, 0.0% two or more races (2000); Density: 59.4 persons per square mile (2000); Age: 22.2% under 18, 22.2% over 64 (2000); Marriage status: 26.1% never married, 65.2% now married, 8.7% widowed, 0.0% divorced (2000); Foreign born: 0.0% (2000); Ancestry (includes multiple ancestries): 81.5% Norwegian, 29.6% German, 18.5% Swedish, 18.5% Irish, 14.8% Czech (2000).
Economy: Grain, potatoes, sunflowers. Employment by occupation: 0.0% management, 0.0% professional, 33.3% services, 11.1% sales, 0.0% farming, 0.0% construction, 55.6% production (2000).
Income: Per capita income: $12,670 (2000); Median household income: $23,750 (2000); Poverty rate: 0.0% (2000).
Taxes: Total city taxes per capita: $49 (1997); City property taxes per capita: $49 (1997).
Education: High school graduation rate: 81.0% (2000); College graduation rate: 9.5% (2000).
Housing: Homeownership rate: 100.0% (2000); Median home value: $30,000 (2000); Median age of housing: 26 years (2000).
Transportation: Commute to work: 77.8% car, 0.0% public transportation, 22.2% walk, 0.0% work from home (2000); Travel time to work: 44.4% less than 15 minutes, 11.1% 15 to 30 minutes, 44.4% 30 to 45 minutes, 0.0% 45 to 60 minutes, 0.0% 60 minutes or more (2000)

WANNASKA (unincorporated postal area, zip code 56761). Covers a land area of 117.746 square miles and a water area of 0.045 square miles. Located at 48.60° N. Lat.; 95.66° W. Long. Elevation is 1,105 feet.
Population: 569 (2000); Race: 99.5% White, 0.0% Black, 0.0% Asian, 0.0% American Indian and Alaska Native, 0.2% Hispanic of any race, 0.4% two or more races (2000); Density: 4.8 persons per square mile (2000); Age: 28.2% under 18, 16.0% over 64 (2000); Marriage status: 17.1% never married, 71.7% now married, 4.9% widowed, 6.3% divorced (2000); Foreign born: 0.0% (2000); Ancestry (includes multiple ancestries): 54.7% Norwegian, 28.1% Swedish, 24.3% German, 4.7% English, 3.4% Irish (2000).
Economy: Employment by occupation: 11.5% management, 14.0% professional, 6.6% services, 20.3% sales, 0.7% farming, 7.3% construction, 39.5% production (2000).
Income: Per capita income: $16,234 (2000); Median household income: $45,357 (2000); Poverty rate: 6.7% (2000).
Education: High school graduation rate: 81.3% (2000); College graduation rate: 7.3% (2000).
Housing: Homeownership rate: 95.4% (2000); Median home value: $66,500 (2000); Median rent: $269 per month (2000); Median age of housing: 29 years (2000).
Transportation: Commute to work: 89.2% car, 1.0% public transportation, 2.1% walk, 7.0% work from home (2000); Travel time to work: 11.7% less than 15 minutes, 41.4% 15 to 30 minutes, 27.1% 30 to 45 minutes, 13.2% 45 to 60 minutes, 6.8% 60 minutes or more (2000)

WARROAD (city). Covers a land area of 2.606 square miles and a water area of 0.137 square miles. Located at 48.90° N. Lat.; 95.32° W. Long. Elevation is 1,070 feet.

History: Settled 1890, Incorporated 1901.
Population: 1,722 (2000); Race: 82.6% White, 0.1% Black, 8.8% Asian, 7.3% American Indian and Alaska Native, 1.4% Hispanic of any race, 1.2% two or more races (2000); Density: 660.8 persons per square mile (2000); Age: 31.7% under 18, 12.0% over 64 (2000); Marriage status: 26.6% never married, 54.7% now married, 9.2% widowed, 9.5% divorced (2000); Foreign born: 6.7% (2000); Ancestry (includes multiple ancestries): 27.4% Norwegian, 24.9% German, 19.9% Other groups, 12.4% Swedish, 8.9% Irish (2000).
Economy: Port of entry. Railroad terminus. Agriculture includes dairying, poultry, cattle, sheep, grain and flax. Manufacturing of apparel, lumber and concrete. Single-family building permits issued: 3 (2001) / 2 (2000); Multi-family building permits issued: 0 (2001) / 0 (2000); Employment by occupation: 5.7% management, 17.1% professional, 13.9% services, 25.0% sales, 0.5% farming, 2.8% construction, 35.0% production (2000).
Income: Per capita income: $16,412 (2000); Median household income: $34,948 (2000); Poverty rate: 8.8% (2000).
Taxes: Total city taxes per capita: $331 (1997); City property taxes per capita: $319 (1997).
Education: High school graduation rate: 80.4% (2000); College graduation rate: 18.4% (2000).

School District(s)

Warroad (PK-12)
2000 Enrollment: 1,431 218-386-1472
Housing: Homeownership rate: 60.3% (2000); Median home value: $76,500 (2000); Median rent: $383 per month (2000); Median age of housing: 25 years (2000).
Safety: Violent crime rate: 28.7 per 10,000 population; Property crime rate: 523.0 per 10,000 population (2001).
Newspapers: The Warroad Pioneer (1 x week)
Transportation: Commute to work: 89.5% car, 0.2% public transportation, 4.6% walk, 2.7% work from home (2000); Travel time to work: 80.8% less than 15 minutes, 11.8% 15 to 30 minutes, 5.6% 30 to 45 minutes, 0.4% 45 to 60 minutes, 1.5% 60 minutes or more (2000)
Airports: Warroad International-Swede Carlson Fiel
Additional Information Contacts
Warroad Chamber of Commerce 218-386-3543

Saint Louis County

Located in northeastern Minnesota; bounded on the north by Rainy Lake, Namakan Lake, Lac La Croix and the Canadian province of Ontario, and on the southeast by Lake Superior; watered by the St. Louis and Little Fork Rivers; includes many lakes, and p art of Superior National Forest. Covers a land area of 6,225.20 square miles, a water area of 634.70 square miles, and is located in the Central Time Zone. The county government was organized in 1855. County seat is Duluth.

Saint Louis County is part of the Duluth-Superior, MN-WI MSA. The entire metro area includes: St. Louis County, MN; Douglas County, WI

Weather Station: Cotton — Elevation: 1,328 feet

	Jan	Feb	Mar	Apr	May	Jun	Jul	Aug	Sep	Oct	Nov	Dec
High	18	26	37	52	na	74	78	76	66	53	35	22
Low	-7	-0	13	26	na	47	52	50	42	32	17	1
Precip	0.8	0.6	1.1	2.0	na	4.3	5.0	3.5	3.2	2.4	1.7	0.8
Snow	11.4	6.7	7.8	3.0	tr	0.0	0.0	0.0	tr	0.7	10.8	10.2

High and Low temperatures in degrees Fahrenheit; Precipitation and Snow in inches

Weather Station: Duluth Harbor Station — Elevation: 606 feet

	Jan	Feb	Mar	Apr	May	Jun	Jul	Aug	Sep	Oct	Nov	Dec
High	19	25	33	45	55	66	74	73	64	52	37	25
Low	3	9	20	32	41	49	58	59	50	40	26	11
Precip	0.9	0.6	1.4	1.5	2.5	3.5	3.6	3.7	3.7	2.2	1.5	0.9
Snow	10.4	na	7.0	1.7	tr	tr	tr	0.0	tr	0.1	4.0	na

High and Low temperatures in degrees Fahrenheit; Precipitation and Snow in inches

Weather Station: Duluth Int'l Airport — Elevation: 1,430 feet

	Jan	Feb	Mar	Apr	May	Jun	Jul	Aug	Sep	Oct	Nov	Dec
High	16	23	33	48	62	71	76	74	64	51	34	21
Low	-1	5	16	29	40	49	55	54	45	35	21	6
Precip	1.1	0.8	1.6	2.2	3.0	4.2	4.2	4.1	4.1	2.6	2.1	1.0
Snow	19.3	11.3	13.6	6.6	0.4	tr	tr	tr	0.1	1.6	15.2	15.2

High and Low temperatures in degrees Fahrenheit; Precipitation and Snow in inches

Weather Station: Hibbing Chisholm-Hibbing Airport — Elevation: 1,345 feet

	Jan	Feb	Mar	Apr	May	Jun	Jul	Aug	Sep	Oct	Nov	Dec
High	16	23	35	51	65	73	77	75	64	52	33	21
Low	-6	1	14	28	39	49	54	51	42	32	17	2
Precip	0.8	0.6	1.0	1.5	2.6	4.2	4.7	3.4	3.2	2.6	1.3	0.8
Snow	15.0	8.5	10.0	4.1	0.3	tr	tr	tr	tr	1.0	11.5	11.6

High and Low temperatures in degrees Fahrenheit; Precipitation and Snow in inches

Weather Station: Tower 3 S — Elevation: 1,459 feet

	Jan	Feb	Mar	Apr	May	Jun	Jul	Aug	Sep	Oct	Nov	Dec
High	16	24	36	51	65	73	78	75	65	52	34	21
Low	-11	-5	9	23	35	44	49	47	38	29	14	-3
Precip	0.8	0.7	1.0	1.6	3.0	4.4	4.4	4.2	4.0	3.0	1.4	0.6
Snow	15.2	9.9	10.8	5.6	0.5	0.0	0.0	0.0	tr	2.6	12.6	11.1

High and Low temperatures in degrees Fahrenheit; Precipitation and Snow in inches

Population: 200,528 (2000); Race: 94.9% White, 0.9% Black, 0.8% Asian, 1.9% American Indian and Alaska Native, 0.8% Hispanic of any race, 1.3% two or more races (2000); Density: 32.2 persons per square mile (2000); Age: 22.4% under 18, 16.1% over 64 (2000).
Religion: Five largest groups: 25.9% Catholic Church, 11.6% Evangelical Lutheran Church in America, 2.5% The United Methodist Church, 1.6% Lutheran Church—Missouri Synod, 1.6% Assemblies of God (2000).
Economy: Unemployment rate: 4.0% (11/2002); Total civilian labor force: 107,449 (11/2002); Leading industries: 22.0% health care and social assistance; 16.0% retail trade; 11.5% accommodation & food services (2000); Companies that employ more than 1,000 persons: 5 (2000); Companies that employ more than 100 persons: 106 (2000); Farms: 713 totaling 155,452 acres (1997); Minority business ownership rate: 2.4% (1997); Women business ownership rate: 25.0% (1997); Retail sales per capita: $9,720 (1997). Single-family building permits issued: 546 (2001) / 500 (2000); Multi-family building permits issued: 14 (2001) / 81 (2000).
Income: Per capita income: $18,982 (2000); Median household income: $36,306 (2000); Poverty rate: 12.1% (2000); Bankruptcy rate: 3.51% (2001).
Taxes: Total county taxes per capita: $384 (2000); County property taxes per capita: $383 (2000).
Education: High school graduation rate: 87.2% (2000); College graduation rate: 21.9% (2000).
Housing: Homeownership rate: 74.7% (2000); Median home value: $75,000 (2000); Median rent: $375 per month (2000); Median age of housing: 46 years (2000).
Health: Birth rate: 103.4 per 10,000 population (1998); Age adjusted death rate: 93.6 per 10,000 population (1999); Age adjusted cancer mortality rate: 208.6 deaths per 100,000 population (1999). Air Quality Index: 97% good, 3% moderate, 0% unhealthy (percent of days in 2000). Number of physicians: 29.1 per 10,000 population (1999); Number of hospital beds: 62.5 per 10,000 population (1999).
Elections: 2000 Presidential election results: 59.8% Gore, 33.0% Bush, 5.9% Nader, 0.9% Buchanan
National and State Parks: Arrowhead Lake State Game Refuge; Bear Head Lake State Park; Burntside State Forest; Canosia State Wildlife Management Area; Cloquet Valley State Forest; Fayal Township State Game Refuge; Hearding Island State Wildlife Management Area; Jeanette State Forest; Kabetogama State Forest; McCarthy Beach State Park; Purvis Ober State Natural Area; Soudan Underground Mine State Park; Sturgeon River State Forest; Superior State Game Refuge; Voyageurs National Park
Additional Information Contacts
St. Louis County Government Offices 218-726-2000
Duluth Area Association of Realtors 218-728-5676
Duluth Chamber of Commerce 218-722-5501
Duluth Convention & Visitors Bureau 218-722-4011
Ely Chamber of Commerce 218-365-6123
Eveleth Chamber of Commerce 218-744-1940
Hermantown Chamber of Commerce 218-727-7667
Hibbing Chamber of Commerce 218-262-3895
Iron Trail Convention Bureau 218-749-8161
Range Association of Realtors 218-262-2564
Superior Area Association of Realtors 218-728-5676
Tower Chamber of Commerce 218-753-2301
Virginia Chamber of Commerce 218-741-2717

Saint Louis County Communities

ALANGO (township). Covers a land area of 36.147 square miles and a water area of 0 square miles. Located at 47.76° N. Lat.; 92.76° W. Long.

Population: 301 (2000); Race: 91.8% White, 0.0% Black, 0.0% Asian, 3.9% American Indian and Alaska Native, 0.7% Hispanic of any race, 3.6% two or more races (2000); Density: 8.3 persons per square mile (2000); Age: 30.7% under 18, 11.4% over 64 (2000); Marriage status: 24.8% never married, 62.0% now married, 6.8% widowed, 6.4% divorced (2000); Foreign born: 4.2% (2000); Ancestry (includes multiple ancestries): 28.8% Finnish, 17.6% Swedish, 17.3% Norwegian, 11.8% German, 11.1% Irish (2000).
Economy: Employment by occupation: 2.5% management, 18.3% professional, 19.2% services, 14.2% sales, 6.7% farming, 13.3% construction, 25.8% production (2000).
Income: Per capita income: $16,399 (2000); Median household income: $37,500 (2000); Poverty rate: 11.8% (2000).
Taxes: Total city taxes per capita: $29 (1997); City property taxes per capita: $29 (1997).
Education: High school graduation rate: 82.3% (2000); College graduation rate: 13.0% (2000).
Housing: Homeownership rate: 92.2% (2000); Median home value: $56,000 (2000); Median rent: $275 per month (2000); Median age of housing: 32 years (2000).
Transportation: Commute to work: 87.5% car, 0.0% public transportation, 1.7% walk, 10.8% work from home (2000); Travel time to work: 29.9% less than 15 minutes, 43.0% 15 to 30 minutes, 22.4% 30 to 45 minutes, 0.9% 45 to 60 minutes, 3.7% 60 minutes or more (2000)

ALBORN (township). Covers a land area of 34.544 square miles and a water area of 0.693 square miles. Located at 46.97° N. Lat.; 92.58° W. Long. Elevation is 1,304 feet.
Population: 399 (2000); Race: 90.7% White, 0.0% Black, 0.5% Asian, 5.3% American Indian and Alaska Native, 1.1% Hispanic of any race, 3.5% two or more races (2000); Density: 11.6 persons per square mile (2000); Age: 21.1% under 18, 12.0% over 64 (2000); Marriage status: 24.0% never married, 62.1% now married, 8.2% widowed, 5.7% divorced (2000); Foreign born: 1.6% (2000); Ancestry (includes multiple ancestries): 22.7% Swedish, 21.9% German, 15.5% Norwegian, 14.1% Other groups, 11.5% Finnish (2000).
Economy: Employment by occupation: 9.5% management, 15.5% professional, 7.1% services, 23.2% sales, 0.0% farming, 18.5% construction, 26.2% production (2000).
Income: Per capita income: $18,953 (2000); Median household income: $42,500 (2000); Poverty rate: 5.3% (2000).
Taxes: Total city taxes per capita: $98 (2000); City property taxes per capita: $98 (2000).
Education: High school graduation rate: 91.0% (2000); College graduation rate: 13.3% (2000).
Housing: Homeownership rate: 90.5% (2000); Median home value: $113,600 (2000); Median rent: $483 per month (2000); Median age of housing: 30 years (2000).
Transportation: Commute to work: 98.8% car, 0.0% public transportation, 0.0% walk, 0.0% work from home (2000); Travel time to work: 1.2% less than 15 minutes, 17.9% 15 to 30 minutes, 50.0% 30 to 45 minutes, 17.9% 45 to 60 minutes, 13.1% 60 minutes or more (2000)

ALDEN (township). Covers a land area of 35.656 square miles and a water area of 0.103 square miles. Located at 47.03° N. Lat.; 91.84° W. Long.
Population: 198 (2000); Race: 96.1% White, 0.0% Black, 0.0% Asian, 3.9% American Indian and Alaska Native, 0.9% Hispanic of any race, 0.0% two or more races (2000); Density: 5.6 persons per square mile (2000); Age: 28.9% under 18, 12.3% over 64 (2000); Marriage status: 17.1% never married, 72.0% now married, 4.0% widowed, 6.9% divorced (2000); Foreign born: 2.2% (2000); Ancestry (includes multiple ancestries): 24.1% German, 18.0% Norwegian, 14.5% Finnish, 13.6% Swedish, 12.3% French (except Basque) (2000).
Economy: Employment by occupation: 9.3% management, 23.7% professional, 23.7% services, 15.5% sales, 2.1% farming, 12.4% construction, 13.4% production (2000).
Income: Per capita income: $17,897 (2000); Median household income: $48,750 (2000); Poverty rate: 7.5% (2000).
Taxes: Total city taxes per capita: $93 (1997); City property taxes per capita: $93 (1997).
Education: High school graduation rate: 87.2% (2000); College graduation rate: 25.0% (2000).
Housing: Homeownership rate: 87.8% (2000); Median home value: $83,300 (2000); Median rent: $158 per month (2000); Median age of housing: 54 years (2000).
Transportation: Commute to work: 97.9% car, 0.0% public transportation, 0.0% walk, 2.1% work from home (2000); Travel time to work: 8.4% less than 15 minutes, 51.6% 15 to 30 minutes, 20.0% 30 to 45 minutes, 11.6% 45 to 60 minutes, 8.4% 60 minutes or more (2000)

ANGORA (township). Aka Shermans Corner. Covers a land area of 36.286 square miles and a water area of 0.100 square miles. Located at 47.76° N. Lat.; 92.64° W. Long. Elevation is 1,349 feet.
Population: 277 (2000); Race: 97.2% White, 0.0% Black, 0.0% Asian, 2.2% American Indian and Alaska Native, 1.6% Hispanic of any race, 0.6% two or more races (2000); Density: 7.6 persons per square mile (2000); Age: 25.3% under 18, 4.4% over 64 (2000); Marriage status: 20.9% never married, 70.8% now married, 0.0% widowed, 8.3% divorced (2000); Foreign born: 1.6% (2000); Ancestry (includes multiple ancestries): 29.7% Finnish, 18.1% Norwegian, 15.6% Swedish, 14.7% German, 14.1% Irish (2000).
Economy: Employment by occupation: 5.3% management, 24.5% professional, 17.2% services, 15.9% sales, 2.0% farming, 12.6% construction, 22.5% production (2000).
Income: Per capita income: $15,279 (2000); Median household income: $38,750 (2000); Poverty rate: 4.4% (2000).
Taxes: Total city taxes per capita: $47 (1997); City property taxes per capita: $47 (1997).
Education: High school graduation rate: 88.8% (2000); College graduation rate: 19.9% (2000).
Housing: Homeownership rate: 90.2% (2000); Median home value: $34,500 (2000); Median rent: $335 per month (2000); Median age of housing: 29 years (2000).
Transportation: Commute to work: 89.4% car, 0.0% public transportation, 0.0% walk, 10.6% work from home (2000); Travel time to work: 34.8% less than 15 minutes, 31.1% 15 to 30 minutes, 23.0% 30 to 45 minutes, 6.7% 45 to 60 minutes, 4.4% 60 minutes or more (2000)

ARNOLD (CDP). Covers a land area of 11.563 square miles and a water area of 0.071 square miles. Located at 46.86° N. Lat.; 92.10° W. Long. Elevation is 1,438 feet.
Population: 3,032 (2000); Race: 97.8% White, 0.3% Black, 0.2% Asian, 0.9% American Indian and Alaska Native, 0.2% Hispanic of any race, 0.9% two or more races (2000); Density: 262.2 persons per square mile (2000); Age: 30.3% under 18, 9.8% over 64 (2000); Marriage status: 22.9% never married, 66.7% now married, 4.3% widowed, 6.1% divorced (2000); Foreign born: 0.9% (2000); Ancestry (includes multiple ancestries): 25.1% German, 22.4% Norwegian, 15.2% Swedish, 10.0% Irish, 9.8% Polish (2000).
Economy: Employment by occupation: 13.0% management, 17.8% professional, 16.6% services, 25.2% sales, 0.9% farming, 12.1% construction, 14.5% production (2000).
Income: Per capita income: $18,104 (2000); Median household income: $46,111 (2000); Poverty rate: 5.2% (2000).
Education: High school graduation rate: 85.9% (2000); College graduation rate: 18.0% (2000).
Housing: Homeownership rate: 93.1% (2000); Median home value: $89,900 (2000); Median rent: $638 per month (2000); Median age of housing: 34 years (2000).
Transportation: Commute to work: 91.0% car, 2.3% public transportation, 0.9% walk, 5.8% work from home (2000); Travel time to work: 31.4% less than 15 minutes, 52.1% 15 to 30 minutes, 13.1% 30 to 45 minutes, 2.1% 45 to 60 minutes, 1.3% 60 minutes or more (2000)

ARROWHEAD (township). Covers a land area of 70.831 square miles and a water area of 0.818 square miles. Located at 46.86° N. Lat.; 92.74° W. Long.
Population: 232 (2000); Race: 100.0% White, 0.0% Black, 0.0% Asian, 0.0% American Indian and Alaska Native, 0.0% Hispanic of any race, 0.0% two or more races (2000); Density: 3.3 persons per square mile (2000); Age: 30.3% under 18, 23.0% over 64 (2000); Marriage status: 15.8% never married, 66.8% now married, 10.5% widowed, 6.8% divorced (2000); Foreign born: 1.2% (2000); Ancestry (includes multiple ancestries): 21.3% Finnish, 17.6% German, 13.1% Swedish, 9.4% Polish, 7.4% Irish (2000).
Economy: Employment by occupation: 4.6% management, 3.1% professional, 16.9% services, 15.4% sales, 9.2% farming, 35.4% construction, 15.4% production (2000).
Income: Per capita income: $12,055 (2000); Median household income: $31,071 (2000); Poverty rate: 27.9% (2000).
Taxes: Total city taxes per capita: $519 (1997); City property taxes per capita: $519 (1997).
Education: High school graduation rate: 72.0% (2000); College graduation rate: 3.1% (2000).

Housing: Homeownership rate: 97.2% (2000); Median home value: $95,000 (2000); Median rent: $275 per month (2000); Median age of housing: 25 years (2000).
Transportation: Commute to work: 72.3% car, 0.0% public transportation, 0.0% walk, 23.1% work from home (2000); Travel time to work: 4.0% less than 15 minutes, 26.0% 15 to 30 minutes, 40.0% 30 to 45 minutes, 18.0% 45 to 60 minutes, 12.0% 60 minutes or more (2000)

AULT (township). Covers a land area of 70.110 square miles and a water area of 1.739 square miles. Located at 47.24° N. Lat.; 91.88° W. Long.
Population: 125 (2000); Race: 100.0% White, 0.0% Black, 0.0% Asian, 0.0% American Indian and Alaska Native, 0.0% Hispanic of any race, 0.0% two or more races (2000); Density: 1.8 persons per square mile (2000); Age: 17.1% under 18, 20.3% over 64 (2000); Marriage status: 20.6% never married, 50.5% now married, 8.4% widowed, 20.6% divorced (2000); Foreign born: 0.0% (2000); Ancestry (includes multiple ancestries): 30.9% Finnish, 21.1% German, 17.9% Irish, 17.1% Swedish, 17.1% Norwegian (2000).
Economy: Employment by occupation: 4.8% management, 14.3% professional, 11.1% services, 22.2% sales, 6.3% farming, 17.5% construction, 23.8% production (2000).
Income: Per capita income: $18,007 (2000); Median household income: $40,179 (2000); Poverty rate: 14.6% (2000).
Taxes: Total city taxes per capita: $149 (1997); City property taxes per capita: $149 (1997).
Education: High school graduation rate: 83.5% (2000); College graduation rate: 11.3% (2000).
Housing: Homeownership rate: 90.0% (2000); Median home value: $58,300 (2000); Median rent: $325 per month (2000); Median age of housing: 28 years (2000).
Transportation: Commute to work: 90.5% car, 0.0% public transportation, 4.8% walk, 4.8% work from home (2000); Travel time to work: 15.0% less than 15 minutes, 15.0% 15 to 30 minutes, 30.0% 30 to 45 minutes, 30.0% 45 to 60 minutes, 10.0% 60 minutes or more (2000)

AURORA (city). Covers a land area of 3.796 square miles and a water area of 0.138 square miles. Located at 47.52° N. Lat.; 92.24° W. Long. Elevation is 1,480 feet.
History: Incorporated 1903.
Population: 1,850 (2000); Race: 98.3% White, 0.2% Black, 0.2% Asian, 0.8% American Indian and Alaska Native, 1.1% Hispanic of any race, 0.5% two or more races (2000); Density: 487.4 persons per square mile (2000); Age: 19.9% under 18, 23.7% over 64 (2000); Marriage status: 18.6% never married, 60.6% now married, 10.2% widowed, 10.5% divorced (2000); Foreign born: 1.4% (2000); Ancestry (includes multiple ancestries): 18.6% German, 17.7% Finnish, 13.6% Norwegian, 11.9% Swedish, 9.1% Slovene (2000).
Economy: Open-pit iron mines nearby. Taconite plant; light manufacturing. Giants Ridge Ski Area to NorthweSaint Single-family building permits issued: 0 (2001) / 0 (2000); Multi-family building permits issued: 0 (2001) / 0 (2000); Employment by occupation: 9.5% management, 19.5% professional, 20.5% services, 15.9% sales, 0.0% farming, 14.8% construction, 19.7% production (2000).
Income: Per capita income: $17,442 (2000); Median household income: $32,094 (2000); Poverty rate: 11.9% (2000).
Taxes: Total city taxes per capita: $206 (1997); City property taxes per capita: $203 (1997).
Education: High school graduation rate: 80.8% (2000); College graduation rate: 18.4% (2000).

School District(s)

Mesabi East (PK-12)
2000 Enrollment: 1,089 218-229-3321
Housing: Homeownership rate: 80.0% (2000); Median home value: $46,900 (2000); Median rent: $271 per month (2000); Median age of housing: 44 years (2000).
Hospitals: White Community Hospital (85 beds)
Safety: Violent crime rate: 42.8 per 10,000 population; Property crime rate: 278.1 per 10,000 population (2001).
Transportation: Commute to work: 84.9% car, 0.5% public transportation, 10.2% walk, 3.2% work from home (2000); Travel time to work: 51.6% less than 15 minutes, 31.9% 15 to 30 minutes, 9.3% 30 to 45 minutes, 4.5% 45 to 60 minutes, 2.6% 60 minutes or more (2000)

BABBITT (city). Covers a land area of 105.651 square miles and a water area of 1.063 square miles. Located at 47.66° N. Lat.; 91.91° W. Long. Elevation is 1,490 feet.
Population: 1,670 (2000); Race: 99.2% White, 0.1% Black, 0.3% Asian, 0.1% American Indian and Alaska Native, 0.0% Hispanic of any race, 0.3% two or more races (2000); Density: 15.8 persons per square mile (2000); Age: 21.1% under 18, 28.6% over 64 (2000); Marriage status: 13.9% never married, 69.2% now married, 9.6% widowed, 7.3% divorced (2000); Foreign born: 0.8% (2000); Ancestry (includes multiple ancestries): 23.7% German, 18.8% Norwegian, 17.4% Finnish, 11.4% Swedish, 10.5% Irish (2000).
Economy: Timber; dairying; cattle; alfalfa; recreation. Manufacturing: consumer goods; taconite plant. Terminus (to Southeast) of Reserve Mining Co. Railroad to Silver Bay iron ore processing plant and loading facilities on Lake Superior. Single-family building permits issued: 1 (2001) / 2 (2000); Multi-family building permits issued: 0 (2001) / 0 (2000); Employment by occupation: 5.7% management, 13.3% professional, 18.2% services, 25.7% sales, 0.3% farming, 12.7% construction, 24.1% production (2000).
Income: Per capita income: $18,853 (2000); Median household income: $33,229 (2000); Poverty rate: 6.1% (2000).
Taxes: Total city taxes per capita: $202 (1997); City property taxes per capita: $198 (1997).
Education: High school graduation rate: 83.0% (2000); College graduation rate: 7.9% (2000).
Housing: Homeownership rate: 89.5% (2000); Median home value: $44,200 (2000); Median rent: $297 per month (2000); Median age of housing: 43 years (2000).
Safety: Violent crime rate: 47.4 per 10,000 population; Property crime rate: 290.3 per 10,000 population (2001).
Newspapers: New Babbitt Weekly News (1 x week)
Transportation: Commute to work: 95.4% car, 0.0% public transportation, 0.7% walk, 2.6% work from home (2000); Travel time to work: 45.2% less than 15 minutes, 23.6% 15 to 30 minutes, 18.0% 30 to 45 minutes, 8.2% 45 to 60 minutes, 4.9% 60 minutes or more (2000)

BALKAN (township). Covers a land area of 64.210 square miles and a water area of 1.056 square miles. Located at 47.51° N. Lat.; 92.87° W. Long.
Population: 811 (2000); Race: 98.5% White, 0.0% Black, 0.0% Asian, 0.0% American Indian and Alaska Native, 0.0% Hispanic of any race, 0.9% two or more races (2000); Density: 12.6 persons per square mile (2000); Age: 20.6% under 18, 11.3% over 64 (2000); Marriage status: 18.9% never married, 65.2% now married, 6.8% widowed, 9.1% divorced (2000); Foreign born: 0.9% (2000); Ancestry (includes multiple ancestries): 22.1% Finnish, 16.8% German, 11.9% Norwegian, 11.1% Italian, 9.8% Swedish (2000).
Economy: Employment by occupation: 11.0% management, 13.5% professional, 13.0% services, 21.8% sales, 0.0% farming, 25.8% construction, 14.8% production (2000).
Income: Per capita income: $21,570 (2000); Median household income: $44,853 (2000); Poverty rate: 4.3% (2000).
Taxes: Total city taxes per capita: $174 (2000); City property taxes per capita: $174 (2000).
Education: High school graduation rate: 90.2% (2000); College graduation rate: 10.6% (2000).
Housing: Homeownership rate: 97.0% (2000); Median home value: $73,200 (2000); Median rent: $175 per month (2000); Median age of housing: 30 years (2000).
Transportation: Commute to work: 96.4% car, 0.5% public transportation, 0.0% walk, 3.1% work from home (2000); Travel time to work: 33.6% less than 15 minutes, 45.0% 15 to 30 minutes, 16.9% 30 to 45 minutes, 2.6% 45 to 60 minutes, 1.9% 60 minutes or more (2000)

BASSETT (township). Covers a land area of 174.521 square miles and a water area of 7.634 square miles. Located at 47.44° N. Lat.; 91.90° W. Long.
Population: 55 (2000); Race: 91.5% White, 0.0% Black, 0.0% Asian, 8.5% American Indian and Alaska Native, 0.0% Hispanic of any race, 0.0% two or more races (2000); Density: 0.3 persons per square mile (2000); Age: 21.3% under 18, 10.6% over 64 (2000); Marriage status: 37.2% never married, 55.8% now married, 0.0% widowed, 7.0% divorced (2000); Foreign born: 10.6% (2000); Ancestry (includes multiple ancestries): 31.9% Swedish, 27.7% Norwegian, 25.5% Finnish, 17.0% German, 12.8% Slovene (2000).
Economy: Employment by occupation: 6.3% management, 9.4% professional, 21.9% services, 28.1% sales, 0.0% farming, 15.6% construction, 18.8% production (2000).
Income: Per capita income: $24,879 (2000); Median household income: $32,500 (2000); Poverty rate: 14.9% (2000).
Taxes: Total city taxes per capita: $135 (1997); City property taxes per capita: $135 (1997).
Education: High school graduation rate: 91.7% (2000); College graduation rate: 8.3% (2000).

Housing: Homeownership rate: 100.0% (2000); Median home value: $28,000 (2000); Median age of housing: 39 years (2000).
Transportation: Commute to work: 100.0% car, 0.0% public transportation, 0.0% walk, 0.0% work from home (2000); Travel time to work: 37.5% less than 15 minutes, 18.8% 15 to 30 minutes, 0.0% 30 to 45 minutes, 12.5% 45 to 60 minutes, 31.3% 60 minutes or more (2000)

BEATTY (township). Covers a land area of 65.215 square miles and a water area of 14.724 square miles. Located at 47.94° N. Lat.; 92.63° W. Long.
Population: 434 (2000); Race: 100.0% White, 0.0% Black, 0.0% Asian, 0.0% American Indian and Alaska Native, 0.0% Hispanic of any race, 0.0% two or more races (2000); Density: 6.7 persons per square mile (2000); Age: 16.5% under 18, 27.5% over 64 (2000); Marriage status: 10.3% never married, 73.3% now married, 8.3% widowed, 8.1% divorced (2000); Foreign born: 0.5% (2000); Ancestry (includes multiple ancestries): 19.7% German, 17.2% Swedish, 16.5% Finnish, 16.5% Norwegian, 13.3% English (2000).
Economy: Employment by occupation: 10.9% management, 32.0% professional, 9.1% services, 20.0% sales, 1.1% farming, 12.6% construction, 14.3% production (2000).
Income: Per capita income: $23,118 (2000); Median household income: $43,542 (2000); Poverty rate: 6.6% (2000).
Taxes: Total city taxes per capita: $153 (1997); City property taxes per capita: $153 (1997).
Education: High school graduation rate: 94.3% (2000); College graduation rate: 34.1% (2000).
Housing: Homeownership rate: 97.0% (2000); Median home value: $197,900 (2000); Median rent: $525 per month (2000); Median age of housing: 29 years (2000).
Transportation: Commute to work: 87.3% car, 1.7% public transportation, 0.0% walk, 11.0% work from home (2000); Travel time to work: 26.0% less than 15 minutes, 29.2% 15 to 30 minutes, 16.9% 30 to 45 minutes, 14.9% 45 to 60 minutes, 13.0% 60 minutes or more (2000)

BIWABIK (city). Covers a land area of 4.773 square miles and a water area of 0.336 square miles. Located at 47.53° N. Lat.; 92.34° W. Long. Elevation is 1,448 feet.
History: The name of Biwabik is derived from the Chippewa word for iron.
Population: 954 (2000); Race: 97.9% White, 0.0% Black, 0.2% Asian, 1.9% American Indian and Alaska Native, 0.0% Hispanic of any race, 0.0% two or more races (2000); Density: 199.9 persons per square mile (2000); Age: 21.0% under 18, 20.0% over 64 (2000); Marriage status: 22.8% never married, 51.3% now married, 12.5% widowed, 13.5% divorced (2000); Foreign born: 1.6% (2000); Ancestry (includes multiple ancestries): 18.7% Finnish, 14.5% German, 14.5% Norwegian, 9.7% Irish, 8.8% Swedish (2000).
Economy: Single-family building permits issued: 0 (2001) / 0 (2000); Multi-family building permits issued: 0 (2001) / 0 (2000); Employment by occupation: 6.7% management, 18.2% professional, 24.1% services, 16.2% sales, 0.0% farming, 19.6% construction, 15.1% production (2000).
Income: Per capita income: $16,182 (2000); Median household income: $28,359 (2000); Poverty rate: 17.0% (2000).
Taxes: Total city taxes per capita: $252 (1997); City property taxes per capita: $237 (1997).
Education: High school graduation rate: 87.5% (2000); College graduation rate: 10.0% (2000).
Housing: Homeownership rate: 82.7% (2000); Median home value: $43,400 (2000); Median rent: $233 per month (2000); Median age of housing: 48 years (2000).
Safety: Violent crime rate: 20.7 per 10,000 population; Property crime rate: 62.2 per 10,000 population (2001).
Newspapers: The Biwabik Times (1 x week)
Transportation: Commute to work: 82.8% car, 2.6% public transportation, 12.6% walk, 2.0% work from home (2000); Travel time to work: 32.6% less than 15 minutes, 52.8% 15 to 30 minutes, 9.4% 30 to 45 minutes, 2.9% 45 to 60 minutes, 2.3% 60 minutes or more (2000)

BIWABIK (township). Covers a land area of 27.123 square miles and a water area of 2.272 square miles. Located at 47.47° N. Lat.; 92.38° W. Long. Elevation is 1,448 feet.
Population: 911 (2000); Race: 98.3% White, 0.0% Black, 0.0% Asian, 1.2% American Indian and Alaska Native, 0.0% Hispanic of any race, 0.3% two or more races (2000); Density: 33.6 persons per square mile (2000); Age: 23.3% under 18, 16.0% over 64 (2000); Marriage status: 22.0% never married, 62.5% now married, 7.6% widowed, 7.9% divorced (2000); Foreign born: 0.2% (2000); Ancestry (includes multiple ancestries): 25.1% Finnish, 21.1% German, 17.0% Norwegian, 15.5% Swedish, 8.1% English (2000).
Economy: Iron mines. Employment by occupation: 7.2% management, 17.6% professional, 18.1% services, 21.2% sales, 0.2% farming, 20.2% construction, 15.4% production (2000).
Income: Per capita income: $19,435 (2000); Median household income: $44,375 (2000); Poverty rate: 8.0% (2000).
Taxes: Total city taxes per capita: $173 (2000); City property taxes per capita: $173 (2000).
Education: High school graduation rate: 88.8% (2000); College graduation rate: 16.8% (2000).
Housing: Homeownership rate: 90.6% (2000); Median home value: $98,300 (2000); Median rent: $250 per month (2000); Median age of housing: 29 years (2000).
Transportation: Commute to work: 95.1% car, 0.7% public transportation, 0.0% walk, 4.1% work from home (2000); Travel time to work: 18.0% less than 15 minutes, 52.9% 15 to 30 minutes, 20.0% 30 to 45 minutes, 5.6% 45 to 60 minutes, 3.5% 60 minutes or more (2000)

BREITUNG (township). Covers a land area of 23.000 square miles and a water area of 15.850 square miles. Located at 47.82° N. Lat.; 92.23° W. Long.
Population: 662 (2000); Race: 98.5% White, 0.0% Black, 0.0% Asian, 0.9% American Indian and Alaska Native, 1.0% Hispanic of any race, 0.6% two or more races (2000); Density: 28.8 persons per square mile (2000); Age: 20.8% under 18, 21.1% over 64 (2000); Marriage status: 24.1% never married, 58.2% now married, 9.6% widowed, 8.0% divorced (2000); Foreign born: 1.3% (2000); Ancestry (includes multiple ancestries): 23.3% Finnish, 16.4% Norwegian, 16.0% German, 12.9% Swedish, 8.6% Slovene (2000).
Economy: Employment by occupation: 9.8% management, 18.6% professional, 16.7% services, 21.8% sales, 0.0% farming, 18.3% construction, 14.8% production (2000).
Income: Per capita income: $20,134 (2000); Median household income: $40,750 (2000); Poverty rate: 17.3% (2000).
Taxes: Total city taxes per capita: $358 (2000); City property taxes per capita: $356 (2000).
Education: High school graduation rate: 89.1% (2000); College graduation rate: 21.8% (2000).
Housing: Homeownership rate: 89.8% (2000); Median home value: $51,300 (2000); Median rent: $288 per month (2000); Median age of housing: 37 years (2000).
Transportation: Commute to work: 90.5% car, 0.0% public transportation, 5.2% walk, 1.6% work from home (2000); Travel time to work: 24.9% less than 15 minutes, 26.6% 15 to 30 minutes, 30.9% 30 to 45 minutes, 10.6% 45 to 60 minutes, 7.0% 60 minutes or more (2000)

BREVATOR (township). Covers a land area of 34.572 square miles and a water area of 1.119 square miles. Located at 46.79° N. Lat.; 92.48° W. Long.
Population: 1,226 (2000); Race: 79.1% White, 0.0% Black, 3.0% Asian, 14.5% American Indian and Alaska Native, 1.5% Hispanic of any race, 2.3% two or more races (2000); Density: 35.5 persons per square mile (2000); Age: 32.8% under 18, 7.0% over 64 (2000); Marriage status: 29.2% never married, 58.2% now married, 5.1% widowed, 7.5% divorced (2000); Foreign born: 2.7% (2000); Ancestry (includes multiple ancestries): 21.0% German, 20.9% Other groups, 17.8% Finnish, 12.5% Swedish, 12.1% Norwegian (2000).
Economy: Employment by occupation: 8.2% management, 9.1% professional, 23.3% services, 26.6% sales, 1.4% farming, 14.7% construction, 16.7% production (2000).
Income: Per capita income: $16,686 (2000); Median household income: $46,944 (2000); Poverty rate: 8.2% (2000).
Taxes: Total city taxes per capita: $45 (1997); City property taxes per capita: $45 (1997).
Education: High school graduation rate: 85.7% (2000); College graduation rate: 10.4% (2000).
Housing: Homeownership rate: 87.0% (2000); Median home value: $90,300 (2000); Median rent: $159 per month (2000); Median age of housing: 29 years (2000).
Transportation: Commute to work: 92.3% car, 0.0% public transportation, 1.1% walk, 5.0% work from home (2000); Travel time to work: 22.8% less than 15 minutes, 45.5% 15 to 30 minutes, 24.6% 30 to 45 minutes, 4.1% 45 to 60 minutes, 3.1% 60 minutes or more (2000)

BRIMSON (unincorporated postal area, zip code 55602). Covers a land area of 218.960 square miles and a water area of 9.221 square miles. Located at 47.30° N. Lat.; 91.87° W. Long. Elevation is 1,516 feet.

Population: 236 (2000); Race: 97.2% White, 0.0% Black, 0.0% Asian, 1.6% American Indian and Alaska Native, 0.0% Hispanic of any race, 1.2% two or more races (2000); Density: 1.1 persons per square mile (2000); Age: 13.0% under 18, 24.3% over 64 (2000); Marriage status: 22.3% never married, 56.3% now married, 4.0% widowed, 17.4% divorced (2000); Foreign born: 0.0% (2000); Ancestry (includes multiple ancestries): 27.1% Finnish, 20.6% Irish, 20.2% German, 18.2% Swedish, 17.0% Norwegian (2000).
Economy: Employment by occupation: 11.9% management, 15.6% professional, 13.8% services, 22.9% sales, 3.7% farming, 15.6% construction, 16.5% production (2000).
Income: Per capita income: $24,272 (2000); Median household income: $38,125 (2000); Poverty rate: 10.5% (2000).
Education: High school graduation rate: 89.0% (2000); College graduation rate: 21.5% (2000).
Housing: Homeownership rate: 95.2% (2000); Median home value: $42,500 (2000); Median rent: $325 per month (2000); Median age of housing: 31 years (2000).
Transportation: Commute to work: 83.5% car, 0.0% public transportation, 5.5% walk, 7.3% work from home (2000); Travel time to work: 18.8% less than 15 minutes, 20.8% 15 to 30 minutes, 20.8% 30 to 45 minutes, 15.8% 45 to 60 minutes, 23.8% 60 minutes or more (2000)

BRITT (unincorporated postal area, zip code 55710). Covers a land area of 102.939 square miles and a water area of 4.135 square miles. Located at 47.65° N. Lat.; 92.66° W. Long. Elevation is 1,477 feet.
Population: 1,498 (2000); Race: 98.5% White, 0.4% Black, 0.0% Asian, 0.5% American Indian and Alaska Native, 0.7% Hispanic of any race, 0.5% two or more races (2000); Density: 14.6 persons per square mile (2000); Age: 24.4% under 18, 8.8% over 64 (2000); Marriage status: 20.5% never married, 70.0% now married, 3.3% widowed, 6.2% divorced (2000); Foreign born: 1.5% (2000); Ancestry (includes multiple ancestries): 21.6% German, 21.2% Finnish, 18.0% Norwegian, 12.4% Swedish, 10.4% Irish (2000).
Economy: Employment by occupation: 7.1% management, 27.0% professional, 11.6% services, 20.2% sales, 0.5% farming, 22.4% construction, 11.1% production (2000).
Income: Per capita income: $20,457 (2000); Median household income: $48,409 (2000); Poverty rate: 5.6% (2000).
Education: High school graduation rate: 89.9% (2000); College graduation rate: 22.2% (2000).
Housing: Homeownership rate: 98.3% (2000); Median home value: $94,900 (2000); Median rent: $365 per month (2000); Median age of housing: 33 years (2000).
Transportation: Commute to work: 94.8% car, 0.0% public transportation, 1.0% walk, 2.9% work from home (2000); Travel time to work: 16.1% less than 15 minutes, 49.6% 15 to 30 minutes, 17.5% 30 to 45 minutes, 6.6% 45 to 60 minutes, 10.1% 60 minutes or more (2000)

BROOKSTON (city). Covers a land area of 0.557 square miles and a water area of 0 square miles. Located at 46.86° N. Lat.; 92.60° W. Long. Elevation is 1,228 feet.
Population: 98 (2000); Race: 94.7% White, 0.0% Black, 0.0% Asian, 0.0% American Indian and Alaska Native, 0.0% Hispanic of any race, 5.3% two or more races (2000); Density: 175.9 persons per square mile (2000); Age: 28.0% under 18, 22.7% over 64 (2000); Marriage status: 7.4% never married, 79.6% now married, 7.4% widowed, 5.6% divorced (2000); Foreign born: 2.7% (2000); Ancestry (includes multiple ancestries): 60.0% Finnish, 17.3% Swedish, 12.0% Irish, 10.7% Danish, 8.0% English (2000).
Economy: Railroad junction to WeSaint Potatoes, oats, alfalfa; livestock; dairying. Employment by occupation: 0.0% management, 14.3% professional, 17.9% services, 32.1% sales, 0.0% farming, 10.7% construction, 25.0% production (2000).
Income: Per capita income: $14,009 (2000); Median household income: $32,917 (2000); Poverty rate: 5.3% (2000).
Taxes: Total city taxes per capita: $28 (1997); City property taxes per capita: $19 (1997).
Education: High school graduation rate: 50.0% (2000); College graduation rate: 0.0% (2000).
Housing: Homeownership rate: 100.0% (2000); Median home value: $75,000 (2000); Median age of housing: 39 years (2000).
Transportation: Commute to work: 46.4% car, 25.0% public transportation, 17.9% walk, 10.7% work from home (2000); Travel time to work: 32.0% less than 15 minutes, 12.0% 15 to 30 minutes, 24.0% 30 to 45 minutes, 12.0% 45 to 60 minutes, 20.0% 60 minutes or more (2000)

BUHL (city). Covers a land area of 3.287 square miles and a water area of 0.242 square miles. Located at 47.49° N. Lat.; 92.77° W. Long. Elevation is 1,533 feet.
Population: 983 (2000); Race: 93.1% White, 0.5% Black, 0.0% Asian, 3.3% American Indian and Alaska Native, 1.2% Hispanic of any race, 2.3% two or more races (2000); Density: 299.0 persons per square mile (2000); Age: 26.3% under 18, 19.3% over 64 (2000); Marriage status: 24.5% never married, 52.0% now married, 13.3% widowed, 10.2% divorced (2000); Foreign born: 3.6% (2000); Ancestry (includes multiple ancestries): 20.7% Finnish, 19.9% German, 9.3% Italian, 8.3% English, 8.0% Irish (2000).
Economy: Single-family building permits issued: 11 (2001) / 4 (2000); Multi-family building permits issued: 0 (2001) / 0 (2000); Employment by occupation: 4.9% management, 12.7% professional, 18.7% services, 23.6% sales, 1.0% farming, 19.0% construction, 20.2% production (2000).
Income: Per capita income: $14,828 (2000); Median household income: $31,574 (2000); Poverty rate: 13.2% (2000).
Taxes: Total city taxes per capita: $109 (1997); City property taxes per capita: $108 (1997).
Education: High school graduation rate: 88.3% (2000); College graduation rate: 10.0% (2000).

School District(s)

Martin Hughes Charter School (08-12)
2000 Enrollment: 64 218-258-8974

Housing: Homeownership rate: 85.0% (2000); Median home value: $40,600 (2000); Median rent: $325 per month (2000); Median age of housing: 55 years (2000).
Transportation: Commute to work: 91.5% car, 0.0% public transportation, 4.0% walk, 4.5% work from home (2000); Travel time to work: 33.3% less than 15 minutes, 58.8% 15 to 30 minutes, 5.8% 30 to 45 minutes, 1.6% 45 to 60 minutes, 0.5% 60 minutes or more (2000)

CAMP 5 (township). Covers a land area of 31.407 square miles and a water area of 3.658 square miles. Located at 48.21° N. Lat.; 92.78° W. Long.
Population: 41 (2000); Race: 100.0% White, 0.0% Black, 0.0% Asian, 0.0% American Indian and Alaska Native, 0.0% Hispanic of any race, 0.0% two or more races (2000); Density: 1.3 persons per square mile (2000); Age: 0.0% under 18, 35.5% over 64 (2000); Marriage status: 0.0% never married, 51.6% now married, 3.2% widowed, 45.2% divorced (2000); Foreign born: 0.0% (2000); Ancestry (includes multiple ancestries): 22.6% Finnish, 19.4% German, 16.1% Polish, 12.9% Norwegian, 6.5% Italian (2000).
Economy: Employment by occupation: 0.0% management, 0.0% professional, 58.3% services, 41.7% sales, 0.0% farming, 0.0% construction, 0.0% production (2000).
Income: Per capita income: $17,784 (2000); Median household income: $21,071 (2000); Poverty rate: 9.7% (2000).
Education: High school graduation rate: 83.9% (2000); College graduation rate: 0.0% (2000).
Housing: Homeownership rate: 100.0% (2000); Median home value: $62,000 (2000); Median age of housing: 19 years (2000).
Transportation: Commute to work: 100.0% car, 0.0% public transportation, 0.0% walk, 0.0% work from home (2000); Travel time to work: 0.0% less than 15 minutes, 0.0% 15 to 30 minutes, 41.7% 30 to 45 minutes, 0.0% 45 to 60 minutes, 58.3% 60 minutes or more (2000)

CANOSIA (township). Covers a land area of 30.124 square miles and a water area of 5.575 square miles. Located at 46.89° N. Lat.; 92.25° W. Long.
Population: 1,998 (2000); Race: 97.8% White, 0.0% Black, 0.2% Asian, 0.6% American Indian and Alaska Native, 1.0% Hispanic of any race, 1.2% two or more races (2000); Density: 66.3 persons per square mile (2000); Age: 26.2% under 18, 8.8% over 64 (2000); Marriage status: 19.9% never married, 66.9% now married, 3.7% widowed, 9.4% divorced (2000); Foreign born: 1.1% (2000); Ancestry (includes multiple ancestries): 22.9% Norwegian, 19.9% German, 18.5% Swedish, 9.7% Finnish, 9.4% Polish (2000).
Economy: Single-family building permits issued: 21 (2001) / 22 (2000); Multi-family building permits issued: 0 (2001) / 2 (2000); Employment by occupation: 15.1% management, 18.5% professional, 12.5% services, 28.9% sales, 0.4% farming, 14.9% construction, 9.7% production (2000).
Income: Per capita income: $21,986 (2000); Median household income: $52,813 (2000); Poverty rate: 3.9% (2000).
Taxes: Total city taxes per capita: $92 (1997); City property taxes per capita: $88 (1997).
Education: High school graduation rate: 90.9% (2000); College graduation rate: 25.3% (2000).

Housing: Homeownership rate: 90.2% (2000); Median home value: $131,600 (2000); Median rent: $482 per month (2000); Median age of housing: 28 years (2000).
Transportation: Commute to work: 94.6% car, 0.2% public transportation, 1.6% walk, 3.6% work from home (2000); Travel time to work: 21.0% less than 15 minutes, 59.2% 15 to 30 minutes, 14.3% 30 to 45 minutes, 2.0% 45 to 60 minutes, 3.6% 60 minutes or more (2000)

CANYON (unincorporated postal area, zip code 55717). Covers a land area of 118.897 square miles and a water area of 2.396 square miles. Located at 47.05° N. Lat.; 92.46° W. Long. Elevation is 1,355 feet.
Population: 376 (2000); Race: 99.4% White, 0.0% Black, 0.0% Asian, 0.6% American Indian and Alaska Native, 1.8% Hispanic of any race, 0.0% two or more races (2000); Density: 3.2 persons per square mile (2000); Age: 17.6% under 18, 14.0% over 64 (2000); Marriage status: 17.5% never married, 73.9% now married, 5.0% widowed, 3.6% divorced (2000); Foreign born: 0.0% (2000); Ancestry (includes multiple ancestries): 29.6% German, 27.5% Swedish, 17.6% Finnish, 14.9% Norwegian, 7.5% Polish (2000).
Economy: Employment by occupation: 9.0% management, 15.7% professional, 13.3% services, 27.1% sales, 3.0% farming, 13.3% construction, 18.7% production (2000).
Income: Per capita income: $21,968 (2000); Median household income: $48,750 (2000); Poverty rate: 6.6% (2000).
Education: High school graduation rate: 94.2% (2000); College graduation rate: 22.9% (2000).
Housing: Homeownership rate: 93.5% (2000); Median home value: $135,000 (2000); Median rent: $675 per month (2000); Median age of housing: 45 years (2000).
Transportation: Commute to work: 91.0% car, 0.0% public transportation, 0.0% walk, 9.0% work from home (2000); Travel time to work: 10.6% less than 15 minutes, 17.2% 15 to 30 minutes, 37.7% 30 to 45 minutes, 25.2% 45 to 60 minutes, 9.3% 60 minutes or more (2000)

CEDAR VALLEY (township). Covers a land area of 68.532 square miles and a water area of 0.857 square miles. Located at 47.10° N. Lat.; 93.00° W. Long.
Population: 232 (2000); Race: 99.2% White, 0.0% Black, 0.8% Asian, 0.0% American Indian and Alaska Native, 0.0% Hispanic of any race, 0.0% two or more races (2000); Density: 3.4 persons per square mile (2000); Age: 27.0% under 18, 12.1% over 64 (2000); Marriage status: 23.1% never married, 72.8% now married, 2.6% widowed, 1.5% divorced (2000); Foreign born: 0.8% (2000); Ancestry (includes multiple ancestries): 45.2% Finnish, 21.4% Norwegian, 19.8% German, 14.9% Swedish, 10.5% United States or American (2000).
Economy: Employment by occupation: 9.5% management, 35.3% professional, 6.9% services, 9.5% sales, 1.7% farming, 23.3% construction, 13.8% production (2000).
Income: Per capita income: $16,569 (2000); Median household income: $42,143 (2000); Poverty rate: 10.1% (2000).
Taxes: Total city taxes per capita: $70 (1997); City property taxes per capita: $70 (1997).
Education: High school graduation rate: 82.8% (2000); College graduation rate: 17.8% (2000).
Housing: Homeownership rate: 95.1% (2000); Median home value: $80,000 (2000); Median rent: $375 per month (2000); Median age of housing: 28 years (2000).
Transportation: Commute to work: 92.2% car, 0.0% public transportation, 0.0% walk, 6.0% work from home (2000); Travel time to work: 3.7% less than 15 minutes, 33.9% 15 to 30 minutes, 32.1% 30 to 45 minutes, 8.3% 45 to 60 minutes, 22.0% 60 minutes or more (2000)

CHERRY (township). Covers a land area of 32.923 square miles and a water area of 0.571 square miles. Located at 47.42° N. Lat.; 92.75° W. Long. Elevation is 1,353 feet.
Population: 915 (2000); Race: 98.4% White, 0.0% Black, 0.8% Asian, 0.0% American Indian and Alaska Native, 0.3% Hispanic of any race, 0.9% two or more races (2000); Density: 27.8 persons per square mile (2000); Age: 27.7% under 18, 10.0% over 64 (2000); Marriage status: 22.6% never married, 65.4% now married, 4.9% widowed, 7.1% divorced (2000); Foreign born: 1.3% (2000); Ancestry (includes multiple ancestries): 33.2% Finnish, 22.5% German, 17.1% Norwegian, 8.6% Swedish, 7.3% English (2000).
Economy: Employment by occupation: 8.3% management, 22.4% professional, 14.9% services, 18.2% sales, 0.0% farming, 21.3% construction, 14.9% production (2000).
Income: Per capita income: $19,186 (2000); Median household income: $50,263 (2000); Poverty rate: 4.6% (2000).
Taxes: Total city taxes per capita: $25 (1997); City property taxes per capita: $25 (1997).
Education: High school graduation rate: 93.0% (2000); College graduation rate: 17.5% (2000).
Housing: Homeownership rate: 97.0% (2000); Median home value: $80,300 (2000); Median rent: $275 per month (2000); Median age of housing: 28 years (2000).
Transportation: Commute to work: 95.6% car, 0.0% public transportation, 0.0% walk, 4.4% work from home (2000); Travel time to work: 21.5% less than 15 minutes, 63.5% 15 to 30 minutes, 8.3% 30 to 45 minutes, 1.6% 45 to 60 minutes, 5.1% 60 minutes or more (2000)

CHISHOLM (city). Covers a land area of 4.395 square miles and a water area of 0.342 square miles. Located at 47.49° N. Lat.; 92.87° W. Long. Elevation is 1,578 feet.
History: Minnesota Museum of Mines here. Incorporated as town 1901, as city 1934.
Population: 4,960 (2000); Race: 98.7% White, 0.0% Black, 0.2% Asian, 0.5% American Indian and Alaska Native, 0.9% Hispanic of any race, 0.5% two or more races (2000); Density: 1,128.6 persons per square mile (2000); Age: 22.6% under 18, 22.3% over 64 (2000); Marriage status: 26.8% never married, 52.0% now married, 9.8% widowed, 11.3% divorced (2000); Foreign born: 0.8% (2000); Ancestry (includes multiple ancestries): 18.6% German, 13.7% Finnish, 11.4% Irish, 11.2% Swedish, 11.2% Norwegian (2000).
Economy: Trading and mining point. Manufacturing: pulpwood, apparel, drill bits, foods; timber; dairying; alfalfa. Iron mines in area. Single-family building permits issued: 4 (2001) / 9 (2000); Multi-family building permits issued: 0 (2001) / 0 (2000); Employment by occupation: 4.7% management, 12.6% professional, 21.7% services, 22.0% sales, 0.0% farming, 17.8% construction, 21.2% production (2000).
Income: Per capita income: $16,204 (2000); Median household income: $28,472 (2000); Poverty rate: 12.1% (2000).
Taxes: Total city taxes per capita: $152 (1997); City property taxes per capita: $143 (1997).
Education: High school graduation rate: 85.6% (2000); College graduation rate: 12.5% (2000).

School District(s)

Chisholm (PK-12)
2000 Enrollment: 916 218-254-5726
Housing: Homeownership rate: 78.1% (2000); Median home value: $47,300 (2000); Median rent: $270 per month (2000); Median age of housing: 60+ years (2000).
Safety: Violent crime rate: 2.0 per 10,000 population; Property crime rate: 225.4 per 10,000 population (2001).
Newspapers: The Chisholm Tribune-Press (1 x week)
Transportation: Commute to work: 90.1% car, 0.3% public transportation, 7.1% walk, 0.9% work from home (2000); Travel time to work: 47.3% less than 15 minutes, 37.9% 15 to 30 minutes, 7.3% 30 to 45 minutes, 2.8% 45 to 60 minutes, 4.7% 60 minutes or more (2000)

CLINTON (township). Covers a land area of 33.208 square miles and a water area of 0.653 square miles. Located at 47.40° N. Lat.; 92.61° W. Long.
Population: 1,036 (2000); Race: 96.1% White, 0.0% Black, 0.4% Asian, 1.3% American Indian and Alaska Native, 2.2% Hispanic of any race, 1.8% two or more races (2000); Density: 31.2 persons per square mile (2000); Age: 23.4% under 18, 10.4% over 64 (2000); Marriage status: 27.0% never married, 57.4% now married, 5.4% widowed, 10.2% divorced (2000); Foreign born: 2.1% (2000); Ancestry (includes multiple ancestries): 29.5% Finnish, 24.2% German, 15.1% Norwegian, 11.0% Swedish, 9.2% Irish (2000).
Economy: Employment by occupation: 6.9% management, 8.8% professional, 14.8% services, 26.0% sales, 2.3% farming, 23.3% construction, 17.9% production (2000).
Income: Per capita income: $18,359 (2000); Median household income: $44,773 (2000); Poverty rate: 6.4% (2000).
Taxes: Total city taxes per capita: $77 (2000); City property taxes per capita: $76 (2000).
Education: High school graduation rate: 89.6% (2000); College graduation rate: 8.9% (2000).
Housing: Homeownership rate: 93.8% (2000); Median home value: $67,800 (2000); Median rent: $250 per month (2000); Median age of housing: 29 years (2000).
Transportation: Commute to work: 94.0% car, 0.0% public transportation, 1.8% walk, 3.5% work from home (2000); Travel time to work: 18.8% less

than 15 minutes, 64.3% 15 to 30 minutes, 11.1% 30 to 45 minutes, 1.6% 45 to 60 minutes, 4.2% 60 minutes or more (2000)

COLVIN (township). Covers a land area of 33.625 square miles and a water area of 2.299 square miles. Located at 47.31° N. Lat.; 92.22° W. Long.
Population: 354 (2000); Race: 93.3% White, 0.0% Black, 0.0% Asian, 3.5% American Indian and Alaska Native, 0.0% Hispanic of any race, 3.2% two or more races (2000); Density: 10.5 persons per square mile (2000); Age: 15.2% under 18, 14.3% over 64 (2000); Marriage status: 22.8% never married, 57.0% now married, 6.8% widowed, 13.4% divorced (2000); Foreign born: 1.8% (2000); Ancestry (includes multiple ancestries): 38.6% Finnish, 23.7% German, 19.9% Swedish, 10.2% Norwegian, 5.6% Other groups (2000).
Economy: Employment by occupation: 5.2% management, 12.8% professional, 12.8% services, 18.0% sales, 1.2% farming, 33.7% construction, 16.3% production (2000).
Income: Per capita income: $17,359 (2000); Median household income: $39,821 (2000); Poverty rate: 16.4% (2000).
Taxes: Total city taxes per capita: $120 (1997); City property taxes per capita: $120 (1997).
Education: High school graduation rate: 88.0% (2000); College graduation rate: 12.7% (2000).
Housing: Homeownership rate: 93.0% (2000); Median home value: $67,500 (2000); Median age of housing: 35 years (2000).
Transportation: Commute to work: 93.0% car, 0.0% public transportation, 0.0% walk, 5.3% work from home (2000); Travel time to work: 9.3% less than 15 minutes, 19.1% 15 to 30 minutes, 45.1% 30 to 45 minutes, 19.1% 45 to 60 minutes, 7.4% 60 minutes or more (2000)

COOK (city). Covers a land area of 0.787 square miles and a water area of 0 square miles. Located at 47.85° N. Lat.; 92.68° W. Long. Elevation is 1,306 feet.
Population: 622 (2000); Race: 99.1% White, 0.0% Black, 0.0% Asian, 0.3% American Indian and Alaska Native, 0.0% Hispanic of any race, 0.5% two or more races (2000); Density: 790.1 persons per square mile (2000); Age: 17.4% under 18, 33.2% over 64 (2000); Marriage status: 20.5% never married, 46.8% now married, 17.9% widowed, 14.8% divorced (2000); Foreign born: 0.7% (2000); Ancestry (includes multiple ancestries): 26.5% Norwegian, 21.7% German, 17.2% Finnish, 15.5% Swedish, 8.1% Irish (2000).
Economy: Single-family building permits issued: 0 (2001) / 0 (2000); Multi-family building permits issued: 0 (2001) / 0 (2000); Employment by occupation: 5.5% management, 20.7% professional, 22.4% services, 19.8% sales, 3.0% farming, 13.1% construction, 15.6% production (2000).
Income: Per capita income: $15,848 (2000); Median household income: $21,607 (2000); Poverty rate: 13.0% (2000).
Taxes: Total city taxes per capita: $199 (1997); City property taxes per capita: $191 (1997).
Education: High school graduation rate: 78.2% (2000); College graduation rate: 13.3% (2000).
Housing: Homeownership rate: 60.4% (2000); Median home value: $49,500 (2000); Median rent: $254 per month (2000); Median age of housing: 40 years (2000).
Hospitals: Cook Hospital (14 beds)
Newspapers: The Cook News-Herald (1 x week)
Transportation: Commute to work: 82.9% car, 0.0% public transportation, 13.7% walk, 3.4% work from home (2000); Travel time to work: 59.7% less than 15 minutes, 19.9% 15 to 30 minutes, 14.2% 30 to 45 minutes, 3.1% 45 to 60 minutes, 3.1% 60 minutes or more (2000)

COTTON (township). Covers a land area of 69.345 square miles and a water area of 2.726 square miles. Located at 47.16° N. Lat.; 92.39° W. Long. Elevation is 1,329 feet.
Population: 506 (2000); Race: 99.3% White, 0.0% Black, 0.0% Asian, 0.4% American Indian and Alaska Native, 0.0% Hispanic of any race, 0.4% two or more races (2000); Density: 7.3 persons per square mile (2000); Age: 27.2% under 18, 14.4% over 64 (2000); Marriage status: 24.9% never married, 61.5% now married, 9.3% widowed, 4.3% divorced (2000); Foreign born: 1.5% (2000); Ancestry (includes multiple ancestries): 23.9% Swedish, 20.0% German, 16.4% Norwegian, 9.1% Finnish, 7.6% Irish (2000).
Economy: Employment by occupation: 7.6% management, 9.3% professional, 23.6% services, 21.1% sales, 0.0% farming, 18.6% construction, 19.8% production (2000).
Income: Per capita income: $16,216 (2000); Median household income: $40,313 (2000); Poverty rate: 5.6% (2000).
Taxes: Total city taxes per capita: $144 (1997); City property taxes per capita: $144 (1997).
Education: High school graduation rate: 94.4% (2000); College graduation rate: 15.1% (2000).
Housing: Homeownership rate: 96.9% (2000); Median home value: $102,100 (2000); Median age of housing: 32 years (2000).
Transportation: Commute to work: 92.3% car, 0.0% public transportation, 0.0% walk, 7.7% work from home (2000); Travel time to work: 12.6% less than 15 minutes, 18.1% 15 to 30 minutes, 21.9% 30 to 45 minutes, 32.1% 45 to 60 minutes, 15.3% 60 minutes or more (2000)

CRANE LAKE (unincorporated postal area, zip code 55725). Covers a land area of 201.943 square miles and a water area of 11.014 square miles. Located at 48.26° N. Lat.; 92.61° W. Long. Elevation is 1,180 feet.
Population: 111 (2000); Race: 96.9% White, 0.0% Black, 0.0% Asian, 0.0% American Indian and Alaska Native, 0.0% Hispanic of any race, 3.1% two or more races (2000); Density: 0.5 persons per square mile (2000); Age: 18.4% under 18, 9.2% over 64 (2000); Marriage status: 8.4% never married, 65.1% now married, 0.0% widowed, 26.5% divorced (2000); Foreign born: 0.0% (2000); Ancestry (includes multiple ancestries): 37.8% Finnish, 35.7% Polish, 19.4% English, 15.3% German, 14.3% Swedish (2000).
Economy: Employment by occupation: 9.4% management, 25.0% professional, 0.0% services, 28.1% sales, 0.0% farming, 37.5% construction, 0.0% production (2000).
Income: Per capita income: $15,136 (2000); Median household income: $30,139 (2000); Poverty rate: 7.1% (2000).
Education: High school graduation rate: 100.0% (2000); College graduation rate: 16.4% (2000).
Housing: Homeownership rate: 86.0% (2000); Median home value: $90,000 (2000); Median age of housing: 26 years (2000).
Transportation: Commute to work: 71.9% car, 0.0% public transportation, 0.0% walk, 28.1% work from home (2000); Travel time to work: 8.7% less than 15 minutes, 34.8% 15 to 30 minutes, 13.0% 30 to 45 minutes, 0.0% 45 to 60 minutes, 43.5% 60 minutes or more (2000)

CULVER (township). Covers a land area of 34.583 square miles and a water area of 0.506 square miles. Located at 46.89° N. Lat.; 92.59° W. Long. Elevation is 1,289 feet.
Population: 285 (2000); Race: 89.4% White, 0.0% Black, 0.0% Asian, 8.0% American Indian and Alaska Native, 0.0% Hispanic of any race, 1.9% two or more races (2000); Density: 8.2 persons per square mile (2000); Age: 29.3% under 18, 15.8% over 64 (2000); Marriage status: 31.5% never married, 53.4% now married, 4.2% widowed, 10.9% divorced (2000); Foreign born: 0.3% (2000); Ancestry (includes multiple ancestries): 20.6% Swedish, 17.0% Finnish, 14.8% Norwegian, 13.5% Polish, 13.2% German (2000).
Economy: Employment by occupation: 4.3% management, 19.6% professional, 15.2% services, 29.0% sales, 0.0% farming, 14.5% construction, 17.4% production (2000).
Income: Per capita income: $15,028 (2000); Median household income: $38,333 (2000); Poverty rate: 12.7% (2000).
Taxes: Total city taxes per capita: $78 (1997); City property taxes per capita: $78 (1997).
Education: High school graduation rate: 84.8% (2000); College graduation rate: 7.9% (2000).
Housing: Homeownership rate: 82.2% (2000); Median home value: $73,800 (2000); Median rent: $331 per month (2000); Median age of housing: 25 years (2000).
Transportation: Commute to work: 94.0% car, 0.0% public transportation, 0.0% walk, 6.0% work from home (2000); Travel time to work: 7.1% less than 15 minutes, 37.3% 15 to 30 minutes, 30.2% 30 to 45 minutes, 20.6% 45 to 60 minutes, 4.8% 60 minutes or more (2000)

DULUTH (city). Covers a land area of 68.008 square miles and a water area of 19.314 square miles. Located at 46.78° N. Lat.; 92.11° W. Long. Elevation is 900 feet.
History: Daniel Greysolon, Sieur Du Luth, for whom the city of Duluth was named, made his first visit here in 1679, exploring trapping and trading possibilities on the western end of Lake Superior. The entire area was then known as Fond du Lac. The first permanent settler in what was to become Duluth was George P. Suntz, who visited in 1852 and returned in 1853 to build a cabin. Rumors of immense copper deposits brought a rush of miners and settlers in the 1850's, and the towns of Duluth, Fond du Lac, Portland, Belville, and Oneota (all later joining into Duluth) were incorporated as separate villages. The railroad arrived in the early 1870's, but economic disaster that hit in 1873 kept Duluth from becoming a city until 1887. By 1900, Duluth had absorbed the other communities along the lake shore. Duluth's protected harbor on Lake Superior made it an important commercial shipping center

Population: 86,918 (2000); Race: 92.7% White, 1.7% Black, 1.4% Asian, 2.2% American Indian and Alaska Native, 1.1% Hispanic of any race, 1.7% two or more races (2000); Density: 1,278.1 persons per square mile (2000); Age: 21.2% under 18, 15.2% over 64 (2000); Marriage status: 33.5% never married, 47.9% now married, 7.2% widowed, 11.4% divorced (2000); Foreign born: 2.8% (2000); Ancestry (includes multiple ancestries): 23.6% German, 16.8% Norwegian, 15.3% Swedish, 10.6% Irish, 7.6% Finnish (2000).
Vital Statistics: Birth rate: 117.2 per 10,000 population (1998)
Economy: Unemployment rate: 3.2% (11/2002); Total civilian labor force: 46,101 (11/2002); Single-family building permits issued: 94 (2001) / 59 (2000); Multi-family building permits issued: 12 (2001) / 46 (2000); Employment by occupation: 11.1% management, 23.2% professional, 19.8% services, 28.1% sales, 0.2% farming, 7.3% construction, 10.4% production (2000).
Income: Per capita income: $18,969 (2000); Median household income: $33,766 (2000); Poverty rate: 15.5% (2000).
Taxes: Total city taxes per capita: $355 (2000); City property taxes per capita: $167 (2000).
Education: High school graduation rate: 87.7% (2000); College graduation rate: 28.2% (2000).

School District(s)

Duluth (PK-12)
2000 Enrollment: 12,430 218-723-4150
Edison Charter School (KG-09)
2000 Enrollment: 817 218-728-9556
Hermantown (PK-12)
2000 Enrollment: 1,955 218-729-9313
Peaks-Duluth (09-12)
2000 Enrollment: 70 218-529-2468

Four-year College(s)

University of Minnesota-Duluth (Public)
2001 Enrollment: 9,380 218-726-8000
2001 Tuition: In-state $4,920; Out-of-state $13,958
The College of Saint Scholastica (Private, Not-for-profit, Roman Catholic)
2001 Enrollment: 2,228 218-723-6000
2001 Tuition: In-state $17,080; Out-of-state $17,080

Two-year College(s)

Lake Superior College (Public)
2001 Enrollment: 3,909 800-432-2884
2001 Tuition: In-state $2,310; Out-of-state $4,620
Duluth Business University Inc (Private, For-profit)
2001 Enrollment: 233 218-722-3361
2001 Tuition: In-state $15,000; Out-of-state $15,000

Housing: Homeownership rate: 64.2% (2000); Median home value: $81,600 (2000); Median rent: $413 per month (2000); Median age of housing: 58 years (2000).
Hospitals: Miller-Dwan Medical Center (165 beds); SMDC Health System (380 beds); Saint Luke's Hospital (267 beds)
Safety: Violent crime rate: 36.2 per 10,000 population; Property crime rate: 575.1 per 10,000 population (2001).
Newspapers: Duluth News-Tribune (7 x week); Direct Mail Advertiser (1 x month); Budgeteer News (2 x week)
Transportation: Commute to work: 86.9% car, 4.2% public transportation, 5.0% walk, 3.1% work from home (2000); Travel time to work: 50.4% less than 15 minutes, 38.9% 15 to 30 minutes, 6.1% 30 to 45 minutes, 1.2% 45 to 60 minutes, 3.4% 60 minutes or more (2000); Amtrak: Service available.
Airports: Duluth International (primary service)

Additional Information Contacts

Duluth Area Association of Realtors 218-728-5676
Duluth Chamber of Commerce 218-722-5501
Duluth Convention & Visitors Bureau. 218-722-4011
Superior Area Association of Realtors. 218-728-5676

DULUTH (township). Covers a land area of 46.487 square miles and a water area of 5.356 square miles. Located at 46.94° N. Lat.; 91.86° W. Long. Elevation is 900 feet.
History: Native Americans found here in the 1670s included the Sieur Duluth for whom the city was named. Permanent settlement began c.1852. The city was at first a trade and shipping center for timber. Discovery of iron (1865) in the Mesabi Range made it thechief shipping point for ore for the nation's steel mills. With the opening of the St. Lawrence Seaway (1959), it became one of the leading ports on the Great Lakes for the export of grain. Incorporated 1870.
Population: 1,723 (2000); Race: 98.6% White, 0.5% Black, 0.0% Asian, 0.2% American Indian and Alaska Native, 0.5% Hispanic of any race, 0.6% two or more races (2000); Density: 37.1 persons per square mile (2000); Age: 25.7% under 18, 11.7% over 64 (2000); Marriage status: 22.5% never married, 66.3% now married, 4.3% widowed, 6.9% divorced (2000); Foreign born: 1.5% (2000); Ancestry (includes multiple ancestries): 24.0% Norwegian, 22.4% Swedish, 22.1% German, 16.3% Finnish, 8.7% Irish (2000).
Economy: A commercial, industrial and cultural center. It is a major port on the Great Lakes, convention center and gateway to resort region. Large amounts of grain, iron ore, oil, and bulk cargo are shipped on lake freighters and ocean vessels. Industry includes fish processing, grain elevator services, specialty fabricating, steel, concrete, piping, chemical lime, paper, hand tools and consumer goods. Tourism and the military air-defense installation at Duluth Int'l Airport are valuable to the economy. Single-family building permits issued: 17 (2001) / 15 (2000); Multi-family building permits issued: 0 (2001) / 0 (2000); Employment by occupation: 11.6% management, 30.1% professional, 18.2% services, 16.1% sales, 0.4% farming, 13.4% construction, 10.3% production (2000).
Income: Per capita income: $23,116 (2000); Median household income: $46,118 (2000); Poverty rate: 4.1% (2000).
Taxes: Total city taxes per capita: $113 (2000); City property taxes per capita: $111 (2000).
Education: High school graduation rate: 92.4% (2000); College graduation rate: 32.4% (2000).
Housing: Homeownership rate: 92.0% (2000); Median home value: $105,400 (2000); Median rent: $458 per month (2000); Median age of housing: 30 years (2000).
Transportation: Commute to work: 91.8% car, 0.0% public transportation, 1.3% walk, 6.2% work from home (2000); Travel time to work: 12.9% less than 15 minutes, 48.1% 15 to 30 minutes, 32.4% 30 to 45 minutes, 3.7% 45 to 60 minutes, 2.9% 60 minutes or more (2000); Amtrak: Service available.

EAGLES NEST (township). Covers a land area of 25.167 square miles and a water area of 4.742 square miles. Located at 47.84° N. Lat.; 92.10° W. Long. Elevation is 1,491 feet.
Population: 169 (2000); Race: 98.9% White, 0.0% Black, 1.1% Asian, 0.0% American Indian and Alaska Native, 0.0% Hispanic of any race, 0.0% two or more races (2000); Density: 6.7 persons per square mile (2000); Age: 13.4% under 18, 25.8% over 64 (2000); Marriage status: 7.5% never married, 76.4% now married, 9.3% widowed, 6.8% divorced (2000); Foreign born: 1.1% (2000); Ancestry (includes multiple ancestries): 17.7% German, 17.2% Swedish, 15.1% Finnish, 14.5% Norwegian, 11.8% English (2000).
Economy: Employment by occupation: 11.8% management, 17.6% professional, 23.5% services, 20.6% sales, 0.0% farming, 14.7% construction, 11.8% production (2000).
Income: Per capita income: $19,568 (2000); Median household income: $36,250 (2000); Poverty rate: 8.6% (2000).
Taxes: Total city taxes per capita: $298 (1997); City property taxes per capita: $298 (1997).
Education: High school graduation rate: 89.8% (2000); College graduation rate: 26.1% (2000).
Housing: Homeownership rate: 100.0% (2000); Median home value: $152,300 (2000); Median age of housing: 29 years (2000).
Transportation: Commute to work: 80.6% car, 0.0% public transportation, 0.0% walk, 16.4% work from home (2000); Travel time to work: 8.9% less than 15 minutes, 46.4% 15 to 30 minutes, 28.6% 30 to 45 minutes, 7.1% 45 to 60 minutes, 8.9% 60 minutes or more (2000)

ELLSBURG (township). Covers a land area of 69.574 square miles and a water area of 2.443 square miles. Located at 47.23° N. Lat.; 92.41° W. Long.
Population: 174 (2000); Race: 89.8% White, 0.0% Black, 6.6% Asian, 0.0% American Indian and Alaska Native, 0.0% Hispanic of any race, 3.6% two or more races (2000); Density: 2.5 persons per square mile (2000); Age: 31.1% under 18, 13.3% over 64 (2000); Marriage status: 17.9% never married, 61.6% now married, 7.3% widowed, 13.2% divorced (2000); Foreign born: 4.6% (2000); Ancestry (includes multiple ancestries): 26.5% German, 20.4% Swedish, 11.7% Irish, 10.2% Other groups, 10.2% Finnish (2000).
Economy: Employment by occupation: 0.0% management, 31.7% professional, 11.1% services, 20.6% sales, 0.0% farming, 23.8% construction, 12.7% production (2000).
Income: Per capita income: $15,582 (2000); Median household income: $39,250 (2000); Poverty rate: 21.4% (2000).
Taxes: Total city taxes per capita: $621 (1997); City property taxes per capita: $621 (1997).
Education: High school graduation rate: 84.0% (2000); College graduation rate: 19.8% (2000).

Housing: Homeownership rate: 100.0% (2000); Median home value: $65,000 (2000); Median age of housing: 42 years (2000).
Transportation: Commute to work: 96.8% car, 0.0% public transportation, 0.0% walk, 0.0% work from home (2000); Travel time to work: 11.3% less than 15 minutes, 9.7% 15 to 30 minutes, 24.2% 30 to 45 minutes, 19.4% 45 to 60 minutes, 35.5% 60 minutes or more (2000)

ELMER (township). Covers a land area of 40.563 square miles and a water area of 0.128 square miles. Located at 47.07° N. Lat.; 92.81° W. Long. Elevation is 912 feet.
Population: 165 (2000); Race: 96.1% White, 2.8% Black, 0.0% Asian, 1.1% American Indian and Alaska Native, 0.0% Hispanic of any race, 0.0% two or more races (2000); Density: 4.1 persons per square mile (2000); Age: 26.0% under 18, 11.6% over 64 (2000); Marriage status: 16.5% never married, 75.5% now married, 5.8% widowed, 2.2% divorced (2000); Foreign born: 0.6% (2000); Ancestry (includes multiple ancestries): 27.1% German, 25.4% Swedish, 23.8% Norwegian, 14.9% Finnish, 12.7% Czechoslovakian (2000).
Economy: Employment by occupation: 20.9% management, 8.1% professional, 17.4% services, 8.1% sales, 4.7% farming, 23.3% construction, 17.4% production (2000).
Income: Per capita income: $17,418 (2000); Median household income: $42,344 (2000); Poverty rate: 19.9% (2000).
Taxes: Total city taxes per capita: $38 (1997); City property taxes per capita: $38 (1997).
Education: High school graduation rate: 83.7% (2000); College graduation rate: 2.4% (2000).
Housing: Homeownership rate: 88.5% (2000); Median home value: $65,000 (2000); Median rent: <$100 per month (2000); Median age of housing: 32 years (2000).
Transportation: Commute to work: 71.6% car, 7.4% public transportation, 0.0% walk, 21.0% work from home (2000); Travel time to work: 14.1% less than 15 minutes, 43.8% 15 to 30 minutes, 7.8% 30 to 45 minutes, 23.4% 45 to 60 minutes, 10.9% 60 minutes or more (2000)

ELY (city). Covers a land area of 2.719 square miles and a water area of 0.003 square miles. Located at 47.90° N. Lat.; 91.85° W. Long. Elevation is 1,417 feet.
History: Ely, established on the shore of Lake Shagawa, developed as the mining capital of the Vermilion Iron Range, as well as a summer resort area.
Population: 3,724 (2000); Race: 97.9% White, 0.2% Black, 0.7% Asian, 0.1% American Indian and Alaska Native, 0.3% Hispanic of any race, 0.9% two or more races (2000); Density: 1,369.5 persons per square mile (2000); Age: 17.7% under 18, 21.7% over 64 (2000); Marriage status: 34.6% never married, 44.8% now married, 12.4% widowed, 8.2% divorced (2000); Foreign born: 1.0% (2000); Ancestry (includes multiple ancestries): 24.9% German, 12.5% Slovene, 11.9% Finnish, 11.2% Irish, 8.9% Norwegian (2000).
Economy: Single-family building permits issued: 7 (2001) / 0 (2000); Multi-family building permits issued: 0 (2001) / 0 (2000); Employment by occupation: 12.1% management, 17.9% professional, 21.4% services, 23.8% sales, 0.4% farming, 14.6% construction, 9.8% production (2000).
Income: Per capita income: $16,855 (2000); Median household income: $27,615 (2000); Poverty rate: 14.5% (2000).
Education: High school graduation rate: 86.0% (2000); College graduation rate: 22.0% (2000).

School District(s)

Ely (PK-12)
2000 Enrollment: 796 218-365-6166

Two-year College(s)

Vermilion Community College (Public)
2001 Enrollment: 857 218-365-7200
2001 Tuition: In-state $2,460; Out-of-state $4,880

Housing: Homeownership rate: 71.7% (2000); Median home value: $56,900 (2000); Median rent: $325 per month (2000); Median age of housing: 58 years (2000).
Hospitals: Ely-Bloomenson Community Hospital and Nursing Home (15 beds)
Safety: Violent crime rate: 21.3 per 10,000 population; Property crime rate: 361.3 per 10,000 population (2001).
Newspapers: Ely Echo (1 x week); North Country Saver (1 x week)
Transportation: Commute to work: 75.2% car, 0.4% public transportation, 15.0% walk, 8.7% work from home (2000); Travel time to work: 65.2% less than 15 minutes, 10.7% 15 to 30 minutes, 8.4% 30 to 45 minutes, 5.9% 45 to 60 minutes, 9.8% 60 minutes or more (2000)
Airports: Ely Municipal
Additional Information Contacts
Ely Chamber of Commerce 218-365-6123

EMBARRASS (township). Covers a land area of 32.692 square miles and a water area of 0.078 square miles. Located at 47.65° N. Lat.; 92.23° W. Long. Elevation is 1,421 feet.
History: The name of Embarrass is from the French and means "obstacle," referring to the floating driftwood that made canoeing difficult on the nearby river.
Population: 691 (2000); Race: 99.3% White, 0.0% Black, 0.0% Asian, 0.0% American Indian and Alaska Native, 0.4% Hispanic of any race, 0.7% two or more races (2000); Density: 21.1 persons per square mile (2000); Age: 22.7% under 18, 16.9% over 64 (2000); Marriage status: 19.2% never married, 61.3% now married, 6.5% widowed, 13.0% divorced (2000); Foreign born: 0.6% (2000); Ancestry (includes multiple ancestries): 29.2% Finnish, 22.3% German, 10.8% Norwegian, 9.0% Swedish, 7.1% Irish (2000).
Economy: Employment by occupation: 12.5% management, 13.5% professional, 14.8% services, 22.6% sales, 1.0% farming, 18.5% construction, 17.2% production (2000).
Income: Per capita income: $17,983 (2000); Median household income: $36,111 (2000); Poverty rate: 8.6% (2000).
Taxes: Total city taxes per capita: $127 (1997); City property taxes per capita: $127 (1997).
Education: High school graduation rate: 82.9% (2000); College graduation rate: 7.7% (2000).
Housing: Homeownership rate: 95.6% (2000); Median home value: $50,000 (2000); Median rent: $175 per month (2000); Median age of housing: 36 years (2000).
Transportation: Commute to work: 92.2% car, 1.7% public transportation, 0.7% walk, 5.1% work from home (2000); Travel time to work: 27.0% less than 15 minutes, 37.4% 15 to 30 minutes, 22.7% 30 to 45 minutes, 9.4% 45 to 60 minutes, 3.6% 60 minutes or more (2000)

EVELETH (city). Covers a land area of 6.326 square miles and a water area of 0.160 square miles. Located at 47.46° N. Lat.; 92.54° W. Long. Elevation is 1,574 feet.
History: Eveleth was named for Edwin Eveleth, a Michigan lumberman. The town was platted in 1893, but grew after 1900 when mining operations began. At one time, half of Minnesota's iron ore came from mines located with a 50-mile radius of Eveleth.
Population: 3,865 (2000); Race: 96.4% White, 0.0% Black, 0.5% Asian, 1.0% American Indian and Alaska Native, 1.5% Hispanic of any race, 1.8% two or more races (2000); Density: 611.0 persons per square mile (2000); Age: 21.7% under 18, 21.2% over 64 (2000); Marriage status: 25.5% never married, 48.9% now married, 13.5% widowed, 12.0% divorced (2000); Foreign born: 1.6% (2000); Ancestry (includes multiple ancestries): 17.8% German, 16.7% Finnish, 14.2% Norwegian, 10.9% Swedish, 9.5% Slovene (2000).
Economy: Single-family building permits issued: 4 (2001) / 0 (2000); Multi-family building permits issued: 0 (2001) / 0 (2000); Employment by occupation: 6.1% management, 16.7% professional, 17.9% services, 28.4% sales, 0.0% farming, 13.4% construction, 17.6% production (2000).
Income: Per capita income: $16,635 (2000); Median household income: $27,736 (2000); Poverty rate: 15.4% (2000).
Taxes: Total city taxes per capita: $148 (1997); City property taxes per capita: $135 (1997).
Education: High school graduation rate: 82.1% (2000); College graduation rate: 12.8% (2000).

School District(s)

Eveleth-Gilbert (PK-12)
2000 Enrollment: 1,460 218-744-7701

Two-year College(s)

Mesabi Range Community and Technical College (Public)
2001 Enrollment: n/a 218-741-3095
2001 Tuition: In-state $2,399; Out-of-state $2,399

Housing: Homeownership rate: 69.9% (2000); Median home value: $46,700 (2000); Median rent: $325 per month (2000); Median age of housing: 60+ years (2000).
Safety: Violent crime rate: 30.7 per 10,000 population; Property crime rate: 581.2 per 10,000 population (2001).
Transportation: Commute to work: 90.8% car, 0.7% public transportation, 6.5% walk, 1.8% work from home (2000); Travel time to work: 63.0% less than 15 minutes, 20.4% 15 to 30 minutes, 11.7% 30 to 45 minutes, 2.6% 45 to 60 minutes, 2.3% 60 minutes or more (2000)
Airports: Eveleth-Virginia Municipal
Additional Information Contacts
Eveleth Chamber of Commerce 218-744-1940

FAIRBANKS (township). Covers a land area of 69.956 square miles and a water area of 1.969 square miles. Located at 47.32° N. Lat.; 91.85° W. Long. Elevation is 1,653 feet.
Population: 68 (2000); Race: 96.2% White, 0.0% Black, 0.0% Asian, 0.0% American Indian and Alaska Native, 0.0% Hispanic of any race, 3.8% two or more races (2000); Density: 1.0 persons per square mile (2000); Age: 6.3% under 18, 29.1% over 64 (2000); Marriage status: 13.2% never married, 64.5% now married, 2.6% widowed, 19.7% divorced (2000); Foreign born: 0.0% (2000); Ancestry (includes multiple ancestries): 27.8% Irish, 24.1% German, 22.8% Swedish, 15.2% Finnish, 12.7% Norwegian (2000).
Economy: Employment by occupation: 26.7% management, 26.7% professional, 10.0% services, 26.7% sales, 0.0% farming, 10.0% construction, 0.0% production (2000).
Income: Per capita income: $24,939 (2000); Median household income: $38,750 (2000); Poverty rate: 3.8% (2000).
Taxes: Total city taxes per capita: $107 (1997); City property taxes per capita: $107 (1997).
Education: High school graduation rate: 90.5% (2000); College graduation rate: 17.6% (2000).
Housing: Homeownership rate: 100.0% (2000); Median home value: $137,500 (2000); Median age of housing: 28 years (2000).
Transportation: Commute to work: 60.0% car, 0.0% public transportation, 10.0% walk, 16.7% work from home (2000); Travel time to work: 12.0% less than 15 minutes, 32.0% 15 to 30 minutes, 24.0% 30 to 45 minutes, 0.0% 45 to 60 minutes, 32.0% 60 minutes or more (2000)

FAYAL (township). Covers a land area of 31.423 square miles and a water area of 3.023 square miles. Located at 47.42° N. Lat.; 92.51° W. Long.
Population: 1,906 (2000); Race: 96.3% White, 0.0% Black, 0.7% Asian, 0.2% American Indian and Alaska Native, 0.9% Hispanic of any race, 2.6% two or more races (2000); Density: 60.7 persons per square mile (2000); Age: 24.6% under 18, 17.3% over 64 (2000); Marriage status: 14.3% never married, 73.8% now married, 5.7% widowed, 6.2% divorced (2000); Foreign born: 2.1% (2000); Ancestry (includes multiple ancestries): 20.9% German, 18.6% Finnish, 11.8% Swedish, 9.8% Slovene, 9.5% Norwegian (2000).
Economy: Employment by occupation: 12.7% management, 19.8% professional, 6.4% services, 26.9% sales, 1.7% farming, 20.9% construction, 11.7% production (2000).
Income: Per capita income: $22,938 (2000); Median household income: $50,665 (2000); Poverty rate: 2.3% (2000).
Taxes: Total city taxes per capita: $110 (2000); City property taxes per capita: $110 (2000).
Education: High school graduation rate: 91.1% (2000); College graduation rate: 24.3% (2000).
Housing: Homeownership rate: 98.6% (2000); Median home value: $95,500 (2000); Median rent: $444 per month (2000); Median age of housing: 35 years (2000).
Transportation: Commute to work: 98.4% car, 0.0% public transportation, 0.4% walk, 1.2% work from home (2000); Travel time to work: 29.9% less than 15 minutes, 47.1% 15 to 30 minutes, 13.6% 30 to 45 minutes, 5.2% 45 to 60 minutes, 4.2% 60 minutes or more (2000)

FIELD (township). Covers a land area of 54.231 square miles and a water area of 0.012 square miles. Located at 47.86° N. Lat.; 92.75° W. Long.
Population: 391 (2000); Race: 97.1% White, 0.5% Black, 0.0% Asian, 1.5% American Indian and Alaska Native, 0.0% Hispanic of any race, 1.0% two or more races (2000); Density: 7.2 persons per square mile (2000); Age: 21.9% under 18, 12.4% over 64 (2000); Marriage status: 17.1% never married, 65.6% now married, 7.2% widowed, 10.2% divorced (2000); Foreign born: 0.5% (2000); Ancestry (includes multiple ancestries): 30.9% German, 23.4% Finnish, 17.5% Norwegian, 17.5% Swedish, 6.8% Irish (2000).
Economy: Employment by occupation: 13.0% management, 18.4% professional, 11.4% services, 23.8% sales, 0.0% farming, 24.3% construction, 9.2% production (2000).
Income: Per capita income: $21,995 (2000); Median household income: $45,333 (2000); Poverty rate: 12.4% (2000).
Taxes: Total city taxes per capita: $30 (1997); City property taxes per capita: $30 (1997).
Education: High school graduation rate: 90.1% (2000); College graduation rate: 8.6% (2000).
Housing: Homeownership rate: 94.0% (2000); Median home value: $58,800 (2000); Median rent: $275 per month (2000); Median age of housing: 37 years (2000).
Transportation: Commute to work: 88.1% car, 1.7% public transportation, 5.7% walk, 4.5% work from home (2000); Travel time to work: 51.8% less than 15 minutes, 10.1% 15 to 30 minutes, 28.6% 30 to 45 minutes, 5.4% 45 to 60 minutes, 4.2% 60 minutes or more (2000)

FINE LAKES (township). Covers a land area of 34.108 square miles and a water area of 1.788 square miles. Located at 46.79° N. Lat.; 92.89° W. Long.
Population: 145 (2000); Race: 98.3% White, 0.0% Black, 0.0% Asian, 1.7% American Indian and Alaska Native, 0.0% Hispanic of any race, 0.0% two or more races (2000); Density: 4.3 persons per square mile (2000); Age: 19.1% under 18, 20.0% over 64 (2000); Marriage status: 7.3% never married, 82.3% now married, 0.0% widowed, 10.4% divorced (2000); Foreign born: 0.0% (2000); Ancestry (includes multiple ancestries): 33.9% Finnish, 24.3% Norwegian, 23.5% German, 17.4% Swedish, 7.8% Polish (2000).
Economy: Employment by occupation: 8.2% management, 12.2% professional, 16.3% services, 16.3% sales, 0.0% farming, 22.4% construction, 24.5% production (2000).
Income: Per capita income: $16,015 (2000); Median household income: $38,750 (2000); Poverty rate: 8.7% (2000).
Taxes: Total city taxes per capita: $471 (1997); City property taxes per capita: $471 (1997).
Education: High school graduation rate: 79.5% (2000); College graduation rate: 10.2% (2000).
Housing: Homeownership rate: 100.0% (2000); Median home value: $103,100 (2000); Median age of housing: 34 years (2000).
Transportation: Commute to work: 100.0% car, 0.0% public transportation, 0.0% walk, 0.0% work from home (2000); Travel time to work: 26.5% less than 15 minutes, 28.6% 15 to 30 minutes, 16.3% 30 to 45 minutes, 18.4% 45 to 60 minutes, 10.2% 60 minutes or more (2000)

FLOODWOOD (city). Covers a land area of 0.444 square miles and a water area of 0 square miles. Located at 46.92° N. Lat.; 92.91° W. Long. Elevation is 1,253 feet.
Population: 503 (2000); Race: 94.9% White, 0.0% Black, 0.6% Asian, 4.5% American Indian and Alaska Native, 0.6% Hispanic of any race, 0.0% two or more races (2000); Density: 1,131.9 persons per square mile (2000); Age: 25.9% under 18, 24.2% over 64 (2000); Marriage status: 30.1% never married, 39.3% now married, 14.5% widowed, 16.1% divorced (2000); Foreign born: 1.4% (2000); Ancestry (includes multiple ancestries): 50.5% Finnish, 23.0% German, 9.4% Polish, 9.4% Swedish, 6.4% Norwegian (2000).
Economy: Single-family building permits issued: 0 (2001) / 0 (2000); Multi-family building permits issued: 0 (2001) / 0 (2000); Employment by occupation: 7.4% management, 8.5% professional, 23.3% services, 23.3% sales, 1.6% farming, 14.8% construction, 21.2% production (2000).
Income: Per capita income: $14,649 (2000); Median household income: $18,977 (2000); Poverty rate: 19.4% (2000).
Taxes: Total city taxes per capita: $207 (1997); City property taxes per capita: $193 (1997).
Education: High school graduation rate: 71.7% (2000); College graduation rate: 6.0% (2000).

School District(s)

Floodwood (PK-12)
2000 Enrollment: 438 218-476-2285
Housing: Homeownership rate: 72.3% (2000); Median home value: $39,300 (2000); Median rent: $242 per month (2000); Median age of housing: 38 years (2000).
Safety: Violent crime rate: 0.0 per 10,000 population; Property crime rate: 315.0 per 10,000 population (2001).
Newspapers: The Forum (1 x week)
Transportation: Commute to work: 74.7% car, 0.0% public transportation, 17.2% walk, 6.5% work from home (2000); Travel time to work: 52.9% less than 15 minutes, 4.6% 15 to 30 minutes, 8.0% 30 to 45 minutes, 14.9% 45 to 60 minutes, 19.5% 60 minutes or more (2000)

FLOODWOOD (township). Covers a land area of 34.842 square miles and a water area of 0.641 square miles. Located at 46.89° N. Lat.; 92.88° W. Long. Elevation is 1,253 feet.
Population: 325 (2000); Race: 98.4% White, 0.0% Black, 0.0% Asian, 0.0% American Indian and Alaska Native, 0.9% Hispanic of any race, 0.6% two or more races (2000); Density: 9.3 persons per square mile (2000); Age: 25.2% under 18, 11.3% over 64 (2000); Marriage status: 24.0% never married, 65.4% now married, 2.8% widowed, 7.9% divorced (2000); Foreign born: 0.9% (2000); Ancestry (includes multiple ancestries): 42.5% Finnish, 22.3% German, 18.2% Irish, 11.0% English, 10.1% Swedish (2000).

Economy: Dairying; poultry; oats, alfalfa. Manufacturing. Employment by occupation: 5.6% management, 11.9% professional, 14.4% services, 21.9% sales, 1.9% farming, 11.3% construction, 33.1% production (2000).
Income: Per capita income: $17,805 (2000); Median household income: $38,906 (2000); Poverty rate: 5.8% (2000).
Taxes: Total city taxes per capita: $85 (1997); City property taxes per capita: $85 (1997).
Education: High school graduation rate: 88.3% (2000); College graduation rate: 10.7% (2000).
Housing: Homeownership rate: 95.7% (2000); Median home value: $62,900 (2000); Median rent: $225 per month (2000); Median age of housing: 40 years (2000).
Transportation: Commute to work: 93.6% car, 0.0% public transportation, 5.8% walk, 0.0% work from home (2000); Travel time to work: 53.8% less than 15 minutes, 11.5% 15 to 30 minutes, 6.4% 30 to 45 minutes, 21.2% 45 to 60 minutes, 7.1% 60 minutes or more (2000)

FORBES (unincorporated postal area, zip code 55738). Covers a land area of 107.526 square miles and a water area of 2.156 square miles. Located at 47.27° N. Lat.; 92.67° W. Long. Elevation is 1,347 feet.
Population: 631 (2000); Race: 94.0% White, 0.0% Black, 0.0% Asian, 2.6% American Indian and Alaska Native, 1.8% Hispanic of any race, 1.9% two or more races (2000); Density: 5.9 persons per square mile (2000); Age: 26.5% under 18, 8.7% over 64 (2000); Marriage status: 18.8% never married, 71.1% now married, 3.0% widowed, 7.1% divorced (2000); Foreign born: 0.5% (2000); Ancestry (includes multiple ancestries): 20.4% Finnish, 18.9% German, 13.1% Norwegian, 8.7% Swedish, 5.2% English (2000).
Economy: Employment by occupation: 9.5% management, 11.0% professional, 21.8% services, 18.9% sales, 1.9% farming, 23.3% construction, 13.6% production (2000).
Income: Per capita income: $16,815 (2000); Median household income: $39,844 (2000); Poverty rate: 13.3% (2000).
Education: High school graduation rate: 90.8% (2000); College graduation rate: 8.0% (2000).
Housing: Homeownership rate: 89.1% (2000); Median home value: $66,300 (2000); Median rent: $243 per month (2000); Median age of housing: 33 years (2000).
Transportation: Commute to work: 90.2% car, 0.0% public transportation, 4.8% walk, 5.1% work from home (2000); Travel time to work: 18.1% less than 15 minutes, 42.5% 15 to 30 minutes, 29.4% 30 to 45 minutes, 7.0% 45 to 60 minutes, 3.0% 60 minutes or more (2000)

FREDENBERG (township). Covers a land area of 25.415 square miles and a water area of 10.494 square miles. Located at 46.98° N. Lat.; 92.23° W. Long. Elevation is 1,393 feet.
Population: 1,156 (2000); Race: 98.9% White, 0.0% Black, 0.0% Asian, 0.0% American Indian and Alaska Native, 1.0% Hispanic of any race, 0.7% two or more races (2000); Density: 45.5 persons per square mile (2000); Age: 23.6% under 18, 8.6% over 64 (2000); Marriage status: 17.6% never married, 71.5% now married, 2.7% widowed, 8.1% divorced (2000); Foreign born: 1.4% (2000); Ancestry (includes multiple ancestries): 22.0% German, 20.0% Swedish, 19.2% Norwegian, 11.0% Polish, 8.8% Irish (2000).
Economy: Employment by occupation: 13.8% management, 22.9% professional, 12.2% services, 27.8% sales, 0.5% farming, 10.7% construction, 12.1% production (2000).
Income: Per capita income: $25,536 (2000); Median household income: $58,750 (2000); Poverty rate: 3.2% (2000).
Taxes: Total city taxes per capita: $101 (1997); City property taxes per capita: $101 (1997).
Education: High school graduation rate: 92.5% (2000); College graduation rate: 28.2% (2000).
Housing: Homeownership rate: 95.5% (2000); Median home value: $163,100 (2000); Median rent: $575 per month (2000); Median age of housing: 24 years (2000).
Transportation: Commute to work: 93.5% car, 0.0% public transportation, 1.4% walk, 4.5% work from home (2000); Travel time to work: 7.8% less than 15 minutes, 36.2% 15 to 30 minutes, 43.6% 30 to 45 minutes, 6.5% 45 to 60 minutes, 5.9% 60 minutes or more (2000)

FRENCH (township). Covers a land area of 33.198 square miles and a water area of 4.119 square miles. Located at 47.66° N. Lat.; 93.02° W. Long.
Population: 354 (2000); Race: 96.6% White, 0.6% Black, 0.0% Asian, 1.5% American Indian and Alaska Native, 0.0% Hispanic of any race, 0.6% two or more races (2000); Density: 10.7 persons per square mile (2000); Age: 21.6% under 18, 13.9% over 64 (2000); Marriage status: 16.4% never married, 68.7% now married, 2.6% widowed, 12.3% divorced (2000); Foreign born: 0.9% (2000); Ancestry (includes multiple ancestries): 27.5% German, 14.8% Italian, 13.6% Irish, 12.0% Finnish, 12.0% Swedish (2000).
Economy: Employment by occupation: 12.1% management, 25.5% professional, 9.6% services, 19.1% sales, 1.9% farming, 19.7% construction, 12.1% production (2000).
Income: Per capita income: $23,856 (2000); Median household income: $49,583 (2000); Poverty rate: 3.7% (2000).
Taxes: Total city taxes per capita: $153 (1997); City property taxes per capita: $153 (1997).
Education: High school graduation rate: 95.0% (2000); College graduation rate: 29.4% (2000).
Housing: Homeownership rate: 100.0% (2000); Median home value: $155,900 (2000); Median age of housing: 37 years (2000).
Transportation: Commute to work: 92.9% car, 0.0% public transportation, 3.9% walk, 1.9% work from home (2000); Travel time to work: 15.1% less than 15 minutes, 45.4% 15 to 30 minutes, 26.3% 30 to 45 minutes, 7.2% 45 to 60 minutes, 5.9% 60 minutes or more (2000)

GILBERT (city). Covers a land area of 11.791 square miles and a water area of 0.792 square miles. Located at 47.48° N. Lat.; 92.46° W. Long. Elevation is 1,624 feet.
History: Incorporated 1909.
Population: 1,847 (2000); Race: 99.1% White, 0.0% Black, 0.0% Asian, 0.0% American Indian and Alaska Native, 0.7% Hispanic of any race, 0.6% two or more races (2000); Density: 156.7 persons per square mile (2000); Age: 21.2% under 18, 21.5% over 64 (2000); Marriage status: 27.0% never married, 54.3% now married, 10.8% widowed, 7.9% divorced (2000); Foreign born: 0.9% (2000); Ancestry (includes multiple ancestries): 22.0% Finnish, 15.8% German, 14.8% Slovene, 11.4% Norwegian, 9.4% Swedish (2000).
Economy: In iron mining area; poultry; oats, alfalfa; dairying; light manufacturing. Virginia-Eveleth Airport to SouthweSaint Superior National Fores to North. Single-family building permits issued: 2 (2001) / 2 (2000); Multi-family building permits issued: 0 (2001) / 0 (2000); Employment by occupation: 6.9% management, 10.8% professional, 23.0% services, 24.8% sales, 0.8% farming, 16.7% construction, 17.0% production (2000).
Income: Per capita income: $17,407 (2000); Median household income: $35,859 (2000); Poverty rate: 13.2% (2000).
Taxes: Total city taxes per capita: $139 (1997); City property taxes per capita: $128 (1997).
Education: High school graduation rate: 88.3% (2000); College graduation rate: 15.0% (2000).
Housing: Homeownership rate: 81.4% (2000); Median home value: $46,100 (2000); Median rent: $318 per month (2000); Median age of housing: 60+ years (2000).
Newspapers: The Gilbert Herald (1 x week); Eveleth Scene (1 x week)
Transportation: Commute to work: 90.9% car, 0.9% public transportation, 5.0% walk, 3.3% work from home (2000); Travel time to work: 60.6% less than 15 minutes, 23.5% 15 to 30 minutes, 11.2% 30 to 45 minutes, 1.6% 45 to 60 minutes, 3.1% 60 minutes or more (2000)

GNESEN (township). Covers a land area of 61.522 square miles and a water area of 10.103 square miles. Located at 47.01° N. Lat.; 92.12° W. Long.
Population: 1,468 (2000); Race: 97.3% White, 0.9% Black, 0.7% Asian, 0.7% American Indian and Alaska Native, 0.3% Hispanic of any race, 0.3% two or more races (2000); Density: 23.9 persons per square mile (2000); Age: 24.8% under 18, 10.2% over 64 (2000); Marriage status: 21.4% never married, 66.7% now married, 4.0% widowed, 8.0% divorced (2000); Foreign born: 0.9% (2000); Ancestry (includes multiple ancestries): 21.1% German, 20.6% Norwegian, 14.8% Swedish, 11.2% Irish, 9.8% Polish (2000).
Economy: Single-family building permits issued: 18 (2001) / 19 (2000); Multi-family building permits issued: 0 (2001) / 0 (2000); Employment by occupation: 13.3% management, 26.2% professional, 11.3% services, 25.5% sales, 0.3% farming, 13.0% construction, 10.5% production (2000).
Income: Per capita income: $26,202 (2000); Median household income: $57,292 (2000); Poverty rate: 4.5% (2000).
Taxes: Total city taxes per capita: $69 (1997); City property taxes per capita: $61 (1997).
Education: High school graduation rate: 92.9% (2000); College graduation rate: 29.2% (2000).
Housing: Homeownership rate: 96.3% (2000); Median home value: $151,600 (2000); Median rent: $413 per month (2000); Median age of housing: 22 years (2000).
Transportation: Commute to work: 93.8% car, 0.7% public transportation, 1.1% walk, 3.5% work from home (2000); Travel time to work: 7.8% less

than 15 minutes, 50.6% 15 to 30 minutes, 33.6% 30 to 45 minutes, 4.9% 45 to 60 minutes, 3.2% 60 minutes or more (2000)

GRAND LAKE (township). Covers a land area of 65.907 square miles and a water area of 5.543 square miles. Located at 46.90° N. Lat.; 92.36° W. Long. Elevation is 1,337 feet.
Population: 2,621 (2000); Race: 95.6% White, 0.2% Black, 0.2% Asian, 1.6% American Indian and Alaska Native, 1.0% Hispanic of any race, 2.2% two or more races (2000); Density: 39.8 persons per square mile (2000); Age: 23.5% under 18, 9.4% over 64 (2000); Marriage status: 19.0% never married, 68.9% now married, 3.2% widowed, 8.9% divorced (2000); Foreign born: 0.9% (2000); Ancestry (includes multiple ancestries): 21.9% German, 20.6% Norwegian, 19.0% Swedish, 10.8% Finnish, 8.3% Polish (2000).
Economy: Employment by occupation: 11.4% management, 21.3% professional, 14.4% services, 28.0% sales, 0.6% farming, 15.6% construction, 8.6% production (2000).
Income: Per capita income: $22,334 (2000); Median household income: $53,900 (2000); Poverty rate: 4.6% (2000).
Taxes: Total city taxes per capita: $33 (1997); City property taxes per capita: $33 (1997).
Education: High school graduation rate: 90.1% (2000); College graduation rate: 19.2% (2000).
Housing: Homeownership rate: 94.8% (2000); Median home value: $131,400 (2000); Median rent: $556 per month (2000); Median age of housing: 31 years (2000).
Transportation: Commute to work: 95.6% car, 0.3% public transportation, 0.9% walk, 3.1% work from home (2000); Travel time to work: 12.4% less than 15 minutes, 49.2% 15 to 30 minutes, 30.2% 30 to 45 minutes, 4.3% 45 to 60 minutes, 3.9% 60 minutes or more (2000)

GREAT SCOTT (township). Covers a land area of 63.107 square miles and a water area of 1.344 square miles. Located at 47.52° N. Lat.; 92.74° W. Long.
Population: 622 (2000); Race: 97.0% White, 0.0% Black, 0.0% Asian, 0.0% American Indian and Alaska Native, 2.8% Hispanic of any race, 2.6% two or more races (2000); Density: 9.9 persons per square mile (2000); Age: 24.6% under 18, 11.2% over 64 (2000); Marriage status: 23.8% never married, 61.3% now married, 4.4% widowed, 10.6% divorced (2000); Foreign born: 1.0% (2000); Ancestry (includes multiple ancestries): 27.7% German, 18.6% Finnish, 11.4% Swedish, 10.1% Irish, 9.7% Slovene (2000).
Economy: Employment by occupation: 11.9% management, 16.6% professional, 21.4% services, 19.3% sales, 0.0% farming, 18.0% construction, 12.9% production (2000).
Income: Per capita income: $18,106 (2000); Median household income: $38,438 (2000); Poverty rate: 12.5% (2000).
Taxes: Total city taxes per capita: $75 (1997); City property taxes per capita: $75 (1997).
Education: High school graduation rate: 90.0% (2000); College graduation rate: 12.4% (2000).
Housing: Homeownership rate: 95.8% (2000); Median home value: $53,500 (2000); Median rent: $375 per month (2000); Median age of housing: 29 years (2000).
Transportation: Commute to work: 94.2% car, 0.0% public transportation, 0.7% walk, 5.1% work from home (2000); Travel time to work: 22.0% less than 15 minutes, 52.7% 15 to 30 minutes, 17.7% 30 to 45 minutes, 0.7% 45 to 60 minutes, 6.9% 60 minutes or more (2000)

GREENWOOD (township). Covers a land area of 58.181 square miles and a water area of 34.077 square miles. Located at 47.87° N. Lat.; 92.38° W. Long.
Population: 905 (2000); Race: 84.1% White, 0.8% Black, 0.0% Asian, 13.5% American Indian and Alaska Native, 0.0% Hispanic of any race, 1.7% two or more races (2000); Density: 15.6 persons per square mile (2000); Age: 16.5% under 18, 21.1% over 64 (2000); Marriage status: 11.3% never married, 72.8% now married, 4.9% widowed, 11.0% divorced (2000); Foreign born: 0.8% (2000); Ancestry (includes multiple ancestries): 17.9% Finnish, 15.8% German, 14.6% Swedish, 12.7% Other groups, 12.1% Norwegian (2000).
Economy: Single-family building permits issued: 25 (2001) / 23 (2000); Multi-family building permits issued: 0 (2001) / 0 (2000); Employment by occupation: 12.4% management, 19.8% professional, 12.7% services, 29.7% sales, 0.0% farming, 15.0% construction, 10.5% production (2000).
Income: Per capita income: $26,433 (2000); Median household income: $47,917 (2000); Poverty rate: 9.1% (2000).
Taxes: Total city taxes per capita: $214 (2000); City property taxes per capita: $197 (2000).
Education: High school graduation rate: 91.9% (2000); College graduation rate: 26.3% (2000).
Housing: Homeownership rate: 92.7% (2000); Median home value: $185,300 (2000); Median rent: $125 per month (2000); Median age of housing: 32 years (2000).
Transportation: Commute to work: 89.8% car, 0.3% public transportation, 1.5% walk, 7.3% work from home (2000); Travel time to work: 17.3% less than 15 minutes, 13.5% 15 to 30 minutes, 42.8% 30 to 45 minutes, 15.4% 45 to 60 minutes, 11.0% 60 minutes or more (2000)

HALDEN (township). Covers a land area of 35.788 square miles and a water area of 0 square miles. Located at 46.91° N. Lat.; 92.97° W. Long.
Population: 154 (2000); Race: 100.0% White, 0.0% Black, 0.0% Asian, 0.0% American Indian and Alaska Native, 0.0% Hispanic of any race, 0.0% two or more races (2000); Density: 4.3 persons per square mile (2000); Age: 27.7% under 18, 10.9% over 64 (2000); Marriage status: 21.2% never married, 65.4% now married, 2.9% widowed, 10.6% divorced (2000); Foreign born: 2.9% (2000); Ancestry (includes multiple ancestries): 32.8% Finnish, 12.4% Swedish, 10.9% Italian, 7.3% German, 6.6% Irish (2000).
Economy: Employment by occupation: 7.5% management, 10.4% professional, 20.9% services, 13.4% sales, 9.0% farming, 17.9% construction, 20.9% production (2000).
Income: Per capita income: $15,844 (2000); Median household income: $35,417 (2000); Poverty rate: 13.1% (2000).
Taxes: Total city taxes per capita: $163 (1997); City property taxes per capita: $163 (1997).
Education: High school graduation rate: 85.3% (2000); College graduation rate: 4.2% (2000).
Housing: Homeownership rate: 100.0% (2000); Median age of housing: 30 years (2000).
Transportation: Commute to work: 91.0% car, 0.0% public transportation, 0.0% walk, 9.0% work from home (2000); Travel time to work: 39.3% less than 15 minutes, 19.7% 15 to 30 minutes, 6.6% 30 to 45 minutes, 23.0% 45 to 60 minutes, 11.5% 60 minutes or more (2000)

HERMANTOWN (city). Covers a land area of 34.333 square miles and a water area of 0.016 square miles. Located at 46.80° N. Lat.; 92.22° W. Long. Elevation is 1,365 feet.
Population: 7,448 (2000); Race: 97.1% White, 0.5% Black, 0.0% Asian, 0.7% American Indian and Alaska Native, 0.4% Hispanic of any race, 1.0% two or more races (2000); Density: 216.9 persons per square mile (2000); Age: 27.4% under 18, 13.9% over 64 (2000); Marriage status: 21.4% never married, 65.7% now married, 6.1% widowed, 6.8% divorced (2000); Foreign born: 0.8% (2000); Ancestry (includes multiple ancestries): 24.6% Norwegian, 21.6% German, 18.7% Swedish, 11.2% Irish, 10.8% Finnish (2000).
Economy: Manufacturing: sheet metal fabrication. Agriculture: dairying; poultry; hay. Duluth Municipal Airport to NortheaSaint Single-family building permits issued: 37 (2001) / 36 (2000); Multi-family building permits issued: 0 (2001) / 5 (2000); Employment by occupation: 11.9% management, 21.6% professional, 14.0% services, 28.6% sales, 0.3% farming, 11.3% construction, 12.2% production (2000).
Income: Per capita income: $20,993 (2000); Median household income: $49,861 (2000); Poverty rate: 4.1% (2000).
Taxes: Total city taxes per capita: $157 (1997); City property taxes per capita: $147 (1997).
Education: High school graduation rate: 87.5% (2000); College graduation rate: 23.5% (2000).
Housing: Homeownership rate: 81.7% (2000); Median home value: $109,600 (2000); Median rent: $630 per month (2000); Median age of housing: 30 years (2000).
Safety: Violent crime rate: 8.0 per 10,000 population; Property crime rate: 377.3 per 10,000 population (2001).
Newspapers: Hermantown Star (1 x week)
Transportation: Commute to work: 94.9% car, 0.0% public transportation, 1.8% walk, 2.8% work from home (2000); Travel time to work: 34.7% less than 15 minutes, 57.0% 15 to 30 minutes, 4.4% 30 to 45 minutes, 1.3% 45 to 60 minutes, 2.7% 60 minutes or more (2000)
Additional Information Contacts
Hermantown Chamber of Commerce. 218-727-7667

HIBBING (city). Covers a land area of 181.677 square miles and a water area of 4.836 square miles. Located at 47.41° N. Lat.; 92.93° W. Long. Elevation is 1,489 feet.
History: Hibbing was platted in 1893 by a lumber company, which set up a portable sawmill here. Progress was slow, for supplies had to be hauled over

rough roads. The village was named for Captain Frank Hibbing, who installed light and water systems that stopped the spread of typhoid, which had been common the first year. When valuable ore was found under Hibbing's streets in 1919, an iron company bought the land and moved the village to its new location.

Population: 17,071 (2000); Race: 97.7% White, 0.5% Black, 0.1% Asian, 0.7% American Indian and Alaska Native, 0.9% Hispanic of any race, 0.7% two or more races (2000); Density: 94.0 persons per square mile (2000); Age: 22.8% under 18, 19.7% over 64 (2000); Marriage status: 23.6% never married, 56.0% now married, 9.5% widowed, 10.8% divorced (2000); Foreign born: 1.0% (2000); Ancestry (includes multiple ancestries): 21.9% German, 13.8% Finnish, 12.8% Norwegian, 10.2% Irish, 10.1% Swedish (2000).

Vital Statistics: Birth rate: 95.5 per 10,000 population (1998)

Economy: Single-family building permits issued: 24 (2001) / 37 (2000); Multi-family building permits issued: 0 (2001) / 18 (2000); Employment by occupation: 8.1% management, 18.3% professional, 18.6% services, 23.9% sales, 0.3% farming, 14.2% construction, 16.5% production (2000).

Income: Per capita income: $18,561 (2000); Median household income: $33,346 (2000); Poverty rate: 11.7% (2000).

Taxes: Total city taxes per capita: $200 (2000); City property taxes per capita: $190 (2000).

Education: High school graduation rate: 84.1% (2000); College graduation rate: 17.3% (2000).

School District(s)

Hibbing (PK-12)
2000 Enrollment: 2,923 218-263-4850

Two-year College(s)

Hibbing Community College-A Technical and Community College (Public)
2001 Enrollment: 1,765 218-262-7200
2001 Tuition: In-state $2,298; Out-of-state $4,596

Housing: Homeownership rate: 74.8% (2000); Median home value: $61,600 (2000); Median rent: $310 per month (2000); Median age of housing: 48 years (2000).

Hospitals: University Medical Center - Mesabi (175 beds)

Safety: Violent crime rate: 12.8 per 10,000 population; Property crime rate: 137.4 per 10,000 population (2001).

Newspapers: Hibbing Daily Tribune (7 x week)

Transportation: Commute to work: 90.7% car, 1.2% public transportation, 4.6% walk, 2.7% work from home (2000); Travel time to work: 57.8% less than 15 minutes, 27.7% 15 to 30 minutes, 7.9% 30 to 45 minutes, 2.1% 45 to 60 minutes, 4.4% 60 minutes or more (2000)

Airports: Chisholm-Hibbing (commercial service)

Additional Information Contacts

Hibbing Chamber of Commerce 218-262-3895
Range Association of Realtors 218-262-2564

HOYT LAKES (city). Covers a land area of 56.047 square miles and a water area of 2.044 square miles. Located at 47.52° N. Lat.; 92.13° W. Long. Elevation is 1,469 feet.

Population: 2,082 (2000); Race: 98.8% White, 1.2% Black, 0.0% Asian, 0.0% American Indian and Alaska Native, 0.0% Hispanic of any race, 0.0% two or more races (2000); Density: 37.1 persons per square mile (2000); Age: 20.1% under 18, 21.2% over 64 (2000); Marriage status: 17.9% never married, 66.6% now married, 8.1% widowed, 7.4% divorced (2000); Foreign born: 1.2% (2000); Ancestry (includes multiple ancestries): 24.3% Norwegian, 22.3% German, 15.4% Finnish, 11.8% Swedish, 10.9% Irish (2000).

Economy: Railroad junction to NortheaSaint Manufacturing of hardwood products. Agriculture: timber, dairying; cattle; oats, alfalfa. Recreation area. Single-family building permits issued: 1 (2001) / 3 (2000); Multi-family building permits issued: 0 (2001) / 0 (2000); Employment by occupation: 7.9% management, 13.9% professional, 18.6% services, 20.4% sales, 0.0% farming, 18.0% construction, 21.1% production (2000).

Income: Per capita income: $18,882 (2000); Median household income: $39,493 (2000); Poverty rate: 8.9% (2000).

Taxes: Total city taxes per capita: $241 (1997); City property taxes per capita: $234 (1997).

Education: High school graduation rate: 88.2% (2000); College graduation rate: 18.2% (2000).

Housing: Homeownership rate: 91.6% (2000); Median home value: $39,100 (2000); Median rent: $269 per month (2000); Median age of housing: 44 years (2000).

Safety: Violent crime rate: 9.5 per 10,000 population; Property crime rate: 61.8 per 10,000 population (2001).

Transportation: Commute to work: 93.3% car, 0.0% public transportation, 3.5% walk, 2.9% work from home (2000); Travel time to work: 48.2% less than 15 minutes, 24.6% 15 to 30 minutes, 14.0% 30 to 45 minutes, 4.7% 45 to 60 minutes, 8.5% 60 minutes or more (2000)

INDUSTRIAL (township). Covers a land area of 35.642 square miles and a water area of 0.437 square miles. Located at 46.89° N. Lat.; 92.48° W. Long.

Population: 628 (2000); Race: 93.5% White, 0.0% Black, 2.8% Asian, 1.3% American Indian and Alaska Native, 0.3% Hispanic of any race, 2.1% two or more races (2000); Density: 17.6 persons per square mile (2000); Age: 26.8% under 18, 10.3% over 64 (2000); Marriage status: 21.3% never married, 63.3% now married, 4.4% widowed, 11.0% divorced (2000); Foreign born: 2.9% (2000); Ancestry (includes multiple ancestries): 29.6% German, 17.0% Swedish, 15.4% Norwegian, 11.9% Finnish, 10.6% French (except Basque) (2000).

Economy: Employment by occupation: 9.8% management, 16.2% professional, 16.6% services, 18.9% sales, 0.0% farming, 17.9% construction, 20.6% production (2000).

Income: Per capita income: $19,355 (2000); Median household income: $43,750 (2000); Poverty rate: 5.8% (2000).

Taxes: Total city taxes per capita: $54 (1997); City property taxes per capita: $54 (1997).

Education: High school graduation rate: 86.4% (2000); College graduation rate: 15.0% (2000).

Housing: Homeownership rate: 92.1% (2000); Median home value: $100,000 (2000); Median rent: $308 per month (2000); Median age of housing: 27 years (2000).

Transportation: Commute to work: 93.8% car, 2.1% public transportation, 0.0% walk, 2.7% work from home (2000); Travel time to work: 6.7% less than 15 minutes, 37.3% 15 to 30 minutes, 33.8% 30 to 45 minutes, 10.2% 45 to 60 minutes, 12.0% 60 minutes or more (2000)

IRON (unincorporated postal area, zip code 55751). Aka Iron Junction. Covers a land area of 81.387 square miles and a water area of 0.807 square miles. Located at 47.42° N. Lat.; 92.68° W. Long.

Population: 1,726 (2000); Race: 97.4% White, 0.0% Black, 0.2% Asian, 0.8% American Indian and Alaska Native, 1.6% Hispanic of any race, 1.2% two or more races (2000); Density: 21.2 persons per square mile (2000); Age: 24.5% under 18, 11.1% over 64 (2000); Marriage status: 25.5% never married, 59.7% now married, 5.7% widowed, 9.2% divorced (2000); Foreign born: 1.4% (2000); Ancestry (includes multiple ancestries): 31.7% Finnish, 22.9% German, 17.6% Norwegian, 10.0% Swedish, 6.4% Irish (2000).

Economy: Railroad junction. Oats, alfalfa; dairying. Manufacturing: electronic ice fishing equipment. Iron mines in area. Employment by occupation: 6.6% management, 11.8% professional, 15.2% services, 24.4% sales, 2.0% farming, 20.5% construction, 19.4% production (2000).

Income: Per capita income: $18,116 (2000); Median household income: $43,854 (2000); Poverty rate: 5.1% (2000).

Education: High school graduation rate: 89.2% (2000); College graduation rate: 10.2% (2000).

Housing: Homeownership rate: 94.6% (2000); Median home value: $65,700 (2000); Median rent: $268 per month (2000); Median age of housing: 30 years (2000).

Transportation: Commute to work: 93.9% car, 0.2% public transportation, 1.3% walk, 4.0% work from home (2000); Travel time to work: 22.0% less than 15 minutes, 57.2% 15 to 30 minutes, 13.8% 30 to 45 minutes, 1.8% 45 to 60 minutes, 5.3% 60 minutes or more (2000)

IRON JUNCTION (city). Aka Iron. Covers a land area of 0.780 square miles and a water area of 0 square miles. Located at 47.41° N. Lat.; 92.60° W. Long. Elevation is 1,384 feet.

Population: 93 (2000); Race: 97.8% White, 0.0% Black, 0.0% Asian, 0.0% American Indian and Alaska Native, 0.0% Hispanic of any race, 2.2% two or more races (2000); Density: 119.3 persons per square mile (2000); Age: 13.0% under 18, 14.1% over 64 (2000); Marriage status: 21.7% never married, 59.0% now married, 8.4% widowed, 10.8% divorced (2000); Foreign born: 2.2% (2000); Ancestry (includes multiple ancestries): 23.9% Norwegian, 17.4% German, 14.1% Finnish, 13.0% Swedish, 8.7% Slovene (2000).

Economy: Employment by occupation: 0.0% management, 19.1% professional, 10.6% services, 23.4% sales, 4.3% farming, 25.5% construction, 17.0% production (2000).

Income: Per capita income: $21,751 (2000); Median household income: $40,938 (2000); Poverty rate: 0.0% (2000).

Taxes: Total city taxes per capita: $22 (1997); City property taxes per capita: $22 (1997).
Education: High school graduation rate: 69.6% (2000); College graduation rate: 15.9% (2000).
Housing: Homeownership rate: 95.7% (2000); Median home value: $37,200 (2000); Median age of housing: 47 years (2000).
Transportation: Commute to work: 100.0% car, 0.0% public transportation, 0.0% walk, 0.0% work from home (2000); Travel time to work: 31.9% less than 15 minutes, 46.8% 15 to 30 minutes, 6.4% 30 to 45 minutes, 8.5% 45 to 60 minutes, 6.4% 60 minutes or more (2000)

KELSEY (township). Covers a land area of 35.254 square miles and a water area of 0.376 square miles. Located at 47.15° N. Lat.; 92.60° W. Long. Elevation is 1,304 feet.
Population: 141 (2000); Race: 98.0% White, 0.0% Black, 0.0% Asian, 0.0% American Indian and Alaska Native, 0.0% Hispanic of any race, 2.0% two or more races (2000); Density: 4.0 persons per square mile (2000); Age: 17.4% under 18, 10.7% over 64 (2000); Marriage status: 21.4% never married, 64.9% now married, 4.6% widowed, 9.2% divorced (2000); Foreign born: 3.4% (2000); Ancestry (includes multiple ancestries): 28.2% German, 20.1% Swedish, 13.4% Norwegian, 8.7% Czech, 7.4% Irish (2000).
Economy: Employment by occupation: 20.8% management, 20.8% professional, 23.6% services, 5.6% sales, 2.8% farming, 15.3% construction, 11.1% production (2000).
Income: Per capita income: $15,419 (2000); Median household income: $39,583 (2000); Poverty rate: 30.9% (2000).
Education: High school graduation rate: 87.5% (2000); College graduation rate: 20.5% (2000).
Housing: Homeownership rate: 100.0% (2000); Median home value: $67,500 (2000); Median age of housing: 27 years (2000).
Transportation: Commute to work: 93.1% car, 0.0% public transportation, 0.0% walk, 6.9% work from home (2000); Travel time to work: 16.4% less than 15 minutes, 14.9% 15 to 30 minutes, 34.3% 30 to 45 minutes, 7.5% 45 to 60 minutes, 26.9% 60 minutes or more (2000)

KINNEY (city). Covers a land area of 4.568 square miles and a water area of 0.281 square miles. Located at 47.51° N. Lat.; 92.73° W. Long. Elevation is 1,545 feet.
Population: 199 (2000); Race: 94.3% White, 0.0% Black, 0.0% Asian, 0.0% American Indian and Alaska Native, 2.8% Hispanic of any race, 5.7% two or more races (2000); Density: 43.6 persons per square mile (2000); Age: 19.3% under 18, 22.7% over 64 (2000); Marriage status: 19.6% never married, 64.9% now married, 4.1% widowed, 11.5% divorced (2000); Foreign born: 0.0% (2000); Ancestry (includes multiple ancestries): 29.5% German, 21.0% Finnish, 11.4% Norwegian, 10.8% Irish, 9.7% Swedish (2000).
Economy: Large open-pit iron mine nearby. Superior National Forest to North. Employment by occupation: 16.4% management, 2.7% professional, 34.2% services, 15.1% sales, 0.0% farming, 11.0% construction, 20.5% production (2000).
Income: Per capita income: $14,756 (2000); Median household income: $25,000 (2000); Poverty rate: 13.6% (2000).
Taxes: Total city taxes per capita: $180 (1997); City property taxes per capita: $176 (1997).
Education: High school graduation rate: 78.8% (2000); College graduation rate: 0.0% (2000).
Housing: Homeownership rate: 90.0% (2000); Median home value: $36,100 (2000); Median rent: $325 per month (2000); Median age of housing: 42 years (2000).
Transportation: Commute to work: 93.2% car, 0.0% public transportation, 2.7% walk, 4.1% work from home (2000); Travel time to work: 34.3% less than 15 minutes, 57.1% 15 to 30 minutes, 2.9% 30 to 45 minutes, 0.0% 45 to 60 minutes, 5.7% 60 minutes or more (2000)

KUGLER (township). Covers a land area of 35.370 square miles and a water area of 0.265 square miles. Located at 47.76° N. Lat.; 92.27° W. Long.
Population: 200 (2000); Race: 96.1% White, 0.0% Black, 1.1% Asian, 1.1% American Indian and Alaska Native, 7.8% Hispanic of any race, 1.7% two or more races (2000); Density: 5.7 persons per square mile (2000); Age: 28.5% under 18, 7.8% over 64 (2000); Marriage status: 19.9% never married, 66.9% now married, 4.4% widowed, 8.8% divorced (2000); Foreign born: 4.5% (2000); Ancestry (includes multiple ancestries): 35.8% Finnish, 22.3% Norwegian, 14.0% Other groups, 14.0% German, 8.9% Swedish (2000).
Economy: Employment by occupation: 10.7% management, 14.3% professional, 10.7% services, 29.8% sales, 0.0% farming, 25.0% construction, 9.5% production (2000).
Income: Per capita income: $16,601 (2000); Median household income: $44,167 (2000); Poverty rate: 12.8% (2000).
Taxes: Total city taxes per capita: $77 (1997); City property taxes per capita: $77 (1997).
Education: High school graduation rate: 95.0% (2000); College graduation rate: 6.7% (2000).
Housing: Homeownership rate: 100.0% (2000); Median home value: $71,800 (2000); Median age of housing: 22 years (2000).
Transportation: Commute to work: 100.0% car, 0.0% public transportation, 0.0% walk, 0.0% work from home (2000); Travel time to work: 19.0% less than 15 minutes, 36.9% 15 to 30 minutes, 35.7% 30 to 45 minutes, 3.6% 45 to 60 minutes, 4.8% 60 minutes or more (2000)

LAKEWOOD (township). Covers a land area of 27.756 square miles and a water area of 0 square miles. Located at 46.89° N. Lat.; 91.99° W. Long. Elevation is 662 feet.
Population: 2,013 (2000); Race: 97.5% White, 0.3% Black, 0.4% Asian, 1.3% American Indian and Alaska Native, 0.7% Hispanic of any race, 0.2% two or more races (2000); Density: 72.5 persons per square mile (2000); Age: 31.2% under 18, 7.0% over 64 (2000); Marriage status: 21.3% never married, 68.3% now married, 3.7% widowed, 6.7% divorced (2000); Foreign born: 1.3% (2000); Ancestry (includes multiple ancestries): 22.3% German, 21.0% Swedish, 20.5% Norwegian, 13.0% Finnish, 9.5% Irish (2000).
Economy: Single-family building permits issued: 13 (2001) / 11 (2000); Multi-family building permits issued: 0 (2001) / 2 (2000); Employment by occupation: 11.8% management, 28.6% professional, 16.1% services, 18.4% sales, 0.2% farming, 14.3% construction, 10.6% production (2000).
Income: Per capita income: $21,086 (2000); Median household income: $51,700 (2000); Poverty rate: 6.3% (2000).
Taxes: Total city taxes per capita: $40 (2000); City property taxes per capita: $38 (2000).
Education: High school graduation rate: 91.2% (2000); College graduation rate: 28.5% (2000).
Housing: Homeownership rate: 96.8% (2000); Median home value: $114,900 (2000); Median rent: $438 per month (2000); Median age of housing: 26 years (2000).
Transportation: Commute to work: 93.4% car, 0.0% public transportation, 0.9% walk, 5.3% work from home (2000); Travel time to work: 8.8% less than 15 minutes, 62.9% 15 to 30 minutes, 19.3% 30 to 45 minutes, 4.2% 45 to 60 minutes, 4.8% 60 minutes or more (2000)

LAVELL (township). Covers a land area of 107.779 square miles and a water area of 0.515 square miles. Located at 47.26° N. Lat.; 92.76° W. Long.
Population: 363 (2000); Race: 93.5% White, 0.0% Black, 0.0% Asian, 1.6% American Indian and Alaska Native, 2.4% Hispanic of any race, 2.4% two or more races (2000); Density: 3.4 persons per square mile (2000); Age: 27.2% under 18, 6.0% over 64 (2000); Marriage status: 24.3% never married, 62.0% now married, 4.8% widowed, 8.9% divorced (2000); Foreign born: 1.4% (2000); Ancestry (includes multiple ancestries): 29.1% German, 28.0% Finnish, 14.9% Norwegian, 12.0% Swedish, 9.5% Irish (2000).
Economy: Employment by occupation: 7.4% management, 16.0% professional, 19.1% services, 15.4% sales, 2.1% farming, 20.7% construction, 19.1% production (2000).
Income: Per capita income: $16,538 (2000); Median household income: $43,056 (2000); Poverty rate: 7.3% (2000).
Taxes: Total city taxes per capita: $222 (1997); City property taxes per capita: $222 (1997).
Education: High school graduation rate: 84.6% (2000); College graduation rate: 8.1% (2000).
Housing: Homeownership rate: 98.5% (2000); Median home value: $23,800 (2000); Median age of housing: 28 years (2000).
Transportation: Commute to work: 91.9% car, 0.0% public transportation, 1.6% walk, 5.9% work from home (2000); Travel time to work: 9.1% less than 15 minutes, 44.0% 15 to 30 minutes, 36.0% 30 to 45 minutes, 7.4% 45 to 60 minutes, 3.4% 60 minutes or more (2000)

LEIDING (township). Covers a land area of 122.522 square miles and a water area of 18.496 square miles. Located at 48.06° N. Lat.; 92.84° W. Long.
Population: 452 (2000); Race: 85.8% White, 0.0% Black, 0.0% Asian, 11.3% American Indian and Alaska Native, 0.0% Hispanic of any race, 1.1% two or more races (2000); Density: 3.7 persons per square mile (2000); Age: 21.4% under 18, 18.0% over 64 (2000); Marriage status: 14.0% never married, 72.1% now married, 3.0% widowed, 11.0% divorced (2000); Foreign born: 0.5% (2000); Ancestry (includes multiple ancestries): 28.2%

German, 18.2% Norwegian, 15.0% Finnish, 11.5% Other groups, 10.5% Polish (2000).
Economy: Employment by occupation: 14.2% management, 15.3% professional, 5.1% services, 18.8% sales, 6.3% farming, 15.3% construction, 25.0% production (2000).
Income: Per capita income: $17,796 (2000); Median household income: $39,464 (2000); Poverty rate: 9.1% (2000).
Taxes: Total city taxes per capita: $77 (1997); City property taxes per capita: $77 (1997).
Education: High school graduation rate: 91.3% (2000); College graduation rate: 17.4% (2000).
Housing: Homeownership rate: 90.1% (2000); Median home value: $76,700 (2000); Median rent: $325 per month (2000); Median age of housing: 28 years (2000).
Transportation: Commute to work: 85.8% car, 0.0% public transportation, 3.6% walk, 8.3% work from home (2000); Travel time to work: 33.5% less than 15 minutes, 22.6% 15 to 30 minutes, 22.6% 30 to 45 minutes, 10.3% 45 to 60 minutes, 11.0% 60 minutes or more (2000)

LEONIDAS (city). Covers a land area of 1.329 square miles and a water area of 0.063 square miles. Located at 47.46° N. Lat.; 92.56° W. Long.
Population: 60 (2000); Race: 97.1% White, 0.0% Black, 0.0% Asian, 0.0% American Indian and Alaska Native, 0.0% Hispanic of any race, 2.9% two or more races (2000); Density: 45.1 persons per square mile (2000); Age: 28.6% under 18, 20.0% over 64 (2000); Marriage status: 8.0% never married, 80.0% now married, 8.0% widowed, 4.0% divorced (2000); Foreign born: 0.0% (2000); Ancestry (includes multiple ancestries): 65.7% Swedish, 48.6% German, 17.1% Finnish, 11.4% Slovene, 2.9% Norwegian (2000).
Economy: Iron mines nearby. Single-family building permits issued: 0 (2001) / 0 (2000); Multi-family building permits issued: 0 (2001) / 0 (2000); Employment by occupation: 12.5% management, 0.0% professional, 18.8% services, 0.0% sales, 0.0% farming, 25.0% construction, 43.8% production (2000).
Income: Per capita income: $15,023 (2000); Median household income: $19,167 (2000); Poverty rate: 14.3% (2000).
Taxes: Total city taxes per capita: $45 (1997); City property taxes per capita: $45 (1997).
Education: High school graduation rate: 83.3% (2000); College graduation rate: 0.0% (2000).
Housing: Homeownership rate: 82.6% (2000); Median home value: $56,100 (2000); Median rent: $375 per month (2000); Median age of housing: 60+ years (2000).
Transportation: Commute to work: 87.5% car, 0.0% public transportation, 12.5% walk, 0.0% work from home (2000); Travel time to work: 12.5% less than 15 minutes, 56.3% 15 to 30 minutes, 18.8% 30 to 45 minutes, 0.0% 45 to 60 minutes, 12.5% 60 minutes or more (2000)

LINDEN GROVE (township). Covers a land area of 35.434 square miles and a water area of 0 square miles. Located at 47.85° N. Lat.; 92.88° W. Long. Elevation is 1,307 feet.
Population: 141 (2000); Race: 96.9% White, 0.0% Black, 0.0% Asian, 1.6% American Indian and Alaska Native, 0.0% Hispanic of any race, 1.6% two or more races (2000); Density: 4.0 persons per square mile (2000); Age: 29.1% under 18, 12.6% over 64 (2000); Marriage status: 9.8% never married, 77.2% now married, 7.6% widowed, 5.4% divorced (2000); Foreign born: 0.0% (2000); Ancestry (includes multiple ancestries): 29.9% Swedish, 23.6% Finnish, 15.7% United States or American, 15.7% German, 12.6% Irish (2000).
Economy: Employment by occupation: 10.7% management, 8.9% professional, 7.1% services, 23.2% sales, 8.9% farming, 30.4% construction, 10.7% production (2000).
Income: Per capita income: $18,004 (2000); Median household income: $38,500 (2000); Poverty rate: 3.1% (2000).
Taxes: Total city taxes per capita: $96 (1997); City property taxes per capita: $96 (1997).
Education: High school graduation rate: 80.5% (2000); College graduation rate: 4.6% (2000).
Housing: Homeownership rate: 79.2% (2000); Median rent: $125 per month (2000); Median age of housing: 39 years (2000).
Transportation: Commute to work: 92.9% car, 0.0% public transportation, 0.0% walk, 7.1% work from home (2000); Travel time to work: 21.2% less than 15 minutes, 46.2% 15 to 30 minutes, 28.8% 30 to 45 minutes, 0.0% 45 to 60 minutes, 3.8% 60 minutes or more (2000)

MAKINEN (unincorporated postal area, zip code 55763). Covers a land area of 86.971 square miles and a water area of 8.811 square miles. Located at 47.31° N. Lat.; 92.20° W. Long. Elevation is 1,405 feet.
Population: 591 (2000); Race: 94.6% White, 0.0% Black, 0.5% Asian, 1.9% American Indian and Alaska Native, 0.0% Hispanic of any race, 3.1% two or more races (2000); Density: 6.8 persons per square mile (2000); Age: 18.5% under 18, 18.6% over 64 (2000); Marriage status: 21.1% never married, 62.4% now married, 4.7% widowed, 11.9% divorced (2000); Foreign born: 1.2% (2000); Ancestry (includes multiple ancestries): 31.4% Finnish, 25.4% German, 14.2% Norwegian, 13.4% Swedish, 7.5% English (2000).
Economy: Employment by occupation: 3.9% management, 16.1% professional, 18.6% services, 22.1% sales, 1.8% farming, 28.9% construction, 8.6% production (2000).
Income: Per capita income: $17,911 (2000); Median household income: $39,688 (2000); Poverty rate: 14.6% (2000).
Education: High school graduation rate: 81.3% (2000); College graduation rate: 16.9% (2000).
Housing: Homeownership rate: 97.6% (2000); Median home value: $72,500 (2000); Median age of housing: 35 years (2000).
Transportation: Commute to work: 96.8% car, 0.0% public transportation, 0.0% walk, 2.1% work from home (2000); Travel time to work: 7.6% less than 15 minutes, 28.3% 15 to 30 minutes, 35.5% 30 to 45 minutes, 14.5% 45 to 60 minutes, 14.1% 60 minutes or more (2000)

MCDAVITT (township). Covers a land area of 71.147 square miles and a water area of 1.225 square miles. Located at 47.29° N. Lat.; 92.63° W. Long.
Population: 487 (2000); Race: 95.9% White, 0.0% Black, 0.0% Asian, 2.2% American Indian and Alaska Native, 1.3% Hispanic of any race, 1.5% two or more races (2000); Density: 6.8 persons per square mile (2000); Age: 26.0% under 18, 9.9% over 64 (2000); Marriage status: 20.1% never married, 69.4% now married, 4.2% widowed, 6.3% divorced (2000); Foreign born: 0.4% (2000); Ancestry (includes multiple ancestries): 20.0% Finnish, 18.7% German, 18.7% Norwegian, 7.3% Swedish, 4.7% Polish (2000).
Economy: Employment by occupation: 13.7% management, 9.6% professional, 14.5% services, 19.7% sales, 0.8% farming, 23.3% construction, 18.5% production (2000).
Income: Per capita income: $16,251 (2000); Median household income: $40,625 (2000); Poverty rate: 14.4% (2000).
Taxes: Total city taxes per capita: $33 (1997); City property taxes per capita: $33 (1997).
Education: High school graduation rate: 93.6% (2000); College graduation rate: 11.8% (2000).
Housing: Homeownership rate: 85.0% (2000); Median home value: $68,300 (2000); Median rent: $250 per month (2000); Median age of housing: 35 years (2000).
Transportation: Commute to work: 86.2% car, 0.8% public transportation, 5.7% walk, 7.3% work from home (2000); Travel time to work: 16.2% less than 15 minutes, 35.8% 15 to 30 minutes, 33.6% 30 to 45 minutes, 8.7% 45 to 60 minutes, 5.7% 60 minutes or more (2000)

MCKINLEY (city). Covers a land area of 0.774 square miles and a water area of 0.026 square miles. Located at 47.51° N. Lat.; 92.41° W. Long. Elevation is 1,438 feet.
Population: 80 (2000); Race: 93.9% White, 0.0% Black, 0.0% Asian, 0.0% American Indian and Alaska Native, 0.0% Hispanic of any race, 6.1% two or more races (2000); Density: 103.3 persons per square mile (2000); Age: 24.4% under 18, 30.5% over 64 (2000); Marriage status: 16.2% never married, 73.5% now married, 5.9% widowed, 4.4% divorced (2000); Foreign born: 0.0% (2000); Ancestry (includes multiple ancestries): 14.6% Slovene, 8.5% Irish, 7.3% German, 7.3% Norwegian, 6.1% English (2000).
Economy: Iron mines in area. Single-family building permits issued: 0 (2001) / 0 (2000); Multi-family building permits issued: 0 (2001) / 0 (2000); Employment by occupation: 0.0% management, 12.9% professional, 35.5% services, 12.9% sales, 0.0% farming, 25.8% construction, 12.9% production (2000).
Income: Per capita income: $14,384 (2000); Median household income: $28,750 (2000); Poverty rate: 30.5% (2000).
Taxes: Total city taxes per capita: $33 (1997); City property taxes per capita: $33 (1997).
Education: High school graduation rate: 86.0% (2000); College graduation rate: 10.5% (2000).
Housing: Homeownership rate: 100.0% (2000); Median home value: $46,300 (2000); Median age of housing: 44 years (2000).
Transportation: Commute to work: 100.0% car, 0.0% public transportation, 0.0% walk, 0.0% work from home (2000); Travel time to work: 0.0% less

than 15 minutes, 93.5% 15 to 30 minutes, 6.5% 30 to 45 minutes, 0.0% 45 to 60 minutes, 0.0% 60 minutes or more (2000)

MEADOWLANDS (city). Covers a land area of 0.381 square miles and a water area of 0 square miles. Located at 47.07° N. Lat.; 92.73° W. Long. Elevation is 1,275 feet.
Population: 111 (2000); Race: 98.0% White, 0.0% Black, 0.0% Asian, 2.0% American Indian and Alaska Native, 0.0% Hispanic of any race, 0.0% two or more races (2000); Density: 291.1 persons per square mile (2000); Age: 25.0% under 18, 26.0% over 64 (2000); Marriage status: 16.9% never married, 54.5% now married, 18.2% widowed, 10.4% divorced (2000); Foreign born: 0.0% (2000); Ancestry (includes multiple ancestries): 28.0% German, 12.0% Czech, 11.0% Swedish, 11.0% Other groups, 7.0% Norwegian (2000).
Economy: Single-family building permits issued: 0 (2001) / 0 (2000); Multi-family building permits issued: 0 (2001) / 0 (2000); Employment by occupation: 6.3% management, 0.0% professional, 43.8% services, 18.8% sales, 0.0% farming, 31.3% construction, 0.0% production (2000).
Income: Per capita income: $11,682 (2000); Median household income: $20,625 (2000); Poverty rate: 14.0% (2000).
Taxes: Total city taxes per capita: $211 (1997); City property taxes per capita: $200 (1997).
Education: High school graduation rate: 61.4% (2000); College graduation rate: 2.9% (2000).

School District(s)

Toivola-Meadowlands Charter School (KG-12)
2000 Enrollment: 0 218-427-2191

Housing: Homeownership rate: 63.5% (2000); Median home value: $34,200 (2000); Median rent: $189 per month (2000); Median age of housing: 46 years (2000).
Transportation: Commute to work: 93.8% car, 0.0% public transportation, 6.3% walk, 0.0% work from home (2000); Travel time to work: 12.5% less than 15 minutes, 25.0% 15 to 30 minutes, 6.3% 30 to 45 minutes, 25.0% 45 to 60 minutes, 31.3% 60 minutes or more (2000)

MEADOWLANDS (township). Covers a land area of 59.857 square miles and a water area of 0.590 square miles. Located at 47.07° N. Lat.; 92.69° W. Long. Elevation is 1,275 feet.
Population: 315 (2000); Race: 97.5% White, 0.0% Black, 0.0% Asian, 1.9% American Indian and Alaska Native, 0.0% Hispanic of any race, 0.6% two or more races (2000); Density: 5.3 persons per square mile (2000); Age: 23.5% under 18, 13.3% over 64 (2000); Marriage status: 14.6% never married, 64.6% now married, 6.3% widowed, 14.6% divorced (2000); Foreign born: 0.0% (2000); Ancestry (includes multiple ancestries): 18.9% Swedish, 14.2% Norwegian, 12.1% Finnish, 7.4% Czechoslovakian, 5.9% Czech (2000).
Economy: Dairying; poultry; oats, alfalfa. Manufacturing: furniture. Employment by occupation: 10.6% management, 12.4% professional, 8.7% services, 15.5% sales, 1.2% farming, 23.6% construction, 28.0% production (2000).
Income: Per capita income: $16,321 (2000); Median household income: $31,250 (2000); Poverty rate: 12.4% (2000).
Taxes: Total city taxes per capita: $61 (1997); City property taxes per capita: $61 (1997).
Education: High school graduation rate: 81.8% (2000); College graduation rate: 11.6% (2000).
Housing: Homeownership rate: 89.4% (2000); Median home value: $34,300 (2000); Median rent: $238 per month (2000); Median age of housing: 39 years (2000).
Transportation: Commute to work: 93.8% car, 0.0% public transportation, 0.0% walk, 3.7% work from home (2000); Travel time to work: 31.0% less than 15 minutes, 3.9% 15 to 30 minutes, 23.2% 30 to 45 minutes, 23.9% 45 to 60 minutes, 18.1% 60 minutes or more (2000)

MIDWAY (township). Covers a land area of 18.010 square miles and a water area of 0 square miles. Located at 46.72° N. Lat.; 92.27° W. Long.
Population: 1,479 (2000); Race: 95.8% White, 0.0% Black, 0.0% Asian, 3.2% American Indian and Alaska Native, 0.9% Hispanic of any race, 1.0% two or more races (2000); Density: 82.1 persons per square mile (2000); Age: 23.4% under 18, 20.9% over 64 (2000); Marriage status: 19.7% never married, 55.6% now married, 16.1% widowed, 8.7% divorced (2000); Foreign born: 0.4% (2000); Ancestry (includes multiple ancestries): 19.7% Swedish, 18.9% German, 15.8% Norwegian, 11.2% Finnish, 10.2% Irish (2000).
Economy: Single-family building permits issued: 9 (2001) / 3 (2000); Multi-family building permits issued: 0 (2001) / 0 (2000); Employment by occupation: 8.0% management, 17.6% professional, 14.9% services, 28.2% sales, 0.5% farming, 17.8% construction, 13.0% production (2000).
Income: Per capita income: $17,487 (2000); Median household income: $42,411 (2000); Poverty rate: 5.4% (2000).
Taxes: Total city taxes per capita: $70 (2000); City property taxes per capita: $64 (2000).
Education: High school graduation rate: 84.3% (2000); College graduation rate: 9.9% (2000).
Housing: Homeownership rate: 94.8% (2000); Median home value: $85,400 (2000); Median rent: $550 per month (2000); Median age of housing: 40 years (2000).
Transportation: Commute to work: 93.0% car, 0.0% public transportation, 1.6% walk, 5.1% work from home (2000); Travel time to work: 27.7% less than 15 minutes, 64.4% 15 to 30 minutes, 5.2% 30 to 45 minutes, 1.2% 45 to 60 minutes, 1.5% 60 minutes or more (2000)

MORCOM (township). Covers a land area of 35.904 square miles and a water area of 0 square miles. Located at 47.78° N. Lat.; 93.00° W. Long.
Population: 115 (2000); Race: 93.4% White, 0.0% Black, 0.0% Asian, 6.6% American Indian and Alaska Native, 0.0% Hispanic of any race, 0.0% two or more races (2000); Density: 3.2 persons per square mile (2000); Age: 31.4% under 18, 17.5% over 64 (2000); Marriage status: 35.4% never married, 50.4% now married, 14.2% widowed, 0.0% divorced (2000); Foreign born: 1.5% (2000); Ancestry (includes multiple ancestries): 28.5% Swedish, 20.4% German, 13.9% Yugoslavian, 13.9% Norwegian, 8.0% Other groups (2000).
Economy: Employment by occupation: 3.9% management, 21.6% professional, 9.8% services, 21.6% sales, 9.8% farming, 23.5% construction, 9.8% production (2000).
Income: Per capita income: $14,721 (2000); Median household income: $35,972 (2000); Poverty rate: 14.6% (2000).
Taxes: Total city taxes per capita: $64 (1997); City property taxes per capita: $64 (1997).
Education: High school graduation rate: 77.5% (2000); College graduation rate: 6.7% (2000).
Housing: Homeownership rate: 87.8% (2000); Median home value: $65,000 (2000); Median rent: $125 per month (2000); Median age of housing: 28 years (2000).
Transportation: Commute to work: 96.1% car, 0.0% public transportation, 0.0% walk, 3.9% work from home (2000); Travel time to work: 0.0% less than 15 minutes, 44.9% 15 to 30 minutes, 18.4% 30 to 45 minutes, 26.5% 45 to 60 minutes, 10.2% 60 minutes or more (2000)

MORSE (township). Covers a land area of 115.613 square miles and a water area of 22.491 square miles. Located at 47.89° N. Lat.; 91.90° W. Long.
Population: 1,229 (2000); Race: 96.2% White, 0.2% Black, 0.3% Asian, 1.9% American Indian and Alaska Native, 0.9% Hispanic of any race, 0.7% two or more races (2000); Density: 10.6 persons per square mile (2000); Age: 20.6% under 18, 18.3% over 64 (2000); Marriage status: 22.9% never married, 64.6% now married, 6.2% widowed, 6.4% divorced (2000); Foreign born: 1.5% (2000); Ancestry (includes multiple ancestries): 27.9% German, 13.6% Finnish, 12.3% Norwegian, 10.7% Swedish, 9.8% English (2000).
Economy: Employment by occupation: 11.1% management, 20.3% professional, 16.6% services, 24.5% sales, 2.4% farming, 16.5% construction, 8.6% production (2000).
Income: Per capita income: $21,503 (2000); Median household income: $36,944 (2000); Poverty rate: 4.4% (2000).
Taxes: Total city taxes per capita: $102 (1997); City property taxes per capita: $102 (1997).
Education: High school graduation rate: 92.2% (2000); College graduation rate: 27.7% (2000).
Housing: Homeownership rate: 93.0% (2000); Median home value: $134,700 (2000); Median rent: $336 per month (2000); Median age of housing: 30 years (2000).
Transportation: Commute to work: 89.2% car, 0.0% public transportation, 2.3% walk, 8.2% work from home (2000); Travel time to work: 47.6% less than 15 minutes, 33.1% 15 to 30 minutes, 5.3% 30 to 45 minutes, 5.0% 45 to 60 minutes, 9.0% 60 minutes or more (2000)

MOUNTAIN IRON (city). Covers a land area of 49.437 square miles and a water area of 2.910 square miles. Located at 47.51° N. Lat.; 92.60° W. Long. Elevation is 1,474 feet.
History: Grew with development of iron deposits. Settled 1890, incorporated 1892.
Population: 2,999 (2000); Race: 97.9% White, 0.0% Black, 0.0% Asian, 1.5% American Indian and Alaska Native, 0.7% Hispanic of any race, 0.6%

two or more races (2000); Density: 60.7 persons per square mile (2000); Age: 22.9% under 18, 15.3% over 64 (2000); Marriage status: 25.6% never married, 58.2% now married, 8.0% widowed, 8.2% divorced (2000); Foreign born: 1.4% (2000); Ancestry (includes multiple ancestries): 28.2% Finnish, 17.1% German, 13.4% Italian, 13.0% Norwegian, 9.5% Swedish (2000).
Economy: Manufacturing: crushers and shovels, taconite, pallets, steel fabrication. Superior National Forest to North. Single-family building permits issued: 11 (2001) / 3 (2000); Multi-family building permits issued: 0 (2001) / 0 (2000); Employment by occupation: 6.2% management, 18.6% professional, 12.5% services, 35.9% sales, 0.3% farming, 15.3% construction, 11.2% production (2000).
Income: Per capita income: $18,761 (2000); Median household income: $35,163 (2000); Poverty rate: 10.7% (2000).
Taxes: Total city taxes per capita: $198 (1997); City property taxes per capita: $188 (1997).
Education: High school graduation rate: 90.6% (2000); College graduation rate: 18.8% (2000).

School District(s)

Mountain Iron-Buhl (PK-12)
2000 Enrollment: 584 218-735-8271
Housing: Homeownership rate: 69.8% (2000); Median home value: $75,400 (2000); Median rent: $409 per month (2000); Median age of housing: 28 years (2000).
Safety: Violent crime rate: 0.0 per 10,000 population; Property crime rate: 29.7 per 10,000 population (2001).
Transportation: Commute to work: 96.3% car, 0.0% public transportation, 2.6% walk, 0.9% work from home (2000); Travel time to work: 62.3% less than 15 minutes, 21.6% 15 to 30 minutes, 9.6% 30 to 45 minutes, 0.0% 45 to 60 minutes, 6.5% 60 minutes or more (2000)

NESS (township). Covers a land area of 34.883 square miles and a water area of 0.344 square miles. Located at 46.99° N. Lat.; 92.75° W. Long.
Population: 60 (2000); Race: 87.1% White, 0.0% Black, 0.0% Asian, 0.0% American Indian and Alaska Native, 12.9% Hispanic of any race, 9.7% two or more races (2000); Density: 1.7 persons per square mile (2000); Age: 16.1% under 18, 12.9% over 64 (2000); Marriage status: 22.4% never married, 46.6% now married, 10.3% widowed, 20.7% divorced (2000); Foreign born: 8.1% (2000); Ancestry (includes multiple ancestries): 32.3% German, 25.8% Other groups, 12.9% United States or American, 8.1% French (except Basque), 8.1% English (2000).
Economy: Employment by occupation: 0.0% management, 22.7% professional, 0.0% services, 40.9% sales, 0.0% farming, 0.0% construction, 36.4% production (2000).
Income: Per capita income: $15,934 (2000); Median household income: $39,167 (2000); Poverty rate: 13.3% (2000).
Taxes: Total city taxes per capita: $52 (1997); City property taxes per capita: $52 (1997).
Education: High school graduation rate: 92.0% (2000); College graduation rate: 8.0% (2000).
Housing: Homeownership rate: 83.3% (2000); Median home value: $55,000 (2000); Median rent: $325 per month (2000); Median age of housing: 32 years (2000).
Transportation: Commute to work: 59.1% car, 0.0% public transportation, 27.3% walk, 0.0% work from home (2000); Travel time to work: 27.3% less than 15 minutes, 9.1% 15 to 30 minutes, 40.9% 30 to 45 minutes, 13.6% 45 to 60 minutes, 9.1% 60 minutes or more (2000)

NEW INDEPENDENCE (township). Covers a land area of 34.836 square miles and a water area of 0.907 square miles. Located at 46.98° N. Lat.; 92.47° W. Long.
Population: 272 (2000); Race: 99.3% White, 0.0% Black, 0.0% Asian, 0.7% American Indian and Alaska Native, 2.2% Hispanic of any race, 0.0% two or more races (2000); Density: 7.8 persons per square mile (2000); Age: 23.6% under 18, 13.7% over 64 (2000); Marriage status: 22.3% never married, 62.9% now married, 6.3% widowed, 8.5% divorced (2000); Foreign born: 0.7% (2000); Ancestry (includes multiple ancestries): 23.6% Swedish, 17.3% Finnish, 17.0% Norwegian, 15.9% German, 10.3% Irish (2000).
Economy: Employment by occupation: 11.3% management, 10.5% professional, 20.3% services, 30.1% sales, 0.0% farming, 14.3% construction, 13.5% production (2000).
Income: Per capita income: $20,738 (2000); Median household income: $50,625 (2000); Poverty rate: 1.8% (2000).
Taxes: Total city taxes per capita: $64 (1997); City property taxes per capita: $64 (1997).
Education: High school graduation rate: 89.9% (2000); College graduation rate: 10.1% (2000).
Housing: Homeownership rate: 96.3% (2000); Median home value: $62,500 (2000); Median rent: $675 per month (2000); Median age of housing: 39 years (2000).
Transportation: Commute to work: 91.0% car, 0.0% public transportation, 0.0% walk, 9.0% work from home (2000); Travel time to work: 6.6% less than 15 minutes, 43.8% 15 to 30 minutes, 37.2% 30 to 45 minutes, 6.6% 45 to 60 minutes, 5.8% 60 minutes or more (2000)

NORMANNA (township). Covers a land area of 36.450 square miles and a water area of 0.040 square miles. Located at 46.98° N. Lat.; 91.97° W. Long.
Population: 637 (2000); Race: 98.9% White, 0.0% Black, 0.0% Asian, 0.8% American Indian and Alaska Native, 1.3% Hispanic of any race, 0.3% two or more races (2000); Density: 17.5 persons per square mile (2000); Age: 29.1% under 18, 7.8% over 64 (2000); Marriage status: 26.1% never married, 64.9% now married, 3.2% widowed, 5.9% divorced (2000); Foreign born: 1.0% (2000); Ancestry (includes multiple ancestries): 24.2% German, 22.6% Swedish, 16.3% Norwegian, 13.8% Finnish, 8.5% Irish (2000).
Economy: Employment by occupation: 6.2% management, 21.7% professional, 17.7% services, 27.3% sales, 0.0% farming, 10.2% construction, 16.8% production (2000).
Income: Per capita income: $19,127 (2000); Median household income: $52,000 (2000); Poverty rate: 3.4% (2000).
Taxes: Total city taxes per capita: $32 (1997); City property taxes per capita: $32 (1997).
Education: High school graduation rate: 93.9% (2000); College graduation rate: 26.1% (2000).
Housing: Homeownership rate: 94.1% (2000); Median home value: $120,500 (2000); Median rent: $325 per month (2000); Median age of housing: 19 years (2000).
Transportation: Commute to work: 95.0% car, 0.0% public transportation, 0.0% walk, 5.0% work from home (2000); Travel time to work: 3.3% less than 15 minutes, 53.3% 15 to 30 minutes, 39.5% 30 to 45 minutes, 1.3% 45 to 60 minutes, 2.6% 60 minutes or more (2000)

NORTH STAR (township). Covers a land area of 33.302 square miles and a water area of 2.277 square miles. Located at 47.05° N. Lat.; 91.99° W. Long.
Population: 203 (2000); Race: 98.1% White, 0.0% Black, 0.0% Asian, 1.9% American Indian and Alaska Native, 0.0% Hispanic of any race, 0.0% two or more races (2000); Density: 6.1 persons per square mile (2000); Age: 24.8% under 18, 5.8% over 64 (2000); Marriage status: 18.4% never married, 58.2% now married, 8.2% widowed, 15.2% divorced (2000); Foreign born: 1.0% (2000); Ancestry (includes multiple ancestries): 21.8% German, 12.6% English, 11.7% Swedish, 11.2% Finnish, 10.7% Irish (2000).
Economy: Employment by occupation: 20.7% management, 23.9% professional, 8.7% services, 35.9% sales, 0.0% farming, 4.3% construction, 6.5% production (2000).
Income: Per capita income: $19,640 (2000); Median household income: $51,875 (2000); Poverty rate: 8.8% (2000).
Taxes: Total city taxes per capita: $226 (1997); City property taxes per capita: $226 (1997).
Education: High school graduation rate: 90.1% (2000); College graduation rate: 31.7% (2000).
Housing: Homeownership rate: 97.3% (2000); Median home value: $134,900 (2000); Median age of housing: 32 years (2000).
Transportation: Commute to work: 96.7% car, 0.0% public transportation, 2.2% walk, 1.1% work from home (2000); Travel time to work: 7.7% less than 15 minutes, 18.7% 15 to 30 minutes, 38.5% 30 to 45 minutes, 11.0% 45 to 60 minutes, 24.2% 60 minutes or more (2000)

NORTHLAND (township). Covers a land area of 34.723 square miles and a water area of 0.669 square miles. Located at 47.05° N. Lat.; 92.47° W. Long.
Population: 161 (2000); Race: 100.0% White, 0.0% Black, 0.0% Asian, 0.0% American Indian and Alaska Native, 0.0% Hispanic of any race, 0.0% two or more races (2000); Density: 4.6 persons per square mile (2000); Age: 24.0% under 18, 6.5% over 64 (2000); Marriage status: 19.2% never married, 70.8% now married, 6.7% widowed, 3.3% divorced (2000); Foreign born: 0.0% (2000); Ancestry (includes multiple ancestries): 27.9% Swedish, 24.7% German, 16.9% Norwegian, 14.9% Finnish, 12.3% Polish (2000).
Economy: Employment by occupation: 6.0% management, 16.9% professional, 14.5% services, 27.7% sales, 6.0% farming, 19.3% construction, 9.6% production (2000).
Income: Per capita income: $21,136 (2000); Median household income: $49,375 (2000); Poverty rate: 15.6% (2000).

Taxes: Total city taxes per capita: $198 (1997); City property taxes per capita: $198 (1997).
Education: High school graduation rate: 92.5% (2000); College graduation rate: 16.0% (2000).
Housing: Homeownership rate: 90.8% (2000); Median home value: $137,500 (2000); Median rent: $675 per month (2000); Median age of housing: 47 years (2000).
Transportation: Commute to work: 91.6% car, 0.0% public transportation, 0.0% walk, 8.4% work from home (2000); Travel time to work: 15.8% less than 15 minutes, 7.9% 15 to 30 minutes, 25.0% 30 to 45 minutes, 40.8% 45 to 60 minutes, 10.5% 60 minutes or more (2000)

ORR (city). Covers a land area of 1.340 square miles and a water area of 0.012 square miles. Located at 48.06° N. Lat.; 92.82° W. Long. Elevation is 1,304 feet.
Population: 249 (2000); Race: 88.5% White, 0.0% Black, 0.0% Asian, 8.6% American Indian and Alaska Native, 3.3% Hispanic of any race, 2.9% two or more races (2000); Density: 185.8 persons per square mile (2000); Age: 22.1% under 18, 24.6% over 64 (2000); Marriage status: 15.5% never married, 66.8% now married, 6.7% widowed, 10.9% divorced (2000); Foreign born: 0.0% (2000); Ancestry (includes multiple ancestries): 19.7% German, 16.0% Irish, 13.5% Other groups, 13.1% Finnish, 10.2% Norwegian (2000).
Economy: Resort area; timber. Manufacturing of wood product. Superior National Forest to East; Voyageurs National Park to North. Single-family building permits issued: 0 (2001) / 0 (2000); Multi-family building permits issued: 0 (2001) / 0 (2000); Employment by occupation: 16.5% management, 7.8% professional, 8.7% services, 30.1% sales, 1.9% farming, 17.5% construction, 17.5% production (2000).
Income: Per capita income: $14,776 (2000); Median household income: $27,222 (2000); Poverty rate: 16.4% (2000).
Education: High school graduation rate: 77.8% (2000); College graduation rate: 7.0% (2000).
Housing: Homeownership rate: 71.8% (2000); Median home value: $54,000 (2000); Median rent: $187 per month (2000); Median age of housing: 32 years (2000).
Transportation: Commute to work: 88.3% car, 0.0% public transportation, 7.8% walk, 3.9% work from home (2000); Travel time to work: 45.5% less than 15 minutes, 26.3% 15 to 30 minutes, 7.1% 30 to 45 minutes, 10.1% 45 to 60 minutes, 11.1% 60 minutes or more (2000)
Airports: Orr Regional

OWENS (township). Covers a land area of 29.490 square miles and a water area of 0.006 square miles. Located at 47.82° N. Lat.; 92.63° W. Long.
Population: 270 (2000); Race: 97.4% White, 0.0% Black, 0.0% Asian, 2.3% American Indian and Alaska Native, 0.0% Hispanic of any race, 0.3% two or more races (2000); Density: 9.2 persons per square mile (2000); Age: 24.2% under 18, 13.6% over 64 (2000); Marriage status: 17.9% never married, 69.9% now married, 3.9% widowed, 8.3% divorced (2000); Foreign born: 0.0% (2000); Ancestry (includes multiple ancestries): 24.5% Swedish, 22.2% Finnish, 19.5% Norwegian, 14.6% German, 13.2% Irish (2000).
Economy: Employment by occupation: 9.3% management, 10.0% professional, 14.3% services, 17.1% sales, 5.0% farming, 23.6% construction, 20.7% production (2000).
Income: Per capita income: $15,892 (2000); Median household income: $40,208 (2000); Poverty rate: 13.1% (2000).
Taxes: Total city taxes per capita: $58 (1997); City property taxes per capita: $58 (1997).
Education: High school graduation rate: 91.9% (2000); College graduation rate: 10.6% (2000).
Housing: Homeownership rate: 85.5% (2000); Median home value: $61,300 (2000); Median rent: $363 per month (2000); Median age of housing: 42 years (2000).
Transportation: Commute to work: 90.6% car, 0.0% public transportation, 1.4% walk, 8.0% work from home (2000); Travel time to work: 53.5% less than 15 minutes, 18.9% 15 to 30 minutes, 15.7% 30 to 45 minutes, 3.1% 45 to 60 minutes, 8.7% 60 minutes or more (2000)

PEQUAYWAN (township). Covers a land area of 33.943 square miles and a water area of 2.194 square miles. Located at 47.18° N. Lat.; 91.88° W. Long.
Population: 133 (2000); Race: 100.0% White, 0.0% Black, 0.0% Asian, 0.0% American Indian and Alaska Native, 0.0% Hispanic of any race, 0.0% two or more races (2000); Density: 3.9 persons per square mile (2000); Age: 25.2% under 18, 13.4% over 64 (2000); Marriage status: 18.8% never married, 72.3% now married, 2.0% widowed, 6.9% divorced (2000); Foreign born: 1.6% (2000); Ancestry (includes multiple ancestries): 27.6% Norwegian, 25.2% German, 16.5% Swedish, 15.0% Finnish, 13.4% Irish (2000).
Economy: Employment by occupation: 17.6% management, 13.7% professional, 17.6% services, 31.4% sales, 0.0% farming, 11.8% construction, 7.8% production (2000).
Income: Per capita income: $20,869 (2000); Median household income: $36,250 (2000); Poverty rate: 14.2% (2000).
Taxes: Total city taxes per capita: $202 (1997); City property taxes per capita: $202 (1997).
Education: High school graduation rate: 97.8% (2000); College graduation rate: 18.7% (2000).
Housing: Homeownership rate: 100.0% (2000); Median home value: $122,100 (2000); Median age of housing: 35 years (2000).
Transportation: Commute to work: 86.3% car, 0.0% public transportation, 0.0% walk, 13.7% work from home (2000); Travel time to work: 0.0% less than 15 minutes, 4.5% 15 to 30 minutes, 34.1% 30 to 45 minutes, 36.4% 45 to 60 minutes, 25.0% 60 minutes or more (2000)

PIKE (township). Covers a land area of 33.596 square miles and a water area of 0.031 square miles. Located at 47.65° N. Lat.; 92.37° W. Long.
Population: 492 (2000); Race: 97.7% White, 0.0% Black, 1.3% Asian, 0.0% American Indian and Alaska Native, 0.0% Hispanic of any race, 1.1% two or more races (2000); Density: 14.6 persons per square mile (2000); Age: 21.7% under 18, 7.9% over 64 (2000); Marriage status: 22.8% never married, 61.9% now married, 2.7% widowed, 12.6% divorced (2000); Foreign born: 1.3% (2000); Ancestry (includes multiple ancestries): 35.7% Finnish, 23.2% German, 7.7% Swedish, 6.2% Norwegian, 5.5% Irish (2000).
Economy: Employment by occupation: 12.8% management, 20.6% professional, 18.3% services, 15.6% sales, 0.0% farming, 13.2% construction, 19.5% production (2000).
Income: Per capita income: $19,701 (2000); Median household income: $41,346 (2000); Poverty rate: 8.1% (2000).
Taxes: Total city taxes per capita: $7 (1997); City property taxes per capita: $7 (1997).
Education: High school graduation rate: 94.8% (2000); College graduation rate: 22.4% (2000).
Housing: Homeownership rate: 96.3% (2000); Median home value: $67,100 (2000); Median rent: $208 per month (2000); Median age of housing: 35 years (2000).
Transportation: Commute to work: 93.3% car, 0.0% public transportation, 0.8% walk, 5.9% work from home (2000); Travel time to work: 9.2% less than 15 minutes, 64.2% 15 to 30 minutes, 19.2% 30 to 45 minutes, 7.1% 45 to 60 minutes, 0.4% 60 minutes or more (2000)

PORTAGE (township). Covers a land area of 137.297 square miles and a water area of 5.802 square miles. Located at 48.13° N. Lat.; 92.60° W. Long.
Population: 177 (2000); Race: 99.4% White, 0.0% Black, 0.0% Asian, 0.6% American Indian and Alaska Native, 0.0% Hispanic of any race, 0.0% two or more races (2000); Density: 1.3 persons per square mile (2000); Age: 23.1% under 18, 24.3% over 64 (2000); Marriage status: 19.6% never married, 63.8% now married, 6.5% widowed, 10.1% divorced (2000); Foreign born: 0.0% (2000); Ancestry (includes multiple ancestries): 30.6% German, 22.5% Polish, 16.8% Finnish, 15.6% Swedish, 10.4% Irish (2000).
Economy: Employment by occupation: 19.4% management, 3.2% professional, 16.1% services, 19.4% sales, 6.5% farming, 27.4% construction, 8.1% production (2000).
Income: Per capita income: $19,107 (2000); Median household income: $28,750 (2000); Poverty rate: 13.9% (2000).
Taxes: Total city taxes per capita: $115 (1997); City property taxes per capita: $115 (1997).
Education: High school graduation rate: 81.5% (2000); College graduation rate: 8.1% (2000).
Housing: Homeownership rate: 89.3% (2000); Median home value: $100,000 (2000); Median age of housing: 32 years (2000).
Transportation: Commute to work: 83.1% car, 0.0% public transportation, 6.8% walk, 10.2% work from home (2000); Travel time to work: 39.6% less than 15 minutes, 22.6% 15 to 30 minutes, 9.4% 30 to 45 minutes, 9.4% 45 to 60 minutes, 18.9% 60 minutes or more (2000)

PRAIRIE LAKE (township). Covers a land area of 35.394 square miles and a water area of 0.293 square miles. Located at 46.79° N. Lat.; 92.97° W. Long.
Population: 51 (2000); Race: 80.0% White, 0.0% Black, 0.0% Asian, 0.0% American Indian and Alaska Native, 0.0% Hispanic of any race, 20.0% two or more races (2000); Density: 1.4 persons per square mile (2000); Age:

48.2% under 18, 9.4% over 64 (2000); Marriage status: 39.1% never married, 32.6% now married, 10.9% widowed, 17.4% divorced (2000); Foreign born: 0.0% (2000); Ancestry (includes multiple ancestries): 49.4% German, 22.4% Finnish, 20.0% Other groups, 10.6% English, 10.6% French (except Basque) (2000).
Economy: Employment by occupation: 0.0% management, 6.3% professional, 43.8% services, 12.5% sales, 9.4% farming, 21.9% construction, 6.3% production (2000).
Income: Per capita income: $8,914 (2000); Median household income: $36,250 (2000); Poverty rate: 32.9% (2000).
Taxes: Total city taxes per capita: $232 (1997); City property taxes per capita: $232 (1997).
Education: High school graduation rate: 88.6% (2000); College graduation rate: 13.6% (2000).
Housing: Homeownership rate: 69.0% (2000); Median home value: $68,300 (2000); Median age of housing: 35 years (2000).
Transportation: Commute to work: 84.4% car, 0.0% public transportation, 0.0% walk, 15.6% work from home (2000); Travel time to work: 11.1% less than 15 minutes, 33.3% 15 to 30 minutes, 25.9% 30 to 45 minutes, 14.8% 45 to 60 minutes, 14.8% 60 minutes or more (2000)

PROCTOR (city). Covers a land area of 3.025 square miles and a water area of 0 square miles. Located at 46.74° N. Lat.; 92.22° W. Long. Elevation is 1,248 feet.
History: Settled 1893.
Population: 2,852 (2000); Race: 96.3% White, 0.2% Black, 0.4% Asian, 0.2% American Indian and Alaska Native, 0.0% Hispanic of any race, 2.5% two or more races (2000); Density: 942.8 persons per square mile (2000); Age: 25.2% under 18, 15.6% over 64 (2000); Marriage status: 27.8% never married, 51.9% now married, 9.0% widowed, 11.3% divorced (2000); Foreign born: 1.5% (2000); Ancestry (includes multiple ancestries): 27.0% German, 20.1% Norwegian, 16.6% Swedish, 12.7% Irish, 9.6% Polish (2000).
Economy: Agriculture to West: vegetables, hay; poultry; dairying. Light manufacturing. Spirit Mt. Ski Area to SouthweSaint Single-family building permits issued: 3 (2001) / 4 (2000); Multi-family building permits issued: 0 (2001) / 0 (2000); Employment by occupation: 8.4% management, 17.0% professional, 19.3% services, 30.7% sales, 1.2% farming, 10.4% construction, 13.0% production (2000).
Income: Per capita income: $18,851 (2000); Median household income: $38,322 (2000); Poverty rate: 5.0% (2000).
Taxes: Total city taxes per capita: $154 (1997); City property taxes per capita: $143 (1997).
Education: High school graduation rate: 89.0% (2000); College graduation rate: 15.9% (2000).

School District(s)

Proctor (PK-12)
2000 Enrollment: 2,044 218-628-4934
Housing: Homeownership rate: 79.8% (2000); Median home value: $72,800 (2000); Median rent: $364 per month (2000); Median age of housing: 46 years (2000).
Safety: Violent crime rate: 13.9 per 10,000 population; Property crime rate: 353.8 per 10,000 population (2001).
Newspapers: Proctor Journal (1 x week)
Transportation: Commute to work: 88.4% car, 3.1% public transportation, 2.8% walk, 3.9% work from home (2000); Travel time to work: 36.8% less than 15 minutes, 53.3% 15 to 30 minutes, 5.4% 30 to 45 minutes, 2.0% 45 to 60 minutes, 2.6% 60 minutes or more (2000)

RICE LAKE (township). Covers a land area of 32.350 square miles and a water area of 1.146 square miles. Located at 46.87° N. Lat.; 92.12° W. Long.
Population: 4,139 (2000); Race: 97.1% White, 0.5% Black, 0.5% Asian, 0.6% American Indian and Alaska Native, 0.2% Hispanic of any race, 1.1% two or more races (2000); Density: 127.9 persons per square mile (2000); Age: 29.4% under 18, 8.5% over 64 (2000); Marriage status: 22.1% never married, 67.5% now married, 3.8% widowed, 6.7% divorced (2000); Foreign born: 1.0% (2000); Ancestry (includes multiple ancestries): 24.6% German, 23.5% Norwegian, 16.3% Swedish, 11.7% Irish, 9.4% Polish (2000).
Economy: Single-family building permits issued: 19 (2001) / 24 (2000); Multi-family building permits issued: 0 (2001) / 4 (2000); Employment by occupation: 13.0% management, 18.4% professional, 16.5% services, 25.2% sales, 0.9% farming, 12.3% construction, 13.7% production (2000).
Income: Per capita income: $18,857 (2000); Median household income: $51,341 (2000); Poverty rate: 5.5% (2000).
Taxes: Total city taxes per capita: $79 (2000); City property taxes per capita: $70 (2000).
Education: High school graduation rate: 86.0% (2000); College graduation rate: 18.0% (2000).
Housing: Homeownership rate: 93.4% (2000); Median home value: $94,400 (2000); Median rent: $613 per month (2000); Median age of housing: 29 years (2000).
Transportation: Commute to work: 90.8% car, 1.6% public transportation, 1.2% walk, 5.7% work from home (2000); Travel time to work: 26.1% less than 15 minutes, 58.7% 15 to 30 minutes, 11.6% 30 to 45 minutes, 1.8% 45 to 60 minutes, 1.8% 60 minutes or more (2000)

SAGINAW (unincorporated postal area, zip code 55779). Covers a land area of 124.269 square miles and a water area of 5.381 square miles. Located at 46.90° N. Lat.; 92.44° W. Long. Elevation is 1,354 feet.
Population: 3,490 (2000); Race: 95.2% White, 0.3% Black, 0.6% Asian, 1.7% American Indian and Alaska Native, 0.5% Hispanic of any race, 2.0% two or more races (2000); Density: 28.1 persons per square mile (2000); Age: 26.5% under 18, 8.1% over 64 (2000); Marriage status: 20.3% never married, 66.7% now married, 3.7% widowed, 9.3% divorced (2000); Foreign born: 1.1% (2000); Ancestry (includes multiple ancestries): 22.2% German, 17.1% Swedish, 15.8% Norwegian, 14.3% Finnish, 9.1% Irish (2000).
Economy: Manufacturing: concrete, drilling equipment. Agriculture: dairying; poultry; hay. Employment by occupation: 10.7% management, 17.6% professional, 16.3% services, 25.4% sales, 0.6% farming, 16.4% construction, 12.8% production (2000).
Income: Per capita income: $19,862 (2000); Median household income: $51,078 (2000); Poverty rate: 5.1% (2000).
Education: High school graduation rate: 88.7% (2000); College graduation rate: 15.1% (2000).
Housing: Homeownership rate: 93.6% (2000); Median home value: $114,100 (2000); Median rent: $379 per month (2000); Median age of housing: 29 years (2000).
Transportation: Commute to work: 94.0% car, 0.5% public transportation, 0.7% walk, 4.4% work from home (2000); Travel time to work: 9.1% less than 15 minutes, 47.2% 15 to 30 minutes, 31.8% 30 to 45 minutes, 6.2% 45 to 60 minutes, 5.7% 60 minutes or more (2000)

SANDY (township). Covers a land area of 30.237 square miles and a water area of 3.322 square miles. Located at 47.66° N. Lat.; 92.50° W. Long.
Population: 382 (2000); Race: 97.6% White, 1.5% Black, 0.0% Asian, 0.0% American Indian and Alaska Native, 0.5% Hispanic of any race, 0.5% two or more races (2000); Density: 12.6 persons per square mile (2000); Age: 22.3% under 18, 12.4% over 64 (2000); Marriage status: 14.1% never married, 69.5% now married, 6.3% widowed, 10.1% divorced (2000); Foreign born: 0.5% (2000); Ancestry (includes multiple ancestries): 29.4% Finnish, 18.7% Norwegian, 15.5% German, 12.9% Swedish, 7.0% Polish (2000).
Economy: Employment by occupation: 4.1% management, 18.8% professional, 12.4% services, 23.9% sales, 2.8% farming, 24.3% construction, 13.8% production (2000).
Income: Per capita income: $20,422 (2000); Median household income: $44,048 (2000); Poverty rate: 4.1% (2000).
Taxes: Total city taxes per capita: $30 (1997); City property taxes per capita: $30 (1997).
Education: High school graduation rate: 89.9% (2000); College graduation rate: 18.6% (2000).
Housing: Homeownership rate: 96.4% (2000); Median home value: $68,100 (2000); Median rent: $300 per month (2000); Median age of housing: 30 years (2000).
Transportation: Commute to work: 97.7% car, 1.4% public transportation, 0.0% walk, 0.9% work from home (2000); Travel time to work: 12.5% less than 15 minutes, 60.2% 15 to 30 minutes, 14.8% 30 to 45 minutes, 6.5% 45 to 60 minutes, 6.0% 60 minutes or more (2000)

SIDE LAKE (unincorporated postal area, zip code 55781). Covers a land area of 18.531 square miles and a water area of 3.157 square miles. Located at 47.55° N. Lat.; 92.99° W. Long.
Population: 408 (2000); Race: 97.6% White, 0.5% Black, 0.0% Asian, 1.3% American Indian and Alaska Native, 0.0% Hispanic of any race, 0.5% two or more races (2000); Density: 22.0 persons per square mile (2000); Age: 19.8% under 18, 14.7% over 64 (2000); Marriage status: 16.9% never married, 70.0% now married, 2.9% widowed, 10.2% divorced (2000); Foreign born: 0.8% (2000); Ancestry (includes multiple ancestries): 23.1% German, 18.0% Italian, 15.3% Irish, 13.1% Finnish, 12.6% Swedish (2000).
Economy: Employment by occupation: 12.4% management, 24.3% professional, 9.0% services, 22.0% sales, 0.0% farming, 20.9% construction, 11.3% production (2000).

Income: Per capita income: $25,590 (2000); Median household income: $51,875 (2000); Poverty rate: 3.2% (2000).
Education: High school graduation rate: 94.3% (2000); College graduation rate: 32.5% (2000).
Housing: Homeownership rate: 100.0% (2000); Median home value: $155,100 (2000); Median age of housing: 35 years (2000).
Transportation: Commute to work: 93.7% car, 0.0% public transportation, 4.6% walk, 0.0% work from home (2000); Travel time to work: 13.1% less than 15 minutes, 45.1% 15 to 30 minutes, 29.7% 30 to 45 minutes, 6.3% 45 to 60 minutes, 5.7% 60 minutes or more (2000)

SOLWAY (township). Covers a land area of 35.538 square miles and a water area of 0.202 square miles. Located at 46.81° N. Lat.; 92.36° W. Long.
Population: 1,842 (2000); Race: 98.2% White, 0.5% Black, 0.1% Asian, 0.3% American Indian and Alaska Native, 0.5% Hispanic of any race, 0.4% two or more races (2000); Density: 51.8 persons per square mile (2000); Age: 26.9% under 18, 8.7% over 64 (2000); Marriage status: 21.3% never married, 66.4% now married, 3.4% widowed, 9.0% divorced (2000); Foreign born: 0.7% (2000); Ancestry (includes multiple ancestries): 21.8% Swedish, 20.5% German, 19.1% Norwegian, 11.8% Finnish, 11.3% Irish (2000).
Economy: Employment by occupation: 7.5% management, 14.7% professional, 16.0% services, 28.9% sales, 0.6% farming, 15.3% construction, 17.0% production (2000).
Income: Per capita income: $18,510 (2000); Median household income: $46,360 (2000); Poverty rate: 4.9% (2000).
Taxes: Total city taxes per capita: $75 (1997); City property taxes per capita: $73 (1997).
Education: High school graduation rate: 90.4% (2000); College graduation rate: 12.5% (2000).
Housing: Homeownership rate: 94.3% (2000); Median home value: $106,300 (2000); Median rent: $408 per month (2000); Median age of housing: 27 years (2000).
Transportation: Commute to work: 95.1% car, 0.2% public transportation, 0.4% walk, 3.2% work from home (2000); Travel time to work: 12.5% less than 15 minutes, 62.1% 15 to 30 minutes, 20.6% 30 to 45 minutes, 1.7% 45 to 60 minutes, 3.0% 60 minutes or more (2000)

STONEY BROOK (township). Covers a land area of 34.983 square miles and a water area of 0.872 square miles. Located at 46.82° N. Lat.; 92.61° W. Long.
Population: 266 (2000); Race: 74.7% White, 0.0% Black, 0.0% Asian, 22.9% American Indian and Alaska Native, 0.0% Hispanic of any race, 2.4% two or more races (2000); Density: 7.6 persons per square mile (2000); Age: 27.4% under 18, 10.6% over 64 (2000); Marriage status: 21.3% never married, 66.2% now married, 4.0% widowed, 8.4% divorced (2000); Foreign born: 2.1% (2000); Ancestry (includes multiple ancestries): 17.8% Finnish, 15.8% German, 15.1% Other groups, 14.7% Swedish, 8.6% English (2000).
Economy: Employment by occupation: 12.8% management, 21.6% professional, 16.8% services, 15.2% sales, 0.0% farming, 12.0% construction, 21.6% production (2000).
Income: Per capita income: $19,369 (2000); Median household income: $53,750 (2000); Poverty rate: 8.9% (2000).
Taxes: Total city taxes per capita: $62 (1997); City property taxes per capita: $62 (1997).
Education: High school graduation rate: 94.2% (2000); College graduation rate: 14.7% (2000).
Housing: Homeownership rate: 81.3% (2000); Median home value: $91,700 (2000); Median rent: $175 per month (2000); Median age of housing: 17 years (2000).
Transportation: Commute to work: 93.6% car, 0.0% public transportation, 0.0% walk, 6.4% work from home (2000); Travel time to work: 10.3% less than 15 minutes, 38.5% 15 to 30 minutes, 47.0% 30 to 45 minutes, 1.7% 45 to 60 minutes, 2.6% 60 minutes or more (2000)

STURGEON (township). Covers a land area of 36.935 square miles and a water area of 0 square miles. Located at 47.77° N. Lat.; 92.88° W. Long. Elevation is 1,296 feet.
Population: 116 (2000); Race: 82.8% White, 0.0% Black, 4.5% Asian, 2.2% American Indian and Alaska Native, 0.0% Hispanic of any race, 8.2% two or more races (2000); Density: 3.1 persons per square mile (2000); Age: 26.1% under 18, 13.4% over 64 (2000); Marriage status: 17.6% never married, 66.7% now married, 4.6% widowed, 11.1% divorced (2000); Foreign born: 2.2% (2000); Ancestry (includes multiple ancestries): 35.8% Finnish, 35.1% Swedish, 16.4% German, 16.4% Irish, 11.9% Norwegian (2000).
Economy: Employment by occupation: 7.6% management, 25.8% professional, 13.6% services, 10.6% sales, 10.6% farming, 27.3% construction, 4.5% production (2000).
Income: Per capita income: $12,677 (2000); Median household income: $35,469 (2000); Poverty rate: 8.2% (2000).
Taxes: Total city taxes per capita: $57 (1997); City property taxes per capita: $57 (1997).
Education: High school graduation rate: 80.2% (2000); College graduation rate: 12.1% (2000).
Housing: Homeownership rate: 96.0% (2000); Median home value: $51,700 (2000); Median age of housing: 43 years (2000).
Transportation: Commute to work: 89.4% car, 0.0% public transportation, 0.0% walk, 10.6% work from home (2000); Travel time to work: 6.8% less than 15 minutes, 39.0% 15 to 30 minutes, 44.1% 30 to 45 minutes, 10.2% 45 to 60 minutes, 0.0% 60 minutes or more (2000)

TOIVOLA (township). Covers a land area of 71.670 square miles and a water area of 0.274 square miles. Located at 47.15° N. Lat.; 92.78° W. Long. Elevation is 1,265 feet.
Population: 196 (2000); Race: 86.4% White, 0.0% Black, 0.0% Asian, 0.0% American Indian and Alaska Native, 0.0% Hispanic of any race, 13.6% two or more races (2000); Density: 2.7 persons per square mile (2000); Age: 25.4% under 18, 16.4% over 64 (2000); Marriage status: 17.1% never married, 59.3% now married, 10.0% widowed, 13.6% divorced (2000); Foreign born: 0.0% (2000); Ancestry (includes multiple ancestries): 25.4% Finnish, 18.1% Other groups, 13.6% Scottish, 12.4% Norwegian, 11.3% Swedish (2000).
Economy: Employment by occupation: 7.1% management, 5.4% professional, 21.4% services, 14.3% sales, 5.4% farming, 25.0% construction, 21.4% production (2000).
Income: Per capita income: $12,252 (2000); Median household income: $27,321 (2000); Poverty rate: 9.2% (2000).
Taxes: Total city taxes per capita: $72 (1997); City property taxes per capita: $72 (1997).
Education: High school graduation rate: 85.9% (2000); College graduation rate: 4.7% (2000).
Housing: Homeownership rate: 96.9% (2000); Median home value: $37,500 (2000); Median age of housing: 51 years (2000).
Transportation: Commute to work: 82.1% car, 0.0% public transportation, 3.6% walk, 7.1% work from home (2000); Travel time to work: 32.7% less than 15 minutes, 0.0% 15 to 30 minutes, 19.2% 30 to 45 minutes, 23.1% 45 to 60 minutes, 25.0% 60 minutes or more (2000)

TOWER (city). Covers a land area of 2.709 square miles and a water area of 0.402 square miles. Located at 47.80° N. Lat.; 92.27° W. Long. Elevation is 1,350 feet.
History: Tower grew as a resort on the shores of Lake Vermilion, with boating and fishing for vacationers.
Population: 479 (2000); Race: 99.4% White, 0.0% Black, 0.0% Asian, 0.0% American Indian and Alaska Native, 0.0% Hispanic of any race, 0.6% two or more races (2000); Density: 176.8 persons per square mile (2000); Age: 22.2% under 18, 19.6% over 64 (2000); Marriage status: 21.6% never married, 54.2% now married, 12.2% widowed, 12.0% divorced (2000); Foreign born: 0.0% (2000); Ancestry (includes multiple ancestries): 30.3% Finnish, 19.0% Norwegian, 16.6% Swedish, 16.2% German, 7.9% Italian (2000).
Economy: Single-family building permits issued: 1 (2001) / 1 (2000); Multi-family building permits issued: 0 (2001) / 0 (2000); Employment by occupation: 6.4% management, 9.8% professional, 23.4% services, 27.7% sales, 0.0% farming, 16.6% construction, 16.2% production (2000).
Income: Per capita income: $17,169 (2000); Median household income: $26,429 (2000); Poverty rate: 10.7% (2000).
Taxes: Total city taxes per capita: $256 (1997); City property taxes per capita: $232 (1997).
Education: High school graduation rate: 88.4% (2000); College graduation rate: 11.3% (2000).
Housing: Homeownership rate: 71.2% (2000); Median home value: $55,800 (2000); Median rent: $314 per month (2000); Median age of housing: 47 years (2000).
Newspapers: The Tower News (1 x week); The Tower & Soudan Timberjay (1 x week); The Cook & Orr Timberjay (1 x week); The Ely Timberjay (1 x week)
Transportation: Commute to work: 84.8% car, 0.0% public transportation, 13.5% walk, 1.7% work from home (2000); Travel time to work: 52.2% less than 15 minutes, 17.7% 15 to 30 minutes, 20.4% 30 to 45 minutes, 7.1% 45 to 60 minutes, 2.7% 60 minutes or more (2000)

Additional Information Contacts
Tower Chamber of Commerce 218-753-2301

VAN BUREN (township). Covers a land area of 35.275 square miles and a water area of 0.310 square miles. Located at 46.97° N. Lat.; 92.84° W. Long.
Population: 175 (2000); Race: 98.8% White, 0.0% Black, 0.0% Asian, 1.2% American Indian and Alaska Native, 0.0% Hispanic of any race, 0.0% two or more races (2000); Density: 5.0 persons per square mile (2000); Age: 24.8% under 18, 9.3% over 64 (2000); Marriage status: 21.7% never married, 65.1% now married, 7.8% widowed, 5.4% divorced (2000); Foreign born: 0.0% (2000); Ancestry (includes multiple ancestries): 37.3% Finnish, 37.3% German, 12.4% Swedish, 11.2% Polish, 7.5% Scottish (2000).
Economy: Employment by occupation: 10.1% management, 7.9% professional, 15.7% services, 22.5% sales, 3.4% farming, 14.6% construction, 25.8% production (2000).
Income: Per capita income: $16,509 (2000); Median household income: $33,250 (2000); Poverty rate: 16.8% (2000).
Taxes: Total city taxes per capita: $138 (1997); City property taxes per capita: $138 (1997).
Education: High school graduation rate: 90.0% (2000); College graduation rate: 12.7% (2000).
Housing: Homeownership rate: 90.9% (2000); Median home value: $68,300 (2000); Median rent: $225 per month (2000); Median age of housing: 26 years (2000).
Transportation: Commute to work: 86.5% car, 1.1% public transportation, 5.6% walk, 4.5% work from home (2000); Travel time to work: 37.6% less than 15 minutes, 16.5% 15 to 30 minutes, 0.0% 30 to 45 minutes, 29.4% 45 to 60 minutes, 16.5% 60 minutes or more (2000)

VERMILION LAKE (township). Covers a land area of 35.762 square miles and a water area of 0.831 square miles. Located at 47.78° N. Lat.; 92.37° W. Long.
Population: 326 (2000); Race: 99.1% White, 0.0% Black, 0.0% Asian, 0.0% American Indian and Alaska Native, 0.0% Hispanic of any race, 0.9% two or more races (2000); Density: 9.1 persons per square mile (2000); Age: 23.1% under 18, 10.1% over 64 (2000); Marriage status: 16.4% never married, 69.8% now married, 4.1% widowed, 9.7% divorced (2000); Foreign born: 0.0% (2000); Ancestry (includes multiple ancestries): 38.9% Finnish, 19.6% German, 11.6% English, 9.8% Norwegian, 6.8% Irish (2000).
Economy: Employment by occupation: 17.7% management, 12.8% professional, 11.0% services, 17.7% sales, 0.6% farming, 23.8% construction, 16.5% production (2000).
Income: Per capita income: $19,855 (2000); Median household income: $51,875 (2000); Poverty rate: 2.4% (2000).
Taxes: Total city taxes per capita: $77 (2000); City property taxes per capita: $74 (2000).
Education: High school graduation rate: 85.1% (2000); College graduation rate: 15.8% (2000).
Housing: Homeownership rate: 100.0% (2000); Median home value: $105,600 (2000); Median age of housing: 34 years (2000).
Transportation: Commute to work: 95.1% car, 0.0% public transportation, 1.2% walk, 3.7% work from home (2000); Travel time to work: 17.9% less than 15 minutes, 34.0% 15 to 30 minutes, 27.6% 30 to 45 minutes, 5.8% 45 to 60 minutes, 14.7% 60 minutes or more (2000)

VIRGINIA (city). Covers a land area of 18.838 square miles and a water area of 0.366 square miles. Located at 47.51° N. Lat.; 92.54° W. Long. Elevation is 1,437 feet.
History: Virginia was platted in 1892 by the Virginia Improvement Company, and named for the home state of the company's president. The mining boom made the land attractive to settlers and investors. Virginia was incorporated as a city in 1894, and became a leading sawmill town. The Missabe Mountain Mine in Virginia was one of the largest open-pit mines in the country.
Population: 9,157 (2000); Race: 95.1% White, 0.7% Black, 0.5% Asian, 3.2% American Indian and Alaska Native, 0.6% Hispanic of any race, 0.5% two or more races (2000); Density: 486.1 persons per square mile (2000); Age: 19.2% under 18, 23.0% over 64 (2000); Marriage status: 26.6% never married, 46.6% now married, 13.9% widowed, 12.9% divorced (2000); Foreign born: 2.1% (2000); Ancestry (includes multiple ancestries): 21.0% Finnish, 17.9% German, 12.2% Norwegian, 11.2% Swedish, 8.7% Italian (2000).
Economy: Single-family building permits issued: 6 (2001) / 7 (2000); Multi-family building permits issued: 0 (2001) / 0 (2000); Employment by occupation: 7.9% management, 19.2% professional, 18.9% services, 28.7% sales, 0.3% farming, 13.0% construction, 11.9% production (2000).
Income: Per capita income: $17,776 (2000); Median household income: $28,873 (2000); Poverty rate: 15.9% (2000).
Taxes: Total city taxes per capita: $215 (2000); City property taxes per capita: $196 (2000).
Education: High school graduation rate: 86.0% (2000); College graduation rate: 17.3% (2000).

School District(s)

Northland Education Cooperative (02-12)
2000 Enrollment: 138 218-742-3972
Saint Louis County (PK-12)
2000 Enrollment: 2,715 218-749-8130
Virginia (PK-12)
2000 Enrollment: 1,826 218-741-6955

Two-year College(s)

Mesabi Range Community and Technical College (Public)
2001 Enrollment: 1,866 218-741-3095
2001 Tuition: In-state $2,399; Out-of-state $2,399
Housing: Homeownership rate: 61.6% (2000); Median home value: $54,000 (2000); Median rent: $302 per month (2000); Median age of housing: 57 years (2000).
Hospitals: Virginia Regional Medical Center (83 beds)
Safety: Violent crime rate: 32.4 per 10,000 population; Property crime rate: 531.6 per 10,000 population (2001).
Newspapers: Saturday Daily News & Tribune; Mesabi Daily News (7 x week)
Transportation: Commute to work: 87.9% car, 1.3% public transportation, 7.4% walk, 2.6% work from home (2000); Travel time to work: 64.7% less than 15 minutes, 19.1% 15 to 30 minutes, 12.9% 30 to 45 minutes, 1.5% 45 to 60 minutes, 1.9% 60 minutes or more (2000)
Additional Information Contacts
Iron Trail Convention Bureau 218-749-8161
Virginia Chamber of Commerce 218-741-2717

WAASA (township). Covers a land area of 35.109 square miles and a water area of 0.241 square miles. Located at 47.66° N. Lat.; 92.11° W. Long.
Population: 304 (2000); Race: 92.6% White, 0.0% Black, 0.0% Asian, 6.1% American Indian and Alaska Native, 0.0% Hispanic of any race, 1.3% two or more races (2000); Density: 8.7 persons per square mile (2000); Age: 22.3% under 18, 12.9% over 64 (2000); Marriage status: 26.6% never married, 62.2% now married, 2.7% widowed, 8.5% divorced (2000); Foreign born: 0.3% (2000); Ancestry (includes multiple ancestries): 27.2% Finnish, 22.3% German, 14.9% Irish, 12.9% Norwegian, 8.4% English (2000).
Economy: Employment by occupation: 6.3% management, 11.1% professional, 16.7% services, 25.4% sales, 0.0% farming, 22.2% construction, 18.3% production (2000).
Income: Per capita income: $15,282 (2000); Median household income: $37,778 (2000); Poverty rate: 16.3% (2000).
Taxes: Total city taxes per capita: $40 (1997); City property taxes per capita: $40 (1997).
Education: High school graduation rate: 78.9% (2000); College graduation rate: 7.8% (2000).
Housing: Homeownership rate: 96.6% (2000); Median home value: $47,800 (2000); Median rent: $275 per month (2000); Median age of housing: 38 years (2000).
Transportation: Commute to work: 96.8% car, 0.0% public transportation, 0.8% walk, 2.4% work from home (2000); Travel time to work: 21.3% less than 15 minutes, 29.5% 15 to 30 minutes, 39.3% 30 to 45 minutes, 1.6% 45 to 60 minutes, 8.2% 60 minutes or more (2000)

WHITE (township). Covers a land area of 109.232 square miles and a water area of 4.218 square miles. Located at 47.49° N. Lat.; 92.24° W. Long.
Population: 3,477 (2000); Race: 98.7% White, 0.1% Black, 0.4% Asian, 0.4% American Indian and Alaska Native, 0.6% Hispanic of any race, 0.3% two or more races (2000); Density: 31.8 persons per square mile (2000); Age: 21.2% under 18, 19.5% over 64 (2000); Marriage status: 18.5% never married, 64.2% now married, 7.8% widowed, 9.5% divorced (2000); Foreign born: 1.3% (2000); Ancestry (includes multiple ancestries): 23.8% Finnish, 22.6% German, 15.3% Norwegian, 11.1% Swedish, 8.7% English (2000).
Economy: Employment by occupation: 7.2% management, 16.8% professional, 18.0% services, 16.9% sales, 0.9% farming, 21.0% construction, 19.1% production (2000).
Income: Per capita income: $19,431 (2000); Median household income: $37,529 (2000); Poverty rate: 10.1% (2000).

Taxes: Total city taxes per capita: $159 (2000); City property taxes per capita: $159 (2000).
Education: High school graduation rate: 81.5% (2000); College graduation rate: 14.6% (2000).
Housing: Homeownership rate: 87.1% (2000); Median home value: $51,800 (2000); Median rent: $281 per month (2000); Median age of housing: 41 years (2000).
Transportation: Commute to work: 90.3% car, 0.3% public transportation, 6.1% walk, 2.4% work from home (2000); Travel time to work: 36.1% less than 15 minutes, 39.0% 15 to 30 minutes, 17.4% 30 to 45 minutes, 3.0% 45 to 60 minutes, 4.5% 60 minutes or more (2000)

WILLOW VALLEY (township). Covers a land area of 34.901 square miles and a water area of 0.005 square miles. Located at 47.95° N. Lat.; 92.88° W. Long.
Population: 139 (2000); Race: 89.5% White, 0.0% Black, 0.0% Asian, 7.3% American Indian and Alaska Native, 0.0% Hispanic of any race, 3.2% two or more races (2000); Density: 4.0 persons per square mile (2000); Age: 32.3% under 18, 16.1% over 64 (2000); Marriage status: 27.7% never married, 56.4% now married, 5.9% widowed, 9.9% divorced (2000); Foreign born: 2.4% (2000); Ancestry (includes multiple ancestries): 24.2% German, 16.1% Norwegian, 11.3% Finnish, 9.7% Other groups, 8.1% United States or American (2000).
Economy: Employment by occupation: 10.9% management, 18.2% professional, 20.0% services, 21.8% sales, 14.5% farming, 7.3% construction, 7.3% production (2000).
Income: Per capita income: $15,012 (2000); Median household income: $30,000 (2000); Poverty rate: 4.0% (2000).
Taxes: Total city taxes per capita: $58 (1997); City property taxes per capita: $58 (1997).
Education: High school graduation rate: 82.9% (2000); College graduation rate: 14.5% (2000).
Housing: Homeownership rate: 84.6% (2000); Median home value: $55,000 (2000); Median rent: $175 per month (2000); Median age of housing: 24 years (2000).
Transportation: Commute to work: 90.9% car, 0.0% public transportation, 0.0% walk, 9.1% work from home (2000); Travel time to work: 20.0% less than 15 minutes, 32.0% 15 to 30 minutes, 16.0% 30 to 45 minutes, 20.0% 45 to 60 minutes, 12.0% 60 minutes or more (2000)

WINTON (city). Covers a land area of 0.130 square miles and a water area of <.001 square miles. Located at 47.92° N. Lat.; 91.80° W. Long. Elevation is 1,335 feet.
Population: 185 (2000); Race: 97.9% White, 0.0% Black, 0.0% Asian, 1.0% American Indian and Alaska Native, 0.0% Hispanic of any race, 1.0% two or more races (2000); Density: 1,421.2 persons per square mile (2000); Age: 20.8% under 18, 14.1% over 64 (2000); Marriage status: 28.2% never married, 60.3% now married, 6.4% widowed, 5.1% divorced (2000); Foreign born: 2.1% (2000); Ancestry (includes multiple ancestries): 24.0% German, 22.4% Finnish, 12.5% Swedish, 8.9% French (except Basque), 8.9% Norwegian (2000).
Economy: Light manufacturing. Boundary Waters Canoe Area to North and East; outfitting point for canoe trips. Single-family building permits issued: 0 (2001) / 0 (2000); Multi-family building permits issued: 2 (2001) / 4 (2000); Employment by occupation: 10.5% management, 10.5% professional, 22.1% services, 32.6% sales, 0.0% farming, 18.9% construction, 5.3% production (2000).
Income: Per capita income: $18,017 (2000); Median household income: $29,063 (2000); Poverty rate: 8.9% (2000).
Taxes: Total city taxes per capita: $88 (1997); City property taxes per capita: $88 (1997).
Education: High school graduation rate: 84.9% (2000); College graduation rate: 12.7% (2000).
Housing: Homeownership rate: 81.2% (2000); Median home value: $48,800 (2000); Median rent: $375 per month (2000); Median age of housing: 57 years (2000).
Transportation: Commute to work: 95.7% car, 0.0% public transportation, 0.0% walk, 4.3% work from home (2000); Travel time to work: 71.9% less than 15 minutes, 12.4% 15 to 30 minutes, 0.0% 30 to 45 minutes, 5.6% 45 to 60 minutes, 10.1% 60 minutes or more (2000)

WUORI (township). Covers a land area of 34.766 square miles and a water area of 0.149 square miles. Located at 47.61° N. Lat.; 92.52° W. Long.
Population: 563 (2000); Race: 98.6% White, 0.0% Black, 0.0% Asian, 0.4% American Indian and Alaska Native, 0.0% Hispanic of any race, 0.6% two or more races (2000); Density: 16.2 persons per square mile (2000); Age: 23.6% under 18, 10.3% over 64 (2000); Marriage status: 22.1% never married, 68.1% now married, 2.8% widowed, 7.0% divorced (2000); Foreign born: 2.1% (2000); Ancestry (includes multiple ancestries): 38.4% Finnish, 19.1% German, 12.9% Norwegian, 12.1% Swedish, 9.2% English (2000).
Economy: Employment by occupation: 6.2% management, 18.9% professional, 21.8% services, 17.1% sales, 0.0% farming, 20.0% construction, 16.0% production (2000).
Income: Per capita income: $19,070 (2000); Median household income: $45,694 (2000); Poverty rate: 3.9% (2000).
Taxes: Total city taxes per capita: $42 (1997); City property taxes per capita: $42 (1997).
Education: High school graduation rate: 90.2% (2000); College graduation rate: 15.2% (2000).
Housing: Homeownership rate: 95.1% (2000); Median home value: $91,700 (2000); Median rent: $338 per month (2000); Median age of housing: 29 years (2000).
Transportation: Commute to work: 94.1% car, 1.1% public transportation, 0.7% walk, 4.0% work from home (2000); Travel time to work: 26.4% less than 15 minutes, 54.0% 15 to 30 minutes, 10.3% 30 to 45 minutes, 4.6% 45 to 60 minutes, 4.6% 60 minutes or more (2000)

Scott County

Located in southern Minnesota; bounded on the north and west by the Minnesota River. Covers a land area of 356.70 square miles, a water area of 11.90 square miles, and is located in the Central Time Zone. The county government was organized in 1853. County seat is Shakopee.

Scott County is part of the Minneapolis-St. Paul, MN-WI MSA. The entire metro area includes: Anoka County, MN; Carver County, MN; Chisago County, MN; Dakota County, MN; Hennepin County, MN; Isanti County, MN; Ramsey County, MN; Scott County, MN; Sherburne County, MN; Washington County, MN; Wright County, MN; Pierce County, WI; St. Croix County, WI

Weather Station: Jordan 1 S — Elevation: 928 feet

	Jan	Feb	Mar	Apr	May	Jun	Jul	Aug	Sep	Oct	Nov	Dec
High	22	28	40	58	71	79	83	80	71	59	40	27
Low	1	8	20	33	46	55	59	56	47	36	22	8
Precip	0.8	0.5	1.6	2.5	3.4	4.4	3.9	4.7	3.1	2.3	1.7	0.7
Snow	na	3.3	3.9	1.5	tr	0.0	0.0	0.0	tr	0.1	2.2	5.3

High and Low temperatures in degrees Fahrenheit; Precipitation and Snow in inches

Population: 89,498 (2000); Race: 93.8% White, 0.7% Black, 2.1% Asian, 0.9% American Indian and Alaska Native, 2.7% Hispanic of any race, 1.0% two or more races (2000); Density: 250.9 persons per square mile (2000); Age: 31.2% under 18, 6.1% over 64 (2000).
Religion: Five largest groups: 24.7% Catholic Church, 9.6% Evangelical Lutheran Church in America, 2.2% Wisconsin Evangelical Lutheran Synod, 1.9% Lutheran Church—Missouri Synod, 1.8% Baptist General Conference (2000).
Economy: Unemployment rate: 3.6% (11/2002); Total civilian labor force: 51,718 (11/2002); Leading industries: 17.0% manufacturing; 15.2% arts, entertainment & recreation; 12.1% construction (2000); Companies that employ more than 1,000 persons: 2 (2000); Companies that employ more than 100 persons: 44 (2000); Farms: 805 totaling 117,830 acres (1997); Minority business ownership rate: 3.1% (1997); Women business ownership rate: 23.7% (1997); Retail sales per capita: $5,493 (1997). Single-family building permits issued: 1,772 (2001) / 1,976 (2000); Multi-family building permits issued: 234 (2001) / 226 (2000).
Income: Per capita income: $26,418 (2000); Median household income: $66,612 (2000); Poverty rate: 3.4% (2000); Bankruptcy rate: 3.29% (2001).
Taxes: Total county taxes per capita: $310 (2000); County property taxes per capita: $299 (2000).
Education: High school graduation rate: 91.0% (2000); College graduation rate: 29.4% (2000).
Housing: Homeownership rate: 86.6% (2000); Median home value: $157,300 (2000); Median rent: $605 per month (2000); Median age of housing: 16 years (2000).
Health: Birth rate: 168.2 per 10,000 population (1998); Age adjusted death rate: 78.5 per 10,000 population (1999); Age adjusted cancer mortality rate: 202.6 deaths per 100,000 population (1999). Number of physicians: 7.7 per 10,000 population (1999); Number of hospital beds: 10.5 per 10,000 population (1999).
Elections: 2000 Presidential election results: 40.0% Gore, 54.7% Bush, 4.2% Nader, 0.7% Buchanan

National and State Parks: Karnitz State Wildlife Management Area; Mahoney State Wildlife Management Area; Michel State Wildlife Management Area; Saint Patrick State Wildlife Management Area

Additional Information Contacts

Scott County Government Offices 952-445-7750
Jordan Chamber of Commerce. 952-492-2355
New Prague Chamber of Commerce 952-758-4360
Prior Lake Chamber of Commerce 952-440-1000
Savage Chamber of Commerce 952-894-8876

Scott County Communities

BELLE PLAINE (city). Covers a land area of 4.063 square miles and a water area of 0.188 square miles. Located at 44.62° N. Lat.; 93.76° W. Long. Elevation is 730 feet.

Population: 3,789 (2000); Race: 97.9% White, 0.1% Black, 0.6% Asian, 0.4% American Indian and Alaska Native, 1.3% Hispanic of any race, 0.7% two or more races (2000); Density: 932.7 persons per square mile (2000); Age: 27.8% under 18, 16.2% over 64 (2000); Marriage status: 27.2% never married, 55.9% now married, 5.7% widowed, 11.2% divorced (2000); Foreign born: 0.6% (2000); Ancestry (includes multiple ancestries): 56.9% German, 16.1% Irish, 12.6% Norwegian, 4.9% Swedish, 4.8% French (except Basque) (2000).

Economy: Employment by occupation: 7.8% management, 11.7% professional, 20.2% services, 26.1% sales, 0.1% farming, 14.4% construction, 19.8% production (2000).

Income: Per capita income: $19,433 (2000); Median household income: $50,272 (2000); Poverty rate: 5.8% (2000).

Taxes: Total city taxes per capita: $185 (1997); City property taxes per capita: $175 (1997).

Education: High school graduation rate: 81.5% (2000); College graduation rate: 17.3% (2000).

School District(s)

Belle Plaine (KG-12)
2000 Enrollment: 1,168 952-873-2400

Housing: Homeownership rate: 78.7% (2000); Median home value: $129,800 (2000); Median rent: $428 per month (2000); Median age of housing: 28 years (2000).

Safety: Violent crime rate: 7.8 per 10,000 population; Property crime rate: 336.8 per 10,000 population (2001).

Newspapers: The Belle Plaine Herald (1 x week)

Transportation: Commute to work: 91.6% car, 0.0% public transportation, 3.5% walk, 4.8% work from home (2000); Travel time to work: 31.2% less than 15 minutes, 30.7% 15 to 30 minutes, 22.1% 30 to 45 minutes, 10.9% 45 to 60 minutes, 5.1% 60 minutes or more (2000)

BELLE PLAINE (township). Covers a land area of 39.213 square miles and a water area of 0 square miles. Located at 44.58° N. Lat.; 93.71° W. Long. Elevation is 730 feet.

History: Plotted 1853.

Population: 806 (2000); Race: 99.0% White, 0.0% Black, 0.0% Asian, 0.8% American Indian and Alaska Native, 1.4% Hispanic of any race, 0.3% two or more races (2000); Density: 20.6 persons per square mile (2000); Age: 31.5% under 18, 13.1% over 64 (2000); Marriage status: 23.3% never married, 69.2% now married, 1.9% widowed, 5.6% divorced (2000); Foreign born: 0.0% (2000); Ancestry (includes multiple ancestries): 63.1% German, 10.0% Irish, 9.0% Polish, 7.8% Norwegian, 4.8% English (2000).

Economy: Livestock; grain; dairying. Manufacturing: fertilizers, printing and publishing, pharmaceuticals. Employment by occupation: 12.8% management, 14.7% professional, 14.9% services, 25.9% sales, 0.5% farming, 19.2% construction, 12.0% production (2000).

Income: Per capita income: $18,621 (2000); Median household income: $51,000 (2000); Poverty rate: 5.3% (2000).

Taxes: Total city taxes per capita: $66 (1997); City property taxes per capita: $66 (1997).

Education: High school graduation rate: 81.9% (2000); College graduation rate: 11.8% (2000).

Housing: Homeownership rate: 89.5% (2000); Median home value: $175,000 (2000); Median rent: $500 per month (2000); Median age of housing: 43 years (2000).

Transportation: Commute to work: 89.1% car, 0.0% public transportation, 1.1% walk, 9.3% work from home (2000); Travel time to work: 29.4% less than 15 minutes, 28.5% 15 to 30 minutes, 28.5% 30 to 45 minutes, 10.6% 45 to 60 minutes, 2.9% 60 minutes or more (2000)

BLAKELEY (township). Covers a land area of 26.897 square miles and a water area of 0.692 square miles. Located at 44.58° N. Lat.; 93.83° W. Long. Elevation is 734 feet.

Population: 496 (2000); Race: 97.1% White, 0.0% Black, 0.9% Asian, 2.0% American Indian and Alaska Native, 0.0% Hispanic of any race, 0.0% two or more races (2000); Density: 18.4 persons per square mile (2000); Age: 27.2% under 18, 9.9% over 64 (2000); Marriage status: 25.1% never married, 63.5% now married, 3.7% widowed, 7.7% divorced (2000); Foreign born: 0.0% (2000); Ancestry (includes multiple ancestries): 56.0% German, 8.8% Irish, 5.8% Norwegian, 5.6% European, 4.9% Swedish (2000).

Economy: Employment by occupation: 17.1% management, 15.0% professional, 13.8% services, 27.2% sales, 1.6% farming, 9.8% construction, 15.4% production (2000).

Income: Per capita income: $22,530 (2000); Median household income: $59,583 (2000); Poverty rate: 3.6% (2000).

Taxes: Total city taxes per capita: $67 (1997); City property taxes per capita: $67 (1997).

Education: High school graduation rate: 87.7% (2000); College graduation rate: 17.1% (2000).

Housing: Homeownership rate: 88.0% (2000); Median home value: $122,100 (2000); Median rent: $550 per month (2000); Median age of housing: 60+ years (2000).

Transportation: Commute to work: 88.1% car, 0.0% public transportation, 0.8% walk, 11.1% work from home (2000); Travel time to work: 30.4% less than 15 minutes, 18.9% 15 to 30 minutes, 33.2% 30 to 45 minutes, 11.5% 45 to 60 minutes, 6.0% 60 minutes or more (2000)

CEDAR LAKE (township). Covers a land area of 35.186 square miles and a water area of 1.149 square miles. Located at 44.58° N. Lat.; 93.47° W. Long. Elevation is 947 feet.

Population: 2,197 (2000); Race: 98.1% White, 0.0% Black, 0.6% Asian, 0.3% American Indian and Alaska Native, 0.9% Hispanic of any race, 0.6% two or more races (2000); Density: 62.4 persons per square mile (2000); Age: 32.2% under 18, 6.3% over 64 (2000); Marriage status: 20.9% never married, 70.9% now married, 1.6% widowed, 6.7% divorced (2000); Foreign born: 1.8% (2000); Ancestry (includes multiple ancestries): 44.2% German, 15.2% Norwegian, 11.7% Irish, 11.5% Czech, 11.0% Swedish (2000).

Economy: Employment by occupation: 15.6% management, 15.6% professional, 11.8% services, 26.2% sales, 0.7% farming, 12.7% construction, 17.5% production (2000).

Income: Per capita income: $28,404 (2000); Median household income: $75,926 (2000); Poverty rate: 2.1% (2000).

Taxes: Total city taxes per capita: $104 (1997); City property taxes per capita: $102 (1997).

Education: High school graduation rate: 91.5% (2000); College graduation rate: 22.9% (2000).

Housing: Homeownership rate: 98.1% (2000); Median home value: $190,000 (2000); Median rent: $1,292 per month (2000); Median age of housing: 21 years (2000).

Transportation: Commute to work: 90.9% car, 0.0% public transportation, 1.0% walk, 7.8% work from home (2000); Travel time to work: 15.9% less than 15 minutes, 29.3% 15 to 30 minutes, 33.0% 30 to 45 minutes, 16.5% 45 to 60 minutes, 5.4% 60 minutes or more (2000)

CREDIT RIVER (township). Covers a land area of 23.446 square miles and a water area of 0.408 square miles. Located at 44.69° N. Lat.; 93.35° W. Long. Elevation is 990 feet.

Population: 3,895 (2000); Race: 97.4% White, 0.0% Black, 1.2% Asian, 0.0% American Indian and Alaska Native, 0.3% Hispanic of any race, 1.4% two or more races (2000); Density: 166.1 persons per square mile (2000); Age: 31.2% under 18, 4.8% over 64 (2000); Marriage status: 18.7% never married, 75.0% now married, 1.2% widowed, 5.1% divorced (2000); Foreign born: 4.7% (2000); Ancestry (includes multiple ancestries): 51.7% German, 14.3% Irish, 11.1% Norwegian, 7.5% Swedish, 7.2% English (2000).

Economy: Employment by occupation: 16.7% management, 20.7% professional, 7.5% services, 31.4% sales, 0.4% farming, 12.0% construction, 11.3% production (2000).

Income: Per capita income: $29,567 (2000); Median household income: $78,501 (2000); Poverty rate: 3.1% (2000).

Taxes: Total city taxes per capita: $57 (2000); City property taxes per capita: $56 (2000).

Education: High school graduation rate: 92.2% (2000); College graduation rate: 30.7% (2000).

Housing: Homeownership rate: 96.0% (2000); Median home value: $171,500 (2000); Median rent: $753 per month (2000); Median age of housing: 21 years (2000).
Transportation: Commute to work: 91.8% car, 0.9% public transportation, 0.3% walk, 7.0% work from home (2000); Travel time to work: 17.2% less than 15 minutes, 47.0% 15 to 30 minutes, 30.6% 30 to 45 minutes, 3.3% 45 to 60 minutes, 2.0% 60 minutes or more (2000)

ELKO (city). Covers a land area of 1.361 square miles and a water area of 0 square miles. Located at 44.56° N. Lat.; 93.32° W. Long. Elevation is 1,132 feet.
Population: 472 (2000); Race: 98.6% White, 0.0% Black, 0.0% Asian, 0.0% American Indian and Alaska Native, 0.6% Hispanic of any race, 1.4% two or more races (2000); Density: 346.8 persons per square mile (2000); Age: 36.6% under 18, 3.0% over 64 (2000); Marriage status: 15.5% never married, 75.5% now married, 2.1% widowed, 7.0% divorced (2000); Foreign born: 0.4% (2000); Ancestry (includes multiple ancestries): 41.4% German, 21.2% Norwegian, 15.8% Irish, 6.9% Swedish, 5.9% Dutch (2000).
Economy: Poultry; grain; dairying; light manufacturing. Race track here. Employment by occupation: 14.1% management, 16.6% professional, 12.6% services, 27.1% sales, 0.0% farming, 10.8% construction, 18.8% production (2000).
Income: Per capita income: $21,827 (2000); Median household income: $67,625 (2000); Poverty rate: 1.2% (2000).
Taxes: Total city taxes per capita: $243 (1997); City property taxes per capita: $208 (1997).
Education: High school graduation rate: 91.9% (2000); College graduation rate: 21.4% (2000).
Housing: Homeownership rate: 98.8% (2000); Median home value: $159,100 (2000); Median rent: $325 per month (2000); Median age of housing: 12 years (2000).
Transportation: Commute to work: 95.6% car, 0.0% public transportation, 0.7% walk, 3.7% work from home (2000); Travel time to work: 14.9% less than 15 minutes, 37.2% 15 to 30 minutes, 31.8% 30 to 45 minutes, 14.6% 45 to 60 minutes, 1.5% 60 minutes or more (2000)

HELENA (township). Covers a land area of 33.494 square miles and a water area of 1.235 square miles. Located at 44.58° N. Lat.; 93.58° W. Long.
Population: 1,440 (2000); Race: 98.9% White, 0.0% Black, 0.7% Asian, 0.0% American Indian and Alaska Native, 1.7% Hispanic of any race, 0.1% two or more races (2000); Density: 43.0 persons per square mile (2000); Age: 35.5% under 18, 8.7% over 64 (2000); Marriage status: 20.3% never married, 71.3% now married, 3.0% widowed, 5.4% divorced (2000); Foreign born: 1.1% (2000); Ancestry (includes multiple ancestries): 53.3% German, 17.8% Czech, 10.9% Norwegian, 8.6% Swedish, 7.5% Irish (2000).
Economy: Employment by occupation: 13.2% management, 20.3% professional, 12.9% services, 24.2% sales, 1.3% farming, 14.1% construction, 14.0% production (2000).
Income: Per capita income: $23,059 (2000); Median household income: $64,250 (2000); Poverty rate: 3.8% (2000).
Taxes: Total city taxes per capita: $119 (2000); City property taxes per capita: $118 (2000).
Education: High school graduation rate: 91.5% (2000); College graduation rate: 23.2% (2000).
Housing: Homeownership rate: 97.8% (2000); Median home value: $172,200 (2000); Median rent: $488 per month (2000); Median age of housing: 27 years (2000).
Transportation: Commute to work: 89.6% car, 0.4% public transportation, 3.3% walk, 6.5% work from home (2000); Travel time to work: 30.6% less than 15 minutes, 24.1% 15 to 30 minutes, 28.2% 30 to 45 minutes, 11.5% 45 to 60 minutes, 5.6% 60 minutes or more (2000)

JACKSON (township). Covers a land area of 6.972 square miles and a water area of 0.192 square miles. Located at 44.77° N. Lat.; 93.55° W. Long.
Population: 1,361 (2000); Race: 79.7% White, 0.0% Black, 1.8% Asian, 1.1% American Indian and Alaska Native, 25.7% Hispanic of any race, 2.7% two or more races (2000); Density: 195.2 persons per square mile (2000); Age: 30.0% under 18, 5.9% over 64 (2000); Marriage status: 25.5% never married, 62.5% now married, 2.5% widowed, 9.4% divorced (2000); Foreign born: 19.7% (2000); Ancestry (includes multiple ancestries): 38.9% German, 27.2% Other groups, 13.7% Irish, 8.0% Norwegian, 5.2% United States or American (2000).
Economy: Employment by occupation: 8.5% management, 10.3% professional, 16.0% services, 27.6% sales, 0.0% farming, 12.0% construction, 25.7% production (2000).
Income: Per capita income: $22,802 (2000); Median household income: $50,263 (2000); Poverty rate: 12.0% (2000).
Taxes: Total city taxes per capita: $178 (2000); City property taxes per capita: $177 (2000).
Education: High school graduation rate: 75.5% (2000); College graduation rate: 13.8% (2000).
Housing: Homeownership rate: 89.2% (2000); Median home value: $210,000 (2000); Median rent: $706 per month (2000); Median age of housing: 16 years (2000).
Transportation: Commute to work: 95.7% car, 1.2% public transportation, 0.1% walk, 2.6% work from home (2000); Travel time to work: 28.4% less than 15 minutes, 46.5% 15 to 30 minutes, 15.3% 30 to 45 minutes, 6.4% 45 to 60 minutes, 3.4% 60 minutes or more (2000)

JORDAN (city). Covers a land area of 2.614 square miles and a water area of 0.023 square miles. Located at 44.66° N. Lat.; 93.63° W. Long. Elevation is 755 feet.
History: Jordan was named for the biblical river. Many of Jordan's early residents were of German descent. A canning factory was an early industry here.
Population: 3,833 (2000); Race: 94.1% White, 0.0% Black, 0.1% Asian, 0.4% American Indian and Alaska Native, 7.3% Hispanic of any race, 0.3% two or more races (2000); Density: 1,466.5 persons per square mile (2000); Age: 33.7% under 18, 6.3% over 64 (2000); Marriage status: 29.3% never married, 54.6% now married, 4.7% widowed, 11.4% divorced (2000); Foreign born: 5.6% (2000); Ancestry (includes multiple ancestries): 47.9% German, 15.0% Norwegian, 12.8% Irish, 8.0% Swedish, 6.6% Other groups (2000).
Economy: Single-family building permits issued: 80 (2001) / 108 (2000); Multi-family building permits issued: 6 (2001) / 0 (2000); Employment by occupation: 12.3% management, 14.7% professional, 15.0% services, 27.5% sales, 0.7% farming, 11.8% construction, 18.0% production (2000).
Income: Per capita income: $17,217 (2000); Median household income: $47,468 (2000); Poverty rate: 4.1% (2000).
Taxes: Total city taxes per capita: $299 (1997); City property taxes per capita: $275 (1997).
Education: High school graduation rate: 88.8% (2000); College graduation rate: 16.4% (2000).

School District(s)

Jordan (PK-12)
2000 Enrollment: 1,336 952-492-6200
Minnesota River Valley Special Education Coop (PK-12)
2000 Enrollment: 372 952-492-3030

Housing: Homeownership rate: 82.3% (2000); Median home value: $126,800 (2000); Median rent: $530 per month (2000); Median age of housing: 23 years (2000).
Safety: Violent crime rate: 33.6 per 10,000 population; Property crime rate: 402.7 per 10,000 population (2001).
Newspapers: Jordan Independent (1 x week)
Transportation: Commute to work: 92.2% car, 0.1% public transportation, 3.9% walk, 3.2% work from home (2000); Travel time to work: 19.7% less than 15 minutes, 39.7% 15 to 30 minutes, 24.1% 30 to 45 minutes, 13.0% 45 to 60 minutes, 3.5% 60 minutes or more (2000)
Additional Information Contacts
Jordan Chamber of Commerce. 952-492-2355

LOUISVILLE (township). Covers a land area of 13.892 square miles and a water area of 0.655 square miles. Located at 44.74° N. Lat.; 93.57° W. Long.
Population: 1,359 (2000); Race: 91.7% White, 0.5% Black, 0.6% Asian, 0.0% American Indian and Alaska Native, 10.4% Hispanic of any race, 0.6% two or more races (2000); Density: 97.8 persons per square mile (2000); Age: 30.7% under 18, 4.9% over 64 (2000); Marriage status: 23.4% never married, 70.3% now married, 1.8% widowed, 4.4% divorced (2000); Foreign born: 8.4% (2000); Ancestry (includes multiple ancestries): 47.3% German, 13.2% Norwegian, 10.9% Irish, 9.7% Other groups, 9.1% Swedish (2000).
Economy: Employment by occupation: 20.1% management, 17.3% professional, 9.8% services, 21.3% sales, 0.6% farming, 14.9% construction, 16.1% production (2000).
Income: Per capita income: $27,069 (2000); Median household income: $79,242 (2000); Poverty rate: 4.3% (2000).
Taxes: Total city taxes per capita: $63 (1997); City property taxes per capita: $61 (1997).
Education: High school graduation rate: 85.6% (2000); College graduation rate: 23.2% (2000).

Housing: Homeownership rate: 91.4% (2000); Median home value: $180,700 (2000); Median rent: $617 per month (2000); Median age of housing: 22 years (2000).
Transportation: Commute to work: 92.5% car, 0.0% public transportation, 0.8% walk, 5.3% work from home (2000); Travel time to work: 30.3% less than 15 minutes, 38.4% 15 to 30 minutes, 22.7% 30 to 45 minutes, 6.6% 45 to 60 minutes, 1.9% 60 minutes or more (2000)

NEW MARKET (city). Covers a land area of 0.630 square miles and a water area of 0 square miles. Located at 44.57° N. Lat.; 93.35° W. Long.
Population: 332 (2000); Race: 100.0% White, 0.0% Black, 0.0% Asian, 0.0% American Indian and Alaska Native, 0.0% Hispanic of any race, 0.0% two or more races (2000); Density: 527.3 persons per square mile (2000); Age: 20.4% under 18, 6.0% over 64 (2000); Marriage status: 25.8% never married, 55.6% now married, 6.5% widowed, 12.1% divorced (2000); Foreign born: 0.0% (2000); Ancestry (includes multiple ancestries): 48.8% German, 22.4% Norwegian, 7.4% Irish, 7.0% Swedish, 6.4% Czech (2000).
Economy: Employment by occupation: 3.5% management, 8.5% professional, 17.0% services, 31.5% sales, 2.0% farming, 17.0% construction, 20.5% production (2000).
Income: Per capita income: $24,302 (2000); Median household income: $53,250 (2000); Poverty rate: 2.7% (2000).
Taxes: Total city taxes per capita: $293 (1997); City property taxes per capita: $276 (1997).
Education: High school graduation rate: 82.5% (2000); College graduation rate: 12.1% (2000).
Housing: Homeownership rate: 94.1% (2000); Median home value: $122,000 (2000); Median rent: $675 per month (2000); Median age of housing: 26 years (2000).
Transportation: Commute to work: 94.4% car, 0.0% public transportation, 3.0% walk, 2.5% work from home (2000); Travel time to work: 14.5% less than 15 minutes, 47.2% 15 to 30 minutes, 25.9% 30 to 45 minutes, 6.7% 45 to 60 minutes, 5.7% 60 minutes or more (2000)

NEW MARKET (township). Covers a land area of 33.767 square miles and a water area of 0.067 square miles. Located at 44.58° N. Lat.; 93.32° W. Long.
Population: 3,057 (2000); Race: 98.5% White, 0.1% Black, 0.0% Asian, 0.4% American Indian and Alaska Native, 0.6% Hispanic of any race, 0.7% two or more races (2000); Density: 90.5 persons per square mile (2000); Age: 32.9% under 18, 4.0% over 64 (2000); Marriage status: 20.9% never married, 71.7% now married, 2.3% widowed, 5.2% divorced (2000); Foreign born: 1.1% (2000); Ancestry (includes multiple ancestries): 40.9% German, 18.8% Norwegian, 14.0% Irish, 9.6% Swedish, 7.2% English (2000).
Economy: Grain; livestock; dairying. Employment by occupation: 18.3% management, 19.9% professional, 9.9% services, 25.4% sales, 0.4% farming, 13.7% construction, 12.4% production (2000).
Income: Per capita income: $31,176 (2000); Median household income: $82,718 (2000); Poverty rate: 2.3% (2000).
Taxes: Total city taxes per capita: $91 (2000); City property taxes per capita: $90 (2000).
Education: High school graduation rate: 92.8% (2000); College graduation rate: 27.5% (2000).
Housing: Homeownership rate: 95.0% (2000); Median home value: $229,200 (2000); Median rent: $409 per month (2000); Median age of housing: 19 years (2000).
Transportation: Commute to work: 89.3% car, 0.3% public transportation, 0.4% walk, 10.0% work from home (2000); Travel time to work: 15.7% less than 15 minutes, 36.9% 15 to 30 minutes, 33.4% 30 to 45 minutes, 8.8% 45 to 60 minutes, 5.2% 60 minutes or more (2000)

NEW PRAGUE (city). Covers a land area of 2.633 square miles and a water area of 0 square miles. Located at 44.54° N. Lat.; 93.57° W. Long.
History: New Prague was founded by a group of Bohemians who had been directed to follow the Mississippi River, but followed the Minnesota River instead. Dairy farming became the principal industry of the area.
Population: 4,559 (2000); Race: 98.8% White, 0.0% Black, 0.1% Asian, 0.1% American Indian and Alaska Native, 0.8% Hispanic of any race, 1.0% two or more races (2000); Density: 1,731.3 persons per square mile (2000); Age: 30.3% under 18, 16.7% over 64 (2000); Marriage status: 23.4% never married, 58.5% now married, 9.8% widowed, 8.3% divorced (2000); Foreign born: 0.4% (2000); Ancestry (includes multiple ancestries): 41.7% German, 24.1% Czech, 14.2% Irish, 11.5% Norwegian, 5.0% Czechoslovakian (2000).
Economy: Single-family building permits issued: 68 (2001) / 40 (2000); Multi-family building permits issued: 73 (2001) / 12 (2000); Employment by occupation: 11.3% management, 17.4% professional, 18.0% services, 26.0% sales, 0.3% farming, 11.5% construction, 15.4% production (2000).
Income: Per capita income: $17,732 (2000); Median household income: $41,750 (2000); Poverty rate: 6.5% (2000).
Taxes: Total city taxes per capita: $273 (1997); City property taxes per capita: $241 (1997).
Education: High school graduation rate: 83.8% (2000); College graduation rate: 20.9% (2000).

School District(s)

New Prague (PK-12)
2000 Enrollment: 2,512 952-758-1700
Housing: Homeownership rate: 75.6% (2000); Median home value: $120,300 (2000); Median rent: $472 per month (2000); Median age of housing: 33 years (2000).
Hospitals: Queen of Peace Hospital (56 beds)
Newspapers: The New Prague Times (1 x week)
Transportation: Commute to work: 89.4% car, 0.4% public transportation, 4.7% walk, 4.3% work from home (2000); Travel time to work: 42.6% less than 15 minutes, 12.4% 15 to 30 minutes, 27.8% 30 to 45 minutes, 13.8% 45 to 60 minutes, 3.4% 60 minutes or more (2000)
Additional Information Contacts
New Prague Chamber of Commerce 952-758-4360

PRIOR LAKE (city). Covers a land area of 13.507 square miles and a water area of 2.532 square miles. Located at 44.72° N. Lat.; 93.43° W. Long. Elevation is 950 feet.
Population: 15,917 (2000); Race: 95.1% White, 0.9% Black, 0.6% Asian, 2.2% American Indian and Alaska Native, 0.9% Hispanic of any race, 0.8% two or more races (2000); Density: 1,178.4 persons per square mile (2000); Age: 30.8% under 18, 4.0% over 64 (2000); Marriage status: 22.6% never married, 66.2% now married, 2.3% widowed, 8.8% divorced (2000); Foreign born: 1.8% (2000); Ancestry (includes multiple ancestries): 40.4% German, 17.6% Norwegian, 15.6% Irish, 10.1% Swedish, 6.8% Other groups (2000).
Vital Statistics: Birth rate: 186.0 per 10,000 population (1998)
Economy: Grain, soybeans; poultry, livestock; dairying. Manufacturing: sand and gravel processing, machining, diverse light manufacturing. Single-family building permits issued: 331 (2001) / 251 (2000); Multi-family building permits issued: 43 (2001) / 24 (2000); Employment by occupation: 20.3% management, 17.5% professional, 12.1% services, 29.3% sales, 0.1% farming, 10.0% construction, 10.7% production (2000).
Income: Per capita income: $32,089 (2000); Median household income: $75,363 (2000); Poverty rate: 3.6% (2000).
Taxes: Total city taxes per capita: $311 (1997); City property taxes per capita: $255 (1997).
Education: High school graduation rate: 93.7% (2000); College graduation rate: 32.8% (2000).

School District(s)

Prior Lake (PK-12)
2000 Enrollment: 4,662 952-447-2185
Housing: Homeownership rate: 87.6% (2000); Median home value: $175,100 (2000); Median rent: $640 per month (2000); Median age of housing: 16 years (2000).
Safety: Violent crime rate: 26.1 per 10,000 population; Property crime rate: 341.2 per 10,000 population (2001).
Newspapers: American (1 x week); Savage Pacer (1 x week)
Transportation: Commute to work: 93.0% car, 1.3% public transportation, 0.5% walk, 4.9% work from home (2000); Travel time to work: 25.4% less than 15 minutes, 36.5% 15 to 30 minutes, 28.0% 30 to 45 minutes, 7.2% 45 to 60 minutes, 2.9% 60 minutes or more (2000)
Additional Information Contacts
Prior Lake Chamber of Commerce 952-440-1000

SAINT LAWRENCE (township). Covers a land area of 14.423 square miles and a water area of 0.469 square miles. Located at 44.65° N. Lat.; 93.69° W. Long.
Population: 472 (2000); Race: 94.3% White, 0.0% Black, 0.0% Asian, 2.3% American Indian and Alaska Native, 3.4% Hispanic of any race, 0.0% two or more races (2000); Density: 32.7 persons per square mile (2000); Age: 31.1% under 18, 3.2% over 64 (2000); Marriage status: 22.8% never married, 67.7% now married, 0.8% widowed, 8.7% divorced (2000); Foreign born: 0.4% (2000); Ancestry (includes multiple ancestries): 60.9% German, 15.1% Irish, 13.5% Swedish, 10.5% Norwegian, 9.2% Polish (2000).
Economy: Employment by occupation: 19.1% management, 11.7% professional, 11.4% services, 19.7% sales, 0.0% farming, 20.1% construction, 18.1% production (2000).

Income: Per capita income: $23,825 (2000); Median household income: $66,750 (2000); Poverty rate: 0.8% (2000).
Education: High school graduation rate: 85.5% (2000); College graduation rate: 17.8% (2000).
Housing: Homeownership rate: 89.8% (2000); Median home value: $140,600 (2000); Median rent: $442 per month (2000); Median age of housing: 23 years (2000).
Transportation: Commute to work: 93.5% car, 0.0% public transportation, 1.7% walk, 2.7% work from home (2000); Travel time to work: 26.9% less than 15 minutes, 33.2% 15 to 30 minutes, 21.9% 30 to 45 minutes, 12.7% 45 to 60 minutes, 5.3% 60 minutes or more (2000)

SAND CREEK (township). Covers a land area of 32.420 square miles and a water area of 0.456 square miles. Located at 44.67° N. Lat.; 93.58° W. Long.
Population: 1,551 (2000); Race: 97.6% White, 1.2% Black, 0.5% Asian, 0.1% American Indian and Alaska Native, 0.6% Hispanic of any race, 0.1% two or more races (2000); Density: 47.8 persons per square mile (2000); Age: 28.4% under 18, 11.4% over 64 (2000); Marriage status: 26.0% never married, 67.8% now married, 2.4% widowed, 3.8% divorced (2000); Foreign born: 1.0% (2000); Ancestry (includes multiple ancestries): 57.3% German, 13.2% Norwegian, 9.5% Irish, 6.8% Czech, 4.3% United States or American (2000).
Economy: Employment by occupation: 12.9% management, 16.5% professional, 11.8% services, 23.8% sales, 1.5% farming, 18.0% construction, 15.5% production (2000).
Income: Per capita income: $23,029 (2000); Median household income: $65,370 (2000); Poverty rate: 2.0% (2000).
Taxes: Total city taxes per capita: $52 (1997); City property taxes per capita: $52 (1997).
Education: High school graduation rate: 85.2% (2000); College graduation rate: 22.4% (2000).
Housing: Homeownership rate: 88.9% (2000); Median home value: $162,500 (2000); Median rent: $525 per month (2000); Median age of housing: 27 years (2000).
Transportation: Commute to work: 88.5% car, 0.0% public transportation, 2.4% walk, 8.8% work from home (2000); Travel time to work: 24.2% less than 15 minutes, 34.5% 15 to 30 minutes, 26.0% 30 to 45 minutes, 9.8% 45 to 60 minutes, 5.4% 60 minutes or more (2000)

SAVAGE (city). Covers a land area of 15.913 square miles and a water area of 0.605 square miles. Located at 44.75° N. Lat.; 93.35° W. Long. Elevation is 720 feet.
Population: 21,115 (2000); Race: 90.8% White, 1.2% Black, 5.2% Asian, 0.6% American Indian and Alaska Native, 1.8% Hispanic of any race, 1.5% two or more races (2000); Density: 1,326.9 persons per square mile (2000); Age: 35.5% under 18, 2.7% over 64 (2000); Marriage status: 17.8% never married, 73.6% now married, 1.7% widowed, 6.9% divorced (2000); Foreign born: 6.1% (2000); Ancestry (includes multiple ancestries): 40.9% German, 19.2% Norwegian, 15.2% Irish, 10.5% Swedish, 9.8% Other groups (2000).
Economy: Agriculture includes corn, oats, barley; livestock, poultry; dairying. Manufacturing: cans, bandsaws, stock products, asphalt, diversified light manufacturing. James W. Wilke Regional Park to Northwest. Single-family building permits issued: 329 (2001) / 506 (2000); Multi-family building permits issued: 0 (2001) / 134 (2000); Employment by occupation: 21.9% management, 22.6% professional, 9.5% services, 26.8% sales, 0.0% farming, 7.6% construction, 11.5% production (2000).
Income: Per capita income: $26,858 (2000); Median household income: $75,097 (2000); Poverty rate: 2.3% (2000).
Taxes: Total city taxes per capita: $279 (2000); City property taxes per capita: $230 (2000).
Education: High school graduation rate: 95.4% (2000); College graduation rate: 41.4% (2000).
Housing: Homeownership rate: 91.2% (2000); Median home value: $168,400 (2000); Median rent: $638 per month (2000); Median age of housing: 10 years (2000).
Safety: Violent crime rate: 10.3 per 10,000 population; Property crime rate: 250.2 per 10,000 population (2001).
Transportation: Commute to work: 93.5% car, 1.3% public transportation, 0.5% walk, 4.3% work from home (2000); Travel time to work: 20.4% less than 15 minutes, 41.9% 15 to 30 minutes, 27.9% 30 to 45 minutes, 7.1% 45 to 60 minutes, 2.6% 60 minutes or more (2000)
Additional Information Contacts
Savage Chamber of Commerce 952-894-8876

SHAKOPEE (city). Covers a land area of 27.003 square miles and a water area of 1.452 square miles. Located at 44.78° N. Lat.; 93.50° W. Long. Elevation is 751 feet.
History: Shakopee was founded in 1851, and named for the Dakota chief Shakpa ("Little Six") whose village was nearby. Many of the early residents were from Germany, perhaps because the gently sloping banks of the Minnesota River here reminded them of the Rhine River valley in their homeland.
Population: 20,568 (2000); Race: 91.6% White, 1.0% Black, 2.5% Asian, 1.0% American Indian and Alaska Native, 4.6% Hispanic of any race, 1.3% two or more races (2000); Density: 761.7 persons per square mile (2000); Age: 27.6% under 18, 7.2% over 64 (2000); Marriage status: 25.5% never married, 61.1% now married, 4.6% widowed, 8.7% divorced (2000); Foreign born: 5.2% (2000); Ancestry (includes multiple ancestries): 47.7% German, 13.5% Norwegian, 13.1% Irish, 10.3% Other groups, 7.1% Swedish (2000).
Vital Statistics: Birth rate: 178.4 per 10,000 population (1998)
Economy: Single-family building permits issued: 676 (2001) / 717 (2000); Multi-family building permits issued: 112 (2001) / 56 (2000); Employment by occupation: 15.7% management, 19.0% professional, 13.6% services, 27.3% sales, 0.2% farming, 8.9% construction, 15.3% production (2000).
Income: Per capita income: $25,128 (2000); Median household income: $59,137 (2000); Poverty rate: 3.5% (2000).
Taxes: Total city taxes per capita: $385 (2000); City property taxes per capita: $259 (2000).
Education: High school graduation rate: 89.4% (2000); College graduation rate: 25.8% (2000).

School District(s)

Shakopee (PK-12)
2000 Enrollment: 4,014 952-496-5005
Housing: Homeownership rate: 79.0% (2000); Median home value: $141,500 (2000); Median rent: $647 per month (2000); Median age of housing: 13 years (2000).
Hospitals: Saint Francis Regional Medical Center (70 beds)
Safety: Violent crime rate: 19.2 per 10,000 population; Property crime rate: 336.7 per 10,000 population (2001).
Newspapers: Shakopee Valley News (1 x week); Mint Shopper (1 x week)
Transportation: Commute to work: 94.8% car, 0.9% public transportation, 1.3% walk, 2.3% work from home (2000); Travel time to work: 32.6% less than 15 minutes, 40.0% 15 to 30 minutes, 18.6% 30 to 45 minutes, 5.9% 45 to 60 minutes, 2.9% 60 minutes or more (2000)

SPRING LAKE (township). Covers a land area of 30.293 square miles and a water area of 1.760 square miles. Located at 44.66° N. Lat.; 93.46° W. Long.
Population: 3,681 (2000); Race: 98.1% White, 0.8% Black, 0.5% Asian, 0.1% American Indian and Alaska Native, 0.4% Hispanic of any race, 0.4% two or more races (2000); Density: 121.5 persons per square mile (2000); Age: 28.4% under 18, 7.0% over 64 (2000); Marriage status: 23.6% never married, 68.7% now married, 2.8% widowed, 4.9% divorced (2000); Foreign born: 1.7% (2000); Ancestry (includes multiple ancestries): 48.3% German, 16.0% Irish, 14.2% Norwegian, 7.8% Swedish, 6.2% English (2000).
Economy: Employment by occupation: 18.2% management, 17.3% professional, 13.2% services, 24.2% sales, 0.0% farming, 14.8% construction, 12.3% production (2000).
Income: Per capita income: $29,562 (2000); Median household income: $80,141 (2000); Poverty rate: 1.5% (2000).
Taxes: Total city taxes per capita: $91 (2000); City property taxes per capita: $82 (2000).
Education: High school graduation rate: 94.2% (2000); College graduation rate: 27.8% (2000).
Housing: Homeownership rate: 98.2% (2000); Median home value: $201,600 (2000); Median rent: $633 per month (2000); Median age of housing: 24 years (2000).
Transportation: Commute to work: 90.8% car, 0.9% public transportation, 0.9% walk, 6.9% work from home (2000); Travel time to work: 19.5% less than 15 minutes, 35.6% 15 to 30 minutes, 29.1% 30 to 45 minutes, 11.3% 45 to 60 minutes, 4.5% 60 minutes or more (2000)

Sherburne County

Located in central Minnesota; bounded on the west and south by the Mississippi River; drained by the Elk River. Covers a land area of 436.30 square miles, a water area of 14.70 square miles, and is located in the Central Time Zone. The county government was organized in 1856. County seat is Elk River.

Sherburne County is part of the Minneapolis-St. Paul, MN-WI MSA. The entire metro area includes: Anoka County, MN; Carver County, MN; Chisago County, MN; Dakota County, MN; Hennepin County, MN; Isanti County, MN; Ramsey County, MN; Scott County, MN; Sherburne County, MN; Washington County, MN; Wright County, MN; Pierce County, WI; St. Croix County, WI

Weather Station: Saint Cloud Municipal Airport — Elevation: 1,026 feet

	Jan	Feb	Mar	Apr	May	Jun	Jul	Aug	Sep	Oct	Nov	Dec
High	19	26	38	55	69	78	82	79	70	57	38	24
Low	-2	6	18	32	44	53	58	56	46	34	20	6
Precip	0.8	0.6	1.5	2.2	3.0	4.5	3.3	4.0	3.0	2.4	1.5	0.7
Snow	10.2	7.0	8.4	2.8	0.1	0.0	0.0	0.0	tr	0.6	9.1	8.4

High and Low temperatures in degrees Fahrenheit; Precipitation and Snow in inches

Weather Station: Santiago 3 E — Elevation: 1,017 feet

	Jan	Feb	Mar	Apr	May	Jun	Jul	Aug	Sep	Oct	Nov	Dec
High	21	29	40	58	72	80	84	81	72	59	39	26
Low	-1	6	19	32	44	53	57	55	46	34	21	6
Precip	1.1	0.8	1.7	2.5	3.3	4.5	4.2	4.6	2.9	2.7	1.8	0.9
Snow	12.5	7.1	8.7	2.3	tr	0.0	0.0	0.0	tr	0.1	8.1	8.5

High and Low temperatures in degrees Fahrenheit; Precipitation and Snow in inches

Population: 64,417 (2000); Race: 96.9% White, 0.7% Black, 0.6% Asian, 0.4% American Indian and Alaska Native, 1.4% Hispanic of any race, 0.9% two or more races (2000); Density: 147.6 persons per square mile (2000); Age: 30.9% under 18, 7.1% over 64 (2000).
Religion: Five largest groups: 18.6% Catholic Church, 12.2% Evangelical Lutheran Church in America, 3.1% Lutheran Church—Missouri Synod, 1.6% The Evangelical Free Church of America, 1.1% The United Methodist Church (2000).
Economy: Unemployment rate: 4.4% (11/2002); Total civilian labor force: 36,471 (11/2002); Leading industries: 23.0% manufacturing; 18.1% retail trade; 12.0% health care and social assistance (2000); Companies that employ more than 1,000 persons: 0 (2000); Companies that employ more than 100 persons: 19 (2000); Farms: 512 totaling 105,042 acres (1997); Minority business ownership rate: 2.8% (1997); Women business ownership rate: 32.5% (1997); Retail sales per capita: $8,672 (1997). Single-family building permits issued: 1,027 (2001) / 1,108 (2000); Multi-family building permits issued: 102 (2001) / 179 (2000).
Income: Per capita income: $21,322 (2000); Median household income: $57,014 (2000); Poverty rate: 4.4% (2000); Bankruptcy rate: 4.43% (2001).
Taxes: Total county taxes per capita: $258 (1997); County property taxes per capita: $252 (1997).
Education: High school graduation rate: 89.9% (2000); College graduation rate: 19.4% (2000).
Housing: Homeownership rate: 84.0% (2000); Median home value: $137,500 (2000); Median rent: $540 per month (2000); Median age of housing: 15 years (2000).
Health: Birth rate: 153.8 per 10,000 population (1998); Age adjusted death rate: 99.0 per 10,000 population (1999); Age adjusted cancer mortality rate: 218.4 deaths per 100,000 population (1999). Number of physicians: 5.0 per 10,000 population (1999); Number of hospital beds: n/a (1999).
Elections: 2000 Presidential election results: 39.3% Gore, 54.5% Bush, 4.9% Nader, 0.9% Buchanan
National and State Parks: Sherburne National Wildlife Refuge
Additional Information Contacts
Sherburne County Government Offices 763-241-2700
Becker Chamber of Commerce 763-261-2420
Big Lake Chamber of Commerce 763-263-7800
Elk River Chamber of Commerce 763-441-3110
Zimmerman Chamber of Commerce 763-856-4404
Zimmerman Greater Chamber of Commerce 763-856-4404

Sherburne County Communities

BALDWIN (township). Covers a land area of 33.615 square miles and a water area of 1.242 square miles. Located at 45.51° N. Lat.; 93.58° W. Long.
Population: 4,672 (2000); Race: 98.2% White, 0.1% Black, 0.1% Asian, 0.0% American Indian and Alaska Native, 1.4% Hispanic of any race, 1.1% two or more races (2000); Density: 139.0 persons per square mile (2000); Age: 31.1% under 18, 3.5% over 64 (2000); Marriage status: 21.0% never married, 68.3% now married, 2.3% widowed, 8.4% divorced (2000); Foreign born: 0.6% (2000); Ancestry (includes multiple ancestries): 49.4% German, 19.6% Norwegian, 10.2% Irish, 9.4% Swedish, 5.9% English (2000).
Economy: Employment by occupation: 13.1% management, 13.1% professional, 11.3% services, 24.8% sales, 0.3% farming, 13.4% construction, 24.0% production (2000).
Income: Per capita income: $20,798 (2000); Median household income: $60,607 (2000); Poverty rate: 2.4% (2000).
Taxes: Total city taxes per capita: $36 (2000); City property taxes per capita: $36 (2000).
Education: High school graduation rate: 93.5% (2000); College graduation rate: 12.3% (2000).
Housing: Homeownership rate: 97.5% (2000); Median home value: $136,900 (2000); Median rent: $511 per month (2000); Median age of housing: 19 years (2000).
Transportation: Commute to work: 94.0% car, 0.0% public transportation, 0.3% walk, 4.7% work from home (2000); Travel time to work: 24.8% less than 15 minutes, 16.8% 15 to 30 minutes, 20.3% 30 to 45 minutes, 17.4% 45 to 60 minutes, 20.8% 60 minutes or more (2000)

BECKER (city). Covers a land area of 8.662 square miles and a water area of 0.429 square miles. Located at 45.39° N. Lat.; 93.87° W. Long. Elevation is 973 feet.
Population: 2,673 (2000); Race: 98.1% White, 0.0% Black, 0.3% Asian, 0.9% American Indian and Alaska Native, 1.7% Hispanic of any race, 0.4% two or more races (2000); Density: 308.6 persons per square mile (2000); Age: 34.2% under 18, 6.4% over 64 (2000); Marriage status: 24.8% never married, 62.3% now married, 2.5% widowed, 10.4% divorced (2000); Foreign born: 0.1% (2000); Ancestry (includes multiple ancestries): 49.1% German, 15.9% Norwegian, 12.6% Irish, 9.8% Swedish, 7.6% Polish (2000).
Economy: Single-family building permits issued: 82 (2001) / 66 (2000); Multi-family building permits issued: 0 (2001) / 0 (2000); Employment by occupation: 11.3% management, 17.9% professional, 14.6% services, 23.2% sales, 1.1% farming, 13.4% construction, 18.5% production (2000).
Income: Per capita income: $19,333 (2000); Median household income: $50,714 (2000); Poverty rate: 4.1% (2000).
Taxes: Total city taxes per capita: $2,105 (2000); City property taxes per capita: $2,071 (2000).
Education: High school graduation rate: 94.5% (2000); College graduation rate: 21.8% (2000).

School District(s)

Becker (PK-12)
2000 Enrollment: 2,112 763-261-4502
Housing: Homeownership rate: 73.3% (2000); Median home value: $130,300 (2000); Median rent: $498 per month (2000); Median age of housing: 8 years (2000).
Safety: Violent crime rate: 0.0 per 10,000 population; Property crime rate: 59.2 per 10,000 population (2001).
Transportation: Commute to work: 94.2% car, 0.0% public transportation, 1.7% walk, 3.6% work from home (2000); Travel time to work: 33.5% less than 15 minutes, 28.6% 15 to 30 minutes, 15.7% 30 to 45 minutes, 13.7% 45 to 60 minutes, 8.5% 60 minutes or more (2000)
Additional Information Contacts
Becker Chamber of Commerce 763-261-2420

BECKER (township). Covers a land area of 55.485 square miles and a water area of 0.345 square miles. Located at 45.40° N. Lat.; 93.83° W. Long. Elevation is 973 feet.
Population: 3,605 (2000); Race: 98.3% White, 0.7% Black, 0.0% Asian, 0.0% American Indian and Alaska Native, 0.3% Hispanic of any race, 0.8% two or more races (2000); Density: 65.0 persons per square mile (2000); Age: 35.1% under 18, 3.3% over 64 (2000); Marriage status: 20.6% never married, 67.3% now married, 3.1% widowed, 9.0% divorced (2000); Foreign born: 0.1% (2000); Ancestry (includes multiple ancestries): 47.8% German, 16.7% Norwegian, 14.1% Swedish, 10.9% Irish, 7.5% Polish (2000).
Economy: Grain, alfalfa, soybeans, potatoes; hogs. Manufacturing: wood products, plastics. Employment by occupation: 12.8% management, 16.7% professional, 10.6% services, 23.7% sales, 0.5% farming, 14.6% construction, 21.1% production (2000).
Income: Per capita income: $23,015 (2000); Median household income: $65,089 (2000); Poverty rate: 2.7% (2000).
Taxes: Total city taxes per capita: $58 (2000); City property taxes per capita: $58 (2000).
Education: High school graduation rate: 94.9% (2000); College graduation rate: 14.1% (2000).
Housing: Homeownership rate: 95.9% (2000); Median home value: $144,700 (2000); Median rent: $528 per month (2000); Median age of housing: 10 years (2000).

Transportation: Commute to work: 94.5% car, 0.2% public transportation, 0.9% walk, 4.1% work from home (2000); Travel time to work: 25.2% less than 15 minutes, 24.2% 15 to 30 minutes, 20.7% 30 to 45 minutes, 15.7% 45 to 60 minutes, 14.3% 60 minutes or more (2000)

BIG LAKE (city). Covers a land area of 3.591 square miles and a water area of 0.791 square miles. Located at 45.34° N. Lat.; 93.75° W. Long. Elevation is 942 feet.

History: Big Lake was settled in 1848 as Humboldt, but its name was changed in 1867 when the railroad arrived. The town developed as a summer resort area.

Population: 6,063 (2000); Race: 98.2% White, 0.1% Black, 0.8% Asian, 0.4% American Indian and Alaska Native, 0.3% Hispanic of any race, 0.4% two or more races (2000); Density: 1,688.4 persons per square mile (2000); Age: 32.9% under 18, 4.6% over 64 (2000); Marriage status: 26.0% never married, 63.8% now married, 3.0% widowed, 7.3% divorced (2000); Foreign born: 0.9% (2000); Ancestry (includes multiple ancestries): 43.6% German, 19.6% Norwegian, 16.6% Swedish, 14.3% Irish, 8.2% Polish (2000).

Economy: Single-family building permits issued: 138 (2001) / 235 (2000); Multi-family building permits issued: 0 (2001) / 65 (2000); Employment by occupation: 10.6% management, 12.5% professional, 12.9% services, 25.9% sales, 0.0% farming, 13.8% construction, 24.2% production (2000).

Income: Per capita income: $18,931 (2000); Median household income: $50,658 (2000); Poverty rate: 4.7% (2000).

Taxes: Total city taxes per capita: $223 (1997); City property taxes per capita: $180 (1997).

Education: High school graduation rate: 88.2% (2000); College graduation rate: 13.5% (2000).

School District(s)

Big Lake (PK-12)
2000 Enrollment: 2,636 763-262-2536

Housing: Homeownership rate: 84.6% (2000); Median home value: $123,900 (2000); Median rent: $486 per month (2000); Median age of housing: 11 years (2000).

Safety: Violent crime rate: 16.3 per 10,000 population; Property crime rate: 270.9 per 10,000 population (2001).

Newspapers: West Sherburne Tribune (1 x week)

Transportation: Commute to work: 95.1% car, 0.4% public transportation, 1.4% walk, 3.0% work from home (2000); Travel time to work: 22.8% less than 15 minutes, 23.1% 15 to 30 minutes, 25.3% 30 to 45 minutes, 17.5% 45 to 60 minutes, 11.3% 60 minutes or more (2000)

Additional Information Contacts

Big Lake Chamber of Commerce. 763-263-7800

BIG LAKE (township). Covers a land area of 42.311 square miles and a water area of 1.514 square miles. Located at 45.34° N. Lat.; 93.71° W. Long. Elevation is 942 feet.

Population: 6,785 (2000); Race: 97.2% White, 0.0% Black, 1.7% Asian, 0.0% American Indian and Alaska Native, 1.5% Hispanic of any race, 0.4% two or more races (2000); Density: 160.4 persons per square mile (2000); Age: 33.7% under 18, 5.4% over 64 (2000); Marriage status: 21.6% never married, 70.0% now married, 3.0% widowed, 5.4% divorced (2000); Foreign born: 1.5% (2000); Ancestry (includes multiple ancestries): 42.6% German, 23.1% Norwegian, 13.4% Swedish, 10.5% Irish, 7.1% Polish (2000).

Economy: Grain, soybeans, potatoes, alfalfa; hogs. Manufacturing: computer parts, oil filters, rubber stamps, ice augers. Employment by occupation: 13.6% management, 15.9% professional, 11.2% services, 25.4% sales, 0.8% farming, 13.7% construction, 19.3% production (2000).

Income: Per capita income: $22,418 (2000); Median household income: $65,185 (2000); Poverty rate: 1.2% (2000).

Taxes: Total city taxes per capita: $79 (2000); City property taxes per capita: $79 (2000).

Education: High school graduation rate: 91.6% (2000); College graduation rate: 18.8% (2000).

Housing: Homeownership rate: 96.1% (2000); Median home value: $155,200 (2000); Median rent: $1,011 per month (2000); Median age of housing: 16 years (2000).

Transportation: Commute to work: 92.3% car, 0.2% public transportation, 0.6% walk, 6.7% work from home (2000); Travel time to work: 25.0% less than 15 minutes, 26.0% 15 to 30 minutes, 18.5% 30 to 45 minutes, 18.9% 45 to 60 minutes, 11.5% 60 minutes or more (2000)

BLUE HILL (township). Covers a land area of 35.733 square miles and a water area of 0.689 square miles. Located at 45.51° N. Lat.; 93.68° W. Long.

Population: 762 (2000); Race: 99.7% White, 0.0% Black, 0.0% Asian, 0.3% American Indian and Alaska Native, 0.0% Hispanic of any race, 0.0% two or more races (2000); Density: 21.3 persons per square mile (2000); Age: 34.0% under 18, 2.4% over 64 (2000); Marriage status: 21.6% never married, 67.3% now married, 1.1% widowed, 10.0% divorced (2000); Foreign born: 0.3% (2000); Ancestry (includes multiple ancestries): 45.8% German, 15.7% Norwegian, 15.2% Irish, 10.9% Swedish, 5.8% English (2000).

Economy: Employment by occupation: 9.1% management, 18.3% professional, 8.9% services, 24.0% sales, 1.0% farming, 16.1% construction, 22.6% production (2000).

Income: Per capita income: $19,609 (2000); Median household income: $57,321 (2000); Poverty rate: 3.7% (2000).

Taxes: Total city taxes per capita: $36 (1997); City property taxes per capita: $36 (1997).

Education: High school graduation rate: 87.3% (2000); College graduation rate: 14.0% (2000).

Housing: Homeownership rate: 95.7% (2000); Median home value: $127,200 (2000); Median rent: $425 per month (2000); Median age of housing: 21 years (2000).

Transportation: Commute to work: 96.1% car, 0.0% public transportation, 0.0% walk, 3.2% work from home (2000); Travel time to work: 13.8% less than 15 minutes, 23.6% 15 to 30 minutes, 23.6% 30 to 45 minutes, 16.1% 45 to 60 minutes, 22.9% 60 minutes or more (2000)

CLEAR LAKE (city). Covers a land area of 0.793 square miles and a water area of 0.013 square miles. Located at 45.44° N. Lat.; 93.99° W. Long. Elevation is 990 feet.

Population: 266 (2000); Race: 98.1% White, 0.0% Black, 0.0% Asian, 0.0% American Indian and Alaska Native, 0.4% Hispanic of any race, 1.9% two or more races (2000); Density: 335.4 persons per square mile (2000); Age: 33.5% under 18, 11.3% over 64 (2000); Marriage status: 24.7% never married, 54.2% now married, 8.9% widowed, 12.1% divorced (2000); Foreign born: 0.0% (2000); Ancestry (includes multiple ancestries): 56.8% German, 11.7% Swedish, 9.8% Polish, 7.5% Norwegian, 7.5% French (except Basque) (2000).

Economy: Single-family building permits issued: 4 (2001) / 2 (2000); Multi-family building permits issued: 0 (2001) / 0 (2000); Employment by occupation: 7.1% management, 12.1% professional, 15.0% services, 27.1% sales, 1.4% farming, 19.3% construction, 17.9% production (2000).

Income: Per capita income: $16,894 (2000); Median household income: $40,625 (2000); Poverty rate: 3.1% (2000).

Taxes: Total city taxes per capita: $97 (1997); City property taxes per capita: $88 (1997).

Education: High school graduation rate: 84.8% (2000); College graduation rate: 11.0% (2000).

Housing: Homeownership rate: 65.0% (2000); Median home value: $89,700 (2000); Median rent: $373 per month (2000); Median age of housing: 38 years (2000).

Transportation: Commute to work: 92.0% car, 0.0% public transportation, 5.8% walk, 0.7% work from home (2000); Travel time to work: 29.4% less than 15 minutes, 44.1% 15 to 30 minutes, 16.9% 30 to 45 minutes, 2.9% 45 to 60 minutes, 6.6% 60 minutes or more (2000)

CLEAR LAKE (township). Covers a land area of 33.655 square miles and a water area of 3.443 square miles. Located at 45.44° N. Lat.; 93.98° W. Long. Elevation is 990 feet.

Population: 1,630 (2000); Race: 98.5% White, 0.7% Black, 0.1% Asian, 0.0% American Indian and Alaska Native, 0.4% Hispanic of any race, 0.6% two or more races (2000); Density: 48.4 persons per square mile (2000); Age: 26.0% under 18, 9.4% over 64 (2000); Marriage status: 18.1% never married, 73.3% now married, 2.1% widowed, 6.5% divorced (2000); Foreign born: 1.4% (2000); Ancestry (includes multiple ancestries): 52.6% German, 11.3% Norwegian, 10.7% Irish, 9.4% English, 9.1% Swedish (2000).

Economy: Agricultural area: grains; livestock. Manufacturing: meat processing, tool and die, industrial valves. Employment by occupation: 19.5% management, 21.6% professional, 8.7% services, 25.3% sales, 1.4% farming, 9.8% construction, 13.7% production (2000).

Income: Per capita income: $29,599 (2000); Median household income: $63,229 (2000); Poverty rate: 0.5% (2000).

Taxes: Total city taxes per capita: $65 (1997); City property taxes per capita: $65 (1997).

Education: High school graduation rate: 94.5% (2000); College graduation rate: 31.0% (2000).

Housing: Homeownership rate: 93.4% (2000); Median home value: $156,900 (2000); Median rent: $475 per month (2000); Median age of housing: 27 years (2000).

Transportation: Commute to work: 95.5% car, 0.1% public transportation, 2.0% walk, 2.4% work from home (2000); Travel time to work: 14.9% less

than 15 minutes, 46.1% 15 to 30 minutes, 20.5% 30 to 45 minutes, 7.8% 45 to 60 minutes, 10.7% 60 minutes or more (2000)

ELK RIVER (city). Covers a land area of 42.659 square miles and a water area of 1.172 square miles. Located at 45.31° N. Lat.; 93.58° W. Long. Elevation is 900 feet.
History: Elk River began with a trading post built in 1848 by Pierre Bottineau, a French trader and guide. Both the village, which was first platted in 1865, and the river were named for the herds of elk that once roamed this area. Elk River was first a lumber town, settled by many people from Maine. Early in the 1900's, however, dairying became the mainstay of the economy.
Population: 16,447 (2000); Race: 97.2% White, 0.2% Black, 0.2% Asian, 0.2% American Indian and Alaska Native, 1.7% Hispanic of any race, 1.1% two or more races (2000); Density: 385.5 persons per square mile (2000); Age: 31.2% under 18, 7.9% over 64 (2000); Marriage status: 23.6% never married, 64.2% now married, 4.8% widowed, 7.4% divorced (2000); Foreign born: 1.6% (2000); Ancestry (includes multiple ancestries): 44.4% German, 17.2% Norwegian, 13.6% Irish, 10.7% Swedish, 6.5% French (except Basque) (2000).
Vital Statistics: Birth rate: 179.4 per 10,000 population (1998)
Economy: Single-family building permits issued: 178 (2001) / 230 (2000); Multi-family building permits issued: 78 (2001) / 82 (2000); Employment by occupation: 13.6% management, 20.5% professional, 12.9% services, 26.7% sales, 0.2% farming, 10.7% construction, 15.4% production (2000).
Income: Per capita income: $21,808 (2000); Median household income: $58,114 (2000); Poverty rate: 3.2% (2000).
Taxes: Total city taxes per capita: $278 (2000); City property taxes per capita: $243 (2000).
Education: High school graduation rate: 89.8% (2000); College graduation rate: 22.6% (2000).

School District(s)

Elk River (PK-12)
2000 Enrollment: 9,315 763-241-3400
Housing: Homeownership rate: 78.2% (2000); Median home value: $144,800 (2000); Median rent: $568 per month (2000); Median age of housing: 14 years (2000).
Safety: Violent crime rate: 15.0 per 10,000 population; Property crime rate: 407.8 per 10,000 population (2001).
Newspapers: Star Shopper (2 x week); Elk River Star News (1 x week)
Transportation: Commute to work: 93.7% car, 0.3% public transportation, 1.8% walk, 4.2% work from home (2000); Travel time to work: 30.2% less than 15 minutes, 22.9% 15 to 30 minutes, 25.0% 30 to 45 minutes, 14.7% 45 to 60 minutes, 7.2% 60 minutes or more (2000)
Additional Information Contacts
Elk River Chamber of Commerce 763-441-3110

HAVEN (township). Covers a land area of 33.471 square miles and a water area of 0.795 square miles. Located at 45.50° N. Lat.; 94.06° W. Long.
Population: 2,024 (2000); Race: 97.3% White, 0.7% Black, 0.5% Asian, 0.0% American Indian and Alaska Native, 0.8% Hispanic of any race, 1.2% two or more races (2000); Density: 60.5 persons per square mile (2000); Age: 30.2% under 18, 9.8% over 64 (2000); Marriage status: 19.3% never married, 73.2% now married, 2.8% widowed, 4.7% divorced (2000); Foreign born: 1.1% (2000); Ancestry (includes multiple ancestries): 55.9% German, 12.5% Norwegian, 11.5% Irish, 10.3% Polish, 9.7% Swedish (2000).
Economy: Employment by occupation: 13.4% management, 21.8% professional, 11.8% services, 26.1% sales, 0.5% farming, 10.2% construction, 16.1% production (2000).
Income: Per capita income: $23,065 (2000); Median household income: $63,906 (2000); Poverty rate: 2.8% (2000).
Taxes: Total city taxes per capita: $29 (1997); City property taxes per capita: $28 (1997).
Education: High school graduation rate: 92.2% (2000); College graduation rate: 28.8% (2000).
Housing: Homeownership rate: 95.5% (2000); Median home value: $131,800 (2000); Median rent: $725 per month (2000); Median age of housing: 22 years (2000).
Transportation: Commute to work: 91.5% car, 0.0% public transportation, 0.9% walk, 7.6% work from home (2000); Travel time to work: 26.5% less than 15 minutes, 50.9% 15 to 30 minutes, 11.6% 30 to 45 minutes, 2.2% 45 to 60 minutes, 8.8% 60 minutes or more (2000)

LIVONIA (township). Covers a land area of 31.843 square miles and a water area of 0.932 square miles. Located at 45.43° N. Lat.; 93.57° W. Long.
Population: 3,917 (2000); Race: 98.1% White, 0.0% Black, 0.2% Asian, 0.8% American Indian and Alaska Native, 1.1% Hispanic of any race, 0.6% two or more races (2000); Density: 123.0 persons per square mile (2000); Age: 35.1% under 18, 6.0% over 64 (2000); Marriage status: 22.5% never married, 69.6% now married, 1.6% widowed, 6.4% divorced (2000); Foreign born: 0.9% (2000); Ancestry (includes multiple ancestries): 46.7% German, 16.6% Norwegian, 12.2% Irish, 11.3% Swedish, 9.4% French (except Basque) (2000).
Economy: Employment by occupation: 10.7% management, 12.9% professional, 11.5% services, 23.3% sales, 1.5% farming, 17.9% construction, 22.3% production (2000).
Income: Per capita income: $22,902 (2000); Median household income: $63,381 (2000); Poverty rate: 1.8% (2000).
Taxes: Total city taxes per capita: $44 (1997); City property taxes per capita: $44 (1997).
Education: High school graduation rate: 89.6% (2000); College graduation rate: 17.8% (2000).
Housing: Homeownership rate: 97.7% (2000); Median home value: $154,500 (2000); Median rent: $663 per month (2000); Median age of housing: 14 years (2000).
Transportation: Commute to work: 94.4% car, 0.0% public transportation, 0.8% walk, 4.4% work from home (2000); Travel time to work: 13.6% less than 15 minutes, 25.2% 15 to 30 minutes, 24.4% 30 to 45 minutes, 23.5% 45 to 60 minutes, 13.3% 60 minutes or more (2000)

ORROCK (township). Covers a land area of 34.897 square miles and a water area of 1.352 square miles. Located at 45.41° N. Lat.; 93.69° W. Long. Elevation is 987 feet.
Population: 2,764 (2000); Race: 98.8% White, 0.0% Black, 0.0% Asian, 0.2% American Indian and Alaska Native, 1.1% Hispanic of any race, 0.0% two or more races (2000); Density: 79.2 persons per square mile (2000); Age: 31.8% under 18, 4.1% over 64 (2000); Marriage status: 19.4% never married, 70.2% now married, 2.0% widowed, 8.4% divorced (2000); Foreign born: 1.7% (2000); Ancestry (includes multiple ancestries): 41.5% German, 16.2% Norwegian, 15.8% Swedish, 13.6% Irish, 7.3% Polish (2000).
Economy: Employment by occupation: 8.7% management, 15.5% professional, 13.3% services, 25.4% sales, 0.1% farming, 17.7% construction, 19.3% production (2000).
Income: Per capita income: $22,540 (2000); Median household income: $60,168 (2000); Poverty rate: 4.5% (2000).
Taxes: Total city taxes per capita: $45 (1997); City property taxes per capita: $45 (1997).
Education: High school graduation rate: 89.3% (2000); College graduation rate: 12.1% (2000).
Housing: Homeownership rate: 95.4% (2000); Median home value: $140,600 (2000); Median rent: $719 per month (2000); Median age of housing: 13 years (2000).
Transportation: Commute to work: 93.4% car, 0.0% public transportation, 0.0% walk, 5.5% work from home (2000); Travel time to work: 10.2% less than 15 minutes, 33.3% 15 to 30 minutes, 16.3% 30 to 45 minutes, 22.0% 45 to 60 minutes, 18.2% 60 minutes or more (2000)

PALMER (township). Covers a land area of 34.917 square miles and a water area of 1.591 square miles. Located at 45.51° N. Lat.; 93.93° W. Long.
Population: 2,414 (2000); Race: 99.0% White, 0.0% Black, 0.4% Asian, 0.0% American Indian and Alaska Native, 0.5% Hispanic of any race, 0.2% two or more races (2000); Density: 69.1 persons per square mile (2000); Age: 29.4% under 18, 9.7% over 64 (2000); Marriage status: 22.0% never married, 69.3% now married, 3.3% widowed, 5.4% divorced (2000); Foreign born: 0.8% (2000); Ancestry (includes multiple ancestries): 53.3% German, 15.4% Polish, 14.8% Norwegian, 11.5% Swedish, 8.9% Irish (2000).
Economy: Employment by occupation: 11.1% management, 16.5% professional, 12.7% services, 24.7% sales, 1.5% farming, 13.0% construction, 20.6% production (2000).
Income: Per capita income: $22,254 (2000); Median household income: $61,125 (2000); Poverty rate: 2.5% (2000).
Taxes: Total city taxes per capita: $66 (1997); City property taxes per capita: $66 (1997).
Education: High school graduation rate: 90.0% (2000); College graduation rate: 18.2% (2000).
Housing: Homeownership rate: 94.8% (2000); Median home value: $140,900 (2000); Median rent: $510 per month (2000); Median age of housing: 24 years (2000).
Transportation: Commute to work: 94.9% car, 0.2% public transportation, 0.5% walk, 4.2% work from home (2000); Travel time to work: 9.3% less than 15 minutes, 43.7% 15 to 30 minutes, 22.4% 30 to 45 minutes, 9.3% 45 to 60 minutes, 15.3% 60 minutes or more (2000)

SANTIAGO (township). Covers a land area of 36.089 square miles and a water area of 0.226 square miles. Located at 45.52° N. Lat.; 93.82° W. Long. Elevation is 1,020 feet.
Population: 1,555 (2000); Race: 98.3% White, 0.4% Black, 0.0% Asian, 0.3% American Indian and Alaska Native, 0.3% Hispanic of any race, 1.0% two or more races (2000); Density: 43.1 persons per square mile (2000); Age: 35.5% under 18, 5.1% over 64 (2000); Marriage status: 26.6% never married, 64.9% now married, 2.3% widowed, 6.3% divorced (2000); Foreign born: 3.6% (2000); Ancestry (includes multiple ancestries): 48.8% German, 16.3% Norwegian, 11.8% Irish, 8.8% Polish, 7.4% Swedish (2000).
Economy: Employment by occupation: 11.8% management, 12.3% professional, 13.4% services, 20.8% sales, 1.1% farming, 13.0% construction, 27.7% production (2000).
Income: Per capita income: $19,029 (2000); Median household income: $58,688 (2000); Poverty rate: 8.5% (2000).
Taxes: Total city taxes per capita: $40 (1997); City property taxes per capita: $40 (1997).
Education: High school graduation rate: 86.5% (2000); College graduation rate: 12.4% (2000).
Housing: Homeownership rate: 97.5% (2000); Median home value: $133,600 (2000); Median rent: $350 per month (2000); Median age of housing: 8 years (2000).
Transportation: Commute to work: 94.6% car, 0.0% public transportation, 0.8% walk, 4.5% work from home (2000); Travel time to work: 10.1% less than 15 minutes, 33.0% 15 to 30 minutes, 21.6% 30 to 45 minutes, 15.1% 45 to 60 minutes, 20.2% 60 minutes or more (2000)

ZIMMERMAN (city). Aka Lake Fremont. Covers a land area of 2.779 square miles and a water area of 0.082 square miles. Located at 45.44° N. Lat.; 93.59° W. Long.
History: Also known as Lake Fremont.
Population: 2,851 (2000); Race: 98.5% White, 0.0% Black, 0.3% Asian, 0.2% American Indian and Alaska Native, 4.6% Hispanic of any race, 1.0% two or more races (2000); Density: 1,026.0 persons per square mile (2000); Age: 36.1% under 18, 4.4% over 64 (2000); Marriage status: 27.9% never married, 56.1% now married, 2.5% widowed, 13.6% divorced (2000); Foreign born: 4.4% (2000); Ancestry (includes multiple ancestries): 40.3% German, 14.3% Norwegian, 11.3% Irish, 9.8% Swedish, 6.9% Polish (2000).
Economy: Agriculture includes grain, soybeans, potatoes; hogs. Manufacturing: Christmas wreaths and trees; diverse light manufacturing. Sherburne National Wildlife Refuge to West. Single-family building permits issued: 65 (2001) / 45 (2000); Multi-family building permits issued: 24 (2001) / 32 (2000); Employment by occupation: 6.1% management, 12.9% professional, 17.0% services, 22.0% sales, 0.2% farming, 15.8% construction, 26.1% production (2000).
Income: Per capita income: $18,528 (2000); Median household income: $49,332 (2000); Poverty rate: 6.3% (2000).
Taxes: Total city taxes per capita: $251 (2000); City property taxes per capita: $217 (2000).
Education: High school graduation rate: 84.2% (2000); College graduation rate: 7.9% (2000).
Housing: Homeownership rate: 88.2% (2000); Median home value: $115,000 (2000); Median rent: $409 per month (2000); Median age of housing: 10 years (2000).
Transportation: Commute to work: 93.4% car, 0.7% public transportation, 1.3% walk, 3.7% work from home (2000); Travel time to work: 15.2% less than 15 minutes, 29.6% 15 to 30 minutes, 25.3% 30 to 45 minutes, 17.1% 45 to 60 minutes, 12.8% 60 minutes or more (2000)
Additional Information Contacts
Zimmerman Chamber of Commerce 763-856-4404
Zimmerman Greater Chamber of Commerce............... 763-856-4404

Sibley County

Located in southern Minnesota; bounded on the east by the Minnesota River; includes several lakes. Covers a land area of 588.60 square miles, a water area of 11.80 square miles, and is located in the Central Time Zone. The county government was organized in 1853. County seat is Gaylord.

Weather Station: Gaylord — Elevation: 1,017 feet

	Jan	Feb	Mar	Apr	May	Jun	Jul	Aug	Sep	Oct	Nov	Dec
High	21	28	40	57	72	81	84	81	73	60	40	27
Low	3	10	22	35	48	58	62	59	49	38	24	10
Precip	0.7	0.6	1.6	2.6	3.4	4.7	3.6	4.4	3.0	2.2	1.7	0.7
Snow	9.1	5.7	9.3	1.8	tr	0.0	0.0	0.0	0.0	0.3	5.4	8.3

High and Low temperatures in degrees Fahrenheit; Precipitation and Snow in inches

Population: 15,356 (2000); Race: 95.4% White, 0.2% Black, 0.3% Asian, 0.4% American Indian and Alaska Native, 5.3% Hispanic of any race, 0.7% two or more races (2000); Density: 26.1 persons per square mile (2000); Age: 27.6% under 18, 16.5% over 64 (2000).
Religion: Five largest groups: 20.1% Evangelical Lutheran Church in America, 16.3% Catholic Church, 16.1% Lutheran Church—Missouri Synod, 10.6% Wisconsin Evangelical Lutheran Synod, 5.0% United Church of Christ (2000).
Economy: Unemployment rate: 4.3% (11/2002); Total civilian labor force: 6,731 (11/2002); Leading industries: 29.9% manufacturing; 15.3% health care and social assistance; 13.7% retail trade (2000); Companies that employ more than 1,000 persons: 0 (2000); Companies that employ more than 100 persons: 4 (2000); Farms: 958 totaling 309,860 acres (1997); Minority business ownership rate: 0.0% (1997); Women business ownership rate: 15.8% (1997); Retail sales per capita: $4,313 (1997). Single-family building permits issued: 54 (2001) / 58 (2000); Multi-family building permits issued: 2 (2001) / 6 (2000).
Income: Per capita income: $18,004 (2000); Median household income: $41,458 (2000); Poverty rate: 8.1% (2000); Bankruptcy rate: 2.44% (2001).
Taxes: Total county taxes per capita: $294 (1997); County property taxes per capita: $288 (1997).
Education: High school graduation rate: 79.2% (2000); College graduation rate: 11.6% (2000).
Housing: Homeownership rate: 80.9% (2000); Median home value: $80,700 (2000); Median rent: $364 per month (2000); Median age of housing: 48 years (2000).
Health: Birth rate: 113.3 per 10,000 population (1998); Age adjusted death rate: 76.0 per 10,000 population (1999); Age adjusted cancer mortality rate: 220.7 deaths per 100,000 population (1999). Number of physicians: 15.0 per 10,000 population (1999); Number of hospital beds: 11.1 per 10,000 population (1999).
Elections: 2000 Presidential election results: 36.6% Gore, 55.7% Bush, 4.9% Nader, 2.1% Buchanan
National and State Parks: Alfsborg State Wildlife Management Area; Altnow Marsh State Wildlife Management Area; Faxon Marsh State Wildlife Management Area; Indian State Wildlife Management Area; Rush River State Wayside
Additional Information Contacts
Sibley County Government Offices.......................... 507-237-4070
Gaylord Chamber of Commerce 507-237-2508
Winthrop Area Chamber of Commerce.................. 507-647-2627

Sibley County Communities

ALFSBORG (township). Covers a land area of 35.046 square miles and a water area of 0.060 square miles. Located at 44.49° N. Lat.; 94.32° W. Long.
Population: 356 (2000); Race: 99.5% White, 0.0% Black, 0.5% Asian, 0.0% American Indian and Alaska Native, 0.0% Hispanic of any race, 0.0% two or more races (2000); Density: 10.2 persons per square mile (2000); Age: 28.2% under 18, 17.1% over 64 (2000); Marriage status: 18.0% never married, 74.2% now married, 2.1% widowed, 5.7% divorced (2000); Foreign born: 0.5% (2000); Ancestry (includes multiple ancestries): 58.5% German, 19.0% Swedish, 8.1% United States or American, 7.0% Irish, 6.0% Norwegian (2000).
Economy: Employment by occupation: 24.5% management, 13.3% professional, 4.3% services, 22.9% sales, 1.1% farming, 9.6% construction, 24.5% production (2000).
Income: Per capita income: $16,517 (2000); Median household income: $42,250 (2000); Poverty rate: 12.2% (2000).
Taxes: Total city taxes per capita: $113 (1997); City property taxes per capita: $113 (1997).
Education: High school graduation rate: 83.5% (2000); College graduation rate: 6.8% (2000).
Housing: Homeownership rate: 87.9% (2000); Median home value: $75,500 (2000); Median rent: $238 per month (2000); Median age of housing: 60+ years (2000).
Transportation: Commute to work: 80.7% car, 1.1% public transportation, 2.1% walk, 15.5% work from home (2000); Travel time to work: 44.3% less

than 15 minutes, 29.1% 15 to 30 minutes, 19.0% 30 to 45 minutes, 3.8% 45 to 60 minutes, 3.8% 60 minutes or more (2000)

ARLINGTON (city). Covers a land area of 1.468 square miles and a water area of 0 square miles. Located at 44.60° N. Lat.; 94.07° W. Long. Elevation is 995 feet.
Population: 2,048 (2000); Race: 95.4% White, 0.0% Black, 0.3% Asian, 0.0% American Indian and Alaska Native, 6.4% Hispanic of any race, 0.9% two or more races (2000); Density: 1,395.1 persons per square mile (2000); Age: 26.7% under 18, 19.1% over 64 (2000); Marriage status: 21.3% never married, 58.4% now married, 14.1% widowed, 6.2% divorced (2000); Foreign born: 3.1% (2000); Ancestry (includes multiple ancestries): 64.5% German, 8.9% Norwegian, 7.8% Other groups, 7.1% Swedish, 7.0% Irish (2000).
Economy: Single-family building permits issued: 9 (2001) / 13 (2000); Multi-family building permits issued: 2 (2001) / 0 (2000); Employment by occupation: 6.1% management, 16.9% professional, 15.0% services, 20.7% sales, 0.7% farming, 10.4% construction, 30.3% production (2000).
Income: Per capita income: $18,458 (2000); Median household income: $37,632 (2000); Poverty rate: 7.5% (2000).
Taxes: Total city taxes per capita: $210 (1997); City property taxes per capita: $208 (1997).
Education: High school graduation rate: 75.4% (2000); College graduation rate: 14.1% (2000).

School District(s)

Sibley East (PK-12)
2000 Enrollment: 1,336 507-964-2292
Housing: Homeownership rate: 70.4% (2000); Median home value: $79,600 (2000); Median rent: $355 per month (2000); Median age of housing: 42 years (2000).
Hospitals: Arlington Municipal Hospital (20 beds)
Newspapers: Arlington Enterprise (1 x week); The Shopper (1 x week)
Transportation: Commute to work: 89.9% car, 0.0% public transportation, 6.0% walk, 3.6% work from home (2000); Travel time to work: 44.0% less than 15 minutes, 21.2% 15 to 30 minutes, 16.9% 30 to 45 minutes, 9.3% 45 to 60 minutes, 8.6% 60 minutes or more (2000)

ARLINGTON (township). Covers a land area of 34.656 square miles and a water area of 0 square miles. Located at 44.58° N. Lat.; 94.07° W. Long. Elevation is 995 feet.
Population: 562 (2000); Race: 100.0% White, 0.0% Black, 0.0% Asian, 0.0% American Indian and Alaska Native, 0.0% Hispanic of any race, 0.0% two or more races (2000); Density: 16.2 persons per square mile (2000); Age: 26.2% under 18, 14.5% over 64 (2000); Marriage status: 22.9% never married, 68.8% now married, 5.3% widowed, 3.0% divorced (2000); Foreign born: 0.4% (2000); Ancestry (includes multiple ancestries): 74.0% German, 10.2% Norwegian, 6.7% Irish, 3.5% Swedish, 2.8% Czech (2000).
Economy: Grain; livestock, poultry; dairying. Manufacturing: concrete products, food processing, electronic wiring. Employment by occupation: 22.0% management, 7.5% professional, 7.5% services, 25.2% sales, 0.3% farming, 9.4% construction, 28.0% production (2000).
Income: Per capita income: $21,144 (2000); Median household income: $51,667 (2000); Poverty rate: 5.8% (2000).
Taxes: Total city taxes per capita: $64 (1997); City property taxes per capita: $64 (1997).
Education: High school graduation rate: 83.5% (2000); College graduation rate: 8.0% (2000).
Housing: Homeownership rate: 93.2% (2000); Median home value: $133,300 (2000); Median rent: $175 per month (2000); Median age of housing: 52 years (2000).
Transportation: Commute to work: 83.3% car, 0.9% public transportation, 2.5% walk, 13.2% work from home (2000); Travel time to work: 48.6% less than 15 minutes, 19.6% 15 to 30 minutes, 12.0% 30 to 45 minutes, 9.1% 45 to 60 minutes, 10.9% 60 minutes or more (2000)

BISMARCK (township). Covers a land area of 36.028 square miles and a water area of 0.062 square miles. Located at 44.59° N. Lat.; 94.44° W. Long.
Population: 376 (2000); Race: 99.2% White, 0.0% Black, 0.0% Asian, 0.0% American Indian and Alaska Native, 0.0% Hispanic of any race, 0.8% two or more races (2000); Density: 10.4 persons per square mile (2000); Age: 36.1% under 18, 14.5% over 64 (2000); Marriage status: 20.6% never married, 68.9% now married, 0.7% widowed, 9.7% divorced (2000); Foreign born: 1.1% (2000); Ancestry (includes multiple ancestries): 69.1% German, 6.3% Swedish, 3.6% Norwegian, 3.0% Scottish, 2.7% English (2000).
Economy: Employment by occupation: 26.8% management, 9.4% professional, 7.9% services, 16.5% sales, 11.0% farming, 15.0% construction, 13.4% production (2000).
Income: Per capita income: $12,727 (2000); Median household income: $29,375 (2000); Poverty rate: 19.2% (2000).
Taxes: Total city taxes per capita: $155 (1997); City property taxes per capita: $155 (1997).
Education: High school graduation rate: 71.9% (2000); College graduation rate: 9.5% (2000).
Housing: Homeownership rate: 89.1% (2000); Median home value: $78,600 (2000); Median rent: $325 per month (2000); Median age of housing: 60+ years (2000).
Transportation: Commute to work: 70.4% car, 0.0% public transportation, 6.4% walk, 17.6% work from home (2000); Travel time to work: 42.7% less than 15 minutes, 26.2% 15 to 30 minutes, 10.7% 30 to 45 minutes, 3.9% 45 to 60 minutes, 16.5% 60 minutes or more (2000)

CORNISH (township). Covers a land area of 35.425 square miles and a water area of 0.105 square miles. Located at 44.49° N. Lat.; 94.43° W. Long.
Population: 267 (2000); Race: 99.3% White, 0.0% Black, 0.0% Asian, 0.0% American Indian and Alaska Native, 0.0% Hispanic of any race, 0.7% two or more races (2000); Density: 7.5 persons per square mile (2000); Age: 25.5% under 18, 19.9% over 64 (2000); Marriage status: 18.5% never married, 69.4% now married, 6.5% widowed, 5.6% divorced (2000); Foreign born: 2.2% (2000); Ancestry (includes multiple ancestries): 65.5% German, 17.6% Swedish, 12.4% Norwegian, 7.5% English, 6.0% Dutch (2000).
Economy: Employment by occupation: 22.7% management, 6.5% professional, 7.8% services, 24.7% sales, 2.6% farming, 9.7% construction, 26.0% production (2000).
Income: Per capita income: $18,561 (2000); Median household income: $48,036 (2000); Poverty rate: 6.0% (2000).
Taxes: Total city taxes per capita: $121 (1997); City property taxes per capita: $121 (1997).
Education: High school graduation rate: 79.5% (2000); College graduation rate: 12.1% (2000).
Housing: Homeownership rate: 80.0% (2000); Median home value: $86,400 (2000); Median rent: $175 per month (2000); Median age of housing: 60+ years (2000).
Transportation: Commute to work: 81.2% car, 0.0% public transportation, 4.5% walk, 14.3% work from home (2000); Travel time to work: 51.5% less than 15 minutes, 29.5% 15 to 30 minutes, 11.4% 30 to 45 minutes, 0.0% 45 to 60 minutes, 7.6% 60 minutes or more (2000)

DRYDEN (township). Covers a land area of 32.905 square miles and a water area of 1.675 square miles. Located at 44.59° N. Lat.; 94.20° W. Long.
Population: 280 (2000); Race: 100.0% White, 0.0% Black, 0.0% Asian, 0.0% American Indian and Alaska Native, 0.0% Hispanic of any race, 0.0% two or more races (2000); Density: 8.5 persons per square mile (2000); Age: 24.5% under 18, 18.9% over 64 (2000); Marriage status: 24.5% never married, 68.9% now married, 4.8% widowed, 1.8% divorced (2000); Foreign born: 0.0% (2000); Ancestry (includes multiple ancestries): 74.8% German, 7.5% Swedish, 6.8% United States or American, 4.3% Norwegian, 4.3% Belgian (2000).
Economy: Employment by occupation: 20.1% management, 10.9% professional, 6.0% services, 22.8% sales, 1.6% farming, 9.2% construction, 29.3% production (2000).
Income: Per capita income: $17,527 (2000); Median household income: $43,750 (2000); Poverty rate: 11.8% (2000).
Taxes: Total city taxes per capita: $79 (1997); City property taxes per capita: $79 (1997).
Education: High school graduation rate: 80.5% (2000); College graduation rate: 7.6% (2000).
Housing: Homeownership rate: 85.7% (2000); Median home value: $107,500 (2000); Median rent: $310 per month (2000); Median age of housing: 60+ years (2000).
Transportation: Commute to work: 76.6% car, 0.0% public transportation, 3.3% walk, 20.1% work from home (2000); Travel time to work: 53.7% less than 15 minutes, 32.7% 15 to 30 minutes, 9.5% 30 to 45 minutes, 1.4% 45 to 60 minutes, 2.7% 60 minutes or more (2000)

FAXON (township). Covers a land area of 20.966 square miles and a water area of 0.505 square miles. Located at 44.65° N. Lat.; 93.80° W. Long.
Population: 598 (2000); Race: 98.9% White, 0.0% Black, 0.3% Asian, 0.0% American Indian and Alaska Native, 0.5% Hispanic of any race, 0.3% two or more races (2000); Density: 28.5 persons per square mile (2000); Age: 34.0% under 18, 5.6% over 64 (2000); Marriage status: 23.0% never married, 70.2%

now married, 1.8% widowed, 5.0% divorced (2000); Foreign born: 0.8% (2000); Ancestry (includes multiple ancestries): 54.6% German, 25.5% Irish, 9.5% Swedish, 6.6% French (except Basque), 6.4% Norwegian (2000).
Economy: Employment by occupation: 12.7% management, 10.4% professional, 13.3% services, 28.3% sales, 0.3% farming, 13.6% construction, 21.4% production (2000).
Income: Per capita income: $19,632 (2000); Median household income: $59,375 (2000); Poverty rate: 1.6% (2000).
Taxes: Total city taxes per capita: $71 (1997); City property taxes per capita: $71 (1997).
Education: High school graduation rate: 87.4% (2000); College graduation rate: 13.4% (2000).
Housing: Homeownership rate: 95.4% (2000); Median home value: $179,900 (2000); Median rent: $488 per month (2000); Median age of housing: 20 years (2000).
Transportation: Commute to work: 90.4% car, 0.6% public transportation, 1.7% walk, 7.3% work from home (2000); Travel time to work: 24.5% less than 15 minutes, 21.0% 15 to 30 minutes, 27.6% 30 to 45 minutes, 17.2% 45 to 60 minutes, 9.7% 60 minutes or more (2000)

GAYLORD (city). Covers a land area of 1.588 square miles and a water area of 0 square miles. Located at 44.55° N. Lat.; 94.22° W. Long. Elevation is 995 feet.
History: Plotted 1881.
Population: 2,279 (2000); Race: 88.2% White, 0.0% Black, 0.0% Asian, 0.0% American Indian and Alaska Native, 18.4% Hispanic of any race, 0.7% two or more races (2000); Density: 1,435.3 persons per square mile (2000); Age: 24.8% under 18, 21.1% over 64 (2000); Marriage status: 17.6% never married, 64.3% now married, 10.5% widowed, 7.6% divorced (2000); Foreign born: 7.8% (2000); Ancestry (includes multiple ancestries): 55.4% German, 15.8% Other groups, 9.4% Norwegian, 6.7% Swedish, 5.4% Irish (2000).
Economy: Trade point in agricultural area: grain; livestock; dairying. Manufacturing: food, building materials. Single-family building permits issued: 4 (2001) / 5 (2000); Multi-family building permits issued: 0 (2001) / 0 (2000); Employment by occupation: 9.6% management, 12.9% professional, 14.5% services, 19.6% sales, 0.9% farming, 7.6% construction, 35.0% production (2000).
Income: Per capita income: $17,048 (2000); Median household income: $39,053 (2000); Poverty rate: 13.6% (2000).
Taxes: Total city taxes per capita: $253 (1997); City property taxes per capita: $244 (1997).
Education: High school graduation rate: 73.7% (2000); College graduation rate: 12.0% (2000).
Housing: Homeownership rate: 72.2% (2000); Median home value: $76,300 (2000); Median rent: $405 per month (2000); Median age of housing: 38 years (2000).
Newspapers: Gaylord Hub (1 x week)
Transportation: Commute to work: 88.6% car, 0.3% public transportation, 3.7% walk, 3.7% work from home (2000); Travel time to work: 54.0% less than 15 minutes, 16.8% 15 to 30 minutes, 18.2% 30 to 45 minutes, 6.1% 45 to 60 minutes, 4.9% 60 minutes or more (2000)
Additional Information Contacts
Gaylord Chamber of Commerce 507-237-2508

GIBBON (city). Covers a land area of 0.888 square miles and a water area of 0 square miles. Located at 44.53° N. Lat.; 94.52° W. Long.
Population: 808 (2000); Race: 93.7% White, 0.5% Black, 0.4% Asian, 1.4% American Indian and Alaska Native, 6.0% Hispanic of any race, 1.5% two or more races (2000); Density: 910.0 persons per square mile (2000); Age: 23.7% under 18, 25.5% over 64 (2000); Marriage status: 19.0% never married, 62.6% now married, 12.1% widowed, 6.2% divorced (2000); Foreign born: 2.4% (2000); Ancestry (includes multiple ancestries): 57.6% German, 11.2% Swedish, 9.4% Norwegian, 8.5% Other groups, 7.7% Irish (2000).
Economy: Agricultural area: poultry, livestock; grain, soybeans, alfalfa; dairying. Manufacturing: feeds, fabricated metal products. Single-family building permits issued: 2 (2001) / 1 (2000); Multi-family building permits issued: 0 (2001) / 2 (2000); Employment by occupation: 13.1% management, 8.8% professional, 11.0% services, 21.7% sales, 1.6% farming, 13.1% construction, 30.6% production (2000).
Income: Per capita income: $17,897 (2000); Median household income: $33,816 (2000); Poverty rate: 7.4% (2000).
Taxes: Total city taxes per capita: $223 (1997); City property taxes per capita: $212 (1997).
Education: High school graduation rate: 78.4% (2000); College graduation rate: 8.3% (2000).

School District(s)

G.F.W. (PK-12)
2000 Enrollment: 988 507-834-9813
Housing: Homeownership rate: 81.5% (2000); Median home value: $51,500 (2000); Median rent: $341 per month (2000); Median age of housing: 51 years (2000).
Newspapers: The Gazette (1 x week)
Transportation: Commute to work: 86.7% car, 0.5% public transportation, 10.6% walk, 2.2% work from home (2000); Travel time to work: 38.2% less than 15 minutes, 31.9% 15 to 30 minutes, 14.7% 30 to 45 minutes, 6.4% 45 to 60 minutes, 8.9% 60 minutes or more (2000)

GRAFTON (township). Covers a land area of 38.983 square miles and a water area of 0.156 square miles. Located at 44.66° N. Lat.; 94.56° W. Long.
Population: 259 (2000); Race: 95.3% White, 0.0% Black, 2.2% Asian, 1.8% American Indian and Alaska Native, 0.0% Hispanic of any race, 0.7% two or more races (2000); Density: 6.6 persons per square mile (2000); Age: 32.1% under 18, 10.1% over 64 (2000); Marriage status: 21.3% never married, 71.6% now married, 4.7% widowed, 2.4% divorced (2000); Foreign born: 3.2% (2000); Ancestry (includes multiple ancestries): 64.3% German, 15.2% Norwegian, 12.6% Swedish, 9.4% Irish, 5.1% Dutch (2000).
Economy: Employment by occupation: 30.3% management, 12.7% professional, 13.4% services, 18.3% sales, 0.0% farming, 6.3% construction, 19.0% production (2000).
Income: Per capita income: $18,045 (2000); Median household income: $45,250 (2000); Poverty rate: 4.3% (2000).
Taxes: Total city taxes per capita: $254 (1997); City property taxes per capita: $254 (1997).
Education: High school graduation rate: 92.3% (2000); College graduation rate: 7.1% (2000).
Housing: Homeownership rate: 90.1% (2000); Median home value: $114,300 (2000); Median rent: $275 per month (2000); Median age of housing: 54 years (2000).
Transportation: Commute to work: 73.9% car, 0.0% public transportation, 0.0% walk, 26.1% work from home (2000); Travel time to work: 35.2% less than 15 minutes, 45.7% 15 to 30 minutes, 19.0% 30 to 45 minutes, 0.0% 45 to 60 minutes, 0.0% 60 minutes or more (2000)

GREEN ISLE (city). Covers a land area of 0.746 square miles and a water area of 0.002 square miles. Located at 44.67° N. Lat.; 94.00° W. Long. Elevation is 1,000 feet.
Population: 334 (2000); Race: 99.4% White, 0.6% Black, 0.0% Asian, 0.0% American Indian and Alaska Native, 1.4% Hispanic of any race, 0.0% two or more races (2000); Density: 447.5 persons per square mile (2000); Age: 25.0% under 18, 14.3% over 64 (2000); Marriage status: 18.1% never married, 70.6% now married, 3.2% widowed, 8.2% divorced (2000); Foreign born: 0.6% (2000); Ancestry (includes multiple ancestries): 67.4% German, 14.6% Irish, 4.2% United States or American, 3.9% Norwegian, 3.1% Other groups (2000).
Economy: Employment by occupation: 14.5% management, 14.0% professional, 11.8% services, 29.0% sales, 1.1% farming, 11.8% construction, 17.7% production (2000).
Income: Per capita income: $25,537 (2000); Median household income: $44,792 (2000); Poverty rate: 2.5% (2000).
Taxes: Total city taxes per capita: $268 (1997); City property taxes per capita: $251 (1997).
Education: High school graduation rate: 78.3% (2000); College graduation rate: 9.4% (2000).
Housing: Homeownership rate: 87.2% (2000); Median home value: $82,800 (2000); Median rent: $514 per month (2000); Median age of housing: 51 years (2000).
Transportation: Commute to work: 92.5% car, 0.0% public transportation, 2.2% walk, 5.4% work from home (2000); Travel time to work: 34.1% less than 15 minutes, 22.7% 15 to 30 minutes, 19.9% 30 to 45 minutes, 8.0% 45 to 60 minutes, 15.3% 60 minutes or more (2000)

GREEN ISLE (township). Covers a land area of 35.489 square miles and a water area of 0.768 square miles. Located at 44.67° N. Lat.; 94.06° W. Long. Elevation is 1,000 feet.
Population: 556 (2000); Race: 99.5% White, 0.5% Black, 0.0% Asian, 0.0% American Indian and Alaska Native, 0.0% Hispanic of any race, 0.0% two or more races (2000); Density: 15.7 persons per square mile (2000); Age: 25.9% under 18, 17.9% over 64 (2000); Marriage status: 25.6% never married, 65.9% now married, 5.8% widowed, 2.7% divorced (2000); Foreign born:

0.3% (2000); Ancestry (includes multiple ancestries): 79.6% German, 5.5% Norwegian, 3.8% Irish, 2.4% Dutch, 2.1% Swedish (2000).
Economy: Agricultural area: grain, soybeans; livestock; dairying. Employment by occupation: 16.3% management, 10.1% professional, 11.5% services, 19.5% sales, 3.0% farming, 16.3% construction, 23.4% production (2000).
Income: Per capita income: $18,371 (2000); Median household income: $49,375 (2000); Poverty rate: 1.7% (2000).
Taxes: Total city taxes per capita: $58 (1997); City property taxes per capita: $58 (1997).
Education: High school graduation rate: 72.3% (2000); College graduation rate: 5.8% (2000).
Housing: Homeownership rate: 86.6% (2000); Median home value: $112,500 (2000); Median rent: $463 per month (2000); Median age of housing: 52 years (2000).
Transportation: Commute to work: 89.0% car, 0.0% public transportation, 2.1% walk, 8.3% work from home (2000); Travel time to work: 31.2% less than 15 minutes, 31.8% 15 to 30 minutes, 22.4% 30 to 45 minutes, 6.8% 45 to 60 minutes, 7.8% 60 minutes or more (2000)

HENDERSON (city). Covers a land area of 1.005 square miles and a water area of 0.021 square miles. Located at 44.52° N. Lat.; 93.90° W. Long. Elevation is 740 feet.
Population: 910 (2000); Race: 93.7% White, 0.0% Black, 0.8% Asian, 1.2% American Indian and Alaska Native, 5.4% Hispanic of any race, 0.9% two or more races (2000); Density: 905.4 persons per square mile (2000); Age: 27.9% under 18, 13.6% over 64 (2000); Marriage status: 28.1% never married, 52.8% now married, 8.7% widowed, 10.4% divorced (2000); Foreign born: 1.9% (2000); Ancestry (includes multiple ancestries): 59.7% German, 14.8% Irish, 8.6% Norwegian, 8.4% Other groups, 5.1% Swedish (2000).
Economy: Single-family building permits issued: 10 (2001) / 8 (2000); Multi-family building permits issued: 0 (2001) / 0 (2000); Employment by occupation: 7.2% management, 11.7% professional, 14.8% services, 13.0% sales, 0.7% farming, 9.1% construction, 43.5% production (2000).
Income: Per capita income: $17,544 (2000); Median household income: $43,125 (2000); Poverty rate: 6.6% (2000).
Taxes: Total city taxes per capita: $157 (1997); City property taxes per capita: $141 (1997).
Education: High school graduation rate: 82.3% (2000); College graduation rate: 10.3% (2000).

School District(s)

Minnesota New Country School (07-12)
2000 Enrollment: 95 507-248-3353
Housing: Homeownership rate: 78.7% (2000); Median home value: $80,500 (2000); Median rent: $348 per month (2000); Median age of housing: 54 years (2000).
Newspapers: Henderson Independent (1 x week)
Transportation: Commute to work: 94.9% car, 0.0% public transportation, 3.1% walk, 2.0% work from home (2000); Travel time to work: 29.8% less than 15 minutes, 33.9% 15 to 30 minutes, 17.7% 30 to 45 minutes, 10.7% 45 to 60 minutes, 8.0% 60 minutes or more (2000)

HENDERSON (township). Covers a land area of 29.945 square miles and a water area of 0.217 square miles. Located at 44.49° N. Lat.; 93.93° W. Long. Elevation is 740 feet.
Population: 700 (2000); Race: 98.1% White, 1.6% Black, 0.0% Asian, 0.0% American Indian and Alaska Native, 2.6% Hispanic of any race, 0.3% two or more races (2000); Density: 23.4 persons per square mile (2000); Age: 34.7% under 18, 9.8% over 64 (2000); Marriage status: 25.7% never married, 63.2% now married, 5.5% widowed, 5.5% divorced (2000); Foreign born: 0.7% (2000); Ancestry (includes multiple ancestries): 72.2% German, 11.5% Irish, 8.8% Norwegian, 3.1% United States or American, 2.8% French (except Basque) (2000).
Economy: Grain; livestock, poultry; dairying. Manufacturing: displays. Employment by occupation: 11.6% management, 13.1% professional, 5.5% services, 22.6% sales, 3.4% farming, 17.1% construction, 26.6% production (2000).
Income: Per capita income: $18,502 (2000); Median household income: $48,167 (2000); Poverty rate: 11.1% (2000).
Taxes: Total city taxes per capita: $62 (1997); City property taxes per capita: $62 (1997).
Education: High school graduation rate: 86.1% (2000); College graduation rate: 15.9% (2000).
Housing: Homeownership rate: 79.7% (2000); Median home value: $118,000 (2000); Median rent: $350 per month (2000); Median age of housing: 45 years (2000).
Transportation: Commute to work: 88.2% car, 0.0% public transportation, 1.9% walk, 9.9% work from home (2000); Travel time to work: 32.4% less than 15 minutes, 32.1% 15 to 30 minutes, 14.8% 30 to 45 minutes, 11.7% 45 to 60 minutes, 9.0% 60 minutes or more (2000)

JESSENLAND (township). Covers a land area of 33.205 square miles and a water area of 1.197 square miles. Located at 44.59° N. Lat.; 93.94° W. Long.
Population: 481 (2000); Race: 96.6% White, 0.0% Black, 0.0% Asian, 0.0% American Indian and Alaska Native, 0.4% Hispanic of any race, 3.0% two or more races (2000); Density: 14.5 persons per square mile (2000); Age: 30.1% under 18, 10.7% over 64 (2000); Marriage status: 22.8% never married, 70.0% now married, 2.7% widowed, 4.6% divorced (2000); Foreign born: 1.0% (2000); Ancestry (includes multiple ancestries): 59.2% German, 14.3% Irish, 6.7% Norwegian, 4.2% English, 3.6% Swedish (2000).
Economy: Employment by occupation: 13.8% management, 9.2% professional, 13.4% services, 19.2% sales, 2.7% farming, 22.2% construction, 19.5% production (2000).
Income: Per capita income: $18,758 (2000); Median household income: $55,000 (2000); Poverty rate: 3.9% (2000).
Taxes: Total city taxes per capita: $25 (1997); City property taxes per capita: $25 (1997).
Education: High school graduation rate: 81.6% (2000); College graduation rate: 12.8% (2000).
Housing: Homeownership rate: 92.2% (2000); Median home value: $121,900 (2000); Median rent: $375 per month (2000); Median age of housing: 60+ years (2000).
Transportation: Commute to work: 88.7% car, 0.0% public transportation, 1.6% walk, 9.8% work from home (2000); Travel time to work: 13.4% less than 15 minutes, 30.3% 15 to 30 minutes, 22.9% 30 to 45 minutes, 16.0% 45 to 60 minutes, 17.3% 60 minutes or more (2000)

KELSO (township). Covers a land area of 35.597 square miles and a water area of 0 square miles. Located at 44.49° N. Lat.; 94.06° W. Long.
Population: 357 (2000); Race: 99.2% White, 0.0% Black, 0.8% Asian, 0.0% American Indian and Alaska Native, 0.6% Hispanic of any race, 0.0% two or more races (2000); Density: 10.0 persons per square mile (2000); Age: 28.2% under 18, 9.4% over 64 (2000); Marriage status: 28.0% never married, 65.1% now married, 4.7% widowed, 2.2% divorced (2000); Foreign born: 0.8% (2000); Ancestry (includes multiple ancestries): 74.0% German, 10.8% Swedish, 7.7% Czech, 5.2% Norwegian, 5.0% Irish (2000).
Economy: Employment by occupation: 25.5% management, 14.2% professional, 10.4% services, 19.8% sales, 0.9% farming, 8.5% construction, 20.8% production (2000).
Income: Per capita income: $17,818 (2000); Median household income: $46,250 (2000); Poverty rate: 6.6% (2000).
Taxes: Total city taxes per capita: $86 (1997); City property taxes per capita: $86 (1997).
Education: High school graduation rate: 87.9% (2000); College graduation rate: 13.4% (2000).
Housing: Homeownership rate: 84.7% (2000); Median home value: $90,000 (2000); Median rent: $425 per month (2000); Median age of housing: 60+ years (2000).
Transportation: Commute to work: 81.2% car, 0.0% public transportation, 2.5% walk, 15.3% work from home (2000); Travel time to work: 31.6% less than 15 minutes, 42.1% 15 to 30 minutes, 7.6% 30 to 45 minutes, 10.5% 45 to 60 minutes, 8.2% 60 minutes or more (2000)

MOLTKE (township). Covers a land area of 39.020 square miles and a water area of 0 square miles. Located at 44.57° N. Lat.; 94.55° W. Long.
Population: 337 (2000); Race: 97.6% White, 0.0% Black, 0.0% Asian, 0.0% American Indian and Alaska Native, 1.2% Hispanic of any race, 1.8% two or more races (2000); Density: 8.6 persons per square mile (2000); Age: 29.4% under 18, 11.9% over 64 (2000); Marriage status: 27.5% never married, 69.8% now married, 1.9% widowed, 0.8% divorced (2000); Foreign born: 0.0% (2000); Ancestry (includes multiple ancestries): 72.7% German, 6.8% United States or American, 5.6% Norwegian, 2.4% Other groups, 2.4% Swedish (2000).
Economy: Employment by occupation: 27.7% management, 12.2% professional, 11.2% services, 19.7% sales, 2.7% farming, 10.6% construction, 16.0% production (2000).
Income: Per capita income: $16,737 (2000); Median household income: $45,234 (2000); Poverty rate: 5.0% (2000).

Taxes: Total city taxes per capita: $136 (1997); City property taxes per capita: $136 (1997).
Education: High school graduation rate: 89.0% (2000); College graduation rate: 10.1% (2000).
Housing: Homeownership rate: 78.8% (2000); Median home value: $95,000 (2000); Median rent: $258 per month (2000); Median age of housing: 60+ years (2000).
Transportation: Commute to work: 74.2% car, 0.0% public transportation, 2.2% walk, 23.6% work from home (2000); Travel time to work: 28.1% less than 15 minutes, 36.0% 15 to 30 minutes, 16.5% 30 to 45 minutes, 10.8% 45 to 60 minutes, 8.6% 60 minutes or more (2000)

NEW AUBURN (city). Covers a land area of 0.494 square miles and a water area of 0 square miles. Located at 44.67° N. Lat.; 94.23° W. Long. Elevation is 1,002 feet.
Population: 488 (2000); Race: 89.1% White, 0.0% Black, 0.0% Asian, 1.3% American Indian and Alaska Native, 11.8% Hispanic of any race, 2.2% two or more races (2000); Density: 987.6 persons per square mile (2000); Age: 36.8% under 18, 8.3% over 64 (2000); Marriage status: 25.0% never married, 61.7% now married, 5.8% widowed, 7.5% divorced (2000); Foreign born: 5.4% (2000); Ancestry (includes multiple ancestries): 50.3% German, 11.5% Other groups, 7.6% Norwegian, 7.6% French (except Basque), 7.0% United States or American (2000).
Economy: Single-family building permits issued: 3 (2001) / 5 (2000); Multi-family building permits issued: 0 (2001) / 0 (2000); Employment by occupation: 11.1% management, 7.0% professional, 11.6% services, 17.6% sales, 0.0% farming, 14.1% construction, 38.7% production (2000).
Income: Per capita income: $13,943 (2000); Median household income: $38,542 (2000); Poverty rate: 13.4% (2000).
Taxes: Total city taxes per capita: $88 (1997); City property taxes per capita: $77 (1997).
Education: High school graduation rate: 75.3% (2000); College graduation rate: 5.7% (2000).
Housing: Homeownership rate: 82.0% (2000); Median home value: $53,500 (2000); Median rent: $354 per month (2000); Median age of housing: 48 years (2000).
Transportation: Commute to work: 94.8% car, 0.0% public transportation, 1.0% walk, 4.2% work from home (2000); Travel time to work: 12.6% less than 15 minutes, 33.3% 15 to 30 minutes, 31.7% 30 to 45 minutes, 9.8% 45 to 60 minutes, 12.6% 60 minutes or more (2000)

NEW AUBURN (township). Covers a land area of 31.969 square miles and a water area of 3.821 square miles. Located at 44.67° N. Lat.; 94.18° W. Long. Elevation is 1,002 feet.
Population: 464 (2000); Race: 95.2% White, 0.0% Black, 0.4% Asian, 2.9% American Indian and Alaska Native, 0.0% Hispanic of any race, 1.0% two or more races (2000); Density: 14.5 persons per square mile (2000); Age: 28.9% under 18, 12.3% over 64 (2000); Marriage status: 20.8% never married, 69.4% now married, 3.8% widowed, 6.0% divorced (2000); Foreign born: 0.8% (2000); Ancestry (includes multiple ancestries): 72.4% German, 8.4% Swedish, 7.5% Irish, 5.4% Norwegian, 3.3% English (2000).
Economy: Livestock; grain, soybeans; dairying. Employment by occupation: 19.2% management, 10.5% professional, 13.0% services, 23.2% sales, 2.9% farming, 12.7% construction, 18.5% production (2000).
Income: Per capita income: $19,149 (2000); Median household income: $48,750 (2000); Poverty rate: 6.9% (2000).
Taxes: Total city taxes per capita: $37 (1997); City property taxes per capita: $37 (1997).
Education: High school graduation rate: 82.0% (2000); College graduation rate: 13.8% (2000).
Housing: Homeownership rate: 93.6% (2000); Median home value: $105,000 (2000); Median rent: $300 per month (2000); Median age of housing: 60+ years (2000).
Transportation: Commute to work: 86.3% car, 0.7% public transportation, 1.8% walk, 11.1% work from home (2000); Travel time to work: 40.2% less than 15 minutes, 22.8% 15 to 30 minutes, 16.2% 30 to 45 minutes, 10.0% 45 to 60 minutes, 10.8% 60 minutes or more (2000)

SEVERANCE (township). Covers a land area of 36.483 square miles and a water area of 1.577 square miles. Located at 44.49° N. Lat.; 94.56° W. Long.
Population: 343 (2000); Race: 95.4% White, 0.0% Black, 2.0% Asian, 0.0% American Indian and Alaska Native, 2.0% Hispanic of any race, 2.6% two or more races (2000); Density: 9.4 persons per square mile (2000); Age: 30.9% under 18, 12.3% over 64 (2000); Marriage status: 29.8% never married, 65.6% now married, 3.4% widowed, 1.1% divorced (2000); Foreign born: 2.0% (2000); Ancestry (includes multiple ancestries): 71.4% German, 17.7% Norwegian, 14.0% Swedish, 9.1% Irish, 5.4% French (except Basque) (2000).
Economy: Employment by occupation: 31.1% management, 12.2% professional, 7.1% services, 14.3% sales, 5.6% farming, 7.1% construction, 22.4% production (2000).
Income: Per capita income: $14,857 (2000); Median household income: $39,063 (2000); Poverty rate: 4.6% (2000).
Taxes: Total city taxes per capita: $168 (1997); City property taxes per capita: $168 (1997).
Education: High school graduation rate: 83.2% (2000); College graduation rate: 15.9% (2000).
Housing: Homeownership rate: 79.3% (2000); Median home value: $88,300 (2000); Median rent: $142 per month (2000); Median age of housing: 60+ years (2000).
Transportation: Commute to work: 77.2% car, 0.0% public transportation, 9.3% walk, 13.5% work from home (2000); Travel time to work: 38.3% less than 15 minutes, 25.7% 15 to 30 minutes, 21.0% 30 to 45 minutes, 3.6% 45 to 60 minutes, 11.4% 60 minutes or more (2000)

SIBLEY (township). Covers a land area of 35.598 square miles and a water area of 0.048 square miles. Located at 44.49° N. Lat.; 94.19° W. Long.
Population: 353 (2000); Race: 100.0% White, 0.0% Black, 0.0% Asian, 0.0% American Indian and Alaska Native, 0.0% Hispanic of any race, 0.0% two or more races (2000); Density: 9.9 persons per square mile (2000); Age: 32.2% under 18, 5.7% over 64 (2000); Marriage status: 25.0% never married, 62.5% now married, 2.7% widowed, 9.8% divorced (2000); Foreign born: 1.7% (2000); Ancestry (includes multiple ancestries): 71.8% German, 9.1% Norwegian, 7.4% Swedish, 5.4% Irish, 3.7% Dutch (2000).
Economy: Employment by occupation: 22.4% management, 14.1% professional, 10.4% services, 18.8% sales, 4.7% farming, 14.1% construction, 15.6% production (2000).
Income: Per capita income: $14,814 (2000); Median household income: $39,125 (2000); Poverty rate: 11.1% (2000).
Taxes: Total city taxes per capita: $107 (1997); City property taxes per capita: $107 (1997).
Education: High school graduation rate: 83.4% (2000); College graduation rate: 12.2% (2000).
Housing: Homeownership rate: 86.1% (2000); Median home value: $98,300 (2000); Median rent: $138 per month (2000); Median age of housing: 60+ years (2000).
Transportation: Commute to work: 81.7% car, 0.0% public transportation, 4.8% walk, 13.4% work from home (2000); Travel time to work: 49.7% less than 15 minutes, 28.0% 15 to 30 minutes, 14.3% 30 to 45 minutes, 3.1% 45 to 60 minutes, 5.0% 60 minutes or more (2000)

TRANSIT (township). Covers a land area of 35.173 square miles and a water area of 0.386 square miles. Located at 44.57° N. Lat.; 94.30° W. Long.
Population: 324 (2000); Race: 98.0% White, 0.0% Black, 0.0% Asian, 1.3% American Indian and Alaska Native, 1.3% Hispanic of any race, 0.0% two or more races (2000); Density: 9.2 persons per square mile (2000); Age: 20.9% under 18, 18.0% over 64 (2000); Marriage status: 25.8% never married, 64.6% now married, 4.2% widowed, 5.4% divorced (2000); Foreign born: 0.0% (2000); Ancestry (includes multiple ancestries): 72.2% German, 8.5% Norwegian, 8.5% Swedish, 2.9% French (except Basque), 2.6% Irish (2000).
Economy: Employment by occupation: 17.9% management, 7.1% professional, 13.1% services, 13.7% sales, 6.0% farming, 11.9% construction, 30.4% production (2000).
Income: Per capita income: $23,658 (2000); Median household income: $34,583 (2000); Poverty rate: 5.3% (2000).
Taxes: Total city taxes per capita: $118 (1997); City property taxes per capita: $118 (1997).
Education: High school graduation rate: 79.7% (2000); College graduation rate: 11.8% (2000).
Housing: Homeownership rate: 91.4% (2000); Median home value: $98,800 (2000); Median rent: $425 per month (2000); Median age of housing: 60+ years (2000).
Transportation: Commute to work: 77.8% car, 0.0% public transportation, 7.6% walk, 14.6% work from home (2000); Travel time to work: 34.2% less than 15 minutes, 37.0% 15 to 30 minutes, 11.6% 30 to 45 minutes, 4.1% 45 to 60 minutes, 13.0% 60 minutes or more (2000)

WASHINGTON LAKE (township). Covers a land area of 34.316 square miles and a water area of 1.090 square miles. Located at 44.68° N. Lat.; 93.95° W. Long.

Population: 506 (2000); Race: 98.6% White, 1.4% Black, 0.0% Asian, 0.0% American Indian and Alaska Native, 0.0% Hispanic of any race, 0.0% two or more races (2000); Density: 14.7 persons per square mile (2000); Age: 26.6% under 18, 10.8% over 64 (2000); Marriage status: 22.6% never married, 67.7% now married, 4.1% widowed, 5.6% divorced (2000); Foreign born: 0.9% (2000); Ancestry (includes multiple ancestries): 79.9% German, 19.6% Irish, 8.1% Norwegian, 4.7% Swedish, 4.1% English (2000).
Economy: Employment by occupation: 17.3% management, 13.0% professional, 11.8% services, 19.7% sales, 1.6% farming, 15.0% construction, 21.7% production (2000).
Income: Per capita income: $17,967 (2000); Median household income: $46,528 (2000); Poverty rate: 9.9% (2000).
Taxes: Total city taxes per capita: $80 (1997); City property taxes per capita: $80 (1997).
Education: High school graduation rate: 87.4% (2000); College graduation rate: 8.5% (2000).
Housing: Homeownership rate: 92.3% (2000); Median home value: $112,500 (2000); Median rent: $475 per month (2000); Median age of housing: 60+ years (2000).
Transportation: Commute to work: 80.7% car, 0.4% public transportation, 5.5% walk, 12.2% work from home (2000); Travel time to work: 21.5% less than 15 minutes, 40.4% 15 to 30 minutes, 25.6% 30 to 45 minutes, 7.2% 45 to 60 minutes, 5.4% 60 minutes or more (2000)

WINTHROP (city). Covers a land area of 1.048 square miles and a water area of 0 square miles. Located at 44.54° N. Lat.; 94.36° W. Long. Elevation is 1,018 feet.
History: Settled 1881, incorporated as village 1884, as city 1910.
Population: 1,367 (2000); Race: 95.8% White, 0.0% Black, 0.0% Asian, 0.5% American Indian and Alaska Native, 4.8% Hispanic of any race, 0.3% two or more races (2000); Density: 1,303.8 persons per square mile (2000); Age: 23.7% under 18, 26.0% over 64 (2000); Marriage status: 20.5% never married, 57.8% now married, 14.1% widowed, 7.6% divorced (2000); Foreign born: 2.0% (2000); Ancestry (includes multiple ancestries): 51.9% German, 15.6% Swedish, 10.0% Norwegian, 6.8% Other groups, 6.0% Irish (2000).
Economy: Agricultural trading point: grain; livestock; dairy products. Manufacturing of dairy products, hardwood. Single-family building permits issued: 1 (2001) / 2 (2000); Multi-family building permits issued: 0 (2001) / 0 (2000); Employment by occupation: 8.9% management, 16.5% professional, 10.7% services, 19.6% sales, 2.4% farming, 7.9% construction, 34.0% production (2000).
Income: Per capita income: $18,188 (2000); Median household income: $34,813 (2000); Poverty rate: 6.1% (2000).
Taxes: Total city taxes per capita: $241 (1997); City property taxes per capita: $238 (1997).
Education: High school graduation rate: 75.5% (2000); College graduation rate: 15.1% (2000).
Housing: Homeownership rate: 79.8% (2000); Median home value: $68,900 (2000); Median rent: $350 per month (2000); Median age of housing: 50 years (2000).
Newspapers: Winthrop News (1 x week)
Transportation: Commute to work: 85.4% car, 0.0% public transportation, 11.6% walk, 2.7% work from home (2000); Travel time to work: 53.6% less than 15 minutes, 21.8% 15 to 30 minutes, 16.2% 30 to 45 minutes, 2.7% 45 to 60 minutes, 5.6% 60 minutes or more (2000)
Additional Information Contacts
Winthrop Area Chamber of Commerce 507-647-2627

Stearns County

Located in central Minnesota; bounded on the east by the Mississippi River; watered by the Sauk River; includes many small lakes. Covers a land area of 1,344.50 square miles, a water area of 45.40 square miles, and is located in the Central Time Zone. The county government was organized in 1855. County seat is St. Cloud.

Stearns County is part of the St. Cloud, MN MSA. The entire metro area includes: Benton County; Stearns County

Weather Station: Collegeville Saint John — Elevation: 1,223 feet

	Jan	Feb	Mar	Apr	May	Jun	Jul	Aug	Sep	Oct	Nov	Dec
High	20	27	39	56	70	78	83	80	71	58	38	25
Low	1	9	20	34	47	56	61	59	50	38	23	9
Precip	0.9	0.7	1.8	2.3	3.5	4.7	3.5	3.8	3.2	2.6	1.7	0.7
Snow	12.2	7.4	9.7	3.2	tr	tr	0.0	0.0	tr	0.4	9.0	8.4

High and Low temperatures in degrees Fahrenheit; Precipitation and Snow in inches

Weather Station: Melrose — Elevation: 1,207 feet

	Jan	Feb	Mar	Apr	May	Jun	Jul	Aug	Sep	Oct	Nov	Dec
High	20	27	39	57	71	79	84	81	71	58	38	25
Low	-1	7	19	33	45	55	60	57	48	36	21	7
Precip	0.9	0.6	1.6	2.2	3.3	4.3	3.4	3.5	2.8	2.5	1.5	0.6
Snow	11.3	6.8	7.9	2.1	tr	0.0	0.0	0.0	0.0	0.4	6.7	6.5

High and Low temperatures in degrees Fahrenheit; Precipitation and Snow in inches

Population: 133,166 (2000); Race: 96.4% White, 0.7% Black, 1.3% Asian, 0.3% American Indian and Alaska Native, 1.2% Hispanic of any race, 1.0% two or more races (2000); Density: 99.0 persons per square mile (2000); Age: 25.7% under 18, 11.0% over 64 (2000).
Religion: Five largest groups: 49.9% Catholic Church, 11.1% Evangelical Lutheran Church in America, 3.6% Lutheran Church—Missouri Synod, 1.7% The United Methodist Church, 1.2% Assemblies of God (2000).
Economy: Unemployment rate: 3.6% (11/2002); Total civilian labor force: 81,214 (11/2002); Leading industries: 19.8% manufacturing; 17.2% retail trade; 14.0% health care and social assistance (2000); Companies that employ more than 1,000 persons: 5 (2000); Companies that employ more than 100 persons: 109 (2000); Farms: 2,982 totaling 646,025 acres (1997); Minority business ownership rate: 0.0% (1997); Women business ownership rate: 24.4% (1997); Retail sales per capita: $12,990 (1997). Single-family building permits issued: 981 (2001) / 849 (2000); Multi-family building permits issued: 87 (2001) / 109 (2000).
Income: Per capita income: $19,211 (2000); Median household income: $42,426 (2000); Poverty rate: 8.7% (2000); Bankruptcy rate: 3.04% (2001).
Taxes: Total county taxes per capita: $217 (2000); County property taxes per capita: $211 (2000).
Education: High school graduation rate: 86.2% (2000); College graduation rate: 22.0% (2000).
Housing: Homeownership rate: 73.8% (2000); Median home value: $100,300 (2000); Median rent: $431 per month (2000); Median age of housing: 26 years (2000).
Health: Birth rate: 121.8 per 10,000 population (1998); Age adjusted death rate: 64.6 per 10,000 population (1999); Age adjusted cancer mortality rate: 164.6 deaths per 100,000 population (1999). Air Quality Index: 100% good, 0% moderate, 0% unhealthy (percent of days in 2000). Number of physicians: 25.5 per 10,000 population (1999); Number of hospital beds: 100.6 per 10,000 population (1999).
Elections: 2000 Presidential election results: 39.7% Gore, 51.9% Bush, 6.1% Nader, 1.8% Buchanan
National and State Parks: Birch Lakes State Forest; Padua State Wildlife Management Area; Tamarack State Wildlife Management Area; Tower State Wildlife Management Area; Zion State Wildlife Management Area
Additional Information Contacts
Stearns County Government Offices 320-656-3600
Albany Chamber of Commerce 320-845-7777
Cold Spring Chamber of Commerce 320-685-4186
Melrose Chamber of Commerce 320-256-7174
Paynesville Area Chamber of Commerce 320-243-3233
Sauk Centre Chamber of Commerce 320-352-5201
St. Cloud Area Association of Realtors 320-253-7149
St. Cloud Chamber of Commerce 320-251-2940

Stearns County Communities

ALBANY (city). Covers a land area of 1.395 square miles and a water area of 0.113 square miles. Located at 45.63° N. Lat.; 94.57° W. Long. Elevation is 1,201 feet.
Population: 1,796 (2000); Race: 98.7% White, 0.2% Black, 0.2% Asian, 0.0% American Indian and Alaska Native, 0.6% Hispanic of any race, 0.9% two or more races (2000); Density: 1,287.6 persons per square mile (2000); Age: 27.5% under 18, 22.5% over 64 (2000); Marriage status: 21.1% never married, 57.0% now married, 12.3% widowed, 9.6% divorced (2000); Foreign born: 0.6% (2000); Ancestry (includes multiple ancestries): 63.0% German, 8.1% Irish, 6.7% Norwegian, 6.6% Polish, 5.0% United States or American (2000).

Economy: Single-family building permits issued: 25 (2001) / 13 (2000); Multi-family building permits issued: 4 (2001) / 0 (2000); Employment by occupation: 8.4% management, 13.3% professional, 22.1% services, 25.7% sales, 0.6% farming, 8.6% construction, 21.4% production (2000).
Income: Per capita income: $16,383 (2000); Median household income: $31,577 (2000); Poverty rate: 10.3% (2000).
Taxes: Total city taxes per capita: $247 (1997); City property taxes per capita: $229 (1997).
Education: High school graduation rate: 72.0% (2000); College graduation rate: 15.9% (2000).

School District(s)

Albany (PK-12)
2000 Enrollment: 1,645 320-845-2171
Housing: Homeownership rate: 69.7% (2000); Median home value: $88,800 (2000); Median rent: $333 per month (2000); Median age of housing: 36 years (2000).
Hospitals: Albany Area Hospital (17 beds)
Newspapers: Stearns Morrison Enterprise (1 x week)
Transportation: Commute to work: 89.3% car, 0.0% public transportation, 4.8% walk, 5.7% work from home (2000); Travel time to work: 47.2% less than 15 minutes, 31.1% 15 to 30 minutes, 13.6% 30 to 45 minutes, 4.5% 45 to 60 minutes, 3.5% 60 minutes or more (2000)
Additional Information Contacts
Albany Chamber of Commerce 320-845-7777

ALBANY (township). Covers a land area of 37.132 square miles and a water area of 0.241 square miles. Located at 45.63° N. Lat.; 94.57° W. Long. Elevation is 1,201 feet.
Population: 884 (2000); Race: 99.0% White, 0.2% Black, 0.0% Asian, 0.2% American Indian and Alaska Native, 0.0% Hispanic of any race, 0.6% two or more races (2000); Density: 23.8 persons per square mile (2000); Age: 32.9% under 18, 10.4% over 64 (2000); Marriage status: 23.5% never married, 67.5% now married, 3.6% widowed, 5.3% divorced (2000); Foreign born: 0.7% (2000); Ancestry (includes multiple ancestries): 73.9% German, 7.6% Polish, 3.1% United States or American, 2.6% Irish, 2.4% Norwegian (2000).
Economy: RR junction. Dairying; poultry, hogs, sheep, cattle; grain; manufacturesfood, consumer goods, machinery. Single-family building permits issued: 10 (2001) / 13 (2000); Multi-family building permits issued: 12 (2001) / 15 (2000); Employment by occupation: 20.3% management, 11.3% professional, 14.6% services, 24.0% sales, 3.9% farming, 9.0% construction, 16.9% production (2000).
Income: Per capita income: $16,572 (2000); Median household income: $47,656 (2000); Poverty rate: 6.8% (2000).
Education: High school graduation rate: 78.8% (2000); College graduation rate: 5.7% (2000).
Housing: Homeownership rate: 91.8% (2000); Median home value: $117,200 (2000); Median rent: $458 per month (2000); Median age of housing: 31 years (2000).
Transportation: Commute to work: 80.3% car, 0.9% public transportation, 4.5% walk, 14.3% work from home (2000); Travel time to work: 43.5% less than 15 minutes, 30.5% 15 to 30 minutes, 19.8% 30 to 45 minutes, 2.3% 45 to 60 minutes, 4.0% 60 minutes or more (2000)

ASHLEY (township). Covers a land area of 41.944 square miles and a water area of 0.112 square miles. Located at 45.73° N. Lat.; 95.07° W. Long.
Population: 244 (2000); Race: 98.6% White, 1.4% Black, 0.0% Asian, 0.0% American Indian and Alaska Native, 0.0% Hispanic of any race, 0.0% two or more races (2000); Density: 5.8 persons per square mile (2000); Age: 29.5% under 18, 17.1% over 64 (2000); Marriage status; 23.8% never married, 64.6% now married, 2.4% widowed, 9.1% divorced (2000); Foreign born: 0.9% (2000); Ancestry (includes multiple ancestries): 70.0% German, 8.3% United States or American, 7.8% Norwegian, 7.4% Dutch, 4.1% Irish (2000).
Economy: Single-family building permits issued: 0 (2001) / 0 (2000); Multi-family building permits issued: 0 (2001) / 0 (2000); Employment by occupation: 24.5% management, 9.8% professional, 7.8% services, 18.6% sales, 6.9% farming, 15.7% construction, 16.7% production (2000).
Income: Per capita income: $15,347 (2000); Median household income: $45,179 (2000); Poverty rate: 8.3% (2000).
Taxes: Total city taxes per capita: $98 (1997); City property taxes per capita: $98 (1997).
Education: High school graduation rate: 75.0% (2000); College graduation rate: 4.4% (2000).
Housing: Homeownership rate: 100.0% (2000); Median home value: $79,400 (2000); Median age of housing: 31 years (2000).
Transportation: Commute to work: 77.5% car, 0.0% public transportation, 0.0% walk, 22.5% work from home (2000); Travel time to work: 41.8% less than 15 minutes, 27.8% 15 to 30 minutes, 21.5% 30 to 45 minutes, 0.0% 45 to 60 minutes, 8.9% 60 minutes or more (2000)

AVON (city). Covers a land area of 1.033 square miles and a water area of 0 square miles. Located at 45.60° N. Lat.; 94.45° W. Long. Elevation is 1,129 feet.
Population: 1,242 (2000); Race: 99.8% White, 0.0% Black, 0.0% Asian, 0.0% American Indian and Alaska Native, 0.5% Hispanic of any race, 0.2% two or more races (2000); Density: 1,201.8 persons per square mile (2000); Age: 29.0% under 18, 12.0% over 64 (2000); Marriage status: 20.1% never married, 68.7% now married, 5.4% widowed, 5.8% divorced (2000); Foreign born: 0.6% (2000); Ancestry (includes multiple ancestries): 66.6% German, 13.7% Polish, 11.4% Irish, 10.9% Norwegian, 3.9% French (except Basque) (2000).
Economy: Single-family building permits issued: 14 (2001) / 14 (2000); Multi-family building permits issued: 0 (2001) / 0 (2000); Employment by occupation: 12.5% management, 17.6% professional, 9.3% services, 28.6% sales, 0.6% farming, 11.2% construction, 20.3% production (2000).
Income: Per capita income: $19,980 (2000); Median household income: $47,721 (2000); Poverty rate: 3.1% (2000).
Taxes: Total city taxes per capita: $312 (1997); City property taxes per capita: $297 (1997).
Education: High school graduation rate: 87.3% (2000); College graduation rate: 22.9% (2000).
Housing: Homeownership rate: 82.8% (2000); Median home value: $106,400 (2000); Median rent: $461 per month (2000); Median age of housing: 22 years (2000).
Transportation: Commute to work: 95.3% car, 0.0% public transportation, 0.6% walk, 3.4% work from home (2000); Travel time to work: 28.1% less than 15 minutes, 45.9% 15 to 30 minutes, 19.3% 30 to 45 minutes, 1.5% 45 to 60 minutes, 5.2% 60 minutes or more (2000)

AVON (township). Covers a land area of 32.286 square miles and a water area of 2.588 square miles. Located at 45.62° N. Lat.; 94.45° W. Long. Elevation is 1,129 feet.
Population: 2,132 (2000); Race: 98.8% White, 0.0% Black, 0.2% Asian, 0.1% American Indian and Alaska Native, 2.9% Hispanic of any race, 0.1% two or more races (2000); Density: 66.0 persons per square mile (2000); Age: 30.8% under 18, 8.0% over 64 (2000); Marriage status: 25.7% never married, 64.7% now married, 3.5% widowed, 6.0% divorced (2000); Foreign born: 2.5% (2000); Ancestry (includes multiple ancestries): 63.9% German, 21.5% Polish, 6.1% Norwegian, 4.5% Irish, 3.4% Other groups (2000).
Economy: Dairying; livestock, poultry; grain, alfalfa, soybeans. Manufacturing: gears, metal fabrication, cabinets. Marl deposits in vicinity. Single-family building permits issued: 17 (2001) / 17 (2000); Multi-family building permits issued: 0 (2001) / 0 (2000); Employment by occupation: 16.2% management, 12.1% professional, 13.6% services, 24.1% sales, 1.2% farming, 12.0% construction, 20.9% production (2000).
Income: Per capita income: $19,944 (2000); Median household income: $51,806 (2000); Poverty rate: 7.0% (2000).
Taxes: Total city taxes per capita: $66 (2000); City property taxes per capita: $64 (2000).
Education: High school graduation rate: 86.4% (2000); College graduation rate: 16.4% (2000).
Housing: Homeownership rate: 89.9% (2000); Median home value: $117,200 (2000); Median rent: $331 per month (2000); Median age of housing: 22 years (2000).
Transportation: Commute to work: 89.6% car, 0.0% public transportation, 1.8% walk, 8.4% work from home (2000); Travel time to work: 25.8% less than 15 minutes, 44.1% 15 to 30 minutes, 24.0% 30 to 45 minutes, 2.7% 45 to 60 minutes, 3.5% 60 minutes or more (2000)

BELGRADE (city). Covers a land area of 1.178 square miles and a water area of 0 square miles. Located at 45.45° N. Lat.; 95.00° W. Long. Elevation is 1,266 feet.
Population: 750 (2000); Race: 100.0% White, 0.0% Black, 0.0% Asian, 0.0% American Indian and Alaska Native, 0.3% Hispanic of any race, 0.0% two or more races (2000); Density: 636.7 persons per square mile (2000); Age: 17.2% under 18, 37.7% over 64 (2000); Marriage status: 19.1% never married, 50.1% now married, 22.6% widowed, 8.2% divorced (2000); Foreign born: 1.3% (2000); Ancestry (includes multiple ancestries): 50.5% German, 29.3% Norwegian, 9.1% Swedish, 7.1% Irish, 3.2% English (2000).
Economy: Grain, soybeans, alfalfa; poultry, cattle, sheep, hogs; dairying. Manufacturing: building materials, steel tanks, crafts. Employment by occupation: 7.8% management, 18.0% professional, 19.6% services, 22.9% sales, 1.6% farming, 7.2% construction, 22.9% production (2000).

Income: Per capita income: $19,293 (2000); Median household income: $22,098 (2000); Poverty rate: 13.6% (2000).
Taxes: Total city taxes per capita: $217 (1997); City property taxes per capita: $209 (1997).
Education: High school graduation rate: 72.3% (2000); College graduation rate: 14.9% (2000).

School District(s)

Belgrade-Brooten-Elrosa (PK-12)
2000 Enrollment: 869 320-254-8213

Housing: Homeownership rate: 73.8% (2000); Median home value: $47,600 (2000); Median rent: $223 per month (2000); Median age of housing: 42 years (2000).
Newspapers: Observer (1 x week)
Transportation: Commute to work: 76.8% car, 0.0% public transportation, 17.6% walk, 3.6% work from home (2000); Travel time to work: 65.4% less than 15 minutes, 12.2% 15 to 30 minutes, 12.2% 30 to 45 minutes, 6.8% 45 to 60 minutes, 3.4% 60 minutes or more (2000)

BROCKWAY (township). Covers a land area of 47.869 square miles and a water area of 0.717 square miles. Located at 45.71° N. Lat.; 94.29° W. Long.
Population: 2,551 (2000); Race: 99.1% White, 0.0% Black, 0.2% Asian, 0.0% American Indian and Alaska Native, 0.0% Hispanic of any race, 0.6% two or more races (2000); Density: 53.3 persons per square mile (2000); Age: 32.4% under 18, 6.4% over 64 (2000); Marriage status: 26.7% never married, 67.3% now married, 1.6% widowed, 4.4% divorced (2000); Foreign born: 0.6% (2000); Ancestry (includes multiple ancestries): 56.9% German, 25.7% Polish, 8.3% Norwegian, 7.8% Irish, 6.7% Swedish (2000).
Economy: Employment by occupation: 15.2% management, 16.2% professional, 11.4% services, 20.3% sales, 1.9% farming, 10.1% construction, 24.9% production (2000).
Income: Per capita income: $22,041 (2000); Median household income: $54,375 (2000); Poverty rate: 4.3% (2000).
Taxes: Total city taxes per capita: $116 (2000); City property taxes per capita: $116 (2000).
Education: High school graduation rate: 85.9% (2000); College graduation rate: 19.0% (2000).
Housing: Homeownership rate: 92.8% (2000); Median home value: $121,300 (2000); Median rent: $371 per month (2000); Median age of housing: 23 years (2000).
Transportation: Commute to work: 91.0% car, 0.0% public transportation, 2.0% walk, 6.7% work from home (2000); Travel time to work: 18.1% less than 15 minutes, 58.1% 15 to 30 minutes, 18.8% 30 to 45 minutes, 0.7% 45 to 60 minutes, 4.3% 60 minutes or more (2000)

BROOTEN (city). Covers a land area of 1.453 square miles and a water area of 0 square miles. Located at 45.50° N. Lat.; 95.12° W. Long. Elevation is 1,314 feet.
Population: 649 (2000); Race: 99.4% White, 0.0% Black, 0.3% Asian, 0.0% American Indian and Alaska Native, 4.2% Hispanic of any race, 0.0% two or more races (2000); Density: 446.7 persons per square mile (2000); Age: 27.3% under 18, 18.3% over 64 (2000); Marriage status: 20.0% never married, 60.8% now married, 8.1% widowed, 11.1% divorced (2000); Foreign born: 3.2% (2000); Ancestry (includes multiple ancestries): 39.8% German, 38.0% Norwegian, 6.2% Dutch, 6.0% Swedish, 5.2% Danish (2000).
Economy: Railroad junction. Agricultural area: dairying; sheep, hogs, cattle, poultry; grain, soybeans. Manufacturing: medical supplies; light manufacturing. Single-family building permits issued: 2 (2001) / 4 (2000); Multi-family building permits issued: 4 (2001) / 0 (2000); Employment by occupation: 7.6% management, 17.4% professional, 19.4% services, 17.1% sales, 1.3% farming, 12.5% construction, 24.7% production (2000).
Income: Per capita income: $17,048 (2000); Median household income: $35,625 (2000); Poverty rate: 12.9% (2000).
Taxes: Total city taxes per capita: $230 (1997); City property taxes per capita: $219 (1997).
Education: High school graduation rate: 81.4% (2000); College graduation rate: 15.7% (2000).
Housing: Homeownership rate: 81.9% (2000); Median home value: $45,000 (2000); Median rent: $221 per month (2000); Median age of housing: 45 years (2000).
Newspapers: Bonanza Valley Voice (1 x week)
Transportation: Commute to work: 90.6% car, 0.0% public transportation, 6.4% walk, 2.0% work from home (2000); Travel time to work: 51.5% less than 15 minutes, 20.3% 15 to 30 minutes, 14.1% 30 to 45 minutes, 5.8% 45 to 60 minutes, 8.2% 60 minutes or more (2000)

COLD SPRING (city). Covers a land area of 2.079 square miles and a water area of 0.021 square miles. Located at 45.45° N. Lat.; 94.43° W. Long. Elevation is 1,091 feet.
Population: 2,975 (2000); Race: 99.3% White, 0.2% Black, 0.2% Asian, 0.0% American Indian and Alaska Native, 0.4% Hispanic of any race, 0.3% two or more races (2000); Density: 1,431.1 persons per square mile (2000); Age: 27.4% under 18, 20.9% over 64 (2000); Marriage status: 25.4% never married, 57.1% now married, 13.0% widowed, 4.5% divorced (2000); Foreign born: 0.8% (2000); Ancestry (includes multiple ancestries): 58.8% German, 8.4% Norwegian, 6.9% United States or American, 5.4% Polish, 5.0% Irish (2000).
Economy: Grain; livestock; dairying; mink. Manufacturing: food and beverages; furniture. Granite quarries nearby. Single-family building permits issued: 40 (2001) / 24 (2000); Multi-family building permits issued: 0 (2001) / 16 (2000); Employment by occupation: 10.6% management, 14.6% professional, 15.1% services, 26.0% sales, 0.4% farming, 8.9% construction, 24.2% production (2000).
Income: Per capita income: $18,308 (2000); Median household income: $37,500 (2000); Poverty rate: 3.3% (2000).
Taxes: Total city taxes per capita: $212 (1997); City property taxes per capita: $198 (1997).
Education: High school graduation rate: 76.7% (2000); College graduation rate: 14.2% (2000).

School District(s)

Rocori (PK-12)
2000 Enrollment: 2,364 320-685-4901

Housing: Homeownership rate: 70.4% (2000); Median home value: $94,900 (2000); Median rent: $420 per month (2000); Median age of housing: 27 years (2000).
Newspapers: Cold Spring Record (1 x week)
Transportation: Commute to work: 86.8% car, 1.3% public transportation, 6.5% walk, 5.0% work from home (2000); Travel time to work: 46.5% less than 15 minutes, 31.0% 15 to 30 minutes, 15.0% 30 to 45 minutes, 6.0% 45 to 60 minutes, 1.5% 60 minutes or more (2000)
Additional Information Contacts
Cold Spring Chamber of Commerce 320-685-4186

COLLEGEVILLE (township). Covers a land area of 31.644 square miles and a water area of 3.453 square miles. Located at 45.55° N. Lat.; 94.44° W. Long. Elevation is 1,094 feet.
History: St. John's University (Roman Catholic) is here.
Population: 3,516 (2000); Race: 97.2% White, 0.7% Black, 1.3% Asian, 0.1% American Indian and Alaska Native, 1.6% Hispanic of any race, 0.4% two or more races (2000); Density: 111.1 persons per square mile (2000); Age: 16.9% under 18, 6.1% over 64 (2000); Marriage status: 57.0% never married, 39.8% now married, 0.9% widowed, 2.3% divorced (2000); Foreign born: 2.7% (2000); Ancestry (includes multiple ancestries): 60.2% German, 12.4% Irish, 12.0% Norwegian, 7.5% Polish, 6.0% Swedish (2000).
Economy: Agriculture and dairying area. Employment by occupation: 11.9% management, 22.7% professional, 19.5% services, 24.0% sales, 0.2% farming, 8.8% construction, 12.8% production (2000).
Income: Per capita income: $18,348 (2000); Median household income: $61,146 (2000); Poverty rate: 6.0% (2000).
Taxes: Total city taxes per capita: $37 (1997); City property taxes per capita: $37 (1997).
Education: High school graduation rate: 90.0% (2000); College graduation rate: 34.6% (2000).

Four-year College(s)

Saint John's University (Private, Not-for-profit, Roman Catholic)
2001 Enrollment: 2,040 320-363-2011
2001 Tuition: In-state $18,015; Out-of-state $18,015

Housing: Homeownership rate: 94.2% (2000); Median home value: $147,300 (2000); Median rent: $446 per month (2000); Median age of housing: 22 years (2000).
Transportation: Commute to work: 61.8% car, 1.6% public transportation, 29.3% walk, 6.6% work from home (2000); Travel time to work: 49.1% less than 15 minutes, 32.6% 15 to 30 minutes, 12.3% 30 to 45 minutes, 1.8% 45 to 60 minutes, 4.3% 60 minutes or more (2000)

CROW LAKE (township). Covers a land area of 33.673 square miles and a water area of 1.440 square miles. Located at 45.47° N. Lat.; 95.07° W. Long.
Population: 345 (2000); Race: 100.0% White, 0.0% Black, 0.0% Asian, 0.0% American Indian and Alaska Native, 0.0% Hispanic of any race, 0.0% two or more races (2000); Density: 10.2 persons per square mile (2000); Age:

33.0% under 18, 9.7% over 64 (2000); Marriage status: 26.0% never married, 66.4% now married, 3.2% widowed, 4.3% divorced (2000); Foreign born: 0.5% (2000); Ancestry (includes multiple ancestries): 40.8% German, 22.3% Norwegian, 13.1% Swedish, 8.0% Irish, 7.2% United States or American (2000).
Economy: Employment by occupation: 16.6% management, 11.8% professional, 7.7% services, 20.1% sales, 4.1% farming, 11.2% construction, 28.4% production (2000).
Income: Per capita income: $19,108 (2000); Median household income: $41,042 (2000); Poverty rate: 7.8% (2000).
Taxes: Total city taxes per capita: $52 (1997); City property taxes per capita: $52 (1997).
Education: High school graduation rate: 85.2% (2000); College graduation rate: 14.4% (2000).
Housing: Homeownership rate: 93.8% (2000); Median home value: $56,300 (2000); Median rent: $475 per month (2000); Median age of housing: 27 years (2000).
Transportation: Commute to work: 93.4% car, 0.0% public transportation, 1.2% walk, 5.4% work from home (2000); Travel time to work: 57.0% less than 15 minutes, 13.3% 15 to 30 minutes, 19.6% 30 to 45 minutes, 2.5% 45 to 60 minutes, 7.6% 60 minutes or more (2000)

CROW RIVER (township). Covers a land area of 34.294 square miles and a water area of 0.009 square miles. Located at 45.44° N. Lat.; 94.94° W. Long.
Population: 352 (2000); Race: 100.0% White, 0.0% Black, 0.0% Asian, 0.0% American Indian and Alaska Native, 0.0% Hispanic of any race, 0.0% two or more races (2000); Density: 10.3 persons per square mile (2000); Age: 32.9% under 18, 7.9% over 64 (2000); Marriage status: 24.7% never married, 67.0% now married, 3.4% widowed, 4.9% divorced (2000); Foreign born: 0.8% (2000); Ancestry (includes multiple ancestries): 66.9% German, 26.7% Norwegian, 11.8% Swedish, 4.5% Irish, 3.7% English (2000).
Economy: Employment by occupation: 24.7% management, 12.1% professional, 9.5% services, 23.7% sales, 5.3% farming, 8.4% construction, 16.3% production (2000).
Income: Per capita income: $13,765 (2000); Median household income: $39,107 (2000); Poverty rate: 12.7% (2000).
Taxes: Total city taxes per capita: $58 (1997); City property taxes per capita: $58 (1997).
Education: High school graduation rate: 81.8% (2000); College graduation rate: 9.8% (2000).
Housing: Homeownership rate: 88.1% (2000); Median home value: $47,500 (2000); Median rent: $400 per month (2000); Median age of housing: 40 years (2000).
Transportation: Commute to work: 78.4% car, 0.0% public transportation, 0.0% walk, 21.6% work from home (2000); Travel time to work: 44.3% less than 15 minutes, 18.8% 15 to 30 minutes, 25.5% 30 to 45 minutes, 0.0% 45 to 60 minutes, 11.4% 60 minutes or more (2000)

EDEN LAKE (township). Covers a land area of 33.809 square miles and a water area of 4.746 square miles. Located at 45.37° N. Lat.; 94.57° W. Long.
Population: 1,526 (2000); Race: 99.0% White, 0.1% Black, 0.0% Asian, 0.0% American Indian and Alaska Native, 0.6% Hispanic of any race, 0.8% two or more races (2000); Density: 45.1 persons per square mile (2000); Age: 30.4% under 18, 11.0% over 64 (2000); Marriage status: 22.4% never married, 69.8% now married, 3.4% widowed, 4.4% divorced (2000); Foreign born: 0.6% (2000); Ancestry (includes multiple ancestries): 66.2% German, 10.3% Norwegian, 8.8% Irish, 5.4% Other groups, 5.2% French (except Basque) (2000).
Economy: Single-family building permits issued: 37 (2001) / 12 (2000); Multi-family building permits issued: 0 (2001) / 0 (2000); Employment by occupation: 15.1% management, 14.2% professional, 10.5% services, 22.3% sales, 3.8% farming, 12.3% construction, 21.7% production (2000).
Income: Per capita income: $17,727 (2000); Median household income: $48,295 (2000); Poverty rate: 5.9% (2000).
Taxes: Total city taxes per capita: $133 (2000); City property taxes per capita: $131 (2000).
Education: High school graduation rate: 84.2% (2000); College graduation rate: 12.3% (2000).
Housing: Homeownership rate: 94.6% (2000); Median home value: $108,600 (2000); Median rent: $475 per month (2000); Median age of housing: 25 years (2000).
Transportation: Commute to work: 89.5% car, 0.0% public transportation, 2.4% walk, 8.0% work from home (2000); Travel time to work: 28.3% less than 15 minutes, 30.5% 15 to 30 minutes, 19.2% 30 to 45 minutes, 10.6% 45 to 60 minutes, 11.3% 60 minutes or more (2000)

ELROSA (city). Covers a land area of 0.128 square miles and a water area of 0 square miles. Located at 45.56° N. Lat.; 94.94° W. Long. Elevation is 1,313 feet.
Population: 166 (2000); Race: 100.0% White, 0.0% Black, 0.0% Asian, 0.0% American Indian and Alaska Native, 0.0% Hispanic of any race, 0.0% two or more races (2000); Density: 1,300.9 persons per square mile (2000); Age: 23.7% under 18, 27.3% over 64 (2000); Marriage status: 21.9% never married, 63.2% now married, 13.2% widowed, 1.8% divorced (2000); Foreign born: 0.0% (2000); Ancestry (includes multiple ancestries): 88.5% German, 5.0% Irish, 4.3% English, 3.6% French (except Basque), 2.2% Swedish (2000).
Economy: Grain, poultry, livestock; dairying. Employment by occupation: 16.4% management, 6.0% professional, 9.0% services, 17.9% sales, 9.0% farming, 9.0% construction, 32.8% production (2000).
Income: Per capita income: $17,227 (2000); Median household income: $34,375 (2000); Poverty rate: 9.4% (2000).
Taxes: Total city taxes per capita: $144 (1997); City property taxes per capita: $125 (1997).
Education: High school graduation rate: 52.6% (2000); College graduation rate: 3.1% (2000).
Housing: Homeownership rate: 100.0% (2000); Median home value: $70,600 (2000); Median age of housing: 38 years (2000).
Transportation: Commute to work: 73.1% car, 0.0% public transportation, 3.0% walk, 23.9% work from home (2000); Travel time to work: 37.3% less than 15 minutes, 51.0% 15 to 30 minutes, 3.9% 30 to 45 minutes, 7.8% 45 to 60 minutes, 0.0% 60 minutes or more (2000)

FAIR HAVEN (township). Covers a land area of 34.000 square miles and a water area of 1.819 square miles. Located at 45.34° N. Lat.; 94.19° W. Long.
Population: 1,458 (2000); Race: 97.1% White, 0.2% Black, 0.8% Asian, 1.0% American Indian and Alaska Native, 0.0% Hispanic of any race, 0.9% two or more races (2000); Density: 42.9 persons per square mile (2000); Age: 29.6% under 18, 9.2% over 64 (2000); Marriage status: 22.4% never married, 67.2% now married, 4.0% widowed, 6.3% divorced (2000); Foreign born: 0.5% (2000); Ancestry (includes multiple ancestries): 56.1% German, 13.5% Norwegian, 10.8% Irish, 8.0% Polish, 7.5% United States or American (2000).
Economy: Single-family building permits issued: 5 (2001) / 5 (2000); Multi-family building permits issued: 0 (2001) / 0 (2000); Employment by occupation: 13.3% management, 10.8% professional, 11.3% services, 24.5% sales, 2.4% farming, 21.1% construction, 16.6% production (2000).
Income: Per capita income: $17,951 (2000); Median household income: $44,808 (2000); Poverty rate: 6.1% (2000).
Taxes: Total city taxes per capita: $107 (1997); City property taxes per capita: $104 (1997).
Education: High school graduation rate: 84.2% (2000); College graduation rate: 11.9% (2000).
Housing: Homeownership rate: 94.3% (2000); Median home value: $113,000 (2000); Median rent: $408 per month (2000); Median age of housing: 27 years (2000).
Transportation: Commute to work: 87.3% car, 0.3% public transportation, 2.7% walk, 9.8% work from home (2000); Travel time to work: 21.4% less than 15 minutes, 30.3% 15 to 30 minutes, 25.7% 30 to 45 minutes, 6.2% 45 to 60 minutes, 16.4% 60 minutes or more (2000)

FARMING (township). Covers a land area of 37.540 square miles and a water area of 1.371 square miles. Located at 45.54° N. Lat.; 94.55° W. Long.
Population: 875 (2000); Race: 99.8% White, 0.0% Black, 0.2% Asian, 0.0% American Indian and Alaska Native, 0.0% Hispanic of any race, 0.0% two or more races (2000); Density: 23.3 persons per square mile (2000); Age: 31.3% under 18, 6.3% over 64 (2000); Marriage status: 31.4% never married, 61.8% now married, 2.4% widowed, 4.4% divorced (2000); Foreign born: 0.6% (2000); Ancestry (includes multiple ancestries): 78.1% German, 5.0% Norwegian, 4.9% Polish, 4.1% United States or American, 4.0% Swedish (2000).
Economy: Single-family building permits issued: 10 (2001) / 10 (2000); Multi-family building permits issued: 0 (2001) / 0 (2000); Employment by occupation: 15.5% management, 11.5% professional, 10.6% services, 16.4% sales, 3.5% farming, 13.1% construction, 29.4% production (2000).
Income: Per capita income: $18,431 (2000); Median household income: $50,170 (2000); Poverty rate: 4.8% (2000).

Taxes: Total city taxes per capita: $138 (2000); City property taxes per capita: $137 (2000).
Education: High school graduation rate: 84.2% (2000); College graduation rate: 8.6% (2000).
Housing: Homeownership rate: 91.3% (2000); Median home value: $109,400 (2000); Median rent: $225 per month (2000); Median age of housing: 27 years (2000).
Transportation: Commute to work: 82.1% car, 0.4% public transportation, 4.6% walk, 11.9% work from home (2000); Travel time to work: 20.0% less than 15 minutes, 44.6% 15 to 30 minutes, 26.8% 30 to 45 minutes, 3.8% 45 to 60 minutes, 4.7% 60 minutes or more (2000)

FREEPORT (city). Covers a land area of 0.883 square miles and a water area of 0.006 square miles. Located at 45.66° N. Lat.; 94.68° W. Long. Elevation is 1,240 feet.
Population: 454 (2000); Race: 98.9% White, 0.0% Black, 0.0% Asian, 0.0% American Indian and Alaska Native, 0.4% Hispanic of any race, 0.8% two or more races (2000); Density: 514.3 persons per square mile (2000); Age: 24.8% under 18, 26.3% over 64 (2000); Marriage status: 19.7% never married, 65.4% now married, 9.8% widowed, 5.0% divorced (2000); Foreign born: 0.4% (2000); Ancestry (includes multiple ancestries): 66.2% German, 7.3% United States or American, 3.2% English, 2.8% Finnish, 1.3% Polish (2000).
Economy: Grain; poultry; dairying. Manufacturing: coal-mining filters, garage doors, machining, aviation fueling equipment, agricultural separating equipment, industrial fans, pipe and duct work, showcase components, special machinery, printing and publishing. Single-family building permits issued: 5 (2001) / 6 (2000); Multi-family building permits issued: 0 (2001) / 0 (2000); Employment by occupation: 13.4% management, 10.7% professional, 16.5% services, 23.0% sales, 4.6% farming, 10.7% construction, 21.1% production (2000).
Income: Per capita income: $15,827 (2000); Median household income: $32,955 (2000); Poverty rate: 7.9% (2000).
Taxes: Total city taxes per capita: $181 (1997); City property taxes per capita: $161 (1997).
Education: High school graduation rate: 70.8% (2000); College graduation rate: 8.1% (2000).
Housing: Homeownership rate: 83.0% (2000); Median home value: $79,800 (2000); Median rent: $300 per month (2000); Median age of housing: 39 years (2000).
Transportation: Commute to work: 88.1% car, 0.0% public transportation, 5.0% walk, 6.9% work from home (2000); Travel time to work: 55.1% less than 15 minutes, 22.6% 15 to 30 minutes, 16.5% 30 to 45 minutes, 3.3% 45 to 60 minutes, 2.5% 60 minutes or more (2000)

GETTY (township). Covers a land area of 36.008 square miles and a water area of 0.145 square miles. Located at 45.63° N. Lat.; 94.94° W. Long.
Population: 405 (2000); Race: 99.3% White, 0.7% Black, 0.0% Asian, 0.0% American Indian and Alaska Native, 0.0% Hispanic of any race, 0.0% two or more races (2000); Density: 11.2 persons per square mile (2000); Age: 39.1% under 18, 8.7% over 64 (2000); Marriage status: 35.6% never married, 59.7% now married, 2.3% widowed, 2.3% divorced (2000); Foreign born: 1.6% (2000); Ancestry (includes multiple ancestries): 68.2% German, 5.2% Norwegian, 4.9% Polish, 3.5% United States or American, 3.3% Irish (2000).
Economy: Single-family building permits issued: 0 (2001) / 0 (2000); Multi-family building permits issued: 0 (2001) / 0 (2000); Employment by occupation: 34.5% management, 4.4% professional, 8.7% services, 18.0% sales, 9.2% farming, 6.3% construction, 18.9% production (2000).
Income: Per capita income: $13,948 (2000); Median household income: $43,839 (2000); Poverty rate: 3.1% (2000).
Taxes: Total city taxes per capita: $60 (1997); City property taxes per capita: $60 (1997).
Education: High school graduation rate: 74.3% (2000); College graduation rate: 5.0% (2000).
Housing: Homeownership rate: 87.1% (2000); Median home value: $73,300 (2000); Median rent: $363 per month (2000); Median age of housing: 48 years (2000).
Transportation: Commute to work: 57.8% car, 0.0% public transportation, 8.5% walk, 32.7% work from home (2000); Travel time to work: 41.0% less than 15 minutes, 44.0% 15 to 30 minutes, 3.7% 30 to 45 minutes, 9.0% 45 to 60 minutes, 2.2% 60 minutes or more (2000)

GREENWALD (city). Covers a land area of 0.772 square miles and a water area of 0 square miles. Located at 45.60° N. Lat.; 94.85° W. Long. Elevation is 1,263 feet.
Population: 201 (2000); Race: 100.0% White, 0.0% Black, 0.0% Asian, 0.0% American Indian and Alaska Native, 0.0% Hispanic of any race, 0.0% two or more races (2000); Density: 260.2 persons per square mile (2000); Age: 15.0% under 18, 21.7% over 64 (2000); Marriage status: 33.7% never married, 56.4% now married, 8.8% widowed, 1.1% divorced (2000); Foreign born: 0.0% (2000); Ancestry (includes multiple ancestries): 95.2% German, 5.3% Irish, 2.9% Norwegian, 2.9% Polish, 1.4% Swedish (2000).
Economy: Poultry, cattle, sheep, hogs; dairying; grain. Manufacturing: livestock feed. Single-family building permits issued: 0 (2001) / 0 (2000); Multi-family building permits issued: 0 (2001) / 0 (2000); Employment by occupation: 8.2% management, 8.2% professional, 13.1% services, 23.0% sales, 0.0% farming, 17.2% construction, 30.3% production (2000).
Income: Per capita income: $17,539 (2000); Median household income: $37,000 (2000); Poverty rate: 2.4% (2000).
Taxes: Total city taxes per capita: $61 (1997); City property taxes per capita: $51 (1997).
Education: High school graduation rate: 70.2% (2000); College graduation rate: 5.7% (2000).
Housing: Homeownership rate: 94.2% (2000); Median home value: $73,800 (2000); Median rent: $458 per month (2000); Median age of housing: 60+ years (2000).
Transportation: Commute to work: 85.3% car, 0.0% public transportation, 9.5% walk, 0.0% work from home (2000); Travel time to work: 35.3% less than 15 minutes, 50.9% 15 to 30 minutes, 7.8% 30 to 45 minutes, 1.7% 45 to 60 minutes, 4.3% 60 minutes or more (2000)

GROVE (township). Covers a land area of 33.270 square miles and a water area of 0.486 square miles. Located at 45.63° N. Lat.; 94.82° W. Long.
Population: 505 (2000); Race: 99.2% White, 0.0% Black, 0.4% Asian, 0.4% American Indian and Alaska Native, 1.5% Hispanic of any race, 0.0% two or more races (2000); Density: 15.2 persons per square mile (2000); Age: 33.8% under 18, 5.1% over 64 (2000); Marriage status: 23.8% never married, 66.7% now married, 3.5% widowed, 6.1% divorced (2000); Foreign born: 0.4% (2000); Ancestry (includes multiple ancestries): 83.9% German, 4.2% Polish, 3.2% Other groups, 3.0% English, 2.8% Norwegian (2000).
Economy: Grain; livestock; dairying. Single-family building permits issued: 1 (2001) / 1 (2000); Multi-family building permits issued: 0 (2001) / 0 (2000); Employment by occupation: 25.3% management, 6.4% professional, 20.1% services, 20.1% sales, 2.0% farming, 10.8% construction, 15.3% production (2000).
Income: Per capita income: $18,533 (2000); Median household income: $45,750 (2000); Poverty rate: 12.6% (2000).
Taxes: Total city taxes per capita: $50 (1997); City property taxes per capita: $50 (1997).
Education: High school graduation rate: 83.3% (2000); College graduation rate: 7.0% (2000).
Housing: Homeownership rate: 91.5% (2000); Median home value: $108,600 (2000); Median rent: $419 per month (2000); Median age of housing: 27 years (2000).
Transportation: Commute to work: 70.2% car, 0.0% public transportation, 6.5% walk, 23.4% work from home (2000); Travel time to work: 55.3% less than 15 minutes, 24.7% 15 to 30 minutes, 11.1% 30 to 45 minutes, 3.2% 45 to 60 minutes, 5.8% 60 minutes or more (2000)

HOLDING (township). Covers a land area of 41.074 square miles and a water area of 0.717 square miles. Located at 45.72° N. Lat.; 94.46° W. Long.
Population: 1,147 (2000); Race: 98.6% White, 0.0% Black, 0.3% Asian, 0.7% American Indian and Alaska Native, 0.2% Hispanic of any race, 0.4% two or more races (2000); Density: 27.9 persons per square mile (2000); Age: 31.4% under 18, 8.7% over 64 (2000); Marriage status: 27.0% never married, 68.6% now married, 2.4% widowed, 1.9% divorced (2000); Foreign born: 0.5% (2000); Ancestry (includes multiple ancestries): 60.6% German, 37.0% Polish, 5.3% Irish, 4.8% Norwegian, 2.7% Swedish (2000).
Economy: Grain; livestock, poultry; dairying; light manufacturing. Single-family building permits issued: 0 (2001) / 10 (2000); Multi-family building permits issued: 0 (2001) / 0 (2000); Employment by occupation: 18.3% management, 10.5% professional, 14.7% services, 17.6% sales, 3.6% farming, 8.1% construction, 27.1% production (2000).
Income: Per capita income: $14,879 (2000); Median household income: $42,212 (2000); Poverty rate: 11.3% (2000).
Taxes: Total city taxes per capita: $123 (2000); City property taxes per capita: $120 (2000).
Education: High school graduation rate: 82.4% (2000); College graduation rate: 9.3% (2000).
Housing: Homeownership rate: 95.6% (2000); Median home value: $97,400 (2000); Median age of housing: 28 years (2000).

Transportation: Commute to work: 77.0% car, 0.3% public transportation, 3.3% walk, 17.3% work from home (2000); Travel time to work: 29.6% less than 15 minutes, 31.1% 15 to 30 minutes, 28.2% 30 to 45 minutes, 5.2% 45 to 60 minutes, 5.8% 60 minutes or more (2000)

HOLDINGFORD (city). Covers a land area of 0.623 square miles and a water area of 0 square miles. Located at 45.73° N. Lat.; 94.47° W. Long. Elevation is 1,210 feet.

Population: 736 (2000); Race: 98.2% White, 0.0% Black, 0.8% Asian, 0.0% American Indian and Alaska Native, 0.0% Hispanic of any race, 1.0% two or more races (2000); Density: 1,182.1 persons per square mile (2000); Age: 27.2% under 18, 21.8% over 64 (2000); Marriage status: 24.6% never married, 54.1% now married, 9.2% widowed, 12.1% divorced (2000); Foreign born: 0.8% (2000); Ancestry (includes multiple ancestries): 51.6% German, 21.3% Polish, 6.9% Norwegian, 5.1% United States or American, 4.8% Irish (2000).

Economy: Single-family building permits issued: 3 (2001) / 4 (2000); Multi-family building permits issued: 0 (2001) / 0 (2000); Employment by occupation: 5.1% management, 13.9% professional, 14.6% services, 26.4% sales, 2.0% farming, 10.5% construction, 27.5% production (2000).

Income: Per capita income: $15,410 (2000); Median household income: $34,000 (2000); Poverty rate: 11.2% (2000).

Taxes: Total city taxes per capita: $325 (1997); City property taxes per capita: $318 (1997).

Education: High school graduation rate: 75.9% (2000); College graduation rate: 8.0% (2000).

School District(s)

Holdingford (PK-12)
2000 Enrollment: 1,075 320-746-2196

Housing: Homeownership rate: 80.8% (2000); Median home value: $77,000 (2000); Median rent: $390 per month (2000); Median age of housing: 36 years (2000).

Transportation: Commute to work: 88.2% car, 0.0% public transportation, 9.4% walk, 2.1% work from home (2000); Travel time to work: 34.5% less than 15 minutes, 23.8% 15 to 30 minutes, 34.9% 30 to 45 minutes, 2.8% 45 to 60 minutes, 3.9% 60 minutes or more (2000)

KIMBALL (city). Aka Kimball Prairie. Covers a land area of 1.383 square miles and a water area of 0 square miles. Located at 45.31° N. Lat.; 94.30° W. Long.

Population: 635 (2000); Race: 99.0% White, 0.2% Black, 0.0% Asian, 0.2% American Indian and Alaska Native, 0.3% Hispanic of any race, 0.7% two or more races (2000); Density: 459.0 persons per square mile (2000); Age: 24.8% under 18, 18.3% over 64 (2000); Marriage status: 28.0% never married, 56.1% now married, 9.0% widowed, 6.9% divorced (2000); Foreign born: 1.2% (2000); Ancestry (includes multiple ancestries): 51.2% German, 21.7% Irish, 12.7% Swedish, 5.6% Norwegian, 5.6% Polish (2000).

Economy: Single-family building permits issued: 2 (2001) / 0 (2000); Multi-family building permits issued: 0 (2001) / 0 (2000); Employment by occupation: 9.2% management, 10.5% professional, 14.9% services, 25.8% sales, 0.3% farming, 9.8% construction, 29.5% production (2000).

Income: Per capita income: $16,971 (2000); Median household income: $34,219 (2000); Poverty rate: 9.1% (2000).

Taxes: Total city taxes per capita: $236 (1997); City property taxes per capita: $232 (1997).

Education: High school graduation rate: 79.7% (2000); College graduation rate: 8.4% (2000).

School District(s)

Kimball (PK-12)
2000 Enrollment: 904 320-398-5585

Housing: Homeownership rate: 66.9% (2000); Median home value: $73,600 (2000); Median rent: $412 per month (2000); Median age of housing: 42 years (2000).

Newspapers: Tri-County News (1 x week)

Transportation: Commute to work: 89.1% car, 0.3% public transportation, 6.5% walk, 4.1% work from home (2000); Travel time to work: 29.8% less than 15 minutes, 35.5% 15 to 30 minutes, 23.8% 30 to 45 minutes, 3.9% 45 to 60 minutes, 7.1% 60 minutes or more (2000)

KRAIN (township). Covers a land area of 43.367 square miles and a water area of 0.729 square miles. Located at 45.72° N. Lat.; 94.56° W. Long.

Population: 901 (2000); Race: 99.4% White, 0.0% Black, 0.0% Asian, 0.2% American Indian and Alaska Native, 0.2% Hispanic of any race, 0.2% two or more races (2000); Density: 20.8 persons per square mile (2000); Age: 31.6% under 18, 8.6% over 64 (2000); Marriage status: 28.2% never married, 66.0% now married, 2.1% widowed, 3.7% divorced (2000); Foreign born: 0.2% (2000); Ancestry (includes multiple ancestries): 69.7% German, 11.7% Polish, 7.7% United States or American, 3.1% English, 3.1% Swedish (2000).

Economy: Employment by occupation: 25.8% management, 6.7% professional, 10.8% services, 18.7% sales, 3.5% farming, 12.5% construction, 22.1% production (2000).

Income: Per capita income: $17,556 (2000); Median household income: $40,550 (2000); Poverty rate: 8.6% (2000).

Taxes: Total city taxes per capita: $87 (1997); City property taxes per capita: $87 (1997).

Education: High school graduation rate: 79.6% (2000); College graduation rate: 6.8% (2000).

Housing: Homeownership rate: 92.8% (2000); Median home value: $102,900 (2000); Median rent: $325 per month (2000); Median age of housing: 33 years (2000).

Transportation: Commute to work: 76.7% car, 0.0% public transportation, 2.3% walk, 21.0% work from home (2000); Travel time to work: 27.8% less than 15 minutes, 31.0% 15 to 30 minutes, 28.3% 30 to 45 minutes, 6.6% 45 to 60 minutes, 6.3% 60 minutes or more (2000)

LAKE GEORGE (township). Covers a land area of 34.636 square miles and a water area of 0.717 square miles. Located at 45.55° N. Lat.; 94.93° W. Long.

Population: 371 (2000); Race: 99.3% White, 0.0% Black, 0.0% Asian, 0.0% American Indian and Alaska Native, 0.5% Hispanic of any race, 0.2% two or more races (2000); Density: 10.7 persons per square mile (2000); Age: 38.4% under 18, 11.1% over 64 (2000); Marriage status: 19.5% never married, 71.0% now married, 3.8% widowed, 5.7% divorced (2000); Foreign born: 0.5% (2000); Ancestry (includes multiple ancestries): 83.0% German, 11.8% Norwegian, 5.2% French (except Basque), 4.7% Dutch, 4.4% Irish (2000).

Economy: Employment by occupation: 38.1% management, 5.7% professional, 11.4% services, 10.8% sales, 6.3% farming, 13.6% construction, 14.2% production (2000).

Income: Per capita income: $13,662 (2000); Median household income: $36,029 (2000); Poverty rate: 18.5% (2000).

Taxes: Total city taxes per capita: $41 (1997); City property taxes per capita: $41 (1997).

Education: High school graduation rate: 79.7% (2000); College graduation rate: 3.4% (2000).

Housing: Homeownership rate: 91.8% (2000); Median home value: $90,800 (2000); Median rent: $275 per month (2000); Median age of housing: 49 years (2000).

Transportation: Commute to work: 61.5% car, 0.0% public transportation, 14.9% walk, 23.6% work from home (2000); Travel time to work: 56.4% less than 15 minutes, 21.8% 15 to 30 minutes, 13.5% 30 to 45 minutes, 3.0% 45 to 60 minutes, 5.3% 60 minutes or more (2000)

LAKE HENRY (city). Covers a land area of 0.139 square miles and a water area of 0 square miles. Located at 45.46° N. Lat.; 94.79° W. Long.

Population: 90 (2000); Race: 99.0% White, 0.0% Black, 0.0% Asian, 0.0% American Indian and Alaska Native, 0.0% Hispanic of any race, 1.0% two or more races (2000); Density: 649.0 persons per square mile (2000); Age: 37.8% under 18, 16.3% over 64 (2000); Marriage status: 24.6% never married, 61.5% now married, 9.2% widowed, 4.6% divorced (2000); Foreign born: 0.0% (2000); Ancestry (includes multiple ancestries): 66.3% German, 8.2% Swedish, 8.2% Polish, 4.1% French (except Basque), 3.1% Norwegian (2000).

Economy: Employment by occupation: 5.4% management, 10.8% professional, 16.2% services, 45.9% sales, 0.0% farming, 16.2% construction, 5.4% production (2000).

Income: Per capita income: $15,694 (2000); Median household income: $38,750 (2000); Poverty rate: 5.3% (2000).

Taxes: Total city taxes per capita: $80 (1997); City property taxes per capita: $57 (1997).

Education: High school graduation rate: 75.9% (2000); College graduation rate: 7.4% (2000).

Housing: Homeownership rate: 100.0% (2000); Median home value: $59,200 (2000); Median age of housing: 35 years (2000).

Transportation: Commute to work: 64.9% car, 0.0% public transportation, 21.6% walk, 13.5% work from home (2000); Travel time to work: 59.4% less than 15 minutes, 12.5% 15 to 30 minutes, 15.6% 30 to 45 minutes, 12.5% 45 to 60 minutes, 0.0% 60 minutes or more (2000)

LAKE HENRY (township). Covers a land area of 35.451 square miles and a water area of 0.111 square miles. Located at 45.46° N. Lat.; 94.83° W. Long.

Population: 330 (2000); Race: 98.1% White, 0.3% Black, 0.0% Asian, 0.0% American Indian and Alaska Native, 0.0% Hispanic of any race, 1.6% two or more races (2000); Density: 9.3 persons per square mile (2000); Age: 33.0% under 18, 5.3% over 64 (2000); Marriage status: 32.3% never married, 61.7% now married, 3.4% widowed, 2.6% divorced (2000); Foreign born: 0.0% (2000); Ancestry (includes multiple ancestries): 76.6% German, 7.2% United States or American, 5.3% Norwegian, 4.0% Irish, 3.1% Other groups (2000).
Economy: Grain; livestock, poultry; dairying. Employment by occupation: 35.6% management, 6.3% professional, 8.6% services, 13.8% sales, 13.2% farming, 9.8% construction, 12.6% production (2000).
Income: Per capita income: $15,036 (2000); Median household income: $42,188 (2000); Poverty rate: 4.7% (2000).
Taxes: Total city taxes per capita: $174 (1997); City property taxes per capita: $174 (1997).
Education: High school graduation rate: 78.8% (2000); College graduation rate: 4.9% (2000).
Housing: Homeownership rate: 91.8% (2000); Median home value: $39,200 (2000); Median rent: $225 per month (2000); Median age of housing: 45 years (2000).
Transportation: Commute to work: 53.8% car, 0.0% public transportation, 10.4% walk, 35.8% work from home (2000); Travel time to work: 47.7% less than 15 minutes, 26.1% 15 to 30 minutes, 8.1% 30 to 45 minutes, 8.1% 45 to 60 minutes, 9.9% 60 minutes or more (2000)

LE SAUK (township). Covers a land area of 14.069 square miles and a water area of 0.385 square miles. Located at 45.61° N. Lat.; 94.21° W. Long.
Population: 1,880 (2000); Race: 99.1% White, 0.0% Black, 0.1% Asian, 0.0% American Indian and Alaska Native, 0.0% Hispanic of any race, 0.8% two or more races (2000); Density: 133.6 persons per square mile (2000); Age: 32.9% under 18, 9.7% over 64 (2000); Marriage status: 19.9% never married, 75.2% now married, 2.4% widowed, 2.5% divorced (2000); Foreign born: 0.1% (2000); Ancestry (includes multiple ancestries): 61.8% German, 12.1% Polish, 9.2% Swedish, 8.9% Norwegian, 6.8% Irish (2000).
Economy: Single-family building permits issued: 3 (2001) / 5 (2000); Multi-family building permits issued: 0 (2001) / 0 (2000); Employment by occupation: 12.5% management, 16.8% professional, 12.9% services, 27.3% sales, 0.7% farming, 8.1% construction, 21.7% production (2000).
Income: Per capita income: $26,510 (2000); Median household income: $60,750 (2000); Poverty rate: 0.9% (2000).
Taxes: Total city taxes per capita: $47 (2000); City property taxes per capita: $39 (2000).
Education: High school graduation rate: 92.8% (2000); College graduation rate: 28.8% (2000).
Housing: Homeownership rate: 92.0% (2000); Median home value: $117,800 (2000); Median rent: $425 per month (2000); Median age of housing: 28 years (2000).
Transportation: Commute to work: 92.1% car, 0.0% public transportation, 1.3% walk, 6.6% work from home (2000); Travel time to work: 32.5% less than 15 minutes, 56.1% 15 to 30 minutes, 5.9% 30 to 45 minutes, 0.6% 45 to 60 minutes, 4.8% 60 minutes or more (2000)

LUXEMBURG (township). Covers a land area of 35.508 square miles and a water area of 0.275 square miles. Located at 45.37° N. Lat.; 94.44° W. Long. Elevation is 1,106 feet.
Population: 689 (2000); Race: 98.9% White, 0.3% Black, 0.0% Asian, 0.9% American Indian and Alaska Native, 0.6% Hispanic of any race, 0.0% two or more races (2000); Density: 19.4 persons per square mile (2000); Age: 29.4% under 18, 5.4% over 64 (2000); Marriage status: 32.1% never married, 64.4% now married, 1.7% widowed, 1.8% divorced (2000); Foreign born: 0.0% (2000); Ancestry (includes multiple ancestries): 80.8% German, 6.0% Polish, 4.5% United States or American, 3.3% Other groups, 2.6% Czech (2000).
Economy: Single-family building permits issued: 0 (2001) / 2 (2000); Multi-family building permits issued: 0 (2001) / 0 (2000); Employment by occupation: 26.9% management, 7.3% professional, 9.8% services, 15.6% sales, 3.7% farming, 10.3% construction, 26.4% production (2000).
Income: Per capita income: $20,067 (2000); Median household income: $57,083 (2000); Poverty rate: 5.9% (2000).
Taxes: Total city taxes per capita: $222 (2000); City property taxes per capita: $221 (2000).
Education: High school graduation rate: 80.6% (2000); College graduation rate: 6.4% (2000).
Housing: Homeownership rate: 91.9% (2000); Median home value: $111,700 (2000); Median rent: $950 per month (2000); Median age of housing: 58 years (2000).
Transportation: Commute to work: 67.0% car, 0.0% public transportation, 2.0% walk, 30.7% work from home (2000); Travel time to work: 37.8% less than 15 minutes, 21.8% 15 to 30 minutes, 24.7% 30 to 45 minutes, 10.2% 45 to 60 minutes, 5.5% 60 minutes or more (2000)

LYNDEN (township). Covers a land area of 23.921 square miles and a water area of 1.579 square miles. Located at 45.39° N. Lat.; 94.10° W. Long.
Population: 1,919 (2000); Race: 98.4% White, 0.2% Black, 0.6% Asian, 0.0% American Indian and Alaska Native, 0.7% Hispanic of any race, 0.4% two or more races (2000); Density: 80.2 persons per square mile (2000); Age: 30.2% under 18, 6.1% over 64 (2000); Marriage status: 22.6% never married, 68.5% now married, 2.4% widowed, 6.5% divorced (2000); Foreign born: 1.0% (2000); Ancestry (includes multiple ancestries): 64.4% German, 10.8% Norwegian, 9.5% Polish, 8.2% Irish, 7.4% Swedish (2000).
Economy: Employment by occupation: 12.6% management, 14.2% professional, 13.4% services, 24.4% sales, 0.6% farming, 13.9% construction, 20.9% production (2000).
Income: Per capita income: $21,405 (2000); Median household income: $57,765 (2000); Poverty rate: 3.2% (2000).
Taxes: Total city taxes per capita: $130 (1997); City property taxes per capita: $126 (1997).
Education: High school graduation rate: 87.1% (2000); College graduation rate: 20.0% (2000).
Housing: Homeownership rate: 95.8% (2000); Median home value: $126,800 (2000); Median rent: $275 per month (2000); Median age of housing: 20 years (2000).
Transportation: Commute to work: 95.2% car, 0.5% public transportation, 0.6% walk, 3.6% work from home (2000); Travel time to work: 18.6% less than 15 minutes, 44.4% 15 to 30 minutes, 20.1% 30 to 45 minutes, 4.3% 45 to 60 minutes, 12.6% 60 minutes or more (2000)

MAINE PRAIRIE (township). Covers a land area of 56.346 square miles and a water area of 2.991 square miles. Located at 45.37° N. Lat.; 94.32° W. Long.
Population: 1,686 (2000); Race: 98.2% White, 0.1% Black, 0.0% Asian, 0.2% American Indian and Alaska Native, 0.6% Hispanic of any race, 1.1% two or more races (2000); Density: 29.9 persons per square mile (2000); Age: 30.5% under 18, 10.0% over 64 (2000); Marriage status: 23.9% never married, 65.7% now married, 6.0% widowed, 4.4% divorced (2000); Foreign born: 0.2% (2000); Ancestry (includes multiple ancestries): 64.6% German, 10.1% Irish, 6.7% Norwegian, 6.6% Swedish, 5.9% Polish (2000).
Economy: Single-family building permits issued: 15 (2001) / 4 (2000); Multi-family building permits issued: 0 (2001) / 0 (2000); Employment by occupation: 16.4% management, 15.5% professional, 10.8% services, 24.5% sales, 2.2% farming, 12.0% construction, 18.5% production (2000).
Income: Per capita income: $19,875 (2000); Median household income: $50,833 (2000); Poverty rate: 3.1% (2000).
Taxes: Total city taxes per capita: $111 (1997); City property taxes per capita: $110 (1997).
Education: High school graduation rate: 87.7% (2000); College graduation rate: 13.8% (2000).
Housing: Homeownership rate: 92.1% (2000); Median home value: $121,500 (2000); Median rent: $340 per month (2000); Median age of housing: 31 years (2000).
Transportation: Commute to work: 88.0% car, 0.0% public transportation, 2.2% walk, 9.7% work from home (2000); Travel time to work: 25.4% less than 15 minutes, 36.6% 15 to 30 minutes, 22.8% 30 to 45 minutes, 5.3% 45 to 60 minutes, 10.0% 60 minutes or more (2000)

MEIRE GROVE (city). Covers a land area of 0.459 square miles and a water area of 0 square miles. Located at 45.62° N. Lat.; 94.86° W. Long.
Population: 149 (2000); Race: 100.0% White, 0.0% Black, 0.0% Asian, 0.0% American Indian and Alaska Native, 0.0% Hispanic of any race, 0.0% two or more races (2000); Density: 324.8 persons per square mile (2000); Age: 30.9% under 18, 21.6% over 64 (2000); Marriage status: 19.1% never married, 56.5% now married, 13.0% widowed, 11.3% divorced (2000); Foreign born: 0.0% (2000); Ancestry (includes multiple ancestries): 79.6% German, 8.6% French (except Basque), 3.7% Other groups, 2.5% English, 1.9% Italian (2000).
Economy: Employment by occupation: 25.8% management, 3.0% professional, 18.2% services, 18.2% sales, 4.5% farming, 3.0% construction, 27.3% production (2000).
Income: Per capita income: $13,559 (2000); Median household income: $24,250 (2000); Poverty rate: 17.3% (2000).
Taxes: Total city taxes per capita: $93 (1997); City property taxes per capita: $76 (1997).
Education: High school graduation rate: 71.7% (2000); College graduation rate: 9.4% (2000).

Housing: Homeownership rate: 76.2% (2000); Median home value: $36,300 (2000); Median rent: $555 per month (2000); Median age of housing: 29 years (2000).
Transportation: Commute to work: 77.0% car, 0.0% public transportation, 21.3% walk, 1.6% work from home (2000); Travel time to work: 63.3% less than 15 minutes, 20.0% 15 to 30 minutes, 16.7% 30 to 45 minutes, 0.0% 45 to 60 minutes, 0.0% 60 minutes or more (2000)

MELROSE (city). Covers a land area of 2.831 square miles and a water area of 0.116 square miles. Located at 45.67° N. Lat.; 94.81° W. Long. Elevation is 1,213 feet.
Population: 3,091 (2000); Race: 97.2% White, 0.7% Black, 0.5% Asian, 0.0% American Indian and Alaska Native, 11.5% Hispanic of any race, 0.3% two or more races (2000); Density: 1,091.8 persons per square mile (2000); Age: 27.9% under 18, 20.8% over 64 (2000); Marriage status: 25.6% never married, 59.3% now married, 11.0% widowed, 4.1% divorced (2000); Foreign born: 9.1% (2000); Ancestry (includes multiple ancestries): 61.7% German, 11.7% Other groups, 5.1% United States or American, 5.0% Norwegian, 4.1% Irish (2000).
Economy: Single-family building permits issued: 25 (2001) / 12 (2000); Multi-family building permits issued: 0 (2001) / 0 (2000); Employment by occupation: 7.4% management, 16.6% professional, 13.9% services, 23.7% sales, 1.5% farming, 7.0% construction, 29.9% production (2000).
Income: Per capita income: $15,510 (2000); Median household income: $34,432 (2000); Poverty rate: 7.6% (2000).
Taxes: Total city taxes per capita: $108 (1997); City property taxes per capita: $96 (1997).
Education: High school graduation rate: 70.7% (2000); College graduation rate: 13.5% (2000).

School District(s)

Melrose (PK-12)
2000 Enrollment: 1,607 320-256-4224
Housing: Homeownership rate: 78.2% (2000); Median home value: $81,600 (2000); Median rent: $372 per month (2000); Median age of housing: 34 years (2000).
Hospitals: Melrose Area Hospital & Pine Villa Care Center (28 beds)
Safety: Violent crime rate: 19.2 per 10,000 population; Property crime rate: 182.5 per 10,000 population (2001).
Newspapers: The Melrose Beacon (1 x week)
Transportation: Commute to work: 84.6% car, 0.4% public transportation, 8.7% walk, 4.8% work from home (2000); Travel time to work: 67.0% less than 15 minutes, 11.4% 15 to 30 minutes, 14.5% 30 to 45 minutes, 3.3% 45 to 60 minutes, 3.8% 60 minutes or more (2000)
Additional Information Contacts
Melrose Chamber of Commerce 320-256-7174

MELROSE (township). Covers a land area of 39.648 square miles and a water area of 0.669 square miles. Located at 45.71° N. Lat.; 94.83° W. Long. Elevation is 1,213 feet.
History: Settled 1857, incorporated as city 1898.
Population: 772 (2000); Race: 100.0% White, 0.0% Black, 0.0% Asian, 0.0% American Indian and Alaska Native, 0.0% Hispanic of any race, 0.0% two or more races (2000); Density: 19.5 persons per square mile (2000); Age: 29.8% under 18, 14.0% over 64 (2000); Marriage status: 25.0% never married, 66.5% now married, 4.6% widowed, 3.9% divorced (2000); Foreign born: 0.3% (2000); Ancestry (includes multiple ancestries): 79.1% German, 8.3% Polish, 6.6% Norwegian, 5.3% United States or American, 2.3% Swedish (2000).
Economy: Trade and shipping point: grain; livestock; dairying. Manufacturing: cheese, feeds, machine parts, furniture; food processing. Single-family building permits issued: 5 (2001) / 4 (2000); Multi-family building permits issued: 0 (2001) / 0 (2000); Employment by occupation: 36.6% management, 10.5% professional, 10.5% services, 12.8% sales, 5.2% farming, 6.8% construction, 17.5% production (2000).
Income: Per capita income: $16,462 (2000); Median household income: $42,589 (2000); Poverty rate: 5.7% (2000).
Taxes: Total city taxes per capita: $55 (1997); City property taxes per capita: $55 (1997).
Education: High school graduation rate: 80.7% (2000); College graduation rate: 10.8% (2000).
Housing: Homeownership rate: 92.5% (2000); Median home value: $116,700 (2000); Median rent: $235 per month (2000); Median age of housing: 29 years (2000).
Transportation: Commute to work: 68.1% car, 0.0% public transportation, 1.8% walk, 30.1% work from home (2000); Travel time to work: 57.7% less than 15 minutes, 21.5% 15 to 30 minutes, 9.8% 30 to 45 minutes, 8.7% 45 to 60 minutes, 2.3% 60 minutes or more (2000)

MILLWOOD (township). Covers a land area of 38.952 square miles and a water area of 2.487 square miles. Located at 45.71° N. Lat.; 94.69° W. Long.
Population: 986 (2000); Race: 100.0% White, 0.0% Black, 0.0% Asian, 0.0% American Indian and Alaska Native, 0.0% Hispanic of any race, 0.0% two or more races (2000); Density: 25.3 persons per square mile (2000); Age: 30.9% under 18, 8.7% over 64 (2000); Marriage status: 25.7% never married, 68.2% now married, 3.3% widowed, 2.8% divorced (2000); Foreign born: 0.2% (2000); Ancestry (includes multiple ancestries): 70.9% German, 5.3% Polish, 3.7% United States or American, 2.9% Dutch, 2.5% Norwegian (2000).
Economy: Employment by occupation: 27.6% management, 7.6% professional, 8.2% services, 16.8% sales, 5.4% farming, 12.6% construction, 21.8% production (2000).
Income: Per capita income: $18,236 (2000); Median household income: $46,071 (2000); Poverty rate: 8.0% (2000).
Taxes: Total city taxes per capita: $141 (1997); City property taxes per capita: $141 (1997).
Education: High school graduation rate: 84.7% (2000); College graduation rate: 10.2% (2000).
Housing: Homeownership rate: 91.8% (2000); Median home value: $118,900 (2000); Median rent: $388 per month (2000); Median age of housing: 31 years (2000).
Transportation: Commute to work: 70.0% car, 0.0% public transportation, 7.4% walk, 21.8% work from home (2000); Travel time to work: 37.1% less than 15 minutes, 34.3% 15 to 30 minutes, 12.5% 30 to 45 minutes, 7.4% 45 to 60 minutes, 8.7% 60 minutes or more (2000)

MUNSON (township). Covers a land area of 34.609 square miles and a water area of 3.024 square miles. Located at 45.44° N. Lat.; 94.55° W. Long.
Population: 1,351 (2000); Race: 99.6% White, 0.1% Black, 0.0% Asian, 0.0% American Indian and Alaska Native, 0.0% Hispanic of any race, 0.1% two or more races (2000); Density: 39.0 persons per square mile (2000); Age: 25.1% under 18, 11.8% over 64 (2000); Marriage status: 20.0% never married, 74.6% now married, 2.0% widowed, 3.4% divorced (2000); Foreign born: 0.5% (2000); Ancestry (includes multiple ancestries): 66.5% German, 8.2% Norwegian, 7.3% Irish, 5.3% Swedish, 4.9% United States or American (2000).
Economy: Single-family building permits issued: 19 (2001) / 14 (2000); Multi-family building permits issued: 0 (2001) / 0 (2000); Employment by occupation: 16.0% management, 13.6% professional, 8.0% services, 23.4% sales, 1.0% farming, 12.3% construction, 25.8% production (2000).
Income: Per capita income: $20,446 (2000); Median household income: $49,539 (2000); Poverty rate: 3.3% (2000).
Taxes: Total city taxes per capita: $128 (1997); City property taxes per capita: $126 (1997).
Education: High school graduation rate: 87.4% (2000); College graduation rate: 14.2% (2000).
Housing: Homeownership rate: 96.2% (2000); Median home value: $120,600 (2000); Median rent: $460 per month (2000); Median age of housing: 28 years (2000).
Transportation: Commute to work: 88.1% car, 0.6% public transportation, 0.7% walk, 10.7% work from home (2000); Travel time to work: 27.4% less than 15 minutes, 23.1% 15 to 30 minutes, 29.1% 30 to 45 minutes, 11.6% 45 to 60 minutes, 8.8% 60 minutes or more (2000)

NEW MUNICH (city). Covers a land area of 0.544 square miles and a water area of 0 square miles. Located at 45.62° N. Lat.; 94.75° W. Long. Elevation is 1,192 feet.
Population: 352 (2000); Race: 98.1% White, 0.0% Black, 0.0% Asian, 1.9% American Indian and Alaska Native, 0.0% Hispanic of any race, 0.0% two or more races (2000); Density: 646.9 persons per square mile (2000); Age: 19.9% under 18, 25.7% over 64 (2000); Marriage status: 24.6% never married, 49.1% now married, 23.4% widowed, 2.9% divorced (2000); Foreign born: 0.0% (2000); Ancestry (includes multiple ancestries): 69.9% German, 10.7% Irish, 6.3% English, 4.9% French Canadian, 4.9% Polish (2000).
Economy: Grain; poultry; dairying. Manufacturing of concrete. Single-family building permits issued: 1 (2001) / 1 (2000); Multi-family building permits issued: 0 (2001) / 0 (2000); Employment by occupation: 6.6% management, 7.7% professional, 8.8% services, 16.5% sales, 3.3% farming, 11.0% construction, 46.2% production (2000).

Income: Per capita income: $15,016 (2000); Median household income: $38,750 (2000); Poverty rate: 14.6% (2000).
Taxes: Total city taxes per capita: $52 (1997); City property taxes per capita: $42 (1997).
Education: High school graduation rate: 69.9% (2000); College graduation rate: 0.0% (2000).
Housing: Homeownership rate: 93.2% (2000); Median home value: $45,000 (2000); Median rent: $225 per month (2000); Median age of housing: 57 years (2000).
Transportation: Commute to work: 88.8% car, 0.0% public transportation, 11.2% walk, 0.0% work from home (2000); Travel time to work: 52.8% less than 15 minutes, 21.3% 15 to 30 minutes, 18.0% 30 to 45 minutes, 7.9% 45 to 60 minutes, 0.0% 60 minutes or more (2000)

NORTH FORK (township). Covers a land area of 34.803 square miles and a water area of 0 square miles. Located at 45.54° N. Lat.; 95.06° W. Long.
Population: 253 (2000); Race: 100.0% White, 0.0% Black, 0.0% Asian, 0.0% American Indian and Alaska Native, 0.0% Hispanic of any race, 0.0% two or more races (2000); Density: 7.3 persons per square mile (2000); Age: 31.4% under 18, 13.6% over 64 (2000); Marriage status: 24.4% never married, 63.9% now married, 3.4% widowed, 8.3% divorced (2000); Foreign born: 1.5% (2000); Ancestry (includes multiple ancestries): 43.9% German, 40.2% Norwegian, 8.0% Irish, 6.8% United States or American, 5.7% French (except Basque) (2000).
Economy: Employment by occupation: 40.3% management, 12.7% professional, 6.0% services, 14.9% sales, 7.5% farming, 9.0% construction, 9.7% production (2000).
Income: Per capita income: $13,326 (2000); Median household income: $30,000 (2000); Poverty rate: 15.2% (2000).
Taxes: Total city taxes per capita: $81 (1997); City property taxes per capita: $81 (1997).
Education: High school graduation rate: 81.7% (2000); College graduation rate: 7.1% (2000).
Housing: Homeownership rate: 89.0% (2000); Median home value: $45,000 (2000); Median rent: $425 per month (2000); Median age of housing: 52 years (2000).
Transportation: Commute to work: 61.2% car, 0.0% public transportation, 6.7% walk, 30.6% work from home (2000); Travel time to work: 46.2% less than 15 minutes, 25.8% 15 to 30 minutes, 11.8% 30 to 45 minutes, 9.7% 45 to 60 minutes, 6.5% 60 minutes or more (2000)

OAK (township). Covers a land area of 33.438 square miles and a water area of 1.147 square miles. Located at 45.62° N. Lat.; 94.70° W. Long.
Population: 608 (2000); Race: 100.0% White, 0.0% Black, 0.0% Asian, 0.0% American Indian and Alaska Native, 0.0% Hispanic of any race, 0.0% two or more races (2000); Density: 18.2 persons per square mile (2000); Age: 36.6% under 18, 7.6% over 64 (2000); Marriage status: 26.3% never married, 68.4% now married, 2.9% widowed, 2.4% divorced (2000); Foreign born: 0.0% (2000); Ancestry (includes multiple ancestries): 71.7% German, 9.0% United States or American, 6.6% Norwegian, 5.7% Irish, 3.5% French (except Basque) (2000).
Economy: Single-family building permits issued: 0 (2001) / 0 (2000); Multi-family building permits issued: 0 (2001) / 0 (2000); Employment by occupation: 34.1% management, 10.2% professional, 7.0% services, 16.9% sales, 7.6% farming, 7.9% construction, 16.3% production (2000).
Income: Per capita income: $16,360 (2000); Median household income: $45,893 (2000); Poverty rate: 3.1% (2000).
Education: High school graduation rate: 84.8% (2000); College graduation rate: 9.8% (2000).
Housing: Homeownership rate: 87.7% (2000); Median home value: $100,800 (2000); Median rent: $188 per month (2000); Median age of housing: 30 years (2000).
Transportation: Commute to work: 64.0% car, 0.0% public transportation, 2.9% walk, 32.2% work from home (2000); Travel time to work: 40.9% less than 15 minutes, 29.1% 15 to 30 minutes, 18.3% 30 to 45 minutes, 4.3% 45 to 60 minutes, 7.4% 60 minutes or more (2000)

PAYNESVILLE (city). Covers a land area of 1.322 square miles and a water area of 0 square miles. Located at 45.37° N. Lat.; 94.72° W. Long. Elevation is 1,280 feet.
Population: 2,267 (2000); Race: 98.7% White, 0.0% Black, 0.3% Asian, 0.3% American Indian and Alaska Native, 0.8% Hispanic of any race, 0.2% two or more races (2000); Density: 1,715.2 persons per square mile (2000); Age: 22.4% under 18, 25.8% over 64 (2000); Marriage status: 19.6% never married, 62.1% now married, 11.2% widowed, 7.0% divorced (2000); Foreign born: 2.4% (2000); Ancestry (includes multiple ancestries): 59.6% German, 16.2% Norwegian, 5.4% English, 5.3% Swedish, 5.2% French (except Basque) (2000).
Economy: Single-family building permits issued: 2 (2001) / 10 (2000); Multi-family building permits issued: 20 (2001) / 8 (2000); Employment by occupation: 8.3% management, 15.5% professional, 14.8% services, 21.0% sales, 3.2% farming, 13.8% construction, 23.4% production (2000).
Income: Per capita income: $17,246 (2000); Median household income: $34,000 (2000); Poverty rate: 8.1% (2000).
Taxes: Total city taxes per capita: $300 (1997); City property taxes per capita: $248 (1997).
Education: High school graduation rate: 76.5% (2000); College graduation rate: 13.3% (2000).

School District(s)

Paynesville (PK-12)
2000 Enrollment: 1,241 320-243-3410
Housing: Homeownership rate: 72.6% (2000); Median home value: $72,500 (2000); Median rent: $360 per month (2000); Median age of housing: 40 years (2000).
Hospitals: Paynesville Area Health Care System (94 beds)
Safety: Violent crime rate: 13.1 per 10,000 population; Property crime rate: 336.1 per 10,000 population (2001).
Newspapers: The Paynesville Press (1 x week)
Transportation: Commute to work: 89.5% car, 0.0% public transportation, 6.5% walk, 3.6% work from home (2000); Travel time to work: 58.2% less than 15 minutes, 12.9% 15 to 30 minutes, 13.9% 30 to 45 minutes, 8.2% 45 to 60 minutes, 6.9% 60 minutes or more (2000)
Additional Information Contacts
Paynesville Area Chamber of Commerce 320-243-3233

PAYNESVILLE (township). Covers a land area of 29.994 square miles and a water area of 4.515 square miles. Located at 45.37° N. Lat.; 94.69° W. Long. Elevation is 1,280 feet.
History: Incorporated 1887.
Population: 1,376 (2000); Race: 98.8% White, 0.1% Black, 0.7% Asian, 0.0% American Indian and Alaska Native, 0.1% Hispanic of any race, 0.3% two or more races (2000); Density: 45.9 persons per square mile (2000); Age: 27.8% under 18, 12.4% over 64 (2000); Marriage status: 19.4% never married, 70.8% now married, 4.3% widowed, 5.5% divorced (2000); Foreign born: 1.0% (2000); Ancestry (includes multiple ancestries): 65.6% German, 16.3% Norwegian, 11.5% Irish, 7.3% Swedish, 4.7% United States or American (2000).
Economy: In agricultural area: grain, alfalfa, soybeans, fruit; cattle, hogs, sheep, poultry. Dairying. Manufacturing: dairy products, fertilizer, apparel, printing and publishing, feeds. Single-family building permits issued: 17 (2001) / 17 (2000); Multi-family building permits issued: 8 (2001) / 6 (2000); Employment by occupation: 11.7% management, 20.6% professional, 14.6% services, 21.9% sales, 2.6% farming, 13.7% construction, 14.9% production (2000).
Income: Per capita income: $19,936 (2000); Median household income: $49,792 (2000); Poverty rate: 5.9% (2000).
Taxes: Total city taxes per capita: $153 (2000); City property taxes per capita: $149 (2000).
Education: High school graduation rate: 87.6% (2000); College graduation rate: 19.9% (2000).
Housing: Homeownership rate: 94.0% (2000); Median home value: $127,600 (2000); Median rent: $411 per month (2000); Median age of housing: 31 years (2000).
Transportation: Commute to work: 85.8% car, 0.0% public transportation, 2.6% walk, 9.1% work from home (2000); Travel time to work: 54.4% less than 15 minutes, 18.7% 15 to 30 minutes, 8.7% 30 to 45 minutes, 10.0% 45 to 60 minutes, 8.2% 60 minutes or more (2000)

PLEASANT LAKE (city). Covers a land area of 0.786 square miles and a water area of 0 square miles. Located at 45.49° N. Lat.; 94.29° W. Long. Elevation is 1,100 feet.
Population: 504 (2000); Race: 97.8% White, 1.0% Black, 1.2% Asian, 0.0% American Indian and Alaska Native, 0.6% Hispanic of any race, 0.0% two or more races (2000); Density: 641.2 persons per square mile (2000); Age: 29.9% under 18, 8.3% over 64 (2000); Marriage status: 19.1% never married, 67.4% now married, 3.8% widowed, 9.7% divorced (2000); Foreign born: 0.8% (2000); Ancestry (includes multiple ancestries): 58.6% German, 12.1% Swedish, 12.1% Polish, 7.9% Norwegian, 4.2% Irish (2000).
Economy: Grain; dairying. Single-family building permits issued: 1 (2001) / 0 (2000); Multi-family building permits issued: 0 (2001) / 0 (2000); Employment by occupation: 25.0% management, 11.8% professional, 10.4%

services, 26.7% sales, 0.0% farming, 12.5% construction, 13.5% production (2000).
Income: Per capita income: $28,811 (2000); Median household income: $56,346 (2000); Poverty rate: 1.4% (2000).
Taxes: Total city taxes per capita: $117 (1997); City property taxes per capita: $94 (1997).
Education: High school graduation rate: 95.3% (2000); College graduation rate: 24.9% (2000).
Housing: Homeownership rate: 92.1% (2000); Median home value: $147,900 (2000); Median rent: $475 per month (2000); Median age of housing: 15 years (2000).
Transportation: Commute to work: 92.3% car, 0.0% public transportation, 1.4% walk, 6.3% work from home (2000); Travel time to work: 20.5% less than 15 minutes, 72.0% 15 to 30 minutes, 4.1% 30 to 45 minutes, 1.5% 45 to 60 minutes, 1.9% 60 minutes or more (2000)

RAYMOND (township). Covers a land area of 35.988 square miles and a water area of 0.167 square miles. Located at 45.62° N. Lat.; 95.07° W. Long.
Population: 255 (2000); Race: 93.3% White, 0.0% Black, 0.0% Asian, 0.0% American Indian and Alaska Native, 3.2% Hispanic of any race, 4.0% two or more races (2000); Density: 7.1 persons per square mile (2000); Age: 41.7% under 18, 5.2% over 64 (2000); Marriage status: 27.4% never married, 64.0% now married, 3.7% widowed, 4.9% divorced (2000); Foreign born: 0.0% (2000); Ancestry (includes multiple ancestries): 52.0% German, 8.7% Norwegian, 7.9% Danish, 7.5% Other groups, 6.7% French (except Basque) (2000).
Economy: Single-family building permits issued: 1 (2001) / 0 (2000); Multi-family building permits issued: 0 (2001) / 0 (2000); Employment by occupation: 49.1% management, 9.6% professional, 8.8% services, 5.3% sales, 4.4% farming, 3.5% construction, 19.3% production (2000).
Income: Per capita income: $15,223 (2000); Median household income: $30,000 (2000); Poverty rate: 16.7% (2000).
Taxes: Total city taxes per capita: $88 (1997); City property taxes per capita: $88 (1997).
Education: High school graduation rate: 80.5% (2000); College graduation rate: 11.3% (2000).
Housing: Homeownership rate: 77.9% (2000); Median home value: $67,500 (2000); Median rent: $375 per month (2000); Median age of housing: 42 years (2000).
Transportation: Commute to work: 52.7% car, 0.0% public transportation, 14.5% walk, 32.7% work from home (2000); Travel time to work: 37.8% less than 15 minutes, 48.6% 15 to 30 minutes, 5.4% 30 to 45 minutes, 2.7% 45 to 60 minutes, 5.4% 60 minutes or more (2000)

RICHMOND (city). Covers a land area of 0.853 square miles and a water area of 0.012 square miles. Located at 45.45° N. Lat.; 94.51° W. Long. Elevation is 1,119 feet.
Population: 1,213 (2000); Race: 99.5% White, 0.0% Black, 0.0% Asian, 0.0% American Indian and Alaska Native, 0.5% Hispanic of any race, 0.2% two or more races (2000); Density: 1,421.5 persons per square mile (2000); Age: 22.9% under 18, 19.7% over 64 (2000); Marriage status: 22.9% never married, 64.6% now married, 7.5% widowed, 5.1% divorced (2000); Foreign born: 0.7% (2000); Ancestry (includes multiple ancestries): 70.5% German, 5.3% Norwegian, 4.4% Polish, 4.3% United States or American, 3.9% Irish (2000).
Economy: In agricultural area. Manufacturing: meat processing, light manufacturing. Granite quarries nearby. Single-family building permits issued: 22 (2001) / 11 (2000); Multi-family building permits issued: 0 (2001) / 0 (2000); Employment by occupation: 6.8% management, 14.4% professional, 12.2% services, 25.1% sales, 0.6% farming, 16.6% construction, 24.3% production (2000).
Income: Per capita income: $15,995 (2000); Median household income: $38,400 (2000); Poverty rate: 6.6% (2000).
Taxes: Total city taxes per capita: $76 (1997); City property taxes per capita: $70 (1997).
Education: High school graduation rate: 73.2% (2000); College graduation rate: 7.4% (2000).
Housing: Homeownership rate: 82.2% (2000); Median home value: $93,800 (2000); Median rent: $300 per month (2000); Median age of housing: 27 years (2000).
Transportation: Commute to work: 90.6% car, 0.0% public transportation, 4.3% walk, 4.8% work from home (2000); Travel time to work: 42.3% less than 15 minutes, 25.8% 15 to 30 minutes, 20.5% 30 to 45 minutes, 7.7% 45 to 60 minutes, 3.8% 60 minutes or more (2000)

ROCKVILLE (city). Covers a land area of 0.657 square miles and a water area of 0 square miles. Located at 45.47° N. Lat.; 94.34° W. Long. Elevation is 1,084 feet.
History: Rockville was established on a granite mountain, which provided the reason for existence of the town that developed around the quarries.
Population: 749 (2000); Race: 95.4% White, 0.3% Black, 0.0% Asian, 0.0% American Indian and Alaska Native, 7.5% Hispanic of any race, 0.0% two or more races (2000); Density: 1,140.7 persons per square mile (2000); Age: 32.7% under 18, 7.4% over 64 (2000); Marriage status: 30.9% never married, 59.8% now married, 2.4% widowed, 6.9% divorced (2000); Foreign born: 3.7% (2000); Ancestry (includes multiple ancestries): 58.1% German, 11.7% Norwegian, 9.1% Other groups, 8.6% Irish, 5.5% Polish (2000).
Economy: Single-family building permits issued: 7 (2001) / 5 (2000); Multi-family building permits issued: 0 (2001) / 24 (2000); Employment by occupation: 9.4% management, 13.3% professional, 12.8% services, 24.8% sales, 1.2% farming, 10.1% construction, 28.4% production (2000).
Income: Per capita income: $16,527 (2000); Median household income: $43,854 (2000); Poverty rate: 4.8% (2000).
Taxes: Total city taxes per capita: $97 (1997); City property taxes per capita: $89 (1997).
Education: High school graduation rate: 87.3% (2000); College graduation rate: 15.7% (2000).
Housing: Homeownership rate: 66.4% (2000); Median home value: $99,800 (2000); Median rent: $401 per month (2000); Median age of housing: 30 years (2000).
Transportation: Commute to work: 95.2% car, 0.0% public transportation, 1.2% walk, 2.7% work from home (2000); Travel time to work: 35.1% less than 15 minutes, 44.0% 15 to 30 minutes, 14.2% 30 to 45 minutes, 1.2% 45 to 60 minutes, 5.5% 60 minutes or more (2000)

ROCKVILLE (township). Covers a land area of 32.537 square miles and a water area of 1.932 square miles. Located at 45.45° N. Lat.; 94.32° W. Long. Elevation is 1,084 feet.
Population: 1,254 (2000); Race: 97.3% White, 0.2% Black, 1.1% Asian, 0.0% American Indian and Alaska Native, 0.0% Hispanic of any race, 1.4% two or more races (2000); Density: 38.5 persons per square mile (2000); Age: 34.2% under 18, 8.4% over 64 (2000); Marriage status: 24.1% never married, 69.9% now married, 3.1% widowed, 2.9% divorced (2000); Foreign born: 0.5% (2000); Ancestry (includes multiple ancestries): 72.1% German, 8.2% Polish, 6.3% United States or American, 6.1% French (except Basque), 6.0% Irish (2000).
Economy: Grain; poultry, livestock; dairying. Granite quarries here. Single-family building permits issued: 3 (2001) / 3 (2000); Multi-family building permits issued: 0 (2001) / 0 (2000); Employment by occupation: 15.7% management, 13.5% professional, 13.5% services, 25.8% sales, 0.3% farming, 11.0% construction, 20.3% production (2000).
Income: Per capita income: $20,703 (2000); Median household income: $61,250 (2000); Poverty rate: 2.0% (2000).
Taxes: Total city taxes per capita: $175 (2000); City property taxes per capita: $170 (2000).
Education: High school graduation rate: 90.2% (2000); College graduation rate: 20.2% (2000).
Housing: Homeownership rate: 95.0% (2000); Median home value: $127,900 (2000); Median rent: $325 per month (2000); Median age of housing: 25 years (2000).
Transportation: Commute to work: 94.2% car, 0.0% public transportation, 1.0% walk, 3.6% work from home (2000); Travel time to work: 22.6% less than 15 minutes, 57.4% 15 to 30 minutes, 13.5% 30 to 45 minutes, 1.6% 45 to 60 minutes, 5.0% 60 minutes or more (2000)

ROSCOE (city). Covers a land area of 0.642 square miles and a water area of 0 square miles. Located at 45.43° N. Lat.; 94.63° W. Long.
Population: 116 (2000); Race: 98.3% White, 0.0% Black, 0.0% Asian, 0.0% American Indian and Alaska Native, 0.0% Hispanic of any race, 1.7% two or more races (2000); Density: 180.7 persons per square mile (2000); Age: 27.4% under 18, 6.8% over 64 (2000); Marriage status: 38.5% never married, 51.9% now married, 5.8% widowed, 3.8% divorced (2000); Foreign born: 0.0% (2000); Ancestry (includes multiple ancestries): 56.4% German, 10.3% Danish, 8.5% United States or American, 5.1% Norwegian, 5.1% Dutch (2000).
Economy: Grain; poultry; dairying. Manufacturing: organs. Employment by occupation: 4.5% management, 14.9% professional, 16.4% services, 14.9% sales, 1.5% farming, 3.0% construction, 44.8% production (2000).
Income: Per capita income: $13,931 (2000); Median household income: $45,714 (2000); Poverty rate: 6.8% (2000).

Taxes: Total city taxes per capita: $101 (1997); City property taxes per capita: $87 (1997).
Education: High school graduation rate: 62.0% (2000); College graduation rate: 2.8% (2000).
Housing: Homeownership rate: 82.1% (2000); Median home value: $59,000 (2000); Median age of housing: 60+ years (2000).
Transportation: Commute to work: 88.1% car, 0.0% public transportation, 7.5% walk, 4.5% work from home (2000); Travel time to work: 28.1% less than 15 minutes, 31.3% 15 to 30 minutes, 14.1% 30 to 45 minutes, 21.9% 45 to 60 minutes, 4.7% 60 minutes or more (2000)

SAINT ANTHONY (city). Covers a land area of 0.490 square miles and a water area of 0 square miles. Located at 45.68° N. Lat.; 94.61° W. Long. Elevation is 1,270 feet.
Population: 90 (2000); Race: 100.0% White, 0.0% Black, 0.0% Asian, 0.0% American Indian and Alaska Native, 0.0% Hispanic of any race, 0.0% two or more races (2000); Density: 183.7 persons per square mile (2000); Age: 26.7% under 18, 16.8% over 64 (2000); Marriage status: 18.2% never married, 71.4% now married, 10.4% widowed, 0.0% divorced (2000); Foreign born: 0.0% (2000); Ancestry (includes multiple ancestries): 79.2% German, 8.9% Irish, 6.9% Norwegian, 4.0% Polish, 4.0% Welsh (2000).
Economy: Single-family building permits issued: 0 (2001) / 0 (2000); Multi-family building permits issued: 0 (2001) / 0 (2000); Employment by occupation: 4.8% management, 19.0% professional, 4.8% services, 31.0% sales, 0.0% farming, 9.5% construction, 31.0% production (2000).
Income: Per capita income: $13,736 (2000); Median household income: $29,107 (2000); Poverty rate: 15.2% (2000).
Education: High school graduation rate: 67.7% (2000); College graduation rate: 12.3% (2000).
Housing: Homeownership rate: 90.0% (2000); Median home value: $38,100 (2000); Median age of housing: 60+ years (2000).
Transportation: Commute to work: 92.5% car, 0.0% public transportation, 2.5% walk, 5.0% work from home (2000); Travel time to work: 23.7% less than 15 minutes, 23.7% 15 to 30 minutes, 42.1% 30 to 45 minutes, 10.5% 45 to 60 minutes, 0.0% 60 minutes or more (2000)

SAINT AUGUSTA (township). Aka Ventura. Covers a land area of 37.642 square miles and a water area of 0.294 square miles. Located at 45.46° N. Lat.; 94.19° W. Long. Elevation is 1,014 feet.
Population: 3,065 (2000); Race: 97.6% White, 0.0% Black, 1.2% Asian, 0.0% American Indian and Alaska Native, 0.0% Hispanic of any race, 1.3% two or more races (2000); Density: 81.4 persons per square mile (2000); Age: 31.5% under 18, 6.3% over 64 (2000); Marriage status: 26.9% never married, 64.5% now married, 2.9% widowed, 5.7% divorced (2000); Foreign born: 1.2% (2000); Ancestry (includes multiple ancestries): 67.7% German, 11.5% Norwegian, 7.6% Irish, 7.1% Polish, 5.3% Swedish (2000).
Economy: Single-family building permits issued: 18 (2001) / 12 (2000); Multi-family building permits issued: 0 (2001) / 0 (2000); Employment by occupation: 10.0% management, 14.2% professional, 11.5% services, 30.6% sales, 1.1% farming, 14.9% construction, 17.7% production (2000).
Income: Per capita income: $21,712 (2000); Median household income: $57,292 (2000); Poverty rate: 2.3% (2000).
Education: High school graduation rate: 89.4% (2000); College graduation rate: 15.7% (2000).
Housing: Homeownership rate: 93.5% (2000); Median home value: $119,200 (2000); Median rent: $311 per month (2000); Median age of housing: 22 years (2000).
Transportation: Commute to work: 93.0% car, 0.4% public transportation, 1.3% walk, 5.3% work from home (2000); Travel time to work: 23.3% less than 15 minutes, 53.8% 15 to 30 minutes, 10.7% 30 to 45 minutes, 1.6% 45 to 60 minutes, 10.5% 60 minutes or more (2000)

SAINT CLOUD (city). Covers a land area of 30.158 square miles and a water area of 0.775 square miles. Located at 45.55° N. Lat.; 94.17° W. Long. Elevation is 1,044 feet.
History: St. Cloud was established at the place where one of the fur trails from the Red River country crossed the Mississippi River. The town was platted in 1853 by John L. Wilson from Maine, who purchased the land from Ole Bergeson, a Norwegian who had settled here earlier in the year. Wilson named the town for the French city about which he had read in Napoleon's biography. For its first two decades, St. Cloud was an outfitting post for the fur trade, and a river shipping point for the furs. Many immigrants from European countries came to St. Cloud in the 1800's for the free land offered by the government. The city was incorporated in 1868. Granite quarrying began in St. Cloud in the 1870's, with the granite used by builders throughout the country, particularly in the construction of public buildings, churches, and bridges.
Population: 59,107 (2000); Race: 92.1% White, 1.9% Black, 2.8% Asian, 0.8% American Indian and Alaska Native, 1.3% Hispanic of any race, 1.8% two or more races (2000); Density: 1,959.9 persons per square mile (2000); Age: 20.7% under 18, 10.2% over 64 (2000); Marriage status: 44.6% never married, 42.9% now married, 4.4% widowed, 8.0% divorced (2000); Foreign born: 3.8% (2000); Ancestry (includes multiple ancestries): 48.8% German, 13.6% Norwegian, 9.6% Irish, 8.0% Other groups, 7.5% Swedish (2000).
Vital Statistics: Birth rate: 122.3 per 10,000 population (1998)
Economy: Unemployment rate: 3.8% (11/2002); Total civilian labor force: 39,464 (11/2002); Single-family building permits issued: 195 (2001) / 185 (2000); Multi-family building permits issued: 30 (2001) / 35 (2000); Employment by occupation: 11.1% management, 19.8% professional, 16.4% services, 30.5% sales, 0.2% farming, 6.7% construction, 15.3% production (2000).
Income: Per capita income: $19,769 (2000); Median household income: $37,346 (2000); Poverty rate: 13.1% (2000).
Education: High school graduation rate: 89.1% (2000); College graduation rate: 29.6% (2000).

School District(s)

Central Minnesota Deaf School (N-N)
2000 Enrollment: n/a 320-203-0552
Central Minnesota Joint Powers District (11-12)
2000 Enrollment: 53 320-202-6803
Correctional Facility - Saint Cloud (KG-12)
2000 Enrollment: 0 320-240-3000
Peaks-St.Cloud (09-12)
2000 Enrollment: 20 218-746-4060
Saint Cloud (PK-12)
2000 Enrollment: 10,803 320-253-9333

Four-year College(s)

Saint Cloud State University (Public)
2001 Enrollment: 15,920 320-255-0121
2001 Tuition: In-state $3,063; Out-of-state $6,648

Two-year College(s)

Saint Cloud Technical College (Public)
2001 Enrollment: 3,172 320-654-5000
2001 Tuition: In-state $2,550; Out-of-state $5,100
Saint Cloud Hospital School of X-ray Technology (Private, Not-for-profit, Roman Catholic)
2001 Enrollment: n/a 320-255-5719
Rasmussen College-Saint Cloud (Private, For-profit)
2001 Enrollment: 387 320-251-5600
2001 Tuition: In-state $18,000; Out-of-state $18,000

Housing: Homeownership rate: 56.0% (2000); Median home value: $94,300 (2000); Median rent: $437 per month (2000); Median age of housing: 27 years (2000).
Hospitals: Saint Cloud Hospital (489 beds); Veterans Affairs Medical Center
Safety: Violent crime rate: 33.5 per 10,000 population; Property crime rate: 451.4 per 10,000 population (2001).
Newspapers: St. Cloud Visitor (1 x week); Saint Cloud Times (7 x week)
Transportation: Commute to work: 88.2% car, 2.6% public transportation, 5.1% walk, 3.0% work from home (2000); Travel time to work: 54.2% less than 15 minutes, 31.3% 15 to 30 minutes, 6.1% 30 to 45 minutes, 2.8% 45 to 60 minutes, 5.7% 60 minutes or more (2000); Amtrak: Service available.
Airports: St Cloud Regional (primary service)
Additional Information Contacts
St. Cloud Area Association of Realtors 320-253-7149
St. Cloud Chamber of Commerce 320-251-2940

SAINT JOSEPH (city). Covers a land area of 1.859 square miles and a water area of 0 square miles. Located at 45.56° N. Lat.; 94.31° W. Long.
Population: 4,681 (2000); Race: 95.9% White, 1.1% Black, 1.3% Asian, 0.2% American Indian and Alaska Native, 1.1% Hispanic of any race, 0.8% two or more races (2000); Density: 2,517.4 persons per square mile (2000); Age: 16.6% under 18, 8.9% over 64 (2000); Marriage status: 59.1% never married, 33.2% now married, 2.2% widowed, 5.5% divorced (2000); Foreign born: 2.9% (2000); Ancestry (includes multiple ancestries): 56.0% German, 17.1% Irish, 9.6% Polish, 9.6% Norwegian, 4.9% Other groups (2000).
Economy: Single-family building permits issued: 52 (2001) / 23 (2000); Multi-family building permits issued: 0 (2001) / 0 (2000); Employment by occupation: 6.4% management, 18.6% professional, 18.6% services, 35.4% sales, 0.6% farming, 7.1% construction, 13.2% production (2000).
Income: Per capita income: $12,011 (2000); Median household income: $38,938 (2000); Poverty rate: 20.8% (2000).

Education: High school graduation rate: 90.3% (2000); College graduation rate: 28.7% (2000).

Four-year College(s)

College of Saint Benedict (Private, Not-for-profit, Roman Catholic)
2001 Enrollment: 2,100 320-363-5011
2001 Tuition: In-state $18,015; Out-of-state $18,015

Housing: Homeownership rate: 73.1% (2000); Median home value: $93,800 (2000); Median rent: $350 per month (2000); Median age of housing: 22 years (2000).
Safety: Violent crime rate: 14.8 per 10,000 population; Property crime rate: 126.8 per 10,000 population (2001).
Newspapers: Sartell Newsleader (1 x week); Saint Joseph Newsleader (1 x week)
Transportation: Commute to work: 71.0% car, 4.2% public transportation, 21.8% walk, 1.6% work from home (2000); Travel time to work: 53.3% less than 15 minutes, 37.2% 15 to 30 minutes, 5.5% 30 to 45 minutes, 1.0% 45 to 60 minutes, 2.9% 60 minutes or more (2000)

SAINT JOSEPH (township). Covers a land area of 33.289 square miles and a water area of 0.516 square miles. Located at 45.53° N. Lat.; 94.30° W. Long.
Population: 2,449 (2000); Race: 96.0% White, 0.1% Black, 3.4% Asian, 0.2% American Indian and Alaska Native, 2.7% Hispanic of any race, 0.4% two or more races (2000); Density: 73.6 persons per square mile (2000); Age: 30.3% under 18, 6.4% over 64 (2000); Marriage status: 32.0% never married, 58.8% now married, 1.9% widowed, 7.2% divorced (2000); Foreign born: 3.8% (2000); Ancestry (includes multiple ancestries): 60.5% German, 9.8% Polish, 9.8% Norwegian, 7.8% Other groups, 7.0% Irish (2000).
Economy: Single-family building permits issued: 11 (2001) / 11 (2000); Multi-family building permits issued: 0 (2001) / 0 (2000); Employment by occupation: 9.2% management, 12.6% professional, 11.6% services, 27.9% sales, 0.0% farming, 11.6% construction, 27.1% production (2000).
Income: Per capita income: $18,384 (2000); Median household income: $45,396 (2000); Poverty rate: 6.3% (2000).
Education: High school graduation rate: 81.2% (2000); College graduation rate: 17.3% (2000).
Housing: Homeownership rate: 88.9% (2000); Median home value: $117,300 (2000); Median rent: $436 per month (2000); Median age of housing: 25 years (2000).
Transportation: Commute to work: 94.4% car, 0.0% public transportation, 1.9% walk, 2.9% work from home (2000); Travel time to work: 31.9% less than 15 minutes, 49.7% 15 to 30 minutes, 9.3% 30 to 45 minutes, 3.4% 45 to 60 minutes, 5.7% 60 minutes or more (2000)

SAINT MARTIN (city). Covers a land area of 0.950 square miles and a water area of 0 square miles. Located at 45.50° N. Lat.; 94.66° W. Long. Elevation is 1,253 feet.
Population: 278 (2000); Race: 98.9% White, 0.0% Black, 0.0% Asian, 0.0% American Indian and Alaska Native, 1.1% Hispanic of any race, 0.0% two or more races (2000); Density: 292.8 persons per square mile (2000); Age: 34.1% under 18, 18.2% over 64 (2000); Marriage status: 32.1% never married, 53.4% now married, 9.8% widowed, 4.7% divorced (2000); Foreign born: 0.0% (2000); Ancestry (includes multiple ancestries): 85.2% German, 6.1% Norwegian, 5.7% Other groups, 5.7% Polish, 4.2% French (except Basque) (2000).
Economy: Single-family building permits issued: 2 (2001) / 2 (2000); Multi-family building permits issued: 0 (2001) / 0 (2000); Employment by occupation: 3.2% management, 7.9% professional, 18.3% services, 31.7% sales, 6.3% farming, 6.3% construction, 26.2% production (2000).
Income: Per capita income: $12,497 (2000); Median household income: $36,786 (2000); Poverty rate: 8.3% (2000).
Education: High school graduation rate: 70.6% (2000); College graduation rate: 0.0% (2000).
Housing: Homeownership rate: 100.0% (2000); Median home value: $78,000 (2000); Median age of housing: 37 years (2000).
Transportation: Commute to work: 88.0% car, 0.0% public transportation, 8.0% walk, 1.6% work from home (2000); Travel time to work: 31.7% less than 15 minutes, 39.8% 15 to 30 minutes, 12.2% 30 to 45 minutes, 15.4% 45 to 60 minutes, 0.8% 60 minutes or more (2000)

SAINT MARTIN (township). Covers a land area of 34.420 square miles and a water area of 0.143 square miles. Located at 45.53° N. Lat.; 94.69° W. Long. Elevation is 1,253 feet.
Population: 472 (2000); Race: 100.0% White, 0.0% Black, 0.0% Asian, 0.0% American Indian and Alaska Native, 0.0% Hispanic of any race, 0.0% two or more races (2000); Density: 13.7 persons per square mile (2000); Age: 40.2% under 18, 11.1% over 64 (2000); Marriage status: 23.8% never married, 74.4% now married, 1.2% widowed, 0.6% divorced (2000); Foreign born: 1.0% (2000); Ancestry (includes multiple ancestries): 82.3% German, 4.8% United States or American, 3.2% Irish, 2.6% Polish, 2.0% English (2000).
Economy: Employment by occupation: 36.0% management, 9.2% professional, 8.8% services, 17.5% sales, 7.9% farming, 9.2% construction, 11.4% production (2000).
Income: Per capita income: $15,123 (2000); Median household income: $40,000 (2000); Poverty rate: 12.1% (2000).
Education: High school graduation rate: 81.0% (2000); College graduation rate: 4.0% (2000).
Housing: Homeownership rate: 92.2% (2000); Median home value: $89,200 (2000); Median age of housing: 58 years (2000).
Transportation: Commute to work: 61.5% car, 0.0% public transportation, 10.2% walk, 26.5% work from home (2000); Travel time to work: 28.3% less than 15 minutes, 32.5% 15 to 30 minutes, 28.9% 30 to 45 minutes, 6.6% 45 to 60 minutes, 3.6% 60 minutes or more (2000)

SAINT ROSA (city). Covers a land area of 0.373 square miles and a water area of 0.003 square miles. Located at 45.73° N. Lat.; 94.71° W. Long.
Population: 44 (2000); Race: 88.6% White, 0.0% Black, 0.0% Asian, 0.0% American Indian and Alaska Native, 6.8% Hispanic of any race, 11.4% two or more races (2000); Density: 118.0 persons per square mile (2000); Age: 29.5% under 18, 13.6% over 64 (2000); Marriage status: 32.4% never married, 55.9% now married, 0.0% widowed, 11.8% divorced (2000); Foreign born: 0.0% (2000); Ancestry (includes multiple ancestries): 72.7% German, 15.9% Polish, 11.4% Norwegian, 11.4% Swedish, 11.4% Irish (2000).
Economy: Employment by occupation: 15.4% management, 23.1% professional, 23.1% services, 23.1% sales, 0.0% farming, 7.7% construction, 7.7% production (2000).
Income: Per capita income: $28,282 (2000); Median household income: $48,125 (2000); Poverty rate: 0.0% (2000).
Education: High school graduation rate: 81.5% (2000); College graduation rate: 14.8% (2000).
Housing: Homeownership rate: 88.2% (2000); Median home value: $97,500 (2000); Median rent: $425 per month (2000); Median age of housing: 27 years (2000).
Transportation: Commute to work: 69.2% car, 0.0% public transportation, 19.2% walk, 11.5% work from home (2000); Travel time to work: 56.5% less than 15 minutes, 26.1% 15 to 30 minutes, 0.0% 30 to 45 minutes, 17.4% 45 to 60 minutes, 0.0% 60 minutes or more (2000)

SAINT STEPHEN (city). Covers a land area of 3.676 square miles and a water area of 0 square miles. Located at 45.70° N. Lat.; 94.27° W. Long.
Population: 860 (2000); Race: 98.5% White, 0.4% Black, 0.0% Asian, 0.0% American Indian and Alaska Native, 0.0% Hispanic of any race, 1.2% two or more races (2000); Density: 233.9 persons per square mile (2000); Age: 31.5% under 18, 6.9% over 64 (2000); Marriage status: 24.0% never married, 69.7% now married, 2.4% widowed, 4.0% divorced (2000); Foreign born: 0.5% (2000); Ancestry (includes multiple ancestries): 63.8% German, 14.8% Polish, 9.0% Slovene, 6.9% Norwegian, 6.8% Irish (2000).
Economy: Employment by occupation: 11.5% management, 14.3% professional, 13.9% services, 25.6% sales, 1.0% farming, 12.7% construction, 21.0% production (2000).
Income: Per capita income: $20,445 (2000); Median household income: $55,078 (2000); Poverty rate: 2.8% (2000).
Education: High school graduation rate: 91.1% (2000); College graduation rate: 10.1% (2000).
Housing: Homeownership rate: 93.4% (2000); Median home value: $103,600 (2000); Median rent: $507 per month (2000); Median age of housing: 17 years (2000).
Transportation: Commute to work: 88.5% car, 0.0% public transportation, 4.3% walk, 6.9% work from home (2000); Travel time to work: 23.0% less than 15 minutes, 57.4% 15 to 30 minutes, 17.6% 30 to 45 minutes, 0.4% 45 to 60 minutes, 1.5% 60 minutes or more (2000)

SAINT WENDEL (township). Covers a land area of 35.765 square miles and a water area of 0.313 square miles. Located at 45.60° N. Lat.; 94.33° W. Long. Elevation is 1,210 feet.
Population: 2,313 (2000); Race: 100.0% White, 0.0% Black, 0.0% Asian, 0.0% American Indian and Alaska Native, 1.2% Hispanic of any race, 0.0% two or more races (2000); Density: 64.7 persons per square mile (2000); Age: 31.6% under 18, 7.1% over 64 (2000); Marriage status: 23.0% never married, 70.6% now married, 2.4% widowed, 4.0% divorced (2000); Foreign born:

0.5% (2000); Ancestry (includes multiple ancestries): 65.5% German, 19.8% Polish, 7.6% Norwegian, 7.4% Irish, 5.7% French (except Basque) (2000).
Economy: Single-family building permits issued: 0 (2001) / 5 (2000); Multi-family building permits issued: 0 (2001) / 0 (2000); Employment by occupation: 11.4% management, 16.9% professional, 14.2% services, 29.5% sales, 0.5% farming, 10.1% construction, 17.4% production (2000).
Income: Per capita income: $20,116 (2000); Median household income: $57,946 (2000); Poverty rate: 2.8% (2000).
Education: High school graduation rate: 89.6% (2000); College graduation rate: 22.3% (2000).
Housing: Homeownership rate: 98.5% (2000); Median home value: $119,300 (2000); Median rent: $261 per month (2000); Median age of housing: 22 years (2000).
Transportation: Commute to work: 91.2% car, 0.0% public transportation, 0.9% walk, 7.4% work from home (2000); Travel time to work: 24.0% less than 15 minutes, 58.5% 15 to 30 minutes, 9.8% 30 to 45 minutes, 1.9% 45 to 60 minutes, 5.7% 60 minutes or more (2000)

SARTELL (city). Covers a land area of 5.901 square miles and a water area of 0.235 square miles. Located at 45.62° N. Lat.; 94.20° W. Long. Elevation is 1,055 feet.
Population: 9,641 (2000); Race: 98.2% White, 0.3% Black, 0.8% Asian, 0.0% American Indian and Alaska Native, 0.6% Hispanic of any race, 0.4% two or more races (2000); Density: 1,633.9 persons per square mile (2000); Age: 31.5% under 18, 8.9% over 64 (2000); Marriage status: 24.5% never married, 63.0% now married, 5.8% widowed, 6.8% divorced (2000); Foreign born: 1.3% (2000); Ancestry (includes multiple ancestries): 54.9% German, 16.9% Norwegian, 12.7% Irish, 10.9% Polish, 6.0% Swedish (2000).
Economy: Agriculture includes grain; livestock, poultry; dairying. Manufacturing: papers for magazine publishing, castings, valves. Single-family building permits issued: 253 (2001) / 258 (2000); Multi-family building permits issued: 0 (2001) / 0 (2000); Employment by occupation: 13.5% management, 22.2% professional, 12.5% services, 26.9% sales, 0.0% farming, 6.9% construction, 18.0% production (2000).
Income: Per capita income: $22,667 (2000); Median household income: $52,531 (2000); Poverty rate: 4.0% (2000).
Taxes: Total city taxes per capita: $141 (1997); City property taxes per capita: $115 (1997).
Education: High school graduation rate: 90.4% (2000); College graduation rate: 30.2% (2000).

School District(s)

Benton-Stearns Ed. Dist. (PK-11)
2000 Enrollment: 60 320-252-8427
Sartell (PK-12)
2000 Enrollment: 2,694 320-253-2440

Housing: Homeownership rate: 77.1% (2000); Median home value: $125,300 (2000); Median rent: $517 per month (2000); Median age of housing: 10 years (2000).
Transportation: Commute to work: 96.2% car, 0.2% public transportation, 0.9% walk, 2.4% work from home (2000); Travel time to work: 37.9% less than 15 minutes, 49.3% 15 to 30 minutes, 5.0% 30 to 45 minutes, 1.6% 45 to 60 minutes, 6.1% 60 minutes or more (2000)

SAUK CENTRE (city). Covers a land area of 3.718 square miles and a water area of 0.254 square miles. Located at 45.73° N. Lat.; 94.95° W. Long. Elevation is 1,246 feet.
History: City was birthplace of Sinclair Lewis, who used it as setting for *Main Street*. Sinclair Lewis Interpretive Center here. Settled 1856, platted 1863, Incorporated as village 1876, as city 1889.
Population: 3,930 (2000); Race: 99.5% White, 0.2% Black, 0.0% Asian, 0.0% American Indian and Alaska Native, 0.2% Hispanic of any race, 0.1% two or more races (2000); Density: 1,057.2 persons per square mile (2000); Age: 25.2% under 18, 22.6% over 64 (2000); Marriage status: 23.2% never married, 61.5% now married, 9.6% widowed, 5.7% divorced (2000); Foreign born: 0.6% (2000); Ancestry (includes multiple ancestries): 59.5% German, 16.3% Norwegian, 7.6% Irish, 4.1% Swedish, 4.0% United States or American (2000).
Economy: Resort and trading point in grain and livestock. Agriculture includes dairying, poultry, grain, soybeans, beans and alfalfa. Manufacturing includes printing and publishing and diversified light manufacturing. Single-family building permits issued: 58 (2001) / 21 (2000); Multi-family building permits issued: 4 (2001) / 0 (2000); Employment by occupation: 11.4% management, 14.6% professional, 15.8% services, 23.8% sales, 2.0% farming, 8.1% construction, 24.3% production (2000).
Income: Per capita income: $18,390 (2000); Median household income: $37,644 (2000); Poverty rate: 5.2% (2000).
Taxes: Total city taxes per capita: $235 (1997); City property taxes per capita: $228 (1997).
Education: High school graduation rate: 78.9% (2000); College graduation rate: 17.7% (2000).

School District(s)

Correctional Facility - Sauk Center (KG-12)
2000 Enrollment: 0 320-325-1100
Sauk Centre (PK-12)
2000 Enrollment: 1,208 320-352-2284
West Central Ed. Dist. (09-12)
2000 Enrollment: 43 320-352-6120

Housing: Homeownership rate: 72.7% (2000); Median home value: $74,500 (2000); Median rent: $363 per month (2000); Median age of housing: 40 years (2000).
Hospitals: Saint Michael's Hospital (28 beds)
Safety: Violent crime rate: 12.6 per 10,000 population; Property crime rate: 385.2 per 10,000 population (2001).
Newspapers: Dairyland Peach (1 x week); Sauk Centre Herald (1 x week)
Transportation: Commute to work: 88.8% car, 2.1% public transportation, 4.9% walk, 3.5% work from home (2000); Travel time to work: 69.5% less than 15 minutes, 15.3% 15 to 30 minutes, 4.9% 30 to 45 minutes, 6.1% 45 to 60 minutes, 4.1% 60 minutes or more (2000)
Additional Information Contacts
Sauk Centre Chamber of Commerce 320-352-5201

SAUK CENTRE (township). Covers a land area of 36.234 square miles and a water area of 1.836 square miles. Located at 45.73° N. Lat.; 94.93° W. Long. Elevation is 1,246 feet.
Population: 996 (2000); Race: 99.1% White, 0.0% Black, 0.2% Asian, 0.2% American Indian and Alaska Native, 0.2% Hispanic of any race, 0.3% two or more races (2000); Density: 27.5 persons per square mile (2000); Age: 29.6% under 18, 11.9% over 64 (2000); Marriage status: 26.3% never married, 60.9% now married, 5.3% widowed, 7.5% divorced (2000); Foreign born: 0.9% (2000); Ancestry (includes multiple ancestries): 65.7% German, 11.1% Norwegian, 9.5% Irish, 3.6% Polish, 3.6% French (except Basque) (2000).
Economy: Single-family building permits issued: 5 (2001) / 12 (2000); Multi-family building permits issued: 0 (2001) / 0 (2000); Employment by occupation: 16.5% management, 12.5% professional, 11.4% services, 27.0% sales, 4.4% farming, 9.5% construction, 18.7% production (2000).
Income: Per capita income: $18,905 (2000); Median household income: $43,365 (2000); Poverty rate: 5.7% (2000).
Taxes: Total city taxes per capita: $43 (1997); City property taxes per capita: $40 (1997).
Education: High school graduation rate: 88.6% (2000); College graduation rate: 11.2% (2000).
Housing: Homeownership rate: 92.8% (2000); Median home value: $110,300 (2000); Median rent: $281 per month (2000); Median age of housing: 24 years (2000).
Transportation: Commute to work: 86.7% car, 0.0% public transportation, 3.1% walk, 10.2% work from home (2000); Travel time to work: 67.3% less than 15 minutes, 17.9% 15 to 30 minutes, 4.5% 30 to 45 minutes, 5.3% 45 to 60 minutes, 4.9% 60 minutes or more (2000)

SPRING HILL (city). Covers a land area of 0.729 square miles and a water area of 0 square miles. Located at 45.52° N. Lat.; 94.83° W. Long. Elevation is 1,255 feet.
Population: 55 (2000); Race: 100.0% White, 0.0% Black, 0.0% Asian, 0.0% American Indian and Alaska Native, 0.0% Hispanic of any race, 0.0% two or more races (2000); Density: 75.4 persons per square mile (2000); Age: 7.1% under 18, 40.5% over 64 (2000); Marriage status: 25.6% never married, 41.0% now married, 33.3% widowed, 0.0% divorced (2000); Foreign born: 0.0% (2000); Ancestry (includes multiple ancestries): 83.3% German (2000).
Economy: Employment by occupation: 18.2% management, 0.0% professional, 18.2% services, 22.7% sales, 0.0% farming, 0.0% construction, 40.9% production (2000).
Income: Per capita income: $16,271 (2000); Median household income: $25,833 (2000); Poverty rate: 11.9% (2000).
Taxes: Total city taxes per capita: $111 (1997); City property taxes per capita: $86 (1997).
Education: High school graduation rate: 40.6% (2000); College graduation rate: 0.0% (2000).
Housing: Homeownership rate: 100.0% (2000); Median home value: $41,000 (2000); Median age of housing: 45 years (2000).
Transportation: Commute to work: 72.7% car, 0.0% public transportation, 9.1% walk, 18.2% work from home (2000); Travel time to work: 22.2% less

than 15 minutes, 44.4% 15 to 30 minutes, 22.2% 30 to 45 minutes, 11.1% 45 to 60 minutes, 0.0% 60 minutes or more (2000)

SPRING HILL (township). Covers a land area of 34.853 square miles and a water area of 0.044 square miles. Located at 45.54° N. Lat.; 94.81° W. Long. Elevation is 1,255 feet.
Population: 438 (2000); Race: 100.0% White, 0.0% Black, 0.0% Asian, 0.0% American Indian and Alaska Native, 0.0% Hispanic of any race, 0.0% two or more races (2000); Density: 12.6 persons per square mile (2000); Age: 36.9% under 18, 5.5% over 64 (2000); Marriage status: 29.6% never married, 69.1% now married, 0.6% widowed, 0.6% divorced (2000); Foreign born: 0.0% (2000); Ancestry (includes multiple ancestries): 76.5% German, 8.4% United States or American, 5.0% Norwegian, 1.6% English, 1.6% French Canadian (2000).
Economy: Grain; livestock. Employment by occupation: 32.5% management, 8.7% professional, 12.1% services, 8.7% sales, 14.3% farming, 4.3% construction, 19.5% production (2000).
Income: Per capita income: $12,267 (2000); Median household income: $41,406 (2000); Poverty rate: 14.8% (2000).
Taxes: Total city taxes per capita: $63 (1997); City property taxes per capita: $63 (1997).
Education: High school graduation rate: 80.7% (2000); College graduation rate: 6.3% (2000).
Housing: Homeownership rate: 86.5% (2000); Median home value: $108,300 (2000); Median rent: $258 per month (2000); Median age of housing: 51 years (2000).
Transportation: Commute to work: 58.9% car, 0.0% public transportation, 8.9% walk, 31.7% work from home (2000); Travel time to work: 31.4% less than 15 minutes, 43.8% 15 to 30 minutes, 9.8% 30 to 45 minutes, 7.2% 45 to 60 minutes, 7.8% 60 minutes or more (2000)

WAITE PARK (city). Covers a land area of 7.810 square miles and a water area of 0 square miles. Located at 45.55° N. Lat.; 94.22° W. Long. Elevation is 1,077 feet.
Population: 6,568 (2000); Race: 94.4% White, 0.3% Black, 3.0% Asian, 0.3% American Indian and Alaska Native, 2.2% Hispanic of any race, 1.5% two or more races (2000); Density: 841.0 persons per square mile (2000); Age: 19.7% under 18, 13.2% over 64 (2000); Marriage status: 40.6% never married, 44.1% now married, 5.6% widowed, 9.8% divorced (2000); Foreign born: 4.0% (2000); Ancestry (includes multiple ancestries): 49.7% German, 12.0% Norwegian, 9.0% Irish, 8.3% Polish, 7.1% Other groups (2000).
Economy: Railroad junction. Agriculture: grain; livestock, poultry. Manufacturing: restaurant fixtures, steel shapes, machining, printing and publishing, stone layout plates, aircraft overhead cranes. Single-family building permits issued: 69 (2001) / 76 (2000); Multi-family building permits issued: 5 (2001) / 5 (2000); Employment by occupation: 9.3% management, 14.2% professional, 16.0% services, 28.2% sales, 0.1% farming, 10.0% construction, 22.3% production (2000).
Income: Per capita income: $17,796 (2000); Median household income: $33,803 (2000); Poverty rate: 12.1% (2000).
Taxes: Total city taxes per capita: $446 (1997); City property taxes per capita: $432 (1997).
Education: High school graduation rate: 85.9% (2000); College graduation rate: 16.1% (2000).
Housing: Homeownership rate: 39.7% (2000); Median home value: $93,900 (2000); Median rent: $525 per month (2000); Median age of housing: 18 years (2000).
Safety: Violent crime rate: 24.1 per 10,000 population; Property crime rate: 762.2 per 10,000 population (2001).
Transportation: Commute to work: 92.3% car, 0.3% public transportation, 2.4% walk, 3.5% work from home (2000); Travel time to work: 54.5% less than 15 minutes, 34.5% 15 to 30 minutes, 4.9% 30 to 45 minutes, 2.0% 45 to 60 minutes, 4.2% 60 minutes or more (2000)

WAKEFIELD (township). Covers a land area of 30.921 square miles and a water area of 2.390 square miles. Located at 45.44° N. Lat.; 94.46° W. Long.
Population: 3,103 (2000); Race: 98.0% White, 0.1% Black, 0.4% Asian, 0.0% American Indian and Alaska Native, 1.2% Hispanic of any race, 1.4% two or more races (2000); Density: 100.4 persons per square mile (2000); Age: 32.7% under 18, 8.8% over 64 (2000); Marriage status: 19.2% never married, 74.4% now married, 2.1% widowed, 4.3% divorced (2000); Foreign born: 1.1% (2000); Ancestry (includes multiple ancestries): 69.2% German, 7.3% Norwegian, 7.0% Polish, 5.1% Irish, 4.7% Swedish (2000).
Economy: Single-family building permits issued: 20 (2001) / 17 (2000); Multi-family building permits issued: 0 (2001) / 0 (2000); Employment by occupation: 12.8% management, 17.5% professional, 12.7% services, 23.6% sales, 0.6% farming, 12.3% construction, 20.5% production (2000).
Income: Per capita income: $21,335 (2000); Median household income: $56,204 (2000); Poverty rate: 4.2% (2000).
Taxes: Total city taxes per capita: $65 (1997); City property taxes per capita: $61 (1997).
Education: High school graduation rate: 92.0% (2000); College graduation rate: 23.3% (2000).
Housing: Homeownership rate: 95.4% (2000); Median home value: $137,000 (2000); Median rent: $425 per month (2000); Median age of housing: 21 years (2000).
Transportation: Commute to work: 90.9% car, 0.0% public transportation, 0.6% walk, 7.5% work from home (2000); Travel time to work: 37.6% less than 15 minutes, 31.4% 15 to 30 minutes, 20.7% 30 to 45 minutes, 4.8% 45 to 60 minutes, 5.6% 60 minutes or more (2000)

ZION (township). Covers a land area of 35.441 square miles and a water area of 0.018 square miles. Located at 45.47° N. Lat.; 94.69° W. Long.
Population: 388 (2000); Race: 98.9% White, 1.1% Black, 0.0% Asian, 0.0% American Indian and Alaska Native, 4.1% Hispanic of any race, 0.0% two or more races (2000); Density: 10.9 persons per square mile (2000); Age: 32.6% under 18, 8.4% over 64 (2000); Marriage status: 31.5% never married, 63.8% now married, 2.9% widowed, 1.8% divorced (2000); Foreign born: 0.5% (2000); Ancestry (includes multiple ancestries): 71.5% German, 5.4% Other groups, 5.4% Irish, 4.6% Polish, 3.0% United States or American (2000).
Economy: Single-family building permits issued: 6 (2001) / 6 (2000); Multi-family building permits issued: 0 (2001) / 0 (2000); Employment by occupation: 30.8% management, 6.6% professional, 13.3% services, 19.4% sales, 6.6% farming, 7.6% construction, 15.6% production (2000).
Income: Per capita income: $15,544 (2000); Median household income: $45,769 (2000); Poverty rate: 9.9% (2000).
Taxes: Total city taxes per capita: $46 (1997); City property taxes per capita: $46 (1997).
Education: High school graduation rate: 85.2% (2000); College graduation rate: 8.7% (2000).
Housing: Homeownership rate: 84.2% (2000); Median home value: $92,500 (2000); Median rent: $368 per month (2000); Median age of housing: 60+ years (2000).
Transportation: Commute to work: 65.4% car, 0.0% public transportation, 8.1% walk, 25.1% work from home (2000); Travel time to work: 36.1% less than 15 minutes, 22.8% 15 to 30 minutes, 15.2% 30 to 45 minutes, 17.1% 45 to 60 minutes, 8.9% 60 minutes or more (2000)

Steele County

Located in southeastern Minnesota; drained by the Straight River. Covers a land area of 429.50 square miles, a water area of 2.60 square miles, and is located in the Central Time Zone. The county government was organized in 1855. County seat is Owatonna.

Weather Station: Owatonna — Elevation: 1,148 feet

	Jan	Feb	Mar	Apr	May	Jun	Jul	Aug	Sep	Oct	Nov	Dec
High	22	29	41	58	72	81	84	82	74	61	41	28
Low	4	10	22	35	47	57	61	59	50	38	24	11
Precip	1.0	0.6	1.9	3.0	3.9	3.8	4.6	4.4	3.3	2.4	1.8	1.0
Snow	10.3	6.0	7.6	2.9	tr	0.0	0.0	0.0	0.0	0.6	5.2	8.3

High and Low temperatures in degrees Fahrenheit; Precipitation and Snow in inches

Population: 33,680 (2000); Race: 95.1% White, 0.9% Black, 0.7% Asian, 0.1% American Indian and Alaska Native, 3.7% Hispanic of any race, 1.5% two or more races (2000); Density: 78.4 persons per square mile (2000); Age: 27.8% under 18, 13.1% over 64 (2000).
Religion: Five largest groups: 28.3% Catholic Church, 27.9% Evangelical Lutheran Church in America, 5.6% Lutheran Church—Missouri Synod, 2.9% The United Methodist Church, 2.8% New Testament Association of Independent Baptist Churches and other Fun
Economy: Unemployment rate: 3.4% (11/2002); Total civilian labor force: 18,952 (11/2002); Leading industries: 39.3% manufacturing; 13.0% retail trade; 12.0% finance & insurance (2000); Companies that employ more than 1,000 persons: 3 (2000); Companies that employ more than 100 persons: 30 (2000); Farms: 774 totaling 226,926 acres (1997); Minority business ownership rate: 0.0% (1997); Women business ownership rate: 20.8% (1997); Retail sales per capita: $8,665 (1997). Single-family building permits issued: 188 (2001) / 173 (2000); Multi-family building permits issued: 0 (2001) / 26 (2000).

Income: Per capita income: $20,328 (2000); Median household income: $46,106 (2000); Poverty rate: 6.2% (2000); Bankruptcy rate: 2.36% (2001).
Taxes: Total county taxes per capita: $190 (1997); County property taxes per capita: $188 (1997).
Education: High school graduation rate: 86.6% (2000); College graduation rate: 20.1% (2000).
Housing: Homeownership rate: 80.2% (2000); Median home value: $102,300 (2000); Median rent: $413 per month (2000); Median age of housing: 36 years (2000).
Health: Birth rate: 122.3 per 10,000 population (1998); Age adjusted death rate: 75.0 per 10,000 population (1999); Age adjusted cancer mortality rate: 205.5 deaths per 100,000 population (1999). Number of physicians: 13.4 per 10,000 population (1999); Number of hospital beds: 10.7 per 10,000 population (1999).
Elections: 2000 Presidential election results: 43.0% Gore, 51.2% Bush, 4.3% Nader, 1.1% Buchanan
National and State Parks: Aurora State Wildlife Management Area; Kaplan Woods State Park; Oak Glen State Wildlife Management Area; Pogones State Wildlife Management Area
Additional Information Contacts
Steele County Government Offices 507-444-7400
Economic Development Authority.................... 507-583-4472
Owatonna Chamber of Commerce.................... 507-451-7970

Steele County Communities

AURORA (township). Covers a land area of 35.960 square miles and a water area of 0.027 square miles. Located at 43.97° N. Lat.; 93.10° W. Long.
Population: 625 (2000); Race: 99.4% White, 0.0% Black, 0.0% Asian, 0.0% American Indian and Alaska Native, 0.8% Hispanic of any race, 0.3% two or more races (2000); Density: 17.4 persons per square mile (2000); Age: 27.2% under 18, 12.9% over 64 (2000); Marriage status: 28.9% never married, 59.8% now married, 4.1% widowed, 7.1% divorced (2000); Foreign born: 0.0% (2000); Ancestry (includes multiple ancestries): 48.0% German, 28.8% Norwegian, 20.9% Czech, 6.6% English, 3.8% Polish (2000).
Economy: Employment by occupation: 19.7% management, 9.6% professional, 9.9% services, 25.2% sales, 2.7% farming, 11.8% construction, 21.1% production (2000).
Income: Per capita income: $17,192 (2000); Median household income: $45,804 (2000); Poverty rate: 5.1% (2000).
Taxes: Total city taxes per capita: $41 (1997); City property taxes per capita: $41 (1997).
Education: High school graduation rate: 84.6% (2000); College graduation rate: 8.8% (2000).
Housing: Homeownership rate: 92.0% (2000); Median home value: $89,500 (2000); Median rent: $465 per month (2000); Median age of housing: 60+ years (2000).
Transportation: Commute to work: 84.2% car, 0.6% public transportation, 4.0% walk, 10.2% work from home (2000); Travel time to work: 22.6% less than 15 minutes, 66.0% 15 to 30 minutes, 6.3% 30 to 45 minutes, 3.8% 45 to 60 minutes, 1.3% 60 minutes or more (2000)

BERLIN (township). Covers a land area of 35.121 square miles and a water area of 0.268 square miles. Located at 43.90° N. Lat.; 93.32° W. Long.
Population: 508 (2000); Race: 99.2% White, 0.4% Black, 0.0% Asian, 0.0% American Indian and Alaska Native, 0.0% Hispanic of any race, 0.4% two or more races (2000); Density: 14.5 persons per square mile (2000); Age: 26.2% under 18, 13.7% over 64 (2000); Marriage status: 19.3% never married, 69.7% now married, 5.4% widowed, 5.7% divorced (2000); Foreign born: 0.0% (2000); Ancestry (includes multiple ancestries): 44.6% Norwegian, 40.1% German, 11.0% Swedish, 10.4% Danish, 9.2% Irish (2000).
Economy: Employment by occupation: 25.4% management, 14.8% professional, 3.7% services, 21.3% sales, 1.2% farming, 13.9% construction, 19.7% production (2000).
Income: Per capita income: $18,764 (2000); Median household income: $47,083 (2000); Poverty rate: 10.7% (2000).
Taxes: Total city taxes per capita: $82 (1997); City property taxes per capita: $82 (1997).
Education: High school graduation rate: 84.0% (2000); College graduation rate: 17.2% (2000).
Housing: Homeownership rate: 93.5% (2000); Median home value: $121,700 (2000); Median rent: $425 per month (2000); Median age of housing: 45 years (2000).
Transportation: Commute to work: 82.1% car, 0.0% public transportation, 2.9% walk, 15.0% work from home (2000); Travel time to work: 36.8% less than 15 minutes, 43.6% 15 to 30 minutes, 13.7% 30 to 45 minutes, 1.0% 45 to 60 minutes, 4.9% 60 minutes or more (2000)

BLOOMING PRAIRIE (city). Covers a land area of 1.353 square miles and a water area of 0 square miles. Located at 43.86° N. Lat.; 93.05° W. Long.
Population: 1,933 (2000); Race: 96.2% White, 0.2% Black, 0.5% Asian, 0.1% American Indian and Alaska Native, 3.6% Hispanic of any race, 0.7% two or more races (2000); Density: 1,428.4 persons per square mile (2000); Age: 25.3% under 18, 22.7% over 64 (2000); Marriage status: 19.6% never married, 61.4% now married, 10.5% widowed, 8.5% divorced (2000); Foreign born: 1.1% (2000); Ancestry (includes multiple ancestries): 37.8% German, 35.7% Norwegian, 11.2% Irish, 7.0% Czech, 6.0% Danish (2000).
Economy: Single-family building permits issued: 4 (2001) / 4 (2000); Multi-family building permits issued: 0 (2001) / 14 (2000); Employment by occupation: 9.8% management, 17.1% professional, 15.9% services, 25.5% sales, 1.3% farming, 8.6% construction, 21.7% production (2000).
Income: Per capita income: $19,343 (2000); Median household income: $40,345 (2000); Poverty rate: 6.6% (2000).
Taxes: Total city taxes per capita: $162 (1997); City property taxes per capita: $155 (1997).
Education: High school graduation rate: 82.5% (2000); College graduation rate: 16.6% (2000).

School District(s)
Blooming Prairie (PK-12)
2000 Enrollment: 840 507-583-4427
Housing: Homeownership rate: 83.7% (2000); Median home value: $82,000 (2000); Median rent: $335 per month (2000); Median age of housing: 47 years (2000).
Safety: Violent crime rate: 10.2 per 10,000 population; Property crime rate: 225.2 per 10,000 population (2001).
Newspapers: Blooming Prairie Times (1 x week)
Transportation: Commute to work: 85.7% car, 0.3% public transportation, 7.6% walk, 5.0% work from home (2000); Travel time to work: 45.2% less than 15 minutes, 30.5% 15 to 30 minutes, 15.6% 30 to 45 minutes, 4.9% 45 to 60 minutes, 3.8% 60 minutes or more (2000)
Additional Information Contacts
Economic Development Authority.................... 507-583-4472

BLOOMING PRAIRIE (township). Covers a land area of 34.449 square miles and a water area of 0.524 square miles. Located at 43.89° N. Lat.; 93.09° W. Long.
Population: 519 (2000); Race: 99.6% White, 0.0% Black, 0.0% Asian, 0.0% American Indian and Alaska Native, 2.3% Hispanic of any race, 0.4% two or more races (2000); Density: 15.1 persons per square mile (2000); Age: 34.2% under 18, 10.8% over 64 (2000); Marriage status: 25.9% never married, 67.8% now married, 3.6% widowed, 2.8% divorced (2000); Foreign born: 0.0% (2000); Ancestry (includes multiple ancestries): 35.4% German, 28.7% Norwegian, 13.1% Danish, 11.0% Czech, 8.2% English (2000).
Economy: Agricultural area: grain, soybeans, peas; livestock, poultry; dairying. Manufacturing: hog and chicken feed, soybean oil. Employment by occupation: 19.4% management, 11.2% professional, 9.4% services, 26.6% sales, 4.3% farming, 9.4% construction, 19.8% production (2000).
Income: Per capita income: $18,189 (2000); Median household income: $45,625 (2000); Poverty rate: 8.6% (2000).
Taxes: Total city taxes per capita: $21 (1997); City property taxes per capita: $21 (1997).
Education: High school graduation rate: 86.9% (2000); College graduation rate: 15.0% (2000).
Housing: Homeownership rate: 89.0% (2000); Median home value: $84,200 (2000); Median rent: $288 per month (2000); Median age of housing: 60+ years (2000).
Transportation: Commute to work: 85.8% car, 0.7% public transportation, 1.5% walk, 12.0% work from home (2000); Travel time to work: 29.0% less than 15 minutes, 49.4% 15 to 30 minutes, 14.9% 30 to 45 minutes, 4.6% 45 to 60 minutes, 2.1% 60 minutes or more (2000)

CLINTON FALLS (township). Covers a land area of 16.070 square miles and a water area of 0.060 square miles. Located at 44.13° N. Lat.; 93.23° W. Long. Elevation is 1,133 feet.
Population: 452 (2000); Race: 96.6% White, 0.0% Black, 0.4% Asian, 0.0% American Indian and Alaska Native, 7.5% Hispanic of any race, 0.9% two or more races (2000); Density: 28.1 persons per square mile (2000); Age: 23.8% under 18, 13.1% over 64 (2000); Marriage status: 20.6% never married, 68.8% now married, 5.2% widowed, 5.5% divorced (2000); Foreign born:

5.4% (2000); Ancestry (includes multiple ancestries): 45.5% German, 16.3% Norwegian, 9.7% Irish, 9.2% Czech, 9.0% Other groups (2000).
Economy: Employment by occupation: 10.3% management, 12.3% professional, 9.6% services, 26.1% sales, 6.5% farming, 12.3% construction, 23.0% production (2000).
Income: Per capita income: $24,864 (2000); Median household income: $46,250 (2000); Poverty rate: 6.9% (2000).
Taxes: Total city taxes per capita: $66 (1997); City property taxes per capita: $66 (1997).
Education: High school graduation rate: 84.5% (2000); College graduation rate: 21.2% (2000).
Housing: Homeownership rate: 91.6% (2000); Median home value: $131,600 (2000); Median rent: $642 per month (2000); Median age of housing: 57 years (2000).
Transportation: Commute to work: 91.6% car, 0.0% public transportation, 1.5% walk, 6.9% work from home (2000); Travel time to work: 51.0% less than 15 minutes, 28.8% 15 to 30 minutes, 3.3% 30 to 45 minutes, 1.6% 45 to 60 minutes, 15.2% 60 minutes or more (2000)

DEERFIELD (township). Covers a land area of 35.593 square miles and a water area of 0.323 square miles. Located at 44.13° N. Lat.; 93.35° W. Long.
Population: 693 (2000); Race: 98.3% White, 0.0% Black, 0.0% Asian, 0.0% American Indian and Alaska Native, 1.6% Hispanic of any race, 0.7% two or more races (2000); Density: 19.5 persons per square mile (2000); Age: 33.8% under 18, 5.6% over 64 (2000); Marriage status: 27.2% never married, 66.7% now married, 2.1% widowed, 4.0% divorced (2000); Foreign born: 0.9% (2000); Ancestry (includes multiple ancestries): 47.5% German, 23.9% Norwegian, 11.0% Irish, 10.6% English, 6.2% Swedish (2000).
Economy: Employment by occupation: 13.1% management, 9.9% professional, 9.9% services, 29.3% sales, 2.1% farming, 10.5% construction, 25.1% production (2000).
Income: Per capita income: $17,872 (2000); Median household income: $52,727 (2000); Poverty rate: 3.0% (2000).
Taxes: Total city taxes per capita: $76 (1997); City property taxes per capita: $76 (1997).
Education: High school graduation rate: 84.8% (2000); College graduation rate: 6.7% (2000).
Housing: Homeownership rate: 91.9% (2000); Median home value: $130,000 (2000); Median rent: $450 per month (2000); Median age of housing: 44 years (2000).
Transportation: Commute to work: 91.0% car, 0.0% public transportation, 4.0% walk, 4.2% work from home (2000); Travel time to work: 35.5% less than 15 minutes, 52.3% 15 to 30 minutes, 7.4% 30 to 45 minutes, 2.2% 45 to 60 minutes, 2.5% 60 minutes or more (2000)

ELLENDALE (city). Covers a land area of 0.890 square miles and a water area of 0 square miles. Located at 43.87° N. Lat.; 93.30° W. Long.
Population: 590 (2000); Race: 99.7% White, 0.0% Black, 0.3% Asian, 0.0% American Indian and Alaska Native, 0.0% Hispanic of any race, 0.0% two or more races (2000); Density: 662.8 persons per square mile (2000); Age: 24.1% under 18, 20.1% over 64 (2000); Marriage status: 23.6% never married, 57.4% now married, 8.1% widowed, 10.9% divorced (2000); Foreign born: 0.7% (2000); Ancestry (includes multiple ancestries): 37.3% German, 28.8% Norwegian, 11.9% Danish, 8.6% Irish, 5.6% Czech (2000).
Economy: Agricultural area: poultry; grain, soybeans; dairying. Manufacturing: electric fence insulations. Single-family building permits issued: 2 (2001) / 2 (2000); Multi-family building permits issued: 0 (2001) / 0 (2000); Employment by occupation: 9.5% management, 14.1% professional, 11.5% services, 29.6% sales, 0.0% farming, 9.9% construction, 25.3% production (2000).
Income: Per capita income: $19,750 (2000); Median household income: $37,750 (2000); Poverty rate: 10.1% (2000).
Taxes: Total city taxes per capita: $66 (1997); City property taxes per capita: $61 (1997).
Education: High school graduation rate: 84.5% (2000); College graduation rate: 16.0% (2000).
Housing: Homeownership rate: 80.2% (2000); Median home value: $74,500 (2000); Median rent: $309 per month (2000); Median age of housing: 46 years (2000).
Newspapers: Ellendale Eagle (1 x week)
Transportation: Commute to work: 91.6% car, 0.0% public transportation, 5.7% walk, 2.3% work from home (2000); Travel time to work: 34.0% less than 15 minutes, 47.8% 15 to 30 minutes, 11.7% 30 to 45 minutes, 4.8% 45 to 60 minutes, 1.7% 60 minutes or more (2000)

HAVANA (township). Covers a land area of 35.001 square miles and a water area of 0.993 square miles. Located at 44.07° N. Lat.; 93.11° W. Long. Elevation is 1,223 feet.
Population: 607 (2000); Race: 96.5% White, 0.3% Black, 0.0% Asian, 0.0% American Indian and Alaska Native, 2.1% Hispanic of any race, 3.2% two or more races (2000); Density: 17.3 persons per square mile (2000); Age: 26.3% under 18, 14.3% over 64 (2000); Marriage status: 17.7% never married, 68.0% now married, 5.4% widowed, 8.9% divorced (2000); Foreign born: 2.1% (2000); Ancestry (includes multiple ancestries): 52.9% German, 23.1% Norwegian, 11.7% Irish, 9.6% Czech, 6.9% English (2000).
Economy: Employment by occupation: 18.1% management, 9.4% professional, 10.3% services, 28.3% sales, 3.6% farming, 11.4% construction, 18.9% production (2000).
Income: Per capita income: $23,720 (2000); Median household income: $52,500 (2000); Poverty rate: 1.0% (2000).
Taxes: Total city taxes per capita: $88 (1997); City property taxes per capita: $88 (1997).
Education: High school graduation rate: 87.9% (2000); College graduation rate: 14.2% (2000).
Housing: Homeownership rate: 84.8% (2000); Median home value: $140,800 (2000); Median rent: $383 per month (2000); Median age of housing: 57 years (2000).
Transportation: Commute to work: 82.9% car, 0.0% public transportation, 2.5% walk, 13.2% work from home (2000); Travel time to work: 33.7% less than 15 minutes, 48.2% 15 to 30 minutes, 9.7% 30 to 45 minutes, 2.9% 45 to 60 minutes, 5.5% 60 minutes or more (2000)

LEMOND (township). Covers a land area of 36.022 square miles and a water area of 0.025 square miles. Located at 43.97° N. Lat.; 93.34° W. Long.
Population: 510 (2000); Race: 95.7% White, 2.1% Black, 1.0% Asian, 0.0% American Indian and Alaska Native, 0.0% Hispanic of any race, 1.2% two or more races (2000); Density: 14.2 persons per square mile (2000); Age: 26.2% under 18, 10.5% over 64 (2000); Marriage status: 25.0% never married, 67.7% now married, 3.2% widowed, 4.1% divorced (2000); Foreign born: 1.0% (2000); Ancestry (includes multiple ancestries): 53.3% German, 26.0% Norwegian, 12.8% Czech, 7.6% Irish, 6.2% Other groups (2000).
Economy: Employment by occupation: 19.8% management, 11.9% professional, 7.5% services, 27.0% sales, 2.7% farming, 11.3% construction, 19.8% production (2000).
Income: Per capita income: $20,188 (2000); Median household income: $47,708 (2000); Poverty rate: 5.8% (2000).
Taxes: Total city taxes per capita: $118 (1997); City property taxes per capita: $118 (1997).
Education: High school graduation rate: 86.2% (2000); College graduation rate: 14.7% (2000).
Housing: Homeownership rate: 90.9% (2000); Median home value: $101,900 (2000); Median rent: $325 per month (2000); Median age of housing: 60+ years (2000).
Transportation: Commute to work: 87.0% car, 0.0% public transportation, 0.7% walk, 12.3% work from home (2000); Travel time to work: 23.7% less than 15 minutes, 55.3% 15 to 30 minutes, 9.3% 30 to 45 minutes, 1.9% 45 to 60 minutes, 9.7% 60 minutes or more (2000)

MEDFORD (city). Covers a land area of 0.681 square miles and a water area of 0 square miles. Located at 44.17° N. Lat.; 93.24° W. Long. Elevation is 1,101 feet.
History: Medford was settled in 1853 on the east bank of the Straight River, the first community in Steele County.
Population: 984 (2000); Race: 91.9% White, 0.0% Black, 0.0% Asian, 0.0% American Indian and Alaska Native, 5.5% Hispanic of any race, 2.6% two or more races (2000); Density: 1,444.9 persons per square mile (2000); Age: 26.4% under 18, 8.9% over 64 (2000); Marriage status: 24.9% never married, 60.2% now married, 5.2% widowed, 9.7% divorced (2000); Foreign born: 4.5% (2000); Ancestry (includes multiple ancestries): 50.8% German, 17.1% Norwegian, 12.7% Irish, 9.5% Other groups, 6.6% Swedish (2000).
Economy: Single-family building permits issued: 12 (2001) / 14 (2000); Multi-family building permits issued: 0 (2001) / 0 (2000); Employment by occupation: 9.3% management, 12.7% professional, 10.4% services, 27.8% sales, 4.2% farming, 7.6% construction, 28.0% production (2000).
Income: Per capita income: $18,886 (2000); Median household income: $50,000 (2000); Poverty rate: 4.4% (2000).
Taxes: Total city taxes per capita: $157 (1997); City property taxes per capita: $152 (1997).
Education: High school graduation rate: 88.6% (2000); College graduation rate: 15.8% (2000).

School District(s)

Medford (PK-12)
2000 Enrollment: 562 507-451-5250

Housing: Homeownership rate: 85.1% (2000); Median home value: $99,700 (2000); Median rent: $308 per month (2000); Median age of housing: 32 years (2000).

Transportation: Commute to work: 94.4% car, 0.0% public transportation, 2.0% walk, 2.9% work from home (2000); Travel time to work: 50.9% less than 15 minutes, 32.4% 15 to 30 minutes, 3.5% 30 to 45 minutes, 8.8% 45 to 60 minutes, 4.4% 60 minutes or more (2000)

MEDFORD (township). Covers a land area of 17.078 square miles and a water area of 0.060 square miles. Located at 44.17° N. Lat.; 93.24° W. Long. Elevation is 1,101 feet.

History: Incorporated 1936.

Population: 681 (2000); Race: 97.7% White, 0.0% Black, 0.6% Asian, 0.3% American Indian and Alaska Native, 1.8% Hispanic of any race, 1.0% two or more races (2000); Density: 39.9 persons per square mile (2000); Age: 29.2% under 18, 11.7% over 64 (2000); Marriage status: 21.1% never married, 62.6% now married, 5.2% widowed, 11.1% divorced (2000); Foreign born: 1.1% (2000); Ancestry (includes multiple ancestries): 41.5% German, 28.5% Norwegian, 11.2% Irish, 7.5% Polish, 5.3% Czech (2000).

Economy: Dairying; poultry; grain, soybeans, beans. Manufacturing: concrete blocks, exercise equipment. Employment by occupation: 13.1% management, 8.8% professional, 13.1% services, 27.7% sales, 0.0% farming, 14.3% construction, 22.9% production (2000).

Income: Per capita income: $19,890 (2000); Median household income: $39,000 (2000); Poverty rate: 4.2% (2000).

Taxes: Total city taxes per capita: $65 (1997); City property taxes per capita: $63 (1997).

Education: High school graduation rate: 86.7% (2000); College graduation rate: 9.3% (2000).

Housing: Homeownership rate: 92.0% (2000); Median home value: $126,100 (2000); Median rent: $350 per month (2000); Median age of housing: 27 years (2000).

Transportation: Commute to work: 88.4% car, 1.6% public transportation, 2.2% walk, 6.6% work from home (2000); Travel time to work: 34.8% less than 15 minutes, 42.5% 15 to 30 minutes, 11.7% 30 to 45 minutes, 3.0% 45 to 60 minutes, 8.0% 60 minutes or more (2000)

MERIDEN (township). Covers a land area of 36.087 square miles and a water area of 0.070 square miles. Located at 44.07° N. Lat.; 93.34° W. Long. Elevation is 1,140 feet.

Population: 631 (2000); Race: 100.0% White, 0.0% Black, 0.0% Asian, 0.0% American Indian and Alaska Native, 0.0% Hispanic of any race, 0.0% two or more races (2000); Density: 17.5 persons per square mile (2000); Age: 24.7% under 18, 14.9% over 64 (2000); Marriage status: 28.6% never married, 57.8% now married, 6.3% widowed, 7.3% divorced (2000); Foreign born: 1.4% (2000); Ancestry (includes multiple ancestries): 52.2% German, 21.2% Norwegian, 12.1% Irish, 7.0% English, 6.4% Czech (2000).

Economy: Employment by occupation: 18.2% management, 15.0% professional, 6.1% services, 20.6% sales, 2.1% farming, 17.9% construction, 20.1% production (2000).

Income: Per capita income: $21,162 (2000); Median household income: $51,477 (2000); Poverty rate: 4.1% (2000).

Taxes: Total city taxes per capita: $78 (1997); City property taxes per capita: $78 (1997).

Education: High school graduation rate: 81.5% (2000); College graduation rate: 14.7% (2000).

Housing: Homeownership rate: 90.6% (2000); Median home value: $112,500 (2000); Median rent: $408 per month (2000); Median age of housing: 60+ years (2000).

Transportation: Commute to work: 85.3% car, 0.0% public transportation, 3.0% walk, 10.9% work from home (2000); Travel time to work: 41.0% less than 15 minutes, 44.0% 15 to 30 minutes, 5.5% 30 to 45 minutes, 5.2% 45 to 60 minutes, 4.3% 60 minutes or more (2000)

MERTON (township). Covers a land area of 35.793 square miles and a water area of 0.099 square miles. Located at 44.15° N. Lat.; 93.10° W. Long. Elevation is 1,260 feet.

Population: 380 (2000); Race: 99.5% White, 0.0% Black, 0.0% Asian, 0.0% American Indian and Alaska Native, 4.0% Hispanic of any race, 0.0% two or more races (2000); Density: 10.6 persons per square mile (2000); Age: 28.3% under 18, 16.3% over 64 (2000); Marriage status: 23.4% never married, 67.7% now married, 2.7% widowed, 6.2% divorced (2000); Foreign born: 0.0% (2000); Ancestry (includes multiple ancestries): 55.6% German, 18.2% Norwegian, 16.8% Czech, 10.7% Irish, 7.8% United States or American (2000).

Economy: Employment by occupation: 21.9% management, 11.2% professional, 12.2% services, 22.4% sales, 5.1% farming, 8.7% construction, 18.4% production (2000).

Income: Per capita income: $21,321 (2000); Median household income: $52,875 (2000); Poverty rate: 2.7% (2000).

Taxes: Total city taxes per capita: $61 (1997); City property taxes per capita: $61 (1997).

Education: High school graduation rate: 81.1% (2000); College graduation rate: 8.8% (2000).

Housing: Homeownership rate: 88.7% (2000); Median home value: $127,900 (2000); Median rent: $525 per month (2000); Median age of housing: 58 years (2000).

Transportation: Commute to work: 84.7% car, 0.0% public transportation, 8.2% walk, 7.1% work from home (2000); Travel time to work: 28.0% less than 15 minutes, 55.5% 15 to 30 minutes, 4.4% 30 to 45 minutes, 4.4% 45 to 60 minutes, 7.7% 60 minutes or more (2000)

OWATONNA (city). Covers a land area of 12.604 square miles and a water area of 0.068 square miles. Located at 44.08° N. Lat.; 93.22° W. Long. Elevation is 1,129 feet.

History: Owatonna grew up around a mineral spring, rich in iron and sulphur, that was reported to have medicinal value similar to the Vichy springs in France. A legend tells that Owatonna was the daughter of Chief Wadena, who brought her here to be healed by the spring waters. Owatonna developed as the center of a dairy farming region, with cooperative creameries producing butter.

Population: 22,434 (2000); Race: 93.9% White, 1.3% Black, 0.8% Asian, 0.1% American Indian and Alaska Native, 4.4% Hispanic of any race, 1.9% two or more races (2000); Density: 1,779.9 persons per square mile (2000); Age: 27.9% under 18, 12.6% over 64 (2000); Marriage status: 23.3% never married, 61.3% now married, 7.0% widowed, 8.4% divorced (2000); Foreign born: 4.5% (2000); Ancestry (includes multiple ancestries): 42.2% German, 19.6% Norwegian, 8.7% Irish, 8.0% Other groups, 6.1% Czech (2000).

Vital Statistics: Birth rate: 132.4 per 10,000 population (1998)

Economy: Single-family building permits issued: 137 (2001) / 137 (2000); Multi-family building permits issued: 0 (2001) / 12 (2000); Employment by occupation: 11.5% management, 18.9% professional, 13.3% services, 28.8% sales, 0.3% farming, 7.4% construction, 19.7% production (2000).

Income: Per capita income: $20,513 (2000); Median household income: $45,660 (2000); Poverty rate: 6.6% (2000).

Taxes: Total city taxes per capita: $211 (2000); City property taxes per capita: $187 (2000).

Education: High school graduation rate: 87.1% (2000); College graduation rate: 23.2% (2000).

School District(s)

Owatonna (PK-12)
2000 Enrollment: 5,110 507-444-8601

Four-year College(s)

Pillsbury Baptist Bible College (Private, Not-for-profit, Baptist)
2001 Enrollment: 222 507-451-2710
2001 Tuition: In-state $5,888; Out-of-state $5,888

Housing: Homeownership rate: 76.5% (2000); Median home value: $104,000 (2000); Median rent: $427 per month (2000); Median age of housing: 31 years (2000).

Hospitals: Owatonna Hospital (77 beds); Owatonna Hospital - Mental Health Unit (10 beds)

Safety: Violent crime rate: 19.0 per 10,000 population; Property crime rate: 357.2 per 10,000 population (2001).

Newspapers: Owatonna People's Press (6 x week)

Transportation: Commute to work: 92.2% car, 0.3% public transportation, 2.5% walk, 3.9% work from home (2000); Travel time to work: 72.7% less than 15 minutes, 15.2% 15 to 30 minutes, 4.1% 30 to 45 minutes, 3.9% 45 to 60 minutes, 4.0% 60 minutes or more (2000)

Additional Information Contacts

Owatonna Chamber of Commerce. 507-451-7970

OWATONNA (township). Covers a land area of 25.088 square miles and a water area of 0.029 square miles. Located at 44.05° N. Lat.; 93.22° W. Long. Elevation is 1,129 feet.

Population: 771 (2000); Race: 96.9% White, 0.0% Black, 3.1% Asian, 0.0% American Indian and Alaska Native, 0.9% Hispanic of any race, 0.0% two or more races (2000); Density: 30.7 persons per square mile (2000); Age: 29.4% under 18, 16.7% over 64 (2000); Marriage status: 22.5% never married, 68.5% now married, 5.3% widowed, 3.6% divorced (2000); Foreign born:

3.0% (2000); Ancestry (includes multiple ancestries): 44.5% German, 19.2% Czech, 17.6% Norwegian, 9.7% Irish, 6.1% Danish (2000).
Economy: Railroad junction. Manufacturing: furniture, consumer goods, electronic equipment, apparel, machinery, printing and publishing. Agriculture: corn, oats, soybeans, peas, alfalfa; poultry, livestock; dairying. Employment by occupation: 18.6% management, 14.9% professional, 9.4% services, 24.6% sales, 2.5% farming, 11.7% construction, 18.4% production (2000).
Income: Per capita income: $24,037 (2000); Median household income: $51,250 (2000); Poverty rate: 2.2% (2000).
Taxes: Total city taxes per capita: $73 (1997); City property taxes per capita: $72 (1997).
Education: High school graduation rate: 89.4% (2000); College graduation rate: 16.6% (2000).
Housing: Homeownership rate: 88.0% (2000); Median home value: $134,800 (2000); Median rent: $400 per month (2000); Median age of housing: 39 years (2000).
Transportation: Commute to work: 87.2% car, 0.0% public transportation, 4.0% walk, 8.8% work from home (2000); Travel time to work: 64.7% less than 15 minutes, 18.7% 15 to 30 minutes, 8.0% 30 to 45 minutes, 2.8% 45 to 60 minutes, 5.8% 60 minutes or more (2000)

SOMERSET (township). Covers a land area of 35.909 square miles and a water area of 0.041 square miles. Located at 43.97° N. Lat.; 93.23° W. Long.
Population: 847 (2000); Race: 99.3% White, 0.0% Black, 0.0% Asian, 0.0% American Indian and Alaska Native, 0.7% Hispanic of any race, 0.2% two or more races (2000); Density: 23.6 persons per square mile (2000); Age: 29.2% under 18, 9.4% over 64 (2000); Marriage status: 18.3% never married, 72.1% now married, 4.4% widowed, 5.2% divorced (2000); Foreign born: 0.9% (2000); Ancestry (includes multiple ancestries): 40.2% German, 20.8% Norwegian, 18.9% Czech, 5.0% United States or American, 3.9% Irish (2000).
Economy: Employment by occupation: 18.8% management, 14.8% professional, 9.2% services, 27.0% sales, 1.4% farming, 11.2% construction, 17.6% production (2000).
Income: Per capita income: $20,704 (2000); Median household income: $55,938 (2000); Poverty rate: 3.3% (2000).
Taxes: Total city taxes per capita: $37 (1997); City property taxes per capita: $37 (1997).
Education: High school graduation rate: 91.4% (2000); College graduation rate: 13.4% (2000).
Housing: Homeownership rate: 90.2% (2000); Median home value: $112,500 (2000); Median rent: $475 per month (2000); Median age of housing: 51 years (2000).
Transportation: Commute to work: 91.7% car, 0.0% public transportation, 1.8% walk, 6.1% work from home (2000); Travel time to work: 33.5% less than 15 minutes, 51.6% 15 to 30 minutes, 8.8% 30 to 45 minutes, 1.7% 45 to 60 minutes, 4.3% 60 minutes or more (2000)

SUMMIT (township). Covers a land area of 35.919 square miles and a water area of 0.029 square miles. Located at 43.90° N. Lat.; 93.21° W. Long.
Population: 515 (2000); Race: 99.0% White, 0.0% Black, 0.2% Asian, 0.0% American Indian and Alaska Native, 0.0% Hispanic of any race, 0.8% two or more races (2000); Density: 14.3 persons per square mile (2000); Age: 30.6% under 18, 13.8% over 64 (2000); Marriage status: 23.7% never married, 66.8% now married, 4.3% widowed, 5.1% divorced (2000); Foreign born: 0.6% (2000); Ancestry (includes multiple ancestries): 28.5% German, 22.2% Norwegian, 20.4% Czech, 8.6% Irish, 4.7% Danish (2000).
Economy: Employment by occupation: 15.4% management, 12.0% professional, 17.0% services, 19.5% sales, 1.7% farming, 12.4% construction, 22.0% production (2000).
Income: Per capita income: $14,977 (2000); Median household income: $38,958 (2000); Poverty rate: 9.3% (2000).
Taxes: Total city taxes per capita: $70 (1997); City property taxes per capita: $70 (1997).
Education: High school graduation rate: 84.8% (2000); College graduation rate: 10.0% (2000).
Housing: Homeownership rate: 90.7% (2000); Median home value: $92,500 (2000); Median rent: $455 per month (2000); Median age of housing: 60+ years (2000).
Transportation: Commute to work: 80.3% car, 0.0% public transportation, 1.7% walk, 16.3% work from home (2000); Travel time to work: 20.5% less than 15 minutes, 69.0% 15 to 30 minutes, 6.5% 30 to 45 minutes, 1.5% 45 to 60 minutes, 2.5% 60 minutes or more (2000)

Stevens County

Located in western Minnesota; drained by the Pomme de Terre River. Covers a land area of 562.10 square miles, a water area of 13.20 square miles, and is located in the Central Time Zone. The county government was organized in 1862. County seat is Morris.

Weather Station: Morris WC Exp. Station Elevation: 1,138 feet

	Jan	Feb	Mar	Apr	May	Jun	Jul	Aug	Sep	Oct	Nov	Dec
High	17	24	36	54	69	77	81	80	70	57	37	23
Low	-2	5	18	33	45	55	59	57	46	34	20	6
Precip	0.8	0.7	1.5	2.1	2.8	3.9	3.9	3.3	2.2	2.4	1.2	0.6
Snow	11.6	7.8	9.7	3.3	tr	0.0	0.0	0.0	tr	0.9	7.3	6.9

High and Low temperatures in degrees Fahrenheit; Precipitation and Snow in inches

Population: 10,053 (2000); Race: 96.0% White, 1.4% Black, 0.6% Asian, 0.7% American Indian and Alaska Native, 1.0% Hispanic of any race, 0.8% two or more races (2000); Density: 17.9 persons per square mile (2000); Age: 21.6% under 18, 16.9% over 64 (2000).
Religion: Five largest groups: 31.3% Evangelical Lutheran Church in America, 19.6% Catholic Church, 5.3% Apostolic Christian Church of America, Inc., 3.7% Wisconsin Evangelical Lutheran Synod, 2.9% The Evangelical Free Church of America (2000).
Economy: Unemployment rate: 2.1% (11/2002); Total civilian labor force: 5,546 (11/2002); Leading industries: 23.9% health care and social assistance; 16.6% retail trade; 12.2% accommodation & food services (2000); Companies that employ more than 1,000 persons: 0 (2000); Companies that employ more than 100 persons: 7 (2000); Farms: 497 totaling 299,346 acres (1997); Minority business ownership rate: 0.0% (1997); Women business ownership rate: 12.2% (1997); Retail sales per capita: $11,839 (1997). Single-family building permits issued: 26 (2001) / 28 (2000); Multi-family building permits issued: 0 (2001) / 0 (2000).
Income: Per capita income: $17,569 (2000); Median household income: $37,267 (2000); Poverty rate: 13.6% (2000); Bankruptcy rate: 2.47% (2001).
Taxes: Total county taxes per capita: $278 (2000); County property taxes per capita: $278 (2000).
Education: High school graduation rate: 84.4% (2000); College graduation rate: 20.6% (2000).
Housing: Homeownership rate: 70.2% (2000); Median home value: $67,100 (2000); Median rent: $323 per month (2000); Median age of housing: 41 years (2000).
Health: Birth rate: 100.5 per 10,000 population (1998); Age adjusted death rate: 63.7 per 10,000 population (1999); Age adjusted cancer mortality rate: 145.5 (Unreliable figure as per CDC) deaths per 100,000 population (1999). Number of physicians: 7.0 per 10,000 population (1999); Number of hospital beds: 598.8 per 10,000 population (1999).
Elections: 2000 Presidential election results: 42.3% Gore, 49.2% Bush, 6.8% Nader, 1.2% Buchanan
National and State Parks: Alberta Marsh State Wildlife Management Area; Benson State Wildlife Management Area; Boekholt Grove State Wildlife Management; Brouillet State Wildlife Management Area; Chokio State Wildlife Management Area; Cin State Wildlife Management Area; Coleman State Wildlife Management Area; Dablow State Wildlife Management Area; Dolven State Wildlife Management Area; Everglade State Wildlife Management Area; Hornings Pit State Wildlife Management Ar; Klason State Wildlife Management Area; Kline State Wildlife Management Area; Macsville State Wildlife Management Area; Mathison State Wildlife Management Area; Muddy Creek State Wildlife Management Area; Reimers State Wildlife Management Area; Robertson State Wildlife Management Area; Selk State Wildlife Management Area; Thedin State Wildlife Management Area; Weiler State Wildlife Management Area; Wilts State Wildlife Management Area
Additional Information Contacts
Stevens County Government Offices 320-589-7409
Morris Area Chamber of Commerce 320-589-1242

Stevens County Communities

ALBERTA (city). Covers a land area of 0.277 square miles and a water area of 0 square miles. Located at 45.57° N. Lat.; 96.04° W. Long.
Population: 142 (2000); Race: 100.0% White, 0.0% Black, 0.0% Asian, 0.0% American Indian and Alaska Native, 0.0% Hispanic of any race, 0.0% two or more races (2000); Density: 513.2 persons per square mile (2000); Age: 33.1% under 18, 8.8% over 64 (2000); Marriage status: 28.6% never married, 60.5% now married, 1.7% widowed, 9.2% divorced (2000); Foreign

born: 1.9% (2000); Ancestry (includes multiple ancestries): 39.4% German, 26.9% Norwegian, 12.5% Irish, 8.8% Danish, 3.8% English (2000).
Economy: Corn, oats, wheat, barley, sunflowers; hogs, cattle. Single-family building permits issued: 0 (2001) / 2 (2000); Multi-family building permits issued: 0 (2001) / 0 (2000); Employment by occupation: 2.3% management, 15.9% professional, 25.0% services, 30.7% sales, 2.3% farming, 6.8% construction, 17.0% production (2000).
Income: Per capita income: $15,296 (2000); Median household income: $43,500 (2000); Poverty rate: 0.0% (2000).
Taxes: Total city taxes per capita: $168 (1997); City property taxes per capita: $153 (1997).
Education: High school graduation rate: 90.7% (2000); College graduation rate: 18.6% (2000).
Housing: Homeownership rate: 87.3% (2000); Median home value: $38,000 (2000); Median rent: $256 per month (2000); Median age of housing: 51 years (2000).
Transportation: Commute to work: 88.4% car, 0.0% public transportation, 9.3% walk, 2.3% work from home (2000); Travel time to work: 56.0% less than 15 minutes, 38.1% 15 to 30 minutes, 3.6% 30 to 45 minutes, 0.0% 45 to 60 minutes, 2.4% 60 minutes or more (2000)

BAKER (township). Covers a land area of 35.420 square miles and a water area of 0.163 square miles. Located at 45.54° N. Lat.; 96.17° W. Long.
Population: 265 (2000); Race: 98.3% White, 0.0% Black, 0.0% Asian, 1.7% American Indian and Alaska Native, 0.0% Hispanic of any race, 0.0% two or more races (2000); Density: 7.5 persons per square mile (2000); Age: 12.9% under 18, 58.1% over 64 (2000); Marriage status: 25.7% never married, 35.3% now married, 39.0% widowed, 0.0% divorced (2000); Foreign born: 0.0% (2000); Ancestry (includes multiple ancestries): 33.2% German, 12.9% Norwegian, 8.3% Irish, 8.3% Danish, 5.0% Swedish (2000).
Economy: Employment by occupation: 27.5% management, 11.8% professional, 9.8% services, 35.3% sales, 0.0% farming, 7.8% construction, 7.8% production (2000).
Income: Per capita income: $14,426 (2000); Median household income: $23,125 (2000); Poverty rate: 24.8% (2000).
Taxes: Total city taxes per capita: $108 (1997); City property taxes per capita: $108 (1997).
Education: High school graduation rate: 77.3% (2000); College graduation rate: 19.7% (2000).
Housing: Homeownership rate: 69.4% (2000); Median home value: $55,000 (2000); Median rent: $138 per month (2000); Median age of housing: 38 years (2000).
Transportation: Commute to work: 96.1% car, 0.0% public transportation, 0.0% walk, 3.9% work from home (2000); Travel time to work: 46.9% less than 15 minutes, 36.7% 15 to 30 minutes, 12.2% 30 to 45 minutes, 4.1% 45 to 60 minutes, 0.0% 60 minutes or more (2000)

CHOKIO (city). Covers a land area of 0.495 square miles and a water area of 0 square miles. Located at 45.57° N. Lat.; 96.17° W. Long. Elevation is 1,124 feet.
Population: 443 (2000); Race: 100.0% White, 0.0% Black, 0.0% Asian, 0.0% American Indian and Alaska Native, 0.0% Hispanic of any race, 0.0% two or more races (2000); Density: 895.8 persons per square mile (2000); Age: 21.2% under 18, 24.5% over 64 (2000); Marriage status: 21.1% never married, 66.2% now married, 6.9% widowed, 5.8% divorced (2000); Foreign born: 1.1% (2000); Ancestry (includes multiple ancestries): 56.5% German, 26.4% Norwegian, 12.1% Irish, 6.5% Swedish, 5.6% Dutch (2000).
Economy: Wheat, corn, oats, barley, soybeans, sunflowers; hogs, cattle; light manufacturing. Single-family building permits issued: 0 (2001) / 3 (2000); Multi-family building permits issued: 0 (2001) / 0 (2000); Employment by occupation: 14.0% management, 14.5% professional, 20.8% services, 27.1% sales, 2.3% farming, 9.0% construction, 12.2% production (2000).
Income: Per capita income: $15,891 (2000); Median household income: $34,107 (2000); Poverty rate: 5.2% (2000).
Taxes: Total city taxes per capita: $67 (1997); City property taxes per capita: $63 (1997).
Education: High school graduation rate: 80.8% (2000); College graduation rate: 12.4% (2000).

School District(s)

Chokio-Alberta (PK-12)
2000 Enrollment: 244 320-324-7131
Housing: Homeownership rate: 85.6% (2000); Median home value: $45,300 (2000); Median rent: $275 per month (2000); Median age of housing: 43 years (2000).
Newspapers: Chokio Review (1 x week)

Transportation: Commute to work: 75.6% car, 0.0% public transportation, 18.1% walk, 4.5% work from home (2000); Travel time to work: 51.2% less than 15 minutes, 42.2% 15 to 30 minutes, 5.7% 30 to 45 minutes, 0.0% 45 to 60 minutes, 0.9% 60 minutes or more (2000)

DARNEN (township). Covers a land area of 32.841 square miles and a water area of 0.329 square miles. Located at 45.55° N. Lat.; 95.92° W. Long.
Population: 325 (2000); Race: 100.0% White, 0.0% Black, 0.0% Asian, 0.0% American Indian and Alaska Native, 0.0% Hispanic of any race, 0.0% two or more races (2000); Density: 9.9 persons per square mile (2000); Age: 30.9% under 18, 11.8% over 64 (2000); Marriage status: 30.3% never married, 64.9% now married, 1.8% widowed, 3.0% divorced (2000); Foreign born: 2.2% (2000); Ancestry (includes multiple ancestries): 34.4% German, 22.3% United States or American, 10.5% Swiss, 8.3% Norwegian, 8.0% Irish (2000).
Economy: Employment by occupation: 25.3% management, 9.0% professional, 10.7% services, 32.6% sales, 2.8% farming, 6.7% construction, 12.9% production (2000).
Income: Per capita income: $22,645 (2000); Median household income: $51,875 (2000); Poverty rate: 3.3% (2000).
Taxes: Total city taxes per capita: $44 (1997); City property taxes per capita: $44 (1997).
Education: High school graduation rate: 85.2% (2000); College graduation rate: 13.9% (2000).
Housing: Homeownership rate: 89.2% (2000); Median home value: $92,500 (2000); Median rent: $271 per month (2000); Median age of housing: 27 years (2000).
Transportation: Commute to work: 82.0% car, 0.0% public transportation, 1.1% walk, 15.7% work from home (2000); Travel time to work: 70.0% less than 15 minutes, 18.0% 15 to 30 minutes, 9.3% 30 to 45 minutes, 0.0% 45 to 60 minutes, 2.7% 60 minutes or more (2000)

DONNELLY (city). Covers a land area of 2.754 square miles and a water area of 0.322 square miles. Located at 45.68° N. Lat.; 96.01° W. Long. Elevation is 1,133 feet.
Population: 254 (2000); Race: 98.3% White, 0.0% Black, 0.0% Asian, 0.0% American Indian and Alaska Native, 0.0% Hispanic of any race, 1.7% two or more races (2000); Density: 92.2 persons per square mile (2000); Age: 20.3% under 18, 21.2% over 64 (2000); Marriage status: 12.1% never married, 71.7% now married, 9.6% widowed, 6.6% divorced (2000); Foreign born: 0.0% (2000); Ancestry (includes multiple ancestries): 50.6% German, 31.1% Norwegian, 13.7% Swedish, 9.5% Irish, 4.1% United States or American (2000).
Economy: Single-family building permits issued: 0 (2001) / 3 (2000); Multi-family building permits issued: 0 (2001) / 0 (2000); Employment by occupation: 16.2% management, 12.7% professional, 16.2% services, 17.6% sales, 4.2% farming, 3.5% construction, 29.6% production (2000).
Income: Per capita income: $22,523 (2000); Median household income: $35,972 (2000); Poverty rate: 2.5% (2000).
Taxes: Total city taxes per capita: $89 (1997); City property taxes per capita: $84 (1997).
Education: High school graduation rate: 84.9% (2000); College graduation rate: 7.8% (2000).
Housing: Homeownership rate: 91.2% (2000); Median home value: $44,500 (2000); Median rent: $275 per month (2000); Median age of housing: 60+ years (2000).
Transportation: Commute to work: 81.4% car, 0.0% public transportation, 10.7% walk, 7.9% work from home (2000); Travel time to work: 51.9% less than 15 minutes, 34.9% 15 to 30 minutes, 7.8% 30 to 45 minutes, 1.6% 45 to 60 minutes, 3.9% 60 minutes or more (2000)

DONNELLY (township). Covers a land area of 33.345 square miles and a water area of 0.724 square miles. Located at 45.72° N. Lat.; 96.07° W. Long. Elevation is 1,133 feet.
Population: 113 (2000); Race: 98.2% White, 0.0% Black, 0.0% Asian, 0.0% American Indian and Alaska Native, 0.0% Hispanic of any race, 1.8% two or more races (2000); Density: 3.4 persons per square mile (2000); Age: 16.7% under 18, 29.8% over 64 (2000); Marriage status: 18.8% never married, 64.4% now married, 9.9% widowed, 6.9% divorced (2000); Foreign born: 0.0% (2000); Ancestry (includes multiple ancestries): 43.0% German, 37.7% Norwegian, 13.2% English, 8.8% Russian, 8.8% Irish (2000).
Economy: Grain, sunflowers; livestock. Manufacturing: fertilizer, draperies. Employment by occupation: 37.3% management, 11.8% professional, 11.8% services, 19.6% sales, 3.9% farming, 7.8% construction, 7.8% production (2000).

Income: Per capita income: $23,295 (2000); Median household income: $44,750 (2000); Poverty rate: 11.4% (2000).
Taxes: Total city taxes per capita: $94 (1997); City property taxes per capita: $94 (1997).
Education: High school graduation rate: 79.3% (2000); College graduation rate: 8.7% (2000).
Housing: Homeownership rate: 92.3% (2000); Median home value: $65,000 (2000); Median rent: $417 per month (2000); Median age of housing: 60+ years (2000).
Transportation: Commute to work: 74.5% car, 0.0% public transportation, 0.0% walk, 25.5% work from home (2000); Travel time to work: 31.6% less than 15 minutes, 57.9% 15 to 30 minutes, 5.3% 30 to 45 minutes, 0.0% 45 to 60 minutes, 5.3% 60 minutes or more (2000)

ELDORADO (township). Covers a land area of 35.849 square miles and a water area of 0.266 square miles. Located at 45.71° N. Lat.; 96.18° W. Long.
Population: 109 (2000); Race: 95.7% White, 0.0% Black, 1.4% Asian, 0.0% American Indian and Alaska Native, 0.0% Hispanic of any race, 2.8% two or more races (2000); Density: 3.0 persons per square mile (2000); Age: 31.2% under 18, 14.2% over 64 (2000); Marriage status: 25.5% never married, 66.4% now married, 3.6% widowed, 4.5% divorced (2000); Foreign born: 1.4% (2000); Ancestry (includes multiple ancestries): 56.0% German, 17.0% Norwegian, 12.1% Swedish, 4.3% Czech, 4.3% Scandinavian (2000).
Economy: Employment by occupation: 35.2% management, 18.3% professional, 9.9% services, 23.9% sales, 2.8% farming, 0.0% construction, 9.9% production (2000).
Income: Per capita income: $15,789 (2000); Median household income: $58,125 (2000); Poverty rate: 13.7% (2000).
Taxes: Total city taxes per capita: $117 (1997); City property taxes per capita: $117 (1997).
Education: High school graduation rate: 90.0% (2000); College graduation rate: 21.1% (2000).
Housing: Homeownership rate: 90.7% (2000); Median home value: $76,300 (2000); Median rent: $275 per month (2000); Median age of housing: 42 years (2000).
Transportation: Commute to work: 73.1% car, 0.0% public transportation, 4.5% walk, 22.4% work from home (2000); Travel time to work: 53.8% less than 15 minutes, 32.7% 15 to 30 minutes, 7.7% 30 to 45 minutes, 0.0% 45 to 60 minutes, 5.8% 60 minutes or more (2000)

EVERGLADE (township). Covers a land area of 36.048 square miles and a water area of 0.051 square miles. Located at 45.63° N. Lat.; 96.18° W. Long.
Population: 128 (2000); Race: 100.0% White, 0.0% Black, 0.0% Asian, 0.0% American Indian and Alaska Native, 0.0% Hispanic of any race, 0.0% two or more races (2000); Density: 3.6 persons per square mile (2000); Age: 29.6% under 18, 16.2% over 64 (2000); Marriage status: 24.3% never married, 67.8% now married, 7.8% widowed, 0.0% divorced (2000); Foreign born: 0.0% (2000); Ancestry (includes multiple ancestries): 64.1% German, 26.1% Norwegian, 7.7% Irish, 7.7% Danish, 6.3% United States or American (2000).
Economy: Employment by occupation: 26.8% management, 11.0% professional, 2.4% services, 35.4% sales, 0.0% farming, 11.0% construction, 13.4% production (2000).
Income: Per capita income: $21,022 (2000); Median household income: $56,042 (2000); Poverty rate: 1.4% (2000).
Taxes: Total city taxes per capita: $165 (1997); City property taxes per capita: $165 (1997).
Education: High school graduation rate: 86.0% (2000); College graduation rate: 20.9% (2000).
Housing: Homeownership rate: 87.8% (2000); Median home value: $73,800 (2000); Median rent: $175 per month (2000); Median age of housing: 60+ years (2000).
Transportation: Commute to work: 70.7% car, 0.0% public transportation, 9.8% walk, 19.5% work from home (2000); Travel time to work: 40.9% less than 15 minutes, 37.9% 15 to 30 minutes, 3.0% 30 to 45 minutes, 4.5% 45 to 60 minutes, 13.6% 60 minutes or more (2000)

FRAMNAS (township). Covers a land area of 33.393 square miles and a water area of 2.678 square miles. Located at 45.61° N. Lat.; 95.83° W. Long.
Population: 318 (2000); Race: 100.0% White, 0.0% Black, 0.0% Asian, 0.0% American Indian and Alaska Native, 0.0% Hispanic of any race, 0.0% two or more races (2000); Density: 9.5 persons per square mile (2000); Age: 30.8% under 18, 10.6% over 64 (2000); Marriage status: 20.9% never married, 73.9% now married, 1.7% widowed, 3.4% divorced (2000); Foreign born: 0.0% (2000); Ancestry (includes multiple ancestries): 40.4% German, 35.3% Norwegian, 14.1% Swedish, 9.9% Irish, 7.1% English (2000).
Economy: Employment by occupation: 24.2% management, 13.1% professional, 17.0% services, 16.3% sales, 2.6% farming, 7.8% construction, 19.0% production (2000).
Income: Per capita income: $16,943 (2000); Median household income: $45,750 (2000); Poverty rate: 6.2% (2000).
Taxes: Total city taxes per capita: $73 (1997); City property taxes per capita: $73 (1997).
Education: High school graduation rate: 91.0% (2000); College graduation rate: 14.4% (2000).
Housing: Homeownership rate: 85.8% (2000); Median home value: $110,000 (2000); Median rent: $275 per month (2000); Median age of housing: 41 years (2000).
Transportation: Commute to work: 77.8% car, 0.0% public transportation, 10.5% walk, 8.5% work from home (2000); Travel time to work: 49.3% less than 15 minutes, 32.1% 15 to 30 minutes, 8.6% 30 to 45 minutes, 0.0% 45 to 60 minutes, 10.0% 60 minutes or more (2000)

HANCOCK (city). Covers a land area of 0.990 square miles and a water area of 0.008 square miles. Located at 45.49° N. Lat.; 95.79° W. Long. Elevation is 1,151 feet.
Population: 717 (2000); Race: 99.1% White, 0.0% Black, 0.0% Asian, 0.0% American Indian and Alaska Native, 0.0% Hispanic of any race, 0.9% two or more races (2000); Density: 724.5 persons per square mile (2000); Age: 22.0% under 18, 17.6% over 64 (2000); Marriage status: 26.0% never married, 59.1% now married, 7.5% widowed, 7.5% divorced (2000); Foreign born: 0.9% (2000); Ancestry (includes multiple ancestries): 47.0% German, 32.6% Norwegian, 6.6% Irish, 6.3% Dutch, 4.3% English (2000).
Economy: Grain, sunflowers, soybeans; cattle, hogs. Manufacturing: concrete products. Single-family building permits issued: 2 (2001) / 2 (2000); Multi-family building permits issued: 0 (2001) / 0 (2000); Employment by occupation: 16.8% management, 11.2% professional, 27.2% services, 17.3% sales, 1.1% farming, 8.0% construction, 18.4% production (2000).
Income: Per capita income: $17,012 (2000); Median household income: $34,583 (2000); Poverty rate: 8.0% (2000).
Taxes: Total city taxes per capita: $150 (1997); City property taxes per capita: $147 (1997).
Education: High school graduation rate: 81.1% (2000); College graduation rate: 9.8% (2000).

School District(s)

Hancock (PK-12)
2000 Enrollment: 241 320-392-5622
Housing: Homeownership rate: 85.6% (2000); Median home value: $40,000 (2000); Median rent: $244 per month (2000); Median age of housing: 55 years (2000).
Newspapers: The Hancock Record (1 x week)
Transportation: Commute to work: 81.8% car, 1.1% public transportation, 9.8% walk, 3.0% work from home (2000); Travel time to work: 53.5% less than 15 minutes, 36.1% 15 to 30 minutes, 7.6% 30 to 45 minutes, 1.1% 45 to 60 minutes, 1.7% 60 minutes or more (2000)

HODGES (township). Covers a land area of 34.147 square miles and a water area of 1.327 square miles. Located at 45.53° N. Lat.; 95.79° W. Long.
Population: 264 (2000); Race: 100.0% White, 0.0% Black, 0.0% Asian, 0.0% American Indian and Alaska Native, 0.0% Hispanic of any race, 0.0% two or more races (2000); Density: 7.7 persons per square mile (2000); Age: 24.5% under 18, 9.4% over 64 (2000); Marriage status: 19.8% never married, 78.7% now married, 0.5% widowed, 1.0% divorced (2000); Foreign born: 0.0% (2000); Ancestry (includes multiple ancestries): 43.8% German, 29.1% Norwegian, 20.0% Dutch, 10.9% Swedish, 9.1% Belgian (2000).
Economy: Single-family building permits issued: 1 (2001) / 1 (2000); Multi-family building permits issued: 0 (2001) / 0 (2000); Employment by occupation: 25.0% management, 13.5% professional, 9.0% services, 26.3% sales, 9.0% farming, 9.6% construction, 7.7% production (2000).
Income: Per capita income: $25,367 (2000); Median household income: $50,833 (2000); Poverty rate: 1.9% (2000).
Taxes: Total city taxes per capita: $51 (1997); City property taxes per capita: $51 (1997).
Education: High school graduation rate: 97.7% (2000); College graduation rate: 18.4% (2000).
Housing: Homeownership rate: 87.1% (2000); Median home value: $77,500 (2000); Median rent: $363 per month (2000); Median age of housing: 60+ years (2000).
Transportation: Commute to work: 76.8% car, 0.0% public transportation, 6.5% walk, 16.8% work from home (2000); Travel time to work: 56.6% less

than 15 minutes, 34.1% 15 to 30 minutes, 5.4% 30 to 45 minutes, 3.9% 45 to 60 minutes, 0.0% 60 minutes or more (2000)

HORTON (township). Covers a land area of 35.834 square miles and a water area of 0.081 square miles. Located at 45.45° N. Lat.; 95.93° W. Long.
Population: 210 (2000); Race: 100.0% White, 0.0% Black, 0.0% Asian, 0.0% American Indian and Alaska Native, 0.0% Hispanic of any race, 0.0% two or more races (2000); Density: 5.9 persons per square mile (2000); Age: 39.3% under 18, 6.6% over 64 (2000); Marriage status: 29.5% never married, 65.3% now married, 3.2% widowed, 2.1% divorced (2000); Foreign born: 0.0% (2000); Ancestry (includes multiple ancestries): 73.5% German, 23.5% Norwegian, 12.9% Irish, 11.0% Swiss, 8.5% Polish (2000).
Economy: Employment by occupation: 31.3% management, 6.9% professional, 6.1% services, 22.9% sales, 8.4% farming, 5.3% construction, 19.1% production (2000).
Income: Per capita income: $13,299 (2000); Median household income: $43,750 (2000); Poverty rate: 4.8% (2000).
Taxes: Total city taxes per capita: $41 (1997); City property taxes per capita: $41 (1997).
Education: High school graduation rate: 89.2% (2000); College graduation rate: 15.1% (2000).
Housing: Homeownership rate: 80.8% (2000); Median home value: $92,500 (2000); Median rent: $358 per month (2000); Median age of housing: 60+ years (2000).
Transportation: Commute to work: 72.5% car, 0.0% public transportation, 3.1% walk, 24.4% work from home (2000); Travel time to work: 31.3% less than 15 minutes, 58.6% 15 to 30 minutes, 8.1% 30 to 45 minutes, 2.0% 45 to 60 minutes, 0.0% 60 minutes or more (2000)

MOORE (township). Covers a land area of 35.313 square miles and a water area of 0 square miles. Located at 45.46° N. Lat.; 95.82° W. Long.
Population: 252 (2000); Race: 99.2% White, 0.0% Black, 0.0% Asian, 0.0% American Indian and Alaska Native, 0.8% Hispanic of any race, 0.0% two or more races (2000); Density: 7.1 persons per square mile (2000); Age: 31.2% under 18, 12.6% over 64 (2000); Marriage status: 31.5% never married, 61.4% now married, 2.5% widowed, 4.6% divorced (2000); Foreign born: 1.6% (2000); Ancestry (includes multiple ancestries): 72.3% German, 17.8% Swiss, 11.5% Norwegian, 4.0% Dutch, 4.0% English (2000).
Economy: Employment by occupation: 48.8% management, 10.9% professional, 3.1% services, 11.6% sales, 2.3% farming, 7.8% construction, 15.5% production (2000).
Income: Per capita income: $17,001 (2000); Median household income: $44,583 (2000); Poverty rate: 2.4% (2000).
Taxes: Total city taxes per capita: $89 (1997); City property taxes per capita: $89 (1997).
Education: High school graduation rate: 89.2% (2000); College graduation rate: 6.8% (2000).
Housing: Homeownership rate: 88.2% (2000); Median home value: $90,600 (2000); Median rent: $175 per month (2000); Median age of housing: 42 years (2000).
Transportation: Commute to work: 61.2% car, 0.0% public transportation, 3.9% walk, 34.9% work from home (2000); Travel time to work: 47.6% less than 15 minutes, 44.0% 15 to 30 minutes, 2.4% 30 to 45 minutes, 1.2% 45 to 60 minutes, 4.8% 60 minutes or more (2000)

MORRIS (city). Covers a land area of 4.283 square miles and a water area of 0.252 square miles. Located at 45.58° N. Lat.; 95.91° W. Long. Elevation is 1,133 feet.
History: Morris developed as a market center for the farms of Stevens County, and as a commercial center for west central Minnesota. Nearby lakes afforded fishing and hunting, especially for wild fowl.
Population: 5,068 (2000); Race: 92.5% White, 2.7% Black, 1.2% Asian, 1.3% American Indian and Alaska Native, 1.9% Hispanic of any race, 1.4% two or more races (2000); Density: 1,183.2 persons per square mile (2000); Age: 16.4% under 18, 16.6% over 64 (2000); Marriage status: 43.8% never married, 42.6% now married, 8.8% widowed, 4.8% divorced (2000); Foreign born: 2.8% (2000); Ancestry (includes multiple ancestries): 45.6% German, 23.4% Norwegian, 10.6% Irish, 8.1% Swedish, 7.9% Other groups (2000).
Economy: Single-family building permits issued: 18 (2001) / 10 (2000); Multi-family building permits issued: 0 (2001) / 0 (2000); Employment by occupation: 10.7% management, 27.7% professional, 19.7% services, 24.5% sales, 1.7% farming, 5.0% construction, 10.7% production (2000).
Income: Per capita income: $16,607 (2000); Median household income: $31,786 (2000); Poverty rate: 22.4% (2000).
Taxes: Total city taxes per capita: $134 (1997); City property taxes per capita: $126 (1997).
Education: High school graduation rate: 82.6% (2000); College graduation rate: 28.0% (2000).

School District(s)

Midwest Special Education Coop (PK-PK)
2000 Enrollment: 5 320-589-4248
Morris (PK-12)
2000 Enrollment: 1,129 320-589-4840

Four-year College(s)

University of Minnesota-Morris (Public)
2001 Enrollment: 1,927 320-589-2211
2001 Tuition: In-state $5,549; Out-of-state $11,097

Housing: Homeownership rate: 53.5% (2000); Median home value: $70,900 (2000); Median rent: $338 per month (2000); Median age of housing: 37 years (2000).
Hospitals: Stevens Community Medical Center (54 beds)
Safety: Violent crime rate: 11.7 per 10,000 population; Property crime rate: 312.4 per 10,000 population (2001).
Newspapers: Morris Tribune (1 x week); Morris Sun (1 x week); Morris Adviser (1 x week)
Transportation: Commute to work: 75.0% car, 3.4% public transportation, 16.4% walk, 3.3% work from home (2000); Travel time to work: 82.9% less than 15 minutes, 9.3% 15 to 30 minutes, 4.8% 30 to 45 minutes, 0.7% 45 to 60 minutes, 2.3% 60 minutes or more (2000)
Additional Information Contacts
Morris Area Chamber of Commerce 320-589-1242

MORRIS (township). Covers a land area of 33.242 square miles and a water area of 0.570 square miles. Located at 45.62° N. Lat.; 95.93° W. Long. Elevation is 1,133 feet.
History: Plotted 1869, incorporated as village 1878, as city 1903.
Population: 574 (2000); Race: 99.2% White, 0.0% Black, 0.5% Asian, 0.3% American Indian and Alaska Native, 0.0% Hispanic of any race, 0.0% two or more races (2000); Density: 17.3 persons per square mile (2000); Age: 33.3% under 18, 12.5% over 64 (2000); Marriage status: 21.3% never married, 71.4% now married, 3.5% widowed, 3.7% divorced (2000); Foreign born: 0.5% (2000); Ancestry (includes multiple ancestries): 57.6% German, 25.9% Norwegian, 15.4% Irish, 7.5% Swedish, 5.0% Dutch (2000).
Economy: Railroad junction. Wheat, corn, oats, barley, soybeans, alfalfa, sunflowers; hogs, cattle, sheep. Manufacturing: truck trailers, bulk ethanol, printing and publishing, belt conveyors. Employment by occupation: 17.2% management, 20.2% professional, 12.6% services, 31.3% sales, 1.2% farming, 7.7% construction, 9.8% production (2000).
Income: Per capita income: $19,630 (2000); Median household income: $49,904 (2000); Poverty rate: 3.9% (2000).
Taxes: Total city taxes per capita: $41 (1997); City property taxes per capita: $41 (1997).
Education: High school graduation rate: 90.4% (2000); College graduation rate: 23.7% (2000).
Housing: Homeownership rate: 92.4% (2000); Median home value: $123,900 (2000); Median rent: $275 per month (2000); Median age of housing: 26 years (2000).
Transportation: Commute to work: 88.4% car, 0.0% public transportation, 2.2% walk, 9.4% work from home (2000); Travel time to work: 85.1% less than 15 minutes, 13.1% 15 to 30 minutes, 0.0% 30 to 45 minutes, 1.7% 45 to 60 minutes, 0.0% 60 minutes or more (2000)

PEPPERTON (township). Covers a land area of 35.661 square miles and a water area of 0.456 square miles. Located at 45.63° N. Lat.; 96.05° W. Long.
Population: 148 (2000); Race: 100.0% White, 0.0% Black, 0.0% Asian, 0.0% American Indian and Alaska Native, 0.0% Hispanic of any race, 0.0% two or more races (2000); Density: 4.2 persons per square mile (2000); Age: 31.6% under 18, 19.5% over 64 (2000); Marriage status: 20.0% never married, 68.0% now married, 7.0% widowed, 5.0% divorced (2000); Foreign born: 0.0% (2000); Ancestry (includes multiple ancestries): 57.9% German, 21.8% Norwegian, 12.8% English, 9.0% Scottish, 8.3% Swedish (2000).
Economy: Employment by occupation: 24.6% management, 17.5% professional, 22.8% services, 19.3% sales, 0.0% farming, 12.3% construction, 3.5% production (2000).
Income: Per capita income: $17,518 (2000); Median household income: $46,250 (2000); Poverty rate: 9.5% (2000).
Education: High school graduation rate: 87.5% (2000); College graduation rate: 15.9% (2000).
Housing: Homeownership rate: 96.2% (2000); Median home value: $80,000 (2000); Median rent: $325 per month (2000); Median age of housing: 45 years (2000).

Transportation: Commute to work: 84.2% car, 0.0% public transportation, 0.0% walk, 15.8% work from home (2000); Travel time to work: 31.3% less than 15 minutes, 60.4% 15 to 30 minutes, 4.2% 30 to 45 minutes, 4.2% 45 to 60 minutes, 0.0% 60 minutes or more (2000)

RENDSVILLE (township). Covers a land area of 34.371 square miles and a water area of 0.585 square miles. Located at 45.71° N. Lat.; 95.95° W. Long.
Population: 177 (2000); Race: 100.0% White, 0.0% Black, 0.0% Asian, 0.0% American Indian and Alaska Native, 0.0% Hispanic of any race, 0.0% two or more races (2000); Density: 5.1 persons per square mile (2000); Age: 15.3% under 18, 14.6% over 64 (2000); Marriage status: 24.6% never married, 62.7% now married, 6.3% widowed, 6.3% divorced (2000); Foreign born: 0.7% (2000); Ancestry (includes multiple ancestries): 45.1% German, 31.9% Norwegian, 11.8% United States or American, 6.3% Swedish, 6.3% English (2000).
Economy: Employment by occupation: 30.0% management, 10.0% professional, 16.7% services, 14.4% sales, 0.0% farming, 10.0% construction, 18.9% production (2000).
Income: Per capita income: $19,554 (2000); Median household income: $41,250 (2000); Poverty rate: 7.7% (2000).
Taxes: Total city taxes per capita: $69 (1997); City property taxes per capita: $69 (1997).
Education: High school graduation rate: 74.5% (2000); College graduation rate: 11.3% (2000).
Housing: Homeownership rate: 86.2% (2000); Median home value: $56,300 (2000); Median rent: $175 per month (2000); Median age of housing: 60+ years (2000).
Transportation: Commute to work: 78.7% car, 0.0% public transportation, 0.0% walk, 21.3% work from home (2000); Travel time to work: 21.4% less than 15 minutes, 65.7% 15 to 30 minutes, 7.1% 30 to 45 minutes, 0.0% 45 to 60 minutes, 5.7% 60 minutes or more (2000)

SCOTT (township). Covers a land area of 33.131 square miles and a water area of 2.198 square miles. Located at 45.55° N. Lat.; 96.06° W. Long.
Population: 150 (2000); Race: 100.0% White, 0.0% Black, 0.0% Asian, 0.0% American Indian and Alaska Native, 0.0% Hispanic of any race, 0.0% two or more races (2000); Density: 4.5 persons per square mile (2000); Age: 28.9% under 18, 22.1% over 64 (2000); Marriage status: 13.4% never married, 83.9% now married, 2.7% widowed, 0.0% divorced (2000); Foreign born: 0.0% (2000); Ancestry (includes multiple ancestries): 52.3% German, 41.6% Norwegian, 10.1% Swedish, 6.7% French (except Basque), 6.0% English (2000).
Economy: Employment by occupation: 15.7% management, 17.1% professional, 24.3% services, 14.3% sales, 0.0% farming, 8.6% construction, 20.0% production (2000).
Income: Per capita income: $28,924 (2000); Median household income: $51,250 (2000); Poverty rate: 10.7% (2000).
Taxes: Total city taxes per capita: $132 (1997); City property taxes per capita: $132 (1997).
Education: High school graduation rate: 88.3% (2000); College graduation rate: 24.3% (2000).
Housing: Homeownership rate: 88.0% (2000); Median home value: $95,000 (2000); Median rent: $175 per month (2000); Median age of housing: 51 years (2000).
Transportation: Commute to work: 89.6% car, 0.0% public transportation, 0.0% walk, 10.4% work from home (2000); Travel time to work: 38.3% less than 15 minutes, 50.0% 15 to 30 minutes, 0.0% 30 to 45 minutes, 8.3% 45 to 60 minutes, 3.3% 60 minutes or more (2000)

STEVENS (township). Covers a land area of 35.766 square miles and a water area of 0.210 square miles. Located at 45.44° N. Lat.; 96.19° W. Long.
Population: 82 (2000); Race: 100.0% White, 0.0% Black, 0.0% Asian, 0.0% American Indian and Alaska Native, 0.0% Hispanic of any race, 0.0% two or more races (2000); Density: 2.3 persons per square mile (2000); Age: 14.5% under 18, 14.5% over 64 (2000); Marriage status: 12.8% never married, 87.2% now married, 0.0% widowed, 0.0% divorced (2000); Foreign born: 0.0% (2000); Ancestry (includes multiple ancestries): 56.4% German, 9.1% Other groups, 9.1% Irish, 9.1% Dutch, 7.3% Norwegian (2000).
Economy: Employment by occupation: 72.0% management, 0.0% professional, 20.0% services, 8.0% sales, 0.0% farming, 0.0% construction, 0.0% production (2000).
Income: Per capita income: $14,798 (2000); Median household income: $35,938 (2000); Poverty rate: 40.0% (2000).
Taxes: Total city taxes per capita: $184 (1997); City property taxes per capita: $184 (1997).
Education: High school graduation rate: 91.5% (2000); College graduation rate: 21.3% (2000).
Housing: Homeownership rate: 76.0% (2000); Median home value: $45,000 (2000); Median rent: $325 per month (2000); Median age of housing: 60+ years (2000).
Transportation: Commute to work: 84.0% car, 0.0% public transportation, 0.0% walk, 16.0% work from home (2000); Travel time to work: 33.3% less than 15 minutes, 33.3% 15 to 30 minutes, 33.3% 30 to 45 minutes, 0.0% 45 to 60 minutes, 0.0% 60 minutes or more (2000)

SWAN LAKE (township). Covers a land area of 33.417 square miles and a water area of 2.634 square miles. Located at 45.72° N. Lat.; 95.82° W. Long.
Population: 210 (2000); Race: 100.0% White, 0.0% Black, 0.0% Asian, 0.0% American Indian and Alaska Native, 0.0% Hispanic of any race, 0.0% two or more races (2000); Density: 6.3 persons per square mile (2000); Age: 27.6% under 18, 12.9% over 64 (2000); Marriage status: 16.6% never married, 72.8% now married, 4.7% widowed, 5.9% divorced (2000); Foreign born: 0.0% (2000); Ancestry (includes multiple ancestries): 48.8% German, 27.2% Norwegian, 21.7% Swedish, 5.5% Irish, 5.1% Scandinavian (2000).
Economy: Employment by occupation: 20.3% management, 20.3% professional, 8.1% services, 26.8% sales, 3.3% farming, 11.4% construction, 9.8% production (2000).
Income: Per capita income: $15,789 (2000); Median household income: $39,375 (2000); Poverty rate: 6.0% (2000).
Taxes: Total city taxes per capita: $69 (1997); City property taxes per capita: $69 (1997).
Education: High school graduation rate: 84.2% (2000); College graduation rate: 23.3% (2000).
Housing: Homeownership rate: 89.2% (2000); Median home value: $95,000 (2000); Median rent: $175 per month (2000); Median age of housing: 45 years (2000).
Transportation: Commute to work: 85.1% car, 0.0% public transportation, 2.5% walk, 12.4% work from home (2000); Travel time to work: 17.0% less than 15 minutes, 61.3% 15 to 30 minutes, 19.8% 30 to 45 minutes, 0.0% 45 to 60 minutes, 1.9% 60 minutes or more (2000)

SYNNES (township). Covers a land area of 35.489 square miles and a water area of 0.316 square miles. Located at 45.45° N. Lat.; 96.06° W. Long.
Population: 104 (2000); Race: 100.0% White, 0.0% Black, 0.0% Asian, 0.0% American Indian and Alaska Native, 0.0% Hispanic of any race, 0.0% two or more races (2000); Density: 2.9 persons per square mile (2000); Age: 28.8% under 18, 14.4% over 64 (2000); Marriage status: 23.8% never married, 67.9% now married, 3.6% widowed, 4.8% divorced (2000); Foreign born: 0.0% (2000); Ancestry (includes multiple ancestries): 54.1% German, 27.9% Norwegian, 14.4% Irish, 7.2% Danish, 6.3% Dutch (2000).
Economy: Employment by occupation: 20.0% management, 5.5% professional, 16.4% services, 29.1% sales, 0.0% farming, 5.5% construction, 23.6% production (2000).
Income: Per capita income: $16,386 (2000); Median household income: $41,250 (2000); Poverty rate: 0.9% (2000).
Taxes: Total city taxes per capita: $100 (1997); City property taxes per capita: $100 (1997).
Education: High school graduation rate: 89.0% (2000); College graduation rate: 1.4% (2000).
Housing: Homeownership rate: 88.2% (2000); Median home value: $106,300 (2000); Median rent: $375 per month (2000); Median age of housing: 45 years (2000).
Transportation: Commute to work: 86.8% car, 0.0% public transportation, 0.0% walk, 13.2% work from home (2000); Travel time to work: 8.7% less than 15 minutes, 78.3% 15 to 30 minutes, 13.0% 30 to 45 minutes, 0.0% 45 to 60 minutes, 0.0% 60 minutes or more (2000)

Swift County

Located in southwestern Minnesota; drained by the Pomme de Terre and Chippewa Rivers. Covers a land area of 743.50 square miles, a water area of 8.80 square miles, and is located in the Central Time Zone. The county government was organized in 1870. County seat is Benson.

Weather Station: Benson Elevation: 1,040 feet

	Jan	Feb	Mar	Apr	May	Jun	Jul	Aug	Sep	Oct	Nov	Dec
High	20	27	39	57	71	79	83	81	72	59	39	25
Low	1	9	21	34	47	57	61	59	49	37	22	8
Precip	0.9	0.7	1.7	2.2	3.0	4.5	4.0	4.0	2.6	2.5	1.5	0.6
Snow	10.2	7.1	8.5	2.0	tr	0.0	0.0	0.0	tr	0.5	6.6	6.5

High and Low temperatures in degrees Fahrenheit; Precipitation and Snow in inches

Population: 11,956 (2000); Race: 91.0% White, 1.9% Black, 1.0% Asian, 0.2% American Indian and Alaska Native, 2.9% Hispanic of any race, 3.2% two or more races (2000); Density: 16.1 persons per square mile (2000); Age: 23.0% under 18, 18.7% over 64 (2000).
Religion: Five largest groups: 35.9% Evangelical Lutheran Church in America, 22.9% Catholic Church, 12.0% Lutheran Church—Missouri Synod, 2.6% United Church of Christ, 2.1% The Evangelical Free Church of America (2000).
Economy: Unemployment rate: 3.6% (11/2002); Total civilian labor force: 5,124 (11/2002); Leading industries: 23.6% manufacturing; 18.3% health care and social assistance; 14.3% retail trade (2000); Companies that employ more than 1,000 persons: 0 (2000); Companies that employ more than 100 persons: 5 (2000); Farms: 739 totaling 388,215 acres (1997); Minority business ownership rate: 0.0% (1997); Women business ownership rate: 13.1% (1997); Retail sales per capita: $6,328 (1997). Single-family building permits issued: 17 (2001) / 16 (2000); Multi-family building permits issued: 10 (2001) / 6 (2000).
Income: Per capita income: $16,360 (2000); Median household income: $34,820 (2000); Poverty rate: 8.4% (2000); Bankruptcy rate: 1.85% (2001).
Taxes: Total county taxes per capita: $151 (2000); County property taxes per capita: $151 (2000).
Education: High school graduation rate: 80.4% (2000); College graduation rate: 14.0% (2000).
Housing: Homeownership rate: 77.1% (2000); Median home value: $58,200 (2000); Median rent: $291 per month (2000); Median age of housing: 50 years (2000).
Health: Birth rate: 115.4 per 10,000 population (1998); Age adjusted death rate: 77.2 per 10,000 population (1999); Age adjusted cancer mortality rate: 167.8 deaths per 100,000 population (1999). Number of physicians: 5.0 per 10,000 population (1999); Number of hospital beds: 101.2 per 10,000 population (1999).
Elections: 2000 Presidential election results: 49.6% Gore, 43.7% Bush, 4.0% Nader, 2.2% Buchanan
National and State Parks: Bench State Wildlife Management Area; Camp Kerk State Wildlife Management Area; Danvers State Wildlife Management Areas; Ehrenberg State Wildlife Management Area; Hayes-Myhre State Wildlife Management Area; Henry X State Wildlife Management Area; Hollerberg Lake State Wildlife Management Ar; Monson Lake Memorial State Park; Monson State Wildlife Management Areas; Shible Lake State Wildlife Management Area
Additional Information Contacts
Swift County Government Offices....................... 320-843-4069
Appleton Chamber of Commerce......................... 320-289-1527
Benson Chamber of Commerce........................... 320-843-3618

Swift County Communities

APPLETON (city). Covers a land area of 1.991 square miles and a water area of 0.067 square miles. Located at 45.20° N. Lat.; 96.02° W. Long. Elevation is 1,016 feet.
History: Settled 1869, laid out 1870, Incorporated 1881.
Population: 2,871 (2000); Race: 66.9% White, 7.6% Black, 3.5% Asian, 0.8% American Indian and Alaska Native, 9.0% Hispanic of any race, 11.9% two or more races (2000); Density: 1,442.2 persons per square mile (2000); Age: 12.3% under 18, 16.6% over 64 (2000); Marriage status: 39.1% never married, 34.5% now married, 10.5% widowed, 15.9% divorced (2000); Foreign born: 2.8% (2000); Ancestry (includes multiple ancestries): 29.9% Other groups, 29.4% German, 17.1% Norwegian, 6.8% Irish, 5.1% English (2000).
Economy: Railroad junction and farm trade center. Agriculture includes grain; livestock, poultry; dairying. Manufacturing includes feeds, heat pumps, grain processing. Hydroelectric plant is here. Single-family building permits issued: 0 (2001) / 0 (2000); Multi-family building permits issued: 0 (2001) / 0 (2000); Employment by occupation: 14.8% management, 13.7% professional, 25.2% services, 23.6% sales, 0.6% farming, 10.2% construction, 12.0% production (2000).
Income: Per capita income: $12,429 (2000); Median household income: $25,950 (2000); Poverty rate: 14.7% (2000).
Taxes: Total city taxes per capita: $257 (1997); City property taxes per capita: $245 (1997).
Education: High school graduation rate: 76.1% (2000); College graduation rate: 9.3% (2000).
Housing: Homeownership rate: 65.3% (2000); Median home value: $43,800 (2000); Median rent: $299 per month (2000); Median age of housing: 52 years (2000).
Hospitals: Appleton Municipal Hospital & Nursing Home (23 beds)
Safety: Violent crime rate: 13.8 per 10,000 population; Property crime rate: 165.4 per 10,000 population (2001).
Transportation: Commute to work: 86.7% car, 0.0% public transportation, 8.5% walk, 3.1% work from home (2000); Travel time to work: 72.4% less than 15 minutes, 12.1% 15 to 30 minutes, 11.3% 30 to 45 minutes, 1.1% 45 to 60 minutes, 3.1% 60 minutes or more (2000)
Additional Information Contacts
Appleton Chamber of Commerce......................... 320-289-1527

APPLETON (township). Covers a land area of 30.820 square miles and a water area of 1.050 square miles. Located at 45.19° N. Lat.; 96.03° W. Long. Elevation is 1,016 feet.
Population: 232 (2000); Race: 92.6% White, 0.8% Black, 3.7% Asian, 0.0% American Indian and Alaska Native, 2.1% Hispanic of any race, 0.8% two or more races (2000); Density: 7.5 persons per square mile (2000); Age: 23.0% under 18, 22.2% over 64 (2000); Marriage status: 23.8% never married, 62.6% now married, 8.7% widowed, 4.9% divorced (2000); Foreign born: 0.0% (2000); Ancestry (includes multiple ancestries): 46.1% Norwegian, 44.0% German, 4.9% United States or American, 3.3% Danish, 2.9% Swedish (2000).
Economy: Employment by occupation: 12.2% management, 12.2% professional, 12.2% services, 39.8% sales, 3.3% farming, 13.0% construction, 7.3% production (2000).
Income: Per capita income: $20,714 (2000); Median household income: $48,125 (2000); Poverty rate: 4.1% (2000).
Taxes: Total city taxes per capita: $57 (1997); City property taxes per capita: $57 (1997).
Education: High school graduation rate: 86.6% (2000); College graduation rate: 22.1% (2000).
Housing: Homeownership rate: 93.7% (2000); Median home value: $75,000 (2000); Median rent: $175 per month (2000); Median age of housing: 38 years (2000).
Transportation: Commute to work: 87.4% car, 0.0% public transportation, 9.2% walk, 3.4% work from home (2000); Travel time to work: 69.6% less than 15 minutes, 17.4% 15 to 30 minutes, 7.0% 30 to 45 minutes, 0.0% 45 to 60 minutes, 6.1% 60 minutes or more (2000)

BENSON (city). Covers a land area of 2.481 square miles and a water area of 0 square miles. Located at 45.31° N. Lat.; 95.60° W. Long. Elevation is 1,049 feet.
History: Benson was settled in 1870 by immigrants attracted to the fertile land. The city became the shipping point for the wheat grown in the area. For a time, Benson was the western terminus of the Great Northern Railway, built by James J. Hill, and as such was a supply center for points north and west.
Population: 3,376 (2000); Race: 99.4% White, 0.0% Black, 0.1% Asian, 0.0% American Indian and Alaska Native, 0.6% Hispanic of any race, 0.4% two or more races (2000); Density: 1,360.5 persons per square mile (2000); Age: 23.1% under 18, 24.6% over 64 (2000); Marriage status: 20.3% never married, 59.3% now married, 14.9% widowed, 5.4% divorced (2000); Foreign born: 1.0% (2000); Ancestry (includes multiple ancestries): 45.6% German, 39.4% Norwegian, 8.4% Irish, 8.1% Swedish, 6.1% English (2000).
Economy: Single-family building permits issued: 8 (2001) / 9 (2000); Multi-family building permits issued: 6 (2001) / 2 (2000); Employment by occupation: 10.8% management, 17.9% professional, 12.6% services, 28.7% sales, 1.1% farming, 8.7% construction, 20.2% production (2000).
Income: Per capita income: $17,269 (2000); Median household income: $32,234 (2000); Poverty rate: 8.0% (2000).
Taxes: Total city taxes per capita: $161 (2000); City property taxes per capita: $147 (2000).
Education: High school graduation rate: 78.6% (2000); College graduation rate: 20.4% (2000).

School District(s)

Benson (PK-12)
2000 Enrollment: 1,184................................ 320-843-2710
Housing: Homeownership rate: 70.5% (2000); Median home value: $64,000 (2000); Median rent: $298 per month (2000); Median age of housing: 45 years (2000).
Hospitals: Swift County-Benson Hospital (31 beds)

Safety: Violent crime rate: 14.7 per 10,000 population; Property crime rate: 316.5 per 10,000 population (2001).
Newspapers: Swift County Monitor News (1 x week)
Transportation: Commute to work: 88.5% car, 1.6% public transportation, 5.5% walk, 2.6% work from home (2000); Travel time to work: 76.7% less than 15 minutes, 9.0% 15 to 30 minutes, 6.7% 30 to 45 minutes, 4.3% 45 to 60 minutes, 3.4% 60 minutes or more (2000)
Additional Information Contacts
Benson Chamber of Commerce 320-843-3618

BENSON (township). Covers a land area of 34.305 square miles and a water area of 1.670 square miles. Located at 45.36° N. Lat.; 95.57° W. Long. Elevation is 1,049 feet.
History: Plotted 1870, incorporated as village 1877, as city 1908.
Population: 367 (2000); Race: 96.5% White, 0.0% Black, 0.0% Asian, 0.0% American Indian and Alaska Native, 3.5% Hispanic of any race, 0.0% two or more races (2000); Density: 10.7 persons per square mile (2000); Age: 30.5% under 18, 19.6% over 64 (2000); Marriage status: 18.8% never married, 75.9% now married, 4.2% widowed, 1.1% divorced (2000); Foreign born: 2.3% (2000); Ancestry (includes multiple ancestries): 48.1% Norwegian, 41.2% German, 7.8% English, 6.6% Irish, 5.2% Swedish (2000).
Economy: Railroad junction and shipping point; grain, sugar beets, beans; dairying; livestock. Manufacturing: apparel, machinery, fertilizers. Employment by occupation: 15.0% management, 22.0% professional, 12.1% services, 24.3% sales, 0.0% farming, 8.1% construction, 18.5% production (2000).
Income: Per capita income: $16,446 (2000); Median household income: $47,143 (2000); Poverty rate: 4.1% (2000).
Taxes: Total city taxes per capita: $41 (1997); City property taxes per capita: $41 (1997).
Education: High school graduation rate: 88.9% (2000); College graduation rate: 20.4% (2000).
Housing: Homeownership rate: 82.0% (2000); Median home value: $82,000 (2000); Median rent: $328 per month (2000); Median age of housing: 35 years (2000).
Transportation: Commute to work: 92.5% car, 0.0% public transportation, 0.0% walk, 7.5% work from home (2000); Travel time to work: 70.0% less than 15 minutes, 9.4% 15 to 30 minutes, 13.1% 30 to 45 minutes, 3.8% 45 to 60 minutes, 3.8% 60 minutes or more (2000)

CAMP LAKE (township). Covers a land area of 35.413 square miles and a water area of 0.415 square miles. Located at 45.38° N. Lat.; 95.42° W. Long.
Population: 222 (2000); Race: 100.0% White, 0.0% Black, 0.0% Asian, 0.0% American Indian and Alaska Native, 0.0% Hispanic of any race, 0.0% two or more races (2000); Density: 6.3 persons per square mile (2000); Age: 20.6% under 18, 23.6% over 64 (2000); Marriage status: 23.3% never married, 65.3% now married, 8.0% widowed, 3.4% divorced (2000); Foreign born: 0.5% (2000); Ancestry (includes multiple ancestries): 56.3% Norwegian, 38.7% German, 11.1% Swedish, 6.5% Irish, 5.5% Other groups (2000).
Economy: Employment by occupation: 33.3% management, 20.3% professional, 13.0% services, 9.8% sales, 9.8% farming, 4.1% construction, 9.8% production (2000).
Income: Per capita income: $17,084 (2000); Median household income: $31,875 (2000); Poverty rate: 6.0% (2000).
Taxes: Total city taxes per capita: $76 (1997); City property taxes per capita: $76 (1997).
Education: High school graduation rate: 80.4% (2000); College graduation rate: 14.7% (2000).
Housing: Homeownership rate: 79.5% (2000); Median home value: $51,300 (2000); Median rent: $175 per month (2000); Median age of housing: 60+ years (2000).
Transportation: Commute to work: 73.2% car, 0.0% public transportation, 4.1% walk, 22.8% work from home (2000); Travel time to work: 26.3% less than 15 minutes, 52.6% 15 to 30 minutes, 8.4% 30 to 45 minutes, 7.4% 45 to 60 minutes, 5.3% 60 minutes or more (2000)

CASHEL (township). Covers a land area of 35.931 square miles and a water area of 0 square miles. Located at 45.20° N. Lat.; 95.54° W. Long.
Population: 143 (2000); Race: 100.0% White, 0.0% Black, 0.0% Asian, 0.0% American Indian and Alaska Native, 2.0% Hispanic of any race, 0.0% two or more races (2000); Density: 4.0 persons per square mile (2000); Age: 23.5% under 18, 24.2% over 64 (2000); Marriage status: 20.5% never married, 77.0% now married, 0.0% widowed, 2.5% divorced (2000); Foreign born: 0.0% (2000); Ancestry (includes multiple ancestries): 68.5% German, 32.2% Norwegian, 12.1% Irish, 8.1% Swedish, 6.0% Polish (2000).
Economy: Employment by occupation: 47.5% management, 13.8% professional, 12.5% services, 13.8% sales, 0.0% farming, 0.0% construction, 12.5% production (2000).
Income: Per capita income: $23,303 (2000); Median household income: $46,250 (2000); Poverty rate: 11.4% (2000).
Taxes: Total city taxes per capita: $89 (1997); City property taxes per capita: $89 (1997).
Education: High school graduation rate: 76.9% (2000); College graduation rate: 14.4% (2000).
Housing: Homeownership rate: 81.5% (2000); Median home value: $75,000 (2000); Median rent: $300 per month (2000); Median age of housing: 60+ years (2000).
Transportation: Commute to work: 63.7% car, 0.0% public transportation, 0.0% walk, 36.3% work from home (2000); Travel time to work: 19.6% less than 15 minutes, 58.8% 15 to 30 minutes, 21.6% 30 to 45 minutes, 0.0% 45 to 60 minutes, 0.0% 60 minutes or more (2000)

CLONTARF (city). Covers a land area of 2.054 square miles and a water area of 0.048 square miles. Located at 45.37° N. Lat.; 95.67° W. Long. Elevation is 1,050 feet.
Population: 173 (2000); Race: 100.0% White, 0.0% Black, 0.0% Asian, 0.0% American Indian and Alaska Native, 5.8% Hispanic of any race, 0.0% two or more races (2000); Density: 84.2 persons per square mile (2000); Age: 34.4% under 18, 6.9% over 64 (2000); Marriage status: 21.2% never married, 58.4% now married, 4.4% widowed, 16.1% divorced (2000); Foreign born: 0.0% (2000); Ancestry (includes multiple ancestries): 46.0% German, 28.0% Irish, 17.5% Norwegian, 9.0% Swedish, 8.5% English (2000).
Economy: Employment by occupation: 7.5% management, 7.5% professional, 6.6% services, 39.6% sales, 0.0% farming, 15.1% construction, 23.6% production (2000).
Income: Per capita income: $17,048 (2000); Median household income: $55,139 (2000); Poverty rate: 4.4% (2000).
Taxes: Total city taxes per capita: $6 (1997); City property taxes per capita: $6 (1997).
Education: High school graduation rate: 86.4% (2000); College graduation rate: 7.6% (2000).
Housing: Homeownership rate: 87.3% (2000); Median home value: $46,400 (2000); Median rent: $213 per month (2000); Median age of housing: 50 years (2000).
Transportation: Commute to work: 89.6% car, 0.0% public transportation, 8.5% walk, 1.9% work from home (2000); Travel time to work: 77.9% less than 15 minutes, 11.5% 15 to 30 minutes, 4.8% 30 to 45 minutes, 5.8% 45 to 60 minutes, 0.0% 60 minutes or more (2000)

CLONTARF (township). Covers a land area of 33.800 square miles and a water area of 0.133 square miles. Located at 45.37° N. Lat.; 95.70° W. Long. Elevation is 1,050 feet.
Population: 80 (2000); Race: 100.0% White, 0.0% Black, 0.0% Asian, 0.0% American Indian and Alaska Native, 0.0% Hispanic of any race, 0.0% two or more races (2000); Density: 2.4 persons per square mile (2000); Age: 19.7% under 18, 22.5% over 64 (2000); Marriage status: 34.4% never married, 57.8% now married, 0.0% widowed, 7.8% divorced (2000); Foreign born: 0.0% (2000); Ancestry (includes multiple ancestries): 69.0% German, 19.7% Irish, 19.7% Norwegian, 16.9% Danish, 14.1% French (except Basque) (2000).
Economy: Grain; poultry; dairying. Manufacturing: fertilizers. Employment by occupation: 30.6% management, 8.3% professional, 19.4% services, 11.1% sales, 0.0% farming, 16.7% construction, 13.9% production (2000).
Income: Per capita income: $15,617 (2000); Median household income: $38,333 (2000); Poverty rate: 11.3% (2000).
Taxes: Total city taxes per capita: $124 (1997); City property taxes per capita: $124 (1997).
Education: High school graduation rate: 80.0% (2000); College graduation rate: 4.0% (2000).
Housing: Homeownership rate: 100.0% (2000); Median home value: $82,500 (2000); Median age of housing: 32 years (2000).
Transportation: Commute to work: 72.2% car, 0.0% public transportation, 8.3% walk, 13.9% work from home (2000); Travel time to work: 48.4% less than 15 minutes, 32.3% 15 to 30 minutes, 12.9% 30 to 45 minutes, 6.5% 45 to 60 minutes, 0.0% 60 minutes or more (2000)

DANVERS (city). Covers a land area of 0.704 square miles and a water area of 0 square miles. Located at 45.28° N. Lat.; 95.75° W. Long. Elevation is 1,027 feet.

Population: 108 (2000); Race: 100.0% White, 0.0% Black, 0.0% Asian, 0.0% American Indian and Alaska Native, 0.0% Hispanic of any race, 0.0% two or more races (2000); Density: 153.4 persons per square mile (2000); Age: 25.9% under 18, 20.0% over 64 (2000); Marriage status: 17.6% never married, 67.6% now married, 11.8% widowed, 2.9% divorced (2000); Foreign born: 0.0% (2000); Ancestry (includes multiple ancestries): 50.6% German, 29.4% Swedish, 28.2% Norwegian, 24.7% Irish, 4.7% French (except Basque) (2000).
Economy: Grain; dairying. Single-family building permits issued: 0 (2001) / 0 (2000); Multi-family building permits issued: 0 (2001) / 0 (2000); Employment by occupation: 28.9% management, 7.9% professional, 7.9% services, 36.8% sales, 0.0% farming, 0.0% construction, 18.4% production (2000).
Income: Per capita income: $23,452 (2000); Median household income: $44,000 (2000); Poverty rate: 4.7% (2000).
Taxes: Total city taxes per capita: $418 (1997); City property taxes per capita: $418 (1997).
Education: High school graduation rate: 80.7% (2000); College graduation rate: 15.8% (2000).
Housing: Homeownership rate: 92.5% (2000); Median home value: $50,800 (2000); Median rent: $225 per month (2000); Median age of housing: 47 years (2000).
Transportation: Commute to work: 86.8% car, 0.0% public transportation, 5.3% walk, 7.9% work from home (2000); Travel time to work: 71.4% less than 15 minutes, 11.4% 15 to 30 minutes, 5.7% 30 to 45 minutes, 0.0% 45 to 60 minutes, 11.4% 60 minutes or more (2000)

DE GRAFF (city). Covers a land area of 0.807 square miles and a water area of 0 square miles. Located at 45.26° N. Lat.; 95.46° W. Long. Elevation is 1,055 feet.
Population: 133 (2000); Race: 100.0% White, 0.0% Black, 0.0% Asian, 0.0% American Indian and Alaska Native, 3.0% Hispanic of any race, 0.0% two or more races (2000); Density: 164.8 persons per square mile (2000); Age: 35.2% under 18, 6.7% over 64 (2000); Marriage status: 27.3% never married, 62.7% now married, 5.5% widowed, 4.5% divorced (2000); Foreign born: 0.0% (2000); Ancestry (includes multiple ancestries): 47.9% German, 27.3% Norwegian, 23.0% Irish, 9.7% French (except Basque), 7.9% United States or American (2000).
Economy: Grain; livestock, poultry; dairying; light manufacturing. Employment by occupation: 12.9% management, 18.8% professional, 9.4% services, 21.2% sales, 0.0% farming, 9.4% construction, 28.2% production (2000).
Income: Per capita income: $14,987 (2000); Median household income: $38,000 (2000); Poverty rate: 9.7% (2000).
Taxes: Total city taxes per capita: $97 (1997); City property taxes per capita: $97 (1997).
Education: High school graduation rate: 80.8% (2000); College graduation rate: 9.1% (2000).
Housing: Homeownership rate: 87.3% (2000); Median home value: $28,100 (2000); Median rent: $194 per month (2000); Median age of housing: 60+ years (2000).
Transportation: Commute to work: 91.8% car, 0.0% public transportation, 2.4% walk, 3.5% work from home (2000); Travel time to work: 51.2% less than 15 minutes, 19.5% 15 to 30 minutes, 29.3% 30 to 45 minutes, 0.0% 45 to 60 minutes, 0.0% 60 minutes or more (2000)

DUBLIN (township). Covers a land area of 34.938 square miles and a water area of 0 square miles. Located at 45.20° N. Lat.; 95.44° W. Long.
Population: 156 (2000); Race: 95.0% White, 0.0% Black, 1.3% Asian, 0.0% American Indian and Alaska Native, 0.0% Hispanic of any race, 3.8% two or more races (2000); Density: 4.5 persons per square mile (2000); Age: 32.1% under 18, 13.8% over 64 (2000); Marriage status: 14.0% never married, 76.9% now married, 5.0% widowed, 4.1% divorced (2000); Foreign born: 1.3% (2000); Ancestry (includes multiple ancestries): 64.8% German, 27.0% Irish, 23.3% Norwegian, 12.6% Swedish, 3.8% Other groups (2000).
Economy: Employment by occupation: 32.9% management, 11.0% professional, 13.7% services, 23.3% sales, 0.0% farming, 9.6% construction, 9.6% production (2000).
Income: Per capita income: $16,553 (2000); Median household income: $45,000 (2000); Poverty rate: 3.3% (2000).
Taxes: Total city taxes per capita: $172 (1997); City property taxes per capita: $172 (1997).
Education: High school graduation rate: 88.0% (2000); College graduation rate: 9.3% (2000).
Housing: Homeownership rate: 84.7% (2000); Median home value: $112,500 (2000); Median age of housing: 59 years (2000).
Transportation: Commute to work: 71.2% car, 0.0% public transportation, 5.5% walk, 23.3% work from home (2000); Travel time to work: 46.4% less than 15 minutes, 19.6% 15 to 30 minutes, 30.4% 30 to 45 minutes, 0.0% 45 to 60 minutes, 3.6% 60 minutes or more (2000)

EDISON (township). Covers a land area of 35.692 square miles and a water area of 0.058 square miles. Located at 45.19° N. Lat.; 95.91° W. Long.
Population: 131 (2000); Race: 100.0% White, 0.0% Black, 0.0% Asian, 0.0% American Indian and Alaska Native, 0.0% Hispanic of any race, 0.0% two or more races (2000); Density: 3.7 persons per square mile (2000); Age: 17.7% under 18, 12.4% over 64 (2000); Marriage status: 19.6% never married, 72.5% now married, 2.9% widowed, 4.9% divorced (2000); Foreign born: 0.0% (2000); Ancestry (includes multiple ancestries): 59.3% Norwegian, 31.9% German, 11.5% Swedish, 8.8% Irish, 2.7% Polish (2000).
Economy: Employment by occupation: 34.4% management, 12.5% professional, 10.9% services, 17.2% sales, 0.0% farming, 3.1% construction, 21.9% production (2000).
Income: Per capita income: $22,796 (2000); Median household income: $39,375 (2000); Poverty rate: 0.9% (2000).
Taxes: Total city taxes per capita: $79 (1997); City property taxes per capita: $79 (1997).
Education: High school graduation rate: 95.3% (2000); College graduation rate: 20.0% (2000).
Housing: Homeownership rate: 94.1% (2000); Median home value: $52,500 (2000); Median rent: <$100 per month (2000); Median age of housing: 60+ years (2000).
Transportation: Commute to work: 75.8% car, 0.0% public transportation, 11.3% walk, 12.9% work from home (2000); Travel time to work: 42.6% less than 15 minutes, 37.0% 15 to 30 minutes, 11.1% 30 to 45 minutes, 0.0% 45 to 60 minutes, 9.3% 60 minutes or more (2000)

FAIRFIELD (township). Covers a land area of 35.904 square miles and a water area of 0.075 square miles. Located at 45.37° N. Lat.; 95.93° W. Long.
Population: 169 (2000); Race: 100.0% White, 0.0% Black, 0.0% Asian, 0.0% American Indian and Alaska Native, 0.0% Hispanic of any race, 0.0% two or more races (2000); Density: 4.7 persons per square mile (2000); Age: 32.5% under 18, 17.8% over 64 (2000); Marriage status: 15.3% never married, 80.5% now married, 4.2% widowed, 0.0% divorced (2000); Foreign born: 0.0% (2000); Ancestry (includes multiple ancestries): 67.5% German, 16.6% Norwegian, 10.8% Irish, 10.2% Swiss, 7.0% English (2000).
Economy: Employment by occupation: 47.7% management, 18.5% professional, 3.1% services, 21.5% sales, 3.1% farming, 1.5% construction, 4.6% production (2000).
Income: Per capita income: $15,387 (2000); Median household income: $38,750 (2000); Poverty rate: 11.7% (2000).
Taxes: Total city taxes per capita: $55 (1997); City property taxes per capita: $55 (1997).
Education: High school graduation rate: 86.5% (2000); College graduation rate: 6.7% (2000).
Housing: Homeownership rate: 93.3% (2000); Median home value: $38,800 (2000); Median rent: $225 per month (2000); Median age of housing: 60+ years (2000).
Transportation: Commute to work: 63.1% car, 0.0% public transportation, 15.4% walk, 21.5% work from home (2000); Travel time to work: 35.3% less than 15 minutes, 49.0% 15 to 30 minutes, 11.8% 30 to 45 minutes, 0.0% 45 to 60 minutes, 3.9% 60 minutes or more (2000)

HAYES (township). Covers a land area of 34.871 square miles and a water area of 1.035 square miles. Located at 45.28° N. Lat.; 95.30° W. Long.
Population: 221 (2000); Race: 100.0% White, 0.0% Black, 0.0% Asian, 0.0% American Indian and Alaska Native, 0.0% Hispanic of any race, 0.0% two or more races (2000); Density: 6.3 persons per square mile (2000); Age: 19.6% under 18, 16.7% over 64 (2000); Marriage status: 21.5% never married, 72.9% now married, 1.7% widowed, 4.0% divorced (2000); Foreign born: 0.0% (2000); Ancestry (includes multiple ancestries): 43.1% Norwegian, 38.2% German, 20.6% Swedish, 9.8% Irish, 8.8% Polish (2000).
Economy: Employment by occupation: 29.5% management, 15.2% professional, 6.7% services, 15.2% sales, 4.8% farming, 11.4% construction, 17.1% production (2000).
Income: Per capita income: $29,279 (2000); Median household income: $39,583 (2000); Poverty rate: 10.8% (2000).
Taxes: Total city taxes per capita: $31 (1997); City property taxes per capita: $31 (1997).
Education: High school graduation rate: 80.8% (2000); College graduation rate: 13.0% (2000).

Housing: Homeownership rate: 82.9% (2000); Median home value: $58,300 (2000); Median rent: $275 per month (2000); Median age of housing: 60+ years (2000).
Transportation: Commute to work: 69.5% car, 0.0% public transportation, 2.9% walk, 27.6% work from home (2000); Travel time to work: 28.9% less than 15 minutes, 40.8% 15 to 30 minutes, 27.6% 30 to 45 minutes, 0.0% 45 to 60 minutes, 2.6% 60 minutes or more (2000)

HEGBERT (township). Covers a land area of 33.315 square miles and a water area of 2.287 square miles. Located at 45.36° N. Lat.; 96.06° W. Long.
Population: 118 (2000); Race: 98.3% White, 0.0% Black, 1.7% Asian, 0.0% American Indian and Alaska Native, 1.7% Hispanic of any race, 0.0% two or more races (2000); Density: 3.5 persons per square mile (2000); Age: 24.8% under 18, 9.1% over 64 (2000); Marriage status: 14.1% never married, 73.9% now married, 8.7% widowed, 3.3% divorced (2000); Foreign born: 1.7% (2000); Ancestry (includes multiple ancestries): 53.7% German, 40.5% Norwegian, 6.6% Swedish, 6.6% Irish, 5.8% Dutch (2000).
Economy: Employment by occupation: 43.9% management, 15.2% professional, 10.6% services, 6.1% sales, 7.6% farming, 7.6% construction, 9.1% production (2000).
Income: Per capita income: $14,562 (2000); Median household income: $36,250 (2000); Poverty rate: 30.6% (2000).
Taxes: Total city taxes per capita: $89 (1997); City property taxes per capita: $89 (1997).
Education: High school graduation rate: 86.8% (2000); College graduation rate: 11.0% (2000).
Housing: Homeownership rate: 89.4% (2000); Median home value: $25,000 (2000); Median age of housing: 60+ years (2000).
Transportation: Commute to work: 72.7% car, 0.0% public transportation, 6.1% walk, 21.2% work from home (2000); Travel time to work: 19.2% less than 15 minutes, 48.1% 15 to 30 minutes, 21.2% 30 to 45 minutes, 3.8% 45 to 60 minutes, 7.7% 60 minutes or more (2000)

HOLLOWAY (city). Covers a land area of 1.381 square miles and a water area of 0 square miles. Located at 45.24° N. Lat.; 95.91° W. Long. Elevation is 1,032 feet.
Population: 112 (2000); Race: 100.0% White, 0.0% Black, 0.0% Asian, 0.0% American Indian and Alaska Native, 0.0% Hispanic of any race, 0.0% two or more races (2000); Density: 81.1 persons per square mile (2000); Age: 22.0% under 18, 25.7% over 64 (2000); Marriage status: 23.0% never married, 56.3% now married, 9.2% widowed, 11.5% divorced (2000); Foreign born: 0.9% (2000); Ancestry (includes multiple ancestries): 67.9% German, 22.9% Norwegian, 12.8% Polish, 7.3% Swedish, 6.4% Other groups (2000).
Economy: Grain; livestock; dairying. Manufacturing: fertilizers. Single-family building permits issued: 0 (2001) / 0 (2000); Multi-family building permits issued: 0 (2001) / 0 (2000); Employment by occupation: 5.4% management, 8.9% professional, 26.8% services, 8.9% sales, 5.4% farming, 7.1% construction, 37.5% production (2000).
Income: Per capita income: $14,882 (2000); Median household income: $31,250 (2000); Poverty rate: 9.2% (2000).
Taxes: Total city taxes per capita: $435 (1997); City property taxes per capita: $426 (1997).
Education: High school graduation rate: 73.6% (2000); College graduation rate: 12.5% (2000).
Housing: Homeownership rate: 76.9% (2000); Median home value: $35,000 (2000); Median rent: $200 per month (2000); Median age of housing: 39 years (2000).
Transportation: Commute to work: 91.1% car, 0.0% public transportation, 5.4% walk, 3.6% work from home (2000); Travel time to work: 51.9% less than 15 minutes, 29.6% 15 to 30 minutes, 3.7% 30 to 45 minutes, 1.9% 45 to 60 minutes, 13.0% 60 minutes or more (2000)

KERKHOVEN (city). Covers a land area of 0.742 square miles and a water area of 0 square miles. Located at 45.19° N. Lat.; 95.31° W. Long. Elevation is 1,109 feet.
Population: 759 (2000); Race: 97.3% White, 0.0% Black, 0.0% Asian, 0.0% American Indian and Alaska Native, 1.8% Hispanic of any race, 1.2% two or more races (2000); Density: 1,023.5 persons per square mile (2000); Age: 27.0% under 18, 21.7% over 64 (2000); Marriage status: 18.1% never married, 65.1% now married, 9.1% widowed, 7.6% divorced (2000); Foreign born: 1.0% (2000); Ancestry (includes multiple ancestries): 40.0% German, 34.9% Norwegian, 19.8% Swedish, 5.2% Irish, 4.7% Other groups (2000).
Economy: Single-family building permits issued: 1 (2001) / 0 (2000); Multi-family building permits issued: 0 (2001) / 4 (2000); Employment by occupation: 12.3% management, 16.9% professional, 13.7% services, 24.3% sales, 2.3% farming, 12.6% construction, 18.0% production (2000).
Income: Per capita income: $16,435 (2000); Median household income: $32,375 (2000); Poverty rate: 9.3% (2000).
Taxes: Total city taxes per capita: $73 (1997); City property taxes per capita: $72 (1997).
Education: High school graduation rate: 80.3% (2000); College graduation rate: 11.9% (2000).

School District(s)

Kerkhoven-Murdock-Sunburg (PK-12)
2000 Enrollment: 664 320-264-1411

Housing: Homeownership rate: 78.9% (2000); Median home value: $59,100 (2000); Median rent: $313 per month (2000); Median age of housing: 42 years (2000).
Newspapers: The Kerkhoven Banner (1 x week)
Transportation: Commute to work: 86.0% car, 0.9% public transportation, 8.3% walk, 2.9% work from home (2000); Travel time to work: 34.4% less than 15 minutes, 44.7% 15 to 30 minutes, 16.8% 30 to 45 minutes, 1.5% 45 to 60 minutes, 2.6% 60 minutes or more (2000)

KERKHOVEN (township). Covers a land area of 35.465 square miles and a water area of 0.473 square miles. Located at 45.36° N. Lat.; 95.33° W. Long. Elevation is 1,109 feet.
Population: 286 (2000); Race: 96.4% White, 0.0% Black, 2.0% Asian, 0.7% American Indian and Alaska Native, 1.6% Hispanic of any race, 0.0% two or more races (2000); Density: 8.1 persons per square mile (2000); Age: 28.7% under 18, 12.7% over 64 (2000); Marriage status: 22.6% never married, 65.4% now married, 8.5% widowed, 3.4% divorced (2000); Foreign born: 2.3% (2000); Ancestry (includes multiple ancestries): 57.3% Norwegian, 27.0% German, 26.7% Swedish, 10.4% Irish, 4.2% Dutch (2000).
Economy: Agriculture: grain; livestock, poultry; dairying. Light manufacturing. Employment by occupation: 20.2% management, 16.7% professional, 13.7% services, 18.5% sales, 1.8% farming, 15.5% construction, 13.7% production (2000).
Income: Per capita income: $13,944 (2000); Median household income: $32,500 (2000); Poverty rate: 3.3% (2000).
Taxes: Total city taxes per capita: $25 (1997); City property taxes per capita: $25 (1997).
Education: High school graduation rate: 77.1% (2000); College graduation rate: 13.0% (2000).
Housing: Homeownership rate: 87.5% (2000); Median home value: $74,200 (2000); Median rent: <$100 per month (2000); Median age of housing: 57 years (2000).
Transportation: Commute to work: 74.1% car, 0.0% public transportation, 1.8% walk, 24.1% work from home (2000); Travel time to work: 17.5% less than 15 minutes, 33.3% 15 to 30 minutes, 33.3% 30 to 45 minutes, 11.9% 45 to 60 minutes, 4.0% 60 minutes or more (2000)

KILDARE (township). Covers a land area of 34.812 square miles and a water area of 0.354 square miles. Located at 45.27° N. Lat.; 95.45° W. Long.
Population: 192 (2000); Race: 95.5% White, 1.5% Black, 0.0% Asian, 0.0% American Indian and Alaska Native, 0.0% Hispanic of any race, 3.0% two or more races (2000); Density: 5.5 persons per square mile (2000); Age: 23.0% under 18, 24.5% over 64 (2000); Marriage status: 31.5% never married, 54.5% now married, 7.3% widowed, 6.7% divorced (2000); Foreign born: 0.0% (2000); Ancestry (includes multiple ancestries): 23.0% German, 21.5% Norwegian, 20.0% Irish, 11.5% French (except Basque), 9.5% Swedish (2000).
Economy: Employment by occupation: 34.3% management, 7.8% professional, 7.8% services, 18.6% sales, 5.9% farming, 4.9% construction, 20.6% production (2000).
Income: Per capita income: $18,827 (2000); Median household income: $39,375 (2000); Poverty rate: 8.0% (2000).
Taxes: Total city taxes per capita: $98 (1997); City property taxes per capita: $98 (1997).
Education: High school graduation rate: 77.1% (2000); College graduation rate: 9.3% (2000).
Housing: Homeownership rate: 81.3% (2000); Median home value: $76,700 (2000); Median rent: $225 per month (2000); Median age of housing: 60+ years (2000).
Transportation: Commute to work: 75.5% car, 0.0% public transportation, 2.0% walk, 19.6% work from home (2000); Travel time to work: 35.4% less than 15 minutes, 40.2% 15 to 30 minutes, 12.2% 30 to 45 minutes, 8.5% 45 to 60 minutes, 3.7% 60 minutes or more (2000)

MARYSLAND (township). Covers a land area of 35.283 square miles and a water area of 0 square miles. Located at 45.27° N. Lat.; 95.81° W. Long.
Population: 102 (2000); Race: 100.0% White, 0.0% Black, 0.0% Asian, 0.0% American Indian and Alaska Native, 0.0% Hispanic of any race, 0.0% two or more races (2000); Density: 2.9 persons per square mile (2000); Age: 27.6% under 18, 13.3% over 64 (2000); Marriage status: 27.6% never married, 61.8% now married, 7.9% widowed, 2.6% divorced (2000); Foreign born: 0.0% (2000); Ancestry (includes multiple ancestries): 46.9% German, 22.4% Norwegian, 12.2% Irish, 10.2% French (except Basque), 7.1% Swedish (2000).
Economy: Employment by occupation: 27.6% management, 15.5% professional, 8.6% services, 20.7% sales, 0.0% farming, 8.6% construction, 19.0% production (2000).
Income: Per capita income: $20,127 (2000); Median household income: $46,250 (2000); Poverty rate: 13.3% (2000).
Taxes: Total city taxes per capita: $115 (1997); City property taxes per capita: $115 (1997).
Education: High school graduation rate: 80.3% (2000); College graduation rate: 11.5% (2000).
Housing: Homeownership rate: 81.0% (2000); Median home value: $100,000 (2000); Median rent: $225 per month (2000); Median age of housing: 47 years (2000).
Transportation: Commute to work: 81.5% car, 0.0% public transportation, 7.4% walk, 11.1% work from home (2000); Travel time to work: 41.7% less than 15 minutes, 33.3% 15 to 30 minutes, 20.8% 30 to 45 minutes, 4.2% 45 to 60 minutes, 0.0% 60 minutes or more (2000)

MOYER (township). Covers a land area of 34.783 square miles and a water area of 0.005 square miles. Located at 45.29° N. Lat.; 95.92° W. Long.
Population: 125 (2000); Race: 100.0% White, 0.0% Black, 0.0% Asian, 0.0% American Indian and Alaska Native, 0.0% Hispanic of any race, 0.0% two or more races (2000); Density: 3.6 persons per square mile (2000); Age: 27.8% under 18, 16.6% over 64 (2000); Marriage status: 28.6% never married, 67.2% now married, 2.5% widowed, 1.7% divorced (2000); Foreign born: 0.0% (2000); Ancestry (includes multiple ancestries): 82.1% German, 30.5% Norwegian, 5.3% Irish, 3.3% Danish, 3.3% Swedish (2000).
Economy: Employment by occupation: 25.0% management, 10.7% professional, 7.1% services, 20.2% sales, 6.0% farming, 13.1% construction, 17.9% production (2000).
Income: Per capita income: $16,497 (2000); Median household income: $41,250 (2000); Poverty rate: 7.3% (2000).
Taxes: Total city taxes per capita: $89 (1997); City property taxes per capita: $89 (1997).
Education: High school graduation rate: 93.1% (2000); College graduation rate: 4.0% (2000).
Housing: Homeownership rate: 82.7% (2000); Median home value: $37,500 (2000); Median age of housing: 60+ years (2000).
Transportation: Commute to work: 79.8% car, 0.0% public transportation, 3.6% walk, 16.7% work from home (2000); Travel time to work: 37.1% less than 15 minutes, 41.4% 15 to 30 minutes, 12.9% 30 to 45 minutes, 0.0% 45 to 60 minutes, 8.6% 60 minutes or more (2000)

MURDOCK (city). Covers a land area of 0.563 square miles and a water area of 0 square miles. Located at 45.22° N. Lat.; 95.39° W. Long. Elevation is 1,090 feet.
Population: 303 (2000); Race: 96.7% White, 0.7% Black, 0.0% Asian, 0.0% American Indian and Alaska Native, 2.7% Hispanic of any race, 1.3% two or more races (2000); Density: 538.5 persons per square mile (2000); Age: 29.8% under 18, 20.7% over 64 (2000); Marriage status: 19.3% never married, 58.7% now married, 12.6% widowed, 9.4% divorced (2000); Foreign born: 0.7% (2000); Ancestry (includes multiple ancestries): 47.5% German, 30.8% Norwegian, 29.4% Irish, 10.4% Swedish, 5.7% Dutch (2000).
Economy: Alfalfa, beans, sugar beets, grain; livestock, poultry; dairying. Single-family building permits issued: 1 (2001) / 0 (2000); Multi-family building permits issued: 4 (2001) / 0 (2000); Employment by occupation: 8.1% management, 8.1% professional, 14.1% services, 28.1% sales, 1.5% farming, 3.7% construction, 36.3% production (2000).
Income: Per capita income: $17,011 (2000); Median household income: $28,750 (2000); Poverty rate: 7.4% (2000).
Taxes: Total city taxes per capita: $158 (1997); City property taxes per capita: $150 (1997).
Education: High school graduation rate: 81.5% (2000); College graduation rate: 12.5% (2000).
Housing: Homeownership rate: 83.8% (2000); Median home value: $47,200 (2000); Median rent: $278 per month (2000); Median age of housing: 55 years (2000).
Transportation: Commute to work: 90.9% car, 0.0% public transportation, 6.1% walk, 3.0% work from home (2000); Travel time to work: 37.5% less than 15 minutes, 39.1% 15 to 30 minutes, 21.1% 30 to 45 minutes, 0.0% 45 to 60 minutes, 2.3% 60 minutes or more (2000)

PILLSBURY (township). Covers a land area of 34.823 square miles and a water area of 0.033 square miles. Located at 45.19° N. Lat.; 95.31° W. Long.
Population: 306 (2000); Race: 94.1% White, 1.5% Black, 0.0% Asian, 0.7% American Indian and Alaska Native, 3.7% Hispanic of any race, 0.0% two or more races (2000); Density: 8.8 persons per square mile (2000); Age: 30.9% under 18, 14.5% over 64 (2000); Marriage status: 21.2% never married, 71.9% now married, 2.5% widowed, 4.4% divorced (2000); Foreign born: 0.0% (2000); Ancestry (includes multiple ancestries): 33.5% Norwegian, 33.1% German, 30.5% Swedish, 5.9% Other groups, 5.6% Irish (2000).
Economy: Employment by occupation: 27.1% management, 19.4% professional, 2.3% services, 21.7% sales, 4.7% farming, 10.1% construction, 14.7% production (2000).
Income: Per capita income: $16,021 (2000); Median household income: $43,125 (2000); Poverty rate: 6.3% (2000).
Taxes: Total city taxes per capita: $64 (1997); City property taxes per capita: $64 (1997).
Education: High school graduation rate: 80.2% (2000); College graduation rate: 12.0% (2000).
Housing: Homeownership rate: 82.8% (2000); Median home value: $95,000 (2000); Median rent: $325 per month (2000); Median age of housing: 54 years (2000).
Transportation: Commute to work: 81.9% car, 0.0% public transportation, 1.6% walk, 16.5% work from home (2000); Travel time to work: 22.6% less than 15 minutes, 48.1% 15 to 30 minutes, 17.9% 30 to 45 minutes, 0.0% 45 to 60 minutes, 11.3% 60 minutes or more (2000)

SHIBLE (township). Covers a land area of 34.941 square miles and a water area of 1.028 square miles. Located at 45.28° N. Lat.; 96.06° W. Long.
Population: 115 (2000); Race: 100.0% White, 0.0% Black, 0.0% Asian, 0.0% American Indian and Alaska Native, 0.0% Hispanic of any race, 0.0% two or more races (2000); Density: 3.3 persons per square mile (2000); Age: 21.6% under 18, 21.6% over 64 (2000); Marriage status: 17.6% never married, 65.7% now married, 12.0% widowed, 4.6% divorced (2000); Foreign born: 0.0% (2000); Ancestry (includes multiple ancestries): 70.9% German, 21.6% Norwegian, 3.7% Irish, 3.0% English, 3.0% Swedish (2000).
Economy: Employment by occupation: 32.1% management, 17.9% professional, 19.2% services, 6.4% sales, 6.4% farming, 11.5% construction, 6.4% production (2000).
Income: Per capita income: $17,639 (2000); Median household income: $35,625 (2000); Poverty rate: 3.0% (2000).
Taxes: Total city taxes per capita: $83 (1997); City property taxes per capita: $83 (1997).
Education: High school graduation rate: 90.3% (2000); College graduation rate: 19.4% (2000).
Housing: Homeownership rate: 89.3% (2000); Median home value: $53,300 (2000); Median rent: $175 per month (2000); Median age of housing: 60+ years (2000).
Transportation: Commute to work: 73.1% car, 0.0% public transportation, 2.6% walk, 24.4% work from home (2000); Travel time to work: 47.5% less than 15 minutes, 15.3% 15 to 30 minutes, 28.8% 30 to 45 minutes, 5.1% 45 to 60 minutes, 3.4% 60 minutes or more (2000)

SIX MILE GROVE (township). Covers a land area of 35.920 square miles and a water area of 0.042 square miles. Located at 45.28° N. Lat.; 95.67° W. Long.
Population: 171 (2000); Race: 100.0% White, 0.0% Black, 0.0% Asian, 0.0% American Indian and Alaska Native, 0.0% Hispanic of any race, 0.0% two or more races (2000); Density: 4.8 persons per square mile (2000); Age: 26.5% under 18, 9.4% over 64 (2000); Marriage status: 15.0% never married, 82.1% now married, 0.0% widowed, 2.9% divorced (2000); Foreign born: 0.0% (2000); Ancestry (includes multiple ancestries): 48.1% Norwegian, 48.1% German, 9.4% Irish, 6.1% French (except Basque), 4.4% Polish (2000).
Economy: Employment by occupation: 13.4% management, 11.6% professional, 17.9% services, 26.8% sales, 2.7% farming, 9.8% construction, 17.9% production (2000).

Income: Per capita income: $20,035 (2000); Median household income: $42,083 (2000); Poverty rate: 0.6% (2000).
Taxes: Total city taxes per capita: $118 (1997); City property taxes per capita: $118 (1997).
Education: High school graduation rate: 87.4% (2000); College graduation rate: 7.9% (2000).
Housing: Homeownership rate: 91.3% (2000); Median home value: $63,800 (2000); Median rent: $275 per month (2000); Median age of housing: 44 years (2000).
Transportation: Commute to work: 94.6% car, 0.0% public transportation, 0.0% walk, 5.4% work from home (2000); Travel time to work: 42.5% less than 15 minutes, 31.1% 15 to 30 minutes, 17.9% 30 to 45 minutes, 1.9% 45 to 60 minutes, 6.6% 60 minutes or more (2000)

SWENODA (township). Covers a land area of 35.776 square miles and a water area of 0 square miles. Located at 45.20° N. Lat.; 95.67° W. Long.
Population: 159 (2000); Race: 100.0% White, 0.0% Black, 0.0% Asian, 0.0% American Indian and Alaska Native, 0.0% Hispanic of any race, 0.0% two or more races (2000); Density: 4.4 persons per square mile (2000); Age: 29.0% under 18, 13.8% over 64 (2000); Marriage status: 16.3% never married, 75.5% now married, 6.1% widowed, 2.0% divorced (2000); Foreign born: 0.0% (2000); Ancestry (includes multiple ancestries): 58.7% Norwegian, 31.9% German, 16.7% English, 10.1% Swedish, 8.7% Irish (2000).
Economy: Employment by occupation: 26.2% management, 10.8% professional, 9.2% services, 13.8% sales, 0.0% farming, 13.8% construction, 26.2% production (2000).
Income: Per capita income: $32,557 (2000); Median household income: $50,179 (2000); Poverty rate: 1.4% (2000).
Taxes: Total city taxes per capita: $105 (1997); City property taxes per capita: $105 (1997).
Education: High school graduation rate: 89.7% (2000); College graduation rate: 10.3% (2000).
Housing: Homeownership rate: 84.3% (2000); Median home value: $53,800 (2000); Median age of housing: 60+ years (2000).
Transportation: Commute to work: 89.2% car, 0.0% public transportation, 0.0% walk, 10.8% work from home (2000); Travel time to work: 17.2% less than 15 minutes, 56.9% 15 to 30 minutes, 10.3% 30 to 45 minutes, 6.9% 45 to 60 minutes, 8.6% 60 minutes or more (2000)

TARA (township). Covers a land area of 35.830 square miles and a water area of 0.049 square miles. Located at 45.36° N. Lat.; 95.82° W. Long.
Population: 121 (2000); Race: 100.0% White, 0.0% Black, 0.0% Asian, 0.0% American Indian and Alaska Native, 0.0% Hispanic of any race, 0.0% two or more races (2000); Density: 3.4 persons per square mile (2000); Age: 35.8% under 18, 7.3% over 64 (2000); Marriage status: 22.3% never married, 74.5% now married, 1.1% widowed, 2.1% divorced (2000); Foreign born: 0.0% (2000); Ancestry (includes multiple ancestries): 64.2% German, 26.0% Norwegian, 11.4% Irish, 9.8% English, 8.1% Scottish (2000).
Economy: Employment by occupation: 39.7% management, 11.0% professional, 5.5% services, 12.3% sales, 2.7% farming, 4.1% construction, 24.7% production (2000).
Income: Per capita income: $15,656 (2000); Median household income: $54,167 (2000); Poverty rate: 0.0% (2000).
Taxes: Total city taxes per capita: $86 (1997); City property taxes per capita: $86 (1997).
Education: High school graduation rate: 90.7% (2000); College graduation rate: 8.0% (2000).
Housing: Homeownership rate: 95.0% (2000); Median home value: $59,000 (2000); Median rent: $225 per month (2000); Median age of housing: 50 years (2000).
Transportation: Commute to work: 75.3% car, 0.0% public transportation, 0.0% walk, 24.7% work from home (2000); Travel time to work: 30.9% less than 15 minutes, 54.5% 15 to 30 minutes, 14.5% 30 to 45 minutes, 0.0% 45 to 60 minutes, 0.0% 60 minutes or more (2000)

TORNING (township). Covers a land area of 34.018 square miles and a water area of 0 square miles. Located at 45.28° N. Lat.; 95.55° W. Long.
Population: 505 (2000); Race: 99.6% White, 0.4% Black, 0.0% Asian, 0.0% American Indian and Alaska Native, 0.0% Hispanic of any race, 0.0% two or more races (2000); Density: 14.8 persons per square mile (2000); Age: 34.0% under 18, 8.7% over 64 (2000); Marriage status: 21.4% never married, 69.6% now married, 3.6% widowed, 5.4% divorced (2000); Foreign born: 0.0% (2000); Ancestry (includes multiple ancestries): 46.4% German, 43.6% Norwegian, 13.8% Irish, 10.0% Swedish, 6.8% Polish (2000).
Economy: Employment by occupation: 14.1% management, 14.5% professional, 10.0% services, 30.1% sales, 0.7% farming, 9.3% construction, 21.2% production (2000).
Income: Per capita income: $15,961 (2000); Median household income: $47,344 (2000); Poverty rate: 7.5% (2000).
Taxes: Total city taxes per capita: $68 (1997); City property taxes per capita: $68 (1997).
Education: High school graduation rate: 88.3% (2000); College graduation rate: 14.6% (2000).
Housing: Homeownership rate: 92.7% (2000); Median home value: $71,300 (2000); Median rent: $242 per month (2000); Median age of housing: 30 years (2000).
Transportation: Commute to work: 91.7% car, 0.0% public transportation, 3.4% walk, 4.2% work from home (2000); Travel time to work: 72.0% less than 15 minutes, 13.8% 15 to 30 minutes, 9.4% 30 to 45 minutes, 2.4% 45 to 60 minutes, 2.4% 60 minutes or more (2000)

WEST BANK (township). Covers a land area of 36.168 square miles and a water area of 0 square miles. Located at 45.18° N. Lat.; 95.78° W. Long.
Population: 200 (2000); Race: 100.0% White, 0.0% Black, 0.0% Asian, 0.0% American Indian and Alaska Native, 0.0% Hispanic of any race, 0.0% two or more races (2000); Density: 5.5 persons per square mile (2000); Age: 36.7% under 18, 11.4% over 64 (2000); Marriage status: 22.1% never married, 70.9% now married, 4.1% widowed, 2.9% divorced (2000); Foreign born: 1.7% (2000); Ancestry (includes multiple ancestries): 57.4% Norwegian, 43.5% German, 10.5% Irish, 7.2% Dutch, 5.1% Swedish (2000).
Economy: Employment by occupation: 28.5% management, 17.1% professional, 10.6% services, 14.6% sales, 8.9% farming, 7.3% construction, 13.0% production (2000).
Income: Per capita income: $14,140 (2000); Median household income: $34,063 (2000); Poverty rate: 4.6% (2000).
Taxes: Total city taxes per capita: $146 (1997); City property taxes per capita: $146 (1997).
Education: High school graduation rate: 89.5% (2000); College graduation rate: 16.1% (2000).
Housing: Homeownership rate: 82.1% (2000); Median home value: $53,000 (2000); Median rent: $125 per month (2000); Median age of housing: 60+ years (2000).
Transportation: Commute to work: 70.7% car, 0.0% public transportation, 8.9% walk, 15.4% work from home (2000); Travel time to work: 42.3% less than 15 minutes, 45.2% 15 to 30 minutes, 5.8% 30 to 45 minutes, 2.9% 45 to 60 minutes, 3.8% 60 minutes or more (2000)

Todd County

Located in west central Minnesota; watered by Long Prairie River; includes Lake Osakis. Covers a land area of 942.00 square miles, a water area of 37.30 square miles, and is located in the Central Time Zone. The county government was organized in 1855. County seat is Long Prairie.

Weather Station: Long Prairie — Elevation: 1,289 feet

	Jan	Feb	Mar	Apr	May	Jun	Jul	Aug	Sep	Oct	Nov	Dec
High	19	27	38	56	70	78	83	80	71	58	38	24
Low	-1	6	18	32	45	54	59	57	47	36	21	6
Precip	1.3	0.8	2.0	2.3	3.1	4.3	4.0	3.5	2.9	2.6	1.7	0.9
Snow	13.0	7.5	10.2	3.0	tr	0.0	0.0	0.0	tr	0.8	8.2	8.5

High and Low temperatures in degrees Fahrenheit; Precipitation and Snow in inches

Population: 24,426 (2000); Race: 97.5% White, 0.2% Black, 0.4% Asian, 0.6% American Indian and Alaska Native, 2.0% Hispanic of any race, 0.8% two or more races (2000); Density: 25.9 persons per square mile (2000); Age: 27.4% under 18, 16.1% over 64 (2000).
Religion: Five largest groups: 29.5% Catholic Church, 11.8% Lutheran Church—Missouri Synod, 11.4% Evangelical Lutheran Church in America, 3.5% The United Methodist Church, 1.9% Assemblies of God (2000).
Economy: Unemployment rate: 5.2% (11/2002); Total civilian labor force: 9,446 (11/2002); Leading industries: 34.6% manufacturing; 15.6% retail trade; 12.2% health care and social assistance (2000); Companies that employ more than 1,000 persons: 0 (2000); Companies that employ more than 100 persons: 6 (2000); Farms: 1,741 totaling 387,462 acres (1997); Minority business ownership rate: 0.0% (1997); Women business ownership rate: 12.4% (1997); Retail sales per capita: $5,168 (1997). Single-family building permits issued: 53 (2001) / 144 (2000); Multi-family building permits issued: 2 (2001) / 2 (2000).
Income: Per capita income: $15,658 (2000); Median household income: $32,281 (2000); Poverty rate: 12.9% (2000); Bankruptcy rate: 2.33% (2001).

Taxes: Total county taxes per capita: $245 (2000); County property taxes per capita: $241 (2000).
Education: High school graduation rate: 79.3% (2000); College graduation rate: 10.0% (2000).
Housing: Homeownership rate: 82.9% (2000); Median home value: $64,400 (2000); Median rent: $277 per month (2000); Median age of housing: 36 years (2000).
Health: Birth rate: 105.2 per 10,000 population (1998); Age adjusted death rate: 72.8 per 10,000 population (1999); Age adjusted cancer mortality rate: 144.9 deaths per 100,000 population (1999). Number of physicians: 5.3 per 10,000 population (1999); Number of hospital beds: 106.4 per 10,000 population (1999).
Elections: 2000 Presidential election results: 37.3% Gore, 54.4% Bush, 4.4% Nader, 3.5% Buchanan
National and State Parks: Buckhead Lake State Wildlife Management Area; Burleele State Wildlife Management Area; Dower State Wildlife Management Area; Hollister State Wildlife Management Area; Iona State Wildlife Management Area; Ireland State Wildlife Management Area; Lawrence State Wildlife Management Area; Long Prairie State Wildlife Management Ar; Oak Ridge State Wildlife Management Area; Osakis State Wildlife Management Area; Randall State Wildlife Management Area; Sheets Lake State Wildlife Management Area; Staples State Wildlife Management Area; Turtle Creek State Wildlife Management Area
Additional Information Contacts
Todd County Government Offices 320-732-4469
Long Prairie Chamber of Commerce 320-732-2514
Staples Motley Area Chamber 218-894-3974

Todd County Communities

BARTLETT (township). Covers a land area of 35.906 square miles and a water area of 0 square miles. Located at 46.32° N. Lat.; 94.97° W. Long.
Population: 348 (2000); Race: 98.8% White, 0.0% Black, 0.3% Asian, 0.0% American Indian and Alaska Native, 0.3% Hispanic of any race, 0.6% two or more races (2000); Density: 9.7 persons per square mile (2000); Age: 19.1% under 18, 16.1% over 64 (2000); Marriage status: 27.9% never married, 62.1% now married, 5.5% widowed, 4.5% divorced (2000); Foreign born: 0.3% (2000); Ancestry (includes multiple ancestries): 48.2% German, 11.2% Norwegian, 9.4% Swedish, 7.6% Czech, 4.2% French (except Basque) (2000).
Economy: Employment by occupation: 14.4% management, 13.4% professional, 11.2% services, 22.5% sales, 4.3% farming, 8.0% construction, 26.2% production (2000).
Income: Per capita income: $16,374 (2000); Median household income: $33,654 (2000); Poverty rate: 13.0% (2000).
Taxes: Total city taxes per capita: $59 (1997); City property taxes per capita: $59 (1997).
Education: High school graduation rate: 76.9% (2000); College graduation rate: 9.0% (2000).
Housing: Homeownership rate: 94.0% (2000); Median home value: $78,300 (2000); Median rent: $275 per month (2000); Median age of housing: 55 years (2000).
Transportation: Commute to work: 85.2% car, 0.0% public transportation, 1.1% walk, 13.7% work from home (2000); Travel time to work: 24.1% less than 15 minutes, 54.4% 15 to 30 minutes, 3.2% 30 to 45 minutes, 7.0% 45 to 60 minutes, 11.4% 60 minutes or more (2000)

BERTHA (city). Covers a land area of 1.026 square miles and a water area of 0 square miles. Located at 46.26° N. Lat.; 95.06° W. Long. Elevation is 1,417 feet.
Population: 470 (2000); Race: 99.1% White, 0.0% Black, 0.0% Asian, 0.0% American Indian and Alaska Native, 0.0% Hispanic of any race, 0.9% two or more races (2000); Density: 458.2 persons per square mile (2000); Age: 22.1% under 18, 23.2% over 64 (2000); Marriage status: 22.7% never married, 51.0% now married, 15.5% widowed, 10.8% divorced (2000); Foreign born: 0.7% (2000); Ancestry (includes multiple ancestries): 46.4% German, 13.6% Norwegian, 10.6% Swedish, 8.7% English, 4.4% Irish (2000).
Economy: Single-family building permits issued: 0 (2001) / 0 (2000); Multi-family building permits issued: 0 (2001) / 0 (2000); Employment by occupation: 5.9% management, 19.5% professional, 16.2% services, 15.7% sales, 1.6% farming, 5.4% construction, 35.7% production (2000).
Income: Per capita income: $14,171 (2000); Median household income: $22,625 (2000); Poverty rate: 16.1% (2000).
Taxes: Total city taxes per capita: $34 (1997); City property taxes per capita: $34 (1997).
Education: High school graduation rate: 83.3% (2000); College graduation rate: 17.0% (2000).

School District(s)

Bertha-Hewitt (PK-12)
2000 Enrollment: 518 218-924-2500
Housing: Homeownership rate: 75.1% (2000); Median home value: $37,100 (2000); Median rent: $197 per month (2000); Median age of housing: 54 years (2000).
Transportation: Commute to work: 75.7% car, 0.0% public transportation, 11.9% walk, 9.2% work from home (2000); Travel time to work: 31.5% less than 15 minutes, 47.0% 15 to 30 minutes, 10.7% 30 to 45 minutes, 7.1% 45 to 60 minutes, 3.6% 60 minutes or more (2000)

BERTHA (township). Covers a land area of 35.433 square miles and a water area of 0 square miles. Located at 46.24° N. Lat.; 95.08° W. Long. Elevation is 1,417 feet.
Population: 397 (2000); Race: 98.1% White, 0.0% Black, 0.5% Asian, 0.0% American Indian and Alaska Native, 0.0% Hispanic of any race, 1.4% two or more races (2000); Density: 11.2 persons per square mile (2000); Age: 32.9% under 18, 13.8% over 64 (2000); Marriage status: 22.9% never married, 68.4% now married, 4.8% widowed, 3.9% divorced (2000); Foreign born: 0.5% (2000); Ancestry (includes multiple ancestries): 66.9% German, 11.9% Swedish, 11.9% Norwegian, 7.4% Irish, 4.5% French (except Basque) (2000).
Economy: Grain, potatoes, beans; livestock, poultry; dairying. Manufacturing: plastic molds, bedding, agricultural trailers. Employment by occupation: 16.1% management, 12.4% professional, 10.8% services, 17.2% sales, 7.0% farming, 11.3% construction, 25.3% production (2000).
Income: Per capita income: $13,151 (2000); Median household income: $31,250 (2000); Poverty rate: 14.0% (2000).
Taxes: Total city taxes per capita: $69 (1997); City property taxes per capita: $69 (1997).
Education: High school graduation rate: 83.5% (2000); College graduation rate: 7.3% (2000).
Housing: Homeownership rate: 91.5% (2000); Median home value: $39,500 (2000); Median age of housing: 60+ years (2000).
Transportation: Commute to work: 88.8% car, 0.0% public transportation, 5.6% walk, 5.6% work from home (2000); Travel time to work: 35.1% less than 15 minutes, 32.1% 15 to 30 minutes, 19.6% 30 to 45 minutes, 10.7% 45 to 60 minutes, 2.4% 60 minutes or more (2000)

BIRCHDALE (township). Covers a land area of 32.873 square miles and a water area of 3.081 square miles. Located at 45.79° N. Lat.; 94.83° W. Long.
Population: 814 (2000); Race: 100.0% White, 0.0% Black, 0.0% Asian, 0.0% American Indian and Alaska Native, 0.2% Hispanic of any race, 0.0% two or more races (2000); Density: 24.8 persons per square mile (2000); Age: 28.3% under 18, 15.7% over 64 (2000); Marriage status: 23.5% never married, 60.7% now married, 5.9% widowed, 10.0% divorced (2000); Foreign born: 0.0% (2000); Ancestry (includes multiple ancestries): 69.8% German, 9.6% Norwegian, 7.2% French (except Basque), 6.1% Swedish, 5.9% Irish (2000).
Economy: Employment by occupation: 15.2% management, 15.4% professional, 14.4% services, 16.7% sales, 4.6% farming, 11.9% construction, 21.8% production (2000).
Income: Per capita income: $22,056 (2000); Median household income: $33,750 (2000); Poverty rate: 10.9% (2000).
Taxes: Total city taxes per capita: $67 (1997); City property taxes per capita: $67 (1997).
Education: High school graduation rate: 81.8% (2000); College graduation rate: 11.9% (2000).
Housing: Homeownership rate: 93.8% (2000); Median home value: $121,200 (2000); Median rent: $192 per month (2000); Median age of housing: 26 years (2000).
Transportation: Commute to work: 89.4% car, 0.0% public transportation, 1.0% walk, 9.0% work from home (2000); Travel time to work: 27.8% less than 15 minutes, 52.4% 15 to 30 minutes, 8.5% 30 to 45 minutes, 6.5% 45 to 60 minutes, 4.8% 60 minutes or more (2000)

BROWERVILLE (city). Covers a land area of 0.698 square miles and a water area of 0 square miles. Located at 46.08° N. Lat.; 94.86° W. Long. Elevation is 1,283 feet.
History: Browerville was named for Abraham D. Brower, a Todd County pioneer, who settled here in 1860. In 1874 John Bassett built a large boat and

began floating wheat from his farm near Browerville down the Long Prairie River to Motley. This led to steamboat transportation on the river.
Population: 735 (2000); Race: 95.1% White, 0.0% Black, 1.6% Asian, 0.0% American Indian and Alaska Native, 3.6% Hispanic of any race, 1.3% two or more races (2000); Density: 1,052.5 persons per square mile (2000); Age: 25.5% under 18, 22.3% over 64 (2000); Marriage status: 23.2% never married, 52.8% now married, 15.0% widowed, 9.1% divorced (2000); Foreign born: 4.6% (2000); Ancestry (includes multiple ancestries): 45.9% German, 22.7% Polish, 14.3% Norwegian, 7.3% English, 6.5% Other groups (2000).
Economy: Single-family building permits issued: 1 (2001) / 5 (2000); Multi-family building permits issued: 0 (2001) / 0 (2000); Employment by occupation: 10.8% management, 19.0% professional, 20.7% services, 12.1% sales, 0.3% farming, 6.6% construction, 30.5% production (2000).
Income: Per capita income: $15,493 (2000); Median household income: $26,250 (2000); Poverty rate: 15.2% (2000).
Taxes: Total city taxes per capita: $172 (1997); City property taxes per capita: $172 (1997).
Education: High school graduation rate: 76.3% (2000); College graduation rate: 14.3% (2000).

School District(s)

Browerville (PK-12)
2000 Enrollment: 517 320-594-2272
Housing: Homeownership rate: 73.6% (2000); Median home value: $56,200 (2000); Median rent: $296 per month (2000); Median age of housing: 49 years (2000).
Newspapers: Todd County Country Courier (1 x month)
Transportation: Commute to work: 85.2% car, 0.0% public transportation, 10.3% walk, 4.5% work from home (2000); Travel time to work: 60.1% less than 15 minutes, 24.1% 15 to 30 minutes, 7.2% 30 to 45 minutes, 1.8% 45 to 60 minutes, 6.8% 60 minutes or more (2000)

BRUCE (township). Covers a land area of 35.237 square miles and a water area of 0.811 square miles. Located at 45.96° N. Lat.; 94.71° W. Long.
Population: 564 (2000); Race: 98.4% White, 0.0% Black, 0.5% Asian, 0.0% American Indian and Alaska Native, 0.4% Hispanic of any race, 1.1% two or more races (2000); Density: 16.0 persons per square mile (2000); Age: 28.3% under 18, 10.0% over 64 (2000); Marriage status: 20.6% never married, 67.0% now married, 6.0% widowed, 6.5% divorced (2000); Foreign born: 1.1% (2000); Ancestry (includes multiple ancestries): 57.7% German, 11.9% Norwegian, 10.6% Polish, 8.6% Irish, 6.0% Swedish (2000).
Economy: Employment by occupation: 5.3% management, 10.3% professional, 16.7% services, 23.6% sales, 2.3% farming, 14.4% construction, 27.4% production (2000).
Income: Per capita income: $15,762 (2000); Median household income: $40,278 (2000); Poverty rate: 11.9% (2000).
Taxes: Total city taxes per capita: $33 (1997); City property taxes per capita: $33 (1997).
Education: High school graduation rate: 76.2% (2000); College graduation rate: 7.7% (2000).
Housing: Homeownership rate: 90.8% (2000); Median home value: $90,400 (2000); Median rent: $350 per month (2000); Median age of housing: 29 years (2000).
Transportation: Commute to work: 84.7% car, 0.0% public transportation, 1.5% walk, 13.0% work from home (2000); Travel time to work: 26.9% less than 15 minutes, 39.2% 15 to 30 minutes, 21.1% 30 to 45 minutes, 7.5% 45 to 60 minutes, 5.3% 60 minutes or more (2000)

BURLEENE (township). Covers a land area of 35.826 square miles and a water area of 0.047 square miles. Located at 46.06° N. Lat.; 95.08° W. Long.
Population: 365 (2000); Race: 100.0% White, 0.0% Black, 0.0% Asian, 0.0% American Indian and Alaska Native, 0.0% Hispanic of any race, 0.0% two or more races (2000); Density: 10.2 persons per square mile (2000); Age: 28.0% under 18, 15.5% over 64 (2000); Marriage status: 24.6% never married, 63.8% now married, 5.1% widowed, 6.5% divorced (2000); Foreign born: 1.7% (2000); Ancestry (includes multiple ancestries): 47.5% German, 17.2% Norwegian, 12.8% Irish, 9.3% Swedish, 5.8% Polish (2000).
Economy: Employment by occupation: 21.7% management, 6.6% professional, 11.4% services, 22.3% sales, 6.6% farming, 14.5% construction, 16.9% production (2000).
Income: Per capita income: $21,204 (2000); Median household income: $32,143 (2000); Poverty rate: 8.5% (2000).
Taxes: Total city taxes per capita: $34 (1997); City property taxes per capita: $34 (1997).
Education: High school graduation rate: 79.8% (2000); College graduation rate: 2.6% (2000).
Housing: Homeownership rate: 94.7% (2000); Median home value: $37,500 (2000); Median age of housing: 53 years (2000).
Transportation: Commute to work: 78.7% car, 0.0% public transportation, 5.5% walk, 15.9% work from home (2000); Travel time to work: 15.2% less than 15 minutes, 51.4% 15 to 30 minutes, 18.1% 30 to 45 minutes, 2.9% 45 to 60 minutes, 12.3% 60 minutes or more (2000)

BURNHAMVILLE (township). Covers a land area of 31.624 square miles and a water area of 3.424 square miles. Located at 45.89° N. Lat.; 94.69° W. Long.
Population: 751 (2000); Race: 99.2% White, 0.0% Black, 0.0% Asian, 0.0% American Indian and Alaska Native, 0.8% Hispanic of any race, 0.8% two or more races (2000); Density: 23.7 persons per square mile (2000); Age: 23.1% under 18, 10.4% over 64 (2000); Marriage status: 21.8% never married, 66.1% now married, 3.5% widowed, 8.6% divorced (2000); Foreign born: 1.1% (2000); Ancestry (includes multiple ancestries): 70.1% German, 10.6% Polish, 10.6% Irish, 9.4% Norwegian, 8.9% Swedish (2000).
Economy: Employment by occupation: 14.7% management, 13.0% professional, 8.1% services, 19.4% sales, 2.2% farming, 15.0% construction, 27.5% production (2000).
Income: Per capita income: $17,978 (2000); Median household income: $41,375 (2000); Poverty rate: 8.1% (2000).
Taxes: Total city taxes per capita: $63 (1997); City property taxes per capita: $63 (1997).
Education: High school graduation rate: 81.3% (2000); College graduation rate: 9.2% (2000).
Housing: Homeownership rate: 89.2% (2000); Median home value: $88,600 (2000); Median rent: $188 per month (2000); Median age of housing: 28 years (2000).
Transportation: Commute to work: 89.7% car, 0.0% public transportation, 4.0% walk, 6.3% work from home (2000); Travel time to work: 28.1% less than 15 minutes, 31.6% 15 to 30 minutes, 25.1% 30 to 45 minutes, 6.1% 45 to 60 minutes, 9.1% 60 minutes or more (2000)

BURTRUM (city). Covers a land area of 0.566 square miles and a water area of 0 square miles. Located at 45.86° N. Lat.; 94.68° W. Long. Elevation is 1,285 feet.
Population: 146 (2000); Race: 98.7% White, 0.0% Black, 0.0% Asian, 0.0% American Indian and Alaska Native, 1.3% Hispanic of any race, 1.3% two or more races (2000); Density: 258.2 persons per square mile (2000); Age: 24.2% under 18, 15.0% over 64 (2000); Marriage status: 23.0% never married, 57.4% now married, 9.8% widowed, 9.8% divorced (2000); Foreign born: 0.0% (2000); Ancestry (includes multiple ancestries): 69.9% German, 15.0% Norwegian, 13.7% Irish, 11.8% Polish, 7.2% United States or American (2000).
Economy: Grain, potatoes, beans; livestock; dairying. Single-family building permits issued: 0 (2001) / 0 (2000); Multi-family building permits issued: 0 (2001) / 0 (2000); Employment by occupation: 2.9% management, 7.1% professional, 27.1% services, 15.7% sales, 5.7% farming, 14.3% construction, 27.1% production (2000).
Income: Per capita income: $13,788 (2000); Median household income: $26,875 (2000); Poverty rate: 12.4% (2000).
Taxes: Total city taxes per capita: $58 (1997); City property taxes per capita: $47 (1997).
Education: High school graduation rate: 71.9% (2000); College graduation rate: 0.0% (2000).
Housing: Homeownership rate: 71.8% (2000); Median home value: $41,300 (2000); Median rent: $232 per month (2000); Median age of housing: 35 years (2000).
Transportation: Commute to work: 90.0% car, 0.0% public transportation, 3.3% walk, 6.7% work from home (2000); Travel time to work: 28.6% less than 15 minutes, 26.8% 15 to 30 minutes, 30.4% 30 to 45 minutes, 12.5% 45 to 60 minutes, 1.8% 60 minutes or more (2000)

CLARISSA (city). Covers a land area of 0.987 square miles and a water area of 0 square miles. Located at 46.13° N. Lat.; 94.95° W. Long. Elevation is 1,332 feet.
Population: 609 (2000); Race: 98.8% White, 0.0% Black, 0.0% Asian, 0.5% American Indian and Alaska Native, 0.0% Hispanic of any race, 0.7% two or more races (2000); Density: 617.0 persons per square mile (2000); Age: 17.2% under 18, 37.8% over 64 (2000); Marriage status: 14.3% never married, 65.0% now married, 14.5% widowed, 6.3% divorced (2000); Foreign born: 0.7% (2000); Ancestry (includes multiple ancestries): 38.4% German, 13.2% Swedish, 12.8% Norwegian, 8.1% Irish, 5.2% Czech (2000).
Economy: Grain, beans, potatoes; livestock, poultry; dairying. Light manufacturing: consumer goods. Single-family building permits issued: 1

(2001) / 3 (2000); Multi-family building permits issued: 0 (2001) / 0 (2000); Employment by occupation: 8.1% management, 18.3% professional, 19.5% services, 17.5% sales, 3.3% farming, 4.1% construction, 29.3% production (2000).
Income: Per capita income: $14,913 (2000); Median household income: $25,125 (2000); Poverty rate: 8.3% (2000).
Taxes: Total city taxes per capita: $84 (1997); City property taxes per capita: $84 (1997).
Education: High school graduation rate: 73.5% (2000); College graduation rate: 11.7% (2000).

School District(s)

Eagle Valley (PK-12)
2000 Enrollment: 446 218-738-6442
Housing: Homeownership rate: 73.5% (2000); Median home value: $46,100 (2000); Median rent: $250 per month (2000); Median age of housing: 42 years (2000).
Newspapers: Independent News Herald (1 x week)
Transportation: Commute to work: 85.5% car, 0.0% public transportation, 5.1% walk, 5.5% work from home (2000); Travel time to work: 41.4% less than 15 minutes, 37.8% 15 to 30 minutes, 10.8% 30 to 45 minutes, 5.0% 45 to 60 minutes, 5.0% 60 minutes or more (2000)

EAGLE BEND (city). Covers a land area of 1.266 square miles and a water area of 0 square miles. Located at 46.16° N. Lat.; 95.03° W. Long. Elevation is 1,369 feet.
Population: 595 (2000); Race: 97.7% White, 0.0% Black, 0.5% Asian, 0.8% American Indian and Alaska Native, 1.1% Hispanic of any race, 0.8% two or more races (2000); Density: 470.1 persons per square mile (2000); Age: 25.5% under 18, 21.0% over 64 (2000); Marriage status: 26.2% never married, 52.5% now married, 8.9% widowed, 12.5% divorced (2000); Foreign born: 1.4% (2000); Ancestry (includes multiple ancestries): 47.5% German, 13.1% Norwegian, 10.0% Swedish, 6.8% English, 6.2% Irish (2000).
Economy: Grain, beans, potatoes; livestock, poultry; dairying. Single-family building permits issued: 8 (2001) / 1 (2000); Multi-family building permits issued: 0 (2001) / 0 (2000); Employment by occupation: 4.9% management, 14.4% professional, 20.6% services, 20.6% sales, 2.0% farming, 13.7% construction, 23.9% production (2000).
Income: Per capita income: $12,517 (2000); Median household income: $27,308 (2000); Poverty rate: 14.9% (2000).
Taxes: Total city taxes per capita: $88 (1997); City property taxes per capita: $85 (1997).
Education: High school graduation rate: 81.6% (2000); College graduation rate: 9.5% (2000).
Housing: Homeownership rate: 76.2% (2000); Median home value: $43,500 (2000); Median rent: $207 per month (2000); Median age of housing: 44 years (2000).
Transportation: Commute to work: 77.7% car, 0.0% public transportation, 14.6% walk, 6.3% work from home (2000); Travel time to work: 50.4% less than 15 minutes, 23.8% 15 to 30 minutes, 13.8% 30 to 45 minutes, 8.9% 45 to 60 minutes, 3.2% 60 minutes or more (2000)

EAGLE VALLEY (township). Covers a land area of 35.132 square miles and a water area of 0 square miles. Located at 46.14° N. Lat.; 94.95° W. Long.
Population: 570 (2000); Race: 99.0% White, 0.0% Black, 0.0% Asian, 0.7% American Indian and Alaska Native, 0.0% Hispanic of any race, 0.3% two or more races (2000); Density: 16.2 persons per square mile (2000); Age: 30.4% under 18, 9.8% over 64 (2000); Marriage status: 24.1% never married, 65.6% now married, 2.6% widowed, 7.7% divorced (2000); Foreign born: 0.0% (2000); Ancestry (includes multiple ancestries): 49.2% German, 18.9% Swedish, 15.4% Norwegian, 8.1% Polish, 6.8% Irish (2000).
Economy: Employment by occupation: 19.8% management, 11.9% professional, 12.2% services, 16.2% sales, 7.9% farming, 6.9% construction, 25.1% production (2000).
Income: Per capita income: $19,877 (2000); Median household income: $35,000 (2000); Poverty rate: 11.1% (2000).
Taxes: Total city taxes per capita: $16 (1997); City property taxes per capita: $16 (1997).
Education: High school graduation rate: 84.6% (2000); College graduation rate: 9.8% (2000).
Housing: Homeownership rate: 91.1% (2000); Median home value: $52,900 (2000); Median rent: $350 per month (2000); Median age of housing: 40 years (2000).
Transportation: Commute to work: 78.7% car, 0.0% public transportation, 2.3% walk, 19.0% work from home (2000); Travel time to work: 54.3% less than 15 minutes, 28.4% 15 to 30 minutes, 11.5% 30 to 45 minutes, 1.2% 45 to 60 minutes, 4.5% 60 minutes or more (2000)

FAWN LAKE (township). Covers a land area of 34.018 square miles and a water area of 1.713 square miles. Located at 46.22° N. Lat.; 94.73° W. Long.
Population: 440 (2000); Race: 98.5% White, 0.4% Black, 0.4% Asian, 0.6% American Indian and Alaska Native, 0.0% Hispanic of any race, 0.0% two or more races (2000); Density: 12.9 persons per square mile (2000); Age: 27.1% under 18, 14.2% over 64 (2000); Marriage status: 22.3% never married, 63.4% now married, 6.7% widowed, 7.5% divorced (2000); Foreign born: 1.5% (2000); Ancestry (includes multiple ancestries): 47.6% German, 12.3% Polish, 10.2% Czech, 9.6% Norwegian, 7.5% Irish (2000).
Economy: Employment by occupation: 12.9% management, 8.3% professional, 17.0% services, 13.7% sales, 7.1% farming, 10.4% construction, 30.7% production (2000).
Income: Per capita income: $15,559 (2000); Median household income: $33,646 (2000); Poverty rate: 10.9% (2000).
Taxes: Total city taxes per capita: $145 (1997); City property taxes per capita: $145 (1997).
Education: High school graduation rate: 80.5% (2000); College graduation rate: 3.9% (2000).
Housing: Homeownership rate: 92.8% (2000); Median home value: $65,800 (2000); Median rent: $275 per month (2000); Median age of housing: 25 years (2000).
Transportation: Commute to work: 80.5% car, 0.8% public transportation, 0.8% walk, 15.8% work from home (2000); Travel time to work: 27.1% less than 15 minutes, 31.0% 15 to 30 minutes, 23.6% 30 to 45 minutes, 6.9% 45 to 60 minutes, 11.3% 60 minutes or more (2000)

GERMANIA (township). Covers a land area of 36.397 square miles and a water area of 0 square miles. Located at 46.23° N. Lat.; 94.96° W. Long.
Population: 474 (2000); Race: 99.1% White, 0.0% Black, 0.0% Asian, 0.2% American Indian and Alaska Native, 0.4% Hispanic of any race, 0.7% two or more races (2000); Density: 13.0 persons per square mile (2000); Age: 39.6% under 18, 9.6% over 64 (2000); Marriage status: 28.7% never married, 65.4% now married, 3.4% widowed, 2.5% divorced (2000); Foreign born: 0.7% (2000); Ancestry (includes multiple ancestries): 54.6% German, 15.9% Dutch, 9.8% French (except Basque), 7.2% Swedish, 7.2% Norwegian (2000).
Economy: Employment by occupation: 14.7% management, 11.7% professional, 12.2% services, 16.2% sales, 4.1% farming, 19.3% construction, 21.8% production (2000).
Income: Per capita income: $10,133 (2000); Median household income: $35,227 (2000); Poverty rate: 18.4% (2000).
Taxes: Total city taxes per capita: $36 (1997); City property taxes per capita: $36 (1997).
Education: High school graduation rate: 76.6% (2000); College graduation rate: 6.4% (2000).
Housing: Homeownership rate: 89.8% (2000); Median home value: $95,000 (2000); Median rent: $175 per month (2000); Median age of housing: 33 years (2000).
Transportation: Commute to work: 64.8% car, 0.0% public transportation, 4.1% walk, 30.1% work from home (2000); Travel time to work: 26.7% less than 15 minutes, 27.4% 15 to 30 minutes, 21.5% 30 to 45 minutes, 11.1% 45 to 60 minutes, 13.3% 60 minutes or more (2000)

GORDON (township). Covers a land area of 27.867 square miles and a water area of 7.053 square miles. Located at 45.88° N. Lat.; 95.08° W. Long.
Population: 545 (2000); Race: 95.4% White, 0.0% Black, 1.6% Asian, 0.4% American Indian and Alaska Native, 0.0% Hispanic of any race, 2.6% two or more races (2000); Density: 19.6 persons per square mile (2000); Age: 23.8% under 18, 19.6% over 64 (2000); Marriage status: 18.7% never married, 70.7% now married, 5.4% widowed, 5.2% divorced (2000); Foreign born: 1.6% (2000); Ancestry (includes multiple ancestries): 48.9% German, 35.7% Norwegian, 8.2% Swedish, 7.5% Other groups, 3.8% English (2000).
Economy: Employment by occupation: 13.5% management, 13.1% professional, 13.1% services, 23.9% sales, 2.3% farming, 12.4% construction, 21.6% production (2000).
Income: Per capita income: $16,908 (2000); Median household income: $39,531 (2000); Poverty rate: 8.6% (2000).
Taxes: Total city taxes per capita: $56 (1997); City property taxes per capita: $56 (1997).
Education: High school graduation rate: 82.6% (2000); College graduation rate: 13.6% (2000).

Housing: Homeownership rate: 91.3% (2000); Median home value: $99,400 (2000); Median rent: $313 per month (2000); Median age of housing: 28 years (2000).
Transportation: Commute to work: 84.0% car, 0.0% public transportation, 2.7% walk, 13.3% work from home (2000); Travel time to work: 21.6% less than 15 minutes, 52.3% 15 to 30 minutes, 20.7% 30 to 45 minutes, 2.3% 45 to 60 minutes, 3.2% 60 minutes or more (2000)

GREY EAGLE (city). Covers a land area of 0.371 square miles and a water area of 0 square miles. Located at 45.82° N. Lat.; 94.74° W. Long. Elevation is 1,222 feet.
Population: 335 (2000); Race: 95.9% White, 1.2% Black, 0.0% Asian, 0.0% American Indian and Alaska Native, 0.0% Hispanic of any race, 2.9% two or more races (2000); Density: 902.8 persons per square mile (2000); Age: 22.5% under 18, 19.3% over 64 (2000); Marriage status: 27.5% never married, 50.4% now married, 14.4% widowed, 7.7% divorced (2000); Foreign born: 2.6% (2000); Ancestry (includes multiple ancestries): 62.3% German, 11.4% Irish, 9.9% Norwegian, 8.5% French (except Basque), 7.0% Swedish (2000).
Economy: Single-family building permits issued: 2 (2001) / 2 (2000); Multi-family building permits issued: 0 (2001) / 0 (2000); Employment by occupation: 12.7% management, 9.6% professional, 12.7% services, 16.6% sales, 1.3% farming, 10.8% construction, 36.3% production (2000).
Income: Per capita income: $15,952 (2000); Median household income: $32,917 (2000); Poverty rate: 12.2% (2000).
Taxes: Total city taxes per capita: $127 (1997); City property taxes per capita: $121 (1997).
Education: High school graduation rate: 71.4% (2000); College graduation rate: 13.7% (2000).
Housing: Homeownership rate: 80.6% (2000); Median home value: $53,300 (2000); Median rent: $250 per month (2000); Median age of housing: 39 years (2000).
Transportation: Commute to work: 81.3% car, 0.0% public transportation, 11.0% walk, 7.7% work from home (2000); Travel time to work: 38.5% less than 15 minutes, 27.3% 15 to 30 minutes, 14.7% 30 to 45 minutes, 14.7% 45 to 60 minutes, 4.9% 60 minutes or more (2000)

GREY EAGLE (township). Covers a land area of 25.069 square miles and a water area of 4.182 square miles. Located at 45.80° N. Lat.; 94.70° W. Long. Elevation is 1,222 feet.
Population: 663 (2000); Race: 98.2% White, 0.0% Black, 0.4% Asian, 0.0% American Indian and Alaska Native, 0.0% Hispanic of any race, 1.0% two or more races (2000); Density: 26.4 persons per square mile (2000); Age: 26.3% under 18, 18.7% over 64 (2000); Marriage status: 17.9% never married, 70.8% now married, 6.0% widowed, 5.3% divorced (2000); Foreign born: 1.0% (2000); Ancestry (includes multiple ancestries): 54.3% German, 11.5% Norwegian, 7.6% Irish, 6.3% United States or American, 5.1% Swedish (2000).
Economy: Lake resort region; poultry; grain, potatoes; dairying. Employment by occupation: 16.8% management, 12.6% professional, 7.0% services, 24.2% sales, 1.4% farming, 6.7% construction, 31.2% production (2000).
Income: Per capita income: $20,151 (2000); Median household income: $41,923 (2000); Poverty rate: 8.8% (2000).
Taxes: Total city taxes per capita: $34 (1997); City property taxes per capita: $34 (1997).
Education: High school graduation rate: 82.6% (2000); College graduation rate: 11.5% (2000).
Housing: Homeownership rate: 90.9% (2000); Median home value: $100,000 (2000); Median rent: $213 per month (2000); Median age of housing: 35 years (2000).
Transportation: Commute to work: 88.7% car, 0.0% public transportation, 2.1% walk, 8.1% work from home (2000); Travel time to work: 22.7% less than 15 minutes, 33.1% 15 to 30 minutes, 20.0% 30 to 45 minutes, 14.2% 45 to 60 minutes, 10.0% 60 minutes or more (2000)

HARTFORD (township). Covers a land area of 35.033 square miles and a water area of 0.283 square miles. Located at 46.06° N. Lat.; 94.84° W. Long.
Population: 677 (2000); Race: 99.3% White, 0.0% Black, 0.0% Asian, 0.0% American Indian and Alaska Native, 0.3% Hispanic of any race, 0.7% two or more races (2000); Density: 19.3 persons per square mile (2000); Age: 33.6% under 18, 10.8% over 64 (2000); Marriage status: 28.5% never married, 62.9% now married, 1.8% widowed, 6.8% divorced (2000); Foreign born: 0.0% (2000); Ancestry (includes multiple ancestries): 61.9% German, 29.3% Polish, 8.8% Norwegian, 5.4% United States or American, 4.3% Danish (2000).
Economy: Employment by occupation: 11.7% management, 8.5% professional, 19.4% services, 18.8% sales, 5.4% farming, 12.8% construction, 23.4% production (2000).
Income: Per capita income: $14,416 (2000); Median household income: $41,250 (2000); Poverty rate: 13.8% (2000).
Taxes: Total city taxes per capita: $74 (1997); City property taxes per capita: $74 (1997).
Education: High school graduation rate: 79.4% (2000); College graduation rate: 6.2% (2000).
Housing: Homeownership rate: 93.0% (2000); Median home value: $75,800 (2000); Median rent: $350 per month (2000); Median age of housing: 53 years (2000).
Transportation: Commute to work: 84.6% car, 0.0% public transportation, 2.3% walk, 13.1% work from home (2000); Travel time to work: 47.2% less than 15 minutes, 31.5% 15 to 30 minutes, 14.8% 30 to 45 minutes, 3.0% 45 to 60 minutes, 3.6% 60 minutes or more (2000)

HEWITT (city). Covers a land area of 2.050 square miles and a water area of 0 square miles. Located at 46.32° N. Lat.; 95.08° W. Long. Elevation is 1,385 feet.
Population: 267 (2000); Race: 99.3% White, 0.0% Black, 0.0% Asian, 0.7% American Indian and Alaska Native, 2.2% Hispanic of any race, 0.0% two or more races (2000); Density: 130.3 persons per square mile (2000); Age: 15.9% under 18, 26.6% over 64 (2000); Marriage status: 20.9% never married, 50.0% now married, 13.5% widowed, 15.7% divorced (2000); Foreign born: 0.0% (2000); Ancestry (includes multiple ancestries): 46.5% German, 18.8% Norwegian, 10.0% Irish, 7.7% French (except Basque), 5.2% Swedish (2000).
Economy: Poultry, livestock; grain, potatoes; dairying. Manufacturing: wood products. Single-family building permits issued: 0 (2001) / 0 (2000); Multi-family building permits issued: 0 (2001) / 0 (2000); Employment by occupation: 4.5% management, 9.1% professional, 10.9% services, 16.4% sales, 3.6% farming, 20.0% construction, 35.5% production (2000).
Income: Per capita income: $12,520 (2000); Median household income: $26,161 (2000); Poverty rate: 13.4% (2000).
Taxes: Total city taxes per capita: $112 (1997); City property taxes per capita: $112 (1997).
Education: High school graduation rate: 69.8% (2000); College graduation rate: 2.0% (2000).
Housing: Homeownership rate: 87.4% (2000); Median home value: $26,300 (2000); Median rent: $217 per month (2000); Median age of housing: 60+ years (2000).
Transportation: Commute to work: 90.0% car, 0.0% public transportation, 3.6% walk, 4.5% work from home (2000); Travel time to work: 32.4% less than 15 minutes, 43.8% 15 to 30 minutes, 21.9% 30 to 45 minutes, 0.0% 45 to 60 minutes, 1.9% 60 minutes or more (2000)

IONA (township). Covers a land area of 35.992 square miles and a water area of 0.211 square miles. Located at 46.06° N. Lat.; 94.95° W. Long.
Population: 416 (2000); Race: 99.1% White, 0.0% Black, 0.9% Asian, 0.0% American Indian and Alaska Native, 0.0% Hispanic of any race, 0.0% two or more races (2000); Density: 11.6 persons per square mile (2000); Age: 34.7% under 18, 10.8% over 64 (2000); Marriage status: 26.5% never married, 61.9% now married, 5.2% widowed, 6.4% divorced (2000); Foreign born: 0.0% (2000); Ancestry (includes multiple ancestries): 51.4% German, 16.4% Polish, 9.7% Norwegian, 9.0% Swedish, 7.2% Irish (2000).
Economy: Employment by occupation: 18.8% management, 6.3% professional, 17.9% services, 12.1% sales, 4.0% farming, 7.1% construction, 33.9% production (2000).
Income: Per capita income: $18,993 (2000); Median household income: $39,167 (2000); Poverty rate: 7.7% (2000).
Taxes: Total city taxes per capita: $101 (2000); City property taxes per capita: $101 (2000).
Education: High school graduation rate: 73.7% (2000); College graduation rate: 4.7% (2000).
Housing: Homeownership rate: 87.9% (2000); Median home value: $24,500 (2000); Median rent: $275 per month (2000); Median age of housing: 54 years (2000).
Transportation: Commute to work: 80.2% car, 0.0% public transportation, 0.9% walk, 18.9% work from home (2000); Travel time to work: 27.8% less than 15 minutes, 46.7% 15 to 30 minutes, 13.3% 30 to 45 minutes, 6.7% 45 to 60 minutes, 5.6% 60 minutes or more (2000)

KANDOTA (township). Covers a land area of 21.783 square miles and a water area of 2.371 square miles. Located at 45.81° N. Lat.; 94.94° W. Long.
Population: 679 (2000); Race: 100.0% White, 0.0% Black, 0.0% Asian, 0.0% American Indian and Alaska Native, 0.0% Hispanic of any race, 0.0% two or more races (2000); Density: 31.2 persons per square mile (2000); Age: 27.7% under 18, 13.0% over 64 (2000); Marriage status: 21.3% never married, 67.9% now married, 2.9% widowed, 7.8% divorced (2000); Foreign born: 1.5% (2000); Ancestry (includes multiple ancestries): 62.0% German, 14.2% Norwegian, 7.5% Swedish, 6.7% United States or American, 5.4% Irish (2000).
Economy: Employment by occupation: 17.6% management, 10.2% professional, 10.8% services, 19.8% sales, 4.3% farming, 13.3% construction, 23.8% production (2000).
Income: Per capita income: $17,798 (2000); Median household income: $43,750 (2000); Poverty rate: 6.9% (2000).
Taxes: Total city taxes per capita: $49 (1997); City property taxes per capita: $49 (1997).
Education: High school graduation rate: 80.7% (2000); College graduation rate: 11.7% (2000).
Housing: Homeownership rate: 95.3% (2000); Median home value: $112,500 (2000); Median rent: $275 per month (2000); Median age of housing: 27 years (2000).
Transportation: Commute to work: 90.6% car, 0.0% public transportation, 1.3% walk, 7.8% work from home (2000); Travel time to work: 37.3% less than 15 minutes, 41.7% 15 to 30 minutes, 7.1% 30 to 45 minutes, 6.1% 45 to 60 minutes, 7.8% 60 minutes or more (2000)

LESLIE (township). Covers a land area of 34.532 square miles and a water area of 1.692 square miles. Located at 45.96° N. Lat.; 95.07° W. Long.
Population: 690 (2000); Race: 97.1% White, 0.0% Black, 0.0% Asian, 1.8% American Indian and Alaska Native, 3.2% Hispanic of any race, 0.6% two or more races (2000); Density: 20.0 persons per square mile (2000); Age: 22.2% under 18, 18.4% over 64 (2000); Marriage status: 18.9% never married, 63.6% now married, 9.8% widowed, 7.8% divorced (2000); Foreign born: 0.3% (2000); Ancestry (includes multiple ancestries): 44.1% German, 11.9% Irish, 10.0% Norwegian, 7.9% Swedish, 7.3% English (2000).
Economy: Employment by occupation: 14.1% management, 11.2% professional, 11.9% services, 19.1% sales, 2.2% farming, 11.9% construction, 29.6% production (2000).
Income: Per capita income: $21,344 (2000); Median household income: $31,324 (2000); Poverty rate: 7.6% (2000).
Taxes: Total city taxes per capita: $61 (1997); City property taxes per capita: $61 (1997).
Education: High school graduation rate: 77.1% (2000); College graduation rate: 5.5% (2000).
Housing: Homeownership rate: 94.0% (2000); Median home value: $94,500 (2000); Median rent: $242 per month (2000); Median age of housing: 26 years (2000).
Transportation: Commute to work: 85.2% car, 0.0% public transportation, 2.9% walk, 11.2% work from home (2000); Travel time to work: 12.6% less than 15 minutes, 46.3% 15 to 30 minutes, 25.2% 30 to 45 minutes, 6.5% 45 to 60 minutes, 9.3% 60 minutes or more (2000)

LITTLE ELK (township). Covers a land area of 34.747 square miles and a water area of 1.244 square miles. Located at 46.04° N. Lat.; 94.71° W. Long.
Population: 340 (2000); Race: 94.1% White, 0.6% Black, 4.1% Asian, 0.0% American Indian and Alaska Native, 0.0% Hispanic of any race, 1.2% two or more races (2000); Density: 9.8 persons per square mile (2000); Age: 31.1% under 18, 11.7% over 64 (2000); Marriage status: 28.8% never married, 64.2% now married, 4.3% widowed, 2.7% divorced (2000); Foreign born: 3.5% (2000); Ancestry (includes multiple ancestries): 56.3% German, 19.9% Polish, 7.3% Other groups, 7.0% Dutch, 6.2% Irish (2000).
Economy: Employment by occupation: 7.2% management, 6.6% professional, 15.1% services, 30.3% sales, 1.3% farming, 8.6% construction, 30.9% production (2000).
Income: Per capita income: $14,850 (2000); Median household income: $37,679 (2000); Poverty rate: 5.9% (2000).
Taxes: Total city taxes per capita: $102 (1997); City property taxes per capita: $102 (1997).
Education: High school graduation rate: 73.1% (2000); College graduation rate: 3.8% (2000).
Housing: Homeownership rate: 90.7% (2000); Median home value: $69,200 (2000); Median rent: $338 per month (2000); Median age of housing: 42 years (2000).
Transportation: Commute to work: 87.6% car, 0.0% public transportation, 0.0% walk, 12.4% work from home (2000); Travel time to work: 9.4% less than 15 minutes, 45.7% 15 to 30 minutes, 16.5% 30 to 45 minutes, 7.1% 45 to 60 minutes, 21.3% 60 minutes or more (2000)

LITTLE SAUK (township). Covers a land area of 34.206 square miles and a water area of 1.610 square miles. Located at 45.88° N. Lat.; 94.95° W. Long. Elevation is 1,260 feet.
Population: 769 (2000); Race: 97.9% White, 0.0% Black, 1.1% Asian, 0.0% American Indian and Alaska Native, 1.5% Hispanic of any race, 0.0% two or more races (2000); Density: 22.5 persons per square mile (2000); Age: 30.5% under 18, 11.1% over 64 (2000); Marriage status: 29.0% never married, 63.2% now married, 4.7% widowed, 3.1% divorced (2000); Foreign born: 2.5% (2000); Ancestry (includes multiple ancestries): 54.5% German, 10.4% Norwegian, 8.3% Swedish, 7.3% Dutch, 4.4% Irish (2000).
Economy: Employment by occupation: 14.6% management, 9.3% professional, 11.0% services, 20.5% sales, 5.9% farming, 10.1% construction, 28.7% production (2000).
Income: Per capita income: $13,119 (2000); Median household income: $39,875 (2000); Poverty rate: 18.4% (2000).
Education: High school graduation rate: 78.9% (2000); College graduation rate: 9.4% (2000).
Housing: Homeownership rate: 96.6% (2000); Median home value: $67,000 (2000); Median rent: $250 per month (2000); Median age of housing: 30 years (2000).
Transportation: Commute to work: 81.8% car, 0.0% public transportation, 5.5% walk, 10.7% work from home (2000); Travel time to work: 35.6% less than 15 minutes, 44.0% 15 to 30 minutes, 9.4% 30 to 45 minutes, 3.2% 45 to 60 minutes, 7.8% 60 minutes or more (2000)

LONG PRAIRIE (city). Covers a land area of 2.365 square miles and a water area of 0.068 square miles. Located at 45.97° N. Lat.; 94.86° W. Long. Elevation is 1,299 feet.
History: Long Prairie began as an Indian agency headquarters established by the government in 1848. It was followed in 1851 by a mission school founded by Francis Vivaldi, an Italian nobleman who had been forced to leave Italy for political reasons. When the government agency was closed in 1855, the land and buildings were purchased by the Long Prairie Land Company, but settlers were not quick to come. For some years the place was known as Liberty Pole.
Population: 3,040 (2000); Race: 95.5% White, 0.3% Black, 0.1% Asian, 0.8% American Indian and Alaska Native, 9.6% Hispanic of any race, 1.2% two or more races (2000); Density: 1,285.2 persons per square mile (2000); Age: 25.8% under 18, 21.5% over 64 (2000); Marriage status: 22.4% never married, 55.8% now married, 12.6% widowed, 9.2% divorced (2000); Foreign born: 7.1% (2000); Ancestry (includes multiple ancestries): 50.0% German, 16.1% Norwegian, 10.4% Other groups, 9.1% Swedish, 5.5% Polish (2000).
Economy: Single-family building permits issued: 2 (2001) / 3 (2000); Multi-family building permits issued: 2 (2001) / 0 (2000); Employment by occupation: 6.9% management, 14.6% professional, 16.3% services, 24.1% sales, 1.7% farming, 9.5% construction, 26.8% production (2000).
Income: Per capita income: $14,386 (2000); Median household income: $28,237 (2000); Poverty rate: 16.4% (2000).
Taxes: Total city taxes per capita: $172 (1997); City property taxes per capita: $163 (1997).
Education: High school graduation rate: 73.6% (2000); College graduation rate: 14.7% (2000).

School District(s)

Long Prairie-Grey Eagle (PK-12)
2000 Enrollment: 1,369 320-732-4195

Housing: Homeownership rate: 66.6% (2000); Median home value: $64,800 (2000); Median rent: $348 per month (2000); Median age of housing: 40 years (2000).
Hospitals: Long Prairie Memorial Hospital & Nursing Home (34 beds)
Safety: Violent crime rate: 22.8 per 10,000 population; Property crime rate: 400.3 per 10,000 population (2001).
Newspapers: The Long Prairie Leader (1 x week)
Transportation: Commute to work: 84.7% car, 0.0% public transportation, 10.5% walk, 2.3% work from home (2000); Travel time to work: 77.1% less than 15 minutes, 9.8% 15 to 30 minutes, 7.7% 30 to 45 minutes, 2.3% 45 to 60 minutes, 3.1% 60 minutes or more (2000)
Additional Information Contacts
Long Prairie Chamber of Commerce 320-732-2514

LONG PRAIRIE (township). Covers a land area of 33.135 square miles and a water area of 0.377 square miles. Located at 45.97° N. Lat.; 94.84° W. Long. Elevation is 1,299 feet.
History: Winnebago Indian Agency here 1848-1855. Plotted 1867, incorporated 1883.
Population: 823 (2000); Race: 97.5% White, 0.0% Black, 0.4% Asian, 0.0% American Indian and Alaska Native, 2.5% Hispanic of any race, 0.8% two or more races (2000); Density: 24.8 persons per square mile (2000); Age: 28.9% under 18, 12.4% over 64 (2000); Marriage status: 18.3% never married, 70.0% now married, 5.5% widowed, 6.1% divorced (2000); Foreign born: 2.4% (2000); Ancestry (includes multiple ancestries): 57.2% German, 11.3% Norwegian, 6.7% Polish, 6.5% Swedish, 5.6% Irish (2000).
Economy: Trading point in agricultural area: grain, potatoes, beans; livestock, poultry; dairying. Manufacturing: animal protein products, food processing, dump trailers, printing and publishing. Employment by occupation: 12.7% management, 19.6% professional, 11.2% services, 18.2% sales, 2.4% farming, 7.7% construction, 28.1% production (2000).
Income: Per capita income: $17,903 (2000); Median household income: $44,792 (2000); Poverty rate: 4.6% (2000).
Taxes: Total city taxes per capita: $48 (1997); City property taxes per capita: $48 (1997).
Education: High school graduation rate: 84.4% (2000); College graduation rate: 18.0% (2000).
Housing: Homeownership rate: 90.9% (2000); Median home value: $86,900 (2000); Median rent: $369 per month (2000); Median age of housing: 37 years (2000).
Transportation: Commute to work: 93.4% car, 0.0% public transportation, 1.5% walk, 4.6% work from home (2000); Travel time to work: 64.1% less than 15 minutes, 16.2% 15 to 30 minutes, 13.7% 30 to 45 minutes, 1.9% 45 to 60 minutes, 4.2% 60 minutes or more (2000)

MORAN (township). Covers a land area of 35.559 square miles and a water area of 0.460 square miles. Located at 46.24° N. Lat.; 94.82° W. Long.
Population: 515 (2000); Race: 99.2% White, 0.4% Black, 0.4% Asian, 0.0% American Indian and Alaska Native, 0.0% Hispanic of any race, 0.0% two or more races (2000); Density: 14.5 persons per square mile (2000); Age: 29.0% under 18, 11.2% over 64 (2000); Marriage status: 17.1% never married, 69.1% now married, 2.7% widowed, 11.1% divorced (2000); Foreign born: 0.0% (2000); Ancestry (includes multiple ancestries): 47.8% German, 16.5% Polish, 11.2% Swedish, 10.6% Czech, 7.8% Norwegian (2000).
Economy: Employment by occupation: 18.8% management, 8.2% professional, 14.9% services, 21.2% sales, 1.9% farming, 10.1% construction, 25.0% production (2000).
Income: Per capita income: $15,144 (2000); Median household income: $27,083 (2000); Poverty rate: 18.0% (2000).
Taxes: Total city taxes per capita: $55 (1997); City property taxes per capita: $55 (1997).
Education: High school graduation rate: 85.1% (2000); College graduation rate: 6.2% (2000).
Housing: Homeownership rate: 93.4% (2000); Median home value: $63,800 (2000); Median rent: $225 per month (2000); Median age of housing: 29 years (2000).
Transportation: Commute to work: 76.2% car, 0.0% public transportation, 5.8% walk, 18.0% work from home (2000); Travel time to work: 16.6% less than 15 minutes, 45.0% 15 to 30 minutes, 21.3% 30 to 45 minutes, 7.7% 45 to 60 minutes, 9.5% 60 minutes or more (2000)

REYNOLDS (township). Aka Gutches Grove. Covers a land area of 35.630 square miles and a water area of 0.426 square miles. Located at 45.98° N. Lat.; 94.94° W. Long.
Population: 688 (2000); Race: 100.0% White, 0.0% Black, 0.0% Asian, 0.0% American Indian and Alaska Native, 0.0% Hispanic of any race, 0.0% two or more races (2000); Density: 19.3 persons per square mile (2000); Age: 35.6% under 18, 11.0% over 64 (2000); Marriage status: 24.1% never married, 64.5% now married, 6.5% widowed, 4.9% divorced (2000); Foreign born: 0.4% (2000); Ancestry (includes multiple ancestries): 67.5% German, 9.8% Swedish, 9.3% Norwegian, 6.1% Polish, 3.9% Irish (2000).
Economy: Employment by occupation: 22.9% management, 9.3% professional, 15.3% services, 13.6% sales, 10.0% farming, 7.6% construction, 21.3% production (2000).
Income: Per capita income: $12,329 (2000); Median household income: $33,393 (2000); Poverty rate: 17.5% (2000).
Taxes: Total city taxes per capita: $29 (1997); City property taxes per capita: $29 (1997).
Education: High school graduation rate: 74.6% (2000); College graduation rate: 8.9% (2000).
Housing: Homeownership rate: 91.0% (2000); Median home value: $82,900 (2000); Median rent: $263 per month (2000); Median age of housing: 29 years (2000).
Transportation: Commute to work: 70.0% car, 0.0% public transportation, 1.3% walk, 25.3% work from home (2000); Travel time to work: 40.6% less than 15 minutes, 35.3% 15 to 30 minutes, 14.3% 30 to 45 minutes, 7.6% 45 to 60 minutes, 2.2% 60 minutes or more (2000)

ROUND PRAIRIE (township). Covers a land area of 35.069 square miles and a water area of 0.961 square miles. Located at 45.88° N. Lat.; 94.82° W. Long. Elevation is 1,337 feet.
Population: 692 (2000); Race: 99.7% White, 0.0% Black, 0.0% Asian, 0.0% American Indian and Alaska Native, 0.7% Hispanic of any race, 0.3% two or more races (2000); Density: 19.7 persons per square mile (2000); Age: 33.0% under 18, 11.5% over 64 (2000); Marriage status: 20.5% never married, 69.9% now married, 2.6% widowed, 7.0% divorced (2000); Foreign born: 0.0% (2000); Ancestry (includes multiple ancestries): 62.7% German, 7.6% Norwegian, 5.5% Irish, 5.4% English, 5.2% Polish (2000).
Economy: Employment by occupation: 16.7% management, 5.3% professional, 11.7% services, 23.7% sales, 4.7% farming, 9.4% construction, 28.7% production (2000).
Income: Per capita income: $13,422 (2000); Median household income: $35,694 (2000); Poverty rate: 17.2% (2000).
Taxes: Total city taxes per capita: $59 (1997); City property taxes per capita: $59 (1997).
Education: High school graduation rate: 82.9% (2000); College graduation rate: 3.7% (2000).
Housing: Homeownership rate: 93.6% (2000); Median home value: $73,600 (2000); Median rent: $350 per month (2000); Median age of housing: 30 years (2000).
Transportation: Commute to work: 76.6% car, 0.0% public transportation, 7.1% walk, 15.7% work from home (2000); Travel time to work: 49.6% less than 15 minutes, 24.6% 15 to 30 minutes, 15.5% 30 to 45 minutes, 4.6% 45 to 60 minutes, 5.6% 60 minutes or more (2000)

STAPLES (city). Covers a land area of 4.534 square miles and a water area of 0.013 square miles. Located at 46.35° N. Lat.; 94.79° W. Long. Elevation is 1,278 feet.
History: Staples developed as a division point on the Northern Pacific Railway. It became the center of a farming district with creameries and cheese factories.
Population: 3,104 (2000); Race: 94.1% White, 1.1% Black, 0.4% Asian, 3.0% American Indian and Alaska Native, 1.9% Hispanic of any race, 0.7% two or more races (2000); Density: 684.5 persons per square mile (2000); Age: 26.6% under 18, 20.4% over 64 (2000); Marriage status: 22.8% never married, 53.0% now married, 12.5% widowed, 11.8% divorced (2000); Foreign born: 1.4% (2000); Ancestry (includes multiple ancestries): 30.3% German, 11.3% Norwegian, 9.6% Irish, 8.4% Swedish, 7.5% Other groups (2000).
Economy: Single-family building permits issued: 8 (2001) / 6 (2000); Multi-family building permits issued: 0 (2001) / 2 (2000); Employment by occupation: 6.8% management, 12.7% professional, 19.8% services, 23.4% sales, 1.8% farming, 9.2% construction, 26.3% production (2000).
Income: Per capita income: $14,244 (2000); Median household income: $25,208 (2000); Poverty rate: 20.3% (2000).
Taxes: Total city taxes per capita: $199 (1997); City property taxes per capita: $187 (1997).
Education: High school graduation rate: 76.5% (2000); College graduation rate: 10.0% (2000).

School District(s)

Freshwater Ed. Dist. (06-12)
2000 Enrollment: 119 218-894-2439
Staples-Motley (PK-12)
2000 Enrollment: 1,623 218-894-2430

Two-year College(s)

Central Lakes College-Staples Campus (Public)
2001 Enrollment: n/a 218-894-5100
2001 Tuition: In-state $2,345; Out-of-state $4,689

Housing: Homeownership rate: 64.1% (2000); Median home value: $51,100 (2000); Median rent: $299 per month (2000); Median age of housing: 43 years (2000).
Hospitals: Lakewood Health System (140 beds)
Safety: Violent crime rate: 38.3 per 10,000 population; Property crime rate: 436.7 per 10,000 population (2001).

Newspapers: The Staples World (1 x week)
Transportation: Commute to work: 88.1% car, 0.2% public transportation, 7.2% walk, 3.0% work from home (2000); Travel time to work: 53.9% less than 15 minutes, 12.8% 15 to 30 minutes, 18.3% 30 to 45 minutes, 6.4% 45 to 60 minutes, 8.7% 60 minutes or more (2000); Amtrak: Service available.
Additional Information Contacts
Staples Motley Area Chamber 218-894-3974

STAPLES (township). Covers a land area of 32.706 square miles and a water area of 1.152 square miles. Located at 46.32° N. Lat.; 94.82° W. Long. Elevation is 1,278 feet.
History: Settled 1881, plotted 1885, incorporated 1906.
Population: 622 (2000); Race: 97.3% White, 0.0% Black, 1.9% Asian, 0.0% American Indian and Alaska Native, 0.8% Hispanic of any race, 0.0% two or more races (2000); Density: 19.0 persons per square mile (2000); Age: 23.3% under 18, 16.0% over 64 (2000); Marriage status: 32.1% never married, 57.5% now married, 2.8% widowed, 7.5% divorced (2000); Foreign born: 0.9% (2000); Ancestry (includes multiple ancestries): 53.2% German, 19.7% Norwegian, 12.2% Irish, 7.2% Polish, 6.1% French (except Basque) (2000).
Economy: Railroad junction. Trade center for agricultural area: grain, potatoes, beans; livestock, poultry; dairying. Manufacturing: machining, printing and publishing. Employment by occupation: 9.1% management, 11.6% professional, 16.4% services, 17.6% sales, 1.3% farming, 9.7% construction, 34.3% production (2000).
Income: Per capita income: $15,711 (2000); Median household income: $40,469 (2000); Poverty rate: 6.3% (2000).
Taxes: Total city taxes per capita: $64 (1997); City property taxes per capita: $64 (1997).
Education: High school graduation rate: 89.7% (2000); College graduation rate: 7.0% (2000).
Housing: Homeownership rate: 90.9% (2000); Median home value: $60,400 (2000); Median rent: $192 per month (2000); Median age of housing: 37 years (2000).
Transportation: Commute to work: 83.8% car, 0.6% public transportation, 3.2% walk, 10.8% work from home (2000); Travel time to work: 42.3% less than 15 minutes, 37.4% 15 to 30 minutes, 3.9% 30 to 45 minutes, 8.9% 45 to 60 minutes, 7.5% 60 minutes or more (2000); Amtrak: Service available.

STOWE PRAIRIE (township). Covers a land area of 33.825 square miles and a water area of 0.057 square miles. Located at 46.33° N. Lat.; 95.09° W. Long.
Population: 529 (2000); Race: 98.3% White, 0.0% Black, 0.0% Asian, 0.0% American Indian and Alaska Native, 0.6% Hispanic of any race, 1.7% two or more races (2000); Density: 15.6 persons per square mile (2000); Age: 34.2% under 18, 8.1% over 64 (2000); Marriage status: 25.3% never married, 62.7% now married, 6.8% widowed, 5.3% divorced (2000); Foreign born: 0.6% (2000); Ancestry (includes multiple ancestries): 49.4% German, 13.0% Irish, 10.0% United States or American, 8.5% Norwegian, 7.5% Polish (2000).
Economy: Employment by occupation: 17.4% management, 9.7% professional, 11.2% services, 13.9% sales, 6.9% farming, 10.0% construction, 30.9% production (2000).
Income: Per capita income: $12,229 (2000); Median household income: $35,750 (2000); Poverty rate: 9.6% (2000).
Taxes: Total city taxes per capita: $34 (1997); City property taxes per capita: $34 (1997).
Education: High school graduation rate: 87.0% (2000); College graduation rate: 10.4% (2000).
Housing: Homeownership rate: 91.8% (2000); Median home value: $51,700 (2000); Median rent: $258 per month (2000); Median age of housing: 60+ years (2000).
Transportation: Commute to work: 78.8% car, 0.0% public transportation, 1.9% walk, 19.3% work from home (2000); Travel time to work: 33.5% less than 15 minutes, 49.3% 15 to 30 minutes, 9.6% 30 to 45 minutes, 4.3% 45 to 60 minutes, 3.3% 60 minutes or more (2000)

TURTLE CREEK (township). Covers a land area of 32.704 square miles and a water area of 3.029 square miles. Located at 46.16° N. Lat.; 94.72° W. Long.
Population: 323 (2000); Race: 95.5% White, 0.0% Black, 0.0% Asian, 0.0% American Indian and Alaska Native, 0.0% Hispanic of any race, 4.5% two or more races (2000); Density: 9.9 persons per square mile (2000); Age: 23.3% under 18, 17.9% over 64 (2000); Marriage status: 14.9% never married, 75.7% now married, 2.0% widowed, 7.5% divorced (2000); Foreign born: 0.0% (2000); Ancestry (includes multiple ancestries): 54.3% German, 25.9% Polish, 11.5% Norwegian, 9.3% Swedish, 6.1% Irish (2000).
Economy: Employment by occupation: 15.4% management, 19.6% professional, 16.1% services, 18.9% sales, 0.0% farming, 11.9% construction, 18.2% production (2000).
Income: Per capita income: $16,896 (2000); Median household income: $31,750 (2000); Poverty rate: 16.0% (2000).
Taxes: Total city taxes per capita: $188 (1997); City property taxes per capita: $188 (1997).
Education: High school graduation rate: 80.7% (2000); College graduation rate: 9.4% (2000).
Housing: Homeownership rate: 90.6% (2000); Median home value: $105,600 (2000); Median rent: $225 per month (2000); Median age of housing: 31 years (2000).
Transportation: Commute to work: 88.7% car, 0.0% public transportation, 2.8% walk, 8.5% work from home (2000); Travel time to work: 17.8% less than 15 minutes, 38.8% 15 to 30 minutes, 23.3% 30 to 45 minutes, 9.3% 45 to 60 minutes, 10.9% 60 minutes or more (2000)

VILLARD (township). Covers a land area of 30.099 square miles and a water area of 1.583 square miles. Located at 46.31° N. Lat.; 94.72° W. Long.
Population: 592 (2000); Race: 98.6% White, 0.0% Black, 0.3% Asian, 0.0% American Indian and Alaska Native, 0.0% Hispanic of any race, 1.0% two or more races (2000); Density: 19.7 persons per square mile (2000); Age: 28.4% under 18, 7.2% over 64 (2000); Marriage status: 25.8% never married, 63.9% now married, 3.3% widowed, 7.0% divorced (2000); Foreign born: 0.0% (2000); Ancestry (includes multiple ancestries): 45.8% German, 22.9% Norwegian, 9.5% Irish, 6.4% Swedish, 5.9% Polish (2000).
Economy: Employment by occupation: 12.3% management, 12.6% professional, 14.7% services, 20.7% sales, 1.4% farming, 10.5% construction, 27.7% production (2000).
Income: Per capita income: $16,025 (2000); Median household income: $40,556 (2000); Poverty rate: 7.9% (2000).
Taxes: Total city taxes per capita: $44 (2000); City property taxes per capita: $42 (2000).
Education: High school graduation rate: 87.2% (2000); College graduation rate: 9.5% (2000).
Housing: Homeownership rate: 90.4% (2000); Median home value: $82,200 (2000); Median rent: $300 per month (2000); Median age of housing: 25 years (2000).
Transportation: Commute to work: 86.5% car, 0.0% public transportation, 1.8% walk, 10.0% work from home (2000); Travel time to work: 45.8% less than 15 minutes, 25.7% 15 to 30 minutes, 10.3% 30 to 45 minutes, 4.7% 45 to 60 minutes, 13.4% 60 minutes or more (2000)

WARD (township). Covers a land area of 35.879 square miles and a water area of 0.425 square miles. Located at 46.14° N. Lat.; 94.83° W. Long.
Population: 471 (2000); Race: 100.0% White, 0.0% Black, 0.0% Asian, 0.0% American Indian and Alaska Native, 2.2% Hispanic of any race, 0.0% two or more races (2000); Density: 13.1 persons per square mile (2000); Age: 25.3% under 18, 18.6% over 64 (2000); Marriage status: 24.4% never married, 66.7% now married, 4.6% widowed, 4.3% divorced (2000); Foreign born: 0.0% (2000); Ancestry (includes multiple ancestries): 39.3% German, 17.8% Polish, 10.6% Norwegian, 10.6% Swedish, 8.2% English (2000).
Economy: Employment by occupation: 15.4% management, 17.8% professional, 10.1% services, 16.6% sales, 3.6% farming, 8.3% construction, 28.4% production (2000).
Income: Per capita income: $15,830 (2000); Median household income: $33,304 (2000); Poverty rate: 1.9% (2000).
Taxes: Total city taxes per capita: $49 (1997); City property taxes per capita: $49 (1997).
Education: High school graduation rate: 83.1% (2000); College graduation rate: 10.0% (2000).
Housing: Homeownership rate: 91.3% (2000); Median home value: $82,500 (2000); Median rent: $608 per month (2000); Median age of housing: 41 years (2000).
Transportation: Commute to work: 85.5% car, 0.0% public transportation, 4.8% walk, 8.5% work from home (2000); Travel time to work: 16.6% less than 15 minutes, 58.9% 15 to 30 minutes, 13.9% 30 to 45 minutes, 4.6% 45 to 60 minutes, 6.0% 60 minutes or more (2000)

WEST UNION (city). Covers a land area of 0.344 square miles and a water area of 0 square miles. Located at 45.79° N. Lat.; 95.08° W. Long. Elevation is 1,337 feet.
Population: 87 (2000); Race: 100.0% White, 0.0% Black, 0.0% Asian, 0.0% American Indian and Alaska Native, 0.0% Hispanic of any race, 0.0% two or more races (2000); Density: 252.8 persons per square mile (2000); Age: 36.3% under 18, 22.0% over 64 (2000); Marriage status: 22.6% never

married, 61.3% now married, 4.8% widowed, 11.3% divorced (2000); Foreign born: 0.0% (2000); Ancestry (includes multiple ancestries): 54.9% German, 12.1% Norwegian, 11.0% Belgian, 8.8% Italian, 7.7% Irish (2000).
Economy: Employment by occupation: 6.7% management, 23.3% professional, 20.0% services, 30.0% sales, 0.0% farming, 0.0% construction, 20.0% production (2000).
Income: Per capita income: $10,441 (2000); Median household income: $24,643 (2000); Poverty rate: 23.1% (2000).
Taxes: Total city taxes per capita: $63 (1997); City property taxes per capita: $48 (1997).
Education: High school graduation rate: 66.1% (2000); College graduation rate: 3.6% (2000).
Housing: Homeownership rate: 90.3% (2000); Median home value: $45,000 (2000); Median rent: $225 per month (2000); Median age of housing: 49 years (2000).
Transportation: Commute to work: 86.7% car, 0.0% public transportation, 0.0% walk, 13.3% work from home (2000); Travel time to work: 38.5% less than 15 minutes, 61.5% 15 to 30 minutes, 0.0% 30 to 45 minutes, 0.0% 45 to 60 minutes, 0.0% 60 minutes or more (2000)

WEST UNION (township). Covers a land area of 28.842 square miles and a water area of 0.815 square miles. Located at 45.80° N. Lat.; 95.06° W. Long. Elevation is 1,337 feet.
Population: 312 (2000); Race: 98.8% White, 0.0% Black, 0.0% Asian, 0.0% American Indian and Alaska Native, 0.0% Hispanic of any race, 1.2% two or more races (2000); Density: 10.8 persons per square mile (2000); Age: 36.8% under 18, 7.3% over 64 (2000); Marriage status: 28.5% never married, 64.3% now married, 3.4% widowed, 3.8% divorced (2000); Foreign born: 0.6% (2000); Ancestry (includes multiple ancestries): 69.9% German, 15.2% Norwegian, 10.9% Swedish, 5.2% Irish, 2.4% Czech (2000).
Economy: Dairying; poultry; grain. Employment by occupation: 32.0% management, 11.8% professional, 7.3% services, 17.4% sales, 11.8% farming, 5.1% construction, 14.6% production (2000).
Income: Per capita income: $15,175 (2000); Median household income: $41,406 (2000); Poverty rate: 7.9% (2000).
Taxes: Total city taxes per capita: $14 (1997); City property taxes per capita: $14 (1997).
Education: High school graduation rate: 85.5% (2000); College graduation rate: 9.5% (2000).
Housing: Homeownership rate: 89.9% (2000); Median home value: $79,200 (2000); Median rent: $275 per month (2000); Median age of housing: 34 years (2000).
Transportation: Commute to work: 63.4% car, 0.0% public transportation, 1.7% walk, 34.9% work from home (2000); Travel time to work: 34.2% less than 15 minutes, 43.9% 15 to 30 minutes, 18.4% 30 to 45 minutes, 1.8% 45 to 60 minutes, 1.8% 60 minutes or more (2000)

WYKEHAM (township). Covers a land area of 34.835 square miles and a water area of 0.155 square miles. Located at 46.14° N. Lat.; 95.07° W. Long.
Population: 436 (2000); Race: 97.9% White, 0.8% Black, 0.0% Asian, 0.3% American Indian and Alaska Native, 0.5% Hispanic of any race, 1.0% two or more races (2000); Density: 12.5 persons per square mile (2000); Age: 26.8% under 18, 14.7% over 64 (2000); Marriage status: 23.9% never married, 70.4% now married, 3.7% widowed, 2.0% divorced (2000); Foreign born: 0.5% (2000); Ancestry (includes multiple ancestries): 50.4% German, 22.8% Norwegian, 8.4% English, 6.6% Polish, 4.5% Czech (2000).
Economy: Employment by occupation: 15.9% management, 10.1% professional, 17.5% services, 18.0% sales, 1.1% farming, 11.1% construction, 26.5% production (2000).
Income: Per capita income: $16,184 (2000); Median household income: $31,250 (2000); Poverty rate: 13.6% (2000).
Taxes: Total city taxes per capita: $42 (1997); City property taxes per capita: $42 (1997).
Education: High school graduation rate: 82.4% (2000); College graduation rate: 5.3% (2000).
Housing: Homeownership rate: 91.4% (2000); Median home value: $57,500 (2000); Median age of housing: 60+ years (2000).
Transportation: Commute to work: 77.8% car, 0.0% public transportation, 2.7% walk, 15.7% work from home (2000); Travel time to work: 25.0% less than 15 minutes, 29.5% 15 to 30 minutes, 19.9% 30 to 45 minutes, 12.8% 45 to 60 minutes, 12.8% 60 minutes or more (2000)

Traverse County

Located in western Minnesota; bounded on the west by the Bois de Sioux River and Lake Traverse and the North and South Dakota borders; watered by the Mustinka River. Covers a land area of 574.10 square miles, a water area of 11.90 square miles, and is located in the Central Time Zone. The county government was organized in 1862. County seat is Wheaton.

Weather Station: Browns Valley — Elevation: 984 feet

	Jan	Feb	Mar	Apr	May	Jun	Jul	Aug	Sep	Oct	Nov	Dec
High	21	27	38	56	71	79	85	82	73	59	39	26
Low	1	8	20	33	46	55	61	58	48	35	21	8
Precip	0.9	0.6	1.7	2.1	2.4	3.4	3.3	2.9	1.9	1.8	1.1	0.5
Snow	10.8	7.6	9.1	2.4	0.0	0.0	0.0	0.0	0.0	0.3	6.8	5.7

High and Low temperatures in degrees Fahrenheit; Precipitation and Snow in inches

Weather Station: Wheaton — Elevation: 1,017 feet

	Jan	Feb	Mar	Apr	May	Jun	Jul	Aug	Sep	Oct	Nov	Dec
High	20	28	39	58	72	80	85	84	74	61	40	26
Low	1	8	20	34	46	56	60	58	48	37	22	8
Precip	0.9	0.5	1.5	2.0	2.6	3.7	3.1	2.5	2.1	1.9	1.1	0.5
Snow	11.0	6.1	8.7	2.3	tr	0.0	0.0	0.0	0.0	0.3	5.4	6.4

High and Low temperatures in degrees Fahrenheit; Precipitation and Snow in inches

Population: 4,134 (2000); Race: 96.6% White, 0.0% Black, 0.3% Asian, 2.3% American Indian and Alaska Native, 1.1% Hispanic of any race, 0.5% two or more races (2000); Density: 7.2 persons per square mile (2000); Age: 25.5% under 18, 26.5% over 64 (2000).
Religion: Five largest groups: 29.4% Catholic Church, 29.1% Lutheran Church—Missouri Synod, 14.6% Evangelical Lutheran Church in America, 6.6% Presbyterian Church (U.S.A.), 6.0% Episcopal Church (2000).
Economy: Unemployment rate: 2.8% (11/2002); Total civilian labor force: 1,593 (11/2002); Leading industries: Companies that employ more than 1,000 persons: 0 (2000); Companies that employ more than 100 persons: 0 (2000); Farms: 385 totaling 315,068 acres (1997); Minority business ownership rate: 0.0% (1997); Women business ownership rate: 0.0% (1997); Retail sales per capita: $7,402 (1997). Single-family building permits issued: 6 (2001) / 6 (2000); Multi-family building permits issued: 0 (2001) / 0 (2000).
Income: Per capita income: $16,378 (2000); Median household income: $30,617 (2000); Poverty rate: 12.0% (2000); Bankruptcy rate: 1.67% (2001).
Taxes: Total county taxes per capita: $415 (1997); County property taxes per capita: $409 (1997).
Education: High school graduation rate: 82.2% (2000); College graduation rate: 10.7% (2000).
Housing: Homeownership rate: 80.5% (2000); Median home value: $34,100 (2000); Median rent: $283 per month (2000); Median age of housing: 50 years (2000).
Health: Birth rate: 94.3 per 10,000 population (1998); Age adjusted death rate: 76.1 per 10,000 population (1999); Age adjusted cancer mortality rate: 169.5 (Unreliable figure as per CDC) deaths per 100,000 population (1999). Number of physicians: 7.3 per 10,000 population (1999); Number of hospital beds: 60.5 per 10,000 population (1999).
Elections: 2000 Presidential election results: 42.0% Gore, 51.0% Bush, 4.1% Nader, 2.6% Buchanan
National and State Parks: Foley State Wildlife Management Area; Reservation Dam State Wildlife Management Ar; White Rock Dam State Wildlife Management Are
Additional Information Contacts
Traverse County Government Offices 320-563-4242
Wheaton Chamber of Commerce 320-563-8794

Traverse County Communities

ARTHUR (township). Covers a land area of 36.049 square miles and a water area of 0.326 square miles. Located at 45.64° N. Lat.; 96.70° W. Long.
Population: 109 (2000); Race: 100.0% White, 0.0% Black, 0.0% Asian, 0.0% American Indian and Alaska Native, 0.0% Hispanic of any race, 0.0% two or more races (2000); Density: 3.0 persons per square mile (2000); Age: 38.0% under 18, 16.3% over 64 (2000); Marriage status: 19.7% never married, 71.2% now married, 9.1% widowed, 0.0% divorced (2000); Foreign born: 0.0% (2000); Ancestry (includes multiple ancestries): 46.7% German, 15.2% French (except Basque), 12.0% Irish, 9.8% Czech, 9.8% Swedish (2000).
Economy: Employment by occupation: 55.2% management, 6.9% professional, 3.4% services, 24.1% sales, 0.0% farming, 6.9% construction, 3.4% production (2000).

Income: Per capita income: $10,334 (2000); Median household income: $31,563 (2000); Poverty rate: 20.7% (2000).
Taxes: Total city taxes per capita: $83 (1997); City property taxes per capita: $83 (1997).
Education: High school graduation rate: 83.6% (2000); College graduation rate: 1.8% (2000).
Housing: Homeownership rate: 86.2% (2000); Median home value: $40,000 (2000); Median age of housing: 60+ years (2000).
Transportation: Commute to work: 51.7% car, 0.0% public transportation, 0.0% walk, 48.3% work from home (2000); Travel time to work: 80.0% less than 15 minutes, 20.0% 15 to 30 minutes, 0.0% 30 to 45 minutes, 0.0% 45 to 60 minutes, 0.0% 60 minutes or more (2000)

BROWNS VALLEY (city). Covers a land area of 0.785 square miles and a water area of 0 square miles. Located at 45.59° N. Lat.; 96.83° W. Long.
History: Remains of Browns Valley man, associated by some anthropologists with Folsom culture, found here 1934.
Population: 690 (2000); Race: 85.0% White, 0.0% Black, 0.3% Asian, 13.2% American Indian and Alaska Native, 2.0% Hispanic of any race, 1.1% two or more races (2000); Density: 878.5 persons per square mile (2000); Age: 24.4% under 18, 26.6% over 64 (2000); Marriage status: 25.0% never married, 51.3% now married, 16.2% widowed, 7.5% divorced (2000); Foreign born: 0.7% (2000); Ancestry (includes multiple ancestries): 41.5% German, 17.8% Other groups, 14.9% Norwegian, 9.0% Polish, 8.0% Irish (2000).
Economy: Grain, soybeans, sunflowers, sugar beets; livestock, poultry; dairying. Manufacturing: fertilizer. Single-family building permits issued: 1 (2001) / 1 (2000); Multi-family building permits issued: 0 (2001) / 0 (2000); Employment by occupation: 9.3% management, 11.1% professional, 21.8% services, 32.5% sales, 3.5% farming, 7.3% construction, 14.5% production (2000).
Income: Per capita income: $15,062 (2000); Median household income: $26,563 (2000); Poverty rate: 14.4% (2000).
Taxes: Total city taxes per capita: $187 (1997); City property taxes per capita: $180 (1997).
Education: High school graduation rate: 74.1% (2000); College graduation rate: 12.0% (2000).

School District(s)

Browns Valley (PK-12)
2000 Enrollment: 169 320-695-2103
Housing: Homeownership rate: 68.9% (2000); Median home value: $19,200 (2000); Median rent: $270 per month (2000); Median age of housing: 58 years (2000).
Newspapers: The Valley News (1 x week)
Transportation: Commute to work: 82.6% car, 0.0% public transportation, 13.1% walk, 3.5% work from home (2000); Travel time to work: 59.9% less than 15 minutes, 18.8% 15 to 30 minutes, 13.6% 30 to 45 minutes, 3.7% 45 to 60 minutes, 4.0% 60 minutes or more (2000)

CLIFTON (township). Covers a land area of 38.326 square miles and a water area of 0 square miles. Located at 45.81° N. Lat.; 96.30° W. Long.
Population: 92 (2000); Race: 100.0% White, 0.0% Black, 0.0% Asian, 0.0% American Indian and Alaska Native, 3.4% Hispanic of any race, 0.0% two or more races (2000); Density: 2.4 persons per square mile (2000); Age: 38.5% under 18, 16.2% over 64 (2000); Marriage status: 19.5% never married, 80.5% now married, 0.0% widowed, 0.0% divorced (2000); Foreign born: 0.0% (2000); Ancestry (includes multiple ancestries): 57.3% German, 18.8% Norwegian, 12.8% Finnish, 10.3% United States or American, 10.3% Polish (2000).
Economy: Employment by occupation: 45.8% management, 4.2% professional, 0.0% services, 16.7% sales, 8.3% farming, 8.3% construction, 16.7% production (2000).
Income: Per capita income: $14,879 (2000); Median household income: $60,714 (2000); Poverty rate: 3.4% (2000).
Taxes: Total city taxes per capita: $184 (1997); City property taxes per capita: $184 (1997).
Education: High school graduation rate: 91.0% (2000); College graduation rate: 19.4% (2000).
Housing: Homeownership rate: 94.3% (2000); Median home value: $35,000 (2000); Median age of housing: 55 years (2000).
Transportation: Commute to work: 56.3% car, 0.0% public transportation, 0.0% walk, 43.8% work from home (2000); Travel time to work: 66.7% less than 15 minutes, 18.5% 15 to 30 minutes, 7.4% 30 to 45 minutes, 3.7% 45 to 60 minutes, 3.7% 60 minutes or more (2000)

CROKE (township). Covers a land area of 35.893 square miles and a water area of 0 square miles. Located at 45.71° N. Lat.; 96.44° W. Long.
Population: 84 (2000); Race: 100.0% White, 0.0% Black, 0.0% Asian, 0.0% American Indian and Alaska Native, 0.0% Hispanic of any race, 0.0% two or more races (2000); Density: 2.3 persons per square mile (2000); Age: 10.2% under 18, 28.4% over 64 (2000); Marriage status: 18.3% never married, 72.0% now married, 4.9% widowed, 4.9% divorced (2000); Foreign born: 0.0% (2000); Ancestry (includes multiple ancestries): 56.8% German, 13.6% Swedish, 11.4% Norwegian, 9.1% Irish, 9.1% French (except Basque) (2000).
Economy: Employment by occupation: 37.5% management, 8.3% professional, 12.5% services, 8.3% sales, 10.4% farming, 10.4% construction, 12.5% production (2000).
Income: Per capita income: $28,122 (2000); Median household income: $38,750 (2000); Poverty rate: 2.3% (2000).
Education: High school graduation rate: 88.7% (2000); College graduation rate: 16.9% (2000).
Housing: Homeownership rate: 90.0% (2000); Median home value: $55,000 (2000); Median age of housing: 60+ years (2000).
Transportation: Commute to work: 54.3% car, 0.0% public transportation, 4.3% walk, 41.3% work from home (2000); Travel time to work: 81.5% less than 15 minutes, 0.0% 15 to 30 minutes, 7.4% 30 to 45 minutes, 0.0% 45 to 60 minutes, 11.1% 60 minutes or more (2000)

DOLLYMOUNT (township). Covers a land area of 38.395 square miles and a water area of 0 square miles. Located at 45.70° N. Lat.; 96.30° W. Long.
Population: 83 (2000); Race: 100.0% White, 0.0% Black, 0.0% Asian, 0.0% American Indian and Alaska Native, 0.0% Hispanic of any race, 0.0% two or more races (2000); Density: 2.2 persons per square mile (2000); Age: 31.6% under 18, 15.2% over 64 (2000); Marriage status: 26.6% never married, 62.5% now married, 3.1% widowed, 7.8% divorced (2000); Foreign born: 0.0% (2000); Ancestry (includes multiple ancestries): 74.7% German, 21.5% Swedish, 11.4% Norwegian, 10.1% Dutch, 3.8% Danish (2000).
Economy: Employment by occupation: 51.6% management, 9.7% professional, 6.5% services, 12.9% sales, 6.5% farming, 6.5% construction, 6.5% production (2000).
Income: Per capita income: $14,587 (2000); Median household income: $42,083 (2000); Poverty rate: 3.8% (2000).
Taxes: Total city taxes per capita: $130 (1997); City property taxes per capita: $130 (1997).
Education: High school graduation rate: 91.5% (2000); College graduation rate: 8.5% (2000).
Housing: Homeownership rate: 72.0% (2000); Median home value: $52,500 (2000); Median rent: $192 per month (2000); Median age of housing: 55 years (2000).
Transportation: Commute to work: 64.5% car, 0.0% public transportation, 0.0% walk, 35.5% work from home (2000); Travel time to work: 55.0% less than 15 minutes, 25.0% 15 to 30 minutes, 10.0% 30 to 45 minutes, 0.0% 45 to 60 minutes, 10.0% 60 minutes or more (2000)

DUMONT (city). Covers a land area of 0.434 square miles and a water area of 0 square miles. Located at 45.71° N. Lat.; 96.42° W. Long.
Population: 122 (2000); Race: 100.0% White, 0.0% Black, 0.0% Asian, 0.0% American Indian and Alaska Native, 0.0% Hispanic of any race, 0.0% two or more races (2000); Density: 281.4 persons per square mile (2000); Age: 27.5% under 18, 25.8% over 64 (2000); Marriage status: 18.9% never married, 64.2% now married, 9.5% widowed, 7.4% divorced (2000); Foreign born: 3.3% (2000); Ancestry (includes multiple ancestries): 60.0% German, 27.5% Irish, 10.0% Swedish, 9.2% Norwegian, 5.0% English (2000).
Economy: Dairy products. Single-family building permits issued: 0 (2001) / 0 (2000); Multi-family building permits issued: 0 (2001) / 0 (2000); Employment by occupation: 24.1% management, 20.7% professional, 25.9% services, 6.9% sales, 5.2% farming, 3.4% construction, 13.8% production (2000).
Income: Per capita income: $23,118 (2000); Median household income: $28,750 (2000); Poverty rate: 20.8% (2000).
Taxes: Total city taxes per capita: $215 (1997); City property taxes per capita: $198 (1997).
Education: High school graduation rate: 71.4% (2000); College graduation rate: 22.6% (2000).
Housing: Homeownership rate: 96.2% (2000); Median home value: $26,000 (2000); Median rent: $125 per month (2000); Median age of housing: 56 years (2000).

Transportation: Commute to work: 94.0% car, 0.0% public transportation, 6.0% walk, 0.0% work from home (2000); Travel time to work: 68.0% less than 15 minutes, 12.0% 15 to 30 minutes, 16.0% 30 to 45 minutes, 0.0% 45 to 60 minutes, 4.0% 60 minutes or more (2000)

FOLSOM (township). Covers a land area of 19.868 square miles and a water area of 1.818 square miles. Located at 45.62° N. Lat.; 96.81° W. Long.
Population: 149 (2000); Race: 100.0% White, 0.0% Black, 0.0% Asian, 0.0% American Indian and Alaska Native, 3.8% Hispanic of any race, 0.0% two or more races (2000); Density: 7.5 persons per square mile (2000); Age: 30.6% under 18, 20.6% over 64 (2000); Marriage status: 12.3% never married, 77.0% now married, 7.4% widowed, 3.3% divorced (2000); Foreign born: 0.0% (2000); Ancestry (includes multiple ancestries): 48.8% German, 26.9% Norwegian, 13.8% Polish, 8.8% Irish, 5.6% Swedish (2000).
Economy: Employment by occupation: 26.9% management, 11.5% professional, 30.8% services, 21.2% sales, 0.0% farming, 5.8% construction, 3.8% production (2000).
Income: Per capita income: $11,613 (2000); Median household income: $22,321 (2000); Poverty rate: 23.8% (2000).
Taxes: Total city taxes per capita: $43 (1997); City property taxes per capita: $43 (1997).
Education: High school graduation rate: 92.7% (2000); College graduation rate: 12.8% (2000).
Housing: Homeownership rate: 92.1% (2000); Median home value: $52,500 (2000); Median rent: $125 per month (2000); Median age of housing: 43 years (2000).
Transportation: Commute to work: 77.1% car, 0.0% public transportation, 4.2% walk, 18.8% work from home (2000); Travel time to work: 79.5% less than 15 minutes, 5.1% 15 to 30 minutes, 10.3% 30 to 45 minutes, 0.0% 45 to 60 minutes, 5.1% 60 minutes or more (2000)

LAKE VALLEY (township). Covers a land area of 58.839 square miles and a water area of 3.100 square miles. Located at 45.80° N. Lat.; 96.51° W. Long.
Population: 276 (2000); Race: 100.0% White, 0.0% Black, 0.0% Asian, 0.0% American Indian and Alaska Native, 0.0% Hispanic of any race, 0.0% two or more races (2000); Density: 4.7 persons per square mile (2000); Age: 36.6% under 18, 19.4% over 64 (2000); Marriage status: 20.8% never married, 66.0% now married, 10.2% widowed, 3.0% divorced (2000); Foreign born: 0.0% (2000); Ancestry (includes multiple ancestries): 69.4% German, 21.6% Swedish, 12.7% Norwegian, 11.2% Irish, 6.0% Czech (2000).
Economy: Single-family building permits issued: 0 (2001) / 0 (2000); Multi-family building permits issued: 0 (2001) / 0 (2000); Employment by occupation: 18.8% management, 21.4% professional, 16.1% services, 25.9% sales, 0.0% farming, 5.4% construction, 12.5% production (2000).
Income: Per capita income: $16,176 (2000); Median household income: $35,625 (2000); Poverty rate: 6.3% (2000).
Taxes: Total city taxes per capita: $49 (1997); City property taxes per capita: $49 (1997).
Education: High school graduation rate: 93.9% (2000); College graduation rate: 9.8% (2000).
Housing: Homeownership rate: 97.9% (2000); Median home value: $77,000 (2000); Median age of housing: 54 years (2000).
Transportation: Commute to work: 90.0% car, 0.0% public transportation, 0.0% walk, 10.0% work from home (2000); Travel time to work: 86.9% less than 15 minutes, 7.1% 15 to 30 minutes, 2.0% 30 to 45 minutes, 4.0% 45 to 60 minutes, 0.0% 60 minutes or more (2000)

LEONARDSVILLE (township). Covers a land area of 38.527 square miles and a water area of 0 square miles. Located at 45.61° N. Lat.; 96.31° W. Long.
Population: 150 (2000); Race: 100.0% White, 0.0% Black, 0.0% Asian, 0.0% American Indian and Alaska Native, 2.2% Hispanic of any race, 0.0% two or more races (2000); Density: 3.9 persons per square mile (2000); Age: 31.3% under 18, 26.1% over 64 (2000); Marriage status: 15.6% never married, 77.1% now married, 7.3% widowed, 0.0% divorced (2000); Foreign born: 3.0% (2000); Ancestry (includes multiple ancestries): 68.7% German, 14.2% Norwegian, 9.7% Irish, 7.5% United States or American, 6.0% Swedish (2000).
Economy: Employment by occupation: 28.0% management, 20.0% professional, 18.0% services, 12.0% sales, 12.0% farming, 2.0% construction, 8.0% production (2000).
Income: Per capita income: $10,125 (2000); Median household income: $26,875 (2000); Poverty rate: 17.2% (2000).
Taxes: Total city taxes per capita: $54 (1997); City property taxes per capita: $54 (1997).
Education: High school graduation rate: 86.7% (2000); College graduation rate: 8.4% (2000).
Housing: Homeownership rate: 93.6% (2000); Median home value: $56,300 (2000); Median rent: $225 per month (2000); Median age of housing: 40 years (2000).
Transportation: Commute to work: 62.0% car, 0.0% public transportation, 4.0% walk, 28.0% work from home (2000); Travel time to work: 33.3% less than 15 minutes, 47.2% 15 to 30 minutes, 0.0% 30 to 45 minutes, 11.1% 45 to 60 minutes, 8.3% 60 minutes or more (2000)

MONSON (township). Covers a land area of 54.192 square miles and a water area of 0.042 square miles. Located at 45.89° N. Lat.; 96.47° W. Long.
Population: 162 (2000); Race: 100.0% White, 0.0% Black, 0.0% Asian, 0.0% American Indian and Alaska Native, 0.0% Hispanic of any race, 0.0% two or more races (2000); Density: 3.0 persons per square mile (2000); Age: 39.2% under 18, 9.7% over 64 (2000); Marriage status: 19.4% never married, 77.4% now married, 1.6% widowed, 1.6% divorced (2000); Foreign born: 0.0% (2000); Ancestry (includes multiple ancestries): 52.2% German, 29.6% Swedish, 8.1% Norwegian, 7.0% Danish, 5.4% Irish (2000).
Economy: Employment by occupation: 23.8% management, 15.5% professional, 14.3% services, 14.3% sales, 7.1% farming, 8.3% construction, 16.7% production (2000).
Income: Per capita income: $13,454 (2000); Median household income: $42,500 (2000); Poverty rate: 7.0% (2000).
Taxes: Total city taxes per capita: $91 (1997); City property taxes per capita: $91 (1997).
Education: High school graduation rate: 90.3% (2000); College graduation rate: 9.7% (2000).
Housing: Homeownership rate: 96.4% (2000); Median home value: $40,000 (2000); Median age of housing: 60+ years (2000).
Transportation: Commute to work: 84.1% car, 0.0% public transportation, 0.0% walk, 15.9% work from home (2000); Travel time to work: 52.2% less than 15 minutes, 29.0% 15 to 30 minutes, 15.9% 30 to 45 minutes, 2.9% 45 to 60 minutes, 0.0% 60 minutes or more (2000)

PARNELL (township). Covers a land area of 36.424 square miles and a water area of 0.027 square miles. Located at 45.63° N. Lat.; 96.58° W. Long.
Population: 62 (2000); Race: 100.0% White, 0.0% Black, 0.0% Asian, 0.0% American Indian and Alaska Native, 0.0% Hispanic of any race, 0.0% two or more races (2000); Density: 1.7 persons per square mile (2000); Age: 27.9% under 18, 27.9% over 64 (2000); Marriage status: 23.5% never married, 62.7% now married, 3.9% widowed, 9.8% divorced (2000); Foreign born: 0.0% (2000); Ancestry (includes multiple ancestries): 60.3% German, 33.8% Irish, 22.1% Swedish, 10.3% English, 4.4% Polish (2000).
Economy: Employment by occupation: 69.2% management, 0.0% professional, 23.1% services, 7.7% sales, 0.0% farming, 0.0% construction, 0.0% production (2000).
Income: Per capita income: $10,887 (2000); Median household income: $30,000 (2000); Poverty rate: 29.4% (2000).
Taxes: Total city taxes per capita: $113 (2000); City property taxes per capita: $113 (2000).
Education: High school graduation rate: 77.6% (2000); College graduation rate: 10.2% (2000).
Housing: Homeownership rate: 87.5% (2000); Median home value: $45,000 (2000); Median age of housing: 60+ years (2000).
Transportation: Commute to work: 57.7% car, 0.0% public transportation, 0.0% walk, 42.3% work from home (2000); Travel time to work: 46.7% less than 15 minutes, 20.0% 15 to 30 minutes, 13.3% 30 to 45 minutes, 20.0% 45 to 60 minutes, 0.0% 60 minutes or more (2000)

REDPATH (township). Covers a land area of 38.948 square miles and a water area of 0 square miles. Located at 45.89° N. Lat.; 96.32° W. Long.
Population: 35 (2000); Race: 100.0% White, 0.0% Black, 0.0% Asian, 0.0% American Indian and Alaska Native, 0.0% Hispanic of any race, 0.0% two or more races (2000); Density: 0.9 persons per square mile (2000); Age: 17.5% under 18, 25.0% over 64 (2000); Marriage status: 22.2% never married, 77.8% now married, 0.0% widowed, 0.0% divorced (2000); Foreign born: 0.0% (2000); Ancestry (includes multiple ancestries): 32.5% German, 20.0% Swedish, 15.0% Irish, 12.5% Scandinavian, 5.0% Danish (2000).
Economy: Employment by occupation: 31.8% management, 18.2% professional, 9.1% services, 9.1% sales, 0.0% farming, 22.7% construction, 9.1% production (2000).
Income: Per capita income: $16,190 (2000); Median household income: $29,375 (2000); Poverty rate: 0.0% (2000).

Taxes: Total city taxes per capita: $131 (1997); City property taxes per capita: $131 (1997).
Education: High school graduation rate: 93.5% (2000); College graduation rate: 19.4% (2000).
Housing: Homeownership rate: 58.8% (2000); Median home value: $60,000 (2000); Median rent: $175 per month (2000); Median age of housing: 42 years (2000).
Transportation: Commute to work: 59.1% car, 0.0% public transportation, 18.2% walk, 22.7% work from home (2000); Travel time to work: 58.8% less than 15 minutes, 41.2% 15 to 30 minutes, 0.0% 30 to 45 minutes, 0.0% 45 to 60 minutes, 0.0% 60 minutes or more (2000)

TARA (township). Covers a land area of 36.179 square miles and a water area of 0.229 square miles. Located at 45.63° N. Lat.; 96.43° W. Long.
Population: 126 (2000); Race: 100.0% White, 0.0% Black, 0.0% Asian, 0.0% American Indian and Alaska Native, 0.0% Hispanic of any race, 0.0% two or more races (2000); Density: 3.5 persons per square mile (2000); Age: 29.4% under 18, 23.0% over 64 (2000); Marriage status: 15.1% never married, 80.6% now married, 2.2% widowed, 2.2% divorced (2000); Foreign born: 0.0% (2000); Ancestry (includes multiple ancestries): 69.8% German, 15.1% Irish, 15.1% Czech, 11.1% Swedish, 2.4% Swiss (2000).
Economy: Employment by occupation: 37.5% management, 7.1% professional, 14.3% services, 16.1% sales, 0.0% farming, 7.1% construction, 17.9% production (2000).
Income: Per capita income: $18,640 (2000); Median household income: $42,813 (2000); Poverty rate: 3.2% (2000).
Taxes: Total city taxes per capita: $61 (1997); City property taxes per capita: $61 (1997).
Education: High school graduation rate: 85.5% (2000); College graduation rate: 2.4% (2000).
Housing: Homeownership rate: 90.7% (2000); Median home value: $28,800 (2000); Median age of housing: 60+ years (2000).
Transportation: Commute to work: 60.7% car, 3.6% public transportation, 3.6% walk, 32.1% work from home (2000); Travel time to work: 31.6% less than 15 minutes, 36.8% 15 to 30 minutes, 28.9% 30 to 45 minutes, 0.0% 45 to 60 minutes, 2.6% 60 minutes or more (2000)

TAYLOR (township). Covers a land area of 51.970 square miles and a water area of 0 square miles. Located at 45.97° N. Lat.; 96.48° W. Long.
Population: 108 (2000); Race: 100.0% White, 0.0% Black, 0.0% Asian, 0.0% American Indian and Alaska Native, 0.0% Hispanic of any race, 0.0% two or more races (2000); Density: 2.1 persons per square mile (2000); Age: 21.5% under 18, 23.4% over 64 (2000); Marriage status: 7.1% never married, 78.6% now married, 7.1% widowed, 7.1% divorced (2000); Foreign born: 0.0% (2000); Ancestry (includes multiple ancestries): 41.1% German, 19.6% Norwegian, 16.8% Irish, 8.4% Swedish, 4.7% Other groups (2000).
Economy: Employment by occupation: 43.2% management, 4.5% professional, 0.0% services, 27.3% sales, 11.4% farming, 4.5% construction, 9.1% production (2000).
Income: Per capita income: $12,813 (2000); Median household income: $28,750 (2000); Poverty rate: 25.2% (2000).
Taxes: Total city taxes per capita: $138 (1997); City property taxes per capita: $138 (1997).
Education: High school graduation rate: 83.5% (2000); College graduation rate: 10.1% (2000).
Housing: Homeownership rate: 86.7% (2000); Median home value: $33,800 (2000); Median age of housing: 44 years (2000).
Transportation: Commute to work: 45.5% car, 0.0% public transportation, 0.0% walk, 54.5% work from home (2000); Travel time to work: 25.0% less than 15 minutes, 30.0% 15 to 30 minutes, 20.0% 30 to 45 minutes, 15.0% 45 to 60 minutes, 10.0% 60 minutes or more (2000)

TINTAH (city). Covers a land area of 0.755 square miles and a water area of 0 square miles. Located at 46.01° N. Lat.; 96.32° W. Long. Elevation is 999 feet.
Population: 79 (2000); Race: 100.0% White, 0.0% Black, 0.0% Asian, 0.0% American Indian and Alaska Native, 7.8% Hispanic of any race, 0.0% two or more races (2000); Density: 104.7 persons per square mile (2000); Age: 12.5% under 18, 35.9% over 64 (2000); Marriage status: 33.3% never married, 50.0% now married, 13.3% widowed, 3.3% divorced (2000); Foreign born: 3.1% (2000); Ancestry (includes multiple ancestries): 54.7% German, 15.6% English, 15.6% Norwegian, 14.1% Polish, 14.1% Irish (2000).
Economy: Single-family building permits issued: 0 (2001) / 0 (2000); Multi-family building permits issued: 0 (2001) / 0 (2000); Employment by occupation: 8.0% management, 0.0% professional, 12.0% services, 0.0% sales, 16.0% farming, 16.0% construction, 48.0% production (2000).
Income: Per capita income: $13,536 (2000); Median household income: $15,500 (2000); Poverty rate: 23.4% (2000).
Taxes: Total city taxes per capita: $86 (1997); City property taxes per capita: $86 (1997).
Education: High school graduation rate: 76.0% (2000); College graduation rate: 8.0% (2000).
Housing: Homeownership rate: 92.1% (2000); Median home value: $20,800 (2000); Median age of housing: 56 years (2000).
Transportation: Commute to work: 80.0% car, 0.0% public transportation, 20.0% walk, 0.0% work from home (2000); Travel time to work: 76.0% less than 15 minutes, 20.0% 15 to 30 minutes, 4.0% 30 to 45 minutes, 0.0% 45 to 60 minutes, 0.0% 60 minutes or more (2000)

TINTAH (township). Covers a land area of 34.938 square miles and a water area of 0 square miles. Located at 45.98° N. Lat.; 96.31° W. Long. Elevation is 999 feet.
Population: 53 (2000); Race: 100.0% White, 0.0% Black, 0.0% Asian, 0.0% American Indian and Alaska Native, 0.0% Hispanic of any race, 0.0% two or more races (2000); Density: 1.5 persons per square mile (2000); Age: 29.5% under 18, 13.6% over 64 (2000); Marriage status: 42.4% never married, 39.4% now married, 18.2% widowed, 0.0% divorced (2000); Foreign born: 0.0% (2000); Ancestry (includes multiple ancestries): 38.6% German, 25.0% Irish, 18.2% Norwegian, 15.9% Italian, 9.1% English (2000).
Economy: Grain, sunflowers; livestock; light manufacturing. Employment by occupation: 50.0% management, 11.1% professional, 0.0% services, 5.6% sales, 22.2% farming, 11.1% construction, 0.0% production (2000).
Income: Per capita income: $14,443 (2000); Median household income: $38,125 (2000); Poverty rate: 22.5% (2000).
Taxes: Total city taxes per capita: $101 (1997); City property taxes per capita: $101 (1997).
Education: High school graduation rate: 92.0% (2000); College graduation rate: 32.0% (2000).
Housing: Homeownership rate: 100.0% (2000); Median home value: $45,000 (2000); Median age of housing: 57 years (2000).
Transportation: Commute to work: 61.1% car, 0.0% public transportation, 0.0% walk, 38.9% work from home (2000); Travel time to work: 54.5% less than 15 minutes, 36.4% 15 to 30 minutes, 9.1% 30 to 45 minutes, 0.0% 45 to 60 minutes, 0.0% 60 minutes or more (2000)

WALLS (township). Covers a land area of 36.105 square miles and a water area of 0.216 square miles. Located at 45.72° N. Lat.; 96.58° W. Long.
Population: 81 (2000); Race: 100.0% White, 0.0% Black, 0.0% Asian, 0.0% American Indian and Alaska Native, 0.0% Hispanic of any race, 0.0% two or more races (2000); Density: 2.2 persons per square mile (2000); Age: 32.7% under 18, 13.9% over 64 (2000); Marriage status: 20.3% never married, 79.7% now married, 0.0% widowed, 0.0% divorced (2000); Foreign born: 0.0% (2000); Ancestry (includes multiple ancestries): 66.3% German, 18.8% Irish, 14.9% Swedish, 9.9% Norwegian, 5.0% United States or American (2000).
Economy: Employment by occupation: 43.1% management, 2.0% professional, 13.7% services, 15.7% sales, 0.0% farming, 21.6% construction, 3.9% production (2000).
Income: Per capita income: $16,820 (2000); Median household income: $50,000 (2000); Poverty rate: 0.0% (2000).
Taxes: Total city taxes per capita: $96 (1997); City property taxes per capita: $96 (1997).
Education: High school graduation rate: 95.2% (2000); College graduation rate: 1.6% (2000).
Housing: Homeownership rate: 58.1% (2000); Median home value: $70,000 (2000); Median rent: $138 per month (2000); Median age of housing: 32 years (2000).
Transportation: Commute to work: 68.6% car, 0.0% public transportation, 7.8% walk, 23.5% work from home (2000); Travel time to work: 74.4% less than 15 minutes, 20.5% 15 to 30 minutes, 5.1% 30 to 45 minutes, 0.0% 45 to 60 minutes, 0.0% 60 minutes or more (2000)

WHEATON (city). Covers a land area of 1.781 square miles and a water area of 0 square miles. Located at 45.80° N. Lat.; 96.49° W. Long. Elevation is 1,019 feet.
History: The country near Wheaton developed an early reputation for water-fowl and pheasant hunting. Many sport clubs were established in the area.
Population: 1,619 (2000); Race: 97.8% White, 0.0% Black, 0.7% Asian, 0.3% American Indian and Alaska Native, 0.8% Hispanic of any race, 0.7%

two or more races (2000); Density: 909.2 persons per square mile (2000); Age: 20.4% under 18, 33.7% over 64 (2000); Marriage status: 18.3% never married, 60.4% now married, 14.1% widowed, 7.2% divorced (2000); Foreign born: 0.8% (2000); Ancestry (includes multiple ancestries): 51.3% German, 15.8% Norwegian, 13.1% Swedish, 8.5% Irish, 4.1% French (except Basque) (2000).
Economy: Single-family building permits issued: 5 (2001) / 5 (2000); Multi-family building permits issued: 0 (2001) / 0 (2000); Employment by occupation: 15.6% management, 14.0% professional, 22.8% services, 19.0% sales, 1.5% farming, 10.3% construction, 16.7% production (2000).
Income: Per capita income: $18,181 (2000); Median household income: $29,219 (2000); Poverty rate: 10.9% (2000).
Taxes: Total city taxes per capita: $170 (1997); City property taxes per capita: $168 (1997).
Education: High school graduation rate: 80.4% (2000); College graduation rate: 10.0% (2000).

School District(s)

Wheaton Area School (PK-12)
2000 Enrollment: 524 320-563-8283
Housing: Homeownership rate: 76.9% (2000); Median home value: $40,200 (2000); Median rent: $316 per month (2000); Median age of housing: 50 years (2000).
Hospitals: Wheaton Community Hospital (25 beds)
Newspapers: Wheaton Gazette (1 x week)
Transportation: Commute to work: 81.5% car, 0.0% public transportation, 12.2% walk, 6.0% work from home (2000); Travel time to work: 79.3% less than 15 minutes, 9.2% 15 to 30 minutes, 6.7% 30 to 45 minutes, 3.4% 45 to 60 minutes, 1.4% 60 minutes or more (2000)
Additional Information Contacts
Wheaton Chamber of Commerce 320-563-8794

WINDSOR (township). Covers a land area of 15.680 square miles and a water area of 6.112 square miles. Located at 45.69° N. Lat.; 96.67° W. Long.
Population: 54 (2000); Race: 100.0% White, 0.0% Black, 0.0% Asian, 0.0% American Indian and Alaska Native, 0.0% Hispanic of any race, 0.0% two or more races (2000); Density: 3.4 persons per square mile (2000); Age: 20.5% under 18, 11.4% over 64 (2000); Marriage status: 37.1% never married, 54.3% now married, 0.0% widowed, 8.6% divorced (2000); Foreign born: 2.3% (2000); Ancestry (includes multiple ancestries): 54.5% German, 13.6% Norwegian, 11.4% English, 11.4% Irish, 6.8% Danish (2000).
Economy: Employment by occupation: 37.5% management, 0.0% professional, 6.3% services, 6.3% sales, 0.0% farming, 25.0% construction, 25.0% production (2000).
Income: Per capita income: $15,582 (2000); Median household income: $26,250 (2000); Poverty rate: 6.8% (2000).
Taxes: Total city taxes per capita: $121 (1997); City property taxes per capita: $121 (1997).
Education: High school graduation rate: 77.1% (2000); College graduation rate: 2.9% (2000).
Housing: Homeownership rate: 75.0% (2000); Median home value: $22,500 (2000); Median age of housing: 34 years (2000).
Transportation: Commute to work: 62.5% car, 0.0% public transportation, 37.5% walk, 0.0% work from home (2000); Travel time to work: 37.5% less than 15 minutes, 37.5% 15 to 30 minutes, 25.0% 30 to 45 minutes, 0.0% 45 to 60 minutes, 0.0% 60 minutes or more (2000)

Wabasha County

Located in southeastern Minnesota; bounded on the east by the Mississippi River and the Wisconsin border; drained by the Zumbro River. Covers a land area of 525.00 square miles, a water area of 24.80 square miles, and is located in the Central Time Zone. The county government was organized in 1849. County seat is Wabasha.
Population: 21,610 (2000); Race: 98.1% White, 0.2% Black, 0.5% Asian, 0.3% American Indian and Alaska Native, 1.6% Hispanic of any race, 0.4% two or more races (2000); Density: 41.2 persons per square mile (2000); Age: 27.1% under 18, 14.9% over 64 (2000).
Religion: Five largest groups: 35.5% Catholic Church, 12.7% Wisconsin Evangelical Lutheran Synod, 11.1% Lutheran Church—Missouri Synod, 9.3% Evangelical Lutheran Church in America, 3.7% United Church of Christ (2000).
Economy: Unemployment rate: 2.9% (11/2002); Total civilian labor force: 12,545 (11/2002); Leading industries: 32.6% manufacturing; 16.3% retail trade; 14.6% health care and social assistance (2000); Companies that employ more than 1,000 persons: 0 (2000); Companies that employ more than 100 persons: 10 (2000); Farms: 963 totaling 253,401 acres (1997); Minority business ownership rate: 0.0% (1997); Women business ownership rate: 24.1% (1997); Retail sales per capita: $6,031 (1997). Single-family building permits issued: 143 (2001) / 119 (2000); Multi-family building permits issued: 24 (2001) / 2 (2000).
Income: Per capita income: $19,664 (2000); Median household income: $42,117 (2000); Poverty rate: 6.0% (2000); Bankruptcy rate: 1.97% (2001).
Taxes: Total county taxes per capita: $259 (1997); County property taxes per capita: $256 (1997).
Education: High school graduation rate: 85.6% (2000); College graduation rate: 16.9% (2000).
Housing: Homeownership rate: 82.5% (2000); Median home value: $95,000 (2000); Median rent: $374 per month (2000); Median age of housing: 35 years (2000).
Health: Birth rate: 107.8 per 10,000 population (1998); Age adjusted death rate: 75.5 per 10,000 population (1999); Age adjusted cancer mortality rate: 220.5 deaths per 100,000 population (1999). Number of physicians: 11.6 per 10,000 population (1999); Number of hospital beds: 123.6 per 10,000 population (1999).
Elections: 2000 Presidential election results: 42.9% Gore, 49.8% Bush, 5.4% Nader, 1.3% Buchanan
National and State Parks: Carley State Park; Mazeppa State Wildlife Management Area; McCarthy Lake State Wildlife Management; Zumbro State Wildlife Management Area
Additional Information Contacts
Wabasha County Government Offices 612-565-2992
Lake City Chamber of Commerce 651-345-4123
Wabasha Chamber of Commerce 651-565-4158

Wabasha County Communities

CHESTER (township). Covers a land area of 35.443 square miles and a water area of 0.034 square miles. Located at 44.31° N. Lat.; 92.47° W. Long.
Population: 470 (2000); Race: 98.7% White, 0.0% Black, 1.3% Asian, 0.0% American Indian and Alaska Native, 0.4% Hispanic of any race, 0.0% two or more races (2000); Density: 13.3 persons per square mile (2000); Age: 27.2% under 18, 11.9% over 64 (2000); Marriage status: 25.4% never married, 65.1% now married, 5.9% widowed, 3.6% divorced (2000); Foreign born: 0.4% (2000); Ancestry (includes multiple ancestries): 56.6% German, 13.6% Norwegian, 10.4% Irish, 5.7% United States or American, 4.0% Swedish (2000).
Economy: Employment by occupation: 24.3% management, 10.8% professional, 10.8% services, 16.6% sales, 9.7% farming, 9.3% construction, 18.5% production (2000).
Income: Per capita income: $20,701 (2000); Median household income: $48,750 (2000); Poverty rate: 3.8% (2000).
Taxes: Total city taxes per capita: $102 (1997); City property taxes per capita: $102 (1997).
Education: High school graduation rate: 83.4% (2000); College graduation rate: 12.7% (2000).
Housing: Homeownership rate: 77.6% (2000); Median home value: $127,800 (2000); Median rent: $363 per month (2000); Median age of housing: 48 years (2000).
Transportation: Commute to work: 69.6% car, 2.3% public transportation, 7.0% walk, 20.2% work from home (2000); Travel time to work: 28.8% less than 15 minutes, 21.0% 15 to 30 minutes, 31.2% 30 to 45 minutes, 12.7% 45 to 60 minutes, 6.3% 60 minutes or more (2000)

ELGIN (city). Covers a land area of 0.654 square miles and a water area of 0 square miles. Located at 44.13° N. Lat.; 92.25° W. Long. Elevation is 1,069 feet.
Population: 826 (2000); Race: 98.7% White, 0.0% Black, 0.3% Asian, 0.6% American Indian and Alaska Native, 1.0% Hispanic of any race, 0.0% two or more races (2000); Density: 1,262.8 persons per square mile (2000); Age: 29.2% under 18, 12.4% over 64 (2000); Marriage status: 24.7% never married, 55.9% now married, 6.4% widowed, 12.9% divorced (2000); Foreign born: 0.3% (2000); Ancestry (includes multiple ancestries): 57.3% German, 16.1% Norwegian, 11.8% Irish, 5.6% United States or American, 4.3% English (2000).
Economy: Single-family building permits issued: 8 (2001) / 9 (2000); Multi-family building permits issued: 0 (2001) / 0 (2000); Employment by occupation: 8.7% management, 21.5% professional, 13.3% services, 20.8% sales, 2.3% farming, 13.6% construction, 19.7% production (2000).
Income: Per capita income: $18,745 (2000); Median household income: $41,184 (2000); Poverty rate: 5.5% (2000).

Taxes: Total city taxes per capita: $159 (1997); City property taxes per capita: $153 (1997).
Education: High school graduation rate: 80.6% (2000); College graduation rate: 16.5% (2000).

School District(s)

Elgin-Millville (PK-12)
2000 Enrollment: 579 507-876-2493
Housing: Homeownership rate: 75.5% (2000); Median home value: $82,800 (2000); Median rent: $381 per month (2000); Median age of housing: 45 years (2000).
Transportation: Commute to work: 90.0% car, 3.3% public transportation, 3.8% walk, 2.4% work from home (2000); Travel time to work: 21.6% less than 15 minutes, 38.3% 15 to 30 minutes, 31.8% 30 to 45 minutes, 4.6% 45 to 60 minutes, 3.6% 60 minutes or more (2000)

ELGIN (township). Covers a land area of 34.976 square miles and a water area of 0.004 square miles. Located at 44.14° N. Lat.; 92.24° W. Long. Elevation is 1,069 feet.
Population: 787 (2000); Race: 98.8% White, 0.0% Black, 1.2% Asian, 0.0% American Indian and Alaska Native, 0.0% Hispanic of any race, 0.0% two or more races (2000); Density: 22.5 persons per square mile (2000); Age: 33.9% under 18, 7.3% over 64 (2000); Marriage status: 24.3% never married, 72.2% now married, 2.1% widowed, 1.3% divorced (2000); Foreign born: 0.7% (2000); Ancestry (includes multiple ancestries): 58.1% German, 16.9% Irish, 13.3% Norwegian, 6.3% United States or American, 5.0% English (2000).
Economy: Dairying. Manufacturing: lumber, cabinet, feeds. Employment by occupation: 17.8% management, 21.0% professional, 11.4% services, 21.4% sales, 8.2% farming, 12.7% construction, 7.6% production (2000).
Income: Per capita income: $19,928 (2000); Median household income: $55,833 (2000); Poverty rate: 0.6% (2000).
Taxes: Total city taxes per capita: $88 (1997); City property taxes per capita: $87 (1997).
Education: High school graduation rate: 92.9% (2000); College graduation rate: 19.1% (2000).
Housing: Homeownership rate: 87.4% (2000); Median home value: $138,100 (2000); Median rent: $329 per month (2000); Median age of housing: 28 years (2000).
Transportation: Commute to work: 80.5% car, 1.2% public transportation, 1.4% walk, 16.8% work from home (2000); Travel time to work: 19.2% less than 15 minutes, 42.1% 15 to 30 minutes, 29.3% 30 to 45 minutes, 4.7% 45 to 60 minutes, 4.7% 60 minutes or more (2000)

GILLFORD (township). Covers a land area of 35.404 square miles and a water area of 0.005 square miles. Located at 44.32° N. Lat.; 92.37° W. Long.
Population: 581 (2000); Race: 99.7% White, 0.0% Black, 0.3% Asian, 0.0% American Indian and Alaska Native, 0.5% Hispanic of any race, 0.0% two or more races (2000); Density: 16.4 persons per square mile (2000); Age: 34.6% under 18, 9.0% over 64 (2000); Marriage status: 25.2% never married, 69.0% now married, 3.5% widowed, 2.3% divorced (2000); Foreign born: 0.9% (2000); Ancestry (includes multiple ancestries): 59.7% German, 13.5% Norwegian, 8.4% Irish, 6.8% English, 4.4% Other groups (2000).
Economy: Employment by occupation: 27.4% management, 12.8% professional, 15.6% services, 15.0% sales, 5.6% farming, 8.7% construction, 15.0% production (2000).
Income: Per capita income: $16,473 (2000); Median household income: $46,917 (2000); Poverty rate: 6.7% (2000).
Taxes: Total city taxes per capita: $67 (1997); City property taxes per capita: $67 (1997).
Education: High school graduation rate: 90.1% (2000); College graduation rate: 12.7% (2000).
Housing: Homeownership rate: 84.2% (2000); Median home value: $125,000 (2000); Median rent: $450 per month (2000); Median age of housing: 54 years (2000).
Transportation: Commute to work: 72.0% car, 1.9% public transportation, 2.5% walk, 23.1% work from home (2000); Travel time to work: 14.6% less than 15 minutes, 40.9% 15 to 30 minutes, 30.4% 30 to 45 minutes, 11.7% 45 to 60 minutes, 2.4% 60 minutes or more (2000)

GLASGOW (township). Covers a land area of 35.193 square miles and a water area of 0.461 square miles. Located at 44.30° N. Lat.; 92.12° W. Long.
Population: 298 (2000); Race: 100.0% White, 0.0% Black, 0.0% Asian, 0.0% American Indian and Alaska Native, 0.0% Hispanic of any race, 0.0% two or more races (2000); Density: 8.5 persons per square mile (2000); Age: 37.9% under 18, 6.1% over 64 (2000); Marriage status: 23.5% never married, 68.7% now married, 2.8% widowed, 5.1% divorced (2000); Foreign born: 0.0% (2000); Ancestry (includes multiple ancestries): 75.9% German, 23.8% Irish, 7.4% Norwegian, 3.9% Swedish, 2.6% Luxemburger (2000).
Economy: Employment by occupation: 36.5% management, 15.0% professional, 12.0% services, 7.2% sales, 7.8% farming, 10.2% construction, 11.4% production (2000).
Income: Per capita income: $16,322 (2000); Median household income: $40,625 (2000); Poverty rate: 1.6% (2000).
Taxes: Total city taxes per capita: $65 (1997); City property taxes per capita: $65 (1997).
Education: High school graduation rate: 89.4% (2000); College graduation rate: 10.1% (2000).
Housing: Homeownership rate: 87.2% (2000); Median home value: $98,300 (2000); Median rent: $275 per month (2000); Median age of housing: 24 years (2000).
Transportation: Commute to work: 60.5% car, 1.2% public transportation, 10.2% walk, 25.7% work from home (2000); Travel time to work: 37.9% less than 15 minutes, 34.7% 15 to 30 minutes, 5.6% 30 to 45 minutes, 13.7% 45 to 60 minutes, 8.1% 60 minutes or more (2000)

GREENFIELD (township). Covers a land area of 32.961 square miles and a water area of 4.869 square miles. Located at 44.31° N. Lat.; 92.00° W. Long.
Population: 1,254 (2000); Race: 99.6% White, 0.2% Black, 0.0% Asian, 0.2% American Indian and Alaska Native, 0.0% Hispanic of any race, 0.0% two or more races (2000); Density: 38.0 persons per square mile (2000); Age: 22.7% under 18, 17.5% over 64 (2000); Marriage status: 18.7% never married, 70.8% now married, 5.6% widowed, 4.9% divorced (2000); Foreign born: 0.0% (2000); Ancestry (includes multiple ancestries): 57.1% German, 20.0% Norwegian, 16.9% Irish, 5.6% Swedish, 5.5% English (2000).
Economy: Employment by occupation: 13.9% management, 24.8% professional, 10.1% services, 21.0% sales, 1.7% farming, 9.3% construction, 19.2% production (2000).
Income: Per capita income: $25,610 (2000); Median household income: $44,643 (2000); Poverty rate: 3.4% (2000).
Taxes: Total city taxes per capita: $85 (1997); City property taxes per capita: $85 (1997).
Education: High school graduation rate: 88.2% (2000); College graduation rate: 20.6% (2000).
Housing: Homeownership rate: 94.5% (2000); Median home value: $123,100 (2000); Median rent: $319 per month (2000); Median age of housing: 25 years (2000).
Transportation: Commute to work: 88.6% car, 1.8% public transportation, 2.9% walk, 6.3% work from home (2000); Travel time to work: 40.9% less than 15 minutes, 24.3% 15 to 30 minutes, 13.3% 30 to 45 minutes, 12.6% 45 to 60 minutes, 8.9% 60 minutes or more (2000)

HAMMOND (city). Covers a land area of 0.104 square miles and a water area of 0.010 square miles. Located at 44.22° N. Lat.; 92.37° W. Long. Elevation is 800 feet.
Population: 198 (2000); Race: 94.7% White, 2.4% Black, 0.0% Asian, 0.0% American Indian and Alaska Native, 1.0% Hispanic of any race, 1.9% two or more races (2000); Density: 1,896.3 persons per square mile (2000); Age: 29.0% under 18, 6.8% over 64 (2000); Marriage status: 25.8% never married, 47.9% now married, 1.2% widowed, 25.2% divorced (2000); Foreign born: 0.5% (2000); Ancestry (includes multiple ancestries): 39.1% German, 23.2% Norwegian, 19.8% Irish, 6.3% English, 4.3% Swedish (2000).
Economy: Grain; livestock. Employment by occupation: 4.3% management, 12.0% professional, 15.4% services, 23.1% sales, 5.1% farming, 11.1% construction, 29.1% production (2000).
Income: Per capita income: $18,531 (2000); Median household income: $39,375 (2000); Poverty rate: 10.8% (2000).
Taxes: Total city taxes per capita: $48 (1997); City property taxes per capita: $38 (1997).
Education: High school graduation rate: 80.0% (2000); College graduation rate: 6.7% (2000).
Housing: Homeownership rate: 79.2% (2000); Median home value: $49,600 (2000); Median rent: $400 per month (2000); Median age of housing: 60+ years (2000).
Transportation: Commute to work: 91.2% car, 0.0% public transportation, 1.8% walk, 2.7% work from home (2000); Travel time to work: 11.8% less than 15 minutes, 41.8% 15 to 30 minutes, 39.1% 30 to 45 minutes, 0.0% 45 to 60 minutes, 7.3% 60 minutes or more (2000)

HIGHLAND (township). Covers a land area of 35.786 square miles and a water area of 0.008 square miles. Located at 44.24° N. Lat.; 92.12° W. Long.

Population: 471 (2000); Race: 99.4% White, 0.0% Black, 0.2% Asian, 0.0% American Indian and Alaska Native, 0.4% Hispanic of any race, 0.4% two or more races (2000); Density: 13.2 persons per square mile (2000); Age: 32.6% under 18, 8.5% over 64 (2000); Marriage status: 30.8% never married, 63.8% now married, 4.8% widowed, 0.6% divorced (2000); Foreign born: 0.6% (2000); Ancestry (includes multiple ancestries): 57.5% German, 18.6% Irish, 6.6% Norwegian, 4.3% United States or American, 4.1% French (except Basque) (2000).
Economy: Employment by occupation: 31.0% management, 8.5% professional, 14.7% services, 18.6% sales, 7.4% farming, 10.1% construction, 9.7% production (2000).
Income: Per capita income: $18,747 (2000); Median household income: $49,375 (2000); Poverty rate: 8.1% (2000).
Taxes: Total city taxes per capita: $86 (1997); City property taxes per capita: $86 (1997).
Education: High school graduation rate: 84.0% (2000); College graduation rate: 6.1% (2000).
Housing: Homeownership rate: 80.8% (2000); Median home value: $120,800 (2000); Median rent: $350 per month (2000); Median age of housing: 60+ years (2000).
Transportation: Commute to work: 67.6% car, 2.3% public transportation, 8.2% walk, 21.9% work from home (2000); Travel time to work: 36.0% less than 15 minutes, 25.0% 15 to 30 minutes, 17.5% 30 to 45 minutes, 12.0% 45 to 60 minutes, 9.5% 60 minutes or more (2000)

HYDE PARK (township). Covers a land area of 15.882 square miles and a water area of 0.168 square miles. Located at 44.25° N. Lat.; 92.37° W. Long.
Population: 275 (2000); Race: 98.9% White, 0.0% Black, 0.0% Asian, 0.0% American Indian and Alaska Native, 1.1% Hispanic of any race, 0.0% two or more races (2000); Density: 17.3 persons per square mile (2000); Age: 26.1% under 18, 13.8% over 64 (2000); Marriage status: 21.0% never married, 63.0% now married, 5.0% widowed, 11.0% divorced (2000); Foreign born: 0.0% (2000); Ancestry (includes multiple ancestries): 42.5% German, 14.2% Norwegian, 11.5% Irish, 5.4% Swedish, 4.2% United States or American (2000).
Economy: Employment by occupation: 8.8% management, 14.6% professional, 19.0% services, 20.4% sales, 3.6% farming, 16.1% construction, 17.5% production (2000).
Income: Per capita income: $28,488 (2000); Median household income: $56,667 (2000); Poverty rate: 2.3% (2000).
Taxes: Total city taxes per capita: $71 (1997); City property taxes per capita: $71 (1997).
Education: High school graduation rate: 87.3% (2000); College graduation rate: 14.9% (2000).
Housing: Homeownership rate: 84.6% (2000); Median home value: $90,000 (2000); Median rent: $242 per month (2000); Median age of housing: 26 years (2000).
Transportation: Commute to work: 90.0% car, 3.8% public transportation, 1.5% walk, 4.6% work from home (2000); Travel time to work: 14.5% less than 15 minutes, 37.9% 15 to 30 minutes, 30.6% 30 to 45 minutes, 10.5% 45 to 60 minutes, 6.5% 60 minutes or more (2000)

KELLOGG (city). Covers a land area of 0.291 square miles and a water area of 0.009 square miles. Located at 44.30° N. Lat.; 91.99° W. Long. Elevation is 700 feet.
Population: 439 (2000); Race: 99.6% White, 0.0% Black, 0.0% Asian, 0.0% American Indian and Alaska Native, 0.0% Hispanic of any race, 0.4% two or more races (2000); Density: 1,511.0 persons per square mile (2000); Age: 28.1% under 18, 15.8% over 64 (2000); Marriage status: 22.3% never married, 56.7% now married, 10.5% widowed, 10.5% divorced (2000); Foreign born: 2.1% (2000); Ancestry (includes multiple ancestries): 47.5% German, 15.0% Norwegian, 14.1% Irish, 9.0% English, 7.1% French (except Basque) (2000).
Economy: Livestock; poultry; dairying; light manufacturing; timber. Lock and Dam No. 4 to Northeast. Single-family building permits issued: 0 (2001) / 3 (2000); Multi-family building permits issued: 0 (2001) / 0 (2000); Employment by occupation: 8.7% management, 7.0% professional, 19.2% services, 18.8% sales, 1.7% farming, 15.7% construction, 28.8% production (2000).
Income: Per capita income: $16,216 (2000); Median household income: $37,885 (2000); Poverty rate: 14.0% (2000).
Taxes: Total city taxes per capita: $86 (1997); City property taxes per capita: $81 (1997).
Education: High school graduation rate: 76.5% (2000); College graduation rate: 8.5% (2000).
Housing: Homeownership rate: 82.1% (2000); Median home value: $71,200 (2000); Median rent: $433 per month (2000); Median age of housing: 44 years (2000).
Transportation: Commute to work: 88.5% car, 0.0% public transportation, 4.0% walk, 7.5% work from home (2000); Travel time to work: 47.8% less than 15 minutes, 18.2% 15 to 30 minutes, 11.5% 30 to 45 minutes, 12.9% 45 to 60 minutes, 9.6% 60 minutes or more (2000)

LAKE (township). Covers a land area of 25.048 square miles and a water area of 4.785 square miles. Located at 44.40° N. Lat.; 92.25° W. Long.
Population: 412 (2000); Race: 99.3% White, 0.0% Black, 0.0% Asian, 0.0% American Indian and Alaska Native, 2.1% Hispanic of any race, 0.7% two or more races (2000); Density: 16.4 persons per square mile (2000); Age: 29.1% under 18, 11.0% over 64 (2000); Marriage status: 18.6% never married, 71.1% now married, 3.2% widowed, 7.1% divorced (2000); Foreign born: 2.8% (2000); Ancestry (includes multiple ancestries): 60.6% German, 18.3% Norwegian, 8.9% Irish, 3.2% English, 3.2% Dutch (2000).
Economy: Employment by occupation: 17.3% management, 14.4% professional, 18.9% services, 19.8% sales, 0.8% farming, 5.3% construction, 23.5% production (2000).
Income: Per capita income: $21,327 (2000); Median household income: $54,688 (2000); Poverty rate: 4.2% (2000).
Taxes: Total city taxes per capita: $79 (1997); City property taxes per capita: $79 (1997).
Education: High school graduation rate: 89.8% (2000); College graduation rate: 20.8% (2000).
Housing: Homeownership rate: 89.3% (2000); Median home value: $137,000 (2000); Median rent: $508 per month (2000); Median age of housing: 29 years (2000).
Transportation: Commute to work: 88.8% car, 0.0% public transportation, 2.5% walk, 5.0% work from home (2000); Travel time to work: 52.6% less than 15 minutes, 17.4% 15 to 30 minutes, 19.1% 30 to 45 minutes, 8.3% 45 to 60 minutes, 2.6% 60 minutes or more (2000)

LAKE CITY (city). Covers a land area of 4.242 square miles and a water area of 0.056 square miles. Located at 44.44° N. Lat.; 92.27° W. Long. Elevation is 701 feet.
History: Lake City began as a trading center with sawmills and flour mills, and later became a resort town on Lake Pepin. An early industry was clamming, with button factories around the lake using the shells. A nursery business was established in Lake City in the late 1860's.
Population: 4,950 (2000); Race: 96.6% White, 0.6% Black, 1.6% Asian, 0.6% American Indian and Alaska Native, 2.2% Hispanic of any race, 0.5% two or more races (2000); Density: 1,166.9 persons per square mile (2000); Age: 22.9% under 18, 19.3% over 64 (2000); Marriage status: 20.3% never married, 63.1% now married, 8.0% widowed, 8.6% divorced (2000); Foreign born: 4.6% (2000); Ancestry (includes multiple ancestries): 52.0% German, 12.4% Norwegian, 10.6% Irish, 7.6% Swedish, 6.1% English (2000).
Economy: Single-family building permits issued: 10 (2001) / 38 (2000); Multi-family building permits issued: 18 (2001) / 0 (2000); Employment by occupation: 10.5% management, 21.4% professional, 16.7% services, 20.9% sales, 0.9% farming, 5.8% construction, 23.8% production (2000).
Income: Per capita income: $20,944 (2000); Median household income: $40,637 (2000); Poverty rate: 6.0% (2000).
Taxes: Total city taxes per capita: $226 (2000); City property taxes per capita: $205 (2000).
Education: High school graduation rate: 84.6% (2000); College graduation rate: 20.6% (2000).

School District(s)

Lake City (PK-12)
2000 Enrollment: 1,524 651-345-2198
Housing: Homeownership rate: 77.9% (2000); Median home value: $99,100 (2000); Median rent: $434 per month (2000); Median age of housing: 36 years (2000).
Hospitals: Lake City Hospital (49 beds)
Safety: Violent crime rate: 24.0 per 10,000 population; Property crime rate: 413.8 per 10,000 population (2001).
Newspapers: The Lake City Shopper (1 x week); The Lake City Graphic (1 x week)
Transportation: Commute to work: 84.0% car, 1.9% public transportation, 7.9% walk, 4.6% work from home (2000); Travel time to work: 59.8% less than 15 minutes, 15.5% 15 to 30 minutes, 10.6% 30 to 45 minutes, 9.0% 45 to 60 minutes, 5.1% 60 minutes or more (2000)
Additional Information Contacts
Lake City Chamber of Commerce 651-345-4123

MAZEPPA (city). Covers a land area of 0.978 square miles and a water area of 0 square miles. Located at 44.27° N. Lat.; 92.54° W. Long. Elevation is 931 feet.
Population: 778 (2000); Race: 96.4% White, 0.0% Black, 0.4% Asian, 2.2% American Indian and Alaska Native, 0.5% Hispanic of any race, 0.8% two or more races (2000); Density: 795.7 persons per square mile (2000); Age: 29.2% under 18, 14.3% over 64 (2000); Marriage status: 23.5% never married, 63.5% now married, 6.5% widowed, 6.5% divorced (2000); Foreign born: 0.6% (2000); Ancestry (includes multiple ancestries): 45.6% German, 13.6% Norwegian, 10.6% Irish, 6.2% Other groups, 6.1% English (2000).
Economy: Single-family building permits issued: 7 (2001) / 4 (2000); Multi-family building permits issued: 0 (2001) / 0 (2000); Employment by occupation: 6.3% management, 12.6% professional, 16.3% services, 25.9% sales, 1.0% farming, 11.3% construction, 26.6% production (2000).
Income: Per capita income: $17,509 (2000); Median household income: $36,375 (2000); Poverty rate: 7.4% (2000).
Taxes: Total city taxes per capita: $49 (1997); City property taxes per capita: $41 (1997).
Education: High school graduation rate: 80.4% (2000); College graduation rate: 11.5% (2000).

School District(s)

Zumbrota-Mazeppa (PK-12)
2000 Enrollment: 1,248 507-732-5107
Housing: Homeownership rate: 84.5% (2000); Median home value: $89,500 (2000); Median rent: $283 per month (2000); Median age of housing: 29 years (2000).
Transportation: Commute to work: 96.2% car, 0.0% public transportation, 2.8% walk, 0.5% work from home (2000); Travel time to work: 19.3% less than 15 minutes, 36.8% 15 to 30 minutes, 35.7% 30 to 45 minutes, 4.1% 45 to 60 minutes, 4.1% 60 minutes or more (2000)

MAZEPPA (township). Covers a land area of 21.796 square miles and a water area of 0.498 square miles. Located at 44.23° N. Lat.; 92.49° W. Long. Elevation is 931 feet.
Population: 743 (2000); Race: 98.8% White, 0.0% Black, 0.3% Asian, 0.7% American Indian and Alaska Native, 0.0% Hispanic of any race, 0.3% two or more races (2000); Density: 34.1 persons per square mile (2000); Age: 30.4% under 18, 7.0% over 64 (2000); Marriage status: 20.2% never married, 67.5% now married, 3.0% widowed, 9.2% divorced (2000); Foreign born: 0.7% (2000); Ancestry (includes multiple ancestries): 47.5% German, 21.8% Norwegian, 14.8% Irish, 7.7% English, 7.1% Swedish (2000).
Economy: Grain; livestock, poultry; dairying. Manufacturing: fabricated metal products, hog troughs. Employment by occupation: 13.1% management, 23.6% professional, 12.4% services, 22.9% sales, 0.5% farming, 14.1% construction, 13.4% production (2000).
Income: Per capita income: $21,390 (2000); Median household income: $54,554 (2000); Poverty rate: 4.5% (2000).
Taxes: Total city taxes per capita: $33 (1997); City property taxes per capita: $31 (1997).
Education: High school graduation rate: 94.6% (2000); College graduation rate: 19.4% (2000).
Housing: Homeownership rate: 93.0% (2000); Median home value: $134,200 (2000); Median rent: $388 per month (2000); Median age of housing: 24 years (2000).
Transportation: Commute to work: 89.6% car, 0.5% public transportation, 2.0% walk, 7.4% work from home (2000); Travel time to work: 10.4% less than 15 minutes, 58.6% 15 to 30 minutes, 22.7% 30 to 45 minutes, 0.8% 45 to 60 minutes, 7.5% 60 minutes or more (2000)

MILLVILLE (city). Covers a land area of 0.145 square miles and a water area of 0.003 square miles. Located at 44.24° N. Lat.; 92.29° W. Long.
Population: 186 (2000); Race: 93.4% White, 0.0% Black, 0.0% Asian, 0.0% American Indian and Alaska Native, 7.7% Hispanic of any race, 0.0% two or more races (2000); Density: 1,279.8 persons per square mile (2000); Age: 27.6% under 18, 7.2% over 64 (2000); Marriage status: 27.0% never married, 58.2% now married, 9.2% widowed, 5.7% divorced (2000); Foreign born: 1.7% (2000); Ancestry (includes multiple ancestries): 54.7% German, 19.9% Irish, 9.9% Other groups, 7.2% Norwegian, 5.5% United States or American (2000).
Economy: Dairying. Single-family building permits issued: 0 (2001) / 0 (2000); Multi-family building permits issued: 0 (2001) / 0 (2000); Employment by occupation: 7.3% management, 11.0% professional, 20.2% services, 28.4% sales, 0.9% farming, 18.3% construction, 13.8% production (2000).
Income: Per capita income: $16,491 (2000); Median household income: $38,125 (2000); Poverty rate: 4.4% (2000).
Taxes: Total city taxes per capita: $50 (1997); City property taxes per capita: $25 (1997).
Education: High school graduation rate: 79.1% (2000); College graduation rate: 8.2% (2000).
Housing: Homeownership rate: 75.4% (2000); Median home value: $81,000 (2000); Median rent: $292 per month (2000); Median age of housing: 49 years (2000).
Transportation: Commute to work: 92.7% car, 0.0% public transportation, 6.4% walk, 0.9% work from home (2000); Travel time to work: 16.7% less than 15 minutes, 16.7% 15 to 30 minutes, 55.6% 30 to 45 minutes, 7.4% 45 to 60 minutes, 3.7% 60 minutes or more (2000)

MINNEISKA (city). Covers a land area of 0.567 square miles and a water area of 0.460 square miles. Located at 44.19° N. Lat.; 91.86° W. Long.
History: Minneiska was settled in 1851. It became a shipping center for wheat from its river port.
Population: 116 (2000); Race: 100.0% White, 0.0% Black, 0.0% Asian, 0.0% American Indian and Alaska Native, 0.0% Hispanic of any race, 0.0% two or more races (2000); Density: 204.6 persons per square mile (2000); Age: 13.6% under 18, 20.0% over 64 (2000); Marriage status: 14.9% never married, 72.3% now married, 4.0% widowed, 8.9% divorced (2000); Foreign born: 4.5% (2000); Ancestry (includes multiple ancestries): 55.5% German, 21.8% Irish, 12.7% English, 10.0% Norwegian, 6.4% Welsh (2000).
Economy: Single-family building permits issued: 1 (2001) / 0 (2000); Multi-family building permits issued: 0 (2001) / 0 (2000); Employment by occupation: 10.0% management, 15.0% professional, 11.7% services, 16.7% sales, 5.0% farming, 20.0% construction, 21.7% production (2000).
Income: Per capita income: $39,223 (2000); Median household income: $43,750 (2000); Poverty rate: 1.8% (2000).
Taxes: Total city taxes per capita: $65 (1997); City property taxes per capita: $52 (1997).
Education: High school graduation rate: 82.0% (2000); College graduation rate: 13.5% (2000).
Housing: Homeownership rate: 86.3% (2000); Median home value: $107,800 (2000); Median rent: $417 per month (2000); Median age of housing: 41 years (2000).
Transportation: Commute to work: 75.9% car, 0.0% public transportation, 8.6% walk, 15.5% work from home (2000); Travel time to work: 14.3% less than 15 minutes, 55.1% 15 to 30 minutes, 6.1% 30 to 45 minutes, 6.1% 45 to 60 minutes, 18.4% 60 minutes or more (2000)

MINNEISKA (township). Covers a land area of 10.683 square miles and a water area of 7.238 square miles. Located at 44.23° N. Lat.; 91.93° W. Long.
Population: 205 (2000); Race: 100.0% White, 0.0% Black, 0.0% Asian, 0.0% American Indian and Alaska Native, 0.0% Hispanic of any race, 0.0% two or more races (2000); Density: 19.2 persons per square mile (2000); Age: 19.2% under 18, 24.5% over 64 (2000); Marriage status: 14.4% never married, 68.0% now married, 0.0% widowed, 17.5% divorced (2000); Foreign born: 0.0% (2000); Ancestry (includes multiple ancestries): 44.1% German, 17.9% Irish, 12.7% Swedish, 12.2% Norwegian, 9.6% Danish (2000).
Economy: Grain; livestock, poultry; dairying. Lock and Dam No. 5 to Southeast. Employment by occupation: 4.6% management, 10.1% professional, 21.1% services, 14.7% sales, 7.3% farming, 22.9% construction, 19.3% production (2000).
Income: Per capita income: $19,001 (2000); Median household income: $35,313 (2000); Poverty rate: 3.5% (2000).
Taxes: Total city taxes per capita: $57 (1997); City property taxes per capita: $57 (1997).
Education: High school graduation rate: 75.3% (2000); College graduation rate: 14.0% (2000).
Housing: Homeownership rate: 94.9% (2000); Median home value: $78,800 (2000); Median rent: $1,125 per month (2000); Median age of housing: 38 years (2000).
Transportation: Commute to work: 93.6% car, 0.0% public transportation, 1.8% walk, 4.6% work from home (2000); Travel time to work: 16.3% less than 15 minutes, 36.5% 15 to 30 minutes, 7.7% 30 to 45 minutes, 26.9% 45 to 60 minutes, 12.5% 60 minutes or more (2000)

MOUNT PLEASANT (township). Covers a land area of 36.001 square miles and a water area of 0 square miles. Located at 44.41° N. Lat.; 92.35° W. Long.

Population: 475 (2000); Race: 98.1% White, 0.0% Black, 1.5% Asian, 0.4% American Indian and Alaska Native, 0.0% Hispanic of any race, 0.0% two or more races (2000); Density: 13.2 persons per square mile (2000); Age: 33.8% under 18, 6.7% over 64 (2000); Marriage status: 26.7% never married, 66.0% now married, 2.9% widowed, 4.4% divorced (2000); Foreign born: 1.5% (2000); Ancestry (includes multiple ancestries): 71.3% German, 14.7% Norwegian, 11.6% Irish, 11.6% Swedish, 2.4% United States or American (2000).
Economy: Employment by occupation: 26.4% management, 10.9% professional, 13.6% services, 16.6% sales, 7.5% farming, 6.8% construction, 18.1% production (2000).
Income: Per capita income: $16,591 (2000); Median household income: $40,625 (2000); Poverty rate: 9.5% (2000).
Taxes: Total city taxes per capita: $69 (1997); City property taxes per capita: $69 (1997).
Education: High school graduation rate: 90.5% (2000); College graduation rate: 12.9% (2000).
Housing: Homeownership rate: 87.0% (2000); Median home value: $142,600 (2000); Median rent: $338 per month (2000); Median age of housing: 40 years (2000).
Transportation: Commute to work: 74.5% car, 0.0% public transportation, 3.5% walk, 20.8% work from home (2000); Travel time to work: 55.6% less than 15 minutes, 27.3% 15 to 30 minutes, 9.8% 30 to 45 minutes, 4.4% 45 to 60 minutes, 2.9% 60 minutes or more (2000)

OAKWOOD (township). Covers a land area of 35.472 square miles and a water area of 0.187 square miles. Located at 44.23° N. Lat.; 92.26° W. Long.
Population: 433 (2000); Race: 100.0% White, 0.0% Black, 0.0% Asian, 0.0% American Indian and Alaska Native, 1.1% Hispanic of any race, 0.0% two or more races (2000); Density: 12.2 persons per square mile (2000); Age: 38.8% under 18, 9.4% over 64 (2000); Marriage status: 25.9% never married, 65.0% now married, 2.0% widowed, 7.1% divorced (2000); Foreign born: 0.0% (2000); Ancestry (includes multiple ancestries): 57.4% German, 11.9% Irish, 8.7% Norwegian, 5.4% Swedish, 4.0% Ukrainian (2000).
Economy: Employment by occupation: 23.7% management, 11.6% professional, 8.8% services, 22.8% sales, 6.0% farming, 15.8% construction, 11.2% production (2000).
Income: Per capita income: $15,316 (2000); Median household income: $39,000 (2000); Poverty rate: 5.4% (2000).
Taxes: Total city taxes per capita: $81 (1997); City property taxes per capita: $81 (1997).
Education: High school graduation rate: 86.6% (2000); College graduation rate: 7.9% (2000).
Housing: Homeownership rate: 82.4% (2000); Median home value: $97,500 (2000); Median rent: $294 per month (2000); Median age of housing: 30 years (2000).
Transportation: Commute to work: 67.3% car, 1.4% public transportation, 1.4% walk, 29.9% work from home (2000); Travel time to work: 28.0% less than 15 minutes, 20.7% 15 to 30 minutes, 33.3% 30 to 45 minutes, 10.0% 45 to 60 minutes, 8.0% 60 minutes or more (2000)

PEPIN (township). Covers a land area of 17.574 square miles and a water area of 3.987 square miles. Located at 44.38° N. Lat.; 92.12° W. Long.
Population: 471 (2000); Race: 99.5% White, 0.0% Black, 0.0% Asian, 0.5% American Indian and Alaska Native, 0.0% Hispanic of any race, 0.0% two or more races (2000); Density: 26.8 persons per square mile (2000); Age: 21.8% under 18, 16.3% over 64 (2000); Marriage status: 19.9% never married, 66.1% now married, 3.4% widowed, 10.6% divorced (2000); Foreign born: 0.0% (2000); Ancestry (includes multiple ancestries): 53.8% German, 16.8% Norwegian, 14.4% Irish, 6.3% English, 4.7% Dutch (2000).
Economy: Employment by occupation: 20.1% management, 21.6% professional, 15.7% services, 17.6% sales, 0.0% farming, 11.3% construction, 13.7% production (2000).
Income: Per capita income: $20,741 (2000); Median household income: $46,563 (2000); Poverty rate: 5.5% (2000).
Taxes: Total city taxes per capita: $61 (1997); City property taxes per capita: $61 (1997).
Education: High school graduation rate: 86.2% (2000); College graduation rate: 18.4% (2000).
Housing: Homeownership rate: 90.6% (2000); Median home value: $89,700 (2000); Median rent: $375 per month (2000); Median age of housing: 37 years (2000).
Transportation: Commute to work: 83.1% car, 0.0% public transportation, 4.6% walk, 10.3% work from home (2000); Travel time to work: 46.3% less than 15 minutes, 31.4% 15 to 30 minutes, 4.6% 30 to 45 minutes, 10.9% 45 to 60 minutes, 6.9% 60 minutes or more (2000)

PLAINVIEW (city). Covers a land area of 2.196 square miles and a water area of 0 square miles. Located at 44.16° N. Lat.; 92.16° W. Long. Elevation is 1,155 feet.
Population: 3,190 (2000); Race: 96.9% White, 0.0% Black, 0.0% Asian, 0.3% American Indian and Alaska Native, 5.5% Hispanic of any race, 0.8% two or more races (2000); Density: 1,452.5 persons per square mile (2000); Age: 29.5% under 18, 15.8% over 64 (2000); Marriage status: 22.4% never married, 62.4% now married, 7.8% widowed, 7.4% divorced (2000); Foreign born: 3.8% (2000); Ancestry (includes multiple ancestries): 46.5% German, 14.4% Irish, 11.1% Norwegian, 8.6% Other groups, 5.1% English (2000).
Economy: Single-family building permits issued: 20 (2001) / 13 (2000); Multi-family building permits issued: 0 (2001) / 0 (2000); Employment by occupation: 7.3% management, 19.8% professional, 15.7% services, 26.5% sales, 2.5% farming, 13.5% construction, 14.6% production (2000).
Income: Per capita income: $16,494 (2000); Median household income: $39,952 (2000); Poverty rate: 6.4% (2000).
Taxes: Total city taxes per capita: $190 (1997); City property taxes per capita: $183 (1997).
Education: High school graduation rate: 85.5% (2000); College graduation rate: 18.9% (2000).

School District(s)

Plainview (PK-12)
2000 Enrollment: 1,233 507-534-3651
Housing: Homeownership rate: 80.9% (2000); Median home value: $89,200 (2000); Median rent: $389 per month (2000); Median age of housing: 32 years (2000).
Newspapers: Plainview News (1 x week)
Transportation: Commute to work: 83.4% car, 3.6% public transportation, 8.5% walk, 3.5% work from home (2000); Travel time to work: 47.9% less than 15 minutes, 11.7% 15 to 30 minutes, 30.9% 30 to 45 minutes, 4.7% 45 to 60 minutes, 4.8% 60 minutes or more (2000)

PLAINVIEW (township). Covers a land area of 33.368 square miles and a water area of 0 square miles. Located at 44.14° N. Lat.; 92.14° W. Long. Elevation is 1,155 feet.
History: Plotted 1857, incorporated 1875.
Population: 498 (2000); Race: 99.3% White, 0.0% Black, 0.0% Asian, 0.0% American Indian and Alaska Native, 0.7% Hispanic of any race, 0.0% two or more races (2000); Density: 14.9 persons per square mile (2000); Age: 33.2% under 18, 12.8% over 64 (2000); Marriage status: 28.6% never married, 64.2% now married, 3.5% widowed, 3.7% divorced (2000); Foreign born: 0.7% (2000); Ancestry (includes multiple ancestries): 59.2% German, 16.1% Irish, 11.1% Norwegian, 7.1% United States or American, 5.6% French (except Basque) (2000).
Economy: Agriculture: grain; livestock, poultry; dairying. Manufacturing: fertilizer, food products, dairy products. Employment by occupation: 23.6% management, 16.6% professional, 6.6% services, 21.3% sales, 8.0% farming, 8.6% construction, 15.3% production (2000).
Income: Per capita income: $19,778 (2000); Median household income: $53,125 (2000); Poverty rate: 2.4% (2000).
Taxes: Total city taxes per capita: $111 (1997); City property taxes per capita: $109 (1997).
Education: High school graduation rate: 94.1% (2000); College graduation rate: 11.1% (2000).
Housing: Homeownership rate: 86.0% (2000); Median home value: $114,600 (2000); Median rent: $313 per month (2000); Median age of housing: 60+ years (2000).
Transportation: Commute to work: 75.8% car, 1.3% public transportation, 2.0% walk, 20.9% work from home (2000); Travel time to work: 39.1% less than 15 minutes, 11.5% 15 to 30 minutes, 34.0% 30 to 45 minutes, 11.1% 45 to 60 minutes, 4.3% 60 minutes or more (2000)

WABASHA (city). Covers a land area of 8.162 square miles and a water area of 1.125 square miles. Located at 44.37° N. Lat.; 92.03° W. Long. Elevation is 708 feet.
History: Wabasha began with a trading post. In 1838 it was called Cratte's Landing for Oliver Cratte, an Englishman who operated a blacksmith shop here. It was later renamed to honor a family of Sioux chiefs.
Population: 2,599 (2000); Race: 98.5% White, 0.5% Black, 0.3% Asian, 0.0% American Indian and Alaska Native, 0.0% Hispanic of any race, 0.5% two or more races (2000); Density: 318.4 persons per square mile (2000); Age: 21.6% under 18, 22.8% over 64 (2000); Marriage status: 20.3% never married, 61.9% now married, 9.1% widowed, 8.6% divorced (2000); Foreign born: 1.0% (2000); Ancestry (includes multiple ancestries): 49.6% German,

14.2% Irish, 13.1% Norwegian, 5.8% English, 5.0% United States or American (2000).
Economy: Single-family building permits issued: 5 (2001) / 11 (2000); Multi-family building permits issued: 6 (2001) / 2 (2000); Employment by occupation: 10.5% management, 19.5% professional, 14.9% services, 24.6% sales, 0.9% farming, 8.5% construction, 21.2% production (2000).
Income: Per capita income: $20,374 (2000); Median household income: $35,291 (2000); Poverty rate: 10.0% (2000).
Taxes: Total city taxes per capita: $172 (1997); City property taxes per capita: $161 (1997).
Education: High school graduation rate: 82.7% (2000); College graduation rate: 17.6% (2000).

School District(s)

Wabasha-Kellogg (PK-12)
2000 Enrollment: 766 651-565-4603

Housing: Homeownership rate: 73.4% (2000); Median home value: $84,000 (2000); Median rent: $313 per month (2000); Median age of housing: 41 years (2000).
Hospitals: Saint Elizabeth Hospital (25 beds)
Safety: Violent crime rate: 19.0 per 10,000 population; Property crime rate: 369.2 per 10,000 population (2001).
Newspapers: Valley Shopper (1 x week); Wabasha County Herald (1 x week); The Star Shopper (1 x week)
Transportation: Commute to work: 84.1% car, 2.0% public transportation, 8.0% walk, 4.7% work from home (2000); Travel time to work: 58.9% less than 15 minutes, 16.0% 15 to 30 minutes, 10.0% 30 to 45 minutes, 6.1% 45 to 60 minutes, 9.0% 60 minutes or more (2000)

Additional Information Contacts

Wabasha Chamber of Commerce. 651-565-4158

WATOPA (township). Covers a land area of 35.416 square miles and a water area of 0.216 square miles. Located at 44.25° N. Lat.; 92.00° W. Long.
Population: 265 (2000); Race: 100.0% White, 0.0% Black, 0.0% Asian, 0.0% American Indian and Alaska Native, 2.1% Hispanic of any race, 0.0% two or more races (2000); Density: 7.5 persons per square mile (2000); Age: 26.8% under 18, 9.8% over 64 (2000); Marriage status: 22.7% never married, 62.7% now married, 5.4% widowed, 9.2% divorced (2000); Foreign born: 0.0% (2000); Ancestry (includes multiple ancestries): 60.9% German, 12.8% Irish, 11.5% Norwegian, 10.2% Polish, 8.1% Dutch (2000).
Economy: Employment by occupation: 17.9% management, 18.7% professional, 9.7% services, 22.4% sales, 2.2% farming, 14.2% construction, 14.9% production (2000).
Income: Per capita income: $21,418 (2000); Median household income: $47,813 (2000); Poverty rate: 2.6% (2000).
Taxes: Total city taxes per capita: $46 (1997); City property taxes per capita: $46 (1997).
Education: High school graduation rate: 83.4% (2000); College graduation rate: 13.9% (2000).
Housing: Homeownership rate: 95.8% (2000); Median home value: $106,300 (2000); Median rent: $300 per month (2000); Median age of housing: 26 years (2000).
Transportation: Commute to work: 91.7% car, 0.0% public transportation, 0.0% walk, 8.3% work from home (2000); Travel time to work: 24.8% less than 15 minutes, 44.6% 15 to 30 minutes, 16.5% 30 to 45 minutes, 9.9% 45 to 60 minutes, 4.1% 60 minutes or more (2000)

WEST ALBANY (township). Covers a land area of 35.572 square miles and a water area of 0.162 square miles. Located at 44.29° N. Lat.; 92.23° W. Long.
Population: 439 (2000); Race: 97.9% White, 0.0% Black, 0.0% Asian, 0.0% American Indian and Alaska Native, 1.9% Hispanic of any race, 0.2% two or more races (2000); Density: 12.3 persons per square mile (2000); Age: 34.8% under 18, 5.4% over 64 (2000); Marriage status: 24.0% never married, 67.9% now married, 3.2% widowed, 4.9% divorced (2000); Foreign born: 2.5% (2000); Ancestry (includes multiple ancestries): 61.0% German, 13.0% Irish, 12.8% Norwegian, 4.1% Swedish, 3.3% English (2000).
Economy: Employment by occupation: 26.8% management, 12.2% professional, 11.0% services, 23.2% sales, 3.9% farming, 9.4% construction, 13.4% production (2000).
Income: Per capita income: $17,768 (2000); Median household income: $48,125 (2000); Poverty rate: 5.8% (2000).
Taxes: Total city taxes per capita: $55 (1997); City property taxes per capita: $55 (1997).
Education: High school graduation rate: 91.0% (2000); College graduation rate: 12.3% (2000).
Housing: Homeownership rate: 79.6% (2000); Median home value: $103,600 (2000); Median rent: $350 per month (2000); Median age of housing: 36 years (2000).
Transportation: Commute to work: 70.3% car, 0.8% public transportation, 3.2% walk, 24.9% work from home (2000); Travel time to work: 19.8% less than 15 minutes, 31.0% 15 to 30 minutes, 25.1% 30 to 45 minutes, 14.4% 45 to 60 minutes, 9.6% 60 minutes or more (2000)

ZUMBRO (township). Covers a land area of 31.670 square miles and a water area of 0.614 square miles. Located at 44.21° N. Lat.; 92.41° W. Long.
Population: 715 (2000); Race: 98.0% White, 0.0% Black, 1.6% Asian, 0.3% American Indian and Alaska Native, 0.0% Hispanic of any race, 0.1% two or more races (2000); Density: 22.6 persons per square mile (2000); Age: 25.1% under 18, 9.1% over 64 (2000); Marriage status: 15.2% never married, 72.3% now married, 3.3% widowed, 9.1% divorced (2000); Foreign born: 1.0% (2000); Ancestry (includes multiple ancestries): 53.0% German, 21.5% Norwegian, 10.6% Irish, 9.6% English, 4.9% Swedish (2000).
Economy: Agriculture includes grain, soybeans; livestock, poultry; dairying. Manufacturing: meat processing, fencing equipment. Employment by occupation: 14.3% management, 18.9% professional, 13.0% services, 18.1% sales, 1.0% farming, 18.4% construction, 16.3% production (2000).
Income: Per capita income: $23,827 (2000); Median household income: $51,477 (2000); Poverty rate: 2.8% (2000).
Taxes: Total city taxes per capita: $84 (1997); City property taxes per capita: $82 (1997).
Education: High school graduation rate: 89.0% (2000); College graduation rate: 17.8% (2000).
Housing: Homeownership rate: 88.8% (2000); Median home value: $144,900 (2000); Median rent: $363 per month (2000); Median age of housing: 26 years (2000).
Transportation: Commute to work: 89.6% car, 1.6% public transportation, 0.0% walk, 8.4% work from home (2000); Travel time to work: 10.3% less than 15 minutes, 51.6% 15 to 30 minutes, 25.4% 30 to 45 minutes, 4.0% 45 to 60 minutes, 8.8% 60 minutes or more (2000)

ZUMBRO FALLS (city). Covers a land area of 0.461 square miles and a water area of 0.019 square miles. Located at 44.28° N. Lat.; 92.42° W. Long. Elevation is 836 feet.
Population: 177 (2000); Race: 100.0% White, 0.0% Black, 0.0% Asian, 0.0% American Indian and Alaska Native, 1.1% Hispanic of any race, 0.0% two or more races (2000); Density: 383.6 persons per square mile (2000); Age: 23.2% under 18, 9.5% over 64 (2000); Marriage status: 22.6% never married, 58.5% now married, 3.7% widowed, 15.2% divorced (2000); Foreign born: 0.0% (2000); Ancestry (includes multiple ancestries): 56.3% German, 16.3% Irish, 10.0% Other groups, 7.9% Norwegian, 6.3% English (2000).
Economy: Single-family building permits issued: 1 (2001) / 0 (2000); Multi-family building permits issued: 0 (2001) / 0 (2000); Employment by occupation: 7.5% management, 12.1% professional, 23.4% services, 16.8% sales, 0.0% farming, 21.5% construction, 18.7% production (2000).
Income: Per capita income: $18,176 (2000); Median household income: $37,188 (2000); Poverty rate: 13.2% (2000).
Taxes: Total city taxes per capita: $92 (1997); City property taxes per capita: $59 (1997).
Education: High school graduation rate: 84.6% (2000); College graduation rate: 5.1% (2000).
Housing: Homeownership rate: 83.3% (2000); Median home value: $66,700 (2000); Median rent: $344 per month (2000); Median age of housing: 60+ years (2000).
Transportation: Commute to work: 92.4% car, 1.9% public transportation, 2.9% walk, 0.0% work from home (2000); Travel time to work: 15.2% less than 15 minutes, 37.1% 15 to 30 minutes, 40.0% 30 to 45 minutes, 3.8% 45 to 60 minutes, 3.8% 60 minutes or more (2000)

Wadena County

Located in west central Minnesota; drained by the Crow Wing River. Covers a land area of 535.00 square miles, a water area of 8.00 square miles, and is located in the Central Time Zone. The county government was organized in 1858. County seat is Wadena.

Weather Station: Wadena 3 S Elevation: 1,348 feet

	Jan	Feb	Mar	Apr	May	Jun	Jul	Aug	Sep	Oct	Nov	Dec
High	16	23	34	52	67	74	79	77	67	55	35	21
Low	-5	1	14	29	42	53	57	55	45	33	18	3
Precip	0.9	0.6	1.6	2.0	2.9	4.2	3.5	3.1	2.6	2.7	1.4	0.6
Snow	12.1	7.0	9.7	3.2	tr	0.0	0.0	0.0	tr	1.3	8.1	6.9

High and Low temperatures in degrees Fahrenheit; Precipitation and Snow in inches

Population: 13,713 (2000); Race: 97.3% White, 0.4% Black, 0.6% Asian, 0.7% American Indian and Alaska Native, 1.1% Hispanic of any race, 0.5% two or more races (2000); Density: 25.6 persons per square mile (2000); Age: 25.8% under 18, 19.7% over 64 (2000).
Religion: Five largest groups: 19.4% Catholic Church, 14.8% Evangelical Lutheran Church in America, 12.7% Lutheran Church—Missouri Synod, 4.8% The United Methodist Church, 3.8% The Christian and Missionary Alliance (2000).
Economy: Unemployment rate: 4.7% (11/2002); Total civilian labor force: 7,174 (11/2002); Leading industries: 34.6% health care and social assistance; 23.8% manufacturing; 12.9% retail trade (2000); Companies that employ more than 1,000 persons: 0 (2000); Companies that employ more than 100 persons: 6 (2000); Farms: 625 totaling 174,833 acres (1997); Minority business ownership rate: 0.0% (1997); Women business ownership rate: 25.8% (1997); Retail sales per capita: $8,078 (1997). Single-family building permits issued: 65 (2001) / 61 (2000); Multi-family building permits issued: 0 (2001) / 4 (2000).
Income: Per capita income: $15,146 (2000); Median household income: $30,651 (2000); Poverty rate: 14.1% (2000); Bankruptcy rate: 2.85% (2001).
Taxes: Total county taxes per capita: $266 (1997); County property taxes per capita: $264 (1997).
Education: High school graduation rate: 79.5% (2000); College graduation rate: 13.4% (2000).
Housing: Homeownership rate: 77.4% (2000); Median home value: $56,900 (2000); Median rent: $267 per month (2000); Median age of housing: 36 years (2000).
Health: Birth rate: 125.4 per 10,000 population (1998); Age adjusted death rate: 96.9 per 10,000 population (1999); Age adjusted cancer mortality rate: 219.4 deaths per 100,000 population (1999). Number of physicians: 9.5 per 10,000 population (1999); Number of hospital beds: 21.9 per 10,000 population (1999).
Elections: 2000 Presidential election results: 35.3% Gore, 58.5% Bush, 4.0% Nader, 1.8% Buchanan
National and State Parks: Dry Sand Lake State Wildlife Management Area; Huntersville State Forest; Lyons State Forest; Strike Lake State Wildlife Management Area
Additional Information Contacts
Wadena County Government Offices 218-631-7650
Wadena Chamber of Commerce 218-631-1345

Wadena County Communities

ALDRICH (city). Covers a land area of 0.475 square miles and a water area of 0 square miles. Located at 46.37° N. Lat.; 94.94° W. Long.
Population: 53 (2000); Race: 100.0% White, 0.0% Black, 0.0% Asian, 0.0% American Indian and Alaska Native, 0.0% Hispanic of any race, 0.0% two or more races (2000); Density: 111.6 persons per square mile (2000); Age: 17.0% under 18, 15.1% over 64 (2000); Marriage status: 37.3% never married, 23.5% now married, 3.9% widowed, 35.3% divorced (2000); Foreign born: 0.0% (2000); Ancestry (includes multiple ancestries): 54.7% German, 22.6% Norwegian, 15.1% Swedish, 9.4% Polish, 9.4% Irish (2000).
Economy: Single-family building permits issued: 0 (2001) / 0 (2000); Multi-family building permits issued: 0 (2001) / 0 (2000); Employment by occupation: 19.0% management, 33.3% professional, 0.0% services, 19.0% sales, 0.0% farming, 19.0% construction, 9.5% production (2000).
Income: Per capita income: $14,598 (2000); Median household income: $30,417 (2000); Poverty rate: 13.2% (2000).
Taxes: Total city taxes per capita: $138 (1997); City property taxes per capita: $77 (1997).
Education: High school graduation rate: 75.0% (2000); College graduation rate: 2.8% (2000).
Housing: Homeownership rate: 87.5% (2000); Median home value: $53,600 (2000); Median rent: $275 per month (2000); Median age of housing: 60+ years (2000).
Transportation: Commute to work: 66.7% car, 0.0% public transportation, 9.5% walk, 23.8% work from home (2000); Travel time to work: 25.0% less than 15 minutes, 62.5% 15 to 30 minutes, 0.0% 30 to 45 minutes, 12.5% 45 to 60 minutes, 0.0% 60 minutes or more (2000)

ALDRICH (township). Covers a land area of 34.498 square miles and a water area of 0 square miles. Located at 46.40° N. Lat.; 94.96° W. Long.
History: Incorporated 1938.
Population: 418 (2000); Race: 98.1% White, 0.0% Black, 1.5% Asian, 0.4% American Indian and Alaska Native, 0.0% Hispanic of any race, 0.0% two or more races (2000); Density: 12.1 persons per square mile (2000); Age: 29.2% under 18, 12.2% over 64 (2000); Marriage status: 24.4% never married, 66.8% now married, 1.1% widowed, 7.7% divorced (2000); Foreign born: 1.5% (2000); Ancestry (includes multiple ancestries): 41.6% German, 12.6% Norwegian, 12.4% Irish, 7.9% English, 7.5% United States or American (2000).
Economy: Grain, beans; livestock, poultry; dairying. Manufactures trailers. Employment by occupation: 15.2% management, 12.5% professional, 14.8% services, 23.4% sales, 3.9% farming, 11.7% construction, 18.4% production (2000).
Income: Per capita income: $13,335 (2000); Median household income: $33,000 (2000); Poverty rate: 7.7% (2000).
Taxes: Total city taxes per capita: $57 (1997); City property taxes per capita: $57 (1997).
Education: High school graduation rate: 87.2% (2000); College graduation rate: 11.8% (2000).
Housing: Homeownership rate: 87.0% (2000); Median home value: $58,800 (2000); Median rent: $192 per month (2000); Median age of housing: 38 years (2000).
Transportation: Commute to work: 77.7% car, 1.2% public transportation, 6.4% walk, 14.7% work from home (2000); Travel time to work: 40.7% less than 15 minutes, 45.3% 15 to 30 minutes, 7.0% 30 to 45 minutes, 2.8% 45 to 60 minutes, 4.2% 60 minutes or more (2000)

BLUEBERRY (township). Covers a land area of 30.130 square miles and a water area of 1.829 square miles. Located at 46.77° N. Lat.; 95.09° W. Long.
Population: 732 (2000); Race: 98.7% White, 0.4% Black, 0.3% Asian, 0.1% American Indian and Alaska Native, 0.3% Hispanic of any race, 0.4% two or more races (2000); Density: 24.3 persons per square mile (2000); Age: 23.5% under 18, 17.3% over 64 (2000); Marriage status: 17.9% never married, 64.4% now married, 6.3% widowed, 11.4% divorced (2000); Foreign born: 1.9% (2000); Ancestry (includes multiple ancestries): 35.7% Finnish, 21.9% German, 16.0% Norwegian, 8.6% Swedish, 6.3% Polish (2000).
Economy: Employment by occupation: 8.4% management, 22.7% professional, 13.3% services, 20.1% sales, 2.9% farming, 12.0% construction, 20.5% production (2000).
Income: Per capita income: $17,780 (2000); Median household income: $35,833 (2000); Poverty rate: 7.9% (2000).
Taxes: Total city taxes per capita: $85 (1997); City property taxes per capita: $85 (1997).
Education: High school graduation rate: 84.0% (2000); College graduation rate: 17.8% (2000).
Housing: Homeownership rate: 86.2% (2000); Median home value: $89,600 (2000); Median rent: $238 per month (2000); Median age of housing: 31 years (2000).
Transportation: Commute to work: 92.5% car, 0.3% public transportation, 3.3% walk, 3.9% work from home (2000); Travel time to work: 44.6% less than 15 minutes, 34.4% 15 to 30 minutes, 8.8% 30 to 45 minutes, 2.4% 45 to 60 minutes, 9.9% 60 minutes or more (2000)

BULLARD (township). Covers a land area of 30.304 square miles and a water area of 0.718 square miles. Located at 46.48° N. Lat.; 94.83° W. Long.
Population: 207 (2000); Race: 93.7% White, 0.0% Black, 0.0% Asian, 2.5% American Indian and Alaska Native, 4.6% Hispanic of any race, 0.0% two or more races (2000); Density: 6.8 persons per square mile (2000); Age: 37.4% under 18, 9.2% over 64 (2000); Marriage status: 24.8% never married, 54.0% now married, 5.0% widowed, 16.1% divorced (2000); Foreign born: 0.0% (2000); Ancestry (includes multiple ancestries): 36.1% German, 10.1% Norwegian, 6.7% Swedish, 6.7% Irish, 5.5% Danish (2000).
Economy: Employment by occupation: 21.6% management, 11.8% professional, 19.6% services, 14.7% sales, 0.0% farming, 8.8% construction, 23.5% production (2000).
Income: Per capita income: $9,559 (2000); Median household income: $23,125 (2000); Poverty rate: 19.2% (2000).
Taxes: Total city taxes per capita: $69 (1997); City property taxes per capita: $69 (1997).
Education: High school graduation rate: 88.8% (2000); College graduation rate: 6.7% (2000).

Housing: Homeownership rate: 94.1% (2000); Median home value: $39,200 (2000); Median rent: $275 per month (2000); Median age of housing: 27 years (2000).
Transportation: Commute to work: 76.0% car, 3.0% public transportation, 5.0% walk, 16.0% work from home (2000); Travel time to work: 20.2% less than 15 minutes, 35.7% 15 to 30 minutes, 28.6% 30 to 45 minutes, 6.0% 45 to 60 minutes, 9.5% 60 minutes or more (2000)

HUNTERSVILLE (township). Covers a land area of 34.850 square miles and a water area of 1.007 square miles. Located at 46.75° N. Lat.; 94.88° W. Long.
Population: 128 (2000); Race: 98.6% White, 0.0% Black, 0.0% Asian, 1.4% American Indian and Alaska Native, 0.0% Hispanic of any race, 0.0% two or more races (2000); Density: 3.7 persons per square mile (2000); Age: 26.5% under 18, 8.2% over 64 (2000); Marriage status: 15.9% never married, 65.5% now married, 4.4% widowed, 14.2% divorced (2000); Foreign born: 0.0% (2000); Ancestry (includes multiple ancestries): 25.9% United States or American, 22.4% German, 18.4% Norwegian, 8.2% English, 6.8% Swedish (2000).
Economy: Employment by occupation: 8.8% management, 14.7% professional, 7.4% services, 19.1% sales, 7.4% farming, 8.8% construction, 33.8% production (2000).
Income: Per capita income: $12,320 (2000); Median household income: $32,500 (2000); Poverty rate: 25.2% (2000).
Taxes: Total city taxes per capita: $56 (1997); City property taxes per capita: $56 (1997).
Education: High school graduation rate: 78.4% (2000); College graduation rate: 4.1% (2000).
Housing: Homeownership rate: 96.6% (2000); Median home value: $112,500 (2000); Median age of housing: 31 years (2000).
Transportation: Commute to work: 95.6% car, 0.0% public transportation, 0.0% walk, 4.4% work from home (2000); Travel time to work: 7.7% less than 15 minutes, 50.8% 15 to 30 minutes, 27.7% 30 to 45 minutes, 0.0% 45 to 60 minutes, 13.8% 60 minutes or more (2000)

LEAF RIVER (township). Covers a land area of 35.173 square miles and a water area of 0 square miles. Located at 46.49° N. Lat.; 95.10° W. Long.
Population: 515 (2000); Race: 95.3% White, 2.4% Black, 0.4% Asian, 1.8% American Indian and Alaska Native, 0.0% Hispanic of any race, 0.0% two or more races (2000); Density: 14.6 persons per square mile (2000); Age: 27.7% under 18, 9.0% over 64 (2000); Marriage status: 14.9% never married, 76.3% now married, 2.6% widowed, 6.3% divorced (2000); Foreign born: 0.4% (2000); Ancestry (includes multiple ancestries): 44.5% German, 11.8% United States or American, 8.5% Norwegian, 7.4% Irish, 5.4% English (2000).
Economy: Employment by occupation: 18.9% management, 13.4% professional, 16.0% services, 21.4% sales, 1.7% farming, 13.9% construction, 14.7% production (2000).
Income: Per capita income: $14,681 (2000); Median household income: $37,292 (2000); Poverty rate: 19.3% (2000).
Taxes: Total city taxes per capita: $32 (1997); City property taxes per capita: $32 (1997).
Education: High school graduation rate: 79.3% (2000); College graduation rate: 14.4% (2000).
Housing: Homeownership rate: 97.3% (2000); Median home value: $55,600 (2000); Median rent: $225 per month (2000); Median age of housing: 40 years (2000).
Transportation: Commute to work: 88.5% car, 0.0% public transportation, 1.7% walk, 8.1% work from home (2000); Travel time to work: 52.8% less than 15 minutes, 29.2% 15 to 30 minutes, 6.9% 30 to 45 minutes, 2.3% 45 to 60 minutes, 8.8% 60 minutes or more (2000)

LYONS (township). Covers a land area of 34.891 square miles and a water area of 0.740 square miles. Located at 46.58° N. Lat.; 94.83° W. Long.
Population: 180 (2000); Race: 92.5% White, 0.0% Black, 0.0% Asian, 1.4% American Indian and Alaska Native, 4.8% Hispanic of any race, 6.2% two or more races (2000); Density: 5.2 persons per square mile (2000); Age: 14.4% under 18, 12.3% over 64 (2000); Marriage status: 9.4% never married, 67.2% now married, 8.6% widowed, 14.8% divorced (2000); Foreign born: 2.1% (2000); Ancestry (includes multiple ancestries): 27.4% German, 13.7% Norwegian, 8.9% Swedish, 8.2% Finnish, 8.2% United States or American (2000).
Economy: Employment by occupation: 8.6% management, 3.7% professional, 17.3% services, 23.5% sales, 8.6% farming, 12.3% construction, 25.9% production (2000).
Income: Per capita income: $20,031 (2000); Median household income: $35,000 (2000); Poverty rate: 24.7% (2000).
Taxes: Total city taxes per capita: $30 (1997); City property taxes per capita: $30 (1997).
Education: High school graduation rate: 79.7% (2000); College graduation rate: 6.5% (2000).
Housing: Homeownership rate: 94.4% (2000); Median home value: $27,500 (2000); Median rent: $325 per month (2000); Median age of housing: 25 years (2000).
Transportation: Commute to work: 85.2% car, 0.0% public transportation, 4.9% walk, 9.9% work from home (2000); Travel time to work: 12.3% less than 15 minutes, 16.4% 15 to 30 minutes, 47.9% 30 to 45 minutes, 17.8% 45 to 60 minutes, 5.5% 60 minutes or more (2000)

MEADOW (township). Covers a land area of 35.904 square miles and a water area of 0.575 square miles. Located at 46.68° N. Lat.; 94.96° W. Long.
Population: 228 (2000); Race: 99.2% White, 0.0% Black, 0.0% Asian, 0.0% American Indian and Alaska Native, 0.0% Hispanic of any race, 0.8% two or more races (2000); Density: 6.4 persons per square mile (2000); Age: 30.3% under 18, 8.6% over 64 (2000); Marriage status: 18.0% never married, 66.3% now married, 7.3% widowed, 8.4% divorced (2000); Foreign born: 0.0% (2000); Ancestry (includes multiple ancestries): 27.0% German, 20.1% Finnish, 18.0% United States or American, 13.5% Norwegian, 6.6% Swedish (2000).
Economy: Employment by occupation: 18.4% management, 6.1% professional, 18.4% services, 24.6% sales, 0.9% farming, 6.1% construction, 25.4% production (2000).
Income: Per capita income: $12,844 (2000); Median household income: $34,500 (2000); Poverty rate: 11.9% (2000).
Taxes: Total city taxes per capita: $59 (1997); City property taxes per capita: $59 (1997).
Education: High school graduation rate: 78.8% (2000); College graduation rate: 7.5% (2000).
Housing: Homeownership rate: 90.9% (2000); Median home value: $32,500 (2000); Median age of housing: 33 years (2000).
Transportation: Commute to work: 81.8% car, 0.0% public transportation, 0.9% walk, 17.3% work from home (2000); Travel time to work: 22.0% less than 15 minutes, 24.2% 15 to 30 minutes, 47.3% 30 to 45 minutes, 2.2% 45 to 60 minutes, 4.4% 60 minutes or more (2000)

MENAHGA (city). Covers a land area of 3.716 square miles and a water area of 0.201 square miles. Located at 46.75° N. Lat.; 95.10° W. Long.
History: Menahga was originally a lumber town, later becoming a trading center and shipping point for wheat, and then a general agricultural and dairying district. Many of the early residents were of Finnish ancestry.
Population: 1,220 (2000); Race: 98.3% White, 0.0% Black, 0.9% Asian, 0.0% American Indian and Alaska Native, 0.5% Hispanic of any race, 0.7% two or more races (2000); Density: 328.3 persons per square mile (2000); Age: 25.0% under 18, 33.0% over 64 (2000); Marriage status: 19.8% never married, 49.4% now married, 18.5% widowed, 12.3% divorced (2000); Foreign born: 2.2% (2000); Ancestry (includes multiple ancestries): 39.3% Finnish, 24.3% German, 16.6% Norwegian, 4.9% Swedish, 4.6% Irish (2000).
Economy: Single-family building permits issued: 9 (2001) / 3 (2000); Multi-family building permits issued: 0 (2001) / 0 (2000); Employment by occupation: 7.0% management, 17.9% professional, 18.1% services, 23.7% sales, 1.4% farming, 9.2% construction, 22.7% production (2000).
Income: Per capita income: $14,360 (2000); Median household income: $22,232 (2000); Poverty rate: 18.7% (2000).
Taxes: Total city taxes per capita: $179 (1997); City property taxes per capita: $178 (1997).
Education: High school graduation rate: 66.3% (2000); College graduation rate: 8.8% (2000).

School District(s)

Menahga (PK-12)
2000 Enrollment: 710 218-564-4141
Housing: Homeownership rate: 74.4% (2000); Median home value: $57,200 (2000); Median rent: $261 per month (2000); Median age of housing: 34 years (2000).
Transportation: Commute to work: 88.5% car, 0.0% public transportation, 3.7% walk, 6.4% work from home (2000); Travel time to work: 57.2% less than 15 minutes, 26.9% 15 to 30 minutes, 7.3% 30 to 45 minutes, 2.6% 45 to 60 minutes, 6.0% 60 minutes or more (2000)

NIMROD (city). Covers a land area of 0.929 square miles and a water area of 0.053 square miles. Located at 46.63° N. Lat.; 94.87° W. Long. Elevation is 1,335 feet.
Population: 75 (2000); Race: 100.0% White, 0.0% Black, 0.0% Asian, 0.0% American Indian and Alaska Native, 0.0% Hispanic of any race, 0.0% two or more races (2000); Density: 80.7 persons per square mile (2000); Age: 25.0% under 18, 19.3% over 64 (2000); Marriage status: 28.0% never married, 57.3% now married, 8.0% widowed, 6.7% divorced (2000); Foreign born: 0.0% (2000); Ancestry (includes multiple ancestries): 36.4% German, 23.9% United States or American, 21.6% Irish, 15.9% Finnish, 13.6% Norwegian (2000).
Economy: Dairying. Single-family building permits issued: 1 (2001) / 1 (2000); Multi-family building permits issued: 0 (2001) / 0 (2000); Employment by occupation: 9.1% management, 0.0% professional, 9.1% services, 54.5% sales, 0.0% farming, 18.2% construction, 9.1% production (2000).
Income: Per capita income: $15,413 (2000); Median household income: $30,313 (2000); Poverty rate: 6.8% (2000).
Taxes: Total city taxes per capita: $123 (1997); City property taxes per capita: $92 (1997).
Education: High school graduation rate: 85.0% (2000); College graduation rate: 0.0% (2000).
Housing: Homeownership rate: 100.0% (2000); Median home value: $36,300 (2000); Median age of housing: 31 years (2000).
Transportation: Commute to work: 77.3% car, 0.0% public transportation, 0.0% walk, 13.6% work from home (2000); Travel time to work: 21.1% less than 15 minutes, 21.1% 15 to 30 minutes, 42.1% 30 to 45 minutes, 15.8% 45 to 60 minutes, 0.0% 60 minutes or more (2000)

NORTH GERMANY (township). Covers a land area of 35.802 square miles and a water area of 0.009 square miles. Located at 46.58° N. Lat.; 94.98° W. Long.
Population: 327 (2000); Race: 99.4% White, 0.0% Black, 0.0% Asian, 0.0% American Indian and Alaska Native, 0.0% Hispanic of any race, 0.6% two or more races (2000); Density: 9.1 persons per square mile (2000); Age: 23.3% under 18, 15.8% over 64 (2000); Marriage status: 28.5% never married, 62.1% now married, 5.8% widowed, 3.6% divorced (2000); Foreign born: 0.0% (2000); Ancestry (includes multiple ancestries): 54.9% German, 15.2% Norwegian, 11.6% Finnish, 6.3% Irish, 6.3% United States or American (2000).
Economy: Employment by occupation: 11.9% management, 15.2% professional, 18.5% services, 11.3% sales, 7.3% farming, 9.9% construction, 25.8% production (2000).
Income: Per capita income: $12,998 (2000); Median household income: $29,167 (2000); Poverty rate: 17.9% (2000).
Taxes: Total city taxes per capita: $33 (1997); City property taxes per capita: $33 (1997).
Education: High school graduation rate: 77.4% (2000); College graduation rate: 7.7% (2000).
Housing: Homeownership rate: 85.3% (2000); Median home value: $71,700 (2000); Median rent: $275 per month (2000); Median age of housing: 38 years (2000).
Transportation: Commute to work: 85.9% car, 0.0% public transportation, 2.0% walk, 12.1% work from home (2000); Travel time to work: 20.6% less than 15 minutes, 48.9% 15 to 30 minutes, 19.1% 30 to 45 minutes, 6.1% 45 to 60 minutes, 5.3% 60 minutes or more (2000)

ORTON (township). Covers a land area of 34.406 square miles and a water area of 0.380 square miles. Located at 46.67° N. Lat.; 94.84° W. Long.
Population: 220 (2000); Race: 100.0% White, 0.0% Black, 0.0% Asian, 0.0% American Indian and Alaska Native, 0.0% Hispanic of any race, 0.0% two or more races (2000); Density: 6.4 persons per square mile (2000); Age: 26.2% under 18, 18.6% over 64 (2000); Marriage status: 23.3% never married, 58.7% now married, 10.5% widowed, 7.6% divorced (2000); Foreign born: 0.0% (2000); Ancestry (includes multiple ancestries): 25.8% German, 24.9% United States or American, 15.4% Finnish, 12.7% Irish, 9.0% Norwegian (2000).
Economy: Employment by occupation: 30.4% management, 2.9% professional, 5.8% services, 10.1% sales, 8.7% farming, 11.6% construction, 30.4% production (2000).
Income: Per capita income: $12,625 (2000); Median household income: $26,875 (2000); Poverty rate: 16.7% (2000).
Taxes: Total city taxes per capita: $50 (1997); City property taxes per capita: $50 (1997).
Education: High school graduation rate: 73.2% (2000); College graduation rate: 10.1% (2000).
Housing: Homeownership rate: 87.2% (2000); Median home value: $75,000 (2000); Median age of housing: 34 years (2000).
Transportation: Commute to work: 68.1% car, 0.0% public transportation, 8.7% walk, 23.2% work from home (2000); Travel time to work: 18.9% less than 15 minutes, 20.8% 15 to 30 minutes, 43.4% 30 to 45 minutes, 9.4% 45 to 60 minutes, 7.5% 60 minutes or more (2000)

RED EYE (township). Covers a land area of 35.074 square miles and a water area of 0.063 square miles. Located at 46.67° N. Lat.; 95.09° W. Long.
Population: 421 (2000); Race: 100.0% White, 0.0% Black, 0.0% Asian, 0.0% American Indian and Alaska Native, 0.0% Hispanic of any race, 0.0% two or more races (2000); Density: 12.0 persons per square mile (2000); Age: 30.3% under 18, 12.5% over 64 (2000); Marriage status: 19.5% never married, 73.5% now married, 2.9% widowed, 4.2% divorced (2000); Foreign born: 0.0% (2000); Ancestry (includes multiple ancestries): 40.6% German, 32.8% Finnish, 15.9% Norwegian, 11.5% Swedish, 5.6% Other groups (2000).
Economy: Employment by occupation: 14.7% management, 13.7% professional, 17.6% services, 21.1% sales, 4.4% farming, 10.8% construction, 17.6% production (2000).
Income: Per capita income: $15,184 (2000); Median household income: $37,500 (2000); Poverty rate: 8.8% (2000).
Taxes: Total city taxes per capita: $59 (1997); City property taxes per capita: $59 (1997).
Education: High school graduation rate: 82.1% (2000); College graduation rate: 5.2% (2000).
Housing: Homeownership rate: 93.7% (2000); Median home value: $53,800 (2000); Median rent: $258 per month (2000); Median age of housing: 36 years (2000).
Transportation: Commute to work: 82.8% car, 0.0% public transportation, 3.0% walk, 14.1% work from home (2000); Travel time to work: 40.0% less than 15 minutes, 30.0% 15 to 30 minutes, 17.1% 30 to 45 minutes, 7.6% 45 to 60 minutes, 5.3% 60 minutes or more (2000)

ROCKWOOD (township). Covers a land area of 34.572 square miles and a water area of 0 square miles. Located at 46.58° N. Lat.; 95.06° W. Long.
Population: 388 (2000); Race: 96.9% White, 0.0% Black, 0.0% Asian, 0.0% American Indian and Alaska Native, 2.6% Hispanic of any race, 0.5% two or more races (2000); Density: 11.2 persons per square mile (2000); Age: 27.3% under 18, 13.4% over 64 (2000); Marriage status: 19.7% never married, 73.6% now married, 4.4% widowed, 2.4% divorced (2000); Foreign born: 1.3% (2000); Ancestry (includes multiple ancestries): 35.3% German, 15.7% United States or American, 13.4% Norwegian, 10.8% Finnish, 10.8% Swedish (2000).
Economy: Employment by occupation: 25.7% management, 13.4% professional, 7.0% services, 18.7% sales, 4.8% farming, 15.5% construction, 15.0% production (2000).
Income: Per capita income: $13,546 (2000); Median household income: $34,625 (2000); Poverty rate: 9.3% (2000).
Taxes: Total city taxes per capita: $13 (1997); City property taxes per capita: $13 (1997).
Education: High school graduation rate: 85.4% (2000); College graduation rate: 9.9% (2000).
Housing: Homeownership rate: 96.4% (2000); Median home value: $74,000 (2000); Median age of housing: 41 years (2000).
Transportation: Commute to work: 63.6% car, 1.1% public transportation, 4.3% walk, 31.0% work from home (2000); Travel time to work: 31.0% less than 15 minutes, 29.5% 15 to 30 minutes, 32.6% 30 to 45 minutes, 1.6% 45 to 60 minutes, 5.4% 60 minutes or more (2000)

SEBEKA (city). Covers a land area of 2.456 square miles and a water area of 0 square miles. Located at 46.62° N. Lat.; 95.09° W. Long. Elevation is 1,385 feet.
Population: 710 (2000); Race: 97.4% White, 0.0% Black, 0.4% Asian, 0.4% American Indian and Alaska Native, 1.4% Hispanic of any race, 0.4% two or more races (2000); Density: 289.1 persons per square mile (2000); Age: 24.0% under 18, 23.9% over 64 (2000); Marriage status: 17.9% never married, 57.8% now married, 14.5% widowed, 9.7% divorced (2000); Foreign born: 2.1% (2000); Ancestry (includes multiple ancestries): 30.5% German, 27.2% Finnish, 12.8% Norwegian, 8.7% Swedish, 6.6% Irish (2000).
Economy: Agriculture: grain; livestock, poultry; dairying. Manufacturing: printing and publishing, ceramics. Employment by occupation: 10.5%

management, 19.0% professional, 17.3% services, 20.9% sales, 0.7% farming, 8.2% construction, 23.5% production (2000).
Income: Per capita income: $14,933 (2000); Median household income: $23,693 (2000); Poverty rate: 17.8% (2000).
Taxes: Total city taxes per capita: $105 (1997); City property taxes per capita: $102 (1997).
Education: High school graduation rate: 76.7% (2000); College graduation rate: 14.3% (2000).

School District(s)

Sebeka (PK-12)
2000 Enrollment: 580 218-837-5101
Housing: Homeownership rate: 75.4% (2000); Median home value: $40,600 (2000); Median rent: $262 per month (2000); Median age of housing: 44 years (2000).
Newspapers: The Review Messenger (1 x week)
Transportation: Commute to work: 86.0% car, 1.0% public transportation, 10.3% walk, 2.7% work from home (2000); Travel time to work: 46.1% less than 15 minutes, 32.8% 15 to 30 minutes, 10.6% 30 to 45 minutes, 4.4% 45 to 60 minutes, 6.1% 60 minutes or more (2000)

SHELL RIVER (township). Covers a land area of 34.776 square miles and a water area of 1.341 square miles. Located at 46.76° N. Lat.; 94.97° W. Long.
Population: 276 (2000); Race: 96.8% White, 0.0% Black, 0.0% Asian, 1.4% American Indian and Alaska Native, 0.7% Hispanic of any race, 1.8% two or more races (2000); Density: 7.9 persons per square mile (2000); Age: 30.4% under 18, 13.9% over 64 (2000); Marriage status: 15.1% never married, 71.7% now married, 2.0% widowed, 11.2% divorced (2000); Foreign born: 0.7% (2000); Ancestry (includes multiple ancestries): 28.6% German, 18.9% Finnish, 11.1% Swedish, 11.1% Norwegian, 10.0% Irish (2000).
Economy: Employment by occupation: 14.8% management, 14.1% professional, 10.9% services, 14.1% sales, 6.3% farming, 18.8% construction, 21.1% production (2000).
Income: Per capita income: $16,529 (2000); Median household income: $30,000 (2000); Poverty rate: 8.3% (2000).
Taxes: Total city taxes per capita: $75 (1997); City property taxes per capita: $75 (1997).
Education: High school graduation rate: 79.6% (2000); College graduation rate: 15.1% (2000).
Housing: Homeownership rate: 85.6% (2000); Median home value: $87,500 (2000); Median rent: $275 per month (2000); Median age of housing: 28 years (2000).
Transportation: Commute to work: 78.9% car, 0.0% public transportation, 7.8% walk, 13.3% work from home (2000); Travel time to work: 42.3% less than 15 minutes, 47.7% 15 to 30 minutes, 4.5% 30 to 45 minutes, 1.8% 45 to 60 minutes, 3.6% 60 minutes or more (2000)

THOMASTOWN (township). Covers a land area of 40.952 square miles and a water area of 1.009 square miles. Located at 46.41° N. Lat.; 94.83° W. Long.
Population: 714 (2000); Race: 99.6% White, 0.0% Black, 0.0% Asian, 0.0% American Indian and Alaska Native, 1.7% Hispanic of any race, 0.4% two or more races (2000); Density: 17.4 persons per square mile (2000); Age: 29.5% under 18, 8.2% over 64 (2000); Marriage status: 22.0% never married, 69.5% now married, 3.2% widowed, 5.3% divorced (2000); Foreign born: 0.7% (2000); Ancestry (includes multiple ancestries): 35.7% German, 16.3% Norwegian, 11.7% Swedish, 11.1% Irish, 8.2% Polish (2000).
Economy: Employment by occupation: 12.8% management, 30.9% professional, 9.6% services, 16.6% sales, 2.6% farming, 9.6% construction, 17.8% production (2000).
Income: Per capita income: $20,017 (2000); Median household income: $48,000 (2000); Poverty rate: 9.5% (2000).
Taxes: Total city taxes per capita: $61 (1997); City property taxes per capita: $61 (1997).
Education: High school graduation rate: 93.0% (2000); College graduation rate: 30.3% (2000).
Housing: Homeownership rate: 95.6% (2000); Median home value: $101,100 (2000); Median rent: $325 per month (2000); Median age of housing: 23 years (2000).
Transportation: Commute to work: 82.4% car, 0.9% public transportation, 4.5% walk, 11.3% work from home (2000); Travel time to work: 54.4% less than 15 minutes, 24.5% 15 to 30 minutes, 9.4% 30 to 45 minutes, 5.7% 45 to 60 minutes, 6.0% 60 minutes or more (2000)

VERNDALE (city). Covers a land area of 0.978 square miles and a water area of 0 square miles. Located at 46.39° N. Lat.; 95.01° W. Long. Elevation is 1,349 feet.
Population: 575 (2000); Race: 94.5% White, 0.0% Black, 0.8% Asian, 3.6% American Indian and Alaska Native, 3.6% Hispanic of any race, 0.0% two or more races (2000); Density: 587.7 persons per square mile (2000); Age: 28.4% under 18, 21.2% over 64 (2000); Marriage status: 21.8% never married, 55.0% now married, 11.0% widowed, 12.3% divorced (2000); Foreign born: 0.9% (2000); Ancestry (includes multiple ancestries): 31.6% German, 15.6% Norwegian, 11.1% Swedish, 8.5% Irish, 7.5% United States or American (2000).
Economy: Agriculture: dairying; poultry; oats, barley, rye. Manufacturing of prefabricated homes. Single-family building permits issued: 4 (2001) / 1 (2000); Multi-family building permits issued: 0 (2001) / 0 (2000); Employment by occupation: 9.0% management, 14.9% professional, 23.1% services, 9.0% sales, 2.7% farming, 7.7% construction, 33.5% production (2000).
Income: Per capita income: $12,448 (2000); Median household income: $26,000 (2000); Poverty rate: 11.8% (2000).
Taxes: Total city taxes per capita: $217 (1997); City property taxes per capita: $215 (1997).
Education: High school graduation rate: 77.2% (2000); College graduation rate: 8.6% (2000).

School District(s)

Verndale (PK-12)
2000 Enrollment: 437 218-445-5184
Housing: Homeownership rate: 71.6% (2000); Median home value: $44,400 (2000); Median rent: $259 per month (2000); Median age of housing: 41 years (2000).
Newspapers: The Verndale Sun (1 x week)
Transportation: Commute to work: 91.3% car, 0.0% public transportation, 6.0% walk, 2.8% work from home (2000); Travel time to work: 45.3% less than 15 minutes, 40.6% 15 to 30 minutes, 3.8% 30 to 45 minutes, 4.7% 45 to 60 minutes, 5.7% 60 minutes or more (2000)

WADENA (city). Covers a land area of 5.247 square miles and a water area of 0 square miles. Located at 46.44° N. Lat.; 95.13° W. Long. Elevation is 1,352 feet.
History: Wadena developed as a distributing center, with a diversified industrial base that included a canning factory and an ice-cream manufacturing plant. The name of Wadena is of Indian origin meaning "a little round hill."
Population: 4,294 (2000); Race: 96.6% White, 0.5% Black, 1.1% Asian, 0.7% American Indian and Alaska Native, 0.9% Hispanic of any race, 0.5% two or more races (2000); Density: 818.4 persons per square mile (2000); Age: 23.7% under 18, 24.1% over 64 (2000); Marriage status: 26.2% never married, 53.2% now married, 11.5% widowed, 9.1% divorced (2000); Foreign born: 0.8% (2000); Ancestry (includes multiple ancestries): 46.0% German, 19.1% Norwegian, 10.6% Swedish, 6.2% Irish, 5.7% United States or American (2000).
Economy: Single-family building permits issued: 11 (2001) / 8 (2000); Multi-family building permits issued: 0 (2001) / 4 (2000); Employment by occupation: 8.4% management, 20.6% professional, 16.6% services, 22.9% sales, 1.3% farming, 8.7% construction, 21.5% production (2000).
Income: Per capita income: $15,452 (2000); Median household income: $26,947 (2000); Poverty rate: 15.6% (2000).
Taxes: Total city taxes per capita: $108 (1997); City property taxes per capita: $97 (1997).
Education: High school graduation rate: 78.5% (2000); College graduation rate: 16.0% (2000).

School District(s)

Leaf River Ed. Dist. (N -N)
2000 Enrollment: n/a 218-631-2281
Wadena-Deer Creek (PK-12)
2000 Enrollment: 1,367 218-631-2155

Two-year College(s)

Northwest Technical College-Wadena (Public)
2001 Enrollment: n/a 218-631-3530
Housing: Homeownership rate: 63.5% (2000); Median home value: $51,200 (2000); Median rent: $258 per month (2000); Median age of housing: 42 years (2000).
Hospitals: Tri-County Hospital (49 beds)
Safety: Violent crime rate: 34.6 per 10,000 population; Property crime rate: 534.6 per 10,000 population (2001).
Newspapers: Wadena Pioneer Journal (1 x week)

Transportation: Commute to work: 88.3% car, 2.3% public transportation, 3.6% walk, 4.3% work from home (2000); Travel time to work: 68.4% less than 15 minutes, 18.7% 15 to 30 minutes, 6.2% 30 to 45 minutes, 4.0% 45 to 60 minutes, 2.7% 60 minutes or more (2000)
Additional Information Contacts
Wadena Chamber of Commerce 218-631-1345

WADENA (township). Covers a land area of 31.414 square miles and a water area of 0.032 square miles. Located at 46.40° N. Lat.; 95.09° W. Long. Elevation is 1,352 feet.
History: Settled 1871, incorporated 1881.
Population: 1,010 (2000); Race: 97.2% White, 0.7% Black, 0.6% Asian, 0.3% American Indian and Alaska Native, 2.0% Hispanic of any race, 0.2% two or more races (2000); Density: 32.2 persons per square mile (2000); Age: 27.8% under 18, 10.8% over 64 (2000); Marriage status: 21.5% never married, 69.4% now married, 3.3% widowed, 5.8% divorced (2000); Foreign born: 1.4% (2000); Ancestry (includes multiple ancestries): 45.1% German, 12.6% Norwegian, 8.9% English, 8.6% Irish, 8.0% United States or American (2000).
Economy: Trading point in grain; livestock, poultry; and dairying area; light manufacturing. Municipal airport to East. Employment by occupation: 14.1% management, 15.3% professional, 12.0% services, 26.9% sales, 3.1% farming, 11.2% construction, 17.5% production (2000).
Income: Per capita income: $16,109 (2000); Median household income: $41,250 (2000); Poverty rate: 9.0% (2000).
Taxes: Total city taxes per capita: $33 (1997); City property taxes per capita: $33 (1997).
Education: High school graduation rate: 90.4% (2000); College graduation rate: 11.6% (2000).
Housing: Homeownership rate: 89.4% (2000); Median home value: $70,000 (2000); Median rent: $314 per month (2000); Median age of housing: 28 years (2000).
Transportation: Commute to work: 87.7% car, 0.0% public transportation, 3.4% walk, 8.1% work from home (2000); Travel time to work: 67.8% less than 15 minutes, 20.8% 15 to 30 minutes, 4.8% 30 to 45 minutes, 0.9% 45 to 60 minutes, 5.7% 60 minutes or more (2000)

WING RIVER (township). Covers a land area of 36.017 square miles and a water area of 0.022 square miles. Located at 46.50° N. Lat.; 94.97° W. Long.
Population: 430 (2000); Race: 99.0% White, 0.5% Black, 0.0% Asian, 0.0% American Indian and Alaska Native, 0.0% Hispanic of any race, 0.5% two or more races (2000); Density: 11.9 persons per square mile (2000); Age: 26.1% under 18, 18.3% over 64 (2000); Marriage status: 16.2% never married, 68.6% now married, 5.4% widowed, 9.8% divorced (2000); Foreign born: 0.0% (2000); Ancestry (includes multiple ancestries): 37.8% German, 18.5% United States or American, 12.0% Norwegian, 6.5% Swedish, 5.5% Polish (2000).
Economy: Employment by occupation: 12.6% management, 9.6% professional, 10.8% services, 24.0% sales, 7.2% farming, 13.8% construction, 22.2% production (2000).
Income: Per capita income: $13,634 (2000); Median household income: $35,469 (2000); Poverty rate: 7.3% (2000).
Taxes: Total city taxes per capita: $56 (1997); City property taxes per capita: $56 (1997).
Education: High school graduation rate: 76.7% (2000); College graduation rate: 8.6% (2000).
Housing: Homeownership rate: 91.1% (2000); Median home value: $62,500 (2000); Median rent: $225 per month (2000); Median age of housing: 34 years (2000).
Transportation: Commute to work: 83.5% car, 1.2% public transportation, 2.4% walk, 11.6% work from home (2000); Travel time to work: 22.1% less than 15 minutes, 62.1% 15 to 30 minutes, 8.3% 30 to 45 minutes, 0.0% 45 to 60 minutes, 7.6% 60 minutes or more (2000)

Waseca County

Located in southern Minnesota; drained by the Le Sueur River; includes Lake Elysian. Covers a land area of 423.30 square miles, a water area of 9.60 square miles, and is located in the Central Time Zone. The county government was organized in 1857. County seat is Waseca.

Weather Station: Waseca Exp. Station — Elevation: 1,151 feet

	Jan	Feb	Mar	Apr	May	Jun	Jul	Aug	Sep	Oct	Nov	Dec
High	20	27	38	55	69	79	82	80	72	59	40	26
Low	1	8	21	35	47	57	61	58	49	36	23	8
Precip	1.3	0.9	2.5	3.3	3.9	4.0	4.5	4.5	3.4	2.6	2.3	1.3
Snow	12.9	7.8	10.2	4.1	tr	0.0	0.0	0.0	0.0	0.6	8.4	10.7

High and Low temperatures in degrees Fahrenheit; Precipitation and Snow in inches

Population: 19,526 (2000); Race: 94.3% White, 2.4% Black, 0.4% Asian, 0.9% American Indian and Alaska Native, 3.0% Hispanic of any race, 0.7% two or more races (2000); Density: 46.1 persons per square mile (2000); Age: 25.8% under 18, 14.2% over 64 (2000).
Religion: Five largest groups: 27.6% Catholic Church, 25.1% Evangelical Lutheran Church in America, 16.7% Lutheran Church—Missouri Synod, 5.2% The United Methodist Church, 1.5% Wisconsin Evangelical Lutheran Synod (2000).
Economy: Unemployment rate: 3.6% (11/2002); Total civilian labor force: 9,208 (11/2002); Leading industries: 41.0% manufacturing; 16.9% health care and social assistance; 11.1% retail trade (2000); Companies that employ more than 1,000 persons: 1 (2000); Companies that employ more than 100 persons: 13 (2000); Farms: 709 totaling 235,351 acres (1997); Minority business ownership rate: 0.0% (1997); Women business ownership rate: 27.1% (1997); Retail sales per capita: $5,748 (1997). Single-family building permits issued: 53 (2001) / 61 (2000); Multi-family building permits issued: 0 (2001) / 35 (2000).
Income: Per capita income: $18,631 (2000); Median household income: $42,440 (2000); Poverty rate: 6.5% (2000); Bankruptcy rate: 3.10% (2001).
Taxes: Total county taxes per capita: $285 (1997); County property taxes per capita: $277 (1997).
Education: High school graduation rate: 84.8% (2000); College graduation rate: 16.2% (2000).
Housing: Homeownership rate: 80.0% (2000); Median home value: $87,700 (2000); Median rent: $349 per month (2000); Median age of housing: 40 years (2000).
Health: Birth rate: 132.1 per 10,000 population (1998); Age adjusted death rate: 77.5 per 10,000 population (1999); Age adjusted cancer mortality rate: 169.7 deaths per 100,000 population (1999). Number of physicians: 10.8 per 10,000 population (1999); Number of hospital beds: 6.1 per 10,000 population (1999).
Elections: 2000 Presidential election results: 41.7% Gore, 52.0% Bush, 4.5% Nader, 1.5% Buchanan
National and State Parks: Mueller State Wildlife Management Area; Stokman State Wildlife Management Area; Teal State Wildlife Management Area
Additional Information Contacts
Waseca County Government Offices 507-835-0630
Janesville Chamber of Commerce 507-234-5110
Waseca Chamber of Commerce 507-835-3260

Waseca County Communities

ALTON (township). Covers a land area of 34.851 square miles and a water area of 1.369 square miles. Located at 44.07° N. Lat.; 93.72° W. Long.
Population: 645 (2000); Race: 84.8% White, 8.9% Black, 0.0% Asian, 6.3% American Indian and Alaska Native, 0.0% Hispanic of any race, 0.0% two or more races (2000); Density: 18.5 persons per square mile (2000); Age: 17.6% under 18, 12.1% over 64 (2000); Marriage status: 40.4% never married, 47.0% now married, 3.0% widowed, 9.6% divorced (2000); Foreign born: 0.3% (2000); Ancestry (includes multiple ancestries): 41.1% German, 9.0% Norwegian, 8.4% Irish, 4.8% United States or American, 3.1% Swedish (2000).
Economy: Employment by occupation: 14.2% management, 12.7% professional, 7.8% services, 27.0% sales, 5.4% farming, 13.7% construction, 19.1% production (2000).
Income: Per capita income: $15,413 (2000); Median household income: $42,500 (2000); Poverty rate: 5.9% (2000).
Taxes: Total city taxes per capita: $52 (1997); City property taxes per capita: $52 (1997).
Education: High school graduation rate: 82.0% (2000); College graduation rate: 7.5% (2000).
Housing: Homeownership rate: 89.2% (2000); Median home value: $82,000 (2000); Median rent: $275 per month (2000); Median age of housing: 60+ years (2000).
Transportation: Commute to work: 86.5% car, 0.0% public transportation, 0.0% walk, 13.5% work from home (2000); Travel time to work: 35.8% less

than 15 minutes, 32.4% 15 to 30 minutes, 25.4% 30 to 45 minutes, 4.0% 45 to 60 minutes, 2.3% 60 minutes or more (2000)

BLOOMING GROVE (township). Covers a land area of 35.560 square miles and a water area of 0.441 square miles. Located at 44.16° N. Lat.; 93.45° W. Long.
Population: 523 (2000); Race: 95.7% White, 0.0% Black, 0.7% Asian, 0.0% American Indian and Alaska Native, 0.0% Hispanic of any race, 3.5% two or more races (2000); Density: 14.7 persons per square mile (2000); Age: 27.6% under 18, 11.4% over 64 (2000); Marriage status: 22.6% never married, 69.9% now married, 3.2% widowed, 4.4% divorced (2000); Foreign born: 1.5% (2000); Ancestry (includes multiple ancestries): 59.2% German, 18.4% Norwegian, 15.5% Irish, 6.9% United States or American, 6.1% Swedish (2000).
Economy: Employment by occupation: 14.0% management, 11.7% professional, 9.7% services, 27.3% sales, 1.6% farming, 12.3% construction, 23.4% production (2000).
Income: Per capita income: $17,916 (2000); Median household income: $45,750 (2000); Poverty rate: 7.3% (2000).
Taxes: Total city taxes per capita: $59 (1997); City property taxes per capita: $59 (1997).
Education: High school graduation rate: 89.6% (2000); College graduation rate: 15.9% (2000).
Housing: Homeownership rate: 89.7% (2000); Median home value: $135,300 (2000); Median rent: $306 per month (2000); Median age of housing: 52 years (2000).
Transportation: Commute to work: 87.0% car, 0.0% public transportation, 1.3% walk, 11.7% work from home (2000); Travel time to work: 43.8% less than 15 minutes, 38.6% 15 to 30 minutes, 13.2% 30 to 45 minutes, 0.7% 45 to 60 minutes, 3.7% 60 minutes or more (2000)

BYRON (township). Covers a land area of 35.952 square miles and a water area of 0.155 square miles. Located at 43.87° N. Lat.; 93.59° W. Long.
Population: 248 (2000); Race: 98.5% White, 0.0% Black, 0.0% Asian, 0.0% American Indian and Alaska Native, 0.0% Hispanic of any race, 1.5% two or more races (2000); Density: 6.9 persons per square mile (2000); Age: 30.8% under 18, 17.6% over 64 (2000); Marriage status: 18.6% never married, 71.4% now married, 2.4% widowed, 7.6% divorced (2000); Foreign born: 1.5% (2000); Ancestry (includes multiple ancestries): 48.4% German, 13.9% Norwegian, 12.5% Irish, 8.8% English, 8.1% Polish (2000).
Economy: Employment by occupation: 20.7% management, 12.9% professional, 5.0% services, 26.4% sales, 5.7% farming, 11.4% construction, 17.9% production (2000).
Income: Per capita income: $18,577 (2000); Median household income: $42,188 (2000); Poverty rate: 7.0% (2000).
Taxes: Total city taxes per capita: $114 (1997); City property taxes per capita: $114 (1997).
Education: High school graduation rate: 90.6% (2000); College graduation rate: 14.6% (2000).
Housing: Homeownership rate: 90.0% (2000); Median home value: $66,900 (2000); Median rent: $175 per month (2000); Median age of housing: 59 years (2000).
Transportation: Commute to work: 85.0% car, 0.0% public transportation, 0.0% walk, 15.0% work from home (2000); Travel time to work: 24.4% less than 15 minutes, 42.9% 15 to 30 minutes, 15.1% 30 to 45 minutes, 13.4% 45 to 60 minutes, 4.2% 60 minutes or more (2000)

FREEDOM (township). Covers a land area of 35.947 square miles and a water area of 0.229 square miles. Located at 43.98° N. Lat.; 93.70° W. Long.
Population: 397 (2000); Race: 99.2% White, 0.0% Black, 0.0% Asian, 0.0% American Indian and Alaska Native, 1.6% Hispanic of any race, 0.8% two or more races (2000); Density: 11.0 persons per square mile (2000); Age: 27.8% under 18, 15.5% over 64 (2000); Marriage status: 25.3% never married, 66.2% now married, 7.1% widowed, 1.4% divorced (2000); Foreign born: 1.1% (2000); Ancestry (includes multiple ancestries): 58.3% German, 12.0% United States or American, 7.9% Irish, 7.9% English, 6.5% Norwegian (2000).
Economy: Employment by occupation: 17.4% management, 10.9% professional, 10.4% services, 20.4% sales, 5.0% farming, 12.9% construction, 22.9% production (2000).
Income: Per capita income: $14,678 (2000); Median household income: $39,375 (2000); Poverty rate: 4.4% (2000).
Taxes: Total city taxes per capita: $71 (1997); City property taxes per capita: $71 (1997).
Education: High school graduation rate: 86.5% (2000); College graduation rate: 12.3% (2000).
Housing: Homeownership rate: 86.2% (2000); Median home value: $93,000 (2000); Median rent: $269 per month (2000); Median age of housing: 58 years (2000).
Transportation: Commute to work: 88.6% car, 0.0% public transportation, 1.0% walk, 10.4% work from home (2000); Travel time to work: 7.5% less than 15 minutes, 49.1% 15 to 30 minutes, 28.3% 30 to 45 minutes, 8.7% 45 to 60 minutes, 6.4% 60 minutes or more (2000)

IOSCO (township). Covers a land area of 35.040 square miles and a water area of 0.705 square miles. Located at 44.15° N. Lat.; 93.59° W. Long.
Population: 598 (2000); Race: 98.9% White, 0.0% Black, 0.0% Asian, 0.0% American Indian and Alaska Native, 0.0% Hispanic of any race, 1.1% two or more races (2000); Density: 17.1 persons per square mile (2000); Age: 27.3% under 18, 6.8% over 64 (2000); Marriage status: 23.6% never married, 69.2% now married, 2.7% widowed, 4.5% divorced (2000); Foreign born: 0.5% (2000); Ancestry (includes multiple ancestries): 68.8% German, 14.1% Irish, 11.1% Norwegian, 6.8% Czech, 6.3% Swedish (2000).
Economy: Employment by occupation: 18.5% management, 18.8% professional, 8.8% services, 24.3% sales, 4.4% farming, 10.8% construction, 14.4% production (2000).
Income: Per capita income: $26,709 (2000); Median household income: $60,750 (2000); Poverty rate: 8.5% (2000).
Taxes: Total city taxes per capita: $62 (1997); City property taxes per capita: $62 (1997).
Education: High school graduation rate: 96.0% (2000); College graduation rate: 24.1% (2000).
Housing: Homeownership rate: 94.7% (2000); Median home value: $139,700 (2000); Median rent: $425 per month (2000); Median age of housing: 28 years (2000).
Transportation: Commute to work: 87.7% car, 0.0% public transportation, 1.7% walk, 10.6% work from home (2000); Travel time to work: 27.1% less than 15 minutes, 36.1% 15 to 30 minutes, 28.0% 30 to 45 minutes, 3.1% 45 to 60 minutes, 5.6% 60 minutes or more (2000)

JANESVILLE (city). Covers a land area of 1.276 square miles and a water area of 0 square miles. Located at 44.11° N. Lat.; 93.70° W. Long. Elevation is 1,069 feet.
Population: 2,109 (2000); Race: 97.7% White, 0.0% Black, 0.4% Asian, 0.4% American Indian and Alaska Native, 1.8% Hispanic of any race, 1.5% two or more races (2000); Density: 1,653.3 persons per square mile (2000); Age: 27.2% under 18, 15.6% over 64 (2000); Marriage status: 22.2% never married, 61.4% now married, 9.9% widowed, 6.4% divorced (2000); Foreign born: 1.2% (2000); Ancestry (includes multiple ancestries): 55.3% German, 13.2% Irish, 11.1% Norwegian, 9.0% United States or American, 3.9% English (2000).
Economy: Single-family building permits issued: 10 (2001) / 10 (2000); Multi-family building permits issued: 0 (2001) / 0 (2000); Employment by occupation: 9.7% management, 13.4% professional, 13.7% services, 30.4% sales, 0.7% farming, 8.9% construction, 23.3% production (2000).
Income: Per capita income: $17,443 (2000); Median household income: $41,667 (2000); Poverty rate: 3.7% (2000).
Taxes: Total city taxes per capita: $100 (1997); City property taxes per capita: $82 (1997).
Education: High school graduation rate: 85.9% (2000); College graduation rate: 17.1% (2000).

School District(s)

Janesville-Waldorf-Pemberton (PK-12)
2000 Enrollment: 602 507-234-5478

Housing: Homeownership rate: 80.5% (2000); Median home value: $84,300 (2000); Median rent: $364 per month (2000); Median age of housing: 37 years (2000).
Safety: Violent crime rate: 14.1 per 10,000 population; Property crime rate: 314.3 per 10,000 population (2001).
Newspapers: Janesville Argus (1 x week)
Transportation: Commute to work: 91.9% car, 0.4% public transportation, 4.3% walk, 3.4% work from home (2000); Travel time to work: 29.1% less than 15 minutes, 54.7% 15 to 30 minutes, 12.4% 30 to 45 minutes, 1.0% 45 to 60 minutes, 2.8% 60 minutes or more (2000)

Additional Information Contacts

Janesville Chamber of Commerce 507-234-5110

JANESVILLE (township). Covers a land area of 30.927 square miles and a water area of 3.771 square miles. Located at 44.14° N. Lat.; 93.69° W. Long. Elevation is 1,069 feet.
History: Plotted 1855, deserted in Sioux outbreak of 1862, incorporated 1870.

Population: 520 (2000); Race: 100.0% White, 0.0% Black, 0.0% Asian, 0.0% American Indian and Alaska Native, 0.0% Hispanic of any race, 0.0% two or more races (2000); Density: 16.8 persons per square mile (2000); Age: 26.7% under 18, 12.5% over 64 (2000); Marriage status: 28.8% never married, 62.5% now married, 5.5% widowed, 3.1% divorced (2000); Foreign born: 1.2% (2000); Ancestry (includes multiple ancestries): 57.7% German, 22.1% Irish, 8.1% Norwegian, 6.0% English, 4.4% French (except Basque) (2000).
Economy: Agriculture: grain, soybeans; livestock, poultry; dairying. Manufacturing: feeds and fertilizers. Employment by occupation: 12.2% management, 17.3% professional, 8.9% services, 25.8% sales, 0.7% farming, 16.6% construction, 18.5% production (2000).
Income: Per capita income: $17,714 (2000); Median household income: $45,667 (2000); Poverty rate: 5.6% (2000).
Taxes: Total city taxes per capita: $61 (1997); City property taxes per capita: $61 (1997).
Education: High school graduation rate: 95.9% (2000); College graduation rate: 15.1% (2000).
Housing: Homeownership rate: 87.0% (2000); Median home value: $119,200 (2000); Median rent: $369 per month (2000); Median age of housing: 35 years (2000).
Transportation: Commute to work: 82.7% car, 0.0% public transportation, 2.2% walk, 15.1% work from home (2000); Travel time to work: 28.3% less than 15 minutes, 48.3% 15 to 30 minutes, 17.8% 30 to 45 minutes, 0.0% 45 to 60 minutes, 5.7% 60 minutes or more (2000)

NEW RICHLAND (city). Covers a land area of 0.598 square miles and a water area of 0 square miles. Located at 43.89° N. Lat.; 93.49° W. Long. Elevation is 1,184 feet.
Population: 1,197 (2000); Race: 99.6% White, 0.0% Black, 0.0% Asian, 0.0% American Indian and Alaska Native, 1.2% Hispanic of any race, 0.1% two or more races (2000); Density: 2,002.8 persons per square mile (2000); Age: 24.2% under 18, 25.8% over 64 (2000); Marriage status: 18.1% never married, 56.3% now married, 18.0% widowed, 7.7% divorced (2000); Foreign born: 0.9% (2000); Ancestry (includes multiple ancestries): 45.1% German, 29.0% Norwegian, 8.9% Irish, 6.9% Swedish, 6.3% United States or American (2000).
Economy: Single-family building permits issued: 1 (2001) / 2 (2000); Multi-family building permits issued: 0 (2001) / 0 (2000); Employment by occupation: 8.2% management, 14.7% professional, 16.3% services, 24.7% sales, 0.5% farming, 8.4% construction, 27.1% production (2000).
Income: Per capita income: $18,106 (2000); Median household income: $36,406 (2000); Poverty rate: 4.7% (2000).
Taxes: Total city taxes per capita: $110 (1997); City property taxes per capita: $102 (1997).
Education: High school graduation rate: 77.5% (2000); College graduation rate: 14.3% (2000).

School District(s)

N.R.H.E.G. (PK-12)
2000 Enrollment: 1,061 507-465-3205
Housing: Homeownership rate: 78.8% (2000); Median home value: $66,500 (2000); Median rent: $298 per month (2000); Median age of housing: 44 years (2000).
Newspapers: New Richland Star (1 x week)
Transportation: Commute to work: 87.7% car, 0.0% public transportation, 8.8% walk, 3.5% work from home (2000); Travel time to work: 38.9% less than 15 minutes, 39.1% 15 to 30 minutes, 16.4% 30 to 45 minutes, 3.1% 45 to 60 minutes, 2.5% 60 minutes or more (2000)

NEW RICHLAND (township). Covers a land area of 35.335 square miles and a water area of 0.155 square miles. Located at 43.89° N. Lat.; 93.47° W. Long. Elevation is 1,184 feet.
Population: 497 (2000); Race: 97.7% White, 0.0% Black, 1.4% Asian, 0.0% American Indian and Alaska Native, 0.8% Hispanic of any race, 1.0% two or more races (2000); Density: 14.1 persons per square mile (2000); Age: 25.3% under 18, 17.8% over 64 (2000); Marriage status: 22.3% never married, 74.0% now married, 1.7% widowed, 1.9% divorced (2000); Foreign born: 1.4% (2000); Ancestry (includes multiple ancestries): 50.7% German, 33.1% Norwegian, 9.9% Swedish, 6.6% Irish, 3.1% English (2000).
Economy: Grain, soybeans; livestock; dairying. Manufacturing: feeds; grain processing. Employment by occupation: 22.6% management, 15.1% professional, 4.5% services, 27.1% sales, 1.7% farming, 9.2% construction, 19.9% production (2000).
Income: Per capita income: $19,156 (2000); Median household income: $51,500 (2000); Poverty rate: 3.1% (2000).
Taxes: Total city taxes per capita: $115 (1997); City property taxes per capita: $115 (1997).
Education: High school graduation rate: 85.2% (2000); College graduation rate: 17.9% (2000).
Housing: Homeownership rate: 93.4% (2000); Median home value: $103,800 (2000); Median rent: $275 per month (2000); Median age of housing: 46 years (2000).
Transportation: Commute to work: 87.6% car, 0.0% public transportation, 0.0% walk, 12.4% work from home (2000); Travel time to work: 27.8% less than 15 minutes, 40.4% 15 to 30 minutes, 22.4% 30 to 45 minutes, 6.3% 45 to 60 minutes, 3.1% 60 minutes or more (2000)

OTISCO (township). Covers a land area of 36.021 square miles and a water area of 0.010 square miles. Located at 43.97° N. Lat.; 93.47° W. Long. Elevation is 1,149 feet.
Population: 629 (2000); Race: 100.0% White, 0.0% Black, 0.0% Asian, 0.0% American Indian and Alaska Native, 0.9% Hispanic of any race, 0.0% two or more races (2000); Density: 17.5 persons per square mile (2000); Age: 32.6% under 18, 10.5% over 64 (2000); Marriage status: 21.2% never married, 70.0% now married, 3.2% widowed, 5.6% divorced (2000); Foreign born: 0.3% (2000); Ancestry (includes multiple ancestries): 54.0% German, 21.5% Norwegian, 12.2% Swedish, 8.7% Irish, 6.2% English (2000).
Economy: Employment by occupation: 15.3% management, 18.9% professional, 8.2% services, 24.9% sales, 0.6% farming, 11.6% construction, 20.6% production (2000).
Income: Per capita income: $17,310 (2000); Median household income: $50,809 (2000); Poverty rate: 2.5% (2000).
Taxes: Total city taxes per capita: $58 (1997); City property taxes per capita: $58 (1997).
Education: High school graduation rate: 91.4% (2000); College graduation rate: 16.6% (2000).
Housing: Homeownership rate: 86.8% (2000); Median home value: $121,300 (2000); Median rent: $425 per month (2000); Median age of housing: 48 years (2000).
Transportation: Commute to work: 83.0% car, 0.0% public transportation, 2.3% walk, 12.5% work from home (2000); Travel time to work: 40.6% less than 15 minutes, 40.9% 15 to 30 minutes, 9.1% 30 to 45 minutes, 1.6% 45 to 60 minutes, 7.8% 60 minutes or more (2000)

SAINT MARY (township). Covers a land area of 35.861 square miles and a water area of 0.031 square miles. Located at 44.07° N. Lat.; 93.58° W. Long.
Population: 504 (2000); Race: 98.0% White, 1.1% Black, 0.0% Asian, 0.4% American Indian and Alaska Native, 1.3% Hispanic of any race, 0.2% two or more races (2000); Density: 14.1 persons per square mile (2000); Age: 32.9% under 18, 11.6% over 64 (2000); Marriage status: 22.7% never married, 72.7% now married, 2.0% widowed, 2.7% divorced (2000); Foreign born: 0.0% (2000); Ancestry (includes multiple ancestries): 61.9% German, 24.5% Irish, 9.7% Norwegian, 6.6% United States or American, 3.8% Other groups (2000).
Economy: Employment by occupation: 17.2% management, 11.7% professional, 12.3% services, 25.6% sales, 3.6% farming, 14.9% construction, 14.9% production (2000).
Income: Per capita income: $14,820 (2000); Median household income: $41,944 (2000); Poverty rate: 3.2% (2000).
Education: High school graduation rate: 87.5% (2000); College graduation rate: 12.2% (2000).
Housing: Homeownership rate: 90.2% (2000); Median home value: $109,100 (2000); Median rent: $363 per month (2000); Median age of housing: 49 years (2000).
Transportation: Commute to work: 79.3% car, 0.0% public transportation, 0.6% walk, 18.8% work from home (2000); Travel time to work: 55.4% less than 15 minutes, 20.3% 15 to 30 minutes, 12.7% 30 to 45 minutes, 5.2% 45 to 60 minutes, 6.4% 60 minutes or more (2000)

VIVIAN (township). Covers a land area of 35.931 square miles and a water area of 0.018 square miles. Located at 43.88° N. Lat.; 93.71° W. Long.
Population: 259 (2000); Race: 99.1% White, 0.0% Black, 0.0% Asian, 0.9% American Indian and Alaska Native, 0.0% Hispanic of any race, 0.0% two or more races (2000); Density: 7.2 persons per square mile (2000); Age: 27.6% under 18, 19.4% over 64 (2000); Marriage status: 24.0% never married, 65.7% now married, 6.3% widowed, 4.0% divorced (2000); Foreign born: 0.0% (2000); Ancestry (includes multiple ancestries): 69.4% German, 9.5% Polish, 8.6% Irish, 6.9% Norwegian, 6.9% English (2000).

Economy: Employment by occupation: 33.3% management, 9.8% professional, 4.9% services, 28.4% sales, 5.9% farming, 6.9% construction, 10.8% production (2000).
Income: Per capita income: $18,016 (2000); Median household income: $39,750 (2000); Poverty rate: 6.9% (2000).
Taxes: Total city taxes per capita: $138 (1997); City property taxes per capita: $138 (1997).
Education: High school graduation rate: 90.0% (2000); College graduation rate: 15.0% (2000).
Housing: Homeownership rate: 88.3% (2000); Median home value: $72,500 (2000); Median rent: $225 per month (2000); Median age of housing: 60+ years (2000).
Transportation: Commute to work: 75.5% car, 0.0% public transportation, 7.8% walk, 16.7% work from home (2000); Travel time to work: 32.9% less than 15 minutes, 29.4% 15 to 30 minutes, 31.8% 30 to 45 minutes, 3.5% 45 to 60 minutes, 2.4% 60 minutes or more (2000)

WALDORF (city). Covers a land area of 0.384 square miles and a water area of 0 square miles. Located at 43.93° N. Lat.; 93.69° W. Long. Elevation is 1,080 feet.
Population: 242 (2000); Race: 100.0% White, 0.0% Black, 0.0% Asian, 0.0% American Indian and Alaska Native, 1.8% Hispanic of any race, 0.0% two or more races (2000); Density: 630.4 persons per square mile (2000); Age: 22.1% under 18, 13.7% over 64 (2000); Marriage status: 23.6% never married, 59.3% now married, 6.0% widowed, 11.1% divorced (2000); Foreign born: 0.0% (2000); Ancestry (includes multiple ancestries): 48.3% German, 11.8% United States or American, 9.2% Norwegian, 9.2% Irish, 5.2% English (2000).
Economy: Dairying; poultry, livestock; grain, soybeans. Single-family building permits issued: 0 (2001) / 0 (2000); Multi-family building permits issued: 0 (2001) / 0 (2000); Employment by occupation: 8.6% management, 16.4% professional, 21.4% services, 19.3% sales, 1.4% farming, 11.4% construction, 21.4% production (2000).
Income: Per capita income: $16,941 (2000); Median household income: $37,500 (2000); Poverty rate: 15.6% (2000).
Taxes: Total city taxes per capita: $92 (1997); City property taxes per capita: $92 (1997).
Education: High school graduation rate: 83.1% (2000); College graduation rate: 9.0% (2000).
Housing: Homeownership rate: 87.0% (2000); Median home value: $61,400 (2000); Median rent: $250 per month (2000); Median age of housing: 48 years (2000).
Transportation: Commute to work: 86.0% car, 0.0% public transportation, 6.6% walk, 5.1% work from home (2000); Travel time to work: 14.7% less than 15 minutes, 44.2% 15 to 30 minutes, 26.4% 30 to 45 minutes, 10.1% 45 to 60 minutes, 4.7% 60 minutes or more (2000)

WASECA (city). Covers a land area of 3.833 square miles and a water area of 1.112 square miles. Located at 44.07° N. Lat.; 93.50° W. Long. Elevation is 1,151 feet.
History: Waseca sprang up in the middle of a wheatfield when the railroad reached this point in 1867, and the new town soon outstripped other older communities in the area. The name of Waseca is of Indian origin meaning "rich or fertile in provisions." The Waseca County Anti-Horse Thief Detective Society, organized in 1864, expanded its range of operations after 1900 to include the protection of automobiles.
Population: 8,493 (2000); Race: 93.4% White, 1.9% Black, 0.6% Asian, 1.0% American Indian and Alaska Native, 4.8% Hispanic of any race, 0.7% two or more races (2000); Density: 2,215.6 persons per square mile (2000); Age: 26.1% under 18, 15.3% over 64 (2000); Marriage status: 26.4% never married, 56.5% now married, 7.4% widowed, 9.7% divorced (2000); Foreign born: 1.9% (2000); Ancestry (includes multiple ancestries): 43.1% German, 20.6% Norwegian, 12.8% Irish, 9.1% Other groups, 5.0% English (2000).
Economy: Single-family building permits issued: 16 (2001) / 24 (2000); Multi-family building permits issued: 0 (2001) / 33 (2000); Employment by occupation: 9.8% management, 13.8% professional, 13.5% services, 23.9% sales, 0.8% farming, 8.6% construction, 29.6% production (2000).
Income: Per capita income: $18,439 (2000); Median household income: $39,554 (2000); Poverty rate: 8.4% (2000).
Taxes: Total city taxes per capita: $219 (2000); City property taxes per capita: $164 (2000).
Education: High school graduation rate: 84.6% (2000); College graduation rate: 17.8% (2000).

School District(s)

Waseca (PK-12)
2000 Enrollment: 2,272 507-835-2500

Housing: Homeownership rate: 73.3% (2000); Median home value: $84,200 (2000); Median rent: $364 per month (2000); Median age of housing: 39 years (2000).
Hospitals: Waseca Medical Center-Mayo Health System (35 beds)
Safety: Violent crime rate: 29.1 per 10,000 population; Property crime rate: 299.4 per 10,000 population (2001).
Newspapers: Waseca County News (2 x week); Waseca Area Shopper (1 x week)
Transportation: Commute to work: 92.4% car, 1.8% public transportation, 3.6% walk, 2.1% work from home (2000); Travel time to work: 70.4% less than 15 minutes, 16.4% 15 to 30 minutes, 7.7% 30 to 45 minutes, 2.1% 45 to 60 minutes, 3.4% 60 minutes or more (2000)
Additional Information Contacts
Waseca Chamber of Commerce 507-835-3260

WILTON (township). Covers a land area of 35.677 square miles and a water area of 0.435 square miles. Located at 43.97° N. Lat.; 93.57° W. Long. Elevation is 1,109 feet.
Population: 392 (2000); Race: 95.7% White, 0.0% Black, 0.0% Asian, 0.0% American Indian and Alaska Native, 5.3% Hispanic of any race, 1.9% two or more races (2000); Density: 11.0 persons per square mile (2000); Age: 33.9% under 18, 10.8% over 64 (2000); Marriage status: 27.3% never married, 60.8% now married, 2.4% widowed, 9.6% divorced (2000); Foreign born: 1.0% (2000); Ancestry (includes multiple ancestries): 72.4% German, 11.5% Irish, 11.3% Norwegian, 6.3% Other groups, 6.0% French (except Basque) (2000).
Economy: Employment by occupation: 17.3% management, 14.2% professional, 13.7% services, 16.8% sales, 2.0% farming, 20.3% construction, 15.7% production (2000).
Income: Per capita income: $17,327 (2000); Median household income: $40,313 (2000); Poverty rate: 8.8% (2000).
Taxes: Total city taxes per capita: $90 (1997); City property taxes per capita: $90 (1997).
Education: High school graduation rate: 86.8% (2000); College graduation rate: 11.2% (2000).
Housing: Homeownership rate: 83.1% (2000); Median home value: $97,100 (2000); Median rent: $235 per month (2000); Median age of housing: 53 years (2000).
Transportation: Commute to work: 88.5% car, 0.0% public transportation, 0.0% walk, 11.5% work from home (2000); Travel time to work: 26.5% less than 15 minutes, 41.8% 15 to 30 minutes, 12.9% 30 to 45 minutes, 10.0% 45 to 60 minutes, 8.8% 60 minutes or more (2000)

WOODVILLE (township). Covers a land area of 30.039 square miles and a water area of 1.126 square miles. Located at 44.07° N. Lat.; 93.47° W. Long.
Population: 2,273 (2000); Race: 83.5% White, 12.6% Black, 0.5% Asian, 2.2% American Indian and Alaska Native, 2.9% Hispanic of any race, 0.4% two or more races (2000); Density: 75.7 persons per square mile (2000); Age: 18.3% under 18, 5.4% over 64 (2000); Marriage status: 24.5% never married, 58.0% now married, 2.2% widowed, 15.3% divorced (2000); Foreign born: 0.9% (2000); Ancestry (includes multiple ancestries): 39.2% German, 12.3% Norwegian, 9.2% Irish, 4.0% Swedish, 3.2% English (2000).
Economy: Employment by occupation: 16.7% management, 18.5% professional, 12.6% services, 24.0% sales, 1.2% farming, 8.8% construction, 18.1% production (2000).
Income: Per capita income: $22,770 (2000); Median household income: $62,250 (2000); Poverty rate: 2.7% (2000).
Taxes: Total city taxes per capita: $37 (2000); City property taxes per capita: $37 (2000).
Education: High school graduation rate: 78.4% (2000); College graduation rate: 13.7% (2000).
Housing: Homeownership rate: 91.0% (2000); Median home value: $144,100 (2000); Median rent: $414 per month (2000); Median age of housing: 25 years (2000).
Transportation: Commute to work: 93.5% car, 0.4% public transportation, 0.3% walk, 4.6% work from home (2000); Travel time to work: 60.9% less than 15 minutes, 24.5% 15 to 30 minutes, 7.9% 30 to 45 minutes, 2.4% 45 to 60 minutes, 4.3% 60 minutes or more (2000)

Washington County

Located in eastern Minnesota; bounded on the east by the St. Croix River and the Wisconsin border, and on the south by the Mississippi River; includes Forest Lake. Covers a land area of 391.70 square miles, a water area of 31.50

square miles, and is located in the Central Time Zone. The county government was organized in 1849. County seat is Stillwater.

Washington County is part of the Minneapolis-St. Paul, MN-WI MSA. The entire metro area includes: Anoka County, MN; Carver County, MN; Chisago County, MN; Dakota County, MN; Hennepin County, MN; Isanti County, MN; Ramsey County, MN; Scott County, MN; Sherburne County, MN; Washington County, MN; Wright County, MN; Pierce County, WI; St. Croix County, WI

Weather Station: Stillwater 1 SE Elevation: 711 feet

	Jan	Feb	Mar	Apr	May	Jun	Jul	Aug	Sep	Oct	Nov	Dec
High	23	30	42	58	72	80	85	82	72	60	41	28
Low	3	10	22	35	48	57	62	60	51	39	25	11
Precip	1.0	0.7	1.8	2.9	3.5	4.8	4.7	4.9	3.7	2.8	2.1	0.9
Snow	11.2	na	na	0.9	0.0	0.0	0.0	0.0	0.0	tr	na	na

High and Low temperatures in degrees Fahrenheit; Precipitation and Snow in inches

Population: 201,130 (2000); Race: 93.6% White, 1.7% Black, 2.2% Asian, 0.4% American Indian and Alaska Native, 2.0% Hispanic of any race, 1.6% two or more races (2000); Density: 513.5 persons per square mile (2000); Age: 29.5% under 18, 7.5% over 64 (2000).
Religion: Five largest groups: 28.8% Catholic Church, 19.2% Evangelical Lutheran Church in America, 2.5% Lutheran Church—Missouri Synod, 1.8% The United Methodist Church, 1.0% Wisconsin Evangelical Lutheran Synod (2000).
Economy: Unemployment rate: 2.9% (11/2002); Total civilian labor force: 123,920 (11/2002); Leading industries: 20.3% manufacturing; 18.1% retail trade; 11.1% accommodation & food services (2000); Companies that employ more than 1,000 persons: 1 (2000); Companies that employ more than 100 persons: 81 (2000); Farms: 653 totaling 89,935 acres (1997); Minority business ownership rate: 3.6% (1997); Women business ownership rate: 30.0% (1997); Retail sales per capita: $8,725 (1997). Single-family building permits issued: 1,514 (2001) / 1,795 (2000); Multi-family building permits issued: 503 (2001) / 436 (2000).
Income: Per capita income: $28,148 (2000); Median household income: $66,305 (2000); Poverty rate: 2.9% (2000); Bankruptcy rate: 3.38% (2001).
Taxes: Total county taxes per capita: $246 (2000); County property taxes per capita: $236 (2000).
Education: High school graduation rate: 94.0% (2000); College graduation rate: 33.9% (2000).
Housing: Homeownership rate: 85.8% (2000); Median home value: $156,200 (2000); Median rent: $649 per month (2000); Median age of housing: 18 years (2000).
Health: Birth rate: 133.6 per 10,000 population (1998); Age adjusted death rate: 83.1 per 10,000 population (1999); Age adjusted cancer mortality rate: 206.7 deaths per 100,000 population (1999). Air Quality Index: 85% good, 15% moderate, 0% unhealthy (percent of days in 2000). Number of physicians: 20.1 per 10,000 population (1999); Number of hospital beds: 3.1 per 10,000 population (1999).
Elections: 2000 Presidential election results: 46.4% Gore, 48.1% Bush, 4.6% Nader, 0.5% Buchanan
National and State Parks: Afton State Park; Rutstrum State Wildlife Management Area; William O'Brien State Park
Additional Information Contacts
Washington County Government Offices 651-430-6017
Cottage Grove Chamber of Commerce 651-458-8334
Forest Lake Area Chamber. 651-464-3200
Stillwater Area Chamber of Commerce 651-439-7700
Stillwater Chamber of Commerce 651-439-4001
Woodbury Chamber of Commerce 651-578-0722

Washington County Communities

AFTON (city). Covers a land area of 25.181 square miles and a water area of 1.191 square miles. Located at 44.90° N. Lat.; 92.81° W. Long.
History: Afton was settled in the late 1830's by French immigrants, and named for the poem by Robert Burns, "Afton Water."
Population: 2,839 (2000); Race: 97.3% White, 0.5% Black, 0.3% Asian, 0.0% American Indian and Alaska Native, 0.2% Hispanic of any race, 1.4% two or more races (2000); Density: 112.7 persons per square mile (2000); Age: 26.9% under 18, 8.2% over 64 (2000); Marriage status: 21.2% never married, 67.8% now married, 3.8% widowed, 7.3% divorced (2000); Foreign born: 1.8% (2000); Ancestry (includes multiple ancestries): 37.2% German, 16.5% Irish, 15.6% English, 12.1% Norwegian, 11.4% Swedish (2000).
Economy: Single-family building permits issued: 9 (2001) / 12 (2000); Multi-family building permits issued: 0 (2001) / 0 (2000); Employment by occupation: 21.6% management, 33.1% professional, 10.0% services, 19.3% sales, 0.1% farming, 4.8% construction, 11.1% production (2000).
Income: Per capita income: $36,338 (2000); Median household income: $89,095 (2000); Poverty rate: 0.6% (2000).
Taxes: Total city taxes per capita: $203 (1997); City property taxes per capita: $181 (1997).
Education: High school graduation rate: 95.4% (2000); College graduation rate: 50.6% (2000).
Housing: Homeownership rate: 98.4% (2000); Median home value: $225,600 (2000); Median rent: $1,125 per month (2000); Median age of housing: 29 years (2000).
Transportation: Commute to work: 93.3% car, 0.8% public transportation, 1.1% walk, 4.5% work from home (2000); Travel time to work: 12.0% less than 15 minutes, 47.5% 15 to 30 minutes, 26.3% 30 to 45 minutes, 9.4% 45 to 60 minutes, 4.7% 60 minutes or more (2000)

BAYPORT (city). Covers a land area of 1.818 square miles and a water area of 0 square miles. Located at 45.01° N. Lat.; 92.78° W. Long. Elevation is 686 feet.
Population: 3,162 (2000); Race: 71.8% White, 17.7% Black, 1.2% Asian, 4.4% American Indian and Alaska Native, 2.8% Hispanic of any race, 4.0% two or more races (2000); Density: 1,739.0 persons per square mile (2000); Age: 12.4% under 18, 10.4% over 64 (2000); Marriage status: 42.4% never married, 38.7% now married, 5.3% widowed, 13.6% divorced (2000); Foreign born: 2.7% (2000); Ancestry (includes multiple ancestries): 24.0% German, 19.2% Other groups, 11.3% Norwegian, 10.1% Irish, 9.4% Swedish (2000).
Economy: Resort area; cattle, sheep; soybeans, corn, oats, alfalfa. Manufacturing: building materials, printing. Minnesota correctional facilities are here and in adjacent Oak Park Heights, to Northwest. Single-family building permits issued: 3 (2001) / 11 (2000); Multi-family building permits issued: 0 (2001) / 0 (2000); Employment by occupation: 11.4% management, 17.3% professional, 15.8% services, 27.5% sales, 0.0% farming, 10.8% construction, 17.3% production (2000).
Income: Per capita income: $18,490 (2000); Median household income: $53,026 (2000); Poverty rate: 3.7% (2000).
Taxes: Total city taxes per capita: $437 (1997); City property taxes per capita: $420 (1997).
Education: High school graduation rate: 81.3% (2000); College graduation rate: 15.2% (2000).
Housing: Homeownership rate: 76.7% (2000); Median home value: $131,600 (2000); Median rent: $585 per month (2000); Median age of housing: 48 years (2000).
Safety: Violent crime rate: 12.5 per 10,000 population; Property crime rate: 162.7 per 10,000 population (2001).
Transportation: Commute to work: 84.7% car, 0.2% public transportation, 8.2% walk, 4.2% work from home (2000); Travel time to work: 51.6% less than 15 minutes, 24.9% 15 to 30 minutes, 15.9% 30 to 45 minutes, 6.2% 45 to 60 minutes, 1.4% 60 minutes or more (2000)

BAYTOWN (township). Covers a land area of 8.189 square miles and a water area of 1.378 square miles. Located at 45.01° N. Lat.; 92.81° W. Long.
Population: 1,533 (2000); Race: 97.6% White, 0.0% Black, 0.9% Asian, 0.2% American Indian and Alaska Native, 1.5% Hispanic of any race, 1.3% two or more races (2000); Density: 187.2 persons per square mile (2000); Age: 31.2% under 18, 6.6% over 64 (2000); Marriage status: 21.3% never married, 71.6% now married, 3.2% widowed, 3.8% divorced (2000); Foreign born: 2.7% (2000); Ancestry (includes multiple ancestries): 48.3% German, 15.1% Irish, 13.1% Norwegian, 11.5% Swedish, 8.2% English (2000).
Economy: Single-family building permits issued: 9 (2001) / 8 (2000); Multi-family building permits issued: 0 (2001) / 0 (2000); Employment by occupation: 27.1% management, 23.8% professional, 11.1% services, 20.3% sales, 0.0% farming, 7.6% construction, 10.0% production (2000).
Income: Per capita income: $38,260 (2000); Median household income: $99,362 (2000); Poverty rate: 1.3% (2000).
Taxes: Total city taxes per capita: $109 (1997); City property taxes per capita: $96 (1997).
Education: High school graduation rate: 96.5% (2000); College graduation rate: 48.3% (2000).
Housing: Homeownership rate: 96.8% (2000); Median home value: $275,000 (2000); Median rent: $713 per month (2000); Median age of housing: 13 years (2000).
Transportation: Commute to work: 93.4% car, 0.5% public transportation, 1.1% walk, 4.4% work from home (2000); Travel time to work: 40.5% less

than 15 minutes, 30.6% 15 to 30 minutes, 21.6% 30 to 45 minutes, 5.7% 45 to 60 minutes, 1.7% 60 minutes or more (2000)

BIRCHWOOD VILLAGE (city). Aka Birchwood. Covers a land area of 0.345 square miles and a water area of 0 square miles. Located at 45.05° N. Lat.; 92.97° W. Long.
Population: 968 (2000); Race: 96.9% White, 1.1% Black, 0.0% Asian, 0.2% American Indian and Alaska Native, 0.3% Hispanic of any race, 1.8% two or more races (2000); Density: 2,808.2 persons per square mile (2000); Age: 25.9% under 18, 11.9% over 64 (2000); Marriage status: 18.2% never married, 68.5% now married, 3.4% widowed, 9.9% divorced (2000); Foreign born: 2.1% (2000); Ancestry (includes multiple ancestries): 40.9% German, 21.0% Irish, 14.8% Swedish, 14.5% English, 14.2% Norwegian (2000).
Economy: Single-family building permits issued: 0 (2001) / 3 (2000); Multi-family building permits issued: 0 (2001) / 0 (2000); Employment by occupation: 19.5% management, 38.5% professional, 10.7% services, 20.1% sales, 0.0% farming, 6.7% construction, 4.4% production (2000).
Income: Per capita income: $40,102 (2000); Median household income: $81,941 (2000); Poverty rate: 2.9% (2000).
Taxes: Total city taxes per capita: $166 (1997); City property taxes per capita: $156 (1997).
Education: High school graduation rate: 97.2% (2000); College graduation rate: 55.4% (2000).
Housing: Homeownership rate: 93.6% (2000); Median home value: $206,100 (2000); Median rent: $636 per month (2000); Median age of housing: 39 years (2000).
Transportation: Commute to work: 90.9% car, 1.9% public transportation, 0.6% walk, 5.8% work from home (2000); Travel time to work: 18.5% less than 15 minutes, 43.4% 15 to 30 minutes, 24.9% 30 to 45 minutes, 9.3% 45 to 60 minutes, 3.9% 60 minutes or more (2000)

COTTAGE GROVE (city). Covers a land area of 33.984 square miles and a water area of 3.937 square miles. Located at 44.82° N. Lat.; 92.93° W. Long. Elevation is 850 feet.
History: Incorporated 1965.
Population: 30,582 (2000); Race: 93.9% White, 2.5% Black, 1.2% Asian, 0.4% American Indian and Alaska Native, 2.0% Hispanic of any race, 1.6% two or more races (2000); Density: 899.9 persons per square mile (2000); Age: 32.6% under 18, 4.8% over 64 (2000); Marriage status: 23.0% never married, 68.9% now married, 2.3% widowed, 5.8% divorced (2000); Foreign born: 2.8% (2000); Ancestry (includes multiple ancestries): 43.3% German, 14.6% Irish, 14.3% Norwegian, 8.7% Swedish, 8.0% Other groups (2000).
Vital Statistics: Birth rate: 163.8 per 10,000 population (1998)
Economy: Cattle, sheep; corn, soybeans. Manufacturing: chemicals, machinery, printing and publishing. Unemployment rate: 2.8% (11/2002); Total civilian labor force: 19,180 (11/2002); Single-family building permits issued: 92 (2001) / 130 (2000); Multi-family building permits issued: 76 (2001) / 13 (2000); Employment by occupation: 13.5% management, 18.8% professional, 12.4% services, 31.3% sales, 0.2% farming, 9.3% construction, 14.5% production (2000).
Income: Per capita income: $23,348 (2000); Median household income: $65,825 (2000); Poverty rate: 2.2% (2000).
Taxes: Total city taxes per capita: $209 (2000); City property taxes per capita: $188 (2000).
Education: High school graduation rate: 94.5% (2000); College graduation rate: 23.9% (2000).

School District(s)

South Washington County (PK-12)
2000 Enrollment: 14,953 651-458-6300

Housing: Homeownership rate: 91.7% (2000); Median home value: $137,300 (2000); Median rent: $752 per month (2000); Median age of housing: 21 years (2000).
Safety: Violent crime rate: 10.4 per 10,000 population; Property crime rate: 236.8 per 10,000 population (2001).
Newspapers: South Washington County Bulletin (1 x week)
Transportation: Commute to work: 94.3% car, 1.4% public transportation, 0.8% walk, 2.9% work from home (2000); Travel time to work: 20.3% less than 15 minutes, 38.8% 15 to 30 minutes, 28.9% 30 to 45 minutes, 8.7% 45 to 60 minutes, 3.3% 60 minutes or more (2000)

Additional Information Contacts

Cottage Grove Chamber of Commerce 651-458-8334

DELLWOOD (city). Covers a land area of 2.758 square miles and a water area of 0.093 square miles. Located at 45.09° N. Lat.; 92.96° W. Long. Elevation is 941 feet.
Population: 1,033 (2000); Race: 99.8% White, 0.0% Black, 0.2% Asian, 0.0% American Indian and Alaska Native, 0.0% Hispanic of any race, 0.0% two or more races (2000); Density: 374.5 persons per square mile (2000); Age: 30.0% under 18, 7.2% over 64 (2000); Marriage status: 23.4% never married, 72.1% now married, 1.5% widowed, 3.0% divorced (2000); Foreign born: 4.5% (2000); Ancestry (includes multiple ancestries): 29.3% German, 16.0% Irish, 15.6% Swedish, 14.6% English, 14.5% Norwegian (2000).
Economy: Agricultural area: cattle, sheep; corn, oats, alfalfa. Northport Airport to Southeast. Single-family building permits issued: 5 (2001) / 10 (2000); Multi-family building permits issued: 0 (2001) / 0 (2000); Employment by occupation: 35.2% management, 26.5% professional, 4.5% services, 27.8% sales, 0.6% farming, 2.1% construction, 3.4% production (2000).
Income: Per capita income: $61,592 (2000); Median household income: $129,136 (2000); Poverty rate: 1.9% (2000).
Taxes: Total city taxes per capita: $357 (1997); City property taxes per capita: $312 (1997).
Education: High school graduation rate: 97.4% (2000); College graduation rate: 66.7% (2000).
Housing: Homeownership rate: 95.4% (2000); Median home value: $416,000 (2000); Median rent: $575 per month (2000); Median age of housing: 26 years (2000).
Transportation: Commute to work: 89.0% car, 1.3% public transportation, 1.3% walk, 8.2% work from home (2000); Travel time to work: 19.9% less than 15 minutes, 46.8% 15 to 30 minutes, 25.5% 30 to 45 minutes, 4.8% 45 to 60 minutes, 3.1% 60 minutes or more (2000)

DENMARK (township). Covers a land area of 28.620 square miles and a water area of 1.810 square miles. Located at 44.80° N. Lat.; 92.82° W. Long.
Population: 1,348 (2000); Race: 97.0% White, 0.0% Black, 1.0% Asian, 0.3% American Indian and Alaska Native, 2.9% Hispanic of any race, 0.1% two or more races (2000); Density: 47.1 persons per square mile (2000); Age: 23.5% under 18, 10.5% over 64 (2000); Marriage status: 22.5% never married, 69.9% now married, 1.9% widowed, 5.7% divorced (2000); Foreign born: 3.7% (2000); Ancestry (includes multiple ancestries): 50.9% German, 13.6% Irish, 13.3% Norwegian, 10.7% Swedish, 8.1% Polish (2000).
Economy: Single-family building permits issued: 24 (2001) / 4 (2000); Multi-family building permits issued: 0 (2001) / 0 (2000); Employment by occupation: 19.9% management, 20.3% professional, 10.0% services, 25.6% sales, 0.8% farming, 9.5% construction, 13.9% production (2000).
Income: Per capita income: $30,069 (2000); Median household income: $74,821 (2000); Poverty rate: 2.7% (2000).
Taxes: Total city taxes per capita: $282 (2000); City property taxes per capita: $272 (2000).
Education: High school graduation rate: 92.4% (2000); College graduation rate: 30.3% (2000).
Housing: Homeownership rate: 95.2% (2000); Median home value: $196,900 (2000); Median rent: $460 per month (2000); Median age of housing: 24 years (2000).
Transportation: Commute to work: 86.4% car, 0.3% public transportation, 1.3% walk, 12.1% work from home (2000); Travel time to work: 23.7% less than 15 minutes, 37.7% 15 to 30 minutes, 26.2% 30 to 45 minutes, 8.9% 45 to 60 minutes, 3.5% 60 minutes or more (2000)

FOREST LAKE (city). Covers a land area of 4.194 square miles and a water area of 0.054 square miles. Located at 45.27° N. Lat.; 92.98° W. Long. Elevation is 909 feet.
History: Forest Lake developed as the center of a popular summer and fishing resort area.
Population: 6,798 (2000); Race: 97.4% White, 0.4% Black, 0.8% Asian, 0.3% American Indian and Alaska Native, 0.9% Hispanic of any race, 0.9% two or more races (2000); Density: 1,620.8 persons per square mile (2000); Age: 25.6% under 18, 13.3% over 64 (2000); Marriage status: 25.5% never married, 56.0% now married, 6.7% widowed, 11.8% divorced (2000); Foreign born: 2.2% (2000); Ancestry (includes multiple ancestries): 34.0% German, 16.0% Swedish, 15.0% Norwegian, 12.4% Irish, 7.1% French (except Basque) (2000).
Economy: Single-family building permits issued: 91 (2001) / 55 (2000); Multi-family building permits issued: 12 (2001) / 8 (2000); Employment by occupation: 9.9% management, 18.3% professional, 15.0% services, 29.1% sales, 0.0% farming, 10.5% construction, 17.2% production (2000).
Income: Per capita income: $20,058 (2000); Median household income: $44,419 (2000); Poverty rate: 6.3% (2000).
Taxes: Total city taxes per capita: $351 (1997); City property taxes per capita: $327 (1997).

Education: High school graduation rate: 88.6% (2000); College graduation rate: 18.0% (2000).

School District(s)

Forest Lake (PK-12)
2000 Enrollment: 7,711 651-982-8100
North Lakes Academy Charter (06-09)
2000 Enrollment: 147 651-982-2773

Housing: Homeownership rate: 60.1% (2000); Median home value: $122,800 (2000); Median rent: $553 per month (2000); Median age of housing: 25 years (2000).
Safety: Violent crime rate: 11.6 per 10,000 population; Property crime rate: 457.0 per 10,000 population (2001).
Newspapers: The Times (1 x week); Saint Croix Valley Peach (1 x week)
Transportation: Commute to work: 92.9% car, 0.7% public transportation, 2.2% walk, 3.7% work from home (2000); Travel time to work: 30.9% less than 15 minutes, 23.0% 15 to 30 minutes, 29.0% 30 to 45 minutes, 10.7% 45 to 60 minutes, 6.5% 60 minutes or more (2000)

Additional Information Contacts

Forest Lake Area Chamber.............................. 651-464-3200

FOREST LAKE (township). Covers a land area of 26.877 square miles and a water area of 4.359 square miles. Located at 45.26° N. Lat.; 92.95° W. Long. Elevation is 909 feet.
Population: 7,642 (2000); Race: 96.4% White, 0.8% Black, 0.5% Asian, 0.4% American Indian and Alaska Native, 1.0% Hispanic of any race, 1.7% two or more races (2000); Density: 284.3 persons per square mile (2000); Age: 26.7% under 18, 7.1% over 64 (2000); Marriage status: 21.4% never married, 69.7% now married, 3.0% widowed, 5.9% divorced (2000); Foreign born: 1.5% (2000); Ancestry (includes multiple ancestries): 40.3% German, 18.6% Norwegian, 15.6% Swedish, 8.7% Irish, 6.5% English (2000).
Economy: Agricultural area; light manufacturing. Forest Lake Airport to South. Single-family building permits issued: 111 (2001) / 64 (2000); Multi-family building permits issued: 0 (2001) / 0 (2000); Employment by occupation: 18.3% management, 22.9% professional, 11.6% services, 23.1% sales, 0.0% farming, 11.2% construction, 12.9% production (2000).
Income: Per capita income: $29,066 (2000); Median household income: $70,671 (2000); Poverty rate: 2.3% (2000).
Taxes: Total city taxes per capita: $172 (2000); City property taxes per capita: $137 (2000).
Education: High school graduation rate: 93.9% (2000); College graduation rate: 28.3% (2000).
Housing: Homeownership rate: 96.4% (2000); Median home value: $168,100 (2000); Median rent: $711 per month (2000); Median age of housing: 22 years (2000).
Transportation: Commute to work: 94.8% car, 0.4% public transportation, 0.5% walk, 3.3% work from home (2000); Travel time to work: 22.7% less than 15 minutes, 25.0% 15 to 30 minutes, 30.4% 30 to 45 minutes, 15.1% 45 to 60 minutes, 6.8% 60 minutes or more (2000)

GRANT (city). Covers a land area of 25.681 square miles and a water area of 1.335 square miles. Located at 45.08° N. Lat.; 92.92° W. Long.
Population: 4,026 (2000); Race: 97.3% White, 0.0% Black, 1.5% Asian, 0.0% American Indian and Alaska Native, 0.9% Hispanic of any race, 0.8% two or more races (2000); Density: 156.8 persons per square mile (2000); Age: 28.5% under 18, 8.1% over 64 (2000); Marriage status: 18.0% never married, 76.1% now married, 2.7% widowed, 3.2% divorced (2000); Foreign born: 3.5% (2000); Ancestry (includes multiple ancestries): 41.6% German, 14.3% Irish, 12.6% Swedish, 11.9% Norwegian, 11.0% English (2000).
Economy: Single-family building permits issued: 17 (2001) / 21 (2000); Multi-family building permits issued: 0 (2001) / 0 (2000); Employment by occupation: 22.1% management, 27.8% professional, 5.9% services, 24.3% sales, 0.0% farming, 10.9% construction, 9.0% production (2000).
Income: Per capita income: $44,486 (2000); Median household income: $98,228 (2000); Poverty rate: 1.8% (2000).
Taxes: Total city taxes per capita: $130 (2000); City property taxes per capita: $98 (2000).
Education: High school graduation rate: 94.5% (2000); College graduation rate: 43.5% (2000).
Housing: Homeownership rate: 97.4% (2000); Median home value: $247,600 (2000); Median age of housing: 22 years (2000).
Transportation: Commute to work: 90.8% car, 1.9% public transportation, 1.0% walk, 6.1% work from home (2000); Travel time to work: 18.8% less than 15 minutes, 43.0% 15 to 30 minutes, 27.8% 30 to 45 minutes, 7.1% 45 to 60 minutes, 3.3% 60 minutes or more (2000)

GREY CLOUD ISLAND (township). Covers a land area of 3.127 square miles and a water area of 0.728 square miles. Located at 44.80° N. Lat.; 92.99° W. Long.
Population: 307 (2000); Race: 98.2% White, 0.0% Black, 0.0% Asian, 0.0% American Indian and Alaska Native, 1.8% Hispanic of any race, 0.6% two or more races (2000); Density: 98.2 persons per square mile (2000); Age: 22.0% under 18, 16.9% over 64 (2000); Marriage status: 23.3% never married, 51.5% now married, 9.6% widowed, 15.6% divorced (2000); Foreign born: 0.6% (2000); Ancestry (includes multiple ancestries): 36.4% German, 11.7% English, 11.1% Irish, 11.1% Norwegian, 9.3% United States or American (2000).
Economy: Single-family building permits issued: 1 (2001) / 1 (2000); Multi-family building permits issued: 0 (2001) / 0 (2000); Employment by occupation: 9.3% management, 22.1% professional, 6.4% services, 36.6% sales, 2.9% farming, 14.0% construction, 8.7% production (2000).
Income: Per capita income: $26,150 (2000); Median household income: $55,714 (2000); Poverty rate: 7.2% (2000).
Taxes: Total city taxes per capita: $95 (1997); City property taxes per capita: $93 (1997).
Education: High school graduation rate: 81.9% (2000); College graduation rate: 18.1% (2000).
Housing: Homeownership rate: 88.6% (2000); Median home value: $154,200 (2000); Median rent: $575 per month (2000); Median age of housing: 43 years (2000).
Transportation: Commute to work: 88.3% car, 2.3% public transportation, 0.0% walk, 8.2% work from home (2000); Travel time to work: 25.5% less than 15 minutes, 28.7% 15 to 30 minutes, 38.9% 30 to 45 minutes, 5.7% 45 to 60 minutes, 1.3% 60 minutes or more (2000)

HUGO (city). Covers a land area of 33.989 square miles and a water area of 2.023 square miles. Located at 45.15° N. Lat.; 92.96° W. Long. Elevation is 935 feet.
Population: 6,363 (2000); Race: 97.0% White, 0.0% Black, 1.8% Asian, 0.0% American Indian and Alaska Native, 2.2% Hispanic of any race, 0.6% two or more races (2000); Density: 187.2 persons per square mile (2000); Age: 33.0% under 18, 4.6% over 64 (2000); Marriage status: 20.4% never married, 70.4% now married, 2.1% widowed, 7.1% divorced (2000); Foreign born: 1.5% (2000); Ancestry (includes multiple ancestries): 41.6% German, 13.7% Norwegian, 12.5% Irish, 11.2% Swedish, 10.8% French (except Basque) (2000).
Economy: Manufacturing: boring equipment, wire forms, plastic molds. Single-family building permits issued: 205 (2001) / 191 (2000); Multi-family building permits issued: 121 (2001) / 140 (2000); Employment by occupation: 18.1% management, 17.5% professional, 14.2% services, 27.7% sales, 0.1% farming, 10.7% construction, 11.7% production (2000).
Income: Per capita income: $24,334 (2000); Median household income: $63,450 (2000); Poverty rate: 1.5% (2000).
Taxes: Total city taxes per capita: $182 (1997); City property taxes per capita: $162 (1997).
Education: High school graduation rate: 95.3% (2000); College graduation rate: 24.7% (2000).
Housing: Homeownership rate: 95.4% (2000); Median home value: $148,800 (2000); Median rent: $457 per month (2000); Median age of housing: 16 years (2000).
Transportation: Commute to work: 94.2% car, 1.2% public transportation, 0.5% walk, 3.2% work from home (2000); Travel time to work: 19.3% less than 15 minutes, 35.7% 15 to 30 minutes, 28.4% 30 to 45 minutes, 11.2% 45 to 60 minutes, 5.3% 60 minutes or more (2000)

LAKE ELMO (city). Covers a land area of 22.846 square miles and a water area of 1.534 square miles. Located at 44.99° N. Lat.; 92.90° W. Long.
Population: 6,863 (2000); Race: 94.0% White, 0.2% Black, 2.6% Asian, 0.5% American Indian and Alaska Native, 1.8% Hispanic of any race, 2.2% two or more races (2000); Density: 300.4 persons per square mile (2000); Age: 29.2% under 18, 7.0% over 64 (2000); Marriage status: 24.9% never married, 67.6% now married, 1.9% widowed, 5.6% divorced (2000); Foreign born: 3.3% (2000); Ancestry (includes multiple ancestries): 43.6% German, 12.1% Norwegian, 11.8% Irish, 9.4% Swedish, 7.3% Other groups (2000).
Economy: Corn, soybeans; cattle, sheep. Manufacturing: wood products, sand and gravel, wood pallets, wood moldings. Lake Elmo Airport to East. Single-family building permits issued: 140 (2001) / 87 (2000); Multi-family building permits issued: 0 (2001) / 2 (2000); Employment by occupation: 21.5% management, 21.7% professional, 11.1% services, 27.0% sales, 0.7% farming, 8.6% construction, 9.4% production (2000).

Income: Per capita income: $33,007 (2000); Median household income: $76,876 (2000); Poverty rate: 7.3% (2000).
Taxes: Total city taxes per capita: $188 (1997); City property taxes per capita: $165 (1997).
Education: High school graduation rate: 93.6% (2000); College graduation rate: 31.9% (2000).
Housing: Homeownership rate: 96.6% (2000); Median home value: $225,900 (2000); Median rent: $498 per month (2000); Median age of housing: 24 years (2000).
Transportation: Commute to work: 93.3% car, 1.0% public transportation, 0.3% walk, 5.3% work from home (2000); Travel time to work: 23.8% less than 15 minutes, 44.5% 15 to 30 minutes, 21.7% 30 to 45 minutes, 5.3% 45 to 60 minutes, 4.7% 60 minutes or more (2000)

LAKE SAINT CROIX BEACH (city). Covers a land area of 0.575 square miles and a water area of 0.419 square miles. Located at 44.92° N. Lat.; 92.77° W. Long. Elevation is 1,000 feet.
Population: 1,140 (2000); Race: 96.5% White, 0.2% Black, 0.3% Asian, 0.8% American Indian and Alaska Native, 1.6% Hispanic of any race, 1.9% two or more races (2000); Density: 1,982.4 persons per square mile (2000); Age: 23.4% under 18, 9.6% over 64 (2000); Marriage status: 23.4% never married, 61.1% now married, 3.4% widowed, 12.1% divorced (2000); Foreign born: 2.0% (2000); Ancestry (includes multiple ancestries): 39.7% German, 16.7% Irish, 16.3% Norwegian, 13.1% Swedish, 9.6% Polish (2000).
Economy: Single-family building permits issued: 1 (2001) / 1 (2000); Multi-family building permits issued: 0 (2001) / 0 (2000); Employment by occupation: 9.3% management, 18.1% professional, 13.8% services, 28.5% sales, 0.4% farming, 11.9% construction, 18.0% production (2000).
Income: Per capita income: $25,776 (2000); Median household income: $60,652 (2000); Poverty rate: 4.0% (2000).
Taxes: Total city taxes per capita: $141 (1997); City property taxes per capita: $138 (1997).
Education: High school graduation rate: 92.0% (2000); College graduation rate: 23.8% (2000).
Housing: Homeownership rate: 90.3% (2000); Median home value: $120,900 (2000); Median rent: $508 per month (2000); Median age of housing: 38 years (2000).
Transportation: Commute to work: 94.2% car, 0.5% public transportation, 1.2% walk, 4.1% work from home (2000); Travel time to work: 20.3% less than 15 minutes, 36.7% 15 to 30 minutes, 27.8% 30 to 45 minutes, 10.8% 45 to 60 minutes, 4.4% 60 minutes or more (2000)

LAKELAND (city). Covers a land area of 2.105 square miles and a water area of 0.823 square miles. Located at 44.95° N. Lat.; 92.77° W. Long.
Population: 1,917 (2000); Race: 96.3% White, 0.0% Black, 0.7% Asian, 0.1% American Indian and Alaska Native, 1.2% Hispanic of any race, 2.8% two or more races (2000); Density: 910.9 persons per square mile (2000); Age: 25.3% under 18, 6.6% over 64 (2000); Marriage status: 22.0% never married, 66.6% now married, 3.5% widowed, 7.9% divorced (2000); Foreign born: 1.4% (2000); Ancestry (includes multiple ancestries): 42.1% German, 17.5% Irish, 16.7% Norwegian, 13.2% Swedish, 7.4% French (except Basque) (2000).
Economy: Manufacturing: plastic products, water agitators, sand and gravel processing, paving machines. Agriculture: cattle, sheep; corn, soybeans. Lower St. Croix National Scenic Riverway on St. Croix River. Single-family building permits issued: 1 (2001) / 3 (2000); Multi-family building permits issued: 0 (2001) / 0 (2000); Employment by occupation: 13.7% management, 25.2% professional, 10.9% services, 24.8% sales, 0.0% farming, 10.4% construction, 15.0% production (2000).
Income: Per capita income: $30,019 (2000); Median household income: $76,530 (2000); Poverty rate: 3.1% (2000).
Taxes: Total city taxes per capita: $125 (1997); City property taxes per capita: $123 (1997).
Education: High school graduation rate: 95.3% (2000); College graduation rate: 29.4% (2000).
Housing: Homeownership rate: 95.1% (2000); Median home value: $151,100 (2000); Median rent: $675 per month (2000); Median age of housing: 26 years (2000).
Transportation: Commute to work: 94.6% car, 0.2% public transportation, 1.2% walk, 3.7% work from home (2000); Travel time to work: 25.9% less than 15 minutes, 37.5% 15 to 30 minutes, 26.0% 30 to 45 minutes, 6.4% 45 to 60 minutes, 4.1% 60 minutes or more (2000)

LAKELAND SHORES (city). Covers a land area of 0.325 square miles and a water area of 0.410 square miles. Located at 44.94° N. Lat.; 92.76° W. Long.
Population: 355 (2000); Race: 95.8% White, 0.0% Black, 1.2% Asian, 0.0% American Indian and Alaska Native, 3.9% Hispanic of any race, 1.2% two or more races (2000); Density: 1,092.8 persons per square mile (2000); Age: 33.2% under 18, 7.8% over 64 (2000); Marriage status: 17.5% never married, 76.0% now married, 2.8% widowed, 3.7% divorced (2000); Foreign born: 5.4% (2000); Ancestry (includes multiple ancestries): 41.9% German, 17.1% Swedish, 14.4% Irish, 10.5% Norwegian, 8.4% Polish (2000).
Economy: Lower St. Croix National Scenic Riverway on St. Croix River. Single-family building permits issued: 0 (2001) / 0 (2000); Multi-family building permits issued: 0 (2001) / 0 (2000); Employment by occupation: 16.0% management, 30.4% professional, 16.6% services, 22.7% sales, 0.0% farming, 5.5% construction, 8.8% production (2000).
Income: Per capita income: $29,789 (2000); Median household income: $80,907 (2000); Poverty rate: 3.9% (2000).
Taxes: Total city taxes per capita: $157 (1997); City property taxes per capita: $154 (1997).
Education: High school graduation rate: 97.1% (2000); College graduation rate: 36.1% (2000).
Housing: Homeownership rate: 97.3% (2000); Median home value: $217,500 (2000); Median age of housing: 15 years (2000).
Transportation: Commute to work: 97.8% car, 0.0% public transportation, 0.0% walk, 2.2% work from home (2000); Travel time to work: 20.6% less than 15 minutes, 21.1% 15 to 30 minutes, 48.0% 30 to 45 minutes, 7.4% 45 to 60 minutes, 2.9% 60 minutes or more (2000)

LANDFALL (city). Covers a land area of 0.078 square miles and a water area of 0.024 square miles. Located at 44.95° N. Lat.; 92.97° W. Long. Elevation is 963 feet.
Population: 700 (2000); Race: 85.8% White, 0.0% Black, 4.1% Asian, 3.8% American Indian and Alaska Native, 4.8% Hispanic of any race, 6.3% two or more races (2000); Density: 8,996.7 persons per square mile (2000); Age: 28.4% under 18, 4.2% over 64 (2000); Marriage status: 35.7% never married, 35.3% now married, 4.0% widowed, 25.0% divorced (2000); Foreign born: 6.3% (2000); Ancestry (includes multiple ancestries): 31.3% German, 18.6% Other groups, 15.9% Irish, 9.5% Norwegian, 8.0% Swedish (2000).
Economy: Single-family building permits issued: 0 (2001) / 0 (2000); Multi-family building permits issued: 0 (2001) / 0 (2000); Employment by occupation: 6.2% management, 5.0% professional, 22.3% services, 27.3% sales, 0.0% farming, 16.4% construction, 22.9% production (2000).
Income: Per capita income: $15,588 (2000); Median household income: $31,136 (2000); Poverty rate: 19.4% (2000).
Taxes: Total city taxes per capita: $920 (1997); City property taxes per capita: $885 (1997).
Education: High school graduation rate: 76.6% (2000); College graduation rate: 4.2% (2000).
Housing: Homeownership rate: 94.4% (2000); Median home value: $112,500 (2000); Median rent: $300 per month (2000); Median age of housing: 25 years (2000).
Transportation: Commute to work: 90.5% car, 4.6% public transportation, 0.9% walk, 2.8% work from home (2000); Travel time to work: 27.7% less than 15 minutes, 41.8% 15 to 30 minutes, 13.5% 30 to 45 minutes, 11.0% 45 to 60 minutes, 6.0% 60 minutes or more (2000)

MAHTOMEDI (city). Covers a land area of 3.609 square miles and a water area of 1.425 square miles. Located at 45.06° N. Lat.; 92.95° W. Long. Elevation is 953 feet.
History: Northeast Metropolitan Technical College is here. Incorporated 1931.
Population: 7,563 (2000); Race: 97.3% White, 0.3% Black, 1.1% Asian, 0.4% American Indian and Alaska Native, 0.8% Hispanic of any race, 0.8% two or more races (2000); Density: 2,095.4 persons per square mile (2000); Age: 34.8% under 18, 7.3% over 64 (2000); Marriage status: 22.9% never married, 65.6% now married, 4.0% widowed, 7.5% divorced (2000); Foreign born: 2.7% (2000); Ancestry (includes multiple ancestries): 39.4% German, 16.8% Norwegian, 16.1% Irish, 14.1% Swedish, 10.2% English (2000).
Economy: Agricultural area: corn, oats, soybeans, alfalfa; cattle, sheep; light manufacturing. Northport Airport to Northeast. Single-family building permits issued: 21 (2001) / 32 (2000); Multi-family building permits issued: 0 (2001) / 139 (2000); Employment by occupation: 18.8% management, 27.4% professional, 10.5% services, 27.9% sales, 0.1% farming, 7.7% construction, 7.6% production (2000).

Income: Per capita income: $28,930 (2000); Median household income: $72,215 (2000); Poverty rate: 2.7% (2000).
Taxes: Total city taxes per capita: $249 (2000); City property taxes per capita: $226 (2000).
Education: High school graduation rate: 95.6% (2000); College graduation rate: 43.7% (2000).

School District(s)

Mahtomedi (PK-12)
2000 Enrollment: 3,048 651-407-2000

Housing: Homeownership rate: 88.7% (2000); Median home value: $180,300 (2000); Median rent: $684 per month (2000); Median age of housing: 18 years (2000).
Transportation: Commute to work: 91.8% car, 2.6% public transportation, 0.8% walk, 4.5% work from home (2000); Travel time to work: 27.3% less than 15 minutes, 39.3% 15 to 30 minutes, 23.3% 30 to 45 minutes, 6.0% 45 to 60 minutes, 4.1% 60 minutes or more (2000)

MARINE ON SAINT CROIX (city). Aka Marine. Covers a land area of 3.941 square miles and a water area of 0.232 square miles. Located at 45.19° N. Lat.; 92.77° W. Long. Elevation is 775 feet.
Population: 602 (2000); Race: 99.7% White, 0.0% Black, 0.0% Asian, 0.0% American Indian and Alaska Native, 0.3% Hispanic of any race, 0.0% two or more races (2000); Density: 152.8 persons per square mile (2000); Age: 25.4% under 18, 15.6% over 64 (2000); Marriage status: 18.1% never married, 65.4% now married, 6.3% widowed, 10.2% divorced (2000); Foreign born: 2.7% (2000); Ancestry (includes multiple ancestries): 39.0% German, 20.9% Swedish, 17.2% Norwegian, 15.6% English, 13.5% Irish (2000).
Economy: Single-family building permits issued: 5 (2001) / 11 (2000); Multi-family building permits issued: 0 (2001) / 0 (2000); Employment by occupation: 23.1% management, 29.3% professional, 15.9% services, 15.5% sales, 0.0% farming, 6.2% construction, 10.0% production (2000).
Income: Per capita income: $32,383 (2000); Median household income: $66,250 (2000); Poverty rate: 2.8% (2000).
Taxes: Total city taxes per capita: $430 (1997); City property taxes per capita: $420 (1997).
Education: High school graduation rate: 94.9% (2000); College graduation rate: 49.7% (2000).
Housing: Homeownership rate: 90.2% (2000); Median home value: $202,300 (2000); Median rent: $540 per month (2000); Median age of housing: 60+ years (2000).
Transportation: Commute to work: 85.6% car, 1.1% public transportation, 6.7% walk, 6.0% work from home (2000); Travel time to work: 19.9% less than 15 minutes, 27.0% 15 to 30 minutes, 25.8% 30 to 45 minutes, 18.4% 45 to 60 minutes, 9.0% 60 minutes or more (2000)

MAY (township). Covers a land area of 35.303 square miles and a water area of 2.311 square miles. Located at 45.16° N. Lat.; 92.83° W. Long.
Population: 2,928 (2000); Race: 98.1% White, 0.0% Black, 1.6% Asian, 0.0% American Indian and Alaska Native, 0.2% Hispanic of any race, 0.1% two or more races (2000); Density: 82.9 persons per square mile (2000); Age: 28.8% under 18, 7.1% over 64 (2000); Marriage status: 21.5% never married, 68.6% now married, 2.7% widowed, 7.2% divorced (2000); Foreign born: 2.3% (2000); Ancestry (includes multiple ancestries): 43.5% German, 18.0% Norwegian, 16.3% Irish, 13.2% Swedish, 8.6% French (except Basque) (2000).
Economy: Single-family building permits issued: 21 (2001) / 14 (2000); Multi-family building permits issued: 0 (2001) / 0 (2000); Employment by occupation: 16.5% management, 27.1% professional, 8.6% services, 24.1% sales, 1.9% farming, 10.2% construction, 11.7% production (2000).
Income: Per capita income: $32,765 (2000); Median household income: $80,374 (2000); Poverty rate: 2.1% (2000).
Taxes: Total city taxes per capita: $52 (2000); City property taxes per capita: $35 (2000).
Education: High school graduation rate: 96.9% (2000); College graduation rate: 38.0% (2000).
Housing: Homeownership rate: 94.0% (2000); Median home value: $234,700 (2000); Median rent: $713 per month (2000); Median age of housing: 25 years (2000).
Transportation: Commute to work: 92.2% car, 0.6% public transportation, 0.5% walk, 6.4% work from home (2000); Travel time to work: 11.6% less than 15 minutes, 33.0% 15 to 30 minutes, 36.0% 30 to 45 minutes, 13.8% 45 to 60 minutes, 5.6% 60 minutes or more (2000)

NEW SCANDIA (township). Covers a land area of 35.964 square miles and a water area of 3.848 square miles. Located at 45.25° N. Lat.; 92.82° W. Long.
Population: 3,692 (2000); Race: 99.2% White, 0.7% Black, 0.0% Asian, 0.0% American Indian and Alaska Native, 0.6% Hispanic of any race, 0.1% two or more races (2000); Density: 102.7 persons per square mile (2000); Age: 25.9% under 18, 9.3% over 64 (2000); Marriage status: 20.7% never married, 68.9% now married, 3.8% widowed, 6.6% divorced (2000); Foreign born: 3.4% (2000); Ancestry (includes multiple ancestries): 36.6% German, 21.6% Swedish, 16.9% Irish, 12.1% Norwegian, 6.0% English (2000).
Economy: Single-family building permits issued: 28 (2001) / 16 (2000); Multi-family building permits issued: 0 (2001) / 0 (2000); Employment by occupation: 16.9% management, 19.2% professional, 10.9% services, 28.5% sales, 0.0% farming, 13.7% construction, 10.7% production (2000).
Income: Per capita income: $27,399 (2000); Median household income: $68,036 (2000); Poverty rate: 2.3% (2000).
Taxes: Total city taxes per capita: $247 (2000); City property taxes per capita: $241 (2000).
Education: High school graduation rate: 92.8% (2000); College graduation rate: 28.0% (2000).
Housing: Homeownership rate: 93.8% (2000); Median home value: $177,700 (2000); Median rent: $540 per month (2000); Median age of housing: 26 years (2000).
Transportation: Commute to work: 92.9% car, 0.0% public transportation, 0.2% walk, 6.9% work from home (2000); Travel time to work: 18.4% less than 15 minutes, 22.7% 15 to 30 minutes, 27.2% 30 to 45 minutes, 21.0% 45 to 60 minutes, 10.7% 60 minutes or more (2000)

NEWPORT (city). Covers a land area of 3.662 square miles and a water area of 0.247 square miles. Located at 44.87° N. Lat.; 93.00° W. Long. Elevation is 743 feet.
Population: 3,715 (2000); Race: 91.4% White, 0.2% Black, 2.3% Asian, 1.6% American Indian and Alaska Native, 4.7% Hispanic of any race, 2.9% two or more races (2000); Density: 1,014.4 persons per square mile (2000); Age: 27.4% under 18, 9.6% over 64 (2000); Marriage status: 26.7% never married, 54.4% now married, 5.9% widowed, 13.0% divorced (2000); Foreign born: 2.6% (2000); Ancestry (includes multiple ancestries): 37.8% German, 14.9% Irish, 13.2% Norwegian, 12.0% Other groups, 7.9% Swedish (2000).
Economy: Manufacturing: consumer goods, wood products, steel. Single-family building permits issued: 7 (2001) / 8 (2000); Multi-family building permits issued: 0 (2001) / 0 (2000); Employment by occupation: 10.6% management, 17.4% professional, 14.0% services, 29.2% sales, 0.0% farming, 10.9% construction, 17.9% production (2000).
Income: Per capita income: $22,310 (2000); Median household income: $45,373 (2000); Poverty rate: 3.7% (2000).
Taxes: Total city taxes per capita: $492 (1997); City property taxes per capita: $467 (1997).
Education: High school graduation rate: 85.3% (2000); College graduation rate: 14.1% (2000).
Housing: Homeownership rate: 66.6% (2000); Median home value: $112,500 (2000); Median rent: $516 per month (2000); Median age of housing: 34 years (2000).
Safety: Violent crime rate: 37.3 per 10,000 population; Property crime rate: 516.6 per 10,000 population (2001).
Transportation: Commute to work: 94.3% car, 2.9% public transportation, 1.7% walk, 1.1% work from home (2000); Travel time to work: 32.1% less than 15 minutes, 43.7% 15 to 30 minutes, 19.1% 30 to 45 minutes, 2.5% 45 to 60 minutes, 2.6% 60 minutes or more (2000)

OAK PARK HEIGHTS (city). Covers a land area of 3.012 square miles and a water area of 0 square miles. Located at 45.03° N. Lat.; 92.81° W. Long.
Population: 3,957 (2000); Race: 90.5% White, 5.9% Black, 0.6% Asian, 0.6% American Indian and Alaska Native, 1.9% Hispanic of any race, 1.6% two or more races (2000); Density: 1,313.6 persons per square mile (2000); Age: 21.7% under 18, 12.5% over 64 (2000); Marriage status: 28.1% never married, 54.2% now married, 6.9% widowed, 10.8% divorced (2000); Foreign born: 1.9% (2000); Ancestry (includes multiple ancestries): 33.6% German, 15.8% Norwegian, 15.7% Swedish, 15.3% Irish, 9.6% English (2000).
Economy: Light manufacturing. Agriculture: cattle, sheep; corn, oats, alfalfa, soybeans. Minnesota Correctional facilities are here and in adjacent Bayport to South. Lower St. Croix National Scenic Riverway on St. Croix River. Single-family building permits issued: 0 (2001) / 11 (2000); Multi-family

building permits issued: 0 (2001) / 0 (2000); Employment by occupation: 14.9% management, 22.0% professional, 14.8% services, 26.3% sales, 0.1% farming, 8.6% construction, 13.2% production (2000).
Income: Per capita income: $23,293 (2000); Median household income: $48,425 (2000); Poverty rate: 3.4% (2000).
Taxes: Total city taxes per capita: $443 (1997); City property taxes per capita: $403 (1997).
Education: High school graduation rate: 90.8% (2000); College graduation rate: 24.3% (2000).
Housing: Homeownership rate: 68.5% (2000); Median home value: $148,400 (2000); Median rent: $575 per month (2000); Median age of housing: 22 years (2000).
Safety: Violent crime rate: 15.0 per 10,000 population; Property crime rate: 590.1 per 10,000 population (2001).
Transportation: Commute to work: 89.0% car, 1.3% public transportation, 4.0% walk, 4.0% work from home (2000); Travel time to work: 46.1% less than 15 minutes, 21.3% 15 to 30 minutes, 21.1% 30 to 45 minutes, 6.6% 45 to 60 minutes, 4.9% 60 minutes or more (2000)

OAKDALE (city). Covers a land area of 11.067 square miles and a water area of 0.205 square miles. Located at 44.98° N. Lat.; 92.96° W. Long. Elevation is 1,074 feet.
Population: 26,653 (2000); Race: 92.2% White, 2.3% Black, 2.2% Asian, 0.3% American Indian and Alaska Native, 2.7% Hispanic of any race, 2.3% two or more races (2000); Density: 2,408.4 persons per square mile (2000); Age: 29.0% under 18, 8.4% over 64 (2000); Marriage status: 25.6% never married, 60.6% now married, 3.9% widowed, 9.9% divorced (2000); Foreign born: 3.0% (2000); Ancestry (includes multiple ancestries): 41.5% German, 15.9% Irish, 14.3% Norwegian, 9.9% Swedish, 8.9% Other groups (2000).
Vital Statistics: Birth rate: 143.0 per 10,000 population (1998)
Economy: Manufacturing: machinery, pressure vessels, plastic products, polyethylene tubing. Unemployment rate: 2.8% (11/2002); Total civilian labor force: 18,135 (11/2002); Single-family building permits issued: 68 (2001) / 84 (2000); Multi-family building permits issued: 278 (2001) / 78 (2000); Employment by occupation: 14.7% management, 20.7% professional, 13.7% services, 32.3% sales, 0.1% farming, 7.3% construction, 11.3% production (2000).
Income: Per capita income: $24,107 (2000); Median household income: $56,299 (2000); Poverty rate: 3.6% (2000).
Taxes: Total city taxes per capita: $201 (1997); City property taxes per capita: $178 (1997).
Education: High school graduation rate: 92.9% (2000); College graduation rate: 24.3% (2000).

Two-year College(s)

Globe College (Private, For-profit)
2001 Enrollment: 774 651-730-5100
2001 Tuition: In-state $9,180; Out-of-state $9,180
Housing: Homeownership rate: 80.7% (2000); Median home value: $137,200 (2000); Median rent: $621 per month (2000); Median age of housing: 15 years (2000).
Safety: Violent crime rate: 24.5 per 10,000 population; Property crime rate: 422.1 per 10,000 population (2001).
Transportation: Commute to work: 94.3% car, 1.7% public transportation, 1.1% walk, 2.2% work from home (2000); Travel time to work: 26.3% less than 15 minutes, 45.1% 15 to 30 minutes, 20.8% 30 to 45 minutes, 5.6% 45 to 60 minutes, 2.2% 60 minutes or more (2000)

PINE SPRINGS (city). Covers a land area of 0.827 square miles and a water area of 0.111 square miles. Located at 45.03° N. Lat.; 92.95° W. Long. Elevation is 960 feet.
Population: 421 (2000); Race: 97.2% White, 1.3% Black, 0.5% Asian, 0.0% American Indian and Alaska Native, 1.8% Hispanic of any race, 0.3% two or more races (2000); Density: 509.0 persons per square mile (2000); Age: 24.7% under 18, 9.5% over 64 (2000); Marriage status: 23.4% never married, 71.1% now married, 0.6% widowed, 4.9% divorced (2000); Foreign born: 1.5% (2000); Ancestry (includes multiple ancestries): 39.3% German, 17.2% Irish, 9.5% English, 9.3% Norwegian, 6.2% Swedish (2000).
Economy: Single-family building permits issued: 3 (2001) / 0 (2000); Multi-family building permits issued: 0 (2001) / 0 (2000); Employment by occupation: 25.6% management, 24.7% professional, 10.1% services, 20.7% sales, 0.0% farming, 7.5% construction, 11.5% production (2000).
Income: Per capita income: $38,383 (2000); Median household income: $102,496 (2000); Poverty rate: 0.5% (2000).
Taxes: Total city taxes per capita: $85 (1997); City property taxes per capita: $80 (1997).
Education: High school graduation rate: 97.3% (2000); College graduation rate: 49.8% (2000).
Housing: Homeownership rate: 100.0% (2000); Median home value: $255,200 (2000); Median age of housing: 20 years (2000).
Transportation: Commute to work: 92.1% car, 2.2% public transportation, 1.8% walk, 4.0% work from home (2000); Travel time to work: 22.0% less than 15 minutes, 43.6% 15 to 30 minutes, 27.5% 30 to 45 minutes, 5.5% 45 to 60 minutes, 1.4% 60 minutes or more (2000)

SAINT MARYS POINT (city). Covers a land area of 0.403 square miles and a water area of 0 square miles. Located at 44.91° N. Lat.; 92.77° W. Long. Elevation is 693 feet.
Population: 344 (2000); Race: 99.2% White, 0.0% Black, 0.0% Asian, 0.0% American Indian and Alaska Native, 0.5% Hispanic of any race, 0.0% two or more races (2000); Density: 853.0 persons per square mile (2000); Age: 32.9% under 18, 8.6% over 64 (2000); Marriage status: 24.2% never married, 58.1% now married, 3.1% widowed, 14.5% divorced (2000); Foreign born: 0.0% (2000); Ancestry (includes multiple ancestries): 36.8% German, 20.6% Norwegian, 14.6% Irish, 11.0% English, 9.7% Swedish (2000).
Economy: Single-family building permits issued: 2 (2001) / 8 (2000); Multi-family building permits issued: 0 (2001) / 0 (2000); Employment by occupation: 18.7% management, 19.2% professional, 11.9% services, 30.1% sales, 0.0% farming, 5.2% construction, 15.0% production (2000).
Income: Per capita income: $36,905 (2000); Median household income: $61,750 (2000); Poverty rate: 5.8% (2000).
Education: High school graduation rate: 92.1% (2000); College graduation rate: 35.1% (2000).
Housing: Homeownership rate: 91.4% (2000); Median home value: $144,000 (2000); Median rent: $388 per month (2000); Median age of housing: 47 years (2000).
Transportation: Commute to work: 99.0% car, 0.0% public transportation, 1.0% walk, 0.0% work from home (2000); Travel time to work: 22.0% less than 15 minutes, 36.1% 15 to 30 minutes, 30.9% 30 to 45 minutes, 7.9% 45 to 60 minutes, 3.1% 60 minutes or more (2000)

SAINT PAUL PARK (city). Covers a land area of 2.378 square miles and a water area of 0.124 square miles. Located at 44.83° N. Lat.; 92.99° W. Long. Elevation is 766 feet.
Population: 5,070 (2000); Race: 95.6% White, 1.6% Black, 0.3% Asian, 0.5% American Indian and Alaska Native, 4.3% Hispanic of any race, 0.9% two or more races (2000); Density: 2,131.6 persons per square mile (2000); Age: 29.0% under 18, 9.3% over 64 (2000); Marriage status: 26.4% never married, 55.7% now married, 5.2% widowed, 12.7% divorced (2000); Foreign born: 1.2% (2000); Ancestry (includes multiple ancestries): 41.6% German, 19.5% Irish, 15.7% Norwegian, 8.6% Swedish, 7.9% Other groups (2000).
Economy: Single-family building permits issued: 2 (2001) / 2 (2000); Multi-family building permits issued: 0 (2001) / 0 (2000); Employment by occupation: 9.9% management, 15.2% professional, 13.4% services, 30.6% sales, 0.0% farming, 12.3% construction, 18.6% production (2000).
Income: Per capita income: $20,234 (2000); Median household income: $50,805 (2000); Poverty rate: 5.5% (2000).
Education: High school graduation rate: 91.7% (2000); College graduation rate: 12.7% (2000).
Housing: Homeownership rate: 86.2% (2000); Median home value: $106,500 (2000); Median rent: $545 per month (2000); Median age of housing: 36 years (2000).
Safety: Violent crime rate: 31.2 per 10,000 population; Property crime rate: 271.3 per 10,000 population (2001).
Transportation: Commute to work: 92.0% car, 1.9% public transportation, 1.9% walk, 3.7% work from home (2000); Travel time to work: 20.9% less than 15 minutes, 43.2% 15 to 30 minutes, 23.2% 30 to 45 minutes, 7.8% 45 to 60 minutes, 4.9% 60 minutes or more (2000)

SCANDIA (unincorporated postal area, zip code 55073). Covers a land area of 27.753 square miles and a water area of 0.722 square miles. Located at 45.27° N. Lat.; 92.83° W. Long.
Population: 2,790 (2000); Race: 98.7% White, 1.0% Black, 0.0% Asian, 0.0% American Indian and Alaska Native, 0.3% Hispanic of any race, 0.3% two or more races (2000); Density: 100.5 persons per square mile (2000); Age: 26.0% under 18, 6.3% over 64 (2000); Marriage status: 21.4% never married, 68.2% now married, 4.4% widowed, 6.0% divorced (2000); Foreign born: 2.4% (2000); Ancestry (includes multiple ancestries): 38.9% German, 21.5% Irish, 18.4% Swedish, 13.1% Norwegian, 5.9% French (except Basque) (2000).

Economy: Employment by occupation: 14.4% management, 19.3% professional, 9.8% services, 27.9% sales, 0.0% farming, 17.9% construction, 10.7% production (2000).
Income: Per capita income: $26,554 (2000); Median household income: $68,073 (2000); Poverty rate: 2.9% (2000).
Education: High school graduation rate: 93.9% (2000); College graduation rate: 25.7% (2000).

School District(s)

Franconia (01-12)
2000 Enrollment: 0 651-257-2898
Housing: Homeownership rate: 91.4% (2000); Median home value: $171,900 (2000); Median rent: $540 per month (2000); Median age of housing: 25 years (2000).
Newspapers: Country Messenger (1 x week)
Transportation: Commute to work: 93.5% car, 0.0% public transportation, 0.3% walk, 6.2% work from home (2000); Travel time to work: 20.6% less than 15 minutes, 22.9% 15 to 30 minutes, 23.3% 30 to 45 minutes, 24.9% 45 to 60 minutes, 8.4% 60 minutes or more (2000)

STILLWATER (city). Covers a land area of 6.472 square miles and a water area of 0.832 square miles. Located at 45.05° N. Lat.; 92.81° W. Long. Elevation is 639 feet.
History: Stillwater was incorporated in 1844 in an area where logging had begun in 1836.
Population: 15,143 (2000); Race: 97.6% White, 0.5% Black, 0.7% Asian, 0.2% American Indian and Alaska Native, 1.2% Hispanic of any race, 0.6% two or more races (2000); Density: 2,340.0 persons per square mile (2000); Age: 27.6% under 18, 11.9% over 64 (2000); Marriage status: 22.8% never married, 62.2% now married, 5.2% widowed, 9.8% divorced (2000); Foreign born: 1.4% (2000); Ancestry (includes multiple ancestries): 39.5% German, 19.0% Irish, 14.8% Swedish, 14.7% Norwegian, 6.9% English (2000).
Vital Statistics: Birth rate: 159.8 per 10,000 population (1998)
Economy: Single-family building permits issued: 198 (2001) / 184 (2000); Multi-family building permits issued: 16 (2001) / 38 (2000); Employment by occupation: 15.4% management, 24.8% professional, 13.8% services, 30.3% sales, 0.1% farming, 5.1% construction, 10.5% production (2000).
Income: Per capita income: $27,163 (2000); Median household income: $57,154 (2000); Poverty rate: 4.3% (2000).
Taxes: Total city taxes per capita: $418 (2000); City property taxes per capita: $392 (2000).
Education: High school graduation rate: 94.9% (2000); College graduation rate: 37.5% (2000).

School District(s)

New Heights Charter School (KG-12)
2000 Enrollment: 113 651-439-1962
Stillwater (PK-12)
2000 Enrollment: 9,026 651-351-8301
Housing: Homeownership rate: 78.4% (2000); Median home value: $156,200 (2000); Median rent: $564 per month (2000); Median age of housing: 29 years (2000).
Hospitals: Lakeview Hospital (90 beds)
Safety: Violent crime rate: 17.0 per 10,000 population; Property crime rate: 272.4 per 10,000 population (2001).
Newspapers: Stillwater Gazette (5 x week); The Extra (1 x week); The Stillwater Courier News (1 x week)
Transportation: Commute to work: 91.9% car, 0.9% public transportation, 2.8% walk, 3.9% work from home (2000); Travel time to work: 42.6% less than 15 minutes, 25.2% 15 to 30 minutes, 19.4% 30 to 45 minutes, 8.8% 45 to 60 minutes, 4.0% 60 minutes or more (2000)

Additional Information Contacts

Stillwater Area Chamber of Commerce 651-439-7700
Stillwater Chamber of Commerce 651-439-4001

STILLWATER (township). Covers a land area of 16.542 square miles and a water area of 0.977 square miles. Located at 45.08° N. Lat.; 92.81° W. Long. Elevation is 639 feet.
History: A convention here drew up (1848) the petition to Congress for Minnesota's territorial organization. The Minnesota State Prison was established here in 1851. Incorporated 1854.
Population: 2,553 (2000); Race: 97.6% White, 0.0% Black, 0.7% Asian, 0.0% American Indian and Alaska Native, 0.5% Hispanic of any race, 1.2% two or more races (2000); Density: 154.3 persons per square mile (2000); Age: 30.7% under 18, 4.8% over 64 (2000); Marriage status: 19.6% never married, 75.1% now married, 1.6% widowed, 3.7% divorced (2000); Foreign born: 1.3% (2000); Ancestry (includes multiple ancestries): 43.9% German, 15.2% Irish, 14.7% Swedish, 14.3% Norwegian, 9.4% English (2000).
Economy: Manufacturing includes boats, fabricated metal products, signs, computer supplies, molding and tools, electronic goods, printing and publishing. Single-family building permits issued: 11 (2001) / 11 (2000); Multi-family building permits issued: 0 (2001) / 0 (2000); Employment by occupation: 22.0% management, 27.8% professional, 8.9% services, 23.6% sales, 0.0% farming, 7.5% construction, 10.2% production (2000).
Income: Per capita income: $36,795 (2000); Median household income: $96,281 (2000); Poverty rate: 0.6% (2000).
Taxes: Total city taxes per capita: $223 (2000); City property taxes per capita: $201 (2000).
Education: High school graduation rate: 96.4% (2000); College graduation rate: 53.2% (2000).
Housing: Homeownership rate: 96.8% (2000); Median home value: $269,200 (2000); Median rent: $725 per month (2000); Median age of housing: 18 years (2000).
Transportation: Commute to work: 92.7% car, 0.2% public transportation, 0.2% walk, 6.9% work from home (2000); Travel time to work: 24.3% less than 15 minutes, 31.9% 15 to 30 minutes, 28.8% 30 to 45 minutes, 12.4% 45 to 60 minutes, 2.6% 60 minutes or more (2000)

WEST LAKELAND (township). Covers a land area of 12.368 square miles and a water area of 0.260 square miles. Located at 44.97° N. Lat.; 92.81° W. Long.
Population: 3,547 (2000); Race: 97.1% White, 0.0% Black, 2.0% Asian, 0.0% American Indian and Alaska Native, 1.9% Hispanic of any race, 0.3% two or more races (2000); Density: 286.8 persons per square mile (2000); Age: 34.4% under 18, 3.6% over 64 (2000); Marriage status: 18.0% never married, 77.4% now married, 1.1% widowed, 3.6% divorced (2000); Foreign born: 2.5% (2000); Ancestry (includes multiple ancestries): 43.0% German, 15.8% Norwegian, 12.3% Swedish, 11.9% Irish, 10.7% English (2000).
Economy: Single-family building permits issued: 36 (2001) / 46 (2000); Multi-family building permits issued: 0 (2001) / 0 (2000); Employment by occupation: 24.4% management, 27.3% professional, 7.1% services, 27.3% sales, 0.0% farming, 5.4% construction, 8.4% production (2000).
Income: Per capita income: $35,764 (2000); Median household income: $96,256 (2000); Poverty rate: 1.0% (2000).
Taxes: Total city taxes per capita: $134 (1997); City property taxes per capita: $55 (1997).
Education: High school graduation rate: 98.0% (2000); College graduation rate: 49.5% (2000).
Housing: Homeownership rate: 98.9% (2000); Median home value: $284,700 (2000); Median rent: $565 per month (2000); Median age of housing: 9 years (2000).
Transportation: Commute to work: 94.1% car, 0.7% public transportation, 0.1% walk, 4.7% work from home (2000); Travel time to work: 23.3% less than 15 minutes, 44.9% 15 to 30 minutes, 24.5% 30 to 45 minutes, 5.3% 45 to 60 minutes, 2.0% 60 minutes or more (2000)

WILLERNIE (city). Covers a land area of 0.128 square miles and a water area of 0.005 square miles. Located at 45.05° N. Lat.; 92.95° W. Long. Elevation is 1,100 feet.
Population: 549 (2000); Race: 93.6% White, 1.3% Black, 0.0% Asian, 0.4% American Indian and Alaska Native, 0.8% Hispanic of any race, 3.6% two or more races (2000); Density: 4,285.3 persons per square mile (2000); Age: 25.3% under 18, 12.6% over 64 (2000); Marriage status: 26.8% never married, 52.8% now married, 5.6% widowed, 14.8% divorced (2000); Foreign born: 0.2% (2000); Ancestry (includes multiple ancestries): 45.6% German, 15.2% Irish, 11.6% French (except Basque), 10.1% Norwegian, 9.6% English (2000).
Economy: Manufacturing of medical supplies. Single-family building permits issued: 0 (2001) / 1 (2000); Multi-family building permits issued: 0 (2001) / 0 (2000); Employment by occupation: 6.8% management, 14.0% professional, 19.5% services, 23.8% sales, 0.0% farming, 16.3% construction, 19.5% production (2000).
Income: Per capita income: $19,541 (2000); Median household income: $42,500 (2000); Poverty rate: 3.9% (2000).
Taxes: Total city taxes per capita: $149 (1997); City property taxes per capita: $133 (1997).
Education: High school graduation rate: 86.9% (2000); College graduation rate: 10.4% (2000).
Housing: Homeownership rate: 86.3% (2000); Median home value: $106,500 (2000); Median rent: $542 per month (2000); Median age of housing: 50 years (2000).
Transportation: Commute to work: 86.3% car, 1.7% public transportation, 6.0% walk, 5.4% work from home (2000); Travel time to work: 29.0% less

than 15 minutes, 43.5% 15 to 30 minutes, 19.4% 30 to 45 minutes, 7.1% 45 to 60 minutes, 1.1% 60 minutes or more (2000)

WOODBURY (city). Covers a land area of 34.995 square miles and a water area of 0.615 square miles. Located at 44.92° N. Lat.; 92.93° W. Long. Elevation is 1,065 feet.
Population: 46,463 (2000); Race: 90.1% White, 2.1% Black, 5.1% Asian, 0.2% American Indian and Alaska Native, 2.3% Hispanic of any race, 1.9% two or more races (2000); Density: 1,327.7 persons per square mile (2000); Age: 30.7% under 18, 6.0% over 64 (2000); Marriage status: 21.7% never married, 68.4% now married, 2.8% widowed, 7.1% divorced (2000); Foreign born: 6.6% (2000); Ancestry (includes multiple ancestries): 37.6% German, 15.8% Irish, 13.7% Norwegian, 11.3% Other groups, 8.8% Swedish (2000).
Vital Statistics: Birth rate: 150.7 per 10,000 population (1998)
Economy: Manufacturing includes electronic equipment, abrasives, printing and publishing, medical products. Unemployment rate: 2.4% (11/2002); Total civilian labor force: 28,559 (11/2002); Single-family building permits issued: 403 (2001) / 766 (2000); Multi-family building permits issued: 0 (2001) / 18 (2000); Employment by occupation: 24.1% management, 28.0% professional, 9.3% services, 26.5% sales, 0.1% farming, 4.9% construction, 7.2% production (2000).
Income: Per capita income: $32,606 (2000); Median household income: $76,109 (2000); Poverty rate: 1.7% (2000).
Taxes: Total city taxes per capita: $328 (2000); City property taxes per capita: $249 (2000).
Education: High school graduation rate: 96.4% (2000); College graduation rate: 49.3% (2000).

School District(s)

Math & Science Academy (06-11)
2000 Enrollment: 211 651-578-7507
Valley Crossing Community Scho (KG-06)
2000 Enrollment: 870 651-702-5700

Housing: Homeownership rate: 85.3% (2000); Median home value: $174,300 (2000); Median rent: $902 per month (2000); Median age of housing: 8 years (2000).
Safety: Violent crime rate: 6.2 per 10,000 population; Property crime rate: 252.8 per 10,000 population (2001).
Newspapers: The Woodbury Bulletin (1 x week)
Transportation: Commute to work: 93.4% car, 1.5% public transportation, 0.6% walk, 4.0% work from home (2000); Travel time to work: 23.3% less than 15 minutes, 42.9% 15 to 30 minutes, 25.4% 30 to 45 minutes, 5.5% 45 to 60 minutes, 2.8% 60 minutes or more (2000)
Additional Information Contacts
Woodbury Chamber of Commerce 651-578-0722

Watonwan County

Located in southern Minnesota; drained by the Watonwan River. Covers a land area of 434.50 square miles, a water area of 5.40 square miles, and is located in the Central Time Zone. The county government was organized in 1860. County seat is St. James.

Weather Station: Saint James Filtration Plant — Elevation: 1,099 feet

	Jan	Feb	Mar	Apr	May	Jun	Jul	Aug	Sep	Oct	Nov	Dec
High	23	29	41	58	72	81	84	81	74	61	41	28
Low	4	11	23	35	48	57	61	59	50	37	24	11
Precip	0.5	0.4	1.7	2.8	3.3	4.4	3.8	3.6	2.9	2.2	1.5	0.6
Snow	9.7	5.5	8.7	2.4	tr	0.0	0.0	0.0	0.0	0.6	6.2	7.7

High and Low temperatures in degrees Fahrenheit; Precipitation and Snow in inches

Population: 11,876 (2000); Race: 88.4% White, 0.9% Black, 0.8% Asian, 0.3% American Indian and Alaska Native, 15.0% Hispanic of any race, 0.6% two or more races (2000); Density: 27.3 persons per square mile (2000); Age: 27.7% under 18, 18.6% over 64 (2000).
Religion: Five largest groups: 35.3% Evangelical Lutheran Church in America, 19.6% Catholic Church, 6.2% Wisconsin Evangelical Lutheran Synod, 5.1% Presbyterian Church (U.S.A.), 4.4% Lutheran Church—Missouri Synod (2000).
Economy: Unemployment rate: 3.5% (11/2002); Total civilian labor force: 5,519 (11/2002); Leading industries: 32.4% manufacturing; 13.5% health care and social assistance; 10.7% retail trade (2000); Companies that employ more than 1,000 persons: 0 (2000); Companies that employ more than 100 persons: 7 (2000); Farms: 576 totaling 255,994 acres (1997); Minority business ownership rate: 0.0% (1997); Women business ownership rate: 18.0% (1997); Retail sales per capita: $4,758 (1997). Single-family building permits issued: 17 (2001) / 15 (2000); Multi-family building permits issued: 0 (2001) / 0 (2000).
Income: Per capita income: $16,413 (2000); Median household income: $35,441 (2000); Poverty rate: 9.8% (2000); Bankruptcy rate: 2.82% (2001).
Taxes: Total county taxes per capita: $298 (1997); County property taxes per capita: $298 (1997).
Education: High school graduation rate: 75.9% (2000); College graduation rate: 13.7% (2000).
Housing: Homeownership rate: 77.0% (2000); Median home value: $56,600 (2000); Median rent: $284 per month (2000); Median age of housing: 50 years (2000).
Health: Birth rate: 140.6 per 10,000 population (1998); Age adjusted death rate: 74.9 per 10,000 population (1999); Age adjusted cancer mortality rate: 160.3 deaths per 100,000 population (1999). Number of physicians: 5.1 per 10,000 population (1999); Number of hospital beds: 41.3 per 10,000 population (1999).
Elections: 2000 Presidential election results: 44.0% Gore, 49.9% Bush, 4.1% Nader, 1.5% Buchanan
National and State Parks: Bergdahl State Wildlife Management Area; Lewisville State Wildlife Management Area; Madelia State Wildlife Management Area; Mulligan State Wildlife Management Area; Rosendale State Wildlife Management Area; Turtle Marsh State Wildlife Management Area; Voss State Wildlife Management Area; Wilson State Wildlife Management Area; Wood Lake State Wildlife Management Area
Additional Information Contacts
Watonwan County Government Offices 507-375-1298
Madelia Chamber of Commerce 507-642-8822
St. James Chamber of Commerce 507-375-3333

Watonwan County Communities

ADRIAN (township). Covers a land area of 34.707 square miles and a water area of 0.874 square miles. Located at 44.06° N. Lat.; 94.78° W. Long.
Population: 173 (2000); Race: 100.0% White, 0.0% Black, 0.0% Asian, 0.0% American Indian and Alaska Native, 0.0% Hispanic of any race, 0.0% two or more races (2000); Density: 5.0 persons per square mile (2000); Age: 19.4% under 18, 26.5% over 64 (2000); Marriage status: 17.2% never married, 72.8% now married, 6.5% widowed, 3.6% divorced (2000); Foreign born: 0.0% (2000); Ancestry (includes multiple ancestries): 44.9% German, 22.4% Swedish, 17.9% Norwegian, 6.6% English, 3.1% Irish (2000).
Economy: Employment by occupation: 24.2% management, 5.1% professional, 16.2% services, 18.2% sales, 10.1% farming, 7.1% construction, 19.2% production (2000).
Income: Per capita income: $22,279 (2000); Median household income: $41,875 (2000); Poverty rate: 5.2% (2000).
Taxes: Total city taxes per capita: $155 (1997); City property taxes per capita: $155 (1997).
Education: High school graduation rate: 80.6% (2000); College graduation rate: 3.2% (2000).
Housing: Homeownership rate: 90.2% (2000); Median home value: $50,000 (2000); Median rent: $200 per month (2000); Median age of housing: 60+ years (2000).
Transportation: Commute to work: 84.8% car, 0.0% public transportation, 0.0% walk, 15.2% work from home (2000); Travel time to work: 22.6% less than 15 minutes, 54.8% 15 to 30 minutes, 11.9% 30 to 45 minutes, 4.8% 45 to 60 minutes, 6.0% 60 minutes or more (2000)

ANTRIM (township). Covers a land area of 35.686 square miles and a water area of 0.117 square miles. Located at 43.88° N. Lat.; 94.41° W. Long.
Population: 291 (2000); Race: 100.0% White, 0.0% Black, 0.0% Asian, 0.0% American Indian and Alaska Native, 0.0% Hispanic of any race, 0.0% two or more races (2000); Density: 8.2 persons per square mile (2000); Age: 28.8% under 18, 21.9% over 64 (2000); Marriage status: 17.1% never married, 68.5% now married, 12.5% widowed, 1.9% divorced (2000); Foreign born: 3.8% (2000); Ancestry (includes multiple ancestries): 68.8% German, 10.1% Irish, 8.7% English, 4.5% Swedish, 3.8% Norwegian (2000).
Economy: Employment by occupation: 16.9% management, 14.2% professional, 18.2% services, 13.5% sales, 7.4% farming, 6.8% construction, 23.0% production (2000).
Income: Per capita income: $21,739 (2000); Median household income: $35,625 (2000); Poverty rate: 12.2% (2000).
Taxes: Total city taxes per capita: $125 (1997); City property taxes per capita: $125 (1997).
Education: High school graduation rate: 76.4% (2000); College graduation rate: 5.1% (2000).

Housing: Homeownership rate: 80.3% (2000); Median home value: $71,000 (2000); Median rent: $188 per month (2000); Median age of housing: 60+ years (2000).
Transportation: Commute to work: 83.6% car, 0.0% public transportation, 4.8% walk, 11.6% work from home (2000); Travel time to work: 41.1% less than 15 minutes, 40.3% 15 to 30 minutes, 10.9% 30 to 45 minutes, 7.8% 45 to 60 minutes, 0.0% 60 minutes or more (2000)

BUTTERFIELD (city). Covers a land area of 0.437 square miles and a water area of 0 square miles. Located at 43.95° N. Lat.; 94.79° W. Long. Elevation is 1,189 feet.
Population: 564 (2000); Race: 86.8% White, 1.9% Black, 7.6% Asian, 0.0% American Indian and Alaska Native, 13.2% Hispanic of any race, 0.5% two or more races (2000); Density: 1,289.9 persons per square mile (2000); Age: 23.8% under 18, 20.5% over 64 (2000); Marriage status: 22.1% never married, 60.9% now married, 9.0% widowed, 8.1% divorced (2000); Foreign born: 17.6% (2000); Ancestry (includes multiple ancestries): 42.5% German, 22.2% Other groups, 13.2% Norwegian, 6.3% Swedish, 3.9% United States or American (2000).
Economy: Single-family building permits issued: 0 (2001) / 0 (2000); Multi-family building permits issued: 0 (2001) / 0 (2000); Employment by occupation: 6.9% management, 9.4% professional, 18.1% services, 12.3% sales, 1.4% farming, 7.2% construction, 44.8% production (2000).
Income: Per capita income: $15,177 (2000); Median household income: $29,904 (2000); Poverty rate: 8.6% (2000).
Taxes: Total city taxes per capita: $73 (1997); City property taxes per capita: $67 (1997).
Education: High school graduation rate: 60.5% (2000); College graduation rate: 9.2% (2000).

School District(s)

Butterfield (KG-12)
2000 Enrollment: 207 507-956-2771
Housing: Homeownership rate: 84.5% (2000); Median home value: $34,900 (2000); Median rent: $225 per month (2000); Median age of housing: 52 years (2000).
Transportation: Commute to work: 81.0% car, 0.0% public transportation, 14.3% walk, 0.7% work from home (2000); Travel time to work: 43.9% less than 15 minutes, 39.5% 15 to 30 minutes, 7.7% 30 to 45 minutes, 5.5% 45 to 60 minutes, 3.3% 60 minutes or more (2000)

BUTTERFIELD (township). Covers a land area of 35.358 square miles and a water area of 0.224 square miles. Located at 43.96° N. Lat.; 94.80° W. Long. Elevation is 1,189 feet.
Population: 297 (2000); Race: 90.9% White, 0.0% Black, 5.0% Asian, 0.0% American Indian and Alaska Native, 8.1% Hispanic of any race, 0.0% two or more races (2000); Density: 8.4 persons per square mile (2000); Age: 33.6% under 18, 8.1% over 64 (2000); Marriage status: 29.2% never married, 66.0% now married, 2.4% widowed, 2.4% divorced (2000); Foreign born: 9.7% (2000); Ancestry (includes multiple ancestries): 57.0% German, 16.8% Norwegian, 12.8% Other groups, 8.4% Swedish, 7.0% United States or American (2000).
Economy: Railroad junction. Grain, soybeans; livestock. Manufacturing: fowl processing. Employment by occupation: 19.3% management, 15.6% professional, 8.1% services, 13.3% sales, 3.7% farming, 9.6% construction, 30.4% production (2000).
Income: Per capita income: $13,524 (2000); Median household income: $36,528 (2000); Poverty rate: 14.8% (2000).
Taxes: Total city taxes per capita: $71 (1997); City property taxes per capita: $71 (1997).
Education: High school graduation rate: 79.9% (2000); College graduation rate: 14.2% (2000).
Housing: Homeownership rate: 68.4% (2000); Median home value: $49,300 (2000); Median rent: $225 per month (2000); Median age of housing: 60+ years (2000).
Transportation: Commute to work: 89.1% car, 0.0% public transportation, 1.6% walk, 9.4% work from home (2000); Travel time to work: 53.4% less than 15 minutes, 33.6% 15 to 30 minutes, 9.5% 30 to 45 minutes, 3.4% 45 to 60 minutes, 0.0% 60 minutes or more (2000)

DARFUR (city). Covers a land area of 0.354 square miles and a water area of 0 square miles. Located at 44.05° N. Lat.; 94.83° W. Long. Elevation is 1,148 feet.
Population: 137 (2000); Race: 100.0% White, 0.0% Black, 0.0% Asian, 0.0% American Indian and Alaska Native, 0.0% Hispanic of any race, 0.0% two or more races (2000); Density: 386.6 persons per square mile (2000); Age: 25.5% under 18, 20.6% over 64 (2000); Marriage status: 23.3% never married, 63.8% now married, 6.9% widowed, 6.0% divorced (2000); Foreign born: 0.0% (2000); Ancestry (includes multiple ancestries): 62.4% German, 24.8% Swedish, 7.1% Norwegian, 5.7% Irish, 5.0% United States or American (2000).
Economy: Manufacturing: chemicals. Single-family building permits issued: 0 (2001) / 0 (2000); Multi-family building permits issued: 0 (2001) / 0 (2000); Employment by occupation: 2.9% management, 2.9% professional, 23.2% services, 14.5% sales, 0.0% farming, 13.0% construction, 43.5% production (2000).
Income: Per capita income: $14,300 (2000); Median household income: $31,563 (2000); Poverty rate: 7.1% (2000).
Taxes: Total city taxes per capita: $146 (1997); City property taxes per capita: $138 (1997).
Education: High school graduation rate: 80.9% (2000); College graduation rate: 7.9% (2000).
Housing: Homeownership rate: 87.3% (2000); Median home value: $18,900 (2000); Median rent: $150 per month (2000); Median age of housing: 60+ years (2000).
Transportation: Commute to work: 81.2% car, 0.0% public transportation, 15.9% walk, 0.0% work from home (2000); Travel time to work: 29.0% less than 15 minutes, 31.9% 15 to 30 minutes, 36.2% 30 to 45 minutes, 2.9% 45 to 60 minutes, 0.0% 60 minutes or more (2000)

FIELDON (township). Covers a land area of 35.712 square miles and a water area of 0.157 square miles. Located at 43.98° N. Lat.; 94.43° W. Long.
Population: 246 (2000); Race: 99.2% White, 0.0% Black, 0.0% Asian, 0.0% American Indian and Alaska Native, 0.0% Hispanic of any race, 0.8% two or more races (2000); Density: 6.9 persons per square mile (2000); Age: 29.4% under 18, 12.5% over 64 (2000); Marriage status: 23.8% never married, 64.6% now married, 4.2% widowed, 7.4% divorced (2000); Foreign born: 0.0% (2000); Ancestry (includes multiple ancestries): 62.5% German, 25.4% Norwegian, 23.8% Irish, 4.8% Swedish, 3.2% Other groups (2000).
Economy: Employment by occupation: 21.5% management, 11.9% professional, 14.8% services, 18.5% sales, 0.0% farming, 14.1% construction, 19.3% production (2000).
Income: Per capita income: $19,001 (2000); Median household income: $54,167 (2000); Poverty rate: 9.7% (2000).
Taxes: Total city taxes per capita: $135 (1997); City property taxes per capita: $135 (1997).
Education: High school graduation rate: 86.1% (2000); College graduation rate: 12.0% (2000).
Housing: Homeownership rate: 80.0% (2000); Median home value: $92,500 (2000); Median rent: $142 per month (2000); Median age of housing: 60+ years (2000).
Transportation: Commute to work: 80.0% car, 0.0% public transportation, 5.9% walk, 11.1% work from home (2000); Travel time to work: 54.2% less than 15 minutes, 10.8% 15 to 30 minutes, 25.8% 30 to 45 minutes, 6.7% 45 to 60 minutes, 2.5% 60 minutes or more (2000)

LA SALLE (city). Covers a land area of 0.090 square miles and a water area of 0 square miles. Located at 44.07° N. Lat.; 94.57° W. Long. Elevation is 1,030 feet.
Population: 90 (2000); Race: 92.6% White, 0.0% Black, 7.4% Asian, 0.0% American Indian and Alaska Native, 0.0% Hispanic of any race, 0.0% two or more races (2000); Density: 1,001.6 persons per square mile (2000); Age: 30.5% under 18, 22.1% over 64 (2000); Marriage status: 30.4% never married, 41.8% now married, 10.1% widowed, 17.7% divorced (2000); Foreign born: 4.2% (2000); Ancestry (includes multiple ancestries): 44.2% Norwegian, 29.5% German, 8.4% French (except Basque), 8.4% Irish, 7.4% Other groups (2000).
Economy: Grain, soybeans; livestock. Manufacturing: feeds. Single-family building permits issued: 0 (2001) / 0 (2000); Multi-family building permits issued: 0 (2001) / 0 (2000); Employment by occupation: 5.9% management, 11.8% professional, 25.5% services, 31.4% sales, 0.0% farming, 3.9% construction, 21.6% production (2000).
Income: Per capita income: $15,941 (2000); Median household income: $29,375 (2000); Poverty rate: 36.3% (2000).
Taxes: Total city taxes per capita: $116 (1997); City property taxes per capita: $105 (1997).
Education: High school graduation rate: 75.0% (2000); College graduation rate: 18.8% (2000).
Housing: Homeownership rate: 90.7% (2000); Median home value: $35,300 (2000); Median rent: $375 per month (2000); Median age of housing: 58 years (2000).
Transportation: Commute to work: 90.2% car, 0.0% public transportation, 7.8% walk, 2.0% work from home (2000); Travel time to work: 44.0% less

than 15 minutes, 36.0% 15 to 30 minutes, 12.0% 30 to 45 minutes, 8.0% 45 to 60 minutes, 0.0% 60 minutes or more (2000)

LEWISVILLE (city). Covers a land area of 0.293 square miles and a water area of 0 square miles. Located at 43.92° N. Lat.; 94.43° W. Long. Elevation is 1,065 feet.
Population: 274 (2000); Race: 93.7% White, 0.0% Black, 0.0% Asian, 0.0% American Indian and Alaska Native, 10.0% Hispanic of any race, 0.0% two or more races (2000); Density: 936.1 persons per square mile (2000); Age: 28.3% under 18, 17.8% over 64 (2000); Marriage status: 20.1% never married, 64.7% now married, 8.3% widowed, 6.9% divorced (2000); Foreign born: 8.6% (2000); Ancestry (includes multiple ancestries): 65.4% German, 17.8% Norwegian, 7.1% Irish, 4.1% Other groups, 3.0% French (except Basque) (2000).
Economy: Grain, soybeans; livestock. Employment by occupation: 11.7% management, 6.7% professional, 17.5% services, 11.7% sales, 6.7% farming, 17.5% construction, 28.3% production (2000).
Income: Per capita income: $12,700 (2000); Median household income: $29,432 (2000); Poverty rate: 15.2% (2000).
Taxes: Total city taxes per capita: $136 (1997); City property taxes per capita: $136 (1997).
Education: High school graduation rate: 69.3% (2000); College graduation rate: 6.6% (2000).
Housing: Homeownership rate: 91.4% (2000); Median home value: $27,300 (2000); Median rent: $150 per month (2000); Median age of housing: 58 years (2000).
Transportation: Commute to work: 93.3% car, 0.0% public transportation, 5.0% walk, 1.7% work from home (2000); Travel time to work: 20.3% less than 15 minutes, 52.5% 15 to 30 minutes, 14.4% 30 to 45 minutes, 1.7% 45 to 60 minutes, 11.0% 60 minutes or more (2000)

LONG LAKE (township). Covers a land area of 34.374 square miles and a water area of 1.266 square miles. Located at 43.88° N. Lat.; 94.68° W. Long.
Population: 346 (2000); Race: 96.5% White, 0.0% Black, 0.0% Asian, 0.0% American Indian and Alaska Native, 3.5% Hispanic of any race, 0.0% two or more races (2000); Density: 10.1 persons per square mile (2000); Age: 22.1% under 18, 23.3% over 64 (2000); Marriage status: 14.5% never married, 75.5% now married, 7.1% widowed, 2.8% divorced (2000); Foreign born: 2.7% (2000); Ancestry (includes multiple ancestries): 54.3% German, 43.7% Norwegian, 13.3% Swedish, 4.1% Irish, 4.1% Other groups (2000).
Economy: Employment by occupation: 16.7% management, 10.9% professional, 7.5% services, 24.1% sales, 0.0% farming, 9.8% construction, 31.0% production (2000).
Income: Per capita income: $20,009 (2000); Median household income: $47,500 (2000); Poverty rate: 8.6% (2000).
Taxes: Total city taxes per capita: $101 (1997); City property taxes per capita: $101 (1997).
Education: High school graduation rate: 81.9% (2000); College graduation rate: 18.1% (2000).
Housing: Homeownership rate: 91.5% (2000); Median home value: $81,700 (2000); Median rent: $288 per month (2000); Median age of housing: 39 years (2000).
Transportation: Commute to work: 93.7% car, 0.0% public transportation, 1.1% walk, 5.2% work from home (2000); Travel time to work: 47.9% less than 15 minutes, 35.2% 15 to 30 minutes, 3.6% 30 to 45 minutes, 10.9% 45 to 60 minutes, 2.4% 60 minutes or more (2000)

MADELIA (city). Covers a land area of 1.247 square miles and a water area of 0 square miles. Located at 44.05° N. Lat.; 94.41° W. Long. Elevation is 1,029 feet.
Population: 2,340 (2000); Race: 83.9% White, 1.2% Black, 0.0% Asian, 0.2% American Indian and Alaska Native, 21.9% Hispanic of any race, 0.7% two or more races (2000); Density: 1,876.4 persons per square mile (2000); Age: 27.1% under 18, 20.5% over 64 (2000); Marriage status: 24.2% never married, 53.8% now married, 13.2% widowed, 8.8% divorced (2000); Foreign born: 9.5% (2000); Ancestry (includes multiple ancestries): 37.2% German, 20.6% Norwegian, 20.3% Other groups, 8.8% Irish, 4.3% English (2000).
Economy: Single-family building permits issued: 4 (2001) / 2 (2000); Multi-family building permits issued: 0 (2001) / 0 (2000); Employment by occupation: 7.2% management, 15.3% professional, 15.6% services, 21.8% sales, 1.4% farming, 5.1% construction, 33.6% production (2000).
Income: Per capita income: $16,266 (2000); Median household income: $34,219 (2000); Poverty rate: 9.7% (2000).
Taxes: Total city taxes per capita: $184 (1997); City property taxes per capita: $180 (1997).
Education: High school graduation rate: 74.9% (2000); College graduation rate: 17.2% (2000).

School District(s)

Madelia (PK-12)
2000 Enrollment: 619 507-642-3232
Housing: Homeownership rate: 67.1% (2000); Median home value: $60,700 (2000); Median rent: $258 per month (2000); Median age of housing: 44 years (2000).
Hospitals: Madelia Community Hospital (25 beds)
Newspapers: Madelia Times-Messenger (1 x week)
Transportation: Commute to work: 82.9% car, 0.0% public transportation, 9.5% walk, 6.7% work from home (2000); Travel time to work: 58.0% less than 15 minutes, 23.3% 15 to 30 minutes, 13.9% 30 to 45 minutes, 2.2% 45 to 60 minutes, 2.6% 60 minutes or more (2000)
Additional Information Contacts
Madelia Chamber of Commerce 507-642-8822

MADELIA (township). Covers a land area of 33.321 square miles and a water area of 1.200 square miles. Located at 44.05° N. Lat.; 94.43° W. Long. Elevation is 1,029 feet.
History: Settled 1855, plotted 1857, incorporated 1873.
Population: 393 (2000); Race: 99.5% White, 0.0% Black, 0.0% Asian, 0.0% American Indian and Alaska Native, 0.5% Hispanic of any race, 0.5% two or more races (2000); Density: 11.8 persons per square mile (2000); Age: 32.7% under 18, 8.4% over 64 (2000); Marriage status: 25.1% never married, 65.0% now married, 6.7% widowed, 3.2% divorced (2000); Foreign born: 0.0% (2000); Ancestry (includes multiple ancestries): 49.3% German, 21.4% Norwegian, 11.3% Irish, 5.8% Swedish, 5.5% United States or American (2000).
Economy: Agricultural area: grain, soybeans; livestock, poultry. Manufacturing: poultry products, building materials, foods; printing and publishing. Employment by occupation: 17.1% management, 17.1% professional, 19.4% services, 18.0% sales, 1.9% farming, 10.0% construction, 16.6% production (2000).
Income: Per capita income: $18,969 (2000); Median household income: $48,542 (2000); Poverty rate: 2.1% (2000).
Taxes: Total city taxes per capita: $146 (1997); City property taxes per capita: $146 (1997).
Education: High school graduation rate: 91.6% (2000); College graduation rate: 18.6% (2000).
Housing: Homeownership rate: 86.8% (2000); Median home value: $84,400 (2000); Median rent: $233 per month (2000); Median age of housing: 60+ years (2000).
Transportation: Commute to work: 88.5% car, 0.0% public transportation, 1.0% walk, 10.5% work from home (2000); Travel time to work: 56.7% less than 15 minutes, 20.9% 15 to 30 minutes, 20.3% 30 to 45 minutes, 1.1% 45 to 60 minutes, 1.1% 60 minutes or more (2000)

NELSON (township). Covers a land area of 35.655 square miles and a water area of 0.007 square miles. Located at 44.06° N. Lat.; 94.67° W. Long.
Population: 309 (2000); Race: 100.0% White, 0.0% Black, 0.0% Asian, 0.0% American Indian and Alaska Native, 0.0% Hispanic of any race, 0.0% two or more races (2000); Density: 8.7 persons per square mile (2000); Age: 28.1% under 18, 18.9% over 64 (2000); Marriage status: 16.1% never married, 72.9% now married, 4.1% widowed, 6.9% divorced (2000); Foreign born: 0.0% (2000); Ancestry (includes multiple ancestries): 58.7% German, 29.5% Norwegian, 20.6% Swedish, 5.7% Irish, 5.0% United States or American (2000).
Economy: Employment by occupation: 15.6% management, 15.6% professional, 4.3% services, 12.1% sales, 7.1% farming, 22.0% construction, 23.4% production (2000).
Income: Per capita income: $19,699 (2000); Median household income: $47,000 (2000); Poverty rate: 2.5% (2000).
Taxes: Total city taxes per capita: $125 (1997); City property taxes per capita: $125 (1997).
Education: High school graduation rate: 90.3% (2000); College graduation rate: 11.2% (2000).
Housing: Homeownership rate: 88.0% (2000); Median home value: $62,500 (2000); Median rent: $325 per month (2000); Median age of housing: 60+ years (2000).
Transportation: Commute to work: 83.0% car, 0.0% public transportation, 0.7% walk, 16.3% work from home (2000); Travel time to work: 30.5% less than 15 minutes, 33.1% 15 to 30 minutes, 18.6% 30 to 45 minutes, 5.9% 45 to 60 minutes, 11.9% 60 minutes or more (2000)

ODIN (city). Covers a land area of 0.363 square miles and a water area of 0 square miles. Located at 43.86° N. Lat.; 94.74° W. Long.
Population: 125 (2000); Race: 100.0% White, 0.0% Black, 0.0% Asian, 0.0% American Indian and Alaska Native, 0.0% Hispanic of any race, 0.0% two or more races (2000); Density: 344.6 persons per square mile (2000); Age: 19.2% under 18, 29.6% over 64 (2000); Marriage status: 11.3% never married, 64.2% now married, 15.1% widowed, 9.4% divorced (2000); Foreign born: 0.0% (2000); Ancestry (includes multiple ancestries): 45.6% German, 40.8% Norwegian, 16.8% Swedish, 4.8% United States or American, 4.8% Scandinavian (2000).
Economy: Employment by occupation: 0.0% management, 29.4% professional, 5.9% services, 25.5% sales, 0.0% farming, 27.5% construction, 11.8% production (2000).
Income: Per capita income: $16,118 (2000); Median household income: $25,625 (2000); Poverty rate: 16.8% (2000).
Taxes: Total city taxes per capita: $109 (1997); City property taxes per capita: $109 (1997).
Education: High school graduation rate: 83.7% (2000); College graduation rate: 12.0% (2000).
Housing: Homeownership rate: 93.8% (2000); Median home value: $30,600 (2000); Median rent: $325 per month (2000); Median age of housing: 60+ years (2000).
Transportation: Commute to work: 88.2% car, 0.0% public transportation, 7.8% walk, 3.9% work from home (2000); Travel time to work: 34.7% less than 15 minutes, 30.6% 15 to 30 minutes, 20.4% 30 to 45 minutes, 0.0% 45 to 60 minutes, 14.3% 60 minutes or more (2000)

ODIN (township). Covers a land area of 34.610 square miles and a water area of 0.897 square miles. Located at 43.88° N. Lat.; 94.80° W. Long.
Population: 206 (2000); Race: 92.4% White, 0.0% Black, 6.6% Asian, 0.0% American Indian and Alaska Native, 0.0% Hispanic of any race, 0.9% two or more races (2000); Density: 6.0 persons per square mile (2000); Age: 23.2% under 18, 16.1% over 64 (2000); Marriage status: 24.3% never married, 62.1% now married, 9.0% widowed, 4.5% divorced (2000); Foreign born: 5.7% (2000); Ancestry (includes multiple ancestries): 31.3% German, 29.4% Norwegian, 28.0% Swedish, 6.6% Other groups, 5.2% Irish (2000).
Economy: Grain, soybeans; livestock. Manufacturing: agricultural equipment parts, feeds. Employment by occupation: 17.5% management, 8.3% professional, 20.0% services, 26.7% sales, 3.3% farming, 3.3% construction, 20.8% production (2000).
Income: Per capita income: $15,830 (2000); Median household income: $38,625 (2000); Poverty rate: 13.3% (2000).
Taxes: Total city taxes per capita: $84 (1997); City property taxes per capita: $84 (1997).
Education: High school graduation rate: 81.8% (2000); College graduation rate: 11.7% (2000).
Housing: Homeownership rate: 73.3% (2000); Median home value: $47,500 (2000); Median rent: $275 per month (2000); Median age of housing: 60+ years (2000).
Transportation: Commute to work: 87.7% car, 0.0% public transportation, 4.4% walk, 5.3% work from home (2000); Travel time to work: 40.7% less than 15 minutes, 48.1% 15 to 30 minutes, 1.9% 30 to 45 minutes, 6.5% 45 to 60 minutes, 2.8% 60 minutes or more (2000)

ORMSBY (city). Covers a land area of 0.358 square miles and a water area of 0 square miles. Located at 43.84° N. Lat.; 94.69° W. Long.
Population: 154 (2000); Race: 100.0% White, 0.0% Black, 0.0% Asian, 0.0% American Indian and Alaska Native, 0.0% Hispanic of any race, 0.0% two or more races (2000); Density: 429.8 persons per square mile (2000); Age: 32.2% under 18, 18.8% over 64 (2000); Marriage status: 15.3% never married, 63.1% now married, 15.3% widowed, 6.3% divorced (2000); Foreign born: 0.0% (2000); Ancestry (includes multiple ancestries): 45.6% German, 34.9% Norwegian, 15.4% Swedish, 13.4% United States or American, 8.7% Irish (2000).
Economy: Single-family building permits issued: 0 (2001) / 0 (2000); Multi-family building permits issued: 0 (2001) / 0 (2000); Employment by occupation: 8.2% management, 0.0% professional, 18.0% services, 31.1% sales, 3.3% farming, 13.1% construction, 26.2% production (2000).
Income: Per capita income: $16,954 (2000); Median household income: $37,500 (2000); Poverty rate: 6.0% (2000).
Taxes: Total city taxes per capita: $160 (1997); City property taxes per capita: $160 (1997).
Education: High school graduation rate: 86.8% (2000); College graduation rate: 7.7% (2000).
Housing: Homeownership rate: 96.7% (2000); Median home value: $46,000 (2000); Median rent: $325 per month (2000); Median age of housing: 50 years (2000).
Transportation: Commute to work: 90.2% car, 0.0% public transportation, 8.2% walk, 1.6% work from home (2000); Travel time to work: 45.0% less than 15 minutes, 23.3% 15 to 30 minutes, 10.0% 30 to 45 minutes, 8.3% 45 to 60 minutes, 13.3% 60 minutes or more (2000)

RIVERDALE (township). Covers a land area of 38.862 square miles and a water area of 0.026 square miles. Located at 44.06° N. Lat.; 94.55° W. Long.
Population: 338 (2000); Race: 99.4% White, 0.0% Black, 0.0% Asian, 0.0% American Indian and Alaska Native, 0.9% Hispanic of any race, 0.6% two or more races (2000); Density: 8.7 persons per square mile (2000); Age: 25.7% under 18, 15.8% over 64 (2000); Marriage status: 23.6% never married, 61.3% now married, 8.9% widowed, 6.3% divorced (2000); Foreign born: 0.6% (2000); Ancestry (includes multiple ancestries): 41.8% German, 26.0% Norwegian, 14.6% Swedish, 6.7% Irish, 5.0% United States or American (2000).
Economy: Employment by occupation: 24.6% management, 11.2% professional, 13.4% services, 21.8% sales, 0.0% farming, 3.4% construction, 25.7% production (2000).
Income: Per capita income: $20,099 (2000); Median household income: $44,423 (2000); Poverty rate: 6.8% (2000).
Taxes: Total city taxes per capita: $75 (1997); City property taxes per capita: $75 (1997).
Education: High school graduation rate: 86.4% (2000); College graduation rate: 14.4% (2000).
Housing: Homeownership rate: 91.8% (2000); Median home value: $81,300 (2000); Median rent: $325 per month (2000); Median age of housing: 52 years (2000).
Transportation: Commute to work: 78.8% car, 0.0% public transportation, 5.0% walk, 14.5% work from home (2000); Travel time to work: 42.5% less than 15 minutes, 33.3% 15 to 30 minutes, 15.0% 30 to 45 minutes, 7.8% 45 to 60 minutes, 1.3% 60 minutes or more (2000)

ROSENDALE (township). Covers a land area of 38.220 square miles and a water area of 0.217 square miles. Located at 43.97° N. Lat.; 94.54° W. Long.
Population: 357 (2000); Race: 97.6% White, 0.3% Black, 2.1% Asian, 0.0% American Indian and Alaska Native, 0.0% Hispanic of any race, 0.0% two or more races (2000); Density: 9.3 persons per square mile (2000); Age: 26.6% under 18, 15.2% over 64 (2000); Marriage status: 23.7% never married, 71.9% now married, 2.6% widowed, 1.9% divorced (2000); Foreign born: 1.5% (2000); Ancestry (includes multiple ancestries): 57.6% German, 25.4% Norwegian, 12.8% Swedish, 8.1% Irish, 5.7% Polish (2000).
Economy: Employment by occupation: 13.0% management, 20.9% professional, 16.4% services, 18.1% sales, 1.1% farming, 10.2% construction, 20.3% production (2000).
Income: Per capita income: $18,004 (2000); Median household income: $45,000 (2000); Poverty rate: 5.1% (2000).
Taxes: Total city taxes per capita: $86 (1997); City property taxes per capita: $86 (1997).
Education: High school graduation rate: 85.8% (2000); College graduation rate: 10.6% (2000).
Housing: Homeownership rate: 93.2% (2000); Median home value: $78,600 (2000); Median rent: $125 per month (2000); Median age of housing: 47 years (2000).
Transportation: Commute to work: 88.1% car, 0.0% public transportation, 2.3% walk, 8.5% work from home (2000); Travel time to work: 52.2% less than 15 minutes, 24.8% 15 to 30 minutes, 10.6% 30 to 45 minutes, 11.8% 45 to 60 minutes, 0.6% 60 minutes or more (2000)

SAINT JAMES (city). Covers a land area of 2.290 square miles and a water area of 0.022 square miles. Located at 43.98° N. Lat.; 94.62° W. Long. Elevation is 1,078 feet.
Population: 4,695 (2000); Race: 82.4% White, 1.3% Black, 0.2% Asian, 0.6% American Indian and Alaska Native, 24.1% Hispanic of any race, 1.0% two or more races (2000); Density: 2,050.3 persons per square mile (2000); Age: 28.0% under 18, 18.7% over 64 (2000); Marriage status: 24.1% never married, 58.1% now married, 9.9% widowed, 7.8% divorced (2000); Foreign born: 11.2% (2000); Ancestry (includes multiple ancestries): 36.0% German, 26.0% Other groups, 19.0% Norwegian, 9.6% Swedish, 6.8% Irish (2000).
Economy: Single-family building permits issued: 6 (2001) / 7 (2000); Multi-family building permits issued: 0 (2001) / 0 (2000); Employment by

occupation: 6.9% management, 18.4% professional, 13.9% services, 18.2% sales, 0.8% farming, 9.0% construction, 32.8% production (2000).
Income: Per capita income: $15,336 (2000); Median household income: $33,196 (2000); Poverty rate: 10.8% (2000).
Education: High school graduation rate: 71.4% (2000); College graduation rate: 13.9% (2000).

School District(s)

Saint James (PK-12)
2000 Enrollment: 1,313 507-375-5974
Housing: Homeownership rate: 72.7% (2000); Median home value: $58,200 (2000); Median rent: $299 per month (2000); Median age of housing: 46 years (2000).
Hospitals: Saint James Health Service (31 beds)
Newspapers: Town & Country Shopper (1 x week); Saint James Plaindealer (1 x week)
Transportation: Commute to work: 89.2% car, 0.3% public transportation, 6.4% walk, 3.0% work from home (2000); Travel time to work: 72.4% less than 15 minutes, 10.7% 15 to 30 minutes, 6.5% 30 to 45 minutes, 4.0% 45 to 60 minutes, 6.4% 60 minutes or more (2000)
Additional Information Contacts
St. James Chamber of Commerce 507-375-3333

SAINT JAMES (township). Covers a land area of 33.592 square miles and a water area of 0.395 square miles. Located at 43.97° N. Lat.; 94.67° W. Long. Elevation is 1,078 feet.
Population: 294 (2000); Race: 99.4% White, 0.0% Black, 0.0% Asian, 0.0% American Indian and Alaska Native, 0.6% Hispanic of any race, 0.6% two or more races (2000); Density: 8.8 persons per square mile (2000); Age: 33.2% under 18, 19.5% over 64 (2000); Marriage status: 14.6% never married, 69.5% now married, 7.1% widowed, 8.8% divorced (2000); Foreign born: 0.6% (2000); Ancestry (includes multiple ancestries): 60.7% German, 26.8% Norwegian, 14.3% Swedish, 6.4% Irish, 6.4% United States or American (2000).
Economy: Employment by occupation: 22.8% management, 16.6% professional, 14.5% services, 19.3% sales, 0.0% farming, 14.5% construction, 12.4% production (2000).
Income: Per capita income: $19,580 (2000); Median household income: $36,806 (2000); Poverty rate: 2.1% (2000).
Education: High school graduation rate: 92.1% (2000); College graduation rate: 17.7% (2000).
Housing: Homeownership rate: 87.9% (2000); Median home value: $104,200 (2000); Median rent: $610 per month (2000); Median age of housing: 60+ years (2000).
Transportation: Commute to work: 88.2% car, 0.0% public transportation, 1.4% walk, 10.4% work from home (2000); Travel time to work: 66.7% less than 15 minutes, 22.5% 15 to 30 minutes, 3.1% 30 to 45 minutes, 3.1% 45 to 60 minutes, 4.7% 60 minutes or more (2000)

SOUTH BRANCH (township). Covers a land area of 39.084 square miles and a water area of 0 square miles. Located at 43.89° N. Lat.; 94.55° W. Long. Elevation is 1,115 feet.
Population: 303 (2000); Race: 99.4% White, 0.0% Black, 0.0% Asian, 0.6% American Indian and Alaska Native, 0.6% Hispanic of any race, 0.0% two or more races (2000); Density: 7.8 persons per square mile (2000); Age: 33.1% under 18, 14.5% over 64 (2000); Marriage status: 17.0% never married, 70.9% now married, 8.7% widowed, 3.5% divorced (2000); Foreign born: 1.9% (2000); Ancestry (includes multiple ancestries): 73.3% German, 18.6% Norwegian, 8.0% Irish, 5.8% English, 5.1% Swedish (2000).
Economy: Employment by occupation: 25.7% management, 13.8% professional, 6.6% services, 21.1% sales, 2.6% farming, 8.6% construction, 21.7% production (2000).
Income: Per capita income: $13,449 (2000); Median household income: $35,625 (2000); Poverty rate: 10.7% (2000).
Taxes: Total city taxes per capita: $116 (1997); City property taxes per capita: $116 (1997).
Education: High school graduation rate: 78.6% (2000); College graduation rate: 12.4% (2000).
Housing: Homeownership rate: 81.6% (2000); Median home value: $78,800 (2000); Median rent: $238 per month (2000); Median age of housing: 60+ years (2000).
Transportation: Commute to work: 77.0% car, 0.7% public transportation, 0.0% walk, 19.7% work from home (2000); Travel time to work: 32.0% less than 15 minutes, 50.0% 15 to 30 minutes, 4.1% 30 to 45 minutes, 9.8% 45 to 60 minutes, 4.1% 60 minutes or more (2000)

Wilkin County

Located in western Minnesota; bounded on the west by the Bois de Sioux River, the Red River of the North, and the North Dakota border; drained by the Otter Tail River. Covers a land area of 751.40 square miles, a water area of 0.20 square miles, and is located in the Central Time Zone. The county government was organized in 1858. County seat is Breckenridge.

Weather Station: Rothsay — Elevation: 1,204 feet

	Jan	Feb	Mar	Apr	May	Jun	Jul	Aug	Sep	Oct	Nov	Dec
High	16	24	36	56	70	78	82	81	71	57	36	22
Low	-3	6	19	33	46	55	59	58	48	36	20	5
Precip	0.7	0.5	1.3	1.6	2.9	3.5	3.8	2.8	2.2	2.2	1.0	0.5
Snow	11.6	6.2	7.9	2.3	tr	0.0	0.0	0.0	tr	0.9	7.9	6.3

High and Low temperatures in degrees Fahrenheit; Precipitation and Snow in inches

Population: 7,138 (2000); Race: 98.3% White, 0.1% Black, 0.2% Asian, 0.6% American Indian and Alaska Native, 1.7% Hispanic of any race, 0.4% two or more races (2000); Density: 9.5 persons per square mile (2000); Age: 27.9% under 18, 16.1% over 64 (2000).
Religion: Five largest groups: 30.2% Evangelical Lutheran Church in America, 21.5% Catholic Church, 8.7% Lutheran Church—Missouri Synod, 5.6% The United Methodist Church, 1.9% American Baptist Churches in the USA (2000).
Economy: Unemployment rate: 2.5% (11/2002); Total civilian labor force: 3,751 (11/2002); Leading industries: 31.7% health care and social assistance; 15.8% retail trade; 15.4% wholesale trade (2000); Companies that employ more than 1,000 persons: 0 (2000); Companies that employ more than 100 persons: 1 (2000); Farms: 441 totaling 457,806 acres (1997); Minority business ownership rate: 0.0% (1997); Women business ownership rate: 0.0% (1997); Retail sales per capita: $5,166 (1997). Single-family building permits issued: 17 (2001) / 14 (2000); Multi-family building permits issued: 0 (2001) / 0 (2000).
Income: Per capita income: $16,873 (2000); Median household income: $38,093 (2000); Poverty rate: 8.1% (2000); Bankruptcy rate: 3.00% (2001).
Taxes: Total county taxes per capita: $416 (2000); County property taxes per capita: $416 (2000).
Education: High school graduation rate: 84.5% (2000); College graduation rate: 14.0% (2000).
Housing: Homeownership rate: 80.6% (2000); Median home value: $64,100 (2000); Median rent: $267 per month (2000); Median age of housing: 44 years (2000).
Health: Birth rate: 130.3 per 10,000 population (1998); Age adjusted death rate: 84.8 per 10,000 population (1999); Age adjusted cancer mortality rate: 231.5 deaths per 100,000 population (1999). Number of physicians: 1.4 per 10,000 population (1999); Number of hospital beds: 239.6 per 10,000 population (1999).
Elections: 2000 Presidential election results: 31.7% Gore, 61.5% Bush, 2.3% Nader, 3.9% Buchanan
National and State Parks: Akron State Wildlife Management Area; Atherton State Wildlife Management Area; Manston State Wildlife Management Area; Rothsay State Wildlife Management Area
Additional Information Contacts
Wilkin County Government Offices 218-643-5072
Breckenridge Chamber of Commerce 218-643-5244

Wilkin County Communities

AKRON (township). Covers a land area of 35.455 square miles and a water area of 0.027 square miles. Located at 46.40° N. Lat.; 96.33° W. Long.
Population: 153 (2000); Race: 98.7% White, 0.0% Black, 0.0% Asian, 0.0% American Indian and Alaska Native, 0.0% Hispanic of any race, 1.3% two or more races (2000); Density: 4.3 persons per square mile (2000); Age: 32.3% under 18, 9.5% over 64 (2000); Marriage status: 24.1% never married, 71.6% now married, 2.6% widowed, 1.7% divorced (2000); Foreign born: 0.0% (2000); Ancestry (includes multiple ancestries): 48.1% Norwegian, 39.2% German, 8.2% Scandinavian, 8.2% Swedish, 8.2% United States or American (2000).
Economy: Employment by occupation: 45.9% management, 18.9% professional, 12.2% services, 5.4% sales, 6.8% farming, 5.4% construction, 5.4% production (2000).
Income: Per capita income: $15,022 (2000); Median household income: $43,125 (2000); Poverty rate: 17.7% (2000).
Taxes: Total city taxes per capita: $54 (1997); City property taxes per capita: $54 (1997).

Education: High school graduation rate: 94.5% (2000); College graduation rate: 11.0% (2000).
Housing: Homeownership rate: 95.7% (2000); Median home value: $73,300 (2000); Median rent: $125 per month (2000); Median age of housing: 42 years (2000).
Transportation: Commute to work: 61.1% car, 0.0% public transportation, 2.8% walk, 36.1% work from home (2000); Travel time to work: 37.0% less than 15 minutes, 32.6% 15 to 30 minutes, 21.7% 30 to 45 minutes, 4.3% 45 to 60 minutes, 4.3% 60 minutes or more (2000)

ANDREA (township). Covers a land area of 35.444 square miles and a water area of 0 square miles. Located at 46.33° N. Lat.; 96.35° W. Long.
Population: 70 (2000); Race: 100.0% White, 0.0% Black, 0.0% Asian, 0.0% American Indian and Alaska Native, 0.0% Hispanic of any race, 0.0% two or more races (2000); Density: 2.0 persons per square mile (2000); Age: 38.7% under 18, 8.0% over 64 (2000); Marriage status: 28.0% never married, 60.0% now married, 12.0% widowed, 0.0% divorced (2000); Foreign born: 0.0% (2000); Ancestry (includes multiple ancestries): 50.7% German, 29.3% Norwegian, 17.3% Swiss, 16.0% Polish, 12.0% United States or American (2000).
Economy: Employment by occupation: 46.7% management, 13.3% professional, 16.7% services, 0.0% sales, 0.0% farming, 10.0% construction, 13.3% production (2000).
Income: Per capita income: $14,048 (2000); Median household income: $43,333 (2000); Poverty rate: 2.7% (2000).
Taxes: Total city taxes per capita: $141 (1997); City property taxes per capita: $141 (1997).
Education: High school graduation rate: 88.9% (2000); College graduation rate: 22.2% (2000).
Housing: Homeownership rate: 82.6% (2000); Median home value: $92,500 (2000); Median rent: $225 per month (2000); Median age of housing: 60+ years (2000).
Transportation: Commute to work: 60.7% car, 0.0% public transportation, 0.0% walk, 39.3% work from home (2000); Travel time to work: 23.5% less than 15 minutes, 23.5% 15 to 30 minutes, 41.2% 30 to 45 minutes, 11.8% 45 to 60 minutes, 0.0% 60 minutes or more (2000)

ATHERTON (township). Covers a land area of 36.100 square miles and a water area of 0 square miles. Located at 46.58° N. Lat.; 96.47° W. Long.
Population: 155 (2000); Race: 100.0% White, 0.0% Black, 0.0% Asian, 0.0% American Indian and Alaska Native, 0.0% Hispanic of any race, 0.0% two or more races (2000); Density: 4.3 persons per square mile (2000); Age: 28.3% under 18, 10.9% over 64 (2000); Marriage status: 14.7% never married, 80.9% now married, 1.5% widowed, 2.9% divorced (2000); Foreign born: 0.0% (2000); Ancestry (includes multiple ancestries): 66.8% German, 37.5% Norwegian, 7.1% French (except Basque), 6.0% Swedish, 5.4% Irish (2000).
Economy: Employment by occupation: 23.4% management, 19.5% professional, 14.3% services, 13.0% sales, 2.6% farming, 13.0% construction, 14.3% production (2000).
Income: Per capita income: $13,929 (2000); Median household income: $40,750 (2000); Poverty rate: 22.8% (2000).
Taxes: Total city taxes per capita: $78 (1997); City property taxes per capita: $78 (1997).
Education: High school graduation rate: 84.6% (2000); College graduation rate: 13.0% (2000).
Housing: Homeownership rate: 93.5% (2000); Median home value: $76,300 (2000); Median age of housing: 37 years (2000).
Transportation: Commute to work: 76.6% car, 0.0% public transportation, 0.0% walk, 23.4% work from home (2000); Travel time to work: 11.9% less than 15 minutes, 18.6% 15 to 30 minutes, 39.0% 30 to 45 minutes, 27.1% 45 to 60 minutes, 3.4% 60 minutes or more (2000)

BRADFORD (township). Covers a land area of 35.523 square miles and a water area of 0 square miles. Located at 46.14° N. Lat.; 96.32° W. Long.
Population: 119 (2000); Race: 100.0% White, 0.0% Black, 0.0% Asian, 0.0% American Indian and Alaska Native, 0.0% Hispanic of any race, 0.0% two or more races (2000); Density: 3.3 persons per square mile (2000); Age: 27.6% under 18, 24.1% over 64 (2000); Marriage status: 17.4% never married, 78.3% now married, 2.2% widowed, 2.2% divorced (2000); Foreign born: 0.0% (2000); Ancestry (includes multiple ancestries): 37.9% German, 26.7% Norwegian, 7.8% European, 5.2% Danish, 4.3% Swedish (2000).
Economy: Employment by occupation: 41.7% management, 22.9% professional, 12.5% services, 8.3% sales, 2.1% farming, 12.5% construction, 0.0% production (2000).
Income: Per capita income: $14,201 (2000); Median household income: $28,750 (2000); Poverty rate: 12.9% (2000).
Taxes: Total city taxes per capita: $64 (1997); City property taxes per capita: $64 (1997).
Education: High school graduation rate: 73.1% (2000); College graduation rate: 11.5% (2000).
Housing: Homeownership rate: 94.9% (2000); Median home value: $71,500 (2000); Median age of housing: 52 years (2000).
Transportation: Commute to work: 89.6% car, 0.0% public transportation, 0.0% walk, 10.4% work from home (2000); Travel time to work: 30.2% less than 15 minutes, 39.5% 15 to 30 minutes, 25.6% 30 to 45 minutes, 0.0% 45 to 60 minutes, 4.7% 60 minutes or more (2000)

BRANDRUP (township). Covers a land area of 54.169 square miles and a water area of 0.018 square miles. Located at 46.15° N. Lat.; 96.48° W. Long.
Population: 172 (2000); Race: 98.9% White, 0.0% Black, 0.0% Asian, 0.0% American Indian and Alaska Native, 0.0% Hispanic of any race, 1.1% two or more races (2000); Density: 3.2 persons per square mile (2000); Age: 41.5% under 18, 13.8% over 64 (2000); Marriage status: 18.8% never married, 75.8% now married, 5.5% widowed, 0.0% divorced (2000); Foreign born: 0.0% (2000); Ancestry (includes multiple ancestries): 51.6% German, 38.3% Norwegian, 6.4% Irish, 5.9% United States or American, 5.3% Russian (2000).
Economy: Employment by occupation: 33.3% management, 17.4% professional, 5.8% services, 21.7% sales, 2.9% farming, 7.2% construction, 11.6% production (2000).
Income: Per capita income: $14,720 (2000); Median household income: $43,333 (2000); Poverty rate: 0.0% (2000).
Education: High school graduation rate: 88.0% (2000); College graduation rate: 12.0% (2000).
Housing: Homeownership rate: 96.6% (2000); Median home value: $97,500 (2000); Median rent: $275 per month (2000); Median age of housing: 56 years (2000).
Transportation: Commute to work: 85.5% car, 0.0% public transportation, 0.0% walk, 14.5% work from home (2000); Travel time to work: 20.3% less than 15 minutes, 72.9% 15 to 30 minutes, 6.8% 30 to 45 minutes, 0.0% 45 to 60 minutes, 0.0% 60 minutes or more (2000)

BRECKENRIDGE (city). Covers a land area of 2.347 square miles and a water area of 0 square miles. Located at 46.26° N. Lat.; 96.58° W. Long. Elevation is 963 feet.
History: Breckenridge was established in 1857 and named for John C. Breckinridge, vice president under James Buchanan (though the spelling was slightly changed). The town was deserted during the Civil War, but revived in 1871 when the Great Northern Railway arrived. Wheat farming began, followed by the raising of other grains and potatoes. Dairying and stock raising also developed, with Breckenridge as the trade and shipping center of the region.
Population: 3,559 (2000); Race: 97.6% White, 0.1% Black, 0.1% Asian, 1.2% American Indian and Alaska Native, 1.9% Hispanic of any race, 0.5% two or more races (2000); Density: 1,516.4 persons per square mile (2000); Age: 26.6% under 18, 18.8% over 64 (2000); Marriage status: 24.2% never married, 55.8% now married, 11.3% widowed, 8.7% divorced (2000); Foreign born: 0.9% (2000); Ancestry (includes multiple ancestries): 49.5% German, 30.1% Norwegian, 9.6% Irish, 7.4% Swedish, 4.9% English (2000).
Economy: Single-family building permits issued: 6 (2001) / 7 (2000); Multi-family building permits issued: 0 (2001) / 0 (2000); Employment by occupation: 10.2% management, 18.8% professional, 18.3% services, 18.6% sales, 3.0% farming, 12.4% construction, 18.6% production (2000).
Income: Per capita income: $17,059 (2000); Median household income: $37,054 (2000); Poverty rate: 9.0% (2000).
Taxes: Total city taxes per capita: $96 (2000); City property taxes per capita: $83 (2000).
Education: High school graduation rate: 82.3% (2000); College graduation rate: 14.7% (2000).

School District(s)

Breckenridge (PK-12)
2000 Enrollment: 931 218-643-2694
Housing: Homeownership rate: 71.7% (2000); Median home value: $67,800 (2000); Median rent: $278 per month (2000); Median age of housing: 39 years (2000).
Hospitals: Saint Francis Medical Center (42 beds)
Safety: Violent crime rate: 2.8 per 10,000 population; Property crime rate: 342.0 per 10,000 population (2001).
Transportation: Commute to work: 88.1% car, 0.6% public transportation, 5.0% walk, 4.5% work from home (2000); Travel time to work: 75.7% less

than 15 minutes, 14.6% 15 to 30 minutes, 3.3% 30 to 45 minutes, 3.3% 45 to 60 minutes, 3.0% 60 minutes or more (2000)

Additional Information Contacts

Breckenridge Chamber of Commerce 218-643-5244

BRECKENRIDGE (township). Covers a land area of 20.962 square miles and a water area of 0.110 square miles. Located at 46.24° N. Lat.; 96.55° W. Long. Elevation is 963 feet.

History: Laid out 1857, Incorporated 1908.

Population: 234 (2000); Race: 100.0% White, 0.0% Black, 0.0% Asian, 0.0% American Indian and Alaska Native, 0.0% Hispanic of any race, 0.0% two or more races (2000); Density: 11.2 persons per square mile (2000); Age: 29.2% under 18, 8.0% over 64 (2000); Marriage status: 13.3% never married, 75.3% now married, 2.4% widowed, 9.0% divorced (2000); Foreign born: 0.0% (2000); Ancestry (includes multiple ancestries): 52.8% German, 25.9% Norwegian, 9.0% Irish, 3.8% Swedish, 2.8% Scandinavian (2000).

Economy: Railroad center, trade and shipping point for agricultural area: grain, sunflowers, sugar beets, potatoes; hogs, poultry. Manufacturing includes chemicals, sunflower seeds. Employment by occupation: 22.4% management, 10.3% professional, 19.0% services, 17.2% sales, 3.4% farming, 6.9% construction, 20.7% production (2000).

Income: Per capita income: $15,068 (2000); Median household income: $34,375 (2000); Poverty rate: 3.0% (2000).

Taxes: Total city taxes per capita: $33 (1997); City property taxes per capita: $33 (1997).

Education: High school graduation rate: 82.6% (2000); College graduation rate: 13.8% (2000).

Housing: Homeownership rate: 94.9% (2000); Median home value: $101,800 (2000); Median rent: $175 per month (2000); Median age of housing: 27 years (2000).

Transportation: Commute to work: 93.1% car, 0.0% public transportation, 3.4% walk, 1.7% work from home (2000); Travel time to work: 67.5% less than 15 minutes, 28.1% 15 to 30 minutes, 0.9% 30 to 45 minutes, 1.8% 45 to 60 minutes, 1.8% 60 minutes or more (2000)

CAMPBELL (city). Covers a land area of 0.236 square miles and a water area of 0 square miles. Located at 46.09° N. Lat.; 96.40° W. Long. Elevation is 984 feet.

Population: 241 (2000); Race: 92.7% White, 0.9% Black, 0.0% Asian, 0.0% American Indian and Alaska Native, 7.3% Hispanic of any race, 0.0% two or more races (2000); Density: 1,020.0 persons per square mile (2000); Age: 29.7% under 18, 15.1% over 64 (2000); Marriage status: 23.8% never married, 56.4% now married, 11.0% widowed, 8.8% divorced (2000); Foreign born: 0.0% (2000); Ancestry (includes multiple ancestries): 42.2% German, 17.2% Other groups, 10.3% Norwegian, 8.2% Irish, 7.3% Dutch (2000).

Economy: Employment by occupation: 10.4% management, 15.1% professional, 23.6% services, 17.0% sales, 1.9% farming, 4.7% construction, 27.4% production (2000).

Income: Per capita income: $15,128 (2000); Median household income: $31,458 (2000); Poverty rate: 14.2% (2000).

Taxes: Total city taxes per capita: $78 (1997); City property taxes per capita: $73 (1997).

Education: High school graduation rate: 87.3% (2000); College graduation rate: 15.5% (2000).

School District(s)

Campbell-Tintah (PK-12)
2000 Enrollment: 167 218-630-5311

Housing: Homeownership rate: 82.8% (2000); Median home value: $35,800 (2000); Median rent: $304 per month (2000); Median age of housing: 60+ years (2000).

Transportation: Commute to work: 81.7% car, 0.0% public transportation, 14.4% walk, 0.0% work from home (2000); Travel time to work: 26.9% less than 15 minutes, 57.7% 15 to 30 minutes, 11.5% 30 to 45 minutes, 0.0% 45 to 60 minutes, 3.8% 60 minutes or more (2000)

CAMPBELL (township). Covers a land area of 50.048 square miles and a water area of 0 square miles. Located at 46.07° N. Lat.; 96.46° W. Long. Elevation is 984 feet.

Population: 99 (2000); Race: 100.0% White, 0.0% Black, 0.0% Asian, 0.0% American Indian and Alaska Native, 0.0% Hispanic of any race, 0.0% two or more races (2000); Density: 2.0 persons per square mile (2000); Age: 27.1% under 18, 16.7% over 64 (2000); Marriage status: 24.0% never married, 70.7% now married, 5.3% widowed, 0.0% divorced (2000); Foreign born: 0.0% (2000); Ancestry (includes multiple ancestries): 40.6% German, 24.0% Norwegian, 13.5% Irish, 7.3% Czech, 6.3% Dutch (2000).

Economy: Grain, sunflowers, sugar beets. Manufacturing of fertilizers. Employment by occupation: 14.6% management, 0.0% professional, 8.3% services, 35.4% sales, 8.3% farming, 4.2% construction, 29.2% production (2000).

Income: Per capita income: $22,936 (2000); Median household income: $54,063 (2000); Poverty rate: 0.0% (2000).

Taxes: Total city taxes per capita: $186 (1997); City property taxes per capita: $186 (1997).

Education: High school graduation rate: 95.2% (2000); College graduation rate: 6.5% (2000).

Housing: Homeownership rate: 100.0% (2000); Median home value: $55,000 (2000); Median age of housing: 60+ years (2000).

Transportation: Commute to work: 89.6% car, 0.0% public transportation, 0.0% walk, 10.4% work from home (2000); Travel time to work: 11.6% less than 15 minutes, 51.2% 15 to 30 minutes, 32.6% 30 to 45 minutes, 4.7% 45 to 60 minutes, 0.0% 60 minutes or more (2000)

CHAMPION (township). Covers a land area of 32.115 square miles and a water area of 0 square miles. Located at 46.06° N. Lat.; 96.35° W. Long.

Population: 73 (2000); Race: 100.0% White, 0.0% Black, 0.0% Asian, 0.0% American Indian and Alaska Native, 0.0% Hispanic of any race, 0.0% two or more races (2000); Density: 2.3 persons per square mile (2000); Age: 20.7% under 18, 13.8% over 64 (2000); Marriage status: 15.3% never married, 76.4% now married, 2.8% widowed, 5.6% divorced (2000); Foreign born: 0.0% (2000); Ancestry (includes multiple ancestries): 62.1% German, 19.5% Norwegian, 11.5% Swedish, 9.2% Dutch, 6.9% Scandinavian (2000).

Economy: Employment by occupation: 29.7% management, 21.6% professional, 0.0% services, 27.0% sales, 5.4% farming, 0.0% construction, 16.2% production (2000).

Income: Per capita income: $15,884 (2000); Median household income: $45,938 (2000); Poverty rate: 0.0% (2000).

Taxes: Total city taxes per capita: $148 (1997); City property taxes per capita: $148 (1997).

Education: High school graduation rate: 79.4% (2000); College graduation rate: 11.1% (2000).

Housing: Homeownership rate: 100.0% (2000); Median home value: $42,500 (2000); Median age of housing: 60+ years (2000).

Transportation: Commute to work: 97.3% car, 0.0% public transportation, 2.7% walk, 0.0% work from home (2000); Travel time to work: 2.7% less than 15 minutes, 27.0% 15 to 30 minutes, 70.3% 30 to 45 minutes, 0.0% 45 to 60 minutes, 0.0% 60 minutes or more (2000)

CONNELLY (township). Covers a land area of 24.575 square miles and a water area of 0 square miles. Located at 46.33° N. Lat.; 96.58° W. Long.

Population: 123 (2000); Race: 98.4% White, 0.0% Black, 0.0% Asian, 0.0% American Indian and Alaska Native, 0.0% Hispanic of any race, 1.6% two or more races (2000); Density: 5.0 persons per square mile (2000); Age: 31.1% under 18, 12.3% over 64 (2000); Marriage status: 22.7% never married, 64.8% now married, 3.4% widowed, 9.1% divorced (2000); Foreign born: 1.6% (2000); Ancestry (includes multiple ancestries): 62.3% German, 27.9% Norwegian, 12.3% Polish, 10.7% Swedish, 9.0% English (2000).

Economy: Employment by occupation: 25.9% management, 24.1% professional, 17.2% services, 6.9% sales, 3.4% farming, 13.8% construction, 8.6% production (2000).

Income: Per capita income: $19,596 (2000); Median household income: $58,000 (2000); Poverty rate: 1.6% (2000).

Taxes: Total city taxes per capita: $50 (1997); City property taxes per capita: $50 (1997).

Education: High school graduation rate: 93.2% (2000); College graduation rate: 12.2% (2000).

Housing: Homeownership rate: 80.0% (2000); Median home value: $131,300 (2000); Median rent: $275 per month (2000); Median age of housing: 42 years (2000).

Transportation: Commute to work: 87.9% car, 0.0% public transportation, 0.0% walk, 12.1% work from home (2000); Travel time to work: 70.6% less than 15 minutes, 19.6% 15 to 30 minutes, 3.9% 30 to 45 minutes, 5.9% 45 to 60 minutes, 0.0% 60 minutes or more (2000)

DEERHORN (township). Covers a land area of 35.984 square miles and a water area of 0 square miles. Located at 46.59° N. Lat.; 96.60° W. Long.

Population: 111 (2000); Race: 100.0% White, 0.0% Black, 0.0% Asian, 0.0% American Indian and Alaska Native, 0.0% Hispanic of any race, 0.0% two or more races (2000); Density: 3.1 persons per square mile (2000); Age: 28.1% under 18, 9.9% over 64 (2000); Marriage status: 17.0% never married, 73.4% now married, 4.3% widowed, 5.3% divorced (2000); Foreign born:

0.0% (2000); Ancestry (includes multiple ancestries): 57.0% German, 43.0% Norwegian, 7.4% Swedish, 7.4% Irish, 5.8% Other groups (2000).
Economy: Employment by occupation: 37.3% management, 13.6% professional, 15.3% services, 25.4% sales, 0.0% farming, 8.5% construction, 0.0% production (2000).
Income: Per capita income: $16,329 (2000); Median household income: $45,625 (2000); Poverty rate: 1.7% (2000).
Taxes: Total city taxes per capita: $131 (1997); City property taxes per capita: $131 (1997).
Education: High school graduation rate: 97.5% (2000); College graduation rate: 9.9% (2000).
Housing: Homeownership rate: 77.3% (2000); Median home value: $77,500 (2000); Median rent: $140 per month (2000); Median age of housing: 41 years (2000).
Transportation: Commute to work: 89.5% car, 0.0% public transportation, 3.5% walk, 7.0% work from home (2000); Travel time to work: 30.2% less than 15 minutes, 7.5% 15 to 30 minutes, 47.2% 30 to 45 minutes, 7.5% 45 to 60 minutes, 7.5% 60 minutes or more (2000)

DORAN (city). Covers a land area of 0.208 square miles and a water area of 0 square miles. Located at 46.18° N. Lat.; 96.48° W. Long. Elevation is 975 feet.
Population: 59 (2000); Race: 98.3% White, 1.7% Black, 0.0% Asian, 0.0% American Indian and Alaska Native, 0.0% Hispanic of any race, 0.0% two or more races (2000); Density: 284.1 persons per square mile (2000); Age: 10.3% under 18, 19.0% over 64 (2000); Marriage status: 20.0% never married, 52.7% now married, 20.0% widowed, 7.3% divorced (2000); Foreign born: 0.0% (2000); Ancestry (includes multiple ancestries): 69.0% German, 17.2% Norwegian, 10.3% United States or American, 6.9% Czech, 5.2% Swedish (2000).
Economy: Grain, sunflowers; livestock. Manufacturing: plant fertilizer. Employment by occupation: 6.7% management, 3.3% professional, 16.7% services, 16.7% sales, 0.0% farming, 13.3% construction, 43.3% production (2000).
Income: Per capita income: $15,959 (2000); Median household income: $26,250 (2000); Poverty rate: 15.5% (2000).
Taxes: Total city taxes per capita: $55 (1997); City property taxes per capita: $55 (1997).
Education: High school graduation rate: 87.0% (2000); College graduation rate: 6.5% (2000).
Housing: Homeownership rate: 100.0% (2000); Median home value: $33,800 (2000); Median age of housing: 60+ years (2000).
Transportation: Commute to work: 100.0% car, 0.0% public transportation, 0.0% walk, 0.0% work from home (2000); Travel time to work: 26.7% less than 15 minutes, 73.3% 15 to 30 minutes, 0.0% 30 to 45 minutes, 0.0% 45 to 60 minutes, 0.0% 60 minutes or more (2000)

FOXHOME (city). Covers a land area of 0.380 square miles and a water area of 0 square miles. Located at 46.27° N. Lat.; 96.30° W. Long. Elevation is 1,029 feet.
Population: 143 (2000); Race: 100.0% White, 0.0% Black, 0.0% Asian, 0.0% American Indian and Alaska Native, 2.9% Hispanic of any race, 0.0% two or more races (2000); Density: 376.0 persons per square mile (2000); Age: 25.7% under 18, 14.7% over 64 (2000); Marriage status: 27.9% never married, 51.4% now married, 3.6% widowed, 17.1% divorced (2000); Foreign born: 0.0% (2000); Ancestry (includes multiple ancestries): 39.0% German, 26.5% Norwegian, 14.7% Irish, 5.9% Swedish, 5.1% United States or American (2000).
Economy: Employment by occupation: 12.3% management, 11.0% professional, 9.6% services, 23.3% sales, 0.0% farming, 5.5% construction, 38.4% production (2000).
Income: Per capita income: $13,654 (2000); Median household income: $29,688 (2000); Poverty rate: 13.2% (2000).
Taxes: Total city taxes per capita: $49 (1997); City property taxes per capita: $43 (1997).
Education: High school graduation rate: 82.3% (2000); College graduation rate: 13.5% (2000).
Housing: Homeownership rate: 98.2% (2000); Median home value: $25,600 (2000); Median age of housing: 36 years (2000).
Transportation: Commute to work: 95.8% car, 0.0% public transportation, 1.4% walk, 2.8% work from home (2000); Travel time to work: 14.3% less than 15 minutes, 52.9% 15 to 30 minutes, 27.1% 30 to 45 minutes, 0.0% 45 to 60 minutes, 5.7% 60 minutes or more (2000)

FOXHOME (township). Covers a land area of 34.966 square miles and a water area of 0 square miles. Located at 46.23° N. Lat.; 96.31° W. Long. Elevation is 1,029 feet.
Population: 102 (2000); Race: 100.0% White, 0.0% Black, 0.0% Asian, 0.0% American Indian and Alaska Native, 0.0% Hispanic of any race, 0.0% two or more races (2000); Density: 2.9 persons per square mile (2000); Age: 32.2% under 18, 12.7% over 64 (2000); Marriage status: 31.2% never married, 60.2% now married, 6.5% widowed, 2.2% divorced (2000); Foreign born: 0.0% (2000); Ancestry (includes multiple ancestries): 52.5% German, 35.6% Norwegian, 12.7% Irish, 8.5% Dutch, 7.6% French (except Basque) (2000).
Economy: Railroad spur terminus from Fergus Falls. Grain, sunflowers, sugar beets; livestock. Manufacturing: fertilizers. Employment by occupation: 35.6% management, 8.9% professional, 15.6% services, 0.0% sales, 4.4% farming, 20.0% construction, 15.6% production (2000).
Income: Per capita income: $23,049 (2000); Median household income: $49,583 (2000); Poverty rate: 1.7% (2000).
Taxes: Total city taxes per capita: $48 (1997); City property taxes per capita: $48 (1997).
Education: High school graduation rate: 82.4% (2000); College graduation rate: 9.5% (2000).
Housing: Homeownership rate: 79.5% (2000); Median home value: $72,500 (2000); Median age of housing: 56 years (2000).
Transportation: Commute to work: 77.8% car, 0.0% public transportation, 4.4% walk, 17.8% work from home (2000); Travel time to work: 32.4% less than 15 minutes, 43.2% 15 to 30 minutes, 5.4% 30 to 45 minutes, 0.0% 45 to 60 minutes, 18.9% 60 minutes or more (2000)

KENT (city). Covers a land area of 0.192 square miles and a water area of 0 square miles. Located at 46.43° N. Lat.; 96.68° W. Long. Elevation is 945 feet.
Population: 120 (2000); Race: 98.5% White, 0.0% Black, 0.0% Asian, 0.0% American Indian and Alaska Native, 5.3% Hispanic of any race, 1.5% two or more races (2000); Density: 624.2 persons per square mile (2000); Age: 42.7% under 18, 3.8% over 64 (2000); Marriage status: 42.1% never married, 37.9% now married, 5.3% widowed, 14.7% divorced (2000); Foreign born: 0.0% (2000); Ancestry (includes multiple ancestries): 39.7% German, 22.9% Norwegian, 7.6% French (except Basque), 6.1% Dutch, 5.3% Italian (2000).
Economy: Grain, sunflowers; livestock. Single-family building permits issued: 0 (2001) / 0 (2000); Multi-family building permits issued: 0 (2001) / 0 (2000); Employment by occupation: 7.9% management, 17.5% professional, 9.5% services, 31.7% sales, 4.8% farming, 17.5% construction, 11.1% production (2000).
Income: Per capita income: $10,595 (2000); Median household income: $30,417 (2000); Poverty rate: 4.7% (2000).
Taxes: Total city taxes per capita: $33 (1997); City property taxes per capita: $33 (1997).
Education: High school graduation rate: 100.0% (2000); College graduation rate: 10.8% (2000).
Housing: Homeownership rate: 78.7% (2000); Median home value: $37,500 (2000); Median rent: $208 per month (2000); Median age of housing: 53 years (2000).
Transportation: Commute to work: 96.8% car, 0.0% public transportation, 3.2% walk, 0.0% work from home (2000); Travel time to work: 11.1% less than 15 minutes, 71.4% 15 to 30 minutes, 7.9% 30 to 45 minutes, 1.6% 45 to 60 minutes, 7.9% 60 minutes or more (2000)

MANSTON (township). Covers a land area of 36.076 square miles and a water area of 0 square miles. Located at 46.49° N. Lat.; 96.47° W. Long.
Population: 62 (2000); Race: 100.0% White, 0.0% Black, 0.0% Asian, 0.0% American Indian and Alaska Native, 0.0% Hispanic of any race, 0.0% two or more races (2000); Density: 1.7 persons per square mile (2000); Age: 24.1% under 18, 8.4% over 64 (2000); Marriage status: 23.9% never married, 71.6% now married, 4.5% widowed, 0.0% divorced (2000); Foreign born: 0.0% (2000); Ancestry (includes multiple ancestries): 55.4% German, 26.5% Norwegian, 22.9% Irish, 6.0% Polish, 4.8% Swedish (2000).
Economy: Employment by occupation: 18.6% management, 32.6% professional, 7.0% services, 30.2% sales, 0.0% farming, 4.7% construction, 7.0% production (2000).
Income: Per capita income: $14,949 (2000); Median household income: $44,375 (2000); Poverty rate: 15.7% (2000).
Taxes: Total city taxes per capita: $215 (1997); City property taxes per capita: $215 (1997).
Education: High school graduation rate: 86.4% (2000); College graduation rate: 11.9% (2000).

Housing: Homeownership rate: 100.0% (2000); Median home value: $65,000 (2000); Median age of housing: 60 years (2000).
Transportation: Commute to work: 83.7% car, 0.0% public transportation, 4.7% walk, 11.6% work from home (2000); Travel time to work: 18.4% less than 15 minutes, 34.2% 15 to 30 minutes, 21.1% 30 to 45 minutes, 26.3% 45 to 60 minutes, 0.0% 60 minutes or more (2000)

MCCAULEYVILLE (township). Covers a land area of 9.940 square miles and a water area of 0 square miles. Located at 46.43° N. Lat.; 96.67° W. Long.
Population: 56 (2000); Race: 100.0% White, 0.0% Black, 0.0% Asian, 0.0% American Indian and Alaska Native, 0.0% Hispanic of any race, 0.0% two or more races (2000); Density: 5.6 persons per square mile (2000); Age: 20.3% under 18, 20.3% over 64 (2000); Marriage status: 27.3% never married, 67.3% now married, 0.0% widowed, 5.5% divorced (2000); Foreign born: 0.0% (2000); Ancestry (includes multiple ancestries): 64.1% German, 21.9% Norwegian, 12.5% French (except Basque), 9.4% Irish, 9.4% Russian (2000).
Economy: Employment by occupation: 16.2% management, 32.4% professional, 16.2% services, 16.2% sales, 0.0% farming, 8.1% construction, 10.8% production (2000).
Income: Per capita income: $21,842 (2000); Median household income: $42,813 (2000); Poverty rate: 5.0% (2000).
Taxes: Total city taxes per capita: $167 (1997); City property taxes per capita: $167 (1997).
Education: High school graduation rate: 80.4% (2000); College graduation rate: 11.8% (2000).
Housing: Homeownership rate: 93.3% (2000); Median home value: $45,000 (2000); Median rent: $125 per month (2000); Median age of housing: 28 years (2000).
Transportation: Commute to work: 78.4% car, 0.0% public transportation, 2.7% walk, 18.9% work from home (2000); Travel time to work: 26.7% less than 15 minutes, 66.7% 15 to 30 minutes, 0.0% 30 to 45 minutes, 6.7% 45 to 60 minutes, 0.0% 60 minutes or more (2000)

MEADOWS (township). Covers a land area of 36.212 square miles and a water area of 0 square miles. Located at 46.42° N. Lat.; 96.46° W. Long.
Population: 65 (2000); Race: 100.0% White, 0.0% Black, 0.0% Asian, 0.0% American Indian and Alaska Native, 0.0% Hispanic of any race, 0.0% two or more races (2000); Density: 1.8 persons per square mile (2000); Age: 25.9% under 18, 19.0% over 64 (2000); Marriage status: 14.6% never married, 81.3% now married, 4.2% widowed, 0.0% divorced (2000); Foreign born: 0.0% (2000); Ancestry (includes multiple ancestries): 56.9% German, 31.0% Norwegian, 12.1% Irish, 5.2% Scotch-Irish, 3.4% French (except Basque) (2000).
Economy: Employment by occupation: 22.6% management, 19.4% professional, 12.9% services, 25.8% sales, 12.9% farming, 6.5% construction, 0.0% production (2000).
Income: Per capita income: $20,797 (2000); Median household income: $39,583 (2000); Poverty rate: 0.0% (2000).
Taxes: Total city taxes per capita: $123 (1997); City property taxes per capita: $123 (1997).
Education: High school graduation rate: 79.1% (2000); College graduation rate: 11.6% (2000).
Housing: Homeownership rate: 100.0% (2000); Median home value: $75,000 (2000); Median age of housing: 56 years (2000).
Transportation: Commute to work: 77.4% car, 0.0% public transportation, 0.0% walk, 22.6% work from home (2000); Travel time to work: 16.7% less than 15 minutes, 37.5% 15 to 30 minutes, 41.7% 30 to 45 minutes, 4.2% 45 to 60 minutes, 0.0% 60 minutes or more (2000)

MITCHELL (township). Covers a land area of 36.446 square miles and a water area of 0 square miles. Located at 46.50° N. Lat.; 96.59° W. Long.
Population: 103 (2000); Race: 97.4% White, 0.0% Black, 0.0% Asian, 2.6% American Indian and Alaska Native, 0.0% Hispanic of any race, 0.0% two or more races (2000); Density: 2.8 persons per square mile (2000); Age: 25.0% under 18, 17.1% over 64 (2000); Marriage status: 23.4% never married, 64.1% now married, 6.3% widowed, 6.3% divorced (2000); Foreign born: 0.0% (2000); Ancestry (includes multiple ancestries): 60.5% German, 42.1% Norwegian, 7.9% Czech, 6.6% French (except Basque), 2.6% Danish (2000).
Economy: Employment by occupation: 17.6% management, 26.5% professional, 8.8% services, 14.7% sales, 5.9% farming, 20.6% construction, 5.9% production (2000).
Income: Per capita income: $21,974 (2000); Median household income: $36,875 (2000); Poverty rate: 5.3% (2000).
Taxes: Total city taxes per capita: $154 (1997); City property taxes per capita: $154 (1997).

Education: High school graduation rate: 85.2% (2000); College graduation rate: 25.9% (2000).
Housing: Homeownership rate: 76.5% (2000); Median home value: $62,500 (2000); Median rent: $525 per month (2000); Median age of housing: 49 years (2000).
Transportation: Commute to work: 88.2% car, 0.0% public transportation, 0.0% walk, 11.8% work from home (2000); Travel time to work: 16.7% less than 15 minutes, 26.7% 15 to 30 minutes, 30.0% 30 to 45 minutes, 20.0% 45 to 60 minutes, 6.7% 60 minutes or more (2000)

NASHUA (city). Covers a land area of 3.452 square miles and a water area of 0 square miles. Located at 46.03° N. Lat.; 96.30° W. Long. Elevation is 1,000 feet.
Population: 69 (2000); Race: 93.6% White, 0.0% Black, 0.0% Asian, 0.0% American Indian and Alaska Native, 19.2% Hispanic of any race, 6.4% two or more races (2000); Density: 20.0 persons per square mile (2000); Age: 37.2% under 18, 5.1% over 64 (2000); Marriage status: 18.9% never married, 67.9% now married, 0.0% widowed, 13.2% divorced (2000); Foreign born: 0.0% (2000); Ancestry (includes multiple ancestries): 41.0% German, 20.5% Other groups, 11.5% Swedish, 10.3% Norwegian, 7.7% Irish (2000).
Economy: Grain, sunflowers; dairying. Employment by occupation: 8.1% management, 2.7% professional, 16.2% services, 10.8% sales, 29.7% farming, 10.8% construction, 21.6% production (2000).
Income: Per capita income: $15,168 (2000); Median household income: $32,500 (2000); Poverty rate: 2.6% (2000).
Taxes: Total city taxes per capita: $65 (1997); City property taxes per capita: $65 (1997).
Education: High school graduation rate: 95.0% (2000); College graduation rate: 0.0% (2000).
Housing: Homeownership rate: 84.6% (2000); Median home value: $15,000 (2000); Median age of housing: 60+ years (2000).
Transportation: Commute to work: 89.2% car, 0.0% public transportation, 5.4% walk, 0.0% work from home (2000); Travel time to work: 43.2% less than 15 minutes, 21.6% 15 to 30 minutes, 29.7% 30 to 45 minutes, 5.4% 45 to 60 minutes, 0.0% 60 minutes or more (2000)

NILSEN (township). Covers a land area of 36.172 square miles and a water area of 0 square miles. Located at 46.31° N. Lat.; 96.45° W. Long.
Population: 59 (2000); Race: 100.0% White, 0.0% Black, 0.0% Asian, 0.0% American Indian and Alaska Native, 0.0% Hispanic of any race, 0.0% two or more races (2000); Density: 1.6 persons per square mile (2000); Age: 13.6% under 18, 11.4% over 64 (2000); Marriage status: 10.0% never married, 85.0% now married, 0.0% widowed, 5.0% divorced (2000); Foreign born: 0.0% (2000); Ancestry (includes multiple ancestries): 84.1% German, 20.5% Irish, 15.9% Swedish, 13.6% English, 11.4% Norwegian (2000).
Economy: Employment by occupation: 22.6% management, 38.7% professional, 0.0% services, 22.6% sales, 0.0% farming, 6.5% construction, 9.7% production (2000).
Income: Per capita income: $38,902 (2000); Median household income: $81,111 (2000); Poverty rate: 9.1% (2000).
Taxes: Total city taxes per capita: $98 (1997); City property taxes per capita: $98 (1997).
Education: High school graduation rate: 86.1% (2000); College graduation rate: 41.7% (2000).
Housing: Homeownership rate: 100.0% (2000); Median home value: $112,500 (2000); Median age of housing: 57 years (2000).
Transportation: Commute to work: 74.2% car, 0.0% public transportation, 0.0% walk, 25.8% work from home (2000); Travel time to work: 0.0% less than 15 minutes, 82.6% 15 to 30 minutes, 0.0% 30 to 45 minutes, 0.0% 45 to 60 minutes, 17.4% 60 minutes or more (2000)

NORDICK (township). Covers a land area of 36.175 square miles and a water area of 0 square miles. Located at 46.40° N. Lat.; 96.60° W. Long.
Population: 118 (2000); Race: 100.0% White, 0.0% Black, 0.0% Asian, 0.0% American Indian and Alaska Native, 0.0% Hispanic of any race, 0.0% two or more races (2000); Density: 3.3 persons per square mile (2000); Age: 36.4% under 18, 10.0% over 64 (2000); Marriage status: 16.2% never married, 73.0% now married, 5.4% widowed, 5.4% divorced (2000); Foreign born: 0.0% (2000); Ancestry (includes multiple ancestries): 54.5% German, 22.7% Norwegian, 12.7% English, 4.5% Polish, 4.5% French (except Basque) (2000).
Economy: Employment by occupation: 38.9% management, 7.4% professional, 3.7% services, 22.2% sales, 0.0% farming, 7.4% construction, 20.4% production (2000).
Income: Per capita income: $15,608 (2000); Median household income: $37,500 (2000); Poverty rate: 0.0% (2000).

Taxes: Total city taxes per capita: $136 (1997); City property taxes per capita: $136 (1997).
Education: High school graduation rate: 84.1% (2000); College graduation rate: 21.7% (2000).
Housing: Homeownership rate: 94.9% (2000); Median home value: $75,000 (2000); Median age of housing: 56 years (2000).
Transportation: Commute to work: 75.9% car, 0.0% public transportation, 5.6% walk, 18.5% work from home (2000); Travel time to work: 18.2% less than 15 minutes, 47.7% 15 to 30 minutes, 15.9% 30 to 45 minutes, 9.1% 45 to 60 minutes, 9.1% 60 minutes or more (2000)

PRAIRIE VIEW (township). Covers a land area of 35.064 square miles and a water area of 0.040 square miles. Located at 46.57° N. Lat.; 96.33° W. Long.
Population: 215 (2000); Race: 98.4% White, 0.0% Black, 1.6% Asian, 0.0% American Indian and Alaska Native, 0.0% Hispanic of any race, 0.0% two or more races (2000); Density: 6.1 persons per square mile (2000); Age: 35.1% under 18, 9.9% over 64 (2000); Marriage status: 30.0% never married, 62.9% now married, 1.4% widowed, 5.7% divorced (2000); Foreign born: 1.6% (2000); Ancestry (includes multiple ancestries): 57.6% Norwegian, 20.9% German, 3.1% French (except Basque), 2.6% United States or American, 1.6% Other groups (2000).
Economy: Employment by occupation: 18.3% management, 17.2% professional, 10.8% services, 17.2% sales, 4.3% farming, 11.8% construction, 20.4% production (2000).
Income: Per capita income: $18,038 (2000); Median household income: $42,500 (2000); Poverty rate: 0.0% (2000).
Taxes: Total city taxes per capita: $58 (1997); City property taxes per capita: $58 (1997).
Education: High school graduation rate: 90.3% (2000); College graduation rate: 13.3% (2000).
Housing: Homeownership rate: 91.7% (2000); Median home value: $85,000 (2000); Median rent: $138 per month (2000); Median age of housing: 60+ years (2000).
Transportation: Commute to work: 79.6% car, 0.0% public transportation, 0.0% walk, 20.4% work from home (2000); Travel time to work: 12.2% less than 15 minutes, 31.1% 15 to 30 minutes, 29.7% 30 to 45 minutes, 25.7% 45 to 60 minutes, 1.4% 60 minutes or more (2000)

ROBERTS (township). Covers a land area of 22.262 square miles and a water area of 0 square miles. Located at 46.50° N. Lat.; 96.70° W. Long.
Population: 118 (2000); Race: 100.0% White, 0.0% Black, 0.0% Asian, 0.0% American Indian and Alaska Native, 0.0% Hispanic of any race, 0.0% two or more races (2000); Density: 5.3 persons per square mile (2000); Age: 38.9% under 18, 7.6% over 64 (2000); Marriage status: 8.5% never married, 86.6% now married, 2.4% widowed, 2.4% divorced (2000); Foreign born: 0.0% (2000); Ancestry (includes multiple ancestries): 55.0% German, 38.9% Norwegian, 15.3% Swedish, 9.9% English, 9.9% Irish (2000).
Economy: Employment by occupation: 36.4% management, 7.3% professional, 9.1% services, 12.7% sales, 0.0% farming, 18.2% construction, 16.4% production (2000).
Income: Per capita income: $11,909 (2000); Median household income: $35,625 (2000); Poverty rate: 8.4% (2000).
Taxes: Total city taxes per capita: $39 (1997); City property taxes per capita: $39 (1997).
Education: High school graduation rate: 94.9% (2000); College graduation rate: 23.1% (2000).
Housing: Homeownership rate: 93.2% (2000); Median home value: $57,500 (2000); Median age of housing: 60+ years (2000).
Transportation: Commute to work: 74.5% car, 0.0% public transportation, 0.0% walk, 25.5% work from home (2000); Travel time to work: 22.0% less than 15 minutes, 34.1% 15 to 30 minutes, 43.9% 30 to 45 minutes, 0.0% 45 to 60 minutes, 0.0% 60 minutes or more (2000)

ROTHSAY (city). Covers a land area of 4.025 square miles and a water area of 0 square miles. Located at 46.47° N. Lat.; 96.28° W. Long. Elevation is 1,209 feet.
Population: 497 (2000); Race: 97.5% White, 0.0% Black, 0.0% Asian, 1.0% American Indian and Alaska Native, 2.5% Hispanic of any race, 1.5% two or more races (2000); Density: 123.5 persons per square mile (2000); Age: 24.8% under 18, 21.5% over 64 (2000); Marriage status: 27.1% never married, 57.0% now married, 11.9% widowed, 4.1% divorced (2000); Foreign born: 1.7% (2000); Ancestry (includes multiple ancestries): 59.8% Norwegian, 36.9% German, 8.1% Swedish, 3.8% Danish, 2.5% Scandinavian (2000).
Economy: Grain; poultry, cattle, sheep; dairying. Manufacturing: fertilizer, meat processing. Single-family building permits issued: 3 (2001) / 1 (2000); Multi-family building permits issued: 0 (2001) / 0 (2000); Employment by occupation: 7.6% management, 9.4% professional, 21.9% services, 26.3% sales, 0.4% farming, 6.7% construction, 27.7% production (2000).
Income: Per capita income: $14,854 (2000); Median household income: $31,058 (2000); Poverty rate: 9.6% (2000).
Taxes: Total city taxes per capita: $100 (1997); City property taxes per capita: $95 (1997).
Education: High school graduation rate: 77.2% (2000); College graduation rate: 8.7% (2000).

School District(s)

Rothsay (KG-12)
2000 Enrollment: 254 218-867-2735
Housing: Homeownership rate: 78.3% (2000); Median home value: $40,800 (2000); Median rent: $286 per month (2000); Median age of housing: 46 years (2000).
Newspapers: Rothsay Regional Report (1 x month)
Transportation: Commute to work: 86.9% car, 0.0% public transportation, 6.3% walk, 6.8% work from home (2000); Travel time to work: 29.6% less than 15 minutes, 39.8% 15 to 30 minutes, 27.2% 30 to 45 minutes, 3.4% 45 to 60 minutes, 0.0% 60 minutes or more (2000)

SUNNYSIDE (township). Covers a land area of 35.617 square miles and a water area of 0 square miles. Located at 46.23° N. Lat.; 96.44° W. Long.
Population: 143 (2000); Race: 97.1% White, 0.0% Black, 2.9% Asian, 0.0% American Indian and Alaska Native, 0.0% Hispanic of any race, 0.0% two or more races (2000); Density: 4.0 persons per square mile (2000); Age: 19.9% under 18, 14.0% over 64 (2000); Marriage status: 20.3% never married, 72.9% now married, 6.8% widowed, 0.0% divorced (2000); Foreign born: 2.9% (2000); Ancestry (includes multiple ancestries): 64.0% German, 16.9% Norwegian, 13.2% Irish, 13.2% United States or American, 5.1% Swedish (2000).
Economy: Employment by occupation: 25.9% management, 12.9% professional, 15.3% services, 10.6% sales, 0.0% farming, 16.5% construction, 18.8% production (2000).
Income: Per capita income: $21,846 (2000); Median household income: $48,125 (2000); Poverty rate: 4.4% (2000).
Taxes: Total city taxes per capita: $72 (1997); City property taxes per capita: $72 (1997).
Education: High school graduation rate: 88.9% (2000); College graduation rate: 10.1% (2000).
Housing: Homeownership rate: 96.6% (2000); Median home value: $75,000 (2000); Median age of housing: 32 years (2000).
Transportation: Commute to work: 83.3% car, 0.0% public transportation, 0.0% walk, 16.7% work from home (2000); Travel time to work: 22.9% less than 15 minutes, 57.1% 15 to 30 minutes, 17.1% 30 to 45 minutes, 2.9% 45 to 60 minutes, 0.0% 60 minutes or more (2000)

TANBERG (township). Covers a land area of 33.268 square miles and a water area of 0 square miles. Located at 46.51° N. Lat.; 96.32° W. Long.
Population: 68 (2000); Race: 100.0% White, 0.0% Black, 0.0% Asian, 0.0% American Indian and Alaska Native, 0.0% Hispanic of any race, 0.0% two or more races (2000); Density: 2.0 persons per square mile (2000); Age: 24.2% under 18, 12.1% over 64 (2000); Marriage status: 16.0% never married, 78.0% now married, 6.0% widowed, 0.0% divorced (2000); Foreign born: 0.0% (2000); Ancestry (includes multiple ancestries): 62.1% Norwegian, 27.3% German, 7.6% Scandinavian, 7.6% Welsh, 6.1% Irish (2000).
Economy: Employment by occupation: 27.6% management, 10.3% professional, 13.8% services, 41.4% sales, 0.0% farming, 0.0% construction, 6.9% production (2000).
Income: Per capita income: $17,429 (2000); Median household income: $45,938 (2000); Poverty rate: 0.0% (2000).
Taxes: Total city taxes per capita: $109 (1997); City property taxes per capita: $109 (1997).
Education: High school graduation rate: 84.0% (2000); College graduation rate: 6.0% (2000).
Housing: Homeownership rate: 100.0% (2000); Median home value: $82,500 (2000); Median age of housing: 38 years (2000).
Transportation: Commute to work: 79.3% car, 0.0% public transportation, 6.9% walk, 13.8% work from home (2000); Travel time to work: 56.0% less than 15 minutes, 36.0% 15 to 30 minutes, 8.0% 30 to 45 minutes, 0.0% 45 to 60 minutes, 0.0% 60 minutes or more (2000)

TENNEY (city). Covers a land area of 0.020 square miles and a water area of 0 square miles. Located at 46.04° N. Lat.; 96.45° W. Long.

Population: 6 (2000); Race: 100.0% White, 0.0% Black, 0.0% Asian, 0.0% American Indian and Alaska Native, 0.0% Hispanic of any race, 0.0% two or more races (2000); Density: 298.0 persons per square mile (2000); Age: 0.0% under 18, 100.0% over 64 (2000); Marriage status: 0.0% never married, 0.0% now married, 100.0% widowed, 0.0% divorced (2000); Foreign born: 0.0% (2000); Ancestry (includes multiple ancestries): 100.0% German (2000).
Economy: Grain. Employment by occupation: 100.0% management, 0.0% professional, 0.0% services, 0.0% sales, 0.0% farming, 0.0% construction, 0.0% production (2000).
Income: Per capita income: $8,000 (2000); Median household income: $8,750 (2000); Poverty rate: 100.0% (2000).
Taxes: Total city taxes per capita: $250 (1997); City property taxes per capita: $250 (1997).
Education: High school graduation rate: 0.0% (2000); College graduation rate: 0.0% (2000).
Housing: Homeownership rate: 100.0% (2000); Median home value: <$10,000 (2000); Median age of housing: 60+ years (2000).
Transportation: Commute to work: 100.0% car, 0.0% public transportation, 0.0% walk, 0.0% work from home (2000); Travel time to work: 100.0% less than 15 minutes, 0.0% 15 to 30 minutes, 0.0% 30 to 45 minutes, 0.0% 45 to 60 minutes, 0.0% 60 minutes or more (2000)

WOLVERTON (city). Covers a land area of 0.284 square miles and a water area of 0 square miles. Located at 46.56° N. Lat.; 96.73° W. Long. Elevation is 926 feet.
Population: 122 (2000); Race: 100.0% White, 0.0% Black, 0.0% Asian, 0.0% American Indian and Alaska Native, 0.0% Hispanic of any race, 0.0% two or more races (2000); Density: 429.4 persons per square mile (2000); Age: 22.1% under 18, 21.4% over 64 (2000); Marriage status: 26.3% never married, 51.8% now married, 12.3% widowed, 9.6% divorced (2000); Foreign born: 0.0% (2000); Ancestry (includes multiple ancestries): 51.4% Norwegian, 48.6% German, 15.7% Swedish, 6.4% Scotch-Irish, 5.7% Irish (2000).
Economy: Employment by occupation: 6.3% management, 21.9% professional, 21.9% services, 18.8% sales, 3.1% farming, 14.1% construction, 14.1% production (2000).
Income: Per capita income: $16,839 (2000); Median household income: $29,063 (2000); Poverty rate: 15.7% (2000).
Taxes: Total city taxes per capita: $103 (1997); City property taxes per capita: $97 (1997).
Education: High school graduation rate: 88.4% (2000); College graduation rate: 23.3% (2000).
Housing: Homeownership rate: 86.9% (2000); Median home value: $41,000 (2000); Median rent: $225 per month (2000); Median age of housing: 48 years (2000).
Transportation: Commute to work: 82.8% car, 0.0% public transportation, 6.3% walk, 10.9% work from home (2000); Travel time to work: 19.3% less than 15 minutes, 28.1% 15 to 30 minutes, 28.1% 30 to 45 minutes, 12.3% 45 to 60 minutes, 12.3% 60 minutes or more (2000)

WOLVERTON (township). Covers a land area of 29.712 square miles and a water area of 0 square miles. Located at 46.60° N. Lat.; 96.71° W. Long. Elevation is 926 feet.
Population: 130 (2000); Race: 100.0% White, 0.0% Black, 0.0% Asian, 0.0% American Indian and Alaska Native, 0.0% Hispanic of any race, 0.0% two or more races (2000); Density: 4.4 persons per square mile (2000); Age: 21.6% under 18, 25.0% over 64 (2000); Marriage status: 12.1% never married, 74.7% now married, 8.8% widowed, 4.4% divorced (2000); Foreign born: 0.0% (2000); Ancestry (includes multiple ancestries): 48.3% Norwegian, 45.7% German, 16.4% Swedish, 8.6% Irish, 3.4% European (2000).
Economy: Agriculture: wheat, sugar beets, potatoes. Manufacturing of fertilizer. Employment by occupation: 3.6% management, 7.3% professional, 18.2% services, 38.2% sales, 0.0% farming, 10.9% construction, 21.8% production (2000).
Income: Per capita income: $18,638 (2000); Median household income: $42,500 (2000); Poverty rate: 0.0% (2000).
Taxes: Total city taxes per capita: $118 (1997); City property taxes per capita: $118 (1997).
Education: High school graduation rate: 90.5% (2000); College graduation rate: 13.1% (2000).
Housing: Homeownership rate: 95.7% (2000); Median home value: $78,300 (2000); Median age of housing: 60+ years (2000).
Transportation: Commute to work: 100.0% car, 0.0% public transportation, 0.0% walk, 0.0% work from home (2000); Travel time to work: 13.2% less than 15 minutes, 22.6% 15 to 30 minutes, 60.4% 30 to 45 minutes, 3.8% 45 to 60 minutes, 0.0% 60 minutes or more (2000)

Winona County

Located in southeastern Minnesota; bounded on the east by the Mississippi River and the Wisconsin border. Covers a land area of 626.30 square miles, a water area of 15.30 square miles, and is located in the Central Time Zone. The county government was organized in 1854. County seat is Winona.
Population: 49,985 (2000); Race: 95.7% White, 0.8% Black, 1.6% Asian, 0.3% American Indian and Alaska Native, 1.4% Hispanic of any race, 1.1% two or more races (2000); Density: 79.8 persons per square mile (2000); Age: 22.8% under 18, 13.1% over 64 (2000).
Religion: Five largest groups: 29.2% Catholic Church, 10.4% Evangelical Lutheran Church in America, 8.8% Wisconsin Evangelical Lutheran Synod, 8.1% Lutheran Church—Missouri Synod, 2.9% The United Methodist Church (2000).
Economy: Unemployment rate: 2.9% (11/2002); Total civilian labor force: 28,418 (11/2002); Leading industries: 30.1% manufacturing; 11.8% health care and social assistance; 11.8% retail trade (2000); Companies that employ more than 1,000 persons: 1 (2000); Companies that employ more than 100 persons: 45 (2000); Farms: 1,044 totaling 289,708 acres (1997); Minority business ownership rate: 5.5% (1997); Women business ownership rate: 23.1% (1997); Retail sales per capita: $7,969 (1997). Single-family building permits issued: 189 (2001) / 152 (2000); Multi-family building permits issued: 16 (2001) / 17 (2000).
Income: Per capita income: $18,077 (2000); Median household income: $38,700 (2000); Poverty rate: 12.0% (2000); Bankruptcy rate: 1.85% (2001).
Taxes: Total county taxes per capita: $234 (2000); County property taxes per capita: $228 (2000).
Education: High school graduation rate: 84.0% (2000); College graduation rate: 23.2% (2000).
Housing: Homeownership rate: 71.0% (2000); Median home value: $95,800 (2000); Median rent: $380 per month (2000); Median age of housing: 41 years (2000).
Health: Birth rate: 113.8 per 10,000 population (1998); Age adjusted death rate: 80.4 per 10,000 population (1999); Age adjusted cancer mortality rate: 209.4 deaths per 100,000 population (1999). Number of physicians: 10.0 per 10,000 population (1999); Number of hospital beds: 15.2 per 10,000 population (1999).
Elections: 2000 Presidential election results: 46.3% Gore, 45.0% Bush, 7.3% Nader, 0.8% Buchanan
National and State Parks: Great River Bluffs State Park; John Latsch State Park; Richard J Dorer Memorial Hardwood State Forest; Whitewater State Park
Additional Information Contacts
Winona County Government Offices.................... 507-457-6350
Winona Chamber of Commerce.......................... 507-452-2272
Winona Visitors Information 507-452-2278

Winona County Communities

ALTURA (city). Covers a land area of 2.969 square miles and a water area of 0 square miles. Located at 44.07° N. Lat.; 91.93° W. Long.
Population: 417 (2000); Race: 98.9% White, 0.5% Black, 0.5% Asian, 0.0% American Indian and Alaska Native, 0.0% Hispanic of any race, 0.0% two or more races (2000); Density: 140.5 persons per square mile (2000); Age: 25.5% under 18, 18.2% over 64 (2000); Marriage status: 22.1% never married, 61.9% now married, 8.3% widowed, 7.6% divorced (2000); Foreign born: 1.6% (2000); Ancestry (includes multiple ancestries): 60.6% German, 19.3% Norwegian, 9.9% Polish, 6.4% Irish, 4.0% Luxemburger (2000).
Economy: Dairying; poultry, livestock; grain. Single-family building permits issued: 4 (2001) / 5 (2000); Multi-family building permits issued: 0 (2001) / 0 (2000); Employment by occupation: 14.0% management, 17.4% professional, 12.1% services, 15.9% sales, 7.2% farming, 9.2% construction, 24.2% production (2000).
Income: Per capita income: $17,199 (2000); Median household income: $38,393 (2000); Poverty rate: 8.7% (2000).
Taxes: Total city taxes per capita: $69 (1997); City property taxes per capita: $53 (1997).
Education: High school graduation rate: 82.0% (2000); College graduation rate: 13.9% (2000).
Housing: Homeownership rate: 81.3% (2000); Median home value: $85,000 (2000); Median rent: $303 per month (2000); Median age of housing: 42 years (2000).

Transportation: Commute to work: 84.7% car, 1.5% public transportation, 4.0% walk, 9.9% work from home (2000); Travel time to work: 32.4% less than 15 minutes, 32.4% 15 to 30 minutes, 20.3% 30 to 45 minutes, 10.4% 45 to 60 minutes, 4.4% 60 minutes or more (2000)

DAKOTA (city). Covers a land area of 0.667 square miles and a water area of 0.317 square miles. Located at 43.91° N. Lat.; 91.36° W. Long. Elevation is 691 feet.
History: Dakota began as a trading post, the headquarters of Jeremiah Tibbitts, who came to this region at the age of 17 and carried on trade up and down the river until 1853.
Population: 329 (2000); Race: 99.4% White, 0.0% Black, 0.0% Asian, 0.0% American Indian and Alaska Native, 0.0% Hispanic of any race, 0.0% two or more races (2000); Density: 493.1 persons per square mile (2000); Age: 32.4% under 18, 17.6% over 64 (2000); Marriage status: 12.1% never married, 66.9% now married, 13.4% widowed, 7.5% divorced (2000); Foreign born: 0.0% (2000); Ancestry (includes multiple ancestries): 47.6% German, 32.4% Norwegian, 10.3% Irish, 8.2% United States or American, 8.2% English (2000).
Economy: Single-family building permits issued: 3 (2001) / 3 (2000); Multi-family building permits issued: 0 (2001) / 0 (2000); Employment by occupation: 4.8% management, 23.8% professional, 18.4% services, 21.8% sales, 2.0% farming, 5.4% construction, 23.8% production (2000).
Income: Per capita income: $17,700 (2000); Median household income: $50,156 (2000); Poverty rate: 4.7% (2000).
Taxes: Total city taxes per capita: $78 (1997); City property taxes per capita: $75 (1997).
Education: High school graduation rate: 78.7% (2000); College graduation rate: 18.5% (2000).
Housing: Homeownership rate: 92.9% (2000); Median home value: $83,800 (2000); Median rent: $515 per month (2000); Median age of housing: 39 years (2000).
Transportation: Commute to work: 91.8% car, 0.0% public transportation, 0.0% walk, 6.1% work from home (2000); Travel time to work: 28.3% less than 15 minutes, 55.8% 15 to 30 minutes, 15.2% 30 to 45 minutes, 0.7% 45 to 60 minutes, 0.0% 60 minutes or more (2000)

DRESBACH (township). Covers a land area of 7.966 square miles and a water area of 1.302 square miles. Located at 43.87° N. Lat.; 91.33° W. Long.
Population: 413 (2000); Race: 99.5% White, 0.0% Black, 0.0% Asian, 0.0% American Indian and Alaska Native, 1.5% Hispanic of any race, 0.5% two or more races (2000); Density: 51.8 persons per square mile (2000); Age: 21.8% under 18, 11.5% over 64 (2000); Marriage status: 18.2% never married, 68.8% now married, 4.4% widowed, 8.5% divorced (2000); Foreign born: 0.5% (2000); Ancestry (includes multiple ancestries): 36.5% German, 18.9% Norwegian, 14.7% Irish, 10.0% United States or American, 5.9% Polish (2000).
Economy: Employment by occupation: 14.6% management, 22.9% professional, 10.7% services, 18.5% sales, 3.4% farming, 5.9% construction, 23.9% production (2000).
Income: Per capita income: $25,648 (2000); Median household income: $47,813 (2000); Poverty rate: 8.6% (2000).
Taxes: Total city taxes per capita: $243 (1997); City property taxes per capita: $243 (1997).
Education: High school graduation rate: 86.1% (2000); College graduation rate: 28.4% (2000).
Housing: Homeownership rate: 90.5% (2000); Median home value: $95,000 (2000); Median rent: $325 per month (2000); Median age of housing: 39 years (2000).
Transportation: Commute to work: 95.1% car, 0.0% public transportation, 2.0% walk, 2.0% work from home (2000); Travel time to work: 27.1% less than 15 minutes, 55.3% 15 to 30 minutes, 9.0% 30 to 45 minutes, 1.0% 45 to 60 minutes, 7.5% 60 minutes or more (2000)

ELBA (city). Covers a land area of 2.039 square miles and a water area of 0 square miles. Located at 44.09° N. Lat.; 92.01° W. Long. Elevation is 740 feet.
Population: 214 (2000); Race: 100.0% White, 0.0% Black, 0.0% Asian, 0.0% American Indian and Alaska Native, 2.9% Hispanic of any race, 0.0% two or more races (2000); Density: 105.0 persons per square mile (2000); Age: 32.5% under 18, 11.0% over 64 (2000); Marriage status: 30.3% never married, 56.6% now married, 4.6% widowed, 8.6% divorced (2000); Foreign born: 1.9% (2000); Ancestry (includes multiple ancestries): 72.2% German, 10.5% Irish, 10.5% Norwegian, 5.7% Danish, 5.3% Luxemburger (2000).
Economy: Single-family building permits issued: 1 (2001) / 1 (2000); Multi-family building permits issued: 0 (2001) / 0 (2000); Employment by occupation: 6.3% management, 4.5% professional, 13.5% services, 27.0% sales, 3.6% farming, 18.9% construction, 26.1% production (2000).
Income: Per capita income: $14,398 (2000); Median household income: $38,750 (2000); Poverty rate: 6.2% (2000).
Taxes: Total city taxes per capita: $49 (1997); City property taxes per capita: $27 (1997).
Education: High school graduation rate: 80.6% (2000); College graduation rate: 6.5% (2000).
Housing: Homeownership rate: 86.3% (2000); Median home value: $75,000 (2000); Median rent: $313 per month (2000); Median age of housing: 28 years (2000).
Transportation: Commute to work: 89.9% car, 0.0% public transportation, 1.8% walk, 8.3% work from home (2000); Travel time to work: 6.0% less than 15 minutes, 31.0% 15 to 30 minutes, 38.0% 30 to 45 minutes, 13.0% 45 to 60 minutes, 12.0% 60 minutes or more (2000)

ELBA (township). Covers a land area of 33.351 square miles and a water area of 0.007 square miles. Located at 44.07° N. Lat.; 92.02° W. Long. Elevation is 740 feet.
Population: 263 (2000); Race: 100.0% White, 0.0% Black, 0.0% Asian, 0.0% American Indian and Alaska Native, 0.0% Hispanic of any race, 0.0% two or more races (2000); Density: 7.9 persons per square mile (2000); Age: 31.6% under 18, 8.9% over 64 (2000); Marriage status: 24.0% never married, 68.6% now married, 2.9% widowed, 4.4% divorced (2000); Foreign born: 0.7% (2000); Ancestry (includes multiple ancestries): 54.6% German, 13.4% Irish, 12.3% Luxemburger, 10.4% English, 7.1% Norwegian (2000).
Economy: Dairying; poultry; grain. Employment by occupation: 21.5% management, 21.5% professional, 1.3% services, 23.5% sales, 2.7% farming, 12.8% construction, 16.8% production (2000).
Income: Per capita income: $18,246 (2000); Median household income: $43,750 (2000); Poverty rate: 3.7% (2000).
Taxes: Total city taxes per capita: $110 (1997); City property taxes per capita: $103 (1997).
Education: High school graduation rate: 86.9% (2000); College graduation rate: 13.1% (2000).
Housing: Homeownership rate: 80.0% (2000); Median home value: $137,500 (2000); Median rent: $375 per month (2000); Median age of housing: 28 years (2000).
Transportation: Commute to work: 74.5% car, 0.0% public transportation, 10.1% walk, 15.4% work from home (2000); Travel time to work: 31.0% less than 15 minutes, 27.0% 15 to 30 minutes, 28.6% 30 to 45 minutes, 8.7% 45 to 60 minutes, 4.8% 60 minutes or more (2000)

FREMONT (township). Covers a land area of 35.895 square miles and a water area of 0 square miles. Located at 43.90° N. Lat.; 91.91° W. Long.
Population: 360 (2000); Race: 100.0% White, 0.0% Black, 0.0% Asian, 0.0% American Indian and Alaska Native, 0.5% Hispanic of any race, 0.0% two or more races (2000); Density: 10.0 persons per square mile (2000); Age: 33.2% under 18, 14.2% over 64 (2000); Marriage status: 23.5% never married, 69.8% now married, 3.6% widowed, 3.2% divorced (2000); Foreign born: 0.0% (2000); Ancestry (includes multiple ancestries): 50.9% German, 39.1% Norwegian, 10.3% Irish, 8.2% United States or American, 6.9% Polish (2000).
Economy: Employment by occupation: 20.6% management, 19.1% professional, 2.9% services, 16.7% sales, 11.8% farming, 7.8% construction, 21.1% production (2000).
Income: Per capita income: $17,365 (2000); Median household income: $44,583 (2000); Poverty rate: 7.4% (2000).
Taxes: Total city taxes per capita: $51 (1997); City property taxes per capita: $51 (1997).
Education: High school graduation rate: 85.3% (2000); College graduation rate: 14.7% (2000).
Housing: Homeownership rate: 77.2% (2000); Median home value: $92,500 (2000); Median rent: $475 per month (2000); Median age of housing: 60+ years (2000).
Transportation: Commute to work: 68.5% car, 2.0% public transportation, 7.4% walk, 22.2% work from home (2000); Travel time to work: 38.0% less than 15 minutes, 25.9% 15 to 30 minutes, 22.2% 30 to 45 minutes, 9.5% 45 to 60 minutes, 4.4% 60 minutes or more (2000)

GOODVIEW (city). Covers a land area of 1.732 square miles and a water area of 0.221 square miles. Located at 44.06° N. Lat.; 91.70° W. Long.
Population: 3,373 (2000); Race: 97.2% White, 0.8% Black, 0.3% Asian, 0.2% American Indian and Alaska Native, 1.1% Hispanic of any race, 1.2% two or more races (2000); Density: 1,947.2 persons per square mile (2000); Age: 25.5% under 18, 10.7% over 64 (2000); Marriage status: 23.4% never

married, 64.1% now married, 4.7% widowed, 7.8% divorced (2000); Foreign born: 1.3% (2000); Ancestry (includes multiple ancestries): 51.1% German, 17.3% Norwegian, 17.3% Polish, 8.4% English, 7.8% Irish (2000).
Economy: Max Conrad Field airport to North. Single-family building permits issued: 3 (2001) / 9 (2000); Multi-family building permits issued: 0 (2001) / 0 (2000); Employment by occupation: 11.6% management, 21.6% professional, 10.2% services, 25.5% sales, 0.0% farming, 6.8% construction, 24.3% production (2000).
Income: Per capita income: $22,488 (2000); Median household income: $43,654 (2000); Poverty rate: 6.2% (2000).
Taxes: Total city taxes per capita: $303 (1997); City property taxes per capita: $297 (1997).
Education: High school graduation rate: 89.6% (2000); College graduation rate: 26.3% (2000).
Housing: Homeownership rate: 77.3% (2000); Median home value: $109,200 (2000); Median rent: $477 per month (2000); Median age of housing: 22 years (2000).
Safety: Violent crime rate: 8.8 per 10,000 population; Property crime rate: 234.7 per 10,000 population (2001).
Transportation: Commute to work: 93.4% car, 1.0% public transportation, 1.6% walk, 3.4% work from home (2000); Travel time to work: 64.6% less than 15 minutes, 23.5% 15 to 30 minutes, 4.8% 30 to 45 minutes, 3.2% 45 to 60 minutes, 3.9% 60 minutes or more (2000)

HART (township). Covers a land area of 35.598 square miles and a water area of 0 square miles. Located at 43.89° N. Lat.; 91.78° W. Long. Elevation is 1,209 feet.
Population: 301 (2000); Race: 99.3% White, 0.0% Black, 0.0% Asian, 0.7% American Indian and Alaska Native, 0.0% Hispanic of any race, 0.0% two or more races (2000); Density: 8.5 persons per square mile (2000); Age: 26.0% under 18, 17.0% over 64 (2000); Marriage status: 20.7% never married, 68.5% now married, 5.0% widowed, 5.9% divorced (2000); Foreign born: 0.0% (2000); Ancestry (includes multiple ancestries): 75.8% German, 36.5% Norwegian, 6.5% Irish, 4.0% Dutch, 2.5% Other groups (2000).
Economy: Employment by occupation: 28.0% management, 6.2% professional, 9.3% services, 19.9% sales, 11.2% farming, 8.7% construction, 16.8% production (2000).
Income: Per capita income: $17,258 (2000); Median household income: $41,250 (2000); Poverty rate: 4.7% (2000).
Taxes: Total city taxes per capita: $87 (1997); City property taxes per capita: $87 (1997).
Education: High school graduation rate: 77.3% (2000); College graduation rate: 5.5% (2000).
Housing: Homeownership rate: 82.2% (2000); Median home value: $97,500 (2000); Median rent: $275 per month (2000); Median age of housing: 60+ years (2000).
Transportation: Commute to work: 73.3% car, 0.6% public transportation, 5.0% walk, 19.9% work from home (2000); Travel time to work: 45.7% less than 15 minutes, 37.2% 15 to 30 minutes, 14.7% 30 to 45 minutes, 2.3% 45 to 60 minutes, 0.0% 60 minutes or more (2000)

HILLSDALE (township). Covers a land area of 16.064 square miles and a water area of 0.015 square miles. Located at 44.02° N. Lat.; 91.78° W. Long.
Population: 945 (2000); Race: 96.1% White, 0.7% Black, 0.6% Asian, 0.0% American Indian and Alaska Native, 2.0% Hispanic of any race, 2.0% two or more races (2000); Density: 58.8 persons per square mile (2000); Age: 31.3% under 18, 7.2% over 64 (2000); Marriage status: 30.1% never married, 52.7% now married, 3.0% widowed, 14.2% divorced (2000); Foreign born: 1.5% (2000); Ancestry (includes multiple ancestries): 44.8% German, 15.3% Norwegian, 11.3% Irish, 9.9% Polish, 8.0% Other groups (2000).
Economy: Single-family building permits issued: 3 (2001) / 2 (2000); Multi-family building permits issued: 0 (2001) / 0 (2000); Employment by occupation: 10.7% management, 11.1% professional, 13.3% services, 17.9% sales, 3.5% farming, 10.7% construction, 32.7% production (2000).
Income: Per capita income: $16,345 (2000); Median household income: $33,750 (2000); Poverty rate: 13.3% (2000).
Taxes: Total city taxes per capita: $29 (1997); City property taxes per capita: $29 (1997).
Education: High school graduation rate: 78.8% (2000); College graduation rate: 13.8% (2000).
Housing: Homeownership rate: 85.3% (2000); Median home value: $120,000 (2000); Median rent: $355 per month (2000); Median age of housing: 23 years (2000).
Transportation: Commute to work: 89.3% car, 0.6% public transportation, 0.8% walk, 7.1% work from home (2000); Travel time to work: 39.9% less than 15 minutes, 41.6% 15 to 30 minutes, 6.6% 30 to 45 minutes, 6.0% 45 to 60 minutes, 6.0% 60 minutes or more (2000)

HOMER (township). Covers a land area of 35.474 square miles and a water area of 1.021 square miles. Located at 44.00° N. Lat.; 91.56° W. Long.
Population: 1,472 (2000); Race: 98.5% White, 0.1% Black, 0.6% Asian, 0.0% American Indian and Alaska Native, 0.5% Hispanic of any race, 0.6% two or more races (2000); Density: 41.5 persons per square mile (2000); Age: 25.5% under 18, 11.0% over 64 (2000); Marriage status: 19.9% never married, 72.2% now married, 2.9% widowed, 4.9% divorced (2000); Foreign born: 1.3% (2000); Ancestry (includes multiple ancestries): 49.4% German, 16.9% Norwegian, 15.3% Polish, 10.4% Irish, 10.2% English (2000).
Economy: Employment by occupation: 17.3% management, 18.9% professional, 9.6% services, 21.0% sales, 0.0% farming, 9.6% construction, 23.6% production (2000).
Income: Per capita income: $22,864 (2000); Median household income: $53,693 (2000); Poverty rate: 2.1% (2000).
Taxes: Total city taxes per capita: $45 (1997); City property taxes per capita: $45 (1997).
Education: High school graduation rate: 88.4% (2000); College graduation rate: 27.3% (2000).
Housing: Homeownership rate: 88.8% (2000); Median home value: $129,900 (2000); Median rent: $388 per month (2000); Median age of housing: 27 years (2000).
Transportation: Commute to work: 94.2% car, 0.0% public transportation, 0.5% walk, 5.1% work from home (2000); Travel time to work: 24.6% less than 15 minutes, 58.2% 15 to 30 minutes, 10.3% 30 to 45 minutes, 3.2% 45 to 60 minutes, 3.7% 60 minutes or more (2000)

LEWISTON (city). Covers a land area of 1.095 square miles and a water area of 0 square miles. Located at 43.98° N. Lat.; 91.86° W. Long. Elevation is 1,211 feet.
History: Lewiston grew up around a stagecoach stop on the route between Winona and Rochester.
Population: 1,484 (2000); Race: 98.9% White, 0.3% Black, 0.4% Asian, 0.0% American Indian and Alaska Native, 1.7% Hispanic of any race, 0.4% two or more races (2000); Density: 1,355.9 persons per square mile (2000); Age: 31.0% under 18, 13.4% over 64 (2000); Marriage status: 24.5% never married, 62.0% now married, 7.2% widowed, 6.4% divorced (2000); Foreign born: 2.6% (2000); Ancestry (includes multiple ancestries): 52.5% German, 17.3% Norwegian, 10.1% United States or American, 7.8% Irish, 6.6% Polish (2000).
Economy: Single-family building permits issued: 11 (2001) / 5 (2000); Multi-family building permits issued: 0 (2001) / 0 (2000); Employment by occupation: 8.9% management, 20.9% professional, 13.1% services, 21.4% sales, 1.7% farming, 8.9% construction, 25.0% production (2000).
Income: Per capita income: $17,666 (2000); Median household income: $43,220 (2000); Poverty rate: 5.7% (2000).
Taxes: Total city taxes per capita: $218 (1997); City property taxes per capita: $211 (1997).
Education: High school graduation rate: 87.0% (2000); College graduation rate: 18.7% (2000).

School District(s)

Lewiston (PK-12)
2000 Enrollment: 838 507-523-2191
Housing: Homeownership rate: 79.2% (2000); Median home value: $93,200 (2000); Median rent: $363 per month (2000); Median age of housing: 32 years (2000).
Newspapers: Lewiston Journal (1 x week)
Transportation: Commute to work: 85.9% car, 1.3% public transportation, 7.6% walk, 4.5% work from home (2000); Travel time to work: 44.8% less than 15 minutes, 29.4% 15 to 30 minutes, 15.7% 30 to 45 minutes, 6.2% 45 to 60 minutes, 3.8% 60 minutes or more (2000)

MINNESOTA CITY (city). Covers a land area of 0.258 square miles and a water area of 0 square miles. Located at 44.09° N. Lat.; 91.75° W. Long. Elevation is 677 feet.
History: Minnesota City was the site of a communal dream of a group of New York mechanics known as the Western Farm and Village Association. They came in 1852, drawn by plans they had seen of a well-built city along the river. They found only wilderness. Many died, and some found their way back to New York. The town of Minnesota City developed later on this site.
Population: 235 (2000); Race: 100.0% White, 0.0% Black, 0.0% Asian, 0.0% American Indian and Alaska Native, 0.0% Hispanic of any race, 0.0% two or more races (2000); Density: 912.0 persons per square mile (2000); Age: 27.0% under 18, 8.1% over 64 (2000); Marriage status: 28.3% never

married, 67.7% now married, 2.0% widowed, 2.0% divorced (2000); Foreign born: 0.0% (2000); Ancestry (includes multiple ancestries): 43.1% German, 21.4% Norwegian, 11.3% Irish, 6.5% United States or American, 4.8% Polish (2000).
Economy: Single-family building permits issued: 0 (2001) / 0 (2000); Multi-family building permits issued: 0 (2001) / 0 (2000); Employment by occupation: 8.3% management, 6.9% professional, 11.8% services, 26.4% sales, 0.0% farming, 12.5% construction, 34.0% production (2000).
Income: Per capita income: $18,430 (2000); Median household income: $46,458 (2000); Poverty rate: 2.5% (2000).
Taxes: Total city taxes per capita: $107 (1997); City property taxes per capita: $98 (1997).
Education: High school graduation rate: 83.6% (2000); College graduation rate: 8.8% (2000).
Housing: Homeownership rate: 81.4% (2000); Median home value: $75,700 (2000); Median rent: $192 per month (2000); Median age of housing: 45 years (2000).
Transportation: Commute to work: 93.1% car, 0.0% public transportation, 3.5% walk, 1.4% work from home (2000); Travel time to work: 45.1% less than 15 minutes, 35.9% 15 to 30 minutes, 12.7% 30 to 45 minutes, 1.4% 45 to 60 minutes, 4.9% 60 minutes or more (2000)

MOUNT VERNON (township). Covers a land area of 35.135 square miles and a water area of 0.234 square miles. Located at 44.15° N. Lat.; 91.89° W. Long.
Population: 297 (2000); Race: 97.0% White, 0.0% Black, 0.7% Asian, 0.0% American Indian and Alaska Native, 0.7% Hispanic of any race, 1.6% two or more races (2000); Density: 8.5 persons per square mile (2000); Age: 27.3% under 18, 10.5% over 64 (2000); Marriage status: 28.5% never married, 60.3% now married, 4.2% widowed, 7.1% divorced (2000); Foreign born: 0.7% (2000); Ancestry (includes multiple ancestries): 53.6% German, 12.5% Irish, 11.5% Luxemburger, 8.9% Norwegian, 6.6% United States or American (2000).
Economy: Employment by occupation: 30.6% management, 13.9% professional, 8.1% services, 12.7% sales, 8.1% farming, 12.1% construction, 14.5% production (2000).
Income: Per capita income: $17,914 (2000); Median household income: $45,781 (2000); Poverty rate: 12.8% (2000).
Taxes: Total city taxes per capita: $48 (1997); City property taxes per capita: $48 (1997).
Education: High school graduation rate: 84.0% (2000); College graduation rate: 10.3% (2000).
Housing: Homeownership rate: 80.6% (2000); Median home value: $87,500 (2000); Median rent: $467 per month (2000); Median age of housing: 33 years (2000).
Transportation: Commute to work: 76.9% car, 0.0% public transportation, 7.5% walk, 15.6% work from home (2000); Travel time to work: 26.7% less than 15 minutes, 36.3% 15 to 30 minutes, 16.4% 30 to 45 minutes, 8.2% 45 to 60 minutes, 12.3% 60 minutes or more (2000)

NEW HARTFORD (township). Covers a land area of 35.109 square miles and a water area of 0.069 square miles. Located at 43.88° N. Lat.; 91.41° W. Long.
Population: 820 (2000); Race: 97.9% White, 0.0% Black, 0.0% Asian, 0.0% American Indian and Alaska Native, 2.1% Hispanic of any race, 0.4% two or more races (2000); Density: 23.4 persons per square mile (2000); Age: 29.0% under 18, 8.8% over 64 (2000); Marriage status: 25.9% never married, 65.6% now married, 2.0% widowed, 6.4% divorced (2000); Foreign born: 2.6% (2000); Ancestry (includes multiple ancestries): 58.2% German, 20.4% Norwegian, 11.1% Irish, 5.7% Dutch, 4.7% Polish (2000).
Economy: Employment by occupation: 23.9% management, 12.7% professional, 6.4% services, 20.4% sales, 4.8% farming, 8.3% construction, 23.5% production (2000).
Income: Per capita income: $18,738 (2000); Median household income: $45,938 (2000); Poverty rate: 7.6% (2000).
Taxes: Total city taxes per capita: $58 (1997); City property taxes per capita: $58 (1997).
Education: High school graduation rate: 85.1% (2000); College graduation rate: 21.7% (2000).
Housing: Homeownership rate: 87.2% (2000); Median home value: $105,700 (2000); Median rent: $450 per month (2000); Median age of housing: 37 years (2000).
Transportation: Commute to work: 82.5% car, 0.0% public transportation, 5.2% walk, 11.7% work from home (2000); Travel time to work: 15.8% less than 15 minutes, 48.7% 15 to 30 minutes, 30.3% 30 to 45 minutes, 2.4% 45 to 60 minutes, 2.8% 60 minutes or more (2000)

NORTON (township). Covers a land area of 32.612 square miles and a water area of 0 square miles. Located at 44.06° N. Lat.; 91.88° W. Long.
Population: 527 (2000); Race: 98.7% White, 0.0% Black, 1.3% Asian, 0.0% American Indian and Alaska Native, 0.0% Hispanic of any race, 0.0% two or more races (2000); Density: 16.2 persons per square mile (2000); Age: 31.8% under 18, 9.1% over 64 (2000); Marriage status: 25.5% never married, 61.3% now married, 5.8% widowed, 7.5% divorced (2000); Foreign born: 0.9% (2000); Ancestry (includes multiple ancestries): 66.7% German, 16.7% Irish, 15.3% Norwegian, 9.5% Polish, 6.9% Luxemburger (2000).
Economy: Employment by occupation: 25.2% management, 12.4% professional, 9.7% services, 20.8% sales, 9.4% farming, 9.7% construction, 12.8% production (2000).
Income: Per capita income: $16,211 (2000); Median household income: $43,636 (2000); Poverty rate: 5.3% (2000).
Taxes: Total city taxes per capita: $48 (1997); City property taxes per capita: $48 (1997).
Education: High school graduation rate: 91.4% (2000); College graduation rate: 16.0% (2000).
Housing: Homeownership rate: 87.5% (2000); Median home value: $108,800 (2000); Median rent: $338 per month (2000); Median age of housing: 43 years (2000).
Transportation: Commute to work: 78.2% car, 0.0% public transportation, 3.7% walk, 18.0% work from home (2000); Travel time to work: 32.4% less than 15 minutes, 50.2% 15 to 30 minutes, 7.5% 30 to 45 minutes, 7.5% 45 to 60 minutes, 2.5% 60 minutes or more (2000)

PLEASANT HILL (township). Covers a land area of 35.721 square miles and a water area of 0 square miles. Located at 43.88° N. Lat.; 91.54° W. Long.
Population: 535 (2000); Race: 98.3% White, 0.0% Black, 1.5% Asian, 0.0% American Indian and Alaska Native, 0.0% Hispanic of any race, 0.2% two or more races (2000); Density: 15.0 persons per square mile (2000); Age: 28.0% under 18, 11.5% over 64 (2000); Marriage status: 27.7% never married, 62.8% now married, 4.7% widowed, 4.9% divorced (2000); Foreign born: 0.4% (2000); Ancestry (includes multiple ancestries): 62.8% German, 17.6% Norwegian, 8.7% Irish, 7.2% Polish, 3.8% Swedish (2000).
Economy: Employment by occupation: 26.6% management, 11.2% professional, 7.1% services, 15.4% sales, 8.3% farming, 4.8% construction, 26.6% production (2000).
Income: Per capita income: $17,447 (2000); Median household income: $40,000 (2000); Poverty rate: 4.7% (2000).
Taxes: Total city taxes per capita: $80 (1997); City property taxes per capita: $80 (1997).
Education: High school graduation rate: 70.3% (2000); College graduation rate: 12.6% (2000).
Housing: Homeownership rate: 87.0% (2000); Median home value: $97,500 (2000); Median rent: $238 per month (2000); Median age of housing: 39 years (2000).
Transportation: Commute to work: 72.9% car, 0.0% public transportation, 0.3% walk, 26.8% work from home (2000); Travel time to work: 18.7% less than 15 minutes, 52.6% 15 to 30 minutes, 21.7% 30 to 45 minutes, 2.6% 45 to 60 minutes, 4.3% 60 minutes or more (2000)

RICHMOND (township). Covers a land area of 16.210 square miles and a water area of 2.433 square miles. Located at 43.97° N. Lat.; 91.42° W. Long.
Population: 729 (2000); Race: 98.2% White, 0.0% Black, 0.7% Asian, 0.0% American Indian and Alaska Native, 0.4% Hispanic of any race, 0.4% two or more races (2000); Density: 45.0 persons per square mile (2000); Age: 25.0% under 18, 7.6% over 64 (2000); Marriage status: 25.2% never married, 64.5% now married, 2.1% widowed, 8.2% divorced (2000); Foreign born: 0.8% (2000); Ancestry (includes multiple ancestries): 58.3% German, 21.2% Norwegian, 13.0% Polish, 11.3% Irish, 6.5% English (2000).
Economy: Employment by occupation: 15.9% management, 19.1% professional, 11.2% services, 19.4% sales, 0.9% farming, 8.4% construction, 25.1% production (2000).
Income: Per capita income: $24,862 (2000); Median household income: $52,386 (2000); Poverty rate: 4.4% (2000).
Taxes: Total city taxes per capita: $59 (1997); City property taxes per capita: $59 (1997).
Education: High school graduation rate: 88.5% (2000); College graduation rate: 24.0% (2000).
Housing: Homeownership rate: 93.8% (2000); Median home value: $114,000 (2000); Median rent: $300 per month (2000); Median age of housing: 24 years (2000).

Transportation: Commute to work: 94.5% car, 0.0% public transportation, 0.0% walk, 4.6% work from home (2000); Travel time to work: 11.1% less than 15 minutes, 72.0% 15 to 30 minutes, 13.5% 30 to 45 minutes, 0.5% 45 to 60 minutes, 2.9% 60 minutes or more (2000)

ROLLINGSTONE (city). Covers a land area of 0.456 square miles and a water area of 0 square miles. Located at 44.09° N. Lat.; 91.82° W. Long. Elevation is 759 feet.
History: Rollingstone was settled by German immigrants who came here before the Civil War. The town was established in an area of many prehistoric mounds.
Population: 697 (2000); Race: 99.6% White, 0.0% Black, 0.4% Asian, 0.0% American Indian and Alaska Native, 0.0% Hispanic of any race, 0.0% two or more races (2000); Density: 1,528.2 persons per square mile (2000); Age: 33.2% under 18, 9.3% over 64 (2000); Marriage status: 21.9% never married, 70.0% now married, 4.5% widowed, 3.5% divorced (2000); Foreign born: 0.7% (2000); Ancestry (includes multiple ancestries): 49.9% German, 15.3% Norwegian, 11.9% Polish, 8.2% Irish, 6.4% Luxemburger (2000).
Economy: Single-family building permits issued: 0 (2001) / 0 (2000); Multi-family building permits issued: 0 (2001) / 0 (2000); Employment by occupation: 10.1% management, 20.3% professional, 14.3% services, 20.8% sales, 1.8% farming, 8.8% construction, 23.9% production (2000).
Income: Per capita income: $17,294 (2000); Median household income: $45,000 (2000); Poverty rate: 2.5% (2000).
Taxes: Total city taxes per capita: $126 (1997); City property taxes per capita: $119 (1997).
Education: High school graduation rate: 91.1% (2000); College graduation rate: 24.4% (2000).
Housing: Homeownership rate: 89.7% (2000); Median home value: $102,900 (2000); Median rent: $267 per month (2000); Median age of housing: 27 years (2000).
Transportation: Commute to work: 92.1% car, 0.0% public transportation, 4.2% walk, 2.9% work from home (2000); Travel time to work: 29.3% less than 15 minutes, 53.7% 15 to 30 minutes, 5.1% 30 to 45 minutes, 6.2% 45 to 60 minutes, 5.7% 60 minutes or more (2000)

ROLLINGSTONE (township). Covers a land area of 30.266 square miles and a water area of 4.142 square miles. Located at 44.09° N. Lat.; 91.75° W. Long. Elevation is 759 feet.
Population: 1,087 (2000); Race: 97.7% White, 0.0% Black, 1.1% Asian, 0.2% American Indian and Alaska Native, 0.2% Hispanic of any race, 1.1% two or more races (2000); Density: 35.9 persons per square mile (2000); Age: 22.5% under 18, 15.0% over 64 (2000); Marriage status: 16.8% never married, 72.7% now married, 5.2% widowed, 5.4% divorced (2000); Foreign born: 2.5% (2000); Ancestry (includes multiple ancestries): 50.6% German, 17.5% Norwegian, 16.7% Polish, 14.1% Irish, 6.1% English (2000).
Economy: Grain; livestock, poultry; dairying; light manufacturing. Employment by occupation: 14.5% management, 13.5% professional, 11.9% services, 23.9% sales, 0.8% farming, 10.2% construction, 25.2% production (2000).
Income: Per capita income: $22,310 (2000); Median household income: $54,250 (2000); Poverty rate: 2.5% (2000).
Taxes: Total city taxes per capita: $40 (1997); City property taxes per capita: $40 (1997).
Education: High school graduation rate: 87.7% (2000); College graduation rate: 18.9% (2000).
Housing: Homeownership rate: 93.2% (2000); Median home value: $118,900 (2000); Median rent: $271 per month (2000); Median age of housing: 33 years (2000).
Transportation: Commute to work: 91.0% car, 0.0% public transportation, 1.0% walk, 7.7% work from home (2000); Travel time to work: 46.6% less than 15 minutes, 39.9% 15 to 30 minutes, 6.9% 30 to 45 minutes, 3.4% 45 to 60 minutes, 3.2% 60 minutes or more (2000)

SAINT CHARLES (city). Covers a land area of 3.278 square miles and a water area of 0 square miles. Located at 43.97° N. Lat.; 92.06° W. Long. Elevation is 1,142 feet.
History: When the site of St. Charles was surveyed in 1854, it is reported that the founders offered an acre lot to any Christian Democrat who would settle here.
Population: 3,295 (2000); Race: 91.9% White, 1.4% Black, 3.5% Asian, 0.7% American Indian and Alaska Native, 3.3% Hispanic of any race, 0.4% two or more races (2000); Density: 1,005.3 persons per square mile (2000); Age: 29.6% under 18, 15.6% over 64 (2000); Marriage status: 21.4% never married, 63.8% now married, 6.2% widowed, 8.6% divorced (2000); Foreign born: 4.4% (2000); Ancestry (includes multiple ancestries): 47.1% German, 20.4% Norwegian, 11.1% Irish, 10.0% Other groups, 7.0% English (2000).
Economy: Single-family building permits issued: 33 (2001) / 24 (2000); Multi-family building permits issued: 0 (2001) / 4 (2000); Employment by occupation: 9.7% management, 18.6% professional, 15.8% services, 27.1% sales, 1.1% farming, 10.6% construction, 17.0% production (2000).
Income: Per capita income: $17,727 (2000); Median household income: $42,813 (2000); Poverty rate: 9.1% (2000).
Education: High school graduation rate: 82.5% (2000); College graduation rate: 19.9% (2000).

School District(s)

Saint Charles (PK-12)
2000 Enrollment: 1,096 507-932-4423
Housing: Homeownership rate: 72.2% (2000); Median home value: $96,600 (2000); Median rent: $383 per month (2000); Median age of housing: 31 years (2000).
Newspapers: Saint Charles Press (1 x week)
Transportation: Commute to work: 87.7% car, 0.8% public transportation, 5.4% walk, 4.6% work from home (2000); Travel time to work: 33.6% less than 15 minutes, 19.8% 15 to 30 minutes, 40.5% 30 to 45 minutes, 3.2% 45 to 60 minutes, 2.9% 60 minutes or more (2000)

SAINT CHARLES (township). Covers a land area of 32.314 square miles and a water area of 0 square miles. Located at 43.96° N. Lat.; 92.02° W. Long. Elevation is 1,142 feet.
Population: 610 (2000); Race: 96.2% White, 0.0% Black, 0.3% Asian, 2.1% American Indian and Alaska Native, 1.2% Hispanic of any race, 0.5% two or more races (2000); Density: 18.9 persons per square mile (2000); Age: 35.4% under 18, 9.4% over 64 (2000); Marriage status: 20.9% never married, 70.1% now married, 2.7% widowed, 6.2% divorced (2000); Foreign born: 1.2% (2000); Ancestry (includes multiple ancestries): 54.6% German, 12.7% Irish, 9.7% Norwegian, 9.4% English, 5.4% United States or American (2000).
Economy: Employment by occupation: 18.4% management, 15.4% professional, 11.0% services, 21.3% sales, 4.4% farming, 14.3% construction, 15.1% production (2000).
Income: Per capita income: $16,209 (2000); Median household income: $51,250 (2000); Poverty rate: 14.8% (2000).
Education: High school graduation rate: 79.6% (2000); College graduation rate: 17.3% (2000).
Housing: Homeownership rate: 84.1% (2000); Median home value: $132,500 (2000); Median rent: $413 per month (2000); Median age of housing: 30 years (2000).
Transportation: Commute to work: 79.6% car, 0.7% public transportation, 4.8% walk, 14.1% work from home (2000); Travel time to work: 29.0% less than 15 minutes, 20.3% 15 to 30 minutes, 37.7% 30 to 45 minutes, 8.2% 45 to 60 minutes, 4.8% 60 minutes or more (2000)

SARATOGA (township). Covers a land area of 35.669 square miles and a water area of 0 square miles. Located at 43.87° N. Lat.; 92.02° W. Long.
Population: 573 (2000); Race: 98.4% White, 0.0% Black, 0.9% Asian, 0.7% American Indian and Alaska Native, 1.1% Hispanic of any race, 0.0% two or more races (2000); Density: 16.1 persons per square mile (2000); Age: 39.1% under 18, 6.2% over 64 (2000); Marriage status: 21.4% never married, 70.0% now married, 3.2% widowed, 5.4% divorced (2000); Foreign born: 1.8% (2000); Ancestry (includes multiple ancestries): 44.8% German, 15.0% Norwegian, 11.0% United States or American, 9.0% Irish, 6.0% English (2000).
Economy: Employment by occupation: 25.8% management, 18.2% professional, 12.9% services, 12.9% sales, 7.2% farming, 11.0% construction, 12.1% production (2000).
Income: Per capita income: $16,518 (2000); Median household income: $44,219 (2000); Poverty rate: 18.7% (2000).
Taxes: Total city taxes per capita: $105 (2000); City property taxes per capita: $105 (2000).
Education: High school graduation rate: 77.7% (2000); College graduation rate: 15.2% (2000).
Housing: Homeownership rate: 86.8% (2000); Median home value: $90,000 (2000); Median rent: $388 per month (2000); Median age of housing: 29 years (2000).
Transportation: Commute to work: 62.5% car, 0.0% public transportation, 7.7% walk, 29.0% work from home (2000); Travel time to work: 32.4% less than 15 minutes, 25.0% 15 to 30 minutes, 32.4% 30 to 45 minutes, 7.4% 45 to 60 minutes, 2.8% 60 minutes or more (2000)

STOCKTON (city). Covers a land area of 1.628 square miles and a water area of 0.002 square miles. Located at 44.02° N. Lat.; 91.77° W. Long. Elevation is 753 feet.
Population: 682 (2000); Race: 98.8% White, 0.0% Black, 0.1% Asian, 0.6% American Indian and Alaska Native, 0.0% Hispanic of any race, 0.4% two or more races (2000); Density: 419.0 persons per square mile (2000); Age: 32.3% under 18, 9.1% over 64 (2000); Marriage status: 29.1% never married, 52.8% now married, 4.0% widowed, 14.1% divorced (2000); Foreign born: 0.3% (2000); Ancestry (includes multiple ancestries): 49.6% German, 21.2% Norwegian, 16.1% Polish, 11.7% Irish, 2.9% United States or American (2000).
Economy: Dairying; poultry, livestock; grain. Manufacturing: tool and die. Single-family building permits issued: 5 (2001) / 3 (2000); Multi-family building permits issued: 2 (2001) / 0 (2000); Employment by occupation: 5.8% management, 12.1% professional, 11.6% services, 27.1% sales, 1.6% farming, 10.8% construction, 31.1% production (2000).
Income: Per capita income: $17,038 (2000); Median household income: $41,250 (2000); Poverty rate: 4.1% (2000).
Taxes: Total city taxes per capita: $104 (1997); City property taxes per capita: $92 (1997).
Education: High school graduation rate: 79.7% (2000); College graduation rate: 8.4% (2000).
Housing: Homeownership rate: 91.6% (2000); Median home value: $94,200 (2000); Median rent: $375 per month (2000); Median age of housing: 24 years (2000).
Transportation: Commute to work: 92.8% car, 1.1% public transportation, 2.1% walk, 2.1% work from home (2000); Travel time to work: 34.0% less than 15 minutes, 49.2% 15 to 30 minutes, 8.7% 30 to 45 minutes, 3.0% 45 to 60 minutes, 5.2% 60 minutes or more (2000)

UTICA (city). Covers a land area of 0.920 square miles and a water area of 0 square miles. Located at 43.97° N. Lat.; 91.95° W. Long.
Population: 230 (2000); Race: 100.0% White, 0.0% Black, 0.0% Asian, 0.0% American Indian and Alaska Native, 0.0% Hispanic of any race, 0.0% two or more races (2000); Density: 250.1 persons per square mile (2000); Age: 24.0% under 18, 13.9% over 64 (2000); Marriage status: 17.8% never married, 62.0% now married, 6.7% widowed, 13.5% divorced (2000); Foreign born: 1.0% (2000); Ancestry (includes multiple ancestries): 60.1% German, 23.6% Norwegian, 9.1% Polish, 6.3% English, 4.3% United States or American (2000).
Economy: Single-family building permits issued: 0 (2001) / 1 (2000); Multi-family building permits issued: 0 (2001) / 0 (2000); Employment by occupation: 1.8% management, 15.5% professional, 10.9% services, 29.1% sales, 1.8% farming, 9.1% construction, 31.8% production (2000).
Income: Per capita income: $19,185 (2000); Median household income: $43,250 (2000); Poverty rate: 3.8% (2000).
Taxes: Total city taxes per capita: $70 (2000); City property taxes per capita: $65 (2000).
Education: High school graduation rate: 77.1% (2000); College graduation rate: 6.1% (2000).
Housing: Homeownership rate: 92.2% (2000); Median home value: $63,300 (2000); Median rent: $425 per month (2000); Median age of housing: 60+ years (2000).
Transportation: Commute to work: 78.2% car, 4.5% public transportation, 3.6% walk, 13.6% work from home (2000); Travel time to work: 29.5% less than 15 minutes, 14.7% 15 to 30 minutes, 30.5% 30 to 45 minutes, 18.9% 45 to 60 minutes, 6.3% 60 minutes or more (2000)

UTICA (township). Covers a land area of 33.879 square miles and a water area of 0 square miles. Located at 43.98° N. Lat.; 91.89° W. Long.
Population: 649 (2000); Race: 100.0% White, 0.0% Black, 0.0% Asian, 0.0% American Indian and Alaska Native, 0.0% Hispanic of any race, 0.0% two or more races (2000); Density: 19.2 persons per square mile (2000); Age: 32.6% under 18, 13.2% over 64 (2000); Marriage status: 21.6% never married, 73.2% now married, 2.6% widowed, 2.6% divorced (2000); Foreign born: 0.0% (2000); Ancestry (includes multiple ancestries): 63.6% German, 23.1% Norwegian, 12.6% Irish, 4.4% Polish, 4.1% English (2000).
Economy: Agriculture: dairying; livestock, poultry; grain. Manufacturing of medical products. Employment by occupation: 20.8% management, 16.7% professional, 8.3% services, 21.7% sales, 9.5% farming, 4.5% construction, 18.5% production (2000).
Income: Per capita income: $17,576 (2000); Median household income: $49,844 (2000); Poverty rate: 8.4% (2000).
Taxes: Total city taxes per capita: $104 (1997); City property taxes per capita: $104 (1997).
Education: High school graduation rate: 85.5% (2000); College graduation rate: 17.4% (2000).
Housing: Homeownership rate: 87.0% (2000); Median home value: $113,200 (2000); Median rent: $328 per month (2000); Median age of housing: 43 years (2000).
Transportation: Commute to work: 76.4% car, 0.0% public transportation, 3.9% walk, 18.1% work from home (2000); Travel time to work: 49.4% less than 15 minutes, 21.0% 15 to 30 minutes, 15.1% 30 to 45 minutes, 11.8% 45 to 60 minutes, 2.6% 60 minutes or more (2000)

WARREN (township). Covers a land area of 35.522 square miles and a water area of 0 square miles. Located at 43.98° N. Lat.; 91.78° W. Long.
Population: 629 (2000); Race: 98.6% White, 0.5% Black, 0.0% Asian, 0.0% American Indian and Alaska Native, 0.3% Hispanic of any race, 0.6% two or more races (2000); Density: 17.7 persons per square mile (2000); Age: 32.6% under 18, 11.2% over 64 (2000); Marriage status: 25.0% never married, 68.2% now married, 3.6% widowed, 3.2% divorced (2000); Foreign born: 0.6% (2000); Ancestry (includes multiple ancestries): 59.8% German, 19.2% Norwegian, 8.0% Polish, 6.2% English, 5.4% Irish (2000).
Economy: Single-family building permits issued: 8 (2001) / 1 (2000); Multi-family building permits issued: 0 (2001) / 0 (2000); Employment by occupation: 23.5% management, 11.7% professional, 9.2% services, 20.9% sales, 6.9% farming, 12.3% construction, 15.5% production (2000).
Income: Per capita income: $15,372 (2000); Median household income: $37,167 (2000); Poverty rate: 7.3% (2000).
Taxes: Total city taxes per capita: $91 (1997); City property taxes per capita: $88 (1997).
Education: High school graduation rate: 80.8% (2000); College graduation rate: 18.0% (2000).
Housing: Homeownership rate: 80.3% (2000); Median home value: $98,500 (2000); Median rent: $335 per month (2000); Median age of housing: 47 years (2000).
Transportation: Commute to work: 78.9% car, 0.6% public transportation, 2.6% walk, 17.5% work from home (2000); Travel time to work: 30.5% less than 15 minutes, 42.2% 15 to 30 minutes, 14.5% 30 to 45 minutes, 7.4% 45 to 60 minutes, 5.3% 60 minutes or more (2000)

WHITEWATER (township). Covers a land area of 35.200 square miles and a water area of 0.129 square miles. Located at 44.15° N. Lat.; 92.01° W. Long.
Population: 202 (2000); Race: 100.0% White, 0.0% Black, 0.0% Asian, 0.0% American Indian and Alaska Native, 0.0% Hispanic of any race, 0.0% two or more races (2000); Density: 5.7 persons per square mile (2000); Age: 39.5% under 18, 8.5% over 64 (2000); Marriage status: 20.4% never married, 72.1% now married, 3.4% widowed, 4.1% divorced (2000); Foreign born: 0.0% (2000); Ancestry (includes multiple ancestries): 71.3% German, 11.2% Irish, 8.5% French (except Basque), 7.2% United States or American, 6.3% Norwegian (2000).
Economy: Employment by occupation: 31.2% management, 15.2% professional, 6.4% services, 17.6% sales, 11.2% farming, 8.0% construction, 10.4% production (2000).
Income: Per capita income: $19,122 (2000); Median household income: $51,875 (2000); Poverty rate: 0.9% (2000).
Taxes: Total city taxes per capita: $75 (1997); City property taxes per capita: $75 (1997).
Education: High school graduation rate: 87.4% (2000); College graduation rate: 18.1% (2000).
Housing: Homeownership rate: 87.5% (2000); Median home value: $87,500 (2000); Median rent: $475 per month (2000); Median age of housing: 60+ years (2000).
Transportation: Commute to work: 69.6% car, 0.0% public transportation, 6.4% walk, 24.0% work from home (2000); Travel time to work: 36.8% less than 15 minutes, 16.8% 15 to 30 minutes, 27.4% 30 to 45 minutes, 11.6% 45 to 60 minutes, 7.4% 60 minutes or more (2000)

WILSON (township). Covers a land area of 34.978 square miles and a water area of 0.003 square miles. Located at 43.99° N. Lat.; 91.63° W. Long. Elevation is 933 feet.
Population: 1,152 (2000); Race: 98.3% White, 0.2% Black, 0.5% Asian, 0.5% American Indian and Alaska Native, 0.2% Hispanic of any race, 0.3% two or more races (2000); Density: 32.9 persons per square mile (2000); Age: 26.5% under 18, 9.4% over 64 (2000); Marriage status: 30.2% never married, 60.3% now married, 3.0% widowed, 6.5% divorced (2000); Foreign born: 2.9% (2000); Ancestry (includes multiple ancestries): 48.7% German, 16.0% Norwegian, 11.5% Polish, 11.0% Irish, 6.6% English (2000).

Economy: Single-family building permits issued: 5 (2001) / 4 (2000); Multi-family building permits issued: 0 (2001) / 0 (2000); Employment by occupation: 17.1% management, 13.7% professional, 11.2% services, 20.1% sales, 3.2% farming, 7.4% construction, 27.2% production (2000).
Income: Per capita income: $25,832 (2000); Median household income: $52,422 (2000); Poverty rate: 2.0% (2000).
Taxes: Total city taxes per capita: $66 (1997); City property taxes per capita: $65 (1997).
Education: High school graduation rate: 88.9% (2000); College graduation rate: 24.5% (2000).
Housing: Homeownership rate: 90.6% (2000); Median home value: $119,600 (2000); Median rent: $468 per month (2000); Median age of housing: 28 years (2000).
Transportation: Commute to work: 84.7% car, 0.3% public transportation, 1.0% walk, 13.5% work from home (2000); Travel time to work: 37.2% less than 15 minutes, 47.4% 15 to 30 minutes, 5.1% 30 to 45 minutes, 4.4% 45 to 60 minutes, 5.8% 60 minutes or more (2000)

WINONA (city). Covers a land area of 18.228 square miles and a water area of 5.332 square miles. Located at 44.04° N. Lat.; 91.64° W. Long. Elevation is 661 feet.
History: The site of Winona was a barren prairie when Orren Smith, captain of a steamboat on this section of the Mississippi River, secured land for a town here in 1851. The village that grew up was platted as Montezuma, but the name was soon changed to Winona, a Sioux name often given to the first-born child in the family. By 1855, Winona had a sawmill, processing lumber floated on rafts down the river from the forests. Though lumber brought the first prosperity, wheat warehousing and marketing soon gained prominence. The railroad joined the river as a means of shipping in the 1860's, replacing it by 1900. The first brickyard opened in Winona in 1870, becoming a major industry along with the quarrying of limestone for building material.
Population: 27,069 (2000); Race: 94.2% White, 1.1% Black, 2.2% Asian, 0.3% American Indian and Alaska Native, 1.6% Hispanic of any race, 1.6% two or more races (2000); Density: 1,485.0 persons per square mile (2000); Age: 17.8% under 18, 14.5% over 64 (2000); Marriage status: 41.8% never married, 42.4% now married, 7.7% widowed, 8.1% divorced (2000); Foreign born: 3.5% (2000); Ancestry (includes multiple ancestries): 43.3% German, 15.5% Norwegian, 14.9% Polish, 13.1% Irish, 6.6% Other groups (2000).
Vital Statistics: Birth rate: 111.6 per 10,000 population (1998)
Economy: Unemployment rate: 3.7% (11/2002); Total civilian labor force: 14,755 (11/2002); Single-family building permits issued: 56 (2001) / 29 (2000); Multi-family building permits issued: 14 (2001) / 13 (2000); Employment by occupation: 9.5% management, 18.8% professional, 19.7% services, 27.2% sales, 0.4% farming, 4.9% construction, 19.5% production (2000).
Income: Per capita income: $16,783 (2000); Median household income: $32,845 (2000); Poverty rate: 17.3% (2000).
Taxes: Total city taxes per capita: $246 (2000); City property taxes per capita: $193 (2000).
Education: High school graduation rate: 82.9% (2000); College graduation rate: 26.3% (2000).

School District(s)

Bluffview Montessori (KG-08)
2000 Enrollment: 175 507-452-2807
Hiawatha Valley Ed. Dist. (06-12)
2000 Enrollment: 61 507-452-1200
Riverway Learning Community Chtr (KG-12)
2000 Enrollment: 54 507-452-1609
Winona (PK-12)
2000 Enrollment: 4,458 507-454-9461

Four-year College(s)

Saint Mary's University of Minnesota (Private, Not-for-profit, Roman Catholic)
2001 Enrollment: 5,008 507-452-4430
2001 Tuition: In-state $14,830; Out-of-state $14,830
Winona State University (Public)
2001 Enrollment: 7,707 507-457-5000
2001 Tuition: In-state $3,110; Out-of-state $6,820

Two-year College(s)

Minnesota State College-Southeast Technical-Winona (Public)
2001 Enrollment: n/a 507-453-2700
2001 Tuition: In-state $2,556; Out-of-state $5,111

Housing: Homeownership rate: 61.0% (2000); Median home value: $89,300 (2000); Median rent: $373 per month (2000); Median age of housing: 54 years (2000).
Hospitals: Community Memorial Hospital (99 beds)
Safety: Violent crime rate: 13.2 per 10,000 population; Property crime rate: 318.0 per 10,000 population (2001).
Newspapers: Winona Daily News (7 x week); Winona Post (2 x week)
Transportation: Commute to work: 83.2% car, 1.3% public transportation, 10.9% walk, 2.5% work from home (2000); Travel time to work: 72.0% less than 15 minutes, 18.1% 15 to 30 minutes, 4.7% 30 to 45 minutes, 2.4% 45 to 60 minutes, 2.7% 60 minutes or more (2000); Amtrak: Service available.
Airports: Winona Municipal-Max Conrad Field
Additional Information Contacts
Winona Chamber of Commerce.......... 507-452-2272
Winona Visitors Information 507-452-2278

WISCOY (township). Covers a land area of 35.720 square miles and a water area of 0 square miles. Located at 43.90° N. Lat.; 91.65° W. Long.
Population: 336 (2000); Race: 98.2% White, 0.0% Black, 0.6% Asian, 0.0% American Indian and Alaska Native, 0.0% Hispanic of any race, 0.0% two or more races (2000); Density: 9.4 persons per square mile (2000); Age: 29.0% under 18, 6.3% over 64 (2000); Marriage status: 18.4% never married, 71.0% now married, 4.5% widowed, 6.1% divorced (2000); Foreign born: 2.1% (2000); Ancestry (includes multiple ancestries): 49.1% German, 14.7% Irish, 13.8% Norwegian, 10.8% Polish, 8.4% United States or American (2000).
Economy: Employment by occupation: 25.7% management, 14.5% professional, 5.0% services, 19.6% sales, 7.3% farming, 8.9% construction, 19.0% production (2000).
Income: Per capita income: $15,814 (2000); Median household income: $36,607 (2000); Poverty rate: 8.1% (2000).
Taxes: Total city taxes per capita: $70 (1997); City property taxes per capita: $70 (1997).
Education: High school graduation rate: 85.3% (2000); College graduation rate: 31.8% (2000).
Housing: Homeownership rate: 87.5% (2000); Median home value: $88,800 (2000); Median rent: $275 per month (2000); Median age of housing: 39 years (2000).
Transportation: Commute to work: 80.4% car, 0.0% public transportation, 1.1% walk, 17.3% work from home (2000); Travel time to work: 13.5% less than 15 minutes, 62.2% 15 to 30 minutes, 15.5% 30 to 45 minutes, 6.1% 45 to 60 minutes, 2.7% 60 minutes or more (2000)

Wright County

Located in south central Minnesota; bounded on the north by the Mississippi River, and on the east by the Crow River; includes Clearwater and Pelican Lakes. Covers a land area of 660.80 square miles, a water area of 53.60 square miles, and is located in the Central Time Zone. The county government was organized in 1855. County seat is Buffalo.

Wright County is part of the Minneapolis-St. Paul, MN-WI MSA. The entire metro area includes: Anoka County, MN; Carver County, MN; Chisago County, MN; Dakota County, MN; Hennepin County, MN; Isanti County, MN; Ramsey County, MN; Scott County, MN; Sherburne County, MN; Washington County, MN; Wright County, MN; Pierce County, WI; St. Croix County, WI

Weather Station: Buffalo Elevation: 977 feet

	Jan	Feb	Mar	Apr	May	Jun	Jul	Aug	Sep	Oct	Nov	Dec
High	21	28	39	57	71	79	84	81	72	59	39	25
Low	1	8	20	34	47	56	61	59	49	37	23	9
Precip	0.8	0.6	1.6	2.4	3.2	4.4	3.8	4.3	3.0	2.3	1.8	0.8
Snow	9.7	6.2	8.8	2.6	0.1	0.0	0.0	0.0	tr	0.2	7.6	8.2

High and Low temperatures in degrees Fahrenheit; Precipitation and Snow in inches

Population: 89,986 (2000); Race: 98.0% White, 0.4% Black, 0.2% Asian, 0.3% American Indian and Alaska Native, 1.1% Hispanic of any race, 0.7% two or more races (2000); Density: 136.2 persons per square mile (2000); Age: 31.2% under 18, 8.8% over 64 (2000).
Religion: Five largest groups: 28.9% Catholic Church, 17.0% Evangelical Lutheran Church in America, 5.1% Lutheran Church—Missouri Synod, 2.4% The United Methodist Church, 2.1% Wisconsin Evangelical Lutheran Synod (2000).
Economy: Unemployment rate: 4.3% (11/2002); Total civilian labor force: 51,446 (11/2002); Leading industries: 21.3% manufacturing; 16.9% retail trade; 14.1% health care and social assistance (2000); Companies that employ more than 1,000 persons: 0 (2000); Companies that employ more than 100 persons: 33 (2000); Farms: 1,422 totaling 251,832 acres (1997); Minority business ownership rate: 2.0% (1997); Women business ownership rate:

29.7% (1997); Retail sales per capita: $8,222 (1997). Single-family building permits issued: 1,660 (2001) / 1,426 (2000); Multi-family building permits issued: 94 (2001) / 146 (2000).
Income: Per capita income: $21,844 (2000); Median household income: $53,945 (2000); Poverty rate: 4.7% (2000); Bankruptcy rate: 3.70% (2001).
Taxes: Total county taxes per capita: $220 (2000); County property taxes per capita: $212 (2000).
Education: High school graduation rate: 88.1% (2000); College graduation rate: 17.9% (2000).
Housing: Homeownership rate: 84.3% (2000); Median home value: $135,300 (2000); Median rent: $480 per month (2000); Median age of housing: 22 years (2000).
Health: Birth rate: 152.3 per 10,000 population (1998); Age adjusted death rate: 82.1 per 10,000 population (1999); Age adjusted cancer mortality rate: 183.5 deaths per 100,000 population (1999). Number of physicians: 6.1 per 10,000 population (1999); Number of hospital beds: 15.6 per 10,000 population (1999).
Elections: 2000 Presidential election results: 38.7% Gore, 55.0% Bush, 4.6% Nader, 1.1% Buchanan
National and State Parks: Albion State Wildlife Management Area; Corinna State Wildlife Management Area; Grass Lake - Stockholm State Wildlife Management Area; Hoglund State Wildlife Management Area; Kelly Meyer State Wildlife Management Area; Lake Maria State Park; Malardi Lake State Wildlife Management Area; Maple Lake State Wildlife Management Area; Otsego State Wildlife Management Area; Suconnix State Wildlife Management Area; Swartout State Wildlife Management Area
Additional Information Contacts
Wright County Government Offices 763-682-3900
Annanadale Area Chamber 320-274-2223
Buffalo Chamber of Commerce 763-682-4902
Delano Chamber of Commerce 763-972-6756
Monticello Area Chamber of Commerce 763-295-2700
Saint Michael Area Chamber 763-497-7848

Wright County Communities

ALBERTVILLE (city). Covers a land area of 4.382 square miles and a water area of 0.316 square miles. Located at 45.23° N. Lat.; 93.66° W. Long. Elevation is 981 feet.
Population: 3,621 (2000); Race: 97.3% White, 1.4% Black, 0.0% Asian, 0.2% American Indian and Alaska Native, 0.7% Hispanic of any race, 1.1% two or more races (2000); Density: 826.3 persons per square mile (2000); Age: 35.9% under 18, 5.3% over 64 (2000); Marriage status: 24.1% never married, 65.0% now married, 2.3% widowed, 8.6% divorced (2000); Foreign born: 1.6% (2000); Ancestry (includes multiple ancestries): 48.1% German, 12.1% Norwegian, 12.1% Irish, 9.3% Swedish, 6.8% French (except Basque) (2000).
Economy: Corn, oats, barley, soybeans, alfalfa; dairying; poultry. Manufactures concrete and steel products, feeds, plastic molds, woodroof trusses. Single-family building permits issued: 178 (2001) / 110 (2000); Multi-family building permits issued: 52 (2001) / 28 (2000); Employment by occupation: 13.4% management, 14.2% professional, 11.4% services, 30.1% sales, 0.5% farming, 14.7% construction, 15.7% production (2000).
Income: Per capita income: $21,424 (2000); Median household income: $58,260 (2000); Poverty rate: 6.9% (2000).
Taxes: Total city taxes per capita: $198 (1997); City property taxes per capita: $167 (1997).
Education: High school graduation rate: 92.9% (2000); College graduation rate: 15.3% (2000).
Housing: Homeownership rate: 78.9% (2000); Median home value: $137,400 (2000); Median rent: $661 per month (2000); Median age of housing: 7 years (2000).
Transportation: Commute to work: 96.6% car, 0.5% public transportation, 0.2% walk, 2.6% work from home (2000); Travel time to work: 19.6% less than 15 minutes, 23.4% 15 to 30 minutes, 33.5% 30 to 45 minutes, 17.6% 45 to 60 minutes, 5.9% 60 minutes or more (2000)

ALBION (township). Covers a land area of 32.494 square miles and a water area of 2.973 square miles. Located at 45.19° N. Lat.; 94.07° W. Long.
Population: 1,146 (2000); Race: 99.3% White, 0.2% Black, 0.0% Asian, 0.0% American Indian and Alaska Native, 1.5% Hispanic of any race, 0.5% two or more races (2000); Density: 35.3 persons per square mile (2000); Age: 29.0% under 18, 11.2% over 64 (2000); Marriage status: 25.5% never married, 65.6% now married, 4.2% widowed, 4.7% divorced (2000); Foreign born: 0.6% (2000); Ancestry (includes multiple ancestries): 52.1% German, 11.8% Swedish, 9.9% Norwegian, 8.2% Irish, 7.3% French (except Basque) (2000).
Economy: Employment by occupation: 12.9% management, 10.7% professional, 13.2% services, 23.4% sales, 0.9% farming, 15.5% construction, 23.5% production (2000).
Income: Per capita income: $22,840 (2000); Median household income: $52,339 (2000); Poverty rate: 4.7% (2000).
Taxes: Total city taxes per capita: $49 (1997); City property taxes per capita: $49 (1997).
Education: High school graduation rate: 83.9% (2000); College graduation rate: 12.2% (2000).
Housing: Homeownership rate: 95.0% (2000); Median home value: $114,600 (2000); Median rent: $438 per month (2000); Median age of housing: 33 years (2000).
Transportation: Commute to work: 86.6% car, 0.0% public transportation, 1.4% walk, 11.7% work from home (2000); Travel time to work: 22.9% less than 15 minutes, 32.0% 15 to 30 minutes, 9.9% 30 to 45 minutes, 14.8% 45 to 60 minutes, 20.5% 60 minutes or more (2000)

ANNANDALE (city). Covers a land area of 2.710 square miles and a water area of 0 square miles. Located at 45.26° N. Lat.; 94.11° W. Long. Elevation is 1,066 feet.
Population: 2,684 (2000); Race: 96.8% White, 0.6% Black, 1.1% Asian, 0.3% American Indian and Alaska Native, 0.8% Hispanic of any race, 0.4% two or more races (2000); Density: 990.3 persons per square mile (2000); Age: 28.3% under 18, 17.1% over 64 (2000); Marriage status: 23.8% never married, 53.4% now married, 12.0% widowed, 10.8% divorced (2000); Foreign born: 2.6% (2000); Ancestry (includes multiple ancestries): 43.7% German, 14.1% Irish, 13.3% Norwegian, 10.2% Swedish, 6.8% Finnish (2000).
Economy: Livestock, poultry; dairying; grain. Manufacturing: construction materials, agricultural equipment, industrial hand tools. Printing and publishing industry. Single-family building permits issued: 28 (2001) / 15 (2000); Multi-family building permits issued: 0 (2001) / 0 (2000); Employment by occupation: 11.5% management, 15.1% professional, 18.9% services, 21.1% sales, 0.7% farming, 12.8% construction, 19.8% production (2000).
Income: Per capita income: $18,876 (2000); Median household income: $37,929 (2000); Poverty rate: 12.1% (2000).
Taxes: Total city taxes per capita: $244 (1997); City property taxes per capita: $229 (1997).
Education: High school graduation rate: 79.8% (2000); College graduation rate: 14.9% (2000).

School District(s)

Annandale (PK-12)
2000 Enrollment: 1,926 320-274-5602
Housing: Homeownership rate: 75.9% (2000); Median home value: $104,700 (2000); Median rent: $373 per month (2000); Median age of housing: 21 years (2000).
Newspapers: Annandale Advocate (1 x week)
Transportation: Commute to work: 94.0% car, 0.0% public transportation, 1.3% walk, 4.0% work from home (2000); Travel time to work: 30.4% less than 15 minutes, 20.7% 15 to 30 minutes, 13.6% 30 to 45 minutes, 10.4% 45 to 60 minutes, 25.0% 60 minutes or more (2000)
Additional Information Contacts
Annanadale Area Chamber 320-274-2223

BUFFALO (city). Covers a land area of 6.025 square miles and a water area of 1.769 square miles. Located at 45.18° N. Lat.; 93.86° W. Long. Elevation is 967 feet.
History: Buffalo was named for the buffalo fish which were found in nearby Buffalo Lake. The ginseng plant, used for its medicinal value, once grew in abundance in this area.
Population: 10,097 (2000); Race: 96.9% White, 0.9% Black, 0.3% Asian, 0.3% American Indian and Alaska Native, 1.5% Hispanic of any race, 1.4% two or more races (2000); Density: 1,675.8 persons per square mile (2000); Age: 29.1% under 18, 11.3% over 64 (2000); Marriage status: 24.4% never married, 58.0% now married, 6.8% widowed, 10.8% divorced (2000); Foreign born: 0.8% (2000); Ancestry (includes multiple ancestries): 42.6% German, 18.1% Norwegian, 12.6% Swedish, 10.9% Irish, 7.1% English (2000).
Economy: Single-family building permits issued: 278 (2001) / 255 (2000); Multi-family building permits issued: 5 (2001) / 48 (2000); Employment by occupation: 13.0% management, 17.4% professional, 14.7% services, 27.0% sales, 0.2% farming, 10.1% construction, 17.6% production (2000).

Income: Per capita income: $21,424 (2000); Median household income: $49,573 (2000); Poverty rate: 5.1% (2000).
Taxes: Total city taxes per capita: $256 (1997); City property taxes per capita: $235 (1997).
Education: High school graduation rate: 87.4% (2000); College graduation rate: 23.2% (2000).

School District(s)

Buffalo (PK-12)
2000 Enrollment: 4,775 612-682-5200
Wright Tech Cntr (07-12)
2000 Enrollment: 114 763-682-4112

Housing: Homeownership rate: 71.8% (2000); Median home value: $129,300 (2000); Median rent: $503 per month (2000); Median age of housing: 20 years (2000).
Hospitals: Buffalo Hospital (65 beds)
Safety: Violent crime rate: 14.7 per 10,000 population; Property crime rate: 426.3 per 10,000 population (2001).
Newspapers: Wright County Journal-Press (1 x week); The Drummer (1 x week)
Transportation: Commute to work: 95.0% car, 0.3% public transportation, 1.1% walk, 2.9% work from home (2000); Travel time to work: 35.4% less than 15 minutes, 18.1% 15 to 30 minutes, 20.6% 30 to 45 minutes, 16.0% 45 to 60 minutes, 9.9% 60 minutes or more (2000)

Additional Information Contacts
Buffalo Chamber of Commerce 763-682-4902

BUFFALO (township). Covers a land area of 26.241 square miles and a water area of 3.028 square miles. Located at 45.19° N. Lat.; 93.83° W. Long. Elevation is 967 feet.
History: Settled c.1855, incorporated 1887.
Population: 1,938 (2000); Race: 99.8% White, 0.0% Black, 0.2% Asian, 0.0% American Indian and Alaska Native, 0.4% Hispanic of any race, 0.0% two or more races (2000); Density: 73.9 persons per square mile (2000); Age: 33.1% under 18, 6.8% over 64 (2000); Marriage status: 21.9% never married, 67.1% now married, 2.9% widowed, 8.1% divorced (2000); Foreign born: 0.5% (2000); Ancestry (includes multiple ancestries): 45.8% German, 14.5% Norwegian, 12.2% Swedish, 6.1% Polish, 5.9% United States or American (2000).
Economy: Livestock, poultry; grain; dairying. Manufacturing: construction materials, feeds, cellulose insulation, machinery, plastic products, printing and publishing. Employment by occupation: 14.8% management, 12.8% professional, 10.9% services, 28.8% sales, 0.5% farming, 12.8% construction, 19.4% production (2000).
Income: Per capita income: $21,972 (2000); Median household income: $59,531 (2000); Poverty rate: 1.9% (2000).
Taxes: Total city taxes per capita: $66 (1997); City property taxes per capita: $66 (1997).
Education: High school graduation rate: 90.7% (2000); College graduation rate: 16.6% (2000).
Housing: Homeownership rate: 93.4% (2000); Median home value: $145,100 (2000); Median rent: $553 per month (2000); Median age of housing: 21 years (2000).
Transportation: Commute to work: 91.2% car, 0.0% public transportation, 1.4% walk, 6.7% work from home (2000); Travel time to work: 31.7% less than 15 minutes, 24.0% 15 to 30 minutes, 21.3% 30 to 45 minutes, 13.1% 45 to 60 minutes, 9.9% 60 minutes or more (2000)

CHATHAM (township). Covers a land area of 15.083 square miles and a water area of 2.267 square miles. Located at 45.17° N. Lat.; 93.94° W. Long.
Population: 1,162 (2000); Race: 98.6% White, 0.0% Black, 0.8% Asian, 0.2% American Indian and Alaska Native, 0.0% Hispanic of any race, 0.4% two or more races (2000); Density: 77.0 persons per square mile (2000); Age: 33.5% under 18, 6.2% over 64 (2000); Marriage status: 23.2% never married, 68.1% now married, 3.7% widowed, 5.0% divorced (2000); Foreign born: 1.0% (2000); Ancestry (includes multiple ancestries): 59.2% German, 18.5% Norwegian, 15.9% Irish, 13.3% Swedish, 6.7% French (except Basque) (2000).
Economy: Employment by occupation: 14.0% management, 21.4% professional, 9.5% services, 24.8% sales, 0.3% farming, 13.4% construction, 16.6% production (2000).
Income: Per capita income: $24,080 (2000); Median household income: $71,250 (2000); Poverty rate: 3.1% (2000).
Taxes: Total city taxes per capita: $29 (2000); City property taxes per capita: $28 (2000).
Education: High school graduation rate: 94.1% (2000); College graduation rate: 27.1% (2000).
Housing: Homeownership rate: 94.1% (2000); Median home value: $178,600 (2000); Median rent: $325 per month (2000); Median age of housing: 20 years (2000).
Transportation: Commute to work: 93.2% car, 0.3% public transportation, 0.5% walk, 6.0% work from home (2000); Travel time to work: 33.7% less than 15 minutes, 16.0% 15 to 30 minutes, 14.2% 30 to 45 minutes, 21.6% 45 to 60 minutes, 14.4% 60 minutes or more (2000)

CLEARWATER (city). Covers a land area of 1.158 square miles and a water area of 0.127 square miles. Located at 45.41° N. Lat.; 94.04° W. Long. Elevation is 960 feet.
Population: 858 (2000); Race: 96.3% White, 0.2% Black, 0.4% Asian, 1.0% American Indian and Alaska Native, 1.1% Hispanic of any race, 1.0% two or more races (2000); Density: 740.9 persons per square mile (2000); Age: 32.5% under 18, 8.8% over 64 (2000); Marriage status: 27.0% never married, 55.7% now married, 5.2% widowed, 12.1% divorced (2000); Foreign born: 1.2% (2000); Ancestry (includes multiple ancestries): 48.6% German, 11.2% Irish, 11.0% Norwegian, 8.1% Swedish, 7.9% English (2000).
Economy: Single-family building permits issued: 8 (2001) / 12 (2000); Multi-family building permits issued: 0 (2001) / 0 (2000); Employment by occupation: 8.3% management, 15.0% professional, 11.1% services, 24.3% sales, 0.0% farming, 15.0% construction, 26.4% production (2000).
Income: Per capita income: $17,325 (2000); Median household income: $41,696 (2000); Poverty rate: 9.3% (2000).
Taxes: Total city taxes per capita: $287 (1997); City property taxes per capita: $252 (1997).
Education: High school graduation rate: 86.7% (2000); College graduation rate: 11.7% (2000).
Housing: Homeownership rate: 73.5% (2000); Median home value: $96,300 (2000); Median rent: $418 per month (2000); Median age of housing: 17 years (2000).
Transportation: Commute to work: 91.3% car, 0.0% public transportation, 4.5% walk, 4.0% work from home (2000); Travel time to work: 27.7% less than 15 minutes, 36.8% 15 to 30 minutes, 13.2% 30 to 45 minutes, 9.6% 45 to 60 minutes, 12.6% 60 minutes or more (2000)

CLEARWATER (township). Covers a land area of 22.413 square miles and a water area of 1.438 square miles. Located at 45.36° N. Lat.; 94.02° W. Long. Elevation is 960 feet.
Population: 1,368 (2000); Race: 98.7% White, 0.0% Black, 0.1% Asian, 0.2% American Indian and Alaska Native, 0.1% Hispanic of any race, 0.8% two or more races (2000); Density: 61.0 persons per square mile (2000); Age: 28.8% under 18, 8.9% over 64 (2000); Marriage status: 20.7% never married, 70.4% now married, 3.0% widowed, 5.9% divorced (2000); Foreign born: 1.1% (2000); Ancestry (includes multiple ancestries): 53.3% German, 13.9% Norwegian, 10.2% Swedish, 8.1% Irish, 7.0% Polish (2000).
Economy: Grain; livestock, poultry; dairying. Manufacturing: plastic vacuum molding, feeds. Employment by occupation: 12.5% management, 16.8% professional, 11.9% services, 24.9% sales, 1.5% farming, 15.2% construction, 17.3% production (2000).
Income: Per capita income: $22,220 (2000); Median household income: $54,688 (2000); Poverty rate: 5.1% (2000).
Taxes: Total city taxes per capita: $119 (2000); City property taxes per capita: $118 (2000).
Education: High school graduation rate: 89.7% (2000); College graduation rate: 19.0% (2000).
Housing: Homeownership rate: 93.5% (2000); Median home value: $124,800 (2000); Median rent: $471 per month (2000); Median age of housing: 24 years (2000).
Transportation: Commute to work: 93.8% car, 0.0% public transportation, 0.8% walk, 4.1% work from home (2000); Travel time to work: 17.9% less than 15 minutes, 36.3% 15 to 30 minutes, 15.4% 30 to 45 minutes, 13.8% 45 to 60 minutes, 16.6% 60 minutes or more (2000)

COKATO (city). Covers a land area of 1.283 square miles and a water area of <.001 square miles. Located at 45.07° N. Lat.; 94.18° W. Long. Elevation is 1,052 feet.
History: Many of the early residents of Cokato were Swedish settlers, but later a number of Finns moved to the area. Early industry in Cokato included a cannery and a produce company dealing largely in poultry and eggs.
Population: 2,727 (2000); Race: 97.8% White, 0.1% Black, 0.8% Asian, 0.3% American Indian and Alaska Native, 1.9% Hispanic of any race, 0.3% two or more races (2000); Density: 2,125.8 persons per square mile (2000); Age: 31.6% under 18, 17.3% over 64 (2000); Marriage status: 22.5% never married, 58.4% now married, 11.2% widowed, 7.9% divorced (2000); Foreign born: 2.5% (2000); Ancestry (includes multiple ancestries): 32.1%

German, 23.8% Finnish, 23.1% Swedish, 13.5% Norwegian, 5.6% Irish (2000).
Economy: Single-family building permits issued: 7 (2001) / 10 (2000); Multi-family building permits issued: 0 (2001) / 0 (2000); Employment by occupation: 6.0% management, 21.6% professional, 13.8% services, 21.3% sales, 1.3% farming, 12.8% construction, 23.3% production (2000).
Income: Per capita income: $17,149 (2000); Median household income: $39,613 (2000); Poverty rate: 7.7% (2000).
Taxes: Total city taxes per capita: $185 (1997); City property taxes per capita: $179 (1997).
Education: High school graduation rate: 82.6% (2000); College graduation rate: 15.0% (2000).

School District(s)

Crow River Special Education Coop (PK-12)
2000 Enrollment: 93 320-587-6790
Dassel-Cokato (PK-12)
2000 Enrollment: 2,270 320-286-4100
Meeker & Wright Special Education Coop (PK-12)
2000 Enrollment: 95 320-286-2129

Housing: Homeownership rate: 69.8% (2000); Median home value: $102,300 (2000); Median rent: $350 per month (2000); Median age of housing: 32 years (2000).
Transportation: Commute to work: 92.4% car, 0.0% public transportation, 3.1% walk, 3.9% work from home (2000); Travel time to work: 52.6% less than 15 minutes, 13.9% 15 to 30 minutes, 13.5% 30 to 45 minutes, 8.7% 45 to 60 minutes, 11.2% 60 minutes or more (2000)

COKATO (township). Covers a land area of 32.991 square miles and a water area of 1.415 square miles. Located at 45.10° N. Lat.; 94.19° W. Long. Elevation is 1,052 feet.
History: Incorporated 1878.
Population: 1,238 (2000); Race: 99.7% White, 0.0% Black, 0.0% Asian, 0.0% American Indian and Alaska Native, 0.2% Hispanic of any race, 0.3% two or more races (2000); Density: 37.5 persons per square mile (2000); Age: 42.3% under 18, 6.8% over 64 (2000); Marriage status: 35.7% never married, 58.3% now married, 2.3% widowed, 3.6% divorced (2000); Foreign born: 1.1% (2000); Ancestry (includes multiple ancestries): 37.1% Finnish, 27.5% German, 21.4% Swedish, 11.5% Norwegian, 9.0% Irish (2000).
Economy: Trading and shipping point in agricultural area: dairying; poultry; vegetables, soybeans, grain, garlic. Manufacturing: prepared foods, animal feeds, fabricated metal products, electronic equipment. Employment by occupation: 9.3% management, 13.7% professional, 18.0% services, 23.3% sales, 3.3% farming, 15.0% construction, 17.4% production (2000).
Income: Per capita income: $15,863 (2000); Median household income: $50,139 (2000); Poverty rate: 5.5% (2000).
Taxes: Total city taxes per capita: $61 (2000); City property taxes per capita: $60 (2000).
Education: High school graduation rate: 91.6% (2000); College graduation rate: 13.9% (2000).
Housing: Homeownership rate: 90.5% (2000); Median home value: $125,900 (2000); Median rent: $371 per month (2000); Median age of housing: 47 years (2000).
Transportation: Commute to work: 92.1% car, 0.4% public transportation, 2.1% walk, 4.7% work from home (2000); Travel time to work: 45.4% less than 15 minutes, 18.9% 15 to 30 minutes, 13.8% 30 to 45 minutes, 5.5% 45 to 60 minutes, 16.5% 60 minutes or more (2000)

CORINNA (township). Covers a land area of 24.850 square miles and a water area of 8.495 square miles. Located at 45.28° N. Lat.; 94.07° W. Long.
Population: 2,457 (2000); Race: 99.2% White, 0.2% Black, 0.1% Asian, 0.0% American Indian and Alaska Native, 1.0% Hispanic of any race, 0.4% two or more races (2000); Density: 98.9 persons per square mile (2000); Age: 23.1% under 18, 14.9% over 64 (2000); Marriage status: 21.2% never married, 65.7% now married, 3.8% widowed, 9.3% divorced (2000); Foreign born: 0.3% (2000); Ancestry (includes multiple ancestries): 44.7% German, 15.1% Swedish, 14.4% Norwegian, 13.5% Irish, 7.7% English (2000).
Economy: Employment by occupation: 12.7% management, 17.1% professional, 11.2% services, 28.8% sales, 0.3% farming, 12.9% construction, 17.0% production (2000).
Income: Per capita income: $28,610 (2000); Median household income: $53,770 (2000); Poverty rate: 5.0% (2000).
Taxes: Total city taxes per capita: $214 (2000); City property taxes per capita: $214 (2000).
Education: High school graduation rate: 92.6% (2000); College graduation rate: 17.9% (2000).
Housing: Homeownership rate: 93.9% (2000); Median home value: $154,200 (2000); Median rent: $481 per month (2000); Median age of housing: 32 years (2000).
Transportation: Commute to work: 92.7% car, 0.9% public transportation, 0.8% walk, 4.4% work from home (2000); Travel time to work: 27.2% less than 15 minutes, 24.9% 15 to 30 minutes, 17.4% 30 to 45 minutes, 10.2% 45 to 60 minutes, 20.2% 60 minutes or more (2000)

DELANO (city). Covers a land area of 2.570 square miles and a water area of 0 square miles. Located at 45.04° N. Lat.; 93.78° W. Long. Elevation is 944 feet.
History: Incorporated 1885.
Population: 3,837 (2000); Race: 98.9% White, 0.0% Black, 0.1% Asian, 0.2% American Indian and Alaska Native, 1.0% Hispanic of any race, 0.7% two or more races (2000); Density: 1,492.8 persons per square mile (2000); Age: 33.0% under 18, 7.1% over 64 (2000); Marriage status: 25.3% never married, 61.0% now married, 6.3% widowed, 7.3% divorced (2000); Foreign born: 0.8% (2000); Ancestry (includes multiple ancestries): 48.1% German, 16.4% Norwegian, 13.1% Swedish, 12.0% Irish, 8.0% Polish (2000).
Economy: Grain, soybeans; livestock, poultry; dairying. Manufacturing: wood products, concrete, chemicals. Single-family building permits issued: 35 (2001) / 24 (2000); Multi-family building permits issued: 0 (2001) / 0 (2000); Employment by occupation: 14.6% management, 18.7% professional, 11.6% services, 26.6% sales, 0.0% farming, 11.2% construction, 17.3% production (2000).
Income: Per capita income: $21,538 (2000); Median household income: $52,917 (2000); Poverty rate: 2.7% (2000).
Taxes: Total city taxes per capita: $139 (1997); City property taxes per capita: $93 (1997).
Education: High school graduation rate: 91.3% (2000); College graduation rate: 23.9% (2000).

School District(s)

Delano (PK-12)
2000 Enrollment: 1,870 763-972-3365

Housing: Homeownership rate: 77.3% (2000); Median home value: $135,100 (2000); Median rent: $451 per month (2000); Median age of housing: 24 years (2000).
Newspapers: Delano Eagle (1 x week)
Transportation: Commute to work: 92.8% car, 0.5% public transportation, 2.7% walk, 3.8% work from home (2000); Travel time to work: 26.8% less than 15 minutes, 25.0% 15 to 30 minutes, 29.5% 30 to 45 minutes, 15.6% 45 to 60 minutes, 3.2% 60 minutes or more (2000)
Additional Information Contacts
Delano Chamber of Commerce 763-972-6756

FRANKLIN (township). Covers a land area of 42.833 square miles and a water area of 1.089 square miles. Located at 45.03° N. Lat.; 93.84° W. Long.
Population: 2,774 (2000); Race: 97.9% White, 0.3% Black, 0.1% Asian, 0.4% American Indian and Alaska Native, 1.9% Hispanic of any race, 0.7% two or more races (2000); Density: 64.8 persons per square mile (2000); Age: 28.8% under 18, 10.6% over 64 (2000); Marriage status: 22.8% never married, 67.8% now married, 5.4% widowed, 4.0% divorced (2000); Foreign born: 1.0% (2000); Ancestry (includes multiple ancestries): 53.1% German, 13.5% Norwegian, 12.7% Polish, 9.8% Swedish, 9.3% Irish (2000).
Economy: Employment by occupation: 15.1% management, 15.2% professional, 10.6% services, 26.4% sales, 1.3% farming, 14.0% construction, 17.3% production (2000).
Income: Per capita income: $27,429 (2000); Median household income: $68,750 (2000); Poverty rate: 1.7% (2000).
Taxes: Total city taxes per capita: $73 (2000); City property taxes per capita: $73 (2000).
Education: High school graduation rate: 89.1% (2000); College graduation rate: 17.2% (2000).
Housing: Homeownership rate: 94.2% (2000); Median home value: $157,200 (2000); Median rent: $525 per month (2000); Median age of housing: 27 years (2000).
Transportation: Commute to work: 90.8% car, 0.7% public transportation, 1.0% walk, 6.5% work from home (2000); Travel time to work: 23.8% less than 15 minutes, 24.0% 15 to 30 minutes, 26.9% 30 to 45 minutes, 16.6% 45 to 60 minutes, 8.6% 60 minutes or more (2000)

FRENCH LAKE (township). Covers a land area of 33.469 square miles and a water area of 2.002 square miles. Located at 45.19° N. Lat.; 94.19° W. Long. Elevation is 1,061 feet.
Population: 1,130 (2000); Race: 99.0% White, 0.4% Black, 0.0% Asian, 0.0% American Indian and Alaska Native, 0.0% Hispanic of any race, 0.6%

two or more races (2000); Density: 33.8 persons per square mile (2000); Age: 30.6% under 18, 13.5% over 64 (2000); Marriage status: 18.5% never married, 71.1% now married, 4.3% widowed, 6.1% divorced (2000); Foreign born: 1.1% (2000); Ancestry (includes multiple ancestries): 35.1% German, 21.6% Finnish, 17.3% Swedish, 14.3% Norwegian, 7.1% Irish (2000).
Economy: Employment by occupation: 15.1% management, 16.7% professional, 9.2% services, 23.0% sales, 2.2% farming, 11.5% construction, 22.3% production (2000).
Income: Per capita income: $23,488 (2000); Median household income: $57,708 (2000); Poverty rate: 8.3% (2000).
Taxes: Total city taxes per capita: $95 (2000); City property taxes per capita: $95 (2000).
Education: High school graduation rate: 81.1% (2000); College graduation rate: 17.4% (2000).
Housing: Homeownership rate: 93.1% (2000); Median home value: $134,600 (2000); Median rent: $325 per month (2000); Median age of housing: 28 years (2000).
Transportation: Commute to work: 89.8% car, 0.0% public transportation, 1.5% walk, 7.5% work from home (2000); Travel time to work: 17.5% less than 15 minutes, 31.8% 15 to 30 minutes, 15.7% 30 to 45 minutes, 11.2% 45 to 60 minutes, 23.8% 60 minutes or more (2000)

HANOVER (city). Covers a land area of 4.892 square miles and a water area of 0.239 square miles. Located at 45.16° N. Lat.; 93.66° W. Long. Elevation is 916 feet.
Population: 1,355 (2000); Race: 98.2% White, 0.0% Black, 1.1% Asian, 0.0% American Indian and Alaska Native, 0.4% Hispanic of any race, 0.4% two or more races (2000); Density: 277.0 persons per square mile (2000); Age: 34.2% under 18, 5.2% over 64 (2000); Marriage status: 19.1% never married, 72.2% now married, 2.8% widowed, 6.0% divorced (2000); Foreign born: 2.0% (2000); Ancestry (includes multiple ancestries): 47.7% German, 21.3% Norwegian, 12.2% Swedish, 9.7% Irish, 6.3% United States or American (2000).
Economy: Single-family building permits issued: 82 (2001) / 64 (2000); Multi-family building permits issued: 0 (2001) / 0 (2000); Employment by occupation: 12.9% management, 20.5% professional, 11.7% services, 27.4% sales, 0.9% farming, 9.8% construction, 16.8% production (2000).
Income: Per capita income: $27,826 (2000); Median household income: $73,667 (2000); Poverty rate: 0.9% (2000).
Taxes: Total city taxes per capita: $145 (1997); City property taxes per capita: $115 (1997).
Education: High school graduation rate: 92.2% (2000); College graduation rate: 23.2% (2000).
Housing: Homeownership rate: 93.4% (2000); Median home value: $170,000 (2000); Median rent: $396 per month (2000); Median age of housing: 13 years (2000).
Transportation: Commute to work: 93.8% car, 0.9% public transportation, 0.7% walk, 4.2% work from home (2000); Travel time to work: 12.5% less than 15 minutes, 27.5% 15 to 30 minutes, 33.9% 30 to 45 minutes, 19.4% 45 to 60 minutes, 6.7% 60 minutes or more (2000)

HOWARD LAKE (city). Covers a land area of 1.319 square miles and a water area of 0.273 square miles. Located at 45.06° N. Lat.; 94.06° W. Long. Elevation is 1,018 feet.
Population: 1,853 (2000); Race: 97.3% White, 0.4% Black, 0.0% Asian, 0.3% American Indian and Alaska Native, 1.9% Hispanic of any race, 1.2% two or more races (2000); Density: 1,405.2 persons per square mile (2000); Age: 28.3% under 18, 14.4% over 64 (2000); Marriage status: 22.8% never married, 59.3% now married, 6.9% widowed, 11.0% divorced (2000); Foreign born: 1.0% (2000); Ancestry (includes multiple ancestries): 51.6% German, 10.8% Swedish, 10.3% Norwegian, 9.3% Irish, 5.1% Other groups (2000).
Economy: Diversified-farming area: poultry; grain, soybeans; dairying. Manufacturing: feeds, kitchen cabinets, pewter awards, egg processing, wooden wagon wheels. Single-family building permits issued: 12 (2001) / 5 (2000); Multi-family building permits issued: 8 (2001) / 0 (2000); Employment by occupation: 7.6% management, 15.7% professional, 10.7% services, 27.0% sales, 1.7% farming, 13.0% construction, 24.3% production (2000).
Income: Per capita income: $17,900 (2000); Median household income: $38,015 (2000); Poverty rate: 9.4% (2000).
Taxes: Total city taxes per capita: $243 (1997); City property taxes per capita: $227 (1997).
Education: High school graduation rate: 81.7% (2000); College graduation rate: 9.4% (2000).

School District(s)

Howard Lake-Waverly-Winsted (PK-12)
2000 Enrollment: 933 320-543-3521
Housing: Homeownership rate: 72.1% (2000); Median home value: $96,400 (2000); Median rent: $431 per month (2000); Median age of housing: 30 years (2000).
Newspapers: Howard Lake - Waverly Herald (1 x week)
Transportation: Commute to work: 92.1% car, 0.0% public transportation, 4.1% walk, 2.7% work from home (2000); Travel time to work: 36.8% less than 15 minutes, 15.8% 15 to 30 minutes, 16.2% 30 to 45 minutes, 15.8% 45 to 60 minutes, 15.4% 60 minutes or more (2000)

MAPLE LAKE (city). Covers a land area of 1.924 square miles and a water area of 0.032 square miles. Located at 45.23° N. Lat.; 94.00° W. Long.
Population: 1,633 (2000); Race: 97.4% White, 0.7% Black, 0.2% Asian, 0.3% American Indian and Alaska Native, 1.5% Hispanic of any race, 1.0% two or more races (2000); Density: 848.9 persons per square mile (2000); Age: 30.8% under 18, 13.3% over 64 (2000); Marriage status: 26.3% never married, 55.6% now married, 8.6% widowed, 9.4% divorced (2000); Foreign born: 1.2% (2000); Ancestry (includes multiple ancestries): 51.3% German, 19.8% Irish, 10.3% Norwegian, 7.3% French (except Basque), 6.1% Swedish (2000).
Economy: Single-family building permits issued: 10 (2001) / 9 (2000); Multi-family building permits issued: 2 (2001) / 0 (2000); Employment by occupation: 10.4% management, 8.5% professional, 17.5% services, 25.8% sales, 1.1% farming, 15.3% construction, 21.5% production (2000).
Income: Per capita income: $17,476 (2000); Median household income: $43,047 (2000); Poverty rate: 5.5% (2000).
Taxes: Total city taxes per capita: $281 (1997); City property taxes per capita: $265 (1997).
Education: High school graduation rate: 83.0% (2000); College graduation rate: 10.2% (2000).

School District(s)

Maple Lake (PK-12)
2000 Enrollment: 910 320-963-3171
Housing: Homeownership rate: 74.8% (2000); Median home value: $104,300 (2000); Median rent: $336 per month (2000); Median age of housing: 29 years (2000).
Newspapers: Maple Lake Messenger (1 x week)
Transportation: Commute to work: 89.4% car, 0.0% public transportation, 5.7% walk, 4.4% work from home (2000); Travel time to work: 33.2% less than 15 minutes, 19.9% 15 to 30 minutes, 13.2% 30 to 45 minutes, 17.5% 45 to 60 minutes, 16.3% 60 minutes or more (2000)

MAPLE LAKE (township). Covers a land area of 31.770 square miles and a water area of 2.881 square miles. Located at 45.23° N. Lat.; 93.94° W. Long.
Population: 2,128 (2000); Race: 97.8% White, 0.2% Black, 0.1% Asian, 0.4% American Indian and Alaska Native, 1.1% Hispanic of any race, 0.9% two or more races (2000); Density: 67.0 persons per square mile (2000); Age: 28.0% under 18, 9.7% over 64 (2000); Marriage status: 20.2% never married, 71.7% now married, 3.1% widowed, 5.0% divorced (2000); Foreign born: 0.7% (2000); Ancestry (includes multiple ancestries): 46.7% German, 16.1% Irish, 11.3% Norwegian, 7.4% Swedish, 7.0% French (except Basque) (2000).
Economy: Grain, soybeans; livestock, poultry; dairying. Manufacturing: metal fabrication; frozen foods, consumer goods, feeds and fertilizers, boats. Employment by occupation: 15.0% management, 17.9% professional, 10.0% services, 27.5% sales, 0.1% farming, 12.0% construction, 17.5% production (2000).
Income: Per capita income: $23,773 (2000); Median household income: $60,208 (2000); Poverty rate: 4.2% (2000).
Taxes: Total city taxes per capita: $109 (2000); City property taxes per capita: $109 (2000).
Education: High school graduation rate: 86.8% (2000); College graduation rate: 14.9% (2000).
Housing: Homeownership rate: 96.4% (2000); Median home value: $146,500 (2000); Median rent: $394 per month (2000); Median age of housing: 28 years (2000).
Transportation: Commute to work: 90.9% car, 0.2% public transportation, 1.6% walk, 6.8% work from home (2000); Travel time to work: 29.1% less than 15 minutes, 25.0% 15 to 30 minutes, 12.7% 30 to 45 minutes, 15.0% 45 to 60 minutes, 18.1% 60 minutes or more (2000)

MARYSVILLE (township). Covers a land area of 32.554 square miles and a water area of 1.336 square miles. Located at 45.09° N. Lat.; 93.94° W. Long.
Population: 2,097 (2000); Race: 97.4% White, 0.0% Black, 0.1% Asian, 1.0% American Indian and Alaska Native, 2.5% Hispanic of any race, 1.1% two or more races (2000); Density: 64.4 persons per square mile (2000); Age: 30.7% under 18, 7.2% over 64 (2000); Marriage status: 25.0% never married, 64.1% now married, 3.3% widowed, 7.6% divorced (2000); Foreign born: 0.9% (2000); Ancestry (includes multiple ancestries): 46.4% German, 14.2% Swedish, 13.8% Norwegian, 13.3% Irish, 7.2% French (except Basque) (2000).
Economy: Employment by occupation: 10.5% management, 13.7% professional, 12.7% services, 23.9% sales, 0.7% farming, 13.3% construction, 25.2% production (2000).
Income: Per capita income: $21,171 (2000); Median household income: $53,011 (2000); Poverty rate: 9.5% (2000).
Taxes: Total city taxes per capita: $40 (1997); City property taxes per capita: $40 (1997).
Education: High school graduation rate: 84.3% (2000); College graduation rate: 11.5% (2000).
Housing: Homeownership rate: 95.3% (2000); Median home value: $135,300 (2000); Median rent: $425 per month (2000); Median age of housing: 25 years (2000).
Transportation: Commute to work: 89.7% car, 0.5% public transportation, 1.4% walk, 7.4% work from home (2000); Travel time to work: 24.0% less than 15 minutes, 25.0% 15 to 30 minutes, 19.0% 30 to 45 minutes, 18.0% 45 to 60 minutes, 13.9% 60 minutes or more (2000)

MIDDLEVILLE (township). Covers a land area of 33.632 square miles and a water area of 1.911 square miles. Located at 45.09° N. Lat.; 94.08° W. Long.
Population: 925 (2000); Race: 97.6% White, 0.0% Black, 1.1% Asian, 0.6% American Indian and Alaska Native, 0.0% Hispanic of any race, 0.6% two or more races (2000); Density: 27.5 persons per square mile (2000); Age: 29.7% under 18, 13.2% over 64 (2000); Marriage status: 22.0% never married, 70.1% now married, 3.0% widowed, 4.9% divorced (2000); Foreign born: 2.8% (2000); Ancestry (includes multiple ancestries): 46.2% German, 17.6% Norwegian, 15.1% Swedish, 8.3% Irish, 6.3% English (2000).
Economy: Single-family building permits issued: 3 (2001) / 7 (2000); Multi-family building permits issued: 0 (2001) / 0 (2000); Employment by occupation: 17.3% management, 14.1% professional, 11.6% services, 23.7% sales, 0.4% farming, 12.9% construction, 20.0% production (2000).
Income: Per capita income: $18,850 (2000); Median household income: $50,833 (2000); Poverty rate: 2.2% (2000).
Taxes: Total city taxes per capita: $88 (1997); City property taxes per capita: $84 (1997).
Education: High school graduation rate: 86.0% (2000); College graduation rate: 14.7% (2000).
Housing: Homeownership rate: 89.0% (2000); Median home value: $137,000 (2000); Median rent: $475 per month (2000); Median age of housing: 43 years (2000).
Transportation: Commute to work: 89.4% car, 0.2% public transportation, 2.3% walk, 8.1% work from home (2000); Travel time to work: 37.7% less than 15 minutes, 23.0% 15 to 30 minutes, 13.4% 30 to 45 minutes, 9.5% 45 to 60 minutes, 16.4% 60 minutes or more (2000)

MONTICELLO (city). Covers a land area of 6.222 square miles and a water area of 0 square miles. Located at 45.30° N. Lat.; 93.79° W. Long. Elevation is 933 feet.
Population: 7,868 (2000); Race: 97.4% White, 0.5% Black, 0.2% Asian, 0.6% American Indian and Alaska Native, 2.1% Hispanic of any race, 0.6% two or more races (2000); Density: 1,264.6 persons per square mile (2000); Age: 31.8% under 18, 8.7% over 64 (2000); Marriage status: 23.9% never married, 60.1% now married, 5.9% widowed, 10.1% divorced (2000); Foreign born: 1.9% (2000); Ancestry (includes multiple ancestries): 46.1% German, 17.3% Norwegian, 13.2% Irish, 10.4% Swedish, 5.8% Polish (2000).
Economy: Single-family building permits issued: 222 (2001) / 148 (2000); Multi-family building permits issued: 20 (2001) / 70 (2000); Employment by occupation: 11.4% management, 17.1% professional, 15.0% services, 29.2% sales, 0.4% farming, 10.2% construction, 16.6% production (2000).
Income: Per capita income: $19,229 (2000); Median household income: $45,384 (2000); Poverty rate: 4.6% (2000).
Taxes: Total city taxes per capita: $734 (1997); City property taxes per capita: $699 (1997).
Education: High school graduation rate: 84.2% (2000); College graduation rate: 21.2% (2000).

School District(s)

Monticello (PK-12)
2000 Enrollment: 3,809 763-271-0300
Housing: Homeownership rate: 72.0% (2000); Median home value: $130,200 (2000); Median rent: $527 per month (2000); Median age of housing: 13 years (2000).
Hospitals: Monticello-Big Lake Community Hospital (39 beds)
Newspapers: Monticello Times (1 x week); Monticello Shopper (1 x week)
Transportation: Commute to work: 94.9% car, 0.3% public transportation, 1.1% walk, 3.0% work from home (2000); Travel time to work: 35.6% less than 15 minutes, 18.8% 15 to 30 minutes, 23.5% 30 to 45 minutes, 15.8% 45 to 60 minutes, 6.3% 60 minutes or more (2000)
Additional Information Contacts
Monticello Area Chamber of Commerce 763-295-2700

MONTICELLO (township). Covers a land area of 40.113 square miles and a water area of 3.334 square miles. Located at 45.27° N. Lat.; 93.80° W. Long. Elevation is 933 feet.
History: Incorporated 1856.
Population: 4,139 (2000); Race: 97.5% White, 1.0% Black, 0.2% Asian, 0.5% American Indian and Alaska Native, 0.8% Hispanic of any race, 0.0% two or more races (2000); Density: 103.2 persons per square mile (2000); Age: 31.0% under 18, 5.9% over 64 (2000); Marriage status: 24.3% never married, 65.2% now married, 3.8% widowed, 6.8% divorced (2000); Foreign born: 1.3% (2000); Ancestry (includes multiple ancestries): 51.1% German, 15.7% Norwegian, 12.5% Irish, 10.5% Swedish, 6.1% Polish (2000).
Economy: Grain, soybeans; livestock; dairying. Manufacturing: molded products, hand tools, cabinets, fabicated structural metals. Sherburn National Wildlife Refuge to Northeast. Nuclear Power Plant. Employment by occupation: 12.6% management, 13.0% professional, 14.1% services, 23.6% sales, 0.7% farming, 11.4% construction, 24.6% production (2000).
Income: Per capita income: $21,154 (2000); Median household income: $57,527 (2000); Poverty rate: 3.6% (2000).
Taxes: Total city taxes per capita: $33 (2000); City property taxes per capita: $33 (2000).
Education: High school graduation rate: 89.1% (2000); College graduation rate: 12.9% (2000).
Housing: Homeownership rate: 95.3% (2000); Median home value: $137,800 (2000); Median rent: $537 per month (2000); Median age of housing: 21 years (2000).
Transportation: Commute to work: 94.7% car, 0.0% public transportation, 1.2% walk, 4.1% work from home (2000); Travel time to work: 32.0% less than 15 minutes, 23.6% 15 to 30 minutes, 20.7% 30 to 45 minutes, 15.3% 45 to 60 minutes, 8.5% 60 minutes or more (2000)

MONTROSE (city). Covers a land area of 0.960 square miles and a water area of 0.010 square miles. Located at 45.06° N. Lat.; 93.91° W. Long.
Population: 1,143 (2000); Race: 98.1% White, 0.2% Black, 0.1% Asian, 0.0% American Indian and Alaska Native, 1.5% Hispanic of any race, 0.2% two or more races (2000); Density: 1,190.4 persons per square mile (2000); Age: 28.9% under 18, 8.7% over 64 (2000); Marriage status: 26.5% never married, 56.0% now married, 5.7% widowed, 11.8% divorced (2000); Foreign born: 0.3% (2000); Ancestry (includes multiple ancestries): 46.6% German, 12.7% Irish, 11.2% Norwegian, 7.5% Swedish, 6.7% Polish (2000).
Economy: Poultry. Dairying. Manufacturing of speaker systems, color dispensers. Single-family building permits issued: 101 (2001) / 42 (2000); Multi-family building permits issued: 0 (2001) / 0 (2000); Employment by occupation: 9.4% management, 12.0% professional, 12.1% services, 23.5% sales, 0.3% farming, 16.9% construction, 25.7% production (2000).
Income: Per capita income: $19,281 (2000); Median household income: $39,583 (2000); Poverty rate: 6.4% (2000).
Taxes: Total city taxes per capita: $134 (1997); City property taxes per capita: $115 (1997).
Education: High school graduation rate: 83.8% (2000); College graduation rate: 10.5% (2000).
Housing: Homeownership rate: 74.4% (2000); Median home value: $105,800 (2000); Median rent: $445 per month (2000); Median age of housing: 19 years (2000).
Transportation: Commute to work: 94.8% car, 0.7% public transportation, 1.5% walk, 2.6% work from home (2000); Travel time to work: 16.0% less than 15 minutes, 28.9% 15 to 30 minutes, 27.1% 30 to 45 minutes, 18.0% 45 to 60 minutes, 10.1% 60 minutes or more (2000)

OTSEGO (city). Covers a land area of 29.370 square miles and a water area of 0.973 square miles. Located at 45.27° N. Lat.; 93.59° W. Long. Elevation is 889 feet.

Population: 6,389 (2000); Race: 97.7% White, 0.6% Black, 0.0% Asian, 0.0% American Indian and Alaska Native, 1.4% Hispanic of any race, 1.3% two or more races (2000); Density: 217.5 persons per square mile (2000); Age: 32.6% under 18, 4.1% over 64 (2000); Marriage status: 24.8% never married, 67.5% now married, 2.3% widowed, 5.4% divorced (2000); Foreign born: 0.5% (2000); Ancestry (includes multiple ancestries): 45.4% German, 18.8% Norwegian, 11.0% Irish, 8.4% Swedish, 5.5% English (2000).

Economy: On fringe of Minneapolis-St. Paul (Twin Cities) urban area. Agriculture includes dairying; poultry, livestock; grain, soybeans. Single-family building permits issued: 48 (2001) / 46 (2000); Multi-family building permits issued: 0 (2001) / 0 (2000); Employment by occupation: 12.3% management, 15.4% professional, 11.2% services, 22.4% sales, 0.0% farming, 14.4% construction, 24.3% production (2000).

Income: Per capita income: $20,209 (2000); Median household income: $57,422 (2000); Poverty rate: 3.2% (2000).

Taxes: Total city taxes per capita: $134 (1997); City property taxes per capita: $125 (1997).

Education: High school graduation rate: 91.2% (2000); College graduation rate: 13.4% (2000).

Housing: Homeownership rate: 96.6% (2000); Median home value: $132,700 (2000); Median rent: $513 per month (2000); Median age of housing: 21 years (2000).

Transportation: Commute to work: 91.4% car, 0.6% public transportation, 1.0% walk, 5.7% work from home (2000); Travel time to work: 24.9% less than 15 minutes, 27.4% 15 to 30 minutes, 26.6% 30 to 45 minutes, 13.5% 45 to 60 minutes, 7.6% 60 minutes or more (2000)

ROCKFORD (city). Covers a land area of 1.724 square miles and a water area of 0.060 square miles. Located at 45.09° N. Lat.; 93.73° W. Long.

Population: 3,484 (2000); Race: 96.1% White, 0.0% Black, 0.3% Asian, 1.5% American Indian and Alaska Native, 1.7% Hispanic of any race, 1.5% two or more races (2000); Density: 2,021.2 persons per square mile (2000); Age: 31.5% under 18, 4.5% over 64 (2000); Marriage status: 24.5% never married, 58.4% now married, 2.7% widowed, 14.4% divorced (2000); Foreign born: 1.4% (2000); Ancestry (includes multiple ancestries): 43.4% German, 20.6% Norwegian, 12.3% Irish, 9.7% Swedish, 6.7% English (2000).

Economy: Single-family building permits issued: 26 (2001) / 63 (2000); Multi-family building permits issued: 7 (2001) / 0 (2000); Employment by occupation: 13.0% management, 15.2% professional, 10.9% services, 27.8% sales, 0.5% farming, 11.6% construction, 21.0% production (2000).

Income: Per capita income: $20,675 (2000); Median household income: $51,349 (2000); Poverty rate: 6.5% (2000).

Taxes: Total city taxes per capita: $232 (1997); City property taxes per capita: $207 (1997).

Education: High school graduation rate: 87.7% (2000); College graduation rate: 14.7% (2000).

School District(s)

Rockford (PK-12)
2000 Enrollment: 1,753 763-477-9165

Housing: Homeownership rate: 81.1% (2000); Median home value: $140,600 (2000); Median rent: $435 per month (2000); Median age of housing: 14 years (2000).

Transportation: Commute to work: 95.9% car, 0.6% public transportation, 1.3% walk, 1.9% work from home (2000); Travel time to work: 19.7% less than 15 minutes, 29.2% 15 to 30 minutes, 30.3% 30 to 45 minutes, 15.7% 45 to 60 minutes, 5.1% 60 minutes or more (2000)

ROCKFORD (township). Covers a land area of 34.726 square miles and a water area of 2.081 square miles. Located at 45.12° N. Lat.; 93.79° W. Long.

Population: 3,444 (2000); Race: 98.2% White, 0.5% Black, 0.5% Asian, 0.0% American Indian and Alaska Native, 0.0% Hispanic of any race, 0.8% two or more races (2000); Density: 99.2 persons per square mile (2000); Age: 28.8% under 18, 6.2% over 64 (2000); Marriage status: 24.6% never married, 65.5% now married, 2.5% widowed, 7.4% divorced (2000); Foreign born: 1.6% (2000); Ancestry (includes multiple ancestries): 52.9% German, 17.4% Irish, 12.5% Norwegian, 12.3% Swedish, 7.3% English (2000).

Economy: Employment by occupation: 16.6% management, 16.5% professional, 10.7% services, 26.4% sales, 0.5% farming, 15.9% construction, 13.4% production (2000).

Income: Per capita income: $30,536 (2000); Median household income: $67,708 (2000); Poverty rate: 1.9% (2000).

Taxes: Total city taxes per capita: $153 (2000); City property taxes per capita: $153 (2000).

Education: High school graduation rate: 90.4% (2000); College graduation rate: 18.5% (2000).

Housing: Homeownership rate: 96.3% (2000); Median home value: $145,100 (2000); Median rent: $308 per month (2000); Median age of housing: 25 years (2000).

Transportation: Commute to work: 90.7% car, 0.2% public transportation, 0.2% walk, 8.9% work from home (2000); Travel time to work: 18.7% less than 15 minutes, 31.7% 15 to 30 minutes, 20.8% 30 to 45 minutes, 22.0% 45 to 60 minutes, 6.9% 60 minutes or more (2000)

SAINT MICHAEL (city). Covers a land area of 32.564 square miles and a water area of 3.842 square miles. Located at 45.20° N. Lat.; 93.67° W. Long.

Population: 9,099 (2000); Race: 99.4% White, 0.0% Black, 0.1% Asian, 0.0% American Indian and Alaska Native, 0.6% Hispanic of any race, 0.4% two or more races (2000); Density: 279.4 persons per square mile (2000); Age: 33.8% under 18, 5.5% over 64 (2000); Marriage status: 21.1% never married, 70.9% now married, 2.3% widowed, 5.8% divorced (2000); Foreign born: 0.1% (2000); Ancestry (includes multiple ancestries): 50.9% German, 13.2% Irish, 11.7% Norwegian, 8.7% Swedish, 6.2% French (except Basque) (2000).

Economy: Single-family building permits issued: 400 (2001) / 398 (2000); Multi-family building permits issued: 0 (2001) / 0 (2000); Employment by occupation: 16.3% management, 16.9% professional, 10.8% services, 29.5% sales, 0.2% farming, 11.0% construction, 15.2% production (2000).

Income: Per capita income: $24,742 (2000); Median household income: $69,903 (2000); Poverty rate: 2.7% (2000).

Education: High school graduation rate: 92.5% (2000); College graduation rate: 22.9% (2000).

School District(s)

Saint Michael-Albertville (PK-12)
2000 Enrollment: 2,879 763-497-3180

Housing: Homeownership rate: 91.0% (2000); Median home value: $156,500 (2000); Median rent: $547 per month (2000); Median age of housing: 11 years (2000).

Transportation: Commute to work: 91.3% car, 0.6% public transportation, 0.9% walk, 6.9% work from home (2000); Travel time to work: 22.4% less than 15 minutes, 28.2% 15 to 30 minutes, 28.2% 30 to 45 minutes, 14.3% 45 to 60 minutes, 7.0% 60 minutes or more (2000)

Additional Information Contacts

Saint Michael Area Chamber 763-497-7848

SILVER CREEK (township). Covers a land area of 36.009 square miles and a water area of 3.178 square miles. Located at 45.33° N. Lat.; 93.96° W. Long. Elevation is 1,013 feet.

Population: 2,332 (2000); Race: 99.3% White, 0.1% Black, 0.1% Asian, 0.0% American Indian and Alaska Native, 0.7% Hispanic of any race, 0.4% two or more races (2000); Density: 64.8 persons per square mile (2000); Age: 30.9% under 18, 7.1% over 64 (2000); Marriage status: 22.5% never married, 68.6% now married, 3.6% widowed, 5.3% divorced (2000); Foreign born: 0.7% (2000); Ancestry (includes multiple ancestries): 45.0% German, 14.9% Norwegian, 14.1% Swedish, 11.5% Irish, 6.3% English (2000).

Economy: Employment by occupation: 15.2% management, 17.8% professional, 12.0% services, 22.7% sales, 1.4% farming, 11.3% construction, 19.6% production (2000).

Income: Per capita income: $23,430 (2000); Median household income: $60,511 (2000); Poverty rate: 3.7% (2000).

Taxes: Total city taxes per capita: $143 (2000); City property taxes per capita: $142 (2000).

Education: High school graduation rate: 89.4% (2000); College graduation rate: 18.0% (2000).

Housing: Homeownership rate: 94.0% (2000); Median home value: $136,400 (2000); Median rent: $488 per month (2000); Median age of housing: 25 years (2000).

Transportation: Commute to work: 93.7% car, 0.0% public transportation, 2.0% walk, 4.0% work from home (2000); Travel time to work: 22.4% less than 15 minutes, 33.3% 15 to 30 minutes, 18.0% 30 to 45 minutes, 12.0% 45 to 60 minutes, 14.3% 60 minutes or more (2000)

SOUTH HAVEN (city). Covers a land area of 0.632 square miles and a water area of 0 square miles. Located at 45.29° N. Lat.; 94.21° W. Long. Elevation is 1,102 feet.

Population: 204 (2000); Race: 96.5% White, 3.5% Black, 0.0% Asian, 0.0% American Indian and Alaska Native, 0.0% Hispanic of any race, 0.0% two or more races (2000); Density: 322.7 persons per square mile (2000); Age: 29.3% under 18, 17.2% over 64 (2000); Marriage status: 28.4% never married, 56.1% now married, 10.3% widowed, 5.2% divorced (2000); Foreign born: 4.5% (2000); Ancestry (includes multiple ancestries): 35.9% German, 14.1% Irish, 11.6% Norwegian, 11.1% Swedish, 7.6% English (2000).
Economy: Corn, oats; livestock, poultry; dairying. Single-family building permits issued: 0 (2001) / 1 (2000); Multi-family building permits issued: 0 (2001) / 0 (2000); Employment by occupation: 8.7% management, 5.8% professional, 8.7% services, 37.7% sales, 4.3% farming, 17.4% construction, 17.4% production (2000).
Income: Per capita income: $12,751 (2000); Median household income: $26,250 (2000); Poverty rate: 12.1% (2000).
Taxes: Total city taxes per capita: $65 (1997); City property taxes per capita: $60 (1997).
Education: High school graduation rate: 72.0% (2000); College graduation rate: 3.4% (2000).
Housing: Homeownership rate: 82.9% (2000); Median home value: $76,700 (2000); Median rent: $375 per month (2000); Median age of housing: 60+ years (2000).
Transportation: Commute to work: 94.2% car, 0.0% public transportation, 5.8% walk, 0.0% work from home (2000); Travel time to work: 27.5% less than 15 minutes, 11.6% 15 to 30 minutes, 17.4% 30 to 45 minutes, 15.9% 45 to 60 minutes, 27.5% 60 minutes or more (2000)

SOUTHSIDE (township). Covers a land area of 24.322 square miles and a water area of 4.060 square miles. Located at 45.27° N. Lat.; 94.19° W. Long.
Population: 1,576 (2000); Race: 99.5% White, 0.1% Black, 0.1% Asian, 0.0% American Indian and Alaska Native, 0.2% Hispanic of any race, 0.1% two or more races (2000); Density: 64.8 persons per square mile (2000); Age: 27.9% under 18, 12.5% over 64 (2000); Marriage status: 20.1% never married, 70.2% now married, 3.5% widowed, 6.1% divorced (2000); Foreign born: 0.4% (2000); Ancestry (includes multiple ancestries): 42.9% German, 16.6% Norwegian, 16.4% Swedish, 10.3% Irish, 7.9% Finnish (2000).
Economy: Employment by occupation: 12.7% management, 19.0% professional, 9.1% services, 23.5% sales, 0.8% farming, 13.2% construction, 21.7% production (2000).
Income: Per capita income: $23,607 (2000); Median household income: $51,875 (2000); Poverty rate: 4.7% (2000).
Taxes: Total city taxes per capita: $89 (1997); City property taxes per capita: $89 (1997).
Education: High school graduation rate: 88.6% (2000); College graduation rate: 22.3% (2000).
Housing: Homeownership rate: 91.5% (2000); Median home value: $148,500 (2000); Median rent: $462 per month (2000); Median age of housing: 33 years (2000).
Transportation: Commute to work: 93.7% car, 0.3% public transportation, 0.7% walk, 5.2% work from home (2000); Travel time to work: 25.4% less than 15 minutes, 21.9% 15 to 30 minutes, 14.8% 30 to 45 minutes, 10.7% 45 to 60 minutes, 27.2% 60 minutes or more (2000)

STOCKHOLM (township). Covers a land area of 34.503 square miles and a water area of 1.050 square miles. Located at 45.02° N. Lat.; 94.19° W. Long.
Population: 805 (2000); Race: 97.8% White, 0.0% Black, 0.0% Asian, 0.0% American Indian and Alaska Native, 1.9% Hispanic of any race, 0.6% two or more races (2000); Density: 23.3 persons per square mile (2000); Age: 37.3% under 18, 9.0% over 64 (2000); Marriage status: 22.4% never married, 69.8% now married, 4.8% widowed, 3.0% divorced (2000); Foreign born: 2.3% (2000); Ancestry (includes multiple ancestries): 35.9% German, 20.6% Swedish, 12.3% Finnish, 10.0% Polish, 6.7% Norwegian (2000).
Economy: Single-family building permits issued: 11 (2001) / 11 (2000); Multi-family building permits issued: 0 (2001) / 0 (2000); Employment by occupation: 8.6% management, 11.3% professional, 13.8% services, 20.4% sales, 2.7% farming, 15.7% construction, 27.5% production (2000).
Income: Per capita income: $17,598 (2000); Median household income: $52,321 (2000); Poverty rate: 3.7% (2000).
Taxes: Total city taxes per capita: $112 (1997); City property taxes per capita: $110 (1997).
Education: High school graduation rate: 86.1% (2000); College graduation rate: 10.3% (2000).
Housing: Homeownership rate: 88.5% (2000); Median home value: $119,000 (2000); Median rent: $450 per month (2000); Median age of housing: 55 years (2000).
Transportation: Commute to work: 93.6% car, 0.0% public transportation, 0.5% walk, 4.2% work from home (2000); Travel time to work: 36.2% less than 15 minutes, 25.1% 15 to 30 minutes, 11.0% 30 to 45 minutes, 10.5% 45 to 60 minutes, 17.2% 60 minutes or more (2000)

VICTOR (township). Covers a land area of 32.390 square miles and a water area of 2.024 square miles. Located at 45.03° N. Lat.; 94.05° W. Long.
Population: 1,069 (2000); Race: 98.1% White, 0.5% Black, 0.0% Asian, 0.0% American Indian and Alaska Native, 1.4% Hispanic of any race, 0.0% two or more races (2000); Density: 33.0 persons per square mile (2000); Age: 34.6% under 18, 8.2% over 64 (2000); Marriage status: 21.6% never married, 67.8% now married, 3.5% widowed, 7.1% divorced (2000); Foreign born: 0.9% (2000); Ancestry (includes multiple ancestries): 53.5% German, 14.3% Irish, 12.3% Norwegian, 9.7% Swedish, 6.9% Polish (2000).
Economy: Employment by occupation: 16.4% management, 12.4% professional, 13.4% services, 24.7% sales, 2.0% farming, 9.9% construction, 21.1% production (2000).
Income: Per capita income: $18,217 (2000); Median household income: $49,514 (2000); Poverty rate: 4.3% (2000).
Taxes: Total city taxes per capita: $67 (1997); City property taxes per capita: $67 (1997).
Education: High school graduation rate: 86.0% (2000); College graduation rate: 16.7% (2000).
Housing: Homeownership rate: 91.0% (2000); Median home value: $139,000 (2000); Median rent: $465 per month (2000); Median age of housing: 34 years (2000).
Transportation: Commute to work: 89.4% car, 0.0% public transportation, 1.4% walk, 8.4% work from home (2000); Travel time to work: 35.1% less than 15 minutes, 19.3% 15 to 30 minutes, 16.3% 30 to 45 minutes, 13.3% 45 to 60 minutes, 16.1% 60 minutes or more (2000)

WAVERLY (city). Covers a land area of 0.832 square miles and a water area of 0.735 square miles. Located at 45.06° N. Lat.; 93.96° W. Long. Elevation is 998 feet.
Population: 732 (2000); Race: 98.8% White, 0.4% Black, 0.3% Asian, 0.0% American Indian and Alaska Native, 0.3% Hispanic of any race, 0.6% two or more races (2000); Density: 879.9 persons per square mile (2000); Age: 29.0% under 18, 11.6% over 64 (2000); Marriage status: 25.4% never married, 58.6% now married, 7.9% widowed, 8.2% divorced (2000); Foreign born: 0.6% (2000); Ancestry (includes multiple ancestries): 50.1% German, 17.9% Irish, 9.8% French (except Basque), 8.8% Norwegian, 8.8% Swedish (2000).
Economy: In grain and livestock area: soybeans; dairying; poultry. Manufacturing: machining. Single-family building permits issued: 0 (2001) / 8 (2000); Multi-family building permits issued: 0 (2001) / 0 (2000); Employment by occupation: 11.1% management, 15.6% professional, 8.4% services, 23.5% sales, 0.0% farming, 15.3% construction, 26.1% production (2000).
Income: Per capita income: $22,552 (2000); Median household income: $52,000 (2000); Poverty rate: 4.2% (2000).
Taxes: Total city taxes per capita: $299 (1997); City property taxes per capita: $276 (1997).
Education: High school graduation rate: 86.8% (2000); College graduation rate: 15.7% (2000).
Housing: Homeownership rate: 80.6% (2000); Median home value: $113,100 (2000); Median rent: $336 per month (2000); Median age of housing: 44 years (2000).
Transportation: Commute to work: 91.1% car, 0.5% public transportation, 2.4% walk, 4.9% work from home (2000); Travel time to work: 24.1% less than 15 minutes, 31.5% 15 to 30 minutes, 18.8% 30 to 45 minutes, 11.1% 45 to 60 minutes, 14.5% 60 minutes or more (2000)

WOODLAND (township). Covers a land area of 34.199 square miles and a water area of 0.792 square miles. Located at 45.02° N. Lat.; 93.95° W. Long.
Population: 1,137 (2000); Race: 99.3% White, 0.0% Black, 0.2% Asian, 0.4% American Indian and Alaska Native, 0.3% Hispanic of any race, 0.2% two or more races (2000); Density: 33.2 persons per square mile (2000); Age: 26.4% under 18, 9.5% over 64 (2000); Marriage status: 24.7% never married, 65.6% now married, 4.0% widowed, 5.7% divorced (2000); Foreign born: 0.2% (2000); Ancestry (includes multiple ancestries): 53.6% German, 13.9% Irish, 12.5% Polish, 11.6% Norwegian, 7.4% Swedish (2000).

Economy: Employment by occupation: 16.7% management, 16.1% professional, 13.5% services, 21.1% sales, 2.6% farming, 15.3% construction, 14.6% production (2000).
Income: Per capita income: $21,813 (2000); Median household income: $58,646 (2000); Poverty rate: 4.5% (2000).
Taxes: Total city taxes per capita: $97 (1997); City property taxes per capita: $97 (1997).
Education: High school graduation rate: 86.4% (2000); College graduation rate: 13.1% (2000).
Housing: Homeownership rate: 89.2% (2000); Median home value: $142,400 (2000); Median rent: $342 per month (2000); Median age of housing: 29 years (2000).
Transportation: Commute to work: 91.9% car, 0.0% public transportation, 0.9% walk, 7.1% work from home (2000); Travel time to work: 16.9% less than 15 minutes, 24.0% 15 to 30 minutes, 23.5% 30 to 45 minutes, 22.8% 45 to 60 minutes, 12.8% 60 minutes or more (2000)

Yellow Medicine County

Located in southwestern Minnesota; bounded on the west by South Dakota, and on the northeast by the Minnesota River; drained by the Lac qui Parle and Yellow Medicine Rivers. Covers a land area of 758.00 square miles, a water area of 5.40 square miles, and is located in the Central Time Zone. The county government was organized in 1871. County seat is Granite Falls.

Weather Station: Canby — Elevation: 1,240 feet

	Jan	Feb	Mar	Apr	May	Jun	Jul	Aug	Sep	Oct	Nov	Dec
High	23	29	40	58	72	81	86	83	74	60	40	28
Low	3	10	22	34	47	57	61	59	49	37	23	10
Precip	0.9	0.7	1.8	2.4	2.9	4.1	3.3	2.8	2.5	2.2	1.6	0.7
Snow	8.7	6.2	9.2	3.2	tr	0.0	0.0	0.0	tr	0.8	8.0	6.2

High and Low temperatures in degrees Fahrenheit; Precipitation and Snow in inches

Population: 11,080 (2000); Race: 95.5% White, 0.2% Black, 0.3% Asian, 2.1% American Indian and Alaska Native, 2.0% Hispanic of any race, 0.8% two or more races (2000); Density: 14.6 persons per square mile (2000); Age: 25.8% under 18, 20.4% over 64 (2000).
Religion: Five largest groups: 45.7% Evangelical Lutheran Church in America, 19.0% Catholic Church, 9.4% Lutheran Church—Missouri Synod, 5.0% Wisconsin Evangelical Lutheran Synod, 2.7% United Church of Christ (2000).
Economy: Unemployment rate: 3.7% (11/2002); Total civilian labor force: 4,690 (11/2002); Leading industries: 20.8% health care and social assistance; 18.7% construction; 13.2% manufacturing (2000); Companies that employ more than 1,000 persons: 0 (2000); Companies that employ more than 100 persons: 6 (2000); Farms: 876 totaling 415,269 acres (1997); Minority business ownership rate: 0.0% (1997); Women business ownership rate: 15.7% (1997); Retail sales per capita: $6,872 (1997). Single-family building permits issued: 35 (2001) / 24 (2000); Multi-family building permits issued: 0 (2001) / 2 (2000).
Income: Per capita income: $17,120 (2000); Median household income: $34,393 (2000); Poverty rate: 10.4% (2000); Bankruptcy rate: 1.85% (2001).
Taxes: Total county taxes per capita: $419 (2000); County property taxes per capita: $417 (2000).
Education: High school graduation rate: 81.9% (2000); College graduation rate: 14.4% (2000).
Housing: Homeownership rate: 79.3% (2000); Median home value: $52,400 (2000); Median rent: $276 per month (2000); Median age of housing: 52 years (2000).
Health: Birth rate: 107.4 per 10,000 population (1998); Age adjusted death rate: 70.9 per 10,000 population (1999); Age adjusted cancer mortality rate: 160.6 deaths per 100,000 population (1999). Number of physicians: 9.0 per 10,000 population (1999); Number of hospital beds: 157.0 per 10,000 population (1999).
Elections: 2000 Presidential election results: 45.8% Gore, 47.1% Bush, 4.2% Nader, 2.2% Buchanan
National and State Parks: Big Rock State Wildlife Management Area; Bohemian State Wildlife Management Area; Clawson State Wildlife Management Area; Lanners State Wildlife Management Area; Miller-Richter State Wildlife Management Ar; Myhre State Wildlife Management Area; Omro State Wildlife Management Area; Oshkosh State Wildlife Management Area; Penthole State Wildlife Management Area; Posen State Wildlife Management Area; Providence State Wildlife Management Area; Saint Leo State Wildlife Management Areas; Sioux Nation State Wildlife Management Area; Stokke State Wildlife Management Area; Tyro State Wildlife Management Area; Upper Sioux Agency State Park; Wood Lake State Monument
Additional Information Contacts
Yellow Medicine County Government Offices 320-564-3132
Canby Chamber of Commerce 507-223-7775
Granite Falls Chamber of Commerce. 320-564-4039

Yellow Medicine County Communities

BURTON (township). Covers a land area of 35.729 square miles and a water area of 0.241 square miles. Located at 44.67° N. Lat.; 96.04° W. Long.
Population: 174 (2000); Race: 100.0% White, 0.0% Black, 0.0% Asian, 0.0% American Indian and Alaska Native, 0.0% Hispanic of any race, 0.0% two or more races (2000); Density: 4.9 persons per square mile (2000); Age: 32.2% under 18, 13.0% over 64 (2000); Marriage status: 23.9% never married, 63.4% now married, 6.0% widowed, 6.7% divorced (2000); Foreign born: 0.0% (2000); Ancestry (includes multiple ancestries): 44.6% German, 23.7% Belgian, 23.2% Norwegian, 7.3% Czech, 6.2% United States or American (2000).
Economy: Employment by occupation: 35.4% management, 12.7% professional, 3.8% services, 16.5% sales, 2.5% farming, 3.8% construction, 25.3% production (2000).
Income: Per capita income: $13,616 (2000); Median household income: $34,500 (2000); Poverty rate: 10.7% (2000).
Taxes: Total city taxes per capita: $64 (1997); City property taxes per capita: $64 (1997).
Education: High school graduation rate: 91.7% (2000); College graduation rate: 9.3% (2000).
Housing: Homeownership rate: 82.8% (2000); Median home value: $58,800 (2000); Median rent: $275 per month (2000); Median age of housing: 60+ years (2000).
Transportation: Commute to work: 69.3% car, 0.0% public transportation, 5.3% walk, 25.3% work from home (2000); Travel time to work: 44.6% less than 15 minutes, 25.0% 15 to 30 minutes, 12.5% 30 to 45 minutes, 3.6% 45 to 60 minutes, 14.3% 60 minutes or more (2000)

CANBY (city). Covers a land area of 2.171 square miles and a water area of 0.007 square miles. Located at 44.71° N. Lat.; 96.27° W. Long. Elevation is 1,243 feet.
History: Incorporated as village 1879, as city 1905.
Population: 1,903 (2000); Race: 97.1% White, 0.6% Black, 0.3% Asian, 0.7% American Indian and Alaska Native, 1.7% Hispanic of any race, 0.9% two or more races (2000); Density: 876.5 persons per square mile (2000); Age: 20.6% under 18, 30.2% over 64 (2000); Marriage status: 25.9% never married, 48.5% now married, 16.2% widowed, 9.4% divorced (2000); Foreign born: 1.2% (2000); Ancestry (includes multiple ancestries): 45.5% German, 31.4% Norwegian, 6.8% Polish, 5.2% Swedish, 4.4% Irish (2000).
Economy: Agricultural area: grain, soybeans, alfalfa, sugar beets; livestock; trade center for farm cooperatives. Manufacturing: fertilizers, steel and aluminum fabrication, machinery. Single-family building permits issued: 4 (2001) / 4 (2000); Multi-family building permits issued: 0 (2001) / 2 (2000); Employment by occupation: 12.5% management, 18.9% professional, 17.4% services, 15.1% sales, 2.3% farming, 13.4% construction, 20.5% production (2000).
Income: Per capita income: $16,269 (2000); Median household income: $27,533 (2000); Poverty rate: 13.5% (2000).
Taxes: Total city taxes per capita: $126 (1997); City property taxes per capita: $122 (1997).
Education: High school graduation rate: 70.9% (2000); College graduation rate: 15.6% (2000).

School District(s)

Canby (PK-12)
2000 Enrollment: 733 507-223-5965
Housing: Homeownership rate: 70.8% (2000); Median home value: $42,500 (2000); Median rent: $260 per month (2000); Median age of housing: 49 years (2000).
Hospitals: Sioux Valley Canby Campus (102 beds)
Newspapers: The Canby News (1 x week)
Transportation: Commute to work: 89.5% car, 0.0% public transportation, 8.5% walk, 1.9% work from home (2000); Travel time to work: 72.9% less than 15 minutes, 12.8% 15 to 30 minutes, 6.8% 30 to 45 minutes, 5.2% 45 to 60 minutes, 2.3% 60 minutes or more (2000)
Additional Information Contacts
Canby Chamber of Commerce. 507-223-7775

CLARKFIELD (city). Covers a land area of 1.082 square miles and a water area of 0 square miles. Located at 44.79° N. Lat.; 95.80° W. Long. Elevation is 1,090 feet.
Population: 944 (2000); Race: 97.1% White, 0.0% Black, 0.3% Asian, 0.9% American Indian and Alaska Native, 1.3% Hispanic of any race, 0.6% two or more races (2000); Density: 872.7 persons per square mile (2000); Age: 22.1% under 18, 30.9% over 64 (2000); Marriage status: 27.3% never married, 52.7% now married, 11.9% widowed, 8.1% divorced (2000); Foreign born: 0.9% (2000); Ancestry (includes multiple ancestries): 49.1% Norwegian, 36.5% German, 8.6% Swedish, 8.1% Irish, 5.8% English (2000).
Economy: Grain, soybeans, sugar beets; livestock. Manufacturing: apparel. Single-family building permits issued: 0 (2001) / 0 (2000); Multi-family building permits issued: 0 (2001) / 0 (2000); Employment by occupation: 12.4% management, 14.7% professional, 18.4% services, 19.7% sales, 1.8% farming, 12.9% construction, 20.0% production (2000).
Income: Per capita income: $17,349 (2000); Median household income: $33,819 (2000); Poverty rate: 12.8% (2000).
Taxes: Total city taxes per capita: $174 (1997); City property taxes per capita: $169 (1997).
Education: High school graduation rate: 76.8% (2000); College graduation rate: 11.4% (2000).
Housing: Homeownership rate: 77.6% (2000); Median home value: $38,400 (2000); Median rent: $274 per month (2000); Median age of housing: 52 years (2000).
Transportation: Commute to work: 88.9% car, 0.0% public transportation, 7.4% walk, 3.7% work from home (2000); Travel time to work: 44.3% less than 15 minutes, 35.5% 15 to 30 minutes, 15.3% 30 to 45 minutes, 0.3% 45 to 60 minutes, 4.6% 60 minutes or more (2000)

ECHO (city). Covers a land area of 1.018 square miles and a water area of 0 square miles. Located at 44.61° N. Lat.; 95.41° W. Long. Elevation is 1,083 feet.
Population: 278 (2000); Race: 95.3% White, 0.0% Black, 0.0% Asian, 1.6% American Indian and Alaska Native, 0.0% Hispanic of any race, 3.1% two or more races (2000); Density: 273.1 persons per square mile (2000); Age: 20.8% under 18, 28.2% over 64 (2000); Marriage status: 21.1% never married, 54.1% now married, 17.7% widowed, 7.2% divorced (2000); Foreign born: 5.9% (2000); Ancestry (includes multiple ancestries): 35.7% Norwegian, 34.1% German, 6.7% Swedish, 4.7% Irish, 4.7% Other groups (2000).
Economy: Single-family building permits issued: 0 (2001) / 0 (2000); Multi-family building permits issued: 0 (2001) / 0 (2000); Employment by occupation: 8.5% management, 13.2% professional, 13.2% services, 17.0% sales, 0.9% farming, 4.7% construction, 42.5% production (2000).
Income: Per capita income: $15,275 (2000); Median household income: $27,656 (2000); Poverty rate: 10.6% (2000).
Taxes: Total city taxes per capita: $179 (1997); City property taxes per capita: $172 (1997).
Education: High school graduation rate: 80.1% (2000); College graduation rate: 15.5% (2000).

School District(s)

E.C.H.O. Charter School (KG-10)
2000 Enrollment: 105 507-925-4143

Housing: Homeownership rate: 76.9% (2000); Median home value: $24,400 (2000); Median rent: $313 per month (2000); Median age of housing: 56 years (2000).
Transportation: Commute to work: 84.9% car, 0.0% public transportation, 11.3% walk, 1.9% work from home (2000); Travel time to work: 36.5% less than 15 minutes, 45.2% 15 to 30 minutes, 13.5% 30 to 45 minutes, 4.8% 45 to 60 minutes, 0.0% 60 minutes or more (2000)

ECHO (township). Covers a land area of 34.856 square miles and a water area of 0.574 square miles. Located at 44.57° N. Lat.; 95.41° W. Long. Elevation is 1,083 feet.
Population: 179 (2000); Race: 100.0% White, 0.0% Black, 0.0% Asian, 0.0% American Indian and Alaska Native, 0.0% Hispanic of any race, 0.0% two or more races (2000); Density: 5.1 persons per square mile (2000); Age: 28.6% under 18, 8.0% over 64 (2000); Marriage status: 23.5% never married, 68.8% now married, 1.2% widowed, 6.5% divorced (2000); Foreign born: 0.0% (2000); Ancestry (includes multiple ancestries): 68.1% German, 29.6% Norwegian, 4.7% French (except Basque), 4.2% Irish, 3.8% Belgian (2000).
Economy: Livestock; grain, soybeans, alfalfa. Manufacturing: fertilizers. Employment by occupation: 28.0% management, 10.3% professional, 7.5% services, 19.6% sales, 0.0% farming, 21.5% construction, 13.1% production (2000).
Income: Per capita income: $16,671 (2000); Median household income: $42,750 (2000); Poverty rate: 12.2% (2000).
Taxes: Total city taxes per capita: $197 (1997); City property taxes per capita: $197 (1997).
Education: High school graduation rate: 94.4% (2000); College graduation rate: 16.0% (2000).
Housing: Homeownership rate: 81.1% (2000); Median home value: $32,500 (2000); Median rent: <$100 per month (2000); Median age of housing: 60+ years (2000).
Transportation: Commute to work: 74.8% car, 0.0% public transportation, 2.8% walk, 22.4% work from home (2000); Travel time to work: 31.3% less than 15 minutes, 32.5% 15 to 30 minutes, 21.7% 30 to 45 minutes, 10.8% 45 to 60 minutes, 3.6% 60 minutes or more (2000)

FLORIDA (township). Covers a land area of 33.414 square miles and a water area of 0 square miles. Located at 44.75° N. Lat.; 96.39° W. Long.
Population: 164 (2000); Race: 100.0% White, 0.0% Black, 0.0% Asian, 0.0% American Indian and Alaska Native, 0.0% Hispanic of any race, 0.0% two or more races (2000); Density: 4.9 persons per square mile (2000); Age: 35.5% under 18, 9.0% over 64 (2000); Marriage status: 20.7% never married, 68.6% now married, 5.0% widowed, 5.8% divorced (2000); Foreign born: 0.0% (2000); Ancestry (includes multiple ancestries): 57.8% German, 14.5% Norwegian, 13.9% Irish, 10.8% Belgian, 10.2% Polish (2000).
Economy: Employment by occupation: 19.2% management, 17.8% professional, 12.3% services, 12.3% sales, 8.2% farming, 5.5% construction, 24.7% production (2000).
Income: Per capita income: $12,349 (2000); Median household income: $30,625 (2000); Poverty rate: 9.6% (2000).
Taxes: Total city taxes per capita: $74 (1997); City property taxes per capita: $74 (1997).
Education: High school graduation rate: 84.8% (2000); College graduation rate: 4.0% (2000).
Housing: Homeownership rate: 85.7% (2000); Median home value: $32,500 (2000); Median rent: $325 per month (2000); Median age of housing: 60+ years (2000).
Transportation: Commute to work: 75.3% car, 0.0% public transportation, 8.2% walk, 13.7% work from home (2000); Travel time to work: 50.8% less than 15 minutes, 22.2% 15 to 30 minutes, 14.3% 30 to 45 minutes, 9.5% 45 to 60 minutes, 3.2% 60 minutes or more (2000)

FORTIER (township). Covers a land area of 33.384 square miles and a water area of 0.097 square miles. Located at 44.67° N. Lat.; 96.38° W. Long.
Population: 116 (2000); Race: 100.0% White, 0.0% Black, 0.0% Asian, 0.0% American Indian and Alaska Native, 0.0% Hispanic of any race, 0.0% two or more races (2000); Density: 3.5 persons per square mile (2000); Age: 20.8% under 18, 18.8% over 64 (2000); Marriage status: 33.7% never married, 57.0% now married, 0.0% widowed, 9.3% divorced (2000); Foreign born: 0.0% (2000); Ancestry (includes multiple ancestries): 36.6% Norwegian, 26.7% German, 9.9% English, 7.9% Swedish, 7.9% Polish (2000).
Economy: Employment by occupation: 26.7% management, 8.3% professional, 8.3% services, 13.3% sales, 0.0% farming, 16.7% construction, 26.7% production (2000).
Income: Per capita income: $20,984 (2000); Median household income: $32,500 (2000); Poverty rate: 15.8% (2000).
Taxes: Total city taxes per capita: $139 (1997); City property taxes per capita: $139 (1997).
Education: High school graduation rate: 69.8% (2000); College graduation rate: 7.9% (2000).
Housing: Homeownership rate: 66.7% (2000); Median home value: $27,500 (2000); Median rent: <$100 per month (2000); Median age of housing: 60+ years (2000).
Transportation: Commute to work: 83.3% car, 0.0% public transportation, 0.0% walk, 16.7% work from home (2000); Travel time to work: 60.0% less than 15 minutes, 34.0% 15 to 30 minutes, 6.0% 30 to 45 minutes, 0.0% 45 to 60 minutes, 0.0% 60 minutes or more (2000)

FRIENDSHIP (township). Covers a land area of 35.092 square miles and a water area of 0.105 square miles. Located at 44.76° N. Lat.; 95.78° W. Long.
Population: 258 (2000); Race: 95.9% White, 0.0% Black, 0.0% Asian, 0.0% American Indian and Alaska Native, 4.1% Hispanic of any race, 0.0% two or more races (2000); Density: 7.4 persons per square mile (2000); Age: 30.3% under 18, 12.2% over 64 (2000); Marriage status: 17.5% never married, 72.0% now married, 3.8% widowed, 6.6% divorced (2000); Foreign born:

1.5% (2000); Ancestry (includes multiple ancestries): 67.9% Norwegian, 35.4% German, 18.8% Swedish, 4.1% Other groups, 3.3% Danish (2000).
Economy: Employment by occupation: 25.9% management, 20.0% professional, 3.0% services, 20.7% sales, 0.0% farming, 14.1% construction, 16.3% production (2000).
Income: Per capita income: $18,718 (2000); Median household income: $42,404 (2000); Poverty rate: 3.0% (2000).
Taxes: Total city taxes per capita: $143 (1997); City property taxes per capita: $143 (1997).
Education: High school graduation rate: 89.9% (2000); College graduation rate: 16.0% (2000).
Housing: Homeownership rate: 83.3% (2000); Median home value: $112,500 (2000); Median rent: $514 per month (2000); Median age of housing: 39 years (2000).
Transportation: Commute to work: 86.4% car, 0.0% public transportation, 3.0% walk, 10.6% work from home (2000); Travel time to work: 46.6% less than 15 minutes, 24.6% 15 to 30 minutes, 22.0% 30 to 45 minutes, 0.0% 45 to 60 minutes, 6.8% 60 minutes or more (2000)

GRANITE FALLS (city). Covers a land area of 3.447 square miles and a water area of 0.243 square miles. Located at 44.81° N. Lat.; 95.54° W. Long. Elevation is 920 feet.
History: The founders of Granite Falls were attracted by the water power provided by the falls on the Minnesota River, where the Northern States Power Company later built a large power plant. The town developed as the center for an agricultural area, and around its granite quarries, which contain rocks dating from the earliest geologic era.
Population: 3,070 (2000); Race: 90.3% White, 1.0% Black, 0.2% Asian, 6.7% American Indian and Alaska Native, 0.8% Hispanic of any race, 1.8% two or more races (2000); Density: 890.5 persons per square mile (2000); Age: 24.3% under 18, 21.8% over 64 (2000); Marriage status: 23.2% never married, 55.9% now married, 13.1% widowed, 7.9% divorced (2000); Foreign born: 0.5% (2000); Ancestry (includes multiple ancestries): 41.6% Norwegian, 34.2% German, 9.8% Swedish, 9.5% Other groups, 8.0% Irish (2000).
Economy: Single-family building permits issued: 15 (2001) / 4 (2000); Multi-family building permits issued: 0 (2001) / 0 (2000); Employment by occupation: 11.7% management, 20.3% professional, 18.6% services, 23.8% sales, 0.6% farming, 6.9% construction, 18.0% production (2000).
Income: Per capita income: $18,356 (2000); Median household income: $32,031 (2000); Poverty rate: 9.7% (2000).
Taxes: Total city taxes per capita: $188 (1997); City property taxes per capita: $181 (1997).
Education: High school graduation rate: 85.2% (2000); College graduation rate: 17.2% (2000).

School District(s)

Yellow Medicine East (PK-12)
2000 Enrollment: 1,245 320-564-4081

Two-year College(s)

Minnesota West Community and Technical College (Public)
2001 Enrollment: 3,155 320-564-4511
2001 Tuition: In-state $2,505; Out-of-state $2,505

Housing: Homeownership rate: 70.1% (2000); Median home value: $64,400 (2000); Median rent: $334 per month (2000); Median age of housing: 37 years (2000).
Hospitals: Granite Falls Municipal Hospital (95 beds)
Newspapers: The Granite Falls-Clarkfield Advocate-Tribune (1 x week)
Transportation: Commute to work: 89.9% car, 0.8% public transportation, 5.2% walk, 3.1% work from home (2000); Travel time to work: 67.1% less than 15 minutes, 21.4% 15 to 30 minutes, 7.8% 30 to 45 minutes, 2.3% 45 to 60 minutes, 1.5% 60 minutes or more (2000)
Additional Information Contacts
Granite Falls Chamber of Commerce. 320-564-4039

HAMMER (township). Covers a land area of 35.692 square miles and a water area of 0 square miles. Located at 44.75° N. Lat.; 96.27° W. Long.
Population: 233 (2000); Race: 100.0% White, 0.0% Black, 0.0% Asian, 0.0% American Indian and Alaska Native, 0.0% Hispanic of any race, 0.0% two or more races (2000); Density: 6.5 persons per square mile (2000); Age: 25.2% under 18, 16.7% over 64 (2000); Marriage status: 18.3% never married, 71.6% now married, 7.2% widowed, 2.9% divorced (2000); Foreign born: 0.8% (2000); Ancestry (includes multiple ancestries): 51.9% German, 30.2% Norwegian, 8.1% Dutch, 7.0% Irish, 5.8% Polish (2000).
Economy: Employment by occupation: 32.0% management, 18.4% professional, 8.0% services, 13.6% sales, 2.4% farming, 12.8% construction, 12.8% production (2000).
Income: Per capita income: $22,013 (2000); Median household income: $44,167 (2000); Poverty rate: 12.4% (2000).
Taxes: Total city taxes per capita: $116 (1997); City property taxes per capita: $116 (1997).
Education: High school graduation rate: 89.8% (2000); College graduation rate: 20.3% (2000).
Housing: Homeownership rate: 93.5% (2000); Median home value: $37,500 (2000); Median rent: <$100 per month (2000); Median age of housing: 48 years (2000).
Transportation: Commute to work: 77.6% car, 0.0% public transportation, 6.4% walk, 16.0% work from home (2000); Travel time to work: 56.2% less than 15 minutes, 27.6% 15 to 30 minutes, 10.5% 30 to 45 minutes, 1.9% 45 to 60 minutes, 3.8% 60 minutes or more (2000)

HANLEY FALLS (city). Covers a land area of 0.264 square miles and a water area of 0 square miles. Located at 44.69° N. Lat.; 95.62° W. Long. Elevation is 1,046 feet.
Population: 323 (2000); Race: 74.1% White, 0.0% Black, 2.5% Asian, 0.6% American Indian and Alaska Native, 37.7% Hispanic of any race, 1.2% two or more races (2000); Density: 1,223.0 persons per square mile (2000); Age: 33.0% under 18, 11.4% over 64 (2000); Marriage status: 26.0% never married, 63.6% now married, 6.1% widowed, 4.3% divorced (2000); Foreign born: 11.7% (2000); Ancestry (includes multiple ancestries): 34.0% Other groups, 23.8% German, 19.4% Norwegian, 6.8% Swedish, 3.4% United States or American (2000).
Economy: Railroad junction. Corn, oats, soybeans; livestock. Single-family building permits issued: 1 (2001) / 0 (2000); Multi-family building permits issued: 0 (2001) / 0 (2000); Employment by occupation: 6.3% management, 11.9% professional, 9.5% services, 7.9% sales, 10.3% farming, 7.9% construction, 46.0% production (2000).
Income: Per capita income: $14,248 (2000); Median household income: $31,667 (2000); Poverty rate: 16.4% (2000).
Taxes: Total city taxes per capita: $239 (1997); City property taxes per capita: $239 (1997).
Education: High school graduation rate: 69.9% (2000); College graduation rate: 5.1% (2000).
Housing: Homeownership rate: 75.0% (2000); Median home value: $29,000 (2000); Median rent: $295 per month (2000); Median age of housing: 52 years (2000).
Transportation: Commute to work: 84.9% car, 1.6% public transportation, 9.5% walk, 4.0% work from home (2000); Travel time to work: 50.4% less than 15 minutes, 25.6% 15 to 30 minutes, 17.4% 30 to 45 minutes, 6.6% 45 to 60 minutes, 0.0% 60 minutes or more (2000)

HAZEL RUN (city). Covers a land area of 0.752 square miles and a water area of 0 square miles. Located at 44.75° N. Lat.; 95.71° W. Long. Elevation is 1,062 feet.
Population: 64 (2000); Race: 100.0% White, 0.0% Black, 0.0% Asian, 0.0% American Indian and Alaska Native, 0.0% Hispanic of any race, 0.0% two or more races (2000); Density: 85.1 persons per square mile (2000); Age: 26.9% under 18, 9.0% over 64 (2000); Marriage status: 26.4% never married, 54.7% now married, 18.9% widowed, 0.0% divorced (2000); Foreign born: 0.0% (2000); Ancestry (includes multiple ancestries): 61.2% Norwegian, 26.9% German, 3.0% French Canadian, 3.0% English, 3.0% Swedish (2000).
Economy: Single-family building permits issued: 0 (2001) / 0 (2000); Multi-family building permits issued: 0 (2001) / 0 (2000); Employment by occupation: 13.3% management, 6.7% professional, 6.7% services, 33.3% sales, 6.7% farming, 10.0% construction, 23.3% production (2000).
Income: Per capita income: $17,125 (2000); Median household income: $24,643 (2000); Poverty rate: 19.4% (2000).
Taxes: Total city taxes per capita: $38 (1997); City property taxes per capita: $38 (1997).
Education: High school graduation rate: 85.0% (2000); College graduation rate: 10.0% (2000).
Housing: Homeownership rate: 76.7% (2000); Median home value: $16,300 (2000); Median rent: $325 per month (2000); Median age of housing: 60+ years (2000).
Transportation: Commute to work: 83.3% car, 0.0% public transportation, 10.0% walk, 0.0% work from home (2000); Travel time to work: 53.3% less than 15 minutes, 46.7% 15 to 30 minutes, 0.0% 30 to 45 minutes, 0.0% 45 to 60 minutes, 0.0% 60 minutes or more (2000)

HAZEL RUN (township). Covers a land area of 35.615 square miles and a water area of 0 square miles. Located at 44.76° N. Lat.; 95.67° W. Long. Elevation is 1,062 feet.

Population: 194 (2000); Race: 98.1% White, 0.0% Black, 0.0% Asian, 1.9% American Indian and Alaska Native, 0.0% Hispanic of any race, 0.0% two or more races (2000); Density: 5.4 persons per square mile (2000); Age: 28.4% under 18, 15.3% over 64 (2000); Marriage status: 25.9% never married, 68.7% now married, 3.6% widowed, 1.8% divorced (2000); Foreign born: 0.0% (2000); Ancestry (includes multiple ancestries): 56.3% Norwegian, 45.6% German, 6.0% English, 5.6% Dutch, 4.7% Swedish (2000).
Economy: Grain; livestock. Employment by occupation: 28.6% management, 24.1% professional, 5.4% services, 11.6% sales, 2.7% farming, 10.7% construction, 17.0% production (2000).
Income: Per capita income: $20,053 (2000); Median household income: $46,406 (2000); Poverty rate: 8.5% (2000).
Taxes: Total city taxes per capita: $137 (1997); City property taxes per capita: $137 (1997).
Education: High school graduation rate: 88.9% (2000); College graduation rate: 11.9% (2000).
Housing: Homeownership rate: 84.2% (2000); Median home value: $88,800 (2000); Median rent: $150 per month (2000); Median age of housing: 60+ years (2000).
Transportation: Commute to work: 80.4% car, 0.0% public transportation, 4.5% walk, 15.2% work from home (2000); Travel time to work: 53.7% less than 15 minutes, 23.2% 15 to 30 minutes, 11.6% 30 to 45 minutes, 4.2% 45 to 60 minutes, 7.4% 60 minutes or more (2000)

LISBON (township). Covers a land area of 35.698 square miles and a water area of 0.025 square miles. Located at 44.85° N. Lat.; 95.79° W. Long.
Population: 217 (2000); Race: 100.0% White, 0.0% Black, 0.0% Asian, 0.0% American Indian and Alaska Native, 0.0% Hispanic of any race, 0.0% two or more races (2000); Density: 6.1 persons per square mile (2000); Age: 25.1% under 18, 15.6% over 64 (2000); Marriage status: 25.7% never married, 67.1% now married, 3.0% widowed, 4.2% divorced (2000); Foreign born: 0.0% (2000); Ancestry (includes multiple ancestries): 58.8% Norwegian, 22.1% German, 4.5% French Canadian, 3.5% Swedish, 3.5% Italian (2000).
Economy: Employment by occupation: 25.9% management, 15.7% professional, 6.5% services, 21.3% sales, 3.7% farming, 14.8% construction, 12.0% production (2000).
Income: Per capita income: $15,221 (2000); Median household income: $33,500 (2000); Poverty rate: 8.5% (2000).
Taxes: Total city taxes per capita: $120 (2000); City property taxes per capita: $120 (2000).
Education: High school graduation rate: 92.1% (2000); College graduation rate: 12.2% (2000).
Housing: Homeownership rate: 88.6% (2000); Median home value: $64,300 (2000); Median rent: $325 per month (2000); Median age of housing: 60+ years (2000).
Transportation: Commute to work: 80.2% car, 0.0% public transportation, 3.8% walk, 16.0% work from home (2000); Travel time to work: 50.6% less than 15 minutes, 43.8% 15 to 30 minutes, 3.4% 30 to 45 minutes, 0.0% 45 to 60 minutes, 2.2% 60 minutes or more (2000)

MINNESOTA FALLS (township). Covers a land area of 31.122 square miles and a water area of 0.272 square miles. Located at 44.76° N. Lat.; 95.55° W. Long.
Population: 361 (2000); Race: 69.3% White, 0.0% Black, 0.6% Asian, 30.1% American Indian and Alaska Native, 2.0% Hispanic of any race, 0.0% two or more races (2000); Density: 11.6 persons per square mile (2000); Age: 28.9% under 18, 16.7% over 64 (2000); Marriage status: 16.5% never married, 69.3% now married, 4.2% widowed, 10.0% divorced (2000); Foreign born: 1.2% (2000); Ancestry (includes multiple ancestries): 37.1% Norwegian, 34.8% Other groups, 22.5% German, 12.9% Swedish, 5.6% Irish (2000).
Economy: Employment by occupation: 15.7% management, 15.0% professional, 25.7% services, 11.4% sales, 0.0% farming, 18.6% construction, 13.6% production (2000).
Income: Per capita income: $17,521 (2000); Median household income: $41,667 (2000); Poverty rate: 15.9% (2000).
Taxes: Total city taxes per capita: $51 (1997); City property taxes per capita: $51 (1997).
Education: High school graduation rate: 87.3% (2000); College graduation rate: 15.2% (2000).
Housing: Homeownership rate: 91.1% (2000); Median home value: $90,700 (2000); Median rent: $325 per month (2000); Median age of housing: 30 years (2000).
Transportation: Commute to work: 81.3% car, 0.0% public transportation, 1.5% walk, 14.9% work from home (2000); Travel time to work: 59.6% less than 15 minutes, 24.6% 15 to 30 minutes, 14.9% 30 to 45 minutes, 0.0% 45 to 60 minutes, 0.9% 60 minutes or more (2000)

NORMAN (township). Covers a land area of 34.904 square miles and a water area of 0.044 square miles. Located at 44.67° N. Lat.; 96.28° W. Long.
Population: 291 (2000); Race: 97.3% White, 0.0% Black, 0.0% Asian, 0.0% American Indian and Alaska Native, 2.7% Hispanic of any race, 0.0% two or more races (2000); Density: 8.3 persons per square mile (2000); Age: 30.2% under 18, 18.9% over 64 (2000); Marriage status: 20.7% never married, 72.1% now married, 3.6% widowed, 3.6% divorced (2000); Foreign born: 2.7% (2000); Ancestry (includes multiple ancestries): 45.7% German, 27.8% Norwegian, 10.0% Polish, 7.2% Belgian, 6.9% English (2000).
Economy: Employment by occupation: 22.4% management, 17.7% professional, 13.6% services, 18.4% sales, 2.7% farming, 5.4% construction, 19.7% production (2000).
Income: Per capita income: $16,936 (2000); Median household income: $43,333 (2000); Poverty rate: 2.1% (2000).
Taxes: Total city taxes per capita: $54 (1997); City property taxes per capita: $54 (1997).
Education: High school graduation rate: 89.9% (2000); College graduation rate: 24.5% (2000).
Housing: Homeownership rate: 93.2% (2000); Median home value: $55,000 (2000); Median rent: $375 per month (2000); Median age of housing: 49 years (2000).
Transportation: Commute to work: 87.6% car, 0.0% public transportation, 1.4% walk, 11.0% work from home (2000); Travel time to work: 71.3% less than 15 minutes, 4.7% 15 to 30 minutes, 17.8% 30 to 45 minutes, 3.1% 45 to 60 minutes, 3.1% 60 minutes or more (2000)

NORMANIA (township). Covers a land area of 35.519 square miles and a water area of 0.754 square miles. Located at 44.66° N. Lat.; 95.79° W. Long.
Population: 188 (2000); Race: 100.0% White, 0.0% Black, 0.0% Asian, 0.0% American Indian and Alaska Native, 0.0% Hispanic of any race, 0.0% two or more races (2000); Density: 5.3 persons per square mile (2000); Age: 29.3% under 18, 15.5% over 64 (2000); Marriage status: 13.4% never married, 78.4% now married, 6.0% widowed, 2.2% divorced (2000); Foreign born: 0.0% (2000); Ancestry (includes multiple ancestries): 47.0% Norwegian, 41.4% German, 18.8% Belgian, 9.9% Swedish, 6.1% Other groups (2000).
Economy: Employment by occupation: 25.3% management, 22.0% professional, 2.2% services, 16.5% sales, 3.3% farming, 15.4% construction, 15.4% production (2000).
Income: Per capita income: $19,067 (2000); Median household income: $36,750 (2000); Poverty rate: 6.1% (2000).
Taxes: Total city taxes per capita: $117 (1997); City property taxes per capita: $117 (1997).
Education: High school graduation rate: 79.3% (2000); College graduation rate: 22.3% (2000).
Housing: Homeownership rate: 88.0% (2000); Median home value: $76,700 (2000); Median rent: $125 per month (2000); Median age of housing: 60+ years (2000).
Transportation: Commute to work: 87.9% car, 0.0% public transportation, 5.5% walk, 6.6% work from home (2000); Travel time to work: 40.0% less than 15 minutes, 41.2% 15 to 30 minutes, 11.8% 30 to 45 minutes, 4.7% 45 to 60 minutes, 2.4% 60 minutes or more (2000)

OMRO (township). Covers a land area of 35.966 square miles and a water area of 0.345 square miles. Located at 44.75° N. Lat.; 96.03° W. Long.
Population: 184 (2000); Race: 100.0% White, 0.0% Black, 0.0% Asian, 0.0% American Indian and Alaska Native, 0.0% Hispanic of any race, 0.0% two or more races (2000); Density: 5.1 persons per square mile (2000); Age: 33.2% under 18, 16.1% over 64 (2000); Marriage status: 27.7% never married, 68.6% now married, 2.2% widowed, 1.5% divorced (2000); Foreign born: 0.0% (2000); Ancestry (includes multiple ancestries): 64.8% German, 37.3% Norwegian, 10.4% Dutch, 6.7% Belgian, 4.7% Swedish (2000).
Economy: Employment by occupation: 22.8% management, 16.3% professional, 9.8% services, 10.9% sales, 1.1% farming, 6.5% construction, 32.6% production (2000).
Income: Per capita income: $11,647 (2000); Median household income: $29,375 (2000); Poverty rate: 15.8% (2000).
Taxes: Total city taxes per capita: $91 (1997); City property taxes per capita: $91 (1997).
Education: High school graduation rate: 74.6% (2000); College graduation rate: 9.6% (2000).

Housing: Homeownership rate: 73.0% (2000); Median home value: $67,500 (2000); Median rent: $175 per month (2000); Median age of housing: 60+ years (2000).
Transportation: Commute to work: 76.1% car, 0.0% public transportation, 0.0% walk, 23.9% work from home (2000); Travel time to work: 20.0% less than 15 minutes, 52.9% 15 to 30 minutes, 12.9% 30 to 45 minutes, 7.1% 45 to 60 minutes, 7.1% 60 minutes or more (2000)

OSHKOSH (township). Covers a land area of 36.284 square miles and a water area of 0 square miles. Located at 44.76° N. Lat.; 96.15° W. Long.
Population: 249 (2000); Race: 97.0% White, 0.0% Black, 0.0% Asian, 0.0% American Indian and Alaska Native, 0.0% Hispanic of any race, 3.0% two or more races (2000); Density: 6.9 persons per square mile (2000); Age: 35.2% under 18, 8.7% over 64 (2000); Marriage status: 25.8% never married, 69.1% now married, 2.6% widowed, 2.6% divorced (2000); Foreign born: 0.8% (2000); Ancestry (includes multiple ancestries): 29.5% Norwegian, 27.3% German, 9.5% Swedish, 9.1% United States or American, 4.2% Other groups (2000).
Economy: Employment by occupation: 20.1% management, 13.7% professional, 12.9% services, 28.8% sales, 2.2% farming, 5.8% construction, 16.5% production (2000).
Income: Per capita income: $14,263 (2000); Median household income: $43,750 (2000); Poverty rate: 10.4% (2000).
Taxes: Total city taxes per capita: $81 (1997); City property taxes per capita: $81 (1997).
Education: High school graduation rate: 83.6% (2000); College graduation rate: 10.5% (2000).
Housing: Homeownership rate: 82.4% (2000); Median home value: $55,000 (2000); Median rent: $183 per month (2000); Median age of housing: 60+ years (2000).
Transportation: Commute to work: 83.9% car, 1.5% public transportation, 0.0% walk, 14.6% work from home (2000); Travel time to work: 54.7% less than 15 minutes, 33.3% 15 to 30 minutes, 10.3% 30 to 45 minutes, 0.0% 45 to 60 minutes, 1.7% 60 minutes or more (2000)

PORTER (city). Covers a land area of 2.229 square miles and a water area of 0.008 square miles. Located at 44.63° N. Lat.; 96.16° W. Long. Elevation is 1,207 feet.
Population: 190 (2000); Race: 97.5% White, 0.0% Black, 0.0% Asian, 0.0% American Indian and Alaska Native, 2.5% Hispanic of any race, 0.0% two or more races (2000); Density: 85.2 persons per square mile (2000); Age: 23.4% under 18, 16.9% over 64 (2000); Marriage status: 15.8% never married, 60.8% now married, 10.1% widowed, 13.3% divorced (2000); Foreign born: 3.5% (2000); Ancestry (includes multiple ancestries): 36.3% German, 33.3% Norwegian, 8.0% Swedish, 7.5% Irish, 5.0% Belgian (2000).
Economy: Grain, soybeans, alfalfa, sugar beets; livestock. Single-family building permits issued: 0 (2001) / 0 (2000); Multi-family building permits issued: 0 (2001) / 0 (2000); Employment by occupation: 6.6% management, 10.4% professional, 20.8% services, 22.6% sales, 1.9% farming, 9.4% construction, 28.3% production (2000).
Income: Per capita income: $12,910 (2000); Median household income: $21,250 (2000); Poverty rate: 18.1% (2000).
Taxes: Total city taxes per capita: $111 (1997); City property taxes per capita: $101 (1997).
Education: High school graduation rate: 89.4% (2000); College graduation rate: 3.5% (2000).
Housing: Homeownership rate: 76.7% (2000); Median home value: $34,000 (2000); Median rent: $144 per month (2000); Median age of housing: 54 years (2000).
Transportation: Commute to work: 90.6% car, 0.0% public transportation, 7.5% walk, 1.9% work from home (2000); Travel time to work: 47.1% less than 15 minutes, 31.7% 15 to 30 minutes, 11.5% 30 to 45 minutes, 3.8% 45 to 60 minutes, 5.8% 60 minutes or more (2000)

POSEN (township). Covers a land area of 35.118 square miles and a water area of 0.971 square miles. Located at 44.59° N. Lat.; 95.53° W. Long.
Population: 234 (2000); Race: 100.0% White, 0.0% Black, 0.0% Asian, 0.0% American Indian and Alaska Native, 0.0% Hispanic of any race, 0.0% two or more races (2000); Density: 6.7 persons per square mile (2000); Age: 26.5% under 18, 19.2% over 64 (2000); Marriage status: 17.3% never married, 74.0% now married, 6.4% widowed, 2.3% divorced (2000); Foreign born: 0.9% (2000); Ancestry (includes multiple ancestries): 71.7% German, 21.9% Norwegian, 6.8% French (except Basque), 4.1% English, 4.1% Belgian (2000).
Economy: Employment by occupation: 34.4% management, 13.6% professional, 12.0% services, 12.8% sales, 1.6% farming, 6.4% construction, 19.2% production (2000).
Income: Per capita income: $20,132 (2000); Median household income: $40,313 (2000); Poverty rate: 8.7% (2000).
Taxes: Total city taxes per capita: $135 (1997); City property taxes per capita: $135 (1997).
Education: High school graduation rate: 79.1% (2000); College graduation rate: 8.1% (2000).
Housing: Homeownership rate: 90.2% (2000); Median home value: $80,000 (2000); Median rent: $125 per month (2000); Median age of housing: 60+ years (2000).
Transportation: Commute to work: 73.6% car, 0.0% public transportation, 2.4% walk, 24.0% work from home (2000); Travel time to work: 49.5% less than 15 minutes, 22.1% 15 to 30 minutes, 28.4% 30 to 45 minutes, 0.0% 45 to 60 minutes, 0.0% 60 minutes or more (2000)

SAINT LEO (city). Covers a land area of 0.262 square miles and a water area of 0 square miles. Located at 44.71° N. Lat.; 96.05° W. Long. Elevation is 1,119 feet.
Population: 106 (2000); Race: 98.1% White, 0.0% Black, 0.0% Asian, 0.0% American Indian and Alaska Native, 0.0% Hispanic of any race, 0.0% two or more races (2000); Density: 404.0 persons per square mile (2000); Age: 16.2% under 18, 36.2% over 64 (2000); Marriage status: 26.0% never married, 58.3% now married, 13.5% widowed, 2.1% divorced (2000); Foreign born: 3.8% (2000); Ancestry (includes multiple ancestries): 48.6% German, 19.0% Belgian, 15.2% Polish, 14.3% Norwegian, 5.7% Italian (2000).
Economy: Single-family building permits issued: 0 (2001) / 0 (2000); Multi-family building permits issued: 0 (2001) / 0 (2000); Employment by occupation: 15.2% management, 10.9% professional, 13.0% services, 30.4% sales, 0.0% farming, 13.0% construction, 17.4% production (2000).
Income: Per capita income: $15,275 (2000); Median household income: $23,125 (2000); Poverty rate: 11.4% (2000).
Education: High school graduation rate: 72.2% (2000); College graduation rate: 0.0% (2000).
Housing: Homeownership rate: 80.8% (2000); Median home value: $36,700 (2000); Median rent: $200 per month (2000); Median age of housing: 49 years (2000).
Transportation: Commute to work: 76.1% car, 0.0% public transportation, 13.0% walk, 10.9% work from home (2000); Travel time to work: 29.3% less than 15 minutes, 53.7% 15 to 30 minutes, 9.8% 30 to 45 minutes, 7.3% 45 to 60 minutes, 0.0% 60 minutes or more (2000)

SANDNES (township). Covers a land area of 36.056 square miles and a water area of 0.010 square miles. Located at 44.67° N. Lat.; 95.64° W. Long.
Population: 197 (2000); Race: 100.0% White, 0.0% Black, 0.0% Asian, 0.0% American Indian and Alaska Native, 0.0% Hispanic of any race, 0.0% two or more races (2000); Density: 5.5 persons per square mile (2000); Age: 28.6% under 18, 12.6% over 64 (2000); Marriage status: 32.3% never married, 62.9% now married, 3.6% widowed, 1.2% divorced (2000); Foreign born: 0.0% (2000); Ancestry (includes multiple ancestries): 49.0% German, 43.2% Norwegian, 11.7% Swedish, 10.7% French (except Basque), 9.2% Belgian (2000).
Economy: Employment by occupation: 19.7% management, 11.5% professional, 10.7% services, 18.9% sales, 4.9% farming, 13.9% construction, 20.5% production (2000).
Income: Per capita income: $15,280 (2000); Median household income: $45,000 (2000); Poverty rate: 2.0% (2000).
Taxes: Total city taxes per capita: $150 (1997); City property taxes per capita: $150 (1997).
Education: High school graduation rate: 90.5% (2000); College graduation rate: 11.1% (2000).
Housing: Homeownership rate: 94.5% (2000); Median home value: $114,100 (2000); Median age of housing: 60+ years (2000).
Transportation: Commute to work: 71.3% car, 0.0% public transportation, 6.6% walk, 22.1% work from home (2000); Travel time to work: 53.7% less than 15 minutes, 32.6% 15 to 30 minutes, 11.6% 30 to 45 minutes, 2.1% 45 to 60 minutes, 0.0% 60 minutes or more (2000)

SIOUX AGENCY (township). Covers a land area of 41.537 square miles and a water area of 0.571 square miles. Located at 44.68° N. Lat.; 95.43° W. Long.
Population: 237 (2000); Race: 100.0% White, 0.0% Black, 0.0% Asian, 0.0% American Indian and Alaska Native, 0.0% Hispanic of any race, 0.0% two or more races (2000); Density: 5.7 persons per square mile (2000); Age:

25.0% under 18, 18.5% over 64 (2000); Marriage status: 18.9% never married, 72.1% now married, 4.7% widowed, 4.2% divorced (2000); Foreign born: 1.7% (2000); Ancestry (includes multiple ancestries): 55.2% Norwegian, 47.8% German, 12.9% Irish, 3.9% English, 3.4% Swedish (2000).
Economy: Employment by occupation: 18.5% management, 5.9% professional, 16.8% services, 21.8% sales, 0.8% farming, 5.0% construction, 31.1% production (2000).
Income: Per capita income: $19,641 (2000); Median household income: $40,139 (2000); Poverty rate: 4.7% (2000).
Taxes: Total city taxes per capita: $73 (1997); City property taxes per capita: $73 (1997).
Education: High school graduation rate: 89.0% (2000); College graduation rate: 17.7% (2000).
Housing: Homeownership rate: 86.5% (2000); Median home value: $88,500 (2000); Median rent: $458 per month (2000); Median age of housing: 60+ years (2000).
Transportation: Commute to work: 95.0% car, 0.0% public transportation, 0.0% walk, 5.0% work from home (2000); Travel time to work: 34.5% less than 15 minutes, 33.6% 15 to 30 minutes, 26.5% 30 to 45 minutes, 4.4% 45 to 60 minutes, 0.9% 60 minutes or more (2000)

STONY RUN (township). Covers a land area of 40.856 square miles and a water area of 0.360 square miles. Located at 44.84° N. Lat.; 95.65° W. Long.
Population: 544 (2000); Race: 95.3% White, 0.4% Black, 1.4% Asian, 0.0% American Indian and Alaska Native, 2.0% Hispanic of any race, 0.5% two or more races (2000); Density: 13.3 persons per square mile (2000); Age: 31.7% under 18, 8.2% over 64 (2000); Marriage status: 20.7% never married, 71.3% now married, 3.0% widowed, 4.9% divorced (2000); Foreign born: 2.1% (2000); Ancestry (includes multiple ancestries): 47.2% Norwegian, 40.1% German, 8.9% Swedish, 5.4% English, 3.6% Irish (2000).
Economy: Employment by occupation: 10.4% management, 18.7% professional, 11.8% services, 28.7% sales, 0.0% farming, 15.9% construction, 14.5% production (2000).
Income: Per capita income: $19,010 (2000); Median household income: $45,469 (2000); Poverty rate: 9.7% (2000).
Taxes: Total city taxes per capita: $56 (1997); City property taxes per capita: $56 (1997).
Education: High school graduation rate: 89.7% (2000); College graduation rate: 18.5% (2000).
Housing: Homeownership rate: 89.0% (2000); Median home value: $92,500 (2000); Median rent: $181 per month (2000); Median age of housing: 30 years (2000).
Transportation: Commute to work: 85.0% car, 0.0% public transportation, 3.2% walk, 11.8% work from home (2000); Travel time to work: 60.3% less than 15 minutes, 27.9% 15 to 30 minutes, 4.5% 30 to 45 minutes, 2.4% 45 to 60 minutes, 4.9% 60 minutes or more (2000)

SWEDE PRAIRIE (township). Covers a land area of 36.305 square miles and a water area of 0.012 square miles. Located at 44.68° N. Lat.; 95.91° W. Long.
Population: 162 (2000); Race: 100.0% White, 0.0% Black, 0.0% Asian, 0.0% American Indian and Alaska Native, 0.0% Hispanic of any race, 0.0% two or more races (2000); Density: 4.5 persons per square mile (2000); Age: 27.1% under 18, 13.5% over 64 (2000); Marriage status: 22.1% never married, 75.0% now married, 1.4% widowed, 1.4% divorced (2000); Foreign born: 0.0% (2000); Ancestry (includes multiple ancestries): 40.0% Norwegian, 28.8% Belgian, 28.2% German, 19.4% Swedish, 5.9% Dutch (2000).
Economy: Employment by occupation: 30.0% management, 11.1% professional, 12.2% services, 16.7% sales, 5.6% farming, 10.0% construction, 14.4% production (2000).
Income: Per capita income: $18,955 (2000); Median household income: $55,250 (2000); Poverty rate: 6.5% (2000).
Taxes: Total city taxes per capita: $73 (1997); City property taxes per capita: $73 (1997).
Education: High school graduation rate: 91.2% (2000); College graduation rate: 5.3% (2000).
Housing: Homeownership rate: 77.6% (2000); Median home value: $62,500 (2000); Median rent: $225 per month (2000); Median age of housing: 60+ years (2000).
Transportation: Commute to work: 68.2% car, 0.0% public transportation, 2.3% walk, 29.5% work from home (2000); Travel time to work: 32.3% less than 15 minutes, 48.4% 15 to 30 minutes, 16.1% 30 to 45 minutes, 3.2% 45 to 60 minutes, 0.0% 60 minutes or more (2000)

TYRO (township). Covers a land area of 36.297 square miles and a water area of 0.025 square miles. Located at 44.75° N. Lat.; 95.91° W. Long.
Population: 208 (2000); Race: 100.0% White, 0.0% Black, 0.0% Asian, 0.0% American Indian and Alaska Native, 0.0% Hispanic of any race, 0.0% two or more races (2000); Density: 5.7 persons per square mile (2000); Age: 30.9% under 18, 14.9% over 64 (2000); Marriage status: 24.2% never married, 69.1% now married, 4.0% widowed, 2.7% divorced (2000); Foreign born: 0.0% (2000); Ancestry (includes multiple ancestries): 55.7% German, 46.4% Norwegian, 12.4% Swedish, 8.2% Belgian, 5.2% Scotch-Irish (2000).
Economy: Employment by occupation: 29.5% management, 9.5% professional, 7.4% services, 21.1% sales, 2.1% farming, 8.4% construction, 22.1% production (2000).
Income: Per capita income: $16,897 (2000); Median household income: $40,909 (2000); Poverty rate: 3.6% (2000).
Taxes: Total city taxes per capita: $175 (1997); City property taxes per capita: $175 (1997).
Education: High school graduation rate: 79.2% (2000); College graduation rate: 14.6% (2000).
Housing: Homeownership rate: 86.7% (2000); Median home value: $68,000 (2000); Median rent: $175 per month (2000); Median age of housing: 60+ years (2000).
Transportation: Commute to work: 84.6% car, 0.0% public transportation, 0.0% walk, 15.4% work from home (2000); Travel time to work: 26.0% less than 15 minutes, 28.6% 15 to 30 minutes, 42.9% 30 to 45 minutes, 0.0% 45 to 60 minutes, 2.6% 60 minutes or more (2000)

WERGELAND (township). Covers a land area of 33.896 square miles and a water area of 0 square miles. Located at 44.66° N. Lat.; 96.16° W. Long.
Population: 201 (2000); Race: 98.4% White, 0.0% Black, 1.6% Asian, 0.0% American Indian and Alaska Native, 0.0% Hispanic of any race, 0.0% two or more races (2000); Density: 5.9 persons per square mile (2000); Age: 32.3% under 18, 10.9% over 64 (2000); Marriage status: 26.4% never married, 65.5% now married, 2.0% widowed, 6.1% divorced (2000); Foreign born: 0.5% (2000); Ancestry (includes multiple ancestries): 52.1% German, 24.0% Norwegian, 13.5% Belgian, 7.8% Swedish, 5.2% United States or American (2000).
Economy: Employment by occupation: 32.0% management, 13.4% professional, 8.2% services, 15.5% sales, 6.2% farming, 9.3% construction, 15.5% production (2000).
Income: Per capita income: $15,341 (2000); Median household income: $43,250 (2000); Poverty rate: 6.8% (2000).
Taxes: Total city taxes per capita: $94 (1997); City property taxes per capita: $94 (1997).
Education: High school graduation rate: 78.8% (2000); College graduation rate: 9.3% (2000).
Housing: Homeownership rate: 84.1% (2000); Median home value: $72,500 (2000); Median rent: $150 per month (2000); Median age of housing: 60+ years (2000).
Transportation: Commute to work: 65.3% car, 0.0% public transportation, 0.0% walk, 31.6% work from home (2000); Travel time to work: 41.8% less than 15 minutes, 34.3% 15 to 30 minutes, 17.9% 30 to 45 minutes, 0.0% 45 to 60 minutes, 6.0% 60 minutes or more (2000)

WOOD LAKE (city). Covers a land area of 0.805 square miles and a water area of 0 square miles. Located at 44.65° N. Lat.; 95.53° W. Long. Elevation is 1,053 feet.
Population: 436 (2000); Race: 99.3% White, 0.2% Black, 0.0% Asian, 0.0% American Indian and Alaska Native, 2.0% Hispanic of any race, 0.5% two or more races (2000); Density: 541.6 persons per square mile (2000); Age: 27.1% under 18, 20.3% over 64 (2000); Marriage status: 20.7% never married, 63.8% now married, 8.7% widowed, 6.8% divorced (2000); Foreign born: 0.5% (2000); Ancestry (includes multiple ancestries): 58.9% German, 28.1% Norwegian, 9.5% Irish, 7.1% United States or American, 4.4% English (2000).
Economy: Single-family building permits issued: 0 (2001) / 0 (2000); Multi-family building permits issued: 0 (2001) / 0 (2000); Employment by occupation: 9.2% management, 18.4% professional, 8.2% services, 27.0% sales, 2.6% farming, 8.7% construction, 26.0% production (2000).
Income: Per capita income: $16,903 (2000); Median household income: $38,203 (2000); Poverty rate: 3.9% (2000).
Taxes: Total city taxes per capita: $160 (1997); City property taxes per capita: $157 (1997).
Education: High school graduation rate: 71.3% (2000); College graduation rate: 10.3% (2000).

Housing: Homeownership rate: 86.4% (2000); Median home value: $36,900 (2000); Median rent: $306 per month (2000); Median age of housing: 57 years (2000).
Newspapers: Wood Lake News (1 x week)
Transportation: Commute to work: 88.1% car, 0.0% public transportation, 11.9% walk, 0.0% work from home (2000); Travel time to work: 44.8% less than 15 minutes, 33.0% 15 to 30 minutes, 11.3% 30 to 45 minutes, 4.6% 45 to 60 minutes, 6.2% 60 minutes or more (2000)

WOOD LAKE (township). Covers a land area of 34.324 square miles and a water area of 0.865 square miles. Located at 44.67° N. Lat.; 95.55° W. Long. Elevation is 1,053 feet.
Population: 220 (2000); Race: 100.0% White, 0.0% Black, 0.0% Asian, 0.0% American Indian and Alaska Native, 0.0% Hispanic of any race, 0.0% two or more races (2000); Density: 6.4 persons per square mile (2000); Age: 30.5% under 18, 12.3% over 64 (2000); Marriage status: 18.4% never married, 74.3% now married, 5.0% widowed, 2.2% divorced (2000); Foreign born: 0.0% (2000); Ancestry (includes multiple ancestries): 58.4% German, 45.3% Norwegian, 11.9% Irish, 9.1% English, 7.0% Scandinavian (2000).
Economy: Agriculture: grain, soybeans, alfalfa: livestock. Manufacturing: furniture, feed milling. Employment by occupation: 27.5% management, 9.9% professional, 18.3% services, 14.5% sales, 3.1% farming, 9.2% construction, 17.6% production (2000).
Income: Per capita income: $15,331 (2000); Median household income: $34,250 (2000); Poverty rate: 9.5% (2000).
Taxes: Total city taxes per capita: $152 (1997); City property taxes per capita: $152 (1997).
Education: High school graduation rate: 92.5% (2000); College graduation rate: 10.3% (2000).
Housing: Homeownership rate: 84.0% (2000); Median home value: $66,300 (2000); Median rent: $250 per month (2000); Median age of housing: 60+ years (2000).
Transportation: Commute to work: 77.1% car, 0.0% public transportation, 0.0% walk, 22.9% work from home (2000); Travel time to work: 66.3% less than 15 minutes, 19.8% 15 to 30 minutes, 11.9% 30 to 45 minutes, 0.0% 45 to 60 minutes, 2.0% 60 minutes or more (2000)

Missouri

The Show Me State

MISSOURI –Metropolitan Areas, Counties, Independent City, and Central Cities

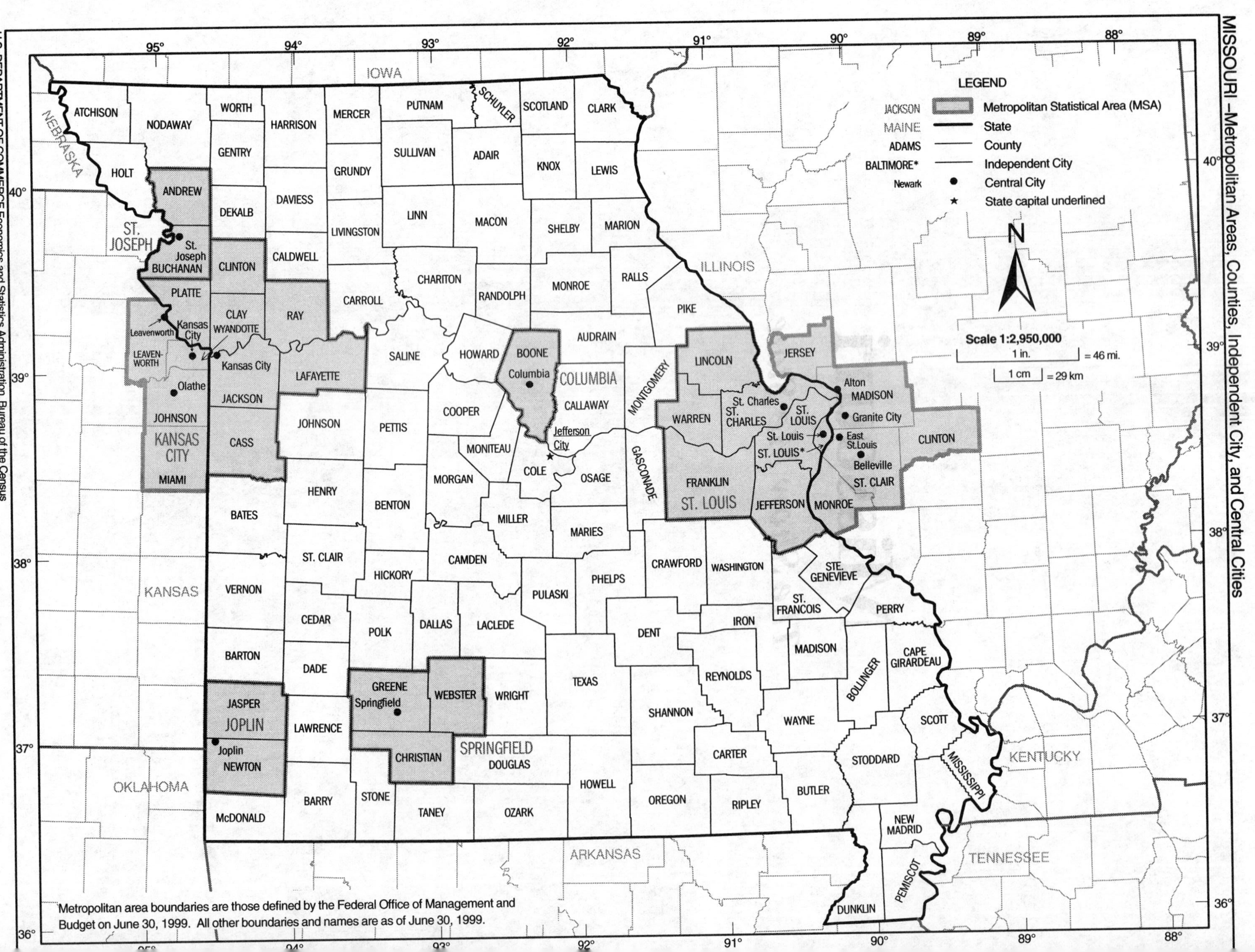

U.S. DEPARTMENT OF COMMERCE Economics and Statistics Administration Bureau of the Census

A

B

C

I

J

K

L

M

CDP = Census Designated Place

N

O

P

Q

R

CDP = Census Designated Place

CDP = Census Designated Place

Y

Z

Adair County

Located in northern Missouri; drained by the Chariton and Salt Rivers. Covers a land area of 567.00 square miles, a water area of 2.30 square miles, and is located in the Central Time Zone. The county government was organized in 1841. County seat is Kirksville.

Weather Station: Kirksville Elevation: 967 feet

	Jan	Feb	Mar	Apr	May	Jun	Jul	Aug	Sep	Oct	Nov	Dec
High	33	39	51	64	73	82	87	85	77	66	50	37
Low	15	21	31	41	52	61	66	63	55	44	32	21
Precip	1.0	1.1	2.5	3.5	5.1	4.3	4.6	4.0	4.3	3.3	2.8	1.7
Snow	6.1	4.8	2.7	1.0	0.0	0.0	0.0	0.0	0.0	tr	1.7	3.6

High and Low temperatures in degrees Fahrenheit; Precipitation and Snow in inches

Population: 24,977 (2000); Race: 95.6% White, 1.2% Black, 1.4% Asian, 0.4% American Indian and Alaska Native, 1.2% Hispanic of any race, 0.9% two or more races (2000); Density: 44.1 persons per square mile (2000); Age: 19.2% under 18, 12.2% over 64 (2000).
Religion: Five largest groups: 10.1% Southern Baptist Convention, 6.0% Catholic Church, 5.5% Christian Church (Disciples of Christ), 5.4% The United Methodist Church, 2.7% The Church of Jesus Christ of Latter-day Saints (2000).
Economy: Unemployment rate: 2.2% (11/2002); Total civilian labor force: 12,707 (11/2002); Leading industries: 20.3% health care and social assistance; 18.4% retail trade; 17.0% manufacturing (2000); Companies that employ more than 1,000 persons: 0 (2000); Companies that employ more than 100 persons: 13 (2000); Farms: 861 totaling 268,101 acres (1997); Minority business ownership rate: 0.0% (1997); Women business ownership rate: 16.7% (1997); Retail sales per capita: $9,255 (1997). Single-family building permits issued: 33 (2001) / 30 (2000); Multi-family building permits issued: 14 (2001) / 81 (2000).
Income: Per capita income: $15,484 (2000); Median household income: $26,677 (2000); Poverty rate: 23.3% (2000); Bankruptcy rate: 2.41% (2001).
Taxes: Total county taxes per capita: $61 (1997); County property taxes per capita: $13 (1997).
Education: High school graduation rate: 84.6% (2000); College graduation rate: 28.5% (2000).
Housing: Homeownership rate: 60.4% (2000); Median home value: $73,900 (2000); Median rent: $329 per month (2000); Median age of housing: 31 years (2000).
Health: Birth rate: 128.1 per 10,000 population (1998); Age adjusted death rate: 95.3 per 10,000 population (1999); Age adjusted cancer mortality rate: 227.4 deaths per 100,000 population (1999). Number of physicians: 3.6 per 10,000 population (1999); Number of hospital beds: 65.7 per 10,000 population (1999).
Elections: 2000 Presidential election results: 38.9% Gore, 57.3% Bush, 2.9% Nader, 0.3% Buchanan
National and State Parks: Sugar Creek State Forest; Thousand Hills State Park
Additional Information Contacts
Adair County Government Offices 660-665-3350
Kirksville Chamber of Commerce 660-665-3766
Northeast Central Board of Realtors 660-665-3400

Adair County Communities

BRASHEAR (city). Covers a land area of 0.351 square miles and a water area of 0 square miles. Located at 40.14° N. Lat.; 92.37° W. Long. Elevation is 875 feet.
Population: 280 (2000); Race: 97.8% White, 2.2% Black, 0.0% Asian, 0.0% American Indian and Alaska Native, 0.7% Hispanic of any race, 0.0% two or more races (2000); Density: 796.7 persons per square mile (2000); Age: 26.4% under 18, 16.1% over 64 (2000); Marriage status: 16.0% never married, 57.1% now married, 11.3% widowed, 15.6% divorced (2000); Foreign born: 0.0% (2000); Ancestry (includes multiple ancestries): 22.7% German, 12.8% Irish, 9.2% United States or American, 5.9% Other groups, 5.5% Italian (2000).
Economy: Single-family building permits issued: 0 (2001) / 0 (2000); Multi-family building permits issued: 0 (2001) / 0 (2000); Employment by occupation: 7.4% management, 11.6% professional, 14.9% services, 25.6% sales, 1.7% farming, 14.0% construction, 24.8% production (2000).
Income: Per capita income: $11,763 (2000); Median household income: $21,750 (2000); Poverty rate: 26.5% (2000).
Taxes: Total city taxes per capita: $146 (2000); City property taxes per capita: $107 (2000).
Education: High school graduation rate: 89.1% (2000); College graduation rate: 10.9% (2000).

School District(s)

Adair Co. R-II (KG-12)
2000 Enrollment: 269 660-323-5272
Housing: Homeownership rate: 74.4% (2000); Median home value: $32,900 (2000); Median rent: $182 per month (2000); Median age of housing: 54 years (2000).
Transportation: Commute to work: 90.1% car, 0.0% public transportation, 4.1% walk, 5.8% work from home (2000); Travel time to work: 19.3% less than 15 minutes, 59.6% 15 to 30 minutes, 15.8% 30 to 45 minutes, 0.0% 45 to 60 minutes, 5.3% 60 minutes or more (2000)

GIBBS (village). Covers a land area of 0.249 square miles and a water area of 0 square miles. Located at 40.09° N. Lat.; 92.41° W. Long. Elevation is 915 feet.
Population: 100 (2000); Race: 100.0% White, 0.0% Black, 0.0% Asian, 0.0% American Indian and Alaska Native, 0.0% Hispanic of any race, 0.0% two or more races (2000); Density: 401.2 persons per square mile (2000); Age: 30.9% under 18, 9.3% over 64 (2000); Marriage status: 26.4% never married, 62.5% now married, 2.8% widowed, 8.3% divorced (2000); Foreign born: 0.0% (2000); Ancestry (includes multiple ancestries): 25.8% United States or American, 22.7% German, 12.4% French (except Basque), 7.2% Irish, 6.2% Other groups (2000).
Economy: Employment by occupation: 0.0% management, 18.4% professional, 36.8% services, 5.3% sales, 5.3% farming, 10.5% construction, 23.7% production (2000).
Income: Per capita income: $9,368 (2000); Median household income: $23,611 (2000); Poverty rate: 37.1% (2000).
Taxes: Total city taxes per capita: $57 (1997); City property taxes per capita: $34 (1997).
Education: High school graduation rate: 75.4% (2000); College graduation rate: 9.8% (2000).
Housing: Homeownership rate: 83.3% (2000); Median home value: $30,000 (2000); Median rent: $288 per month (2000); Median age of housing: 60+ years (2000).
Transportation: Commute to work: 100.0% car, 0.0% public transportation, 0.0% walk, 0.0% work from home (2000); Travel time to work: 10.5% less than 15 minutes, 65.8% 15 to 30 minutes, 15.8% 30 to 45 minutes, 0.0% 45 to 60 minutes, 7.9% 60 minutes or more (2000)

KIRKSVILLE (city). Covers a land area of 10.460 square miles and a water area of 0.044 square miles. Located at 40.19° N. Lat.; 92.58° W. Long. Elevation is 982 feet.
History: Kirksville was founded in 1841, the year that Adair County was organized. Local legend relates that Jesse Kirk and his wife, operators of a tavern, invited the county commissioners to a turkey dinner on the condition that the town be named for them.
Population: 16,988 (2000); Race: 94.1% White, 1.7% Black, 1.9% Asian, 0.4% American Indian and Alaska Native, 1.4% Hispanic of any race, 1.3% two or more races (2000); Density: 1,624.0 persons per square mile (2000); Age: 15.4% under 18, 11.9% over 64 (2000); Marriage status: 49.9% never married, 35.8% now married, 6.4% widowed, 7.8% divorced (2000); Foreign born: 2.5% (2000); Ancestry (includes multiple ancestries): 26.4% German, 14.8% Irish, 12.3% English, 10.4% Other groups, 9.9% United States or American (2000).
Vital Statistics: Birth rate: 130.1 per 10,000 population (1998)
Economy: Single-family building permits issued: 33 (2001) / 30 (2000); Multi-family building permits issued: 14 (2001) / 81 (2000); Employment by occupation: 8.2% management, 28.8% professional, 19.3% services, 24.2% sales, 0.4% farming, 6.3% construction, 12.8% production (2000).
Income: Per capita income: $14,388 (2000); Median household income: $22,836 (2000); Poverty rate: 30.6% (2000).
Taxes: Total city taxes per capita: $438 (2000); City property taxes per capita: $60 (2000).
Education: High school graduation rate: 84.8% (2000); College graduation rate: 33.3% (2000).

School District(s)

Kirksville R-III (PK-12)
2000 Enrollment: 2,363 660-665-7774

Four-year College(s)

Kirksville College of Osteopathic Medicine (Private, Not-for-profit)
2001 Enrollment: 1,140 660-626-2121
Truman State University (Public)
2001 Enrollment: 6,005 660-785-4000
2001 Tuition: In-state $3,800; Out-of-state $6,928

Two-year College(s)

Northeast Missouri Bible College (Private, Not-for-profit, Undenominational)
2001 Enrollment: n/a 660-665-2323

Housing: Homeownership rate: 47.6% (2000); Median home value: $73,700 (2000); Median rent: $335 per month (2000); Median age of housing: 32 years (2000).
Hospitals: Northeast Regional Medical Center (164 beds)
Safety: Violent crime rate: 36.3 per 10,000 population; Property crime rate: 334.6 per 10,000 population (2001).
Newspapers: Kirksville Daily Express & News (6 x week); Kirksville Crier (1 x week)
Transportation: Commute to work: 79.9% car, 0.5% public transportation, 15.0% walk, 2.5% work from home (2000); Travel time to work: 81.4% less than 15 minutes, 11.1% 15 to 30 minutes, 3.4% 30 to 45 minutes, 1.7% 45 to 60 minutes, 2.4% 60 minutes or more (2000)
Airports: Kirksville Regional
Additional Information Contacts
Kirksville Chamber of Commerce 660-665-3766
Northeast Central Board of Realtors 660-665-3400

MILLARD (village). Covers a land area of 0.124 square miles and a water area of 0 square miles. Located at 40.10° N. Lat.; 92.54° W. Long. Elevation is 970 feet.
Population: 75 (2000); Race: 100.0% White, 0.0% Black, 0.0% Asian, 0.0% American Indian and Alaska Native, 0.0% Hispanic of any race, 0.0% two or more races (2000); Density: 606.5 persons per square mile (2000); Age: 0.0% under 18, 18.3% over 64 (2000); Marriage status: 5.0% never married, 63.3% now married, 11.7% widowed, 20.0% divorced (2000); Foreign born: 0.0% (2000); Ancestry (includes multiple ancestries): 16.7% German, 10.0% United States or American, 8.3% Dutch, 3.3% British, 3.3% Irish (2000).
Economy: Employment by occupation: 6.5% management, 12.9% professional, 29.0% services, 16.1% sales, 0.0% farming, 12.9% construction, 22.6% production (2000).
Income: Per capita income: $16,458 (2000); Median household income: $25,833 (2000); Poverty rate: 18.3% (2000).
Taxes: Total city taxes per capita: $14 (1997); City property taxes per capita: $0 (1997).
Education: High school graduation rate: 81.7% (2000); College graduation rate: 13.3% (2000).
Housing: Homeownership rate: 87.5% (2000); Median home value: $55,000 (2000); Median rent: $175 per month (2000); Median age of housing: 34 years (2000).
Transportation: Commute to work: 93.5% car, 0.0% public transportation, 0.0% walk, 6.5% work from home (2000); Travel time to work: 44.8% less than 15 minutes, 55.2% 15 to 30 minutes, 0.0% 30 to 45 minutes, 0.0% 45 to 60 minutes, 0.0% 60 minutes or more (2000)

NOVINGER (city). Covers a land area of 0.806 square miles and a water area of 0.016 square miles. Located at 40.23° N. Lat.; 92.70° W. Long. Elevation is 790 feet.
History: Settled 1830s; platted 1888. Former coal-mining town; population peaked c.1900 at c.5,000 inhabitants.
Population: 534 (2000); Race: 99.3% White, 0.0% Black, 0.0% Asian, 0.7% American Indian and Alaska Native, 1.1% Hispanic of any race, 0.0% two or more races (2000); Density: 662.7 persons per square mile (2000); Age: 27.4% under 18, 14.2% over 64 (2000); Marriage status: 21.6% never married, 57.1% now married, 10.8% widowed, 10.6% divorced (2000); Foreign born: 0.4% (2000); Ancestry (includes multiple ancestries): 21.0% United States or American, 17.1% German, 16.9% Irish, 11.0% Other groups, 6.7% English (2000).
Economy: Corn, soybeans; cattle, hogs, poultry. Employment by occupation: 8.4% management, 11.4% professional, 29.1% services, 11.0% sales, 0.0% farming, 10.5% construction, 29.5% production (2000).
Income: Per capita income: $10,586 (2000); Median household income: $20,990 (2000); Poverty rate: 15.6% (2000).
Taxes: Total city taxes per capita: $44 (1997); City property taxes per capita: $15 (1997).
Education: High school graduation rate: 71.3% (2000); College graduation rate: 6.0% (2000).

School District(s)

Adair Co. R-I (PK-12)
2000 Enrollment: 324 660-488-6411

Housing: Homeownership rate: 75.0% (2000); Median home value: $26,100 (2000); Median rent: $231 per month (2000); Median age of housing: 60+ years (2000).
Transportation: Commute to work: 96.2% car, 0.0% public transportation, 0.0% walk, 2.1% work from home (2000); Travel time to work: 32.8% less than 15 minutes, 44.5% 15 to 30 minutes, 14.8% 30 to 45 minutes, 3.1% 45 to 60 minutes, 4.8% 60 minutes or more (2000)

Andrew County

Located in northwestern Missouri; bounded on the west by the Nodaway River, and on the southwest by the Missouri River. Covers a land area of 435.20 square miles, a water area of 1.30 square miles, and is located in the Central Time Zone. The county government was organized in 1841. County seat is Savannah.

Andrew County is part of the St. Joseph, MO MSA. The entire metro area includes: Andrew County; Buchanan County

Population: 16,492 (2000); Race: 98.0% White, 0.4% Black, 0.3% Asian, 0.2% American Indian and Alaska Native, 1.4% Hispanic of any race, 0.6% two or more races (2000); Density: 37.9 persons per square mile (2000); Age: 26.2% under 18, 14.4% over 64 (2000).
Religion: Five largest groups: 13.0% Southern Baptist Convention, 9.1% Christian Church (Disciples of Christ), 6.0% The United Methodist Church, 5.5% The Church of Jesus Christ of Latter-day Saints, 2.5% United Church of Christ (2000).
Economy: Unemployment rate: 4.3% (11/2002); Total civilian labor force: 8,298 (11/2002); Leading industries: 45.9% retail trade; 14.9% health care and social assistance; 7.9% accommodation & food services (2000); Companies that employ more than 1,000 persons: 0 (2000); Companies that employ more than 100 persons: 3 (2000); Farms: 820 totaling 226,725 acres (1997); Minority business ownership rate: 0.0% (1997); Women business ownership rate: 28.0% (1997); Retail sales per capita: $5,648 (1997). Single-family building permits issued: 17 (2001) / 17 (2000); Multi-family building permits issued: 0 (2001) / 22 (2000).
Income: Per capita income: $19,375 (2000); Median household income: $40,688 (2000); Poverty rate: 8.2% (2000); Bankruptcy rate: 3.50% (2001).
Taxes: Total county taxes per capita: $105 (2000); County property taxes per capita: $62 (2000).
Education: High school graduation rate: 84.7% (2000); College graduation rate: 18.8% (2000).
Housing: Homeownership rate: 80.0% (2000); Median home value: $89,000 (2000); Median rent: $341 per month (2000); Median age of housing: 28 years (2000).
Health: Birth rate: 104.9 per 10,000 population (1998); Age adjusted death rate: 82.9 per 10,000 population (1999); Age adjusted cancer mortality rate: 190.3 deaths per 100,000 population (1999). Number of physicians: 61.2 per 10,000 population (1999); Number of hospital beds: 386.9 per 10,000 population (1999).
Elections: 2000 Presidential election results: 38.4% Gore, 58.5% Bush, 1.8% Nader, 0.7% Buchanan
National and State Parks: Eva Neely Davis Memorial State Forest
Additional Information Contacts
Andrew County Government Offices. 816-324-3624
Savannah Chamber of Commerce 816-324-3976

Andrew County Communities

AMAZONIA (village). Covers a land area of 0.353 square miles and a water area of 0 square miles. Located at 39.88° N. Lat.; 94.89° W. Long. Elevation is 835 feet.
Population: 277 (2000); Race: 100.0% White, 0.0% Black, 0.0% Asian, 0.0% American Indian and Alaska Native, 0.0% Hispanic of any race, 0.0% two or more races (2000); Density: 785.1 persons per square mile (2000); Age: 25.3% under 18, 7.6% over 64 (2000); Marriage status: 18.7% never married, 67.6% now married, 5.5% widowed, 8.2% divorced (2000); Foreign born: 0.0% (2000); Ancestry (includes multiple ancestries): 26.0% German, 11.2% Irish, 9.7% English, 7.2% United States or American, 5.4% Other groups (2000).
Economy: Employment by occupation: 9.6% management, 5.5% professional, 21.9% services, 23.3% sales, 3.4% farming, 13.0% construction, 23.3% production (2000).
Income: Per capita income: $17,609 (2000); Median household income: $36,250 (2000); Poverty rate: 12.0% (2000).
Taxes: Total city taxes per capita: $171 (1997); City property taxes per capita: $36 (1997).

Education: High school graduation rate: 72.8% (2000); College graduation rate: 5.6% (2000).
Housing: Homeownership rate: 87.3% (2000); Median home value: $48,800 (2000); Median rent: $263 per month (2000); Median age of housing: 40 years (2000).
Transportation: Commute to work: 93.8% car, 0.0% public transportation, 3.4% walk, 1.4% work from home (2000); Travel time to work: 25.9% less than 15 minutes, 52.4% 15 to 30 minutes, 14.0% 30 to 45 minutes, 4.2% 45 to 60 minutes, 3.5% 60 minutes or more (2000)

BOLCKOW (city). Covers a land area of 0.325 square miles and a water area of 0 square miles. Located at 40.11° N. Lat.; 94.82° W. Long. Elevation is 948 feet.
Population: 234 (2000); Race: 97.3% White, 0.0% Black, 0.9% Asian, 0.9% American Indian and Alaska Native, 0.0% Hispanic of any race, 0.9% two or more races (2000); Density: 720.2 persons per square mile (2000); Age: 22.8% under 18, 5.9% over 64 (2000); Marriage status: 17.0% never married, 60.8% now married, 4.0% widowed, 18.2% divorced (2000); Foreign born: 1.8% (2000); Ancestry (includes multiple ancestries): 14.6% German, 14.2% United States or American, 9.6% Other groups, 9.1% Irish, 7.3% English (2000).
Economy: Employment by occupation: 4.6% management, 5.6% professional, 19.4% services, 20.4% sales, 0.0% farming, 24.1% construction, 25.9% production (2000).
Income: Per capita income: $13,028 (2000); Median household income: $26,250 (2000); Poverty rate: 15.5% (2000).
Taxes: Total city taxes per capita: $50 (1997); City property taxes per capita: $15 (1997).
Education: High school graduation rate: 85.1% (2000); College graduation rate: 3.5% (2000).
Housing: Homeownership rate: 83.3% (2000); Median home value: $26,700 (2000); Median rent: $225 per month (2000); Median age of housing: 60+ years (2000).
Transportation: Commute to work: 93.6% car, 0.0% public transportation, 0.0% walk, 6.4% work from home (2000); Travel time to work: 9.7% less than 15 minutes, 35.0% 15 to 30 minutes, 42.7% 30 to 45 minutes, 8.7% 45 to 60 minutes, 3.9% 60 minutes or more (2000)

COSBY (village). Covers a land area of 0.094 square miles and a water area of 0 square miles. Located at 39.86° N. Lat.; 94.68° W. Long. Elevation is 938 feet.
Population: 143 (2000); Race: 100.0% White, 0.0% Black, 0.0% Asian, 0.0% American Indian and Alaska Native, 0.0% Hispanic of any race, 0.0% two or more races (2000); Density: 1,525.5 persons per square mile (2000); Age: 20.7% under 18, 6.3% over 64 (2000); Marriage status: 24.7% never married, 64.5% now married, 2.2% widowed, 8.6% divorced (2000); Foreign born: 0.0% (2000); Ancestry (includes multiple ancestries): 41.4% German, 17.1% Irish, 15.3% United States or American, 5.4% English, 2.7% Dutch (2000).
Economy: Meat processing. Employment by occupation: 10.8% management, 15.4% professional, 12.3% services, 36.9% sales, 0.0% farming, 3.1% construction, 21.5% production (2000).
Income: Per capita income: $19,121 (2000); Median household income: $35,938 (2000); Poverty rate: 4.5% (2000).
Taxes: Total city taxes per capita: $80 (1997); City property taxes per capita: $16 (1997).
Education: High school graduation rate: 82.5% (2000); College graduation rate: 15.0% (2000).

School District(s)

Avenue City R-IX (KG-08)
2000 Enrollment: 132 816-662-2305

Housing: Homeownership rate: 88.7% (2000); Median home value: $43,000 (2000); Median rent: $313 per month (2000); Median age of housing: 60+ years (2000).
Transportation: Commute to work: 98.5% car, 0.0% public transportation, 0.0% walk, 1.5% work from home (2000); Travel time to work: 7.8% less than 15 minutes, 68.8% 15 to 30 minutes, 18.8% 30 to 45 minutes, 0.0% 45 to 60 minutes, 4.7% 60 minutes or more (2000)

COUNTRY CLUB (village). Aka Country Club Village. Covers a land area of 1.168 square miles and a water area of 0 square miles. Located at 39.82° N. Lat.; 94.82° W. Long.
Population: 1,846 (2000); Race: 97.2% White, 0.9% Black, 0.4% Asian, 0.4% American Indian and Alaska Native, 1.9% Hispanic of any race, 0.5% two or more races (2000); Density: 1,580.3 persons per square mile (2000); Age: 28.1% under 18, 9.4% over 64 (2000); Marriage status: 21.6% never married, 63.1% now married, 4.0% widowed, 11.4% divorced (2000); Foreign born: 1.1% (2000); Ancestry (includes multiple ancestries): 29.9% German, 18.6% Irish, 10.2% Other groups, 9.1% United States or American, 7.9% English (2000).
Economy: Residential suburb. Single-family building permits issued: 5 (2001) / 4 (2000); Multi-family building permits issued: 0 (2001) / 4 (2000); Employment by occupation: 12.8% management, 18.9% professional, 14.6% services, 30.9% sales, 0.4% farming, 10.3% construction, 12.2% production (2000).
Income: Per capita income: $19,871 (2000); Median household income: $45,987 (2000); Poverty rate: 3.1% (2000).
Taxes: Total city taxes per capita: $40 (1997); City property taxes per capita: $26 (1997).
Education: High school graduation rate: 90.4% (2000); College graduation rate: 27.4% (2000).
Housing: Homeownership rate: 73.8% (2000); Median home value: $94,600 (2000); Median rent: $452 per month (2000); Median age of housing: 25 years (2000).
Transportation: Commute to work: 95.7% car, 0.2% public transportation, 0.7% walk, 2.3% work from home (2000); Travel time to work: 37.3% less than 15 minutes, 49.4% 15 to 30 minutes, 5.9% 30 to 45 minutes, 3.5% 45 to 60 minutes, 3.9% 60 minutes or more (2000)

FILLMORE (city). Covers a land area of 0.139 square miles and a water area of 0 square miles. Located at 40.02° N. Lat.; 94.97° W. Long. Elevation is 764 feet.
Population: 211 (2000); Race: 95.1% White, 0.0% Black, 0.0% Asian, 0.9% American Indian and Alaska Native, 0.9% Hispanic of any race, 4.0% two or more races (2000); Density: 1,520.0 persons per square mile (2000); Age: 32.6% under 18, 9.8% over 64 (2000); Marriage status: 31.0% never married, 55.7% now married, 3.2% widowed, 10.1% divorced (2000); Foreign born: 0.0% (2000); Ancestry (includes multiple ancestries): 17.0% United States or American, 10.7% German, 5.8% Irish, 5.4% English, 3.1% Scotch-Irish (2000).
Economy: Employment by occupation: 10.2% management, 9.3% professional, 11.1% services, 9.3% sales, 4.6% farming, 24.1% construction, 31.5% production (2000).
Income: Per capita income: $13,047 (2000); Median household income: $31,750 (2000); Poverty rate: 15.2% (2000).
Taxes: Total city taxes per capita: $23 (1997); City property taxes per capita: $23 (1997).
Education: High school graduation rate: 77.8% (2000); College graduation rate: 9.5% (2000).
Housing: Homeownership rate: 80.7% (2000); Median home value: $40,000 (2000); Median rent: $238 per month (2000); Median age of housing: 60+ years (2000).
Transportation: Commute to work: 93.5% car, 0.0% public transportation, 0.0% walk, 0.0% work from home (2000); Travel time to work: 9.3% less than 15 minutes, 38.9% 15 to 30 minutes, 26.9% 30 to 45 minutes, 0.9% 45 to 60 minutes, 24.1% 60 minutes or more (2000)

HELENA (unincorporated postal area, zip code 64459). Covers a land area of 23.874 square miles and a water area of 0 square miles. Located at 39.91° N. Lat.; 94.64° W. Long. Elevation is 1,066 feet.
Population: 553 (2000); Race: 100.0% White, 0.0% Black, 0.0% Asian, 0.0% American Indian and Alaska Native, 1.5% Hispanic of any race, 0.0% two or more races (2000); Density: 23.2 persons per square mile (2000); Age: 20.7% under 18, 14.2% over 64 (2000); Marriage status: 20.3% never married, 63.4% now married, 4.1% widowed, 12.2% divorced (2000); Foreign born: 0.0% (2000); Ancestry (includes multiple ancestries): 30.1% German, 10.5% English, 10.3% United States or American, 5.7% Irish, 4.1% Swiss (2000).
Economy: Employment by occupation: 22.8% management, 4.4% professional, 8.4% services, 20.4% sales, 0.8% farming, 31.2% construction, 12.0% production (2000).
Income: Per capita income: $17,066 (2000); Median household income: $33,088 (2000); Poverty rate: 8.1% (2000).
Education: High school graduation rate: 86.6% (2000); College graduation rate: 15.0% (2000).
Housing: Homeownership rate: 87.4% (2000); Median home value: $66,500 (2000); Median rent: $241 per month (2000); Median age of housing: 41 years (2000).
Transportation: Commute to work: 94.3% car, 0.0% public transportation, 0.0% walk, 5.7% work from home (2000); Travel time to work: 8.6% less than 15 minutes, 41.4% 15 to 30 minutes, 34.5% 30 to 45 minutes, 0.0% 45 to 60 minutes, 15.5% 60 minutes or more (2000)

REA (city). Covers a land area of 0.121 square miles and a water area of 0 square miles. Located at 40.06° N. Lat.; 94.76° W. Long. Elevation is 1,059 feet.
Population: 56 (2000); Race: 100.0% White, 0.0% Black, 0.0% Asian, 0.0% American Indian and Alaska Native, 0.0% Hispanic of any race, 0.0% two or more races (2000); Density: 461.2 persons per square mile (2000); Age: 26.1% under 18, 15.2% over 64 (2000); Marriage status: 0.0% never married, 76.5% now married, 5.9% widowed, 17.6% divorced (2000); Foreign born: 0.0% (2000); Ancestry (includes multiple ancestries): 21.7% European, 19.6% English, 19.6% German, 15.2% United States or American, 8.7% Irish (2000).
Economy: Corn, soybeans, wheat; cattle. Employment by occupation: 14.3% management, 14.3% professional, 14.3% services, 4.8% sales, 9.5% farming, 19.0% construction, 23.8% production (2000).
Income: Per capita income: $13,639 (2000); Median household income: $31,250 (2000); Poverty rate: 4.3% (2000).
Education: High school graduation rate: 73.5% (2000); College graduation rate: 11.8% (2000).
Housing: Homeownership rate: 90.9% (2000); Median home value: $37,500 (2000); Median rent: $225 per month (2000); Median age of housing: 50 years (2000).
Transportation: Commute to work: 76.2% car, 9.5% public transportation, 14.3% walk, 0.0% work from home (2000); Travel time to work: 23.8% less than 15 minutes, 33.3% 15 to 30 minutes, 42.9% 30 to 45 minutes, 0.0% 45 to 60 minutes, 0.0% 60 minutes or more (2000)

ROSENDALE (city). Covers a land area of 0.311 square miles and a water area of 0 square miles. Located at 40.04° N. Lat.; 94.82° W. Long. Elevation is 909 feet.
Population: 180 (2000); Race: 98.8% White, 0.0% Black, 0.0% Asian, 0.0% American Indian and Alaska Native, 0.0% Hispanic of any race, 1.3% two or more races (2000); Density: 578.4 persons per square mile (2000); Age: 30.0% under 18, 12.5% over 64 (2000); Marriage status: 22.4% never married, 65.6% now married, 4.0% widowed, 8.0% divorced (2000); Foreign born: 0.0% (2000); Ancestry (includes multiple ancestries): 26.9% German, 11.3% Other groups, 9.4% United States or American, 9.4% Irish, 8.1% Scottish (2000).
Economy: Employment by occupation: 18.8% management, 5.0% professional, 28.7% services, 13.8% sales, 2.5% farming, 17.5% construction, 13.8% production (2000).
Income: Per capita income: $12,847 (2000); Median household income: $26,731 (2000); Poverty rate: 11.9% (2000).
Taxes: Total city taxes per capita: $32 (1997); City property taxes per capita: $11 (1997).
Education: High school graduation rate: 78.9% (2000); College graduation rate: 10.5% (2000).

School District(s)

North Andrew Co. R-VI (KG-12)
2000 Enrollment: 362 816-567-2965
Housing: Homeownership rate: 80.0% (2000); Median home value: $24,000 (2000); Median rent: $200 per month (2000); Median age of housing: 60+ years (2000).
Transportation: Commute to work: 96.3% car, 0.0% public transportation, 3.8% walk, 0.0% work from home (2000); Travel time to work: 20.0% less than 15 minutes, 28.7% 15 to 30 minutes, 31.3% 30 to 45 minutes, 5.0% 45 to 60 minutes, 15.0% 60 minutes or more (2000)

SAVANNAH (city). Covers a land area of 3.126 square miles and a water area of 0.003 square miles. Located at 39.94° N. Lat.; 94.83° W. Long. Elevation is 1,115 feet.
History: Savannah was platted in 1841, the year Andrew County was created, and named for Savannah, Georgia. At the start of the Civil War there were two newspapers published in Savannah, one strongly pro-slavery, the other strongly abolitionist. Union troops destroyed the plant of the pro-slavery Northwest Democrat. A short time later, Confederate troops confiscated the type of the abolitionist Plain Dealer and melted it down for bullets.
Population: 4,762 (2000); Race: 98.1% White, 0.1% Black, 0.2% Asian, 0.0% American Indian and Alaska Native, 2.0% Hispanic of any race, 0.2% two or more races (2000); Density: 1,523.2 persons per square mile (2000); Age: 26.3% under 18, 20.9% over 64 (2000); Marriage status: 19.1% never married, 57.0% now married, 11.5% widowed, 12.4% divorced (2000); Foreign born: 0.8% (2000); Ancestry (includes multiple ancestries): 21.8% German, 14.8% United States or American, 10.6% Irish, 10.5% English, 8.2% Other groups (2000).
Economy: Single-family building permits issued: 12 (2001) / 13 (2000); Multi-family building permits issued: 0 (2001) / 18 (2000); Employment by occupation: 10.5% management, 13.8% professional, 19.7% services, 26.6% sales, 0.3% farming, 9.1% construction, 20.0% production (2000).
Income: Per capita income: $17,809 (2000); Median household income: $32,996 (2000); Poverty rate: 11.8% (2000).
Taxes: Total city taxes per capita: $137 (1997); City property taxes per capita: $76 (1997).
Education: High school graduation rate: 83.8% (2000); College graduation rate: 16.1% (2000).

School District(s)

Savannah R-III (PK-12)
2000 Enrollment: 2,417 816-324-3144
Housing: Homeownership rate: 68.3% (2000); Median home value: $81,200 (2000); Median rent: $345 per month (2000); Median age of housing: 28 years (2000).
Safety: Violent crime rate: 0.0 per 10,000 population; Property crime rate: 75.1 per 10,000 population (2001).
Newspapers: Savannah Reporter (1 x week)
Transportation: Commute to work: 91.4% car, 0.0% public transportation, 3.3% walk, 3.6% work from home (2000); Travel time to work: 26.6% less than 15 minutes, 47.2% 15 to 30 minutes, 14.3% 30 to 45 minutes, 2.0% 45 to 60 minutes, 10.0% 60 minutes or more (2000)
Additional Information Contacts
Savannah Chamber of Commerce 816-324-3976

Atchison County

Located in northwestern Missouri; bounded on the west by the Missouri River and the Nebraska border. Covers a land area of 544.70 square miles, a water area of 2.60 square miles, and is located in the Central Time Zone. The county government was organized in 1845. County seat is Rock Port.
Population: 6,430 (2000); Race: 96.6% White, 2.2% Black, 0.2% Asian, 0.2% American Indian and Alaska Native, 0.4% Hispanic of any race, 0.4% two or more races (2000); Density: 11.8 persons per square mile (2000); Age: 24.1% under 18, 21.1% over 64 (2000).
Religion: Five largest groups: 21.8% The United Methodist Church, 20.9% Southern Baptist Convention, 14.1% Evangelical Lutheran Church in America, 5.3% Christian Church (Disciples of Christ), 4.8% Presbyterian Church (U.S.A.) (2000).
Economy: Unemployment rate: 2.6% (11/2002); Total civilian labor force: 2,775 (11/2002); Leading industries: 30.4% health care and social assistance; 19.7% retail trade; 12.5% accommodation & food services (2000); Companies that employ more than 1,000 persons: 0 (2000); Companies that employ more than 100 persons: 1 (2000); Farms: 471 totaling 294,149 acres (1997); Minority business ownership rate: 0.0% (1997); Women business ownership rate: 29.8% (1997); Retail sales per capita: $8,389 (1997). Single-family building permits issued: 2 (2001) / 6 (2000); Multi-family building permits issued: 0 (2001) / 0 (2000).
Income: Per capita income: $16,956 (2000); Median household income: $30,959 (2000); Poverty rate: 11.6% (2000); Bankruptcy rate: 3.39% (2001).
Taxes: Total county taxes per capita: $219 (2000); County property taxes per capita: $137 (2000).
Education: High school graduation rate: 80.0% (2000); College graduation rate: 16.6% (2000).
Housing: Homeownership rate: 69.2% (2000); Median home value: $49,800 (2000); Median rent: $224 per month (2000); Median age of housing: 52 years (2000).
Health: Birth rate: 105.8 per 10,000 population (1998); Age adjusted death rate: 91.6 per 10,000 population (1999); Age adjusted cancer mortality rate: 192.8 deaths per 100,000 population (1999). Number of physicians: 4.7 per 10,000 population (1999); Number of hospital beds: 38.9 per 10,000 population (1999).
Elections: 2000 Presidential election results: 35.3% Gore, 62.6% Bush, 1.2% Nader, 0.6% Buchanan
Additional Information Contacts
Atchison County Government Offices 660-744-6214
Tarkio Chamber of Commerce 660-736-5772

Atchison County Communities

FAIRFAX (city). Covers a land area of 0.479 square miles and a water area of 0 square miles. Located at 40.34° N. Lat.; 95.39° W. Long. Elevation is 905 feet.

Population: 645 (2000); Race: 97.8% White, 0.9% Black, 0.3% Asian, 0.3% American Indian and Alaska Native, 0.0% Hispanic of any race, 0.0% two or more races (2000); Density: 1,345.4 persons per square mile (2000); Age: 23.5% under 18, 20.6% over 64 (2000); Marriage status: 17.5% never married, 63.5% now married, 12.3% widowed, 6.7% divorced (2000); Foreign born: 0.5% (2000); Ancestry (includes multiple ancestries): 24.1% United States or American, 18.4% German, 11.2% Irish, 9.8% English, 7.4% Other groups (2000).
Economy: Soybeans, corn, wheat; hogs, cattle. Employment by occupation: 8.6% management, 18.2% professional, 22.5% services, 22.8% sales, 4.3% farming, 8.3% construction, 15.1% production (2000).
Income: Per capita income: $16,417 (2000); Median household income: $30,156 (2000); Poverty rate: 8.7% (2000).
Taxes: Total city taxes per capita: $147 (1997); City property taxes per capita: $43 (1997).
Education: High school graduation rate: 81.8% (2000); College graduation rate: 18.6% (2000).

School District(s)

Fairfax R-III (PK-12)
2000 Enrollment: 190 660-686-2421

Housing: Homeownership rate: 72.2% (2000); Median home value: $40,700 (2000); Median rent: $208 per month (2000); Median age of housing: 48 years (2000).
Hospitals: Community Hospital Association (49 beds)
Newspapers: The Fairfax Forum (1 x week)
Transportation: Commute to work: 88.3% car, 0.0% public transportation, 7.1% walk, 2.2% work from home (2000); Travel time to work: 56.8% less than 15 minutes, 18.3% 15 to 30 minutes, 14.5% 30 to 45 minutes, 4.1% 45 to 60 minutes, 6.3% 60 minutes or more (2000)

ROCK PORT (city). Aka Rockport. Covers a land area of 2.856 square miles and a water area of 0 square miles. Located at 40.41° N. Lat.; 95.52° W. Long. Elevation is 840 feet.
History: Rock Port was platted in 1851 as the seat of Atchison County, succeeding Linden.
Population: 1,395 (2000); Race: 98.5% White, 0.3% Black, 0.1% Asian, 0.3% American Indian and Alaska Native, 0.4% Hispanic of any race, 0.6% two or more races (2000); Density: 488.5 persons per square mile (2000); Age: 17.0% under 18, 30.8% over 64 (2000); Marriage status: 15.6% never married, 59.9% now married, 14.4% widowed, 10.1% divorced (2000); Foreign born: 0.2% (2000); Ancestry (includes multiple ancestries): 28.1% German, 14.2% United States or American, 11.6% English, 10.5% Irish, 4.0% Dutch (2000).
Economy: Single-family building permits issued: 1 (2001) / 3 (2000); Multi-family building permits issued: 0 (2001) / 0 (2000); Employment by occupation: 11.8% management, 16.5% professional, 18.4% services, 24.9% sales, 3.4% farming, 8.9% construction, 16.0% production (2000).
Income: Per capita income: $18,322 (2000); Median household income: $28,571 (2000); Poverty rate: 11.6% (2000).
Taxes: Total city taxes per capita: $355 (1997); City property taxes per capita: $161 (1997).
Education: High school graduation rate: 76.8% (2000); College graduation rate: 13.1% (2000).

School District(s)

Rock Port R-II (KG-12)
2000 Enrollment: 411 660-744-6298

Housing: Homeownership rate: 68.3% (2000); Median home value: $56,300 (2000); Median rent: $194 per month (2000); Median age of housing: 44 years (2000).
Newspapers: Atchison County Mail (1 x week)
Transportation: Commute to work: 89.4% car, 0.0% public transportation, 7.4% walk, 2.7% work from home (2000); Travel time to work: 59.7% less than 15 minutes, 26.3% 15 to 30 minutes, 5.8% 30 to 45 minutes, 3.1% 45 to 60 minutes, 5.0% 60 minutes or more (2000)

TARKIO (city). Covers a land area of 1.384 square miles and a water area of 0 square miles. Located at 40.44° N. Lat.; 95.38° W. Long. Elevation is 940 feet.
History: Tarkio was laid out in 1880 along the Big Tarkio River, and became known as the center of the corn belt. The name is of Indian origin meaning "walnut." Tarkio citizens built a courthouse in 1882, thinking they could lure the county seat away from Rock Port. They were unsuccessful, so used the new building to establish Tarkio Valley College and Normal Institute in 1883.
Population: 1,935 (2000); Race: 92.2% White, 6.6% Black, 0.0% Asian, 0.0% American Indian and Alaska Native, 0.2% Hispanic of any race, 0.9% two or more races (2000); Density: 1,397.9 persons per square mile (2000); Age: 29.3% under 18, 19.4% over 64 (2000); Marriage status: 18.9% never married, 56.0% now married, 13.3% widowed, 11.9% divorced (2000); Foreign born: 0.2% (2000); Ancestry (includes multiple ancestries): 23.2% German, 14.7% Irish, 10.2% English, 9.7% United States or American, 4.6% Other groups (2000).
Economy: Single-family building permits issued: 1 (2001) / 3 (2000); Multi-family building permits issued: 0 (2001) / 0 (2000); Employment by occupation: 7.9% management, 20.0% professional, 17.7% services, 20.2% sales, 1.5% farming, 8.3% construction, 24.3% production (2000).
Income: Per capita income: $14,160 (2000); Median household income: $28,144 (2000); Poverty rate: 16.3% (2000).
Taxes: Total city taxes per capita: $174 (1997); City property taxes per capita: $72 (1997).
Education: High school graduation rate: 72.5% (2000); College graduation rate: 19.5% (2000).

School District(s)

Tarkio R-I (KG-12)
2000 Enrollment: 602 660-736-4161

Housing: Homeownership rate: 69.8% (2000); Median home value: $50,300 (2000); Median rent: $241 per month (2000); Median age of housing: 53 years (2000).
Newspapers: The Tarkio Avalanche (1 x week)
Transportation: Commute to work: 94.0% car, 0.0% public transportation, 2.3% walk, 3.5% work from home (2000); Travel time to work: 60.8% less than 15 minutes, 21.3% 15 to 30 minutes, 10.8% 30 to 45 minutes, 4.5% 45 to 60 minutes, 2.5% 60 minutes or more (2000)

Additional Information Contacts

Tarkio Chamber of Commerce. 660-736-5772

WATSON (village). Covers a land area of 0.106 square miles and a water area of 0 square miles. Located at 40.47° N. Lat.; 95.62° W. Long. Elevation is 894 feet.
Population: 121 (2000); Race: 100.0% White, 0.0% Black, 0.0% Asian, 0.0% American Indian and Alaska Native, 0.0% Hispanic of any race, 0.0% two or more races (2000); Density: 1,136.4 persons per square mile (2000); Age: 24.4% under 18, 13.3% over 64 (2000); Marriage status: 29.3% never married, 56.9% now married, 0.0% widowed, 13.8% divorced (2000); Foreign born: 0.0% (2000); Ancestry (includes multiple ancestries): 32.6% United States or American, 25.2% German, 12.6% Irish, 8.9% French Canadian, 8.1% Other groups (2000).
Economy: Single-family building permits issued: 0 (2001) / 0 (2000); Multi-family building permits issued: 0 (2001) / 0 (2000); Employment by occupation: 8.5% management, 0.0% professional, 11.9% services, 16.9% sales, 3.4% farming, 25.4% construction, 33.9% production (2000).
Income: Per capita income: $13,753 (2000); Median household income: $27,750 (2000); Poverty rate: 7.4% (2000).
Taxes: Total city taxes per capita: $50 (2000); City property taxes per capita: $33 (2000).
Education: High school graduation rate: 77.6% (2000); College graduation rate: 2.4% (2000).
Housing: Homeownership rate: 90.0% (2000); Median home value: $28,300 (2000); Median rent: $250 per month (2000); Median age of housing: 60+ years (2000).
Transportation: Commute to work: 96.6% car, 0.0% public transportation, 0.0% walk, 3.4% work from home (2000); Travel time to work: 21.1% less than 15 minutes, 26.3% 15 to 30 minutes, 31.6% 30 to 45 minutes, 14.0% 45 to 60 minutes, 7.0% 60 minutes or more (2000)

WESTBORO (city). Covers a land area of 0.202 square miles and a water area of 0 square miles. Located at 40.53° N. Lat.; 95.32° W. Long. Elevation is 980 feet.
Population: 163 (2000); Race: 95.0% White, 0.0% Black, 1.1% Asian, 0.0% American Indian and Alaska Native, 3.9% Hispanic of any race, 0.0% two or more races (2000); Density: 808.8 persons per square mile (2000); Age: 35.2% under 18, 7.8% over 64 (2000); Marriage status: 19.2% never married, 70.0% now married, 9.2% widowed, 1.5% divorced (2000); Foreign born: 2.8% (2000); Ancestry (includes multiple ancestries): 20.1% German, 16.2% Other groups, 10.1% United States or American, 9.5% Irish, 7.3% Norwegian (2000).
Economy: Employment by occupation: 10.8% management, 14.0% professional, 11.8% services, 15.1% sales, 5.4% farming, 17.2% construction, 25.8% production (2000).
Income: Per capita income: $12,466 (2000); Median household income: $31,563 (2000); Poverty rate: 8.4% (2000).

Taxes: Total city taxes per capita: $102 (1997); City property taxes per capita: $85 (1997).
Education: High school graduation rate: 77.0% (2000); College graduation rate: 5.3% (2000).
Housing: Homeownership rate: 88.2% (2000); Median home value: $19,400 (2000); Median rent: $275 per month (2000); Median age of housing: 60+ years (2000).
Transportation: Commute to work: 89.9% car, 0.0% public transportation, 0.0% walk, 10.1% work from home (2000); Travel time to work: 32.5% less than 15 minutes, 30.0% 15 to 30 minutes, 30.0% 30 to 45 minutes, 1.3% 45 to 60 minutes, 6.3% 60 minutes or more (2000)

Audrain County

Located in central Missouri; drained by the South Fork of the Salt River and the West Fork of the Cuivre River. Covers a land area of 693.10 square miles, a water area of 3.70 square miles, and is located in the Central Time Zone. The county government was organized in 1836. County seat is Mexico.

Weather Station: Mexico Elevation: 800 feet

	Jan	Feb	Mar	Apr	May	Jun	Jul	Aug	Sep	Oct	Nov	Dec
High	35	41	53	65	75	84	89	87	79	68	53	41
Low	16	20	30	42	52	61	66	63	55	43	32	21
Precip	1.7	1.7	3.1	4.1	5.3	4.3	3.5	3.5	3.9	3.1	3.6	2.6
Snow	7.1	5.8	3.3	0.4	0.0	0.0	0.0	0.0	0.0	tr	1.7	4.2

High and Low temperatures in degrees Fahrenheit; Precipitation and Snow in inches

Weather Station: Vandalia Elevation: 757 feet

	Jan	Feb	Mar	Apr	May	Jun	Jul	Aug	Sep	Oct	Nov	Dec
High	35	42	54	65	75	84	89	87	80	68	53	42
Low	17	22	32	42	52	62	66	64	55	44	34	24
Precip	1.8	1.8	3.1	3.9	5.1	4.2	4.1	3.9	3.4	2.8	3.3	2.4
Snow	5.5	4.6	2.7	0.7	0.0	0.0	0.0	0.0	0.0	tr	1.7	4.4

High and Low temperatures in degrees Fahrenheit; Precipitation and Snow in inches

Population: 25,853 (2000); Race: 91.1% White, 6.6% Black, 0.4% Asian, 0.4% American Indian and Alaska Native, 0.5% Hispanic of any race, 1.4% two or more races (2000); Density: 37.3 persons per square mile (2000); Age: 24.6% under 18, 17.2% over 64 (2000).
Religion: Five largest groups: 25.4% Southern Baptist Convention, 13.6% Catholic Church, 7.5% Christian Church (Disciples of Christ), 5.9% Christian Churches and Churches of Christ, 5.1% Presbyterian Church (U.S.A.) (2000).
Economy: Unemployment rate: 4.2% (11/2002); Total civilian labor force: 13,226 (11/2002); Leading industries: 31.7% manufacturing; 18.3% retail trade; 17.9% health care and social assistance (2000); Companies that employ more than 1,000 persons: 0 (2000); Companies that employ more than 100 persons: 15 (2000); Farms: 1,005 totaling 382,474 acres (1997); Minority business ownership rate: 12.3% (1997); Women business ownership rate: 15.8% (1997); Retail sales per capita: $7,096 (1997). Single-family building permits issued: 20 (2001) / 17 (2000); Multi-family building permits issued: 0 (2001) / 3 (2000).
Income: Per capita income: $16,441 (2000); Median household income: $32,057 (2000); Poverty rate: 14.8% (2000); Bankruptcy rate: 4.66% (2001).
Taxes: Total county taxes per capita: $154 (2000); County property taxes per capita: $30 (2000).
Education: High school graduation rate: 75.1% (2000); College graduation rate: 12.7% (2000).
Housing: Homeownership rate: 74.1% (2000); Median home value: $62,400 (2000); Median rent: $283 per month (2000); Median age of housing: 38 years (2000).
Health: Birth rate: 139.3 per 10,000 population (1998); Age adjusted death rate: 107.8 per 10,000 population (1999); Age adjusted cancer mortality rate: 296.1 deaths per 100,000 population (1999). Number of physicians: 15.9 per 10,000 population (1999); Number of hospital beds: 59.6 per 10,000 population (1999).
Elections: 2000 Presidential election results: 45.6% Gore, 52.6% Bush, 1.1% Nader, 0.4% Buchanan
Additional Information Contacts
Audrain County Government Offices 573-473-5820
Audrain County Board of Realtors...................... 573-581-1363
Mexico Chamber of Commerce.......................... 573-581-2765

Audrain County Communities

BENTON CITY (village). Covers a land area of 0.104 square miles and a water area of 0 square miles. Located at 39.13° N. Lat.; 91.76° W. Long. Elevation is 822 feet.
Population: 122 (2000); Race: 93.7% White, 0.0% Black, 0.0% Asian, 1.6% American Indian and Alaska Native, 0.0% Hispanic of any race, 4.7% two or more races (2000); Density: 1,177.0 persons per square mile (2000); Age: 19.7% under 18, 12.6% over 64 (2000); Marriage status: 8.6% never married, 79.0% now married, 0.0% widowed, 12.4% divorced (2000); Foreign born: 0.0% (2000); Ancestry (includes multiple ancestries): 18.1% United States or American, 12.6% Irish, 11.0% German, 7.1% Other groups, 6.3% English (2000).
Economy: Employment by occupation: 0.0% management, 8.0% professional, 21.3% services, 14.7% sales, 0.0% farming, 13.3% construction, 42.7% production (2000).
Income: Per capita income: $16,112 (2000); Median household income: $41,250 (2000); Poverty rate: 0.0% (2000).
Education: High school graduation rate: 64.5% (2000); College graduation rate: 0.0% (2000).
Housing: Homeownership rate: 81.3% (2000); Median home value: $43,800 (2000); Median rent: $375 per month (2000); Median age of housing: 42 years (2000).
Transportation: Commute to work: 94.7% car, 0.0% public transportation, 0.0% walk, 0.0% work from home (2000); Travel time to work: 14.7% less than 15 minutes, 76.0% 15 to 30 minutes, 4.0% 30 to 45 minutes, 2.7% 45 to 60 minutes, 2.7% 60 minutes or more (2000)

FARBER (city). Covers a land area of 0.285 square miles and a water area of 0 square miles. Located at 39.27° N. Lat.; 91.57° W. Long. Elevation is 767 feet.
Population: 411 (2000); Race: 99.8% White, 0.0% Black, 0.2% Asian, 0.0% American Indian and Alaska Native, 0.0% Hispanic of any race, 0.0% two or more races (2000); Density: 1,444.3 persons per square mile (2000); Age: 22.0% under 18, 14.0% over 64 (2000); Marriage status: 26.9% never married, 56.7% now married, 4.8% widowed, 11.6% divorced (2000); Foreign born: 0.2% (2000); Ancestry (includes multiple ancestries): 41.2% United States or American, 14.2% German, 11.0% Irish, 4.6% English, 4.1% Other groups (2000).
Economy: Soybeans; cattle, hogs. Manufacturing: fire bricks. Single-family building permits issued: 0 (2001) / 0 (2000); Multi-family building permits issued: 0 (2001) / 0 (2000); Employment by occupation: 3.4% management, 12.7% professional, 15.6% services, 17.3% sales, 1.7% farming, 11.0% construction, 38.4% production (2000).
Income: Per capita income: $16,622 (2000); Median household income: $36,250 (2000); Poverty rate: 10.6% (2000).
Taxes: Total city taxes per capita: $87 (1997); City property taxes per capita: $55 (1997).
Education: High school graduation rate: 75.9% (2000); College graduation rate: 4.6% (2000).
Housing: Homeownership rate: 74.6% (2000); Median home value: $33,500 (2000); Median rent: $265 per month (2000); Median age of housing: 38 years (2000).
Transportation: Commute to work: 97.4% car, 0.0% public transportation, 0.9% walk, 0.9% work from home (2000); Travel time to work: 45.6% less than 15 minutes, 18.6% 15 to 30 minutes, 24.8% 30 to 45 minutes, 5.3% 45 to 60 minutes, 5.8% 60 minutes or more (2000)

LADDONIA (city). Covers a land area of 0.552 square miles and a water area of 0 square miles. Located at 39.24° N. Lat.; 91.64° W. Long. Elevation is 775 feet.
History: Laddonia originated as a railroad camp in 1871, and was named for Amos Ladd, one of the founders of the town. The town was sometimes referred to as Mutton Town for the herds of sheep awaiting shipment here.
Population: 620 (2000); Race: 98.6% White, 0.0% Black, 0.8% Asian, 0.0% American Indian and Alaska Native, 0.8% Hispanic of any race, 0.6% two or more races (2000); Density: 1,123.7 persons per square mile (2000); Age: 25.5% under 18, 14.4% over 64 (2000); Marriage status: 23.3% never married, 56.9% now married, 7.8% widowed, 12.0% divorced (2000); Foreign born: 0.3% (2000); Ancestry (includes multiple ancestries): 24.2% United States or American, 19.9% German, 9.3% Irish, 9.0% Other groups, 6.2% English (2000).
Economy: Single-family building permits issued: 0 (2001) / 0 (2000); Multi-family building permits issued: 0 (2001) / 0 (2000); Employment by occupation: 9.8% management, 9.8% professional, 20.3% services, 16.1% sales, 0.0% farming, 10.1% construction, 33.9% production (2000).

Income: Per capita income: $17,516 (2000); Median household income: $31,250 (2000); Poverty rate: 4.4% (2000).
Taxes: Total city taxes per capita: $138 (1997); City property taxes per capita: $53 (1997).
Education: High school graduation rate: 72.0% (2000); College graduation rate: 8.2% (2000).

School District(s)

Community R-VI (KG-12)
2000 Enrollment: 388 573-492-6223

Housing: Homeownership rate: 77.8% (2000); Median home value: $40,900 (2000); Median rent: $232 per month (2000); Median age of housing: 38 years (2000).
Transportation: Commute to work: 93.9% car, 0.0% public transportation, 1.3% walk, 3.2% work from home (2000); Travel time to work: 23.7% less than 15 minutes, 32.6% 15 to 30 minutes, 24.3% 30 to 45 minutes, 8.6% 45 to 60 minutes, 10.9% 60 minutes or more (2000)

MARTINSBURG (town). Covers a land area of 0.260 square miles and a water area of 0 square miles. Located at 39.10° N. Lat.; 91.64° W. Long. Elevation is 807 feet.
Population: 326 (2000); Race: 97.0% White, 1.6% Black, 0.0% Asian, 0.0% American Indian and Alaska Native, 0.7% Hispanic of any race, 1.3% two or more races (2000); Density: 1,255.3 persons per square mile (2000); Age: 20.7% under 18, 21.7% over 64 (2000); Marriage status: 15.3% never married, 70.6% now married, 3.5% widowed, 10.6% divorced (2000); Foreign born: 0.3% (2000); Ancestry (includes multiple ancestries): 44.7% German, 12.8% United States or American, 8.6% Irish, 6.3% English, 5.3% Other groups (2000).
Economy: Grain; livestock; lumber. Employment by occupation: 17.9% management, 3.2% professional, 12.2% services, 28.2% sales, 1.3% farming, 14.7% construction, 22.4% production (2000).
Income: Per capita income: $17,562 (2000); Median household income: $31,442 (2000); Poverty rate: 4.6% (2000).
Taxes: Total city taxes per capita: $169 (1997); City property taxes per capita: $39 (1997).
Education: High school graduation rate: 71.5% (2000); College graduation rate: 3.9% (2000).
Housing: Homeownership rate: 85.3% (2000); Median home value: $61,400 (2000); Median rent: $319 per month (2000); Median age of housing: 34 years (2000).
Transportation: Commute to work: 87.8% car, 0.0% public transportation, 8.3% walk, 3.8% work from home (2000); Travel time to work: 42.7% less than 15 minutes, 30.7% 15 to 30 minutes, 12.7% 30 to 45 minutes, 8.0% 45 to 60 minutes, 6.0% 60 minutes or more (2000)

MEXICO (city). Covers a land area of 11.369 square miles and a water area of 0.336 square miles. Located at 39.16° N. Lat.; 91.88° W. Long. Elevation is 802 feet.
History: Mexico had its beginnings in 1837 as the seat of the new Audrain County. The town site was in the Salt River settlement, where fine horses and horse racing were traditions. During the Civil War, Union troops were quartered in the town, where residents primarily supported the Confederacy. In the early 1900's, deposits of fire clay were discovered and clay refractories were founded.
Population: 11,320 (2000); Race: 88.8% White, 8.2% Black, 0.7% Asian, 0.3% American Indian and Alaska Native, 0.8% Hispanic of any race, 1.6% two or more races (2000); Density: 995.7 persons per square mile (2000); Age: 23.8% under 18, 21.4% over 64 (2000); Marriage status: 20.4% never married, 54.8% now married, 12.4% widowed, 12.4% divorced (2000); Foreign born: 1.1% (2000); Ancestry (includes multiple ancestries): 20.4% German, 14.8% United States or American, 13.0% Other groups, 10.2% English, 9.4% Irish (2000).
Vital Statistics: Birth rate: 132.5 per 10,000 population (1998)
Economy: Single-family building permits issued: 9 (2001) / 13 (2000); Multi-family building permits issued: 0 (2001) / 3 (2000); Employment by occupation: 10.7% management, 18.3% professional, 14.0% services, 25.8% sales, 0.0% farming, 7.7% construction, 23.4% production (2000).
Income: Per capita income: $17,845 (2000); Median household income: $30,714 (2000); Poverty rate: 13.8% (2000).
Taxes: Total city taxes per capita: $301 (1997); City property taxes per capita: $60 (1997).
Education: High school graduation rate: 76.2% (2000); College graduation rate: 15.2% (2000).

School District(s)

Mexico 59 (PK-12)
2000 Enrollment: 2,660 573-581-3773

Housing: Homeownership rate: 66.3% (2000); Median home value: $63,600 (2000); Median rent: $285 per month (2000); Median age of housing: 42 years (2000).
Safety: Violent crime rate: 16.7 per 10,000 population; Property crime rate: 309.0 per 10,000 population (2001).
Newspapers: Mexico Ledger (6 x week)
Transportation: Commute to work: 94.5% car, 0.6% public transportation, 1.3% walk, 3.0% work from home (2000); Travel time to work: 66.5% less than 15 minutes, 17.4% 15 to 30 minutes, 7.5% 30 to 45 minutes, 5.3% 45 to 60 minutes, 3.3% 60 minutes or more (2000)
Airports: Mexico Memorial
Additional Information Contacts
Audrain County Board of Realtors.............................. 573-581-1363
Mexico Chamber of Commerce.............................. 573-581-2765

RUSH HILL (village). Covers a land area of 0.176 square miles and a water area of 0 square miles. Located at 39.21° N. Lat.; 91.72° W. Long. Elevation is 787 feet.
Population: 130 (2000); Race: 100.0% White, 0.0% Black, 0.0% Asian, 0.0% American Indian and Alaska Native, 1.6% Hispanic of any race, 0.0% two or more races (2000); Density: 737.8 persons per square mile (2000); Age: 21.8% under 18, 23.4% over 64 (2000); Marriage status: 8.1% never married, 71.7% now married, 12.1% widowed, 8.1% divorced (2000); Foreign born: 0.0% (2000); Ancestry (includes multiple ancestries): 24.2% German, 13.7% United States or American, 12.9% Other groups, 12.1% Irish, 11.3% English (2000).
Economy: Wheat, soybeans; cattle. Employment by occupation: 9.4% management, 13.2% professional, 26.4% services, 9.4% sales, 0.0% farming, 15.1% construction, 26.4% production (2000).
Income: Per capita income: $14,523 (2000); Median household income: $26,250 (2000); Poverty rate: 11.5% (2000).
Taxes: Total city taxes per capita: $76 (1997); City property taxes per capita: $25 (1997).
Education: High school graduation rate: 61.1% (2000); College graduation rate: 2.2% (2000).
Housing: Homeownership rate: 88.2% (2000); Median home value: $34,600 (2000); Median age of housing: 33 years (2000).
Transportation: Commute to work: 90.6% car, 5.7% public transportation, 0.0% walk, 3.8% work from home (2000); Travel time to work: 25.5% less than 15 minutes, 52.9% 15 to 30 minutes, 3.9% 30 to 45 minutes, 0.0% 45 to 60 minutes, 17.6% 60 minutes or more (2000)

THOMPSON (unincorporated postal area, zip code 65285). Covers a land area of 63.739 square miles and a water area of 0.384 square miles. Located at 39.20° N. Lat.; 91.99° W. Long. Elevation is 840 feet.
Population: 738 (2000); Race: 98.9% White, 0.0% Black, 0.0% Asian, 0.0% American Indian and Alaska Native, 0.0% Hispanic of any race, 1.1% two or more races (2000); Density: 11.6 persons per square mile (2000); Age: 29.3% under 18, 15.4% over 64 (2000); Marriage status: 13.6% never married, 72.5% now married, 5.4% widowed, 8.5% divorced (2000); Foreign born: 0.0% (2000); Ancestry (includes multiple ancestries): 24.8% Irish, 24.0% German, 13.3% United States or American, 10.9% Other groups, 7.5% English (2000).
Economy: Employment by occupation: 10.8% management, 17.4% professional, 13.5% services, 21.3% sales, 3.3% farming, 11.4% construction, 22.2% production (2000).
Income: Per capita income: $12,675 (2000); Median household income: $30,954 (2000); Poverty rate: 9.9% (2000).
Education: High school graduation rate: 78.0% (2000); College graduation rate: 16.8% (2000).
Housing: Homeownership rate: 84.5% (2000); Median home value: $101,800 (2000); Median rent: $175 per month (2000); Median age of housing: 33 years (2000).
Transportation: Commute to work: 92.4% car, 0.0% public transportation, 0.0% walk, 7.6% work from home (2000); Travel time to work: 22.5% less than 15 minutes, 55.6% 15 to 30 minutes, 9.9% 30 to 45 minutes, 8.9% 45 to 60 minutes, 3.0% 60 minutes or more (2000)

VANDALIA (city). Covers a land area of 2.262 square miles and a water area of 0 square miles. Located at 39.30° N. Lat.; 91.48° W. Long. Elevation is 763 feet.
History: Vandalia was laid out about 1871 by Aaron McPike, Judge Caldwell, Amos Ladd, and Colonel Haden, and incorporated in 1874. It grew as an agricultural community, and as a manufacturer of clay products using local clay.

Population: 2,529 (2000); Race: 87.6% White, 9.6% Black, 0.0% Asian, 0.0% American Indian and Alaska Native, 0.0% Hispanic of any race, 2.8% two or more races (2000); Density: 1,117.8 persons per square mile (2000); Age: 23.4% under 18, 23.5% over 64 (2000); Marriage status: 21.5% never married, 53.9% now married, 13.7% widowed, 10.9% divorced (2000); Foreign born: 0.2% (2000); Ancestry (includes multiple ancestries): 17.8% German, 15.4% Other groups, 14.7% United States or American, 12.7% Irish, 10.3% English (2000).
Economy: Single-family building permits issued: 11 (2001) / 4 (2000); Multi-family building permits issued: 0 (2001) / 0 (2000); Employment by occupation: 4.2% management, 20.1% professional, 16.9% services, 22.7% sales, 0.6% farming, 10.2% construction, 25.2% production (2000).
Income: Per capita income: $14,859 (2000); Median household income: $25,213 (2000); Poverty rate: 18.0% (2000).
Taxes: Total city taxes per capita: $21 (1997); City property taxes per capita: $5 (1997).
Education: High school graduation rate: 69.0% (2000); College graduation rate: 11.5% (2000).

School District(s)

Van-Far R-I (KG-12)
2000 Enrollment: 633 573-594-6111

Housing: Homeownership rate: 75.0% (2000); Median home value: $45,000 (2000); Median rent: $276 per month (2000); Median age of housing: 44 years (2000).
Safety: Violent crime rate: 7.9 per 10,000 population; Property crime rate: 23.6 per 10,000 population (2001).
Newspapers: The Vandalia Leader-Press (1 x week)
Transportation: Commute to work: 96.0% car, 0.0% public transportation, 2.5% walk, 0.9% work from home (2000); Travel time to work: 64.2% less than 15 minutes, 17.1% 15 to 30 minutes, 12.3% 30 to 45 minutes, 3.5% 45 to 60 minutes, 2.9% 60 minutes or more (2000)

VANDIVER (village). Covers a land area of 0.303 square miles and a water area of 0 square miles. Located at 39.16° N. Lat.; 91.84° W. Long. Elevation is 810 feet.
Population: 83 (2000); Race: 96.2% White, 0.0% Black, 0.0% Asian, 1.3% American Indian and Alaska Native, 0.0% Hispanic of any race, 2.6% two or more races (2000); Density: 273.6 persons per square mile (2000); Age: 26.9% under 18, 19.2% over 64 (2000); Marriage status: 6.7% never married, 73.3% now married, 8.3% widowed, 11.7% divorced (2000); Foreign born: 2.6% (2000); Ancestry (includes multiple ancestries): 33.3% German, 21.8% English, 19.2% United States or American, 10.3% Other groups, 9.0% Irish (2000).
Economy: Employment by occupation: 5.7% management, 11.4% professional, 22.9% services, 22.9% sales, 0.0% farming, 14.3% construction, 22.9% production (2000).
Income: Per capita income: $17,501 (2000); Median household income: $44,583 (2000); Poverty rate: 12.8% (2000).
Taxes: Total city taxes per capita: $1,432 (1997); City property taxes per capita: $108 (1997).
Education: High school graduation rate: 92.9% (2000); College graduation rate: 19.6% (2000).
Housing: Homeownership rate: 87.1% (2000); Median home value: $78,300 (2000); Median rent: $300 per month (2000); Median age of housing: 31 years (2000).
Transportation: Commute to work: 91.4% car, 0.0% public transportation, 0.0% walk, 8.6% work from home (2000); Travel time to work: 62.5% less than 15 minutes, 3.1% 15 to 30 minutes, 0.0% 30 to 45 minutes, 15.6% 45 to 60 minutes, 18.8% 60 minutes or more (2000)

Barry County

Located in southwestern Missouri, in the Ozarks; bounded on the south by Arkansas; drained by the White River; includes part of Mark Twain National Forest. Covers a land area of 779.10 square miles, a water area of 11.80 square miles, and is located in the Central Time Zone. The county government was organized in 1835. County seat is Cassville.

Weather Station: Cassville Ranger Station — Elevation: 1,338 feet

	Jan	Feb	Mar	Apr	May	Jun	Jul	Aug	Sep	Oct	Nov	Dec
High	42	48	58	68	75	84	88	89	81	70	na	na
Low	19	24	34	42	52	61	65	63	56	43	na	na
Precip	2.0	2.4	4.3	4.8	4.9	4.6	3.4	3.5	4.8	3.4	4.4	3.5
Snow	2.4	2.6	2.9	0.3	0.0	0.0	0.0	0.0	0.0	0.0	0.7	2.0

High and Low temperatures in degrees Fahrenheit; Precipitation and Snow in inches

Weather Station: Monett 4 SW — Elevation: 1,377 feet

	Jan	Feb	Mar	Apr	May	Jun	Jul	Aug	Sep	Oct	Nov	Dec
High	41	48	57	67	74	83	89	88	79	69	56	45
Low	22	28	36	45	54	62	68	66	58	47	36	27
Precip	2.0	2.1	4.1	4.6	5.0	5.4	3.1	3.7	5.0	3.9	4.3	2.9
Snow	4.6	3.3	2.0	tr	0.0	0.0	0.0	0.0	0.0	tr	1.1	1.8

High and Low temperatures in degrees Fahrenheit; Precipitation and Snow in inches

Population: 34,010 (2000); Race: 93.5% White, 0.2% Black, 0.3% Asian, 0.8% American Indian and Alaska Native, 5.1% Hispanic of any race, 1.7% two or more races (2000); Density: 43.7 persons per square mile (2000); Age: 26.2% under 18, 16.1% over 64 (2000).
Religion: Five largest groups: 33.3% Southern Baptist Convention, 6.9% Catholic Church, 5.4% The United Methodist Church, 2.6% Christian Churches and Churches of Christ, 2.0% Assemblies of God (2000).
Economy: Unemployment rate: 4.8% (11/2002); Total civilian labor force: 15,327 (11/2002); Leading industries: 50.9% manufacturing; 11.2% retail trade; 7.1% health care and social assistance (2000); Companies that employ more than 1,000 persons: 1 (2000); Companies that employ more than 100 persons: 17 (2000); Farms: 1,598 totaling 285,169 acres (1997); Minority business ownership rate: 0.0% (1997); Women business ownership rate: 30.2% (1997); Retail sales per capita: $7,801 (1997). Single-family building permits issued: 80 (2001) / 65 (2000); Multi-family building permits issued: 21 (2001) / 18 (2000).
Income: Per capita income: $14,980 (2000); Median household income: $28,906 (2000); Poverty rate: 16.6% (2000); Bankruptcy rate: 3.98% (2001).
Taxes: Total county taxes per capita: $152 (2000); County property taxes per capita: $67 (2000).
Education: High school graduation rate: 75.7% (2000); College graduation rate: 10.7% (2000).
Housing: Homeownership rate: 75.7% (2000); Median home value: $70,600 (2000); Median rent: $285 per month (2000); Median age of housing: 25 years (2000).
Health: Birth rate: 133.2 per 10,000 population (1998); Age adjusted death rate: 91.3 per 10,000 population (1999); Age adjusted cancer mortality rate: 210.6 deaths per 100,000 population (1999). Number of physicians: 6.2 per 10,000 population (1999); Number of hospital beds: 20.9 per 10,000 population (1999).
Elections: 2000 Presidential election results: 33.4% Gore, 63.8% Bush, 1.6% Nader, 0.8% Buchanan
National and State Parks: Roaring River State Park; Washburn Tower Site State Public Hunting Grounds
Additional Information Contacts
Barry County Government Offices 417-847-2613
Cassville Chamber of Commerce. 417-847-2814
Monett Chamber of Commerce 417-235-7919
Shell Knob Chamber of Commerce 417-858-3300
Southwest Missouri Board of Realtors. 417-235-8181

Barry County Communities

ARROW POINT (village). Covers a land area of 0.518 square miles and a water area of 0.049 square miles. Located at 36.54° N. Lat.; 93.61° W. Long. Elevation is 1,061 feet.
Population: 133 (2000); Race: 86.4% White, 0.0% Black, 0.0% Asian, 0.0% American Indian and Alaska Native, 13.6% Hispanic of any race, 1.5% two or more races (2000); Density: 256.6 persons per square mile (2000); Age: 23.5% under 18, 15.2% over 64 (2000); Marriage status: 17.7% never married, 69.9% now married, 1.8% widowed, 10.6% divorced (2000); Foreign born: 7.6% (2000); Ancestry (includes multiple ancestries): 20.5% Other groups, 17.4% German, 10.6% English, 9.1% Irish, 4.5% French (except Basque) (2000).
Economy: Employment by occupation: 0.0% management, 0.0% professional, 13.2% services, 44.7% sales, 5.3% farming, 13.2% construction, 23.7% production (2000).
Income: Per capita income: $11,014 (2000); Median household income: $21,429 (2000); Poverty rate: 34.1% (2000).
Education: High school graduation rate: 69.5% (2000); College graduation rate: 9.5% (2000).
Housing: Homeownership rate: 98.3% (2000); Median home value: $100,000 (2000); Median rent: $275 per month (2000); Median age of housing: 13 years (2000).
Transportation: Commute to work: 94.7% car, 0.0% public transportation, 0.0% walk, 5.3% work from home (2000); Travel time to work: 11.1% less than 15 minutes, 55.6% 15 to 30 minutes, 33.3% 30 to 45 minutes, 0.0% 45 to 60 minutes, 0.0% 60 minutes or more (2000)

BUTTERFIELD (village). Covers a land area of 0.419 square miles and a water area of 0 square miles. Located at 36.74° N. Lat.; 93.90° W. Long. Elevation is 1,528 feet.
Population: 397 (2000); Race: 90.3% White, 0.0% Black, 0.5% Asian, 0.0% American Indian and Alaska Native, 18.7% Hispanic of any race, 0.5% two or more races (2000); Density: 947.6 persons per square mile (2000); Age: 37.6% under 18, 3.6% over 64 (2000); Marriage status: 33.7% never married, 54.3% now married, 2.2% widowed, 9.8% divorced (2000); Foreign born: 12.5% (2000); Ancestry (includes multiple ancestries): 24.0% Other groups, 12.0% United States or American, 8.2% English, 6.6% German, 5.9% Irish (2000).
Economy: Employment by occupation: 1.5% management, 2.5% professional, 17.4% services, 18.9% sales, 0.5% farming, 9.5% construction, 49.8% production (2000).
Income: Per capita income: $9,460 (2000); Median household income: $24,706 (2000); Poverty rate: 19.9% (2000).
Taxes: Total city taxes per capita: $30 (1997); City property taxes per capita: $3 (1997).
Education: High school graduation rate: 70.1% (2000); College graduation rate: 1.5% (2000).
Housing: Homeownership rate: 75.9% (2000); Median home value: $49,500 (2000); Median rent: $290 per month (2000); Median age of housing: 26 years (2000).
Transportation: Commute to work: 98.5% car, 0.0% public transportation, 0.0% walk, 0.0% work from home (2000); Travel time to work: 44.3% less than 15 minutes, 34.8% 15 to 30 minutes, 12.9% 30 to 45 minutes, 0.0% 45 to 60 minutes, 8.0% 60 minutes or more (2000)

CASSVILLE (city). Covers a land area of 2.763 square miles and a water area of 0 square miles. Located at 36.68° N. Lat.; 93.86° W. Long. Elevation is 1,324 feet.
History: Cassville was platted in 1845 as the seat of Barry County. The community developed as a fishing center and a shipping point for livestock, poultry, and dairy products. During the Civil War, Cassville was attacked by both Union and Confederate forces.
Population: 2,890 (2000); Race: 93.1% White, 0.4% Black, 0.0% Asian, 0.9% American Indian and Alaska Native, 3.3% Hispanic of any race, 3.6% two or more races (2000); Density: 1,046.0 persons per square mile (2000); Age: 24.4% under 18, 18.6% over 64 (2000); Marriage status: 18.5% never married, 56.8% now married, 11.5% widowed, 13.2% divorced (2000); Foreign born: 1.7% (2000); Ancestry (includes multiple ancestries): 15.6% German, 14.7% Other groups, 13.4% English, 12.0% United States or American, 9.9% Irish (2000).
Economy: Single-family building permits issued: 23 (2001) / 22 (2000); Multi-family building permits issued: 6 (2001) / 6 (2000); Employment by occupation: 7.8% management, 13.6% professional, 15.7% services, 19.9% sales, 2.4% farming, 10.0% construction, 30.6% production (2000).
Income: Per capita income: $16,660 (2000); Median household income: $27,351 (2000); Poverty rate: 15.4% (2000).
Taxes: Total city taxes per capita: $357 (1997); City property taxes per capita: $28 (1997).
Education: High school graduation rate: 77.0% (2000); College graduation rate: 14.4% (2000).

School District(s)

Cassville R-IV (PK-12)
2000 Enrollment: 1,993 417-847-2221
Housing: Homeownership rate: 65.3% (2000); Median home value: $66,800 (2000); Median rent: $284 per month (2000); Median age of housing: 32 years (2000).
Hospitals: Saint John's County Hospital (18 beds)
Newspapers: Cassville Democrat (1 x week); Barry County Advertiser (1 x week)
Transportation: Commute to work: 95.6% car, 0.4% public transportation, 1.2% walk, 2.0% work from home (2000); Travel time to work: 63.9% less than 15 minutes, 17.9% 15 to 30 minutes, 6.4% 30 to 45 minutes, 5.3% 45 to 60 minutes, 6.5% 60 minutes or more (2000)
Additional Information Contacts
Cassville Chamber of Commerce. 417-847-2814

CHAIN-O-LAKES (village). Covers a land area of 0.084 square miles and a water area of 0 square miles. Located at 36.53° N. Lat.; 93.72° W. Long. Elevation is 1,000 feet.
Population: 127 (2000); Race: 98.4% White, 0.0% Black, 0.0% Asian, 0.0% American Indian and Alaska Native, 0.0% Hispanic of any race, 1.6% two or more races (2000); Density: 1,505.9 persons per square mile (2000); Age: 10.9% under 18, 38.8% over 64 (2000); Marriage status: 12.6% never married, 63.0% now married, 10.1% widowed, 14.3% divorced (2000); Foreign born: 1.6% (2000); Ancestry (includes multiple ancestries): 24.8% English, 21.7% German, 14.0% Irish, 8.5% Swedish, 7.8% Other groups (2000).
Economy: Recreational area. Residential. Single-family building permits issued: 0 (2001) / 1 (2000); Multi-family building permits issued: 0 (2001) / 0 (2000); Employment by occupation: 13.6% management, 6.8% professional, 22.7% services, 25.0% sales, 0.0% farming, 18.2% construction, 13.6% production (2000).
Income: Per capita income: $14,944 (2000); Median household income: $25,714 (2000); Poverty rate: 7.8% (2000).
Taxes: Total city taxes per capita: $74 (1997); City property taxes per capita: $74 (1997).
Education: High school graduation rate: 90.2% (2000); College graduation rate: 3.6% (2000).
Housing: Homeownership rate: 93.8% (2000); Median home value: $94,400 (2000); Median rent: $300 per month (2000); Median age of housing: 23 years (2000).
Transportation: Commute to work: 100.0% car, 0.0% public transportation, 0.0% walk, 0.0% work from home (2000); Travel time to work: 25.0% less than 15 minutes, 42.5% 15 to 30 minutes, 25.0% 30 to 45 minutes, 0.0% 45 to 60 minutes, 7.5% 60 minutes or more (2000)

EAGLE ROCK (unincorporated postal area, zip code 65641). Covers a land area of 57.837 square miles and a water area of 0.005 square miles. Located at 36.53° N. Lat.; 93.73° W. Long. Elevation is 931 feet.
Population: 1,378 (2000); Race: 94.6% White, 0.5% Black, 0.0% Asian, 0.0% American Indian and Alaska Native, 4.0% Hispanic of any race, 0.9% two or more races (2000); Density: 23.8 persons per square mile (2000); Age: 19.3% under 18, 23.5% over 64 (2000); Marriage status: 8.7% never married, 69.3% now married, 7.7% widowed, 14.2% divorced (2000); Foreign born: 5.6% (2000); Ancestry (includes multiple ancestries): 23.6% German, 14.4% Irish, 14.4% United States or American, 12.1% English, 11.7% Other groups (2000).
Economy: Employment by occupation: 6.7% management, 6.7% professional, 14.2% services, 27.4% sales, 0.8% farming, 10.7% construction, 33.6% production (2000).
Income: Per capita income: $15,758 (2000); Median household income: $30,208 (2000); Poverty rate: 19.0% (2000).
Education: High school graduation rate: 83.2% (2000); College graduation rate: 14.8% (2000).
Housing: Homeownership rate: 85.6% (2000); Median home value: $87,200 (2000); Median rent: $290 per month (2000); Median age of housing: 21 years (2000).
Transportation: Commute to work: 90.8% car, 0.0% public transportation, 3.4% walk, 4.0% work from home (2000); Travel time to work: 19.3% less than 15 minutes, 36.8% 15 to 30 minutes, 31.0% 30 to 45 minutes, 5.1% 45 to 60 minutes, 7.9% 60 minutes or more (2000)

EMERALD BEACH (village). Covers a land area of 0.715 square miles and a water area of 0 square miles. Located at 36.57° N. Lat.; 93.67° W. Long. Elevation is 1,025 feet.
Population: 250 (2000); Race: 99.2% White, 0.0% Black, 0.0% Asian, 0.8% American Indian and Alaska Native, 0.0% Hispanic of any race, 0.0% two or more races (2000); Density: 349.8 persons per square mile (2000); Age: 11.7% under 18, 23.4% over 64 (2000); Marriage status: 11.2% never married, 73.4% now married, 6.0% widowed, 9.4% divorced (2000); Foreign born: 0.0% (2000); Ancestry (includes multiple ancestries): 19.5% German, 17.2% English, 11.7% Other groups, 7.8% Irish, 7.4% United States or American (2000).
Economy: Single-family building permits issued: 7 (2001) / 4 (2000); Multi-family building permits issued: 0 (2001) / 0 (2000); Employment by occupation: 8.8% management, 4.4% professional, 19.5% services, 26.5% sales, 1.8% farming, 21.2% construction, 17.7% production (2000).
Income: Per capita income: $16,267 (2000); Median household income: $32,813 (2000); Poverty rate: 12.9% (2000).
Taxes: Total city taxes per capita: $108 (1997); City property taxes per capita: $104 (1997).
Education: High school graduation rate: 87.0% (2000); College graduation rate: 14.4% (2000).
Housing: Homeownership rate: 97.5% (2000); Median home value: $91,700 (2000); Median rent: $325 per month (2000); Median age of housing: 14 years (2000).
Transportation: Commute to work: 91.7% car, 0.0% public transportation, 0.0% walk, 8.3% work from home (2000); Travel time to work: 18.2% less

than 15 minutes, 13.1% 15 to 30 minutes, 35.4% 30 to 45 minutes, 15.2% 45 to 60 minutes, 18.2% 60 minutes or more (2000)

EXETER (city). Covers a land area of 0.795 square miles and a water area of 0 square miles. Located at 36.67° N. Lat.; 93.94° W. Long. Elevation is 1,559 feet.
Population: 707 (2000); Race: 93.2% White, 0.0% Black, 0.0% Asian, 1.7% American Indian and Alaska Native, 6.4% Hispanic of any race, 0.9% two or more races (2000); Density: 889.0 persons per square mile (2000); Age: 28.1% under 18, 12.5% over 64 (2000); Marriage status: 21.8% never married, 54.0% now married, 10.1% widowed, 14.2% divorced (2000); Foreign born: 3.4% (2000); Ancestry (includes multiple ancestries): 21.0% Other groups, 13.6% United States or American, 12.4% German, 11.9% English, 10.4% Irish (2000).
Economy: Employment by occupation: 5.3% management, 9.7% professional, 14.5% services, 17.9% sales, 0.0% farming, 8.2% construction, 44.3% production (2000).
Income: Per capita income: $11,600 (2000); Median household income: $25,438 (2000); Poverty rate: 18.6% (2000).
Taxes: Total city taxes per capita: $129 (1997); City property taxes per capita: $30 (1997).
Education: High school graduation rate: 64.8% (2000); College graduation rate: 5.0% (2000).

School District(s)

Exeter R-VI (PK-12)
2000 Enrollment: 341 417-835-2922
Housing: Homeownership rate: 65.8% (2000); Median home value: $49,900 (2000); Median rent: $276 per month (2000); Median age of housing: 26 years (2000).
Transportation: Commute to work: 89.6% car, 0.0% public transportation, 2.9% walk, 4.5% work from home (2000); Travel time to work: 55.1% less than 15 minutes, 29.3% 15 to 30 minutes, 8.2% 30 to 45 minutes, 5.8% 45 to 60 minutes, 1.7% 60 minutes or more (2000)

GOLDEN (unincorporated postal area, zip code 65658). Covers a land area of 20.135 square miles and a water area of 0.008 square miles. Located at 36.55° N. Lat.; 93.64° W. Long. Elevation is 1,155 feet.
Population: 1,019 (2000); Race: 97.6% White, 0.0% Black, 0.0% Asian, 0.2% American Indian and Alaska Native, 1.8% Hispanic of any race, 0.6% two or more races (2000); Density: 50.6 persons per square mile (2000); Age: 19.8% under 18, 20.4% over 64 (2000); Marriage status: 8.9% never married, 76.6% now married, 6.0% widowed, 8.6% divorced (2000); Foreign born: 1.0% (2000); Ancestry (includes multiple ancestries): 20.1% English, 17.6% German, 12.7% Other groups, 10.6% United States or American, 5.1% Irish (2000).
Economy: Employment by occupation: 7.1% management, 9.8% professional, 8.2% services, 27.0% sales, 1.1% farming, 17.8% construction, 29.0% production (2000).
Income: Per capita income: $13,707 (2000); Median household income: $29,167 (2000); Poverty rate: 17.9% (2000).
Education: High school graduation rate: 81.6% (2000); College graduation rate: 13.3% (2000).
Housing: Homeownership rate: 90.5% (2000); Median home value: $89,000 (2000); Median rent: $282 per month (2000); Median age of housing: 13 years (2000).
Transportation: Commute to work: 87.5% car, 0.0% public transportation, 1.8% walk, 6.4% work from home (2000); Travel time to work: 29.4% less than 15 minutes, 23.9% 15 to 30 minutes, 28.8% 30 to 45 minutes, 8.8% 45 to 60 minutes, 9.2% 60 minutes or more (2000)

MONETT (city). Covers a land area of 6.510 square miles and a water area of 0 square miles. Located at 36.92° N. Lat.; 93.92° W. Long. Elevation is 1,317 feet.
History: Monett was incorporated in 1887 as a railroad town, and developed as the shipping center of the berry-growing region.
Population: 7,396 (2000); Race: 88.5% White, 0.1% Black, 0.6% Asian, 0.6% American Indian and Alaska Native, 10.9% Hispanic of any race, 1.2% two or more races (2000); Density: 1,136.2 persons per square mile (2000); Age: 27.8% under 18, 17.8% over 64 (2000); Marriage status: 18.8% never married, 58.7% now married, 9.0% widowed, 13.5% divorced (2000); Foreign born: 7.0% (2000); Ancestry (includes multiple ancestries): 19.4% Other groups, 17.5% United States or American, 13.4% German, 11.2% English, 8.2% Irish (2000).
Economy: Single-family building permits issued: 50 (2001) / 38 (2000); Multi-family building permits issued: 15 (2001) / 12 (2000); Employment by occupation: 8.5% management, 18.0% professional, 13.4% services, 24.0% sales, 2.1% farming, 8.3% construction, 25.6% production (2000).
Income: Per capita income: $17,048 (2000); Median household income: $30,764 (2000); Poverty rate: 15.0% (2000).
Taxes: Total city taxes per capita: $202 (2000); City property taxes per capita: $32 (2000).
Education: High school graduation rate: 75.2% (2000); College graduation rate: 14.3% (2000).

School District(s)

Monett R-I (PK-12)
2000 Enrollment: 2,004 417-235-7422
Housing: Homeownership rate: 61.8% (2000); Median home value: $67,700 (2000); Median rent: $317 per month (2000); Median age of housing: 40 years (2000).
Hospitals: Cox-Monett Hospital (78 beds)
Safety: Violent crime rate: 17.5 per 10,000 population; Property crime rate: 405.8 per 10,000 population (2001).
Newspapers: The Monett Times (5 x week)
Transportation: Commute to work: 92.2% car, 0.6% public transportation, 3.1% walk, 2.4% work from home (2000); Travel time to work: 72.6% less than 15 minutes, 16.2% 15 to 30 minutes, 5.2% 30 to 45 minutes, 3.3% 45 to 60 minutes, 2.7% 60 minutes or more (2000)
Airports: Monett Municipal
Additional Information Contacts
Monett Chamber of Commerce 417-235-7919
Southwest Missouri Board of Realtors. 417-235-8181

PURDY (city). Covers a land area of 0.650 square miles and a water area of 0 square miles. Located at 36.81° N. Lat.; 93.92° W. Long. Elevation is 1,485 feet.
Population: 1,103 (2000); Race: 78.0% White, 0.0% Black, 0.4% Asian, 0.6% American Indian and Alaska Native, 20.0% Hispanic of any race, 4.0% two or more races (2000); Density: 1,697.4 persons per square mile (2000); Age: 29.4% under 18, 17.2% over 64 (2000); Marriage status: 19.4% never married, 57.3% now married, 11.6% widowed, 11.6% divorced (2000); Foreign born: 12.6% (2000); Ancestry (includes multiple ancestries): 30.3% Other groups, 16.4% United States or American, 12.6% German, 10.6% Irish, 8.7% English (2000).
Economy: Apples, peaches, vegetables; dairying. Manufacturing of drill bits. Employment by occupation: 4.7% management, 12.6% professional, 7.7% services, 25.3% sales, 2.8% farming, 9.4% construction, 37.5% production (2000).
Income: Per capita income: $10,662 (2000); Median household income: $24,318 (2000); Poverty rate: 20.2% (2000).
Taxes: Total city taxes per capita: $90 (1997); City property taxes per capita: $28 (1997).
Education: High school graduation rate: 66.5% (2000); College graduation rate: 8.1% (2000).

School District(s)

Purdy R-II (PK-12)
2000 Enrollment: 701 417-442-3216
Housing: Homeownership rate: 63.2% (2000); Median home value: $51,200 (2000); Median rent: $255 per month (2000); Median age of housing: 29 years (2000).
Transportation: Commute to work: 98.5% car, 0.0% public transportation, 0.0% walk, 1.0% work from home (2000); Travel time to work: 48.5% less than 15 minutes, 39.0% 15 to 30 minutes, 4.7% 30 to 45 minutes, 2.0% 45 to 60 minutes, 5.9% 60 minutes or more (2000)

SELIGMAN (city). Covers a land area of 1.206 square miles and a water area of 0 square miles. Located at 36.52° N. Lat.; 93.93° W. Long. Elevation is 1,540 feet.
Population: 877 (2000); Race: 89.1% White, 0.0% Black, 0.0% Asian, 4.1% American Indian and Alaska Native, 6.1% Hispanic of any race, 4.9% two or more races (2000); Density: 727.0 persons per square mile (2000); Age: 32.1% under 18, 9.5% over 64 (2000); Marriage status: 24.3% never married, 51.7% now married, 7.5% widowed, 16.5% divorced (2000); Foreign born: 2.2% (2000); Ancestry (includes multiple ancestries): 23.2% Other groups, 16.3% Irish, 12.3% United States or American, 8.1% German, 5.9% English (2000).
Economy: Employment by occupation: 3.1% management, 4.8% professional, 16.8% services, 19.3% sales, 2.8% farming, 19.9% construction, 33.3% production (2000).
Income: Per capita income: $10,918 (2000); Median household income: $25,313 (2000); Poverty rate: 26.8% (2000).

Taxes: Total city taxes per capita: $223 (1997); City property taxes per capita: $32 (1997).
Education: High school graduation rate: 57.1% (2000); College graduation rate: 2.8% (2000).
Housing: Homeownership rate: 70.6% (2000); Median home value: $46,700 (2000); Median rent: $268 per month (2000); Median age of housing: 27 years (2000).
Transportation: Commute to work: 94.2% car, 0.6% public transportation, 1.2% walk, 2.3% work from home (2000); Travel time to work: 17.1% less than 15 minutes, 21.8% 15 to 30 minutes, 35.4% 30 to 45 minutes, 14.7% 45 to 60 minutes, 10.9% 60 minutes or more (2000)

SHELL KNOB (CDP). Covers a land area of 8.210 square miles and a water area of 2.579 square miles. Located at 36.60° N. Lat.; 93.59° W. Long. Elevation is 1,143 feet.
Population: 1,393 (2000); Race: 99.1% White, 0.0% Black, 0.0% Asian, 0.0% American Indian and Alaska Native, 0.0% Hispanic of any race, 0.9% two or more races (2000); Density: 169.7 persons per square mile (2000); Age: 13.7% under 18, 38.6% over 64 (2000); Marriage status: 8.6% never married, 68.9% now married, 12.5% widowed, 10.0% divorced (2000); Foreign born: 0.0% (2000); Ancestry (includes multiple ancestries): 17.5% German, 17.0% English, 15.7% United States or American, 11.8% Irish, 5.2% Other groups (2000).
Economy: Employment by occupation: 6.6% management, 17.6% professional, 17.1% services, 21.5% sales, 1.2% farming, 14.2% construction, 21.8% production (2000).
Income: Per capita income: $18,111 (2000); Median household income: $29,896 (2000); Poverty rate: 12.1% (2000).
Education: High school graduation rate: 79.1% (2000); College graduation rate: 13.7% (2000).

School District(s)

Shell Knob 78 (KG-08)
2000 Enrollment: 237 417-858-6743
Housing: Homeownership rate: 87.7% (2000); Median home value: $94,700 (2000); Median rent: $334 per month (2000); Median age of housing: 24 years (2000).
Transportation: Commute to work: 91.8% car, 0.0% public transportation, 1.0% walk, 2.2% work from home (2000); Travel time to work: 41.8% less than 15 minutes, 21.7% 15 to 30 minutes, 14.0% 30 to 45 minutes, 7.1% 45 to 60 minutes, 15.3% 60 minutes or more (2000)
Additional Information Contacts
Shell Knob Chamber of Commerce 417-858-3300

WASHBURN (city). Covers a land area of 0.839 square miles and a water area of 0 square miles. Located at 36.58° N. Lat.; 93.96° W. Long. Elevation is 1,467 feet.
Population: 448 (2000); Race: 96.9% White, 0.0% Black, 0.0% Asian, 2.0% American Indian and Alaska Native, 1.8% Hispanic of any race, 1.1% two or more races (2000); Density: 534.2 persons per square mile (2000); Age: 27.6% under 18, 15.7% over 64 (2000); Marriage status: 24.9% never married, 57.7% now married, 5.6% widowed, 11.8% divorced (2000); Foreign born: 0.7% (2000); Ancestry (includes multiple ancestries): 21.3% United States or American, 15.5% Other groups, 9.4% English, 9.4% German, 8.7% Irish (2000).
Economy: Single-family building permits issued: 0 (2001) / 0 (2000); Multi-family building permits issued: 0 (2001) / 0 (2000); Employment by occupation: 4.8% management, 7.1% professional, 16.7% services, 19.0% sales, 0.5% farming, 8.6% construction, 43.3% production (2000).
Income: Per capita income: $12,401 (2000); Median household income: $27,417 (2000); Poverty rate: 13.7% (2000).
Taxes: Total city taxes per capita: $103 (1997); City property taxes per capita: $50 (1997).
Education: High school graduation rate: 73.0% (2000); College graduation rate: 5.8% (2000).

School District(s)

Southwest R-V (PK-12)
2000 Enrollment: 934 417-826-5410
Housing: Homeownership rate: 71.5% (2000); Median home value: $54,800 (2000); Median rent: $335 per month (2000); Median age of housing: 27 years (2000).
Transportation: Commute to work: 92.3% car, 0.0% public transportation, 2.4% walk, 5.3% work from home (2000); Travel time to work: 28.4% less than 15 minutes, 26.9% 15 to 30 minutes, 17.8% 30 to 45 minutes, 20.8% 45 to 60 minutes, 6.1% 60 minutes or more (2000)

WHEATON (city). Covers a land area of 0.508 square miles and a water area of 0 square miles. Located at 36.76° N. Lat.; 94.05° W. Long. Elevation is 1,380 feet.
Population: 721 (2000); Race: 91.3% White, 0.0% Black, 0.4% Asian, 0.7% American Indian and Alaska Native, 9.7% Hispanic of any race, 0.7% two or more races (2000); Density: 1,420.3 persons per square mile (2000); Age: 27.0% under 18, 16.9% over 64 (2000); Marriage status: 19.2% never married, 58.6% now married, 10.7% widowed, 11.5% divorced (2000); Foreign born: 6.6% (2000); Ancestry (includes multiple ancestries): 20.8% United States or American, 19.7% Other groups, 10.8% German, 7.7% Irish, 5.2% English (2000).
Economy: Fruit, vegetables; dairying; cattle; poultry processing. Employment by occupation: 7.8% management, 7.8% professional, 14.2% services, 22.6% sales, 1.7% farming, 8.8% construction, 37.2% production (2000).
Income: Per capita income: $11,124 (2000); Median household income: $21,354 (2000); Poverty rate: 20.8% (2000).
Taxes: Total city taxes per capita: $145 (1997); City property taxes per capita: $34 (1997).
Education: High school graduation rate: 70.4% (2000); College graduation rate: 4.6% (2000).

School District(s)

Wheaton R-III (KG-12)
2000 Enrollment: 437 417-652-3914
Housing: Homeownership rate: 65.6% (2000); Median home value: $43,700 (2000); Median rent: $254 per month (2000); Median age of housing: 31 years (2000).
Transportation: Commute to work: 92.5% car, 0.0% public transportation, 2.4% walk, 2.4% work from home (2000); Travel time to work: 22.0% less than 15 minutes, 40.8% 15 to 30 minutes, 22.0% 30 to 45 minutes, 7.7% 45 to 60 minutes, 7.7% 60 minutes or more (2000)

Barton County

Located in southwestern Missouri; bounded on the west by Kansas; drained by a branch of the Spring River. Covers a land area of 594.20 square miles, a water area of 2.50 square miles, and is located in the Central Time Zone. The county government was organized in 1855. County seat is Lamar.

Weather Station: Lamar Elevation: 977 feet

	Jan	Feb	Mar	Apr	May	Jun	Jul	Aug	Sep	Oct	Nov	Dec
High	40	47	57	68	75	84	89	89	80	71	56	45
Low	20	25	34	44	54	63	68	66	57	46	35	25
Precip	1.9	2.1	4.0	4.7	5.3	5.4	4.4	3.7	5.5	4.2	4.3	2.9
Snow	4.2	2.9	1.9	tr	0.0	0.0	0.0	0.0	0.0	tr	0.9	2.8

High and Low temperatures in degrees Fahrenheit; Precipitation and Snow in inches

Population: 12,541 (2000); Race: 96.7% White, 0.1% Black, 0.4% Asian, 0.6% American Indian and Alaska Native, 1.2% Hispanic of any race, 2.2% two or more races (2000); Density: 21.1 persons per square mile (2000); Age: 27.4% under 18, 16.5% over 64 (2000).
Religion: Five largest groups: 17.0% Southern Baptist Convention, 11.2% Christian Churches and Churches of Christ, 11.2% The United Methodist Church, 2.5% National Association of Free Will Baptists, 1.6% Catholic Church (2000).
Economy: Unemployment rate: 3.9% (11/2002); Total civilian labor force: 6,781 (11/2002); Leading industries: 42.8% manufacturing; 14.6% health care and social assistance; 13.2% retail trade (2000); Companies that employ more than 1,000 persons: 1 (2000); Companies that employ more than 100 persons: 7 (2000); Farms: 896 totaling 335,182 acres (1997); Minority business ownership rate: 0.0% (1997); Women business ownership rate: 18.7% (1997); Retail sales per capita: $6,577 (1997). Single-family building permits issued: 16 (2001) / 13 (2000); Multi-family building permits issued: 0 (2001) / 0 (2000).
Income: Per capita income: $13,987 (2000); Median household income: $29,275 (2000); Poverty rate: 13.0% (2000); Bankruptcy rate: 3.67% (2001).
Taxes: Total county taxes per capita: $73 (1997); County property taxes per capita: $4 (1997).
Education: High school graduation rate: 77.3% (2000); College graduation rate: 10.6% (2000).
Housing: Homeownership rate: 73.4% (2000); Median home value: $55,800 (2000); Median rent: $264 per month (2000); Median age of housing: 37 years (2000).
Health: Birth rate: 142.7 per 10,000 population (1998); Age adjusted death rate: 79.5 per 10,000 population (1999); Age adjusted cancer mortality rate: 175.4 deaths per 100,000 population (1999). Number of physicians: 2.4 per

10,000 population (1999); Number of hospital beds: 33.5 per 10,000 population (1999).
Elections: 2000 Presidential election results: 26.5% Gore, 71.5% Bush, 1.4% Nader, 0.3% Buchanan
National and State Parks: Hunkah Prairie State Wildlife Area; Lester R Davis Memorial State Forest
Additional Information Contacts
Barton County Government Offices. 417-682-3529
Barton County Chamber of Commerce 417-682-3595

Barton County Communities

BURGESS (town). Covers a land area of 0.075 square miles and a water area of 0 square miles. Located at 37.55° N. Lat.; 94.61° W. Long. Elevation is 892 feet.
Population: 70 (2000); Race: 100.0% White, 0.0% Black, 0.0% Asian, 0.0% American Indian and Alaska Native, 0.0% Hispanic of any race, 0.0% two or more races (2000); Density: 932.2 persons per square mile (2000); Age: 27.5% under 18, 8.7% over 64 (2000); Marriage status: 24.1% never married, 59.3% now married, 11.1% widowed, 5.6% divorced (2000); Foreign born: 0.0% (2000); Ancestry (includes multiple ancestries): 31.9% United States or American, 27.5% Other groups, 5.8% English, 2.9% French (except Basque) (2000).
Economy: Employment by occupation: 0.0% management, 3.7% professional, 18.5% services, 37.0% sales, 0.0% farming, 3.7% construction, 37.0% production (2000).
Income: Per capita income: $7,409 (2000); Median household income: $19,375 (2000); Poverty rate: 17.4% (2000).
Taxes: Total city taxes per capita: $10 (1997); City property taxes per capita: $10 (1997).
Education: High school graduation rate: 80.0% (2000); College graduation rate: 7.5% (2000).
Housing: Homeownership rate: 66.7% (2000); Median home value: $12,900 (2000); Median rent: $225 per month (2000); Median age of housing: 60+ years (2000).
Transportation: Commute to work: 76.9% car, 0.0% public transportation, 0.0% walk, 23.1% work from home (2000); Travel time to work: 0.0% less than 15 minutes, 20.0% 15 to 30 minutes, 40.0% 30 to 45 minutes, 0.0% 45 to 60 minutes, 40.0% 60 minutes or more (2000)

GOLDEN CITY (city). Covers a land area of 1.027 square miles and a water area of 0 square miles. Located at 37.39° N. Lat.; 94.09° W. Long. Elevation is 1,060 feet.
Population: 884 (2000); Race: 96.7% White, 0.0% Black, 0.2% Asian, 2.2% American Indian and Alaska Native, 2.7% Hispanic of any race, 0.7% two or more races (2000); Density: 861.1 persons per square mile (2000); Age: 25.2% under 18, 18.2% over 64 (2000); Marriage status: 19.0% never married, 55.0% now married, 11.8% widowed, 14.2% divorced (2000); Foreign born: 1.3% (2000); Ancestry (includes multiple ancestries): 23.7% German, 21.5% United States or American, 16.3% Other groups, 14.9% Irish, 9.7% English (2000).
Economy: Corn, wheat, sorghum, hay, soybeans; cattle; manufacturing: business forms. Employment by occupation: 11.7% management, 8.7% professional, 15.4% services, 20.6% sales, 3.5% farming, 7.0% construction, 33.1% production (2000).
Income: Per capita income: $11,192 (2000); Median household income: $21,793 (2000); Poverty rate: 23.2% (2000).
Taxes: Total city taxes per capita: $231 (1997); City property taxes per capita: $32 (1997).
Education: High school graduation rate: 68.7% (2000); College graduation rate: 3.7% (2000).

School District(s)

Golden City R-III (PK-12)
2000 Enrollment: 318 417-537-4900
Housing: Homeownership rate: 66.7% (2000); Median home value: $41,100 (2000); Median rent: $210 per month (2000); Median age of housing: 58 years (2000).
Transportation: Commute to work: 91.6% car, 0.0% public transportation, 3.5% walk, 2.2% work from home (2000); Travel time to work: 37.4% less than 15 minutes, 31.0% 15 to 30 minutes, 22.2% 30 to 45 minutes, 5.3% 45 to 60 minutes, 4.2% 60 minutes or more (2000)

LAMAR (city). Covers a land area of 3.833 square miles and a water area of 0.303 square miles. Located at 37.49° N. Lat.; 94.27° W. Long. Elevation is 958 feet.
History: Lamar was founded in 1856 and named for Mirabeau B. Lamar, president of the Texas Republic from 1838 to 1841.
Population: 4,425 (2000); Race: 96.9% White, 0.2% Black, 0.7% Asian, 0.3% American Indian and Alaska Native, 0.9% Hispanic of any race, 1.9% two or more races (2000); Density: 1,154.5 persons per square mile (2000); Age: 25.1% under 18, 21.8% over 64 (2000); Marriage status: 18.1% never married, 53.7% now married, 13.2% widowed, 15.0% divorced (2000); Foreign born: 0.8% (2000); Ancestry (includes multiple ancestries): 24.3% German, 15.8% Irish, 14.0% United States or American, 12.3% Other groups, 11.7% English (2000).
Economy: Single-family building permits issued: 16 (2001) / 13 (2000); Multi-family building permits issued: 0 (2001) / 0 (2000); Employment by occupation: 7.9% management, 10.9% professional, 15.6% services, 24.8% sales, 0.0% farming, 9.9% construction, 30.9% production (2000).
Income: Per capita income: $15,684 (2000); Median household income: $29,296 (2000); Poverty rate: 12.1% (2000).
Taxes: Total city taxes per capita: $292 (2000); City property taxes per capita: $59 (2000).
Education: High school graduation rate: 75.3% (2000); College graduation rate: 10.5% (2000).

School District(s)

Lamar R-I (PK-12)
2000 Enrollment: 1,343 417-682-3527
Housing: Homeownership rate: 67.3% (2000); Median home value: $61,200 (2000); Median rent: $276 per month (2000); Median age of housing: 39 years (2000).
Hospitals: Barton County Memorial Hospital (49 beds)
Newspapers: Lamar Democrat (2 x week)
Transportation: Commute to work: 93.1% car, 0.0% public transportation, 2.6% walk, 2.9% work from home (2000); Travel time to work: 78.1% less than 15 minutes, 10.7% 15 to 30 minutes, 5.5% 30 to 45 minutes, 2.5% 45 to 60 minutes, 3.3% 60 minutes or more (2000)
Additional Information Contacts
Barton County Chamber of Commerce 417-682-3595

LAMAR HEIGHTS (village). Covers a land area of 0.803 square miles and a water area of 0 square miles. Located at 37.49° N. Lat.; 94.29° W. Long. Elevation is 971 feet.
Population: 216 (2000); Race: 87.9% White, 0.0% Black, 2.5% Asian, 0.0% American Indian and Alaska Native, 8.8% Hispanic of any race, 8.8% two or more races (2000); Density: 269.1 persons per square mile (2000); Age: 29.3% under 18, 12.6% over 64 (2000); Marriage status: 28.3% never married, 52.2% now married, 4.9% widowed, 14.7% divorced (2000); Foreign born: 2.5% (2000); Ancestry (includes multiple ancestries): 19.7% United States or American, 18.4% Other groups, 18.4% German, 8.4% English, 3.8% Irish (2000).
Economy: Residential and commercial area. Employment by occupation: 5.8% management, 12.5% professional, 22.1% services, 24.0% sales, 3.8% farming, 8.7% construction, 23.1% production (2000).
Income: Per capita income: $16,018 (2000); Median household income: $30,625 (2000); Poverty rate: 18.3% (2000).
Taxes: Total city taxes per capita: $104 (1997); City property taxes per capita: $88 (1997).
Education: High school graduation rate: 82.4% (2000); College graduation rate: 13.4% (2000).
Housing: Homeownership rate: 59.6% (2000); Median home value: $112,500 (2000); Median rent: $254 per month (2000); Median age of housing: 19 years (2000).
Transportation: Commute to work: 92.9% car, 0.0% public transportation, 3.0% walk, 4.0% work from home (2000); Travel time to work: 66.3% less than 15 minutes, 6.3% 15 to 30 minutes, 14.7% 30 to 45 minutes, 9.5% 45 to 60 minutes, 3.2% 60 minutes or more (2000)

LIBERAL (city). Covers a land area of 0.837 square miles and a water area of 0.007 square miles. Located at 37.55° N. Lat.; 94.52° W. Long. Elevation is 894 feet.
History: Liberal was founded in 1880 by G.H. Walser, a disciple of Robert C. Ingersoll, who laid out the town as a refuge for free-thinkers. In 1881 an addition to Liberal was established by H.H. Waggoner, who invited only orthodox Christians to move in. The Liberalites erected a barbed wire fence between the two settlements. After Walser's death in 1910, the town became more diversified in its character.
Population: 779 (2000); Race: 98.2% White, 0.0% Black, 0.6% Asian, 0.8% American Indian and Alaska Native, 1.4% Hispanic of any race, 0.4% two or more races (2000); Density: 930.7 persons per square mile (2000); Age: 29.5% under 18, 17.2% over 64 (2000); Marriage status: 17.6% never

married, 58.7% now married, 12.5% widowed, 11.1% divorced (2000); Foreign born: 0.9% (2000); Ancestry (includes multiple ancestries): 14.1% Other groups, 13.5% United States or American, 12.6% German, 11.9% Irish, 8.3% English (2000).
Economy: Employment by occupation: 8.2% management, 13.8% professional, 19.6% services, 21.1% sales, 2.3% farming, 10.3% construction, 24.6% production (2000).
Income: Per capita income: $11,246 (2000); Median household income: $24,375 (2000); Poverty rate: 19.6% (2000).
Taxes: Total city taxes per capita: $45 (1997); City property taxes per capita: $17 (1997).
Education: High school graduation rate: 78.9% (2000); College graduation rate: 13.3% (2000).

School District(s)

Liberal R-II (KG-12)
2000 Enrollment: 507 417-843-5115
Housing: Homeownership rate: 69.9% (2000); Median home value: $36,800 (2000); Median rent: $237 per month (2000); Median age of housing: 47 years (2000).
Newspapers: Liberal News (1 x week)
Transportation: Commute to work: 96.1% car, 0.0% public transportation, 1.5% walk, 2.4% work from home (2000); Travel time to work: 25.5% less than 15 minutes, 33.2% 15 to 30 minutes, 28.3% 30 to 45 minutes, 6.2% 45 to 60 minutes, 6.8% 60 minutes or more (2000)

MILFORD (village). Covers a land area of 0.040 square miles and a water area of 0 square miles. Located at 37.58° N. Lat.; 94.15° W. Long. Elevation is 924 feet.
Population: 52 (2000); Race: 95.0% White, 0.0% Black, 0.0% Asian, 0.0% American Indian and Alaska Native, 0.0% Hispanic of any race, 5.0% two or more races (2000); Density: 1,288.2 persons per square mile (2000); Age: 15.0% under 18, 25.0% over 64 (2000); Marriage status: 29.4% never married, 61.8% now married, 0.0% widowed, 8.8% divorced (2000); Foreign born: 0.0% (2000); Ancestry (includes multiple ancestries): 30.0% Irish, 12.5% United States or American, 12.5% Swedish, 10.0% Dutch, 5.0% Other groups (2000).
Economy: Employment by occupation: 0.0% management, 5.0% professional, 0.0% services, 30.0% sales, 0.0% farming, 0.0% construction, 65.0% production (2000).
Income: Per capita income: $12,303 (2000); Median household income: $26,875 (2000); Poverty rate: 20.0% (2000).
Education: High school graduation rate: 58.6% (2000); College graduation rate: 13.8% (2000).
Housing: Homeownership rate: 84.2% (2000); Median home value: $36,700 (2000); Median rent: $275 per month (2000); Median age of housing: 28 years (2000).
Transportation: Commute to work: 100.0% car, 0.0% public transportation, 0.0% walk, 0.0% work from home (2000); Travel time to work: 25.0% less than 15 minutes, 50.0% 15 to 30 minutes, 15.0% 30 to 45 minutes, 10.0% 45 to 60 minutes, 0.0% 60 minutes or more (2000)

MINDENMINES (city). Aka Minden Mines. Covers a land area of 3.776 square miles and a water area of 0.010 square miles. Located at 37.47° N. Lat.; 94.58° W. Long. Elevation is 968 feet.
History: In a former strip coal-mining area.
Population: 409 (2000); Race: 95.1% White, 0.0% Black, 0.0% Asian, 2.8% American Indian and Alaska Native, 0.0% Hispanic of any race, 2.1% two or more races (2000); Density: 108.3 persons per square mile (2000); Age: 37.6% under 18, 13.1% over 64 (2000); Marriage status: 26.7% never married, 60.1% now married, 4.0% widowed, 9.2% divorced (2000); Foreign born: 0.7% (2000); Ancestry (includes multiple ancestries): 20.4% United States or American, 12.2% German, 11.7% Other groups, 8.9% Irish, 7.3% English (2000).
Economy: Oil field. Wheat, corn, sorghum; cattle. Employment by occupation: 7.5% management, 1.5% professional, 26.1% services, 12.7% sales, 0.0% farming, 13.4% construction, 38.8% production (2000).
Income: Per capita income: $9,560 (2000); Median household income: $22,125 (2000); Poverty rate: 15.6% (2000).
Taxes: Total city taxes per capita: $35 (1997); City property taxes per capita: $16 (1997).
Education: High school graduation rate: 60.3% (2000); College graduation rate: 5.7% (2000).
Housing: Homeownership rate: 70.2% (2000); Median home value: $26,600 (2000); Median rent: $264 per month (2000); Median age of housing: 45 years (2000).
Transportation: Commute to work: 94.0% car, 0.0% public transportation, 1.5% walk, 4.5% work from home (2000); Travel time to work: 31.3% less than 15 minutes, 44.5% 15 to 30 minutes, 21.9% 30 to 45 minutes, 2.3% 45 to 60 minutes, 0.0% 60 minutes or more (2000)

Bates County

Located in western Missouri; bounded on the west by Kansas; drained by the Marais des Cygnes and South Grand Rivers. Covers a land area of 848.50 square miles, a water area of 2.90 square miles, and is located in the Central Time Zone. The county government was organized in 1841. County seat is Butler.

Weather Station: Butler Elevation: 787 feet

	Jan	Feb	Mar	Apr	May	Jun	Jul	Aug	Sep	Oct	Nov	Dec
High	40	48	58	69	77	85	91	89	82	71	56	44
Low	19	25	34	44	53	63	68	65	57	45	34	24
Precip	1.7	1.7	3.1	4.2	5.0	5.3	3.9	3.9	4.6	3.6	3.3	2.0
Snow	4.6	2.3	1.0	tr	0.0	0.0	0.0	0.0	0.0	0.0	0.6	1.5

High and Low temperatures in degrees Fahrenheit; Precipitation and Snow in inches

Population: 16,653 (2000); Race: 97.4% White, 0.4% Black, 0.4% Asian, 0.4% American Indian and Alaska Native, 1.0% Hispanic of any race, 0.8% two or more races (2000); Density: 19.6 persons per square mile (2000); Age: 26.6% under 18, 17.4% over 64 (2000).
Religion: Five largest groups: 19.1% Southern Baptist Convention, 10.9% Christian Churches and Churches of Christ, 8.4% The United Methodist Church, 5.4% Christian Church (Disciples of Christ), 2.4% Catholic Church (2000).
Economy: Unemployment rate: 6.6% (11/2002); Total civilian labor force: 7,038 (11/2002); Leading industries: 20.0% retail trade; 19.3% health care and social assistance; 12.4% manufacturing (2000); Companies that employ more than 1,000 persons: 0 (2000); Companies that employ more than 100 persons: 4 (2000); Farms: 1,250 totaling 444,769 acres (1997); Minority business ownership rate: 0.0% (1997); Women business ownership rate: 20.0% (1997); Retail sales per capita: $5,172 (1997). Single-family building permits issued: 6 (2001) / 0 (2000); Multi-family building permits issued: 20 (2001) / 0 (2000).
Income: Per capita income: $15,477 (2000); Median household income: $30,731 (2000); Poverty rate: 14.5% (2000); Bankruptcy rate: 3.64% (2001).
Taxes: Total county taxes per capita: $123 (2000); County property taxes per capita: $22 (2000).
Education: High school graduation rate: 76.9% (2000); College graduation rate: 10.1% (2000).
Housing: Homeownership rate: 75.0% (2000); Median home value: $58,000 (2000); Median rent: $286 per month (2000); Median age of housing: 35 years (2000).
Health: Birth rate: 120.7 per 10,000 population (1998); Age adjusted death rate: 93.8 per 10,000 population (1999); Age adjusted cancer mortality rate: 194.0 deaths per 100,000 population (1999). Number of physicians: 3.6 per 10,000 population (1999); Number of hospital beds: 28.8 per 10,000 population (1999).
Elections: 2000 Presidential election results: 43.5% Gore, 54.5% Bush, 1.1% Nader, 0.4% Buchanan

Additional Information Contacts

Bates County Government Offices. 660-679-3371
Butler Chamber of Commerce 660-679-3380

Bates County Communities

ADRIAN (city). Covers a land area of 1.867 square miles and a water area of 0.072 square miles. Located at 38.39° N. Lat.; 94.35° W. Long. Elevation is 871 feet.
History: Adrian was founded in 1880 and named for the Michigan home of some of its early settlers. The town was a shipping center for grain and poultry.
Population: 1,780 (2000); Race: 98.9% White, 0.0% Black, 0.0% Asian, 0.3% American Indian and Alaska Native, 1.4% Hispanic of any race, 0.7% two or more races (2000); Density: 953.6 persons per square mile (2000); Age: 27.0% under 18, 20.5% over 64 (2000); Marriage status: 16.0% never married, 61.7% now married, 12.0% widowed, 10.3% divorced (2000); Foreign born: 0.2% (2000); Ancestry (includes multiple ancestries): 17.4% United States or American, 16.6% German, 11.8% Irish, 8.6% English, 8.5% Other groups (2000).

Economy: Employment by occupation: 10.3% management, 15.7% professional, 16.9% services, 23.6% sales, 0.9% farming, 14.7% construction, 17.9% production (2000).
Income: Per capita income: $15,856 (2000); Median household income: $31,436 (2000); Poverty rate: 12.8% (2000).
Taxes: Total city taxes per capita: $118 (1997); City property taxes per capita: $46 (1997).
Education: High school graduation rate: 80.3% (2000); College graduation rate: 8.8% (2000).

School District(s)

Adrian R-III (KG-12)
2000 Enrollment: 687 816-297-2710
Housing: Homeownership rate: 69.7% (2000); Median home value: $62,400 (2000); Median rent: $294 per month (2000); Median age of housing: 34 years (2000).
Newspapers: The Adrian Journal (1 x week)
Transportation: Commute to work: 93.9% car, 0.1% public transportation, 2.7% walk, 2.6% work from home (2000); Travel time to work: 27.2% less than 15 minutes, 22.9% 15 to 30 minutes, 10.0% 30 to 45 minutes, 16.6% 45 to 60 minutes, 23.3% 60 minutes or more (2000)

AMORET (city). Covers a land area of 0.215 square miles and a water area of 0 square miles. Located at 38.25° N. Lat.; 94.58° W. Long. Elevation is 852 feet.
Population: 211 (2000); Race: 97.8% White, 0.0% Black, 0.0% Asian, 0.0% American Indian and Alaska Native, 0.9% Hispanic of any race, 1.3% two or more races (2000); Density: 980.2 persons per square mile (2000); Age: 31.0% under 18, 11.1% over 64 (2000); Marriage status: 21.1% never married, 56.0% now married, 5.1% widowed, 17.7% divorced (2000); Foreign born: 0.9% (2000); Ancestry (includes multiple ancestries): 21.2% Irish, 17.7% United States or American, 15.0% German, 9.3% English, 8.0% Dutch (2000).
Economy: Employment by occupation: 1.2% management, 4.7% professional, 14.0% services, 17.4% sales, 2.3% farming, 16.3% construction, 44.2% production (2000).
Income: Per capita income: $10,071 (2000); Median household income: $26,250 (2000); Poverty rate: 23.9% (2000).
Taxes: Total city taxes per capita: $9 (1997); City property taxes per capita: $9 (1997).
Education: High school graduation rate: 64.4% (2000); College graduation rate: 1.5% (2000).

School District(s)

Miami R-I (PK-12)
2000 Enrollment: 320 660-267-3480
Housing: Homeownership rate: 84.8% (2000); Median home value: $27,700 (2000); Median rent: $325 per month (2000); Median age of housing: 44 years (2000).
Transportation: Commute to work: 89.3% car, 2.4% public transportation, 2.4% walk, 3.6% work from home (2000); Travel time to work: 8.6% less than 15 minutes, 45.7% 15 to 30 minutes, 9.9% 30 to 45 minutes, 8.6% 45 to 60 minutes, 27.2% 60 minutes or more (2000)

AMSTERDAM (city). Covers a land area of 0.584 square miles and a water area of 0 square miles. Located at 38.35° N. Lat.; 94.58° W. Long. Elevation is 885 feet.
Population: 281 (2000); Race: 99.3% White, 0.0% Black, 0.0% Asian, 0.0% American Indian and Alaska Native, 0.0% Hispanic of any race, 0.7% two or more races (2000); Density: 480.9 persons per square mile (2000); Age: 29.0% under 18, 14.9% over 64 (2000); Marriage status: 25.5% never married, 55.3% now married, 13.0% widowed, 6.3% divorced (2000); Foreign born: 0.7% (2000); Ancestry (includes multiple ancestries): 18.2% United States or American, 13.8% English, 9.3% Irish, 8.2% German, 5.2% Other groups (2000).
Economy: Sorghum, hay, corn; cattle. Employment by occupation: 6.3% management, 11.6% professional, 6.3% services, 22.3% sales, 0.0% farming, 31.3% construction, 22.3% production (2000).
Income: Per capita income: $11,670 (2000); Median household income: $29,821 (2000); Poverty rate: 16.0% (2000).
Taxes: Total city taxes per capita: $102 (1997); City property taxes per capita: $43 (1997).
Education: High school graduation rate: 77.2% (2000); College graduation rate: 4.9% (2000).
Housing: Homeownership rate: 79.6% (2000); Median home value: $46,300 (2000); Median rent: $281 per month (2000); Median age of housing: 33 years (2000).
Transportation: Commute to work: 90.2% car, 0.0% public transportation, 6.3% walk, 3.6% work from home (2000); Travel time to work: 22.2% less than 15 minutes, 8.3% 15 to 30 minutes, 10.2% 30 to 45 minutes, 25.9% 45 to 60 minutes, 33.3% 60 minutes or more (2000)

BUTLER (city). Covers a land area of 3.863 square miles and a water area of 0 square miles. Located at 38.25° N. Lat.; 94.33° W. Long. Elevation is 863 feet.
History: Butler was platted in 1854 and named for William O. Butler, an officer in the Mexican War. The town was devastated during the Civil War, and gradually rebuilt afterwards.
Population: 4,209 (2000); Race: 95.9% White, 1.2% Black, 0.9% Asian, 0.0% American Indian and Alaska Native, 1.3% Hispanic of any race, 1.0% two or more races (2000); Density: 1,089.5 persons per square mile (2000); Age: 24.2% under 18, 24.9% over 64 (2000); Marriage status: 17.7% never married, 55.8% now married, 12.7% widowed, 13.9% divorced (2000); Foreign born: 1.5% (2000); Ancestry (includes multiple ancestries): 16.6% German, 15.2% United States or American, 12.7% Irish, 11.1% English, 11.1% Other groups (2000).
Economy: Single-family building permits issued: 6 (2001) / 0 (2000); Multi-family building permits issued: 20 (2001) / 0 (2000); Employment by occupation: 4.4% management, 15.8% professional, 22.1% services, 24.0% sales, 1.8% farming, 13.8% construction, 18.1% production (2000).
Income: Per capita income: $15,237 (2000); Median household income: $25,531 (2000); Poverty rate: 19.4% (2000).
Taxes: Total city taxes per capita: $219 (2000); City property taxes per capita: $50 (2000).
Education: High school graduation rate: 73.0% (2000); College graduation rate: 12.7% (2000).

School District(s)

Ballard R-II (KG-12)
2000 Enrollment: 154 816-297-2656
Butler R-V (PK-12)
2000 Enrollment: 1,227 660-679-0653
Housing: Homeownership rate: 62.6% (2000); Median home value: $57,300 (2000); Median rent: $296 per month (2000); Median age of housing: 42 years (2000).
Hospitals: Bates County Memorial Hospital (60 beds)
Safety: Violent crime rate: 59.0 per 10,000 population; Property crime rate: 661.2 per 10,000 population (2001).
Newspapers: News-Xpress (1 x week)
Transportation: Commute to work: 88.7% car, 0.0% public transportation, 7.0% walk, 1.4% work from home (2000); Travel time to work: 53.4% less than 15 minutes, 10.7% 15 to 30 minutes, 10.8% 30 to 45 minutes, 8.9% 45 to 60 minutes, 16.3% 60 minutes or more (2000)
Additional Information Contacts
Butler Chamber of Commerce 660-679-3380

FOSTER (village). Covers a land area of 0.468 square miles and a water area of 0.005 square miles. Located at 38.16° N. Lat.; 94.50° W. Long. Elevation is 842 feet.
History: Former coal-mining area.
Population: 130 (2000); Race: 95.8% White, 0.0% Black, 0.0% Asian, 2.1% American Indian and Alaska Native, 0.0% Hispanic of any race, 2.1% two or more races (2000); Density: 277.5 persons per square mile (2000); Age: 40.3% under 18, 7.6% over 64 (2000); Marriage status: 16.1% never married, 64.5% now married, 11.8% widowed, 7.5% divorced (2000); Foreign born: 0.0% (2000); Ancestry (includes multiple ancestries): 18.1% United States or American, 11.8% Other groups, 9.7% German, 6.3% Italian, 3.5% Irish (2000).
Economy: Employment by occupation: 3.3% management, 16.7% professional, 25.0% services, 10.0% sales, 6.7% farming, 18.3% construction, 20.0% production (2000).
Income: Per capita income: $15,631 (2000); Median household income: $28,750 (2000); Poverty rate: 12.5% (2000).
Taxes: Total city taxes per capita: $94 (1997); City property taxes per capita: $70 (1997).
Education: High school graduation rate: 72.8% (2000); College graduation rate: 18.5% (2000).
Housing: Homeownership rate: 77.4% (2000); Median home value: $45,000 (2000); Median rent: $175 per month (2000); Median age of housing: 47 years (2000).
Transportation: Commute to work: 90.0% car, 0.0% public transportation, 8.3% walk, 1.7% work from home (2000); Travel time to work: 23.7% less than 15 minutes, 23.7% 15 to 30 minutes, 15.3% 30 to 45 minutes, 22.0% 45 to 60 minutes, 15.3% 60 minutes or more (2000)

HUME (town). Covers a land area of 0.682 square miles and a water area of 0 square miles. Located at 38.09° N. Lat.; 94.58° W. Long. Elevation is 894 feet.

Population: 337 (2000); Race: 95.3% White, 0.0% Black, 0.6% Asian, 0.9% American Indian and Alaska Native, 2.5% Hispanic of any race, 1.3% two or more races (2000); Density: 494.2 persons per square mile (2000); Age: 27.5% under 18, 12.5% over 64 (2000); Marriage status: 15.6% never married, 67.5% now married, 6.6% widowed, 10.3% divorced (2000); Foreign born: 1.3% (2000); Ancestry (includes multiple ancestries): 22.5% United States or American, 15.9% Irish, 11.6% Other groups, 8.1% German, 7.2% English (2000).

Economy: Agriculture. Employment by occupation: 6.7% management, 17.5% professional, 17.5% services, 16.7% sales, 0.0% farming, 24.2% construction, 17.5% production (2000).

Income: Per capita income: $11,176 (2000); Median household income: $25,250 (2000); Poverty rate: 12.6% (2000).

Taxes: Total city taxes per capita: $89 (1997); City property taxes per capita: $56 (1997).

Education: High school graduation rate: 81.8% (2000); College graduation rate: 4.9% (2000).

School District(s)

Hume R-VIII (KG-12)
2000 Enrollment: 136 660-643-7411

Housing: Homeownership rate: 74.6% (2000); Median home value: $27,500 (2000); Median rent: $189 per month (2000); Median age of housing: 54 years (2000).

Transportation: Commute to work: 96.6% car, 0.0% public transportation, 1.7% walk, 1.7% work from home (2000); Travel time to work: 25.4% less than 15 minutes, 20.2% 15 to 30 minutes, 26.3% 30 to 45 minutes, 14.9% 45 to 60 minutes, 13.2% 60 minutes or more (2000)

MERWIN (village). Covers a land area of 0.145 square miles and a water area of 0 square miles. Located at 38.40° N. Lat.; 94.59° W. Long. Elevation is 883 feet.

Population: 83 (2000); Race: 94.9% White, 0.0% Black, 0.0% Asian, 0.0% American Indian and Alaska Native, 3.1% Hispanic of any race, 3.1% two or more races (2000); Density: 572.7 persons per square mile (2000); Age: 27.6% under 18, 14.3% over 64 (2000); Marriage status: 13.2% never married, 60.5% now married, 11.8% widowed, 14.5% divorced (2000); Foreign born: 0.0% (2000); Ancestry (includes multiple ancestries): 20.4% Other groups, 19.4% Irish, 16.3% United States or American, 13.3% German, 11.2% Dutch (2000).

Economy: Employment by occupation: 0.0% management, 8.8% professional, 5.9% services, 17.6% sales, 0.0% farming, 38.2% construction, 29.4% production (2000).

Income: Per capita income: $10,038 (2000); Median household income: $23,125 (2000); Poverty rate: 27.4% (2000).

Taxes: Total city taxes per capita: $24 (1997); City property taxes per capita: $24 (1997).

Education: High school graduation rate: 63.5% (2000); College graduation rate: 6.3% (2000).

Housing: Homeownership rate: 78.4% (2000); Median home value: $18,600 (2000); Median rent: $213 per month (2000); Median age of housing: 42 years (2000).

Transportation: Commute to work: 100.0% car, 0.0% public transportation, 0.0% walk, 0.0% work from home (2000); Travel time to work: 5.9% less than 15 minutes, 23.5% 15 to 30 minutes, 29.4% 30 to 45 minutes, 5.9% 45 to 60 minutes, 35.3% 60 minutes or more (2000)

PASSAIC (town). Covers a land area of 0.071 square miles and a water area of 0 square miles. Located at 38.32° N. Lat.; 94.34° W. Long. Elevation is 865 feet.

Population: 40 (2000); Race: 100.0% White, 0.0% Black, 0.0% Asian, 0.0% American Indian and Alaska Native, 11.1% Hispanic of any race, 0.0% two or more races (2000); Density: 562.5 persons per square mile (2000); Age: 46.3% under 18, 3.7% over 64 (2000); Marriage status: 44.8% never married, 20.7% now married, 13.8% widowed, 20.7% divorced (2000); Foreign born: 3.7% (2000); Ancestry (includes multiple ancestries): 57.4% United States or American, 5.6% Polish, 3.7% French Canadian, 3.7% German, 3.7% French (except Basque) (2000).

Economy: Employment by occupation: 17.4% management, 0.0% professional, 17.4% services, 8.7% sales, 0.0% farming, 30.4% construction, 26.1% production (2000).

Income: Per capita income: $17,024 (2000); Median household income: $36,250 (2000); Poverty rate: 29.6% (2000).

Taxes: Total city taxes per capita: $24 (1997); City property taxes per capita: $24 (1997).

Education: High school graduation rate: 62.5% (2000); College graduation rate: 0.0% (2000).

Housing: Homeownership rate: 73.3% (2000); Median home value: $38,100 (2000); Median rent: $250 per month (2000); Median age of housing: 52 years (2000).

Transportation: Commute to work: 90.5% car, 0.0% public transportation, 0.0% walk, 9.5% work from home (2000); Travel time to work: 36.8% less than 15 minutes, 26.3% 15 to 30 minutes, 21.1% 30 to 45 minutes, 15.8% 45 to 60 minutes, 0.0% 60 minutes or more (2000)

RICH HILL (city). Covers a land area of 1.372 square miles and a water area of 0 square miles. Located at 38.09° N. Lat.; 94.36° W. Long. Elevation is 801 feet.

History: Rich Hill was named by its first postmaster, E.W. Ratekin, for its location on a hill underlaid with coal. The town was founded in the early 1880's.

Population: 1,461 (2000); Race: 96.8% White, 0.3% Black, 0.1% Asian, 1.5% American Indian and Alaska Native, 1.6% Hispanic of any race, 0.8% two or more races (2000); Density: 1,064.8 persons per square mile (2000); Age: 25.9% under 18, 18.4% over 64 (2000); Marriage status: 18.9% never married, 56.5% now married, 12.1% widowed, 12.5% divorced (2000); Foreign born: 0.3% (2000); Ancestry (includes multiple ancestries): 18.0% Other groups, 16.3% German, 12.7% United States or American, 9.7% Irish, 6.8% English (2000).

Economy: Employment by occupation: 6.8% management, 10.2% professional, 18.6% services, 21.2% sales, 2.1% farming, 15.1% construction, 26.1% production (2000).

Income: Per capita income: $15,356 (2000); Median household income: $22,964 (2000); Poverty rate: 19.0% (2000).

Taxes: Total city taxes per capita: $117 (1997); City property taxes per capita: $26 (1997).

Education: High school graduation rate: 64.9% (2000); College graduation rate: 9.0% (2000).

School District(s)

Rich Hill R-IV (KG-12)
2000 Enrollment: 510 417-395-2418

Housing: Homeownership rate: 73.4% (2000); Median home value: $34,700 (2000); Median rent: $223 per month (2000); Median age of housing: 39 years (2000).

Safety: Violent crime rate: 88.4 per 10,000 population; Property crime rate: 265.3 per 10,000 population (2001).

Newspapers: Rich Hill Mining Review (1 x week)

Transportation: Commute to work: 94.2% car, 0.0% public transportation, 1.3% walk, 3.1% work from home (2000); Travel time to work: 31.9% less than 15 minutes, 37.5% 15 to 30 minutes, 12.1% 30 to 45 minutes, 5.2% 45 to 60 minutes, 13.4% 60 minutes or more (2000)

ROCKVILLE (city). Covers a land area of 0.321 square miles and a water area of 0 square miles. Located at 38.07° N. Lat.; 94.08° W. Long. Elevation is 784 feet.

Population: 162 (2000); Race: 100.0% White, 0.0% Black, 0.0% Asian, 0.0% American Indian and Alaska Native, 1.9% Hispanic of any race, 0.0% two or more races (2000); Density: 504.8 persons per square mile (2000); Age: 18.5% under 18, 22.2% over 64 (2000); Marriage status: 16.9% never married, 54.9% now married, 11.3% widowed, 16.9% divorced (2000); Foreign born: 0.0% (2000); Ancestry (includes multiple ancestries): 23.5% German, 12.3% United States or American, 12.3% Irish, 10.5% Other groups, 8.6% English (2000).

Economy: Corn, wheat, sorghum; cattle. Employment by occupation: 0.0% management, 3.6% professional, 14.3% services, 10.7% sales, 3.6% farming, 19.6% construction, 48.2% production (2000).

Income: Per capita income: $12,730 (2000); Median household income: $19,219 (2000); Poverty rate: 32.1% (2000).

Taxes: Total city taxes per capita: $54 (1997); City property taxes per capita: $25 (1997).

Education: High school graduation rate: 64.7% (2000); College graduation rate: 6.7% (2000).

Housing: Homeownership rate: 71.6% (2000); Median home value: $32,500 (2000); Median rent: $218 per month (2000); Median age of housing: 57 years (2000).

Transportation: Commute to work: 96.1% car, 0.0% public transportation, 3.9% walk, 0.0% work from home (2000); Travel time to work: 60.8% less than 15 minutes, 19.6% 15 to 30 minutes, 3.9% 30 to 45 minutes, 13.7% 45 to 60 minutes, 2.0% 60 minutes or more (2000)

Benton County

Located in central Missouri, in the Ozarks; drained by the Osage, South Grand, and Pomme de Terre Rivers; crossed by the Lake of the Ozarks. Covers a land area of 705.50 square miles, a water area of 47.00 square miles, and is located in the Central Time Zone. The county government was organized in 1835. County seat is Warsaw.

Population: 17,180 (2000); Race: 97.6% White, 0.3% Black, 0.1% Asian, 0.6% American Indian and Alaska Native, 0.8% Hispanic of any race, 1.2% two or more races (2000); Density: 24.4 persons per square mile (2000); Age: 20.5% under 18, 22.4% over 64 (2000).

Religion: Five largest groups: 18.2% Southern Baptist Convention, 10.3% Lutheran Church—Missouri Synod, 7.8% The United Methodist Church, 4.1% Evangelical Lutheran Church in America, 2.9% Catholic Church (2000).

Economy: Unemployment rate: 6.7% (11/2002); Total civilian labor force: 6,272 (11/2002); Leading industries: 26.1% retail trade; 16.4% accommodation & food services; 13.5% manufacturing (2000); Companies that employ more than 1,000 persons: 0 (2000); Companies that employ more than 100 persons: 2 (2000); Farms: 804 totaling 232,412 acres (1997); Minority business ownership rate: 0.0% (1997); Women business ownership rate: 15.5% (1997); Retail sales per capita: $5,987 (1997). Single-family building permits issued: 8 (2001) / 5 (2000); Multi-family building permits issued: 0 (2001) / 0 (2000).

Income: Per capita income: $15,457 (2000); Median household income: $26,646 (2000); Poverty rate: 15.7% (2000); Bankruptcy rate: 3.02% (2001).

Taxes: Total county taxes per capita: $108 (2000); County property taxes per capita: $27 (2000).

Education: High school graduation rate: 71.8% (2000); College graduation rate: 8.8% (2000).

Housing: Homeownership rate: 82.2% (2000); Median home value: $65,700 (2000); Median rent: $281 per month (2000); Median age of housing: 24 years (2000).

Health: Birth rate: 89.1 per 10,000 population (1998); Age adjusted death rate: 98.5 per 10,000 population (1999); Age adjusted cancer mortality rate: 288.7 deaths per 100,000 population (1999). Number of physicians: 1.7 per 10,000 population (1999); Number of hospital beds: n/a (1999).

Elections: 2000 Presidential election results: 41.8% Gore, 56.0% Bush, 1.3% Nader, 0.5% Buchanan

National and State Parks: Big Buffalo Creek State Wildlife Area; Brush Creek State Wildlife Management Area; Harry S Truman State Park; Leesville State Wildlife Management Area; Little Tebo Creek State Wildlife Management Area; Mount Hulda State Wildlife Area; Tebo Islands State Wildlife Management Area

Additional Information Contacts

Benton County Government Offices 660-438-7406
Warsaw Area Chamber of Commerce 660-438-5922

Benton County Communities

COLE CAMP (city). Covers a land area of 0.979 square miles and a water area of 0 square miles. Located at 38.45° N. Lat.; 93.20° W. Long. Elevation is 1,018 feet.

History: Settled by German immigrants, 1830s.

Population: 1,028 (2000); Race: 97.7% White, 0.2% Black, 0.5% Asian, 0.0% American Indian and Alaska Native, 0.9% Hispanic of any race, 1.4% two or more races (2000); Density: 1,050.6 persons per square mile (2000); Age: 19.4% under 18, 29.0% over 64 (2000); Marriage status: 16.3% never married, 58.1% now married, 16.7% widowed, 8.9% divorced (2000); Foreign born: 0.7% (2000); Ancestry (includes multiple ancestries): 52.7% German, 10.2% Irish, 6.7% United States or American, 6.4% Other groups, 3.7% English (2000).

Economy: Corn, wheat; hogs, cattle. Single-family building permits issued: 0 (2001) / 0 (2000); Multi-family building permits issued: 0 (2001) / 0 (2000); Employment by occupation: 10.2% management, 18.2% professional, 17.5% services, 27.1% sales, 0.6% farming, 9.7% construction, 16.7% production (2000).

Income: Per capita income: $17,280 (2000); Median household income: $26,190 (2000); Poverty rate: 6.2% (2000).

Taxes: Total city taxes per capita: $203 (1997); City property taxes per capita: $34 (1997).

Education: High school graduation rate: 71.0% (2000); College graduation rate: 14.8% (2000).

School District(s)

Cole Camp R-I (PK-12)
2000 Enrollment: 791 660-668-4427

Housing: Homeownership rate: 78.4% (2000); Median home value: $64,100 (2000); Median rent: $254 per month (2000); Median age of housing: 47 years (2000).

Newspapers: Cole Camp Courier (1 x week)

Transportation: Commute to work: 91.7% car, 0.0% public transportation, 3.5% walk, 2.8% work from home (2000); Travel time to work: 37.6% less than 15 minutes, 27.1% 15 to 30 minutes, 27.7% 30 to 45 minutes, 4.5% 45 to 60 minutes, 3.1% 60 minutes or more (2000)

EDWARDS (unincorporated postal area, zip code 65326). Covers a land area of 145.181 square miles and a water area of 0.179 square miles. Located at 38.20° N. Lat.; 93.14° W. Long. Elevation is 801 feet.

Population: 1,873 (2000); Race: 96.4% White, 0.4% Black, 0.2% Asian, 0.7% American Indian and Alaska Native, 0.4% Hispanic of any race, 2.1% two or more races (2000); Density: 12.9 persons per square mile (2000); Age: 11.2% under 18, 33.1% over 64 (2000); Marriage status: 8.0% never married, 68.6% now married, 10.1% widowed, 13.2% divorced (2000); Foreign born: 0.7% (2000); Ancestry (includes multiple ancestries): 17.3% English, 13.3% German, 11.5% Irish, 10.5% Other groups, 8.7% United States or American (2000).

Economy: Employment by occupation: 12.3% management, 12.5% professional, 13.0% services, 25.6% sales, 0.0% farming, 20.8% construction, 15.9% production (2000).

Income: Per capita income: $14,744 (2000); Median household income: $21,473 (2000); Poverty rate: 19.2% (2000).

Education: High school graduation rate: 72.0% (2000); College graduation rate: 7.9% (2000).

Housing: Homeownership rate: 88.1% (2000); Median home value: $65,700 (2000); Median rent: $312 per month (2000); Median age of housing: 27 years (2000).

Transportation: Commute to work: 81.3% car, 0.0% public transportation, 2.9% walk, 14.7% work from home (2000); Travel time to work: 17.4% less than 15 minutes, 37.3% 15 to 30 minutes, 26.2% 30 to 45 minutes, 6.0% 45 to 60 minutes, 13.1% 60 minutes or more (2000)

IONIA (town). Covers a land area of 0.153 square miles and a water area of 0 square miles. Located at 38.50° N. Lat.; 93.32° W. Long. Elevation is 958 feet.

Population: 108 (2000); Race: 100.0% White, 0.0% Black, 0.0% Asian, 0.0% American Indian and Alaska Native, 0.0% Hispanic of any race, 0.0% two or more races (2000); Density: 703.6 persons per square mile (2000); Age: 27.6% under 18, 24.5% over 64 (2000); Marriage status: 12.8% never married, 57.7% now married, 16.7% widowed, 12.8% divorced (2000); Foreign born: 0.0% (2000); Ancestry (includes multiple ancestries): 31.6% Irish, 18.4% Other groups, 16.3% English, 13.3% German, 6.1% Scottish (2000).

Economy: Single-family building permits issued: 0 (2001) / 0 (2000); Multi-family building permits issued: 0 (2001) / 0 (2000); Employment by occupation: 9.1% management, 3.0% professional, 30.3% services, 27.3% sales, 0.0% farming, 9.1% construction, 21.2% production (2000).

Income: Per capita income: $12,317 (2000); Median household income: $21,250 (2000); Poverty rate: 27.6% (2000).

Taxes: Total city taxes per capita: $21 (1997); City property taxes per capita: $21 (1997).

Education: High school graduation rate: 67.8% (2000); College graduation rate: 10.2% (2000).

Housing: Homeownership rate: 90.0% (2000); Median home value: $30,300 (2000); Median rent: $375 per month (2000); Median age of housing: 29 years (2000).

Transportation: Commute to work: 93.9% car, 0.0% public transportation, 0.0% walk, 0.0% work from home (2000); Travel time to work: 24.2% less than 15 minutes, 39.4% 15 to 30 minutes, 21.2% 30 to 45 minutes, 0.0% 45 to 60 minutes, 15.2% 60 minutes or more (2000)

LINCOLN (city). Covers a land area of 0.951 square miles and a water area of 0.032 square miles. Located at 38.39° N. Lat.; 93.33° W. Long. Elevation is 963 feet.

History: Lincoln was incorporated in 1869 as an outgrowth of an older settlement that grew up around Wiley Vincent's tavern on the Springfield Road.

Population: 1,026 (2000); Race: 96.0% White, 0.8% Black, 0.0% Asian, 0.1% American Indian and Alaska Native, 3.2% Hispanic of any race, 2.7% two or more races (2000); Density: 1,079.2 persons per square mile (2000);

Age: 25.9% under 18, 28.1% over 64 (2000); Marriage status: 16.9% never married, 60.8% now married, 13.6% widowed, 8.7% divorced (2000); Foreign born: 1.5% (2000); Ancestry (includes multiple ancestries): 21.8% German, 14.3% United States or American, 14.1% English, 12.8% Irish, 7.2% Other groups (2000).
Economy: Single-family building permits issued: 2 (2001) / 2 (2000); Multi-family building permits issued: 0 (2001) / 0 (2000); Employment by occupation: 6.3% management, 14.8% professional, 20.6% services, 24.2% sales, 0.0% farming, 12.5% construction, 21.6% production (2000).
Income: Per capita income: $13,803 (2000); Median household income: $25,595 (2000); Poverty rate: 10.2% (2000).
Taxes: Total city taxes per capita: $165 (1997); City property taxes per capita: $35 (1997).
Education: High school graduation rate: 71.3% (2000); College graduation rate: 9.5% (2000).

School District(s)

Lincoln R-II (KG-12)
2000 Enrollment: 576 660-547-3514
Housing: Homeownership rate: 76.8% (2000); Median home value: $64,500 (2000); Median rent: $273 per month (2000); Median age of housing: 29 years (2000).
Newspapers: The Lincoln New Era (1 x week)
Transportation: Commute to work: 91.9% car, 0.5% public transportation, 2.4% walk, 4.2% work from home (2000); Travel time to work: 48.5% less than 15 minutes, 23.6% 15 to 30 minutes, 23.6% 30 to 45 minutes, 1.6% 45 to 60 minutes, 2.7% 60 minutes or more (2000)

MORA (unincorporated postal area, zip code 65345). Covers a land area of 40.470 square miles and a water area of 0.020 square miles. Located at 38.55° N. Lat.; 93.11° W. Long. Elevation is 1,015 feet.
Population: 485 (2000); Race: 97.2% White, 0.0% Black, 0.0% Asian, 1.8% American Indian and Alaska Native, 1.0% Hispanic of any race, 0.0% two or more races (2000); Density: 12.0 persons per square mile (2000); Age: 27.0% under 18, 11.5% over 64 (2000); Marriage status: 17.4% never married, 73.1% now married, 6.0% widowed, 3.5% divorced (2000); Foreign born: 1.0% (2000); Ancestry (includes multiple ancestries): 52.7% German, 16.0% Other groups, 8.7% United States or American, 7.9% English, 2.5% Irish (2000).
Economy: Employment by occupation: 9.2% management, 16.5% professional, 6.0% services, 18.3% sales, 2.3% farming, 16.5% construction, 31.2% production (2000).
Income: Per capita income: $16,607 (2000); Median household income: $44,732 (2000); Poverty rate: 6.1% (2000).
Education: High school graduation rate: 67.4% (2000); College graduation rate: 4.1% (2000).
Housing: Homeownership rate: 93.6% (2000); Median home value: $70,400 (2000); Median rent: $275 per month (2000); Median age of housing: 40 years (2000).
Transportation: Commute to work: 87.6% car, 2.8% public transportation, 0.0% walk, 9.6% work from home (2000); Travel time to work: 14.2% less than 15 minutes, 44.7% 15 to 30 minutes, 26.9% 30 to 45 minutes, 3.0% 45 to 60 minutes, 11.2% 60 minutes or more (2000)

WARSAW (city). Covers a land area of 1.980 square miles and a water area of 0.189 square miles. Located at 38.24° N. Lat.; 93.37° W. Long. Elevation is 709 feet.
History: Warsaw was platted by the county commissioners in 1813 as the seat of Benton County. The town, on the banks of the Osage River, became a shipping point for the area. The building of Bagnell Dam about 1930 created Lake of the Ozarks and gave Warsaw a tourist industry.
Population: 2,070 (2000); Race: 97.2% White, 0.2% Black, 0.2% Asian, 0.0% American Indian and Alaska Native, 2.3% Hispanic of any race, 1.3% two or more races (2000); Density: 1,045.5 persons per square mile (2000); Age: 20.2% under 18, 26.8% over 64 (2000); Marriage status: 18.6% never married, 55.7% now married, 13.2% widowed, 12.5% divorced (2000); Foreign born: 1.0% (2000); Ancestry (includes multiple ancestries): 24.1% German, 14.5% Irish, 14.4% United States or American, 11.3% English, 10.2% Other groups (2000).
Economy: Single-family building permits issued: 6 (2001) / 3 (2000); Multi-family building permits issued: 0 (2001) / 0 (2000); Employment by occupation: 11.9% management, 20.7% professional, 18.7% services, 22.3% sales, 1.0% farming, 10.9% construction, 14.6% production (2000).
Income: Per capita income: $15,262 (2000); Median household income: $23,583 (2000); Poverty rate: 18.5% (2000).
Taxes: Total city taxes per capita: $196 (1997); City property taxes per capita: $69 (1997).
Education: High school graduation rate: 67.8% (2000); College graduation rate: 11.5% (2000).

School District(s)

Warsaw R-IX (PK-12)
2000 Enrollment: 1,398 660-438-7120
Housing: Homeownership rate: 62.0% (2000); Median home value: $64,800 (2000); Median rent: $267 per month (2000); Median age of housing: 30 years (2000).
Safety: Violent crime rate: 52.8 per 10,000 population; Property crime rate: 201.6 per 10,000 population (2001).
Newspapers: Benton County Enterprise (1 x week)
Transportation: Commute to work: 92.5% car, 0.6% public transportation, 4.3% walk, 2.5% work from home (2000); Travel time to work: 61.2% less than 15 minutes, 9.6% 15 to 30 minutes, 10.6% 30 to 45 minutes, 8.9% 45 to 60 minutes, 9.8% 60 minutes or more (2000)
Additional Information Contacts
Warsaw Area Chamber of Commerce 660-438-5922

Bollinger County

Located in southeastern Missouri; crossed by the Castor and Whitewater Rivers. Covers a land area of 620.70 square miles, a water area of 0.50 square miles, and is located in the Central Time Zone. The county government was organized in 1851. County seat is Marble Hill.

Weather Station: Marble Hill — Elevation: 387 feet

	Jan	Feb	Mar	Apr	May	Jun	Jul	Aug	Sep	Oct	Nov	Dec
High	42	49	59	70	78	85	89	88	82	72	57	46
Low	21	26	35	43	53	61	65	63	56	43	34	26
Precip	3.2	3.1	5.0	4.7	4.6	4.1	4.1	3.8	3.6	3.5	4.7	4.3
Snow	4.3	4.6	2.1	tr	0.0	0.0	0.0	0.0	0.0	0.1	0.6	1.8

High and Low temperatures in degrees Fahrenheit; Precipitation and Snow in inches

Population: 12,029 (2000); Race: 97.8% White, 0.0% Black, 0.1% Asian, 0.8% American Indian and Alaska Native, 0.6% Hispanic of any race, 1.3% two or more races (2000); Density: 19.4 persons per square mile (2000); Age: 26.2% under 18, 14.7% over 64 (2000).
Religion: Five largest groups: 22.7% Southern Baptist Convention, 7.9% Catholic Church, 5.6% The United Methodist Church, 2.0% The Church of Jesus Christ of Latter-day Saints, 1.6% Evangelical Lutheran Church in America (2000).
Economy: Unemployment rate: 4.9% (11/2002); Total civilian labor force: 5,290 (11/2002); Leading industries: 24.5% retail trade; 20.6% manufacturing; 17.4% health care and social assistance (2000); Companies that employ more than 1,000 persons: 0 (2000); Companies that employ more than 100 persons: 1 (2000); Farms: 832 totaling 209,202 acres (1997); Minority business ownership rate: 0.0% (1997); Women business ownership rate: 0.0% (1997); Retail sales per capita: $3,536 (1997). Single-family building permits issued: 3 (2001) / 2 (2000); Multi-family building permits issued: 2 (2001) / 0 (2000).
Income: Per capita income: $13,641 (2000); Median household income: $30,462 (2000); Poverty rate: 13.8% (2000); Bankruptcy rate: 4.75% (2001).
Taxes: Total county taxes per capita: $76 (1997); County property taxes per capita: $32 (1997).
Education: High school graduation rate: 70.7% (2000); College graduation rate: 6.9% (2000).
Housing: Homeownership rate: 81.6% (2000); Median home value: $58,400 (2000); Median rent: $256 per month (2000); Median age of housing: 26 years (2000).
Health: Birth rate: 99.8 per 10,000 population (1998); Age adjusted death rate: 103.8 per 10,000 population (1999); Age adjusted cancer mortality rate: 254.5 deaths per 100,000 population (1999). Number of physicians: 1.7 per 10,000 population (1999); Number of hospital beds: n/a (1999).
Elections: 2000 Presidential election results: 32.0% Gore, 65.9% Bush, 0.8% Nader, 0.6% Buchanan
National and State Parks: Castor River State Forest; Club Creek State Forest; Dark Cypress Swamp State Wildlife Area; Duck Creek State Wildlife Management Area; Duck Creek State Wildlife Refuge; Grassy Tower Site State Public Hunting Area; Sank State Wildlife Area
Additional Information Contacts
Bollinger County Government Offices 573-238-2126

Bollinger County Communities

GIPSY (unincorporated postal area, zip code 63750). Covers a land area of 20.310 square miles and a water area of 0.006 square miles. Located at 37.14° N. Lat.; 90.18° W. Long. Elevation is 410 feet.
Population: 131 (2000); Race: 100.0% White, 0.0% Black, 0.0% Asian, 0.0% American Indian and Alaska Native, 0.0% Hispanic of any race, 0.0% two or more races (2000); Density: 6.4 persons per square mile (2000); Age: 20.5% under 18, 30.8% over 64 (2000); Marriage status: 11.8% never married, 67.7% now married, 12.9% widowed, 7.5% divorced (2000); Foreign born: 0.0% (2000); Ancestry (includes multiple ancestries): 24.8% German, 13.7% Irish, 8.5% Russian, 8.5% United States or American, 7.7% English (2000).
Economy: Employment by occupation: 0.0% management, 26.9% professional, 19.2% services, 11.5% sales, 0.0% farming, 11.5% construction, 30.8% production (2000).
Income: Per capita income: $10,232 (2000); Median household income: $14,000 (2000); Poverty rate: 44.4% (2000).
Education: High school graduation rate: 54.0% (2000); College graduation rate: 8.0% (2000).
Housing: Homeownership rate: 83.0% (2000); Median home value: $55,000 (2000); Median rent: $175 per month (2000); Median age of housing: 20 years (2000).
Transportation: Commute to work: 100.0% car, 0.0% public transportation, 0.0% walk, 0.0% work from home (2000); Travel time to work: 19.2% less than 15 minutes, 53.8% 15 to 30 minutes, 0.0% 30 to 45 minutes, 7.7% 45 to 60 minutes, 19.2% 60 minutes or more (2000)

GLEN ALLEN (town). Covers a land area of 0.059 square miles and a water area of 0 square miles. Located at 37.31° N. Lat.; 90.02° W. Long. Elevation is 459 feet.
Population: 145 (2000); Race: 96.6% White, 0.0% Black, 0.0% Asian, 3.4% American Indian and Alaska Native, 11.6% Hispanic of any race, 0.0% two or more races (2000); Density: 2,477.4 persons per square mile (2000); Age: 35.6% under 18, 4.1% over 64 (2000); Marriage status: 24.5% never married, 54.1% now married, 13.3% widowed, 8.2% divorced (2000); Foreign born: 0.0% (2000); Ancestry (includes multiple ancestries): 20.5% Other groups, 20.5% German, 17.1% United States or American, 10.3% English, 5.5% Irish (2000).
Economy: Employment by occupation: 4.3% management, 4.3% professional, 17.0% services, 14.9% sales, 4.3% farming, 21.3% construction, 34.0% production (2000).
Income: Per capita income: $15,079 (2000); Median household income: $15,000 (2000); Poverty rate: 30.8% (2000).
Education: High school graduation rate: 65.4% (2000); College graduation rate: 7.4% (2000).
Housing: Homeownership rate: 62.0% (2000); Median home value: $25,500 (2000); Median rent: $318 per month (2000); Median age of housing: 49 years (2000).
Transportation: Commute to work: 85.1% car, 0.0% public transportation, 2.1% walk, 12.8% work from home (2000); Travel time to work: 36.6% less than 15 minutes, 26.8% 15 to 30 minutes, 4.9% 30 to 45 minutes, 26.8% 45 to 60 minutes, 4.9% 60 minutes or more (2000)

GRASSY (unincorporated postal area, zip code 63753). Covers a land area of 28.593 square miles and a water area of 0.034 square miles. Located at 37.21° N. Lat.; 90.13° W. Long. Elevation is 706 feet.
Population: 259 (2000); Race: 100.0% White, 0.0% Black, 0.0% Asian, 0.0% American Indian and Alaska Native, 0.0% Hispanic of any race, 0.0% two or more races (2000); Density: 9.1 persons per square mile (2000); Age: 36.1% under 18, 13.5% over 64 (2000); Marriage status: 19.9% never married, 72.2% now married, 4.6% widowed, 3.2% divorced (2000); Foreign born: 0.0% (2000); Ancestry (includes multiple ancestries): 24.3% German, 9.7% United States or American, 9.0% Other groups, 8.3% Irish, 6.9% European (2000).
Economy: Employment by occupation: 17.6% management, 4.9% professional, 9.8% services, 15.7% sales, 3.9% farming, 25.5% construction, 22.5% production (2000).
Income: Per capita income: $11,160 (2000); Median household income: $32,500 (2000); Poverty rate: 9.0% (2000).
Education: High school graduation rate: 65.7% (2000); College graduation rate: 4.1% (2000).
Housing: Homeownership rate: 81.4% (2000); Median home value: $81,900 (2000); Median rent: $144 per month (2000); Median age of housing: 24 years (2000).
Transportation: Commute to work: 95.7% car, 0.0% public transportation, 0.0% walk, 4.3% work from home (2000); Travel time to work: 31.5% less than 15 minutes, 14.6% 15 to 30 minutes, 11.2% 30 to 45 minutes, 19.1% 45 to 60 minutes, 23.6% 60 minutes or more (2000)

LEOPOLD (unincorporated postal area, zip code 63760). Covers a land area of 32.209 square miles and a water area of 0.028 square miles. Located at 37.24° N. Lat.; 89.88° W. Long. Elevation is 639 feet.
Population: 646 (2000); Race: 98.9% White, 0.0% Black, 0.3% Asian, 0.0% American Indian and Alaska Native, 0.0% Hispanic of any race, 0.8% two or more races (2000); Density: 20.1 persons per square mile (2000); Age: 26.1% under 18, 14.3% over 64 (2000); Marriage status: 19.8% never married, 66.8% now married, 8.9% widowed, 4.5% divorced (2000); Foreign born: 0.0% (2000); Ancestry (includes multiple ancestries): 51.2% German, 16.2% Dutch, 8.8% United States or American, 5.8% Other groups, 4.0% English (2000).
Economy: Employment by occupation: 8.6% management, 14.6% professional, 8.9% services, 27.9% sales, 0.5% farming, 14.1% construction, 25.5% production (2000).
Income: Per capita income: $16,376 (2000); Median household income: $38,333 (2000); Poverty rate: 6.4% (2000).
Education: High school graduation rate: 75.3% (2000); College graduation rate: 11.1% (2000).

School District(s)

Leopold R-III (KG-12)
2000 Enrollment: 233 573-238-2211
Housing: Homeownership rate: 88.0% (2000); Median home value: $84,300 (2000); Median rent: $281 per month (2000); Median age of housing: 27 years (2000).
Transportation: Commute to work: 92.1% car, 0.5% public transportation, 3.2% walk, 4.2% work from home (2000); Travel time to work: 19.2% less than 15 minutes, 22.5% 15 to 30 minutes, 29.4% 30 to 45 minutes, 18.4% 45 to 60 minutes, 10.4% 60 minutes or more (2000)

MARBLE HILL (city). Covers a land area of 1.605 square miles and a water area of 0 square miles. Located at 37.30° N. Lat.; 89.97° W. Long. Elevation is 485 feet.
History: Annexed adjacent Lutesville in 1986.
Population: 1,502 (2000); Race: 97.3% White, 0.0% Black, 0.0% Asian, 1.8% American Indian and Alaska Native, 0.7% Hispanic of any race, 0.9% two or more races (2000); Density: 935.9 persons per square mile (2000); Age: 26.4% under 18, 19.7% over 64 (2000); Marriage status: 19.2% never married, 54.2% now married, 12.6% widowed, 14.0% divorced (2000); Foreign born: 0.0% (2000); Ancestry (includes multiple ancestries): 16.0% German, 14.3% English, 14.2% Irish, 12.4% Other groups, 11.2% United States or American (2000).
Economy: Corn, wheat; livestock; timber; manufacturing: headwear. Single-family building permits issued: 3 (2001) / 2 (2000); Multi-family building permits issued: 2 (2001) / 0 (2000); Employment by occupation: 6.5% management, 12.1% professional, 16.6% services, 19.0% sales, 0.3% farming, 10.0% construction, 35.5% production (2000).
Income: Per capita income: $12,857 (2000); Median household income: $22,163 (2000); Poverty rate: 19.6% (2000).
Taxes: Total city taxes per capita: $238 (1997); City property taxes per capita: $30 (1997).
Education: High school graduation rate: 64.3% (2000); College graduation rate: 8.9% (2000).

School District(s)

Woodland R-IV (PK-12)
2000 Enrollment: 954 573-238-3343
Housing: Homeownership rate: 60.6% (2000); Median home value: $45,900 (2000); Median rent: $268 per month (2000); Median age of housing: 36 years (2000).
Newspapers: The Banner-Press (1 x week)
Transportation: Commute to work: 93.6% car, 0.5% public transportation, 3.3% walk, 1.3% work from home (2000); Travel time to work: 42.7% less than 15 minutes, 12.2% 15 to 30 minutes, 18.3% 30 to 45 minutes, 20.2% 45 to 60 minutes, 6.7% 60 minutes or more (2000)

PATTON (unincorporated postal area, zip code 63662). Covers a land area of 66.761 square miles and a water area of 0.040 square miles. Located at 37.51° N. Lat.; 90.02° W. Long. Elevation is 623 feet.
Population: 1,162 (2000); Race: 98.4% White, 0.0% Black, 0.6% Asian, 0.0% American Indian and Alaska Native, 0.0% Hispanic of any race, 1.0% two or more races (2000); Density: 17.4 persons per square mile (2000); Age: 28.7% under 18, 12.7% over 64 (2000); Marriage status: 19.4% never married, 65.7% now married, 6.1% widowed, 8.8% divorced (2000); Foreign born: 0.6% (2000); Ancestry (includes multiple ancestries): 24.7% German,

14.2% Irish, 14.0% United States or American, 10.2% Other groups, 6.7% English (2000).
Economy: Employment by occupation: 6.3% management, 7.6% professional, 15.6% services, 20.2% sales, 1.3% farming, 17.9% construction, 31.0% production (2000).
Income: Per capita income: $14,294 (2000); Median household income: $33,487 (2000); Poverty rate: 12.1% (2000).
Education: High school graduation rate: 72.9% (2000); College graduation rate: 3.5% (2000).

School District(s)

Meadow Heights R-II (KG-12)
2000 Enrollment: 623 573-866-0060
Housing: Homeownership rate: 89.5% (2000); Median home value: $54,800 (2000); Median rent: $343 per month (2000); Median age of housing: 25 years (2000).
Transportation: Commute to work: 87.4% car, 0.0% public transportation, 5.8% walk, 5.5% work from home (2000); Travel time to work: 21.7% less than 15 minutes, 13.5% 15 to 30 minutes, 33.2% 30 to 45 minutes, 20.7% 45 to 60 minutes, 10.9% 60 minutes or more (2000)

SEDGEWICKVILLE (village). Covers a land area of 0.632 square miles and a water area of 0 square miles. Located at 37.51° N. Lat.; 89.90° W. Long. Elevation is 642 feet.
Population: 197 (2000); Race: 100.0% White, 0.0% Black, 0.0% Asian, 0.0% American Indian and Alaska Native, 4.8% Hispanic of any race, 0.0% two or more races (2000); Density: 311.5 persons per square mile (2000); Age: 41.4% under 18, 7.0% over 64 (2000); Marriage status: 17.1% never married, 71.8% now married, 6.8% widowed, 4.3% divorced (2000); Foreign born: 0.0% (2000); Ancestry (includes multiple ancestries): 24.2% German, 11.8% United States or American, 10.2% Other groups, 9.7% Irish, 3.2% Italian (2000).
Economy: Light manufacturing. Single-family building permits issued: 0 (2001) / 0 (2000); Multi-family building permits issued: 0 (2001) / 0 (2000); Employment by occupation: 2.6% management, 6.6% professional, 7.9% services, 27.6% sales, 2.6% farming, 6.6% construction, 46.1% production (2000).
Income: Per capita income: $11,962 (2000); Median household income: $35,156 (2000); Poverty rate: 14.0% (2000).
Taxes: Total city taxes per capita: $14 (1997); City property taxes per capita: $14 (1997).
Education: High school graduation rate: 78.0% (2000); College graduation rate: 7.0% (2000).
Housing: Homeownership rate: 92.4% (2000); Median home value: $47,000 (2000); Median rent: $325 per month (2000); Median age of housing: 45 years (2000).
Transportation: Commute to work: 100.0% car, 0.0% public transportation, 0.0% walk, 0.0% work from home (2000); Travel time to work: 17.6% less than 15 minutes, 25.7% 15 to 30 minutes, 37.8% 30 to 45 minutes, 8.1% 45 to 60 minutes, 10.8% 60 minutes or more (2000)

STURDIVANT (unincorporated postal area, zip code 63782). Covers a land area of 17.492 square miles and a water area of 0.011 square miles. Located at 37.10° N. Lat.; 90.02° W. Long. Elevation is 349 feet.
Population: 375 (2000); Race: 99.4% White, 0.0% Black, 0.3% Asian, 0.3% American Indian and Alaska Native, 0.3% Hispanic of any race, 0.0% two or more races (2000); Density: 21.4 persons per square mile (2000); Age: 27.7% under 18, 6.4% over 64 (2000); Marriage status: 25.8% never married, 66.8% now married, 2.1% widowed, 5.3% divorced (2000); Foreign born: 0.0% (2000); Ancestry (includes multiple ancestries): 20.9% Irish, 19.6% German, 19.6% Other groups, 16.5% United States or American, 4.5% English (2000).
Economy: Employment by occupation: 3.1% management, 6.2% professional, 12.3% services, 19.8% sales, 3.1% farming, 22.8% construction, 32.7% production (2000).
Income: Per capita income: $13,229 (2000); Median household income: $32,344 (2000); Poverty rate: 17.6% (2000).
Education: High school graduation rate: 69.3% (2000); College graduation rate: 5.3% (2000).
Housing: Homeownership rate: 82.9% (2000); Median home value: $52,100 (2000); Median rent: $271 per month (2000); Median age of housing: 24 years (2000).
Transportation: Commute to work: 98.8% car, 0.0% public transportation, 0.0% walk, 1.3% work from home (2000); Travel time to work: 13.3% less than 15 minutes, 31.6% 15 to 30 minutes, 19.0% 30 to 45 minutes, 20.3% 45 to 60 minutes, 15.8% 60 minutes or more (2000)

ZALMA (village). Covers a land area of 0.144 square miles and a water area of 0 square miles. Located at 37.14° N. Lat.; 90.07° W. Long. Elevation is 375 feet.
Population: 93 (2000); Race: 98.2% White, 0.0% Black, 0.0% Asian, 1.8% American Indian and Alaska Native, 0.0% Hispanic of any race, 0.0% two or more races (2000); Density: 645.6 persons per square mile (2000); Age: 26.8% under 18, 9.8% over 64 (2000); Marriage status: 18.8% never married, 45.9% now married, 10.6% widowed, 24.7% divorced (2000); Foreign born: 0.0% (2000); Ancestry (includes multiple ancestries): 18.8% Irish, 15.2% German, 10.7% United States or American, 9.8% Other groups, 9.8% French Canadian (2000).
Economy: Corn, wheat, soybeans; cattle. Employment by occupation: 7.7% management, 0.0% professional, 21.2% services, 30.8% sales, 0.0% farming, 21.2% construction, 19.2% production (2000).
Income: Per capita income: $10,842 (2000); Median household income: $21,250 (2000); Poverty rate: 35.7% (2000).
Taxes: Total city taxes per capita: $79 (1997); City property taxes per capita: $79 (1997).
Education: High school graduation rate: 72.9% (2000); College graduation rate: 4.3% (2000).

School District(s)

Zalma R-V (KG-12)
2000 Enrollment: 262 573-722-3320
Housing: Homeownership rate: 79.1% (2000); Median home value: $55,000 (2000); Median rent: $192 per month (2000); Median age of housing: 37 years (2000).
Transportation: Commute to work: 86.5% car, 0.0% public transportation, 9.6% walk, 3.8% work from home (2000); Travel time to work: 18.0% less than 15 minutes, 18.0% 15 to 30 minutes, 20.0% 30 to 45 minutes, 28.0% 45 to 60 minutes, 16.0% 60 minutes or more (2000)

Boone County

Located in central Missouri, bounded on the southwest by the Missouri River. Covers a land area of 685.40 square miles, a water area of 5.90 square miles, and is located in the Central Time Zone. The county government was organized in 1820. County seat is Columbia.

Boone County is part of the Columbia, MO MSA. The entire metro area includes: Boone County

Weather Station: Columbia Regional Airport — Elevation: 889 feet

	Jan	Feb	Mar	Apr	May	Jun	Jul	Aug	Sep	Oct	Nov	Dec
High	36	43	54	65	74	83	88	87	79	67	53	41
Low	19	24	34	44	53	62	67	65	57	45	34	24
Precip	1.7	2.1	3.2	4.4	5.0	3.9	3.7	3.6	3.7	3.2	3.5	2.5
Snow	7.0	7.2	3.5	0.8	tr	tr	tr	0.0	0.0	tr	2.3	4.5

High and Low temperatures in degrees Fahrenheit; Precipitation and Snow in inches

Population: 135,454 (2000); Race: 85.9% White, 8.4% Black, 2.9% Asian, 0.5% American Indian and Alaska Native, 1.9% Hispanic of any race, 1.8% two or more races (2000); Density: 197.6 persons per square mile (2000); Age: 22.8% under 18, 8.6% over 64 (2000).
Religion: Five largest groups: 11.5% Southern Baptist Convention, 6.9% Catholic Church, 4.5% Christian Church (Disciples of Christ), 4.0% The United Methodist Church, 1.4% Lutheran Church—Missouri Synod (2000).
Economy: Unemployment rate: 1.8% (11/2002); Total civilian labor force: 87,039 (11/2002); Leading industries: 21.5% health care and social assistance; 14.7% retail trade; 10.5% accommodation & food services (2000); Companies that employ more than 1,000 persons: 7 (2000); Companies that employ more than 100 persons: 84 (2000); Farms: 1,227 totaling 249,849 acres (1997); Minority business ownership rate: 5.6% (1997); Women business ownership rate: 27.3% (1997); Retail sales per capita: $11,495 (1997). Single-family building permits issued: 1,049 (2001) / 899 (2000); Multi-family building permits issued: 140 (2001) / 364 (2000).
Income: Per capita income: $19,844 (2000); Median household income: $37,485 (2000); Poverty rate: 14.5% (2000); Bankruptcy rate: 4.09% (2001).
Taxes: Total county taxes per capita: $166 (2000); County property taxes per capita: $33 (2000).
Education: High school graduation rate: 89.2% (2000); College graduation rate: 41.7% (2000).
Housing: Homeownership rate: 57.5% (2000); Median home value: $107,400 (2000); Median rent: $421 per month (2000); Median age of housing: 22 years (2000).
Health: Birth rate: 126.1 per 10,000 population (1998); Age adjusted death rate: 85.9 per 10,000 population (1999); Age adjusted cancer mortality rate:

220.0 deaths per 100,000 population (1999). Number of physicians: 75.7 per 10,000 population (1999); Number of hospital beds: 88.7 per 10,000 population (1999).
Elections: 2000 Presidential election results: 48.3% Gore, 47.7% Bush, 3.2% Nader, 0.3% Buchanan
National and State Parks: Charles W Green State Wildlife Management Area; Finger Lakes State Park; Rock Bridge Memorial State Park
Additional Information Contacts
Boone County Government Offices 573-886-4305
Centralia Chamber of Commerce 573-682-2272
Columbia Board of Realtors 573-446-2400
Columbia Chamber of Commerce 573-874-1132
Missouri Association of Realtors 573-445-8400
Southern Boone Chamber of Commerce 573-657-5555

Boone County Communities

ASHLAND (city). Covers a land area of 0.887 square miles and a water area of 0 square miles. Located at 38.77° N. Lat.; 92.25° W. Long. Elevation is 902 feet.
History: Ashland was founded in 1853 at the western edge of Two-Mile Prairie, a landmark for pioneers in the late 1800's.
Population: 1,869 (2000); Race: 97.7% White, 0.4% Black, 0.4% Asian, 0.3% American Indian and Alaska Native, 1.0% Hispanic of any race, 0.7% two or more races (2000); Density: 2,106.7 persons per square mile (2000); Age: 28.0% under 18, 14.6% over 64 (2000); Marriage status: 19.9% never married, 51.6% now married, 11.5% widowed, 17.0% divorced (2000); Foreign born: 0.5% (2000); Ancestry (includes multiple ancestries): 21.6% German, 14.4% United States or American, 13.0% English, 10.9% Other groups, 8.3% Irish (2000).
Economy: Employment by occupation: 8.4% management, 20.2% professional, 20.3% services, 26.2% sales, 0.3% farming, 10.7% construction, 13.9% production (2000).
Income: Per capita income: $15,938 (2000); Median household income: $34,750 (2000); Poverty rate: 10.3% (2000).
Taxes: Total city taxes per capita: $235 (1997); City property taxes per capita: $26 (1997).
Education: High school graduation rate: 84.3% (2000); College graduation rate: 22.9% (2000).

School District(s)

Southern Boone Co. R-I (PK-12)
2000 Enrollment: 1,219 573-657-2147
Housing: Homeownership rate: 58.7% (2000); Median home value: $94,200 (2000); Median rent: $430 per month (2000); Median age of housing: 16 years (2000).
Newspapers: Boone County Journal (1 x week)
Transportation: Commute to work: 92.6% car, 0.0% public transportation, 2.3% walk, 3.9% work from home (2000); Travel time to work: 22.8% less than 15 minutes, 56.1% 15 to 30 minutes, 17.2% 30 to 45 minutes, 0.7% 45 to 60 minutes, 3.2% 60 minutes or more (2000)
Additional Information Contacts
Southern Boone Chamber of Commerce 573-657-5555

CENTRALIA (city). Covers a land area of 2.530 square miles and a water area of 0 square miles. Located at 39.21° N. Lat.; 92.13° W. Long. Elevation is 891 feet.
History: Centralia was established in 1857 on the route of the North Missouri Railroad, which was completed to this point in 1859. The town later developed around the A.B. Chance Manufacturing Company which produced telephone-pole anchors.
Population: 3,774 (2000); Race: 97.4% White, 0.7% Black, 0.0% Asian, 0.1% American Indian and Alaska Native, 0.0% Hispanic of any race, 1.8% two or more races (2000); Density: 1,492.0 persons per square mile (2000); Age: 28.3% under 18, 18.0% over 64 (2000); Marriage status: 18.3% never married, 61.0% now married, 11.5% widowed, 9.2% divorced (2000); Foreign born: 0.3% (2000); Ancestry (includes multiple ancestries): 23.3% United States or American, 17.6% German, 9.8% English, 9.2% Irish, 5.4% Other groups (2000).
Economy: Employment by occupation: 8.5% management, 16.7% professional, 17.3% services, 21.8% sales, 0.9% farming, 10.9% construction, 23.8% production (2000).
Income: Per capita income: $17,583 (2000); Median household income: $34,475 (2000); Poverty rate: 4.5% (2000).
Taxes: Total city taxes per capita: $259 (1997); City property taxes per capita: $91 (1997).
Education: High school graduation rate: 82.1% (2000); College graduation rate: 12.6% (2000).

School District(s)

Centralia R-VI (PK-12)
2000 Enrollment: 1,302 573-682-3561
Housing: Homeownership rate: 69.6% (2000); Median home value: $65,000 (2000); Median rent: $312 per month (2000); Median age of housing: 37 years (2000).
Safety: Violent crime rate: 84.3 per 10,000 population; Property crime rate: 402.9 per 10,000 population (2001).
Newspapers: The Centralia Fireside Guard (1 x week)
Transportation: Commute to work: 92.1% car, 0.0% public transportation, 2.0% walk, 5.2% work from home (2000); Travel time to work: 45.8% less than 15 minutes, 24.1% 15 to 30 minutes, 23.1% 30 to 45 minutes, 6.5% 45 to 60 minutes, 0.4% 60 minutes or more (2000)
Additional Information Contacts
Centralia Chamber of Commerce 573-682-2272

COLUMBIA (city). Covers a land area of 53.069 square miles and a water area of 0.270 square miles. Located at 38.94° N. Lat.; 92.33° W. Long. Elevation is 758 feet.
History: Columbia's origins are in the town of Smithton, established in 1819 by the Smithton Land Company . When the location was moved to secure a more adequate water supply, the town was named Columbia. Columbia was incorporated in 1826. Many of Columbia's residents were from Virginia and Kentucky, and they placed great value on education. By collecting almost $118,000 in subscriptions, the residents secured the state university in 1839.
Population: 84,531 (2000); Race: 82.1% White, 10.7% Black, 4.2% Asian, 0.5% American Indian and Alaska Native, 2.1% Hispanic of any race, 1.8% two or more races (2000); Density: 1,592.8 persons per square mile (2000); Age: 19.5% under 18, 8.7% over 64 (2000); Marriage status: 43.9% never married, 43.0% now married, 4.2% widowed, 9.0% divorced (2000); Foreign born: 6.4% (2000); Ancestry (includes multiple ancestries): 25.6% German, 19.7% Other groups, 13.4% Irish, 12.9% English, 7.2% United States or American (2000).
Vital Statistics: Birth rate: 131.4 per 10,000 population (1998)
Economy: Unemployment rate: 1.9% (11/2002); Total civilian labor force: 52,200 (11/2002); Single-family building permits issued: 640 (2001) / 516 (2000); Multi-family building permits issued: 110 (2001) / 346 (2000); Employment by occupation: 12.0% management, 33.5% professional, 15.9% services, 26.9% sales, 0.5% farming, 4.0% construction, 7.2% production (2000).
Income: Per capita income: $19,507 (2000); Median household income: $33,729 (2000); Poverty rate: 19.2% (2000).
Taxes: Total city taxes per capita: $423 (2000); City property taxes per capita: $62 (2000).
Education: High school graduation rate: 91.1% (2000); College graduation rate: 50.5% (2000).

School District(s)

Columbia 93 (PK-12)
2000 Enrollment: 16,178 573-886-2100

Four-year College(s)

Columbia College (Private, Not-for-profit, Christian Church (Disciples of Christ))
2001 Enrollment: 8,564 573-875-8700
2001 Tuition: In-state $10,506; Out-of-state $10,506
University of Missouri-Columbia (Public)
2001 Enrollment: 23,667 573-882-2121
2001 Tuition: In-state $4,245; Out-of-state $12,690
Stephens College (Private, Not-for-profit)
2001 Enrollment: 669 573-442-2211
2001 Tuition: In-state $16,245; Out-of-state $16,245
Housing: Homeownership rate: 47.2% (2000); Median home value: $118,500 (2000); Median rent: $427 per month (2000); Median age of housing: 23 years (2000).
Hospitals: Boone Hospital Center (367 beds); Columbia Regional Hospital (255 beds); Ellis Fischel Cancer Hospital (60 beds); Harry S Truman Memorial Veterans' Hospital; Mid Missouri Mental Health Center (69 beds); University of Missouri Hospital and Clinics (495 beds)
Safety: Violent crime rate: 51.6 per 10,000 population; Property crime rate: 406.6 per 10,000 population (2001).
Newspapers: Columbia Missourian (6 x week); Columbia Daily Tribune (7 x week)
Transportation: Commute to work: 86.8% car, 1.1% public transportation, 7.0% walk, 2.9% work from home (2000); Travel time to work: 56.9% less

than 15 minutes, 31.7% 15 to 30 minutes, 7.0% 30 to 45 minutes, 2.4% 45 to 60 minutes, 2.0% 60 minutes or more (2000)
Airports: Columbia Regional (primary service)
Additional Information Contacts
Columbia Board of Realtors.......................... 573-446-2400
Columbia Chamber of Commerce....................... 573-874-1132
Missouri Association of Realtors.................... 573-445-8400

HALLSVILLE (city). Covers a land area of 0.733 square miles and a water area of 0 square miles. Located at 39.11° N. Lat.; 92.22° W. Long. Elevation is 910 feet.
Population: 978 (2000); Race: 95.6% White, 0.2% Black, 0.0% Asian, 0.8% American Indian and Alaska Native, 0.7% Hispanic of any race, 2.9% two or more races (2000); Density: 1,334.2 persons per square mile (2000); Age: 25.6% under 18, 13.7% over 64 (2000); Marriage status: 14.9% never married, 61.9% now married, 10.9% widowed, 12.2% divorced (2000); Foreign born: 0.0% (2000); Ancestry (includes multiple ancestries): 18.9% German, 14.9% English, 12.0% Other groups, 11.5% United States or American, 11.3% Irish (2000).
Economy: Corn, hay; cattle. Employment by occupation: 11.3% management, 19.5% professional, 12.8% services, 27.3% sales, 0.6% farming, 13.2% construction, 15.2% production (2000).
Income: Per capita income: $18,282 (2000); Median household income: $35,536 (2000); Poverty rate: 6.6% (2000).
Taxes: Total city taxes per capita: $193 (1997); City property taxes per capita: $71 (1997).
Education: High school graduation rate: 86.3% (2000); College graduation rate: 15.6% (2000).

School District(s)
Boone Co. R-IV (PK-12)
2000 Enrollment: 1,196 573-696-5512
Housing: Homeownership rate: 76.9% (2000); Median home value: $70,400 (2000); Median rent: $318 per month (2000); Median age of housing: 29 years (2000).
Transportation: Commute to work: 94.4% car, 0.0% public transportation, 2.1% walk, 2.7% work from home (2000); Travel time to work: 15.5% less than 15 minutes, 53.4% 15 to 30 minutes, 22.8% 30 to 45 minutes, 3.0% 45 to 60 minutes, 5.4% 60 minutes or more (2000)

HARRISBURG (town). Covers a land area of 0.693 square miles and a water area of 0.002 square miles. Located at 39.14° N. Lat.; 92.46° W. Long. Elevation is 841 feet.
Population: 184 (2000); Race: 90.7% White, 0.0% Black, 0.0% Asian, 0.0% American Indian and Alaska Native, 0.0% Hispanic of any race, 9.3% two or more races (2000); Density: 265.7 persons per square mile (2000); Age: 28.4% under 18, 13.1% over 64 (2000); Marriage status: 26.5% never married, 58.5% now married, 6.1% widowed, 8.8% divorced (2000); Foreign born: 0.0% (2000); Ancestry (includes multiple ancestries): 19.1% Irish, 18.0% United States or American, 16.4% Other groups, 13.1% German, 9.3% English (2000).
Economy: Coal mining. Employment by occupation: 8.4% management, 15.7% professional, 12.0% services, 25.3% sales, 2.4% farming, 15.7% construction, 20.5% production (2000).
Income: Per capita income: $14,298 (2000); Median household income: $40,714 (2000); Poverty rate: 18.0% (2000).
Taxes: Total city taxes per capita: $245 (1997); City property taxes per capita: $16 (1997).
Education: High school graduation rate: 83.8% (2000); College graduation rate: 11.7% (2000).

School District(s)
Harrisburg R-VIII (KG-12)
2000 Enrollment: 570 573-875-5604
Housing: Homeownership rate: 61.5% (2000); Median home value: $75,000 (2000); Median rent: $350 per month (2000); Median age of housing: 28 years (2000).
Transportation: Commute to work: 86.7% car, 0.0% public transportation, 6.0% walk, 4.8% work from home (2000); Travel time to work: 8.9% less than 15 minutes, 19.0% 15 to 30 minutes, 57.0% 30 to 45 minutes, 8.9% 45 to 60 minutes, 6.3% 60 minutes or more (2000)

HARTSBURG (town). Covers a land area of 0.081 square miles and a water area of 0 square miles. Located at 38.69° N. Lat.; 92.31° W. Long. Elevation is 564 feet.
History: Flooding in 1993 severely damaged town.
Population: 108 (2000); Race: 78.8% White, 0.0% Black, 0.0% Asian, 2.9% American Indian and Alaska Native, 0.0% Hispanic of any race, 18.3% two or more races (2000); Density: 1,327.0 persons per square mile (2000); Age: 20.2% under 18, 20.2% over 64 (2000); Marriage status: 17.9% never married, 58.3% now married, 11.9% widowed, 11.9% divorced (2000); Foreign born: 0.0% (2000); Ancestry (includes multiple ancestries): 32.7% German, 26.9% United States or American, 9.6% Other groups, 3.8% Irish, 2.9% French (except Basque) (2000).
Economy: Pumpkins, corn, soybeans; cattle. Employment by occupation: 19.2% management, 11.5% professional, 17.3% services, 28.8% sales, 3.8% farming, 9.6% construction, 9.6% production (2000).
Income: Per capita income: $16,739 (2000); Median household income: $32,500 (2000); Poverty rate: 5.8% (2000).
Taxes: Total city taxes per capita: $34 (1997); City property taxes per capita: $14 (1997).
Education: High school graduation rate: 89.0% (2000); College graduation rate: 13.7% (2000).
Housing: Homeownership rate: 59.2% (2000); Median home value: $82,000 (2000); Median rent: $350 per month (2000); Median age of housing: 60+ years (2000).
Transportation: Commute to work: 100.0% car, 0.0% public transportation, 0.0% walk, 0.0% work from home (2000); Travel time to work: 7.7% less than 15 minutes, 71.2% 15 to 30 minutes, 21.2% 30 to 45 minutes, 0.0% 45 to 60 minutes, 0.0% 60 minutes or more (2000)

MCBAINE (town). Covers a land area of 0.232 square miles and a water area of 0.003 square miles. Located at 38.88° N. Lat.; 92.44° W. Long. Elevation is 571 feet.
Population: 17 (2000); Race: 100.0% White, 0.0% Black, 0.0% Asian, 0.0% American Indian and Alaska Native, 0.0% Hispanic of any race, 0.0% two or more races (2000); Density: 73.2 persons per square mile (2000); Age: 29.4% under 18, 0.0% over 64 (2000); Marriage status: 50.0% never married, 8.3% now married, 0.0% widowed, 41.7% divorced (2000); Foreign born: 0.0% (2000); Ancestry (includes multiple ancestries): 64.7% Other groups, 35.3% German, 11.8% Irish (2000).
Economy: Employment by occupation: 0.0% management, 50.0% professional, 50.0% services, 0.0% sales, 0.0% farming, 0.0% construction, 0.0% production (2000).
Income: Per capita income: $10,112 (2000); Median household income: $21,875 (2000); Poverty rate: 35.3% (2000).
Education: High school graduation rate: 70.0% (2000); College graduation rate: 0.0% (2000).
Housing: Homeownership rate: 55.6% (2000); Median rent: $225 per month (2000); Median age of housing: 24 years (2000).
Transportation: Commute to work: 100.0% car, 0.0% public transportation, 0.0% walk, 0.0% work from home (2000); Travel time to work: 50.0% less than 15 minutes, 25.0% 15 to 30 minutes, 0.0% 30 to 45 minutes, 25.0% 45 to 60 minutes, 0.0% 60 minutes or more (2000)

ROCHEPORT (city). Covers a land area of 0.268 square miles and a water area of 0 square miles. Located at 38.97° N. Lat.; 92.56° W. Long. Elevation is 597 feet.
History: A ferry was established near Rocheport in 1819 by John Gray, and a town was platted in 1825. Rocheport suffered from a recurring cholera epidemic in the 1850's, and from repeated plundering during the Civil War.
Population: 208 (2000); Race: 92.2% White, 5.9% Black, 0.0% Asian, 0.0% American Indian and Alaska Native, 0.0% Hispanic of any race, 2.0% two or more races (2000); Density: 774.7 persons per square mile (2000); Age: 15.7% under 18, 27.9% over 64 (2000); Marriage status: 23.9% never married, 57.8% now married, 8.9% widowed, 9.4% divorced (2000); Foreign born: 0.0% (2000); Ancestry (includes multiple ancestries): 19.1% Other groups, 18.6% German, 16.2% United States or American, 13.2% Irish, 6.4% English (2000).
Economy: Employment by occupation: 9.2% management, 22.0% professional, 10.1% services, 19.3% sales, 1.8% farming, 12.8% construction, 24.8% production (2000).
Income: Per capita income: $21,483 (2000); Median household income: $32,188 (2000); Poverty rate: 4.9% (2000).
Taxes: Total city taxes per capita: $42 (1997); City property taxes per capita: $10 (1997).
Education: High school graduation rate: 74.6% (2000); College graduation rate: 25.4% (2000).
Housing: Homeownership rate: 75.0% (2000); Median home value: $63,600 (2000); Median rent: $308 per month (2000); Median age of housing: 47 years (2000).
Transportation: Commute to work: 86.5% car, 0.0% public transportation, 0.0% walk, 13.5% work from home (2000); Travel time to work: 23.3% less

than 15 minutes, 57.8% 15 to 30 minutes, 6.7% 30 to 45 minutes, 0.0% 45 to 60 minutes, 12.2% 60 minutes or more (2000)

STURGEON (city). Covers a land area of 0.631 square miles and a water area of 0 square miles. Located at 39.23° N. Lat.; 92.28° W. Long. Elevation is 851 feet.
History: Amish community to North.
Population: 944 (2000); Race: 97.2% White, 0.0% Black, 0.0% Asian, 1.2% American Indian and Alaska Native, 1.7% Hispanic of any race, 0.6% two or more races (2000); Density: 1,494.9 persons per square mile (2000); Age: 23.9% under 18, 16.1% over 64 (2000); Marriage status: 17.7% never married, 58.4% now married, 9.9% widowed, 14.1% divorced (2000); Foreign born: 0.0% (2000); Ancestry (includes multiple ancestries): 17.4% German, 17.2% United States or American, 12.6% Irish, 9.1% English, 5.8% Other groups (2000).
Economy: Corn, soybeans; cattle. Employment by occupation: 7.5% management, 11.9% professional, 16.9% services, 31.7% sales, 0.0% farming, 10.7% construction, 21.2% production (2000).
Income: Per capita income: $15,830 (2000); Median household income: $33,173 (2000); Poverty rate: 8.6% (2000).
Taxes: Total city taxes per capita: $121 (1997); City property taxes per capita: $18 (1997).
Education: High school graduation rate: 73.4% (2000); College graduation rate: 9.6% (2000).

School District(s)

Sturgeon R-V (KG-12)
2000 Enrollment: 504 573-687-3515

Housing: Homeownership rate: 72.9% (2000); Median home value: $59,700 (2000); Median rent: $267 per month (2000); Median age of housing: 34 years (2000).
Transportation: Commute to work: 96.5% car, 0.0% public transportation, 0.5% walk, 3.0% work from home (2000); Travel time to work: 16.5% less than 15 minutes, 28.0% 15 to 30 minutes, 43.1% 30 to 45 minutes, 6.9% 45 to 60 minutes, 5.5% 60 minutes or more (2000)

Buchanan County

Located in northwestern Missouri; bounded on the west by the Missouri River. Covers a land area of 409.70 square miles, a water area of 4.80 square miles, and is located in the Central Time Zone. The county government was organized in 1838. County seat is St. Joseph.

Buchanan County is part of the St. Joseph, MO MSA. The entire metro area includes: Andrew County; Buchanan County

Population: 85,998 (2000); Race: 92.7% White, 4.2% Black, 0.3% Asian, 0.5% American Indian and Alaska Native, 2.5% Hispanic of any race, 1.5% two or more races (2000); Density: 209.9 persons per square mile (2000); Age: 24.3% under 18, 15.0% over 64 (2000).
Religion: Five largest groups: 16.7% Southern Baptist Convention, 12.6% Catholic Church, 6.4% The United Methodist Church, 3.9% Independent, Charismatic Churches, 3.0% Christian Churches and Churches of Christ (2000).
Economy: Unemployment rate: 5.6% (11/2002); Total civilian labor force: 41,985 (11/2002); Leading industries: 18.3% manufacturing; 16.6% health care and social assistance; 12.4% retail trade (2000); Companies that employ more than 1,000 persons: 1 (2000); Companies that employ more than 100 persons: 57 (2000); Farms: 776 totaling 181,502 acres (1997); Minority business ownership rate: 2.2% (1997); Women business ownership rate: 31.7% (1997); Retail sales per capita: $9,756 (1997). Single-family building permits issued: 161 (2001) / 207 (2000); Multi-family building permits issued: 50 (2001) / 40 (2000).
Income: Per capita income: $17,882 (2000); Median household income: $34,704 (2000); Poverty rate: 12.2% (2000); Bankruptcy rate: 5.08% (2001).
Taxes: Total county taxes per capita: $157 (2000); County property taxes per capita: $28 (2000).
Education: High school graduation rate: 81.5% (2000); College graduation rate: 16.9% (2000).
Housing: Homeownership rate: 67.5% (2000); Median home value: $72,700 (2000); Median rent: $347 per month (2000); Median age of housing: 44 years (2000).
Health: Birth rate: 136.3 per 10,000 population (1998); Age adjusted death rate: 95.4 per 10,000 population (1999); Age adjusted cancer mortality rate: 212.7 deaths per 100,000 population (1999). Air Quality Index: 91% good, 9% moderate, 0% unhealthy (percent of days in 2000). Number of physicians: 6.0 per 10,000 population (1999); Number of hospital beds: n/a (1999).
Elections: 2000 Presidential election results: 49.2% Gore, 47.3% Bush, 2.2% Nader, 0.8% Buchanan
National and State Parks: Bluffwoods State Forest; Lewis and Clark State Park; Pigeon Hill State Wildlife Area
Additional Information Contacts
Buchanan County Government Offices 816-271-1503
St. Joseph Area Chamber of Commerce 816-232-4461
St. Joseph Convention & Visitors Bureau 816-233-6688
St. Joseph Downtown Partnership 816-233-9192
St. Joseph Regional Association of Realtors 816-233-9009

Buchanan County Communities

AGENCY (village). Covers a land area of 1.937 square miles and a water area of 0 square miles. Located at 39.64° N. Lat.; 94.74° W. Long. Elevation is 835 feet.
History: Once known as Agency Ford, a ferry was established here in 1839 by Robert Gilmore. The town was platted in 1863. The Ratcliffe Manufacturing Plant, producer of wooden stirrups, was opened in the late 1870's.
Population: 599 (2000); Race: 97.0% White, 0.0% Black, 2.2% Asian, 0.0% American Indian and Alaska Native, 0.5% Hispanic of any race, 0.8% two or more races (2000); Density: 309.3 persons per square mile (2000); Age: 28.8% under 18, 5.6% over 64 (2000); Marriage status: 20.1% never married, 62.8% now married, 6.3% widowed, 10.7% divorced (2000); Foreign born: 1.3% (2000); Ancestry (includes multiple ancestries): 26.1% German, 15.9% United States or American, 14.7% Other groups, 10.3% Irish, 7.3% English (2000).
Economy: Single-family building permits issued: 2 (2001) / 0 (2000); Multi-family building permits issued: 0 (2001) / 0 (2000); Employment by occupation: 11.8% management, 14.6% professional, 20.2% services, 24.4% sales, 0.0% farming, 10.4% construction, 18.5% production (2000).
Income: Per capita income: $20,304 (2000); Median household income: $49,375 (2000); Poverty rate: 6.1% (2000).
Taxes: Total city taxes per capita: $47 (1997); City property taxes per capita: $26 (1997).
Education: High school graduation rate: 86.7% (2000); College graduation rate: 15.1% (2000).
Housing: Homeownership rate: 82.2% (2000); Median home value: $96,500 (2000); Median rent: $391 per month (2000); Median age of housing: 20 years (2000).
Transportation: Commute to work: 96.3% car, 0.0% public transportation, 0.0% walk, 2.3% work from home (2000); Travel time to work: 21.1% less than 15 minutes, 60.1% 15 to 30 minutes, 5.8% 30 to 45 minutes, 10.1% 45 to 60 minutes, 2.9% 60 minutes or more (2000)

DE KALB (town). Covers a land area of 0.253 square miles and a water area of 0 square miles. Located at 39.58° N. Lat.; 94.92° W. Long. Elevation is 1,138 feet.
Population: 257 (2000); Race: 98.3% White, 0.0% Black, 0.0% Asian, 0.9% American Indian and Alaska Native, 0.9% Hispanic of any race, 0.9% two or more races (2000); Density: 1,017.0 persons per square mile (2000); Age: 16.2% under 18, 16.7% over 64 (2000); Marriage status: 20.1% never married, 60.3% now married, 9.8% widowed, 9.8% divorced (2000); Foreign born: 0.9% (2000); Ancestry (includes multiple ancestries): 15.4% German, 12.8% United States or American, 9.0% Irish, 9.0% English, 3.4% Other groups (2000).
Economy: Tobacco, corn, cattle. Employment by occupation: 9.2% management, 20.2% professional, 17.4% services, 17.4% sales, 0.0% farming, 12.8% construction, 22.9% production (2000).
Income: Per capita income: $18,880 (2000); Median household income: $38,750 (2000); Poverty rate: 3.0% (2000).
Taxes: Total city taxes per capita: $52 (1997); City property taxes per capita: $26 (1997).
Education: High school graduation rate: 79.4% (2000); College graduation rate: 9.7% (2000).

School District(s)

Buchanan Co. R-IV (KG-12)
2000 Enrollment: 397 816-685-3160

Housing: Homeownership rate: 83.8% (2000); Median home value: $59,000 (2000); Median rent: $300 per month (2000); Median age of housing: 57 years (2000).

Transportation: Commute to work: 95.4% car, 0.0% public transportation, 2.8% walk, 0.0% work from home (2000); Travel time to work: 13.8% less than 15 minutes, 27.5% 15 to 30 minutes, 45.0% 30 to 45 minutes, 6.4% 45 to 60 minutes, 7.3% 60 minutes or more (2000)

EASTON (city). Covers a land area of 0.605 square miles and a water area of 0 square miles. Located at 39.72° N. Lat.; 94.64° W. Long. Elevation is 925 feet.

Population: 258 (2000); Race: 97.6% White, 0.0% Black, 0.0% Asian, 0.0% American Indian and Alaska Native, 2.8% Hispanic of any race, 0.8% two or more races (2000); Density: 426.3 persons per square mile (2000); Age: 29.3% under 18, 8.4% over 64 (2000); Marriage status: 24.9% never married, 56.1% now married, 9.5% widowed, 9.5% divorced (2000); Foreign born: 0.0% (2000); Ancestry (includes multiple ancestries): 27.7% German, 18.1% Irish, 13.7% English, 7.6% United States or American, 7.6% Other groups (2000).

Economy: Single-family building permits issued: 0 (2001) / 2 (2000); Multi-family building permits issued: 0 (2001) / 0 (2000); Employment by occupation: 6.9% management, 6.0% professional, 16.4% services, 31.9% sales, 0.0% farming, 19.8% construction, 19.0% production (2000).

Income: Per capita income: $14,865 (2000); Median household income: $31,750 (2000); Poverty rate: 4.8% (2000).

Taxes: Total city taxes per capita: $36 (1997); City property taxes per capita: $13 (1997).

Education: High school graduation rate: 80.7% (2000); College graduation rate: 7.5% (2000).

Housing: Homeownership rate: 81.0% (2000); Median home value: $56,000 (2000); Median rent: $177 per month (2000); Median age of housing: 36 years (2000).

Transportation: Commute to work: 94.0% car, 0.0% public transportation, 3.4% walk, 2.6% work from home (2000); Travel time to work: 20.4% less than 15 minutes, 48.7% 15 to 30 minutes, 20.4% 30 to 45 minutes, 6.2% 45 to 60 minutes, 4.4% 60 minutes or more (2000)

FAUCETT (unincorporated postal area, zip code 64448). Covers a land area of 37.930 square miles and a water area of 0 square miles. Located at 39.60° N. Lat.; 94.81° W. Long. Elevation is 968 feet.

History: Faucett developed in the mid-1800's as the center of a tobacco industry.

Population: 1,133 (2000); Race: 96.8% White, 0.0% Black, 0.0% Asian, 0.0% American Indian and Alaska Native, 2.4% Hispanic of any race, 2.1% two or more races (2000); Density: 29.9 persons per square mile (2000); Age: 29.1% under 18, 10.6% over 64 (2000); Marriage status: 22.6% never married, 61.9% now married, 4.2% widowed, 11.3% divorced (2000); Foreign born: 0.3% (2000); Ancestry (includes multiple ancestries): 18.1% German, 14.2% United States or American, 9.2% Irish, 6.8% Other groups, 6.6% English (2000).

Economy: Employment by occupation: 12.7% management, 12.9% professional, 10.3% services, 23.8% sales, 1.3% farming, 19.2% construction, 19.8% production (2000).

Income: Per capita income: $17,593 (2000); Median household income: $44,643 (2000); Poverty rate: 7.4% (2000).

Education: High school graduation rate: 86.7% (2000); College graduation rate: 12.7% (2000).

School District(s)

Mid-Buchanan Co. R-V (KG-12)
2000 Enrollment: 750 816-238-1646

Housing: Homeownership rate: 83.3% (2000); Median home value: $89,200 (2000); Median rent: $335 per month (2000); Median age of housing: 28 years (2000).

Transportation: Commute to work: 96.2% car, 0.0% public transportation, 0.3% walk, 3.5% work from home (2000); Travel time to work: 12.3% less than 15 minutes, 50.5% 15 to 30 minutes, 21.1% 30 to 45 minutes, 8.6% 45 to 60 minutes, 7.5% 60 minutes or more (2000)

LEWIS AND CLARK VILLAGE (town). Covers a land area of 0.601 square miles and a water area of 0.102 square miles. Located at 39.54° N. Lat.; 95.04° W. Long. Elevation is 782 feet.

Population: 155 (2000); Race: 98.8% White, 0.0% Black, 0.0% Asian, 0.0% American Indian and Alaska Native, 0.0% Hispanic of any race, 1.2% two or more races (2000); Density: 257.9 persons per square mile (2000); Age: 20.2% under 18, 13.5% over 64 (2000); Marriage status: 21.2% never married, 62.8% now married, 5.8% widowed, 10.2% divorced (2000); Foreign born: 1.8% (2000); Ancestry (includes multiple ancestries): 31.9% German, 14.1% United States or American, 8.6% Dutch, 7.4% Irish, 6.7% Other groups (2000).

Economy: Single-family building permits issued: 0 (2001) / 0 (2000); Multi-family building permits issued: 0 (2001) / 0 (2000); Employment by occupation: 4.5% management, 14.8% professional, 12.5% services, 12.5% sales, 0.0% farming, 12.5% construction, 43.2% production (2000).

Income: Per capita income: $19,050 (2000); Median household income: $42,000 (2000); Poverty rate: 10.6% (2000).

Taxes: Total city taxes per capita: $81 (1997); City property taxes per capita: $52 (1997).

Education: High school graduation rate: 86.5% (2000); College graduation rate: 9.0% (2000).

Housing: Homeownership rate: 83.3% (2000); Median home value: $97,500 (2000); Median rent: $342 per month (2000); Median age of housing: 34 years (2000).

Transportation: Commute to work: 96.6% car, 0.0% public transportation, 0.0% walk, 0.0% work from home (2000); Travel time to work: 23.9% less than 15 minutes, 37.5% 15 to 30 minutes, 25.0% 30 to 45 minutes, 4.5% 45 to 60 minutes, 9.1% 60 minutes or more (2000)

RUSHVILLE (town). Covers a land area of 0.226 square miles and a water area of 0 square miles. Located at 39.58° N. Lat.; 95.02° W. Long. Elevation is 812 feet.

Population: 280 (2000); Race: 99.7% White, 0.0% Black, 0.0% Asian, 0.0% American Indian and Alaska Native, 0.7% Hispanic of any race, 0.3% two or more races (2000); Density: 1,236.4 persons per square mile (2000); Age: 30.7% under 18, 14.9% over 64 (2000); Marriage status: 18.4% never married, 61.8% now married, 10.1% widowed, 9.7% divorced (2000); Foreign born: 0.0% (2000); Ancestry (includes multiple ancestries): 19.5% United States or American, 17.2% Irish, 13.5% German, 6.6% English, 6.3% Other groups (2000).

Economy: Corn, soybeans, oats; livestock. Single-family building permits issued: 0 (2001) / 0 (2000); Multi-family building permits issued: 0 (2001) / 0 (2000); Employment by occupation: 12.8% management, 9.6% professional, 16.0% services, 18.4% sales, 1.6% farming, 11.2% construction, 30.4% production (2000).

Income: Per capita income: $15,147 (2000); Median household income: $31,875 (2000); Poverty rate: 11.2% (2000).

Taxes: Total city taxes per capita: $44 (1997); City property taxes per capita: $27 (1997).

Education: High school graduation rate: 71.4% (2000); College graduation rate: 1.7% (2000).

Housing: Homeownership rate: 76.5% (2000); Median home value: $50,000 (2000); Median rent: $286 per month (2000); Median age of housing: 49 years (2000).

Transportation: Commute to work: 94.4% car, 0.0% public transportation, 1.6% walk, 2.4% work from home (2000); Travel time to work: 18.0% less than 15 minutes, 42.6% 15 to 30 minutes, 18.9% 30 to 45 minutes, 12.3% 45 to 60 minutes, 8.2% 60 minutes or more (2000)

SAINT JOSEPH (city). Covers a land area of 43.842 square miles and a water area of 0.658 square miles. Located at 39.75° N. Lat.; 94.83° W. Long. Elevation is 885 feet.

History: Joseph Robidoux first visited the site of St. Joseph while on a trading expedition up the Missouri River in 1799. He established Robidoux's Post here in 1827 for the American Fur Company. Settlers flooded in when the 1836 Platte Purchase by the Federal government opened the area for settlement. Hemp cultivation was an important crop. In 1843 Robidoux platted the town and named it St. Joseph, after his patron saint. Later in the 1840's, streams of immigrants passed through St. Joseph on their way to the riches of the west, including James W. Marshall who discovered gold at Sutter's Mill in California.

Population: 73,990 (2000); Race: 91.8% White, 4.9% Black, 0.3% Asian, 0.6% American Indian and Alaska Native, 2.6% Hispanic of any race, 1.6% two or more races (2000); Density: 1,687.7 persons per square mile (2000); Age: 24.0% under 18, 15.4% over 64 (2000); Marriage status: 26.0% never married, 52.9% now married, 8.1% widowed, 13.0% divorced (2000); Foreign born: 1.0% (2000); Ancestry (includes multiple ancestries): 20.5% German, 13.4% Irish, 13.4% Other groups, 10.6% United States or American, 10.0% English (2000).

Vital Statistics: Birth rate: 145.8 per 10,000 population (1998)

Economy: Unemployment rate: 5.9% (11/2002); Total civilian labor force: 35,723 (11/2002); Single-family building permits issued: 104 (2001) / 146 (2000); Multi-family building permits issued: 50 (2001) / 40 (2000); Employment by occupation: 10.1% management, 17.0% professional, 18.1% services, 27.5% sales, 0.2% farming, 9.4% construction, 17.7% production (2000).

Income: Per capita income: $17,445 (2000); Median household income: $32,663 (2000); Poverty rate: 13.0% (2000).
Education: High school graduation rate: 80.9% (2000); College graduation rate: 17.1% (2000).

School District(s)

Saint Joseph (PK-12)
2000 Enrollment: 12,045 816-671-4000

Four-year College(s)

Missouri Western State College (Public)
2001 Enrollment: 5,102 816-271-4200
2001 Tuition: In-state $2,928; Out-of-state $5,394

Two-year College(s)

Hillyard Technical Center (Public)
2001 Enrollment: 110 816-671-4170
Vatterott College (Private, For-profit)
2001 Enrollment: 398 816-364-5399
2001 Tuition: In-state $6,570; Out-of-state $6,570

Housing: Homeownership rate: 64.8% (2000); Median home value: $69,600 (2000); Median rent: $348 per month (2000); Median age of housing: 46 years (2000).
Hospitals: Heartland Health (690 beds); Northwest Missouri Psychiatric Rehabilitation Center
Safety: Violent crime rate: 23.4 per 10,000 population; Property crime rate: 563.2 per 10,000 population (2001).
Newspapers: Saint Joseph Daily Courier (5 x week); Buchanan County News (1 x week); The Saint Joseph Telegraph (1 x week); St. Joseph News-Press (7 x week)
Transportation: Commute to work: 94.3% car, 0.9% public transportation, 2.0% walk, 2.0% work from home (2000); Travel time to work: 54.1% less than 15 minutes, 30.9% 15 to 30 minutes, 5.8% 30 to 45 minutes, 4.3% 45 to 60 minutes, 4.9% 60 minutes or more (2000); Amtrak: Service available.
Airports: Rosecrans Memorial
Additional Information Contacts
St. Joseph Area Chamber of Commerce 816-232-4461
St. Joseph Convention & Visitors Bureau 816-233-6688
St. Joseph Downtown Partnership 816-233-9192
St. Joseph Regional Association of Realtors 816-233-9009

Butler County

Located in southeastern Missouri, in the Ozark region; bounded on the east by the St. Francis River, and on the south by Arkansas; includes part of Clark National Forest. Covers a land area of 697.50 square miles, a water area of 1.40 square miles, and is located in the Central Time Zone. The county government was organized in 1849. County seat is Poplar Bluff.

Weather Station: Wappapello Dam Elevation: 410 feet

	Jan	Feb	Mar	Apr	May	Jun	Jul	Aug	Sep	Oct	Nov	Dec
High	41	48	58	70	78	86	91	89	82	71	58	47
Low	22	27	36	47	56	65	69	67	59	47	37	28
Precip	3.5	3.3	4.8	4.8	4.5	3.9	3.8	3.3	3.6	3.6	5.0	4.0
Snow	2.6	1.8	0.9	0.0	0.0	0.0	0.0	0.0	0.0	0.0	0.3	0.7

High and Low temperatures in degrees Fahrenheit; Precipitation and Snow in inches

Population: 40,867 (2000); Race: 92.1% White, 5.2% Black, 0.6% Asian, 0.5% American Indian and Alaska Native, 0.9% Hispanic of any race, 1.1% two or more races (2000); Density: 58.6 persons per square mile (2000); Age: 24.1% under 18, 16.7% over 64 (2000).
Religion: Five largest groups: 15.8% Southern Baptist Convention, 3.4% Catholic Church, 2.8% The United Methodist Church, 1.7% Christian Church (Disciples of Christ), 1.6% Churches of Christ (2000).
Economy: Unemployment rate: 5.3% (11/2002); Total civilian labor force: 18,754 (11/2002); Leading industries: 23.6% manufacturing; 21.5% health care and social assistance; 16.4% retail trade (2000); Companies that employ more than 1,000 persons: 2 (2000); Companies that employ more than 100 persons: 20 (2000); Farms: 678 totaling 255,067 acres (1997); Minority business ownership rate: 0.0% (1997); Women business ownership rate: 19.9% (1997); Retail sales per capita: $10,544 (1997). Single-family building permits issued: 27 (2001) / 22 (2000); Multi-family building permits issued: 6 (2001) / 0 (2000).
Income: Per capita income: $15,721 (2000); Median household income: $27,228 (2000); Poverty rate: 18.6% (2000); Bankruptcy rate: 4.44% (2001).
Taxes: Total county taxes per capita: $114 (2000); County property taxes per capita: $11 (2000).
Education: High school graduation rate: 70.5% (2000); College graduation rate: 11.6% (2000).
Housing: Homeownership rate: 68.9% (2000); Median home value: $59,400 (2000); Median rent: $273 per month (2000); Median age of housing: 28 years (2000).
Health: Birth rate: 134.1 per 10,000 population (1998); Age adjusted death rate: 111.5 per 10,000 population (1999); Age adjusted cancer mortality rate: 236.3 deaths per 100,000 population (1999). Number of physicians: 22.3 per 10,000 population (1999); Number of hospital beds: 90.8 per 10,000 population (1999).
Elections: 2000 Presidential election results: 34.7% Gore, 63.3% Bush, 1.0% Nader, 0.5% Buchanan
National and State Parks: Poplar Bluff State Forest; State Public Hunting Area
Additional Information Contacts
Butler County Government Offices 573-686-8050
Poplar Bluff Chamber of Commerce 573-785-7761
Three Rivers Board of Realtors 573-686-0575

Butler County Communities

BROSELEY (unincorporated postal area, zip code 63932). Covers a land area of 53.312 square miles and a water area of 0.039 square miles. Located at 36.68° N. Lat.; 90.23° W. Long. Elevation is 320 feet.
Population: 1,362 (2000); Race: 88.6% White, 10.0% Black, 0.0% Asian, 0.0% American Indian and Alaska Native, 0.8% Hispanic of any race, 1.4% two or more races (2000); Density: 25.5 persons per square mile (2000); Age: 24.6% under 18, 13.7% over 64 (2000); Marriage status: 25.8% never married, 57.9% now married, 6.2% widowed, 10.1% divorced (2000); Foreign born: 0.0% (2000); Ancestry (includes multiple ancestries): 25.1% United States or American, 21.1% Other groups, 16.0% Irish, 11.8% German, 5.4% Dutch (2000).
Economy: Employment by occupation: 11.1% management, 11.7% professional, 18.7% services, 16.7% sales, 4.6% farming, 12.7% construction, 24.6% production (2000).
Income: Per capita income: $15,008 (2000); Median household income: $29,539 (2000); Poverty rate: 18.3% (2000).
Education: High school graduation rate: 62.9% (2000); College graduation rate: 7.6% (2000).

School District(s)

Twin Rivers R-X (KG-12)
2000 Enrollment: 1,085 573-328-4321

Housing: Homeownership rate: 84.5% (2000); Median home value: $47,600 (2000); Median rent: $208 per month (2000); Median age of housing: 28 years (2000).
Transportation: Commute to work: 92.0% car, 0.0% public transportation, 0.0% walk, 5.6% work from home (2000); Travel time to work: 16.1% less than 15 minutes, 44.1% 15 to 30 minutes, 29.3% 30 to 45 minutes, 4.7% 45 to 60 minutes, 5.9% 60 minutes or more (2000)

FISK (city). Covers a land area of 0.330 square miles and a water area of 0 square miles. Located at 36.78° N. Lat.; 90.20° W. Long. Elevation is 328 feet.
History: Fisk developed as an important rice shipping point. The Roy Utley Rice Farm was a principal producer.
Population: 363 (2000); Race: 98.9% White, 0.0% Black, 0.0% Asian, 1.1% American Indian and Alaska Native, 1.4% Hispanic of any race, 0.0% two or more races (2000); Density: 1,099.8 persons per square mile (2000); Age: 25.0% under 18, 19.0% over 64 (2000); Marriage status: 14.5% never married, 52.3% now married, 13.8% widowed, 19.4% divorced (2000); Foreign born: 0.0% (2000); Ancestry (includes multiple ancestries): 45.9% United States or American, 9.0% German, 6.5% English, 5.7% Other groups, 3.3% Italian (2000).
Economy: Employment by occupation: 7.2% management, 9.6% professional, 20.0% services, 15.2% sales, 0.0% farming, 5.6% construction, 42.4% production (2000).
Income: Per capita income: $11,577 (2000); Median household income: $19,886 (2000); Poverty rate: 30.7% (2000).
Taxes: Total city taxes per capita: $208 (1997); City property taxes per capita: $80 (1997).
Education: High school graduation rate: 58.3% (2000); College graduation rate: 7.4% (2000).
Housing: Homeownership rate: 58.5% (2000); Median home value: $35,500 (2000); Median rent: $197 per month (2000); Median age of housing: 37 years (2000).
Transportation: Commute to work: 92.7% car, 0.0% public transportation, 0.0% walk, 0.0% work from home (2000); Travel time to work: 24.4% less

than 15 minutes, 55.3% 15 to 30 minutes, 13.8% 30 to 45 minutes, 1.6% 45 to 60 minutes, 4.9% 60 minutes or more (2000)

HARVIELL (unincorporated postal area, zip code 63945). Covers a land area of 38.740 square miles and a water area of 0.025 square miles. Located at 36.63° N. Lat.; 90.52° W. Long. Elevation is 318 feet.
Population: 1,171 (2000); Race: 97.8% White, 0.0% Black, 0.0% Asian, 2.2% American Indian and Alaska Native, 0.4% Hispanic of any race, 0.0% two or more races (2000); Density: 30.2 persons per square mile (2000); Age: 27.4% under 18, 8.3% over 64 (2000); Marriage status: 19.6% never married, 62.9% now married, 4.9% widowed, 12.6% divorced (2000); Foreign born: 0.0% (2000); Ancestry (includes multiple ancestries): 21.7% United States or American, 16.0% Other groups, 11.6% German, 7.5% Irish, 5.3% English (2000).
Economy: Employment by occupation: 10.6% management, 21.7% professional, 9.9% services, 18.6% sales, 0.0% farming, 8.7% construction, 30.5% production (2000).
Income: Per capita income: $12,708 (2000); Median household income: $28,462 (2000); Poverty rate: 14.4% (2000).
Education: High school graduation rate: 68.8% (2000); College graduation rate: 9.2% (2000).
Housing: Homeownership rate: 81.0% (2000); Median home value: $61,700 (2000); Median rent: $183 per month (2000); Median age of housing: 19 years (2000).
Transportation: Commute to work: 96.2% car, 1.4% public transportation, 0.0% walk, 0.0% work from home (2000); Travel time to work: 21.2% less than 15 minutes, 55.3% 15 to 30 minutes, 13.6% 30 to 45 minutes, 1.7% 45 to 60 minutes, 8.1% 60 minutes or more (2000)

NEELYVILLE (city). Covers a land area of 1.162 square miles and a water area of 0 square miles. Located at 36.55° N. Lat.; 90.51° W. Long. Elevation is 305 feet.
History: Neelyville was founded in the early 1870's as a timber shipping point on the Missouri Pacific Railroad. Near Neelyville, several hundred prehistoric earthen mounds have yielded well-preserved artifacts.
Population: 487 (2000); Race: 85.0% White, 13.6% Black, 0.0% Asian, 0.8% American Indian and Alaska Native, 2.3% Hispanic of any race, 0.2% two or more races (2000); Density: 419.3 persons per square mile (2000); Age: 32.6% under 18, 6.6% over 64 (2000); Marriage status: 21.8% never married, 54.7% now married, 8.9% widowed, 14.6% divorced (2000); Foreign born: 0.0% (2000); Ancestry (includes multiple ancestries): 34.5% United States or American, 19.9% Other groups, 10.7% German, 6.2% Irish, 2.7% English (2000).
Economy: Single-family building permits issued: 0 (2001) / 0 (2000); Multi-family building permits issued: 0 (2001) / 0 (2000); Employment by occupation: 5.0% management, 11.5% professional, 13.0% services, 16.0% sales, 2.0% farming, 9.0% construction, 43.5% production (2000).
Income: Per capita income: $10,598 (2000); Median household income: $21,719 (2000); Poverty rate: 25.7% (2000).
Taxes: Total city taxes per capita: $67 (1997); City property taxes per capita: $19 (1997).
Education: High school graduation rate: 61.2% (2000); College graduation rate: 3.6% (2000).

School District(s)

Neelyville R-IV (PK-12)
2000 Enrollment: 676 573-989-3813

Housing: Homeownership rate: 66.5% (2000); Median home value: $35,300 (2000); Median rent: $175 per month (2000); Median age of housing: 28 years (2000).
Transportation: Commute to work: 96.9% car, 0.0% public transportation, 1.0% walk, 1.0% work from home (2000); Travel time to work: 26.8% less than 15 minutes, 45.4% 15 to 30 minutes, 14.9% 30 to 45 minutes, 4.1% 45 to 60 minutes, 8.8% 60 minutes or more (2000)

POPLAR BLUFF (city). Covers a land area of 11.572 square miles and a water area of 0 square miles. Located at 36.76° N. Lat.; 90.40° W. Long. Elevation is 340 feet.
History: Poplar Bluff was founded in 1850 by a commission appointed to select a site for a county seat. The spot chosen was a grove of poplar trees on the bluffs along the Black River. Lumbering activity began in 1873 with the completion of the Iron Mountain Railroad.
Population: 16,651 (2000); Race: 87.3% White, 9.6% Black, 0.7% Asian, 0.4% American Indian and Alaska Native, 1.2% Hispanic of any race, 1.4% two or more races (2000); Density: 1,438.9 persons per square mile (2000); Age: 24.0% under 18, 19.5% over 64 (2000); Marriage status: 19.8% never married, 52.7% now married, 12.6% widowed, 14.9% divorced (2000); Foreign born: 1.7% (2000); Ancestry (includes multiple ancestries): 19.8% Other groups, 15.4% United States or American, 11.9% German, 10.7% Irish, 8.3% English (2000).
Vital Statistics: Birth rate: 167.0 per 10,000 population (1998)
Economy: Single-family building permits issued: 27 (2001) / 22 (2000); Multi-family building permits issued: 6 (2001) / 0 (2000); Employment by occupation: 9.1% management, 19.0% professional, 19.7% services, 24.4% sales, 0.5% farming, 6.4% construction, 20.9% production (2000).
Income: Per capita income: $13,996 (2000); Median household income: $22,068 (2000); Poverty rate: 24.4% (2000).
Taxes: Total city taxes per capita: $538 (2000); City property taxes per capita: $67 (2000).
Education: High school graduation rate: 67.9% (2000); College graduation rate: 12.2% (2000).

School District(s)

Poplar Bluff R-I (PK-12)
2000 Enrollment: 4,836 573-785-7751

Two-year College(s)

Three Rivers Community College (Public)
2001 Enrollment: 2,812 573-840-9600
2001 Tuition: In-state $2,664; Out-of-state $5,328

Housing: Homeownership rate: 54.8% (2000); Median home value: $50,200 (2000); Median rent: $270 per month (2000); Median age of housing: 36 years (2000).
Hospitals: John J. Pershing Veterans Affairs Medical Center (16 beds)
Safety: Violent crime rate: 29.2 per 10,000 population; Property crime rate: 471.5 per 10,000 population (2001).
Newspapers: Daily American Republic (6 x week)
Transportation: Commute to work: 92.4% car, 2.6% public transportation, 2.0% walk, 2.1% work from home (2000); Travel time to work: 66.6% less than 15 minutes, 24.2% 15 to 30 minutes, 4.7% 30 to 45 minutes, 1.5% 45 to 60 minutes, 3.0% 60 minutes or more (2000); Amtrak: Service available.
Airports: Poplar Bluff Municipal
Additional Information Contacts
Poplar Bluff Chamber of Commerce 573-785-7761
Three Rivers Board of Realtors 573-686-0575

QULIN (city). Covers a land area of 0.446 square miles and a water area of 0 square miles. Located at 36.59° N. Lat.; 90.24° W. Long. Elevation is 316 feet.
Population: 467 (2000); Race: 97.6% White, 0.0% Black, 0.0% Asian, 0.9% American Indian and Alaska Native, 0.2% Hispanic of any race, 1.5% two or more races (2000); Density: 1,047.2 persons per square mile (2000); Age: 25.5% under 18, 16.9% over 64 (2000); Marriage status: 22.2% never married, 48.9% now married, 13.2% widowed, 15.7% divorced (2000); Foreign born: 0.2% (2000); Ancestry (includes multiple ancestries): 34.9% United States or American, 11.8% Other groups, 10.5% German, 8.1% Irish, 3.4% Dutch (2000).
Economy: Manufacturing of concrete. Rice, wheat, corn. Single-family building permits issued: 0 (2001) / 0 (2000); Multi-family building permits issued: 0 (2001) / 0 (2000); Employment by occupation: 5.0% management, 4.4% professional, 21.9% services, 16.9% sales, 1.3% farming, 13.1% construction, 37.5% production (2000).
Income: Per capita income: $9,594 (2000); Median household income: $15,714 (2000); Poverty rate: 28.1% (2000).
Taxes: Total city taxes per capita: $126 (1997); City property taxes per capita: $17 (1997).
Education: High school graduation rate: 46.4% (2000); College graduation rate: 1.9% (2000).
Housing: Homeownership rate: 66.3% (2000); Median home value: $32,300 (2000); Median rent: $208 per month (2000); Median age of housing: 30 years (2000).
Transportation: Commute to work: 91.8% car, 0.0% public transportation, 5.0% walk, 1.9% work from home (2000); Travel time to work: 25.6% less than 15 minutes, 36.5% 15 to 30 minutes, 33.3% 30 to 45 minutes, 2.6% 45 to 60 minutes, 1.9% 60 minutes or more (2000)

Caldwell County

Located in northwestern Missouri; crossed by Shoal Creek. Covers a land area of 429.30 square miles, a water area of 0.40 square miles, and is located in the Central Time Zone. The county government was organized in 1836. County seat is Kingston.

Weather Station: Hamilton 2 W — Elevation: 898 feet

	Jan	Feb	Mar	Apr	May	Jun	Jul	Aug	Sep	Oct	Nov	Dec
High	34	40	52	64	73	83	88	86	78	67	51	39
Low	12	17	28	39	50	59	64	62	52	39	29	18
Precip	1.1	1.2	2.7	3.7	4.9	4.1	3.8	3.8	4.8	3.2	2.4	1.7
Snow	2.9	3.1	1.7	tr	0.0	0.0	0.0	0.0	0.0	tr	0.5	1.8

High and Low temperatures in degrees Fahrenheit; Precipitation and Snow in inches

Population: 8,969 (2000); Race: 98.1% White, 0.1% Black, 0.1% Asian, 0.2% American Indian and Alaska Native, 0.6% Hispanic of any race, 1.3% two or more races (2000); Density: 20.9 persons per square mile (2000); Age: 27.1% under 18, 16.9% over 64 (2000).
Religion: Five largest groups: 26.4% Southern Baptist Convention, 14.1% The United Methodist Church, 4.6% The Church of Jesus Christ of Latter-day Saints, 4.2% Christian Churches and Churches of Christ, 2.1% Community of Christ (2000).
Economy: Unemployment rate: 6.2% (11/2002); Total civilian labor force: 3,461 (11/2002); Leading industries: 20.0% health care and social assistance; 18.8% retail trade; 17.8% construction (2000); Companies that employ more than 1,000 persons: 0 (2000); Companies that employ more than 100 persons: 0 (2000); Farms: 845 totaling 227,016 acres (1997); Minority business ownership rate: 0.0% (1997); Women business ownership rate: 26.1% (1997); Retail sales per capita: $2,912 (1997). Single-family building permits issued: 0 (2001) / 2 (2000); Multi-family building permits issued: 0 (2001) / 0 (2000).
Income: Per capita income: $15,343 (2000); Median household income: $31,240 (2000); Poverty rate: 11.9% (2000); Bankruptcy rate: 3.68% (2001).
Taxes: Total county taxes per capita: $70 (2000); County property taxes per capita: $0 (2000).
Education: High school graduation rate: 81.5% (2000); College graduation rate: 11.7% (2000).
Housing: Homeownership rate: 77.4% (2000); Median home value: $53,800 (2000); Median rent: $252 per month (2000); Median age of housing: 31 years (2000).
Health: Birth rate: 113.7 per 10,000 population (1998); Age adjusted death rate: 105.5 per 10,000 population (1999); Age adjusted cancer mortality rate: 219.8 deaths per 100,000 population (1999). Number of physicians: 3.3 per 10,000 population (1999); Number of hospital beds: n/a (1999).
Elections: 2000 Presidential election results: 38.7% Gore, 57.7% Bush, 2.0% Nader, 0.9% Buchanan
National and State Parks: Bonanza State Wildlife Area
Additional Information Contacts
Caldwell County Government Offices 816-586-2571

Caldwell County Communities

BRAYMER (city). Covers a land area of 0.563 square miles and a water area of 0 square miles. Located at 39.58° N. Lat.; 93.79° W. Long. Elevation is 761 feet.
Population: 910 (2000); Race: 98.8% White, 0.0% Black, 0.2% Asian, 0.0% American Indian and Alaska Native, 0.0% Hispanic of any race, 1.0% two or more races (2000); Density: 1,617.1 persons per square mile (2000); Age: 27.9% under 18, 17.7% over 64 (2000); Marriage status: 18.0% never married, 56.2% now married, 13.2% widowed, 12.6% divorced (2000); Foreign born: 0.4% (2000); Ancestry (includes multiple ancestries): 14.7% German, 10.8% Irish, 10.4% United States or American, 9.8% Other groups, 7.8% English (2000).
Economy: Agriculture: feed mill; sheep, cattle, hogs. Employment by occupation: 7.6% management, 12.9% professional, 21.5% services, 20.5% sales, 1.8% farming, 15.0% construction, 20.7% production (2000).
Income: Per capita income: $14,518 (2000); Median household income: $26,667 (2000); Poverty rate: 12.4% (2000).
Taxes: Total city taxes per capita: $187 (2000); City property taxes per capita: $55 (2000).
Education: High school graduation rate: 80.6% (2000); College graduation rate: 8.9% (2000).

School District(s)

Braymer C-4 (PK-12)
2000 Enrollment: 427 660-645-2284
Housing: Homeownership rate: 71.8% (2000); Median home value: $44,200 (2000); Median rent: $253 per month (2000); Median age of housing: 52 years (2000).
Newspapers: Braymer Bee (1 x week)
Transportation: Commute to work: 91.2% car, 0.0% public transportation, 4.3% walk, 4.0% work from home (2000); Travel time to work: 25.0% less than 15 minutes, 10.3% 15 to 30 minutes, 18.1% 30 to 45 minutes, 17.2% 45 to 60 minutes, 29.4% 60 minutes or more (2000)

BRECKENRIDGE (city). Covers a land area of 0.552 square miles and a water area of 0 square miles. Located at 39.76° N. Lat.; 93.80° W. Long. Elevation is 927 feet.
History: Breckenridge was platted in 1858 and named for John C. Breckenridge, vice-president under James Buchanan and candidate for president against Abraham Lincoln in 1860. The town developed as a farm trading center.
Population: 454 (2000); Race: 96.7% White, 0.0% Black, 0.0% Asian, 1.6% American Indian and Alaska Native, 0.0% Hispanic of any race, 1.8% two or more races (2000); Density: 822.1 persons per square mile (2000); Age: 30.1% under 18, 15.0% over 64 (2000); Marriage status: 19.5% never married, 52.3% now married, 15.8% widowed, 12.5% divorced (2000); Foreign born: 0.0% (2000); Ancestry (includes multiple ancestries): 23.4% United States or American, 12.5% Irish, 10.0% Other groups, 9.8% English, 5.1% German (2000).
Economy: Employment by occupation: 14.0% management, 15.2% professional, 9.8% services, 20.1% sales, 7.3% farming, 11.0% construction, 22.6% production (2000).
Income: Per capita income: $12,468 (2000); Median household income: $23,625 (2000); Poverty rate: 23.2% (2000).
Taxes: Total city taxes per capita: $114 (1997); City property taxes per capita: $34 (1997).
Education: High school graduation rate: 68.8% (2000); College graduation rate: 6.6% (2000).

School District(s)

Breckenridge R-I (PK-12)
2000 Enrollment: 121 660-644-5715
Housing: Homeownership rate: 70.2% (2000); Median home value: $37,300 (2000); Median rent: $271 per month (2000); Median age of housing: 38 years (2000).
Transportation: Commute to work: 94.3% car, 0.0% public transportation, 3.8% walk, 1.9% work from home (2000); Travel time to work: 31.0% less than 15 minutes, 27.7% 15 to 30 minutes, 25.8% 30 to 45 minutes, 10.3% 45 to 60 minutes, 5.2% 60 minutes or more (2000)

COWGILL (city). Covers a land area of 0.233 square miles and a water area of 0 square miles. Located at 39.56° N. Lat.; 93.92° W. Long. Elevation is 965 feet.
Population: 247 (2000); Race: 97.2% White, 0.0% Black, 0.8% Asian, 0.0% American Indian and Alaska Native, 1.2% Hispanic of any race, 0.8% two or more races (2000); Density: 1,060.7 persons per square mile (2000); Age: 29.0% under 18, 18.7% over 64 (2000); Marriage status: 17.0% never married, 60.6% now married, 12.2% widowed, 10.1% divorced (2000); Foreign born: 0.8% (2000); Ancestry (includes multiple ancestries): 17.1% German, 14.7% Irish, 13.1% English, 11.1% Other groups, 10.7% United States or American (2000).
Economy: Employment by occupation: 7.5% management, 2.2% professional, 11.8% services, 24.7% sales, 0.0% farming, 19.4% construction, 34.4% production (2000).
Income: Per capita income: $11,356 (2000); Median household income: $21,563 (2000); Poverty rate: 21.9% (2000).
Taxes: Total city taxes per capita: $37 (1997); City property taxes per capita: $11 (1997).
Education: High school graduation rate: 71.3% (2000); College graduation rate: 1.9% (2000).

School District(s)

Cowgill R-VI (KG-08)
2000 Enrollment: 61 660-255-4415
Housing: Homeownership rate: 67.6% (2000); Median home value: $29,500 (2000); Median rent: $221 per month (2000); Median age of housing: 59 years (2000).
Transportation: Commute to work: 95.6% car, 0.0% public transportation, 0.0% walk, 4.4% work from home (2000); Travel time to work: 8.0% less than 15 minutes, 17.2% 15 to 30 minutes, 23.0% 30 to 45 minutes, 19.5% 45 to 60 minutes, 32.2% 60 minutes or more (2000)

HAMILTON (city). Covers a land area of 1.365 square miles and a water area of 0 square miles. Located at 39.74° N. Lat.; 93.99° W. Long. Elevation is 994 feet.
History: Hamilton was founded in 1855 and incorporated in 1868. It developed as a grain and livestock center.
Population: 1,813 (2000); Race: 98.0% White, 0.1% Black, 0.1% Asian, 0.0% American Indian and Alaska Native, 0.2% Hispanic of any race, 1.5%

two or more races (2000); Density: 1,327.9 persons per square mile (2000); Age: 27.1% under 18, 21.0% over 64 (2000); Marriage status: 17.2% never married, 59.0% now married, 10.8% widowed, 13.1% divorced (2000); Foreign born: 0.6% (2000); Ancestry (includes multiple ancestries): 18.8% German, 14.7% United States or American, 12.4% English, 12.0% Irish, 9.4% Other groups (2000).
Economy: Single-family building permits issued: 0 (2001) / 2 (2000); Multi-family building permits issued: 0 (2001) / 0 (2000); Employment by occupation: 6.3% management, 14.2% professional, 20.8% services, 20.2% sales, 1.1% farming, 16.9% construction, 20.4% production (2000).
Income: Per capita income: $14,484 (2000); Median household income: $25,972 (2000); Poverty rate: 16.1% (2000).
Taxes: Total city taxes per capita: $117 (1997); City property taxes per capita: $27 (1997).
Education: High school graduation rate: 82.5% (2000); College graduation rate: 15.4% (2000).

School District(s)

Hamilton R-II (PK-12)
2000 Enrollment: 718 816-583-2134
New York R-IV (KG-08)
2000 Enrollment: 48 816-583-2563

Housing: Homeownership rate: 64.3% (2000); Median home value: $57,600 (2000); Median rent: $265 per month (2000); Median age of housing: 40 years (2000).
Safety: Violent crime rate: 76.8 per 10,000 population; Property crime rate: 263.2 per 10,000 population (2001).
Newspapers: Hamilton Advocate (1 x week)
Transportation: Commute to work: 93.7% car, 0.4% public transportation, 2.0% walk, 3.6% work from home (2000); Travel time to work: 35.1% less than 15 minutes, 26.3% 15 to 30 minutes, 9.7% 30 to 45 minutes, 13.6% 45 to 60 minutes, 15.4% 60 minutes or more (2000)

KIDDER (city). Covers a land area of 0.408 square miles and a water area of 0 square miles. Located at 39.78° N. Lat.; 94.10° W. Long. Elevation is 1,009 feet.
Population: 271 (2000); Race: 99.3% White, 0.7% Black, 0.0% Asian, 0.0% American Indian and Alaska Native, 0.0% Hispanic of any race, 0.0% two or more races (2000); Density: 663.7 persons per square mile (2000); Age: 29.0% under 18, 14.0% over 64 (2000); Marriage status: 20.3% never married, 64.7% now married, 6.3% widowed, 8.7% divorced (2000); Foreign born: 0.7% (2000); Ancestry (includes multiple ancestries): 17.6% German, 17.6% United States or American, 16.9% Irish, 11.0% English, 8.5% Other groups (2000).
Economy: Livestock area: cattle, hogs. Employment by occupation: 7.8% management, 17.2% professional, 19.8% services, 26.7% sales, 1.7% farming, 21.6% construction, 5.2% production (2000).
Income: Per capita income: $13,424 (2000); Median household income: $26,771 (2000); Poverty rate: 22.1% (2000).
Taxes: Total city taxes per capita: $103 (1997); City property taxes per capita: $24 (1997).
Education: High school graduation rate: 85.5% (2000); College graduation rate: 9.9% (2000).
Housing: Homeownership rate: 77.7% (2000); Median home value: $48,100 (2000); Median rent: $219 per month (2000); Median age of housing: 46 years (2000).
Transportation: Commute to work: 91.2% car, 0.0% public transportation, 1.8% walk, 4.4% work from home (2000); Travel time to work: 14.7% less than 15 minutes, 36.7% 15 to 30 minutes, 9.2% 30 to 45 minutes, 8.3% 45 to 60 minutes, 31.2% 60 minutes or more (2000)

KINGSTON (city). Covers a land area of 0.581 square miles and a water area of 0 square miles. Located at 39.64° N. Lat.; 94.03° W. Long. Elevation is 912 feet.
History: Kingston was named for Judge Austin A. King, governor of Missouri from 1848 to 1852.
Population: 287 (2000); Race: 98.2% White, 1.1% Black, 0.0% Asian, 0.0% American Indian and Alaska Native, 0.0% Hispanic of any race, 0.7% two or more races (2000); Density: 493.9 persons per square mile (2000); Age: 25.1% under 18, 14.3% over 64 (2000); Marriage status: 16.1% never married, 56.7% now married, 12.4% widowed, 14.7% divorced (2000); Foreign born: 0.0% (2000); Ancestry (includes multiple ancestries): 26.5% United States or American, 18.6% German, 14.0% English, 13.3% Irish, 4.3% Dutch (2000).
Economy: Employment by occupation: 8.5% management, 6.4% professional, 26.2% services, 27.7% sales, 4.3% farming, 12.1% construction, 14.9% production (2000).
Income: Per capita income: $11,867 (2000); Median household income: $23,889 (2000); Poverty rate: 17.2% (2000).
Taxes: Total city taxes per capita: $69 (1997); City property taxes per capita: $21 (1997).
Education: High school graduation rate: 74.4% (2000); College graduation rate: 5.6% (2000).

School District(s)

Kingston 42 (PK-08)
2000 Enrollment: 51 816-586-3111

Housing: Homeownership rate: 75.8% (2000); Median home value: $36,000 (2000); Median rent: $220 per month (2000); Median age of housing: 46 years (2000).
Transportation: Commute to work: 98.6% car, 0.0% public transportation, 1.4% walk, 0.0% work from home (2000); Travel time to work: 34.0% less than 15 minutes, 19.1% 15 to 30 minutes, 22.7% 30 to 45 minutes, 11.3% 45 to 60 minutes, 12.8% 60 minutes or more (2000)

POLO (city). Covers a land area of 0.578 square miles and a water area of 0 square miles. Located at 39.55° N. Lat.; 94.03° W. Long. Elevation is 1,000 feet.
Population: 582 (2000); Race: 99.3% White, 0.0% Black, 0.0% Asian, 0.0% American Indian and Alaska Native, 1.8% Hispanic of any race, 0.3% two or more races (2000); Density: 1,006.4 persons per square mile (2000); Age: 25.0% under 18, 18.5% over 64 (2000); Marriage status: 17.7% never married, 56.2% now married, 14.9% widowed, 11.3% divorced (2000); Foreign born: 0.3% (2000); Ancestry (includes multiple ancestries): 15.9% German, 13.5% Irish, 11.5% United States or American, 8.8% English, 8.2% Other groups (2000).
Economy: Corn, wheat; cattle, hogs. Employment by occupation: 6.6% management, 10.3% professional, 16.1% services, 19.4% sales, 0.7% farming, 11.4% construction, 35.5% production (2000).
Income: Per capita income: $15,868 (2000); Median household income: $34,250 (2000); Poverty rate: 7.1% (2000).
Taxes: Total city taxes per capita: $48 (2000); City property taxes per capita: $15 (2000).
Education: High school graduation rate: 73.6% (2000); College graduation rate: 6.5% (2000).

School District(s)

Mirabile C-1 (KG-08)
2000 Enrollment: 39 816-586-4129
Polo R-VII (KG-12)
2000 Enrollment: 392 660-354-2326

Housing: Homeownership rate: 77.1% (2000); Median home value: $59,100 (2000); Median rent: $250 per month (2000); Median age of housing: 43 years (2000).
Transportation: Commute to work: 95.6% car, 0.0% public transportation, 2.6% walk, 0.7% work from home (2000); Travel time to work: 14.1% less than 15 minutes, 11.2% 15 to 30 minutes, 30.1% 30 to 45 minutes, 27.1% 45 to 60 minutes, 17.5% 60 minutes or more (2000)

Callaway County

Located in central Missouri; bounded on the south by the Missouri River. Covers a land area of 838.80 square miles, a water area of 8.20 square miles, and is located in the Central Time Zone. The county government was organized in 1820. County seat is Fulton.

Weather Station: Fulton — Elevation: 869 feet

	Jan	Feb	Mar	Apr	May	Jun	Jul	Aug	Sep	Oct	Nov	Dec
High	36	43	54	65	74	83	88	87	79	68	53	41
Low	18	22	32	42	52	61	66	64	56	44	33	23
Precip	1.8	2.1	3.1	4.1	5.1	3.9	4.0	3.5	3.9	3.2	3.8	2.7
Snow	6.9	5.9	3.3	0.6	0.0	0.0	0.0	0.0	0.0	tr	1.6	4.4

High and Low temperatures in degrees Fahrenheit; Precipitation and Snow in inches

Population: 40,766 (2000); Race: 91.8% White, 5.4% Black, 0.5% Asian, 0.5% American Indian and Alaska Native, 1.0% Hispanic of any race, 1.3% two or more races (2000); Density: 48.6 persons per square mile (2000); Age: 25.4% under 18, 10.9% over 64 (2000).
Religion: Five largest groups: 15.4% Southern Baptist Convention, 4.5% The United Methodist Church, 4.2% Catholic Church, 3.5% Christian Church (Disciples of Christ), 1.8% Presbyterian Church (U.S.A.) (2000).
Economy: Unemployment rate: 3.2% (11/2002); Total civilian labor force: 21,923 (11/2002); Leading industries: 19.7% health care and social assistance; 19.0% manufacturing; 12.5% retail trade (2000); Companies that employ more than 1,000 persons: 1 (2000); Companies that employ more

than 100 persons: 11 (2000); Farms: 1,338 totaling 330,471 acres (1997); Minority business ownership rate: 5.7% (1997); Women business ownership rate: 29.3% (1997); Retail sales per capita: $5,639 (1997). Single-family building permits issued: 33 (2001) / 38 (2000); Multi-family building permits issued: 54 (2001) / 86 (2000).
Income: Per capita income: $17,005 (2000); Median household income: $39,110 (2000); Poverty rate: 8.5% (2000); Bankruptcy rate: 5.44% (2001).
Taxes: Total county taxes per capita: $366 (2000); County property taxes per capita: $76 (2000).
Education: High school graduation rate: 78.9% (2000); College graduation rate: 16.5% (2000).
Housing: Homeownership rate: 76.8% (2000); Median home value: $85,800 (2000); Median rent: $312 per month (2000); Median age of housing: 22 years (2000).
Health: Birth rate: 111.6 per 10,000 population (1998); Age adjusted death rate: 92.3 per 10,000 population (1999); Age adjusted cancer mortality rate: 219.3 deaths per 100,000 population (1999). Number of physicians: 6.6 per 10,000 population (1999); Number of hospital beds: 131.5 per 10,000 population (1999).
Elections: 2000 Presidential election results: 43.8% Gore, 53.8% Bush, 1.4% Nader, 0.5% Buchanan
National and State Parks: Little Dixie State Wildlife Management Area; Whetstone Creek State Wildlife Area
Additional Information Contacts
Callaway County Government Offices 573-642-0780
Fulton Chamber of Commerce 573-642-3055

Callaway County Communities

AUXVASSE (city). Covers a land area of 0.664 square miles and a water area of 0 square miles. Located at 39.01° N. Lat.; 91.89° W. Long. Elevation is 870 feet.
History: Auxvasse was founded in 1871 by J.A. Harrison. An early agricultural trading center, Auxvasse produced mules and horses for sale.
Population: 901 (2000); Race: 95.0% White, 2.3% Black, 0.0% Asian, 0.6% American Indian and Alaska Native, 0.0% Hispanic of any race, 1.6% two or more races (2000); Density: 1,356.6 persons per square mile (2000); Age: 28.1% under 18, 16.1% over 64 (2000); Marriage status: 21.3% never married, 53.0% now married, 12.9% widowed, 12.8% divorced (2000); Foreign born: 0.0% (2000); Ancestry (includes multiple ancestries): 18.6% German, 13.8% English, 11.7% Other groups, 11.1% United States or American, 8.1% Irish (2000).
Economy: Employment by occupation: 5.7% management, 11.8% professional, 12.3% services, 30.9% sales, 0.7% farming, 18.0% construction, 20.7% production (2000).
Income: Per capita income: $15,785 (2000); Median household income: $33,875 (2000); Poverty rate: 11.4% (2000).
Taxes: Total city taxes per capita: $45 (1997); City property taxes per capita: $26 (1997).
Education: High school graduation rate: 76.5% (2000); College graduation rate: 9.6% (2000).
Housing: Homeownership rate: 69.9% (2000); Median home value: $54,400 (2000); Median rent: $274 per month (2000); Median age of housing: 36 years (2000).
Transportation: Commute to work: 93.4% car, 0.0% public transportation, 1.4% walk, 1.8% work from home (2000); Travel time to work: 27.7% less than 15 minutes, 42.4% 15 to 30 minutes, 21.2% 30 to 45 minutes, 4.7% 45 to 60 minutes, 4.0% 60 minutes or more (2000)

FULTON (city). Covers a land area of 11.310 square miles and a water area of 0.045 square miles. Located at 38.85° N. Lat.; 91.94° W. Long. Elevation is 770 feet.
History: Fulton was founded as the seat of Callaway County in 1825, and first named Volney for Count Constantin Volney, a French scientist. The name was soon changed to honor Robert Fulton, American marine engineer. The land on which the town was located was donated by Geroge Nichols, who settled here in 1824.
Population: 12,128 (2000); Race: 81.9% White, 14.8% Black, 1.0% Asian, 0.5% American Indian and Alaska Native, 1.1% Hispanic of any race, 1.3% two or more races (2000); Density: 1,072.3 persons per square mile (2000); Age: 18.0% under 18, 13.7% over 64 (2000); Marriage status: 34.1% never married, 43.0% now married, 8.6% widowed, 14.2% divorced (2000); Foreign born: 1.5% (2000); Ancestry (includes multiple ancestries): 22.3% German, 21.0% Other groups, 11.6% Irish, 9.8% English, 9.1% United States or American (2000).
Vital Statistics: Birth rate: 85.8 per 10,000 population (1998)
Economy: Single-family building permits issued: 20 (2001) / 30 (2000); Multi-family building permits issued: 28 (2001) / 68 (2000); Employment by occupation: 12.4% management, 22.1% professional, 21.6% services, 23.9% sales, 0.4% farming, 7.0% construction, 12.5% production (2000).
Income: Per capita income: $14,489 (2000); Median household income: $32,635 (2000); Poverty rate: 11.9% (2000).
Taxes: Total city taxes per capita: $211 (2000); City property taxes per capita: $26 (2000).
Education: High school graduation rate: 74.1% (2000); College graduation rate: 17.8% (2000).

School District(s)

Fulton 58 (PK-12)
2000 Enrollment: 2,450 573-642-2206

Four-year College(s)

Westminster College (Private, Not-for-profit, Presbyterian Church (USA))
2001 Enrollment: 750 573-642-3361
2001 Tuition: In-state $14,630; Out-of-state $14,630
William Woods University (Private, Not-for-profit, Christian Church (Disciples of Christ))
2001 Enrollment: 1,659 573-642-2251
2001 Tuition: In-state $13,500; Out-of-state $13,500
Housing: Homeownership rate: 56.9% (2000); Median home value: $74,500 (2000); Median rent: $292 per month (2000); Median age of housing: 35 years (2000).
Hospitals: Fulton State Hospital (508 beds)
Safety: Violent crime rate: 15.6 per 10,000 population; Property crime rate: 243.4 per 10,000 population (2001).
Newspapers: The Fulton Sun (5 x week)
Transportation: Commute to work: 90.8% car, 1.0% public transportation, 6.0% walk, 1.8% work from home (2000); Travel time to work: 60.9% less than 15 minutes, 18.5% 15 to 30 minutes, 13.8% 30 to 45 minutes, 2.9% 45 to 60 minutes, 3.9% 60 minutes or more (2000)
Airports: Elton Hensley Memorial
Additional Information Contacts
Fulton Chamber of Commerce 573-642-3055

HOLTS SUMMIT (city). Covers a land area of 3.311 square miles and a water area of 0.019 square miles. Located at 38.64° N. Lat.; 92.11° W. Long. Elevation is 845 feet.
Population: 2,935 (2000); Race: 94.4% White, 2.2% Black, 0.3% Asian, 0.9% American Indian and Alaska Native, 3.3% Hispanic of any race, 1.8% two or more races (2000); Density: 886.3 persons per square mile (2000); Age: 29.6% under 18, 8.9% over 64 (2000); Marriage status: 23.0% never married, 52.7% now married, 9.2% widowed, 15.2% divorced (2000); Foreign born: 1.8% (2000); Ancestry (includes multiple ancestries): 31.6% German, 15.0% United States or American, 11.8% Other groups, 11.4% Irish, 10.3% English (2000).
Economy: Manufacturing: utility trailers, light manufacturing. Single-family building permits issued: 12 (2001) / 5 (2000); Multi-family building permits issued: 20 (2001) / 14 (2000); Employment by occupation: 9.6% management, 16.8% professional, 18.1% services, 28.0% sales, 0.0% farming, 9.8% construction, 17.8% production (2000).
Income: Per capita income: $16,633 (2000); Median household income: $35,313 (2000); Poverty rate: 11.2% (2000).
Taxes: Total city taxes per capita: $171 (1997); City property taxes per capita: $0 (1997).
Education: High school graduation rate: 78.3% (2000); College graduation rate: 19.8% (2000).
Housing: Homeownership rate: 77.9% (2000); Median home value: $85,900 (2000); Median rent: $343 per month (2000); Median age of housing: 18 years (2000).
Safety: Violent crime rate: 61.0 per 10,000 population; Property crime rate: 13.5 per 10,000 population (2001).
Transportation: Commute to work: 96.6% car, 0.0% public transportation, 0.0% walk, 2.1% work from home (2000); Travel time to work: 34.2% less than 15 minutes, 53.6% 15 to 30 minutes, 8.9% 30 to 45 minutes, 1.9% 45 to 60 minutes, 1.3% 60 minutes or more (2000)

KINGDOM CITY (village). Aka McCredie. Covers a land area of 1.354 square miles and a water area of 0.005 square miles. Located at 38.94° N. Lat.; 91.93° W. Long. Elevation is 862 feet.
History: Kingdom City was named for an incident that occurred in 1861, when Union forces from Pike County prepared to invade Callway County, a Confederate stronghold. Callaway's Colonel Jefferson F. Jones assembled some old men and boys and armed them with makeshift weapons, including a

"cannon" made of a painted log. The Union commander, thinking he faced a formidable foe, agreed to retreat if Jones would disband his force. The agreement held, and this independent action caused Callaway County to be known as "The Kingdom."
Population: 121 (2000); Race: 84.2% White, 14.0% Black, 0.0% Asian, 1.8% American Indian and Alaska Native, 0.0% Hispanic of any race, 0.0% two or more races (2000); Density: 89.3 persons per square mile (2000); Age: 21.9% under 18, 15.8% over 64 (2000); Marriage status: 8.7% never married, 75.0% now married, 3.3% widowed, 13.0% divorced (2000); Foreign born: 0.0% (2000); Ancestry (includes multiple ancestries): 18.4% Irish, 17.5% Other groups, 15.8% United States or American, 15.8% German, 14.0% French (except Basque) (2000).
Economy: Employment by occupation: 3.3% management, 6.7% professional, 15.0% services, 26.7% sales, 0.0% farming, 8.3% construction, 40.0% production (2000).
Income: Per capita income: $16,978 (2000); Median household income: $35,417 (2000); Poverty rate: 0.0% (2000).
Taxes: Total city taxes per capita: $2,413 (1997); City property taxes per capita: $87 (1997).
Education: High school graduation rate: 69.7% (2000); College graduation rate: 9.0% (2000).

School District(s)

North Callaway Co. R-I (PK-12)
2000 Enrollment: 1,324 573-386-2214
Housing: Homeownership rate: 78.2% (2000); Median home value: $85,000 (2000); Median rent: $238 per month (2000); Median age of housing: 26 years (2000).
Transportation: Commute to work: 83.1% car, 6.8% public transportation, 6.8% walk, 3.4% work from home (2000); Travel time to work: 36.8% less than 15 minutes, 45.6% 15 to 30 minutes, 14.0% 30 to 45 minutes, 0.0% 45 to 60 minutes, 3.5% 60 minutes or more (2000)

LAKE MYKEE TOWN (village). Covers a land area of 0.195 square miles and a water area of 0.059 square miles. Located at 38.67° N. Lat.; 92.10° W. Long. Elevation is 844 feet.
Population: 326 (2000); Race: 95.1% White, 0.0% Black, 0.0% Asian, 1.8% American Indian and Alaska Native, 3.7% Hispanic of any race, 0.0% two or more races (2000); Density: 1,672.2 persons per square mile (2000); Age: 29.4% under 18, 8.0% over 64 (2000); Marriage status: 16.4% never married, 74.0% now married, 5.2% widowed, 4.4% divorced (2000); Foreign born: 1.5% (2000); Ancestry (includes multiple ancestries): 29.4% German, 22.1% United States or American, 12.3% Other groups, 7.1% English, 6.1% Irish (2000).
Economy: Employment by occupation: 15.3% management, 23.5% professional, 12.4% services, 26.5% sales, 0.0% farming, 7.6% construction, 14.7% production (2000).
Income: Per capita income: $20,374 (2000); Median household income: $56,667 (2000); Poverty rate: 3.7% (2000).
Taxes: Total city taxes per capita: $44 (1997); City property taxes per capita: $44 (1997).
Education: High school graduation rate: 91.5% (2000); College graduation rate: 25.9% (2000).
Housing: Homeownership rate: 95.7% (2000); Median home value: $118,400 (2000); Median rent: $575 per month (2000); Median age of housing: 14 years (2000).
Transportation: Commute to work: 100.0% car, 0.0% public transportation, 0.0% walk, 0.0% work from home (2000); Travel time to work: 22.8% less than 15 minutes, 58.7% 15 to 30 minutes, 15.0% 30 to 45 minutes, 3.6% 45 to 60 minutes, 0.0% 60 minutes or more (2000)

MOKANE (city). Covers a land area of 0.299 square miles and a water area of 0 square miles. Located at 38.67° N. Lat.; 91.87° W. Long. Elevation is 534 feet.
Population: 188 (2000); Race: 100.0% White, 0.0% Black, 0.0% Asian, 0.0% American Indian and Alaska Native, 0.0% Hispanic of any race, 0.0% two or more races (2000); Density: 628.6 persons per square mile (2000); Age: 30.8% under 18, 10.1% over 64 (2000); Marriage status: 27.6% never married, 58.6% now married, 5.9% widowed, 7.9% divorced (2000); Foreign born: 0.0% (2000); Ancestry (includes multiple ancestries): 25.3% German, 24.2% United States or American, 20.7% Irish, 17.7% Other groups, 6.1% English (2000).
Economy: Grain, livestock. Employment by occupation: 11.9% management, 9.9% professional, 16.8% services, 24.8% sales, 0.0% farming, 10.9% construction, 25.7% production (2000).
Income: Per capita income: $20,175 (2000); Median household income: $55,625 (2000); Poverty rate: 14.1% (2000).
Taxes: Total city taxes per capita: $45 (1997); City property taxes per capita: $25 (1997).
Education: High school graduation rate: 74.8% (2000); College graduation rate: 20.9% (2000).

School District(s)

South Callaway Co. R-II (PK-12)
2000 Enrollment: 984 573-676-5211
Housing: Homeownership rate: 81.2% (2000); Median home value: $46,600 (2000); Median rent: $256 per month (2000); Median age of housing: 60+ years (2000).
Transportation: Commute to work: 100.0% car, 0.0% public transportation, 0.0% walk, 0.0% work from home (2000); Travel time to work: 20.0% less than 15 minutes, 35.8% 15 to 30 minutes, 27.4% 30 to 45 minutes, 13.7% 45 to 60 minutes, 3.2% 60 minutes or more (2000)

NEW BLOOMFIELD (city). Covers a land area of 0.475 square miles and a water area of 0 square miles. Located at 38.71° N. Lat.; 92.09° W. Long. Elevation is 841 feet.
Population: 599 (2000); Race: 95.1% White, 0.0% Black, 0.0% Asian, 0.0% American Indian and Alaska Native, 1.3% Hispanic of any race, 2.2% two or more races (2000); Density: 1,261.3 persons per square mile (2000); Age: 32.2% under 18, 15.5% over 64 (2000); Marriage status: 24.7% never married, 50.3% now married, 13.4% widowed, 11.6% divorced (2000); Foreign born: 1.0% (2000); Ancestry (includes multiple ancestries): 32.0% German, 17.3% United States or American, 14.5% English, 13.1% Irish, 12.0% Other groups (2000).
Economy: Single-family building permits issued: 1 (2001) / 3 (2000); Multi-family building permits issued: 6 (2001) / 4 (2000); Employment by occupation: 9.0% management, 12.1% professional, 14.8% services, 34.1% sales, 1.0% farming, 14.1% construction, 14.8% production (2000).
Income: Per capita income: $15,180 (2000); Median household income: $32,969 (2000); Poverty rate: 9.1% (2000).
Taxes: Total city taxes per capita: $128 (1997); City property taxes per capita: $20 (1997).
Education: High school graduation rate: 78.9% (2000); College graduation rate: 14.2% (2000).

School District(s)

New Bloomfield R-III (KG-12)
2000 Enrollment: 678 573-491-3700
Housing: Homeownership rate: 60.2% (2000); Median home value: $71,300 (2000); Median rent: $298 per month (2000); Median age of housing: 32 years (2000).
Transportation: Commute to work: 93.6% car, 0.0% public transportation, 2.5% walk, 0.4% work from home (2000); Travel time to work: 20.1% less than 15 minutes, 59.1% 15 to 30 minutes, 13.3% 30 to 45 minutes, 2.5% 45 to 60 minutes, 5.0% 60 minutes or more (2000)

PORTLAND (unincorporated postal area, zip code 65067). Covers a land area of 46.936 square miles and a water area of 0.115 square miles. Located at 38.75° N. Lat.; 91.69° W. Long. Elevation is 541 feet.
Population: 412 (2000); Race: 96.2% White, 0.0% Black, 0.0% Asian, 3.8% American Indian and Alaska Native, 0.0% Hispanic of any race, 0.0% two or more races (2000); Density: 8.8 persons per square mile (2000); Age: 28.9% under 18, 5.1% over 64 (2000); Marriage status: 19.9% never married, 63.4% now married, 6.5% widowed, 10.3% divorced (2000); Foreign born: 0.0% (2000); Ancestry (includes multiple ancestries): 32.7% German, 19.9% Other groups, 12.3% United States or American, 9.0% Irish, 4.6% French (except Basque) (2000).
Economy: Employment by occupation: 4.7% management, 0.0% professional, 20.2% services, 24.0% sales, 0.0% farming, 28.7% construction, 22.5% production (2000).
Income: Per capita income: $11,996 (2000); Median household income: $23,424 (2000); Poverty rate: 26.9% (2000).
Education: High school graduation rate: 59.5% (2000); College graduation rate: 0.0% (2000).
Housing: Homeownership rate: 79.1% (2000); Median home value: $74,000 (2000); Median rent: $398 per month (2000); Median age of housing: 26 years (2000).
Transportation: Commute to work: 94.6% car, 0.0% public transportation, 0.0% walk, 5.4% work from home (2000); Travel time to work: 0.0% less than 15 minutes, 27.0% 15 to 30 minutes, 47.5% 30 to 45 minutes, 5.7% 45 to 60 minutes, 19.7% 60 minutes or more (2000)

STEEDMAN (unincorporated postal area, zip code 65077). Covers a land area of 37.161 square miles and a water area of 0.216 square miles. Located at 38.78° N. Lat.; 91.80° W. Long. Elevation is 560 feet.

Population: 554 (2000); Race: 98.8% White, 0.0% Black, 1.2% Asian, 0.0% American Indian and Alaska Native, 0.0% Hispanic of any race, 0.0% two or more races (2000); Density: 14.9 persons per square mile (2000); Age: 20.9% under 18, 9.8% over 64 (2000); Marriage status: 29.1% never married, 56.9% now married, 1.6% widowed, 12.4% divorced (2000); Foreign born: 1.2% (2000); Ancestry (includes multiple ancestries): 31.1% German, 15.9% United States or American, 11.9% English, 11.5% Irish, 8.2% Other groups (2000).
Economy: Employment by occupation: 3.2% management, 21.5% professional, 9.6% services, 14.3% sales, 0.0% farming, 25.9% construction, 25.5% production (2000).
Income: Per capita income: $17,727 (2000); Median household income: $34,792 (2000); Poverty rate: 1.8% (2000).
Education: High school graduation rate: 59.2% (2000); College graduation rate: 13.4% (2000).
Housing: Homeownership rate: 93.5% (2000); Median home value: $55,400 (2000); Median rent: $325 per month (2000); Median age of housing: 16 years (2000).
Transportation: Commute to work: 100.0% car, 0.0% public transportation, 0.0% walk, 0.0% work from home (2000); Travel time to work: 12.1% less than 15 minutes, 24.2% 15 to 30 minutes, 29.6% 30 to 45 minutes, 13.8% 45 to 60 minutes, 20.4% 60 minutes or more (2000)

TEBBETTS (unincorporated postal area, zip code 65080). Covers a land area of 39.890 square miles and a water area of 0.041 square miles. Located at 38.63° N. Lat.; 91.97° W. Long. Elevation is 580 feet.
Population: 762 (2000); Race: 98.1% White, 0.8% Black, 0.0% Asian, 0.0% American Indian and Alaska Native, 0.0% Hispanic of any race, 1.1% two or more races (2000); Density: 19.1 persons per square mile (2000); Age: 28.6% under 18, 11.1% over 64 (2000); Marriage status: 20.0% never married, 67.1% now married, 4.5% widowed, 8.3% divorced (2000); Foreign born: 1.2% (2000); Ancestry (includes multiple ancestries): 30.3% German, 16.7% United States or American, 8.1% English, 7.2% Polish, 6.0% Italian (2000).
Economy: Employment by occupation: 14.4% management, 13.1% professional, 13.4% services, 24.0% sales, 2.1% farming, 14.4% construction, 18.6% production (2000).
Income: Per capita income: $23,698 (2000); Median household income: $37,383 (2000); Poverty rate: 8.9% (2000).
Education: High school graduation rate: 84.6% (2000); College graduation rate: 8.2% (2000).
Housing: Homeownership rate: 95.9% (2000); Median home value: $75,000 (2000); Median rent: $225 per month (2000); Median age of housing: 24 years (2000).
Transportation: Commute to work: 92.5% car, 0.0% public transportation, 3.5% walk, 4.0% work from home (2000); Travel time to work: 20.1% less than 15 minutes, 37.9% 15 to 30 minutes, 30.9% 30 to 45 minutes, 2.5% 45 to 60 minutes, 8.6% 60 minutes or more (2000)

WILLIAMSBURG (unincorporated postal area, zip code 63388). Covers a land area of 55.505 square miles and a water area of 0.518 square miles. Located at 38.88° N. Lat.; 91.76° W. Long. Elevation is 826 feet.
History: Williamsburg was platted in 1837, and grew around an area of stock raising and horse breeding when settlers from Kentucky and Tennessee made their home here.
Population: 636 (2000); Race: 92.7% White, 7.3% Black, 0.0% Asian, 0.0% American Indian and Alaska Native, 0.0% Hispanic of any race, 0.0% two or more races (2000); Density: 11.5 persons per square mile (2000); Age: 19.3% under 18, 16.9% over 64 (2000); Marriage status: 7.1% never married, 64.0% now married, 17.5% widowed, 11.4% divorced (2000); Foreign born: 0.0% (2000); Ancestry (includes multiple ancestries): 15.4% English, 14.0% German, 13.3% Irish, 11.8% Other groups, 10.9% European (2000).
Economy: Employment by occupation: 5.1% management, 14.9% professional, 29.8% services, 15.2% sales, 7.0% farming, 14.9% construction, 13.0% production (2000).
Income: Per capita income: $17,024 (2000); Median household income: $38,289 (2000); Poverty rate: 0.0% (2000).
Education: High school graduation rate: 75.5% (2000); College graduation rate: 20.0% (2000).
Housing: Homeownership rate: 96.2% (2000); Median home value: $58,400 (2000); Median rent: $525 per month (2000); Median age of housing: 25 years (2000).
Transportation: Commute to work: 82.2% car, 0.0% public transportation, 10.8% walk, 7.0% work from home (2000); Travel time to work: 13.7% less than 15 minutes, 29.7% 15 to 30 minutes, 33.4% 30 to 45 minutes, 6.8% 45 to 60 minutes, 16.4% 60 minutes or more (2000)

Camden County

Located in central Missouri, in the Ozarks; crossed by Lake of the Ozarks; drained by the Niangua River. Covers a land area of 655.10 square miles, a water area of 53.70 square miles, and is located in the Central Time Zone. The county government was organized in 1841. County seat is Camdenton.
Population: 37,051 (2000); Race: 97.5% White, 0.3% Black, 0.2% Asian, 0.5% American Indian and Alaska Native, 0.6% Hispanic of any race, 1.2% two or more races (2000); Density: 56.6 persons per square mile (2000); Age: 20.2% under 18, 18.9% over 64 (2000).
Religion: Five largest groups: 13.7% Southern Baptist Convention, 4.7% Catholic Church, 3.6% Christian Church (Disciples of Christ), 3.2% The United Methodist Church, 2.0% Lutheran Church—Missouri Synod (2000).
Economy: Unemployment rate: 6.7% (11/2002); Total civilian labor force: 16,515 (11/2002); Leading industries: 22.2% retail trade; 18.7% accommodation & food services; 13.2% construction (2000); Companies that employ more than 1,000 persons: 0 (2000); Companies that employ more than 100 persons: 12 (2000); Farms: 584 totaling 172,273 acres (1997); Minority business ownership rate: 0.0% (1997); Women business ownership rate: 23.1% (1997); Retail sales per capita: $13,150 (1997). Single-family building permits issued: 25 (2001) / 25 (2000); Multi-family building permits issued: 88 (2001) / 97 (2000).
Income: Per capita income: $20,197 (2000); Median household income: $35,840 (2000); Poverty rate: 11.4% (2000); Bankruptcy rate: 4.50% (2001).
Taxes: Total county taxes per capita: $121 (2000); County property taxes per capita: $14 (2000).
Education: High school graduation rate: 82.9% (2000); College graduation rate: 17.7% (2000).
Housing: Homeownership rate: 82.3% (2000); Median home value: $124,300 (2000); Median rent: $359 per month (2000); Median age of housing: 17 years (2000).
Health: Birth rate: 91.0 per 10,000 population (1998); Age adjusted death rate: 88.9 per 10,000 population (1999); Age adjusted cancer mortality rate: 191.0 deaths per 100,000 population (1999). Number of physicians: 9.4 per 10,000 population (1999); Number of hospital beds: 28.1 per 10,000 population (1999).
Elections: 2000 Presidential election results: 37.0% Gore, 60.6% Bush, 1.5% Nader, 0.5% Buchanan
National and State Parks: Camdenton Towersite State Wildlife Management Area; Fiery Fork State Forest; Ganter State Public Hunting Area; Ha Ha Tonka State Park; Lake of the Ozarks State Park; Mansfield Forest State Wildlife Management Area; Moles Cave State Wildlife Area
Additional Information Contacts
Camden County Government Offices 573-346-4440
Camdenton Chamber of Commerce.................... 573-346-2227
Lake of Ozarks West Chamber 573-374-5500
Lake of The Ozarks Convention 573-348-1599

Camden County Communities

CAMDENTON (city). Covers a land area of 3.494 square miles and a water area of 0 square miles. Located at 38.00° N. Lat.; 92.74° W. Long. Elevation is 1,043 feet.
History: Camdenton was established in 1929 by residents of a town which was inundated by waters of the Lake of the Ozarks, formed by the construction of Bagnell Dam.
Population: 2,779 (2000); Race: 92.6% White, 0.7% Black, 0.0% Asian, 1.0% American Indian and Alaska Native, 2.1% Hispanic of any race, 4.1% two or more races (2000); Density: 795.3 persons per square mile (2000); Age: 25.6% under 18, 15.2% over 64 (2000); Marriage status: 22.4% never married, 50.1% now married, 10.4% widowed, 17.2% divorced (2000); Foreign born: 2.3% (2000); Ancestry (includes multiple ancestries): 23.4% German, 15.7% Irish, 15.1% Other groups, 14.4% English, 11.3% United States or American (2000).
Economy: Single-family building permits issued: 3 (2001) / 3 (2000); Multi-family building permits issued: 2 (2001) / 32 (2000); Employment by occupation: 7.1% management, 13.3% professional, 24.9% services, 27.9% sales, 0.0% farming, 12.2% construction, 14.5% production (2000).
Income: Per capita income: $14,040 (2000); Median household income: $26,649 (2000); Poverty rate: 17.1% (2000).
Taxes: Total city taxes per capita: $1,035 (2000); City property taxes per capita: $0 (2000).
Education: High school graduation rate: 79.0% (2000); College graduation rate: 11.5% (2000).

School District(s)
Camdenton R-III (PK-12)
2000 Enrollment: 4,080 573-346-9215
Housing: Homeownership rate: 51.9% (2000); Median home value: $68,700 (2000); Median rent: $304 per month (2000); Median age of housing: 26 years (2000).
Newspapers: Lake Sun Leader (5 x week)
Transportation: Commute to work: 90.9% car, 0.0% public transportation, 2.2% walk, 4.3% work from home (2000); Travel time to work: 54.8% less than 15 minutes, 31.5% 15 to 30 minutes, 7.7% 30 to 45 minutes, 2.9% 45 to 60 minutes, 3.1% 60 minutes or more (2000)
Additional Information Contacts
Camdenton Chamber of Commerce 573-346-2227

CLIMAX SPRINGS (village). Covers a land area of 0.272 square miles and a water area of 0 square miles. Located at 38.10° N. Lat.; 93.05° W. Long. Elevation is 966 feet.
Population: 80 (2000); Race: 100.0% White, 0.0% Black, 0.0% Asian, 0.0% American Indian and Alaska Native, 0.0% Hispanic of any race, 0.0% two or more races (2000); Density: 294.6 persons per square mile (2000); Age: 18.9% under 18, 17.9% over 64 (2000); Marriage status: 22.5% never married, 43.8% now married, 14.6% widowed, 19.1% divorced (2000); Foreign born: 0.0% (2000); Ancestry (includes multiple ancestries): 22.1% United States or American, 11.6% Other groups, 10.5% English, 8.4% Danish, 8.4% Irish (2000).
Economy: Manufacturing: bearings. Employment by occupation: 7.9% management, 21.1% professional, 23.7% services, 5.3% sales, 0.0% farming, 10.5% construction, 31.6% production (2000).
Income: Per capita income: $13,620 (2000); Median household income: $30,000 (2000); Poverty rate: 8.4% (2000).
Taxes: Total city taxes per capita: $9 (1997); City property taxes per capita: $0 (1997).
Education: High school graduation rate: 75.7% (2000); College graduation rate: 10.0% (2000).

School District(s)
Climax Springs R-IV (PK-12)
2000 Enrollment: 265 573-347-3905
Housing: Homeownership rate: 83.3% (2000); Median home value: $32,500 (2000); Median rent: $225 per month (2000); Median age of housing: 30 years (2000).
Transportation: Commute to work: 100.0% car, 0.0% public transportation, 0.0% walk, 0.0% work from home (2000); Travel time to work: 42.1% less than 15 minutes, 7.9% 15 to 30 minutes, 39.5% 30 to 45 minutes, 10.5% 45 to 60 minutes, 0.0% 60 minutes or more (2000)

LINN CREEK (city). Covers a land area of 1.107 square miles and a water area of <.001 square miles. Located at 38.04° N. Lat.; 92.69° W. Long. Elevation is 682 feet.
History: Linn Creek's original site on the Osage River was inundated when Bagnell Dam created the Lake of the Ozarks. Half of the residents opted to establish a new town of Linn Creek in the valley. The other half moved to a nearby bluff and founded Camdenton.
Population: 280 (2000); Race: 98.5% White, 1.5% Black, 0.0% Asian, 0.0% American Indian and Alaska Native, 2.9% Hispanic of any race, 0.0% two or more races (2000); Density: 252.9 persons per square mile (2000); Age: 30.9% under 18, 8.7% over 64 (2000); Marriage status: 18.8% never married, 59.4% now married, 11.4% widowed, 10.4% divorced (2000); Foreign born: 2.2% (2000); Ancestry (includes multiple ancestries): 14.2% United States or American, 13.1% German, 11.6% Other groups, 9.5% English, 5.5% Irish (2000).
Economy: Employment by occupation: 7.6% management, 12.9% professional, 17.4% services, 32.6% sales, 0.0% farming, 14.4% construction, 15.2% production (2000).
Income: Per capita income: $11,009 (2000); Median household income: $22,125 (2000); Poverty rate: 19.9% (2000).
Taxes: Total city taxes per capita: $271 (1997); City property taxes per capita: $0 (1997).
Education: High school graduation rate: 62.4% (2000); College graduation rate: 11.8% (2000).
Housing: Homeownership rate: 50.5% (2000); Median home value: $54,000 (2000); Median rent: $453 per month (2000); Median age of housing: 25 years (2000).
Transportation: Commute to work: 91.4% car, 0.0% public transportation, 4.7% walk, 3.9% work from home (2000); Travel time to work: 60.2% less than 15 minutes, 30.1% 15 to 30 minutes, 3.3% 30 to 45 minutes, 4.9% 45 to 60 minutes, 1.6% 60 minutes or more (2000)

MACKS CREEK (city). Covers a land area of 0.936 square miles and a water area of 0.010 square miles. Located at 37.96° N. Lat.; 92.97° W. Long. Elevation is 875 feet.
Population: 267 (2000); Race: 99.3% White, 0.0% Black, 0.7% Asian, 0.0% American Indian and Alaska Native, 0.0% Hispanic of any race, 0.0% two or more races (2000); Density: 285.2 persons per square mile (2000); Age: 30.7% under 18, 10.6% over 64 (2000); Marriage status: 14.1% never married, 62.8% now married, 9.5% widowed, 13.6% divorced (2000); Foreign born: 0.7% (2000); Ancestry (includes multiple ancestries): 30.7% United States or American, 8.0% German, 5.1% French (except Basque), 5.1% English, 4.7% Other groups (2000).
Economy: Tunnel Dam hydroelectric power station on Niangua River to East. Timber; cattle. Recreational area. Employment by occupation: 3.7% management, 11.9% professional, 20.2% services, 16.5% sales, 0.0% farming, 25.7% construction, 22.0% production (2000).
Income: Per capita income: $9,053 (2000); Median household income: $21,875 (2000); Poverty rate: 22.3% (2000).
Taxes: Total city taxes per capita: $21 (1997); City property taxes per capita: $0 (1997).
Education: High school graduation rate: 74.5% (2000); College graduation rate: 3.0% (2000).

School District(s)
Macks Creek R-V (PK-12)
2000 Enrollment: 407 573-363-5909
Housing: Homeownership rate: 68.2% (2000); Median home value: $50,000 (2000); Median rent: $197 per month (2000); Median age of housing: 29 years (2000).
Transportation: Commute to work: 98.1% car, 0.0% public transportation, 0.0% walk, 1.9% work from home (2000); Travel time to work: 22.9% less than 15 minutes, 34.3% 15 to 30 minutes, 21.9% 30 to 45 minutes, 11.4% 45 to 60 minutes, 9.5% 60 minutes or more (2000)

MONTREAL (unincorporated postal area, zip code 65591). Covers a land area of 51.377 square miles and a water area of 0 square miles. Located at 37.98° N. Lat.; 92.59° W. Long. Elevation is 1,060 feet.
Population: 834 (2000); Race: 99.6% White, 0.0% Black, 0.4% Asian, 0.0% American Indian and Alaska Native, 0.0% Hispanic of any race, 0.0% two or more races (2000); Density: 16.2 persons per square mile (2000); Age: 25.4% under 18, 12.0% over 64 (2000); Marriage status: 16.2% never married, 67.1% now married, 5.3% widowed, 11.4% divorced (2000); Foreign born: 0.4% (2000); Ancestry (includes multiple ancestries): 17.7% United States or American, 15.3% German, 10.6% English, 9.2% Irish, 7.5% Other groups (2000).
Economy: Employment by occupation: 12.3% management, 6.8% professional, 13.5% services, 16.8% sales, 0.8% farming, 26.6% construction, 23.3% production (2000).
Income: Per capita income: $15,160 (2000); Median household income: $36,250 (2000); Poverty rate: 5.0% (2000).
Education: High school graduation rate: 89.5% (2000); College graduation rate: 5.4% (2000).
Housing: Homeownership rate: 86.5% (2000); Median home value: $36,300 (2000); Median rent: $464 per month (2000); Median age of housing: 18 years (2000).
Transportation: Commute to work: 91.6% car, 0.0% public transportation, 1.8% walk, 6.6% work from home (2000); Travel time to work: 9.8% less than 15 minutes, 52.3% 15 to 30 minutes, 26.4% 30 to 45 minutes, 5.7% 45 to 60 minutes, 5.7% 60 minutes or more (2000)

OSAGE BEACH (city). Covers a land area of 9.395 square miles and a water area of 0.710 square miles. Located at 38.13° N. Lat.; 92.64° W. Long. Elevation is 895 feet.
History: Osage Beach was platted by real estate promoters when Bagnell Dam was first proposed in 1928. The town developed as a resort center on the Lake of the Ozarks.
Population: 3,662 (2000); Race: 96.6% White, 0.8% Black, 0.2% Asian, 1.4% American Indian and Alaska Native, 1.1% Hispanic of any race, 0.7% two or more races (2000); Density: 389.8 persons per square mile (2000); Age: 15.2% under 18, 20.0% over 64 (2000); Marriage status: 18.7% never married, 59.0% now married, 10.3% widowed, 12.0% divorced (2000); Foreign born: 1.4% (2000); Ancestry (includes multiple ancestries): 23.7% German, 15.2% English, 13.4% Irish, 12.2% United States or American, 8.0% Other groups (2000).
Economy: Single-family building permits issued: 22 (2001) / 22 (2000); Multi-family building permits issued: 86 (2001) / 65 (2000); Employment by

occupation: 16.4% management, 17.2% professional, 16.1% services, 33.4% sales, 0.0% farming, 9.5% construction, 7.5% production (2000).
Income: Per capita income: $22,685 (2000); Median household income: $38,448 (2000); Poverty rate: 6.7% (2000).
Taxes: Total city taxes per capita: $2,114 (2000); City property taxes per capita: $0 (2000).
Education: High school graduation rate: 85.7% (2000); College graduation rate: 23.7% (2000).
Housing: Homeownership rate: 67.6% (2000); Median home value: $133,800 (2000); Median rent: $387 per month (2000); Median age of housing: 14 years (2000).
Hospitals: Lake Regional Health Systems
Safety: Violent crime rate: n/a; Property crime rate: 835.8 per 10,000 population (2001).
Transportation: Commute to work: 90.8% car, 0.0% public transportation, 5.1% walk, 2.9% work from home (2000); Travel time to work: 55.6% less than 15 minutes, 27.9% 15 to 30 minutes, 7.3% 30 to 45 minutes, 4.9% 45 to 60 minutes, 4.3% 60 minutes or more (2000)
Additional Information Contacts
Lake of The Ozarks Convention 573-348-1599

ROACH (unincorporated postal area, zip code 65787). Covers a land area of 44.672 square miles and a water area of 0.053 square miles. Located at 38.06° N. Lat.; 92.88° W. Long. Elevation is 991 feet.
Population: 1,104 (2000); Race: 100.0% White, 0.0% Black, 0.0% Asian, 0.0% American Indian and Alaska Native, 0.0% Hispanic of any race, 0.0% two or more races (2000); Density: 24.7 persons per square mile (2000); Age: 12.8% under 18, 29.1% over 64 (2000); Marriage status: 9.2% never married, 79.2% now married, 7.0% widowed, 4.6% divorced (2000); Foreign born: 0.7% (2000); Ancestry (includes multiple ancestries): 29.7% German, 15.7% Irish, 13.3% English, 8.2% United States or American, 7.2% Other groups (2000).
Economy: Employment by occupation: 10.5% management, 24.5% professional, 8.9% services, 23.7% sales, 1.0% farming, 14.3% construction, 17.1% production (2000).
Income: Per capita income: $22,028 (2000); Median household income: $37,132 (2000); Poverty rate: 9.3% (2000).
Education: High school graduation rate: 81.4% (2000); College graduation rate: 15.8% (2000).
Housing: Homeownership rate: 95.6% (2000); Median home value: $137,200 (2000); Median rent: $275 per month (2000); Median age of housing: 20 years (2000).
Transportation: Commute to work: 94.5% car, 0.0% public transportation, 0.0% walk, 5.5% work from home (2000); Travel time to work: 8.3% less than 15 minutes, 42.8% 15 to 30 minutes, 36.9% 30 to 45 minutes, 10.0% 45 to 60 minutes, 1.9% 60 minutes or more (2000)

STOUTLAND (village). Covers a land area of 0.597 square miles and a water area of 0 square miles. Located at 37.81° N. Lat.; 92.51° W. Long. Elevation is 1,171 feet.
Population: 177 (2000); Race: 93.6% White, 0.0% Black, 0.0% Asian, 0.0% American Indian and Alaska Native, 0.0% Hispanic of any race, 6.4% two or more races (2000); Density: 296.7 persons per square mile (2000); Age: 21.9% under 18, 13.7% over 64 (2000); Marriage status: 20.2% never married, 54.5% now married, 10.7% widowed, 14.6% divorced (2000); Foreign born: 1.4% (2000); Ancestry (includes multiple ancestries): 26.5% Other groups, 21.0% United States or American, 17.4% German, 9.1% Irish, 6.4% English (2000).
Economy: Employment by occupation: 13.4% management, 18.8% professional, 14.3% services, 11.6% sales, 0.0% farming, 9.8% construction, 32.1% production (2000).
Income: Per capita income: $15,476 (2000); Median household income: $31,250 (2000); Poverty rate: 5.5% (2000).
Taxes: Total city taxes per capita: $42 (1997); City property taxes per capita: $25 (1997).
Education: High school graduation rate: 72.7% (2000); College graduation rate: 17.3% (2000).

School District(s)

Stoutland R-II (PK-12)
2000 Enrollment: 589 417-286-3984
Housing: Homeownership rate: 82.2% (2000); Median home value: $39,400 (2000); Median rent: $225 per month (2000); Median age of housing: 45 years (2000).
Transportation: Commute to work: 87.3% car, 0.0% public transportation, 8.2% walk, 0.0% work from home (2000); Travel time to work: 29.1% less than 15 minutes, 32.7% 15 to 30 minutes, 26.4% 30 to 45 minutes, 7.3% 45 to 60 minutes, 4.5% 60 minutes or more (2000)

SUNRISE BEACH (village). Covers a land area of 4.433 square miles and a water area of <.001 square miles. Located at 38.18° N. Lat.; 92.77° W. Long. Elevation is 853 feet.
Population: 368 (2000); Race: 91.4% White, 0.0% Black, 0.0% Asian, 3.9% American Indian and Alaska Native, 2.9% Hispanic of any race, 2.3% two or more races (2000); Density: 83.0 persons per square mile (2000); Age: 10.7% under 18, 36.5% over 64 (2000); Marriage status: 13.8% never married, 59.3% now married, 9.0% widowed, 17.8% divorced (2000); Foreign born: 1.6% (2000); Ancestry (includes multiple ancestries): 21.4% German, 19.3% United States or American, 12.5% Other groups, 8.3% English, 8.1% Irish (2000).
Economy: Employment by occupation: 11.2% management, 4.2% professional, 27.3% services, 33.6% sales, 0.0% farming, 18.2% construction, 5.6% production (2000).
Income: Per capita income: $17,382 (2000); Median household income: $27,679 (2000); Poverty rate: 10.7% (2000).
Taxes: Total city taxes per capita: $394 (1997); City property taxes per capita: $29 (1997).
Education: High school graduation rate: 82.6% (2000); College graduation rate: 5.6% (2000).
Housing: Homeownership rate: 88.6% (2000); Median home value: $127,500 (2000); Median rent: $263 per month (2000); Median age of housing: 19 years (2000).
Transportation: Commute to work: 90.8% car, 0.0% public transportation, 4.3% walk, 5.0% work from home (2000); Travel time to work: 61.9% less than 15 minutes, 14.9% 15 to 30 minutes, 11.9% 30 to 45 minutes, 3.7% 45 to 60 minutes, 7.5% 60 minutes or more (2000)
Additional Information Contacts
Lake of Ozarks West Chamber 573-374-5500

VILLAGE OF FOUR SEASONS (village). Covers a land area of 4.467 square miles and a water area of 0.081 square miles. Located at 38.20° N. Lat.; 92.71° W. Long.
Population: 1,493 (2000); Race: 98.8% White, 0.0% Black, 0.0% Asian, 0.0% American Indian and Alaska Native, 1.1% Hispanic of any race, 1.2% two or more races (2000); Density: 334.2 persons per square mile (2000); Age: 20.9% under 18, 16.5% over 64 (2000); Marriage status: 15.3% never married, 72.6% now married, 4.0% widowed, 8.1% divorced (2000); Foreign born: 1.4% (2000); Ancestry (includes multiple ancestries): 27.7% German, 17.0% Irish, 14.4% English, 7.9% United States or American, 5.6% Other groups (2000).
Economy: Employment by occupation: 23.7% management, 20.2% professional, 13.2% services, 32.6% sales, 0.3% farming, 5.5% construction, 4.5% production (2000).
Income: Per capita income: $36,593 (2000); Median household income: $59,063 (2000); Poverty rate: 10.7% (2000).
Education: High school graduation rate: 95.6% (2000); College graduation rate: 41.1% (2000).
Housing: Homeownership rate: 83.5% (2000); Median home value: $237,100 (2000); Median rent: $442 per month (2000); Median age of housing: 12 years (2000).
Transportation: Commute to work: 91.0% car, 0.0% public transportation, 0.6% walk, 7.2% work from home (2000); Travel time to work: 31.7% less than 15 minutes, 47.8% 15 to 30 minutes, 8.2% 30 to 45 minutes, 5.7% 45 to 60 minutes, 6.6% 60 minutes or more (2000)

Cape Girardeau County

Located in southeastern Missouri; bounded on the east by the Mississippi River; crossed by the Whitewater River. Covers a land area of 578.60 square miles, a water area of 7.70 square miles, and is located in the Central Time Zone. The county government was organized in 1812. County seat is Jackson.

Weather Station: Jackson — Elevation: 439 feet

	Jan	Feb	Mar	Apr	May	Jun	Jul	Aug	Sep	Oct	Nov	Dec
High	42	48	59	71	79	88	91	90	83	72	57	46
Low	23	28	37	46	55	64	68	66	58	46	37	28
Precip	3.0	3.3	4.9	4.9	5.1	4.0	3.8	3.4	3.5	3.3	4.7	3.8
Snow	na	3.2	2.1	tr	0.0	0.0	0.0	0.0	0.0	tr	0.5	1.3

High and Low temperatures in degrees Fahrenheit; Precipitation and Snow in inches

Population: 68,693 (2000); Race: 92.1% White, 5.3% Black, 0.6% Asian, 0.3% American Indian and Alaska Native, 0.7% Hispanic of any race, 1.3%

two or more races (2000); Density: 118.7 persons per square mile (2000); Age: 23.4% under 18, 13.7% over 64 (2000).
Religion: Five largest groups: 15.3% Catholic Church, 14.5% Southern Baptist Convention, 11.2% Lutheran Church—Missouri Synod, 8.2% The United Methodist Church, 3.5% Assemblies of God (2000).
Economy: Unemployment rate: 3.6% (11/2002); Total civilian labor force: 36,864 (11/2002); Leading industries: 20.6% health care and social assistance; 17.6% retail trade; 17.5% manufacturing (2000); Companies that employ more than 1,000 persons: 3 (2000); Companies that employ more than 100 persons: 51 (2000); Farms: 1,161 totaling 260,931 acres (1997); Minority business ownership rate: 4.2% (1997); Women business ownership rate: 22.7% (1997); Retail sales per capita: $14,537 (1997). Single-family building permits issued: 151 (2001) / 150 (2000); Multi-family building permits issued: 46 (2001) / 180 (2000).
Income: Per capita income: $18,593 (2000); Median household income: $36,458 (2000); Poverty rate: 11.1% (2000); Bankruptcy rate: 4.24% (2001).
Taxes: Total county taxes per capita: $86 (2000); County property taxes per capita: $13 (2000).
Education: High school graduation rate: 81.1% (2000); College graduation rate: 24.2% (2000).
Housing: Homeownership rate: 68.4% (2000); Median home value: $94,700 (2000); Median rent: $351 per month (2000); Median age of housing: 27 years (2000).
Health: Birth rate: 113.3 per 10,000 population (1998); Age adjusted death rate: 96.0 per 10,000 population (1999); Age adjusted cancer mortality rate: 203.7 deaths per 100,000 population (1999). Number of physicians: 29.0 per 10,000 population (1999); Number of hospital beds: 70.9 per 10,000 population (1999).
Elections: 2000 Presidential election results: 31.3% Gore, 66.4% Bush, 1.3% Nader, 0.5% Buchanan
National and State Parks: Bollinger Mill State Park; Trail Of Tears State Park
Additional Information Contacts
Cape Girardeau County Government Offices 573-243-1052
Cape Girardeau Chamber of Commerce 573-335-3312
Cape Girardeau County Board of Realtors. 573-335-7969
Jackson Chamber of Commerce. 573-243-8131

Cape Girardeau County Communities

ALLENVILLE (village). Covers a land area of 0.174 square miles and a water area of 0 square miles. Located at 37.22° N. Lat.; 89.75° W. Long. Elevation is 352 feet.
Population: 104 (2000); Race: 100.0% White, 0.0% Black, 0.0% Asian, 0.0% American Indian and Alaska Native, 0.0% Hispanic of any race, 0.0% two or more races (2000); Density: 598.2 persons per square mile (2000); Age: 18.4% under 18, 22.4% over 64 (2000); Marriage status: 22.0% never married, 51.2% now married, 14.6% widowed, 12.2% divorced (2000); Foreign born: 2.0% (2000); Ancestry (includes multiple ancestries): 30.6% United States or American, 12.2% Irish, 10.2% German, 8.2% Other groups, 2.0% English (2000).
Economy: Employment by occupation: 0.0% management, 10.3% professional, 10.3% services, 35.9% sales, 7.7% farming, 0.0% construction, 35.9% production (2000).
Income: Per capita income: $15,993 (2000); Median household income: $19,583 (2000); Poverty rate: 21.9% (2000).
Taxes: Total city taxes per capita: $13 (1997); City property taxes per capita: $13 (1997).
Education: High school graduation rate: 44.8% (2000); College graduation rate: 3.4% (2000).
Housing: Homeownership rate: 79.5% (2000); Median home value: $27,500 (2000); Median rent: $225 per month (2000); Median age of housing: 33 years (2000).
Transportation: Commute to work: 84.6% car, 0.0% public transportation, 5.1% walk, 5.1% work from home (2000); Travel time to work: 21.6% less than 15 minutes, 43.2% 15 to 30 minutes, 10.8% 30 to 45 minutes, 5.4% 45 to 60 minutes, 18.9% 60 minutes or more (2000)

BURFORDVILLE (unincorporated postal area, zip code 63739). Covers a land area of 16.790 square miles and a water area of 0.035 square miles. Located at 37.36° N. Lat.; 89.79° W. Long. Elevation is 410 feet.
History: Burfordville was established on the Whitewater River, and grew around the Bollinger Mill, built about 1800, which ground the grain of farmers from a wide area. The mill was operated by Major George Frederick Bollinger who brought a group of German immigrants to settle at Burfordville in 1800.
Population: 621 (2000); Race: 100.0% White, 0.0% Black, 0.0% Asian, 0.0% American Indian and Alaska Native, 0.0% Hispanic of any race, 0.0% two or more races (2000); Density: 37.0 persons per square mile (2000); Age: 25.8% under 18, 7.2% over 64 (2000); Marriage status: 23.1% never married, 67.1% now married, 3.0% widowed, 6.9% divorced (2000); Foreign born: 0.0% (2000); Ancestry (includes multiple ancestries): 18.7% German, 18.3% United States or American, 16.1% Irish, 12.5% English, 8.0% Other groups (2000).
Economy: Employment by occupation: 12.8% management, 13.7% professional, 16.1% services, 25.3% sales, 0.0% farming, 11.9% construction, 20.2% production (2000).
Income: Per capita income: $20,386 (2000); Median household income: $49,375 (2000); Poverty rate: 10.6% (2000).
Education: High school graduation rate: 76.4% (2000); College graduation rate: 16.7% (2000).
Housing: Homeownership rate: 94.1% (2000); Median home value: $121,400 (2000); Median age of housing: 22 years (2000).
Transportation: Commute to work: 96.1% car, 0.0% public transportation, 3.0% walk, 0.9% work from home (2000); Travel time to work: 13.2% less than 15 minutes, 48.3% 15 to 30 minutes, 29.4% 30 to 45 minutes, 3.6% 45 to 60 minutes, 5.4% 60 minutes or more (2000)

CAPE GIRARDEAU (city). Covers a land area of 24.270 square miles and a water area of 0.052 square miles. Located at 37.30° N. Lat.; 89.54° W. Long. Elevation is 354 feet.
History: The town of Cape Girardeau was platted in 1806, but its history goes back to 1720 when a French ensign named Girardot is thought to have settled near the site. In 1792 Louis Lorimier was granted land here by the Spanish government, and built a trading post. Other settlers came from Kentucky, Virginia, Tennessee, and the Carolinas. When the Spanish surrendered the area to the United States in 1804, Cape Girardeau was designated the seat of government for the district, an honor which it lost in 1815. The city's location at the confluence of the Ohio and Mississippi Rivers provided power for the sawmills and flour mills that flourished.
Population: 35,349 (2000); Race: 87.2% White, 9.4% Black, 0.9% Asian, 0.5% American Indian and Alaska Native, 0.9% Hispanic of any race, 1.6% two or more races (2000); Density: 1,456.5 persons per square mile (2000); Age: 20.5% under 18, 15.4% over 64 (2000); Marriage status: 32.6% never married, 49.2% now married, 8.3% widowed, 9.9% divorced (2000); Foreign born: 2.0% (2000); Ancestry (includes multiple ancestries): 28.1% German, 15.1% Other groups, 10.7% Irish, 10.6% United States or American, 8.0% English (2000).
Vital Statistics: Birth rate: 116.8 per 10,000 population (1998)
Economy: Unemployment rate: 4.2% (11/2002); Total civilian labor force: 20,509 (11/2002); Single-family building permits issued: 66 (2001) / 63 (2000); Multi-family building permits issued: 38 (2001) / 154 (2000); Employment by occupation: 10.6% management, 22.5% professional, 18.2% services, 28.2% sales, 0.1% farming, 6.8% construction, 13.6% production (2000).
Income: Per capita income: $18,918 (2000); Median household income: $32,452 (2000); Poverty rate: 15.2% (2000).
Taxes: Total city taxes per capita: $607 (2000); City property taxes per capita: $46 (2000).
Education: High school graduation rate: 81.6% (2000); College graduation rate: 29.3% (2000).

School District(s)
Cape Girardeau 63 (PK-12)
2000 Enrollment: 4,070 573-335-1867
Nell Holcomb R-IV (KG-08)
2000 Enrollment: 300 573-334-3644

Four-year College(s)
Stage One (Private, For-profit)
2001 Enrollment: n/a 314-335-5078
Southeast Missouri State University (Public)
2001 Enrollment: 9,348 573-651-2000
2001 Tuition: In-state $3,234; Out-of-state $6,069

Two-year College(s)
Metro Business College of Cape Girardeau (Private, For-profit)
2001 Enrollment: 91 573-334-9181
2001 Tuition: In-state $7,785; Out-of-state $7,785
Southeast Missouri Hospital College of Nursing (Private, Not-for-profit)
2001 Enrollment: 96 573-334-6825
2001 Tuition: In-state $8,000; Out-of-state $8,000

Housing: Homeownership rate: 57.3% (2000); Median home value: $90,800 (2000); Median rent: $348 per month (2000); Median age of housing: 32 years (2000).
Hospitals: Saint Francis Medical Center (264 beds); Southeast Missouri Hospital (269 beds)
Safety: Violent crime rate: 16.9 per 10,000 population; Property crime rate: 696.2 per 10,000 population (2001).
Newspapers: Jackson USA Signal (1 x week); Southeast Missourian (7 x week); Big Nickel Advertiser (1 x week)
Transportation: Commute to work: 91.6% car, 0.7% public transportation, 5.2% walk, 1.8% work from home (2000); Travel time to work: 59.9% less than 15 minutes, 29.4% 15 to 30 minutes, 5.3% 30 to 45 minutes, 2.0% 45 to 60 minutes, 3.4% 60 minutes or more (2000)
Airports: Cape Girardeau Regional (commercial service)
Additional Information Contacts
Cape Girardeau Chamber of Commerce 573-335-3312
Cape Girardeau County Board of Realtors. 573-335-7969

DAISY (unincorporated postal area, zip code 63743). Covers a land area of 2.344 square miles and a water area of 0 square miles. Located at 37.52° N. Lat.; 89.81° W. Long. Elevation is 590 feet.
Population: 46 (2000); Race: 100.0% White, 0.0% Black, 0.0% Asian, 0.0% American Indian and Alaska Native, 0.0% Hispanic of any race, 0.0% two or more races (2000); Density: 19.6 persons per square mile (2000); Age: 29.7% under 18, 10.8% over 64 (2000); Marriage status: 11.1% never married, 88.9% now married, 0.0% widowed, 0.0% divorced (2000); Foreign born: 0.0% (2000); Ancestry (includes multiple ancestries): 51.4% German, 13.5% Irish, 5.4% Other groups, 5.4% Ukrainian, 5.4% French (except Basque) (2000).
Economy: Employment by occupation: 12.5% management, 25.0% professional, 12.5% services, 12.5% sales, 0.0% farming, 25.0% construction, 12.5% production (2000).
Income: Per capita income: $13,946 (2000); Median household income: $51,250 (2000); Poverty rate: 32.4% (2000).
Education: High school graduation rate: 83.3% (2000); College graduation rate: 0.0% (2000).
Housing: Homeownership rate: 100.0% (2000); Median home value: $55,000 (2000); Median age of housing: 33 years (2000).
Transportation: Commute to work: 100.0% car, 0.0% public transportation, 0.0% walk, 0.0% work from home (2000); Travel time to work: 0.0% less than 15 minutes, 50.0% 15 to 30 minutes, 50.0% 30 to 45 minutes, 0.0% 45 to 60 minutes, 0.0% 60 minutes or more (2000)

DELTA (city). Covers a land area of 0.440 square miles and a water area of 0 square miles. Located at 37.19° N. Lat.; 89.73° W. Long. Elevation is 340 feet.
History: Delta grew around a farming community, as a shipping point for produce.
Population: 517 (2000); Race: 98.1% White, 0.0% Black, 0.0% Asian, 0.0% American Indian and Alaska Native, 0.9% Hispanic of any race, 1.9% two or more races (2000); Density: 1,175.0 persons per square mile (2000); Age: 27.0% under 18, 15.3% over 64 (2000); Marriage status: 20.9% never married, 59.0% now married, 9.2% widowed, 10.9% divorced (2000); Foreign born: 0.0% (2000); Ancestry (includes multiple ancestries): 21.2% United States or American, 18.1% German, 10.4% Other groups, 9.1% Irish, 4.5% French (except Basque) (2000).
Economy: Single-family building permits issued: 0 (2001) / 0 (2000); Multi-family building permits issued: 0 (2001) / 0 (2000); Employment by occupation: 3.6% management, 10.0% professional, 16.3% services, 26.2% sales, 0.9% farming, 10.9% construction, 32.1% production (2000).
Income: Per capita income: $13,622 (2000); Median household income: $25,417 (2000); Poverty rate: 17.1% (2000).
Taxes: Total city taxes per capita: $84 (1997); City property taxes per capita: $26 (1997).
Education: High school graduation rate: 62.8% (2000); College graduation rate: 3.4% (2000).

School District(s)

Delta R-V (KG-12)
2000 Enrollment: 312 573-794-2500
Housing: Homeownership rate: 70.7% (2000); Median home value: $46,700 (2000); Median rent: $229 per month (2000); Median age of housing: 31 years (2000).
Transportation: Commute to work: 93.2% car, 0.0% public transportation, 1.8% walk, 3.6% work from home (2000); Travel time to work: 14.1% less than 15 minutes, 48.4% 15 to 30 minutes, 21.6% 30 to 45 minutes, 6.6% 45 to 60 minutes, 9.4% 60 minutes or more (2000)

DUTCHTOWN (village). Covers a land area of 0.495 square miles and a water area of 0 square miles. Located at 37.25° N. Lat.; 89.65° W. Long. Elevation is 350 feet.
Population: 99 (2000); Race: 98.0% White, 0.0% Black, 2.0% Asian, 0.0% American Indian and Alaska Native, 0.0% Hispanic of any race, 0.0% two or more races (2000); Density: 200.1 persons per square mile (2000); Age: 19.0% under 18, 19.0% over 64 (2000); Marriage status: 28.1% never married, 61.8% now married, 3.4% widowed, 6.7% divorced (2000); Foreign born: 0.0% (2000); Ancestry (includes multiple ancestries): 36.0% German, 18.0% Irish, 17.0% Other groups, 9.0% Scottish, 8.0% Swedish (2000).
Economy: Employment by occupation: 7.7% management, 13.5% professional, 19.2% services, 23.1% sales, 0.0% farming, 15.4% construction, 21.2% production (2000).
Income: Per capita income: $14,033 (2000); Median household income: $23,750 (2000); Poverty rate: 15.0% (2000).
Taxes: Total city taxes per capita: $283 (2000); City property taxes per capita: $40 (2000).
Education: High school graduation rate: 71.2% (2000); College graduation rate: 9.1% (2000).
Housing: Homeownership rate: 86.0% (2000); Median home value: $71,000 (2000); Median rent: $375 per month (2000); Median age of housing: 35 years (2000).
Transportation: Commute to work: 88.5% car, 0.0% public transportation, 5.8% walk, 5.8% work from home (2000); Travel time to work: 20.4% less than 15 minutes, 63.3% 15 to 30 minutes, 10.2% 30 to 45 minutes, 6.1% 45 to 60 minutes, 0.0% 60 minutes or more (2000)

FRIEDHEIM (unincorporated postal area, zip code 63747). Covers a land area of 21.301 square miles and a water area of 0.007 square miles. Located at 37.55° N. Lat.; 89.80° W. Long. Elevation is 550 feet.
Population: 388 (2000); Race: 100.0% White, 0.0% Black, 0.0% Asian, 0.0% American Indian and Alaska Native, 0.0% Hispanic of any race, 0.0% two or more races (2000); Density: 18.2 persons per square mile (2000); Age: 31.5% under 18, 9.3% over 64 (2000); Marriage status: 15.5% never married, 77.8% now married, 4.9% widowed, 1.8% divorced (2000); Foreign born: 0.0% (2000); Ancestry (includes multiple ancestries): 41.9% German, 24.3% United States or American, 5.2% Irish, 5.2% English, 3.1% Other groups (2000).
Economy: Employment by occupation: 16.1% management, 6.8% professional, 10.7% services, 23.9% sales, 2.0% farming, 10.7% construction, 29.8% production (2000).
Income: Per capita income: $14,300 (2000); Median household income: $39,583 (2000); Poverty rate: 7.2% (2000).
Education: High school graduation rate: 79.8% (2000); College graduation rate: 15.8% (2000).
Housing: Homeownership rate: 80.0% (2000); Median home value: $68,000 (2000); Median rent: $375 per month (2000); Median age of housing: 32 years (2000).
Transportation: Commute to work: 88.7% car, 0.0% public transportation, 1.0% walk, 10.3% work from home (2000); Travel time to work: 20.9% less than 15 minutes, 28.6% 15 to 30 minutes, 36.8% 30 to 45 minutes, 4.4% 45 to 60 minutes, 9.3% 60 minutes or more (2000)

GORDONVILLE (village). Covers a land area of 0.806 square miles and a water area of 0 square miles. Located at 37.31° N. Lat.; 89.67° W. Long. Elevation is 395 feet.
Population: 425 (2000); Race: 98.6% White, 0.0% Black, 0.5% Asian, 0.2% American Indian and Alaska Native, 0.7% Hispanic of any race, 0.7% two or more races (2000); Density: 527.1 persons per square mile (2000); Age: 27.3% under 18, 12.6% over 64 (2000); Marriage status: 20.2% never married, 70.1% now married, 4.8% widowed, 4.8% divorced (2000); Foreign born: 2.0% (2000); Ancestry (includes multiple ancestries): 40.3% German, 13.3% United States or American, 10.8% Irish, 9.5% English, 4.7% Dutch (2000).
Economy: Corn, soybeans; hogs. Manufacturing: advertising specialties. Employment by occupation: 15.9% management, 13.1% professional, 16.7% services, 25.3% sales, 0.8% farming, 12.7% construction, 15.5% production (2000).
Income: Per capita income: $20,763 (2000); Median household income: $53,125 (2000); Poverty rate: 3.9% (2000).
Taxes: Total city taxes per capita: $69 (1997); City property taxes per capita: $36 (1997).
Education: High school graduation rate: 88.4% (2000); College graduation rate: 24.1% (2000).

Housing: Homeownership rate: 91.1% (2000); Median home value: $98,500 (2000); Median rent: $325 per month (2000); Median age of housing: 22 years (2000).
Transportation: Commute to work: 95.5% car, 0.0% public transportation, 2.5% walk, 2.1% work from home (2000); Travel time to work: 22.8% less than 15 minutes, 65.0% 15 to 30 minutes, 6.3% 30 to 45 minutes, 4.6% 45 to 60 minutes, 1.3% 60 minutes or more (2000)

JACKSON (city). Covers a land area of 10.123 square miles and a water area of 0.007 square miles. Located at 37.38° N. Lat.; 89.65° W. Long. Elevation is 497 feet.
History: Jackson was platted in 1814 as the seat of Cape Girardeau County, and named for General Andrew Jackson. A cholera epidemic in 1849 followed by the Civil War resulted in slow growth for Jackson, which later developed as a trading and milling center for an agricultural area.
Population: 11,947 (2000); Race: 96.3% White, 1.7% Black, 0.5% Asian, 0.1% American Indian and Alaska Native, 0.6% Hispanic of any race, 1.2% two or more races (2000); Density: 1,180.2 persons per square mile (2000); Age: 26.1% under 18, 14.1% over 64 (2000); Marriage status: 19.7% never married, 62.2% now married, 8.4% widowed, 9.7% divorced (2000); Foreign born: 0.9% (2000); Ancestry (includes multiple ancestries): 33.3% German, 13.7% United States or American, 9.0% Other groups, 8.8% Irish, 7.3% English (2000).
Economy: Single-family building permits issued: 85 (2001) / 87 (2000); Multi-family building permits issued: 8 (2001) / 26 (2000); Employment by occupation: 10.4% management, 22.3% professional, 12.1% services, 28.5% sales, 0.5% farming, 10.1% construction, 16.0% production (2000).
Income: Per capita income: $18,799 (2000); Median household income: $40,412 (2000); Poverty rate: 6.7% (2000).
Taxes: Total city taxes per capita: $275 (2000); City property taxes per capita: $80 (2000).
Education: High school graduation rate: 81.4% (2000); College graduation rate: 23.7% (2000).

School District(s)

Jackson R-II (PK-12)
2000 Enrollment: 4,608 573-243-9501
Housing: Homeownership rate: 71.5% (2000); Median home value: $96,100 (2000); Median rent: $359 per month (2000); Median age of housing: 25 years (2000).
Safety: Violent crime rate: 25.0 per 10,000 population; Property crime rate: 267.9 per 10,000 population (2001).
Newspapers: Cash-Book Journal (1 x week)
Transportation: Commute to work: 95.2% car, 0.1% public transportation, 0.9% walk, 3.0% work from home (2000); Travel time to work: 34.9% less than 15 minutes, 47.3% 15 to 30 minutes, 10.5% 30 to 45 minutes, 2.9% 45 to 60 minutes, 4.4% 60 minutes or more (2000)
Additional Information Contacts
Jackson Chamber of Commerce. 573-243-8131

MILLERSVILLE (unincorporated postal area, zip code 63766). Covers a land area of 41.056 square miles and a water area of 0.049 square miles. Located at 37.43° N. Lat.; 89.85° W. Long. Elevation is 485 feet.
Population: 944 (2000); Race: 100.0% White, 0.0% Black, 0.0% Asian, 0.0% American Indian and Alaska Native, 0.0% Hispanic of any race, 0.0% two or more races (2000); Density: 23.0 persons per square mile (2000); Age: 28.3% under 18, 14.5% over 64 (2000); Marriage status: 11.1% never married, 75.4% now married, 6.6% widowed, 6.9% divorced (2000); Foreign born: 0.7% (2000); Ancestry (includes multiple ancestries): 31.2% German, 15.7% Irish, 15.4% English, 10.9% United States or American, 9.5% Other groups (2000).
Economy: Employment by occupation: 4.4% management, 7.9% professional, 25.4% services, 26.3% sales, 0.0% farming, 15.4% construction, 20.5% production (2000).
Income: Per capita income: $15,819 (2000); Median household income: $34,857 (2000); Poverty rate: 10.7% (2000).
Education: High school graduation rate: 86.2% (2000); College graduation rate: 14.6% (2000).
Housing: Homeownership rate: 85.6% (2000); Median home value: $87,800 (2000); Median rent: $295 per month (2000); Median age of housing: 23 years (2000).
Transportation: Commute to work: 99.3% car, 0.0% public transportation, 0.0% walk, 0.7% work from home (2000); Travel time to work: 8.2% less than 15 minutes, 33.1% 15 to 30 minutes, 35.4% 30 to 45 minutes, 10.3% 45 to 60 minutes, 13.1% 60 minutes or more (2000)

OAK RIDGE (town). Covers a land area of 0.368 square miles and a water area of 0 square miles. Located at 37.50° N. Lat.; 89.73° W. Long. Elevation is 610 feet.
Population: 202 (2000); Race: 97.2% White, 1.9% Black, 0.0% Asian, 0.9% American Indian and Alaska Native, 0.0% Hispanic of any race, 0.0% two or more races (2000); Density: 549.3 persons per square mile (2000); Age: 20.6% under 18, 14.0% over 64 (2000); Marriage status: 8.6% never married, 71.3% now married, 5.7% widowed, 14.4% divorced (2000); Foreign born: 0.0% (2000); Ancestry (includes multiple ancestries): 35.5% German, 11.7% Irish, 7.5% Other groups, 5.1% Dutch, 4.7% English (2000).
Economy: Employment by occupation: 10.3% management, 15.5% professional, 16.4% services, 13.8% sales, 0.0% farming, 13.8% construction, 30.2% production (2000).
Income: Per capita income: $18,310 (2000); Median household income: $32,188 (2000); Poverty rate: 4.7% (2000).
Taxes: Total city taxes per capita: $37 (1997); City property taxes per capita: $37 (1997).
Education: High school graduation rate: 66.9% (2000); College graduation rate: 14.7% (2000).

School District(s)

Oak Ridge R-VI (PK-12)
2000 Enrollment: 390 573-266-3218
Housing: Homeownership rate: 91.7% (2000); Median home value: $38,300 (2000); Median rent: $335 per month (2000); Median age of housing: 54 years (2000).
Transportation: Commute to work: 92.1% car, 0.0% public transportation, 1.8% walk, 3.5% work from home (2000); Travel time to work: 18.2% less than 15 minutes, 23.6% 15 to 30 minutes, 48.2% 30 to 45 minutes, 10.0% 45 to 60 minutes, 0.0% 60 minutes or more (2000)

OLD APPLETON (town). Aka Appleton. Covers a land area of 0.123 square miles and a water area of 0 square miles. Located at 37.59° N. Lat.; 89.70° W. Long.
History: Old Appleton was established in the 1820's when Appleton Mill was built on Apple Creek. Among the early residents were many Roman Catholic families from Kentucky and a group of German immigrants from Baden.
Population: 82 (2000); Race: 100.0% White, 0.0% Black, 0.0% Asian, 0.0% American Indian and Alaska Native, 0.0% Hispanic of any race, 0.0% two or more races (2000); Density: 665.8 persons per square mile (2000); Age: 24.6% under 18, 3.1% over 64 (2000); Marriage status: 12.2% never married, 79.6% now married, 4.1% widowed, 4.1% divorced (2000); Foreign born: 0.0% (2000); Ancestry (includes multiple ancestries): 53.8% German, 30.8% United States or American, 10.8% French (except Basque), 9.2% Austrian, 7.7% Irish (2000).
Economy: Employment by occupation: 11.1% management, 0.0% professional, 0.0% services, 41.7% sales, 0.0% farming, 8.3% construction, 38.9% production (2000).
Income: Per capita income: $20,894 (2000); Median household income: $47,500 (2000); Poverty rate: 0.0% (2000).
Taxes: Total city taxes per capita: $11 (1997); City property taxes per capita: $11 (1997).
Education: High school graduation rate: 88.9% (2000); College graduation rate: 11.1% (2000).
Housing: Homeownership rate: 70.8% (2000); Median home value: $55,000 (2000); Median age of housing: 47 years (2000).
Transportation: Commute to work: 83.9% car, 0.0% public transportation, 0.0% walk, 6.5% work from home (2000); Travel time to work: 10.3% less than 15 minutes, 34.5% 15 to 30 minutes, 34.5% 30 to 45 minutes, 20.7% 45 to 60 minutes, 0.0% 60 minutes or more (2000)

POCAHONTAS (town). Covers a land area of 0.099 square miles and a water area of 0 square miles. Located at 37.50° N. Lat.; 89.63° W. Long. Elevation is 575 feet.
Population: 127 (2000); Race: 100.0% White, 0.0% Black, 0.0% Asian, 0.0% American Indian and Alaska Native, 0.0% Hispanic of any race, 0.0% two or more races (2000); Density: 1,280.9 persons per square mile (2000); Age: 35.5% under 18, 7.5% over 64 (2000); Marriage status: 21.6% never married, 67.6% now married, 5.4% widowed, 5.4% divorced (2000); Foreign born: 0.0% (2000); Ancestry (includes multiple ancestries): 48.6% German, 23.4% Irish, 11.2% Dutch, 5.6% English, 3.7% United States or American (2000).
Economy: Employment by occupation: 6.0% management, 12.0% professional, 18.0% services, 16.0% sales, 0.0% farming, 16.0% construction, 32.0% production (2000).

Income: Per capita income: $13,650 (2000); Median household income: $36,250 (2000); Poverty rate: 3.7% (2000).
Taxes: Total city taxes per capita: $15 (1997); City property taxes per capita: $15 (1997).
Education: High school graduation rate: 69.4% (2000); College graduation rate: 3.2% (2000).
Housing: Homeownership rate: 95.0% (2000); Median home value: $52,500 (2000); Median rent: $375 per month (2000); Median age of housing: 46 years (2000).
Transportation: Commute to work: 86.0% car, 0.0% public transportation, 6.0% walk, 8.0% work from home (2000); Travel time to work: 21.7% less than 15 minutes, 56.5% 15 to 30 minutes, 21.7% 30 to 45 minutes, 0.0% 45 to 60 minutes, 0.0% 60 minutes or more (2000)

WHITEWATER (town). Aka White Water. Covers a land area of 0.200 square miles and a water area of 0 square miles. Located at 37.23° N. Lat.; 89.79° W. Long. Elevation is 370 feet.
Population: 113 (2000); Race: 96.0% White, 0.0% Black, 1.6% Asian, 0.0% American Indian and Alaska Native, 4.0% Hispanic of any race, 2.4% two or more races (2000); Density: 564.0 persons per square mile (2000); Age: 22.6% under 18, 23.4% over 64 (2000); Marriage status: 12.5% never married, 69.8% now married, 9.4% widowed, 8.3% divorced (2000); Foreign born: 1.6% (2000); Ancestry (includes multiple ancestries): 15.3% United States or American, 11.3% German, 11.3% Other groups, 8.9% English, 7.3% Irish (2000).
Economy: Employment by occupation: 9.1% management, 13.6% professional, 4.5% services, 15.9% sales, 4.5% farming, 0.0% construction, 52.3% production (2000).
Income: Per capita income: $11,533 (2000); Median household income: $26,750 (2000); Poverty rate: 30.6% (2000).
Taxes: Total city taxes per capita: $55 (1997); City property taxes per capita: $55 (1997).
Education: High school graduation rate: 74.4% (2000); College graduation rate: 14.1% (2000).
Housing: Homeownership rate: 89.6% (2000); Median home value: $43,600 (2000); Median rent: $250 per month (2000); Median age of housing: 40 years (2000).
Transportation: Commute to work: 100.0% car, 0.0% public transportation, 0.0% walk, 0.0% work from home (2000); Travel time to work: 11.4% less than 15 minutes, 47.7% 15 to 30 minutes, 36.4% 30 to 45 minutes, 0.0% 45 to 60 minutes, 4.5% 60 minutes or more (2000)

Carroll County

Located in northwest central Missouri; bounded on the south by the Missouri River, and on the east by the Grand River. Covers a land area of 694.70 square miles, a water area of 7.60 square miles, and is located in the Central Time Zone. The county government was organized in 1833. County seat is Carrollton.

Weather Station: Carrollton — Elevation: 702 feet

	Jan	Feb	Mar	Apr	May	Jun	Jul	Aug	Sep	Oct	Nov	Dec
High	36	43	55	67	77	86	90	88	80	68	52	41
Low	18	23	33	43	53	63	67	65	56	45	33	23
Precip	1.5	1.6	2.9	4.2	5.1	4.5	4.2	4.1	4.7	3.5	3.0	2.2
Snow	7.5	6.1	3.2	0.7	0.0	0.0	0.0	0.0	0.0	0.2	1.4	3.7

High and Low temperatures in degrees Fahrenheit; Precipitation and Snow in inches

Population: 10,285 (2000); Race: 97.1% White, 1.4% Black, 0.0% Asian, 0.6% American Indian and Alaska Native, 1.1% Hispanic of any race, 0.8% two or more races (2000); Density: 14.8 persons per square mile (2000); Age: 25.1% under 18, 20.1% over 64 (2000).
Religion: Five largest groups: 37.8% Southern Baptist Convention, 11.6% The United Methodist Church, 6.7% Lutheran Church—Missouri Synod, 6.1% Christian Church (Disciples of Christ), 5.8% Catholic Church (2000).
Economy: Unemployment rate: 5.1% (11/2002); Total civilian labor force: 5,013 (11/2002); Leading industries: 25.4% manufacturing; 14.1% retail trade; 9.6% health care and social assistance (2000); Companies that employ more than 1,000 persons: 0 (2000); Companies that employ more than 100 persons: 3 (2000); Farms: 952 totaling 395,657 acres (1997); Minority business ownership rate: 0.0% (1997); Women business ownership rate: 16.8% (1997); Retail sales per capita: $3,556 (1997). Single-family building permits issued: 1 (2001) / 6 (2000); Multi-family building permits issued: 0 (2001) / 0 (2000).
Income: Per capita income: $15,522 (2000); Median household income: $30,643 (2000); Poverty rate: 13.7% (2000); Bankruptcy rate: 2.54% (2001).
Taxes: Total county taxes per capita: $62 (1997); County property taxes per capita: $36 (1997).
Education: High school graduation rate: 79.1% (2000); College graduation rate: 14.0% (2000).
Housing: Homeownership rate: 74.0% (2000); Median home value: $48,900 (2000); Median rent: $229 per month (2000); Median age of housing: 44 years (2000).
Health: Birth rate: 126.4 per 10,000 population (1998); Age adjusted death rate: 85.3 per 10,000 population (1999); Age adjusted cancer mortality rate: 276.4 deaths per 100,000 population (1999). Number of physicians: 1.0 per 10,000 population (1999); Number of hospital beds: 48.6 per 10,000 population (1999).
Elections: 2000 Presidential election results: 35.4% Gore, 62.9% Bush, 1.2% Nader, 0.3% Buchanan
Additional Information Contacts
Carroll County Government Offices 660-542-0615

Carroll County Communities

BOGARD (city). Covers a land area of 0.546 square miles and a water area of 0 square miles. Located at 39.45° N. Lat.; 93.52° W. Long. Elevation is 865 feet.
Population: 234 (2000); Race: 100.0% White, 0.0% Black, 0.0% Asian, 0.0% American Indian and Alaska Native, 0.8% Hispanic of any race, 0.0% two or more races (2000); Density: 429.0 persons per square mile (2000); Age: 19.6% under 18, 29.0% over 64 (2000); Marriage status: 10.7% never married, 69.4% now married, 13.6% widowed, 6.3% divorced (2000); Foreign born: 0.8% (2000); Ancestry (includes multiple ancestries): 22.0% German, 15.1% Irish, 11.4% United States or American, 11.4% English, 8.2% Other groups (2000).
Economy: Corn; hogs, cattle. Employment by occupation: 12.4% management, 1.9% professional, 11.4% services, 21.0% sales, 3.8% farming, 9.5% construction, 40.0% production (2000).
Income: Per capita income: $17,208 (2000); Median household income: $22,639 (2000); Poverty rate: 13.1% (2000).
Taxes: Total city taxes per capita: $49 (1997); City property taxes per capita: $18 (1997).
Education: High school graduation rate: 70.4% (2000); College graduation rate: 3.7% (2000).
Housing: Homeownership rate: 87.0% (2000); Median home value: $20,500 (2000); Median rent: $205 per month (2000); Median age of housing: 60+ years (2000).
Transportation: Commute to work: 90.5% car, 1.9% public transportation, 0.0% walk, 5.7% work from home (2000); Travel time to work: 6.1% less than 15 minutes, 43.4% 15 to 30 minutes, 18.2% 30 to 45 minutes, 17.2% 45 to 60 minutes, 15.2% 60 minutes or more (2000)

BOSWORTH (city). Covers a land area of 0.553 square miles and a water area of 0 square miles. Located at 39.47° N. Lat.; 93.33° W. Long. Elevation is 765 feet.
Population: 382 (2000); Race: 100.0% White, 0.0% Black, 0.0% Asian, 0.0% American Indian and Alaska Native, 0.0% Hispanic of any race, 0.0% two or more races (2000); Density: 691.0 persons per square mile (2000); Age: 31.6% under 18, 12.8% over 64 (2000); Marriage status: 19.7% never married, 62.8% now married, 8.0% widowed, 9.5% divorced (2000); Foreign born: 0.0% (2000); Ancestry (includes multiple ancestries): 25.5% United States or American, 15.4% German, 8.8% English, 6.9% Other groups, 5.3% Irish (2000).
Economy: Wheat, corn, soybeans; hogs. Manufacturing: apparel. Employment by occupation: 4.6% management, 7.8% professional, 19.0% services, 14.4% sales, 4.6% farming, 11.1% construction, 38.6% production (2000).
Income: Per capita income: $11,526 (2000); Median household income: $25,357 (2000); Poverty rate: 15.4% (2000).
Taxes: Total city taxes per capita: $71 (1997); City property taxes per capita: $41 (1997).
Education: High school graduation rate: 73.6% (2000); College graduation rate: 5.6% (2000).

School District(s)

Bosworth R-V (PK-12)
2000 Enrollment: 177 660-534-7311
Housing: Homeownership rate: 88.1% (2000); Median home value: $19,300 (2000); Median rent: $175 per month (2000); Median age of housing: 60+ years (2000).

Transportation: Commute to work: 94.7% car, 0.7% public transportation, 0.7% walk, 2.6% work from home (2000); Travel time to work: 16.9% less than 15 minutes, 31.1% 15 to 30 minutes, 15.5% 30 to 45 minutes, 5.4% 45 to 60 minutes, 31.1% 60 minutes or more (2000)

CARROLLTON (city). Covers a land area of 4.264 square miles and a water area of 0.013 square miles. Located at 39.35° N. Lat.; 93.49° W. Long. Elevation is 754 feet.
History: The first settlers in Carrollton were John Standley and his seven sons, who came in 1819. When Carroll County (named for Charles Carroll, a signer of the Declaration of Independence) was organized in 1833, Standley donated land for the county seat.
Population: 4,122 (2000); Race: 95.7% White, 2.5% Black, 0.1% Asian, 0.5% American Indian and Alaska Native, 1.9% Hispanic of any race, 0.9% two or more races (2000); Density: 966.7 persons per square mile (2000); Age: 23.4% under 18, 23.9% over 64 (2000); Marriage status: 14.7% never married, 58.9% now married, 14.3% widowed, 12.1% divorced (2000); Foreign born: 0.5% (2000); Ancestry (includes multiple ancestries): 23.7% German, 14.1% United States or American, 13.0% English, 10.5% Irish, 8.6% Other groups (2000).
Economy: Single-family building permits issued: 1 (2001) / 6 (2000); Multi-family building permits issued: 0 (2001) / 0 (2000); Employment by occupation: 11.7% management, 15.8% professional, 16.3% services, 17.9% sales, 1.3% farming, 8.1% construction, 28.8% production (2000).
Income: Per capita income: $15,295 (2000); Median household income: $27,161 (2000); Poverty rate: 16.1% (2000).
Taxes: Total city taxes per capita: $305 (1997); City property taxes per capita: $102 (1997).
Education: High school graduation rate: 73.4% (2000); College graduation rate: 13.9% (2000).

School District(s)

Carrollton R-VII (PK-12)
2000 Enrollment: 1,076 660-542-2769

Housing: Homeownership rate: 64.0% (2000); Median home value: $55,200 (2000); Median rent: $240 per month (2000); Median age of housing: 41 years (2000).
Hospitals: Carroll County Memorial Hospital (77 beds)
Newspapers: Carrollton Daily Democrat (2 x week)
Transportation: Commute to work: 95.1% car, 0.0% public transportation, 1.6% walk, 2.2% work from home (2000); Travel time to work: 63.0% less than 15 minutes, 11.1% 15 to 30 minutes, 12.5% 30 to 45 minutes, 6.7% 45 to 60 minutes, 6.7% 60 minutes or more (2000)

DE WITT (city). Covers a land area of 0.247 square miles and a water area of 0 square miles. Located at 39.38° N. Lat.; 93.22° W. Long. Elevation is 782 feet.
History: De Witt was platted along the Missouri River in 1837. The town became the center of a conflict in 1838 when the residents resisted the purchase of lots by Mormons, who wanted to create a Mormon settlement. The Mormons agreed to leave.
Population: 120 (2000); Race: 88.2% White, 2.0% Black, 0.0% Asian, 5.9% American Indian and Alaska Native, 0.0% Hispanic of any race, 3.9% two or more races (2000); Density: 486.5 persons per square mile (2000); Age: 22.5% under 18, 11.8% over 64 (2000); Marriage status: 21.3% never married, 68.8% now married, 0.0% widowed, 10.0% divorced (2000); Foreign born: 0.0% (2000); Ancestry (includes multiple ancestries): 27.5% German, 22.5% Other groups, 18.6% Irish, 11.8% English, 7.8% United States or American (2000).
Economy: Employment by occupation: 6.9% management, 15.5% professional, 15.5% services, 10.3% sales, 0.0% farming, 13.8% construction, 37.9% production (2000).
Income: Per capita income: $15,030 (2000); Median household income: $28,500 (2000); Poverty rate: 6.9% (2000).
Taxes: Total city taxes per capita: $73 (1997); City property taxes per capita: $40 (1997).
Education: High school graduation rate: 81.5% (2000); College graduation rate: 9.2% (2000).
Housing: Homeownership rate: 79.1% (2000); Median home value: $17,500 (2000); Median rent: $163 per month (2000); Median age of housing: 60+ years (2000).
Transportation: Commute to work: 96.6% car, 0.0% public transportation, 0.0% walk, 3.4% work from home (2000); Travel time to work: 21.4% less than 15 minutes, 30.4% 15 to 30 minutes, 39.3% 30 to 45 minutes, 3.6% 45 to 60 minutes, 5.4% 60 minutes or more (2000)

HALE (city). Covers a land area of 0.550 square miles and a water area of 0 square miles. Located at 39.60° N. Lat.; 93.34° W. Long. Elevation is 765 feet.
Population: 473 (2000); Race: 98.4% White, 0.0% Black, 0.0% Asian, 0.6% American Indian and Alaska Native, 1.8% Hispanic of any race, 1.0% two or more races (2000); Density: 859.8 persons per square mile (2000); Age: 31.8% under 18, 18.1% over 64 (2000); Marriage status: 17.8% never married, 63.1% now married, 8.3% widowed, 10.8% divorced (2000); Foreign born: 1.6% (2000); Ancestry (includes multiple ancestries): 27.0% United States or American, 17.8% German, 9.9% Irish, 5.9% Other groups, 3.7% English (2000).
Economy: Wheat, corn, soybeans; hogs, cattle; feed and fertilizer. Employment by occupation: 8.1% management, 11.9% professional, 13.3% services, 20.5% sales, 0.0% farming, 11.4% construction, 34.8% production (2000).
Income: Per capita income: $12,180 (2000); Median household income: $27,885 (2000); Poverty rate: 19.1% (2000).
Taxes: Total city taxes per capita: $110 (1997); City property taxes per capita: $48 (1997).
Education: High school graduation rate: 77.2% (2000); College graduation rate: 8.6% (2000).

School District(s)

Hale R-I (PK-12)
2000 Enrollment: 177 660-565-2417

Housing: Homeownership rate: 81.1% (2000); Median home value: $26,800 (2000); Median rent: $210 per month (2000); Median age of housing: 52 years (2000).
Transportation: Commute to work: 91.0% car, 0.0% public transportation, 5.7% walk, 3.3% work from home (2000); Travel time to work: 28.6% less than 15 minutes, 15.8% 15 to 30 minutes, 39.4% 30 to 45 minutes, 4.4% 45 to 60 minutes, 11.8% 60 minutes or more (2000)

NORBORNE (city). Covers a land area of 0.626 square miles and a water area of 0 square miles. Located at 39.30° N. Lat.; 93.67° W. Long. Elevation is 692 feet.
History: Laid out 1868.
Population: 805 (2000); Race: 94.3% White, 3.6% Black, 0.0% Asian, 2.0% American Indian and Alaska Native, 2.9% Hispanic of any race, 0.0% two or more races (2000); Density: 1,285.0 persons per square mile (2000); Age: 24.7% under 18, 20.5% over 64 (2000); Marriage status: 14.1% never married, 59.5% now married, 13.7% widowed, 12.7% divorced (2000); Foreign born: 0.0% (2000); Ancestry (includes multiple ancestries): 30.3% German, 14.0% English, 13.3% Irish, 12.8% United States or American, 12.2% Other groups (2000).
Economy: Wheat, corn, soybeans; hogs, cattle. Employment by occupation: 14.6% management, 11.0% professional, 14.3% services, 15.6% sales, 5.5% farming, 18.8% construction, 20.1% production (2000).
Income: Per capita income: $14,526 (2000); Median household income: $25,208 (2000); Poverty rate: 15.8% (2000).
Taxes: Total city taxes per capita: $148 (1997); City property taxes per capita: $45 (1997).
Education: High school graduation rate: 80.3% (2000); College graduation rate: 10.1% (2000).

School District(s)

Norborne R-VIII (PK-12)
2000 Enrollment: 237 660-593-3319

Housing: Homeownership rate: 72.8% (2000); Median home value: $41,900 (2000); Median rent: $213 per month (2000); Median age of housing: 51 years (2000).
Newspapers: Norborne Democrat-Leader (1 x week)
Transportation: Commute to work: 95.0% car, 0.0% public transportation, 3.7% walk, 1.3% work from home (2000); Travel time to work: 34.1% less than 15 minutes, 23.3% 15 to 30 minutes, 13.9% 30 to 45 minutes, 4.7% 45 to 60 minutes, 24.0% 60 minutes or more (2000)

TINA (village). Covers a land area of 0.346 square miles and a water area of 0 square miles. Located at 39.53° N. Lat.; 93.43° W. Long. Elevation is 722 feet.
Population: 193 (2000); Race: 100.0% White, 0.0% Black, 0.0% Asian, 0.0% American Indian and Alaska Native, 0.0% Hispanic of any race, 0.0% two or more races (2000); Density: 557.1 persons per square mile (2000); Age: 27.2% under 18, 18.8% over 64 (2000); Marriage status: 22.6% never married, 65.8% now married, 8.4% widowed, 3.2% divorced (2000); Foreign born: 2.5% (2000); Ancestry (includes multiple ancestries): 22.3% United

States or American, 13.4% German, 11.9% English, 9.9% Irish, 6.4% French (except Basque) (2000).
Economy: Employment by occupation: 2.4% management, 6.1% professional, 8.5% services, 36.6% sales, 0.0% farming, 22.0% construction, 24.4% production (2000).
Income: Per capita income: $11,485 (2000); Median household income: $29,167 (2000); Poverty rate: 8.9% (2000).
Taxes: Total city taxes per capita: $36 (1997); City property taxes per capita: $10 (1997).
Education: High school graduation rate: 78.0% (2000); College graduation rate: 3.9% (2000).

School District(s)

Tina-Avalon R-II (PK-12)
2000 Enrollment: 209 660-622-4211
Housing: Homeownership rate: 76.6% (2000); Median home value: $38,800 (2000); Median rent: $208 per month (2000); Median age of housing: 46 years (2000).
Transportation: Commute to work: 96.3% car, 0.0% public transportation, 0.0% walk, 1.2% work from home (2000); Travel time to work: 28.4% less than 15 minutes, 29.6% 15 to 30 minutes, 14.8% 30 to 45 minutes, 7.4% 45 to 60 minutes, 19.8% 60 minutes or more (2000)

Carter County

Located in southern Missouri, in the Ozarks; drained by the Current River; includes part of Clark National Forest. Covers a land area of 507.60 square miles, a water area of 1.40 square miles, and is located in the Central Time Zone. The county government was organized in 1859. County seat is Van Buren.
Population: 5,941 (2000); Race: 95.5% White, 0.1% Black, 0.1% Asian, 1.6% American Indian and Alaska Native, 1.0% Hispanic of any race, 2.5% two or more races (2000); Density: 11.7 persons per square mile (2000); Age: 25.2% under 18, 15.9% over 64 (2000).
Religion: Five largest groups: 21.3% Southern Baptist Convention, 5.0% Assemblies of God, 2.4% Catholic Church, 2.1% Baptist Missionary Association of America, 1.6% Church of God of Prophecy (2000).
Economy: Unemployment rate: 5.9% (11/2002); Total civilian labor force: 2,592 (11/2002); Leading industries: 31.2% manufacturing; 21.6% retail trade; 11.4% health care and social assistance (2000); Companies that employ more than 1,000 persons: 0 (2000); Companies that employ more than 100 persons: 0 (2000); Farms: 202 totaling 62,899 acres (1997); Minority business ownership rate: 0.0% (1997); Women business ownership rate: 17.1% (1997); Retail sales per capita: $2,829 (1997). Single-family building permits issued: 4 (2001) / 1 (2000); Multi-family building permits issued: 0 (2001) / 0 (2000).
Income: Per capita income: $13,349 (2000); Median household income: $22,863 (2000); Poverty rate: 25.2% (2000); Bankruptcy rate: 3.42% (2001).
Taxes: Total county taxes per capita: $35 (1997); County property taxes per capita: $14 (1997).
Education: High school graduation rate: 66.6% (2000); College graduation rate: 10.8% (2000).
Housing: Homeownership rate: 76.7% (2000); Median home value: $51,900 (2000); Median rent: $216 per month (2000); Median age of housing: 25 years (2000).
Health: Birth rate: 149.8 per 10,000 population (1998); Age adjusted death rate: 113.4 per 10,000 population (1999); Age adjusted cancer mortality rate: 175.0 (Unreliable figure as per CDC) deaths per 100,000 population (1999). Number of physicians: n/a (1999); Number of hospital beds: n/a (1999).
Elections: 2000 Presidential election results: 35.5% Gore, 61.6% Bush, 1.4% Nader, 0.9% Buchanan
National and State Parks: Big Spring State Park; Mark Twain National Forest; Miller Community Lake State Wildlife Area; Ozark National Scenic Riverways; Peck Ranch State Wildlife Management Area
Additional Information Contacts
Carter County Government Offices 573-323-4527
Van Buren Chamber of Commerce 573-323-4782

Carter County Communities

ELLSINORE (city). Aka Elsinore. Covers a land area of 0.437 square miles and a water area of 0 square miles. Located at 36.93° N. Lat.; 90.74° W. Long. Elevation is 711 feet.
History: Ellsinore grew up around a sawmill within the Clark National Forest.
Population: 363 (2000); Race: 98.0% White, 0.0% Black, 0.0% Asian, 0.0% American Indian and Alaska Native, 0.8% Hispanic of any race, 2.0% two or more races (2000); Density: 830.7 persons per square mile (2000); Age: 24.6% under 18, 27.2% over 64 (2000); Marriage status: 13.7% never married, 50.5% now married, 21.1% widowed, 14.7% divorced (2000); Foreign born: 0.0% (2000); Ancestry (includes multiple ancestries): 18.1% Irish, 15.3% German, 14.4% Other groups, 14.2% English, 12.5% United States or American (2000).
Economy: Employment by occupation: 3.4% management, 18.6% professional, 8.5% services, 13.6% sales, 0.0% farming, 10.2% construction, 45.8% production (2000).
Income: Per capita income: $11,444 (2000); Median household income: $17,143 (2000); Poverty rate: 19.7% (2000).
Taxes: Total city taxes per capita: $263 (1997); City property taxes per capita: $210 (1997).
Education: High school graduation rate: 62.2% (2000); College graduation rate: 8.8% (2000).

School District(s)

East Carter Co. R-II (PK-12)
2000 Enrollment: 800 573-322-5625
Housing: Homeownership rate: 54.8% (2000); Median home value: $40,000 (2000); Median rent: $225 per month (2000); Median age of housing: 32 years (2000).
Transportation: Commute to work: 93.2% car, 0.0% public transportation, 2.5% walk, 0.0% work from home (2000); Travel time to work: 54.2% less than 15 minutes, 4.2% 15 to 30 minutes, 26.3% 30 to 45 minutes, 4.2% 45 to 60 minutes, 11.0% 60 minutes or more (2000)

FREMONT (unincorporated postal area, zip code 63941). Covers a land area of 178.414 square miles and a water area of 0.033 square miles. Located at 36.91° N. Lat.; 91.15° W. Long. Elevation is 621 feet.
Population: 536 (2000); Race: 94.3% White, 0.0% Black, 0.4% Asian, 0.6% American Indian and Alaska Native, 2.1% Hispanic of any race, 4.7% two or more races (2000); Density: 3.0 persons per square mile (2000); Age: 22.5% under 18, 23.3% over 64 (2000); Marriage status: 22.3% never married, 58.7% now married, 8.1% widowed, 10.9% divorced (2000); Foreign born: 0.4% (2000); Ancestry (includes multiple ancestries): 27.3% United States or American, 19.9% Irish, 16.5% German, 9.5% Other groups, 5.3% Dutch (2000).
Economy: In Ozark region, in Mark Twain National Forest. Employment by occupation: 3.2% management, 23.7% professional, 15.1% services, 21.5% sales, 7.5% farming, 5.9% construction, 23.1% production (2000).
Income: Per capita income: $11,763 (2000); Median household income: $22,857 (2000); Poverty rate: 26.3% (2000).
Education: High school graduation rate: 66.8% (2000); College graduation rate: 11.1% (2000).
Housing: Homeownership rate: 76.2% (2000); Median home value: $50,800 (2000); Median rent: $290 per month (2000); Median age of housing: 29 years (2000).
Transportation: Commute to work: 94.6% car, 0.0% public transportation, 0.0% walk, 0.0% work from home (2000); Travel time to work: 37.1% less than 15 minutes, 22.0% 15 to 30 minutes, 11.3% 30 to 45 minutes, 15.6% 45 to 60 minutes, 14.0% 60 minutes or more (2000)

GRANDIN (city). Covers a land area of 0.398 square miles and a water area of 0 square miles. Located at 36.83° N. Lat.; 90.82° W. Long. Elevation is 585 feet.
History: Grandin was founded in 1887 by the Missouri Lumber and Mining Company, and developed around a large lumber mill. When the company closed down in 1910, the former employees built their own mill and continued the industry.
Population: 236 (2000); Race: 96.3% White, 0.0% Black, 0.0% Asian, 0.0% American Indian and Alaska Native, 0.0% Hispanic of any race, 3.7% two or more races (2000); Density: 592.2 persons per square mile (2000); Age: 21.2% under 18, 10.8% over 64 (2000); Marriage status: 14.6% never married, 65.8% now married, 2.0% widowed, 17.6% divorced (2000); Foreign born: 0.0% (2000); Ancestry (includes multiple ancestries): 24.1% Other groups, 16.2% Irish, 15.4% German, 10.4% United States or American, 6.6% English (2000).
Economy: Employment by occupation: 0.0% management, 9.8% professional, 16.3% services, 13.0% sales, 4.3% farming, 18.5% construction, 38.0% production (2000).
Income: Per capita income: $10,497 (2000); Median household income: $19,844 (2000); Poverty rate: 28.6% (2000).
Taxes: Total city taxes per capita: $238 (1997); City property taxes per capita: $19 (1997).

Education: High school graduation rate: 48.0% (2000); College graduation rate: 7.4% (2000).
Housing: Homeownership rate: 60.9% (2000); Median home value: $27,800 (2000); Median rent: $187 per month (2000); Median age of housing: 29 years (2000).
Transportation: Commute to work: 92.4% car, 3.3% public transportation, 2.2% walk, 2.2% work from home (2000); Travel time to work: 13.3% less than 15 minutes, 21.1% 15 to 30 minutes, 33.3% 30 to 45 minutes, 17.8% 45 to 60 minutes, 14.4% 60 minutes or more (2000)

VAN BUREN (town). Covers a land area of 2.000 square miles and a water area of 0 square miles. Located at 37.00° N. Lat.; 91.01° W. Long. Elevation is 475 feet.
History: Van Buren developed as a fishing resort on the Current River, and as the seat of Carter County since 1859. Before the formation of Carter County, Van Buren was the seat of Ripley County.
Population: 845 (2000); Race: 96.6% White, 0.0% Black, 0.0% Asian, 1.4% American Indian and Alaska Native, 0.9% Hispanic of any race, 2.1% two or more races (2000); Density: 422.6 persons per square mile (2000); Age: 22.7% under 18, 25.7% over 64 (2000); Marriage status: 18.6% never married, 53.6% now married, 15.9% widowed, 11.9% divorced (2000); Foreign born: 0.0% (2000); Ancestry (includes multiple ancestries): 12.2% United States or American, 12.1% German, 8.6% Other groups, 8.6% Irish, 8.4% English (2000).
Economy: Single-family building permits issued: 4 (2001) / 1 (2000); Multi-family building permits issued: 0 (2001) / 0 (2000); Employment by occupation: 12.6% management, 18.4% professional, 15.2% services, 22.0% sales, 0.0% farming, 14.1% construction, 17.7% production (2000).
Income: Per capita income: $13,061 (2000); Median household income: $19,766 (2000); Poverty rate: 25.0% (2000).
Taxes: Total city taxes per capita: $72 (1997); City property taxes per capita: $10 (1997).
Education: High school graduation rate: 66.5% (2000); College graduation rate: 11.9% (2000).

School District(s)

Van Buren R-I (PK-12)
2000 Enrollment: 543 573-323-4281
Housing: Homeownership rate: 68.8% (2000); Median home value: $56,900 (2000); Median rent: $220 per month (2000); Median age of housing: 34 years (2000).
Newspapers: The Current Local (1 x week)
Transportation: Commute to work: 88.7% car, 0.0% public transportation, 5.3% walk, 4.5% work from home (2000); Travel time to work: 66.1% less than 15 minutes, 10.6% 15 to 30 minutes, 7.9% 30 to 45 minutes, 5.9% 45 to 60 minutes, 9.4% 60 minutes or more (2000)
Additional Information Contacts
Van Buren Chamber of Commerce 573-323-4782

Cass County

Located in western Missouri; bounded on the west by Kansas; drained by the South Grand River. Covers a land area of 699.00 square miles, a water area of 3.70 square miles, and is located in the Central Time Zone. The county government was organized in 1835. County seat is Harrisonville.

Cass County is part of the Kansas City, MO-KS MSA. The entire metro area includes: Johnson County, KS; Leavenworth County, KS; Miami County, KS; Wyandotte County, KS; Cass County, MO; Clay County, MO; Clinton County, MO; Jackson County, MO; Lafayette County, MO; Platte County, MO; Ray County, MO

Population: 82,092 (2000); Race: 95.4% White, 1.6% Black, 0.4% Asian, 0.5% American Indian and Alaska Native, 2.0% Hispanic of any race, 1.5% two or more races (2000); Density: 117.4 persons per square mile (2000); Age: 28.3% under 18, 11.7% over 64 (2000).
Religion: Five largest groups: 17.8% Southern Baptist Convention, 5.8% Catholic Church, 5.3% The United Methodist Church, 3.7% Christian Church (Disciples of Christ), 1.2% Church of the Nazarene (2000).
Economy: Unemployment rate: 4.1% (11/2002); Total civilian labor force: 47,921 (11/2002); Leading industries: 22.0% retail trade; 15.3% construction; 14.6% health care and social assistance (2000); Companies that employ more than 1,000 persons: 0 (2000); Companies that employ more than 100 persons: 17 (2000); Farms: 1,519 totaling 310,479 acres (1997); Minority business ownership rate: 6.0% (1997); Women business ownership rate: 25.4% (1997); Retail sales per capita: $6,315 (1997). Single-family building permits issued: 648 (2001) / 637 (2000); Multi-family building permits issued: 355 (2001) / 174 (2000).
Income: Per capita income: $21,073 (2000); Median household income: $49,562 (2000); Poverty rate: 5.8% (2000); Bankruptcy rate: 4.88% (2001).
Taxes: Total county taxes per capita: $115 (2000); County property taxes per capita: $106 (2000).
Education: High school graduation rate: 86.7% (2000); College graduation rate: 17.7% (2000).
Housing: Homeownership rate: 79.6% (2000); Median home value: $104,200 (2000); Median rent: $418 per month (2000); Median age of housing: 21 years (2000).
Health: Birth rate: 142.4 per 10,000 population (1998); Age adjusted death rate: 83.2 per 10,000 population (1999); Age adjusted cancer mortality rate: 211.4 deaths per 100,000 population (1999). Air Quality Index: 64% good, 36% moderate, 0% unhealthy (percent of days in 2000). Number of physicians: 4.6 per 10,000 population (1999); Number of hospital beds: 10.2 per 10,000 population (1999).
Elections: 2000 Presidential election results: 41.6% Gore, 56.1% Bush, 1.4% Nader, 0.4% Buchanan
Additional Information Contacts
Cass County Government Offices 816-380-8100
Belton Chamber of Commerce 816-331-2420
Harrisonville Area Chamber 816-380-5271
Pleasant Hill Chamber of Commerce 816-987-2595
Raymore Chamber of Commerce 816-322-0599

Cass County Communities

ARCHIE (city). Covers a land area of 1.024 square miles and a water area of 0.002 square miles. Located at 38.48° N. Lat.; 94.35° W. Long. Elevation is 832 feet.
Population: 890 (2000); Race: 99.0% White, 0.0% Black, 0.0% Asian, 0.8% American Indian and Alaska Native, 0.0% Hispanic of any race, 0.2% two or more races (2000); Density: 868.8 persons per square mile (2000); Age: 28.2% under 18, 17.6% over 64 (2000); Marriage status: 15.8% never married, 65.1% now married, 9.5% widowed, 9.6% divorced (2000); Foreign born: 0.1% (2000); Ancestry (includes multiple ancestries): 21.5% German, 20.6% Irish, 12.0% English, 10.4% United States or American, 8.6% Other groups (2000).
Economy: Cattle; hay, wheat, sorghum. Single-family building permits issued: 3 (2001) / 3 (2000); Multi-family building permits issued: 4 (2001) / 0 (2000); Employment by occupation: 11.4% management, 18.1% professional, 9.7% services, 25.2% sales, 0.7% farming, 16.3% construction, 18.6% production (2000).
Income: Per capita income: $17,051 (2000); Median household income: $36,944 (2000); Poverty rate: 5.7% (2000).
Taxes: Total city taxes per capita: $152 (1997); City property taxes per capita: $47 (1997).
Education: High school graduation rate: 82.7% (2000); College graduation rate: 12.1% (2000).

School District(s)

Cass Co. R-V (KG-12)
2000 Enrollment: 496 816-293-5312
Housing: Homeownership rate: 71.2% (2000); Median home value: $75,100 (2000); Median rent: $302 per month (2000); Median age of housing: 29 years (2000).
Transportation: Commute to work: 95.8% car, 0.0% public transportation, 2.7% walk, 1.5% work from home (2000); Travel time to work: 26.3% less than 15 minutes, 21.0% 15 to 30 minutes, 19.9% 30 to 45 minutes, 12.4% 45 to 60 minutes, 20.5% 60 minutes or more (2000)

BALDWIN PARK (village). Covers a land area of 0.070 square miles and a water area of 0.042 square miles. Located at 38.79° N. Lat.; 94.24° W. Long. Elevation is 900 feet.
Population: 115 (2000); Race: 100.0% White, 0.0% Black, 0.0% Asian, 0.0% American Indian and Alaska Native, 0.7% Hispanic of any race, 0.0% two or more races (2000); Density: 1,639.7 persons per square mile (2000); Age: 36.4% under 18, 0.0% over 64 (2000); Marriage status: 42.5% never married, 42.5% now married, 1.9% widowed, 13.2% divorced (2000); Foreign born: 0.0% (2000); Ancestry (includes multiple ancestries): 22.9% German, 12.9% Irish, 9.3% Dutch, 6.4% English, 4.3% United States or American (2000).
Economy: Single-family building permits issued: 0 (2001) / 0 (2000); Multi-family building permits issued: 0 (2001) / 0 (2000); Employment by

occupation: 8.1% management, 10.8% professional, 13.5% services, 23.0% sales, 0.0% farming, 14.9% construction, 29.7% production (2000).
Income: Per capita income: $22,489 (2000); Median household income: $40,208 (2000); Poverty rate: 8.8% (2000).
Taxes: Total city taxes per capita: $110 (1997); City property taxes per capita: $20 (1997).
Education: High school graduation rate: 73.2% (2000); College graduation rate: 2.4% (2000).
Housing: Homeownership rate: 66.7% (2000); Median home value: $41,300 (2000); Median rent: $366 per month (2000); Median age of housing: 41 years (2000).
Transportation: Commute to work: 86.5% car, 2.7% public transportation, 10.8% walk, 0.0% work from home (2000); Travel time to work: 17.6% less than 15 minutes, 18.9% 15 to 30 minutes, 44.6% 30 to 45 minutes, 14.9% 45 to 60 minutes, 4.1% 60 minutes or more (2000)

BELTON (city). Covers a land area of 13.396 square miles and a water area of 0.043 square miles. Located at 38.81° N. Lat.; 94.53° W. Long. Elevation is 1,102 feet.
History: Belton was platted in 1871. Carry Nation, the militant prohibitionist, lived for a time in Belton with her parents, George and Mary Campbell Moore.
Population: 21,730 (2000); Race: 92.2% White, 3.9% Black, 0.4% Asian, 0.5% American Indian and Alaska Native, 4.0% Hispanic of any race, 1.9% two or more races (2000); Density: 1,622.2 persons per square mile (2000); Age: 29.6% under 18, 10.2% over 64 (2000); Marriage status: 21.6% never married, 60.1% now married, 6.1% widowed, 12.3% divorced (2000); Foreign born: 2.9% (2000); Ancestry (includes multiple ancestries): 22.5% German, 15.4% Irish, 15.0% Other groups, 12.3% United States or American, 10.9% English (2000).
Vital Statistics: Birth rate: 175.8 per 10,000 population (1998)
Economy: Single-family building permits issued: 86 (2001) / 147 (2000); Multi-family building permits issued: 210 (2001) / 60 (2000); Employment by occupation: 11.5% management, 16.6% professional, 14.7% services, 29.0% sales, 0.5% farming, 12.2% construction, 15.6% production (2000).
Income: Per capita income: $18,572 (2000); Median household income: $45,581 (2000); Poverty rate: 7.9% (2000).
Taxes: Total city taxes per capita: $414 (2000); City property taxes per capita: $121 (2000).
Education: High school graduation rate: 84.7% (2000); College graduation rate: 14.6% (2000).

School District(s)

Belton 124 (PK-12)
2000 Enrollment: 4,560 816-348-1000
Housing: Homeownership rate: 73.4% (2000); Median home value: $90,000 (2000); Median rent: $458 per month (2000); Median age of housing: 23 years (2000).
Hospitals: Research Belton Hospital (75 beds)
Safety: Violent crime rate: 28.8 per 10,000 population; Property crime rate: 384.7 per 10,000 population (2001).
Newspapers: The Star Herald (1 x week)
Transportation: Commute to work: 94.8% car, 0.4% public transportation, 0.7% walk, 2.8% work from home (2000); Travel time to work: 24.1% less than 15 minutes, 32.2% 15 to 30 minutes, 30.1% 30 to 45 minutes, 10.5% 45 to 60 minutes, 3.1% 60 minutes or more (2000)
Additional Information Contacts
Belton Chamber of Commerce 816-331-2420

CLEVELAND (city). Covers a land area of 1.570 square miles and a water area of 0 square miles. Located at 38.67° N. Lat.; 94.59° W. Long. Elevation is 980 feet.
Population: 592 (2000); Race: 94.0% White, 0.8% Black, 0.3% Asian, 3.9% American Indian and Alaska Native, 2.9% Hispanic of any race, 1.0% two or more races (2000); Density: 377.1 persons per square mile (2000); Age: 29.4% under 18, 6.3% over 64 (2000); Marriage status: 20.2% never married, 65.5% now married, 4.5% widowed, 9.8% divorced (2000); Foreign born: 1.3% (2000); Ancestry (includes multiple ancestries): 20.2% German, 17.9% Other groups, 13.6% Irish, 10.5% English, 9.4% United States or American (2000).
Economy: Twenty-eight miles South of downtown Kansas City, on Kansas border. Agricultural area. Manufacturing: pipe organs. Single-family building permits issued: 6 (2001) / 7 (2000); Multi-family building permits issued: 0 (2001) / 0 (2000); Employment by occupation: 16.2% management, 16.5% professional, 9.2% services, 19.8% sales, 0.3% farming, 14.5% construction, 23.4% production (2000).
Income: Per capita income: $19,064 (2000); Median household income: $54,722 (2000); Poverty rate: 4.9% (2000).
Taxes: Total city taxes per capita: $127 (1997); City property taxes per capita: $42 (1997).
Education: High school graduation rate: 79.0% (2000); College graduation rate: 13.0% (2000).

School District(s)

Midway R-I (KG-12)
2000 Enrollment: 556 816-250-2994
Housing: Homeownership rate: 88.6% (2000); Median home value: $112,000 (2000); Median rent: $439 per month (2000); Median age of housing: 25 years (2000).
Transportation: Commute to work: 97.7% car, 0.0% public transportation, 0.0% walk, 1.3% work from home (2000); Travel time to work: 8.2% less than 15 minutes, 29.6% 15 to 30 minutes, 35.4% 30 to 45 minutes, 21.1% 45 to 60 minutes, 5.8% 60 minutes or more (2000)

CREIGHTON (city). Covers a land area of 0.296 square miles and a water area of 0 square miles. Located at 38.49° N. Lat.; 94.07° W. Long. Elevation is 775 feet.
Population: 322 (2000); Race: 96.7% White, 0.6% Black, 0.0% Asian, 0.0% American Indian and Alaska Native, 1.2% Hispanic of any race, 2.1% two or more races (2000); Density: 1,086.7 persons per square mile (2000); Age: 28.8% under 18, 12.2% over 64 (2000); Marriage status: 19.5% never married, 59.0% now married, 5.6% widowed, 15.9% divorced (2000); Foreign born: 0.6% (2000); Ancestry (includes multiple ancestries): 20.8% United States or American, 19.9% German, 6.8% Other groups, 6.5% English, 6.5% Irish (2000).
Economy: Single-family building permits issued: 2 (2001) / 5 (2000); Multi-family building permits issued: 0 (2001) / 0 (2000); Employment by occupation: 16.5% management, 5.0% professional, 10.1% services, 21.6% sales, 0.7% farming, 27.3% construction, 18.7% production (2000).
Income: Per capita income: $20,369 (2000); Median household income: $41,071 (2000); Poverty rate: 12.9% (2000).
Taxes: Total city taxes per capita: $78 (1997); City property taxes per capita: $27 (1997).
Education: High school graduation rate: 76.4% (2000); College graduation rate: 5.3% (2000).

School District(s)

Sherwood Cass R-VIII (PK-12)
2000 Enrollment: 920 660-499-2239
Housing: Homeownership rate: 72.6% (2000); Median home value: $49,200 (2000); Median rent: $225 per month (2000); Median age of housing: 43 years (2000).
Transportation: Commute to work: 94.2% car, 4.3% public transportation, 1.4% walk, 0.0% work from home (2000); Travel time to work: 17.3% less than 15 minutes, 20.9% 15 to 30 minutes, 10.8% 30 to 45 minutes, 12.9% 45 to 60 minutes, 38.1% 60 minutes or more (2000)

DREXEL (city). Covers a land area of 0.749 square miles and a water area of 0.032 square miles. Located at 38.48° N. Lat.; 94.60° W. Long. Elevation is 992 feet.
Population: 1,090 (2000); Race: 97.5% White, 0.0% Black, 0.0% Asian, 1.3% American Indian and Alaska Native, 2.0% Hispanic of any race, 1.3% two or more races (2000); Density: 1,454.6 persons per square mile (2000); Age: 29.0% under 18, 13.4% over 64 (2000); Marriage status: 15.2% never married, 65.8% now married, 8.2% widowed, 10.8% divorced (2000); Foreign born: 0.0% (2000); Ancestry (includes multiple ancestries): 20.3% German, 14.4% Irish, 12.9% English, 10.8% Other groups, 8.4% United States or American (2000).
Economy: Wheat, soybeans; livestock; gas wells, oil field. Single-family building permits issued: 6 (2001) / 0 (2000); Multi-family building permits issued: 0 (2001) / 2 (2000); Employment by occupation: 12.8% management, 14.0% professional, 12.2% services, 24.2% sales, 1.0% farming, 24.2% construction, 11.4% production (2000).
Income: Per capita income: $17,207 (2000); Median household income: $39,219 (2000); Poverty rate: 7.1% (2000).
Taxes: Total city taxes per capita: $140 (1997); City property taxes per capita: $109 (1997).
Education: High school graduation rate: 79.7% (2000); College graduation rate: 10.7% (2000).

School District(s)

Drexel R-IV (KG-12)
2000 Enrollment: 377 816-657-4715

Housing: Homeownership rate: 67.9% (2000); Median home value: $71,000 (2000); Median rent: $266 per month (2000); Median age of housing: 32 years (2000).
Newspapers: Drexel Star (1 x week)
Transportation: Commute to work: 96.4% car, 0.0% public transportation, 2.0% walk, 1.6% work from home (2000); Travel time to work: 20.7% less than 15 minutes, 16.2% 15 to 30 minutes, 19.9% 30 to 45 minutes, 29.0% 45 to 60 minutes, 14.2% 60 minutes or more (2000)

EAST LYNNE (city). Covers a land area of 0.281 square miles and a water area of 0 square miles. Located at 38.66° N. Lat.; 94.23° W. Long. Elevation is 855 feet.
Population: 300 (2000); Race: 96.0% White, 0.0% Black, 0.0% Asian, 1.3% American Indian and Alaska Native, 3.4% Hispanic of any race, 2.7% two or more races (2000); Density: 1,066.9 persons per square mile (2000); Age: 33.2% under 18, 8.1% over 64 (2000); Marriage status: 21.8% never married, 60.5% now married, 4.5% widowed, 13.2% divorced (2000); Foreign born: 0.0% (2000); Ancestry (includes multiple ancestries): 21.1% Irish, 17.8% German, 14.1% English, 11.7% Other groups, 8.7% United States or American (2000).
Economy: Employment by occupation: 7.4% management, 1.5% professional, 27.2% services, 19.9% sales, 1.5% farming, 22.8% construction, 19.9% production (2000).
Income: Per capita income: $14,055 (2000); Median household income: $38,472 (2000); Poverty rate: 6.1% (2000).
Taxes: Total city taxes per capita: $45 (1997); City property taxes per capita: $45 (1997).
Education: High school graduation rate: 76.9% (2000); College graduation rate: 7.5% (2000).

School District(s)

East Lynne 40 (KG-08)
2000 Enrollment: 165 816-626-3511

Housing: Homeownership rate: 74.1% (2000); Median home value: $55,800 (2000); Median rent: $195 per month (2000); Median age of housing: 35 years (2000).
Transportation: Commute to work: 92.4% car, 0.0% public transportation, 1.5% walk, 4.6% work from home (2000); Travel time to work: 21.6% less than 15 minutes, 24.8% 15 to 30 minutes, 10.4% 30 to 45 minutes, 20.8% 45 to 60 minutes, 22.4% 60 minutes or more (2000)

FREEMAN (city). Covers a land area of 0.465 square miles and a water area of 0 square miles. Located at 38.61° N. Lat.; 94.50° W. Long. Elevation is 349 feet.
Population: 521 (2000); Race: 98.9% White, 0.0% Black, 0.0% Asian, 1.1% American Indian and Alaska Native, 0.0% Hispanic of any race, 0.0% two or more races (2000); Density: 1,121.2 persons per square mile (2000); Age: 32.8% under 18, 11.5% over 64 (2000); Marriage status: 17.8% never married, 66.5% now married, 6.5% widowed, 9.3% divorced (2000); Foreign born: 0.4% (2000); Ancestry (includes multiple ancestries): 15.1% United States or American, 14.0% German, 9.8% English, 8.0% Irish, 6.4% Other groups (2000).
Economy: Single-family building permits issued: 1 (2001) / 4 (2000); Multi-family building permits issued: 4 (2001) / 0 (2000); Employment by occupation: 7.9% management, 8.3% professional, 12.6% services, 30.0% sales, 0.7% farming, 23.5% construction, 17.0% production (2000).
Income: Per capita income: $17,450 (2000); Median household income: $46,339 (2000); Poverty rate: 9.1% (2000).
Taxes: Total city taxes per capita: $102 (1997); City property taxes per capita: $26 (1997).
Education: High school graduation rate: 87.5% (2000); College graduation rate: 8.5% (2000).
Housing: Homeownership rate: 85.2% (2000); Median home value: $66,400 (2000); Median rent: $431 per month (2000); Median age of housing: 46 years (2000).
Transportation: Commute to work: 95.7% car, 0.7% public transportation, 0.0% walk, 2.2% work from home (2000); Travel time to work: 16.2% less than 15 minutes, 21.0% 15 to 30 minutes, 27.7% 30 to 45 minutes, 26.6% 45 to 60 minutes, 8.5% 60 minutes or more (2000)

GARDEN CITY (city). Covers a land area of 1.726 square miles and a water area of 0 square miles. Located at 38.55° N. Lat.; 94.18° W. Long. Elevation is 916 feet.
Population: 1,500 (2000); Race: 97.0% White, 0.6% Black, 0.0% Asian, 0.6% American Indian and Alaska Native, 1.6% Hispanic of any race, 1.5% two or more races (2000); Density: 869.0 persons per square mile (2000); Age: 29.3% under 18, 11.1% over 64 (2000); Marriage status: 21.3% never married, 57.8% now married, 8.7% widowed, 12.1% divorced (2000); Foreign born: 0.1% (2000); Ancestry (includes multiple ancestries): 19.0% German, 13.9% Irish, 13.2% United States or American, 11.5% Other groups, 7.8% English (2000).
Economy: Corn, soybeans, sorghum, wheat; cattle. Limestone quarry. Single-family building permits issued: 17 (2001) / 5 (2000); Multi-family building permits issued: 16 (2001) / 0 (2000); Employment by occupation: 9.4% management, 12.0% professional, 14.3% services, 22.3% sales, 1.7% farming, 18.6% construction, 21.7% production (2000).
Income: Per capita income: $19,695 (2000); Median household income: $37,461 (2000); Poverty rate: 8.0% (2000).
Taxes: Total city taxes per capita: $121 (1997); City property taxes per capita: $25 (1997).
Education: High school graduation rate: 81.5% (2000); College graduation rate: 11.7% (2000).
Housing: Homeownership rate: 70.4% (2000); Median home value: $77,800 (2000); Median rent: $330 per month (2000); Median age of housing: 29 years (2000).
Transportation: Commute to work: 96.4% car, 0.0% public transportation, 0.7% walk, 1.9% work from home (2000); Travel time to work: 19.5% less than 15 minutes, 27.1% 15 to 30 minutes, 12.2% 30 to 45 minutes, 19.8% 45 to 60 minutes, 21.3% 60 minutes or more (2000)

GUNN CITY (village). Covers a land area of 0.081 square miles and a water area of 0 square miles. Located at 38.66° N. Lat.; 94.16° W. Long. Elevation is 858 feet.
Population: 85 (2000); Race: 100.0% White, 0.0% Black, 0.0% Asian, 0.0% American Indian and Alaska Native, 0.0% Hispanic of any race, 0.0% two or more races (2000); Density: 1,054.6 persons per square mile (2000); Age: 37.0% under 18, 11.1% over 64 (2000); Marriage status: 7.2% never married, 78.3% now married, 2.9% widowed, 11.6% divorced (2000); Foreign born: 0.0% (2000); Ancestry (includes multiple ancestries): 23.1% United States or American, 15.7% European, 15.7% Other groups, 13.9% German, 7.4% Scotch-Irish (2000).
Economy: Employment by occupation: 13.9% management, 5.6% professional, 36.1% services, 16.7% sales, 2.8% farming, 11.1% construction, 13.9% production (2000).
Income: Per capita income: $11,144 (2000); Median household income: $28,333 (2000); Poverty rate: 22.2% (2000).
Taxes: Total city taxes per capita: $63 (1997); City property taxes per capita: $13 (1997).
Education: High school graduation rate: 58.8% (2000); College graduation rate: 4.4% (2000).
Housing: Homeownership rate: 72.2% (2000); Median home value: $60,000 (2000); Median rent: $567 per month (2000); Median age of housing: 22 years (2000).
Transportation: Commute to work: 88.9% car, 0.0% public transportation, 0.0% walk, 11.1% work from home (2000); Travel time to work: 18.8% less than 15 minutes, 12.5% 15 to 30 minutes, 46.9% 30 to 45 minutes, 12.5% 45 to 60 minutes, 9.4% 60 minutes or more (2000)

HARRISONVILLE (city). Covers a land area of 8.642 square miles and a water area of 0.096 square miles. Located at 38.65° N. Lat.; 94.34° W. Long. Elevation is 904 feet.
History: Harrisonville was the boyhood home of Cole Younger, whose father operated a livery stable in the town. Cole Younger and Frank James were the apparent organizers of the gorup which, under the leadership of Jesse James, became the most notorious band of outlaws in American history. Wounded and captured after a bank robbery in Minnesota, Cole Younger was later pardoned and had a career as a lecturer and as a performer with a Wild West show.
Population: 8,946 (2000); Race: 95.5% White, 0.9% Black, 1.0% Asian, 0.5% American Indian and Alaska Native, 1.0% Hispanic of any race, 1.7% two or more races (2000); Density: 1,035.2 persons per square mile (2000); Age: 27.1% under 18, 15.6% over 64 (2000); Marriage status: 23.2% never married, 54.1% now married, 8.9% widowed, 13.8% divorced (2000); Foreign born: 1.6% (2000); Ancestry (includes multiple ancestries): 20.0% German, 19.7% United States or American, 13.0% Irish, 11.7% Other groups, 10.1% English (2000).
Economy: Single-family building permits issued: 40 (2001) / 28 (2000); Multi-family building permits issued: 18 (2001) / 32 (2000); Employment by occupation: 9.7% management, 14.2% professional, 15.7% services, 28.0% sales, 0.0% farming, 12.8% construction, 19.6% production (2000).
Income: Per capita income: $17,280 (2000); Median household income: $39,498 (2000); Poverty rate: 6.5% (2000).

Taxes: Total city taxes per capita: $475 (2000); City property taxes per capita: $78 (2000).
Education: High school graduation rate: 83.0% (2000); College graduation rate: 12.4% (2000).

School District(s)

Harrisonville R-IX (PK-12)
2000 Enrollment: 2,445 816-380-2727

Housing: Homeownership rate: 65.7% (2000); Median home value: $85,900 (2000); Median rent: $378 per month (2000); Median age of housing: 26 years (2000).
Hospitals: Cass Medical Center (49 beds)
Newspapers: The Cass County Democrat-Missourian (1 x week)
Transportation: Commute to work: 95.0% car, 0.0% public transportation, 1.4% walk, 2.6% work from home (2000); Travel time to work: 38.8% less than 15 minutes, 18.7% 15 to 30 minutes, 19.4% 30 to 45 minutes, 15.6% 45 to 60 minutes, 7.5% 60 minutes or more (2000)
Additional Information Contacts
Harrisonville Area Chamber 816-380-5271

LAKE ANNETTE (city). Covers a land area of 0.158 square miles and a water area of 0.061 square miles. Located at 38.65° N. Lat.; 94.50° W. Long. Elevation is 870 feet.
Population: 163 (2000); Race: 93.8% White, 0.0% Black, 1.4% Asian, 4.8% American Indian and Alaska Native, 2.8% Hispanic of any race, 0.0% two or more races (2000); Density: 1,033.5 persons per square mile (2000); Age: 16.6% under 18, 13.1% over 64 (2000); Marriage status: 20.5% never married, 51.2% now married, 9.4% widowed, 18.9% divorced (2000); Foreign born: 4.1% (2000); Ancestry (includes multiple ancestries): 22.8% Other groups, 19.3% German, 15.9% English, 13.8% Irish, 4.1% Norwegian (2000).
Economy: Single-family building permits issued: 0 (2001) / 0 (2000); Multi-family building permits issued: 0 (2001) / 0 (2000); Employment by occupation: 10.0% management, 5.7% professional, 14.3% services, 28.6% sales, 5.7% farming, 18.6% construction, 17.1% production (2000).
Income: Per capita income: $18,623 (2000); Median household income: $22,292 (2000); Poverty rate: 23.4% (2000).
Taxes: Total city taxes per capita: $90 (1997); City property taxes per capita: $90 (1997).
Education: High school graduation rate: 58.7% (2000); College graduation rate: 12.8% (2000).
Housing: Homeownership rate: 74.0% (2000); Median home value: $37,900 (2000); Median rent: $406 per month (2000); Median age of housing: 30 years (2000).
Transportation: Commute to work: 97.1% car, 0.0% public transportation, 2.9% walk, 0.0% work from home (2000); Travel time to work: 8.8% less than 15 minutes, 22.1% 15 to 30 minutes, 11.8% 30 to 45 minutes, 33.8% 45 to 60 minutes, 23.5% 60 minutes or more (2000)

LAKE WINNEBAGO (city). Covers a land area of 1.885 square miles and a water area of 0.416 square miles. Located at 38.82° N. Lat.; 94.36° W. Long. Elevation is 950 feet.
Population: 902 (2000); Race: 98.5% White, 0.0% Black, 0.4% Asian, 0.3% American Indian and Alaska Native, 2.5% Hispanic of any race, 0.2% two or more races (2000); Density: 478.6 persons per square mile (2000); Age: 17.2% under 18, 12.5% over 64 (2000); Marriage status: 13.7% never married, 74.7% now married, 4.6% widowed, 7.0% divorced (2000); Foreign born: 1.7% (2000); Ancestry (includes multiple ancestries): 28.1% German, 19.9% English, 14.2% Irish, 11.8% United States or American, 7.0% Other groups (2000).
Economy: Single-family building permits issued: 18 (2001) / 13 (2000); Multi-family building permits issued: 0 (2001) / 0 (2000); Employment by occupation: 23.8% management, 23.4% professional, 7.3% services, 33.9% sales, 0.0% farming, 5.0% construction, 6.5% production (2000).
Income: Per capita income: $41,891 (2000); Median household income: $78,478 (2000); Poverty rate: 1.6% (2000).
Taxes: Total city taxes per capita: $99 (1997); City property taxes per capita: $23 (1997).
Education: High school graduation rate: 96.6% (2000); College graduation rate: 42.7% (2000).
Housing: Homeownership rate: 96.9% (2000); Median home value: $233,700 (2000); Median age of housing: 24 years (2000).
Safety: Violent crime rate: 0.0 per 10,000 population; Property crime rate: 77.1 per 10,000 population (2001).
Transportation: Commute to work: 92.3% car, 0.4% public transportation, 0.0% walk, 6.7% work from home (2000); Travel time to work: 9.3% less than 15 minutes, 42.2% 15 to 30 minutes, 30.3% 30 to 45 minutes, 10.6% 45 to 60 minutes, 7.6% 60 minutes or more (2000)

PECULIAR (city). Covers a land area of 3.496 square miles and a water area of 0.046 square miles. Located at 38.72° N. Lat.; 94.45° W. Long. Elevation is 1,004 feet.
History: The story behind the naming of Peculiar claims that a group of spiritualists under the leadership of Jane Hawkins came to Cass County in search of a home. When shown a particular farm by George Moore (Carry Nation's father), Mrs. Hawkins exclaimed: "That's peculiar! It is the very place I saw in a vision in Connecticut." The spiritualists bought the farm and laid out a town in 1868 which they named Peculiar.
Population: 2,604 (2000); Race: 97.6% White, 0.3% Black, 0.7% Asian, 0.3% American Indian and Alaska Native, 1.5% Hispanic of any race, 1.0% two or more races (2000); Density: 744.8 persons per square mile (2000); Age: 31.3% under 18, 9.5% over 64 (2000); Marriage status: 18.6% never married, 62.9% now married, 6.1% widowed, 12.4% divorced (2000); Foreign born: 0.7% (2000); Ancestry (includes multiple ancestries): 19.9% German, 17.3% United States or American, 15.2% Irish, 11.4% English, 10.0% Other groups (2000).
Economy: Single-family building permits issued: 21 (2001) / 60 (2000); Multi-family building permits issued: 34 (2001) / 18 (2000); Employment by occupation: 10.8% management, 15.5% professional, 16.2% services, 24.8% sales, 0.4% farming, 16.7% construction, 15.7% production (2000).
Income: Per capita income: $19,104 (2000); Median household income: $44,769 (2000); Poverty rate: 7.5% (2000).
Taxes: Total city taxes per capita: $137 (1997); City property taxes per capita: $13 (1997).
Education: High school graduation rate: 85.4% (2000); College graduation rate: 13.5% (2000).
Housing: Homeownership rate: 73.6% (2000); Median home value: $96,900 (2000); Median rent: $376 per month (2000); Median age of housing: 21 years (2000).
Transportation: Commute to work: 95.6% car, 0.5% public transportation, 1.4% walk, 2.3% work from home (2000); Travel time to work: 16.9% less than 15 minutes, 29.8% 15 to 30 minutes, 31.4% 30 to 45 minutes, 14.6% 45 to 60 minutes, 7.3% 60 minutes or more (2000)

PLEASANT HILL (city). Covers a land area of 4.493 square miles and a water area of 0.023 square miles. Located at 38.79° N. Lat.; 94.26° W. Long. Elevation is 909 feet.
History: Laid out 1843.
Population: 5,582 (2000); Race: 96.6% White, 0.0% Black, 0.8% Asian, 0.4% American Indian and Alaska Native, 2.1% Hispanic of any race, 1.6% two or more races (2000); Density: 1,242.3 persons per square mile (2000); Age: 30.1% under 18, 11.5% over 64 (2000); Marriage status: 17.5% never married, 64.6% now married, 6.5% widowed, 11.4% divorced (2000); Foreign born: 1.6% (2000); Ancestry (includes multiple ancestries): 20.5% German, 13.9% Irish, 13.3% United States or American, 12.7% Other groups, 9.1% English (2000).
Economy: Railroad junction. Agriculture. Manufacturing: treated lumber, wood products, furniture. Single-family building permits issued: 71 (2001) / 62 (2000); Multi-family building permits issued: 37 (2001) / 2 (2000); Employment by occupation: 13.4% management, 15.9% professional, 17.1% services, 22.3% sales, 0.4% farming, 13.8% construction, 17.1% production (2000).
Income: Per capita income: $21,623 (2000); Median household income: $48,915 (2000); Poverty rate: 5.5% (2000).
Taxes: Total city taxes per capita: $153 (1997); City property taxes per capita: $37 (1997).
Education: High school graduation rate: 88.7% (2000); College graduation rate: 20.4% (2000).

School District(s)

Pleasant Hill R-III (PK-12)
2000 Enrollment: 1,819 816-540-3161

Housing: Homeownership rate: 72.8% (2000); Median home value: $94,300 (2000); Median rent: $433 per month (2000); Median age of housing: 22 years (2000).
Safety: Violent crime rate: 1.8 per 10,000 population; Property crime rate: 270.7 per 10,000 population (2001).
Newspapers: Pleasant Hill Times (1 x week); Penny Saver (1 x week)
Transportation: Commute to work: 95.1% car, 0.1% public transportation, 2.6% walk, 1.9% work from home (2000); Travel time to work: 22.2% less than 15 minutes, 32.6% 15 to 30 minutes, 20.6% 30 to 45 minutes, 15.7% 45 to 60 minutes, 8.8% 60 minutes or more (2000)
Additional Information Contacts

Pleasant Hill Chamber of Commerce.................... 816-987-2595

RAYMORE (city). Covers a land area of 16.993 square miles and a water area of 0.112 square miles. Located at 38.80° N. Lat.; 94.46° W. Long. Elevation is 1,104 feet.
Population: 11,146 (2000); Race: 94.7% White, 2.0% Black, 0.5% Asian, 0.5% American Indian and Alaska Native, 1.5% Hispanic of any race, 2.2% two or more races (2000); Density: 655.9 persons per square mile (2000); Age: 29.2% under 18, 14.0% over 64 (2000); Marriage status: 13.2% never married, 72.8% now married, 7.3% widowed, 6.6% divorced (2000); Foreign born: 1.3% (2000); Ancestry (includes multiple ancestries): 25.7% German, 16.0% Irish, 15.2% English, 11.4% Other groups, 10.4% United States or American (2000).
Economy: Manufacturing of automotive regulators. Single-family building permits issued: 254 (2001) / 173 (2000); Multi-family building permits issued: 32 (2001) / 60 (2000); Employment by occupation: 15.5% management, 23.2% professional, 9.0% services, 31.8% sales, 0.0% farming, 11.4% construction, 9.0% production (2000).
Income: Per capita income: $22,496 (2000); Median household income: $56,007 (2000); Poverty rate: 3.1% (2000).
Taxes: Total city taxes per capita: $444 (2000); City property taxes per capita: $132 (2000).
Education: High school graduation rate: 91.1% (2000); College graduation rate: 26.8% (2000).

School District(s)

Raymore-Peculiar R-II (PK-12)
2000 Enrollment: 4,217 816-331-0050

Housing: Homeownership rate: 82.5% (2000); Median home value: $121,000 (2000); Median rent: $620 per month (2000); Median age of housing: 11 years (2000).
Transportation: Commute to work: 95.9% car, 0.0% public transportation, 0.7% walk, 2.9% work from home (2000); Travel time to work: 16.0% less than 15 minutes, 32.6% 15 to 30 minutes, 32.1% 30 to 45 minutes, 15.6% 45 to 60 minutes, 3.7% 60 minutes or more (2000)
Additional Information Contacts
Raymore Chamber of Commerce......................... 816-322-0599

STRASBURG (city). Covers a land area of 0.219 square miles and a water area of 0 square miles. Located at 38.76° N. Lat.; 94.16° W. Long. Elevation is 840 feet.
Population: 136 (2000); Race: 100.0% White, 0.0% Black, 0.0% Asian, 0.0% American Indian and Alaska Native, 0.0% Hispanic of any race, 0.0% two or more races (2000); Density: 619.6 persons per square mile (2000); Age: 40.6% under 18, 14.3% over 64 (2000); Marriage status: 20.0% never married, 66.7% now married, 5.6% widowed, 7.8% divorced (2000); Foreign born: 0.0% (2000); Ancestry (includes multiple ancestries): 28.6% Irish, 26.3% German, 8.3% United States or American, 6.0% English, 3.8% Norwegian (2000).
Economy: Employment by occupation: 2.2% management, 0.0% professional, 10.9% services, 21.7% sales, 0.0% farming, 23.9% construction, 41.3% production (2000).
Income: Per capita income: $10,655 (2000); Median household income: $30,417 (2000); Poverty rate: 30.1% (2000).
Taxes: Total city taxes per capita: $8 (1997); City property taxes per capita: $8 (1997).
Education: High school graduation rate: 64.8% (2000); College graduation rate: 4.2% (2000).

School District(s)

Strasburg C-3 (KG-08)
2000 Enrollment: 123 816-680-3333

Housing: Homeownership rate: 73.9% (2000); Median home value: $60,000 (2000); Median rent: $275 per month (2000); Median age of housing: 43 years (2000).
Transportation: Commute to work: 100.0% car, 0.0% public transportation, 0.0% walk, 0.0% work from home (2000); Travel time to work: 28.3% less than 15 minutes, 17.4% 15 to 30 minutes, 19.6% 30 to 45 minutes, 13.0% 45 to 60 minutes, 21.7% 60 minutes or more (2000)

WEST LINE (village). Covers a land area of 0.124 square miles and a water area of 0 square miles. Located at 38.63° N. Lat.; 94.58° W. Long. Elevation is 915 feet.
Population: 95 (2000); Race: 97.5% White, 0.0% Black, 0.0% Asian, 0.0% American Indian and Alaska Native, 0.0% Hispanic of any race, 2.5% two or more races (2000); Density: 768.0 persons per square mile (2000); Age: 8.8% under 18, 16.3% over 64 (2000); Marriage status: 32.9% never married, 50.7% now married, 9.6% widowed, 6.8% divorced (2000); Foreign born: 0.0% (2000); Ancestry (includes multiple ancestries): 18.8% German, 13.8% English, 13.8% United States or American, 10.0% Irish, 8.8% Other groups (2000).
Economy: Single-family building permits issued: 0 (2001) / 0 (2000); Multi-family building permits issued: 0 (2001) / 0 (2000); Employment by occupation: 6.7% management, 11.1% professional, 11.1% services, 26.7% sales, 2.2% farming, 33.3% construction, 8.9% production (2000).
Income: Per capita income: $24,831 (2000); Median household income: $46,250 (2000); Poverty rate: 6.3% (2000).
Taxes: Total city taxes per capita: $37 (1997); City property taxes per capita: $18 (1997).
Education: High school graduation rate: 73.8% (2000); College graduation rate: 3.3% (2000).
Housing: Homeownership rate: 94.7% (2000); Median home value: $42,500 (2000); Median rent: $175 per month (2000); Median age of housing: 46 years (2000).
Transportation: Commute to work: 100.0% car, 0.0% public transportation, 0.0% walk, 0.0% work from home (2000); Travel time to work: 9.1% less than 15 minutes, 25.0% 15 to 30 minutes, 18.2% 30 to 45 minutes, 11.4% 45 to 60 minutes, 36.4% 60 minutes or more (2000)

Cedar County

Located in western Missouri, in the Ozarks; drained by the Sac River. Covers a land area of 475.90 square miles, a water area of 22.60 square miles, and is located in the Central Time Zone. The county government was organized in 1845. County seat is Stockton.

Weather Station: Stockton Dam Elevation: 921 feet

	Jan	Feb	Mar	Apr	May	Jun	Jul	Aug	Sep	Oct	Nov	Dec
High	40	46	57	67	76	84	90	90	81	70	56	45
Low	21	25	34	44	54	64	69	67	59	46	36	26
Precip	1.8	2.3	3.5	4.0	5.1	4.7	3.7	4.0	4.6	4.3	3.7	2.7
Snow	3.2	2.4	0.8	tr	0.0	0.0	0.0	0.0	0.0	0.0	0.8	1.2

High and Low temperatures in degrees Fahrenheit; Precipitation and Snow in inches

Population: 13,733 (2000); Race: 96.6% White, 0.4% Black, 0.6% Asian, 0.4% American Indian and Alaska Native, 0.4% Hispanic of any race, 1.6% two or more races (2000); Density: 28.9 persons per square mile (2000); Age: 24.6% under 18, 20.8% over 64 (2000).
Religion: Five largest groups: 18.4% Southern Baptist Convention, 8.5% Christian Churches and Churches of Christ, 4.3% The United Methodist Church, 3.4% Christian Church (Disciples of Christ), 2.7% Catholic Church (2000).
Economy: Unemployment rate: 6.3% (11/2002); Total civilian labor force: 5,165 (11/2002); Leading industries: 23.1% health care and social assistance; 19.1% manufacturing; 18.6% retail trade (2000); Companies that employ more than 1,000 persons: 0 (2000); Companies that employ more than 100 persons: 4 (2000); Farms: 865 totaling 203,685 acres (1997); Minority business ownership rate: 0.0% (1997); Women business ownership rate: 18.3% (1997); Retail sales per capita: $5,357 (1997). Single-family building permits issued: 5 (2001) / 10 (2000); Multi-family building permits issued: 24 (2001) / 2 (2000).
Income: Per capita income: $14,356 (2000); Median household income: $26,694 (2000); Poverty rate: 17.4% (2000); Bankruptcy rate: 2.73% (2001).
Taxes: Total county taxes per capita: $59 (1997); County property taxes per capita: $15 (1997).
Education: High school graduation rate: 74.0% (2000); College graduation rate: 10.0% (2000).
Housing: Homeownership rate: 78.3% (2000); Median home value: $57,900 (2000); Median rent: $228 per month (2000); Median age of housing: 26 years (2000).
Health: Birth rate: 111.4 per 10,000 population (1998); Age adjusted death rate: 108.0 per 10,000 population (1999); Age adjusted cancer mortality rate: 227.3 deaths per 100,000 population (1999). Air Quality Index: 56% good, 44% moderate, 0% unhealthy (percent of days in 2000). Number of physicians: 2.9 per 10,000 population (1999); Number of hospital beds: 24.8 per 10,000 population (1999).
Elections: 2000 Presidential election results: 35.0% Gore, 62.3% Bush, 1.4% Nader, 0.8% Buchanan
National and State Parks: Stockton State Park
Additional Information Contacts
El Dorado Springs Chamber of Commerce 417-876-4154
Stockton Chamber of Commerce......................... 417-276-5213

Cedar County Communities

EL DORADO SPRINGS (city). Aka Eldorado Springs. Covers a land area of 3.080 square miles and a water area of 0.006 square miles. Located at 37.87° N. Lat.; 94.02° W. Long. Elevation is 901 feet.
History: El Dorado Springs was founded in 1881 after Mrs. Joshua Hightower found her health improved by drinking the waters of the local springs. The town that grew up around a hotel became a popular health spa.
Population: 3,775 (2000); Race: 96.2% White, 0.0% Black, 1.2% Asian, 0.7% American Indian and Alaska Native, 0.3% Hispanic of any race, 1.8% two or more races (2000); Density: 1,225.7 persons per square mile (2000); Age: 22.2% under 18, 24.9% over 64 (2000); Marriage status: 15.7% never married, 59.0% now married, 12.7% widowed, 12.6% divorced (2000); Foreign born: 1.6% (2000); Ancestry (includes multiple ancestries): 15.7% Other groups, 15.3% German, 14.4% Irish, 13.9% United States or American, 9.4% English (2000).
Economy: Single-family building permits issued: 1 (2001) / 2 (2000); Multi-family building permits issued: 24 (2001) / 0 (2000); Employment by occupation: 7.8% management, 13.4% professional, 22.3% services, 18.7% sales, 1.0% farming, 14.4% construction, 22.4% production (2000).
Income: Per capita income: $12,575 (2000); Median household income: $20,789 (2000); Poverty rate: 24.9% (2000).
Taxes: Total city taxes per capita: $180 (1997); City property taxes per capita: $8 (1997).
Education: High school graduation rate: 70.1% (2000); College graduation rate: 8.5% (2000).

School District(s)

El Dorado Springs R-II (PK-12)
2000 Enrollment: 1,324 417-876-3112
Housing: Homeownership rate: 64.8% (2000); Median home value: $47,700 (2000); Median rent: $215 per month (2000); Median age of housing: 36 years (2000).
Hospitals: Cedar County Memorial Hospital (34 beds)
Newspapers: The Star (1 x week); El Dorado Springs Sun (1 x week)
Transportation: Commute to work: 93.0% car, 0.9% public transportation, 2.5% walk, 2.2% work from home (2000); Travel time to work: 56.6% less than 15 minutes, 18.1% 15 to 30 minutes, 16.0% 30 to 45 minutes, 3.3% 45 to 60 minutes, 5.9% 60 minutes or more (2000)
Additional Information Contacts
El Dorado Springs Chamber of Commerce 417-876-4154

JERICO SPRINGS (village). Covers a land area of 0.674 square miles and a water area of 0 square miles. Located at 37.62° N. Lat.; 94.00° W. Long. Elevation is 1,020 feet.
History: Former health springs resort. Plotted 1882.
Population: 259 (2000); Race: 100.0% White, 0.0% Black, 0.0% Asian, 0.0% American Indian and Alaska Native, 1.9% Hispanic of any race, 0.0% two or more races (2000); Density: 384.0 persons per square mile (2000); Age: 34.1% under 18, 11.6% over 64 (2000); Marriage status: 10.5% never married, 69.1% now married, 11.6% widowed, 8.8% divorced (2000); Foreign born: 0.0% (2000); Ancestry (includes multiple ancestries): 30.0% United States or American, 22.1% German, 11.6% Irish, 8.2% Norwegian, 7.9% Other groups (2000).
Economy: Soybeans, corn, wheat; cattle. Employment by occupation: 3.9% management, 9.8% professional, 9.8% services, 15.7% sales, 5.9% farming, 14.7% construction, 40.2% production (2000).
Income: Per capita income: $11,094 (2000); Median household income: $22,188 (2000); Poverty rate: 12.4% (2000).
Taxes: Total city taxes per capita: $31 (1997); City property taxes per capita: $15 (1997).
Education: High school graduation rate: 75.9% (2000); College graduation rate: 3.1% (2000).
Housing: Homeownership rate: 88.8% (2000); Median home value: $34,800 (2000); Median rent: $275 per month (2000); Median age of housing: 50 years (2000).
Transportation: Commute to work: 98.1% car, 0.0% public transportation, 0.0% walk, 1.9% work from home (2000); Travel time to work: 1.9% less than 15 minutes, 33.0% 15 to 30 minutes, 60.2% 30 to 45 minutes, 2.9% 45 to 60 minutes, 1.9% 60 minutes or more (2000)

STOCKTON (city). Covers a land area of 2.127 square miles and a water area of 0 square miles. Located at 37.69° N. Lat.; 93.79° W. Long. Elevation is 965 feet.
Population: 1,960 (2000); Race: 95.7% White, 0.4% Black, 1.4% Asian, 0.3% American Indian and Alaska Native, 1.4% Hispanic of any race, 1.7% two or more races (2000); Density: 921.7 persons per square mile (2000); Age: 28.0% under 18, 24.7% over 64 (2000); Marriage status: 21.3% never married, 55.8% now married, 12.9% widowed, 10.0% divorced (2000); Foreign born: 2.5% (2000); Ancestry (includes multiple ancestries): 20.2% German, 19.5% United States or American, 12.4% Irish, 10.8% English, 10.6% Other groups (2000).
Economy: Corn, soybeans, wheat; cattle. Manufacturing: walnuts and walnut shell processing; feeds, gear boxes. Stockton Dam on East side of city. Single-family building permits issued: 3 (2001) / 7 (2000); Multi-family building permits issued: 0 (2001) / 2 (2000); Employment by occupation: 8.1% management, 17.9% professional, 19.1% services, 19.8% sales, 1.6% farming, 14.4% construction, 19.1% production (2000).
Income: Per capita income: $14,540 (2000); Median household income: $25,353 (2000); Poverty rate: 14.8% (2000).
Taxes: Total city taxes per capita: $264 (1997); City property taxes per capita: $111 (1997).
Education: High school graduation rate: 74.0% (2000); College graduation rate: 14.1% (2000).

School District(s)

Stockton R-I (KG-12)
2000 Enrollment: 1,075 417-276-5143
Housing: Homeownership rate: 71.5% (2000); Median home value: $60,700 (2000); Median rent: $250 per month (2000); Median age of housing: 26 years (2000).
Safety: Violent crime rate: 5.1 per 10,000 population; Property crime rate: 243.4 per 10,000 population (2001).
Newspapers: Cedar County Republican (1 x week)
Transportation: Commute to work: 88.1% car, 0.0% public transportation, 1.5% walk, 8.0% work from home (2000); Travel time to work: 62.6% less than 15 minutes, 5.1% 15 to 30 minutes, 14.8% 30 to 45 minutes, 7.0% 45 to 60 minutes, 10.4% 60 minutes or more (2000)
Additional Information Contacts
Stockton Chamber of Commerce 417-276-5213

UMBER VIEW HEIGHTS (village). Covers a land area of 0.068 square miles and a water area of 0 square miles. Located at 37.62° N. Lat.; 93.80° W. Long. Elevation is 1,050 feet.
Population: 52 (2000); Race: 100.0% White, 0.0% Black, 0.0% Asian, 0.0% American Indian and Alaska Native, 0.0% Hispanic of any race, 0.0% two or more races (2000); Density: 768.0 persons per square mile (2000); Age: 14.6% under 18, 35.4% over 64 (2000); Marriage status: 12.2% never married, 80.5% now married, 0.0% widowed, 7.3% divorced (2000); Foreign born: 0.0% (2000); Ancestry (includes multiple ancestries): 14.6% Norwegian, 14.6% German, 14.6% French (except Basque), 14.6% Swedish, 12.5% Irish (2000).
Economy: Single-family building permits issued: 1 (2001) / 1 (2000); Multi-family building permits issued: 0 (2001) / 0 (2000); Employment by occupation: 31.6% management, 21.1% professional, 0.0% services, 31.6% sales, 0.0% farming, 15.8% construction, 0.0% production (2000).
Income: Per capita income: $18,050 (2000); Median household income: $36,563 (2000); Poverty rate: 10.9% (2000).
Taxes: Total city taxes per capita: $26 (1997); City property taxes per capita: $26 (1997).
Education: High school graduation rate: 100.0% (2000); College graduation rate: 19.5% (2000).
Housing: Homeownership rate: 91.7% (2000); Median home value: $112,500 (2000); Median age of housing: 23 years (2000).
Transportation: Commute to work: 84.2% car, 0.0% public transportation, 0.0% walk, 15.8% work from home (2000); Travel time to work: 81.3% less than 15 minutes, 0.0% 15 to 30 minutes, 0.0% 30 to 45 minutes, 0.0% 45 to 60 minutes, 18.8% 60 minutes or more (2000)

Chariton County

Located in north central Missouri; bounded on the south by the Missouri River, and on the west by the Grand River. Covers a land area of 755.90 square miles, a water area of 12.40 square miles, and is located in the Central Time Zone. The county government was organized in 1820. County seat is Keytesville.

Weather Station: Brunswick Elevation: 659 feet

	Jan	Feb	Mar	Apr	May	Jun	Jul	Aug	Sep	Oct	Nov	Dec
High	35	41	53	65	74	83	88	86	78	67	52	40
Low	16	21	31	42	52	62	66	64	55	43	32	22
Precip	1.6	1.5	2.7	3.7	5.0	4.3	3.7	3.9	4.0	3.3	3.2	1.9
Snow	na	na	1.8	tr	0.0	0.0	0.0	0.0	0.0	tr	1.1	2.3

High and Low temperatures in degrees Fahrenheit; Precipitation and Snow in inches

Weather Station: Salisbury Elevation: 728 feet

	Jan	Feb	Mar	Apr	May	Jun	Jul	Aug	Sep	Oct	Nov	Dec
High	35	42	54	65	75	84	88	87	79	68	53	41
Low	16	22	32	42	52	62	66	63	55	44	33	23
Precip	1.6	1.7	2.8	4.0	5.2	4.4	3.9	3.9	4.7	3.3	3.2	2.3
Snow	7.2	5.0	2.8	0.6	0.0	0.0	0.0	0.0	0.0	tr	1.5	4.1

High and Low temperatures in degrees Fahrenheit; Precipitation and Snow in inches

Population: 8,438 (2000); Race: 96.5% White, 2.9% Black, 0.1% Asian, 0.1% American Indian and Alaska Native, 0.3% Hispanic of any race, 0.3% two or more races (2000); Density: 11.2 persons per square mile (2000); Age: 23.8% under 18, 22.4% over 64 (2000).
Religion: Five largest groups: 21.0% Catholic Church, 15.9% Southern Baptist Convention, 14.1% The United Methodist Church, 10.9% Lutheran Church—Missouri Synod, 6.5% Christian Church (Disciples of Christ) (2000).
Economy: Unemployment rate: 6.4% (11/2002); Total civilian labor force: 4,220 (11/2002); Leading industries: 18.7% retail trade; 16.4% manufacturing; 9.9% wholesale trade (2000); Companies that employ more than 1,000 persons: 0 (2000); Companies that employ more than 100 persons: 2 (2000); Farms: 1,071 totaling 414,379 acres (1997); Minority business ownership rate: 0.0% (1997); Women business ownership rate: 55.1% (1997); Retail sales per capita: $5,437 (1997). Single-family building permits issued: 4 (2001) / 4 (2000); Multi-family building permits issued: 0 (2001) / 0 (2000).
Income: Per capita income: $15,515 (2000); Median household income: $32,285 (2000); Poverty rate: 11.6% (2000); Bankruptcy rate: 1.74% (2001).
Taxes: Total county taxes per capita: $83 (2000); County property taxes per capita: $31 (2000).
Education: High school graduation rate: 79.6% (2000); College graduation rate: 11.4% (2000).
Housing: Homeownership rate: 80.5% (2000); Median home value: $43,800 (2000); Median rent: $201 per month (2000); Median age of housing: 40 years (2000).
Health: Birth rate: 90.1 per 10,000 population (1998); Age adjusted death rate: 98.9 per 10,000 population (1999); Age adjusted cancer mortality rate: 215.3 deaths per 100,000 population (1999). Number of physicians: 2.4 per 10,000 population (1999); Number of hospital beds: n/a (1999).
Elections: 2000 Presidential election results: 43.1% Gore, 55.4% Bush, 0.7% Nader, 0.6% Buchanan
National and State Parks: Fountain Grove State Wildlife Area; Swan Lake National Wildlife Refuge; Swan Lake National Wildlife Refuge Habitat Trail
Additional Information Contacts
Chariton County Government Offices 660-288-3273

Chariton County Communities

BRUNSWICK (city). Covers a land area of 1.191 square miles and a water area of 0.053 square miles. Located at 39.42° N. Lat.; 93.12° W. Long. Elevation is 648 feet.
History: Brunswick was laid out in 1836 along the Grand River by Reverend James Keyte, and named for his former home in England, Brunswick Terrace. Although the town had promise as a river port when it was established, in 1875 the river changed its course and left Brunswick a mile inland.
Population: 925 (2000); Race: 84.1% White, 15.9% Black, 0.0% Asian, 0.0% American Indian and Alaska Native, 0.7% Hispanic of any race, 0.0% two or more races (2000); Density: 776.8 persons per square mile (2000); Age: 16.6% under 18, 31.6% over 64 (2000); Marriage status: 20.3% never married, 52.9% now married, 17.7% widowed, 9.1% divorced (2000); Foreign born: 0.7% (2000); Ancestry (includes multiple ancestries): 22.6% German, 18.2% United States or American, 18.0% Other groups, 7.9% Irish, 6.3% English (2000).
Economy: Employment by occupation: 6.1% management, 18.3% professional, 14.3% services, 19.3% sales, 1.6% farming, 15.6% construction, 24.9% production (2000).
Income: Per capita income: $18,516 (2000); Median household income: $27,969 (2000); Poverty rate: 17.7% (2000).
Taxes: Total city taxes per capita: $24 (1997); City property taxes per capita: $17 (1997).
Education: High school graduation rate: 72.2% (2000); College graduation rate: 9.5% (2000).

School District(s)

Brunswick R-II (PK-12)
2000 Enrollment: 300 660-548-3550
Housing: Homeownership rate: 67.4% (2000); Median home value: $28,900 (2000); Median rent: $199 per month (2000); Median age of housing: 45 years (2000).
Newspapers: The Brunswicker (1 x week)
Transportation: Commute to work: 93.3% car, 0.0% public transportation, 2.7% walk, 1.6% work from home (2000); Travel time to work: 43.6% less than 15 minutes, 13.1% 15 to 30 minutes, 22.3% 30 to 45 minutes, 9.3% 45 to 60 minutes, 11.7% 60 minutes or more (2000)

DALTON (town). Covers a land area of 0.177 square miles and a water area of 0 square miles. Located at 39.39° N. Lat.; 92.99° W. Long. Elevation is 725 feet.
Population: 27 (2000); Race: 0.0% White, 100.0% Black, 0.0% Asian, 0.0% American Indian and Alaska Native, 0.0% Hispanic of any race, 0.0% two or more races (2000); Density: 152.5 persons per square mile (2000); Age: 0.0% under 18, 30.8% over 64 (2000); Marriage status: 23.1% never married, 69.2% now married, 7.7% widowed, 0.0% divorced (2000); Foreign born: 0.0% (2000); Ancestry (includes multiple ancestries): 69.2% Other groups, 7.7% United States or American (2000).
Economy: Employment by occupation: 0.0% management, 0.0% professional, 0.0% services, 0.0% sales, 0.0% farming, 0.0% construction, 100.0% production (2000).
Income: Per capita income: $19,492 (2000); Median household income: $42,500 (2000); Poverty rate: 0.0% (2000).
Taxes: Total city taxes per capita: $79 (1997); City property taxes per capita: $26 (1997).
Education: High school graduation rate: 76.9% (2000); College graduation rate: 0.0% (2000).
Housing: Homeownership rate: 100.0% (2000); Median home value: $50,000 (2000); Median age of housing: 37 years (2000).
Transportation: Commute to work: 100.0% car, 0.0% public transportation, 0.0% walk, 0.0% work from home (2000); Travel time to work: 0.0% less than 15 minutes, 0.0% 15 to 30 minutes, 100.0% 30 to 45 minutes, 0.0% 45 to 60 minutes, 0.0% 60 minutes or more (2000)

KEYTESVILLE (city). Covers a land area of 0.697 square miles and a water area of 0 square miles. Located at 39.43° N. Lat.; 92.93° W. Long. Elevation is 709 feet.
History: Keytesville was platted in 1830 by Reverend James Keyte, and named for him. This was the home of Confederate General Sterling Price, who had been elected governor of Missouri in 1852. Granted a tract of land near Cordova, Mexico, by Emperor Maximilian after the Civil War ended, Price tried to establish a colony there for ex-Confederate soldiers. When that failed, he returned to Missouri in 1866.
Population: 533 (2000); Race: 92.7% White, 3.4% Black, 0.0% Asian, 0.0% American Indian and Alaska Native, 0.0% Hispanic of any race, 3.6% two or more races (2000); Density: 764.8 persons per square mile (2000); Age: 21.2% under 18, 25.6% over 64 (2000); Marriage status: 15.7% never married, 55.9% now married, 18.1% widowed, 10.3% divorced (2000); Foreign born: 0.4% (2000); Ancestry (includes multiple ancestries): 25.8% United States or American, 19.1% German, 14.0% Other groups, 11.3% Irish, 6.5% English (2000).
Economy: Employment by occupation: 3.0% management, 12.9% professional, 16.8% services, 22.0% sales, 0.4% farming, 6.9% construction, 37.9% production (2000).
Income: Per capita income: $14,699 (2000); Median household income: $25,000 (2000); Poverty rate: 16.4% (2000).
Taxes: Total city taxes per capita: $87 (1997); City property taxes per capita: $31 (1997).
Education: High school graduation rate: 74.5% (2000); College graduation rate: 10.9% (2000).

School District(s)

Keytesville R-III (PK-12)
2000 Enrollment: 225 660-288-3767
Housing: Homeownership rate: 67.9% (2000); Median home value: $31,400 (2000); Median rent: $197 per month (2000); Median age of housing: 42 years (2000).
Transportation: Commute to work: 94.4% car, 0.0% public transportation, 2.2% walk, 2.2% work from home (2000); Travel time to work: 44.9% less

than 15 minutes, 15.4% 15 to 30 minutes, 14.5% 30 to 45 minutes, 15.0% 45 to 60 minutes, 10.1% 60 minutes or more (2000)

MENDON (city). Covers a land area of 0.178 square miles and a water area of 0 square miles. Located at 39.59° N. Lat.; 93.13° W. Long. Elevation is 703 feet.
Population: 208 (2000); Race: 100.0% White, 0.0% Black, 0.0% Asian, 0.0% American Indian and Alaska Native, 0.0% Hispanic of any race, 0.0% two or more races (2000); Density: 1,171.6 persons per square mile (2000); Age: 26.0% under 18, 18.8% over 64 (2000); Marriage status: 11.0% never married, 68.6% now married, 9.9% widowed, 10.5% divorced (2000); Foreign born: 0.0% (2000); Ancestry (includes multiple ancestries): 19.7% German, 19.7% Irish, 16.6% United States or American, 12.6% English, 6.7% Swedish (2000).
Economy: Corn, wheat, soybeans. Dairying; livestock raising. Swan Lake National Wildlife Refuge on North side. Employment by occupation: 11.1% management, 14.8% professional, 9.9% services, 24.7% sales, 2.5% farming, 6.2% construction, 30.9% production (2000).
Income: Per capita income: $14,537 (2000); Median household income: $31,875 (2000); Poverty rate: 7.6% (2000).
Taxes: Total city taxes per capita: $65 (1997); City property taxes per capita: $25 (1997).
Education: High school graduation rate: 79.2% (2000); College graduation rate: 8.7% (2000).

School District(s)

Northwestern R-I (PK-12)
2000 Enrollment: 228 660-272-3201
Housing: Homeownership rate: 88.4% (2000); Median home value: $18,800 (2000); Median rent: $225 per month (2000); Median age of housing: 60+ years (2000).
Transportation: Commute to work: 87.7% car, 0.0% public transportation, 9.9% walk, 2.5% work from home (2000); Travel time to work: 29.1% less than 15 minutes, 44.3% 15 to 30 minutes, 17.7% 30 to 45 minutes, 8.9% 45 to 60 minutes, 0.0% 60 minutes or more (2000)

ROTHVILLE (village). Covers a land area of 0.251 square miles and a water area of 0 square miles. Located at 39.65° N. Lat.; 93.06° W. Long. Elevation is 743 feet.
Population: 93 (2000); Race: 100.0% White, 0.0% Black, 0.0% Asian, 0.0% American Indian and Alaska Native, 0.0% Hispanic of any race, 0.0% two or more races (2000); Density: 370.3 persons per square mile (2000); Age: 34.3% under 18, 12.7% over 64 (2000); Marriage status: 24.7% never married, 57.1% now married, 5.2% widowed, 13.0% divorced (2000); Foreign born: 2.9% (2000); Ancestry (includes multiple ancestries): 17.6% German, 16.7% United States or American, 5.9% Irish, 5.9% Other groups, 2.0% Scotch-Irish (2000).
Economy: Employment by occupation: 0.0% management, 20.9% professional, 18.6% services, 25.6% sales, 0.0% farming, 0.0% construction, 34.9% production (2000).
Income: Per capita income: $10,226 (2000); Median household income: $26,786 (2000); Poverty rate: 10.8% (2000).
Taxes: Total city taxes per capita: $38 (1997); City property taxes per capita: $10 (1997).
Education: High school graduation rate: 75.4% (2000); College graduation rate: 3.1% (2000).
Housing: Homeownership rate: 85.4% (2000); Median home value: $18,900 (2000); Median rent: $175 per month (2000); Median age of housing: 60+ years (2000).
Transportation: Commute to work: 90.2% car, 0.0% public transportation, 4.9% walk, 4.9% work from home (2000); Travel time to work: 10.3% less than 15 minutes, 74.4% 15 to 30 minutes, 10.3% 30 to 45 minutes, 0.0% 45 to 60 minutes, 5.1% 60 minutes or more (2000)

SALISBURY (city). Covers a land area of 1.353 square miles and a water area of 0 square miles. Located at 39.42° N. Lat.; 92.80° W. Long. Elevation is 735 feet.
History: Settled 1877, incorporated 1891.
Population: 1,726 (2000); Race: 96.2% White, 3.2% Black, 0.0% Asian, 0.0% American Indian and Alaska Native, 0.6% Hispanic of any race, 0.2% two or more races (2000); Density: 1,276.0 persons per square mile (2000); Age: 23.8% under 18, 22.2% over 64 (2000); Marriage status: 21.3% never married, 59.2% now married, 11.7% widowed, 7.8% divorced (2000); Foreign born: 0.5% (2000); Ancestry (includes multiple ancestries): 32.9% German, 16.3% United States or American, 11.2% Irish, 7.9% English, 5.8% Other groups (2000).
Economy: Agriculture: corn, wheat, soybeans; cattle, hogs. Manufacturing: air pollution filters, metal fabrication, flour, feed. Former coal mines. Single-family building permits issued: 4 (2001) / 4 (2000); Multi-family building permits issued: 0 (2001) / 0 (2000); Employment by occupation: 11.9% management, 15.2% professional, 15.1% services, 21.3% sales, 1.4% farming, 12.8% construction, 22.2% production (2000).
Income: Per capita income: $15,163 (2000); Median household income: $30,729 (2000); Poverty rate: 10.0% (2000).
Taxes: Total city taxes per capita: $308 (1997); City property taxes per capita: $69 (1997).
Education: High school graduation rate: 81.6% (2000); College graduation rate: 11.8% (2000).

School District(s)

Salisbury R-IV (KG-12)
2000 Enrollment: 593 660-388-6699
Housing: Homeownership rate: 80.7% (2000); Median home value: $47,200 (2000); Median rent: $197 per month (2000); Median age of housing: 40 years (2000).
Newspapers: Salisbury Press-Spectator (1 x week)
Transportation: Commute to work: 91.9% car, 0.0% public transportation, 2.8% walk, 4.1% work from home (2000); Travel time to work: 55.8% less than 15 minutes, 18.9% 15 to 30 minutes, 13.8% 30 to 45 minutes, 2.3% 45 to 60 minutes, 9.3% 60 minutes or more (2000)

SUMNER (town). Covers a land area of 0.258 square miles and a water area of 0 square miles. Located at 39.65° N. Lat.; 93.24° W. Long. Elevation is 682 feet.
History: Fountain Grove State Wildlife Refuge to Northwest; 40 foot statue of a wild goose.
Population: 142 (2000); Race: 98.4% White, 1.6% Black, 0.0% Asian, 0.0% American Indian and Alaska Native, 0.0% Hispanic of any race, 0.0% two or more races (2000); Density: 549.7 persons per square mile (2000); Age: 27.0% under 18, 30.3% over 64 (2000); Marriage status: 23.4% never married, 37.2% now married, 23.4% widowed, 16.0% divorced (2000); Foreign born: 2.5% (2000); Ancestry (includes multiple ancestries): 15.6% United States or American, 15.6% Irish, 11.5% German, 9.8% English, 1.6% Welsh (2000).
Economy: Grain; corn, soybeans, livestock. Railroad junction. Swan Lake National Wildlife Refuge to Southeast. Employment by occupation: 12.1% management, 6.1% professional, 18.2% services, 21.2% sales, 0.0% farming, 0.0% construction, 42.4% production (2000).
Income: Per capita income: $21,025 (2000); Median household income: $14,792 (2000); Poverty rate: 32.5% (2000).
Taxes: Total city taxes per capita: $92 (1997); City property taxes per capita: $56 (1997).
Education: High school graduation rate: 54.7% (2000); College graduation rate: 0.0% (2000).
Housing: Homeownership rate: 91.9% (2000); Median home value: <$10,000 (2000); Median rent: $125 per month (2000); Median age of housing: 53 years (2000).
Transportation: Commute to work: 84.8% car, 0.0% public transportation, 6.1% walk, 9.1% work from home (2000); Travel time to work: 20.0% less than 15 minutes, 60.0% 15 to 30 minutes, 6.7% 30 to 45 minutes, 6.7% 45 to 60 minutes, 6.7% 60 minutes or more (2000)

TRIPLETT (city). Covers a land area of 0.229 square miles and a water area of 0 square miles. Located at 39.49° N. Lat.; 93.19° W. Long. Elevation is 662 feet.
Population: 64 (2000); Race: 88.6% White, 0.0% Black, 0.0% Asian, 11.4% American Indian and Alaska Native, 0.0% Hispanic of any race, 0.0% two or more races (2000); Density: 279.9 persons per square mile (2000); Age: 9.1% under 18, 20.5% over 64 (2000); Marriage status: 14.6% never married, 68.3% now married, 17.1% widowed, 0.0% divorced (2000); Foreign born: 0.0% (2000); Ancestry (includes multiple ancestries): 40.9% German, 13.6% Irish, 9.1% Other groups, 9.1% United States or American, 4.5% English (2000).
Economy: Corn, soybeans. Employment by occupation: 22.2% management, 11.1% professional, 11.1% services, 11.1% sales, 0.0% farming, 5.6% construction, 38.9% production (2000).
Income: Per capita income: $12,773 (2000); Median household income: $18,750 (2000); Poverty rate: 47.7% (2000).
Taxes: Total city taxes per capita: $73 (1997); City property taxes per capita: $55 (1997).
Education: High school graduation rate: 64.9% (2000); College graduation rate: 5.4% (2000).

Housing: Homeownership rate: 89.5% (2000); Median home value: $16,900 (2000); Median rent: $275 per month (2000); Median age of housing: 55 years (2000).
Transportation: Commute to work: 88.9% car, 0.0% public transportation, 0.0% walk, 11.1% work from home (2000); Travel time to work: 18.8% less than 15 minutes, 43.8% 15 to 30 minutes, 0.0% 30 to 45 minutes, 37.5% 45 to 60 minutes, 0.0% 60 minutes or more (2000)

Christian County

Located in southwestern Missouri, in the Ozarks; includes part of Mark Twain National Forest. Covers a land area of 563.20 square miles, a water area of 0.90 square miles, and is located in the Central Time Zone. The county government was organized in 1859. County seat is Ozark.

Christian County is part of the Springfield, MO MSA. The entire metro area includes: Christian County; Greene County; Webster County

Weather Station: Billings 2 N Elevation: 1,351 feet

	Jan	Feb	Mar	Apr	May	Jun	Jul	Aug	Sep	Oct	Nov	Dec
High	40	47	56	67	75	83	89	89	na	na	56	45
Low	19	24	33	42	52	61	66	64	na	na	33	24
Precip	2.0	1.9	3.7	4.1	4.4	4.6	3.3	3.7	5.0	3.4	4.3	3.1
Snow	6.2	4.0	3.6	0.5	0.0	0.0	0.0	0.0	0.0	tr	1.4	2.8

High and Low temperatures in degrees Fahrenheit; Precipitation and Snow in inches

Population: 54,285 (2000); Race: 97.3% White, 0.2% Black, 0.3% Asian, 0.8% American Indian and Alaska Native, 1.2% Hispanic of any race, 1.1% two or more races (2000); Density: 96.4 persons per square mile (2000); Age: 27.8% under 18, 10.6% over 64 (2000).
Religion: Five largest groups: 18.0% Southern Baptist Convention, 4.3% Catholic Church, 3.8% Assemblies of God, 2.2% The United Methodist Church, 2.0% Christian Church (Disciples of Christ) (2000).
Economy: Unemployment rate: 4.5% (11/2002); Total civilian labor force: 30,432 (11/2002); Leading industries: 25.6% manufacturing; 18.2% retail trade; 13.7% construction (2000); Companies that employ more than 1,000 persons: 0 (2000); Companies that employ more than 100 persons: 10 (2000); Farms: 1,209 totaling 202,863 acres (1997); Minority business ownership rate: 0.0% (1997); Women business ownership rate: 25.6% (1997); Retail sales per capita: $5,268 (1997). Single-family building permits issued: 535 (2001) / 472 (2000); Multi-family building permits issued: 90 (2001) / 73 (2000).
Income: Per capita income: $18,422 (2000); Median household income: $38,085 (2000); Poverty rate: 9.1% (2000); Bankruptcy rate: 6.09% (2001).
Taxes: Total county taxes per capita: $71 (2000); County property taxes per capita: $9 (2000).
Education: High school graduation rate: 85.9% (2000); College graduation rate: 20.9% (2000).
Housing: Homeownership rate: 75.9% (2000); Median home value: $97,900 (2000); Median rent: $411 per month (2000); Median age of housing: 12 years (2000).
Health: Birth rate: 129.3 per 10,000 population (1998); Age adjusted death rate: 89.0 per 10,000 population (1999); Age adjusted cancer mortality rate: 179.0 deaths per 100,000 population (1999). Number of physicians: 4.8 per 10,000 population (1999); Number of hospital beds: n/a (1999).
Elections: 2000 Presidential election results: 34.0% Gore, 63.8% Bush, 1.2% Nader, 0.6% Buchanan

Additional Information Contacts

Christian County Government Offices 417-581-6360
Nixa Chamber of Commerce 417-725-1545
Ozark Chamber of Commerce 417-581-6139

Christian County Communities

BILLINGS (city). Covers a land area of 0.779 square miles and a water area of 0 square miles. Located at 37.06° N. Lat.; 93.55° W. Long. Elevation is 1,368 feet.
History: Billings developed as a strawberry-growing town on a southern branch of the St. Louis-San Francisco Railway.
Population: 1,091 (2000); Race: 98.4% White, 0.0% Black, 0.3% Asian, 0.0% American Indian and Alaska Native, 0.2% Hispanic of any race, 1.3% two or more races (2000); Density: 1,400.0 persons per square mile (2000); Age: 26.7% under 18, 15.7% over 64 (2000); Marriage status: 19.2% never married, 57.0% now married, 11.2% widowed, 12.6% divorced (2000); Foreign born: 0.0% (2000); Ancestry (includes multiple ancestries): 22.7% German, 14.5% English, 12.9% Other groups, 12.6% United States or American, 12.2% Irish (2000).
Economy: Single-family building permits issued: 2 (2001) / 3 (2000); Multi-family building permits issued: 4 (2001) / 0 (2000); Employment by occupation: 12.4% management, 14.5% professional, 13.1% services, 25.7% sales, 0.0% farming, 10.0% construction, 24.3% production (2000).
Income: Per capita income: $16,503 (2000); Median household income: $28,207 (2000); Poverty rate: 15.1% (2000).
Taxes: Total city taxes per capita: $54 (1997); City property taxes per capita: $31 (1997).
Education: High school graduation rate: 82.8% (2000); College graduation rate: 12.8% (2000).

School District(s)

Billings R-IV (PK-12)
2000 Enrollment: 488 417-744-2623

Housing: Homeownership rate: 67.4% (2000); Median home value: $70,900 (2000); Median rent: $331 per month (2000); Median age of housing: 30 years (2000).
Transportation: Commute to work: 93.8% car, 0.0% public transportation, 3.0% walk, 3.2% work from home (2000); Travel time to work: 26.2% less than 15 minutes, 20.0% 15 to 30 minutes, 46.8% 30 to 45 minutes, 5.4% 45 to 60 minutes, 1.7% 60 minutes or more (2000)

BRUNER (unincorporated postal area, zip code 65620). Covers a land area of 20.051 square miles and a water area of 0.024 square miles. Located at 37.02° N. Lat.; 92.95° W. Long. Elevation is 1,468 feet.
Population: 379 (2000); Race: 97.3% White, 0.0% Black, 0.0% Asian, 2.7% American Indian and Alaska Native, 0.0% Hispanic of any race, 0.0% two or more races (2000); Density: 18.9 persons per square mile (2000); Age: 31.3% under 18, 3.0% over 64 (2000); Marriage status: 16.6% never married, 72.5% now married, 1.7% widowed, 9.3% divorced (2000); Foreign born: 0.0% (2000); Ancestry (includes multiple ancestries): 18.5% Other groups, 14.5% German, 14.5% Irish, 12.3% English, 10.6% United States or American (2000).
Economy: Employment by occupation: 6.1% management, 5.0% professional, 11.6% services, 14.4% sales, 10.5% farming, 16.6% construction, 35.9% production (2000).
Income: Per capita income: $11,542 (2000); Median household income: $26,875 (2000); Poverty rate: 14.7% (2000).
Education: High school graduation rate: 70.8% (2000); College graduation rate: 1.6% (2000).
Housing: Homeownership rate: 83.1% (2000); Median home value: $85,000 (2000); Median rent: $288 per month (2000); Median age of housing: 18 years (2000).
Transportation: Commute to work: 87.2% car, 0.0% public transportation, 2.2% walk, 10.6% work from home (2000); Travel time to work: 16.9% less than 15 minutes, 21.3% 15 to 30 minutes, 40.0% 30 to 45 minutes, 14.4% 45 to 60 minutes, 7.5% 60 minutes or more (2000)

CHADWICK (unincorporated postal area, zip code 65629). Covers a land area of 69.866 square miles and a water area of 0 square miles. Located at 36.89° N. Lat.; 93.00° W. Long. Elevation is 1,330 feet.
Population: 781 (2000); Race: 98.4% White, 0.0% Black, 0.0% Asian, 0.0% American Indian and Alaska Native, 0.9% Hispanic of any race, 1.6% two or more races (2000); Density: 11.2 persons per square mile (2000); Age: 26.2% under 18, 11.0% over 64 (2000); Marriage status: 19.1% never married, 62.3% now married, 7.7% widowed, 10.9% divorced (2000); Foreign born: 0.3% (2000); Ancestry (includes multiple ancestries): 33.7% United States or American, 14.8% German, 10.2% Other groups, 7.5% Irish, 5.6% English (2000).
Economy: Employment by occupation: 5.7% management, 9.2% professional, 13.0% services, 22.2% sales, 1.4% farming, 14.1% construction, 34.4% production (2000).
Income: Per capita income: $13,115 (2000); Median household income: $28,173 (2000); Poverty rate: 17.7% (2000).
Education: High school graduation rate: 71.7% (2000); College graduation rate: 6.8% (2000).

School District(s)

Chadwick R-I (KG-12)
2000 Enrollment: 258 417-634-3588

Housing: Homeownership rate: 81.4% (2000); Median home value: $51,700 (2000); Median rent: $261 per month (2000); Median age of housing: 29 years (2000).
Transportation: Commute to work: 95.3% car, 0.0% public transportation, 1.6% walk, 3.0% work from home (2000); Travel time to work: 8.8% less

than 15 minutes, 20.4% 15 to 30 minutes, 31.2% 30 to 45 minutes, 29.7% 45 to 60 minutes, 9.9% 60 minutes or more (2000)

CHESTNUTRIDGE (unincorporated postal area, zip code 65630). Covers a land area of 8.727 square miles and a water area of 0 square miles. Located at 36.82° N. Lat.; 93.20° W. Long. Elevation is 1,322 feet.
Population: 159 (2000); Race: 90.1% White, 0.0% Black, 0.0% Asian, 0.0% American Indian and Alaska Native, 0.0% Hispanic of any race, 9.9% two or more races (2000); Density: 18.2 persons per square mile (2000); Age: 30.3% under 18, 7.9% over 64 (2000); Marriage status: 31.9% never married, 48.1% now married, 8.9% widowed, 11.1% divorced (2000); Foreign born: 18.4% (2000); Ancestry (includes multiple ancestries): 21.7% French (except Basque), 17.1% German, 13.2% Canadian, 12.5% Irish, 11.8% European (2000).
Economy: Employment by occupation: 36.1% management, 11.5% professional, 0.0% services, 39.3% sales, 0.0% farming, 0.0% construction, 13.1% production (2000).
Income: Per capita income: $13,319 (2000); Median household income: $45,875 (2000); Poverty rate: 9.9% (2000).
Education: High school graduation rate: 91.5% (2000); College graduation rate: 26.4% (2000).
Housing: Homeownership rate: 83.7% (2000); Median home value: $108,600 (2000); Median rent: $175 per month (2000); Median age of housing: 8 years (2000).
Transportation: Commute to work: 100.0% car, 0.0% public transportation, 0.0% walk, 0.0% work from home (2000); Travel time to work: 0.0% less than 15 minutes, 24.6% 15 to 30 minutes, 63.9% 30 to 45 minutes, 0.0% 45 to 60 minutes, 11.5% 60 minutes or more (2000)

CLEVER (city). Covers a land area of 0.639 square miles and a water area of 0 square miles. Located at 37.02° N. Lat.; 93.47° W. Long. Elevation is 1,398 feet.
Population: 1,010 (2000); Race: 97.0% White, 0.0% Black, 0.4% Asian, 0.2% American Indian and Alaska Native, 1.5% Hispanic of any race, 2.1% two or more races (2000); Density: 1,581.7 persons per square mile (2000); Age: 30.8% under 18, 11.0% over 64 (2000); Marriage status: 16.3% never married, 66.1% now married, 7.0% widowed, 10.6% divorced (2000); Foreign born: 0.9% (2000); Ancestry (includes multiple ancestries): 15.1% United States or American, 14.5% Other groups, 13.4% German, 10.8% Irish, 7.7% English (2000).
Economy: Limestone quarry. Single-family building permits issued: 18 (2001) / 27 (2000); Multi-family building permits issued: 0 (2001) / 0 (2000); Employment by occupation: 7.2% management, 11.4% professional, 16.3% services, 29.5% sales, 0.4% farming, 8.8% construction, 26.3% production (2000).
Income: Per capita income: $14,958 (2000); Median household income: $32,798 (2000); Poverty rate: 6.0% (2000).
Taxes: Total city taxes per capita: $127 (1997); City property taxes per capita: $55 (1997).
Education: High school graduation rate: 81.7% (2000); College graduation rate: 13.3% (2000).

School District(s)

Clever R-V (PK-12)
2000 Enrollment: 623 417-743-4800

Housing: Homeownership rate: 76.5% (2000); Median home value: $72,300 (2000); Median rent: $410 per month (2000); Median age of housing: 19 years (2000).
Transportation: Commute to work: 95.3% car, 0.0% public transportation, 1.4% walk, 1.4% work from home (2000); Travel time to work: 14.6% less than 15 minutes, 29.0% 15 to 30 minutes, 39.9% 30 to 45 minutes, 12.6% 45 to 60 minutes, 3.9% 60 minutes or more (2000)

FREMONT HILLS (city). Covers a land area of 0.520 square miles and a water area of 0 square miles. Located at 37.06° N. Lat.; 93.25° W. Long. Elevation is 1,298 feet.
Population: 597 (2000); Race: 97.3% White, 0.0% Black, 1.7% Asian, 0.3% American Indian and Alaska Native, 0.3% Hispanic of any race, 0.7% two or more races (2000); Density: 1,147.0 persons per square mile (2000); Age: 23.5% under 18, 6.7% over 64 (2000); Marriage status: 13.0% never married, 81.4% now married, 2.1% widowed, 3.5% divorced (2000); Foreign born: 1.5% (2000); Ancestry (includes multiple ancestries): 20.5% English, 16.5% German, 14.8% United States or American, 13.6% Irish, 7.4% Other groups (2000).
Economy: Employment by occupation: 30.4% management, 26.1% professional, 4.3% services, 31.3% sales, 0.0% farming, 2.3% construction, 5.5% production (2000).
Income: Per capita income: $39,895 (2000); Median household income: $87,863 (2000); Poverty rate: 3.5% (2000).
Taxes: Total city taxes per capita: $323 (1997); City property taxes per capita: $191 (1997).
Education: High school graduation rate: 94.9% (2000); College graduation rate: 49.1% (2000).
Housing: Homeownership rate: 85.7% (2000); Median home value: $244,000 (2000); Median rent: $468 per month (2000); Median age of housing: 10 years (2000).
Transportation: Commute to work: 92.7% car, 0.0% public transportation, 0.6% walk, 6.4% work from home (2000); Travel time to work: 22.7% less than 15 minutes, 66.0% 15 to 30 minutes, 8.4% 30 to 45 minutes, 1.2% 45 to 60 minutes, 1.6% 60 minutes or more (2000)

GARRISON (unincorporated postal area, zip code 65657). Covers a land area of 17.900 square miles and a water area of 0 square miles. Located at 36.83° N. Lat.; 93.00° W. Long. Elevation is 891 feet.
Population: 135 (2000); Race: 90.0% White, 0.0% Black, 0.0% Asian, 1.8% American Indian and Alaska Native, 0.0% Hispanic of any race, 8.2% two or more races (2000); Density: 7.5 persons per square mile (2000); Age: 27.3% under 18, 12.7% over 64 (2000); Marriage status: 22.1% never married, 57.0% now married, 9.3% widowed, 11.6% divorced (2000); Foreign born: 0.0% (2000); Ancestry (includes multiple ancestries): 30.0% United States or American, 20.9% Other groups, 10.9% German, 7.3% Irish, 7.3% English (2000).
Economy: Employment by occupation: 13.0% management, 6.5% professional, 8.7% services, 10.9% sales, 0.0% farming, 21.7% construction, 39.1% production (2000).
Income: Per capita income: $11,682 (2000); Median household income: $26,250 (2000); Poverty rate: 23.6% (2000).
Education: High school graduation rate: 80.0% (2000); College graduation rate: 10.0% (2000).
Housing: Homeownership rate: 71.4% (2000); Median home value: $42,500 (2000); Median rent: $292 per month (2000); Median age of housing: 30 years (2000).
Transportation: Commute to work: 90.9% car, 0.0% public transportation, 0.0% walk, 9.1% work from home (2000); Travel time to work: 15.0% less than 15 minutes, 12.5% 15 to 30 minutes, 15.0% 30 to 45 minutes, 27.5% 45 to 60 minutes, 30.0% 60 minutes or more (2000)

HIGHLANDVILLE (city). Covers a land area of 4.977 square miles and a water area of 0.007 square miles. Located at 36.94° N. Lat.; 93.28° W. Long. Elevation is 1,380 feet.
Population: 872 (2000); Race: 96.6% White, 0.0% Black, 0.0% Asian, 0.2% American Indian and Alaska Native, 1.1% Hispanic of any race, 3.2% two or more races (2000); Density: 175.2 persons per square mile (2000); Age: 26.9% under 18, 6.8% over 64 (2000); Marriage status: 27.0% never married, 56.4% now married, 5.3% widowed, 11.3% divorced (2000); Foreign born: 1.1% (2000); Ancestry (includes multiple ancestries): 19.6% United States or American, 13.9% Other groups, 13.3% English, 11.3% German, 8.6% Irish (2000).
Economy: Employment by occupation: 5.7% management, 12.4% professional, 16.7% services, 23.0% sales, 1.2% farming, 23.4% construction, 17.5% production (2000).
Income: Per capita income: $12,442 (2000); Median household income: $31,767 (2000); Poverty rate: 17.9% (2000).
Education: High school graduation rate: 77.5% (2000); College graduation rate: 4.9% (2000).
Housing: Homeownership rate: 70.5% (2000); Median home value: $83,300 (2000); Median rent: $330 per month (2000); Median age of housing: 23 years (2000).
Transportation: Commute to work: 93.2% car, 0.0% public transportation, 3.4% walk, 2.9% work from home (2000); Travel time to work: 17.3% less than 15 minutes, 35.1% 15 to 30 minutes, 33.6% 30 to 45 minutes, 8.0% 45 to 60 minutes, 6.0% 60 minutes or more (2000)

NIXA (city). Covers a land area of 6.157 square miles and a water area of 0 square miles. Located at 37.04° N. Lat.; 93.29° W. Long. Elevation is 1,295 feet.
Population: 12,124 (2000); Race: 97.1% White, 0.7% Black, 0.3% Asian, 0.2% American Indian and Alaska Native, 1.3% Hispanic of any race, 1.4% two or more races (2000); Density: 1,969.1 persons per square mile (2000); Age: 27.7% under 18, 11.8% over 64 (2000); Marriage status: 16.8% never married, 65.0% now married, 5.2% widowed, 13.0% divorced (2000); Foreign born: 0.7% (2000); Ancestry (includes multiple ancestries): 20.8%

German, 16.2% United States or American, 15.0% Irish, 10.6% English, 10.4% Other groups (2000).
Economy: Fruit; dairying. Manufacturing: plastic molding, deodorants, lamps, fixtures, aluminum and sand castings, furniture, pottery. Single-family building permits issued: 237 (2001) / 171 (2000); Multi-family building permits issued: 42 (2001) / 40 (2000); Employment by occupation: 12.1% management, 16.6% professional, 13.6% services, 33.4% sales, 0.5% farming, 11.8% construction, 11.9% production (2000).
Income: Per capita income: $17,774 (2000); Median household income: $37,655 (2000); Poverty rate: 9.7% (2000).
Taxes: Total city taxes per capita: $215 (2000); City property taxes per capita: $24 (2000).
Education: High school graduation rate: 88.5% (2000); College graduation rate: 21.9% (2000).

School District(s)

Nixa R-II (PK-12)
2000 Enrollment: 3,780 417-725-7400
Housing: Homeownership rate: 68.5% (2000); Median home value: $90,800 (2000); Median rent: $498 per month (2000); Median age of housing: 6 years (2000).
Newspapers: Nixa News-Enterprise (1 x week)
Transportation: Commute to work: 96.8% car, 0.0% public transportation, 0.9% walk, 1.8% work from home (2000); Travel time to work: 25.2% less than 15 minutes, 44.0% 15 to 30 minutes, 24.0% 30 to 45 minutes, 3.0% 45 to 60 minutes, 3.8% 60 minutes or more (2000)
Additional Information Contacts
Nixa Chamber of Commerce 417-725-1545

OLDFIELD (unincorporated postal area, zip code 65720). Covers a land area of 35.932 square miles and a water area of 0 square miles. Located at 36.93° N. Lat.; 92.93° W. Long. Elevation is 1,380 feet.
Population: 463 (2000); Race: 97.3% White, 0.0% Black, 0.6% Asian, 0.8% American Indian and Alaska Native, 0.0% Hispanic of any race, 1.2% two or more races (2000); Density: 12.9 persons per square mile (2000); Age: 27.2% under 18, 15.1% over 64 (2000); Marriage status: 19.4% never married, 60.7% now married, 7.3% widowed, 12.6% divorced (2000); Foreign born: 1.9% (2000); Ancestry (includes multiple ancestries): 16.7% German, 15.3% English, 11.8% Other groups, 11.5% United States or American, 5.8% Irish (2000).
Economy: Employment by occupation: 10.6% management, 5.1% professional, 10.1% services, 16.2% sales, 1.0% farming, 13.6% construction, 43.4% production (2000).
Income: Per capita income: $12,072 (2000); Median household income: $26,944 (2000); Poverty rate: 10.6% (2000).
Education: High school graduation rate: 69.5% (2000); College graduation rate: 3.7% (2000).
Housing: Homeownership rate: 83.6% (2000); Median home value: $71,400 (2000); Median rent: $158 per month (2000); Median age of housing: 27 years (2000).
Transportation: Commute to work: 92.0% car, 1.0% public transportation, 0.0% walk, 7.0% work from home (2000); Travel time to work: 12.4% less than 15 minutes, 17.7% 15 to 30 minutes, 26.3% 30 to 45 minutes, 26.3% 45 to 60 minutes, 17.2% 60 minutes or more (2000)

OZARK (city). Covers a land area of 7.546 square miles and a water area of 0.035 square miles. Located at 37.02° N. Lat.; 93.21° W. Long. Elevation is 1,178 feet.
History: Ozark was platted in 1843 and became the trading center of a tomato-growing region.
Population: 9,665 (2000); Race: 96.3% White, 0.1% Black, 0.8% Asian, 0.9% American Indian and Alaska Native, 1.2% Hispanic of any race, 1.6% two or more races (2000); Density: 1,280.8 persons per square mile (2000); Age: 28.9% under 18, 9.2% over 64 (2000); Marriage status: 19.2% never married, 61.9% now married, 6.8% widowed, 12.1% divorced (2000); Foreign born: 1.0% (2000); Ancestry (includes multiple ancestries): 18.4% German, 13.9% United States or American, 13.1% English, 11.1% Other groups, 10.9% Irish (2000).
Economy: Single-family building permits issued: 278 (2001) / 271 (2000); Multi-family building permits issued: 44 (2001) / 33 (2000); Employment by occupation: 13.8% management, 17.0% professional, 14.3% services, 28.9% sales, 0.3% farming, 10.9% construction, 14.8% production (2000).
Income: Per capita income: $15,912 (2000); Median household income: $34,210 (2000); Poverty rate: 11.7% (2000).
Taxes: Total city taxes per capita: $254 (1997); City property taxes per capita: $60 (1997).
Education: High school graduation rate: 85.6% (2000); College graduation rate: 23.9% (2000).

School District(s)

Ozark R-VI (PK-12)
2000 Enrollment: 3,571 417-581-7694
Housing: Homeownership rate: 62.3% (2000); Median home value: $91,900 (2000); Median rent: $406 per month (2000); Median age of housing: 8 years (2000).
Newspapers: Christian County Headliner News (1 x week); Pennysaver (1 x week)
Transportation: Commute to work: 95.1% car, 0.0% public transportation, 0.7% walk, 3.6% work from home (2000); Travel time to work: 31.2% less than 15 minutes, 43.6% 15 to 30 minutes, 17.8% 30 to 45 minutes, 3.1% 45 to 60 minutes, 4.3% 60 minutes or more (2000)
Additional Information Contacts
Ozark Chamber of Commerce 417-581-6139

SPARTA (city). Covers a land area of 0.877 square miles and a water area of 0 square miles. Located at 37.00° N. Lat.; 93.08° W. Long. Elevation is 1,407 feet.
Population: 1,144 (2000); Race: 95.9% White, 0.6% Black, 0.0% Asian, 1.0% American Indian and Alaska Native, 0.7% Hispanic of any race, 1.9% two or more races (2000); Density: 1,304.3 persons per square mile (2000); Age: 29.0% under 18, 15.4% over 64 (2000); Marriage status: 14.6% never married, 59.9% now married, 10.8% widowed, 14.8% divorced (2000); Foreign born: 0.7% (2000); Ancestry (includes multiple ancestries): 22.5% United States or American, 12.7% English, 11.1% Other groups, 10.4% German, 9.9% Irish (2000).
Economy: Plotted 1885. Employment by occupation: 8.2% management, 7.3% professional, 16.1% services, 30.0% sales, 0.2% farming, 12.6% construction, 25.6% production (2000).
Income: Per capita income: $11,869 (2000); Median household income: $22,768 (2000); Poverty rate: 18.7% (2000).
Taxes: Total city taxes per capita: $96 (1997); City property taxes per capita: $19 (1997).
Education: High school graduation rate: 70.3% (2000); College graduation rate: 4.2% (2000).

School District(s)

Sparta R-III (PK-12)
2000 Enrollment: 677 417-634-4284
Housing: Homeownership rate: 64.0% (2000); Median home value: $63,800 (2000); Median rent: $325 per month (2000); Median age of housing: 20 years (2000).
Transportation: Commute to work: 96.0% car, 0.0% public transportation, 1.1% walk, 1.3% work from home (2000); Travel time to work: 18.6% less than 15 minutes, 27.4% 15 to 30 minutes, 37.2% 30 to 45 minutes, 12.6% 45 to 60 minutes, 4.3% 60 minutes or more (2000)

SPOKANE (CDP). Covers a land area of 0.790 square miles and a water area of 0 square miles. Located at 36.86° N. Lat.; 93.30° W. Long. Elevation is 1,340 feet.
Population: 133 (2000); Race: 72.9% White, 10.3% Black, 0.0% Asian, 12.9% American Indian and Alaska Native, 0.0% Hispanic of any race, 3.9% two or more races (2000); Density: 168.4 persons per square mile (2000); Age: 57.4% under 18, 0.0% over 64 (2000); Marriage status: 22.8% never married, 77.2% now married, 0.0% widowed, 0.0% divorced (2000); Foreign born: 0.0% (2000); Ancestry (includes multiple ancestries): 38.1% Other groups, 10.3% German, 7.1% European, 3.9% English, 3.2% French (except Basque) (2000).
Economy: Employment by occupation: 8.3% management, 10.0% professional, 28.3% services, 21.7% sales, 0.0% farming, 11.7% construction, 20.0% production (2000).
Income: Per capita income: $17,157 (2000); Median household income: $35,417 (2000); Poverty rate: 0.0% (2000).
Education: High school graduation rate: 90.2% (2000); College graduation rate: 19.7% (2000).

School District(s)

Spokane R-VII (PK-12)
2000 Enrollment: 750 417-443-3502
Housing: Homeownership rate: 52.5% (2000); Median home value: $145,800 (2000); Median rent: $348 per month (2000); Median age of housing: 23 years (2000).
Transportation: Commute to work: 91.7% car, 0.0% public transportation, 0.0% walk, 8.3% work from home (2000); Travel time to work: 41.8% less than 15 minutes, 34.5% 15 to 30 minutes, 0.0% 30 to 45 minutes, 23.6% 45 to 60 minutes, 0.0% 60 minutes or more (2000)

Clark County

Located in northeastern Missouri; bounded on the east by the Mississippi River and the Illinois border, and on the north and northeast by the Des Moines River and the Iowa border; drained by the Fox and Wyaconda Rivers. Covers a land area of 507.30 square miles, a water area of 4.60 square miles, and is located in the Central Time Zone. The county government was organized in 1836. County seat is Kahoka.

Population: 7,416 (2000); Race: 98.5% White, 0.2% Black, 0.1% Asian, 0.2% American Indian and Alaska Native, 0.4% Hispanic of any race, 1.0% two or more races (2000); Density: 14.6 persons per square mile (2000); Age: 25.0% under 18, 16.7% over 64 (2000).

Religion: Five largest groups: 20.5% Southern Baptist Convention, 8.0% The United Methodist Church, 7.6% Christian Church (Disciples of Christ), 5.8% United Church of Christ, 4.8% Catholic Church (2000).

Economy: Unemployment rate: 5.5% (11/2002); Total civilian labor force: 3,879 (11/2002); Leading industries: 32.4% retail trade; 17.7% wholesale trade; 8.5% health care and social assistance (2000); Companies that employ more than 1,000 persons: 0 (2000); Companies that employ more than 100 persons: 0 (2000); Farms: 634 totaling 248,397 acres (1997); Minority business ownership rate: 0.0% (1997); Women business ownership rate: 0.0% (1997); Retail sales per capita: $5,892 (1997). Single-family building permits issued: 7 (2001) / 4 (2000); Multi-family building permits issued: 0 (2001) / 0 (2000).

Income: Per capita income: $15,988 (2000); Median household income: $29,457 (2000); Poverty rate: 14.1% (2000); Bankruptcy rate: 2.55% (2001).

Taxes: Total county taxes per capita: $196 (2000); County property taxes per capita: $85 (2000).

Education: High school graduation rate: 79.6% (2000); College graduation rate: 10.7% (2000).

Housing: Homeownership rate: 78.5% (2000); Median home value: $51,300 (2000); Median rent: $230 per month (2000); Median age of housing: 33 years (2000).

Health: Birth rate: 103.8 per 10,000 population (1998); Age adjusted death rate: 93.7 per 10,000 population (1999); Age adjusted cancer mortality rate: 220.9 deaths per 100,000 population (1999). Number of physicians: n/a (1999); Number of hospital beds: n/a (1999).

Elections: 2000 Presidential election results: 47.7% Gore, 50.0% Bush, 1.4% Nader, 0.5% Buchanan

National and State Parks: Athens State Park; Charlie Heath State Forest and Memorial Wildlife Area

Additional Information Contacts

Clark County Government Offices. 660-727-3283
Kahoka Chamber of Commerce. 660-727-3143

Clark County Communities

ALEXANDRIA (city). Covers a land area of 0.374 square miles and a water area of 0.011 square miles. Located at 40.36° N. Lat.; 91.45° W. Long. Elevation is 485 feet.

History: Alexandria was named in 1839 for a Mississippi River ferryman who had settled here about 1824. The town developed as a pork-packing center in the 1860's and 1870's.

Population: 166 (2000); Race: 100.0% White, 0.0% Black, 0.0% Asian, 0.0% American Indian and Alaska Native, 0.0% Hispanic of any race, 0.0% two or more races (2000); Density: 443.7 persons per square mile (2000); Age: 22.9% under 18, 19.1% over 64 (2000); Marriage status: 17.8% never married, 72.6% now married, 4.5% widowed, 5.1% divorced (2000); Foreign born: 0.0% (2000); Ancestry (includes multiple ancestries): 19.7% German, 19.7% Irish, 9.6% United States or American, 9.0% Other groups, 4.8% English (2000).

Economy: Employment by occupation: 0.0% management, 0.0% professional, 19.4% services, 16.4% sales, 0.0% farming, 20.9% construction, 43.3% production (2000).

Income: Per capita income: $13,404 (2000); Median household income: $30,000 (2000); Poverty rate: 6.4% (2000).

Taxes: Total city taxes per capita: $70 (1997); City property taxes per capita: $20 (1997).

Education: High school graduation rate: 61.7% (2000); College graduation rate: 1.6% (2000).

Housing: Homeownership rate: 77.1% (2000); Median home value: $45,400 (2000); Median rent: $271 per month (2000); Median age of housing: 18 years (2000).

Transportation: Commute to work: 95.5% car, 0.0% public transportation, 4.5% walk, 0.0% work from home (2000); Travel time to work: 38.8% less than 15 minutes, 31.3% 15 to 30 minutes, 17.9% 30 to 45 minutes, 0.0% 45 to 60 minutes, 11.9% 60 minutes or more (2000)

KAHOKA (city). Covers a land area of 1.531 square miles and a water area of 0.026 square miles. Located at 40.42° N. Lat.; 91.72° W. Long. Elevation is 703 feet.

History: Kahoka was platted in 1856, and developed as a grain center and as the seat of Clark County. The Anti-Horse Thief Association was organized in 1854 in Kahoka, to combat criminals who brought stolen goods over the state line from Illinois and Iowa. The name of Kahoka was taken from that of the Gawakie Indians.

Population: 2,241 (2000); Race: 97.0% White, 0.6% Black, 0.1% Asian, 0.8% American Indian and Alaska Native, 1.1% Hispanic of any race, 1.5% two or more races (2000); Density: 1,464.0 persons per square mile (2000); Age: 24.4% under 18, 23.8% over 64 (2000); Marriage status: 20.2% never married, 56.1% now married, 15.7% widowed, 8.0% divorced (2000); Foreign born: 0.2% (2000); Ancestry (includes multiple ancestries): 24.5% German, 14.8% United States or American, 10.0% English, 10.0% Irish, 7.7% Other groups (2000).

Economy: Single-family building permits issued: 7 (2001) / 4 (2000); Multi-family building permits issued: 0 (2001) / 0 (2000); Employment by occupation: 6.6% management, 14.8% professional, 12.8% services, 24.9% sales, 0.5% farming, 12.1% construction, 28.2% production (2000).

Income: Per capita income: $14,928 (2000); Median household income: $24,384 (2000); Poverty rate: 17.4% (2000).

Taxes: Total city taxes per capita: $80 (1997); City property taxes per capita: $50 (1997).

Education: High school graduation rate: 80.0% (2000); College graduation rate: 11.0% (2000).

School District(s)

Clark Co. R-I (PK-12)
2000 Enrollment: 1,079 660-727-2377

Housing: Homeownership rate: 68.5% (2000); Median home value: $51,100 (2000); Median rent: $239 per month (2000); Median age of housing: 39 years (2000).

Newspapers: The Media (1 x week)

Transportation: Commute to work: 89.7% car, 0.8% public transportation, 5.4% walk, 3.5% work from home (2000); Travel time to work: 53.0% less than 15 minutes, 17.8% 15 to 30 minutes, 16.2% 30 to 45 minutes, 4.3% 45 to 60 minutes, 8.6% 60 minutes or more (2000)

Additional Information Contacts

Kahoka Chamber of Commerce 660-727-3143

LURAY (village). Covers a land area of 0.196 square miles and a water area of 0 square miles. Located at 40.45° N. Lat.; 91.88° W. Long. Elevation is 745 feet.

Population: 102 (2000); Race: 100.0% White, 0.0% Black, 0.0% Asian, 0.0% American Indian and Alaska Native, 0.0% Hispanic of any race, 0.0% two or more races (2000); Density: 519.7 persons per square mile (2000); Age: 42.2% under 18, 3.6% over 64 (2000); Marriage status: 13.2% never married, 39.6% now married, 1.9% widowed, 45.3% divorced (2000); Foreign born: 0.0% (2000); Ancestry (includes multiple ancestries): 15.7% United States or American, 8.4% German, 8.4% English, 4.8% Swedish, 4.8% Scottish (2000).

Economy: Employment by occupation: 4.7% management, 4.7% professional, 14.0% services, 14.0% sales, 0.0% farming, 16.3% construction, 46.5% production (2000).

Income: Per capita income: $10,927 (2000); Median household income: $23,125 (2000); Poverty rate: 27.7% (2000).

Taxes: Total city taxes per capita: $56 (1997); City property taxes per capita: $14 (1997).

Education: High school graduation rate: 80.4% (2000); College graduation rate: 0.0% (2000).

School District(s)

Luray 33 (KG-08)
2000 Enrollment: 54 660-866-2222

Housing: Homeownership rate: 80.6% (2000); Median home value: $14,000 (2000); Median rent: $138 per month (2000); Median age of housing: 60+ years (2000).

Transportation: Commute to work: 84.6% car, 0.0% public transportation, 10.3% walk, 5.1% work from home (2000); Travel time to work: 16.2% less than 15 minutes, 27.0% 15 to 30 minutes, 32.4% 30 to 45 minutes, 13.5% 45 to 60 minutes, 10.8% 60 minutes or more (2000)

REVERE (town). Covers a land area of 0.187 square miles and a water area of 0 square miles. Located at 40.49° N. Lat.; 91.67° W. Long. Elevation is 680 feet.
Population: 121 (2000); Race: 100.0% White, 0.0% Black, 0.0% Asian, 0.0% American Indian and Alaska Native, 0.0% Hispanic of any race, 0.0% two or more races (2000); Density: 647.8 persons per square mile (2000); Age: 32.3% under 18, 7.1% over 64 (2000); Marriage status: 12.5% never married, 75.0% now married, 4.5% widowed, 8.0% divorced (2000); Foreign born: 0.0% (2000); Ancestry (includes multiple ancestries): 35.4% United States or American, 9.4% Other groups, 7.9% Irish, 3.1% German, 1.6% Norwegian (2000).
Economy: Single-family building permits issued: 0 (2001) / 0 (2000); Multi-family building permits issued: 0 (2001) / 0 (2000); Employment by occupation: 0.0% management, 5.9% professional, 23.5% services, 17.6% sales, 0.0% farming, 17.6% construction, 35.3% production (2000).
Income: Per capita income: $10,635 (2000); Median household income: $25,625 (2000); Poverty rate: 13.4% (2000).
Taxes: Total city taxes per capita: $142 (1997); City property taxes per capita: $50 (1997).
Education: High school graduation rate: 68.1% (2000); College graduation rate: 5.8% (2000).

School District(s)

Revere C-3 (KG-12)
2000 Enrollment: 82 660-948-2621
Housing: Homeownership rate: 87.5% (2000); Median home value: $22,800 (2000); Median rent: $175 per month (2000); Median age of housing: 60+ years (2000).
Transportation: Commute to work: 93.2% car, 0.0% public transportation, 0.0% walk, 2.3% work from home (2000); Travel time to work: 4.7% less than 15 minutes, 32.6% 15 to 30 minutes, 53.5% 30 to 45 minutes, 0.0% 45 to 60 minutes, 9.3% 60 minutes or more (2000)

WAYLAND (city). Covers a land area of 0.274 square miles and a water area of 0 square miles. Located at 40.39° N. Lat.; 91.58° W. Long. Elevation is 535 feet.
Population: 425 (2000); Race: 98.2% White, 0.0% Black, 0.5% Asian, 0.0% American Indian and Alaska Native, 0.0% Hispanic of any race, 1.4% two or more races (2000); Density: 1,549.6 persons per square mile (2000); Age: 21.1% under 18, 24.5% over 64 (2000); Marriage status: 21.0% never married, 48.9% now married, 14.2% widowed, 15.8% divorced (2000); Foreign born: 0.5% (2000); Ancestry (includes multiple ancestries): 29.5% German, 17.4% United States or American, 16.9% Irish, 12.1% English, 7.3% Other groups (2000).
Economy: Single-family building permits issued: 0 (2001) / 0 (2000); Multi-family building permits issued: 0 (2001) / 0 (2000); Employment by occupation: 5.9% management, 3.2% professional, 24.7% services, 15.1% sales, 0.0% farming, 10.8% construction, 40.3% production (2000).
Income: Per capita income: $11,240 (2000); Median household income: $19,034 (2000); Poverty rate: 19.5% (2000).
Taxes: Total city taxes per capita: $122 (1997); City property taxes per capita: $37 (1997).
Education: High school graduation rate: 65.1% (2000); College graduation rate: 3.7% (2000).
Housing: Homeownership rate: 68.9% (2000); Median home value: $42,100 (2000); Median rent: $208 per month (2000); Median age of housing: 37 years (2000).
Transportation: Commute to work: 81.0% car, 0.0% public transportation, 11.4% walk, 3.3% work from home (2000); Travel time to work: 25.8% less than 15 minutes, 52.2% 15 to 30 minutes, 12.4% 30 to 45 minutes, 3.9% 45 to 60 minutes, 5.6% 60 minutes or more (2000)

WYACONDA (city). Covers a land area of 0.646 square miles and a water area of 0 square miles. Located at 40.39° N. Lat.; 91.92° W. Long. Elevation is 756 feet.
Population: 310 (2000); Race: 99.3% White, 0.0% Black, 0.0% Asian, 0.0% American Indian and Alaska Native, 0.0% Hispanic of any race, 0.7% two or more races (2000); Density: 479.8 persons per square mile (2000); Age: 19.5% under 18, 18.8% over 64 (2000); Marriage status: 19.7% never married, 59.0% now married, 7.7% widowed, 13.7% divorced (2000); Foreign born: 0.0% (2000); Ancestry (includes multiple ancestries): 17.0% German, 14.1% United States or American, 13.7% Other groups, 13.4% English, 10.8% Irish (2000).
Economy: Agriculture: corn, soybeans; hogs; cattle. Manufacturing of fertilizer. Single-family building permits issued: 0 (2001) / 0 (2000); Multi-family building permits issued: 0 (2001) / 0 (2000); Employment by occupation: 7.5% management, 7.5% professional, 25.5% services, 10.4% sales, 0.0% farming, 16.0% construction, 33.0% production (2000).
Income: Per capita income: $12,913 (2000); Median household income: $20,893 (2000); Poverty rate: 24.1% (2000).
Taxes: Total city taxes per capita: $112 (1997); City property taxes per capita: $68 (1997).
Education: High school graduation rate: 75.5% (2000); College graduation rate: 7.6% (2000).

School District(s)

Wyaconda C-1 (KG-12)
2000 Enrollment: 87 660-479-5431
Housing: Homeownership rate: 67.2% (2000); Median home value: $15,400 (2000); Median rent: $200 per month (2000); Median age of housing: 60+ years (2000).
Transportation: Commute to work: 89.7% car, 0.0% public transportation, 7.5% walk, 2.8% work from home (2000); Travel time to work: 26.9% less than 15 minutes, 17.3% 15 to 30 minutes, 15.4% 30 to 45 minutes, 26.0% 45 to 60 minutes, 14.4% 60 minutes or more (2000)

Clay County

Located in western Missouri; bounded on the south by the Missouri River. Covers a land area of 396.30 square miles, a water area of 12.50 square miles, and is located in the Central Time Zone. The county government was organized in 1822. County seat is Liberty.

Clay County is part of the Kansas City, MO-KS MSA. The entire metro area includes: Johnson County, KS; Leavenworth County, KS; Miami County, KS; Wyandotte County, KS; Cass County, MO; Clay County, MO; Clinton County, MO; Jackson County, MO; Lafayette County, MO; Platte County, MO; Ray County, MO

Population: 184,006 (2000); Race: 92.4% White, 2.5% Black, 1.2% Asian, 0.5% American Indian and Alaska Native, 3.5% Hispanic of any race, 2.3% two or more races (2000); Density: 464.3 persons per square mile (2000); Age: 25.8% under 18, 10.8% over 64 (2000).
Religion: Five largest groups: 14.4% Southern Baptist Convention, 12.7% Catholic Church, 4.9% The United Methodist Church, 3.5% Christian Church (Disciples of Christ), 2.4% Assemblies of God (2000).
Economy: Unemployment rate: 3.7% (11/2002); Total civilian labor force: 112,583 (11/2002); Leading industries: 16.9% manufacturing; 15.0% retail trade; 13.2% accommodation & food services (2000); Companies that employ more than 1,000 persons: 8 (2000); Companies that employ more than 100 persons: 118 (2000); Farms: 634 totaling 134,156 acres (1997); Minority business ownership rate: 4.2% (1997); Women business ownership rate: 26.6% (1997); Retail sales per capita: $14,230 (1997). Single-family building permits issued: 551 (2001) / 660 (2000); Multi-family building permits issued: 27 (2001) / 3 (2000).
Income: Per capita income: $23,144 (2000); Median household income: $48,347 (2000); Poverty rate: 5.5% (2000); Bankruptcy rate: 5.26% (2001).
Taxes: Total county taxes per capita: $140 (2000); County property taxes per capita: $22 (2000).
Education: High school graduation rate: 88.7% (2000); College graduation rate: 24.9% (2000).
Housing: Homeownership rate: 70.7% (2000); Median home value: $104,900 (2000); Median rent: $488 per month (2000); Median age of housing: 27 years (2000).
Health: Birth rate: 139.2 per 10,000 population (1998); Age adjusted death rate: 88.7 per 10,000 population (1999); Age adjusted cancer mortality rate: 198.9 deaths per 100,000 population (1999). Air Quality Index: 66% good, 34% moderate, 0% unhealthy (percent of days in 2000). Number of physicians: 17.0 per 10,000 population (1999); Number of hospital beds: 37.6 per 10,000 population (1999).
Elections: 2000 Presidential election results: 48.8% Gore, 48.8% Bush, 1.8% Nader, 0.3% Buchanan
National and State Parks: Watkins Mill State Park
Additional Information Contacts
Clay County Government Offices 816-792-7733
Excelsior Springs Chamber of Commerce 816-630-6161
Gladstone Chamber of Commerce 816-436-4523
Kearney Chamber of Commerce 816-628-4229
Liberty Area Chamber/Commerce 816-781-5200
Smithville Chamber of Commerce 816-532-0946

Clay County Communities

AVONDALE (city). Covers a land area of 0.132 square miles and a water area of 0 square miles. Located at 39.15° N. Lat.; 94.54° W. Long. Elevation is 840 feet.
Population: 529 (2000); Race: 95.5% White, 0.8% Black, 0.0% Asian, 0.0% American Indian and Alaska Native, 2.9% Hispanic of any race, 2.1% two or more races (2000); Density: 3,996.3 persons per square mile (2000); Age: 23.6% under 18, 14.8% over 64 (2000); Marriage status: 20.4% never married, 54.0% now married, 4.4% widowed, 21.1% divorced (2000); Foreign born: 1.2% (2000); Ancestry (includes multiple ancestries): 25.7% United States or American, 14.8% Irish, 14.6% German, 11.1% Other groups, 9.0% English (2000).
Economy: Suburb of downtown Kansas City. Single-family building permits issued: 0 (2001) / 0 (2000); Multi-family building permits issued: 0 (2001) / 0 (2000); Employment by occupation: 9.5% management, 10.7% professional, 17.7% services, 31.7% sales, 0.0% farming, 14.8% construction, 15.6% production (2000).
Income: Per capita income: $17,372 (2000); Median household income: $37,159 (2000); Poverty rate: 10.1% (2000).
Taxes: Total city taxes per capita: $70 (1997); City property taxes per capita: $23 (1997).
Education: High school graduation rate: 74.0% (2000); College graduation rate: 10.1% (2000).
Housing: Homeownership rate: 67.0% (2000); Median home value: $73,900 (2000); Median rent: $418 per month (2000); Median age of housing: 46 years (2000).
Transportation: Commute to work: 94.1% car, 0.8% public transportation, 2.1% walk, 1.3% work from home (2000); Travel time to work: 44.3% less than 15 minutes, 37.9% 15 to 30 minutes, 10.6% 30 to 45 minutes, 3.4% 45 to 60 minutes, 3.8% 60 minutes or more (2000)

BIRMINGHAM (village). Covers a land area of 0.510 square miles and a water area of 0 square miles. Located at 39.16° N. Lat.; 94.45° W. Long. Elevation is 734 feet.
Population: 214 (2000); Race: 98.2% White, 0.0% Black, 0.0% Asian, 0.0% American Indian and Alaska Native, 0.0% Hispanic of any race, 1.8% two or more races (2000); Density: 419.5 persons per square mile (2000); Age: 35.6% under 18, 8.2% over 64 (2000); Marriage status: 21.9% never married, 61.3% now married, 6.5% widowed, 10.3% divorced (2000); Foreign born: 0.0% (2000); Ancestry (includes multiple ancestries): 27.4% United States or American, 18.3% German, 7.3% English, 5.9% French (except Basque), 5.5% Irish (2000).
Economy: Suburb of downtown Kansas City. Single-family building permits issued: 0 (2001) / 0 (2000); Multi-family building permits issued: 0 (2001) / 0 (2000); Employment by occupation: 9.5% management, 7.1% professional, 4.8% services, 32.1% sales, 0.0% farming, 29.8% construction, 16.7% production (2000).
Income: Per capita income: $16,420 (2000); Median household income: $36,563 (2000); Poverty rate: 5.1% (2000).
Taxes: Total city taxes per capita: $236 (1997); City property taxes per capita: $17 (1997).
Education: High school graduation rate: 72.6% (2000); College graduation rate: 0.0% (2000).
Housing: Homeownership rate: 73.5% (2000); Median home value: $65,000 (2000); Median rent: $340 per month (2000); Median age of housing: 49 years (2000).
Transportation: Commute to work: 97.6% car, 0.0% public transportation, 0.0% walk, 2.4% work from home (2000); Travel time to work: 18.3% less than 15 minutes, 39.0% 15 to 30 minutes, 26.8% 30 to 45 minutes, 3.7% 45 to 60 minutes, 12.2% 60 minutes or more (2000)

CLAYCOMO (village). Covers a land area of 2.504 square miles and a water area of 0 square miles. Located at 39.20° N. Lat.; 94.48° W. Long. Elevation is 835 feet.
History: Town's name derived from the combination of Clay county and Mo.
Population: 1,267 (2000); Race: 94.4% White, 2.2% Black, 1.3% Asian, 0.9% American Indian and Alaska Native, 1.8% Hispanic of any race, 1.0% two or more races (2000); Density: 506.0 persons per square mile (2000); Age: 23.5% under 18, 14.9% over 64 (2000); Marriage status: 25.4% never married, 52.0% now married, 7.8% widowed, 14.7% divorced (2000); Foreign born: 0.6% (2000); Ancestry (includes multiple ancestries): 21.1% German, 20.4% United States or American, 12.6% Other groups, 10.4% English, 9.3% Irish (2000).
Economy: Manufacturing: ornamental iron products. Single-family building permits issued: 0 (2001) / 0 (2000); Multi-family building permits issued: 0 (2001) / 0 (2000); Employment by occupation: 7.2% management, 8.8% professional, 13.1% services, 31.5% sales, 0.0% farming, 14.9% construction, 24.4% production (2000).
Income: Per capita income: $20,000 (2000); Median household income: $39,271 (2000); Poverty rate: 4.7% (2000).
Taxes: Total city taxes per capita: $545 (2000); City property taxes per capita: $105 (2000).
Education: High school graduation rate: 78.8% (2000); College graduation rate: 4.9% (2000).
Housing: Homeownership rate: 61.0% (2000); Median home value: $80,400 (2000); Median rent: $376 per month (2000); Median age of housing: 38 years (2000).
Safety: Violent crime rate: 39.2 per 10,000 population; Property crime rate: 807.8 per 10,000 population (2001).
Transportation: Commute to work: 95.9% car, 0.0% public transportation, 1.5% walk, 2.7% work from home (2000); Travel time to work: 35.4% less than 15 minutes, 48.3% 15 to 30 minutes, 15.3% 30 to 45 minutes, 0.0% 45 to 60 minutes, 0.9% 60 minutes or more (2000)

EXCELSIOR SPRINGS (city). Covers a land area of 9.817 square miles and a water area of 0.024 square miles. Located at 39.34° N. Lat.; 94.23° W. Long. Elevation is 770 feet.
History: Excelsior Springs developed about 1880 as a health spa around the Old Siloam mineral springs. Other springs were soon developed, and the town became a major resort. In the 1900's the Mineral Water System, a division of the city government, was established to dispense the waters from a central point.
Population: 10,847 (2000); Race: 92.8% White, 3.2% Black, 0.2% Asian, 0.8% American Indian and Alaska Native, 1.9% Hispanic of any race, 2.8% two or more races (2000); Density: 1,104.9 persons per square mile (2000); Age: 27.9% under 18, 13.1% over 64 (2000); Marriage status: 22.5% never married, 57.5% now married, 7.0% widowed, 13.0% divorced (2000); Foreign born: 1.7% (2000); Ancestry (includes multiple ancestries): 18.3% German, 17.4% Other groups, 13.6% United States or American, 11.0% Irish, 8.8% English (2000).
Vital Statistics: Birth rate: 177.0 per 10,000 population (1998)
Economy: Single-family building permits issued: 26 (2001) / 49 (2000); Multi-family building permits issued: 0 (2001) / 0 (2000); Employment by occupation: 8.2% management, 11.4% professional, 18.2% services, 27.2% sales, 0.5% farming, 10.2% construction, 24.3% production (2000).
Income: Per capita income: $17,718 (2000); Median household income: $36,657 (2000); Poverty rate: 12.2% (2000).
Taxes: Total city taxes per capita: $284 (2000); City property taxes per capita: $69 (2000).
Education: High school graduation rate: 78.6% (2000); College graduation rate: 11.3% (2000).

School District(s)

Excelsior Springs 40 (PK-12)
2000 Enrollment: 3,311 816-630-9200

Housing: Homeownership rate: 66.1% (2000); Median home value: $82,900 (2000); Median rent: $390 per month (2000); Median age of housing: 33 years (2000).
Hospitals: Excelsior Springs Medical Center (109 beds)
Safety: Violent crime rate: 9.2 per 10,000 population; Property crime rate: 507.6 per 10,000 population (2001).
Newspapers: Excelsior Spring Standard (2 x week); Standard (3 x week)
Transportation: Commute to work: 93.9% car, 0.8% public transportation, 3.3% walk, 0.9% work from home (2000); Travel time to work: 37.0% less than 15 minutes, 24.2% 15 to 30 minutes, 24.0% 30 to 45 minutes, 10.2% 45 to 60 minutes, 4.6% 60 minutes or more (2000)

Additional Information Contacts

Excelsior Springs Chamber of Commerce 816-630-6161

GLADSTONE (city). Aka Linden. Covers a land area of 7.996 square miles and a water area of 0 square miles. Located at 39.21° N. Lat.; 94.56° W. Long. Elevation is 940 feet.
History: Founded c.1878, incorporated 1952.
Population: 26,365 (2000); Race: 93.3% White, 1.6% Black, 0.9% Asian, 0.9% American Indian and Alaska Native, 3.6% Hispanic of any race, 2.3% two or more races (2000); Density: 3,297.2 persons per square mile (2000); Age: 21.0% under 18, 15.9% over 64 (2000); Marriage status: 22.7% never married, 58.2% now married, 7.0% widowed, 12.1% divorced (2000); Foreign born: 2.0% (2000); Ancestry (includes multiple ancestries): 25.1%

German, 17.1% Irish, 13.7% English, 12.6% Other groups, 9.5% United States or American (2000).
Vital Statistics: Birth rate: 102.4 per 10,000 population (1998)
Economy: The city has diverse light industries. Unemployment rate: 2.8% (11/2002); Total civilian labor force: 20,023 (11/2002); Single-family building permits issued: 28 (2001) / 46 (2000); Multi-family building permits issued: 25 (2001) / 3 (2000); Employment by occupation: 12.6% management, 18.4% professional, 13.1% services, 34.2% sales, 0.1% farming, 9.0% construction, 12.5% production (2000).
Income: Per capita income: $25,105 (2000); Median household income: $46,333 (2000); Poverty rate: 4.7% (2000).
Taxes: Total city taxes per capita: $406 (2000); City property taxes per capita: $63 (2000).
Education: High school graduation rate: 90.3% (2000); College graduation rate: 25.1% (2000).
Housing: Homeownership rate: 68.8% (2000); Median home value: $100,100 (2000); Median rent: $488 per month (2000); Median age of housing: 30 years (2000).
Safety: Violent crime rate: 19.2 per 10,000 population; Property crime rate: 338.9 per 10,000 population (2001).
Transportation: Commute to work: 95.2% car, 0.5% public transportation, 0.5% walk, 3.2% work from home (2000); Travel time to work: 26.2% less than 15 minutes, 48.5% 15 to 30 minutes, 18.5% 30 to 45 minutes, 3.7% 45 to 60 minutes, 3.1% 60 minutes or more (2000)
Additional Information Contacts
Gladstone Chamber of Commerce 816-436-4523

GLENAIRE (city). Covers a land area of 0.297 square miles and a water area of 0 square miles. Located at 39.22° N. Lat.; 94.45° W. Long. Elevation is 800 feet.
Population: 553 (2000); Race: 95.0% White, 0.0% Black, 0.9% Asian, 0.0% American Indian and Alaska Native, 0.7% Hispanic of any race, 4.1% two or more races (2000); Density: 1,861.8 persons per square mile (2000); Age: 24.0% under 18, 15.7% over 64 (2000); Marriage status: 23.2% never married, 64.1% now married, 5.4% widowed, 7.3% divorced (2000); Foreign born: 1.4% (2000); Ancestry (includes multiple ancestries): 23.8% German, 18.6% English, 12.5% Irish, 9.8% United States or American, 7.2% Other groups (2000).
Economy: Single-family building permits issued: 5 (2001) / 6 (2000); Multi-family building permits issued: 0 (2001) / 0 (2000); Employment by occupation: 11.9% management, 13.9% professional, 12.9% services, 27.4% sales, 0.0% farming, 14.9% construction, 19.1% production (2000).
Income: Per capita income: $21,133 (2000); Median household income: $54,327 (2000); Poverty rate: 3.8% (2000).
Taxes: Total city taxes per capita: $66 (1997); City property taxes per capita: $27 (1997).
Education: High school graduation rate: 86.0% (2000); College graduation rate: 17.0% (2000).
Housing: Homeownership rate: 88.2% (2000); Median home value: $100,000 (2000); Median rent: $470 per month (2000); Median age of housing: 35 years (2000).
Transportation: Commute to work: 96.7% car, 0.7% public transportation, 0.0% walk, 2.7% work from home (2000); Travel time to work: 36.3% less than 15 minutes, 45.5% 15 to 30 minutes, 12.0% 30 to 45 minutes, 4.8% 45 to 60 minutes, 1.4% 60 minutes or more (2000)

HOLT (city). Covers a land area of 0.362 square miles and a water area of 0 square miles. Located at 39.45° N. Lat.; 94.33° W. Long. Elevation is 860 feet.
Population: 405 (2000); Race: 95.0% White, 0.0% Black, 0.9% Asian, 1.3% American Indian and Alaska Native, 0.0% Hispanic of any race, 2.9% two or more races (2000); Density: 1,119.4 persons per square mile (2000); Age: 34.4% under 18, 12.9% over 64 (2000); Marriage status: 21.9% never married, 50.8% now married, 8.9% widowed, 18.4% divorced (2000); Foreign born: 1.1% (2000); Ancestry (includes multiple ancestries): 35.1% United States or American, 21.7% Irish, 17.5% German, 8.1% French Canadian, 5.5% French (except Basque) (2000).
Economy: Single-family building permits issued: 0 (2001) / 10 (2000); Multi-family building permits issued: 0 (2001) / 0 (2000); Employment by occupation: 6.4% management, 7.4% professional, 20.7% services, 21.3% sales, 0.0% farming, 23.4% construction, 20.7% production (2000).
Income: Per capita income: $16,841 (2000); Median household income: $38,438 (2000); Poverty rate: 16.6% (2000).
Taxes: Total city taxes per capita: $255 (1997); City property taxes per capita: $53 (1997).
Education: High school graduation rate: 77.0% (2000); College graduation rate: 6.7% (2000).
Housing: Homeownership rate: 69.3% (2000); Median home value: $79,600 (2000); Median rent: $289 per month (2000); Median age of housing: 36 years (2000).
Transportation: Commute to work: 86.3% car, 0.0% public transportation, 8.7% walk, 1.6% work from home (2000); Travel time to work: 16.1% less than 15 minutes, 33.9% 15 to 30 minutes, 27.8% 30 to 45 minutes, 10.0% 45 to 60 minutes, 12.2% 60 minutes or more (2000)

KEARNEY (city). Covers a land area of 6.568 square miles and a water area of 0 square miles. Located at 39.36° N. Lat.; 94.36° W. Long. Elevation is 849 feet.
History: A major center of mule breeding and raising in early 20th century. Outlaw Jesse James' birthplace and farm on East side of town. Platted 1867.
Population: 5,472 (2000); Race: 98.6% White, 0.2% Black, 0.0% Asian, 0.2% American Indian and Alaska Native, 0.2% Hispanic of any race, 1.0% two or more races (2000); Density: 833.2 persons per square mile (2000); Age: 33.7% under 18, 8.8% over 64 (2000); Marriage status: 17.1% never married, 67.0% now married, 5.8% widowed, 10.1% divorced (2000); Foreign born: 0.1% (2000); Ancestry (includes multiple ancestries): 23.5% German, 16.2% English, 13.4% Irish, 7.8% United States or American, 7.5% Other groups (2000).
Economy: Ships livestock, grain; coal mines; light manufacturing. Single-family building permits issued: 123 (2001) / 129 (2000); Multi-family building permits issued: 0 (2001) / 0 (2000); Employment by occupation: 13.6% management, 19.6% professional, 12.6% services, 29.7% sales, 0.2% farming, 9.8% construction, 14.5% production (2000).
Income: Per capita income: $21,147 (2000); Median household income: $56,603 (2000); Poverty rate: 2.5% (2000).
Taxes: Total city taxes per capita: $319 (2000); City property taxes per capita: $77 (2000).
Education: High school graduation rate: 91.3% (2000); College graduation rate: 24.2% (2000).

School District(s)

Kearney R-I (PK-12)
2000 Enrollment: 3,105 816-628-4116
Housing: Homeownership rate: 74.6% (2000); Median home value: $114,000 (2000); Median rent: $469 per month (2000); Median age of housing: 8 years (2000).
Safety: Violent crime rate: 7.3 per 10,000 population; Property crime rate: 159.8 per 10,000 population (2001).
Newspapers: The Kearney Courier (1 x week)
Transportation: Commute to work: 96.7% car, 0.0% public transportation, 0.0% walk, 2.9% work from home (2000); Travel time to work: 28.8% less than 15 minutes, 35.2% 15 to 30 minutes, 24.1% 30 to 45 minutes, 7.2% 45 to 60 minutes, 4.7% 60 minutes or more (2000)
Additional Information Contacts
Kearney Chamber of Commerce 816-628-4229

LIBERTY (city). Covers a land area of 26.953 square miles and a water area of 0.058 square miles. Located at 39.24° N. Lat.; 94.42° W. Long. Elevation is 889 feet.
History: Liberty was platted in 1822 and grew as a trade center for the northwest Missouri area. During the Civil War, Liberty was the center of guerilla skirmishes that culminated in 1866 with the robbing of the Clay County Savings Association, an act attributed to Jesse and Frank James.
Population: 26,232 (2000); Race: 94.0% White, 2.4% Black, 0.5% Asian, 0.4% American Indian and Alaska Native, 3.0% Hispanic of any race, 1.8% two or more races (2000); Density: 973.3 persons per square mile (2000); Age: 27.6% under 18, 10.7% over 64 (2000); Marriage status: 23.2% never married, 58.8% now married, 6.5% widowed, 11.5% divorced (2000); Foreign born: 1.4% (2000); Ancestry (includes multiple ancestries): 25.1% German, 13.9% Irish, 13.7% English, 12.7% Other groups, 9.9% United States or American (2000).
Vital Statistics: Birth rate: 133.0 per 10,000 population (1998)
Economy: Unemployment rate: 3.4% (11/2002); Total civilian labor force: 14,496 (11/2002); Single-family building permits issued: 181 (2001) / 208 (2000); Multi-family building permits issued: 2 (2001) / 0 (2000); Employment by occupation: 16.0% management, 21.9% professional, 13.7% services, 29.5% sales, 0.2% farming, 7.7% construction, 11.0% production (2000).
Income: Per capita income: $23,415 (2000); Median household income: $52,745 (2000); Poverty rate: 5.0% (2000).
Taxes: Total city taxes per capita: $411 (2000); City property taxes per capita: $149 (2000).

Education: High school graduation rate: 90.4% (2000); College graduation rate: 32.0% (2000).

School District(s)

Liberty 53 (PK-12)
2000 Enrollment: 6,921 816-415-5300

Four-year College(s)

William Jewell College (Private, Not-for-profit, Baptist)
2001 Enrollment: 1,369 816-781-7700
2001 Tuition: In-state $14,450; Out-of-state $14,450

Housing: Homeownership rate: 73.2% (2000); Median home value: $121,600 (2000); Median rent: $466 per month (2000); Median age of housing: 22 years (2000).

Hospitals: Liberty Hospital (202 beds)

Newspapers: Liberty Tribune (2 x week); Liberty Sun-News (1 x week)

Transportation: Commute to work: 93.6% car, 0.3% public transportation, 2.0% walk, 3.5% work from home (2000); Travel time to work: 35.7% less than 15 minutes, 37.5% 15 to 30 minutes, 19.3% 30 to 45 minutes, 4.8% 45 to 60 minutes, 2.7% 60 minutes or more (2000)

Additional Information Contacts

Liberty Area Chamber/Commerce 816-781-5200

MISSOURI CITY (city). Covers a land area of 1.015 square miles and a water area of 0.113 square miles. Located at 39.23° N. Lat.; 94.30° W. Long. Elevation is 725 feet.

Population: 295 (2000); Race: 98.4% White, 0.3% Black, 0.0% Asian, 0.7% American Indian and Alaska Native, 1.3% Hispanic of any race, 0.7% two or more races (2000); Density: 290.5 persons per square mile (2000); Age: 21.4% under 18, 6.3% over 64 (2000); Marriage status: 30.5% never married, 44.8% now married, 4.6% widowed, 20.1% divorced (2000); Foreign born: 0.7% (2000); Ancestry (includes multiple ancestries): 22.7% German, 17.8% Other groups, 15.1% United States or American, 13.8% Irish, 10.9% English (2000).

Economy: Concrete and crushed limestone. Single-family building permits issued: 0 (2001) / 0 (2000); Multi-family building permits issued: 0 (2001) / 0 (2000); Employment by occupation: 12.7% management, 6.4% professional, 9.2% services, 35.3% sales, 0.0% farming, 16.8% construction, 19.7% production (2000).

Income: Per capita income: $17,693 (2000); Median household income: $41,875 (2000); Poverty rate: 7.6% (2000).

Taxes: Total city taxes per capita: $29 (1997); City property taxes per capita: $29 (1997).

Education: High school graduation rate: 75.8% (2000); College graduation rate: 1.9% (2000).

School District(s)

Missouri City 56 (KG-08)
2000 Enrollment: 61 816-750-4391

Housing: Homeownership rate: 78.2% (2000); Median home value: $68,000 (2000); Median rent: $339 per month (2000); Median age of housing: 35 years (2000).

Transportation: Commute to work: 93.3% car, 0.0% public transportation, 1.2% walk, 0.0% work from home (2000); Travel time to work: 5.5% less than 15 minutes, 37.2% 15 to 30 minutes, 38.4% 30 to 45 minutes, 11.0% 45 to 60 minutes, 7.9% 60 minutes or more (2000)

MOSBY (city). Aka Moseby. Covers a land area of 1.539 square miles and a water area of 0 square miles. Located at 39.31° N. Lat.; 94.30° W. Long. Elevation is 1,012 feet.

Population: 242 (2000); Race: 95.9% White, 0.0% Black, 0.0% Asian, 1.6% American Indian and Alaska Native, 0.8% Hispanic of any race, 1.6% two or more races (2000); Density: 157.3 persons per square mile (2000); Age: 37.0% under 18, 11.4% over 64 (2000); Marriage status: 35.4% never married, 48.9% now married, 6.2% widowed, 9.6% divorced (2000); Foreign born: 0.0% (2000); Ancestry (includes multiple ancestries): 22.0% Irish, 18.7% German, 15.4% United States or American, 14.6% Other groups, 14.6% English (2000).

Economy: Single-family building permits issued: 0 (2001) / 0 (2000); Multi-family building permits issued: 0 (2001) / 0 (2000); Employment by occupation: 0.9% management, 6.3% professional, 22.3% services, 26.8% sales, 0.9% farming, 18.8% construction, 24.1% production (2000).

Income: Per capita income: $12,617 (2000); Median household income: $33,333 (2000); Poverty rate: 18.7% (2000).

Taxes: Total city taxes per capita: $360 (1997); City property taxes per capita: $236 (1997).

Education: High school graduation rate: 66.4% (2000); College graduation rate: 5.3% (2000).

Housing: Homeownership rate: 70.5% (2000); Median home value: $37,500 (2000); Median rent: $297 per month (2000); Median age of housing: 45 years (2000).

Transportation: Commute to work: 95.5% car, 0.0% public transportation, 0.0% walk, 1.8% work from home (2000); Travel time to work: 18.5% less than 15 minutes, 18.5% 15 to 30 minutes, 27.8% 30 to 45 minutes, 13.9% 45 to 60 minutes, 21.3% 60 minutes or more (2000)

NORTH KANSAS CITY (city). Covers a land area of 4.365 square miles and a water area of 0.275 square miles. Located at 39.13° N. Lat.; 94.57° W. Long. Elevation is 745 feet.

History: North Kansas City was founded in 1912 by the North Kansas City Development Company, as an industrial development on the north bank of the Missouri River.

Population: 4,714 (2000); Race: 82.7% White, 4.9% Black, 2.3% Asian, 0.3% American Indian and Alaska Native, 8.1% Hispanic of any race, 6.5% two or more races (2000); Density: 1,080.0 persons per square mile (2000); Age: 17.6% under 18, 14.3% over 64 (2000); Marriage status: 35.9% never married, 35.7% now married, 9.0% widowed, 19.3% divorced (2000); Foreign born: 17.4% (2000); Ancestry (includes multiple ancestries): 20.5% Other groups, 16.0% German, 11.4% Irish, 8.3% United States or American, 6.8% English (2000).

Economy: Single-family building permits issued: 0 (2001) / 1 (2000); Multi-family building permits issued: 0 (2001) / 0 (2000); Employment by occupation: 6.1% management, 13.6% professional, 20.2% services, 33.4% sales, 0.0% farming, 5.5% construction, 21.2% production (2000).

Income: Per capita income: $18,967 (2000); Median household income: $28,674 (2000); Poverty rate: 12.5% (2000).

Taxes: Total city taxes per capita: $3,562 (2000); City property taxes per capita: $306 (2000).

Education: High school graduation rate: 79.3% (2000); College graduation rate: 13.4% (2000).

Two-year College(s)

Sanford-Brown College (Private, For-profit)
2001 Enrollment: 360 816-472-0275
2001 Tuition: In-state $3,000; Out-of-state $3,000

Housing: Homeownership rate: 23.6% (2000); Median home value: $78,100 (2000); Median rent: $429 per month (2000); Median age of housing: 48 years (2000).

Hospitals: North Kansas City Hospital (350 beds)

Safety: Violent crime rate: 128.6 per 10,000 population; Property crime rate: 1,218.6 per 10,000 population (2001).

Transportation: Commute to work: 88.9% car, 3.0% public transportation, 3.0% walk, 2.7% work from home (2000); Travel time to work: 39.8% less than 15 minutes, 44.7% 15 to 30 minutes, 9.9% 30 to 45 minutes, 4.0% 45 to 60 minutes, 1.6% 60 minutes or more (2000)

OAKS (village). Covers a land area of 0.095 square miles and a water area of 0 square miles. Located at 39.19° N. Lat.; 94.57° W. Long. Elevation is 982 feet.

Population: 136 (2000); Race: 94.4% White, 1.4% Black, 0.0% Asian, 0.0% American Indian and Alaska Native, 1.4% Hispanic of any race, 2.1% two or more races (2000); Density: 1,429.2 persons per square mile (2000); Age: 25.9% under 18, 10.5% over 64 (2000); Marriage status: 18.4% never married, 76.3% now married, 1.8% widowed, 3.5% divorced (2000); Foreign born: 2.1% (2000); Ancestry (includes multiple ancestries): 21.7% German, 16.8% English, 9.8% French (except Basque), 7.7% Polish, 6.3% Irish (2000).

Economy: Single-family building permits issued: 0 (2001) / 0 (2000); Multi-family building permits issued: 0 (2001) / 0 (2000); Employment by occupation: 32.4% management, 28.2% professional, 0.0% services, 36.6% sales, 0.0% farming, 1.4% construction, 1.4% production (2000).

Income: Per capita income: $26,823 (2000); Median household income: $72,500 (2000); Poverty rate: 2.1% (2000).

Taxes: Total city taxes per capita: $15 (1997); City property taxes per capita: $15 (1997).

Education: High school graduation rate: 95.8% (2000); College graduation rate: 54.7% (2000).

Housing: Homeownership rate: 100.0% (2000); Median home value: $155,600 (2000); Median age of housing: 53 years (2000).

Transportation: Commute to work: 93.0% car, 0.0% public transportation, 0.0% walk, 7.0% work from home (2000); Travel time to work: 33.3% less than 15 minutes, 48.5% 15 to 30 minutes, 7.6% 30 to 45 minutes, 4.5% 45 to 60 minutes, 6.1% 60 minutes or more (2000)

OAKVIEW (village). Covers a land area of 0.173 square miles and a water area of 0 square miles. Located at 39.20° N. Lat.; 94.57° W. Long. Elevation is 1,003 feet.
Population: 386 (2000); Race: 95.3% White, 2.0% Black, 0.0% Asian, 0.5% American Indian and Alaska Native, 5.4% Hispanic of any race, 1.5% two or more races (2000); Density: 2,236.8 persons per square mile (2000); Age: 23.7% under 18, 15.8% over 64 (2000); Marriage status: 19.5% never married, 56.8% now married, 11.7% widowed, 12.0% divorced (2000); Foreign born: 1.0% (2000); Ancestry (includes multiple ancestries): 24.9% Irish, 24.7% German, 14.8% Other groups, 8.1% English, 7.9% Polish (2000).
Economy: Single-family building permits issued: 0 (2001) / 0 (2000); Multi-family building permits issued: 0 (2001) / 0 (2000); Employment by occupation: 11.2% management, 25.7% professional, 8.3% services, 29.6% sales, 0.0% farming, 10.7% construction, 14.6% production (2000).
Income: Per capita income: $22,344 (2000); Median household income: $46,786 (2000); Poverty rate: 4.9% (2000).
Taxes: Total city taxes per capita: $336 (1997); City property taxes per capita: $56 (1997).
Education: High school graduation rate: 84.0% (2000); College graduation rate: 18.1% (2000).
Housing: Homeownership rate: 91.0% (2000); Median home value: $87,800 (2000); Median rent: $620 per month (2000); Median age of housing: 45 years (2000).
Safety: Violent crime rate: 180.4 per 10,000 population; Property crime rate: 206.2 per 10,000 population (2001).
Transportation: Commute to work: 96.1% car, 0.0% public transportation, 1.5% walk, 2.5% work from home (2000); Travel time to work: 30.2% less than 15 minutes, 53.3% 15 to 30 minutes, 12.1% 30 to 45 minutes, 1.0% 45 to 60 minutes, 3.5% 60 minutes or more (2000)

OAKWOOD (village). Covers a land area of 0.199 square miles and a water area of 0 square miles. Located at 39.19° N. Lat.; 94.57° W. Long. Elevation is 400 feet.
Population: 197 (2000); Race: 98.4% White, 0.0% Black, 0.0% Asian, 0.0% American Indian and Alaska Native, 1.0% Hispanic of any race, 1.6% two or more races (2000); Density: 989.5 persons per square mile (2000); Age: 19.2% under 18, 22.3% over 64 (2000); Marriage status: 12.1% never married, 73.3% now married, 7.9% widowed, 6.7% divorced (2000); Foreign born: 0.5% (2000); Ancestry (includes multiple ancestries): 23.3% German, 22.8% English, 16.1% United States or American, 8.8% Other groups, 6.7% French (except Basque) (2000).
Economy: Single-family building permits issued: 0 (2001) / 0 (2000); Multi-family building permits issued: 0 (2001) / 0 (2000); Employment by occupation: 12.4% management, 18.0% professional, 7.9% services, 48.3% sales, 0.0% farming, 7.9% construction, 5.6% production (2000).
Income: Per capita income: $35,242 (2000); Median household income: $81,412 (2000); Poverty rate: 0.0% (2000).
Taxes: Total city taxes per capita: $84 (1997); City property taxes per capita: $42 (1997).
Education: High school graduation rate: 92.7% (2000); College graduation rate: 44.7% (2000).
Housing: Homeownership rate: 100.0% (2000); Median home value: $191,400 (2000); Median age of housing: 40 years (2000).
Transportation: Commute to work: 90.2% car, 0.0% public transportation, 3.3% walk, 6.5% work from home (2000); Travel time to work: 30.2% less than 15 minutes, 52.3% 15 to 30 minutes, 7.0% 30 to 45 minutes, 2.3% 45 to 60 minutes, 8.1% 60 minutes or more (2000)

OAKWOOD PARK (village). Covers a land area of 0.082 square miles and a water area of 0 square miles. Located at 39.20° N. Lat.; 94.57° W. Long. Elevation is 993 feet.
Population: 183 (2000); Race: 95.2% White, 0.0% Black, 1.2% Asian, 1.8% American Indian and Alaska Native, 1.2% Hispanic of any race, 1.8% two or more races (2000); Density: 2,242.8 persons per square mile (2000); Age: 14.5% under 18, 23.6% over 64 (2000); Marriage status: 23.5% never married, 58.4% now married, 6.0% widowed, 12.1% divorced (2000); Foreign born: 2.4% (2000); Ancestry (includes multiple ancestries): 40.6% German, 27.9% Irish, 11.5% Other groups, 9.7% English, 4.8% Swedish (2000).
Economy: Single-family building permits issued: 0 (2001) / 0 (2000); Multi-family building permits issued: 0 (2001) / 0 (2000); Employment by occupation: 21.5% management, 18.3% professional, 8.6% services, 33.3% sales, 0.0% farming, 10.8% construction, 7.5% production (2000).
Income: Per capita income: $27,990 (2000); Median household income: $51,875 (2000); Poverty rate: 1.2% (2000).
Taxes: Total city taxes per capita: $73 (1997); City property taxes per capita: $28 (1997).
Education: High school graduation rate: 88.4% (2000); College graduation rate: 40.6% (2000).
Housing: Homeownership rate: 89.5% (2000); Median home value: $95,700 (2000); Median rent: $700 per month (2000); Median age of housing: 46 years (2000).
Transportation: Commute to work: 91.4% car, 0.0% public transportation, 0.0% walk, 8.6% work from home (2000); Travel time to work: 16.5% less than 15 minutes, 58.8% 15 to 30 minutes, 16.5% 30 to 45 minutes, 8.2% 45 to 60 minutes, 0.0% 60 minutes or more (2000)

PLEASANT VALLEY (city). Covers a land area of 1.298 square miles and a water area of 0 square miles. Located at 39.22° N. Lat.; 94.47° W. Long. Elevation is 770 feet.
Population: 3,321 (2000); Race: 93.2% White, 0.8% Black, 0.1% Asian, 0.3% American Indian and Alaska Native, 4.5% Hispanic of any race, 2.9% two or more races (2000); Density: 2,559.5 persons per square mile (2000); Age: 22.5% under 18, 11.1% over 64 (2000); Marriage status: 21.0% never married, 54.2% now married, 9.0% widowed, 15.8% divorced (2000); Foreign born: 0.5% (2000); Ancestry (includes multiple ancestries): 27.9% German, 19.3% Irish, 14.5% Other groups, 11.0% United States or American, 8.7% English (2000).
Economy: Single-family building permits issued: 1 (2001) / 0 (2000); Multi-family building permits issued: 0 (2001) / 0 (2000); Employment by occupation: 10.0% management, 11.6% professional, 11.1% services, 38.1% sales, 0.0% farming, 11.2% construction, 18.0% production (2000).
Income: Per capita income: $26,084 (2000); Median household income: $48,684 (2000); Poverty rate: 4.6% (2000).
Taxes: Total city taxes per capita: $310 (1997); City property taxes per capita: $58 (1997).
Education: High school graduation rate: 87.6% (2000); College graduation rate: 13.3% (2000).
Housing: Homeownership rate: 67.5% (2000); Median home value: $102,800 (2000); Median rent: $504 per month (2000); Median age of housing: 20 years (2000).
Transportation: Commute to work: 96.4% car, 0.0% public transportation, 0.3% walk, 2.9% work from home (2000); Travel time to work: 28.7% less than 15 minutes, 49.8% 15 to 30 minutes, 16.2% 30 to 45 minutes, 3.1% 45 to 60 minutes, 2.3% 60 minutes or more (2000)

PRATHERSVILLE (village). Covers a land area of 2.237 square miles and a water area of 0 square miles. Located at 39.31° N. Lat.; 94.27° W. Long. Elevation is 748 feet.
Population: 111 (2000); Race: 100.0% White, 0.0% Black, 0.0% Asian, 0.0% American Indian and Alaska Native, 0.0% Hispanic of any race, 0.0% two or more races (2000); Density: 49.6 persons per square mile (2000); Age: 16.0% under 18, 31.2% over 64 (2000); Marriage status: 14.8% never married, 73.1% now married, 6.5% widowed, 5.6% divorced (2000); Foreign born: 0.0% (2000); Ancestry (includes multiple ancestries): 44.0% German, 35.2% Irish, 12.0% English, 7.2% Scottish, 6.4% Italian (2000).
Economy: Single-family building permits issued: 1 (2001) / 0 (2000); Multi-family building permits issued: 0 (2001) / 0 (2000); Employment by occupation: 27.1% management, 12.5% professional, 6.3% services, 27.1% sales, 0.0% farming, 10.4% construction, 16.7% production (2000).
Income: Per capita income: $20,745 (2000); Median household income: $34,063 (2000); Poverty rate: 4.0% (2000).
Taxes: Total city taxes per capita: $79 (1997); City property taxes per capita: $43 (1997).
Education: High school graduation rate: 84.8% (2000); College graduation rate: 14.1% (2000).
Housing: Homeownership rate: 96.0% (2000); Median home value: $94,100 (2000); Median rent: $525 per month (2000); Median age of housing: 44 years (2000).
Transportation: Commute to work: 95.8% car, 0.0% public transportation, 0.0% walk, 4.2% work from home (2000); Travel time to work: 28.3% less than 15 minutes, 21.7% 15 to 30 minutes, 30.4% 30 to 45 minutes, 6.5% 45 to 60 minutes, 13.0% 60 minutes or more (2000)

RANDOLPH (village). Aka East Kansas City. Covers a land area of 0.341 square miles and a water area of 0 square miles. Located at 39.15° N. Lat.; 94.49° W. Long. Elevation is 768 feet.
Population: 47 (2000); Race: 92.9% White, 0.0% Black, 0.0% Asian, 0.0% American Indian and Alaska Native, 0.0% Hispanic of any race, 7.1% two or

more races (2000); Density: 137.7 persons per square mile (2000); Age: 4.8% under 18, 26.2% over 64 (2000); Marriage status: 35.7% never married, 50.0% now married, 4.8% widowed, 9.5% divorced (2000); Foreign born: 4.8% (2000); Ancestry (includes multiple ancestries): 26.2% Irish, 14.3% German, 11.9% United States or American, 11.9% English, 7.1% Norwegian (2000).
Economy: Employment by occupation: 11.5% management, 7.7% professional, 7.7% services, 38.5% sales, 0.0% farming, 3.8% construction, 30.8% production (2000).
Income: Per capita income: $23,067 (2000); Median household income: $53,750 (2000); Poverty rate: 0.0% (2000).
Taxes: Total city taxes per capita: $1,805 (1997); City property taxes per capita: $260 (1997).
Education: High school graduation rate: 79.4% (2000); College graduation rate: 14.7% (2000).
Housing: Homeownership rate: 78.9% (2000); Median home value: $71,300 (2000); Median rent: $550 per month (2000); Median age of housing: 46 years (2000).
Transportation: Commute to work: 100.0% car, 0.0% public transportation, 0.0% walk, 0.0% work from home (2000); Travel time to work: 15.4% less than 15 minutes, 38.5% 15 to 30 minutes, 46.2% 30 to 45 minutes, 0.0% 45 to 60 minutes, 0.0% 60 minutes or more (2000)

SMITHVILLE (city). Covers a land area of 13.712 square miles and a water area of 0.065 square miles. Located at 39.38° N. Lat.; 94.57° W. Long. Elevation is 815 feet.
Population: 5,514 (2000); Race: 97.4% White, 0.1% Black, 0.3% Asian, 0.6% American Indian and Alaska Native, 1.9% Hispanic of any race, 0.8% two or more races (2000); Density: 402.1 persons per square mile (2000); Age: 28.0% under 18, 11.7% over 64 (2000); Marriage status: 18.1% never married, 64.5% now married, 6.0% widowed, 11.4% divorced (2000); Foreign born: 1.1% (2000); Ancestry (includes multiple ancestries): 22.8% German, 13.7% United States or American, 13.5% Irish, 11.4% English, 10.5% Other groups (2000).
Economy: Wheat, corn, fruit; livestock, poultry. Smithville Dam and Lake on East side. Single-family building permits issued: 75 (2001) / 78 (2000); Multi-family building permits issued: 0 (2001) / 0 (2000); Employment by occupation: 14.7% management, 17.1% professional, 13.0% services, 31.2% sales, 0.1% farming, 11.2% construction, 12.7% production (2000).
Income: Per capita income: $22,669 (2000); Median household income: $52,639 (2000); Poverty rate: 4.0% (2000).
Taxes: Total city taxes per capita: $184 (2000); City property taxes per capita: $0 (2000).
Education: High school graduation rate: 89.2% (2000); College graduation rate: 20.9% (2000).

School District(s)

Smithville R-II (PK-12)
2000 Enrollment: 1,639 816-532-0406
Housing: Homeownership rate: 77.5% (2000); Median home value: $118,000 (2000); Median rent: $403 per month (2000); Median age of housing: 10 years (2000).
Safety: Violent crime rate: 12.6 per 10,000 population; Property crime rate: 248.7 per 10,000 population (2001).
Newspapers: The Smithville Lake Herald (1 x week)
Transportation: Commute to work: 95.7% car, 0.1% public transportation, 0.9% walk, 2.5% work from home (2000); Travel time to work: 21.7% less than 15 minutes, 36.6% 15 to 30 minutes, 28.6% 30 to 45 minutes, 9.8% 45 to 60 minutes, 3.3% 60 minutes or more (2000)
Additional Information Contacts
Smithville Chamber of Commerce 816-532-0946

Clinton County

Located in northwestern Missouri; drained by the Little Platte River. Covers a land area of 418.80 square miles, a water area of 4.70 square miles, and is located in the Central Time Zone. The county government was organized in 1833. County seat is Plattsburg.

Clinton County is part of the Kansas City, MO-KS MSA. The entire metro area includes: Johnson County, KS; Leavenworth County, KS; Miami County, KS; Wyandotte County, KS; Cass County, MO; Clay County, MO; Clinton County, MO; Jackson County, MO; Lafayette County, MO; Platte County, MO; Ray County, MO

Population: 18,979 (2000); Race: 96.6% White, 1.2% Black, 0.2% Asian, 0.5% American Indian and Alaska Native, 1.3% Hispanic of any race, 1.3% two or more races (2000); Density: 45.3 persons per square mile (2000); Age: 26.8% under 18, 14.1% over 64 (2000).
Religion: Five largest groups: 19.7% Southern Baptist Convention, 9.5% Christian Church (Disciples of Christ), 8.4% The United Methodist Church, 5.9% Catholic Church, 2.7% Community of Christ (2000).
Economy: Unemployment rate: 4.7% (11/2002); Total civilian labor force: 10,395 (11/2002); Leading industries: 25.7% health care and social assistance; 23.8% retail trade; 11.4% accommodation & food services (2000); Companies that employ more than 1,000 persons: 0 (2000); Companies that employ more than 100 persons: 3 (2000); Farms: 768 totaling 216,483 acres (1997); Minority business ownership rate: 0.0% (1997); Women business ownership rate: 16.9% (1997); Retail sales per capita: $6,927 (1997). Single-family building permits issued: 177 (2001) / 166 (2000); Multi-family building permits issued: 8 (2001) / 14 (2000).
Income: Per capita income: $19,056 (2000); Median household income: $41,629 (2000); Poverty rate: 9.3% (2000); Bankruptcy rate: 4.18% (2001).
Taxes: Total county taxes per capita: $91 (1997); County property taxes per capita: $47 (1997).
Education: High school graduation rate: 86.1% (2000); College graduation rate: 14.5% (2000).
Housing: Homeownership rate: 79.0% (2000); Median home value: $86,400 (2000); Median rent: $341 per month (2000); Median age of housing: 28 years (2000).
Health: Birth rate: 129.1 per 10,000 population (1998); Age adjusted death rate: 83.8 per 10,000 population (1999); Age adjusted cancer mortality rate: 186.2 deaths per 100,000 population (1999). Number of physicians: 4.2 per 10,000 population (1999); Number of hospital beds: 25.3 per 10,000 population (1999).
Elections: 2000 Presidential election results: 46.8% Gore, 50.7% Bush, 1.5% Nader, 0.5% Buchanan
National and State Parks: Smithville Lake State Wildlife Area; Wallace State Park
Additional Information Contacts
Clinton County Government Offices 816-539-3713
Cameron Chamber of Commerce 816-632-2005
Lathrop Chamber of Commerce 816-528-4251
Plattsburg Chamber of Commerce 816-539-2649

Clinton County Communities

CAMERON (city). Covers a land area of 5.326 square miles and a water area of 0.026 square miles. Located at 39.74° N. Lat.; 94.24° W. Long. Elevation is 1,037 feet.
History: Cameron was platted in 1855 and named for Colonel Elisha Cameron, father-in-law of Samuel McCorkle, one of the town's founders. Early industries here included garment factories.
Population: 8,312 (2000); Race: 85.0% White, 12.0% Black, 0.5% Asian, 0.6% American Indian and Alaska Native, 1.3% Hispanic of any race, 1.8% two or more races (2000); Density: 1,560.6 persons per square mile (2000); Age: 18.0% under 18, 14.2% over 64 (2000); Marriage status: 25.7% never married, 46.1% now married, 8.3% widowed, 19.9% divorced (2000); Foreign born: 1.1% (2000); Ancestry (includes multiple ancestries): 17.5% German, 15.6% Other groups, 11.4% Irish, 11.2% United States or American, 9.1% English (2000).
Economy: Single-family building permits issued: 26 (2001) / 27 (2000); Multi-family building permits issued: 4 (2001) / 10 (2000); Employment by occupation: 9.4% management, 22.7% professional, 20.6% services, 23.1% sales, 0.5% farming, 10.1% construction, 13.6% production (2000).
Income: Per capita income: $12,375 (2000); Median household income: $32,136 (2000); Poverty rate: 12.0% (2000).
Taxes: Total city taxes per capita: $101 (2000); City property taxes per capita: $21 (2000).
Education: High school graduation rate: 78.8% (2000); College graduation rate: 11.3% (2000).

School District(s)

Cameron R-I (PK-12)
2000 Enrollment: 1,625 816-632-2170
Housing: Homeownership rate: 64.1% (2000); Median home value: $77,300 (2000); Median rent: $317 per month (2000); Median age of housing: 33 years (2000).
Hospitals: Cameron Community Hospital (57 beds)
Safety: Violent crime rate: 25.1 per 10,000 population; Property crime rate: 270.2 per 10,000 population (2001).

Newspapers: The Citizen Observer (1 x week); Cameron Shopper (1 x week)
Transportation: Commute to work: 88.6% car, 1.0% public transportation, 3.4% walk, 5.1% work from home (2000); Travel time to work: 58.6% less than 15 minutes, 4.7% 15 to 30 minutes, 15.9% 30 to 45 minutes, 10.0% 45 to 60 minutes, 10.7% 60 minutes or more (2000)
Additional Information Contacts
Cameron Chamber of Commerce 816-632-2005

GOWER (city). Covers a land area of 0.999 square miles and a water area of 0 square miles. Located at 39.61° N. Lat.; 94.59° W. Long. Elevation is 941 feet.
Population: 1,399 (2000); Race: 99.4% White, 0.3% Black, 0.0% Asian, 0.0% American Indian and Alaska Native, 1.1% Hispanic of any race, 0.3% two or more races (2000); Density: 1,399.9 persons per square mile (2000); Age: 29.8% under 18, 12.3% over 64 (2000); Marriage status: 20.5% never married, 64.2% now married, 7.6% widowed, 7.6% divorced (2000); Foreign born: 0.2% (2000); Ancestry (includes multiple ancestries): 21.2% German, 12.4% Irish, 11.3% English, 10.5% United States or American, 7.1% Other groups (2000).
Economy: Agriculture: corn, hay; cattle. Manufacturing: concrete. Single-family building permits issued: 8 (2001) / 3 (2000); Multi-family building permits issued: 0 (2001) / 0 (2000); Employment by occupation: 13.4% management, 18.7% professional, 14.4% services, 22.3% sales, 0.3% farming, 12.2% construction, 18.7% production (2000).
Income: Per capita income: $19,408 (2000); Median household income: $48,125 (2000); Poverty rate: 3.8% (2000).
Taxes: Total city taxes per capita: $105 (1997); City property taxes per capita: $37 (1997).
Education: High school graduation rate: 89.1% (2000); College graduation rate: 20.2% (2000).

School District(s)
East Buchanan Co. C-1 (PK-12)
2000 Enrollment: 752 816-424-6466
Housing: Homeownership rate: 80.4% (2000); Median home value: $81,800 (2000); Median rent: $363 per month (2000); Median age of housing: 29 years (2000).
Transportation: Commute to work: 93.6% car, 0.7% public transportation, 1.8% walk, 2.8% work from home (2000); Travel time to work: 21.5% less than 15 minutes, 34.4% 15 to 30 minutes, 24.3% 30 to 45 minutes, 8.6% 45 to 60 minutes, 11.2% 60 minutes or more (2000)

LATHROP (city). Covers a land area of 1.387 square miles and a water area of 0 square miles. Located at 39.54° N. Lat.; 94.33° W. Long. Elevation is 1,069 feet.
History: Lathrop was known as a mule breeding center. The British government sent buyers here to purchase mules for its army during the Boer War.
Population: 2,092 (2000); Race: 95.9% White, 1.2% Black, 0.2% Asian, 0.2% American Indian and Alaska Native, 0.4% Hispanic of any race, 2.2% two or more races (2000); Density: 1,508.5 persons per square mile (2000); Age: 30.4% under 18, 10.8% over 64 (2000); Marriage status: 20.8% never married, 61.4% now married, 6.1% widowed, 11.7% divorced (2000); Foreign born: 0.6% (2000); Ancestry (includes multiple ancestries): 15.6% German, 14.6% United States or American, 11.2% English, 9.9% Irish, 9.1% Other groups (2000).
Economy: Single-family building permits issued: 12 (2001) / 14 (2000); Multi-family building permits issued: 2 (2001) / 0 (2000); Employment by occupation: 8.4% management, 10.4% professional, 15.0% services, 31.0% sales, 0.4% farming, 13.7% construction, 21.0% production (2000).
Income: Per capita income: $17,189 (2000); Median household income: $39,537 (2000); Poverty rate: 10.9% (2000).
Taxes: Total city taxes per capita: $298 (1997); City property taxes per capita: $69 (1997).
Education: High school graduation rate: 81.8% (2000); College graduation rate: 11.8% (2000).

School District(s)
Lathrop R-II (PK-12)
2000 Enrollment: 894 816-528-7500
Housing: Homeownership rate: 71.0% (2000); Median home value: $81,300 (2000); Median rent: $353 per month (2000); Median age of housing: 27 years (2000).
Transportation: Commute to work: 95.8% car, 0.2% public transportation, 2.6% walk, 1.2% work from home (2000); Travel time to work: 22.8% less than 15 minutes, 20.0% 15 to 30 minutes, 26.0% 30 to 45 minutes, 21.7% 45 to 60 minutes, 9.5% 60 minutes or more (2000)
Additional Information Contacts
Lathrop Chamber of Commerce 816-528-4251

PLATTSBURG (city). Covers a land area of 3.540 square miles and a water area of 0.026 square miles. Located at 39.56° N. Lat.; 94.45° W. Long. Elevation is 953 feet.
History: Plattsburg was laid out on the site selected by commissioners for the county seat when Clay County was organized in 1833. The town was first called Concord, then Springfield, but became Plattsburg in 1835, named for Plattsburg in Clinton County, New York. It is said that John Livingston, an early settler, killed 48 black bears in Plattsburg during his first year.
Population: 2,354 (2000); Race: 90.8% White, 6.7% Black, 0.6% Asian, 0.0% American Indian and Alaska Native, 0.4% Hispanic of any race, 1.8% two or more races (2000); Density: 665.1 persons per square mile (2000); Age: 27.1% under 18, 16.6% over 64 (2000); Marriage status: 20.1% never married, 57.8% now married, 9.6% widowed, 12.5% divorced (2000); Foreign born: 0.9% (2000); Ancestry (includes multiple ancestries): 20.1% German, 14.3% Irish, 13.8% United States or American, 13.1% Other groups, 11.0% English (2000).
Economy: Single-family building permits issued: 16 (2001) / 10 (2000); Multi-family building permits issued: 2 (2001) / 4 (2000); Employment by occupation: 11.8% management, 16.1% professional, 17.6% services, 24.4% sales, 0.0% farming, 12.0% construction, 18.2% production (2000).
Income: Per capita income: $19,212 (2000); Median household income: $37,417 (2000); Poverty rate: 12.3% (2000).
Taxes: Total city taxes per capita: $205 (1997); City property taxes per capita: $78 (1997).
Education: High school graduation rate: 81.3% (2000); College graduation rate: 17.7% (2000).

School District(s)
Clinton Co. R-III (KG-12)
2000 Enrollment: 816 816-539-2183
Housing: Homeownership rate: 71.0% (2000); Median home value: $89,200 (2000); Median rent: $295 per month (2000); Median age of housing: 32 years (2000).
Safety: Violent crime rate: 38.0 per 10,000 population; Property crime rate: 177.3 per 10,000 population (2001).
Newspapers: The Clinton County Leader (1 x week)
Transportation: Commute to work: 90.7% car, 0.3% public transportation, 3.1% walk, 4.5% work from home (2000); Travel time to work: 37.3% less than 15 minutes, 8.2% 15 to 30 minutes, 21.3% 30 to 45 minutes, 17.5% 45 to 60 minutes, 15.7% 60 minutes or more (2000)
Additional Information Contacts
Plattsburg Chamber of Commerce 816-539-2649

TRIMBLE (city). Covers a land area of 0.489 square miles and a water area of 0 square miles. Located at 39.47° N. Lat.; 94.56° W. Long. Elevation is 931 feet.
Population: 451 (2000); Race: 97.4% White, 0.0% Black, 1.1% Asian, 0.0% American Indian and Alaska Native, 0.4% Hispanic of any race, 1.1% two or more races (2000); Density: 923.0 persons per square mile (2000); Age: 29.2% under 18, 9.8% over 64 (2000); Marriage status: 18.4% never married, 55.0% now married, 9.8% widowed, 16.7% divorced (2000); Foreign born: 1.1% (2000); Ancestry (includes multiple ancestries): 23.3% German, 15.9% Other groups, 14.4% United States or American, 9.8% Irish, 9.4% English (2000).
Economy: Single-family building permits issued: 4 (2001) / 4 (2000); Multi-family building permits issued: 0 (2001) / 0 (2000); Employment by occupation: 10.3% management, 12.3% professional, 12.8% services, 23.2% sales, 0.0% farming, 26.1% construction, 15.3% production (2000).
Income: Per capita income: $17,715 (2000); Median household income: $38,571 (2000); Poverty rate: 10.7% (2000).
Taxes: Total city taxes per capita: $62 (1997); City property taxes per capita: $19 (1997).
Education: High school graduation rate: 86.2% (2000); College graduation rate: 12.0% (2000).
Housing: Homeownership rate: 75.4% (2000); Median home value: $86,700 (2000); Median rent: $363 per month (2000); Median age of housing: 23 years (2000).
Transportation: Commute to work: 97.0% car, 0.0% public transportation, 0.0% walk, 3.0% work from home (2000); Travel time to work: 9.7% less than 15 minutes, 19.0% 15 to 30 minutes, 41.0% 30 to 45 minutes, 25.1% 45 to 60 minutes, 5.1% 60 minutes or more (2000)

TURNEY (village). Covers a land area of 0.476 square miles and a water area of 0 square miles. Located at 39.63° N. Lat.; 94.32° W. Long. Elevation is 1,056 feet.

Population: 155 (2000); Race: 98.1% White, 0.0% Black, 1.3% Asian, 0.0% American Indian and Alaska Native, 0.0% Hispanic of any race, 0.0% two or more races (2000); Density: 325.9 persons per square mile (2000); Age: 26.4% under 18, 12.6% over 64 (2000); Marriage status: 20.8% never married, 65.6% now married, 5.6% widowed, 8.0% divorced (2000); Foreign born: 1.3% (2000); Ancestry (includes multiple ancestries): 37.7% United States or American, 15.1% German, 13.2% Other groups, 8.2% Irish, 5.0% French (except Basque) (2000).
Economy: Employment by occupation: 6.2% management, 4.9% professional, 28.4% services, 22.2% sales, 0.0% farming, 19.8% construction, 18.5% production (2000).
Income: Per capita income: $14,221 (2000); Median household income: $36,528 (2000); Poverty rate: 9.6% (2000).
Taxes: Total city taxes per capita: $17 (1997); City property taxes per capita: $0 (1997).
Education: High school graduation rate: 81.5% (2000); College graduation rate: 7.4% (2000).
Housing: Homeownership rate: 81.4% (2000); Median home value: $56,000 (2000); Median rent: $375 per month (2000); Median age of housing: 27 years (2000).
Transportation: Commute to work: 93.2% car, 0.0% public transportation, 4.1% walk, 2.7% work from home (2000); Travel time to work: 5.6% less than 15 minutes, 26.4% 15 to 30 minutes, 33.3% 30 to 45 minutes, 26.4% 45 to 60 minutes, 8.3% 60 minutes or more (2000)

Cole County

Located in central Missouri, in the Ozarks; bounded on the north by the Missouri River, and on the east by the Osage River. Covers a land area of 391.40 square miles, a water area of 7.60 square miles, and is located in the Central Time Zone. The county government was organized in 1820. County seat is Jefferson City.

Weather Station: Jefferson City Water Plant — Elevation: 669 feet

	Jan	Feb	Mar	Apr	May	Jun	Jul	Aug	Sep	Oct	Nov	Dec
High	39	45	56	67	76	84	90	88	81	70	55	44
Low	18	23	32	42	52	62	66	64	55	43	33	23
Precip	1.6	1.9	3.2	4.0	4.8	4.1	3.6	3.3	3.7	3.3	3.5	2.6
Snow	5.5	3.7	1.9	0.2	0.0	0.0	0.0	0.0	0.0	0.0	1.1	2.6

High and Low temperatures in degrees Fahrenheit; Precipitation and Snow in inches

Population: 71,397 (2000); Race: 87.0% White, 9.6% Black, 0.9% Asian, 0.3% American Indian and Alaska Native, 1.1% Hispanic of any race, 1.5% two or more races (2000); Density: 182.4 persons per square mile (2000); Age: 24.1% under 18, 11.3% over 64 (2000).
Religion: Five largest groups: 36.7% Catholic Church, 14.3% Southern Baptist Convention, 5.1% Lutheran Church—Missouri Synod, 3.4% The United Methodist Church, 2.3% Christian Churches and Churches of Christ (2000).
Economy: Unemployment rate: 2.6% (11/2002); Total civilian labor force: 40,802 (11/2002); Leading industries: 14.9% health care and social assistance; 14.4% retail trade; 11.5% wholesale trade (2000); Companies that employ more than 1,000 persons: 3 (2000); Companies that employ more than 100 persons: 47 (2000); Farms: 1,045 totaling 179,018 acres (1997); Minority business ownership rate: 4.1% (1997); Women business ownership rate: 25.7% (1997); Retail sales per capita: $11,108 (1997). Single-family building permits issued: 368 (2001) / 447 (2000); Multi-family building permits issued: 168 (2001) / 184 (2000).
Income: Per capita income: $20,739 (2000); Median household income: $42,924 (2000); Poverty rate: 8.7% (2000); Bankruptcy rate: 3.71% (2001).
Taxes: Total county taxes per capita: $147 (2000); County property taxes per capita: $85 (2000).
Education: High school graduation rate: 85.3% (2000); College graduation rate: 27.4% (2000).
Housing: Homeownership rate: 67.8% (2000); Median home value: $97,200 (2000); Median rent: $360 per month (2000); Median age of housing: 26 years (2000).
Health: Birth rate: 126.2 per 10,000 population (1998); Age adjusted death rate: 96.0 per 10,000 population (1999); Age adjusted cancer mortality rate: 236.5 deaths per 100,000 population (1999). Number of physicians: 19.2 per 10,000 population (1999); Number of hospital beds: 42.2 per 10,000 population (1999).
Elections: 2000 Presidential election results: 36.8% Gore, 61.5% Bush, 1.1% Nader, 0.3% Buchanan

National and State Parks: Jefferson Landing State Historic Site; Mari-Osa State Wildlife Area; Pikes Camp State Wildlife Area; Scrivner Road State Wildlife Area

Additional Information Contacts

Cole County Government Offices 573-634-9100
Jefferson City Area Board of Realtors 573-636-6721
Jefferson City Chamber of Commerce 573-634-3511
Jefferson City Convention 573-632-2820
Jefferson City Convention & Visitors Bureau 573-632-2820

Cole County Communities

CENTERTOWN (town). Covers a land area of 0.901 square miles and a water area of 0 square miles. Located at 38.61° N. Lat.; 92.41° W. Long. Elevation is 848 feet.
Population: 257 (2000); Race: 96.3% White, 0.0% Black, 1.7% Asian, 0.0% American Indian and Alaska Native, 0.0% Hispanic of any race, 2.0% two or more races (2000); Density: 285.4 persons per square mile (2000); Age: 18.9% under 18, 15.2% over 64 (2000); Marriage status: 23.4% never married, 57.3% now married, 6.5% widowed, 12.9% divorced (2000); Foreign born: 1.7% (2000); Ancestry (includes multiple ancestries): 26.7% German, 13.5% United States or American, 9.5% Irish, 5.7% Other groups, 5.7% French (except Basque) (2000).
Economy: Employment by occupation: 9.6% management, 11.5% professional, 10.9% services, 41.0% sales, 0.0% farming, 12.8% construction, 14.1% production (2000).
Income: Per capita income: $17,321 (2000); Median household income: $39,750 (2000); Poverty rate: 3.7% (2000).
Taxes: Total city taxes per capita: $103 (1997); City property taxes per capita: $38 (1997).
Education: High school graduation rate: 79.1% (2000); College graduation rate: 7.9% (2000).
Housing: Homeownership rate: 76.2% (2000); Median home value: $58,300 (2000); Median rent: $270 per month (2000); Median age of housing: 39 years (2000).
Transportation: Commute to work: 95.4% car, 0.0% public transportation, 2.0% walk, 2.6% work from home (2000); Travel time to work: 2.0% less than 15 minutes, 67.8% 15 to 30 minutes, 20.8% 30 to 45 minutes, 0.0% 45 to 60 minutes, 9.4% 60 minutes or more (2000)

EUGENE (unincorporated postal area, zip code 65032). Covers a land area of 51.145 square miles and a water area of 0.067 square miles. Located at 38.39° N. Lat.; 92.36° W. Long. Elevation is 840 feet.
Population: 1,427 (2000); Race: 99.8% White, 0.0% Black, 0.0% Asian, 0.0% American Indian and Alaska Native, 0.1% Hispanic of any race, 0.1% two or more races (2000); Density: 27.9 persons per square mile (2000); Age: 30.7% under 18, 10.7% over 64 (2000); Marriage status: 20.1% never married, 66.2% now married, 6.9% widowed, 6.9% divorced (2000); Foreign born: 1.0% (2000); Ancestry (includes multiple ancestries): 35.0% German, 12.1% United States or American, 11.2% Other groups, 6.8% English, 6.0% Irish (2000).
Economy: Employment by occupation: 7.6% management, 15.5% professional, 11.1% services, 27.2% sales, 1.8% farming, 12.9% construction, 23.9% production (2000).
Income: Per capita income: $17,298 (2000); Median household income: $41,563 (2000); Poverty rate: 7.2% (2000).
Education: High school graduation rate: 81.7% (2000); College graduation rate: 10.1% (2000).

School District(s)

Cole Co. R-V (KG-12)
2000 Enrollment: 769 573-498-4000

Housing: Homeownership rate: 90.3% (2000); Median home value: $95,900 (2000); Median rent: $214 per month (2000); Median age of housing: 24 years (2000).
Transportation: Commute to work: 93.4% car, 0.0% public transportation, 1.9% walk, 4.4% work from home (2000); Travel time to work: 12.4% less than 15 minutes, 30.8% 15 to 30 minutes, 34.5% 30 to 45 minutes, 16.8% 45 to 60 minutes, 5.5% 60 minutes or more (2000)

HENLEY (unincorporated postal area, zip code 65040). Covers a land area of 44.410 square miles and a water area of 0.151 square miles. Located at 38.35° N. Lat.; 92.31° W. Long. Elevation is 595 feet.
History: Former railroad bridge over Osage River.
Population: 1,265 (2000); Race: 100.0% White, 0.0% Black, 0.0% Asian, 0.0% American Indian and Alaska Native, 0.9% Hispanic of any race, 0.0%

two or more races (2000); Density: 28.5 persons per square mile (2000); Age: 30.7% under 18, 6.7% over 64 (2000); Marriage status: 21.5% never married, 65.4% now married, 6.8% widowed, 6.3% divorced (2000); Foreign born: 0.0% (2000); Ancestry (includes multiple ancestries): 41.6% German, 14.6% United States or American, 10.7% Irish, 9.8% Other groups, 4.2% English (2000).
Economy: Employment by occupation: 14.6% management, 8.8% professional, 11.2% services, 35.1% sales, 1.0% farming, 18.3% construction, 11.0% production (2000).
Income: Per capita income: $17,687 (2000); Median household income: $45,417 (2000); Poverty rate: 4.4% (2000).
Education: High school graduation rate: 85.5% (2000); College graduation rate: 13.5% (2000).
Housing: Homeownership rate: 86.6% (2000); Median home value: $88,300 (2000); Median rent: $259 per month (2000); Median age of housing: 30 years (2000).
Transportation: Commute to work: 96.2% car, 0.0% public transportation, 1.4% walk, 1.4% work from home (2000); Travel time to work: 13.6% less than 15 minutes, 36.5% 15 to 30 minutes, 32.8% 30 to 45 minutes, 7.5% 45 to 60 minutes, 9.6% 60 minutes or more (2000)

JEFFERSON CITY (city). Covers a land area of 27.252 square miles and a water area of 1.018 square miles. Located at 38.57° N. Lat.; 92.18° W. Long. Elevation is 702 feet.
History: When Jefferson City was declared the capital of Missouri in 1821, the community consisted of only two or three buildings. A town was platted in 1822, and a capitol building erected in 1823, but when the town was incorporated in 1825 there were just 31 families living here. A series of disasters began with the burning of the capitol building in 1837 and the loss of all the state records, followed by a deadly outbreak of cholera in 1849. When the first train approached Jefferson City in 1855, a trestle across the Gasconade River collapsed, killing and injuring scores of people. At the start of the Civil War, a Missouri convention voted to remain in the Union. The Missouri governor, however, favored secession and refused to respond to President Lincoln's call for troops.
Population: 39,636 (2000); Race: 81.8% White, 14.0% Black, 1.4% Asian, 0.4% American Indian and Alaska Native, 1.2% Hispanic of any race, 1.9% two or more races (2000); Density: 1,454.4 persons per square mile (2000); Age: 20.2% under 18, 14.1% over 64 (2000); Marriage status: 28.4% never married, 50.5% now married, 7.2% widowed, 13.9% divorced (2000); Foreign born: 2.9% (2000); Ancestry (includes multiple ancestries): 31.4% German, 18.1% Other groups, 10.1% Irish, 10.0% English, 9.4% United States or American (2000).
Economy: Unemployment rate: 3.0% (11/2002); Total civilian labor force: 22,460 (11/2002); Single-family building permits issued: 140 (2001) / 152 (2000); Multi-family building permits issued: 77 (2001) / 21 (2000); Employment by occupation: 16.1% management, 23.6% professional, 13.3% services, 30.6% sales, 0.3% farming, 6.2% construction, 10.1% production (2000).
Income: Per capita income: $21,268 (2000); Median household income: $39,628 (2000); Poverty rate: 11.5% (2000).
Taxes: Total city taxes per capita: $535 (2000); City property taxes per capita: $95 (2000).
Education: High school graduation rate: 85.1% (2000); College graduation rate: 30.8% (2000).

School District(s)

Cole Co. R-II (KG-12)
2000 Enrollment: 594 573-636-2020
Division of Youth Services (UG-UG)
2000 Enrollment: 1,003 573-751-2799
Jefferson City (PK-12)
2000 Enrollment: 8,476 573-659-3000
State Schools Severely Handicp (PK-12)
2000 Enrollment: 1,376 573-751-4427

Four-year College(s)

Lincoln University (Public, Historically black)
2001 Enrollment: 3,332 573-681-5000
2001 Tuition: In-state $2,568; Out-of-state $5,136

Two-year College(s)

Nichols Career Center (Public)
2001 Enrollment: 72 573-659-3100
Metro Business College (Private, For-profit)
2001 Enrollment: 138 573-635-6600
2001 Tuition: In-state $7,785; Out-of-state $7,785

Housing: Homeownership rate: 58.8% (2000); Median home value: $98,700 (2000); Median rent: $353 per month (2000); Median age of housing: 32 years (2000).
Hospitals: Capital Region Medical Center (134 beds); Jefferson City Corrections Center Infirmary (23 beds); Saint Marys Health Center (167 beds)
Safety: Violent crime rate: 76.0 per 10,000 population; Property crime rate: 339.8 per 10,000 population (2001).
Newspapers: The Sunday News Tribune; Post-Tribune (7 x week); Daily Capital News (7 x week); Word and Way (1 x week); The Catholic Missourian (1 x week)
Transportation: Commute to work: 93.4% car, 1.7% public transportation, 2.2% walk, 2.3% work from home (2000); Travel time to work: 60.2% less than 15 minutes, 29.9% 15 to 30 minutes, 5.5% 30 to 45 minutes, 2.4% 45 to 60 minutes, 2.0% 60 minutes or more (2000); Amtrak: Service available.
Airports: Jefferson City Memorial
Additional Information Contacts
Jefferson City Area Board of Realtors 573-636-6721
Jefferson City Chamber of Commerce 573-634-3511
Jefferson City Convention 573-632-2820
Jefferson City Convention & Visitors Bureau 573-632-2820

LOHMAN (city). Covers a land area of 0.447 square miles and a water area of 0 square miles. Located at 38.54° N. Lat.; 92.36° W. Long. Elevation is 649 feet.
Population: 168 (2000); Race: 100.0% White, 0.0% Black, 0.0% Asian, 0.0% American Indian and Alaska Native, 0.0% Hispanic of any race, 0.0% two or more races (2000); Density: 376.0 persons per square mile (2000); Age: 26.5% under 18, 13.2% over 64 (2000); Marriage status: 23.7% never married, 72.4% now married, 2.6% widowed, 1.3% divorced (2000); Foreign born: 1.1% (2000); Ancestry (includes multiple ancestries): 38.6% German, 25.4% United States or American, 9.5% Irish, 5.3% Other groups, 4.8% Dutch (2000).
Economy: In agricultural area: grain, soybeans; hogs, cattle. Employment by occupation: 7.8% management, 23.3% professional, 9.5% services, 31.9% sales, 0.0% farming, 12.1% construction, 15.5% production (2000).
Income: Per capita income: $22,666 (2000); Median household income: $54,583 (2000); Poverty rate: 3.7% (2000).
Taxes: Total city taxes per capita: $41 (1997); City property taxes per capita: $18 (1997).
Education: High school graduation rate: 83.8% (2000); College graduation rate: 25.6% (2000).
Housing: Homeownership rate: 89.1% (2000); Median home value: $92,100 (2000); Median rent: $338 per month (2000); Median age of housing: 53 years (2000).
Transportation: Commute to work: 92.1% car, 0.0% public transportation, 3.5% walk, 4.4% work from home (2000); Travel time to work: 22.9% less than 15 minutes, 65.1% 15 to 30 minutes, 7.3% 30 to 45 minutes, 2.8% 45 to 60 minutes, 1.8% 60 minutes or more (2000)

RUSSELLVILLE (city). Covers a land area of 0.755 square miles and a water area of 0 square miles. Located at 38.51° N. Lat.; 92.43° W. Long. Elevation is 888 feet.
Population: 758 (2000); Race: 96.1% White, 0.0% Black, 0.0% Asian, 3.5% American Indian and Alaska Native, 2.4% Hispanic of any race, 0.4% two or more races (2000); Density: 1,003.4 persons per square mile (2000); Age: 31.0% under 18, 11.4% over 64 (2000); Marriage status: 22.8% never married, 58.1% now married, 7.5% widowed, 11.6% divorced (2000); Foreign born: 0.0% (2000); Ancestry (includes multiple ancestries): 37.8% German, 14.8% Other groups, 12.0% Irish, 9.0% United States or American, 7.0% English (2000).
Economy: Corn, hay; cattle. Employment by occupation: 14.6% management, 13.1% professional, 17.4% services, 29.7% sales, 1.0% farming, 14.1% construction, 10.0% production (2000).
Income: Per capita income: $14,812 (2000); Median household income: $34,408 (2000); Poverty rate: 9.5% (2000).
Taxes: Total city taxes per capita: $72 (1997); City property taxes per capita: $9 (1997).
Education: High school graduation rate: 81.1% (2000); College graduation rate: 16.1% (2000).

School District(s)

Cole Co. R-I (KG-12)
2000 Enrollment: 702 573-782-3534

Housing: Homeownership rate: 68.9% (2000); Median home value: $70,900 (2000); Median rent: $304 per month (2000); Median age of housing: 34 years (2000).

Transportation: Commute to work: 91.9% car, 0.0% public transportation, 4.7% walk, 2.1% work from home (2000); Travel time to work: 20.1% less than 15 minutes, 54.8% 15 to 30 minutes, 18.2% 30 to 45 minutes, 2.1% 45 to 60 minutes, 4.8% 60 minutes or more (2000)

SAINT MARTINS (city). Covers a land area of 1.589 square miles and a water area of 0.007 square miles. Located at 38.59° N. Lat.; 92.33° W. Long. Elevation is 780 feet.

Population: 1,023 (2000); Race: 95.6% White, 1.1% Black, 0.3% Asian, 0.2% American Indian and Alaska Native, 1.5% Hispanic of any race, 1.7% two or more races (2000); Density: 643.8 persons per square mile (2000); Age: 30.6% under 18, 8.9% over 64 (2000); Marriage status: 20.5% never married, 59.7% now married, 9.4% widowed, 10.4% divorced (2000); Foreign born: 1.0% (2000); Ancestry (includes multiple ancestries): 38.9% German, 10.3% United States or American, 9.6% Irish, 8.9% Other groups, 6.1% English (2000).

Economy: Single-family building permits issued: 12 (2001) / 18 (2000); Multi-family building permits issued: 0 (2001) / 0 (2000); Employment by occupation: 12.5% management, 15.2% professional, 15.0% services, 33.2% sales, 0.6% farming, 9.3% construction, 14.2% production (2000).

Income: Per capita income: $23,900 (2000); Median household income: $41,389 (2000); Poverty rate: 8.8% (2000).

Education: High school graduation rate: 80.2% (2000); College graduation rate: 16.6% (2000).

Housing: Homeownership rate: 72.7% (2000); Median home value: $98,400 (2000); Median rent: $348 per month (2000); Median age of housing: 21 years (2000).

Transportation: Commute to work: 93.5% car, 0.8% public transportation, 1.3% walk, 3.6% work from home (2000); Travel time to work: 31.9% less than 15 minutes, 52.4% 15 to 30 minutes, 8.7% 30 to 45 minutes, 4.8% 45 to 60 minutes, 2.2% 60 minutes or more (2000)

SAINT THOMAS (town). Covers a land area of 1.175 square miles and a water area of 0 square miles. Located at 38.37° N. Lat.; 92.21° W. Long. Elevation is 775 feet.

Population: 287 (2000); Race: 100.0% White, 0.0% Black, 0.0% Asian, 0.0% American Indian and Alaska Native, 0.0% Hispanic of any race, 0.0% two or more races (2000); Density: 244.2 persons per square mile (2000); Age: 24.3% under 18, 19.2% over 64 (2000); Marriage status: 27.4% never married, 61.2% now married, 7.3% widowed, 4.1% divorced (2000); Foreign born: 0.0% (2000); Ancestry (includes multiple ancestries): 80.1% German, 2.9% English, 2.2% French (except Basque), 1.8% Dutch, 1.8% United States or American (2000).

Economy: Employment by occupation: 12.0% management, 12.0% professional, 6.7% services, 36.7% sales, 0.7% farming, 16.0% construction, 16.0% production (2000).

Income: Per capita income: $18,134 (2000); Median household income: $43,571 (2000); Poverty rate: 6.2% (2000).

Education: High school graduation rate: 74.4% (2000); College graduation rate: 16.7% (2000).

Housing: Homeownership rate: 86.2% (2000); Median home value: $79,200 (2000); Median rent: $188 per month (2000); Median age of housing: 28 years (2000).

Transportation: Commute to work: 88.7% car, 0.0% public transportation, 3.3% walk, 6.0% work from home (2000); Travel time to work: 10.6% less than 15 minutes, 27.7% 15 to 30 minutes, 47.5% 30 to 45 minutes, 6.4% 45 to 60 minutes, 7.8% 60 minutes or more (2000)

TAOS (city). Covers a land area of 2.251 square miles and a water area of 0.102 square miles. Located at 38.50° N. Lat.; 92.08° W. Long. Elevation is 728 feet.

History: Taos was established around a church built in 1840 by Father Helias D'Huddeghem who had come from Belgium as a Jesuit missionary. In 1847 a group of Belgian craftsmen settled at Taos, contributing to the prosperity of the community.

Population: 870 (2000); Race: 99.7% White, 0.0% Black, 0.0% Asian, 0.2% American Indian and Alaska Native, 0.2% Hispanic of any race, 0.1% two or more races (2000); Density: 386.5 persons per square mile (2000); Age: 27.9% under 18, 14.4% over 64 (2000); Marriage status: 20.1% never married, 68.2% now married, 5.6% widowed, 6.1% divorced (2000); Foreign born: 0.0% (2000); Ancestry (includes multiple ancestries): 57.6% German, 11.9% United States or American, 10.4% Irish, 5.6% Other groups, 4.9% French (except Basque) (2000).

Economy: Employment by occupation: 9.0% management, 11.1% professional, 18.0% services, 34.1% sales, 0.4% farming, 14.9% construction, 12.6% production (2000).

Income: Per capita income: $18,481 (2000); Median household income: $50,333 (2000); Poverty rate: 2.3% (2000).

Taxes: Total city taxes per capita: $106 (1997); City property taxes per capita: $19 (1997).

Education: High school graduation rate: 79.5% (2000); College graduation rate: 11.2% (2000).

Housing: Homeownership rate: 84.2% (2000); Median home value: $84,000 (2000); Median rent: $182 per month (2000); Median age of housing: 25 years (2000).

Transportation: Commute to work: 91.1% car, 0.2% public transportation, 1.3% walk, 6.4% work from home (2000); Travel time to work: 15.6% less than 15 minutes, 64.5% 15 to 30 minutes, 13.6% 30 to 45 minutes, 2.3% 45 to 60 minutes, 4.1% 60 minutes or more (2000)

WARDSVILLE (village). Covers a land area of 2.426 square miles and a water area of 0.041 square miles. Located at 38.49° N. Lat.; 92.17° W. Long. Elevation is 803 feet.

Population: 976 (2000); Race: 99.2% White, 0.0% Black, 0.0% Asian, 0.0% American Indian and Alaska Native, 0.2% Hispanic of any race, 0.6% two or more races (2000); Density: 402.4 persons per square mile (2000); Age: 31.8% under 18, 9.6% over 64 (2000); Marriage status: 21.8% never married, 69.7% now married, 4.5% widowed, 4.1% divorced (2000); Foreign born: 0.2% (2000); Ancestry (includes multiple ancestries): 56.8% German, 11.5% United States or American, 4.7% Irish, 4.5% Other groups, 4.5% English (2000).

Economy: Cattle; hay. Employment by occupation: 16.1% management, 19.6% professional, 7.8% services, 32.0% sales, 0.0% farming, 15.9% construction, 8.7% production (2000).

Income: Per capita income: $21,925 (2000); Median household income: $57,813 (2000); Poverty rate: 1.9% (2000).

Taxes: Total city taxes per capita: $64 (1997); City property taxes per capita: $29 (1997).

Education: High school graduation rate: 84.3% (2000); College graduation rate: 20.0% (2000).

Housing: Homeownership rate: 81.5% (2000); Median home value: $136,200 (2000); Median rent: $453 per month (2000); Median age of housing: 13 years (2000).

Transportation: Commute to work: 95.3% car, 0.0% public transportation, 0.7% walk, 3.9% work from home (2000); Travel time to work: 26.5% less than 15 minutes, 57.9% 15 to 30 minutes, 6.8% 30 to 45 minutes, 4.7% 45 to 60 minutes, 4.1% 60 minutes or more (2000)

Cooper County

Located in central Missouri; bounded on the north by the Missouri River; drained by the Lamine and Blackwater Rivers. Covers a land area of 565.00 square miles, a water area of 5.20 square miles, and is located in the Central Time Zone. The county government was organized in 1818. County seat is Boonville.

Weather Station: Boonville — Elevation: 669 feet

	Jan	Feb	Mar	Apr	May	Jun	Jul	Aug	Sep	Oct	Nov	Dec
High	36	42	54	65	75	84	89	88	80	68	53	41
Low	18	23	33	44	54	63	68	65	57	45	34	24
Precip	1.6	1.8	3.1	4.3	5.4	4.7	3.7	4.2	4.4	3.5	3.8	2.6
Snow	7.2	6.1	2.9	0.4	0.0	0.0	0.0	0.0	0.0	tr	1.5	3.9

High and Low temperatures in degrees Fahrenheit; Precipitation and Snow in inches

Population: 16,670 (2000); Race: 88.4% White, 9.6% Black, 0.2% Asian, 0.2% American Indian and Alaska Native, 0.5% Hispanic of any race, 1.2% two or more races (2000); Density: 29.5 persons per square mile (2000); Age: 22.8% under 18, 15.4% over 64 (2000).

Religion: Five largest groups: 17.5% Catholic Church, 15.7% Southern Baptist Convention, 6.2% The United Methodist Church, 5.7% Lutheran Church—Missouri Synod, 3.3% United Church of Christ (2000).

Economy: Unemployment rate: 4.0% (11/2002); Total civilian labor force: 7,814 (11/2002); Leading industries: 21.8% retail trade; 17.2% health care and social assistance; 15.3% manufacturing (2000); Companies that employ more than 1,000 persons: 0 (2000); Companies that employ more than 100 persons: 5 (2000); Farms: 879 totaling 301,692 acres (1997); Minority business ownership rate: 0.0% (1997); Women business ownership rate: 14.5% (1997); Retail sales per capita: $6,010 (1997). Single-family building permits issued: 22 (2001) / 20 (2000); Multi-family building permits issued: 10 (2001) / 55 (2000).

Income: Per capita income: $15,648 (2000); Median household income: $35,313 (2000); Poverty rate: 10.7% (2000); Bankruptcy rate: 3.81% (2001).

Taxes: Total county taxes per capita: $185 (2000); County property taxes per capita: $70 (2000).
Education: High school graduation rate: 80.3% (2000); College graduation rate: 13.7% (2000).
Housing: Homeownership rate: 74.2% (2000); Median home value: $74,200 (2000); Median rent: $307 per month (2000); Median age of housing: 36 years (2000).
Health: Birth rate: 123.0 per 10,000 population (1998); Age adjusted death rate: 86.4 per 10,000 population (1999); Age adjusted cancer mortality rate: 227.9 deaths per 100,000 population (1999). Number of physicians: 5.4 per 10,000 population (1999); Number of hospital beds: 29.4 per 10,000 population (1999).
Elections: 2000 Presidential election results: 37.8% Gore, 60.0% Bush, 1.2% Nader, 0.7% Buchanan
National and State Parks: Prairie Home State Wildlife Area
Additional Information Contacts
Cooper County Government Offices 660-882-2114
Boonville Chamber of Commerce 660-882-2721

Cooper County Communities

BLACKWATER (city). Covers a land area of 0.326 square miles and a water area of 0 square miles. Located at 38.97° N. Lat.; 92.99° W. Long. Elevation is 610 feet.
Population: 199 (2000); Race: 93.4% White, 6.6% Black, 0.0% Asian, 0.0% American Indian and Alaska Native, 1.2% Hispanic of any race, 0.0% two or more races (2000); Density: 611.1 persons per square mile (2000); Age: 17.5% under 18, 21.1% over 64 (2000); Marriage status: 19.7% never married, 55.1% now married, 10.2% widowed, 15.0% divorced (2000); Foreign born: 0.0% (2000); Ancestry (includes multiple ancestries): 28.3% German, 16.3% United States or American, 16.3% English, 10.2% Irish, 6.0% Other groups (2000).
Economy: Employment by occupation: 5.8% management, 17.4% professional, 27.5% services, 13.0% sales, 0.0% farming, 23.2% construction, 13.0% production (2000).
Income: Per capita income: $13,186 (2000); Median household income: $25,481 (2000); Poverty rate: 21.1% (2000).
Taxes: Total city taxes per capita: $174 (1997); City property taxes per capita: $123 (1997).
Education: High school graduation rate: 68.0% (2000); College graduation rate: 10.4% (2000).

School District(s)

Blackwater R-II (PK-08)
2000 Enrollment: 130 660-846-2461
Housing: Homeownership rate: 85.5% (2000); Median home value: $37,000 (2000); Median rent: $225 per month (2000); Median age of housing: 60+ years (2000).
Transportation: Commute to work: 92.8% car, 0.0% public transportation, 4.3% walk, 0.0% work from home (2000); Travel time to work: 27.5% less than 15 minutes, 21.7% 15 to 30 minutes, 27.5% 30 to 45 minutes, 14.5% 45 to 60 minutes, 8.7% 60 minutes or more (2000)

BOONVILLE (city). Covers a land area of 6.888 square miles and a water area of 0.461 square miles. Located at 38.96° N. Lat.; 92.74° W. Long. Elevation is 660 feet.
History: Boonville was settled in 1810 by Hannah Cole, a widow who brought her nine children with her and built a cabin on the bluffs overlooking the Missouri River. Through Boonville came prairie schooners which had crossed the river by ferry and were starting out over the western plains.
Population: 8,202 (2000); Race: 79.6% White, 18.1% Black, 0.3% Asian, 0.3% American Indian and Alaska Native, 0.4% Hispanic of any race, 1.6% two or more races (2000); Density: 1,190.8 persons per square mile (2000); Age: 20.0% under 18, 15.9% over 64 (2000); Marriage status: 33.7% never married, 46.4% now married, 10.2% widowed, 9.8% divorced (2000); Foreign born: 0.4% (2000); Ancestry (includes multiple ancestries): 24.2% German, 17.4% Other groups, 13.1% United States or American, 10.2% Irish, 7.1% English (2000).
Economy: Single-family building permits issued: 22 (2001) / 20 (2000); Multi-family building permits issued: 10 (2001) / 55 (2000); Employment by occupation: 7.7% management, 14.9% professional, 22.1% services, 25.8% sales, 0.6% farming, 9.1% construction, 19.7% production (2000).
Income: Per capita income: $14,854 (2000); Median household income: $33,440 (2000); Poverty rate: 11.3% (2000).
Taxes: Total city taxes per capita: $241 (1997); City property taxes per capita: $39 (1997).
Education: High school graduation rate: 77.0% (2000); College graduation rate: 13.1% (2000).

School District(s)

Boonville R-I (PK-12)
2000 Enrollment: 1,451 660-882-7474
Housing: Homeownership rate: 64.3% (2000); Median home value: $74,200 (2000); Median rent: $328 per month (2000); Median age of housing: 41 years (2000).
Hospitals: Cooper County Memorial Hospital (70 beds)
Newspapers: Boonville Daily News (5 x week); The Record (1 x week)
Transportation: Commute to work: 93.2% car, 0.4% public transportation, 3.4% walk, 1.7% work from home (2000); Travel time to work: 63.4% less than 15 minutes, 12.9% 15 to 30 minutes, 16.9% 30 to 45 minutes, 3.6% 45 to 60 minutes, 3.2% 60 minutes or more (2000)
Additional Information Contacts
Boonville Chamber of Commerce 660-882-2721

BUNCETON (city). Covers a land area of 0.945 square miles and a water area of 0.003 square miles. Located at 38.78° N. Lat.; 92.79° W. Long. Elevation is 770 feet.
Population: 348 (2000); Race: 93.4% White, 5.8% Black, 0.0% Asian, 0.0% American Indian and Alaska Native, 0.0% Hispanic of any race, 0.8% two or more races (2000); Density: 368.1 persons per square mile (2000); Age: 24.4% under 18, 11.4% over 64 (2000); Marriage status: 24.7% never married, 47.8% now married, 7.2% widowed, 20.3% divorced (2000); Foreign born: 1.1% (2000); Ancestry (includes multiple ancestries): 31.9% German, 19.9% Irish, 16.3% Other groups, 12.7% English, 9.1% United States or American (2000).
Economy: Wheat, corn; cattle. Employment by occupation: 5.9% management, 12.4% professional, 18.9% services, 17.3% sales, 1.1% farming, 14.1% construction, 30.3% production (2000).
Income: Per capita income: $13,202 (2000); Median household income: $27,917 (2000); Poverty rate: 11.1% (2000).
Taxes: Total city taxes per capita: $55 (1997); City property taxes per capita: $22 (1997).
Education: High school graduation rate: 78.3% (2000); College graduation rate: 7.7% (2000).

School District(s)

Cooper Co. R-IV (KG-12)
2000 Enrollment: 178 660-427-5347
Housing: Homeownership rate: 78.9% (2000); Median home value: $43,300 (2000); Median rent: $268 per month (2000); Median age of housing: 41 years (2000).
Transportation: Commute to work: 94.0% car, 0.0% public transportation, 6.0% walk, 0.0% work from home (2000); Travel time to work: 20.8% less than 15 minutes, 45.9% 15 to 30 minutes, 9.8% 30 to 45 minutes, 15.3% 45 to 60 minutes, 8.2% 60 minutes or more (2000)

OTTERVILLE (city). Covers a land area of 0.489 square miles and a water area of 0 square miles. Located at 38.70° N. Lat.; 93.00° W. Long. Elevation is 722 feet.
Population: 476 (2000); Race: 99.4% White, 0.0% Black, 0.0% Asian, 0.4% American Indian and Alaska Native, 0.6% Hispanic of any race, 0.0% two or more races (2000); Density: 972.5 persons per square mile (2000); Age: 23.9% under 18, 16.2% over 64 (2000); Marriage status: 23.5% never married, 53.0% now married, 9.7% widowed, 13.8% divorced (2000); Foreign born: 0.4% (2000); Ancestry (includes multiple ancestries): 44.1% German, 14.5% English, 8.2% Irish, 6.9% Other groups, 4.6% United States or American (2000).
Economy: Cattle; corn, wheat; lumber. Employment by occupation: 7.9% management, 13.3% professional, 26.7% services, 20.8% sales, 1.7% farming, 9.6% construction, 20.0% production (2000).
Income: Per capita income: $12,741 (2000); Median household income: $27,031 (2000); Poverty rate: 14.3% (2000).
Taxes: Total city taxes per capita: $118 (1997); City property taxes per capita: $39 (1997).
Education: High school graduation rate: 77.7% (2000); College graduation rate: 9.1% (2000).

School District(s)

Otterville R-VI (KG-12)
2000 Enrollment: 299 660-366-4391
Housing: Homeownership rate: 79.2% (2000); Median home value: $48,100 (2000); Median rent: $236 per month (2000); Median age of housing: 49 years (2000).
Transportation: Commute to work: 89.1% car, 0.8% public transportation, 5.9% walk, 2.9% work from home (2000); Travel time to work: 29.4% less

than 15 minutes, 45.9% 15 to 30 minutes, 14.3% 30 to 45 minutes, 3.0% 45 to 60 minutes, 7.4% 60 minutes or more (2000)

PILOT GROVE (city). Covers a land area of 0.419 square miles and a water area of 0 square miles. Located at 38.87° N. Lat.; 92.91° W. Long. Elevation is 845 feet.

History: Platted 1873.

Population: 723 (2000); Race: 99.2% White, 0.6% Black, 0.0% Asian, 0.0% American Indian and Alaska Native, 0.0% Hispanic of any race, 0.3% two or more races (2000); Density: 1,724.8 persons per square mile (2000); Age: 21.0% under 18, 25.8% over 64 (2000); Marriage status: 22.6% never married, 54.1% now married, 14.1% widowed, 9.1% divorced (2000); Foreign born: 0.3% (2000); Ancestry (includes multiple ancestries): 50.8% German, 8.5% United States or American, 6.8% Irish, 4.5% Other groups, 3.5% English (2000).

Economy: Wheat, corn; cattle. Employment by occupation: 8.8% management, 11.4% professional, 15.7% services, 28.1% sales, 0.7% farming, 19.3% construction, 16.0% production (2000).

Income: Per capita income: $14,857 (2000); Median household income: $31,354 (2000); Poverty rate: 7.0% (2000).

Taxes: Total city taxes per capita: $172 (1997); City property taxes per capita: $30 (1997).

Education: High school graduation rate: 77.2% (2000); College graduation rate: 4.9% (2000).

School District(s)

Pilot Grove C-4 (KG-12)
2000 Enrollment: 296 660-834-6915

Housing: Homeownership rate: 74.8% (2000); Median home value: $61,500 (2000); Median rent: $191 per month (2000); Median age of housing: 34 years (2000).

Transportation: Commute to work: 93.8% car, 0.0% public transportation, 3.3% walk, 2.0% work from home (2000); Travel time to work: 24.5% less than 15 minutes, 24.8% 15 to 30 minutes, 21.5% 30 to 45 minutes, 17.8% 45 to 60 minutes, 11.4% 60 minutes or more (2000)

PRAIRIE HOME (city). Covers a land area of 0.391 square miles and a water area of 0 square miles. Located at 38.81° N. Lat.; 92.59° W. Long. Elevation is 895 feet.

Population: 220 (2000); Race: 97.7% White, 0.0% Black, 0.0% Asian, 0.0% American Indian and Alaska Native, 2.7% Hispanic of any race, 2.3% two or more races (2000); Density: 562.2 persons per square mile (2000); Age: 31.1% under 18, 16.2% over 64 (2000); Marriage status: 17.2% never married, 56.2% now married, 12.4% widowed, 14.2% divorced (2000); Foreign born: 1.4% (2000); Ancestry (includes multiple ancestries): 25.2% German, 17.6% United States or American, 14.9% English, 11.3% Irish, 9.9% Other groups (2000).

Economy: Corn, soybeans; cattle. Employment by occupation: 6.5% management, 14.1% professional, 16.3% services, 22.8% sales, 0.0% farming, 26.1% construction, 14.1% production (2000).

Income: Per capita income: $15,182 (2000); Median household income: $29,375 (2000); Poverty rate: 6.0% (2000).

Taxes: Total city taxes per capita: $39 (1997); City property taxes per capita: $17 (1997).

Education: High school graduation rate: 82.3% (2000); College graduation rate: 8.8% (2000).

School District(s)

Prairie Home R-V (KG-12)
2000 Enrollment: 165 660-841-5296

Housing: Homeownership rate: 72.7% (2000); Median home value: $51,000 (2000); Median rent: $196 per month (2000); Median age of housing: 54 years (2000).

Transportation: Commute to work: 89.9% car, 0.0% public transportation, 0.0% walk, 10.1% work from home (2000); Travel time to work: 13.8% less than 15 minutes, 35.0% 15 to 30 minutes, 32.5% 30 to 45 minutes, 16.3% 45 to 60 minutes, 2.5% 60 minutes or more (2000)

WOOLDRIDGE (village). Covers a land area of 0.062 square miles and a water area of 0 square miles. Located at 38.90° N. Lat.; 92.52° W. Long. Elevation is 600 feet.

History: Severely damaged by flood of 1993.

Population: 47 (2000); Race: 81.5% White, 18.5% Black, 0.0% Asian, 0.0% American Indian and Alaska Native, 0.0% Hispanic of any race, 0.0% two or more races (2000); Density: 761.3 persons per square mile (2000); Age: 38.9% under 18, 0.0% over 64 (2000); Marriage status: 38.5% never married, 43.6% now married, 5.1% widowed, 12.8% divorced (2000); Foreign born: 0.0% (2000); Ancestry (includes multiple ancestries): 24.1% United States or American, 16.7% German, 13.0% African, 7.4% Irish, 7.4% Scottish (2000).

Economy: Corn, soybeans, cattle. Employment by occupation: 7.7% management, 7.7% professional, 19.2% services, 19.2% sales, 0.0% farming, 23.1% construction, 23.1% production (2000).

Income: Per capita income: $13,781 (2000); Median household income: $45,000 (2000); Poverty rate: 29.6% (2000).

Taxes: Total city taxes per capita: $53 (1997); City property taxes per capita: $18 (1997).

Education: High school graduation rate: 86.2% (2000); College graduation rate: 6.9% (2000).

Housing: Homeownership rate: 85.0% (2000); Median home value: $73,600 (2000); Median rent: $175 per month (2000); Median age of housing: 60+ years (2000).

Transportation: Commute to work: 100.0% car, 0.0% public transportation, 0.0% walk, 0.0% work from home (2000); Travel time to work: 0.0% less than 15 minutes, 50.0% 15 to 30 minutes, 30.8% 30 to 45 minutes, 19.2% 45 to 60 minutes, 0.0% 60 minutes or more (2000)

Crawford County

Located in east central Missouri, in the Ozarks; drained by the Meramec River; includes part of Clark National Forest. Covers a land area of 742.50 square miles, a water area of 1.30 square miles, and is located in the Central Time Zone. The county government was organized in 1829. County seat is Steelville.

Weather Station: Steelville 2 N — Elevation: 698 feet

	Jan	Feb	Mar	Apr	May	Jun	Jul	Aug	Sep	Oct	Nov	Dec
High	40	47	57	69	77	84	89	88	80	70	56	45
Low	16	20	29	38	47	57	62	60	52	39	30	21
Precip	2.1	2.3	3.5	4.3	4.6	3.9	3.8	3.7	3.7	3.4	3.9	2.9
Snow	5.1	3.4	1.9	0.1	0.0	0.0	0.0	0.0	0.0	tr	0.8	2.6

High and Low temperatures in degrees Fahrenheit; Precipitation and Snow in inches

Population: 22,804 (2000); Race: 98.1% White, 0.1% Black, 0.2% Asian, 0.3% American Indian and Alaska Native, 1.1% Hispanic of any race, 1.2% two or more races (2000); Density: 30.7 persons per square mile (2000); Age: 26.1% under 18, 15.8% over 64 (2000).

Religion: Five largest groups: 18.3% Southern Baptist Convention, 4.3% Catholic Church, 2.6% Church of God (Cleveland, Tennessee), 2.4% Lutheran Church—Missouri Synod, 2.3% The United Methodist Church (2000).

Economy: Unemployment rate: 5.8% (11/2002); Total civilian labor force: 10,254 (11/2002); Leading industries: 30.8% manufacturing; 21.0% retail trade; 11.2% health care and social assistance (2000); Companies that employ more than 1,000 persons: 0 (2000); Companies that employ more than 100 persons: 9 (2000); Farms: 691 totaling 182,123 acres (1997); Minority business ownership rate: 0.0% (1997); Women business ownership rate: 23.2% (1997); Retail sales per capita: $10,222 (1997). Single-family building permits issued: 23 (2001) / 19 (2000); Multi-family building permits issued: 6 (2001) / 0 (2000).

Income: Per capita income: $14,825 (2000); Median household income: $30,860 (2000); Poverty rate: 16.3% (2000); Bankruptcy rate: 4.37% (2001).

Taxes: Total county taxes per capita: $67 (1997); County property taxes per capita: $15 (1997).

Education: High school graduation rate: 69.4% (2000); College graduation rate: 8.4% (2000).

Housing: Homeownership rate: 76.7% (2000); Median home value: $66,100 (2000); Median rent: $283 per month (2000); Median age of housing: 27 years (2000).

Health: Birth rate: 123.2 per 10,000 population (1998); Age adjusted death rate: 93.7 per 10,000 population (1999); Age adjusted cancer mortality rate: 192.1 deaths per 100,000 population (1999). Number of physicians: 2.2 per 10,000 population (1999); Number of hospital beds: n/a (1999).

Elections: 2000 Presidential election results: 40.4% Gore, 57.3% Bush, 1.2% Nader, 0.7% Buchanan

National and State Parks: Crooked Creek State Forest; Dillard Mill State Historic Site; Gibbs State Wildlife Area; Huzzah State Wildlife Management Area; Richter State Wildlife Area; Woodson K Woods State Memorial Wildlife Area

Additional Information Contacts

Crawford County Government Offices 573-775-2376
Cuba Chamber of Commerce 573-885-2531
Steelville Chamber of Commerce 573-775-5533

Crawford County Communities

BOURBON (city). Covers a land area of 1.187 square miles and a water area of 0 square miles. Located at 38.15° N. Lat.; 91.24° W. Long. Elevation is 932 feet.
Population: 1,348 (2000); Race: 98.6% White, 0.0% Black, 0.0% Asian, 0.4% American Indian and Alaska Native, 0.2% Hispanic of any race, 1.0% two or more races (2000); Density: 1,135.9 persons per square mile (2000); Age: 28.4% under 18, 13.3% over 64 (2000); Marriage status: 19.9% never married, 57.3% now married, 7.4% widowed, 15.5% divorced (2000); Foreign born: 0.2% (2000); Ancestry (includes multiple ancestries): 23.5% German, 15.6% Irish, 14.6% United States or American, 8.3% Other groups, 6.5% English (2000).
Economy: Grain; livestock. Single-family building permits issued: 4 (2001) / 4 (2000); Multi-family building permits issued: 0 (2001) / 0 (2000); Employment by occupation: 4.0% management, 10.1% professional, 16.8% services, 22.7% sales, 0.0% farming, 17.5% construction, 28.9% production (2000).
Income: Per capita income: $12,992 (2000); Median household income: $30,240 (2000); Poverty rate: 14.2% (2000).
Taxes: Total city taxes per capita: $162 (1997); City property taxes per capita: $31 (1997).
Education: High school graduation rate: 73.2% (2000); College graduation rate: 9.7% (2000).

School District(s)

Crawford Co. R-I (PK-12)
2000 Enrollment: 1,006 573-732-4426
Housing: Homeownership rate: 63.9% (2000); Median home value: $58,100 (2000); Median rent: $265 per month (2000); Median age of housing: 32 years (2000).
Transportation: Commute to work: 93.8% car, 0.0% public transportation, 3.2% walk, 2.1% work from home (2000); Travel time to work: 45.6% less than 15 minutes, 24.1% 15 to 30 minutes, 12.6% 30 to 45 minutes, 5.4% 45 to 60 minutes, 12.4% 60 minutes or more (2000)

CHERRYVILLE (unincorporated postal area, zip code 65446). Covers a land area of 29.279 square miles and a water area of 0.021 square miles. Located at 37.81° N. Lat.; 91.26° W. Long. Elevation is 1,020 feet.
History: Former iron mines.
Population: 376 (2000); Race: 97.7% White, 0.0% Black, 1.1% Asian, 0.0% American Indian and Alaska Native, 0.0% Hispanic of any race, 1.1% two or more races (2000); Density: 12.8 persons per square mile (2000); Age: 24.4% under 18, 16.7% over 64 (2000); Marriage status: 18.2% never married, 65.0% now married, 8.2% widowed, 8.6% divorced (2000); Foreign born: 1.1% (2000); Ancestry (includes multiple ancestries): 23.2% United States or American, 15.6% English, 11.9% Irish, 9.1% German, 8.2% Other groups (2000).
Economy: Employment by occupation: 2.5% management, 11.5% professional, 19.1% services, 12.7% sales, 3.8% farming, 15.3% construction, 35.0% production (2000).
Income: Per capita income: $11,888 (2000); Median household income: $29,453 (2000); Poverty rate: 15.6% (2000).
Education: High school graduation rate: 65.3% (2000); College graduation rate: 5.2% (2000).
Housing: Homeownership rate: 83.1% (2000); Median home value: $48,600 (2000); Median rent: $261 per month (2000); Median age of housing: 36 years (2000).
Transportation: Commute to work: 100.0% car, 0.0% public transportation, 0.0% walk, 0.0% work from home (2000); Travel time to work: 7.6% less than 15 minutes, 29.9% 15 to 30 minutes, 26.1% 30 to 45 minutes, 16.6% 45 to 60 minutes, 19.7% 60 minutes or more (2000)

COOK STATION (unincorporated postal area, zip code 65449). Covers a land area of 54.576 square miles and a water area of 0.062 square miles. Located at 37.85° N. Lat.; 91.49° W. Long. Elevation is 892 feet.
Population: 452 (2000); Race: 98.8% White, 0.0% Black, 0.0% Asian, 0.0% American Indian and Alaska Native, 0.0% Hispanic of any race, 1.2% two or more races (2000); Density: 8.3 persons per square mile (2000); Age: 22.1% under 18, 17.2% over 64 (2000); Marriage status: 16.8% never married, 73.4% now married, 4.5% widowed, 5.3% divorced (2000); Foreign born: 0.0% (2000); Ancestry (includes multiple ancestries): 21.9% United States or American, 19.7% German, 10.4% Irish, 7.6% English, 6.3% Dutch (2000).
Economy: Employment by occupation: 4.3% management, 18.4% professional, 10.3% services, 22.2% sales, 4.3% farming, 17.9% construction, 22.6% production (2000).
Income: Per capita income: $12,125 (2000); Median household income: $29,300 (2000); Poverty rate: 16.8% (2000).
Education: High school graduation rate: 70.2% (2000); College graduation rate: 2.9% (2000).
Housing: Homeownership rate: 82.5% (2000); Median home value: $67,500 (2000); Median rent: $196 per month (2000); Median age of housing: 36 years (2000).
Transportation: Commute to work: 90.6% car, 0.0% public transportation, 5.6% walk, 3.8% work from home (2000); Travel time to work: 5.8% less than 15 minutes, 31.6% 15 to 30 minutes, 48.0% 30 to 45 minutes, 12.0% 45 to 60 minutes, 2.7% 60 minutes or more (2000)

CUBA (city). Covers a land area of 2.949 square miles and a water area of 0 square miles. Located at 38.06° N. Lat.; 91.40° W. Long. Elevation is 1,015 feet.
History: Cuba began in 1857 when M.W. Trask and W.H. Ferguson, anticipating the construction of the St. Louis-San Francisco Railway, laid out a townsite.
Population: 3,230 (2000); Race: 97.4% White, 0.2% Black, 0.4% Asian, 0.6% American Indian and Alaska Native, 1.6% Hispanic of any race, 1.0% two or more races (2000); Density: 1,095.4 persons per square mile (2000); Age: 28.6% under 18, 19.3% over 64 (2000); Marriage status: 20.7% never married, 54.4% now married, 12.9% widowed, 12.0% divorced (2000); Foreign born: 1.0% (2000); Ancestry (includes multiple ancestries): 18.3% United States or American, 17.4% German, 12.5% Irish, 8.2% English, 8.2% Other groups (2000).
Economy: Single-family building permits issued: 15 (2001) / 11 (2000); Multi-family building permits issued: 6 (2001) / 0 (2000); Employment by occupation: 8.6% management, 11.7% professional, 20.2% services, 18.6% sales, 0.0% farming, 11.0% construction, 29.9% production (2000).
Income: Per capita income: $12,665 (2000); Median household income: $24,127 (2000); Poverty rate: 20.1% (2000).
Taxes: Total city taxes per capita: $238 (1997); City property taxes per capita: $0 (1997).
Education: High school graduation rate: 63.6% (2000); College graduation rate: 9.1% (2000).

School District(s)

Crawford Co. R-II (KG-12)
2000 Enrollment: 1,472 573-885-2534
Housing: Homeownership rate: 59.1% (2000); Median home value: $60,400 (2000); Median rent: $304 per month (2000); Median age of housing: 32 years (2000).
Newspapers: Extra Plan (1 x week); The Cuba Free Press (1 x week)
Transportation: Commute to work: 92.9% car, 0.7% public transportation, 3.4% walk, 2.7% work from home (2000); Travel time to work: 59.1% less than 15 minutes, 19.9% 15 to 30 minutes, 9.3% 30 to 45 minutes, 4.3% 45 to 60 minutes, 7.4% 60 minutes or more (2000)

Additional Information Contacts

Cuba Chamber of Commerce 573-885-2531

DAVISVILLE (unincorporated postal area, zip code 65456). Covers a land area of 80.955 square miles and a water area of 0.013 square miles. Located at 37.78° N. Lat.; 91.19° W. Long. Elevation is 840 feet.
Population: 619 (2000); Race: 98.6% White, 0.0% Black, 0.0% Asian, 0.0% American Indian and Alaska Native, 0.0% Hispanic of any race, 1.4% two or more races (2000); Density: 7.6 persons per square mile (2000); Age: 21.5% under 18, 14.5% over 64 (2000); Marriage status: 14.7% never married, 73.1% now married, 6.1% widowed, 6.1% divorced (2000); Foreign born: 0.0% (2000); Ancestry (includes multiple ancestries): 24.7% United States or American, 14.5% English, 14.4% German, 9.2% Irish, 4.3% Other groups (2000).
Economy: Employment by occupation: 10.0% management, 21.6% professional, 19.1% services, 8.3% sales, 2.5% farming, 18.7% construction, 19.9% production (2000).
Income: Per capita income: $14,022 (2000); Median household income: $26,023 (2000); Poverty rate: 17.0% (2000).
Education: High school graduation rate: 78.3% (2000); College graduation rate: 9.5% (2000).
Housing: Homeownership rate: 88.6% (2000); Median home value: $48,100 (2000); Median rent: $131 per month (2000); Median age of housing: 28 years (2000).
Transportation: Commute to work: 91.1% car, 0.0% public transportation, 1.3% walk, 7.6% work from home (2000); Travel time to work: 15.5% less than 15 minutes, 22.8% 15 to 30 minutes, 27.4% 30 to 45 minutes, 14.2% 45 to 60 minutes, 20.1% 60 minutes or more (2000)

LEASBURG (village). Covers a land area of 0.431 square miles and a water area of 0 square miles. Located at 38.09° N. Lat.; 91.29° W. Long. Elevation is 1,025 feet.
History: Leasburg was established near several large caves: Cathedral Cave, Missouri Caverns, and Onondaga Cave.
Population: 323 (2000); Race: 98.2% White, 0.0% Black, 0.9% Asian, 0.0% American Indian and Alaska Native, 0.6% Hispanic of any race, 0.3% two or more races (2000); Density: 750.2 persons per square mile (2000); Age: 17.9% under 18, 19.4% over 64 (2000); Marriage status: 18.6% never married, 56.9% now married, 13.9% widowed, 10.6% divorced (2000); Foreign born: 0.9% (2000); Ancestry (includes multiple ancestries): 19.7% Irish, 15.2% German, 8.2% Other groups, 7.6% United States or American, 7.3% English (2000).
Economy: Employment by occupation: 5.0% management, 6.7% professional, 15.1% services, 24.4% sales, 0.0% farming, 23.5% construction, 25.2% production (2000).
Income: Per capita income: $11,878 (2000); Median household income: $19,750 (2000); Poverty rate: 21.0% (2000).
Taxes: Total city taxes per capita: $12 (1997); City property taxes per capita: $12 (1997).
Education: High school graduation rate: 54.4% (2000); College graduation rate: 4.2% (2000).
Housing: Homeownership rate: 67.1% (2000); Median home value: $43,800 (2000); Median rent: $210 per month (2000); Median age of housing: 33 years (2000).
Transportation: Commute to work: 98.3% car, 0.0% public transportation, 0.0% walk, 1.7% work from home (2000); Travel time to work: 24.8% less than 15 minutes, 42.7% 15 to 30 minutes, 3.4% 30 to 45 minutes, 1.7% 45 to 60 minutes, 27.4% 60 minutes or more (2000)

SAINT CLOUD (village). Covers a land area of 1.239 square miles and a water area of 0 square miles. Located at 38.17° N. Lat.; 91.20° W. Long. Elevation is 960 feet.
Population: 56 (2000); Race: 100.0% White, 0.0% Black, 0.0% Asian, 0.0% American Indian and Alaska Native, 44.2% Hispanic of any race, 0.0% two or more races (2000); Density: 45.2 persons per square mile (2000); Age: 40.4% under 18, 17.3% over 64 (2000); Marriage status: 6.3% never married, 84.4% now married, 0.0% widowed, 9.4% divorced (2000); Foreign born: 34.6% (2000); Ancestry (includes multiple ancestries): 44.2% Other groups, 25.0% United States or American, 5.8% Irish, 3.8% Swiss, 3.8% German (2000).
Economy: Employment by occupation: 17.6% management, 5.9% professional, 0.0% services, 17.6% sales, 23.5% farming, 11.8% construction, 23.5% production (2000).
Income: Per capita income: $8,081 (2000); Median household income: $23,750 (2000); Poverty rate: 48.1% (2000).
Education: High school graduation rate: 77.8% (2000); College graduation rate: 0.0% (2000).
Housing: Homeownership rate: 59.1% (2000); Median home value: $65,000 (2000); Median rent: $275 per month (2000); Median age of housing: 16 years (2000).
Transportation: Commute to work: 64.7% car, 0.0% public transportation, 23.5% walk, 11.8% work from home (2000); Travel time to work: 73.3% less than 15 minutes, 13.3% 15 to 30 minutes, 6.7% 30 to 45 minutes, 0.0% 45 to 60 minutes, 6.7% 60 minutes or more (2000)

STEELVILLE (city). Covers a land area of 2.604 square miles and a water area of 0 square miles. Located at 37.96° N. Lat.; 91.35° W. Long. Elevation is 750 feet.
History: The first settler here was William Britton, who built a log house and a grist mill on Yadkin Creek in 1833. The town of Steelville was named for James Steel, who arrived two years later. The area became the center of iron mining activities, but later turned to agriculture.
Population: 1,429 (2000); Race: 98.3% White, 0.5% Black, 0.0% Asian, 0.0% American Indian and Alaska Native, 0.0% Hispanic of any race, 0.7% two or more races (2000); Density: 548.8 persons per square mile (2000); Age: 24.4% under 18, 23.9% over 64 (2000); Marriage status: 20.7% never married, 53.0% now married, 13.9% widowed, 12.5% divorced (2000); Foreign born: 0.6% (2000); Ancestry (includes multiple ancestries): 15.1% German, 13.2% United States or American, 12.3% Irish, 11.9% Other groups, 11.9% English (2000).
Economy: Single-family building permits issued: 4 (2001) / 4 (2000); Multi-family building permits issued: 0 (2001) / 0 (2000); Employment by occupation: 7.8% management, 13.1% professional, 21.3% services, 20.3% sales, 0.9% farming, 10.2% construction, 26.4% production (2000).
Income: Per capita income: $12,550 (2000); Median household income: $19,596 (2000); Poverty rate: 25.5% (2000).
Taxes: Total city taxes per capita: $246 (1997); City property taxes per capita: $83 (1997).
Education: High school graduation rate: 63.9% (2000); College graduation rate: 10.6% (2000).

School District(s)

Steelville R-III (PK-12)
2000 Enrollment: 991 573-775-2175

Housing: Homeownership rate: 59.5% (2000); Median home value: $55,000 (2000); Median rent: $228 per month (2000); Median age of housing: 41 years (2000).
Newspapers: The Steelville Star/Crawford Mirror (1 x week)
Transportation: Commute to work: 89.9% car, 0.0% public transportation, 4.5% walk, 3.6% work from home (2000); Travel time to work: 59.1% less than 15 minutes, 15.1% 15 to 30 minutes, 13.7% 30 to 45 minutes, 4.9% 45 to 60 minutes, 7.2% 60 minutes or more (2000)
Additional Information Contacts
Steelville Chamber of Commerce 573-775-5533

Dade County

Located in southwestern Missouri, in the Ozarks; drained by the Sac River. Covers a land area of 490.30 square miles, a water area of 16.00 square miles, and is located in the Central Time Zone. The county government was organized in 1841. County seat is Greenfield.

Weather Station: Lockwood — Elevation: 1,079 feet

	Jan	Feb	Mar	Apr	May	Jun	Jul	Aug	Sep	Oct	Nov	Dec
High	42	48	58	69	77	85	91	90	81	71	57	46
Low	22	27	36	45	54	63	68	66	58	47	36	27
Precip	1.9	2.2	3.7	4.5	4.9	5.1	3.9	3.9	5.1	4.0	4.2	3.0
Snow	5.4	3.8	3.6	tr	0.0	0.0	0.0	0.0	0.0	tr	0.9	2.8

High and Low temperatures in degrees Fahrenheit; Precipitation and Snow in inches

Population: 7,923 (2000); Race: 97.3% White, 0.1% Black, 0.1% Asian, 0.6% American Indian and Alaska Native, 0.7% Hispanic of any race, 1.7% two or more races (2000); Density: 16.2 persons per square mile (2000); Age: 24.3% under 18, 20.3% over 64 (2000).
Religion: Five largest groups: 31.3% Southern Baptist Convention, 7.9% Lutheran Church—Missouri Synod, 4.3% Christian Churches and Churches of Christ, 3.7% The United Methodist Church, 3.7% Christian Church (Disciples of Christ) (2000).
Economy: Unemployment rate: 4.2% (11/2002); Total civilian labor force: 3,344 (11/2002); Leading industries: 24.6% manufacturing; 22.0% wholesale trade; 9.6% retail trade (2000); Companies that employ more than 1,000 persons: 0 (2000); Companies that employ more than 100 persons: 1 (2000); Farms: 808 totaling 249,096 acres (1997); Minority business ownership rate: 0.0% (1997); Women business ownership rate: 0.0% (1997); Retail sales per capita: $2,648 (1997). Single-family building permits issued: 0 (2001) / 0 (2000); Multi-family building permits issued: 0 (2001) / 0 (2000).
Income: Per capita income: $14,254 (2000); Median household income: $29,097 (2000); Poverty rate: 13.4% (2000); Bankruptcy rate: 3.62% (2001).
Taxes: Total county taxes per capita: $53 (1997); County property taxes per capita: $6 (1997).
Education: High school graduation rate: 78.5% (2000); College graduation rate: 9.9% (2000).
Housing: Homeownership rate: 78.8% (2000); Median home value: $54,500 (2000); Median rent: $223 per month (2000); Median age of housing: 36 years (2000).
Health: Birth rate: 112.3 per 10,000 population (1998); Age adjusted death rate: 89.3 per 10,000 population (1999); Age adjusted cancer mortality rate: 182.9 deaths per 100,000 population (1999). Number of physicians: 2.5 per 10,000 population (1999); Number of hospital beds: n/a (1999).
Elections: 2000 Presidential election results: 31.8% Gore, 65.8% Bush, 1.1% Nader, 0.8% Buchanan
Additional Information Contacts
Dade County Government Offices 417-637-2724
Greenfield Chamber of Commerce 417-637-9736

Dade County Communities

ARCOLA (village). Covers a land area of 0.290 square miles and a water area of 0 square miles. Located at 37.54° N. Lat.; 93.87° W. Long. Elevation is 1,050 feet.

Population: 45 (2000); Race: 100.0% White, 0.0% Black, 0.0% Asian, 0.0% American Indian and Alaska Native, 0.0% Hispanic of any race, 0.0% two or more races (2000); Density: 155.0 persons per square mile (2000); Age: 21.3% under 18, 36.2% over 64 (2000); Marriage status: 5.4% never married, 48.6% now married, 24.3% widowed, 21.6% divorced (2000); Foreign born: 0.0% (2000); Ancestry (includes multiple ancestries): 21.3% French Canadian, 17.0% United States or American, 14.9% Irish, 14.9% Other groups, 14.9% English (2000).
Economy: Employment by occupation: 14.3% management, 0.0% professional, 0.0% services, 14.3% sales, 0.0% farming, 14.3% construction, 57.1% production (2000).
Income: Per capita income: $13,123 (2000); Median household income: $15,938 (2000); Poverty rate: 34.0% (2000).
Taxes: Total city taxes per capita: $103 (1997); City property taxes per capita: $103 (1997).
Education: High school graduation rate: 81.1% (2000); College graduation rate: 5.4% (2000).
Housing: Homeownership rate: 85.7% (2000); Median home value: $50,000 (2000); Median rent: $125 per month (2000); Median age of housing: 47 years (2000).
Transportation: Commute to work: 100.0% car, 0.0% public transportation, 0.0% walk, 0.0% work from home (2000); Travel time to work: 28.6% less than 15 minutes, 50.0% 15 to 30 minutes, 21.4% 30 to 45 minutes, 0.0% 45 to 60 minutes, 0.0% 60 minutes or more (2000)

DADEVILLE (village). Covers a land area of 0.993 square miles and a water area of 0 square miles. Located at 37.47° N. Lat.; 93.67° W. Long. Elevation is 1,085 feet.
Population: 224 (2000); Race: 96.9% White, 0.0% Black, 0.0% Asian, 0.9% American Indian and Alaska Native, 0.0% Hispanic of any race, 2.2% two or more races (2000); Density: 225.5 persons per square mile (2000); Age: 29.8% under 18, 19.6% over 64 (2000); Marriage status: 11.9% never married, 77.4% now married, 6.0% widowed, 4.8% divorced (2000); Foreign born: 1.3% (2000); Ancestry (includes multiple ancestries): 17.8% German, 14.2% United States or American, 7.1% Scotch-Irish, 5.8% English, 4.4% Other groups (2000).
Economy: Soybeans, hay, wheat; dairying; cattle. Employment by occupation: 4.3% management, 21.3% professional, 21.3% services, 21.3% sales, 0.0% farming, 4.3% construction, 27.7% production (2000).
Income: Per capita income: $11,135 (2000); Median household income: $27,000 (2000); Poverty rate: 16.0% (2000).
Taxes: Total city taxes per capita: $160 (1997); City property taxes per capita: $13 (1997).
Education: High school graduation rate: 76.9% (2000); College graduation rate: 12.9% (2000).

School District(s)

Dadeville R-II (KG-12)
2000 Enrollment: 197 417-995-2201
Housing: Homeownership rate: 81.9% (2000); Median home value: $54,300 (2000); Median rent: $218 per month (2000); Median age of housing: 32 years (2000).
Transportation: Commute to work: 92.6% car, 0.0% public transportation, 2.1% walk, 5.3% work from home (2000); Travel time to work: 21.3% less than 15 minutes, 27.0% 15 to 30 minutes, 25.8% 30 to 45 minutes, 13.5% 45 to 60 minutes, 12.4% 60 minutes or more (2000)

EVERTON (city). Covers a land area of 0.343 square miles and a water area of 0 square miles. Located at 37.34° N. Lat.; 93.70° W. Long. Elevation is 1,038 feet.
Population: 322 (2000); Race: 98.4% White, 0.0% Black, 0.0% Asian, 0.0% American Indian and Alaska Native, 0.7% Hispanic of any race, 1.6% two or more races (2000); Density: 939.3 persons per square mile (2000); Age: 25.2% under 18, 16.7% over 64 (2000); Marriage status: 23.8% never married, 50.8% now married, 12.1% widowed, 13.3% divorced (2000); Foreign born: 0.7% (2000); Ancestry (includes multiple ancestries): 20.3% German, 13.4% Irish, 12.1% English, 10.2% United States or American, 6.2% Other groups (2000).
Economy: Wheat, hay; cattle; dairying. Employment by occupation: 8.0% management, 8.0% professional, 15.2% services, 11.2% sales, 4.0% farming, 12.0% construction, 41.6% production (2000).
Income: Per capita income: $11,464 (2000); Median household income: $30,208 (2000); Poverty rate: 20.3% (2000).
Taxes: Total city taxes per capita: $37 (1997); City property taxes per capita: $37 (1997).
Education: High school graduation rate: 67.0% (2000); College graduation rate: 5.6% (2000).

School District(s)

Everton R-III (KG-12)
2000 Enrollment: 219 417-535-2221
Housing: Homeownership rate: 78.9% (2000); Median home value: $40,800 (2000); Median rent: $263 per month (2000); Median age of housing: 48 years (2000).
Transportation: Commute to work: 92.7% car, 3.2% public transportation, 0.0% walk, 4.0% work from home (2000); Travel time to work: 10.9% less than 15 minutes, 16.0% 15 to 30 minutes, 38.7% 30 to 45 minutes, 25.2% 45 to 60 minutes, 9.2% 60 minutes or more (2000)

GREENFIELD (city). Covers a land area of 1.100 square miles and a water area of 0 square miles. Located at 37.41° N. Lat.; 93.84° W. Long. Elevation is 1,087 feet.
History: Settled 1841.
Population: 1,358 (2000); Race: 95.9% White, 0.4% Black, 0.1% Asian, 0.9% American Indian and Alaska Native, 0.9% Hispanic of any race, 2.1% two or more races (2000); Density: 1,235.0 persons per square mile (2000); Age: 22.5% under 18, 25.5% over 64 (2000); Marriage status: 15.1% never married, 55.6% now married, 15.0% widowed, 14.2% divorced (2000); Foreign born: 0.9% (2000); Ancestry (includes multiple ancestries): 16.3% United States or American, 13.7% German, 10.0% English, 9.7% Other groups, 9.1% Irish (2000).
Economy: Wheat, hay, soybeans; dairying; cattle. Manufacturing: apparel, animal feed, grass seed. Single-family building permits issued: 0 (2001) / 0 (2000); Multi-family building permits issued: 0 (2001) / 0 (2000); Employment by occupation: 7.4% management, 10.4% professional, 20.0% services, 16.1% sales, 1.4% farming, 11.0% construction, 33.6% production (2000).
Income: Per capita income: $14,051 (2000); Median household income: $22,336 (2000); Poverty rate: 18.6% (2000).
Taxes: Total city taxes per capita: $313 (1997); City property taxes per capita: $108 (1997).
Education: High school graduation rate: 71.2% (2000); College graduation rate: 7.5% (2000).

School District(s)

Greenfield R-IV (KG-12)
2000 Enrollment: 507 417-637-5321
Housing: Homeownership rate: 63.5% (2000); Median home value: $54,000 (2000); Median rent: $219 per month (2000); Median age of housing: 36 years (2000).
Newspapers: Vedette (1 x week)
Transportation: Commute to work: 86.8% car, 0.0% public transportation, 8.1% walk, 3.3% work from home (2000); Travel time to work: 53.8% less than 15 minutes, 12.9% 15 to 30 minutes, 8.2% 30 to 45 minutes, 13.5% 45 to 60 minutes, 11.6% 60 minutes or more (2000)
Additional Information Contacts
Greenfield Chamber of Commerce 417-637-9736

LOCKWOOD (city). Covers a land area of 0.924 square miles and a water area of 0.017 square miles. Located at 37.38° N. Lat.; 93.95° W. Long. Elevation is 1,085 feet.
Population: 989 (2000); Race: 96.8% White, 0.0% Black, 0.0% Asian, 1.3% American Indian and Alaska Native, 0.3% Hispanic of any race, 1.5% two or more races (2000); Density: 1,070.3 persons per square mile (2000); Age: 23.6% under 18, 22.5% over 64 (2000); Marriage status: 19.9% never married, 59.1% now married, 10.5% widowed, 10.6% divorced (2000); Foreign born: 0.2% (2000); Ancestry (includes multiple ancestries): 24.1% German, 14.7% United States or American, 10.6% Other groups, 10.4% Irish, 9.1% English (2000).
Economy: Corn, sorghum, wheat, cattle; light manufacturing; limestone quarries. Employment by occupation: 6.2% management, 12.8% professional, 19.5% services, 23.4% sales, 1.5% farming, 7.1% construction, 29.6% production (2000).
Income: Per capita income: $13,439 (2000); Median household income: $26,125 (2000); Poverty rate: 15.8% (2000).
Taxes: Total city taxes per capita: $117 (1997); City property taxes per capita: $26 (1997).
Education: High school graduation rate: 75.0% (2000); College graduation rate: 14.3% (2000).

School District(s)

Lockwood R-I (KG-12)
2000 Enrollment: 370 417-232-4513
Housing: Homeownership rate: 72.0% (2000); Median home value: $48,600 (2000); Median rent: $221 per month (2000); Median age of housing: 50 years (2000).

Transportation: Commute to work: 93.5% car, 0.0% public transportation, 5.0% walk, 0.5% work from home (2000); Travel time to work: 52.8% less than 15 minutes, 15.8% 15 to 30 minutes, 18.3% 30 to 45 minutes, 5.3% 45 to 60 minutes, 8.0% 60 minutes or more (2000)

SOUTH GREENFIELD (village). Covers a land area of 0.170 square miles and a water area of 0 square miles. Located at 37.37° N. Lat.; 93.84° W. Long. Elevation is 943 feet.
Population: 136 (2000); Race: 98.3% White, 0.0% Black, 0.0% Asian, 0.0% American Indian and Alaska Native, 0.0% Hispanic of any race, 1.7% two or more races (2000); Density: 798.1 persons per square mile (2000); Age: 28.3% under 18, 11.7% over 64 (2000); Marriage status: 33.0% never married, 56.4% now married, 7.4% widowed, 3.2% divorced (2000); Foreign born: 0.0% (2000); Ancestry (includes multiple ancestries): 15.0% Other groups, 9.2% United States or American, 8.3% German, 5.8% Swedish, 5.0% Scotch-Irish (2000).
Economy: Wheat, corn, hay; dairying; cattle. Employment by occupation: 5.8% management, 15.4% professional, 13.5% services, 19.2% sales, 0.0% farming, 15.4% construction, 30.8% production (2000).
Income: Per capita income: $10,241 (2000); Median household income: $19,000 (2000); Poverty rate: 30.0% (2000).
Taxes: Total city taxes per capita: $43 (1997); City property taxes per capita: $17 (1997).
Education: High school graduation rate: 65.3% (2000); College graduation rate: 5.6% (2000).
Housing: Homeownership rate: 72.9% (2000); Median home value: $24,400 (2000); Median rent: $225 per month (2000); Median age of housing: 60+ years (2000).
Transportation: Commute to work: 96.2% car, 0.0% public transportation, 3.8% walk, 0.0% work from home (2000); Travel time to work: 44.2% less than 15 minutes, 28.8% 15 to 30 minutes, 11.5% 30 to 45 minutes, 9.6% 45 to 60 minutes, 5.8% 60 minutes or more (2000)

Dallas County

Located in southwest central Missouri, in the Ozarks; drained by the Niangua and Little Niangua Rivers. Covers a land area of 541.50 square miles, a water area of 1.30 square miles, and is located in the Central Time Zone. The county government was organized in 1841. County seat is Buffalo.

Weather Station: Buffalo 3 S — Elevation: 1,148 feet

	Jan	Feb	Mar	Apr	May	Jun	Jul	Aug	Sep	Oct	Nov	Dec
High	41	48	59	69	76	83	89	88	80	69	55	46
Low	21	26	35	44	53	61	66	64	57	46	35	25
Precip	1.9	2.1	3.6	4.3	4.9	4.2	3.0	3.9	4.9	4.1	4.4	2.8
Snow	5.1	3.8	2.6	0.2	0.0	0.0	0.0	0.0	0.0	tr	1.4	3.0

High and Low temperatures in degrees Fahrenheit; Precipitation and Snow in inches

Population: 15,661 (2000); Race: 97.6% White, 0.1% Black, 0.1% Asian, 0.7% American Indian and Alaska Native, 0.9% Hispanic of any race, 1.1% two or more races (2000); Density: 28.9 persons per square mile (2000); Age: 27.2% under 18, 15.2% over 64 (2000).
Religion: Five largest groups: 16.1% Southern Baptist Convention, 4.7% National Association of Free Will Baptists, 3.0% The United Methodist Church, 2.8% Christian Church (Disciples of Christ), 1.7% Amish; Other Groups (2000).
Economy: Unemployment rate: 6.9% (11/2002); Total civilian labor force: 5,735 (11/2002); Leading industries: 28.6% health care and social assistance; 19.4% manufacturing; 16.0% retail trade (2000); Companies that employ more than 1,000 persons: 0 (2000); Companies that employ more than 100 persons: 3 (2000); Farms: 1,130 totaling 221,713 acres (1997); Minority business ownership rate: 0.0% (1997); Women business ownership rate: 13.7% (1997); Retail sales per capita: $5,371 (1997). Single-family building permits issued: -1 (2001) / -1 (2000); Multi-family building permits issued: -1 (2001) / -1 (2000).
Income: Per capita income: $15,106 (2000); Median household income: $27,346 (2000); Poverty rate: 17.9% (2000); Bankruptcy rate: 3.76% (2001).
Taxes: Total county taxes per capita: $103 (2000); County property taxes per capita: $6 (2000).
Education: High school graduation rate: 72.8% (2000); College graduation rate: 9.5% (2000).
Housing: Homeownership rate: 79.2% (2000); Median home value: $72,300 (2000); Median rent: $263 per month (2000); Median age of housing: 27 years (2000).
Health: Birth rate: 122.6 per 10,000 population (1998); Age adjusted death rate: 97.1 per 10,000 population (1999); Age adjusted cancer mortality rate: 222.2 deaths per 100,000 population (1999). Number of physicians: 0.6 per 10,000 population (1999); Number of hospital beds: n/a (1999).
Elections: 2000 Presidential election results: 37.2% Gore, 59.9% Bush, 1.2% Nader, 1.2% Buchanan
National and State Parks: Bennett Spring State Park; Bennett Spring State Public Access Area; Hackler Ford State Forest; Lead Mine State Forest
Additional Information Contacts
Dallas County Government Offices 417-345-2632
Buffalo Chamber of Commerce 417-345-2852

Dallas County Communities

BUFFALO (city). Covers a land area of 2.198 square miles and a water area of 0 square miles. Located at 37.64° N. Lat.; 93.09° W. Long. Elevation is 1,200 feet.
History: Settled 1839, incorporated 1854.
Population: 2,781 (2000); Race: 98.0% White, 0.4% Black, 0.0% Asian, 1.5% American Indian and Alaska Native, 0.5% Hispanic of any race, 0.0% two or more races (2000); Density: 1,265.1 persons per square mile (2000); Age: 25.6% under 18, 22.5% over 64 (2000); Marriage status: 18.5% never married, 53.6% now married, 12.0% widowed, 15.9% divorced (2000); Foreign born: 0.5% (2000); Ancestry (includes multiple ancestries): 17.2% United States or American, 14.1% Other groups, 13.2% German, 12.0% English, 11.4% Irish (2000).
Economy: Wheat, corn, sorghum; poultry; dairying. Manufacturing: apparel, poultry processing. Employment by occupation: 5.7% management, 16.0% professional, 20.0% services, 20.5% sales, 0.0% farming, 11.3% construction, 26.6% production (2000).
Income: Per capita income: $11,942 (2000); Median household income: $19,632 (2000); Poverty rate: 28.9% (2000).
Taxes: Total city taxes per capita: $244 (1997); City property taxes per capita: $49 (1997).
Education: High school graduation rate: 73.2% (2000); College graduation rate: 8.4% (2000).

School District(s)

Dallas Co. R-I (PK-12)
2000 Enrollment: 2,179 417-345-2222
Housing: Homeownership rate: 52.4% (2000); Median home value: $66,200 (2000); Median rent: $269 per month (2000); Median age of housing: 32 years (2000).
Newspapers: Buffalo Reflex (1 x week); Dallas County Shopper (1 x week); Dallas County Courier (1 x week)
Transportation: Commute to work: 92.5% car, 0.0% public transportation, 4.4% walk, 0.7% work from home (2000); Travel time to work: 48.2% less than 15 minutes, 14.7% 15 to 30 minutes, 14.3% 30 to 45 minutes, 15.6% 45 to 60 minutes, 7.2% 60 minutes or more (2000)
Additional Information Contacts
Buffalo Chamber of Commerce 417-345-2852

LONG LANE (unincorporated postal area, zip code 65590). Covers a land area of 80.402 square miles and a water area of 0.209 square miles. Located at 37.61° N. Lat.; 92.94° W. Long. Elevation is 1,139 feet.
Population: 1,565 (2000); Race: 98.4% White, 0.0% Black, 0.0% Asian, 0.0% American Indian and Alaska Native, 0.0% Hispanic of any race, 1.6% two or more races (2000); Density: 19.5 persons per square mile (2000); Age: 27.8% under 18, 10.3% over 64 (2000); Marriage status: 21.2% never married, 66.7% now married, 3.0% widowed, 9.1% divorced (2000); Foreign born: 0.8% (2000); Ancestry (includes multiple ancestries): 22.2% German, 15.6% United States or American, 14.9% Other groups, 13.0% English, 12.4% Irish (2000).
Economy: Employment by occupation: 8.3% management, 7.2% professional, 12.3% services, 19.6% sales, 1.4% farming, 21.7% construction, 29.4% production (2000).
Income: Per capita income: $12,489 (2000); Median household income: $28,672 (2000); Poverty rate: 11.2% (2000).
Education: High school graduation rate: 76.0% (2000); College graduation rate: 5.2% (2000).
Housing: Homeownership rate: 88.7% (2000); Median home value: $60,400 (2000); Median age of housing: 25 years (2000).
Transportation: Commute to work: 97.0% car, 0.0% public transportation, 0.0% walk, 3.0% work from home (2000); Travel time to work: 6.5% less than 15 minutes, 33.8% 15 to 30 minutes, 21.7% 30 to 45 minutes, 11.6% 45 to 60 minutes, 26.3% 60 minutes or more (2000)

LOUISBURG (village). Covers a land area of 0.462 square miles and a water area of 0 square miles. Located at 37.75° N. Lat.; 93.14° W. Long. Elevation is 1,175 feet.
Population: 147 (2000); Race: 100.0% White, 0.0% Black, 0.0% Asian, 0.0% American Indian and Alaska Native, 0.0% Hispanic of any race, 0.0% two or more races (2000); Density: 318.4 persons per square mile (2000); Age: 18.8% under 18, 34.4% over 64 (2000); Marriage status: 10.6% never married, 74.0% now married, 8.7% widowed, 6.7% divorced (2000); Foreign born: 0.0% (2000); Ancestry (includes multiple ancestries): 25.0% United States or American, 18.8% Irish, 18.0% English, 14.1% German, 13.3% Other groups (2000).
Economy: Employment by occupation: 0.0% management, 14.7% professional, 17.6% services, 20.6% sales, 0.0% farming, 20.6% construction, 26.5% production (2000).
Income: Per capita income: $11,952 (2000); Median household income: $28,438 (2000); Poverty rate: 20.3% (2000).
Taxes: Total city taxes per capita: $23 (1997); City property taxes per capita: $0 (1997).
Education: High school graduation rate: 58.6% (2000); College graduation rate: 3.4% (2000).
Housing: Homeownership rate: 75.0% (2000); Median home value: $48,800 (2000); Median rent: $272 per month (2000); Median age of housing: 43 years (2000).
Transportation: Commute to work: 85.3% car, 0.0% public transportation, 0.0% walk, 14.7% work from home (2000); Travel time to work: 6.9% less than 15 minutes, 37.9% 15 to 30 minutes, 10.3% 30 to 45 minutes, 31.0% 45 to 60 minutes, 13.8% 60 minutes or more (2000)

TUNAS (unincorporated postal area, zip code 65764). Covers a land area of 100.889 square miles and a water area of 0.359 square miles. Located at 37.82° N. Lat.; 92.98° W. Long. Elevation is 915 feet.
Population: 1,265 (2000); Race: 100.0% White, 0.0% Black, 0.0% Asian, 0.0% American Indian and Alaska Native, 0.4% Hispanic of any race, 0.0% two or more races (2000); Density: 12.5 persons per square mile (2000); Age: 27.9% under 18, 14.2% over 64 (2000); Marriage status: 17.1% never married, 69.6% now married, 8.6% widowed, 4.8% divorced (2000); Foreign born: 0.7% (2000); Ancestry (includes multiple ancestries): 17.2% German, 16.4% United States or American, 10.5% English, 6.0% Other groups, 5.1% Irish (2000).
Economy: Employment by occupation: 16.1% management, 11.7% professional, 13.0% services, 18.6% sales, 7.1% farming, 11.0% construction, 22.5% production (2000).
Income: Per capita income: $9,935 (2000); Median household income: $18,705 (2000); Poverty rate: 36.6% (2000).
Education: High school graduation rate: 59.0% (2000); College graduation rate: 9.9% (2000).
Housing: Homeownership rate: 89.9% (2000); Median home value: $52,000 (2000); Median rent: $135 per month (2000); Median age of housing: 32 years (2000).
Transportation: Commute to work: 83.9% car, 0.0% public transportation, 0.0% walk, 13.2% work from home (2000); Travel time to work: 11.8% less than 15 minutes, 31.8% 15 to 30 minutes, 21.1% 30 to 45 minutes, 18.6% 45 to 60 minutes, 16.6% 60 minutes or more (2000)

URBANA (city). Covers a land area of 0.955 square miles and a water area of 0 square miles. Located at 37.84° N. Lat.; 93.16° W. Long. Elevation is 1,055 feet.
Population: 407 (2000); Race: 98.1% White, 0.0% Black, 0.0% Asian, 0.2% American Indian and Alaska Native, 1.2% Hispanic of any race, 1.7% two or more races (2000); Density: 426.2 persons per square mile (2000); Age: 26.6% under 18, 17.9% over 64 (2000); Marriage status: 23.0% never married, 47.6% now married, 16.1% widowed, 13.2% divorced (2000); Foreign born: 0.0% (2000); Ancestry (includes multiple ancestries): 17.4% United States or American, 13.8% German, 13.8% Irish, 9.7% Other groups, 9.4% English (2000).
Economy: Employment by occupation: 7.4% management, 11.5% professional, 22.3% services, 16.9% sales, 1.4% farming, 21.6% construction, 18.9% production (2000).
Income: Per capita income: $16,824 (2000); Median household income: $19,236 (2000); Poverty rate: 16.5% (2000).
Taxes: Total city taxes per capita: $115 (1997); City property taxes per capita: $35 (1997).
Education: High school graduation rate: 64.9% (2000); College graduation rate: 4.6% (2000).

School District(s)

Hickory Co. R-I (KG-12)
2000 Enrollment: 791 417-993-4241
Housing: Homeownership rate: 64.7% (2000); Median home value: $38,800 (2000); Median rent: $232 per month (2000); Median age of housing: 36 years (2000).
Transportation: Commute to work: 85.6% car, 1.4% public transportation, 8.2% walk, 4.8% work from home (2000); Travel time to work: 28.1% less than 15 minutes, 23.0% 15 to 30 minutes, 15.1% 30 to 45 minutes, 17.3% 45 to 60 minutes, 16.5% 60 minutes or more (2000)

WINDYVILLE (unincorporated postal area, zip code 65783). Covers a land area of 11.360 square miles and a water area of 0.078 square miles. Located at 37.71° N. Lat.; 92.92° W. Long. Elevation is 1,078 feet.
Population: 153 (2000); Race: 82.4% White, 1.8% Black, 0.0% Asian, 3.6% American Indian and Alaska Native, 0.0% Hispanic of any race, 12.2% two or more races (2000); Density: 13.5 persons per square mile (2000); Age: 31.1% under 18, 4.5% over 64 (2000); Marriage status: 14.3% never married, 77.1% now married, 5.7% widowed, 2.9% divorced (2000); Foreign born: 0.0% (2000); Ancestry (includes multiple ancestries): 14.0% Other groups, 10.8% Irish, 10.4% German, 9.9% English, 8.6% European (2000).
Economy: Employment by occupation: 19.2% management, 6.7% professional, 13.5% services, 20.2% sales, 0.0% farming, 9.6% construction, 30.8% production (2000).
Income: Per capita income: $17,057 (2000); Median household income: $48,000 (2000); Poverty rate: 0.0% (2000).
Education: High school graduation rate: 83.7% (2000); College graduation rate: 12.1% (2000).
Housing: Homeownership rate: 74.5% (2000); Median home value: $71,400 (2000); Median rent: $275 per month (2000); Median age of housing: 7 years (2000).
Transportation: Commute to work: 81.7% car, 0.0% public transportation, 10.6% walk, 0.0% work from home (2000); Travel time to work: 10.6% less than 15 minutes, 15.4% 15 to 30 minutes, 58.7% 30 to 45 minutes, 0.0% 45 to 60 minutes, 15.4% 60 minutes or more (2000)

Daviess County

Located in northwestern Missouri; drained by the Grand River. Covers a land area of 567.00 square miles, a water area of 2.10 square miles, and is located in the Central Time Zone. The county government was organized in 1836. County seat is Gallatin.
Population: 8,016 (2000); Race: 99.2% White, 0.0% Black, 0.0% Asian, 0.1% American Indian and Alaska Native, 0.4% Hispanic of any race, 0.3% two or more races (2000); Density: 14.1 persons per square mile (2000); Age: 27.1% under 18, 17.6% over 64 (2000).
Religion: Five largest groups: 32.2% Southern Baptist Convention, 8.3% Christian Church (Disciples of Christ), 8.2% The United Methodist Church, 5.1% Old Order Amish Church, 3.1% The Church of Jesus Christ of Latter-day Saints (2000).
Economy: Unemployment rate: 4.5% (11/2002); Total civilian labor force: 3,542 (11/2002); Leading industries: 34.8% manufacturing; 19.6% retail trade; 12.2% wholesale trade (2000); Companies that employ more than 1,000 persons: 0 (2000); Companies that employ more than 100 persons: 1 (2000); Farms: 886 totaling 301,788 acres (1997); Minority business ownership rate: 0.0% (1997); Women business ownership rate: 0.0% (1997); Retail sales per capita: $3,178 (1997). Single-family building permits issued: 6 (2001) / 2 (2000); Multi-family building permits issued: 0 (2001) / 0 (2000).
Income: Per capita income: $15,953 (2000); Median household income: $30,855 (2000); Poverty rate: 15.2% (2000); Bankruptcy rate: 3.09% (2001).
Taxes: Total county taxes per capita: $91 (1997); County property taxes per capita: $36 (1997).
Education: High school graduation rate: 79.1% (2000); College graduation rate: 12.0% (2000).
Housing: Homeownership rate: 76.8% (2000); Median home value: $56,700 (2000); Median rent: $242 per month (2000); Median age of housing: 35 years (2000).
Health: Birth rate: 144.7 per 10,000 population (1998); Age adjusted death rate: 89.3 per 10,000 population (1999); Age adjusted cancer mortality rate: 158.9 (Unreliable figure as per CDC) deaths per 100,000 population (1999). Number of physicians: 1.2 per 10,000 population (1999); Number of hospital beds: n/a (1999).
Elections: 2000 Presidential election results: 39.1% Gore, 57.6% Bush, 1.7% Nader, 1.0% Buchanan

Additional Information Contacts
Daviess County Government Offices 660-663-2641
Jamesport Community Association 660-684-4146

Daviess County Communities

ALTAMONT (village). Covers a land area of 0.257 square miles and a water area of 0 square miles. Located at 39.88° N. Lat.; 94.08° W. Long. Elevation is 1,004 feet.
Population: 218 (2000); Race: 99.1% White, 0.0% Black, 0.0% Asian, 0.0% American Indian and Alaska Native, 0.0% Hispanic of any race, 0.9% two or more races (2000); Density: 847.6 persons per square mile (2000); Age: 35.5% under 18, 5.1% over 64 (2000); Marriage status: 16.1% never married, 72.0% now married, 4.2% widowed, 7.7% divorced (2000); Foreign born: 0.0% (2000); Ancestry (includes multiple ancestries): 22.1% United States or American, 16.6% Irish, 15.7% German, 4.6% English, 3.2% Other groups (2000).
Economy: Cattle, hogs; dairy farms. Employment by occupation: 1.9% management, 14.6% professional, 21.4% services, 18.4% sales, 0.0% farming, 21.4% construction, 22.3% production (2000).
Income: Per capita income: $9,953 (2000); Median household income: $26,250 (2000); Poverty rate: 21.7% (2000).
Taxes: Total city taxes per capita: $31 (1997); City property taxes per capita: $16 (1997).
Education: High school graduation rate: 77.2% (2000); College graduation rate: 2.0% (2000).
Housing: Homeownership rate: 78.5% (2000); Median home value: $30,000 (2000); Median rent: $288 per month (2000); Median age of housing: 36 years (2000).
Transportation: Commute to work: 90.3% car, 1.0% public transportation, 2.9% walk, 5.8% work from home (2000); Travel time to work: 25.8% less than 15 minutes, 32.0% 15 to 30 minutes, 9.3% 30 to 45 minutes, 8.2% 45 to 60 minutes, 24.7% 60 minutes or more (2000)

COFFEY (city). Aka Salem. Covers a land area of 0.202 square miles and a water area of 0 square miles. Located at 40.10° N. Lat.; 94.00° W. Long. Elevation is 290 feet.
Population: 140 (2000); Race: 96.9% White, 0.0% Black, 0.0% Asian, 1.5% American Indian and Alaska Native, 3.1% Hispanic of any race, 1.5% two or more races (2000); Density: 692.4 persons per square mile (2000); Age: 20.0% under 18, 29.2% over 64 (2000); Marriage status: 21.1% never married, 56.9% now married, 11.9% widowed, 10.1% divorced (2000); Foreign born: 0.0% (2000); Ancestry (includes multiple ancestries): 26.2% United States or American, 16.2% German, 6.9% Irish, 5.4% French Canadian, 5.4% French (except Basque) (2000).
Economy: Employment by occupation: 0.0% management, 20.0% professional, 13.3% services, 31.1% sales, 8.9% farming, 13.3% construction, 13.3% production (2000).
Income: Per capita income: $11,415 (2000); Median household income: $15,000 (2000); Poverty rate: 43.1% (2000).
Taxes: Total city taxes per capita: $30 (1997); City property taxes per capita: $23 (1997).
Education: High school graduation rate: 61.3% (2000); College graduation rate: 7.5% (2000).
Housing: Homeownership rate: 86.4% (2000); Median home value: $26,300 (2000); Median rent: $175 per month (2000); Median age of housing: 47 years (2000).
Transportation: Commute to work: 100.0% car, 0.0% public transportation, 0.0% walk, 0.0% work from home (2000); Travel time to work: 13.3% less than 15 minutes, 60.0% 15 to 30 minutes, 8.9% 30 to 45 minutes, 4.4% 45 to 60 minutes, 13.3% 60 minutes or more (2000)

GALLATIN (city). Covers a land area of 2.795 square miles and a water area of 0.006 square miles. Located at 39.91° N. Lat.; 93.96° W. Long. Elevation is 931 feet.
History: Gallatin was platted in 1837 and named for Albert Gallatin, Secretary of the Treasury (1801-1913).
Population: 1,789 (2000); Race: 99.3% White, 0.0% Black, 0.2% Asian, 0.0% American Indian and Alaska Native, 0.2% Hispanic of any race, 0.4% two or more races (2000); Density: 640.1 persons per square mile (2000); Age: 27.0% under 18, 20.9% over 64 (2000); Marriage status: 19.3% never married, 58.0% now married, 14.6% widowed, 8.2% divorced (2000); Foreign born: 0.1% (2000); Ancestry (includes multiple ancestries): 20.8% United States or American, 12.0% German, 11.5% English, 9.2% Irish, 4.3% Other groups (2000).
Economy: Single-family building permits issued: 6 (2001) / 2 (2000); Multi-family building permits issued: 0 (2001) / 0 (2000); Employment by occupation: 8.7% management, 17.7% professional, 17.2% services, 24.4% sales, 2.0% farming, 12.5% construction, 17.5% production (2000).
Income: Per capita income: $17,092 (2000); Median household income: $29,234 (2000); Poverty rate: 14.3% (2000).
Taxes: Total city taxes per capita: $189 (1997); City property taxes per capita: $21 (1997).
Education: High school graduation rate: 82.5% (2000); College graduation rate: 17.3% (2000).

School District(s)
Gallatin R-V (PK-12)
2000 Enrollment: 614 660-663-2171
Housing: Homeownership rate: 67.7% (2000); Median home value: $57,800 (2000); Median rent: $240 per month (2000); Median age of housing: 39 years (2000).
Safety: Violent crime rate: 11.1 per 10,000 population; Property crime rate: 133.3 per 10,000 population (2001).
Newspapers: Pony Express Advertising Shopper (1 x week); Gallatin North Missourian (1 x week)
Transportation: Commute to work: 88.9% car, 0.0% public transportation, 7.4% walk, 3.0% work from home (2000); Travel time to work: 52.0% less than 15 minutes, 16.4% 15 to 30 minutes, 13.6% 30 to 45 minutes, 5.6% 45 to 60 minutes, 12.5% 60 minutes or more (2000)

JAMESON (town). Covers a land area of 0.222 square miles and a water area of 0 square miles. Located at 40.00° N. Lat.; 93.98° W. Long. Elevation is 797 feet.
History: Mormon Shrine of Adam-ondi-Ahman to South.
Population: 120 (2000); Race: 99.2% White, 0.0% Black, 0.0% Asian, 0.0% American Indian and Alaska Native, 0.0% Hispanic of any race, 0.8% two or more races (2000); Density: 541.7 persons per square mile (2000); Age: 20.3% under 18, 14.6% over 64 (2000); Marriage status: 18.3% never married, 49.0% now married, 9.6% widowed, 23.1% divorced (2000); Foreign born: 0.0% (2000); Ancestry (includes multiple ancestries): 19.5% United States or American, 14.6% English, 10.6% Irish, 7.3% German, 5.7% Other groups (2000).
Economy: Employment by occupation: 8.8% management, 0.0% professional, 26.3% services, 19.3% sales, 5.3% farming, 15.8% construction, 24.6% production (2000).
Income: Per capita income: $10,351 (2000); Median household income: $21,750 (2000); Poverty rate: 17.9% (2000).
Taxes: Total city taxes per capita: $13 (1997); City property taxes per capita: $13 (1997).
Education: High school graduation rate: 77.2% (2000); College graduation rate: 0.0% (2000).

School District(s)
North Daviess R-III (KG-12)
2000 Enrollment: 120 660-828-4123
Housing: Homeownership rate: 80.7% (2000); Median home value: $29,600 (2000); Median rent: $255 per month (2000); Median age of housing: 60+ years (2000).
Transportation: Commute to work: 100.0% car, 0.0% public transportation, 0.0% walk, 0.0% work from home (2000); Travel time to work: 17.5% less than 15 minutes, 26.3% 15 to 30 minutes, 35.1% 30 to 45 minutes, 10.5% 45 to 60 minutes, 10.5% 60 minutes or more (2000)

JAMESPORT (city). Covers a land area of 0.564 square miles and a water area of 0 square miles. Located at 39.97° N. Lat.; 93.80° W. Long. Elevation is 990 feet.
History: Large Amish community established 1953. Platted 1857.
Population: 505 (2000); Race: 99.6% White, 0.0% Black, 0.0% Asian, 0.0% American Indian and Alaska Native, 0.4% Hispanic of any race, 0.0% two or more races (2000); Density: 895.0 persons per square mile (2000); Age: 22.8% under 18, 19.4% over 64 (2000); Marriage status: 22.4% never married, 58.0% now married, 10.2% widowed, 9.3% divorced (2000); Foreign born: 0.0% (2000); Ancestry (includes multiple ancestries): 13.3% German, 9.5% United States or American, 7.5% English, 6.0% Other groups, 3.6% Irish (2000).
Economy: Corn, soybeans, wheat; cattle, hogs; concrete. Numerous antique shops. Employment by occupation: 5.5% management, 9.0% professional, 15.4% services, 27.4% sales, 9.0% farming, 10.0% construction, 23.9% production (2000).
Income: Per capita income: $13,043 (2000); Median household income: $22,321 (2000); Poverty rate: 22.8% (2000).

Taxes: Total city taxes per capita: $118 (1997); City property taxes per capita: $40 (1997).
Education: High school graduation rate: 64.3% (2000); College graduation rate: 7.2% (2000).

School District(s)

Tri-County R-VII (PK-12)
2000 Enrollment: 215 660-684-6118

Housing: Homeownership rate: 75.0% (2000); Median home value: $35,700 (2000); Median rent: $271 per month (2000); Median age of housing: 47 years (2000).
Newspapers: Tri-County Weekly (1 x week)
Transportation: Commute to work: 80.1% car, 0.5% public transportation, 12.4% walk, 4.5% work from home (2000); Travel time to work: 39.1% less than 15 minutes, 29.7% 15 to 30 minutes, 13.0% 30 to 45 minutes, 3.6% 45 to 60 minutes, 14.6% 60 minutes or more (2000)
Additional Information Contacts
Jamesport Community Association 660-684-4146

LOCK SPRINGS (village). Covers a land area of 0.122 square miles and a water area of 0 square miles. Located at 39.84° N. Lat.; 93.77° W. Long. Elevation is 717 feet.
History: Damaged by flooding in 1993.
Population: 69 (2000); Race: 80.2% White, 0.0% Black, 0.0% Asian, 0.0% American Indian and Alaska Native, 0.0% Hispanic of any race, 0.0% two or more races (2000); Density: 564.5 persons per square mile (2000); Age: 34.6% under 18, 17.3% over 64 (2000); Marriage status: 17.2% never married, 58.6% now married, 17.2% widowed, 6.9% divorced (2000); Foreign born: 0.0% (2000); Ancestry (includes multiple ancestries): 30.9% German, 23.5% Other groups, 11.1% Irish, 4.9% Scottish, 4.9% Dutch (2000).
Economy: Employment by occupation: 14.8% management, 7.4% professional, 22.2% services, 11.1% sales, 0.0% farming, 11.1% construction, 33.3% production (2000).
Income: Per capita income: $10,816 (2000); Median household income: $21,500 (2000); Poverty rate: 37.0% (2000).
Education: High school graduation rate: 82.0% (2000); College graduation rate: 4.0% (2000).
Housing: Homeownership rate: 78.6% (2000); Median home value: $13,300 (2000); Median rent: $125 per month (2000); Median age of housing: 60+ years (2000).
Transportation: Commute to work: 100.0% car, 0.0% public transportation, 0.0% walk, 0.0% work from home (2000); Travel time to work: 22.2% less than 15 minutes, 37.0% 15 to 30 minutes, 22.2% 30 to 45 minutes, 18.5% 45 to 60 minutes, 0.0% 60 minutes or more (2000)

PATTONSBURG (city). Covers a land area of 1.342 square miles and a water area of 0.008 square miles. Located at 40.05° N. Lat.; 94.12° W. Long. Elevation is 776 feet.
History: Pattonsburg was platted in 1845 at a spot two miles north of its later site, and when the Chillicothe & Omaha Railroad was built in 1871, the residents moved to meet it. The early economy of the town depended on the dairy products of the surrounding farms, and on a cannery.
Population: 261 (2000); Race: 100.0% White, 0.0% Black, 0.0% Asian, 0.0% American Indian and Alaska Native, 3.9% Hispanic of any race, 0.0% two or more races (2000); Density: 194.5 persons per square mile (2000); Age: 28.6% under 18, 18.0% over 64 (2000); Marriage status: 33.0% never married, 44.3% now married, 10.3% widowed, 12.4% divorced (2000); Foreign born: 0.0% (2000); Ancestry (includes multiple ancestries): 25.1% United States or American, 8.6% English, 7.1% German, 6.7% Other groups, 2.4% Irish (2000).
Economy: Employment by occupation: 3.9% management, 16.5% professional, 20.4% services, 29.1% sales, 1.9% farming, 16.5% construction, 11.7% production (2000).
Income: Per capita income: $20,779 (2000); Median household income: $30,500 (2000); Poverty rate: 26.3% (2000).
Taxes: Total city taxes per capita: $66 (1997); City property taxes per capita: $17 (1997).
Education: High school graduation rate: 79.0% (2000); College graduation rate: 20.4% (2000).

School District(s)

Pattonsburg R-II (PK-12)
2000 Enrollment: 236 660-367-2111

Housing: Homeownership rate: 71.4% (2000); Median home value: $59,500 (2000); Median rent: $214 per month (2000); Median age of housing: 5 years (2000).
Transportation: Commute to work: 92.2% car, 1.9% public transportation, 0.0% walk, 5.8% work from home (2000); Travel time to work: 35.1% less than 15 minutes, 45.4% 15 to 30 minutes, 15.5% 30 to 45 minutes, 2.1% 45 to 60 minutes, 2.1% 60 minutes or more (2000)

WINSTON (village). Covers a land area of 0.309 square miles and a water area of 0 square miles. Located at 39.87° N. Lat.; 94.14° W. Long. Elevation is 1,063 feet.
History: Winston was the scene in 1881 of a holdup of the Chicago, Rock Island & Pacific Railroad train, in which the bandits got away with between $8,000 and $10,000. Frank and Jesse James were later charged with the holdup.
Population: 247 (2000); Race: 97.5% White, 0.0% Black, 0.0% Asian, 0.0% American Indian and Alaska Native, 1.3% Hispanic of any race, 2.5% two or more races (2000); Density: 798.8 persons per square mile (2000); Age: 27.1% under 18, 11.7% over 64 (2000); Marriage status: 22.2% never married, 62.2% now married, 6.7% widowed, 8.9% divorced (2000); Foreign born: 0.0% (2000); Ancestry (includes multiple ancestries): 22.1% German, 13.8% Irish, 13.8% Dutch, 12.9% United States or American, 10.4% English (2000).
Economy: Employment by occupation: 4.7% management, 17.0% professional, 9.4% services, 24.5% sales, 0.0% farming, 13.2% construction, 31.1% production (2000).
Income: Per capita income: $13,283 (2000); Median household income: $30,125 (2000); Poverty rate: 8.9% (2000).
Taxes: Total city taxes per capita: $20 (1997); City property taxes per capita: $20 (1997).
Education: High school graduation rate: 75.4% (2000); College graduation rate: 7.7% (2000).

School District(s)

Winston R-VI (PK-12)
2000 Enrollment: 197 660-749-5456

Housing: Homeownership rate: 74.0% (2000); Median home value: $38,100 (2000); Median rent: $321 per month (2000); Median age of housing: 52 years (2000).
Transportation: Commute to work: 94.2% car, 0.0% public transportation, 1.0% walk, 1.9% work from home (2000); Travel time to work: 29.4% less than 15 minutes, 30.4% 15 to 30 minutes, 19.6% 30 to 45 minutes, 12.7% 45 to 60 minutes, 7.8% 60 minutes or more (2000)

De Kalb County

Located in northwestern Missouri; drained by branches of the Grand and Platte Rivers. Covers a land area of 424.20 square miles, a water area of 1.60 square miles, and is located in the Central Time Zone. The county government was organized in 1845. County seat is Maysville.
Population: 11,597 (2000); Race: 89.1% White, 8.6% Black, 0.4% Asian, 0.4% American Indian and Alaska Native, 0.9% Hispanic of any race, 1.2% two or more races (2000); Density: 27.3 persons per square mile (2000); Age: 20.6% under 18, 14.0% over 64 (2000).
Religion: Five largest groups: 16.7% Southern Baptist Convention, 6.7% The United Methodist Church, 3.8% Christian Churches and Churches of Christ, 2.8% Assemblies of God, 2.2% Community of Christ (2000).
Economy: Unemployment rate: 4.4% (11/2002); Total civilian labor force: 4,332 (11/2002); Leading industries: 18.7% health care and social assistance; 15.8% accommodation & food services; 15.0% retail trade (2000); Companies that employ more than 1,000 persons: 0 (2000); Companies that employ more than 100 persons: 1 (2000); Farms: 769 totaling 215,215 acres (1997); Minority business ownership rate: 0.0% (1997); Women business ownership rate: 27.3% (1997); Retail sales per capita: $4,063 (1997). Single-family building permits issued: 0 (2001) / 0 (2000); Multi-family building permits issued: 0 (2001) / 0 (2000).
Income: Per capita income: $12,687 (2000); Median household income: $31,654 (2000); Poverty rate: 10.8% (2000); Bankruptcy rate: 2.64% (2001).
Taxes: Total county taxes per capita: $37 (1997); County property taxes per capita: $2 (1997).
Education: High school graduation rate: 77.0% (2000); College graduation rate: 10.7% (2000).
Housing: Homeownership rate: 73.4% (2000); Median home value: $64,800 (2000); Median rent: $244 per month (2000); Median age of housing: 30 years (2000).
Health: Birth rate: 93.1 per 10,000 population (1998); Age adjusted death rate: 114.2 per 10,000 population (1999); Age adjusted cancer mortality rate: 298.7 deaths per 100,000 population (1999). Number of physicians: 0.9 per 10,000 population (1999); Number of hospital beds: n/a (1999).

Elections: 2000 Presidential election results: 38.6% Gore, 58.4% Bush, 1.6% Nader, 1.0% Buchanan
National and State Parks: Pony Express State Wildlife Area
Additional Information Contacts
De Kalb County Government Offices 816-449-5402

De Kalb County Communities

AMITY (town). Covers a land area of 0.215 square miles and a water area of 0 square miles. Located at 39.86° N. Lat.; 94.43° W. Long. Elevation is 1,030 feet.
Population: 70 (2000); Race: 94.8% White, 0.0% Black, 0.0% Asian, 0.0% American Indian and Alaska Native, 0.0% Hispanic of any race, 5.2% two or more races (2000); Density: 324.9 persons per square mile (2000); Age: 27.3% under 18, 24.7% over 64 (2000); Marriage status: 8.6% never married, 81.0% now married, 6.9% widowed, 3.4% divorced (2000); Foreign born: 0.0% (2000); Ancestry (includes multiple ancestries): 24.7% German, 18.2% Other groups, 15.6% Irish, 3.9% Polish, 2.6% French (except Basque) (2000).
Economy: Employment by occupation: 0.0% management, 6.3% professional, 31.3% services, 21.9% sales, 0.0% farming, 21.9% construction, 18.8% production (2000).
Income: Per capita income: $11,388 (2000); Median household income: $25,625 (2000); Poverty rate: 18.2% (2000).
Taxes: Total city taxes per capita: $29 (1997); City property taxes per capita: $10 (1997).
Education: High school graduation rate: 78.2% (2000); College graduation rate: 7.3% (2000).
Housing: Homeownership rate: 81.3% (2000); Median home value: $40,000 (2000); Median rent: $363 per month (2000); Median age of housing: 60+ years (2000).
Transportation: Commute to work: 100.0% car, 0.0% public transportation, 0.0% walk, 0.0% work from home (2000); Travel time to work: 0.0% less than 15 minutes, 18.8% 15 to 30 minutes, 31.3% 30 to 45 minutes, 6.3% 45 to 60 minutes, 43.8% 60 minutes or more (2000)

CLARKSDALE (city). Covers a land area of 0.320 square miles and a water area of 0 square miles. Located at 39.81° N. Lat.; 94.55° W. Long. Elevation is 942 feet.
Population: 351 (2000); Race: 98.4% White, 0.0% Black, 0.0% Asian, 0.0% American Indian and Alaska Native, 1.6% Hispanic of any race, 0.0% two or more races (2000); Density: 1,097.1 persons per square mile (2000); Age: 31.1% under 18, 12.5% over 64 (2000); Marriage status: 17.5% never married, 62.2% now married, 9.1% widowed, 11.3% divorced (2000); Foreign born: 0.0% (2000); Ancestry (includes multiple ancestries): 18.4% German, 17.0% Irish, 11.7% United States or American, 9.0% English, 6.6% Other groups (2000).
Economy: Employment by occupation: 7.4% management, 7.4% professional, 20.0% services, 26.3% sales, 0.0% farming, 17.1% construction, 21.7% production (2000).
Income: Per capita income: $13,394 (2000); Median household income: $34,375 (2000); Poverty rate: 9.7% (2000).
Taxes: Total city taxes per capita: $111 (1997); City property taxes per capita: $79 (1997).
Education: High school graduation rate: 75.9% (2000); College graduation rate: 7.4% (2000).
Housing: Homeownership rate: 80.0% (2000); Median home value: $49,100 (2000); Median rent: $242 per month (2000); Median age of housing: 35 years (2000).
Transportation: Commute to work: 92.9% car, 0.0% public transportation, 0.0% walk, 7.1% work from home (2000); Travel time to work: 2.5% less than 15 minutes, 53.5% 15 to 30 minutes, 29.3% 30 to 45 minutes, 5.1% 45 to 60 minutes, 9.6% 60 minutes or more (2000)

MAYSVILLE (city). Covers a land area of 1.137 square miles and a water area of 0 square miles. Located at 39.88° N. Lat.; 94.36° W. Long. Elevation is 974 feet.
Population: 1,212 (2000); Race: 98.8% White, 0.0% Black, 0.0% Asian, 0.6% American Indian and Alaska Native, 0.7% Hispanic of any race, 0.1% two or more races (2000); Density: 1,065.9 persons per square mile (2000); Age: 31.9% under 18, 19.4% over 64 (2000); Marriage status: 19.4% never married, 58.0% now married, 12.6% widowed, 10.0% divorced (2000); Foreign born: 0.2% (2000); Ancestry (includes multiple ancestries): 20.4% German, 12.4% United States or American, 12.0% Irish, 10.3% English, 9.0% Other groups (2000).
Economy: Single-family building permits issued: 0 (2001) / 0 (2000); Multi-family building permits issued: 0 (2001) / 0 (2000); Employment by occupation: 7.5% management, 19.5% professional, 18.8% services, 25.5% sales, 0.8% farming, 15.3% construction, 12.6% production (2000).
Income: Per capita income: $11,871 (2000); Median household income: $27,727 (2000); Poverty rate: 16.6% (2000).
Taxes: Total city taxes per capita: $188 (1997); City property taxes per capita: $22 (1997).
Education: High school graduation rate: 77.4% (2000); College graduation rate: 13.5% (2000).

School District(s)

Maysville R-I (KG-12)
2000 Enrollment: 768 816-449-2308
Housing: Homeownership rate: 69.8% (2000); Median home value: $51,900 (2000); Median rent: $242 per month (2000); Median age of housing: 36 years (2000).
Newspapers: De Kalb County Record-Herald (1 x week)
Transportation: Commute to work: 91.1% car, 0.4% public transportation, 6.1% walk, 1.7% work from home (2000); Travel time to work: 50.0% less than 15 minutes, 16.3% 15 to 30 minutes, 16.7% 30 to 45 minutes, 4.7% 45 to 60 minutes, 12.2% 60 minutes or more (2000)

OSBORN (city). Covers a land area of 0.573 square miles and a water area of 0 square miles. Located at 39.74° N. Lat.; 94.35° W. Long.
Population: 455 (2000); Race: 98.9% White, 0.4% Black, 0.0% Asian, 0.0% American Indian and Alaska Native, 0.4% Hispanic of any race, 0.7% two or more races (2000); Density: 794.5 persons per square mile (2000); Age: 29.2% under 18, 14.8% over 64 (2000); Marriage status: 17.8% never married, 63.6% now married, 6.1% widowed, 12.5% divorced (2000); Foreign born: 0.4% (2000); Ancestry (includes multiple ancestries): 17.8% German, 16.2% United States or American, 13.3% English, 7.2% Other groups, 7.2% Irish (2000).
Economy: Employment by occupation: 6.0% management, 13.6% professional, 10.1% services, 27.1% sales, 2.5% farming, 17.6% construction, 23.1% production (2000).
Income: Per capita income: $16,230 (2000); Median household income: $32,344 (2000); Poverty rate: 9.9% (2000).
Taxes: Total city taxes per capita: $51 (1997); City property taxes per capita: $26 (1997).
Education: High school graduation rate: 81.8% (2000); College graduation rate: 10.0% (2000).

School District(s)

Osborn R-O (KG-12)
2000 Enrollment: 180 816-675-2217
Housing: Homeownership rate: 69.6% (2000); Median home value: $55,300 (2000); Median rent: $247 per month (2000); Median age of housing: 36 years (2000).
Transportation: Commute to work: 92.2% car, 2.6% public transportation, 1.0% walk, 2.6% work from home (2000); Travel time to work: 28.7% less than 15 minutes, 33.0% 15 to 30 minutes, 26.6% 30 to 45 minutes, 4.8% 45 to 60 minutes, 6.9% 60 minutes or more (2000)

STEWARTSVILLE (city). Covers a land area of 0.974 square miles and a water area of 0 square miles. Located at 39.75° N. Lat.; 94.49° W. Long. Elevation is 958 feet.
Population: 759 (2000); Race: 95.9% White, 2.5% Black, 0.0% Asian, 0.0% American Indian and Alaska Native, 1.6% Hispanic of any race, 0.5% two or more races (2000); Density: 779.5 persons per square mile (2000); Age: 29.7% under 18, 14.9% over 64 (2000); Marriage status: 22.4% never married, 57.0% now married, 7.4% widowed, 13.2% divorced (2000); Foreign born: 0.3% (2000); Ancestry (includes multiple ancestries): 23.6% German, 13.1% United States or American, 12.3% Irish, 10.1% Other groups, 7.6% English (2000).
Economy: Employment by occupation: 9.6% management, 19.6% professional, 22.0% services, 18.6% sales, 0.0% farming, 9.0% construction, 21.1% production (2000).
Income: Per capita income: $14,509 (2000); Median household income: $35,063 (2000); Poverty rate: 7.6% (2000).
Taxes: Total city taxes per capita: $67 (1997); City property taxes per capita: $32 (1997).
Education: High school graduation rate: 83.8% (2000); College graduation rate: 14.1% (2000).

School District(s)

Stewartsville C-2 (KG-12)
2000 Enrollment: 309 816-669-3792

Housing: Homeownership rate: 75.9% (2000); Median home value: $64,800 (2000); Median rent: $303 per month (2000); Median age of housing: 32 years (2000).
Transportation: Commute to work: 95.6% car, 0.0% public transportation, 1.6% walk, 1.6% work from home (2000); Travel time to work: 13.1% less than 15 minutes, 46.8% 15 to 30 minutes, 14.4% 30 to 45 minutes, 6.4% 45 to 60 minutes, 19.2% 60 minutes or more (2000)

UNION STAR (town). Covers a land area of 0.259 square miles and a water area of 0 square miles. Located at 39.98° N. Lat.; 94.59° W. Long. Elevation is 1,034 feet.
Population: 433 (2000); Race: 94.6% White, 0.0% Black, 0.7% Asian, 3.6% American Indian and Alaska Native, 0.0% Hispanic of any race, 1.0% two or more races (2000); Density: 1,672.0 persons per square mile (2000); Age: 27.0% under 18, 19.0% over 64 (2000); Marriage status: 16.5% never married, 59.3% now married, 14.3% widowed, 9.9% divorced (2000); Foreign born: 2.2% (2000); Ancestry (includes multiple ancestries): 19.5% German, 16.3% English, 15.6% Irish, 15.3% United States or American, 11.4% Other groups (2000).
Economy: Employment by occupation: 8.5% management, 12.5% professional, 14.0% services, 31.0% sales, 0.0% farming, 12.5% construction, 21.5% production (2000).
Income: Per capita income: $13,057 (2000); Median household income: $24,875 (2000); Poverty rate: 8.6% (2000).
Taxes: Total city taxes per capita: $120 (1997); City property taxes per capita: $80 (1997).
Education: High school graduation rate: 82.4% (2000); College graduation rate: 12.5% (2000).

School District(s)

Union Star R-II (KG-12)
2000 Enrollment: 187 816-593-2294

Housing: Homeownership rate: 73.4% (2000); Median home value: $41,600 (2000); Median rent: $242 per month (2000); Median age of housing: 57 years (2000).
Transportation: Commute to work: 95.0% car, 0.0% public transportation, 2.0% walk, 2.0% work from home (2000); Travel time to work: 16.3% less than 15 minutes, 27.6% 15 to 30 minutes, 45.4% 30 to 45 minutes, 3.6% 45 to 60 minutes, 7.1% 60 minutes or more (2000)

WEATHERBY (town). Covers a land area of 0.120 square miles and a water area of 0 square miles. Located at 39.90° N. Lat.; 94.24° W. Long. Elevation is 885 feet.
Population: 123 (2000); Race: 100.0% White, 0.0% Black, 0.0% Asian, 0.0% American Indian and Alaska Native, 0.0% Hispanic of any race, 0.0% two or more races (2000); Density: 1,027.2 persons per square mile (2000); Age: 30.3% under 18, 13.2% over 64 (2000); Marriage status: 26.2% never married, 54.1% now married, 4.9% widowed, 14.8% divorced (2000); Foreign born: 0.0% (2000); Ancestry (includes multiple ancestries): 22.4% German, 10.5% United States or American, 10.5% English, 6.6% Other groups, 5.3% Polish (2000).
Economy: Employment by occupation: 5.7% management, 11.4% professional, 20.0% services, 25.7% sales, 0.0% farming, 14.3% construction, 22.9% production (2000).
Income: Per capita income: $9,475 (2000); Median household income: $19,375 (2000); Poverty rate: 21.1% (2000).
Taxes: Total city taxes per capita: $93 (1997); City property taxes per capita: $31 (1997).
Education: High school graduation rate: 58.7% (2000); College graduation rate: 6.5% (2000).
Housing: Homeownership rate: 69.4% (2000); Median home value: $18,000 (2000); Median rent: $239 per month (2000); Median age of housing: 60+ years (2000).
Transportation: Commute to work: 100.0% car, 0.0% public transportation, 0.0% walk, 0.0% work from home (2000); Travel time to work: 37.1% less than 15 minutes, 20.0% 15 to 30 minutes, 25.7% 30 to 45 minutes, 2.9% 45 to 60 minutes, 14.3% 60 minutes or more (2000)

Dent County

Located in southeast central Missouri, in the Ozarks; drained by the Meramec River; includes part of Clark National Forest. Covers a land area of 753.50 square miles, a water area of 1.00 square miles, and is located in the Central Time Zone. The county government was organized in 1851. County seat is Salem.

Population: 14,927 (2000); Race: 97.6% White, 0.4% Black, 0.2% Asian, 0.9% American Indian and Alaska Native, 0.9% Hispanic of any race, 0.9% two or more races (2000); Density: 19.8 persons per square mile (2000); Age: 24.7% under 18, 17.8% over 64 (2000).
Religion: Five largest groups: 43.8% Southern Baptist Convention, 4.1% Assemblies of God, 3.8% Catholic Church, 3.7% The United Methodist Church, 3.3% Christian Churches and Churches of Christ (2000).
Economy: Unemployment rate: 7.4% (11/2002); Total civilian labor force: 5,234 (11/2002); Leading industries: 22.8% manufacturing; 17.8% retail trade; 13.3% health care and social assistance (2000); Companies that employ more than 1,000 persons: 0 (2000); Companies that employ more than 100 persons: 7 (2000); Farms: 727 totaling 221,967 acres (1997); Minority business ownership rate: 0.0% (1997); Women business ownership rate: 20.2% (1997); Retail sales per capita: $7,485 (1997). Single-family building permits issued: 6 (2001) / 3 (2000); Multi-family building permits issued: 0 (2001) / 0 (2000).
Income: Per capita income: $14,463 (2000); Median household income: $27,193 (2000); Poverty rate: 17.2% (2000); Bankruptcy rate: 3.89% (2001).
Taxes: Total county taxes per capita: $83 (1997); County property taxes per capita: $33 (1997).
Education: High school graduation rate: 66.3% (2000); College graduation rate: 10.1% (2000).
Housing: Homeownership rate: 74.1% (2000); Median home value: $61,000 (2000); Median rent: $254 per month (2000); Median age of housing: 28 years (2000).
Health: Birth rate: 112.6 per 10,000 population (1998); Age adjusted death rate: 103.0 per 10,000 population (1999); Age adjusted cancer mortality rate: 245.6 deaths per 100,000 population (1999). Number of physicians: 4.7 per 10,000 population (1999); Number of hospital beds: 28.8 per 10,000 population (1999).
Elections: 2000 Presidential election results: 30.7% Gore, 66.7% Bush, 1.1% Nader, 0.8% Buchanan
National and State Parks: Cedar Grove State Forest; Indian Trail State Forest; Montauk State Park; Richard F Clement Memorial State Forest and Wildlife Mgmt Area
Additional Information Contacts
Dent County Government Offices 573-729-4144
Salem Chamber of Commerce 573-729-6900

Dent County Communities

BOSS (unincorporated postal area, zip code 65440). Covers a land area of 103.419 square miles and a water area of 0.146 square miles. Located at 37.61° N. Lat.; 91.17° W. Long. Elevation is 1,122 feet.
Population: 634 (2000); Race: 99.2% White, 0.0% Black, 0.0% Asian, 0.8% American Indian and Alaska Native, 0.0% Hispanic of any race, 0.0% two or more races (2000); Density: 6.1 persons per square mile (2000); Age: 20.8% under 18, 19.9% over 64 (2000); Marriage status: 21.0% never married, 61.4% now married, 8.5% widowed, 9.1% divorced (2000); Foreign born: 1.0% (2000); Ancestry (includes multiple ancestries): 17.4% United States or American, 10.7% Irish, 10.3% German, 8.5% English, 5.0% Other groups (2000).
Economy: Employment by occupation: 4.3% management, 4.7% professional, 17.1% services, 22.6% sales, 2.1% farming, 23.9% construction, 25.2% production (2000).
Income: Per capita income: $15,017 (2000); Median household income: $27,500 (2000); Poverty rate: 17.9% (2000).
Education: High school graduation rate: 58.3% (2000); College graduation rate: 2.6% (2000).
Housing: Homeownership rate: 80.3% (2000); Median home value: $42,900 (2000); Median rent: $275 per month (2000); Median age of housing: 31 years (2000).
Transportation: Commute to work: 93.4% car, 1.3% public transportation, 2.7% walk, 1.8% work from home (2000); Travel time to work: 30.6% less than 15 minutes, 39.6% 15 to 30 minutes, 17.1% 30 to 45 minutes, 3.2% 45 to 60 minutes, 9.5% 60 minutes or more (2000)

JADWIN (unincorporated postal area, zip code 65501). Covers a land area of 32.723 square miles and a water area of 0 square miles. Located at 37.46° N. Lat.; 91.54° W. Long. Elevation is 1,318 feet.
Population: 197 (2000); Race: 97.0% White, 0.0% Black, 0.0% Asian, 0.0% American Indian and Alaska Native, 0.0% Hispanic of any race, 3.0% two or more races (2000); Density: 6.0 persons per square mile (2000); Age: 24.7% under 18, 20.7% over 64 (2000); Marriage status: 13.5% never married, 71.6% now married, 7.1% widowed, 7.7% divorced (2000); Foreign born:

0.0% (2000); Ancestry (includes multiple ancestries): 18.7% Other groups, 15.2% United States or American, 7.6% German, 7.1% Irish, 6.6% Norwegian (2000).
Economy: Employment by occupation: 9.7% management, 12.5% professional, 19.4% services, 22.2% sales, 9.7% farming, 9.7% construction, 16.7% production (2000).
Income: Per capita income: $11,344 (2000); Median household income: $25,833 (2000); Poverty rate: 15.6% (2000).
Education: High school graduation rate: 67.8% (2000); College graduation rate: 10.5% (2000).
Housing: Homeownership rate: 93.5% (2000); Median home value: $85,000 (2000); Median rent: $325 per month (2000); Median age of housing: 20 years (2000).
Transportation: Commute to work: 94.2% car, 0.0% public transportation, 0.0% walk, 5.8% work from home (2000); Travel time to work: 12.3% less than 15 minutes, 35.4% 15 to 30 minutes, 24.6% 30 to 45 minutes, 0.0% 45 to 60 minutes, 27.7% 60 minutes or more (2000)

LECOMA (unincorporated postal area, zip code 65540). Covers a land area of 27.138 square miles and a water area of 0.033 square miles. Located at 37.76° N. Lat.; 91.75° W. Long. Elevation is 1,176 feet.
Population: 379 (2000); Race: 98.7% White, 0.0% Black, 0.0% Asian, 0.0% American Indian and Alaska Native, 0.0% Hispanic of any race, 1.3% two or more races (2000); Density: 14.0 persons per square mile (2000); Age: 22.0% under 18, 9.8% over 64 (2000); Marriage status: 11.3% never married, 82.4% now married, 3.0% widowed, 3.3% divorced (2000); Foreign born: 0.8% (2000); Ancestry (includes multiple ancestries): 32.8% United States or American, 15.1% German, 10.8% English, 5.6% Irish, 3.4% Other groups (2000).
Economy: Employment by occupation: 9.4% management, 12.9% professional, 4.1% services, 18.2% sales, 0.0% farming, 31.8% construction, 23.5% production (2000).
Income: Per capita income: $17,308 (2000); Median household income: $24,167 (2000); Poverty rate: 11.4% (2000).
Education: High school graduation rate: 65.9% (2000); College graduation rate: 14.3% (2000).
Housing: Homeownership rate: 87.4% (2000); Median home value: $48,300 (2000); Median rent: $380 per month (2000); Median age of housing: 27 years (2000).
Transportation: Commute to work: 95.3% car, 0.0% public transportation, 0.0% walk, 4.7% work from home (2000); Travel time to work: 4.3% less than 15 minutes, 41.4% 15 to 30 minutes, 43.2% 30 to 45 minutes, 4.3% 45 to 60 minutes, 6.8% 60 minutes or more (2000)

LENOX (unincorporated postal area, zip code 65541). Covers a land area of 15.833 square miles and a water area of 0.005 square miles. Located at 37.62° N. Lat.; 91.76° W. Long. Elevation is 1,275 feet.
Population: 233 (2000); Race: 93.2% White, 0.0% Black, 0.0% Asian, 0.0% American Indian and Alaska Native, 6.4% Hispanic of any race, 6.8% two or more races (2000); Density: 14.7 persons per square mile (2000); Age: 31.5% under 18, 12.3% over 64 (2000); Marriage status: 27.1% never married, 63.3% now married, 1.7% widowed, 7.9% divorced (2000); Foreign born: 5.0% (2000); Ancestry (includes multiple ancestries): 19.2% United States or American, 19.2% English, 11.4% Irish, 7.8% German, 5.5% Other groups (2000).
Economy: Employment by occupation: 0.0% management, 0.0% professional, 31.6% services, 32.9% sales, 0.0% farming, 6.6% construction, 28.9% production (2000).
Income: Per capita income: $13,030 (2000); Median household income: $33,173 (2000); Poverty rate: 21.9% (2000).
Education: High school graduation rate: 72.5% (2000); College graduation rate: 5.1% (2000).
Housing: Homeownership rate: 100.0% (2000); Median home value: $54,600 (2000); Median age of housing: 29 years (2000).
Transportation: Commute to work: 89.5% car, 6.6% public transportation, 0.0% walk, 3.9% work from home (2000); Travel time to work: 12.3% less than 15 minutes, 45.2% 15 to 30 minutes, 35.6% 30 to 45 minutes, 0.0% 45 to 60 minutes, 6.8% 60 minutes or more (2000)

SALEM (city). Covers a land area of 3.020 square miles and a water area of 0 square miles. Located at 37.64° N. Lat.; 91.53° W. Long. Elevation is 1,182 feet.
History: Salem was founded in 1851 by Joseph Milsaps. Salem developed as a mining and shipping center, and as the gateway to the Big Springs Country.
Population: 4,854 (2000); Race: 98.4% White, 1.1% Black, 0.0% Asian, 0.3% American Indian and Alaska Native, 1.4% Hispanic of any race, 0.1% two or more races (2000); Density: 1,607.4 persons per square mile (2000); Age: 24.3% under 18, 23.0% over 64 (2000); Marriage status: 18.9% never married, 55.5% now married, 14.4% widowed, 11.2% divorced (2000); Foreign born: 0.5% (2000); Ancestry (includes multiple ancestries): 19.4% United States or American, 16.2% German, 13.0% Irish, 11.5% English, 11.5% Other groups (2000).
Economy: Single-family building permits issued: 6 (2001) / 3 (2000); Multi-family building permits issued: 0 (2001) / 0 (2000); Employment by occupation: 7.0% management, 15.1% professional, 17.4% services, 24.5% sales, 1.2% farming, 11.6% construction, 23.0% production (2000).
Income: Per capita income: $12,766 (2000); Median household income: $21,648 (2000); Poverty rate: 17.4% (2000).
Taxes: Total city taxes per capita: $310 (1997); City property taxes per capita: $58 (1997).
Education: High school graduation rate: 60.0% (2000); College graduation rate: 9.8% (2000).

School District(s)

Dent-Phelps R-III (PK-08)
2000 Enrollment: 316 573-729-4680
Green Forest R-II (KG-08)
2000 Enrollment: 248 573-729-3902
North Wood R-IV (PK-08)
2000 Enrollment: 243 573-729-4607
Oak Hill R-I (KG-08)
2000 Enrollment: 160 573-729-5618
Salem R-80 (PK-12)
2000 Enrollment: 1,604 573-729-6642

Housing: Homeownership rate: 56.7% (2000); Median home value: $55,600 (2000); Median rent: $250 per month (2000); Median age of housing: 37 years (2000).
Hospitals: Salem Memorial District Hospital (59 beds)
Newspapers: The Salem News (2 x week)
Transportation: Commute to work: 95.0% car, 0.0% public transportation, 1.6% walk, 2.1% work from home (2000); Travel time to work: 61.0% less than 15 minutes, 14.5% 15 to 30 minutes, 12.2% 30 to 45 minutes, 5.7% 45 to 60 minutes, 6.6% 60 minutes or more (2000)
Additional Information Contacts
Salem Chamber of Commerce 573-729-6900

Douglas County

Located in southern Missouri, in the Ozarks; drained by the North Fork of the White River. Covers a land area of 814.50 square miles, a water area of 0.10 square miles, and is located in the Central Time Zone. The county government was organized in 1857. County seat is Ava.
Population: 13,084 (2000); Race: 97.0% White, 0.0% Black, 0.1% Asian, 0.8% American Indian and Alaska Native, 0.8% Hispanic of any race, 1.8% two or more races (2000); Density: 16.1 persons per square mile (2000); Age: 25.8% under 18, 17.0% over 64 (2000).
Religion: Five largest groups: 6.1% Southern Baptist Convention, 4.3% Church of the Nazarene, 3.6% The Church of Jesus Christ of Latter-day Saints, 2.3% The United Methodist Church, 2.1% Catholic Church (2000).
Economy: Unemployment rate: 9.9% (11/2002); Total civilian labor force: 4,872 (11/2002); Leading industries: 32.1% manufacturing; 16.7% retail trade; 12.3% health care and social assistance (2000); Companies that employ more than 1,000 persons: 0 (2000); Companies that employ more than 100 persons: 2 (2000); Farms: 1,206 totaling 301,564 acres (1997); Minority business ownership rate: 0.0% (1997); Women business ownership rate: 13.0% (1997); Retail sales per capita: $3,790 (1997). Single-family building permits issued: 4 (2001) / 12 (2000); Multi-family building permits issued: 0 (2001) / 0 (2000).
Income: Per capita income: $13,785 (2000); Median household income: $25,918 (2000); Poverty rate: 17.5% (2000); Bankruptcy rate: 3.77% (2001).
Taxes: Total county taxes per capita: $76 (1997); County property taxes per capita: $32 (1997).
Education: High school graduation rate: 69.7% (2000); College graduation rate: 9.9% (2000).
Housing: Homeownership rate: 79.0% (2000); Median home value: $54,100 (2000); Median rent: $229 per month (2000); Median age of housing: 27 years (2000).
Health: Birth rate: 99.4 per 10,000 population (1998); Age adjusted death rate: 90.2 per 10,000 population (1999); Age adjusted cancer mortality rate: 200.4 deaths per 100,000 population (1999). Number of physicians: 0.8 per 10,000 population (1999); Number of hospital beds: n/a (1999).

Elections: 2000 Presidential election results: 29.3% Gore, 68.2% Bush, 1.0% Nader, 1.0% Buchanan
National and State Parks: Rippee State Wildlife Management Area
Additional Information Contacts
Douglas County Government Offices 417-683-4714
Ava Area Chamber of Commerce 417-683-4594

Douglas County Communities

AVA (city). Covers a land area of 3.105 square miles and a water area of 0 square miles. Located at 36.95° N. Lat.; 92.66° W. Long. Elevation is 1,283 feet.
History: Trappist monastery 20 mi 32 km Sotheast. Founded 1864.
Population: 3,021 (2000); Race: 97.1% White, 0.0% Black, 0.0% Asian, 1.2% American Indian and Alaska Native, 1.8% Hispanic of any race, 1.6% two or more races (2000); Density: 973.0 persons per square mile (2000); Age: 24.6% under 18, 22.4% over 64 (2000); Marriage status: 15.8% never married, 55.7% now married, 14.7% widowed, 13.8% divorced (2000); Foreign born: 1.1% (2000); Ancestry (includes multiple ancestries): 19.1% United States or American, 11.0% German, 10.8% Other groups, 9.4% English, 9.3% Irish (2000).
Economy: Resort, timber, and agricultural region; fruit; lumber. Manufacturing: electrical motors, apparel, sports protective gear. Single-family building permits issued: 4 (2001) / 12 (2000); Multi-family building permits issued: 0 (2001) / 0 (2000); Employment by occupation: 6.8% management, 16.2% professional, 14.1% services, 24.0% sales, 0.7% farming, 8.9% construction, 29.4% production (2000).
Income: Per capita income: $13,307 (2000); Median household income: $22,331 (2000); Poverty rate: 21.7% (2000).
Education: High school graduation rate: 63.3% (2000); College graduation rate: 10.8% (2000).

School District(s)

Ava R-I (PK-12)
2000 Enrollment: 1,643 417-683-4717
Plainview R-VIII (KG-08)
2000 Enrollment: 88 417-683-2046

Housing: Homeownership rate: 61.1% (2000); Median home value: $52,300 (2000); Median rent: $231 per month (2000); Median age of housing: 31 years (2000).
Newspapers: Douglas County Herald (1 x week)
Transportation: Commute to work: 93.1% car, 0.0% public transportation, 2.5% walk, 3.4% work from home (2000); Travel time to work: 57.6% less than 15 minutes, 9.1% 15 to 30 minutes, 8.9% 30 to 45 minutes, 6.3% 45 to 60 minutes, 18.1% 60 minutes or more (2000)
Additional Information Contacts
Ava Area Chamber of Commerce 417-683-4594

DRURY (unincorporated postal area, zip code 65638). Covers a land area of 58.089 square miles and a water area of 0 square miles. Located at 36.85° N. Lat.; 92.33° W. Long. Elevation is 1,218 feet.
Population: 462 (2000); Race: 94.6% White, 0.0% Black, 0.0% Asian, 1.0% American Indian and Alaska Native, 3.9% Hispanic of any race, 4.4% two or more races (2000); Density: 8.0 persons per square mile (2000); Age: 16.5% under 18, 20.0% over 64 (2000); Marriage status: 15.9% never married, 65.9% now married, 7.4% widowed, 10.7% divorced (2000); Foreign born: 1.0% (2000); Ancestry (includes multiple ancestries): 16.3% Irish, 15.8% English, 11.9% German, 10.7% United States or American, 10.5% Other groups (2000).
Economy: Employment by occupation: 24.7% management, 11.2% professional, 8.8% services, 16.7% sales, 5.6% farming, 13.0% construction, 20.0% production (2000).
Income: Per capita income: $14,870 (2000); Median household income: $26,382 (2000); Poverty rate: 12.2% (2000).
Education: High school graduation rate: 73.2% (2000); College graduation rate: 9.5% (2000).
Housing: Homeownership rate: 81.1% (2000); Median home value: $95,000 (2000); Median rent: $425 per month (2000); Median age of housing: 26 years (2000).
Transportation: Commute to work: 72.4% car, 0.0% public transportation, 6.2% walk, 19.5% work from home (2000); Travel time to work: 24.3% less than 15 minutes, 27.2% 15 to 30 minutes, 24.9% 30 to 45 minutes, 14.8% 45 to 60 minutes, 8.9% 60 minutes or more (2000)

SQUIRES (unincorporated postal area, zip code 65755). Covers a land area of 39.520 square miles and a water area of 0 square miles. Located at 36.80° N. Lat.; 92.62° W. Long. Elevation is 380 feet.
Population: 467 (2000); Race: 98.6% White, 0.0% Black, 0.5% Asian, 0.0% American Indian and Alaska Native, 0.0% Hispanic of any race, 0.8% two or more races (2000); Density: 11.8 persons per square mile (2000); Age: 19.3% under 18, 20.2% over 64 (2000); Marriage status: 13.0% never married, 70.5% now married, 8.1% widowed, 8.4% divorced (2000); Foreign born: 0.0% (2000); Ancestry (includes multiple ancestries): 16.1% English, 13.1% German, 12.8% United States or American, 7.1% Irish, 5.7% Swedish (2000).
Economy: Employment by occupation: 20.8% management, 5.4% professional, 4.6% services, 30.0% sales, 6.2% farming, 6.2% construction, 26.9% production (2000).
Income: Per capita income: $14,922 (2000); Median household income: $28,125 (2000); Poverty rate: 17.2% (2000).
Education: High school graduation rate: 64.7% (2000); College graduation rate: 5.9% (2000).
Housing: Homeownership rate: 93.3% (2000); Median home value: $12,800 (2000); Median age of housing: 22 years (2000).
Transportation: Commute to work: 82.3% car, 0.0% public transportation, 0.0% walk, 13.8% work from home (2000); Travel time to work: 20.5% less than 15 minutes, 58.9% 15 to 30 minutes, 7.1% 30 to 45 minutes, 6.3% 45 to 60 minutes, 7.1% 60 minutes or more (2000)

VANZANT (unincorporated postal area, zip code 65768). Covers a land area of 44.827 square miles and a water area of 0 square miles. Located at 36.91° N. Lat.; 92.25° W. Long. Elevation is 1,170 feet.
Population: 383 (2000); Race: 98.5% White, 0.0% Black, 0.0% Asian, 0.5% American Indian and Alaska Native, 0.0% Hispanic of any race, 1.0% two or more races (2000); Density: 8.5 persons per square mile (2000); Age: 16.8% under 18, 14.9% over 64 (2000); Marriage status: 16.8% never married, 74.5% now married, 4.1% widowed, 4.7% divorced (2000); Foreign born: 0.0% (2000); Ancestry (includes multiple ancestries): 13.9% United States or American, 11.5% English, 11.0% German, 7.8% Irish, 7.6% Other groups (2000).
Economy: Employment by occupation: 15.7% management, 3.7% professional, 14.1% services, 22.5% sales, 10.5% farming, 11.5% construction, 22.0% production (2000).
Income: Per capita income: $16,338 (2000); Median household income: $32,083 (2000); Poverty rate: 14.4% (2000).
Education: High school graduation rate: 73.9% (2000); College graduation rate: 7.1% (2000).
Housing: Homeownership rate: 94.2% (2000); Median home value: $68,300 (2000); Median rent: $275 per month (2000); Median age of housing: 29 years (2000).
Transportation: Commute to work: 77.8% car, 0.0% public transportation, 3.2% walk, 16.9% work from home (2000); Travel time to work: 19.7% less than 15 minutes, 19.1% 15 to 30 minutes, 46.5% 30 to 45 minutes, 7.0% 45 to 60 minutes, 7.6% 60 minutes or more (2000)

Dunklin County

Located in southeastern Missouri; bounded on the west by the St. Francis River and the Missouri border, on the south by the Arkansas border, and on the east by the Mississippi River and the Tennessee border. Covers a land area of 545.60 square miles, a water area of 1.50 square miles, and is located in the Central Time Zone. The county government was organized in 1845. County seat is Kennett.

Weather Station: Kennett Radio KBOA — Elevation: 269 feet

	Jan	Feb	Mar	Apr	May	Jun	Jul	Aug	Sep	Oct	Nov	Dec
High	44	51	60	71	80	89	93	91	84	74	60	49
Low	25	30	39	48	57	65	69	67	59	47	38	30
Precip	3.3	3.7	4.9	5.1	5.3	4.1	3.6	2.8	3.5	4.1	4.7	4.6
Snow	3.9	3.1	0.6	tr	0.0	0.0	0.0	0.0	0.0	0.0	0.3	0.9

High and Low temperatures in degrees Fahrenheit; Precipitation and Snow in inches

Population: 33,155 (2000); Race: 88.7% White, 8.9% Black, 0.3% Asian, 0.3% American Indian and Alaska Native, 2.2% Hispanic of any race, 1.0% two or more races (2000); Density: 60.8 persons per square mile (2000); Age: 26.0% under 18, 16.6% over 64 (2000).
Religion: Five largest groups: 34.4% Southern Baptist Convention, 4.6% The United Methodist Church, 3.6% Churches of Christ, 3.1% Catholic Church, 2.9% Assemblies of God (2000).

Economy: Unemployment rate: 7.0% (11/2002); Total civilian labor force: 13,526 (11/2002); Leading industries: 23.3% health care and social assistance; 21.4% retail trade; 15.0% manufacturing (2000); Companies that employ more than 1,000 persons: 0 (2000); Companies that employ more than 100 persons: 11 (2000); Farms: 473 totaling 313,147 acres (1997); Minority business ownership rate: 4.6% (1997); Women business ownership rate: 22.0% (1997); Retail sales per capita: $7,811 (1997). Single-family building permits issued: 26 (2001) / 34 (2000); Multi-family building permits issued: 53 (2001) / 14 (2000).
Income: Per capita income: $13,561 (2000); Median household income: $24,878 (2000); Poverty rate: 24.5% (2000); Bankruptcy rate: 4.90% (2001).
Taxes: Total county taxes per capita: $42 (1997); County property taxes per capita: $41 (1997).
Education: High school graduation rate: 63.7% (2000); College graduation rate: 9.1% (2000).
Housing: Homeownership rate: 65.9% (2000); Median home value: $48,500 (2000); Median rent: $221 per month (2000); Median age of housing: 34 years (2000).
Health: Birth rate: 144.2 per 10,000 population (1998); Age adjusted death rate: 119.9 per 10,000 population (1999); Age adjusted cancer mortality rate: 232.9 deaths per 100,000 population (1999). Number of physicians: 9.7 per 10,000 population (1999); Number of hospital beds: 35.0 per 10,000 population (1999).
Elections: 2000 Presidential election results: 47.0% Gore, 51.6% Bush, 0.7% Nader, 0.4% Buchanan
National and State Parks: Ben Cash Memorial State Wildlife Area; Hornersville Swamp State Wildlife Area; Warbler Woods State Natural Area; Wilhelmina State Forest
Additional Information Contacts
Dunklin County Government Offices 573-888-2796
Kennett Chamber of Commerce.......................... 573-888-5828
Malden Chamber of Commerce.......................... 573-276-4519

Dunklin County Communities

ARBYRD (city). Covers a land area of 0.998 square miles and a water area of 0 square miles. Located at 36.05° N. Lat.; 90.23° W. Long. Elevation is 247 feet.
History: Arbyrd grew around the Arbyrd Compress, which processed cotton for shipping.
Population: 528 (2000); Race: 100.0% White, 0.0% Black, 0.0% Asian, 0.0% American Indian and Alaska Native, 1.0% Hispanic of any race, 0.0% two or more races (2000); Density: 528.8 persons per square mile (2000); Age: 24.2% under 18, 18.0% over 64 (2000); Marriage status: 13.9% never married, 58.9% now married, 11.8% widowed, 15.4% divorced (2000); Foreign born: 0.0% (2000); Ancestry (includes multiple ancestries): 22.1% United States or American, 18.2% Other groups, 16.7% Irish, 5.8% German, 5.8% English (2000).
Economy: Single-family building permits issued: 0 (2001) / 2 (2000); Multi-family building permits issued: 0 (2001) / 0 (2000); Employment by occupation: 8.0% management, 6.4% professional, 19.3% services, 18.2% sales, 4.3% farming, 13.4% construction, 30.5% production (2000).
Income: Per capita income: $12,504 (2000); Median household income: $25,438 (2000); Poverty rate: 23.8% (2000).
Taxes: Total city taxes per capita: $100 (1997); City property taxes per capita: $24 (1997).
Education: High school graduation rate: 58.8% (2000); College graduation rate: 5.0% (2000).
Housing: Homeownership rate: 72.2% (2000); Median home value: $29,700 (2000); Median rent: $223 per month (2000); Median age of housing: 46 years (2000).
Transportation: Commute to work: 91.4% car, 0.0% public transportation, 3.2% walk, 4.3% work from home (2000); Travel time to work: 27.9% less than 15 minutes, 36.9% 15 to 30 minutes, 23.5% 30 to 45 minutes, 5.6% 45 to 60 minutes, 6.1% 60 minutes or more (2000)

CAMPBELL (city). Covers a land area of 1.274 square miles and a water area of 0 square miles. Located at 36.49° N. Lat.; 90.07° W. Long. Elevation is 317 feet.
History: Incorporated 1900.
Population: 1,883 (2000); Race: 98.3% White, 0.0% Black, 0.0% Asian, 1.0% American Indian and Alaska Native, 1.7% Hispanic of any race, 0.0% two or more races (2000); Density: 1,477.9 persons per square mile (2000); Age: 23.9% under 18, 22.0% over 64 (2000); Marriage status: 14.9% never married, 53.7% now married, 13.1% widowed, 18.3% divorced (2000); Foreign born: 0.8% (2000); Ancestry (includes multiple ancestries): 27.1% United States or American, 13.5% Other groups, 10.8% Irish, 9.3% German, 3.5% Dutch (2000).
Economy: Cotton, rice, soybeans, peaches. Employment by occupation: 5.8% management, 12.5% professional, 10.2% services, 22.5% sales, 2.8% farming, 16.1% construction, 30.1% production (2000).
Income: Per capita income: $14,026 (2000); Median household income: $21,838 (2000); Poverty rate: 20.2% (2000).
Taxes: Total city taxes per capita: $80 (1997); City property taxes per capita: $18 (1997).
Education: High school graduation rate: 59.1% (2000); College graduation rate: 6.5% (2000).

School District(s)

Campbell R-II (KG-12)
2000 Enrollment: 684 573-246-2133
Housing: Homeownership rate: 60.7% (2000); Median home value: $33,600 (2000); Median rent: $199 per month (2000); Median age of housing: 37 years (2000).
Transportation: Commute to work: 92.9% car, 0.0% public transportation, 3.4% walk, 2.0% work from home (2000); Travel time to work: 35.2% less than 15 minutes, 36.1% 15 to 30 minutes, 15.6% 30 to 45 minutes, 6.3% 45 to 60 minutes, 6.8% 60 minutes or more (2000)

CARDWELL (city). Covers a land area of 0.633 square miles and a water area of 0 square miles. Located at 36.04° N. Lat.; 90.29° W. Long. Elevation is 249 feet.
History: Cardwell was platted in 1896 by the Burtig brothers from Arkansas, and named for a bank cashier, Frank Cardwell. The town grew around the railroad as a timbering center.
Population: 789 (2000); Race: 98.0% White, 0.0% Black, 0.5% Asian, 1.5% American Indian and Alaska Native, 1.1% Hispanic of any race, 0.0% two or more races (2000); Density: 1,246.1 persons per square mile (2000); Age: 25.1% under 18, 16.6% over 64 (2000); Marriage status: 16.1% never married, 54.1% now married, 12.6% widowed, 17.3% divorced (2000); Foreign born: 1.9% (2000); Ancestry (includes multiple ancestries): 33.2% United States or American, 12.8% Other groups, 10.8% Irish, 7.4% German, 3.7% English (2000).
Economy: Single-family building permits issued: 0 (2001) / 1 (2000); Multi-family building permits issued: 0 (2001) / 0 (2000); Employment by occupation: 10.7% management, 8.8% professional, 22.8% services, 14.3% sales, 3.3% farming, 9.2% construction, 30.9% production (2000).
Income: Per capita income: $12,207 (2000); Median household income: $21,042 (2000); Poverty rate: 27.0% (2000).
Taxes: Total city taxes per capita: $135 (1997); City property taxes per capita: $33 (1997).
Education: High school graduation rate: 53.9% (2000); College graduation rate: 7.0% (2000).

School District(s)

Southland C-9 (PK-12)
2000 Enrollment: 379 573-654-3574
Housing: Homeownership rate: 69.1% (2000); Median home value: $30,400 (2000); Median rent: $199 per month (2000); Median age of housing: 40 years (2000).
Transportation: Commute to work: 89.0% car, 0.0% public transportation, 3.3% walk, 4.4% work from home (2000); Travel time to work: 31.2% less than 15 minutes, 46.9% 15 to 30 minutes, 13.1% 30 to 45 minutes, 3.8% 45 to 60 minutes, 5.0% 60 minutes or more (2000)

CLARKTON (city). Covers a land area of 1.125 square miles and a water area of 0 square miles. Located at 36.45° N. Lat.; 89.96° W. Long. Elevation is 282 feet.
History: Clarkton was platted in 1860 and named for Henry E. Clark, one of the contractors of the plank road between Weaverville and Clarkton.
Population: 1,330 (2000); Race: 90.8% White, 5.9% Black, 0.0% Asian, 0.2% American Indian and Alaska Native, 3.9% Hispanic of any race, 1.4% two or more races (2000); Density: 1,182.1 persons per square mile (2000); Age: 31.6% under 18, 13.4% over 64 (2000); Marriage status: 21.4% never married, 54.1% now married, 13.5% widowed, 11.0% divorced (2000); Foreign born: 2.5% (2000); Ancestry (includes multiple ancestries): 24.3% United States or American, 16.0% Other groups, 7.4% Irish, 2.6% German, 2.6% English (2000).
Economy: Single-family building permits issued: 0 (2001) / 0 (2000); Multi-family building permits issued: 0 (2001) / 0 (2000); Employment by occupation: 6.8% management, 6.8% professional, 19.2% services, 15.6% sales, 2.9% farming, 12.2% construction, 36.6% production (2000).

Income: Per capita income: $9,292 (2000); Median household income: $16,250 (2000); Poverty rate: 40.0% (2000).
Taxes: Total city taxes per capita: $92 (1997); City property taxes per capita: $22 (1997).
Education: High school graduation rate: 49.0% (2000); College graduation rate: 3.9% (2000).

School District(s)

Clarkton C-4 (PK-12)
2000 Enrollment: 359 573-448-3712
Housing: Homeownership rate: 57.0% (2000); Median home value: $28,000 (2000); Median rent: $179 per month (2000); Median age of housing: 28 years (2000).
Transportation: Commute to work: 91.8% car, 0.0% public transportation, 3.4% walk, 2.5% work from home (2000); Travel time to work: 24.8% less than 15 minutes, 39.3% 15 to 30 minutes, 18.2% 30 to 45 minutes, 7.9% 45 to 60 minutes, 9.8% 60 minutes or more (2000)

HOLCOMB (city). Covers a land area of 0.610 square miles and a water area of 0 square miles. Located at 36.40° N. Lat.; 90.02° W. Long. Elevation is 239 feet.
History: Holcomb was platted about 1870 and named for Louis Holcomb, an early settler. The town grew as a shipping center for cotton, melons, and strawberries.
Population: 696 (2000); Race: 98.2% White, 0.0% Black, 0.0% Asian, 0.0% American Indian and Alaska Native, 0.7% Hispanic of any race, 1.1% two or more races (2000); Density: 1,140.1 persons per square mile (2000); Age: 29.7% under 18, 15.9% over 64 (2000); Marriage status: 17.6% never married, 61.2% now married, 6.8% widowed, 14.3% divorced (2000); Foreign born: 0.1% (2000); Ancestry (includes multiple ancestries): 22.4% United States or American, 9.9% Other groups, 8.9% Irish, 4.2% Dutch, 3.2% German (2000).
Economy: Employment by occupation: 6.8% management, 7.9% professional, 15.8% services, 21.1% sales, 3.8% farming, 11.3% construction, 33.5% production (2000).
Income: Per capita income: $11,699 (2000); Median household income: $25,163 (2000); Poverty rate: 20.1% (2000).
Taxes: Total city taxes per capita: $139 (1997); City property taxes per capita: $33 (1997).
Education: High school graduation rate: 57.5% (2000); College graduation rate: 3.3% (2000).

School District(s)

Holcomb R-III (PK-12)
2000 Enrollment: 532 573-792-3631
Housing: Homeownership rate: 71.3% (2000); Median home value: $38,600 (2000); Median rent: $180 per month (2000); Median age of housing: 33 years (2000).
Transportation: Commute to work: 87.0% car, 0.0% public transportation, 3.8% walk, 5.0% work from home (2000); Travel time to work: 20.9% less than 15 minutes, 57.8% 15 to 30 minutes, 6.0% 30 to 45 minutes, 6.4% 45 to 60 minutes, 8.8% 60 minutes or more (2000)

HORNERSVILLE (city). Covers a land area of 0.792 square miles and a water area of 0 square miles. Located at 36.04° N. Lat.; 90.11° W. Long. Elevation is 248 feet.
Population: 686 (2000); Race: 97.5% White, 0.0% Black, 0.0% Asian, 0.4% American Indian and Alaska Native, 4.2% Hispanic of any race, 0.9% two or more races (2000); Density: 865.8 persons per square mile (2000); Age: 30.6% under 18, 15.2% over 64 (2000); Marriage status: 21.5% never married, 54.6% now married, 11.3% widowed, 12.5% divorced (2000); Foreign born: 2.3% (2000); Ancestry (includes multiple ancestries): 32.0% United States or American, 18.6% Other groups, 7.2% Irish, 3.3% German, 3.2% English (2000).
Economy: Soybeans, cotton, corn. Manufacturing: barbecue sauce. Employment by occupation: 6.1% management, 7.3% professional, 16.6% services, 18.2% sales, 3.2% farming, 15.8% construction, 32.8% production (2000).
Income: Per capita income: $11,589 (2000); Median household income: $22,000 (2000); Poverty rate: 28.9% (2000).
Taxes: Total city taxes per capita: $121 (1997); City property taxes per capita: $42 (1997).
Education: High school graduation rate: 57.3% (2000); College graduation rate: 6.8% (2000).
Housing: Homeownership rate: 65.6% (2000); Median home value: $35,500 (2000); Median rent: $147 per month (2000); Median age of housing: 43 years (2000).
Transportation: Commute to work: 91.7% car, 0.0% public transportation, 4.6% walk, 1.7% work from home (2000); Travel time to work: 35.4% less than 15 minutes, 29.1% 15 to 30 minutes, 21.9% 30 to 45 minutes, 8.9% 45 to 60 minutes, 4.6% 60 minutes or more (2000)

KENNETT (city). Covers a land area of 6.657 square miles and a water area of 0 square miles. Located at 36.23° N. Lat.; 90.05° W. Long. Elevation is 267 feet.
History: Kennett was established on the site of the village of Chief Chilletecaux, who sold his pole house to Howard Moore. Moore built a grist mill here, and when the town was platted in 1846 it was named for him. In 1849, however, the name was changed to Butler and, a few years later, to Kennett, in honor of Dr. Luther M. Kennett, mayor of St. Louis from 1849 to 1852. Kennett developed as a cotton town.
Population: 11,260 (2000); Race: 84.2% White, 13.4% Black, 0.5% Asian, 0.2% American Indian and Alaska Native, 0.9% Hispanic of any race, 1.7% two or more races (2000); Density: 1,691.4 persons per square mile (2000); Age: 26.9% under 18, 16.1% over 64 (2000); Marriage status: 19.6% never married, 57.3% now married, 11.4% widowed, 11.8% divorced (2000); Foreign born: 0.9% (2000); Ancestry (includes multiple ancestries): 22.9% United States or American, 21.4% Other groups, 11.3% Irish, 7.0% German, 6.2% English (2000).
Vital Statistics: Birth rate: 153.6 per 10,000 population (1998)
Economy: Single-family building permits issued: 20 (2001) / 23 (2000); Multi-family building permits issued: 49 (2001) / 14 (2000); Employment by occupation: 7.5% management, 17.5% professional, 14.7% services, 25.3% sales, 0.5% farming, 8.8% construction, 25.6% production (2000).
Income: Per capita income: $14,397 (2000); Median household income: $26,088 (2000); Poverty rate: 26.1% (2000).
Taxes: Total city taxes per capita: $171 (2000); City property taxes per capita: $37 (2000).
Education: High school graduation rate: 65.9% (2000); College graduation rate: 11.9% (2000).

School District(s)

Kennett 39 (PK-12)
2000 Enrollment: 2,174 573-717-1100
Housing: Homeownership rate: 59.7% (2000); Median home value: $63,300 (2000); Median rent: $255 per month (2000); Median age of housing: 36 years (2000).
Hospitals: Twin Rivers Regional Medical Center (116 beds)
Safety: Violent crime rate: 34.4 per 10,000 population; Property crime rate: 339.0 per 10,000 population (2001).
Newspapers: The Daily Dunklin Democrat (5 x week)
Transportation: Commute to work: 93.1% car, 1.4% public transportation, 1.9% walk, 2.1% work from home (2000); Travel time to work: 67.9% less than 15 minutes, 12.1% 15 to 30 minutes, 8.7% 30 to 45 minutes, 8.0% 45 to 60 minutes, 3.4% 60 minutes or more (2000)
Additional Information Contacts
Kennett Chamber of Commerce 573-888-5828

MALDEN (city). Covers a land area of 6.207 square miles and a water area of 0 square miles. Located at 36.57° N. Lat.; 89.97° W. Long. Elevation is 289 feet.
History: Howard Moore built a house here in 1829, but it was 1877 when the town of Malden was platted under the direction of Major George B. Clark, construction engineer for the Little River Valley & Arkansas Railroad. The town was named for Malden, Massachusetts. Malden's location on the railroad made it a major cotton shipping center.
Population: 4,782 (2000); Race: 75.2% White, 23.4% Black, 0.0% Asian, 0.3% American Indian and Alaska Native, 0.5% Hispanic of any race, 1.1% two or more races (2000); Density: 770.4 persons per square mile (2000); Age: 26.7% under 18, 17.6% over 64 (2000); Marriage status: 23.9% never married, 53.9% now married, 11.9% widowed, 10.3% divorced (2000); Foreign born: 0.4% (2000); Ancestry (includes multiple ancestries): 25.2% Other groups, 16.4% United States or American, 7.9% Irish, 7.6% English, 6.8% German (2000).
Economy: Single-family building permits issued: 6 (2001) / 8 (2000); Multi-family building permits issued: 4 (2001) / 0 (2000); Employment by occupation: 9.8% management, 11.6% professional, 17.1% services, 21.9% sales, 2.4% farming, 12.0% construction, 25.1% production (2000).
Income: Per capita income: $12,475 (2000); Median household income: $22,910 (2000); Poverty rate: 27.8% (2000).
Taxes: Total city taxes per capita: $292 (2000); City property taxes per capita: $36 (2000).
Education: High school graduation rate: 61.6% (2000); College graduation rate: 8.3% (2000).

School District(s)

Malden R-I (PK-12)
2000 Enrollment: 1,235 573-276-5794

Housing: Homeownership rate: 59.0% (2000); Median home value: $43,600 (2000); Median rent: $214 per month (2000); Median age of housing: 35 years (2000).
Safety: Violent crime rate: 66.5 per 10,000 population; Property crime rate: 397.0 per 10,000 population (2001).
Newspapers: Delta News Citizen (1 x week)
Transportation: Commute to work: 93.6% car, 0.0% public transportation, 3.3% walk, 1.9% work from home (2000); Travel time to work: 59.6% less than 15 minutes, 16.1% 15 to 30 minutes, 17.3% 30 to 45 minutes, 4.3% 45 to 60 minutes, 2.7% 60 minutes or more (2000)
Additional Information Contacts
Malden Chamber of Commerce 573-276-4519

RIVES (town). Covers a land area of 0.396 square miles and a water area of 0 square miles. Located at 36.09° N. Lat.; 90.01° W. Long. Elevation is 244 feet.
Population: 88 (2000); Race: 100.0% White, 0.0% Black, 0.0% Asian, 0.0% American Indian and Alaska Native, 0.0% Hispanic of any race, 0.0% two or more races (2000); Density: 222.1 persons per square mile (2000); Age: 21.3% under 18, 20.0% over 64 (2000); Marriage status: 16.9% never married, 69.2% now married, 7.7% widowed, 6.2% divorced (2000); Foreign born: 0.0% (2000); Ancestry (includes multiple ancestries): 26.7% United States or American, 9.3% German, 9.3% Other groups, 8.0% English, 2.7% Irish (2000).
Economy: Employment by occupation: 0.0% management, 0.0% professional, 27.3% services, 6.1% sales, 0.0% farming, 15.2% construction, 51.5% production (2000).
Income: Per capita income: $12,111 (2000); Median household income: $28,125 (2000); Poverty rate: 18.7% (2000).
Education: High school graduation rate: 45.1% (2000); College graduation rate: 0.0% (2000).
Housing: Homeownership rate: 76.5% (2000); Median home value: $24,000 (2000); Median rent: $275 per month (2000); Median age of housing: 33 years (2000).
Transportation: Commute to work: 100.0% car, 0.0% public transportation, 0.0% walk, 0.0% work from home (2000); Travel time to work: 3.0% less than 15 minutes, 33.3% 15 to 30 minutes, 63.6% 30 to 45 minutes, 0.0% 45 to 60 minutes, 0.0% 60 minutes or more (2000)

SENATH (city). Covers a land area of 1.907 square miles and a water area of 0.017 square miles. Located at 36.13° N. Lat.; 90.16° W. Long. Elevation is 256 feet.
History: Senath was established by its first postmaster, A.W. Douglass, in 1882, and named for his wife, Senath Hale Douglass. The community developed around the cotton industry.
Population: 1,650 (2000); Race: 90.3% White, 0.4% Black, 0.1% Asian, 0.4% American Indian and Alaska Native, 13.2% Hispanic of any race, 0.2% two or more races (2000); Density: 865.3 persons per square mile (2000); Age: 25.7% under 18, 23.9% over 64 (2000); Marriage status: 20.5% never married, 51.2% now married, 16.0% widowed, 12.2% divorced (2000); Foreign born: 8.7% (2000); Ancestry (includes multiple ancestries): 28.4% United States or American, 23.8% Other groups, 9.5% Irish, 5.3% German, 3.9% English (2000).
Economy: Employment by occupation: 4.0% management, 11.9% professional, 18.8% services, 19.1% sales, 7.2% farming, 7.8% construction, 31.3% production (2000).
Income: Per capita income: $11,434 (2000); Median household income: $20,938 (2000); Poverty rate: 29.5% (2000).
Taxes: Total city taxes per capita: $117 (1997); City property taxes per capita: $26 (1997).
Education: High school graduation rate: 51.7% (2000); College graduation rate: 8.3% (2000).

School District(s)

Senath-Hornersville C-8 (PK-12)
2000 Enrollment: 882 573-738-2669

Housing: Homeownership rate: 65.7% (2000); Median home value: $42,400 (2000); Median rent: $199 per month (2000); Median age of housing: 33 years (2000).
Transportation: Commute to work: 97.1% car, 0.0% public transportation, 1.0% walk, 1.0% work from home (2000); Travel time to work: 35.1% less than 15 minutes, 33.0% 15 to 30 minutes, 16.1% 30 to 45 minutes, 9.3% 45 to 60 minutes, 6.4% 60 minutes or more (2000)

Franklin County

Located in east central Missouri, in the Ozarks; bounded on the north by the Missouri River; drained by the Meramec River. Covers a land area of 922.80 square miles, a water area of 7.80 square miles, and is located in the Central Time Zone. The county government was organized in 1818. County seat is Union.

Franklin County is part of the St. Louis, MO-IL MSA. The entire metro area includes: Clinton County, IL; Jersey County, IL; Madison County, IL; Monroe County, IL; St. Clair County, IL; Crawford County, MO (pt.)**; Franklin County, MO; Jefferson County, MO; Lincoln County, MO; St. Charles County, MO; St. Louis County, MO; Warren County, MO; St. Louis city, MO

Weather Station: Union Elevation: 538 feet

	Jan	Feb	Mar	Apr	May	Jun	Jul	Aug	Sep	Oct	Nov	Dec
High	41	48	58	70	78	86	91	89	82	71	57	45
Low	20	24	34	43	52	61	66	64	56	44	34	25
Precip	2.2	2.3	3.8	4.2	4.2	4.1	3.7	3.7	3.9	3.3	4.1	3.1
Snow	5.7	4.4	2.7	0.6	0.0	0.0	0.0	0.0	0.0	tr	1.4	3.6

High and Low temperatures in degrees Fahrenheit; Precipitation and Snow in inches

Population: 93,807 (2000); Race: 97.2% White, 0.9% Black, 0.3% Asian, 0.3% American Indian and Alaska Native, 0.6% Hispanic of any race, 1.0% two or more races (2000); Density: 101.7 persons per square mile (2000); Age: 27.4% under 18, 12.1% over 64 (2000).
Religion: Five largest groups: 25.6% Catholic Church, 12.0% Southern Baptist Convention, 4.2% United Church of Christ, 3.3% Lutheran Church—Missouri Synod, 2.5% Baptist Missionary Association of America (2000).
Economy: Unemployment rate: 4.8% (11/2002); Total civilian labor force: 48,266 (11/2002); Leading industries: 33.7% manufacturing; 15.6% retail trade; 9.9% health care and social assistance (2000); Companies that employ more than 1,000 persons: 0 (2000); Companies that employ more than 100 persons: 57 (2000); Farms: 1,592 totaling 289,608 acres (1997); Minority business ownership rate: 2.2% (1997); Women business ownership rate: 26.7% (1997); Retail sales per capita: $8,846 (1997). Single-family building permits issued: 519 (2001) / 533 (2000); Multi-family building permits issued: 116 (2001) / 46 (2000).
Income: Per capita income: $19,705 (2000); Median household income: $43,474 (2000); Poverty rate: 7.0% (2000); Bankruptcy rate: 5.41% (2001).
Taxes: Total county taxes per capita: $162 (2000); County property taxes per capita: $48 (2000).
Education: High school graduation rate: 77.7% (2000); College graduation rate: 12.8% (2000).
Housing: Homeownership rate: 78.0% (2000); Median home value: $96,400 (2000); Median rent: $375 per month (2000); Median age of housing: 25 years (2000).
Health: Birth rate: 135.5 per 10,000 population (1998); Age adjusted death rate: 98.2 per 10,000 population (1999); Age adjusted cancer mortality rate: 221.0 deaths per 100,000 population (1999). Number of physicians: 10.6 per 10,000 population (1999); Number of hospital beds: 4.9 per 10,000 population (1999).
Elections: 2000 Presidential election results: 41.3% Gore, 55.8% Bush, 1.7% Nader, 0.7% Buchanan
National and State Parks: Meramec State Park
Additional Information Contacts
Franklin County Government Offices 636-583-6355
Franklin County Board of Realtors 636-583-6008
Gerald Chamber of Commerce. 573-764-4627
New Haven Chamber of Commerce 573-237-3830
Pacific Chamber of Commerce 636-257-5156
St. Clair Chamber of Commerce 636-629-1889
Sullivan Area Chamber of Commerce 573-468-3314
Union Chamber of Commerce 636-583-8979
Washington Chamber of Commerce 636-239-2715

Franklin County Communities

BEAUFORT (unincorporated postal area, zip code 63013). Covers a land area of 42.764 square miles and a water area of 0.026 square miles. Located at 38.41° N. Lat.; 91.16° W. Long. Elevation is 882 feet.
Population: 1,636 (2000); Race: 99.4% White, 0.0% Black, 0.0% Asian, 0.0% American Indian and Alaska Native, 0.0% Hispanic of any race, 0.6% two or more races (2000); Density: 38.3 persons per square mile (2000); Age:

26.7% under 18, 9.3% over 64 (2000); Marriage status: 23.3% never married, 65.1% now married, 3.5% widowed, 8.1% divorced (2000); Foreign born: 0.0% (2000); Ancestry (includes multiple ancestries): 45.0% German, 16.8% United States or American, 9.0% Other groups, 6.2% Irish, 4.5% English (2000).
Economy: Employment by occupation: 9.7% management, 12.1% professional, 19.0% services, 15.0% sales, 1.7% farming, 11.4% construction, 31.1% production (2000).
Income: Per capita income: $17,120 (2000); Median household income: $45,077 (2000); Poverty rate: 3.3% (2000).
Education: High school graduation rate: 78.9% (2000); College graduation rate: 8.1% (2000).
Housing: Homeownership rate: 88.4% (2000); Median home value: $113,500 (2000); Median rent: $413 per month (2000); Median age of housing: 22 years (2000).
Transportation: Commute to work: 93.5% car, 0.5% public transportation, 0.0% walk, 6.0% work from home (2000); Travel time to work: 11.5% less than 15 minutes, 42.3% 15 to 30 minutes, 20.1% 30 to 45 minutes, 10.7% 45 to 60 minutes, 15.3% 60 minutes or more (2000)

BERGER (city). Covers a land area of 0.300 square miles and a water area of 0 square miles. Located at 38.67° N. Lat.; 91.33° W. Long. Elevation is 512 feet.
Population: 206 (2000); Race: 100.0% White, 0.0% Black, 0.0% Asian, 0.0% American Indian and Alaska Native, 0.0% Hispanic of any race, 0.0% two or more races (2000); Density: 686.7 persons per square mile (2000); Age: 25.0% under 18, 22.1% over 64 (2000); Marriage status: 24.2% never married, 50.3% now married, 15.2% widowed, 10.3% divorced (2000); Foreign born: 0.0% (2000); Ancestry (includes multiple ancestries): 64.4% German, 12.0% Irish, 11.1% English, 5.3% Other groups, 3.8% French (except Basque) (2000).
Economy: Dairying; corn, wheat, soybeans, grapes; cattle; light manufacturing; wineries. Employment by occupation: 7.1% management, 8.0% professional, 16.1% services, 13.4% sales, 2.7% farming, 9.8% construction, 42.9% production (2000).
Income: Per capita income: $18,460 (2000); Median household income: $32,083 (2000); Poverty rate: 5.8% (2000).
Taxes: Total city taxes per capita: $235 (1997); City property taxes per capita: $18 (1997).
Education: High school graduation rate: 66.9% (2000); College graduation rate: 7.2% (2000).
Housing: Homeownership rate: 80.9% (2000); Median home value: $47,600 (2000); Median rent: $369 per month (2000); Median age of housing: 60+ years (2000).
Transportation: Commute to work: 97.2% car, 0.0% public transportation, 0.0% walk, 2.8% work from home (2000); Travel time to work: 25.2% less than 15 minutes, 35.0% 15 to 30 minutes, 15.5% 30 to 45 minutes, 20.4% 45 to 60 minutes, 3.9% 60 minutes or more (2000)

CATAWISSA (unincorporated postal area, zip code 63015). Covers a land area of 20.505 square miles and a water area of 0.140 square miles. Located at 38.40° N. Lat.; 90.74° W. Long. Elevation is 530 feet.
Population: 2,201 (2000); Race: 100.0% White, 0.0% Black, 0.0% Asian, 0.0% American Indian and Alaska Native, 0.3% Hispanic of any race, 0.0% two or more races (2000); Density: 107.3 persons per square mile (2000); Age: 31.2% under 18, 10.0% over 64 (2000); Marriage status: 23.2% never married, 62.0% now married, 4.7% widowed, 10.1% divorced (2000); Foreign born: 0.0% (2000); Ancestry (includes multiple ancestries): 23.7% German, 12.0% United States or American, 9.8% Irish, 6.9% French (except Basque), 6.9% English (2000).
Economy: Employment by occupation: 6.4% management, 10.0% professional, 11.1% services, 23.6% sales, 1.2% farming, 23.5% construction, 24.2% production (2000).
Income: Per capita income: $18,285 (2000); Median household income: $46,979 (2000); Poverty rate: 10.5% (2000).
Education: High school graduation rate: 65.9% (2000); College graduation rate: 3.1% (2000).
Housing: Homeownership rate: 88.0% (2000); Median home value: $100,300 (2000); Median rent: $346 per month (2000); Median age of housing: 23 years (2000).
Transportation: Commute to work: 94.1% car, 0.0% public transportation, 0.5% walk, 3.2% work from home (2000); Travel time to work: 9.9% less than 15 minutes, 31.9% 15 to 30 minutes, 13.5% 30 to 45 minutes, 29.2% 45 to 60 minutes, 15.5% 60 minutes or more (2000)

GERALD (city). Covers a land area of 1.402 square miles and a water area of 0.009 square miles. Located at 38.40° N. Lat.; 91.33° W. Long. Elevation is 895 feet.
Population: 1,171 (2000); Race: 96.8% White, 0.0% Black, 1.5% Asian, 0.2% American Indian and Alaska Native, 1.2% Hispanic of any race, 0.7% two or more races (2000); Density: 835.0 persons per square mile (2000); Age: 27.1% under 18, 17.2% over 64 (2000); Marriage status: 22.3% never married, 59.9% now married, 6.2% widowed, 11.7% divorced (2000); Foreign born: 1.3% (2000); Ancestry (includes multiple ancestries): 35.4% German, 15.8% Irish, 11.4% Other groups, 5.9% English, 5.5% United States or American (2000).
Economy: Grain products, livestock. Manufacturing: fabricated metal products, paint, apparel. Single-family building permits issued: 10 (2001) / 4 (2000); Multi-family building permits issued: 4 (2001) / 0 (2000); Employment by occupation: 4.3% management, 11.6% professional, 15.4% services, 19.9% sales, 0.0% farming, 13.0% construction, 35.7% production (2000).
Income: Per capita income: $14,095 (2000); Median household income: $29,095 (2000); Poverty rate: 10.6% (2000).
Taxes: Total city taxes per capita: $183 (1997); City property taxes per capita: $29 (1997).
Education: High school graduation rate: 65.2% (2000); College graduation rate: 5.3% (2000).
Housing: Homeownership rate: 73.5% (2000); Median home value: $73,900 (2000); Median rent: $287 per month (2000); Median age of housing: 29 years (2000).
Transportation: Commute to work: 93.1% car, 0.7% public transportation, 4.5% walk, 1.1% work from home (2000); Travel time to work: 34.2% less than 15 minutes, 25.3% 15 to 30 minutes, 21.9% 30 to 45 minutes, 5.1% 45 to 60 minutes, 13.4% 60 minutes or more (2000)
Additional Information Contacts
Gerald Chamber of Commerce. 573-764-4627

GRAY SUMMIT (CDP). Covers a land area of 7.435 square miles and a water area of 0.019 square miles. Located at 38.49° N. Lat.; 90.81° W. Long. Elevation is 750 feet.
History: Gray Summit developed around the junction of the Missouri Pacific Railroad with the Wagon Road and the State Road to Jefferson City. It was named for Daniel Gray, who settled here in 1845, with the "Summit" added because it was one of the highest points on the railroad route.
Population: 2,640 (2000); Race: 98.4% White, 0.1% Black, 0.2% Asian, 0.0% American Indian and Alaska Native, 0.0% Hispanic of any race, 0.6% two or more races (2000); Density: 355.1 persons per square mile (2000); Age: 28.8% under 18, 8.8% over 64 (2000); Marriage status: 22.6% never married, 64.4% now married, 2.3% widowed, 10.7% divorced (2000); Foreign born: 0.5% (2000); Ancestry (includes multiple ancestries): 30.4% German, 20.1% Irish, 12.6% English, 11.6% Other groups, 8.1% United States or American (2000).
Economy: Employment by occupation: 6.7% management, 14.3% professional, 15.6% services, 23.7% sales, 0.0% farming, 20.3% construction, 19.5% production (2000).
Income: Per capita income: $17,503 (2000); Median household income: $46,648 (2000); Poverty rate: 5.1% (2000).
Education: High school graduation rate: 77.9% (2000); College graduation rate: 4.4% (2000).
Housing: Homeownership rate: 83.4% (2000); Median home value: $95,300 (2000); Median rent: $352 per month (2000); Median age of housing: 23 years (2000).
Transportation: Commute to work: 98.3% car, 0.0% public transportation, 0.0% walk, 1.4% work from home (2000); Travel time to work: 19.7% less than 15 minutes, 33.0% 15 to 30 minutes, 20.5% 30 to 45 minutes, 16.5% 45 to 60 minutes, 10.3% 60 minutes or more (2000)

LABADIE (unincorporated postal area, zip code 63055). Covers a land area of 30.550 square miles and a water area of 0.211 square miles. Located at 38.53° N. Lat.; 90.84° W. Long. Elevation is 526 feet.
Population: 1,767 (2000); Race: 99.5% White, 0.0% Black, 0.0% Asian, 0.0% American Indian and Alaska Native, 0.6% Hispanic of any race, 0.5% two or more races (2000); Density: 57.8 persons per square mile (2000); Age: 25.7% under 18, 8.4% over 64 (2000); Marriage status: 17.0% never married, 74.8% now married, 2.0% widowed, 6.1% divorced (2000); Foreign born: 1.4% (2000); Ancestry (includes multiple ancestries): 47.2% German, 15.7% Irish, 8.2% English, 7.5% French (except Basque), 5.6% Italian (2000).

Economy: Employment by occupation: 13.6% management, 28.7% professional, 11.7% services, 25.0% sales, 0.0% farming, 14.1% construction, 7.0% production (2000).
Income: Per capita income: $28,639 (2000); Median household income: $62,083 (2000); Poverty rate: 4.0% (2000).
Education: High school graduation rate: 85.7% (2000); College graduation rate: 25.9% (2000).
Housing: Homeownership rate: 88.6% (2000); Median home value: $152,000 (2000); Median rent: $573 per month (2000); Median age of housing: 25 years (2000).
Transportation: Commute to work: 91.8% car, 1.2% public transportation, 0.8% walk, 6.1% work from home (2000); Travel time to work: 21.9% less than 15 minutes, 23.2% 15 to 30 minutes, 24.5% 30 to 45 minutes, 16.2% 45 to 60 minutes, 14.1% 60 minutes or more (2000)

LESLIE (village). Covers a land area of 0.162 square miles and a water area of 0 square miles. Located at 38.41° N. Lat.; 91.23° W. Long. Elevation is 825 feet.
Population: 87 (2000); Race: 100.0% White, 0.0% Black, 0.0% Asian, 0.0% American Indian and Alaska Native, 0.0% Hispanic of any race, 0.0% two or more races (2000); Density: 535.5 persons per square mile (2000); Age: 34.0% under 18, 9.6% over 64 (2000); Marriage status: 15.6% never married, 46.9% now married, 14.1% widowed, 23.4% divorced (2000); Foreign born: 0.0% (2000); Ancestry (includes multiple ancestries): 57.4% German, 23.4% Irish, 11.7% United States or American, 3.2% Scottish, 2.1% English (2000).
Economy: Hay, cattle. Employment by occupation: 12.8% management, 5.1% professional, 7.7% services, 15.4% sales, 0.0% farming, 17.9% construction, 41.0% production (2000).
Income: Per capita income: $13,140 (2000); Median household income: $29,250 (2000); Poverty rate: 12.4% (2000).
Taxes: Total city taxes per capita: $45 (1997); City property taxes per capita: $19 (1997).
Education: High school graduation rate: 84.0% (2000); College graduation rate: 6.0% (2000).
Housing: Homeownership rate: 56.4% (2000); Median home value: $53,800 (2000); Median rent: $360 per month (2000); Median age of housing: 38 years (2000).
Transportation: Commute to work: 100.0% car, 0.0% public transportation, 0.0% walk, 0.0% work from home (2000); Travel time to work: 10.3% less than 15 minutes, 43.6% 15 to 30 minutes, 20.5% 30 to 45 minutes, 10.3% 45 to 60 minutes, 15.4% 60 minutes or more (2000)

LONEDELL (unincorporated postal area, zip code 63060). Covers a land area of 49.172 square miles and a water area of 0.101 square miles. Located at 38.24° N. Lat.; 90.85° W. Long. Elevation is 575 feet.
Population: 2,467 (2000); Race: 95.1% White, 2.7% Black, 0.1% Asian, 0.0% American Indian and Alaska Native, 0.4% Hispanic of any race, 2.2% two or more races (2000); Density: 50.2 persons per square mile (2000); Age: 28.7% under 18, 8.6% over 64 (2000); Marriage status: 20.1% never married, 69.4% now married, 1.8% widowed, 8.7% divorced (2000); Foreign born: 0.0% (2000); Ancestry (includes multiple ancestries): 27.7% German, 13.2% Irish, 9.5% United States or American, 8.1% Other groups, 7.4% English (2000).
Economy: Employment by occupation: 7.5% management, 12.7% professional, 18.2% services, 16.2% sales, 0.7% farming, 23.1% construction, 21.6% production (2000).
Income: Per capita income: $17,940 (2000); Median household income: $46,800 (2000); Poverty rate: 6.5% (2000).
Education: High school graduation rate: 74.6% (2000); College graduation rate: 8.4% (2000).

School District(s)

Lonedell R-XIV (KG-08)
2000 Enrollment: 484 636-629-0401

Housing: Homeownership rate: 86.9% (2000); Median home value: $72,700 (2000); Median rent: $348 per month (2000); Median age of housing: 24 years (2000).
Transportation: Commute to work: 94.8% car, 0.4% public transportation, 0.8% walk, 3.9% work from home (2000); Travel time to work: 4.7% less than 15 minutes, 19.2% 15 to 30 minutes, 21.8% 30 to 45 minutes, 20.0% 45 to 60 minutes, 34.3% 60 minutes or more (2000)

LUEBBERING (unincorporated postal area, zip code 63061). Covers a land area of 5.252 square miles and a water area of 0.023 square miles. Located at 38.25° N. Lat.; 90.80° W. Long. Elevation is 759 feet.
Population: 259 (2000); Race: 100.0% White, 0.0% Black, 0.0% Asian, 0.0% American Indian and Alaska Native, 0.0% Hispanic of any race, 0.0% two or more races (2000); Density: 49.3 persons per square mile (2000); Age: 20.6% under 18, 7.3% over 64 (2000); Marriage status: 24.5% never married, 60.1% now married, 6.9% widowed, 8.5% divorced (2000); Foreign born: 0.9% (2000); Ancestry (includes multiple ancestries): 30.3% German, 15.1% United States or American, 12.4% Irish, 11.0% English, 7.8% Other groups (2000).
Economy: Employment by occupation: 12.4% management, 8.6% professional, 18.1% services, 14.3% sales, 0.0% farming, 18.1% construction, 28.6% production (2000).
Income: Per capita income: $20,363 (2000); Median household income: $41,786 (2000); Poverty rate: 4.8% (2000).
Education: High school graduation rate: 66.4% (2000); College graduation rate: 3.4% (2000).
Housing: Homeownership rate: 90.8% (2000); Median home value: $108,900 (2000); Median rent: $275 per month (2000); Median age of housing: 19 years (2000).
Transportation: Commute to work: 95.1% car, 1.9% public transportation, 1.0% walk, 1.9% work from home (2000); Travel time to work: 5.0% less than 15 minutes, 5.9% 15 to 30 minutes, 41.6% 30 to 45 minutes, 19.8% 45 to 60 minutes, 27.7% 60 minutes or more (2000)

MIRAMIGUOA PARK (village). Covers a land area of 0.385 square miles and a water area of 0 square miles. Located at 38.23° N. Lat.; 91.06° W. Long. Elevation is 630 feet.
Population: 127 (2000); Race: 98.6% White, 0.0% Black, 0.0% Asian, 0.0% American Indian and Alaska Native, 0.0% Hispanic of any race, 1.4% two or more races (2000); Density: 329.8 persons per square mile (2000); Age: 32.4% under 18, 8.5% over 64 (2000); Marriage status: 25.5% never married, 43.6% now married, 7.3% widowed, 23.6% divorced (2000); Foreign born: 0.0% (2000); Ancestry (includes multiple ancestries): 19.7% Irish, 19.7% United States or American, 16.2% German, 13.4% French (except Basque), 12.0% Other groups (2000).
Economy: Employment by occupation: 5.0% management, 10.0% professional, 16.7% services, 20.0% sales, 1.7% farming, 15.0% construction, 31.7% production (2000).
Income: Per capita income: $12,141 (2000); Median household income: $28,750 (2000); Poverty rate: 21.4% (2000).
Education: High school graduation rate: 65.2% (2000); College graduation rate: 4.5% (2000).
Housing: Homeownership rate: 96.2% (2000); Median home value: $46,500 (2000); Median age of housing: 31 years (2000).
Transportation: Commute to work: 90.0% car, 0.0% public transportation, 0.0% walk, 10.0% work from home (2000); Travel time to work: 14.8% less than 15 minutes, 20.4% 15 to 30 minutes, 0.0% 30 to 45 minutes, 13.0% 45 to 60 minutes, 51.9% 60 minutes or more (2000)

NEW HAVEN (city). Covers a land area of 2.854 square miles and a water area of 0.151 square miles. Located at 38.60° N. Lat.; 91.21° W. Long. Elevation is 660 feet.
History: Laid out 1856. Settled by German immigrants, 1840s.
Population: 1,867 (2000); Race: 98.6% White, 0.4% Black, 0.1% Asian, 0.1% American Indian and Alaska Native, 0.5% Hispanic of any race, 0.8% two or more races (2000); Density: 654.2 persons per square mile (2000); Age: 28.2% under 18, 17.0% over 64 (2000); Marriage status: 20.0% never married, 57.8% now married, 12.1% widowed, 10.0% divorced (2000); Foreign born: 0.4% (2000); Ancestry (includes multiple ancestries): 48.6% German, 11.5% Irish, 7.8% Other groups, 6.7% English, 5.7% United States or American (2000).
Economy: Corn, soybeans; dairying; cattle. Manufacturing: grain products, apparel, fabricated metal, sporting equipment. Single-family building permits issued: 8 (2001) / 12 (2000); Multi-family building permits issued: 0 (2001) / 0 (2000); Employment by occupation: 8.8% management, 12.1% professional, 16.9% services, 19.8% sales, 0.2% farming, 10.8% construction, 31.4% production (2000).
Income: Per capita income: $16,503 (2000); Median household income: $36,681 (2000); Poverty rate: 4.7% (2000).
Taxes: Total city taxes per capita: $264 (1997); City property taxes per capita: $111 (1997).
Education: High school graduation rate: 74.4% (2000); College graduation rate: 8.9% (2000).

School District(s)

Franklin Co. R-II (KG-08)
2000 Enrollment: 189 573-237-2414
New Haven (KG-12)
2000 Enrollment: 485 573-237-3231

Housing: Homeownership rate: 71.8% (2000); Median home value: $78,300 (2000); Median rent: $355 per month (2000); Median age of housing: 34 years (2000).
Newspapers: New Haven Leader (1 x week)
Transportation: Commute to work: 95.0% car, 0.5% public transportation, 0.7% walk, 3.0% work from home (2000); Travel time to work: 39.9% less than 15 minutes, 31.7% 15 to 30 minutes, 12.3% 30 to 45 minutes, 4.7% 45 to 60 minutes, 11.4% 60 minutes or more (2000)
Additional Information Contacts
New Haven Chamber of Commerce 573-237-3830

OAK GROVE (village). Covers a land area of 0.525 square miles and a water area of 0 square miles. Located at 38.22° N. Lat.; 91.15° W. Long. Elevation is 958 feet.
Population: 382 (2000); Race: 98.1% White, 0.0% Black, 0.0% Asian, 0.6% American Indian and Alaska Native, 0.6% Hispanic of any race, 0.6% two or more races (2000); Density: 727.5 persons per square mile (2000); Age: 21.2% under 18, 17.6% over 64 (2000); Marriage status: 19.0% never married, 54.7% now married, 10.5% widowed, 15.9% divorced (2000); Foreign born: 0.0% (2000); Ancestry (includes multiple ancestries): 23.4% United States or American, 16.0% German, 11.2% Other groups, 9.6% Irish, 9.0% French (except Basque) (2000).
Economy: Employment by occupation: 5.7% management, 9.3% professional, 11.4% services, 25.0% sales, 0.0% farming, 20.0% construction, 28.6% production (2000).
Income: Per capita income: $15,390 (2000); Median household income: $35,357 (2000); Poverty rate: 13.4% (2000).
Taxes: Total city taxes per capita: $356 (1997); City property taxes per capita: $14 (1997).
Education: High school graduation rate: 66.0% (2000); College graduation rate: 1.9% (2000).
Housing: Homeownership rate: 73.2% (2000); Median home value: $71,400 (2000); Median rent: $296 per month (2000); Median age of housing: 23 years (2000).
Transportation: Commute to work: 89.3% car, 0.0% public transportation, 7.9% walk, 2.9% work from home (2000); Travel time to work: 48.5% less than 15 minutes, 22.1% 15 to 30 minutes, 6.6% 30 to 45 minutes, 8.1% 45 to 60 minutes, 14.7% 60 minutes or more (2000)

PACIFIC (city). Covers a land area of 5.422 square miles and a water area of 0.006 square miles. Located at 38.48° N. Lat.; 90.75° W. Long. Elevation is 466 feet.
History: Pacific was platted in 1852 and called Franklin. When the town was incorporated in 1859, the name was changed to Pacific. Silica mines were an early source of revenue for the town.
Population: 5,482 (2000); Race: 93.6% White, 3.0% Black, 0.4% Asian, 0.6% American Indian and Alaska Native, 1.1% Hispanic of any race, 1.7% two or more races (2000); Density: 1,011.0 persons per square mile (2000); Age: 26.8% under 18, 12.5% over 64 (2000); Marriage status: 25.0% never married, 52.0% now married, 8.9% widowed, 14.0% divorced (2000); Foreign born: 1.0% (2000); Ancestry (includes multiple ancestries): 31.2% German, 16.4% Irish, 14.8% United States or American, 12.6% Other groups, 10.8% English (2000).
Economy: Single-family building permits issued: 35 (2001) / 42 (2000); Multi-family building permits issued: 4 (2001) / 8 (2000); Employment by occupation: 8.3% management, 12.5% professional, 20.2% services, 25.6% sales, 0.0% farming, 11.1% construction, 22.3% production (2000).
Income: Per capita income: $17,865 (2000); Median household income: $39,554 (2000); Poverty rate: 14.7% (2000).
Taxes: Total city taxes per capita: $436 (2000); City property taxes per capita: $53 (2000).
Education: High school graduation rate: 74.4% (2000); College graduation rate: 11.1% (2000).

School District(s)

Meramec Valley R-III (PK-12)
2000 Enrollment: 4,014 636-271-1400
Housing: Homeownership rate: 61.9% (2000); Median home value: $87,200 (2000); Median rent: $374 per month (2000); Median age of housing: 27 years (2000).
Safety: Violent crime rate: 83.4 per 10,000 population; Property crime rate: 386.1 per 10,000 population (2001).
Newspapers: Tri-County Journal (1 x week)
Transportation: Commute to work: 96.3% car, 0.4% public transportation, 1.3% walk, 1.1% work from home (2000); Travel time to work: 30.4% less than 15 minutes, 24.6% 15 to 30 minutes, 24.5% 30 to 45 minutes, 13.7% 45 to 60 minutes, 6.8% 60 minutes or more (2000)
Additional Information Contacts
Pacific Chamber of Commerce 636-257-5156

PARKWAY (village). Covers a land area of 0.308 square miles and a water area of 0 square miles. Located at 38.33° N. Lat.; 90.96° W. Long. Elevation is 748 feet.
Population: 280 (2000); Race: 97.8% White, 0.0% Black, 0.0% Asian, 0.0% American Indian and Alaska Native, 0.4% Hispanic of any race, 0.7% two or more races (2000); Density: 908.8 persons per square mile (2000); Age: 21.7% under 18, 18.1% over 64 (2000); Marriage status: 16.2% never married, 68.6% now married, 5.2% widowed, 10.0% divorced (2000); Foreign born: 1.1% (2000); Ancestry (includes multiple ancestries): 23.1% United States or American, 21.3% German, 9.0% Other groups, 8.7% Irish, 7.2% French (except Basque) (2000).
Economy: Employment by occupation: 5.4% management, 14.0% professional, 18.6% services, 31.0% sales, 0.0% farming, 13.2% construction, 17.8% production (2000).
Income: Per capita income: $16,535 (2000); Median household income: $28,929 (2000); Poverty rate: 4.0% (2000).
Taxes: Total city taxes per capita: $71 (1997); City property taxes per capita: $23 (1997).
Education: High school graduation rate: 72.5% (2000); College graduation rate: 8.3% (2000).
Housing: Homeownership rate: 73.9% (2000); Median home value: $74,200 (2000); Median rent: $336 per month (2000); Median age of housing: 43 years (2000).
Transportation: Commute to work: 96.1% car, 0.0% public transportation, 3.9% walk, 0.0% work from home (2000); Travel time to work: 38.6% less than 15 minutes, 20.5% 15 to 30 minutes, 15.0% 30 to 45 minutes, 10.2% 45 to 60 minutes, 15.7% 60 minutes or more (2000)

ROBERTSVILLE (unincorporated postal area, zip code 63072). Covers a land area of 38.350 square miles and a water area of 0.144 square miles. Located at 38.36° N. Lat.; 90.81° W. Long. Elevation is 510 feet.
Population: 2,915 (2000); Race: 92.9% White, 2.7% Black, 0.4% Asian, 0.8% American Indian and Alaska Native, 0.7% Hispanic of any race, 3.0% two or more races (2000); Density: 76.0 persons per square mile (2000); Age: 26.1% under 18, 6.2% over 64 (2000); Marriage status: 23.0% never married, 58.6% now married, 4.7% widowed, 13.7% divorced (2000); Foreign born: 0.7% (2000); Ancestry (includes multiple ancestries): 31.8% German, 18.7% Irish, 16.6% Other groups, 10.0% English, 7.3% United States or American (2000).
Economy: Employment by occupation: 11.5% management, 11.0% professional, 13.1% services, 25.1% sales, 0.0% farming, 14.0% construction, 25.2% production (2000).
Income: Per capita income: $21,017 (2000); Median household income: $52,263 (2000); Poverty rate: 9.2% (2000).
Education: High school graduation rate: 73.4% (2000); College graduation rate: 8.1% (2000).
Housing: Homeownership rate: 90.4% (2000); Median home value: $95,600 (2000); Median rent: $429 per month (2000); Median age of housing: 21 years (2000).
Transportation: Commute to work: 95.7% car, 0.0% public transportation, 1.2% walk, 1.9% work from home (2000); Travel time to work: 4.5% less than 15 minutes, 18.2% 15 to 30 minutes, 28.8% 30 to 45 minutes, 24.5% 45 to 60 minutes, 24.1% 60 minutes or more (2000)

SAINT CLAIR (city). Covers a land area of 3.126 square miles and a water area of 0.010 square miles. Located at 38.35° N. Lat.; 90.98° W. Long. Elevation is 769 feet.
History: St. Clair was settled in 1843 by B.J. Inge, and was known as Traveler's Repose, which made it occasionally mistaken for a cemetery or a tavern. The name was changed in 1859 to St. Clair for an engineer of the Southwestern Branch Railroad.
Population: 4,390 (2000); Race: 98.5% White, 0.0% Black, 0.8% Asian, 0.3% American Indian and Alaska Native, 0.4% Hispanic of any race, 0.5% two or more races (2000); Density: 1,404.3 persons per square mile (2000); Age: 28.5% under 18, 14.3% over 64 (2000); Marriage status: 22.4% never married, 54.3% now married, 11.4% widowed, 11.9% divorced (2000); Foreign born: 1.0% (2000); Ancestry (includes multiple ancestries): 25.3% German, 16.0% Irish, 15.6% United States or American, 9.4% English, 8.1% Other groups (2000).
Economy: Single-family building permits issued: 7 (2001) / 13 (2000); Multi-family building permits issued: 24 (2001) / 0 (2000); Employment by occupation: 7.4% management, 12.5% professional, 14.5% services, 19.5% sales, 0.0% farming, 12.9% construction, 33.2% production (2000).

Income: Per capita income: $18,101 (2000); Median household income: $35,716 (2000); Poverty rate: 10.6% (2000).
Education: High school graduation rate: 69.0% (2000); College graduation rate: 9.1% (2000).

School District(s)

Saint Clair R-XIII (PK-12)
2000 Enrollment: 2,475 636-629-3500

Housing: Homeownership rate: 61.4% (2000); Median home value: $67,200 (2000); Median rent: $339 per month (2000); Median age of housing: 27 years (2000).
Transportation: Commute to work: 96.0% car, 0.0% public transportation, 1.4% walk, 1.8% work from home (2000); Travel time to work: 30.3% less than 15 minutes, 30.8% 15 to 30 minutes, 14.0% 30 to 45 minutes, 10.3% 45 to 60 minutes, 14.5% 60 minutes or more (2000)
Additional Information Contacts
St. Clair Chamber of Commerce 636-629-1889

SULLIVAN (city). Covers a land area of 7.666 square miles and a water area of 0 square miles. Located at 38.21° N. Lat.; 91.16° W. Long. Elevation is 987 feet.
History: Sullivan was established in 1856 as Mt. Helicon, but the name was changed by railway officials in 1860 to honor Stephen Sullivan, who had donated the land for the right of way. Sullivan was the birthplace of George Hearst (1820-1891), who became a U.S. Senator and the father of publisher William Randolph Hearst.
Population: 6,351 (2000); Race: 98.2% White, 0.0% Black, 0.2% Asian, 0.9% American Indian and Alaska Native, 0.6% Hispanic of any race, 0.6% two or more races (2000); Density: 828.4 persons per square mile (2000); Age: 24.7% under 18, 19.9% over 64 (2000); Marriage status: 18.2% never married, 57.4% now married, 10.9% widowed, 13.5% divorced (2000); Foreign born: 0.7% (2000); Ancestry (includes multiple ancestries): 21.3% German, 13.6% United States or American, 10.3% Irish, 8.1% Other groups, 7.3% English (2000).
Economy: Single-family building permits issued: 26 (2001) / 21 (2000); Multi-family building permits issued: 8 (2001) / 2 (2000); Employment by occupation: 8.4% management, 13.7% professional, 12.5% services, 22.9% sales, 0.0% farming, 15.1% construction, 27.5% production (2000).
Income: Per capita income: $17,518 (2000); Median household income: $30,046 (2000); Poverty rate: 11.0% (2000).
Taxes: Total city taxes per capita: $223 (2000); City property taxes per capita: $30 (2000).
Education: High school graduation rate: 70.6% (2000); College graduation rate: 9.8% (2000).

School District(s)

Spring Bluff R-XV (KG-08)
2000 Enrollment: 229 573-457-8302
Strain-Japan R-XVI (KG-08)
2000 Enrollment: 92 573-627-3243
Sullivan C-2 (PK-12)
2000 Enrollment: 2,145 573-468-5171

Housing: Homeownership rate: 61.8% (2000); Median home value: $75,300 (2000); Median rent: $332 per month (2000); Median age of housing: 34 years (2000).
Safety: Violent crime rate: 6.3 per 10,000 population; Property crime rate: 388.1 per 10,000 population (2001).
Newspapers: Sullivan Independent News (1 x week)
Transportation: Commute to work: 95.1% car, 0.7% public transportation, 1.3% walk, 1.7% work from home (2000); Travel time to work: 52.0% less than 15 minutes, 14.4% 15 to 30 minutes, 14.8% 30 to 45 minutes, 6.8% 45 to 60 minutes, 12.0% 60 minutes or more (2000)
Additional Information Contacts
Sullivan Area Chamber of Commerce 573-468-3314

UNION (city). Covers a land area of 8.081 square miles and a water area of 0 square miles. Located at 38.44° N. Lat.; 91.00° W. Long. Elevation is 545 feet.
History: Union was platted in 1826 by a commission appointed to locate a new seat for Franklin County. A shoe factory was an early industry here.
Population: 7,757 (2000); Race: 96.9% White, 0.5% Black, 0.2% Asian, 0.1% American Indian and Alaska Native, 1.0% Hispanic of any race, 1.6% two or more races (2000); Density: 959.9 persons per square mile (2000); Age: 26.6% under 18, 13.3% over 64 (2000); Marriage status: 26.5% never married, 53.1% now married, 7.6% widowed, 12.9% divorced (2000); Foreign born: 0.6% (2000); Ancestry (includes multiple ancestries): 39.9% German, 11.6% Irish, 10.3% Other groups, 8.2% United States or American, 7.8% English (2000).
Economy: Single-family building permits issued: 53 (2001) / 65 (2000); Multi-family building permits issued: 50 (2001) / 16 (2000); Employment by occupation: 9.3% management, 9.9% professional, 14.8% services, 22.4% sales, 0.5% farming, 12.2% construction, 30.9% production (2000).
Income: Per capita income: $16,885 (2000); Median household income: $39,596 (2000); Poverty rate: 7.2% (2000).
Taxes: Total city taxes per capita: $458 (2000); City property taxes per capita: $98 (2000).
Education: High school graduation rate: 73.7% (2000); College graduation rate: 10.9% (2000).

School District(s)

Union R-XI (KG-12)
2000 Enrollment: 3,064 636-583-8626

Two-year College(s)

East Central College (Public)
2001 Enrollment: 3,462 636-583-5193
2001 Tuition: In-state $1,560; Out-of-state $2,280

Housing: Homeownership rate: 71.8% (2000); Median home value: $86,800 (2000); Median rent: $410 per month (2000); Median age of housing: 31 years (2000).
Safety: Violent crime rate: 24.3 per 10,000 population; Property crime rate: 594.5 per 10,000 population (2001).
Newspapers: Union Missourian (2 x week)
Transportation: Commute to work: 95.2% car, 0.2% public transportation, 1.1% walk, 2.4% work from home (2000); Travel time to work: 41.7% less than 15 minutes, 25.6% 15 to 30 minutes, 12.4% 30 to 45 minutes, 12.1% 45 to 60 minutes, 8.3% 60 minutes or more (2000)
Additional Information Contacts
Franklin County Board of Realtors 636-583-6008
Union Chamber of Commerce 636-583-8979

VILLA RIDGE (CDP). Covers a land area of 4.934 square miles and a water area of 0.058 square miles. Located at 38.47° N. Lat.; 90.88° W. Long. Elevation is 637 feet.
Population: 2,417 (2000); Race: 91.7% White, 5.9% Black, 0.0% Asian, 0.0% American Indian and Alaska Native, 0.8% Hispanic of any race, 2.3% two or more races (2000); Density: 489.9 persons per square mile (2000); Age: 26.3% under 18, 12.8% over 64 (2000); Marriage status: 22.0% never married, 65.7% now married, 3.2% widowed, 9.2% divorced (2000); Foreign born: 0.0% (2000); Ancestry (includes multiple ancestries): 34.8% German, 20.6% Irish, 16.1% Other groups, 13.4% United States or American, 13.3% English (2000).
Economy: Employment by occupation: 11.3% management, 12.4% professional, 17.4% services, 21.8% sales, 0.7% farming, 14.0% construction, 22.3% production (2000).
Income: Per capita income: $18,378 (2000); Median household income: $45,045 (2000); Poverty rate: 4.7% (2000).
Education: High school graduation rate: 74.9% (2000); College graduation rate: 9.7% (2000).
Housing: Homeownership rate: 81.5% (2000); Median home value: $114,000 (2000); Median rent: $660 per month (2000); Median age of housing: 18 years (2000).
Transportation: Commute to work: 92.6% car, 0.8% public transportation, 0.0% walk, 5.2% work from home (2000); Travel time to work: 9.0% less than 15 minutes, 39.3% 15 to 30 minutes, 26.1% 30 to 45 minutes, 11.5% 45 to 60 minutes, 14.2% 60 minutes or more (2000)

WASHINGTON (city). Covers a land area of 8.550 square miles and a water area of 0.493 square miles. Located at 38.55° N. Lat.; 91.01° W. Long. Elevation is 568 feet.
History: Washington was platted in 1828 by William G. Owens, and grew as a river port. In 1833, twelve families from Hanover, Germany, arrived in St. Louis, planning to go on to the Illinois country. When they failed to find a boat heading that direction, they decided to settle in Washington. During the 1850's they were joined by other German immigrants.
Population: 13,243 (2000); Race: 97.6% White, 1.3% Black, 0.3% Asian, 0.2% American Indian and Alaska Native, 0.6% Hispanic of any race, 0.3% two or more races (2000); Density: 1,548.9 persons per square mile (2000); Age: 25.1% under 18, 16.7% over 64 (2000); Marriage status: 24.0% never married, 58.6% now married, 8.7% widowed, 8.7% divorced (2000); Foreign born: 1.4% (2000); Ancestry (includes multiple ancestries): 49.6% German, 11.7% Irish, 9.9% English, 8.1% Other groups, 6.5% United States or American (2000).
Vital Statistics: Birth rate: 161.6 per 10,000 population (1998)
Economy: Single-family building permits issued: 68 (2001) / 64 (2000); Multi-family building permits issued: 26 (2001) / 20 (2000); Employment by

occupation: 11.1% management, 18.2% professional, 13.1% services, 24.1% sales, 0.2% farming, 11.1% construction, 22.2% production (2000).
Income: Per capita income: $22,360 (2000); Median household income: $43,417 (2000); Poverty rate: 5.0% (2000).
Taxes: Total city taxes per capita: $478 (2000); City property taxes per capita: $83 (2000).
Education: High school graduation rate: 83.7% (2000); College graduation rate: 20.0% (2000).

School District(s)

Washington (PK-12)
2000 Enrollment: 3,886 636-239-2727

Two-year College(s)

Four Rivers Area Vocational Technical School (Public)
2001 Enrollment: 29 636-239-7777
2001 Tuition: In-state $4,675; Out-of-state $4,675

Housing: Homeownership rate: 69.7% (2000); Median home value: $100,600 (2000); Median rent: $408 per month (2000); Median age of housing: 28 years (2000).
Hospitals: Saint John's Mercy Hospital (187 beds)
Newspapers: Saint Clair Missourian (2 x week); Washington Missourian (2 x week)
Transportation: Commute to work: 94.5% car, 0.7% public transportation, 2.5% walk, 1.8% work from home (2000); Travel time to work: 53.9% less than 15 minutes, 19.5% 15 to 30 minutes, 8.5% 30 to 45 minutes, 8.6% 45 to 60 minutes, 9.4% 60 minutes or more (2000); Amtrak: Service available.
Additional Information Contacts
Washington Chamber of Commerce 636-239-2715

Gasconade County

Located in east central Missouri, in the Ozarks; bounded on the north by the Missouri River; drained by the Gasconade and Bourbeuse Rivers. Covers a land area of 520.70 square miles, a water area of 5.40 square miles, and is located in the Central Time Zone. The county government was organized in 1820. County seat is Hermann.
Population: 15,342 (2000); Race: 98.6% White, 0.1% Black, 0.1% Asian, 0.1% American Indian and Alaska Native, 0.4% Hispanic of any race, 0.8% two or more races (2000); Density: 29.5 persons per square mile (2000); Age: 24.7% under 18, 18.9% over 64 (2000).
Religion: Five largest groups: 16.3% United Church of Christ, 14.7% Catholic Church, 14.6% Southern Baptist Convention, 4.6% Lutheran Church—Missouri Synod, 4.0% The United Methodist Church (2000).
Economy: Unemployment rate: 4.7% (11/2002); Total civilian labor force: 7,142 (11/2002); Leading industries: 37.8% manufacturing; 15.9% retail trade; 10.0% health care and social assistance (2000); Companies that employ more than 1,000 persons: 0 (2000); Companies that employ more than 100 persons: 6 (2000); Farms: 762 totaling 187,925 acres (1997); Minority business ownership rate: 0.0% (1997); Women business ownership rate: 28.3% (1997); Retail sales per capita: $6,120 (1997). Single-family building permits issued: 10 (2001) / 11 (2000); Multi-family building permits issued: 0 (2001) / 0 (2000).
Income: Per capita income: $17,319 (2000); Median household income: $35,047 (2000); Poverty rate: 9.5% (2000); Bankruptcy rate: 4.26% (2001).
Taxes: Total county taxes per capita: $122 (1997); County property taxes per capita: $42 (1997).
Education: High school graduation rate: 74.0% (2000); College graduation rate: 10.4% (2000).
Housing: Homeownership rate: 80.3% (2000); Median home value: $70,500 (2000); Median rent: $267 per month (2000); Median age of housing: 32 years (2000).
Health: Birth rate: 108.2 per 10,000 population (1998); Age adjusted death rate: 85.0 per 10,000 population (1999); Age adjusted cancer mortality rate: 156.7 deaths per 100,000 population (1999). Number of physicians: 3.3 per 10,000 population (1999); Number of hospital beds: 28.7 per 10,000 population (1999).
Elections: 2000 Presidential election results: 34.1% Gore, 63.2% Bush, 1.7% Nader, 0.7% Buchanan
Additional Information Contacts
Gasconade County Government Offices 573-486-5427
Hermann Chamber of Commerce......................... 573-486-2313
Owensville Chamber of Commerce 573-437-4270

Gasconade County Communities

BLAND (city). Covers a land area of 0.642 square miles and a water area of 0 square miles. Located at 38.30° N. Lat.; 91.63° W. Long. Elevation is 1,023 feet.
Population: 565 (2000); Race: 96.9% White, 0.0% Black, 0.0% Asian, 0.0% American Indian and Alaska Native, 0.0% Hispanic of any race, 3.1% two or more races (2000); Density: 880.6 persons per square mile (2000); Age: 30.2% under 18, 15.7% over 64 (2000); Marriage status: 17.8% never married, 52.7% now married, 13.6% widowed, 15.8% divorced (2000); Foreign born: 0.0% (2000); Ancestry (includes multiple ancestries): 36.3% German, 20.8% Irish, 14.1% English, 8.7% Other groups, 5.6% United States or American (2000).
Economy: Manufacturing: pool tables. Employment by occupation: 2.5% management, 7.1% professional, 15.1% services, 22.2% sales, 0.8% farming, 10.9% construction, 41.4% production (2000).
Income: Per capita income: $13,102 (2000); Median household income: $26,667 (2000); Poverty rate: 11.5% (2000).
Taxes: Total city taxes per capita: $334 (1997); City property taxes per capita: $67 (1997).
Education: High school graduation rate: 69.2% (2000); College graduation rate: 6.1% (2000).
Housing: Homeownership rate: 65.3% (2000); Median home value: $39,400 (2000); Median rent: $243 per month (2000); Median age of housing: 52 years (2000).
Transportation: Commute to work: 95.8% car, 0.0% public transportation, 1.7% walk, 0.8% work from home (2000); Travel time to work: 36.6% less than 15 minutes, 31.5% 15 to 30 minutes, 9.8% 30 to 45 minutes, 5.1% 45 to 60 minutes, 17.0% 60 minutes or more (2000)

GASCONADE (city). Covers a land area of 0.209 square miles and a water area of 0 square miles. Located at 38.67° N. Lat.; 91.55° W. Long. Elevation is 527 feet.
Population: 267 (2000); Race: 93.2% White, 0.0% Black, 0.0% Asian, 4.3% American Indian and Alaska Native, 0.0% Hispanic of any race, 2.5% two or more races (2000); Density: 1,280.5 persons per square mile (2000); Age: 30.1% under 18, 18.3% over 64 (2000); Marriage status: 24.9% never married, 54.5% now married, 10.5% widowed, 10.0% divorced (2000); Foreign born: 0.7% (2000); Ancestry (includes multiple ancestries): 39.1% German, 15.4% Other groups, 10.8% United States or American, 9.0% Irish, 2.5% British (2000).
Economy: Single-family building permits issued: 0 (2001) / 1 (2000); Multi-family building permits issued: 0 (2001) / 0 (2000); Employment by occupation: 1.7% management, 13.2% professional, 12.4% services, 23.1% sales, 5.0% farming, 4.1% construction, 40.5% production (2000).
Income: Per capita income: $13,131 (2000); Median household income: $27,404 (2000); Poverty rate: 25.4% (2000).
Taxes: Total city taxes per capita: $92 (1997); City property taxes per capita: $17 (1997).
Education: High school graduation rate: 60.2% (2000); College graduation rate: 3.4% (2000).
Housing: Homeownership rate: 84.0% (2000); Median home value: $27,000 (2000); Median rent: $190 per month (2000); Median age of housing: 46 years (2000).
Transportation: Commute to work: 96.6% car, 0.0% public transportation, 3.4% walk, 0.0% work from home (2000); Travel time to work: 10.9% less than 15 minutes, 48.7% 15 to 30 minutes, 11.8% 30 to 45 minutes, 18.5% 45 to 60 minutes, 10.1% 60 minutes or more (2000)

HERMANN (city). Covers a land area of 2.302 square miles and a water area of 0.172 square miles. Located at 38.69° N. Lat.; 91.43° W. Long. Elevation is 519 feet.
History: Hermann was selected by the German Settlement Society of Philadelphia in 1837 as the site of a German colony. In 1839 the colony separated from the Society. Grape growing, begun in 1844, brought recognition when a Hermann citizen received the New York State Fair award in 1853 for the best Catawba wine made west of the Mississippi River.
Population: 2,674 (2000); Race: 98.8% White, 0.3% Black, 0.1% Asian, 0.0% American Indian and Alaska Native, 0.1% Hispanic of any race, 0.3% two or more races (2000); Density: 1,161.5 persons per square mile (2000); Age: 22.3% under 18, 25.9% over 64 (2000); Marriage status: 18.2% never married, 59.6% now married, 13.7% widowed, 8.5% divorced (2000); Foreign born: 0.5% (2000); Ancestry (includes multiple ancestries): 54.2% German, 8.7% English, 8.5% Irish, 7.0% United States or American, 6.1% French (except Basque) (2000).

Economy: Employment by occupation: 9.6% management, 15.2% professional, 16.5% services, 18.0% sales, 0.5% farming, 11.2% construction, 29.0% production (2000).
Income: Per capita income: $19,428 (2000); Median household income: $35,634 (2000); Poverty rate: 6.7% (2000).
Taxes: Total city taxes per capita: $226 (1997); City property taxes per capita: $30 (1997).
Education: High school graduation rate: 74.2% (2000); College graduation rate: 16.8% (2000).

School District(s)

Gasconade Co. R-I (KG-12)
2000 Enrollment: 1,118 573-486-2116
Housing: Homeownership rate: 70.3% (2000); Median home value: $76,100 (2000); Median rent: $313 per month (2000); Median age of housing: 44 years (2000).
Hospitals: Hermann Area District Hospital (44 beds)
Safety: Violent crime rate: 74.3 per 10,000 population; Property crime rate: 338.3 per 10,000 population (2001).
Newspapers: The Advertiser-Courier (1 x week)
Transportation: Commute to work: 91.1% car, 0.0% public transportation, 3.0% walk, 4.8% work from home (2000); Travel time to work: 56.9% less than 15 minutes, 13.3% 15 to 30 minutes, 15.5% 30 to 45 minutes, 6.2% 45 to 60 minutes, 8.0% 60 minutes or more (2000); Amtrak: Service available.
Additional Information Contacts
Hermann Chamber of Commerce. 573-486-2313

MORRISON (city). Covers a land area of 0.453 square miles and a water area of 0 square miles. Located at 38.67° N. Lat.; 91.63° W. Long. Elevation is 530 feet.
History: Damged by flood of 1993.
Population: 123 (2000); Race: 92.9% White, 4.7% Black, 0.0% Asian, 0.0% American Indian and Alaska Native, 7.1% Hispanic of any race, 2.4% two or more races (2000); Density: 271.2 persons per square mile (2000); Age: 25.2% under 18, 12.6% over 64 (2000); Marriage status: 18.6% never married, 54.9% now married, 5.9% widowed, 20.6% divorced (2000); Foreign born: 2.4% (2000); Ancestry (includes multiple ancestries): 43.3% German, 21.3% Other groups, 18.1% United States or American, 11.8% Irish, 3.9% British (2000).
Economy: Corn, soybeans, cattle. Employment by occupation: 0.0% management, 29.0% professional, 0.0% services, 30.6% sales, 0.0% farming, 12.9% construction, 27.4% production (2000).
Income: Per capita income: $14,194 (2000); Median household income: $31,607 (2000); Poverty rate: 7.1% (2000).
Taxes: Total city taxes per capita: $150 (1997); City property taxes per capita: $24 (1997).
Education: High school graduation rate: 65.1% (2000); College graduation rate: 4.8% (2000).
Housing: Homeownership rate: 81.1% (2000); Median home value: $26,400 (2000); Median rent: $244 per month (2000); Median age of housing: 60+ years (2000).
Transportation: Commute to work: 96.8% car, 0.0% public transportation, 1.6% walk, 1.6% work from home (2000); Travel time to work: 21.3% less than 15 minutes, 11.5% 15 to 30 minutes, 27.9% 30 to 45 minutes, 1.6% 45 to 60 minutes, 37.7% 60 minutes or more (2000)

MOUNT STERLING (unincorporated postal area, zip code 65062). Covers a land area of 2.632 square miles and a water area of 0 square miles. Located at 38.49° N. Lat.; 91.66° W. Long. Elevation is 591 feet.
Population: 8 (2000); Race: 100.0% White, 0.0% Black, 0.0% Asian, 0.0% American Indian and Alaska Native, 0.0% Hispanic of any race, 0.0% two or more races (2000); Density: 3.0 persons per square mile (2000); Age: 0.0% under 18, 100.0% over 64 (2000); Marriage status: 0.0% never married, 100.0% now married, 0.0% widowed, 0.0% divorced (2000); Foreign born: 0.0% (2000); Ancestry (includes multiple ancestries): 58.3% Scotch-Irish, 41.7% Welsh (2000).
Economy: Income: Per capita income: $33,125 (2000); Median household income: $68,750 (2000); Poverty rate: 0.0% (2000).
Education: High school graduation rate: 41.7% (2000); College graduation rate: 0.0% (2000).
Housing: Homeownership rate: 100.0% (2000); Median age of housing: 4 years (2000).

OWENSVILLE (city). Covers a land area of 2.020 square miles and a water area of 0 square miles. Located at 38.34° N. Lat.; 91.50° W. Long. Elevation is 935 feet.
History: Incorporated 1900.
Population: 2,500 (2000); Race: 98.9% White, 0.0% Black, 0.0% Asian, 0.0% American Indian and Alaska Native, 0.4% Hispanic of any race, 0.9% two or more races (2000); Density: 1,237.5 persons per square mile (2000); Age: 24.5% under 18, 24.7% over 64 (2000); Marriage status: 16.6% never married, 59.1% now married, 12.5% widowed, 11.9% divorced (2000); Foreign born: 0.7% (2000); Ancestry (includes multiple ancestries): 39.9% German, 12.0% English, 11.5% Irish, 8.7% United States or American, 4.1% Other groups (2000).
Economy: Corn; cattle, poultry. Manufacturing: printing, signs, store fixtures, hats; clay. Single-family building permits issued: 10 (2001) / 10 (2000); Multi-family building permits issued: 0 (2001) / 0 (2000); Employment by occupation: 6.1% management, 10.4% professional, 12.5% services, 23.0% sales, 0.0% farming, 9.7% construction, 38.2% production (2000).
Income: Per capita income: $15,208 (2000); Median household income: $26,913 (2000); Poverty rate: 15.6% (2000).
Taxes: Total city taxes per capita: $493 (1997); City property taxes per capita: $86 (1997).
Education: High school graduation rate: 68.7% (2000); College graduation rate: 9.0% (2000).

School District(s)

Gasconade Co. R-II (KG-12)
2000 Enrollment: 2,002 573-437-2177
Housing: Homeownership rate: 65.9% (2000); Median home value: $64,000 (2000); Median rent: $247 per month (2000); Median age of housing: 44 years (2000).
Newspapers: Owensville Republican (1 x week)
Transportation: Commute to work: 93.7% car, 0.3% public transportation, 0.3% walk, 4.5% work from home (2000); Travel time to work: 58.7% less than 15 minutes, 10.9% 15 to 30 minutes, 9.1% 30 to 45 minutes, 7.0% 45 to 60 minutes, 14.4% 60 minutes or more (2000)
Additional Information Contacts
Owensville Chamber of Commerce. 573-437-4270

ROSEBUD (city). Covers a land area of 0.325 square miles and a water area of 0 square miles. Located at 38.38° N. Lat.; 91.40° W. Long. Elevation is 883 feet.
History: Settled 1840s.
Population: 364 (2000); Race: 96.6% White, 0.5% Black, 0.5% Asian, 0.5% American Indian and Alaska Native, 0.0% Hispanic of any race, 1.9% two or more races (2000); Density: 1,119.4 persons per square mile (2000); Age: 26.3% under 18, 17.8% over 64 (2000); Marriage status: 24.9% never married, 58.0% now married, 9.2% widowed, 7.9% divorced (2000); Foreign born: 0.5% (2000); Ancestry (includes multiple ancestries): 56.5% German, 11.7% Irish, 11.1% Other groups, 4.8% English, 4.5% Polish (2000).
Economy: Corn, hay; cattle. Machine tools. Employment by occupation: 6.4% management, 7.5% professional, 20.8% services, 13.3% sales, 0.0% farming, 9.8% construction, 42.2% production (2000).
Income: Per capita income: $18,513 (2000); Median household income: $29,688 (2000); Poverty rate: 23.3% (2000).
Taxes: Total city taxes per capita: $189 (1997); City property taxes per capita: $74 (1997).
Education: High school graduation rate: 68.5% (2000); College graduation rate: 5.0% (2000).
Housing: Homeownership rate: 80.1% (2000); Median home value: $57,500 (2000); Median rent: $272 per month (2000); Median age of housing: 37 years (2000).
Transportation: Commute to work: 84.1% car, 0.0% public transportation, 8.5% walk, 3.0% work from home (2000); Travel time to work: 49.7% less than 15 minutes, 15.1% 15 to 30 minutes, 12.6% 30 to 45 minutes, 13.2% 45 to 60 minutes, 9.4% 60 minutes or more (2000)

Gentry County

Located in northwestern Missouri; drained by the Grand River. Covers a land area of 491.50 square miles, a water area of 0.30 square miles, and is located in the Central Time Zone. The county government was organized in 1845. County seat is Albany.
Population: 6,861 (2000); Race: 98.8% White, 0.1% Black, 0.1% Asian, 0.4% American Indian and Alaska Native, 0.2% Hispanic of any race, 0.5% two or more races (2000); Density: 14.0 persons per square mile (2000); Age: 26.0% under 18, 21.7% over 64 (2000).
Religion: Five largest groups: 41.8% Southern Baptist Convention, 13.1% The United Methodist Church, 9.0% Christian Church (Disciples of Christ), 6.1% Catholic Church, 2.9% Presbyterian Church (U.S.A.) (2000).

Economy: Unemployment rate: 3.4% (11/2002); Total civilian labor force: 3,734 (11/2002); Leading industries: 28.0% health care and social assistance; 17.8% manufacturing; 16.7% retail trade (2000); Companies that employ more than 1,000 persons: 0 (2000); Companies that employ more than 100 persons: 2 (2000); Farms: 667 totaling 248,593 acres (1997); Minority business ownership rate: 0.0% (1997); Women business ownership rate: 0.0% (1997); Retail sales per capita: $5,938 (1997). Single-family building permits issued: 8 (2001) / 4 (2000); Multi-family building permits issued: 0 (2001) / 0 (2000).
Income: Per capita income: $15,879 (2000); Median household income: $28,750 (2000); Poverty rate: 12.0% (2000); Bankruptcy rate: 3.32% (2001).
Taxes: Total county taxes per capita: $78 (1997); County property taxes per capita: $42 (1997).
Education: High school graduation rate: 81.8% (2000); College graduation rate: 14.5% (2000).
Housing: Homeownership rate: 74.5% (2000); Median home value: $47,200 (2000); Median rent: $227 per month (2000); Median age of housing: 46 years (2000).
Health: Birth rate: 100.6 per 10,000 population (1998); Age adjusted death rate: 79.8 per 10,000 population (1999); Age adjusted cancer mortality rate: 215.5 deaths per 100,000 population (1999). Number of physicians: 2.9 per 10,000 population (1999); Number of hospital beds: 51.0 per 10,000 population (1999).
Elections: 2000 Presidential election results: 40.9% Gore, 57.0% Bush, 1.3% Nader, 0.5% Buchanan
National and State Parks: Elam Bend State Wildlife Area
Additional Information Contacts
Gentry County Government Offices 660-726-3525

Gentry County Communities

ALBANY (city). Covers a land area of 2.450 square miles and a water area of 0 square miles. Located at 40.24° N. Lat.; 94.33° W. Long. Elevation is 915 feet.
History: Founded c.1845.
Population: 1,937 (2000); Race: 99.0% White, 0.2% Black, 0.2% Asian, 0.4% American Indian and Alaska Native, 0.0% Hispanic of any race, 0.2% two or more races (2000); Density: 790.6 persons per square mile (2000); Age: 21.9% under 18, 25.5% over 64 (2000); Marriage status: 17.4% never married, 59.9% now married, 14.4% widowed, 8.3% divorced (2000); Foreign born: 0.7% (2000); Ancestry (includes multiple ancestries): 21.5% United States or American, 19.4% German, 11.2% English, 9.3% Irish, 4.7% Other groups (2000).
Economy: Corn, soybeans; cattle, hogs; manufactures automatic controls. Single-family building permits issued: 8 (2001) / 3 (2000); Multi-family building permits issued: 0 (2001) / 0 (2000); Employment by occupation: 11.3% management, 19.7% professional, 17.9% services, 26.4% sales, 2.9% farming, 5.1% construction, 16.8% production (2000).
Income: Per capita income: $17,552 (2000); Median household income: $25,912 (2000); Poverty rate: 11.1% (2000).
Taxes: Total city taxes per capita: $250 (1997); City property taxes per capita: $148 (1997).
Education: High school graduation rate: 79.1% (2000); College graduation rate: 20.4% (2000).

School District(s)

Albany R-III (PK-12)
2000 Enrollment: 573 660-726-3911
Housing: Homeownership rate: 68.9% (2000); Median home value: $57,000 (2000); Median rent: $234 per month (2000); Median age of housing: 40 years (2000).
Hospitals: Gentry County Memorial Hospital (45 beds)
Newspapers: Gentry County Shopper (1 x week); The Albany Ledger (1 x week)
Transportation: Commute to work: 95.2% car, 0.0% public transportation, 1.5% walk, 3.3% work from home (2000); Travel time to work: 64.1% less than 15 minutes, 18.7% 15 to 30 minutes, 8.5% 30 to 45 minutes, 5.3% 45 to 60 minutes, 3.4% 60 minutes or more (2000)

DARLINGTON (village). Covers a land area of 0.410 square miles and a water area of 0 square miles. Located at 40.19° N. Lat.; 94.39° W. Long. Elevation is 836 feet.
Population: 113 (2000); Race: 97.0% White, 0.0% Black, 0.0% Asian, 3.0% American Indian and Alaska Native, 0.0% Hispanic of any race, 0.0% two or more races (2000); Density: 275.7 persons per square mile (2000); Age: 37.4% under 18, 16.2% over 64 (2000); Marriage status: 11.9% never married, 85.1% now married, 3.0% widowed, 0.0% divorced (2000); Foreign born: 0.0% (2000); Ancestry (includes multiple ancestries): 31.3% United States or American, 16.2% English, 16.2% Other groups, 9.1% German, 9.1% Irish (2000).
Economy: Employment by occupation: 10.3% management, 7.7% professional, 28.2% services, 2.6% sales, 0.0% farming, 15.4% construction, 35.9% production (2000).
Income: Per capita income: $9,586 (2000); Median household income: $31,250 (2000); Poverty rate: 18.2% (2000).
Taxes: Total city taxes per capita: $9 (1997); City property taxes per capita: $9 (1997).
Education: High school graduation rate: 85.7% (2000); College graduation rate: 0.0% (2000).
Housing: Homeownership rate: 91.7% (2000); Median home value: $16,100 (2000); Median rent: $125 per month (2000); Median age of housing: 60+ years (2000).
Transportation: Commute to work: 94.4% car, 0.0% public transportation, 0.0% walk, 5.6% work from home (2000); Travel time to work: 14.7% less than 15 minutes, 50.0% 15 to 30 minutes, 5.9% 30 to 45 minutes, 11.8% 45 to 60 minutes, 17.6% 60 minutes or more (2000)

GENTRY (village). Covers a land area of 0.227 square miles and a water area of 0 square miles. Located at 40.33° N. Lat.; 94.42° W. Long. Elevation is 888 feet.
Population: 101 (2000); Race: 100.0% White, 0.0% Black, 0.0% Asian, 0.0% American Indian and Alaska Native, 0.0% Hispanic of any race, 0.0% two or more races (2000); Density: 445.7 persons per square mile (2000); Age: 45.7% under 18, 5.7% over 64 (2000); Marriage status: 23.2% never married, 60.9% now married, 4.3% widowed, 11.6% divorced (2000); Foreign born: 0.0% (2000); Ancestry (includes multiple ancestries): 22.9% English, 15.2% Irish, 9.5% German, 8.6% European, 5.7% Other groups (2000).
Economy: Employment by occupation: 5.3% management, 0.0% professional, 26.3% services, 26.3% sales, 0.0% farming, 23.7% construction, 18.4% production (2000).
Income: Per capita income: $8,501 (2000); Median household income: $20,000 (2000); Poverty rate: 17.1% (2000).
Taxes: Total city taxes per capita: $49 (1997); City property taxes per capita: $29 (1997).
Education: High school graduation rate: 77.8% (2000); College graduation rate: 3.7% (2000).
Housing: Homeownership rate: 82.9% (2000); Median home value: $17,500 (2000); Median rent: $250 per month (2000); Median age of housing: 60+ years (2000).
Transportation: Commute to work: 86.8% car, 0.0% public transportation, 7.9% walk, 5.3% work from home (2000); Travel time to work: 11.1% less than 15 minutes, 27.8% 15 to 30 minutes, 36.1% 30 to 45 minutes, 16.7% 45 to 60 minutes, 8.3% 60 minutes or more (2000)

KING CITY (city). Covers a land area of 1.381 square miles and a water area of 0 square miles. Located at 40.05° N. Lat.; 94.52° W. Long. Elevation is 1,106 feet.
History: Plotted 1869.
Population: 1,012 (2000); Race: 99.3% White, 0.3% Black, 0.1% Asian, 0.3% American Indian and Alaska Native, 0.3% Hispanic of any race, 0.0% two or more races (2000); Density: 732.8 persons per square mile (2000); Age: 27.7% under 18, 20.5% over 64 (2000); Marriage status: 17.5% never married, 65.5% now married, 9.6% widowed, 7.4% divorced (2000); Foreign born: 1.7% (2000); Ancestry (includes multiple ancestries): 18.3% United States or American, 14.4% German, 10.6% English, 9.6% Irish, 5.0% Other groups (2000).
Economy: Corn, soybeans, wheat; cattle, hogs; native bluestem prairie sod and seed. Single-family building permits issued: 0 (2001) / 1 (2000); Multi-family building permits issued: 0 (2001) / 0 (2000); Employment by occupation: 9.5% management, 14.2% professional, 21.7% services, 17.7% sales, 2.5% farming, 17.0% construction, 17.5% production (2000).
Income: Per capita income: $14,177 (2000); Median household income: $24,605 (2000); Poverty rate: 16.0% (2000).
Taxes: Total city taxes per capita: $101 (1997); City property taxes per capita: $52 (1997).
Education: High school graduation rate: 82.1% (2000); College graduation rate: 13.7% (2000).

School District(s)

King City R-I (PK-12)
2000 Enrollment: 412 660-535-4319

Housing: Homeownership rate: 68.3% (2000); Median home value: $38,900 (2000); Median rent: $230 per month (2000); Median age of housing: 46 years (2000).
Newspapers: The Tri-County News (1 x week)
Transportation: Commute to work: 94.3% car, 0.0% public transportation, 3.2% walk, 1.7% work from home (2000); Travel time to work: 39.8% less than 15 minutes, 11.4% 15 to 30 minutes, 23.6% 30 to 45 minutes, 17.3% 45 to 60 minutes, 7.9% 60 minutes or more (2000)

MCFALL (city). Covers a land area of 0.310 square miles and a water area of 0 square miles. Located at 40.11° N. Lat.; 94.22° W. Long. Elevation is 994 feet.
Population: 135 (2000); Race: 100.0% White, 0.0% Black, 0.0% Asian, 0.0% American Indian and Alaska Native, 0.0% Hispanic of any race, 0.0% two or more races (2000); Density: 436.0 persons per square mile (2000); Age: 29.6% under 18, 20.4% over 64 (2000); Marriage status: 11.2% never married, 53.6% now married, 17.6% widowed, 17.6% divorced (2000); Foreign born: 0.0% (2000); Ancestry (includes multiple ancestries): 11.7% United States or American, 11.7% Irish, 7.4% German, 4.9% Welsh, 3.7% Other groups (2000).
Economy: Corn, soybeans; hogs, cattle. Employment by occupation: 24.6% management, 6.6% professional, 14.8% services, 4.9% sales, 6.6% farming, 16.4% construction, 26.2% production (2000).
Income: Per capita income: $28,852 (2000); Median household income: $24,750 (2000); Poverty rate: 18.0% (2000).
Taxes: Total city taxes per capita: $21 (1997); City property taxes per capita: $0 (1997).
Education: High school graduation rate: 59.6% (2000); College graduation rate: 5.8% (2000).
Housing: Homeownership rate: 63.6% (2000); Median home value: $22,500 (2000); Median rent: $200 per month (2000); Median age of housing: 53 years (2000).
Transportation: Commute to work: 86.9% car, 0.0% public transportation, 6.6% walk, 1.6% work from home (2000); Travel time to work: 33.3% less than 15 minutes, 35.0% 15 to 30 minutes, 21.7% 30 to 45 minutes, 1.7% 45 to 60 minutes, 8.3% 60 minutes or more (2000)

STANBERRY (city). Covers a land area of 1.319 square miles and a water area of 0 square miles. Located at 40.21° N. Lat.; 94.53° W. Long. Elevation is 886 feet.
Population: 1,243 (2000); Race: 98.3% White, 0.0% Black, 0.0% Asian, 0.0% American Indian and Alaska Native, 0.0% Hispanic of any race, 1.4% two or more races (2000); Density: 942.5 persons per square mile (2000); Age: 24.8% under 18, 27.3% over 64 (2000); Marriage status: 17.6% never married, 62.4% now married, 13.9% widowed, 6.0% divorced (2000); Foreign born: 0.7% (2000); Ancestry (includes multiple ancestries): 24.9% German, 13.3% United States or American, 13.1% Irish, 10.0% English, 7.5% Other groups (2000).
Economy: Corn, soybeans; hogs, cattle; light manufacturing. Employment by occupation: 8.7% management, 17.5% professional, 18.8% services, 18.6% sales, 1.0% farming, 10.7% construction, 24.7% production (2000).
Income: Per capita income: $13,736 (2000); Median household income: $30,417 (2000); Poverty rate: 8.8% (2000).
Taxes: Total city taxes per capita: $96 (1997); City property taxes per capita: $24 (1997).
Education: High school graduation rate: 78.7% (2000); College graduation rate: 11.7% (2000).

School District(s)

Stanberry R-II (PK-12)
2000 Enrollment: 390 660-783-2136
Housing: Homeownership rate: 76.4% (2000); Median home value: $44,100 (2000); Median rent: $212 per month (2000); Median age of housing: 52 years (2000).
Transportation: Commute to work: 92.5% car, 0.4% public transportation, 4.0% walk, 2.3% work from home (2000); Travel time to work: 54.9% less than 15 minutes, 17.3% 15 to 30 minutes, 12.8% 30 to 45 minutes, 7.7% 45 to 60 minutes, 7.3% 60 minutes or more (2000)

Greene County

Located in southwestern Missouri, in the Ozarks; drained by the James, Sac, Little Sac, and Pomme de Terre Rivers. Covers a land area of 675.00 square miles, a water area of 2.80 square miles, and is located in the Central Time Zone. The county government was organized in 1833. County seat is Springfield.

Greene County is part of the Springfield, MO MSA. The entire metro area includes: Christian County; Greene County; Webster County

Weather Station: Springfield Regional Airport — Elevation: 1,256 feet

	Jan	Feb	Mar	Apr	May	Jun	Jul	Aug	Sep	Oct	Nov	Dec
High	41	47	57	67	75	84	89	89	80	69	56	46
Low	22	26	35	44	54	62	67	66	58	46	36	26
Precip	2.1	2.2	3.9	4.5	4.5	5.0	3.4	3.5	5.1	3.5	4.4	3.2
Snow	6.6	4.4	3.6	0.4	tr	tr	tr	0.0	0.0	tr	1.7	3.3

High and Low temperatures in degrees Fahrenheit; Precipitation and Snow in inches

Population: 240,391 (2000); Race: 93.5% White, 2.1% Black, 0.9% Asian, 0.8% American Indian and Alaska Native, 1.7% Hispanic of any race, 2.0% two or more races (2000); Density: 356.1 persons per square mile (2000); Age: 22.2% under 18, 13.7% over 64 (2000).
Religion: Five largest groups: 21.6% Southern Baptist Convention, 7.5% Assemblies of God, 6.0% Catholic Church, 5.3% The United Methodist Church, 1.8% Presbyterian Church (U.S.A.) (2000).
Economy: Unemployment rate: 3.3% (11/2002); Total civilian labor force: 133,657 (11/2002); Leading industries: 16.2% health care and social assistance; 14.9% retail trade; 13.5% manufacturing (2000); Companies that employ more than 1,000 persons: 9 (2000); Companies that employ more than 100 persons: 197 (2000); Farms: 1,997 totaling 277,043 acres (1997); Minority business ownership rate: 3.6% (1997); Women business ownership rate: 22.1% (1997); Retail sales per capita: $14,503 (1997). Single-family building permits issued: 1,485 (2001) / 1,311 (2000); Multi-family building permits issued: 256 (2001) / 603 (2000).
Income: Per capita income: $19,185 (2000); Median household income: $34,157 (2000); Poverty rate: 12.1% (2000); Bankruptcy rate: 5.42% (2001).
Taxes: Total county taxes per capita: $138 (2000); County property taxes per capita: $32 (2000).
Education: High school graduation rate: 84.7% (2000); College graduation rate: 24.2% (2000).
Housing: Homeownership rate: 63.6% (2000); Median home value: $88,200 (2000); Median rent: $388 per month (2000); Median age of housing: 26 years (2000).
Health: Birth rate: 132.4 per 10,000 population (1998); Age adjusted death rate: 94.8 per 10,000 population (1999); Age adjusted cancer mortality rate: 223.7 deaths per 100,000 population (1999). Air Quality Index: 70% good, 30% moderate, 0% unhealthy (percent of days in 2000). Number of physicians: 29.2 per 10,000 population (1999); Number of hospital beds: 85.8 per 10,000 population (1999).
Elections: 2000 Presidential election results: 39.9% Gore, 57.5% Bush, 1.7% Nader, 0.5% Buchanan
National and State Parks: Wilsons Creek National Battlefield
Additional Information Contacts
Greene County Government Offices 417-868-4000
Greater Springfield Board of Realtors 417-883-1226
Springfield Area Chamber of Commerce 417-862-5567
Springfield Convention & Visitors Bureau 417-881-5300
Strafford Chamber of Commerce 417-736-4422

Greene County Communities

ASH GROVE (city). Covers a land area of 1.188 square miles and a water area of 0 square miles. Located at 37.31° N. Lat.; 93.58° W. Long. Elevation is 1,042 feet.
History: Ash Grove was settled and named in 1837 by Colonel Nathan Boone, the youngest son of Daniel Boone.
Population: 1,430 (2000); Race: 96.8% White, 0.0% Black, 0.3% Asian, 1.2% American Indian and Alaska Native, 0.8% Hispanic of any race, 1.2% two or more races (2000); Density: 1,204.1 persons per square mile (2000); Age: 26.7% under 18, 16.9% over 64 (2000); Marriage status: 15.1% never married, 65.0% now married, 9.2% widowed, 10.7% divorced (2000); Foreign born: 0.6% (2000); Ancestry (includes multiple ancestries): 21.9% United States or American, 14.9% German, 12.6% Irish, 9.1% English, 9.0% Other groups (2000).
Economy: Employment by occupation: 6.6% management, 17.1% professional, 20.1% services, 20.1% sales, 0.6% farming, 10.3% construction, 25.2% production (2000).
Income: Per capita income: $15,548 (2000); Median household income: $31,250 (2000); Poverty rate: 13.4% (2000).
Taxes: Total city taxes per capita: $24 (1997); City property taxes per capita: $18 (1997).

Education: High school graduation rate: 78.0% (2000); College graduation rate: 13.1% (2000).

School District(s)

Ash Grove R-IV (PK-12)
2000 Enrollment: 861 417-751-2534

Housing: Homeownership rate: 65.6% (2000); Median home value: $69,100 (2000); Median rent: $295 per month (2000); Median age of housing: 41 years (2000).

Newspapers: Ash Grove Commonwealth (1 x week)

Transportation: Commute to work: 92.8% car, 0.0% public transportation, 5.0% walk, 2.0% work from home (2000); Travel time to work: 32.1% less than 15 minutes, 16.6% 15 to 30 minutes, 35.4% 30 to 45 minutes, 10.7% 45 to 60 minutes, 5.2% 60 minutes or more (2000)

BATTLEFIELD (city). Covers a land area of 1.984 square miles and a water area of 0 square miles. Located at 37.12° N. Lat.; 93.36° W. Long. Elevation is 1,275 feet.

History: Wilson's Creek National Battlefield is to West.

Population: 2,385 (2000); Race: 96.0% White, 0.0% Black, 0.2% Asian, 0.3% American Indian and Alaska Native, 3.5% Hispanic of any race, 1.7% two or more races (2000); Density: 1,202.4 persons per square mile (2000); Age: 29.0% under 18, 5.6% over 64 (2000); Marriage status: 20.3% never married, 70.9% now married, 2.3% widowed, 6.6% divorced (2000); Foreign born: 0.9% (2000); Ancestry (includes multiple ancestries): 17.3% German, 15.3% United States or American, 13.0% English, 12.4% Other groups, 10.6% Irish (2000).

Economy: Light manufacturing. Employment by occupation: 14.7% management, 17.1% professional, 13.4% services, 26.4% sales, 0.0% farming, 10.7% construction, 17.8% production (2000).

Income: Per capita income: $20,656 (2000); Median household income: $47,788 (2000); Poverty rate: 2.4% (2000).

Taxes: Total city taxes per capita: $80 (1997); City property taxes per capita: $18 (1997).

Education: High school graduation rate: 90.1% (2000); College graduation rate: 19.0% (2000).

Housing: Homeownership rate: 86.6% (2000); Median home value: $85,400 (2000); Median rent: $384 per month (2000); Median age of housing: 19 years (2000).

Transportation: Commute to work: 95.4% car, 0.0% public transportation, 0.7% walk, 3.3% work from home (2000); Travel time to work: 19.6% less than 15 minutes, 59.7% 15 to 30 minutes, 13.7% 30 to 45 minutes, 2.2% 45 to 60 minutes, 4.8% 60 minutes or more (2000)

BOIS D'ARC (unincorporated postal area, zip code 65612). Covers a land area of 34.886 square miles and a water area of 0.027 square miles. Located at 37.21° N. Lat.; 93.53° W. Long. Elevation is 1,205 feet.

Population: 1,264 (2000); Race: 95.1% White, 0.0% Black, 0.0% Asian, 0.0% American Indian and Alaska Native, 1.2% Hispanic of any race, 4.9% two or more races (2000); Density: 36.2 persons per square mile (2000); Age: 28.4% under 18, 10.0% over 64 (2000); Marriage status: 18.3% never married, 68.1% now married, 5.8% widowed, 7.8% divorced (2000); Foreign born: 0.5% (2000); Ancestry (includes multiple ancestries): 17.2% Irish, 16.4% United States or American, 15.8% German, 13.6% Other groups, 12.8% English (2000).

Economy: Employment by occupation: 8.8% management, 12.4% professional, 21.3% services, 30.4% sales, 0.6% farming, 7.0% construction, 19.5% production (2000).

Income: Per capita income: $14,728 (2000); Median household income: $42,276 (2000); Poverty rate: 10.3% (2000).

Education: High school graduation rate: 83.1% (2000); College graduation rate: 11.9% (2000).

Housing: Homeownership rate: 76.1% (2000); Median home value: $80,800 (2000); Median rent: $388 per month (2000); Median age of housing: 28 years (2000).

Transportation: Commute to work: 97.0% car, 0.0% public transportation, 0.6% walk, 2.3% work from home (2000); Travel time to work: 12.6% less than 15 minutes, 35.2% 15 to 30 minutes, 40.0% 30 to 45 minutes, 7.0% 45 to 60 minutes, 5.3% 60 minutes or more (2000)

BROOKLINE (village). Covers a land area of 4.009 square miles and a water area of 0 square miles. Located at 37.17° N. Lat.; 93.41° W. Long. Elevation is 1,286 feet.

Population: 326 (2000); Race: 98.4% White, 0.0% Black, 0.0% Asian, 0.0% American Indian and Alaska Native, 0.0% Hispanic of any race, 1.6% two or more races (2000); Density: 81.3 persons per square mile (2000); Age: 22.0% under 18, 19.1% over 64 (2000); Marriage status: 17.5% never married, 55.5% now married, 10.3% widowed, 16.7% divorced (2000); Foreign born: 0.0% (2000); Ancestry (includes multiple ancestries): 15.9% German, 15.6% Other groups, 15.0% United States or American, 12.1% English, 10.8% Irish (2000).

Economy: Employment by occupation: 19.7% management, 12.4% professional, 13.9% services, 26.3% sales, 0.0% farming, 8.8% construction, 19.0% production (2000).

Income: Per capita income: $17,130 (2000); Median household income: $29,750 (2000); Poverty rate: 13.2% (2000).

Taxes: Total city taxes per capita: $76 (1997); City property taxes per capita: $25 (1997).

Education: High school graduation rate: 77.6% (2000); College graduation rate: 18.5% (2000).

Housing: Homeownership rate: 86.5% (2000); Median home value: $91,700 (2000); Median rent: $338 per month (2000); Median age of housing: 44 years (2000).

Transportation: Commute to work: 82.5% car, 0.0% public transportation, 0.7% walk, 15.3% work from home (2000); Travel time to work: 30.2% less than 15 minutes, 52.6% 15 to 30 minutes, 10.3% 30 to 45 minutes, 1.7% 45 to 60 minutes, 5.2% 60 minutes or more (2000)

BROOKLINE STATION (unincorporated postal area, zip code 65619). Aka Brookline. Covers a land area of 21.221 square miles and a water area of 0.024 square miles. Located at 37.13° N. Lat.; 93.38° W. Long.

Population: 4,213 (2000); Race: 96.2% White, 0.1% Black, 0.3% Asian, 0.6% American Indian and Alaska Native, 1.6% Hispanic of any race, 1.9% two or more races (2000); Density: 198.5 persons per square mile (2000); Age: 25.2% under 18, 8.5% over 64 (2000); Marriage status: 19.3% never married, 67.5% now married, 4.4% widowed, 8.8% divorced (2000); Foreign born: 0.7% (2000); Ancestry (includes multiple ancestries): 21.7% German, 16.0% United States or American, 13.2% Other groups, 12.2% English, 11.6% Irish (2000).

Economy: Employment by occupation: 13.3% management, 18.2% professional, 12.8% services, 28.2% sales, 0.0% farming, 11.9% construction, 15.7% production (2000).

Income: Per capita income: $19,146 (2000); Median household income: $44,410 (2000); Poverty rate: 3.9% (2000).

Education: High school graduation rate: 87.1% (2000); College graduation rate: 23.0% (2000).

Housing: Homeownership rate: 87.7% (2000); Median home value: $89,900 (2000); Median rent: $414 per month (2000); Median age of housing: 19 years (2000).

Transportation: Commute to work: 95.2% car, 0.0% public transportation, 0.8% walk, 3.6% work from home (2000); Travel time to work: 19.5% less than 15 minutes, 62.8% 15 to 30 minutes, 12.1% 30 to 45 minutes, 2.1% 45 to 60 minutes, 3.5% 60 minutes or more (2000)

FAIR GROVE (city). Covers a land area of 3.100 square miles and a water area of 0 square miles. Located at 37.38° N. Lat.; 93.15° W. Long. Elevation is 1,209 feet.

Population: 1,107 (2000); Race: 97.9% White, 0.0% Black, 0.0% Asian, 0.2% American Indian and Alaska Native, 0.0% Hispanic of any race, 1.9% two or more races (2000); Density: 357.1 persons per square mile (2000); Age: 31.1% under 18, 10.9% over 64 (2000); Marriage status: 17.4% never married, 62.9% now married, 7.4% widowed, 12.4% divorced (2000); Foreign born: 0.0% (2000); Ancestry (includes multiple ancestries): 19.5% German, 15.1% Other groups, 13.9% Irish, 13.2% English, 10.7% United States or American (2000).

Economy: Satellite community of Springfield. Agricultural area. Light manufacturing. Single-family building permits issued: 18 (2001) / 21 (2000); Multi-family building permits issued: 4 (2001) / 0 (2000); Employment by occupation: 8.6% management, 11.6% professional, 12.9% services, 31.6% sales, 0.0% farming, 11.6% construction, 23.7% production (2000).

Income: Per capita income: $16,765 (2000); Median household income: $36,761 (2000); Poverty rate: 6.8% (2000).

Taxes: Total city taxes per capita: $161 (1997); City property taxes per capita: $0 (1997).

Education: High school graduation rate: 87.3% (2000); College graduation rate: 9.9% (2000).

School District(s)

Fair Grove R-X (KG-12)
2000 Enrollment: 1,013 417-759-2233

Housing: Homeownership rate: 79.4% (2000); Median home value: $76,000 (2000); Median rent: $258 per month (2000); Median age of housing: 24 years (2000).

Transportation: Commute to work: 93.7% car, 0.0% public transportation, 1.5% walk, 3.0% work from home (2000); Travel time to work: 16.8% less than 15 minutes, 44.0% 15 to 30 minutes, 31.7% 30 to 45 minutes, 3.4% 45 to 60 minutes, 4.0% 60 minutes or more (2000)

REPUBLIC (city). Covers a land area of 5.595 square miles and a water area of 0 square miles. Located at 37.12° N. Lat.; 93.47° W. Long. Elevation is 1,309 feet.

History: Republic developed as the center of a fruit and vegetable district, shipping apples, strawberries, grapes, and tomatoes. Nearby, Wilson's Creek Battlefield was the site of the most important Civil War engagement in Missouri, which occurred in 1861.

Population: 8,438 (2000); Race: 96.8% White, 0.0% Black, 0.2% Asian, 1.3% American Indian and Alaska Native, 0.6% Hispanic of any race, 1.4% two or more races (2000); Density: 1,508.1 persons per square mile (2000); Age: 28.3% under 18, 12.8% over 64 (2000); Marriage status: 17.8% never married, 62.4% now married, 7.5% widowed, 12.2% divorced (2000); Foreign born: 0.3% (2000); Ancestry (includes multiple ancestries): 18.1% German, 14.6% United States or American, 12.5% English, 12.5% Other groups, 11.2% Irish (2000).

Economy: Single-family building permits issued: 182 (2001) / 152 (2000); Multi-family building permits issued: 109 (2001) / 6 (2000); Employment by occupation: 8.9% management, 13.7% professional, 16.5% services, 29.5% sales, 0.2% farming, 9.0% construction, 22.2% production (2000).

Income: Per capita income: $15,212 (2000); Median household income: $34,611 (2000); Poverty rate: 6.7% (2000).

Taxes: Total city taxes per capita: $169 (1997); City property taxes per capita: $65 (1997).

Education: High school graduation rate: 82.2% (2000); College graduation rate: 15.2% (2000).

School District(s)

Republic R-III (PK-12)
2000 Enrollment: 3,039 417-732-3605

Housing: Homeownership rate: 75.9% (2000); Median home value: $81,500 (2000); Median rent: $396 per month (2000); Median age of housing: 19 years (2000).

Safety: Violent crime rate: 25.9 per 10,000 population; Property crime rate: 332.2 per 10,000 population (2001).

Newspapers: The Republic Monitor (1 x week)

Transportation: Commute to work: 96.3% car, 0.1% public transportation, 0.1% walk, 3.0% work from home (2000); Travel time to work: 23.8% less than 15 minutes, 42.7% 15 to 30 minutes, 24.5% 30 to 45 minutes, 3.2% 45 to 60 minutes, 5.8% 60 minutes or more (2000)

SPRINGFIELD (city). Covers a land area of 73.155 square miles and a water area of 0.639 square miles. Located at 37.19° N. Lat.; 93.28° W. Long. Elevation is 1,300 feet.

History: Springfield grew up around a claim staked in 1830 near a spring by John Polk Campbell and his brother, Madison. When Green County was organized in 1833, Campbell was made county clerk and the county seat was established in his log cabin. The town was first incorporated in 1838, and received a charter in 1847. Stockbreeders looking for good grazing and grain-producing land came to Springfield, which was a depot on the Butterfield Stage Line. During the Civil War, Springfield was sympathetic to the Confederates, who held the town briefly in 1861-1862. "Wild Bill" Hickok served at the Union headquarters in Springfield as a scout and spy, and remained here as a resident after the war.

Population: 151,580 (2000); Race: 91.6% White, 3.1% Black, 1.2% Asian, 0.9% American Indian and Alaska Native, 2.2% Hispanic of any race, 2.3% two or more races (2000); Density: 2,072.0 persons per square mile (2000); Age: 19.9% under 18, 15.0% over 64 (2000); Marriage status: 31.4% never married, 47.8% now married, 7.1% widowed, 13.7% divorced (2000); Foreign born: 2.4% (2000); Ancestry (includes multiple ancestries): 18.7% German, 16.1% Other groups, 12.8% Irish, 11.4% United States or American, 10.9% English (2000).

Vital Statistics: Birth rate: 145.3 per 10,000 population (1998)

Economy: Unemployment rate: 3.7% (11/2002); Total civilian labor force: 89,071 (11/2002); Single-family building permits issued: 404 (2001) / 377 (2000); Multi-family building permits issued: 129 (2001) / 567 (2000); Employment by occupation: 10.3% management, 17.4% professional, 18.6% services, 30.3% sales, 0.2% farming, 7.8% construction, 15.5% production (2000).

Income: Per capita income: $17,711 (2000); Median household income: $29,563 (2000); Poverty rate: 15.9% (2000).

Taxes: Total city taxes per capita: $501 (2000); City property taxes per capita: $72 (2000).

Education: High school graduation rate: 82.8% (2000); College graduation rate: 23.0% (2000).

School District(s)

Heart of the Ozarks Tech Comm (09-12)
2000 Enrollment: n/a 417-895-7000

Springfield R-XII (PK-12)
2000 Enrollment: 24,630 417-864-3800

Four-year College(s)

Assemblies of God Theological Seminary (Private, Not-for-profit, Assemblies of God Church)
2001 Enrollment: 426 417-268-1000

Baptist Bible College (Private, Not-for-profit, Baptist)
2001 Enrollment: 763 417-268-6060
2001 Tuition: In-state $3,206; Out-of-state $3,206

Lester L Cox College of Nursing and Health Science (Private, Not-for-profit)
2001 Enrollment: 312 417-269-3401
2001 Tuition: In-state $6,288; Out-of-state $6,288

Central Bible College (Private, Not-for-profit, Assemblies of God Church)
2001 Enrollment: 805 417-833-2551
2001 Tuition: In-state $5,920; Out-of-state $5,920

Drury University (Private, Not-for-profit)
2001 Enrollment: 4,243 417-873-7879
2001 Tuition: In-state $11,690; Out-of-state $11,690

Evangel University (Private, Not-for-profit, Assemblies of God Church)
2001 Enrollment: 1,521 417-865-2811
2001 Tuition: In-state $9,620; Out-of-state $9,620

Forest Institute of Professional Psychology (Private, Not-for-profit)
2001 Enrollment: 242 417-823-3477

Cox Health Systems School of Radiologic Technology (Private, Not-for-profit)
2001 Enrollment: 40 417-269-4074
2001 Tuition: In-state $1,200; Out-of-state $1,200

Springfield College (Private, For-profit)
2001 Enrollment: 455 417-864-7220
2001 Tuition: In-state $8,976; Out-of-state $8,976

Southwest Missouri State University (Public)
2001 Enrollment: 18,252 417-836-5000
2001 Tuition: In-state $3,330; Out-of-state $6,660

Berean University (Private, Not-for-profit, Assemblies of God Church)
2001 Enrollment: n/a 417-862-9533

Lester E Cox Medical Center-School of Med Tech (Private, Not-for-profit)
2001 Enrollment: 6 417-269-6633

Pacific International University (Private, Not-for-profit, Seventh Day Adventists)
2001 Enrollment: 2,700 417-831-7515

Two-year College(s)

Ozarks Technical Community College (Public)
2001 Enrollment: 7,571 417-895-7000
2001 Tuition: In-state $1,824; Out-of-state $2,544

Saint John's Regional Health Center-School of Rad Techn (Private, Not-for-profit, Roman Catholic)
2001 Enrollment: 35 417-885-2982

Vatterott College (Private, For-profit)
2001 Enrollment: 236 417-831-8116

Housing: Homeownership rate: 53.6% (2000); Median home value: $79,800 (2000); Median rent: $384 per month (2000); Median age of housing: 30 years (2000).

Hospitals: Cox Medical Centers - North and South & Walnut Lawn (800 beds); Lakeland Regional Hospital (133 beds); Saint John's Regional Health Center (866 beds); US Medical Center for Federal Prisoners (800 beds)

Safety: Violent crime rate: 64.8 per 10,000 population; Property crime rate: 862.3 per 10,000 population (2001).

Newspapers: Daily Events (5 x week); The News-Leader (7 x week)

Transportation: Commute to work: 91.1% car, 1.3% public transportation, 3.6% walk, 2.6% work from home (2000); Travel time to work: 45.3% less than 15 minutes, 43.2% 15 to 30 minutes, 7.2% 30 to 45 minutes, 1.7% 45 to 60 minutes, 2.7% 60 minutes or more (2000)

Airports: Springfield-Branson Regional (primary service); Downtown (primary service)

Additional Information Contacts

Greater Springfield Board of Realtors 417-883-1226
Springfield Area Chamber of Commerce. 417-862-5567
Springfield Convention & Visitors Bureau 417-881-5300

STRAFFORD (city). Covers a land area of 2.336 square miles and a water area of 0 square miles. Located at 37.27° N. Lat.; 93.12° W. Long. Elevation is 1,482 feet.
History: Strafford was settled on land that once belonged to the Kickapoo Indians.
Population: 1,845 (2000); Race: 97.7% White, 0.2% Black, 0.2% Asian, 0.8% American Indian and Alaska Native, 1.3% Hispanic of any race, 0.7% two or more races (2000); Density: 789.9 persons per square mile (2000); Age: 28.7% under 18, 8.9% over 64 (2000); Marriage status: 19.0% never married, 61.3% now married, 5.7% widowed, 13.9% divorced (2000); Foreign born: 0.6% (2000); Ancestry (includes multiple ancestries): 21.6% United States or American, 14.0% German, 12.1% Other groups, 8.2% Irish, 7.3% English (2000).
Economy: Employment by occupation: 7.3% management, 12.8% professional, 13.5% services, 28.8% sales, 0.5% farming, 12.1% construction, 25.0% production (2000).
Income: Per capita income: $14,858 (2000); Median household income: $36,111 (2000); Poverty rate: 12.3% (2000).
Taxes: Total city taxes per capita: $238 (1997); City property taxes per capita: $31 (1997).
Education: High school graduation rate: 75.9% (2000); College graduation rate: 10.1% (2000).

School District(s)

Strafford R-VI (PK-12)
2000 Enrollment: 1,115 417-736-7000
Housing: Homeownership rate: 70.1% (2000); Median home value: $83,400 (2000); Median rent: $344 per month (2000); Median age of housing: 16 years (2000).
Transportation: Commute to work: 96.1% car, 0.0% public transportation, 0.9% walk, 1.4% work from home (2000); Travel time to work: 20.8% less than 15 minutes, 49.9% 15 to 30 minutes, 21.5% 30 to 45 minutes, 4.5% 45 to 60 minutes, 3.3% 60 minutes or more (2000)
Additional Information Contacts
Strafford Chamber of Commerce 417-736-4422

WALNUT GROVE (city). Covers a land area of 0.560 square miles and a water area of 0 square miles. Located at 37.41° N. Lat.; 93.54° W. Long. Elevation is 1,208 feet.
Population: 630 (2000); Race: 98.4% White, 0.0% Black, 0.0% Asian, 1.3% American Indian and Alaska Native, 0.0% Hispanic of any race, 0.3% two or more races (2000); Density: 1,124.1 persons per square mile (2000); Age: 27.6% under 18, 16.6% over 64 (2000); Marriage status: 17.6% never married, 58.3% now married, 15.9% widowed, 8.3% divorced (2000); Foreign born: 0.3% (2000); Ancestry (includes multiple ancestries): 24.5% United States or American, 11.3% German, 9.0% Other groups, 8.9% Irish, 7.2% English (2000).
Economy: Employment by occupation: 13.1% management, 11.2% professional, 13.1% services, 18.4% sales, 0.0% farming, 11.2% construction, 33.0% production (2000).
Income: Per capita income: $16,019 (2000); Median household income: $31,563 (2000); Poverty rate: 12.8% (2000).
Taxes: Total city taxes per capita: $137 (1997); City property taxes per capita: $53 (1997).
Education: High school graduation rate: 78.1% (2000); College graduation rate: 13.9% (2000).

School District(s)

Walnut Grove R-V (KG-12)
2000 Enrollment: 326 417-788-2543
Housing: Homeownership rate: 74.8% (2000); Median home value: $56,300 (2000); Median rent: $331 per month (2000); Median age of housing: 36 years (2000).
Transportation: Commute to work: 96.2% car, 0.0% public transportation, 3.1% walk, 0.8% work from home (2000); Travel time to work: 18.5% less than 15 minutes, 19.6% 15 to 30 minutes, 41.9% 30 to 45 minutes, 14.6% 45 to 60 minutes, 5.4% 60 minutes or more (2000)

WILLARD (city). Covers a land area of 5.551 square miles and a water area of 0 square miles. Located at 37.29° N. Lat.; 93.42° W. Long. Elevation is 1,235 feet.
Population: 3,193 (2000); Race: 97.7% White, 0.2% Black, 0.0% Asian, 0.5% American Indian and Alaska Native, 0.9% Hispanic of any race, 1.2% two or more races (2000); Density: 575.2 persons per square mile (2000); Age: 32.1% under 18, 9.0% over 64 (2000); Marriage status: 18.9% never married, 65.1% now married, 5.6% widowed, 10.4% divorced (2000); Foreign born: 1.2% (2000); Ancestry (includes multiple ancestries): 21.5% German, 20.3% United States or American, 13.1% Irish, 11.7% Other groups, 9.4% English (2000).
Economy: Dairying; cattle, poultry, hogs; strawberries, hay. Manufacturing: wood products, cut stone, limestone. Employment by occupation: 9.0% management, 19.6% professional, 15.8% services, 28.7% sales, 0.3% farming, 9.2% construction, 17.4% production (2000).
Income: Per capita income: $15,253 (2000); Median household income: $39,565 (2000); Poverty rate: 9.6% (2000).
Taxes: Total city taxes per capita: $159 (1997); City property taxes per capita: $39 (1997).
Education: High school graduation rate: 88.4% (2000); College graduation rate: 17.4% (2000).

School District(s)

Willard R-II (PK-12)
2000 Enrollment: 3,165 417-742-2584
Housing: Homeownership rate: 76.2% (2000); Median home value: $82,100 (2000); Median rent: $337 per month (2000); Median age of housing: 21 years (2000).
Newspapers: Willard Cross Country Times (1 x week)
Transportation: Commute to work: 96.2% car, 0.0% public transportation, 1.0% walk, 2.6% work from home (2000); Travel time to work: 20.1% less than 15 minutes, 55.0% 15 to 30 minutes, 17.2% 30 to 45 minutes, 3.8% 45 to 60 minutes, 3.8% 60 minutes or more (2000)

Grundy County

Located in northern Missouri; drained by the Thompson and Weldon Rivers. Covers a land area of 435.80 square miles, a water area of 2.20 square miles, and is located in the Central Time Zone. The county government was organized in 1841. County seat is Trenton.

Weather Station: Spickard — Elevation: 872 feet

	Jan	Feb	Mar	Apr	May	Jun	Jul	Aug	Sep	Oct	Nov	Dec
High	33	39	51	64	73	83	88	86	78	67	50	38
Low	13	19	29	40	51	60	65	62	53	41	30	18
Precip	1.0	1.0	2.6	3.5	4.9	4.2	4.9	3.8	4.1	3.2	2.4	1.6
Snow	5.6	4.3	2.9	0.3	0.0	0.0	0.0	0.0	0.0	0.0	0.8	3.0

High and Low temperatures in degrees Fahrenheit; Precipitation and Snow in inches

Population: 10,432 (2000); Race: 97.5% White, 0.1% Black, 0.2% Asian, 0.4% American Indian and Alaska Native, 2.5% Hispanic of any race, 1.2% two or more races (2000); Density: 23.9 persons per square mile (2000); Age: 23.2% under 18, 20.5% over 64 (2000).
Religion: Five largest groups: 35.9% Southern Baptist Convention, 11.0% Christian Church (Disciples of Christ), 9.4% The United Methodist Church, 5.2% Christian Churches and Churches of Christ, 3.0% Assemblies of God (2000).
Economy: Unemployment rate: 4.2% (11/2002); Total civilian labor force: 4,735 (11/2002); Leading industries: 51.0% manufacturing; 13.3% health care and social assistance; 12.1% retail trade (2000); Companies that employ more than 1,000 persons: 0 (2000); Companies that employ more than 100 persons: 5 (2000); Farms: 667 totaling 221,866 acres (1997); Minority business ownership rate: 0.0% (1997); Women business ownership rate: 30.4% (1997); Retail sales per capita: $6,430 (1997). Single-family building permits issued: 20 (2001) / 20 (2000); Multi-family building permits issued: 0 (2001) / 0 (2000).
Income: Per capita income: $15,432 (2000); Median household income: $27,333 (2000); Poverty rate: 15.8% (2000); Bankruptcy rate: 3.13% (2001).
Taxes: Total county taxes per capita: $82 (1997); County property taxes per capita: $9 (1997).
Education: High school graduation rate: 79.0% (2000); College graduation rate: 12.5% (2000).
Housing: Homeownership rate: 71.8% (2000); Median home value: $42,500 (2000); Median rent: $240 per month (2000); Median age of housing: 42 years (2000).
Health: Birth rate: 125.6 per 10,000 population (1998); Age adjusted death rate: 77.2 per 10,000 population (1999); Age adjusted cancer mortality rate: 182.5 deaths per 100,000 population (1999). Number of physicians: 4.8 per 10,000 population (1999); Number of hospital beds: 32.6 per 10,000 population (1999).
Elections: 2000 Presidential election results: 33.2% Gore, 63.2% Bush, 2.2% Nader, 0.6% Buchanan
National and State Parks: Crowder State Park
Additional Information Contacts
Grundy County Government Offices 660-359-6305
North Central Board of Realtors 660-359-2224

Trenton Chamber of Commerce. 660-359-4324

Grundy County Communities

BRIMSON (village). Covers a land area of 0.085 square miles and a water area of 0 square miles. Located at 40.14° N. Lat.; 93.73° W. Long. Elevation is 776 feet.
Population: 63 (2000); Race: 100.0% White, 0.0% Black, 0.0% Asian, 0.0% American Indian and Alaska Native, 0.0% Hispanic of any race, 0.0% two or more races (2000); Density: 737.9 persons per square mile (2000); Age: 17.1% under 18, 29.3% over 64 (2000); Marriage status: 0.0% never married, 47.1% now married, 20.6% widowed, 32.4% divorced (2000); Foreign born: 0.0% (2000); Ancestry (includes multiple ancestries): 7.3% Dutch, 7.3% French (except Basque), 7.3% Irish, 4.9% Other groups, 4.9% United States or American (2000).
Economy: Employment by occupation: 0.0% management, 25.0% professional, 0.0% services, 6.3% sales, 0.0% farming, 0.0% construction, 68.8% production (2000).
Income: Per capita income: $13,368 (2000); Median household income: $19,000 (2000); Poverty rate: 12.2% (2000).
Taxes: Total city taxes per capita: $14 (1997); City property taxes per capita: $0 (1997).
Education: High school graduation rate: 67.6% (2000); College graduation rate: 11.8% (2000).
Housing: Homeownership rate: 92.3% (2000); Median home value: <$10,000 (2000); Median rent: $225 per month (2000); Median age of housing: 60+ years (2000).
Transportation: Commute to work: 81.3% car, 0.0% public transportation, 0.0% walk, 18.8% work from home (2000); Travel time to work: 15.4% less than 15 minutes, 15.4% 15 to 30 minutes, 38.5% 30 to 45 minutes, 15.4% 45 to 60 minutes, 15.4% 60 minutes or more (2000)

GALT (city). Covers a land area of 0.287 square miles and a water area of 0 square miles. Located at 40.12° N. Lat.; 93.38° W. Long. Elevation is 840 feet.
Population: 275 (2000); Race: 95.5% White, 0.0% Black, 0.7% Asian, 1.0% American Indian and Alaska Native, 0.7% Hispanic of any race, 2.8% two or more races (2000); Density: 957.3 persons per square mile (2000); Age: 30.1% under 18, 18.0% over 64 (2000); Marriage status: 23.0% never married, 47.9% now married, 15.2% widowed, 13.8% divorced (2000); Foreign born: 0.7% (2000); Ancestry (includes multiple ancestries): 17.6% United States or American, 17.3% Irish, 13.8% German, 12.1% English, 9.3% Dutch (2000).
Economy: Corn, wheat; cattle. Employment by occupation: 6.6% management, 8.2% professional, 18.9% services, 13.9% sales, 5.7% farming, 10.7% construction, 36.1% production (2000).
Income: Per capita income: $10,493 (2000); Median household income: $24,375 (2000); Poverty rate: 23.7% (2000).
Taxes: Total city taxes per capita: $20 (1997); City property taxes per capita: $20 (1997).
Education: High school graduation rate: 78.2% (2000); College graduation rate: 2.4% (2000).

School District(s)

Grundy Co R-V (PK-12)
2000 Enrollment: 281 660-673-6511
Housing: Homeownership rate: 69.1% (2000); Median home value: $19,000 (2000); Median rent: $220 per month (2000); Median age of housing: 47 years (2000).
Transportation: Commute to work: 95.9% car, 0.0% public transportation, 1.7% walk, 1.7% work from home (2000); Travel time to work: 16.0% less than 15 minutes, 59.7% 15 to 30 minutes, 14.3% 30 to 45 minutes, 0.0% 45 to 60 minutes, 10.1% 60 minutes or more (2000)

LAREDO (city). Covers a land area of 0.274 square miles and a water area of 0 square miles. Located at 40.02° N. Lat.; 93.44° W. Long. Elevation is 808 feet.
Population: 250 (2000); Race: 97.9% White, 0.0% Black, 0.0% Asian, 0.0% American Indian and Alaska Native, 0.0% Hispanic of any race, 2.1% two or more races (2000); Density: 913.8 persons per square mile (2000); Age: 19.1% under 18, 26.8% over 64 (2000); Marriage status: 20.7% never married, 54.5% now married, 15.7% widowed, 9.1% divorced (2000); Foreign born: 0.0% (2000); Ancestry (includes multiple ancestries): 16.2% United States or American, 7.7% German, 6.8% Other groups, 4.3% Irish, 3.4% English (2000).
Economy: Corn, wheat; cattle. Employment by occupation: 4.2% management, 10.4% professional, 20.8% services, 15.6% sales, 9.4% farming, 13.5% construction, 26.0% production (2000).
Income: Per capita income: $12,451 (2000); Median household income: $20,536 (2000); Poverty rate: 19.6% (2000).
Taxes: Total city taxes per capita: $94 (1997); City property taxes per capita: $89 (1997).
Education: High school graduation rate: 65.7% (2000); College graduation rate: 1.7% (2000).

School District(s)

Laredo R-VII (PK-08)
2000 Enrollment: 59 660-286-2225
Housing: Homeownership rate: 67.5% (2000); Median home value: $13,300 (2000); Median rent: $173 per month (2000); Median age of housing: 60+ years (2000).
Transportation: Commute to work: 93.8% car, 0.0% public transportation, 6.3% walk, 0.0% work from home (2000); Travel time to work: 21.9% less than 15 minutes, 54.2% 15 to 30 minutes, 19.8% 30 to 45 minutes, 4.2% 45 to 60 minutes, 0.0% 60 minutes or more (2000)

SPICKARD (city). Aka Spickardsville. Covers a land area of 0.633 square miles and a water area of 0 square miles. Located at 40.24° N. Lat.; 93.59° W. Long. Elevation is 802 feet.
Population: 315 (2000); Race: 97.2% White, 0.0% Black, 0.0% Asian, 0.0% American Indian and Alaska Native, 2.2% Hispanic of any race, 2.2% two or more races (2000); Density: 497.5 persons per square mile (2000); Age: 32.3% under 18, 14.7% over 64 (2000); Marriage status: 22.2% never married, 56.1% now married, 8.3% widowed, 13.5% divorced (2000); Foreign born: 0.6% (2000); Ancestry (includes multiple ancestries): 17.2% English, 14.1% Irish, 13.8% United States or American, 12.2% German, 9.1% Dutch (2000).
Economy: Employment by occupation: 5.4% management, 16.1% professional, 15.2% services, 16.1% sales, 4.5% farming, 17.0% construction, 25.9% production (2000).
Income: Per capita income: $12,761 (2000); Median household income: $18,194 (2000); Poverty rate: 40.4% (2000).
Taxes: Total city taxes per capita: $84 (1997); City property taxes per capita: $28 (1997).
Education: High school graduation rate: 68.4% (2000); College graduation rate: 7.3% (2000).

School District(s)

Spickard R-II (KG-08)
2000 Enrollment: 62 660-485-6121
Housing: Homeownership rate: 71.2% (2000); Median home value: $11,700 (2000); Median rent: $214 per month (2000); Median age of housing: 56 years (2000).
Transportation: Commute to work: 93.8% car, 0.0% public transportation, 3.6% walk, 2.7% work from home (2000); Travel time to work: 32.1% less than 15 minutes, 36.7% 15 to 30 minutes, 3.7% 30 to 45 minutes, 5.5% 45 to 60 minutes, 22.0% 60 minutes or more (2000)

TINDALL (town). Covers a land area of 0.131 square miles and a water area of 0 square miles. Located at 40.16° N. Lat.; 93.61° W. Long. Elevation is 787 feet.
Population: 65 (2000); Race: 100.0% White, 0.0% Black, 0.0% Asian, 0.0% American Indian and Alaska Native, 0.0% Hispanic of any race, 0.0% two or more races (2000); Density: 496.9 persons per square mile (2000); Age: 30.9% under 18, 16.2% over 64 (2000); Marriage status: 14.9% never married, 48.9% now married, 21.3% widowed, 14.9% divorced (2000); Foreign born: 0.0% (2000); Ancestry (includes multiple ancestries): 26.5% German, 16.2% English, 4.4% United States or American, 4.4% Dutch, 4.4% Irish (2000).
Economy: Employment by occupation: 0.0% management, 16.1% professional, 29.0% services, 9.7% sales, 3.2% farming, 25.8% construction, 16.1% production (2000).
Income: Per capita income: $10,721 (2000); Median household income: $16,563 (2000); Poverty rate: 14.8% (2000).
Taxes: Total city taxes per capita: $43 (1997); City property taxes per capita: $43 (1997).
Education: High school graduation rate: 80.0% (2000); College graduation rate: 17.8% (2000).
Housing: Homeownership rate: 93.9% (2000); Median home value: $31,300 (2000); Median rent: $125 per month (2000); Median age of housing: 31 years (2000).
Transportation: Commute to work: 100.0% car, 0.0% public transportation, 0.0% walk, 0.0% work from home (2000); Travel time to work: 45.2% less

than 15 minutes, 45.2% 15 to 30 minutes, 9.7% 30 to 45 minutes, 0.0% 45 to 60 minutes, 0.0% 60 minutes or more (2000)

TRENTON (city). Covers a land area of 5.834 square miles and a water area of 0.291 square miles. Located at 40.07° N. Lat.; 93.61° W. Long. Elevation is 841 feet.
History: First known as Bluff Grove or Lomax's Store when it was settled in 1834, Trenton was platted in 1841 when Grundy County was organized. It was probably named for Trenton, New Jersey. From 1897 to 1905, Trenton was the site of a socialist movement known as the Ruskin Hall movement in England, a cooperative experiment in education and business.
Population: 6,216 (2000); Race: 97.0% White, 0.0% Black, 0.3% Asian, 0.3% American Indian and Alaska Native, 3.6% Hispanic of any race, 1.5% two or more races (2000); Density: 1,065.5 persons per square mile (2000); Age: 21.9% under 18, 23.6% over 64 (2000); Marriage status: 17.7% never married, 58.0% now married, 12.6% widowed, 11.6% divorced (2000); Foreign born: 1.9% (2000); Ancestry (includes multiple ancestries): 18.6% United States or American, 11.1% English, 10.4% German, 10.2% Other groups, 7.2% Irish (2000).
Economy: Single-family building permits issued: 20 (2001) / 20 (2000); Multi-family building permits issued: 0 (2001) / 0 (2000); Employment by occupation: 10.5% management, 12.3% professional, 21.1% services, 20.5% sales, 3.2% farming, 10.2% construction, 22.3% production (2000).
Income: Per capita income: $15,834 (2000); Median household income: $25,733 (2000); Poverty rate: 17.1% (2000).
Taxes: Total city taxes per capita: $211 (2000); City property taxes per capita: $57 (2000).
Education: High school graduation rate: 78.7% (2000); College graduation rate: 13.5% (2000).

School District(s)

Pleasant View R-VI (PK-08)
2000 Enrollment: 131 660-359-3438
Trenton R-IX (PK-12)
2000 Enrollment: 1,287 660-359-3994

Two-year College(s)

North Central Missouri College (Public)
2001 Enrollment: 1,348 660-359-3948
2001 Tuition: In-state $1,890; Out-of-state $2,760

Housing: Homeownership rate: 66.1% (2000); Median home value: $47,800 (2000); Median rent: $251 per month (2000); Median age of housing: 43 years (2000).
Safety: Violent crime rate: 3.2 per 10,000 population; Property crime rate: 410.9 per 10,000 population (2001).
Newspapers: Republican-Times (5 x week)
Transportation: Commute to work: 90.8% car, 0.6% public transportation, 3.6% walk, 4.0% work from home (2000); Travel time to work: 70.8% less than 15 minutes, 13.4% 15 to 30 minutes, 8.2% 30 to 45 minutes, 3.6% 45 to 60 minutes, 4.0% 60 minutes or more (2000)

Additional Information Contacts

North Central Board of Realtors 660-359-2224
Trenton Chamber of Commerce. 660-359-4324

Harrison County

Located in northwestern Missouri; bounded on the north by Iowa. Covers a land area of 725.10 square miles, a water area of 1.30 square miles, and is located in the Central Time Zone. The county government was organized in 1845. County seat is Bethany.

Weather Station: Bethany Elevation: 948 feet

	Jan	Feb	Mar	Apr	May	Jun	Jul	Aug	Sep	Oct	Nov	Dec
High	33	40	51	64	74	83	88	86	78	66	50	38
Low	14	20	30	41	52	61	66	63	54	42	31	20
Precip	1.1	1.2	2.6	3.6	4.7	4.0	5.2	4.4	4.3	3.1	2.4	1.5
Snow	8.1	5.9	3.3	1.6	0.0	0.0	0.0	0.0	0.0	tr	1.7	4.9

High and Low temperatures in degrees Fahrenheit; Precipitation and Snow in inches

Population: 8,850 (2000); Race: 98.4% White, 0.3% Black, 0.4% Asian, 0.1% American Indian and Alaska Native, 0.6% Hispanic of any race, 0.7% two or more races (2000); Density: 12.2 persons per square mile (2000); Age: 23.9% under 18, 22.1% over 64 (2000).
Religion: Five largest groups: 30.1% Southern Baptist Convention, 14.8% The United Methodist Church, 11.6% Christian Church (Disciples of Christ), 2.7% Assemblies of God, 2.0% Catholic Church (2000).
Economy: Unemployment rate: 4.6% (11/2002); Total civilian labor force: 3,954 (11/2002); Leading industries: 31.1% retail trade; 22.8% health care and social assistance; 14.0% accommodation & food services (2000); Companies that employ more than 1,000 persons: 0 (2000); Companies that employ more than 100 persons: 5 (2000); Farms: 901 totaling 387,360 acres (1997); Minority business ownership rate: 0.0% (1997); Women business ownership rate: 21.4% (1997); Retail sales per capita: $10,991 (1997). Single-family building permits issued: 4 (2001) / 11 (2000); Multi-family building permits issued: 0 (2001) / 0 (2000).
Income: Per capita income: $14,192 (2000); Median household income: $28,707 (2000); Poverty rate: 13.5% (2000); Bankruptcy rate: 4.00% (2001).
Taxes: Total county taxes per capita: $96 (2000); County property taxes per capita: $29 (2000).
Education: High school graduation rate: 80.1% (2000); College graduation rate: 9.3% (2000).
Housing: Homeownership rate: 74.7% (2000); Median home value: $41,500 (2000); Median rent: $230 per month (2000); Median age of housing: 46 years (2000).
Health: Birth rate: 128.8 per 10,000 population (1998); Age adjusted death rate: 83.9 per 10,000 population (1999); Age adjusted cancer mortality rate: 203.7 deaths per 100,000 population (1999). Number of physicians: 9.0 per 10,000 population (1999); Number of hospital beds: 22.6 per 10,000 population (1999).
Elections: 2000 Presidential election results: 33.3% Gore, 63.9% Bush, 1.6% Nader, 0.6% Buchanan
National and State Parks: Grand Trace State Forest; Wayne Helton Memorial State Wildlife Area

Additional Information Contacts

Harrison County Government Offices 660-425-6424
Bethany Chamber of Commerce 660-425-6358

Harrison County Communities

BETHANY (city). Covers a land area of 4.434 square miles and a water area of 0.014 square miles. Located at 40.26° N. Lat.; 94.03° W. Long. Elevation is 904 feet.
History: John Seehorn Allen settled near here in 1840, and platted the town of Bethany in 1845 when Harrison County was organized. Allen later served as Circuit and County Clerk.
Population: 3,087 (2000); Race: 98.0% White, 0.5% Black, 0.6% Asian, 0.1% American Indian and Alaska Native, 0.4% Hispanic of any race, 0.8% two or more races (2000); Density: 696.2 persons per square mile (2000); Age: 20.8% under 18, 29.3% over 64 (2000); Marriage status: 15.9% never married, 57.6% now married, 15.3% widowed, 11.2% divorced (2000); Foreign born: 1.0% (2000); Ancestry (includes multiple ancestries): 16.2% United States or American, 15.4% German, 14.7% English, 6.6% Irish, 4.5% Other groups (2000).
Economy: Single-family building permits issued: 4 (2001) / 11 (2000); Multi-family building permits issued: 0 (2001) / 0 (2000); Employment by occupation: 11.1% management, 14.6% professional, 22.1% services, 22.3% sales, 1.8% farming, 10.2% construction, 17.9% production (2000).
Income: Per capita income: $15,189 (2000); Median household income: $28,050 (2000); Poverty rate: 13.0% (2000).
Taxes: Total city taxes per capita: $282 (1997); City property taxes per capita: $82 (1997).
Education: High school graduation rate: 77.3% (2000); College graduation rate: 9.5% (2000).

School District(s)

South Harrison Co. R-II (PK-12)
2000 Enrollment: 857 660-425-8044

Housing: Homeownership rate: 66.2% (2000); Median home value: $60,600 (2000); Median rent: $255 per month (2000); Median age of housing: 38 years (2000).
Hospitals: Harrison County Community Hospital (23 beds)
Newspapers: Bethany Republican-Clipper (1 x week); Harrison County Advisor (1 x week)
Transportation: Commute to work: 90.3% car, 0.8% public transportation, 6.4% walk, 1.2% work from home (2000); Travel time to work: 75.2% less than 15 minutes, 10.2% 15 to 30 minutes, 4.2% 30 to 45 minutes, 5.3% 45 to 60 minutes, 5.0% 60 minutes or more (2000)

Additional Information Contacts

Bethany Chamber of Commerce 660-425-6358

BLYTHEDALE (village). Covers a land area of 0.309 square miles and a water area of 0 square miles. Located at 40.47° N. Lat.; 93.92° W. Long. Elevation is 1,087 feet.

Population: 233 (2000); Race: 97.9% White, 0.0% Black, 2.1% Asian, 0.0% American Indian and Alaska Native, 2.1% Hispanic of any race, 0.0% two or more races (2000); Density: 754.3 persons per square mile (2000); Age: 29.9% under 18, 12.8% over 64 (2000); Marriage status: 20.7% never married, 54.5% now married, 10.8% widowed, 14.1% divorced (2000); Foreign born: 2.8% (2000); Ancestry (includes multiple ancestries): 34.0% United States or American, 10.4% English, 6.9% Other groups, 6.9% Irish, 2.8% French Canadian (2000).
Economy: Employment by occupation: 17.4% management, 1.7% professional, 28.7% services, 15.7% sales, 3.5% farming, 8.7% construction, 24.3% production (2000).
Income: Per capita income: $11,281 (2000); Median household income: $25,417 (2000); Poverty rate: 32.4% (2000).
Taxes: Total city taxes per capita: $113 (1997); City property taxes per capita: $18 (1997).
Education: High school graduation rate: 78.3% (2000); College graduation rate: 4.0% (2000).
Housing: Homeownership rate: 80.4% (2000); Median home value: $19,300 (2000); Median rent: $143 per month (2000); Median age of housing: 48 years (2000).
Transportation: Commute to work: 97.4% car, 0.0% public transportation, 0.0% walk, 1.7% work from home (2000); Travel time to work: 43.4% less than 15 minutes, 34.5% 15 to 30 minutes, 8.0% 30 to 45 minutes, 7.1% 45 to 60 minutes, 7.1% 60 minutes or more (2000)

CAINSVILLE (city). Aka Cainesville. Covers a land area of 1.374 square miles and a water area of 0 square miles. Located at 40.43° N. Lat.; 93.77° W. Long. Elevation is 860 feet.
History: Sometimes spelled Cainesville.
Population: 370 (2000); Race: 94.3% White, 0.0% Black, 0.0% Asian, 0.0% American Indian and Alaska Native, 4.1% Hispanic of any race, 2.6% two or more races (2000); Density: 269.2 persons per square mile (2000); Age: 21.2% under 18, 21.2% over 64 (2000); Marriage status: 19.4% never married, 59.6% now married, 11.4% widowed, 9.6% divorced (2000); Foreign born: 2.3% (2000); Ancestry (includes multiple ancestries): 24.4% United States or American, 8.5% English, 8.3% German, 7.5% Irish, 3.4% Other groups (2000).
Economy: Corn, soybeans, wheat; cattle; limestone, rock quarries. Employment by occupation: 13.4% management, 12.4% professional, 21.0% services, 18.3% sales, 5.9% farming, 11.8% construction, 17.2% production (2000).
Income: Per capita income: $12,046 (2000); Median household income: $21,250 (2000); Poverty rate: 21.5% (2000).
Taxes: Total city taxes per capita: $46 (1997); City property taxes per capita: $46 (1997).
Education: High school graduation rate: 77.9% (2000); College graduation rate: 6.0% (2000).

School District(s)

Cainsville R-I (KG-12)
2000 Enrollment: 110 660-893-5213
Housing: Homeownership rate: 83.9% (2000); Median home value: $19,800 (2000); Median rent: $189 per month (2000); Median age of housing: 60+ years (2000).
Transportation: Commute to work: 91.8% car, 0.0% public transportation, 3.3% walk, 3.8% work from home (2000); Travel time to work: 20.0% less than 15 minutes, 23.4% 15 to 30 minutes, 41.1% 30 to 45 minutes, 5.7% 45 to 60 minutes, 9.7% 60 minutes or more (2000)

EAGLEVILLE (town). Covers a land area of 1.020 square miles and a water area of 0 square miles. Located at 40.46° N. Lat.; 93.98° W. Long. Elevation is 1,097 feet.
Population: 321 (2000); Race: 96.6% White, 0.0% Black, 0.0% Asian, 1.7% American Indian and Alaska Native, 5.1% Hispanic of any race, 1.4% two or more races (2000); Density: 314.8 persons per square mile (2000); Age: 20.1% under 18, 28.3% over 64 (2000); Marriage status: 18.3% never married, 58.9% now married, 9.3% widowed, 13.4% divorced (2000); Foreign born: 0.3% (2000); Ancestry (includes multiple ancestries): 16.7% German, 14.3% English, 14.3% Irish, 14.0% United States or American, 7.5% Other groups (2000).
Economy: Employment by occupation: 15.4% management, 10.0% professional, 25.4% services, 20.0% sales, 1.5% farming, 16.2% construction, 11.5% production (2000).
Income: Per capita income: $15,299 (2000); Median household income: $24,821 (2000); Poverty rate: 17.4% (2000).
Taxes: Total city taxes per capita: $7 (1997); City property taxes per capita: $7 (1997).
Education: High school graduation rate: 82.8% (2000); College graduation rate: 8.4% (2000).

School District(s)

North Harrison R-III (PK-12)
2000 Enrollment: 250 660-867-5222
Housing: Homeownership rate: 67.6% (2000); Median home value: $28,300 (2000); Median rent: $218 per month (2000); Median age of housing: 38 years (2000).
Transportation: Commute to work: 89.8% car, 0.0% public transportation, 4.7% walk, 5.5% work from home (2000); Travel time to work: 34.7% less than 15 minutes, 42.1% 15 to 30 minutes, 12.4% 30 to 45 minutes, 1.7% 45 to 60 minutes, 9.1% 60 minutes or more (2000)

GILMAN CITY (city). Covers a land area of 0.854 square miles and a water area of 0 square miles. Located at 40.14° N. Lat.; 93.87° W. Long. Elevation is 979 feet.
Population: 380 (2000); Race: 99.5% White, 0.0% Black, 0.0% Asian, 0.5% American Indian and Alaska Native, 0.0% Hispanic of any race, 0.0% two or more races (2000); Density: 444.9 persons per square mile (2000); Age: 24.9% under 18, 19.7% over 64 (2000); Marriage status: 21.7% never married, 56.6% now married, 10.7% widowed, 11.0% divorced (2000); Foreign born: 0.5% (2000); Ancestry (includes multiple ancestries): 16.5% German, 15.2% English, 14.7% Irish, 14.2% United States or American, 4.7% Other groups (2000).
Economy: Corn, wheat; sheep, cattle. Employment by occupation: 7.7% management, 16.8% professional, 20.6% services, 17.4% sales, 5.8% farming, 12.9% construction, 18.7% production (2000).
Income: Per capita income: $12,413 (2000); Median household income: $26,042 (2000); Poverty rate: 9.8% (2000).
Taxes: Total city taxes per capita: $23 (1997); City property taxes per capita: $18 (1997).
Education: High school graduation rate: 77.2% (2000); College graduation rate: 13.1% (2000).

School District(s)

Gilman City R-IV (PK-12)
2000 Enrollment: 158 660-876-5221
Housing: Homeownership rate: 89.2% (2000); Median home value: $28,200 (2000); Median rent: $221 per month (2000); Median age of housing: 60+ years (2000).
Transportation: Commute to work: 91.9% car, 0.0% public transportation, 2.7% walk, 1.4% work from home (2000); Travel time to work: 28.8% less than 15 minutes, 45.9% 15 to 30 minutes, 13.7% 30 to 45 minutes, 4.1% 45 to 60 minutes, 7.5% 60 minutes or more (2000)

HATFIELD (unincorporated postal area, zip code 64458). Covers a land area of 67.919 square miles and a water area of 0.016 square miles. Located at 40.52° N. Lat.; 94.15° W. Long. Elevation is 1,152 feet.
Population: 229 (2000); Race: 100.0% White, 0.0% Black, 0.0% Asian, 0.0% American Indian and Alaska Native, 0.0% Hispanic of any race, 0.0% two or more races (2000); Density: 3.4 persons per square mile (2000); Age: 29.7% under 18, 14.8% over 64 (2000); Marriage status: 21.7% never married, 64.0% now married, 7.5% widowed, 6.8% divorced (2000); Foreign born: 0.0% (2000); Ancestry (includes multiple ancestries): 26.3% German, 11.5% United States or American, 10.0% Scottish, 9.1% Irish, 8.6% English (2000).
Economy: Employment by occupation: 22.6% management, 7.5% professional, 22.6% services, 15.1% sales, 1.9% farming, 10.4% construction, 19.8% production (2000).
Income: Per capita income: $13,958 (2000); Median household income: $32,500 (2000); Poverty rate: 12.9% (2000).
Education: High school graduation rate: 76.8% (2000); College graduation rate: 4.9% (2000).
Housing: Homeownership rate: 75.6% (2000); Median home value: $27,500 (2000); Median rent: $192 per month (2000); Median age of housing: 50 years (2000).
Transportation: Commute to work: 80.0% car, 3.8% public transportation, 0.0% walk, 14.3% work from home (2000); Travel time to work: 16.7% less than 15 minutes, 46.7% 15 to 30 minutes, 7.8% 30 to 45 minutes, 20.0% 45 to 60 minutes, 8.9% 60 minutes or more (2000)

MARTINSVILLE (unincorporated postal area, zip code 64467). Covers a land area of 45.904 square miles and a water area of 0.008 square miles. Located at 40.39° N. Lat.; 94.15° W. Long. Elevation is 1,076 feet.
Population: 179 (2000); Race: 100.0% White, 0.0% Black, 0.0% Asian, 0.0% American Indian and Alaska Native, 0.0% Hispanic of any race, 0.0% two or more races (2000); Density: 3.9 persons per square mile (2000); Age:

27.5% under 18, 13.5% over 64 (2000); Marriage status: 23.2% never married, 61.9% now married, 5.2% widowed, 9.7% divorced (2000); Foreign born: 0.0% (2000); Ancestry (includes multiple ancestries): 23.3% Other groups, 13.0% German, 12.4% United States or American, 10.4% English (2000).
Economy: Rural community. Employment by occupation: 15.8% management, 2.6% professional, 51.8% services, 3.5% sales, 0.0% farming, 6.1% construction, 20.2% production (2000).
Income: Per capita income: $15,989 (2000); Median household income: $42,292 (2000); Poverty rate: 0.0% (2000).
Education: High school graduation rate: 78.6% (2000); College graduation rate: 3.6% (2000).
Housing: Homeownership rate: 63.5% (2000); Median home value: $45,000 (2000); Median age of housing: 60+ years (2000).
Transportation: Commute to work: 89.6% car, 0.0% public transportation, 0.0% walk, 10.4% work from home (2000); Travel time to work: 18.9% less than 15 minutes, 21.1% 15 to 30 minutes, 37.9% 30 to 45 minutes, 6.3% 45 to 60 minutes, 15.8% 60 minutes or more (2000)

MOUNT MORIAH (town). Covers a land area of 1.024 square miles and a water area of 0 square miles. Located at 40.33° N. Lat.; 93.79° W. Long. Elevation is 820 feet.
Population: 143 (2000); Race: 91.5% White, 0.0% Black, 0.0% Asian, 0.0% American Indian and Alaska Native, 0.0% Hispanic of any race, 8.5% two or more races (2000); Density: 139.7 persons per square mile (2000); Age: 32.3% under 18, 24.4% over 64 (2000); Marriage status: 17.6% never married, 50.4% now married, 16.0% widowed, 16.0% divorced (2000); Foreign born: 0.0% (2000); Ancestry (includes multiple ancestries): 23.2% German, 12.8% English, 12.8% United States or American, 10.4% Irish, 7.3% Scotch-Irish (2000).
Economy: Employment by occupation: 8.6% management, 8.6% professional, 27.6% services, 8.6% sales, 0.0% farming, 24.1% construction, 22.4% production (2000).
Income: Per capita income: $9,346 (2000); Median household income: $24,063 (2000); Poverty rate: 12.2% (2000).
Taxes: Total city taxes per capita: $57 (1997); City property taxes per capita: $57 (1997).
Education: High school graduation rate: 70.0% (2000); College graduation rate: 1.8% (2000).
Housing: Homeownership rate: 78.0% (2000); Median home value: $16,700 (2000); Median rent: $117 per month (2000); Median age of housing: 60 years (2000).
Transportation: Commute to work: 93.1% car, 0.0% public transportation, 0.0% walk, 3.4% work from home (2000); Travel time to work: 12.5% less than 15 minutes, 51.8% 15 to 30 minutes, 16.1% 30 to 45 minutes, 3.6% 45 to 60 minutes, 16.1% 60 minutes or more (2000)

NEW HAMPTON (city). Covers a land area of 0.696 square miles and a water area of 0 square miles. Located at 40.26° N. Lat.; 94.19° W. Long. Elevation is 958 feet.
Population: 349 (2000); Race: 100.0% White, 0.0% Black, 0.0% Asian, 0.0% American Indian and Alaska Native, 0.0% Hispanic of any race, 0.0% two or more races (2000); Density: 501.3 persons per square mile (2000); Age: 26.0% under 18, 20.0% over 64 (2000); Marriage status: 18.9% never married, 57.4% now married, 13.7% widowed, 10.0% divorced (2000); Foreign born: 0.0% (2000); Ancestry (includes multiple ancestries): 14.3% United States or American, 13.4% German, 10.0% English, 8.0% Irish, 6.3% Other groups (2000).
Economy: Corn, wheat, soybeans; cattle. Employment by occupation: 5.2% management, 13.9% professional, 22.5% services, 24.9% sales, 4.0% farming, 5.8% construction, 23.7% production (2000).
Income: Per capita income: $13,450 (2000); Median household income: $32,917 (2000); Poverty rate: 10.9% (2000).
Taxes: Total city taxes per capita: $28 (1997); City property taxes per capita: $28 (1997).
Education: High school graduation rate: 79.7% (2000); College graduation rate: 7.4% (2000).
Housing: Homeownership rate: 72.7% (2000); Median home value: $26,700 (2000); Median rent: $221 per month (2000); Median age of housing: 60+ years (2000).
Transportation: Commute to work: 95.3% car, 0.0% public transportation, 3.0% walk, 0.0% work from home (2000); Travel time to work: 34.3% less than 15 minutes, 42.0% 15 to 30 minutes, 6.5% 30 to 45 minutes, 5.9% 45 to 60 minutes, 11.2% 60 minutes or more (2000)

RIDGEWAY (city). Covers a land area of 1.141 square miles and a water area of 0.021 square miles. Located at 40.37° N. Lat.; 93.93° W. Long. Elevation is 1,057 feet.
Population: 530 (2000); Race: 100.0% White, 0.0% Black, 0.0% Asian, 0.0% American Indian and Alaska Native, 0.0% Hispanic of any race, 0.0% two or more races (2000); Density: 464.5 persons per square mile (2000); Age: 21.8% under 18, 25.8% over 64 (2000); Marriage status: 23.9% never married, 55.3% now married, 11.7% widowed, 9.1% divorced (2000); Foreign born: 0.0% (2000); Ancestry (includes multiple ancestries): 15.3% United States or American, 10.0% German, 9.5% English, 5.3% Irish, 4.7% Scotch-Irish (2000).
Economy: Corn, soybeans; cattle. Employment by occupation: 3.8% management, 10.8% professional, 27.6% services, 18.9% sales, 4.9% farming, 14.1% construction, 20.0% production (2000).
Income: Per capita income: $12,551 (2000); Median household income: $19,844 (2000); Poverty rate: 22.7% (2000).
Taxes: Total city taxes per capita: $66 (1997); City property taxes per capita: $52 (1997).
Education: High school graduation rate: 68.5% (2000); College graduation rate: 5.9% (2000).

School District(s)

Ridgeway R-V (PK-12)
2000 Enrollment: 129 660-872-6813
Housing: Homeownership rate: 76.0% (2000); Median home value: $30,600 (2000); Median rent: $185 per month (2000); Median age of housing: 55 years (2000).
Transportation: Commute to work: 88.6% car, 0.0% public transportation, 3.8% walk, 3.8% work from home (2000); Travel time to work: 28.7% less than 15 minutes, 45.5% 15 to 30 minutes, 7.9% 30 to 45 minutes, 4.5% 45 to 60 minutes, 13.5% 60 minutes or more (2000)

Henry County

Located in west central Missouri; drained by the South Grand River. Covers a land area of 702.50 square miles, a water area of 30.10 square miles, and is located in the Central Time Zone. The county government was organized in 1834. County seat is Clinton.

Weather Station: Clinton — Elevation: 800 feet

	Jan	Feb	Mar	Apr	May	Jun	Jul	Aug	Sep	Oct	Nov	Dec
High	38	45	56	67	76	84	90	89	80	70	55	43
Low	17	22	32	42	52	62	67	64	56	43	33	23
Precip	1.6	2.0	3.3	4.3	5.6	5.1	3.8	4.0	4.7	3.7	3.7	2.2
Snow	6.3	3.6	1.7	tr	0.0	0.0	0.0	0.0	0.0	tr	1.3	2.4

High and Low temperatures in degrees Fahrenheit; Precipitation and Snow in inches

Weather Station: Windsor — Elevation: 839 feet

	Jan	Feb	Mar	Apr	May	Jun	Jul	Aug	Sep	Oct	Nov	Dec
High	36	44	55	66	75	83	89	88	80	69	54	43
Low	16	22	32	42	52	61	66	63	55	43	33	23
Precip	1.6	1.8	3.1	4.1	4.8	4.6	3.7	3.6	4.6	3.7	3.5	2.1
Snow	5.5	4.5	1.7	0.1	0.0	0.0	0.0	0.0	0.0	0.0	1.0	3.4

High and Low temperatures in degrees Fahrenheit; Precipitation and Snow in inches

Population: 21,997 (2000); Race: 96.7% White, 1.0% Black, 0.2% Asian, 0.5% American Indian and Alaska Native, 1.0% Hispanic of any race, 1.0% two or more races (2000); Density: 31.3 persons per square mile (2000); Age: 23.7% under 18, 18.3% over 64 (2000).
Religion: Five largest groups: 31.1% Southern Baptist Convention, 8.4% The United Methodist Church, 6.0% Catholic Church, 5.9% Christian Church (Disciples of Christ), 3.0% Assemblies of God (2000).
Economy: Unemployment rate: 5.9% (11/2002); Total civilian labor force: 9,781 (11/2002); Leading industries: 28.3% manufacturing; 19.5% health care and social assistance; 17.8% retail trade (2000); Companies that employ more than 1,000 persons: 0 (2000); Companies that employ more than 100 persons: 11 (2000); Farms: 938 totaling 315,460 acres (1997); Minority business ownership rate: 0.0% (1997); Women business ownership rate: 26.2% (1997); Retail sales per capita: $8,393 (1997). Single-family building permits issued: 27 (2001) / 23 (2000); Multi-family building permits issued: 39 (2001) / 30 (2000).
Income: Per capita income: $16,468 (2000); Median household income: $30,949 (2000); Poverty rate: 14.3% (2000); Bankruptcy rate: 4.03% (2001).
Taxes: Total county taxes per capita: $53 (2000); County property taxes per capita: $7 (2000).
Education: High school graduation rate: 77.3% (2000); College graduation rate: 11.7% (2000).

Housing: Homeownership rate: 73.0% (2000); Median home value: $64,200 (2000); Median rent: $276 per month (2000); Median age of housing: 32 years (2000).
Health: Birth rate: 114.1 per 10,000 population (1998); Age adjusted death rate: 98.0 per 10,000 population (1999); Age adjusted cancer mortality rate: 185.7 deaths per 100,000 population (1999). Number of physicians: 5.9 per 10,000 population (1999); Number of hospital beds: 66.8 per 10,000 population (1999).
Elections: 2000 Presidential election results: 45.6% Gore, 52.4% Bush, 1.3% Nader, 0.4% Buchanan
National and State Parks: Brownington State Wildlife Area; Montrose State Wildlife Area; Poague State Wildlife Area; Urich State Wildlife Area
Additional Information Contacts
Henry County Government Offices 660-885-6963
Clinton Chamber of Commerce 660-885-8168
Windsor Chamber of Commerce 660-647-2318

Henry County Communities

BLAIRSTOWN (city). Covers a land area of 0.247 square miles and a water area of 0 square miles. Located at 38.55° N. Lat.; 93.95° W. Long. Elevation is 760 feet.
Population: 141 (2000); Race: 91.0% White, 0.0% Black, 0.0% Asian, 0.0% American Indian and Alaska Native, 0.0% Hispanic of any race, 1.9% two or more races (2000); Density: 569.7 persons per square mile (2000); Age: 33.3% under 18, 12.2% over 64 (2000); Marriage status: 25.2% never married, 47.8% now married, 8.7% widowed, 18.3% divorced (2000); Foreign born: 2.6% (2000); Ancestry (includes multiple ancestries): 15.4% United States or American, 14.1% Other groups, 14.1% German, 4.5% English, 4.5% Irish (2000).
Economy: Agriculture. Employment by occupation: 4.5% management, 0.0% professional, 9.1% services, 13.6% sales, 0.0% farming, 31.8% construction, 40.9% production (2000).
Income: Per capita income: $9,613 (2000); Median household income: $21,250 (2000); Poverty rate: 21.2% (2000).
Taxes: Total city taxes per capita: $16 (1997); City property taxes per capita: $10 (1997).
Education: High school graduation rate: 55.1% (2000); College graduation rate: 0.0% (2000).
Housing: Homeownership rate: 80.0% (2000); Median home value: $18,800 (2000); Median rent: <$100 per month (2000); Median age of housing: 60+ years (2000).
Transportation: Commute to work: 95.2% car, 0.0% public transportation, 0.0% walk, 0.0% work from home (2000); Travel time to work: 4.8% less than 15 minutes, 40.5% 15 to 30 minutes, 11.9% 30 to 45 minutes, 28.6% 45 to 60 minutes, 14.3% 60 minutes or more (2000)

BROWNINGTON (town). Covers a land area of 0.147 square miles and a water area of 0 square miles. Located at 38.24° N. Lat.; 93.72° W. Long. Elevation is 721 feet.
Population: 119 (2000); Race: 88.0% White, 0.0% Black, 0.0% Asian, 0.0% American Indian and Alaska Native, 0.0% Hispanic of any race, 12.0% two or more races (2000); Density: 811.1 persons per square mile (2000); Age: 25.6% under 18, 21.1% over 64 (2000); Marriage status: 21.0% never married, 52.4% now married, 17.1% widowed, 9.5% divorced (2000); Foreign born: 0.0% (2000); Ancestry (includes multiple ancestries): 20.3% Other groups, 16.5% Irish, 15.8% United States or American, 7.5% English, 6.8% German (2000).
Economy: Coal in area; corn, sorghum; cattle. Employment by occupation: 0.0% management, 20.0% professional, 20.0% services, 16.0% sales, 0.0% farming, 8.0% construction, 36.0% production (2000).
Income: Per capita income: $8,174 (2000); Median household income: $17,250 (2000); Poverty rate: 21.1% (2000).
Education: High school graduation rate: 48.9% (2000); College graduation rate: 2.1% (2000).
Housing: Homeownership rate: 91.3% (2000); Median home value: $36,500 (2000); Median rent: $275 per month (2000); Median age of housing: 50 years (2000).
Transportation: Commute to work: 100.0% car, 0.0% public transportation, 0.0% walk, 0.0% work from home (2000); Travel time to work: 0.0% less than 15 minutes, 52.0% 15 to 30 minutes, 24.0% 30 to 45 minutes, 12.0% 45 to 60 minutes, 12.0% 60 minutes or more (2000)

CALHOUN (city). Covers a land area of 0.989 square miles and a water area of 0.009 square miles. Located at 38.46° N. Lat.; 93.62° W. Long. Elevation is 792 feet.
Population: 491 (2000); Race: 98.4% White, 0.0% Black, 0.0% Asian, 0.4% American Indian and Alaska Native, 0.0% Hispanic of any race, 1.2% two or more races (2000); Density: 496.5 persons per square mile (2000); Age: 30.8% under 18, 12.0% over 64 (2000); Marriage status: 18.4% never married, 56.0% now married, 13.9% widowed, 11.7% divorced (2000); Foreign born: 0.4% (2000); Ancestry (includes multiple ancestries): 23.2% German, 17.3% English, 14.5% United States or American, 14.1% Irish, 12.2% Other groups (2000).
Economy: Soybeans, corn, wheat; cattle. Former coal-mining center. Employment by occupation: 10.9% management, 12.9% professional, 15.4% services, 14.4% sales, 0.0% farming, 11.9% construction, 34.3% production (2000).
Income: Per capita income: $11,326 (2000); Median household income: $25,417 (2000); Poverty rate: 26.5% (2000).
Taxes: Total city taxes per capita: $11 (1997); City property taxes per capita: $11 (1997).
Education: High school graduation rate: 67.8% (2000); College graduation rate: 8.6% (2000).

School District(s)

Calhoun R-VIII (PK-12)
2000 Enrollment: 235 660-694-3422
Housing: Homeownership rate: 75.5% (2000); Median home value: $41,000 (2000); Median rent: $178 per month (2000); Median age of housing: 50 years (2000).
Transportation: Commute to work: 94.9% car, 0.0% public transportation, 3.6% walk, 1.5% work from home (2000); Travel time to work: 29.4% less than 15 minutes, 45.4% 15 to 30 minutes, 9.8% 30 to 45 minutes, 5.2% 45 to 60 minutes, 10.3% 60 minutes or more (2000)

CLINTON (city). Covers a land area of 9.241 square miles and a water area of 0.023 square miles. Located at 38.37° N. Lat.; 93.77° W. Long. Elevation is 803 feet.
History: Clinton was chosen as the seat of Henry County in 1836, and the first lots were sold in the spring of 1837. The town grew slowly until about 1870, when the introduction of large-scale dairy and poultry farms and the opening of coal mines in the vicinity brought prosperity.
Population: 9,311 (2000); Race: 95.7% White, 1.9% Black, 0.2% Asian, 0.5% American Indian and Alaska Native, 1.1% Hispanic of any race, 1.1% two or more races (2000); Density: 1,007.6 persons per square mile (2000); Age: 23.1% under 18, 21.4% over 64 (2000); Marriage status: 18.4% never married, 57.0% now married, 10.3% widowed, 14.3% divorced (2000); Foreign born: 0.7% (2000); Ancestry (includes multiple ancestries): 20.9% United States or American, 16.2% German, 11.2% Other groups, 10.3% Irish, 9.9% English (2000).
Economy: Single-family building permits issued: 17 (2001) / 13 (2000); Multi-family building permits issued: 0 (2001) / 0 (2000); Employment by occupation: 8.0% management, 15.6% professional, 16.9% services, 27.5% sales, 0.9% farming, 10.1% construction, 20.9% production (2000).
Income: Per capita income: $16,282 (2000); Median household income: $28,079 (2000); Poverty rate: 15.5% (2000).
Taxes: Total city taxes per capita: $386 (2000); City property taxes per capita: $52 (2000).
Education: High school graduation rate: 75.3% (2000); College graduation rate: 12.0% (2000).

School District(s)

Clinton (PK-12)
2000 Enrollment: 1,983 660-885-2237
Davis R-XII (KG-08)
2000 Enrollment: 48 660-885-2629
Leesville R-IX (KG-08)
2000 Enrollment: 97 660-477-3406
Housing: Homeownership rate: 62.8% (2000); Median home value: $69,200 (2000); Median rent: $282 per month (2000); Median age of housing: 35 years (2000).
Hospitals: Golden Valley Memorial Hospital (106 beds)
Newspapers: Clinton Daily Democrat (5 x week); The Kayo (1 x week); Clinton Eye (1 x week)
Transportation: Commute to work: 96.5% car, 0.0% public transportation, 1.2% walk, 1.9% work from home (2000); Travel time to work: 69.1% less than 15 minutes, 13.3% 15 to 30 minutes, 4.4% 30 to 45 minutes, 3.0% 45 to 60 minutes, 10.2% 60 minutes or more (2000)
Airports: Clinton Memorial

Additional Information Contacts
Clinton Chamber of Commerce 660-885-8168

DEEPWATER (city). Covers a land area of 0.854 square miles and a water area of 0.001 square miles. Located at 38.26° N. Lat.; 93.77° W. Long. Elevation is 230 feet.
Population: 507 (2000); Race: 97.2% White, 0.4% Black, 0.0% Asian, 1.8% American Indian and Alaska Native, 1.2% Hispanic of any race, 0.6% two or more races (2000); Density: 593.9 persons per square mile (2000); Age: 25.9% under 18, 13.6% over 64 (2000); Marriage status: 16.1% never married, 53.7% now married, 13.9% widowed, 16.3% divorced (2000); Foreign born: 0.8% (2000); Ancestry (includes multiple ancestries): 16.4% Irish, 14.8% German, 12.6% English, 8.7% Other groups, 6.5% United States or American (2000).
Economy: Single-family building permits issued: 0 (2001) / 0 (2000); Multi-family building permits issued: 0 (2001) / 0 (2000); Employment by occupation: 4.9% management, 4.9% professional, 21.9% services, 20.8% sales, 0.0% farming, 6.6% construction, 41.0% production (2000).
Income: Per capita income: $11,721 (2000); Median household income: $24,722 (2000); Poverty rate: 20.9% (2000).
Taxes: Total city taxes per capita: $84 (1997); City property taxes per capita: $26 (1997).
Education: High school graduation rate: 67.2% (2000); College graduation rate: 6.3% (2000).

School District(s)

Lakeland R-III (PK-12)
2000 Enrollment: 511 417-644-2223

Housing: Homeownership rate: 66.4% (2000); Median home value: $33,600 (2000); Median rent: $245 per month (2000); Median age of housing: 52 years (2000).
Transportation: Commute to work: 93.8% car, 0.0% public transportation, 2.3% walk, 2.8% work from home (2000); Travel time to work: 22.2% less than 15 minutes, 46.2% 15 to 30 minutes, 6.4% 30 to 45 minutes, 4.1% 45 to 60 minutes, 21.1% 60 minutes or more (2000)

HARTWELL (village). Covers a land area of 0.477 square miles and a water area of 0 square miles. Located at 38.43° N. Lat.; 93.93° W. Long. Elevation is 763 feet.
Population: 16 (2000); Race: 100.0% White, 0.0% Black, 0.0% Asian, 0.0% American Indian and Alaska Native, 0.0% Hispanic of any race, 0.0% two or more races (2000); Density: 33.6 persons per square mile (2000); Age: 60.0% under 18, 0.0% over 64 (2000); Marriage status: 0.0% never married, 100.0% now married, 0.0% widowed, 0.0% divorced (2000); Foreign born: 0.0% (2000); Ancestry (includes multiple ancestries): 92.0% United States or American, 8.0% German, 8.0% Irish (2000).
Economy: Employment by occupation: 0.0% management, 0.0% professional, 28.6% services, 28.6% sales, 42.9% farming, 0.0% construction, 0.0% production (2000).
Income: Per capita income: $4,216 (2000); Median household income: $9,375 (2000); Poverty rate: 44.0% (2000).
Education: High school graduation rate: 50.0% (2000); College graduation rate: 0.0% (2000).
Housing: Homeownership rate: 100.0% (2000); Median home value: $45,000 (2000); Median age of housing: 7 years (2000).
Transportation: Commute to work: 100.0% car, 0.0% public transportation, 0.0% walk, 0.0% work from home (2000); Travel time to work: 42.9% less than 15 minutes, 0.0% 15 to 30 minutes, 28.6% 30 to 45 minutes, 28.6% 45 to 60 minutes, 0.0% 60 minutes or more (2000)

LA DUE (village). Covers a land area of 0.081 square miles and a water area of 0 square miles. Located at 38.31° N. Lat.; 93.87° W. Long. Elevation is 745 feet.
Population: 39 (2000); Race: 95.7% White, 0.0% Black, 0.0% Asian, 4.3% American Indian and Alaska Native, 0.0% Hispanic of any race, 0.0% two or more races (2000); Density: 483.5 persons per square mile (2000); Age: 30.4% under 18, 21.7% over 64 (2000); Marriage status: 20.0% never married, 48.6% now married, 8.6% widowed, 22.9% divorced (2000); Foreign born: 0.0% (2000); Ancestry (includes multiple ancestries): 45.7% United States or American, 19.6% Other groups, 10.9% Irish, 10.9% German, 6.5% Scottish (2000).
Economy: Employment by occupation: 18.8% management, 0.0% professional, 31.3% services, 12.5% sales, 0.0% farming, 25.0% construction, 12.5% production (2000).
Income: Per capita income: $9,120 (2000); Median household income: $23,750 (2000); Poverty rate: 45.7% (2000).
Education: High school graduation rate: 56.7% (2000); College graduation rate: 0.0% (2000).
Housing: Homeownership rate: 100.0% (2000); Median home value: $19,200 (2000); Median age of housing: 28 years (2000).
Transportation: Commute to work: 87.5% car, 0.0% public transportation, 12.5% walk, 0.0% work from home (2000); Travel time to work: 31.3% less than 15 minutes, 25.0% 15 to 30 minutes, 25.0% 30 to 45 minutes, 0.0% 45 to 60 minutes, 18.8% 60 minutes or more (2000)

MONTROSE (city). Covers a land area of 0.574 square miles and a water area of 0 square miles. Located at 38.25° N. Lat.; 93.98° W. Long. Elevation is 836 feet.
Population: 417 (2000); Race: 99.2% White, 0.0% Black, 0.0% Asian, 0.0% American Indian and Alaska Native, 0.0% Hispanic of any race, 0.8% two or more races (2000); Density: 726.4 persons per square mile (2000); Age: 17.3% under 18, 22.5% over 64 (2000); Marriage status: 25.9% never married, 49.8% now married, 10.3% widowed, 14.0% divorced (2000); Foreign born: 0.0% (2000); Ancestry (includes multiple ancestries): 34.7% German, 13.6% United States or American, 12.7% Irish, 8.7% English, 5.4% Other groups (2000).
Economy: Corn, wheat, soybeans; cattle. Manufacturing: lead castings, fishing lures. Strip coal mining. Coal-fired electric power generating plant (Kansas City). Employment by occupation: 10.9% management, 12.5% professional, 13.6% services, 27.7% sales, 2.2% farming, 12.5% construction, 20.7% production (2000).
Income: Per capita income: $15,062 (2000); Median household income: $21,563 (2000); Poverty rate: 16.8% (2000).
Taxes: Total city taxes per capita: $87 (1997); City property taxes per capita: $55 (1997).
Education: High school graduation rate: 73.9% (2000); College graduation rate: 9.2% (2000).

School District(s)

Montrose R-XIV (KG-12)
2000 Enrollment: 123 660-693-4812

Housing: Homeownership rate: 73.0% (2000); Median home value: $40,400 (2000); Median rent: $199 per month (2000); Median age of housing: 42 years (2000).
Transportation: Commute to work: 87.8% car, 0.0% public transportation, 5.0% walk, 6.1% work from home (2000); Travel time to work: 35.9% less than 15 minutes, 21.8% 15 to 30 minutes, 26.5% 30 to 45 minutes, 5.3% 45 to 60 minutes, 10.6% 60 minutes or more (2000)

TIGHTWAD (village). Covers a land area of 1.000 square miles and a water area of 0.007 square miles. Located at 38.30° N. Lat.; 93.55° W. Long. Elevation is 872 feet.
History: Of interest is the Bank of Tightwad.
Population: 63 (2000); Race: 92.6% White, 0.0% Black, 0.0% Asian, 0.0% American Indian and Alaska Native, 0.0% Hispanic of any race, 7.4% two or more races (2000); Density: 63.0 persons per square mile (2000); Age: 16.7% under 18, 25.9% over 64 (2000); Marriage status: 20.4% never married, 34.7% now married, 16.3% widowed, 28.6% divorced (2000); Foreign born: 0.0% (2000); Ancestry (includes multiple ancestries): 20.4% United States or American, 18.5% Other groups, 18.5% French (except Basque), 13.0% English, 11.1% German (2000).
Economy: Employment by occupation: 0.0% management, 24.0% professional, 20.0% services, 28.0% sales, 0.0% farming, 16.0% construction, 12.0% production (2000).
Income: Per capita income: $18,981 (2000); Median household income: $24,375 (2000); Poverty rate: 16.7% (2000).
Education: High school graduation rate: 63.4% (2000); College graduation rate: 19.5% (2000).
Housing: Homeownership rate: 83.3% (2000); Median home value: $57,800 (2000); Median rent: $325 per month (2000); Median age of housing: 25 years (2000).
Transportation: Commute to work: 100.0% car, 0.0% public transportation, 0.0% walk, 0.0% work from home (2000); Travel time to work: 22.7% less than 15 minutes, 59.1% 15 to 30 minutes, 0.0% 30 to 45 minutes, 9.1% 45 to 60 minutes, 9.1% 60 minutes or more (2000)

URICH (city). Covers a land area of 0.411 square miles and a water area of 0 square miles. Located at 38.46° N. Lat.; 94.00° W. Long. Elevation is 785 feet.
Population: 499 (2000); Race: 99.2% White, 0.6% Black, 0.0% Asian, 0.0% American Indian and Alaska Native, 1.6% Hispanic of any race, 0.2% two or more races (2000); Density: 1,215.2 persons per square mile (2000); Age: 27.0% under 18, 16.0% over 64 (2000); Marriage status: 24.2% never

married, 50.8% now married, 10.3% widowed, 14.7% divorced (2000); Foreign born: 0.4% (2000); Ancestry (includes multiple ancestries): 21.7% United States or American, 20.5% German, 17.4% English, 13.1% Irish, 5.1% Other groups (2000).
Economy: Soybeans, corn, wheat; cattle; meat processing. Employment by occupation: 1.4% management, 10.7% professional, 18.1% services, 25.6% sales, 0.9% farming, 18.6% construction, 24.7% production (2000).
Income: Per capita income: $14,250 (2000); Median household income: $30,197 (2000); Poverty rate: 15.2% (2000).
Taxes: Total city taxes per capita: $162 (1997); City property taxes per capita: $58 (1997).
Education: High school graduation rate: 75.9% (2000); College graduation rate: 8.9% (2000).
Housing: Homeownership rate: 74.1% (2000); Median home value: $45,000 (2000); Median rent: $238 per month (2000); Median age of housing: 40 years (2000).
Transportation: Commute to work: 93.5% car, 0.9% public transportation, 2.8% walk, 2.8% work from home (2000); Travel time to work: 14.9% less than 15 minutes, 29.3% 15 to 30 minutes, 17.3% 30 to 45 minutes, 14.9% 45 to 60 minutes, 23.6% 60 minutes or more (2000)

WINDSOR (city). Covers a land area of 2.356 square miles and a water area of 0.024 square miles. Located at 38.53° N. Lat.; 93.52° W. Long. Elevation is 915 feet.
History: Settled 1855, incorporated 1873.
Population: 3,087 (2000); Race: 97.8% White, 0.4% Black, 0.0% Asian, 0.7% American Indian and Alaska Native, 0.0% Hispanic of any race, 1.1% two or more races (2000); Density: 1,310.5 persons per square mile (2000); Age: 25.6% under 18, 19.5% over 64 (2000); Marriage status: 14.7% never married, 60.6% now married, 10.3% widowed, 14.5% divorced (2000); Foreign born: 0.9% (2000); Ancestry (includes multiple ancestries): 24.3% German, 16.2% United States or American, 13.3% English, 11.7% Irish, 4.6% Other groups (2000).
Economy: Corn, wheat, soybeans; cattle. Manufacturing: metal fabrication. Single-family building permits issued: 10 (2001) / 10 (2000); Multi-family building permits issued: 39 (2001) / 30 (2000); Employment by occupation: 8.8% management, 18.9% professional, 13.1% services, 19.6% sales, 0.6% farming, 9.9% construction, 29.0% production (2000).
Income: Per capita income: $16,052 (2000); Median household income: $29,922 (2000); Poverty rate: 16.5% (2000).
Taxes: Total city taxes per capita: $284 (1997); City property taxes per capita: $81 (1997).
Education: High school graduation rate: 74.5% (2000); College graduation rate: 9.5% (2000).

School District(s)

Henry Co. R-I (PK-12)
2000 Enrollment: 744 660-647-3533

Housing: Homeownership rate: 71.8% (2000); Median home value: $53,100 (2000); Median rent: $294 per month (2000); Median age of housing: 38 years (2000).
Hospitals: Royal Oaks Hospital (41 beds)
Safety: Violent crime rate: 19.3 per 10,000 population; Property crime rate: 212.5 per 10,000 population (2001).
Newspapers: The Windsor Review (1 x week); Benton County Shoppers Guide (1 x week)
Transportation: Commute to work: 92.9% car, 0.0% public transportation, 4.0% walk, 2.3% work from home (2000); Travel time to work: 37.9% less than 15 minutes, 18.5% 15 to 30 minutes, 26.4% 30 to 45 minutes, 3.7% 45 to 60 minutes, 13.4% 60 minutes or more (2000)
Additional Information Contacts
Windsor Chamber of Commerce 660-647-2318

Hickory County

Located in central Missouri, in the Ozarks; drained by Pomme de Terre and Little Niangua Rivers. Covers a land area of 398.60 square miles, a water area of 13.10 square miles, and is located in the Central Time Zone. The county government was organized in 1845. County seat is Hermitage.

Weather Station: Pomme De Terre Dam Elevation: 898 feet

	Jan	Feb	Mar	Apr	May	Jun	Jul	Aug	Sep	Oct	Nov	Dec
High	na	na	56	67	76	84	90	89	81	70	55	na
Low	na	24	33	44	53	63	68	66	58	46	35	na
Precip	1.7	2.0	3.3	4.2	5.0	4.0	3.8	3.2	4.5	3.8	3.4	2.5
Snow	na	na	1.0	0.1	0.0	0.0	0.0	0.0	0.0	0.0	0.5	1.6

High and Low temperatures in degrees Fahrenheit; Precipitation and Snow in inches

Population: 8,940 (2000); Race: 96.0% White, 0.0% Black, 0.2% Asian, 0.9% American Indian and Alaska Native, 0.8% Hispanic of any race, 2.4% two or more races (2000); Density: 22.4 persons per square mile (2000); Age: 19.9% under 18, 26.0% over 64 (2000).
Religion: Five largest groups: 17.1% Southern Baptist Convention, 4.0% The United Methodist Church, 3.2% Assemblies of God, 2.7% Catholic Church, 1.8% Christian Church (Disciples of Christ) (2000).
Economy: Unemployment rate: 7.6% (11/2002); Total civilian labor force: 2,448 (11/2002); Leading industries: 21.5% accommodation & food services; 20.3% retail trade; 12.8% construction (2000); Companies that employ more than 1,000 persons: 0 (2000); Companies that employ more than 100 persons: 0 (2000); Farms: 521 totaling 171,780 acres (1997); Minority business ownership rate: 0.0% (1997); Women business ownership rate: 24.4% (1997); Retail sales per capita: $2,618 (1997). Single-family building permits issued: 0 (2001) / 0 (2000); Multi-family building permits issued: 0 (2001) / 0 (2000).
Income: Per capita income: $13,536 (2000); Median household income: $25,346 (2000); Poverty rate: 19.7% (2000); Bankruptcy rate: 4.28% (2001).
Taxes: Total county taxes per capita: $82 (1997); County property taxes per capita: $30 (1997).
Education: High school graduation rate: 73.4% (2000); College graduation rate: 7.7% (2000).
Housing: Homeownership rate: 84.5% (2000); Median home value: $62,600 (2000); Median rent: $244 per month (2000); Median age of housing: 23 years (2000).
Health: Birth rate: 78.3 per 10,000 population (1998); Age adjusted death rate: 94.0 per 10,000 population (1999); Age adjusted cancer mortality rate: 241.5 deaths per 100,000 population (1999). Number of physicians: 1.1 per 10,000 population (1999); Number of hospital beds: n/a (1999).
Elections: 2000 Presidential election results: 46.3% Gore, 51.3% Bush, 1.3% Nader, 0.8% Buchanan
National and State Parks: Pomme de Terre State Wildlife Management Area
Additional Information Contacts
Hickory County Government Offices 417-745-6450
Pomme De Terre Lake Chambers 417-852-4100

Hickory County Communities

CROSS TIMBERS (city). Covers a land area of 0.450 square miles and a water area of 0 square miles. Located at 38.02° N. Lat.; 93.22° W. Long. Elevation is 1,035 feet.
History: Cross Timbers was named in 1871 for the intersection of two timber belts. Legend tells of a Lost Silver Mine here, flooded by its owner when he feared the Union troops would seize it during the Civil War.
Population: 185 (2000); Race: 99.4% White, 0.0% Black, 0.0% Asian, 0.0% American Indian and Alaska Native, 0.0% Hispanic of any race, 0.6% two or more races (2000); Density: 411.1 persons per square mile (2000); Age: 28.4% under 18, 25.0% over 64 (2000); Marriage status: 22.3% never married, 45.3% now married, 19.4% widowed, 12.9% divorced (2000); Foreign born: 0.0% (2000); Ancestry (includes multiple ancestries): 15.3% Other groups, 12.5% United States or American, 11.4% German, 7.4% English, 6.3% Irish (2000).
Economy: Employment by occupation: 12.3% management, 12.3% professional, 22.8% services, 5.3% sales, 0.0% farming, 14.0% construction, 33.3% production (2000).
Income: Per capita income: $10,413 (2000); Median household income: $12,917 (2000); Poverty rate: 42.6% (2000).
Taxes: Total city taxes per capita: $21 (1997); City property taxes per capita: $11 (1997).
Education: High school graduation rate: 72.3% (2000); College graduation rate: 3.4% (2000).
Housing: Homeownership rate: 68.6% (2000); Median home value: $43,600 (2000); Median rent: $256 per month (2000); Median age of housing: 41 years (2000).
Transportation: Commute to work: 100.0% car, 0.0% public transportation, 0.0% walk, 0.0% work from home (2000); Travel time to work: 5.3% less than 15 minutes, 28.1% 15 to 30 minutes, 43.9% 30 to 45 minutes, 3.5% 45 to 60 minutes, 19.3% 60 minutes or more (2000)

HERMITAGE (city). Covers a land area of 1.202 square miles and a water area of 0.021 square miles. Located at 37.94° N. Lat.; 93.31° W. Long. Elevation is 822 feet.
History: Hermitage was settled by Thomas Davis, who came before the site was selected as the seat of Hickory County in 1845. Hermitage was named

for the home of Andrew Jackson in Tennessee. W.E. Dorman established an ox-mill here to grind wheat and corn.
Population: 406 (2000); Race: 94.2% White, 0.0% Black, 0.0% Asian, 1.0% American Indian and Alaska Native, 0.5% Hispanic of any race, 4.8% two or more races (2000); Density: 337.9 persons per square mile (2000); Age: 25.4% under 18, 22.2% over 64 (2000); Marriage status: 20.4% never married, 57.1% now married, 10.3% widowed, 12.2% divorced (2000); Foreign born: 0.7% (2000); Ancestry (includes multiple ancestries): 23.2% United States or American, 15.9% German, 15.2% Irish, 13.8% English, 8.2% Other groups (2000).
Economy: Employment by occupation: 3.8% management, 23.1% professional, 20.0% services, 15.4% sales, 3.1% farming, 13.8% construction, 20.8% production (2000).
Income: Per capita income: $12,944 (2000); Median household income: $23,958 (2000); Poverty rate: 18.6% (2000).
Taxes: Total city taxes per capita: $64 (1997); City property taxes per capita: $28 (1997).
Education: High school graduation rate: 65.5% (2000); College graduation rate: 12.5% (2000).

School District(s)

Hermitage R-IV (KG-12)
2000 Enrollment: 324 417-745-6418
Housing: Homeownership rate: 67.0% (2000); Median home value: $62,700 (2000); Median rent: $244 per month (2000); Median age of housing: 27 years (2000).
Newspapers: The Index (1 x week)
Transportation: Commute to work: 87.7% car, 0.0% public transportation, 8.5% walk, 3.1% work from home (2000); Travel time to work: 63.5% less than 15 minutes, 8.7% 15 to 30 minutes, 15.9% 30 to 45 minutes, 4.8% 45 to 60 minutes, 7.1% 60 minutes or more (2000)

PITTSBURG (unincorporated postal area, zip code 65724). Covers a land area of 22.709 square miles and a water area of 0 square miles. Located at 37.85° N. Lat.; 93.31° W. Long. Elevation is 1,035 feet.
Population: 1,369 (2000); Race: 93.6% White, 0.0% Black, 0.0% Asian, 1.1% American Indian and Alaska Native, 3.4% Hispanic of any race, 1.9% two or more races (2000); Density: 60.3 persons per square mile (2000); Age: 12.0% under 18, 26.9% over 64 (2000); Marriage status: 8.9% never married, 70.8% now married, 10.6% widowed, 9.7% divorced (2000); Foreign born: 2.9% (2000); Ancestry (includes multiple ancestries): 19.0% German, 15.1% Irish, 12.6% English, 12.4% United States or American, 7.7% Other groups (2000).
Economy: Employment by occupation: 6.5% management, 14.3% professional, 16.5% services, 23.5% sales, 1.7% farming, 16.9% construction, 20.6% production (2000).
Income: Per capita income: $15,129 (2000); Median household income: $23,875 (2000); Poverty rate: 21.1% (2000).
Education: High school graduation rate: 77.9% (2000); College graduation rate: 13.1% (2000).
Housing: Homeownership rate: 84.3% (2000); Median home value: $68,500 (2000); Median rent: $273 per month (2000); Median age of housing: 23 years (2000).
Transportation: Commute to work: 93.8% car, 0.0% public transportation, 2.7% walk, 1.7% work from home (2000); Travel time to work: 27.2% less than 15 minutes, 26.6% 15 to 30 minutes, 17.8% 30 to 45 minutes, 9.6% 45 to 60 minutes, 18.8% 60 minutes or more (2000)
Additional Information Contacts
Pomme De Terre Lake Chambers 417-852-4100

PRESTON (town). Covers a land area of 0.170 square miles and a water area of 0 square miles. Located at 37.94° N. Lat.; 93.21° W. Long. Elevation is 1,046 feet.
Population: 113 (2000); Race: 100.0% White, 0.0% Black, 0.0% Asian, 0.0% American Indian and Alaska Native, 0.0% Hispanic of any race, 0.0% two or more races (2000); Density: 666.4 persons per square mile (2000); Age: 29.7% under 18, 19.5% over 64 (2000); Marriage status: 16.7% never married, 52.2% now married, 18.9% widowed, 12.2% divorced (2000); Foreign born: 0.0% (2000); Ancestry (includes multiple ancestries): 25.4% German, 20.3% English, 17.8% Irish, 17.8% United States or American, 8.5% Other groups (2000).
Economy: Employment by occupation: 0.0% management, 17.9% professional, 10.7% services, 17.9% sales, 0.0% farming, 14.3% construction, 39.3% production (2000).
Income: Per capita income: $11,318 (2000); Median household income: $19,583 (2000); Poverty rate: 30.5% (2000).
Taxes: Total city taxes per capita: $19 (1997); City property taxes per capita: $0 (1997).
Education: High school graduation rate: 71.8% (2000); College graduation rate: 8.5% (2000).
Housing: Homeownership rate: 65.3% (2000); Median home value: $50,000 (2000); Median rent: $275 per month (2000); Median age of housing: 47 years (2000).
Transportation: Commute to work: 100.0% car, 0.0% public transportation, 0.0% walk, 0.0% work from home (2000); Travel time to work: 30.8% less than 15 minutes, 0.0% 15 to 30 minutes, 61.5% 30 to 45 minutes, 0.0% 45 to 60 minutes, 7.7% 60 minutes or more (2000)

QUINCY (unincorporated postal area, zip code 65735). Covers a land area of 26.620 square miles and a water area of 0.019 square miles. Located at 38.06° N. Lat.; 93.48° W. Long. Elevation is 303 feet.
Population: 191 (2000); Race: 95.7% White, 0.0% Black, 0.0% Asian, 0.0% American Indian and Alaska Native, 0.0% Hispanic of any race, 4.3% two or more races (2000); Density: 7.2 persons per square mile (2000); Age: 22.7% under 18, 21.1% over 64 (2000); Marriage status: 4.9% never married, 69.9% now married, 16.1% widowed, 9.1% divorced (2000); Foreign born: 2.2% (2000); Ancestry (includes multiple ancestries): 24.3% United States or American, 9.2% Irish, 5.9% French (except Basque), 4.9% German, 2.7% Austrian (2000).
Economy: Employment by occupation: 19.0% management, 9.5% professional, 23.8% services, 7.1% sales, 9.5% farming, 11.9% construction, 19.0% production (2000).
Income: Per capita income: $10,622 (2000); Median household income: $17,321 (2000); Poverty rate: 6.5% (2000).
Education: High school graduation rate: 56.9% (2000); College graduation rate: 4.4% (2000).
Housing: Homeownership rate: 95.7% (2000); Median home value: $35,000 (2000); Median age of housing: 30 years (2000).
Transportation: Commute to work: 90.5% car, 0.0% public transportation, 0.0% walk, 9.5% work from home (2000); Travel time to work: 28.9% less than 15 minutes, 13.2% 15 to 30 minutes, 34.2% 30 to 45 minutes, 10.5% 45 to 60 minutes, 13.2% 60 minutes or more (2000)

WEAUBLEAU (city). Covers a land area of 0.877 square miles and a water area of 0 square miles. Located at 37.89° N. Lat.; 93.54° W. Long. Elevation is 980 feet.
Population: 518 (2000); Race: 97.8% White, 0.0% Black, 0.0% Asian, 0.7% American Indian and Alaska Native, 1.1% Hispanic of any race, 1.5% two or more races (2000); Density: 590.8 persons per square mile (2000); Age: 26.4% under 18, 23.8% over 64 (2000); Marriage status: 13.9% never married, 56.0% now married, 14.2% widowed, 15.9% divorced (2000); Foreign born: 0.0% (2000); Ancestry (includes multiple ancestries): 14.0% United States or American, 12.3% Irish, 10.2% English, 8.9% German, 6.5% Other groups (2000).
Economy: Hay, wheat; cattle. Single-family building permits issued: 0 (2001) / 0 (2000); Multi-family building permits issued: 0 (2001) / 0 (2000); Employment by occupation: 6.8% management, 4.9% professional, 19.1% services, 14.8% sales, 2.5% farming, 15.4% construction, 36.4% production (2000).
Income: Per capita income: $9,952 (2000); Median household income: $18,750 (2000); Poverty rate: 27.3% (2000).
Taxes: Total city taxes per capita: $96 (1997); City property taxes per capita: $14 (1997).
Education: High school graduation rate: 69.3% (2000); College graduation rate: 5.3% (2000).

School District(s)

Weaubleau R-III (PK-12)
2000 Enrollment: 460 417-428-3317
Housing: Homeownership rate: 71.2% (2000); Median home value: $38,000 (2000); Median rent: $174 per month (2000); Median age of housing: 33 years (2000).
Transportation: Commute to work: 95.0% car, 0.0% public transportation, 3.8% walk, 1.3% work from home (2000); Travel time to work: 39.5% less than 15 minutes, 19.7% 15 to 30 minutes, 21.0% 30 to 45 minutes, 1.3% 45 to 60 minutes, 18.5% 60 minutes or more (2000)

WHEATLAND (city). Covers a land area of 0.355 square miles and a water area of 0 square miles. Located at 37.94° N. Lat.; 93.40° W. Long. Elevation is 1,030 feet.
Population: 388 (2000); Race: 97.8% White, 0.2% Black, 0.0% Asian, 0.0% American Indian and Alaska Native, 0.0% Hispanic of any race, 2.0% two or more races (2000); Density: 1,093.8 persons per square mile (2000); Age:

27.5% under 18, 25.5% over 64 (2000); Marriage status: 20.3% never married, 50.2% now married, 17.8% widowed, 11.7% divorced (2000); Foreign born: 0.2% (2000); Ancestry (includes multiple ancestries): 18.4% German, 14.7% Other groups, 9.8% United States or American, 8.6% Irish, 4.7% English (2000).
Economy: Employment by occupation: 7.5% management, 0.8% professional, 31.7% services, 17.5% sales, 0.0% farming, 25.8% construction, 16.7% production (2000).
Income: Per capita income: $10,025 (2000); Median household income: $17,500 (2000); Poverty rate: 28.1% (2000).
Taxes: Total city taxes per capita: $34 (1997); City property taxes per capita: $10 (1997).
Education: High school graduation rate: 60.2% (2000); College graduation rate: 1.5% (2000).

School District(s)

Wheatland R-II (KG-12)
2000 Enrollment: 317 417-282-6433
Housing: Homeownership rate: 63.1% (2000); Median home value: $41,000 (2000); Median rent: $213 per month (2000); Median age of housing: 31 years (2000).
Transportation: Commute to work: 92.2% car, 0.0% public transportation, 2.6% walk, 5.2% work from home (2000); Travel time to work: 44.0% less than 15 minutes, 22.0% 15 to 30 minutes, 18.3% 30 to 45 minutes, 0.9% 45 to 60 minutes, 14.7% 60 minutes or more (2000)

Holt County

Located in northwestern Missouri; bounded on the west and south by the Missouri River and the Nebraska and Kansas borders, and on the east by the Nodaway River; drained by the Tarkio River. Covers a land area of 461.90 square miles, a water area of 7.20 square miles, and is located in the Central Time Zone. The county government was organized in 1841. County seat is Oregon.
Population: 5,351 (2000); Race: 98.5% White, 0.0% Black, 0.1% Asian, 0.5% American Indian and Alaska Native, 0.3% Hispanic of any race, 0.7% two or more races (2000); Density: 11.6 persons per square mile (2000); Age: 23.7% under 18, 21.5% over 64 (2000).
Religion: Five largest groups: 18.5% The United Methodist Church, 13.2% Christian Churches and Churches of Christ, 8.3% Christian Church (Disciples of Christ), 7.5% Lutheran Church—Missouri Synod, 7.4% Southern Baptist Convention (2000).
Economy: Unemployment rate: 4.5% (11/2002); Total civilian labor force: 2,422 (11/2002); Leading industries: 24.3% retail trade; 15.7% health care and social assistance; 15.6% accommodation & food services (2000); Companies that employ more than 1,000 persons: 0 (2000); Companies that employ more than 100 persons: 0 (2000); Farms: 465 totaling 231,040 acres (1997); Minority business ownership rate: 0.0% (1997); Women business ownership rate: 0.0% (1997); Retail sales per capita: $6,990 (1997). Single-family building permits issued: 6 (2001) / 4 (2000); Multi-family building permits issued: 0 (2001) / 0 (2000).
Income: Per capita income: $15,876 (2000); Median household income: $29,461 (2000); Poverty rate: 13.0% (2000); Bankruptcy rate: 4.11% (2001).
Taxes: Total county taxes per capita: $276 (2000); County property taxes per capita: $99 (2000).
Education: High school graduation rate: 81.9% (2000); College graduation rate: 11.7% (2000).
Housing: Homeownership rate: 74.4% (2000); Median home value: $50,100 (2000); Median rent: $206 per month (2000); Median age of housing: 47 years (2000).
Health: Birth rate: 97.2 per 10,000 population (1998); Age adjusted death rate: 85.0 per 10,000 population (1999); Age adjusted cancer mortality rate: 164.5 (Unreliable figure as per CDC) deaths per 100,000 population (1999). Number of physicians: 3.7 per 10,000 population (1999); Number of hospital beds: n/a (1999).
Elections: 2000 Presidential election results: 32.7% Gore, 65.3% Bush, 0.9% Nader, 0.8% Buchanan
National and State Parks: Big Lake State Park; Squaw Creek National Wildlife Refuge; Thurnau State Wildlife Area
Additional Information Contacts
Holt County Government Offices 660-446-3303
Mound City Chamber of Commerce 660-442-3262

Holt County Communities

BIG LAKE (village). Covers a land area of 1.694 square miles and a water area of 0.960 square miles. Located at 40.07° N. Lat.; 95.35° W. Long. Elevation is 365 feet.
Population: 127 (2000); Race: 97.9% White, 0.0% Black, 1.4% Asian, 0.7% American Indian and Alaska Native, 0.0% Hispanic of any race, 0.0% two or more races (2000); Density: 75.0 persons per square mile (2000); Age: 18.9% under 18, 24.5% over 64 (2000); Marriage status: 17.5% never married, 61.9% now married, 13.5% widowed, 7.1% divorced (2000); Foreign born: 1.4% (2000); Ancestry (includes multiple ancestries): 29.4% German, 16.8% Irish, 11.9% United States or American, 9.8% English, 9.1% Swedish (2000).
Economy: Single-family building permits issued: 4 (2001) / 2 (2000); Multi-family building permits issued: 0 (2001) / 0 (2000); Employment by occupation: 1.8% management, 7.3% professional, 21.8% services, 30.9% sales, 1.8% farming, 14.5% construction, 21.8% production (2000).
Income: Per capita income: $27,243 (2000); Median household income: $29,583 (2000); Poverty rate: 5.9% (2000).
Taxes: Total city taxes per capita: $53 (1997); City property taxes per capita: $53 (1997).
Education: High school graduation rate: 85.8% (2000); College graduation rate: 7.1% (2000).
Housing: Homeownership rate: 100.0% (2000); Median home value: $65,000 (2000); Median age of housing: 36 years (2000).
Transportation: Commute to work: 92.7% car, 0.0% public transportation, 0.0% walk, 7.3% work from home (2000); Travel time to work: 9.8% less than 15 minutes, 49.0% 15 to 30 minutes, 13.7% 30 to 45 minutes, 15.7% 45 to 60 minutes, 11.8% 60 minutes or more (2000)

BIGELOW (village). Covers a land area of 0.091 square miles and a water area of 0 square miles. Located at 40.11° N. Lat.; 95.29° W. Long. Elevation is 858 feet.
Population: 38 (2000); Race: 95.2% White, 0.0% Black, 0.0% Asian, 0.0% American Indian and Alaska Native, 0.0% Hispanic of any race, 4.8% two or more races (2000); Density: 415.9 persons per square mile (2000); Age: 21.4% under 18, 38.1% over 64 (2000); Marriage status: 0.0% never married, 51.5% now married, 9.1% widowed, 39.4% divorced (2000); Foreign born: 0.0% (2000); Ancestry (includes multiple ancestries): 35.7% English, 9.5% United States or American, 9.5% Scotch-Irish, 7.1% Dutch, 4.8% Irish (2000).
Economy: Squaw Creek National Wildlife Refuge nearby. Employment by occupation: 0.0% management, 0.0% professional, 52.0% services, 12.0% sales, 8.0% farming, 12.0% construction, 16.0% production (2000).
Income: Per capita income: $13,067 (2000); Median household income: $23,750 (2000); Poverty rate: 31.0% (2000).
Taxes: Total city taxes per capita: $121 (1997); City property taxes per capita: $30 (1997).
Education: High school graduation rate: 48.4% (2000); College graduation rate: 0.0% (2000).
Housing: Homeownership rate: 77.8% (2000); Median home value: <$10,000 (2000); Median rent: $175 per month (2000); Median age of housing: 60 years (2000).
Transportation: Commute to work: 88.0% car, 0.0% public transportation, 8.0% walk, 0.0% work from home (2000); Travel time to work: 36.0% less than 15 minutes, 32.0% 15 to 30 minutes, 0.0% 30 to 45 minutes, 8.0% 45 to 60 minutes, 24.0% 60 minutes or more (2000)

CORNING (town). Covers a land area of 0.111 square miles and a water area of 0 square miles. Located at 40.24° N. Lat.; 95.45° W. Long. Elevation is 875 feet.
History: Flooded 1993.
Population: 21 (2000); Race: 100.0% White, 0.0% Black, 0.0% Asian, 0.0% American Indian and Alaska Native, 0.0% Hispanic of any race, 0.0% two or more races (2000); Density: 188.9 persons per square mile (2000); Age: 20.0% under 18, 16.0% over 64 (2000); Marriage status: 4.8% never married, 85.7% now married, 9.5% widowed, 0.0% divorced (2000); Foreign born: 0.0% (2000); Ancestry (includes multiple ancestries): 28.0% Dutch, 12.0% Irish, 8.0% Other groups (2000).
Economy: Employment by occupation: 0.0% management, 18.2% professional, 0.0% services, 0.0% sales, 0.0% farming, 0.0% construction, 81.8% production (2000).
Income: Per capita income: $10,132 (2000); Median household income: $23,750 (2000); Poverty rate: 24.0% (2000).
Taxes: Total city taxes per capita: $34 (1997); City property taxes per capita: $11 (1997).
Education: High school graduation rate: 55.0% (2000); College graduation rate: 0.0% (2000).

Housing: Homeownership rate: 83.3% (2000); Median home value: $53,300 (2000); Median age of housing: 52 years (2000).
Transportation: Commute to work: 72.7% car, 0.0% public transportation, 0.0% walk, 0.0% work from home (2000); Travel time to work: 0.0% less than 15 minutes, 54.5% 15 to 30 minutes, 45.5% 30 to 45 minutes, 0.0% 45 to 60 minutes, 0.0% 60 minutes or more (2000)

CRAIG (city). Covers a land area of 0.276 square miles and a water area of 0 square miles. Located at 40.19° N. Lat.; 95.37° W. Long. Elevation is 868 feet.
History: Major flooding in area in 1993.
Population: 309 (2000); Race: 100.0% White, 0.0% Black, 0.0% Asian, 0.0% American Indian and Alaska Native, 0.0% Hispanic of any race, 0.0% two or more races (2000); Density: 1,120.0 persons per square mile (2000); Age: 26.5% under 18, 16.6% over 64 (2000); Marriage status: 21.9% never married, 55.5% now married, 11.3% widowed, 11.3% divorced (2000); Foreign born: 0.0% (2000); Ancestry (includes multiple ancestries): 25.9% German, 22.0% United States or American, 5.8% Irish, 4.2% English, 1.0% Norwegian (2000).
Economy: Corn, wheat; hogs, cattle. Employment by occupation: 1.8% management, 11.9% professional, 19.3% services, 16.5% sales, 1.8% farming, 22.0% construction, 26.6% production (2000).
Income: Per capita income: $10,719 (2000); Median household income: $22,500 (2000); Poverty rate: 17.9% (2000).
Taxes: Total city taxes per capita: $198 (1997); City property taxes per capita: $152 (1997).
Education: High school graduation rate: 70.2% (2000); College graduation rate: 3.7% (2000).

School District(s)

Craig R-III (KG-12)
2000 Enrollment: 158 660-683-5351
Housing: Homeownership rate: 84.7% (2000); Median home value: $22,300 (2000); Median rent: $300 per month (2000); Median age of housing: 55 years (2000).
Transportation: Commute to work: 98.2% car, 0.0% public transportation, 1.8% walk, 0.0% work from home (2000); Travel time to work: 35.8% less than 15 minutes, 19.3% 15 to 30 minutes, 18.3% 30 to 45 minutes, 12.8% 45 to 60 minutes, 13.8% 60 minutes or more (2000)

FOREST CITY (city). Covers a land area of 0.976 square miles and a water area of 0 square miles. Located at 39.98° N. Lat.; 95.19° W. Long. Elevation is 856 feet.
History: Laid out in 1857, Forest City was an important port on the Missouri River until the 1868 flood, when the river formed a new channel away from the town.
Population: 338 (2000); Race: 94.8% White, 0.0% Black, 0.0% Asian, 0.9% American Indian and Alaska Native, 0.0% Hispanic of any race, 4.3% two or more races (2000); Density: 346.3 persons per square mile (2000); Age: 26.0% under 18, 12.7% over 64 (2000); Marriage status: 19.5% never married, 60.2% now married, 10.5% widowed, 9.8% divorced (2000); Foreign born: 0.0% (2000); Ancestry (includes multiple ancestries): 26.0% United States or American, 21.7% German, 9.8% Irish, 7.2% Dutch, 5.2% English (2000).
Economy: Employment by occupation: 6.3% management, 15.2% professional, 26.6% services, 12.0% sales, 0.0% farming, 10.1% construction, 29.7% production (2000).
Income: Per capita income: $18,671 (2000); Median household income: $31,016 (2000); Poverty rate: 4.4% (2000).
Taxes: Total city taxes per capita: $130 (2000); City property taxes per capita: $74 (2000).
Education: High school graduation rate: 85.3% (2000); College graduation rate: 6.7% (2000).
Housing: Homeownership rate: 78.7% (2000); Median home value: $43,200 (2000); Median rent: $182 per month (2000); Median age of housing: 47 years (2000).
Transportation: Commute to work: 98.7% car, 0.0% public transportation, 0.0% walk, 1.3% work from home (2000); Travel time to work: 41.1% less than 15 minutes, 15.2% 15 to 30 minutes, 25.2% 30 to 45 minutes, 11.3% 45 to 60 minutes, 7.3% 60 minutes or more (2000)

FORTESCUE (town). Covers a land area of 0.076 square miles and a water area of 0 square miles. Located at 40.05° N. Lat.; 95.31° W. Long. Elevation is 860 feet.
History: Area flooded 1993.
Population: 51 (2000); Race: 100.0% White, 0.0% Black, 0.0% Asian, 0.0% American Indian and Alaska Native, 0.0% Hispanic of any race, 0.0% two or more races (2000); Density: 674.1 persons per square mile (2000); Age: 45.9% under 18, 0.0% over 64 (2000); Marriage status: 53.7% never married, 34.1% now married, 0.0% widowed, 12.2% divorced (2000); Foreign born: 0.0% (2000); Ancestry (includes multiple ancestries): 83.6% United States or American, 9.8% German, 6.6% Irish, 3.3% English (2000).
Economy: Manufacturing: lead alloys and smelting. Employment by occupation: 0.0% management, 13.3% professional, 30.0% services, 0.0% sales, 6.7% farming, 20.0% construction, 30.0% production (2000).
Income: Per capita income: $5,695 (2000); Median household income: $26,250 (2000); Poverty rate: 29.5% (2000).
Taxes: Total city taxes per capita: $10,667 (1997); City property taxes per capita: $0 (1997).
Education: High school graduation rate: 76.7% (2000); College graduation rate: 16.7% (2000).
Housing: Homeownership rate: 80.0% (2000); Median home value: $13,800 (2000); Median rent: $325 per month (2000); Median age of housing: 48 years (2000).
Transportation: Commute to work: 90.0% car, 0.0% public transportation, 0.0% walk, 10.0% work from home (2000); Travel time to work: 33.3% less than 15 minutes, 37.0% 15 to 30 minutes, 22.2% 30 to 45 minutes, 7.4% 45 to 60 minutes, 0.0% 60 minutes or more (2000)

MAITLAND (city). Covers a land area of 0.290 square miles and a water area of 0 square miles. Located at 40.20° N. Lat.; 95.07° W. Long. Elevation is 940 feet.
Population: 342 (2000); Race: 100.0% White, 0.0% Black, 0.0% Asian, 0.0% American Indian and Alaska Native, 0.0% Hispanic of any race, 0.0% two or more races (2000); Density: 1,179.7 persons per square mile (2000); Age: 31.6% under 18, 14.2% over 64 (2000); Marriage status: 21.4% never married, 57.5% now married, 9.5% widowed, 11.5% divorced (2000); Foreign born: 0.0% (2000); Ancestry (includes multiple ancestries): 20.9% United States or American, 15.9% German, 10.3% English, 9.1% Irish, 7.4% Other groups (2000).
Economy: Corn; cattle, hogs. Single-family building permits issued: 0 (2001) / 1 (2000); Multi-family building permits issued: 0 (2001) / 0 (2000); Employment by occupation: 10.3% management, 14.7% professional, 20.5% services, 17.9% sales, 0.0% farming, 15.4% construction, 21.2% production (2000).
Income: Per capita income: $13,743 (2000); Median household income: $31,250 (2000); Poverty rate: 10.9% (2000).
Taxes: Total city taxes per capita: $10 (1997); City property taxes per capita: $10 (1997).
Education: High school graduation rate: 82.8% (2000); College graduation rate: 9.6% (2000).
Housing: Homeownership rate: 78.7% (2000); Median home value: $32,500 (2000); Median rent: $166 per month (2000); Median age of housing: 58 years (2000).
Transportation: Commute to work: 86.0% car, 0.0% public transportation, 6.7% walk, 7.3% work from home (2000); Travel time to work: 30.2% less than 15 minutes, 23.7% 15 to 30 minutes, 30.9% 30 to 45 minutes, 3.6% 45 to 60 minutes, 11.5% 60 minutes or more (2000)

MOUND CITY (city). Covers a land area of 1.295 square miles and a water area of 0 square miles. Located at 40.13° N. Lat.; 95.23° W. Long. Elevation is 890 feet.
History: Mound City was first known as Jackson's Point, a stopping place on the stage route from St. Joseph to Council Bluffs. Mound City was platted in 1857, and named for a low hill upon which the city was built.
Population: 1,193 (2000); Race: 97.5% White, 0.0% Black, 0.0% Asian, 1.1% American Indian and Alaska Native, 1.0% Hispanic of any race, 0.6% two or more races (2000); Density: 921.4 persons per square mile (2000); Age: 20.0% under 18, 30.1% over 64 (2000); Marriage status: 16.3% never married, 57.6% now married, 15.0% widowed, 11.1% divorced (2000); Foreign born: 0.3% (2000); Ancestry (includes multiple ancestries): 23.8% German, 14.3% English, 11.6% United States or American, 10.1% Irish, 5.1% Other groups (2000).
Economy: Single-family building permits issued: 2 (2001) / 1 (2000); Multi-family building permits issued: 0 (2001) / 0 (2000); Employment by occupation: 10.4% management, 15.2% professional, 22.8% services, 23.2% sales, 0.6% farming, 8.8% construction, 19.0% production (2000).
Income: Per capita income: $15,985 (2000); Median household income: $24,219 (2000); Poverty rate: 12.5% (2000).
Taxes: Total city taxes per capita: $256 (1997); City property taxes per capita: $138 (1997).
Education: High school graduation rate: 77.0% (2000); College graduation rate: 11.7% (2000).

School District(s)

Mound City R-II (PK-12)
2000 Enrollment: 342 660-442-3737

Housing: Homeownership rate: 65.5% (2000); Median home value: $57,900 (2000); Median rent: $206 per month (2000); Median age of housing: 46 years (2000).

Newspapers: Mound City News (1 x week)

Transportation: Commute to work: 88.2% car, 0.0% public transportation, 6.9% walk, 3.2% work from home (2000); Travel time to work: 52.8% less than 15 minutes, 17.6% 15 to 30 minutes, 15.7% 30 to 45 minutes, 8.8% 45 to 60 minutes, 5.0% 60 minutes or more (2000)

Additional Information Contacts

Mound City Chamber of Commerce 660-442-3262

OREGON (city). Covers a land area of 1.004 square miles and a water area of 0 square miles. Located at 39.98° N. Lat.; 95.14° W. Long. Elevation is 1,094 feet.

History: Oregon was laid out in 1841 as the seat of the newly-organized Holt County. The town was named for the Oregon territory which was being settled about that time.

Population: 935 (2000); Race: 98.2% White, 0.0% Black, 0.0% Asian, 0.5% American Indian and Alaska Native, 0.0% Hispanic of any race, 1.3% two or more races (2000); Density: 931.0 persons per square mile (2000); Age: 27.0% under 18, 22.2% over 64 (2000); Marriage status: 18.2% never married, 59.0% now married, 10.5% widowed, 12.2% divorced (2000); Foreign born: 0.7% (2000); Ancestry (includes multiple ancestries): 25.4% German, 17.9% United States or American, 9.7% English, 7.3% Irish, 3.6% Scotch-Irish (2000).

Economy: Employment by occupation: 17.5% management, 20.2% professional, 14.7% services, 18.9% sales, 1.6% farming, 12.9% construction, 14.3% production (2000).

Income: Per capita income: $15,441 (2000); Median household income: $34,250 (2000); Poverty rate: 7.5% (2000).

Taxes: Total city taxes per capita: $91 (1997); City property taxes per capita: $53 (1997).

Education: High school graduation rate: 81.4% (2000); College graduation rate: 18.8% (2000).

School District(s)

South Holt Co. R-I (PK-12)
2000 Enrollment: 411 660-446-2282

Housing: Homeownership rate: 76.4% (2000); Median home value: $59,600 (2000); Median rent: $228 per month (2000); Median age of housing: 43 years (2000).

Newspapers: Times Observer (1 x week)

Transportation: Commute to work: 96.5% car, 0.0% public transportation, 0.5% walk, 3.0% work from home (2000); Travel time to work: 49.4% less than 15 minutes, 14.7% 15 to 30 minutes, 26.6% 30 to 45 minutes, 4.5% 45 to 60 minutes, 4.8% 60 minutes or more (2000)

Howard County

Located in central Missouri; bounded on the west and south by the Missouri River. Covers a land area of 465.70 square miles, a water area of 4.80 square miles, and is located in the Central Time Zone. The county government was organized in 1816. County seat is Fayette.

Weather Station: New Franklin 1 W Elevation: 639 feet

	Jan	Feb	Mar	Apr	May	Jun	Jul	Aug	Sep	Oct	Nov	Dec
High	37	44	55	66	76	85	90	88	80	69	54	42
Low	18	23	33	43	54	63	67	65	56	45	34	24
Precip	1.6	1.7	3.0	4.0	4.9	4.0	3.4	4.2	4.0	3.2	2.9	2.1
Snow	na	3.9	1.4	0.1	0.0	0.0	0.0	0.0	0.0	0.0	1.1	2.3

High and Low temperatures in degrees Fahrenheit; Precipitation and Snow in inches

Population: 10,212 (2000); Race: 91.4% White, 6.3% Black, 0.2% Asian, 0.4% American Indian and Alaska Native, 1.1% Hispanic of any race, 1.1% two or more races (2000); Density: 21.9 persons per square mile (2000); Age: 23.9% under 18, 16.2% over 64 (2000).

Religion: Five largest groups: 21.0% Southern Baptist Convention, 10.3% The United Methodist Church, 8.3% Catholic Church, 7.6% Christian Church (Disciples of Christ), 2.4% United Church of Christ (2000).

Economy: Unemployment rate: 4.4% (11/2002); Total civilian labor force: 4,330 (11/2002); Leading industries: 19.5% manufacturing; 17.2% health care and social assistance; 9.8% retail trade (2000); Companies that employ more than 1,000 persons: 0 (2000); Companies that employ more than 100 persons: 2 (2000); Farms: 709 totaling 242,364 acres (1997); Minority business ownership rate: 0.0% (1997); Women business ownership rate: 13.9% (1997); Retail sales per capita: $2,544 (1997). Single-family building permits issued: 3 (2001) / 3 (2000); Multi-family building permits issued: 16 (2001) / 0 (2000).

Income: Per capita income: $15,198 (2000); Median household income: $31,614 (2000); Poverty rate: 11.6% (2000); Bankruptcy rate: 3.16% (2001).

Taxes: Total county taxes per capita: $127 (2000); County property taxes per capita: $71 (2000).

Education: High school graduation rate: 81.3% (2000); College graduation rate: 17.9% (2000).

Housing: Homeownership rate: 75.2% (2000); Median home value: $59,500 (2000); Median rent: $251 per month (2000); Median age of housing: 38 years (2000).

Health: Birth rate: 100.9 per 10,000 population (1998); Age adjusted death rate: 94.2 per 10,000 population (1999); Age adjusted cancer mortality rate: 181.1 deaths per 100,000 population (1999). Number of physicians: 5.9 per 10,000 population (1999); Number of hospital beds: n/a (1999).

Elections: 2000 Presidential election results: 43.1% Gore, 53.5% Bush, 1.8% Nader, 1.0% Buchanan

National and State Parks: Boonslick State Park; Rudolf Bennitt State Wildlife Area

Additional Information Contacts

Howard County Government Offices. 660-248-3400
Fayette Chamber of Commerce 660-248-2200

Howard County Communities

ARMSTRONG (city). Covers a land area of 0.843 square miles and a water area of 0 square miles. Located at 39.26° N. Lat.; 92.70° W. Long. Elevation is 830 feet.

Population: 287 (2000); Race: 91.3% White, 4.2% Black, 0.8% Asian, 0.0% American Indian and Alaska Native, 1.1% Hispanic of any race, 3.8% two or more races (2000); Density: 340.5 persons per square mile (2000); Age: 29.4% under 18, 24.5% over 64 (2000); Marriage status: 21.1% never married, 61.3% now married, 7.0% widowed, 10.6% divorced (2000); Foreign born: 1.5% (2000); Ancestry (includes multiple ancestries): 26.4% German, 17.0% English, 12.8% Irish, 11.7% Other groups, 7.9% United States or American (2000).

Economy: Corn, soybeans; hogs, cattle. Employment by occupation: 13.1% management, 10.3% professional, 14.0% services, 14.0% sales, 2.8% farming, 17.8% construction, 28.0% production (2000).

Income: Per capita income: $13,055 (2000); Median household income: $24,167 (2000); Poverty rate: 16.5% (2000).

Taxes: Total city taxes per capita: $121 (1997); City property taxes per capita: $38 (1997).

Education: High school graduation rate: 75.6% (2000); College graduation rate: 11.9% (2000).

Housing: Homeownership rate: 83.2% (2000); Median home value: $29,400 (2000); Median rent: $238 per month (2000); Median age of housing: 59 years (2000).

Transportation: Commute to work: 93.5% car, 0.0% public transportation, 4.7% walk, 1.9% work from home (2000); Travel time to work: 29.5% less than 15 minutes, 27.6% 15 to 30 minutes, 21.9% 30 to 45 minutes, 12.4% 45 to 60 minutes, 8.6% 60 minutes or more (2000)

FAYETTE (city). Covers a land area of 2.228 square miles and a water area of 0 square miles. Located at 39.14° N. Lat.; 92.68° W. Long. Elevation is 700 feet.

History: Fayette was designated as the seat of Howard County in 1823, and became the political and social, though not the commercial, center of the county.

Population: 2,793 (2000); Race: 79.8% White, 15.4% Black, 0.7% Asian, 1.0% American Indian and Alaska Native, 2.1% Hispanic of any race, 2.1% two or more races (2000); Density: 1,253.6 persons per square mile (2000); Age: 17.9% under 18, 18.1% over 64 (2000); Marriage status: 43.8% never married, 40.8% now married, 6.7% widowed, 8.8% divorced (2000); Foreign born: 2.0% (2000); Ancestry (includes multiple ancestries): 19.6% Other groups, 18.2% German, 10.0% English, 8.9% Irish, 6.0% United States or American (2000).

Economy: Single-family building permits issued: 1 (2001) / 3 (2000); Multi-family building permits issued: 16 (2001) / 0 (2000); Employment by occupation: 8.8% management, 19.9% professional, 25.9% services, 25.4% sales, 1.2% farming, 8.5% construction, 10.3% production (2000).

Income: Per capita income: $13,451 (2000); Median household income: $27,276 (2000); Poverty rate: 15.6% (2000).

Taxes: Total city taxes per capita: $301 (2000); City property taxes per capita: $178 (2000).
Education: High school graduation rate: 76.5% (2000); College graduation rate: 24.8% (2000).

School District(s)

Fayette R-III (KG-12)
2000 Enrollment: 718 660-248-2153

Four-year College(s)

Central Methodist College (Private, Not-for-profit, United Methodist)
2001 Enrollment: 1,279 660-248-3391
2001 Tuition: In-state $11,950; Out-of-state $11,950
Housing: Homeownership rate: 63.4% (2000); Median home value: $58,300 (2000); Median rent: $264 per month (2000); Median age of housing: 54 years (2000).
Safety: Violent crime rate: 14.2 per 10,000 population; Property crime rate: 103.2 per 10,000 population (2001).
Newspapers: The Fayette Advertiser (1 x week); The Democrat-Leader (1 x week)
Transportation: Commute to work: 76.5% car, 0.0% public transportation, 15.8% walk, 7.0% work from home (2000); Travel time to work: 50.7% less than 15 minutes, 14.0% 15 to 30 minutes, 21.2% 30 to 45 minutes, 11.2% 45 to 60 minutes, 2.9% 60 minutes or more (2000)
Additional Information Contacts
Fayette Chamber of Commerce 660-248-2200

FRANKLIN (city). Covers a land area of 0.229 square miles and a water area of 0.003 square miles. Located at 39.01° N. Lat.; 92.75° W. Long. Elevation is 590 feet.
History: Former railroad junction. Original East terminus of the Santa Fe Trail. It has the same name as the town established in 1816, 2 miles away on the Missouri River, which was destroyed by floods in the 1820s.
Population: 112 (2000); Race: 100.0% White, 0.0% Black, 0.0% Asian, 0.0% American Indian and Alaska Native, 0.0% Hispanic of any race, 0.0% two or more races (2000); Density: 490.1 persons per square mile (2000); Age: 27.7% under 18, 7.9% over 64 (2000); Marriage status: 10.4% never married, 55.8% now married, 7.8% widowed, 26.0% divorced (2000); Foreign born: 0.0% (2000); Ancestry (includes multiple ancestries): 29.7% Other groups, 18.8% United States or American, 13.9% German, 12.9% Irish, 5.9% Dutch (2000).
Economy: Employment by occupation: 10.0% management, 5.0% professional, 25.0% services, 12.5% sales, 0.0% farming, 12.5% construction, 35.0% production (2000).
Income: Per capita income: $15,104 (2000); Median household income: $28,542 (2000); Poverty rate: 20.8% (2000).
Taxes: Total city taxes per capita: $47 (1997); City property taxes per capita: $21 (1997).
Education: High school graduation rate: 70.4% (2000); College graduation rate: 2.8% (2000).
Housing: Homeownership rate: 95.7% (2000); Median home value: $32,500 (2000); Median rent: $375 per month (2000); Median age of housing: 29 years (2000).
Transportation: Commute to work: 88.9% car, 0.0% public transportation, 11.1% walk, 0.0% work from home (2000); Travel time to work: 30.6% less than 15 minutes, 19.4% 15 to 30 minutes, 50.0% 30 to 45 minutes, 0.0% 45 to 60 minutes, 0.0% 60 minutes or more (2000)

GLASGOW (city). Covers a land area of 1.335 square miles and a water area of 0.088 square miles. Located at 39.22° N. Lat.; 92.84° W. Long. Elevation is 650 feet.
History: Glasgow was laid out in 1836, after three earlier attempts to establish a river port in the vicinity had failed, and named for James Glasgow, a St. Louis merchant. Glasgow suffered during the Civil War because of divided loyalties. The bridge across the Missouri River built by the Chicago & Alton Railroad in 1879 was the first all-steel railway bridge in the world, and was used until 1922.
Population: 1,263 (2000); Race: 90.6% White, 8.3% Black, 0.0% Asian, 0.2% American Indian and Alaska Native, 0.0% Hispanic of any race, 0.9% two or more races (2000); Density: 946.1 persons per square mile (2000); Age: 26.0% under 18, 18.1% over 64 (2000); Marriage status: 23.5% never married, 58.4% now married, 6.8% widowed, 11.3% divorced (2000); Foreign born: 0.0% (2000); Ancestry (includes multiple ancestries): 32.3% German, 13.9% United States or American, 10.1% Irish, 10.0% Other groups, 5.3% English (2000).
Economy: Single-family building permits issued: 2 (2001) / 0 (2000); Multi-family building permits issued: 0 (2001) / 0 (2000); Employment by occupation: 7.6% management, 15.3% professional, 18.6% services, 19.4% sales, 2.8% farming, 11.6% construction, 24.6% production (2000).
Income: Per capita income: $14,544 (2000); Median household income: $30,242 (2000); Poverty rate: 10.8% (2000).
Taxes: Total city taxes per capita: $614 (2000); City property taxes per capita: $223 (2000).
Education: High school graduation rate: 82.9% (2000); College graduation rate: 16.2% (2000).

School District(s)

Howard Co. R-II (PK-12)
2000 Enrollment: 380 660-338-2012
Housing: Homeownership rate: 72.6% (2000); Median home value: $52,400 (2000); Median rent: $211 per month (2000); Median age of housing: 45 years (2000).
Newspapers: The Glasgow Missourian (1 x week)
Transportation: Commute to work: 92.8% car, 0.5% public transportation, 3.4% walk, 3.4% work from home (2000); Travel time to work: 47.1% less than 15 minutes, 19.8% 15 to 30 minutes, 18.0% 30 to 45 minutes, 6.4% 45 to 60 minutes, 8.7% 60 minutes or more (2000)

NEW FRANKLIN (city). Covers a land area of 1.334 square miles and a water area of 0 square miles. Located at 39.01° N. Lat.; 92.73° W. Long. Elevation is 645 feet.
History: New Franklin was laid out in 1828 by James Alcorn, a Revolutionary War soldier. The town grew when the Missouri-Kansas-Texas Railroad shops were built nearby.
Population: 1,145 (2000); Race: 97.9% White, 0.4% Black, 0.0% Asian, 0.1% American Indian and Alaska Native, 1.5% Hispanic of any race, 1.5% two or more races (2000); Density: 858.6 persons per square mile (2000); Age: 25.6% under 18, 21.0% over 64 (2000); Marriage status: 16.4% never married, 57.1% now married, 15.3% widowed, 11.2% divorced (2000); Foreign born: 0.9% (2000); Ancestry (includes multiple ancestries): 28.2% German, 14.1% Irish, 11.7% United States or American, 10.6% Other groups, 8.5% English (2000).
Economy: Single-family building permits issued: 0 (2001) / 0 (2000); Multi-family building permits issued: 0 (2001) / 0 (2000); Employment by occupation: 9.4% management, 11.7% professional, 19.4% services, 26.0% sales, 1.1% farming, 12.5% construction, 19.8% production (2000).
Income: Per capita income: $14,657 (2000); Median household income: $30,357 (2000); Poverty rate: 13.7% (2000).
Taxes: Total city taxes per capita: $226 (1997); City property taxes per capita: $44 (1997).
Education: High school graduation rate: 78.7% (2000); College graduation rate: 10.7% (2000).

School District(s)

New Franklin R-I (PK-12)
2000 Enrollment: 486 660-848-2141
Housing: Homeownership rate: 68.0% (2000); Median home value: $57,900 (2000); Median rent: $247 per month (2000); Median age of housing: 39 years (2000).
Transportation: Commute to work: 90.5% car, 0.4% public transportation, 4.7% walk, 4.1% work from home (2000); Travel time to work: 35.8% less than 15 minutes, 23.9% 15 to 30 minutes, 21.7% 30 to 45 minutes, 11.3% 45 to 60 minutes, 7.3% 60 minutes or more (2000)

Howell County

Located in southern Missouri, in the Ozarks; bounded on the south by Arkansas; drained by the Eleven Point River; includes part of Mark Twain National Forest. Covers a land area of 927.70 square miles, a water area of 0.60 square miles, and is located in the Central Time Zone. The county government was organized in 1857. County seat is West Plains.

Weather Station: West Plains — Elevation: 1,007 feet

	Jan	Feb	Mar	Apr	May	Jun	Jul	Aug	Sep	Oct	Nov	Dec
High	43	49	58	69	76	84	90	88	80	71	57	47
Low	21	26	34	43	52	61	66	64	57	44	34	26
Precip	2.6	2.9	4.9	4.6	4.5	4.3	3.1	3.3	4.1	3.6	4.8	4.0
Snow	3.7	3.4	2.6	0.2	0.0	0.0	0.0	0.0	0.0	tr	0.7	1.9

High and Low temperatures in degrees Fahrenheit; Precipitation and Snow in inches

Weather Station: Willow Springs Radio KUKU Elevation: 1,309 feet

	Jan	Feb	Mar	Apr	May	Jun	Jul	Aug	Sep	Oct	Nov	Dec
High	42	48	58	68	76	83	89	88	80	70	56	46
Low	22	26	35	44	52	61	65	64	57	45	35	26
Precip	2.1	2.3	4.2	4.6	4.8	4.0	3.2	3.0	3.5	3.8	4.2	3.5
Snow	3.9	2.1	2.4	0.3	0.0	0.0	0.0	0.0	0.0	tr	0.6	1.6

High and Low temperatures in degrees Fahrenheit; Precipitation and Snow in inches

Population: 37,238 (2000); Race: 96.2% White, 0.2% Black, 0.6% Asian, 0.9% American Indian and Alaska Native, 1.1% Hispanic of any race, 1.6% two or more races (2000); Density: 40.1 persons per square mile (2000); Age: 25.9% under 18, 16.8% over 64 (2000).
Religion: Five largest groups: 23.2% Southern Baptist Convention, 4.3% Churches of Christ, 3.4% Catholic Church, 3.3% Christian Churches and Churches of Christ, 2.7% Assemblies of God (2000).
Economy: Unemployment rate: 4.5% (11/2002); Total civilian labor force: 16,908 (11/2002); Leading industries: 29.6% manufacturing; 20.4% health care and social assistance; 17.0% retail trade (2000); Companies that employ more than 1,000 persons: 1 (2000); Companies that employ more than 100 persons: 21 (2000); Farms: 1,637 totaling 386,796 acres (1997); Minority business ownership rate: 3.0% (1997); Women business ownership rate: 18.7% (1997); Retail sales per capita: $9,894 (1997). Single-family building permits issued: 45 (2001) / 61 (2000); Multi-family building permits issued: 2 (2001) / 2 (2000).
Income: Per capita income: $13,959 (2000); Median household income: $25,628 (2000); Poverty rate: 18.7% (2000); Bankruptcy rate: 3.43% (2001).
Taxes: Total county taxes per capita: $114 (2000); County property taxes per capita: $64 (2000).
Education: High school graduation rate: 73.4% (2000); College graduation rate: 10.9% (2000).
Housing: Homeownership rate: 73.5% (2000); Median home value: $67,700 (2000); Median rent: $263 per month (2000); Median age of housing: 24 years (2000).
Health: Birth rate: 132.7 per 10,000 population (1998); Age adjusted death rate: 101.1 per 10,000 population (1999); Age adjusted cancer mortality rate: 223.4 deaths per 100,000 population (1999). Number of physicians: 12.9 per 10,000 population (1999); Number of hospital beds: 36.0 per 10,000 population (1999).
Elections: 2000 Presidential election results: 33.0% Gore, 64.1% Bush, 1.4% Nader, 1.0% Buchanan
National and State Parks: Dean Davis State Wildlife Area; White River State Forest
Additional Information Contacts
Howell County Government Offices 417-256-2591
Mountain View Chamber of Commerce 417-934-2794
West Plains Board of Realtors 417-256-6988
West Plains Chamber of Commerce 417-256-4433
Willow Springs Chamber 417-469-5519

Howell County Communities

BRANDSVILLE (city). Covers a land area of 0.473 square miles and a water area of 0 square miles. Located at 36.65° N. Lat.; 91.69° W. Long. Elevation is 949 feet.
History: Brandsville grew as a trading center for farmers.
Population: 174 (2000); Race: 96.4% White, 0.0% Black, 0.0% Asian, 1.5% American Indian and Alaska Native, 0.0% Hispanic of any race, 2.1% two or more races (2000); Density: 367.7 persons per square mile (2000); Age: 32.5% under 18, 7.2% over 64 (2000); Marriage status: 27.5% never married, 53.5% now married, 5.6% widowed, 13.4% divorced (2000); Foreign born: 0.0% (2000); Ancestry (includes multiple ancestries): 21.6% United States or American, 18.6% German, 18.0% Irish, 12.4% English, 6.7% Other groups (2000).
Economy: Employment by occupation: 5.6% management, 7.9% professional, 4.5% services, 22.5% sales, 6.7% farming, 24.7% construction, 28.1% production (2000).
Income: Per capita income: $12,024 (2000); Median household income: $27,188 (2000); Poverty rate: 21.4% (2000).
Taxes: Total city taxes per capita: $22 (1997); City property taxes per capita: $0 (1997).
Education: High school graduation rate: 82.9% (2000); College graduation rate: 6.3% (2000).
Housing: Homeownership rate: 88.7% (2000); Median home value: $36,700 (2000); Median rent: $235 per month (2000); Median age of housing: 29 years (2000).
Transportation: Commute to work: 83.9% car, 0.0% public transportation, 9.2% walk, 3.4% work from home (2000); Travel time to work: 21.4% less than 15 minutes, 71.4% 15 to 30 minutes, 4.8% 30 to 45 minutes, 0.0% 45 to 60 minutes, 2.4% 60 minutes or more (2000)

CAULFIELD (unincorporated postal area, zip code 65626). Covers a land area of 102.298 square miles and a water area of 0 square miles. Located at 36.61° N. Lat.; 92.14° W. Long. Elevation is 1,029 feet.
Population: 1,678 (2000); Race: 97.4% White, 0.0% Black, 0.1% Asian, 1.3% American Indian and Alaska Native, 0.1% Hispanic of any race, 1.3% two or more races (2000); Density: 16.4 persons per square mile (2000); Age: 27.9% under 18, 13.2% over 64 (2000); Marriage status: 18.8% never married, 62.3% now married, 8.5% widowed, 10.4% divorced (2000); Foreign born: 0.3% (2000); Ancestry (includes multiple ancestries): 28.0% United States or American, 8.5% German, 8.4% Other groups, 6.6% Irish, 5.1% English (2000).
Economy: Employment by occupation: 9.7% management, 6.4% professional, 18.6% services, 20.3% sales, 2.7% farming, 12.5% construction, 29.7% production (2000).
Income: Per capita income: $12,787 (2000); Median household income: $23,125 (2000); Poverty rate: 25.9% (2000).
Education: High school graduation rate: 67.1% (2000); College graduation rate: 4.9% (2000).
Housing: Homeownership rate: 85.0% (2000); Median home value: $43,500 (2000); Median rent: $217 per month (2000); Median age of housing: 22 years (2000).
Transportation: Commute to work: 91.4% car, 0.8% public transportation, 2.8% walk, 3.3% work from home (2000); Travel time to work: 17.9% less than 15 minutes, 23.1% 15 to 30 minutes, 39.8% 30 to 45 minutes, 15.2% 45 to 60 minutes, 4.0% 60 minutes or more (2000)

MOODY (unincorporated postal area, zip code 65777). Covers a land area of 17.511 square miles and a water area of 0 square miles. Located at 36.52° N. Lat.; 91.98° W. Long. Elevation is 975 feet.
Population: 337 (2000); Race: 100.0% White, 0.0% Black, 0.0% Asian, 0.0% American Indian and Alaska Native, 0.0% Hispanic of any race, 0.0% two or more races (2000); Density: 19.2 persons per square mile (2000); Age: 19.3% under 18, 14.8% over 64 (2000); Marriage status: 21.9% never married, 65.8% now married, 1.7% widowed, 10.6% divorced (2000); Foreign born: 0.0% (2000); Ancestry (includes multiple ancestries): 31.8% German, 14.2% English, 11.9% French (except Basque), 11.1% Irish, 11.1% United States or American (2000).
Economy: Employment by occupation: 12.2% management, 20.7% professional, 3.7% services, 14.6% sales, 3.0% farming, 25.6% construction, 20.1% production (2000).
Income: Per capita income: $11,831 (2000); Median household income: $23,750 (2000); Poverty rate: 10.8% (2000).
Education: High school graduation rate: 75.7% (2000); College graduation rate: 8.4% (2000).
Housing: Homeownership rate: 79.3% (2000); Median home value: $40,400 (2000); Median rent: $375 per month (2000); Median age of housing: 26 years (2000).
Transportation: Commute to work: 91.5% car, 0.0% public transportation, 0.0% walk, 8.5% work from home (2000); Travel time to work: 25.3% less than 15 minutes, 24.7% 15 to 30 minutes, 37.3% 30 to 45 minutes, 12.7% 45 to 60 minutes, 0.0% 60 minutes or more (2000)

MOUNTAIN VIEW (city). Covers a land area of 3.675 square miles and a water area of 0 square miles. Located at 36.99° N. Lat.; 91.70° W. Long. Elevation is 1,144 feet.
History: Mountain View grew around a mill that began producing railroad ties, staves, and finished lumber in 1878.
Population: 2,430 (2000); Race: 95.4% White, 0.0% Black, 0.0% Asian, 1.4% American Indian and Alaska Native, 1.3% Hispanic of any race, 2.3% two or more races (2000); Density: 661.2 persons per square mile (2000); Age: 24.0% under 18, 24.4% over 64 (2000); Marriage status: 15.4% never married, 59.5% now married, 15.3% widowed, 9.8% divorced (2000); Foreign born: 1.6% (2000); Ancestry (includes multiple ancestries): 15.5% German, 13.1% Irish, 11.3% English, 11.2% United States or American, 10.3% Other groups (2000).
Economy: Single-family building permits issued: 17 (2001) / 17 (2000); Multi-family building permits issued: 0 (2001) / 0 (2000); Employment by occupation: 5.3% management, 20.2% professional, 13.5% services, 19.2% sales, 1.3% farming, 10.5% construction, 30.0% production (2000).
Income: Per capita income: $14,022 (2000); Median household income: $22,308 (2000); Poverty rate: 24.3% (2000).

Taxes: Total city taxes per capita: $205 (1997); City property taxes per capita: $79 (1997).
Education: High school graduation rate: 70.6% (2000); College graduation rate: 11.7% (2000).

School District(s)

Mountain View-Birch Tree R-III (PK-12)
2000 Enrollment: 1,380 417-934-2020
Housing: Homeownership rate: 64.2% (2000); Median home value: $59,600 (2000); Median rent: $204 per month (2000); Median age of housing: 24 years (2000).
Hospitals: St Francis Hospital (42 beds)
Newspapers: Mountain View Standard News (1 x week)
Transportation: Commute to work: 92.0% car, 0.0% public transportation, 2.4% walk, 3.1% work from home (2000); Travel time to work: 63.5% less than 15 minutes, 10.6% 15 to 30 minutes, 12.7% 30 to 45 minutes, 5.3% 45 to 60 minutes, 7.9% 60 minutes or more (2000)
Additional Information Contacts
Mountain View Chamber of Commerce 417-934-2794

PEACE VALLEY (unincorporated postal area, zip code 65788). Covers a land area of 27.732 square miles and a water area of 0 square miles. Located at 36.80° N. Lat.; 91.71° W. Long. Elevation is 1,093 feet.
Population: 447 (2000); Race: 97.6% White, 0.0% Black, 0.0% Asian, 1.2% American Indian and Alaska Native, 0.0% Hispanic of any race, 1.2% two or more races (2000); Density: 16.1 persons per square mile (2000); Age: 30.2% under 18, 10.2% over 64 (2000); Marriage status: 14.8% never married, 68.8% now married, 9.0% widowed, 7.4% divorced (2000); Foreign born: 2.9% (2000); Ancestry (includes multiple ancestries): 17.4% Other groups, 13.6% United States or American, 10.2% Irish, 4.5% English, 4.5% German (2000).
Economy: Employment by occupation: 3.8% management, 1.6% professional, 24.0% services, 23.5% sales, 3.8% farming, 10.4% construction, 32.8% production (2000).
Income: Per capita income: $12,037 (2000); Median household income: $28,417 (2000); Poverty rate: 6.9% (2000).
Education: High school graduation rate: 64.7% (2000); College graduation rate: 0.0% (2000).
Housing: Homeownership rate: 81.0% (2000); Median home value: $36,900 (2000); Median rent: $294 per month (2000); Median age of housing: 26 years (2000).
Transportation: Commute to work: 90.0% car, 0.0% public transportation, 0.0% walk, 7.2% work from home (2000); Travel time to work: 5.4% less than 15 minutes, 55.1% 15 to 30 minutes, 34.1% 30 to 45 minutes, 0.0% 45 to 60 minutes, 5.4% 60 minutes or more (2000)

POMONA (unincorporated postal area, zip code 65789). Covers a land area of 74.105 square miles and a water area of 0 square miles. Located at 36.85° N. Lat.; 91.89° W. Long. Elevation is 1,241 feet.
Population: 1,889 (2000); Race: 95.2% White, 2.5% Black, 0.9% Asian, 0.0% American Indian and Alaska Native, 0.2% Hispanic of any race, 1.4% two or more races (2000); Density: 25.5 persons per square mile (2000); Age: 29.1% under 18, 10.4% over 64 (2000); Marriage status: 19.3% never married, 70.9% now married, 3.4% widowed, 6.4% divorced (2000); Foreign born: 1.3% (2000); Ancestry (includes multiple ancestries): 18.5% United States or American, 16.7% German, 11.4% Other groups, 8.0% Irish, 4.1% English (2000).
Economy: Employment by occupation: 7.2% management, 12.1% professional, 18.9% services, 17.8% sales, 2.8% farming, 14.9% construction, 26.3% production (2000).
Income: Per capita income: $14,445 (2000); Median household income: $26,250 (2000); Poverty rate: 14.5% (2000).
Education: High school graduation rate: 70.5% (2000); College graduation rate: 6.5% (2000).
Housing: Homeownership rate: 83.8% (2000); Median home value: $63,800 (2000); Median rent: $285 per month (2000); Median age of housing: 22 years (2000).
Transportation: Commute to work: 92.9% car, 0.6% public transportation, 0.7% walk, 4.6% work from home (2000); Travel time to work: 19.4% less than 15 minutes, 50.7% 15 to 30 minutes, 17.0% 30 to 45 minutes, 3.5% 45 to 60 minutes, 9.3% 60 minutes or more (2000)

POTTERSVILLE (unincorporated postal area, zip code 65790). Covers a land area of 52.343 square miles and a water area of 0 square miles. Located at 36.67° N. Lat.; 92.10° W. Long. Elevation is 962 feet.
Population: 646 (2000); Race: 96.8% White, 0.0% Black, 2.7% Asian, 0.2% American Indian and Alaska Native, 0.3% Hispanic of any race, 0.0% two or more races (2000); Density: 12.3 persons per square mile (2000); Age: 19.7% under 18, 19.2% over 64 (2000); Marriage status: 14.4% never married, 76.0% now married, 4.4% widowed, 5.2% divorced (2000); Foreign born: 1.5% (2000); Ancestry (includes multiple ancestries): 16.1% United States or American, 12.9% Other groups, 11.9% English, 7.8% German, 6.5% Irish (2000).
Economy: Employment by occupation: 13.6% management, 5.4% professional, 14.3% services, 23.3% sales, 7.9% farming, 15.4% construction, 20.1% production (2000).
Income: Per capita income: $11,712 (2000); Median household income: $26,500 (2000); Poverty rate: 22.8% (2000).
Education: High school graduation rate: 66.8% (2000); College graduation rate: 8.6% (2000).
Housing: Homeownership rate: 88.6% (2000); Median home value: $66,800 (2000); Median rent: $225 per month (2000); Median age of housing: 26 years (2000).
Transportation: Commute to work: 89.6% car, 1.1% public transportation, 0.0% walk, 7.9% work from home (2000); Travel time to work: 13.6% less than 15 minutes, 49.8% 15 to 30 minutes, 30.7% 30 to 45 minutes, 1.6% 45 to 60 minutes, 4.3% 60 minutes or more (2000)

WEST PLAINS (city). Covers a land area of 12.362 square miles and a water area of 0.021 square miles. Located at 36.73° N. Lat.; 91.86° W. Long. Elevation is 991 feet.
History: West Plains was laid out in 1858 as the seat of Howell County, named for Josiah Howell who was one of the first residents in West Plains. The town grew as the center of an agricultural area, with creameries and livestock shipping pens.
Population: 10,866 (2000); Race: 96.2% White, 0.2% Black, 1.1% Asian, 0.6% American Indian and Alaska Native, 2.1% Hispanic of any race, 1.2% two or more races (2000); Density: 879.0 persons per square mile (2000); Age: 24.3% under 18, 21.5% over 64 (2000); Marriage status: 16.6% never married, 60.4% now married, 11.7% widowed, 11.4% divorced (2000); Foreign born: 1.5% (2000); Ancestry (includes multiple ancestries): 14.7% United States or American, 14.0% German, 13.5% Other groups, 11.3% Irish, 8.4% English (2000).
Economy: Single-family building permits issued: 28 (2001) / 44 (2000); Multi-family building permits issued: 2 (2001) / 2 (2000); Employment by occupation: 10.1% management, 16.7% professional, 16.0% services, 26.7% sales, 0.3% farming, 5.6% construction, 24.4% production (2000).
Income: Per capita income: $15,019 (2000); Median household income: $24,122 (2000); Poverty rate: 19.0% (2000).
Taxes: Total city taxes per capita: $394 (2000); City property taxes per capita: $0 (2000).
Education: High school graduation rate: 74.0% (2000); College graduation rate: 13.4% (2000).

School District(s)

Fairview R-XI (PK-08)
2000 Enrollment: 586 417-256-1063
Glenwood R-VIII (PK-08)
2000 Enrollment: 278 417-256-4849
Howell Valley R-I (KG-08)
2000 Enrollment: 216 417-256-2268
Junction Hill C-12 (PK-08)
2000 Enrollment: 302 417-256-4265
Richards R-V (PK-08)
2000 Enrollment: 552 417-256-5239
West Plains R-VII (PK-12)
2000 Enrollment: 2,714 417-256-6150

Two-year College(s)

Southwest Missouri State University-West Plains (Public)
2001 Enrollment: 1,653 417-255-7255
2001 Tuition: In-state $2,280; Out-of-state $4,560
Housing: Homeownership rate: 61.1% (2000); Median home value: $70,300 (2000); Median rent: $276 per month (2000); Median age of housing: 27 years (2000).
Hospitals: Ozarks Medical Center (114 beds)
Safety: Violent crime rate: 52.1 per 10,000 population; Property crime rate: 572.6 per 10,000 population (2001).
Newspapers: West Plains Daily Quill (5 x week)
Transportation: Commute to work: 94.4% car, 0.5% public transportation, 2.0% walk, 2.2% work from home (2000); Travel time to work: 72.0% less than 15 minutes, 16.5% 15 to 30 minutes, 5.8% 30 to 45 minutes, 1.3% 45 to 60 minutes, 4.3% 60 minutes or more (2000)
Additional Information Contacts
West Plains Board of Realtors 417-256-6988

West Plains Chamber of Commerce 417-256-4433

WILLOW SPRINGS (city). Covers a land area of 3.278 square miles and a water area of 0.016 square miles. Located at 36.99° N. Lat.; 91.96° W. Long. Elevation is 1,257 feet.
History: Willow Springs developed around several sawmills, and as a dairy and poultry center.
Population: 2,147 (2000); Race: 96.6% White, 0.6% Black, 0.4% Asian, 0.4% American Indian and Alaska Native, 0.7% Hispanic of any race, 1.7% two or more races (2000); Density: 654.9 persons per square mile (2000); Age: 22.7% under 18, 27.9% over 64 (2000); Marriage status: 16.9% never married, 56.2% now married, 16.1% widowed, 10.8% divorced (2000); Foreign born: 0.8% (2000); Ancestry (includes multiple ancestries): 16.4% United States or American, 10.5% Irish, 9.9% German, 9.2% Other groups, 9.2% English (2000).
Economy: Single-family building permits issued: 0 (2001) / 0 (2000); Multi-family building permits issued: 0 (2001) / 0 (2000); Employment by occupation: 7.4% management, 16.6% professional, 16.9% services, 26.1% sales, 1.6% farming, 8.8% construction, 22.6% production (2000).
Income: Per capita income: $13,681 (2000); Median household income: $19,894 (2000); Poverty rate: 26.0% (2000).
Taxes: Total city taxes per capita: $21 (1997); City property taxes per capita: $6 (1997).
Education: High school graduation rate: 64.6% (2000); College graduation rate: 11.1% (2000).

School District(s)

Willow Springs R-IV (PK-12)
2000 Enrollment: 1,336 417-469-3260
Housing: Homeownership rate: 62.4% (2000); Median home value: $49,400 (2000); Median rent: $191 per month (2000); Median age of housing: 39 years (2000).
Transportation: Commute to work: 90.6% car, 0.0% public transportation, 5.3% walk, 3.7% work from home (2000); Travel time to work: 57.9% less than 15 minutes, 18.1% 15 to 30 minutes, 16.7% 30 to 45 minutes, 0.9% 45 to 60 minutes, 6.5% 60 minutes or more (2000)
Additional Information Contacts
Willow Springs Chamber 417-469-5519

Iron County

Located in southeast central Missouri, partly in the St. Francois Mountains; includes Taum Sauk Mountain, the highest point in the state (1,772 ft), and parts of Clark National Forest. Covers a land area of 551.30 square miles, a water area of 0.70 square miles, and is located in the Central Time Zone. The county government was organized in 1857. County seat is Ironton.

Weather Station: Arcadia — Elevation: 1,069 feet

	Jan	Feb	Mar	Apr	May	Jun	Jul	Aug	Sep	Oct	Nov	Dec
High	41	48	59	71	77	84	89	88	80	70	56	46
Low	21	25	34	44	52	60	64	63	55	44	35	27
Precip	2.4	2.5	4.2	4.7	5.1	4.1	3.6	4.6	3.9	3.6	5.6	3.7
Snow	4.3	3.5	1.8	0.6	0.0	0.0	0.0	0.0	0.0	tr	1.1	1.9

High and Low temperatures in degrees Fahrenheit; Precipitation and Snow in inches

Population: 10,697 (2000); Race: 96.5% White, 1.5% Black, 0.1% Asian, 0.5% American Indian and Alaska Native, 0.5% Hispanic of any race, 1.3% two or more races (2000); Density: 19.4 persons per square mile (2000); Age: 24.9% under 18, 17.1% over 64 (2000).
Religion: Five largest groups: 24.9% Southern Baptist Convention, 4.6% The United Methodist Church, 3.4% Catholic Church, 3.0% Assemblies of God, 1.9% Church of the Nazarene (2000).
Economy: Unemployment rate: 7.7% (11/2002); Total civilian labor force: 5,266 (11/2002); Leading industries: 20.0% health care and social assistance; 16.7% manufacturing; 16.3% retail trade (2000); Companies that employ more than 1,000 persons: 0 (2000); Companies that employ more than 100 persons: 4 (2000); Farms: 274 totaling 62,537 acres (1997); Minority business ownership rate: 0.0% (1997); Women business ownership rate: 13.4% (1997); Retail sales per capita: $5,109 (1997). Single-family building permits issued: 2 (2001) / 2 (2000); Multi-family building permits issued: 0 (2001) / 0 (2000).
Income: Per capita income: $14,227 (2000); Median household income: $26,080 (2000); Poverty rate: 19.0% (2000); Bankruptcy rate: 4.25% (2001).
Taxes: Total county taxes per capita: $92 (1997); County property taxes per capita: $63 (1997).
Education: High school graduation rate: 65.2% (2000); College graduation rate: 8.4% (2000).
Housing: Homeownership rate: 75.9% (2000); Median home value: $51,800 (2000); Median rent: $258 per month (2000); Median age of housing: 29 years (2000).
Health: Birth rate: 118.7 per 10,000 population (1998); Age adjusted death rate: 136.6 per 10,000 population (1999); Age adjusted cancer mortality rate: 355.1 deaths per 100,000 population (1999). Air Quality Index: 92% good, 8% moderate, 0% unhealthy (percent of days in 2000). Number of physicians: 6.5 per 10,000 population (1999); Number of hospital beds: n/a (1999).
Elections: 2000 Presidential election results: 46.3% Gore, 50.7% Bush, 1.5% Nader, 0.9% Buchanan
National and State Parks: Elephant Rocks State Park; Johnson Shut-Ins State Park
Additional Information Contacts
Iron County Government Offices 573-546-2912
Arcadia Valley Chamber of Commerce 573-546-7117
Viburnum Chamber of Commerce 573-244-3200

Iron County Communities

ANNAPOLIS (city). Covers a land area of 0.380 square miles and a water area of 0 square miles. Located at 37.36° N. Lat.; 90.69° W. Long. Elevation is 655 feet.
Population: 310 (2000); Race: 98.1% White, 0.0% Black, 0.0% Asian, 1.0% American Indian and Alaska Native, 0.0% Hispanic of any race, 1.0% two or more races (2000); Density: 815.5 persons per square mile (2000); Age: 26.3% under 18, 23.7% over 64 (2000); Marriage status: 20.2% never married, 51.9% now married, 15.2% widowed, 12.8% divorced (2000); Foreign born: 0.0% (2000); Ancestry (includes multiple ancestries): 24.0% United States or American, 15.7% Irish, 14.1% German, 8.3% English, 3.5% Other groups (2000).
Economy: Rhyolite quarry; manufactures roofing granules. Employment by occupation: 9.7% management, 24.3% professional, 9.7% services, 17.5% sales, 4.9% farming, 6.8% construction, 27.2% production (2000).
Income: Per capita income: $10,015 (2000); Median household income: $16,389 (2000); Poverty rate: 22.1% (2000).
Taxes: Total city taxes per capita: $206 (1997); City property taxes per capita: $43 (1997).
Education: High school graduation rate: 65.7% (2000); College graduation rate: 12.3% (2000).

School District(s)

South Iron Co. R-I (PK-12)
2000 Enrollment: 453 573-598-4241
Housing: Homeownership rate: 60.3% (2000); Median home value: $42,000 (2000); Median rent: $237 per month (2000); Median age of housing: 39 years (2000).
Transportation: Commute to work: 83.8% car, 0.0% public transportation, 14.1% walk, 0.0% work from home (2000); Travel time to work: 48.5% less than 15 minutes, 13.1% 15 to 30 minutes, 23.2% 30 to 45 minutes, 4.0% 45 to 60 minutes, 11.1% 60 minutes or more (2000)

ARCADIA (city). Aka Arcadia-Ironton. Covers a land area of 0.837 square miles and a water area of 0 square miles. Located at 37.58° N. Lat.; 90.62° W. Long. Elevation is 915 feet.
History: Arcadia was platted in 1849 and grew as a resort village surrounded by mountain streams and woodlands.
Population: 567 (2000); Race: 96.4% White, 0.0% Black, 0.0% Asian, 1.0% American Indian and Alaska Native, 0.0% Hispanic of any race, 2.6% two or more races (2000); Density: 677.6 persons per square mile (2000); Age: 21.7% under 18, 26.5% over 64 (2000); Marriage status: 16.8% never married, 59.5% now married, 13.8% widowed, 9.9% divorced (2000); Foreign born: 0.7% (2000); Ancestry (includes multiple ancestries): 19.6% Irish, 15.4% Other groups, 15.3% German, 10.4% English, 9.9% French (except Basque) (2000).
Economy: Single-family building permits issued: 0 (2001) / 0 (2000); Multi-family building permits issued: 0 (2001) / 0 (2000); Employment by occupation: 11.3% management, 17.4% professional, 22.5% services, 26.3% sales, 0.5% farming, 11.3% construction, 10.8% production (2000).
Income: Per capita income: $15,374 (2000); Median household income: $24,333 (2000); Poverty rate: 21.3% (2000).
Taxes: Total city taxes per capita: $223 (1997); City property taxes per capita: $32 (1997).
Education: High school graduation rate: 69.9% (2000); College graduation rate: 10.5% (2000).

Housing: Homeownership rate: 63.8% (2000); Median home value: $67,100 (2000); Median rent: $253 per month (2000); Median age of housing: 37 years (2000).
Transportation: Commute to work: 93.4% car, 0.0% public transportation, 4.3% walk, 2.4% work from home (2000); Travel time to work: 54.4% less than 15 minutes, 5.3% 15 to 30 minutes, 25.7% 30 to 45 minutes, 4.9% 45 to 60 minutes, 9.7% 60 minutes or more (2000)

BELLEVIEW (unincorporated postal area, zip code 63623). Covers a land area of 107.923 square miles and a water area of 0.007 square miles. Located at 37.68° N. Lat.; 90.88° W. Long. Elevation is 1,050 feet.
Population: 823 (2000); Race: 96.8% White, 0.7% Black, 0.0% Asian, 0.2% American Indian and Alaska Native, 0.0% Hispanic of any race, 2.2% two or more races (2000); Density: 7.6 persons per square mile (2000); Age: 21.2% under 18, 19.4% over 64 (2000); Marriage status: 23.0% never married, 59.6% now married, 8.8% widowed, 8.5% divorced (2000); Foreign born: 0.6% (2000); Ancestry (includes multiple ancestries): 20.0% United States or American, 14.4% Irish, 13.1% German, 10.1% Other groups, 7.3% French (except Basque) (2000).
Economy: Employment by occupation: 9.2% management, 14.0% professional, 19.9% services, 19.2% sales, 0.7% farming, 12.9% construction, 24.0% production (2000).
Income: Per capita income: $16,080 (2000); Median household income: $26,250 (2000); Poverty rate: 12.3% (2000).
Education: High school graduation rate: 58.8% (2000); College graduation rate: 4.8% (2000).

School District(s)

Belleview R-III (PK-08)
2000 Enrollment: 176 573-697-5702
Housing: Homeownership rate: 85.9% (2000); Median home value: $40,800 (2000); Median rent: $225 per month (2000); Median age of housing: 31 years (2000).
Transportation: Commute to work: 90.6% car, 1.1% public transportation, 0.8% walk, 6.4% work from home (2000); Travel time to work: 18.5% less than 15 minutes, 32.5% 15 to 30 minutes, 25.3% 30 to 45 minutes, 6.4% 45 to 60 minutes, 17.3% 60 minutes or more (2000)

BIXBY (unincorporated postal area, zip code 65439). Covers a land area of 34.380 square miles and a water area of 0.015 square miles. Located at 37.67° N. Lat.; 91.11° W. Long. Elevation is 1,410 feet.
Population: 310 (2000); Race: 100.0% White, 0.0% Black, 0.0% Asian, 0.0% American Indian and Alaska Native, 4.7% Hispanic of any race, 0.0% two or more races (2000); Density: 9.0 persons per square mile (2000); Age: 18.3% under 18, 12.0% over 64 (2000); Marriage status: 16.3% never married, 70.4% now married, 3.1% widowed, 10.1% divorced (2000); Foreign born: 1.0% (2000); Ancestry (includes multiple ancestries): 20.0% Irish, 18.7% United States or American, 17.3% English, 10.7% Other groups, 10.7% German (2000).
Economy: Employment by occupation: 4.6% management, 9.2% professional, 21.6% services, 22.2% sales, 6.5% farming, 9.2% construction, 26.8% production (2000).
Income: Per capita income: $11,795 (2000); Median household income: $23,125 (2000); Poverty rate: 13.3% (2000).
Education: High school graduation rate: 57.6% (2000); College graduation rate: 6.7% (2000).
Housing: Homeownership rate: 83.1% (2000); Median home value: $47,500 (2000); Median rent: $150 per month (2000); Median age of housing: 24 years (2000).
Transportation: Commute to work: 85.6% car, 0.0% public transportation, 9.8% walk, 0.0% work from home (2000); Travel time to work: 56.2% less than 15 minutes, 20.9% 15 to 30 minutes, 14.4% 30 to 45 minutes, 5.9% 45 to 60 minutes, 2.6% 60 minutes or more (2000)

DES ARC (village). Covers a land area of 0.210 square miles and a water area of 0 square miles. Located at 37.28° N. Lat.; 90.63° W. Long. Elevation is 555 feet.
Population: 187 (2000); Race: 96.7% White, 2.3% Black, 0.0% Asian, 0.9% American Indian and Alaska Native, 0.0% Hispanic of any race, 0.0% two or more races (2000); Density: 889.6 persons per square mile (2000); Age: 27.7% under 18, 18.8% over 64 (2000); Marriage status: 7.6% never married, 73.9% now married, 6.4% widowed, 12.1% divorced (2000); Foreign born: 0.0% (2000); Ancestry (includes multiple ancestries): 14.6% United States or American, 13.1% Irish, 10.3% Other groups, 8.5% German, 8.0% English (2000).
Economy: Employment by occupation: 3.3% management, 11.5% professional, 21.3% services, 13.1% sales, 8.2% farming, 18.0% construction, 24.6% production (2000).
Income: Per capita income: $10,461 (2000); Median household income: $22,917 (2000); Poverty rate: 29.1% (2000).
Taxes: Total city taxes per capita: $40 (1997); City property taxes per capita: $11 (1997).
Education: High school graduation rate: 49.4% (2000); College graduation rate: 3.2% (2000).
Housing: Homeownership rate: 74.1% (2000); Median home value: $32,200 (2000); Median rent: $183 per month (2000); Median age of housing: 60+ years (2000).
Transportation: Commute to work: 84.7% car, 0.0% public transportation, 11.9% walk, 0.0% work from home (2000); Travel time to work: 15.3% less than 15 minutes, 50.8% 15 to 30 minutes, 8.5% 30 to 45 minutes, 16.9% 45 to 60 minutes, 8.5% 60 minutes or more (2000)

IRONTON (city). Covers a land area of 1.358 square miles and a water area of 0.044 square miles. Located at 37.60° N. Lat.; 90.63° W. Long. Elevation is 910 feet.
History: Ironton was founded in 1857 as the county seat when Iron County was organized. An early interest in mining was soon replaced by tourist activities.
Population: 1,471 (2000); Race: 93.6% White, 4.3% Black, 0.0% Asian, 0.5% American Indian and Alaska Native, 1.1% Hispanic of any race, 1.2% two or more races (2000); Density: 1,083.2 persons per square mile (2000); Age: 23.2% under 18, 18.6% over 64 (2000); Marriage status: 27.6% never married, 50.2% now married, 11.7% widowed, 10.5% divorced (2000); Foreign born: 0.5% (2000); Ancestry (includes multiple ancestries): 16.8% German, 15.6% Other groups, 13.5% Irish, 10.3% English, 9.8% United States or American (2000).
Economy: Single-family building permits issued: 0 (2001) / 2 (2000); Multi-family building permits issued: 0 (2001) / 0 (2000); Employment by occupation: 6.9% management, 20.1% professional, 20.8% services, 18.8% sales, 0.0% farming, 12.9% construction, 20.5% production (2000).
Income: Per capita income: $14,710 (2000); Median household income: $23,808 (2000); Poverty rate: 22.9% (2000).
Taxes: Total city taxes per capita: $272 (1997); City property taxes per capita: $47 (1997).
Education: High school graduation rate: 68.1% (2000); College graduation rate: 11.1% (2000).

School District(s)

Arcadia Valley R-II (PK-12)
2000 Enrollment: 1,223 573-546-7313
Housing: Homeownership rate: 67.2% (2000); Median home value: $56,900 (2000); Median rent: $258 per month (2000); Median age of housing: 39 years (2000).
Safety: Violent crime rate: 67.6 per 10,000 population; Property crime rate: 358.1 per 10,000 population (2001).
Newspapers: Mountain Echo (1 x week)
Transportation: Commute to work: 94.7% car, 0.0% public transportation, 3.7% walk, 1.3% work from home (2000); Travel time to work: 47.2% less than 15 minutes, 18.3% 15 to 30 minutes, 19.8% 30 to 45 minutes, 5.2% 45 to 60 minutes, 9.4% 60 minutes or more (2000)
Additional Information Contacts
Arcadia Valley Chamber of Commerce 573-546-7117

MIDDLE BROOK (unincorporated postal area, zip code 63656). Aka Middlebrook. Covers a land area of 55.208 square miles and a water area of 0.225 square miles. Located at 37.61° N. Lat.; 90.77° W. Long.
Population: 470 (2000); Race: 97.2% White, 0.0% Black, 0.0% Asian, 0.0% American Indian and Alaska Native, 0.0% Hispanic of any race, 2.8% two or more races (2000); Density: 8.5 persons per square mile (2000); Age: 22.8% under 18, 10.9% over 64 (2000); Marriage status: 15.2% never married, 68.5% now married, 7.2% widowed, 9.0% divorced (2000); Foreign born: 0.0% (2000); Ancestry (includes multiple ancestries): 16.6% United States or American, 11.1% German, 10.7% Irish, 9.2% Other groups, 9.0% French (except Basque) (2000).
Economy: Employment by occupation: 7.4% management, 12.5% professional, 23.9% services, 25.0% sales, 2.8% farming, 13.6% construction, 14.8% production (2000).
Income: Per capita income: $19,833 (2000); Median household income: $36,944 (2000); Poverty rate: 11.7% (2000).
Education: High school graduation rate: 69.3% (2000); College graduation rate: 14.2% (2000).

Housing: Homeownership rate: 89.8% (2000); Median home value: $32,500 (2000); Median rent: $331 per month (2000); Median age of housing: 25 years (2000).
Transportation: Commute to work: 96.6% car, 0.0% public transportation, 0.0% walk, 3.4% work from home (2000); Travel time to work: 12.4% less than 15 minutes, 36.5% 15 to 30 minutes, 30.6% 30 to 45 minutes, 7.6% 45 to 60 minutes, 12.9% 60 minutes or more (2000)

PILOT KNOB (city). Covers a land area of 0.867 square miles and a water area of 0 square miles. Located at 37.62° N. Lat.; 90.64° W. Long. Elevation is 962 feet.
History: Pilot Knob was named for the 600-foot mountain that rises above the town. The mountain was once thought to be composed of solid iron, but after about fifty years, mining was no longer productive here and the community turned to agriculture.
Population: 697 (2000); Race: 94.2% White, 3.1% Black, 1.0% Asian, 0.7% American Indian and Alaska Native, 0.0% Hispanic of any race, 0.9% two or more races (2000); Density: 803.7 persons per square mile (2000); Age: 24.8% under 18, 15.6% over 64 (2000); Marriage status: 24.3% never married, 49.9% now married, 11.2% widowed, 14.6% divorced (2000); Foreign born: 0.9% (2000); Ancestry (includes multiple ancestries): 20.3% Other groups, 20.2% United States or American, 15.4% German, 10.1% English, 8.5% Irish (2000).
Economy: Single-family building permits issued: 2 (2001) / 0 (2000); Multi-family building permits issued: 0 (2001) / 0 (2000); Employment by occupation: 6.5% management, 11.8% professional, 27.6% services, 20.3% sales, 0.0% farming, 10.6% construction, 23.2% production (2000).
Income: Per capita income: $12,487 (2000); Median household income: $19,702 (2000); Poverty rate: 27.0% (2000).
Taxes: Total city taxes per capita: $249 (1997); City property taxes per capita: $20 (1997).
Education: High school graduation rate: 64.6% (2000); College graduation rate: 4.4% (2000).
Housing: Homeownership rate: 55.2% (2000); Median home value: $41,800 (2000); Median rent: $252 per month (2000); Median age of housing: 31 years (2000).
Transportation: Commute to work: 94.9% car, 0.0% public transportation, 2.6% walk, 1.3% work from home (2000); Travel time to work: 47.4% less than 15 minutes, 22.8% 15 to 30 minutes, 17.7% 30 to 45 minutes, 3.4% 45 to 60 minutes, 8.6% 60 minutes or more (2000)

VIBURNUM (city). Covers a land area of 1.722 square miles and a water area of 0.007 square miles. Located at 37.71° N. Lat.; 91.12° W. Long. Elevation is 1,270 feet.
History: Located in the "New Lead Belt," discovered in 1955.
Population: 825 (2000); Race: 98.8% White, 0.0% Black, 0.2% Asian, 1.0% American Indian and Alaska Native, 0.4% Hispanic of any race, 0.0% two or more races (2000); Density: 479.0 persons per square mile (2000); Age: 32.4% under 18, 16.9% over 64 (2000); Marriage status: 18.5% never married, 62.8% now married, 11.6% widowed, 7.1% divorced (2000); Foreign born: 1.3% (2000); Ancestry (includes multiple ancestries): 16.6% German, 14.0% Irish, 10.3% United States or American, 9.1% Other groups, 8.0% English (2000).
Economy: In a unit of the Mark Twain National Forest. 90% of US lead mined here. Employment by occupation: 9.4% management, 24.4% professional, 14.7% services, 21.6% sales, 1.6% farming, 13.1% construction, 15.3% production (2000).
Income: Per capita income: $15,085 (2000); Median household income: $34,107 (2000); Poverty rate: 13.6% (2000).
Taxes: Total city taxes per capita: $397 (1997); City property taxes per capita: $266 (1997).
Education: High school graduation rate: 70.3% (2000); College graduation rate: 15.2% (2000).

School District(s)

Iron Co. C-4 (PK-12)
2000 Enrollment: 569 573-244-5422

Housing: Homeownership rate: 71.9% (2000); Median home value: $54,800 (2000); Median rent: $250 per month (2000); Median age of housing: 27 years (2000).
Transportation: Commute to work: 97.4% car, 0.0% public transportation, 1.6% walk, 1.0% work from home (2000); Travel time to work: 68.4% less than 15 minutes, 11.3% 15 to 30 minutes, 11.0% 30 to 45 minutes, 5.2% 45 to 60 minutes, 4.2% 60 minutes or more (2000)
Additional Information Contacts
Viburnum Chamber of Commerce 573-244-3200

VULCAN (unincorporated postal area, zip code 63675). Covers a land area of 21.824 square miles and a water area of 0 square miles. Located at 37.32° N. Lat.; 90.68° W. Long. Elevation is 558 feet.
Population: 157 (2000); Race: 100.0% White, 0.0% Black, 0.0% Asian, 0.0% American Indian and Alaska Native, 0.0% Hispanic of any race, 0.0% two or more races (2000); Density: 7.2 persons per square mile (2000); Age: 19.5% under 18, 20.1% over 64 (2000); Marriage status: 25.9% never married, 60.0% now married, 6.7% widowed, 7.4% divorced (2000); Foreign born: 0.0% (2000); Ancestry (includes multiple ancestries): 19.5% United States or American, 19.5% German, 17.6% English, 8.8% Irish, 3.8% French (except Basque) (2000).
Economy: Employment by occupation: 11.8% management, 10.3% professional, 20.6% services, 14.7% sales, 11.8% farming, 10.3% construction, 20.6% production (2000).
Income: Per capita income: $17,302 (2000); Median household income: $28,750 (2000); Poverty rate: 15.1% (2000).
Education: High school graduation rate: 60.0% (2000); College graduation rate: 10.9% (2000).
Housing: Homeownership rate: 75.3% (2000); Median home value: $46,300 (2000); Median rent: $238 per month (2000); Median age of housing: 31 years (2000).
Transportation: Commute to work: 90.9% car, 0.0% public transportation, 0.0% walk, 9.1% work from home (2000); Travel time to work: 46.7% less than 15 minutes, 16.7% 15 to 30 minutes, 15.0% 30 to 45 minutes, 6.7% 45 to 60 minutes, 15.0% 60 minutes or more (2000)

Jackson County

Located in western Missouri; bounded on the west by Kansas, and on the north by the Missouri River, with the Kansas River entering the Missouri in the northwest. Covers a land area of 604.80 square miles, a water area of 11.60 square miles, and is located in the Central Time Zone. The county government was organized in 1826. County seat is Independence.

Jackson County is part of the Kansas City, MO-KS MSA. The entire metro area includes: Johnson County, KS; Leavenworth County, KS; Miami County, KS; Wyandotte County, KS; Cass County, MO; Clay County, MO; Clinton County, MO; Jackson County, MO; Lafayette County, MO; Platte County, MO; Ray County, MO

Weather Station: Lees Summit Reed Wildlife Refuge Elevation: 997 feet

	Jan	Feb	Mar	Apr	May	Jun	Jul	Aug	Sep	Oct	Nov	Dec
High	38	45	56	67	76	85	90	88	80	70	54	42
Low	17	23	32	43	53	61	66	64	56	44	33	23
Precip	1.3	1.5	2.8	4.0	5.2	5.4	4.1	4.0	4.9	3.5	2.9	1.9
Snow	5.6	5.1	1.8	0.3	0.0	0.0	0.0	0.0	0.0	tr	0.7	2.3

High and Low temperatures in degrees Fahrenheit; Precipitation and Snow in inches

Population: 654,880 (2000); Race: 70.1% White, 22.9% Black, 1.3% Asian, 0.5% American Indian and Alaska Native, 5.3% Hispanic of any race, 2.5% two or more races (2000); Density: 1,082.7 persons per square mile (2000); Age: 25.7% under 18, 12.5% over 64 (2000).
Religion: Five largest groups: 15.4% Catholic Church, 11.5% Southern Baptist Convention, 4.2% The United Methodist Church, 3.1% Christian Church (Disciples of Christ), 2.3% Assemblies of God (2000).
Economy: Unemployment rate: 5.8% (11/2002); Total civilian labor force: 384,380 (11/2002); Leading industries: 12.2% health care and social assistance; 10.4% retail trade; 9.8% manufacturing (2000); Companies that employ more than 1,000 persons: 29 (2000); Companies that employ more than 100 persons: 603 (2000); Farms: 765 totaling 150,581 acres (1997); Minority business ownership rate: 11.1% (1997); Women business ownership rate: 25.0% (1997); Retail sales per capita: $11,066 (1997). Single-family building permits issued: 3,376 (2001) / 3,086 (2000); Multi-family building permits issued: 1,822 (2001) / 1,261 (2000).
Income: Per capita income: $20,788 (2000); Median household income: $39,277 (2000); Poverty rate: 11.9% (2000); Bankruptcy rate: 6.08% (2001).
Taxes: Total county taxes per capita: $204 (2000); County property taxes per capita: $99 (2000).
Education: High school graduation rate: 83.4% (2000); College graduation rate: 23.4% (2000).
Housing: Homeownership rate: 62.9% (2000); Median home value: $85,000 (2000); Median rent: $432 per month (2000); Median age of housing: 37 years (2000).
Health: Birth rate: 152.4 per 10,000 population (1998); Age adjusted death rate: 93.7 per 10,000 population (1999); Infant mortality rate: 8.7 per 1,000

live births (1998); Age adjusted cancer mortality rate: 207.6 deaths per 100,000 population (1999). Air Quality Index: 100% good, 0% moderate, 0% unhealthy (percent of days in 2000). Number of physicians: 24.9 per 10,000 population (1999); Number of hospital beds: 61.4 per 10,000 population (1999).
Elections: 2000 Presidential election results: 59.0% Gore, 38.4% Bush, 1.9% Nader, 0.3% Buchanan
Additional Information Contacts
Jackson County Government Offices 816-881-3333
Blue Springs Chamber of Commerce 816-229-8558
Grain Valley Chamber of Commerce 816-443-2627
Grandview Chamber of Commerce 816-761-6505
Hispanic Chamber of Commerce 816-472-6767
Independence Chamber of Commerce 816-252-4745
Kansas City Chamber of Commerce 816-221-2424
Kansas City Convention & Visitors Bureau 816-221-5242
Lees Summit Chamber of Commerce 816-524-2424
North Kansas City Business 816-472-7700

Jackson County Communities

BLUE SPRINGS (city). Covers a land area of 18.194 square miles and a water area of 0.027 square miles. Located at 39.01° N. Lat.; 94.27° W. Long. Elevation is 972 feet.
Population: 48,080 (2000); Race: 92.9% White, 2.9% Black, 1.0% Asian, 0.7% American Indian and Alaska Native, 2.4% Hispanic of any race, 1.7% two or more races (2000); Density: 2,642.7 persons per square mile (2000); Age: 29.2% under 18, 7.4% over 64 (2000); Marriage status: 21.7% never married, 63.4% now married, 4.2% widowed, 10.7% divorced (2000); Foreign born: 1.7% (2000); Ancestry (includes multiple ancestries): 25.4% German, 14.6% Irish, 14.1% English, 13.1% Other groups, 8.6% United States or American (2000).
Vital Statistics: Birth rate: 147.3 per 10,000 population (1998)
Economy: Agriculture to East: wheat, corn; dairy farms. Manufacturing: fabricated metal products, tool and die, apparel, transportation equipment, paper products. Unemployment rate: 3.3% (11/2002); Total civilian labor force: 25,177 (11/2002); Single-family building permits issued: 307 (2001) / 306 (2000); Multi-family building permits issued: 44 (2001) / 114 (2000); Employment by occupation: 15.5% management, 20.9% professional, 12.1% services, 30.1% sales, 0.1% farming, 10.1% construction, 11.1% production (2000).
Income: Per capita income: $23,444 (2000); Median household income: $55,402 (2000); Poverty rate: 4.8% (2000).
Taxes: Total city taxes per capita: $315 (2000); City property taxes per capita: $74 (2000).
Education: High school graduation rate: 92.4% (2000); College graduation rate: 27.4% (2000).

School District(s)

Blue Springs R-IV (PK-12)
2000 Enrollment: 12,685 816-224-1300
Housing: Homeownership rate: 74.1% (2000); Median home value: $108,300 (2000); Median rent: $543 per month (2000); Median age of housing: 19 years (2000).
Hospitals: Saint Mary's Hospital of Blue Springs (130 beds)
Safety: Violent crime rate: 20.5 per 10,000 population; Property crime rate: 433.1 per 10,000 population (2001).
Newspapers: The Blue Springs Examiner (6 x week)
Transportation: Commute to work: 94.6% car, 0.4% public transportation, 0.6% walk, 3.9% work from home (2000); Travel time to work: 24.1% less than 15 minutes, 29.8% 15 to 30 minutes, 32.0% 30 to 45 minutes, 10.8% 45 to 60 minutes, 3.3% 60 minutes or more (2000)
Additional Information Contacts
Blue Springs Chamber of Commerce 816-229-8558

BUCKNER (city). Covers a land area of 1.708 square miles and a water area of 0.003 square miles. Located at 39.13° N. Lat.; 94.19° W. Long. Elevation is 752 feet.
History: Buckner began as a station on the Missouri Pacific Railroad in 1875.
Population: 2,725 (2000); Race: 95.3% White, 0.1% Black, 0.1% Asian, 0.4% American Indian and Alaska Native, 2.2% Hispanic of any race, 2.6% two or more races (2000); Density: 1,595.3 persons per square mile (2000); Age: 31.1% under 18, 9.8% over 64 (2000); Marriage status: 20.4% never married, 60.0% now married, 6.1% widowed, 13.6% divorced (2000); Foreign born: 0.8% (2000); Ancestry (includes multiple ancestries): 21.8% German, 15.1% Irish, 12.0% United States or American, 11.7% English, 9.6% Other groups (2000).
Economy: Single-family building permits issued: 19 (2001) / 2 (2000); Multi-family building permits issued: 0 (2001) / 0 (2000); Employment by occupation: 6.5% management, 13.4% professional, 16.3% services, 25.2% sales, 0.2% farming, 16.8% construction, 21.7% production (2000).
Income: Per capita income: $16,748 (2000); Median household income: $40,577 (2000); Poverty rate: 8.4% (2000).
Taxes: Total city taxes per capita: $165 (1997); City property taxes per capita: $37 (1997).
Education: High school graduation rate: 79.6% (2000); College graduation rate: 8.3% (2000).
Housing: Homeownership rate: 73.2% (2000); Median home value: $71,600 (2000); Median rent: $337 per month (2000); Median age of housing: 30 years (2000).
Transportation: Commute to work: 97.0% car, 0.2% public transportation, 0.2% walk, 1.7% work from home (2000); Travel time to work: 18.6% less than 15 minutes, 31.5% 15 to 30 minutes, 26.4% 30 to 45 minutes, 16.1% 45 to 60 minutes, 7.3% 60 minutes or more (2000)

GRAIN VALLEY (city). Covers a land area of 4.800 square miles and a water area of 0.006 square miles. Located at 39.00° N. Lat.; 94.20° W. Long. Elevation is 793 feet.
Population: 5,160 (2000); Race: 95.8% White, 0.8% Black, 0.6% Asian, 0.0% American Indian and Alaska Native, 2.8% Hispanic of any race, 1.9% two or more races (2000); Density: 1,075.0 persons per square mile (2000); Age: 32.2% under 18, 4.7% over 64 (2000); Marriage status: 19.9% never married, 67.4% now married, 3.6% widowed, 9.1% divorced (2000); Foreign born: 0.7% (2000); Ancestry (includes multiple ancestries): 24.0% German, 14.5% Other groups, 12.5% Irish, 11.8% United States or American, 7.8% English (2000).
Economy: Sorghum, wheat, corn; cattle. Manufacturing: railroad communications equipment. Single-family building permits issued: 146 (2001) / 198 (2000); Multi-family building permits issued: 52 (2001) / 24 (2000); Employment by occupation: 11.5% management, 17.1% professional, 13.1% services, 27.6% sales, 0.2% farming, 16.4% construction, 14.1% production (2000).
Income: Per capita income: $20,265 (2000); Median household income: $50,118 (2000); Poverty rate: 4.4% (2000).
Taxes: Total city taxes per capita: $197 (1997); City property taxes per capita: $101 (1997).
Education: High school graduation rate: 89.1% (2000); College graduation rate: 18.1% (2000).

School District(s)

Grain Valley R-V (PK-12)
2000 Enrollment: 1,735 816-847-5006
Housing: Homeownership rate: 74.9% (2000); Median home value: $102,800 (2000); Median rent: $573 per month (2000); Median age of housing: 4 years (2000).
Safety: Violent crime rate: 9.6 per 10,000 population; Property crime rate: 306.2 per 10,000 population (2001).
Transportation: Commute to work: 96.9% car, 0.0% public transportation, 0.5% walk, 1.9% work from home (2000); Travel time to work: 25.9% less than 15 minutes, 28.2% 15 to 30 minutes, 26.3% 30 to 45 minutes, 13.3% 45 to 60 minutes, 6.3% 60 minutes or more (2000)
Additional Information Contacts
Grain Valley Chamber of Commerce 816-443-2627

GRANDVIEW (city). Covers a land area of 14.728 square miles and a water area of 0.142 square miles. Located at 38.88° N. Lat.; 94.52° W. Long. Elevation is 1,049 feet.
History: Harry S. Truman farm nearby. Incorporated 1912.
Population: 24,881 (2000); Race: 59.7% White, 33.4% Black, 0.7% Asian, 0.4% American Indian and Alaska Native, 4.5% Hispanic of any race, 3.8% two or more races (2000); Density: 1,689.4 persons per square mile (2000); Age: 26.8% under 18, 9.9% over 64 (2000); Marriage status: 29.5% never married, 52.3% now married, 5.2% widowed, 13.0% divorced (2000); Foreign born: 3.8% (2000); Ancestry (includes multiple ancestries): 41.8% Other groups, 17.2% German, 10.8% Irish, 8.7% English, 5.9% United States or American (2000).
Vital Statistics: Birth rate: 160.0 per 10,000 population (1998)
Economy: Manufacturing: hardware, chemicals, transportation equipment, apparel, steel fabrication, food processing, consumer goods, machinery. Richards-Gebaur Airport, former A.F.B. nearby. Unemployment rate: 4.4% (11/2002); Total civilian labor force: 16,809 (11/2002); Single-family building permits issued: 24 (2001) / 8 (2000); Multi-family building permits

issued: 444 (2001) / 18 (2000); Employment by occupation: 12.6% management, 16.9% professional, 16.5% services, 29.8% sales, 0.0% farming, 10.3% construction, 13.8% production (2000).
Income: Per capita income: $19,079 (2000); Median household income: $40,003 (2000); Poverty rate: 8.4% (2000).
Taxes: Total city taxes per capita: $445 (2000); City property taxes per capita: $133 (2000).
Education: High school graduation rate: 84.3% (2000); College graduation rate: 19.3% (2000).

School District(s)

Grandview C-4 (PK-12)
2000 Enrollment: 4,279 816-316-5000
Housing: Homeownership rate: 61.4% (2000); Median home value: $78,100 (2000); Median rent: $441 per month (2000); Median age of housing: 29 years (2000).
Newspapers: Jackson County Advocate (1 x week)
Transportation: Commute to work: 95.2% car, 0.7% public transportation, 1.2% walk, 1.7% work from home (2000); Travel time to work: 26.0% less than 15 minutes, 39.5% 15 to 30 minutes, 23.8% 30 to 45 minutes, 6.7% 45 to 60 minutes, 3.9% 60 minutes or more (2000)
Additional Information Contacts
Grandview Chamber of Commerce 816-761-6505

GREENWOOD (city). Covers a land area of 4.040 square miles and a water area of 0 square miles. Located at 38.85° N. Lat.; 94.34° W. Long. Elevation is 953 feet.
Population: 3,952 (2000); Race: 93.1% White, 1.6% Black, 0.0% Asian, 1.6% American Indian and Alaska Native, 2.6% Hispanic of any race, 1.9% two or more races (2000); Density: 978.3 persons per square mile (2000); Age: 32.0% under 18, 5.1% over 64 (2000); Marriage status: 18.3% never married, 68.9% now married, 1.8% widowed, 11.0% divorced (2000); Foreign born: 2.1% (2000); Ancestry (includes multiple ancestries): 26.7% German, 18.3% Other groups, 17.4% Irish, 12.5% English, 7.1% United States or American (2000).
Economy: Single-family building permits issued: 57 (2001) / 82 (2000); Multi-family building permits issued: 0 (2001) / 0 (2000); Employment by occupation: 17.2% management, 18.1% professional, 10.0% services, 29.8% sales, 0.0% farming, 16.0% construction, 8.9% production (2000).
Income: Per capita income: $21,586 (2000); Median household income: $62,574 (2000); Poverty rate: 3.9% (2000).
Taxes: Total city taxes per capita: $40 (1997); City property taxes per capita: $25 (1997).
Education: High school graduation rate: 93.5% (2000); College graduation rate: 27.1% (2000).
Housing: Homeownership rate: 93.2% (2000); Median home value: $113,400 (2000); Median rent: $528 per month (2000); Median age of housing: 7 years (2000).
Transportation: Commute to work: 96.9% car, 0.0% public transportation, 0.0% walk, 2.6% work from home (2000); Travel time to work: 18.2% less than 15 minutes, 24.7% 15 to 30 minutes, 31.0% 30 to 45 minutes, 19.6% 45 to 60 minutes, 6.5% 60 minutes or more (2000)

INDEPENDENCE (city). Covers a land area of 78.328 square miles and a water area of 0.126 square miles. Located at 39.08° N. Lat.; 94.40° W. Long. Elevation is 1,033 feet.
History: Independence was settled about 1825, and platted as the seat of Jackson County in 1827. In 1830, Samuel Weston opened a blacksmith shop and wagon factory, and Independence soon became a starting point for immigrants heading west and southwest. The first overland mail stagecoach lines into the far west were started from Independence in 1846, and in 1850 Samuel H. Woodson received the government contract to establish a monthly mail stage service to Salt Lake City.
Population: 113,288 (2000); Race: 91.8% White, 2.3% Black, 0.9% Asian, 0.5% American Indian and Alaska Native, 3.5% Hispanic of any race, 2.6% two or more races (2000); Density: 1,446.3 persons per square mile (2000); Age: 23.8% under 18, 15.5% over 64 (2000); Marriage status: 22.9% never married, 55.3% now married, 7.8% widowed, 14.0% divorced (2000); Foreign born: 2.6% (2000); Ancestry (includes multiple ancestries): 20.8% German, 15.8% Other groups, 13.7% Irish, 13.1% English, 10.2% United States or American (2000).
Vital Statistics: Birth rate: 141.5 per 10,000 population (1998)
Economy: Unemployment rate: 4.8% (11/2002); Total civilian labor force: 69,189 (11/2002); Single-family building permits issued: 363 (2001) / 376 (2000); Multi-family building permits issued: 94 (2001) / 0 (2000); Employment by occupation: 10.6% management, 15.3% professional, 14.0% services, 31.7% sales, 0.1% farming, 10.8% construction, 17.4% production (2000).
Income: Per capita income: $19,384 (2000); Median household income: $38,012 (2000); Poverty rate: 8.6% (2000).
Taxes: Total city taxes per capita: $363 (2000); City property taxes per capita: $64 (2000).
Education: High school graduation rate: 82.9% (2000); College graduation rate: 15.2% (2000).

School District(s)

Fort Osage R-I (PK-12)
2000 Enrollment: 4,908 816-650-7000
Independence 30 (PK-12)
2000 Enrollment: 11,225 816-521-2700

Four-year College(s)

Graceland University-Independence (Private, Not-for-profit, Reorganized Latter Day Saints Church)
2001 Enrollment: n/a 816-833-0524
2001 Tuition: In-state $13,025; Out-of-state $13,025
Housing: Homeownership rate: 67.8% (2000); Median home value: $77,000 (2000); Median rent: $409 per month (2000); Median age of housing: 36 years (2000).
Hospitals: Independence Regional Health Center (363 beds); Medical Center of Independence (205 beds)
Safety: Violent crime rate: 58.6 per 10,000 population; Property crime rate: 721.2 per 10,000 population (2001).
Newspapers: The Examiner (6 x week); The Examiner Extra (1 x week)
Transportation: Commute to work: 95.4% car, 0.8% public transportation, 0.9% walk, 2.1% work from home (2000); Travel time to work: 23.0% less than 15 minutes, 41.7% 15 to 30 minutes, 26.2% 30 to 45 minutes, 5.9% 45 to 60 minutes, 3.2% 60 minutes or more (2000); Amtrak: Service available.
Additional Information Contacts
Independence Chamber of Commerce 816-252-4745

KANSAS CITY (city). Covers a land area of 313.544 square miles and a water area of 4.471 square miles. Located at 39.07° N. Lat.; 94.55° W. Long. Elevation is 882 feet.
History: Kansas City had its origins in two frontier settlements, the Missouri River town of Kansas, and the town of Westport, four miles to the south on the Santa Fe Trail. The town of Kansas was first a trading post established in 1821 by Francois Chouteau of the American Fur Company and called Westport Landing. The town of Westport grew from a store operated in 1832 by John Calvin McCoy to supply travelers on the Santa Fe Trail. Westport Landing was platted in 1838 and renamed Kansas, and soon encompassed the trail trade from the other Westport. When a charter of incorporation was obtained in 1853, it named the City of Kansas. Kansas City developed as a crossroads and market place for the western half of the United States.
Population: 441,545 (2000); Race: 60.8% White, 30.7% Black, 1.9% Asian, 0.5% American Indian and Alaska Native, 6.9% Hispanic of any race, 2.7% two or more races (2000); Density: 1,408.2 persons per square mile (2000); Age: 25.3% under 18, 11.7% over 64 (2000); Marriage status: 32.5% never married, 47.8% now married, 6.6% widowed, 13.1% divorced (2000); Foreign born: 5.8% (2000); Ancestry (includes multiple ancestries): 37.7% Other groups, 15.4% German, 10.3% Irish, 8.1% English, 5.8% United States or American (2000).
Vital Statistics: Birth rate: 162.9 per 10,000 population (1998)
Economy: Unemployment rate: 6.3% (11/2002); Total civilian labor force: 274,924 (11/2002); Single-family building permits issued: 1,208 (2001) / 1,117 (2000); Multi-family building permits issued: 973 (2001) / 751 (2000); Employment by occupation: 13.7% management, 20.4% professional, 16.2% services, 28.6% sales, 0.1% farming, 7.9% construction, 13.0% production (2000).
Income: Per capita income: $20,753 (2000); Median household income: $37,198 (2000); Poverty rate: 14.3% (2000).
Taxes: Total city taxes per capita: $1,161 (2000); City property taxes per capita: $175 (2000).
Education: High school graduation rate: 82.5% (2000); College graduation rate: 25.7% (2000).

School District(s)

Center 58 (PK-12)
2000 Enrollment: 2,725 816-349-3300
Hickman Mills C-1 (PK-12)
2000 Enrollment: 7,532 816-316-7000
Kansas City 33 (PK-12)
2000 Enrollment: 37,298 816-418-7000
North Kansas City 74 (PK-12)
2000 Enrollment: 17,258 816-413-5000

Park Hill (PK-12)
2000 Enrollment: 9,067 816-741-1521

Four-year College(s)

Avila College (Private, Not-for-profit, Roman Catholic)
2001 Enrollment: 1,644 816-942-8400
2001 Tuition: In-state $13,150; Out-of-state $13,150
Calvary Bible College and Theological Seminary (Private, Not-for-profit, Other Protestant)
2001 Enrollment: 306 816-322-0110
2001 Tuition: In-state $4,860; Out-of-state $4,860
Cleveland Chiropractic College (Private, Not-for-profit)
2001 Enrollment: 494 816-501-0100
2001 Tuition: In-state $3,498; Out-of-state $3,498
DeVry Institute of Technology (Private, For-profit)
2001 Enrollment: 2,620 816-941-0430
2001 Tuition: In-state $8,740; Out-of-state $8,740
Finlay Engineering College (Private, For-profit)
2001 Enrollment: n/a 816-523-6030
Kansas City Art Institute (Private, Not-for-profit)
2001 Enrollment: 531 816-802-3469
2001 Tuition: In-state $17,974; Out-of-state $17,974
Midwestern Baptist Theological Seminary (Private, Not-for-profit, Southern Baptist)
2001 Enrollment: 447 816-414-3700
2001 Tuition: In-state $2,040; Out-of-state $2,040
University of Missouri-Kansas City (Public)
2001 Enrollment: 12,969 816-235-1000
2001 Tuition: In-state $4,245; Out-of-state $12,690
Nazarene Theological Seminary (Private, Not-for-profit, Church of the Nazarene)
2001 Enrollment: 399 816-333-6254
Research College of Nursing (Private, Not-for-profit)
2001 Enrollment: 163 816-276-4700
2001 Tuition: In-state $14,800; Out-of-state $14,800
Rockhurst University (Private, Not-for-profit, Roman Catholic)
2001 Enrollment: 2,730 816-501-4000
2001 Tuition: In-state $14,800; Out-of-state $14,800
Saint Paul School of Theology (Private, Not-for-profit, United Methodist)
2001 Enrollment: 328 816-483-9600
Saint Luke's College (Private, Not-for-profit, Protestant Episcopal)
2001 Enrollment: 115 816-932-2233
2001 Tuition: In-state $7,700; Out-of-state $7,700
Truman Medical Center School for Nurse Anesthetists (Public)
2001 Enrollment: n/a 816-556-3000
University of Health Sciences-College of Osteopathy (Private, Not-for-profit)
2001 Enrollment: 891 816-283-2000
Western Baptist Bible College (Private, Not-for-profit, Baptist)
2001 Enrollment: n/a 816-842-4195
National American University (Private, For-profit)
2001 Enrollment: 331 605-394-4800
2001 Tuition: In-state $9,360; Out-of-state $9,360
Keller Graduate School of Management Inc (Private, For-profit)
2001 Enrollment: 296 816-941-0367

Two-year College(s)

Electronics Institute (Private, For-profit)
2001 Enrollment: 294 816-331-5700
2001 Tuition: In-state $7,776; Out-of-state $7,776
Metropolitan Community College (Public)
2001 Enrollment: 5,045 816-437-3000
2001 Tuition: In-state $2,790; Out-of-state $3,900
Metropolitan Community Colleges (Public)
2001 Enrollment: 4,376 816-759-4000
2001 Tuition: In-state $2,790; Out-of-state $3,900
Research Medical Center School of Nuclear Med Techn (Private, Not-for-profit)
2001 Enrollment: 6 816-276-4235
Research Medical Center School of Radiologic Techn (Private, Not-for-profit)
2001 Enrollment: 28 816-276-4000
Vatterott College (Private, For-profit)
2001 Enrollment: 562 816-861-1000

Housing: Homeownership rate: 57.7% (2000); Median home value: $84,000 (2000); Median rent: $445 per month (2000); Median age of housing: 40 years (2000).
Hospitals: Baptist-Lutheran Medical Center (354 beds); Children's Mercy Hospitals and Clinics (187 beds); Crittenton/Saint Luke's Shawnee Mission Health System (67 beds); Kindred Hospital-Kansas City (167 beds); Rehabilitation Institute (40 beds); Research Medical Center (536 beds); Research Psychiatric Center (100 beds); Saint Joseph Health Center (300 beds); Saint Luke's Hospital (642 beds); Saint Luke's Northland Hospital (55 beds); Swope Ridge Geriatric Center (240 beds); Truman Medical Center - Lakewood (304 beds); Truman Medical Center-Hospital Hill; Two Rivers Psychiatric Hospital (80 beds); Veterans Affairs Medical Center (213 beds); Western Missouri Mental Health Center (110 beds)
Safety: Violent crime rate: 159.4 per 10,000 population; Property crime rate: 965.1 per 10,000 population (2001).
Newspapers: Press Dispatch-Tribune (2 x week); Platte County Sun-Gazette (1 x week); Gladstone/Northland Sun-News (1 x week); Clay Sun Chronicle (1 x week); The Kansas City Star (7 x week); The Daily Record (5 x week); Missouri State Post (1 x week); Dos Mundos (2 x month); The Call (1 x week); Kansas City Globe (1 x week); Pitch Weekly (1 x week); The Catholic Key (1 x week); The Northeast News (1 x week)
Transportation: Commute to work: 90.6% car, 3.8% public transportation, 2.3% walk, 2.6% work from home (2000); Travel time to work: 27.7% less than 15 minutes, 46.8% 15 to 30 minutes, 18.8% 30 to 45 minutes, 3.4% 45 to 60 minutes, 3.3% 60 minutes or more (2000); Amtrak: Service available.
Airports: Kansas City International (primary service/medium hub); Charles B. Wheeler Downtown (primary service/medium hub)
Additional Information Contacts
Hispanic Chamber of Commerce 816-472-6767
Kansas City Chamber of Commerce 816-221-2424
Kansas City Convention & Visitors Bureau. 816-221-5242
North Kansas City Business 816-472-7700

LAKE LOTAWANA (city). Aka Lotawana Lake. Covers a land area of 1.522 square miles and a water area of 0.806 square miles. Located at 38.92° N. Lat.; 94.25° W. Long. Elevation is 940 feet.
Population: 1,872 (2000); Race: 95.7% White, 0.4% Black, 0.7% Asian, 1.2% American Indian and Alaska Native, 1.3% Hispanic of any race, 2.0% two or more races (2000); Density: 1,230.3 persons per square mile (2000); Age: 18.3% under 18, 13.4% over 64 (2000); Marriage status: 19.5% never married, 67.1% now married, 2.9% widowed, 10.6% divorced (2000); Foreign born: 1.8% (2000); Ancestry (includes multiple ancestries): 28.8% German, 14.5% English, 14.4% Irish, 12.3% Other groups, 6.8% United States or American (2000).
Economy: Single-family building permits issued: 21 (2001) / 20 (2000); Multi-family building permits issued: 0 (2001) / 0 (2000); Employment by occupation: 19.0% management, 23.2% professional, 8.9% services, 29.2% sales, 0.0% farming, 12.3% construction, 7.5% production (2000).
Income: Per capita income: $38,125 (2000); Median household income: $65,750 (2000); Poverty rate: 4.3% (2000).
Taxes: Total city taxes per capita: $265 (1997); City property taxes per capita: $111 (1997).
Education: High school graduation rate: 93.1% (2000); College graduation rate: 35.1% (2000).
Housing: Homeownership rate: 88.9% (2000); Median home value: $176,900 (2000); Median rent: $543 per month (2000); Median age of housing: 41 years (2000).
Safety: Violent crime rate: 21.2 per 10,000 population; Property crime rate: 180.5 per 10,000 population (2001).
Transportation: Commute to work: 92.7% car, 0.0% public transportation, 0.7% walk, 5.3% work from home (2000); Travel time to work: 13.0% less than 15 minutes, 30.6% 15 to 30 minutes, 33.0% 30 to 45 minutes, 16.4% 45 to 60 minutes, 7.0% 60 minutes or more (2000)

LAKE TAPAWINGO (city). Covers a land area of 0.343 square miles and a water area of 0.127 square miles. Located at 39.02° N. Lat.; 94.30° W. Long. Elevation is 849 feet.
Population: 843 (2000); Race: 98.2% White, 0.0% Black, 0.5% Asian, 0.0% American Indian and Alaska Native, 2.2% Hispanic of any race, 0.8% two or more races (2000); Density: 2,454.6 persons per square mile (2000); Age: 18.9% under 18, 14.5% over 64 (2000); Marriage status: 15.9% never married, 69.9% now married, 2.9% widowed, 11.3% divorced (2000); Foreign born: 1.4% (2000); Ancestry (includes multiple ancestries): 27.5% German, 23.0% Irish, 17.6% English, 6.3% Other groups, 6.0% United States or American (2000).
Economy: Employment by occupation: 16.7% management, 25.5% professional, 7.7% services, 28.6% sales, 0.0% farming, 12.3% construction, 9.2% production (2000).
Income: Per capita income: $32,141 (2000); Median household income: $73,500 (2000); Poverty rate: 3.3% (2000).

Taxes: Total city taxes per capita: $226 (1997); City property taxes per capita: $203 (1997).
Education: High school graduation rate: 93.0% (2000); College graduation rate: 32.8% (2000).
Housing: Homeownership rate: 91.9% (2000); Median home value: $149,000 (2000); Median rent: $581 per month (2000); Median age of housing: 49 years (2000).
Transportation: Commute to work: 92.6% car, 0.0% public transportation, 0.0% walk, 5.7% work from home (2000); Travel time to work: 29.7% less than 15 minutes, 35.7% 15 to 30 minutes, 26.7% 30 to 45 minutes, 4.5% 45 to 60 minutes, 3.4% 60 minutes or more (2000)

LEE'S SUMMIT (city). Aka Lees Summit. Covers a land area of 59.513 square miles and a water area of 2.160 square miles. Located at 38.92° N. Lat.; 94.37° W. Long.
History: Lee's Summit was laid out in 1865 by William B. Howard, when the railroad provided a boxcar for a depot. Painted on the side of the boxcar was "Lee's Summit" referring to Dr. Pleasant Lea, who had a home nearby. The mis-spelling was never corrected.
Population: 70,700 (2000); Race: 93.2% White, 3.5% Black, 0.7% Asian, 0.5% American Indian and Alaska Native, 2.0% Hispanic of any race, 1.4% two or more races (2000); Density: 1,188.0 persons per square mile (2000); Age: 29.3% under 18, 10.1% over 64 (2000); Marriage status: 19.7% never married, 65.1% now married, 5.5% widowed, 9.7% divorced (2000); Foreign born: 2.0% (2000); Ancestry (includes multiple ancestries): 27.9% German, 15.0% Irish, 14.4% English, 12.0% Other groups, 9.0% United States or American (2000).
Vital Statistics: Birth rate: 151.3 per 10,000 population (1998)
Economy: Unemployment rate: 3.1% (11/2002); Total civilian labor force: 29,202 (11/2002); Single-family building permits issued: 893 (2001) / 776 (2000); Multi-family building permits issued: 50 (2001) / 268 (2000); Employment by occupation: 19.1% management, 25.5% professional, 10.7% services, 28.3% sales, 0.1% farming, 7.7% construction, 8.6% production (2000).
Income: Per capita income: $26,891 (2000); Median household income: $60,905 (2000); Poverty rate: 3.8% (2000).
Education: High school graduation rate: 93.1% (2000); College graduation rate: 37.3% (2000).

School District(s)

Lee's Summit R-VII (PK-12)
2000 Enrollment: 14,340 816-986-1000

Two-year College(s)

Metropolitan Community College (Public)
2001 Enrollment: 5,792 816-672-2000
2001 Tuition: In-state $2,790; Out-of-state $3,900
Housing: Homeownership rate: 75.7% (2000); Median home value: $131,500 (2000); Median rent: $561 per month (2000); Median age of housing: 16 years (2000).
Safety: Violent crime rate: 9.4 per 10,000 population; Property crime rate: 271.0 per 10,000 population (2001).
Newspapers: Lees Summit Journal (2 x week); Metro Voice (1 x month)
Transportation: Commute to work: 95.5% car, 0.2% public transportation, 0.6% walk, 3.6% work from home (2000); Travel time to work: 25.8% less than 15 minutes, 32.6% 15 to 30 minutes, 29.5% 30 to 45 minutes, 9.0% 45 to 60 minutes, 3.1% 60 minutes or more (2000); Amtrak: Service available.
Airports: Lee's Summit Municipal
Additional Information Contacts
Lees Summit Chamber of Commerce 816-524-2424

LEVASY (city). Covers a land area of 0.577 square miles and a water area of 0 square miles. Located at 39.13° N. Lat.; 94.13° W. Long. Elevation is 710 feet.
History: Fort Osage National Historic Landmark to North.
Population: 108 (2000); Race: 100.0% White, 0.0% Black, 0.0% Asian, 0.0% American Indian and Alaska Native, 0.0% Hispanic of any race, 0.0% two or more races (2000); Density: 187.1 persons per square mile (2000); Age: 25.4% under 18, 11.0% over 64 (2000); Marriage status: 15.7% never married, 68.5% now married, 0.0% widowed, 15.7% divorced (2000); Foreign born: 0.0% (2000); Ancestry (includes multiple ancestries): 43.2% German, 30.5% Irish, 17.8% Other groups, 11.9% Dutch, 7.6% French (except Basque) (2000).
Economy: Soybeans, wheat, corn; cattle. Single-family building permits issued: 0 (2001) / 0 (2000); Multi-family building permits issued: 0 (2001) / 0 (2000); Employment by occupation: 0.0% management, 28.6% professional, 22.4% services, 12.2% sales, 0.0% farming, 14.3% construction, 22.4% production (2000).
Income: Per capita income: $17,016 (2000); Median household income: $51,250 (2000); Poverty rate: 5.1% (2000).
Taxes: Total city taxes per capita: $130 (1997); City property taxes per capita: $89 (1997).
Education: High school graduation rate: 85.3% (2000); College graduation rate: 24.0% (2000).
Housing: Homeownership rate: 83.7% (2000); Median home value: $60,000 (2000); Median rent: $385 per month (2000); Median age of housing: 57 years (2000).
Transportation: Commute to work: 95.9% car, 0.0% public transportation, 0.0% walk, 4.1% work from home (2000); Travel time to work: 12.8% less than 15 minutes, 12.8% 15 to 30 minutes, 48.9% 30 to 45 minutes, 25.5% 45 to 60 minutes, 0.0% 60 minutes or more (2000)

LONE JACK (city). Aka Lonejack. Covers a land area of 3.838 square miles and a water area of 0 square miles. Located at 38.87° N. Lat.; 94.18° W. Long. Elevation is 1,015 feet.
History: Lone Jack was named for a blackjack tree near a spring which served as a prairie landmark. The town was the scene of a battle between Union and Confederate forces in 1862, which resulted in a Union retreat. Union and Confederate dead were buried in separate but unmarked trenches in Soldiers Cemetery.
Population: 528 (2000); Race: 96.3% White, 0.4% Black, 0.0% Asian, 0.7% American Indian and Alaska Native, 0.9% Hispanic of any race, 1.7% two or more races (2000); Density: 137.6 persons per square mile (2000); Age: 27.6% under 18, 9.9% over 64 (2000); Marriage status: 22.7% never married, 65.2% now married, 5.7% widowed, 6.4% divorced (2000); Foreign born: 0.4% (2000); Ancestry (includes multiple ancestries): 19.6% German, 18.1% Irish, 10.3% English, 9.3% Other groups, 7.8% United States or American (2000).
Economy: Single-family building permits issued: 6 (2001) / 5 (2000); Multi-family building permits issued: 0 (2001) / 0 (2000); Employment by occupation: 7.2% management, 17.2% professional, 10.7% services, 33.7% sales, 0.0% farming, 19.2% construction, 12.0% production (2000).
Income: Per capita income: $20,558 (2000); Median household income: $51,154 (2000); Poverty rate: 3.6% (2000).
Taxes: Total city taxes per capita: $192 (1997); City property taxes per capita: $50 (1997).
Education: High school graduation rate: 88.9% (2000); College graduation rate: 15.7% (2000).

School District(s)

Lone Jack C-6 (KG-12)
2000 Enrollment: 484 816-697-3539
Housing: Homeownership rate: 78.3% (2000); Median home value: $100,000 (2000); Median rent: $395 per month (2000); Median age of housing: 23 years (2000).
Transportation: Commute to work: 94.5% car, 0.0% public transportation, 3.1% walk, 2.4% work from home (2000); Travel time to work: 9.9% less than 15 minutes, 35.9% 15 to 30 minutes, 31.7% 30 to 45 minutes, 18.3% 45 to 60 minutes, 4.2% 60 minutes or more (2000)

OAK GROVE (city). Covers a land area of 4.854 square miles and a water area of 0.019 square miles. Located at 39.00° N. Lat.; 94.12° W. Long. Elevation is 873 feet.
Population: 5,535 (2000); Race: 97.1% White, 1.0% Black, 0.0% Asian, 0.0% American Indian and Alaska Native, 2.5% Hispanic of any race, 0.5% two or more races (2000); Density: 1,140.3 persons per square mile (2000); Age: 31.6% under 18, 9.4% over 64 (2000); Marriage status: 20.4% never married, 58.6% now married, 6.4% widowed, 14.5% divorced (2000); Foreign born: 1.5% (2000); Ancestry (includes multiple ancestries): 18.3% German, 11.7% United States or American, 10.9% Irish, 10.6% Other groups, 8.5% English (2000).
Economy: Corn, wheat, sorghum; cattle. Single-family building permits issued: 146 (2001) / 36 (2000); Multi-family building permits issued: 123 (2001) / 74 (2000); Employment by occupation: 5.4% management, 17.5% professional, 12.2% services, 30.7% sales, 0.0% farming, 17.8% construction, 16.5% production (2000).
Income: Per capita income: $17,738 (2000); Median household income: $44,952 (2000); Poverty rate: 10.1% (2000).
Taxes: Total city taxes per capita: $294 (2000); City property taxes per capita: $84 (2000).
Education: High school graduation rate: 81.2% (2000); College graduation rate: 10.6% (2000).

School District(s)

Oak Grove R-VI (PK-12)
2000 Enrollment: 1,920 816-690-4156

Housing: Homeownership rate: 68.2% (2000); Median home value: $83,900 (2000); Median rent: $461 per month (2000); Median age of housing: 23 years (2000).
Newspapers: Town & Country News (1 x week)
Transportation: Commute to work: 91.8% car, 0.7% public transportation, 3.4% walk, 4.1% work from home (2000); Travel time to work: 27.6% less than 15 minutes, 23.2% 15 to 30 minutes, 24.0% 30 to 45 minutes, 21.1% 45 to 60 minutes, 4.1% 60 minutes or more (2000)

RAYTOWN (city). Covers a land area of 9.911 square miles and a water area of 0.030 square miles. Located at 38.99° N. Lat.; 94.46° W. Long. Elevation is 1,015 feet.
History: Raytown began as a postal station and assembly place for wagon trains on the Santa Fe Trail.
Population: 30,388 (2000); Race: 83.5% White, 11.8% Black, 0.9% Asian, 0.3% American Indian and Alaska Native, 2.4% Hispanic of any race, 2.5% two or more races (2000); Density: 3,065.9 persons per square mile (2000); Age: 22.6% under 18, 19.1% over 64 (2000); Marriage status: 21.8% never married, 55.5% now married, 8.7% widowed, 14.0% divorced (2000); Foreign born: 2.0% (2000); Ancestry (includes multiple ancestries): 20.7% German, 19.7% Other groups, 13.3% Irish, 12.3% English, 9.9% United States or American (2000).
Vital Statistics: Birth rate: 128.3 per 10,000 population (1998)
Economy: Unemployment rate: 3.4% (11/2002); Total civilian labor force: 19,092 (11/2002); Single-family building permits issued: 30 (2001) / 29 (2000); Multi-family building permits issued: 42 (2001) / 10 (2000); Employment by occupation: 12.9% management, 17.5% professional, 13.6% services, 32.0% sales, 0.0% farming, 10.1% construction, 14.0% production (2000).
Income: Per capita income: $21,634 (2000); Median household income: $41,949 (2000); Poverty rate: 5.0% (2000).
Taxes: Total city taxes per capita: $260 (2000); City property taxes per capita: $44 (2000).
Education: High school graduation rate: 87.3% (2000); College graduation rate: 19.5% (2000).

School District(s)

Raytown C-2 (PK-12)
2000 Enrollment: 8,509 816-737-6200
Housing: Homeownership rate: 73.9% (2000); Median home value: $79,600 (2000); Median rent: $451 per month (2000); Median age of housing: 38 years (2000).
Safety: Violent crime rate: 26.5 per 10,000 population; Property crime rate: 372.9 per 10,000 population (2001).
Newspapers: Raytown Dispatch Tribune (1 x week); Raytown Post (1 x week)
Transportation: Commute to work: 95.6% car, 0.4% public transportation, 1.3% walk, 2.1% work from home (2000); Travel time to work: 23.8% less than 15 minutes, 48.9% 15 to 30 minutes, 21.3% 30 to 45 minutes, 3.8% 45 to 60 minutes, 2.1% 60 minutes or more (2000)

RIVER BEND (village). Covers a land area of 1.321 square miles and a water area of 0.440 square miles. Located at 39.18° N. Lat.; 94.39° W. Long. Elevation is 733 feet.
Population: 10 (2000); Race: 100.0% White, 0.0% Black, 0.0% Asian, 0.0% American Indian and Alaska Native, 0.0% Hispanic of any race, 0.0% two or more races (2000); Density: 7.6 persons per square mile (2000); Age: 0.0% under 18, 40.0% over 64 (2000); Marriage status: 0.0% never married, 100.0% now married, 0.0% widowed, 0.0% divorced (2000); Foreign born: 0.0% (2000); Ancestry (includes multiple ancestries): 40.0% Italian, 30.0% German, 20.0% French (except Basque), 20.0% Irish, 10.0% Greek (2000).
Economy: Single-family building permits issued: 0 (2001) / 0 (2000); Multi-family building permits issued: 0 (2001) / 0 (2000); Employment by occupation: 0.0% management, 0.0% professional, 0.0% services, 20.0% sales, 0.0% farming, 20.0% construction, 60.0% production (2000).
Income: Per capita income: $27,820 (2000); Median household income: $70,000 (2000); Poverty rate: 0.0% (2000).
Taxes: Total city taxes per capita: $273 (1997); City property taxes per capita: $273 (1997).
Education: High school graduation rate: 100.0% (2000); College graduation rate: 0.0% (2000).
Housing: Homeownership rate: 20.0% (2000); Median rent: $575 per month (2000); Median age of housing: 52 years (2000).
Transportation: Commute to work: 100.0% car, 0.0% public transportation, 0.0% walk, 0.0% work from home (2000); Travel time to work: 0.0% less than 15 minutes, 20.0% 15 to 30 minutes, 80.0% 30 to 45 minutes, 0.0% 45 to 60 minutes, 0.0% 60 minutes or more (2000)

SIBLEY (village). Covers a land area of 1.042 square miles and a water area of 0 square miles. Located at 39.18° N. Lat.; 94.19° W. Long. Elevation is 809 feet.
History: Sibley was named for Major George C. Sibley, early factor of Fort Osage and a surveyor of the Santa Fe Trail. Fort Osage was established near the site of Sibley in 1808 under the direction of William Clark, of the Lewis and Clark Expedition, as a military and trading post.
Population: 347 (2000); Race: 96.0% White, 1.4% Black, 0.0% Asian, 0.0% American Indian and Alaska Native, 5.2% Hispanic of any race, 2.0% two or more races (2000); Density: 332.9 persons per square mile (2000); Age: 25.5% under 18, 13.8% over 64 (2000); Marriage status: 14.8% never married, 67.8% now married, 9.3% widowed, 8.1% divorced (2000); Foreign born: 0.6% (2000); Ancestry (includes multiple ancestries): 18.1% Other groups, 17.5% German, 17.5% United States or American, 8.3% Irish, 6.0% English (2000).
Economy: Employment by occupation: 7.5% management, 6.8% professional, 8.1% services, 28.0% sales, 0.0% farming, 23.0% construction, 26.7% production (2000).
Income: Per capita income: $17,100 (2000); Median household income: $45,000 (2000); Poverty rate: 5.4% (2000).
Taxes: Total city taxes per capita: $20 (1997); City property taxes per capita: $10 (1997).
Education: High school graduation rate: 81.3% (2000); College graduation rate: 4.5% (2000).
Housing: Homeownership rate: 91.0% (2000); Median home value: $78,900 (2000); Median rent: $360 per month (2000); Median age of housing: 41 years (2000).
Transportation: Commute to work: 94.4% car, 0.0% public transportation, 3.1% walk, 2.5% work from home (2000); Travel time to work: 22.9% less than 15 minutes, 20.4% 15 to 30 minutes, 22.3% 30 to 45 minutes, 28.0% 45 to 60 minutes, 6.4% 60 minutes or more (2000)

SUGAR CREEK (city). Covers a land area of 8.255 square miles and a water area of 0.684 square miles. Located at 39.11° N. Lat.; 94.43° W. Long. Elevation is 820 feet.
History: Incorporated 1920.
Population: 3,839 (2000); Race: 93.8% White, 0.0% Black, 0.0% Asian, 0.7% American Indian and Alaska Native, 4.4% Hispanic of any race, 3.0% two or more races (2000); Density: 465.0 persons per square mile (2000); Age: 21.3% under 18, 14.6% over 64 (2000); Marriage status: 23.6% never married, 53.1% now married, 7.3% widowed, 16.0% divorced (2000); Foreign born: 2.1% (2000); Ancestry (includes multiple ancestries): 20.6% German, 15.3% Irish, 13.0% Other groups, 12.5% United States or American, 11.0% English (2000).
Economy: Oil refinery, cement plant. Manufacturing of cement, asphalt. Single-family building permits issued: 3 (2001) / 0 (2000); Multi-family building permits issued: 0 (2001) / 0 (2000); Employment by occupation: 7.6% management, 10.7% professional, 13.1% services, 33.7% sales, 0.0% farming, 18.0% construction, 16.9% production (2000).
Income: Per capita income: $20,784 (2000); Median household income: $39,967 (2000); Poverty rate: 10.8% (2000).
Taxes: Total city taxes per capita: $372 (1997); City property taxes per capita: $33 (1997).
Education: High school graduation rate: 78.4% (2000); College graduation rate: 9.9% (2000).
Housing: Homeownership rate: 67.0% (2000); Median home value: $64,900 (2000); Median rent: $407 per month (2000); Median age of housing: 45 years (2000).
Safety: Violent crime rate: 54.4 per 10,000 population; Property crime rate: 473.7 per 10,000 population (2001).
Transportation: Commute to work: 97.0% car, 0.3% public transportation, 0.8% walk, 1.1% work from home (2000); Travel time to work: 25.4% less than 15 minutes, 40.9% 15 to 30 minutes, 23.3% 30 to 45 minutes, 7.0% 45 to 60 minutes, 3.4% 60 minutes or more (2000)

UNITY VILLAGE (village). Aka Unity. Covers a land area of 1.902 square miles and a water area of 0.064 square miles. Located at 38.94° N. Lat.; 94.39° W. Long. Elevation is 952 feet.
Population: 140 (2000); Race: 88.4% White, 11.6% Black, 0.0% Asian, 0.0% American Indian and Alaska Native, 8.2% Hispanic of any race, 0.0% two or more races (2000); Density: 73.6 persons per square mile (2000); Age: 1.0% under 18, 13.0% over 64 (2000); Marriage status: 8.3% never married, 39.5% now married, 13.2% widowed, 39.0% divorced (2000); Foreign born: 10.1% (2000); Ancestry (includes multiple ancestries): 32.4% German, 25.6% Irish, 15.0% Welsh, 9.7% Other groups, 9.7% English (2000).

Economy: Single-family building permits issued: 0 (2001) / 0 (2000); Multi-family building permits issued: 0 (2001) / 0 (2000); Employment by occupation: 47.1% management, 26.1% professional, 2.6% services, 13.1% sales, 0.0% farming, 2.6% construction, 8.5% production (2000).
Income: Per capita income: $31,836 (2000); Median household income: $29,583 (2000); Poverty rate: 11.9% (2000).
Taxes: Total city taxes per capita: $15 (1997); City property taxes per capita: $15 (1997).
Education: High school graduation rate: 100.0% (2000); College graduation rate: 54.1% (2000).
Housing: Homeownership rate: 8.9% (2000); Median home value: $112,500 (2000); Median rent: $461 per month (2000); Median age of housing: 33 years (2000).
Transportation: Commute to work: 61.4% car, 0.0% public transportation, 11.1% walk, 8.5% work from home (2000); Travel time to work: 59.3% less than 15 minutes, 26.4% 15 to 30 minutes, 7.1% 30 to 45 minutes, 7.1% 45 to 60 minutes, 0.0% 60 minutes or more (2000)

Jasper County

Located in southwestern Missouri, in the Ozarks; bounded on the west by Kansas; drained by the Spring River. Covers a land area of 639.70 square miles, a water area of 1.60 square miles, and is located in the Central Time Zone. The county government was organized in 1841. County seat is Carthage.

Jasper County is part of the Joplin, MO MSA. The entire metro area includes: Jasper County; Newton County

Weather Station: Joplin Municipal Airport Elevation: 977 feet

	Jan	Feb	Mar	Apr	May	Jun	Jul	Aug	Sep	Oct	Nov	Dec
High	42	48	59	69	77	85	90	89	81	71	57	47
Low	23	28	37	47	56	65	70	68	59	48	37	28
Precip	1.8	2.2	3.6	4.6	5.1	5.4	3.3	3.9	5.4	3.9	4.0	3.0
Snow	4.5	3.3	2.1	tr	tr	0.0	0.0	tr	tr	tr	0.6	2.6

High and Low temperatures in degrees Fahrenheit; Precipitation and Snow in inches

Population: 104,686 (2000); Race: 92.5% White, 1.3% Black, 0.6% Asian, 1.4% American Indian and Alaska Native, 3.7% Hispanic of any race, 2.4% two or more races (2000); Density: 163.6 persons per square mile (2000); Age: 25.7% under 18, 13.8% over 64 (2000).
Religion: Five largest groups: 19.5% Southern Baptist Convention, 9.0% Christian Churches and Churches of Christ, 6.7% The United Methodist Church, 5.2% Catholic Church, 4.0% Independent, Non-Charismatic Churches (2000).
Economy: Unemployment rate: 4.6% (11/2002); Total civilian labor force: 53,931 (11/2002); Leading industries: 20.6% manufacturing; 15.4% retail trade; 12.6% health care and social assistance (2000); Companies that employ more than 1,000 persons: 5 (2000); Companies that employ more than 100 persons: 85 (2000); Farms: 1,355 totaling 271,040 acres (1997); Minority business ownership rate: 4.9% (1997); Women business ownership rate: 20.3% (1997); Retail sales per capita: $11,656 (1997). Single-family building permits issued: 367 (2001) / 363 (2000); Multi-family building permits issued: 25 (2001) / 81 (2000).
Income: Per capita income: $16,227 (2000); Median household income: $31,323 (2000); Poverty rate: 14.5% (2000); Bankruptcy rate: 5.32% (2001).
Taxes: Total county taxes per capita: $131 (2000); County property taxes per capita: $41 (2000).
Education: High school graduation rate: 79.5% (2000); College graduation rate: 16.5% (2000).
Housing: Homeownership rate: 67.0% (2000); Median home value: $67,700 (2000); Median rent: $344 per month (2000); Median age of housing: 33 years (2000).
Health: Birth rate: 150.6 per 10,000 population (1998); Age adjusted death rate: 100.6 per 10,000 population (1999); Age adjusted cancer mortality rate: 253.7 deaths per 100,000 population (1999). Air Quality Index: 82% good, 17% moderate, 1% unhealthy (percent of days in 2000). Number of physicians: 22.3 per 10,000 population (1999); Number of hospital beds: 40.2 per 10,000 population (1999).
Elections: 2000 Presidential election results: 31.3% Gore, 66.4% Bush, 1.5% Nader, 0.3% Buchanan
National and State Parks: Wah-Sha-She Prairie State Wildlife Area
Additional Information Contacts
Jasper County Government Offices 417-358-0421
Carthage Board of Realtors 417-358-4041
Carthage Chamber of Commerce 417-358-2373
Joplin Area Chamber of Commerce 417-624-4150
Joplin Board of Realtors 417-782-6161
Webb City Chamber of Commerce 417-673-1154

Jasper County Communities

AIRPORT DRIVE (village). Covers a land area of 1.988 square miles and a water area of 0 square miles. Located at 37.14° N. Lat.; 94.51° W. Long. Elevation is 964 feet.
Population: 622 (2000); Race: 98.3% White, 0.0% Black, 0.0% Asian, 1.2% American Indian and Alaska Native, 1.0% Hispanic of any race, 0.0% two or more races (2000); Density: 312.9 persons per square mile (2000); Age: 15.2% under 18, 16.8% over 64 (2000); Marriage status: 21.0% never married, 60.6% now married, 6.3% widowed, 12.1% divorced (2000); Foreign born: 1.2% (2000); Ancestry (includes multiple ancestries): 21.9% United States or American, 18.2% German, 12.5% English, 11.1% Irish, 6.1% Other groups (2000).
Economy: Residential suburb of downtown Joplin. Single-family building permits issued: 2 (2001) / 2 (2000); Multi-family building permits issued: 0 (2001) / 0 (2000); Employment by occupation: 12.5% management, 23.9% professional, 12.5% services, 26.6% sales, 0.0% farming, 9.8% construction, 14.8% production (2000).
Income: Per capita income: $19,678 (2000); Median household income: $38,750 (2000); Poverty rate: 6.8% (2000).
Taxes: Total city taxes per capita: $183 (1997); City property taxes per capita: $0 (1997).
Education: High school graduation rate: 95.8% (2000); College graduation rate: 25.6% (2000).
Housing: Homeownership rate: 75.7% (2000); Median home value: $91,300 (2000); Median rent: $409 per month (2000); Median age of housing: 33 years (2000).
Transportation: Commute to work: 94.6% car, 0.0% public transportation, 0.7% walk, 4.7% work from home (2000); Travel time to work: 40.8% less than 15 minutes, 47.9% 15 to 30 minutes, 8.1% 30 to 45 minutes, 1.8% 45 to 60 minutes, 1.4% 60 minutes or more (2000)

ALBA (city). Covers a land area of 0.327 square miles and a water area of 0 square miles. Located at 37.23° N. Lat.; 94.41° W. Long. Elevation is 989 feet.
Population: 588 (2000); Race: 87.6% White, 0.7% Black, 0.0% Asian, 6.5% American Indian and Alaska Native, 0.5% Hispanic of any race, 5.2% two or more races (2000); Density: 1,796.2 persons per square mile (2000); Age: 28.9% under 18, 5.9% over 64 (2000); Marriage status: 27.7% never married, 58.0% now married, 3.8% widowed, 10.4% divorced (2000); Foreign born: 0.3% (2000); Ancestry (includes multiple ancestries): 16.3% German, 16.2% Other groups, 15.5% English, 11.7% Irish, 9.8% United States or American (2000).
Economy: Wheat, hay, soybeans; cattle. Employment by occupation: 6.5% management, 9.0% professional, 27.2% services, 20.1% sales, 2.2% farming, 9.3% construction, 25.8% production (2000).
Income: Per capita income: $11,588 (2000); Median household income: $30,333 (2000); Poverty rate: 15.2% (2000).
Taxes: Total city taxes per capita: $93 (1997); City property taxes per capita: $32 (1997).
Education: High school graduation rate: 80.1% (2000); College graduation rate: 8.3% (2000).
Housing: Homeownership rate: 87.8% (2000); Median home value: $49,000 (2000); Median rent: $417 per month (2000); Median age of housing: 32 years (2000).
Transportation: Commute to work: 90.9% car, 0.0% public transportation, 9.1% walk, 0.0% work from home (2000); Travel time to work: 24.6% less than 15 minutes, 52.2% 15 to 30 minutes, 20.3% 30 to 45 minutes, 1.1% 45 to 60 minutes, 1.8% 60 minutes or more (2000)

ASBURY (city). Covers a land area of 0.352 square miles and a water area of 0 square miles. Located at 37.27° N. Lat.; 94.60° W. Long. Elevation is 902 feet.
Population: 218 (2000); Race: 98.6% White, 0.0% Black, 0.0% Asian, 1.4% American Indian and Alaska Native, 0.0% Hispanic of any race, 0.0% two or more races (2000); Density: 618.4 persons per square mile (2000); Age: 23.0% under 18, 9.1% over 64 (2000); Marriage status: 14.8% never married, 69.1% now married, 8.0% widowed, 8.0% divorced (2000); Foreign born: 0.0% (2000); Ancestry (includes multiple ancestries): 21.5% English, 9.6% German, 7.7% United States or American, 5.7% Irish, 3.3% Dutch (2000).

Economy: Wheat, soybeans. Employment by occupation: 14.9% management, 4.0% professional, 5.9% services, 40.6% sales, 0.0% farming, 14.9% construction, 19.8% production (2000).
Income: Per capita income: $15,205 (2000); Median household income: $28,125 (2000); Poverty rate: 10.0% (2000).
Taxes: Total city taxes per capita: $17 (1997); City property taxes per capita: $17 (1997).
Education: High school graduation rate: 82.9% (2000); College graduation rate: 13.6% (2000).
Housing: Homeownership rate: 76.7% (2000); Median home value: $35,400 (2000); Median rent: $269 per month (2000); Median age of housing: 57 years (2000).
Transportation: Commute to work: 100.0% car, 0.0% public transportation, 0.0% walk, 0.0% work from home (2000); Travel time to work: 11.1% less than 15 minutes, 37.4% 15 to 30 minutes, 32.3% 30 to 45 minutes, 8.1% 45 to 60 minutes, 11.1% 60 minutes or more (2000)

AVILLA (town). Covers a land area of 0.201 square miles and a water area of 0 square miles. Located at 37.19° N. Lat.; 94.12° W. Long. Elevation is 1,117 feet.
Population: 137 (2000); Race: 93.4% White, 0.0% Black, 0.0% Asian, 0.0% American Indian and Alaska Native, 0.0% Hispanic of any race, 6.6% two or more races (2000); Density: 680.9 persons per square mile (2000); Age: 22.6% under 18, 11.3% over 64 (2000); Marriage status: 18.6% never married, 60.5% now married, 4.7% widowed, 16.3% divorced (2000); Foreign born: 0.0% (2000); Ancestry (includes multiple ancestries): 18.9% Other groups, 11.3% German, 9.4% Irish, 8.5% English, 5.7% French (except Basque) (2000).
Economy: Employment by occupation: 4.9% management, 0.0% professional, 22.0% services, 14.6% sales, 4.9% farming, 12.2% construction, 41.5% production (2000).
Income: Per capita income: $11,673 (2000); Median household income: $21,750 (2000); Poverty rate: 18.9% (2000).
Taxes: Total city taxes per capita: $25 (1997); City property taxes per capita: $6 (1997).
Education: High school graduation rate: 64.8% (2000); College graduation rate: 0.0% (2000).

School District(s)

Avilla R-XIII (PK-08)
2000 Enrollment: 153 417-246-5330
Housing: Homeownership rate: 60.9% (2000); Median home value: $45,000 (2000); Median rent: $175 per month (2000); Median age of housing: 49 years (2000).
Transportation: Commute to work: 100.0% car, 0.0% public transportation, 0.0% walk, 0.0% work from home (2000); Travel time to work: 21.1% less than 15 minutes, 18.4% 15 to 30 minutes, 50.0% 30 to 45 minutes, 5.3% 45 to 60 minutes, 5.3% 60 minutes or more (2000)

BROOKLYN HEIGHTS (town). Covers a land area of 0.119 square miles and a water area of 0 square miles. Located at 37.16° N. Lat.; 94.38° W. Long. Elevation is 992 feet.
Population: 125 (2000); Race: 91.0% White, 0.0% Black, 0.0% Asian, 0.0% American Indian and Alaska Native, 9.0% Hispanic of any race, 0.0% two or more races (2000); Density: 1,046.6 persons per square mile (2000); Age: 20.0% under 18, 23.0% over 64 (2000); Marriage status: 17.4% never married, 61.6% now married, 15.1% widowed, 5.8% divorced (2000); Foreign born: 2.0% (2000); Ancestry (includes multiple ancestries): 40.0% United States or American, 12.0% German, 9.0% Other groups, 7.0% Irish, 5.0% English (2000).
Economy: Employment by occupation: 0.0% management, 17.1% professional, 9.8% services, 31.7% sales, 0.0% farming, 14.6% construction, 26.8% production (2000).
Income: Per capita income: $12,458 (2000); Median household income: $31,875 (2000); Poverty rate: 21.0% (2000).
Taxes: Total city taxes per capita: $71 (1997); City property taxes per capita: $71 (1997).
Education: High school graduation rate: 73.0% (2000); College graduation rate: 14.9% (2000).
Housing: Homeownership rate: 86.4% (2000); Median home value: $67,500 (2000); Median rent: $350 per month (2000); Median age of housing: 42 years (2000).
Transportation: Commute to work: 100.0% car, 0.0% public transportation, 0.0% walk, 0.0% work from home (2000); Travel time to work: 42.1% less than 15 minutes, 31.6% 15 to 30 minutes, 7.9% 30 to 45 minutes, 7.9% 45 to 60 minutes, 10.5% 60 minutes or more (2000)

CARL JUNCTION (city). Covers a land area of 4.881 square miles and a water area of 0.137 square miles. Located at 37.17° N. Lat.; 94.55° W. Long. Elevation is 895 feet.
Population: 5,294 (2000); Race: 98.3% White, 0.0% Black, 0.0% Asian, 0.7% American Indian and Alaska Native, 2.0% Hispanic of any race, 0.8% two or more races (2000); Density: 1,084.6 persons per square mile (2000); Age: 29.9% under 18, 8.4% over 64 (2000); Marriage status: 19.6% never married, 66.8% now married, 5.8% widowed, 7.8% divorced (2000); Foreign born: 0.8% (2000); Ancestry (includes multiple ancestries): 18.3% German, 17.4% United States or American, 13.8% English, 13.5% Irish, 10.1% Other groups (2000).
Economy: Dairying; wheat, soybeans, corn; light manufacturing. Single-family building permits issued: 60 (2001) / 70 (2000); Multi-family building permits issued: 0 (2001) / 0 (2000); Employment by occupation: 15.6% management, 21.3% professional, 8.7% services, 28.3% sales, 0.0% farming, 5.1% construction, 21.0% production (2000).
Income: Per capita income: $18,291 (2000); Median household income: $42,575 (2000); Poverty rate: 5.1% (2000).
Taxes: Total city taxes per capita: $146 (1997); City property taxes per capita: $71 (1997).
Education: High school graduation rate: 88.8% (2000); College graduation rate: 23.4% (2000).

School District(s)

Carl Junction R-I (PK-12)
2000 Enrollment: 2,626 417-649-7026
Housing: Homeownership rate: 81.5% (2000); Median home value: $77,000 (2000); Median rent: $410 per month (2000); Median age of housing: 23 years (2000).
Transportation: Commute to work: 94.7% car, 0.0% public transportation, 1.3% walk, 3.6% work from home (2000); Travel time to work: 26.3% less than 15 minutes, 55.8% 15 to 30 minutes, 9.7% 30 to 45 minutes, 4.1% 45 to 60 minutes, 4.1% 60 minutes or more (2000)

CARTERVILLE (city). Covers a land area of 2.608 square miles and a water area of 0 square miles. Located at 37.14° N. Lat.; 94.44° W. Long. Elevation is 985 feet.
History: Carterville was surveyed in 1875 and incorporated in 1877. It was the center of a prosperous lead and zinc mining area until the close of World War I.
Population: 1,850 (2000); Race: 96.1% White, 0.1% Black, 0.0% Asian, 0.4% American Indian and Alaska Native, 1.3% Hispanic of any race, 2.9% two or more races (2000); Density: 709.4 persons per square mile (2000); Age: 29.0% under 18, 10.5% over 64 (2000); Marriage status: 20.3% never married, 58.2% now married, 6.7% widowed, 14.9% divorced (2000); Foreign born: 0.4% (2000); Ancestry (includes multiple ancestries): 25.2% United States or American, 14.2% Other groups, 10.7% German, 8.2% Irish, 6.6% English (2000).
Economy: Employment by occupation: 6.4% management, 10.0% professional, 15.1% services, 26.8% sales, 0.6% farming, 12.1% construction, 29.1% production (2000).
Income: Per capita income: $12,924 (2000); Median household income: $29,595 (2000); Poverty rate: 13.5% (2000).
Taxes: Total city taxes per capita: $166 (1997); City property taxes per capita: $27 (1997).
Education: High school graduation rate: 71.6% (2000); College graduation rate: 6.3% (2000).
Housing: Homeownership rate: 77.2% (2000); Median home value: $45,500 (2000); Median rent: $303 per month (2000); Median age of housing: 46 years (2000).
Safety: Violent crime rate: 26.9 per 10,000 population; Property crime rate: 290.2 per 10,000 population (2001).
Transportation: Commute to work: 95.7% car, 0.3% public transportation, 1.0% walk, 1.7% work from home (2000); Travel time to work: 32.1% less than 15 minutes, 48.7% 15 to 30 minutes, 15.7% 30 to 45 minutes, 1.8% 45 to 60 minutes, 1.8% 60 minutes or more (2000)

CARTHAGE (city). Covers a land area of 9.538 square miles and a water area of 0.037 square miles. Located at 37.16° N. Lat.; 94.31° W. Long. Elevation is 1,002 feet.
History: Carthage was platted in 1842 and named for the ancient commercial center of Northern Africa. Marble quarries opened in the 1880's established an economic base for Carthage, which was supplemented by dairying in the region. Carthage was the birthplace of Belle Starr (1846-1889), who served as a spy for the Confederates and later became a member of Quantrill's band of outlaws. After marrying Sam Starr, Belle organized her own band of bandits.

Population: 12,668 (2000); Race: 86.1% White, 1.9% Black, 1.1% Asian, 1.9% American Indian and Alaska Native, 12.3% Hispanic of any race, 2.6% two or more races (2000); Density: 1,328.2 persons per square mile (2000); Age: 25.8% under 18, 17.8% over 64 (2000); Marriage status: 21.1% never married, 56.6% now married, 11.1% widowed, 11.2% divorced (2000); Foreign born: 9.1% (2000); Ancestry (includes multiple ancestries): 24.6% Other groups, 15.6% German, 11.9% United States or American, 9.8% Irish, 9.4% English (2000).
Vital Statistics: Birth rate: 171.3 per 10,000 population (1998)
Economy: Single-family building permits issued: 34 (2001) / 42 (2000); Multi-family building permits issued: 2 (2001) / 4 (2000); Employment by occupation: 8.9% management, 14.0% professional, 16.5% services, 21.4% sales, 0.9% farming, 10.2% construction, 28.0% production (2000).
Income: Per capita income: $15,281 (2000); Median household income: $28,557 (2000); Poverty rate: 19.2% (2000).
Taxes: Total city taxes per capita: $354 (2000); City property taxes per capita: $46 (2000).
Education: High school graduation rate: 72.0% (2000); College graduation rate: 14.3% (2000).

School District(s)

Carthage R-IX (PK-12)
2000 Enrollment: 3,686 417-359-7000

Housing: Homeownership rate: 63.3% (2000); Median home value: $57,400 (2000); Median rent: $320 per month (2000); Median age of housing: 48 years (2000).
Hospitals: McCune-Brooks Hospital (59 beds)
Newspapers: Carthage Press (6 x week)
Transportation: Commute to work: 91.5% car, 0.0% public transportation, 4.4% walk, 2.6% work from home (2000); Travel time to work: 54.7% less than 15 minutes, 26.0% 15 to 30 minutes, 14.1% 30 to 45 minutes, 2.7% 45 to 60 minutes, 2.5% 60 minutes or more (2000)
Additional Information Contacts
Carthage Board of Realtors 417-358-4041
Carthage Chamber of Commerce 417-358-2373

CARYTOWN (city). Covers a land area of 14.388 square miles and a water area of 0 square miles. Located at 37.26° N. Lat.; 94.33° W. Long. Elevation is 920 feet.
Population: 217 (2000); Race: 96.1% White, 0.0% Black, 0.0% Asian, 3.9% American Indian and Alaska Native, 0.0% Hispanic of any race, 0.0% two or more races (2000); Density: 15.1 persons per square mile (2000); Age: 17.0% under 18, 13.6% over 64 (2000); Marriage status: 15.6% never married, 68.9% now married, 8.3% widowed, 7.2% divorced (2000); Foreign born: 0.0% (2000); Ancestry (includes multiple ancestries): 19.4% United States or American, 17.0% German, 15.0% English, 13.6% Other groups, 7.8% Irish (2000).
Economy: Employment by occupation: 9.8% management, 9.8% professional, 12.7% services, 25.5% sales, 2.0% farming, 8.8% construction, 31.4% production (2000).
Income: Per capita income: $13,852 (2000); Median household income: $27,292 (2000); Poverty rate: 7.8% (2000).
Taxes: Total city taxes per capita: $32 (1997); City property taxes per capita: $6 (1997).
Education: High school graduation rate: 81.5% (2000); College graduation rate: 11.0% (2000).
Housing: Homeownership rate: 82.6% (2000); Median home value: $61,900 (2000); Median rent: $250 per month (2000); Median age of housing: 34 years (2000).
Transportation: Commute to work: 94.1% car, 0.0% public transportation, 0.0% walk, 3.9% work from home (2000); Travel time to work: 28.6% less than 15 minutes, 54.1% 15 to 30 minutes, 7.1% 30 to 45 minutes, 8.2% 45 to 60 minutes, 2.0% 60 minutes or more (2000)

DUENWEG (city). Covers a land area of 0.530 square miles and a water area of 0 square miles. Located at 37.07° N. Lat.; 94.41° W. Long. Elevation is 1,074 feet.
Population: 1,034 (2000); Race: 95.2% White, 0.7% Black, 0.0% Asian, 1.5% American Indian and Alaska Native, 0.9% Hispanic of any race, 2.2% two or more races (2000); Density: 1,949.7 persons per square mile (2000); Age: 29.1% under 18, 9.0% over 64 (2000); Marriage status: 19.0% never married, 57.2% now married, 6.2% widowed, 17.6% divorced (2000); Foreign born: 0.6% (2000); Ancestry (includes multiple ancestries): 16.2% English, 14.2% German, 11.7% Other groups, 10.8% United States or American, 8.0% Irish (2000).
Economy: Residential and commercial area. Light manufacturing. Single-family building permits issued: 1 (2001) / 3 (2000); Multi-family building permits issued: 0 (2001) / 0 (2000); Employment by occupation: 7.5% management, 7.1% professional, 19.2% services, 26.9% sales, 0.8% farming, 12.1% construction, 26.3% production (2000).
Income: Per capita income: $12,342 (2000); Median household income: $25,350 (2000); Poverty rate: 16.0% (2000).
Taxes: Total city taxes per capita: $151 (1997); City property taxes per capita: $46 (1997).
Education: High school graduation rate: 77.1% (2000); College graduation rate: 6.0% (2000).
Housing: Homeownership rate: 66.6% (2000); Median home value: $51,600 (2000); Median rent: $308 per month (2000); Median age of housing: 24 years (2000).
Transportation: Commute to work: 94.7% car, 0.4% public transportation, 0.4% walk, 3.5% work from home (2000); Travel time to work: 27.2% less than 15 minutes, 56.5% 15 to 30 minutes, 12.3% 30 to 45 minutes, 1.5% 45 to 60 minutes, 2.5% 60 minutes or more (2000)

DUQUESNE (village). Covers a land area of 1.876 square miles and a water area of 0 square miles. Located at 37.07° N. Lat.; 94.46° W. Long. Elevation is 1,072 feet.
Population: 1,640 (2000); Race: 91.6% White, 0.7% Black, 2.4% Asian, 2.8% American Indian and Alaska Native, 1.2% Hispanic of any race, 2.1% two or more races (2000); Density: 874.4 persons per square mile (2000); Age: 24.1% under 18, 14.3% over 64 (2000); Marriage status: 18.8% never married, 61.0% now married, 7.5% widowed, 12.7% divorced (2000); Foreign born: 2.8% (2000); Ancestry (includes multiple ancestries): 16.7% German, 15.7% Other groups, 12.1% Irish, 11.6% United States or American, 10.7% English (2000).
Economy: Residential suburb of downtown Joplin. Single-family building permits issued: 7 (2001) / 7 (2000); Multi-family building permits issued: 3 (2001) / 3 (2000); Employment by occupation: 13.4% management, 15.3% professional, 15.4% services, 25.6% sales, 0.0% farming, 8.7% construction, 21.6% production (2000).
Income: Per capita income: $16,815 (2000); Median household income: $37,188 (2000); Poverty rate: 7.7% (2000).
Taxes: Total city taxes per capita: $92 (1997); City property taxes per capita: $0 (1997).
Education: High school graduation rate: 81.8% (2000); College graduation rate: 17.6% (2000).
Housing: Homeownership rate: 73.7% (2000); Median home value: $78,900 (2000); Median rent: $391 per month (2000); Median age of housing: 27 years (2000).
Transportation: Commute to work: 94.0% car, 0.2% public transportation, 2.3% walk, 2.0% work from home (2000); Travel time to work: 51.0% less than 15 minutes, 39.2% 15 to 30 minutes, 5.2% 30 to 45 minutes, 1.4% 45 to 60 minutes, 3.2% 60 minutes or more (2000)

FIDELITY (town). Covers a land area of 0.967 square miles and a water area of 0 square miles. Located at 37.07° N. Lat.; 94.31° W. Long. Elevation is 1,121 feet.
Population: 252 (2000); Race: 100.0% White, 0.0% Black, 0.0% Asian, 0.0% American Indian and Alaska Native, 0.0% Hispanic of any race, 0.0% two or more races (2000); Density: 260.5 persons per square mile (2000); Age: 37.1% under 18, 6.8% over 64 (2000); Marriage status: 22.9% never married, 50.5% now married, 8.0% widowed, 18.6% divorced (2000); Foreign born: 1.1% (2000); Ancestry (includes multiple ancestries): 25.0% United States or American, 15.0% German, 6.1% Other groups, 5.7% English, 2.1% Irish (2000).
Economy: Wheat, hay; cattle. Employment by occupation: 6.0% management, 9.0% professional, 14.0% services, 22.0% sales, 0.0% farming, 13.0% construction, 36.0% production (2000).
Income: Per capita income: $9,810 (2000); Median household income: $27,250 (2000); Poverty rate: 44.9% (2000).
Taxes: Total city taxes per capita: $15 (1997); City property taxes per capita: $15 (1997).
Education: High school graduation rate: 82.1% (2000); College graduation rate: 2.9% (2000).
Housing: Homeownership rate: 57.9% (2000); Median home value: $64,700 (2000); Median rent: $329 per month (2000); Median age of housing: 31 years (2000).
Transportation: Commute to work: 99.0% car, 0.0% public transportation, 0.0% walk, 1.0% work from home (2000); Travel time to work: 29.5% less than 15 minutes, 56.8% 15 to 30 minutes, 7.4% 30 to 45 minutes, 0.0% 45 to 60 minutes, 6.3% 60 minutes or more (2000)

JASPER (city). Covers a land area of 1.097 square miles and a water area of 0.021 square miles. Located at 37.33° N. Lat.; 94.30° W. Long. Elevation is 946 feet.

Population: 1,011 (2000); Race: 97.1% White, 0.3% Black, 0.0% Asian, 0.7% American Indian and Alaska Native, 1.1% Hispanic of any race, 1.9% two or more races (2000); Density: 921.8 persons per square mile (2000); Age: 28.5% under 18, 17.2% over 64 (2000); Marriage status: 18.1% never married, 59.4% now married, 9.9% widowed, 12.6% divorced (2000); Foreign born: 0.2% (2000); Ancestry (includes multiple ancestries): 15.8% Other groups, 15.3% German, 13.4% United States or American, 10.5% Irish, 6.4% English (2000).

Economy: Agriculture: wheat, soybeans; dairying; cattle. Manufacturing: popcorn, auto parts. Employment by occupation: 8.1% management, 9.7% professional, 15.2% services, 19.7% sales, 0.5% farming, 15.6% construction, 31.3% production (2000).

Income: Per capita income: $17,067 (2000); Median household income: $27,650 (2000); Poverty rate: 12.4% (2000).

Taxes: Total city taxes per capita: $191 (1997); City property taxes per capita: $47 (1997).

Education: High school graduation rate: 75.3% (2000); College graduation rate: 8.7% (2000).

School District(s)

Jasper Co. R-V (PK-12)
2000 Enrollment: 517 417-394-2416

Housing: Homeownership rate: 68.5% (2000); Median home value: $48,300 (2000); Median rent: $235 per month (2000); Median age of housing: 38 years (2000).

Transportation: Commute to work: 92.3% car, 0.2% public transportation, 4.8% walk, 1.2% work from home (2000); Travel time to work: 32.5% less than 15 minutes, 48.5% 15 to 30 minutes, 12.9% 30 to 45 minutes, 4.4% 45 to 60 minutes, 1.7% 60 minutes or more (2000)

JOPLIN (city). Covers a land area of 31.416 square miles and a water area of 0.081 square miles. Located at 37.07° N. Lat.; 94.51° W. Long. Elevation is 1,005 feet.

History: Joplin was built on top of the mines that gave it prosperity. The first settler was John C. Cox from Tennessee, who built a cabin in 1838. He was followed by Harris G. Joplin, a Methodist minister, and by 1841 a settlement had grown up around their cabins. Joplin was appointed postmaster and the community was named Blytheville for Billy Blythe, a popular Cherokee who lived nearby. Lead deposits were discovered about 1849; by 1870 there were several large mining companies and several new towns laid out, with intense rivalries between them. In 1873 the towns were joined in incorporation as the City of Joplin. The arrival of the railroads in the 1880's made possible the shipping of lead and the development of the zinc industry.

Population: 45,504 (2000); Race: 91.2% White, 2.3% Black, 0.8% Asian, 1.7% American Indian and Alaska Native, 2.7% Hispanic of any race, 2.6% two or more races (2000); Density: 1,448.4 persons per square mile (2000); Age: 23.2% under 18, 15.6% over 64 (2000); Marriage status: 23.4% never married, 55.8% now married, 7.8% widowed, 13.0% divorced (2000); Foreign born: 1.9% (2000); Ancestry (includes multiple ancestries): 17.1% German, 16.5% Other groups, 12.6% United States or American, 12.0% Irish, 9.7% English (2000).

Vital Statistics: Birth rate: 174.5 per 10,000 population (1998)

Economy: Unemployment rate: 5.2% (11/2002); Total civilian labor force: 24,460 (11/2002); Single-family building permits issued: 217 (2001) / 172 (2000); Multi-family building permits issued: 0 (2001) / 60 (2000); Employment by occupation: 10.2% management, 18.6% professional, 16.0% services, 28.4% sales, 0.2% farming, 7.8% construction, 18.8% production (2000).

Income: Per capita income: $17,738 (2000); Median household income: $30,555 (2000); Poverty rate: 14.8% (2000).

Taxes: Total city taxes per capita: $460 (2000); City property taxes per capita: $23 (2000).

Education: High school graduation rate: 81.5% (2000); College graduation rate: 20.7% (2000).

School District(s)

Joplin R-VIII (PK-12)
2000 Enrollment: 7,341 417-625-5200

Four-year College(s)

Missouri Southern State College (Public)
2001 Enrollment: 5,899 417-625-6772
2001 Tuition: In-state $2,700; Out-of-state $5,400

Ozark Christian College (Private, Not-for-profit, Other Protestant)
2001 Enrollment: 744 417-624-2518
2001 Tuition: In-state $4,640; Out-of-state $4,640

Messenger College (Private, Not-for-profit, Seventh Day Adventists)
2001 Enrollment: 100 417-624-7070
2001 Tuition: In-state $4,200; Out-of-state $4,200

Two-year College(s)

Vatterott College (Private, For-profit)
2001 Enrollment: 214 417-781-5633

Housing: Homeownership rate: 57.6% (2000); Median home value: $67,300 (2000); Median rent: $359 per month (2000); Median age of housing: 37 years (2000).

Hospitals: Freeman Health System (203 beds); Saint John's Regional Medical Center (367 beds)

Safety: Violent crime rate: 46.5 per 10,000 population; Property crime rate: 830.2 per 10,000 population (2001).

Newspapers: The Joplin Globe (7 x week)

Transportation: Commute to work: 93.5% car, 0.4% public transportation, 2.5% walk, 2.4% work from home (2000); Travel time to work: 57.2% less than 15 minutes, 31.2% 15 to 30 minutes, 6.8% 30 to 45 minutes, 2.6% 45 to 60 minutes, 2.3% 60 minutes or more (2000)

Airports: Joplin Regional (primary service)

Additional Information Contacts

Joplin Area Chamber of Commerce 417-624-4150
Joplin Board of Realtors 417-782-6161

LA RUSSELL (city). Covers a land area of 0.341 square miles and a water area of 0 square miles. Located at 37.14° N. Lat.; 94.06° W. Long. Elevation is 1,060 feet.

Population: 138 (2000); Race: 90.5% White, 0.0% Black, 4.8% Asian, 4.8% American Indian and Alaska Native, 0.0% Hispanic of any race, 0.0% two or more races (2000); Density: 405.2 persons per square mile (2000); Age: 34.1% under 18, 7.9% over 64 (2000); Marriage status: 13.8% never married, 70.1% now married, 4.6% widowed, 11.5% divorced (2000); Foreign born: 4.8% (2000); Ancestry (includes multiple ancestries): 33.3% United States or American, 15.1% German, 12.7% Other groups, 6.3% English, 6.3% Polish (2000).

Economy: Wheat, hay, sorghum; cattle. Employment by occupation: 14.0% management, 4.0% professional, 16.0% services, 38.0% sales, 0.0% farming, 14.0% construction, 14.0% production (2000).

Income: Per capita income: $10,451 (2000); Median household income: $28,000 (2000); Poverty rate: 26.6% (2000).

Taxes: Total city taxes per capita: $40 (1997); City property taxes per capita: $8 (1997).

Education: High school graduation rate: 76.9% (2000); College graduation rate: 9.0% (2000).

Housing: Homeownership rate: 85.4% (2000); Median home value: $38,100 (2000); Median rent: $292 per month (2000); Median age of housing: 42 years (2000).

Transportation: Commute to work: 100.0% car, 0.0% public transportation, 0.0% walk, 0.0% work from home (2000); Travel time to work: 16.0% less than 15 minutes, 50.0% 15 to 30 minutes, 28.0% 30 to 45 minutes, 0.0% 45 to 60 minutes, 6.0% 60 minutes or more (2000)

NECK CITY (city). Aka Neck. Covers a land area of 0.104 square miles and a water area of 0 square miles. Located at 37.25° N. Lat.; 94.44° W. Long. Elevation is 934 feet.

Population: 119 (2000); Race: 91.0% White, 0.0% Black, 0.0% Asian, 6.7% American Indian and Alaska Native, 0.0% Hispanic of any race, 2.2% two or more races (2000); Density: 1,149.6 persons per square mile (2000); Age: 28.1% under 18, 9.0% over 64 (2000); Marriage status: 30.1% never married, 52.1% now married, 5.5% widowed, 12.3% divorced (2000); Foreign born: 0.0% (2000); Ancestry (includes multiple ancestries): 27.0% Other groups, 23.6% German, 20.2% United States or American, 9.0% Polish, 6.7% Irish (2000).

Economy: Employment by occupation: 8.2% management, 8.2% professional, 18.4% services, 24.5% sales, 0.0% farming, 12.2% construction, 28.6% production (2000).

Income: Per capita income: $12,454 (2000); Median household income: $29,375 (2000); Poverty rate: 3.4% (2000).

Taxes: Total city taxes per capita: $34 (1997); City property taxes per capita: $7 (1997).

Education: High school graduation rate: 68.4% (2000); College graduation rate: 0.0% (2000).

Housing: Homeownership rate: 85.3% (2000); Median home value: $36,700 (2000); Median rent: $292 per month (2000); Median age of housing: 39 years (2000).
Transportation: Commute to work: 87.2% car, 0.0% public transportation, 4.3% walk, 0.0% work from home (2000); Travel time to work: 8.5% less than 15 minutes, 63.8% 15 to 30 minutes, 14.9% 30 to 45 minutes, 12.8% 45 to 60 minutes, 0.0% 60 minutes or more (2000)

ORONOGO (city). Covers a land area of 2.016 square miles and a water area of 0.027 square miles. Located at 37.19° N. Lat.; 94.46° W. Long. Elevation is 915 feet.
History: Oronogo developed around the Oronogo Circle Mine, which produced about thirty million dollars worth of lead and zinc ore during its prime period of operation, when it made millionaires of several men.
Population: 976 (2000); Race: 96.6% White, 0.0% Black, 0.0% Asian, 1.8% American Indian and Alaska Native, 0.0% Hispanic of any race, 1.6% two or more races (2000); Density: 484.1 persons per square mile (2000); Age: 36.2% under 18, 7.9% over 64 (2000); Marriage status: 16.6% never married, 67.5% now married, 3.9% widowed, 12.0% divorced (2000); Foreign born: 0.5% (2000); Ancestry (includes multiple ancestries): 19.6% United States or American, 18.6% Other groups, 14.6% English, 13.0% Irish, 11.5% German (2000).
Economy: Employment by occupation: 8.8% management, 13.4% professional, 16.4% services, 29.2% sales, 0.0% farming, 9.6% construction, 22.6% production (2000).
Income: Per capita income: $11,626 (2000); Median household income: $33,839 (2000); Poverty rate: 19.4% (2000).
Taxes: Total city taxes per capita: $93 (1997); City property taxes per capita: $21 (1997).
Education: High school graduation rate: 76.9% (2000); College graduation rate: 13.3% (2000).
Housing: Homeownership rate: 81.4% (2000); Median home value: $72,200 (2000); Median rent: $295 per month (2000); Median age of housing: 18 years (2000).
Transportation: Commute to work: 92.8% car, 0.0% public transportation, 0.9% walk, 5.1% work from home (2000); Travel time to work: 29.6% less than 15 minutes, 50.6% 15 to 30 minutes, 15.4% 30 to 45 minutes, 2.7% 45 to 60 minutes, 1.7% 60 minutes or more (2000)

PURCELL (city). Covers a land area of 0.417 square miles and a water area of 0 square miles. Located at 37.24° N. Lat.; 94.43° W. Long. Elevation is 965 feet.
Population: 357 (2000); Race: 96.4% White, 0.0% Black, 0.0% Asian, 3.1% American Indian and Alaska Native, 1.4% Hispanic of any race, 0.6% two or more races (2000); Density: 856.0 persons per square mile (2000); Age: 32.7% under 18, 10.3% over 64 (2000); Marriage status: 13.4% never married, 70.1% now married, 6.3% widowed, 10.2% divorced (2000); Foreign born: 1.1% (2000); Ancestry (includes multiple ancestries): 31.6% United States or American, 16.2% German, 10.3% Irish, 7.5% English, 5.3% Other groups (2000).
Economy: Wheat, soybeans, sorghum; cattle. Employment by occupation: 3.2% management, 10.4% professional, 21.4% services, 20.1% sales, 0.0% farming, 18.2% construction, 26.6% production (2000).
Income: Per capita income: $10,866 (2000); Median household income: $31,964 (2000); Poverty rate: 5.4% (2000).
Taxes: Total city taxes per capita: $36 (1997); City property taxes per capita: $13 (1997).
Education: High school graduation rate: 73.4% (2000); College graduation rate: 3.7% (2000).
Housing: Homeownership rate: 86.6% (2000); Median home value: $43,500 (2000); Median rent: $300 per month (2000); Median age of housing: 41 years (2000).
Transportation: Commute to work: 98.7% car, 0.0% public transportation, 0.0% walk, 1.3% work from home (2000); Travel time to work: 16.0% less than 15 minutes, 54.7% 15 to 30 minutes, 28.7% 30 to 45 minutes, 0.7% 45 to 60 minutes, 0.0% 60 minutes or more (2000)

REEDS (town). Covers a land area of 0.151 square miles and a water area of 0 square miles. Located at 37.11° N. Lat.; 94.16° W. Long. Elevation is 1,118 feet.
Population: 103 (2000); Race: 98.9% White, 0.0% Black, 0.0% Asian, 0.0% American Indian and Alaska Native, 0.0% Hispanic of any race, 1.1% two or more races (2000); Density: 681.8 persons per square mile (2000); Age: 24.2% under 18, 11.6% over 64 (2000); Marriage status: 1.4% never married, 83.3% now married, 2.8% widowed, 12.5% divorced (2000); Foreign born: 0.0% (2000); Ancestry (includes multiple ancestries): 34.7% United States or American, 21.1% Irish, 16.8% Other groups, 11.6% Dutch, 3.2% French (except Basque) (2000).
Economy: Employment by occupation: 21.1% management, 5.3% professional, 7.9% services, 13.2% sales, 0.0% farming, 28.9% construction, 23.7% production (2000).
Income: Per capita income: $18,279 (2000); Median household income: $25,625 (2000); Poverty rate: 11.6% (2000).
Taxes: Total city taxes per capita: $16 (1997); City property taxes per capita: $0 (1997).
Education: High school graduation rate: 49.3% (2000); College graduation rate: 0.0% (2000).
Housing: Homeownership rate: 92.5% (2000); Median home value: $31,700 (2000); Median age of housing: 39 years (2000).
Transportation: Commute to work: 100.0% car, 0.0% public transportation, 0.0% walk, 0.0% work from home (2000); Travel time to work: 23.5% less than 15 minutes, 41.2% 15 to 30 minutes, 29.4% 30 to 45 minutes, 5.9% 45 to 60 minutes, 0.0% 60 minutes or more (2000)

SARCOXIE (city). Covers a land area of 1.079 square miles and a water area of 0 square miles. Located at 37.06° N. Lat.; 94.12° W. Long. Elevation is 1,089 feet.
History: Laid out 1834.
Population: 1,354 (2000); Race: 95.4% White, 0.0% Black, 0.1% Asian, 1.2% American Indian and Alaska Native, 1.4% Hispanic of any race, 3.1% two or more races (2000); Density: 1,254.6 persons per square mile (2000); Age: 25.7% under 18, 20.7% over 64 (2000); Marriage status: 17.2% never married, 59.8% now married, 11.5% widowed, 11.4% divorced (2000); Foreign born: 0.5% (2000); Ancestry (includes multiple ancestries): 16.9% German, 16.0% United States or American, 15.2% Other groups, 13.1% Irish, 9.1% English (2000).
Economy: Apples, peaches, vegetables, wheat, hay; dairying; cattle. Manufacturing: boots, furniture panels. Single-family building permits issued: 0 (2001) / 1 (2000); Multi-family building permits issued: 0 (2001) / 0 (2000); Employment by occupation: 5.1% management, 11.7% professional, 17.5% services, 15.6% sales, 1.7% farming, 9.7% construction, 38.6% production (2000).
Income: Per capita income: $13,531 (2000); Median household income: $25,000 (2000); Poverty rate: 16.8% (2000).
Taxes: Total city taxes per capita: $227 (1997); City property taxes per capita: $66 (1997).
Education: High school graduation rate: 69.8% (2000); College graduation rate: 10.4% (2000).

School District(s)

Sarcoxie R-II (KG-12)
2000 Enrollment: 740 417-548-3134

Housing: Homeownership rate: 70.2% (2000); Median home value: $52,200 (2000); Median rent: $257 per month (2000); Median age of housing: 39 years (2000).
Newspapers: Leader-Journal (1 x week); Sarcoxie Record (1 x week)
Transportation: Commute to work: 95.9% car, 0.0% public transportation, 2.2% walk, 1.5% work from home (2000); Travel time to work: 33.9% less than 15 minutes, 36.2% 15 to 30 minutes, 19.1% 30 to 45 minutes, 6.6% 45 to 60 minutes, 4.2% 60 minutes or more (2000)

WACO (town). Covers a land area of 0.256 square miles and a water area of 0 square miles. Located at 37.24° N. Lat.; 94.59° W. Long. Elevation is 905 feet.
Population: 86 (2000); Race: 100.0% White, 0.0% Black, 0.0% Asian, 0.0% American Indian and Alaska Native, 0.0% Hispanic of any race, 0.0% two or more races (2000); Density: 336.0 persons per square mile (2000); Age: 22.9% under 18, 13.5% over 64 (2000); Marriage status: 23.8% never married, 57.5% now married, 2.5% widowed, 16.3% divorced (2000); Foreign born: 0.0% (2000); Ancestry (includes multiple ancestries): 32.3% United States or American, 12.5% German, 12.5% Irish, 8.3% English, 4.2% Dutch West Indian (2000).
Economy: Employment by occupation: 2.0% management, 16.3% professional, 4.1% services, 28.6% sales, 0.0% farming, 14.3% construction, 34.7% production (2000).
Income: Per capita income: $13,071 (2000); Median household income: $31,250 (2000); Poverty rate: 7.3% (2000).
Taxes: Total city taxes per capita: $32 (1997); City property taxes per capita: $11 (1997).
Education: High school graduation rate: 65.6% (2000); College graduation rate: 4.9% (2000).
Housing: Homeownership rate: 81.1% (2000); Median home value: $49,200 (2000); Median age of housing: 32 years (2000).

Transportation: Commute to work: 93.9% car, 0.0% public transportation, 6.1% walk, 0.0% work from home (2000); Travel time to work: 10.2% less than 15 minutes, 46.9% 15 to 30 minutes, 38.8% 30 to 45 minutes, 4.1% 45 to 60 minutes, 0.0% 60 minutes or more (2000)

WEBB CITY (city). Covers a land area of 7.445 square miles and a water area of 0 square miles. Located at 37.14° N. Lat.; 94.46° W. Long. Elevation is 999 feet.
History: Webb City was platted in 1875 by John C. Webb, who two years earlier had uncovered a chunk of lead on his farm here. That discovery led to a lead and zinc mining boom that lasted for more than forty years.
Population: 9,812 (2000); Race: 93.4% White, 0.6% Black, 0.6% Asian, 0.8% American Indian and Alaska Native, 3.3% Hispanic of any race, 3.3% two or more races (2000); Density: 1,318.0 persons per square mile (2000); Age: 27.7% under 18, 13.9% over 64 (2000); Marriage status: 22.7% never married, 57.8% now married, 6.9% widowed, 12.5% divorced (2000); Foreign born: 1.8% (2000); Ancestry (includes multiple ancestries): 18.0% Other groups, 17.2% German, 12.6% Irish, 11.7% United States or American, 10.4% English (2000).
Economy: Single-family building permits issued: 46 (2001) / 66 (2000); Multi-family building permits issued: 20 (2001) / 14 (2000); Employment by occupation: 8.1% management, 15.2% professional, 15.9% services, 28.8% sales, 0.0% farming, 8.7% construction, 23.3% production (2000).
Income: Per capita income: $15,589 (2000); Median household income: $29,849 (2000); Poverty rate: 15.7% (2000).
Taxes: Total city taxes per capita: $186 (1997); City property taxes per capita: $32 (1997).
Education: High school graduation rate: 80.3% (2000); College graduation rate: 15.6% (2000).

School District(s)

Webb City R-VII (PK-12)
2000 Enrollment: 3,534 417-673-6000

Housing: Homeownership rate: 65.1% (2000); Median home value: $70,300 (2000); Median rent: $338 per month (2000); Median age of housing: 35 years (2000).
Safety: Violent crime rate: 18.2 per 10,000 population; Property crime rate: 360.6 per 10,000 population (2001).
Newspapers: Webb City Sentinel (1 x week)
Transportation: Commute to work: 96.4% car, 0.5% public transportation, 1.4% walk, 1.5% work from home (2000); Travel time to work: 40.1% less than 15 minutes, 44.6% 15 to 30 minutes, 10.4% 30 to 45 minutes, 1.8% 45 to 60 minutes, 3.1% 60 minutes or more (2000)
Additional Information Contacts
Webb City Chamber of Commerce 417-673-1154

Jefferson County

Located in eastern Missouri; bounded on the east by the Mississippi River and the Illinois border, and on the northeast by the Meramec River; drained by the Big River. Covers a land area of 656.80 square miles, a water area of 7.30 square miles, and is located in the Central Time Zone. The county government was organized in 1818. County seat is Hillsboro.

Jefferson County is part of the St. Louis, MO-IL MSA. The entire metro area includes: Clinton County, IL; Jersey County, IL; Madison County, IL; Monroe County, IL; St. Clair County, IL; Crawford County, MO (pt.)**; Franklin County, MO; Jefferson County, MO; Lincoln County, MO; St. Charles County, MO; St. Louis County, MO; Warren County, MO; St. Louis city, MO

Population: 198,099 (2000); Race: 97.5% White, 0.7% Black, 0.4% Asian, 0.3% American Indian and Alaska Native, 0.9% Hispanic of any race, 1.0% two or more races (2000); Density: 301.6 persons per square mile (2000); Age: 27.9% under 18, 9.2% over 64 (2000).
Religion: Five largest groups: 15.7% Catholic Church, 13.3% Southern Baptist Convention, 3.2% Lutheran Church—Missouri Synod, 1.7% The United Methodist Church, 1.1% United Church of Christ (2000).
Economy: Unemployment rate: 4.6% (11/2002); Total civilian labor force: 105,625 (11/2002); Leading industries: 18.2% retail trade; 15.0% manufacturing; 14.4% health care and social assistance (2000); Companies that employ more than 1,000 persons: 1 (2000); Companies that employ more than 100 persons: 52 (2000); Farms: 659 totaling 109,430 acres (1997); Minority business ownership rate: 2.6% (1997); Women business ownership rate: 29.8% (1997); Retail sales per capita: $5,757 (1997). Single-family building permits issued: 1,403 (2001) / 1,242 (2000); Multi-family building permits issued: 67 (2001) / 30 (2000).
Income: Per capita income: $19,435 (2000); Median household income: $46,338 (2000); Poverty rate: 6.8% (2000); Bankruptcy rate: 6.82% (2001).
Taxes: Total county taxes per capita: $130 (2000); County property taxes per capita: $17 (2000).
Education: High school graduation rate: 79.4% (2000); College graduation rate: 12.1% (2000).
Housing: Homeownership rate: 83.4% (2000); Median home value: $99,200 (2000); Median rent: $400 per month (2000); Median age of housing: 23 years (2000).
Health: Birth rate: 139.3 per 10,000 population (1998); Age adjusted death rate: 108.6 per 10,000 population (1999); Age adjusted cancer mortality rate: 222.6 deaths per 100,000 population (1999). Air Quality Index: 67% good, 33% moderate, 0% unhealthy (percent of days in 2000). Number of physicians: 4.5 per 10,000 population (1999); Number of hospital beds: 11.9 per 10,000 population (1999).
Elections: 2000 Presidential election results: 50.0% Gore, 47.6% Bush, 1.5% Nader, 0.4% Buchanan
National and State Parks: Mastodon State Park
Additional Information Contacts
Jefferson County Government Offices.................... 636-797-5555
Arnold Chamber of Commerce 636-296-1910
De Soto Chamber of Commerce 636-586-3050
Festus Chamber of Commerce......................... 636-937-7697
Hillsboro Chamber of Commerce 636-789-4920
Jefferson County Board of Realtors...................... 636-797-4514
Jefferson County Growth & Development................ 636-797-4311
Kimmswick Vistors Center 636-464-6464

Jefferson County Communities

ARNOLD (city). Covers a land area of 11.248 square miles and a water area of 0.334 square miles. Located at 38.43° N. Lat.; 90.36° W. Long. Elevation is 605 feet.
History: Parts of city were damaged by a catastrophic flood in 1993.
Population: 19,965 (2000); Race: 97.8% White, 0.1% Black, 0.3% Asian, 0.4% American Indian and Alaska Native, 1.0% Hispanic of any race, 0.9% two or more races (2000); Density: 1,775.0 persons per square mile (2000); Age: 25.5% under 18, 12.6% over 64 (2000); Marriage status: 22.6% never married, 58.2% now married, 7.0% widowed, 12.1% divorced (2000); Foreign born: 1.0% (2000); Ancestry (includes multiple ancestries): 36.4% German, 16.5% Irish, 11.1% United States or American, 9.0% Other groups, 8.8% English (2000).
Vital Statistics: Birth rate: 146.8 per 10,000 population (1998)
Economy: Manufacturing: metal and glass products, medical supplies, transportation equipment, machinery, electronics. Single-family building permits issued: 39 (2001) / 33 (2000); Multi-family building permits issued: 0 (2001) / 0 (2000); Employment by occupation: 10.7% management, 13.6% professional, 15.3% services, 31.1% sales, 0.1% farming, 12.1% construction, 17.1% production (2000).
Income: Per capita income: $20,378 (2000); Median household income: $47,188 (2000); Poverty rate: 4.4% (2000).
Taxes: Total city taxes per capita: $330 (2000); City property taxes per capita: $31 (2000).
Education: High school graduation rate: 79.2% (2000); College graduation rate: 11.5% (2000).

School District(s)

Fox C-6 (PK-12)
2000 Enrollment: 11,124 636-296-8000

Two-year College(s)

Itt Technical Institute (Private, For-profit)
2001 Enrollment: 484 636-464-6600
2001 Tuition: In-state $11,304; Out-of-state $11,304

Housing: Homeownership rate: 82.0% (2000); Median home value: $97,300 (2000); Median rent: $480 per month (2000); Median age of housing: 28 years (2000).
Safety: Violent crime rate: 84.6 per 10,000 population; Property crime rate: 516.2 per 10,000 population (2001).
Transportation: Commute to work: 97.3% car, 0.3% public transportation, 0.5% walk, 1.5% work from home (2000); Travel time to work: 21.5% less than 15 minutes, 34.1% 15 to 30 minutes, 29.4% 30 to 45 minutes, 10.7% 45 to 60 minutes, 4.3% 60 minutes or more (2000)
Additional Information Contacts
Arnold Chamber of Commerce 636-296-1910

BARNHART (CDP). Covers a land area of 5.139 square miles and a water area of 0.143 square miles. Located at 38.33° N. Lat.; 90.40° W. Long. Elevation is 435 feet.
Population: 6,108 (2000); Race: 96.9% White, 0.7% Black, 0.4% Asian, 0.0% American Indian and Alaska Native, 1.8% Hispanic of any race, 1.9% two or more races (2000); Density: 1,188.5 persons per square mile (2000); Age: 30.8% under 18, 5.5% over 64 (2000); Marriage status: 22.8% never married, 64.0% now married, 2.4% widowed, 10.8% divorced (2000); Foreign born: 1.0% (2000); Ancestry (includes multiple ancestries): 38.8% German, 17.5% Irish, 10.6% English, 10.3% Other groups, 8.1% United States or American (2000).
Economy: Manufacturing: medical supplies. Employment by occupation: 11.1% management, 17.7% professional, 13.2% services, 29.9% sales, 0.0% farming, 12.6% construction, 15.6% production (2000).
Income: Per capita income: $20,940 (2000); Median household income: $56,559 (2000); Poverty rate: 2.6% (2000).
Education: High school graduation rate: 89.3% (2000); College graduation rate: 17.2% (2000).
Housing: Homeownership rate: 93.1% (2000); Median home value: $99,400 (2000); Median rent: $379 per month (2000); Median age of housing: 20 years (2000).
Transportation: Commute to work: 96.7% car, 0.4% public transportation, 0.8% walk, 2.1% work from home (2000); Travel time to work: 15.0% less than 15 minutes, 26.9% 15 to 30 minutes, 27.3% 30 to 45 minutes, 21.4% 45 to 60 minutes, 9.4% 60 minutes or more (2000)

BYRNES MILL (city). Covers a land area of 4.958 square miles and a water area of 0.137 square miles. Located at 38.43° N. Lat.; 90.57° W. Long. Elevation is 458 feet.
Population: 2,376 (2000); Race: 98.0% White, 0.2% Black, 0.2% Asian, 0.8% American Indian and Alaska Native, 1.4% Hispanic of any race, 0.2% two or more races (2000); Density: 479.2 persons per square mile (2000); Age: 29.4% under 18, 5.4% over 64 (2000); Marriage status: 22.6% never married, 61.1% now married, 3.2% widowed, 13.1% divorced (2000); Foreign born: 1.2% (2000); Ancestry (includes multiple ancestries): 30.9% German, 15.3% Irish, 11.5% English, 9.6% Other groups, 7.8% United States or American (2000).
Economy: Residential suburb of downtown St. Louis. Single-family building permits issued: 11 (2001) / 33 (2000); Multi-family building permits issued: 0 (2001) / 0 (2000); Employment by occupation: 10.8% management, 15.1% professional, 11.5% services, 32.4% sales, 0.4% farming, 12.0% construction, 17.7% production (2000).
Income: Per capita income: $20,278 (2000); Median household income: $51,211 (2000); Poverty rate: 7.4% (2000).
Taxes: Total city taxes per capita: $117 (1997); City property taxes per capita: $38 (1997).
Education: High school graduation rate: 82.0% (2000); College graduation rate: 10.1% (2000).
Housing: Homeownership rate: 90.9% (2000); Median home value: $121,600 (2000); Median rent: $403 per month (2000); Median age of housing: 15 years (2000).
Transportation: Commute to work: 96.1% car, 0.5% public transportation, 0.9% walk, 2.5% work from home (2000); Travel time to work: 15.0% less than 15 minutes, 29.6% 15 to 30 minutes, 34.0% 30 to 45 minutes, 15.4% 45 to 60 minutes, 6.0% 60 minutes or more (2000)

CEDAR HILL (CDP). Covers a land area of 2.296 square miles and a water area of 0 square miles. Located at 38.35° N. Lat.; 90.64° W. Long. Elevation is 550 feet.
Population: 1,703 (2000); Race: 98.1% White, 0.0% Black, 0.0% Asian, 1.6% American Indian and Alaska Native, 1.8% Hispanic of any race, 0.2% two or more races (2000); Density: 741.6 persons per square mile (2000); Age: 23.3% under 18, 8.7% over 64 (2000); Marriage status: 27.7% never married, 56.4% now married, 5.0% widowed, 10.8% divorced (2000); Foreign born: 0.5% (2000); Ancestry (includes multiple ancestries): 27.4% United States or American, 25.3% German, 15.4% Irish, 9.6% English, 6.3% French (except Basque) (2000).
Economy: Employment by occupation: 9.6% management, 8.6% professional, 21.8% services, 20.7% sales, 0.0% farming, 17.1% construction, 22.1% production (2000).
Income: Per capita income: $15,599 (2000); Median household income: $35,481 (2000); Poverty rate: 12.9% (2000).
Education: High school graduation rate: 66.9% (2000); College graduation rate: 7.1% (2000).
Housing: Homeownership rate: 85.7% (2000); Median home value: $87,300 (2000); Median rent: $315 per month (2000); Median age of housing: 26 years (2000).
Transportation: Commute to work: 98.4% car, 0.0% public transportation, 1.0% walk, 0.6% work from home (2000); Travel time to work: 21.7% less than 15 minutes, 25.4% 15 to 30 minutes, 28.0% 30 to 45 minutes, 9.9% 45 to 60 minutes, 14.9% 60 minutes or more (2000)

CEDAR HILL LAKES (village). Covers a land area of 0.249 square miles and a water area of 0.029 square miles. Located at 38.32° N. Lat.; 90.65° W. Long. Elevation is 650 feet.
Population: 229 (2000); Race: 98.1% White, 0.0% Black, 0.5% Asian, 1.4% American Indian and Alaska Native, 0.0% Hispanic of any race, 0.0% two or more races (2000); Density: 921.4 persons per square mile (2000); Age: 27.8% under 18, 5.6% over 64 (2000); Marriage status: 27.4% never married, 53.6% now married, 6.7% widowed, 12.3% divorced (2000); Foreign born: 0.5% (2000); Ancestry (includes multiple ancestries): 24.1% United States or American, 21.8% German, 16.7% Irish, 12.0% Other groups, 6.5% French (except Basque) (2000).
Economy: Single-family building permits issued: 0 (2001) / 0 (2000); Multi-family building permits issued: 0 (2001) / 0 (2000); Employment by occupation: 4.7% management, 4.7% professional, 10.4% services, 39.6% sales, 0.0% farming, 24.5% construction, 16.0% production (2000).
Income: Per capita income: $20,222 (2000); Median household income: $54,375 (2000); Poverty rate: 5.6% (2000).
Taxes: Total city taxes per capita: $88 (1997); City property taxes per capita: $55 (1997).
Education: High school graduation rate: 79.9% (2000); College graduation rate: 7.9% (2000).
Housing: Homeownership rate: 95.1% (2000); Median home value: $67,500 (2000); Median rent: $333 per month (2000); Median age of housing: 38 years (2000).
Transportation: Commute to work: 93.2% car, 0.0% public transportation, 0.0% walk, 1.9% work from home (2000); Travel time to work: 5.0% less than 15 minutes, 21.8% 15 to 30 minutes, 27.7% 30 to 45 minutes, 22.8% 45 to 60 minutes, 22.8% 60 minutes or more (2000)

CRYSTAL CITY (city). Covers a land area of 3.736 square miles and a water area of 0.006 square miles. Located at 38.22° N. Lat.; 90.38° W. Long. Elevation is 432 feet.
History: Crystal City originated as a factory town planned and built by the Pittsburgh Plate Glass Company. Glass production began in Crystal City about 1872, when all of the operations were done by hand.
Population: 4,247 (2000); Race: 91.0% White, 5.2% Black, 1.1% Asian, 0.5% American Indian and Alaska Native, 0.5% Hispanic of any race, 1.7% two or more races (2000); Density: 1,136.7 persons per square mile (2000); Age: 23.3% under 18, 20.6% over 64 (2000); Marriage status: 20.5% never married, 55.3% now married, 10.9% widowed, 13.3% divorced (2000); Foreign born: 1.0% (2000); Ancestry (includes multiple ancestries): 26.2% German, 14.7% Other groups, 11.6% English, 11.5% United States or American, 10.7% French (except Basque) (2000).
Economy: Single-family building permits issued: 44 (2001) / 59 (2000); Multi-family building permits issued: 0 (2001) / 0 (2000); Employment by occupation: 8.9% management, 17.4% professional, 13.9% services, 29.0% sales, 0.0% farming, 13.1% construction, 17.7% production (2000).
Income: Per capita income: $17,816 (2000); Median household income: $36,117 (2000); Poverty rate: 15.2% (2000).
Taxes: Total city taxes per capita: $262 (1997); City property taxes per capita: $109 (1997).
Education: High school graduation rate: 78.2% (2000); College graduation rate: 18.6% (2000).

School District(s)

Crystal City 47 (KG-12)
2000 Enrollment: 698 636-937-4411
Housing: Homeownership rate: 73.3% (2000); Median home value: $85,400 (2000); Median rent: $311 per month (2000); Median age of housing: 45 years (2000).
Hospitals: Jefferson Memorial Hospital (210 beds)
Safety: Violent crime rate: 42.1 per 10,000 population; Property crime rate: 330.0 per 10,000 population (2001).
Transportation: Commute to work: 96.0% car, 0.0% public transportation, 1.2% walk, 2.8% work from home (2000); Travel time to work: 43.2% less than 15 minutes, 19.8% 15 to 30 minutes, 15.4% 30 to 45 minutes, 14.2% 45 to 60 minutes, 7.5% 60 minutes or more (2000)

DE SOTO (city). Covers a land area of 3.809 square miles and a water area of 0 square miles. Located at 38.14° N. Lat.; 90.55° W. Long. Elevation is 503 feet.

History: Isaac van Metre built the first house on the site of De Soto in 1803, but the town was not founded until 1857 when the St. Louis & Iron Mountain Railroad was completed through Jefferson County, and De Soto became a shipping point for lead mined nearby.

Population: 6,375 (2000); Race: 98.3% White, 1.2% Black, 0.0% Asian, 0.0% American Indian and Alaska Native, 1.0% Hispanic of any race, 0.5% two or more races (2000); Density: 1,673.6 persons per square mile (2000); Age: 25.2% under 18, 19.1% over 64 (2000); Marriage status: 22.6% never married, 55.7% now married, 10.8% widowed, 11.0% divorced (2000); Foreign born: 0.3% (2000); Ancestry (includes multiple ancestries): 22.7% German, 15.0% Irish, 13.7% Other groups, 12.3% French (except Basque), 9.6% United States or American (2000).

Economy: Single-family building permits issued: 17 (2001) / 12 (2000); Multi-family building permits issued: 67 (2001) / 0 (2000); Employment by occupation: 3.9% management, 15.0% professional, 17.0% services, 23.4% sales, 0.7% farming, 19.1% construction, 20.9% production (2000).

Income: Per capita income: $14,971 (2000); Median household income: $30,725 (2000); Poverty rate: 14.7% (2000).

Taxes: Total city taxes per capita: $230 (1997); City property taxes per capita: $49 (1997).

Education: High school graduation rate: 72.3% (2000); College graduation rate: 6.9% (2000).

School District(s)

Desoto 73 (PK-12)
2000 Enrollment: 3,016 636-586-1000
Sunrise R-IX (PK-08)
2000 Enrollment: 382 636-586-6660

Housing: Homeownership rate: 62.5% (2000); Median home value: $67,200 (2000); Median rent: $312 per month (2000); Median age of housing: 46 years (2000).

Safety: Violent crime rate: 59.2 per 10,000 population; Property crime rate: 495.8 per 10,000 population (2001).

Transportation: Commute to work: 94.5% car, 0.0% public transportation, 2.3% walk, 2.7% work from home (2000); Travel time to work: 32.0% less than 15 minutes, 23.0% 15 to 30 minutes, 10.2% 30 to 45 minutes, 13.9% 45 to 60 minutes, 20.9% 60 minutes or more (2000)

Additional Information Contacts

De Soto Chamber of Commerce 636-586-3050

DITTMER (unincorporated postal area, zip code 63023). Covers a land area of 62.420 square miles and a water area of 0.138 square miles. Located at 38.28° N. Lat.; 90.70° W. Long. Elevation is 720 feet.

Population: 5,253 (2000); Race: 97.2% White, 0.7% Black, 0.2% Asian, 0.0% American Indian and Alaska Native, 0.3% Hispanic of any race, 1.7% two or more races (2000); Density: 84.2 persons per square mile (2000); Age: 27.1% under 18, 8.1% over 64 (2000); Marriage status: 20.5% never married, 63.9% now married, 4.6% widowed, 11.0% divorced (2000); Foreign born: 1.5% (2000); Ancestry (includes multiple ancestries): 35.6% German, 16.5% Irish, 12.5% United States or American, 8.4% Other groups, 7.0% English (2000).

Economy: Employment by occupation: 5.1% management, 13.7% professional, 14.1% services, 23.2% sales, 1.0% farming, 19.6% construction, 23.4% production (2000).

Income: Per capita income: $16,980 (2000); Median household income: $42,833 (2000); Poverty rate: 6.6% (2000).

Education: High school graduation rate: 73.9% (2000); College graduation rate: 8.3% (2000).

Housing: Homeownership rate: 88.4% (2000); Median home value: $88,700 (2000); Median rent: $435 per month (2000); Median age of housing: 22 years (2000).

Transportation: Commute to work: 95.1% car, 0.0% public transportation, 1.3% walk, 2.4% work from home (2000); Travel time to work: 10.2% less than 15 minutes, 17.1% 15 to 30 minutes, 24.8% 30 to 45 minutes, 25.8% 45 to 60 minutes, 22.1% 60 minutes or more (2000)

FESTUS (city). Covers a land area of 4.782 square miles and a water area of 0 square miles. Located at 38.21° N. Lat.; 90.40° W. Long. Elevation is 425 feet.

History: Festus, platted in 1878 when it was called Tanglefoot, developed as the commercial and residential neighbor of industrial Crystal City. The name of Festus was chosen at random from the Bible.

Population: 9,660 (2000); Race: 92.5% White, 4.3% Black, 1.4% Asian, 0.1% American Indian and Alaska Native, 1.0% Hispanic of any race, 1.3% two or more races (2000); Density: 2,020.2 persons per square mile (2000); Age: 25.5% under 18, 16.0% over 64 (2000); Marriage status: 20.4% never married, 58.4% now married, 9.0% widowed, 12.2% divorced (2000); Foreign born: 1.8% (2000); Ancestry (includes multiple ancestries): 26.6% German, 14.3% Irish, 13.7% Other groups, 11.9% United States or American, 10.7% French (except Basque) (2000).

Economy: Single-family building permits issued: 39 (2001) / 38 (2000); Multi-family building permits issued: 0 (2001) / 12 (2000); Employment by occupation: 10.8% management, 13.2% professional, 15.0% services, 30.7% sales, 0.0% farming, 12.5% construction, 17.9% production (2000).

Income: Per capita income: $19,035 (2000); Median household income: $36,687 (2000); Poverty rate: 10.2% (2000).

Taxes: Total city taxes per capita: $328 (1997); City property taxes per capita: $52 (1997).

Education: High school graduation rate: 76.5% (2000); College graduation rate: 12.2% (2000).

School District(s)

Festus R-VI (KG-12)
2000 Enrollment: 2,571 636-937-4920
Jefferson Co. R-VII (KG-08)
2000 Enrollment: 684 636-937-9188

Housing: Homeownership rate: 65.1% (2000); Median home value: $87,300 (2000); Median rent: $383 per month (2000); Median age of housing: 34 years (2000).

Safety: Violent crime rate: 101.9 per 10,000 population; Property crime rate: 303.5 per 10,000 population (2001).

Newspapers: Jefferson County Journal (2 x week); News Democrat Journal (2 x week); Meramec Journal (2 x week)

Transportation: Commute to work: 95.0% car, 0.3% public transportation, 2.6% walk, 1.5% work from home (2000); Travel time to work: 36.3% less than 15 minutes, 21.8% 15 to 30 minutes, 17.1% 30 to 45 minutes, 16.4% 45 to 60 minutes, 8.4% 60 minutes or more (2000)

Additional Information Contacts

Festus Chamber of Commerce 636-937-7697

FLETCHER (unincorporated postal area, zip code 63030). Covers a land area of 19.149 square miles and a water area of 0.060 square miles. Located at 38.12° N. Lat.; 90.74° W. Long. Elevation is 572 feet.

Population: 346 (2000); Race: 99.5% White, 0.0% Black, 0.0% Asian, 0.0% American Indian and Alaska Native, 0.0% Hispanic of any race, 0.5% two or more races (2000); Density: 18.1 persons per square mile (2000); Age: 27.9% under 18, 3.0% over 64 (2000); Marriage status: 29.2% never married, 55.5% now married, 4.7% widowed, 10.6% divorced (2000); Foreign born: 0.0% (2000); Ancestry (includes multiple ancestries): 36.9% German, 17.8% French (except Basque), 13.1% United States or American, 13.1% Irish, 9.6% Scottish (2000).

Economy: Employment by occupation: 5.3% management, 8.0% professional, 30.0% services, 11.3% sales, 0.0% farming, 18.7% construction, 26.7% production (2000).

Income: Per capita income: $16,981 (2000); Median household income: $30,417 (2000); Poverty rate: 16.4% (2000).

Education: High school graduation rate: 56.2% (2000); College graduation rate: 0.0% (2000).

Housing: Homeownership rate: 87.9% (2000); Median home value: $78,000 (2000); Median rent: $356 per month (2000); Median age of housing: 20 years (2000).

Transportation: Commute to work: 87.4% car, 0.0% public transportation, 5.6% walk, 3.5% work from home (2000); Travel time to work: 10.9% less than 15 minutes, 20.3% 15 to 30 minutes, 23.2% 30 to 45 minutes, 25.4% 45 to 60 minutes, 20.3% 60 minutes or more (2000)

GRUBVILLE (unincorporated postal area, zip code 63041). Covers a land area of 6.777 square miles and a water area of 0.021 square miles. Located at 38.28° N. Lat.; 90.76° W. Long. Elevation is 901 feet.

Population: 310 (2000); Race: 95.5% White, 0.0% Black, 0.0% Asian, 0.0% American Indian and Alaska Native, 0.0% Hispanic of any race, 4.5% two or more races (2000); Density: 45.7 persons per square mile (2000); Age: 24.3% under 18, 7.8% over 64 (2000); Marriage status: 20.9% never married, 68.4% now married, 4.9% widowed, 5.8% divorced (2000); Foreign born: 0.0% (2000); Ancestry (includes multiple ancestries): 54.5% German, 18.3% Other groups, 11.2% United States or American, 6.7% Swedish, 5.2% Irish (2000).

Economy: Employment by occupation: 2.1% management, 21.3% professional, 22.0% services, 23.4% sales, 0.0% farming, 18.4% construction, 12.8% production (2000).

Income: Per capita income: $21,063 (2000); Median household income: $57,604 (2000); Poverty rate: 2.6% (2000).
Education: High school graduation rate: 81.6% (2000); College graduation rate: 21.8% (2000).
Housing: Homeownership rate: 97.9% (2000); Median home value: $125,800 (2000); Median age of housing: 13 years (2000).
Transportation: Commute to work: 100.0% car, 0.0% public transportation, 0.0% walk, 0.0% work from home (2000); Travel time to work: 0.0% less than 15 minutes, 9.2% 15 to 30 minutes, 22.0% 30 to 45 minutes, 42.6% 45 to 60 minutes, 26.2% 60 minutes or more (2000)

HERCULANEUM (city). Covers a land area of 3.438 square miles and a water area of 0.047 square miles. Located at 38.25° N. Lat.; 90.38° W. Long. Elevation is 422 feet.
History: Herculaneum was platted and named in 1808 by Moses Austin and Samuel Hammond. The town grew around the St. Joseph Lead Company smelters at the mouth of Joachim Creek.
Population: 2,805 (2000); Race: 97.5% White, 2.3% Black, 0.0% Asian, 0.0% American Indian and Alaska Native, 0.5% Hispanic of any race, 0.2% two or more races (2000); Density: 815.8 persons per square mile (2000); Age: 23.8% under 18, 23.4% over 64 (2000); Marriage status: 18.2% never married, 62.4% now married, 11.0% widowed, 8.5% divorced (2000); Foreign born: 0.2% (2000); Ancestry (includes multiple ancestries): 23.0% German, 13.4% United States or American, 11.1% Irish, 10.9% French (except Basque), 8.4% Other groups (2000).
Economy: Single-family building permits issued: 50 (2001) / 59 (2000); Multi-family building permits issued: 0 (2001) / 0 (2000); Employment by occupation: 9.0% management, 17.1% professional, 14.1% services, 24.8% sales, 0.3% farming, 11.3% construction, 23.4% production (2000).
Income: Per capita income: $18,613 (2000); Median household income: $40,365 (2000); Poverty rate: 5.7% (2000).
Taxes: Total city taxes per capita: $81 (1997); City property taxes per capita: $18 (1997).
Education: High school graduation rate: 72.9% (2000); College graduation rate: 14.2% (2000).

School District(s)

Dunklin R-V (PK-12)
2000 Enrollment: 1,501 636-479-5604

Housing: Homeownership rate: 80.1% (2000); Median home value: $87,400 (2000); Median rent: $494 per month (2000); Median age of housing: 36 years (2000).
Transportation: Commute to work: 96.5% car, 0.3% public transportation, 0.4% walk, 1.6% work from home (2000); Travel time to work: 25.1% less than 15 minutes, 23.5% 15 to 30 minutes, 25.8% 30 to 45 minutes, 17.7% 45 to 60 minutes, 8.0% 60 minutes or more (2000)

HIGH RIDGE (CDP). Covers a land area of 3.992 square miles and a water area of 0 square miles. Located at 38.46° N. Lat.; 90.52° W. Long. Elevation is 927 feet.
Population: 4,236 (2000); Race: 99.1% White, 0.2% Black, 0.0% Asian, 0.1% American Indian and Alaska Native, 1.5% Hispanic of any race, 0.6% two or more races (2000); Density: 1,061.0 persons per square mile (2000); Age: 29.3% under 18, 8.1% over 64 (2000); Marriage status: 22.4% never married, 59.0% now married, 5.4% widowed, 13.3% divorced (2000); Foreign born: 1.3% (2000); Ancestry (includes multiple ancestries): 33.2% German, 18.6% Irish, 9.6% English, 7.8% United States or American, 7.1% Other groups (2000).
Economy: Residential and manufacturing suburb. Manufacturing: fabricated metal products, electronic equipment, machinery. Employment by occupation: 10.7% management, 14.5% professional, 14.3% services, 26.9% sales, 0.0% farming, 15.5% construction, 18.2% production (2000).
Income: Per capita income: $17,959 (2000); Median household income: $46,742 (2000); Poverty rate: 5.4% (2000).
Education: High school graduation rate: 80.7% (2000); College graduation rate: 11.1% (2000).

School District(s)

Northwest R-I (PK-12)
2000 Enrollment: 7,828 636-677-3473

Housing: Homeownership rate: 85.6% (2000); Median home value: $88,600 (2000); Median rent: $442 per month (2000); Median age of housing: 28 years (2000).
Transportation: Commute to work: 96.2% car, 0.0% public transportation, 0.5% walk, 3.0% work from home (2000); Travel time to work: 11.9% less than 15 minutes, 37.4% 15 to 30 minutes, 37.4% 30 to 45 minutes, 9.9% 45 to 60 minutes, 3.4% 60 minutes or more (2000)

HILLSBORO (city). Covers a land area of 2.388 square miles and a water area of 0 square miles. Located at 38.23° N. Lat.; 90.56° W. Long. Elevation is 802 feet.
History: Seat of Jefferson College. Plotted 1839.
Population: 1,675 (2000); Race: 96.2% White, 2.1% Black, 0.3% Asian, 0.2% American Indian and Alaska Native, 1.6% Hispanic of any race, 1.1% two or more races (2000); Density: 701.4 persons per square mile (2000); Age: 32.9% under 18, 7.3% over 64 (2000); Marriage status: 32.1% never married, 50.5% now married, 5.0% widowed, 12.3% divorced (2000); Foreign born: 0.8% (2000); Ancestry (includes multiple ancestries): 30.0% German, 14.1% Irish, 12.4% United States or American, 12.1% Other groups, 11.8% French (except Basque) (2000).
Economy: Light manufacturing. Semi-urban development in area; satellite community of St. Louis. Single-family building permits issued: 3 (2001) / 4 (2000); Multi-family building permits issued: 0 (2001) / 4 (2000); Employment by occupation: 7.7% management, 19.9% professional, 16.5% services, 23.3% sales, 0.0% farming, 11.7% construction, 20.8% production (2000).
Income: Per capita income: $15,585 (2000); Median household income: $36,850 (2000); Poverty rate: 14.3% (2000).
Taxes: Total city taxes per capita: $163 (1997); City property taxes per capita: $31 (1997).
Education: High school graduation rate: 75.6% (2000); College graduation rate: 15.6% (2000).

School District(s)

Grandview R-II (KG-12)
2000 Enrollment: 951 636-944-3941
Hillsboro R-III (PK-12)
2000 Enrollment: 3,633 636-789-3378
Jefferson Community College (09-12)
2000 Enrollment: n/a 314-789-3951

Two-year College(s)

Jefferson College (Public)
2001 Enrollment: 3,899 636-797-3000
2001 Tuition: In-state $2,010; Out-of-state $2,700

Housing: Homeownership rate: 54.3% (2000); Median home value: $93,800 (2000); Median rent: $421 per month (2000); Median age of housing: 29 years (2000).
Transportation: Commute to work: 96.3% car, 0.0% public transportation, 1.0% walk, 1.8% work from home (2000); Travel time to work: 30.9% less than 15 minutes, 22.1% 15 to 30 minutes, 17.6% 30 to 45 minutes, 16.4% 45 to 60 minutes, 13.2% 60 minutes or more (2000)

Additional Information Contacts

Hillsboro Chamber of Commerce 636-789-4920
Jefferson County Board of Realtors 636-797-4514
Jefferson County Growth & Development. 636-797-4311

HORINE (CDP). Covers a land area of 0.830 square miles and a water area of 0.016 square miles. Located at 38.26° N. Lat.; 90.43° W. Long. Elevation is 420 feet.
Population: 923 (2000); Race: 100.0% White, 0.0% Black, 0.0% Asian, 0.0% American Indian and Alaska Native, 0.0% Hispanic of any race, 0.0% two or more races (2000); Density: 1,112.2 persons per square mile (2000); Age: 25.8% under 18, 5.5% over 64 (2000); Marriage status: 19.6% never married, 63.1% now married, 6.7% widowed, 10.6% divorced (2000); Foreign born: 1.8% (2000); Ancestry (includes multiple ancestries): 24.0% German, 10.7% Irish, 8.1% French (except Basque), 7.2% United States or American, 6.0% Other groups (2000).
Economy: Employment by occupation: 5.5% management, 7.9% professional, 19.4% services, 32.3% sales, 0.0% farming, 22.3% construction, 12.6% production (2000).
Income: Per capita income: $17,366 (2000); Median household income: $41,676 (2000); Poverty rate: 3.7% (2000).
Education: High school graduation rate: 80.0% (2000); College graduation rate: 7.2% (2000).
Housing: Homeownership rate: 90.7% (2000); Median home value: $72,600 (2000); Median rent: $312 per month (2000); Median age of housing: 34 years (2000).
Transportation: Commute to work: 94.1% car, 0.0% public transportation, 4.1% walk, 1.8% work from home (2000); Travel time to work: 31.2% less than 15 minutes, 31.0% 15 to 30 minutes, 11.5% 30 to 45 minutes, 18.3% 45 to 60 minutes, 8.0% 60 minutes or more (2000)

HOUSE SPRINGS (unincorporated postal area, zip code 63051). Covers a land area of 43.158 square miles and a water area of 0.126 square miles. Located at 38.40° N. Lat.; 90.57° W. Long. Elevation is 474 feet.
Population: 13,230 (2000); Race: 97.2% White, 0.2% Black, 0.4% Asian, 0.4% American Indian and Alaska Native, 0.6% Hispanic of any race, 1.6% two or more races (2000); Density: 306.5 persons per square mile (2000); Age: 29.9% under 18, 6.7% over 64 (2000); Marriage status: 22.7% never married, 60.1% now married, 4.6% widowed, 12.5% divorced (2000); Foreign born: 0.8% (2000); Ancestry (includes multiple ancestries): 31.4% German, 16.6% Irish, 10.9% United States or American, 10.2% Other groups, 8.1% English (2000).
Economy: Light manufacturing. Employment by occupation: 9.3% management, 11.6% professional, 14.2% services, 27.6% sales, 0.1% farming, 16.1% construction, 21.2% production (2000).
Income: Per capita income: $18,252 (2000); Median household income: $46,961 (2000); Poverty rate: 5.3% (2000).
Education: High school graduation rate: 76.9% (2000); College graduation rate: 8.7% (2000).
Housing: Homeownership rate: 88.3% (2000); Median home value: $98,400 (2000); Median rent: $387 per month (2000); Median age of housing: 20 years (2000).
Transportation: Commute to work: 97.3% car, 0.2% public transportation, 0.9% walk, 1.5% work from home (2000); Travel time to work: 14.9% less than 15 minutes, 26.7% 15 to 30 minutes, 30.9% 30 to 45 minutes, 18.2% 45 to 60 minutes, 9.3% 60 minutes or more (2000)

IMPERIAL (CDP). Covers a land area of 5.383 square miles and a water area of 0.741 square miles. Located at 38.37° N. Lat.; 90.37° W. Long. Elevation is 446 feet.
History: Mastodon State Park.
Population: 4,373 (2000); Race: 97.7% White, 0.2% Black, 0.3% Asian, 0.2% American Indian and Alaska Native, 1.6% Hispanic of any race, 1.2% two or more races (2000); Density: 812.4 persons per square mile (2000); Age: 28.6% under 18, 8.3% over 64 (2000); Marriage status: 23.5% never married, 60.8% now married, 5.6% widowed, 10.0% divorced (2000); Foreign born: 0.6% (2000); Ancestry (includes multiple ancestries): 35.8% German, 14.9% Irish, 12.3% United States or American, 8.5% English, 7.2% Other groups (2000).
Economy: Manufacturing: chemicals, transportation equipment. Employment by occupation: 12.9% management, 15.2% professional, 16.1% services, 29.2% sales, 0.0% farming, 10.9% construction, 15.8% production (2000).
Income: Per capita income: $20,431 (2000); Median household income: $49,565 (2000); Poverty rate: 9.8% (2000).
Education: High school graduation rate: 84.5% (2000); College graduation rate: 14.2% (2000).

School District(s)

Windsor C-1 (PK-12)
2000 Enrollment: 3,017 636-464-4400
Housing: Homeownership rate: 85.8% (2000); Median home value: $98,400 (2000); Median rent: $441 per month (2000); Median age of housing: 19 years (2000).
Transportation: Commute to work: 94.8% car, 0.0% public transportation, 1.9% walk, 3.3% work from home (2000); Travel time to work: 23.4% less than 15 minutes, 28.3% 15 to 30 minutes, 32.6% 30 to 45 minutes, 11.4% 45 to 60 minutes, 4.3% 60 minutes or more (2000)
Additional Information Contacts
Kimmswick Vistors Center 636-464-6464

KIMMSWICK (city). Covers a land area of 0.079 square miles and a water area of 0 square miles. Located at 38.36° N. Lat.; 90.36° W. Long. Elevation is 411 feet.
History: Kimmswick was laid out in 1857 by Theodore Kimm as a port on the Mississippi River. It became a smelting and shipping point for iron mined at Pilot Knob and Iron Mountain, and later turned to farming and resort activities.
Population: 94 (2000); Race: 92.0% White, 2.0% Black, 0.0% Asian, 0.0% American Indian and Alaska Native, 0.0% Hispanic of any race, 6.0% two or more races (2000); Density: 1,186.5 persons per square mile (2000); Age: 24.0% under 18, 14.0% over 64 (2000); Marriage status: 33.3% never married, 52.4% now married, 4.8% widowed, 9.5% divorced (2000); Foreign born: 0.0% (2000); Ancestry (includes multiple ancestries): 35.0% United States or American, 20.0% Irish, 7.0% French (except Basque), 7.0% Other groups, 6.0% English (2000).
Economy: Single-family building permits issued: 0 (2001) / 0 (2000); Multi-family building permits issued: 0 (2001) / 0 (2000); Employment by occupation: 16.4% management, 9.0% professional, 20.9% services, 32.8% sales, 0.0% farming, 9.0% construction, 11.9% production (2000).
Income: Per capita income: $23,359 (2000); Median household income: $54,688 (2000); Poverty rate: 7.0% (2000).
Taxes: Total city taxes per capita: $441 (1997); City property taxes per capita: $0 (1997).
Education: High school graduation rate: 78.5% (2000); College graduation rate: 13.8% (2000).
Housing: Homeownership rate: 88.2% (2000); Median home value: $121,400 (2000); Median rent: $425 per month (2000); Median age of housing: 60+ years (2000).
Transportation: Commute to work: 89.6% car, 0.0% public transportation, 1.5% walk, 9.0% work from home (2000); Travel time to work: 27.9% less than 15 minutes, 36.1% 15 to 30 minutes, 29.5% 30 to 45 minutes, 6.6% 45 to 60 minutes, 0.0% 60 minutes or more (2000)

MURPHY (CDP). Covers a land area of 3.965 square miles and a water area of 0.047 square miles. Located at 38.49° N. Lat.; 90.48° W. Long. Elevation is 570 feet.
Population: 9,048 (2000); Race: 98.2% White, 0.1% Black, 0.2% Asian, 0.1% American Indian and Alaska Native, 1.3% Hispanic of any race, 1.3% two or more races (2000); Density: 2,281.9 persons per square mile (2000); Age: 24.9% under 18, 10.8% over 64 (2000); Marriage status: 23.8% never married, 58.1% now married, 4.9% widowed, 13.2% divorced (2000); Foreign born: 0.9% (2000); Ancestry (includes multiple ancestries): 33.3% German, 19.7% Irish, 9.3% English, 8.0% United States or American, 7.5% Other groups (2000).
Economy: Employment by occupation: 10.3% management, 10.0% professional, 15.5% services, 30.1% sales, 0.0% farming, 11.8% construction, 22.4% production (2000).
Income: Per capita income: $20,374 (2000); Median household income: $42,430 (2000); Poverty rate: 5.8% (2000).
Education: High school graduation rate: 77.8% (2000); College graduation rate: 9.6% (2000).
Housing: Homeownership rate: 89.8% (2000); Median home value: $96,400 (2000); Median rent: $395 per month (2000); Median age of housing: 25 years (2000).
Transportation: Commute to work: 96.0% car, 0.3% public transportation, 0.6% walk, 2.9% work from home (2000); Travel time to work: 20.9% less than 15 minutes, 35.3% 15 to 30 minutes, 30.5% 30 to 45 minutes, 9.0% 45 to 60 minutes, 4.3% 60 minutes or more (2000)

OLYMPIAN VILLAGE (city). Covers a land area of 0.562 square miles and a water area of 0 square miles. Located at 38.13° N. Lat.; 90.45° W. Long. Elevation is 600 feet.
Population: 669 (2000); Race: 97.4% White, 0.0% Black, 0.9% Asian, 0.0% American Indian and Alaska Native, 1.5% Hispanic of any race, 1.4% two or more races (2000); Density: 1,190.1 persons per square mile (2000); Age: 27.1% under 18, 3.9% over 64 (2000); Marriage status: 31.8% never married, 55.2% now married, 2.5% widowed, 10.5% divorced (2000); Foreign born: 0.5% (2000); Ancestry (includes multiple ancestries): 20.6% United States or American, 15.9% German, 12.8% Other groups, 12.7% Irish, 8.8% English (2000).
Economy: Single-family building permits issued: 4 (2001) / 3 (2000); Multi-family building permits issued: 0 (2001) / 0 (2000); Employment by occupation: 4.2% management, 10.2% professional, 28.9% services, 23.2% sales, 0.0% farming, 15.0% construction, 18.4% production (2000).
Income: Per capita income: $14,928 (2000); Median household income: $41,447 (2000); Poverty rate: 10.2% (2000).
Taxes: Total city taxes per capita: $106 (1997); City property taxes per capita: $33 (1997).
Education: High school graduation rate: 74.1% (2000); College graduation rate: 3.4% (2000).
Housing: Homeownership rate: 90.7% (2000); Median home value: $72,800 (2000); Median rent: $236 per month (2000); Median age of housing: 26 years (2000).
Transportation: Commute to work: 98.5% car, 0.0% public transportation, 0.0% walk, 1.5% work from home (2000); Travel time to work: 12.3% less than 15 minutes, 30.9% 15 to 30 minutes, 17.4% 30 to 45 minutes, 20.4% 45 to 60 minutes, 18.9% 60 minutes or more (2000)

PARKDALE (village). Covers a land area of 0.127 square miles and a water area of 0 square miles. Located at 38.48° N. Lat.; 90.52° W. Long. Elevation is 750 feet.
Population: 205 (2000); Race: 100.0% White, 0.0% Black, 0.0% Asian, 0.0% American Indian and Alaska Native, 0.0% Hispanic of any race, 0.0%

two or more races (2000); Density: 1,616.4 persons per square mile (2000); Age: 27.6% under 18, 8.3% over 64 (2000); Marriage status: 24.4% never married, 58.5% now married, 7.3% widowed, 9.8% divorced (2000); Foreign born: 0.0% (2000); Ancestry (includes multiple ancestries): 29.5% German, 19.8% Irish, 14.7% United States or American, 12.4% English, 9.2% French (except Basque) (2000).
Economy: Single-family building permits issued: 0 (2001) / 0 (2000); Multi-family building permits issued: 0 (2001) / 0 (2000); Employment by occupation: 2.8% management, 15.7% professional, 20.4% services, 26.9% sales, 0.0% farming, 13.0% construction, 21.3% production (2000).
Income: Per capita income: $17,783 (2000); Median household income: $52,000 (2000); Poverty rate: 3.7% (2000).
Taxes: Total city taxes per capita: $15 (1997); City property taxes per capita: $5 (1997).
Education: High school graduation rate: 87.2% (2000); College graduation rate: 9.8% (2000).
Housing: Homeownership rate: 97.5% (2000); Median home value: $92,800 (2000); Median age of housing: 42 years (2000).
Transportation: Commute to work: 100.0% car, 0.0% public transportation, 0.0% walk, 0.0% work from home (2000); Travel time to work: 12.0% less than 15 minutes, 31.5% 15 to 30 minutes, 29.6% 30 to 45 minutes, 23.1% 45 to 60 minutes, 3.7% 60 minutes or more (2000)

PEVELY (city). Covers a land area of 3.324 square miles and a water area of 0.092 square miles. Located at 38.28° N. Lat.; 90.39° W. Long. Elevation is 440 feet.
Population: 3,768 (2000); Race: 97.1% White, 1.8% Black, 0.5% Asian, 0.2% American Indian and Alaska Native, 0.3% Hispanic of any race, 0.4% two or more races (2000); Density: 1,133.7 persons per square mile (2000); Age: 31.1% under 18, 7.7% over 64 (2000); Marriage status: 23.9% never married, 53.6% now married, 5.7% widowed, 16.8% divorced (2000); Foreign born: 0.8% (2000); Ancestry (includes multiple ancestries): 25.4% German, 14.9% Irish, 14.2% United States or American, 12.4% Other groups, 10.9% French (except Basque) (2000).
Economy: Manufacturing: fabricated metal products, steel castings, plastic foam insulation, glass products. Single-family building permits issued: 40 (2001) / 26 (2000); Multi-family building permits issued: 0 (2001) / 0 (2000); Employment by occupation: 5.3% management, 10.2% professional, 14.4% services, 28.2% sales, 0.0% farming, 18.7% construction, 23.1% production (2000).
Income: Per capita income: $14,403 (2000); Median household income: $34,916 (2000); Poverty rate: 19.6% (2000).
Taxes: Total city taxes per capita: $495 (1997); City property taxes per capita: $166 (1997).
Education: High school graduation rate: 72.3% (2000); College graduation rate: 5.7% (2000).
Housing: Homeownership rate: 72.0% (2000); Median home value: $80,200 (2000); Median rent: $304 per month (2000); Median age of housing: 20 years (2000).
Safety: Violent crime rate: 10.6 per 10,000 population; Property crime rate: 255.9 per 10,000 population (2001).
Transportation: Commute to work: 97.6% car, 0.0% public transportation, 1.0% walk, 1.1% work from home (2000); Travel time to work: 17.4% less than 15 minutes, 27.6% 15 to 30 minutes, 28.4% 30 to 45 minutes, 13.8% 45 to 60 minutes, 12.7% 60 minutes or more (2000)

SCOTSDALE (town). Covers a land area of 0.804 square miles and a water area of 0 square miles. Located at 38.40° N. Lat.; 90.58° W. Long. Elevation is 550 feet.
Population: 211 (2000); Race: 99.5% White, 0.0% Black, 0.5% Asian, 0.0% American Indian and Alaska Native, 0.0% Hispanic of any race, 0.0% two or more races (2000); Density: 262.4 persons per square mile (2000); Age: 39.1% under 18, 2.3% over 64 (2000); Marriage status: 29.3% never married, 66.2% now married, 1.3% widowed, 3.2% divorced (2000); Foreign born: 0.0% (2000); Ancestry (includes multiple ancestries): 47.0% German, 22.3% Irish, 21.9% English, 8.8% French (except Basque), 7.9% Polish (2000).
Economy: Employment by occupation: 2.9% management, 11.5% professional, 9.6% services, 30.8% sales, 0.0% farming, 18.3% construction, 26.9% production (2000).
Income: Per capita income: $16,304 (2000); Median household income: $53,750 (2000); Poverty rate: 14.0% (2000).
Taxes: Total city taxes per capita: $23 (1997); City property taxes per capita: $23 (1997).
Education: High school graduation rate: 80.3% (2000); College graduation rate: 22.1% (2000).
Housing: Homeownership rate: 83.3% (2000); Median home value: $95,600 (2000); Median rent: $413 per month (2000); Median age of housing: 22 years (2000).
Transportation: Commute to work: 87.0% car, 0.0% public transportation, 4.0% walk, 9.0% work from home (2000); Travel time to work: 25.3% less than 15 minutes, 17.6% 15 to 30 minutes, 36.3% 30 to 45 minutes, 14.3% 45 to 60 minutes, 6.6% 60 minutes or more (2000)

Johnson County

Located in west central Missouri; drained by the Blackwater River. Covers a land area of 830.40 square miles, a water area of 2.60 square miles, and is located in the Central Time Zone. The county government was organized in 1834. County seat is Warrensburg.
Population: 48,258 (2000); Race: 90.2% White, 4.0% Black, 1.2% Asian, 0.7% American Indian and Alaska Native, 3.1% Hispanic of any race, 2.3% two or more races (2000); Density: 58.1 persons per square mile (2000); Age: 25.2% under 18, 9.4% over 64 (2000).
Religion: Five largest groups: 20.4% Southern Baptist Convention, 5.1% The United Methodist Church, 3.5% Catholic Church, 2.7% The Church of Jesus Christ of Latter-day Saints, 2.6% Christian Churches and Churches of Christ (2000).
Economy: Unemployment rate: 3.8% (11/2002); Total civilian labor force: 22,570 (11/2002); Leading industries: 21.2% manufacturing; 17.9% retail trade; 16.2% accommodation & food services (2000); Companies that employ more than 1,000 persons: 0 (2000); Companies that employ more than 100 persons: 12 (2000); Farms: 1,626 totaling 399,600 acres (1997); Minority business ownership rate: 5.1% (1997); Women business ownership rate: 22.1% (1997); Retail sales per capita: $5,169 (1997). Single-family building permits issued: 63 (2001) / 49 (2000); Multi-family building permits issued: 89 (2001) / 24 (2000).
Income: Per capita income: $16,037 (2000); Median household income: $35,391 (2000); Poverty rate: 14.9% (2000); Bankruptcy rate: 3.96% (2001).
Taxes: Total county taxes per capita: $118 (2000); County property taxes per capita: $33 (2000).
Education: High school graduation rate: 86.0% (2000); College graduation rate: 23.2% (2000).
Housing: Homeownership rate: 61.5% (2000); Median home value: $86,500 (2000); Median rent: $385 per month (2000); Median age of housing: 24 years (2000).
Health: Birth rate: 139.5 per 10,000 population (1998); Age adjusted death rate: 91.2 per 10,000 population (1999); Age adjusted cancer mortality rate: 171.4 deaths per 100,000 population (1999). Number of physicians: 8.7 per 10,000 population (1999); Number of hospital beds: 13.9 per 10,000 population (1999).
Elections: 2000 Presidential election results: 41.3% Gore, 55.6% Bush, 1.9% Nader, 0.4% Buchanan
National and State Parks: Knob Noster State Park; Ralph and Martha Perry Memorial State Wildlife Area
Additional Information Contacts
Johnson County Government Offices 660-747-2112
Holden Chamber of Commerce 816-732-6844
Midwest Missouri Board of Realtors 660-429-5518
Warrensburg Chamber of Commerce...................... 660-747-3168

Johnson County Communities

CENTERVIEW (city). Covers a land area of 0.116 square miles and a water area of 0 square miles. Located at 38.74° N. Lat.; 93.84° W. Long. Elevation is 865 feet.
Population: 249 (2000); Race: 87.0% White, 0.0% Black, 0.0% Asian, 5.0% American Indian and Alaska Native, 2.5% Hispanic of any race, 5.9% two or more races (2000); Density: 2,148.1 persons per square mile (2000); Age: 30.3% under 18, 10.1% over 64 (2000); Marriage status: 28.7% never married, 51.6% now married, 5.9% widowed, 13.8% divorced (2000); Foreign born: 0.0% (2000); Ancestry (includes multiple ancestries): 30.7% Other groups, 20.2% Irish, 13.4% German, 6.3% English, 5.9% United States or American (2000).
Economy: Employment by occupation: 4.6% management, 8.0% professional, 26.4% services, 9.2% sales, 4.6% farming, 20.7% construction, 26.4% production (2000).
Income: Per capita income: $12,696 (2000); Median household income: $28,333 (2000); Poverty rate: 28.6% (2000).
Taxes: Total city taxes per capita: $30 (1997); City property taxes per capita: $4 (1997).

Education: High school graduation rate: 67.4% (2000); College graduation rate: 5.7% (2000).

School District(s)

Johnson Co. R-VII (PK-12)
2000 Enrollment: 629 660-656-3316

Housing: Homeownership rate: 64.3% (2000); Median home value: $44,500 (2000); Median rent: $375 per month (2000); Median age of housing: 38 years (2000).

Transportation: Commute to work: 90.4% car, 0.0% public transportation, 7.2% walk, 2.4% work from home (2000); Travel time to work: 32.1% less than 15 minutes, 32.1% 15 to 30 minutes, 13.6% 30 to 45 minutes, 8.6% 45 to 60 minutes, 13.6% 60 minutes or more (2000)

CHILHOWEE (town). Covers a land area of 0.383 square miles and a water area of 0 square miles. Located at 38.58° N. Lat.; 93.85° W. Long. Elevation is 885 feet.

Population: 329 (2000); Race: 98.8% White, 0.0% Black, 0.0% Asian, 0.6% American Indian and Alaska Native, 0.0% Hispanic of any race, 0.6% two or more races (2000); Density: 858.6 persons per square mile (2000); Age: 23.1% under 18, 21.9% over 64 (2000); Marriage status: 19.0% never married, 53.5% now married, 13.8% widowed, 13.8% divorced (2000); Foreign born: 0.0% (2000); Ancestry (includes multiple ancestries): 20.1% German, 10.8% Other groups, 10.5% English, 10.2% United States or American, 4.5% Canadian (2000).

Economy: Corn, soybeans, hay; cattle. Employment by occupation: 8.0% management, 6.4% professional, 13.6% services, 24.0% sales, 0.0% farming, 19.2% construction, 28.8% production (2000).

Income: Per capita income: $14,850 (2000); Median household income: $29,688 (2000); Poverty rate: 9.3% (2000).

Taxes: Total city taxes per capita: $137 (1997); City property taxes per capita: $22 (1997).

Education: High school graduation rate: 74.2% (2000); College graduation rate: 4.4% (2000).

School District(s)

Chilhowee R-IV (KG-12)
2000 Enrollment: 168 660-678-2511

Shawnee R-III (KG-08)
2000 Enrollment: 67 660-885-3620

Housing: Homeownership rate: 68.2% (2000); Median home value: $40,400 (2000); Median rent: $209 per month (2000); Median age of housing: 36 years (2000).

Transportation: Commute to work: 95.3% car, 0.0% public transportation, 4.7% walk, 0.0% work from home (2000); Travel time to work: 16.5% less than 15 minutes, 29.9% 15 to 30 minutes, 33.9% 30 to 45 minutes, 2.4% 45 to 60 minutes, 17.3% 60 minutes or more (2000)

HOLDEN (city). Covers a land area of 2.412 square miles and a water area of 0.008 square miles. Located at 38.71° N. Lat.; 93.99° W. Long. Elevation is 770 feet.

History: Holden was the home of Carry Nation when she was the bride of Dr. William Gloyd, a physician and an alcoholic. After less than a year of marriage, Carry went home to her family in Belton. After Gloyd died of alcoholism, Carry returned to Holden to teach in the public school. Four years later she was dismissed, reportedly because of an argument over the pronunication of the letter "a." Carry later married David Nation and moved to Texas.

Population: 2,510 (2000); Race: 94.0% White, 2.2% Black, 0.0% Asian, 1.0% American Indian and Alaska Native, 1.0% Hispanic of any race, 2.5% two or more races (2000); Density: 1,040.8 persons per square mile (2000); Age: 31.2% under 18, 13.4% over 64 (2000); Marriage status: 21.3% never married, 55.9% now married, 10.6% widowed, 12.3% divorced (2000); Foreign born: 0.5% (2000); Ancestry (includes multiple ancestries): 14.8% German, 12.8% Irish, 12.3% United States or American, 11.6% Other groups, 9.0% English (2000).

Economy: Employment by occupation: 9.0% management, 12.5% professional, 14.9% services, 21.8% sales, 1.7% farming, 16.9% construction, 23.3% production (2000).

Income: Per capita income: $13,537 (2000); Median household income: $30,255 (2000); Poverty rate: 12.5% (2000).

Taxes: Total city taxes per capita: $164 (1997); City property taxes per capita: $37 (1997).

Education: High school graduation rate: 78.2% (2000); College graduation rate: 13.2% (2000).

School District(s)

Holden R-III (PK-12)
2000 Enrollment: 1,449 816-732-5568

Housing: Homeownership rate: 68.6% (2000); Median home value: $56,700 (2000); Median rent: $328 per month (2000); Median age of housing: 38 years (2000).

Newspapers: Holden Image (1 x week)

Transportation: Commute to work: 94.1% car, 0.3% public transportation, 1.5% walk, 4.1% work from home (2000); Travel time to work: 34.1% less than 15 minutes, 13.4% 15 to 30 minutes, 16.8% 30 to 45 minutes, 19.2% 45 to 60 minutes, 16.4% 60 minutes or more (2000)

Additional Information Contacts

Holden Chamber of Commerce 816-732-6844

KINGSVILLE (city). Covers a land area of 0.299 square miles and a water area of 0 square miles. Located at 38.74° N. Lat.; 94.06° W. Long. Elevation is 914 feet.

Population: 257 (2000); Race: 96.8% White, 0.0% Black, 0.0% Asian, 1.4% American Indian and Alaska Native, 0.0% Hispanic of any race, 1.8% two or more races (2000); Density: 858.8 persons per square mile (2000); Age: 28.0% under 18, 12.4% over 64 (2000); Marriage status: 11.0% never married, 70.3% now married, 7.2% widowed, 11.5% divorced (2000); Foreign born: 0.0% (2000); Ancestry (includes multiple ancestries): 19.1% German, 11.3% United States or American, 8.2% English, 7.1% Other groups, 3.5% Dutch (2000).

Economy: Manufacturing: aluminum mold castings, casting machines. Employment by occupation: 8.1% management, 15.4% professional, 11.8% services, 15.4% sales, 0.0% farming, 19.9% construction, 29.4% production (2000).

Income: Per capita income: $15,879 (2000); Median household income: $37,031 (2000); Poverty rate: 8.2% (2000).

Taxes: Total city taxes per capita: $23 (1997); City property taxes per capita: $17 (1997).

Education: High school graduation rate: 77.8% (2000); College graduation rate: 13.1% (2000).

School District(s)

Kingsville R-I (KG-12)
2000 Enrollment: 291 816-597-3422

Housing: Homeownership rate: 82.1% (2000); Median home value: $57,100 (2000); Median rent: $345 per month (2000); Median age of housing: 32 years (2000).

Transportation: Commute to work: 91.6% car, 0.0% public transportation, 8.4% walk, 0.0% work from home (2000); Travel time to work: 34.4% less than 15 minutes, 9.2% 15 to 30 minutes, 26.0% 30 to 45 minutes, 19.1% 45 to 60 minutes, 11.5% 60 minutes or more (2000)

KNOB NOSTER (city). Aka Knobnoster. Covers a land area of 1.732 square miles and a water area of 0.010 square miles. Located at 38.76° N. Lat.; 93.55° W. Long. Elevation is 793 feet.

Population: 2,462 (2000); Race: 68.4% White, 9.3% Black, 1.3% Asian, 3.3% American Indian and Alaska Native, 17.6% Hispanic of any race, 3.3% two or more races (2000); Density: 1,421.8 persons per square mile (2000); Age: 25.9% under 18, 8.2% over 64 (2000); Marriage status: 30.5% never married, 54.7% now married, 4.6% widowed, 10.3% divorced (2000); Foreign born: 14.2% (2000); Ancestry (includes multiple ancestries): 28.8% Other groups, 15.4% German, 11.9% Irish, 9.1% United States or American, 8.8% English (2000).

Economy: Grain; livestock, egg processing. Whiteman Air Force Base (former Minuteman missile site, now bomber base) to Southwest. Single-family building permits issued: 1 (2001) / 1 (2000); Multi-family building permits issued: 8 (2001) / 10 (2000); Employment by occupation: 8.1% management, 13.0% professional, 20.9% services, 18.1% sales, 1.8% farming, 12.3% construction, 25.9% production (2000).

Income: Per capita income: $15,702 (2000); Median household income: $30,869 (2000); Poverty rate: 17.0% (2000).

Taxes: Total city taxes per capita: $21 (1997); City property taxes per capita: $5 (1997).

Education: High school graduation rate: 79.1% (2000); College graduation rate: 15.5% (2000).

School District(s)

Knob Noster R-VIII (PK-12)
2000 Enrollment: 2,014 660-563-3186

Housing: Homeownership rate: 44.6% (2000); Median home value: $70,500 (2000); Median rent: $323 per month (2000); Median age of housing: 27 years (2000).

Newspapers: Knob Noster Item (1 x week)

Transportation: Commute to work: 95.0% car, 0.2% public transportation, 2.0% walk, 1.5% work from home (2000); Travel time to work: 45.1% less

than 15 minutes, 37.1% 15 to 30 minutes, 9.6% 30 to 45 minutes, 2.6% 45 to 60 minutes, 5.6% 60 minutes or more (2000)
Airports: Whiteman AFB

LA TOUR (village). Aka Latour. Covers a land area of 0.111 square miles and a water area of 0 square miles. Located at 38.63° N. Lat.; 94.10° W. Long.
Population: 65 (2000); Race: 100.0% White, 0.0% Black, 0.0% Asian, 0.0% American Indian and Alaska Native, 0.0% Hispanic of any race, 0.0% two or more races (2000); Density: 583.4 persons per square mile (2000); Age: 30.2% under 18, 15.9% over 64 (2000); Marriage status: 17.4% never married, 56.5% now married, 8.7% widowed, 17.4% divorced (2000); Foreign born: 0.0% (2000); Ancestry (includes multiple ancestries): 17.5% German, 17.5% United States or American, 11.1% Dutch, 11.1% Other groups, 9.5% French (except Basque) (2000).
Economy: Employment by occupation: 8.0% management, 12.0% professional, 8.0% services, 16.0% sales, 0.0% farming, 12.0% construction, 44.0% production (2000).
Income: Per capita income: $15,684 (2000); Median household income: $38,250 (2000); Poverty rate: 21.3% (2000).
Education: High school graduation rate: 47.5% (2000); College graduation rate: 5.0% (2000).
Housing: Homeownership rate: 73.9% (2000); Median home value: $23,800 (2000); Median rent: $125 per month (2000); Median age of housing: 60+ years (2000).
Transportation: Commute to work: 100.0% car, 0.0% public transportation, 0.0% walk, 0.0% work from home (2000); Travel time to work: 0.0% less than 15 minutes, 32.0% 15 to 30 minutes, 24.0% 30 to 45 minutes, 32.0% 45 to 60 minutes, 12.0% 60 minutes or more (2000)

LEETON (city). Covers a land area of 0.507 square miles and a water area of 0 square miles. Located at 38.58° N. Lat.; 93.69° W. Long. Elevation is 955 feet.
Population: 619 (2000); Race: 99.4% White, 0.5% Black, 0.0% Asian, 0.0% American Indian and Alaska Native, 0.2% Hispanic of any race, 0.2% two or more races (2000); Density: 1,220.2 persons per square mile (2000); Age: 31.0% under 18, 10.3% over 64 (2000); Marriage status: 25.5% never married, 51.7% now married, 5.9% widowed, 16.9% divorced (2000); Foreign born: 1.7% (2000); Ancestry (includes multiple ancestries): 22.9% United States or American, 19.8% German, 11.5% Irish, 10.9% English, 7.2% Other groups (2000).
Economy: Single-family building permits issued: 2 (2001) / 0 (2000); Multi-family building permits issued: 0 (2001) / 0 (2000); Employment by occupation: 6.9% management, 13.8% professional, 17.5% services, 17.1% sales, 0.0% farming, 10.5% construction, 34.2% production (2000).
Income: Per capita income: $13,207 (2000); Median household income: $29,063 (2000); Poverty rate: 14.4% (2000).
Taxes: Total city taxes per capita: $196 (1997); City property taxes per capita: $54 (1997).
Education: High school graduation rate: 84.2% (2000); College graduation rate: 5.5% (2000).

School District(s)

Leeton R-X (PK-12)
2000 Enrollment: 378 660-653-2301
Housing: Homeownership rate: 66.9% (2000); Median home value: $50,800 (2000); Median rent: $262 per month (2000); Median age of housing: 34 years (2000).
Transportation: Commute to work: 93.2% car, 0.0% public transportation, 5.7% walk, 1.1% work from home (2000); Travel time to work: 14.8% less than 15 minutes, 39.7% 15 to 30 minutes, 26.7% 30 to 45 minutes, 8.3% 45 to 60 minutes, 10.5% 60 minutes or more (2000)

WARRENSBURG (city). Covers a land area of 8.429 square miles and a water area of 0.063 square miles. Located at 38.76° N. Lat.; 93.73° W. Long. Elevation is 880 feet.
History: Warrensburg was settled in 1833 by Martin Warren, a Revolutionary War veteran from Kentucky. The site was selected in 1836 as the seat of Johnson County, and the town was named for the first settler. The completion of the Pacific Railroad to Warrensburg in 1864 brought a period of growth.
Population: 16,340 (2000); Race: 87.2% White, 6.3% Black, 2.5% Asian, 0.5% American Indian and Alaska Native, 2.9% Hispanic of any race, 2.7% two or more races (2000); Density: 1,938.5 persons per square mile (2000); Age: 18.4% under 18, 10.4% over 64 (2000); Marriage status: 45.9% never married, 41.5% now married, 4.9% widowed, 7.8% divorced (2000); Foreign born: 4.5% (2000); Ancestry (includes multiple ancestries): 26.0% German, 16.2% Other groups, 14.3% Irish, 11.1% English, 8.7% United States or American (2000).
Vital Statistics: Birth rate: 127.3 per 10,000 population (1998)
Economy: Single-family building permits issued: 60 (2001) / 48 (2000); Multi-family building permits issued: 81 (2001) / 14 (2000); Employment by occupation: 7.8% management, 23.3% professional, 23.5% services, 27.8% sales, 0.4% farming, 6.4% construction, 10.8% production (2000).
Income: Per capita income: $14,714 (2000); Median household income: $29,332 (2000); Poverty rate: 24.3% (2000).
Taxes: Total city taxes per capita: $217 (1997); City property taxes per capita: $31 (1997).
Education: High school graduation rate: 88.9% (2000); College graduation rate: 37.2% (2000).

School District(s)

Warrensburg R-VI (PK-12)
2000 Enrollment: 3,211 660-747-7823

Four-year College(s)

Central Missouri State University (Public)
2001 Enrollment: 10,822 660-543-4111
2001 Tuition: In-state $3,450; Out-of-state $6,900
Housing: Homeownership rate: 42.5% (2000); Median home value: $91,600 (2000); Median rent: $405 per month (2000); Median age of housing: 26 years (2000).
Hospitals: Western Missouri Medical Center (92 beds)
Safety: Violent crime rate: 26.8 per 10,000 population; Property crime rate: 418.5 per 10,000 population (2001).
Newspapers: Daily Star-Journal (5 x week); Warrensburg Gazette (1 x week)
Transportation: Commute to work: 86.9% car, 0.2% public transportation, 9.6% walk, 2.3% work from home (2000); Travel time to work: 60.3% less than 15 minutes, 19.5% 15 to 30 minutes, 8.0% 30 to 45 minutes, 3.9% 45 to 60 minutes, 8.3% 60 minutes or more (2000); Amtrak: Service available.
Airports: Skyhaven
Additional Information Contacts
Midwest Missouri Board of Realtors 660-429-5518
Warrensburg Chamber of Commerce 660-747-3168

WHITEMAN AFB (CDP). Covers a land area of 5.170 square miles and a water area of 0 square miles. Located at 38.73° N. Lat.; 93.55° W. Long.
Population: 3,814 (2000); Race: 82.2% White, 7.4% Black, 1.6% Asian, 1.1% American Indian and Alaska Native, 6.7% Hispanic of any race, 4.0% two or more races (2000); Density: 737.7 persons per square mile (2000); Age: 37.4% under 18, 0.0% over 64 (2000); Marriage status: 27.5% never married, 67.8% now married, 0.2% widowed, 4.6% divorced (2000); Foreign born: 3.6% (2000); Ancestry (includes multiple ancestries): 24.1% German, 21.7% Other groups, 13.9% Irish, 8.7% English, 8.1% United States or American (2000).
Economy: Employment by occupation: 14.1% management, 10.6% professional, 30.9% services, 26.0% sales, 1.6% farming, 5.4% construction, 11.4% production (2000).
Income: Per capita income: $11,538 (2000); Median household income: $33,664 (2000); Poverty rate: 7.3% (2000).
Education: High school graduation rate: 96.0% (2000); College graduation rate: 16.8% (2000).
Housing: Homeownership rate: 0.0% (2000); Median rent: $472 per month (2000); Median age of housing: 38 years (2000).
Transportation: Commute to work: 88.0% car, 0.3% public transportation, 6.0% walk, 4.2% work from home (2000); Travel time to work: 81.1% less than 15 minutes, 13.5% 15 to 30 minutes, 4.2% 30 to 45 minutes, 0.3% 45 to 60 minutes, 0.9% 60 minutes or more (2000)

Knox County

Located in northeastern Missouri; drained by the Salt, Middle and South Fabius Rivers Covers a land area of 505.70 square miles, a water area of 1.10 square miles, and is located in the Central Time Zone. The county government was organized in 1845. County seat is Edina.
Population: 4,361 (2000); Race: 98.6% White, 0.3% Black, 0.3% Asian, 0.0% American Indian and Alaska Native, 0.4% Hispanic of any race, 0.8% two or more races (2000); Density: 8.6 persons per square mile (2000); Age: 24.8% under 18, 21.3% over 64 (2000).
Religion: Five largest groups: 16.2% Southern Baptist Convention, 14.1% The United Methodist Church, 13.0% Catholic Church, 7.5% Assemblies of God, 6.7% Christian Churches and Churches of Christ (2000).

Economy: Unemployment rate: 2.6% (11/2002); Total civilian labor force: 2,026 (11/2002); Leading industries: 17.8% retail trade; except pub other services; Health car 10.5% (2000); Companies that employ more than 1,000 persons: 0 (2000); Companies that employ more than 100 persons: 0 (2000); Farms: 602 totaling 280,699 acres (1997); Minority business ownership rate: 0.0% (1997); Women business ownership rate: 0.0% (1997); Retail sales per capita: $4,693 (1997). Single-family building permits issued: 4 (2001) / 2 (2000); Multi-family building permits issued: 0 (2001) / 0 (2000).
Income: Per capita income: $13,075 (2000); Median household income: $27,124 (2000); Poverty rate: 18.0% (2000); Bankruptcy rate: 2.07% (2001).
Taxes: Total county taxes per capita: $183 (2000); County property taxes per capita: $92 (2000).
Education: High school graduation rate: 80.0% (2000); College graduation rate: 12.8% (2000).
Housing: Homeownership rate: 77.1% (2000); Median home value: $37,800 (2000); Median rent: $190 per month (2000); Median age of housing: 45 years (2000).
Health: Birth rate: 146.8 per 10,000 population (1998); Age adjusted death rate: 111.7 per 10,000 population (1999); Age adjusted cancer mortality rate: 305.7 (Unreliable figure as per CDC) deaths per 100,000 population (1999). Number of physicians: n/a (1999); Number of hospital beds: n/a (1999).
Elections: 2000 Presidential election results: 38.3% Gore, 59.7% Bush, 1.2% Nader, 0.4% Buchanan
Additional Information Contacts
Knox County Government Offices. 660-397-2184

Knox County Communities

BARING (city). Covers a land area of 0.127 square miles and a water area of 0 square miles. Located at 40.24° N. Lat.; 92.20° W. Long. Elevation is 825 feet.
Population: 159 (2000); Race: 100.0% White, 0.0% Black, 0.0% Asian, 0.0% American Indian and Alaska Native, 0.0% Hispanic of any race, 0.0% two or more races (2000); Density: 1,254.6 persons per square mile (2000); Age: 27.0% under 18, 23.9% over 64 (2000); Marriage status: 14.5% never married, 69.4% now married, 11.3% widowed, 4.8% divorced (2000); Foreign born: 0.0% (2000); Ancestry (includes multiple ancestries): 28.2% United States or American, 19.0% German, 11.0% English, 7.4% Irish, 6.7% Swedish (2000).
Economy: Employment by occupation: 4.3% management, 11.6% professional, 24.6% services, 14.5% sales, 2.9% farming, 8.7% construction, 33.3% production (2000).
Income: Per capita income: $11,980 (2000); Median household income: $27,500 (2000); Poverty rate: 14.1% (2000).
Taxes: Total city taxes per capita: $51 (1997); City property taxes per capita: $34 (1997).
Education: High school graduation rate: 80.6% (2000); College graduation rate: 7.4% (2000).
Housing: Homeownership rate: 75.7% (2000); Median home value: $25,400 (2000); Median rent: $214 per month (2000); Median age of housing: 52 years (2000).
Transportation: Commute to work: 83.3% car, 0.0% public transportation, 6.1% walk, 10.6% work from home (2000); Travel time to work: 16.9% less than 15 minutes, 27.1% 15 to 30 minutes, 33.9% 30 to 45 minutes, 8.5% 45 to 60 minutes, 13.6% 60 minutes or more (2000)

EDINA (city). Covers a land area of 1.311 square miles and a water area of 0 square miles. Located at 40.16° N. Lat.; 92.17° W. Long. Elevation is 816 feet.
History: Incorporated 1857.
Population: 1,233 (2000); Race: 98.0% White, 0.0% Black, 0.0% Asian, 0.2% American Indian and Alaska Native, 0.8% Hispanic of any race, 1.8% two or more races (2000); Density: 940.7 persons per square mile (2000); Age: 24.2% under 18, 24.9% over 64 (2000); Marriage status: 19.4% never married, 56.6% now married, 12.9% widowed, 11.1% divorced (2000); Foreign born: 0.5% (2000); Ancestry (includes multiple ancestries): 22.2% United States or American, 18.3% German, 11.4% Irish, 11.0% English, 6.2% Other groups (2000).
Economy: Corn, soybeans; cattle, hogs; lumber. Manufacturing: crushed stone, leather products. Single-family building permits issued: 4 (2001) / 2 (2000); Multi-family building permits issued: 0 (2001) / 0 (2000); Employment by occupation: 6.0% management, 16.1% professional, 19.2% services, 29.5% sales, 2.6% farming, 15.0% construction, 11.5% production (2000).
Income: Per capita income: $12,863 (2000); Median household income: $24,900 (2000); Poverty rate: 19.1% (2000).
Taxes: Total city taxes per capita: $357 (1997); City property taxes per capita: $58 (1997).
Education: High school graduation rate: 80.8% (2000); College graduation rate: 14.3% (2000).

School District(s)

Knox Co. R-I (PK-12)
2000 Enrollment: 684 660-397-2228
Housing: Homeownership rate: 65.1% (2000); Median home value: $53,600 (2000); Median rent: $198 per month (2000); Median age of housing: 44 years (2000).
Newspapers: The Sentinel Advertiser (1 x week); The Edina Sentinel (1 x week)
Transportation: Commute to work: 91.9% car, 0.4% public transportation, 5.0% walk, 2.2% work from home (2000); Travel time to work: 60.0% less than 15 minutes, 13.0% 15 to 30 minutes, 23.6% 30 to 45 minutes, 1.1% 45 to 60 minutes, 2.3% 60 minutes or more (2000)

HURDLAND (city). Covers a land area of 0.329 square miles and a water area of 0 square miles. Located at 40.15° N. Lat.; 92.30° W. Long. Elevation is 889 feet.
Population: 239 (2000); Race: 97.5% White, 0.0% Black, 0.0% Asian, 0.0% American Indian and Alaska Native, 0.0% Hispanic of any race, 2.5% two or more races (2000); Density: 725.5 persons per square mile (2000); Age: 23.3% under 18, 15.0% over 64 (2000); Marriage status: 22.5% never married, 57.5% now married, 8.5% widowed, 11.5% divorced (2000); Foreign born: 0.0% (2000); Ancestry (includes multiple ancestries): 18.3% German, 15.0% United States or American, 11.3% Irish, 7.5% Other groups, 3.8% French (except Basque) (2000).
Economy: Agriculture. Employment by occupation: 3.3% management, 6.6% professional, 18.2% services, 24.0% sales, 0.0% farming, 18.2% construction, 29.8% production (2000).
Income: Per capita income: $11,584 (2000); Median household income: $25,625 (2000); Poverty rate: 24.6% (2000).
Taxes: Total city taxes per capita: $29 (1997); City property taxes per capita: $29 (1997).
Education: High school graduation rate: 62.8% (2000); College graduation rate: 2.6% (2000).
Housing: Homeownership rate: 92.5% (2000); Median home value: $24,300 (2000); Median rent: $225 per month (2000); Median age of housing: 38 years (2000).
Transportation: Commute to work: 93.4% car, 0.0% public transportation, 1.7% walk, 5.0% work from home (2000); Travel time to work: 23.5% less than 15 minutes, 28.7% 15 to 30 minutes, 36.5% 30 to 45 minutes, 1.7% 45 to 60 minutes, 9.6% 60 minutes or more (2000)

KNOX CITY (city). Aka Knox. Covers a land area of 0.210 square miles and a water area of 0 square miles. Located at 40.14° N. Lat.; 92.01° W. Long. Elevation is 765 feet.
Population: 223 (2000); Race: 100.0% White, 0.0% Black, 0.0% Asian, 0.0% American Indian and Alaska Native, 2.3% Hispanic of any race, 0.0% two or more races (2000); Density: 1,062.5 persons per square mile (2000); Age: 15.6% under 18, 23.3% over 64 (2000); Marriage status: 25.0% never married, 55.4% now married, 12.5% widowed, 7.1% divorced (2000); Foreign born: 0.0% (2000); Ancestry (includes multiple ancestries): 24.5% German, 22.6% United States or American, 8.9% Irish, 6.2% English, 4.7% Other groups (2000).
Economy: Grain; livestock; lumber. Employment by occupation: 10.3% management, 4.3% professional, 15.5% services, 23.3% sales, 1.7% farming, 16.4% construction, 28.4% production (2000).
Income: Per capita income: $10,696 (2000); Median household income: $18,417 (2000); Poverty rate: 16.0% (2000).
Education: High school graduation rate: 74.0% (2000); College graduation rate: 3.5% (2000).
Housing: Homeownership rate: 80.2% (2000); Median home value: $19,000 (2000); Median rent: $175 per month (2000); Median age of housing: 60+ years (2000).
Transportation: Commute to work: 98.3% car, 0.0% public transportation, 1.7% walk, 0.0% work from home (2000); Travel time to work: 25.0% less than 15 minutes, 28.4% 15 to 30 minutes, 7.8% 30 to 45 minutes, 12.9% 45 to 60 minutes, 25.9% 60 minutes or more (2000)

NEWARK (village). Covers a land area of 0.324 square miles and a water area of 0 square miles. Located at 39.99° N. Lat.; 91.97° W. Long. Elevation is 692 feet.

Population: 100 (2000); Race: 98.7% White, 0.0% Black, 1.3% Asian, 0.0% American Indian and Alaska Native, 0.0% Hispanic of any race, 0.0% two or more races (2000); Density: 308.8 persons per square mile (2000); Age: 27.6% under 18, 21.1% over 64 (2000); Marriage status: 12.7% never married, 63.6% now married, 14.5% widowed, 9.1% divorced (2000); Foreign born: 0.0% (2000); Ancestry (includes multiple ancestries): 26.3% United States or American, 11.8% German, 11.8% Other groups, 7.9% Irish, 3.9% English (2000).
Economy: Limestone quarry. Employment by occupation: 14.7% management, 23.5% professional, 0.0% services, 8.8% sales, 0.0% farming, 8.8% construction, 44.1% production (2000).
Income: Per capita income: $10,634 (2000); Median household income: $20,250 (2000); Poverty rate: 13.2% (2000).
Taxes: Total city taxes per capita: $37 (1997); City property taxes per capita: $25 (1997).
Education: High school graduation rate: 70.0% (2000); College graduation rate: 18.0% (2000).
Housing: Homeownership rate: 71.4% (2000); Median home value: $28,800 (2000); Median rent: $225 per month (2000); Median age of housing: 55 years (2000).
Transportation: Commute to work: 85.3% car, 0.0% public transportation, 5.9% walk, 8.8% work from home (2000); Travel time to work: 22.6% less than 15 minutes, 16.1% 15 to 30 minutes, 12.9% 30 to 45 minutes, 6.5% 45 to 60 minutes, 41.9% 60 minutes or more (2000)

NOVELTY (village). Covers a land area of 0.277 square miles and a water area of 0 square miles. Located at 40.01° N. Lat.; 92.20° W. Long. Elevation is 832 feet.
Population: 119 (2000); Race: 100.0% White, 0.0% Black, 0.0% Asian, 0.0% American Indian and Alaska Native, 0.0% Hispanic of any race, 0.0% two or more races (2000); Density: 430.2 persons per square mile (2000); Age: 15.3% under 18, 24.3% over 64 (2000); Marriage status: 25.5% never married, 51.0% now married, 17.6% widowed, 5.9% divorced (2000); Foreign born: 0.0% (2000); Ancestry (includes multiple ancestries): 36.9% United States or American, 21.6% German, 16.2% Irish, 9.9% English, 5.4% European (2000).
Economy: Lumber. Employment by occupation: 1.4% management, 16.2% professional, 17.6% services, 31.1% sales, 6.8% farming, 12.2% construction, 14.9% production (2000).
Income: Per capita income: $17,046 (2000); Median household income: $29,583 (2000); Poverty rate: 9.9% (2000).
Taxes: Total city taxes per capita: $80 (1997); City property taxes per capita: $43 (1997).
Education: High school graduation rate: 89.5% (2000); College graduation rate: 8.1% (2000).
Housing: Homeownership rate: 94.7% (2000); Median home value: $29,400 (2000); Median rent: <$100 per month (2000); Median age of housing: 60+ years (2000).
Transportation: Commute to work: 88.7% car, 0.0% public transportation, 2.8% walk, 5.6% work from home (2000); Travel time to work: 19.4% less than 15 minutes, 23.9% 15 to 30 minutes, 38.8% 30 to 45 minutes, 17.9% 45 to 60 minutes, 0.0% 60 minutes or more (2000)

PLEVNA (unincorporated postal area, zip code 63464). Covers a land area of 4.750 square miles and a water area of 0 square miles. Located at 39.97° N. Lat.; 92.06° W. Long. Elevation is 792 feet.
Population: 43 (2000); Race: 100.0% White, 0.0% Black, 0.0% Asian, 0.0% American Indian and Alaska Native, 0.0% Hispanic of any race, 0.0% two or more races (2000); Density: 9.1 persons per square mile (2000); Age: 18.8% under 18, 27.1% over 64 (2000); Marriage status: 0.0% never married, 51.3% now married, 23.1% widowed, 25.6% divorced (2000); Foreign born: 0.0% (2000); Ancestry (includes multiple ancestries): 47.9% German, 45.8% Irish, 43.8% English, 8.3% French (except Basque) (2000).
Economy: Employment by occupation: 0.0% management, 0.0% professional, 0.0% services, 0.0% sales, 0.0% farming, 100.0% construction, 0.0% production (2000).
Income: Per capita income: $12,154 (2000); Median household income: $20,577 (2000); Poverty rate: 20.8% (2000).
Education: High school graduation rate: 89.7% (2000); College graduation rate: 0.0% (2000).
Housing: Homeownership rate: 100.0% (2000); Median home value: $17,500 (2000); Median age of housing: 60+ years (2000).
Transportation: Commute to work: 100.0% car, 0.0% public transportation, 0.0% walk, 0.0% work from home (2000); Travel time to work: 100.0% less than 15 minutes, 0.0% 15 to 30 minutes, 0.0% 30 to 45 minutes, 0.0% 45 to 60 minutes, 0.0% 60 minutes or more (2000)

Laclede County

Located in south central Missouri, in the Ozarks; drained by the Gasconade River; includes part of Mark Twain National Forest. Covers a land area of 765.90 square miles, a water area of 2.10 square miles, and is located in the Central Time Zone. The county government was organized in 1849. County seat is Lebanon.

Weather Station: Lebanon 2 W — Elevation: 1,276 feet

	Jan	Feb	Mar	Apr	May	Jun	Jul	Aug	Sep	Oct	Nov	Dec
High	41	48	58	69	77	85	90	89	80	70	56	46
Low	21	26	35	45	53	62	67	65	57	46	36	26
Precip	1.8	2.1	3.6	4.5	4.6	4.2	3.7	3.3	4.5	3.8	4.3	2.6
Snow	5.2	3.2	1.8	0.2	0.0	0.0	0.0	0.0	0.0	tr	1.3	1.9

High and Low temperatures in degrees Fahrenheit; Precipitation and Snow in inches

Population: 32,513 (2000); Race: 96.8% White, 0.3% Black, 0.1% Asian, 0.4% American Indian and Alaska Native, 1.4% Hispanic of any race, 1.4% two or more races (2000); Density: 42.5 persons per square mile (2000); Age: 26.7% under 18, 14.2% over 64 (2000).
Religion: Five largest groups: 22.2% Southern Baptist Convention, 4.7% The United Methodist Church, 4.1% Christian Churches and Churches of Christ, 3.6% National Association of Free Will Baptists, 2.9% Assemblies of God (2000).
Economy: Unemployment rate: 5.3% (11/2002); Total civilian labor force: 15,796 (11/2002); Leading industries: 46.1% manufacturing; 16.9% retail trade; 8.7% accommodation & food services (2000); Companies that employ more than 1,000 persons: 1 (2000); Companies that employ more than 100 persons: 17 (2000); Farms: 1,300 totaling 317,051 acres (1997); Minority business ownership rate: 0.0% (1997); Women business ownership rate: 21.6% (1997); Retail sales per capita: $10,468 (1997). Single-family building permits issued: 69 (2001) / 76 (2000); Multi-family building permits issued: 24 (2001) / 30 (2000).
Income: Per capita income: $15,572 (2000); Median household income: $29,562 (2000); Poverty rate: 14.3% (2000); Bankruptcy rate: 4.80% (2001).
Taxes: Total county taxes per capita: $56 (2000); County property taxes per capita: $8 (2000).
Education: High school graduation rate: 72.9% (2000); College graduation rate: 11.3% (2000).
Housing: Homeownership rate: 72.8% (2000); Median home value: $73,000 (2000); Median rent: $281 per month (2000); Median age of housing: 24 years (2000).
Health: Birth rate: 132.6 per 10,000 population (1998); Age adjusted death rate: 101.7 per 10,000 population (1999); Age adjusted cancer mortality rate: 249.3 deaths per 100,000 population (1999). Number of physicians: 7.1 per 10,000 population (1999); Number of hospital beds: 12.6 per 10,000 population (1999).
Elections: 2000 Presidential election results: 32.1% Gore, 65.6% Bush, 1.1% Nader, 0.8% Buchanan
National and State Parks: Bear Creek State Forest; Coffin State Forest; Flatwoods Church State Forest; Osage Fork State Forest
Additional Information Contacts
Laclede County Government Offices 417-532-2471
Lebanon Board of Realtors 417-533-7697
Lebanon Chamber of Commerce 417-588-3256

Laclede County Communities

CONWAY (city). Covers a land area of 1.821 square miles and a water area of 0.009 square miles. Located at 37.50° N. Lat.; 92.82° W. Long. Elevation is 1,405 feet.
Population: 743 (2000); Race: 95.4% White, 0.1% Black, 0.0% Asian, 0.8% American Indian and Alaska Native, 3.2% Hispanic of any race, 0.8% two or more races (2000); Density: 408.0 persons per square mile (2000); Age: 26.9% under 18, 15.3% over 64 (2000); Marriage status: 18.0% never married, 59.7% now married, 10.2% widowed, 12.1% divorced (2000); Foreign born: 0.0% (2000); Ancestry (includes multiple ancestries): 19.1% United States or American, 12.7% Irish, 12.6% Other groups, 12.3% German, 7.3% English (2000).
Economy: Wheat, corn, hay; cattle. Employment by occupation: 3.6% management, 6.7% professional, 19.5% services, 22.8% sales, 0.9% farming, 15.8% construction, 30.7% production (2000).
Income: Per capita income: $11,623 (2000); Median household income: $21,736 (2000); Poverty rate: 18.6% (2000).
Taxes: Total city taxes per capita: $75 (1997); City property taxes per capita: $3 (1997).

Education: High school graduation rate: 74.6% (2000); College graduation rate: 6.6% (2000).

School District(s)

Laclede Co. R-I (PK-12)
2000 Enrollment: 920 417-589-2951

Housing: Homeownership rate: 73.1% (2000); Median home value: $40,700 (2000); Median rent: $195 per month (2000); Median age of housing: 29 years (2000).

Transportation: Commute to work: 92.6% car, 0.0% public transportation, 2.8% walk, 2.8% work from home (2000); Travel time to work: 30.1% less than 15 minutes, 41.8% 15 to 30 minutes, 13.6% 30 to 45 minutes, 4.4% 45 to 60 minutes, 10.1% 60 minutes or more (2000)

ELDRIDGE (unincorporated postal area, zip code 65463). Covers a land area of 69.055 square miles and a water area of 0.226 square miles. Located at 37.84° N. Lat.; 92.78° W. Long. Elevation is 1,194 feet.

Population: 960 (2000); Race: 98.7% White, 0.0% Black, 0.3% Asian, 0.0% American Indian and Alaska Native, 0.0% Hispanic of any race, 0.9% two or more races (2000); Density: 13.9 persons per square mile (2000); Age: 27.8% under 18, 15.0% over 64 (2000); Marriage status: 14.8% never married, 70.9% now married, 6.8% widowed, 7.6% divorced (2000); Foreign born: 0.3% (2000); Ancestry (includes multiple ancestries): 29.1% United States or American, 16.9% German, 10.0% English, 9.0% Irish, 7.0% Other groups (2000).

Economy: Employment by occupation: 4.5% management, 1.6% professional, 12.5% services, 18.8% sales, 0.0% farming, 9.3% construction, 53.4% production (2000).

Income: Per capita income: $11,239 (2000); Median household income: $24,167 (2000); Poverty rate: 18.3% (2000).

Education: High school graduation rate: 57.6% (2000); College graduation rate: 8.1% (2000).

Housing: Homeownership rate: 86.3% (2000); Median home value: $59,400 (2000); Median rent: $222 per month (2000); Median age of housing: 25 years (2000).

Transportation: Commute to work: 93.6% car, 0.0% public transportation, 0.0% walk, 6.4% work from home (2000); Travel time to work: 9.2% less than 15 minutes, 47.4% 15 to 30 minutes, 17.4% 30 to 45 minutes, 20.5% 45 to 60 minutes, 5.5% 60 minutes or more (2000)

FALCON (unincorporated postal area, zip code 65470). Covers a land area of 112.467 square miles and a water area of 0.526 square miles. Located at 37.53° N. Lat.; 92.39° W. Long. Elevation is 1,158 feet.

Population: 996 (2000); Race: 95.1% White, 0.0% Black, 0.6% Asian, 1.4% American Indian and Alaska Native, 1.2% Hispanic of any race, 2.6% two or more races (2000); Density: 8.9 persons per square mile (2000); Age: 20.8% under 18, 12.8% over 64 (2000); Marriage status: 13.0% never married, 70.5% now married, 4.9% widowed, 11.5% divorced (2000); Foreign born: 0.5% (2000); Ancestry (includes multiple ancestries): 34.4% United States or American, 14.9% Irish, 11.2% German, 6.8% Other groups, 6.4% English (2000).

Economy: Employment by occupation: 16.5% management, 14.0% professional, 13.1% services, 11.8% sales, 5.3% farming, 9.5% construction, 29.8% production (2000).

Income: Per capita income: $13,970 (2000); Median household income: $26,780 (2000); Poverty rate: 20.6% (2000).

Education: High school graduation rate: 73.5% (2000); College graduation rate: 6.2% (2000).

School District(s)

Gasconade C-4 (KG-08)
2000 Enrollment: 116 417-532-4821

Housing: Homeownership rate: 82.5% (2000); Median home value: $64,100 (2000); Median rent: $304 per month (2000); Median age of housing: 26 years (2000).

Transportation: Commute to work: 82.6% car, 0.0% public transportation, 0.6% walk, 12.3% work from home (2000); Travel time to work: 13.8% less than 15 minutes, 20.8% 15 to 30 minutes, 40.9% 30 to 45 minutes, 14.3% 45 to 60 minutes, 10.2% 60 minutes or more (2000)

LEBANON (city). Covers a land area of 13.628 square miles and a water area of 0.031 square miles. Located at 37.67° N. Lat.; 92.66° W. Long. Elevation is 1,265 feet.

History: Lebanon had its beginning when Laclede County was formed in 1849. During the Civil War, Lebanon was on the line of march for both Union and Confederate armies, and was occupied alternately by the North and the South. In 1868 the railroad line was built a mile from the town, and the town picked itself up and moved over to the railroad.

Population: 12,155 (2000); Race: 96.1% White, 0.7% Black, 0.1% Asian, 0.7% American Indian and Alaska Native, 1.9% Hispanic of any race, 1.3% two or more races (2000); Density: 891.9 persons per square mile (2000); Age: 25.6% under 18, 17.3% over 64 (2000); Marriage status: 20.7% never married, 57.3% now married, 10.2% widowed, 11.8% divorced (2000); Foreign born: 1.3% (2000); Ancestry (includes multiple ancestries): 19.2% United States or American, 17.1% German, 13.9% Other groups, 12.9% Irish, 7.3% English (2000).

Economy: Single-family building permits issued: 69 (2001) / 76 (2000); Multi-family building permits issued: 24 (2001) / 30 (2000); Employment by occupation: 8.3% management, 13.9% professional, 14.7% services, 24.4% sales, 0.2% farming, 8.1% construction, 30.5% production (2000).

Income: Per capita income: $16,636 (2000); Median household income: $27,668 (2000); Poverty rate: 15.2% (2000).

Taxes: Total city taxes per capita: $551 (2000); City property taxes per capita: $55 (2000).

Education: High school graduation rate: 72.3% (2000); College graduation rate: 12.4% (2000).

School District(s)

Laclede Co. C-5 (PK-08)
2000 Enrollment: 542 417-532-4837

Lebanon R-III (PK-12)
2000 Enrollment: 4,393 417-532-9141

Housing: Homeownership rate: 56.7% (2000); Median home value: $68,300 (2000); Median rent: $283 per month (2000); Median age of housing: 27 years (2000).

Hospitals: Breech Regional Medical Center (41 beds)

Safety: Violent crime rate: 93.2 per 10,000 population; Property crime rate: 715.5 per 10,000 population (2001).

Newspapers: The Lebanon Daily Record (6 x week)

Transportation: Commute to work: 93.4% car, 0.7% public transportation, 2.4% walk, 3.1% work from home (2000); Travel time to work: 71.4% less than 15 minutes, 17.2% 15 to 30 minutes, 5.1% 30 to 45 minutes, 2.9% 45 to 60 minutes, 3.4% 60 minutes or more (2000)

Additional Information Contacts

Lebanon Board of Realtors.................................. 417-533-7697
Lebanon Chamber of Commerce 417-588-3256

LYNCHBURG (unincorporated postal area, zip code 65543). Covers a land area of 48.802 square miles and a water area of 0 square miles. Located at 37.47° N. Lat.; 92.29° W. Long. Elevation is 1,383 feet.

Population: 279 (2000); Race: 100.0% White, 0.0% Black, 0.0% Asian, 0.0% American Indian and Alaska Native, 0.0% Hispanic of any race, 0.0% two or more races (2000); Density: 5.7 persons per square mile (2000); Age: 36.1% under 18, 15.7% over 64 (2000); Marriage status: 9.2% never married, 80.9% now married, 8.6% widowed, 1.3% divorced (2000); Foreign born: 0.0% (2000); Ancestry (includes multiple ancestries): 28.7% Other groups, 17.8% Irish, 11.3% German, 10.9% English, 7.0% United States or American (2000).

Economy: Employment by occupation: 11.7% management, 9.6% professional, 43.6% services, 25.5% sales, 0.0% farming, 3.2% construction, 6.4% production (2000).

Income: Per capita income: $11,204 (2000); Median household income: $18,967 (2000); Poverty rate: 5.2% (2000).

Education: High school graduation rate: 49.7% (2000); College graduation rate: 6.1% (2000).

Housing: Homeownership rate: 88.0% (2000); Median home value: $23,000 (2000); Median rent: $125 per month (2000); Median age of housing: 32 years (2000).

Transportation: Commute to work: 67.0% car, 0.0% public transportation, 0.0% walk, 30.9% work from home (2000); Travel time to work: 16.9% less than 15 minutes, 4.6% 15 to 30 minutes, 43.1% 30 to 45 minutes, 30.8% 45 to 60 minutes, 4.6% 60 minutes or more (2000)

PHILLIPSBURG (village). Covers a land area of 0.510 square miles and a water area of 0 square miles. Located at 37.55° N. Lat.; 92.78° W. Long. Elevation is 1,412 feet.

Population: 201 (2000); Race: 89.6% White, 3.6% Black, 0.0% Asian, 3.1% American Indian and Alaska Native, 0.0% Hispanic of any race, 3.6% two or more races (2000); Density: 394.4 persons per square mile (2000); Age: 31.6% under 18, 11.9% over 64 (2000); Marriage status: 27.1% never married, 56.3% now married, 6.9% widowed, 9.7% divorced (2000); Foreign born: 0.0% (2000); Ancestry (includes multiple ancestries): 20.7% United States or American, 15.5% Other groups, 9.8% English, 7.8% German, 7.3% Irish (2000).

Economy: Employment by occupation: 5.7% management, 5.7% professional, 14.3% services, 32.9% sales, 5.7% farming, 4.3% construction, 31.4% production (2000).
Income: Per capita income: $9,083 (2000); Median household income: $21,875 (2000); Poverty rate: 40.4% (2000).
Taxes: Total city taxes per capita: $27 (1997); City property taxes per capita: $11 (1997).
Education: High school graduation rate: 69.0% (2000); College graduation rate: 8.0% (2000).
Housing: Homeownership rate: 73.6% (2000); Median home value: $43,800 (2000); Median rent: $304 per month (2000); Median age of housing: 36 years (2000).
Transportation: Commute to work: 94.3% car, 0.0% public transportation, 2.9% walk, 2.9% work from home (2000); Travel time to work: 10.3% less than 15 minutes, 73.5% 15 to 30 minutes, 0.0% 30 to 45 minutes, 16.2% 45 to 60 minutes, 0.0% 60 minutes or more (2000)

TWIN BRIDGES (village). Covers a land area of 8.518 square miles and a water area of 0.050 square miles. Located at 37.53° N. Lat.; 92.58° W. Long. Elevation is 1,240 feet.
Population: 42 (2000); Race: 100.0% White, 0.0% Black, 0.0% Asian, 0.0% American Indian and Alaska Native, 0.0% Hispanic of any race, 0.0% two or more races (2000); Density: 4.9 persons per square mile (2000); Age: 37.5% under 18, 0.0% over 64 (2000); Marriage status: 18.8% never married, 81.3% now married, 0.0% widowed, 0.0% divorced (2000); Foreign born: 0.0% (2000); Ancestry (includes multiple ancestries): 25.0% Irish, 25.0% United States or American, 12.5% German, 12.5% Hungarian, 8.3% English (2000).
Economy: Employment by occupation: 7.7% management, 15.4% professional, 15.4% services, 15.4% sales, 7.7% farming, 0.0% construction, 38.5% production (2000).
Income: Per capita income: $11,925 (2000); Median household income: $31,875 (2000); Poverty rate: 0.0% (2000).
Taxes: Total city taxes per capita: $106 (1997); City property taxes per capita: $106 (1997).
Education: High school graduation rate: 92.3% (2000); College graduation rate: 15.4% (2000).
Housing: Homeownership rate: 44.4% (2000); Median rent: $425 per month (2000); Median age of housing: 35 years (2000).
Transportation: Commute to work: 92.3% car, 0.0% public transportation, 0.0% walk, 7.7% work from home (2000); Travel time to work: 25.0% less than 15 minutes, 50.0% 15 to 30 minutes, 8.3% 30 to 45 minutes, 16.7% 45 to 60 minutes, 0.0% 60 minutes or more (2000)

Lafayette County

Located in west central Missouri; bounded on the north by the Missouri River. Covers a land area of 629.30 square miles, a water area of 9.50 square miles, and is located in the Central Time Zone. The county government was organized in 1820. County seat is Lexington.

Lafayette County is part of the Kansas City, MO-KS MSA. The entire metro area includes: Johnson County, KS; Leavenworth County, KS; Miami County, KS; Wyandotte County, KS; Cass County, MO; Clay County, MO; Clinton County, MO; Jackson County, MO; Lafayette County, MO; Platte County, MO; Ray County, MO

Weather Station: Lexington 3 NE — Elevation: 823 feet

	Jan	Feb	Mar	Apr	May	Jun	Jul	Aug	Sep	Oct	Nov	Dec
High	36	42	54	66	75	84	89	87	79	68	53	41
Low	17	22	32	43	53	62	67	64	56	44	33	23
Precip	1.5	1.5	2.7	3.8	5.0	4.2	4.6	3.9	4.9	3.4	2.9	2.0
Snow	6.4	4.8	2.6	0.7	0.0	0.0	0.0	0.0	0.0	tr	1.1	3.1

High and Low temperatures in degrees Fahrenheit; Precipitation and Snow in inches

Population: 32,960 (2000); Race: 95.4% White, 2.2% Black, 0.2% Asian, 0.2% American Indian and Alaska Native, 1.0% Hispanic of any race, 1.6% two or more races (2000); Density: 52.4 persons per square mile (2000); Age: 26.0% under 18, 15.4% over 64 (2000).
Religion: Five largest groups: 19.4% Southern Baptist Convention, 12.8% Lutheran Church—Missouri Synod, 6.6% The United Methodist Church, 6.3% United Church of Christ, 4.5% Catholic Church (2000).
Economy: Unemployment rate: 4.2% (11/2002); Total civilian labor force: 17,294 (11/2002); Leading industries: 23.4% retail trade; 19.8% manufacturing; 12.2% accommodation & food services (2000); Companies that employ more than 1,000 persons: 0 (2000); Companies that employ more than 100 persons: 11 (2000); Farms: 1,215 totaling 349,265 acres (1997); Minority business ownership rate: 0.0% (1997); Women business ownership rate: 16.4% (1997); Retail sales per capita: $6,200 (1997). Single-family building permits issued: 34 (2001) / 16 (2000); Multi-family building permits issued: 3 (2001) / 0 (2000).
Income: Per capita income: $18,493 (2000); Median household income: $38,235 (2000); Poverty rate: 8.8% (2000); Bankruptcy rate: 3.88% (2001).
Taxes: Total county taxes per capita: $97 (2000); County property taxes per capita: $18 (2000).
Education: High school graduation rate: 79.9% (2000); College graduation rate: 13.8% (2000).
Housing: Homeownership rate: 75.4% (2000); Median home value: $74,400 (2000); Median rent: $304 per month (2000); Median age of housing: 31 years (2000).
Health: Birth rate: 118.3 per 10,000 population (1998); Age adjusted death rate: 90.4 per 10,000 population (1999); Age adjusted cancer mortality rate: 158.2 deaths per 100,000 population (1999). Number of physicians: 3.6 per 10,000 population (1999); Number of hospital beds: 10.0 per 10,000 population (1999).
Elections: 2000 Presidential election results: 43.7% Gore, 54.1% Bush, 1.4% Nader, 0.5% Buchanan

Additional Information Contacts
Lafayette County Government Offices 660-259-4315
Concordia Chamber of Commerce. 660-463-2454
Higginsville Chamber of Commerce 660-584-3030
Lexington Area Chamber. 660-259-3082
Odessa Chamber of Commerce 816-633-4044

Lafayette County Communities

ALMA (city). Covers a land area of 0.270 square miles and a water area of 0 square miles. Located at 39.09° N. Lat.; 93.54° W. Long. Elevation is 805 feet.
Population: 399 (2000); Race: 100.0% White, 0.0% Black, 0.0% Asian, 0.0% American Indian and Alaska Native, 0.0% Hispanic of any race, 0.0% two or more races (2000); Density: 1,476.7 persons per square mile (2000); Age: 14.9% under 18, 19.1% over 64 (2000); Marriage status: 24.2% never married, 59.7% now married, 13.8% widowed, 2.3% divorced (2000); Foreign born: 0.0% (2000); Ancestry (includes multiple ancestries): 59.0% German, 7.0% English, 6.7% Irish, 4.4% Scotch-Irish, 3.1% French (except Basque) (2000).
Economy: Corn, wheat, cattle, hogs; meat processing. Single-family building permits issued: 0 (2001) / 0 (2000); Multi-family building permits issued: 0 (2001) / 0 (2000); Employment by occupation: 10.3% management, 17.9% professional, 20.5% services, 19.7% sales, 0.9% farming, 11.1% construction, 19.7% production (2000).
Income: Per capita income: $24,000 (2000); Median household income: $37,426 (2000); Poverty rate: 4.1% (2000).
Taxes: Total city taxes per capita: $111 (1997); City property taxes per capita: $47 (1997).
Education: High school graduation rate: 82.6% (2000); College graduation rate: 16.0% (2000).

School District(s)
Santa Fe R-X (PK-12)
2000 Enrollment: 399 660-674-2236
Housing: Homeownership rate: 86.2% (2000); Median home value: $59,800 (2000); Median rent: $256 per month (2000); Median age of housing: 51 years (2000).
Newspapers: The Santa Fe Times (1 x week)
Transportation: Commute to work: 90.0% car, 0.0% public transportation, 5.2% walk, 4.8% work from home (2000); Travel time to work: 37.7% less than 15 minutes, 31.8% 15 to 30 minutes, 12.3% 30 to 45 minutes, 5.0% 45 to 60 minutes, 13.2% 60 minutes or more (2000)

AULLVILLE (village). Covers a land area of 0.253 square miles and a water area of 0 square miles. Located at 39.01° N. Lat.; 93.67° W. Long. Elevation is 728 feet.
Population: 86 (2000); Race: 82.9% White, 0.0% Black, 6.1% Asian, 2.4% American Indian and Alaska Native, 0.0% Hispanic of any race, 8.5% two or more races (2000); Density: 340.5 persons per square mile (2000); Age: 30.5% under 18, 9.8% over 64 (2000); Marriage status: 32.2% never married, 39.0% now married, 8.5% widowed, 20.3% divorced (2000); Foreign born: 2.4% (2000); Ancestry (includes multiple ancestries): 22.0% Irish, 19.5% German, 19.5% Other groups, 14.6% English, 11.0% United States or American (2000).

Economy: Employment by occupation: 2.6% management, 0.0% professional, 51.3% services, 7.7% sales, 0.0% farming, 25.6% construction, 12.8% production (2000).
Income: Per capita income: $13,339 (2000); Median household income: $33,542 (2000); Poverty rate: 15.2% (2000).
Taxes: Total city taxes per capita: $53 (1997); City property taxes per capita: $13 (1997).
Education: High school graduation rate: 81.4% (2000); College graduation rate: 7.0% (2000).
Housing: Homeownership rate: 87.9% (2000); Median home value: $37,500 (2000); Median rent: $175 per month (2000); Median age of housing: 29 years (2000).
Transportation: Commute to work: 100.0% car, 0.0% public transportation, 0.0% walk, 0.0% work from home (2000); Travel time to work: 10.3% less than 15 minutes, 74.4% 15 to 30 minutes, 2.6% 30 to 45 minutes, 5.1% 45 to 60 minutes, 7.7% 60 minutes or more (2000)

BATES CITY (city). Covers a land area of 0.869 square miles and a water area of 0 square miles. Located at 39.00° N. Lat.; 94.06° W. Long. Elevation is 880 feet.
Population: 245 (2000); Race: 100.0% White, 0.0% Black, 0.0% Asian, 0.0% American Indian and Alaska Native, 0.0% Hispanic of any race, 0.0% two or more races (2000); Density: 281.9 persons per square mile (2000); Age: 17.1% under 18, 5.2% over 64 (2000); Marriage status: 15.2% never married, 70.5% now married, 2.3% widowed, 12.0% divorced (2000); Foreign born: 0.4% (2000); Ancestry (includes multiple ancestries): 17.9% German, 15.1% United States or American, 12.3% English, 11.1% Irish, 11.1% Other groups (2000).
Economy: Manufacturing: consumer goods. Employment by occupation: 7.8% management, 18.8% professional, 23.4% services, 18.8% sales, 0.0% farming, 13.6% construction, 17.5% production (2000).
Income: Per capita income: $19,950 (2000); Median household income: $43,125 (2000); Poverty rate: 11.2% (2000).
Taxes: Total city taxes per capita: $389 (1997); City property taxes per capita: $23 (1997).
Education: High school graduation rate: 80.8% (2000); College graduation rate: 7.3% (2000).
Housing: Homeownership rate: 57.4% (2000); Median home value: $75,000 (2000); Median rent: $283 per month (2000); Median age of housing: 26 years (2000).
Transportation: Commute to work: 92.1% car, 0.0% public transportation, 5.3% walk, 2.6% work from home (2000); Travel time to work: 32.7% less than 15 minutes, 21.1% 15 to 30 minutes, 11.6% 30 to 45 minutes, 17.7% 45 to 60 minutes, 17.0% 60 minutes or more (2000)

CONCORDIA (city). Covers a land area of 1.681 square miles and a water area of 0.004 square miles. Located at 38.98° N. Lat.; 93.56° W. Long. Elevation is 787 feet.
History: Concordia was settled about 1839 by Heinrich Dierking and the town was platted in 1868, with many of the early residents being of German descent. The Concordia Creamery Company was established in 1892, an early example of a cooperative creamery.
Population: 2,360 (2000); Race: 98.4% White, 0.1% Black, 0.0% Asian, 0.6% American Indian and Alaska Native, 0.7% Hispanic of any race, 0.5% two or more races (2000); Density: 1,404.0 persons per square mile (2000); Age: 23.7% under 18, 24.7% over 64 (2000); Marriage status: 20.9% never married, 57.8% now married, 12.3% widowed, 9.1% divorced (2000); Foreign born: 0.5% (2000); Ancestry (includes multiple ancestries): 54.0% German, 9.9% United States or American, 9.8% Irish, 6.5% English, 5.5% Other groups (2000).
Economy: Single-family building permits issued: 3 (2001) / 1 (2000); Multi-family building permits issued: 0 (2001) / 0 (2000); Employment by occupation: 9.4% management, 14.5% professional, 18.1% services, 24.7% sales, 0.2% farming, 12.0% construction, 21.1% production (2000).
Income: Per capita income: $16,813 (2000); Median household income: $33,906 (2000); Poverty rate: 10.0% (2000).
Taxes: Total city taxes per capita: $312 (1997); City property taxes per capita: $43 (1997).
Education: High school graduation rate: 70.9% (2000); College graduation rate: 15.8% (2000).

School District(s)

Concordia R-II (PK-12)
2000 Enrollment: 505 660-463-7235

Housing: Homeownership rate: 66.2% (2000); Median home value: $74,500 (2000); Median rent: $261 per month (2000); Median age of housing: 35 years (2000).
Newspapers: The Concordian (1 x week)
Transportation: Commute to work: 90.7% car, 0.2% public transportation, 5.0% walk, 3.4% work from home (2000); Travel time to work: 57.2% less than 15 minutes, 12.8% 15 to 30 minutes, 12.1% 30 to 45 minutes, 6.9% 45 to 60 minutes, 11.0% 60 minutes or more (2000)
Additional Information Contacts
Concordia Chamber of Commerce. 660-463-2454

CORDER (city). Covers a land area of 0.351 square miles and a water area of 0 square miles. Located at 39.09° N. Lat.; 93.63° W. Long. Elevation is 868 feet.
Population: 427 (2000); Race: 98.4% White, 0.7% Black, 0.0% Asian, 0.0% American Indian and Alaska Native, 1.2% Hispanic of any race, 0.9% two or more races (2000); Density: 1,215.1 persons per square mile (2000); Age: 20.6% under 18, 18.2% over 64 (2000); Marriage status: 22.5% never married, 52.8% now married, 10.8% widowed, 13.8% divorced (2000); Foreign born: 1.2% (2000); Ancestry (includes multiple ancestries): 34.1% German, 11.7% Other groups, 9.1% English, 9.1% Irish, 7.5% United States or American (2000).
Economy: Corn, wheat; cattle. Employment by occupation: 7.9% management, 12.0% professional, 19.0% services, 23.6% sales, 2.8% farming, 12.5% construction, 22.2% production (2000).
Income: Per capita income: $17,897 (2000); Median household income: $32,727 (2000); Poverty rate: 10.7% (2000).
Taxes: Total city taxes per capita: $80 (1997); City property taxes per capita: $41 (1997).
Education: High school graduation rate: 75.0% (2000); College graduation rate: 7.6% (2000).
Housing: Homeownership rate: 75.7% (2000); Median home value: $43,200 (2000); Median rent: $283 per month (2000); Median age of housing: 60+ years (2000).
Transportation: Commute to work: 86.7% car, 0.0% public transportation, 6.7% walk, 4.8% work from home (2000); Travel time to work: 58.0% less than 15 minutes, 14.5% 15 to 30 minutes, 14.5% 30 to 45 minutes, 2.0% 45 to 60 minutes, 11.0% 60 minutes or more (2000)

DOVER (town). Covers a land area of 0.192 square miles and a water area of 0 square miles. Located at 39.19° N. Lat.; 93.68° W. Long. Elevation is 817 feet.
History: Dover was platted in 1835 in an area called Terre Beau or Terre Bonne by early French traders, either for its beauty or for its trading advantages.
Population: 108 (2000); Race: 87.6% White, 5.2% Black, 0.0% Asian, 0.0% American Indian and Alaska Native, 7.2% Hispanic of any race, 0.0% two or more races (2000); Density: 562.4 persons per square mile (2000); Age: 18.6% under 18, 20.6% over 64 (2000); Marriage status: 23.9% never married, 54.5% now married, 13.6% widowed, 8.0% divorced (2000); Foreign born: 7.2% (2000); Ancestry (includes multiple ancestries): 15.5% United States or American, 13.4% Other groups, 13.4% Irish, 8.2% Scotch-Irish, 4.1% French (except Basque) (2000).
Economy: Employment by occupation: 3.9% management, 0.0% professional, 15.7% services, 41.2% sales, 0.0% farming, 5.9% construction, 33.3% production (2000).
Income: Per capita income: $40,768 (2000); Median household income: $39,688 (2000); Poverty rate: 0.0% (2000).
Taxes: Total city taxes per capita: $41 (1997); City property taxes per capita: $8 (1997).
Education: High school graduation rate: 63.0% (2000); College graduation rate: 0.0% (2000).
Housing: Homeownership rate: 83.3% (2000); Median home value: $37,500 (2000); Median rent: $258 per month (2000); Median age of housing: 53 years (2000).
Transportation: Commute to work: 84.3% car, 0.0% public transportation, 0.0% walk, 0.0% work from home (2000); Travel time to work: 37.3% less than 15 minutes, 11.8% 15 to 30 minutes, 7.8% 30 to 45 minutes, 7.8% 45 to 60 minutes, 35.3% 60 minutes or more (2000)

HIGGINSVILLE (city). Covers a land area of 3.685 square miles and a water area of 0.019 square miles. Located at 39.06° N. Lat.; 93.72° W. Long. Elevation is 836 feet.
History: Laid out 1869. Confederate Memorial State Historic Site with cemetery.
Population: 4,682 (2000); Race: 91.5% White, 6.0% Black, 0.0% Asian, 0.3% American Indian and Alaska Native, 1.0% Hispanic of any race, 2.0% two or more races (2000); Density: 1,270.6 persons per square mile (2000); Age: 24.4% under 18, 21.1% over 64 (2000); Marriage status: 20.3% never

married, 57.1% now married, 13.0% widowed, 9.5% divorced (2000); Foreign born: 0.4% (2000); Ancestry (includes multiple ancestries): 35.0% German, 12.5% Other groups, 10.8% Irish, 10.2% English, 9.3% United States or American (2000).
Economy: Wheat, corn, soybeans; cattle, hogs. Limestone quarry. Manufacturing: electronic equipment, plastic products. Single-family building permits issued: 11 (2001) / 12 (2000); Multi-family building permits issued: 3 (2001) / 0 (2000); Employment by occupation: 10.4% management, 13.5% professional, 23.0% services, 21.5% sales, 0.9% farming, 9.7% construction, 21.0% production (2000).
Income: Per capita income: $17,982 (2000); Median household income: $31,497 (2000); Poverty rate: 8.4% (2000).
Taxes: Total city taxes per capita: $152 (2000); City property taxes per capita: $46 (2000).
Education: High school graduation rate: 76.0% (2000); College graduation rate: 17.2% (2000).

School District(s)

Lafayette Co. C-1 (PK-12)
2000 Enrollment: 1,056 660-584-3631

Housing: Homeownership rate: 68.1% (2000); Median home value: $67,700 (2000); Median rent: $252 per month (2000); Median age of housing: 38 years (2000).
Newspapers: Higginsville Advance (2 x week)
Transportation: Commute to work: 92.6% car, 0.0% public transportation, 3.3% walk, 2.6% work from home (2000); Travel time to work: 55.0% less than 15 minutes, 10.8% 15 to 30 minutes, 11.6% 30 to 45 minutes, 7.3% 45 to 60 minutes, 15.3% 60 minutes or more (2000)
Additional Information Contacts
Higginsville Chamber of Commerce 660-584-3030

LAKE LAFAYETTE (city). Covers a land area of 0.639 square miles and a water area of 0.119 square miles. Located at 38.94° N. Lat.; 93.97° W. Long. Elevation is 890 feet.
Population: 346 (2000); Race: 91.4% White, 5.2% Black, 2.0% Asian, 0.0% American Indian and Alaska Native, 0.0% Hispanic of any race, 1.4% two or more races (2000); Density: 541.3 persons per square mile (2000); Age: 21.6% under 18, 8.6% over 64 (2000); Marriage status: 18.6% never married, 52.3% now married, 7.2% widowed, 21.9% divorced (2000); Foreign born: 2.0% (2000); Ancestry (includes multiple ancestries): 22.1% United States or American, 21.0% German, 16.7% Irish, 10.6% Other groups, 5.7% English (2000).
Economy: Employment by occupation: 3.0% management, 1.2% professional, 15.8% services, 24.8% sales, 1.2% farming, 17.6% construction, 36.4% production (2000).
Income: Per capita income: $19,683 (2000); Median household income: $30,750 (2000); Poverty rate: 13.2% (2000).
Taxes: Total city taxes per capita: $43 (1997); City property taxes per capita: $40 (1997).
Education: High school graduation rate: 72.2% (2000); College graduation rate: 3.7% (2000).
Housing: Homeownership rate: 82.6% (2000); Median home value: $50,000 (2000); Median rent: $308 per month (2000); Median age of housing: 23 years (2000).
Transportation: Commute to work: 98.8% car, 0.0% public transportation, 0.0% walk, 0.0% work from home (2000); Travel time to work: 16.6% less than 15 minutes, 23.3% 15 to 30 minutes, 28.8% 30 to 45 minutes, 12.3% 45 to 60 minutes, 19.0% 60 minutes or more (2000)

LEXINGTON (city). Covers a land area of 3.480 square miles and a water area of 0.178 square miles. Located at 39.18° N. Lat.; 93.87° W. Long. Elevation is 849 feet.
History: Lexington grew up around William Jack's Ferry, established in 1819. The town was platted in 1822 and named for Lexington, Kentucky, former home of many of its settlers. That same year John Aull of Delaware opened a store, where he and his brothers James and Robert developed a business outfitting travelers.
Population: 4,453 (2000); Race: 91.0% White, 5.6% Black, 0.4% Asian, 0.1% American Indian and Alaska Native, 1.8% Hispanic of any race, 2.1% two or more races (2000); Density: 1,279.7 persons per square mile (2000); Age: 25.4% under 18, 17.5% over 64 (2000); Marriage status: 20.7% never married, 53.3% now married, 12.1% widowed, 14.0% divorced (2000); Foreign born: 1.7% (2000); Ancestry (includes multiple ancestries): 24.2% German, 14.0% Other groups, 12.4% Irish, 11.5% English, 9.6% United States or American (2000).
Economy: Single-family building permits issued: 2 (2001) / 3 (2000); Multi-family building permits issued: 0 (2001) / 0 (2000); Employment by occupation: 10.1% management, 17.6% professional, 19.8% services, 22.9% sales, 0.2% farming, 12.1% construction, 17.3% production (2000).
Income: Per capita income: $17,879 (2000); Median household income: $32,759 (2000); Poverty rate: 14.9% (2000).
Taxes: Total city taxes per capita: $282 (1997); City property taxes per capita: $33 (1997).
Education: High school graduation rate: 76.9% (2000); College graduation rate: 17.0% (2000).

School District(s)

Lexington R-V (PK-12)
2000 Enrollment: 1,168 660-259-4369

Two-year College(s)

Wentworth Military Academy (Private, Not-for-profit)
2001 Enrollment: 312 660-259-2221
2001 Tuition: In-state $10,815; Out-of-state $10,815

Housing: Homeownership rate: 66.9% (2000); Median home value: $63,100 (2000); Median rent: $306 per month (2000); Median age of housing: 44 years (2000).
Hospitals: Lafayette Regional Health Center (49 beds)
Safety: Violent crime rate: 149.6 per 10,000 population; Property crime rate: 567.0 per 10,000 population (2001).
Newspapers: Dollar Saver Shopper (1 x week); Lexington News (2 x week)
Transportation: Commute to work: 94.9% car, 0.2% public transportation, 2.0% walk, 1.9% work from home (2000); Travel time to work: 46.5% less than 15 minutes, 16.2% 15 to 30 minutes, 10.5% 30 to 45 minutes, 11.4% 45 to 60 minutes, 15.4% 60 minutes or more (2000)
Additional Information Contacts
Lexington Area Chamber 660-259-3082

MAYVIEW (city). Covers a land area of 0.156 square miles and a water area of 0 square miles. Located at 39.05° N. Lat.; 93.83° W. Long. Elevation is 900 feet.
Population: 294 (2000); Race: 83.5% White, 9.6% Black, 0.0% Asian, 1.4% American Indian and Alaska Native, 3.4% Hispanic of any race, 2.7% two or more races (2000); Density: 1,885.9 persons per square mile (2000); Age: 40.5% under 18, 7.9% over 64 (2000); Marriage status: 26.1% never married, 65.7% now married, 1.4% widowed, 6.8% divorced (2000); Foreign born: 0.0% (2000); Ancestry (includes multiple ancestries): 33.3% Other groups, 22.0% German, 10.3% Irish, 10.0% United States or American, 4.1% Scotch-Irish (2000).
Economy: Corn, soybeans; cattle. Employment by occupation: 7.6% management, 1.5% professional, 19.7% services, 28.8% sales, 0.8% farming, 15.9% construction, 25.8% production (2000).
Income: Per capita income: $10,784 (2000); Median household income: $25,313 (2000); Poverty rate: 14.1% (2000).
Taxes: Total city taxes per capita: $87 (1997); City property taxes per capita: $17 (1997).
Education: High school graduation rate: 60.5% (2000); College graduation rate: 1.9% (2000).
Housing: Homeownership rate: 83.0% (2000); Median home value: $29,300 (2000); Median rent: $290 per month (2000); Median age of housing: 58 years (2000).
Transportation: Commute to work: 88.2% car, 0.0% public transportation, 3.9% walk, 6.3% work from home (2000); Travel time to work: 10.9% less than 15 minutes, 59.7% 15 to 30 minutes, 13.4% 30 to 45 minutes, 8.4% 45 to 60 minutes, 7.6% 60 minutes or more (2000)

NAPOLEON (city). Covers a land area of 1.744 square miles and a water area of 0 square miles. Located at 39.13° N. Lat.; 94.07° W. Long. Elevation is 768 feet.
History: Napoleon was laid out in 1836 as Poston's Landing, but the name was changed to Napoleon sometime before the Civil War.
Population: 208 (2000); Race: 98.7% White, 0.0% Black, 0.0% Asian, 0.0% American Indian and Alaska Native, 0.0% Hispanic of any race, 1.3% two or more races (2000); Density: 119.3 persons per square mile (2000); Age: 16.6% under 18, 12.1% over 64 (2000); Marriage status: 21.6% never married, 67.4% now married, 3.2% widowed, 7.9% divorced (2000); Foreign born: 0.0% (2000); Ancestry (includes multiple ancestries): 31.4% German, 21.1% Irish, 13.0% English, 12.6% United States or American, 12.6% Other groups (2000).
Economy: Employment by occupation: 11.3% management, 1.7% professional, 9.6% services, 33.9% sales, 1.7% farming, 10.4% construction, 31.3% production (2000).
Income: Per capita income: $17,546 (2000); Median household income: $36,875 (2000); Poverty rate: 7.6% (2000).

Taxes: Total city taxes per capita: $4 (1997); City property taxes per capita: $4 (1997).
Education: High school graduation rate: 80.0% (2000); College graduation rate: 4.7% (2000).
Housing: Homeownership rate: 85.3% (2000); Median home value: $58,200 (2000); Median rent: $388 per month (2000); Median age of housing: 54 years (2000).
Transportation: Commute to work: 94.5% car, 0.0% public transportation, 3.6% walk, 1.8% work from home (2000); Travel time to work: 16.7% less than 15 minutes, 18.5% 15 to 30 minutes, 33.3% 30 to 45 minutes, 15.7% 45 to 60 minutes, 15.7% 60 minutes or more (2000)

ODESSA (city). Covers a land area of 3.487 square miles and a water area of <.001 square miles. Located at 38.99° N. Lat.; 93.95° W. Long. Elevation is 935 feet.
History: Odessa was platted in 1878 by A.R. Patterson and John Kirkpatrick after the Chicago & Alton Railroad arrived in the area. The town was called Kirkpatrick until its founder objected, saying: "It never will amount to anything and I don't want it named for me." The name of Odessa was suggested because the rolling wheat fields reminded the railroad president of the country around Odessa, Russia.
Population: 4,818 (2000); Race: 97.0% White, 0.8% Black, 0.1% Asian, 0.0% American Indian and Alaska Native, 0.5% Hispanic of any race, 2.1% two or more races (2000); Density: 1,381.7 persons per square mile (2000); Age: 27.9% under 18, 14.6% over 64 (2000); Marriage status: 20.7% never married, 62.4% now married, 5.6% widowed, 11.3% divorced (2000); Foreign born: 0.4% (2000); Ancestry (includes multiple ancestries): 19.9% German, 15.3% United States or American, 12.1% Irish, 8.8% Other groups, 8.5% English (2000).
Economy: Employment by occupation: 6.8% management, 14.1% professional, 12.9% services, 30.4% sales, 0.0% farming, 13.7% construction, 22.0% production (2000).
Income: Per capita income: $17,455 (2000); Median household income: $34,007 (2000); Poverty rate: 9.9% (2000).
Taxes: Total city taxes per capita: $282 (1997); City property taxes per capita: $32 (1997).
Education: High school graduation rate: 78.9% (2000); College graduation rate: 12.9% (2000).

School District(s)

Odessa R-VII (PK-12)
2000 Enrollment: 2,385 816-230-5316
Housing: Homeownership rate: 67.2% (2000); Median home value: $85,200 (2000); Median rent: $379 per month (2000); Median age of housing: 23 years (2000).
Safety: Violent crime rate: 14.4 per 10,000 population; Property crime rate: 484.7 per 10,000 population (2001).
Newspapers: The Odessan (1 x week)
Transportation: Commute to work: 96.4% car, 0.0% public transportation, 1.6% walk, 1.3% work from home (2000); Travel time to work: 36.2% less than 15 minutes, 14.4% 15 to 30 minutes, 20.1% 30 to 45 minutes, 18.7% 45 to 60 minutes, 10.6% 60 minutes or more (2000)
Additional Information Contacts
Odessa Chamber of Commerce 816-633-4044

WAVERLY (city). Covers a land area of 0.999 square miles and a water area of 0.128 square miles. Located at 39.20° N. Lat.; 93.52° W. Long. Elevation is 825 feet.
History: Platted as Middletown in 1845, the settlement was renamed Waverly in 1848. The town developed as a port along the Missouri River.
Population: 806 (2000); Race: 97.8% White, 0.0% Black, 0.0% Asian, 0.0% American Indian and Alaska Native, 1.5% Hispanic of any race, 1.4% two or more races (2000); Density: 806.8 persons per square mile (2000); Age: 27.5% under 18, 17.8% over 64 (2000); Marriage status: 17.6% never married, 65.5% now married, 7.9% widowed, 9.1% divorced (2000); Foreign born: 0.1% (2000); Ancestry (includes multiple ancestries): 29.1% German, 13.8% United States or American, 11.1% Irish, 10.3% English, 7.5% Other groups (2000).
Economy: Employment by occupation: 8.7% management, 13.4% professional, 19.1% services, 20.4% sales, 2.5% farming, 16.9% construction, 19.1% production (2000).
Income: Per capita income: $17,066 (2000); Median household income: $36,806 (2000); Poverty rate: 10.4% (2000).
Taxes: Total city taxes per capita: $151 (1997); City property taxes per capita: $33 (1997).
Education: High school graduation rate: 76.4% (2000); College graduation rate: 9.4% (2000).
Housing: Homeownership rate: 74.8% (2000); Median home value: $51,900 (2000); Median rent: $255 per month (2000); Median age of housing: 41 years (2000).
Transportation: Commute to work: 97.8% car, 0.0% public transportation, 0.5% walk, 1.1% work from home (2000); Travel time to work: 35.5% less than 15 minutes, 28.4% 15 to 30 minutes, 7.7% 30 to 45 minutes, 7.2% 45 to 60 minutes, 21.2% 60 minutes or more (2000)

WELLINGTON (city). Covers a land area of 1.098 square miles and a water area of 0.027 square miles. Located at 39.13° N. Lat.; 93.98° W. Long. Elevation is 790 feet.
History: Wellington was platted in 1837 at a location along the Missouri River.
Population: 784 (2000); Race: 99.5% White, 0.1% Black, 0.0% Asian, 0.4% American Indian and Alaska Native, 0.8% Hispanic of any race, 0.0% two or more races (2000); Density: 714.0 persons per square mile (2000); Age: 23.7% under 18, 16.0% over 64 (2000); Marriage status: 23.2% never married, 57.3% now married, 9.6% widowed, 9.9% divorced (2000); Foreign born: 0.3% (2000); Ancestry (includes multiple ancestries): 26.0% German, 20.8% United States or American, 13.4% Other groups, 10.9% Irish, 8.8% English (2000).
Economy: Employment by occupation: 8.2% management, 11.5% professional, 15.6% services, 27.6% sales, 0.0% farming, 15.9% construction, 21.2% production (2000).
Income: Per capita income: $17,997 (2000); Median household income: $32,500 (2000); Poverty rate: 6.7% (2000).
Taxes: Total city taxes per capita: $59 (1997); City property taxes per capita: $21 (1997).
Education: High school graduation rate: 82.6% (2000); College graduation rate: 12.9% (2000).

School District(s)

Wellington-Napoleon R-IX (KG-12)
2000 Enrollment: 420 816-934-2531
Housing: Homeownership rate: 76.1% (2000); Median home value: $64,900 (2000); Median rent: $275 per month (2000); Median age of housing: 41 years (2000).
Transportation: Commute to work: 95.8% car, 0.0% public transportation, 1.6% walk, 2.6% work from home (2000); Travel time to work: 19.9% less than 15 minutes, 26.1% 15 to 30 minutes, 18.8% 30 to 45 minutes, 14.2% 45 to 60 minutes, 21.0% 60 minutes or more (2000)

Lawrence County

Located in southwestern Missouri, in the Ozarks; drained by the Spring River. Covers a land area of 613.10 square miles, a water area of 0.30 square miles, and is located in the Central Time Zone. The county government was organized in 1845. County seat is Mount Vernon.

Weather Station: Mount Vernon M U SW Center Elevation: 1,187 feet

	Jan	Feb	Mar	Apr	May	Jun	Jul	Aug	Sep	Oct	Nov	Dec
High	41	47	57	67	75	83	89	88	80	69	56	46
Low	20	25	34	44	53	62	66	65	57	45	35	25
Precip	1.9	1.9	3.8	4.2	4.7	5.3	3.2	4.0	5.6	3.6	4.4	2.9
Snow	na	3.3	2.4	tr	0.0	0.0	0.0	0.0	0.0	0.0	0.8	2.4

High and Low temperatures in degrees Fahrenheit; Precipitation and Snow in inches

Population: 35,204 (2000); Race: 95.6% White, 0.1% Black, 0.1% Asian, 0.7% American Indian and Alaska Native, 3.5% Hispanic of any race, 1.4% two or more races (2000); Density: 57.4 persons per square mile (2000); Age: 27.2% under 18, 15.6% over 64 (2000).
Religion: Five largest groups: 26.0% Southern Baptist Convention, 5.8% Catholic Church, 5.7% The United Methodist Church, 3.4% Lutheran Church—Missouri Synod, 1.9% Assemblies of God (2000).
Economy: Unemployment rate: 4.2% (11/2002); Total civilian labor force: 15,817 (11/2002); Leading industries: 22.5% manufacturing; 15.9% retail trade; 15.5% health care and social assistance (2000); Companies that employ more than 1,000 persons: 0 (2000); Companies that employ more than 100 persons: 12 (2000); Farms: 1,733 totaling 337,988 acres (1997); Minority business ownership rate: 0.0% (1997); Women business ownership rate: 23.0% (1997); Retail sales per capita: $8,260 (1997). Single-family building permits issued: 29 (2001) / 25 (2000); Multi-family building permits issued: 12 (2001) / 18 (2000).
Income: Per capita income: $15,399 (2000); Median household income: $31,239 (2000); Poverty rate: 14.1% (2000); Bankruptcy rate: 5.37% (2001).
Taxes: Total county taxes per capita: $65 (1997); County property taxes per capita: $10 (1997).

Education: High school graduation rate: 77.4% (2000); College graduation rate: 12.1% (2000).
Housing: Homeownership rate: 74.3% (2000); Median home value: $65,500 (2000); Median rent: $309 per month (2000); Median age of housing: 30 years (2000).
Health: Birth rate: 132.4 per 10,000 population (1998); Age adjusted death rate: 90.9 per 10,000 population (1999); Age adjusted cancer mortality rate: 197.9 deaths per 100,000 population (1999). Number of physicians: 4.8 per 10,000 population (1999); Number of hospital beds: 46.0 per 10,000 population (1999).
Elections: 2000 Presidential election results: 32.8% Gore, 64.4% Bush, 1.4% Nader, 0.9% Buchanan
Additional Information Contacts
Lawrence County Government Offices 417-466-3666
Aurora Chamber of Commerce 417-678-4150
Mt Vernon Chamber of Commerce 417-466-7654

Lawrence County Communities

AURORA (city). Covers a land area of 5.485 square miles and a water area of 0.006 square miles. Located at 36.97° N. Lat.; 93.72° W. Long. Elevation is 1,368 feet.
History: Aurora was platted in 1872. Lead and zinc deposits provided a period of growth for Aurora in the 1880's and 1890's. Industry that developed in the early 1900's included flour and feed mills, a shoe factory, and the Midwest Map Company.
Population: 7,014 (2000); Race: 96.8% White, 0.0% Black, 0.1% Asian, 1.2% American Indian and Alaska Native, 3.0% Hispanic of any race, 1.3% two or more races (2000); Density: 1,278.7 persons per square mile (2000); Age: 27.4% under 18, 18.4% over 64 (2000); Marriage status: 16.6% never married, 61.1% now married, 9.0% widowed, 13.2% divorced (2000); Foreign born: 2.3% (2000); Ancestry (includes multiple ancestries): 14.8% United States or American, 13.9% German, 13.6% English, 13.3% Other groups, 11.4% Irish (2000).
Economy: Single-family building permits issued: 7 (2001) / 11 (2000); Multi-family building permits issued: 0 (2001) / 0 (2000); Employment by occupation: 9.6% management, 15.1% professional, 15.7% services, 22.5% sales, 1.2% farming, 10.1% construction, 25.8% production (2000).
Income: Per capita income: $13,410 (2000); Median household income: $25,118 (2000); Poverty rate: 18.2% (2000).
Taxes: Total city taxes per capita: $283 (2000); City property taxes per capita: $42 (2000).
Education: High school graduation rate: 73.4% (2000); College graduation rate: 10.8% (2000).
School District(s)
Aurora R-VIII (PK-12)
2000 Enrollment: 2,036 417-678-3373
Housing: Homeownership rate: 68.1% (2000); Median home value: $59,900 (2000); Median rent: $276 per month (2000); Median age of housing: 36 years (2000).
Hospitals: Aurora Community Hospital (59 beds)
Safety: Violent crime rate: 42.5 per 10,000 population; Property crime rate: 425.1 per 10,000 population (2001).
Newspapers: Aurora Advertiser/Marionville Free Press (3 x week)
Transportation: Commute to work: 96.6% car, 0.0% public transportation, 0.6% walk, 2.1% work from home (2000); Travel time to work: 43.0% less than 15 minutes, 28.7% 15 to 30 minutes, 13.9% 30 to 45 minutes, 6.8% 45 to 60 minutes, 7.5% 60 minutes or more (2000)
Additional Information Contacts
Aurora Chamber of Commerce 417-678-4150

FREISTATT (village). Covers a land area of 0.183 square miles and a water area of 0 square miles. Located at 37.02° N. Lat.; 93.89° W. Long. Elevation is 1,338 feet.
History: Settled by Germans.
Population: 184 (2000); Race: 90.2% White, 0.0% Black, 0.0% Asian, 0.0% American Indian and Alaska Native, 1.6% Hispanic of any race, 6.0% two or more races (2000); Density: 1,007.6 persons per square mile (2000); Age: 27.7% under 18, 27.2% over 64 (2000); Marriage status: 15.1% never married, 60.4% now married, 6.5% widowed, 18.0% divorced (2000); Foreign born: 0.0% (2000); Ancestry (includes multiple ancestries): 37.5% German, 23.4% Other groups, 4.3% Irish, 4.3% United States or American, 2.7% Czech (2000).
Economy: Employment by occupation: 4.9% management, 7.4% professional, 13.6% services, 23.5% sales, 4.9% farming, 12.3% construction, 33.3% production (2000).
Income: Per capita income: $10,757 (2000); Median household income: $21,750 (2000); Poverty rate: 18.1% (2000).
Taxes: Total city taxes per capita: $40 (1997); City property taxes per capita: $6 (1997).
Education: High school graduation rate: 80.3% (2000); College graduation rate: 1.6% (2000).
Housing: Homeownership rate: 60.5% (2000); Median home value: $60,700 (2000); Median rent: $193 per month (2000); Median age of housing: 49 years (2000).
Transportation: Commute to work: 79.2% car, 0.0% public transportation, 6.5% walk, 14.3% work from home (2000); Travel time to work: 33.3% less than 15 minutes, 56.1% 15 to 30 minutes, 3.0% 30 to 45 minutes, 6.1% 45 to 60 minutes, 1.5% 60 minutes or more (2000)

HALLTOWN (village). Covers a land area of 0.208 square miles and a water area of 0 square miles. Located at 37.19° N. Lat.; 93.62° W. Long. Elevation is 1,175 feet.
History: Plotted 1887.
Population: 189 (2000); Race: 100.0% White, 0.0% Black, 0.0% Asian, 0.0% American Indian and Alaska Native, 0.0% Hispanic of any race, 0.0% two or more races (2000); Density: 908.0 persons per square mile (2000); Age: 38.9% under 18, 6.9% over 64 (2000); Marriage status: 20.3% never married, 58.7% now married, 9.8% widowed, 11.2% divorced (2000); Foreign born: 0.0% (2000); Ancestry (includes multiple ancestries): 32.5% Irish, 26.1% United States or American, 13.3% Other groups, 11.8% German, 5.9% Dutch (2000).
Economy: Employment by occupation: 7.5% management, 8.6% professional, 24.7% services, 24.7% sales, 0.0% farming, 20.4% construction, 14.0% production (2000).
Income: Per capita income: $10,301 (2000); Median household income: $30,833 (2000); Poverty rate: 11.3% (2000).
Taxes: Total city taxes per capita: $6 (1997); City property taxes per capita: $6 (1997).
Education: High school graduation rate: 74.5% (2000); College graduation rate: 3.9% (2000).
Housing: Homeownership rate: 67.6% (2000); Median home value: $68,300 (2000); Median rent: $323 per month (2000); Median age of housing: 58 years (2000).
Transportation: Commute to work: 94.6% car, 0.0% public transportation, 2.2% walk, 3.2% work from home (2000); Travel time to work: 23.3% less than 15 minutes, 41.1% 15 to 30 minutes, 26.7% 30 to 45 minutes, 6.7% 45 to 60 minutes, 2.2% 60 minutes or more (2000)

HOBERG (village). Covers a land area of 0.058 square miles and a water area of 0 square miles. Located at 37.06° N. Lat.; 93.84° W. Long. Elevation is 1,162 feet.
Population: 60 (2000); Race: 100.0% White, 0.0% Black, 0.0% Asian, 0.0% American Indian and Alaska Native, 0.0% Hispanic of any race, 0.0% two or more races (2000); Density: 1,032.2 persons per square mile (2000); Age: 24.5% under 18, 13.2% over 64 (2000); Marriage status: 11.9% never married, 76.2% now married, 4.8% widowed, 7.1% divorced (2000); Foreign born: 0.0% (2000); Ancestry (includes multiple ancestries): 20.8% Irish, 18.9% German, 17.0% English, 11.3% Dutch, 5.7% Other groups (2000).
Economy: Employment by occupation: 0.0% management, 0.0% professional, 19.0% services, 14.3% sales, 0.0% farming, 28.6% construction, 38.1% production (2000).
Income: Per capita income: $10,121 (2000); Median household income: $21,250 (2000); Poverty rate: 32.1% (2000).
Taxes: Total city taxes per capita: $15 (1997); City property taxes per capita: $15 (1997).
Education: High school graduation rate: 48.5% (2000); College graduation rate: 0.0% (2000).
Housing: Homeownership rate: 40.0% (2000); Median home value: $15,000 (2000); Median rent: $225 per month (2000); Median age of housing: 41 years (2000).
Transportation: Commute to work: 95.2% car, 0.0% public transportation, 0.0% walk, 4.8% work from home (2000); Travel time to work: 0.0% less than 15 minutes, 40.0% 15 to 30 minutes, 35.0% 30 to 45 minutes, 15.0% 45 to 60 minutes, 10.0% 60 minutes or more (2000)

MARIONVILLE (city). Covers a land area of 1.385 square miles and a water area of 0 square miles. Located at 37.00° N. Lat.; 93.63° W. Long. Elevation is 1,359 feet.

History: Marionville was settled about 1854, and grew around a flour mill and a sawmill, as well as having a brief mining period.
Population: 2,113 (2000); Race: 98.1% White, 0.0% Black, 0.0% Asian, 0.9% American Indian and Alaska Native, 0.8% Hispanic of any race, 0.9% two or more races (2000); Density: 1,525.6 persons per square mile (2000); Age: 24.2% under 18, 23.2% over 64 (2000); Marriage status: 16.9% never married, 62.4% now married, 10.5% widowed, 10.3% divorced (2000); Foreign born: 0.0% (2000); Ancestry (includes multiple ancestries): 14.4% United States or American, 12.6% Irish, 11.5% Other groups, 11.5% German, 9.1% English (2000).
Economy: Single-family building permits issued: 3 (2001) / 3 (2000); Multi-family building permits issued: 0 (2001) / 0 (2000); Employment by occupation: 5.7% management, 11.5% professional, 23.8% services, 18.9% sales, 2.3% farming, 11.7% construction, 26.1% production (2000).
Income: Per capita income: $13,552 (2000); Median household income: $25,078 (2000); Poverty rate: 22.0% (2000).
Taxes: Total city taxes per capita: $289 (1997); City property taxes per capita: $117 (1997).
Education: High school graduation rate: 75.6% (2000); College graduation rate: 7.8% (2000).

School District(s)

Marionville R-IX (PK-12)
2000 Enrollment: 767 417-258-7755
Housing: Homeownership rate: 60.5% (2000); Median home value: $54,600 (2000); Median rent: $338 per month (2000); Median age of housing: 28 years (2000).
Transportation: Commute to work: 92.4% car, 0.0% public transportation, 1.3% walk, 3.8% work from home (2000); Travel time to work: 33.8% less than 15 minutes, 20.5% 15 to 30 minutes, 25.0% 30 to 45 minutes, 11.4% 45 to 60 minutes, 9.4% 60 minutes or more (2000)

MILLER (city). Covers a land area of 0.757 square miles and a water area of 0 square miles. Located at 37.21° N. Lat.; 93.84° W. Long. Elevation is 1,305 feet.
Population: 754 (2000); Race: 97.5% White, 0.0% Black, 0.5% Asian, 0.0% American Indian and Alaska Native, 1.6% Hispanic of any race, 1.3% two or more races (2000); Density: 995.8 persons per square mile (2000); Age: 29.0% under 18, 16.7% over 64 (2000); Marriage status: 20.2% never married, 52.5% now married, 13.1% widowed, 14.2% divorced (2000); Foreign born: 0.5% (2000); Ancestry (includes multiple ancestries): 18.1% German, 15.1% United States or American, 12.5% Irish, 12.0% English, 7.6% Other groups (2000).
Economy: Flour mills. Corn, hay, cattle, dairying. Employment by occupation: 5.9% management, 13.0% professional, 18.0% services, 16.1% sales, 0.9% farming, 13.0% construction, 33.1% production (2000).
Income: Per capita income: $12,680 (2000); Median household income: $24,722 (2000); Poverty rate: 20.2% (2000).
Taxes: Total city taxes per capita: $103 (1997); City property taxes per capita: $21 (1997).
Education: High school graduation rate: 77.2% (2000); College graduation rate: 8.7% (2000).

School District(s)

Miller R-II (PK-12)
2000 Enrollment: 721 417-452-3515
Housing: Homeownership rate: 68.2% (2000); Median home value: $49,900 (2000); Median rent: $253 per month (2000); Median age of housing: 42 years (2000).
Newspapers: The Miller Press (1 x week)
Transportation: Commute to work: 92.0% car, 0.0% public transportation, 4.8% walk, 1.6% work from home (2000); Travel time to work: 26.9% less than 15 minutes, 34.3% 15 to 30 minutes, 22.7% 30 to 45 minutes, 10.7% 45 to 60 minutes, 5.5% 60 minutes or more (2000)

MOUNT VERNON (city). Covers a land area of 3.423 square miles and a water area of 0 square miles. Located at 37.10° N. Lat.; 93.81° W. Long. Elevation is 1,200 feet.
History: Laid out 1845.
Population: 4,017 (2000); Race: 96.7% White, 1.0% Black, 0.0% Asian, 0.2% American Indian and Alaska Native, 0.0% Hispanic of any race, 2.0% two or more races (2000); Density: 1,173.4 persons per square mile (2000); Age: 23.8% under 18, 23.8% over 64 (2000); Marriage status: 14.7% never married, 59.3% now married, 11.2% widowed, 14.9% divorced (2000); Foreign born: 0.3% (2000); Ancestry (includes multiple ancestries): 17.8% German, 16.3% Irish, 15.5% United States or American, 13.0% English, 11.6% Other groups (2000).
Economy: Wheat, corn, produce; dairying; cattle. Manufacturing: woodburning stoves, apparel, aluminum cans, motor vehicle equipment. Missouri Rehabilitation Center and Missouri Veterans' Home. Single-family building permits issued: 19 (2001) / 6 (2000); Multi-family building permits issued: 12 (2001) / 18 (2000); Employment by occupation: 6.6% management, 20.3% professional, 15.9% services, 25.0% sales, 0.9% farming, 8.3% construction, 23.1% production (2000).
Income: Per capita income: $16,210 (2000); Median household income: $28,628 (2000); Poverty rate: 13.7% (2000).
Taxes: Total city taxes per capita: $1,820 (2000); City property taxes per capita: $311 (2000).
Education: High school graduation rate: 76.9% (2000); College graduation rate: 12.4% (2000).

School District(s)

Mount Vernon R-V (KG-12)
2000 Enrollment: 1,431 417-466-7573
Housing: Homeownership rate: 63.2% (2000); Median home value: $68,000 (2000); Median rent: $292 per month (2000); Median age of housing: 35 years (2000).
Hospitals: Missouri Rehabilitation Center (136 beds)
Newspapers: The Lawrence County Record (1 x week)
Transportation: Commute to work: 90.7% car, 0.6% public transportation, 4.6% walk, 3.1% work from home (2000); Travel time to work: 61.4% less than 15 minutes, 12.9% 15 to 30 minutes, 13.4% 30 to 45 minutes, 8.8% 45 to 60 minutes, 3.5% 60 minutes or more (2000)
Additional Information Contacts
Mt Vernon Chamber of Commerce 417-466-7654

PIERCE CITY (city). Aka Peirce City. Covers a land area of 1.222 square miles and a water area of 0 square miles. Located at 36.94° N. Lat.; 94.00° W. Long. Elevation is 1,199 feet.
History: Founded c.1870.
Population: 1,385 (2000); Race: 94.6% White, 0.0% Black, 0.1% Asian, 2.3% American Indian and Alaska Native, 1.0% Hispanic of any race, 2.6% two or more races (2000); Density: 1,133.3 persons per square mile (2000); Age: 25.9% under 18, 10.9% over 64 (2000); Marriage status: 19.5% never married, 56.3% now married, 10.0% widowed, 14.3% divorced (2000); Foreign born: 0.4% (2000); Ancestry (includes multiple ancestries): 18.5% German, 15.8% Other groups, 14.2% United States or American, 12.7% Irish, 11.4% English (2000).
Economy: Corn, wheat, fruit; dairying; cattle; lime products. Single-family building permits issued: 0 (2001) / 5 (2000); Multi-family building permits issued: 0 (2001) / 0 (2000); Employment by occupation: 4.3% management, 15.3% professional, 15.8% services, 22.6% sales, 0.0% farming, 11.2% construction, 30.7% production (2000).
Income: Per capita income: $12,310 (2000); Median household income: $24,186 (2000); Poverty rate: 20.6% (2000).
Taxes: Total city taxes per capita: $54 (1997); City property taxes per capita: $31 (1997).
Education: High school graduation rate: 74.8% (2000); College graduation rate: 8.4% (2000).

School District(s)

Pierce City R-VI (KG-12)
2000 Enrollment: 676 417-476-2555
Housing: Homeownership rate: 62.8% (2000); Median home value: $48,200 (2000); Median rent: $291 per month (2000); Median age of housing: 49 years (2000).
Transportation: Commute to work: 96.1% car, 0.0% public transportation, 1.3% walk, 1.3% work from home (2000); Travel time to work: 34.1% less than 15 minutes, 39.1% 15 to 30 minutes, 16.0% 30 to 45 minutes, 6.0% 45 to 60 minutes, 4.8% 60 minutes or more (2000)

STOTTS CITY (city). Covers a land area of 0.514 square miles and a water area of 0 square miles. Located at 37.10° N. Lat.; 93.94° W. Long. Elevation is 1,148 feet.
Population: 250 (2000); Race: 87.5% White, 0.0% Black, 2.5% Asian, 5.0% American Indian and Alaska Native, 12.9% Hispanic of any race, 5.0% two or more races (2000); Density: 486.2 persons per square mile (2000); Age: 24.2% under 18, 17.1% over 64 (2000); Marriage status: 18.3% never married, 62.8% now married, 9.9% widowed, 8.9% divorced (2000); Foreign born: 8.3% (2000); Ancestry (includes multiple ancestries): 28.7% Other groups, 16.7% United States or American, 5.0% Irish, 4.2% German, 3.3% English (2000).
Economy: Fruit, vegetables; dairying; cattle. Employment by occupation: 5.6% management, 9.3% professional, 23.1% services, 19.4% sales, 4.6% farming, 13.9% construction, 24.1% production (2000).

Income: Per capita income: $8,942 (2000); Median household income: $18,958 (2000); Poverty rate: 24.6% (2000).
Taxes: Total city taxes per capita: $24 (1997); City property taxes per capita: $24 (1997).
Education: High school graduation rate: 65.0% (2000); College graduation rate: 3.5% (2000).
Housing: Homeownership rate: 75.0% (2000); Median home value: $20,000 (2000); Median rent: $316 per month (2000); Median age of housing: 39 years (2000).
Transportation: Commute to work: 86.6% car, 0.0% public transportation, 5.2% walk, 8.2% work from home (2000); Travel time to work: 21.3% less than 15 minutes, 47.2% 15 to 30 minutes, 21.3% 30 to 45 minutes, 4.5% 45 to 60 minutes, 5.6% 60 minutes or more (2000)

VERONA (town). Covers a land area of 0.870 square miles and a water area of 0 square miles. Located at 36.96° N. Lat.; 93.79° W. Long. Elevation is 1,275 feet.
History: Verona was platted in 1868 as a shipping point on the railroad for strawberries grown in the area.
Population: 714 (2000); Race: 73.2% White, 0.0% Black, 0.0% Asian, 1.0% American Indian and Alaska Native, 30.9% Hispanic of any race, 1.8% two or more races (2000); Density: 820.3 persons per square mile (2000); Age: 30.6% under 18, 10.4% over 64 (2000); Marriage status: 23.4% never married, 56.6% now married, 8.6% widowed, 11.4% divorced (2000); Foreign born: 22.3% (2000); Ancestry (includes multiple ancestries): 38.1% Other groups, 15.4% German, 9.9% United States or American, 9.0% Irish, 7.2% English (2000).
Economy: Single-family building permits issued: 0 (2001) / 0 (2000); Multi-family building permits issued: 0 (2001) / 0 (2000); Employment by occupation: 5.0% management, 5.4% professional, 20.2% services, 15.5% sales, 6.0% farming, 8.8% construction, 39.1% production (2000).
Income: Per capita income: $11,750 (2000); Median household income: $27,813 (2000); Poverty rate: 26.4% (2000).
Taxes: Total city taxes per capita: $80 (1997); City property taxes per capita: $28 (1997).
Education: High school graduation rate: 60.4% (2000); College graduation rate: 5.3% (2000).

School District(s)

Verona R-VII (KG-12)
2000 Enrollment: 356 417-498-2274

Housing: Homeownership rate: 68.4% (2000); Median home value: $44,000 (2000); Median rent: $294 per month (2000); Median age of housing: 35 years (2000).
Transportation: Commute to work: 94.6% car, 0.0% public transportation, 1.0% walk, 3.5% work from home (2000); Travel time to work: 27.6% less than 15 minutes, 44.1% 15 to 30 minutes, 14.8% 30 to 45 minutes, 7.6% 45 to 60 minutes, 5.9% 60 minutes or more (2000)

Lewis County

Located in northeastern Missouri; bounded on the east by the Mississippi River and the Illinois border; drained by the Wyaconda River and North and Middle Fabius Rivers. Covers a land area of 505.00 square miles, a water area of 5.80 square miles, and is located in the Central Time Zone. The county government was organized in 1833. County seat is Monticello.

Weather Station: Canton Lock & Dam 20 Elevation: 488 feet

	Jan	Feb	Mar	Apr	May	Jun	Jul	Aug	Sep	Oct	Nov	Dec
High	34	39	52	64	75	84	89	86	79	68	52	39
Low	16	21	31	43	54	63	67	65	56	44	33	22
Precip	1.5	1.6	2.9	3.6	5.3	3.6	4.2	3.9	4.5	2.7	3.2	2.1
Snow	na	na	1.1	tr	0.0	0.0	0.0	0.0	0.0	0.0	0.4	na

High and Low temperatures in degrees Fahrenheit; Precipitation and Snow in inches

Weather Station: Steffenville Elevation: 688 feet

	Jan	Feb	Mar	Apr	May	Jun	Jul	Aug	Sep	Oct	Nov	Dec
High	34	40	53	65	74	83	88	86	79	67	52	39
Low	16	21	31	42	52	61	66	63	55	44	33	22
Precip	1.3	1.4	2.7	3.4	4.9	3.4	3.9	3.6	4.0	3.0	3.1	2.0
Snow	7.0	5.2	2.4	0.8	0.0	0.0	0.0	0.0	0.0	tr	1.4	3.9

High and Low temperatures in degrees Fahrenheit; Precipitation and Snow in inches

Population: 10,494 (2000); Race: 95.7% White, 2.4% Black, 0.3% Asian, 0.2% American Indian and Alaska Native, 0.3% Hispanic of any race, 1.2% two or more races (2000); Density: 20.8 persons per square mile (2000); Age: 25.1% under 18, 16.1% over 64 (2000).
Religion: Five largest groups: 33.7% Southern Baptist Convention, 7.8% Christian Church (Disciples of Christ), 6.8% Catholic Church, 6.6% The United Methodist Church, 2.4% Christian Churches and Churches of Christ (2000).
Economy: Unemployment rate: 3.3% (11/2002); Total civilian labor force: 6,020 (11/2002); Leading industries: 19.8% retail trade; 18.1% health care and social assistance; 5.1% finance & insurance (2000); Companies that employ more than 1,000 persons: 0 (2000); Companies that employ more than 100 persons: 5 (2000); Farms: 719 totaling 268,595 acres (1997); Minority business ownership rate: 0.0% (1997); Women business ownership rate: 22.7% (1997); Retail sales per capita: $4,652 (1997). Single-family building permits issued: 8 (2001) / 2 (2000); Multi-family building permits issued: 0 (2001) / 6 (2000).
Income: Per capita income: $14,746 (2000); Median household income: $30,651 (2000); Poverty rate: 16.1% (2000); Bankruptcy rate: 4.64% (2001).
Taxes: Total county taxes per capita: $86 (1997); County property taxes per capita: $39 (1997).
Education: High school graduation rate: 79.5% (2000); College graduation rate: 13.0% (2000).
Housing: Homeownership rate: 76.5% (2000); Median home value: $52,400 (2000); Median rent: $228 per month (2000); Median age of housing: 36 years (2000).
Health: Birth rate: 142.0 per 10,000 population (1998); Age adjusted death rate: 87.1 per 10,000 population (1999); Age adjusted cancer mortality rate: 216.1 deaths per 100,000 population (1999). Number of physicians: 1.9 per 10,000 population (1999); Number of hospital beds: n/a (1999).
Elections: 2000 Presidential election results: 45.1% Gore, 53.3% Bush, 0.8% Nader, 0.6% Buchanan
National and State Parks: Wakonda State Park
Additional Information Contacts
Lewis County Government Offices 573-767-5205

Lewis County Communities

CANTON (city). Covers a land area of 2.287 square miles and a water area of 0.257 square miles. Located at 40.13° N. Lat.; 91.52° W. Long. Elevation is 590 feet.
History: Canton was established in 1830 and named for Canton, Ohio. In 1853, Culver-Stockton College (originally Christian University) was founded by the Disciples of Christ church, and became the first college west of the Mississippi to receive a charter as a coeducational institution.
Population: 2,557 (2000); Race: 94.4% White, 2.0% Black, 1.1% Asian, 0.4% American Indian and Alaska Native, 0.2% Hispanic of any race, 1.8% two or more races (2000); Density: 1,118.1 persons per square mile (2000); Age: 20.9% under 18, 13.6% over 64 (2000); Marriage status: 30.5% never married, 52.1% now married, 8.2% widowed, 9.3% divorced (2000); Foreign born: 1.3% (2000); Ancestry (includes multiple ancestries): 29.2% German, 12.3% Irish, 8.8% Other groups, 8.5% United States or American, 8.3% English (2000).
Economy: Single-family building permits issued: 8 (2001) / 2 (2000); Multi-family building permits issued: 0 (2001) / 6 (2000); Employment by occupation: 8.8% management, 23.8% professional, 18.8% services, 22.6% sales, 0.2% farming, 6.7% construction, 19.1% production (2000).
Income: Per capita income: $14,663 (2000); Median household income: $26,983 (2000); Poverty rate: 16.8% (2000).
Taxes: Total city taxes per capita: $184 (1997); City property taxes per capita: $50 (1997).
Education: High school graduation rate: 80.8% (2000); College graduation rate: 25.0% (2000).

School District(s)

Canton R-V (PK-12)
2000 Enrollment: 618 573-288-5216

Four-year College(s)

Culver-Stockton College (Private, Not-for-profit, Christian Church (Disciples of Christ))
2001 Enrollment: 821 217-231-6000
2001 Tuition: In-state $11,200; Out-of-state $11,200

Housing: Homeownership rate: 63.8% (2000); Median home value: $57,500 (2000); Median rent: $249 per month (2000); Median age of housing: 44 years (2000).
Safety: Violent crime rate: 101.0 per 10,000 population; Property crime rate: 380.9 per 10,000 population (2001).
Newspapers: Canton Press-News Journal (1 x week)
Transportation: Commute to work: 77.0% car, 0.0% public transportation, 18.9% walk, 2.9% work from home (2000); Travel time to work: 69.3% less

than 15 minutes, 11.9% 15 to 30 minutes, 14.7% 30 to 45 minutes, 2.3% 45 to 60 minutes, 1.8% 60 minutes or more (2000)

DURHAM (unincorporated postal area, zip code 63438). Covers a land area of 14.454 square miles and a water area of 0.012 square miles. Located at 39.95° N. Lat.; 91.70° W. Long. Elevation is 649 feet.
Population: 518 (2000); Race: 100.0% White, 0.0% Black, 0.0% Asian, 0.0% American Indian and Alaska Native, 0.9% Hispanic of any race, 0.0% two or more races (2000); Density: 35.8 persons per square mile (2000); Age: 20.7% under 18, 16.9% over 64 (2000); Marriage status: 17.4% never married, 67.5% now married, 4.9% widowed, 10.2% divorced (2000); Foreign born: 0.9% (2000); Ancestry (includes multiple ancestries): 27.2% German, 15.8% Irish, 8.0% English, 6.5% United States or American, 6.0% French (except Basque) (2000).
Economy: Employment by occupation: 6.6% management, 7.0% professional, 13.5% services, 18.3% sales, 0.9% farming, 12.7% construction, 41.0% production (2000).
Income: Per capita income: $13,402 (2000); Median household income: $31,324 (2000); Poverty rate: 20.3% (2000).
Education: High school graduation rate: 82.8% (2000); College graduation rate: 6.6% (2000).
Housing: Homeownership rate: 87.5% (2000); Median home value: $52,100 (2000); Median rent: $294 per month (2000); Median age of housing: 28 years (2000).
Transportation: Commute to work: 98.3% car, 0.0% public transportation, 0.0% walk, 1.7% work from home (2000); Travel time to work: 5.8% less than 15 minutes, 29.3% 15 to 30 minutes, 53.8% 30 to 45 minutes, 8.4% 45 to 60 minutes, 2.7% 60 minutes or more (2000)

EWING (city). Covers a land area of 0.629 square miles and a water area of 0 square miles. Located at 40.00° N. Lat.; 91.71° W. Long. Elevation is 690 feet.
Population: 464 (2000); Race: 97.1% White, 0.0% Black, 0.0% Asian, 0.8% American Indian and Alaska Native, 0.0% Hispanic of any race, 2.1% two or more races (2000); Density: 737.1 persons per square mile (2000); Age: 29.8% under 18, 15.7% over 64 (2000); Marriage status: 16.4% never married, 64.1% now married, 12.3% widowed, 7.2% divorced (2000); Foreign born: 0.4% (2000); Ancestry (includes multiple ancestries): 30.6% German, 10.9% English, 9.4% United States or American, 7.3% Irish, 4.2% Other groups (2000).
Economy: Employment by occupation: 8.8% management, 12.4% professional, 13.3% services, 23.9% sales, 0.0% farming, 7.5% construction, 34.1% production (2000).
Income: Per capita income: $14,115 (2000); Median household income: $30,000 (2000); Poverty rate: 13.8% (2000).
Taxes: Total city taxes per capita: $100 (1997); City property taxes per capita: $34 (1997).
Education: High school graduation rate: 80.0% (2000); College graduation rate: 9.8% (2000).

School District(s)

Lewis Co. C-1 (PK-12)
2000 Enrollment: 1,103 573-209-3217
Housing: Homeownership rate: 65.3% (2000); Median home value: $52,300 (2000); Median rent: $257 per month (2000); Median age of housing: 28 years (2000).
Transportation: Commute to work: 91.5% car, 0.0% public transportation, 5.4% walk, 3.1% work from home (2000); Travel time to work: 30.4% less than 15 minutes, 15.2% 15 to 30 minutes, 37.8% 30 to 45 minutes, 12.9% 45 to 60 minutes, 3.7% 60 minutes or more (2000)

LA BELLE (city). Covers a land area of 0.636 square miles and a water area of 0.004 square miles. Located at 40.11° N. Lat.; 91.91° W. Long. Elevation is 738 feet.
Population: 669 (2000); Race: 91.3% White, 7.1% Black, 0.0% Asian, 0.0% American Indian and Alaska Native, 0.3% Hispanic of any race, 1.6% two or more races (2000); Density: 1,052.6 persons per square mile (2000); Age: 21.8% under 18, 29.2% over 64 (2000); Marriage status: 17.5% never married, 51.2% now married, 19.0% widowed, 12.4% divorced (2000); Foreign born: 0.3% (2000); Ancestry (includes multiple ancestries): 14.9% German, 14.4% United States or American, 8.8% Other groups, 8.3% English, 6.7% Irish (2000).
Economy: Corn, soybeans; hogs; lumber. Employment by occupation: 5.9% management, 10.2% professional, 16.9% services, 21.6% sales, 3.8% farming, 10.2% construction, 31.4% production (2000).
Income: Per capita income: $12,424 (2000); Median household income: $21,477 (2000); Poverty rate: 28.5% (2000).
Taxes: Total city taxes per capita: $110 (1997); City property taxes per capita: $56 (1997).
Education: High school graduation rate: 63.0% (2000); College graduation rate: 7.1% (2000).
Housing: Homeownership rate: 76.0% (2000); Median home value: $26,500 (2000); Median rent: $188 per month (2000); Median age of housing: 55 years (2000).
Newspapers: La Belle Star (1 x week)
Transportation: Commute to work: 92.2% car, 0.9% public transportation, 6.5% walk, 0.0% work from home (2000); Travel time to work: 42.4% less than 15 minutes, 19.5% 15 to 30 minutes, 10.0% 30 to 45 minutes, 20.8% 45 to 60 minutes, 7.4% 60 minutes or more (2000)

LA GRANGE (city). Covers a land area of 1.389 square miles and a water area of 0.285 square miles. Located at 40.04° N. Lat.; 91.50° W. Long. Elevation is 490 feet.
History: La Grange was platted in 1830 and incorporated in 1838. The town began as a trading post established by Godfrey Le Sieur at the mouth of the Wyaconda River in the late 1700's, when the area was under Spanish rule. Many of the early residents came from Kentucky and Tennessee, and a diversified industrial base was established early.
Population: 1,000 (2000); Race: 89.8% White, 9.0% Black, 0.0% Asian, 0.2% American Indian and Alaska Native, 0.3% Hispanic of any race, 0.7% two or more races (2000); Density: 719.7 persons per square mile (2000); Age: 22.0% under 18, 18.0% over 64 (2000); Marriage status: 19.6% never married, 53.5% now married, 10.5% widowed, 16.4% divorced (2000); Foreign born: 0.0% (2000); Ancestry (includes multiple ancestries): 25.7% German, 10.6% Other groups, 10.3% Irish, 6.7% United States or American, 4.5% English (2000).
Economy: Employment by occupation: 6.2% management, 8.9% professional, 14.1% services, 22.2% sales, 2.1% farming, 8.3% construction, 38.3% production (2000).
Income: Per capita income: $15,399 (2000); Median household income: $30,938 (2000); Poverty rate: 12.2% (2000).
Taxes: Total city taxes per capita: $24 (1997); City property taxes per capita: $18 (1997).
Education: High school graduation rate: 80.7% (2000); College graduation rate: 6.3% (2000).
Housing: Homeownership rate: 73.5% (2000); Median home value: $44,900 (2000); Median rent: $232 per month (2000); Median age of housing: 43 years (2000).
Transportation: Commute to work: 93.1% car, 0.0% public transportation, 2.3% walk, 4.6% work from home (2000); Travel time to work: 23.6% less than 15 minutes, 35.8% 15 to 30 minutes, 34.5% 30 to 45 minutes, 5.0% 45 to 60 minutes, 1.1% 60 minutes or more (2000)

LEWISTOWN (town). Covers a land area of 0.450 square miles and a water area of 0 square miles. Located at 40.08° N. Lat.; 91.81° W. Long. Elevation is 725 feet.
Population: 595 (2000); Race: 99.3% White, 0.0% Black, 0.0% Asian, 0.0% American Indian and Alaska Native, 1.5% Hispanic of any race, 0.0% two or more races (2000); Density: 1,321.9 persons per square mile (2000); Age: 29.1% under 18, 20.6% over 64 (2000); Marriage status: 14.1% never married, 60.2% now married, 16.0% widowed, 9.7% divorced (2000); Foreign born: 0.7% (2000); Ancestry (includes multiple ancestries): 24.7% German, 18.5% United States or American, 12.8% English, 12.8% Irish, 5.2% Other groups (2000).
Economy: Agriculture. Employment by occupation: 8.5% management, 10.0% professional, 19.6% services, 20.4% sales, 0.8% farming, 13.8% construction, 26.9% production (2000).
Income: Per capita income: $12,655 (2000); Median household income: $22,188 (2000); Poverty rate: 22.1% (2000).
Taxes: Total city taxes per capita: $209 (1997); City property taxes per capita: $82 (1997).
Education: High school graduation rate: 78.6% (2000); College graduation rate: 6.6% (2000).
Housing: Homeownership rate: 66.7% (2000); Median home value: $40,200 (2000); Median rent: $210 per month (2000); Median age of housing: 36 years (2000).
Transportation: Commute to work: 92.5% car, 0.0% public transportation, 1.6% walk, 4.7% work from home (2000); Travel time to work: 37.9% less than 15 minutes, 10.3% 15 to 30 minutes, 28.0% 30 to 45 minutes, 16.5% 45 to 60 minutes, 7.4% 60 minutes or more (2000)

MAYWOOD (unincorporated postal area, zip code 63454). Covers a land area of 34.888 square miles and a water area of 0.038 square miles. Located at 39.93° N. Lat.; 91.63° W. Long. Elevation is 516 feet.
Population: 869 (2000); Race: 99.2% White, 0.5% Black, 0.0% Asian, 0.0% American Indian and Alaska Native, 0.5% Hispanic of any race, 0.0% two or more races (2000); Density: 24.9 persons per square mile (2000); Age: 24.2% under 18, 12.0% over 64 (2000); Marriage status: 16.3% never married, 66.1% now married, 6.1% widowed, 11.5% divorced (2000); Foreign born: 0.0% (2000); Ancestry (includes multiple ancestries): 32.1% German, 13.3% United States or American, 11.7% Irish, 11.5% English, 4.5% Other groups (2000).
Economy: Employment by occupation: 10.1% management, 7.1% professional, 11.1% services, 28.5% sales, 0.9% farming, 12.7% construction, 29.5% production (2000).
Income: Per capita income: $17,175 (2000); Median household income: $35,313 (2000); Poverty rate: 9.8% (2000).
Education: High school graduation rate: 78.3% (2000); College graduation rate: 7.5% (2000).
Housing: Homeownership rate: 86.3% (2000); Median home value: $71,000 (2000); Median rent: $171 per month (2000); Median age of housing: 36 years (2000).
Transportation: Commute to work: 94.5% car, 0.5% public transportation, 0.0% walk, 5.0% work from home (2000); Travel time to work: 7.6% less than 15 minutes, 48.7% 15 to 30 minutes, 31.3% 30 to 45 minutes, 7.3% 45 to 60 minutes, 5.1% 60 minutes or more (2000)

MONTICELLO (village). Covers a land area of 0.262 square miles and a water area of 0 square miles. Located at 40.11° N. Lat.; 91.71° W. Long. Elevation is 480 feet.
Population: 126 (2000); Race: 98.2% White, 0.0% Black, 0.0% Asian, 1.8% American Indian and Alaska Native, 0.0% Hispanic of any race, 0.0% two or more races (2000); Density: 481.5 persons per square mile (2000); Age: 15.6% under 18, 9.2% over 64 (2000); Marriage status: 14.1% never married, 55.4% now married, 10.9% widowed, 19.6% divorced (2000); Foreign born: 1.8% (2000); Ancestry (includes multiple ancestries): 33.0% German, 12.8% United States or American, 9.2% English, 4.6% Scottish, 4.6% Dutch (2000).
Economy: Corn, soybeans; cattle, hogs. Employment by occupation: 17.7% management, 11.3% professional, 22.6% services, 9.7% sales, 0.0% farming, 19.4% construction, 19.4% production (2000).
Income: Per capita income: $16,592 (2000); Median household income: $25,625 (2000); Poverty rate: 11.8% (2000).
Taxes: Total city taxes per capita: $46 (1997); City property taxes per capita: $19 (1997).
Education: High school graduation rate: 80.5% (2000); College graduation rate: 11.0% (2000).
Housing: Homeownership rate: 100.0% (2000); Median home value: $42,100 (2000); Median age of housing: 48 years (2000).
Transportation: Commute to work: 88.5% car, 0.0% public transportation, 11.5% walk, 0.0% work from home (2000); Travel time to work: 37.7% less than 15 minutes, 29.5% 15 to 30 minutes, 8.2% 30 to 45 minutes, 24.6% 45 to 60 minutes, 0.0% 60 minutes or more (2000)

WILLIAMSTOWN (unincorporated postal area, zip code 63473). Covers a land area of 62.563 square miles and a water area of 0.403 square miles. Located at 40.24° N. Lat.; 91.77° W. Long. Elevation is 721 feet.
Population: 282 (2000); Race: 100.0% White, 0.0% Black, 0.0% Asian, 0.0% American Indian and Alaska Native, 0.0% Hispanic of any race, 0.0% two or more races (2000); Density: 4.5 persons per square mile (2000); Age: 15.8% under 18, 18.8% over 64 (2000); Marriage status: 29.3% never married, 57.9% now married, 5.1% widowed, 7.7% divorced (2000); Foreign born: 0.0% (2000); Ancestry (includes multiple ancestries): 28.6% German, 23.4% Irish, 18.8% English, 13.2% United States or American, 4.9% Dutch (2000).
Economy: Employment by occupation: 21.7% management, 9.6% professional, 8.9% services, 19.7% sales, 8.3% farming, 0.0% construction, 31.8% production (2000).
Income: Per capita income: $15,713 (2000); Median household income: $19,821 (2000); Poverty rate: 16.4% (2000).
Education: High school graduation rate: 73.3% (2000); College graduation rate: 17.9% (2000).
Housing: Homeownership rate: 76.1% (2000); Median home value: $17,100 (2000); Median rent: $221 per month (2000); Median age of housing: 36 years (2000).
Transportation: Commute to work: 79.0% car, 0.0% public transportation, 4.5% walk, 16.6% work from home (2000); Travel time to work: 27.5% less than 15 minutes, 36.6% 15 to 30 minutes, 15.3% 30 to 45 minutes, 16.0% 45 to 60 minutes, 4.6% 60 minutes or more (2000)

Lincoln County

Located in eastern Missouri; bounded on the east by the Mississippi River and the Illinois border; drained by the Cuivre River. Covers a land area of 630.50 square miles, a water area of 9.90 square miles, and is located in the Central Time Zone. The county government was organized in 1818. County seat is Troy.

Lincoln County is part of the St. Louis, MO-IL MSA. The entire metro area includes: Clinton County, IL; Jersey County, IL; Madison County, IL; Monroe County, IL; St. Clair County, IL; Crawford County, MO (pt.)**; Franklin County, MO; Jefferson County, MO; Lincoln County, MO; St. Charles County, MO; St. Louis County, MO; Warren County, MO; St. Louis city, MO

Weather Station: Elsberry 1 S Elevation: 449 feet

	Jan	Feb	Mar	Apr	May	Jun	Jul	Aug	Sep	Oct	Nov	Dec
High	37	44	56	68	77	86	90	88	80	69	55	42
Low	17	22	32	42	52	61	66	63	55	43	33	23
Precip	2.0	2.0	3.5	4.0	4.2	3.4	3.3	3.3	3.4	2.9	3.5	3.0
Snow	6.8	4.6	2.9	0.7	0.0	0.0	0.0	0.0	0.0	tr	1.2	4.0

High and Low temperatures in degrees Fahrenheit; Precipitation and Snow in inches

Population: 38,944 (2000); Race: 95.9% White, 2.0% Black, 0.1% Asian, 0.4% American Indian and Alaska Native, 1.0% Hispanic of any race, 1.2% two or more races (2000); Density: 61.8 persons per square mile (2000); Age: 30.0% under 18, 10.8% over 64 (2000).
Religion: Five largest groups: 15.0% Catholic Church, 11.6% Southern Baptist Convention, 5.0% The United Methodist Church, 2.7% Christian Church (Disciples of Christ), 1.7% Lutheran Church—Missouri Synod (2000).
Economy: Unemployment rate: 5.2% (11/2002); Total civilian labor force: 19,056 (11/2002); Leading industries: 20.2% retail trade; 17.5% manufacturing; 12.9% construction (2000); Companies that employ more than 1,000 persons: 0 (2000); Companies that employ more than 100 persons: 7 (2000); Farms: 989 totaling 262,362 acres (1997); Minority business ownership rate: 0.0% (1997); Women business ownership rate: 27.0% (1997); Retail sales per capita: $6,647 (1997). Single-family building permits issued: 117 (2001) / 112 (2000); Multi-family building permits issued: 0 (2001) / 2 (2000).
Income: Per capita income: $17,149 (2000); Median household income: $42,592 (2000); Poverty rate: 8.3% (2000); Bankruptcy rate: 5.67% (2001).
Taxes: Total county taxes per capita: $157 (2000); County property taxes per capita: $31 (2000).
Education: High school graduation rate: 76.4% (2000); College graduation rate: 9.7% (2000).
Housing: Homeownership rate: 80.8% (2000); Median home value: $102,200 (2000); Median rent: $353 per month (2000); Median age of housing: 19 years (2000).
Health: Birth rate: 126.6 per 10,000 population (1998); Age adjusted death rate: 91.0 per 10,000 population (1999); Age adjusted cancer mortality rate: 194.1 deaths per 100,000 population (1999). Air Quality Index: 100% good, 0% moderate, 0% unhealthy (percent of days in 2000). Number of physicians: 3.3 per 10,000 population (1999); Number of hospital beds: 7.2 per 10,000 population (1999).
Elections: 2000 Presidential election results: 43.7% Gore, 53.7% Bush, 1.4% Nader, 0.6% Buchanan
National and State Parks: Cuivre River State Park; David Kessler Memorial State Wildlife Area; Vonaventure State Memorial Forest And; White Memorial State Wildlife Area; William Logan State Wildlife Area
Additional Information Contacts
Lincoln County Government Offices 636-528-6300
East Central Board of Realtors 636-462-2872
Troy Chamber of Commerce 636-462-8769

Lincoln County Communities

CAVE (town). Covers a land area of 0.988 square miles and a water area of 0 square miles. Located at 39.02° N. Lat.; 91.05° W. Long. Elevation is 500 feet.
Population: 7 (2000); Race: 100.0% White, 0.0% Black, 0.0% Asian, 0.0% American Indian and Alaska Native, 0.0% Hispanic of any race, 0.0% two or more races (2000); Density: 7.1 persons per square mile (2000); Age: 80.0%

under 18, 0.0% over 64 (2000); Marriage status: 0.0% never married, 0.0% now married, 0.0% widowed, 100.0% divorced (2000); Foreign born: 0.0% (2000); Ancestry (includes multiple ancestries): 100.0% German (2000).
Economy: Employment by occupation: 0.0% management, 0.0% professional, 0.0% services, 100.0% sales, 0.0% farming, 0.0% construction, 0.0% production (2000).
Income: Per capita income: $8,120 (2000); Median household income: $41,250 (2000); Poverty rate: 0.0% (2000).
Taxes: Total city taxes per capita: $10,667 (1997); City property taxes per capita: $83 (1997).
Education: High school graduation rate: 100.0% (2000); College graduation rate: 0.0% (2000).
Housing: Homeownership rate: 0.0% (2000); Median age of housing: 60 years (2000).
Transportation: Commute to work: 100.0% car, 0.0% public transportation, 0.0% walk, 0.0% work from home (2000); Travel time to work: 0.0% less than 15 minutes, 0.0% 15 to 30 minutes, 100.0% 30 to 45 minutes, 0.0% 45 to 60 minutes, 0.0% 60 minutes or more (2000)

CHAIN OF ROCKS (village). Covers a land area of 0.172 square miles and a water area of 0 square miles. Located at 38.91° N. Lat.; 90.80° W. Long. Elevation is 438 feet.
Population: 91 (2000); Race: 100.0% White, 0.0% Black, 0.0% Asian, 0.0% American Indian and Alaska Native, 0.0% Hispanic of any race, 0.0% two or more races (2000); Density: 528.1 persons per square mile (2000); Age: 21.2% under 18, 13.6% over 64 (2000); Marriage status: 28.8% never married, 44.2% now married, 9.6% widowed, 17.3% divorced (2000); Foreign born: 0.0% (2000); Ancestry (includes multiple ancestries): 53.0% German, 28.8% Irish, 10.6% United States or American, 3.0% English, 3.0% Scottish (2000).
Economy: Employment by occupation: 9.7% management, 0.0% professional, 22.6% services, 35.5% sales, 0.0% farming, 19.4% construction, 12.9% production (2000).
Income: Per capita income: $18,848 (2000); Median household income: $31,250 (2000); Poverty rate: 13.6% (2000).
Taxes: Total city taxes per capita: $363 (2000); City property taxes per capita: $88 (2000).
Education: High school graduation rate: 66.7% (2000); College graduation rate: 11.1% (2000).
Housing: Homeownership rate: 81.8% (2000); Median home value: $105,000 (2000); Median rent: $325 per month (2000); Median age of housing: 32 years (2000).
Transportation: Commute to work: 100.0% car, 0.0% public transportation, 0.0% walk, 0.0% work from home (2000); Travel time to work: 21.4% less than 15 minutes, 57.1% 15 to 30 minutes, 0.0% 30 to 45 minutes, 7.1% 45 to 60 minutes, 14.3% 60 minutes or more (2000)

ELSBERRY (city). Covers a land area of 1.168 square miles and a water area of 0 square miles. Located at 39.16° N. Lat.; 90.78° W. Long. Elevation is 450 feet.
History: Established 1871.
Population: 2,047 (2000); Race: 95.3% White, 2.3% Black, 0.6% Asian, 1.0% American Indian and Alaska Native, 1.7% Hispanic of any race, 0.3% two or more races (2000); Density: 1,751.9 persons per square mile (2000); Age: 32.6% under 18, 13.3% over 64 (2000); Marriage status: 24.1% never married, 53.9% now married, 7.5% widowed, 14.6% divorced (2000); Foreign born: 0.6% (2000); Ancestry (includes multiple ancestries): 22.3% German, 19.4% United States or American, 12.2% Irish, 11.3% Other groups, 10.3% English (2000).
Economy: Corn, soybeans, apples; hogs, cattle; light manufacturing; limestone products. Has a U.S. nursery (plant materials center). Employment by occupation: 10.9% management, 9.6% professional, 15.3% services, 19.6% sales, 2.8% farming, 15.6% construction, 26.2% production (2000).
Income: Per capita income: $14,615 (2000); Median household income: $27,917 (2000); Poverty rate: 14.7% (2000).
Taxes: Total city taxes per capita: $164 (1997); City property taxes per capita: $37 (1997).
Education: High school graduation rate: 69.8% (2000); College graduation rate: 8.5% (2000).

School District(s)

Elsberry R-II (KG-12)
2000 Enrollment: 915 573-898-5554
Housing: Homeownership rate: 70.1% (2000); Median home value: $65,900 (2000); Median rent: $339 per month (2000); Median age of housing: 40 years (2000).
Newspapers: The Elsberry Democrat (1 x week)
Transportation: Commute to work: 92.9% car, 0.0% public transportation, 3.7% walk, 1.0% work from home (2000); Travel time to work: 36.6% less than 15 minutes, 13.2% 15 to 30 minutes, 25.7% 30 to 45 minutes, 12.2% 45 to 60 minutes, 12.3% 60 minutes or more (2000)

FOLEY (city). Covers a land area of 0.147 square miles and a water area of 0 square miles. Located at 39.04° N. Lat.; 90.74° W. Long. Elevation is 450 feet.
Population: 178 (2000); Race: 96.3% White, 0.0% Black, 0.0% Asian, 0.0% American Indian and Alaska Native, 1.6% Hispanic of any race, 2.1% two or more races (2000); Density: 1,214.9 persons per square mile (2000); Age: 37.6% under 18, 12.7% over 64 (2000); Marriage status: 29.5% never married, 42.6% now married, 10.9% widowed, 17.1% divorced (2000); Foreign born: 1.6% (2000); Ancestry (includes multiple ancestries): 17.5% German, 12.7% Irish, 12.7% United States or American, 11.6% Other groups, 3.7% English (2000).
Economy: Single-family building permits issued: 0 (2001) / 0 (2000); Multi-family building permits issued: 0 (2001) / 0 (2000); Employment by occupation: 9.7% management, 4.2% professional, 18.1% services, 16.7% sales, 5.6% farming, 27.8% construction, 18.1% production (2000).
Income: Per capita income: $9,902 (2000); Median household income: $29,000 (2000); Poverty rate: 16.9% (2000).
Taxes: Total city taxes per capita: $117 (1997); City property taxes per capita: $18 (1997).
Education: High school graduation rate: 57.4% (2000); College graduation rate: 0.9% (2000).
Housing: Homeownership rate: 73.1% (2000); Median home value: $33,200 (2000); Median rent: $367 per month (2000); Median age of housing: 44 years (2000).
Transportation: Commute to work: 88.9% car, 0.0% public transportation, 4.2% walk, 6.9% work from home (2000); Travel time to work: 16.4% less than 15 minutes, 22.4% 15 to 30 minutes, 16.4% 30 to 45 minutes, 29.9% 45 to 60 minutes, 14.9% 60 minutes or more (2000)

FOUNTAIN N' LAKES (village). Covers a land area of 0.143 square miles and a water area of 0 square miles. Located at 38.96° N. Lat.; 90.85° W. Long. Elevation is 605 feet.
Population: 129 (2000); Race: 98.3% White, 0.0% Black, 0.0% Asian, 1.7% American Indian and Alaska Native, 0.0% Hispanic of any race, 0.0% two or more races (2000); Density: 904.1 persons per square mile (2000); Age: 25.2% under 18, 9.6% over 64 (2000); Marriage status: 27.8% never married, 51.1% now married, 5.6% widowed, 15.6% divorced (2000); Foreign born: 0.0% (2000); Ancestry (includes multiple ancestries): 17.4% Irish, 13.9% Other groups, 10.4% German, 7.8% United States or American, 2.6% French (except Basque) (2000).
Economy: Employment by occupation: 1.9% management, 3.8% professional, 23.1% services, 13.5% sales, 0.0% farming, 13.5% construction, 44.2% production (2000).
Income: Per capita income: $14,108 (2000); Median household income: $30,313 (2000); Poverty rate: 15.7% (2000).
Taxes: Total city taxes per capita: $178 (2000); City property taxes per capita: $39 (2000).
Education: High school graduation rate: 56.6% (2000); College graduation rate: 2.6% (2000).
Housing: Homeownership rate: 85.1% (2000); Median rent: $225 per month (2000); Median age of housing: 18 years (2000).
Transportation: Commute to work: 100.0% car, 0.0% public transportation, 0.0% walk, 0.0% work from home (2000); Travel time to work: 3.8% less than 15 minutes, 13.5% 15 to 30 minutes, 30.8% 30 to 45 minutes, 26.9% 45 to 60 minutes, 25.0% 60 minutes or more (2000)

HAWK POINT (city). Covers a land area of 0.252 square miles and a water area of 0 square miles. Located at 38.97° N. Lat.; 91.13° W. Long. Elevation is 730 feet.
History: Hawk Point was settled in the early 1840's as a Bohemian community in the timber lands of the Cuivre River Valley.
Population: 459 (2000); Race: 98.4% White, 0.0% Black, 0.0% Asian, 0.0% American Indian and Alaska Native, 0.0% Hispanic of any race, 1.6% two or more races (2000); Density: 1,820.8 persons per square mile (2000); Age: 30.7% under 18, 21.5% over 64 (2000); Marriage status: 26.0% never married, 43.8% now married, 15.7% widowed, 14.5% divorced (2000); Foreign born: 0.5% (2000); Ancestry (includes multiple ancestries): 33.9% German, 12.9% Irish, 12.2% United States or American, 9.5% Other groups, 8.3% Czech (2000).
Economy: Single-family building permits issued: 2 (2001) / 0 (2000); Multi-family building permits issued: 0 (2001) / 0 (2000); Employment by

occupation: 0.0% management, 6.4% professional, 11.7% services, 21.6% sales, 0.0% farming, 18.1% construction, 42.1% production (2000).
Income: Per capita income: $14,823 (2000); Median household income: $29,286 (2000); Poverty rate: 9.6% (2000).
Taxes: Total city taxes per capita: $133 (1997); City property taxes per capita: $23 (1997).
Education: High school graduation rate: 67.0% (2000); College graduation rate: 1.9% (2000).
Housing: Homeownership rate: 67.0% (2000); Median home value: $76,100 (2000); Median rent: $317 per month (2000); Median age of housing: 23 years (2000).
Transportation: Commute to work: 90.8% car, 0.0% public transportation, 3.1% walk, 3.7% work from home (2000); Travel time to work: 14.0% less than 15 minutes, 34.4% 15 to 30 minutes, 20.4% 30 to 45 minutes, 15.3% 45 to 60 minutes, 15.9% 60 minutes or more (2000)

MOSCOW MILLS (city). Covers a land area of 1.874 square miles and a water area of 0 square miles. Located at 38.94° N. Lat.; 90.92° W. Long. Elevation is 530 feet.
History: Moscow Mills began as a farm village overlooking the Cuivre River. It was platted in 1821.
Population: 1,742 (2000); Race: 92.6% White, 4.8% Black, 0.2% Asian, 0.0% American Indian and Alaska Native, 0.8% Hispanic of any race, 2.3% two or more races (2000); Density: 929.3 persons per square mile (2000); Age: 34.2% under 18, 5.4% over 64 (2000); Marriage status: 25.1% never married, 52.9% now married, 3.8% widowed, 18.2% divorced (2000); Foreign born: 1.0% (2000); Ancestry (includes multiple ancestries): 28.2% German, 22.2% United States or American, 15.9% Other groups, 10.0% Irish, 4.6% English (2000).
Economy: Employment by occupation: 6.7% management, 8.5% professional, 14.1% services, 26.7% sales, 0.3% farming, 18.5% construction, 25.2% production (2000).
Income: Per capita income: $14,555 (2000); Median household income: $37,067 (2000); Poverty rate: 8.7% (2000).
Taxes: Total city taxes per capita: $252 (1997); City property taxes per capita: $27 (1997).
Education: High school graduation rate: 75.4% (2000); College graduation rate: 5.7% (2000).
Housing: Homeownership rate: 79.7% (2000); Median home value: $78,800 (2000); Median rent: $394 per month (2000); Median age of housing: 6 years (2000).
Transportation: Commute to work: 96.3% car, 1.3% public transportation, 2.3% walk, 0.1% work from home (2000); Travel time to work: 27.9% less than 15 minutes, 27.7% 15 to 30 minutes, 22.7% 30 to 45 minutes, 11.4% 45 to 60 minutes, 10.3% 60 minutes or more (2000)

OLD MONROE (city). Covers a land area of 0.151 square miles and a water area of 0 square miles. Located at 38.93° N. Lat.; 90.74° W. Long. Elevation is 438 feet.
Population: 250 (2000); Race: 99.2% White, 0.0% Black, 0.0% Asian, 0.0% American Indian and Alaska Native, 0.0% Hispanic of any race, 0.8% two or more races (2000); Density: 1,654.1 persons per square mile (2000); Age: 26.3% under 18, 21.9% over 64 (2000); Marriage status: 30.1% never married, 51.8% now married, 10.4% widowed, 7.8% divorced (2000); Foreign born: 0.0% (2000); Ancestry (includes multiple ancestries): 31.2% German, 13.4% Dutch, 11.7% United States or American, 8.1% Irish, 7.7% English (2000).
Economy: Lumber; fertilizers and feed. Single-family building permits issued: 1 (2001) / 0 (2000); Multi-family building permits issued: 0 (2001) / 0 (2000); Employment by occupation: 5.3% management, 10.5% professional, 13.2% services, 22.8% sales, 0.0% farming, 17.5% construction, 30.7% production (2000).
Income: Per capita income: $15,457 (2000); Median household income: $31,429 (2000); Poverty rate: 4.5% (2000).
Taxes: Total city taxes per capita: $240 (1997); City property taxes per capita: $8 (1997).
Education: High school graduation rate: 70.5% (2000); College graduation rate: 10.2% (2000).
Housing: Homeownership rate: 72.5% (2000); Median home value: $77,000 (2000); Median rent: $408 per month (2000); Median age of housing: 52 years (2000).
Transportation: Commute to work: 95.4% car, 0.0% public transportation, 1.8% walk, 2.8% work from home (2000); Travel time to work: 15.1% less than 15 minutes, 54.7% 15 to 30 minutes, 14.2% 30 to 45 minutes, 15.1% 45 to 60 minutes, 0.9% 60 minutes or more (2000)

OLNEY (unincorporated postal area, zip code 63370). Covers a land area of 1.769 square miles and a water area of 0 square miles. Located at 39.08° N. Lat.; 91.22° W. Long. Elevation is 710 feet.
Population: 41 (2000); Race: 100.0% White, 0.0% Black, 0.0% Asian, 0.0% American Indian and Alaska Native, 0.0% Hispanic of any race, 0.0% two or more races (2000); Density: 23.2 persons per square mile (2000); Age: 0.0% under 18, 0.0% over 64 (2000); Marriage status: 72.5% never married, 27.5% now married, 0.0% widowed, 0.0% divorced (2000); Foreign born: 0.0% (2000); Ancestry (includes multiple ancestries): 72.5% German, 15.0% English (2000).
Economy: Employment by occupation: 0.0% management, 0.0% professional, 0.0% services, 82.9% sales, 0.0% farming, 0.0% construction, 17.1% production (2000).
Income: Per capita income: $20,180 (2000); Median household income: $48,542 (2000); Poverty rate: 0.0% (2000).
Education: High school graduation rate: 100.0% (2000); College graduation rate: 0.0% (2000).
Housing: Homeownership rate: 64.7% (2000); Median home value: $187,500 (2000); Median age of housing: 32 years (2000).
Transportation: Commute to work: 100.0% car, 0.0% public transportation, 0.0% walk, 0.0% work from home (2000); Travel time to work: 0.0% less than 15 minutes, 14.3% 15 to 30 minutes, 85.7% 30 to 45 minutes, 0.0% 45 to 60 minutes, 0.0% 60 minutes or more (2000)

SILEX (village). Covers a land area of 0.192 square miles and a water area of 0 square miles. Located at 39.12° N. Lat.; 91.05° W. Long. Elevation is 508 feet.
Population: 206 (2000); Race: 95.2% White, 0.0% Black, 0.0% Asian, 1.0% American Indian and Alaska Native, 2.9% Hispanic of any race, 1.0% two or more races (2000); Density: 1,074.5 persons per square mile (2000); Age: 23.1% under 18, 13.5% over 64 (2000); Marriage status: 25.9% never married, 54.2% now married, 3.0% widowed, 16.9% divorced (2000); Foreign born: 0.0% (2000); Ancestry (includes multiple ancestries): 31.7% United States or American, 22.6% Irish, 16.3% German, 11.1% English, 5.8% Other groups (2000).
Economy: Single-family building permits issued: 0 (2001) / 0 (2000); Multi-family building permits issued: 0 (2001) / 0 (2000); Employment by occupation: 6.7% management, 6.7% professional, 14.4% services, 12.2% sales, 0.0% farming, 28.9% construction, 31.1% production (2000).
Income: Per capita income: $12,529 (2000); Median household income: $24,531 (2000); Poverty rate: 12.5% (2000).
Taxes: Total city taxes per capita: $75 (1997); City property taxes per capita: $5 (1997).
Education: High school graduation rate: 68.1% (2000); College graduation rate: 9.6% (2000).

School District(s)

Silex R-I (KG-12)
2000 Enrollment: 371 573-384-5227
Housing: Homeownership rate: 73.2% (2000); Median home value: $38,800 (2000); Median rent: $338 per month (2000); Median age of housing: 60+ years (2000).
Transportation: Commute to work: 95.5% car, 0.0% public transportation, 0.0% walk, 3.4% work from home (2000); Travel time to work: 32.9% less than 15 minutes, 15.3% 15 to 30 minutes, 31.8% 30 to 45 minutes, 7.1% 45 to 60 minutes, 12.9% 60 minutes or more (2000)

TROY (city). Covers a land area of 5.938 square miles and a water area of 0.010 square miles. Located at 38.97° N. Lat.; 90.97° W. Long. Elevation is 545 feet.
History: Troy was platted in 1819 and named for Troy, New York. The town was located on the site of Woods' Fort, built during the War of 1812. In 1828 Troy became the seat of Lincoln County.
Population: 6,737 (2000); Race: 94.4% White, 2.3% Black, 0.0% Asian, 1.1% American Indian and Alaska Native, 1.5% Hispanic of any race, 2.0% two or more races (2000); Density: 1,134.5 persons per square mile (2000); Age: 30.9% under 18, 13.4% over 64 (2000); Marriage status: 22.8% never married, 56.2% now married, 8.8% widowed, 12.2% divorced (2000); Foreign born: 0.3% (2000); Ancestry (includes multiple ancestries): 27.0% German, 12.9% Irish, 11.6% Other groups, 10.5% United States or American, 8.3% English (2000).
Economy: Single-family building permits issued: 114 (2001) / 112 (2000); Multi-family building permits issued: 0 (2001) / 2 (2000); Employment by occupation: 8.4% management, 18.5% professional, 17.3% services, 24.7% sales, 0.3% farming, 12.2% construction, 18.7% production (2000).

Income: Per capita income: $17,666 (2000); Median household income: $40,332 (2000); Poverty rate: 11.0% (2000).
Taxes: Total city taxes per capita: $486 (2000); City property taxes per capita: $42 (2000).
Education: High school graduation rate: 78.3% (2000); College graduation rate: 14.9% (2000).

School District(s)

Troy R-III (KG-12)
2000 Enrollment: 4,484 636-462-6098
Housing: Homeownership rate: 64.6% (2000); Median home value: $92,900 (2000); Median rent: $373 per month (2000); Median age of housing: 17 years (2000).
Newspapers: Troy Free Press (1 x week); Lincoln County Journal (1 x week)
Transportation: Commute to work: 94.9% car, 0.0% public transportation, 0.8% walk, 4.1% work from home (2000); Travel time to work: 44.6% less than 15 minutes, 24.6% 15 to 30 minutes, 17.8% 30 to 45 minutes, 8.6% 45 to 60 minutes, 4.3% 60 minutes or more (2000)

Additional Information Contacts

East Central Board of Realtors 636-462-2872
Troy Chamber of Commerce 636-462-8769

TRUXTON (village). Covers a land area of 0.245 square miles and a water area of 0 square miles. Located at 39.00° N. Lat.; 91.24° W. Long. Elevation is 738 feet.
Population: 96 (2000); Race: 98.3% White, 0.0% Black, 0.0% Asian, 0.0% American Indian and Alaska Native, 0.0% Hispanic of any race, 1.7% two or more races (2000); Density: 392.1 persons per square mile (2000); Age: 17.4% under 18, 19.1% over 64 (2000); Marriage status: 25.3% never married, 67.4% now married, 0.0% widowed, 7.4% divorced (2000); Foreign born: 3.5% (2000); Ancestry (includes multiple ancestries): 27.8% German, 22.6% Other groups, 14.8% United States or American, 13.9% Irish, 8.7% English (2000).
Economy: Employment by occupation: 17.8% management, 8.9% professional, 17.8% services, 22.2% sales, 0.0% farming, 0.0% construction, 33.3% production (2000).
Income: Per capita income: $15,901 (2000); Median household income: $40,625 (2000); Poverty rate: 7.0% (2000).
Taxes: Total city taxes per capita: $29 (1997); City property taxes per capita: $10 (1997).
Education: High school graduation rate: 55.3% (2000); College graduation rate: 0.0% (2000).
Housing: Homeownership rate: 71.4% (2000); Median home value: $52,500 (2000); Median rent: $238 per month (2000); Median age of housing: 60+ years (2000).
Transportation: Commute to work: 84.1% car, 0.0% public transportation, 0.0% walk, 15.9% work from home (2000); Travel time to work: 5.4% less than 15 minutes, 27.0% 15 to 30 minutes, 43.2% 30 to 45 minutes, 5.4% 45 to 60 minutes, 18.9% 60 minutes or more (2000)

WHITESIDE (village). Covers a land area of 0.091 square miles and a water area of <.001 square miles. Located at 39.18° N. Lat.; 91.01° W. Long. Elevation is 795 feet.
Population: 67 (2000); Race: 100.0% White, 0.0% Black, 0.0% Asian, 0.0% American Indian and Alaska Native, 0.0% Hispanic of any race, 0.0% two or more races (2000); Density: 737.7 persons per square mile (2000); Age: 28.1% under 18, 15.6% over 64 (2000); Marriage status: 17.3% never married, 55.8% now married, 9.6% widowed, 17.3% divorced (2000); Foreign born: 0.0% (2000); Ancestry (includes multiple ancestries): 17.2% German, 15.6% United States or American, 9.4% Italian, 4.7% Irish, 4.7% Polish (2000).
Economy: Employment by occupation: 12.0% management, 8.0% professional, 20.0% services, 0.0% sales, 0.0% farming, 16.0% construction, 44.0% production (2000).
Income: Per capita income: $16,297 (2000); Median household income: $41,250 (2000); Poverty rate: 12.5% (2000).
Taxes: Total city taxes per capita: $11 (1997); City property taxes per capita: $11 (1997).
Education: High school graduation rate: 65.9% (2000); College graduation rate: 14.6% (2000).
Housing: Homeownership rate: 75.0% (2000); Median home value: $55,000 (2000); Median rent: $375 per month (2000); Median age of housing: 54 years (2000).
Transportation: Commute to work: 100.0% car, 0.0% public transportation, 0.0% walk, 0.0% work from home (2000); Travel time to work: 34.8% less than 15 minutes, 8.7% 15 to 30 minutes, 17.4% 30 to 45 minutes, 39.1% 45 to 60 minutes, 0.0% 60 minutes or more (2000)

WINFIELD (city). Covers a land area of 0.559 square miles and a water area of 0 square miles. Located at 38.99° N. Lat.; 90.74° W. Long. Elevation is 446 feet.
Population: 723 (2000); Race: 97.0% White, 0.1% Black, 1.1% Asian, 1.1% American Indian and Alaska Native, 0.4% Hispanic of any race, 0.7% two or more races (2000); Density: 1,293.5 persons per square mile (2000); Age: 28.6% under 18, 12.2% over 64 (2000); Marriage status: 26.9% never married, 51.6% now married, 6.3% widowed, 15.2% divorced (2000); Foreign born: 0.0% (2000); Ancestry (includes multiple ancestries): 29.2% German, 19.3% United States or American, 16.5% Irish, 9.2% Other groups, 7.4% English (2000).
Economy: Manufacturing of apparel, furniture. Lock and Dam No. 25 (Winfield Dam). Employment by occupation: 4.5% management, 8.0% professional, 14.9% services, 19.6% sales, 0.0% farming, 23.2% construction, 29.8% production (2000).
Income: Per capita income: $17,740 (2000); Median household income: $36,167 (2000); Poverty rate: 15.8% (2000).
Taxes: Total city taxes per capita: $213 (1997); City property taxes per capita: $17 (1997).
Education: High school graduation rate: 62.5% (2000); College graduation rate: 7.1% (2000).

School District(s)

Winfield R-IV (PK-12)
2000 Enrollment: 1,532 636-668-8188
Housing: Homeownership rate: 54.9% (2000); Median home value: $77,100 (2000); Median rent: $340 per month (2000); Median age of housing: 21 years (2000).
Transportation: Commute to work: 95.7% car, 0.6% public transportation, 3.6% walk, 0.0% work from home (2000); Travel time to work: 18.5% less than 15 minutes, 25.2% 15 to 30 minutes, 30.4% 30 to 45 minutes, 18.5% 45 to 60 minutes, 7.3% 60 minutes or more (2000)

Linn County

Located in north central Missouri; crossed by Locust Creek. Covers a land area of 620.40 square miles, a water area of 1.10 square miles, and is located in the Central Time Zone. The county government was organized in 1837. County seat is Linneus.

Weather Station: Brookfield Elevation: 764 feet

	Jan	Feb	Mar	Apr	May	Jun	Jul	Aug	Sep	Oct	Nov	Dec
High	34	42	54	66	75	84	89	87	80	68	52	39
Low	17	22	32	43	53	63	67	65	57	45	33	23
Precip	1.5	1.4	2.7	3.8	5.0	4.0	4.6	4.1	4.6	3.4	2.9	2.0
Snow	4.8	3.2	1.7	0.5	0.0	0.0	0.0	0.0	0.0	tr	1.2	2.4

High and Low temperatures in degrees Fahrenheit; Precipitation and Snow in inches

Population: 13,754 (2000); Race: 97.8% White, 0.9% Black, 0.2% Asian, 0.4% American Indian and Alaska Native, 0.7% Hispanic of any race, 0.7% two or more races (2000); Density: 22.2 persons per square mile (2000); Age: 25.2% under 18, 20.5% over 64 (2000).
Religion: Five largest groups: 32.9% Southern Baptist Convention, 15.0% The United Methodist Church, 7.4% Christian Church (Disciples of Christ), 6.3% Catholic Church, 1.5% Assemblies of God (2000).
Economy: Unemployment rate: 9.7% (11/2002); Total civilian labor force: 6,330 (11/2002); Leading industries: 46.4% manufacturing; 14.3% retail trade; 12.4% health care and social assistance (2000); Companies that employ more than 1,000 persons: 1 (2000); Companies that employ more than 100 persons: 7 (2000); Farms: 933 totaling 346,184 acres (1997); Minority business ownership rate: 0.0% (1997); Women business ownership rate: 21.2% (1997); Retail sales per capita: $5,766 (1997). Single-family building permits issued: 6 (2001) / 6 (2000); Multi-family building permits issued: 4 (2001) / 4 (2000).
Income: Per capita income: $15,378 (2000); Median household income: $28,242 (2000); Poverty rate: 14.9% (2000); Bankruptcy rate: 3.41% (2001).
Taxes: Total county taxes per capita: $47 (2000); County property taxes per capita: $7 (2000).
Education: High school graduation rate: 80.0% (2000); College graduation rate: 10.8% (2000).
Housing: Homeownership rate: 77.0% (2000); Median home value: $42,200 (2000); Median rent: $203 per month (2000); Median age of housing: 44 years (2000).
Health: Birth rate: 122.2 per 10,000 population (1998); Age adjusted death rate: 94.0 per 10,000 population (1999); Age adjusted cancer mortality rate: 190.5 deaths per 100,000 population (1999). Number of physicians: 3.6 per

10,000 population (1999); Number of hospital beds: 21.1 per 10,000 population (1999).
Elections: 2000 Presidential election results: 44.0% Gore, 54.0% Bush, 1.1% Nader, 0.5% Buchanan
National and State Parks: Pershing State Park
Additional Information Contacts
Linn County Government Offices 660-895-5417
Brookfield Chamber of Commerce 660-258-7255

Linn County Communities

BROOKFIELD (city). Covers a land area of 4.296 square miles and a water area of 0.004 square miles. Located at 39.78° N. Lat.; 93.07° W. Long. Elevation is 767 feet.
History: Brookfield was platted in 1859 when Major Josiah Hunt planned the town as a shipping point on the new Hannibal & St. Joseph Railroad. Many of the early residents here were Irish workmen who had been employed by the railroad.
Population: 4,769 (2000); Race: 96.4% White, 2.2% Black, 0.0% Asian, 0.6% American Indian and Alaska Native, 1.4% Hispanic of any race, 0.7% two or more races (2000); Density: 1,110.2 persons per square mile (2000); Age: 23.4% under 18, 25.1% over 64 (2000); Marriage status: 17.8% never married, 51.9% now married, 16.4% widowed, 13.9% divorced (2000); Foreign born: 0.8% (2000); Ancestry (includes multiple ancestries): 24.1% German, 15.1% United States or American, 14.1% Irish, 11.1% English, 8.1% Other groups (2000).
Economy: Single-family building permits issued: 4 (2001) / 4 (2000); Multi-family building permits issued: 4 (2001) / 4 (2000); Employment by occupation: 7.1% management, 16.8% professional, 15.0% services, 22.6% sales, 1.2% farming, 8.3% construction, 29.1% production (2000).
Income: Per capita income: $14,842 (2000); Median household income: $25,753 (2000); Poverty rate: 19.1% (2000).
Taxes: Total city taxes per capita: $441 (2000); City property taxes per capita: $39 (2000).
Education: High school graduation rate: 77.5% (2000); College graduation rate: 9.8% (2000).

School District(s)

Brookfield R-III (PK-12)
2000 Enrollment: 1,283 660-258-7443
Housing: Homeownership rate: 71.6% (2000); Median home value: $44,800 (2000); Median rent: $199 per month (2000); Median age of housing: 45 years (2000).
Hospitals: General JJ Pershing Memorial Hospital (57 beds)
Safety: Violent crime rate: 12.5 per 10,000 population; Property crime rate: 260.5 per 10,000 population (2001).
Newspapers: News-Bulletin (5 x week)
Transportation: Commute to work: 91.5% car, 0.9% public transportation, 2.5% walk, 3.3% work from home (2000); Travel time to work: 69.9% less than 15 minutes, 15.1% 15 to 30 minutes, 4.7% 30 to 45 minutes, 3.4% 45 to 60 minutes, 6.9% 60 minutes or more (2000)
Additional Information Contacts
Brookfield Chamber of Commerce 660-258-7255

BROWNING (city). Covers a land area of 0.524 square miles and a water area of 0 square miles. Located at 40.03° N. Lat.; 93.16° W. Long. Elevation is 765 feet.
Population: 317 (2000); Race: 97.8% White, 0.0% Black, 0.0% Asian, 0.0% American Indian and Alaska Native, 0.0% Hispanic of any race, 2.2% two or more races (2000); Density: 604.5 persons per square mile (2000); Age: 18.1% under 18, 28.7% over 64 (2000); Marriage status: 21.9% never married, 52.6% now married, 13.1% widowed, 12.4% divorced (2000); Foreign born: 0.0% (2000); Ancestry (includes multiple ancestries): 19.4% United States or American, 17.5% German, 10.3% Irish, 9.4% Other groups, 8.4% English (2000).
Economy: Employment by occupation: 4.3% management, 10.3% professional, 15.4% services, 14.5% sales, 10.3% farming, 11.1% construction, 34.2% production (2000).
Income: Per capita income: $11,266 (2000); Median household income: $19,167 (2000); Poverty rate: 26.9% (2000).
Taxes: Total city taxes per capita: $50 (1997); City property taxes per capita: $12 (1997).
Education: High school graduation rate: 62.9% (2000); College graduation rate: 3.0% (2000).
Housing: Homeownership rate: 81.4% (2000); Median home value: $18,600 (2000); Median rent: $181 per month (2000); Median age of housing: 60+ years (2000).
Transportation: Commute to work: 93.7% car, 0.0% public transportation, 0.9% walk, 5.4% work from home (2000); Travel time to work: 11.4% less than 15 minutes, 57.1% 15 to 30 minutes, 16.2% 30 to 45 minutes, 11.4% 45 to 60 minutes, 3.8% 60 minutes or more (2000)

BUCKLIN (city). Covers a land area of 1.184 square miles and a water area of 0 square miles. Located at 39.78° N. Lat.; 92.88° W. Long. Elevation is 910 feet.
Population: 524 (2000); Race: 98.0% White, 0.0% Black, 0.0% Asian, 0.0% American Indian and Alaska Native, 3.3% Hispanic of any race, 0.7% two or more races (2000); Density: 442.6 persons per square mile (2000); Age: 21.5% under 18, 27.2% over 64 (2000); Marriage status: 14.2% never married, 56.5% now married, 15.6% widowed, 13.7% divorced (2000); Foreign born: 0.6% (2000); Ancestry (includes multiple ancestries): 19.6% German, 11.5% Irish, 10.0% United States or American, 7.8% Other groups, 5.9% English (2000).
Economy: Corn, wheat, soybeans; sheep, cattle. Railroad junction. Single-family building permits issued: 0 (2001) / 0 (2000); Multi-family building permits issued: 0 (2001) / 0 (2000); Employment by occupation: 9.6% management, 12.8% professional, 17.8% services, 21.9% sales, 0.9% farming, 10.0% construction, 26.9% production (2000).
Income: Per capita income: $13,709 (2000); Median household income: $21,490 (2000); Poverty rate: 20.0% (2000).
Taxes: Total city taxes per capita: $170 (1997); City property taxes per capita: $90 (1997).
Education: High school graduation rate: 74.2% (2000); College graduation rate: 11.2% (2000).

School District(s)

Bucklin R-II (PK-12)
2000 Enrollment: 190 660-695-3225
Housing: Homeownership rate: 76.2% (2000); Median home value: $27,700 (2000); Median rent: $191 per month (2000); Median age of housing: 47 years (2000).
Transportation: Commute to work: 92.1% car, 0.0% public transportation, 6.1% walk, 1.9% work from home (2000); Travel time to work: 36.2% less than 15 minutes, 43.3% 15 to 30 minutes, 10.5% 30 to 45 minutes, 0.0% 45 to 60 minutes, 10.0% 60 minutes or more (2000)

LACLEDE (city). Covers a land area of 1.245 square miles and a water area of 0.013 square miles. Located at 39.78° N. Lat.; 93.17° W. Long. Elevation is 794 feet.
History: Laclede was the boyhood home of General John J. Pershing, who was born near here in 1860 and had a long and distinguished military career, including being commander-in-chief of the American Expeditionary Forces during World War I.
Population: 415 (2000); Race: 97.7% White, 1.2% Black, 0.0% Asian, 0.5% American Indian and Alaska Native, 0.5% Hispanic of any race, 0.7% two or more races (2000); Density: 333.3 persons per square mile (2000); Age: 24.2% under 18, 18.0% over 64 (2000); Marriage status: 16.8% never married, 61.4% now married, 12.8% widowed, 9.1% divorced (2000); Foreign born: 0.7% (2000); Ancestry (includes multiple ancestries): 23.0% United States or American, 14.1% German, 11.5% Irish, 8.5% English, 8.3% Other groups (2000).
Economy: Employment by occupation: 2.3% management, 7.0% professional, 25.1% services, 11.7% sales, 0.0% farming, 18.7% construction, 35.1% production (2000).
Income: Per capita income: $11,890 (2000); Median household income: $24,688 (2000); Poverty rate: 19.8% (2000).
Taxes: Total city taxes per capita: $69 (1997); City property taxes per capita: $34 (1997).
Education: High school graduation rate: 68.0% (2000); College graduation rate: 2.9% (2000).
Housing: Homeownership rate: 68.6% (2000); Median home value: $24,500 (2000); Median rent: $186 per month (2000); Median age of housing: 36 years (2000).
Transportation: Commute to work: 97.0% car, 0.0% public transportation, 2.4% walk, 0.6% work from home (2000); Travel time to work: 31.5% less than 15 minutes, 42.3% 15 to 30 minutes, 11.3% 30 to 45 minutes, 0.0% 45 to 60 minutes, 14.9% 60 minutes or more (2000)

LINNEUS (city). Covers a land area of 1.082 square miles and a water area of 0 square miles. Located at 39.87° N. Lat.; 93.18° W. Long. Elevation is 837 feet.

Population: 369 (2000); Race: 97.8% White, 2.2% Black, 0.0% Asian, 0.0% American Indian and Alaska Native, 0.0% Hispanic of any race, 0.0% two or more races (2000); Density: 341.0 persons per square mile (2000); Age: 24.9% under 18, 19.6% over 64 (2000); Marriage status: 24.6% never married, 54.7% now married, 11.1% widowed, 9.7% divorced (2000); Foreign born: 0.0% (2000); Ancestry (includes multiple ancestries): 18.2% German, 17.4% United States or American, 8.6% Irish, 8.0% Other groups, 7.5% English (2000).
Economy: Corn, wheat, soybeans; sheep, cattle, hogs. Employment by occupation: 8.5% management, 13.7% professional, 9.8% services, 22.9% sales, 1.3% farming, 14.4% construction, 29.4% production (2000).
Income: Per capita income: $12,437 (2000); Median household income: $26,250 (2000); Poverty rate: 20.8% (2000).
Taxes: Total city taxes per capita: $198 (1997); City property taxes per capita: $154 (1997).
Education: High school graduation rate: 75.5% (2000); College graduation rate: 7.5% (2000).
Housing: Homeownership rate: 79.6% (2000); Median home value: $31,000 (2000); Median rent: $173 per month (2000); Median age of housing: 58 years (2000).
Transportation: Commute to work: 96.7% car, 0.0% public transportation, 0.7% walk, 2.0% work from home (2000); Travel time to work: 24.7% less than 15 minutes, 40.0% 15 to 30 minutes, 24.0% 30 to 45 minutes, 5.3% 45 to 60 minutes, 6.0% 60 minutes or more (2000)

MARCELINE (city). Covers a land area of 3.250 square miles and a water area of 0.028 square miles. Located at 39.71° N. Lat.; 92.94° W. Long. Elevation is 860 feet.
History: Marceline began as a freight division point on the Atchison, Topeka & Santa Fe Railroad. This was the boyhood home of Walt Disney, creator of animated cartoons, who is said to have painted cartoons with tar on his grandfather's white barn door when he was about ten.
Population: 2,558 (2000); Race: 99.1% White, 0.0% Black, 0.7% Asian, 0.1% American Indian and Alaska Native, 0.3% Hispanic of any race, 0.1% two or more races (2000); Density: 787.1 persons per square mile (2000); Age: 26.6% under 18, 19.7% over 64 (2000); Marriage status: 18.9% never married, 54.2% now married, 12.2% widowed, 14.8% divorced (2000); Foreign born: 0.9% (2000); Ancestry (includes multiple ancestries): 21.6% German, 14.9% Irish, 12.2% United States or American, 8.7% English, 6.3% Other groups (2000).
Economy: Single-family building permits issued: 2 (2001) / 2 (2000); Multi-family building permits issued: 0 (2001) / 0 (2000); Employment by occupation: 11.0% management, 12.7% professional, 10.7% services, 23.3% sales, 1.6% farming, 9.0% construction, 31.7% production (2000).
Income: Per capita income: $15,086 (2000); Median household income: $25,164 (2000); Poverty rate: 13.1% (2000).
Taxes: Total city taxes per capita: $174 (1997); City property taxes per capita: $72 (1997).
Education: High school graduation rate: 77.9% (2000); College graduation rate: 10.2% (2000).

School District(s)

Marceline R-V (KG-12)
2000 Enrollment: 775 660-376-3371
Housing: Homeownership rate: 73.7% (2000); Median home value: $41,000 (2000); Median rent: $223 per month (2000); Median age of housing: 48 years (2000).
Newspapers: The Marceline Press (1 x week)
Transportation: Commute to work: 92.3% car, 0.0% public transportation, 2.7% walk, 4.1% work from home (2000); Travel time to work: 60.3% less than 15 minutes, 29.9% 15 to 30 minutes, 3.4% 30 to 45 minutes, 1.7% 45 to 60 minutes, 4.7% 60 minutes or more (2000)

MEADVILLE (city). Covers a land area of 0.409 square miles and a water area of 0 square miles. Located at 39.78° N. Lat.; 93.30° W. Long. Elevation is 756 feet.
Population: 457 (2000); Race: 98.3% White, 0.4% Black, 0.4% Asian, 0.0% American Indian and Alaska Native, 0.8% Hispanic of any race, 0.8% two or more races (2000); Density: 1,118.4 persons per square mile (2000); Age: 27.0% under 18, 21.5% over 64 (2000); Marriage status: 17.0% never married, 63.8% now married, 12.4% widowed, 6.8% divorced (2000); Foreign born: 1.7% (2000); Ancestry (includes multiple ancestries): 20.3% United States or American, 14.6% German, 9.3% English, 8.0% Irish, 4.0% European (2000).
Economy: Corn, wheat, soybeans; cattle. Employment by occupation: 7.1% management, 21.0% professional, 11.6% services, 22.8% sales, 1.8% farming, 13.8% construction, 21.9% production (2000).
Income: Per capita income: $14,427 (2000); Median household income: $32,841 (2000); Poverty rate: 6.1% (2000).
Taxes: Total city taxes per capita: $53 (1997); City property taxes per capita: $24 (1997).
Education: High school graduation rate: 87.0% (2000); College graduation rate: 15.6% (2000).

School District(s)

Meadville R-IV (PK-12)
2000 Enrollment: 306 660-938-4111
Housing: Homeownership rate: 83.6% (2000); Median home value: $41,100 (2000); Median rent: $186 per month (2000); Median age of housing: 39 years (2000).
Transportation: Commute to work: 95.0% car, 0.0% public transportation, 1.8% walk, 3.2% work from home (2000); Travel time to work: 36.6% less than 15 minutes, 52.1% 15 to 30 minutes, 5.2% 30 to 45 minutes, 1.4% 45 to 60 minutes, 4.7% 60 minutes or more (2000)

NEW BOSTON (unincorporated postal area, zip code 63557). Covers a land area of 72.142 square miles and a water area of 0.014 square miles. Located at 39.96° N. Lat.; 92.88° W. Long. Elevation is 960 feet.
Population: 278 (2000); Race: 100.0% White, 0.0% Black, 0.0% Asian, 0.0% American Indian and Alaska Native, 0.0% Hispanic of any race, 0.0% two or more races (2000); Density: 3.9 persons per square mile (2000); Age: 24.6% under 18, 19.9% over 64 (2000); Marriage status: 13.7% never married, 78.0% now married, 4.8% widowed, 3.5% divorced (2000); Foreign born: 0.0% (2000); Ancestry (includes multiple ancestries): 22.8% German, 17.4% Irish, 8.5% English, 8.2% United States or American, 6.0% Other groups (2000).
Economy: Employment by occupation: 24.6% management, 14.8% professional, 7.7% services, 30.3% sales, 2.8% farming, 11.3% construction, 8.5% production (2000).
Income: Per capita income: $15,692 (2000); Median household income: $33,068 (2000); Poverty rate: 7.9% (2000).
Education: High school graduation rate: 82.5% (2000); College graduation rate: 10.5% (2000).
Housing: Homeownership rate: 90.3% (2000); Median home value: $27,500 (2000); Median rent: <$100 per month (2000); Median age of housing: 46 years (2000).
Transportation: Commute to work: 78.7% car, 0.0% public transportation, 2.9% walk, 16.9% work from home (2000); Travel time to work: 15.9% less than 15 minutes, 34.5% 15 to 30 minutes, 31.0% 30 to 45 minutes, 9.7% 45 to 60 minutes, 8.8% 60 minutes or more (2000)

PURDIN (city). Covers a land area of 0.311 square miles and a water area of 0 square miles. Located at 39.95° N. Lat.; 93.16° W. Long. Elevation is 886 feet.
Population: 223 (2000); Race: 99.2% White, 0.0% Black, 0.0% Asian, 0.0% American Indian and Alaska Native, 0.8% Hispanic of any race, 0.8% two or more races (2000); Density: 717.1 persons per square mile (2000); Age: 33.3% under 18, 16.5% over 64 (2000); Marriage status: 15.7% never married, 62.4% now married, 13.5% widowed, 8.4% divorced (2000); Foreign born: 0.0% (2000); Ancestry (includes multiple ancestries): 13.7% German, 13.3% Irish, 11.2% English, 8.8% United States or American, 5.2% Other groups (2000).
Economy: Employment by occupation: 4.7% management, 19.8% professional, 22.1% services, 15.1% sales, 0.0% farming, 9.3% construction, 29.1% production (2000).
Income: Per capita income: $9,636 (2000); Median household income: $19,750 (2000); Poverty rate: 28.1% (2000).
Taxes: Total city taxes per capita: $18 (1997); City property taxes per capita: $18 (1997).
Education: High school graduation rate: 65.8% (2000); College graduation rate: 5.2% (2000).

School District(s)

Linn Co. R-I (PK-12)
2000 Enrollment: 309 660-244-5035
Housing: Homeownership rate: 72.5% (2000); Median home value: $16,300 (2000); Median rent: $163 per month (2000); Median age of housing: 60+ years (2000).
Transportation: Commute to work: 90.5% car, 3.6% public transportation, 2.4% walk, 3.6% work from home (2000); Travel time to work: 24.7% less than 15 minutes, 39.5% 15 to 30 minutes, 28.4% 30 to 45 minutes, 0.0% 45 to 60 minutes, 7.4% 60 minutes or more (2000)

Livingston County

Located in north central Missouri; drained by the Grand River. Covers a land area of 534.50 square miles, a water area of 4.00 square miles, and is located in the Central Time Zone. The county government was organized in 1837. County seat is Chillicothe.
Population: 14,558 (2000); Race: 96.0% White, 2.3% Black, 0.2% Asian, 0.4% American Indian and Alaska Native, 0.5% Hispanic of any race, 1.0% two or more races (2000); Density: 27.2 persons per square mile (2000); Age: 24.0% under 18, 19.0% over 64 (2000).
Religion: Five largest groups: 39.3% Southern Baptist Convention, 11.4% The United Methodist Church, 8.5% Catholic Church, 4.0% Christian Church (Disciples of Christ), 2.0% Assemblies of God (2000).
Economy: Unemployment rate: 3.8% (11/2002); Total civilian labor force: 7,245 (11/2002); Leading industries: 20.6% retail trade; 16.9% manufacturing; 15.9% health care and social assistance (2000); Companies that employ more than 1,000 persons: 0 (2000); Companies that employ more than 100 persons: 7 (2000); Farms: 738 totaling 272,817 acres (1997); Minority business ownership rate: 0.0% (1997); Women business ownership rate: 18.4% (1997); Retail sales per capita: $10,562 (1997). Single-family building permits issued: 27 (2001) / 34 (2000); Multi-family building permits issued: 16 (2001) / 0 (2000).
Income: Per capita income: $16,685 (2000); Median household income: $32,290 (2000); Poverty rate: 12.4% (2000); Bankruptcy rate: 2.89% (2001).
Taxes: Total county taxes per capita: $57 (1997); County property taxes per capita: $4 (1997).
Education: High school graduation rate: 80.6% (2000); College graduation rate: 13.1% (2000).
Housing: Homeownership rate: 70.8% (2000); Median home value: $61,400 (2000); Median rent: $249 per month (2000); Median age of housing: 38 years (2000).
Health: Birth rate: 126.4 per 10,000 population (1998); Age adjusted death rate: 97.3 per 10,000 population (1999); Age adjusted cancer mortality rate: 213.7 deaths per 100,000 population (1999). Number of physicians: 6.9 per 10,000 population (1999); Number of hospital beds: 55.0 per 10,000 population (1999).
Elections: 2000 Presidential election results: 38.6% Gore, 59.1% Bush, 1.6% Nader, 0.4% Buchanan
National and State Parks: Poosey State Forest
Additional Information Contacts
Livingston County Government Offices 660-646-2293
Chillicothe Area Chamber of Commerce. 660-646-4050

Livingston County Communities

CHILLICOTHE (city). Covers a land area of 6.541 square miles and a water area of 0.015 square miles. Located at 39.79° N. Lat.; 93.55° W. Long. Elevation is 798 feet.
History: Chillicothe was platted in 1837 and named for Chillicothe, Ohio. The name is of Shawnee origin meaning "the big town where we live." Chillicothe began to live up to its name when the Hannibal & St. Joseph Railroad was completed in 1859. Chillicothe was the home of Earl Sawyer Sloan who concocted a compound that became world-known as Sloan's Liniment.
Population: 8,968 (2000); Race: 93.6% White, 3.8% Black, 0.2% Asian, 0.5% American Indian and Alaska Native, 0.7% Hispanic of any race, 1.6% two or more races (2000); Density: 1,370.9 persons per square mile (2000); Age: 22.3% under 18, 21.8% over 64 (2000); Marriage status: 18.5% never married, 58.3% now married, 10.6% widowed, 12.6% divorced (2000); Foreign born: 0.5% (2000); Ancestry (includes multiple ancestries): 19.4% German, 18.2% United States or American, 12.7% Other groups, 11.9% English, 11.0% Irish (2000).
Economy: Single-family building permits issued: 4 (2001) / 14 (2000); Multi-family building permits issued: 16 (2001) / 0 (2000); Employment by occupation: 9.3% management, 17.0% professional, 20.4% services, 25.9% sales, 0.8% farming, 8.5% construction, 18.2% production (2000).
Income: Per capita income: $16,172 (2000); Median household income: $30,053 (2000); Poverty rate: 13.4% (2000).
Taxes: Total city taxes per capita: $424 (2000); City property taxes per capita: $63 (2000).
Education: High school graduation rate: 79.1% (2000); College graduation rate: 13.3% (2000).

School District(s)

Chillicothe R-II (PK-12)
2000 Enrollment: 2,114 660-646-4566

Housing: Homeownership rate: 64.2% (2000); Median home value: $62,400 (2000); Median rent: $255 per month (2000); Median age of housing: 40 years (2000).
Hospitals: Hedrick Medical Center (49 beds)
Safety: Violent crime rate: 10.0 per 10,000 population; Property crime rate: 317.0 per 10,000 population (2001).
Newspapers: Chillicothe Constitution-Tribune (5 x week); Chillicothe Constitution-Tribune Extra (1 x week)
Transportation: Commute to work: 90.9% car, 0.7% public transportation, 3.9% walk, 3.0% work from home (2000); Travel time to work: 78.5% less than 15 minutes, 9.1% 15 to 30 minutes, 7.0% 30 to 45 minutes, 1.8% 45 to 60 minutes, 3.6% 60 minutes or more (2000)
Additional Information Contacts
Chillicothe Area Chamber of Commerce. 660-646-4050

CHULA (city). Covers a land area of 0.166 square miles and a water area of 0 square miles. Located at 39.92° N. Lat.; 93.47° W. Long. Elevation is 748 feet.
Population: 198 (2000); Race: 100.0% White, 0.0% Black, 0.0% Asian, 0.0% American Indian and Alaska Native, 0.0% Hispanic of any race, 0.0% two or more races (2000); Density: 1,192.1 persons per square mile (2000); Age: 38.4% under 18, 10.5% over 64 (2000); Marriage status: 25.6% never married, 54.5% now married, 7.1% widowed, 12.8% divorced (2000); Foreign born: 0.0% (2000); Ancestry (includes multiple ancestries): 28.3% United States or American, 11.9% German, 9.6% Other groups, 5.5% French (except Basque), 5.0% Welsh (2000).
Economy: Employment by occupation: 0.0% management, 17.0% professional, 25.0% services, 14.8% sales, 0.0% farming, 20.5% construction, 22.7% production (2000).
Income: Per capita income: $11,920 (2000); Median household income: $30,208 (2000); Poverty rate: 21.5% (2000).
Taxes: Total city taxes per capita: $90 (1997); City property taxes per capita: $56 (1997).
Education: High school graduation rate: 79.5% (2000); College graduation rate: 4.3% (2000).

School District(s)

Livingston Co. R-III (PK-08)
2000 Enrollment: 75 660-639-3135

Housing: Homeownership rate: 65.7% (2000); Median home value: $14,100 (2000); Median rent: $261 per month (2000); Median age of housing: 60+ years (2000).
Transportation: Commute to work: 90.4% car, 0.0% public transportation, 2.4% walk, 4.8% work from home (2000); Travel time to work: 10.1% less than 15 minutes, 50.6% 15 to 30 minutes, 10.1% 30 to 45 minutes, 10.1% 45 to 60 minutes, 19.0% 60 minutes or more (2000)

DAWN (unincorporated postal area, zip code 64638). Covers a land area of 90.141 square miles and a water area of 0.070 square miles. Located at 39.61° N. Lat.; 93.62° W. Long. Elevation is 763 feet.
Population: 640 (2000); Race: 99.2% White, 0.0% Black, 0.0% Asian, 0.8% American Indian and Alaska Native, 0.0% Hispanic of any race, 0.0% two or more races (2000); Density: 7.1 persons per square mile (2000); Age: 27.7% under 18, 13.9% over 64 (2000); Marriage status: 20.1% never married, 70.6% now married, 4.6% widowed, 4.6% divorced (2000); Foreign born: 0.0% (2000); Ancestry (includes multiple ancestries): 19.0% German, 14.0% United States or American, 13.5% Welsh, 12.0% English, 8.7% Irish (2000).
Economy: Employment by occupation: 26.3% management, 12.7% professional, 15.5% services, 13.6% sales, 3.5% farming, 12.0% construction, 16.5% production (2000).
Income: Per capita income: $15,074 (2000); Median household income: $36,375 (2000); Poverty rate: 7.6% (2000).
Education: High school graduation rate: 87.0% (2000); College graduation rate: 17.9% (2000).
Housing: Homeownership rate: 74.8% (2000); Median home value: $27,100 (2000); Median rent: $173 per month (2000); Median age of housing: 40 years (2000).
Transportation: Commute to work: 90.2% car, 0.0% public transportation, 2.3% walk, 6.9% work from home (2000); Travel time to work: 28.1% less than 15 minutes, 37.9% 15 to 30 minutes, 16.1% 30 to 45 minutes, 5.3% 45 to 60 minutes, 12.6% 60 minutes or more (2000)

LUDLOW (town). Covers a land area of 0.131 square miles and a water area of 0 square miles. Located at 39.65° N. Lat.; 93.70° W. Long. Elevation is 745 feet.
Population: 204 (2000); Race: 100.0% White, 0.0% Black, 0.0% Asian, 0.0% American Indian and Alaska Native, 0.0% Hispanic of any race, 0.0%

two or more races (2000); Density: 1,562.3 persons per square mile (2000); Age: 36.8% under 18, 13.7% over 64 (2000); Marriage status: 24.5% never married, 52.4% now married, 7.5% widowed, 15.6% divorced (2000); Foreign born: 0.0% (2000); Ancestry (includes multiple ancestries): 32.1% German, 28.3% United States or American, 17.0% Irish, 13.2% Other groups, 12.3% English (2000).
Economy: Employment by occupation: 2.9% management, 8.8% professional, 33.8% services, 22.1% sales, 0.0% farming, 8.8% construction, 23.5% production (2000).
Income: Per capita income: $10,118 (2000); Median household income: $19,688 (2000); Poverty rate: 27.4% (2000).
Taxes: Total city taxes per capita: $56 (1997); City property taxes per capita: $21 (1997).
Education: High school graduation rate: 65.5% (2000); College graduation rate: 0.0% (2000).

School District(s)

Southwest Livingston Co. R-I (KG-12)
2000 Enrollment: 242 660-738-4433
Housing: Homeownership rate: 75.7% (2000); Median home value: $17,300 (2000); Median rent: $314 per month (2000); Median age of housing: 59 years (2000).
Transportation: Commute to work: 90.6% car, 0.0% public transportation, 3.1% walk, 1.6% work from home (2000); Travel time to work: 12.7% less than 15 minutes, 38.1% 15 to 30 minutes, 12.7% 30 to 45 minutes, 7.9% 45 to 60 minutes, 28.6% 60 minutes or more (2000)

MOORESVILLE (village). Covers a land area of 0.182 square miles and a water area of 0 square miles. Located at 39.74° N. Lat.; 93.71° W. Long. Elevation is 920 feet.
History: Mooresville was named for W.B. Moore, a Kentuckian who surveyed the site in 1860. The medicinal properties of a nearby spring, discovered by Moore, gained national attention at the Chicago World's Fair in 1893.
Population: 89 (2000); Race: 100.0% White, 0.0% Black, 0.0% Asian, 0.0% American Indian and Alaska Native, 0.0% Hispanic of any race, 0.0% two or more races (2000); Density: 489.8 persons per square mile (2000); Age: 8.1% under 18, 43.2% over 64 (2000); Marriage status: 12.5% never married, 66.7% now married, 15.3% widowed, 5.6% divorced (2000); Foreign born: 0.0% (2000); Ancestry (includes multiple ancestries): 31.1% English, 25.7% Irish, 25.7% German, 10.8% United States or American, 8.1% Dutch (2000).
Economy: Employment by occupation: 6.3% management, 21.9% professional, 18.8% services, 25.0% sales, 0.0% farming, 6.3% construction, 21.9% production (2000).
Income: Per capita income: $16,282 (2000); Median household income: $21,875 (2000); Poverty rate: 2.7% (2000).
Taxes: Total city taxes per capita: $10 (1997); City property taxes per capita: $10 (1997).
Education: High school graduation rate: 75.0% (2000); College graduation rate: 10.9% (2000).
Housing: Homeownership rate: 84.1% (2000); Median home value: $31,900 (2000); Median rent: $125 per month (2000); Median age of housing: 55 years (2000).
Transportation: Commute to work: 100.0% car, 0.0% public transportation, 0.0% walk, 0.0% work from home (2000); Travel time to work: 18.8% less than 15 minutes, 40.6% 15 to 30 minutes, 28.1% 30 to 45 minutes, 0.0% 45 to 60 minutes, 12.5% 60 minutes or more (2000)

UTICA (village). Covers a land area of 0.882 square miles and a water area of 0 square miles. Located at 39.74° N. Lat.; 93.62° W. Long. Elevation is 764 feet.
Population: 274 (2000); Race: 99.3% White, 0.0% Black, 0.0% Asian, 0.0% American Indian and Alaska Native, 0.7% Hispanic of any race, 0.0% two or more races (2000); Density: 310.7 persons per square mile (2000); Age: 22.6% under 18, 21.2% over 64 (2000); Marriage status: 23.3% never married, 63.4% now married, 3.9% widowed, 9.5% divorced (2000); Foreign born: 0.0% (2000); Ancestry (includes multiple ancestries): 25.2% German, 19.7% Irish, 13.1% United States or American, 12.8% Scotch-Irish, 8.8% English (2000).
Economy: Employment by occupation: 9.6% management, 5.9% professional, 27.4% services, 18.5% sales, 1.5% farming, 14.1% construction, 23.0% production (2000).
Income: Per capita income: $16,860 (2000); Median household income: $38,750 (2000); Poverty rate: 9.6% (2000).
Education: High school graduation rate: 75.8% (2000); College graduation rate: 7.7% (2000).
Housing: Homeownership rate: 92.1% (2000); Median home value: $28,300 (2000); Median rent: $125 per month (2000); Median age of housing: 38 years (2000).
Transportation: Commute to work: 87.2% car, 2.3% public transportation, 3.0% walk, 2.3% work from home (2000); Travel time to work: 53.1% less than 15 minutes, 34.6% 15 to 30 minutes, 0.0% 30 to 45 minutes, 4.6% 45 to 60 minutes, 7.7% 60 minutes or more (2000)

WHEELING (city). Covers a land area of 0.321 square miles and a water area of 0 square miles. Located at 39.78° N. Lat.; 93.38° W. Long. Elevation is 749 feet.
Population: 268 (2000); Race: 99.3% White, 0.0% Black, 0.0% Asian, 0.7% American Indian and Alaska Native, 0.0% Hispanic of any race, 0.0% two or more races (2000); Density: 835.6 persons per square mile (2000); Age: 31.3% under 18, 20.9% over 64 (2000); Marriage status: 12.7% never married, 62.4% now married, 10.2% widowed, 14.7% divorced (2000); Foreign born: 0.0% (2000); Ancestry (includes multiple ancestries): 28.0% United States or American, 14.2% German, 11.2% Irish, 10.4% Other groups, 10.1% English (2000).
Economy: Employment by occupation: 12.3% management, 5.7% professional, 17.9% services, 23.6% sales, 4.7% farming, 14.2% construction, 21.7% production (2000).
Income: Per capita income: $13,150 (2000); Median household income: $26,154 (2000); Poverty rate: 23.7% (2000).
Taxes: Total city taxes per capita: $42 (1997); City property taxes per capita: $10 (1997).
Education: High school graduation rate: 79.2% (2000); College graduation rate: 5.2% (2000).
Housing: Homeownership rate: 67.3% (2000); Median home value: $44,000 (2000); Median rent: $200 per month (2000); Median age of housing: 37 years (2000).
Transportation: Commute to work: 90.6% car, 0.0% public transportation, 0.0% walk, 6.6% work from home (2000); Travel time to work: 24.2% less than 15 minutes, 46.5% 15 to 30 minutes, 6.1% 30 to 45 minutes, 10.1% 45 to 60 minutes, 13.1% 60 minutes or more (2000)

Macon County

Located in north central Missouri; drained by the Chariton River. Covers a land area of 803.80 square miles, a water area of 8.80 square miles, and is located in the Central Time Zone. The county government was organized in 1837. County seat is Macon.
Population: 15,762 (2000); Race: 96.5% White, 2.3% Black, 0.1% Asian, 0.4% American Indian and Alaska Native, 0.5% Hispanic of any race, 0.6% two or more races (2000); Density: 19.6 persons per square mile (2000); Age: 24.1% under 18, 19.1% over 64 (2000).
Religion: Five largest groups: 28.1% Southern Baptist Convention, 10.7% Christian Churches and Churches of Christ, 8.2% Christian Church (Disciples of Christ), 7.6% Catholic Church, 4.5% The United Methodist Church (2000).
Economy: Unemployment rate: 5.5% (11/2002); Total civilian labor force: 6,179 (11/2002); Leading industries: 18.9% retail trade; 12.6% health care and social assistance; 11.5% accommodation & food services (2000); Companies that employ more than 1,000 persons: 0 (2000); Companies that employ more than 100 persons: 6 (2000); Farms: 1,155 totaling 380,527 acres (1997); Minority business ownership rate: 0.0% (1997); Women business ownership rate: 17.5% (1997); Retail sales per capita: $5,599 (1997). Single-family building permits issued: 7 (2001) / 11 (2000); Multi-family building permits issued: 0 (2001) / 0 (2000).
Income: Per capita income: $16,189 (2000); Median household income: $30,195 (2000); Poverty rate: 12.5% (2000); Bankruptcy rate: 2.94% (2001).
Taxes: Total county taxes per capita: $150 (2000); County property taxes per capita: $62 (2000).
Education: High school graduation rate: 77.8% (2000); College graduation rate: 13.0% (2000).
Housing: Homeownership rate: 75.9% (2000); Median home value: $55,900 (2000); Median rent: $226 per month (2000); Median age of housing: 37 years (2000).
Health: Birth rate: 133.9 per 10,000 population (1998); Age adjusted death rate: 85.9 per 10,000 population (1999); Age adjusted cancer mortality rate: 169.4 deaths per 100,000 population (1999). Number of physicians: 4.4 per 10,000 population (1999); Number of hospital beds: 17.8 per 10,000 population (1999).
Elections: 2000 Presidential election results: 39.3% Gore, 59.0% Bush, 1.1% Nader, 0.5% Buchanan

National and State Parks: Atlanta State Wildlife Area; Griffith State Wildlife Area; Redman State Wildlife Area
Additional Information Contacts
Macon County Government Offices 660-385-2913
Macon Chamber of Commerce 660-385-2811

Macon County Communities

ANABEL (unincorporated postal area, zip code 63431). Covers a land area of 45.701 square miles and a water area of 0 square miles. Located at 39.75° N. Lat.; 92.32° W. Long. Elevation is 838 feet.
Population: 385 (2000); Race: 96.5% White, 3.5% Black, 0.0% Asian, 0.0% American Indian and Alaska Native, 0.0% Hispanic of any race, 0.0% two or more races (2000); Density: 8.4 persons per square mile (2000); Age: 20.6% under 18, 10.8% over 64 (2000); Marriage status: 15.9% never married, 76.4% now married, 1.7% widowed, 6.0% divorced (2000); Foreign born: 0.0% (2000); Ancestry (includes multiple ancestries): 34.2% German, 24.8% English, 13.6% Italian, 10.3% Irish, 5.2% United States or American (2000).
Economy: Employment by occupation: 16.5% management, 9.5% professional, 10.7% services, 24.0% sales, 0.8% farming, 15.7% construction, 22.7% production (2000).
Income: Per capita income: $15,226 (2000); Median household income: $29,702 (2000); Poverty rate: 4.0% (2000).
Education: High school graduation rate: 70.2% (2000); College graduation rate: 17.0% (2000).
Housing: Homeownership rate: 79.5% (2000); Median home value: $46,400 (2000); Median rent: $225 per month (2000); Median age of housing: 31 years (2000).
Transportation: Commute to work: 90.4% car, 0.0% public transportation, 3.5% walk, 6.1% work from home (2000); Travel time to work: 25.1% less than 15 minutes, 55.3% 15 to 30 minutes, 13.5% 30 to 45 minutes, 1.4% 45 to 60 minutes, 4.7% 60 minutes or more (2000)

ATLANTA (city). Covers a land area of 0.342 square miles and a water area of 0 square miles. Located at 39.89° N. Lat.; 92.48° W. Long. Elevation is 905 feet.
History: Atlanta was platted in 1858.
Population: 450 (2000); Race: 100.0% White, 0.0% Black, 0.0% Asian, 0.0% American Indian and Alaska Native, 0.0% Hispanic of any race, 0.0% two or more races (2000); Density: 1,314.2 persons per square mile (2000); Age: 26.5% under 18, 13.5% over 64 (2000); Marriage status: 18.8% never married, 65.4% now married, 7.2% widowed, 8.6% divorced (2000); Foreign born: 0.2% (2000); Ancestry (includes multiple ancestries): 28.3% United States or American, 16.4% German, 12.4% English, 6.0% Other groups, 6.0% Irish (2000).
Economy: Employment by occupation: 5.9% management, 8.2% professional, 24.2% services, 20.5% sales, 0.0% farming, 12.3% construction, 28.8% production (2000).
Income: Per capita income: $14,940 (2000); Median household income: $33,571 (2000); Poverty rate: 9.1% (2000).
Taxes: Total city taxes per capita: $138 (1997); City property taxes per capita: $82 (1997).
Education: High school graduation rate: 78.9% (2000); College graduation rate: 12.5% (2000).

School District(s)

Atlanta C-3 (KG-12)
2000 Enrollment: 241 660-239-4212
Housing: Homeownership rate: 81.5% (2000); Median home value: $32,100 (2000); Median rent: $200 per month (2000); Median age of housing: 55 years (2000).
Transportation: Commute to work: 95.9% car, 0.0% public transportation, 0.0% walk, 4.1% work from home (2000); Travel time to work: 32.7% less than 15 minutes, 42.8% 15 to 30 minutes, 14.9% 30 to 45 minutes, 6.7% 45 to 60 minutes, 2.9% 60 minutes or more (2000)

BEVIER (city). Covers a land area of 0.862 square miles and a water area of 0 square miles. Located at 39.74° N. Lat.; 92.56° W. Long. Elevation is 791 feet.
History: Bevier grew up around the coal mines, established after Alex Rector discovered coal here in 1860 while digging a well.
Population: 723 (2000); Race: 96.6% White, 0.3% Black, 0.0% Asian, 1.8% American Indian and Alaska Native, 0.3% Hispanic of any race, 1.1% two or more races (2000); Density: 838.6 persons per square mile (2000); Age: 26.4% under 18, 18.7% over 64 (2000); Marriage status: 18.7% never married, 54.6% now married, 11.9% widowed, 14.7% divorced (2000); Foreign born: 1.0% (2000); Ancestry (includes multiple ancestries): 27.4% German, 14.6% United States or American, 13.2% Other groups, 13.2% Irish, 10.0% English (2000).
Economy: Employment by occupation: 4.4% management, 8.9% professional, 19.3% services, 17.1% sales, 0.0% farming, 10.4% construction, 39.9% production (2000).
Income: Per capita income: $13,099 (2000); Median household income: $28,250 (2000); Poverty rate: 7.6% (2000).
Taxes: Total city taxes per capita: $28 (1997); City property taxes per capita: $28 (1997).
Education: High school graduation rate: 65.6% (2000); College graduation rate: 5.3% (2000).

School District(s)

Bevier C-4 (KG-12)
2000 Enrollment: 267 660-773-6611
Housing: Homeownership rate: 78.5% (2000); Median home value: $33,600 (2000); Median rent: $223 per month (2000); Median age of housing: 44 years (2000).
Transportation: Commute to work: 94.2% car, 0.0% public transportation, 2.6% walk, 2.6% work from home (2000); Travel time to work: 45.2% less than 15 minutes, 32.8% 15 to 30 minutes, 12.1% 30 to 45 minutes, 4.9% 45 to 60 minutes, 4.9% 60 minutes or more (2000)

CALLAO (city). Covers a land area of 0.502 square miles and a water area of 0 square miles. Located at 39.76° N. Lat.; 92.62° W. Long. Elevation is 819 feet.
History: Callao was platted in 1858 and named by the first postmaster, who pointed his finger at random on a map of South America and landed on the Peruvian seaport of that name. The town was incorporated in 1889.
Population: 291 (2000); Race: 97.1% White, 0.0% Black, 1.5% Asian, 0.7% American Indian and Alaska Native, 1.8% Hispanic of any race, 0.7% two or more races (2000); Density: 580.0 persons per square mile (2000); Age: 20.1% under 18, 19.0% over 64 (2000); Marriage status: 23.6% never married, 52.9% now married, 7.6% widowed, 16.0% divorced (2000); Foreign born: 1.5% (2000); Ancestry (includes multiple ancestries): 23.0% German, 11.3% English, 10.2% Irish, 9.1% United States or American, 5.8% Other groups (2000).
Economy: Single-family building permits issued: 0 (2001) / 0 (2000); Multi-family building permits issued: 0 (2001) / 0 (2000); Employment by occupation: 1.6% management, 18.0% professional, 9.8% services, 21.3% sales, 1.6% farming, 23.0% construction, 24.6% production (2000).
Income: Per capita income: $12,573 (2000); Median household income: $24,659 (2000); Poverty rate: 26.1% (2000).
Taxes: Total city taxes per capita: $131 (1997); City property taxes per capita: $51 (1997).
Education: High school graduation rate: 66.1% (2000); College graduation rate: 11.8% (2000).

School District(s)

Callao C-8 (KG-08)
2000 Enrollment: 77 660-768-5541
Housing: Homeownership rate: 83.3% (2000); Median home value: $18,500 (2000); Median rent: $213 per month (2000); Median age of housing: 60+ years (2000).
Transportation: Commute to work: 88.0% car, 0.0% public transportation, 6.0% walk, 6.0% work from home (2000); Travel time to work: 31.8% less than 15 minutes, 31.8% 15 to 30 minutes, 19.1% 30 to 45 minutes, 10.0% 45 to 60 minutes, 7.3% 60 minutes or more (2000)

ELMER (city). Covers a land area of 0.244 square miles and a water area of 0 square miles. Located at 39.95° N. Lat.; 92.64° W. Long. Elevation is 737 feet.
Population: 98 (2000); Race: 100.0% White, 0.0% Black, 0.0% Asian, 0.0% American Indian and Alaska Native, 0.0% Hispanic of any race, 0.0% two or more races (2000); Density: 402.0 persons per square mile (2000); Age: 20.7% under 18, 16.3% over 64 (2000); Marriage status: 21.1% never married, 43.4% now married, 23.7% widowed, 11.8% divorced (2000); Foreign born: 0.0% (2000); Ancestry (includes multiple ancestries): 12.0% German, 10.9% English, 8.7% Irish, 6.5% United States or American, 4.3% Scottish (2000).
Economy: Employment by occupation: 0.0% management, 8.5% professional, 12.8% services, 21.3% sales, 6.4% farming, 23.4% construction, 27.7% production (2000).
Income: Per capita income: $9,834 (2000); Median household income: $16,250 (2000); Poverty rate: 29.5% (2000).
Taxes: Total city taxes per capita: $67 (1997); City property taxes per capita: $22 (1997).

Education: High school graduation rate: 56.5% (2000); College graduation rate: 8.1% (2000).
Housing: Homeownership rate: 80.9% (2000); Median home value: $10,000 (2000); Median rent: $125 per month (2000); Median age of housing: 60+ years (2000).
Transportation: Commute to work: 97.9% car, 0.0% public transportation, 0.0% walk, 2.1% work from home (2000); Travel time to work: 4.3% less than 15 minutes, 28.3% 15 to 30 minutes, 45.7% 30 to 45 minutes, 4.3% 45 to 60 minutes, 17.4% 60 minutes or more (2000)

ETHEL (town). Covers a land area of 0.238 square miles and a water area of 0 square miles. Located at 39.89° N. Lat.; 92.74° W. Long. Elevation is 850 feet.
Population: 100 (2000); Race: 100.0% White, 0.0% Black, 0.0% Asian, 0.0% American Indian and Alaska Native, 0.0% Hispanic of any race, 0.0% two or more races (2000); Density: 419.3 persons per square mile (2000); Age: 10.3% under 18, 34.0% over 64 (2000); Marriage status: 15.4% never married, 64.8% now married, 11.0% widowed, 8.8% divorced (2000); Foreign born: 0.0% (2000); Ancestry (includes multiple ancestries): 26.8% Irish, 24.7% German, 14.4% English, 10.3% Scotch-Irish, 6.2% United States or American (2000).
Economy: Employment by occupation: 30.0% management, 25.0% professional, 0.0% services, 15.0% sales, 0.0% farming, 10.0% construction, 20.0% production (2000).
Income: Per capita income: $16,126 (2000); Median household income: $22,500 (2000); Poverty rate: 18.6% (2000).
Taxes: Total city taxes per capita: $41 (1997); City property taxes per capita: $0 (1997).
Education: High school graduation rate: 70.9% (2000); College graduation rate: 19.0% (2000).
Housing: Homeownership rate: 84.8% (2000); Median home value: $14,200 (2000); Median rent: $175 per month (2000); Median age of housing: 60+ years (2000).
Transportation: Commute to work: 100.0% car, 0.0% public transportation, 0.0% walk, 0.0% work from home (2000); Travel time to work: 0.0% less than 15 minutes, 23.5% 15 to 30 minutes, 29.4% 30 to 45 minutes, 0.0% 45 to 60 minutes, 47.1% 60 minutes or more (2000)

EXCELLO (unincorporated postal area, zip code 65247). Covers a land area of 46.548 square miles and a water area of 0.026 square miles. Located at 39.62° N. Lat.; 92.49° W. Long. Elevation is 868 feet.
Population: 567 (2000); Race: 100.0% White, 0.0% Black, 0.0% Asian, 0.0% American Indian and Alaska Native, 2.0% Hispanic of any race, 0.0% two or more races (2000); Density: 12.2 persons per square mile (2000); Age: 31.0% under 18, 10.8% over 64 (2000); Marriage status: 22.3% never married, 57.2% now married, 7.1% widowed, 13.4% divorced (2000); Foreign born: 0.0% (2000); Ancestry (includes multiple ancestries): 28.1% German, 14.3% United States or American, 9.4% Irish, 9.2% Italian, 8.0% Other groups (2000).
Economy: Employment by occupation: 9.7% management, 12.4% professional, 12.1% services, 25.0% sales, 2.9% farming, 23.2% construction, 14.7% production (2000).
Income: Per capita income: $14,101 (2000); Median household income: $29,609 (2000); Poverty rate: 16.4% (2000).
Education: High school graduation rate: 77.7% (2000); College graduation rate: 14.3% (2000).
Housing: Homeownership rate: 89.8% (2000); Median home value: $71,100 (2000); Median rent: $246 per month (2000); Median age of housing: 35 years (2000).
Transportation: Commute to work: 97.9% car, 0.6% public transportation, 0.0% walk, 1.5% work from home (2000); Travel time to work: 12.0% less than 15 minutes, 59.7% 15 to 30 minutes, 18.8% 30 to 45 minutes, 2.2% 45 to 60 minutes, 7.4% 60 minutes or more (2000)

LA PLATA (city). Covers a land area of 1.219 square miles and a water area of 0 square miles. Located at 40.02° N. Lat.; 92.49° W. Long. Elevation is 941 feet.
History: La Plata was laid out in 1855 at the place where the Wabash and Santa Fe railroad lines crossed.
Population: 1,486 (2000); Race: 99.3% White, 0.0% Black, 0.1% Asian, 0.0% American Indian and Alaska Native, 0.1% Hispanic of any race, 0.5% two or more races (2000); Density: 1,219.0 persons per square mile (2000); Age: 25.2% under 18, 26.9% over 64 (2000); Marriage status: 18.9% never married, 53.7% now married, 17.6% widowed, 9.8% divorced (2000); Foreign born: 0.4% (2000); Ancestry (includes multiple ancestries): 15.3% German, 14.1% United States or American, 10.7% English, 10.3% Irish, 4.4% Other groups (2000).
Economy: Single-family building permits issued: 0 (2001) / 2 (2000); Multi-family building permits issued: 0 (2001) / 0 (2000); Employment by occupation: 7.7% management, 16.6% professional, 20.4% services, 22.8% sales, 0.7% farming, 14.0% construction, 17.8% production (2000).
Income: Per capita income: $19,675 (2000); Median household income: $29,583 (2000); Poverty rate: 14.1% (2000).
Taxes: Total city taxes per capita: $225 (1997); City property taxes per capita: $55 (1997).
Education: High school graduation rate: 75.6% (2000); College graduation rate: 11.4% (2000).

School District(s)

La Plata R-II (KG-12)
2000 Enrollment: 407 660-332-7001

Housing: Homeownership rate: 64.8% (2000); Median home value: $51,500 (2000); Median rent: $224 per month (2000); Median age of housing: 39 years (2000).
Newspapers: The Home Press (1 x week)
Transportation: Commute to work: 94.0% car, 0.0% public transportation, 4.7% walk, 0.9% work from home (2000); Travel time to work: 30.3% less than 15 minutes, 46.2% 15 to 30 minutes, 13.5% 30 to 45 minutes, 2.5% 45 to 60 minutes, 7.6% 60 minutes or more (2000); Amtrak: Service available.

MACON (city). Covers a land area of 6.127 square miles and a water area of 0.291 square miles. Located at 39.74° N. Lat.; 92.47° W. Long. Elevation is 872 feet.
History: Macon was named for Nathaniel Macon (1757-1837), Revolutionary War soldier and U.S. senator from North Carolina. The town was incorporated as Macon City in 1859 when the communities of Macon and Hudson were combined.
Population: 5,538 (2000); Race: 92.7% White, 5.8% Black, 0.3% Asian, 0.4% American Indian and Alaska Native, 0.4% Hispanic of any race, 0.8% two or more races (2000); Density: 903.9 persons per square mile (2000); Age: 22.6% under 18, 24.3% over 64 (2000); Marriage status: 20.0% never married, 50.9% now married, 14.6% widowed, 14.5% divorced (2000); Foreign born: 0.4% (2000); Ancestry (includes multiple ancestries): 18.8% German, 14.7% United States or American, 13.4% English, 13.4% Irish, 11.4% Other groups (2000).
Economy: Single-family building permits issued: 7 (2001) / 9 (2000); Multi-family building permits issued: 0 (2001) / 0 (2000); Employment by occupation: 10.2% management, 14.4% professional, 21.8% services, 23.1% sales, 1.3% farming, 8.6% construction, 20.6% production (2000).
Income: Per capita income: $16,679 (2000); Median household income: $26,738 (2000); Poverty rate: 12.8% (2000).
Taxes: Total city taxes per capita: $294 (2000); City property taxes per capita: $39 (2000).
Education: High school graduation rate: 78.8% (2000); College graduation rate: 14.9% (2000).

School District(s)

Macon Co. R-I (PK-12)
2000 Enrollment: 1,336 660-385-5719

Housing: Homeownership rate: 66.8% (2000); Median home value: $65,400 (2000); Median rent: $230 per month (2000); Median age of housing: 40 years (2000).
Hospitals: Samaritan Memorial Hospital (48 beds)
Safety: Violent crime rate: 79.0 per 10,000 population; Property crime rate: 278.2 per 10,000 population (2001).
Newspapers: Macon Chronicle-Herald (4 x week); The Journal (3 x week)
Transportation: Commute to work: 89.8% car, 0.0% public transportation, 3.3% walk, 6.1% work from home (2000); Travel time to work: 67.2% less than 15 minutes, 13.1% 15 to 30 minutes, 11.2% 30 to 45 minutes, 3.6% 45 to 60 minutes, 4.9% 60 minutes or more (2000)
Airports: Macon-Fower Memorial
Additional Information Contacts
Macon Chamber of Commerce 660-385-2811

NEW CAMBRIA (city). Covers a land area of 0.674 square miles and a water area of 0 square miles. Located at 39.77° N. Lat.; 92.75° W. Long. Elevation is 855 feet.
History: New Cambria was settled in 1864 as Stockton, but the name was changed in 1880 by Welshmen who came to the town.
Population: 222 (2000); Race: 98.1% White, 0.0% Black, 0.0% Asian, 0.0% American Indian and Alaska Native, 0.9% Hispanic of any race, 1.9% two or more races (2000); Density: 329.2 persons per square mile (2000); Age: 22.2% under 18, 23.1% over 64 (2000); Marriage status: 22.3% never

married, 57.0% now married, 17.3% widowed, 3.4% divorced (2000); Foreign born: 0.0% (2000); Ancestry (includes multiple ancestries): 24.5% English, 22.7% United States or American, 12.0% German, 9.3% Welsh, 6.5% Irish (2000).
Economy: Employment by occupation: 12.4% management, 3.1% professional, 13.4% services, 33.0% sales, 2.1% farming, 10.3% construction, 25.8% production (2000).
Income: Per capita income: $14,331 (2000); Median household income: $25,536 (2000); Poverty rate: 6.1% (2000).
Taxes: Total city taxes per capita: $59 (1997); City property taxes per capita: $23 (1997).
Education: High school graduation rate: 80.4% (2000); College graduation rate: 5.4% (2000).

School District(s)

Macon Co. R-IV (KG-12)
2000 Enrollment: 164 660-226-5615

Housing: Homeownership rate: 76.6% (2000); Median home value: $21,300 (2000); Median rent: $133 per month (2000); Median age of housing: 60+ years (2000).
Transportation: Commute to work: 83.8% car, 0.0% public transportation, 0.0% walk, 11.1% work from home (2000); Travel time to work: 14.8% less than 15 minutes, 36.4% 15 to 30 minutes, 22.7% 30 to 45 minutes, 8.0% 45 to 60 minutes, 18.2% 60 minutes or more (2000)

SOUTH GIFFORD (village). Covers a land area of 0.209 square miles and a water area of 0 square miles. Located at 40.02° N. Lat.; 92.68° W. Long.
Population: 72 (2000); Race: 100.0% White, 0.0% Black, 0.0% Asian, 0.0% American Indian and Alaska Native, 0.0% Hispanic of any race, 0.0% two or more races (2000); Density: 345.2 persons per square mile (2000); Age: 37.5% under 18, 6.3% over 64 (2000); Marriage status: 40.4% never married, 46.8% now married, 2.1% widowed, 10.6% divorced (2000); Foreign born: 0.0% (2000); Ancestry (includes multiple ancestries): 21.9% German, 21.9% United States or American, 15.6% Irish, 3.1% Scotch-Irish, 3.1% Croatian (2000).
Economy: Employment by occupation: 9.7% management, 6.5% professional, 29.0% services, 6.5% sales, 0.0% farming, 19.4% construction, 29.0% production (2000).
Income: Per capita income: $9,225 (2000); Median household income: $22,500 (2000); Poverty rate: 28.1% (2000).
Taxes: Total city taxes per capita: $32 (1997); City property taxes per capita: $0 (1997).
Education: High school graduation rate: 61.1% (2000); College graduation rate: 5.6% (2000).
Housing: Homeownership rate: 68.2% (2000); Median home value: $36,300 (2000); Median rent: $415 per month (2000); Median age of housing: 60 years (2000).
Transportation: Commute to work: 93.5% car, 0.0% public transportation, 0.0% walk, 6.5% work from home (2000); Travel time to work: 0.0% less than 15 minutes, 41.4% 15 to 30 minutes, 27.6% 30 to 45 minutes, 17.2% 45 to 60 minutes, 13.8% 60 minutes or more (2000)

Madison County

Located in southeastern Missouri, partly in the St. Francois Mountains; drained by the St. Francis and Castor Rivers; includes part of Clark National Forest. Covers a land area of 496.70 square miles, a water area of 0.90 square miles, and is located in the Central Time Zone. The county government was organized in 1818. County seat is Fredericktown.

Weather Station: Fredericktown Elevation: 698 feet

	Jan	Feb	Mar	Apr	May	Jun	Jul	Aug	Sep	Oct	Nov	Dec
High	41	47	57	68	77	85	90	88	81	70	56	45
Low	19	23	32	42	51	59	64	62	54	41	33	24
Precip	2.7	2.5	4.2	4.6	4.7	3.8	3.7	4.1	3.3	3.2	4.7	3.9
Snow	5.1	3.9	2.2	0.2	0.0	0.0	0.0	0.0	0.0	0.1	0.9	2.2

High and Low temperatures in degrees Fahrenheit; Precipitation and Snow in inches

Population: 11,800 (2000); Race: 97.6% White, 0.1% Black, 0.5% Asian, 0.2% American Indian and Alaska Native, 0.4% Hispanic of any race, 1.3% two or more races (2000); Density: 23.8 persons per square mile (2000); Age: 24.5% under 18, 18.0% over 64 (2000).
Religion: Five largest groups: 22.1% Southern Baptist Convention, 10.1% Independent, Non-Charismatic Churches, 7.0% National Association of Free Will Baptists, 4.0% The United Methodist Church, 3.9% Catholic Church (2000).
Economy: Unemployment rate: 7.5% (11/2002); Total civilian labor force: 4,375 (11/2002); Leading industries: 20.3% manufacturing; 18.0% retail trade; 16.0% health care and social assistance (2000); Companies that employ more than 1,000 persons: 0 (2000); Companies that employ more than 100 persons: 5 (2000); Farms: 386 totaling 110,092 acres (1997); Minority business ownership rate: 0.0% (1997); Women business ownership rate: 18.6% (1997); Retail sales per capita: $5,481 (1997). Single-family building permits issued: 1 (2001) / 8 (2000); Multi-family building permits issued: 0 (2001) / 0 (2000).
Income: Per capita income: $13,215 (2000); Median household income: $25,601 (2000); Poverty rate: 17.2% (2000); Bankruptcy rate: 4.66% (2001).
Taxes: Total county taxes per capita: $143 (2000); County property taxes per capita: $73 (2000).
Education: High school graduation rate: 68.6% (2000); College graduation rate: 7.8% (2000).
Housing: Homeownership rate: 76.0% (2000); Median home value: $54,800 (2000); Median rent: $258 per month (2000); Median age of housing: 31 years (2000).
Health: Birth rate: 123.7 per 10,000 population (1998); Age adjusted death rate: 104.8 per 10,000 population (1999); Age adjusted cancer mortality rate: 273.8 deaths per 100,000 population (1999). Number of physicians: 11.0 per 10,000 population (1999); Number of hospital beds: 118.6 per 10,000 population (1999).
Elections: 2000 Presidential election results: 41.8% Gore, 56.3% Bush, 1.0% Nader, 0.6% Buchanan

Additional Information Contacts

Madison County Government Offices 573-783-2176
Fredericktown Chamber of Commerce 573-783-2604

Madison County Communities

COBALT (village). Covers a land area of 0.145 square miles and a water area of 0 square miles. Located at 37.54° N. Lat.; 90.28° W. Long.
Population: 189 (2000); Race: 100.0% White, 0.0% Black, 0.0% Asian, 0.0% American Indian and Alaska Native, 0.0% Hispanic of any race, 0.0% two or more races (2000); Density: 1,300.8 persons per square mile (2000); Age: 22.1% under 18, 14.7% over 64 (2000); Marriage status: 11.8% never married, 66.0% now married, 7.8% widowed, 14.4% divorced (2000); Foreign born: 0.0% (2000); Ancestry (includes multiple ancestries): 33.2% United States or American, 16.3% Irish, 8.4% English, 6.3% Other groups, 5.3% German (2000).
Economy: Employment by occupation: 0.0% management, 2.6% professional, 18.4% services, 23.7% sales, 0.0% farming, 15.8% construction, 39.5% production (2000).
Income: Per capita income: $9,361 (2000); Median household income: $20,962 (2000); Poverty rate: 8.4% (2000).
Taxes: Total city taxes per capita: $19 (1997); City property taxes per capita: $19 (1997).
Education: High school graduation rate: 48.9% (2000); College graduation rate: 2.3% (2000).
Housing: Homeownership rate: 67.4% (2000); Median home value: $28,800 (2000); Median rent: $200 per month (2000); Median age of housing: 40 years (2000).
Transportation: Commute to work: 100.0% car, 0.0% public transportation, 0.0% walk, 0.0% work from home (2000); Travel time to work: 51.4% less than 15 minutes, 2.7% 15 to 30 minutes, 16.2% 30 to 45 minutes, 12.2% 45 to 60 minutes, 17.6% 60 minutes or more (2000)

FREDERICKTOWN (city). Covers a land area of 4.270 square miles and a water area of 0.142 square miles. Located at 37.55° N. Lat.; 90.29° W. Long. Elevation is 743 feet.
History: The first village here was erected by Creole settlers in 1800 and called St. Michael. It was almost destroyed by flood in 1814. In 1819 Fredericktown was established as the seat of the newly-organized Madison County, and it soon encompassed the village of St. Michael. The railroad arrived in 1872 to boost commerce, which was dependent on dairy farming and lead mining.
Population: 3,928 (2000); Race: 97.7% White, 0.0% Black, 1.4% Asian, 0.1% American Indian and Alaska Native, 0.2% Hispanic of any race, 0.7% two or more races (2000); Density: 919.9 persons per square mile (2000); Age: 22.9% under 18, 24.6% over 64 (2000); Marriage status: 17.9% never married, 53.0% now married, 15.0% widowed, 14.1% divorced (2000); Foreign born: 1.3% (2000); Ancestry (includes multiple ancestries): 19.4% United States or American, 16.4% German, 14.3% Irish, 10.4% Other groups, 7.4% English (2000).

Economy: Single-family building permits issued: 1 (2001) / 8 (2000); Multi-family building permits issued: 0 (2001) / 0 (2000); Employment by occupation: 4.8% management, 14.5% professional, 16.7% services, 21.6% sales, 2.0% farming, 13.8% construction, 26.7% production (2000).
Income: Per capita income: $13,512 (2000); Median household income: $21,354 (2000); Poverty rate: 22.3% (2000).
Taxes: Total city taxes per capita: $79 (2000); City property taxes per capita: $72 (2000).
Education: High school graduation rate: 65.0% (2000); College graduation rate: 8.5% (2000).

School District(s)

Fredericktown R-I (PK-12)
2000 Enrollment: 1,914 573-783-2570
Housing: Homeownership rate: 64.8% (2000); Median home value: $50,300 (2000); Median rent: $264 per month (2000); Median age of housing: 41 years (2000).
Hospitals: Madison Medical Center
Newspapers: The Democrat-News (1 x week)
Transportation: Commute to work: 96.7% car, 0.0% public transportation, 1.0% walk, 1.0% work from home (2000); Travel time to work: 53.0% less than 15 minutes, 15.0% 15 to 30 minutes, 13.9% 30 to 45 minutes, 6.2% 45 to 60 minutes, 11.9% 60 minutes or more (2000)
Additional Information Contacts
Fredericktown Chamber of Commerce 573-783-2604

JUNCTION CITY (village). Covers a land area of 0.356 square miles and a water area of 0 square miles. Located at 37.57° N. Lat.; 90.28° W. Long. Elevation is 745 feet.
Population: 319 (2000); Race: 98.4% White, 0.0% Black, 0.0% Asian, 0.0% American Indian and Alaska Native, 0.0% Hispanic of any race, 1.0% two or more races (2000); Density: 894.9 persons per square mile (2000); Age: 26.0% under 18, 26.6% over 64 (2000); Marriage status: 20.0% never married, 45.7% now married, 13.9% widowed, 20.4% divorced (2000); Foreign born: 0.0% (2000); Ancestry (includes multiple ancestries): 16.4% German, 15.1% United States or American, 11.8% Other groups, 11.5% Irish, 6.3% English (2000).
Economy: Employment by occupation: 4.0% management, 11.1% professional, 12.1% services, 24.2% sales, 1.0% farming, 15.2% construction, 32.3% production (2000).
Income: Per capita income: $11,561 (2000); Median household income: $15,833 (2000); Poverty rate: 37.3% (2000).
Taxes: Total city taxes per capita: $9 (1997); City property taxes per capita: $9 (1997).
Education: High school graduation rate: 51.2% (2000); College graduation rate: 6.1% (2000).
Housing: Homeownership rate: 40.4% (2000); Median home value: $47,500 (2000); Median rent: $224 per month (2000); Median age of housing: 24 years (2000).
Transportation: Commute to work: 89.5% car, 0.0% public transportation, 3.2% walk, 5.3% work from home (2000); Travel time to work: 42.2% less than 15 minutes, 10.0% 15 to 30 minutes, 20.0% 30 to 45 minutes, 14.4% 45 to 60 minutes, 13.3% 60 minutes or more (2000)

MARQUAND (city). Covers a land area of 0.242 square miles and a water area of 0 square miles. Located at 37.42° N. Lat.; 90.16° W. Long. Elevation is 571 feet.
Population: 251 (2000); Race: 96.3% White, 0.0% Black, 0.9% Asian, 0.0% American Indian and Alaska Native, 0.9% Hispanic of any race, 2.8% two or more races (2000); Density: 1,035.6 persons per square mile (2000); Age: 23.5% under 18, 18.4% over 64 (2000); Marriage status: 23.8% never married, 50.6% now married, 14.0% widowed, 11.6% divorced (2000); Foreign born: 1.8% (2000); Ancestry (includes multiple ancestries): 27.2% German, 14.3% Other groups, 12.9% Irish, 12.0% United States or American, 5.1% French (except Basque) (2000).
Economy: Cattle; timber. Surrounded by Mark Twain National Forest. Employment by occupation: 2.7% management, 12.0% professional, 24.0% services, 22.7% sales, 1.3% farming, 6.7% construction, 30.7% production (2000).
Income: Per capita income: $8,533 (2000); Median household income: $19,861 (2000); Poverty rate: 32.5% (2000).
Taxes: Total city taxes per capita: $94 (1997); City property taxes per capita: $25 (1997).
Education: High school graduation rate: 60.0% (2000); College graduation rate: 4.8% (2000).

School District(s)

Marquand-Zion R-VI (KG-12)
2000 Enrollment: 201 573-783-3388
Housing: Homeownership rate: 60.9% (2000); Median home value: $26,300 (2000); Median rent: $207 per month (2000); Median age of housing: 48 years (2000).
Transportation: Commute to work: 68.5% car, 0.0% public transportation, 2.7% walk, 16.4% work from home (2000); Travel time to work: 21.3% less than 15 minutes, 32.8% 15 to 30 minutes, 3.3% 30 to 45 minutes, 23.0% 45 to 60 minutes, 19.7% 60 minutes or more (2000)

Maries County

Located in central Missouri, in the Ozarks; drained by the Gasconade River. Covers a land area of 527.70 square miles, a water area of 2.20 square miles, and is located in the Central Time Zone. The county government was organized in 1855. County seat is Vienna.

Weather Station: Vienna 2 WNW — Elevation: 767 feet

	Jan	Feb	Mar	Apr	May	Jun	Jul	Aug	Sep	Oct	Nov	Dec
High	39	45	56	67	76	83	89	88	80	69	55	44
Low	18	23	32	42	51	60	65	63	54	42	33	23
Precip	2.0	2.2	3.7	4.3	4.9	4.5	3.9	3.8	4.1	3.5	4.1	3.1
Snow	5.6	3.6	2.7	0.3	0.0	0.0	0.0	0.0	0.0	0.0	1.7	3.6

High and Low temperatures in degrees Fahrenheit; Precipitation and Snow in inches

Population: 8,903 (2000); Race: 97.5% White, 0.2% Black, 0.0% Asian, 0.3% American Indian and Alaska Native, 0.8% Hispanic of any race, 2.0% two or more races (2000); Density: 16.9 persons per square mile (2000); Age: 26.0% under 18, 15.9% over 64 (2000).
Religion: Five largest groups: 28.4% Southern Baptist Convention, 8.9% Catholic Church, 5.2% Christian Churches and Churches of Christ, 4.6% The United Methodist Church, 3.5% Churches of Christ (2000).
Economy: Unemployment rate: 3.3% (11/2002); Total civilian labor force: 4,809 (11/2002); Leading industries: 23.5% manufacturing; 21.1% retail trade; 11.1% transportation & warehousing (2000); Companies that employ more than 1,000 persons: 0 (2000); Companies that employ more than 100 persons: 0 (2000); Farms: 817 totaling 228,892 acres (1997); Minority business ownership rate: 0.0% (1997); Women business ownership rate: 41.2% (1997); Retail sales per capita: $3,778 (1997). Single-family building permits issued: -1 (2001) / -1 (2000); Multi-family building permits issued: -1 (2001) / -1 (2000).
Income: Per capita income: $15,662 (2000); Median household income: $31,925 (2000); Poverty rate: 13.1% (2000); Bankruptcy rate: 2.10% (2001).
Taxes: Total county taxes per capita: $90 (1997); County property taxes per capita: $47 (1997).
Education: High school graduation rate: 74.5% (2000); College graduation rate: 11.0% (2000).
Housing: Homeownership rate: 81.5% (2000); Median home value: $64,400 (2000); Median rent: $264 per month (2000); Median age of housing: 29 years (2000).
Health: Birth rate: 115.7 per 10,000 population (1998); Age adjusted death rate: 83.6 per 10,000 population (1999); Age adjusted cancer mortality rate: 207.0 deaths per 100,000 population (1999). Number of physicians: 2.2 per 10,000 population (1999); Number of hospital beds: n/a (1999).
Elections: 2000 Presidential election results: 40.3% Gore, 57.5% Bush, 0.8% Nader, 0.7% Buchanan
National and State Parks: Ringuelin Trail Community Lake State Wildlife Area
Additional Information Contacts
Maries County Government Offices 573-422-3388

Maries County Communities

BELLE (city). Covers a land area of 1.265 square miles and a water area of 0 square miles. Located at 38.28° N. Lat.; 91.72° W. Long. Elevation is 1,039 feet.
Population: 1,344 (2000); Race: 96.7% White, 0.2% Black, 0.0% Asian, 0.6% American Indian and Alaska Native, 0.6% Hispanic of any race, 2.5% two or more races (2000); Density: 1,062.1 persons per square mile (2000); Age: 23.8% under 18, 20.7% over 64 (2000); Marriage status: 18.5% never married, 52.6% now married, 16.0% widowed, 12.9% divorced (2000); Foreign born: 0.3% (2000); Ancestry (includes multiple ancestries): 21.8% German, 17.7% United States or American, 10.9% Other groups, 9.0% Irish, 7.6% English (2000).

Economy: Agriculture: cattle; dairying; timber. Light manufacturing. Employment by occupation: 10.6% management, 14.0% professional, 18.6% services, 19.5% sales, 0.0% farming, 10.3% construction, 27.0% production (2000).
Income: Per capita income: $17,785 (2000); Median household income: $24,091 (2000); Poverty rate: 19.3% (2000).
Taxes: Total city taxes per capita: $225 (1997); City property taxes per capita: $54 (1997).
Education: High school graduation rate: 68.2% (2000); College graduation rate: 11.2% (2000).

School District(s)

Maries Co. R-II (PK-12)
2000 Enrollment: 871 573-859-3800

Housing: Homeownership rate: 66.1% (2000); Median home value: $50,400 (2000); Median rent: $261 per month (2000); Median age of housing: 36 years (2000).
Newspapers: Maries County Gazette (1 x week); The Belle Banner (1 x week); The Bland Courier (1 x week)
Transportation: Commute to work: 93.0% car, 0.4% public transportation, 4.2% walk, 1.8% work from home (2000); Travel time to work: 36.8% less than 15 minutes, 20.5% 15 to 30 minutes, 13.9% 30 to 45 minutes, 17.7% 45 to 60 minutes, 11.1% 60 minutes or more (2000)

BRINKTOWN (unincorporated postal area, zip code 65443). Covers a land area of 9.049 square miles and a water area of 0 square miles. Located at 38.12° N. Lat.; 92.08° W. Long. Elevation is 1,055 feet.
Population: 134 (2000); Race: 100.0% White, 0.0% Black, 0.0% Asian, 0.0% American Indian and Alaska Native, 0.0% Hispanic of any race, 0.0% two or more races (2000); Density: 14.8 persons per square mile (2000); Age: 14.6% under 18, 34.4% over 64 (2000); Marriage status: 26.4% never married, 66.7% now married, 6.9% widowed, 0.0% divorced (2000); Foreign born: 7.3% (2000); Ancestry (includes multiple ancestries): 24.0% German, 15.6% Irish, 11.5% Dutch, 11.5% English, 5.2% Norwegian (2000).
Economy: Employment by occupation: 9.8% management, 18.0% professional, 34.4% services, 8.2% sales, 8.2% farming, 13.1% construction, 8.2% production (2000).
Income: Per capita income: $21,269 (2000); Median household income: $47,917 (2000); Poverty rate: 15.6% (2000).
Education: High school graduation rate: 67.6% (2000); College graduation rate: 6.8% (2000).
Housing: Homeownership rate: 70.8% (2000); Median home value: $32,500 (2000); Median rent: $225 per month (2000); Median age of housing: 60+ years (2000).
Transportation: Commute to work: 62.3% car, 0.0% public transportation, 29.5% walk, 8.2% work from home (2000); Travel time to work: 33.9% less than 15 minutes, 8.9% 15 to 30 minutes, 19.6% 30 to 45 minutes, 0.0% 45 to 60 minutes, 37.5% 60 minutes or more (2000)

VICHY (unincorporated postal area, zip code 65580). Covers a land area of 54.123 square miles and a water area of 0.028 square miles. Located at 38.10° N. Lat.; 91.77° W. Long. Elevation is 1,118 feet.
History: Vichy was platted in 1880 and named for the French resort and spa town. The town suffered in 1886 when a tornado destroyed most of the buildings.
Population: 801 (2000); Race: 97.6% White, 0.6% Black, 0.0% Asian, 0.0% American Indian and Alaska Native, 0.0% Hispanic of any race, 1.8% two or more races (2000); Density: 14.8 persons per square mile (2000); Age: 20.0% under 18, 21.8% over 64 (2000); Marriage status: 15.4% never married, 65.7% now married, 7.8% widowed, 11.1% divorced (2000); Foreign born: 0.7% (2000); Ancestry (includes multiple ancestries): 18.9% English, 18.5% German, 13.1% United States or American, 6.7% Irish, 6.5% Other groups (2000).
Economy: Employment by occupation: 12.2% management, 7.4% professional, 14.3% services, 30.2% sales, 2.3% farming, 14.1% construction, 19.6% production (2000).
Income: Per capita income: $16,805 (2000); Median household income: $33,142 (2000); Poverty rate: 9.4% (2000).
Education: High school graduation rate: 73.9% (2000); College graduation rate: 7.5% (2000).
Housing: Homeownership rate: 86.6% (2000); Median home value: $71,900 (2000); Median rent: $300 per month (2000); Median age of housing: 20 years (2000).
Transportation: Commute to work: 90.1% car, 0.9% public transportation, 0.9% walk, 6.3% work from home (2000); Travel time to work: 16.8% less than 15 minutes, 41.9% 15 to 30 minutes, 21.1% 30 to 45 minutes, 6.3% 45 to 60 minutes, 14.0% 60 minutes or more (2000)

Airports: Rolla National

VIENNA (city). Covers a land area of 1.057 square miles and a water area of 0 square miles. Located at 38.18° N. Lat.; 91.94° W. Long. Elevation is 873 feet.
History: Vienna was settled in 1855 by German and Irish immigrants. The name was suggested by Judge E.G. Latham, who wanted the town called Vie Anna for a woman of his family who had recently died. Vienna was accepted as a compromise.
Population: 628 (2000); Race: 99.4% White, 0.0% Black, 0.0% Asian, 0.0% American Indian and Alaska Native, 0.0% Hispanic of any race, 0.6% two or more races (2000); Density: 594.0 persons per square mile (2000); Age: 21.7% under 18, 28.1% over 64 (2000); Marriage status: 22.8% never married, 48.0% now married, 17.4% widowed, 11.8% divorced (2000); Foreign born: 0.5% (2000); Ancestry (includes multiple ancestries): 29.8% German, 15.7% Irish, 12.7% English, 12.4% United States or American, 7.8% Other groups (2000).
Economy: Employment by occupation: 5.7% management, 16.0% professional, 12.7% services, 26.2% sales, 0.0% farming, 15.2% construction, 24.2% production (2000).
Income: Per capita income: $13,682 (2000); Median household income: $23,456 (2000); Poverty rate: 8.1% (2000).
Taxes: Total city taxes per capita: $151 (1997); City property taxes per capita: $33 (1997).
Education: High school graduation rate: 56.9% (2000); College graduation rate: 12.2% (2000).

School District(s)

Maries Co. R-I (KG-12)
2000 Enrollment: 568 573-422-3304

Housing: Homeownership rate: 57.0% (2000); Median home value: $56,800 (2000); Median rent: $262 per month (2000); Median age of housing: 29 years (2000).
Transportation: Commute to work: 91.3% car, 0.0% public transportation, 5.4% walk, 2.1% work from home (2000); Travel time to work: 38.0% less than 15 minutes, 15.2% 15 to 30 minutes, 21.9% 30 to 45 minutes, 19.4% 45 to 60 minutes, 5.5% 60 minutes or more (2000)

Marion County

Located in northeastern Missouri; bounded on the east by the Mississippi River and the Illinois border; drained by the North and South Fabius Rivers. Covers a land area of 438.10 square miles, a water area of 6.00 square miles, and is located in the Central Time Zone. The county government was organized in 1826. County seat is Palmyra.

Weather Station: Hannibal Water Works — Elevation: 711 feet

	Jan	Feb	Mar	Apr	May	Jun	Jul	Aug	Sep	Oct	Nov	Dec
High	33	40	51	64	74	83	87	85	78	66	51	38
Low	16	21	32	43	53	62	67	65	56	44	33	22
Precip	1.7	2.1	3.2	4.0	4.9	3.5	4.3	4.3	3.5	3.2	3.5	2.6
Snow	7.2	5.5	3.1	1.0	0.0	0.0	0.0	0.0	0.0	tr	1.4	4.6

High and Low temperatures in degrees Fahrenheit; Precipitation and Snow in inches

Population: 28,289 (2000); Race: 93.8% White, 4.2% Black, 0.1% Asian, 0.1% American Indian and Alaska Native, 0.9% Hispanic of any race, 1.4% two or more races (2000); Density: 64.6 persons per square mile (2000); Age: 25.8% under 18, 16.7% over 64 (2000).
Religion: Five largest groups: 20.3% Southern Baptist Convention, 11.4% Catholic Church, 7.2% Lutheran Church—Missouri Synod, 6.0% The United Methodist Church, 5.5% Christian Church (Disciples of Christ) (2000).
Economy: Unemployment rate: 4.4% (11/2002); Total civilian labor force: 15,244 (11/2002); Leading industries: 26.2% manufacturing; 16.4% health care and social assistance; 16.1% retail trade (2000); Companies that employ more than 1,000 persons: 0 (2000); Companies that employ more than 100 persons: 18 (2000); Farms: 695 totaling 221,353 acres (1997); Minority business ownership rate: 0.0% (1997); Women business ownership rate: 24.3% (1997); Retail sales per capita: $10,744 (1997). Single-family building permits issued: 66 (2001) / 55 (2000); Multi-family building permits issued: 10 (2001) / 52 (2000).
Income: Per capita income: $16,964 (2000); Median household income: $31,774 (2000); Poverty rate: 12.1% (2000); Bankruptcy rate: 5.73% (2001).
Taxes: Total county taxes per capita: $171 (2000); County property taxes per capita: $67 (2000).
Education: High school graduation rate: 79.4% (2000); College graduation rate: 15.6% (2000).

Housing: Homeownership rate: 70.4% (2000); Median home value: $66,600 (2000); Median rent: $283 per month (2000); Median age of housing: 41 years (2000).
Health: Birth rate: 141.8 per 10,000 population (1998); Age adjusted death rate: 93.2 per 10,000 population (1999); Age adjusted cancer mortality rate: 201.4 deaths per 100,000 population (1999). Number of physicians: 17.3 per 10,000 population (1999); Number of hospital beds: 37.1 per 10,000 population (1999).
Elections: 2000 Presidential election results: 42.6% Gore, 55.9% Bush, 0.7% Nader, 0.4% Buchanan
National and State Parks: Elmslie Memorial State Forest
Additional Information Contacts
Marion County Government Offices 573-769-2549
Hannibal Chamber of Commerce. 573-221-1101
Mark Twain Board of Realtors. 573-221-8030

Marion County Communities

HANNIBAL (city). Covers a land area of 14.611 square miles and a water area of 0.472 square miles. Located at 39.70° N. Lat.; 91.37° W. Long. Elevation is 491 feet.
History: Hannibal was platted in 1819 at the mouth of Bear Creek on the Mississippi River, and lots were offered for sale in St. Louis. In 1838 the Hannibal Company was formed and the town was incorporated. It soon became a river port, with tobacco factories, flour mills, and a port-packing plant. Hannibal was the boyhood home of Mark Twain, whose family moved here in 1839. Many of the incidents attributed to Tom Sawyer and Huckleberry Finn actually happened to the young Samuel Clemens while he was growing up in Hannibal.
Population: 17,757 (2000); Race: 91.5% White, 6.0% Black, 0.1% Asian, 0.2% American Indian and Alaska Native, 1.2% Hispanic of any race, 1.9% two or more races (2000); Density: 1,215.3 persons per square mile (2000); Age: 26.6% under 18, 16.5% over 64 (2000); Marriage status: 22.0% never married, 56.5% now married, 10.0% widowed, 11.4% divorced (2000); Foreign born: 1.1% (2000); Ancestry (includes multiple ancestries): 19.6% German, 17.0% United States or American, 13.6% Other groups, 11.7% Irish, 10.7% English (2000).
Vital Statistics: Birth rate: 135.2 per 10,000 population (1998)
Economy: Single-family building permits issued: 25 (2001) / 20 (2000); Multi-family building permits issued: 10 (2001) / 52 (2000); Employment by occupation: 7.5% management, 16.5% professional, 17.7% services, 24.4% sales, 0.4% farming, 9.7% construction, 23.8% production (2000).
Income: Per capita income: $16,902 (2000); Median household income: $29,892 (2000); Poverty rate: 14.1% (2000).
Taxes: Total city taxes per capita: $467 (2000); City property taxes per capita: $164 (2000).
Education: High school graduation rate: 77.0% (2000); College graduation rate: 15.6% (2000).

School District(s)

Hannibal 60 (PK-12)
2000 Enrollment: 3,821 573-221-1258

Four-year College(s)

Hannibal-LaGrange College (Private, Not-for-profit, Southern Baptist)
2001 Enrollment: 1,099 573-221-3675
2001 Tuition: In-state $8,859; Out-of-state $8,859
Housing: Homeownership rate: 67.5% (2000); Median home value: $56,500 (2000); Median rent: $290 per month (2000); Median age of housing: 48 years (2000).
Hospitals: Hannibal Regional Hospital (105 beds)
Safety: Violent crime rate: 81.2 per 10,000 population; Property crime rate: 472.4 per 10,000 population (2001).
Newspapers: Hannibal Courier-Post (6 x week); The Salt River Journal (1 x week)
Transportation: Commute to work: 94.7% car, 0.7% public transportation, 2.4% walk, 1.5% work from home (2000); Travel time to work: 67.0% less than 15 minutes, 20.6% 15 to 30 minutes, 7.7% 30 to 45 minutes, 2.4% 45 to 60 minutes, 2.3% 60 minutes or more (2000)
Airports: Hannibal Municipal
Additional Information Contacts
Hannibal Chamber of Commerce. 573-221-1101
Mark Twain Board of Realtors. 573-221-8030

PALMYRA (city). Covers a land area of 2.223 square miles and a water area of 0 square miles. Located at 39.79° N. Lat.; 91.52° W. Long. Elevation is 641 feet.
History: Palmyra was platted in 1819 and named for the Syrian city built by King Solomon, also founded in the wilderness. The town grew up around a large spring, the water of which was later piped to the Palmyra power plant.
Population: 3,467 (2000); Race: 95.8% White, 3.0% Black, 0.0% Asian, 0.1% American Indian and Alaska Native, 0.5% Hispanic of any race, 0.4% two or more races (2000); Density: 1,559.9 persons per square mile (2000); Age: 24.6% under 18, 20.5% over 64 (2000); Marriage status: 18.5% never married, 61.6% now married, 10.3% widowed, 9.5% divorced (2000); Foreign born: 0.5% (2000); Ancestry (includes multiple ancestries): 29.0% German, 14.6% United States or American, 9.2% English, 9.2% Irish, 7.8% Other groups (2000).
Economy: Single-family building permits issued: 6 (2001) / 9 (2000); Multi-family building permits issued: 0 (2001) / 0 (2000); Employment by occupation: 8.9% management, 13.2% professional, 14.3% services, 25.0% sales, 0.3% farming, 12.7% construction, 25.6% production (2000).
Income: Per capita income: $15,625 (2000); Median household income: $31,284 (2000); Poverty rate: 8.1% (2000).
Taxes: Total city taxes per capita: $182 (1997); City property taxes per capita: $39 (1997).
Education: High school graduation rate: 80.3% (2000); College graduation rate: 12.9% (2000).

School District(s)

Palmyra R-I (PK-12)
2000 Enrollment: 1,153 573-769-2066
Housing: Homeownership rate: 70.3% (2000); Median home value: $72,300 (2000); Median rent: $237 per month (2000); Median age of housing: 42 years (2000).
Newspapers: Palmyra Spectator (1 x week)
Transportation: Commute to work: 93.9% car, 0.0% public transportation, 2.2% walk, 2.6% work from home (2000); Travel time to work: 50.6% less than 15 minutes, 33.1% 15 to 30 minutes, 10.7% 30 to 45 minutes, 1.8% 45 to 60 minutes, 3.8% 60 minutes or more (2000)

PHILADELPHIA (unincorporated postal area, zip code 63463). Covers a land area of 43.928 square miles and a water area of 0.027 square miles. Located at 39.81° N. Lat.; 91.74° W. Long. Elevation is 705 feet.
Population: 643 (2000); Race: 98.9% White, 0.0% Black, 0.0% Asian, 0.0% American Indian and Alaska Native, 0.0% Hispanic of any race, 0.3% two or more races (2000); Density: 14.6 persons per square mile (2000); Age: 33.8% under 18, 9.4% over 64 (2000); Marriage status: 17.9% never married, 71.4% now married, 5.1% widowed, 5.6% divorced (2000); Foreign born: 0.3% (2000); Ancestry (includes multiple ancestries): 27.7% German, 16.8% United States or American, 16.1% Irish, 13.0% English, 6.5% Other groups (2000).
Economy: Employment by occupation: 11.7% management, 16.3% professional, 9.2% services, 18.4% sales, 1.8% farming, 13.8% construction, 28.7% production (2000).
Income: Per capita income: $12,892 (2000); Median household income: $32,411 (2000); Poverty rate: 9.2% (2000).
Education: High school graduation rate: 77.4% (2000); College graduation rate: 12.6% (2000).

School District(s)

Marion Co. R-II (PK-12)
2000 Enrollment: 288 573-439-5913
Housing: Homeownership rate: 78.6% (2000); Median home value: $61,400 (2000); Median rent: $217 per month (2000); Median age of housing: 26 years (2000).
Transportation: Commute to work: 95.0% car, 0.0% public transportation, 0.0% walk, 4.6% work from home (2000); Travel time to work: 16.0% less than 15 minutes, 34.2% 15 to 30 minutes, 28.6% 30 to 45 minutes, 18.6% 45 to 60 minutes, 2.6% 60 minutes or more (2000)

TAYLOR (unincorporated postal area, zip code 63471). Covers a land area of 41.828 square miles and a water area of 0.131 square miles. Located at 39.92° N. Lat.; 91.49° W. Long. Elevation is 489 feet.
History: Taylor grew as a farming community.
Population: 662 (2000); Race: 100.0% White, 0.0% Black, 0.0% Asian, 0.0% American Indian and Alaska Native, 0.0% Hispanic of any race, 0.0% two or more races (2000); Density: 15.8 persons per square mile (2000); Age: 27.3% under 18, 11.9% over 64 (2000); Marriage status: 11.2% never married, 76.7% now married, 3.5% widowed, 8.6% divorced (2000); Foreign born: 0.0% (2000); Ancestry (includes multiple ancestries): 33.6% United States or American, 18.0% German, 5.9% English, 5.1% Irish, 4.6% Dutch (2000).

Economy: Employment by occupation: 11.6% management, 8.8% professional, 21.8% services, 24.9% sales, 2.5% farming, 12.2% construction, 18.1% production (2000).
Income: Per capita income: $20,846 (2000); Median household income: $35,962 (2000); Poverty rate: 10.5% (2000).
Education: High school graduation rate: 85.4% (2000); College graduation rate: 12.1% (2000).
Housing: Homeownership rate: 80.0% (2000); Median home value: $81,900 (2000); Median rent: $388 per month (2000); Median age of housing: 22 years (2000).
Transportation: Commute to work: 92.5% car, 0.0% public transportation, 1.4% walk, 6.1% work from home (2000); Travel time to work: 18.1% less than 15 minutes, 47.2% 15 to 30 minutes, 24.5% 30 to 45 minutes, 3.1% 45 to 60 minutes, 7.1% 60 minutes or more (2000)

McDonald County

Located in southwestern Missouri, in the Ozarks; bounded on the west by Oklahoma, and on the south by Arkansas; drained by the Elk River. Covers a land area of 539.50 square miles, a water area of 0.20 square miles, and is located in the Central Time Zone. The county government was organized in 1849. County seat is Pineville.

Weather Station: Anderson — Elevation: 1,049 feet

	Jan	Feb	Mar	Apr	May	Jun	Jul	Aug	Sep	Oct	Nov	Dec
High	45	51	60	70	76	84	89	88	80	71	58	49
Low	22	27	35	44	53	62	66	64	57	45	35	26
Precip	2.0	2.0	3.7	4.2	4.7	4.5	3.1	3.7	5.0	3.6	4.3	3.0
Snow	4.5	3.0	2.8	tr	0.0	0.0	0.0	0.0	0.0	tr	1.1	2.3

High and Low temperatures in degrees Fahrenheit; Precipitation and Snow in inches

Population: 21,681 (2000); Race: 89.0% White, 0.1% Black, 0.2% Asian, 2.7% American Indian and Alaska Native, 9.4% Hispanic of any race, 3.9% two or more races (2000); Density: 40.2 persons per square mile (2000); Age: 28.8% under 18, 11.2% over 64 (2000).
Religion: Five largest groups: 21.4% Southern Baptist Convention, 3.9% The United Methodist Church, 3.2% Catholic Church, 1.5% Church of the Nazarene, 1.5% Christian Churches and Churches of Christ (2000).
Economy: Unemployment rate: 6.4% (11/2002); Total civilian labor force: 8,151 (11/2002); Leading industries: 61.8% manufacturing; 9.9% retail trade; 5.2% accommodation & food services (2000); Companies that employ more than 1,000 persons: 1 (2000); Companies that employ more than 100 persons: 8 (2000); Farms: 1,078 totaling 231,648 acres (1997); Minority business ownership rate: 0.0% (1997); Women business ownership rate: 19.4% (1997); Retail sales per capita: $4,191 (1997). Single-family building permits issued: 9 (2001) / 3 (2000); Multi-family building permits issued: 4 (2001) / 4 (2000).
Income: Per capita income: $13,175 (2000); Median household income: $27,010 (2000); Poverty rate: 20.7% (2000); Bankruptcy rate: 3.33% (2001).
Taxes: Total county taxes per capita: $52 (2000); County property taxes per capita: $25 (2000).
Education: High school graduation rate: 69.4% (2000); College graduation rate: 7.0% (2000).
Housing: Homeownership rate: 71.5% (2000); Median home value: $55,800 (2000); Median rent: $297 per month (2000); Median age of housing: 26 years (2000).
Health: Birth rate: 176.2 per 10,000 population (1998); Age adjusted death rate: 98.4 per 10,000 population (1999); Age adjusted cancer mortality rate: 210.1 deaths per 100,000 population (1999). Number of physicians: 1.4 per 10,000 population (1999); Number of hospital beds: n/a (1999).
Elections: 2000 Presidential election results: 28.6% Gore, 68.3% Bush, 1.6% Nader, 0.8% Buchanan
National and State Parks: Elkhorn Tower State Public Hunting Grounds; Elkhorn Tower State Public Hunting Grounds; Huckleberry Ridge State Forest; Powell Tower Site State Public Hunting Grounds
Additional Information Contacts
McDonald County Government Offices 417-223-4717

McDonald County Communities

ANDERSON (city). Covers a land area of 1.923 square miles and a water area of 0 square miles. Located at 36.65° N. Lat.; 94.44° W. Long. Elevation is 890 feet.
History: Anderson developed as an outfitting point for fishing parties.
Population: 1,856 (2000); Race: 90.3% White, 0.0% Black, 0.6% Asian, 3.4% American Indian and Alaska Native, 4.0% Hispanic of any race, 2.6% two or more races (2000); Density: 965.4 persons per square mile (2000); Age: 28.2% under 18, 16.2% over 64 (2000); Marriage status: 20.3% never married, 55.0% now married, 9.8% widowed, 14.9% divorced (2000); Foreign born: 3.2% (2000); Ancestry (includes multiple ancestries): 23.4% United States or American, 19.5% Other groups, 13.6% German, 12.4% Irish, 7.6% English (2000).
Economy: Single-family building permits issued: 6 (2001) / 3 (2000); Multi-family building permits issued: 0 (2001) / 0 (2000); Employment by occupation: 5.9% management, 12.7% professional, 16.5% services, 25.2% sales, 2.5% farming, 12.1% construction, 25.2% production (2000).
Income: Per capita income: $12,967 (2000); Median household income: $23,966 (2000); Poverty rate: 25.1% (2000).
Taxes: Total city taxes per capita: $181 (1997); City property taxes per capita: $44 (1997).
Education: High school graduation rate: 70.2% (2000); College graduation rate: 9.5% (2000).

School District(s)

Mcdonald Co. R-I (PK-12)
2000 Enrollment: 3,440 417-845-3321

Housing: Homeownership rate: 60.1% (2000); Median home value: $55,500 (2000); Median rent: $278 per month (2000); Median age of housing: 29 years (2000).
Newspapers: Anderson Graphic (2 x week)
Transportation: Commute to work: 92.2% car, 0.5% public transportation, 3.0% walk, 4.0% work from home (2000); Travel time to work: 38.3% less than 15 minutes, 27.4% 15 to 30 minutes, 20.9% 30 to 45 minutes, 9.1% 45 to 60 minutes, 4.2% 60 minutes or more (2000)

GOODMAN (town). Covers a land area of 1.284 square miles and a water area of 0 square miles. Located at 36.74° N. Lat.; 94.41° W. Long. Elevation is 1,254 feet.
Population: 1,183 (2000); Race: 93.7% White, 0.0% Black, 0.1% Asian, 1.5% American Indian and Alaska Native, 0.4% Hispanic of any race, 4.4% two or more races (2000); Density: 921.4 persons per square mile (2000); Age: 29.5% under 18, 15.7% over 64 (2000); Marriage status: 15.0% never married, 59.8% now married, 10.6% widowed, 14.6% divorced (2000); Foreign born: 0.5% (2000); Ancestry (includes multiple ancestries): 20.9% United States or American, 13.0% Other groups, 12.6% Irish, 12.2% German, 5.6% English (2000).
Economy: Employment by occupation: 7.4% management, 7.8% professional, 15.6% services, 24.6% sales, 2.3% farming, 10.9% construction, 31.6% production (2000).
Income: Per capita income: $11,052 (2000); Median household income: $26,349 (2000); Poverty rate: 18.3% (2000).
Taxes: Total city taxes per capita: $92 (1997); City property taxes per capita: $23 (1997).
Education: High school graduation rate: 74.0% (2000); College graduation rate: 4.5% (2000).
Housing: Homeownership rate: 75.7% (2000); Median home value: $46,000 (2000); Median rent: $297 per month (2000); Median age of housing: 28 years (2000).
Newspapers: Goodman News Dispatch (1 x week)
Transportation: Commute to work: 93.4% car, 0.6% public transportation, 1.9% walk, 0.8% work from home (2000); Travel time to work: 27.2% less than 15 minutes, 41.1% 15 to 30 minutes, 13.1% 30 to 45 minutes, 9.8% 45 to 60 minutes, 8.9% 60 minutes or more (2000)

LANAGAN (town). Covers a land area of 0.965 square miles and a water area of 0 square miles. Located at 36.60° N. Lat.; 94.45° W. Long. Elevation is 868 feet.
History: Lanagan grew up around a well of sulphur water that attracted visitors.
Population: 411 (2000); Race: 88.4% White, 0.5% Black, 0.0% Asian, 4.5% American Indian and Alaska Native, 11.2% Hispanic of any race, 3.3% two or more races (2000); Density: 426.1 persons per square mile (2000); Age: 24.7% under 18, 14.5% over 64 (2000); Marriage status: 18.5% never married, 61.4% now married, 10.9% widowed, 9.1% divorced (2000); Foreign born: 6.7% (2000); Ancestry (includes multiple ancestries): 27.8% Other groups, 23.8% United States or American, 15.0% Irish, 12.4% English, 10.0% German (2000).
Economy: Employment by occupation: 3.8% management, 4.4% professional, 18.4% services, 15.8% sales, 3.8% farming, 7.0% construction, 46.8% production (2000).
Income: Per capita income: $9,776 (2000); Median household income: $20,125 (2000); Poverty rate: 34.9% (2000).

Taxes: Total city taxes per capita: $152 (1997); City property taxes per capita: $47 (1997).
Education: High school graduation rate: 58.4% (2000); College graduation rate: 5.2% (2000).
Housing: Homeownership rate: 57.9% (2000); Median home value: $29,300 (2000); Median rent: $225 per month (2000); Median age of housing: 40 years (2000).
Transportation: Commute to work: 94.2% car, 0.0% public transportation, 2.6% walk, 1.3% work from home (2000); Travel time to work: 22.7% less than 15 minutes, 38.3% 15 to 30 minutes, 17.5% 30 to 45 minutes, 11.7% 45 to 60 minutes, 9.7% 60 minutes or more (2000)

NOEL (city). Covers a land area of 2.001 square miles and a water area of 0.057 square miles. Located at 36.54° N. Lat.; 94.48° W. Long. Elevation is 830 feet.
History: Plotted 1891.
Population: 1,480 (2000); Race: 66.0% White, 0.2% Black, 0.9% Asian, 3.2% American Indian and Alaska Native, 40.4% Hispanic of any race, 4.5% two or more races (2000); Density: 739.7 persons per square mile (2000); Age: 28.4% under 18, 11.3% over 64 (2000); Marriage status: 26.7% never married, 52.2% now married, 5.7% widowed, 15.5% divorced (2000); Foreign born: 22.1% (2000); Ancestry (includes multiple ancestries): 46.4% Other groups, 15.2% United States or American, 9.5% German, 8.4% Irish, 5.0% English (2000).
Economy: Sport fishing; berries, chickens, dairying. Manufacturing: poultry processing, wood products. Single-family building permits issued: 3 (2001) / 0 (2000); Multi-family building permits issued: 0 (2001) / 0 (2000); Employment by occupation: 5.4% management, 5.1% professional, 16.9% services, 16.2% sales, 1.5% farming, 12.1% construction, 42.7% production (2000).
Income: Per capita income: $11,166 (2000); Median household income: $27,386 (2000); Poverty rate: 21.0% (2000).
Taxes: Total city taxes per capita: $294 (1997); City property taxes per capita: $0 (1997).
Education: High school graduation rate: 53.9% (2000); College graduation rate: 6.7% (2000).
Housing: Homeownership rate: 46.0% (2000); Median home value: $53,200 (2000); Median rent: $275 per month (2000); Median age of housing: 34 years (2000).
Transportation: Commute to work: 92.1% car, 0.5% public transportation, 4.5% walk, 1.2% work from home (2000); Travel time to work: 53.1% less than 15 minutes, 24.2% 15 to 30 minutes, 11.6% 30 to 45 minutes, 5.0% 45 to 60 minutes, 6.1% 60 minutes or more (2000)

PINEVILLE (town). Covers a land area of 0.702 square miles and a water area of 0 square miles. Located at 36.59° N. Lat.; 94.38° W. Long. Elevation is 899 feet.
History: Pineville was established in 1847. In 1938, Hollywood came to Pineville to film "Jesse James."
Population: 768 (2000); Race: 97.4% White, 0.0% Black, 0.0% Asian, 1.0% American Indian and Alaska Native, 3.6% Hispanic of any race, 0.6% two or more races (2000); Density: 1,094.0 persons per square mile (2000); Age: 27.9% under 18, 13.3% over 64 (2000); Marriage status: 18.3% never married, 59.8% now married, 5.4% widowed, 16.5% divorced (2000); Foreign born: 2.5% (2000); Ancestry (includes multiple ancestries): 23.7% United States or American, 13.8% Other groups, 13.4% German, 12.8% Irish, 9.6% English (2000).
Economy: Employment by occupation: 18.9% management, 8.2% professional, 12.3% services, 28.9% sales, 1.3% farming, 8.8% construction, 21.7% production (2000).
Income: Per capita income: $13,414 (2000); Median household income: $24,886 (2000); Poverty rate: 23.2% (2000).
Taxes: Total city taxes per capita: $151 (1997); City property taxes per capita: $45 (1997).
Education: High school graduation rate: 77.1% (2000); College graduation rate: 13.3% (2000).
Housing: Homeownership rate: 57.7% (2000); Median home value: $64,400 (2000); Median rent: $289 per month (2000); Median age of housing: 40 years (2000).
Newspapers: McDonald County Press (1 x week); McDonald County News-Gazette (2 x week)
Transportation: Commute to work: 90.5% car, 0.0% public transportation, 6.3% walk, 1.9% work from home (2000); Travel time to work: 31.6% less than 15 minutes, 32.9% 15 to 30 minutes, 24.2% 30 to 45 minutes, 9.4% 45 to 60 minutes, 1.9% 60 minutes or more (2000)

POWELL (unincorporated postal area, zip code 65730). Covers a land area of 12.219 square miles and a water area of 0 square miles. Located at 36.61° N. Lat.; 94.15° W. Long. Elevation is 998 feet.
Population: 158 (2000); Race: 100.0% White, 0.0% Black, 0.0% Asian, 0.0% American Indian and Alaska Native, 0.0% Hispanic of any race, 0.0% two or more races (2000); Density: 12.9 persons per square mile (2000); Age: 0.0% under 18, 21.6% over 64 (2000); Marriage status: 37.8% never married, 29.7% now married, 12.2% widowed, 20.3% divorced (2000); Foreign born: 0.0% (2000); Ancestry (includes multiple ancestries): 39.2% United States or American, 39.2% Other groups, 10.8% French Canadian (2000).
Economy: Employment by occupation: 0.0% management, 0.0% professional, 34.6% services, 65.4% sales, 0.0% farming, 0.0% construction, 0.0% production (2000).
Income: Per capita income: $13,385 (2000); Median household income: $25,313 (2000); Poverty rate: 20.3% (2000).
Education: High school graduation rate: 73.7% (2000); College graduation rate: 19.3% (2000).
Housing: Homeownership rate: 84.1% (2000); Median home value: $40,900 (2000); Median age of housing: 44 years (2000).
Transportation: Commute to work: 100.0% car, 0.0% public transportation, 0.0% walk, 0.0% work from home (2000); Travel time to work: 0.0% less than 15 minutes, 34.6% 15 to 30 minutes, 65.4% 30 to 45 minutes, 0.0% 45 to 60 minutes, 0.0% 60 minutes or more (2000)

ROCKY COMFORT (unincorporated postal area, zip code 64861). Covers a land area of 56.675 square miles and a water area of 0.024 square miles. Located at 36.71° N. Lat.; 94.14° W. Long. Elevation is 1,331 feet.
History: Settled c. 1860.
Population: 1,052 (2000); Race: 96.9% White, 0.0% Black, 0.0% Asian, 1.9% American Indian and Alaska Native, 0.9% Hispanic of any race, 1.2% two or more races (2000); Density: 18.6 persons per square mile (2000); Age: 24.5% under 18, 16.6% over 64 (2000); Marriage status: 17.5% never married, 62.3% now married, 8.5% widowed, 11.7% divorced (2000); Foreign born: 0.4% (2000); Ancestry (includes multiple ancestries): 32.8% United States or American, 16.5% Other groups, 9.1% Irish, 6.8% French (except Basque), 4.3% German (2000).
Economy: Employment by occupation: 16.9% management, 4.1% professional, 14.6% services, 16.6% sales, 4.3% farming, 16.6% construction, 26.8% production (2000).
Income: Per capita income: $21,315 (2000); Median household income: $29,063 (2000); Poverty rate: 23.8% (2000).
Education: High school graduation rate: 65.3% (2000); College graduation rate: 3.7% (2000).
Housing: Homeownership rate: 80.6% (2000); Median home value: $60,500 (2000); Median rent: $228 per month (2000); Median age of housing: 39 years (2000).
Transportation: Commute to work: 81.4% car, 0.0% public transportation, 6.9% walk, 11.7% work from home (2000); Travel time to work: 28.5% less than 15 minutes, 15.9% 15 to 30 minutes, 22.9% 30 to 45 minutes, 23.1% 45 to 60 minutes, 9.5% 60 minutes or more (2000)

SOUTH WEST CITY (town). Covers a land area of 1.393 square miles and a water area of 0.023 square miles. Located at 36.51° N. Lat.; 94.61° W. Long. Elevation is 949 feet.
Population: 855 (2000); Race: 70.4% White, 0.2% Black, 0.0% Asian, 6.6% American Indian and Alaska Native, 44.6% Hispanic of any race, 3.6% two or more races (2000); Density: 613.6 persons per square mile (2000); Age: 38.0% under 18, 6.6% over 64 (2000); Marriage status: 25.8% never married, 55.7% now married, 3.8% widowed, 14.7% divorced (2000); Foreign born: 28.0% (2000); Ancestry (includes multiple ancestries): 56.4% Other groups, 10.6% United States or American, 4.6% Irish, 4.4% English, 4.1% German (2000).
Economy: Corn, hay; cattle, poultry. Single-family building permits issued: 0 (2001) / 0 (2000); Multi-family building permits issued: 4 (2001) / 4 (2000); Employment by occupation: 6.9% management, 8.0% professional, 17.8% services, 14.0% sales, 2.9% farming, 8.9% construction, 41.5% production (2000).
Income: Per capita income: $9,526 (2000); Median household income: $22,721 (2000); Poverty rate: 40.2% (2000).
Taxes: Total city taxes per capita: $338 (1997); City property taxes per capita: $78 (1997).
Education: High school graduation rate: 54.2% (2000); College graduation rate: 7.3% (2000).

Housing: Homeownership rate: 56.1% (2000); Median home value: $56,000 (2000); Median rent: $312 per month (2000); Median age of housing: 31 years (2000).
Newspapers: South West City Republic (2 x week)
Transportation: Commute to work: 92.8% car, 0.0% public transportation, 1.2% walk, 3.6% work from home (2000); Travel time to work: 43.9% less than 15 minutes, 36.1% 15 to 30 minutes, 12.1% 30 to 45 minutes, 5.9% 45 to 60 minutes, 1.9% 60 minutes or more (2000)

Mercer County

Located in northern Missouri; bounded on the north by Iowa; drained by the Weldon River. Covers a land area of 454.20 square miles, a water area of 1.00 square miles, and is located in the Central Time Zone. The county government was organized in 1845. County seat is Princeton.

Weather Station: Princeton 6 SW — Elevation: 977 feet

	Jan	Feb	Mar	Apr	May	Jun	Jul	Aug	Sep	Oct	Nov	Dec
High	33	39	52	64	73	83	87	85	77	66	50	37
Low	14	19	30	41	51	60	65	62	54	42	30	19
Precip	0.9	1.1	2.4	3.6	4.6	4.0	5.0	4.0	4.1	3.1	2.2	1.5
Snow	na	na	0.5	0.7	0.0	0.0	0.0	0.0	0.0	tr	0.7	na

High and Low temperatures in degrees Fahrenheit; Precipitation and Snow in inches

Population: 3,757 (2000); Race: 99.4% White, 0.0% Black, 0.1% Asian, 0.1% American Indian and Alaska Native, 0.2% Hispanic of any race, 0.3% two or more races (2000); Density: 8.3 persons per square mile (2000); Age: 22.8% under 18, 21.9% over 64 (2000).
Religion: Five largest groups: 51.8% Southern Baptist Convention, 11.9% The United Methodist Church, 6.6% Christian Church (Disciples of Christ), 4.9% Christian Churches and Churches of Christ, 2.2% Assemblies of God (2000).
Economy: Unemployment rate: 5.9% (11/2002); Total civilian labor force: 1,519 (11/2002); Leading industries: 22.4% retail trade; 12.7% health care and social assistance; 9.7% construction (2000); Companies that employ more than 1,000 persons: 0 (2000); Companies that employ more than 100 persons: 0 (2000); Farms: 539 totaling 229,598 acres (1997); Minority business ownership rate: 0.0% (1997); Women business ownership rate: 0.0% (1997); Retail sales per capita: $4,365 (1997). Single-family building permits issued: 3 (2001) / 0 (2000); Multi-family building permits issued: 0 (2001) / 0 (2000).
Income: Per capita income: $15,140 (2000); Median household income: $29,640 (2000); Poverty rate: 13.3% (2000); Bankruptcy rate: 4.03% (2001).
Taxes: Total county taxes per capita: $112 (1997); County property taxes per capita: $58 (1997).
Education: High school graduation rate: 82.5% (2000); College graduation rate: 12.2% (2000).
Housing: Homeownership rate: 76.8% (2000); Median home value: $32,300 (2000); Median rent: $197 per month (2000); Median age of housing: 36 years (2000).
Health: Birth rate: 130.4 per 10,000 population (1998); Age adjusted death rate: 74.8 per 10,000 population (1999); Age adjusted cancer mortality rate: 98.4 (Unreliable figure as per CDC) deaths per 100,000 population (1999). Number of physicians: 2.7 per 10,000 population (1999); Number of hospital beds: n/a (1999).
Elections: 2000 Presidential election results: 30.1% Gore, 67.9% Bush, 1.1% Nader, 0.5% Buchanan
National and State Parks: Lake Paho State Wildlife Area
Additional Information Contacts
Mercer County Government Offices 660-748-3425

Mercer County Communities

MERCER (town). Covers a land area of 0.354 square miles and a water area of 0 square miles. Located at 40.51° N. Lat.; 93.52° W. Long. Elevation is 1,074 feet.
Population: 342 (2000); Race: 99.7% White, 0.0% Black, 0.0% Asian, 0.0% American Indian and Alaska Native, 0.8% Hispanic of any race, 0.0% two or more races (2000); Density: 966.3 persons per square mile (2000); Age: 21.5% under 18, 24.1% over 64 (2000); Marriage status: 21.5% never married, 54.6% now married, 14.9% widowed, 8.9% divorced (2000); Foreign born: 0.3% (2000); Ancestry (includes multiple ancestries): 18.7% United States or American, 11.9% Irish, 7.6% Other groups, 7.1% German, 4.0% English (2000).
Economy: Employment by occupation: 13.0% management, 10.7% professional, 30.2% services, 13.6% sales, 8.9% farming, 5.9% construction, 17.8% production (2000).
Income: Per capita income: $13,493 (2000); Median household income: $23,906 (2000); Poverty rate: 26.3% (2000).
Taxes: Total city taxes per capita: $59 (1997); City property taxes per capita: $56 (1997).
Education: High school graduation rate: 67.3% (2000); College graduation rate: 8.2% (2000).

School District(s)

North Mercer Co. R-III (PK-12)
2000 Enrollment: 238 660-382-4214

Housing: Homeownership rate: 75.9% (2000); Median home value: $25,400 (2000); Median rent: $181 per month (2000); Median age of housing: 46 years (2000).
Transportation: Commute to work: 89.9% car, 0.0% public transportation, 5.0% walk, 3.1% work from home (2000); Travel time to work: 37.0% less than 15 minutes, 26.6% 15 to 30 minutes, 20.1% 30 to 45 minutes, 8.4% 45 to 60 minutes, 7.8% 60 minutes or more (2000)

PRINCETON (city). Covers a land area of 1.585 square miles and a water area of 0.013 square miles. Located at 40.39° N. Lat.; 93.58° W. Long. Elevation is 932 feet.
History: Princeton was platted in 1846 and incorporated in 1853. It was named for the Battle of Princeton (New Jersey) in which General Hugh Mercer, for whom the county was named, fought with General George Washington. Martha Canary (1850-1903), known as Calamity Jane, was born in Princeton.
Population: 1,047 (2000); Race: 100.0% White, 0.0% Black, 0.0% Asian, 0.0% American Indian and Alaska Native, 0.4% Hispanic of any race, 0.0% two or more races (2000); Density: 660.5 persons per square mile (2000); Age: 24.2% under 18, 26.5% over 64 (2000); Marriage status: 16.3% never married, 49.9% now married, 17.0% widowed, 16.8% divorced (2000); Foreign born: 0.1% (2000); Ancestry (includes multiple ancestries): 20.4% German, 17.2% United States or American, 12.3% English, 10.2% Irish, 5.0% Other groups (2000).
Economy: Single-family building permits issued: 3 (2001) / 0 (2000); Multi-family building permits issued: 0 (2001) / 0 (2000); Employment by occupation: 12.6% management, 19.5% professional, 13.9% services, 20.1% sales, 8.1% farming, 8.6% construction, 17.1% production (2000).
Income: Per capita income: $15,485 (2000); Median household income: $27,059 (2000); Poverty rate: 17.3% (2000).
Taxes: Total city taxes per capita: $133 (1997); City property taxes per capita: $57 (1997).
Education: High school graduation rate: 84.7% (2000); College graduation rate: 16.8% (2000).

School District(s)

Princeton R-V (PK-12)
2000 Enrollment: 425 660-748-3211

Housing: Homeownership rate: 65.6% (2000); Median home value: $33,800 (2000); Median rent: $189 per month (2000); Median age of housing: 45 years (2000).
Newspapers: The Post-Telegraph (1 x week)
Transportation: Commute to work: 90.8% car, 0.0% public transportation, 4.6% walk, 3.7% work from home (2000); Travel time to work: 54.5% less than 15 minutes, 16.1% 15 to 30 minutes, 16.5% 30 to 45 minutes, 9.0% 45 to 60 minutes, 3.8% 60 minutes or more (2000)

SOUTH LINEVILLE (town). Covers a land area of 0.058 square miles and a water area of 0 square miles. Located at 40.57° N. Lat.; 93.52° W. Long. Elevation is 1,093 feet.
Population: 37 (2000); Race: 100.0% White, 0.0% Black, 0.0% Asian, 0.0% American Indian and Alaska Native, 0.0% Hispanic of any race, 0.0% two or more races (2000); Density: 636.8 persons per square mile (2000); Age: 28.9% under 18, 18.4% over 64 (2000); Marriage status: 0.0% never married, 81.5% now married, 11.1% widowed, 7.4% divorced (2000); Foreign born: 0.0% (2000); Ancestry (includes multiple ancestries): 28.9% German, 23.7% Norwegian, 15.8% United States or American, 5.3% Irish, 5.3% Welsh (2000).
Economy: Employment by occupation: 12.5% management, 0.0% professional, 50.0% services, 12.5% sales, 0.0% farming, 0.0% construction, 25.0% production (2000).
Income: Per capita income: $9,153 (2000); Median household income: $26,875 (2000); Poverty rate: 15.8% (2000).
Taxes: Total city taxes per capita: $23 (1997); City property taxes per capita: $23 (1997).

Education: High school graduation rate: 72.7% (2000); College graduation rate: 0.0% (2000).
Housing: Homeownership rate: 100.0% (2000); Median home value: $27,500 (2000); Median age of housing: 60+ years (2000).
Transportation: Commute to work: 68.8% car, 0.0% public transportation, 18.8% walk, 12.5% work from home (2000); Travel time to work: 21.4% less than 15 minutes, 28.6% 15 to 30 minutes, 21.4% 30 to 45 minutes, 0.0% 45 to 60 minutes, 28.6% 60 minutes or more (2000)

Miller County

Located in central Missouri, in the Ozarks; drained by the Osage River. Covers a land area of 592.30 square miles, a water area of 7.70 square miles, and is located in the Central Time Zone. The county government was organized in 1837. County seat is Tuscumbia.

Weather Station: Eldon — Elevation: 928 feet

	Jan	Feb	Mar	Apr	May	Jun	Jul	Aug	Sep	Oct	Nov	Dec
High	40	47	57	68	76	85	90	89	80	70	55	44
Low	19	24	34	44	54	63	68	65	57	46	35	24
Precip	1.7	1.9	3.2	4.3	5.2	4.4	3.7	3.4	4.5	3.6	3.7	2.7
Snow	4.1	3.4	1.9	0.2	0.0	0.0	0.0	0.0	0.0	tr	1.3	3.0

High and Low temperatures in degrees Fahrenheit; Precipitation and Snow in inches

Weather Station: Lakeside — Elevation: 590 feet

	Jan	Feb	Mar	Apr	May	Jun	Jul	Aug	Sep	Oct	Nov	Dec
High	40	47	57	68	76	84	90	89	80	70	57	46
Low	20	24	33	43	52	62	66	65	57	45	36	26
Precip	1.7	1.8	3.3	4.3	5.0	4.1	3.8	3.7	4.2	3.6	3.7	2.5
Snow	4.0	3.0	1.1	0.1	0.0	0.0	0.0	0.0	0.0	0.0	0.7	2.2

High and Low temperatures in degrees Fahrenheit; Precipitation and Snow in inches

Population: 23,564 (2000); Race: 97.3% White, 0.2% Black, 0.4% Asian, 0.5% American Indian and Alaska Native, 1.1% Hispanic of any race, 1.3% two or more races (2000); Density: 39.8 persons per square mile (2000); Age: 26.3% under 18, 15.3% over 64 (2000).
Religion: Five largest groups: 25.3% Southern Baptist Convention, 16.0% Catholic Church, 3.5% Christian Churches and Churches of Christ, 2.8% The United Methodist Church, 1.9% Churches of Christ (2000).
Economy: Unemployment rate: 6.4% (11/2002); Total civilian labor force: 10,985 (11/2002); Leading industries: 21.2% manufacturing; 17.7% retail trade; 14.9% accommodation & food services (2000); Companies that employ more than 1,000 persons: 0 (2000); Companies that employ more than 100 persons: 7 (2000); Farms: 1,067 totaling 254,520 acres (1997); Minority business ownership rate: 0.0% (1997); Women business ownership rate: 16.6% (1997); Retail sales per capita: $9,233 (1997). Single-family building permits issued: 22 (2001) / 11 (2000); Multi-family building permits issued: 62 (2001) / 44 (2000).
Income: Per capita income: $15,144 (2000); Median household income: $30,977 (2000); Poverty rate: 14.2% (2000); Bankruptcy rate: 5.21% (2001).
Taxes: Total county taxes per capita: $93 (2000); County property taxes per capita: $11 (2000).
Education: High school graduation rate: 73.9% (2000); College graduation rate: 11.4% (2000).
Housing: Homeownership rate: 75.0% (2000); Median home value: $69,900 (2000); Median rent: $280 per month (2000); Median age of housing: 23 years (2000).
Health: Birth rate: 146.0 per 10,000 population (1998); Age adjusted death rate: 86.4 per 10,000 population (1999); Age adjusted cancer mortality rate: 214.4 deaths per 100,000 population (1999). Number of physicians: 1.7 per 10,000 population (1999); Number of hospital beds: n/a (1999).
Elections: 2000 Presidential election results: 34.4% Gore, 63.5% Bush, 1.4% Nader, 0.4% Buchanan
National and State Parks: Boeckman Bridge State Wildlife Area; Kings Bluff State Wildlife Area; Madden Ford Access State Wildlife Area; Osage-Tavern State Wildlife Area; Rocky Mount Towersite State Wildlife Area; Saline Valley State Wildlife Area; Wilson Camp State Wildlife Area
Additional Information Contacts
Miller County Government Offices 573-369-2317
Bagnell Dam Association of Realtors 573-348-4288
Eldon Chamber of Commerce 573-392-3752
Lake Ozark Chamber of Commerce 573-964-0174

Miller County Communities

BAGNELL (town). Covers a land area of 0.469 square miles and a water area of 0.138 square miles. Located at 38.22° N. Lat.; 92.60° W. Long. Elevation is 586 feet.
History: Bagnell was named for William Bagnell, the railroad contractor. The town grew with the building of Bagnell Dam on the Osage River in 1929.
Population: 86 (2000); Race: 94.4% White, 0.0% Black, 0.0% Asian, 5.6% American Indian and Alaska Native, 1.1% Hispanic of any race, 0.0% two or more races (2000); Density: 183.3 persons per square mile (2000); Age: 24.7% under 18, 20.2% over 64 (2000); Marriage status: 22.5% never married, 53.5% now married, 12.7% widowed, 11.3% divorced (2000); Foreign born: 0.0% (2000); Ancestry (includes multiple ancestries): 37.1% United States or American, 16.9% Irish, 14.6% English, 13.5% German, 6.7% Other groups (2000).
Economy: Employment by occupation: 13.6% management, 4.5% professional, 25.0% services, 29.5% sales, 0.0% farming, 6.8% construction, 20.5% production (2000).
Income: Per capita income: $14,633 (2000); Median household income: $25,313 (2000); Poverty rate: 2.2% (2000).
Taxes: Total city taxes per capita: $40 (1997); City property taxes per capita: $10 (1997).
Education: High school graduation rate: 58.6% (2000); College graduation rate: 5.2% (2000).
Housing: Homeownership rate: 57.1% (2000); Median home value: $57,500 (2000); Median rent: $290 per month (2000); Median age of housing: 24 years (2000).
Transportation: Commute to work: 70.5% car, 0.0% public transportation, 15.9% walk, 13.6% work from home (2000); Travel time to work: 44.7% less than 15 minutes, 44.7% 15 to 30 minutes, 10.5% 30 to 45 minutes, 0.0% 45 to 60 minutes, 0.0% 60 minutes or more (2000)

BRUMLEY (town). Covers a land area of 0.483 square miles and a water area of 0 square miles. Located at 38.08° N. Lat.; 92.48° W. Long. Elevation is 751 feet.
Population: 102 (2000); Race: 89.5% White, 0.0% Black, 0.0% Asian, 1.1% American Indian and Alaska Native, 0.0% Hispanic of any race, 9.5% two or more races (2000); Density: 211.3 persons per square mile (2000); Age: 26.3% under 18, 22.1% over 64 (2000); Marriage status: 12.9% never married, 57.1% now married, 14.3% widowed, 15.7% divorced (2000); Foreign born: 0.0% (2000); Ancestry (includes multiple ancestries): 21.1% German, 16.8% Other groups, 5.3% Scottish, 4.2% United States or American, 3.2% Irish (2000).
Economy: Hay, cattle. Employment by occupation: 9.8% management, 7.3% professional, 24.4% services, 26.8% sales, 2.4% farming, 9.8% construction, 19.5% production (2000).
Income: Per capita income: $10,468 (2000); Median household income: $22,500 (2000); Poverty rate: 15.8% (2000).
Taxes: Total city taxes per capita: $189 (1997); City property taxes per capita: $22 (1997).
Education: High school graduation rate: 70.3% (2000); College graduation rate: 7.8% (2000).
Housing: Homeownership rate: 71.4% (2000); Median home value: $35,000 (2000); Median rent: $156 per month (2000); Median age of housing: 26 years (2000).
Transportation: Commute to work: 90.2% car, 0.0% public transportation, 0.0% walk, 0.0% work from home (2000); Travel time to work: 31.7% less than 15 minutes, 29.3% 15 to 30 minutes, 34.1% 30 to 45 minutes, 0.0% 45 to 60 minutes, 4.9% 60 minutes or more (2000)

ELDON (city). Covers a land area of 3.375 square miles and a water area of 0 square miles. Located at 38.34° N. Lat.; 92.58° W. Long. Elevation is 933 feet.
History: Eldon was platted in 1882, and developed as a division point on the Rock Island Railway after 1903. The town experienced greater growth after the construction of Bagnell Dam in 1929.
Population: 4,895 (2000); Race: 97.1% White, 0.0% Black, 1.2% Asian, 0.0% American Indian and Alaska Native, 1.9% Hispanic of any race, 1.6% two or more races (2000); Density: 1,450.2 persons per square mile (2000); Age: 22.6% under 18, 22.8% over 64 (2000); Marriage status: 15.7% never married, 54.0% now married, 16.7% widowed, 13.6% divorced (2000); Foreign born: 1.0% (2000); Ancestry (includes multiple ancestries): 17.5% United States or American, 16.2% German, 10.6% Irish, 10.4% English, 9.0% Other groups (2000).
Economy: Single-family building permits issued: 16 (2001) / 5 (2000); Multi-family building permits issued: 0 (2001) / 0 (2000); Employment by

occupation: 7.5% management, 15.3% professional, 23.0% services, 21.1% sales, 0.3% farming, 10.2% construction, 22.5% production (2000).
Income: Per capita income: $15,015 (2000); Median household income: $27,103 (2000); Poverty rate: 15.8% (2000).
Taxes: Total city taxes per capita: $372 (1997); City property taxes per capita: $33 (1997).
Education: High school graduation rate: 70.1% (2000); College graduation rate: 11.6% (2000).

School District(s)

Eldon R-I (PK-12)
2000 Enrollment: 2,102 573-392-8000

Two-year College(s)

Tri-County Technical School (Public)
2001 Enrollment: 52 573-392-8060

Housing: Homeownership rate: 57.4% (2000); Median home value: $58,400 (2000); Median rent: $279 per month (2000); Median age of housing: 30 years (2000).
Safety: Violent crime rate: 28.4 per 10,000 population; Property crime rate: 621.3 per 10,000 population (2001).
Newspapers: Miller County Autogram Sentinel (1 x week); Advertiser (2 x week)
Transportation: Commute to work: 93.8% car, 0.5% public transportation, 1.3% walk, 3.2% work from home (2000); Travel time to work: 46.0% less than 15 minutes, 27.6% 15 to 30 minutes, 18.4% 30 to 45 minutes, 5.4% 45 to 60 minutes, 2.7% 60 minutes or more (2000)

Additional Information Contacts

Eldon Chamber of Commerce 573-392-3752

IBERIA (city). Covers a land area of 0.899 square miles and a water area of 0 square miles. Located at 38.08° N. Lat.; 92.29° W. Long. Elevation is 932 feet.
Population: 605 (2000); Race: 96.2% White, 0.2% Black, 0.0% Asian, 1.2% American Indian and Alaska Native, 0.8% Hispanic of any race, 2.0% two or more races (2000); Density: 672.8 persons per square mile (2000); Age: 19.3% under 18, 20.9% over 64 (2000); Marriage status: 21.6% never married, 53.3% now married, 14.2% widowed, 11.0% divorced (2000); Foreign born: 0.0% (2000); Ancestry (includes multiple ancestries): 22.7% United States or American, 18.3% German, 15.2% Irish, 12.5% English, 9.1% Other groups (2000).
Economy: Hay; cattle, turkeys. Manufacturing: apparel, wood products. Single-family building permits issued: 0 (2001) / 0 (2000); Multi-family building permits issued: 0 (2001) / 0 (2000); Employment by occupation: 3.8% management, 22.2% professional, 19.9% services, 21.5% sales, 2.3% farming, 16.5% construction, 13.8% production (2000).
Income: Per capita income: $12,918 (2000); Median household income: $22,337 (2000); Poverty rate: 17.8% (2000).
Taxes: Total city taxes per capita: $249 (1997); City property taxes per capita: $20 (1997).
Education: High school graduation rate: 63.0% (2000); College graduation rate: 14.2% (2000).

School District(s)

Iberia R-V (PK-12)
2000 Enrollment: 787 573-793-6818

Housing: Homeownership rate: 65.1% (2000); Median home value: $45,400 (2000); Median rent: $238 per month (2000); Median age of housing: 39 years (2000).
Transportation: Commute to work: 94.8% car, 0.0% public transportation, 4.4% walk, 0.8% work from home (2000); Travel time to work: 36.1% less than 15 minutes, 12.4% 15 to 30 minutes, 24.9% 30 to 45 minutes, 17.7% 45 to 60 minutes, 8.8% 60 minutes or more (2000)

KAISER (unincorporated postal area, zip code 65047). Covers a land area of 33.220 square miles and a water area of 0.096 square miles. Located at 38.14° N. Lat.; 92.58° W. Long. Elevation is 913 feet.
Population: 1,271 (2000); Race: 93.7% White, 0.0% Black, 0.2% Asian, 1.2% American Indian and Alaska Native, 1.2% Hispanic of any race, 4.9% two or more races (2000); Density: 38.3 persons per square mile (2000); Age: 30.6% under 18, 13.6% over 64 (2000); Marriage status: 20.9% never married, 60.0% now married, 7.8% widowed, 11.3% divorced (2000); Foreign born: 0.7% (2000); Ancestry (includes multiple ancestries): 30.9% German, 14.4% United States or American, 14.0% English, 12.2% Other groups, 9.9% Irish (2000).
Economy: Employment by occupation: 11.9% management, 5.0% professional, 24.5% services, 22.6% sales, 1.4% farming, 15.8% construction, 18.8% production (2000).
Income: Per capita income: $16,911 (2000); Median household income: $27,614 (2000); Poverty rate: 17.2% (2000).
Education: High school graduation rate: 80.7% (2000); College graduation rate: 14.9% (2000).
Housing: Homeownership rate: 75.0% (2000); Median home value: $107,700 (2000); Median rent: $273 per month (2000); Median age of housing: 15 years (2000).
Transportation: Commute to work: 93.3% car, 1.3% public transportation, 1.1% walk, 3.7% work from home (2000); Travel time to work: 38.6% less than 15 minutes, 48.4% 15 to 30 minutes, 5.6% 30 to 45 minutes, 4.8% 45 to 60 minutes, 2.5% 60 minutes or more (2000)

LAKE OZARK (city). Covers a land area of 7.036 square miles and a water area of 0.725 square miles. Located at 38.20° N. Lat.; 92.62° W. Long. Elevation is 703 feet.
History: Lake Ozark developed as a service center for people vacationing in the Lake of the Ozarks area.
Population: 1,489 (2000); Race: 94.4% White, 0.5% Black, 0.6% Asian, 1.9% American Indian and Alaska Native, 2.1% Hispanic of any race, 2.3% two or more races (2000); Density: 211.6 persons per square mile (2000); Age: 21.8% under 18, 11.0% over 64 (2000); Marriage status: 22.4% never married, 55.0% now married, 4.7% widowed, 18.0% divorced (2000); Foreign born: 1.8% (2000); Ancestry (includes multiple ancestries): 33.8% German, 17.6% Irish, 13.6% English, 12.1% Other groups, 7.4% United States or American (2000).
Economy: Single-family building permits issued: 0 (2001) / 0 (2000); Multi-family building permits issued: 0 (2001) / 0 (2000); Employment by occupation: 13.1% management, 13.1% professional, 15.5% services, 33.8% sales, 0.0% farming, 12.8% construction, 11.7% production (2000).
Income: Per capita income: $20,830 (2000); Median household income: $37,386 (2000); Poverty rate: 13.1% (2000).
Taxes: Total city taxes per capita: $121 (1997); City property taxes per capita: $17 (1997).
Education: High school graduation rate: 87.2% (2000); College graduation rate: 21.3% (2000).

School District(s)

School of the Osage R-II (PK-12)
2000 Enrollment: 1,665 573-365-4091

Housing: Homeownership rate: 70.0% (2000); Median home value: $109,200 (2000); Median rent: $349 per month (2000); Median age of housing: 13 years (2000).
Safety: Violent crime rate: 113.5 per 10,000 population; Property crime rate: 660.9 per 10,000 population (2001).
Transportation: Commute to work: 87.4% car, 0.0% public transportation, 4.4% walk, 6.4% work from home (2000); Travel time to work: 40.6% less than 15 minutes, 42.3% 15 to 30 minutes, 9.4% 30 to 45 minutes, 2.5% 45 to 60 minutes, 5.2% 60 minutes or more (2000)

Additional Information Contacts

Bagnell Dam Association of Realtors 573-348-4288
Lake Ozark Chamber of Commerce. 573-964-0174

LAKESIDE (city). Covers a land area of 0.349 square miles and a water area of 0.306 square miles. Located at 38.20° N. Lat.; 92.62° W. Long. Elevation is 836 feet.
History: Lakeside was built by the Union Electric Light and Power Company, which operated Bagnell Dam.
Population: 37 (2000); Race: 100.0% White, 0.0% Black, 0.0% Asian, 0.0% American Indian and Alaska Native, 0.0% Hispanic of any race, 0.0% two or more races (2000); Density: 106.0 persons per square mile (2000); Age: 27.8% under 18, 0.0% over 64 (2000); Marriage status: 11.1% never married, 88.9% now married, 0.0% widowed, 0.0% divorced (2000); Foreign born: 0.0% (2000); Ancestry (includes multiple ancestries): 66.7% German, 33.3% English, 22.2% Swedish, 11.1% Irish, 5.6% French (except Basque) (2000).
Economy: Employment by occupation: 20.8% management, 12.5% professional, 8.3% services, 12.5% sales, 0.0% farming, 29.2% construction, 16.7% production (2000).
Income: Per capita income: $32,786 (2000); Median household income: $69,375 (2000); Poverty rate: 0.0% (2000).
Taxes: Total city taxes per capita: $500 (1997); City property taxes per capita: $0 (1997).
Education: High school graduation rate: 100.0% (2000); College graduation rate: 26.9% (2000).
Housing: Homeownership rate: 11.1% (2000); Median rent: <$100 per month (2000); Median age of housing: 60+ years (2000).
Transportation: Commute to work: 87.5% car, 0.0% public transportation, 0.0% walk, 12.5% work from home (2000); Travel time to work: 90.5% less

than 15 minutes, 9.5% 15 to 30 minutes, 0.0% 30 to 45 minutes, 0.0% 45 to 60 minutes, 0.0% 60 minutes or more (2000)

OLEAN (town). Covers a land area of 0.170 square miles and a water area of 0 square miles. Located at 38.41° N. Lat.; 92.52° W. Long. Elevation is 769 feet.

Population: 157 (2000); Race: 98.8% White, 1.2% Black, 0.0% Asian, 0.0% American Indian and Alaska Native, 0.0% Hispanic of any race, 0.0% two or more races (2000); Density: 922.0 persons per square mile (2000); Age: 31.7% under 18, 16.2% over 64 (2000); Marriage status: 30.6% never married, 33.1% now married, 17.7% widowed, 18.5% divorced (2000); Foreign born: 0.0% (2000); Ancestry (includes multiple ancestries): 36.5% United States or American, 9.0% German, 6.6% English, 4.8% Other groups, 4.2% French (except Basque) (2000).
Economy: Employment by occupation: 0.0% management, 0.0% professional, 25.0% services, 38.3% sales, 0.0% farming, 15.0% construction, 21.7% production (2000).
Income: Per capita income: $10,296 (2000); Median household income: $18,333 (2000); Poverty rate: 24.0% (2000).
Taxes: Total city taxes per capita: $35 (1997); City property taxes per capita: $9 (1997).
Education: High school graduation rate: 55.6% (2000); College graduation rate: 2.0% (2000).
Housing: Homeownership rate: 60.0% (2000); Median home value: $45,000 (2000); Median rent: $282 per month (2000); Median age of housing: 60+ years (2000).
Transportation: Commute to work: 100.0% car, 0.0% public transportation, 0.0% walk, 0.0% work from home (2000); Travel time to work: 25.0% less than 15 minutes, 46.7% 15 to 30 minutes, 25.0% 30 to 45 minutes, 3.3% 45 to 60 minutes, 0.0% 60 minutes or more (2000)

SAINT ELIZABETH (village). Covers a land area of 0.906 square miles and a water area of 0 square miles. Located at 38.25° N. Lat.; 92.26° W. Long. Elevation is 812 feet.

Population: 297 (2000); Race: 100.0% White, 0.0% Black, 0.0% Asian, 0.0% American Indian and Alaska Native, 1.6% Hispanic of any race, 0.0% two or more races (2000); Density: 327.7 persons per square mile (2000); Age: 24.0% under 18, 34.5% over 64 (2000); Marriage status: 18.4% never married, 68.6% now married, 9.8% widowed, 3.3% divorced (2000); Foreign born: 0.7% (2000); Ancestry (includes multiple ancestries): 68.4% German, 9.2% Irish, 7.2% United States or American, 3.0% English, 2.6% Dutch (2000).
Economy: Employment by occupation: 11.5% management, 20.8% professional, 10.0% services, 31.5% sales, 0.8% farming, 12.3% construction, 13.1% production (2000).
Income: Per capita income: $13,882 (2000); Median household income: $39,375 (2000); Poverty rate: 2.7% (2000).
Education: High school graduation rate: 57.9% (2000); College graduation rate: 12.4% (2000).

School District(s)

Saint Elizabeth R-IV (KG-12)
2000 Enrollment: 266 573-493-2246

Housing: Homeownership rate: 70.8% (2000); Median home value: $77,500 (2000); Median rent: $197 per month (2000); Median age of housing: 33 years (2000).
Transportation: Commute to work: 86.9% car, 0.0% public transportation, 6.9% walk, 6.2% work from home (2000); Travel time to work: 29.5% less than 15 minutes, 3.3% 15 to 30 minutes, 26.2% 30 to 45 minutes, 32.0% 45 to 60 minutes, 9.0% 60 minutes or more (2000)

TUSCUMBIA (town). Covers a land area of 0.353 square miles and a water area of 0 square miles. Located at 38.23° N. Lat.; 92.46° W. Long. Elevation is 742 feet.

History: The site of Tuscumbia was first settled by J.P. and J.B. Harrison, who built a trading post near a spring. When Miller County was organized in 1837, the house of William Miller was selected as the county seat. The second court, however, moved the seat to the Harrison brothers' store. The town was laid out on land donated by the Harrisons, and was probably named for Tuscumbia, Alabama.
Population: 218 (2000); Race: 95.3% White, 4.7% Black, 0.0% Asian, 0.0% American Indian and Alaska Native, 0.0% Hispanic of any race, 0.0% two or more races (2000); Density: 617.2 persons per square mile (2000); Age: 6.6% under 18, 9.0% over 64 (2000); Marriage status: 41.3% never married, 24.4% now married, 6.5% widowed, 27.9% divorced (2000); Foreign born: 0.0% (2000); Ancestry (includes multiple ancestries): 15.6% United States or American, 15.6% German, 8.5% Other groups, 5.7% English, 4.7% French (except Basque) (2000).
Economy: Employment by occupation: 11.1% management, 4.4% professional, 55.6% services, 13.3% sales, 0.0% farming, 6.7% construction, 8.9% production (2000).
Income: Per capita income: $8,117 (2000); Median household income: $19,375 (2000); Poverty rate: 19.3% (2000).
Taxes: Total city taxes per capita: $26 (1997); City property taxes per capita: $7 (1997).
Education: High school graduation rate: 68.8% (2000); College graduation rate: 1.4% (2000).

School District(s)

Miller Co. R-III (KG-12)
2000 Enrollment: 294 573-369-2375

Housing: Homeownership rate: 75.7% (2000); Median home value: $32,500 (2000); Median rent: $263 per month (2000); Median age of housing: 48 years (2000).
Transportation: Commute to work: 95.6% car, 0.0% public transportation, 0.0% walk, 4.4% work from home (2000); Travel time to work: 46.5% less than 15 minutes, 25.6% 15 to 30 minutes, 16.3% 30 to 45 minutes, 0.0% 45 to 60 minutes, 11.6% 60 minutes or more (2000)

ULMAN (unincorporated postal area, zip code 65083). Covers a land area of 11.678 square miles and a water area of 0 square miles. Located at 38.14° N. Lat.; 92.43° W. Long. Elevation is 940 feet.

Population: 292 (2000); Race: 100.0% White, 0.0% Black, 0.0% Asian, 0.0% American Indian and Alaska Native, 0.0% Hispanic of any race, 0.0% two or more races (2000); Density: 25.0 persons per square mile (2000); Age: 29.3% under 18, 10.5% over 64 (2000); Marriage status: 26.5% never married, 62.4% now married, 7.2% widowed, 3.9% divorced (2000); Foreign born: 0.0% (2000); Ancestry (includes multiple ancestries): 16.6% German, 15.7% United States or American, 15.2% Other groups, 5.0% Italian, 4.4% Dutch (2000).
Economy: Employment by occupation: 15.3% management, 8.0% professional, 19.0% services, 12.3% sales, 1.2% farming, 23.3% construction, 20.9% production (2000).
Income: Per capita income: $12,319 (2000); Median household income: $31,538 (2000); Poverty rate: 6.4% (2000).
Education: High school graduation rate: 79.7% (2000); College graduation rate: 4.4% (2000).
Housing: Homeownership rate: 73.9% (2000); Median home value: $67,000 (2000); Median rent: $157 per month (2000); Median age of housing: 24 years (2000).
Transportation: Commute to work: 96.9% car, 0.0% public transportation, 1.2% walk, 1.8% work from home (2000); Travel time to work: 27.5% less than 15 minutes, 36.9% 15 to 30 minutes, 25.6% 30 to 45 minutes, 1.3% 45 to 60 minutes, 8.8% 60 minutes or more (2000)

Mississippi County

Located in southeastern Missouri; bounded on the east by the Mississippi River and the Illinois border. Covers a land area of 413.20 square miles, a water area of 15.70 square miles, and is located in the Central Time Zone. The county government was organized in 1845. County seat is Charleston.
Population: 13,427 (2000); Race: 77.4% White, 21.1% Black, 0.4% Asian, 0.4% American Indian and Alaska Native, 0.3% Hispanic of any race, 0.5% two or more races (2000); Density: 32.5 persons per square mile (2000); Age: 26.4% under 18, 15.9% over 64 (2000).
Religion: Five largest groups: 25.3% Southern Baptist Convention, 6.4% The United Methodist Church, 3.5% Christian Churches and Churches of Christ, 3.2% Catholic Church, 2.4% Assemblies of God (2000).
Economy: Unemployment rate: 7.6% (11/2002); Total civilian labor force: 5,903 (11/2002); Leading industries: 21.1% retail trade; 17.3% manufacturing; 14.2% transportation & warehousing (2000); Companies that employ more than 1,000 persons: 0 (2000); Companies that employ more than 100 persons: 3 (2000); Farms: 267 totaling 263,623 acres (1997); Minority business ownership rate: 0.0% (1997); Women business ownership rate: 25.3% (1997); Retail sales per capita: $7,021 (1997). Single-family building permits issued: 13 (2001) / 15 (2000); Multi-family building permits issued: 0 (2001) / 8 (2000).
Income: Per capita income: $13,038 (2000); Median household income: $23,012 (2000); Poverty rate: 23.7% (2000); Bankruptcy rate: 4.58% (2001).
Taxes: Total county taxes per capita: $198 (2000); County property taxes per capita: $56 (2000).

Education: High school graduation rate: 61.1% (2000); College graduation rate: 9.6% (2000).
Housing: Homeownership rate: 63.5% (2000); Median home value: $47,000 (2000); Median rent: $220 per month (2000); Median age of housing: 36 years (2000).
Health: Birth rate: 162.4 per 10,000 population (1998); Age adjusted death rate: 112.0 per 10,000 population (1999); Age adjusted cancer mortality rate: 339.5 deaths per 100,000 population (1999). Number of physicians: 2.2 per 10,000 population (1999); Number of hospital beds: n/a (1999).
Elections: 2000 Presidential election results: 52.9% Gore, 45.9% Bush, 0.6% Nader, 0.5% Buchanan
National and State Parks: Big Oak Tree State Park; Towosahgy State Park
Additional Information Contacts
Mississippi County Government Offices 573-683-2146
Charleston Chamber of Commerce 573-683-6509
East Prairie Chamber of Commerce 573-649-5243

Mississippi County Communities

ANNISTON (town). Covers a land area of 0.397 square miles and a water area of 0 square miles. Located at 36.82° N. Lat.; 89.32° W. Long. Elevation is 312 feet.
Population: 285 (2000); Race: 98.6% White, 0.0% Black, 0.0% Asian, 0.0% American Indian and Alaska Native, 0.7% Hispanic of any race, 0.7% two or more races (2000); Density: 717.9 persons per square mile (2000); Age: 23.8% under 18, 17.5% over 64 (2000); Marriage status: 15.5% never married, 66.5% now married, 7.7% widowed, 10.3% divorced (2000); Foreign born: 0.0% (2000); Ancestry (includes multiple ancestries): 17.5% Other groups, 16.1% Irish, 10.5% United States or American, 9.8% German, 3.8% English (2000).
Economy: Employment by occupation: 1.7% management, 3.4% professional, 18.8% services, 26.5% sales, 6.8% farming, 5.1% construction, 37.6% production (2000).
Income: Per capita income: $9,626 (2000); Median household income: $22,232 (2000); Poverty rate: 15.4% (2000).
Taxes: Total city taxes per capita: $22 (1997); City property taxes per capita: $18 (1997).
Education: High school graduation rate: 54.4% (2000); College graduation rate: 0.0% (2000).
Housing: Homeownership rate: 76.7% (2000); Median home value: $23,500 (2000); Median rent: $233 per month (2000); Median age of housing: 38 years (2000).
Transportation: Commute to work: 97.4% car, 1.7% public transportation, 0.0% walk, 0.9% work from home (2000); Travel time to work: 32.5% less than 15 minutes, 37.7% 15 to 30 minutes, 18.4% 30 to 45 minutes, 3.5% 45 to 60 minutes, 7.9% 60 minutes or more (2000)

BERTRAND (city). Covers a land area of 0.664 square miles and a water area of 0 square miles. Located at 36.91° N. Lat.; 89.44° W. Long. Elevation is 325 feet.
History: Bertrand was laid out in 1859 by H.J. Deal along the Missouri Pacific Railroad line.
Population: 740 (2000); Race: 96.0% White, 2.3% Black, 0.0% Asian, 0.3% American Indian and Alaska Native, 0.3% Hispanic of any race, 1.4% two or more races (2000); Density: 1,115.2 persons per square mile (2000); Age: 16.3% under 18, 23.2% over 64 (2000); Marriage status: 14.7% never married, 60.2% now married, 15.3% widowed, 9.7% divorced (2000); Foreign born: 0.3% (2000); Ancestry (includes multiple ancestries): 16.5% United States or American, 9.2% Other groups, 7.6% Irish, 6.1% German, 3.8% English (2000).
Economy: Single-family building permits issued: 2 (2001) / 0 (2000); Multi-family building permits issued: 0 (2001) / 0 (2000); Employment by occupation: 10.2% management, 7.3% professional, 13.1% services, 31.3% sales, 0.0% farming, 14.1% construction, 24.0% production (2000).
Income: Per capita income: $15,346 (2000); Median household income: $26,023 (2000); Poverty rate: 15.4% (2000).
Taxes: Total city taxes per capita: $46 (1997); City property taxes per capita: $19 (1997).
Education: High school graduation rate: 60.3% (2000); College graduation rate: 3.3% (2000).
Housing: Homeownership rate: 69.7% (2000); Median home value: $55,200 (2000); Median rent: $231 per month (2000); Median age of housing: 26 years (2000).
Transportation: Commute to work: 93.5% car, 0.0% public transportation, 1.9% walk, 1.9% work from home (2000); Travel time to work: 28.5% less than 15 minutes, 50.3% 15 to 30 minutes, 14.9% 30 to 45 minutes, 2.0% 45 to 60 minutes, 4.3% 60 minutes or more (2000)

CHARLESTON (city). Covers a land area of 4.677 square miles and a water area of 0 square miles. Located at 36.92° N. Lat.; 89.34° W. Long. Elevation is 323 feet.
History: Charleston was platted in 1837 by John Rodney in a prairie area popular for its buffalo herds. Charleston grew as a trading and shipping center for the cotton plantations developed in the lowlands area.
Population: 4,732 (2000); Race: 51.1% White, 47.4% Black, 0.9% Asian, 0.2% American Indian and Alaska Native, 0.3% Hispanic of any race, 0.0% two or more races (2000); Density: 1,011.8 persons per square mile (2000); Age: 30.0% under 18, 15.3% over 64 (2000); Marriage status: 28.7% never married, 50.2% now married, 12.5% widowed, 8.6% divorced (2000); Foreign born: 1.0% (2000); Ancestry (includes multiple ancestries): 45.7% Other groups, 9.4% United States or American, 6.1% German, 6.0% English, 4.7% Irish (2000).
Economy: Single-family building permits issued: 4 (2001) / 3 (2000); Multi-family building permits issued: 0 (2001) / 8 (2000); Employment by occupation: 9.1% management, 14.0% professional, 24.2% services, 21.7% sales, 2.6% farming, 8.4% construction, 19.9% production (2000).
Income: Per capita income: $12,876 (2000); Median household income: $21,812 (2000); Poverty rate: 26.0% (2000).
Taxes: Total city taxes per capita: $572 (1997); City property taxes per capita: $67 (1997).
Education: High school graduation rate: 66.3% (2000); College graduation rate: 14.0% (2000).

School District(s)
Charleston R-I (PK-12)
2000 Enrollment: 1,365 573-683-3776
Housing: Homeownership rate: 59.1% (2000); Median home value: $47,200 (2000); Median rent: $195 per month (2000); Median age of housing: 38 years (2000).
Safety: Violent crime rate: 88.2 per 10,000 population; Property crime rate: 518.8 per 10,000 population (2001).
Newspapers: Charleston Enterprise Courier (1 x week)
Transportation: Commute to work: 91.1% car, 0.3% public transportation, 3.7% walk, 2.9% work from home (2000); Travel time to work: 57.2% less than 15 minutes, 29.5% 15 to 30 minutes, 7.4% 30 to 45 minutes, 2.2% 45 to 60 minutes, 3.8% 60 minutes or more (2000)
Additional Information Contacts
Charleston Chamber of Commerce 573-683-6509

EAST PRAIRIE (city). Covers a land area of 1.277 square miles and a water area of 0 square miles. Located at 36.78° N. Lat.; 89.38° W. Long. Elevation is 307 feet.
Population: 3,227 (2000); Race: 95.3% White, 2.9% Black, 0.2% Asian, 0.5% American Indian and Alaska Native, 0.5% Hispanic of any race, 1.2% two or more races (2000); Density: 2,526.0 persons per square mile (2000); Age: 26.6% under 18, 16.0% over 64 (2000); Marriage status: 21.9% never married, 48.8% now married, 14.6% widowed, 14.8% divorced (2000); Foreign born: 0.7% (2000); Ancestry (includes multiple ancestries): 18.3% Irish, 17.2% Other groups, 16.0% United States or American, 9.3% English, 7.6% German (2000).
Economy: Single-family building permits issued: 6 (2001) / 10 (2000); Multi-family building permits issued: 0 (2001) / 0 (2000); Employment by occupation: 6.3% management, 11.0% professional, 14.1% services, 21.7% sales, 4.1% farming, 12.0% construction, 30.7% production (2000).
Income: Per capita income: $10,912 (2000); Median household income: $19,825 (2000); Poverty rate: 30.1% (2000).
Taxes: Total city taxes per capita: $251 (1997); City property taxes per capita: $38 (1997).
Education: High school graduation rate: 53.0% (2000); College graduation rate: 6.0% (2000).

School District(s)
East Prairie R-II (PK-12)
2000 Enrollment: 1,159 573-649-3562
Housing: Homeownership rate: 58.1% (2000); Median home value: $38,100 (2000); Median rent: $251 per month (2000); Median age of housing: 41 years (2000).
Transportation: Commute to work: 96.1% car, 0.0% public transportation, 0.5% walk, 1.7% work from home (2000); Travel time to work: 44.4% less than 15 minutes, 29.3% 15 to 30 minutes, 15.9% 30 to 45 minutes, 4.0% 45 to 60 minutes, 6.5% 60 minutes or more (2000)
Additional Information Contacts
East Prairie Chamber of Commerce 573-649-5243

PINHOOK (village). Covers a land area of 0.143 square miles and a water area of 0 square miles. Located at 36.73° N. Lat.; 89.26° W. Long. Elevation is 301 feet.
Population: 48 (2000); Race: 0.0% White, 100.0% Black, 0.0% Asian, 0.0% American Indian and Alaska Native, 0.0% Hispanic of any race, 0.0% two or more races (2000); Density: 336.1 persons per square mile (2000); Age: 25.0% under 18, 21.4% over 64 (2000); Marriage status: 31.8% never married, 47.7% now married, 9.1% widowed, 11.4% divorced (2000); Foreign born: 0.0% (2000); Ancestry (includes multiple ancestries): 94.6% Other groups, 8.9% English (2000).
Economy: Employment by occupation: 0.0% management, 17.9% professional, 17.9% services, 10.7% sales, 3.6% farming, 7.1% construction, 42.9% production (2000).
Income: Per capita income: $10,114 (2000); Median household income: $15,417 (2000); Poverty rate: 55.4% (2000).
Education: High school graduation rate: 69.2% (2000); College graduation rate: 2.6% (2000).
Housing: Homeownership rate: 94.7% (2000); Median home value: $55,000 (2000); Median age of housing: 24 years (2000).
Transportation: Commute to work: 84.6% car, 0.0% public transportation, 0.0% walk, 7.7% work from home (2000); Travel time to work: 16.7% less than 15 minutes, 20.8% 15 to 30 minutes, 37.5% 30 to 45 minutes, 25.0% 45 to 60 minutes, 0.0% 60 minutes or more (2000)

WILSON CITY (village). Covers a land area of 0.078 square miles and a water area of 0 square miles. Located at 36.92° N. Lat.; 89.22° W. Long. Elevation is 313 feet.
Population: 165 (2000); Race: 0.0% White, 98.2% Black, 0.0% Asian, 0.0% American Indian and Alaska Native, 0.0% Hispanic of any race, 1.8% two or more races (2000); Density: 2,128.6 persons per square mile (2000); Age: 32.0% under 18, 13.6% over 64 (2000); Marriage status: 42.2% never married, 33.5% now married, 11.2% widowed, 13.0% divorced (2000); Foreign born: 0.0% (2000); Ancestry (includes multiple ancestries): 87.7% Other groups, 2.6% African (2000).
Economy: Single-family building permits issued: 1 (2001) / 1 (2000); Multi-family building permits issued: 0 (2001) / 0 (2000); Employment by occupation: 2.4% management, 8.3% professional, 25.0% services, 25.0% sales, 11.9% farming, 10.7% construction, 16.7% production (2000).
Income: Per capita income: $11,068 (2000); Median household income: $15,417 (2000); Poverty rate: 39.5% (2000).
Education: High school graduation rate: 35.2% (2000); College graduation rate: 3.4% (2000).
Housing: Homeownership rate: 66.3% (2000); Median home value: $11,900 (2000); Median rent: $129 per month (2000); Median age of housing: 52 years (2000).
Transportation: Commute to work: 88.1% car, 7.1% public transportation, 4.8% walk, 0.0% work from home (2000); Travel time to work: 52.4% less than 15 minutes, 10.7% 15 to 30 minutes, 17.9% 30 to 45 minutes, 4.8% 45 to 60 minutes, 14.3% 60 minutes or more (2000)

WYATT (city). Covers a land area of 1.150 square miles and a water area of 0.074 square miles. Located at 36.91° N. Lat.; 89.21° W. Long. Elevation is 318 feet.
Population: 364 (2000); Race: 92.3% White, 7.1% Black, 0.0% Asian, 0.0% American Indian and Alaska Native, 0.0% Hispanic of any race, 0.6% two or more races (2000); Density: 316.7 persons per square mile (2000); Age: 22.6% under 18, 27.2% over 64 (2000); Marriage status: 12.4% never married, 62.2% now married, 15.8% widowed, 9.7% divorced (2000); Foreign born: 0.0% (2000); Ancestry (includes multiple ancestries): 13.3% United States or American, 13.3% Other groups, 11.8% Irish, 8.4% German, 4.0% French (except Basque) (2000).
Economy: Single-family building permits issued: 0 (2001) / 1 (2000); Multi-family building permits issued: 0 (2001) / 0 (2000); Employment by occupation: 13.0% management, 6.1% professional, 20.0% services, 30.4% sales, 3.5% farming, 5.2% construction, 21.7% production (2000).
Income: Per capita income: $13,646 (2000); Median household income: $19,444 (2000); Poverty rate: 20.2% (2000).
Taxes: Total city taxes per capita: $134 (1997); City property taxes per capita: $27 (1997).
Education: High school graduation rate: 56.3% (2000); College graduation rate: 4.0% (2000).
Housing: Homeownership rate: 73.5% (2000); Median home value: $40,800 (2000); Median rent: $171 per month (2000); Median age of housing: 45 years (2000).
Transportation: Commute to work: 92.8% car, 0.0% public transportation, 5.4% walk, 0.0% work from home (2000); Travel time to work: 29.7% less than 15 minutes, 28.8% 15 to 30 minutes, 33.3% 30 to 45 minutes, 6.3% 45 to 60 minutes, 1.8% 60 minutes or more (2000)

Moniteau County

Located in central Missouri; bounded on the northeast by the Missouri River. Covers a land area of 416.50 square miles, a water area of 2.30 square miles, and is located in the Central Time Zone. The county government was organized in 1845. County seat is California.

Weather Station: California — Elevation: 869 feet

	Jan	Feb	Mar	Apr	May	Jun	Jul	Aug	Sep	Oct	Nov	Dec
High	40	47	58	68	76	85	90	89	81	71	56	44
Low	20	25	35	45	55	64	68	67	58	46	36	26
Precip	1.5	1.8	3.2	4.3	5.3	3.8	3.7	3.4	4.1	3.4	3.5	2.3
Snow	3.9	4.1	1.4	0.2	0.0	0.0	0.0	0.0	0.0	0.0	1.1	2.3

High and Low temperatures in degrees Fahrenheit; Precipitation and Snow in inches

Population: 14,827 (2000); Race: 93.8% White, 3.3% Black, 0.4% Asian, 0.4% American Indian and Alaska Native, 2.7% Hispanic of any race, 0.9% two or more races (2000); Density: 35.6 persons per square mile (2000); Age: 25.8% under 18, 14.0% over 64 (2000).
Religion: Five largest groups: 33.8% Southern Baptist Convention, 11.7% Catholic Church, 6.4% United Church of Christ, 4.9% The United Methodist Church, 2.9% Christian Church (Disciples of Christ) (2000).
Economy: Unemployment rate: 3.4% (11/2002); Total civilian labor force: 7,518 (11/2002); Leading industries: 33.1% manufacturing; 18.2% retail trade; 8.7% health care and social assistance (2000); Companies that employ more than 1,000 persons: 0 (2000); Companies that employ more than 100 persons: 3 (2000); Farms: 1,024 totaling 222,758 acres (1997); Minority business ownership rate: 0.0% (1997); Women business ownership rate: 15.7% (1997); Retail sales per capita: $8,208 (1997). Single-family building permits issued: 9 (2001) / 4 (2000); Multi-family building permits issued: 0 (2001) / 0 (2000).
Income: Per capita income: $16,609 (2000); Median household income: $37,168 (2000); Poverty rate: 9.9% (2000); Bankruptcy rate: 4.53% (2001).
Taxes: Total county taxes per capita: $62 (1997); County property taxes per capita: $37 (1997).
Education: High school graduation rate: 77.6% (2000); College graduation rate: 13.0% (2000).
Housing: Homeownership rate: 77.7% (2000); Median home value: $69,900 (2000); Median rent: $285 per month (2000); Median age of housing: 32 years (2000).
Health: Birth rate: 135.6 per 10,000 population (1998); Age adjusted death rate: 106.5 per 10,000 population (1999); Age adjusted cancer mortality rate: 272.8 deaths per 100,000 population (1999). Number of physicians: 2.0 per 10,000 population (1999); Number of hospital beds: n/a (1999).
Elections: 2000 Presidential election results: 35.9% Gore, 62.1% Bush, 1.0% Nader, 0.7% Buchanan
Additional Information Contacts
Moniteau County Government Offices 573-796-4661
California Chamber of Commerce 573-796-3040
Tipton Chamber of Commerce 660-433-6377

Moniteau County Communities

CALIFORNIA (city). Covers a land area of 2.995 square miles and a water area of 0.012 square miles. Located at 38.63° N. Lat.; 92.56° W. Long. Elevation is 874 feet.
History: California developed along the Missouri Pacific Railroad line built in the 1850's. The town was named for someone called "California" Wilson, who requested that his nickname be memorialized. When Moniteau County was organized in 1845, land donated for the county seat was called Boonesborough. The post office was moved from the old town, and in 1847 the name of California replaced that of Boonesborough.
Population: 4,005 (2000); Race: 94.7% White, 0.5% Black, 0.0% Asian, 0.3% American Indian and Alaska Native, 8.3% Hispanic of any race, 0.7% two or more races (2000); Density: 1,337.3 persons per square mile (2000); Age: 24.8% under 18, 19.7% over 64 (2000); Marriage status: 22.0% never married, 55.6% now married, 12.8% widowed, 9.5% divorced (2000); Foreign born: 4.1% (2000); Ancestry (includes multiple ancestries): 29.1% German, 17.4% United States or American, 13.3% Other groups, 8.2% Irish, 7.7% English (2000).

Economy: Employment by occupation: 9.3% management, 15.7% professional, 17.8% services, 22.7% sales, 0.7% farming, 13.7% construction, 20.2% production (2000).
Income: Per capita income: $17,533 (2000); Median household income: $31,736 (2000); Poverty rate: 12.0% (2000).
Taxes: Total city taxes per capita: $151 (1997); City property taxes per capita: $109 (1997).
Education: High school graduation rate: 77.2% (2000); College graduation rate: 13.0% (2000).

School District(s)

Moniteau Co. R-I (KG-12)
2000 Enrollment: 1,333 573-796-2145
Housing: Homeownership rate: 65.6% (2000); Median home value: $67,000 (2000); Median rent: $304 per month (2000); Median age of housing: 35 years (2000).
Safety: Violent crime rate: 101.7 per 10,000 population; Property crime rate: 245.7 per 10,000 population (2001).
Newspapers: California Democrat (1 x week)
Transportation: Commute to work: 91.6% car, 0.0% public transportation, 4.8% walk, 2.9% work from home (2000); Travel time to work: 45.4% less than 15 minutes, 23.3% 15 to 30 minutes, 23.3% 30 to 45 minutes, 6.0% 45 to 60 minutes, 1.9% 60 minutes or more (2000)
Additional Information Contacts
California Chamber of Commerce 573-796-3040

CLARKSBURG (city). Covers a land area of 0.577 square miles and a water area of 0 square miles. Located at 38.66° N. Lat.; 92.66° W. Long. Elevation is 897 feet.
Population: 375 (2000); Race: 99.4% White, 0.0% Black, 0.0% Asian, 0.0% American Indian and Alaska Native, 3.1% Hispanic of any race, 0.6% two or more races (2000); Density: 649.9 persons per square mile (2000); Age: 36.1% under 18, 9.7% over 64 (2000); Marriage status: 25.2% never married, 53.7% now married, 7.4% widowed, 13.6% divorced (2000); Foreign born: 1.1% (2000); Ancestry (includes multiple ancestries): 19.6% German, 18.8% Other groups, 15.1% United States or American, 11.6% Irish, 7.4% English (2000).
Economy: Soybeans, corn; cattle, poultry. Employment by occupation: 3.7% management, 6.7% professional, 36.0% services, 11.0% sales, 0.0% farming, 13.4% construction, 29.3% production (2000).
Income: Per capita income: $11,903 (2000); Median household income: $28,750 (2000); Poverty rate: 8.3% (2000).
Taxes: Total city taxes per capita: $44 (1997); City property taxes per capita: $13 (1997).
Education: High school graduation rate: 64.9% (2000); College graduation rate: 2.5% (2000).

School District(s)

Clarksburg C-2 (KG-08)
2000 Enrollment: 136 573-787-3511
Housing: Homeownership rate: 76.7% (2000); Median home value: $35,500 (2000); Median rent: $161 per month (2000); Median age of housing: 54 years (2000).
Transportation: Commute to work: 95.5% car, 1.3% public transportation, 0.0% walk, 1.9% work from home (2000); Travel time to work: 27.0% less than 15 minutes, 39.5% 15 to 30 minutes, 20.4% 30 to 45 minutes, 9.2% 45 to 60 minutes, 3.9% 60 minutes or more (2000)

FORTUNA (unincorporated postal area, zip code 65034). Covers a land area of 34.010 square miles and a water area of 0.020 square miles. Located at 38.56° N. Lat.; 92.80° W. Long. Elevation is 961 feet.
Population: 584 (2000); Race: 99.1% White, 0.0% Black, 0.0% Asian, 0.0% American Indian and Alaska Native, 1.7% Hispanic of any race, 0.9% two or more races (2000); Density: 17.2 persons per square mile (2000); Age: 27.9% under 18, 10.1% over 64 (2000); Marriage status: 25.8% never married, 54.9% now married, 7.2% widowed, 12.1% divorced (2000); Foreign born: 0.0% (2000); Ancestry (includes multiple ancestries): 20.7% United States or American, 17.3% German, 8.5% Swiss, 7.2% English, 4.4% Other groups (2000).
Economy: Employment by occupation: 15.8% management, 2.8% professional, 12.7% services, 19.0% sales, 10.1% farming, 15.5% construction, 24.1% production (2000).
Income: Per capita income: $14,223 (2000); Median household income: $35,833 (2000); Poverty rate: 23.3% (2000).
Education: High school graduation rate: 59.5% (2000); College graduation rate: 6.5% (2000).
Housing: Homeownership rate: 86.6% (2000); Median home value: $52,500 (2000); Median rent: $242 per month (2000); Median age of housing: 38 years (2000).
Transportation: Commute to work: 70.7% car, 0.0% public transportation, 3.9% walk, 15.8% work from home (2000); Travel time to work: 32.1% less than 15 minutes, 30.9% 15 to 30 minutes, 13.7% 30 to 45 minutes, 14.5% 45 to 60 minutes, 8.8% 60 minutes or more (2000)

JAMESTOWN (town). Covers a land area of 1.002 square miles and a water area of 0 square miles. Located at 38.76° N. Lat.; 92.47° W. Long. Elevation is 865 feet.
Population: 382 (2000); Race: 97.5% White, 0.0% Black, 0.5% Asian, 0.0% American Indian and Alaska Native, 0.5% Hispanic of any race, 2.0% two or more races (2000); Density: 381.2 persons per square mile (2000); Age: 25.0% under 18, 15.4% over 64 (2000); Marriage status: 19.7% never married, 56.5% now married, 8.9% widowed, 14.9% divorced (2000); Foreign born: 1.0% (2000); Ancestry (includes multiple ancestries): 26.3% German, 22.0% United States or American, 9.3% Other groups, 9.1% Irish, 3.8% English (2000).
Economy: Cattle, hogs, corn. Single-family building permits issued: 0 (2001) / 0 (2000); Multi-family building permits issued: 0 (2001) / 0 (2000); Employment by occupation: 9.7% management, 7.0% professional, 12.4% services, 31.2% sales, 0.5% farming, 14.0% construction, 25.3% production (2000).
Income: Per capita income: $16,498 (2000); Median household income: $31,667 (2000); Poverty rate: 8.1% (2000).
Taxes: Total city taxes per capita: $52 (1997); City property taxes per capita: $48 (1997).
Education: High school graduation rate: 79.6% (2000); College graduation rate: 13.8% (2000).

School District(s)

Moniteau Co. C-1 (KG-12)
2000 Enrollment: 207 660-849-2141
Housing: Homeownership rate: 76.3% (2000); Median home value: $63,600 (2000); Median rent: $275 per month (2000); Median age of housing: 34 years (2000).
Transportation: Commute to work: 91.1% car, 0.0% public transportation, 1.1% walk, 5.6% work from home (2000); Travel time to work: 11.2% less than 15 minutes, 21.3% 15 to 30 minutes, 45.0% 30 to 45 minutes, 13.0% 45 to 60 minutes, 9.5% 60 minutes or more (2000)

LATHAM (unincorporated postal area, zip code 65050). Covers a land area of 19.006 square miles and a water area of 0.019 square miles. Located at 38.54° N. Lat.; 92.69° W. Long. Elevation is 884 feet.
Population: 567 (2000); Race: 100.0% White, 0.0% Black, 0.0% Asian, 0.0% American Indian and Alaska Native, 0.0% Hispanic of any race, 0.0% two or more races (2000); Density: 29.8 persons per square mile (2000); Age: 44.6% under 18, 6.0% over 64 (2000); Marriage status: 26.9% never married, 64.7% now married, 3.1% widowed, 5.3% divorced (2000); Foreign born: 0.0% (2000); Ancestry (includes multiple ancestries): 29.1% German, 14.5% Swiss, 13.4% United States or American, 4.8% Other groups, 3.7% Irish (2000).
Economy: Employment by occupation: 22.5% management, 8.4% professional, 15.0% services, 12.8% sales, 3.5% farming, 9.7% construction, 28.2% production (2000).
Income: Per capita income: $11,154 (2000); Median household income: $31,442 (2000); Poverty rate: 19.4% (2000).
Education: High school graduation rate: 57.0% (2000); College graduation rate: 7.2% (2000).

School District(s)

Moniteau Co. R-V (KG-08)
2000 Enrollment: 52 660-458-6271
Housing: Homeownership rate: 88.4% (2000); Median home value: $55,000 (2000); Median rent: $225 per month (2000); Median age of housing: 30 years (2000).
Transportation: Commute to work: 68.3% car, 0.0% public transportation, 1.8% walk, 22.0% work from home (2000); Travel time to work: 13.6% less than 15 minutes, 37.9% 15 to 30 minutes, 20.9% 30 to 45 minutes, 12.4% 45 to 60 minutes, 15.3% 60 minutes or more (2000)

LUPUS (town). Covers a land area of 0.192 square miles and a water area of 0 square miles. Located at 38.84° N. Lat.; 92.45° W. Long. Elevation is 574 feet.
Population: 29 (2000); Race: 100.0% White, 0.0% Black, 0.0% Asian, 0.0% American Indian and Alaska Native, 0.0% Hispanic of any race, 0.0% two or more races (2000); Density: 150.8 persons per square mile (2000); Age:

17.6% under 18, 35.3% over 64 (2000); Marriage status: 0.0% never married, 0.0% now married, 42.9% widowed, 57.1% divorced (2000); Foreign born: 0.0% (2000); Ancestry (includes multiple ancestries): 47.1% Irish, 41.2% United States or American, 23.5% German, 23.5% English, 11.8% Other groups (2000).
Economy: Employment by occupation: 25.0% management, 25.0% professional, 0.0% services, 25.0% sales, 0.0% farming, 0.0% construction, 25.0% production (2000).
Income: Per capita income: $19,341 (2000); Median household income: $18,750 (2000); Poverty rate: 0.0% (2000).
Taxes: Total city taxes per capita: $24 (1997); City property taxes per capita: $24 (1997).
Education: High school graduation rate: 85.7% (2000); College graduation rate: 0.0% (2000).
Housing: Homeownership rate: 100.0% (2000); Median home value: $28,000 (2000); Median age of housing: 60+ years (2000).
Transportation: Commute to work: 75.0% car, 0.0% public transportation, 0.0% walk, 25.0% work from home (2000); Travel time to work: 0.0% less than 15 minutes, 33.3% 15 to 30 minutes, 33.3% 30 to 45 minutes, 33.3% 45 to 60 minutes, 0.0% 60 minutes or more (2000)

TIPTON (city). Covers a land area of 2.098 square miles and a water area of 0.006 square miles. Located at 38.65° N. Lat.; 92.77° W. Long. Elevation is 926 feet.
History: Tipton was platted in 1858 on land donated by Tipton Sealey. The town developed as the terminus of the Pacific Railroad and the starting point of the Overland Mail. Jesse James is said to have operated a livery stable here for about a year, sometime after the Civil War.
Population: 3,261 (2000); Race: 81.9% White, 14.3% Black, 1.2% Asian, 0.9% American Indian and Alaska Native, 0.9% Hispanic of any race, 1.7% two or more races (2000); Density: 1,554.6 persons per square mile (2000); Age: 16.9% under 18, 14.3% over 64 (2000); Marriage status: 27.5% never married, 48.2% now married, 7.9% widowed, 16.4% divorced (2000); Foreign born: 0.7% (2000); Ancestry (includes multiple ancestries): 23.7% German, 18.6% Other groups, 11.9% United States or American, 11.0% Irish, 5.1% English (2000).
Economy: Single-family building permits issued: 9 (2001) / 4 (2000); Multi-family building permits issued: 0 (2001) / 0 (2000); Employment by occupation: 11.2% management, 11.0% professional, 22.8% services, 25.4% sales, 1.3% farming, 12.3% construction, 15.8% production (2000).
Income: Per capita income: $15,987 (2000); Median household income: $32,155 (2000); Poverty rate: 10.2% (2000).
Taxes: Total city taxes per capita: $495 (1997); City property taxes per capita: $165 (1997).
Education: High school graduation rate: 72.9% (2000); College graduation rate: 8.5% (2000).

School District(s)

Moniteau Co. R-VI (KG-12)
2000 Enrollment: 604 660-433-5520

Housing: Homeownership rate: 74.5% (2000); Median home value: $68,800 (2000); Median rent: $261 per month (2000); Median age of housing: 34 years (2000).
Newspapers: Tipton Times (1 x week)
Transportation: Commute to work: 94.4% car, 0.2% public transportation, 2.6% walk, 2.0% work from home (2000); Travel time to work: 60.1% less than 15 minutes, 12.1% 15 to 30 minutes, 12.4% 30 to 45 minutes, 9.1% 45 to 60 minutes, 6.3% 60 minutes or more (2000)
Additional Information Contacts
Tipton Chamber of Commerce 660-433-6377

Monroe County

Located in northeast central Missouri; drained by the Salt River. Covers a land area of 646.00 square miles, a water area of 24.20 square miles, and is located in the Central Time Zone. The county government was organized in 1831. County seat is Paris.
Population: 9,311 (2000); Race: 94.7% White, 4.1% Black, 0.3% Asian, 0.6% American Indian and Alaska Native, 0.3% Hispanic of any race, 0.3% two or more races (2000); Density: 14.4 persons per square mile (2000); Age: 25.9% under 18, 17.7% over 64 (2000).
Religion: Five largest groups: 19.9% Southern Baptist Convention, 15.6% Christian Church (Disciples of Christ), 14.4% Catholic Church, 7.1% The United Methodist Church, 2.1% Lutheran Church—Missouri Synod (2000).
Economy: Unemployment rate: 6.4% (11/2002); Total civilian labor force: 3,652 (11/2002); Leading industries: 13.2% retail trade; 11.8% health care and social assistance; 6.4% accommodation & food services (2000); Companies that employ more than 1,000 persons: 0 (2000); Companies that employ more than 100 persons: 2 (2000); Farms: 886 totaling 328,200 acres (1997); Minority business ownership rate: 0.0% (1997); Women business ownership rate: 22.6% (1997); Retail sales per capita: $5,238 (1997). Single-family building permits issued: 49 (2001) / 34 (2000); Multi-family building permits issued: 0 (2001) / 0 (2000).
Income: Per capita income: $14,695 (2000); Median household income: $30,871 (2000); Poverty rate: 11.9% (2000); Bankruptcy rate: 4.55% (2001).
Taxes: Total county taxes per capita: $102 (1997); County property taxes per capita: $36 (1997).
Education: High school graduation rate: 78.7% (2000); College graduation rate: 9.5% (2000).
Housing: Homeownership rate: 78.5% (2000); Median home value: $55,300 (2000); Median rent: $236 per month (2000); Median age of housing: 30 years (2000).
Health: Birth rate: 117.1 per 10,000 population (1998); Age adjusted death rate: 84.2 per 10,000 population (1999); Age adjusted cancer mortality rate: 267.1 deaths per 100,000 population (1999). Air Quality Index: 71% good, 29% moderate, 0% unhealthy (percent of days in 2000). Number of physicians: 1.1 per 10,000 population (1999); Number of hospital beds: n/a (1999).
Elections: 2000 Presidential election results: 45.4% Gore, 53.1% Bush, 0.5% Nader, 0.6% Buchanan
National and State Parks: Mark Twain Birthplace State Historic Site; Mark Twain State Park
Additional Information Contacts
Monroe County Government Offices 660-327-5106
Monroe City Area Chamber 573-735-4391
Monroe City Chamber of Commerce 573-735-4220
Paris Chamber of Commerce 660-327-4450

Monroe County Communities

HOLLIDAY (village). Covers a land area of 0.260 square miles and a water area of 0 square miles. Located at 39.49° N. Lat.; 92.13° W. Long. Elevation is 788 feet.
Population: 129 (2000); Race: 100.0% White, 0.0% Black, 0.0% Asian, 0.0% American Indian and Alaska Native, 1.4% Hispanic of any race, 0.0% two or more races (2000); Density: 496.2 persons per square mile (2000); Age: 18.1% under 18, 21.5% over 64 (2000); Marriage status: 13.1% never married, 76.2% now married, 4.9% widowed, 5.7% divorced (2000); Foreign born: 0.0% (2000); Ancestry (includes multiple ancestries): 19.4% Irish, 15.3% English, 13.9% German, 13.2% United States or American, 9.7% Dutch (2000).
Economy: Employment by occupation: 2.9% management, 11.4% professional, 27.1% services, 10.0% sales, 0.0% farming, 17.1% construction, 31.4% production (2000).
Income: Per capita income: $13,266 (2000); Median household income: $26,250 (2000); Poverty rate: 15.3% (2000).
Taxes: Total city taxes per capita: $29 (1997); City property taxes per capita: $7 (1997).
Education: High school graduation rate: 78.8% (2000); College graduation rate: 0.0% (2000).

School District(s)

Holliday C-2 (PK-08)
2000 Enrollment: 64 660-266-3412

Housing: Homeownership rate: 81.5% (2000); Median home value: $27,900 (2000); Median rent: $225 per month (2000); Median age of housing: 49 years (2000).
Transportation: Commute to work: 85.3% car, 0.0% public transportation, 10.3% walk, 4.4% work from home (2000); Travel time to work: 20.0% less than 15 minutes, 32.3% 15 to 30 minutes, 18.5% 30 to 45 minutes, 4.6% 45 to 60 minutes, 24.6% 60 minutes or more (2000)

MADISON (city). Covers a land area of 0.446 square miles and a water area of 0 square miles. Located at 39.47° N. Lat.; 92.21° W. Long. Elevation is 796 feet.
History: Madison was settled by people from Kentucky in the late 1830's. The area developed with an interest in horses, but drawing its revenue from livestock and poultry raising.
Population: 586 (2000); Race: 99.1% White, 0.0% Black, 0.0% Asian, 0.0% American Indian and Alaska Native, 1.2% Hispanic of any race, 0.4% two or more races (2000); Density: 1,314.3 persons per square mile (2000); Age: 21.3% under 18, 16.9% over 64 (2000); Marriage status: 14.9% never

married, 64.7% now married, 9.1% widowed, 11.3% divorced (2000); Foreign born: 0.5% (2000); Ancestry (includes multiple ancestries): 17.3% German, 13.9% Irish, 12.9% United States or American, 9.9% English, 7.9% Other groups (2000).
Economy: Single-family building permits issued: 0 (2001) / 0 (2000); Multi-family building permits issued: 0 (2001) / 0 (2000); Employment by occupation: 5.7% management, 10.2% professional, 19.4% services, 28.3% sales, 0.0% farming, 10.6% construction, 25.8% production (2000).
Income: Per capita income: $15,128 (2000); Median household income: $28,125 (2000); Poverty rate: 14.7% (2000).
Taxes: Total city taxes per capita: $175 (1997); City property taxes per capita: $37 (1997).
Education: High school graduation rate: 79.0% (2000); College graduation rate: 5.9% (2000).

School District(s)

Madison C-3 (KG-12)
2000 Enrollment: 291 660-291-5115
Middle Grove C-1 (KG-08)
2000 Enrollment: 43 660-291-8583

Housing: Homeownership rate: 82.0% (2000); Median home value: $41,600 (2000); Median rent: $227 per month (2000); Median age of housing: 44 years (2000).
Transportation: Commute to work: 94.2% car, 0.0% public transportation, 3.3% walk, 2.5% work from home (2000); Travel time to work: 25.7% less than 15 minutes, 49.1% 15 to 30 minutes, 12.6% 30 to 45 minutes, 3.0% 45 to 60 minutes, 9.7% 60 minutes or more (2000)

MONROE CITY (city). Covers a land area of 3.092 square miles and a water area of 0.041 square miles. Located at 39.65° N. Lat.; 91.73° W. Long.
History: Monroe City was platted in 1857 by E.B. Talcott as a shipping point on the Hannibal & St. Joseph Railroad for the grain and livestock raised in the surrounding area. The town was incorporated in 1869. In 1898 the Henderson Produce Company began developing the poultry industry here.
Population: 2,588 (2000); Race: 88.0% White, 10.0% Black, 0.6% Asian, 0.3% American Indian and Alaska Native, 0.6% Hispanic of any race, 0.6% two or more races (2000); Density: 837.1 persons per square mile (2000); Age: 28.1% under 18, 18.9% over 64 (2000); Marriage status: 23.5% never married, 52.8% now married, 12.6% widowed, 11.1% divorced (2000); Foreign born: 0.5% (2000); Ancestry (includes multiple ancestries): 19.1% German, 15.3% Other groups, 14.3% United States or American, 13.5% English, 12.3% Irish (2000).
Economy: Single-family building permits issued: 6 (2001) / 12 (2000); Multi-family building permits issued: 0 (2001) / 0 (2000); Employment by occupation: 9.0% management, 13.0% professional, 18.4% services, 19.6% sales, 1.0% farming, 8.5% construction, 30.5% production (2000).
Income: Per capita income: $14,937 (2000); Median household income: $30,377 (2000); Poverty rate: 11.0% (2000).
Taxes: Total city taxes per capita: $298 (1997); City property taxes per capita: $69 (1997).
Education: High school graduation rate: 80.1% (2000); College graduation rate: 12.7% (2000).

School District(s)

Monroe City R-I (PK-12)
2000 Enrollment: 818 573-735-4631

Housing: Homeownership rate: 70.1% (2000); Median home value: $67,200 (2000); Median rent: $250 per month (2000); Median age of housing: 34 years (2000).
Transportation: Commute to work: 92.2% car, 0.0% public transportation, 3.8% walk, 2.8% work from home (2000); Travel time to work: 64.3% less than 15 minutes, 17.1% 15 to 30 minutes, 12.4% 30 to 45 minutes, 4.0% 45 to 60 minutes, 2.2% 60 minutes or more (2000)

Additional Information Contacts

Monroe City Area Chamber 573-735-4391
Monroe City Chamber of Commerce 573-735-4220

PARIS (city). Covers a land area of 1.245 square miles and a water area of 0 square miles. Located at 39.48° N. Lat.; 92.00° W. Long. Elevation is 696 feet.
History: Paris was platted as the seat of Monroe County in 1831. The early residents, many from Kentucky and Tennessee, laid out a race track and raised horses that made racing history here.
Population: 1,529 (2000); Race: 89.9% White, 7.7% Black, 0.0% Asian, 2.0% American Indian and Alaska Native, 0.1% Hispanic of any race, 0.3% two or more races (2000); Density: 1,228.5 persons per square mile (2000); Age: 21.5% under 18, 27.5% over 64 (2000); Marriage status: 18.2% never married, 56.3% now married, 16.3% widowed, 9.1% divorced (2000); Foreign born: 0.3% (2000); Ancestry (includes multiple ancestries): 19.9% German, 14.6% United States or American, 11.3% English, 10.5% Other groups, 8.8% Irish (2000).
Economy: Single-family building permits issued: 0 (2001) / 0 (2000); Multi-family building permits issued: 0 (2001) / 0 (2000); Employment by occupation: 9.7% management, 12.6% professional, 22.5% services, 21.5% sales, 1.8% farming, 10.5% construction, 21.3% production (2000).
Income: Per capita income: $14,980 (2000); Median household income: $29,556 (2000); Poverty rate: 10.4% (2000).
Taxes: Total city taxes per capita: $181 (1997); City property taxes per capita: $44 (1997).
Education: High school graduation rate: 74.4% (2000); College graduation rate: 11.7% (2000).

School District(s)

Paris R-II (KG-12)
2000 Enrollment: 606 660-327-4112

Housing: Homeownership rate: 73.2% (2000); Median home value: $47,500 (2000); Median rent: $204 per month (2000); Median age of housing: 42 years (2000).
Newspapers: Monroe County Appeal (1 x week)
Transportation: Commute to work: 91.6% car, 0.3% public transportation, 3.5% walk, 2.0% work from home (2000); Travel time to work: 48.3% less than 15 minutes, 12.2% 15 to 30 minutes, 26.2% 30 to 45 minutes, 7.4% 45 to 60 minutes, 6.0% 60 minutes or more (2000)

Additional Information Contacts

Paris Chamber of Commerce 660-327-4450

SANTA FE (unincorporated postal area, zip code 65282). Covers a land area of 13.719 square miles and a water area of 0 square miles. Located at 39.36° N. Lat.; 91.81° W. Long. Elevation is 718 feet.
Population: 153 (2000); Race: 100.0% White, 0.0% Black, 0.0% Asian, 0.0% American Indian and Alaska Native, 0.0% Hispanic of any race, 0.0% two or more races (2000); Density: 11.2 persons per square mile (2000); Age: 28.1% under 18, 19.2% over 64 (2000); Marriage status: 21.5% never married, 65.3% now married, 6.9% widowed, 6.3% divorced (2000); Foreign born: 0.0% (2000); Ancestry (includes multiple ancestries): 28.1% United States or American, 13.2% Other groups, 13.2% Irish, 10.2% German, 7.2% Scottish (2000).
Economy: Employment by occupation: 0.0% management, 0.0% professional, 14.0% services, 44.2% sales, 0.0% farming, 0.0% construction, 41.9% production (2000).
Income: Per capita income: $11,043 (2000); Median household income: $37,857 (2000); Poverty rate: 13.2% (2000).
Education: High school graduation rate: 73.5% (2000); College graduation rate: 0.0% (2000).
Housing: Homeownership rate: 79.7% (2000); Median home value: $85,000 (2000); Median rent: $425 per month (2000); Median age of housing: 30 years (2000).
Transportation: Commute to work: 100.0% car, 0.0% public transportation, 0.0% walk, 0.0% work from home (2000); Travel time to work: 0.0% less than 15 minutes, 0.0% 15 to 30 minutes, 67.4% 30 to 45 minutes, 32.6% 45 to 60 minutes, 0.0% 60 minutes or more (2000)

STOUTSVILLE (village). Covers a land area of 0.798 square miles and a water area of 0 square miles. Located at 39.55° N. Lat.; 91.85° W. Long. Elevation is 613 feet.
Population: 44 (2000); Race: 90.7% White, 0.0% Black, 0.0% Asian, 9.3% American Indian and Alaska Native, 0.0% Hispanic of any race, 0.0% two or more races (2000); Density: 55.1 persons per square mile (2000); Age: 4.7% under 18, 41.9% over 64 (2000); Marriage status: 9.8% never married, 68.3% now married, 0.0% widowed, 22.0% divorced (2000); Foreign born: 0.0% (2000); Ancestry (includes multiple ancestries): 23.3% German, 14.0% Other groups, 9.3% Irish, 9.3% Scotch-Irish, 4.7% United States or American (2000).
Economy: Employment by occupation: 0.0% management, 0.0% professional, 14.3% services, 57.1% sales, 0.0% farming, 14.3% construction, 14.3% production (2000).
Income: Per capita income: $18,165 (2000); Median household income: $31,875 (2000); Poverty rate: 4.9% (2000).
Education: High school graduation rate: 84.6% (2000); College graduation rate: 15.4% (2000).
Housing: Homeownership rate: 95.5% (2000); Median home value: $30,000 (2000); Median rent: $425 per month (2000); Median age of housing: 23 years (2000).
Transportation: Commute to work: 100.0% car, 0.0% public transportation, 0.0% walk, 0.0% work from home (2000); Travel time to work: 42.9% less

than 15 minutes, 0.0% 15 to 30 minutes, 28.6% 30 to 45 minutes, 28.6% 45 to 60 minutes, 0.0% 60 minutes or more (2000)

Montgomery County

Located in east central Missouri; bounded on the south by the Missouri River; drained by the Loutre River. Covers a land area of 537.50 square miles, a water area of 2.90 square miles, and is located in the Central Time Zone. The county government was organized in 1818. County seat is Montgomery City.
Population: 12,136 (2000); Race: 95.9% White, 1.6% Black, 0.8% Asian, 0.2% American Indian and Alaska Native, 1.1% Hispanic of any race, 1.3% two or more races (2000); Density: 22.6 persons per square mile (2000); Age: 25.3% under 18, 17.4% over 64 (2000).
Religion: Five largest groups: 15.3% Southern Baptist Convention, 11.1% Catholic Church, 10.8% The United Methodist Church, 6.8% The Church of Jesus Christ of Latter-day Saints, 5.4% Lutheran Church—Missouri Synod (2000).
Economy: Unemployment rate: 4.7% (11/2002); Total civilian labor force: 5,902 (11/2002); Leading industries: 26.7% manufacturing; 16.1% retail trade; 10.7% health care and social assistance (2000); Companies that employ more than 1,000 persons: 0 (2000); Companies that employ more than 100 persons: 4 (2000); Farms: 765 totaling 247,776 acres (1997); Minority business ownership rate: 0.0% (1997); Women business ownership rate: 10.3% (1997); Retail sales per capita: $6,303 (1997). Single-family building permits issued: 21 (2001) / 19 (2000); Multi-family building permits issued: 6 (2001) / 4 (2000).
Income: Per capita income: $15,092 (2000); Median household income: $32,772 (2000); Poverty rate: 11.8% (2000); Bankruptcy rate: 4.31% (2001).
Taxes: Total county taxes per capita: $104 (2000); County property taxes per capita: $33 (2000).
Education: High school graduation rate: 71.1% (2000); College graduation rate: 9.9% (2000).
Housing: Homeownership rate: 78.7% (2000); Median home value: $59,300 (2000); Median rent: $270 per month (2000); Median age of housing: 34 years (2000).
Health: Birth rate: 112.1 per 10,000 population (1998); Age adjusted death rate: 105.9 per 10,000 population (1999); Age adjusted cancer mortality rate: 273.7 deaths per 100,000 population (1999). Number of physicians: 3.3 per 10,000 population (1999); Number of hospital beds: n/a (1999).
Elections: 2000 Presidential election results: 39.5% Gore, 58.6% Bush, 1.3% Nader, 0.4% Buchanan
National and State Parks: Baldwin State Wildlife Area; Danville State Wildlife Area; Graham Cave State Park; Marshall I Diggs State Wildlife Management A; Mineola State Wildlife Area; Thornhill and Schulz State Wildlife Area; Wellsville Lake State Wildlife Management Ar
Additional Information Contacts
Montgomery County Government Offices. 573-564-3357

Montgomery County Communities

BELLFLOWER (city). Covers a land area of 0.549 square miles and a water area of 0 square miles. Located at 39.00° N. Lat.; 91.35° W. Long. Elevation is 765 feet.
Population: 427 (2000); Race: 98.8% White, 0.0% Black, 0.0% Asian, 0.0% American Indian and Alaska Native, 1.7% Hispanic of any race, 0.0% two or more races (2000); Density: 777.6 persons per square mile (2000); Age: 45.0% under 18, 6.2% over 64 (2000); Marriage status: 23.1% never married, 58.0% now married, 5.3% widowed, 13.6% divorced (2000); Foreign born: 0.0% (2000); Ancestry (includes multiple ancestries): 28.7% German, 17.1% Irish, 13.0% Other groups, 12.1% United States or American, 4.7% French (except Basque) (2000).
Economy: Cattle; corn, soybeans. Employment by occupation: 7.4% management, 5.5% professional, 8.0% services, 20.9% sales, 1.2% farming, 9.2% construction, 47.9% production (2000).
Income: Per capita income: $11,257 (2000); Median household income: $33,594 (2000); Poverty rate: 14.8% (2000).
Taxes: Total city taxes per capita: $105 (1997); City property taxes per capita: $16 (1997).
Education: High school graduation rate: 69.9% (2000); College graduation rate: 5.3% (2000).
Housing: Homeownership rate: 76.8% (2000); Median home value: $43,200 (2000); Median rent: $275 per month (2000); Median age of housing: 42 years (2000).
Transportation: Commute to work: 95.0% car, 1.2% public transportation, 2.5% walk, 1.2% work from home (2000); Travel time to work: 13.2% less than 15 minutes, 41.5% 15 to 30 minutes, 25.2% 30 to 45 minutes, 11.3% 45 to 60 minutes, 8.8% 60 minutes or more (2000)

HIGH HILL (city). Covers a land area of 0.460 square miles and a water area of 0 square miles. Located at 38.87° N. Lat.; 91.38° W. Long. Elevation is 894 feet.
Population: 231 (2000); Race: 93.0% White, 0.0% Black, 2.3% Asian, 0.0% American Indian and Alaska Native, 0.0% Hispanic of any race, 4.7% two or more races (2000); Density: 502.2 persons per square mile (2000); Age: 17.8% under 18, 25.2% over 64 (2000); Marriage status: 19.8% never married, 58.8% now married, 8.6% widowed, 12.8% divorced (2000); Foreign born: 1.9% (2000); Ancestry (includes multiple ancestries): 29.4% German, 14.5% Irish, 12.6% English, 9.8% Other groups, 5.6% French (except Basque) (2000).
Economy: Fire-clay. Employment by occupation: 3.6% management, 12.5% professional, 13.4% services, 30.4% sales, 1.8% farming, 9.8% construction, 28.6% production (2000).
Income: Per capita income: $18,155 (2000); Median household income: $31,429 (2000); Poverty rate: 10.7% (2000).
Taxes: Total city taxes per capita: $170 (1997); City property taxes per capita: $37 (1997).
Education: High school graduation rate: 61.9% (2000); College graduation rate: 8.4% (2000).
Housing: Homeownership rate: 86.8% (2000); Median home value: $51,400 (2000); Median rent: $163 per month (2000); Median age of housing: 27 years (2000).
Transportation: Commute to work: 91.1% car, 0.0% public transportation, 4.5% walk, 1.8% work from home (2000); Travel time to work: 30.0% less than 15 minutes, 27.3% 15 to 30 minutes, 17.3% 30 to 45 minutes, 18.2% 45 to 60 minutes, 7.3% 60 minutes or more (2000)

JONESBURG (city). Covers a land area of 1.256 square miles and a water area of 0 square miles. Located at 38.85° N. Lat.; 91.31° W. Long. Elevation is 897 feet.
History: In 1828 James Jones came from North Carolina and built a log house here. He opened the Cross Keys Tavern, a stopping place on the Boon's Lick Trail, in 1834. When the town was platted in 1858, it was named for Jones.
Population: 695 (2000); Race: 97.5% White, 0.7% Black, 0.0% Asian, 0.0% American Indian and Alaska Native, 1.4% Hispanic of any race, 1.8% two or more races (2000); Density: 553.3 persons per square mile (2000); Age: 25.3% under 18, 19.1% over 64 (2000); Marriage status: 19.6% never married, 45.7% now married, 17.7% widowed, 17.0% divorced (2000); Foreign born: 0.0% (2000); Ancestry (includes multiple ancestries): 28.2% German, 17.3% United States or American, 12.2% Other groups, 11.3% Irish, 6.7% English (2000).
Economy: Single-family building permits issued: 1 (2001) / 3 (2000); Multi-family building permits issued: 0 (2001) / 0 (2000); Employment by occupation: 5.3% management, 7.9% professional, 13.2% services, 21.4% sales, 0.0% farming, 14.8% construction, 37.4% production (2000).
Income: Per capita income: $13,230 (2000); Median household income: $26,875 (2000); Poverty rate: 16.8% (2000).
Taxes: Total city taxes per capita: $184 (1997); City property taxes per capita: $31 (1997).
Education: High school graduation rate: 60.3% (2000); College graduation rate: 5.7% (2000).
Housing: Homeownership rate: 67.2% (2000); Median home value: $72,000 (2000); Median rent: $258 per month (2000); Median age of housing: 35 years (2000).
Transportation: Commute to work: 91.3% car, 0.0% public transportation, 4.8% walk, 1.9% work from home (2000); Travel time to work: 40.2% less than 15 minutes, 29.7% 15 to 30 minutes, 11.4% 30 to 45 minutes, 10.5% 45 to 60 minutes, 8.2% 60 minutes or more (2000)

MCKITTRICK (town). Covers a land area of 0.163 square miles and a water area of 0 square miles. Located at 38.73° N. Lat.; 91.44° W. Long. Elevation is 550 feet.
History: Flooded in 1993.
Population: 72 (2000); Race: 100.0% White, 0.0% Black, 0.0% Asian, 0.0% American Indian and Alaska Native, 0.0% Hispanic of any race, 0.0% two or more races (2000); Density: 440.7 persons per square mile (2000); Age: 8.6% under 18, 41.4% over 64 (2000); Marriage status: 7.5% never married, 81.1% now married, 7.5% widowed, 3.8% divorced (2000); Foreign born: 0.0% (2000); Ancestry (includes multiple ancestries): 65.5% German, 17.2% Scotch-Irish, 8.6% United States or American, 5.2% Czech, 3.4% English (2000).

Economy: Feed mill. Employment by occupation: 0.0% management, 20.7% professional, 6.9% services, 13.8% sales, 0.0% farming, 27.6% construction, 31.0% production (2000).
Income: Per capita income: $17,105 (2000); Median household income: $37,750 (2000); Poverty rate: 0.0% (2000).
Taxes: Total city taxes per capita: $10,657 (1997); City property taxes per capita: $0 (1997).
Education: High school graduation rate: 55.8% (2000); College graduation rate: 0.0% (2000).
Housing: Homeownership rate: 100.0% (2000); Median home value: $48,800 (2000); Median age of housing: 60+ years (2000).
Transportation: Commute to work: 100.0% car, 0.0% public transportation, 0.0% walk, 0.0% work from home (2000); Travel time to work: 42.3% less than 15 minutes, 15.4% 15 to 30 minutes, 42.3% 30 to 45 minutes, 0.0% 45 to 60 minutes, 0.0% 60 minutes or more (2000)

MIDDLETOWN (town). Covers a land area of 0.321 square miles and a water area of 0 square miles. Located at 39.12° N. Lat.; 91.41° W. Long. Elevation is 713 feet.
Population: 199 (2000); Race: 100.0% White, 0.0% Black, 0.0% Asian, 0.0% American Indian and Alaska Native, 0.0% Hispanic of any race, 0.0% two or more races (2000); Density: 620.3 persons per square mile (2000); Age: 17.3% under 18, 20.0% over 64 (2000); Marriage status: 16.6% never married, 49.0% now married, 19.7% widowed, 14.6% divorced (2000); Foreign born: 1.1% (2000); Ancestry (includes multiple ancestries): 20.5% German, 20.0% United States or American, 17.8% English, 12.4% Irish, 5.9% Other groups (2000).
Economy: Agriculture. Employment by occupation: 10.9% management, 10.9% professional, 10.9% services, 23.4% sales, 0.0% farming, 4.7% construction, 39.1% production (2000).
Income: Per capita income: $11,756 (2000); Median household income: $19,500 (2000); Poverty rate: 35.1% (2000).
Taxes: Total city taxes per capita: $114 (1997); City property taxes per capita: $22 (1997).
Education: High school graduation rate: 54.6% (2000); College graduation rate: 5.0% (2000).
Housing: Homeownership rate: 91.0% (2000); Median home value: $33,500 (2000); Median rent: $225 per month (2000); Median age of housing: 36 years (2000).
Transportation: Commute to work: 87.5% car, 0.0% public transportation, 6.3% walk, 3.1% work from home (2000); Travel time to work: 16.1% less than 15 minutes, 54.8% 15 to 30 minutes, 17.7% 30 to 45 minutes, 0.0% 45 to 60 minutes, 11.3% 60 minutes or more (2000)

MONTGOMERY CITY (city). Aka Montgomery. Covers a land area of 2.844 square miles and a water area of 0 square miles. Located at 38.97° N. Lat.; 91.50° W. Long. Elevation is 816 feet.
History: Laid out 1853.
Population: 2,442 (2000); Race: 95.9% White, 1.7% Black, 0.2% Asian, 0.4% American Indian and Alaska Native, 1.5% Hispanic of any race, 1.1% two or more races (2000); Density: 858.6 persons per square mile (2000); Age: 24.8% under 18, 15.1% over 64 (2000); Marriage status: 22.9% never married, 53.9% now married, 9.5% widowed, 13.7% divorced (2000); Foreign born: 0.5% (2000); Ancestry (includes multiple ancestries): 27.9% German, 15.0% English, 9.7% United States or American, 9.0% Irish, 7.3% Other groups (2000).
Economy: Corn, wheat, soybeans; cattle. Manufacturing: commercial printing, toll booths, feeds, apparel. Single-family building permits issued: 14 (2001) / 13 (2000); Multi-family building permits issued: 6 (2001) / 0 (2000); Employment by occupation: 5.0% management, 18.3% professional, 19.5% services, 24.3% sales, 0.4% farming, 9.4% construction, 23.1% production (2000).
Income: Per capita income: $15,735 (2000); Median household income: $30,446 (2000); Poverty rate: 14.0% (2000).
Taxes: Total city taxes per capita: $171 (1997); City property taxes per capita: $0 (1997).
Education: High school graduation rate: 79.6% (2000); College graduation rate: 15.7% (2000).

School District(s)

Montgomery Co. R-II (PK-12)
2000 Enrollment: 1,431 573-564-2278
Housing: Homeownership rate: 71.3% (2000); Median home value: $64,800 (2000); Median rent: $301 per month (2000); Median age of housing: 37 years (2000).
Safety: Violent crime rate: 24.4 per 10,000 population; Property crime rate: 244.2 per 10,000 population (2001).
Newspapers: Montgomery Standard (1 x week)
Transportation: Commute to work: 91.9% car, 0.0% public transportation, 3.7% walk, 3.8% work from home (2000); Travel time to work: 49.9% less than 15 minutes, 18.3% 15 to 30 minutes, 15.0% 30 to 45 minutes, 6.5% 45 to 60 minutes, 10.2% 60 minutes or more (2000)

NEW FLORENCE (city). Covers a land area of 1.621 square miles and a water area of 0 square miles. Located at 38.91° N. Lat.; 91.44° W. Long. Elevation is 875 feet.
Population: 764 (2000); Race: 98.3% White, 0.3% Black, 0.0% Asian, 0.0% American Indian and Alaska Native, 0.0% Hispanic of any race, 1.4% two or more races (2000); Density: 471.3 persons per square mile (2000); Age: 27.2% under 18, 23.9% over 64 (2000); Marriage status: 20.4% never married, 49.7% now married, 19.5% widowed, 10.4% divorced (2000); Foreign born: 0.6% (2000); Ancestry (includes multiple ancestries): 27.7% German, 17.3% United States or American, 14.5% Irish, 12.0% English, 8.1% Other groups (2000).
Economy: Agriculture: corn, wheat, soybeans; hogs. Manufacturing: barrel staves, wine, champagne. Limestone quarries. Single-family building permits issued: 6 (2001) / 3 (2000); Multi-family building permits issued: 0 (2001) / 4 (2000); Employment by occupation: 5.8% management, 5.5% professional, 24.2% services, 18.8% sales, 1.7% farming, 11.6% construction, 32.4% production (2000).
Income: Per capita income: $12,367 (2000); Median household income: $30,156 (2000); Poverty rate: 22.2% (2000).
Taxes: Total city taxes per capita: $91 (1997); City property taxes per capita: $53 (1997).
Education: High school graduation rate: 54.9% (2000); College graduation rate: 2.9% (2000).
Housing: Homeownership rate: 80.4% (2000); Median home value: $51,700 (2000); Median rent: $294 per month (2000); Median age of housing: 39 years (2000).
Transportation: Commute to work: 95.5% car, 0.7% public transportation, 1.0% walk, 1.0% work from home (2000); Travel time to work: 37.5% less than 15 minutes, 25.4% 15 to 30 minutes, 14.5% 30 to 45 minutes, 9.9% 45 to 60 minutes, 12.7% 60 minutes or more (2000)

RHINELAND (town). Covers a land area of 0.341 square miles and a water area of 0 square miles. Located at 38.71° N. Lat.; 91.51° W. Long. Elevation is 517 feet.
History: River flooding in 1993 destroyed town; relocated onto adjacent bluffs.
Population: 176 (2000); Race: 97.8% White, 0.0% Black, 0.0% Asian, 0.0% American Indian and Alaska Native, 3.8% Hispanic of any race, 2.2% two or more races (2000); Density: 515.4 persons per square mile (2000); Age: 31.7% under 18, 15.3% over 64 (2000); Marriage status: 23.7% never married, 50.4% now married, 14.8% widowed, 11.1% divorced (2000); Foreign born: 0.0% (2000); Ancestry (includes multiple ancestries): 61.7% German, 9.3% Irish, 6.6% United States or American, 6.0% English, 4.9% French (except Basque) (2000).
Economy: Soybeans, corn, wheat; cattle. Employment by occupation: 13.3% management, 8.2% professional, 10.2% services, 14.3% sales, 2.0% farming, 29.6% construction, 22.4% production (2000).
Income: Per capita income: $16,989 (2000); Median household income: $37,000 (2000); Poverty rate: 8.8% (2000).
Taxes: Total city taxes per capita: $101 (1997); City property taxes per capita: $57 (1997).
Education: High school graduation rate: 71.4% (2000); College graduation rate: 12.4% (2000).
Housing: Homeownership rate: 80.6% (2000); Median home value: $82,500 (2000); Median rent: $288 per month (2000); Median age of housing: 39 years (2000).
Transportation: Commute to work: 95.9% car, 0.0% public transportation, 0.0% walk, 4.1% work from home (2000); Travel time to work: 37.2% less than 15 minutes, 25.5% 15 to 30 minutes, 2.1% 30 to 45 minutes, 8.5% 45 to 60 minutes, 26.6% 60 minutes or more (2000)

WELLSVILLE (city). Covers a land area of 1.423 square miles and a water area of 0 square miles. Located at 39.07° N. Lat.; 91.56° W. Long. Elevation is 815 feet.
History: Laid out 1856.
Population: 1,423 (2000); Race: 93.8% White, 5.0% Black, 0.0% Asian, 0.1% American Indian and Alaska Native, 0.6% Hispanic of any race, 1.1% two or more races (2000); Density: 999.8 persons per square mile (2000); Age: 26.9% under 18, 20.6% over 64 (2000); Marriage status: 23.0% never married, 52.0% now married, 15.6% widowed, 9.3% divorced (2000);

Foreign born: 0.2% (2000); Ancestry (includes multiple ancestries): 20.1% German, 10.4% Other groups, 8.4% United States or American, 8.1% English, 8.1% Irish (2000).
Economy: Corn, soybeans; hogs, cattle; manufacturing of bricks, cement. Employment by occupation: 4.6% management, 18.3% professional, 18.3% services, 20.0% sales, 0.6% farming, 9.1% construction, 29.2% production (2000).
Income: Per capita income: $11,817 (2000); Median household income: $27,260 (2000); Poverty rate: 20.3% (2000).
Taxes: Total city taxes per capita: $81 (1997); City property taxes per capita: $15 (1997).
Education: High school graduation rate: 62.4% (2000); College graduation rate: 7.7% (2000).

School District(s)

Wellsville Middletown R-I (PK-12)
2000 Enrollment: 550 573-684-2428
Housing: Homeownership rate: 69.5% (2000); Median home value: $39,000 (2000); Median rent: $251 per month (2000); Median age of housing: 40 years (2000).
Newspapers: Optic-News (1 x week)
Transportation: Commute to work: 94.5% car, 0.0% public transportation, 2.1% walk, 1.9% work from home (2000); Travel time to work: 44.2% less than 15 minutes, 18.7% 15 to 30 minutes, 21.2% 30 to 45 minutes, 6.4% 45 to 60 minutes, 9.5% 60 minutes or more (2000)

Morgan County

Located in central Missouri, in the Ozarks; drained by the Lamine River; includes part of Lake of the Ozarks. Covers a land area of 597.40 square miles, a water area of 16.50 square miles, and is located in the Central Time Zone. The county government was organized in 1833. County seat is Versailles.

Weather Station: Versailles — Elevation: 1,026 feet

	Jan	Feb	Mar	Apr	May	Jun	Jul	Aug	Sep	Oct	Nov	Dec
High	40	47	58	68	76	83	89	87	79	69	56	45
Low	20	25	34	44	53	62	67	65	57	46	35	25
Precip	1.8	2.0	3.3	4.5	5.2	4.1	3.9	3.8	4.1	4.0	3.8	2.6
Snow	na	2.1	0.5	tr	0.0	0.0	0.0	0.0	0.0	tr	1.1	1.2

High and Low temperatures in degrees Fahrenheit; Precipitation and Snow in inches

Population: 19,309 (2000); Race: 97.2% White, 0.5% Black, 0.1% Asian, 0.5% American Indian and Alaska Native, 0.9% Hispanic of any race, 1.6% two or more races (2000); Density: 32.3 persons per square mile (2000); Age: 23.8% under 18, 19.6% over 64 (2000).
Religion: Five largest groups: 20.3% Southern Baptist Convention, 8.5% The United Methodist Church, 5.0% Catholic Church, 3.3% Assemblies of God, 2.8% The Church of Jesus Christ of Latter-day Saints (2000).
Economy: Unemployment rate: 6.9% (11/2002); Total civilian labor force: 7,965 (11/2002); Leading industries: 27.4% retail trade; 23.8% manufacturing; 11.5% accommodation & food services (2000); Companies that employ more than 1,000 persons: 0 (2000); Companies that employ more than 100 persons: 3 (2000); Farms: 869 totaling 202,467 acres (1997); Minority business ownership rate: 0.0% (1997); Women business ownership rate: 25.1% (1997); Retail sales per capita: $8,081 (1997). Single-family building permits issued: -1 (2001) / -1 (2000); Multi-family building permits issued: -1 (2001) / -1 (2000).
Income: Per capita income: $15,950 (2000); Median household income: $30,659 (2000); Poverty rate: 16.2% (2000); Bankruptcy rate: 4.37% (2001).
Taxes: Total county taxes per capita: $73 (2000); County property taxes per capita: $24 (2000).
Education: High school graduation rate: 74.5% (2000); College graduation rate: 10.7% (2000).
Housing: Homeownership rate: 82.9% (2000); Median home value: $79,500 (2000); Median rent: $273 per month (2000); Median age of housing: 23 years (2000).
Health: Birth rate: 106.7 per 10,000 population (1998); Age adjusted death rate: 92.4 per 10,000 population (1999); Age adjusted cancer mortality rate: 215.2 deaths per 100,000 population (1999). Number of physicians: 1.6 per 10,000 population (1999); Number of hospital beds: n/a (1999).
Elections: 2000 Presidential election results: 41.1% Gore, 56.6% Bush, 1.1% Nader, 0.7% Buchanan
National and State Parks: Carpenter Memorial State Wildlife Area; Proctor Towersite State Wildlife Area
Additional Information Contacts
Morgan County Government Offices. 573-378-4644
Lake of The Ozarks Board of Realtors. 573-374-6646

Morgan County Communities

BARNETT (city). Covers a land area of 0.273 square miles and a water area of 0 square miles. Located at 38.37° N. Lat.; 92.67° W. Long. Elevation is 970 feet.
Population: 207 (2000); Race: 98.5% White, 0.0% Black, 0.0% Asian, 0.5% American Indian and Alaska Native, 1.0% Hispanic of any race, 0.0% two or more races (2000); Density: 757.6 persons per square mile (2000); Age: 27.4% under 18, 14.7% over 64 (2000); Marriage status: 26.8% never married, 50.3% now married, 6.0% widowed, 16.8% divorced (2000); Foreign born: 0.0% (2000); Ancestry (includes multiple ancestries): 11.7% German, 7.6% Irish, 6.6% Other groups, 6.1% United States or American, 3.0% Dutch (2000).
Economy: Employment by occupation: 7.3% management, 11.0% professional, 24.4% services, 19.5% sales, 0.0% farming, 18.3% construction, 19.5% production (2000).
Income: Per capita income: $11,499 (2000); Median household income: $26,023 (2000); Poverty rate: 12.7% (2000).
Taxes: Total city taxes per capita: $33 (1997); City property taxes per capita: $25 (1997).
Education: High school graduation rate: 58.1% (2000); College graduation rate: 4.0% (2000).
Housing: Homeownership rate: 78.1% (2000); Median home value: $27,500 (2000); Median rent: $258 per month (2000); Median age of housing: 45 years (2000).
Transportation: Commute to work: 94.9% car, 0.0% public transportation, 0.0% walk, 5.1% work from home (2000); Travel time to work: 27.0% less than 15 minutes, 29.7% 15 to 30 minutes, 25.7% 30 to 45 minutes, 6.8% 45 to 60 minutes, 10.8% 60 minutes or more (2000)

FLORENCE (unincorporated postal area, zip code 65329). Covers a land area of 23.835 square miles and a water area of 0 square miles. Located at 38.60° N. Lat.; 92.97° W. Long. Elevation is 942 feet.
Population: 363 (2000); Race: 98.7% White, 0.0% Black, 0.0% Asian, 1.3% American Indian and Alaska Native, 0.0% Hispanic of any race, 0.0% two or more races (2000); Density: 15.2 persons per square mile (2000); Age: 32.8% under 18, 9.0% over 64 (2000); Marriage status: 17.3% never married, 57.5% now married, 12.8% widowed, 12.4% divorced (2000); Foreign born: 0.0% (2000); Ancestry (includes multiple ancestries): 45.2% German, 14.8% Dutch, 11.9% English, 8.7% Irish, 8.2% United States or American (2000).
Economy: Employment by occupation: 24.7% management, 13.3% professional, 13.3% services, 10.8% sales, 0.0% farming, 18.4% construction, 19.6% production (2000).
Income: Per capita income: $14,029 (2000); Median household income: $32,500 (2000); Poverty rate: 24.9% (2000).
Education: High school graduation rate: 71.3% (2000); College graduation rate: 16.1% (2000).
Housing: Homeownership rate: 88.8% (2000); Median home value: $91,500 (2000); Median rent: $225 per month (2000); Median age of housing: 24 years (2000).
Transportation: Commute to work: 79.7% car, 3.2% public transportation, 10.1% walk, 7.0% work from home (2000); Travel time to work: 21.1% less than 15 minutes, 29.9% 15 to 30 minutes, 30.6% 30 to 45 minutes, 4.1% 45 to 60 minutes, 14.3% 60 minutes or more (2000)

GRAVOIS MILLS (town). Covers a land area of 0.775 square miles and a water area of 0.077 square miles. Located at 38.30° N. Lat.; 92.82° W. Long. Elevation is 667 feet.
History: Gravois Mills was platted in 1884. Near here, Josiah S. Walton began operating a water-driven grist mill about 1835, and in 1870 the Hume brothers built a woolen mill. A sawmill was added in 1895 by Asa Webster.
Population: 208 (2000); Race: 93.2% White, 0.0% Black, 0.0% Asian, 0.0% American Indian and Alaska Native, 0.0% Hispanic of any race, 6.8% two or more races (2000); Density: 268.4 persons per square mile (2000); Age: 22.4% under 18, 20.8% over 64 (2000); Marriage status: 15.5% never married, 60.0% now married, 9.0% widowed, 15.5% divorced (2000); Foreign born: 0.0% (2000); Ancestry (includes multiple ancestries): 33.3% United States or American, 12.5% Irish, 11.5% German, 5.2% English, 3.1% Italian (2000).
Economy: Employment by occupation: 6.0% management, 8.3% professional, 28.6% services, 28.6% sales, 0.0% farming, 16.7% construction, 11.9% production (2000).

Income: Per capita income: $13,060 (2000); Median household income: $24,167 (2000); Poverty rate: 26.0% (2000).
Taxes: Total city taxes per capita: $160 (1997); City property taxes per capita: $0 (1997).
Education: High school graduation rate: 69.4% (2000); College graduation rate: 8.2% (2000).
Housing: Homeownership rate: 73.7% (2000); Median home value: $65,000 (2000); Median rent: $293 per month (2000); Median age of housing: 29 years (2000).
Transportation: Commute to work: 85.7% car, 0.0% public transportation, 3.6% walk, 10.7% work from home (2000); Travel time to work: 54.7% less than 15 minutes, 33.3% 15 to 30 minutes, 12.0% 30 to 45 minutes, 0.0% 45 to 60 minutes, 0.0% 60 minutes or more (2000)

LAURIE (village). Covers a land area of 5.262 square miles and a water area of 0 square miles. Located at 38.20° N. Lat.; 92.82° W. Long. Elevation is 965 feet.
Population: 663 (2000); Race: 97.2% White, 0.7% Black, 0.0% Asian, 0.9% American Indian and Alaska Native, 1.2% Hispanic of any race, 1.2% two or more races (2000); Density: 126.0 persons per square mile (2000); Age: 15.9% under 18, 40.9% over 64 (2000); Marriage status: 8.8% never married, 53.7% now married, 25.0% widowed, 12.4% divorced (2000); Foreign born: 0.3% (2000); Ancestry (includes multiple ancestries): 18.0% United States or American, 17.1% German, 11.0% Irish, 6.7% Other groups, 6.7% English (2000).
Economy: Employment by occupation: 9.5% management, 9.9% professional, 18.6% services, 36.0% sales, 0.0% farming, 12.6% construction, 13.4% production (2000).
Income: Per capita income: $18,023 (2000); Median household income: $24,333 (2000); Poverty rate: 12.4% (2000).
Taxes: Total city taxes per capita: $151 (1997); City property taxes per capita: $35 (1997).
Education: High school graduation rate: 72.4% (2000); College graduation rate: 7.0% (2000).
Housing: Homeownership rate: 63.5% (2000); Median home value: $108,200 (2000); Median rent: $302 per month (2000); Median age of housing: 14 years (2000).
Transportation: Commute to work: 81.1% car, 0.0% public transportation, 13.3% walk, 5.6% work from home (2000); Travel time to work: 59.6% less than 15 minutes, 18.3% 15 to 30 minutes, 15.3% 30 to 45 minutes, 2.1% 45 to 60 minutes, 4.7% 60 minutes or more (2000)
Additional Information Contacts
Lake of The Ozarks Board of Realtors.................... 573-374-6646

ROCKY MOUNT (unincorporated postal area, zip code 65072). Covers a land area of 18.913 square miles and a water area of 0.034 square miles. Located at 38.24° N. Lat.; 92.71° W. Long. Elevation is 865 feet.
Population: 1,609 (2000); Race: 98.4% White, 0.0% Black, 1.0% Asian, 0.0% American Indian and Alaska Native, 0.0% Hispanic of any race, 0.6% two or more races (2000); Density: 85.1 persons per square mile (2000); Age: 14.6% under 18, 28.0% over 64 (2000); Marriage status: 7.7% never married, 73.8% now married, 10.9% widowed, 7.6% divorced (2000); Foreign born: 3.8% (2000); Ancestry (includes multiple ancestries): 24.7% German, 14.5% Irish, 9.7% United States or American, 8.4% English, 7.4% Other groups (2000).
Economy: Employment by occupation: 19.2% management, 8.6% professional, 15.0% services, 31.8% sales, 0.0% farming, 15.6% construction, 9.7% production (2000).
Income: Per capita income: $21,470 (2000); Median household income: $32,000 (2000); Poverty rate: 13.0% (2000).
Education: High school graduation rate: 82.8% (2000); College graduation rate: 8.8% (2000).
Housing: Homeownership rate: 90.3% (2000); Median home value: $125,900 (2000); Median rent: $407 per month (2000); Median age of housing: 21 years (2000).
Transportation: Commute to work: 91.0% car, 0.0% public transportation, 5.3% walk, 3.7% work from home (2000); Travel time to work: 14.7% less than 15 minutes, 48.4% 15 to 30 minutes, 24.0% 30 to 45 minutes, 9.4% 45 to 60 minutes, 3.6% 60 minutes or more (2000)

STOVER (city). Covers a land area of 0.874 square miles and a water area of 0 square miles. Located at 38.44° N. Lat.; 92.99° W. Long. Elevation is 1,052 feet.
Population: 968 (2000); Race: 98.0% White, 0.0% Black, 0.0% Asian, 0.7% American Indian and Alaska Native, 2.7% Hispanic of any race, 0.5% two or more races (2000); Density: 1,107.1 persons per square mile (2000); Age: 22.0% under 18, 26.8% over 64 (2000); Marriage status: 13.5% never married, 64.5% now married, 12.9% widowed, 9.1% divorced (2000); Foreign born: 0.5% (2000); Ancestry (includes multiple ancestries): 25.4% German, 13.5% Irish, 11.0% English, 9.9% Other groups, 7.8% United States or American (2000).
Economy: Corn, wheat; cattle, poultry; light manufacturing. Employment by occupation: 5.6% management, 11.5% professional, 20.7% services, 20.7% sales, 3.8% farming, 8.3% construction, 29.3% production (2000).
Income: Per capita income: $14,978 (2000); Median household income: $26,078 (2000); Poverty rate: 15.5% (2000).
Taxes: Total city taxes per capita: $189 (1997); City property taxes per capita: $21 (1997).
Education: High school graduation rate: 63.6% (2000); College graduation rate: 8.3% (2000).

School District(s)
Morgan Co. R-I (PK-12)
2000 Enrollment: 704 573-377-2217
Housing: Homeownership rate: 65.6% (2000); Median home value: $45,000 (2000); Median rent: $252 per month (2000); Median age of housing: 41 years (2000).
Newspapers: Morgan County Press (1 x week)
Transportation: Commute to work: 89.9% car, 1.5% public transportation, 2.5% walk, 5.2% work from home (2000); Travel time to work: 48.9% less than 15 minutes, 14.2% 15 to 30 minutes, 10.0% 30 to 45 minutes, 12.0% 45 to 60 minutes, 14.9% 60 minutes or more (2000)

SYRACUSE (city). Covers a land area of 0.381 square miles and a water area of 0 square miles. Located at 38.67° N. Lat.; 92.87° W. Long. Elevation is 912 feet.
History: Syracuse was laid out in 1859, and was well settled when the first Missouri Pacific train came through a few months later. Syracuse was a station for the Overland Mail Company as well as for other stage lines.
Population: 172 (2000); Race: 100.0% White, 0.0% Black, 0.0% Asian, 0.0% American Indian and Alaska Native, 0.0% Hispanic of any race, 0.0% two or more races (2000); Density: 451.9 persons per square mile (2000); Age: 25.7% under 18, 6.1% over 64 (2000); Marriage status: 15.3% never married, 72.2% now married, 2.8% widowed, 9.7% divorced (2000); Foreign born: 0.0% (2000); Ancestry (includes multiple ancestries): 12.3% United States or American, 11.7% German, 10.6% Other groups, 9.5% French (except Basque), 8.4% Irish (2000).
Economy: Employment by occupation: 4.9% management, 2.9% professional, 31.4% services, 21.6% sales, 0.0% farming, 8.8% construction, 30.4% production (2000).
Income: Per capita income: $18,463 (2000); Median household income: $34,773 (2000); Poverty rate: 4.5% (2000).
Taxes: Total city taxes per capita: $39 (1997); City property taxes per capita: $19 (1997).
Education: High school graduation rate: 69.4% (2000); College graduation rate: 4.1% (2000).
Housing: Homeownership rate: 88.9% (2000); Median home value: $29,400 (2000); Median rent: $275 per month (2000); Median age of housing: 43 years (2000).
Transportation: Commute to work: 100.0% car, 0.0% public transportation, 0.0% walk, 0.0% work from home (2000); Travel time to work: 41.2% less than 15 minutes, 24.5% 15 to 30 minutes, 17.6% 30 to 45 minutes, 14.7% 45 to 60 minutes, 2.0% 60 minutes or more (2000)

VERSAILLES (city). Covers a land area of 2.300 square miles and a water area of 0.008 square miles. Located at 38.43° N. Lat.; 92.84° W. Long. Elevation is 1,036 feet.
History: Versailles became the seat of Morgan County in 1834, succeeding the first seat of Millville. The town developed as a trading center for farmers and a service center for tourists.
Population: 2,565 (2000); Race: 95.9% White, 2.0% Black, 0.0% Asian, 1.2% American Indian and Alaska Native, 1.5% Hispanic of any race, 0.9% two or more races (2000); Density: 1,115.2 persons per square mile (2000); Age: 25.0% under 18, 24.6% over 64 (2000); Marriage status: 17.8% never married, 52.9% now married, 16.6% widowed, 12.6% divorced (2000); Foreign born: 0.4% (2000); Ancestry (includes multiple ancestries): 19.1% German, 16.5% Other groups, 14.4% United States or American, 14.2% English, 10.0% Irish (2000).
Economy: Employment by occupation: 4.7% management, 16.8% professional, 20.6% services, 17.6% sales, 0.2% farming, 8.3% construction, 31.7% production (2000).
Income: Per capita income: $14,200 (2000); Median household income: $23,672 (2000); Poverty rate: 16.5% (2000).

Taxes: Total city taxes per capita: $322 (1997); City property taxes per capita: $62 (1997).
Education: High school graduation rate: 75.7% (2000); College graduation rate: 9.5% (2000).

School District(s)

Morgan Co. R-II (PK-12)
2000 Enrollment: 1,622 573-378-4231
Housing: Homeownership rate: 65.9% (2000); Median home value: $55,500 (2000); Median rent: $260 per month (2000); Median age of housing: 35 years (2000).
Newspapers: The Versailles Leader-Statesman (1 x week); Highway Five Beacon (1 x week)
Transportation: Commute to work: 90.5% car, 0.0% public transportation, 4.8% walk, 3.1% work from home (2000); Travel time to work: 57.4% less than 15 minutes, 19.8% 15 to 30 minutes, 10.2% 30 to 45 minutes, 4.8% 45 to 60 minutes, 7.8% 60 minutes or more (2000)

New Madrid County

Located in southeastern Missouri; bounded on the east by the Mississippi River and the Tennessee border; crossed by the Little River. Covers a land area of 678.00 square miles, a water area of 20.00 square miles, and is located in the Central Time Zone. The county government was organized in 1812. County seat is New Madrid.

Weather Station: New Madrid Elevation: 308 feet

	Jan	Feb	Mar	Apr	May	Jun	Jul	Aug	Sep	Oct	Nov	Dec
High	41	47	57	69	78	87	91	89	83	72	57	47
Low	25	29	38	47	57	66	70	67	59	47	38	29
Precip	3.2	3.7	4.8	5.5	5.1	4.3	4.0	2.7	3.4	3.9	4.9	4.9
Snow	1.9	1.7	0.3	0.0	0.0	0.0	0.0	0.0	0.0	0.0	tr	0.4

High and Low temperatures in degrees Fahrenheit; Precipitation and Snow in inches

Population: 19,760 (2000); Race: 83.1% White, 15.7% Black, 0.1% Asian, 0.1% American Indian and Alaska Native, 0.8% Hispanic of any race, 0.8% two or more races (2000); Density: 29.1 persons per square mile (2000); Age: 26.4% under 18, 15.4% over 64 (2000).
Religion: Five largest groups: 30.9% Southern Baptist Convention, 4.3% Catholic Church, 3.6% The United Methodist Church, 2.8% Baptist Missionary Association of America, 2.1% Assemblies of God (2000).
Economy: Unemployment rate: 9.4% (11/2002); Total civilian labor force: 8,689 (11/2002); Leading industries: 41.2% manufacturing; 18.9% retail trade; 9.1% health care and social assistance (2000); Companies that employ more than 1,000 persons: 2 (2000); Companies that employ more than 100 persons: 8 (2000); Farms: 429 totaling 385,766 acres (1997); Minority business ownership rate: 0.0% (1997); Women business ownership rate: 38.0% (1997); Retail sales per capita: $7,072 (1997). Single-family building permits issued: 19 (2001) / 15 (2000); Multi-family building permits issued: 0 (2001) / 0 (2000).
Income: Per capita income: $14,204 (2000); Median household income: $26,826 (2000); Poverty rate: 22.1% (2000); Bankruptcy rate: 4.06% (2001).
Taxes: Total county taxes per capita: $144 (2000); County property taxes per capita: $98 (2000).
Education: High school graduation rate: 63.6% (2000); College graduation rate: 9.6% (2000).
Housing: Homeownership rate: 66.1% (2000); Median home value: $48,100 (2000); Median rent: $222 per month (2000); Median age of housing: 30 years (2000).
Health: Birth rate: 133.6 per 10,000 population (1998); Age adjusted death rate: 117.3 per 10,000 population (1999); Age adjusted cancer mortality rate: 181.2 deaths per 100,000 population (1999). Number of physicians: 13.2 per 10,000 population (1999); Number of hospital beds: n/a (1999).
Elections: 2000 Presidential election results: 51.5% Gore, 47.0% Bush, 0.6% Nader, 0.6% Buchanan
National and State Parks: Hunter-Dawson State Park
Additional Information Contacts
New Madrid County Government Offices 573-748-2524
New Madrid Chamber of Commerce 573-748-5300

New Madrid County Communities

CANALOU (city). Covers a land area of 0.252 square miles and a water area of 0 square miles. Located at 36.75° N. Lat.; 89.68° W. Long. Elevation is 289 feet.
Population: 348 (2000); Race: 98.4% White, 0.3% Black, 0.0% Asian, 0.0% American Indian and Alaska Native, 0.0% Hispanic of any race, 1.3% two or more races (2000); Density: 1,380.1 persons per square mile (2000); Age: 30.9% under 18, 10.5% over 64 (2000); Marriage status: 19.0% never married, 59.1% now married, 10.3% widowed, 11.6% divorced (2000); Foreign born: 0.0% (2000); Ancestry (includes multiple ancestries): 23.6% United States or American, 13.7% Other groups, 13.1% Irish, 6.4% German, 4.5% Dutch (2000).
Economy: Cotton, rice, soybeans. Single-family building permits issued: 0 (2001) / 0 (2000); Multi-family building permits issued: 0 (2001) / 0 (2000); Employment by occupation: 6.1% management, 4.5% professional, 23.5% services, 18.2% sales, 6.1% farming, 8.3% construction, 33.3% production (2000).
Income: Per capita income: $9,660 (2000); Median household income: $21,250 (2000); Poverty rate: 27.4% (2000).
Taxes: Total city taxes per capita: $53 (1997); City property taxes per capita: $33 (1997).
Education: High school graduation rate: 41.6% (2000); College graduation rate: 2.2% (2000).
Housing: Homeownership rate: 87.5% (2000); Median home value: $26,100 (2000); Median rent: $213 per month (2000); Median age of housing: 31 years (2000).
Transportation: Commute to work: 90.2% car, 0.0% public transportation, 1.6% walk, 4.1% work from home (2000); Travel time to work: 20.5% less than 15 minutes, 59.0% 15 to 30 minutes, 17.9% 30 to 45 minutes, 2.6% 45 to 60 minutes, 0.0% 60 minutes or more (2000)

CATRON (town). Covers a land area of 0.396 square miles and a water area of 0 square miles. Located at 36.61° N. Lat.; 89.70° W. Long. Elevation is 285 feet.
Population: 68 (2000); Race: 62.7% White, 37.3% Black, 0.0% Asian, 0.0% American Indian and Alaska Native, 0.0% Hispanic of any race, 0.0% two or more races (2000); Density: 171.6 persons per square mile (2000); Age: 30.7% under 18, 16.0% over 64 (2000); Marriage status: 23.3% never married, 51.7% now married, 15.0% widowed, 10.0% divorced (2000); Foreign born: 0.0% (2000); Ancestry (includes multiple ancestries): 30.7% Other groups, 10.7% Irish, 8.0% United States or American, 8.0% English, 5.3% African (2000).
Economy: Rice, cotton, soybeans. Employment by occupation: 20.8% management, 12.5% professional, 8.3% services, 29.2% sales, 0.0% farming, 0.0% construction, 29.2% production (2000).
Income: Per capita income: $9,909 (2000); Median household income: $21,250 (2000); Poverty rate: 42.7% (2000).
Taxes: Total city taxes per capita: $37 (1997); City property taxes per capita: $37 (1997).
Education: High school graduation rate: 55.3% (2000); College graduation rate: 4.3% (2000).
Housing: Homeownership rate: 100.0% (2000); Median home value: $18,800 (2000); Median age of housing: 26 years (2000).
Transportation: Commute to work: 91.7% car, 0.0% public transportation, 8.3% walk, 0.0% work from home (2000); Travel time to work: 8.3% less than 15 minutes, 41.7% 15 to 30 minutes, 25.0% 30 to 45 minutes, 8.3% 45 to 60 minutes, 16.7% 60 minutes or more (2000)

GIDEON (city). Covers a land area of 1.799 square miles and a water area of 0 square miles. Located at 36.45° N. Lat.; 89.91° W. Long. Elevation is 269 feet.
History: Incorporated 1909.
Population: 1,113 (2000); Race: 99.8% White, 0.0% Black, 0.0% Asian, 0.0% American Indian and Alaska Native, 0.4% Hispanic of any race, 0.2% two or more races (2000); Density: 618.6 persons per square mile (2000); Age: 26.6% under 18, 19.7% over 64 (2000); Marriage status: 17.8% never married, 54.9% now married, 13.4% widowed, 13.8% divorced (2000); Foreign born: 0.2% (2000); Ancestry (includes multiple ancestries): 29.4% United States or American, 11.9% Other groups, 10.5% Irish, 9.9% English, 5.2% German (2000).
Economy: Rice, soybeans; cattle. Single-family building permits issued: 0 (2001) / 1 (2000); Multi-family building permits issued: 0 (2001) / 0 (2000); Employment by occupation: 6.5% management, 9.2% professional, 16.2% services, 16.4% sales, 3.0% farming, 12.2% construction, 36.5% production (2000).
Income: Per capita income: $13,556 (2000); Median household income: $22,208 (2000); Poverty rate: 25.5% (2000).
Taxes: Total city taxes per capita: $1,124 (1997); City property taxes per capita: $1,068 (1997).
Education: High school graduation rate: 54.8% (2000); College graduation rate: 7.8% (2000).

School District(s)

Gideon 37 (KG-12)
 2000 Enrollment: 374 573-448-3911

Housing: Homeownership rate: 65.7% (2000); Median home value: $32,400 (2000); Median rent: $148 per month (2000); Median age of housing: 42 years (2000).
Transportation: Commute to work: 93.9% car, 0.0% public transportation, 3.5% walk, 0.9% work from home (2000); Travel time to work: 34.9% less than 15 minutes, 39.6% 15 to 30 minutes, 12.5% 30 to 45 minutes, 10.1% 45 to 60 minutes, 2.8% 60 minutes or more (2000)

HOWARDVILLE (city). Covers a land area of 0.230 square miles and a water area of 0 square miles. Located at 36.56° N. Lat.; 89.59° W. Long. Elevation is 292 feet.
Population: 342 (2000); Race: 3.5% White, 96.5% Black, 0.0% Asian, 0.0% American Indian and Alaska Native, 0.0% Hispanic of any race, 0.0% two or more races (2000); Density: 1,490.0 persons per square mile (2000); Age: 33.1% under 18, 10.7% over 64 (2000); Marriage status: 53.0% never married, 28.5% now married, 9.6% widowed, 8.8% divorced (2000); Foreign born: 0.0% (2000); Ancestry (includes multiple ancestries): 72.6% Other groups, 2.9% German, 1.7% Scottish, 1.7% African, 0.6% English (2000).
Economy: Residential and commercial area. Single-family building permits issued: 0 (2001) / 1 (2000); Multi-family building permits issued: 0 (2001) / 0 (2000); Employment by occupation: 2.2% management, 12.0% professional, 46.7% services, 17.4% sales, 1.1% farming, 0.0% construction, 20.7% production (2000).
Income: Per capita income: $6,588 (2000); Median household income: $9,671 (2000); Poverty rate: 58.5% (2000).
Taxes: Total city taxes per capita: $29 (1997); City property taxes per capita: $15 (1997).
Education: High school graduation rate: 45.7% (2000); College graduation rate: 1.7% (2000).
Housing: Homeownership rate: 45.9% (2000); Median home value: $30,600 (2000); Median rent: $125 per month (2000); Median age of housing: 27 years (2000).
Transportation: Commute to work: 87.6% car, 0.0% public transportation, 10.1% walk, 0.0% work from home (2000); Travel time to work: 53.9% less than 15 minutes, 15.7% 15 to 30 minutes, 25.8% 30 to 45 minutes, 2.2% 45 to 60 minutes, 2.2% 60 minutes or more (2000)

LILBOURN (city). Covers a land area of 0.879 square miles and a water area of 0 square miles. Located at 36.59° N. Lat.; 89.61° W. Long. Elevation is 287 feet.
History: Incorporated as city 1910.
Population: 1,303 (2000); Race: 62.7% White, 35.7% Black, 0.0% Asian, 0.0% American Indian and Alaska Native, 1.0% Hispanic of any race, 1.6% two or more races (2000); Density: 1,482.6 persons per square mile (2000); Age: 33.7% under 18, 12.5% over 64 (2000); Marriage status: 26.4% never married, 52.5% now married, 8.4% widowed, 12.7% divorced (2000); Foreign born: 0.0% (2000); Ancestry (includes multiple ancestries): 34.3% Other groups, 15.8% United States or American, 6.0% German, 5.9% Irish, 5.6% English (2000).
Economy: Cotton, rice, wheat, soybeans; lumber mills. Employment by occupation: 10.5% management, 12.7% professional, 22.9% services, 17.9% sales, 2.6% farming, 6.0% construction, 27.4% production (2000).
Income: Per capita income: $13,460 (2000); Median household income: $23,512 (2000); Poverty rate: 25.0% (2000).
Taxes: Total city taxes per capita: $266 (1997); City property taxes per capita: $69 (1997).
Education: High school graduation rate: 57.3% (2000); College graduation rate: 6.8% (2000).
Housing: Homeownership rate: 71.2% (2000); Median home value: $39,900 (2000); Median rent: $172 per month (2000); Median age of housing: 29 years (2000).
Transportation: Commute to work: 90.5% car, 0.0% public transportation, 3.6% walk, 2.0% work from home (2000); Travel time to work: 44.7% less than 15 minutes, 29.0% 15 to 30 minutes, 19.8% 30 to 45 minutes, 2.7% 45 to 60 minutes, 3.9% 60 minutes or more (2000)

MARSTON (city). Covers a land area of 1.102 square miles and a water area of 0 square miles. Located at 36.51° N. Lat.; 89.61° W. Long. Elevation is 289 feet.
Population: 610 (2000); Race: 74.6% White, 24.4% Black, 0.0% Asian, 0.2% American Indian and Alaska Native, 0.9% Hispanic of any race, 0.3% two or more races (2000); Density: 553.7 persons per square mile (2000); Age: 27.6% under 18, 16.2% over 64 (2000); Marriage status: 21.2% never married, 47.0% now married, 13.5% widowed, 18.3% divorced (2000); Foreign born: 1.1% (2000); Ancestry (includes multiple ancestries): 23.9% Other groups, 14.3% United States or American, 9.9% Irish, 3.8% French (except Basque), 3.8% Hungarian (2000).
Economy: Soybeans, rice, cotton; rice milling. Single-family building permits issued: 2 (2001) / 0 (2000); Multi-family building permits issued: 0 (2001) / 0 (2000); Employment by occupation: 2.0% management, 11.8% professional, 18.7% services, 17.7% sales, 2.5% farming, 10.8% construction, 36.5% production (2000).
Income: Per capita income: $13,820 (2000); Median household income: $20,375 (2000); Poverty rate: 31.0% (2000).
Taxes: Total city taxes per capita: $157 (1997); City property taxes per capita: $22 (1997).
Education: High school graduation rate: 59.2% (2000); College graduation rate: 5.9% (2000).
Housing: Homeownership rate: 59.8% (2000); Median home value: $28,700 (2000); Median rent: $248 per month (2000); Median age of housing: 27 years (2000).
Transportation: Commute to work: 96.0% car, 0.0% public transportation, 1.5% walk, 1.5% work from home (2000); Travel time to work: 58.7% less than 15 minutes, 26.5% 15 to 30 minutes, 12.2% 30 to 45 minutes, 0.0% 45 to 60 minutes, 2.6% 60 minutes or more (2000)

MATTHEWS (city). Covers a land area of 1.103 square miles and a water area of 0 square miles. Located at 36.75° N. Lat.; 89.58° W. Long. Elevation is 310 feet.
Population: 605 (2000); Race: 98.1% White, 0.3% Black, 0.0% Asian, 0.0% American Indian and Alaska Native, 2.0% Hispanic of any race, 0.0% two or more races (2000); Density: 548.6 persons per square mile (2000); Age: 26.0% under 18, 16.4% over 64 (2000); Marriage status: 14.2% never married, 65.8% now married, 10.8% widowed, 9.1% divorced (2000); Foreign born: 1.2% (2000); Ancestry (includes multiple ancestries): 22.8% United States or American, 15.3% Irish, 13.5% Other groups, 12.1% German, 8.4% English (2000).
Economy: Soybeans, cotton, corn. Single-family building permits issued: 0 (2001) / 0 (2000); Multi-family building permits issued: 0 (2001) / 0 (2000); Employment by occupation: 8.3% management, 9.8% professional, 17.7% services, 18.5% sales, 2.0% farming, 22.4% construction, 21.3% production (2000).
Income: Per capita income: $13,426 (2000); Median household income: $28,083 (2000); Poverty rate: 9.1% (2000).
Taxes: Total city taxes per capita: $127 (1997); City property taxes per capita: $56 (1997).
Education: High school graduation rate: 69.4% (2000); College graduation rate: 6.6% (2000).
Housing: Homeownership rate: 70.8% (2000); Median home value: $52,500 (2000); Median rent: $218 per month (2000); Median age of housing: 30 years (2000).
Transportation: Commute to work: 97.5% car, 0.0% public transportation, 0.8% walk, 0.8% work from home (2000); Travel time to work: 40.6% less than 15 minutes, 40.2% 15 to 30 minutes, 13.0% 30 to 45 minutes, 1.7% 45 to 60 minutes, 4.6% 60 minutes or more (2000)

MOREHOUSE (city). Covers a land area of 0.818 square miles and a water area of 0 square miles. Located at 36.84° N. Lat.; 89.69° W. Long. Elevation is 302 feet.
History: Morehouse was established as a shipping point for lumber on the Cairo branch of the Iron Mountain Railway.
Population: 1,015 (2000); Race: 96.9% White, 1.0% Black, 0.0% Asian, 0.0% American Indian and Alaska Native, 1.4% Hispanic of any race, 1.6% two or more races (2000); Density: 1,240.9 persons per square mile (2000); Age: 23.5% under 18, 17.0% over 64 (2000); Marriage status: 16.0% never married, 63.9% now married, 10.8% widowed, 9.3% divorced (2000); Foreign born: 0.7% (2000); Ancestry (includes multiple ancestries): 25.8% United States or American, 18.1% Other groups, 10.5% Irish, 5.8% English, 3.9% German (2000).
Economy: Employment by occupation: 6.2% management, 11.1% professional, 22.2% services, 15.7% sales, 2.7% farming, 9.5% construction, 32.6% production (2000).
Income: Per capita income: $12,691 (2000); Median household income: $24,931 (2000); Poverty rate: 13.2% (2000).
Taxes: Total city taxes per capita: $152 (1997); City property taxes per capita: $37 (1997).
Education: High school graduation rate: 53.8% (2000); College graduation rate: 2.4% (2000).

Housing: Homeownership rate: 78.4% (2000); Median home value: $23,700 (2000); Median rent: $242 per month (2000); Median age of housing: 40 years (2000).
Transportation: Commute to work: 92.5% car, 0.0% public transportation, 2.3% walk, 1.8% work from home (2000); Travel time to work: 40.7% less than 15 minutes, 46.7% 15 to 30 minutes, 6.3% 30 to 45 minutes, 3.5% 45 to 60 minutes, 2.8% 60 minutes or more (2000)

NEW MADRID (city). Covers a land area of 4.516 square miles and a water area of 0 square miles. Located at 36.58° N. Lat.; 89.53° W. Long. Elevation is 305 feet.
History: New Madrid had its beginnings in a fur-trading post founded about 1783 by Francois and Joseph Le Sieur, Canadian trappers and traders. In 1789 the site of New Madrid was chosen by Colonel George Morgan for a town to be built with the approval of the Spanish authorities. A series of earthquakes and the shifting course and flooding of the Mississippi River caused the town to be relocated several times.
Population: 3,334 (2000); Race: 72.8% White, 25.8% Black, 0.4% Asian, 0.4% American Indian and Alaska Native, 0.2% Hispanic of any race, 0.6% two or more races (2000); Density: 738.3 persons per square mile (2000); Age: 28.2% under 18, 14.6% over 64 (2000); Marriage status: 25.4% never married, 55.1% now married, 8.7% widowed, 10.7% divorced (2000); Foreign born: 0.8% (2000); Ancestry (includes multiple ancestries): 25.0% United States or American, 20.9% Other groups, 10.0% English, 7.4% Irish, 7.3% German (2000).
Economy: Single-family building permits issued: 9 (2001) / 6 (2000); Multi-family building permits issued: 0 (2001) / 0 (2000); Employment by occupation: 12.1% management, 17.2% professional, 17.2% services, 20.7% sales, 0.7% farming, 9.8% construction, 22.4% production (2000).
Income: Per capita income: $14,639 (2000); Median household income: $27,422 (2000); Poverty rate: 25.0% (2000).
Taxes: Total city taxes per capita: $127 (1997); City property taxes per capita: $38 (1997).
Education: High school graduation rate: 70.5% (2000); College graduation rate: 15.3% (2000).

School District(s)

New Madrid Co. R-I (PK-12)
2000 Enrollment: 2,030 573-688-2161
Housing: Homeownership rate: 62.3% (2000); Median home value: $57,400 (2000); Median rent: $223 per month (2000); Median age of housing: 28 years (2000).
Newspapers: The Weekly Record (1 x week)
Transportation: Commute to work: 95.1% car, 0.4% public transportation, 0.6% walk, 2.4% work from home (2000); Travel time to work: 61.5% less than 15 minutes, 22.1% 15 to 30 minutes, 9.0% 30 to 45 minutes, 2.0% 45 to 60 minutes, 5.5% 60 minutes or more (2000)
Additional Information Contacts
New Madrid Chamber of Commerce 573-748-5300

NORTH LILBOURN (village). Covers a land area of 0.173 square miles and a water area of 0 square miles. Located at 36.60° N. Lat.; 89.62° W. Long. Elevation is 283 feet.
Population: 95 (2000); Race: 2.0% White, 98.0% Black, 0.0% Asian, 0.0% American Indian and Alaska Native, 0.0% Hispanic of any race, 0.0% two or more races (2000); Density: 550.3 persons per square mile (2000); Age: 24.5% under 18, 20.6% over 64 (2000); Marriage status: 51.1% never married, 24.5% now married, 14.9% widowed, 9.6% divorced (2000); Foreign born: 0.0% (2000); Ancestry (includes multiple ancestries): 82.4% Other groups, 2.0% German, 2.0% Dutch (2000).
Economy: Employment by occupation: 0.0% management, 0.0% professional, 5.6% services, 0.0% sales, 0.0% farming, 11.1% construction, 83.3% production (2000).
Income: Per capita income: $7,654 (2000); Median household income: $11,563 (2000); Poverty rate: 38.2% (2000).
Education: High school graduation rate: 37.8% (2000); College graduation rate: 4.1% (2000).
Housing: Homeownership rate: 43.5% (2000); Median home value: $12,500 (2000); Median rent: $145 per month (2000); Median age of housing: 34 years (2000).
Transportation: Commute to work: 100.0% car, 0.0% public transportation, 0.0% walk, 0.0% work from home (2000); Travel time to work: 11.1% less than 15 minutes, 55.6% 15 to 30 minutes, 22.2% 30 to 45 minutes, 11.1% 45 to 60 minutes, 0.0% 60 minutes or more (2000)

PARMA (city). Covers a land area of 0.643 square miles and a water area of 0 square miles. Located at 36.61° N. Lat.; 89.81° W. Long. Elevation is 281 feet.
History: Incorporated 1906.
Population: 852 (2000); Race: 52.0% White, 46.1% Black, 0.0% Asian, 0.4% American Indian and Alaska Native, 0.0% Hispanic of any race, 1.5% two or more races (2000); Density: 1,325.6 persons per square mile (2000); Age: 29.6% under 18, 18.1% over 64 (2000); Marriage status: 28.2% never married, 54.0% now married, 8.6% widowed, 9.2% divorced (2000); Foreign born: 0.9% (2000); Ancestry (includes multiple ancestries): 40.2% Other groups, 17.4% United States or American, 6.4% Irish, 3.5% German, 3.3% English (2000).
Economy: Cotton, rice, corn, soybeans. Employment by occupation: 9.3% management, 9.3% professional, 20.9% services, 15.5% sales, 2.3% farming, 10.9% construction, 31.8% production (2000).
Income: Per capita income: $11,031 (2000); Median household income: $18,804 (2000); Poverty rate: 34.1% (2000).
Taxes: Total city taxes per capita: $82 (1997); City property taxes per capita: $15 (1997).
Education: High school graduation rate: 52.0% (2000); College graduation rate: 4.3% (2000).
Housing: Homeownership rate: 60.4% (2000); Median home value: $26,200 (2000); Median rent: $176 per month (2000); Median age of housing: 34 years (2000).
Transportation: Commute to work: 89.4% car, 0.8% public transportation, 6.9% walk, 2.9% work from home (2000); Travel time to work: 26.5% less than 15 minutes, 31.5% 15 to 30 minutes, 30.7% 30 to 45 minutes, 5.9% 45 to 60 minutes, 5.5% 60 minutes or more (2000)

PORTAGEVILLE (city). Covers a land area of 2.005 square miles and a water area of 0 square miles. Located at 36.43° N. Lat.; 89.70° W. Long. Elevation is 281 feet.
History: Portageville developed as the center of a cotton-producing area. The Portageville Compress and Warehouse Company plant used hydraulic pressure to compress bales of ginned cotton for shipment.
Population: 3,295 (2000); Race: 81.9% White, 17.2% Black, 0.0% Asian, 0.2% American Indian and Alaska Native, 0.4% Hispanic of any race, 0.7% two or more races (2000); Density: 1,643.5 persons per square mile (2000); Age: 27.8% under 18, 16.3% over 64 (2000); Marriage status: 23.1% never married, 54.5% now married, 12.9% widowed, 9.5% divorced (2000); Foreign born: 0.0% (2000); Ancestry (includes multiple ancestries): 21.5% Other groups, 16.3% United States or American, 9.0% Irish, 7.8% German, 6.1% English (2000).
Economy: Single-family building permits issued: 5 (2001) / 7 (2000); Multi-family building permits issued: 0 (2001) / 0 (2000); Employment by occupation: 6.5% management, 15.6% professional, 16.5% services, 26.0% sales, 1.6% farming, 7.5% construction, 26.3% production (2000).
Income: Per capita income: $15,114 (2000); Median household income: $26,729 (2000); Poverty rate: 27.0% (2000).
Taxes: Total city taxes per capita: $261 (1997); City property taxes per capita: $40 (1997).
Education: High school graduation rate: 64.5% (2000); College graduation rate: 12.2% (2000).

School District(s)

Portageville (PK-12)
2000 Enrollment: 924 573-379-3855
Housing: Homeownership rate: 57.5% (2000); Median home value: $60,200 (2000); Median rent: $212 per month (2000); Median age of housing: 33 years (2000).
Newspapers: Missourian News (1 x week)
Transportation: Commute to work: 95.4% car, 0.0% public transportation, 2.4% walk, 0.9% work from home (2000); Travel time to work: 66.7% less than 15 minutes, 22.4% 15 to 30 minutes, 6.9% 30 to 45 minutes, 2.1% 45 to 60 minutes, 1.9% 60 minutes or more (2000)

RISCO (city). Covers a land area of 0.477 square miles and a water area of 0 square miles. Located at 36.55° N. Lat.; 89.82° W. Long. Elevation is 277 feet.
Population: 392 (2000); Race: 99.5% White, 0.0% Black, 0.0% Asian, 0.0% American Indian and Alaska Native, 0.0% Hispanic of any race, 0.5% two or more races (2000); Density: 821.3 persons per square mile (2000); Age: 23.3% under 18, 13.3% over 64 (2000); Marriage status: 23.2% never married, 57.3% now married, 10.2% widowed, 9.3% divorced (2000); Foreign born: 0.0% (2000); Ancestry (includes multiple ancestries): 26.0%

United States or American, 12.8% German, 11.5% Other groups, 10.8% Irish, 8.0% English (2000).
Economy: Cotton gin. Single-family building permits issued: 3 (2001) / 0 (2000); Multi-family building permits issued: 0 (2001) / 0 (2000); Employment by occupation: 8.6% management, 12.6% professional, 10.3% services, 22.4% sales, 2.3% farming, 8.6% construction, 35.1% production (2000).
Income: Per capita income: $13,777 (2000); Median household income: $26,827 (2000); Poverty rate: 14.2% (2000).
Taxes: Total city taxes per capita: $205 (1997); City property taxes per capita: $42 (1997).
Education: High school graduation rate: 64.3% (2000); College graduation rate: 8.7% (2000).

School District(s)

Risco R-II (KG-12)
2000 Enrollment: 207 573-396-5568

Housing: Homeownership rate: 75.4% (2000); Median home value: $30,500 (2000); Median rent: $230 per month (2000); Median age of housing: 42 years (2000).
Transportation: Commute to work: 95.3% car, 0.6% public transportation, 1.7% walk, 2.3% work from home (2000); Travel time to work: 23.2% less than 15 minutes, 44.0% 15 to 30 minutes, 17.9% 30 to 45 minutes, 10.7% 45 to 60 minutes, 4.2% 60 minutes or more (2000)

TALLAPOOSA (city). Aka Tallipoosa. Covers a land area of 0.427 square miles and a water area of 0 square miles. Located at 36.50° N. Lat.; 89.81° W. Long. Elevation is 273 feet.
Population: 204 (2000); Race: 96.8% White, 0.0% Black, 0.0% Asian, 0.0% American Indian and Alaska Native, 1.1% Hispanic of any race, 2.1% two or more races (2000); Density: 477.7 persons per square mile (2000); Age: 30.3% under 18, 17.6% over 64 (2000); Marriage status: 29.3% never married, 44.3% now married, 11.4% widowed, 15.0% divorced (2000); Foreign born: 0.0% (2000); Ancestry (includes multiple ancestries): 14.9% Other groups, 11.7% United States or American, 9.6% Irish, 9.0% German, 6.9% English (2000).
Economy: Employment by occupation: 9.5% management, 4.8% professional, 9.5% services, 11.9% sales, 4.8% farming, 14.3% construction, 45.2% production (2000).
Income: Per capita income: $6,377 (2000); Median household income: $14,375 (2000); Poverty rate: 48.4% (2000).
Taxes: Total city taxes per capita: $39 (1997); City property taxes per capita: $11 (1997).
Education: High school graduation rate: 44.1% (2000); College graduation rate: 1.8% (2000).
Housing: Homeownership rate: 59.1% (2000); Median home value: $20,000 (2000); Median rent: $161 per month (2000); Median age of housing: 29 years (2000).
Transportation: Commute to work: 90.5% car, 0.0% public transportation, 9.5% walk, 0.0% work from home (2000); Travel time to work: 14.3% less than 15 minutes, 31.0% 15 to 30 minutes, 35.7% 30 to 45 minutes, 14.3% 45 to 60 minutes, 4.8% 60 minutes or more (2000)

Newton County

Located in southwestern Missouri, in the Ozarks; bounded on the west by Oklahoma and Kansas. Covers a land area of 626.40 square miles, a water area of 0.20 square miles, and is located in the Central Time Zone. The county government was organized in 1838. County seat is Neosho.

Newton County is part of the Joplin, MO MSA. The entire metro area includes: Jasper County; Newton County

Weather Station: Neosho — Elevation: 1,010 feet

	Jan	Feb	Mar	Apr	May	Jun	Jul	Aug	Sep	Oct	Nov	Dec
High	44	51	60	71	78	85	91	90	82	72	58	49
Low	22	27	35	44	54	62	67	64	57	45	35	27
Precip	2.0	2.2	3.9	4.5	5.0	4.9	3.2	3.7	5.2	4.1	4.4	3.0
Snow	4.2	2.6	3.4	tr	0.0	0.0	0.0	0.0	0.0	tr	0.7	1.9

High and Low temperatures in degrees Fahrenheit; Precipitation and Snow in inches

Population: 52,636 (2000); Race: 93.3% White, 0.5% Black, 0.3% Asian, 2.2% American Indian and Alaska Native, 1.9% Hispanic of any race, 2.3% two or more races (2000); Density: 84.0 persons per square mile (2000); Age: 26.2% under 18, 14.1% over 64 (2000).

Religion: Five largest groups: 25.1% Southern Baptist Convention, 3.5% Christian Churches and Churches of Christ, 3.4% Churches of Christ, 2.5% Catholic Church, 2.4% The United Methodist Church (2000).
Economy: Unemployment rate: 6.1% (11/2002); Total civilian labor force: 27,444 (11/2002); Leading industries: 27.6% manufacturing; 24.9% health care and social assistance; 10.6% accommodation & food services (2000); Companies that employ more than 1,000 persons: 2 (2000); Companies that employ more than 100 persons: 19 (2000); Farms: 1,622 totaling 255,605 acres (1997); Minority business ownership rate: 0.0% (1997); Women business ownership rate: 32.9% (1997); Retail sales per capita: $6,016 (1997). Single-family building permits issued: 44 (2001) / 37 (2000); Multi-family building permits issued: 68 (2001) / 0 (2000).
Income: Per capita income: $17,502 (2000); Median household income: $35,041 (2000); Poverty rate: 11.6% (2000); Bankruptcy rate: 4.51% (2001).
Taxes: Total county taxes per capita: $84 (2000); County property taxes per capita: $8 (2000).
Education: High school graduation rate: 79.8% (2000); College graduation rate: 16.1% (2000).
Housing: Homeownership rate: 76.6% (2000); Median home value: $74,200 (2000); Median rent: $320 per month (2000); Median age of housing: 26 years (2000).
Health: Birth rate: 142.1 per 10,000 population (1998); Age adjusted death rate: 101.9 per 10,000 population (1999); Age adjusted cancer mortality rate: 270.6 deaths per 100,000 population (1999). Number of physicians: 4.2 per 10,000 population (1999); Number of hospital beds: 65.5 per 10,000 population (1999).
Elections: 2000 Presidential election results: 30.5% Gore, 67.3% Bush, 1.5% Nader, 0.4% Buchanan
National and State Parks: George Washington Carver National Monument
Additional Information Contacts
Newton County Government Offices 417-451-8220
Granby Economic Development 417-472-7120
Neosho Chamber of Commerce 417-451-1925
Newton Mc Donald Counties Board of Realtors 417-451-5152
Seneca Chamber of Commerce 417-776-2100

Newton County Communities

CLIFF VILLAGE (village). Covers a land area of 0.040 square miles and a water area of 0 square miles. Located at 37.02° N. Lat.; 94.51° W. Long. Elevation is 955 feet.
Population: 33 (2000); Race: 93.6% White, 2.1% Black, 0.0% Asian, 0.0% American Indian and Alaska Native, 0.0% Hispanic of any race, 0.0% two or more races (2000); Density: 824.2 persons per square mile (2000); Age: 21.3% under 18, 6.4% over 64 (2000); Marriage status: 19.0% never married, 57.1% now married, 7.1% widowed, 16.7% divorced (2000); Foreign born: 0.0% (2000); Ancestry (includes multiple ancestries): 25.5% English, 17.0% United States or American, 14.9% German, 10.6% Other groups, 6.4% Scottish (2000).
Economy: Employment by occupation: 8.3% management, 8.3% professional, 29.2% services, 12.5% sales, 0.0% farming, 25.0% construction, 16.7% production (2000).
Income: Per capita income: $19,243 (2000); Median household income: $33,750 (2000); Poverty rate: 0.0% (2000).
Taxes: Total city taxes per capita: $50 (1997); City property taxes per capita: $0 (1997).
Education: High school graduation rate: 60.0% (2000); College graduation rate: 8.6% (2000).
Housing: Homeownership rate: 100.0% (2000); Median home value: $69,000 (2000); Median age of housing: 54 years (2000).
Transportation: Commute to work: 100.0% car, 0.0% public transportation, 0.0% walk, 0.0% work from home (2000); Travel time to work: 87.5% less than 15 minutes, 12.5% 15 to 30 minutes, 0.0% 30 to 45 minutes, 0.0% 45 to 60 minutes, 0.0% 60 minutes or more (2000)

DENNIS ACRES (village). Covers a land area of 0.047 square miles and a water area of 0 square miles. Located at 37.04° N. Lat.; 94.50° W. Long. Elevation is 1,060 feet.
Population: 68 (2000); Race: 61.7% White, 0.0% Black, 0.0% Asian, 0.0% American Indian and Alaska Native, 17.3% Hispanic of any race, 16.0% two or more races (2000); Density: 1,455.7 persons per square mile (2000); Age: 44.4% under 18, 4.9% over 64 (2000); Marriage status: 23.4% never married, 66.0% now married, 6.4% widowed, 4.3% divorced (2000); Foreign born: 13.6% (2000); Ancestry (includes multiple ancestries): 30.9% Irish, 28.4%

Other groups, 27.2% United States or American, 12.3% German, 2.5% Scotch-Irish (2000).
Economy: Surrounded by city of Joplin. Employment by occupation: 0.0% management, 5.7% professional, 22.9% services, 2.9% sales, 11.4% farming, 25.7% construction, 31.4% production (2000).
Income: Per capita income: $8,709 (2000); Median household income: $28,125 (2000); Poverty rate: 17.1% (2000).
Taxes: Total city taxes per capita: $6 (1997); City property taxes per capita: $0 (1997).
Education: High school graduation rate: 61.0% (2000); College graduation rate: 0.0% (2000).
Housing: Homeownership rate: 33.3% (2000); Median home value: $42,500 (2000); Median rent: $305 per month (2000); Median age of housing: 36 years (2000).
Transportation: Commute to work: 81.8% car, 0.0% public transportation, 0.0% walk, 18.2% work from home (2000); Travel time to work: 70.4% less than 15 minutes, 18.5% 15 to 30 minutes, 11.1% 30 to 45 minutes, 0.0% 45 to 60 minutes, 0.0% 60 minutes or more (2000)

DIAMOND (town). Covers a land area of 0.664 square miles and a water area of 0 square miles. Located at 36.99° N. Lat.; 94.31° W. Long. Elevation is 1,180 feet.
History: It was near Diamond that George Washington Carver was born about 1864. Carver became a teacher at Tuskegee Institute, winning fame for his agricultural experiments.
Population: 807 (2000); Race: 95.2% White, 0.0% Black, 1.6% Asian, 1.8% American Indian and Alaska Native, 0.9% Hispanic of any race, 1.1% two or more races (2000); Density: 1,215.2 persons per square mile (2000); Age: 28.8% under 18, 11.4% over 64 (2000); Marriage status: 16.8% never married, 69.0% now married, 6.0% widowed, 8.2% divorced (2000); Foreign born: 1.3% (2000); Ancestry (includes multiple ancestries): 32.0% United States or American, 15.5% Other groups, 14.5% German, 4.9% Irish, 4.9% English (2000).
Economy: Single-family building permits issued: 0 (2001) / 0 (2000); Multi-family building permits issued: 0 (2001) / 0 (2000); Employment by occupation: 6.1% management, 8.6% professional, 16.9% services, 25.8% sales, 0.6% farming, 12.7% construction, 29.4% production (2000).
Income: Per capita income: $13,581 (2000); Median household income: $29,000 (2000); Poverty rate: 11.5% (2000).
Taxes: Total city taxes per capita: $104 (1997); City property taxes per capita: $12 (1997).
Education: High school graduation rate: 80.6% (2000); College graduation rate: 9.4% (2000).

School District(s)

Diamond R-IV (KG-12)
2000 Enrollment: 820 417-325-5186
Housing: Homeownership rate: 65.9% (2000); Median home value: $54,600 (2000); Median rent: $283 per month (2000); Median age of housing: 30 years (2000).
Transportation: Commute to work: 92.3% car, 0.0% public transportation, 2.6% walk, 2.9% work from home (2000); Travel time to work: 17.9% less than 15 minutes, 57.1% 15 to 30 minutes, 17.1% 30 to 45 minutes, 4.4% 45 to 60 minutes, 3.5% 60 minutes or more (2000)

FAIRVIEW (town). Covers a land area of 0.479 square miles and a water area of 0 square miles. Located at 36.81° N. Lat.; 94.08° W. Long. Elevation is 1,305 feet.
Population: 395 (2000); Race: 96.8% White, 0.5% Black, 0.0% Asian, 1.0% American Indian and Alaska Native, 0.0% Hispanic of any race, 1.7% two or more races (2000); Density: 824.5 persons per square mile (2000); Age: 35.4% under 18, 13.7% over 64 (2000); Marriage status: 22.5% never married, 62.8% now married, 6.8% widowed, 7.8% divorced (2000); Foreign born: 0.2% (2000); Ancestry (includes multiple ancestries): 14.0% German, 13.2% English, 12.7% Irish, 11.2% United States or American, 8.7% Other groups (2000).
Economy: Employment by occupation: 4.9% management, 8.6% professional, 17.9% services, 27.8% sales, 1.2% farming, 15.4% construction, 24.1% production (2000).
Income: Per capita income: $12,198 (2000); Median household income: $27,250 (2000); Poverty rate: 20.4% (2000).
Taxes: Total city taxes per capita: $50 (1997); City property taxes per capita: $22 (1997).
Education: High school graduation rate: 65.0% (2000); College graduation rate: 8.0% (2000).
Housing: Homeownership rate: 81.6% (2000); Median home value: $49,800 (2000); Median rent: $188 per month (2000); Median age of housing: 37 years (2000).
Transportation: Commute to work: 92.1% car, 0.0% public transportation, 1.2% walk, 4.2% work from home (2000); Travel time to work: 15.8% less than 15 minutes, 40.5% 15 to 30 minutes, 27.8% 30 to 45 minutes, 12.0% 45 to 60 minutes, 3.8% 60 minutes or more (2000)

GRANBY (city). Covers a land area of 4.436 square miles and a water area of 0 square miles. Located at 36.91° N. Lat.; 94.25° W. Long. Elevation is 1,120 feet.
History: Lead was discovered in Granby in 1853 by William Foster, a Cornish miner. Several thousand prospectors arrived during the next few years, when lead and zinc were produced in great quantities.
Population: 2,121 (2000); Race: 96.0% White, 0.1% Black, 0.3% Asian, 1.8% American Indian and Alaska Native, 0.7% Hispanic of any race, 1.3% two or more races (2000); Density: 478.1 persons per square mile (2000); Age: 25.6% under 18, 15.0% over 64 (2000); Marriage status: 16.6% never married, 55.5% now married, 12.1% widowed, 15.8% divorced (2000); Foreign born: 0.5% (2000); Ancestry (includes multiple ancestries): 25.2% United States or American, 14.7% German, 14.2% Other groups, 12.6% Irish, 6.9% English (2000).
Economy: Employment by occupation: 6.4% management, 9.1% professional, 13.8% services, 19.7% sales, 1.2% farming, 10.5% construction, 39.3% production (2000).
Income: Per capita income: $13,371 (2000); Median household income: $28,625 (2000); Poverty rate: 16.1% (2000).
Taxes: Total city taxes per capita: $225 (1997); City property taxes per capita: $29 (1997).
Education: High school graduation rate: 70.8% (2000); College graduation rate: 5.9% (2000).

School District(s)

East Newton Co. R-VI (KG-12)
2000 Enrollment: 1,513 417-472-6231
Housing: Homeownership rate: 74.9% (2000); Median home value: $41,800 (2000); Median rent: $286 per month (2000); Median age of housing: 35 years (2000).
Newspapers: Newton County News (1 x week)
Transportation: Commute to work: 96.5% car, 0.0% public transportation, 1.4% walk, 2.1% work from home (2000); Travel time to work: 21.2% less than 15 minutes, 44.2% 15 to 30 minutes, 21.8% 30 to 45 minutes, 5.5% 45 to 60 minutes, 7.3% 60 minutes or more (2000)
Additional Information Contacts
Granby Economic Development 417-472-7120

GRAND FALLS PLAZA (town). Covers a land area of 0.094 square miles and a water area of 0 square miles. Located at 37.03° N. Lat.; 94.54° W. Long. Elevation is 892 feet.
Population: 104 (2000); Race: 95.1% White, 0.0% Black, 0.0% Asian, 1.0% American Indian and Alaska Native, 0.0% Hispanic of any race, 3.9% two or more races (2000); Density: 1,105.9 persons per square mile (2000); Age: 34.3% under 18, 9.8% over 64 (2000); Marriage status: 15.8% never married, 72.4% now married, 5.3% widowed, 6.6% divorced (2000); Foreign born: 2.0% (2000); Ancestry (includes multiple ancestries): 26.5% German, 10.8% United States or American, 8.8% Other groups, 4.9% Scottish, 3.9% English (2000).
Economy: Employment by occupation: 13.2% management, 18.9% professional, 9.4% services, 45.3% sales, 0.0% farming, 11.3% construction, 1.9% production (2000).
Income: Per capita income: $15,341 (2000); Median household income: $48,250 (2000); Poverty rate: 8.8% (2000).
Education: High school graduation rate: 81.5% (2000); College graduation rate: 20.0% (2000).
Housing: Homeownership rate: 84.6% (2000); Median home value: $84,700 (2000); Median rent: $675 per month (2000); Median age of housing: 25 years (2000).
Transportation: Commute to work: 100.0% car, 0.0% public transportation, 0.0% walk, 0.0% work from home (2000); Travel time to work: 36.2% less than 15 minutes, 57.4% 15 to 30 minutes, 6.4% 30 to 45 minutes, 0.0% 45 to 60 minutes, 0.0% 60 minutes or more (2000)

LEAWOOD (village). Covers a land area of 1.452 square miles and a water area of 0 square miles. Located at 37.03° N. Lat.; 94.49° W. Long. Elevation is 1,005 feet.
Population: 904 (2000); Race: 93.2% White, 1.0% Black, 1.0% Asian, 0.4% American Indian and Alaska Native, 3.3% Hispanic of any race, 2.3% two or

more races (2000); Density: 622.5 persons per square mile (2000); Age: 27.1% under 18, 8.2% over 64 (2000); Marriage status: 21.2% never married, 69.4% now married, 3.7% widowed, 5.6% divorced (2000); Foreign born: 2.3% (2000); Ancestry (includes multiple ancestries): 20.4% German, 15.9% Irish, 15.7% English, 12.8% Other groups, 10.9% United States or American (2000).
Economy: Employment by occupation: 17.2% management, 27.7% professional, 15.3% services, 27.1% sales, 0.0% farming, 5.8% construction, 6.9% production (2000).
Income: Per capita income: $36,196 (2000); Median household income: $62,250 (2000); Poverty rate: 8.4% (2000).
Taxes: Total city taxes per capita: $24 (1997); City property taxes per capita: $0 (1997).
Education: High school graduation rate: 93.4% (2000); College graduation rate: 42.8% (2000).
Housing: Homeownership rate: 87.4% (2000); Median home value: $143,000 (2000); Median rent: $306 per month (2000); Median age of housing: 21 years (2000).
Transportation: Commute to work: 94.3% car, 0.0% public transportation, 1.1% walk, 3.3% work from home (2000); Travel time to work: 44.9% less than 15 minutes, 43.8% 15 to 30 minutes, 4.5% 30 to 45 minutes, 0.9% 45 to 60 minutes, 5.9% 60 minutes or more (2000)

LOMA LINDA (town). Covers a land area of 3.594 square miles and a water area of 0 square miles. Located at 36.99° N. Lat.; 94.59° W. Long. Elevation is 1,020 feet.
Population: 507 (2000); Race: 94.4% White, 1.7% Black, 0.4% Asian, 2.5% American Indian and Alaska Native, 1.3% Hispanic of any race, 1.0% two or more races (2000); Density: 141.1 persons per square mile (2000); Age: 21.3% under 18, 15.9% over 64 (2000); Marriage status: 14.1% never married, 69.6% now married, 2.3% widowed, 14.1% divorced (2000); Foreign born: 1.0% (2000); Ancestry (includes multiple ancestries): 23.6% German, 13.8% Other groups, 13.0% Irish, 12.8% English, 8.4% United States or American (2000).
Economy: Single-family building permits issued: 0 (2001) / 0 (2000); Multi-family building permits issued: 0 (2001) / 0 (2000); Employment by occupation: 26.8% management, 23.6% professional, 4.7% services, 26.4% sales, 0.7% farming, 8.7% construction, 9.1% production (2000).
Income: Per capita income: $28,583 (2000); Median household income: $53,750 (2000); Poverty rate: 1.4% (2000).
Education: High school graduation rate: 94.6% (2000); College graduation rate: 33.7% (2000).
Housing: Homeownership rate: 87.1% (2000); Median home value: $156,500 (2000); Median rent: $500 per month (2000); Median age of housing: 9 years (2000).
Transportation: Commute to work: 89.7% car, 0.7% public transportation, 0.7% walk, 5.9% work from home (2000); Travel time to work: 16.9% less than 15 minutes, 71.0% 15 to 30 minutes, 5.9% 30 to 45 minutes, 0.0% 45 to 60 minutes, 6.3% 60 minutes or more (2000)

NEOSHO (city). Covers a land area of 14.931 square miles and a water area of 0 square miles. Located at 36.85° N. Lat.; 94.37° W. Long. Elevation is 1,035 feet.
History: Neosho was platted in 1839 by James Wilson. The name is of Osage origin meaning "clear water" for the spring that was near the center of the town. Early development of the town was around the lead mines. Neosho was the home of Colonel Maecenas E. Benton, a Missouri representative in Congress, and of his son, Thomas Hart Benton, painter, and author of "An Artist in America" (1937).
Population: 10,505 (2000); Race: 91.1% White, 1.1% Black, 0.1% Asian, 1.8% American Indian and Alaska Native, 3.8% Hispanic of any race, 1.7% two or more races (2000); Density: 703.6 persons per square mile (2000); Age: 26.4% under 18, 18.1% over 64 (2000); Marriage status: 18.4% never married, 58.6% now married, 9.5% widowed, 13.5% divorced (2000); Foreign born: 2.8% (2000); Ancestry (includes multiple ancestries): 18.0% Other groups, 15.5% German, 15.2% United States or American, 11.1% Irish, 9.7% English (2000).
Economy: Single-family building permits issued: 28 (2001) / 29 (2000); Multi-family building permits issued: 68 (2001) / 0 (2000); Employment by occupation: 9.1% management, 17.7% professional, 12.8% services, 25.7% sales, 0.7% farming, 8.0% construction, 25.9% production (2000).
Income: Per capita income: $15,847 (2000); Median household income: $31,225 (2000); Poverty rate: 12.8% (2000).
Taxes: Total city taxes per capita: $383 (2000); City property taxes per capita: $114 (2000).
Education: High school graduation rate: 78.1% (2000); College graduation rate: 18.0% (2000).

School District(s)

Crowder College (09-12)
2000 Enrollment: n/a 417-451-3584
Neosho R-V (PK-12)
2000 Enrollment: 4,114 417-451-8600
Westview C-6 (KG-08)
2000 Enrollment: 176 417-776-2425

Four-year College(s)

Ozark Bible Institute and College (Private, Not-for-profit, Assemblies of God Church)
2001 Enrollment: n/a 417-451-2057

Two-year College(s)

Crowder College (Public)
2001 Enrollment: 2,012 417-451-3223
2001 Tuition: In-state $1,980; Out-of-state $2,610
Housing: Homeownership rate: 63.7% (2000); Median home value: $64,700 (2000); Median rent: $309 per month (2000); Median age of housing: 36 years (2000).
Safety: Violent crime rate: 39.7 per 10,000 population; Property crime rate: 581.8 per 10,000 population (2001).
Newspapers: Neosho Daily News (6 x week)
Transportation: Commute to work: 94.2% car, 0.6% public transportation, 1.5% walk, 2.3% work from home (2000); Travel time to work: 57.7% less than 15 minutes, 23.6% 15 to 30 minutes, 12.2% 30 to 45 minutes, 2.9% 45 to 60 minutes, 3.6% 60 minutes or more (2000)
Additional Information Contacts
Neosho Chamber of Commerce 417-451-1925
Newton Mc Donald Counties Board of Realtors 417-451-5152

NEWTONIA (town). Covers a land area of 0.329 square miles and a water area of 0 square miles. Located at 36.87° N. Lat.; 94.18° W. Long. Elevation is 1,203 feet.
History: Civil War battle, Sept. 30, 1862.
Population: 231 (2000); Race: 92.8% White, 0.0% Black, 0.0% Asian, 3.6% American Indian and Alaska Native, 2.4% Hispanic of any race, 0.4% two or more races (2000); Density: 702.0 persons per square mile (2000); Age: 34.4% under 18, 12.4% over 64 (2000); Marriage status: 17.8% never married, 61.7% now married, 11.1% widowed, 9.4% divorced (2000); Foreign born: 2.4% (2000); Ancestry (includes multiple ancestries): 24.0% United States or American, 23.2% Other groups, 17.2% German, 9.2% Irish, 7.2% English (2000).
Economy: Employment by occupation: 6.3% management, 8.3% professional, 7.3% services, 18.8% sales, 8.3% farming, 12.5% construction, 38.5% production (2000).
Income: Per capita income: $13,088 (2000); Median household income: $34,375 (2000); Poverty rate: 15.3% (2000).
Taxes: Total city taxes per capita: $37 (1997); City property taxes per capita: $9 (1997).
Education: High school graduation rate: 67.1% (2000); College graduation rate: 9.8% (2000).
Housing: Homeownership rate: 84.1% (2000); Median home value: $37,900 (2000); Median rent: $275 per month (2000); Median age of housing: 48 years (2000).
Transportation: Commute to work: 96.9% car, 0.0% public transportation, 0.0% walk, 0.0% work from home (2000); Travel time to work: 10.4% less than 15 minutes, 47.9% 15 to 30 minutes, 26.0% 30 to 45 minutes, 9.4% 45 to 60 minutes, 6.3% 60 minutes or more (2000)

REDINGS MILL (village). Covers a land area of 0.206 square miles and a water area of 0 square miles. Located at 37.01° N. Lat.; 94.51° W. Long. Elevation is 1,050 feet.
Population: 159 (2000); Race: 90.9% White, 0.0% Black, 0.0% Asian, 4.6% American Indian and Alaska Native, 0.0% Hispanic of any race, 4.6% two or more races (2000); Density: 773.1 persons per square mile (2000); Age: 18.9% under 18, 10.3% over 64 (2000); Marriage status: 14.3% never married, 66.2% now married, 8.4% widowed, 11.0% divorced (2000); Foreign born: 1.1% (2000); Ancestry (includes multiple ancestries): 37.1% German, 31.4% Irish, 28.0% English, 9.7% Other groups, 5.7% Scottish (2000).
Economy: Employment by occupation: 9.5% management, 29.8% professional, 17.9% services, 28.6% sales, 0.0% farming, 7.1% construction, 7.1% production (2000).
Income: Per capita income: $18,629 (2000); Median household income: $35,938 (2000); Poverty rate: 4.6% (2000).

Taxes: Total city taxes per capita: $142 (1997); City property taxes per capita: $0 (1997).
Education: High school graduation rate: 88.1% (2000); College graduation rate: 25.4% (2000).
Housing: Homeownership rate: 87.7% (2000); Median home value: $80,000 (2000); Median rent: $525 per month (2000); Median age of housing: 40 years (2000).
Transportation: Commute to work: 93.8% car, 0.0% public transportation, 0.0% walk, 6.2% work from home (2000); Travel time to work: 26.3% less than 15 minutes, 61.8% 15 to 30 minutes, 7.9% 30 to 45 minutes, 0.0% 45 to 60 minutes, 3.9% 60 minutes or more (2000)

RITCHEY (town). Covers a land area of 0.051 square miles and a water area of 0 square miles. Located at 36.94° N. Lat.; 94.18° W. Long. Elevation is 1,086 feet.
Population: 76 (2000); Race: 84.1% White, 0.0% Black, 2.9% Asian, 5.8% American Indian and Alaska Native, 7.2% Hispanic of any race, 7.2% two or more races (2000); Density: 1,487.7 persons per square mile (2000); Age: 17.4% under 18, 5.8% over 64 (2000); Marriage status: 11.9% never married, 55.9% now married, 10.2% widowed, 22.0% divorced (2000); Foreign born: 2.9% (2000); Ancestry (includes multiple ancestries): 29.0% Other groups, 24.6% United States or American, 7.2% German, 4.3% Irish, 2.9% Dutch (2000).
Economy: Employment by occupation: 0.0% management, 15.6% professional, 9.4% services, 18.8% sales, 6.3% farming, 18.8% construction, 31.3% production (2000).
Income: Per capita income: $13,048 (2000); Median household income: $17,500 (2000); Poverty rate: 10.1% (2000).
Taxes: Total city taxes per capita: $16 (1997); City property taxes per capita: $16 (1997).
Education: High school graduation rate: 69.2% (2000); College graduation rate: 11.5% (2000).
Housing: Homeownership rate: 86.1% (2000); Median home value: $17,500 (2000); Median rent: $338 per month (2000); Median age of housing: 60+ years (2000).
Transportation: Commute to work: 95.8% car, 0.0% public transportation, 0.0% walk, 4.2% work from home (2000); Travel time to work: 0.0% less than 15 minutes, 56.5% 15 to 30 minutes, 30.4% 30 to 45 minutes, 0.0% 45 to 60 minutes, 13.0% 60 minutes or more (2000)

SAGINAW (village). Covers a land area of 0.819 square miles and a water area of 0 square miles. Located at 37.02° N. Lat.; 94.47° W. Long. Elevation is 938 feet.
Population: 276 (2000); Race: 94.3% White, 0.0% Black, 0.8% Asian, 0.0% American Indian and Alaska Native, 2.3% Hispanic of any race, 4.9% two or more races (2000); Density: 337.2 persons per square mile (2000); Age: 26.6% under 18, 11.8% over 64 (2000); Marriage status: 18.4% never married, 57.5% now married, 9.0% widowed, 15.1% divorced (2000); Foreign born: 0.8% (2000); Ancestry (includes multiple ancestries): 22.1% German, 19.0% Irish, 18.3% Other groups, 12.2% English, 11.0% United States or American (2000).
Economy: Single-family building permits issued: 2 (2001) / 1 (2000); Multi-family building permits issued: 0 (2001) / 0 (2000); Employment by occupation: 8.1% management, 23.0% professional, 9.6% services, 23.0% sales, 0.0% farming, 15.6% construction, 20.7% production (2000).
Income: Per capita income: $22,639 (2000); Median household income: $42,083 (2000); Poverty rate: 9.1% (2000).
Taxes: Total city taxes per capita: $99 (1997); City property taxes per capita: $43 (1997).
Education: High school graduation rate: 93.0% (2000); College graduation rate: 19.9% (2000).
Housing: Homeownership rate: 77.6% (2000); Median home value: $77,600 (2000); Median rent: $288 per month (2000); Median age of housing: 23 years (2000).
Transportation: Commute to work: 92.6% car, 0.0% public transportation, 1.5% walk, 3.0% work from home (2000); Travel time to work: 40.5% less than 15 minutes, 42.7% 15 to 30 minutes, 6.1% 30 to 45 minutes, 3.1% 45 to 60 minutes, 7.6% 60 minutes or more (2000)

SENECA (city). Covers a land area of 1.734 square miles and a water area of 0 square miles. Located at 36.84° N. Lat.; 94.61° W. Long. Elevation is 853 feet.
History: Seneca was platted in 1868, and developed as the center of tripoli deposits, used for scouring and polishing and as filter stone for water systems. In the 1920's the Barnsdall Tripoli Company began using tripoli as part of a concrete mixture.
Population: 2,135 (2000); Race: 89.2% White, 0.0% Black, 0.7% Asian, 5.2% American Indian and Alaska Native, 1.4% Hispanic of any race, 4.1% two or more races (2000); Density: 1,231.2 persons per square mile (2000); Age: 27.3% under 18, 20.1% over 64 (2000); Marriage status: 18.6% never married, 58.9% now married, 12.2% widowed, 10.3% divorced (2000); Foreign born: 0.9% (2000); Ancestry (includes multiple ancestries): 14.0% Other groups, 13.4% United States or American, 11.8% German, 10.2% Irish, 7.6% English (2000).
Economy: Single-family building permits issued: 10 (2001) / 5 (2000); Multi-family building permits issued: 0 (2001) / 0 (2000); Employment by occupation: 8.3% management, 12.3% professional, 21.6% services, 23.9% sales, 0.0% farming, 10.4% construction, 23.4% production (2000).
Income: Per capita income: $14,525 (2000); Median household income: $29,441 (2000); Poverty rate: 14.1% (2000).
Taxes: Total city taxes per capita: $201 (1997); City property taxes per capita: $32 (1997).
Education: High school graduation rate: 78.6% (2000); College graduation rate: 12.3% (2000).

School District(s)

Seneca R-VII (PK-12)
2000 Enrollment: 1,729 417-776-3426

Housing: Homeownership rate: 69.2% (2000); Median home value: $60,000 (2000); Median rent: $284 per month (2000); Median age of housing: 37 years (2000).
Newspapers: News-Dispatch (1 x week)
Transportation: Commute to work: 93.0% car, 0.0% public transportation, 4.0% walk, 2.3% work from home (2000); Travel time to work: 35.9% less than 15 minutes, 29.5% 15 to 30 minutes, 28.9% 30 to 45 minutes, 2.2% 45 to 60 minutes, 3.6% 60 minutes or more (2000)
Additional Information Contacts
Seneca Chamber of Commerce 417-776-2100

SHOAL CREEK DRIVE (village). Covers a land area of 0.470 square miles and a water area of 0 square miles. Located at 37.03° N. Lat.; 94.52° W. Long. Elevation is 1,032 feet.
History: Incorporated 1958.
Population: 346 (2000); Race: 93.9% White, 1.5% Black, 0.6% Asian, 2.1% American Indian and Alaska Native, 0.0% Hispanic of any race, 1.8% two or more races (2000); Density: 735.6 persons per square mile (2000); Age: 31.8% under 18, 15.3% over 64 (2000); Marriage status: 21.4% never married, 60.3% now married, 5.6% widowed, 12.7% divorced (2000); Foreign born: 0.6% (2000); Ancestry (includes multiple ancestries): 21.7% German, 18.3% Irish, 17.4% United States or American, 12.8% Other groups, 7.3% English (2000).
Economy: Single-family building permits issued: 2 (2001) / 0 (2000); Multi-family building permits issued: 0 (2001) / 0 (2000); Employment by occupation: 9.2% management, 20.2% professional, 16.6% services, 31.3% sales, 0.0% farming, 7.4% construction, 15.3% production (2000).
Income: Per capita income: $21,253 (2000); Median household income: $39,167 (2000); Poverty rate: 7.5% (2000).
Taxes: Total city taxes per capita: $20 (1997); City property taxes per capita: $10 (1997).
Education: High school graduation rate: 87.1% (2000); College graduation rate: 18.6% (2000).
Housing: Homeownership rate: 91.3% (2000); Median home value: $70,400 (2000); Median rent: $350 per month (2000); Median age of housing: 41 years (2000).
Transportation: Commute to work: 96.2% car, 0.0% public transportation, 1.3% walk, 2.5% work from home (2000); Travel time to work: 42.2% less than 15 minutes, 47.4% 15 to 30 minutes, 5.8% 30 to 45 minutes, 1.3% 45 to 60 minutes, 3.2% 60 minutes or more (2000)

SHOAL CREEK ESTATES (town). Covers a land area of 0.104 square miles and a water area of 0 square miles. Located at 37.01° N. Lat.; 94.49° W. Long. Elevation is 1,035 feet.
Population: 51 (2000); Race: 97.7% White, 0.0% Black, 0.0% Asian, 2.3% American Indian and Alaska Native, 0.0% Hispanic of any race, 0.0% two or more races (2000); Density: 489.1 persons per square mile (2000); Age: 15.9% under 18, 25.0% over 64 (2000); Marriage status: 7.5% never married, 85.0% now married, 0.0% widowed, 7.5% divorced (2000); Foreign born: 20.5% (2000); Ancestry (includes multiple ancestries): 29.5% United States or American, 15.9% Canadian, 11.4% Lithuanian, 9.1% German, 6.8% Irish (2000).
Economy: Employment by occupation: 50.0% management, 26.9% professional, 0.0% services, 23.1% sales, 0.0% farming, 0.0% construction, 0.0% production (2000).

Income: Per capita income: $41,970 (2000); Median household income: $77,394 (2000); Poverty rate: 0.0% (2000).
Taxes: Total city taxes per capita: $261 (1997); City property taxes per capita: $261 (1997).
Education: High school graduation rate: 97.3% (2000); College graduation rate: 24.3% (2000).
Housing: Homeownership rate: 100.0% (2000); Median home value: $200,000 (2000); Median age of housing: 22 years (2000).
Transportation: Commute to work: 88.5% car, 0.0% public transportation, 0.0% walk, 11.5% work from home (2000); Travel time to work: 60.9% less than 15 minutes, 30.4% 15 to 30 minutes, 8.7% 30 to 45 minutes, 0.0% 45 to 60 minutes, 0.0% 60 minutes or more (2000)

SILVER CREEK (village). Covers a land area of 0.783 square miles and a water area of 0 square miles. Located at 37.03° N. Lat.; 94.47° W. Long. Elevation is 1,035 feet.
Population: 608 (2000); Race: 97.5% White, 0.0% Black, 0.0% Asian, 0.3% American Indian and Alaska Native, 0.3% Hispanic of any race, 2.2% two or more races (2000); Density: 776.2 persons per square mile (2000); Age: 19.3% under 18, 20.3% over 64 (2000); Marriage status: 14.7% never married, 65.8% now married, 9.1% widowed, 10.3% divorced (2000); Foreign born: 0.5% (2000); Ancestry (includes multiple ancestries): 28.4% German, 19.2% Irish, 13.1% English, 9.9% United States or American, 9.1% Other groups (2000).
Economy: Single-family building permits issued: 2 (2001) / 2 (2000); Multi-family building permits issued: 0 (2001) / 0 (2000); Employment by occupation: 16.2% management, 24.3% professional, 10.9% services, 36.3% sales, 0.4% farming, 5.6% construction, 6.3% production (2000).
Income: Per capita income: $24,677 (2000); Median household income: $45,781 (2000); Poverty rate: 3.2% (2000).
Taxes: Total city taxes per capita: $26 (1997); City property taxes per capita: $14 (1997).
Education: High school graduation rate: 89.9% (2000); College graduation rate: 29.7% (2000).
Housing: Homeownership rate: 94.5% (2000); Median home value: $115,800 (2000); Median rent: $542 per month (2000); Median age of housing: 25 years (2000).
Transportation: Commute to work: 93.7% car, 1.5% public transportation, 0.7% walk, 4.1% work from home (2000); Travel time to work: 29.2% less than 15 minutes, 54.6% 15 to 30 minutes, 13.1% 30 to 45 minutes, 1.5% 45 to 60 minutes, 1.5% 60 minutes or more (2000)

STARK CITY (town). Covers a land area of 0.122 square miles and a water area of 0 square miles. Located at 36.86° N. Lat.; 94.18° W. Long. Elevation is 1,224 feet.
Population: 156 (2000); Race: 86.5% White, 0.0% Black, 0.0% Asian, 7.1% American Indian and Alaska Native, 0.0% Hispanic of any race, 6.4% two or more races (2000); Density: 1,278.5 persons per square mile (2000); Age: 20.6% under 18, 17.7% over 64 (2000); Marriage status: 15.3% never married, 57.6% now married, 10.2% widowed, 16.9% divorced (2000); Foreign born: 0.0% (2000); Ancestry (includes multiple ancestries): 27.0% Other groups, 14.2% German, 12.8% United States or American, 8.5% English, 4.3% Irish (2000).
Economy: Employment by occupation: 4.8% management, 12.7% professional, 12.7% services, 6.3% sales, 4.8% farming, 25.4% construction, 33.3% production (2000).
Income: Per capita income: $13,311 (2000); Median household income: $25,000 (2000); Poverty rate: 15.9% (2000).
Taxes: Total city taxes per capita: $15 (1997); City property taxes per capita: $0 (1997).
Education: High school graduation rate: 67.6% (2000); College graduation rate: 1.9% (2000).
Housing: Homeownership rate: 82.3% (2000); Median home value: $34,500 (2000); Median rent: $258 per month (2000); Median age of housing: 46 years (2000).
Transportation: Commute to work: 96.8% car, 0.0% public transportation, 0.0% walk, 3.2% work from home (2000); Travel time to work: 18.3% less than 15 minutes, 43.3% 15 to 30 minutes, 30.0% 30 to 45 minutes, 8.3% 45 to 60 minutes, 0.0% 60 minutes or more (2000)

STELLA (town). Covers a land area of 0.154 square miles and a water area of 0 square miles. Located at 36.76° N. Lat.; 94.19° W. Long. Elevation is 1,147 feet.
Population: 178 (2000); Race: 94.1% White, 0.0% Black, 0.0% Asian, 0.0% American Indian and Alaska Native, 7.1% Hispanic of any race, 2.4% two or more races (2000); Density: 1,152.7 persons per square mile (2000); Age: 34.3% under 18, 16.0% over 64 (2000); Marriage status: 12.8% never married, 56.4% now married, 7.7% widowed, 23.1% divorced (2000); Foreign born: 0.0% (2000); Ancestry (includes multiple ancestries): 19.5% Other groups, 16.0% German, 8.3% United States or American, 5.3% English, 3.6% Irish (2000).
Economy: Employment by occupation: 8.4% management, 12.0% professional, 12.0% services, 19.3% sales, 0.0% farming, 8.4% construction, 39.8% production (2000).
Income: Per capita income: $11,799 (2000); Median household income: $25,781 (2000); Poverty rate: 12.4% (2000).
Taxes: Total city taxes per capita: $43 (1997); City property taxes per capita: $14 (1997).
Education: High school graduation rate: 75.5% (2000); College graduation rate: 1.0% (2000).
Housing: Homeownership rate: 86.1% (2000); Median home value: $31,300 (2000); Median rent: $233 per month (2000); Median age of housing: 55 years (2000).
Transportation: Commute to work: 92.8% car, 0.0% public transportation, 0.0% walk, 2.4% work from home (2000); Travel time to work: 8.6% less than 15 minutes, 25.9% 15 to 30 minutes, 30.9% 30 to 45 minutes, 12.3% 45 to 60 minutes, 22.2% 60 minutes or more (2000)

WENTWORTH (village). Covers a land area of 0.196 square miles and a water area of 0 square miles. Located at 36.99° N. Lat.; 94.07° W. Long. Elevation is 1,222 feet.
Population: 141 (2000); Race: 98.5% White, 0.0% Black, 0.0% Asian, 0.0% American Indian and Alaska Native, 0.0% Hispanic of any race, 0.0% two or more races (2000); Density: 718.5 persons per square mile (2000); Age: 23.9% under 18, 20.1% over 64 (2000); Marriage status: 20.4% never married, 62.0% now married, 4.6% widowed, 13.0% divorced (2000); Foreign born: 0.0% (2000); Ancestry (includes multiple ancestries): 19.4% Irish, 17.2% German, 10.4% Other groups, 9.0% English, 8.2% Polish (2000).
Economy: Employment by occupation: 3.4% management, 16.9% professional, 22.0% services, 15.3% sales, 0.0% farming, 13.6% construction, 28.8% production (2000).
Income: Per capita income: $12,051 (2000); Median household income: $19,063 (2000); Poverty rate: 32.8% (2000).
Taxes: Total city taxes per capita: $34 (1997); City property taxes per capita: $14 (1997).
Education: High school graduation rate: 78.7% (2000); College graduation rate: 11.2% (2000).
Housing: Homeownership rate: 85.0% (2000); Median home value: $35,000 (2000); Median rent: $250 per month (2000); Median age of housing: 57 years (2000).
Transportation: Commute to work: 92.9% car, 0.0% public transportation, 0.0% walk, 3.6% work from home (2000); Travel time to work: 14.8% less than 15 minutes, 50.0% 15 to 30 minutes, 24.1% 30 to 45 minutes, 7.4% 45 to 60 minutes, 3.7% 60 minutes or more (2000)

Nodaway County

Located in northwestern Missouri; bounded on the north by Iowa; drained by the Nodaway, Little Platte, and One Hundred and Two Rivers. Covers a land area of 876.60 square miles, a water area of 1.10 square miles, and is located in the Central Time Zone. The county government was organized in 1845. County seat is Maryville.

Weather Station: Conception — Elevation: 1,105 feet

	Jan	Feb	Mar	Apr	May	Jun	Jul	Aug	Sep	Oct	Nov	Dec
High	32	38	50	63	73	83	88	86	78	66	49	37
Low	13	19	29	41	52	61	65	63	54	42	30	19
Precip	0.8	1.1	2.6	3.4	4.9	4.1	4.9	4.2	4.5	2.8	2.4	1.3
Snow	6.2	5.3	3.9	1.2	0.0	0.0	0.0	0.0	0.0	tr	1.4	3.9

High and Low temperatures in degrees Fahrenheit; Precipitation and Snow in inches

Weather Station: Maryville 2 E — Elevation: 984 feet

	Jan	Feb	Mar	Apr	May	Jun	Jul	Aug	Sep	Oct	Nov	Dec
High	32	39	50	63	73	83	88	85	78	66	50	37
Low	12	17	27	38	50	59	64	61	52	40	28	17
Precip	0.9	0.9	2.3	3.2	4.7	4.1	5.1	3.9	4.2	3.0	2.3	1.3
Snow	4.8	3.4	2.5	0.9	0.0	0.0	0.0	0.0	0.0	tr	0.8	3.6

High and Low temperatures in degrees Fahrenheit; Precipitation and Snow in inches

Population: 21,912 (2000); Race: 96.8% White, 1.4% Black, 0.9% Asian, 0.2% American Indian and Alaska Native, 0.5% Hispanic of any race, 0.6%

two or more races (2000); Density: 25.0 persons per square mile (2000); Age: 19.3% under 18, 13.8% over 64 (2000).
Religion: Five largest groups: 16.5% Catholic Church, 11.0% The United Methodist Church, 10.1% Southern Baptist Convention, 7.7% Christian Church (Disciples of Christ), 3.3% Christian Churches and Churches of Christ (2000).
Economy: Unemployment rate: 1.5% (11/2002); Total civilian labor force: 13,278 (11/2002); Leading industries: 28.2% manufacturing; 16.9% retail trade; 14.2% health care and social assistance (2000); Companies that employ more than 1,000 persons: 0 (2000); Companies that employ more than 100 persons: 14 (2000); Farms: 1,257 totaling 491,992 acres (1997); Minority business ownership rate: 0.0% (1997); Women business ownership rate: 22.9% (1997); Retail sales per capita: $6,119 (1997). Single-family building permits issued: 20 (2001) / 23 (2000); Multi-family building permits issued: 51 (2001) / 36 (2000).
Income: Per capita income: $15,384 (2000); Median household income: $31,781 (2000); Poverty rate: 16.5% (2000); Bankruptcy rate: 2.22% (2001).
Taxes: Total county taxes per capita: $76 (2000); County property taxes per capita: $4 (2000).
Education: High school graduation rate: 87.1% (2000); College graduation rate: 23.6% (2000).
Housing: Homeownership rate: 63.8% (2000); Median home value: $71,100 (2000); Median rent: $321 per month (2000); Median age of housing: 36 years (2000).
Health: Birth rate: 95.8 per 10,000 population (1998); Age adjusted death rate: 77.9 per 10,000 population (1999); Age adjusted cancer mortality rate: 189.5 deaths per 100,000 population (1999). Number of physicians: 10.5 per 10,000 population (1999); Number of hospital beds: 24.2 per 10,000 population (1999).
Elections: 2000 Presidential election results: 39.3% Gore, 57.0% Bush, 2.4% Nader, 0.7% Buchanan
Additional Information Contacts
Nodaway County Government Offices 660-582-2251
Maryville Chamber of Commerce 816-582-8643
Northwest Missouri Board of Realtors.................. 816-582-8848

Nodaway County Communities

ARKOE (town). Covers a land area of 0.136 square miles and a water area of 0 square miles. Located at 40.25° N. Lat.; 94.82° W. Long. Elevation is 978 feet.
Population: 58 (2000); Race: 100.0% White, 0.0% Black, 0.0% Asian, 0.0% American Indian and Alaska Native, 0.0% Hispanic of any race, 0.0% two or more races (2000); Density: 425.4 persons per square mile (2000); Age: 30.4% under 18, 12.5% over 64 (2000); Marriage status: 20.9% never married, 48.8% now married, 9.3% widowed, 20.9% divorced (2000); Foreign born: 0.0% (2000); Ancestry (includes multiple ancestries): 41.1% United States or American, 23.2% German, 10.7% Irish, 8.9% French (except Basque), 3.6% Scottish (2000).
Economy: Employment by occupation: 6.1% management, 0.0% professional, 15.2% services, 12.1% sales, 0.0% farming, 30.3% construction, 36.4% production (2000).
Income: Per capita income: $13,725 (2000); Median household income: $40,000 (2000); Poverty rate: 14.3% (2000).
Taxes: Total city taxes per capita: $46 (1997); City property taxes per capita: $31 (1997).
Education: High school graduation rate: 70.6% (2000); College graduation rate: 0.0% (2000).
Housing: Homeownership rate: 90.5% (2000); Median home value: $36,300 (2000); Median rent: $225 per month (2000); Median age of housing: 21 years (2000).
Transportation: Commute to work: 100.0% car, 0.0% public transportation, 0.0% walk, 0.0% work from home (2000); Travel time to work: 29.4% less than 15 minutes, 44.1% 15 to 30 minutes, 0.0% 30 to 45 minutes, 0.0% 45 to 60 minutes, 26.5% 60 minutes or more (2000)

BARNARD (city). Covers a land area of 0.155 square miles and a water area of 0 square miles. Located at 40.17° N. Lat.; 94.82° W. Long. Elevation is 958 feet.
Population: 257 (2000); Race: 100.0% White, 0.0% Black, 0.0% Asian, 0.0% American Indian and Alaska Native, 0.0% Hispanic of any race, 0.0% two or more races (2000); Density: 1,654.3 persons per square mile (2000); Age: 24.0% under 18, 19.9% over 64 (2000); Marriage status: 9.9% never married, 71.3% now married, 10.5% widowed, 8.2% divorced (2000); Foreign born: 0.0% (2000); Ancestry (includes multiple ancestries): 24.9% German, 22.6% United States or American, 13.6% Irish, 5.4% Scotch-Irish, 4.5% English (2000).
Economy: Employment by occupation: 7.8% management, 7.8% professional, 14.4% services, 17.8% sales, 1.1% farming, 13.3% construction, 37.8% production (2000).
Income: Per capita income: $16,868 (2000); Median household income: $35,000 (2000); Poverty rate: 10.9% (2000).
Taxes: Total city taxes per capita: $87 (1997); City property taxes per capita: $52 (1997).
Education: High school graduation rate: 76.9% (2000); College graduation rate: 5.6% (2000).
School District(s)
South Nodaway Co. R-IV (PK-12)
2000 Enrollment: 237 660-652-3221
Housing: Homeownership rate: 71.6% (2000); Median home value: $34,200 (2000); Median rent: $166 per month (2000); Median age of housing: 56 years (2000).
Transportation: Commute to work: 88.6% car, 3.4% public transportation, 2.3% walk, 0.0% work from home (2000); Travel time to work: 13.6% less than 15 minutes, 53.4% 15 to 30 minutes, 21.6% 30 to 45 minutes, 8.0% 45 to 60 minutes, 3.4% 60 minutes or more (2000)

BURLINGTON JUNCTION (city). Covers a land area of 1.121 square miles and a water area of 0 square miles. Located at 40.44° N. Lat.; 95.06° W. Long. Elevation is 944 feet.
Population: 632 (2000); Race: 98.6% White, 0.0% Black, 0.0% Asian, 0.8% American Indian and Alaska Native, 0.0% Hispanic of any race, 0.6% two or more races (2000); Density: 563.8 persons per square mile (2000); Age: 28.4% under 18, 16.6% over 64 (2000); Marriage status: 18.2% never married, 67.1% now married, 9.0% widowed, 5.7% divorced (2000); Foreign born: 0.0% (2000); Ancestry (includes multiple ancestries): 17.7% German, 16.0% Irish, 15.7% English, 9.4% United States or American, 4.2% Other groups (2000).
Economy: Corn, soybeans, wheat; cattle, hogs. Employment by occupation: 9.1% management, 11.1% professional, 26.1% services, 13.2% sales, 1.4% farming, 12.5% construction, 26.5% production (2000).
Income: Per capita income: $13,065 (2000); Median household income: $29,722 (2000); Poverty rate: 12.0% (2000).
Taxes: Total city taxes per capita: $47 (1997); City property taxes per capita: $26 (1997).
Education: High school graduation rate: 79.3% (2000); College graduation rate: 8.2% (2000).
School District(s)
West Nodaway Co. R-I (PK-12)
2000 Enrollment: 401 660-725-4613
Housing: Homeownership rate: 75.4% (2000); Median home value: $36,400 (2000); Median rent: $223 per month (2000); Median age of housing: 60+ years (2000).
Transportation: Commute to work: 90.1% car, 0.0% public transportation, 7.4% walk, 2.5% work from home (2000); Travel time to work: 32.9% less than 15 minutes, 33.9% 15 to 30 minutes, 24.5% 30 to 45 minutes, 3.6% 45 to 60 minutes, 5.1% 60 minutes or more (2000)

CLEARMONT (city). Covers a land area of 0.169 square miles and a water area of 0 square miles. Located at 40.50° N. Lat.; 95.03° W. Long. Elevation is 970 feet.
Population: 191 (2000); Race: 100.0% White, 0.0% Black, 0.0% Asian, 0.0% American Indian and Alaska Native, 0.0% Hispanic of any race, 0.0% two or more races (2000); Density: 1,133.0 persons per square mile (2000); Age: 15.3% under 18, 36.7% over 64 (2000); Marriage status: 15.2% never married, 57.3% now married, 20.5% widowed, 7.0% divorced (2000); Foreign born: 0.0% (2000); Ancestry (includes multiple ancestries): 20.9% German, 14.3% English, 13.3% Irish, 8.2% United States or American, 3.6% Danish (2000).
Economy: Soybeans, grain; livestock. Employment by occupation: 5.5% management, 17.8% professional, 20.5% services, 24.7% sales, 0.0% farming, 13.7% construction, 17.8% production (2000).
Income: Per capita income: $14,642 (2000); Median household income: $17,361 (2000); Poverty rate: 19.9% (2000).
Taxes: Total city taxes per capita: $48 (1997); City property taxes per capita: $24 (1997).
Education: High school graduation rate: 78.9% (2000); College graduation rate: 9.2% (2000).
Housing: Homeownership rate: 65.4% (2000); Median home value: $31,900 (2000); Median rent: $250 per month (2000); Median age of housing: 60+ years (2000).

Transportation: Commute to work: 84.5% car, 0.0% public transportation, 12.7% walk, 2.8% work from home (2000); Travel time to work: 47.8% less than 15 minutes, 21.7% 15 to 30 minutes, 27.5% 30 to 45 minutes, 0.0% 45 to 60 minutes, 2.9% 60 minutes or more (2000)

CLYDE (village). Covers a land area of 0.172 square miles and a water area of 0 square miles. Located at 40.26° N. Lat.; 94.66° W. Long. Elevation is 986 feet.
Population: 74 (2000); Race: 94.9% White, 0.0% Black, 0.0% Asian, 5.1% American Indian and Alaska Native, 0.0% Hispanic of any race, 0.0% two or more races (2000); Density: 430.4 persons per square mile (2000); Age: 22.8% under 18, 5.1% over 64 (2000); Marriage status: 26.5% never married, 70.6% now married, 2.9% widowed, 0.0% divorced (2000); Foreign born: 0.0% (2000); Ancestry (includes multiple ancestries): 49.4% German, 20.3% Irish, 11.4% English, 7.6% Other groups, 7.6% French (except Basque) (2000).
Economy: Employment by occupation: 16.3% management, 11.6% professional, 9.3% services, 11.6% sales, 0.0% farming, 14.0% construction, 37.2% production (2000).
Income: Per capita income: $15,684 (2000); Median household income: $36,250 (2000); Poverty rate: 13.9% (2000).
Taxes: Total city taxes per capita: $30 (1997); City property taxes per capita: $15 (1997).
Education: High school graduation rate: 74.0% (2000); College graduation rate: 20.0% (2000).
Housing: Homeownership rate: 92.0% (2000); Median home value: $68,800 (2000); Median age of housing: 22 years (2000).
Transportation: Commute to work: 90.7% car, 0.0% public transportation, 4.7% walk, 4.7% work from home (2000); Travel time to work: 53.7% less than 15 minutes, 26.8% 15 to 30 minutes, 12.2% 30 to 45 minutes, 7.3% 45 to 60 minutes, 0.0% 60 minutes or more (2000)

CONCEPTION (unincorporated postal area, zip code 64433). Covers a land area of 3.022 square miles and a water area of 0.012 square miles. Located at 40.24° N. Lat.; 94.68° W. Long. Elevation is 1,115 feet.
History: Conception was established in 1860 by leaders of the Reading Colony, a settlement of Irish Catholics who had come from Reading, Pennsylvania. The group was formed to provide for railroad workers who lost their jobs in the depression of 1857.
Population: 190 (2000); Race: 83.6% White, 0.0% Black, 13.1% Asian, 0.0% American Indian and Alaska Native, 3.3% Hispanic of any race, 3.3% two or more races (2000); Density: 62.9 persons per square mile (2000); Age: 7.1% under 18, 13.7% over 64 (2000); Marriage status: 86.5% never married, 4.7% now married, 4.7% widowed, 4.1% divorced (2000); Foreign born: 16.4% (2000); Ancestry (includes multiple ancestries): 25.7% German, 19.7% Irish, 19.7% United States or American, 13.1% Other groups, 12.0% Polish (2000).
Economy: Corn, soybeans; cattle. Employment by occupation: 6.4% management, 45.5% professional, 15.5% services, 14.5% sales, 0.0% farming, 10.9% construction, 7.3% production (2000).
Income: Per capita income: $9,037 (2000); Median household income: $20,625 (2000); Poverty rate: 20.8% (2000).
Education: High school graduation rate: 100.0% (2000); College graduation rate: 39.3% (2000).

Four-year College(s)

Conception Seminary College (Private, Not-for-profit, Roman Catholic)
2001 Enrollment: 90 816-944-2218
2001 Tuition: In-state $9,312; Out-of-state $9,312

Housing: Homeownership rate: 100.0% (2000); Median home value: $30,800 (2000); Median age of housing: 58 years (2000).
Transportation: Commute to work: 14.2% car, 0.0% public transportation, 56.6% walk, 29.2% work from home (2000); Travel time to work: 85.3% less than 15 minutes, 8.0% 15 to 30 minutes, 4.0% 30 to 45 minutes, 0.0% 45 to 60 minutes, 2.7% 60 minutes or more (2000)

CONCEPTION JUNCTION (town). Covers a land area of 0.313 square miles and a water area of 0 square miles. Located at 40.26° N. Lat.; 94.69° W. Long. Elevation is 1,001 feet.
Population: 202 (2000); Race: 99.1% White, 0.0% Black, 0.0% Asian, 0.0% American Indian and Alaska Native, 0.9% Hispanic of any race, 0.9% two or more races (2000); Density: 644.4 persons per square mile (2000); Age: 31.8% under 18, 13.1% over 64 (2000); Marriage status: 21.3% never married, 55.0% now married, 11.3% widowed, 12.5% divorced (2000); Foreign born: 0.9% (2000); Ancestry (includes multiple ancestries): 41.1% German, 10.7% United States or American, 8.4% Irish, 6.5% English, 5.1% Scotch-Irish (2000).
Economy: Employment by occupation: 7.8% management, 8.8% professional, 37.3% services, 5.9% sales, 2.0% farming, 5.9% construction, 32.4% production (2000).
Income: Per capita income: $12,563 (2000); Median household income: $29,219 (2000); Poverty rate: 15.3% (2000).
Taxes: Total city taxes per capita: $57 (1997); City property taxes per capita: $26 (1997).
Education: High school graduation rate: 77.1% (2000); College graduation rate: 9.9% (2000).

School District(s)

Jefferson C-123 (KG-12)
2000 Enrollment: 167 660-944-2316

Housing: Homeownership rate: 70.7% (2000); Median home value: $38,300 (2000); Median rent: $209 per month (2000); Median age of housing: 47 years (2000).
Transportation: Commute to work: 99.0% car, 0.0% public transportation, 1.0% walk, 0.0% work from home (2000); Travel time to work: 34.3% less than 15 minutes, 41.2% 15 to 30 minutes, 11.8% 30 to 45 minutes, 4.9% 45 to 60 minutes, 7.8% 60 minutes or more (2000)

ELMO (city). Covers a land area of 0.215 square miles and a water area of 0 square miles. Located at 40.51° N. Lat.; 95.11° W. Long. Elevation is 1,020 feet.
Population: 166 (2000); Race: 97.5% White, 0.0% Black, 0.0% Asian, 0.0% American Indian and Alaska Native, 0.0% Hispanic of any race, 2.5% two or more races (2000); Density: 771.2 persons per square mile (2000); Age: 24.8% under 18, 30.6% over 64 (2000); Marriage status: 21.6% never married, 44.0% now married, 20.0% widowed, 14.4% divorced (2000); Foreign born: 0.0% (2000); Ancestry (includes multiple ancestries): 15.9% German, 14.0% United States or American, 8.9% Irish, 6.4% Other groups, 5.1% English (2000).
Economy: Grain, livestock. Employment by occupation: 7.8% management, 7.8% professional, 23.5% services, 13.7% sales, 0.0% farming, 13.7% construction, 33.3% production (2000).
Income: Per capita income: $12,966 (2000); Median household income: $20,833 (2000); Poverty rate: 24.2% (2000).
Taxes: Total city taxes per capita: $47 (1997); City property taxes per capita: $23 (1997).
Education: High school graduation rate: 74.5% (2000); College graduation rate: 18.2% (2000).
Housing: Homeownership rate: 72.2% (2000); Median home value: $12,000 (2000); Median rent: $206 per month (2000); Median age of housing: 60+ years (2000).
Transportation: Commute to work: 100.0% car, 0.0% public transportation, 0.0% walk, 0.0% work from home (2000); Travel time to work: 31.4% less than 15 minutes, 25.5% 15 to 30 minutes, 23.5% 30 to 45 minutes, 7.8% 45 to 60 minutes, 11.8% 60 minutes or more (2000)

GRAHAM (town). Covers a land area of 0.260 square miles and a water area of 0 square miles. Located at 40.20° N. Lat.; 95.03° W. Long. Elevation is 955 feet.
Population: 191 (2000); Race: 96.2% White, 1.6% Black, 0.0% Asian, 0.0% American Indian and Alaska Native, 0.0% Hispanic of any race, 2.2% two or more races (2000); Density: 733.6 persons per square mile (2000); Age: 26.5% under 18, 15.1% over 64 (2000); Marriage status: 17.6% never married, 58.1% now married, 11.5% widowed, 12.8% divorced (2000); Foreign born: 0.0% (2000); Ancestry (includes multiple ancestries): 19.5% German, 13.5% English, 10.8% United States or American, 9.2% Irish, 8.1% Scotch-Irish (2000).
Economy: Manufacturing: concrete. Employment by occupation: 7.9% management, 9.0% professional, 25.8% services, 11.2% sales, 2.2% farming, 7.9% construction, 36.0% production (2000).
Income: Per capita income: $13,816 (2000); Median household income: $24,306 (2000); Poverty rate: 21.6% (2000).
Taxes: Total city taxes per capita: $20 (1997); City property taxes per capita: $0 (1997).
Education: High school graduation rate: 83.6% (2000); College graduation rate: 4.7% (2000).

School District(s)

Nodaway-Holt R-VII (PK-12)
2000 Enrollment: 319 660-939-2137

Housing: Homeownership rate: 86.1% (2000); Median home value: $20,800 (2000); Median rent: $139 per month (2000); Median age of housing: 47 years (2000).
Transportation: Commute to work: 87.5% car, 0.0% public transportation, 5.7% walk, 4.5% work from home (2000); Travel time to work: 22.6% less

than 15 minutes, 51.2% 15 to 30 minutes, 10.7% 30 to 45 minutes, 7.1% 45 to 60 minutes, 8.3% 60 minutes or more (2000)

GUILFORD (town). Covers a land area of 0.077 square miles and a water area of 0 square miles. Located at 40.16° N. Lat.; 94.73° W. Long. Elevation is 290 feet.
Population: 87 (2000); Race: 100.0% White, 0.0% Black, 0.0% Asian, 0.0% American Indian and Alaska Native, 5.1% Hispanic of any race, 0.0% two or more races (2000); Density: 1,130.5 persons per square mile (2000); Age: 27.6% under 18, 20.4% over 64 (2000); Marriage status: 26.7% never married, 47.7% now married, 3.5% widowed, 22.1% divorced (2000); Foreign born: 0.0% (2000); Ancestry (includes multiple ancestries): 24.5% English, 21.4% German, 13.3% Irish, 9.2% Danish, 9.2% Swedish (2000).
Economy: Employment by occupation: 0.0% management, 14.0% professional, 25.6% services, 9.3% sales, 0.0% farming, 32.6% construction, 18.6% production (2000).
Income: Per capita income: $9,391 (2000); Median household income: $20,625 (2000); Poverty rate: 28.6% (2000).
Taxes: Total city taxes per capita: $91 (1997); City property taxes per capita: $68 (1997).
Education: High school graduation rate: 80.3% (2000); College graduation rate: 4.9% (2000).
Housing: Homeownership rate: 80.6% (2000); Median home value: <$10,000 (2000); Median age of housing: 60+ years (2000).
Transportation: Commute to work: 83.7% car, 0.0% public transportation, 9.3% walk, 0.0% work from home (2000); Travel time to work: 9.3% less than 15 minutes, 25.6% 15 to 30 minutes, 37.2% 30 to 45 minutes, 7.0% 45 to 60 minutes, 20.9% 60 minutes or more (2000)

HOPKINS (city). Covers a land area of 0.722 square miles and a water area of 0 square miles. Located at 40.55° N. Lat.; 94.81° W. Long. Elevation is 1,046 feet.
Population: 579 (2000); Race: 99.1% White, 0.0% Black, 0.0% Asian, 0.0% American Indian and Alaska Native, 0.9% Hispanic of any race, 0.9% two or more races (2000); Density: 801.5 persons per square mile (2000); Age: 27.9% under 18, 15.2% over 64 (2000); Marriage status: 15.5% never married, 66.7% now married, 7.5% widowed, 10.3% divorced (2000); Foreign born: 0.2% (2000); Ancestry (includes multiple ancestries): 18.9% German, 15.2% United States or American, 14.5% English, 11.8% Irish, 8.1% Other groups (2000).
Economy: Corn, wheat, soybeans; hogs, cattle. Manufacturing: corrugated metal pipe. Employment by occupation: 3.5% management, 12.4% professional, 14.3% services, 17.4% sales, 0.0% farming, 12.8% construction, 39.5% production (2000).
Income: Per capita income: $13,378 (2000); Median household income: $28,194 (2000); Poverty rate: 14.5% (2000).
Taxes: Total city taxes per capita: $85 (1997); City property taxes per capita: $60 (1997).
Education: High school graduation rate: 75.5% (2000); College graduation rate: 7.5% (2000).

School District(s)

North Nodaway Co. R-VI (PK-12)
2000 Enrollment: 274 660-778-3411
Housing: Homeownership rate: 78.9% (2000); Median home value: $24,700 (2000); Median rent: $196 per month (2000); Median age of housing: 60+ years (2000).
Newspapers: The Hopkins Journal (1 x week)
Transportation: Commute to work: 93.4% car, 0.8% public transportation, 2.3% walk, 1.2% work from home (2000); Travel time to work: 21.7% less than 15 minutes, 45.5% 15 to 30 minutes, 24.1% 30 to 45 minutes, 4.7% 45 to 60 minutes, 4.0% 60 minutes or more (2000)

MARYVILLE (city). Covers a land area of 5.032 square miles and a water area of 0.053 square miles. Located at 40.34° N. Lat.; 94.87° W. Long. Elevation is 1,136 feet.
History: Maryville was named for Mary Graham, an early resident whose husband was a prominent politican and lawyer in the town. Maryville was the home of Albert P. Morehouse, who became a governor of Missouri.
Population: 10,581 (2000); Race: 96.0% White, 1.7% Black, 1.4% Asian, 0.2% American Indian and Alaska Native, 0.6% Hispanic of any race, 0.6% two or more races (2000); Density: 2,102.8 persons per square mile (2000); Age: 14.1% under 18, 12.2% over 64 (2000); Marriage status: 48.2% never married, 38.6% now married, 7.5% widowed, 5.7% divorced (2000); Foreign born: 2.3% (2000); Ancestry (includes multiple ancestries): 29.0% German, 16.0% Irish, 13.5% English, 7.9% United States or American, 5.7% Other groups (2000).
Vital Statistics: Birth rate: 87.9 per 10,000 population (1998)
Economy: Single-family building permits issued: 20 (2001) / 23 (2000); Multi-family building permits issued: 51 (2001) / 36 (2000); Employment by occupation: 9.5% management, 26.6% professional, 19.9% services, 24.8% sales, 0.5% farming, 5.3% construction, 13.4% production (2000).
Income: Per capita income: $15,483 (2000); Median household income: $29,043 (2000); Poverty rate: 23.6% (2000).
Taxes: Total city taxes per capita: $347 (2000); City property taxes per capita: $80 (2000).
Education: High school graduation rate: 87.6% (2000); College graduation rate: 35.5% (2000).

School District(s)

Maryville R-II (PK-12)
2000 Enrollment: 1,385 660-562-3255

Four-year College(s)

Northwest Missouri State University (Public)
2001 Enrollment: 6,625 660-562-1212
2001 Tuition: In-state $2,468; Out-of-state $4,935
Housing: Homeownership rate: 48.1% (2000); Median home value: $86,500 (2000); Median rent: $343 per month (2000); Median age of housing: 33 years (2000).
Hospitals: Saint Francis Hospital & Health Services (81 beds)
Safety: Violent crime rate: 1.9 per 10,000 population; Property crime rate: 140.0 per 10,000 population (2001).
Newspapers: Maryville Daily Forum (5 x week); Penny Press 2 (1 x week); Country Shopper (1 x week)
Transportation: Commute to work: 85.8% car, 0.4% public transportation, 11.7% walk, 0.7% work from home (2000); Travel time to work: 83.6% less than 15 minutes, 8.9% 15 to 30 minutes, 3.4% 30 to 45 minutes, 1.3% 45 to 60 minutes, 2.8% 60 minutes or more (2000)
Additional Information Contacts
Maryville Chamber of Commerce 816-582-8643
Northwest Missouri Board of Realtors 816-582-8848

PARNELL (city). Covers a land area of 0.292 square miles and a water area of 0 square miles. Located at 40.43° N. Lat.; 94.62° W. Long. Elevation is 1,060 feet.
Population: 197 (2000); Race: 100.0% White, 0.0% Black, 0.0% Asian, 0.0% American Indian and Alaska Native, 0.0% Hispanic of any race, 0.0% two or more races (2000); Density: 674.4 persons per square mile (2000); Age: 19.1% under 18, 21.6% over 64 (2000); Marriage status: 34.3% never married, 40.7% now married, 18.0% widowed, 7.0% divorced (2000); Foreign born: 0.0% (2000); Ancestry (includes multiple ancestries): 25.6% German, 14.1% United States or American, 13.1% Irish, 6.0% Other groups, 3.5% Italian (2000).
Economy: Corn, wheat, soybeans; hogs, cattle. Employment by occupation: 5.9% management, 13.9% professional, 19.8% services, 12.9% sales, 0.0% farming, 10.9% construction, 36.6% production (2000).
Income: Per capita income: $13,467 (2000); Median household income: $23,281 (2000); Poverty rate: 13.6% (2000).
Taxes: Total city taxes per capita: $33 (1997); City property taxes per capita: $7 (1997).
Education: High school graduation rate: 78.0% (2000); College graduation rate: 11.0% (2000).
Housing: Homeownership rate: 65.3% (2000); Median home value: <$10,000 (2000); Median rent: $145 per month (2000); Median age of housing: 60+ years (2000).
Transportation: Commute to work: 96.1% car, 0.0% public transportation, 1.9% walk, 1.9% work from home (2000); Travel time to work: 12.9% less than 15 minutes, 39.6% 15 to 30 minutes, 37.6% 30 to 45 minutes, 0.0% 45 to 60 minutes, 9.9% 60 minutes or more (2000)

PICKERING (town). Covers a land area of 0.183 square miles and a water area of 0 square miles. Located at 40.45° N. Lat.; 94.84° W. Long. Elevation is 1,022 feet.
Population: 154 (2000); Race: 97.9% White, 0.0% Black, 0.0% Asian, 0.0% American Indian and Alaska Native, 0.0% Hispanic of any race, 2.1% two or more races (2000); Density: 839.7 persons per square mile (2000); Age: 16.1% under 18, 23.1% over 64 (2000); Marriage status: 15.7% never married, 74.0% now married, 7.9% widowed, 2.4% divorced (2000); Foreign born: 0.0% (2000); Ancestry (includes multiple ancestries): 18.9% United States or American, 18.2% German, 9.8% Irish, 7.7% English, 7.0% Dutch (2000).
Economy: Employment by occupation: 10.8% management, 5.4% professional, 16.2% services, 13.5% sales, 4.1% farming, 20.3% construction, 29.7% production (2000).

Income: Per capita income: $16,125 (2000); Median household income: $29,167 (2000); Poverty rate: 14.1% (2000).
Taxes: Total city taxes per capita: $67 (1997); City property taxes per capita: $43 (1997).
Education: High school graduation rate: 65.4% (2000); College graduation rate: 17.3% (2000).
Housing: Homeownership rate: 79.7% (2000); Median home value: $31,500 (2000); Median rent: $225 per month (2000); Median age of housing: 60+ years (2000).
Transportation: Commute to work: 95.8% car, 0.0% public transportation, 2.8% walk, 1.4% work from home (2000); Travel time to work: 32.4% less than 15 minutes, 50.7% 15 to 30 minutes, 8.5% 30 to 45 minutes, 5.6% 45 to 60 minutes, 2.8% 60 minutes or more (2000)

QUITMAN (town). Covers a land area of 0.139 square miles and a water area of 0 square miles. Located at 40.37° N. Lat.; 95.07° W. Long. Elevation is 913 feet.
Population: 46 (2000); Race: 100.0% White, 0.0% Black, 0.0% Asian, 0.0% American Indian and Alaska Native, 0.0% Hispanic of any race, 0.0% two or more races (2000); Density: 331.1 persons per square mile (2000); Age: 30.6% under 18, 6.5% over 64 (2000); Marriage status: 24.0% never married, 44.0% now married, 6.0% widowed, 26.0% divorced (2000); Foreign born: 0.0% (2000); Ancestry (includes multiple ancestries): 22.6% United States or American, 9.7% German, 8.1% Scottish, 8.1% Dutch, 4.8% Other groups (2000).
Economy: Employment by occupation: 5.9% management, 8.8% professional, 11.8% services, 5.9% sales, 0.0% farming, 14.7% construction, 52.9% production (2000).
Income: Per capita income: $11,644 (2000); Median household income: $29,375 (2000); Poverty rate: 21.0% (2000).
Taxes: Total city taxes per capita: $44 (1997); City property taxes per capita: $22 (1997).
Education: High school graduation rate: 78.0% (2000); College graduation rate: 0.0% (2000).
Housing: Homeownership rate: 95.8% (2000); Median home value: $22,500 (2000); Median rent: $125 per month (2000); Median age of housing: 18 years (2000).
Transportation: Commute to work: 91.2% car, 0.0% public transportation, 0.0% walk, 8.8% work from home (2000); Travel time to work: 0.0% less than 15 minutes, 54.8% 15 to 30 minutes, 22.6% 30 to 45 minutes, 0.0% 45 to 60 minutes, 22.6% 60 minutes or more (2000)

RAVENWOOD (town). Covers a land area of 0.270 square miles and a water area of 0 square miles. Located at 40.35° N. Lat.; 94.67° W. Long. Elevation is 1,030 feet.
Population: 448 (2000); Race: 96.9% White, 0.0% Black, 0.4% Asian, 0.4% American Indian and Alaska Native, 0.8% Hispanic of any race, 2.3% two or more races (2000); Density: 1,660.1 persons per square mile (2000); Age: 26.8% under 18, 15.5% over 64 (2000); Marriage status: 26.4% never married, 52.5% now married, 11.7% widowed, 9.4% divorced (2000); Foreign born: 1.2% (2000); Ancestry (includes multiple ancestries): 19.8% United States or American, 16.5% German, 7.8% Irish, 6.8% English, 4.3% Other groups (2000).
Economy: Corn, wheat; cattle. Employment by occupation: 4.8% management, 8.6% professional, 21.2% services, 20.4% sales, 1.5% farming, 20.8% construction, 22.7% production (2000).
Income: Per capita income: $16,136 (2000); Median household income: $31,250 (2000); Poverty rate: 8.9% (2000).
Taxes: Total city taxes per capita: $48 (1997); City property taxes per capita: $48 (1997).
Education: High school graduation rate: 89.6% (2000); College graduation rate: 9.3% (2000).

School District(s)

Northeast Nodaway Co. R-V (PK-12)
2000 Enrollment: 270 660-937-3125

Housing: Homeownership rate: 67.2% (2000); Median home value: $47,900 (2000); Median rent: $259 per month (2000); Median age of housing: 29 years (2000).
Transportation: Commute to work: 92.1% car, 0.0% public transportation, 5.6% walk, 2.2% work from home (2000); Travel time to work: 32.2% less than 15 minutes, 56.7% 15 to 30 minutes, 4.2% 30 to 45 minutes, 1.9% 45 to 60 minutes, 5.0% 60 minutes or more (2000)

SKIDMORE (city). Covers a land area of 0.323 square miles and a water area of 0 square miles. Located at 40.28° N. Lat.; 95.07° W. Long. Elevation is 925 feet.
Population: 342 (2000); Race: 99.4% White, 0.6% Black, 0.0% Asian, 0.0% American Indian and Alaska Native, 0.0% Hispanic of any race, 0.0% two or more races (2000); Density: 1,058.8 persons per square mile (2000); Age: 20.9% under 18, 16.9% over 64 (2000); Marriage status: 17.8% never married, 61.1% now married, 11.1% widowed, 10.0% divorced (2000); Foreign born: 0.0% (2000); Ancestry (includes multiple ancestries): 25.2% United States or American, 12.0% English, 10.7% Irish, 8.6% German, 6.4% Other groups (2000).
Economy: Corn, wheat, soybeans; cattle, hogs. Employment by occupation: 2.7% management, 14.9% professional, 23.6% services, 17.6% sales, 1.4% farming, 10.8% construction, 29.1% production (2000).
Income: Per capita income: $13,881 (2000); Median household income: $30,500 (2000); Poverty rate: 22.1% (2000).
Taxes: Total city taxes per capita: $28 (1997); City property taxes per capita: $26 (1997).
Education: High school graduation rate: 80.3% (2000); College graduation rate: 3.9% (2000).
Housing: Homeownership rate: 85.1% (2000); Median home value: $22,300 (2000); Median rent: $325 per month (2000); Median age of housing: 60+ years (2000).
Transportation: Commute to work: 97.3% car, 0.0% public transportation, 2.7% walk, 0.0% work from home (2000); Travel time to work: 10.8% less than 15 minutes, 52.0% 15 to 30 minutes, 15.5% 30 to 45 minutes, 8.8% 45 to 60 minutes, 12.8% 60 minutes or more (2000)

Oregon County

Located in southern Missouri, in the Ozarks; bounded on the south by Arkansas; drained by Eleven Point and Spring Rivers; includes part of Clark National Forest. Covers a land area of 791.40 square miles, a water area of 0.20 square miles, and is located in the Central Time Zone. The county government was organized in 1845. County seat is Alton.
Population: 10,344 (2000); Race: 94.6% White, 0.1% Black, 0.1% Asian, 1.7% American Indian and Alaska Native, 1.0% Hispanic of any race, 3.3% two or more races (2000); Density: 13.1 persons per square mile (2000); Age: 24.2% under 18, 17.9% over 64 (2000).
Religion: Five largest groups: 21.0% Southern Baptist Convention, 20.1% National Association of Free Will Baptists, 5.7% Churches of Christ, 5.1% Assemblies of God, 3.2% The United Methodist Church (2000).
Economy: Unemployment rate: 3.4% (11/2002); Total civilian labor force: 4,209 (11/2002); Leading industries: 25.4% retail trade; 20.2% manufacturing; 13.9% health care and social assistance (2000); Companies that employ more than 1,000 persons: 0 (2000); Companies that employ more than 100 persons: 1 (2000); Farms: 798 totaling 248,024 acres (1997); Minority business ownership rate: 0.0% (1997); Women business ownership rate: 15.2% (1997); Retail sales per capita: $5,715 (1997). Single-family building permits issued: 2 (2001) / 0 (2000); Multi-family building permits issued: 0 (2001) / 0 (2000).
Income: Per capita income: $12,812 (2000); Median household income: $22,359 (2000); Poverty rate: 22.0% (2000); Bankruptcy rate: 2.70% (2001).
Taxes: Total county taxes per capita: $79 (1997); County property taxes per capita: $15 (1997).
Education: High school graduation rate: 72.0% (2000); College graduation rate: 9.1% (2000).
Housing: Homeownership rate: 78.3% (2000); Median home value: $45,900 (2000); Median rent: $244 per month (2000); Median age of housing: 31 years (2000).
Health: Birth rate: 118.9 per 10,000 population (1998); Age adjusted death rate: 103.1 per 10,000 population (1999); Age adjusted cancer mortality rate: 184.0 deaths per 100,000 population (1999). Number of physicians: n/a (1999); Number of hospital beds: n/a (1999).
Elections: 2000 Presidential election results: 37.0% Gore, 59.6% Bush, 1.4% Nader, 1.2% Buchanan
National and State Parks: Eleven Point National Scenic River; Grand Gulf State Park
Additional Information Contacts
Oregon County Government Offices 417-778-4096

Oregon County Communities

ALTON (city). Covers a land area of 0.838 square miles and a water area of 0 square miles. Located at 36.69° N. Lat.; 91.39° W. Long. Elevation is 779 feet.
History: Alton was settled about 1815 by Thomas Hatcher, and grew as a farm trading center. In 1859, Alton succeeded Thomasville as the seat of

Oregon County. To prevent the destruction of county records during the Civil War, Major M.G. Norman hid them in a cave on Piney Creek, where they remained from 1862 to 1865 and so were preserved when the courthouse was burned.

Population: 668 (2000); Race: 97.0% White, 0.6% Black, 0.0% Asian, 0.9% American Indian and Alaska Native, 0.9% Hispanic of any race, 1.5% two or more races (2000); Density: 797.2 persons per square mile (2000); Age: 23.6% under 18, 21.2% over 64 (2000); Marriage status: 16.7% never married, 51.3% now married, 16.1% widowed, 15.9% divorced (2000); Foreign born: 0.3% (2000); Ancestry (includes multiple ancestries): 18.7% United States or American, 9.9% Irish, 8.8% English, 8.3% Other groups, 6.2% German (2000).

Economy: Single-family building permits issued: 0 (2001) / 0 (2000); Multi-family building permits issued: 0 (2001) / 0 (2000); Employment by occupation: 6.5% management, 14.1% professional, 23.8% services, 19.8% sales, 4.8% farming, 4.8% construction, 26.2% production (2000).

Income: Per capita income: $10,071 (2000); Median household income: $16,667 (2000); Poverty rate: 27.4% (2000).

Taxes: Total city taxes per capita: $218 (1997); City property taxes per capita: $25 (1997).

Education: High school graduation rate: 68.8% (2000); College graduation rate: 9.4% (2000).

School District(s)

Alton R-IV (PK-12)
2000 Enrollment: 724 417-778-7216

Housing: Homeownership rate: 58.1% (2000); Median home value: $42,100 (2000); Median rent: $225 per month (2000); Median age of housing: 40 years (2000).

Transportation: Commute to work: 92.6% car, 0.0% public transportation, 2.0% walk, 5.3% work from home (2000); Travel time to work: 61.0% less than 15 minutes, 8.2% 15 to 30 minutes, 16.5% 30 to 45 minutes, 9.1% 45 to 60 minutes, 5.2% 60 minutes or more (2000)

COUCH (unincorporated postal area, zip code 65690). Covers a land area of 48.193 square miles and a water area of 0.020 square miles. Located at 36.58° N. Lat.; 91.30° W. Long. Elevation is 670 feet.

Population: 494 (2000); Race: 95.3% White, 0.0% Black, 0.4% Asian, 1.0% American Indian and Alaska Native, 0.8% Hispanic of any race, 3.3% two or more races (2000); Density: 10.3 persons per square mile (2000); Age: 19.5% under 18, 22.6% over 64 (2000); Marriage status: 19.6% never married, 59.6% now married, 11.2% widowed, 9.7% divorced (2000); Foreign born: 1.2% (2000); Ancestry (includes multiple ancestries): 16.8% German, 14.4% English, 14.2% Irish, 11.5% United States or American, 8.2% Other groups (2000).

Economy: Employment by occupation: 15.7% management, 11.2% professional, 11.2% services, 17.3% sales, 5.6% farming, 10.2% construction, 28.9% production (2000).

Income: Per capita income: $17,067 (2000); Median household income: $23,015 (2000); Poverty rate: 23.8% (2000).

Education: High school graduation rate: 72.9% (2000); College graduation rate: 10.3% (2000).

Housing: Homeownership rate: 82.7% (2000); Median home value: $18,800 (2000); Median rent: $219 per month (2000); Median age of housing: 33 years (2000).

Transportation: Commute to work: 90.8% car, 0.0% public transportation, 2.1% walk, 7.2% work from home (2000); Travel time to work: 16.6% less than 15 minutes, 32.0% 15 to 30 minutes, 20.4% 30 to 45 minutes, 13.3% 45 to 60 minutes, 17.7% 60 minutes or more (2000)

KOSHKONONG (town). Covers a land area of 0.188 square miles and a water area of 0 square miles. Located at 36.59° N. Lat.; 91.64° W. Long. Elevation is 970 feet.

History: Koshkonong developed along the railroad line as a shipping point for farm produce.

Population: 205 (2000); Race: 93.7% White, 0.0% Black, 0.0% Asian, 2.9% American Indian and Alaska Native, 3.9% Hispanic of any race, 3.4% two or more races (2000); Density: 1,087.6 persons per square mile (2000); Age: 36.2% under 18, 15.0% over 64 (2000); Marriage status: 23.8% never married, 59.4% now married, 4.4% widowed, 12.5% divorced (2000); Foreign born: 0.5% (2000); Ancestry (includes multiple ancestries): 26.1% English, 21.3% Irish, 16.4% United States or American, 9.7% Other groups, 8.7% German (2000).

Economy: Employment by occupation: 6.5% management, 11.3% professional, 17.7% services, 12.9% sales, 0.0% farming, 16.1% construction, 35.5% production (2000).

Income: Per capita income: $7,893 (2000); Median household income: $15,341 (2000); Poverty rate: 44.6% (2000).

Taxes: Total city taxes per capita: $44 (2000); City property taxes per capita: $10 (2000).

Education: High school graduation rate: 50.8% (2000); College graduation rate: 9.2% (2000).

School District(s)

Oregon-Howell R-III (PK-12)
2000 Enrollment: 312 417-867-5601

Housing: Homeownership rate: 72.1% (2000); Median home value: $16,300 (2000); Median rent: $267 per month (2000); Median age of housing: 56 years (2000).

Transportation: Commute to work: 86.4% car, 0.0% public transportation, 3.4% walk, 10.2% work from home (2000); Travel time to work: 20.8% less than 15 minutes, 58.5% 15 to 30 minutes, 11.3% 30 to 45 minutes, 7.5% 45 to 60 minutes, 1.9% 60 minutes or more (2000)

MYRTLE (unincorporated postal area, zip code 65778). Covers a land area of 34.749 square miles and a water area of 0 square miles. Located at 36.53° N. Lat.; 91.29° W. Long. Elevation is 566 feet.

Population: 551 (2000); Race: 95.0% White, 0.0% Black, 0.0% Asian, 2.1% American Indian and Alaska Native, 0.4% Hispanic of any race, 2.5% two or more races (2000); Density: 15.9 persons per square mile (2000); Age: 25.4% under 18, 16.1% over 64 (2000); Marriage status: 14.3% never married, 72.5% now married, 4.8% widowed, 8.4% divorced (2000); Foreign born: 0.0% (2000); Ancestry (includes multiple ancestries): 19.5% Other groups, 15.4% United States or American, 15.0% German, 12.0% English, 9.5% Irish (2000).

Economy: Employment by occupation: 9.1% management, 8.6% professional, 11.4% services, 16.8% sales, 6.8% farming, 13.6% construction, 33.6% production (2000).

Income: Per capita income: $11,605 (2000); Median household income: $22,250 (2000); Poverty rate: 28.5% (2000).

Education: High school graduation rate: 75.3% (2000); College graduation rate: 7.9% (2000).

School District(s)

Couch R-I (PK-12)
2000 Enrollment: 293 417-938-4211

Housing: Homeownership rate: 78.4% (2000); Median home value: $35,000 (2000); Median rent: $264 per month (2000); Median age of housing: 31 years (2000).

Transportation: Commute to work: 90.2% car, 0.0% public transportation, 2.8% walk, 6.1% work from home (2000); Travel time to work: 28.9% less than 15 minutes, 23.4% 15 to 30 minutes, 15.9% 30 to 45 minutes, 18.4% 45 to 60 minutes, 13.4% 60 minutes or more (2000)

THAYER (city). Covers a land area of 2.172 square miles and a water area of 0 square miles. Located at 36.52° N. Lat.; 91.54° W. Long. Elevation is 532 feet.

History: Thayer was established when the railroad was built through the area, and grew as a shipping center for timber and dairy products.

Population: 2,201 (2000); Race: 96.8% White, 0.2% Black, 0.2% Asian, 1.0% American Indian and Alaska Native, 0.5% Hispanic of any race, 1.8% two or more races (2000); Density: 1,013.2 persons per square mile (2000); Age: 24.4% under 18, 23.2% over 64 (2000); Marriage status: 17.9% never married, 59.7% now married, 11.5% widowed, 10.9% divorced (2000); Foreign born: 0.7% (2000); Ancestry (includes multiple ancestries): 17.9% United States or American, 15.3% Irish, 13.1% Other groups, 11.0% German, 10.0% English (2000).

Economy: Single-family building permits issued: 2 (2001) / 0 (2000); Multi-family building permits issued: 0 (2001) / 0 (2000); Employment by occupation: 6.6% management, 15.4% professional, 15.2% services, 24.5% sales, 2.5% farming, 10.9% construction, 24.9% production (2000).

Income: Per capita income: $12,278 (2000); Median household income: $18,648 (2000); Poverty rate: 27.2% (2000).

Taxes: Total city taxes per capita: $40 (1997); City property taxes per capita: $25 (1997).

Education: High school graduation rate: 67.8% (2000); College graduation rate: 7.4% (2000).

School District(s)

Thayer R-II (PK-12)
2000 Enrollment: 655 417-264-7261

Housing: Homeownership rate: 66.3% (2000); Median home value: $50,900 (2000); Median rent: $236 per month (2000); Median age of housing: 40 years (2000).

Newspapers: The South Missourian News (1 x week)

Transportation: Commute to work: 92.3% car, 0.0% public transportation, 3.3% walk, 3.8% work from home (2000); Travel time to work: 63.4% less than 15 minutes, 13.8% 15 to 30 minutes, 14.9% 30 to 45 minutes, 2.1% 45 to 60 minutes, 5.8% 60 minutes or more (2000)

Osage County

Located in central Missouri, in the Ozarks; bounded on the north by the Missouri River, and on the west by the Osage River; drained by the Gasconade River. Covers a land area of 606.10 square miles, a water area of 7.30 square miles, and is located in the Central Time Zone. The county government was organized in 1841. County seat is Linn.

Weather Station: Freedom Elevation: 744 feet

	Jan	Feb	Mar	Apr	May	Jun	Jul	Aug	Sep	Oct	Nov	Dec
High	40	47	57	68	76	84	90	88	81	70	56	45
Low	19	24	33	43	52	61	65	63	55	44	34	24
Precip	1.6	2.0	3.3	3.9	4.8	4.3	3.2	3.7	4.1	3.4	3.7	2.8
Snow	3.8	4.5	1.4	tr	0.0	0.0	0.0	0.0	0.0	0.0	1.5	na

High and Low temperatures in degrees Fahrenheit; Precipitation and Snow in inches

Population: 13,062 (2000); Race: 98.7% White, 0.1% Black, 0.1% Asian, 0.4% American Indian and Alaska Native, 0.3% Hispanic of any race, 0.6% two or more races (2000); Density: 21.6 persons per square mile (2000); Age: 26.4% under 18, 14.7% over 64 (2000).
Religion: Five largest groups: 52.1% Catholic Church, 8.6% Southern Baptist Convention, 3.4% Christian Churches and Churches of Christ, 3.0% The United Methodist Church, 1.7% Pentecostal Church of God (2000).
Economy: Unemployment rate: 4.1% (11/2002); Total civilian labor force: 7,549 (11/2002); Leading industries: 37.7% manufacturing; 14.6% retail trade; 7.2% construction (2000); Companies that employ more than 1,000 persons: 0 (2000); Companies that employ more than 100 persons: 4 (2000); Farms: 1,147 totaling 304,823 acres (1997); Minority business ownership rate: 0.0% (1997); Women business ownership rate: 19.4% (1997); Retail sales per capita: $7,367 (1997). Single-family building permits issued: -1 (2001) / -1 (2000); Multi-family building permits issued: -1 (2001) / -1 (2000).
Income: Per capita income: $17,245 (2000); Median household income: $39,565 (2000); Poverty rate: 8.3% (2000); Bankruptcy rate: 2.06% (2001).
Taxes: Total county taxes per capita: $66 (1997); County property taxes per capita: $34 (1997).
Education: High school graduation rate: 75.2% (2000); College graduation rate: 10.4% (2000).
Housing: Homeownership rate: 83.0% (2000); Median home value: $81,400 (2000); Median rent: $249 per month (2000); Median age of housing: 28 years (2000).
Health: Birth rate: 130.2 per 10,000 population (1998); Age adjusted death rate: 110.2 per 10,000 population (1999); Age adjusted cancer mortality rate: 185.2 deaths per 100,000 population (1999). Number of physicians: 1.5 per 10,000 population (1999); Number of hospital beds: n/a (1999).
Elections: 2000 Presidential election results: 31.4% Gore, 67.2% Bush, 0.8% Nader, 0.4% Buchanan
National and State Parks: Painted Rock State Forest
Additional Information Contacts
Osage County Government Offices 573-897-2139

Osage County Communities

ARGYLE (town). Covers a land area of 0.401 square miles and a water area of 0 square miles. Located at 38.29° N. Lat.; 92.02° W. Long. Elevation is 719 feet.
Population: 164 (2000); Race: 100.0% White, 0.0% Black, 0.0% Asian, 0.0% American Indian and Alaska Native, 0.0% Hispanic of any race, 0.0% two or more races (2000); Density: 409.2 persons per square mile (2000); Age: 19.5% under 18, 32.1% over 64 (2000); Marriage status: 16.4% never married, 65.6% now married, 15.6% widowed, 2.3% divorced (2000); Foreign born: 0.0% (2000); Ancestry (includes multiple ancestries): 85.5% German, 7.5% English, 3.1% United States or American, 3.1% Swedish, 2.5% Irish (2000).
Economy: Employment by occupation: 17.6% management, 14.9% professional, 12.2% services, 10.8% sales, 8.1% farming, 4.1% construction, 32.4% production (2000).
Income: Per capita income: $12,274 (2000); Median household income: $23,750 (2000); Poverty rate: 15.7% (2000).
Taxes: Total city taxes per capita: $76 (1997); City property taxes per capita: $11 (1997).
Education: High school graduation rate: 65.2% (2000); College graduation rate: 8.0% (2000).
Housing: Homeownership rate: 78.5% (2000); Median home value: $52,000 (2000); Median rent: $167 per month (2000); Median age of housing: 47 years (2000).
Transportation: Commute to work: 97.3% car, 0.0% public transportation, 0.0% walk, 2.7% work from home (2000); Travel time to work: 18.1% less than 15 minutes, 50.0% 15 to 30 minutes, 9.7% 30 to 45 minutes, 22.2% 45 to 60 minutes, 0.0% 60 minutes or more (2000)

BONNOTS MILL (unincorporated postal area, zip code 65016). Covers a land area of 44.685 square miles and a water area of 0 square miles. Located at 38.57° N. Lat.; 91.90° W. Long. Elevation is 530 feet.
History: Bonnots Mill began in 1852 when Felix Bonnot established a mill and laid out a settlement. The town was first known as Dauphine, as many of the early residents were French.
Population: 1,265 (2000); Race: 100.0% White, 0.0% Black, 0.0% Asian, 0.0% American Indian and Alaska Native, 0.3% Hispanic of any race, 0.0% two or more races (2000); Density: 28.3 persons per square mile (2000); Age: 24.7% under 18, 12.5% over 64 (2000); Marriage status: 23.5% never married, 63.6% now married, 5.9% widowed, 7.0% divorced (2000); Foreign born: 0.0% (2000); Ancestry (includes multiple ancestries): 68.0% German, 6.7% Irish, 5.8% French (except Basque), 4.9% United States or American, 2.6% English (2000).
Economy: Employment by occupation: 14.2% management, 11.1% professional, 10.3% services, 27.7% sales, 1.8% farming, 11.9% construction, 23.0% production (2000).
Income: Per capita income: $19,177 (2000); Median household income: $43,558 (2000); Poverty rate: 3.6% (2000).
Education: High school graduation rate: 81.3% (2000); College graduation rate: 11.8% (2000).
Housing: Homeownership rate: 92.8% (2000); Median home value: $100,200 (2000); Median rent: $256 per month (2000); Median age of housing: 25 years (2000).
Transportation: Commute to work: 94.2% car, 0.0% public transportation, 0.9% walk, 4.3% work from home (2000); Travel time to work: 16.8% less than 15 minutes, 31.5% 15 to 30 minutes, 35.3% 30 to 45 minutes, 12.0% 45 to 60 minutes, 4.5% 60 minutes or more (2000)

CHAMOIS (city). Covers a land area of 0.360 square miles and a water area of 0.021 square miles. Located at 38.67° N. Lat.; 91.77° W. Long. Elevation is 530 feet.
History: Area damaged in flood of 1993.
Population: 456 (2000); Race: 98.1% White, 0.0% Black, 0.0% Asian, 0.4% American Indian and Alaska Native, 2.1% Hispanic of any race, 1.5% two or more races (2000); Density: 1,268.3 persons per square mile (2000); Age: 29.9% under 18, 18.1% over 64 (2000); Marriage status: 18.6% never married, 58.5% now married, 15.8% widowed, 7.2% divorced (2000); Foreign born: 1.9% (2000); Ancestry (includes multiple ancestries): 46.9% German, 11.7% Other groups, 10.4% Irish, 7.5% United States or American, 7.0% English (2000).
Economy: Agriculture: grain; dairying; livestock. Manufacturing: uniforms. Large coal-fueled electric power plant. Employment by occupation: 5.9% management, 15.0% professional, 12.3% services, 25.7% sales, 2.1% farming, 8.6% construction, 30.5% production (2000).
Income: Per capita income: $12,226 (2000); Median household income: $26,563 (2000); Poverty rate: 17.9% (2000).
Taxes: Total city taxes per capita: $42 (2000); City property taxes per capita: $0 (2000).
Education: High school graduation rate: 65.6% (2000); College graduation rate: 8.8% (2000).

School District(s)

Osage Co. R-I (KG-12)
2000 Enrollment: 249 573-763-5666
Housing: Homeownership rate: 77.9% (2000); Median home value: $31,300 (2000); Median rent: $203 per month (2000); Median age of housing: 51 years (2000).
Transportation: Commute to work: 89.4% car, 0.0% public transportation, 2.2% walk, 7.2% work from home (2000); Travel time to work: 37.1% less than 15 minutes, 14.4% 15 to 30 minutes, 10.8% 30 to 45 minutes, 16.2% 45 to 60 minutes, 21.6% 60 minutes or more (2000)

FREEBURG (village). Covers a land area of 0.824 square miles and a water area of 0 square miles. Located at 38.31° N. Lat.; 91.92° W. Long. Elevation is 899 feet.

History: Freeburg was settled by German immigrants in the 1880's. The town grew with the building of the Rock Island Railroad in 1902, which ran through a tunnel beneath the town.
Population: 423 (2000); Race: 100.0% White, 0.0% Black, 0.0% Asian, 0.0% American Indian and Alaska Native, 1.0% Hispanic of any race, 0.0% two or more races (2000); Density: 513.1 persons per square mile (2000); Age: 20.5% under 18, 15.9% over 64 (2000); Marriage status: 27.8% never married, 52.8% now married, 9.0% widowed, 10.4% divorced (2000); Foreign born: 0.0% (2000); Ancestry (includes multiple ancestries): 44.0% German, 12.8% United States or American, 4.8% Other groups, 4.6% Irish, 2.9% Italian (2000).
Economy: Employment by occupation: 13.7% management, 1.7% professional, 12.0% services, 35.0% sales, 0.0% farming, 7.3% construction, 30.3% production (2000).
Income: Per capita income: $20,071 (2000); Median household income: $31,429 (2000); Poverty rate: 9.2% (2000).
Taxes: Total city taxes per capita: $210 (1997); City property taxes per capita: $0 (1997).
Education: High school graduation rate: 74.1% (2000); College graduation rate: 9.6% (2000).
Housing: Homeownership rate: 74.3% (2000); Median home value: $63,800 (2000); Median rent: $183 per month (2000); Median age of housing: 38 years (2000).
Transportation: Commute to work: 87.0% car, 0.0% public transportation, 11.3% walk, 1.7% work from home (2000); Travel time to work: 43.2% less than 15 minutes, 15.0% 15 to 30 minutes, 26.4% 30 to 45 minutes, 9.3% 45 to 60 minutes, 6.2% 60 minutes or more (2000)

KOELTZTOWN (unincorporated postal area, zip code 65048). Covers a land area of 21.527 square miles and a water area of 0.041 square miles. Located at 38.36° N. Lat.; 92.00° W. Long. Elevation is 930 feet.
Population: 144 (2000); Race: 100.0% White, 0.0% Black, 0.0% Asian, 0.0% American Indian and Alaska Native, 0.0% Hispanic of any race, 0.0% two or more races (2000); Density: 6.7 persons per square mile (2000); Age: 27.1% under 18, 7.5% over 64 (2000); Marriage status: 31.1% never married, 64.2% now married, 4.7% widowed, 0.0% divorced (2000); Foreign born: 0.0% (2000); Ancestry (includes multiple ancestries): 53.4% German, 6.8% United States or American (2000).
Economy: Employment by occupation: 18.4% management, 15.8% professional, 5.3% services, 18.4% sales, 0.0% farming, 19.7% construction, 22.4% production (2000).
Income: Per capita income: $11,482 (2000); Median household income: $33,250 (2000); Poverty rate: 46.6% (2000).
Education: High school graduation rate: 65.8% (2000); College graduation rate: 11.8% (2000).
Housing: Homeownership rate: 89.8% (2000); Median home value: $96,000 (2000); Median age of housing: 20 years (2000).
Transportation: Commute to work: 88.2% car, 0.0% public transportation, 0.0% walk, 11.8% work from home (2000); Travel time to work: 23.9% less than 15 minutes, 14.9% 15 to 30 minutes, 25.4% 30 to 45 minutes, 26.9% 45 to 60 minutes, 9.0% 60 minutes or more (2000)

LINN (city). Covers a land area of 0.877 square miles and a water area of 0 square miles. Located at 38.48° N. Lat.; 91.84° W. Long. Elevation is 850 feet.
History: Linn was created by the county court in 1842 as Linville. Intended to honor U.S. Senator Lewis F. Linn, the name was later changed to Linn.
Population: 1,354 (2000); Race: 97.1% White, 0.8% Black, 0.5% Asian, 0.7% American Indian and Alaska Native, 0.9% Hispanic of any race, 0.5% two or more races (2000); Density: 1,543.3 persons per square mile (2000); Age: 26.6% under 18, 22.9% over 64 (2000); Marriage status: 26.1% never married, 52.4% now married, 12.8% widowed, 8.7% divorced (2000); Foreign born: 1.7% (2000); Ancestry (includes multiple ancestries): 41.9% German, 13.7% United States or American, 9.8% Irish, 8.7% English, 7.8% Other groups (2000).
Economy: Employment by occupation: 12.6% management, 13.6% professional, 18.7% services, 24.1% sales, 0.2% farming, 11.5% construction, 19.3% production (2000).
Income: Per capita income: $13,840 (2000); Median household income: $27,656 (2000); Poverty rate: 17.1% (2000).
Taxes: Total city taxes per capita: $93 (1997); City property taxes per capita: $46 (1997).
Education: High school graduation rate: 73.4% (2000); College graduation rate: 15.3% (2000).

School District(s)

Osage Co. R-II (PK-12)
2000 Enrollment: 685 573-897-4200

Two-year College(s)

Linn State Technical College (Public)
2001 Enrollment: 816 573-897-5000
2001 Tuition: In-state $2,940; Out-of-state $5,880
Housing: Homeownership rate: 57.3% (2000); Median home value: $67,200 (2000); Median rent: $229 per month (2000); Median age of housing: 35 years (2000).
Newspapers: Unterrified Democrat (1 x week)
Transportation: Commute to work: 89.0% car, 0.4% public transportation, 4.8% walk, 5.8% work from home (2000); Travel time to work: 35.7% less than 15 minutes, 21.1% 15 to 30 minutes, 32.2% 30 to 45 minutes, 4.5% 45 to 60 minutes, 6.6% 60 minutes or more (2000)

LOOSE CREEK (unincorporated postal area, zip code 65054). Covers a land area of 17.070 square miles and a water area of 0 square miles. Located at 38.48° N. Lat.; 91.95° W. Long. Elevation is 819 feet.
Population: 554 (2000); Race: 100.0% White, 0.0% Black, 0.0% Asian, 0.0% American Indian and Alaska Native, 0.0% Hispanic of any race, 0.0% two or more races (2000); Density: 32.5 persons per square mile (2000); Age: 32.3% under 18, 8.5% over 64 (2000); Marriage status: 23.5% never married, 63.7% now married, 3.1% widowed, 9.7% divorced (2000); Foreign born: 1.0% (2000); Ancestry (includes multiple ancestries): 63.0% German, 12.0% United States or American, 11.0% Irish, 3.5% Welsh, 2.8% French (except Basque) (2000).
Economy: Employment by occupation: 5.4% management, 15.1% professional, 13.0% services, 24.3% sales, 3.8% farming, 16.7% construction, 21.8% production (2000).
Income: Per capita income: $23,969 (2000); Median household income: $50,385 (2000); Poverty rate: 5.5% (2000).
Education: High school graduation rate: 78.2% (2000); College graduation rate: 15.5% (2000).
Housing: Homeownership rate: 78.0% (2000); Median home value: $101,500 (2000); Median rent: $290 per month (2000); Median age of housing: 25 years (2000).
Transportation: Commute to work: 90.4% car, 0.0% public transportation, 2.1% walk, 4.2% work from home (2000); Travel time to work: 20.1% less than 15 minutes, 47.6% 15 to 30 minutes, 24.0% 30 to 45 minutes, 8.3% 45 to 60 minutes, 0.0% 60 minutes or more (2000)

META (city). Covers a land area of 0.335 square miles and a water area of 0 square miles. Located at 38.31° N. Lat.; 92.16° W. Long. Elevation is 610 feet.
Population: 249 (2000); Race: 98.0% White, 0.0% Black, 1.2% Asian, 0.8% American Indian and Alaska Native, 0.0% Hispanic of any race, 0.0% two or more races (2000); Density: 742.7 persons per square mile (2000); Age: 27.8% under 18, 17.1% over 64 (2000); Marriage status: 22.0% never married, 57.1% now married, 17.3% widowed, 3.7% divorced (2000); Foreign born: 1.2% (2000); Ancestry (includes multiple ancestries): 39.7% German, 14.7% United States or American, 11.1% Scotch-Irish, 6.3% Irish, 6.0% Other groups (2000).
Economy: Pet food; charcoal products. Employment by occupation: 17.7% management, 8.0% professional, 6.2% services, 33.6% sales, 0.0% farming, 11.5% construction, 23.0% production (2000).
Income: Per capita income: $13,902 (2000); Median household income: $35,208 (2000); Poverty rate: 16.7% (2000).
Taxes: Total city taxes per capita: $349 (2000); City property taxes per capita: $76 (2000).
Education: High school graduation rate: 73.6% (2000); College graduation rate: 8.6% (2000).
Housing: Homeownership rate: 80.0% (2000); Median home value: $52,000 (2000); Median rent: $266 per month (2000); Median age of housing: 47 years (2000).
Transportation: Commute to work: 89.3% car, 0.0% public transportation, 5.4% walk, 5.4% work from home (2000); Travel time to work: 18.9% less than 15 minutes, 9.4% 15 to 30 minutes, 40.6% 30 to 45 minutes, 21.7% 45 to 60 minutes, 9.4% 60 minutes or more (2000)

WESTPHALIA (city). Covers a land area of 0.506 square miles and a water area of 0 square miles. Located at 38.44° N. Lat.; 91.99° W. Long. Elevation is 622 feet.
History: Westphalia was settled in 1835 on the Big Maries River, mainly by German immigrants. The town was laid out by Father Ferdinand Benoit

Marie Guislain Helias d'Huddleghem (Father Helias), who conducted missionary activities from here throughout central Missouri.
Population: 320 (2000); Race: 96.0% White, 0.0% Black, 1.1% Asian, 0.0% American Indian and Alaska Native, 0.0% Hispanic of any race, 2.9% two or more races (2000); Density: 631.9 persons per square mile (2000); Age: 26.7% under 18, 21.6% over 64 (2000); Marriage status: 25.5% never married, 55.5% now married, 14.5% widowed, 4.5% divorced (2000); Foreign born: 0.0% (2000); Ancestry (includes multiple ancestries): 73.6% German, 7.7% Irish, 4.4% United States or American, 2.2% Swedish, 1.1% Scandinavian (2000).
Economy: Employment by occupation: 9.8% management, 15.4% professional, 18.7% services, 26.0% sales, 0.0% farming, 13.8% construction, 16.3% production (2000).
Income: Per capita income: $18,496 (2000); Median household income: $35,833 (2000); Poverty rate: 6.2% (2000).
Taxes: Total city taxes per capita: $143 (1997); City property taxes per capita: $0 (1997).
Education: High school graduation rate: 80.0% (2000); College graduation rate: 18.9% (2000).

School District(s)

Osage Co. R-III (PK-12)
2000 Enrollment: 813 573-455-2375

Housing: Homeownership rate: 75.6% (2000); Median home value: $87,100 (2000); Median rent: $252 per month (2000); Median age of housing: 43 years (2000).
Transportation: Commute to work: 90.2% car, 0.0% public transportation, 7.3% walk, 2.4% work from home (2000); Travel time to work: 24.2% less than 15 minutes, 45.0% 15 to 30 minutes, 27.5% 30 to 45 minutes, 0.0% 45 to 60 minutes, 3.3% 60 minutes or more (2000)

Ozark County

Located in southern Missouri, in the Ozarks; bounded on the south by Arkansas; drained by the North Fork of the White River; includes part of Mark Twain National Forest. Covers a land area of 742.10 square miles, a water area of 12.90 square miles, and is located in the Central Time Zone. The county government was organized in 1841. County seat is Gainesville.

Weather Station: Dora — Elevation: 987 feet

	Jan	Feb	Mar	Apr	May	Jun	Jul	Aug	Sep	Oct	Nov	Dec
High	43	50	59	70	76	84	90	89	81	71	58	48
Low	20	24	33	42	52	61	65	64	56	43	33	25
Precip	2.3	2.6	4.0	4.5	4.8	4.1	3.2	3.1	4.3	3.7	4.9	3.7
Snow	4.6	3.0	2.0	0.3	0.0	0.0	0.0	0.0	0.0	tr	0.7	2.1

High and Low temperatures in degrees Fahrenheit; Precipitation and Snow in inches

Population: 9,542 (2000); Race: 97.0% White, 0.1% Black, 0.1% Asian, 0.5% American Indian and Alaska Native, 1.2% Hispanic of any race, 1.7% two or more races (2000); Density: 12.9 persons per square mile (2000); Age: 21.9% under 18, 19.5% over 64 (2000).
Religion: Five largest groups: 5.9% Southern Baptist Convention, 5.7% Churches of Christ, 3.9% Assemblies of God, 2.5% Christian Church (Disciples of Christ), 2.2% The United Methodist Church (2000).
Economy: Unemployment rate: 5.3% (11/2002); Total civilian labor force: 4,321 (11/2002); Leading industries: 34.5% retail trade; 13.8% manufacturing; 9.3% accommodation & food services (2000); Companies that employ more than 1,000 persons: 0 (2000); Companies that employ more than 100 persons: 0 (2000); Farms: 781 totaling 252,722 acres (1997); Minority business ownership rate: 0.0% (1997); Women business ownership rate: 14.4% (1997); Retail sales per capita: $4,105 (1997). Single-family building permits issued: 2 (2001) / 5 (2000); Multi-family building permits issued: 0 (2001) / 0 (2000).
Income: Per capita income: $14,133 (2000); Median household income: $25,861 (2000); Poverty rate: 21.6% (2000); Bankruptcy rate: 3.46% (2001).
Taxes: Total county taxes per capita: $134 (2000); County property taxes per capita: $60 (2000).
Education: High school graduation rate: 73.0% (2000); College graduation rate: 8.3% (2000).
Housing: Homeownership rate: 81.6% (2000); Median home value: $62,600 (2000); Median rent: $250 per month (2000); Median age of housing: 25 years (2000).
Health: Birth rate: 112.1 per 10,000 population (1998); Age adjusted death rate: 89.8 per 10,000 population (1999); Age adjusted cancer mortality rate: 194.1 deaths per 100,000 population (1999). Number of physicians: n/a (1999); Number of hospital beds: n/a (1999).
Elections: 2000 Presidential election results: 33.4% Gore, 62.1% Bush, 2.8% Nader, 1.3% Buchanan
National and State Parks: Caney Mountain State Game Refuge
Additional Information Contacts
Ozark County Government Offices 417-679-3516
Gainesville Chamber of Commerce 417-679-4913

Ozark County Communities

BAKERSFIELD (village). Covers a land area of 1.421 square miles and a water area of 0 square miles. Located at 36.52° N. Lat.; 92.14° W. Long. Elevation is 718 feet.
Population: 285 (2000); Race: 94.5% White, 0.0% Black, 0.0% Asian, 0.0% American Indian and Alaska Native, 5.1% Hispanic of any race, 0.3% two or more races (2000); Density: 200.6 persons per square mile (2000); Age: 27.4% under 18, 16.4% over 64 (2000); Marriage status: 11.8% never married, 74.5% now married, 5.5% widowed, 8.2% divorced (2000); Foreign born: 1.4% (2000); Ancestry (includes multiple ancestries): 9.9% Irish, 9.9% United States or American, 4.5% English, 3.1% Other groups, 2.7% German (2000).
Economy: Cattle; timber, wood products. Employment by occupation: 3.6% management, 19.4% professional, 19.4% services, 16.5% sales, 0.0% farming, 10.8% construction, 30.2% production (2000).
Income: Per capita income: $10,752 (2000); Median household income: $20,139 (2000); Poverty rate: 20.9% (2000).
Taxes: Total city taxes per capita: $40 (1997); City property taxes per capita: $40 (1997).
Education: High school graduation rate: 65.1% (2000); College graduation rate: 4.8% (2000).

School District(s)

Bakersfield R-IV (PK-12)
2000 Enrollment: 395 417-284-7333

Housing: Homeownership rate: 64.7% (2000); Median home value: $43,000 (2000); Median rent: $246 per month (2000); Median age of housing: 33 years (2000).
Transportation: Commute to work: 94.8% car, 0.0% public transportation, 5.2% walk, 0.0% work from home (2000); Travel time to work: 30.6% less than 15 minutes, 10.4% 15 to 30 minutes, 48.5% 30 to 45 minutes, 6.7% 45 to 60 minutes, 3.7% 60 minutes or more (2000)

BRIXEY (unincorporated postal area, zip code 65618). Covers a land area of 26.422 square miles and a water area of 0 square miles. Located at 36.75° N. Lat.; 92.38° W. Long. Elevation is 990 feet.
Population: 158 (2000); Race: 100.0% White, 0.0% Black, 0.0% Asian, 0.0% American Indian and Alaska Native, 0.0% Hispanic of any race, 0.0% two or more races (2000); Density: 6.0 persons per square mile (2000); Age: 10.8% under 18, 16.5% over 64 (2000); Marriage status: 13.7% never married, 63.4% now married, 10.6% widowed, 12.4% divorced (2000); Foreign born: 0.0% (2000); Ancestry (includes multiple ancestries): 23.9% Other groups, 14.2% English, 14.2% Irish, 12.5% Scotch-Irish, 4.0% German (2000).
Economy: Employment by occupation: 18.8% management, 10.0% professional, 20.0% services, 0.0% sales, 2.5% farming, 13.8% construction, 35.0% production (2000).
Income: Per capita income: $14,873 (2000); Median household income: $25,000 (2000); Poverty rate: 8.5% (2000).
Education: High school graduation rate: 77.5% (2000); College graduation rate: 4.9% (2000).
Housing: Homeownership rate: 100.0% (2000); Median home value: $162,500 (2000); Median age of housing: 27 years (2000).
Transportation: Commute to work: 77.5% car, 0.0% public transportation, 8.8% walk, 13.8% work from home (2000); Travel time to work: 44.9% less than 15 minutes, 5.8% 15 to 30 minutes, 24.6% 30 to 45 minutes, 14.5% 45 to 60 minutes, 10.1% 60 minutes or more (2000)

DORA (unincorporated postal area, zip code 65637). Covers a land area of 96.779 square miles and a water area of 0 square miles. Located at 36.75° N. Lat.; 92.17° W. Long. Elevation is 1,042 feet.
Population: 1,162 (2000); Race: 94.2% White, 0.0% Black, 0.0% Asian, 0.5% American Indian and Alaska Native, 1.3% Hispanic of any race, 5.0% two or more races (2000); Density: 12.0 persons per square mile (2000); Age: 24.6% under 18, 14.7% over 64 (2000); Marriage status: 20.8% never married, 66.4% now married, 6.8% widowed, 6.1% divorced (2000); Foreign born: 0.5% (2000); Ancestry (includes multiple ancestries): 30.3% United

States or American, 9.5% Other groups, 8.8% Irish, 8.6% English, 6.4% German (2000).
Economy: Employment by occupation: 12.9% management, 8.2% professional, 13.0% services, 18.5% sales, 7.1% farming, 13.6% construction, 26.8% production (2000).
Income: Per capita income: $12,041 (2000); Median household income: $25,043 (2000); Poverty rate: 21.5% (2000).
Education: High school graduation rate: 78.0% (2000); College graduation rate: 8.8% (2000).

School District(s)

Dora R-III (PK-12)
2000 Enrollment: 313 417-261-2346
Housing: Homeownership rate: 81.7% (2000); Median home value: $50,600 (2000); Median rent: $221 per month (2000); Median age of housing: 24 years (2000).
Transportation: Commute to work: 89.6% car, 0.4% public transportation, 2.0% walk, 7.6% work from home (2000); Travel time to work: 20.3% less than 15 minutes, 21.3% 15 to 30 minutes, 38.6% 30 to 45 minutes, 13.5% 45 to 60 minutes, 6.4% 60 minutes or more (2000)

GAINESVILLE (city). Covers a land area of 2.641 square miles and a water area of 0 square miles. Located at 36.60° N. Lat.; 92.43° W. Long. Elevation is 759 feet.
Population: 632 (2000); Race: 96.9% White, 0.0% Black, 0.0% Asian, 0.9% American Indian and Alaska Native, 1.5% Hispanic of any race, 1.9% two or more races (2000); Density: 239.3 persons per square mile (2000); Age: 24.5% under 18, 22.4% over 64 (2000); Marriage status: 12.8% never married, 62.9% now married, 12.4% widowed, 12.0% divorced (2000); Foreign born: 0.9% (2000); Ancestry (includes multiple ancestries): 19.7% United States or American, 16.7% German, 13.2% Irish, 8.5% English, 7.6% Other groups (2000).
Economy: Lumber products. Manufacturing: wood products. Tourism center for recreation on nearby lakes. Single-family building permits issued: 1 (2001) / 1 (2000); Multi-family building permits issued: 0 (2001) / 0 (2000); Employment by occupation: 8.5% management, 18.5% professional, 12.7% services, 20.0% sales, 0.8% farming, 8.8% construction, 30.8% production (2000).
Income: Per capita income: $14,566 (2000); Median household income: $23,083 (2000); Poverty rate: 18.4% (2000).
Taxes: Total city taxes per capita: $338 (1997); City property taxes per capita: $79 (1997).
Education: High school graduation rate: 73.8% (2000); College graduation rate: 11.4% (2000).

School District(s)

Gainesville R-V (PK-12)
2000 Enrollment: 759 417-679-4260
Housing: Homeownership rate: 61.8% (2000); Median home value: $46,800 (2000); Median rent: $233 per month (2000); Median age of housing: 35 years (2000).
Newspapers: Ozark County Times (1 x week)
Transportation: Commute to work: 95.4% car, 0.8% public transportation, 3.1% walk, 0.8% work from home (2000); Travel time to work: 51.2% less than 15 minutes, 6.2% 15 to 30 minutes, 27.5% 30 to 45 minutes, 12.0% 45 to 60 minutes, 3.1% 60 minutes or more (2000)
Additional Information Contacts
Gainesville Chamber of Commerce 417-679-4913

ISABELLA (unincorporated postal area, zip code 65676). Covers a land area of 18.547 square miles and a water area of 0 square miles. Located at 36.57° N. Lat.; 92.62° W. Long. Elevation is 958 feet.
Population: 549 (2000); Race: 100.0% White, 0.0% Black, 0.0% Asian, 0.0% American Indian and Alaska Native, 0.0% Hispanic of any race, 0.0% two or more races (2000); Density: 29.6 persons per square mile (2000); Age: 17.0% under 18, 18.0% over 64 (2000); Marriage status: 13.5% never married, 71.5% now married, 6.6% widowed, 8.4% divorced (2000); Foreign born: 4.0% (2000); Ancestry (includes multiple ancestries): 19.4% German, 15.8% Other groups, 14.6% United States or American, 8.2% English, 6.6% Irish (2000).
Economy: Employment by occupation: 22.5% management, 5.6% professional, 15.7% services, 19.1% sales, 1.1% farming, 7.9% construction, 28.1% production (2000).
Income: Per capita income: $18,450 (2000); Median household income: $28,214 (2000); Poverty rate: 18.9% (2000).
Education: High school graduation rate: 71.1% (2000); College graduation rate: 8.9% (2000).
Housing: Homeownership rate: 87.3% (2000); Median home value: $96,900 (2000); Median rent: $260 per month (2000); Median age of housing: 24 years (2000).
Transportation: Commute to work: 79.1% car, 0.0% public transportation, 7.6% walk, 13.4% work from home (2000); Travel time to work: 20.1% less than 15 minutes, 32.9% 15 to 30 minutes, 18.8% 30 to 45 minutes, 9.4% 45 to 60 minutes, 18.8% 60 minutes or more (2000)

NOBLE (unincorporated postal area, zip code 65715). Covers a land area of 18.294 square miles and a water area of 0 square miles. Located at 36.73° N. Lat.; 92.58° W. Long. Elevation is 1,040 feet.
Population: 146 (2000); Race: 91.3% White, 0.0% Black, 0.0% Asian, 0.0% American Indian and Alaska Native, 0.0% Hispanic of any race, 8.7% two or more races (2000); Density: 8.0 persons per square mile (2000); Age: 28.3% under 18, 26.8% over 64 (2000); Marriage status: 15.7% never married, 45.4% now married, 13.0% widowed, 25.9% divorced (2000); Foreign born: 1.4% (2000); Ancestry (includes multiple ancestries): 22.5% German, 14.5% European, 13.0% United States or American, 10.1% Scotch-Irish, 9.4% Other groups (2000).
Economy: Employment by occupation: 29.8% management, 0.0% professional, 0.0% services, 34.0% sales, 6.4% farming, 4.3% construction, 25.5% production (2000).
Income: Per capita income: $10,478 (2000); Median household income: $16,953 (2000); Poverty rate: 20.3% (2000).
Education: High school graduation rate: 91.3% (2000); College graduation rate: 0.0% (2000).
Housing: Homeownership rate: 84.4% (2000); Median home value: $71,000 (2000); Median age of housing: 52 years (2000).
Transportation: Commute to work: 100.0% car, 0.0% public transportation, 0.0% walk, 0.0% work from home (2000); Travel time to work: 17.0% less than 15 minutes, 53.2% 15 to 30 minutes, 0.0% 30 to 45 minutes, 14.9% 45 to 60 minutes, 14.9% 60 minutes or more (2000)

PONTIAC (unincorporated postal area, zip code 65729). Covers a land area of 9.446 square miles and a water area of 0.004 square miles. Located at 36.52° N. Lat.; 92.59° W. Long. Elevation is 825 feet.
Population: 223 (2000); Race: 100.0% White, 0.0% Black, 0.0% Asian, 0.0% American Indian and Alaska Native, 0.0% Hispanic of any race, 0.0% two or more races (2000); Density: 23.6 persons per square mile (2000); Age: 11.4% under 18, 43.1% over 64 (2000); Marriage status: 13.3% never married, 63.8% now married, 14.8% widowed, 8.2% divorced (2000); Foreign born: 0.0% (2000); Ancestry (includes multiple ancestries): 19.9% English, 19.9% German, 12.3% Irish, 11.8% Other groups, 4.7% French (except Basque) (2000).
Economy: Employment by occupation: 17.9% management, 17.9% professional, 10.7% services, 17.9% sales, 0.0% farming, 23.2% construction, 12.5% production (2000).
Income: Per capita income: $27,499 (2000); Median household income: $21,094 (2000); Poverty rate: 14.7% (2000).
Education: High school graduation rate: 72.1% (2000); College graduation rate: 17.5% (2000).
Housing: Homeownership rate: 81.9% (2000); Median home value: $85,000 (2000); Median rent: $291 per month (2000); Median age of housing: 23 years (2000).
Transportation: Commute to work: 100.0% car, 0.0% public transportation, 0.0% walk, 0.0% work from home (2000); Travel time to work: 8.9% less than 15 minutes, 50.0% 15 to 30 minutes, 39.3% 30 to 45 minutes, 0.0% 45 to 60 minutes, 1.8% 60 minutes or more (2000)

SUNDOWN (village). Aka Theodosia Hills. Covers a land area of 1.072 square miles and a water area of 0 square miles. Located at 36.56° N. Lat.; 92.63° W. Long. Elevation is 860 feet.
Population: 38 (2000); Race: 100.0% White, 0.0% Black, 0.0% Asian, 0.0% American Indian and Alaska Native, 0.0% Hispanic of any race, 0.0% two or more races (2000); Density: 35.4 persons per square mile (2000); Age: 25.7% under 18, 31.4% over 64 (2000); Marriage status: 16.1% never married, 71.0% now married, 12.9% widowed, 0.0% divorced (2000); Foreign born: 8.6% (2000); Ancestry (includes multiple ancestries): 37.1% German, 25.7% United States or American, 11.4% Irish, 5.7% French (except Basque), 5.7% Other groups (2000).
Economy: Employment by occupation: 28.6% management, 0.0% professional, 28.6% services, 0.0% sales, 0.0% farming, 0.0% construction, 42.9% production (2000).
Income: Per capita income: $15,360 (2000); Median household income: $24,500 (2000); Poverty rate: 8.6% (2000).

Taxes: Total city taxes per capita: $105 (1997); City property taxes per capita: $105 (1997).
Education: High school graduation rate: 76.9% (2000); College graduation rate: 15.4% (2000).
Housing: Homeownership rate: 100.0% (2000); Median home value: $102,100 (2000); Median age of housing: 25 years (2000).
Transportation: Commute to work: 100.0% car, 0.0% public transportation, 0.0% walk, 0.0% work from home (2000); Travel time to work: 57.1% less than 15 minutes, 0.0% 15 to 30 minutes, 0.0% 30 to 45 minutes, 0.0% 45 to 60 minutes, 42.9% 60 minutes or more (2000)

TECUMSEH (unincorporated postal area, zip code 65760). Covers a land area of 35.636 square miles and a water area of 0 square miles. Located at 36.60° N. Lat.; 92.26° W. Long. Elevation is 600 feet.
Population: 624 (2000); Race: 97.9% White, 0.5% Black, 0.0% Asian, 0.3% American Indian and Alaska Native, 2.2% Hispanic of any race, 1.2% two or more races (2000); Density: 17.5 persons per square mile (2000); Age: 20.5% under 18, 18.6% over 64 (2000); Marriage status: 15.9% never married, 67.1% now married, 6.3% widowed, 10.6% divorced (2000); Foreign born: 2.9% (2000); Ancestry (includes multiple ancestries): 17.9% German, 11.9% United States or American, 9.1% English, 8.1% Irish, 6.7% Other groups (2000).
Economy: Employment by occupation: 6.0% management, 10.3% professional, 27.8% services, 21.0% sales, 2.8% farming, 14.7% construction, 17.5% production (2000).
Income: Per capita income: $12,700 (2000); Median household income: $25,083 (2000); Poverty rate: 21.5% (2000).
Education: High school graduation rate: 79.4% (2000); College graduation rate: 4.9% (2000).
Housing: Homeownership rate: 82.0% (2000); Median home value: $66,400 (2000); Median rent: $239 per month (2000); Median age of housing: 19 years (2000).
Transportation: Commute to work: 86.7% car, 0.8% public transportation, 0.8% walk, 8.1% work from home (2000); Travel time to work: 18.9% less than 15 minutes, 30.3% 15 to 30 minutes, 27.2% 30 to 45 minutes, 19.7% 45 to 60 minutes, 3.9% 60 minutes or more (2000)

THEODOSIA (village). Aka Lutie. Covers a land area of 1.346 square miles and a water area of 0.195 square miles. Located at 36.57° N. Lat.; 92.66° W. Long. Elevation is 890 feet.
Population: 240 (2000); Race: 99.2% White, 0.0% Black, 0.0% Asian, 0.0% American Indian and Alaska Native, 1.2% Hispanic of any race, 0.8% two or more races (2000); Density: 178.3 persons per square mile (2000); Age: 23.2% under 18, 26.3% over 64 (2000); Marriage status: 11.6% never married, 64.4% now married, 8.8% widowed, 15.3% divorced (2000); Foreign born: 0.0% (2000); Ancestry (includes multiple ancestries): 20.5% German, 13.1% Other groups, 12.0% English, 10.4% United States or American, 10.0% Irish (2000).
Economy: Single-family building permits issued: 1 (2001) / 4 (2000); Multi-family building permits issued: 0 (2001) / 0 (2000); Employment by occupation: 17.9% management, 23.9% professional, 14.9% services, 16.4% sales, 0.0% farming, 13.4% construction, 13.4% production (2000).
Income: Per capita income: $13,149 (2000); Median household income: $23,750 (2000); Poverty rate: 28.8% (2000).
Taxes: Total city taxes per capita: $181 (1997); City property taxes per capita: $26 (1997).
Education: High school graduation rate: 66.8% (2000); College graduation rate: 13.9% (2000).

School District(s)

Lutie R-VI (PK-12)
2000 Enrollment: 258 417-273-4274
Housing: Homeownership rate: 78.9% (2000); Median home value: $59,700 (2000); Median rent: $333 per month (2000); Median age of housing: 25 years (2000).
Transportation: Commute to work: 68.7% car, 0.0% public transportation, 16.4% walk, 14.9% work from home (2000); Travel time to work: 54.4% less than 15 minutes, 19.3% 15 to 30 minutes, 3.5% 30 to 45 minutes, 5.3% 45 to 60 minutes, 17.5% 60 minutes or more (2000)

THORNFIELD (unincorporated postal area, zip code 65762). Covers a land area of 69.473 square miles and a water area of 0 square miles. Located at 36.68° N. Lat.; 92.66° W. Long. Elevation is 805 feet.
Population: 453 (2000); Race: 99.1% White, 0.0% Black, 0.6% Asian, 0.0% American Indian and Alaska Native, 0.0% Hispanic of any race, 0.2% two or more races (2000); Density: 6.5 persons per square mile (2000); Age: 24.7% under 18, 15.8% over 64 (2000); Marriage status: 14.3% never married, 70.5% now married, 5.1% widowed, 10.0% divorced (2000); Foreign born: 1.3% (2000); Ancestry (includes multiple ancestries): 18.6% German, 14.9% United States or American, 11.3% Irish, 7.1% English, 2.8% Other groups (2000).
Economy: Employment by occupation: 18.9% management, 13.9% professional, 14.9% services, 17.9% sales, 6.5% farming, 12.4% construction, 15.4% production (2000).
Income: Per capita income: $12,353 (2000); Median household income: $27,917 (2000); Poverty rate: 12.4% (2000).
Education: High school graduation rate: 75.6% (2000); College graduation rate: 9.2% (2000).

School District(s)

Thornfield R-I (KG-08)
2000 Enrollment: 80 417-265-3212
Housing: Homeownership rate: 83.8% (2000); Median home value: $55,000 (2000); Median rent: $170 per month (2000); Median age of housing: 26 years (2000).
Transportation: Commute to work: 86.7% car, 0.0% public transportation, 0.0% walk, 10.3% work from home (2000); Travel time to work: 24.2% less than 15 minutes, 26.4% 15 to 30 minutes, 31.3% 30 to 45 minutes, 5.5% 45 to 60 minutes, 12.6% 60 minutes or more (2000)

UDALL (unincorporated postal area, zip code 65766). Covers a land area of 8.995 square miles and a water area of 0 square miles. Located at 36.54° N. Lat.; 92.25° W. Long. Elevation is 845 feet.
Population: 148 (2000); Race: 97.6% White, 0.0% Black, 0.0% Asian, 0.0% American Indian and Alaska Native, 0.0% Hispanic of any race, 2.4% two or more races (2000); Density: 16.5 persons per square mile (2000); Age: 9.6% under 18, 23.2% over 64 (2000); Marriage status: 13.3% never married, 77.0% now married, 5.3% widowed, 4.4% divorced (2000); Foreign born: 0.0% (2000); Ancestry (includes multiple ancestries): 21.6% Irish, 20.8% United States or American, 14.4% Other groups, 9.6% Dutch, 7.2% German (2000).
Economy: Employment by occupation: 2.9% management, 5.7% professional, 2.9% services, 20.0% sales, 2.9% farming, 17.1% construction, 48.6% production (2000).
Income: Per capita income: $12,200 (2000); Median household income: $21,250 (2000); Poverty rate: 25.6% (2000).
Education: High school graduation rate: 63.0% (2000); College graduation rate: 8.0% (2000).
Housing: Homeownership rate: 87.3% (2000); Median home value: $46,700 (2000); Median rent: $213 per month (2000); Median age of housing: 24 years (2000).
Transportation: Commute to work: 93.3% car, 0.0% public transportation, 6.7% walk, 0.0% work from home (2000); Travel time to work: 23.3% less than 15 minutes, 10.0% 15 to 30 minutes, 6.7% 30 to 45 minutes, 56.7% 45 to 60 minutes, 3.3% 60 minutes or more (2000)

WASOLA (unincorporated postal area, zip code 65773). Covers a land area of 78.294 square miles and a water area of 0 square miles. Located at 36.75° N. Lat.; 92.53° W. Long. Elevation is 1,294 feet.
Population: 778 (2000); Race: 95.2% White, 0.0% Black, 0.0% Asian, 0.8% American Indian and Alaska Native, 0.1% Hispanic of any race, 2.9% two or more races (2000); Density: 9.9 persons per square mile (2000); Age: 20.8% under 18, 23.6% over 64 (2000); Marriage status: 12.0% never married, 71.0% now married, 8.1% widowed, 8.9% divorced (2000); Foreign born: 0.8% (2000); Ancestry (includes multiple ancestries): 24.6% United States or American, 13.1% Other groups, 11.7% German, 9.0% Irish, 7.3% English (2000).
Economy: Employment by occupation: 20.4% management, 13.5% professional, 16.5% services, 17.3% sales, 2.7% farming, 14.6% construction, 15.0% production (2000).
Income: Per capita income: $10,193 (2000); Median household income: $19,917 (2000); Poverty rate: 38.7% (2000).
Education: High school graduation rate: 62.2% (2000); College graduation rate: 6.8% (2000).
Housing: Homeownership rate: 81.3% (2000); Median home value: $58,300 (2000); Median rent: $213 per month (2000); Median age of housing: 32 years (2000).
Transportation: Commute to work: 83.7% car, 0.0% public transportation, 2.4% walk, 13.9% work from home (2000); Travel time to work: 24.9% less than 15 minutes, 46.1% 15 to 30 minutes, 9.2% 30 to 45 minutes, 2.8% 45 to 60 minutes, 17.1% 60 minutes or more (2000)

ZANONI (unincorporated postal area, zip code 65784). Covers a land area of 3.873 square miles and a water area of 0 square miles. Located at 36.69° N. Lat.; 92.32° W. Long. Elevation is 710 feet.
Population: 34 (2000); Race: 100.0% White, 0.0% Black, 0.0% Asian, 0.0% American Indian and Alaska Native, 0.0% Hispanic of any race, 0.0% two or more races (2000); Density: 8.8 persons per square mile (2000); Age: 41.7% under 18, 0.0% over 64 (2000); Marriage status: 0.0% never married, 85.7% now married, 0.0% widowed, 14.3% divorced (2000); Foreign born: 0.0% (2000); Ancestry (includes multiple ancestries): 45.8% Other groups, 25.0% German, 16.7% Irish, 8.3% United States or American (2000).
Economy: Employment by occupation: 0.0% management, 18.2% professional, 27.3% services, 0.0% sales, 36.4% farming, 0.0% construction, 18.2% production (2000).
Income: Per capita income: $8,983 (2000); Median household income: $22,083 (2000); Poverty rate: 0.0% (2000).
Education: High school graduation rate: 63.6% (2000); College graduation rate: 0.0% (2000).
Housing: Homeownership rate: 87.5% (2000); Median rent: $275 per month (2000); Median age of housing: 32 years (2000).
Transportation: Commute to work: 100.0% car, 0.0% public transportation, 0.0% walk, 0.0% work from home (2000); Travel time to work: 36.4% less than 15 minutes, 18.2% 15 to 30 minutes, 45.5% 30 to 45 minutes, 0.0% 45 to 60 minutes, 0.0% 60 minutes or more (2000)

Pemiscot County

Located in southeastern Missouri; bounded on the east by the Mississippi River and the Tennessee border. Covers a land area of 493.10 square miles, a water area of 19.30 square miles, and is located in the Central Time Zone. The county government was organized in 1851. County seat is Caruthersville.

Weather Station: Caruthersville — Elevation: 278 feet

	Jan	Feb	Mar	Apr	May	Jun	Jul	Aug	Sep	Oct	Nov	Dec
High	43	49	59	70	79	87	90	89	82	72	59	48
Low	26	30	38	48	58	66	70	68	60	48	39	31
Precip	3.4	3.8	4.8	5.1	4.9	4.6	3.9	3.1	3.2	3.7	4.8	4.8
Snow	2.1	1.8	0.4	tr	0.0	0.0	0.0	0.0	0.0	tr	0.2	0.4

High and Low temperatures in degrees Fahrenheit; Precipitation and Snow in inches

Weather Station: Portageville — Elevation: 278 feet

	Jan	Feb	Mar	Apr	May	Jun	Jul	Aug	Sep	Oct	Nov	Dec
High	42	48	57	69	78	87	90	88	82	72	58	47
Low	26	30	39	48	58	66	70	68	60	48	40	31
Precip	3.1	3.5	4.5	5.2	4.8	4.4	3.5	2.9	3.3	3.7	4.4	4.4
Snow	3.8	3.0	1.3	tr	0.0	0.0	0.0	0.0	0.0	tr	0.3	1.3

High and Low temperatures in degrees Fahrenheit; Precipitation and Snow in inches

Population: 20,047 (2000); Race: 71.4% White, 27.3% Black, 0.2% Asian, 0.1% American Indian and Alaska Native, 1.5% Hispanic of any race, 0.6% two or more races (2000); Density: 40.7 persons per square mile (2000); Age: 29.9% under 18, 15.1% over 64 (2000).
Religion: Five largest groups: 43.1% Southern Baptist Convention, 4.6% The United Methodist Church, 2.9% Churches of Christ, 1.8% Presbyterian Church (U.S.A.), 1.7% The Wesleyan Church (2000).
Economy: Unemployment rate: 10.2% (11/2002); Total civilian labor force: 7,944 (11/2002); Leading industries: 24.5% health care and social assistance; 20.3% manufacturing; 15.5% retail trade (2000); Companies that employ more than 1,000 persons: 0 (2000); Companies that employ more than 100 persons: 4 (2000); Farms: 306 totaling 295,743 acres (1997); Minority business ownership rate: 37.3% (1997); Women business ownership rate: 30.2% (1997); Retail sales per capita: $6,025 (1997). Single-family building permits issued: 12 (2001) / 26 (2000); Multi-family building permits issued: 0 (2001) / 10 (2000).
Income: Per capita income: $12,968 (2000); Median household income: $21,911 (2000); Poverty rate: 30.4% (2000); Bankruptcy rate: 4.64% (2001).
Taxes: Total county taxes per capita: $84 (2000); County property taxes per capita: $44 (2000).
Education: High school graduation rate: 58.2% (2000); College graduation rate: 8.4% (2000).
Housing: Homeownership rate: 58.4% (2000); Median home value: $44,200 (2000); Median rent: $199 per month (2000); Median age of housing: 33 years (2000).
Health: Birth rate: 174.6 per 10,000 population (1998); Age adjusted death rate: 128.7 per 10,000 population (1999); Age adjusted cancer mortality rate: 233.2 deaths per 100,000 population (1999). Number of physicians: 8.0 per 10,000 population (1999); Number of hospital beds: 84.3 per 10,000 population (1999).
Elections: 2000 Presidential election results: 53.6% Gore, 45.4% Bush, 0.6% Nader, 0.3% Buchanan
Additional Information Contacts
Pemiscot County Government Offices. 573-333-4203
Caruthersville Chamber of Commerce. 573-333-1222
Hayti Chamber of Commerce. 573-359-0632

Pemiscot County Communities

BRAGG CITY (town). Covers a land area of 0.205 square miles and a water area of 0 square miles. Located at 36.26° N. Lat.; 89.91° W. Long. Elevation is 263 feet.
Population: 189 (2000); Race: 93.1% White, 0.0% Black, 4.8% Asian, 2.2% American Indian and Alaska Native, 3.0% Hispanic of any race, 0.0% two or more races (2000); Density: 923.5 persons per square mile (2000); Age: 29.0% under 18, 16.5% over 64 (2000); Marriage status: 15.1% never married, 63.8% now married, 9.2% widowed, 11.9% divorced (2000); Foreign born: 6.9% (2000); Ancestry (includes multiple ancestries): 41.6% United States or American, 17.7% Other groups, 15.6% Irish, 12.6% English, 3.9% German (2000).
Economy: Rice, cotton, broom corn, soybeans. Employment by occupation: 2.7% management, 9.6% professional, 16.4% services, 20.5% sales, 5.5% farming, 11.0% construction, 34.2% production (2000).
Income: Per capita income: $12,214 (2000); Median household income: $26,042 (2000); Poverty rate: 18.8% (2000).
Taxes: Total city taxes per capita: $43 (1997); City property taxes per capita: $0 (1997).
Education: High school graduation rate: 47.7% (2000); College graduation rate: 5.9% (2000).
Housing: Homeownership rate: 88.9% (2000); Median home value: $30,600 (2000); Median rent: $200 per month (2000); Median age of housing: 36 years (2000).
Transportation: Commute to work: 90.4% car, 0.0% public transportation, 2.7% walk, 0.0% work from home (2000); Travel time to work: 12.3% less than 15 minutes, 65.8% 15 to 30 minutes, 16.4% 30 to 45 minutes, 2.7% 45 to 60 minutes, 2.7% 60 minutes or more (2000)

CARUTHERSVILLE (city). Covers a land area of 5.237 square miles and a water area of 0.009 square miles. Located at 36.18° N. Lat.; 89.66° W. Long. Elevation is 282 feet.
History: Caruthersville began as La Petite Prairie, a French trading post settled about 1794 by fur trader Francois Le Sieur, who also established a post at New Madrid. John Hardeman Walker and his family came here from Tennessee in 1810. It was Walker who campaigned to have the southeastern "boot heel" included in the state of Missouri. In 1857 Walker and George W. Bushey platted the town and named it for Samuel Caruthers, a Madison County lawyer and judge.
Population: 6,760 (2000); Race: 66.8% White, 32.1% Black, 0.0% Asian, 0.2% American Indian and Alaska Native, 2.3% Hispanic of any race, 0.7% two or more races (2000); Density: 1,290.8 persons per square mile (2000); Age: 32.5% under 18, 14.1% over 64 (2000); Marriage status: 27.6% never married, 50.0% now married, 10.6% widowed, 11.8% divorced (2000); Foreign born: 0.5% (2000); Ancestry (includes multiple ancestries): 34.3% Other groups, 19.4% United States or American, 6.3% Irish, 6.1% German, 3.9% English (2000).
Economy: Single-family building permits issued: 4 (2001) / 9 (2000); Multi-family building permits issued: 0 (2001) / 10 (2000); Employment by occupation: 6.4% management, 11.6% professional, 22.3% services, 24.4% sales, 0.8% farming, 7.8% construction, 26.6% production (2000).
Income: Per capita income: $12,034 (2000); Median household income: $19,601 (2000); Poverty rate: 35.7% (2000).
Taxes: Total city taxes per capita: $141 (1997); City property taxes per capita: $47 (1997).
Education: High school graduation rate: 58.6% (2000); College graduation rate: 8.3% (2000).

School District(s)

Caruthersville 18 (PK-12)
2000 Enrollment: 1,569 573-333-6100
Pemiscot Co. R-III (KG-08)
2000 Enrollment: 155 573-333-1856
Housing: Homeownership rate: 51.5% (2000); Median home value: $45,100 (2000); Median rent: $233 per month (2000); Median age of housing: 35 years (2000).

Newspapers: The Bootheel Beacon (1 x week); The Thursday Democrat-Argus (1 x week)
Transportation: Commute to work: 92.8% car, 0.7% public transportation, 2.0% walk, 2.3% work from home (2000); Travel time to work: 58.4% less than 15 minutes, 25.6% 15 to 30 minutes, 10.5% 30 to 45 minutes, 2.9% 45 to 60 minutes, 2.6% 60 minutes or more (2000)
Airports: Caruthersville Memorial
Additional Information Contacts
Caruthersville Chamber of Commerce.......................573-333-1222

COOTER (city). Covers a land area of 0.295 square miles and a water area of 0 square miles. Located at 36.04° N. Lat.; 89.81° W. Long. Elevation is 258 feet.
Population: 440 (2000); Race: 99.1% White, 0.0% Black, 0.0% Asian, 0.5% American Indian and Alaska Native, 0.5% Hispanic of any race, 0.5% two or more races (2000); Density: 1,492.5 persons per square mile (2000); Age: 24.2% under 18, 16.7% over 64 (2000); Marriage status: 14.7% never married, 64.0% now married, 9.5% widowed, 11.8% divorced (2000); Foreign born: 0.0% (2000); Ancestry (includes multiple ancestries): 21.5% United States or American, 13.5% English, 13.2% Irish, 8.0% Other groups, 2.1% Italian (2000).
Economy: Cotton, rice, corn, soybeans. Employment by occupation: 5.2% management, 19.2% professional, 16.3% services, 17.4% sales, 4.1% farming, 18.0% construction, 19.8% production (2000).
Income: Per capita income: $13,267 (2000); Median household income: $28,750 (2000); Poverty rate: 20.6% (2000).
Taxes: Total city taxes per capita: $80 (1997); City property taxes per capita: $28 (1997).
Education: High school graduation rate: 62.8% (2000); College graduation rate: 11.3% (2000).

School District(s)

Cooter R-IV (KG-12)
2000 Enrollment: 257.......................573-695-3312
Housing: Homeownership rate: 70.3% (2000); Median home value: $38,800 (2000); Median rent: $211 per month (2000); Median age of housing: 35 years (2000).
Transportation: Commute to work: 86.0% car, 0.0% public transportation, 7.6% walk, 5.2% work from home (2000); Travel time to work: 27.6% less than 15 minutes, 49.1% 15 to 30 minutes, 14.7% 30 to 45 minutes, 4.9% 45 to 60 minutes, 3.7% 60 minutes or more (2000)

GOBLER (unincorporated postal area, zip code 63849). Covers a land area of 26.653 square miles and a water area of 0 square miles. Located at 36.12° N. Lat.; 89.99° W. Long. Elevation is 255 feet.
Population: 227 (2000); Race: 61.0% White, 37.7% Black, 0.0% Asian, 0.0% American Indian and Alaska Native, 0.0% Hispanic of any race, 1.3% two or more races (2000); Density: 8.5 persons per square mile (2000); Age: 25.6% under 18, 10.7% over 64 (2000); Marriage status: 29.7% never married, 51.2% now married, 9.4% widowed, 9.8% divorced (2000); Foreign born: 0.0% (2000); Ancestry (includes multiple ancestries): 25.3% Other groups, 14.3% United States or American, 13.0% English, 7.8% German, 7.1% Italian (2000).
Economy: Employment by occupation: 11.9% management, 0.7% professional, 19.9% services, 24.5% sales, 4.0% farming, 6.6% construction, 32.5% production (2000).
Income: Per capita income: $11,623 (2000); Median household income: $26,964 (2000); Poverty rate: 24.8% (2000).
Education: High school graduation rate: 65.8% (2000); College graduation rate: 1.1% (2000).
Housing: Homeownership rate: 74.5% (2000); Median home value: $62,100 (2000); Median rent: $189 per month (2000); Median age of housing: 29 years (2000).
Transportation: Commute to work: 97.4% car, 0.0% public transportation, 0.0% walk, 1.3% work from home (2000); Travel time to work: 22.1% less than 15 minutes, 44.3% 15 to 30 minutes, 23.5% 30 to 45 minutes, 8.7% 45 to 60 minutes, 1.3% 60 minutes or more (2000)

HAYTI (city). Covers a land area of 2.212 square miles and a water area of 0 square miles. Located at 36.23° N. Lat.; 89.74° W. Long. Elevation is 273 feet.
History: Hayti grew as a cotton town around a railroad shipping center.
Population: 3,207 (2000); Race: 52.9% White, 44.9% Black, 0.3% Asian, 0.0% American Indian and Alaska Native, 1.0% Hispanic of any race, 1.3% two or more races (2000); Density: 1,450.1 persons per square mile (2000); Age: 28.5% under 18, 19.8% over 64 (2000); Marriage status: 26.1% never married, 47.6% now married, 14.9% widowed, 11.4% divorced (2000); Foreign born: 2.2% (2000); Ancestry (includes multiple ancestries): 45.6% Other groups, 10.9% United States or American, 6.1% Irish, 4.0% English, 1.8% German (2000).
Economy: Single-family building permits issued: 1 (2001) / 8 (2000); Multi-family building permits issued: 0 (2001) / 0 (2000); Employment by occupation: 6.9% management, 14.8% professional, 24.4% services, 23.1% sales, 0.0% farming, 8.9% construction, 21.9% production (2000).
Income: Per capita income: $13,265 (2000); Median household income: $15,384 (2000); Poverty rate: 38.3% (2000).
Taxes: Total city taxes per capita: $382 (1997); City property taxes per capita: $0 (1997).
Education: High school graduation rate: 51.8% (2000); College graduation rate: 7.4% (2000).

School District(s)

Hayti R-II (PK-12)
2000 Enrollment: 990.......................573-359-6500
Pemiscot Co. Spec. School Dist. (11-12)
2000 Enrollment: 0.......................573-359-0021
Housing: Homeownership rate: 51.3% (2000); Median home value: $39,300 (2000); Median rent: $180 per month (2000); Median age of housing: 33 years (2000).
Hospitals: Pemiscot Memorial Hospital (245 beds)
Transportation: Commute to work: 98.4% car, 0.0% public transportation, 1.0% walk, 0.2% work from home (2000); Travel time to work: 57.0% less than 15 minutes, 25.4% 15 to 30 minutes, 13.8% 30 to 45 minutes, 1.4% 45 to 60 minutes, 2.4% 60 minutes or more (2000)
Additional Information Contacts
Hayti Chamber of Commerce.......................573-359-0632

HAYTI HEIGHTS (city). Covers a land area of 0.988 square miles and a water area of 0 square miles. Located at 36.23° N. Lat.; 89.77° W. Long. Elevation is 268 feet.
Population: 771 (2000); Race: 0.4% White, 99.1% Black, 0.0% Asian, 0.0% American Indian and Alaska Native, 0.0% Hispanic of any race, 0.5% two or more races (2000); Density: 780.0 persons per square mile (2000); Age: 45.8% under 18, 7.5% over 64 (2000); Marriage status: 43.5% never married, 35.8% now married, 9.9% widowed, 10.8% divorced (2000); Foreign born: 0.0% (2000); Ancestry (includes multiple ancestries): 67.0% Other groups, 9.7% United States or American, 3.2% African (2000).
Economy: Single-family building permits issued: 4 (2001) / 4 (2000); Multi-family building permits issued: 0 (2001) / 0 (2000); Employment by occupation: 9.0% management, 4.9% professional, 34.0% services, 19.4% sales, 4.9% farming, 1.4% construction, 26.4% production (2000).
Income: Per capita income: $6,398 (2000); Median household income: $12,011 (2000); Poverty rate: 57.7% (2000).
Taxes: Total city taxes per capita: $151 (1997); City property taxes per capita: $46 (1997).
Education: High school graduation rate: 38.4% (2000); College graduation rate: 2.1% (2000).
Housing: Homeownership rate: 52.6% (2000); Median home value: $22,300 (2000); Median rent: $167 per month (2000); Median age of housing: 24 years (2000).
Transportation: Commute to work: 90.8% car, 0.0% public transportation, 1.4% walk, 0.7% work from home (2000); Travel time to work: 36.2% less than 15 minutes, 25.5% 15 to 30 minutes, 22.0% 30 to 45 minutes, 8.5% 45 to 60 minutes, 7.8% 60 minutes or more (2000)

HAYWARD (town). Covers a land area of 0.236 square miles and a water area of 0 square miles. Located at 36.39° N. Lat.; 89.66° W. Long. Elevation is 282 feet.
Population: 123 (2000); Race: 100.0% White, 0.0% Black, 0.0% Asian, 0.0% American Indian and Alaska Native, 0.0% Hispanic of any race, 0.0% two or more races (2000); Density: 521.2 persons per square mile (2000); Age: 31.8% under 18, 11.4% over 64 (2000); Marriage status: 27.0% never married, 64.0% now married, 6.0% widowed, 3.0% divorced (2000); Foreign born: 0.0% (2000); Ancestry (includes multiple ancestries): 19.7% United States or American, 17.4% Other groups, 10.6% French (except Basque), 6.8% Irish, 5.3% English (2000).
Economy: Employment by occupation: 1.9% management, 5.6% professional, 20.4% services, 20.4% sales, 9.3% farming, 18.5% construction, 24.1% production (2000).
Income: Per capita income: $12,720 (2000); Median household income: $34,375 (2000); Poverty rate: 1.6% (2000).
Taxes: Total city taxes per capita: $183 (1997); City property taxes per capita: $183 (1997).

Education: High school graduation rate: 74.0% (2000); College graduation rate: 0.0% (2000).
Housing: Homeownership rate: 95.8% (2000); Median home value: $37,500 (2000); Median age of housing: 25 years (2000).
Transportation: Commute to work: 98.1% car, 0.0% public transportation, 0.0% walk, 1.9% work from home (2000); Travel time to work: 47.1% less than 15 minutes, 45.1% 15 to 30 minutes, 7.8% 30 to 45 minutes, 0.0% 45 to 60 minutes, 0.0% 60 minutes or more (2000)

HOLLAND (town). Covers a land area of 0.173 square miles and a water area of 0 square miles. Located at 36.05° N. Lat.; 89.87° W. Long. Elevation is 257 feet.
History: Holland developed as a shipping point for cotton, alfalfa, corn, and melons.
Population: 246 (2000); Race: 93.1% White, 6.5% Black, 0.0% Asian, 0.4% American Indian and Alaska Native, 0.4% Hispanic of any race, 0.0% two or more races (2000); Density: 1,424.3 persons per square mile (2000); Age: 33.5% under 18, 9.4% over 64 (2000); Marriage status: 13.4% never married, 69.8% now married, 5.8% widowed, 11.0% divorced (2000); Foreign born: 0.4% (2000); Ancestry (includes multiple ancestries): 35.5% Other groups, 23.3% United States or American, 6.5% Irish, 4.9% English, 1.6% Italian (2000).
Economy: Employment by occupation: 8.9% management, 7.9% professional, 10.9% services, 24.8% sales, 0.0% farming, 19.8% construction, 27.7% production (2000).
Income: Per capita income: $12,524 (2000); Median household income: $35,278 (2000); Poverty rate: 12.7% (2000).
Taxes: Total city taxes per capita: $61 (1997); City property taxes per capita: $16 (1997).
Education: High school graduation rate: 61.9% (2000); College graduation rate: 6.1% (2000).
Housing: Homeownership rate: 72.6% (2000); Median home value: $41,000 (2000); Median rent: $225 per month (2000); Median age of housing: 29 years (2000).
Transportation: Commute to work: 99.0% car, 0.0% public transportation, 0.0% walk, 1.0% work from home (2000); Travel time to work: 33.3% less than 15 minutes, 47.5% 15 to 30 minutes, 12.1% 30 to 45 minutes, 2.0% 45 to 60 minutes, 5.1% 60 minutes or more (2000)

HOMESTOWN (city). Covers a land area of 0.125 square miles and a water area of 0 square miles. Located at 36.33° N. Lat.; 89.82° W. Long. Elevation is 269 feet.
Population: 181 (2000); Race: 0.0% White, 100.0% Black, 0.0% Asian, 0.0% American Indian and Alaska Native, 0.0% Hispanic of any race, 0.0% two or more races (2000); Density: 1,452.6 persons per square mile (2000); Age: 35.4% under 18, 7.3% over 64 (2000); Marriage status: 30.4% never married, 51.3% now married, 8.7% widowed, 9.6% divorced (2000); Foreign born: 0.0% (2000); Ancestry (includes multiple ancestries): 60.7% Other groups, 5.6% African, 1.1% Canadian (2000).
Economy: Employment by occupation: 2.2% management, 13.0% professional, 10.9% services, 21.7% sales, 6.5% farming, 6.5% construction, 39.1% production (2000).
Income: Per capita income: $6,780 (2000); Median household income: $12,143 (2000); Poverty rate: 52.8% (2000).
Taxes: Total city taxes per capita: $4 (1997); City property taxes per capita: $4 (1997).
Education: High school graduation rate: 42.2% (2000); College graduation rate: 4.4% (2000).
Housing: Homeownership rate: 58.2% (2000); Median home value: $23,300 (2000); Median rent: $169 per month (2000); Median age of housing: 41 years (2000).
Transportation: Commute to work: 89.1% car, 0.0% public transportation, 4.3% walk, 6.5% work from home (2000); Travel time to work: 11.6% less than 15 minutes, 65.1% 15 to 30 minutes, 11.6% 30 to 45 minutes, 2.3% 45 to 60 minutes, 9.3% 60 minutes or more (2000)

NORTH WARDELL (village). Covers a land area of 0.095 square miles and a water area of 0 square miles. Located at 36.35° N. Lat.; 89.81° W. Long. Elevation is 268 feet.
Population: 170 (2000); Race: 100.0% White, 0.0% Black, 0.0% Asian, 0.0% American Indian and Alaska Native, 0.0% Hispanic of any race, 0.0% two or more races (2000); Density: 1,784.0 persons per square mile (2000); Age: 21.9% under 18, 22.7% over 64 (2000); Marriage status: 17.1% never married, 53.3% now married, 16.2% widowed, 13.3% divorced (2000); Foreign born: 0.0% (2000); Ancestry (includes multiple ancestries): 22.7% United States or American, 12.5% Irish, 9.4% English, 8.6% Other groups, 1.6% German (2000).
Economy: Employment by occupation: 0.0% management, 13.0% professional, 9.3% services, 20.4% sales, 0.0% farming, 16.7% construction, 40.7% production (2000).
Income: Per capita income: $13,172 (2000); Median household income: $27,692 (2000); Poverty rate: 16.4% (2000).
Taxes: Total city taxes per capita: $7 (1997); City property taxes per capita: $7 (1997).
Education: High school graduation rate: 64.4% (2000); College graduation rate: 2.3% (2000).
Housing: Homeownership rate: 77.4% (2000); Median home value: $31,600 (2000); Median rent: $275 per month (2000); Median age of housing: 38 years (2000).
Transportation: Commute to work: 94.2% car, 0.0% public transportation, 5.8% walk, 0.0% work from home (2000); Travel time to work: 11.5% less than 15 minutes, 65.4% 15 to 30 minutes, 21.2% 30 to 45 minutes, 1.9% 45 to 60 minutes, 0.0% 60 minutes or more (2000)

PASCOLA (village). Covers a land area of 0.239 square miles and a water area of 0 square miles. Located at 36.26° N. Lat.; 89.82° W. Long. Elevation is 268 feet.
Population: 138 (2000); Race: 100.0% White, 0.0% Black, 0.0% Asian, 0.0% American Indian and Alaska Native, 0.0% Hispanic of any race, 0.0% two or more races (2000); Density: 576.3 persons per square mile (2000); Age: 4.0% under 18, 37.6% over 64 (2000); Marriage status: 15.2% never married, 58.6% now married, 12.1% widowed, 14.1% divorced (2000); Foreign born: 0.0% (2000); Ancestry (includes multiple ancestries): 26.7% United States or American, 6.9% Other groups, 5.9% Irish, 4.0% Polish (2000).
Economy: Soybeans, cotton, corn. Employment by occupation: 0.0% management, 0.0% professional, 21.1% services, 10.5% sales, 21.1% farming, 18.4% construction, 28.9% production (2000).
Income: Per capita income: $14,229 (2000); Median household income: $18,438 (2000); Poverty rate: 22.8% (2000).
Taxes: Total city taxes per capita: $48 (1997); City property taxes per capita: $32 (1997).
Education: High school graduation rate: 24.7% (2000); College graduation rate: 0.0% (2000).
Housing: Homeownership rate: 74.5% (2000); Median home value: $30,500 (2000); Median rent: $150 per month (2000); Median age of housing: 29 years (2000).
Transportation: Commute to work: 97.4% car, 0.0% public transportation, 2.6% walk, 0.0% work from home (2000); Travel time to work: 18.4% less than 15 minutes, 68.4% 15 to 30 minutes, 13.2% 30 to 45 minutes, 0.0% 45 to 60 minutes, 0.0% 60 minutes or more (2000)

STEELE (city). Covers a land area of 1.877 square miles and a water area of 0 square miles. Located at 36.08° N. Lat.; 89.82° W. Long. Elevation is 258 feet.
History: Steele grew around the St. Louis-San Francisco Railway station built in 1901.
Population: 2,263 (2000); Race: 81.5% White, 17.6% Black, 0.4% Asian, 0.0% American Indian and Alaska Native, 0.0% Hispanic of any race, 0.6% two or more races (2000); Density: 1,205.9 persons per square mile (2000); Age: 30.0% under 18, 15.6% over 64 (2000); Marriage status: 21.2% never married, 52.6% now married, 12.9% widowed, 13.3% divorced (2000); Foreign born: 0.4% (2000); Ancestry (includes multiple ancestries): 33.5% United States or American, 19.2% Other groups, 7.0% Irish, 5.2% German, 5.1% English (2000).
Economy: Single-family building permits issued: 3 (2001) / 5 (2000); Multi-family building permits issued: 0 (2001) / 0 (2000); Employment by occupation: 7.4% management, 16.0% professional, 15.3% services, 15.0% sales, 2.7% farming, 11.8% construction, 31.7% production (2000).
Income: Per capita income: $13,695 (2000); Median household income: $20,958 (2000); Poverty rate: 31.3% (2000).
Taxes: Total city taxes per capita: $155 (1997); City property taxes per capita: $26 (1997).
Education: High school graduation rate: 53.4% (2000); College graduation rate: 9.2% (2000).

School District(s)

South Pemiscot Co. R-V (KG-12)
2000 Enrollment: 827 573-695-4426

Housing: Homeownership rate: 55.1% (2000); Median home value: $45,300 (2000); Median rent: $174 per month (2000); Median age of housing: 33 years (2000).

Newspapers: The Steele Enterprise (1 x week)
Transportation: Commute to work: 93.2% car, 0.7% public transportation, 3.0% walk, 1.4% work from home (2000); Travel time to work: 35.9% less than 15 minutes, 51.2% 15 to 30 minutes, 10.3% 30 to 45 minutes, 0.4% 45 to 60 minutes, 2.1% 60 minutes or more (2000)

WARDELL (town). Covers a land area of 0.195 square miles and a water area of 0 square miles. Located at 36.35° N. Lat.; 89.81° W. Long. Elevation is 272 feet.
Population: 278 (2000); Race: 89.5% White, 5.8% Black, 0.0% Asian, 0.0% American Indian and Alaska Native, 4.7% Hispanic of any race, 0.0% two or more races (2000); Density: 1,423.3 persons per square mile (2000); Age: 29.2% under 18, 13.2% over 64 (2000); Marriage status: 27.5% never married, 52.4% now married, 4.3% widowed, 15.9% divorced (2000); Foreign born: 0.0% (2000); Ancestry (includes multiple ancestries): 38.3% United States or American, 12.5% Other groups, 9.2% English, 7.1% German, 4.4% Irish (2000).
Economy: Single-family building permits issued: 0 (2001) / 0 (2000); Multi-family building permits issued: 0 (2001) / 0 (2000); Employment by occupation: 5.3% management, 14.4% professional, 20.5% services, 23.5% sales, 3.8% farming, 12.1% construction, 20.5% production (2000).
Income: Per capita income: $9,829 (2000); Median household income: $20,208 (2000); Poverty rate: 22.0% (2000).
Taxes: Total city taxes per capita: $123 (1997); City property taxes per capita: $19 (1997).
Education: High school graduation rate: 59.4% (2000); College graduation rate: 7.3% (2000).

School District(s)

North Pemiscot Co. R-I (KG-12)
2000 Enrollment: 442 573-628-3471

Housing: Homeownership rate: 64.3% (2000); Median home value: $36,100 (2000); Median rent: $188 per month (2000); Median age of housing: 41 years (2000).
Transportation: Commute to work: 97.7% car, 0.0% public transportation, 2.3% walk, 0.0% work from home (2000); Travel time to work: 25.8% less than 15 minutes, 53.0% 15 to 30 minutes, 17.4% 30 to 45 minutes, 3.8% 45 to 60 minutes, 0.0% 60 minutes or more (2000)

Perry County

Located in eastern Missouri; bounded on the east by the Mississippi River and the Illinois border. Covers a land area of 474.70 square miles, a water area of 9.60 square miles, and is located in the Central Time Zone. The county government was organized in 1820. County seat is Perryville.
Population: 18,132 (2000); Race: 97.5% White, 0.2% Black, 0.7% Asian, 0.3% American Indian and Alaska Native, 1.0% Hispanic of any race, 1.0% two or more races (2000); Density: 38.2 persons per square mile (2000); Age: 26.0% under 18, 15.7% over 64 (2000).
Religion: Five largest groups: 45.8% Catholic Church, 22.6% Lutheran Church—Missouri Synod, 3.5% Southern Baptist Convention, 2.3% The United Methodist Church, 1.0% Presbyterian Church (U.S.A.) (2000).
Economy: Unemployment rate: 2.9% (11/2002); Total civilian labor force: 10,254 (11/2002); Leading industries: 41.9% manufacturing; 11.7% retail trade; 9.8% health care and social assistance (2000); Companies that employ more than 1,000 persons: 1 (2000); Companies that employ more than 100 persons: 12 (2000); Farms: 857 totaling 201,396 acres (1997); Minority business ownership rate: 0.0% (1997); Women business ownership rate: 17.0% (1997); Retail sales per capita: $9,722 (1997). Single-family building permits issued: 47 (2001) / 57 (2000); Multi-family building permits issued: 4 (2001) / 0 (2000).
Income: Per capita income: $16,554 (2000); Median household income: $36,632 (2000); Poverty rate: 9.0% (2000); Bankruptcy rate: 5.03% (2001).
Taxes: Total county taxes per capita: $181 (2000); County property taxes per capita: $86 (2000).
Education: High school graduation rate: 71.2% (2000); College graduation rate: 9.9% (2000).
Housing: Homeownership rate: 79.9% (2000); Median home value: $80,000 (2000); Median rent: $340 per month (2000); Median age of housing: 31 years (2000).
Health: Birth rate: 117.5 per 10,000 population (1998); Age adjusted death rate: 84.9 per 10,000 population (1999); Age adjusted cancer mortality rate: 175.1 deaths per 100,000 population (1999). Number of physicians: 6.6 per 10,000 population (1999); Number of hospital beds: 25.9 per 10,000 population (1999).
Elections: 2000 Presidential election results: 30.2% Gore, 67.6% Bush, 1.0% Nader, 0.7% Buchanan
National and State Parks: County Lake State Wildlife Management Area
Additional Information Contacts
Perry County Government Offices....................... 573-547-4242
Perryville Chamber of Commerce 573-547-6062

Perry County Communities

ALTENBURG (city). Covers a land area of 0.956 square miles and a water area of 0 square miles. Located at 37.63° N. Lat.; 89.58° W. Long. Elevation is 570 feet.
History: Altenburg was founded by Lutheran immigrants under the leadership of Martin Stephan, a pastor from Dresden. The colonists were unused to the heavy farm work, and the early years were made more difficult by the expulsion of their leader, whom they accused of high living and dictatorial conduct.
Population: 309 (2000); Race: 100.0% White, 0.0% Black, 0.0% Asian, 0.0% American Indian and Alaska Native, 0.0% Hispanic of any race, 0.0% two or more races (2000); Density: 323.4 persons per square mile (2000); Age: 21.6% under 18, 16.5% over 64 (2000); Marriage status: 18.4% never married, 62.7% now married, 11.8% widowed, 7.0% divorced (2000); Foreign born: 0.0% (2000); Ancestry (includes multiple ancestries): 68.3% German, 9.4% United States or American, 5.0% Irish, 4.7% Other groups, 2.2% English (2000).
Economy: Single-family building permits issued: 1 (2001) / 2 (2000); Multi-family building permits issued: 0 (2001) / 0 (2000); Employment by occupation: 3.1% management, 12.5% professional, 14.4% services, 28.1% sales, 0.0% farming, 11.9% construction, 30.0% production (2000).
Income: Per capita income: $19,174 (2000); Median household income: $40,417 (2000); Poverty rate: 5.0% (2000).
Taxes: Total city taxes per capita: $31 (1997); City property taxes per capita: $16 (1997).
Education: High school graduation rate: 76.2% (2000); College graduation rate: 6.7% (2000).

School District(s)

Altenburg 48 (KG-08)
2000 Enrollment: 141 573-824-5857

Housing: Homeownership rate: 88.2% (2000); Median home value: $62,500 (2000); Median rent: $179 per month (2000); Median age of housing: 54 years (2000).
Transportation: Commute to work: 96.9% car, 0.0% public transportation, 3.1% walk, 0.0% work from home (2000); Travel time to work: 34.4% less than 15 minutes, 19.4% 15 to 30 minutes, 35.6% 30 to 45 minutes, 6.9% 45 to 60 minutes, 3.8% 60 minutes or more (2000)

BIEHLE (village). Covers a land area of 0.097 square miles and a water area of 0 square miles. Located at 37.60° N. Lat.; 89.84° W. Long. Elevation is 465 feet.
Population: 11 (2000); Race: 100.0% White, 0.0% Black, 0.0% Asian, 0.0% American Indian and Alaska Native, 0.0% Hispanic of any race, 0.0% two or more races (2000); Density: 113.1 persons per square mile (2000); Age: 0.0% under 18, 27.3% over 64 (2000); Marriage status: 27.3% never married, 72.7% now married, 0.0% widowed, 0.0% divorced (2000); Foreign born: 0.0% (2000); Ancestry (includes multiple ancestries): 100.0% German, 27.3% French (except Basque) (2000).
Economy: Employment by occupation: 25.0% management, 0.0% professional, 0.0% services, 75.0% sales, 0.0% farming, 0.0% construction, 0.0% production (2000).
Income: Per capita income: $23,000 (2000); Median household income: $31,875 (2000); Poverty rate: 0.0% (2000).
Taxes: Total city taxes per capita: $11,778 (1997); City property taxes per capita: $0 (1997).
Education: High school graduation rate: 72.7% (2000); College graduation rate: 0.0% (2000).
Housing: Homeownership rate: 50.0% (2000); Median home value: $95,000 (2000); Median rent: $125 per month (2000); Median age of housing: 36 years (2000).
Transportation: Commute to work: 62.5% car, 0.0% public transportation, 37.5% walk, 0.0% work from home (2000); Travel time to work: 100.0% less than 15 minutes, 0.0% 15 to 30 minutes, 0.0% 30 to 45 minutes, 0.0% 45 to 60 minutes, 0.0% 60 minutes or more (2000)

FROHNA (city). Covers a land area of 0.587 square miles and a water area of 0 square miles. Located at 37.64° N. Lat.; 89.61° W. Long. Elevation is 580 feet.
History: Hilly area settled by Germans in 1830s. Laid out as a German *Strassendorf* (street village).
Population: 192 (2000); Race: 100.0% White, 0.0% Black, 0.0% Asian, 0.0% American Indian and Alaska Native, 0.0% Hispanic of any race, 0.0% two or more races (2000); Density: 327.3 persons per square mile (2000); Age: 24.9% under 18, 20.4% over 64 (2000); Marriage status: 20.4% never married, 61.1% now married, 9.3% widowed, 9.3% divorced (2000); Foreign born: 0.0% (2000); Ancestry (includes multiple ancestries): 72.6% German, 3.5% Dutch, 3.0% United States or American, 2.0% Irish, 1.0% French (except Basque) (2000).
Economy: Dairying; cattle; timber. Manufacturing: hardwood and softwood lumber. Single-family building permits issued: 0 (2001) / 3 (2000); Multi-family building permits issued: 0 (2001) / 0 (2000); Employment by occupation: 15.6% management, 6.4% professional, 19.3% services, 11.9% sales, 5.5% farming, 15.6% construction, 25.7% production (2000).
Income: Per capita income: $17,400 (2000); Median household income: $41,635 (2000); Poverty rate: 7.0% (2000).
Taxes: Total city taxes per capita: $390 (1997); City property taxes per capita: $24 (1997).
Education: High school graduation rate: 66.2% (2000); College graduation rate: 5.9% (2000).
Housing: Homeownership rate: 88.8% (2000); Median home value: $60,000 (2000); Median rent: $275 per month (2000); Median age of housing: 50 years (2000).
Transportation: Commute to work: 94.5% car, 0.0% public transportation, 5.5% walk, 0.0% work from home (2000); Travel time to work: 42.2% less than 15 minutes, 10.1% 15 to 30 minutes, 33.9% 30 to 45 minutes, 4.6% 45 to 60 minutes, 9.2% 60 minutes or more (2000)

LONGTOWN (town). Covers a land area of 0.128 square miles and a water area of 0 square miles. Located at 37.67° N. Lat.; 89.77° W. Long. Elevation is 665 feet.
Population: 76 (2000); Race: 96.8% White, 0.0% Black, 0.0% Asian, 0.0% American Indian and Alaska Native, 3.2% Hispanic of any race, 0.0% two or more races (2000); Density: 595.4 persons per square mile (2000); Age: 12.7% under 18, 9.5% over 64 (2000); Marriage status: 23.3% never married, 51.7% now married, 10.0% widowed, 15.0% divorced (2000); Foreign born: 0.0% (2000); Ancestry (includes multiple ancestries): 30.2% United States or American, 30.2% German, 7.9% Irish, 6.3% Other groups, 4.8% English (2000).
Economy: Employment by occupation: 5.0% management, 10.0% professional, 17.5% services, 10.0% sales, 0.0% farming, 25.0% construction, 32.5% production (2000).
Income: Per capita income: $22,724 (2000); Median household income: $55,000 (2000); Poverty rate: 7.9% (2000).
Taxes: Total city taxes per capita: $19 (1997); City property taxes per capita: $19 (1997).
Education: High school graduation rate: 81.6% (2000); College graduation rate: 0.0% (2000).
Housing: Homeownership rate: 71.0% (2000); Median home value: $64,000 (2000); Median rent: $225 per month (2000); Median age of housing: 60+ years (2000).
Transportation: Commute to work: 100.0% car, 0.0% public transportation, 0.0% walk, 0.0% work from home (2000); Travel time to work: 52.5% less than 15 minutes, 15.0% 15 to 30 minutes, 20.0% 30 to 45 minutes, 2.5% 45 to 60 minutes, 10.0% 60 minutes or more (2000)

PERRYVILLE (city). Covers a land area of 7.589 square miles and a water area of 0.152 square miles. Located at 37.72° N. Lat.; 89.87° W. Long. Elevation is 580 feet.
History: Perryville was platted as the seat of Perry County in 1822. There had been American settlers here since 1801, when Isadore Moore developed a farm near the forks of Cinque Hommes and Saline Creeks. Ferdinand Rozier, former partner of John James Audubon, operated a store in Perryville.
Population: 7,667 (2000); Race: 96.9% White, 0.2% Black, 1.5% Asian, 0.4% American Indian and Alaska Native, 1.0% Hispanic of any race, 0.6% two or more races (2000); Density: 1,010.3 persons per square mile (2000); Age: 24.6% under 18, 19.5% over 64 (2000); Marriage status: 23.0% never married, 56.8% now married, 11.0% widowed, 9.2% divorced (2000); Foreign born: 1.6% (2000); Ancestry (includes multiple ancestries): 43.2% German, 11.9% United States or American, 10.1% Irish, 9.5% French (except Basque), 9.4% Other groups (2000).
Economy: Single-family building permits issued: 15 (2001) / 21 (2000); Multi-family building permits issued: 4 (2001) / 0 (2000); Employment by occupation: 11.4% management, 12.7% professional, 18.0% services, 22.5% sales, 0.8% farming, 10.2% construction, 24.5% production (2000).
Income: Per capita income: $16,630 (2000); Median household income: $33,934 (2000); Poverty rate: 11.0% (2000).
Taxes: Total city taxes per capita: $464 (2000); City property taxes per capita: $98 (2000).
Education: High school graduation rate: 68.8% (2000); College graduation rate: 12.9% (2000).

School District(s)

Perry Co. 32 (PK-12)
2000 Enrollment: 2,320 573-547-7500
Housing: Homeownership rate: 71.0% (2000); Median home value: $77,100 (2000); Median rent: $357 per month (2000); Median age of housing: 37 years (2000).
Hospitals: Perry County Memorial Hospital (25 beds)
Newspapers: The Perry County Republic Monitor (2 x week)
Transportation: Commute to work: 93.0% car, 1.4% public transportation, 1.7% walk, 2.8% work from home (2000); Travel time to work: 64.7% less than 15 minutes, 18.5% 15 to 30 minutes, 7.6% 30 to 45 minutes, 3.8% 45 to 60 minutes, 5.4% 60 minutes or more (2000)
Additional Information Contacts
Perryville Chamber of Commerce 573-547-6062

UNIONTOWN (unincorporated postal area, zip code 63783). Covers a land area of 6.141 square miles and a water area of 0 square miles. Located at 37.60° N. Lat.; 89.67° W. Long. Elevation is 576 feet.
Population: 161 (2000); Race: 98.8% White, 0.0% Black, 0.0% Asian, 0.0% American Indian and Alaska Native, 0.0% Hispanic of any race, 1.2% two or more races (2000); Density: 26.2 persons per square mile (2000); Age: 20.9% under 18, 19.8% over 64 (2000); Marriage status: 29.1% never married, 60.1% now married, 5.4% widowed, 5.4% divorced (2000); Foreign born: 0.0% (2000); Ancestry (includes multiple ancestries): 53.5% German, 12.8% United States or American, 5.2% English, 4.1% Irish, 4.1% French (except Basque) (2000).
Economy: Employment by occupation: 11.8% management, 17.6% professional, 20.6% services, 15.7% sales, 0.0% farming, 15.7% construction, 18.6% production (2000).
Income: Per capita income: $15,860 (2000); Median household income: $41,563 (2000); Poverty rate: 0.0% (2000).
Education: High school graduation rate: 72.6% (2000); College graduation rate: 11.1% (2000).
Housing: Homeownership rate: 100.0% (2000); Median home value: $82,500 (2000); Median age of housing: 30 years (2000).
Transportation: Commute to work: 92.2% car, 0.0% public transportation, 0.0% walk, 6.9% work from home (2000); Travel time to work: 9.5% less than 15 minutes, 49.5% 15 to 30 minutes, 20.0% 30 to 45 minutes, 13.7% 45 to 60 minutes, 7.4% 60 minutes or more (2000)

Pettis County

Located in central Missouri; crossed by the Lamine River. Covers a land area of 684.80 square miles, a water area of 1.50 square miles, and is located in the Central Time Zone. The county government was organized in 1833. County seat is Sedalia.

Weather Station: Sedalia Water Plant — Elevation: 777 feet

	Jan	Feb	Mar	Apr	May	Jun	Jul	Aug	Sep	Oct	Nov	Dec
High	37	43	54	65	74	83	89	87	79	68	54	42
Low	16	21	31	41	51	61	65	63	54	42	32	22
Precip	1.6	1.7	3.0	4.2	5.3	5.0	4.3	3.6	4.1	3.6	3.5	2.3
Snow	4.3	3.4	1.0	0.5	0.0	0.0	0.0	0.0	0.0	0.0	1.1	1.5

High and Low temperatures in degrees Fahrenheit; Precipitation and Snow in inches

Population: 39,403 (2000); Race: 92.3% White, 3.2% Black, 0.4% Asian, 0.3% American Indian and Alaska Native, 3.5% Hispanic of any race, 1.7% two or more races (2000); Density: 57.5 persons per square mile (2000); Age: 26.3% under 18, 15.5% over 64 (2000).
Religion: Five largest groups: 25.5% Southern Baptist Convention, 8.4% Catholic Church, 7.5% The United Methodist Church, 4.7% Lutheran Church—Missouri Synod, 2.8% Christian Church (Disciples of Christ) (2000).
Economy: Unemployment rate: 4.9% (11/2002); Total civilian labor force: 20,823 (11/2002); Leading industries: 33.5% manufacturing; 13.3% retail trade; 12.6% health care and social assistance (2000); Companies that employ

more than 1,000 persons: 1 (2000); Companies that employ more than 100 persons: 24 (2000); Farms: 1,249 totaling 366,132 acres (1997); Minority business ownership rate: 0.0% (1997); Women business ownership rate: 25.5% (1997); Retail sales per capita: $9,646 (1997). Single-family building permits issued: 22 (2001) / 14 (2000); Multi-family building permits issued: 8 (2001) / 2 (2000).

Income: Per capita income: $16,251 (2000); Median household income: $31,822 (2000); Poverty rate: 12.8% (2000); Bankruptcy rate: 3.88% (2001).

Taxes: Total county taxes per capita: $92 (2000); County property taxes per capita: $35 (2000).

Education: High school graduation rate: 78.3% (2000); College graduation rate: 15.0% (2000).

Housing: Homeownership rate: 72.5% (2000); Median home value: $66,400 (2000); Median rent: $326 per month (2000); Median age of housing: 36 years (2000).

Health: Birth rate: 139.3 per 10,000 population (1998); Age adjusted death rate: 93.2 per 10,000 population (1999); Age adjusted cancer mortality rate: 246.5 deaths per 100,000 population (1999). Number of physicians: 11.2 per 10,000 population (1999); Number of hospital beds: 41.4 per 10,000 population (1999).

Elections: 2000 Presidential election results: 37.2% Gore, 60.5% Bush, 1.4% Nader, 0.4% Buchanan

Additional Information Contacts

Pettis County Government Offices. 660-826-5395
Sedalia Chamber of Commerce 660-826-2222
Sedalia Convention & Visitors Bureau 660-827-5295
Sedalia-Warsaw Board of Realtors 660-826-3149

Pettis County Communities

GREEN RIDGE (city). Covers a land area of 0.444 square miles and a water area of 0.054 square miles. Located at 38.62° N. Lat.; 93.41° W. Long. Elevation is 905 feet.

Population: 445 (2000); Race: 96.0% White, 0.0% Black, 0.4% Asian, 0.0% American Indian and Alaska Native, 2.1% Hispanic of any race, 1.9% two or more races (2000); Density: 1,002.0 persons per square mile (2000); Age: 31.5% under 18, 13.8% over 64 (2000); Marriage status: 17.9% never married, 63.0% now married, 8.3% widowed, 10.8% divorced (2000); Foreign born: 1.0% (2000); Ancestry (includes multiple ancestries): 23.0% German, 14.4% United States or American, 12.3% Other groups, 9.0% English, 7.9% Irish (2000).

Economy: Cattle; wheat, corn, hay, sorghum. Single-family building permits issued: 1 (2001) / 0 (2000); Multi-family building permits issued: 0 (2001) / 0 (2000); Employment by occupation: 11.7% management, 10.2% professional, 11.7% services, 31.6% sales, 2.9% farming, 14.6% construction, 17.5% production (2000).

Income: Per capita income: $14,942 (2000); Median household income: $36,750 (2000); Poverty rate: 10.7% (2000).

Taxes: Total city taxes per capita: $154 (1997); City property taxes per capita: $122 (1997).

Education: High school graduation rate: 81.4% (2000); College graduation rate: 12.7% (2000).

School District(s)

Green Ridge R-VIII (KG-12)
2000 Enrollment: 375 660-527-3315

Housing: Homeownership rate: 84.1% (2000); Median home value: $58,700 (2000); Median rent: $228 per month (2000); Median age of housing: 40 years (2000).

Transportation: Commute to work: 97.6% car, 1.0% public transportation, 0.0% walk, 1.4% work from home (2000); Travel time to work: 11.7% less than 15 minutes, 61.0% 15 to 30 minutes, 13.2% 30 to 45 minutes, 4.4% 45 to 60 minutes, 9.8% 60 minutes or more (2000)

HOUSTONIA (city). Covers a land area of 0.197 square miles and a water area of 0 square miles. Located at 38.89° N. Lat.; 93.35° W. Long. Elevation is 759 feet.

Population: 275 (2000); Race: 100.0% White, 0.0% Black, 0.0% Asian, 0.0% American Indian and Alaska Native, 0.0% Hispanic of any race, 0.0% two or more races (2000); Density: 1,395.8 persons per square mile (2000); Age: 33.4% under 18, 8.1% over 64 (2000); Marriage status: 25.8% never married, 55.9% now married, 7.9% widowed, 10.5% divorced (2000); Foreign born: 0.0% (2000); Ancestry (includes multiple ancestries): 22.3% United States or American, 20.9% German, 16.9% Irish, 13.5% Other groups, 5.1% English (2000).

Economy: Employment by occupation: 7.8% management, 14.0% professional, 18.6% services, 14.0% sales, 0.0% farming, 10.1% construction, 35.7% production (2000).

Income: Per capita income: $12,490 (2000); Median household income: $34,219 (2000); Poverty rate: 24.7% (2000).

Taxes: Total city taxes per capita: $50 (1997); City property taxes per capita: $23 (1997).

Education: High school graduation rate: 61.2% (2000); College graduation rate: 7.6% (2000).

Housing: Homeownership rate: 89.2% (2000); Median home value: $39,300 (2000); Median rent: $213 per month (2000); Median age of housing: 50 years (2000).

Transportation: Commute to work: 92.1% car, 0.0% public transportation, 3.2% walk, 3.2% work from home (2000); Travel time to work: 10.7% less than 15 minutes, 31.1% 15 to 30 minutes, 36.9% 30 to 45 minutes, 3.3% 45 to 60 minutes, 18.0% 60 minutes or more (2000)

HUGHESVILLE (village). Covers a land area of 0.114 square miles and a water area of 0 square miles. Located at 38.83° N. Lat.; 93.29° W. Long. Elevation is 808 feet.

Population: 174 (2000); Race: 100.0% White, 0.0% Black, 0.0% Asian, 0.0% American Indian and Alaska Native, 0.0% Hispanic of any race, 0.0% two or more races (2000); Density: 1,527.5 persons per square mile (2000); Age: 19.1% under 18, 10.2% over 64 (2000); Marriage status: 18.0% never married, 67.7% now married, 6.0% widowed, 8.3% divorced (2000); Foreign born: 0.0% (2000); Ancestry (includes multiple ancestries): 17.2% German, 14.0% English, 12.7% Other groups, 7.6% Irish, 4.5% Norwegian (2000).

Economy: Employment by occupation: 10.1% management, 15.7% professional, 16.9% services, 27.0% sales, 2.2% farming, 2.2% construction, 25.8% production (2000).

Income: Per capita income: $14,576 (2000); Median household income: $30,833 (2000); Poverty rate: 5.7% (2000).

Taxes: Total city taxes per capita: $33 (1997); City property taxes per capita: $17 (1997).

Education: High school graduation rate: 79.2% (2000); College graduation rate: 6.9% (2000).

School District(s)

Pettis Co. R-V (KG-12)
2000 Enrollment: 445 660-827-0772

Housing: Homeownership rate: 80.3% (2000); Median home value: $42,200 (2000); Median rent: $225 per month (2000); Median age of housing: 40 years (2000).

Transportation: Commute to work: 94.4% car, 0.0% public transportation, 4.5% walk, 1.1% work from home (2000); Travel time to work: 21.6% less than 15 minutes, 63.6% 15 to 30 minutes, 6.8% 30 to 45 minutes, 2.3% 45 to 60 minutes, 5.7% 60 minutes or more (2000)

LA MONTE (city). Covers a land area of 1.141 square miles and a water area of 0 square miles. Located at 38.77° N. Lat.; 93.42° W. Long. Elevation is 860 feet.

Population: 1,064 (2000); Race: 88.6% White, 1.9% Black, 1.1% Asian, 0.5% American Indian and Alaska Native, 8.8% Hispanic of any race, 4.3% two or more races (2000); Density: 932.2 persons per square mile (2000); Age: 25.0% under 18, 14.5% over 64 (2000); Marriage status: 20.4% never married, 62.8% now married, 7.1% widowed, 9.7% divorced (2000); Foreign born: 6.9% (2000); Ancestry (includes multiple ancestries): 20.4% Other groups, 18.4% United States or American, 17.2% German, 8.7% Irish, 7.0% English (2000).

Economy: Soybeans, corn; cattle; wood products. Single-family building permits issued: 0 (2001) / 0 (2000); Multi-family building permits issued: 0 (2001) / 0 (2000); Employment by occupation: 7.1% management, 9.6% professional, 20.0% services, 20.8% sales, 1.8% farming, 10.1% construction, 30.6% production (2000).

Income: Per capita income: $13,153 (2000); Median household income: $28,688 (2000); Poverty rate: 21.4% (2000).

Taxes: Total city taxes per capita: $24 (1997); City property taxes per capita: $18 (1997).

Education: High school graduation rate: 78.5% (2000); College graduation rate: 8.2% (2000).

School District(s)

La Monte R-IV (PK-12)
2000 Enrollment: 375 660-347-5439

Housing: Homeownership rate: 60.7% (2000); Median home value: $48,900 (2000); Median rent: $282 per month (2000); Median age of housing: 33 years (2000).

Transportation: Commute to work: 94.8% car, 0.0% public transportation, 1.4% walk, 3.8% work from home (2000); Travel time to work: 24.0% less than 15 minutes, 62.0% 15 to 30 minutes, 10.4% 30 to 45 minutes, 1.0% 45 to 60 minutes, 2.7% 60 minutes or more (2000)

SEDALIA (city). Covers a land area of 11.959 square miles and a water area of 0 square miles. Located at 38.70° N. Lat.; 93.23° W. Long. Elevation is 919 feet.

History: Sedalia was platted in 1857 by George R. Smith, a member of the state legislature, who called the town Sedville for his daughter Sarah, whom he called "Sed." In 1860 Smith replatted the town as Sedalia. During the Civil War, Sedalia was a military post. In 1864 the town was incorporated, the county seat was moved here from Georgetown, and George Smith became the first mayor.

Population: 20,339 (2000); Race: 88.9% White, 5.0% Black, 0.4% Asian, 0.3% American Indian and Alaska Native, 5.4% Hispanic of any race, 1.9% two or more races (2000); Density: 1,700.8 persons per square mile (2000); Age: 25.0% under 18, 17.6% over 64 (2000); Marriage status: 23.0% never married, 52.8% now married, 10.3% widowed, 13.9% divorced (2000); Foreign born: 3.4% (2000); Ancestry (includes multiple ancestries): 21.5% German, 16.7% Other groups, 11.6% United States or American, 9.8% Irish, 9.1% English (2000).

Vital Statistics: Birth rate: 163.7 per 10,000 population (1998)

Economy: Single-family building permits issued: 21 (2001) / 14 (2000); Multi-family building permits issued: 8 (2001) / 2 (2000); Employment by occupation: 8.9% management, 14.7% professional, 15.7% services, 21.2% sales, 0.6% farming, 10.5% construction, 28.4% production (2000).

Income: Per capita income: $15,931 (2000); Median household income: $28,641 (2000); Poverty rate: 15.3% (2000).

Taxes: Total city taxes per capita: $348 (2000); City property taxes per capita: $78 (2000).

Education: High school graduation rate: 75.4% (2000); College graduation rate: 14.4% (2000).

School District(s)

Pettis Co. R-XII (PK-08)
2000 Enrollment: 146 660-826-5385
Sedalia 200 (PK-12)
2000 Enrollment: 4,288 660-829-6450
State Fair Community College (09-12)
2000 Enrollment: n/a 660-530-5800

Two-year College(s)

State Fair Community College (Public)
2001 Enrollment: 3,355 660-530-5800
2001 Tuition: In-state $1,950; Out-of-state $2,670

Housing: Homeownership rate: 64.0% (2000); Median home value: $59,600 (2000); Median rent: $326 per month (2000); Median age of housing: 44 years (2000).

Hospitals: Bothwell Regional Health Center (170 beds)

Safety: Violent crime rate: 82.6 per 10,000 population; Property crime rate: 775.0 per 10,000 population (2001).

Newspapers: Central Missouri News (1 x week); The Sedalia Democrat (7 x week)

Transportation: Commute to work: 93.1% car, 0.7% public transportation, 2.3% walk, 2.6% work from home (2000); Travel time to work: 63.2% less than 15 minutes, 23.8% 15 to 30 minutes, 7.0% 30 to 45 minutes, 1.1% 45 to 60 minutes, 4.9% 60 minutes or more (2000); Amtrak: Service available.

Airports: Sedalia Memorial

Additional Information Contacts

Sedalia Chamber of Commerce 660-826-2222
Sedalia Convention & Visitors Bureau 660-827-5295
Sedalia-Warsaw Board of Realtors 660-826-3149

SMITHTON (city). Covers a land area of 0.291 square miles and a water area of 0 square miles. Located at 38.68° N. Lat.; 93.09° W. Long. Elevation is 888 feet.

History: Smithton was platted in 1859 by William E. Combs, and named in honor of General George R. Smith, founder of Sedalia. Smithton was the home of Colonel Louis M. Monsees, a mule breeder who won prizes at the St. Louis Exposition in 1904, where the term "Missouri Mule" originated.

Population: 510 (2000); Race: 95.2% White, 3.6% Black, 0.4% Asian, 0.8% American Indian and Alaska Native, 0.0% Hispanic of any race, 0.0% two or more races (2000); Density: 1,751.4 persons per square mile (2000); Age: 30.3% under 18, 9.6% over 64 (2000); Marriage status: 19.6% never married, 58.4% now married, 5.8% widowed, 16.2% divorced (2000); Foreign born: 4.0% (2000); Ancestry (includes multiple ancestries): 27.3% German, 10.6% United States or American, 7.0% Other groups, 7.0% Irish, 6.8% Scottish (2000).

Economy: Single-family building permits issued: 0 (2001) / 0 (2000); Multi-family building permits issued: 0 (2001) / 0 (2000); Employment by occupation: 7.9% management, 19.0% professional, 15.4% services, 24.5% sales, 1.6% farming, 12.6% construction, 19.0% production (2000).

Income: Per capita income: $16,320 (2000); Median household income: $32,321 (2000); Poverty rate: 6.3% (2000).

Taxes: Total city taxes per capita: $396 (1997); City property taxes per capita: $265 (1997).

Education: High school graduation rate: 83.5% (2000); College graduation rate: 13.0% (2000).

School District(s)

Smithton R-VI (KG-12)
2000 Enrollment: 592 660-343-5316

Housing: Homeownership rate: 83.5% (2000); Median home value: $53,300 (2000); Median rent: $329 per month (2000); Median age of housing: 46 years (2000).

Transportation: Commute to work: 92.5% car, 0.8% public transportation, 4.0% walk, 2.8% work from home (2000); Travel time to work: 28.5% less than 15 minutes, 54.1% 15 to 30 minutes, 9.8% 30 to 45 minutes, 2.4% 45 to 60 minutes, 5.3% 60 minutes or more (2000)

Phelps County

Located in central Missouri, in the Ozarks; drained by the Meramec and Gasconade Rivers; includes part of Mark Twain National Forest. Covers a land area of 672.90 square miles, a water area of 1.40 square miles, and is located in the Central Time Zone. The county government was organized in 1857. County seat is Rolla.

Weather Station: Rolla Univ. of Missouri — Elevation: 1,164 feet

	Jan	Feb	Mar	Apr	May	Jun	Jul	Aug	Sep	Oct	Nov	Dec
High	40	46	55	66	75	84	89	88	79	69	55	43
Low	21	26	34	45	54	63	68	66	58	47	36	26
Precip	2.3	2.3	3.6	4.4	4.9	4.1	4.5	3.9	3.9	3.5	4.5	3.4
Snow	6.3	4.8	2.9	0.5	0.0	0.0	0.0	0.0	0.0	tr	1.7	4.2

High and Low temperatures in degrees Fahrenheit; Precipitation and Snow in inches

Population: 39,825 (2000); Race: 93.1% White, 1.7% Black, 2.1% Asian, 0.7% American Indian and Alaska Native, 1.2% Hispanic of any race, 1.7% two or more races (2000); Density: 59.2 persons per square mile (2000); Age: 23.9% under 18, 13.9% over 64 (2000).

Religion: Five largest groups: 17.4% Southern Baptist Convention, 5.2% Catholic Church, 4.9% Christian Churches and Churches of Christ, 2.8% The United Methodist Church, 2.7% Assemblies of God (2000).

Economy: Unemployment rate: 2.9% (11/2002); Total civilian labor force: 21,691 (11/2002); Leading industries: 22.5% health care and social assistance; 21.1% retail trade; 14.2% manufacturing (2000); Companies that employ more than 1,000 persons: 0 (2000); Companies that employ more than 100 persons: 14 (2000); Farms: 758 totaling 196,197 acres (1997); Minority business ownership rate: 5.8% (1997); Women business ownership rate: 23.2% (1997); Retail sales per capita: $9,823 (1997). Single-family building permits issued: 81 (2001) / 68 (2000); Multi-family building permits issued: 196 (2001) / 98 (2000).

Income: Per capita income: $16,084 (2000); Median household income: $29,378 (2000); Poverty rate: 16.4% (2000); Bankruptcy rate: 3.67% (2001).

Taxes: Total county taxes per capita: $75 (2000); County property taxes per capita: $22 (2000).

Education: High school graduation rate: 79.0% (2000); College graduation rate: 21.1% (2000).

Housing: Homeownership rate: 65.6% (2000); Median home value: $74,800 (2000); Median rent: $314 per month (2000); Median age of housing: 25 years (2000).

Health: Birth rate: 117.3 per 10,000 population (1998); Age adjusted death rate: 106.9 per 10,000 population (1999); Age adjusted cancer mortality rate: 247.5 deaths per 100,000 population (1999). Number of physicians: 14.6 per 10,000 population (1999); Number of hospital beds: 52.0 per 10,000 population (1999).

Elections: 2000 Presidential election results: 38.8% Gore, 58.5% Bush, 1.6% Nader, 0.5% Buchanan

National and State Parks: Asher State Wildlife Management Area; Dry Fork State Wildlife Area

Additional Information Contacts

Phelps County Government Offices 573-364-1891
Rolla Chamber of Commerce 573-364-3577

South Central Board of Realtors 573-368-2800

Phelps County Communities

BEULAH (unincorporated postal area, zip code 65436). Covers a land area of 23.645 square miles and a water area of 0 square miles. Located at 37.62° N. Lat.; 91.96° W. Long. Elevation is 1,130 feet.
Population: 108 (2000); Race: 95.5% White, 0.0% Black, 0.0% Asian, 0.0% American Indian and Alaska Native, 0.0% Hispanic of any race, 4.5% two or more races (2000); Density: 4.6 persons per square mile (2000); Age: 29.5% under 18, 17.0% over 64 (2000); Marriage status: 18.6% never married, 50.0% now married, 15.1% widowed, 16.3% divorced (2000); Foreign born: 8.9% (2000); Ancestry (includes multiple ancestries): 47.3% United States or American, 18.8% German, 9.8% European, 8.9% English, 8.0% Other groups (2000).
Economy: Employment by occupation: 9.8% management, 19.5% professional, 24.4% services, 0.0% sales, 0.0% farming, 12.2% construction, 34.1% production (2000).
Income: Per capita income: $11,191 (2000); Median household income: $20,313 (2000); Poverty rate: 57.1% (2000).
Education: High school graduation rate: 74.3% (2000); College graduation rate: 21.6% (2000).
Housing: Homeownership rate: 79.1% (2000); Median home value: $55,000 (2000); Median rent: $205 per month (2000); Median age of housing: 26 years (2000).
Transportation: Commute to work: 78.0% car, 0.0% public transportation, 0.0% walk, 22.0% work from home (2000); Travel time to work: 12.5% less than 15 minutes, 31.3% 15 to 30 minutes, 28.1% 30 to 45 minutes, 0.0% 45 to 60 minutes, 28.1% 60 minutes or more (2000)

DOOLITTLE (city). Covers a land area of 2.461 square miles and a water area of 0 square miles. Located at 37.94° N. Lat.; 91.88° W. Long. Elevation is 1,008 feet.
Population: 644 (2000); Race: 97.0% White, 0.0% Black, 0.0% Asian, 0.5% American Indian and Alaska Native, 0.3% Hispanic of any race, 2.6% two or more races (2000); Density: 261.6 persons per square mile (2000); Age: 23.5% under 18, 17.9% over 64 (2000); Marriage status: 21.9% never married, 62.0% now married, 6.3% widowed, 9.8% divorced (2000); Foreign born: 0.9% (2000); Ancestry (includes multiple ancestries): 18.2% German, 17.9% United States or American, 12.9% Irish, 11.1% Other groups, 7.1% English (2000).
Economy: On North edge of Mark Twain National Forest. Timber. Recreation. Employment by occupation: 10.9% management, 21.7% professional, 16.5% services, 27.6% sales, 0.0% farming, 5.9% construction, 17.4% production (2000).
Income: Per capita income: $20,727 (2000); Median household income: $32,813 (2000); Poverty rate: 6.7% (2000).
Taxes: Total city taxes per capita: $74 (1997); City property taxes per capita: $16 (1997).
Education: High school graduation rate: 78.7% (2000); College graduation rate: 11.1% (2000).
Housing: Homeownership rate: 84.2% (2000); Median home value: $64,000 (2000); Median rent: $293 per month (2000); Median age of housing: 29 years (2000).
Transportation: Commute to work: 96.3% car, 0.0% public transportation, 1.2% walk, 1.9% work from home (2000); Travel time to work: 43.4% less than 15 minutes, 41.8% 15 to 30 minutes, 8.5% 30 to 45 minutes, 2.5% 45 to 60 minutes, 3.8% 60 minutes or more (2000)

DUKE (unincorporated postal area, zip code 65461). Covers a land area of 13.344 square miles and a water area of 0.298 square miles. Located at 37.68° N. Lat.; 92.04° W. Long. Elevation is 1,115 feet.
Population: 83 (2000); Race: 100.0% White, 0.0% Black, 0.0% Asian, 0.0% American Indian and Alaska Native, 0.0% Hispanic of any race, 0.0% two or more races (2000); Density: 6.2 persons per square mile (2000); Age: 27.8% under 18, 28.9% over 64 (2000); Marriage status: 38.1% never married, 26.2% now married, 11.9% widowed, 23.8% divorced (2000); Foreign born: 4.4% (2000); Ancestry (includes multiple ancestries): 23.3% French (except Basque), 22.2% English, 15.6% German, 11.1% Other groups, 6.7% Scotch-Irish (2000).
Economy: Employment by occupation: 0.0% management, 0.0% professional, 9.1% services, 36.4% sales, 0.0% farming, 15.2% construction, 39.4% production (2000).
Income: Per capita income: $36,193 (2000); Median household income: $21,750 (2000); Poverty rate: 38.9% (2000).
Education: High school graduation rate: 64.9% (2000); College graduation rate: 0.0% (2000).
Housing: Homeownership rate: 85.3% (2000); Median home value: $127,500 (2000); Median age of housing: 52 years (2000).
Transportation: Commute to work: 68.2% car, 0.0% public transportation, 0.0% walk, 0.0% work from home (2000); Travel time to work: 36.4% less than 15 minutes, 45.5% 15 to 30 minutes, 18.2% 30 to 45 minutes, 0.0% 45 to 60 minutes, 0.0% 60 minutes or more (2000)

EDGAR SPRINGS (city). Covers a land area of 0.487 square miles and a water area of 0 square miles. Located at 37.70° N. Lat.; 91.86° W. Long. Elevation is 1,205 feet.
History: Edgar Springs developed as a lumber mill town. Reforestation efforts were centered at the Licking Nursery, operated by the U.S. Forest Service.
Population: 190 (2000); Race: 99.5% White, 0.0% Black, 0.5% Asian, 0.0% American Indian and Alaska Native, 0.0% Hispanic of any race, 0.0% two or more races (2000); Density: 390.3 persons per square mile (2000); Age: 28.9% under 18, 17.2% over 64 (2000); Marriage status: 15.2% never married, 57.6% now married, 15.9% widowed, 11.3% divorced (2000); Foreign born: 0.0% (2000); Ancestry (includes multiple ancestries): 30.9% German, 12.3% Other groups, 11.8% English, 10.3% Irish, 6.9% United States or American (2000).
Economy: Single-family building permits issued: 0 (2001) / 0 (2000); Multi-family building permits issued: 0 (2001) / 0 (2000); Employment by occupation: 9.2% management, 15.8% professional, 10.5% services, 26.3% sales, 0.0% farming, 15.8% construction, 22.4% production (2000).
Income: Per capita income: $12,672 (2000); Median household income: $30,000 (2000); Poverty rate: 4.9% (2000).
Taxes: Total city taxes per capita: $96 (1997); City property taxes per capita: $41 (1997).
Education: High school graduation rate: 68.4% (2000); College graduation rate: 7.4% (2000).

School District(s)

Phelps Co. R-III (PK-08)
2000 Enrollment: 216 573-435-6293

Housing: Homeownership rate: 81.5% (2000); Median home value: $43,700 (2000); Median rent: $213 per month (2000); Median age of housing: 39 years (2000).
Transportation: Commute to work: 84.4% car, 2.6% public transportation, 7.8% walk, 5.2% work from home (2000); Travel time to work: 20.5% less than 15 minutes, 21.9% 15 to 30 minutes, 34.2% 30 to 45 minutes, 5.5% 45 to 60 minutes, 17.8% 60 minutes or more (2000)

JEROME (unincorporated postal area, zip code 65529). Covers a land area of 0.605 square miles and a water area of 0 square miles. Located at 37.92° N. Lat.; 91.98° W. Long. Elevation is 710 feet.
History: Jerome developed as a fishing resort on the Gasconade River.
Population: 240 (2000); Race: 97.0% White, 0.0% Black, 0.0% Asian, 0.0% American Indian and Alaska Native, 0.0% Hispanic of any race, 3.0% two or more races (2000); Density: 396.6 persons per square mile (2000); Age: 28.9% under 18, 14.7% over 64 (2000); Marriage status: 19.8% never married, 65.6% now married, 6.8% widowed, 7.8% divorced (2000); Foreign born: 0.0% (2000); Ancestry (includes multiple ancestries): 22.0% United States or American, 17.7% Irish, 12.9% Other groups, 11.2% German, 7.3% Dutch (2000).
Economy: Employment by occupation: 6.1% management, 13.6% professional, 0.0% services, 16.7% sales, 0.0% farming, 40.9% construction, 22.7% production (2000).
Income: Per capita income: $13,837 (2000); Median household income: $21,597 (2000); Poverty rate: 23.3% (2000).
Education: High school graduation rate: 65.8% (2000); College graduation rate: 0.0% (2000).
Housing: Homeownership rate: 66.0% (2000); Median home value: $49,300 (2000); Median rent: $266 per month (2000); Median age of housing: 36 years (2000).
Transportation: Commute to work: 100.0% car, 0.0% public transportation, 0.0% walk, 0.0% work from home (2000); Travel time to work: 15.2% less than 15 minutes, 54.5% 15 to 30 minutes, 13.6% 30 to 45 minutes, 0.0% 45 to 60 minutes, 16.7% 60 minutes or more (2000)

NEWBURG (city). Covers a land area of 0.617 square miles and a water area of 0 square miles. Located at 37.91° N. Lat.; 91.90° W. Long. Elevation is 711 feet.

History: Newburg was settled in 1823 by William Coppedge, who manufactured powder using saltpetre from a nearby cave. The town was platted in 1883 when the railroad planned a division point here.
Population: 484 (2000); Race: 97.1% White, 0.0% Black, 0.0% Asian, 0.0% American Indian and Alaska Native, 0.9% Hispanic of any race, 2.6% two or more races (2000); Density: 784.9 persons per square mile (2000); Age: 18.5% under 18, 21.4% over 64 (2000); Marriage status: 23.1% never married, 50.9% now married, 11.8% widowed, 14.2% divorced (2000); Foreign born: 0.4% (2000); Ancestry (includes multiple ancestries): 30.6% United States or American, 14.1% German, 11.9% Other groups, 8.8% English, 6.6% Irish (2000).
Economy: Single-family building permits issued: 0 (2001) / 0 (2000); Multi-family building permits issued: 0 (2001) / 0 (2000); Employment by occupation: 5.1% management, 10.1% professional, 31.6% services, 17.1% sales, 1.9% farming, 14.6% construction, 19.6% production (2000).
Income: Per capita income: $11,092 (2000); Median household income: $18,000 (2000); Poverty rate: 29.7% (2000).
Taxes: Total city taxes per capita: $184 (1997); City property taxes per capita: $31 (1997).
Education: High school graduation rate: 58.4% (2000); College graduation rate: 2.9% (2000).

School District(s)

Newburg R-II (PK-12)
2000 Enrollment: 511 573-762-2211

Housing: Homeownership rate: 60.3% (2000); Median home value: $27,300 (2000); Median rent: $192 per month (2000); Median age of housing: 48 years (2000).
Transportation: Commute to work: 88.0% car, 0.7% public transportation, 2.0% walk, 2.0% work from home (2000); Travel time to work: 18.4% less than 15 minutes, 59.2% 15 to 30 minutes, 15.6% 30 to 45 minutes, 3.4% 45 to 60 minutes, 3.4% 60 minutes or more (2000)

ROLLA (city). Covers a land area of 11.297 square miles and a water area of 0.008 square miles. Located at 37.94° N. Lat.; 91.76° W. Long. Elevation is 1,119 feet.
History: Rolla began in 1855 as a construction center for the St. Louis-San Francisco Railway crews. The town that developed was named for Raleigh, North Carolina, the former home of railroad official E.W. Bishop. The revised spelling reflected Bishop's pronunciation of the name. The Missouri School of Mines opened in Rolla in 1871.
Population: 16,367 (2000); Race: 88.5% White, 3.3% Black, 4.1% Asian, 1.3% American Indian and Alaska Native, 2.1% Hispanic of any race, 1.6% two or more races (2000); Density: 1,448.7 persons per square mile (2000); Age: 20.2% under 18, 13.1% over 64 (2000); Marriage status: 31.2% never married, 51.2% now married, 8.0% widowed, 9.6% divorced (2000); Foreign born: 7.6% (2000); Ancestry (includes multiple ancestries): 23.4% German, 15.9% Other groups, 12.5% Irish, 10.8% English, 10.2% United States or American (2000).
Vital Statistics: Birth rate: 135.6 per 10,000 population (1998)
Economy: Single-family building permits issued: 57 (2001) / 60 (2000); Multi-family building permits issued: 160 (2001) / 78 (2000); Employment by occupation: 9.3% management, 27.9% professional, 17.3% services, 26.5% sales, 0.2% farming, 7.3% construction, 11.7% production (2000).
Income: Per capita income: $15,916 (2000); Median household income: $26,479 (2000); Poverty rate: 22.0% (2000).
Taxes: Total city taxes per capita: $659 (2000); City property taxes per capita: $49 (2000).
Education: High school graduation rate: 82.5% (2000); College graduation rate: 27.9% (2000).

School District(s)

Rolla 31 (PK-12)
2000 Enrollment: 4,105 573-458-0100

Four-year College(s)

University of Missouri-Rolla (Public)
2001 Enrollment: 4,883 573-341-4111
2001 Tuition: In-state $4,245; Out-of-state $12,690

Two-year College(s)

Rolla Technical Institute (Public)
2001 Enrollment: 364 573-458-0150
2001 Tuition: In-state $4,515; Out-of-state $4,515
Metro Business College (Private, For-profit)
2001 Enrollment: 90 573-364-8464
2001 Tuition: In-state $7,785; Out-of-state $7,785

Housing: Homeownership rate: 47.4% (2000); Median home value: $78,700 (2000); Median rent: $331 per month (2000); Median age of housing: 26 years (2000).
Hospitals: Phelps County Regional Medical Center (232 beds)
Safety: Violent crime rate: 26.7 per 10,000 population; Property crime rate: 569.0 per 10,000 population (2001).
Newspapers: Rolla Daily News (6 x week)
Transportation: Commute to work: 83.5% car, 0.7% public transportation, 10.9% walk, 3.0% work from home (2000); Travel time to work: 74.8% less than 15 minutes, 12.3% 15 to 30 minutes, 7.0% 30 to 45 minutes, 2.6% 45 to 60 minutes, 3.3% 60 minutes or more (2000)
Airports: Rolla National
Additional Information Contacts
Rolla Chamber of Commerce. 573-364-3577
South Central Board of Realtors 573-368-2800

SAINT JAMES (city). Covers a land area of 2.792 square miles and a water area of 0.006 square miles. Located at 37.99° N. Lat.; 91.61° W. Long. Elevation is 1,088 feet.
History: St. James was platted in 1859 by John Wood in anticipation of the westward extension of the railroad which would serve as a shipping station for the nearby Meramec Iron Works. When the iron mines closed, St. James turned to lumber, agriculture, and wine making. It was incorporated as a town in 1870.
Population: 3,704 (2000); Race: 93.8% White, 0.7% Black, 0.1% Asian, 0.0% American Indian and Alaska Native, 0.4% Hispanic of any race, 4.8% two or more races (2000); Density: 1,326.4 persons per square mile (2000); Age: 24.6% under 18, 25.0% over 64 (2000); Marriage status: 18.2% never married, 54.8% now married, 14.4% widowed, 12.6% divorced (2000); Foreign born: 0.6% (2000); Ancestry (includes multiple ancestries): 21.2% German, 15.1% Irish, 13.8% United States or American, 9.1% Other groups, 9.1% English (2000).
Economy: Single-family building permits issued: 24 (2001) / 8 (2000); Multi-family building permits issued: 36 (2001) / 20 (2000); Employment by occupation: 8.9% management, 22.5% professional, 19.9% services, 21.8% sales, 0.0% farming, 10.0% construction, 16.9% production (2000).
Income: Per capita income: $14,509 (2000); Median household income: $24,629 (2000); Poverty rate: 17.2% (2000).
Education: High school graduation rate: 71.2% (2000); College graduation rate: 12.9% (2000).

School District(s)

Saint James R-I (PK-12)
2000 Enrollment: 1,843 573-265-3261

Housing: Homeownership rate: 60.5% (2000); Median home value: $65,800 (2000); Median rent: $294 per month (2000); Median age of housing: 30 years (2000).
Newspapers: Leader-Journal (1 x week)
Transportation: Commute to work: 91.1% car, 0.6% public transportation, 3.8% walk, 3.3% work from home (2000); Travel time to work: 50.3% less than 15 minutes, 32.0% 15 to 30 minutes, 7.7% 30 to 45 minutes, 1.5% 45 to 60 minutes, 8.4% 60 minutes or more (2000)

Pike County

Located in eastern Missouri; bounded on the east by the Mississippi River and the Illinois border; crossed by the Salt River. Covers a land area of 672.80 square miles, a water area of 12.00 square miles, and is located in the Central Time Zone. The county government was organized in 1818. County seat is Bowling Green.
Population: 18,351 (2000); Race: 88.7% White, 8.3% Black, 0.6% Asian, 0.2% American Indian and Alaska Native, 1.6% Hispanic of any race, 1.4% two or more races (2000); Density: 27.3 persons per square mile (2000); Age: 23.5% under 18, 14.6% over 64 (2000).
Religion: Five largest groups: 25.6% Southern Baptist Convention, 9.1% Catholic Church, 5.3% Christian Church (Disciples of Christ), 4.0% Presbyterian Church (U.S.A.), 2.3% The United Methodist Church (2000).
Economy: Unemployment rate: 4.6% (11/2002); Total civilian labor force: 7,777 (11/2002); Leading industries: 21.6% manufacturing; 17.4% health care and social assistance; 15.9% retail trade (2000); Companies that employ more than 1,000 persons: 0 (2000); Companies that employ more than 100 persons: 3 (2000); Farms: 944 totaling 316,743 acres (1997); Minority business ownership rate: 0.0% (1997); Women business ownership rate: 14.0% (1997); Retail sales per capita: $5,354 (1997). Single-family building permits issued: 7 (2001) / 13 (2000); Multi-family building permits issued: 0 (2001) / 0 (2000).
Income: Per capita income: $14,462 (2000); Median household income: $32,373 (2000); Poverty rate: 15.5% (2000); Bankruptcy rate: 3.61% (2001).

Taxes: Total county taxes per capita: $130 (2000); County property taxes per capita: $65 (2000).
Education: High school graduation rate: 76.0% (2000); College graduation rate: 10.2% (2000).
Housing: Homeownership rate: 74.1% (2000); Median home value: $63,400 (2000); Median rent: $260 per month (2000); Median age of housing: 34 years (2000).
Health: Birth rate: 122.1 per 10,000 population (1998); Age adjusted death rate: 91.7 per 10,000 population (1999); Age adjusted cancer mortality rate: 203.2 deaths per 100,000 population (1999). Number of physicians: 4.4 per 10,000 population (1999); Number of hospital beds: 13.6 per 10,000 population (1999).
Elections: 2000 Presidential election results: 48.4% Gore, 49.6% Bush, 1.1% Nader, 0.5% Buchanan
National and State Parks: Clarence Cannon National Wildlife Refuge; Clarksville State Game Refuge; Ranacker State Wildlife Area; Ted Shanks State Wildlife Management Area; Upper Mississippi River State Wildlife Manag
Additional Information Contacts
Pike County Government Offices 573-324-2412
Bowling Green Chamber of Commerce 573-324-6800
Louisiana Chamber of Commerce 573-754-5921

Pike County Communities

ANNADA (village). Covers a land area of 0.061 square miles and a water area of 0 square miles. Located at 39.26° N. Lat.; 90.82° W. Long. Elevation is 449 feet.
History: Annada was named for Anna and Ada Jamison, daughters of early settler Carson Jamison. Annada was situated near Saltpetre Bluff, where residents got saltpetre for manufacturing gunpowder.
Population: 48 (2000); Race: 100.0% White, 0.0% Black, 0.0% Asian, 0.0% American Indian and Alaska Native, 0.0% Hispanic of any race, 0.0% two or more races (2000); Density: 790.5 persons per square mile (2000); Age: 23.1% under 18, 30.8% over 64 (2000); Marriage status: 26.5% never married, 38.2% now married, 17.6% widowed, 17.6% divorced (2000); Foreign born: 0.0% (2000); Ancestry (includes multiple ancestries): 46.2% United States or American, 17.9% German, 15.4% English, 5.1% Other groups, 5.1% Scottish (2000).
Economy: Employment by occupation: 0.0% management, 18.8% professional, 0.0% services, 18.8% sales, 12.5% farming, 12.5% construction, 37.5% production (2000).
Income: Per capita income: $15,423 (2000); Median household income: $25,500 (2000); Poverty rate: 15.4% (2000).
Taxes: Total city taxes per capita: $29 (1997); City property taxes per capita: $14 (1997).
Education: High school graduation rate: 80.0% (2000); College graduation rate: 26.7% (2000).
Housing: Homeownership rate: 66.7% (2000); Median home value: $26,300 (2000); Median rent: $225 per month (2000); Median age of housing: 58 years (2000).
Transportation: Commute to work: 100.0% car, 0.0% public transportation, 0.0% walk, 0.0% work from home (2000); Travel time to work: 21.4% less than 15 minutes, 7.1% 15 to 30 minutes, 35.7% 30 to 45 minutes, 14.3% 45 to 60 minutes, 21.4% 60 minutes or more (2000)

ASHBURN (town). Covers a land area of 0.132 square miles and a water area of 0 square miles. Located at 39.54° N. Lat.; 91.17° W. Long. Elevation is 805 feet.
Population: 51 (2000); Race: 100.0% White, 0.0% Black, 0.0% Asian, 0.0% American Indian and Alaska Native, 0.0% Hispanic of any race, 0.0% two or more races (2000); Density: 385.2 persons per square mile (2000); Age: 18.5% under 18, 0.0% over 64 (2000); Marriage status: 0.0% never married, 100.0% now married, 0.0% widowed, 0.0% divorced (2000); Foreign born: 0.0% (2000)
Economy: Employment by occupation: 0.0% management, 0.0% professional, 0.0% services, 0.0% sales, 0.0% farming, 0.0% construction, 100.0% production (2000).
Income: Per capita income: $7,569 (2000); Median household income: $11,797 (2000); Poverty rate: 72.2% (2000).
Education: High school graduation rate: 74.2% (2000); College graduation rate: 0.0% (2000).
Housing: Homeownership rate: 35.0% (2000); Median home value: $45,000 (2000); Median rent: $175 per month (2000); Median age of housing: 31 years (2000).
Transportation: Commute to work: 100.0% car, 0.0% public transportation, 0.0% walk, 0.0% work from home (2000); Travel time to work: 0.0% less than 15 minutes, 100.0% 15 to 30 minutes, 0.0% 30 to 45 minutes, 0.0% 45 to 60 minutes, 0.0% 60 minutes or more (2000)

BOWLING GREEN (city). Covers a land area of 1.944 square miles and a water area of 0 square miles. Located at 39.34° N. Lat.; 91.20° W. Long. Elevation is 899 feet.
History: Bowling Green was platted in 1826 and named for the Kentucky home of many of the town's early residents. Bowling Green was the home of James Beauchamp Clark (1850-1921), Missouri representative to the U.S. Congress and Speaker of the House for eight years.
Population: 3,260 (2000); Race: 91.0% White, 7.4% Black, 0.0% Asian, 0.4% American Indian and Alaska Native, 0.7% Hispanic of any race, 1.3% two or more races (2000); Density: 1,677.0 persons per square mile (2000); Age: 27.4% under 18, 17.8% over 64 (2000); Marriage status: 20.6% never married, 46.9% now married, 13.6% widowed, 18.9% divorced (2000); Foreign born: 0.2% (2000); Ancestry (includes multiple ancestries): 25.9% German, 23.0% United States or American, 16.3% Other groups, 10.9% English, 9.4% Irish (2000).
Economy: Single-family building permits issued: 7 (2001) / 9 (2000); Multi-family building permits issued: 0 (2001) / 0 (2000); Employment by occupation: 7.3% management, 10.6% professional, 27.5% services, 22.6% sales, 1.0% farming, 11.7% construction, 19.2% production (2000).
Income: Per capita income: $14,670 (2000); Median household income: $27,287 (2000); Poverty rate: 13.1% (2000).
Taxes: Total city taxes per capita: $166 (1997); City property taxes per capita: $26 (1997).
Education: High school graduation rate: 77.9% (2000); College graduation rate: 10.2% (2000).

School District(s)

Bowling Green R-I (KG-12)
2000 Enrollment: 1,518 573-324-5441
Housing: Homeownership rate: 59.7% (2000); Median home value: $62,800 (2000); Median rent: $278 per month (2000); Median age of housing: 34 years (2000).
Safety: Violent crime rate: 54.9 per 10,000 population; Property crime rate: 167.7 per 10,000 population (2001).
Newspapers: The Bowling Green Times (1 x week)
Transportation: Commute to work: 92.6% car, 0.3% public transportation, 2.5% walk, 2.5% work from home (2000); Travel time to work: 54.9% less than 15 minutes, 19.7% 15 to 30 minutes, 12.9% 30 to 45 minutes, 8.0% 45 to 60 minutes, 4.5% 60 minutes or more (2000)
Additional Information Contacts
Bowling Green Chamber of Commerce 573-324-6800

CLARKSVILLE (city). Covers a land area of 0.462 square miles and a water area of 0.360 square miles. Located at 39.36° N. Lat.; 90.90° W. Long. Elevation is 480 feet.
History: Clarksville was settled in 1816 on a bluff above the Mississippi River. In the 1850's the community was called Appleton, because of the quantity of apples shipped each fall. It was also known for its rattlesnakes, with reports that as many as 9,000 rattlesnakes were killed in one day on the annual spring snake hunt.
Population: 490 (2000); Race: 92.3% White, 4.4% Black, 0.4% Asian, 0.0% American Indian and Alaska Native, 1.5% Hispanic of any race, 2.3% two or more races (2000); Density: 1,060.2 persons per square mile (2000); Age: 25.0% under 18, 18.3% over 64 (2000); Marriage status: 19.8% never married, 49.2% now married, 12.8% widowed, 18.2% divorced (2000); Foreign born: 0.6% (2000); Ancestry (includes multiple ancestries): 25.4% German, 17.7% Other groups, 14.0% United States or American, 13.3% Irish, 10.0% English (2000).
Economy: Employment by occupation: 5.2% management, 23.5% professional, 17.4% services, 17.8% sales, 1.9% farming, 10.8% construction, 23.5% production (2000).
Income: Per capita income: $14,728 (2000); Median household income: $23,611 (2000); Poverty rate: 22.2% (2000).
Taxes: Total city taxes per capita: $185 (1997); City property taxes per capita: $30 (1997).
Education: High school graduation rate: 77.2% (2000); College graduation rate: 16.5% (2000).

School District(s)

Pike Co. R-III (PK-12)
2000 Enrollment: 608 573-242-3546

Housing: Homeownership rate: 60.2% (2000); Median home value: $58,400 (2000); Median rent: $257 per month (2000); Median age of housing: 39 years (2000).
Transportation: Commute to work: 81.7% car, 0.0% public transportation, 10.1% walk, 5.8% work from home (2000); Travel time to work: 43.4% less than 15 minutes, 29.6% 15 to 30 minutes, 3.6% 30 to 45 minutes, 7.1% 45 to 60 minutes, 16.3% 60 minutes or more (2000)

CURRYVILLE (city). Covers a land area of 0.276 square miles and a water area of 0 square miles. Located at 39.34° N. Lat.; 91.34° W. Long. Elevation is 816 feet.
Population: 251 (2000); Race: 91.9% White, 2.4% Black, 0.0% Asian, 2.4% American Indian and Alaska Native, 0.0% Hispanic of any race, 3.2% two or more races (2000); Density: 909.2 persons per square mile (2000); Age: 20.2% under 18, 9.7% over 64 (2000); Marriage status: 16.9% never married, 61.4% now married, 7.7% widowed, 14.0% divorced (2000); Foreign born: 0.0% (2000); Ancestry (includes multiple ancestries): 23.5% United States or American, 18.6% Other groups, 15.0% English, 12.1% German, 8.9% Irish (2000).
Economy: Amish community nearby. Single-family building permits issued: 0 (2001) / 1 (2000); Multi-family building permits issued: 0 (2001) / 0 (2000); Employment by occupation: 1.7% management, 1.7% professional, 25.4% services, 20.3% sales, 2.5% farming, 19.5% construction, 28.8% production (2000).
Income: Per capita income: $13,032 (2000); Median household income: $27,500 (2000); Poverty rate: 22.7% (2000).
Taxes: Total city taxes per capita: $56 (1997); City property taxes per capita: $24 (1997).
Education: High school graduation rate: 73.7% (2000); College graduation rate: 2.3% (2000).
Housing: Homeownership rate: 78.1% (2000); Median home value: $28,200 (2000); Median rent: $306 per month (2000); Median age of housing: 31 years (2000).
Transportation: Commute to work: 94.1% car, 0.0% public transportation, 4.2% walk, 1.7% work from home (2000); Travel time to work: 37.9% less than 15 minutes, 39.7% 15 to 30 minutes, 9.5% 30 to 45 minutes, 9.5% 45 to 60 minutes, 3.4% 60 minutes or more (2000)

EOLIA (village). Covers a land area of 1.226 square miles and a water area of 0 square miles. Located at 39.23° N. Lat.; 91.01° W. Long. Elevation is 833 feet.
Population: 435 (2000); Race: 93.0% White, 5.6% Black, 0.0% Asian, 0.0% American Indian and Alaska Native, 1.8% Hispanic of any race, 1.1% two or more races (2000); Density: 354.7 persons per square mile (2000); Age: 26.1% under 18, 13.3% over 64 (2000); Marriage status: 24.3% never married, 57.3% now married, 8.8% widowed, 9.6% divorced (2000); Foreign born: 0.0% (2000); Ancestry (includes multiple ancestries): 31.9% United States or American, 16.0% German, 12.6% Other groups, 8.8% Irish, 8.1% English (2000).
Economy: Employment by occupation: 6.3% management, 20.3% professional, 13.0% services, 20.8% sales, 1.0% farming, 9.7% construction, 29.0% production (2000).
Income: Per capita income: $14,445 (2000); Median household income: $35,104 (2000); Poverty rate: 17.8% (2000).
Taxes: Total city taxes per capita: $69 (1997); City property taxes per capita: $37 (1997).
Education: High school graduation rate: 80.6% (2000); College graduation rate: 9.2% (2000).
Housing: Homeownership rate: 78.5% (2000); Median home value: $65,400 (2000); Median rent: $250 per month (2000); Median age of housing: 29 years (2000).
Transportation: Commute to work: 95.7% car, 0.0% public transportation, 1.9% walk, 2.4% work from home (2000); Travel time to work: 17.8% less than 15 minutes, 36.1% 15 to 30 minutes, 16.8% 30 to 45 minutes, 9.9% 45 to 60 minutes, 19.3% 60 minutes or more (2000)

FRANKFORD (city). Covers a land area of 0.471 square miles and a water area of 0 square miles. Located at 39.49° N. Lat.; 91.32° W. Long. Elevation is 600 feet.
Population: 351 (2000); Race: 97.3% White, 1.8% Black, 0.0% Asian, 0.0% American Indian and Alaska Native, 0.0% Hispanic of any race, 0.9% two or more races (2000); Density: 745.2 persons per square mile (2000); Age: 22.9% under 18, 13.1% over 64 (2000); Marriage status: 20.8% never married, 62.4% now married, 6.2% widowed, 10.6% divorced (2000); Foreign born: 0.6% (2000); Ancestry (includes multiple ancestries): 15.9% German, 13.4% United States or American, 8.2% Irish, 7.3% Other groups, 5.8% English (2000).
Economy: Corn, wheat, soybeans; hogs. Wood products; limestone quarry. Employment by occupation: 12.0% management, 9.5% professional, 9.5% services, 19.0% sales, 1.9% farming, 12.0% construction, 36.1% production (2000).
Income: Per capita income: $14,892 (2000); Median household income: $26,406 (2000); Poverty rate: 13.1% (2000).
Taxes: Total city taxes per capita: $69 (1997); City property taxes per capita: $37 (1997).
Education: High school graduation rate: 72.2% (2000); College graduation rate: 9.4% (2000).
Housing: Homeownership rate: 82.1% (2000); Median home value: $40,900 (2000); Median rent: $306 per month (2000); Median age of housing: 48 years (2000).
Transportation: Commute to work: 91.8% car, 0.0% public transportation, 1.9% walk, 1.3% work from home (2000); Travel time to work: 14.1% less than 15 minutes, 48.7% 15 to 30 minutes, 17.9% 30 to 45 minutes, 3.8% 45 to 60 minutes, 15.4% 60 minutes or more (2000)

LOUISIANA (city). Covers a land area of 3.130 square miles and a water area of 0.289 square miles. Located at 39.44° N. Lat.; 91.05° W. Long. Elevation is 1,477 feet.
History: Louisiana was laid out in 1818 by Samuel K. Caldwell and Joel Shaw, and named for the state of Louisiana. First a port on the Mississippi River at the mouth of Noix Creek, the community later turned to agriculture and industry.
Population: 3,863 (2000); Race: 90.4% White, 5.7% Black, 0.9% Asian, 0.3% American Indian and Alaska Native, 3.7% Hispanic of any race, 0.9% two or more races (2000); Density: 1,234.4 persons per square mile (2000); Age: 25.0% under 18, 19.8% over 64 (2000); Marriage status: 24.6% never married, 53.9% now married, 9.8% widowed, 11.8% divorced (2000); Foreign born: 4.5% (2000); Ancestry (includes multiple ancestries): 17.2% United States or American, 16.3% German, 15.8% Other groups, 13.6% Irish, 9.5% English (2000).
Economy: Single-family building permits issued: 0 (2001) / 3 (2000); Multi-family building permits issued: 0 (2001) / 0 (2000); Employment by occupation: 10.6% management, 13.8% professional, 16.9% services, 18.9% sales, 2.1% farming, 8.7% construction, 29.1% production (2000).
Income: Per capita income: $15,623 (2000); Median household income: $30,467 (2000); Poverty rate: 20.4% (2000).
Taxes: Total city taxes per capita: $345 (1997); City property taxes per capita: $55 (1997).
Education: High school graduation rate: 70.3% (2000); College graduation rate: 12.5% (2000).

School District(s)

Boncl R-X (KG-08)
2000 Enrollment: 47 573-754-5412
Louisiana R-II (KG-12)
2000 Enrollment: 788 573-754-4261

Housing: Homeownership rate: 67.3% (2000); Median home value: $53,900 (2000); Median rent: $245 per month (2000); Median age of housing: 44 years (2000).
Hospitals: Pike County Memorial Hospital (45 beds)
Safety: Violent crime rate: 36.0 per 10,000 population; Property crime rate: 450.2 per 10,000 population (2001).
Newspapers: The Louisiana Press-Journal (1 x week)
Transportation: Commute to work: 84.9% car, 4.1% public transportation, 7.7% walk, 2.3% work from home (2000); Travel time to work: 59.9% less than 15 minutes, 16.7% 15 to 30 minutes, 9.6% 30 to 45 minutes, 2.9% 45 to 60 minutes, 10.9% 60 minutes or more (2000)

Additional Information Contacts

Louisiana Chamber of Commerce 573-754-5921

PAYNESVILLE (village). Covers a land area of 0.263 square miles and a water area of 0 square miles. Located at 39.26° N. Lat.; 90.90° W. Long. Elevation is 555 feet.
Population: 91 (2000); Race: 76.6% White, 23.4% Black, 0.0% Asian, 0.0% American Indian and Alaska Native, 0.0% Hispanic of any race, 0.0% two or more races (2000); Density: 345.7 persons per square mile (2000); Age: 22.1% under 18, 13.0% over 64 (2000); Marriage status: 29.7% never married, 50.0% now married, 14.1% widowed, 6.3% divorced (2000); Foreign born: 0.0% (2000); Ancestry (includes multiple ancestries): 31.2% United States or American, 20.8% English, 13.0% Other groups, 13.0% German (2000).

Economy: Employment by occupation: 14.3% management, 57.1% professional, 0.0% services, 7.1% sales, 10.7% farming, 0.0% construction, 10.7% production (2000).
Income: Per capita income: $11,783 (2000); Median household income: $25,625 (2000); Poverty rate: 14.3% (2000).
Taxes: Total city taxes per capita: $11 (2000); City property taxes per capita: $11 (2000).
Education: High school graduation rate: 78.3% (2000); College graduation rate: 26.7% (2000).
Housing: Homeownership rate: 73.3% (2000); Median home value: $58,800 (2000); Median rent: $200 per month (2000); Median age of housing: 43 years (2000).
Transportation: Commute to work: 100.0% car, 0.0% public transportation, 0.0% walk, 0.0% work from home (2000); Travel time to work: 32.1% less than 15 minutes, 14.3% 15 to 30 minutes, 3.6% 30 to 45 minutes, 21.4% 45 to 60 minutes, 28.6% 60 minutes or more (2000)

TARRANTS (village). Covers a land area of 0.044 square miles and a water area of 0 square miles. Located at 39.35° N. Lat.; 91.18° W. Long. Elevation is 715 feet.
Population: 30 (2000); Race: 63.2% White, 36.8% Black, 0.0% Asian, 0.0% American Indian and Alaska Native, 0.0% Hispanic of any race, 0.0% two or more races (2000); Density: 689.3 persons per square mile (2000); Age: 0.0% under 18, 47.4% over 64 (2000); Marriage status: 0.0% never married, 100.0% now married, 0.0% widowed, 0.0% divorced (2000); Foreign born: 0.0% (2000); Ancestry (includes multiple ancestries): 36.8% Other groups, 34.2% German, 15.8% Scotch-Irish, 13.2% Irish, 13.2% French (except Basque) (2000).
Economy: Employment by occupation: 31.6% management, 0.0% professional, 31.6% services, 0.0% sales, 0.0% farming, 36.8% construction, 0.0% production (2000).
Income: Per capita income: $11,358 (2000); Median household income: $20,833 (2000); Poverty rate: 0.0% (2000).
Education: High school graduation rate: 71.1% (2000); College graduation rate: 0.0% (2000).
Housing: Homeownership rate: 63.6% (2000); Median home value: $27,500 (2000); Median rent: $125 per month (2000); Median age of housing: 56 years (2000).
Transportation: Commute to work: 31.6% car, 0.0% public transportation, 0.0% walk, 68.4% work from home (2000); Travel time to work: 100.0% less than 15 minutes, 0.0% 15 to 30 minutes, 0.0% 30 to 45 minutes, 0.0% 45 to 60 minutes, 0.0% 60 minutes or more (2000)

Platte County

Located in western Missouri; bounded on the south and west by the Missouri River; drained by the Little Platte River. Covers a land area of 420.30 square miles, a water area of 6.90 square miles, and is located in the Central Time Zone. The county government was organized in 1838. County seat is Platte City.

Platte County is part of the Kansas City, MO-KS MSA. The entire metro area includes: Johnson County, KS; Leavenworth County, KS; Miami County, KS; Wyandotte County, KS; Cass County, MO; Clay County, MO; Clinton County, MO; Jackson County, MO; Lafayette County, MO; Platte County, MO; Ray County, MO

Weather Station: Kansas City Int'l Airport — Elevation: 971 feet

	Jan	Feb	Mar	Apr	May	Jun	Jul	Aug	Sep	Oct	Nov	Dec
High	35	42	54	65	74	83	89	87	78	67	52	40
Low	18	23	33	44	54	63	68	66	57	46	34	23
Precip	1.2	1.3	2.5	3.6	5.5	4.5	4.4	3.7	4.8	3.4	2.3	1.6
Snow	5.9	5.0	2.6	0.9	tr	tr	tr	0.0	tr	0.3	1.4	4.0

High and Low temperatures in degrees Fahrenheit; Precipitation and Snow in inches

Population: 73,781 (2000); Race: 91.3% White, 3.2% Black, 1.5% Asian, 0.6% American Indian and Alaska Native, 3.0% Hispanic of any race, 2.1% two or more races (2000); Density: 175.5 persons per square mile (2000); Age: 25.7% under 18, 8.8% over 64 (2000).
Religion: Five largest groups: 12.1% Catholic Church, 8.6% Southern Baptist Convention, 5.0% The United Methodist Church, 4.0% Christian Church (Disciples of Christ), 2.1% Independent, Charismatic Churches (2000).
Economy: Unemployment rate: 3.8% (11/2002); Total civilian labor force: 46,721 (11/2002); Leading industries: 18.7% transportation & warehousing; 11.3% accommodation & food services; 10.4% finance & insurance (2000); Companies that employ more than 1,000 persons: 3 (2000); Companies that employ more than 100 persons: 55 (2000); Farms: 714 totaling 180,455 acres (1997); Minority business ownership rate: 5.6% (1997); Women business ownership rate: 24.9% (1997); Retail sales per capita: $8,451 (1997). Single-family building permits issued: 375 (2001) / 379 (2000); Multi-family building permits issued: 150 (2001) / 88 (2000).
Income: Per capita income: $26,356 (2000); Median household income: $55,849 (2000); Poverty rate: 4.8% (2000); Bankruptcy rate: 3.81% (2001).
Taxes: Total county taxes per capita: $169 (2000); County property taxes per capita: $28 (2000).
Education: High school graduation rate: 91.8% (2000); College graduation rate: 33.3% (2000).
Housing: Homeownership rate: 67.4% (2000); Median home value: $126,700 (2000); Median rent: $558 per month (2000); Median age of housing: 20 years (2000).
Health: Birth rate: 133.2 per 10,000 population (1998); Age adjusted death rate: 80.8 per 10,000 population (1999); Age adjusted cancer mortality rate: 198.0 deaths per 100,000 population (1999). Air Quality Index: 74% good, 26% moderate, 0% unhealthy (percent of days in 2000). Number of physicians: 14.4 per 10,000 population (1999); Number of hospital beds: 21.1 per 10,000 population (1999).
Elections: 2000 Presidential election results: 45.0% Gore, 52.2% Bush, 1.9% Nader, 0.3% Buchanan
National and State Parks: Little Bean Marsh State Natural History Area; Weston Bend State Park
Additional Information Contacts
Platte County Government Offices 816-858-2232
Parkville Chamber of Commerce 816-587-2700
Platte City Chamber of Commerce 816-858-5270
Weston Chamber of Commerce 816-640-2909
Weston Development Council 816-640-2909

Platte County Communities

CAMDEN POINT (city). Covers a land area of 0.586 square miles and a water area of 0 square miles. Located at 39.45° N. Lat.; 94.74° W. Long. Elevation is 233 feet.
Population: 484 (2000); Race: 99.8% White, 0.0% Black, 0.0% Asian, 0.0% American Indian and Alaska Native, 0.4% Hispanic of any race, 0.2% two or more races (2000); Density: 826.3 persons per square mile (2000); Age: 29.9% under 18, 3.5% over 64 (2000); Marriage status: 17.8% never married, 68.9% now married, 1.9% widowed, 11.4% divorced (2000); Foreign born: 1.2% (2000); Ancestry (includes multiple ancestries): 23.0% German, 13.1% United States or American, 10.2% Irish, 9.5% English, 7.5% French (except Basque) (2000).
Economy: Single-family building permits issued: 7 (2001) / 6 (2000); Multi-family building permits issued: 0 (2001) / 0 (2000); Employment by occupation: 15.2% management, 24.6% professional, 7.2% services, 26.5% sales, 0.8% farming, 10.2% construction, 15.5% production (2000).
Income: Per capita income: $22,429 (2000); Median household income: $55,089 (2000); Poverty rate: 5.0% (2000).
Taxes: Total city taxes per capita: $60 (1997); City property taxes per capita: $34 (1997).
Education: High school graduation rate: 96.4% (2000); College graduation rate: 25.0% (2000).
Housing: Homeownership rate: 91.8% (2000); Median home value: $111,300 (2000); Median rent: $505 per month (2000); Median age of housing: 20 years (2000).
Transportation: Commute to work: 99.6% car, 0.0% public transportation, 0.0% walk, 0.0% work from home (2000); Travel time to work: 18.3% less than 15 minutes, 37.8% 15 to 30 minutes, 33.2% 30 to 45 minutes, 8.8% 45 to 60 minutes, 1.9% 60 minutes or more (2000)

DEARBORN (city). Covers a land area of 0.859 square miles and a water area of 0.013 square miles. Located at 39.52° N. Lat.; 94.76° W. Long. Elevation is 905 feet.
History: Dearborn was the scene of annual fox hunts conducted by a fox hunters' association.
Population: 529 (2000); Race: 95.8% White, 0.0% Black, 0.0% Asian, 0.0% American Indian and Alaska Native, 1.9% Hispanic of any race, 2.3% two or more races (2000); Density: 615.9 persons per square mile (2000); Age: 24.5% under 18, 15.4% over 64 (2000); Marriage status: 20.8% never married, 52.1% now married, 12.1% widowed, 15.0% divorced (2000); Foreign born: 0.0% (2000); Ancestry (includes multiple ancestries): 18.7%

German, 14.7% United States or American, 10.0% English, 8.9% Irish, 8.9% Other groups (2000).
Economy: Single-family building permits issued: 1 (2001) / 2 (2000); Multi-family building permits issued: 0 (2001) / 0 (2000); Employment by occupation: 10.1% management, 15.5% professional, 18.9% services, 18.1% sales, 0.0% farming, 16.8% construction, 20.6% production (2000).
Income: Per capita income: $17,537 (2000); Median household income: $34,861 (2000); Poverty rate: 11.4% (2000).
Taxes: Total city taxes per capita: $209 (1997); City property taxes per capita: $11 (1997).
Education: High school graduation rate: 79.6% (2000); College graduation rate: 11.2% (2000).

School District(s)

North Platte Co. R-I (PK-12)
2000 Enrollment: 710 816-450-3511

Housing: Homeownership rate: 63.0% (2000); Median home value: $69,500 (2000); Median rent: $280 per month (2000); Median age of housing: 46 years (2000).
Transportation: Commute to work: 97.5% car, 0.0% public transportation, 0.8% walk, 1.7% work from home (2000); Travel time to work: 25.6% less than 15 minutes, 42.7% 15 to 30 minutes, 27.4% 30 to 45 minutes, 3.0% 45 to 60 minutes, 1.3% 60 minutes or more (2000)

EDGERTON (city). Covers a land area of 0.375 square miles and a water area of 0 square miles. Located at 39.50° N. Lat.; 94.63° W. Long. Elevation is 835 feet.
Population: 533 (2000); Race: 97.4% White, 0.0% Black, 0.0% Asian, 1.2% American Indian and Alaska Native, 0.0% Hispanic of any race, 1.4% two or more races (2000); Density: 1,422.4 persons per square mile (2000); Age: 26.3% under 18, 11.0% over 64 (2000); Marriage status: 15.9% never married, 67.1% now married, 7.3% widowed, 9.8% divorced (2000); Foreign born: 0.4% (2000); Ancestry (includes multiple ancestries): 25.5% German, 12.8% Irish, 11.8% United States or American, 6.5% Other groups, 5.9% English (2000).
Economy: Corn, tobacco; cattle. Single-family building permits issued: 2 (2001) / 0 (2000); Multi-family building permits issued: 0 (2001) / 0 (2000); Employment by occupation: 10.0% management, 15.0% professional, 15.7% services, 29.3% sales, 0.0% farming, 13.0% construction, 17.0% production (2000).
Income: Per capita income: $18,444 (2000); Median household income: $42,411 (2000); Poverty rate: 9.8% (2000).
Taxes: Total city taxes per capita: $67 (1997); City property taxes per capita: $32 (1997).
Education: High school graduation rate: 84.7% (2000); College graduation rate: 9.7% (2000).
Housing: Homeownership rate: 86.6% (2000); Median home value: $74,800 (2000); Median rent: $403 per month (2000); Median age of housing: 50 years (2000).
Transportation: Commute to work: 95.7% car, 0.0% public transportation, 4.3% walk, 0.0% work from home (2000); Travel time to work: 16.1% less than 15 minutes, 26.4% 15 to 30 minutes, 27.4% 30 to 45 minutes, 20.7% 45 to 60 minutes, 9.4% 60 minutes or more (2000)

FARLEY (village). Covers a land area of 0.750 square miles and a water area of 0 square miles. Located at 39.28° N. Lat.; 94.83° W. Long. Elevation is 765 feet.
Population: 226 (2000); Race: 100.0% White, 0.0% Black, 0.0% Asian, 0.0% American Indian and Alaska Native, 0.0% Hispanic of any race, 0.0% two or more races (2000); Density: 301.3 persons per square mile (2000); Age: 24.2% under 18, 12.3% over 64 (2000); Marriage status: 12.4% never married, 71.2% now married, 6.2% widowed, 10.2% divorced (2000); Foreign born: 1.8% (2000); Ancestry (includes multiple ancestries): 51.1% German, 28.3% Irish, 9.6% English, 4.6% French (except Basque), 3.7% Scottish (2000).
Economy: Tobacco, corn, wheat; cattle. Employment by occupation: 19.0% management, 18.2% professional, 10.7% services, 28.1% sales, 0.0% farming, 11.6% construction, 12.4% production (2000).
Income: Per capita income: $25,118 (2000); Median household income: $56,406 (2000); Poverty rate: 3.2% (2000).
Taxes: Total city taxes per capita: $23 (1997); City property taxes per capita: $23 (1997).
Education: High school graduation rate: 93.8% (2000); College graduation rate: 18.1% (2000).
Housing: Homeownership rate: 96.7% (2000); Median home value: $92,800 (2000); Median rent: $375 per month (2000); Median age of housing: 32 years (2000).
Transportation: Commute to work: 98.3% car, 0.0% public transportation, 1.7% walk, 0.0% work from home (2000); Travel time to work: 9.1% less than 15 minutes, 40.5% 15 to 30 minutes, 42.1% 30 to 45 minutes, 8.3% 45 to 60 minutes, 0.0% 60 minutes or more (2000)

FERRELVIEW (village). Covers a land area of 0.106 square miles and a water area of 0 square miles. Located at 39.31° N. Lat.; 94.66° W. Long. Elevation is 955 feet.
Population: 593 (2000); Race: 87.7% White, 2.3% Black, 0.7% Asian, 0.0% American Indian and Alaska Native, 5.1% Hispanic of any race, 8.0% two or more races (2000); Density: 5,586.5 persons per square mile (2000); Age: 26.9% under 18, 5.1% over 64 (2000); Marriage status: 26.0% never married, 42.7% now married, 5.5% widowed, 25.8% divorced (2000); Foreign born: 2.8% (2000); Ancestry (includes multiple ancestries): 17.6% Other groups, 16.8% German, 16.1% United States or American, 9.5% Irish, 9.0% English (2000).
Economy: Surrounded by Kansas City. Kansas City International Airport. Single-family building permits issued: 0 (2001) / 0 (2000); Multi-family building permits issued: 0 (2001) / 0 (2000); Employment by occupation: 7.3% management, 8.7% professional, 16.6% services, 26.5% sales, 0.0% farming, 11.3% construction, 29.6% production (2000).
Income: Per capita income: $17,190 (2000); Median household income: $32,750 (2000); Poverty rate: 5.6% (2000).
Taxes: Total city taxes per capita: $72 (1997); City property taxes per capita: $10 (1997).
Education: High school graduation rate: 87.6% (2000); College graduation rate: 14.6% (2000).
Housing: Homeownership rate: 51.1% (2000); Median home value: $80,500 (2000); Median rent: $376 per month (2000); Median age of housing: 23 years (2000).
Transportation: Commute to work: 96.0% car, 0.0% public transportation, 2.0% walk, 1.4% work from home (2000); Travel time to work: 47.9% less than 15 minutes, 34.7% 15 to 30 minutes, 12.3% 30 to 45 minutes, 3.2% 45 to 60 minutes, 2.0% 60 minutes or more (2000)

HOUSTON LAKE (city). Covers a land area of 0.138 square miles and a water area of 0.033 square miles. Located at 39.19° N. Lat.; 94.62° W. Long. Elevation is 845 feet.
Population: 284 (2000); Race: 96.9% White, 0.0% Black, 0.0% Asian, 0.0% American Indian and Alaska Native, 2.4% Hispanic of any race, 2.0% two or more races (2000); Density: 2,055.1 persons per square mile (2000); Age: 16.9% under 18, 19.6% over 64 (2000); Marriage status: 26.0% never married, 48.4% now married, 8.1% widowed, 17.5% divorced (2000); Foreign born: 0.4% (2000); Ancestry (includes multiple ancestries): 20.4% German, 18.8% Irish, 15.7% English, 14.9% United States or American, 5.1% French (except Basque) (2000).
Economy: Single-family building permits issued: 0 (2001) / 0 (2000); Multi-family building permits issued: 0 (2001) / 0 (2000); Employment by occupation: 13.2% management, 20.6% professional, 8.8% services, 33.8% sales, 0.0% farming, 13.2% construction, 10.3% production (2000).
Income: Per capita income: $24,471 (2000); Median household income: $53,750 (2000); Poverty rate: 4.0% (2000).
Taxes: Total city taxes per capita: $132 (1997); City property taxes per capita: $52 (1997).
Education: High school graduation rate: 91.2% (2000); College graduation rate: 14.7% (2000).
Housing: Homeownership rate: 91.1% (2000); Median home value: $85,000 (2000); Median rent: $517 per month (2000); Median age of housing: 46 years (2000).
Transportation: Commute to work: 92.5% car, 1.5% public transportation, 0.0% walk, 6.0% work from home (2000); Travel time to work: 33.6% less than 15 minutes, 40.0% 15 to 30 minutes, 22.4% 30 to 45 minutes, 1.6% 45 to 60 minutes, 2.4% 60 minutes or more (2000)

IATAN (village). Covers a land area of 0.039 square miles and a water area of 0 square miles. Located at 39.47° N. Lat.; 94.98° W. Long. Elevation is 815 feet.
Population: 54 (2000); Race: 100.0% White, 0.0% Black, 0.0% Asian, 0.0% American Indian and Alaska Native, 0.0% Hispanic of any race, 0.0% two or more races (2000); Density: 1,399.0 persons per square mile (2000); Age: 52.5% under 18, 0.0% over 64 (2000); Marriage status: 27.8% never married, 36.1% now married, 8.3% widowed, 27.8% divorced (2000); Foreign born: 0.0% (2000); Ancestry (includes multiple ancestries): 60.7% United States or American, 11.5% Irish, 4.9% Scotch-Irish (2000).

Economy: Employment by occupation: 8.0% management, 0.0% professional, 40.0% services, 28.0% sales, 0.0% farming, 16.0% construction, 8.0% production (2000).
Income: Per capita income: $8,895 (2000); Median household income: $35,625 (2000); Poverty rate: 16.4% (2000).
Taxes: Total city taxes per capita: $35 (1997); City property taxes per capita: $18 (1997).
Education: High school graduation rate: 61.5% (2000); College graduation rate: 0.0% (2000).
Housing: Homeownership rate: 50.0% (2000); Median home value: $43,000 (2000); Median rent: $338 per month (2000); Median age of housing: 60+ years (2000).
Transportation: Commute to work: 100.0% car, 0.0% public transportation, 0.0% walk, 0.0% work from home (2000); Travel time to work: 0.0% less than 15 minutes, 28.0% 15 to 30 minutes, 72.0% 30 to 45 minutes, 0.0% 45 to 60 minutes, 0.0% 60 minutes or more (2000)

LAKE WAUKOMIS (city). Covers a land area of 0.265 square miles and a water area of 0.162 square miles. Located at 39.23° N. Lat.; 94.63° W. Long. Elevation is 1,000 feet.
Population: 917 (2000); Race: 99.0% White, 0.0% Black, 0.0% Asian, 0.0% American Indian and Alaska Native, 1.0% Hispanic of any race, 0.5% two or more races (2000); Density: 3,460.2 persons per square mile (2000); Age: 18.0% under 18, 18.6% over 64 (2000); Marriage status: 15.8% never married, 66.4% now married, 5.9% widowed, 11.8% divorced (2000); Foreign born: 1.7% (2000); Ancestry (includes multiple ancestries): 28.7% German, 25.6% English, 16.9% Irish, 6.4% United States or American, 4.8% French (except Basque) (2000).
Economy: Single-family building permits issued: 1 (2001) / 2 (2000); Multi-family building permits issued: 0 (2001) / 0 (2000); Employment by occupation: 15.5% management, 21.7% professional, 10.9% services, 30.7% sales, 0.0% farming, 7.3% construction, 13.8% production (2000).
Income: Per capita income: $30,840 (2000); Median household income: $60,357 (2000); Poverty rate: 1.0% (2000).
Taxes: Total city taxes per capita: $121 (1997); City property taxes per capita: $25 (1997).
Education: High school graduation rate: 93.5% (2000); College graduation rate: 32.3% (2000).
Housing: Homeownership rate: 93.2% (2000); Median home value: $130,000 (2000); Median rent: $778 per month (2000); Median age of housing: 36 years (2000).
Transportation: Commute to work: 96.7% car, 0.6% public transportation, 0.0% walk, 2.2% work from home (2000); Travel time to work: 21.4% less than 15 minutes, 52.9% 15 to 30 minutes, 15.8% 30 to 45 minutes, 2.8% 45 to 60 minutes, 7.0% 60 minutes or more (2000)

NORTHMOOR (city). Covers a land area of 0.240 square miles and a water area of 0 square miles. Located at 39.18° N. Lat.; 94.60° W. Long. Elevation is 742 feet.
Population: 399 (2000); Race: 96.2% White, 0.0% Black, 0.0% Asian, 0.0% American Indian and Alaska Native, 3.3% Hispanic of any race, 2.3% two or more races (2000); Density: 1,663.8 persons per square mile (2000); Age: 25.7% under 18, 11.8% over 64 (2000); Marriage status: 27.7% never married, 46.1% now married, 9.0% widowed, 17.1% divorced (2000); Foreign born: 3.3% (2000); Ancestry (includes multiple ancestries): 21.2% United States or American, 19.4% German, 18.6% Other groups, 12.6% Irish, 4.8% Hungarian (2000).
Economy: Single-family building permits issued: 2 (2001) / 1 (2000); Multi-family building permits issued: 0 (2001) / 0 (2000); Employment by occupation: 10.2% management, 7.1% professional, 18.8% services, 23.4% sales, 0.0% farming, 20.3% construction, 20.3% production (2000).
Income: Per capita income: $14,263 (2000); Median household income: $27,250 (2000); Poverty rate: 13.5% (2000).
Taxes: Total city taxes per capita: $359 (1997); City property taxes per capita: $23 (1997).
Education: High school graduation rate: 75.6% (2000); College graduation rate: 3.8% (2000).
Housing: Homeownership rate: 65.9% (2000); Median home value: $70,300 (2000); Median rent: $432 per month (2000); Median age of housing: 36 years (2000).
Transportation: Commute to work: 95.9% car, 0.0% public transportation, 2.6% walk, 0.0% work from home (2000); Travel time to work: 44.1% less than 15 minutes, 38.5% 15 to 30 minutes, 15.9% 30 to 45 minutes, 0.0% 45 to 60 minutes, 1.5% 60 minutes or more (2000)

PARKVILLE (city). Covers a land area of 6.916 square miles and a water area of 0.556 square miles. Located at 39.19° N. Lat.; 94.68° W. Long. Elevation is 830 feet.
History: In the early 1840's, Parkville was an important town on the Missouri River. The town was founded by George S. Park, a slaveholder with abolitionist sentiments, who published a newspaper of influence in the 1850's. Members of the Platte County Self-Defensive League destroyed the presses and type, and forced Park and his partner to leave town. Park later returned to Parkville at the request of the residents, and in 1875 founded Park College to provide an education for students without funds by arranging for jobs on the college campus.
Population: 4,059 (2000); Race: 89.6% White, 5.3% Black, 0.4% Asian, 1.0% American Indian and Alaska Native, 0.7% Hispanic of any race, 2.9% two or more races (2000); Density: 586.9 persons per square mile (2000); Age: 22.9% under 18, 7.9% over 64 (2000); Marriage status: 26.1% never married, 62.2% now married, 4.4% widowed, 7.4% divorced (2000); Foreign born: 3.3% (2000); Ancestry (includes multiple ancestries): 20.7% German, 20.4% Irish, 13.1% English, 11.7% Other groups, 7.5% United States or American (2000).
Economy: Single-family building permits issued: 100 (2001) / 124 (2000); Multi-family building permits issued: 0 (2001) / 0 (2000); Employment by occupation: 26.1% management, 24.9% professional, 10.5% services, 24.7% sales, 0.0% farming, 7.0% construction, 6.7% production (2000).
Income: Per capita income: $33,119 (2000); Median household income: $68,600 (2000); Poverty rate: 6.5% (2000).
Taxes: Total city taxes per capita: $360 (2000); City property taxes per capita: $0 (2000).
Education: High school graduation rate: 93.4% (2000); College graduation rate: 45.3% (2000).

Four-year College(s)

Park University (Private, Not-for-profit)
2001 Enrollment: 9,482 816-741-2000
2001 Tuition: In-state $4,816; Out-of-state $4,816

Housing: Homeownership rate: 68.2% (2000); Median home value: $202,200 (2000); Median rent: $429 per month (2000); Median age of housing: 20 years (2000).
Safety: Violent crime rate: 4.9 per 10,000 population; Property crime rate: 264.4 per 10,000 population (2001).
Newspapers: Platte County Gazette (1 x week)
Transportation: Commute to work: 92.0% car, 0.0% public transportation, 3.2% walk, 3.0% work from home (2000); Travel time to work: 25.5% less than 15 minutes, 49.7% 15 to 30 minutes, 18.1% 30 to 45 minutes, 5.9% 45 to 60 minutes, 0.8% 60 minutes or more (2000)

Additional Information Contacts

Parkville Chamber of Commerce 816-587-2700

PLATTE CITY (city). Covers a land area of 3.370 square miles and a water area of 0.040 square miles. Located at 39.36° N. Lat.; 94.77° W. Long. Elevation is 810 feet.
History: Platte City had its beginnings when Zadoc Martin built a ferry at the Platte River crossing of the military road between Liberty Landing and Fort Leavenworth. The town that grew up around his ferry and flour mill was called Martinville, but the name was changed to Platte City in 1839 when it was chosen as the seat of Platte County.
Population: 3,866 (2000); Race: 91.1% White, 4.7% Black, 0.9% Asian, 0.4% American Indian and Alaska Native, 2.1% Hispanic of any race, 2.0% two or more races (2000); Density: 1,147.2 persons per square mile (2000); Age: 27.7% under 18, 10.3% over 64 (2000); Marriage status: 21.7% never married, 60.7% now married, 4.8% widowed, 12.8% divorced (2000); Foreign born: 2.0% (2000); Ancestry (includes multiple ancestries): 20.8% German, 13.1% United States or American, 12.0% English, 12.0% Other groups, 10.7% Irish (2000).
Economy: Single-family building permits issued: 20 (2001) / 44 (2000); Multi-family building permits issued: 148 (2001) / 84 (2000); Employment by occupation: 15.0% management, 15.6% professional, 15.3% services, 32.7% sales, 0.0% farming, 9.2% construction, 12.2% production (2000).
Income: Per capita income: $20,288 (2000); Median household income: $46,379 (2000); Poverty rate: 6.2% (2000).
Taxes: Total city taxes per capita: $1,089 (1997); City property taxes per capita: $463 (1997).
Education: High school graduation rate: 88.7% (2000); College graduation rate: 23.9% (2000).

School District(s)

Platte Co. R-III (PK-12)
2000 Enrollment: 2,080 816-858-5420

Housing: Homeownership rate: 50.6% (2000); Median home value: $111,500 (2000); Median rent: $480 per month (2000); Median age of housing: 21 years (2000).
Safety: Violent crime rate: 43.7 per 10,000 population; Property crime rate: 303.3 per 10,000 population (2001).
Newspapers: The Platte County Citizen (1 x week); The Landmark (1 x week)
Transportation: Commute to work: 94.9% car, 0.0% public transportation, 0.4% walk, 4.6% work from home (2000); Travel time to work: 24.0% less than 15 minutes, 46.2% 15 to 30 minutes, 23.1% 30 to 45 minutes, 4.3% 45 to 60 minutes, 2.4% 60 minutes or more (2000)
Additional Information Contacts
Platte City Chamber of Commerce 816-858-5270

PLATTE WOODS (city). Covers a land area of 0.377 square miles and a water area of 0 square miles. Located at 39.22° N. Lat.; 94.65° W. Long. Elevation is 1,010 feet.
Population: 474 (2000); Race: 95.9% White, 1.4% Black, 0.8% Asian, 0.0% American Indian and Alaska Native, 0.0% Hispanic of any race, 1.9% two or more races (2000); Density: 1,257.1 persons per square mile (2000); Age: 19.6% under 18, 17.6% over 64 (2000); Marriage status: 20.9% never married, 62.1% now married, 8.0% widowed, 9.0% divorced (2000); Foreign born: 1.7% (2000); Ancestry (includes multiple ancestries): 33.7% German, 19.8% English, 14.5% Irish, 9.7% United States or American, 6.8% Scotch-Irish (2000).
Economy: Single-family building permits issued: 0 (2001) / 0 (2000); Multi-family building permits issued: 0 (2001) / 0 (2000); Employment by occupation: 19.8% management, 30.4% professional, 4.9% services, 25.5% sales, 0.0% farming, 6.1% construction, 13.3% production (2000).
Income: Per capita income: $32,704 (2000); Median household income: $64,375 (2000); Poverty rate: 1.7% (2000).
Taxes: Total city taxes per capita: $259 (1997); City property taxes per capita: $76 (1997).
Education: High school graduation rate: 95.5% (2000); College graduation rate: 44.7% (2000).
Housing: Homeownership rate: 71.1% (2000); Median home value: $155,300 (2000); Median rent: $750 per month (2000); Median age of housing: 35 years (2000).
Transportation: Commute to work: 86.9% car, 0.0% public transportation, 3.8% walk, 6.9% work from home (2000); Travel time to work: 43.4% less than 15 minutes, 43.4% 15 to 30 minutes, 10.7% 30 to 45 minutes, 0.8% 45 to 60 minutes, 1.7% 60 minutes or more (2000)

RIDGELY (village). Covers a land area of 1.062 square miles and a water area of 0 square miles. Located at 39.45° N. Lat.; 94.63° W. Long. Elevation is 955 feet.
Population: 64 (2000); Race: 100.0% White, 0.0% Black, 0.0% Asian, 0.0% American Indian and Alaska Native, 0.0% Hispanic of any race, 0.0% two or more races (2000); Density: 60.3 persons per square mile (2000); Age: 39.4% under 18, 15.5% over 64 (2000); Marriage status: 19.6% never married, 67.4% now married, 8.7% widowed, 4.3% divorced (2000); Foreign born: 0.0% (2000); Ancestry (includes multiple ancestries): 35.2% Irish, 25.4% United States or American, 22.5% German, 14.1% Armenian, 4.2% Danish (2000).
Economy: Single-family building permits issued: 0 (2001) / 1 (2000); Multi-family building permits issued: 0 (2001) / 0 (2000); Employment by occupation: 18.5% management, 33.3% professional, 7.4% services, 14.8% sales, 0.0% farming, 7.4% construction, 18.5% production (2000).
Income: Per capita income: $14,017 (2000); Median household income: $29,000 (2000); Poverty rate: 0.0% (2000).
Taxes: Total city taxes per capita: $15 (1997); City property taxes per capita: $15 (1997).
Education: High school graduation rate: 90.7% (2000); College graduation rate: 37.2% (2000).
Housing: Homeownership rate: 85.2% (2000); Median home value: $78,800 (2000); Median rent: $225 per month (2000); Median age of housing: 27 years (2000).
Transportation: Commute to work: 100.0% car, 0.0% public transportation, 0.0% walk, 0.0% work from home (2000); Travel time to work: 0.0% less than 15 minutes, 59.3% 15 to 30 minutes, 33.3% 30 to 45 minutes, 7.4% 45 to 60 minutes, 0.0% 60 minutes or more (2000)

RIVERSIDE (city). Covers a land area of 5.327 square miles and a water area of 0.341 square miles. Located at 39.17° N. Lat.; 94.62° W. Long. Elevation is 775 feet.
Population: 2,979 (2000); Race: 82.0% White, 6.0% Black, 3.9% Asian, 1.1% American Indian and Alaska Native, 6.7% Hispanic of any race, 2.2% two or more races (2000); Density: 559.2 persons per square mile (2000); Age: 22.2% under 18, 13.3% over 64 (2000); Marriage status: 24.2% never married, 49.9% now married, 6.3% widowed, 19.6% divorced (2000); Foreign born: 9.9% (2000); Ancestry (includes multiple ancestries): 16.8% German, 13.9% Other groups, 13.2% United States or American, 11.4% English, 9.5% Irish (2000).
Economy: Manufacturing: pressure sensitive paper, automobile seats, cranes, foam cushions. Single-family building permits issued: 2 (2001) / 1 (2000); Multi-family building permits issued: 0 (2001) / 0 (2000); Employment by occupation: 13.0% management, 13.6% professional, 20.4% services, 30.3% sales, 0.1% farming, 8.5% construction, 14.1% production (2000).
Income: Per capita income: $17,771 (2000); Median household income: $34,679 (2000); Poverty rate: 10.3% (2000).
Taxes: Total city taxes per capita: $567 (2000); City property taxes per capita: $0 (2000).
Education: High school graduation rate: 78.9% (2000); College graduation rate: 20.2% (2000).
Housing: Homeownership rate: 30.3% (2000); Median home value: $114,200 (2000); Median rent: $427 per month (2000); Median age of housing: 31 years (2000).
Safety: Violent crime rate: 103.4 per 10,000 population; Property crime rate: 877.5 per 10,000 population (2001).
Transportation: Commute to work: 98.0% car, 0.0% public transportation, 1.0% walk, 1.0% work from home (2000); Travel time to work: 27.1% less than 15 minutes, 50.4% 15 to 30 minutes, 14.8% 30 to 45 minutes, 4.6% 45 to 60 minutes, 3.0% 60 minutes or more (2000)

TRACY (city). Covers a land area of 0.216 square miles and a water area of 0.003 square miles. Located at 39.37° N. Lat.; 94.79° W. Long. Elevation is 865 feet.
History: Tracy developed on the north bank of the Platte River. The first Platte County Fair was held here in 1888.
Population: 213 (2000); Race: 98.1% White, 0.0% Black, 0.0% Asian, 0.0% American Indian and Alaska Native, 0.0% Hispanic of any race, 1.9% two or more races (2000); Density: 987.4 persons per square mile (2000); Age: 19.9% under 18, 11.4% over 64 (2000); Marriage status: 15.9% never married, 61.4% now married, 5.7% widowed, 17.0% divorced (2000); Foreign born: 1.9% (2000); Ancestry (includes multiple ancestries): 21.8% English, 21.3% Irish, 20.4% German, 13.3% European, 5.2% Swedish (2000).
Economy: Single-family building permits issued: 0 (2001) / 0 (2000); Multi-family building permits issued: 0 (2001) / 0 (2000); Employment by occupation: 15.7% management, 5.5% professional, 15.0% services, 37.0% sales, 0.0% farming, 11.8% construction, 15.0% production (2000).
Income: Per capita income: $21,082 (2000); Median household income: $51,250 (2000); Poverty rate: 9.0% (2000).
Taxes: Total city taxes per capita: $203 (1997); City property taxes per capita: $29 (1997).
Education: High school graduation rate: 71.3% (2000); College graduation rate: 8.1% (2000).
Housing: Homeownership rate: 92.8% (2000); Median home value: $93,200 (2000); Median rent: $267 per month (2000); Median age of housing: 30 years (2000).
Transportation: Commute to work: 90.4% car, 0.0% public transportation, 0.0% walk, 4.8% work from home (2000); Travel time to work: 32.8% less than 15 minutes, 43.7% 15 to 30 minutes, 11.8% 30 to 45 minutes, 3.4% 45 to 60 minutes, 8.4% 60 minutes or more (2000)

WEATHERBY LAKE (city). Covers a land area of 1.035 square miles and a water area of 0.296 square miles. Located at 39.23° N. Lat.; 94.69° W. Long. Elevation is 930 feet.
Population: 1,873 (2000); Race: 95.4% White, 0.4% Black, 4.0% Asian, 0.0% American Indian and Alaska Native, 0.8% Hispanic of any race, 0.2% two or more races (2000); Density: 1,810.5 persons per square mile (2000); Age: 24.1% under 18, 9.3% over 64 (2000); Marriage status: 17.9% never married, 73.1% now married, 3.9% widowed, 5.0% divorced (2000); Foreign born: 6.6% (2000); Ancestry (includes multiple ancestries): 27.9% German, 18.6% English, 11.2% Irish, 10.1% United States or American, 7.4% Other groups (2000).
Economy: Kansas City International Airport to North. Single-family building permits issued: 5 (2001) / 1 (2000); Multi-family building permits issued: 0 (2001) / 0 (2000); Employment by occupation: 24.7% management, 25.6% professional, 10.4% services, 27.3% sales, 0.6% farming, 6.2% construction, 5.1% production (2000).

Income: Per capita income: $37,722 (2000); Median household income: $88,030 (2000); Poverty rate: 1.5% (2000).
Taxes: Total city taxes per capita: $250 (1997); City property taxes per capita: $148 (1997).
Education: High school graduation rate: 96.3% (2000); College graduation rate: 49.2% (2000).
Housing: Homeownership rate: 95.5% (2000); Median home value: $211,500 (2000); Median rent: $575 per month (2000); Median age of housing: 23 years (2000).
Transportation: Commute to work: 85.2% car, 0.4% public transportation, 0.0% walk, 13.6% work from home (2000); Travel time to work: 33.1% less than 15 minutes, 41.4% 15 to 30 minutes, 21.0% 30 to 45 minutes, 3.5% 45 to 60 minutes, 1.0% 60 minutes or more (2000)

WESTON (city). Covers a land area of 1.640 square miles and a water area of 0 square miles. Located at 39.41° N. Lat.; 94.89° W. Long. Elevation is 795 feet.
History: Weston began when Joseph Moore laid out a few streets in 1837 and sold lots. The rest of the town was laid out the next year by Bela M. Hughes. Shipping on the Missouri River made the town an active port. Ben Holladay (1819-1897), a developer of overland stagecoach service, was a resident of Weston.
Population: 1,631 (2000); Race: 96.2% White, 0.0% Black, 0.0% Asian, 0.6% American Indian and Alaska Native, 2.2% Hispanic of any race, 1.8% two or more races (2000); Density: 994.8 persons per square mile (2000); Age: 25.3% under 18, 14.0% over 64 (2000); Marriage status: 18.3% never married, 59.4% now married, 8.4% widowed, 14.0% divorced (2000); Foreign born: 0.3% (2000); Ancestry (includes multiple ancestries): 22.3% German, 18.1% Irish, 12.4% English, 11.5% United States or American, 9.5% Other groups (2000).
Economy: Single-family building permits issued: 1 (2001) / 0 (2000); Multi-family building permits issued: 2 (2001) / 4 (2000); Employment by occupation: 15.3% management, 14.2% professional, 16.3% services, 27.8% sales, 1.2% farming, 11.6% construction, 13.5% production (2000).
Income: Per capita income: $20,794 (2000); Median household income: $43,214 (2000); Poverty rate: 7.1% (2000).
Taxes: Total city taxes per capita: $169 (1997); City property taxes per capita: $49 (1997).
Education: High school graduation rate: 89.0% (2000); College graduation rate: 22.3% (2000).

School District(s)

West Platte Co. R-II (KG-12)
2000 Enrollment: 711 816-640-2236

Housing: Homeownership rate: 63.8% (2000); Median home value: $94,400 (2000); Median rent: $452 per month (2000); Median age of housing: 35 years (2000).
Safety: Violent crime rate: 12.2 per 10,000 population; Property crime rate: 97.5 per 10,000 population (2001).
Newspapers: Weston Chronicle (1 x week)
Transportation: Commute to work: 93.6% car, 0.2% public transportation, 3.2% walk, 2.4% work from home (2000); Travel time to work: 24.4% less than 15 minutes, 38.8% 15 to 30 minutes, 21.6% 30 to 45 minutes, 9.9% 45 to 60 minutes, 5.3% 60 minutes or more (2000)

Additional Information Contacts

Weston Chamber of Commerce 816-640-2909
Weston Development Council 816-640-2909

Polk County

Located in southwest central Missouri, in the Ozarks; drained by the Pomme de Terre and Little Sac Rivers. Covers a land area of 637.20 square miles, a water area of 5.30 square miles, and is located in the Central Time Zone. The county government was organized in 1835. County seat is Bolivar.

Weather Station: Bolivar 1 NE — Elevation: 1,033 feet

	Jan	Feb	Mar	Apr	May	Jun	Jul	Aug	Sep	Oct	Nov	Dec
High	41	47	57	67	76	84	90	89	81	70	56	46
Low	18	23	33	43	52	61	65	63	55	43	33	24
Precip	2.0	2.3	3.9	4.6	5.1	4.7	3.6	3.4	4.8	4.3	4.2	3.1
Snow	na	na	tr	0.0	0.0	0.0	0.0	0.0	0.0	0.0	0.0	na

High and Low temperatures in degrees Fahrenheit; Precipitation and Snow in inches

Population: 26,992 (2000); Race: 97.6% White, 0.3% Black, 0.4% Asian, 0.5% American Indian and Alaska Native, 1.4% Hispanic of any race, 0.9% two or more races (2000); Density: 42.4 persons per square mile (2000); Age: 25.6% under 18, 15.3% over 64 (2000).
Religion: Five largest groups: 21.9% Southern Baptist Convention, 5.5% The United Methodist Church, 4.6% Assemblies of God, 2.3% Catholic Church, 1.6% The Church of Jesus Christ of Latter-day Saints (2000).
Economy: Unemployment rate: 3.9% (11/2002); Total civilian labor force: 12,590 (11/2002); Leading industries: 24.5% health care and social assistance; 13.9% retail trade; 13.4% manufacturing (2000); Companies that employ more than 1,000 persons: 0 (2000); Companies that employ more than 100 persons: 11 (2000); Farms: 1,575 totaling 347,688 acres (1997); Minority business ownership rate: 0.0% (1997); Women business ownership rate: 25.9% (1997); Retail sales per capita: $6,586 (1997). Single-family building permits issued: 36 (2001) / 40 (2000); Multi-family building permits issued: 52 (2001) / 26 (2000).
Income: Per capita income: $13,645 (2000); Median household income: $29,656 (2000); Poverty rate: 16.3% (2000); Bankruptcy rate: 3.49% (2001).
Taxes: Total county taxes per capita: $51 (2000); County property taxes per capita: $18 (2000).
Education: High school graduation rate: 77.5% (2000); College graduation rate: 14.6% (2000).
Housing: Homeownership rate: 73.0% (2000); Median home value: $77,000 (2000); Median rent: $296 per month (2000); Median age of housing: 25 years (2000).
Health: Birth rate: 132.6 per 10,000 population (1998); Age adjusted death rate: 98.7 per 10,000 population (1999); Age adjusted cancer mortality rate: 220.6 deaths per 100,000 population (1999). Number of physicians: 8.9 per 10,000 population (1999); Number of hospital beds: 27.4 per 10,000 population (1999).
Elections: 2000 Presidential election results: 35.0% Gore, 62.5% Bush, 1.2% Nader, 0.8% Buchanan

Additional Information Contacts

Polk County Government Offices 417-326-4031
Bolivar Chamber of Commerce 417-326-4118
Ozarks Board of Realtors 417-326-7639

Polk County Communities

ALDRICH (village). Covers a land area of 0.162 square miles and a water area of 0 square miles. Located at 37.54° N. Lat.; 93.55° W. Long. Elevation is 900 feet.
Population: 75 (2000); Race: 97.2% White, 0.0% Black, 0.0% Asian, 0.0% American Indian and Alaska Native, 0.0% Hispanic of any race, 2.8% two or more races (2000); Density: 463.8 persons per square mile (2000); Age: 23.9% under 18, 16.9% over 64 (2000); Marriage status: 16.7% never married, 75.9% now married, 3.7% widowed, 3.7% divorced (2000); Foreign born: 0.0% (2000); Ancestry (includes multiple ancestries): 26.8% United States or American, 18.3% German, 18.3% English, 12.7% French (except Basque), 11.3% Irish (2000).
Economy: Employment by occupation: 2.9% management, 5.9% professional, 20.6% services, 14.7% sales, 0.0% farming, 50.0% construction, 5.9% production (2000).
Income: Per capita income: $11,717 (2000); Median household income: $28,125 (2000); Poverty rate: 4.5% (2000).
Taxes: Total city taxes per capita: $37 (1997); City property taxes per capita: $12 (1997).
Education: High school graduation rate: 86.0% (2000); College graduation rate: 14.0% (2000).
Housing: Homeownership rate: 75.8% (2000); Median home value: $57,500 (2000); Median rent: $200 per month (2000); Median age of housing: 48 years (2000).
Transportation: Commute to work: 100.0% car, 0.0% public transportation, 0.0% walk, 0.0% work from home (2000); Travel time to work: 8.8% less than 15 minutes, 50.0% 15 to 30 minutes, 20.6% 30 to 45 minutes, 17.6% 45 to 60 minutes, 2.9% 60 minutes or more (2000)

BOLIVAR (city). Covers a land area of 6.267 square miles and a water area of 0 square miles. Located at 37.61° N. Lat.; 93.41° W. Long. Elevation is 1,056 feet.
History: Seat of Southwest Baptist College. Statue of Simon Bolivar dedicated here (1948) by president of Venezuela.
Population: 9,143 (2000); Race: 96.6% White, 0.5% Black, 1.0% Asian, 0.6% American Indian and Alaska Native, 0.7% Hispanic of any race, 0.9% two or more races (2000); Density: 1,458.8 persons per square mile (2000); Age: 19.1% under 18, 19.5% over 64 (2000); Marriage status: 30.3% never married, 53.4% now married, 8.1% widowed, 8.1% divorced (2000); Foreign born: 2.5% (2000); Ancestry (includes multiple ancestries): 16.2% German,

14.0% English, 12.7% United States or American, 12.4% Irish, 10.2% Other groups (2000).
Economy: Cattle; grain center. Light manufacturing: transportation equipment. Single-family building permits issued: 36 (2001) / 40 (2000); Multi-family building permits issued: 52 (2001) / 26 (2000); Employment by occupation: 8.9% management, 24.9% professional, 18.6% services, 24.5% sales, 0.7% farming, 5.4% construction, 17.1% production (2000).
Income: Per capita income: $13,654 (2000); Median household income: $24,609 (2000); Poverty rate: 19.8% (2000).
Taxes: Total city taxes per capita: $257 (2000); City property taxes per capita: $33 (2000).
Education: High school graduation rate: 77.6% (2000); College graduation rate: 21.6% (2000).

School District(s)

Bolivar R-I (PK-12)
2000 Enrollment: 2,400 417-326-5291

Four-year College(s)

Southwest Baptist University (Private, Not-for-profit, Southern Baptist)
2001 Enrollment: 3,564 800-526-5859
2001 Tuition: In-state $10,000; Out-of-state $10,000
Housing: Homeownership rate: 55.5% (2000); Median home value: $80,300 (2000); Median rent: $311 per month (2000); Median age of housing: 24 years (2000).
Hospitals: Citizens Memorial Hospital (74 beds)
Safety: Violent crime rate: 32.6 per 10,000 population; Property crime rate: 431.6 per 10,000 population (2001).
Newspapers: Herald-Free Press (1 x week)
Transportation: Commute to work: 87.8% car, 0.0% public transportation, 8.3% walk, 3.1% work from home (2000); Travel time to work: 65.2% less than 15 minutes, 10.9% 15 to 30 minutes, 11.3% 30 to 45 minutes, 9.4% 45 to 60 minutes, 3.2% 60 minutes or more (2000)
Additional Information Contacts
Bolivar Chamber of Commerce 417-326-4118
Ozarks Board of Realtors 417-326-7639

BRIGHTON (unincorporated postal area, zip code 65617). Covers a land area of 28.071 square miles and a water area of 0 square miles. Located at 37.43° N. Lat.; 93.34° W. Long. Elevation is 1,179 feet.
Population: 1,377 (2000); Race: 93.4% White, 1.0% Black, 0.0% Asian, 0.0% American Indian and Alaska Native, 5.1% Hispanic of any race, 4.3% two or more races (2000); Density: 49.1 persons per square mile (2000); Age: 34.1% under 18, 6.3% over 64 (2000); Marriage status: 15.9% never married, 71.5% now married, 1.6% widowed, 11.0% divorced (2000); Foreign born: 4.0% (2000); Ancestry (includes multiple ancestries): 17.3% Other groups, 16.1% Irish, 15.4% German, 10.4% English, 9.2% United States or American (2000).
Economy: Employment by occupation: 8.6% management, 11.7% professional, 8.8% services, 30.6% sales, 1.4% farming, 15.4% construction, 23.5% production (2000).
Income: Per capita income: $13,505 (2000); Median household income: $40,170 (2000); Poverty rate: 10.1% (2000).
Education: High school graduation rate: 81.5% (2000); College graduation rate: 12.9% (2000).
Housing: Homeownership rate: 83.1% (2000); Median home value: $92,900 (2000); Median rent: $294 per month (2000); Median age of housing: 24 years (2000).
Transportation: Commute to work: 95.1% car, 0.0% public transportation, 0.8% walk, 4.1% work from home (2000); Travel time to work: 7.1% less than 15 minutes, 32.3% 15 to 30 minutes, 42.4% 30 to 45 minutes, 14.0% 45 to 60 minutes, 4.2% 60 minutes or more (2000)

DUNNEGAN (unincorporated postal area, zip code 65640). Covers a land area of 45.060 square miles and a water area of 0 square miles. Located at 37.70° N. Lat.; 93.56° W. Long. Elevation is 932 feet.
Population: 763 (2000); Race: 96.5% White, 0.0% Black, 0.3% Asian, 3.2% American Indian and Alaska Native, 0.0% Hispanic of any race, 0.0% two or more races (2000); Density: 16.9 persons per square mile (2000); Age: 17.5% under 18, 20.0% over 64 (2000); Marriage status: 19.0% never married, 68.1% now married, 8.6% widowed, 4.3% divorced (2000); Foreign born: 1.5% (2000); Ancestry (includes multiple ancestries): 26.4% United States or American, 12.5% German, 11.6% Irish, 11.0% English, 9.6% Other groups (2000).
Economy: Employment by occupation: 19.2% management, 16.0% professional, 20.4% services, 21.1% sales, 4.4% farming, 6.0% construction, 12.9% production (2000).
Income: Per capita income: $13,965 (2000); Median household income: $23,281 (2000); Poverty rate: 18.9% (2000).
Education: High school graduation rate: 65.9% (2000); College graduation rate: 9.7% (2000).
Housing: Homeownership rate: 92.3% (2000); Median home value: $21,300 (2000); Median rent: $175 per month (2000); Median age of housing: 29 years (2000).
Transportation: Commute to work: 89.7% car, 0.0% public transportation, 2.9% walk, 7.4% work from home (2000); Travel time to work: 8.0% less than 15 minutes, 52.1% 15 to 30 minutes, 16.3% 30 to 45 minutes, 9.7% 45 to 60 minutes, 13.9% 60 minutes or more (2000)

FAIR PLAY (city). Covers a land area of 0.300 square miles and a water area of 0 square miles. Located at 37.63° N. Lat.; 93.57° W. Long. Elevation is 994 feet.
Population: 418 (2000); Race: 100.0% White, 0.0% Black, 0.0% Asian, 0.0% American Indian and Alaska Native, 1.5% Hispanic of any race, 0.0% two or more races (2000); Density: 1,392.5 persons per square mile (2000); Age: 36.0% under 18, 12.1% over 64 (2000); Marriage status: 16.5% never married, 63.1% now married, 13.6% widowed, 6.8% divorced (2000); Foreign born: 0.0% (2000); Ancestry (includes multiple ancestries): 23.2% United States or American, 10.6% German, 9.9% Irish, 9.9% English, 8.9% Other groups (2000).
Economy: Dairy and poultry market; wheat, soybeans; cattle. Employment by occupation: 7.2% management, 3.2% professional, 25.6% services, 20.8% sales, 0.0% farming, 16.0% construction, 27.2% production (2000).
Income: Per capita income: $9,151 (2000); Median household income: $20,438 (2000); Poverty rate: 29.9% (2000).
Taxes: Total city taxes per capita: $69 (1997); City property taxes per capita: $34 (1997).
Education: High school graduation rate: 65.2% (2000); College graduation rate: 6.3% (2000).

School District(s)

Fair Play R-II (KG-12)
2000 Enrollment: 385 417-654-2231
Housing: Homeownership rate: 74.0% (2000); Median home value: $36,500 (2000); Median rent: $227 per month (2000); Median age of housing: 41 years (2000).
Transportation: Commute to work: 92.0% car, 0.0% public transportation, 2.4% walk, 5.6% work from home (2000); Travel time to work: 19.5% less than 15 minutes, 45.8% 15 to 30 minutes, 6.8% 30 to 45 minutes, 8.5% 45 to 60 minutes, 19.5% 60 minutes or more (2000)

FLEMINGTON (village). Covers a land area of 0.327 square miles and a water area of 0 square miles. Located at 37.80° N. Lat.; 93.50° W. Long. Elevation is 1,128 feet.
Population: 124 (2000); Race: 93.5% White, 0.0% Black, 0.0% Asian, 6.5% American Indian and Alaska Native, 1.4% Hispanic of any race, 0.0% two or more races (2000); Density: 379.8 persons per square mile (2000); Age: 22.5% under 18, 8.0% over 64 (2000); Marriage status: 15.0% never married, 62.8% now married, 4.4% widowed, 17.7% divorced (2000); Foreign born: 3.6% (2000); Ancestry (includes multiple ancestries): 23.9% Other groups, 15.9% United States or American, 13.8% Irish, 12.3% German, 11.6% English (2000).
Economy: Hay; cattle. Employment by occupation: 3.9% management, 3.9% professional, 7.8% services, 37.3% sales, 0.0% farming, 29.4% construction, 17.6% production (2000).
Income: Per capita income: $11,499 (2000); Median household income: $23,438 (2000); Poverty rate: 27.5% (2000).
Taxes: Total city taxes per capita: $13 (1997); City property taxes per capita: $0 (1997).
Education: High school graduation rate: 70.1% (2000); College graduation rate: 3.1% (2000).
Housing: Homeownership rate: 86.2% (2000); Median home value: $28,500 (2000); Median rent: $150 per month (2000); Median age of housing: 53 years (2000).
Transportation: Commute to work: 85.7% car, 0.0% public transportation, 4.1% walk, 10.2% work from home (2000); Travel time to work: 20.5% less than 15 minutes, 20.5% 15 to 30 minutes, 22.7% 30 to 45 minutes, 18.2% 45 to 60 minutes, 18.2% 60 minutes or more (2000)

GOODSON (unincorporated postal area, zip code 65659). Covers a land area of 21.395 square miles and a water area of 0 square miles. Located at 37.74° N. Lat.; 93.24° W. Long. Elevation is 1,065 feet.
Population: 357 (2000); Race: 98.1% White, 0.0% Black, 0.0% Asian, 0.0% American Indian and Alaska Native, 11.7% Hispanic of any race, 0.5% two

or more races (2000); Density: 16.7 persons per square mile (2000); Age: 29.9% under 18, 9.2% over 64 (2000); Marriage status: 10.4% never married, 77.8% now married, 5.1% widowed, 6.7% divorced (2000); Foreign born: 1.9% (2000); Ancestry (includes multiple ancestries): 18.0% German, 14.8% Other groups, 12.1% English, 9.7% United States or American, 8.3% Italian (2000).
Economy: Employment by occupation: 10.3% management, 10.3% professional, 14.1% services, 19.5% sales, 5.4% farming, 7.0% construction, 33.5% production (2000).
Income: Per capita income: $11,129 (2000); Median household income: $22,031 (2000); Poverty rate: 27.9% (2000).
Education: High school graduation rate: 82.0% (2000); College graduation rate: 7.0% (2000).
Housing: Homeownership rate: 88.2% (2000); Median home value: $24,700 (2000); Median rent: $225 per month (2000); Median age of housing: 22 years (2000).
Transportation: Commute to work: 88.1% car, 0.0% public transportation, 0.0% walk, 5.4% work from home (2000); Travel time to work: 1.7% less than 15 minutes, 36.6% 15 to 30 minutes, 29.1% 30 to 45 minutes, 15.4% 45 to 60 minutes, 17.1% 60 minutes or more (2000)

HALFWAY (village). Aka Half Way. Covers a land area of 2.136 square miles and a water area of 0 square miles. Located at 37.61° N. Lat.; 93.23° W. Long. Elevation is 1,090 feet.
Population: 176 (2000); Race: 84.0% White, 0.0% Black, 1.0% Asian, 2.5% American Indian and Alaska Native, 4.5% Hispanic of any race, 3.5% two or more races (2000); Density: 82.4 persons per square mile (2000); Age: 30.0% under 18, 4.5% over 64 (2000); Marriage status: 34.6% never married, 50.3% now married, 9.2% widowed, 5.9% divorced (2000); Foreign born: 1.0% (2000); Ancestry (includes multiple ancestries): 29.5% United States or American, 16.5% Other groups, 9.0% English, 6.5% German, 6.0% Irish (2000).
Economy: Employment by occupation: 9.5% management, 17.9% professional, 17.9% services, 16.8% sales, 0.0% farming, 10.5% construction, 27.4% production (2000).
Income: Per capita income: $14,551 (2000); Median household income: $32,813 (2000); Poverty rate: 20.5% (2000).
Education: High school graduation rate: 77.6% (2000); College graduation rate: 11.2% (2000).

School District(s)

Halfway R-III (KG-12)
2000 Enrollment: 298 417-445-2351
Housing: Homeownership rate: 79.1% (2000); Median home value: $65,000 (2000); Median rent: $325 per month (2000); Median age of housing: 46 years (2000).
Transportation: Commute to work: 94.6% car, 0.0% public transportation, 0.0% walk, 4.3% work from home (2000); Travel time to work: 28.4% less than 15 minutes, 31.8% 15 to 30 minutes, 18.2% 30 to 45 minutes, 14.8% 45 to 60 minutes, 6.8% 60 minutes or more (2000)

HUMANSVILLE (city). Covers a land area of 1.191 square miles and a water area of 0 square miles. Located at 37.79° N. Lat.; 93.57° W. Long. Elevation is 965 feet.
Population: 946 (2000); Race: 99.2% White, 0.0% Black, 0.0% Asian, 0.0% American Indian and Alaska Native, 0.2% Hispanic of any race, 0.8% two or more races (2000); Density: 794.0 persons per square mile (2000); Age: 23.1% under 18, 26.1% over 64 (2000); Marriage status: 21.6% never married, 48.7% now married, 16.8% widowed, 13.0% divorced (2000); Foreign born: 0.7% (2000); Ancestry (includes multiple ancestries): 22.2% United States or American, 13.7% German, 11.5% Irish, 7.0% Other groups, 6.7% English (2000).
Economy: Corn, soybeans; cattle. Manufacturing: boxes. Employment by occupation: 7.5% management, 7.2% professional, 25.2% services, 21.0% sales, 3.6% farming, 9.0% construction, 26.4% production (2000).
Income: Per capita income: $11,051 (2000); Median household income: $19,821 (2000); Poverty rate: 18.7% (2000).
Taxes: Total city taxes per capita: $101 (1997); City property taxes per capita: $17 (1997).
Education: High school graduation rate: 68.5% (2000); College graduation rate: 5.0% (2000).

School District(s)

Humansville R-IV (PK-12)
2000 Enrollment: 476 417-754-2535
Housing: Homeownership rate: 68.5% (2000); Median home value: $39,600 (2000); Median rent: $219 per month (2000); Median age of housing: 52 years (2000).
Newspapers: Humansville Star-Leader (1 x week)
Transportation: Commute to work: 91.5% car, 0.0% public transportation, 5.8% walk, 0.6% work from home (2000); Travel time to work: 39.9% less than 15 minutes, 30.5% 15 to 30 minutes, 12.5% 30 to 45 minutes, 4.9% 45 to 60 minutes, 12.2% 60 minutes or more (2000)

MORRISVILLE (town). Covers a land area of 0.306 square miles and a water area of 0 square miles. Located at 37.48° N. Lat.; 93.42° W. Long. Elevation is 1,165 feet.
Population: 344 (2000); Race: 96.4% White, 1.3% Black, 0.0% Asian, 0.0% American Indian and Alaska Native, 4.9% Hispanic of any race, 2.3% two or more races (2000); Density: 1,125.5 persons per square mile (2000); Age: 29.8% under 18, 11.3% over 64 (2000); Marriage status: 25.2% never married, 45.0% now married, 11.3% widowed, 18.5% divorced (2000); Foreign born: 0.0% (2000); Ancestry (includes multiple ancestries): 24.9% United States or American, 17.2% Other groups, 11.7% German, 10.7% English, 9.1% Irish (2000).
Economy: Employment by occupation: 3.1% management, 18.1% professional, 17.3% services, 22.0% sales, 0.0% farming, 11.0% construction, 28.3% production (2000).
Income: Per capita income: $11,440 (2000); Median household income: $23,906 (2000); Poverty rate: 27.9% (2000).
Taxes: Total city taxes per capita: $33 (1997); City property taxes per capita: $15 (1997).
Education: High school graduation rate: 79.8% (2000); College graduation rate: 8.2% (2000).

School District(s)

Marion C. Early R-V (KG-12)
2000 Enrollment: 629 417-376-2255
Housing: Homeownership rate: 59.5% (2000); Median home value: $65,500 (2000); Median rent: $261 per month (2000); Median age of housing: 34 years (2000).
Transportation: Commute to work: 95.2% car, 0.0% public transportation, 0.0% walk, 3.2% work from home (2000); Travel time to work: 6.7% less than 15 minutes, 32.5% 15 to 30 minutes, 37.5% 30 to 45 minutes, 12.5% 45 to 60 minutes, 10.8% 60 minutes or more (2000)

PLEASANT HOPE (city). Covers a land area of 0.839 square miles and a water area of 0 square miles. Located at 37.46° N. Lat.; 93.27° W. Long. Elevation is 1,110 feet.
Population: 548 (2000); Race: 97.7% White, 0.0% Black, 0.2% Asian, 0.5% American Indian and Alaska Native, 2.5% Hispanic of any race, 0.0% two or more races (2000); Density: 653.0 persons per square mile (2000); Age: 32.4% under 18, 7.7% over 64 (2000); Marriage status: 21.8% never married, 55.3% now married, 11.2% widowed, 11.7% divorced (2000); Foreign born: 0.5% (2000); Ancestry (includes multiple ancestries): 21.7% German, 14.9% Irish, 14.3% United States or American, 14.0% Other groups, 7.3% Dutch (2000).
Economy: Hay; cattle. Employment by occupation: 9.9% management, 9.1% professional, 18.6% services, 26.1% sales, 1.2% farming, 12.6% construction, 22.5% production (2000).
Income: Per capita income: $12,657 (2000); Median household income: $31,250 (2000); Poverty rate: 16.7% (2000).
Taxes: Total city taxes per capita: $72 (1997); City property taxes per capita: $0 (1997).
Education: High school graduation rate: 83.1% (2000); College graduation rate: 10.6% (2000).

School District(s)

Pleasant Hope R-VI (KG-12)
2000 Enrollment: 905 417-267-2850
Housing: Homeownership rate: 69.6% (2000); Median home value: $78,600 (2000); Median rent: $319 per month (2000); Median age of housing: 21 years (2000).
Transportation: Commute to work: 95.3% car, 0.0% public transportation, 1.6% walk, 0.8% work from home (2000); Travel time to work: 20.3% less than 15 minutes, 18.7% 15 to 30 minutes, 39.8% 30 to 45 minutes, 17.9% 45 to 60 minutes, 3.2% 60 minutes or more (2000)

POLK (unincorporated postal area, zip code 65727). Covers a land area of 10.135 square miles and a water area of 0 square miles. Located at 37.79° N. Lat.; 93.27° W. Long. Elevation is 1,042 feet.
Population: 157 (2000); Race: 100.0% White, 0.0% Black, 0.0% Asian, 0.0% American Indian and Alaska Native, 0.0% Hispanic of any race, 0.0% two or more races (2000); Density: 15.5 persons per square mile (2000); Age: 16.0% under 18, 21.3% over 64 (2000); Marriage status: 10.1% never married, 78.5% now married, 0.0% widowed, 11.4% divorced (2000);

Foreign born: 0.0% (2000); Ancestry (includes multiple ancestries): 40.4% United States or American, 21.3% German, 8.5% Irish, 6.4% English, 6.4% Swiss (2000).
Economy: Employment by occupation: 0.0% management, 15.2% professional, 21.7% services, 0.0% sales, 0.0% farming, 28.3% construction, 34.8% production (2000).
Income: Per capita income: $15,564 (2000); Median household income: $26,538 (2000); Poverty rate: 0.0% (2000).
Education: High school graduation rate: 100.0% (2000); College graduation rate: 16.5% (2000).
Housing: Homeownership rate: 100.0% (2000); Median home value: $38,000 (2000); Median age of housing: 19 years (2000).
Transportation: Commute to work: 100.0% car, 0.0% public transportation, 0.0% walk, 0.0% work from home (2000); Travel time to work: 17.4% less than 15 minutes, 26.1% 15 to 30 minutes, 10.9% 30 to 45 minutes, 10.9% 45 to 60 minutes, 34.8% 60 minutes or more (2000)

Pulaski County

Located in central Missouri, in the Ozarks; drained by the Gasconade River; includes part of Mark Twain National Forest. Covers a land area of 547.00 square miles, a water area of 4.40 square miles, and is located in the Central Time Zone. The county government was organized in 1833. County seat is Waynesville.

Weather Station: Waynesville 2 W Elevation: 889 feet

	Jan	Feb	Mar	Apr	May	Jun	Jul	Aug	Sep	Oct	Nov	Dec
High	44	50	60	71	77	84	89	88	81	72	58	48
Low	19	23	32	41	51	60	64	62	55	43	33	24
Precip	2.2	2.4	4.1	4.2	4.7	4.3	3.7	3.7	4.3	3.9	4.3	3.3
Snow	7.7	4.6	3.2	0.4	0.0	0.0	0.0	0.0	0.0	tr	1.8	2.5

High and Low temperatures in degrees Fahrenheit; Precipitation and Snow in inches

Population: 41,165 (2000); Race: 78.4% White, 12.0% Black, 2.2% Asian, 1.2% American Indian and Alaska Native, 6.0% Hispanic of any race, 3.2% two or more races (2000); Density: 75.3 persons per square mile (2000); Age: 27.5% under 18, 7.9% over 64 (2000).
Religion: Five largest groups: 29.5% Southern Baptist Convention, 3.9% Christian Churches and Churches of Christ, 1.8% Catholic Church, 1.7% The United Methodist Church, 1.1% Assemblies of God (2000).
Economy: Unemployment rate: 4.2% (11/2002); Total civilian labor force: 13,042 (11/2002); Leading industries: 24.8% retail trade; 20.9% accommodation & food services; 17.0% health care and social assistance (2000); Companies that employ more than 1,000 persons: 0 (2000); Companies that employ more than 100 persons: 4 (2000); Farms: 539 totaling 139,681 acres (1997); Minority business ownership rate: 7.0% (1997); Women business ownership rate: 16.7% (1997); Retail sales per capita: $4,723 (1997). Single-family building permits issued: 8 (2001) / 5 (2000); Multi-family building permits issued: 0 (2001) / 2 (2000).
Income: Per capita income: $14,586 (2000); Median household income: $34,247 (2000); Poverty rate: 10.3% (2000); Bankruptcy rate: 4.56% (2001).
Taxes: Total county taxes per capita: $72 (1997); County property taxes per capita: $17 (1997).
Education: High school graduation rate: 85.1% (2000); College graduation rate: 18.8% (2000).
Housing: Homeownership rate: 58.0% (2000); Median home value: $78,300 (2000); Median rent: $357 per month (2000); Median age of housing: 25 years (2000).
Health: Birth rate: 153.5 per 10,000 population (1998); Age adjusted death rate: 103.7 per 10,000 population (1999); Age adjusted cancer mortality rate: 259.0 deaths per 100,000 population (1999). Number of physicians: 2.9 per 10,000 population (1999); Number of hospital beds: 23.6 per 10,000 population (1999).
Elections: 2000 Presidential election results: 36.1% Gore, 62.0% Bush, 1.1% Nader, 0.4% Buchanan
National and State Parks: Big Piney National Scenic Trail; Fort Leonard Wood State Wildlife Management Area; Lone Star Tract State Forest
Additional Information Contacts
Pulaski County Government Offices 573-774-4701
Pulaski County Board of Realtors 573-336-7225
Richland Chamber of Commerce 573-765-4450
St. Robert Chamber of Commerce 573-336-5121

Pulaski County Communities

CROCKER (city). Covers a land area of 1.190 square miles and a water area of 0 square miles. Located at 37.95° N. Lat.; 92.26° W. Long. Elevation is 1,124 feet.
Population: 1,033 (2000); Race: 97.5% White, 0.5% Black, 0.0% Asian, 1.4% American Indian and Alaska Native, 0.0% Hispanic of any race, 0.6% two or more races (2000); Density: 868.4 persons per square mile (2000); Age: 30.1% under 18, 13.9% over 64 (2000); Marriage status: 19.4% never married, 61.5% now married, 9.1% widowed, 10.0% divorced (2000); Foreign born: 0.6% (2000); Ancestry (includes multiple ancestries): 17.1% United States or American, 15.6% German, 13.2% Other groups, 10.2% Irish, 6.4% English (2000).
Economy: Cattle; timber. Manufacturing: building materials. Single-family building permits issued: 0 (2001) / 0 (2000); Multi-family building permits issued: 0 (2001) / 0 (2000); Employment by occupation: 4.4% management, 10.2% professional, 29.6% services, 26.0% sales, 0.2% farming, 13.8% construction, 15.8% production (2000).
Income: Per capita income: $13,401 (2000); Median household income: $29,583 (2000); Poverty rate: 17.5% (2000).
Taxes: Total city taxes per capita: $226 (1997); City property taxes per capita: $203 (1997).
Education: High school graduation rate: 73.7% (2000); College graduation rate: 7.4% (2000).

School District(s)

Crocker R-II (PK-12)
2000 Enrollment: 571 573-736-2215
Housing: Homeownership rate: 66.0% (2000); Median home value: $55,900 (2000); Median rent: $232 per month (2000); Median age of housing: 39 years (2000).
Transportation: Commute to work: 96.7% car, 0.0% public transportation, 0.9% walk, 1.9% work from home (2000); Travel time to work: 30.8% less than 15 minutes, 29.4% 15 to 30 minutes, 20.5% 30 to 45 minutes, 11.2% 45 to 60 minutes, 8.1% 60 minutes or more (2000)

DEVILS ELBOW (unincorporated postal area, zip code 65457). Covers a land area of 11.360 square miles and a water area of 0.355 square miles. Located at 37.82° N. Lat.; 92.05° W. Long. Elevation is 755 feet.
Population: 163 (2000); Race: 100.0% White, 0.0% Black, 0.0% Asian, 0.0% American Indian and Alaska Native, 0.0% Hispanic of any race, 0.0% two or more races (2000); Density: 14.3 persons per square mile (2000); Age: 39.2% under 18, 8.2% over 64 (2000); Marriage status: 30.5% never married, 44.1% now married, 13.6% widowed, 11.9% divorced (2000); Foreign born: 8.2% (2000); Ancestry (includes multiple ancestries): 15.5% Finnish, 12.4% Irish, 8.2% German, 7.2% Scottish (2000).
Economy: Employment by occupation: 0.0% management, 0.0% professional, 100.0% services, 0.0% sales, 0.0% farming, 0.0% construction, 0.0% production (2000).
Income: Per capita income: $7,166 (2000); Median household income: $15,250 (2000); Poverty rate: 48.5% (2000).
Education: High school graduation rate: 100.0% (2000); College graduation rate: 0.0% (2000).
Housing: Homeownership rate: 39.0% (2000); Median home value: $75,000 (2000); Median rent: $213 per month (2000); Median age of housing: 29 years (2000).
Transportation: Commute to work: 100.0% car, 0.0% public transportation, 0.0% walk, 0.0% work from home (2000); Travel time to work: 0.0% less than 15 minutes, 100.0% 15 to 30 minutes, 0.0% 30 to 45 minutes, 0.0% 45 to 60 minutes, 0.0% 60 minutes or more (2000)

DIXON (city). Covers a land area of 1.016 square miles and a water area of 0 square miles. Located at 37.99° N. Lat.; 92.09° W. Long. Elevation is 1,167 feet.
Population: 1,570 (2000); Race: 96.5% White, 0.0% Black, 0.6% Asian, 0.3% American Indian and Alaska Native, 2.3% Hispanic of any race, 1.1% two or more races (2000); Density: 1,545.8 persons per square mile (2000); Age: 27.3% under 18, 21.3% over 64 (2000); Marriage status: 17.8% never married, 57.1% now married, 13.5% widowed, 11.7% divorced (2000); Foreign born: 2.4% (2000); Ancestry (includes multiple ancestries): 23.5% United States or American, 16.4% German, 13.0% Other groups, 10.1% Irish, 9.1% English (2000).
Economy: Ships livestock; dairying; cattle, poultry; light manufacturing. Employment by occupation: 3.7% management, 20.1% professional, 22.4% services, 17.9% sales, 0.6% farming, 15.5% construction, 19.8% production (2000).
Income: Per capita income: $12,405 (2000); Median household income: $21,821 (2000); Poverty rate: 23.5% (2000).

Taxes: Total city taxes per capita: $115 (1997); City property taxes per capita: $48 (1997).
Education: High school graduation rate: 68.7% (2000); College graduation rate: 9.2% (2000).

School District(s)

Dixon R-I (PK-12)
2000 Enrollment: 1,134 573-759-7163

Four-year College(s)

Biblical Life College and Seminary (Private, Not-for-profit, Other Protestant)
2001 Enrollment: n/a 314-759-6238
Housing: Homeownership rate: 58.8% (2000); Median home value: $57,000 (2000); Median rent: $229 per month (2000); Median age of housing: 34 years (2000).
Newspapers: Dixon Pilot (1 x week)
Transportation: Commute to work: 94.2% car, 0.0% public transportation, 1.6% walk, 2.9% work from home (2000); Travel time to work: 31.6% less than 15 minutes, 15.4% 15 to 30 minutes, 30.7% 30 to 45 minutes, 12.6% 45 to 60 minutes, 9.7% 60 minutes or more (2000)

FORT LEONARD WOOD (CDP). Covers a land area of 97.171 square miles and a water area of 0.425 square miles. Located at 37.73° N. Lat.; 92.11° W. Long.
Population: 13,666 (2000); Race: 65.0% White, 21.4% Black, 2.9% Asian, 1.2% American Indian and Alaska Native, 11.6% Hispanic of any race, 4.1% two or more races (2000); Density: 140.6 persons per square mile (2000); Age: 27.9% under 18, 0.0% over 64 (2000); Marriage status: 42.8% never married, 54.0% now married, 0.2% widowed, 3.1% divorced (2000); Foreign born: 5.0% (2000); Ancestry (includes multiple ancestries): 40.3% Other groups, 16.5% German, 10.3% Irish, 7.6% United States or American, 4.6% English (2000).
Economy: Employment by occupation: 5.9% management, 26.0% professional, 21.1% services, 28.6% sales, 0.7% farming, 7.7% construction, 10.0% production (2000).
Income: Per capita income: $11,652 (2000); Median household income: $33,891 (2000); Poverty rate: 4.1% (2000).
Education: High school graduation rate: 97.0% (2000); College graduation rate: 26.0% (2000).
Housing: Homeownership rate: 0.2% (2000); Median home value: $65,000 (2000); Median rent: $556 per month (2000); Median age of housing: 33 years (2000).
Hospitals: General Leonard Wood Army Community Hospital (75 beds)
Transportation: Commute to work: 52.6% car, 5.3% public transportation, 33.1% walk, 1.9% work from home (2000); Travel time to work: 76.2% less than 15 minutes, 17.9% 15 to 30 minutes, 3.1% 30 to 45 minutes, 0.8% 45 to 60 minutes, 2.0% 60 minutes or more (2000)
Airports: Waynesville Regional Airport at Forney F (commercial service)

LAQUEY (unincorporated postal area, zip code 65534). Covers a land area of 42.149 square miles and a water area of 0.006 square miles. Located at 37.68° N. Lat.; 92.28° W. Long. Elevation is 1,065 feet.
Population: 723 (2000); Race: 98.5% White, 0.0% Black, 1.5% Asian, 0.0% American Indian and Alaska Native, 0.0% Hispanic of any race, 0.0% two or more races (2000); Density: 17.2 persons per square mile (2000); Age: 29.1% under 18, 12.2% over 64 (2000); Marriage status: 17.5% never married, 69.6% now married, 5.7% widowed, 7.1% divorced (2000); Foreign born: 2.4% (2000); Ancestry (includes multiple ancestries): 21.3% United States or American, 17.7% German, 12.2% Irish, 9.3% English, 4.8% Other groups (2000).
Economy: Employment by occupation: 8.9% management, 16.7% professional, 18.5% services, 9.2% sales, 8.0% farming, 7.1% construction, 31.5% production (2000).
Income: Per capita income: $14,012 (2000); Median household income: $25,000 (2000); Poverty rate: 15.0% (2000).
Education: High school graduation rate: 61.8% (2000); College graduation rate: 6.9% (2000).

School District(s)

Laquey R-V (PK-12)
2000 Enrollment: 653 573-765-3716
Housing: Homeownership rate: 95.2% (2000); Median home value: $82,200 (2000); Median rent: $425 per month (2000); Median age of housing: 20 years (2000).
Transportation: Commute to work: 89.3% car, 0.0% public transportation, 3.3% walk, 4.5% work from home (2000); Travel time to work: 13.1% less than 15 minutes, 52.0% 15 to 30 minutes, 27.1% 30 to 45 minutes, 5.3% 45 to 60 minutes, 2.5% 60 minutes or more (2000)

RICHLAND (city). Covers a land area of 2.269 square miles and a water area of 0.019 square miles. Located at 37.85° N. Lat.; 92.40° W. Long. Elevation is 1,135 feet.
History: Founded c.1870.
Population: 1,805 (2000); Race: 97.6% White, 0.0% Black, 0.3% Asian, 1.0% American Indian and Alaska Native, 1.2% Hispanic of any race, 0.9% two or more races (2000); Density: 795.7 persons per square mile (2000); Age: 24.1% under 18, 20.4% over 64 (2000); Marriage status: 16.5% never married, 55.1% now married, 13.5% widowed, 14.9% divorced (2000); Foreign born: 1.5% (2000); Ancestry (includes multiple ancestries): 16.5% United States or American, 13.1% German, 12.0% Irish, 11.2% Other groups, 7.7% English (2000).
Economy: Grain, hay; cattle. Manufacturing: boats, apparel. Single-family building permits issued: 2 (2001) / 0 (2000); Multi-family building permits issued: 0 (2001) / 2 (2000); Employment by occupation: 7.2% management, 12.8% professional, 20.8% services, 24.5% sales, 0.6% farming, 9.9% construction, 24.2% production (2000).
Income: Per capita income: $14,209 (2000); Median household income: $22,821 (2000); Poverty rate: 23.5% (2000).
Taxes: Total city taxes per capita: $166 (1997); City property taxes per capita: $26 (1997).
Education: High school graduation rate: 75.9% (2000); College graduation rate: 11.9% (2000).

School District(s)

Pulaski Co. R-IV (PK-12)
2000 Enrollment: 651 573-765-3241
Housing: Homeownership rate: 66.3% (2000); Median home value: $54,400 (2000); Median rent: $197 per month (2000); Median age of housing: 36 years (2000).
Newspapers: Richland Mirror (1 x week)
Transportation: Commute to work: 94.6% car, 0.0% public transportation, 2.7% walk, 2.8% work from home (2000); Travel time to work: 36.6% less than 15 minutes, 17.8% 15 to 30 minutes, 27.3% 30 to 45 minutes, 9.5% 45 to 60 minutes, 8.8% 60 minutes or more (2000)
Additional Information Contacts
Richland Chamber of Commerce 573-765-4450

SAINT ROBERT (city). Covers a land area of 7.205 square miles and a water area of 0 square miles. Located at 37.82° N. Lat.; 92.13° W. Long. Elevation is 1,040 feet.
Population: 2,760 (2000); Race: 63.2% White, 19.5% Black, 5.1% Asian, 1.5% American Indian and Alaska Native, 7.8% Hispanic of any race, 5.9% two or more races (2000); Density: 383.0 persons per square mile (2000); Age: 26.5% under 18, 6.6% over 64 (2000); Marriage status: 21.8% never married, 58.4% now married, 5.0% widowed, 14.8% divorced (2000); Foreign born: 7.3% (2000); Ancestry (includes multiple ancestries): 40.4% Other groups, 20.4% German, 10.2% Irish, 7.2% United States or American, 3.8% English (2000).
Economy: Employment by occupation: 10.7% management, 21.4% professional, 29.6% services, 22.4% sales, 0.0% farming, 7.6% construction, 8.4% production (2000).
Income: Per capita income: $17,650 (2000); Median household income: $33,080 (2000); Poverty rate: 11.3% (2000).
Education: High school graduation rate: 86.1% (2000); College graduation rate: 22.1% (2000).
Housing: Homeownership rate: 42.5% (2000); Median home value: $96,700 (2000); Median rent: $375 per month (2000); Median age of housing: 16 years (2000).
Newspapers: The Daily Guide (5 x week)
Transportation: Commute to work: 91.7% car, 1.1% public transportation, 3.0% walk, 3.0% work from home (2000); Travel time to work: 43.4% less than 15 minutes, 41.0% 15 to 30 minutes, 9.5% 30 to 45 minutes, 1.5% 45 to 60 minutes, 4.7% 60 minutes or more (2000)
Additional Information Contacts
St. Robert Chamber of Commerce 573-336-5121

WAYNESVILLE (city). Covers a land area of 6.226 square miles and a water area of 0.015 square miles. Located at 37.82° N. Lat.; 92.21° W. Long. Elevation is 805 feet.
History: Waynesville was settled in 1831 by G.W. Gibson. In 1835 James A. Bates opened a store here that served also as a temporary courthouse for Pulaski County. The town was platted in 1839 and named for "Mad Anthony" Wayne.
Population: 3,507 (2000); Race: 82.1% White, 9.9% Black, 2.0% Asian, 0.4% American Indian and Alaska Native, 2.8% Hispanic of any race, 3.5%

two or more races (2000); Density: 563.3 persons per square mile (2000); Age: 27.1% under 18, 12.4% over 64 (2000); Marriage status: 20.6% never married, 61.8% now married, 6.9% widowed, 10.6% divorced (2000); Foreign born: 6.0% (2000); Ancestry (includes multiple ancestries): 22.5% Other groups, 19.3% German, 13.1% English, 10.4% United States or American, 10.0% Irish (2000).
Economy: Single-family building permits issued: 6 (2001) / 5 (2000); Multi-family building permits issued: 0 (2001) / 0 (2000); Employment by occupation: 7.3% management, 29.3% professional, 22.9% services, 20.1% sales, 0.6% farming, 9.6% construction, 10.2% production (2000).
Income: Per capita income: $19,117 (2000); Median household income: $41,250 (2000); Poverty rate: 11.3% (2000).
Taxes: Total city taxes per capita: $168 (1997); City property taxes per capita: $44 (1997).
Education: High school graduation rate: 89.0% (2000); College graduation rate: 26.8% (2000).

School District(s)

Waynesville R-VI (PK-12)
2000 Enrollment: 5,207 573-774-6497

Two-year College(s)

Waynesville Technical Academy (Public)
2001 Enrollment: 31 573-774-6106

Housing: Homeownership rate: 59.5% (2000); Median home value: $87,500 (2000); Median rent: $369 per month (2000); Median age of housing: 24 years (2000).
Newspapers: The Fort Leonard Wood Constitution (1 x week)
Transportation: Commute to work: 97.1% car, 0.0% public transportation, 0.8% walk, 1.6% work from home (2000); Travel time to work: 34.2% less than 15 minutes, 52.1% 15 to 30 minutes, 9.1% 30 to 45 minutes, 1.5% 45 to 60 minutes, 3.1% 60 minutes or more (2000)
Additional Information Contacts
Pulaski County Board of Realtors 573-336-7225

Putnam County

Located in northern Missouri; bounded on the east by the Chariton River, and on the north by Iowa. Covers a land area of 517.90 square miles, a water area of 1.80 square miles, and is located in the Central Time Zone. The county government was organized in 1845. County seat is Unionville.
Population: 5,223 (2000); Race: 98.7% White, 0.1% Black, 0.1% Asian, 0.1% American Indian and Alaska Native, 0.7% Hispanic of any race, 0.9% two or more races (2000); Density: 10.1 persons per square mile (2000); Age: 24.0% under 18, 20.6% over 64 (2000).
Religion: Five largest groups: 28.7% Southern Baptist Convention, 13.0% Christian Churches and Churches of Christ, 5.1% The United Methodist Church, 1.9% Churches of Christ, 1.7% Assemblies of God (2000).
Economy: Unemployment rate: 3.8% (11/2002); Total civilian labor force: 1,934 (11/2002); Leading industries: 21.5% retail trade; 16.7% health care and social assistance; 14.5% wholesale trade (2000); Companies that employ more than 1,000 persons: 0 (2000); Companies that employ more than 100 persons: 0 (2000); Farms: 615 totaling 261,360 acres (1997); Minority business ownership rate: 0.0% (1997); Women business ownership rate: 32.4% (1997); Retail sales per capita: $3,572 (1997). Single-family building permits issued: 3 (2001) / 4 (2000); Multi-family building permits issued: 0 (2001) / 0 (2000).
Income: Per capita income: $14,647 (2000); Median household income: $26,282 (2000); Poverty rate: 16.0% (2000); Bankruptcy rate: 2.86% (2001).
Taxes: Total county taxes per capita: $101 (1997); County property taxes per capita: $41 (1997).
Education: High school graduation rate: 80.0% (2000); College graduation rate: 11.2% (2000).
Housing: Homeownership rate: 77.2% (2000); Median home value: $44,500 (2000); Median rent: $194 per month (2000); Median age of housing: 30 years (2000).
Health: Birth rate: 116.8 per 10,000 population (1998); Age adjusted death rate: 106.2 per 10,000 population (1999); Age adjusted cancer mortality rate: 217.8 (Unreliable figure as per CDC) deaths per 100,000 population (1999). Number of physicians: n/a (1999); Number of hospital beds: 49.8 per 10,000 population (1999).
Elections: 2000 Presidential election results: 30.3% Gore, 68.3% Bush, 0.8% Nader, 0.6% Buchanan
Additional Information Contacts
Putnam County Government Offices 660-947-2674

Putnam County Communities

LIVONIA (village). Covers a land area of 0.266 square miles and a water area of 0 square miles. Located at 40.49° N. Lat.; 92.69° W. Long. Elevation is 830 feet.
Population: 114 (2000); Race: 95.3% White, 0.0% Black, 0.0% Asian, 3.1% American Indian and Alaska Native, 0.0% Hispanic of any race, 1.6% two or more races (2000); Density: 428.8 persons per square mile (2000); Age: 34.6% under 18, 15.0% over 64 (2000); Marriage status: 27.3% never married, 51.5% now married, 10.1% widowed, 11.1% divorced (2000); Foreign born: 0.0% (2000); Ancestry (includes multiple ancestries): 22.8% German, 21.3% Irish, 11.8% Dutch, 7.1% English, 6.3% Other groups (2000).
Economy: Employment by occupation: 15.8% management, 13.2% professional, 18.4% services, 15.8% sales, 7.9% farming, 21.1% construction, 7.9% production (2000).
Income: Per capita income: $8,633 (2000); Median household income: $22,813 (2000); Poverty rate: 35.4% (2000).
Taxes: Total city taxes per capita: $8 (1997); City property taxes per capita: $8 (1997).
Education: High school graduation rate: 69.9% (2000); College graduation rate: 5.5% (2000).
Housing: Homeownership rate: 77.6% (2000); Median home value: $19,700 (2000); Median rent: $225 per month (2000); Median age of housing: 60+ years (2000).
Transportation: Commute to work: 100.0% car, 0.0% public transportation, 0.0% walk, 0.0% work from home (2000); Travel time to work: 5.3% less than 15 minutes, 57.9% 15 to 30 minutes, 18.4% 30 to 45 minutes, 0.0% 45 to 60 minutes, 18.4% 60 minutes or more (2000)

LUCERNE (village). Covers a land area of 0.249 square miles and a water area of 0 square miles. Located at 40.46° N. Lat.; 93.29° W. Long. Elevation is 965 feet.
Population: 92 (2000); Race: 100.0% White, 0.0% Black, 0.0% Asian, 0.0% American Indian and Alaska Native, 0.0% Hispanic of any race, 0.0% two or more races (2000); Density: 369.5 persons per square mile (2000); Age: 9.0% under 18, 32.6% over 64 (2000); Marriage status: 21.7% never married, 57.8% now married, 12.0% widowed, 8.4% divorced (2000); Foreign born: 0.0% (2000); Ancestry (includes multiple ancestries): 15.7% Irish, 11.2% United States or American, 10.1% Other groups, 9.0% German, 7.9% Dutch (2000).
Economy: Employment by occupation: 9.1% management, 31.8% professional, 27.3% services, 9.1% sales, 9.1% farming, 13.6% construction, 0.0% production (2000).
Income: Per capita income: $11,046 (2000); Median household income: $16,500 (2000); Poverty rate: 41.2% (2000).
Taxes: Total city taxes per capita: $60 (1997); City property taxes per capita: $20 (1997).
Education: High school graduation rate: 75.6% (2000); College graduation rate: 6.4% (2000).
Housing: Homeownership rate: 68.2% (2000); Median home value: $14,300 (2000); Median rent: $225 per month (2000); Median age of housing: 60+ years (2000).
Transportation: Commute to work: 90.9% car, 0.0% public transportation, 9.1% walk, 0.0% work from home (2000); Travel time to work: 18.2% less than 15 minutes, 59.1% 15 to 30 minutes, 18.2% 30 to 45 minutes, 0.0% 45 to 60 minutes, 4.5% 60 minutes or more (2000)

POWERSVILLE (village). Covers a land area of 0.561 square miles and a water area of 0 square miles. Located at 40.55° N. Lat.; 93.30° W. Long. Elevation is 968 feet.
Population: 86 (2000); Race: 100.0% White, 0.0% Black, 0.0% Asian, 0.0% American Indian and Alaska Native, 0.0% Hispanic of any race, 0.0% two or more races (2000); Density: 153.3 persons per square mile (2000); Age: 18.2% under 18, 20.5% over 64 (2000); Marriage status: 6.7% never married, 77.3% now married, 14.7% widowed, 1.3% divorced (2000); Foreign born: 0.0% (2000); Ancestry (includes multiple ancestries): 14.8% English, 12.5% Irish, 11.4% German, 10.2% Other groups, 6.8% French (except Basque) (2000).
Economy: Employment by occupation: 4.3% management, 4.3% professional, 21.3% services, 10.6% sales, 8.5% farming, 17.0% construction, 34.0% production (2000).
Income: Per capita income: $13,795 (2000); Median household income: $25,750 (2000); Poverty rate: 6.8% (2000).

Taxes: Total city taxes per capita: $13 (1997); City property taxes per capita: $13 (1997).
Education: High school graduation rate: 81.4% (2000); College graduation rate: 0.0% (2000).
Housing: Homeownership rate: 85.0% (2000); Median home value: $12,500 (2000); Median rent: $125 per month (2000); Median age of housing: 60+ years (2000).
Transportation: Commute to work: 83.0% car, 0.0% public transportation, 8.5% walk, 4.3% work from home (2000); Travel time to work: 51.1% less than 15 minutes, 28.9% 15 to 30 minutes, 4.4% 30 to 45 minutes, 0.0% 45 to 60 minutes, 15.6% 60 minutes or more (2000)

UNIONVILLE (city). Covers a land area of 1.991 square miles and a water area of 0 square miles. Located at 40.47° N. Lat.; 93.00° W. Long. Elevation is 1,067 feet.
History: Incorporated c.1855.
Population: 2,041 (2000); Race: 98.5% White, 0.1% Black, 0.2% Asian, 0.0% American Indian and Alaska Native, 0.8% Hispanic of any race, 1.2% two or more races (2000); Density: 1,025.0 persons per square mile (2000); Age: 24.6% under 18, 24.9% over 64 (2000); Marriage status: 19.3% never married, 53.7% now married, 14.5% widowed, 12.4% divorced (2000); Foreign born: 0.6% (2000); Ancestry (includes multiple ancestries): 17.6% United States or American, 16.5% German, 12.7% English, 10.0% Other groups, 8.5% Irish (2000).
Economy: Corn, wheat, soybeans; cattle, sheep; coal mining to East. Manufacturing of labels and decals. Single-family building permits issued: 3 (2001) / 3 (2000); Multi-family building permits issued: 0 (2001) / 0 (2000); Employment by occupation: 12.4% management, 13.3% professional, 16.6% services, 20.1% sales, 5.8% farming, 11.7% construction, 20.1% production (2000).
Income: Per capita income: $11,881 (2000); Median household income: $19,978 (2000); Poverty rate: 18.6% (2000).
Taxes: Total city taxes per capita: $174 (1997); City property taxes per capita: $73 (1997).
Education: High school graduation rate: 74.6% (2000); College graduation rate: 9.5% (2000).

School District(s)

Putnam Co. R-I (PK-12)
2000 Enrollment: 839 660-947-3361

Housing: Homeownership rate: 67.0% (2000); Median home value: $44,000 (2000); Median rent: $192 per month (2000); Median age of housing: 36 years (2000).
Hospitals: Putnam County Memorial Hospital (40 beds)
Newspapers: Unionville Republican (1 x week)
Transportation: Commute to work: 91.5% car, 0.0% public transportation, 3.0% walk, 4.8% work from home (2000); Travel time to work: 58.3% less than 15 minutes, 13.3% 15 to 30 minutes, 18.8% 30 to 45 minutes, 2.8% 45 to 60 minutes, 6.8% 60 minutes or more (2000)

WORTHINGTON (village). Covers a land area of 0.122 square miles and a water area of 0 square miles. Located at 40.40° N. Lat.; 92.68° W. Long. Elevation is 810 feet.
Population: 89 (2000); Race: 100.0% White, 0.0% Black, 0.0% Asian, 0.0% American Indian and Alaska Native, 0.0% Hispanic of any race, 0.0% two or more races (2000); Density: 726.8 persons per square mile (2000); Age: 23.2% under 18, 14.7% over 64 (2000); Marriage status: 25.0% never married, 48.7% now married, 6.6% widowed, 19.7% divorced (2000); Foreign born: 0.0% (2000); Ancestry (includes multiple ancestries): 22.1% German, 20.0% United States or American, 3.2% Irish, 3.2% English, 2.1% Norwegian (2000).
Economy: Employment by occupation: 6.9% management, 0.0% professional, 20.7% services, 13.8% sales, 3.4% farming, 6.9% construction, 48.3% production (2000).
Income: Per capita income: $7,396 (2000); Median household income: $11,964 (2000); Poverty rate: 42.1% (2000).
Education: High school graduation rate: 46.7% (2000); College graduation rate: 0.0% (2000).
Housing: Homeownership rate: 65.1% (2000); Median home value: $13,800 (2000); Median rent: <$100 per month (2000); Median age of housing: 45 years (2000).
Transportation: Commute to work: 93.1% car, 0.0% public transportation, 0.0% walk, 6.9% work from home (2000); Travel time to work: 7.4% less than 15 minutes, 25.9% 15 to 30 minutes, 25.9% 30 to 45 minutes, 25.9% 45 to 60 minutes, 14.8% 60 minutes or more (2000)

Ralls County

Located in northeastern Missouri; bounded on the east by the Mississippi River and the Illinois border; drained by the Salt River. Covers a land area of 471.00 square miles, a water area of 12.80 square miles, and is located in the Central Time Zone. The county government was organized in 1820. County seat is New London.

Weather Station: Saverton Lock & Dam 22 — Elevation: 469 feet

	Jan	Feb	Mar	Apr	May	Jun	Jul	Aug	Sep	Oct	Nov	Dec
High	35	40	52	65	75	84	89	86	79	67	52	40
Low	18	22	32	44	54	63	68	66	58	46	35	24
Precip	1.4	1.7	3.0	3.9	4.8	3.4	3.7	3.8	4.0	3.0	3.2	2.3
Snow	3.0	3.4	1.8	0.1	0.0	0.0	0.0	0.0	0.0	tr	0.4	2.7

High and Low temperatures in degrees Fahrenheit; Precipitation and Snow in inches

Population: 9,626 (2000); Race: 98.1% White, 0.9% Black, 0.2% Asian, 0.1% American Indian and Alaska Native, 0.5% Hispanic of any race, 0.5% two or more races (2000); Density: 20.4 persons per square mile (2000); Age: 25.2% under 18, 14.3% over 64 (2000).
Religion: Five largest groups: 25.9% Southern Baptist Convention, 7.8% Christian Church (Disciples of Christ), 3.6% Catholic Church, 2.7% The United Methodist Church, 1.5% Christian Churches and Churches of Christ (2000).
Economy: Unemployment rate: 4.9% (11/2002); Total civilian labor force: 5,365 (11/2002); Leading industries: 52.2% manufacturing; 10.9% health care and social assistance; 8.6% retail trade (2000); Companies that employ more than 1,000 persons: 0 (2000); Companies that employ more than 100 persons: 5 (2000); Farms: 550 totaling 231,817 acres (1997); Minority business ownership rate: 0.0% (1997); Women business ownership rate: 23.6% (1997); Retail sales per capita: $2,646 (1997). Single-family building permits issued: 2 (2001) / 2 (2000); Multi-family building permits issued: 0 (2001) / 0 (2000).
Income: Per capita income: $16,456 (2000); Median household income: $37,094 (2000); Poverty rate: 8.7% (2000); Bankruptcy rate: 3.11% (2001).
Taxes: Total county taxes per capita: $138 (2000); County property taxes per capita: $64 (2000).
Education: High school graduation rate: 78.7% (2000); College graduation rate: 12.3% (2000).
Housing: Homeownership rate: 82.3% (2000); Median home value: $67,400 (2000); Median rent: $285 per month (2000); Median age of housing: 25 years (2000).
Health: Birth rate: 89.3 per 10,000 population (1998); Age adjusted death rate: 89.1 per 10,000 population (1999); Age adjusted cancer mortality rate: 300.9 deaths per 100,000 population (1999). Number of physicians: 2.1 per 10,000 population (1999); Number of hospital beds: n/a (1999).
Elections: 2000 Presidential election results: 44.8% Gore, 53.9% Bush, 0.8% Nader, 0.2% Buchanan

Additional Information Contacts

Ralls County Government Offices 573-985-7111
Perry Chamber of Commerce 573-565-2245

Ralls County Communities

CENTER (city). Covers a land area of 0.397 square miles and a water area of 0 square miles. Located at 39.50° N. Lat.; 91.52° W. Long. Elevation is 719 feet.
Population: 644 (2000); Race: 99.1% White, 0.0% Black, 0.0% Asian, 0.0% American Indian and Alaska Native, 1.4% Hispanic of any race, 0.9% two or more races (2000); Density: 1,621.4 persons per square mile (2000); Age: 26.1% under 18, 23.1% over 64 (2000); Marriage status: 16.6% never married, 58.5% now married, 11.5% widowed, 13.4% divorced (2000); Foreign born: 0.0% (2000); Ancestry (includes multiple ancestries): 20.0% United States or American, 17.1% German, 8.9% Irish, 7.8% English, 5.4% Other groups (2000).
Economy: Corn, soybeans; hogs. Single-family building permits issued: 0 (2001) / 0 (2000); Multi-family building permits issued: 0 (2001) / 0 (2000); Employment by occupation: 8.0% management, 11.2% professional, 24.3% services, 16.7% sales, 4.4% farming, 9.2% construction, 26.3% production (2000).
Income: Per capita income: $11,598 (2000); Median household income: $21,964 (2000); Poverty rate: 26.4% (2000).
Education: High school graduation rate: 69.1% (2000); College graduation rate: 7.3% (2000).

School District(s)

Ralls Co. R-II (KG-12)
2000 Enrollment: 908 573-267-3397

Housing: Homeownership rate: 61.0% (2000); Median home value: $42,800 (2000); Median rent: $272 per month (2000); Median age of housing: 31 years (2000).

Transportation: Commute to work: 96.3% car, 0.0% public transportation, 1.6% walk, 2.0% work from home (2000); Travel time to work: 38.2% less than 15 minutes, 37.8% 15 to 30 minutes, 17.4% 30 to 45 minutes, 2.1% 45 to 60 minutes, 4.6% 60 minutes or more (2000)

NEW LONDON (city). Covers a land area of 0.703 square miles and a water area of 0.001 square miles. Located at 39.58° N. Lat.; 91.39° W. Long. Elevation is 650 feet.

History: New London was founded in 1819 by William Jamieson, an engineer from England, and developed as a trading and shipping point for farm produce.

Population: 1,001 (2000); Race: 91.2% White, 7.3% Black, 0.6% Asian, 0.0% American Indian and Alaska Native, 1.3% Hispanic of any race, 0.4% two or more races (2000); Density: 1,424.1 persons per square mile (2000); Age: 23.8% under 18, 15.1% over 64 (2000); Marriage status: 24.4% never married, 54.9% now married, 10.3% widowed, 10.4% divorced (2000); Foreign born: 0.8% (2000); Ancestry (includes multiple ancestries): 21.9% United States or American, 16.9% German, 11.7% Other groups, 9.0% Irish, 8.0% English (2000).

Economy: Single-family building permits issued: 1 (2001) / 0 (2000); Multi-family building permits issued: 0 (2001) / 0 (2000); Employment by occupation: 7.4% management, 13.7% professional, 14.9% services, 26.9% sales, 0.4% farming, 10.2% construction, 26.5% production (2000).

Income: Per capita income: $14,360 (2000); Median household income: $28,875 (2000); Poverty rate: 13.6% (2000).

Taxes: Total city taxes per capita: $99 (1997); City property taxes per capita: $19 (1997).

Education: High school graduation rate: 72.4% (2000); College graduation rate: 7.4% (2000).

Housing: Homeownership rate: 77.3% (2000); Median home value: $54,300 (2000); Median rent: $237 per month (2000); Median age of housing: 35 years (2000).

Newspapers: Ralls County Herald-Enterprise (1 x week)

Transportation: Commute to work: 94.3% car, 0.0% public transportation, 3.6% walk, 2.1% work from home (2000); Travel time to work: 40.7% less than 15 minutes, 40.0% 15 to 30 minutes, 10.2% 30 to 45 minutes, 2.2% 45 to 60 minutes, 6.9% 60 minutes or more (2000)

PERRY (city). Covers a land area of 1.227 square miles and a water area of 0.033 square miles. Located at 39.42° N. Lat.; 91.67° W. Long. Elevation is 683 feet.

Population: 666 (2000); Race: 98.8% White, 0.0% Black, 0.0% Asian, 0.6% American Indian and Alaska Native, 0.0% Hispanic of any race, 0.6% two or more races (2000); Density: 542.7 persons per square mile (2000); Age: 17.4% under 18, 29.3% over 64 (2000); Marriage status: 17.8% never married, 51.9% now married, 20.1% widowed, 10.2% divorced (2000); Foreign born: 0.3% (2000); Ancestry (includes multiple ancestries): 16.3% Irish, 15.5% German, 15.2% United States or American, 9.6% English, 3.2% Scotch-Irish (2000).

Economy: Corn, soybeans; cattle, hogs; coal. Single-family building permits issued: 1 (2001) / 2 (2000); Multi-family building permits issued: 0 (2001) / 0 (2000); Employment by occupation: 4.2% management, 16.2% professional, 24.0% services, 20.4% sales, 0.9% farming, 13.5% construction, 21.0% production (2000).

Income: Per capita income: $18,304 (2000); Median household income: $30,625 (2000); Poverty rate: 7.4% (2000).

Taxes: Total city taxes per capita: $508 (1997); City property taxes per capita: $0 (1997).

Education: High school graduation rate: 73.6% (2000); College graduation rate: 14.6% (2000).

Housing: Homeownership rate: 75.4% (2000); Median home value: $51,500 (2000); Median rent: $220 per month (2000); Median age of housing: 48 years (2000).

Transportation: Commute to work: 93.7% car, 0.6% public transportation, 2.4% walk, 3.3% work from home (2000); Travel time to work: 49.5% less than 15 minutes, 18.3% 15 to 30 minutes, 22.9% 30 to 45 minutes, 4.3% 45 to 60 minutes, 5.0% 60 minutes or more (2000)

Additional Information Contacts

Perry Chamber of Commerce. 573-565-2245

RENSSELAER (village). Covers a land area of 1.965 square miles and a water area of 0.043 square miles. Located at 39.67° N. Lat.; 91.54° W. Long. Elevation is 724 feet.

Population: 145 (2000); Race: 100.0% White, 0.0% Black, 0.0% Asian, 0.0% American Indian and Alaska Native, 1.9% Hispanic of any race, 0.0% two or more races (2000); Density: 73.8 persons per square mile (2000); Age: 20.0% under 18, 5.6% over 64 (2000); Marriage status: 17.0% never married, 65.2% now married, 3.0% widowed, 14.8% divorced (2000); Foreign born: 0.0% (2000); Ancestry (includes multiple ancestries): 30.0% United States or American, 10.0% Irish, 9.4% German, 6.3% English, 5.0% Other groups (2000).

Economy: Employment by occupation: 8.0% management, 6.9% professional, 6.9% services, 24.1% sales, 0.0% farming, 10.3% construction, 43.7% production (2000).

Income: Per capita income: $18,103 (2000); Median household income: $55,179 (2000); Poverty rate: 4.4% (2000).

Taxes: Total city taxes per capita: $31 (1997); City property taxes per capita: $10 (1997).

Education: High school graduation rate: 70.6% (2000); College graduation rate: 2.5% (2000).

Housing: Homeownership rate: 91.5% (2000); Median home value: $87,200 (2000); Median rent: $350 per month (2000); Median age of housing: 20 years (2000).

Transportation: Commute to work: 100.0% car, 0.0% public transportation, 0.0% walk, 0.0% work from home (2000); Travel time to work: 27.5% less than 15 minutes, 32.5% 15 to 30 minutes, 11.3% 30 to 45 minutes, 11.3% 45 to 60 minutes, 17.5% 60 minutes or more (2000)

Randolph County

Located in north central Missouri; drained by tributaries of the Chariton and Salt Rivers. Covers a land area of 482.30 square miles, a water area of 5.30 square miles, and is located in the Central Time Zone. The county government was organized in 1829. County seat is Huntsville.

Weather Station: Moberly Elevation: 839 feet

	Jan	Feb	Mar	Apr	May	Jun	Jul	Aug	Sep	Oct	Nov	Dec
High	36	42	54	67	76	84	89	87	79	68	53	41
Low	18	24	34	44	54	63	68	66	58	47	35	24
Precip	1.7	1.8	3.1	4.2	5.0	4.1	3.9	3.7	4.3	3.2	3.0	2.3
Snow	7.1	5.0	2.0	0.4	0.0	0.0	0.0	0.0	0.0	tr	1.1	2.9

High and Low temperatures in degrees Fahrenheit; Precipitation and Snow in inches

Population: 24,663 (2000); Race: 90.4% White, 6.3% Black, 0.7% Asian, 0.5% American Indian and Alaska Native, 1.1% Hispanic of any race, 1.8% two or more races (2000); Density: 51.1 persons per square mile (2000); Age: 23.8% under 18, 14.9% over 64 (2000).

Religion: Five largest groups: 23.9% Southern Baptist Convention, 6.7% Catholic Church, 6.5% Christian Church (Disciples of Christ), 5.3% The United Methodist Church, 4.7% Christian Churches and Churches of Christ (2000).

Economy: Unemployment rate: 4.5% (11/2002); Total civilian labor force: 10,684 (11/2002); Leading industries: 20.7% manufacturing; 16.5% retail trade; 15.0% health care and social assistance (2000); Companies that employ more than 1,000 persons: 0 (2000); Companies that employ more than 100 persons: 12 (2000); Farms: 801 totaling 229,860 acres (1997); Minority business ownership rate: 0.0% (1997); Women business ownership rate: 30.0% (1997); Retail sales per capita: $8,839 (1997). Single-family building permits issued: 9 (2001) / 21 (2000); Multi-family building permits issued: 0 (2001) / 0 (2000).

Income: Per capita income: $15,010 (2000); Median household income: $31,464 (2000); Poverty rate: 12.5% (2000); Bankruptcy rate: 3.81% (2001).

Taxes: Total county taxes per capita: $106 (2000); County property taxes per capita: $64 (2000).

Education: High school graduation rate: 77.1% (2000); College graduation rate: 11.7% (2000).

Housing: Homeownership rate: 72.0% (2000); Median home value: $49,300 (2000); Median rent: $280 per month (2000); Median age of housing: 36 years (2000).

Health: Birth rate: 131.8 per 10,000 population (1998); Age adjusted death rate: 114.2 per 10,000 population (1999); Age adjusted cancer mortality rate: 226.5 deaths per 100,000 population (1999). Number of physicians: 5.3 per 10,000 population (1999); Number of hospital beds: 37.3 per 10,000 population (1999).

Elections: 2000 Presidential election results: 44.8% Gore, 52.7% Bush, 1.2% Nader, 0.7% Buchanan

Additional Information Contacts

Randolph County Government Offices 660-277-4717
Moberly Chamber of Commerce 660-263-6070
Randolph County Board of Realtors 660-263-4400

Randolph County Communities

CAIRO (village). Covers a land area of 0.268 square miles and a water area of 0 square miles. Located at 39.51° N. Lat.; 92.44° W. Long. Elevation is 864 feet.

History: Cairo was platted in 1860 when the railroad was built through the district.

Population: 293 (2000); Race: 100.0% White, 0.0% Black, 0.0% Asian, 0.0% American Indian and Alaska Native, 0.0% Hispanic of any race, 0.0% two or more races (2000); Density: 1,093.2 persons per square mile (2000); Age: 29.4% under 18, 12.1% over 64 (2000); Marriage status: 19.7% never married, 55.7% now married, 8.3% widowed, 16.2% divorced (2000); Foreign born: 0.0% (2000); Ancestry (includes multiple ancestries): 25.2% English, 23.0% German, 17.9% Irish, 10.5% United States or American, 7.3% Other groups (2000).

Economy: Single-family building permits issued: 0 (2001) / 0 (2000); Multi-family building permits issued: 0 (2001) / 0 (2000); Employment by occupation: 8.3% management, 12.8% professional, 7.1% services, 34.6% sales, 0.0% farming, 11.5% construction, 25.6% production (2000).

Income: Per capita income: $14,905 (2000); Median household income: $35,000 (2000); Poverty rate: 10.2% (2000).

Taxes: Total city taxes per capita: $66 (1997); City property taxes per capita: $29 (1997).

Education: High school graduation rate: 86.1% (2000); College graduation rate: 11.3% (2000).

School District(s)

Northeast Randolph Co. R-IV (PK-12)
2000 Enrollment: 428 660-263-2788

Housing: Homeownership rate: 70.5% (2000); Median home value: $35,400 (2000); Median rent: $221 per month (2000); Median age of housing: 40 years (2000).

Transportation: Commute to work: 95.5% car, 0.0% public transportation, 0.0% walk, 3.2% work from home (2000); Travel time to work: 43.7% less than 15 minutes, 40.4% 15 to 30 minutes, 3.3% 30 to 45 minutes, 9.9% 45 to 60 minutes, 2.6% 60 minutes or more (2000)

CLARK (city). Covers a land area of 0.234 square miles and a water area of 0 square miles. Located at 39.28° N. Lat.; 92.34° W. Long. Elevation is 867 feet.

Population: 275 (2000); Race: 93.1% White, 0.0% Black, 0.0% Asian, 4.6% American Indian and Alaska Native, 1.6% Hispanic of any race, 2.3% two or more races (2000); Density: 1,176.0 persons per square mile (2000); Age: 28.3% under 18, 8.2% over 64 (2000); Marriage status: 14.0% never married, 66.8% now married, 9.2% widowed, 10.0% divorced (2000); Foreign born: 0.0% (2000); Ancestry (includes multiple ancestries): 16.1% Irish, 12.8% United States or American, 12.5% English, 12.2% German, 8.6% Other groups (2000).

Economy: Lumber. Amish area to East. Employment by occupation: 5.2% management, 9.6% professional, 26.7% services, 21.5% sales, 0.0% farming, 13.3% construction, 23.7% production (2000).

Income: Per capita income: $11,704 (2000); Median household income: $31,875 (2000); Poverty rate: 18.8% (2000).

Taxes: Total city taxes per capita: $61 (1997); City property taxes per capita: $27 (1997).

Education: High school graduation rate: 71.9% (2000); College graduation rate: 8.1% (2000).

Housing: Homeownership rate: 78.6% (2000); Median home value: $29,600 (2000); Median rent: $295 per month (2000); Median age of housing: 35 years (2000).

Transportation: Commute to work: 95.3% car, 0.0% public transportation, 1.6% walk, 3.1% work from home (2000); Travel time to work: 8.1% less than 15 minutes, 43.9% 15 to 30 minutes, 39.0% 30 to 45 minutes, 6.5% 45 to 60 minutes, 2.4% 60 minutes or more (2000)

CLIFTON HILL (city). Aka Clifton. Covers a land area of 0.131 square miles and a water area of 0 square miles. Located at 39.43° N. Lat.; 92.66° W. Long. Elevation is 722 feet.

Population: 124 (2000); Race: 100.0% White, 0.0% Black, 0.0% Asian, 0.0% American Indian and Alaska Native, 0.0% Hispanic of any race, 0.0% two or more races (2000); Density: 944.8 persons per square mile (2000); Age: 34.1% under 18, 15.4% over 64 (2000); Marriage status: 4.8% never married, 75.9% now married, 12.0% widowed, 7.2% divorced (2000); Foreign born: 0.0% (2000); Ancestry (includes multiple ancestries): 28.5% German, 18.7% Irish, 18.7% United States or American, 17.9% English, 4.9% Other groups (2000).

Economy: Grain; lumber; pecans. Bison ranch to South. Employment by occupation: 14.0% management, 20.9% professional, 11.6% services, 16.3% sales, 0.0% farming, 14.0% construction, 23.3% production (2000).

Income: Per capita income: $11,637 (2000); Median household income: $26,250 (2000); Poverty rate: 20.8% (2000).

Taxes: Total city taxes per capita: $66 (1997); City property taxes per capita: $19 (1997).

Education: High school graduation rate: 72.8% (2000); College graduation rate: 19.8% (2000).

Housing: Homeownership rate: 91.7% (2000); Median home value: $27,000 (2000); Median rent: $150 per month (2000); Median age of housing: 57 years (2000).

Transportation: Commute to work: 86.0% car, 0.0% public transportation, 9.3% walk, 4.7% work from home (2000); Travel time to work: 19.5% less than 15 minutes, 58.5% 15 to 30 minutes, 14.6% 30 to 45 minutes, 0.0% 45 to 60 minutes, 7.3% 60 minutes or more (2000)

HIGBEE (city). Covers a land area of 0.429 square miles and a water area of 0 square miles. Located at 39.30° N. Lat.; 92.51° W. Long. Elevation is 870 feet.

History: Former coal-mining area.

Population: 623 (2000); Race: 95.2% White, 1.6% Black, 0.0% Asian, 1.0% American Indian and Alaska Native, 1.7% Hispanic of any race, 1.9% two or more races (2000); Density: 1,453.6 persons per square mile (2000); Age: 25.8% under 18, 18.9% over 64 (2000); Marriage status: 21.8% never married, 54.8% now married, 9.5% widowed, 13.9% divorced (2000); Foreign born: 0.3% (2000); Ancestry (includes multiple ancestries): 19.7% United States or American, 15.9% Irish, 12.4% English, 11.9% Other groups, 9.5% German (2000).

Economy: Corn, wheat, soybeans; cattle. Manufacturing: wine barrels. Employment by occupation: 4.7% management, 9.3% professional, 19.5% services, 14.4% sales, 0.8% farming, 12.7% construction, 38.6% production (2000).

Income: Per capita income: $16,709 (2000); Median household income: $26,813 (2000); Poverty rate: 13.3% (2000).

Taxes: Total city taxes per capita: $119 (1997); City property taxes per capita: $0 (1997).

Education: High school graduation rate: 65.5% (2000); College graduation rate: 5.4% (2000).

School District(s)

Higbee R-VIII (KG-12)
2000 Enrollment: 216 660-456-7277

Housing: Homeownership rate: 75.4% (2000); Median home value: $22,500 (2000); Median rent: $187 per month (2000); Median age of housing: 57 years (2000).

Transportation: Commute to work: 94.9% car, 0.0% public transportation, 3.0% walk, 0.0% work from home (2000); Travel time to work: 18.2% less than 15 minutes, 44.5% 15 to 30 minutes, 24.2% 30 to 45 minutes, 4.7% 45 to 60 minutes, 8.5% 60 minutes or more (2000)

HUNTSVILLE (city). Covers a land area of 2.367 square miles and a water area of 0 square miles. Located at 39.43° N. Lat.; 92.54° W. Long. Elevation is 800 feet.

History: Huntsville was platted in 1831 and named for Daniel Hunt, one of the first settlers in the vicinity and one of the donors of the town site. Early industry in Huntsville was coal mining.

Population: 1,553 (2000); Race: 89.7% White, 6.3% Black, 0.0% Asian, 1.3% American Indian and Alaska Native, 0.3% Hispanic of any race, 2.7% two or more races (2000); Density: 656.1 persons per square mile (2000); Age: 28.1% under 18, 13.1% over 64 (2000); Marriage status: 23.0% never married, 54.8% now married, 9.3% widowed, 12.9% divorced (2000); Foreign born: 0.4% (2000); Ancestry (includes multiple ancestries): 21.3% United States or American, 20.6% German, 14.9% Other groups, 14.2% English, 10.1% Irish (2000).

Economy: Single-family building permits issued: 0 (2001) / 0 (2000); Multi-family building permits issued: 0 (2001) / 0 (2000); Employment by occupation: 8.3% management, 12.7% professional, 21.1% services, 23.3% sales, 0.4% farming, 10.2% construction, 24.0% production (2000).

Income: Per capita income: $13,939 (2000); Median household income: $30,524 (2000); Poverty rate: 9.0% (2000).
Taxes: Total city taxes per capita: $105 (1997); City property taxes per capita: $37 (1997).
Education: High school graduation rate: 79.5% (2000); College graduation rate: 9.2% (2000).

School District(s)

Westran R-I (PK-12)
2000 Enrollment: 704 660-277-4429
Housing: Homeownership rate: 73.7% (2000); Median home value: $48,000 (2000); Median rent: $258 per month (2000); Median age of housing: 35 years (2000).
Transportation: Commute to work: 95.2% car, 0.0% public transportation, 1.3% walk, 2.3% work from home (2000); Travel time to work: 35.5% less than 15 minutes, 44.1% 15 to 30 minutes, 4.8% 30 to 45 minutes, 7.7% 45 to 60 minutes, 7.9% 60 minutes or more (2000)

JACKSONVILLE (village). Covers a land area of 0.113 square miles and a water area of 0 square miles. Located at 39.58° N. Lat.; 92.47° W. Long. Elevation is 867 feet.
History: Jacksonville was founded as a railroad stop in 1858, and named for Hancock Jackson, a governor of Missouri.
Population: 163 (2000); Race: 100.0% White, 0.0% Black, 0.0% Asian, 0.0% American Indian and Alaska Native, 1.9% Hispanic of any race, 0.0% two or more races (2000); Density: 1,439.7 persons per square mile (2000); Age: 42.0% under 18, 8.6% over 64 (2000); Marriage status: 22.1% never married, 58.7% now married, 11.5% widowed, 7.7% divorced (2000); Foreign born: 0.0% (2000); Ancestry (includes multiple ancestries): 26.5% German, 17.9% United States or American, 14.2% Other groups, 6.2% English, 6.2% French (except Basque) (2000).
Economy: Employment by occupation: 3.0% management, 16.4% professional, 22.4% services, 22.4% sales, 0.0% farming, 10.4% construction, 25.4% production (2000).
Income: Per capita income: $10,626 (2000); Median household income: $24,500 (2000); Poverty rate: 7.6% (2000).
Education: High school graduation rate: 83.1% (2000); College graduation rate: 4.5% (2000).
Housing: Homeownership rate: 85.7% (2000); Median home value: $35,000 (2000); Median rent: $288 per month (2000); Median age of housing: 42 years (2000).
Transportation: Commute to work: 92.5% car, 0.0% public transportation, 3.0% walk, 0.0% work from home (2000); Travel time to work: 13.4% less than 15 minutes, 73.1% 15 to 30 minutes, 4.5% 30 to 45 minutes, 6.0% 45 to 60 minutes, 3.0% 60 minutes or more (2000)

MOBERLY (city). Covers a land area of 11.554 square miles and a water area of 0.055 square miles. Located at 39.42° N. Lat.; 92.43° W. Long. Elevation is 875 feet.
History: Moberly was founded by the Chariton & Randolph County Railroad company in 1858, when they invited residents of nearby Allen to move to the new town. Only one, Patrick Lynch, accepted the offer and until 1866 he was the only resident of Moberly. The town was incorporated in 1873.
Population: 11,945 (2000); Race: 90.0% White, 6.3% Black, 1.4% Asian, 0.3% American Indian and Alaska Native, 1.5% Hispanic of any race, 1.6% two or more races (2000); Density: 1,033.8 persons per square mile (2000); Age: 24.6% under 18, 19.1% over 64 (2000); Marriage status: 21.7% never married, 54.3% now married, 11.6% widowed, 12.4% divorced (2000); Foreign born: 2.3% (2000); Ancestry (includes multiple ancestries): 18.2% German, 14.2% United States or American, 13.0% Other groups, 9.3% English, 9.2% Irish (2000).
Vital Statistics: Birth rate: 164.1 per 10,000 population (1998)
Economy: Single-family building permits issued: 9 (2001) / 21 (2000); Multi-family building permits issued: 0 (2001) / 0 (2000); Employment by occupation: 10.2% management, 17.2% professional, 19.0% services, 23.8% sales, 0.4% farming, 7.3% construction, 22.1% production (2000).
Income: Per capita income: $15,478 (2000); Median household income: $28,519 (2000); Poverty rate: 15.0% (2000).
Taxes: Total city taxes per capita: $592 (2000); City property taxes per capita: $74 (2000).
Education: High school graduation rate: 76.3% (2000); College graduation rate: 14.7% (2000).

School District(s)

Moberly (PK-12)
2000 Enrollment: 2,292 660-269-2600

Four-year College(s)

Central Christian College of the Bible (Private, Not-for-profit, Christian Churches and Churches of Christ)
2001 Enrollment: 191 660-263-3900
2001 Tuition: In-state $4,200; Out-of-state $4,200

Two-year College(s)

Moberly Area Community College (Public)
2001 Enrollment: 3,269 660-263-4110
2001 Tuition: In-state $2,070; Out-of-state $3,480
Housing: Homeownership rate: 62.6% (2000); Median home value: $47,500 (2000); Median rent: $287 per month (2000); Median age of housing: 44 years (2000).
Hospitals: Moberly Regional Medical Center (114 beds)
Safety: Violent crime rate: 41.6 per 10,000 population; Property crime rate: 599.1 per 10,000 population (2001).
Newspapers: Moberly Monitor-Index & Democrat (6 x week)
Transportation: Commute to work: 94.8% car, 0.7% public transportation, 1.6% walk, 1.9% work from home (2000); Travel time to work: 67.0% less than 15 minutes, 12.2% 15 to 30 minutes, 8.7% 30 to 45 minutes, 6.8% 45 to 60 minutes, 5.4% 60 minutes or more (2000)
Airports: Omar N Bradley
Additional Information Contacts
Moberly Chamber of Commerce 660-263-6070
Randolph County Board of Realtors 660-263-4400

RENICK (village). Covers a land area of 0.200 square miles and a water area of 0 square miles. Located at 39.34° N. Lat.; 92.41° W. Long. Elevation is 874 feet.
Population: 221 (2000); Race: 93.9% White, 0.8% Black, 0.0% Asian, 0.0% American Indian and Alaska Native, 0.0% Hispanic of any race, 5.3% two or more races (2000); Density: 1,105.4 persons per square mile (2000); Age: 32.4% under 18, 5.7% over 64 (2000); Marriage status: 18.3% never married, 56.1% now married, 12.2% widowed, 13.3% divorced (2000); Foreign born: 2.0% (2000); Ancestry (includes multiple ancestries): 33.6% German, 18.0% United States or American, 11.1% Other groups, 8.6% Irish, 7.8% Swedish (2000).
Economy: Moberly State Correctional Center (penitentiary). Employment by occupation: 11.7% management, 8.1% professional, 21.6% services, 24.3% sales, 0.0% farming, 13.5% construction, 20.7% production (2000).
Income: Per capita income: $12,549 (2000); Median household income: $30,313 (2000); Poverty rate: 10.8% (2000).
Taxes: Total city taxes per capita: $395 (1997); City property taxes per capita: $29 (1997).
Education: High school graduation rate: 66.7% (2000); College graduation rate: 5.3% (2000).

School District(s)

Renick R-V (PK-08)
2000 Enrollment: 167 660-263-4886
Housing: Homeownership rate: 90.5% (2000); Median home value: $41,400 (2000); Median rent: $250 per month (2000); Median age of housing: 22 years (2000).
Transportation: Commute to work: 99.1% car, 0.0% public transportation, 0.0% walk, 0.0% work from home (2000); Travel time to work: 27.1% less than 15 minutes, 47.7% 15 to 30 minutes, 18.7% 30 to 45 minutes, 6.5% 45 to 60 minutes, 0.0% 60 minutes or more (2000)

Ray County

Located in northwestern Missouri; bounded on the south by the Missouri River; drained by the Crooked River. Covers a land area of 569.50 square miles, a water area of 4.10 square miles, and is located in the Central Time Zone. The county government was organized in 1820. County seat is Richmond.

Ray County is part of the Kansas City, MO-KS MSA. The entire metro area includes: Johnson County, KS; Leavenworth County, KS; Miami County, KS; Wyandotte County, KS; Cass County, MO; Clay County, MO; Clinton County, MO; Jackson County, MO; Lafayette County, MO; Platte County, MO; Ray County, MO

Population: 23,354 (2000); Race: 96.7% White, 1.2% Black, 0.1% Asian, 0.3% American Indian and Alaska Native, 1.2% Hispanic of any race, 1.0% two or more races (2000); Density: 41.0 persons per square mile (2000); Age: 27.6% under 18, 12.7% over 64 (2000).

Religion: Five largest groups: 25.2% Southern Baptist Convention, 7.4% The United Methodist Church, 4.5% Christian Union, 4.3% Christian Church (Disciples of Christ), 2.5% Assemblies of God (2000).
Economy: Unemployment rate: 4.1% (11/2002); Total civilian labor force: 11,931 (11/2002); Leading industries: 16.1% manufacturing; 16.0% retail trade; 14.8% health care and social assistance (2000); Companies that employ more than 1,000 persons: 0 (2000); Companies that employ more than 100 persons: 6 (2000); Farms: 1,075 totaling 274,349 acres (1997); Minority business ownership rate: 0.0% (1997); Women business ownership rate: 26.5% (1997); Retail sales per capita: $4,714 (1997). Single-family building permits issued: 101 (2001) / 95 (2000); Multi-family building permits issued: 6 (2001) / 4 (2000).
Income: Per capita income: $18,685 (2000); Median household income: $41,886 (2000); Poverty rate: 6.8% (2000); Bankruptcy rate: 4.14% (2001).
Taxes: Total county taxes per capita: $117 (2000); County property taxes per capita: $38 (2000).
Education: High school graduation rate: 79.3% (2000); College graduation rate: 10.8% (2000).
Housing: Homeownership rate: 79.5% (2000); Median home value: $81,000 (2000); Median rent: $336 per month (2000); Median age of housing: 29 years (2000).
Health: Birth rate: 131.9 per 10,000 population (1998); Age adjusted death rate: 100.0 per 10,000 population (1999); Age adjusted cancer mortality rate: 293.2 deaths per 100,000 population (1999). Number of physicians: 2.1 per 10,000 population (1999); Number of hospital beds: 21.4 per 10,000 population (1999).
Elections: 2000 Presidential election results: 51.0% Gore, 46.3% Bush, 1.5% Nader, 0.5% Buchanan

Additional Information Contacts

Ray County Government Offices........................ 816-776-3184
Richmond Chamber of Commerce........................ 816-776-6916

Ray County Communities

CAMDEN (city). Covers a land area of 0.755 square miles and a water area of 0 square miles. Located at 39.19° N. Lat.; 94.02° W. Long. Elevation is 713 feet.
History: Plotted 1838.
Population: 209 (2000); Race: 99.5% White, 0.0% Black, 0.0% Asian, 0.0% American Indian and Alaska Native, 0.0% Hispanic of any race, 0.5% two or more races (2000); Density: 277.0 persons per square mile (2000); Age: 25.5% under 18, 14.7% over 64 (2000); Marriage status: 18.0% never married, 61.5% now married, 9.3% widowed, 11.2% divorced (2000); Foreign born: 0.0% (2000); Ancestry (includes multiple ancestries): 52.9% United States or American, 15.2% German, 7.4% Irish, 4.9% Swedish, 4.9% English (2000).
Economy: Soybeans, wheat; hogs, cattle. Employment by occupation: 12.4% management, 5.6% professional, 18.0% services, 18.0% sales, 2.2% farming, 20.2% construction, 23.6% production (2000).
Income: Per capita income: $13,194 (2000); Median household income: $25,833 (2000); Poverty rate: 9.8% (2000).
Taxes: Total city taxes per capita: $36 (1997); City property taxes per capita: $36 (1997).
Education: High school graduation rate: 79.4% (2000); College graduation rate: 2.3% (2000).
Housing: Homeownership rate: 89.5% (2000); Median home value: $41,300 (2000); Median rent: $275 per month (2000); Median age of housing: 42 years (2000).
Transportation: Commute to work: 97.8% car, 0.0% public transportation, 0.0% walk, 2.2% work from home (2000); Travel time to work: 19.5% less than 15 minutes, 12.6% 15 to 30 minutes, 17.2% 30 to 45 minutes, 43.7% 45 to 60 minutes, 6.9% 60 minutes or more (2000)

CRYSTAL LAKES (city). Covers a land area of 1.005 square miles and a water area of 0.218 square miles. Located at 39.35° N. Lat.; 94.18° W. Long. Elevation is 945 feet.
Population: 383 (2000); Race: 100.0% White, 0.0% Black, 0.0% Asian, 0.0% American Indian and Alaska Native, 0.2% Hispanic of any race, 0.0% two or more races (2000); Density: 381.0 persons per square mile (2000); Age: 30.1% under 18, 4.0% over 64 (2000); Marriage status: 17.0% never married, 65.2% now married, 4.6% widowed, 13.1% divorced (2000); Foreign born: 0.9% (2000); Ancestry (includes multiple ancestries): 21.1% Irish, 18.2% German, 15.4% United States or American, 11.8% Other groups, 10.9% English (2000).
Economy: Single-family building permits issued: 3 (2001) / 5 (2000); Multi-family building permits issued: 0 (2001) / 0 (2000); Employment by occupation: 7.6% management, 6.8% professional, 10.4% services, 22.4% sales, 1.2% farming, 16.8% construction, 34.8% production (2000).
Income: Per capita income: $20,288 (2000); Median household income: $52,125 (2000); Poverty rate: 2.9% (2000).
Taxes: Total city taxes per capita: $100 (1997); City property taxes per capita: $66 (1997).
Education: High school graduation rate: 85.2% (2000); College graduation rate: 9.9% (2000).
Housing: Homeownership rate: 89.4% (2000); Median home value: $95,000 (2000); Median rent: $538 per month (2000); Median age of housing: 16 years (2000).
Transportation: Commute to work: 95.1% car, 0.0% public transportation, 0.0% walk, 4.9% work from home (2000); Travel time to work: 20.3% less than 15 minutes, 26.7% 15 to 30 minutes, 30.6% 30 to 45 minutes, 15.5% 45 to 60 minutes, 6.9% 60 minutes or more (2000)

ELMIRA (village). Covers a land area of 0.247 square miles and a water area of 0 square miles. Located at 39.50° N. Lat.; 94.15° W. Long. Elevation is 958 feet.
Population: 82 (2000); Race: 100.0% White, 0.0% Black, 0.0% Asian, 0.0% American Indian and Alaska Native, 0.0% Hispanic of any race, 0.0% two or more races (2000); Density: 331.3 persons per square mile (2000); Age: 37.5% under 18, 6.3% over 64 (2000); Marriage status: 21.5% never married, 66.2% now married, 10.8% widowed, 1.5% divorced (2000); Foreign born: 0.0% (2000); Ancestry (includes multiple ancestries): 18.8% English, 14.6% German, 10.4% Other groups, 7.3% Irish, 6.3% European (2000).
Economy: Employment by occupation: 0.0% management, 0.0% professional, 25.7% services, 22.9% sales, 0.0% farming, 20.0% construction, 31.4% production (2000).
Income: Per capita income: $14,785 (2000); Median household income: $49,375 (2000); Poverty rate: 20.2% (2000).
Taxes: Total city taxes per capita: $26 (1997); City property taxes per capita: $0 (1997).
Education: High school graduation rate: 76.9% (2000); College graduation rate: 0.0% (2000).
Housing: Homeownership rate: 90.3% (2000); Median home value: $23,800 (2000); Median rent: $238 per month (2000); Median age of housing: 45 years (2000).
Transportation: Commute to work: 97.1% car, 0.0% public transportation, 0.0% walk, 0.0% work from home (2000); Travel time to work: 8.6% less than 15 minutes, 28.6% 15 to 30 minutes, 17.1% 30 to 45 minutes, 25.7% 45 to 60 minutes, 20.0% 60 minutes or more (2000)

EXCELSIOR ESTATES (village). Covers a land area of 0.224 square miles and a water area of 0 square miles. Located at 39.39° N. Lat.; 94.21° W. Long.
Population: 263 (2000); Race: 98.1% White, 0.8% Black, 0.0% Asian, 1.1% American Indian and Alaska Native, 0.0% Hispanic of any race, 0.0% two or more races (2000); Density: 1,173.1 persons per square mile (2000); Age: 34.6% under 18, 7.2% over 64 (2000); Marriage status: 18.8% never married, 60.4% now married, 2.6% widowed, 18.2% divorced (2000); Foreign born: 0.0% (2000); Ancestry (includes multiple ancestries): 14.1% German, 12.2% United States or American, 11.4% Irish, 9.1% English, 5.3% Scotch-Irish (2000).
Economy: Employment by occupation: 2.9% management, 5.9% professional, 17.6% services, 17.6% sales, 0.0% farming, 12.7% construction, 43.1% production (2000).
Income: Per capita income: $13,286 (2000); Median household income: $26,667 (2000); Poverty rate: 16.9% (2000).
Taxes: Total city taxes per capita: $80 (1997); City property taxes per capita: $15 (1997).
Education: High school graduation rate: 71.2% (2000); College graduation rate: 3.1% (2000).
Housing: Homeownership rate: 78.9% (2000); Median home value: $55,000 (2000); Median rent: $368 per month (2000); Median age of housing: 25 years (2000).
Transportation: Commute to work: 94.8% car, 0.0% public transportation, 0.0% walk, 3.1% work from home (2000); Travel time to work: 8.5% less than 15 minutes, 45.7% 15 to 30 minutes, 19.1% 30 to 45 minutes, 10.6% 45 to 60 minutes, 16.0% 60 minutes or more (2000)

FLEMING (city). Covers a land area of 0.541 square miles and a water area of 0 square miles. Located at 39.19° N. Lat.; 94.05° W. Long. Elevation is 760 feet.

Population: 122 (2000); Race: 98.4% White, 0.0% Black, 0.0% Asian, 0.0% American Indian and Alaska Native, 0.0% Hispanic of any race, 1.6% two or more races (2000); Density: 225.6 persons per square mile (2000); Age: 31.2% under 18, 8.0% over 64 (2000); Marriage status: 20.2% never married, 58.5% now married, 9.6% widowed, 11.7% divorced (2000); Foreign born: 1.6% (2000); Ancestry (includes multiple ancestries): 36.8% United States or American, 7.2% German, 4.8% Irish, 4.0% French (except Basque), 3.2% English (2000).
Economy: Employment by occupation: 12.5% management, 0.0% professional, 0.0% services, 31.3% sales, 0.0% farming, 14.6% construction, 41.7% production (2000).
Income: Per capita income: $15,697 (2000); Median household income: $35,625 (2000); Poverty rate: 11.2% (2000).
Taxes: Total city taxes per capita: $28 (1997); City property taxes per capita: $0 (1997).
Education: High school graduation rate: 62.7% (2000); College graduation rate: 0.0% (2000).
Housing: Homeownership rate: 93.5% (2000); Median home value: $45,000 (2000); Median age of housing: 30 years (2000).
Transportation: Commute to work: 95.8% car, 0.0% public transportation, 0.0% walk, 4.2% work from home (2000); Travel time to work: 17.4% less than 15 minutes, 21.7% 15 to 30 minutes, 28.3% 30 to 45 minutes, 32.6% 45 to 60 minutes, 0.0% 60 minutes or more (2000)

HARDIN (city). Covers a land area of 0.619 square miles and a water area of 0 square miles. Located at 39.27° N. Lat.; 93.83° W. Long. Elevation is 695 feet.
History: Town and surrounding farmland damaged in 1993 flood.
Population: 614 (2000); Race: 97.7% White, 0.0% Black, 0.0% Asian, 1.0% American Indian and Alaska Native, 0.0% Hispanic of any race, 1.3% two or more races (2000); Density: 992.0 persons per square mile (2000); Age: 28.6% under 18, 17.2% over 64 (2000); Marriage status: 15.9% never married, 64.8% now married, 10.2% widowed, 9.1% divorced (2000); Foreign born: 0.2% (2000); Ancestry (includes multiple ancestries): 35.4% United States or American, 9.5% German, 9.1% English, 7.9% Irish, 5.3% Other groups (2000).
Economy: Corn, wheat, soybeans; hogs, cattle; grain elevators. Single-family building permits issued: 1 (2001) / 0 (2000); Multi-family building permits issued: 0 (2001) / 0 (2000); Employment by occupation: 6.4% management, 10.0% professional, 17.9% services, 24.7% sales, 3.6% farming, 16.3% construction, 21.1% production (2000).
Income: Per capita income: $14,676 (2000); Median household income: $35,000 (2000); Poverty rate: 6.1% (2000).
Taxes: Total city taxes per capita: $70 (1997); City property taxes per capita: $23 (1997).
Education: High school graduation rate: 76.4% (2000); College graduation rate: 7.8% (2000).

School District(s)

Hardin-Central C-2 (KG-12)
2000 Enrollment: 203 660-398-4394

Housing: Homeownership rate: 78.2% (2000); Median home value: $48,200 (2000); Median rent: $307 per month (2000); Median age of housing: 60+ years (2000).
Transportation: Commute to work: 93.7% car, 0.0% public transportation, 2.0% walk, 3.5% work from home (2000); Travel time to work: 24.5% less than 15 minutes, 26.9% 15 to 30 minutes, 10.6% 30 to 45 minutes, 18.0% 45 to 60 minutes, 20.0% 60 minutes or more (2000)

HENRIETTA (city). Covers a land area of 0.597 square miles and a water area of 0 square miles. Located at 39.23° N. Lat.; 93.93° W. Long. Elevation is 702 feet.
History: Damaged during 1993 flood.
Population: 457 (2000); Race: 85.9% White, 8.6% Black, 0.0% Asian, 0.0% American Indian and Alaska Native, 5.9% Hispanic of any race, 0.0% two or more races (2000); Density: 765.0 persons per square mile (2000); Age: 19.7% under 18, 9.5% over 64 (2000); Marriage status: 26.1% never married, 47.2% now married, 6.2% widowed, 20.5% divorced (2000); Foreign born: 5.9% (2000); Ancestry (includes multiple ancestries): 17.5% Other groups, 14.3% German, 14.1% Irish, 12.9% United States or American, 7.3% English (2000).
Economy: Soybeans, corn; livestock. Manufacturing: aluminum granules. Employment by occupation: 0.8% management, 12.7% professional, 7.1% services, 23.0% sales, 1.6% farming, 16.7% construction, 38.1% production (2000).
Income: Per capita income: $16,129 (2000); Median household income: $33,750 (2000); Poverty rate: 11.3% (2000).
Taxes: Total city taxes per capita: $186 (1997); City property taxes per capita: $67 (1997).
Education: High school graduation rate: 64.9% (2000); College graduation rate: 3.8% (2000).
Housing: Homeownership rate: 71.0% (2000); Median home value: $50,600 (2000); Median rent: $325 per month (2000); Median age of housing: 47 years (2000).
Transportation: Commute to work: 93.7% car, 3.2% public transportation, 3.2% walk, 0.0% work from home (2000); Travel time to work: 30.2% less than 15 minutes, 17.5% 15 to 30 minutes, 15.9% 30 to 45 minutes, 15.9% 45 to 60 minutes, 20.6% 60 minutes or more (2000)

HOMESTEAD (village). Covers a land area of 0.190 square miles and a water area of 0 square miles. Located at 39.36° N. Lat.; 94.19° W. Long. Elevation is 930 feet.
Population: 181 (2000); Race: 95.1% White, 1.8% Black, 0.0% Asian, 0.0% American Indian and Alaska Native, 0.0% Hispanic of any race, 3.1% two or more races (2000); Density: 954.5 persons per square mile (2000); Age: 29.3% under 18, 14.7% over 64 (2000); Marriage status: 20.7% never married, 59.8% now married, 2.9% widowed, 16.7% divorced (2000); Foreign born: 0.0% (2000); Ancestry (includes multiple ancestries): 14.2% Irish, 8.9% United States or American, 8.0% English, 8.0% German, 7.6% Other groups (2000).
Economy: Single-family building permits issued: 0 (2001) / 1 (2000); Multi-family building permits issued: 0 (2001) / 0 (2000); Employment by occupation: 2.0% management, 12.1% professional, 11.1% services, 24.2% sales, 0.0% farming, 17.2% construction, 33.3% production (2000).
Income: Per capita income: $14,324 (2000); Median household income: $36,250 (2000); Poverty rate: 8.9% (2000).
Taxes: Total city taxes per capita: $37 (1997); City property taxes per capita: $5 (1997).
Education: High school graduation rate: 81.3% (2000); College graduation rate: 5.0% (2000).
Housing: Homeownership rate: 81.3% (2000); Median home value: $87,500 (2000); Median rent: $325 per month (2000); Median age of housing: 18 years (2000).
Transportation: Commute to work: 100.0% car, 0.0% public transportation, 0.0% walk, 0.0% work from home (2000); Travel time to work: 15.8% less than 15 minutes, 32.6% 15 to 30 minutes, 24.2% 30 to 45 minutes, 18.9% 45 to 60 minutes, 8.4% 60 minutes or more (2000)

LAWSON (city). Covers a land area of 2.787 square miles and a water area of 0.060 square miles. Located at 39.43° N. Lat.; 94.20° W. Long. Elevation is 1,060 feet.
Population: 2,336 (2000); Race: 97.7% White, 0.6% Black, 0.5% Asian, 0.2% American Indian and Alaska Native, 0.9% Hispanic of any race, 0.9% two or more races (2000); Density: 838.3 persons per square mile (2000); Age: 32.8% under 18, 12.4% over 64 (2000); Marriage status: 20.5% never married, 62.2% now married, 8.0% widowed, 9.3% divorced (2000); Foreign born: 0.3% (2000); Ancestry (includes multiple ancestries): 21.7% German, 19.1% United States or American, 13.4% Irish, 12.6% English, 8.6% Other groups (2000).
Economy: Single-family building permits issued: 13 (2001) / 4 (2000); Multi-family building permits issued: 0 (2001) / 0 (2000); Employment by occupation: 9.0% management, 14.2% professional, 16.5% services, 27.5% sales, 0.0% farming, 12.4% construction, 20.4% production (2000).
Income: Per capita income: $17,438 (2000); Median household income: $41,875 (2000); Poverty rate: 7.0% (2000).
Taxes: Total city taxes per capita: $289 (1997); City property taxes per capita: $116 (1997).
Education: High school graduation rate: 86.7% (2000); College graduation rate: 13.6% (2000).

School District(s)

Lawson R-Xiv (PK-12)
2000 Enrollment: 1,286 816-580-7277

Housing: Homeownership rate: 75.4% (2000); Median home value: $83,500 (2000); Median rent: $349 per month (2000); Median age of housing: 27 years (2000).
Newspapers: The Lawson Review (1 x week)
Transportation: Commute to work: 96.2% car, 0.2% public transportation, 0.8% walk, 2.1% work from home (2000); Travel time to work: 26.8% less than 15 minutes, 21.2% 15 to 30 minutes, 27.6% 30 to 45 minutes, 18.6% 45 to 60 minutes, 5.8% 60 minutes or more (2000)

ORRICK (city). Covers a land area of 1.368 square miles and a water area of 0 square miles. Located at 39.21° N. Lat.; 94.12° W. Long. Elevation is 716 feet.
History: Plotted 1873.
Population: 889 (2000); Race: 96.6% White, 0.3% Black, 0.0% Asian, 0.0% American Indian and Alaska Native, 1.0% Hispanic of any race, 3.1% two or more races (2000); Density: 649.9 persons per square mile (2000); Age: 30.2% under 18, 11.8% over 64 (2000); Marriage status: 25.8% never married, 58.0% now married, 6.1% widowed, 10.0% divorced (2000); Foreign born: 0.0% (2000); Ancestry (includes multiple ancestries): 32.9% United States or American, 15.6% German, 11.5% Irish, 8.8% Other groups, 6.2% English (2000).
Economy: Agriculture: corn, wheat, soybeans; hogs. Manufacturing: plastic molding. Single-family building permits issued: 0 (2001) / 0 (2000); Multi-family building permits issued: 0 (2001) / 0 (2000); Employment by occupation: 6.3% management, 11.0% professional, 14.5% services, 23.4% sales, 0.0% farming, 15.6% construction, 29.2% production (2000).
Income: Per capita income: $15,215 (2000); Median household income: $37,500 (2000); Poverty rate: 10.0% (2000).
Taxes: Total city taxes per capita: $106 (1997); City property taxes per capita: $34 (1997).
Education: High school graduation rate: 75.6% (2000); College graduation rate: 7.3% (2000).

School District(s)

Orrick R-XI (KG-12)
2000 Enrollment: 449 816-496-2336
Housing: Homeownership rate: 70.2% (2000); Median home value: $59,500 (2000); Median rent: $293 per month (2000); Median age of housing: 38 years (2000).
Transportation: Commute to work: 94.1% car, 0.4% public transportation, 2.4% walk, 1.3% work from home (2000); Travel time to work: 21.3% less than 15 minutes, 17.6% 15 to 30 minutes, 32.4% 30 to 45 minutes, 18.4% 45 to 60 minutes, 10.2% 60 minutes or more (2000)

RAYVILLE (village). Covers a land area of 0.244 square miles and a water area of 0 square miles. Located at 39.34° N. Lat.; 94.06° W. Long. Elevation is 975 feet.
Population: 204 (2000); Race: 95.1% White, 0.0% Black, 0.0% Asian, 0.0% American Indian and Alaska Native, 0.0% Hispanic of any race, 4.9% two or more races (2000); Density: 836.7 persons per square mile (2000); Age: 22.4% under 18, 15.1% over 64 (2000); Marriage status: 17.1% never married, 48.8% now married, 13.4% widowed, 20.7% divorced (2000); Foreign born: 0.0% (2000); Ancestry (includes multiple ancestries): 38.0% German, 22.9% Irish, 22.0% Other groups, 5.9% English, 4.9% United States or American (2000).
Economy: Employment by occupation: 0.0% management, 8.1% professional, 12.2% services, 23.0% sales, 0.0% farming, 12.2% construction, 44.6% production (2000).
Income: Per capita income: $12,769 (2000); Median household income: $32,750 (2000); Poverty rate: 15.6% (2000).
Taxes: Total city taxes per capita: $79 (1997); City property taxes per capita: $51 (1997).
Education: High school graduation rate: 47.9% (2000); College graduation rate: 0.0% (2000).
Housing: Homeownership rate: 88.0% (2000); Median home value: $35,500 (2000); Median rent: $275 per month (2000); Median age of housing: 51 years (2000).
Transportation: Commute to work: 100.0% car, 0.0% public transportation, 0.0% walk, 0.0% work from home (2000); Travel time to work: 6.8% less than 15 minutes, 24.7% 15 to 30 minutes, 26.0% 30 to 45 minutes, 20.5% 45 to 60 minutes, 21.9% 60 minutes or more (2000)

RICHMOND (city). Covers a land area of 5.755 square miles and a water area of 0.020 square miles. Located at 39.27° N. Lat.; 93.97° W. Long. Elevation is 826 feet.
History: Richmond was platted in 1827 and named for Richmond, Virginia. The town grew in an area that combined agriculture and coal mining for its revenue.
Population: 6,116 (2000); Race: 94.8% White, 3.4% Black, 0.0% Asian, 0.0% American Indian and Alaska Native, 1.7% Hispanic of any race, 1.3% two or more races (2000); Density: 1,062.7 persons per square mile (2000); Age: 26.8% under 18, 17.0% over 64 (2000); Marriage status: 20.1% never married, 56.4% now married, 10.6% widowed, 12.9% divorced (2000); Foreign born: 0.3% (2000); Ancestry (includes multiple ancestries): 21.3% German, 19.1% United States or American, 9.9% English, 8.3% Irish, 7.6% Other groups (2000).
Economy: Single-family building permits issued: 9 (2001) / 9 (2000); Multi-family building permits issued: 0 (2001) / 0 (2000); Employment by occupation: 9.7% management, 13.4% professional, 17.7% services, 22.6% sales, 0.0% farming, 11.3% construction, 25.2% production (2000).
Income: Per capita income: $18,021 (2000); Median household income: $33,514 (2000); Poverty rate: 10.7% (2000).
Taxes: Total city taxes per capita: $209 (1997); City property taxes per capita: $26 (1997).
Education: High school graduation rate: 73.7% (2000); College graduation rate: 11.6% (2000).

School District(s)

Richmond R-XVI (PK-12)
2000 Enrollment: 1,833 816-776-6912
Housing: Homeownership rate: 64.0% (2000); Median home value: $74,800 (2000); Median rent: $336 per month (2000); Median age of housing: 36 years (2000).
Hospitals: Ray County Memorial Hospital (63 beds)
Safety: Violent crime rate: 29.2 per 10,000 population; Property crime rate: 529.7 per 10,000 population (2001).
Newspapers: The Daily News (5 x week)
Transportation: Commute to work: 93.5% car, 1.1% public transportation, 2.6% walk, 1.9% work from home (2000); Travel time to work: 42.8% less than 15 minutes, 12.6% 15 to 30 minutes, 12.5% 30 to 45 minutes, 14.0% 45 to 60 minutes, 18.0% 60 minutes or more (2000)
Additional Information Contacts
Richmond Chamber of Commerce.............................. 816-776-6916

WOODS HEIGHTS (city). Aka Wood Heights. Covers a land area of 2.250 square miles and a water area of 0.006 square miles. Located at 39.33° N. Lat.; 94.16° W. Long.
Population: 742 (2000); Race: 97.2% White, 0.6% Black, 0.4% Asian, 0.0% American Indian and Alaska Native, 2.6% Hispanic of any race, 1.0% two or more races (2000); Density: 329.8 persons per square mile (2000); Age: 29.1% under 18, 10.3% over 64 (2000); Marriage status: 19.8% never married, 68.5% now married, 4.2% widowed, 7.5% divorced (2000); Foreign born: 0.1% (2000); Ancestry (includes multiple ancestries): 18.8% Other groups, 16.7% German, 15.9% United States or American, 11.6% Irish, 9.2% English (2000).
Economy: Residential, agricultural area. Single-family building permits issued: 3 (2001) / 6 (2000); Multi-family building permits issued: 0 (2001) / 0 (2000); Employment by occupation: 10.4% management, 8.1% professional, 13.2% services, 28.7% sales, 0.3% farming, 12.4% construction, 27.0% production (2000).
Income: Per capita income: $18,120 (2000); Median household income: $51,250 (2000); Poverty rate: 2.2% (2000).
Taxes: Total city taxes per capita: $105 (1997); City property taxes per capita: $18 (1997).
Education: High school graduation rate: 85.5% (2000); College graduation rate: 10.3% (2000).
Housing: Homeownership rate: 93.1% (2000); Median home value: $88,200 (2000); Median rent: $513 per month (2000); Median age of housing: 26 years (2000).
Transportation: Commute to work: 93.8% car, 0.0% public transportation, 2.3% walk, 4.0% work from home (2000); Travel time to work: 19.5% less than 15 minutes, 28.6% 15 to 30 minutes, 26.8% 30 to 45 minutes, 16.8% 45 to 60 minutes, 8.3% 60 minutes or more (2000)

Reynolds County

Located in southeastern Missouri, in the Ozarks; drained by the Black River; includes part of Clark National Forest. Covers a land area of 811.20 square miles, a water area of 3.20 square miles, and is located in the Central Time Zone. The county government was organized in 1845. County seat is Centerville.
Population: 6,689 (2000); Race: 94.9% White, 0.6% Black, 0.2% Asian, 2.3% American Indian and Alaska Native, 1.0% Hispanic of any race, 1.8% two or more races (2000); Density: 8.2 persons per square mile (2000); Age: 23.9% under 18, 16.3% over 64 (2000).
Religion: Five largest groups: 33.8% Southern Baptist Convention, 3.5% Baptist Missionary Association of America, 1.8% The United Methodist Church, 1.6% Assemblies of God, 1.2% Catholic Church (2000).
Economy: Unemployment rate: 10.6% (11/2002); Total civilian labor force: 1,764 (11/2002); Leading industries: 29.5% manufacturing; 15.1% health

care and social assistance; 7.7% retail trade (2000); Companies that employ more than 1,000 persons: 0 (2000); Companies that employ more than 100 persons: 5 (2000); Farms: 302 totaling 113,214 acres (1997); Minority business ownership rate: 0.0% (1997); Women business ownership rate: 0.0% (1997); Retail sales per capita: $2,864 (1997). Single-family building permits issued: -1 (2001) / -1 (2000); Multi-family building permits issued: -1 (2001) / -1 (2000).
Income: Per capita income: $13,065 (2000); Median household income: $25,867 (2000); Poverty rate: 20.1% (2000); Bankruptcy rate: 2.99% (2001).
Taxes: Total county taxes per capita: $65 (1997); County property taxes per capita: $65 (1997).
Education: High school graduation rate: 65.2% (2000); College graduation rate: 7.5% (2000).
Housing: Homeownership rate: 77.1% (2000); Median home value: $47,200 (2000); Median rent: $228 per month (2000); Median age of housing: 28 years (2000).
Health: Birth rate: 121.1 per 10,000 population (1998); Age adjusted death rate: 90.2 per 10,000 population (1999); Age adjusted cancer mortality rate: 279.4 deaths per 100,000 population (1999). Number of physicians: 3.0 per 10,000 population (1999); Number of hospital beds: 37.4 per 10,000 population (1999).
Elections: 2000 Presidential election results: 41.5% Gore, 56.3% Bush, 1.3% Nader, 0.5% Buchanan
National and State Parks: Bozarth State Forest; Clearwater Lake State Wildlife Management Area; Deer Run State Forest; Dickens Valley State Forest; Graves Mountain State Forest; Logan Creek State Forest; Paint Rock State Forest; Riverside State Forest; Webb Creek State Forest
Additional Information Contacts
Reynolds County Government Offices 573-648-2494
Ellington Chamber of Commerce. 573-663-7997

Reynolds County Communities

BLACK (unincorporated postal area, zip code 63625). Covers a land area of 77.983 square miles and a water area of 0.036 square miles. Located at 37.53° N. Lat.; 90.96° W. Long. Elevation is 803 feet.
Population: 538 (2000); Race: 90.2% White, 8.1% Black, 0.6% Asian, 0.4% American Indian and Alaska Native, 0.6% Hispanic of any race, 0.8% two or more races (2000); Density: 6.9 persons per square mile (2000); Age: 25.6% under 18, 13.8% over 64 (2000); Marriage status: 23.8% never married, 65.4% now married, 5.9% widowed, 4.9% divorced (2000); Foreign born: 2.2% (2000); Ancestry (includes multiple ancestries): 16.3% Other groups, 12.4% United States or American, 11.0% English, 9.3% German, 7.3% Irish (2000).
Economy: Employment by occupation: 12.6% management, 11.4% professional, 24.0% services, 9.7% sales, 1.7% farming, 20.0% construction, 20.6% production (2000).
Income: Per capita income: $13,559 (2000); Median household income: $32,500 (2000); Poverty rate: 20.8% (2000).
Education: High school graduation rate: 69.8% (2000); College graduation rate: 11.1% (2000).
Housing: Homeownership rate: 87.4% (2000); Median home value: $61,300 (2000); Median rent: $244 per month (2000); Median age of housing: 28 years (2000).
Transportation: Commute to work: 87.9% car, 0.0% public transportation, 8.7% walk, 2.3% work from home (2000); Travel time to work: 32.0% less than 15 minutes, 39.1% 15 to 30 minutes, 8.3% 30 to 45 minutes, 7.7% 45 to 60 minutes, 13.0% 60 minutes or more (2000)

BUNKER (city). Covers a land area of 0.645 square miles and a water area of 0 square miles. Located at 37.45° N. Lat.; 91.21° W. Long. Elevation is 1,355 feet.
Population: 427 (2000); Race: 94.0% White, 0.0% Black, 0.0% Asian, 1.2% American Indian and Alaska Native, 0.0% Hispanic of any race, 4.8% two or more races (2000); Density: 661.8 persons per square mile (2000); Age: 26.8% under 18, 10.6% over 64 (2000); Marriage status: 21.0% never married, 50.5% now married, 9.5% widowed, 19.0% divorced (2000); Foreign born: 0.0% (2000); Ancestry (includes multiple ancestries): 22.7% United States or American, 19.1% Other groups, 17.1% Irish, 11.1% German, 3.4% English (2000).
Economy: Employment by occupation: 6.6% management, 3.8% professional, 15.3% services, 7.7% sales, 8.2% farming, 14.2% construction, 44.3% production (2000).
Income: Per capita income: $9,671 (2000); Median household income: $19,659 (2000); Poverty rate: 32.3% (2000).
Taxes: Total city taxes per capita: $51 (1997); City property taxes per capita: $13 (1997).
Education: High school graduation rate: 63.4% (2000); College graduation rate: 3.3% (2000).

School District(s)

Bunker R-III (KG-12)
2000 Enrollment: 305 573-689-2507
Housing: Homeownership rate: 66.5% (2000); Median home value: $39,400 (2000); Median rent: $192 per month (2000); Median age of housing: 32 years (2000).
Transportation: Commute to work: 80.1% car, 0.0% public transportation, 11.4% walk, 5.1% work from home (2000); Travel time to work: 65.3% less than 15 minutes, 14.4% 15 to 30 minutes, 7.8% 30 to 45 minutes, 7.8% 45 to 60 minutes, 4.8% 60 minutes or more (2000)

CENTERVILLE (city). Covers a land area of 0.320 square miles and a water area of 0 square miles. Located at 37.43° N. Lat.; 90.96° W. Long. Elevation is 742 feet.
Population: 171 (2000); Race: 93.2% White, 0.0% Black, 0.0% Asian, 6.8% American Indian and Alaska Native, 0.0% Hispanic of any race, 0.0% two or more races (2000); Density: 534.3 persons per square mile (2000); Age: 14.2% under 18, 17.6% over 64 (2000); Marriage status: 12.3% never married, 71.4% now married, 7.1% widowed, 9.1% divorced (2000); Foreign born: 0.0% (2000); Ancestry (includes multiple ancestries): 15.9% Irish, 11.9% German, 10.8% United States or American, 8.0% Other groups, 5.7% English (2000).
Economy: Timber; tourist and recreation area. Employment by occupation: 15.1% management, 26.4% professional, 11.3% services, 0.0% sales, 0.0% farming, 18.9% construction, 28.3% production (2000).
Income: Per capita income: $13,207 (2000); Median household income: $23,864 (2000); Poverty rate: 21.1% (2000).
Taxes: Total city taxes per capita: $116 (1997); City property taxes per capita: $20 (1997).
Education: High school graduation rate: 70.9% (2000); College graduation rate: 2.4% (2000).

School District(s)

Centerville R-I (KG-08)
2000 Enrollment: 75 573-648-2285
Housing: Homeownership rate: 68.9% (2000); Median home value: $35,400 (2000); Median rent: $207 per month (2000); Median age of housing: 43 years (2000).
Transportation: Commute to work: 77.4% car, 0.0% public transportation, 11.3% walk, 11.3% work from home (2000); Travel time to work: 23.4% less than 15 minutes, 40.4% 15 to 30 minutes, 23.4% 30 to 45 minutes, 0.0% 45 to 60 minutes, 12.8% 60 minutes or more (2000)

ELLINGTON (city). Covers a land area of 1.411 square miles and a water area of 0 square miles. Located at 37.23° N. Lat.; 90.97° W. Long. Elevation is 662 feet.
History: Ellington developed as a shipping point for fruit, dairy, and poultry products.
Population: 1,045 (2000); Race: 95.6% White, 0.0% Black, 1.2% Asian, 0.4% American Indian and Alaska Native, 2.9% Hispanic of any race, 1.9% two or more races (2000); Density: 740.8 persons per square mile (2000); Age: 27.4% under 18, 19.2% over 64 (2000); Marriage status: 17.2% never married, 56.2% now married, 13.8% widowed, 12.9% divorced (2000); Foreign born: 1.3% (2000); Ancestry (includes multiple ancestries): 20.9% United States or American, 13.4% Other groups, 7.5% German, 7.5% Irish, 6.9% English (2000).
Economy: Employment by occupation: 9.5% management, 17.5% professional, 13.4% services, 20.8% sales, 1.8% farming, 9.8% construction, 27.3% production (2000).
Income: Per capita income: $12,026 (2000); Median household income: $21,836 (2000); Poverty rate: 21.2% (2000).
Taxes: Total city taxes per capita: $207 (1997); City property taxes per capita: $0 (1997).
Education: High school graduation rate: 60.5% (2000); College graduation rate: 8.2% (2000).

School District(s)

Southern Reynolds Co. R-II (PK-12)
2000 Enrollment: 588 573-663-3591
Housing: Homeownership rate: 47.7% (2000); Median home value: $43,400 (2000); Median rent: $235 per month (2000); Median age of housing: 34 years (2000).
Hospitals: Reynolds County Memorial Hospital (25 beds)
Newspapers: Reynolds County Courier (1 x week)

Transportation: Commute to work: 94.3% car, 0.0% public transportation, 3.3% walk, 2.1% work from home (2000); Travel time to work: 57.4% less than 15 minutes, 16.7% 15 to 30 minutes, 15.8% 30 to 45 minutes, 4.6% 45 to 60 minutes, 5.5% 60 minutes or more (2000)
Additional Information Contacts
Ellington Chamber of Commerce........................ 573-663-7997

LESTERVILLE (unincorporated postal area, zip code 63654). Covers a land area of 68.816 square miles and a water area of 0.376 square miles. Located at 37.47° N. Lat.; 90.83° W. Long. Elevation is 712 feet.
History: Lesterville developed as a trading center in a wooded district, and as the gateway to the Black River.
Population: 542 (2000); Race: 96.6% White, 0.0% Black, 0.0% Asian, 1.3% American Indian and Alaska Native, 0.0% Hispanic of any race, 2.1% two or more races (2000); Density: 7.9 persons per square mile (2000); Age: 18.8% under 18, 20.3% over 64 (2000); Marriage status: 16.9% never married, 62.5% now married, 9.1% widowed, 11.5% divorced (2000); Foreign born: 0.0% (2000); Ancestry (includes multiple ancestries): 19.6% German, 17.1% Irish, 16.7% United States or American, 14.3% English, 11.6% Other groups (2000).
Economy: Employment by occupation: 7.8% management, 18.3% professional, 19.3% services, 12.4% sales, 4.6% farming, 15.1% construction, 22.5% production (2000).
Income: Per capita income: $16,336 (2000); Median household income: $28,472 (2000); Poverty rate: 13.3% (2000).
Education: High school graduation rate: 78.5% (2000); College graduation rate: 12.0% (2000).

School District(s)

Lesterville R-IV (PK-12)
2000 Enrollment: 295 573-637-2201
Housing: Homeownership rate: 77.4% (2000); Median home value: $61,800 (2000); Median rent: $281 per month (2000); Median age of housing: 34 years (2000).
Transportation: Commute to work: 92.1% car, 0.9% public transportation, 2.8% walk, 4.2% work from home (2000); Travel time to work: 37.2% less than 15 minutes, 30.4% 15 to 30 minutes, 13.0% 30 to 45 minutes, 10.1% 45 to 60 minutes, 9.2% 60 minutes or more (2000)

REDFORD (unincorporated postal area, zip code 63665). Covers a land area of 75.070 square miles and a water area of 0 square miles. Located at 37.31° N. Lat.; 90.84° W. Long. Elevation is 695 feet.
Population: 306 (2000); Race: 98.5% White, 0.0% Black, 0.0% Asian, 1.5% American Indian and Alaska Native, 0.0% Hispanic of any race, 0.0% two or more races (2000); Density: 4.1 persons per square mile (2000); Age: 21.3% under 18, 12.1% over 64 (2000); Marriage status: 15.4% never married, 70.9% now married, 6.6% widowed, 7.0% divorced (2000); Foreign born: 0.0% (2000); Ancestry (includes multiple ancestries): 29.8% United States or American, 11.8% Irish, 10.3% English, 8.5% Other groups, 7.0% German (2000).
Economy: Employment by occupation: 8.2% management, 13.3% professional, 16.3% services, 6.1% sales, 2.0% farming, 19.4% construction, 34.7% production (2000).
Income: Per capita income: $16,232 (2000); Median household income: $36,875 (2000); Poverty rate: 2.2% (2000).
Education: High school graduation rate: 71.3% (2000); College graduation rate: 5.6% (2000).
Housing: Homeownership rate: 89.1% (2000); Median home value: $62,500 (2000); Median rent: $275 per month (2000); Median age of housing: 27 years (2000).
Transportation: Commute to work: 95.9% car, 0.0% public transportation, 0.0% walk, 2.0% work from home (2000); Travel time to work: 20.8% less than 15 minutes, 59.4% 15 to 30 minutes, 10.4% 30 to 45 minutes, 8.3% 45 to 60 minutes, 1.0% 60 minutes or more (2000)

Ripley County

Located in southern Missouri, in the Ozarks; bounded on the south by Arkansas; drained by the Current and Little Black Rivers; includes part of Clark National Forest. Covers a land area of 629.50 square miles, a water area of 2.20 square miles, and is located in the Central Time Zone. The county government was organized in 1833. County seat is Doniphan.

Weather Station: Doniphan — Elevation: 328 feet

	Jan	Feb	Mar	Apr	May	Jun	Jul	Aug	Sep	Oct	Nov	Dec
High	44	51	60	71	79	87	92	90	83	73	59	48
Low	20	24	33	43	52	61	65	63	55	42	33	24
Precip	3.4	3.3	5.0	5.3	4.9	3.1	3.5	4.0	3.8	3.6	5.4	4.4
Snow	4.3	3.8	2.2	tr	0.0	0.0	0.0	0.0	0.0	tr	0.7	1.1

High and Low temperatures in degrees Fahrenheit; Precipitation and Snow in inches

Population: 13,509 (2000); Race: 97.6% White, 0.1% Black, 0.4% Asian, 1.0% American Indian and Alaska Native, 1.0% Hispanic of any race, 0.6% two or more races (2000); Density: 21.5 persons per square mile (2000); Age: 24.8% under 18, 17.3% over 64 (2000).
Religion: Five largest groups: 9.9% Southern Baptist Convention, 3.4% Churches of Christ, 2.8% Baptist Missionary Association of America, 2.7% Church of God (Anderson, Indiana), 1.8% The United Methodist Church (2000).
Economy: Unemployment rate: 6.2% (11/2002); Total civilian labor force: 5,206 (11/2002); Leading industries: 27.5% manufacturing; 24.4% health care and social assistance; 22.6% retail trade (2000); Companies that employ more than 1,000 persons: 0 (2000); Companies that employ more than 100 persons: 4 (2000); Farms: 472 totaling 151,963 acres (1997); Minority business ownership rate: 0.0% (1997); Women business ownership rate: 11.2% (1997); Retail sales per capita: $4,929 (1997). Single-family building permits issued: 1 (2001) / 3 (2000); Multi-family building permits issued: 0 (2001) / 0 (2000).
Income: Per capita income: $12,889 (2000); Median household income: $22,761 (2000); Poverty rate: 22.0% (2000); Bankruptcy rate: 3.96% (2001).
Taxes: Total county taxes per capita: $45 (1997); County property taxes per capita: $20 (1997).
Education: High school graduation rate: 62.1% (2000); College graduation rate: 7.8% (2000).
Housing: Homeownership rate: 78.0% (2000); Median home value: $49,100 (2000); Median rent: $216 per month (2000); Median age of housing: 25 years (2000).
Health: Birth rate: 129.5 per 10,000 population (1998); Age adjusted death rate: 103.8 per 10,000 population (1999); Age adjusted cancer mortality rate: 213.7 deaths per 100,000 population (1999). Number of physicians: 4.4 per 10,000 population (1999); Number of hospital beds: 19.2 per 10,000 population (1999).
Elections: 2000 Presidential election results: 35.9% Gore, 61.6% Bush, 1.2% Nader, 0.6% Buchanan
National and State Parks: Fourche Creek State Forest; Little Black State Forest; State Public Hunting Area
Additional Information Contacts
Ripley County Government Offices........................ 573-996-3215
Ripley County Chamber of Commerce 573-996-2212

Ripley County Communities

DONIPHAN (city). Covers a land area of 1.368 square miles and a water area of 0 square miles. Located at 36.62° N. Lat.; 90.82° W. Long. Elevation is 402 feet.
History: Doniphan was settled about 1847 on the north bank of the Current River, and named for Colonel Alexander Doniphan of Mexican War fame. A grist and carding mill had been built on the river in 1819 by Lemuel Kittrell. Doniphan later became a starting point for fishing and float trips on the Current River.
Population: 1,932 (2000); Race: 98.8% White, 0.0% Black, 0.4% Asian, 0.0% American Indian and Alaska Native, 1.2% Hispanic of any race, 0.5% two or more races (2000); Density: 1,412.5 persons per square mile (2000); Age: 23.0% under 18, 29.4% over 64 (2000); Marriage status: 17.1% never married, 48.5% now married, 18.3% widowed, 16.1% divorced (2000); Foreign born: 1.0% (2000); Ancestry (includes multiple ancestries): 16.5% United States or American, 14.7% Irish, 10.5% English, 9.6% Other groups, 7.0% German (2000).
Economy: Single-family building permits issued: 1 (2001) / 3 (2000); Multi-family building permits issued: 0 (2001) / 0 (2000); Employment by occupation: 6.3% management, 18.5% professional, 20.2% services, 23.0% sales, 3.1% farming, 6.1% construction, 22.8% production (2000).
Income: Per capita income: $14,407 (2000); Median household income: $19,696 (2000); Poverty rate: 25.9% (2000).
Taxes: Total city taxes per capita: $81 (1997); City property taxes per capita: $17 (1997).
Education: High school graduation rate: 60.7% (2000); College graduation rate: 12.3% (2000).

School District(s)

Doniphan R-I (PK-12)
2000 Enrollment: 1,672 573-996-3819
Ripley Co. R-IV (KG-08)
2000 Enrollment: 166 573-996-7118

Four-year College(s)

Western States University for Professional Studies (Private, For-profit)
2001 Enrollment: n/a 573-996-7388

Housing: Homeownership rate: 54.3% (2000); Median home value: $55,600 (2000); Median rent: $226 per month (2000); Median age of housing: 35 years (2000).
Hospitals: Ripley County Memorial Hospital (30 beds)
Newspapers: The Prospect News (1 x week)
Transportation: Commute to work: 93.3% car, 1.3% public transportation, 4.0% walk, 0.7% work from home (2000); Travel time to work: 70.0% less than 15 minutes, 6.5% 15 to 30 minutes, 10.6% 30 to 45 minutes, 7.9% 45 to 60 minutes, 5.0% 60 minutes or more (2000)
Additional Information Contacts
Ripley County Chamber of Commerce 573-996-2212

FAIRDEALING (unincorporated postal area, zip code 63939). Covers a land area of 38.951 square miles and a water area of 0.030 square miles. Located at 36.64° N. Lat.; 90.68° W. Long. Elevation is 458 feet.
Population: 1,381 (2000); Race: 99.5% White, 0.0% Black, 0.0% Asian, 0.0% American Indian and Alaska Native, 0.8% Hispanic of any race, 0.5% two or more races (2000); Density: 35.5 persons per square mile (2000); Age: 22.7% under 18, 19.5% over 64 (2000); Marriage status: 13.3% never married, 69.8% now married, 8.0% widowed, 8.8% divorced (2000); Foreign born: 0.8% (2000); Ancestry (includes multiple ancestries): 21.7% United States or American, 10.2% Irish, 10.0% English, 9.1% German, 6.6% Other groups (2000).
Economy: Employment by occupation: 8.8% management, 18.2% professional, 12.1% services, 18.2% sales, 0.0% farming, 12.6% construction, 30.1% production (2000).
Income: Per capita income: $12,815 (2000); Median household income: $24,142 (2000); Poverty rate: 14.6% (2000).
Education: High school graduation rate: 66.6% (2000); College graduation rate: 6.1% (2000).
Housing: Homeownership rate: 88.0% (2000); Median home value: $61,500 (2000); Median rent: $146 per month (2000); Median age of housing: 22 years (2000).
Transportation: Commute to work: 93.3% car, 0.0% public transportation, 3.5% walk, 3.2% work from home (2000); Travel time to work: 19.2% less than 15 minutes, 38.2% 15 to 30 minutes, 32.6% 30 to 45 minutes, 5.0% 45 to 60 minutes, 5.0% 60 minutes or more (2000)

GATEWOOD (unincorporated postal area, zip code 63942). Covers a land area of 92.727 square miles and a water area of 0 square miles. Located at 36.54° N. Lat.; 91.05° W. Long. Elevation is 543 feet.
Population: 672 (2000); Race: 98.1% White, 0.0% Black, 0.0% Asian, 0.9% American Indian and Alaska Native, 1.3% Hispanic of any race, 1.0% two or more races (2000); Density: 7.2 persons per square mile (2000); Age: 21.8% under 18, 14.0% over 64 (2000); Marriage status: 18.0% never married, 68.1% now married, 6.9% widowed, 6.9% divorced (2000); Foreign born: 0.3% (2000); Ancestry (includes multiple ancestries): 16.7% United States or American, 15.5% Irish, 14.6% German, 11.9% English, 10.1% Other groups (2000).
Economy: Employment by occupation: 10.7% management, 13.7% professional, 9.3% services, 12.6% sales, 6.3% farming, 6.3% construction, 41.1% production (2000).
Income: Per capita income: $14,619 (2000); Median household income: $26,696 (2000); Poverty rate: 22.1% (2000).
Education: High school graduation rate: 67.2% (2000); College graduation rate: 5.8% (2000).

School District(s)

Ripley Co. R-III (KG-08)
2000 Enrollment: 106 573-255-3213

Housing: Homeownership rate: 87.4% (2000); Median home value: $40,700 (2000); Median rent: $118 per month (2000); Median age of housing: 23 years (2000).
Transportation: Commute to work: 91.1% car, 0.0% public transportation, 0.0% walk, 6.6% work from home (2000); Travel time to work: 23.1% less than 15 minutes, 33.5% 15 to 30 minutes, 16.5% 30 to 45 minutes, 9.1% 45 to 60 minutes, 17.8% 60 minutes or more (2000)

NAYLOR (city). Covers a land area of 0.542 square miles and a water area of 0 square miles. Located at 36.57° N. Lat.; 90.60° W. Long. Elevation is 304 feet.
Population: 610 (2000); Race: 94.8% White, 0.5% Black, 1.0% Asian, 1.0% American Indian and Alaska Native, 1.5% Hispanic of any race, 2.1% two or more races (2000); Density: 1,124.6 persons per square mile (2000); Age: 25.4% under 18, 20.5% over 64 (2000); Marriage status: 15.4% never married, 60.4% now married, 13.1% widowed, 11.0% divorced (2000); Foreign born: 1.0% (2000); Ancestry (includes multiple ancestries): 22.9% United States or American, 14.1% English, 11.5% Other groups, 9.7% Irish, 7.1% German (2000).
Economy: Fruit; timber; cattle. Manufacturing of apparel. Single-family building permits issued: 0 (2001) / 0 (2000); Multi-family building permits issued: 0 (2001) / 0 (2000); Employment by occupation: 2.2% management, 12.2% professional, 15.7% services, 19.2% sales, 2.2% farming, 5.2% construction, 43.2% production (2000).
Income: Per capita income: $18,402 (2000); Median household income: $20,900 (2000); Poverty rate: 24.1% (2000).
Taxes: Total city taxes per capita: $90 (1997); City property taxes per capita: $17 (1997).
Education: High school graduation rate: 55.6% (2000); College graduation rate: 3.9% (2000).

School District(s)

Naylor R-II (KG-12)
2000 Enrollment: 381 573-399-2505

Housing: Homeownership rate: 77.7% (2000); Median home value: $31,100 (2000); Median rent: $186 per month (2000); Median age of housing: 35 years (2000).
Transportation: Commute to work: 95.2% car, 0.9% public transportation, 1.3% walk, 0.4% work from home (2000); Travel time to work: 17.1% less than 15 minutes, 35.1% 15 to 30 minutes, 38.2% 30 to 45 minutes, 5.3% 45 to 60 minutes, 4.4% 60 minutes or more (2000)

OXLY (unincorporated postal area, zip code 63955). Covers a land area of 7.765 square miles and a water area of 0 square miles. Located at 36.60° N. Lat.; 90.68° W. Long. Elevation is 320 feet.
Population: 263 (2000); Race: 98.0% White, 0.0% Black, 0.0% Asian, 0.0% American Indian and Alaska Native, 0.0% Hispanic of any race, 2.0% two or more races (2000); Density: 33.9 persons per square mile (2000); Age: 27.0% under 18, 8.9% over 64 (2000); Marriage status: 19.3% never married, 47.9% now married, 14.1% widowed, 18.8% divorced (2000); Foreign born: 0.8% (2000); Ancestry (includes multiple ancestries): 29.4% Irish, 17.3% Other groups, 15.7% United States or American, 12.1% English, 7.3% German (2000).
Economy: Employment by occupation: 5.7% management, 21.8% professional, 9.2% services, 19.5% sales, 0.0% farming, 3.4% construction, 40.2% production (2000).
Income: Per capita income: $8,613 (2000); Median household income: $15,750 (2000); Poverty rate: 47.6% (2000).
Education: High school graduation rate: 38.7% (2000); College graduation rate: 3.1% (2000).
Housing: Homeownership rate: 90.4% (2000); Median home value: $31,800 (2000); Median rent: $144 per month (2000); Median age of housing: 31 years (2000).
Transportation: Commute to work: 100.0% car, 0.0% public transportation, 0.0% walk, 0.0% work from home (2000); Travel time to work: 6.9% less than 15 minutes, 36.8% 15 to 30 minutes, 41.4% 30 to 45 minutes, 14.9% 45 to 60 minutes, 0.0% 60 minutes or more (2000)

Saint Charles County

Located in eastern Missouri; bounded on the east by the Mississippi River and the Illinois border, and on the south by the Missouri River. Covers a land area of 560.40 square miles, a water area of 31.90 square miles, and is located in the Central Time Zone. The county government was organized in 1812. County seat is St. Charles.

Saint Charles County is part of the St. Louis, MO-IL MSA. The entire metro area includes: Clinton County, IL; Jersey County, IL; Madison County, IL; Monroe County, IL; St. Clair County, IL; Crawford County, MO (pt.)**; Franklin County, MO; Jefferson County, MO; Lincoln County, MO; St. Charles County, MO; St. Louis County, MO; Warren County, MO; St. Louis city, MO

Population: 283,883 (2000); Race: 94.8% White, 2.4% Black, 0.8% Asian, 0.3% American Indian and Alaska Native, 1.6% Hispanic of any race, 1.3% two or more races (2000); Density: 506.6 persons per square mile (2000); Age: 28.9% under 18, 8.7% over 64 (2000).
Religion: Five largest groups: 27.8% Catholic Church, 7.2% Southern Baptist Convention, 3.9% Lutheran Church—Missouri Synod, 2.3% The United Methodist Church, 1.8% United Church of Christ (2000).
Economy: Unemployment rate: 3.5% (11/2002); Total civilian labor force: 162,526 (11/2002); Leading industries: 16.2% manufacturing; 15.9% retail trade; 10.9% accommodation & food services (2000); Companies that employ more than 1,000 persons: 8 (2000); Companies that employ more than 100 persons: 146 (2000); Farms: 680 totaling 187,097 acres (1997); Minority business ownership rate: 3.6% (1997); Women business ownership rate: 33.6% (1997); Retail sales per capita: $8,879 (1997). Single-family building permits issued: 3,202 (2001) / 2,963 (2000); Multi-family building permits issued: 647 (2001) / 1,038 (2000).
Income: Per capita income: $23,592 (2000); Median household income: $57,258 (2000); Poverty rate: 4.0% (2000); Bankruptcy rate: 4.61% (2001).
Taxes: Total county taxes per capita: $123 (2000); County property taxes per capita: $42 (2000).
Education: High school graduation rate: 89.1% (2000); College graduation rate: 26.3% (2000).
Housing: Homeownership rate: 82.0% (2000); Median home value: $126,200 (2000); Median rent: $529 per month (2000); Median age of housing: 16 years (2000).
Health: Birth rate: 144.5 per 10,000 population (1998); Age adjusted death rate: 88.5 per 10,000 population (1999); Age adjusted cancer mortality rate: 210.4 deaths per 100,000 population (1999). Air Quality Index: 48% good, 51% moderate, 2% unhealthy (percent of days in 2000). Number of physicians: 9.2 per 10,000 population (1999); Number of hospital beds: 21.6 per 10,000 population (1999).
Elections: 2000 Presidential election results: 41.8% Gore, 56.0% Bush, 1.5% Nader, 0.3% Buchanan
National and State Parks: Fort Zumwalt State Park
Additional Information Contacts
St. Charles County Government Offices 636-949-7520
Chamber Spotlight 636-939-9515
Lake St. Louis Chamber of Commerce 636-561-9999
New Melle Chamber of Commerce 636-828-5600
O Fallon Chamber of Commerce 636-240-1818
St. Charles Chamber of Commerce 636-946-0633
St. Charles County Association of Realtors 636-946-4022
St. Peters Chamber of Commerce 636-447-3336
Wentzville Chamber of Commerce 636-327-6914

Saint Charles County Communities

AUGUSTA (town). Covers a land area of 0.263 square miles and a water area of 0 square miles. Located at 38.57° N. Lat.; 90.88° W. Long. Elevation is 560 feet.
History: Augusta was laid out in 1836 by Leonard Harold. First called Mount Pleasant, the name was changed to Augusta to honor Harold's wife.
Population: 218 (2000); Race: 100.0% White, 0.0% Black, 0.0% Asian, 0.0% American Indian and Alaska Native, 0.0% Hispanic of any race, 0.0% two or more races (2000); Density: 829.7 persons per square mile (2000); Age: 16.8% under 18, 20.9% over 64 (2000); Marriage status: 23.9% never married, 55.9% now married, 8.5% widowed, 11.7% divorced (2000); Foreign born: 0.9% (2000); Ancestry (includes multiple ancestries): 52.3% German, 11.8% English, 10.0% Irish, 5.9% United States or American, 5.9% French (except Basque) (2000).
Economy: Employment by occupation: 13.9% management, 13.1% professional, 24.6% services, 27.0% sales, 0.0% farming, 8.2% construction, 13.1% production (2000).
Income: Per capita income: $21,065 (2000); Median household income: $35,000 (2000); Poverty rate: 2.3% (2000).
Taxes: Total city taxes per capita: $184 (1997); City property taxes per capita: $30 (1997).
Education: High school graduation rate: 82.5% (2000); College graduation rate: 17.5% (2000).
Housing: Homeownership rate: 84.6% (2000); Median home value: $91,200 (2000); Median rent: $338 per month (2000); Median age of housing: 42 years (2000).
Transportation: Commute to work: 93.4% car, 0.0% public transportation, 3.3% walk, 3.3% work from home (2000); Travel time to work: 22.9% less than 15 minutes, 17.8% 15 to 30 minutes, 31.4% 30 to 45 minutes, 16.9% 45 to 60 minutes, 11.0% 60 minutes or more (2000)

COTTLEVILLE (city). Covers a land area of 3.905 square miles and a water area of 0 square miles. Located at 38.75° N. Lat.; 90.65° W. Long. Elevation is 490 feet.
History: Cottleville was established in 1840 by Lorenzo Cottle, who was joined by many German immigrants during the next twenty years.
Population: 1,928 (2000); Race: 95.8% White, 1.1% Black, 1.7% Asian, 0.0% American Indian and Alaska Native, 1.1% Hispanic of any race, 1.5% two or more races (2000); Density: 493.7 persons per square mile (2000); Age: 33.6% under 18, 4.7% over 64 (2000); Marriage status: 18.6% never married, 74.0% now married, 1.6% widowed, 5.8% divorced (2000); Foreign born: 2.6% (2000); Ancestry (includes multiple ancestries): 48.3% German, 24.0% Irish, 14.5% English, 10.0% Other groups, 6.7% United States or American (2000).
Economy: Single-family building permits issued: 69 (2001) / 50 (2000); Multi-family building permits issued: 0 (2001) / 0 (2000); Employment by occupation: 20.5% management, 25.0% professional, 8.7% services, 31.0% sales, 0.0% farming, 5.4% construction, 9.5% production (2000).
Income: Per capita income: $26,729 (2000); Median household income: $74,200 (2000); Poverty rate: 1.7% (2000).
Taxes: Total city taxes per capita: $177 (1997); City property taxes per capita: $41 (1997).
Education: High school graduation rate: 91.6% (2000); College graduation rate: 35.0% (2000).
Housing: Homeownership rate: 94.3% (2000); Median home value: $176,300 (2000); Median rent: $319 per month (2000); Median age of housing: 7 years (2000).
Transportation: Commute to work: 93.0% car, 0.8% public transportation, 1.4% walk, 4.1% work from home (2000); Travel time to work: 24.2% less than 15 minutes, 27.3% 15 to 30 minutes, 28.0% 30 to 45 minutes, 14.0% 45 to 60 minutes, 6.4% 60 minutes or more (2000)

DARDENNE PRAIRIE (town). Covers a land area of 4.365 square miles and a water area of 0 square miles. Located at 38.75° N. Lat.; 90.73° W. Long. Elevation is 610 feet.
Population: 4,384 (2000); Race: 96.0% White, 1.1% Black, 1.8% Asian, 0.0% American Indian and Alaska Native, 0.1% Hispanic of any race, 1.0% two or more races (2000); Density: 1,004.3 persons per square mile (2000); Age: 32.8% under 18, 5.2% over 64 (2000); Marriage status: 14.6% never married, 81.1% now married, 0.8% widowed, 3.6% divorced (2000); Foreign born: 2.2% (2000); Ancestry (includes multiple ancestries): 37.3% German, 19.5% Irish, 9.0% Other groups, 7.0% Italian, 7.0% English (2000).
Economy: Employment by occupation: 21.9% management, 26.2% professional, 8.4% services, 24.5% sales, 0.0% farming, 10.3% construction, 8.7% production (2000).
Income: Per capita income: $29,325 (2000); Median household income: $77,086 (2000); Poverty rate: 0.7% (2000).
Taxes: Total city taxes per capita: $43 (1997); City property taxes per capita: $39 (1997).
Education: High school graduation rate: 95.4% (2000); College graduation rate: 37.6% (2000).
Housing: Homeownership rate: 98.0% (2000); Median home value: $179,200 (2000); Median rent: $275 per month (2000); Median age of housing: 3 years (2000).
Transportation: Commute to work: 94.5% car, 0.0% public transportation, 0.0% walk, 4.2% work from home (2000); Travel time to work: 11.0% less than 15 minutes, 29.0% 15 to 30 minutes, 37.5% 30 to 45 minutes, 17.8% 45 to 60 minutes, 4.7% 60 minutes or more (2000)

DEFIANCE (unincorporated postal area, zip code 63341). Covers a land area of 56.392 square miles and a water area of 0.498 square miles. Located at 38.68° N. Lat.; 90.78° W. Long. Elevation is 485 feet.
History: Near Defiance was the home of Nathan Boone, where Daniel Boone often came to visit his son, and where the famed frontiersman died of a fever in 1820.
Population: 3,154 (2000); Race: 99.5% White, 0.2% Black, 0.3% Asian, 0.0% American Indian and Alaska Native, 0.2% Hispanic of any race, 0.0% two or more races (2000); Density: 55.9 persons per square mile (2000); Age: 25.2% under 18, 8.3% over 64 (2000); Marriage status: 15.8% never married, 75.4% now married, 3.8% widowed, 5.0% divorced (2000); Foreign born: 0.8% (2000); Ancestry (includes multiple ancestries): 44.2% German, 20.1% Irish, 12.1% English, 8.2% United States or American, 5.6% Other groups (2000).

Economy: Employment by occupation: 17.8% management, 22.0% professional, 8.5% services, 27.8% sales, 0.0% farming, 13.6% construction, 10.4% production (2000).
Income: Per capita income: $28,868 (2000); Median household income: $69,602 (2000); Poverty rate: 2.7% (2000).
Education: High school graduation rate: 93.6% (2000); College graduation rate: 32.2% (2000).
Housing: Homeownership rate: 93.0% (2000); Median home value: $218,400 (2000); Median rent: $340 per month (2000); Median age of housing: 11 years (2000).
Transportation: Commute to work: 93.4% car, 0.0% public transportation, 0.8% walk, 4.0% work from home (2000); Travel time to work: 7.3% less than 15 minutes, 18.7% 15 to 30 minutes, 35.8% 30 to 45 minutes, 27.5% 45 to 60 minutes, 10.7% 60 minutes or more (2000)

FLINT HILL (city). Covers a land area of 2.490 square miles and a water area of 0 square miles. Located at 38.85° N. Lat.; 90.86° W. Long. Elevation is 516 feet.
Population: 379 (2000); Race: 98.9% White, 0.0% Black, 0.0% Asian, 0.0% American Indian and Alaska Native, 0.3% Hispanic of any race, 1.1% two or more races (2000); Density: 152.2 persons per square mile (2000); Age: 30.6% under 18, 14.5% over 64 (2000); Marriage status: 21.7% never married, 70.6% now married, 3.7% widowed, 4.0% divorced (2000); Foreign born: 0.6% (2000); Ancestry (includes multiple ancestries): 52.1% German, 14.8% English, 11.7% Irish, 7.2% French (except Basque), 7.2% United States or American (2000).
Economy: Single-family building permits issued: 3 (2001) / 1 (2000); Multi-family building permits issued: 0 (2001) / 0 (2000); Employment by occupation: 21.1% management, 8.8% professional, 15.2% services, 26.9% sales, 0.0% farming, 15.2% construction, 12.9% production (2000).
Income: Per capita income: $21,194 (2000); Median household income: $47,500 (2000); Poverty rate: 2.2% (2000).
Taxes: Total city taxes per capita: $298 (1997); City property taxes per capita: $196 (1997).
Education: High school graduation rate: 93.8% (2000); College graduation rate: 20.5% (2000).
Housing: Homeownership rate: 84.8% (2000); Median home value: $228,400 (2000); Median rent: $375 per month (2000); Median age of housing: 12 years (2000).
Transportation: Commute to work: 94.1% car, 0.6% public transportation, 3.5% walk, 1.8% work from home (2000); Travel time to work: 27.5% less than 15 minutes, 35.3% 15 to 30 minutes, 19.8% 30 to 45 minutes, 16.8% 45 to 60 minutes, 0.6% 60 minutes or more (2000)

FORISTELL (city). Covers a land area of 4.970 square miles and a water area of 0.067 square miles. Located at 38.81° N. Lat.; 90.95° W. Long. Elevation is 707 feet.
Population: 331 (2000); Race: 94.2% White, 0.0% Black, 0.0% Asian, 0.0% American Indian and Alaska Native, 3.4% Hispanic of any race, 5.8% two or more races (2000); Density: 66.6 persons per square mile (2000); Age: 25.0% under 18, 13.7% over 64 (2000); Marriage status: 18.4% never married, 72.5% now married, 4.3% widowed, 4.7% divorced (2000); Foreign born: 0.0% (2000); Ancestry (includes multiple ancestries): 40.5% German, 24.1% Irish, 12.8% French (except Basque), 10.1% English, 5.8% Other groups (2000).
Economy: Commercial highway services. Agricultural area; manufacturing: corrugated cartons, machining. Employment by occupation: 4.8% management, 15.6% professional, 12.6% services, 26.9% sales, 1.2% farming, 21.6% construction, 17.4% production (2000).
Income: Per capita income: $22,331 (2000); Median household income: $52,386 (2000); Poverty rate: 8.9% (2000).
Taxes: Total city taxes per capita: $650 (2000); City property taxes per capita: $0 (2000).
Education: High school graduation rate: 73.3% (2000); College graduation rate: 13.8% (2000).
Housing: Homeownership rate: 83.9% (2000); Median home value: $128,800 (2000); Median rent: $450 per month (2000); Median age of housing: 33 years (2000).
Transportation: Commute to work: 93.4% car, 0.0% public transportation, 4.2% walk, 2.4% work from home (2000); Travel time to work: 28.2% less than 15 minutes, 38.0% 15 to 30 minutes, 20.9% 30 to 45 minutes, 9.8% 45 to 60 minutes, 3.1% 60 minutes or more (2000)

JOSEPHVILLE (village). Covers a land area of 1.567 square miles and a water area of 0 square miles. Located at 38.83° N. Lat.; 90.79° W. Long. Elevation is 618 feet.
Population: 270 (2000); Race: 100.0% White, 0.0% Black, 0.0% Asian, 0.0% American Indian and Alaska Native, 0.0% Hispanic of any race, 0.0% two or more races (2000); Density: 172.3 persons per square mile (2000); Age: 40.7% under 18, 6.1% over 64 (2000); Marriage status: 25.4% never married, 59.7% now married, 3.9% widowed, 11.0% divorced (2000); Foreign born: 0.0% (2000); Ancestry (includes multiple ancestries): 58.9% German, 18.2% Irish, 9.3% French (except Basque), 3.6% English, 3.2% United States or American (2000).
Economy: Employment by occupation: 6.9% management, 9.0% professional, 19.4% services, 31.3% sales, 1.4% farming, 21.5% construction, 10.4% production (2000).
Income: Per capita income: $16,363 (2000); Median household income: $52,500 (2000); Poverty rate: 1.8% (2000).
Taxes: Total city taxes per capita: $389 (1997); City property taxes per capita: $24 (1997).
Education: High school graduation rate: 85.3% (2000); College graduation rate: 10.7% (2000).
Housing: Homeownership rate: 78.8% (2000); Median home value: $128,100 (2000); Median rent: $432 per month (2000); Median age of housing: 35 years (2000).
Transportation: Commute to work: 92.1% car, 0.0% public transportation, 1.4% walk, 6.4% work from home (2000); Travel time to work: 19.1% less than 15 minutes, 42.0% 15 to 30 minutes, 16.0% 30 to 45 minutes, 16.8% 45 to 60 minutes, 6.1% 60 minutes or more (2000)

LAKE SAINT LOUIS (city). Covers a land area of 7.481 square miles and a water area of 0.844 square miles. Located at 38.78° N. Lat.; 90.78° W. Long. Elevation is 545 feet.
Population: 10,169 (2000); Race: 96.7% White, 1.5% Black, 0.4% Asian, 0.2% American Indian and Alaska Native, 1.2% Hispanic of any race, 1.0% two or more races (2000); Density: 1,359.3 persons per square mile (2000); Age: 24.3% under 18, 12.1% over 64 (2000); Marriage status: 17.7% never married, 70.9% now married, 3.8% widowed, 7.6% divorced (2000); Foreign born: 3.7% (2000); Ancestry (includes multiple ancestries): 40.5% German, 18.5% Irish, 15.1% English, 7.5% Other groups, 5.7% Italian (2000).
Economy: Single-family building permits issued: 187 (2001) / 138 (2000); Multi-family building permits issued: 45 (2001) / 6 (2000); Employment by occupation: 17.3% management, 23.2% professional, 10.1% services, 32.4% sales, 0.0% farming, 6.0% construction, 11.1% production (2000).
Income: Per capita income: $32,064 (2000); Median household income: $68,830 (2000); Poverty rate: 3.9% (2000).
Taxes: Total city taxes per capita: $240 (2000); City property taxes per capita: $132 (2000).
Education: High school graduation rate: 94.4% (2000); College graduation rate: 37.7% (2000).
Housing: Homeownership rate: 81.6% (2000); Median home value: $167,600 (2000); Median rent: $537 per month (2000); Median age of housing: 16 years (2000).
Hospitals: Saint Joseph Hospital West (100 beds)
Safety: Violent crime rate: 11.7 per 10,000 population; Property crime rate: 138.8 per 10,000 population (2001).
Transportation: Commute to work: 93.7% car, 0.0% public transportation, 0.1% walk, 5.3% work from home (2000); Travel time to work: 23.1% less than 15 minutes, 30.6% 15 to 30 minutes, 29.5% 30 to 45 minutes, 11.1% 45 to 60 minutes, 5.7% 60 minutes or more (2000)
Additional Information Contacts
Lake St. Louis Chamber of Commerce 636-561-9999

NEW MELLE (city). Covers a land area of 0.354 square miles and a water area of 0 square miles. Located at 38.71° N. Lat.; 90.88° W. Long. Elevation is 789 feet.
Population: 124 (2000); Race: 94.6% White, 0.0% Black, 2.3% Asian, 0.0% American Indian and Alaska Native, 0.0% Hispanic of any race, 3.1% two or more races (2000); Density: 349.8 persons per square mile (2000); Age: 11.5% under 18, 20.8% over 64 (2000); Marriage status: 18.3% never married, 70.4% now married, 6.1% widowed, 5.2% divorced (2000); Foreign born: 2.3% (2000); Ancestry (includes multiple ancestries): 59.2% German, 18.5% English, 18.5% Polish, 13.8% Irish, 10.8% Other groups (2000).
Economy: Employment by occupation: 7.7% management, 21.5% professional, 15.4% services, 24.6% sales, 0.0% farming, 15.4% construction, 15.4% production (2000).
Income: Per capita income: $29,965 (2000); Median household income: $55,417 (2000); Poverty rate: 3.1% (2000).
Taxes: Total city taxes per capita: $118 (1997); City property taxes per capita: $0 (1997).

Education: High school graduation rate: 65.1% (2000); College graduation rate: 15.1% (2000).
Housing: Homeownership rate: 89.1% (2000); Median home value: $119,600 (2000); Median rent: $458 per month (2000); Median age of housing: 39 years (2000).
Transportation: Commute to work: 72.3% car, 0.0% public transportation, 16.9% walk, 10.8% work from home (2000); Travel time to work: 34.5% less than 15 minutes, 17.2% 15 to 30 minutes, 15.5% 30 to 45 minutes, 25.9% 45 to 60 minutes, 6.9% 60 minutes or more (2000)
Additional Information Contacts
New Melle Chamber of Commerce 636-828-5600

O'FALLON (city). Covers a land area of 22.468 square miles and a water area of 0.007 square miles. Located at 38.78° N. Lat.; 90.70° W. Long. Elevation is 543 feet.
History: O'Fallon was founded in 1857 and named for Major John O'Fallon, St. Louis capitalist and director of the North Missouri Railway. The town was established on the site of Fort Zumwalt, built during the War of 1812.
Population: 46,169 (2000); Race: 95.4% White, 2.1% Black, 1.2% Asian, 0.1% American Indian and Alaska Native, 1.3% Hispanic of any race, 0.9% two or more races (2000); Density: 2,054.9 persons per square mile (2000); Age: 33.4% under 18, 6.5% over 64 (2000); Marriage status: 19.5% never married, 69.3% now married, 3.5% widowed, 7.6% divorced (2000); Foreign born: 2.1% (2000); Ancestry (includes multiple ancestries): 37.1% German, 18.1% Irish, 9.7% Other groups, 8.9% English, 8.1% United States or American (2000).
Vital Statistics: Birth rate: 166.4 per 10,000 population (1998)
Economy: Unemployment rate: 4.0% (11/2002); Total civilian labor force: 14,249 (11/2002); Single-family building permits issued: 1,372 (2001) / 1,446 (2000); Multi-family building permits issued: 4 (2001) / 792 (2000); Employment by occupation: 16.0% management, 19.9% professional, 12.6% services, 28.6% sales, 0.0% farming, 10.3% construction, 12.6% production (2000).
Income: Per capita income: $21,774 (2000); Median household income: $60,179 (2000); Poverty rate: 3.3% (2000).
Taxes: Total city taxes per capita: $367 (2000); City property taxes per capita: $113 (2000).
Education: High school graduation rate: 90.4% (2000); College graduation rate: 27.2% (2000).

School District(s)
Fort Zumwalt R-II (KG-12)
2000 Enrollment: 16,521 636-272-6620
Housing: Homeownership rate: 89.6% (2000); Median home value: $135,800 (2000); Median rent: $527 per month (2000); Median age of housing: 7 years (2000).
Newspapers: O'Fallon Journal (3 x week)
Transportation: Commute to work: 94.8% car, 0.3% public transportation, 1.0% walk, 3.3% work from home (2000); Travel time to work: 21.2% less than 15 minutes, 30.2% 15 to 30 minutes, 29.5% 30 to 45 minutes, 13.4% 45 to 60 minutes, 5.7% 60 minutes or more (2000)
Additional Information Contacts
O Fallon Chamber of Commerce 636-240-1818

PORTAGE DES SIOUX (city). Covers a land area of 0.471 square miles and a water area of 0.035 square miles. Located at 38.92° N. Lat.; 90.34° W. Long. Elevation is 435 feet.
Population: 351 (2000); Race: 100.0% White, 0.0% Black, 0.0% Asian, 0.0% American Indian and Alaska Native, 1.3% Hispanic of any race, 0.0% two or more races (2000); Density: 745.3 persons per square mile (2000); Age: 19.4% under 18, 23.5% over 64 (2000); Marriage status: 16.3% never married, 65.8% now married, 5.3% widowed, 12.5% divorced (2000); Foreign born: 1.6% (2000); Ancestry (includes multiple ancestries): 39.8% German, 16.8% Irish, 10.1% United States or American, 8.5% Other groups, 6.2% Italian (2000).
Economy: Employment by occupation: 13.1% management, 6.6% professional, 10.6% services, 26.8% sales, 0.0% farming, 13.6% construction, 29.3% production (2000).
Income: Per capita income: $18,693 (2000); Median household income: $38,333 (2000); Poverty rate: 2.3% (2000).
Taxes: Total city taxes per capita: $103 (1997); City property taxes per capita: $38 (1997).
Education: High school graduation rate: 66.1% (2000); College graduation rate: 4.1% (2000).
Housing: Homeownership rate: 80.7% (2000); Median home value: $81,100 (2000); Median rent: $404 per month (2000); Median age of housing: 43 years (2000).
Transportation: Commute to work: 95.9% car, 0.0% public transportation, 3.1% walk, 0.0% work from home (2000); Travel time to work: 19.9% less than 15 minutes, 35.2% 15 to 30 minutes, 22.4% 30 to 45 minutes, 16.3% 45 to 60 minutes, 6.1% 60 minutes or more (2000)

SAINT CHARLES (city). Covers a land area of 20.363 square miles and a water area of 0.482 square miles. Located at 38.78° N. Lat.; 90.51° W. Long. Elevation is 536 feet.
History: St. Charles dates from 1787 when August Chouteau surveyed the settlement where Louis Blanchette had built a cabin in 1769. The community first had a French name, Les Petities Cotes, and then a Spanish name, San Carlos del Misuri, Anglicized after 1803 to St. Charles. The Daniel Boone family were among the settlers here in the 1790's. After this area became American territory in 1803, Lewis and Clark made it their headquarters for their explorations of the west.
Population: 60,321 (2000); Race: 93.1% White, 3.4% Black, 0.8% Asian, 0.8% American Indian and Alaska Native, 2.4% Hispanic of any race, 1.3% two or more races (2000); Density: 2,962.4 persons per square mile (2000); Age: 23.2% under 18, 12.3% over 64 (2000); Marriage status: 25.2% never married, 57.5% now married, 6.5% widowed, 10.7% divorced (2000); Foreign born: 2.6% (2000); Ancestry (includes multiple ancestries): 37.9% German, 15.7% Irish, 12.0% Other groups, 9.8% English, 7.1% United States or American (2000).
Vital Statistics: Birth rate: 202.4 per 10,000 population (1998)
Economy: Unemployment rate: 3.5% (11/2002); Total civilian labor force: 43,335 (11/2002); Single-family building permits issued: 183 (2001) / 270 (2000); Multi-family building permits issued: 0 (2001) / 0 (2000); Employment by occupation: 14.4% management, 20.1% professional, 14.2% services, 28.6% sales, 0.1% farming, 9.8% construction, 12.8% production (2000).
Income: Per capita income: $23,607 (2000); Median household income: $47,782 (2000); Poverty rate: 6.3% (2000).
Education: High school graduation rate: 86.4% (2000); College graduation rate: 26.6% (2000).

School District(s)
Francis Howell R-III (PK-12)
2000 Enrollment: 19,497 636-441-0088
Saint Charles Co. R-V (KG-12)
2000 Enrollment: 1,206 636-250-5000
Saint Charles R-VI (KG-12)
2000 Enrollment: 6,190 636-724-5840

Four-year College(s)
Lindenwood University (Private, Not-for-profit)
2001 Enrollment: 6,446 636-949-2000
2001 Tuition: In-state $11,200; Out-of-state $11,200

Two-year College(s)
Sanford-Brown College (Private, For-profit)
2001 Enrollment: 220 636-949-2620
Housing: Homeownership rate: 64.8% (2000); Median home value: $121,300 (2000); Median rent: $507 per month (2000); Median age of housing: 21 years (2000).
Hospitals: Saint Joseph Health Center (342 beds)
Safety: Violent crime rate: 28.8 per 10,000 population; Property crime rate: 287.5 per 10,000 population (2001).
Newspapers: Saint Charles County Business Record (5 x week); St. Peters Journal (3 x week); St. Charles Journal (3 x week)
Transportation: Commute to work: 94.9% car, 0.5% public transportation, 1.4% walk, 2.6% work from home (2000); Travel time to work: 28.3% less than 15 minutes, 42.1% 15 to 30 minutes, 21.1% 30 to 45 minutes, 5.5% 45 to 60 minutes, 2.9% 60 minutes or more (2000)
Additional Information Contacts
St. Charles Chamber of Commerce 636-946-0633
St. Charles County Association of Realtors 636-946-4022

SAINT PAUL (city). Covers a land area of 6.721 square miles and a water area of 0 square miles. Located at 38.85° N. Lat.; 90.73° W. Long. Elevation is 520 feet.
Population: 1,634 (2000); Race: 97.5% White, 0.0% Black, 0.0% Asian, 0.7% American Indian and Alaska Native, 0.5% Hispanic of any race, 1.4% two or more races (2000); Density: 243.1 persons per square mile (2000); Age: 33.2% under 18, 9.0% over 64 (2000); Marriage status: 26.1% never married, 67.7% now married, 3.2% widowed, 3.0% divorced (2000); Foreign born: 1.0% (2000); Ancestry (includes multiple ancestries): 50.0% German, 17.6% Irish, 6.6% English, 5.6% French (except Basque), 4.9% Other groups (2000).

Economy: Employment by occupation: 10.6% management, 14.3% professional, 11.6% services, 33.2% sales, 0.2% farming, 19.9% construction, 10.2% production (2000).
Income: Per capita income: $22,216 (2000); Median household income: $67,841 (2000); Poverty rate: 1.3% (2000).
Education: High school graduation rate: 85.7% (2000); College graduation rate: 16.5% (2000).
Housing: Homeownership rate: 96.4% (2000); Median home value: $183,000 (2000); Median rent: $575 per month (2000); Median age of housing: 15 years (2000).
Transportation: Commute to work: 95.5% car, 0.0% public transportation, 0.3% walk, 3.7% work from home (2000); Travel time to work: 19.5% less than 15 minutes, 42.9% 15 to 30 minutes, 25.6% 30 to 45 minutes, 7.8% 45 to 60 minutes, 4.2% 60 minutes or more (2000)

SAINT PETERS (city). Covers a land area of 21.184 square miles and a water area of <.001 square miles. Located at 38.77° N. Lat.; 90.60° W. Long. Elevation is 435 feet.
History: St. Peters was platted as a village in 1868, though the parish was established in 1820.
Population: 51,381 (2000); Race: 94.7% White, 2.0% Black, 1.3% Asian, 0.2% American Indian and Alaska Native, 1.3% Hispanic of any race, 1.4% two or more races (2000); Density: 2,425.5 persons per square mile (2000); Age: 30.1% under 18, 7.6% over 64 (2000); Marriage status: 22.3% never married, 63.1% now married, 4.9% widowed, 9.8% divorced (2000); Foreign born: 1.8% (2000); Ancestry (includes multiple ancestries): 39.2% German, 18.3% Irish, 11.8% English, 9.9% Other groups, 7.3% Italian (2000).
Vital Statistics: Birth rate: 143.1 per 10,000 population (1998)
Economy: Unemployment rate: 3.1% (11/2002); Total civilian labor force: 34,981 (11/2002); Single-family building permits issued: 143 (2001) / 85 (2000); Multi-family building permits issued: 588 (2001) / 228 (2000); Employment by occupation: 15.2% management, 20.6% professional, 11.9% services, 30.8% sales, 0.0% farming, 9.5% construction, 11.8% production (2000).
Income: Per capita income: $22,792 (2000); Median household income: $57,898 (2000); Poverty rate: 2.7% (2000).
Education: High school graduation rate: 91.4% (2000); College graduation rate: 27.2% (2000).

Two-year College(s)

Saint Charles County Community College (Public)
2001 Enrollment: 6,171 636-922-8380
Housing: Homeownership rate: 85.5% (2000); Median home value: $115,100 (2000); Median rent: $551 per month (2000); Median age of housing: 16 years (2000).
Hospitals: Barnes-Jewish Saint Peters Hospital (111 beds)
Transportation: Commute to work: 96.0% car, 0.3% public transportation, 0.4% walk, 2.6% work from home (2000); Travel time to work: 21.7% less than 15 minutes, 36.8% 15 to 30 minutes, 27.9% 30 to 45 minutes, 9.3% 45 to 60 minutes, 4.2% 60 minutes or more (2000)
Additional Information Contacts
Chamber Spotlight 636-939-9515
St. Peters Chamber of Commerce 636-447-3336

WELDON SPRING (city). Covers a land area of 7.913 square miles and a water area of 0.431 square miles. Located at 38.71° N. Lat.; 90.64° W. Long. Elevation is 410 feet.
History: Weldon Spring was settled about 1859 by German families, and named for John and Joseph Weldon, early residents.
Population: 5,270 (2000); Race: 95.5% White, 1.8% Black, 1.2% Asian, 0.2% American Indian and Alaska Native, 0.9% Hispanic of any race, 0.9% two or more races (2000); Density: 666.0 persons per square mile (2000); Age: 25.7% under 18, 17.2% over 64 (2000); Marriage status: 14.9% never married, 74.1% now married, 6.3% widowed, 4.7% divorced (2000); Foreign born: 2.7% (2000); Ancestry (includes multiple ancestries): 39.2% German, 13.4% Irish, 12.2% English, 7.3% Other groups, 6.7% Italian (2000).
Economy: Employment by occupation: 25.6% management, 24.5% professional, 9.2% services, 29.6% sales, 0.4% farming, 5.5% construction, 5.2% production (2000).
Income: Per capita income: $40,810 (2000); Median household income: $87,998 (2000); Poverty rate: 4.4% (2000).
Taxes: Total city taxes per capita: $77 (1997); City property taxes per capita: $0 (1997).
Education: High school graduation rate: 88.8% (2000); College graduation rate: 38.0% (2000).
Housing: Homeownership rate: 88.2% (2000); Median home value: $252,900 (2000); Median rent: $1,696 per month (2000); Median age of housing: 7 years (2000).
Transportation: Commute to work: 92.6% car, 0.0% public transportation, 0.4% walk, 6.8% work from home (2000); Travel time to work: 13.8% less than 15 minutes, 33.7% 15 to 30 minutes, 29.7% 30 to 45 minutes, 15.0% 45 to 60 minutes, 7.8% 60 minutes or more (2000)

WELDON SPRING HEIGHTS (town). Covers a land area of 0.090 square miles and a water area of 0 square miles. Located at 38.70° N. Lat.; 90.68° W. Long. Elevation is 615 feet.
Population: 79 (2000); Race: 100.0% White, 0.0% Black, 0.0% Asian, 0.0% American Indian and Alaska Native, 2.4% Hispanic of any race, 0.0% two or more races (2000); Density: 880.5 persons per square mile (2000); Age: 23.2% under 18, 30.5% over 64 (2000); Marriage status: 3.1% never married, 80.0% now married, 12.3% widowed, 4.6% divorced (2000); Foreign born: 0.0% (2000); Ancestry (includes multiple ancestries): 61.0% German, 42.7% Irish, 18.3% English, 8.5% French (except Basque), 6.1% Scotch-Irish (2000).
Economy: Single-family building permits issued: 0 (2001) / 0 (2000); Multi-family building permits issued: 0 (2001) / 0 (2000); Employment by occupation: 20.7% management, 27.6% professional, 0.0% services, 34.5% sales, 0.0% farming, 3.4% construction, 13.8% production (2000).
Income: Per capita income: $25,627 (2000); Median household income: $60,625 (2000); Poverty rate: 4.9% (2000).
Taxes: Total city taxes per capita: $481 (2000); City property taxes per capita: $0 (2000).
Education: High school graduation rate: 95.2% (2000); College graduation rate: 52.4% (2000).
Housing: Homeownership rate: 100.0% (2000); Median home value: $250,000 (2000); Median age of housing: 54 years (2000).
Transportation: Commute to work: 93.1% car, 0.0% public transportation, 0.0% walk, 6.9% work from home (2000); Travel time to work: 7.4% less than 15 minutes, 51.9% 15 to 30 minutes, 25.9% 30 to 45 minutes, 14.8% 45 to 60 minutes, 0.0% 60 minutes or more (2000)

WENTZVILLE (city). Covers a land area of 14.400 square miles and a water area of 0.014 square miles. Located at 38.81° N. Lat.; 90.85° W. Long. Elevation is 603 feet.
History: Wentzville was founded in 1855 and named for the chief engineer of the St. Louis, Kansas City & Northern Railway. During the 1870's, Wentzville was a tobacco manufacturing center.
Population: 6,896 (2000); Race: 84.1% White, 12.8% Black, 0.3% Asian, 0.1% American Indian and Alaska Native, 1.9% Hispanic of any race, 2.3% two or more races (2000); Density: 478.9 persons per square mile (2000); Age: 32.1% under 18, 10.9% over 64 (2000); Marriage status: 25.2% never married, 58.8% now married, 7.1% widowed, 8.9% divorced (2000); Foreign born: 1.8% (2000); Ancestry (includes multiple ancestries): 33.0% German, 18.1% Other groups, 13.8% Irish, 9.0% United States or American, 7.1% English (2000).
Economy: Single-family building permits issued: 734 (2001) / 481 (2000); Multi-family building permits issued: 0 (2001) / 0 (2000); Employment by occupation: 10.1% management, 14.3% professional, 16.5% services, 30.3% sales, 0.0% farming, 15.8% construction, 13.0% production (2000).
Income: Per capita income: $18,039 (2000); Median household income: $47,232 (2000); Poverty rate: 11.6% (2000).
Taxes: Total city taxes per capita: $1,089 (1997); City property taxes per capita: $464 (1997).
Education: High school graduation rate: 79.7% (2000); College graduation rate: 14.5% (2000).

School District(s)

Wentzville R-IV (PK-12)
2000 Enrollment: 6,105 636-327-3800
Housing: Homeownership rate: 68.9% (2000); Median home value: $113,100 (2000); Median rent: $382 per month (2000); Median age of housing: 18 years (2000).
Hospitals: Crossroads Regional Hospital (94 beds)
Safety: Violent crime rate: 49.0 per 10,000 population; Property crime rate: 585.1 per 10,000 population (2001).
Newspapers: Wentzville Journal (3 x week)
Transportation: Commute to work: 94.8% car, 0.0% public transportation, 2.6% walk, 2.4% work from home (2000); Travel time to work: 36.1% less than 15 minutes, 25.0% 15 to 30 minutes, 22.7% 30 to 45 minutes, 11.9% 45 to 60 minutes, 4.3% 60 minutes or more (2000)
Additional Information Contacts
Wentzville Chamber of Commerce 636-327-6914

WEST ALTON (city). Aka Westalton. Covers a land area of 28.362 square miles and a water area of 8.564 square miles. Located at 38.86° N. Lat.; 90.22° W. Long. Elevation is 432 feet.
Population: 573 (2000); Race: 99.4% White, 0.0% Black, 0.0% Asian, 0.0% American Indian and Alaska Native, 0.0% Hispanic of any race, 0.6% two or more races (2000); Density: 20.2 persons per square mile (2000); Age: 24.3% under 18, 13.3% over 64 (2000); Marriage status: 27.1% never married, 51.5% now married, 9.9% widowed, 11.5% divorced (2000); Foreign born: 0.0% (2000); Ancestry (includes multiple ancestries): 40.2% German, 9.3% United States or American, 9.1% Other groups, 9.1% Irish, 6.9% English (2000).
Economy: Employment by occupation: 8.0% management, 6.3% professional, 16.8% services, 28.6% sales, 0.0% farming, 18.5% construction, 21.8% production (2000).
Income: Per capita income: $18,975 (2000); Median household income: $36,094 (2000); Poverty rate: 7.7% (2000).
Taxes: Total city taxes per capita: $18,476 (2000); City property taxes per capita: $4,920 (2000).
Education: High school graduation rate: 70.3% (2000); College graduation rate: 5.1% (2000).
Housing: Homeownership rate: 87.1% (2000); Median home value: $67,200 (2000); Median rent: $300 per month (2000); Median age of housing: 41 years (2000).
Transportation: Commute to work: 92.6% car, 0.0% public transportation, 4.3% walk, 3.0% work from home (2000); Travel time to work: 15.7% less than 15 minutes, 31.8% 15 to 30 minutes, 29.6% 30 to 45 minutes, 17.9% 45 to 60 minutes, 4.9% 60 minutes or more (2000)

Saint Clair County

Located in western Missouri; drained by the Osage and Sac Rivers. Covers a land area of 676.70 square miles, a water area of 25.20 square miles, and is located in the Central Time Zone. The county government was organized in 1841. County seat is Osceola.

Weather Station: Appleton City — Elevation: 797 feet

	Jan	Feb	Mar	Apr	May	Jun	Jul	Aug	Sep	Oct	Nov	Dec
High	40	46	58	68	77	85	91	90	81	70	55	44
Low	19	24	34	44	53	63	67	65	57	45	34	24
Precip	1.6	1.8	3.2	4.3	5.0	4.7	3.6	3.8	4.6	3.9	3.5	2.3
Snow	5.9	4.1	1.9	0.1	0.0	0.0	0.0	0.0	0.0	tr	1.0	3.0

High and Low temperatures in degrees Fahrenheit; Precipitation and Snow in inches

Weather Station: Osceola — Elevation: 764 feet

	Jan	Feb	Mar	Apr	May	Jun	Jul	Aug	Sep	Oct	Nov	Dec
High	40	47	58	69	77	85	91	90	81	70	56	45
Low	21	26	35	45	54	63	68	66	58	46	36	26
Precip	1.7	2.0	3.0	4.4	4.7	4.5	3.3	4.1	4.3	4.0	3.6	2.5
Snow	5.9	4.3	1.8	0.3	0.0	0.0	0.0	0.0	0.0	tr	1.1	2.9

High and Low temperatures in degrees Fahrenheit; Precipitation and Snow in inches

Population: 9,652 (2000); Race: 97.2% White, 0.1% Black, 0.3% Asian, 0.9% American Indian and Alaska Native, 1.5% Hispanic of any race, 1.2% two or more races (2000); Density: 14.3 persons per square mile (2000); Age: 23.1% under 18, 21.2% over 64 (2000).
Religion: Five largest groups: 28.4% Southern Baptist Convention, 5.8% The United Methodist Church, 4.9% Christian Church (Disciples of Christ), 2.4% Christian Churches and Churches of Christ, 1.8% Assemblies of God (2000).
Economy: Unemployment rate: 5.1% (11/2002); Total civilian labor force: 4,148 (11/2002); Leading industries: 39.5% health care and social assistance; 20.6% retail trade; 8.7% accommodation & food services (2000); Companies that employ more than 1,000 persons: 0 (2000); Companies that employ more than 100 persons: 1 (2000); Farms: 778 totaling 262,963 acres (1997); Minority business ownership rate: 0.0% (1997); Women business ownership rate: 0.0% (1997); Retail sales per capita: $4,663 (1997). Single-family building permits issued: -1 (2001) / -1 (2000); Multi-family building permits issued: -1 (2001) / -1 (2000).
Income: Per capita income: $14,025 (2000); Median household income: $25,321 (2000); Poverty rate: 19.6% (2000); Bankruptcy rate: 2.04% (2001).
Taxes: Total county taxes per capita: $83 (2000); County property taxes per capita: $62 (2000).
Education: High school graduation rate: 73.1% (2000); College graduation rate: 9.0% (2000).
Housing: Homeownership rate: 79.5% (2000); Median home value: $48,500 (2000); Median rent: $214 per month (2000); Median age of housing: 30 years (2000).
Health: Birth rate: 94.3 per 10,000 population (1998); Age adjusted death rate: 82.0 per 10,000 population (1999); Age adjusted cancer mortality rate: 188.0 deaths per 100,000 population (1999). Number of physicians: 8.3 per 10,000 population (1999); Number of hospital beds: 74.6 per 10,000 population (1999).
Elections: 2000 Presidential election results: 39.4% Gore, 57.6% Bush, 1.7% Nader, 0.8% Buchanan
National and State Parks: Birdsong State Wildlife Area; Gallinipper Creek State Wildlife Area; Kings Prairie State Public Access; Sac-Osage State Wildlife Area; Turkey Creek State Wildlife Area; Weaubleau Creek State Wildlife Area
Additional Information Contacts
St. Clair County Government Offices 660-646-2315
Osceola Chamber of Commerce. 417-646-8020

Saint Clair County Communities

APPLETON CITY (city). Covers a land area of 1.146 square miles and a water area of 0 square miles. Located at 38.19° N. Lat.; 94.02° W. Long. Elevation is 836 feet.
History: Incorporated 1871.
Population: 1,314 (2000); Race: 97.3% White, 0.2% Black, 0.2% Asian, 0.2% American Indian and Alaska Native, 1.3% Hispanic of any race, 1.6% two or more races (2000); Density: 1,147.0 persons per square mile (2000); Age: 28.7% under 18, 28.4% over 64 (2000); Marriage status: 21.2% never married, 50.9% now married, 17.6% widowed, 10.3% divorced (2000); Foreign born: 0.9% (2000); Ancestry (includes multiple ancestries): 26.1% United States or American, 11.8% German, 9.7% Irish, 7.7% English, 7.5% Other groups (2000).
Economy: Agriculture: corn, sorghum, sweet corn; cattle. Manufactures uniforms. Employment by occupation: 8.3% management, 13.5% professional, 17.3% services, 23.3% sales, 2.1% farming, 11.7% construction, 23.8% production (2000).
Income: Per capita income: $12,566 (2000); Median household income: $23,674 (2000); Poverty rate: 23.1% (2000).
Taxes: Total city taxes per capita: $94 (1997); City property taxes per capita: $47 (1997).
Education: High school graduation rate: 66.5% (2000); College graduation rate: 8.6% (2000).

School District(s)

Appleton City R-II (KG-12)
2000 Enrollment: 427 660-476-2161
Hudson R-IX (KG-08)
2000 Enrollment: 49 660-476-5467

Housing: Homeownership rate: 68.3% (2000); Median home value: $47,000 (2000); Median rent: $201 per month (2000); Median age of housing: 37 years (2000).
Hospitals: Ellett Memorial Hospital (25 beds)
Newspapers: Appleton City Journal (1 x week)
Transportation: Commute to work: 92.4% car, 0.0% public transportation, 3.0% walk, 3.2% work from home (2000); Travel time to work: 54.6% less than 15 minutes, 9.2% 15 to 30 minutes, 20.8% 30 to 45 minutes, 2.9% 45 to 60 minutes, 12.5% 60 minutes or more (2000)

COLLINS (village). Covers a land area of 0.153 square miles and a water area of 0 square miles. Located at 37.89° N. Lat.; 93.62° W. Long. Elevation is 851 feet.
Population: 176 (2000); Race: 100.0% White, 0.0% Black, 0.0% Asian, 0.0% American Indian and Alaska Native, 0.0% Hispanic of any race, 0.0% two or more races (2000); Density: 1,154.0 persons per square mile (2000); Age: 31.8% under 18, 10.9% over 64 (2000); Marriage status: 19.0% never married, 62.0% now married, 4.9% widowed, 14.1% divorced (2000); Foreign born: 1.0% (2000); Ancestry (includes multiple ancestries): 27.9% United States or American, 12.9% English, 9.0% German, 8.0% Irish, 5.0% Other groups (2000).
Economy: Employment by occupation: 7.1% management, 9.5% professional, 27.4% services, 15.5% sales, 3.6% farming, 17.9% construction, 19.0% production (2000).
Income: Per capita income: $10,344 (2000); Median household income: $22,292 (2000); Poverty rate: 30.7% (2000).
Taxes: Total city taxes per capita: $229 (1997); City property taxes per capita: $0 (1997).

Education: High school graduation rate: 75.2% (2000); College graduation rate: 5.0% (2000).
Housing: Homeownership rate: 74.7% (2000); Median home value: $42,500 (2000); Median rent: $229 per month (2000); Median age of housing: 36 years (2000).
Transportation: Commute to work: 90.2% car, 0.0% public transportation, 2.4% walk, 4.9% work from home (2000); Travel time to work: 43.6% less than 15 minutes, 17.9% 15 to 30 minutes, 15.4% 30 to 45 minutes, 3.8% 45 to 60 minutes, 19.2% 60 minutes or more (2000)

GERSTER (town). Covers a land area of 0.079 square miles and a water area of 0 square miles. Located at 37.95° N. Lat.; 93.57° W. Long. Elevation is 804 feet.
Population: 35 (2000); Race: 94.3% White, 0.0% Black, 0.0% Asian, 5.7% American Indian and Alaska Native, 0.0% Hispanic of any race, 0.0% two or more races (2000); Density: 444.6 persons per square mile (2000); Age: 40.0% under 18, 0.0% over 64 (2000); Marriage status: 22.2% never married, 44.4% now married, 0.0% widowed, 33.3% divorced (2000); Foreign born: 0.0% (2000); Ancestry (includes multiple ancestries): 22.9% United States or American, 14.3% Irish, 11.4% Other groups, 8.6% German (2000).
Economy: Employment by occupation: 0.0% management, 0.0% professional, 55.6% services, 0.0% sales, 0.0% farming, 44.4% construction, 0.0% production (2000).
Income: Per capita income: $5,289 (2000); Median household income: $14,167 (2000); Poverty rate: 74.3% (2000).
Taxes: Total city taxes per capita: $24 (1997); City property taxes per capita: $0 (1997).
Education: High school graduation rate: 63.2% (2000); College graduation rate: 0.0% (2000).
Housing: Homeownership rate: 61.5% (2000); Median home value: $16,300 (2000); Median rent: $358 per month (2000); Median age of housing: 50 years (2000).
Transportation: Commute to work: 100.0% car, 0.0% public transportation, 0.0% walk, 0.0% work from home (2000); Travel time to work: 0.0% less than 15 minutes, 55.6% 15 to 30 minutes, 33.3% 30 to 45 minutes, 0.0% 45 to 60 minutes, 11.1% 60 minutes or more (2000)

LOWRY CITY (city). Covers a land area of 1.022 square miles and a water area of 0 square miles. Located at 38.14° N. Lat.; 93.72° W. Long. Elevation is 885 feet.
Population: 728 (2000); Race: 96.5% White, 0.0% Black, 0.0% Asian, 2.5% American Indian and Alaska Native, 6.0% Hispanic of any race, 0.7% two or more races (2000); Density: 712.6 persons per square mile (2000); Age: 22.0% under 18, 30.1% over 64 (2000); Marriage status: 21.7% never married, 47.3% now married, 18.6% widowed, 12.4% divorced (2000); Foreign born: 0.4% (2000); Ancestry (includes multiple ancestries): 22.6% United States or American, 15.2% Other groups, 10.0% Irish, 9.3% German, 5.2% English (2000).
Economy: Corn, hay; cattle. Employment by occupation: 5.3% management, 15.4% professional, 19.5% services, 22.0% sales, 0.4% farming, 17.9% construction, 19.5% production (2000).
Income: Per capita income: $10,968 (2000); Median household income: $19,438 (2000); Poverty rate: 22.1% (2000).
Taxes: Total city taxes per capita: $136 (1997); City property taxes per capita: $27 (1997).
Education: High school graduation rate: 57.1% (2000); College graduation rate: 6.5% (2000).
Housing: Homeownership rate: 62.0% (2000); Median home value: $38,500 (2000); Median rent: $223 per month (2000); Median age of housing: 34 years (2000).
Transportation: Commute to work: 94.1% car, 0.0% public transportation, 4.2% walk, 0.4% work from home (2000); Travel time to work: 45.8% less than 15 minutes, 27.7% 15 to 30 minutes, 9.2% 30 to 45 minutes, 2.9% 45 to 60 minutes, 14.3% 60 minutes or more (2000)

OSCEOLA (city). Covers a land area of 0.932 square miles and a water area of 0.023 square miles. Located at 38.04° N. Lat.; 93.70° W. Long. Elevation is 763 feet.
History: During the winter of 1835 Sanders Nance built a cabin here. Other settlers moved in and a town was laid out, named for the Seminole chief Osceola. Its location on the Osage River made Osceola a prosperous port.
Population: 835 (2000); Race: 96.3% White, 0.5% Black, 0.0% Asian, 0.2% American Indian and Alaska Native, 3.4% Hispanic of any race, 2.6% two or more races (2000); Density: 896.1 persons per square mile (2000); Age: 23.3% under 18, 22.9% over 64 (2000); Marriage status: 20.5% never married, 48.9% now married, 14.2% widowed, 16.4% divorced (2000); Foreign born: 0.0% (2000); Ancestry (includes multiple ancestries): 16.5% United States or American, 11.1% German, 9.4% English, 9.0% Other groups, 7.4% Irish (2000).
Economy: Employment by occupation: 4.8% management, 16.1% professional, 25.8% services, 21.3% sales, 0.0% farming, 10.0% construction, 21.9% production (2000).
Income: Per capita income: $17,247 (2000); Median household income: $21,563 (2000); Poverty rate: 19.1% (2000).
Taxes: Total city taxes per capita: $151 (1997); City property taxes per capita: $34 (1997).
Education: High school graduation rate: 70.9% (2000); College graduation rate: 9.8% (2000).

School District(s)

Osceola (KG-12)
2000 Enrollment: 504 417-646-8143

Housing: Homeownership rate: 62.0% (2000); Median home value: $44,800 (2000); Median rent: $196 per month (2000); Median age of housing: 39 years (2000).
Hospitals: Sac-Osage Hospital (47 beds)
Newspapers: Saint Clair County Courier (1 x week)
Transportation: Commute to work: 97.6% car, 0.0% public transportation, 2.1% walk, 0.3% work from home (2000); Travel time to work: 56.4% less than 15 minutes, 10.0% 15 to 30 minutes, 18.6% 30 to 45 minutes, 4.1% 45 to 60 minutes, 11.0% 60 minutes or more (2000)
Additional Information Contacts
Osceola Chamber of Commerce. 417-646-8020

ROSCOE (village). Covers a land area of 1.430 square miles and a water area of 0.232 square miles. Located at 37.97° N. Lat.; 93.81° W. Long. Elevation is 763 feet.
Population: 112 (2000); Race: 100.0% White, 0.0% Black, 0.0% Asian, 0.0% American Indian and Alaska Native, 0.0% Hispanic of any race, 0.0% two or more races (2000); Density: 78.3 persons per square mile (2000); Age: 18.9% under 18, 34.4% over 64 (2000); Marriage status: 7.0% never married, 60.0% now married, 17.0% widowed, 16.0% divorced (2000); Foreign born: 0.0% (2000); Ancestry (includes multiple ancestries): 22.1% United States or American, 21.3% German, 10.7% Other groups, 9.0% English, 6.6% Irish (2000).
Economy: Employment by occupation: 10.5% management, 5.3% professional, 21.1% services, 10.5% sales, 0.0% farming, 2.6% construction, 50.0% production (2000).
Income: Per capita income: $11,377 (2000); Median household income: $30,278 (2000); Poverty rate: 19.7% (2000).
Taxes: Total city taxes per capita: $19 (1997); City property taxes per capita: $19 (1997).
Education: High school graduation rate: 60.6% (2000); College graduation rate: 0.0% (2000).

School District(s)

Roscoe C-1 (KG-08)
2000 Enrollment: 64 417-646-2376

Housing: Homeownership rate: 85.7% (2000); Median home value: $37,800 (2000); Median rent: $125 per month (2000); Median age of housing: 56 years (2000).
Transportation: Commute to work: 94.7% car, 0.0% public transportation, 0.0% walk, 5.3% work from home (2000); Travel time to work: 19.4% less than 15 minutes, 30.6% 15 to 30 minutes, 16.7% 30 to 45 minutes, 16.7% 45 to 60 minutes, 16.7% 60 minutes or more (2000)

VISTA (village). Covers a land area of 0.131 square miles and a water area of 0 square miles. Located at 37.98° N. Lat.; 93.66° W. Long. Elevation is 870 feet.
Population: 55 (2000); Race: 95.0% White, 0.0% Black, 0.0% Asian, 5.0% American Indian and Alaska Native, 0.0% Hispanic of any race, 0.0% two or more races (2000); Density: 419.4 persons per square mile (2000); Age: 20.0% under 18, 25.0% over 64 (2000); Marriage status: 0.0% never married, 93.8% now married, 6.3% widowed, 0.0% divorced (2000); Foreign born: 0.0% (2000); Ancestry (includes multiple ancestries): 22.5% United States or American, 15.0% Irish, 5.0% Other groups, 5.0% German, 5.0% English (2000).
Economy: Employment by occupation: 0.0% management, 0.0% professional, 0.0% services, 10.0% sales, 0.0% farming, 30.0% construction, 60.0% production (2000).
Income: Per capita income: $12,068 (2000); Median household income: $30,000 (2000); Poverty rate: 15.0% (2000).
Taxes: Total city taxes per capita: $19 (1997); City property taxes per capita: $0 (1997).

Education: High school graduation rate: 71.9% (2000); College graduation rate: 0.0% (2000).
Housing: Homeownership rate: 100.0% (2000); Median home value: $27,500 (2000); Median age of housing: 57 years (2000).
Transportation: Commute to work: 100.0% car, 0.0% public transportation, 0.0% walk, 0.0% work from home (2000); Travel time to work: 10.0% less than 15 minutes, 10.0% 15 to 30 minutes, 20.0% 30 to 45 minutes, 60.0% 45 to 60 minutes, 0.0% 60 minutes or more (2000)

Saint Francois County

Located in eastern Missouri, partly in the St. Francois Mountains; drained by the Big and St. Francis Rivers; includes part of Clark National Forest. Covers a land area of 449.50 square miles, a water area of 2.90 square miles, and is located in the Central Time Zone. The county government was organized in 1821. County seat is Farmington.

Weather Station: Farmington Elevation: 898 feet

	Jan	Feb	Mar	Apr	May	Jun	Jul	Aug	Sep	Oct	Nov	Dec
High	39	45	55	67	75	83	88	87	79	68	55	44
Low	19	23	33	43	51	60	65	62	55	43	33	24
Precip	2.3	2.4	4.0	4.2	4.4	3.5	3.7	4.1	3.5	3.0	4.4	3.5
Snow	3.4	4.2	2.3	0.1	0.0	0.0	0.0	0.0	0.0	tr	0.9	2.2

High and Low temperatures in degrees Fahrenheit; Precipitation and Snow in inches

Population: 55,641 (2000); Race: 96.0% White, 2.1% Black, 0.5% Asian, 0.3% American Indian and Alaska Native, 0.7% Hispanic of any race, 0.9% two or more races (2000); Density: 123.8 persons per square mile (2000); Age: 23.9% under 18, 15.0% over 64 (2000).
Religion: Five largest groups: 23.2% Southern Baptist Convention, 7.6% Catholic Church, 4.2% The United Methodist Church, 2.7% Assemblies of God, 2.7% Lutheran Church—Missouri Synod (2000).
Economy: Unemployment rate: 7.1% (11/2002); Total civilian labor force: 24,025 (11/2002); Leading industries: 26.3% health care and social assistance; 18.1% retail trade; 14.7% manufacturing (2000); Companies that employ more than 1,000 persons: 0 (2000); Companies that employ more than 100 persons: 22 (2000); Farms: 649 totaling 112,842 acres (1997); Minority business ownership rate: 0.0% (1997); Women business ownership rate: 15.4% (1997); Retail sales per capita: $8,053 (1997). Single-family building permits issued: 154 (2001) / 122 (2000); Multi-family building permits issued: 46 (2001) / 118 (2000).
Income: Per capita income: $15,273 (2000); Median household income: $31,199 (2000); Poverty rate: 14.9% (2000); Bankruptcy rate: 5.58% (2001).
Taxes: Total county taxes per capita: $59 (2000); County property taxes per capita: $9 (2000).
Education: High school graduation rate: 72.4% (2000); College graduation rate: 10.2% (2000).
Housing: Homeownership rate: 73.2% (2000); Median home value: $68,200 (2000); Median rent: $321 per month (2000); Median age of housing: 27 years (2000).
Health: Birth rate: 122.0 per 10,000 population (1998); Age adjusted death rate: 113.1 per 10,000 population (1999); Age adjusted cancer mortality rate: 265.0 deaths per 100,000 population (1999). Number of physicians: 10.1 per 10,000 population (1999); Number of hospital beds: 83.9 per 10,000 population (1999).
Elections: 2000 Presidential election results: 48.2% Gore, 49.5% Bush, 1.4% Nader, 0.5% Buchanan
National and State Parks: Saint Francois State Park; Saint Joe State Park
Additional Information Contacts
St. Francois County Government Offices 573-756-3623
Bonne Terre Chamber of Commerce 573-358-4000
Desloge Chamber of Commerce 573-431-3006
Farmington Chamber of Commerce 573-756-3615
Leadington Chamber of Commerce 573-431-7424
Mineral Area Board of Realtors 573-756-5576
Park Hills Chamber of Commerce 573-431-1051

Saint Francois County Communities

BISMARCK (city). Covers a land area of 0.995 square miles and a water area of 0 square miles. Located at 37.76° N. Lat.; 90.62° W. Long. Elevation is 1,025 feet.
History: Laid out 1868.
Population: 1,470 (2000); Race: 99.3% White, 0.0% Black, 0.0% Asian, 0.0% American Indian and Alaska Native, 0.6% Hispanic of any race, 0.7% two or more races (2000); Density: 1,477.1 persons per square mile (2000); Age: 25.9% under 18, 15.3% over 64 (2000); Marriage status: 22.6% never married, 59.5% now married, 8.8% widowed, 9.1% divorced (2000); Foreign born: 0.3% (2000); Ancestry (includes multiple ancestries): 23.4% United States or American, 13.7% German, 13.4% Irish, 7.8% English, 6.5% Other groups (2000).
Economy: Agriculture: cattle. Manufacturing: machinery; lumber products; former important iron and lead mining. Railroad junction. Employment by occupation: 6.4% management, 13.1% professional, 26.5% services, 19.3% sales, 1.1% farming, 13.8% construction, 19.8% production (2000).
Income: Per capita income: $12,150 (2000); Median household income: $24,583 (2000); Poverty rate: 20.9% (2000).
Taxes: Total city taxes per capita: $101 (1997); City property taxes per capita: $17 (1997).
Education: High school graduation rate: 67.4% (2000); College graduation rate: 6.2% (2000).

School District(s)
Bismarck R-V (KG-12)
2000 Enrollment: 685 573-734-6111
Housing: Homeownership rate: 72.0% (2000); Median home value: $47,300 (2000); Median rent: $244 per month (2000); Median age of housing: 39 years (2000).
Transportation: Commute to work: 96.2% car, 0.5% public transportation, 0.7% walk, 2.5% work from home (2000); Travel time to work: 22.1% less than 15 minutes, 41.4% 15 to 30 minutes, 13.2% 30 to 45 minutes, 8.0% 45 to 60 minutes, 15.2% 60 minutes or more (2000)

BLACKWELL (unincorporated postal area, zip code 63626). Covers a land area of 7.962 square miles and a water area of 0.168 square miles. Located at 38.05° N. Lat.; 90.64° W. Long. Elevation is 588 feet.
Population: 142 (2000); Race: 100.0% White, 0.0% Black, 0.0% Asian, 0.0% American Indian and Alaska Native, 0.0% Hispanic of any race, 0.0% two or more races (2000); Density: 17.8 persons per square mile (2000); Age: 35.0% under 18, 17.5% over 64 (2000); Marriage status: 25.0% never married, 62.2% now married, 12.8% widowed, 0.0% divorced (2000); Foreign born: 0.0% (2000); Ancestry (includes multiple ancestries): 20.9% United States or American, 18.0% Irish, 13.1% Italian, 13.1% Other groups, 8.3% Dutch (2000).
Economy: Employment by occupation: 33.8% management, 26.2% professional, 0.0% services, 10.8% sales, 0.0% farming, 0.0% construction, 29.2% production (2000).
Income: Per capita income: $13,661 (2000); Median household income: $40,179 (2000); Poverty rate: 24.3% (2000).
Education: High school graduation rate: 57.3% (2000); College graduation rate: 22.2% (2000).
Housing: Homeownership rate: 86.4% (2000); Median home value: <$10,000 (2000); Median rent: $175 per month (2000); Median age of housing: 15 years (2000).
Transportation: Commute to work: 100.0% car, 0.0% public transportation, 0.0% walk, 0.0% work from home (2000); Travel time to work: 0.0% less than 15 minutes, 35.4% 15 to 30 minutes, 12.3% 30 to 45 minutes, 12.3% 45 to 60 minutes, 40.0% 60 minutes or more (2000)

BONNE TERRE (city). Covers a land area of 4.039 square miles and a water area of 0.067 square miles. Located at 37.92° N. Lat.; 90.55° W. Long. Elevation is 830 feet.
History: Bonne Terre began as a lead-mining town around the operations of the St. Joseph Lead Company. Bonne Terre was incorporated in 1864.
Population: 4,039 (2000); Race: 99.7% White, 0.0% Black, 0.0% Asian, 0.0% American Indian and Alaska Native, 0.1% Hispanic of any race, 0.3% two or more races (2000); Density: 1,000.0 persons per square mile (2000); Age: 26.9% under 18, 16.2% over 64 (2000); Marriage status: 20.5% never married, 56.1% now married, 8.6% widowed, 14.7% divorced (2000); Foreign born: 0.7% (2000); Ancestry (includes multiple ancestries): 18.8% German, 18.8% United States or American, 12.6% Irish, 10.5% French (except Basque), 8.1% Other groups (2000).
Economy: Single-family building permits issued: 4 (2001) / 6 (2000); Multi-family building permits issued: 12 (2001) / 8 (2000); Employment by occupation: 10.7% management, 9.7% professional, 15.3% services, 26.4% sales, 0.7% farming, 14.7% construction, 22.4% production (2000).
Income: Per capita income: $15,062 (2000); Median household income: $29,929 (2000); Poverty rate: 15.4% (2000).
Taxes: Total city taxes per capita: $199 (1997); City property taxes per capita: $46 (1997).
Education: High school graduation rate: 69.2% (2000); College graduation rate: 6.0% (2000).

School District(s)

North Saint Francois Co. R-I (PK-12)
2000 Enrollment: 3,231 573-358-2247

Housing: Homeownership rate: 66.6% (2000); Median home value: $54,600 (2000); Median rent: $298 per month (2000); Median age of housing: 49 years (2000).

Safety: Violent crime rate: 22.1 per 10,000 population; Property crime rate: 228.8 per 10,000 population (2001).

Transportation: Commute to work: 96.1% car, 0.0% public transportation, 2.4% walk, 0.7% work from home (2000); Travel time to work: 30.4% less than 15 minutes, 29.2% 15 to 30 minutes, 10.6% 30 to 45 minutes, 7.3% 45 to 60 minutes, 22.5% 60 minutes or more (2000)

Additional Information Contacts

Bonne Terre Chamber of Commerce 573-358-4000

DESLOGE (city). Covers a land area of 2.655 square miles and a water area of 0 square miles. Located at 37.87° N. Lat.; 90.52° W. Long. Elevation is 805 feet.

History: Incorporated 1940.

Population: 4,802 (2000); Race: 98.6% White, 0.3% Black, 0.8% Asian, 0.0% American Indian and Alaska Native, 0.3% Hispanic of any race, 0.3% two or more races (2000); Density: 1,808.8 persons per square mile (2000); Age: 24.8% under 18, 16.1% over 64 (2000); Marriage status: 22.4% never married, 54.7% now married, 10.0% widowed, 12.9% divorced (2000); Foreign born: 0.7% (2000); Ancestry (includes multiple ancestries): 16.5% United States or American, 13.5% German, 12.2% Irish, 8.8% French (except Basque), 7.1% Other groups (2000).

Economy: Former lead-mining area. Light manufacturing. Single-family building permits issued: 8 (2001) / 7 (2000); Multi-family building permits issued: 4 (2001) / 2 (2000); Employment by occupation: 7.8% management, 14.6% professional, 21.3% services, 23.8% sales, 0.0% farming, 15.4% construction, 17.0% production (2000).

Income: Per capita income: $16,235 (2000); Median household income: $31,956 (2000); Poverty rate: 10.2% (2000).

Taxes: Total city taxes per capita: $153 (1997); City property taxes per capita: $37 (1997).

Education: High school graduation rate: 76.2% (2000); College graduation rate: 10.8% (2000).

Housing: Homeownership rate: 69.5% (2000); Median home value: $65,200 (2000); Median rent: $339 per month (2000); Median age of housing: 28 years (2000).

Transportation: Commute to work: 92.8% car, 0.5% public transportation, 1.7% walk, 4.7% work from home (2000); Travel time to work: 43.5% less than 15 minutes, 29.7% 15 to 30 minutes, 4.7% 30 to 45 minutes, 6.1% 45 to 60 minutes, 16.1% 60 minutes or more (2000)

Additional Information Contacts

Desloge Chamber of Commerce 573-431-3006

DOE RUN (unincorporated postal area, zip code 63637). Covers a land area of 12.033 square miles and a water area of 0.032 square miles. Located at 37.73° N. Lat.; 90.51° W. Long. Elevation is 940 feet.

Population: 807 (2000); Race: 98.8% White, 0.0% Black, 0.0% Asian, 0.8% American Indian and Alaska Native, 0.0% Hispanic of any race, 0.4% two or more races (2000); Density: 67.1 persons per square mile (2000); Age: 34.2% under 18, 9.8% over 64 (2000); Marriage status: 28.5% never married, 54.1% now married, 4.7% widowed, 12.7% divorced (2000); Foreign born: 0.4% (2000); Ancestry (includes multiple ancestries): 49.5% United States or American, 9.0% German, 7.8% Irish, 5.4% Other groups, 4.0% Swedish (2000).

Economy: Employment by occupation: 15.7% management, 16.9% professional, 18.5% services, 22.7% sales, 0.0% farming, 8.3% construction, 17.9% production (2000).

Income: Per capita income: $10,776 (2000); Median household income: $30,625 (2000); Poverty rate: 17.5% (2000).

Education: High school graduation rate: 72.4% (2000); College graduation rate: 9.7% (2000).

Housing: Homeownership rate: 79.3% (2000); Median home value: $37,100 (2000); Median rent: $234 per month (2000); Median age of housing: 28 years (2000).

Transportation: Commute to work: 86.3% car, 7.5% public transportation, 0.7% walk, 4.9% work from home (2000); Travel time to work: 28.2% less than 15 minutes, 40.5% 15 to 30 minutes, 21.6% 30 to 45 minutes, 3.4% 45 to 60 minutes, 6.2% 60 minutes or more (2000)

FARMINGTON (city). Covers a land area of 8.954 square miles and a water area of 0.044 square miles. Located at 37.78° N. Lat.; 90.42° W. Long. Elevation is 918 feet.

History: Farmington was settled in 1799 by William Murphy. The town was incorporated in 1823, two years after it was named the seat of St. Francois County.

Population: 13,924 (2000); Race: 89.4% White, 7.6% Black, 1.2% Asian, 0.4% American Indian and Alaska Native, 0.8% Hispanic of any race, 1.3% two or more races (2000); Density: 1,555.0 persons per square mile (2000); Age: 19.2% under 18, 17.0% over 64 (2000); Marriage status: 24.2% never married, 52.4% now married, 8.1% widowed, 15.3% divorced (2000); Foreign born: 1.6% (2000); Ancestry (includes multiple ancestries): 15.4% German, 14.1% Other groups, 13.1% United States or American, 11.1% Irish, 9.1% English (2000).

Vital Statistics: Birth rate: 117.8 per 10,000 population (1998)

Economy: Single-family building permits issued: 41 (2001) / 42 (2000); Multi-family building permits issued: 18 (2001) / 12 (2000); Employment by occupation: 10.9% management, 20.9% professional, 21.2% services, 24.1% sales, 0.9% farming, 7.3% construction, 14.6% production (2000).

Income: Per capita income: $14,706 (2000); Median household income: $30,251 (2000); Poverty rate: 12.4% (2000).

Taxes: Total city taxes per capita: $253 (2000); City property taxes per capita: $33 (2000).

Education: High school graduation rate: 72.0% (2000); College graduation rate: 12.7% (2000).

School District(s)

Farmington R-VII (PK-12)
2000 Enrollment: 3,643 573-701-1300

Two-year College(s)

Mineral Area Regional Medical Center-School of Rad Techn (Private, Not-for-profit)
2001 Enrollment: 25 573-756-4581
2001 Tuition: In-state $1,350; Out-of-state $1,350

Housing: Homeownership rate: 62.3% (2000); Median home value: $81,300 (2000); Median rent: $367 per month (2000); Median age of housing: 27 years (2000).

Hospitals: Mineral Area Regional Medical Center (145 beds); Parkland Health Center (130 beds); Southeast Missouri Mental Health Center (184 beds)

Safety: Violent crime rate: 94.9 per 10,000 population; Property crime rate: 414.7 per 10,000 population (2001).

Newspapers: Farmington Press (7 x week)

Transportation: Commute to work: 94.2% car, 0.7% public transportation, 2.0% walk, 2.7% work from home (2000); Travel time to work: 64.0% less than 15 minutes, 18.3% 15 to 30 minutes, 5.8% 30 to 45 minutes, 2.1% 45 to 60 minutes, 9.8% 60 minutes or more (2000)

Additional Information Contacts

Farmington Chamber of Commerce 573-756-3615
Mineral Area Board of Realtors 573-756-5576

FRENCH VILLAGE (unincorporated postal area, zip code 63036). Covers a land area of 30.677 square miles and a water area of 0.408 square miles. Located at 37.97° N. Lat.; 90.34° W. Long. Elevation is 903 feet.

Population: 961 (2000); Race: 98.5% White, 0.0% Black, 0.0% Asian, 0.0% American Indian and Alaska Native, 0.0% Hispanic of any race, 1.5% two or more races (2000); Density: 31.3 persons per square mile (2000); Age: 21.0% under 18, 18.2% over 64 (2000); Marriage status: 18.9% never married, 63.7% now married, 3.3% widowed, 14.1% divorced (2000); Foreign born: 0.7% (2000); Ancestry (includes multiple ancestries): 22.8% German, 17.8% United States or American, 13.2% Irish, 13.0% Other groups, 10.0% French (except Basque) (2000).

Economy: Employment by occupation: 6.7% management, 4.7% professional, 24.4% services, 18.4% sales, 1.8% farming, 14.0% construction, 30.0% production (2000).

Income: Per capita income: $16,260 (2000); Median household income: $37,778 (2000); Poverty rate: 12.5% (2000).

Education: High school graduation rate: 67.3% (2000); College graduation rate: 2.8% (2000).

Housing: Homeownership rate: 92.6% (2000); Median home value: $76,000 (2000); Median rent: $325 per month (2000); Median age of housing: 17 years (2000).

Transportation: Commute to work: 88.7% car, 1.4% public transportation, 0.0% walk, 6.3% work from home (2000); Travel time to work: 11.1% less than 15 minutes, 29.9% 15 to 30 minutes, 13.3% 30 to 45 minutes, 8.7% 45 to 60 minutes, 37.1% 60 minutes or more (2000)

IRON MOUNTAIN LAKE (city). Covers a land area of 1.970 square miles and a water area of 0.115 square miles. Located at 37.68° N. Lat.; 90.62° W. Long. Elevation is 1,055 feet.
Population: 693 (2000); Race: 97.2% White, 0.0% Black, 0.0% Asian, 0.1% American Indian and Alaska Native, 1.7% Hispanic of any race, 2.7% two or more races (2000); Density: 351.8 persons per square mile (2000); Age: 28.1% under 18, 13.8% over 64 (2000); Marriage status: 16.7% never married, 61.3% now married, 6.7% widowed, 15.4% divorced (2000); Foreign born: 0.8% (2000); Ancestry (includes multiple ancestries): 19.5% United States or American, 18.8% Other groups, 16.1% Irish, 10.7% German, 4.9% English (2000).
Economy: Single-family building permits issued: 0 (2001) / 0 (2000); Multi-family building permits issued: 0 (2001) / 0 (2000); Employment by occupation: 4.3% management, 7.6% professional, 26.7% services, 13.8% sales, 1.4% farming, 23.3% construction, 22.9% production (2000).
Income: Per capita income: $9,399 (2000); Median household income: $19,583 (2000); Poverty rate: 34.9% (2000).
Taxes: Total city taxes per capita: $38 (1997); City property taxes per capita: $13 (1997).
Education: High school graduation rate: 55.2% (2000); College graduation rate: 1.7% (2000).
Housing: Homeownership rate: 82.4% (2000); Median home value: $28,400 (2000); Median rent: $254 per month (2000); Median age of housing: 33 years (2000).
Transportation: Commute to work: 98.1% car, 0.0% public transportation, 0.0% walk, 1.0% work from home (2000); Travel time to work: 7.3% less than 15 minutes, 34.1% 15 to 30 minutes, 21.5% 30 to 45 minutes, 4.4% 45 to 60 minutes, 32.7% 60 minutes or more (2000)

LEADINGTON (city). Covers a land area of 0.681 square miles and a water area of 0 square miles. Located at 37.83° N. Lat.; 90.48° W. Long. Elevation is 840 feet.
Population: 206 (2000); Race: 99.0% White, 1.0% Black, 0.0% Asian, 0.0% American Indian and Alaska Native, 0.0% Hispanic of any race, 0.0% two or more races (2000); Density: 302.5 persons per square mile (2000); Age: 19.8% under 18, 24.8% over 64 (2000); Marriage status: 22.9% never married, 46.9% now married, 11.4% widowed, 18.9% divorced (2000); Foreign born: 0.0% (2000); Ancestry (includes multiple ancestries): 20.3% United States or American, 18.8% German, 10.4% Irish, 8.9% Other groups, 7.9% English (2000).
Economy: Employment by occupation: 14.5% management, 16.1% professional, 9.7% services, 33.9% sales, 0.0% farming, 4.8% construction, 21.0% production (2000).
Income: Per capita income: $13,336 (2000); Median household income: $19,722 (2000); Poverty rate: 13.9% (2000).
Taxes: Total city taxes per capita: $1,218 (1997); City property taxes per capita: $41 (1997).
Education: High school graduation rate: 60.7% (2000); College graduation rate: 5.2% (2000).
Housing: Homeownership rate: 51.6% (2000); Median home value: $54,300 (2000); Median rent: $211 per month (2000); Median age of housing: 35 years (2000).
Transportation: Commute to work: 91.9% car, 0.0% public transportation, 0.0% walk, 0.0% work from home (2000); Travel time to work: 40.3% less than 15 minutes, 17.7% 15 to 30 minutes, 12.9% 30 to 45 minutes, 12.9% 45 to 60 minutes, 16.1% 60 minutes or more (2000)

LEADWOOD (city). Covers a land area of 1.157 square miles and a water area of 0 square miles. Located at 37.86° N. Lat.; 90.59° W. Long. Elevation is 805 feet.
History: Former mining town.
Population: 1,160 (2000); Race: 99.3% White, 0.0% Black, 0.0% Asian, 0.3% American Indian and Alaska Native, 0.0% Hispanic of any race, 0.4% two or more races (2000); Density: 1,002.5 persons per square mile (2000); Age: 29.6% under 18, 11.5% over 64 (2000); Marriage status: 21.3% never married, 60.1% now married, 7.4% widowed, 11.1% divorced (2000); Foreign born: 0.3% (2000); Ancestry (includes multiple ancestries): 17.3% United States or American, 14.8% Other groups, 11.8% German, 11.3% Irish, 7.3% English (2000).
Economy: Sand and gravel. Single-family building permits issued: 0 (2001) / 0 (2000); Multi-family building permits issued: 0 (2001) / 0 (2000); Employment by occupation: 3.3% management, 11.1% professional, 14.1% services, 20.3% sales, 2.6% farming, 24.4% construction, 24.2% production (2000).
Income: Per capita income: $11,402 (2000); Median household income: $25,391 (2000); Poverty rate: 19.6% (2000).
Taxes: Total city taxes per capita: $96 (1997); City property taxes per capita: $24 (1997).
Education: High school graduation rate: 69.8% (2000); College graduation rate: 7.0% (2000).

School District(s)

West Saint Francois Co. R-IV (PK-12)
2000 Enrollment: 1,029 573-562-7535
Housing: Homeownership rate: 79.4% (2000); Median home value: $35,300 (2000); Median rent: $258 per month (2000); Median age of housing: 56 years (2000).
Transportation: Commute to work: 94.8% car, 0.0% public transportation, 1.8% walk, 1.8% work from home (2000); Travel time to work: 28.8% less than 15 minutes, 30.1% 15 to 30 minutes, 12.7% 30 to 45 minutes, 7.9% 45 to 60 minutes, 20.6% 60 minutes or more (2000)

PARK HILLS (city). Aka Elvins. Covers a land area of 20.029 square miles and a water area of 0.117 square miles. Located at 37.84° N. Lat.; 90.51° W. Long. Elevation is 740 feet.
History: Located in lead-mining belt, Park Hills was created in 1993 with the merger of towns of Flat River, Elvins, Rivermines and Esther.
Population: 7,861 (2000); Race: 97.0% White, 0.6% Black, 0.4% Asian, 0.0% American Indian and Alaska Native, 1.2% Hispanic of any race, 1.3% two or more races (2000); Density: 392.5 persons per square mile (2000); Age: 26.6% under 18, 13.7% over 64 (2000); Marriage status: 22.9% never married, 53.1% now married, 8.3% widowed, 15.7% divorced (2000); Foreign born: 1.5% (2000); Ancestry (includes multiple ancestries): 19.0% United States or American, 13.6% Other groups, 12.5% Irish, 10.9% German, 8.2% French (except Basque) (2000).
Economy: Located in lead-mining belt. Chickens, cattle, hogs, hay, lead, sand and gravel. Manufacturing includes printing and publishing, glass products and concrete products. Single-family building permits issued: 26 (2001) / 13 (2000); Multi-family building permits issued: 12 (2001) / 96 (2000); Employment by occupation: 3.3% management, 15.5% professional, 22.1% services, 24.7% sales, 0.0% farming, 11.1% construction, 23.2% production (2000).
Income: Per capita income: $13,048 (2000); Median household income: $25,277 (2000); Poverty rate: 21.1% (2000).
Taxes: Total city taxes per capita: $280 (2000); City property taxes per capita: $32 (2000).
Education: High school graduation rate: 69.5% (2000); College graduation rate: 9.6% (2000).

School District(s)

Central R-III (PK-12)
2000 Enrollment: 1,860 573-431-2616

Two-year College(s)

Mineral Area College (Public)
2001 Enrollment: 2,878 573-431-4593
2001 Tuition: In-state $1,980; Out-of-state $2,610
Housing: Homeownership rate: 59.2% (2000); Median home value: $53,900 (2000); Median rent: $306 per month (2000); Median age of housing: 41 years (2000).
Newspapers: The Daily Journal (7 x week)
Transportation: Commute to work: 96.0% car, 0.7% public transportation, 0.9% walk, 1.5% work from home (2000); Travel time to work: 43.4% less than 15 minutes, 30.4% 15 to 30 minutes, 5.5% 30 to 45 minutes, 5.6% 45 to 60 minutes, 15.0% 60 minutes or more (2000)
Additional Information Contacts
Leadington Chamber of Commerce 573-431-7424
Park Hills Chamber of Commerce 573-431-1051

VALLES MINES (unincorporated postal area, zip code 63087). Covers a land area of 21.661 square miles and a water area of 0.050 square miles. Located at 38.00° N. Lat.; 90.44° W. Long.
Population: 915 (2000); Race: 99.4% White, 0.0% Black, 0.0% Asian, 0.0% American Indian and Alaska Native, 0.0% Hispanic of any race, 0.6% two or more races (2000); Density: 42.2 persons per square mile (2000); Age: 30.9% under 18, 10.2% over 64 (2000); Marriage status: 22.7% never married, 64.9% now married, 4.0% widowed, 8.4% divorced (2000); Foreign born: 2.2% (2000); Ancestry (includes multiple ancestries): 21.9% German, 15.9% United States or American, 15.2% Irish, 14.3% Other groups, 7.5% French (except Basque) (2000).
Economy: Employment by occupation: 19.4% management, 5.5% professional, 21.4% services, 11.7% sales, 5.5% farming, 14.9% construction, 21.7% production (2000).

Income: Per capita income: $12,610 (2000); Median household income: $27,464 (2000); Poverty rate: 20.3% (2000).
Education: High school graduation rate: 70.3% (2000); College graduation rate: 3.1% (2000).
Housing: Homeownership rate: 72.1% (2000); Median home value: $69,400 (2000); Median rent: $263 per month (2000); Median age of housing: 19 years (2000).
Transportation: Commute to work: 88.3% car, 0.0% public transportation, 0.0% walk, 11.7% work from home (2000); Travel time to work: 15.8% less than 15 minutes, 34.1% 15 to 30 minutes, 12.8% 30 to 45 minutes, 9.5% 45 to 60 minutes, 27.8% 60 minutes or more (2000)

Saint Louis County

Located in eastern Missouri; bounded on the east by the Mississippi River and the Illinois border, on the northwest by the Missouri River, and on the southeast and southwest by the Meramec River. Covers a land area of 507.80 square miles, a water area of 15.90 square miles, and is located in the Central Time Zone. The county government was organized in 1812. County seat is Clayton.

Saint Louis County is part of the St. Louis, MO-IL MSA. The entire metro area includes: Clinton County, IL; Jersey County, IL; Madison County, IL; Monroe County, IL; St. Clair County, IL; Crawford County, MO (pt.)**; Franklin County, MO; Jefferson County, MO; Lincoln County, MO; St. Charles County, MO; St. Louis County, MO; Warren County, MO; St. Louis city, MO

Weather Station: Saint Louis Lambert Int'l Arpt. Elevation: 567 feet

	Jan	Feb	Mar	Apr	May	Jun	Jul	Aug	Sep	Oct	Nov	Dec
High	38	44	55	67	76	85	89	87	80	68	54	43
Low	21	26	36	46	56	66	70	68	60	48	37	27
Precip	2.1	2.2	3.6	3.9	4.0	3.7	3.9	3.1	3.1	2.8	3.6	2.9
Snow	7.0	4.8	3.2	0.8	tr	tr	tr	0.0	0.0	tr	1.5	4.3

High and Low temperatures in degrees Fahrenheit; Precipitation and Snow in inches

Population: 1,016,315 (2000); Race: 76.9% White, 18.9% Black, 2.1% Asian, 0.2% American Indian and Alaska Native, 1.4% Hispanic of any race, 1.4% two or more races (2000); Density: 2,001.4 persons per square mile (2000); Age: 25.2% under 18, 14.1% over 64 (2000).
Religion: Five largest groups: 29.6% Catholic Church, 5.1% Southern Baptist Convention, 4.6% Jewish estimate, 3.9% Lutheran Church—Missouri Synod, 2.3% The United Methodist Church (2000).
Economy: Unemployment rate: 4.2% (11/2002); Total civilian labor force: 561,893 (11/2002); Leading industries: 12.6% retail trade; 11.9% health care and social assistance; 10.1% manufacturing (2000); Companies that employ more than 1,000 persons: 39 (2000); Companies that employ more than 100 persons: 966 (2000); Farms: 291 totaling 45,019 acres (1997); Minority business ownership rate: 9.6% (1997); Women business ownership rate: 27.1% (1997); Retail sales per capita: $12,364 (1997). Single-family building permits issued: 1,868 (2001) / 1,993 (2000); Multi-family building permits issued: 586 (2001) / 698 (2000).
Income: Per capita income: $27,595 (2000); Median household income: $50,532 (2000); Poverty rate: 6.9% (2000); Bankruptcy rate: 6.50% (2001).
Taxes: Total county taxes per capita: $379 (2000); County property taxes per capita: $87 (2000).
Education: High school graduation rate: 88.0% (2000); College graduation rate: 35.4% (2000).
Housing: Homeownership rate: 74.1% (2000); Median home value: $116,600 (2000); Median rent: $505 per month (2000); Median age of housing: 34 years (2000).
Health: Birth rate: 126.2 per 10,000 population (1998); Age adjusted death rate: 89.9 per 10,000 population (1999); Infant mortality rate: 8.5 per 1,000 live births (1998); Age adjusted cancer mortality rate: 205.7 deaths per 100,000 population (1999). Air Quality Index: 65% good, 35% moderate, 0% unhealthy (percent of days in 2000). Number of physicians: 65.5 per 10,000 population (1999); Number of hospital beds: 7.5 per 10,000 population (1999).
Elections: 2000 Presidential election results: 51.5% Gore, 46.2% Bush, 1.7% Nader, 0.2% Buchanan
National and State Parks: Babler State Park; Castlewood State Park
Additional Information Contacts
St. Louis County Government Offices 314-615-5432
Chesterfield Chamber of Commerce 636-532-3399
Crestwood-Sunset Hills Chamber 314-843-8545
Eureka Chamber of Commerce 636-938-6062
Fenton Chamber of Commerce 636-343-3839
Ferguson Chamber of Commerce 314-521-6000
Florissant Chamber of Commerce 314-831-3500
Kirkwood Area Chamber of Commerce 314-821-4161
Overland Chamber of Commerce 314-423-9913
Town & Country Chamber of Commerce 636-230-0289
Webster Groves Chamber of Commerce 314-962-4142
West County Chamber of Commerce 636-458-6200

Saint Louis County Communities

AFFTON (CDP). Covers a land area of 4.584 square miles and a water area of 0 square miles. Located at 38.55° N. Lat.; 90.32° W. Long. Elevation is 609 feet.
Population: 20,535 (2000); Race: 96.9% White, 0.3% Black, 1.5% Asian, 0.2% American Indian and Alaska Native, 1.0% Hispanic of any race, 0.8% two or more races (2000); Density: 4,480.1 persons per square mile (2000); Age: 22.2% under 18, 19.1% over 64 (2000); Marriage status: 24.7% never married, 57.5% now married, 8.7% widowed, 9.2% divorced (2000); Foreign born: 4.6% (2000); Ancestry (includes multiple ancestries): 43.0% German, 19.8% Irish, 9.3% Italian, 8.9% English, 6.6% United States or American (2000).
Economy: Manufactures food, machinery, consumer goods, medical equipment. Grant's Farm tourist attraction in adjacent Grantwood Village. Employment by occupation: 14.4% management, 19.8% professional, 13.1% services, 32.0% sales, 0.0% farming, 8.3% construction, 12.5% production (2000).
Income: Per capita income: $22,059 (2000); Median household income: $43,327 (2000); Poverty rate: 3.6% (2000).
Education: High school graduation rate: 83.8% (2000); College graduation rate: 21.3% (2000).
Housing: Homeownership rate: 79.7% (2000); Median home value: $97,000 (2000); Median rent: $440 per month (2000); Median age of housing: 43 years (2000).
Transportation: Commute to work: 96.1% car, 0.9% public transportation, 0.6% walk, 2.1% work from home (2000); Travel time to work: 21.5% less than 15 minutes, 48.6% 15 to 30 minutes, 22.9% 30 to 45 minutes, 4.3% 45 to 60 minutes, 2.7% 60 minutes or more (2000)
Additional Information Contacts
Affton Chamber of Commerce 314-849-6499

BALLWIN (city). Covers a land area of 8.952 square miles and a water area of 0 square miles. Located at 38.59° N. Lat.; 90.54° W. Long. Elevation is 659 feet.
Population: 31,283 (2000); Race: 93.7% White, 1.1% Black, 2.9% Asian, 0.2% American Indian and Alaska Native, 1.6% Hispanic of any race, 1.8% two or more races (2000); Density: 3,494.6 persons per square mile (2000); Age: 27.0% under 18, 12.0% over 64 (2000); Marriage status: 20.8% never married, 66.9% now married, 4.7% widowed, 7.5% divorced (2000); Foreign born: 5.1% (2000); Ancestry (includes multiple ancestries): 39.8% German, 21.3% Irish, 13.1% English, 8.3% Other groups, 7.7% Italian (2000).
Vital Statistics: Birth rate: 61.7 per 10,000 population (1998)
Economy: Mainly residential and commercial with some light industry. Manufacturing: machinery. Unemployment rate: 2.1% (11/2002); Total civilian labor force: 12,958 (11/2002); Single-family building permits issued: 22 (2001) / 82 (2000); Multi-family building permits issued: 0 (2001) / 0 (2000); Employment by occupation: 21.1% management, 25.7% professional, 11.6% services, 29.9% sales, 0.1% farming, 5.0% construction, 6.6% production (2000).
Income: Per capita income: $29,520 (2000); Median household income: $66,458 (2000); Poverty rate: 3.2% (2000).
Taxes: Total city taxes per capita: $68 (2000); City property taxes per capita: $0 (2000).
Education: High school graduation rate: 94.9% (2000); College graduation rate: 46.7% (2000).
Housing: Homeownership rate: 82.9% (2000); Median home value: $157,300 (2000); Median rent: $617 per month (2000); Median age of housing: 27 years (2000).
Transportation: Commute to work: 94.0% car, 0.6% public transportation, 0.7% walk, 4.1% work from home (2000); Travel time to work: 20.9% less than 15 minutes, 33.5% 15 to 30 minutes, 30.7% 30 to 45 minutes, 10.0% 45 to 60 minutes, 4.8% 60 minutes or more (2000)
Additional Information Contacts
West County Chamber of Commerce 636-458-6200

BEL-NOR (village). Covers a land area of 0.625 square miles and a water area of 0 square miles. Located at 38.70° N. Lat.; 90.31° W. Long. Elevation is 638 feet.
History: Incorporated 1937.
Population: 1,598 (2000); Race: 57.3% White, 37.3% Black, 1.7% Asian, 0.7% American Indian and Alaska Native, 1.0% Hispanic of any race, 2.7% two or more races (2000); Density: 2,555.5 persons per square mile (2000); Age: 20.4% under 18, 16.2% over 64 (2000); Marriage status: 21.3% never married, 63.0% now married, 6.7% widowed, 9.0% divorced (2000); Foreign born: 3.5% (2000); Ancestry (includes multiple ancestries): 41.1% Other groups, 24.9% German, 14.4% Irish, 10.0% English, 3.8% United States or American (2000).
Economy: Single-family building permits issued: 0 (2001) / 0 (2000); Multi-family building permits issued: 0 (2001) / 0 (2000); Employment by occupation: 19.0% management, 32.9% professional, 6.5% services, 28.0% sales, 0.0% farming, 5.1% construction, 8.5% production (2000).
Income: Per capita income: $26,534 (2000); Median household income: $57,857 (2000); Poverty rate: 4.0% (2000).
Education: High school graduation rate: 91.7% (2000); College graduation rate: 47.1% (2000).
Housing: Homeownership rate: 96.1% (2000); Median home value: $102,800 (2000); Median rent: $375 per month (2000); Median age of housing: 52 years (2000).
Safety: Violent crime rate: 64.3 per 10,000 population; Property crime rate: 355.6 per 10,000 population (2001).
Transportation: Commute to work: 86.4% car, 7.7% public transportation, 2.7% walk, 2.6% work from home (2000); Travel time to work: 17.7% less than 15 minutes, 52.9% 15 to 30 minutes, 22.7% 30 to 45 minutes, 3.0% 45 to 60 minutes, 3.7% 60 minutes or more (2000)

BEL-RIDGE (village). Covers a land area of 0.811 square miles and a water area of 0 square miles. Located at 38.71° N. Lat.; 90.32° W. Long. Elevation is 590 feet.
Population: 3,082 (2000); Race: 20.2% White, 75.6% Black, 0.0% Asian, 0.0% American Indian and Alaska Native, 1.5% Hispanic of any race, 3.8% two or more races (2000); Density: 3,799.0 persons per square mile (2000); Age: 32.3% under 18, 5.3% over 64 (2000); Marriage status: 40.9% never married, 35.6% now married, 7.0% widowed, 16.6% divorced (2000); Foreign born: 0.5% (2000); Ancestry (includes multiple ancestries): 70.6% Other groups, 5.8% German, 3.6% English, 2.6% African, 2.2% Irish (2000).
Economy: Residential suburb of Saint Louis. Single-family building permits issued: 0 (2001) / 0 (2000); Multi-family building permits issued: 0 (2001) / 0 (2000); Employment by occupation: 7.4% management, 14.2% professional, 25.4% services, 21.5% sales, 0.0% farming, 7.6% construction, 23.9% production (2000).
Income: Per capita income: $13,073 (2000); Median household income: $27,500 (2000); Poverty rate: 16.7% (2000).
Education: High school graduation rate: 73.9% (2000); College graduation rate: 6.1% (2000).
Housing: Homeownership rate: 55.0% (2000); Median home value: $49,000 (2000); Median rent: $409 per month (2000); Median age of housing: 42 years (2000).
Safety: Violent crime rate: 90.3 per 10,000 population; Property crime rate: 857.8 per 10,000 population (2001).
Transportation: Commute to work: 88.5% car, 9.3% public transportation, 1.4% walk, 0.0% work from home (2000); Travel time to work: 19.3% less than 15 minutes, 42.2% 15 to 30 minutes, 26.4% 30 to 45 minutes, 6.6% 45 to 60 minutes, 5.4% 60 minutes or more (2000)

BELLA VILLA (city). Covers a land area of 0.126 square miles and a water area of 0 square miles. Located at 38.54° N. Lat.; 90.28° W. Long. Elevation is 475 feet.
Population: 687 (2000); Race: 95.8% White, 0.3% Black, 1.1% Asian, 0.0% American Indian and Alaska Native, 2.6% Hispanic of any race, 0.9% two or more races (2000); Density: 5,468.3 persons per square mile (2000); Age: 13.2% under 18, 21.7% over 64 (2000); Marriage status: 25.9% never married, 47.4% now married, 13.0% widowed, 13.7% divorced (2000); Foreign born: 5.1% (2000); Ancestry (includes multiple ancestries): 48.1% German, 19.2% Irish, 7.2% English, 6.9% Other groups, 5.9% Polish (2000).
Economy: Residential suburb of Saint Louis. Single-family building permits issued: 0 (2001) / 0 (2000); Multi-family building permits issued: 0 (2001) / 0 (2000); Employment by occupation: 9.5% management, 24.9% professional, 12.8% services, 25.8% sales, 0.0% farming, 9.8% construction, 17.2% production (2000).
Income: Per capita income: $21,692 (2000); Median household income: $36,827 (2000); Poverty rate: 7.2% (2000).
Taxes: Total city taxes per capita: $56 (1997); City property taxes per capita: $9 (1997).
Education: High school graduation rate: 77.9% (2000); College graduation rate: 19.8% (2000).
Housing: Homeownership rate: 86.9% (2000); Median home value: $79,400 (2000); Median rent: $542 per month (2000); Median age of housing: 51 years (2000).
Transportation: Commute to work: 97.9% car, 1.5% public transportation, 0.6% walk, 0.0% work from home (2000); Travel time to work: 25.1% less than 15 minutes, 38.4% 15 to 30 minutes, 30.5% 30 to 45 minutes, 3.9% 45 to 60 minutes, 2.1% 60 minutes or more (2000)

BELLEFONTAINE NEIGHBORS (city). Covers a land area of 4.380 square miles and a water area of 0 square miles. Located at 38.74° N. Lat.; 90.22° W. Long. Elevation is 453 feet.
History: Founded c.1819, incorporated 1950.
Population: 11,271 (2000); Race: 51.5% White, 45.9% Black, 0.4% Asian, 0.2% American Indian and Alaska Native, 0.4% Hispanic of any race, 1.1% two or more races (2000); Density: 2,573.2 persons per square mile (2000); Age: 23.2% under 18, 18.1% over 64 (2000); Marriage status: 33.1% never married, 47.9% now married, 9.3% widowed, 9.7% divorced (2000); Foreign born: 0.6% (2000); Ancestry (includes multiple ancestries): 42.1% Other groups, 20.3% German, 11.4% Irish, 4.5% Italian, 3.9% English (2000).
Vital Statistics: Birth rate: 122.4 per 10,000 population (1998)
Economy: Single-family building permits issued: 0 (2001) / 0 (2000); Multi-family building permits issued: 0 (2001) / 0 (2000); Employment by occupation: 10.0% management, 18.8% professional, 14.3% services, 33.3% sales, 0.0% farming, 9.2% construction, 14.3% production (2000).
Income: Per capita income: $18,911 (2000); Median household income: $40,007 (2000); Poverty rate: 6.5% (2000).
Taxes: Total city taxes per capita: $118 (1997); City property taxes per capita: $0 (1997).
Education: High school graduation rate: 76.3% (2000); College graduation rate: 14.1% (2000).
Housing: Homeownership rate: 91.5% (2000); Median home value: $62,500 (2000); Median rent: $521 per month (2000); Median age of housing: 44 years (2000).
Safety: Violent crime rate: 30.9 per 10,000 population; Property crime rate: 559.1 per 10,000 population (2001).
Transportation: Commute to work: 93.0% car, 3.6% public transportation, 0.6% walk, 2.0% work from home (2000); Travel time to work: 16.5% less than 15 minutes, 41.0% 15 to 30 minutes, 29.7% 30 to 45 minutes, 8.3% 45 to 60 minutes, 4.5% 60 minutes or more (2000)

BELLERIVE (village). Covers a land area of 0.356 square miles and a water area of 0 square miles. Located at 38.71° N. Lat.; 90.31° W. Long. Elevation is 668 feet.
History: Site of University of Missouri, Saint Louis.
Population: 254 (2000); Race: 73.2% White, 25.9% Black, 0.0% Asian, 0.0% American Indian and Alaska Native, 0.9% Hispanic of any race, 0.0% two or more races (2000); Density: 713.0 persons per square mile (2000); Age: 28.9% under 18, 11.4% over 64 (2000); Marriage status: 14.9% never married, 77.6% now married, 0.6% widowed, 6.9% divorced (2000); Foreign born: 1.8% (2000); Ancestry (includes multiple ancestries): 35.5% German, 21.9% Other groups, 19.3% Irish, 7.0% European, 5.7% Polish (2000).
Economy: Residential suburb of Saint Louis. Employment by occupation: 29.1% management, 41.0% professional, 0.9% services, 16.2% sales, 0.0% farming, 8.5% construction, 4.3% production (2000).
Income: Per capita income: $42,336 (2000); Median household income: $87,400 (2000); Poverty rate: 5.3% (2000).
Taxes: Total city taxes per capita: $153 (1997); City property taxes per capita: $117 (1997).
Education: High school graduation rate: 100.0% (2000); College graduation rate: 67.8% (2000).
Housing: Homeownership rate: 92.6% (2000); Median home value: $181,800 (2000); Median rent: $565 per month (2000); Median age of housing: 48 years (2000).
Transportation: Commute to work: 96.6% car, 2.6% public transportation, 0.0% walk, 0.9% work from home (2000); Travel time to work: 25.2% less than 15 minutes, 56.5% 15 to 30 minutes, 14.8% 30 to 45 minutes, 1.7% 45 to 60 minutes, 1.7% 60 minutes or more (2000)

BERKELEY (city). Covers a land area of 4.931 square miles and a water area of 0.004 square miles. Located at 38.74° N. Lat.; 90.33° W. Long. Elevation is 535 feet.
History: Incorporated 1937.
Population: 10,063 (2000); Race: 20.2% White, 77.3% Black, 0.2% Asian, 0.2% American Indian and Alaska Native, 1.0% Hispanic of any race, 1.8% two or more races (2000); Density: 2,040.6 persons per square mile (2000); Age: 32.1% under 18, 11.2% over 64 (2000); Marriage status: 35.9% never married, 41.8% now married, 7.9% widowed, 14.4% divorced (2000); Foreign born: 0.8% (2000); Ancestry (includes multiple ancestries): 67.7% Other groups, 7.5% German, 5.0% Irish, 2.6% United States or American, 1.9% English (2000).
Vital Statistics: Birth rate: 201.7 per 10,000 population (1998)
Economy: Manufacturing: pharmaceuticals, truck lifts, plastic products, airplanes; outdoor advertising; steel fabrication. Single-family building permits issued: 0 (2001) / 1 (2000); Multi-family building permits issued: 0 (2001) / 0 (2000); Employment by occupation: 5.9% management, 12.2% professional, 22.2% services, 32.9% sales, 0.0% farming, 6.4% construction, 20.3% production (2000).
Income: Per capita income: $13,788 (2000); Median household income: $32,219 (2000); Poverty rate: 19.3% (2000).
Taxes: Total city taxes per capita: $443 (2000); City property taxes per capita: $209 (2000).
Education: High school graduation rate: 76.4% (2000); College graduation rate: 9.1% (2000).
Housing: Homeownership rate: 63.7% (2000); Median home value: $51,200 (2000); Median rent: $455 per month (2000); Median age of housing: 42 years (2000).
Transportation: Commute to work: 92.0% car, 5.6% public transportation, 0.7% walk, 1.1% work from home (2000); Travel time to work: 21.0% less than 15 minutes, 47.9% 15 to 30 minutes, 24.1% 30 to 45 minutes, 3.9% 45 to 60 minutes, 3.0% 60 minutes or more (2000)

BEVERLY HILLS (city). Covers a land area of 0.088 square miles and a water area of 0 square miles. Located at 38.69° N. Lat.; 90.29° W. Long. Elevation is 640 feet.
Population: 603 (2000); Race: 3.0% White, 97.0% Black, 0.0% Asian, 0.0% American Indian and Alaska Native, 0.0% Hispanic of any race, 0.0% two or more races (2000); Density: 6,882.0 persons per square mile (2000); Age: 26.9% under 18, 13.5% over 64 (2000); Marriage status: 33.4% never married, 42.4% now married, 9.4% widowed, 14.8% divorced (2000); Foreign born: 1.2% (2000); Ancestry (includes multiple ancestries): 79.4% Other groups, 2.0% African, 1.0% English, 0.8% United States or American, 0.7% French (except Basque) (2000).
Economy: Residential suburb of downtown Saint Louis. Single-family building permits issued: 0 (2001) / 0 (2000); Multi-family building permits issued: 0 (2001) / 0 (2000); Employment by occupation: 4.7% management, 15.6% professional, 21.8% services, 31.5% sales, 0.0% farming, 6.6% construction, 19.8% production (2000).
Income: Per capita income: $14,411 (2000); Median household income: $30,060 (2000); Poverty rate: 18.0% (2000).
Taxes: Total city taxes per capita: $91 (1997); City property taxes per capita: $52 (1997).
Education: High school graduation rate: 71.0% (2000); College graduation rate: 10.3% (2000).
Housing: Homeownership rate: 76.7% (2000); Median home value: $45,200 (2000); Median rent: $339 per month (2000); Median age of housing: 50 years (2000).
Transportation: Commute to work: 89.6% car, 9.6% public transportation, 0.0% walk, 0.8% work from home (2000); Travel time to work: 13.8% less than 15 minutes, 47.8% 15 to 30 minutes, 21.5% 30 to 45 minutes, 5.3% 45 to 60 minutes, 11.7% 60 minutes or more (2000)

BLACK JACK (city). Aka Blackjack. Covers a land area of 2.660 square miles and a water area of 0.007 square miles. Located at 38.79° N. Lat.; 90.26° W. Long. Elevation is 596 feet.
History: Named for early African-American resident whose simple gravemarker is in cemetery to WeSaint
Population: 6,792 (2000); Race: 26.2% White, 72.2% Black, 0.0% Asian, 0.0% American Indian and Alaska Native, 0.4% Hispanic of any race, 1.1% two or more races (2000); Density: 2,553.3 persons per square mile (2000); Age: 25.4% under 18, 13.1% over 64 (2000); Marriage status: 28.2% never married, 51.8% now married, 9.0% widowed, 10.9% divorced (2000); Foreign born: 1.2% (2000); Ancestry (includes multiple ancestries): 66.2% Other groups, 11.4% German, 3.3% Irish, 2.8% English, 1.6% Italian (2000).
Economy: Single-family building permits issued: 45 (2001) / 38 (2000); Multi-family building permits issued: 0 (2001) / 0 (2000); Employment by occupation: 11.4% management, 23.6% professional, 10.2% services, 32.9% sales, 0.0% farming, 7.5% construction, 14.3% production (2000).
Income: Per capita income: $22,705 (2000); Median household income: $51,806 (2000); Poverty rate: 4.7% (2000).
Taxes: Total city taxes per capita: $12 (1997); City property taxes per capita: $0 (1997).
Education: High school graduation rate: 86.4% (2000); College graduation rate: 32.2% (2000).
Housing: Homeownership rate: 75.1% (2000); Median home value: $98,800 (2000); Median rent: $456 per month (2000); Median age of housing: 24 years (2000).
Transportation: Commute to work: 95.1% car, 2.1% public transportation, 0.7% walk, 1.2% work from home (2000); Travel time to work: 11.4% less than 15 minutes, 35.8% 15 to 30 minutes, 38.8% 30 to 45 minutes, 10.0% 45 to 60 minutes, 4.0% 60 minutes or more (2000)

BRECKENRIDGE HILLS (city). Covers a land area of 0.818 square miles and a water area of 0 square miles. Located at 38.71° N. Lat.; 90.36° W. Long. Elevation is 600 feet.
Population: 4,817 (2000); Race: 64.0% White, 30.4% Black, 0.4% Asian, 0.6% American Indian and Alaska Native, 3.2% Hispanic of any race, 2.6% two or more races (2000); Density: 5,890.1 persons per square mile (2000); Age: 31.9% under 18, 7.8% over 64 (2000); Marriage status: 34.7% never married, 45.1% now married, 5.4% widowed, 14.8% divorced (2000); Foreign born: 3.4% (2000); Ancestry (includes multiple ancestries): 31.6% Other groups, 23.6% German, 9.9% Irish, 5.7% United States or American, 4.3% English (2000).
Economy: Residential suburb of Saint Louis. Single-family building permits issued: 0 (2001) / 0 (2000); Multi-family building permits issued: 0 (2001) / 0 (2000); Employment by occupation: 12.3% management, 13.1% professional, 17.0% services, 26.7% sales, 0.0% farming, 12.7% construction, 18.3% production (2000).
Income: Per capita income: $16,847 (2000); Median household income: $34,671 (2000); Poverty rate: 17.3% (2000).
Taxes: Total city taxes per capita: $49 (1997); City property taxes per capita: $9 (1997).
Education: High school graduation rate: 77.6% (2000); College graduation rate: 9.5% (2000).
Housing: Homeownership rate: 51.4% (2000); Median home value: $55,400 (2000); Median rent: $393 per month (2000); Median age of housing: 43 years (2000).
Safety: Violent crime rate: 51.6 per 10,000 population; Property crime rate: 569.4 per 10,000 population (2001).
Transportation: Commute to work: 94.5% car, 1.6% public transportation, 1.6% walk, 2.3% work from home (2000); Travel time to work: 27.3% less than 15 minutes, 45.2% 15 to 30 minutes, 18.6% 30 to 45 minutes, 5.4% 45 to 60 minutes, 3.4% 60 minutes or more (2000)

BRENTWOOD (city). Covers a land area of 1.948 square miles and a water area of 0 square miles. Located at 38.61° N. Lat.; 90.34° W. Long. Elevation is 493 feet.
History: Brentwood was formed by the joining of three subdivisions: Berry Place, Maddenville, and Brentwood. The three were incorporated under the name of Brentwood about 1900.
Population: 7,693 (2000); Race: 92.3% White, 2.6% Black, 3.4% Asian, 0.2% American Indian and Alaska Native, 1.4% Hispanic of any race, 1.1% two or more races (2000); Density: 3,948.4 persons per square mile (2000); Age: 20.2% under 18, 13.8% over 64 (2000); Marriage status: 34.7% never married, 46.4% now married, 8.1% widowed, 10.8% divorced (2000); Foreign born: 4.6% (2000); Ancestry (includes multiple ancestries): 35.8% German, 18.8% Irish, 13.1% English, 10.5% Other groups, 6.9% Italian (2000).
Economy: Single-family building permits issued: 0 (2001) / 0 (2000); Multi-family building permits issued: 0 (2001) / 0 (2000); Employment by occupation: 22.8% management, 34.8% professional, 9.3% services, 24.6% sales, 0.0% farming, 2.3% construction, 6.2% production (2000).
Income: Per capita income: $30,645 (2000); Median household income: $50,643 (2000); Poverty rate: 5.5% (2000).
Taxes: Total city taxes per capita: $507 (2000); City property taxes per capita: $111 (2000).
Education: High school graduation rate: 92.0% (2000); College graduation rate: 55.1% (2000).

School District(s)

Brentwood (PK-12)
2000 Enrollment: 945 314-962-4507

Housing: Homeownership rate: 78.5% (2000); Median home value: $123,600 (2000); Median rent: $682 per month (2000); Median age of housing: 46 years (2000).
Safety: Violent crime rate: 23.3 per 10,000 population; Property crime rate: 387.6 per 10,000 population (2001).
Newspapers: Saint Louis Watchman Advocate (5 x week); Saint Charles Watchman (5 x week); Saint Louis Watchman Legals (5 x week)
Transportation: Commute to work: 93.9% car, 1.1% public transportation, 0.8% walk, 3.7% work from home (2000); Travel time to work: 32.9% less than 15 minutes, 53.0% 15 to 30 minutes, 10.9% 30 to 45 minutes, 1.4% 45 to 60 minutes, 1.8% 60 minutes or more (2000)

BRIDGETON (city). Covers a land area of 14.573 square miles and a water area of 0.671 square miles. Located at 38.75° N. Lat.; 90.41° W. Long. Elevation is 580 feet.
History: Bridgeton, established on the route of French and Spanish trails of the 1700's, was first known as Village a Robert, then as Marais des Liards, and later as Owens Station. In 1794, Lewis Rogers, who had married the daughter of a Shawnee chief and become chief of the tribe himself, brought his group across the Mississippi River and settled at Bridgeton.
Population: 15,550 (2000); Race: 85.8% White, 9.5% Black, 1.7% Asian, 0.2% American Indian and Alaska Native, 2.0% Hispanic of any race, 1.8% two or more races (2000); Density: 1,067.1 persons per square mile (2000); Age: 21.7% under 18, 16.2% over 64 (2000); Marriage status: 24.7% never married, 56.3% now married, 7.6% widowed, 11.4% divorced (2000); Foreign born: 3.7% (2000); Ancestry (includes multiple ancestries): 31.7% German, 19.3% Irish, 14.6% Other groups, 10.0% English, 6.3% Italian (2000).
Vital Statistics: Birth rate: 92.6 per 10,000 population (1998)
Economy: Single-family building permits issued: 35 (2001) / 21 (2000); Multi-family building permits issued: 2 (2001) / 3 (2000); Employment by occupation: 13.3% management, 21.5% professional, 13.6% services, 31.9% sales, 0.1% farming, 8.4% construction, 11.2% production (2000).
Income: Per capita income: $23,955 (2000); Median household income: $49,216 (2000); Poverty rate: 4.9% (2000).
Taxes: Total city taxes per capita: $298 (2000); City property taxes per capita: $32 (2000).
Education: High school graduation rate: 86.8% (2000); College graduation rate: 26.2% (2000).
Housing: Homeownership rate: 69.3% (2000); Median home value: $114,400 (2000); Median rent: $524 per month (2000); Median age of housing: 32 years (2000).
Transportation: Commute to work: 93.4% car, 1.6% public transportation, 0.9% walk, 3.3% work from home (2000); Travel time to work: 33.2% less than 15 minutes, 43.1% 15 to 30 minutes, 17.3% 30 to 45 minutes, 3.4% 45 to 60 minutes, 3.0% 60 minutes or more (2000)

CALVERTON PARK (village). Covers a land area of 0.419 square miles and a water area of 0 square miles. Located at 38.76° N. Lat.; 90.31° W. Long. Elevation is 620 feet.
Population: 1,322 (2000); Race: 70.3% White, 26.8% Black, 0.0% Asian, 0.4% American Indian and Alaska Native, 1.7% Hispanic of any race, 2.3% two or more races (2000); Density: 3,154.5 persons per square mile (2000); Age: 27.8% under 18, 14.0% over 64 (2000); Marriage status: 29.2% never married, 53.8% now married, 3.8% widowed, 13.3% divorced (2000); Foreign born: 0.0% (2000); Ancestry (includes multiple ancestries): 34.2% Other groups, 27.3% German, 13.3% Irish, 8.1% English, 4.4% Italian (2000).
Economy: Residential suburb of downtown Saint Louis. Employment by occupation: 10.8% management, 15.4% professional, 14.2% services, 33.4% sales, 0.0% farming, 10.0% construction, 16.3% production (2000).
Income: Per capita income: $25,723 (2000); Median household income: $44,632 (2000); Poverty rate: 9.1% (2000).
Taxes: Total city taxes per capita: $71 (1997); City property taxes per capita: $35 (1997).
Education: High school graduation rate: 82.9% (2000); College graduation rate: 22.9% (2000).
Housing: Homeownership rate: 85.7% (2000); Median home value: $61,300 (2000); Median rent: $505 per month (2000); Median age of housing: 43 years (2000).
Safety: Violent crime rate: 37.6 per 10,000 population; Property crime rate: 90.2 per 10,000 population (2001).
Transportation: Commute to work: 95.1% car, 2.2% public transportation, 0.0% walk, 2.7% work from home (2000); Travel time to work: 22.3% less than 15 minutes, 43.5% 15 to 30 minutes, 21.4% 30 to 45 minutes, 9.0% 45 to 60 minutes, 3.8% 60 minutes or more (2000)

CASTLE POINT (CDP). Covers a land area of 0.685 square miles and a water area of 0 square miles. Located at 38.75° N. Lat.; 90.24° W. Long. Elevation is 501 feet.
Population: 4,559 (2000); Race: 11.5% White, 86.8% Black, 0.4% Asian, 0.7% American Indian and Alaska Native, 0.2% Hispanic of any race, 0.6% two or more races (2000); Density: 6,653.9 persons per square mile (2000); Age: 34.3% under 18, 9.3% over 64 (2000); Marriage status: 39.6% never married, 42.8% now married, 6.7% widowed, 10.9% divorced (2000); Foreign born: 0.5% (2000); Ancestry (includes multiple ancestries): 74.1% Other groups, 2.8% German, 2.8% African, 1.7% United States or American, 1.5% French (except Basque) (2000).
Economy: Employment by occupation: 12.5% management, 6.5% professional, 29.8% services, 28.6% sales, 0.0% farming, 6.8% construction, 15.8% production (2000).
Income: Per capita income: $11,386 (2000); Median household income: $31,081 (2000); Poverty rate: 24.6% (2000).
Education: High school graduation rate: 67.9% (2000); College graduation rate: 7.4% (2000).
Housing: Homeownership rate: 72.4% (2000); Median home value: $55,600 (2000); Median rent: $381 per month (2000); Median age of housing: 38 years (2000).
Transportation: Commute to work: 81.1% car, 13.9% public transportation, 3.5% walk, 0.8% work from home (2000); Travel time to work: 10.2% less than 15 minutes, 34.1% 15 to 30 minutes, 36.5% 30 to 45 minutes, 5.8% 45 to 60 minutes, 13.4% 60 minutes or more (2000)

CHAMP (village). Covers a land area of 0.836 square miles and a water area of 0 square miles. Located at 38.74° N. Lat.; 90.45° W. Long. Elevation is 607 feet.
History: Established here in early 1960s with the aspiration of attracting the Olympic Games and major industries; neither succeeded.
Population: 12 (2000); Race: 100.0% White, 0.0% Black, 0.0% Asian, 0.0% American Indian and Alaska Native, 0.0% Hispanic of any race, 0.0% two or more races (2000); Density: 14.4 persons per square mile (2000); Age: 52.4% under 18, 0.0% over 64 (2000); Marriage status: 37.5% never married, 62.5% now married, 0.0% widowed, 0.0% divorced (2000); Foreign born: 0.0% (2000); Ancestry (includes multiple ancestries): 100.0% Irish, 76.2% English (2000).
Economy: Single-family building permits issued: 1 (2001) / 1 (2000); Multi-family building permits issued: 0 (2001) / 0 (2000); Employment by occupation: 100.0% management, 0.0% professional, 0.0% services, 0.0% sales, 0.0% farming, 0.0% construction, 0.0% production (2000).
Income: Per capita income: $18,762 (2000); Median household income: $75,487 (2000); Poverty rate: 0.0% (2000).
Taxes: Total city taxes per capita: $3,300 (1997); City property taxes per capita: $100 (1997).
Education: High school graduation rate: 100.0% (2000); College graduation rate: 50.0% (2000).
Housing: Homeownership rate: 0.0% (2000); Median rent: $425 per month (2000); Median age of housing: 35 years (2000).
Transportation: Commute to work: 50.0% car, 0.0% public transportation, 0.0% walk, 50.0% work from home (2000); Travel time to work: 100.0% less than 15 minutes, 0.0% 15 to 30 minutes, 0.0% 30 to 45 minutes, 0.0% 45 to 60 minutes, 0.0% 60 minutes or more (2000)

CHARLACK (city). Covers a land area of 0.262 square miles and a water area of 0 square miles. Located at 38.70° N. Lat.; 90.34° W. Long. Elevation is 598 feet.
Population: 1,431 (2000); Race: 61.1% White, 32.8% Black, 0.4% Asian, 1.0% American Indian and Alaska Native, 1.4% Hispanic of any race, 4.4% two or more races (2000); Density: 5,463.1 persons per square mile (2000); Age: 28.6% under 18, 8.7% over 64 (2000); Marriage status: 38.6% never married, 42.0% now married, 5.0% widowed, 14.5% divorced (2000); Foreign born: 2.1% (2000); Ancestry (includes multiple ancestries): 31.4% Other groups, 24.5% German, 14.3% Irish, 8.8% United States or American, 6.7% English (2000).
Economy: Residential suburb of downtown Saint Louis. Single-family building permits issued: 0 (2001) / 0 (2000); Multi-family building permits issued: 0 (2001) / 0 (2000); Employment by occupation: 7.8% management, 14.7% professional, 17.9% services, 35.5% sales, 0.0% farming, 12.5% construction, 11.6% production (2000).

Income: Per capita income: $18,147 (2000); Median household income: $36,493 (2000); Poverty rate: 11.5% (2000).
Taxes: Total city taxes per capita: $234 (1997); City property taxes per capita: $21 (1997).
Education: High school graduation rate: 80.0% (2000); College graduation rate: 16.9% (2000).
Housing: Homeownership rate: 53.2% (2000); Median home value: $63,900 (2000); Median rent: $480 per month (2000); Median age of housing: 50 years (2000).
Transportation: Commute to work: 89.9% car, 3.8% public transportation, 3.4% walk, 2.0% work from home (2000); Travel time to work: 30.0% less than 15 minutes, 43.0% 15 to 30 minutes, 18.4% 30 to 45 minutes, 4.9% 45 to 60 minutes, 3.7% 60 minutes or more (2000)

CHESTERFIELD (city). Covers a land area of 31.507 square miles and a water area of 1.223 square miles. Located at 38.65° N. Lat.; 90.55° W. Long. Elevation is 470 feet.
History: Though protected by levee, this area was inundated by 1993 flood, causing extensive damage to the airport and businesses. The levee and airport have been rebuilt and businesses have returned. Established 1988.
Population: 46,802 (2000); Race: 90.8% White, 2.3% Black, 5.2% Asian, 0.1% American Indian and Alaska Native, 1.4% Hispanic of any race, 1.0% two or more races (2000); Density: 1,485.4 persons per square mile (2000); Age: 24.7% under 18, 14.6% over 64 (2000); Marriage status: 19.3% never married, 66.5% now married, 7.2% widowed, 7.0% divorced (2000); Foreign born: 8.0% (2000); Ancestry (includes multiple ancestries): 31.0% German, 16.0% Irish, 13.3% English, 11.8% Other groups, 6.3% United States or American (2000).
Vital Statistics: Birth rate: 68.2 per 10,000 population (1998)
Economy: Manufacturing includes apparel, fabricated metal products, paper products, construction materials, plastic products. Unemployment rate: 2.1% (11/2002); Total civilian labor force: 20,866 (11/2002); Employment by occupation: 26.9% management, 30.7% professional, 6.8% services, 30.2% sales, 0.0% farming, 1.8% construction, 3.6% production (2000).
Income: Per capita income: $43,288 (2000); Median household income: $83,802 (2000); Poverty rate: 2.6% (2000).
Taxes: Total city taxes per capita: $163 (2000); City property taxes per capita: $63 (2000).
Education: High school graduation rate: 95.9% (2000); College graduation rate: 60.6% (2000).

School District(s)

Parkway C-2 (PK-12)
2000 Enrollment: 20,433 314-415-8100

Four-year College(s)

Logan College of Chiropractic (Private, Not-for-profit)
2001 Enrollment: 821 363-227-2100
2001 Tuition: In-state $3,040; Out-of-state $3,040

Housing: Homeownership rate: 78.1% (2000); Median home value: $238,300 (2000); Median rent: $754 per month (2000); Median age of housing: 20 years (2000).
Hospitals: Saint Luke's Hospital (493 beds)
Transportation: Commute to work: 92.6% car, 0.3% public transportation, 0.8% walk, 5.6% work from home (2000); Travel time to work: 25.1% less than 15 minutes, 38.3% 15 to 30 minutes, 28.4% 30 to 45 minutes, 6.2% 45 to 60 minutes, 2.0% 60 minutes or more (2000)
Additional Information Contacts
Chesterfield Chamber of Commerce 636-532-3399
Town & Country Chamber of Commerce 636-230-0289

CLARKSON VALLEY (city). Covers a land area of 2.688 square miles and a water area of 0.052 square miles. Located at 38.61° N. Lat.; 90.58° W. Long. Elevation is 595 feet.
Population: 2,675 (2000); Race: 93.6% White, 0.9% Black, 2.5% Asian, 0.8% American Indian and Alaska Native, 0.9% Hispanic of any race, 2.0% two or more races (2000); Density: 995.1 persons per square mile (2000); Age: 26.5% under 18, 7.9% over 64 (2000); Marriage status: 17.3% never married, 78.2% now married, 1.6% widowed, 2.9% divorced (2000); Foreign born: 4.6% (2000); Ancestry (includes multiple ancestries): 30.7% German, 18.4% Irish, 11.9% English, 10.7% Italian, 9.4% Other groups (2000).
Economy: Residential suburb. Single-family building permits issued: 1 (2001) / 4 (2000); Multi-family building permits issued: 0 (2001) / 0 (2000); Employment by occupation: 33.0% management, 20.0% professional, 3.3% services, 32.8% sales, 0.6% farming, 3.2% construction, 7.0% production (2000).
Income: Per capita income: $63,563 (2000); Median household income: $153,933 (2000); Poverty rate: 0.4% (2000).
Taxes: Total city taxes per capita: $476 (2000); City property taxes per capita: $101 (2000).
Education: High school graduation rate: 96.3% (2000); College graduation rate: 60.7% (2000).
Housing: Homeownership rate: 100.0% (2000); Median home value: $412,400 (2000); Median age of housing: 18 years (2000).
Safety: Violent crime rate: 22.3 per 10,000 population; Property crime rate: 174.7 per 10,000 population (2001).
Transportation: Commute to work: 91.8% car, 0.0% public transportation, 0.7% walk, 6.8% work from home (2000); Travel time to work: 19.7% less than 15 minutes, 31.1% 15 to 30 minutes, 31.9% 30 to 45 minutes, 10.3% 45 to 60 minutes, 7.0% 60 minutes or more (2000)

CLAYTON (city). Covers a land area of 2.483 square miles and a water area of 0 square miles. Located at 38.64° N. Lat.; 90.33° W. Long. Elevation is 570 feet.
History: Incorporated 1919.
Population: 12,825 (2000); Race: 83.9% White, 8.2% Black, 6.1% Asian, 0.4% American Indian and Alaska Native, 1.2% Hispanic of any race, 1.2% two or more races (2000); Density: 5,164.4 persons per square mile (2000); Age: 20.9% under 18, 13.6% over 64 (2000); Marriage status: 31.4% never married, 52.8% now married, 6.0% widowed, 9.7% divorced (2000); Foreign born: 8.3% (2000); Ancestry (includes multiple ancestries): 24.4% German, 14.0% English, 13.1% Irish, 11.1% Other groups, 7.6% Russian (2000).
Vital Statistics: Birth rate: 88.9 per 10,000 population (1998)
Economy: Single-family building permits issued: 6 (2001) / 17 (2000); Multi-family building permits issued: 110 (2001) / 22 (2000); Employment by occupation: 24.9% management, 45.0% professional, 5.9% services, 21.6% sales, 0.0% farming, 1.4% construction, 1.1% production (2000).
Income: Per capita income: $48,055 (2000); Median household income: $64,184 (2000); Poverty rate: 7.7% (2000).
Taxes: Total city taxes per capita: $568 (2000); City property taxes per capita: $272 (2000).
Education: High school graduation rate: 96.5% (2000); College graduation rate: 69.7% (2000).

School District(s)

Clayton (PK-12)
2000 Enrollment: 2,452 314-726-5210

Housing: Homeownership rate: 54.7% (2000); Median home value: $425,000 (2000); Median rent: $623 per month (2000); Median age of housing: 56 years (2000).
Safety: Violent crime rate: 16.3 per 10,000 population; Property crime rate: 361.1 per 10,000 population (2001).
Newspapers: Saint Louis Countian (5 x week); Jefferson Watchman (1 x week); Franklin County Watchman (1 x week)
Transportation: Commute to work: 89.0% car, 1.0% public transportation, 4.5% walk, 4.7% work from home (2000); Travel time to work: 44.2% less than 15 minutes, 43.0% 15 to 30 minutes, 9.6% 30 to 45 minutes, 1.5% 45 to 60 minutes, 1.6% 60 minutes or more (2000)

CONCORD (CDP). Covers a land area of 5.513 square miles and a water area of 0 square miles. Located at 38.51° N. Lat.; 90.35° W. Long. Elevation is 620 feet.
Population: 16,689 (2000); Race: 99.0% White, 0.0% Black, 0.5% Asian, 0.0% American Indian and Alaska Native, 0.5% Hispanic of any race, 0.4% two or more races (2000); Density: 3,027.0 persons per square mile (2000); Age: 20.2% under 18, 21.6% over 64 (2000); Marriage status: 20.9% never married, 62.4% now married, 7.8% widowed, 8.9% divorced (2000); Foreign born: 2.8% (2000); Ancestry (includes multiple ancestries): 49.2% German, 18.3% Irish, 9.0% English, 6.8% United States or American, 5.9% French (except Basque) (2000).
Economy: Employment by occupation: 19.7% management, 22.6% professional, 11.8% services, 30.7% sales, 0.1% farming, 7.9% construction, 7.4% production (2000).
Income: Per capita income: $26,933 (2000); Median household income: $55,275 (2000); Poverty rate: 1.7% (2000).
Education: High school graduation rate: 89.5% (2000); College graduation rate: 29.7% (2000).
Housing: Homeownership rate: 89.0% (2000); Median home value: $133,300 (2000); Median rent: $614 per month (2000); Median age of housing: 33 years (2000).
Transportation: Commute to work: 96.1% car, 0.4% public transportation, 0.1% walk, 2.9% work from home (2000); Travel time to work: 23.1% less than 15 minutes, 41.1% 15 to 30 minutes, 27.8% 30 to 45 minutes, 5.4% 45 to 60 minutes, 2.6% 60 minutes or more (2000)

COOL VALLEY (city). Covers a land area of 0.482 square miles and a water area of 0 square miles. Located at 38.72° N. Lat.; 90.30° W. Long. Elevation is 595 feet.
Population: 1,081 (2000); Race: 20.8% White, 75.5% Black, 0.4% Asian, 0.2% American Indian and Alaska Native, 0.6% Hispanic of any race, 3.1% two or more races (2000); Density: 2,244.1 persons per square mile (2000); Age: 32.0% under 18, 7.1% over 64 (2000); Marriage status: 34.4% never married, 42.8% now married, 8.7% widowed, 14.1% divorced (2000); Foreign born: 0.7% (2000); Ancestry (includes multiple ancestries): 67.2% Other groups, 5.8% Irish, 5.5% German, 2.0% French (except Basque), 1.9% Italian (2000).
Economy: University of Missouri, Saint Louis campus to South. Single-family building permits issued: 0 (2001) / 0 (2000); Multi-family building permits issued: 0 (2001) / 0 (2000); Employment by occupation: 5.5% management, 13.9% professional, 23.6% services, 30.7% sales, 0.0% farming, 6.1% construction, 20.2% production (2000).
Income: Per capita income: $20,847 (2000); Median household income: $42,727 (2000); Poverty rate: 10.4% (2000).
Taxes: Total city taxes per capita: $20 (1997); City property taxes per capita: $18 (1997).
Education: High school graduation rate: 79.3% (2000); College graduation rate: 12.3% (2000).
Housing: Homeownership rate: 77.3% (2000); Median home value: $60,200 (2000); Median rent: $489 per month (2000); Median age of housing: 44 years (2000).
Safety: Violent crime rate: 147.1 per 10,000 population; Property crime rate: 1,277.6 per 10,000 population (2001).
Transportation: Commute to work: 91.1% car, 5.1% public transportation, 2.0% walk, 1.4% work from home (2000); Travel time to work: 20.4% less than 15 minutes, 45.6% 15 to 30 minutes, 27.0% 30 to 45 minutes, 5.0% 45 to 60 minutes, 2.0% 60 minutes or more (2000)

COUNTRY CLUB HILLS (city). Covers a land area of 0.178 square miles and a water area of 0 square miles. Located at 38.72° N. Lat.; 90.27° W. Long. Elevation is 545 feet.
Population: 1,381 (2000); Race: 15.5% White, 81.2% Black, 0.0% Asian, 0.7% American Indian and Alaska Native, 0.0% Hispanic of any race, 2.2% two or more races (2000); Density: 7,761.7 persons per square mile (2000); Age: 30.5% under 18, 7.9% over 64 (2000); Marriage status: 42.4% never married, 38.0% now married, 6.0% widowed, 13.6% divorced (2000); Foreign born: 0.6% (2000); Ancestry (includes multiple ancestries): 71.4% Other groups, 4.8% German, 4.1% United States or American, 3.4% Irish, 1.7% Italian (2000).
Economy: Residential suburb of Saint Louis. Single-family building permits issued: 0 (2001) / 0 (2000); Multi-family building permits issued: 0 (2001) / 0 (2000); Employment by occupation: 4.7% management, 16.2% professional, 19.7% services, 36.6% sales, 0.0% farming, 4.2% construction, 18.6% production (2000).
Income: Per capita income: $15,374 (2000); Median household income: $27,955 (2000); Poverty rate: 14.7% (2000).
Taxes: Total city taxes per capita: $71 (1997); City property taxes per capita: $35 (1997).
Education: High school graduation rate: 79.9% (2000); College graduation rate: 8.0% (2000).
Housing: Homeownership rate: 80.8% (2000); Median home value: $45,000 (2000); Median rent: $458 per month (2000); Median age of housing: 47 years (2000).
Safety: Violent crime rate: 50.4 per 10,000 population; Property crime rate: 359.7 per 10,000 population (2001).
Transportation: Commute to work: 88.0% car, 9.4% public transportation, 0.8% walk, 1.8% work from home (2000); Travel time to work: 7.7% less than 15 minutes, 48.2% 15 to 30 minutes, 26.1% 30 to 45 minutes, 4.8% 45 to 60 minutes, 13.2% 60 minutes or more (2000)

COUNTRY LIFE ACRES (village). Covers a land area of 0.112 square miles and a water area of 0 square miles. Located at 38.62° N. Lat.; 90.45° W. Long. Elevation is 660 feet.
Population: 81 (2000); Race: 96.7% White, 0.0% Black, 3.3% Asian, 0.0% American Indian and Alaska Native, 0.0% Hispanic of any race, 0.0% two or more races (2000); Density: 725.5 persons per square mile (2000); Age: 20.0% under 18, 13.3% over 64 (2000); Marriage status: 21.6% never married, 58.8% now married, 15.7% widowed, 3.9% divorced (2000); Foreign born: 16.7% (2000); Ancestry (includes multiple ancestries): 36.7% German, 18.3% Italian, 15.0% Other groups, 6.7% Irish, 3.3% Dutch (2000).
Economy: Residential suburb of Saint Louis. Single-family building permits issued: 0 (2001) / 1 (2000); Multi-family building permits issued: 0 (2001) / 0 (2000); Employment by occupation: 42.3% management, 11.5% professional, 7.7% services, 38.5% sales, 0.0% farming, 0.0% construction, 0.0% production (2000).
Income: Per capita income: $100,617 (2000); Median household income: $193,271 (2000); Poverty rate: 3.3% (2000).
Taxes: Total city taxes per capita: $245 (1997); City property taxes per capita: $224 (1997).
Education: High school graduation rate: 92.5% (2000); College graduation rate: 45.0% (2000).
Housing: Homeownership rate: 100.0% (2000); Median home value: $875,000 (2000); Median age of housing: 30 years (2000).
Transportation: Commute to work: 80.8% car, 0.0% public transportation, 0.0% walk, 19.2% work from home (2000); Travel time to work: 19.0% less than 15 minutes, 33.3% 15 to 30 minutes, 38.1% 30 to 45 minutes, 0.0% 45 to 60 minutes, 9.5% 60 minutes or more (2000)

CRESTWOOD (city). Covers a land area of 3.599 square miles and a water area of 0 square miles. Located at 38.55° N. Lat.; 90.37° W. Long. Elevation is 621 feet.
History: The Thomas Sappington House (1808; restored 1965) is a worthy example of Federal architecture. Incorporated as a city 1949.
Population: 11,863 (2000); Race: 96.0% White, 0.8% Black, 1.0% Asian, 0.3% American Indian and Alaska Native, 0.6% Hispanic of any race, 1.7% two or more races (2000); Density: 3,296.2 persons per square mile (2000); Age: 20.2% under 18, 25.1% over 64 (2000); Marriage status: 20.1% never married, 62.4% now married, 9.1% widowed, 8.5% divorced (2000); Foreign born: 4.0% (2000); Ancestry (includes multiple ancestries): 46.0% German, 20.7% Irish, 12.0% English, 8.0% Italian, 5.3% Other groups (2000).
Vital Statistics: Birth rate: 76.7 per 10,000 population (1998)
Economy: Mostly residential with some light industry. Manufacturing: printing, machining. Employment by occupation: 15.6% management, 30.4% professional, 9.5% services, 30.4% sales, 0.0% farming, 6.0% construction, 8.2% production (2000).
Income: Per capita income: $26,793 (2000); Median household income: $54,185 (2000); Poverty rate: 2.4% (2000).
Taxes: Total city taxes per capita: $208 (2000); City property taxes per capita: $45 (2000).
Education: High school graduation rate: 91.7% (2000); College graduation rate: 36.7% (2000).
Housing: Homeownership rate: 91.1% (2000); Median home value: $130,800 (2000); Median rent: $480 per month (2000); Median age of housing: 41 years (2000).
Safety: Violent crime rate: 14.2 per 10,000 population; Property crime rate: 728.9 per 10,000 population (2001).
Transportation: Commute to work: 97.6% car, 0.5% public transportation, 1.0% walk, 1.0% work from home (2000); Travel time to work: 26.8% less than 15 minutes, 46.2% 15 to 30 minutes, 19.8% 30 to 45 minutes, 4.0% 45 to 60 minutes, 3.2% 60 minutes or more (2000)

CREVE COEUR (city). Covers a land area of 10.130 square miles and a water area of 0 square miles. Located at 38.66° N. Lat.; 90.44° W. Long. Elevation is 644 feet.
History: Missouri Baptist College.
Population: 16,500 (2000); Race: 90.3% White, 2.8% Black, 5.4% Asian, 0.2% American Indian and Alaska Native, 2.6% Hispanic of any race, 0.8% two or more races (2000); Density: 1,628.9 persons per square mile (2000); Age: 20.5% under 18, 19.9% over 64 (2000); Marriage status: 23.3% never married, 62.8% now married, 8.1% widowed, 5.8% divorced (2000); Foreign born: 9.1% (2000); Ancestry (includes multiple ancestries): 22.9% German, 17.8% Other groups, 12.8% Irish, 9.3% English, 9.2% Russian (2000).
Vital Statistics: Birth rate: 47.9 per 10,000 population (1998)
Economy: Mostly residential suburb, 17 miles Northwest of Saint Louis. Manufacturing: consumer goods. Major hospital center; Monsanto Corporation World Headquarters (chemicals). Single-family building permits issued: 39 (2001) / 38 (2000); Multi-family building permits issued: 0 (2001) / 0 (2000); Employment by occupation: 22.4% management, 39.8% professional, 7.9% services, 25.1% sales, 0.0% farming, 2.1% construction, 2.8% production (2000).
Income: Per capita income: $47,905 (2000); Median household income: $75,032 (2000); Poverty rate: 2.9% (2000).
Taxes: Total city taxes per capita: $563 (2000); City property taxes per capita: $23 (2000).
Education: High school graduation rate: 96.6% (2000); College graduation rate: 62.9% (2000).

Housing: Homeownership rate: 70.7% (2000); Median home value: $277,400 (2000); Median rent: $701 per month (2000); Median age of housing: 27 years (2000).
Safety: Violent crime rate: 13.9 per 10,000 population; Property crime rate: 212.0 per 10,000 population (2001).
Transportation: Commute to work: 90.9% car, 0.9% public transportation, 2.0% walk, 5.6% work from home (2000); Travel time to work: 30.4% less than 15 minutes, 46.3% 15 to 30 minutes, 16.9% 30 to 45 minutes, 2.0% 45 to 60 minutes, 4.3% 60 minutes or more (2000)

CRYSTAL LAKE PARK (city). Covers a land area of 0.095 square miles and a water area of 0 square miles. Located at 38.62° N. Lat.; 90.43° W. Long. Elevation is 610 feet.
Population: 457 (2000); Race: 97.3% White, 0.0% Black, 1.8% Asian, 0.0% American Indian and Alaska Native, 1.3% Hispanic of any race, 0.9% two or more races (2000); Density: 4,787.5 persons per square mile (2000); Age: 21.4% under 18, 25.8% over 64 (2000); Marriage status: 11.5% never married, 65.0% now married, 7.5% widowed, 16.0% divorced (2000); Foreign born: 6.9% (2000); Ancestry (includes multiple ancestries): 21.2% German, 20.7% English, 15.4% Irish, 8.0% United States or American, 8.0% Polish (2000).
Economy: Residential suburb of downtown Saint Louis. Single-family building permits issued: 0 (2001) / 0 (2000); Multi-family building permits issued: 0 (2001) / 0 (2000); Employment by occupation: 25.1% management, 32.5% professional, 4.4% services, 33.0% sales, 0.0% farming, 1.0% construction, 3.9% production (2000).
Income: Per capita income: $55,596 (2000); Median household income: $78,441 (2000); Poverty rate: 3.1% (2000).
Taxes: Total city taxes per capita: $268 (1997); City property taxes per capita: $207 (1997).
Education: High school graduation rate: 96.8% (2000); College graduation rate: 57.1% (2000).
Housing: Homeownership rate: 90.9% (2000); Median home value: $221,800 (2000); Median rent: $788 per month (2000); Median age of housing: 29 years (2000).
Transportation: Commute to work: 95.0% car, 1.5% public transportation, 0.0% walk, 3.5% work from home (2000); Travel time to work: 28.0% less than 15 minutes, 52.3% 15 to 30 minutes, 16.1% 30 to 45 minutes, 1.0% 45 to 60 minutes, 2.6% 60 minutes or more (2000)

DELLWOOD (city). Covers a land area of 1.029 square miles and a water area of 0 square miles. Located at 38.75° N. Lat.; 90.27° W. Long. Elevation is 537 feet.
Population: 5,255 (2000); Race: 46.4% White, 51.3% Black, 0.3% Asian, 0.2% American Indian and Alaska Native, 0.1% Hispanic of any race, 1.6% two or more races (2000); Density: 5,108.2 persons per square mile (2000); Age: 30.5% under 18, 12.1% over 64 (2000); Marriage status: 28.8% never married, 50.7% now married, 6.7% widowed, 13.7% divorced (2000); Foreign born: 1.0% (2000); Ancestry (includes multiple ancestries): 52.4% Other groups, 17.9% German, 11.8% Irish, 5.4% Italian, 4.7% English (2000).
Economy: Bordered on all sides except East by city of Ferguson. Single-family building permits issued: 0 (2001) / 0 (2000); Multi-family building permits issued: 0 (2001) / 0 (2000); Employment by occupation: 12.7% management, 15.9% professional, 17.6% services, 26.1% sales, 0.0% farming, 9.4% construction, 18.2% production (2000).
Income: Per capita income: $16,856 (2000); Median household income: $43,210 (2000); Poverty rate: 3.0% (2000).
Taxes: Total city taxes per capita: $232 (1997); City property taxes per capita: $89 (1997).
Education: High school graduation rate: 85.1% (2000); College graduation rate: 14.0% (2000).
Housing: Homeownership rate: 96.1% (2000); Median home value: $62,900 (2000); Median rent: $606 per month (2000); Median age of housing: 40 years (2000).
Safety: Violent crime rate: 41.6 per 10,000 population; Property crime rate: 279.9 per 10,000 population (2001).
Transportation: Commute to work: 95.4% car, 1.2% public transportation, 1.1% walk, 1.2% work from home (2000); Travel time to work: 16.4% less than 15 minutes, 40.4% 15 to 30 minutes, 33.2% 30 to 45 minutes, 5.1% 45 to 60 minutes, 5.0% 60 minutes or more (2000)

DES PERES (city). Covers a land area of 4.396 square miles and a water area of 0 square miles. Located at 38.59° N. Lat.; 90.44° W. Long. Elevation is 615 feet.
History: Incorporated 1934.
Population: 8,592 (2000); Race: 95.9% White, 0.9% Black, 2.1% Asian, 0.4% American Indian and Alaska Native, 1.3% Hispanic of any race, 0.7% two or more races (2000); Density: 1,954.3 persons per square mile (2000); Age: 27.8% under 18, 14.5% over 64 (2000); Marriage status: 19.3% never married, 71.0% now married, 5.1% widowed, 4.6% divorced (2000); Foreign born: 2.4% (2000); Ancestry (includes multiple ancestries): 40.4% German, 26.0% Irish, 16.4% English, 6.2% Other groups, 5.7% Italian (2000).
Economy: Manufacturing: chemicals, printing and publishing. Single-family building permits issued: 25 (2001) / 27 (2000); Multi-family building permits issued: 0 (2001) / 0 (2000); Employment by occupation: 27.5% management, 30.0% professional, 6.0% services, 29.7% sales, 0.0% farming, 3.4% construction, 3.3% production (2000).
Income: Per capita income: $40,916 (2000); Median household income: $96,433 (2000); Poverty rate: 1.5% (2000).
Taxes: Total city taxes per capita: $191 (2000); City property taxes per capita: $54 (2000).
Education: High school graduation rate: 95.2% (2000); College graduation rate: 62.6% (2000).
Housing: Homeownership rate: 95.7% (2000); Median home value: $253,500 (2000); Median rent: $768 per month (2000); Median age of housing: 29 years (2000).
Safety: Violent crime rate: 13.9 per 10,000 population; Property crime rate: 220.9 per 10,000 population (2001).
Transportation: Commute to work: 94.7% car, 0.0% public transportation, 0.7% walk, 4.6% work from home (2000); Travel time to work: 25.1% less than 15 minutes, 53.5% 15 to 30 minutes, 16.5% 30 to 45 minutes, 2.7% 45 to 60 minutes, 2.2% 60 minutes or more (2000)

EDMUNDSON (city). Covers a land area of 0.278 square miles and a water area of 0 square miles. Located at 38.73° N. Lat.; 90.36° W. Long. Elevation is 578 feet.
Population: 840 (2000); Race: 71.4% White, 18.6% Black, 0.7% Asian, 0.0% American Indian and Alaska Native, 7.1% Hispanic of any race, 3.8% two or more races (2000); Density: 3,018.0 persons per square mile (2000); Age: 32.0% under 18, 8.9% over 64 (2000); Marriage status: 31.7% never married, 46.9% now married, 4.2% widowed, 17.2% divorced (2000); Foreign born: 6.9% (2000); Ancestry (includes multiple ancestries): 28.9% Other groups, 24.1% German, 18.0% Irish, 10.3% English, 7.9% United States or American (2000).
Economy: Single-family building permits issued: 0 (2001) / 0 (2000); Multi-family building permits issued: 0 (2001) / 0 (2000); Employment by occupation: 8.5% management, 14.1% professional, 22.6% services, 23.9% sales, 0.5% farming, 8.5% construction, 21.9% production (2000).
Income: Per capita income: $14,123 (2000); Median household income: $37,083 (2000); Poverty rate: 20.3% (2000).
Taxes: Total city taxes per capita: $263 (1997); City property taxes per capita: $77 (1997).
Education: High school graduation rate: 76.7% (2000); College graduation rate: 9.5% (2000).
Housing: Homeownership rate: 60.2% (2000); Median home value: $52,500 (2000); Median rent: $406 per month (2000); Median age of housing: 40 years (2000).
Safety: Violent crime rate: 307.7 per 10,000 population; Property crime rate: 1,159.8 per 10,000 population (2001).
Transportation: Commute to work: 95.6% car, 1.3% public transportation, 0.8% walk, 1.3% work from home (2000); Travel time to work: 24.6% less than 15 minutes, 48.4% 15 to 30 minutes, 21.5% 30 to 45 minutes, 4.5% 45 to 60 minutes, 1.0% 60 minutes or more (2000)

ELLISVILLE (city). Covers a land area of 4.348 square miles and a water area of 0 square miles. Located at 38.59° N. Lat.; 90.58° W. Long. Elevation is 730 feet.
History: Ellisville was settled about 1836 by Captain Harvey Ferris, who came from Kentucky. The town was named for Vespuccio Ellis, a former U.S. Consul to Venezuela, who developed the town.
Population: 9,104 (2000); Race: 93.9% White, 2.5% Black, 2.4% Asian, 0.3% American Indian and Alaska Native, 1.0% Hispanic of any race, 0.5% two or more races (2000); Density: 2,094.1 persons per square mile (2000); Age: 26.0% under 18, 14.5% over 64 (2000); Marriage status: 20.2% never married, 64.3% now married, 7.4% widowed, 8.1% divorced (2000); Foreign born: 3.7% (2000); Ancestry (includes multiple ancestries): 40.7% German, 18.1% Irish, 14.3% English, 7.8% Other groups, 7.5% Italian (2000).
Economy: Single-family building permits issued: 27 (2001) / 38 (2000); Multi-family building permits issued: 0 (2001) / 0 (2000); Employment by occupation: 21.6% management, 24.3% professional, 10.7% services, 31.1% sales, 0.4% farming, 5.9% construction, 6.0% production (2000).

Income: Per capita income: $27,379 (2000); Median household income: $65,016 (2000); Poverty rate: 3.5% (2000).
Taxes: Total city taxes per capita: $251 (2000); City property taxes per capita: $22 (2000).
Education: High school graduation rate: 90.5% (2000); College graduation rate: 37.9% (2000).
Housing: Homeownership rate: 86.4% (2000); Median home value: $151,900 (2000); Median rent: $694 per month (2000); Median age of housing: 24 years (2000).
Safety: Violent crime rate: 7.6 per 10,000 population; Property crime rate: 123.4 per 10,000 population (2001).
Transportation: Commute to work: 93.1% car, 0.4% public transportation, 1.2% walk, 5.0% work from home (2000); Travel time to work: 25.4% less than 15 minutes, 30.0% 15 to 30 minutes, 28.1% 30 to 45 minutes, 11.6% 45 to 60 minutes, 4.9% 60 minutes or more (2000)

EUREKA (city). Covers a land area of 10.052 square miles and a water area of 0.061 square miles. Located at 38.50° N. Lat.; 90.64° W. Long. Elevation is 458 feet.
History: Eureka began as a railroad construction camp in 1853. The town was laid out in 1858 and developed as a crossroads trading center.
Population: 7,676 (2000); Race: 96.6% White, 0.3% Black, 1.3% Asian, 0.2% American Indian and Alaska Native, 1.2% Hispanic of any race, 1.0% two or more races (2000); Density: 763.7 persons per square mile (2000); Age: 31.1% under 18, 8.6% over 64 (2000); Marriage status: 19.3% never married, 70.7% now married, 4.1% widowed, 5.9% divorced (2000); Foreign born: 1.7% (2000); Ancestry (includes multiple ancestries): 38.3% German, 19.4% Irish, 11.6% United States or American, 10.2% English, 7.4% Other groups (2000).
Economy: Single-family building permits issued: 108 (2001) / 144 (2000); Multi-family building permits issued: 0 (2001) / 0 (2000); Employment by occupation: 17.3% management, 22.2% professional, 17.0% services, 27.1% sales, 0.2% farming, 10.1% construction, 6.0% production (2000).
Income: Per capita income: $27,553 (2000); Median household income: $74,301 (2000); Poverty rate: 2.2% (2000).
Taxes: Total city taxes per capita: $163 (2000); City property taxes per capita: $70 (2000).
Education: High school graduation rate: 86.7% (2000); College graduation rate: 38.6% (2000).

School District(s)

Rockwood R-VI (KG-12)
2000 Enrollment: 21,203 636-938-2200
Housing: Homeownership rate: 88.9% (2000); Median home value: $141,500 (2000); Median rent: $401 per month (2000); Median age of housing: 13 years (2000).
Transportation: Commute to work: 93.9% car, 0.0% public transportation, 0.8% walk, 4.6% work from home (2000); Travel time to work: 17.6% less than 15 minutes, 31.3% 15 to 30 minutes, 34.9% 30 to 45 minutes, 10.4% 45 to 60 minutes, 5.8% 60 minutes or more (2000)
Additional Information Contacts
Eureka Chamber of Commerce 636-938-6062

FENTON (city). Covers a land area of 6.135 square miles and a water area of 0.305 square miles. Located at 38.52° N. Lat.; 90.44° W. Long. Elevation is 435 feet.
Population: 4,360 (2000); Race: 98.2% White, 0.0% Black, 1.2% Asian, 0.2% American Indian and Alaska Native, 0.7% Hispanic of any race, 0.3% two or more races (2000); Density: 710.7 persons per square mile (2000); Age: 25.4% under 18, 12.4% over 64 (2000); Marriage status: 18.4% never married, 69.5% now married, 3.5% widowed, 8.6% divorced (2000); Foreign born: 1.5% (2000); Ancestry (includes multiple ancestries): 45.3% German, 19.4% Irish, 16.5% English, 7.8% Italian, 7.2% United States or American (2000).
Economy: Manufacturing: metal products, telecommunications equipment, machinery, transportation equipment, baked specialties, food products, medical supplies, fireproofing materials, consumer goods. Weiss Airport. Single-family building permits issued: 11 (2001) / 9 (2000); Multi-family building permits issued: 0 (2001) / 0 (2000); Employment by occupation: 24.0% management, 18.2% professional, 9.3% services, 31.3% sales, 0.0% farming, 7.1% construction, 10.1% production (2000).
Income: Per capita income: $29,658 (2000); Median household income: $74,708 (2000); Poverty rate: 2.1% (2000).
Taxes: Total city taxes per capita: $603 (2000); City property taxes per capita: $0 (2000).
Education: High school graduation rate: 90.1% (2000); College graduation rate: 32.1% (2000).

Two-year College(s)

Sanford-Brown College (Private, For-profit)
2001 Enrollment: 366 636-349-4900
Housing: Homeownership rate: 85.3% (2000); Median home value: $164,200 (2000); Median rent: $722 per month (2000); Median age of housing: 17 years (2000).
Transportation: Commute to work: 97.4% car, 0.4% public transportation, 0.0% walk, 1.4% work from home (2000); Travel time to work: 25.6% less than 15 minutes, 36.1% 15 to 30 minutes, 29.0% 30 to 45 minutes, 4.0% 45 to 60 minutes, 5.3% 60 minutes or more (2000)
Additional Information Contacts
Fenton Chamber of Commerce 636-343-3839

FERGUSON (city). Covers a land area of 6.189 square miles and a water area of 0.010 square miles. Located at 38.74° N. Lat.; 90.29° W. Long. Elevation is 508 feet.
History: Incorporated 1894.
Population: 22,406 (2000); Race: 45.0% White, 53.0% Black, 0.2% Asian, 0.3% American Indian and Alaska Native, 1.4% Hispanic of any race, 0.9% two or more races (2000); Density: 3,620.6 persons per square mile (2000); Age: 29.9% under 18, 13.0% over 64 (2000); Marriage status: 32.7% never married, 47.3% now married, 8.0% widowed, 12.0% divorced (2000); Foreign born: 1.6% (2000); Ancestry (includes multiple ancestries): 48.4% Other groups, 16.0% German, 8.6% Irish, 5.9% English, 3.3% French (except Basque) (2000).
Vital Statistics: Birth rate: 154.9 per 10,000 population (1998)
Economy: Primarily residential. Light manufacturing. Single-family building permits issued: 0 (2001) / 0 (2000); Multi-family building permits issued: 0 (2001) / 0 (2000); Employment by occupation: 10.2% management, 19.5% professional, 19.4% services, 28.3% sales, 0.0% farming, 7.0% construction, 15.6% production (2000).
Income: Per capita income: $17,661 (2000); Median household income: $35,647 (2000); Poverty rate: 11.6% (2000).
Taxes: Total city taxes per capita: $172 (2000); City property taxes per capita: $85 (2000).
Education: High school graduation rate: 81.2% (2000); College graduation rate: 18.2% (2000).
Housing: Homeownership rate: 66.2% (2000); Median home value: $64,600 (2000); Median rent: $462 per month (2000); Median age of housing: 43 years (2000).
Transportation: Commute to work: 92.4% car, 4.3% public transportation, 1.8% walk, 1.3% work from home (2000); Travel time to work: 19.8% less than 15 minutes, 48.0% 15 to 30 minutes, 23.0% 30 to 45 minutes, 5.3% 45 to 60 minutes, 4.0% 60 minutes or more (2000)
Additional Information Contacts
Ferguson Chamber of Commerce. 314-521-6000

FLORDELL HILLS (city). Covers a land area of 0.115 square miles and a water area of 0 square miles. Located at 38.71° N. Lat.; 90.26° W. Long. Elevation is 493 feet.
Population: 931 (2000); Race: 22.7% White, 74.9% Black, 0.0% Asian, 1.3% American Indian and Alaska Native, 1.1% Hispanic of any race, 0.0% two or more races (2000); Density: 8,111.7 persons per square mile (2000); Age: 27.6% under 18, 9.7% over 64 (2000); Marriage status: 42.2% never married, 32.7% now married, 8.2% widowed, 16.9% divorced (2000); Foreign born: 0.6% (2000); Ancestry (includes multiple ancestries): 68.7% Other groups, 7.8% German, 3.8% Italian, 2.1% United States or American, 1.8% Irish (2000).
Economy: Single-family building permits issued: 0 (2001) / 0 (2000); Multi-family building permits issued: 0 (2001) / 0 (2000); Employment by occupation: 11.1% management, 10.9% professional, 16.3% services, 30.4% sales, 0.0% farming, 9.1% construction, 22.2% production (2000).
Income: Per capita income: $14,539 (2000); Median household income: $31,875 (2000); Poverty rate: 21.0% (2000).
Taxes: Total city taxes per capita: $73 (1997); City property taxes per capita: $19 (1997).
Education: High school graduation rate: 73.8% (2000); College graduation rate: 5.8% (2000).
Housing: Homeownership rate: 69.7% (2000); Median home value: $44,200 (2000); Median rent: $416 per month (2000); Median age of housing: 53 years (2000).
Safety: Violent crime rate: 96.1 per 10,000 population; Property crime rate: 298.8 per 10,000 population (2001).
Transportation: Commute to work: 93.2% car, 5.3% public transportation, 0.3% walk, 0.0% work from home (2000); Travel time to work: 11.6% less

than 15 minutes, 46.2% 15 to 30 minutes, 25.5% 30 to 45 minutes, 10.6% 45 to 60 minutes, 6.1% 60 minutes or more (2000)

FLORISSANT (city). Aka Saint Ferdinand. Covers a land area of 11.367 square miles and a water area of 0.328 square miles. Located at 38.79° N. Lat.; 90.32° W. Long. Elevation is 578 feet.

History: Named Florissant (flowering) by its first French settlers, and called St. Ferdinand by Spanish authorities, the village was known as St. Ferdinand de Florissant until 1939, when it officially became Florissant. The village was established here about 1785, with Francois Dunegant (called Beaurosier) as civil and military commandante.

Population: 50,497 (2000); Race: 85.9% White, 11.3% Black, 0.5% Asian, 0.3% American Indian and Alaska Native, 1.2% Hispanic of any race, 1.5% two or more races (2000); Density: 4,442.4 persons per square mile (2000); Age: 25.0% under 18, 17.0% over 64 (2000); Marriage status: 24.6% never married, 54.9% now married, 9.3% widowed, 11.2% divorced (2000); Foreign born: 1.3% (2000); Ancestry (includes multiple ancestries): 34.2% German, 20.3% Irish, 16.1% Other groups, 9.0% English, 7.2% Italian (2000).

Vital Statistics: Birth rate: 123.8 per 10,000 population (1998)

Economy: Unemployment rate: 3.2% (11/2002); Total civilian labor force: 29,187 (11/2002); Single-family building permits issued: 6 (2001) / 2 (2000); Multi-family building permits issued: 0 (2001) / 0 (2000); Employment by occupation: 10.8% management, 19.0% professional, 13.5% services, 32.0% sales, 0.0% farming, 10.6% construction, 14.0% production (2000).

Income: Per capita income: $20,622 (2000); Median household income: $44,462 (2000); Poverty rate: 4.0% (2000).

Taxes: Total city taxes per capita: $63 (2000); City property taxes per capita: $0 (2000).

Education: High school graduation rate: 85.9% (2000); College graduation rate: 17.4% (2000).

School District(s)

Ferguson-Florissant R-II (PK-12)
2000 Enrollment: 11,792 314-506-9000

Hazelwood (PK-12)
2000 Enrollment: 18,855 314-953-5000

Four-year College(s)

Saint Louis Christian College (Private, Not-for-profit, Christian Churches and Churches of Christ)
2001 Enrollment: 221 314-837-6777
2001 Tuition: In-state $5,824; Out-of-state $5,824

Housing: Homeownership rate: 76.8% (2000); Median home value: $75,300 (2000); Median rent: $493 per month (2000); Median age of housing: 38 years (2000).

Hospitals: Christian Hospital Northwest (223 beds)

Safety: Violent crime rate: 10.8 per 10,000 population; Property crime rate: 249.0 per 10,000 population (2001).

Transportation: Commute to work: 95.1% car, 1.4% public transportation, 1.0% walk, 2.0% work from home (2000); Travel time to work: 24.2% less than 15 minutes, 40.8% 15 to 30 minutes, 26.1% 30 to 45 minutes, 5.4% 45 to 60 minutes, 3.4% 60 minutes or more (2000)

Additional Information Contacts

Florissant Chamber of Commerce 314-831-3500

FRONTENAC (city). Covers a land area of 2.852 square miles and a water area of 0 square miles. Located at 38.63° N. Lat.; 90.41° W. Long. Elevation is 575 feet.

Population: 3,483 (2000); Race: 97.4% White, 0.1% Black, 0.9% Asian, 0.1% American Indian and Alaska Native, 1.4% Hispanic of any race, 1.3% two or more races (2000); Density: 1,221.3 persons per square mile (2000); Age: 29.5% under 18, 20.2% over 64 (2000); Marriage status: 13.3% never married, 75.5% now married, 6.7% widowed, 4.4% divorced (2000); Foreign born: 2.9% (2000); Ancestry (includes multiple ancestries): 32.2% German, 18.5% Irish, 14.7% English, 6.1% Italian, 5.7% United States or American (2000).

Economy: Exclusive shopping district. Single-family building permits issued: 9 (2001) / 11 (2000); Multi-family building permits issued: 0 (2001) / 0 (2000); Employment by occupation: 32.3% management, 43.3% professional, 2.4% services, 19.9% sales, 0.0% farming, 0.7% construction, 1.4% production (2000).

Income: Per capita income: $64,532 (2000); Median household income: $119,508 (2000); Poverty rate: 1.2% (2000).

Taxes: Total city taxes per capita: $543 (1997); City property taxes per capita: $241 (1997).

Education: High school graduation rate: 98.4% (2000); College graduation rate: 71.1% (2000).

Housing: Homeownership rate: 97.5% (2000); Median home value: $444,400 (2000); Median rent: $908 per month (2000); Median age of housing: 38 years (2000).

Safety: Violent crime rate: 14.3 per 10,000 population; Property crime rate: 262.6 per 10,000 population (2001).

Transportation: Commute to work: 91.1% car, 0.1% public transportation, 0.2% walk, 8.1% work from home (2000); Travel time to work: 22.9% less than 15 minutes, 55.3% 15 to 30 minutes, 14.2% 30 to 45 minutes, 3.3% 45 to 60 minutes, 4.3% 60 minutes or more (2000)

GLASGOW VILLAGE (CDP). Covers a land area of 0.926 square miles and a water area of 0 square miles. Located at 38.75° N. Lat.; 90.19° W. Long. Elevation is 498 feet.

Population: 5,234 (2000); Race: 56.7% White, 39.5% Black, 1.0% Asian, 0.0% American Indian and Alaska Native, 1.0% Hispanic of any race, 2.6% two or more races (2000); Density: 5,649.3 persons per square mile (2000); Age: 33.6% under 18, 14.8% over 64 (2000); Marriage status: 30.1% never married, 51.6% now married, 7.9% widowed, 10.4% divorced (2000); Foreign born: 1.1% (2000); Ancestry (includes multiple ancestries): 38.4% Other groups, 23.4% German, 15.4% Irish, 7.3% Italian, 5.8% United States or American (2000).

Economy: Employment by occupation: 9.4% management, 14.5% professional, 18.4% services, 27.3% sales, 0.0% farming, 9.9% construction, 20.6% production (2000).

Income: Per capita income: $17,667 (2000); Median household income: $36,213 (2000); Poverty rate: 13.0% (2000).

Education: High school graduation rate: 75.9% (2000); College graduation rate: 8.1% (2000).

Housing: Homeownership rate: 79.9% (2000); Median home value: $52,500 (2000); Median rent: $449 per month (2000); Median age of housing: 44 years (2000).

Transportation: Commute to work: 98.0% car, 0.6% public transportation, 0.5% walk, 0.4% work from home (2000); Travel time to work: 14.9% less than 15 minutes, 48.7% 15 to 30 minutes, 29.0% 30 to 45 minutes, 4.4% 45 to 60 minutes, 3.1% 60 minutes or more (2000)

GLEN ECHO PARK (village). Covers a land area of 0.031 square miles and a water area of 0 square miles. Located at 38.70° N. Lat.; 90.29° W. Long. Elevation is 630 feet.

Population: 166 (2000); Race: 8.2% White, 91.8% Black, 0.0% Asian, 0.0% American Indian and Alaska Native, 0.0% Hispanic of any race, 0.0% two or more races (2000); Density: 5,416.5 persons per square mile (2000); Age: 22.0% under 18, 22.6% over 64 (2000); Marriage status: 23.9% never married, 56.0% now married, 6.0% widowed, 14.2% divorced (2000); Foreign born: 2.5% (2000); Ancestry (includes multiple ancestries): 81.1% Other groups, 5.0% English, 3.1% German, 2.5% African, 1.9% Dutch (2000).

Economy: Employment by occupation: 6.1% management, 22.7% professional, 10.6% services, 31.8% sales, 0.0% farming, 3.0% construction, 25.8% production (2000).

Income: Per capita income: $24,564 (2000); Median household income: $51,250 (2000); Poverty rate: 0.0% (2000).

Taxes: Total city taxes per capita: $13 (1997); City property taxes per capita: $4 (1997).

Education: High school graduation rate: 82.4% (2000); College graduation rate: 26.1% (2000).

Housing: Homeownership rate: 100.0% (2000); Median home value: $79,200 (2000); Median age of housing: 60+ years (2000).

Transportation: Commute to work: 93.9% car, 6.1% public transportation, 0.0% walk, 0.0% work from home (2000); Travel time to work: 13.6% less than 15 minutes, 56.1% 15 to 30 minutes, 25.8% 30 to 45 minutes, 0.0% 45 to 60 minutes, 4.5% 60 minutes or more (2000)

GLENCOE (unincorporated postal area, zip code 63038). Covers a land area of 20.975 square miles and a water area of 0 square miles. Located at 38.57° N. Lat.; 90.66° W. Long. Elevation is 453 feet.

Population: 5,066 (2000); Race: 94.2% White, 1.9% Black, 1.8% Asian, 0.3% American Indian and Alaska Native, 1.7% Hispanic of any race, 1.1% two or more races (2000); Density: 241.5 persons per square mile (2000); Age: 32.0% under 18, 6.4% over 64 (2000); Marriage status: 17.9% never married, 75.8% now married, 2.3% widowed, 4.0% divorced (2000); Foreign born: 2.5% (2000); Ancestry (includes multiple ancestries): 39.5% German, 18.9% Irish, 15.3% English, 7.3% Other groups, 6.6% Italian (2000).

Economy: Employment by occupation: 26.5% management, 29.3% professional, 7.0% services, 27.9% sales, 0.4% farming, 5.3% construction, 3.7% production (2000).

Income: Per capita income: $45,935 (2000); Median household income: $97,670 (2000); Poverty rate: 2.0% (2000).
Education: High school graduation rate: 94.9% (2000); College graduation rate: 55.3% (2000).
Housing: Homeownership rate: 96.3% (2000); Median home value: $294,100 (2000); Median rent: $618 per month (2000); Median age of housing: 11 years (2000).
Transportation: Commute to work: 92.8% car, 0.3% public transportation, 0.6% walk, 5.9% work from home (2000); Travel time to work: 17.5% less than 15 minutes, 30.4% 15 to 30 minutes, 31.8% 30 to 45 minutes, 16.8% 45 to 60 minutes, 3.5% 60 minutes or more (2000)

GLENDALE (city). Covers a land area of 1.289 square miles and a water area of 0 square miles. Located at 38.59° N. Lat.; 90.38° W. Long. Elevation is 585 feet.
Population: 5,767 (2000); Race: 99.4% White, 0.2% Black, 0.0% Asian, 0.0% American Indian and Alaska Native, 2.0% Hispanic of any race, 0.4% two or more races (2000); Density: 4,474.6 persons per square mile (2000); Age: 28.0% under 18, 14.5% over 64 (2000); Marriage status: 18.4% never married, 68.0% now married, 6.9% widowed, 6.6% divorced (2000); Foreign born: 2.6% (2000); Ancestry (includes multiple ancestries): 39.7% German, 23.3% Irish, 16.2% English, 9.6% United States or American, 7.5% Italian (2000).
Economy: Single-family building permits issued: 2 (2001) / 6 (2000); Multi-family building permits issued: 0 (2001) / 0 (2000); Employment by occupation: 26.0% management, 37.4% professional, 5.1% services, 26.3% sales, 0.0% farming, 2.2% construction, 3.0% production (2000).
Income: Per capita income: $35,136 (2000); Median household income: $75,279 (2000); Poverty rate: 0.4% (2000).
Taxes: Total city taxes per capita: $179 (2000); City property taxes per capita: $83 (2000).
Education: High school graduation rate: 97.5% (2000); College graduation rate: 67.3% (2000).
Housing: Homeownership rate: 96.1% (2000); Median home value: $197,300 (2000); Median rent: $813 per month (2000); Median age of housing: 52 years (2000).
Safety: Violent crime rate: 10.3 per 10,000 population; Property crime rate: 25.8 per 10,000 population (2001).
Transportation: Commute to work: 95.3% car, 0.0% public transportation, 0.6% walk, 3.8% work from home (2000); Travel time to work: 26.1% less than 15 minutes, 57.9% 15 to 30 minutes, 14.3% 30 to 45 minutes, 1.2% 45 to 60 minutes, 0.6% 60 minutes or more (2000)

GRANTWOOD VILLAGE (town). Covers a land area of 0.838 square miles and a water area of 0 square miles. Located at 38.55° N. Lat.; 90.34° W. Long. Elevation is 500 feet.
Population: 883 (2000); Race: 98.6% White, 0.0% Black, 0.8% Asian, 0.0% American Indian and Alaska Native, 1.3% Hispanic of any race, 0.6% two or more races (2000); Density: 1,054.1 persons per square mile (2000); Age: 22.5% under 18, 28.4% over 64 (2000); Marriage status: 15.4% never married, 69.2% now married, 8.4% widowed, 7.0% divorced (2000); Foreign born: 2.9% (2000); Ancestry (includes multiple ancestries): 51.3% German, 25.9% Irish, 14.3% English, 9.4% Italian, 5.0% French (except Basque) (2000).
Economy: Employment by occupation: 24.2% management, 26.8% professional, 6.0% services, 36.2% sales, 0.9% farming, 3.7% construction, 2.3% production (2000).
Income: Per capita income: $52,008 (2000); Median household income: $91,754 (2000); Poverty rate: 1.8% (2000).
Taxes: Total city taxes per capita: $72 (1997); City property taxes per capita: $54 (1997).
Education: High school graduation rate: 93.0% (2000); College graduation rate: 51.3% (2000).
Housing: Homeownership rate: 97.1% (2000); Median home value: $235,800 (2000); Median age of housing: 42 years (2000).
Transportation: Commute to work: 93.8% car, 0.9% public transportation, 1.4% walk, 4.0% work from home (2000); Travel time to work: 25.7% less than 15 minutes, 48.2% 15 to 30 minutes, 18.9% 30 to 45 minutes, 3.0% 45 to 60 minutes, 4.1% 60 minutes or more (2000)

GREEN PARK (city). Covers a land area of 1.397 square miles and a water area of 0 square miles. Located at 38.52° N. Lat.; 90.33° W. Long. Elevation is 550 feet.
Population: 2,666 (2000); Race: 97.6% White, 0.0% Black, 0.8% Asian, 0.1% American Indian and Alaska Native, 1.0% Hispanic of any race, 1.2% two or more races (2000); Density: 1,909.0 persons per square mile (2000); Age: 20.9% under 18, 22.8% over 64 (2000); Marriage status: 18.1% never married, 61.9% now married, 11.6% widowed, 8.4% divorced (2000); Foreign born: 3.1% (2000); Ancestry (includes multiple ancestries): 45.8% German, 15.5% Irish, 11.4% English, 9.7% United States or American, 6.9% Italian (2000).
Economy: Employment by occupation: 14.3% management, 16.0% professional, 16.0% services, 34.7% sales, 0.0% farming, 8.2% construction, 10.7% production (2000).
Income: Per capita income: $20,414 (2000); Median household income: $49,069 (2000); Poverty rate: 3.1% (2000).
Taxes: Total city taxes per capita: $97 (1997); City property taxes per capita: $66 (1997).
Education: High school graduation rate: 81.1% (2000); College graduation rate: 17.4% (2000).
Housing: Homeownership rate: 86.4% (2000); Median home value: $102,000 (2000); Median rent: $526 per month (2000); Median age of housing: 36 years (2000).
Transportation: Commute to work: 95.1% car, 0.3% public transportation, 1.4% walk, 2.8% work from home (2000); Travel time to work: 25.0% less than 15 minutes, 46.0% 15 to 30 minutes, 21.5% 30 to 45 minutes, 4.7% 45 to 60 minutes, 2.8% 60 minutes or more (2000)

GREENDALE (city). Covers a land area of 0.207 square miles and a water area of 0 square miles. Located at 38.69° N. Lat.; 90.31° W. Long. Elevation is 618 feet.
Population: 722 (2000); Race: 34.4% White, 63.3% Black, 0.0% Asian, 0.0% American Indian and Alaska Native, 3.3% Hispanic of any race, 1.6% two or more races (2000); Density: 3,480.3 persons per square mile (2000); Age: 22.0% under 18, 16.6% over 64 (2000); Marriage status: 33.2% never married, 43.9% now married, 10.2% widowed, 12.6% divorced (2000); Foreign born: 0.9% (2000); Ancestry (includes multiple ancestries): 58.6% Other groups, 15.3% German, 6.3% English, 5.7% Irish, 2.6% Polish (2000).
Economy: Single-family building permits issued: 0 (2001) / 0 (2000); Multi-family building permits issued: 0 (2001) / 0 (2000); Employment by occupation: 12.9% management, 26.0% professional, 14.4% services, 26.0% sales, 0.0% farming, 5.9% construction, 14.9% production (2000).
Income: Per capita income: $23,284 (2000); Median household income: $46,083 (2000); Poverty rate: 3.4% (2000).
Taxes: Total city taxes per capita: $90 (2000); City property taxes per capita: $12 (2000).
Education: High school graduation rate: 85.5% (2000); College graduation rate: 32.2% (2000).
Housing: Homeownership rate: 87.5% (2000); Median home value: $73,500 (2000); Median rent: $434 per month (2000); Median age of housing: 50 years (2000).
Transportation: Commute to work: 89.3% car, 7.8% public transportation, 0.5% walk, 1.6% work from home (2000); Travel time to work: 17.5% less than 15 minutes, 47.4% 15 to 30 minutes, 28.6% 30 to 45 minutes, 2.4% 45 to 60 minutes, 4.2% 60 minutes or more (2000)

GROVER (unincorporated postal area, zip code 63040). Covers a land area of 4.606 square miles and a water area of 0 square miles. Located at 38.57° N. Lat.; 90.61° W. Long. Elevation is 794 feet.
Population: 8,300 (2000); Race: 94.2% White, 0.6% Black, 3.2% Asian, 0.4% American Indian and Alaska Native, 1.5% Hispanic of any race, 0.9% two or more races (2000); Density: 1,801.9 persons per square mile (2000); Age: 33.5% under 18, 5.4% over 64 (2000); Marriage status: 16.5% never married, 73.9% now married, 3.0% widowed, 6.7% divorced (2000); Foreign born: 4.7% (2000); Ancestry (includes multiple ancestries): 36.1% German, 20.2% Irish, 11.4% English, 8.7% Italian, 8.1% Other groups (2000).
Economy: Employment by occupation: 25.7% management, 28.9% professional, 7.7% services, 28.7% sales, 0.2% farming, 4.0% construction, 4.8% production (2000).
Income: Per capita income: $30,695 (2000); Median household income: $78,767 (2000); Poverty rate: 2.2% (2000).
Education: High school graduation rate: 97.0% (2000); College graduation rate: 55.9% (2000).
Housing: Homeownership rate: 85.9% (2000); Median home value: $204,500 (2000); Median rent: $863 per month (2000); Median age of housing: 8 years (2000).
Transportation: Commute to work: 92.2% car, 0.6% public transportation, 0.3% walk, 6.8% work from home (2000); Travel time to work: 19.3% less than 15 minutes, 28.8% 15 to 30 minutes, 30.2% 30 to 45 minutes, 15.2% 45 to 60 minutes, 6.5% 60 minutes or more (2000)

HANLEY HILLS (village). Covers a land area of 0.371 square miles and a water area of 0 square miles. Located at 38.68° N. Lat.; 90.32° W. Long. Elevation is 545 feet.

Population: 2,124 (2000); Race: 21.5% White, 76.1% Black, 0.1% Asian, 0.1% American Indian and Alaska Native, 0.8% Hispanic of any race, 2.0% two or more races (2000); Density: 5,721.9 persons per square mile (2000); Age: 28.6% under 18, 9.0% over 64 (2000); Marriage status: 38.9% never married, 38.0% now married, 9.6% widowed, 13.5% divorced (2000); Foreign born: 1.5% (2000); Ancestry (includes multiple ancestries): 62.3% Other groups, 8.3% German, 4.0% Irish, 3.1% English, 2.8% United States or American (2000).

Economy: Employment by occupation: 7.4% management, 12.5% professional, 20.1% services, 37.7% sales, 0.0% farming, 4.8% construction, 17.5% production (2000).

Income: Per capita income: $15,906 (2000); Median household income: $33,802 (2000); Poverty rate: 9.3% (2000).

Taxes: Total city taxes per capita: $22 (1997); City property taxes per capita: $13 (1997).

Education: High school graduation rate: 81.8% (2000); College graduation rate: 13.0% (2000).

Housing: Homeownership rate: 79.3% (2000); Median home value: $47,400 (2000); Median rent: $476 per month (2000); Median age of housing: 47 years (2000).

Transportation: Commute to work: 89.5% car, 7.4% public transportation, 2.3% walk, 0.6% work from home (2000); Travel time to work: 15.4% less than 15 minutes, 47.7% 15 to 30 minutes, 28.5% 30 to 45 minutes, 2.8% 45 to 60 minutes, 5.6% 60 minutes or more (2000)

HAZELWOOD (city). Covers a land area of 15.884 square miles and a water area of 0.944 square miles. Located at 38.77° N. Lat.; 90.36° W. Long. Elevation is 565 feet.

History: Incorporated as a village 1949, city charter approved 1969.

Population: 26,206 (2000); Race: 80.2% White, 15.6% Black, 1.9% Asian, 0.0% American Indian and Alaska Native, 1.6% Hispanic of any race, 1.5% two or more races (2000); Density: 1,649.9 persons per square mile (2000); Age: 24.4% under 18, 11.1% over 64 (2000); Marriage status: 29.6% never married, 50.3% now married, 6.7% widowed, 13.4% divorced (2000); Foreign born: 3.1% (2000); Ancestry (includes multiple ancestries): 30.1% German, 22.7% Other groups, 17.7% Irish, 8.3% English, 6.4% United States or American (2000).

Vital Statistics: Birth rate: 70.2 per 10,000 population (1998)

Economy: On North side of Lambert-Saint Louis Airport. Has a diverse manufacturing base: aircraft, motor vehicles, microbiology instrumentation, plastic products, utility receptacles, power tools, paper goods, foods and beverages, medical equipment, chemicalspublishing. Unemployment rate: 3.7% (11/2002); Total civilian labor force: 15,818 (11/2002); Single-family building permits issued: 24 (2001) / 17 (2000); Multi-family building permits issued: 0 (2001) / 0 (2000); Employment by occupation: 14.4% management, 18.8% professional, 12.3% services, 31.7% sales, 0.1% farming, 8.6% construction, 14.1% production (2000).

Income: Per capita income: $22,311 (2000); Median household income: $45,110 (2000); Poverty rate: 6.3% (2000).

Taxes: Total city taxes per capita: $322 (2000); City property taxes per capita: $47 (2000).

Education: High school graduation rate: 87.4% (2000); College graduation rate: 22.5% (2000).

Two-year College(s)

Sanford-Brown College (Private, For-profit)
2001 Enrollment: 395 314-731-1101

Housing: Homeownership rate: 65.0% (2000); Median home value: $82,700 (2000); Median rent: $511 per month (2000); Median age of housing: 32 years (2000).

Hospitals: DePaul Health Center (538 beds)

Transportation: Commute to work: 94.7% car, 1.9% public transportation, 1.1% walk, 1.8% work from home (2000); Travel time to work: 25.4% less than 15 minutes, 44.8% 15 to 30 minutes, 22.6% 30 to 45 minutes, 4.6% 45 to 60 minutes, 2.7% 60 minutes or more (2000)

HILLSDALE (village). Covers a land area of 0.349 square miles and a water area of 0 square miles. Located at 38.68° N. Lat.; 90.28° W. Long. Elevation is 570 feet.

Population: 1,477 (2000); Race: 2.3% White, 97.1% Black, 0.0% Asian, 0.1% American Indian and Alaska Native, 0.0% Hispanic of any race, 0.0% two or more races (2000); Density: 4,226.3 persons per square mile (2000); Age: 33.5% under 18, 8.1% over 64 (2000); Marriage status: 50.6% never married, 30.2% now married, 8.7% widowed, 10.5% divorced (2000); Foreign born: 0.7% (2000); Ancestry (includes multiple ancestries): 80.1% Other groups, 1.0% German, 0.6% United States or American, 0.5% African, 0.3% Brazilian (2000).

Economy: Single-family building permits issued: 0 (2001) / 0 (2000); Multi-family building permits issued: 0 (2001) / 0 (2000); Employment by occupation: 3.9% management, 11.3% professional, 33.3% services, 22.8% sales, 0.0% farming, 4.6% construction, 24.1% production (2000).

Income: Per capita income: $9,776 (2000); Median household income: $22,159 (2000); Poverty rate: 30.7% (2000).

Taxes: Total city taxes per capita: $64 (1997); City property taxes per capita: $20 (1997).

Education: High school graduation rate: 64.5% (2000); College graduation rate: 1.9% (2000).

Housing: Homeownership rate: 52.0% (2000); Median home value: $31,900 (2000); Median rent: $379 per month (2000); Median age of housing: 51 years (2000).

Transportation: Commute to work: 82.9% car, 14.9% public transportation, 0.0% walk, 2.3% work from home (2000); Travel time to work: 7.6% less than 15 minutes, 35.9% 15 to 30 minutes, 39.2% 30 to 45 minutes, 8.5% 45 to 60 minutes, 8.8% 60 minutes or more (2000)

HUNTLEIGH (city). Covers a land area of 0.996 square miles and a water area of 0 square miles. Located at 38.61° N. Lat.; 90.41° W. Long. Elevation is 557 feet.

Population: 323 (2000); Race: 99.3% White, 0.0% Black, 0.0% Asian, 0.0% American Indian and Alaska Native, 2.6% Hispanic of any race, 0.7% two or more races (2000); Density: 324.4 persons per square mile (2000); Age: 25.6% under 18, 23.6% over 64 (2000); Marriage status: 19.5% never married, 76.8% now married, 3.3% widowed, 0.4% divorced (2000); Foreign born: 1.6% (2000); Ancestry (includes multiple ancestries): 28.2% German, 20.0% Irish, 15.1% English, 12.5% Italian, 8.2% Greek (2000).

Economy: Single-family building permits issued: 1 (2001) / 3 (2000); Multi-family building permits issued: 0 (2001) / 0 (2000); Employment by occupation: 32.5% management, 25.2% professional, 6.5% services, 34.1% sales, 0.0% farming, 0.0% construction, 1.6% production (2000).

Income: Per capita income: $104,420 (2000); Median household income: $200,001 (2000); Poverty rate: 1.3% (2000).

Taxes: Total city taxes per capita: $19 (1997); City property taxes per capita: $11 (1997).

Education: High school graduation rate: 98.0% (2000); College graduation rate: 70.1% (2000).

Housing: Homeownership rate: 96.5% (2000); Median home value: $896,400 (2000); Median rent: $775 per month (2000); Median age of housing: 42 years (2000).

Transportation: Commute to work: 91.0% car, 0.8% public transportation, 0.0% walk, 8.2% work from home (2000); Travel time to work: 28.6% less than 15 minutes, 58.9% 15 to 30 minutes, 10.7% 30 to 45 minutes, 0.0% 45 to 60 minutes, 1.8% 60 minutes or more (2000)

JENNINGS (city). Covers a land area of 3.689 square miles and a water area of 0 square miles. Located at 38.72° N. Lat.; 90.26° W. Long. Elevation is 517 feet.

Population: 15,469 (2000); Race: 21.0% White, 76.2% Black, 0.6% Asian, 0.5% American Indian and Alaska Native, 1.8% Hispanic of any race, 1.3% two or more races (2000); Density: 4,193.3 persons per square mile (2000); Age: 31.0% under 18, 11.1% over 64 (2000); Marriage status: 39.6% never married, 38.7% now married, 7.6% widowed, 14.1% divorced (2000); Foreign born: 1.1% (2000); Ancestry (includes multiple ancestries): 66.6% Other groups, 8.1% German, 5.7% Irish, 2.2% United States or American, 1.8% African (2000).

Vital Statistics: Birth rate: 150.0 per 10,000 population (1998)

Economy: Manufacturing: signs, blowpipes; food products. Single-family building permits issued: 10 (2001) / 11 (2000); Multi-family building permits issued: 0 (2001) / 0 (2000); Employment by occupation: 6.2% management, 13.1% professional, 24.9% services, 32.1% sales, 0.2% farming, 5.9% construction, 17.5% production (2000).

Income: Per capita income: $15,820 (2000); Median household income: $29,196 (2000); Poverty rate: 19.0% (2000).

Taxes: Total city taxes per capita: $148 (1997); City property taxes per capita: $54 (1997).

Education: High school graduation rate: 76.2% (2000); College graduation rate: 9.5% (2000).

School District(s)

Jennings (PK-12)
2000 Enrollment: 3,158 314-653-8000

Housing: Homeownership rate: 69.1% (2000); Median home value: $50,300 (2000); Median rent: $344 per month (2000); Median age of housing: 46 years (2000).
Safety: Violent crime rate: 102.2 per 10,000 population; Property crime rate: 807.6 per 10,000 population (2001).
Newspapers: Community News (1 x week)
Transportation: Commute to work: 90.0% car, 6.5% public transportation, 1.1% walk, 1.7% work from home (2000); Travel time to work: 16.9% less than 15 minutes, 47.6% 15 to 30 minutes, 22.7% 30 to 45 minutes, 6.5% 45 to 60 minutes, 6.4% 60 minutes or more (2000)

KINLOCH (city). Covers a land area of 0.728 square miles and a water area of 0 square miles. Located at 38.74° N. Lat.; 90.32° W. Long. Elevation is 610 feet.
Population: 449 (2000); Race: 0.0% White, 100.0% Black, 0.0% Asian, 0.0% American Indian and Alaska Native, 1.3% Hispanic of any race, 0.0% two or more races (2000); Density: 616.5 persons per square mile (2000); Age: 40.9% under 18, 5.7% over 64 (2000); Marriage status: 62.1% never married, 18.2% now married, 8.8% widowed, 10.9% divorced (2000); Foreign born: 0.0% (2000); Ancestry (includes multiple ancestries): 81.0% Other groups, 1.3% United States or American, 0.4% African (2000).
Economy: Single-family building permits issued: 0 (2001) / 0 (2000); Multi-family building permits issued: 0 (2001) / 0 (2000); Employment by occupation: 1.1% management, 6.6% professional, 35.2% services, 29.7% sales, 0.0% farming, 7.7% construction, 19.8% production (2000).
Income: Per capita income: $8,798 (2000); Median household income: $10,156 (2000); Poverty rate: 58.5% (2000).
Taxes: Total city taxes per capita: $103 (1997); City property taxes per capita: $50 (1997).
Education: High school graduation rate: 53.1% (2000); College graduation rate: 0.0% (2000).
Housing: Homeownership rate: 24.8% (2000); Median home value: $60,000 (2000); Median rent: $164 per month (2000); Median age of housing: 25 years (2000).
Transportation: Commute to work: 76.9% car, 8.8% public transportation, 7.7% walk, 6.6% work from home (2000); Travel time to work: 42.4% less than 15 minutes, 44.7% 15 to 30 minutes, 3.5% 30 to 45 minutes, 7.1% 45 to 60 minutes, 2.4% 60 minutes or more (2000)

KIRKWOOD (city). Covers a land area of 9.227 square miles and a water area of 0.049 square miles. Located at 38.58° N. Lat.; 90.41° W. Long. Elevation is 660 feet.
History: Kirkwood was platted in 1853 by a group of St. Louis businessmen, who planned the town as a residential community for families who wanted to get away from the big city. The town was incorporated in 1865 and named for James P. Kirkwood, a chief engineer of the Missouri Pacific Railroad.
Population: 27,324 (2000); Race: 90.6% White, 7.3% Black, 0.5% Asian, 0.2% American Indian and Alaska Native, 1.2% Hispanic of any race, 1.2% two or more races (2000); Density: 2,961.3 persons per square mile (2000); Age: 22.9% under 18, 18.4% over 64 (2000); Marriage status: 24.6% never married, 56.3% now married, 9.0% widowed, 10.1% divorced (2000); Foreign born: 1.6% (2000); Ancestry (includes multiple ancestries): 36.1% German, 20.7% Irish, 15.5% English, 11.5% Other groups, 4.6% French (except Basque) (2000).
Vital Statistics: Birth rate: 120.8 per 10,000 population (1998)
Economy: Unemployment rate: 2.9% (11/2002); Total civilian labor force: 15,031 (11/2002); Single-family building permits issued: 45 (2001) / 47 (2000); Multi-family building permits issued: 28 (2001) / 64 (2000); Employment by occupation: 21.2% management, 31.5% professional, 10.2% services, 26.5% sales, 0.0% farming, 5.0% construction, 5.6% production (2000).
Income: Per capita income: $32,012 (2000); Median household income: $55,122 (2000); Poverty rate: 4.6% (2000).
Taxes: Total city taxes per capita: $253 (2000); City property taxes per capita: $65 (2000).
Education: High school graduation rate: 94.2% (2000); College graduation rate: 51.5% (2000).

School District(s)

Kirkwood R-VII (KG-12)
2000 Enrollment: 4,984 314-213-6101

Two-year College(s)

Saint Louis Community College-Meramec (Public)
2001 Enrollment: 12,296 314-984-7500
2001 Tuition: In-state $1,530; Out-of-state $1,950

Housing: Homeownership rate: 77.2% (2000); Median home value: $160,500 (2000); Median rent: $583 per month (2000); Median age of housing: 44 years (2000).
Safety: Violent crime rate: 13.1 per 10,000 population; Property crime rate: 238.3 per 10,000 population (2001).
Transportation: Commute to work: 92.3% car, 1.0% public transportation, 1.8% walk, 4.5% work from home (2000); Travel time to work: 26.9% less than 15 minutes, 50.5% 15 to 30 minutes, 17.7% 30 to 45 minutes, 2.3% 45 to 60 minutes, 2.6% 60 minutes or more (2000); Amtrak: Service available.

Additional Information Contacts

Kirkwood Area Chamber of Commerce 314-821-4161

LADUE (city). Covers a land area of 8.591 square miles and a water area of 0 square miles. Located at 38.63° N. Lat.; 90.38° W. Long. Elevation is 545 feet.
History: Incorporated 1936 as a consolidation of former towns of Ladue, Deer Creek, and McKnight.
Population: 8,645 (2000); Race: 95.6% White, 1.4% Black, 1.9% Asian, 0.1% American Indian and Alaska Native, 0.3% Hispanic of any race, 0.9% two or more races (2000); Density: 1,006.2 persons per square mile (2000); Age: 24.8% under 18, 22.3% over 64 (2000); Marriage status: 15.2% never married, 73.8% now married, 7.7% widowed, 3.3% divorced (2000); Foreign born: 4.7% (2000); Ancestry (includes multiple ancestries): 27.9% German, 19.2% English, 15.7% Irish, 7.9% United States or American, 6.2% French (except Basque) (2000).
Economy: Manufacturing: vending machines. Limestone quarry. Single-family building permits issued: 15 (2001) / 22 (2000); Multi-family building permits issued: 0 (2001) / 0 (2000); Employment by occupation: 36.2% management, 32.9% professional, 4.3% services, 23.8% sales, 0.0% farming, 0.7% construction, 2.1% production (2000).
Income: Per capita income: $89,623 (2000); Median household income: $141,720 (2000); Poverty rate: 2.1% (2000).
Taxes: Total city taxes per capita: $403 (1997); City property taxes per capita: $211 (1997).
Education: High school graduation rate: 98.4% (2000); College graduation rate: 71.8% (2000).
Housing: Homeownership rate: 90.9% (2000); Median home value: $585,300 (2000); Median rent: $2,000+ per month (2000); Median age of housing: 46 years (2000).
Safety: Violent crime rate: 17.2 per 10,000 population; Property crime rate: 177.1 per 10,000 population (2001).
Transportation: Commute to work: 88.2% car, 0.1% public transportation, 0.9% walk, 10.2% work from home (2000); Travel time to work: 38.6% less than 15 minutes, 47.4% 15 to 30 minutes, 11.0% 30 to 45 minutes, 0.8% 45 to 60 minutes, 2.3% 60 minutes or more (2000)

LAKESHIRE (city). Covers a land area of 0.214 square miles and a water area of 0 square miles. Located at 38.53° N. Lat.; 90.33° W. Long. Elevation is 397 feet.
Population: 1,375 (2000); Race: 97.5% White, 0.5% Black, 0.0% Asian, 0.2% American Indian and Alaska Native, 1.7% Hispanic of any race, 1.4% two or more races (2000); Density: 6,436.4 persons per square mile (2000); Age: 18.1% under 18, 16.6% over 64 (2000); Marriage status: 30.5% never married, 40.9% now married, 10.4% widowed, 18.2% divorced (2000); Foreign born: 2.2% (2000); Ancestry (includes multiple ancestries): 43.4% German, 17.8% Irish, 9.6% French (except Basque), 8.0% English, 8.0% Italian (2000).
Economy: Single-family building permits issued: 0 (2001) / 0 (2000); Multi-family building permits issued: 0 (2001) / 0 (2000); Employment by occupation: 13.9% management, 24.3% professional, 9.9% services, 37.4% sales, 0.0% farming, 8.0% construction, 6.6% production (2000).
Income: Per capita income: $26,269 (2000); Median household income: $34,970 (2000); Poverty rate: 3.9% (2000).
Taxes: Total city taxes per capita: $104 (1997); City property taxes per capita: $46 (1997).
Education: High school graduation rate: 91.7% (2000); College graduation rate: 27.5% (2000).
Housing: Homeownership rate: 27.2% (2000); Median home value: $144,700 (2000); Median rent: $451 per month (2000); Median age of housing: 34 years (2000).
Transportation: Commute to work: 97.0% car, 0.5% public transportation, 0.1% walk, 2.1% work from home (2000); Travel time to work: 13.1% less than 15 minutes, 49.6% 15 to 30 minutes, 31.4% 30 to 45 minutes, 4.2% 45 to 60 minutes, 1.8% 60 minutes or more (2000)

LEMAY (CDP). Aka Luxemburg. Covers a land area of 4.348 square miles and a water area of 0.186 square miles. Located at 38.53° N. Lat.; 90.28° W. Long. Elevation is 470 feet.

Population: 17,215 (2000); Race: 96.3% White, 0.6% Black, 0.6% Asian, 0.3% American Indian and Alaska Native, 1.7% Hispanic of any race, 1.6% two or more races (2000); Density: 3,959.0 persons per square mile (2000); Age: 22.8% under 18, 20.4% over 64 (2000); Marriage status: 24.8% never married, 49.8% now married, 10.9% widowed, 14.6% divorced (2000); Foreign born: 2.8% (2000); Ancestry (includes multiple ancestries): 37.8% German, 16.4% Irish, 11.0% Other groups, 7.0% French (except Basque), 6.6% United States or American (2000).

Economy: Employment by occupation: 10.0% management, 11.9% professional, 17.5% services, 28.8% sales, 0.0% farming, 12.8% construction, 19.0% production (2000).

Income: Per capita income: $18,730 (2000); Median household income: $34,559 (2000); Poverty rate: 10.4% (2000).

Education: High school graduation rate: 70.5% (2000); College graduation rate: 11.3% (2000).

Housing: Homeownership rate: 77.5% (2000); Median home value: $71,800 (2000); Median rent: $407 per month (2000); Median age of housing: 47 years (2000).

Transportation: Commute to work: 95.4% car, 2.0% public transportation, 0.8% walk, 1.2% work from home (2000); Travel time to work: 21.9% less than 15 minutes, 44.1% 15 to 30 minutes, 23.5% 30 to 45 minutes, 6.6% 45 to 60 minutes, 3.9% 60 minutes or more (2000)

Additional Information Contacts

Lemay Chamber of Commerce 314-631-2796

MACKENZIE (village). Covers a land area of 0.026 square miles and a water area of 0 square miles. Located at 38.58° N. Lat.; 90.31° W. Long. Elevation is 412 feet.

Population: 137 (2000); Race: 98.5% White, 0.0% Black, 1.5% Asian, 0.0% American Indian and Alaska Native, 0.0% Hispanic of any race, 0.0% two or more races (2000); Density: 5,316.5 persons per square mile (2000); Age: 11.7% under 18, 16.8% over 64 (2000); Marriage status: 24.4% never married, 50.4% now married, 4.9% widowed, 20.3% divorced (2000); Foreign born: 1.5% (2000); Ancestry (includes multiple ancestries): 35.8% German, 29.2% Irish, 10.9% Italian, 9.5% United States or American, 6.6% Czech (2000).

Economy: Single-family building permits issued: 0 (2001) / 0 (2000); Multi-family building permits issued: 0 (2001) / 0 (2000); Employment by occupation: 24.1% management, 28.9% professional, 13.3% services, 14.5% sales, 0.0% farming, 10.8% construction, 8.4% production (2000).

Income: Per capita income: $29,732 (2000); Median household income: $45,357 (2000); Poverty rate: 5.1% (2000).

Education: High school graduation rate: 88.7% (2000); College graduation rate: 42.6% (2000).

Housing: Homeownership rate: 95.6% (2000); Median home value: $88,400 (2000); Median rent: $788 per month (2000); Median age of housing: 52 years (2000).

Transportation: Commute to work: 95.2% car, 0.0% public transportation, 0.0% walk, 4.8% work from home (2000); Travel time to work: 31.6% less than 15 minutes, 35.4% 15 to 30 minutes, 30.4% 30 to 45 minutes, 2.5% 45 to 60 minutes, 0.0% 60 minutes or more (2000)

MANCHESTER (city). Covers a land area of 4.997 square miles and a water area of 0 square miles. Located at 38.58° N. Lat.; 90.50° W. Long. Elevation is 582 feet.

History: Manchester was settled about 1795 and named, perhaps, for an early settler known as "old Mr. Manchester." The town's growth was slow. In 1838 it listed only "12 log houses, 1 tavern and 2 stores."

Population: 19,161 (2000); Race: 90.3% White, 3.1% Black, 4.9% Asian, 0.0% American Indian and Alaska Native, 1.1% Hispanic of any race, 1.6% two or more races (2000); Density: 3,834.6 persons per square mile (2000); Age: 27.1% under 18, 10.1% over 64 (2000); Marriage status: 23.2% never married, 64.7% now married, 4.8% widowed, 7.2% divorced (2000); Foreign born: 7.2% (2000); Ancestry (includes multiple ancestries): 39.0% German, 17.1% Irish, 15.0% English, 12.1% Other groups, 6.1% United States or American (2000).

Economy: Employment by occupation: 21.4% management, 31.9% professional, 9.1% services, 28.5% sales, 0.1% farming, 4.1% construction, 5.0% production (2000).

Income: Per capita income: $27,663 (2000); Median household income: $64,381 (2000); Poverty rate: 3.0% (2000).

Taxes: Total city taxes per capita: $203 (1997); City property taxes per capita: $69 (1997).

Education: High school graduation rate: 95.5% (2000); College graduation rate: 52.9% (2000).

Housing: Homeownership rate: 80.5% (2000); Median home value: $144,800 (2000); Median rent: $620 per month (2000); Median age of housing: 24 years (2000).

Safety: Violent crime rate: 6.7 per 10,000 population; Property crime rate: 102.2 per 10,000 population (2001).

Transportation: Commute to work: 95.0% car, 0.4% public transportation, 0.4% walk, 3.9% work from home (2000); Travel time to work: 20.9% less than 15 minutes, 43.4% 15 to 30 minutes, 27.6% 30 to 45 minutes, 5.5% 45 to 60 minutes, 2.6% 60 minutes or more (2000)

MAPLEWOOD (city). Covers a land area of 1.547 square miles and a water area of 0 square miles. Located at 38.61° N. Lat.; 90.32° W. Long. Elevation is 508 feet.

History: Maplewood was established on a Spanish land grant made in 1785 to Charles Gratiot. The town was incorporated in 1908, and developed as a residential community.

Population: 9,228 (2000); Race: 77.1% White, 14.7% Black, 4.0% Asian, 0.6% American Indian and Alaska Native, 2.3% Hispanic of any race, 3.0% two or more races (2000); Density: 5,963.8 persons per square mile (2000); Age: 17.8% under 18, 9.4% over 64 (2000); Marriage status: 41.6% never married, 39.5% now married, 5.4% widowed, 13.4% divorced (2000); Foreign born: 6.6% (2000); Ancestry (includes multiple ancestries): 26.4% German, 22.8% Other groups, 15.0% Irish, 9.9% English, 6.0% United States or American (2000).

Economy: Single-family building permits issued: 1 (2001) / 0 (2000); Multi-family building permits issued: 0 (2001) / 0 (2000); Employment by occupation: 11.0% management, 25.4% professional, 17.6% services, 26.9% sales, 0.2% farming, 6.6% construction, 12.1% production (2000).

Income: Per capita income: $19,087 (2000); Median household income: $29,151 (2000); Poverty rate: 14.1% (2000).

Taxes: Total city taxes per capita: $395 (2000); City property taxes per capita: $176 (2000).

Education: High school graduation rate: 85.0% (2000); College graduation rate: 27.4% (2000).

School District(s)

Maplewood-Richmond Heights (PK-12)
2000 Enrollment: 1,151 314-644-4400

Housing: Homeownership rate: 41.8% (2000); Median home value: $70,800 (2000); Median rent: $348 per month (2000); Median age of housing: 52 years (2000).

Safety: Violent crime rate: 50.6 per 10,000 population; Property crime rate: 476.0 per 10,000 population (2001).

Transportation: Commute to work: 92.3% car, 3.4% public transportation, 2.6% walk, 1.3% work from home (2000); Travel time to work: 29.4% less than 15 minutes, 50.0% 15 to 30 minutes, 15.2% 30 to 45 minutes, 3.0% 45 to 60 minutes, 2.4% 60 minutes or more (2000)

MARLBOROUGH (village). Covers a land area of 0.227 square miles and a water area of 0 square miles. Located at 38.56° N. Lat.; 90.33° W. Long. Elevation is 528 feet.

History: Watson Road (old Route 66) runs length of town; known for its old motels, restaurants, and drive-in theatres.

Population: 2,235 (2000); Race: 78.2% White, 7.3% Black, 10.4% Asian, 0.0% American Indian and Alaska Native, 5.0% Hispanic of any race, 1.7% two or more races (2000); Density: 9,829.4 persons per square mile (2000); Age: 13.1% under 18, 13.6% over 64 (2000); Marriage status: 44.3% never married, 34.2% now married, 4.4% widowed, 17.2% divorced (2000); Foreign born: 15.3% (2000); Ancestry (includes multiple ancestries): 30.0% German, 23.8% Other groups, 15.8% Irish, 6.2% United States or American, 5.9% English (2000).

Economy: Residential and commercial suburb of Saint Louis. Employment by occupation: 11.8% management, 24.1% professional, 21.3% services, 25.5% sales, 0.0% farming, 7.0% construction, 10.2% production (2000).

Income: Per capita income: $18,442 (2000); Median household income: $25,386 (2000); Poverty rate: 15.4% (2000).

Taxes: Total city taxes per capita: $21 (1997); City property taxes per capita: $5 (1997).

Education: High school graduation rate: 86.6% (2000); College graduation rate: 30.2% (2000).

Housing: Homeownership rate: 16.8% (2000); Median home value: $93,600 (2000); Median rent: $465 per month (2000); Median age of housing: 34 years (2000).

Transportation: Commute to work: 93.0% car, 2.3% public transportation, 2.0% walk, 2.0% work from home (2000); Travel time to work: 30.8% less than 15 minutes, 39.7% 15 to 30 minutes, 20.9% 30 to 45 minutes, 6.1% 45 to 60 minutes, 2.6% 60 minutes or more (2000)

MARYLAND HEIGHTS (city). Covers a land area of 21.385 square miles and a water area of 2.186 square miles. Located at 38.72° N. Lat.; 90.44° W. Long. Elevation is 525 feet.
Population: 25,756 (2000); Race: 84.9% White, 5.5% Black, 6.9% Asian, 0.2% American Indian and Alaska Native, 2.4% Hispanic of any race, 1.4% two or more races (2000); Density: 1,204.4 persons per square mile (2000); Age: 21.7% under 18, 9.5% over 64 (2000); Marriage status: 32.4% never married, 51.5% now married, 5.1% widowed, 11.0% divorced (2000); Foreign born: 10.2% (2000); Ancestry (includes multiple ancestries): 32.4% German, 18.1% Other groups, 16.8% Irish, 10.6% English, 5.5% French (except Basque) (2000).
Vital Statistics: Birth rate: 118.8 per 10,000 population (1998)
Economy: Unemployment rate: 2.5% (11/2002); Total civilian labor force: 17,548 (11/2002); Single-family building permits issued: 59 (2001) / 72 (2000); Multi-family building permits issued: 0 (2001) / 0 (2000); Employment by occupation: 17.5% management, 26.3% professional, 11.2% services, 28.7% sales, 0.3% farming, 6.4% construction, 9.6% production (2000).
Income: Per capita income: $24,918 (2000); Median household income: $48,689 (2000); Poverty rate: 5.3% (2000).
Taxes: Total city taxes per capita: $190 (2000); City property taxes per capita: $0 (2000).
Education: High school graduation rate: 88.2% (2000); College graduation rate: 38.7% (2000).
Housing: Homeownership rate: 63.0% (2000); Median home value: $107,900 (2000); Median rent: $588 per month (2000); Median age of housing: 28 years (2000).
Safety: Violent crime rate: 17.0 per 10,000 population; Property crime rate: 446.5 per 10,000 population (2001).
Transportation: Commute to work: 94.9% car, 1.1% public transportation, 0.8% walk, 2.9% work from home (2000); Travel time to work: 29.2% less than 15 minutes, 46.4% 15 to 30 minutes, 18.1% 30 to 45 minutes, 4.2% 45 to 60 minutes, 2.2% 60 minutes or more (2000)
Additional Information Contacts
Maryland Heights Chamber of Commerce 314-576-6603

MEHLVILLE (CDP). Covers a land area of 7.365 square miles and a water area of 0.207 square miles. Located at 38.50° N. Lat.; 90.31° W. Long. Elevation is 638 feet.
Population: 28,822 (2000); Race: 94.6% White, 1.5% Black, 2.5% Asian, 0.1% American Indian and Alaska Native, 1.7% Hispanic of any race, 0.8% two or more races (2000); Density: 3,913.6 persons per square mile (2000); Age: 21.2% under 18, 17.6% over 64 (2000); Marriage status: 25.7% never married, 53.9% now married, 8.4% widowed, 12.0% divorced (2000); Foreign born: 6.6% (2000); Ancestry (includes multiple ancestries): 41.8% German, 19.1% Irish, 8.6% Other groups, 8.3% English, 6.6% French (except Basque) (2000).
Economy: Employment by occupation: 13.7% management, 20.8% professional, 12.3% services, 32.0% sales, 0.0% farming, 9.0% construction, 12.3% production (2000).
Income: Per capita income: $23,125 (2000); Median household income: $43,734 (2000); Poverty rate: 5.6% (2000).
Education: High school graduation rate: 84.7% (2000); College graduation rate: 22.5% (2000).
Housing: Homeownership rate: 67.8% (2000); Median home value: $109,200 (2000); Median rent: $471 per month (2000); Median age of housing: 31 years (2000).
Transportation: Commute to work: 94.6% car, 0.7% public transportation, 1.4% walk, 2.7% work from home (2000); Travel time to work: 22.7% less than 15 minutes, 39.5% 15 to 30 minutes, 27.0% 30 to 45 minutes, 7.8% 45 to 60 minutes, 3.0% 60 minutes or more (2000)

MOLINE ACRES (city). Covers a land area of 0.564 square miles and a water area of 0 square miles. Located at 38.74° N. Lat.; 90.24° W. Long. Elevation is 478 feet.
Population: 2,662 (2000); Race: 13.0% White, 84.5% Black, 0.0% Asian, 0.8% American Indian and Alaska Native, 0.8% Hispanic of any race, 1.7% two or more races (2000); Density: 4,720.6 persons per square mile (2000); Age: 37.5% under 18, 8.2% over 64 (2000); Marriage status: 41.1% never married, 34.5% now married, 4.5% widowed, 19.9% divorced (2000); Foreign born: 0.5% (2000); Ancestry (includes multiple ancestries): 67.9% Other groups, 5.8% German, 3.7% African, 2.6% English, 2.5% Irish (2000).
Economy: Single-family building permits issued: 0 (2001) / 0 (2000); Multi-family building permits issued: 0 (2001) / 0 (2000); Employment by occupation: 7.9% management, 14.1% professional, 18.4% services, 37.0% sales, 0.0% farming, 6.5% construction, 16.1% production (2000).
Income: Per capita income: $12,739 (2000); Median household income: $32,229 (2000); Poverty rate: 19.4% (2000).
Taxes: Total city taxes per capita: $74 (1997); City property taxes per capita: $0 (1997).
Education: High school graduation rate: 76.3% (2000); College graduation rate: 10.5% (2000).
Housing: Homeownership rate: 71.7% (2000); Median home value: $57,900 (2000); Median rent: $415 per month (2000); Median age of housing: 39 years (2000).
Transportation: Commute to work: 93.5% car, 5.4% public transportation, 0.0% walk, 1.2% work from home (2000); Travel time to work: 9.3% less than 15 minutes, 44.7% 15 to 30 minutes, 27.2% 30 to 45 minutes, 7.8% 45 to 60 minutes, 11.1% 60 minutes or more (2000)

NORMANDY (city). Aka Berdell Hills. Covers a land area of 1.823 square miles and a water area of 0 square miles. Located at 38.71° N. Lat.; 90.30° W. Long. Elevation is 595 feet.
History: University of Missouri campus in adjacent Bellerive. Incorporated since 1940.
Population: 5,153 (2000); Race: 26.1% White, 69.4% Black, 1.9% Asian, 0.0% American Indian and Alaska Native, 1.4% Hispanic of any race, 1.9% two or more races (2000); Density: 2,826.3 persons per square mile (2000); Age: 26.5% under 18, 8.1% over 64 (2000); Marriage status: 44.7% never married, 34.9% now married, 5.9% widowed, 14.4% divorced (2000); Foreign born: 4.4% (2000); Ancestry (includes multiple ancestries): 66.0% Other groups, 9.0% German, 6.5% Irish, 2.7% English, 2.1% French (except Basque) (2000).
Economy: Served by Metrolink light railroad. Single-family building permits issued: 0 (2001) / 0 (2000); Multi-family building permits issued: 0 (2001) / 0 (2000); Employment by occupation: 8.9% management, 20.7% professional, 18.9% services, 31.1% sales, 0.2% farming, 7.2% construction, 13.1% production (2000).
Income: Per capita income: $14,399 (2000); Median household income: $25,802 (2000); Poverty rate: 24.1% (2000).
Taxes: Total city taxes per capita: $222 (1997); City property taxes per capita: $24 (1997).
Education: High school graduation rate: 84.2% (2000); College graduation rate: 22.0% (2000).
Housing: Homeownership rate: 42.0% (2000); Median home value: $60,300 (2000); Median rent: $391 per month (2000); Median age of housing: 41 years (2000).
Safety: Violent crime rate: 77.1 per 10,000 population; Property crime rate: 495.7 per 10,000 population (2001).
Transportation: Commute to work: 87.1% car, 7.2% public transportation, 2.8% walk, 1.1% work from home (2000); Travel time to work: 21.3% less than 15 minutes, 53.4% 15 to 30 minutes, 20.8% 30 to 45 minutes, 3.0% 45 to 60 minutes, 1.5% 60 minutes or more (2000)

NORTHWOODS (city). Covers a land area of 0.709 square miles and a water area of 0 square miles. Located at 38.70° N. Lat.; 90.28° W. Long. Elevation is 550 feet.
History: Incorporated 1939.
Population: 4,643 (2000); Race: 6.3% White, 93.5% Black, 0.0% Asian, 0.0% American Indian and Alaska Native, 0.0% Hispanic of any race, 0.2% two or more races (2000); Density: 6,545.7 persons per square mile (2000); Age: 20.9% under 18, 16.7% over 64 (2000); Marriage status: 32.5% never married, 47.6% now married, 9.2% widowed, 10.6% divorced (2000); Foreign born: 0.0% (2000); Ancestry (includes multiple ancestries): 76.8% Other groups, 1.4% Irish, 1.1% United States or American, 1.0% German, 0.7% Polish (2000).
Economy: Single-family building permits issued: 0 (2001) / 0 (2000); Multi-family building permits issued: 0 (2001) / 0 (2000); Employment by occupation: 7.2% management, 18.1% professional, 21.4% services, 33.2% sales, 0.0% farming, 4.5% construction, 15.6% production (2000).
Income: Per capita income: $19,803 (2000); Median household income: $37,938 (2000); Poverty rate: 10.2% (2000).
Taxes: Total city taxes per capita: $144 (1997); City property taxes per capita: $16 (1997).
Education: High school graduation rate: 79.2% (2000); College graduation rate: 14.4% (2000).

Housing: Homeownership rate: 88.5% (2000); Median home value: $54,900 (2000); Median rent: $502 per month (2000); Median age of housing: 47 years (2000).
Safety: Violent crime rate: 72.8 per 10,000 population; Property crime rate: 207.6 per 10,000 population (2001).
Transportation: Commute to work: 93.2% car, 4.9% public transportation, 0.9% walk, 0.5% work from home (2000); Travel time to work: 13.2% less than 15 minutes, 57.3% 15 to 30 minutes, 16.5% 30 to 45 minutes, 8.6% 45 to 60 minutes, 4.3% 60 minutes or more (2000)

NORWOOD COURT (town). Covers a land area of 0.136 square miles and a water area of 0 square miles. Located at 38.71° N. Lat.; 90.28° W. Long. Elevation is 622 feet.
Population: 1,061 (2000); Race: 3.2% White, 95.0% Black, 0.0% Asian, 1.0% American Indian and Alaska Native, 0.0% Hispanic of any race, 0.4% two or more races (2000); Density: 7,783.2 persons per square mile (2000); Age: 22.4% under 18, 6.5% over 64 (2000); Marriage status: 52.5% never married, 26.8% now married, 3.6% widowed, 17.1% divorced (2000); Foreign born: 0.9% (2000); Ancestry (includes multiple ancestries): 84.2% Other groups, 1.6% United States or American, 1.3% Scotch-Irish, 0.7% African, 0.5% Ethiopian (2000).
Economy: Employment by occupation: 3.5% management, 19.6% professional, 18.3% services, 35.1% sales, 0.0% farming, 3.3% construction, 20.3% production (2000).
Income: Per capita income: $19,684 (2000); Median household income: $28,375 (2000); Poverty rate: 13.9% (2000).
Taxes: Total city taxes per capita: $4 (1997); City property taxes per capita: $0 (1997).
Education: High school graduation rate: 91.6% (2000); College graduation rate: 14.9% (2000).
Housing: Homeownership rate: 11.7% (2000); Median home value: $75,500 (2000); Median rent: $438 per month (2000); Median age of housing: 28 years (2000).
Transportation: Commute to work: 94.0% car, 4.4% public transportation, 0.0% walk, 0.0% work from home (2000); Travel time to work: 19.1% less than 15 minutes, 42.9% 15 to 30 minutes, 30.5% 30 to 45 minutes, 3.7% 45 to 60 minutes, 3.7% 60 minutes or more (2000)

OAKLAND (city). Covers a land area of 0.605 square miles and a water area of 0 square miles. Located at 38.57° N. Lat.; 90.38° W. Long. Elevation is 616 feet.
Population: 1,540 (2000); Race: 96.7% White, 2.0% Black, 0.3% Asian, 0.1% American Indian and Alaska Native, 1.3% Hispanic of any race, 0.5% two or more races (2000); Density: 2,545.7 persons per square mile (2000); Age: 17.1% under 18, 38.4% over 64 (2000); Marriage status: 12.9% never married, 73.0% now married, 8.3% widowed, 5.7% divorced (2000); Foreign born: 2.3% (2000); Ancestry (includes multiple ancestries): 30.0% German, 14.8% Irish, 13.8% English, 5.1% Other groups, 3.8% French (except Basque) (2000).
Economy: Single-family building permits issued: 2 (2001) / 6 (2000); Multi-family building permits issued: 0 (2001) / 0 (2000); Employment by occupation: 20.8% management, 30.6% professional, 7.2% services, 31.6% sales, 0.5% farming, 3.5% construction, 5.7% production (2000).
Income: Per capita income: $27,583 (2000); Median household income: $65,000 (2000); Poverty rate: 3.1% (2000).
Taxes: Total city taxes per capita: $206 (1997); City property taxes per capita: $138 (1997).
Education: High school graduation rate: 88.1% (2000); College graduation rate: 38.4% (2000).
Housing: Homeownership rate: 92.4% (2000); Median home value: $154,400 (2000); Median rent: $663 per month (2000); Median age of housing: 48 years (2000).
Safety: Violent crime rate: 0.0 per 10,000 population; Property crime rate: 284.1 per 10,000 population (2001).
Transportation: Commute to work: 91.9% car, 1.5% public transportation, 0.0% walk, 5.2% work from home (2000); Travel time to work: 23.6% less than 15 minutes, 53.9% 15 to 30 minutes, 17.9% 30 to 45 minutes, 2.9% 45 to 60 minutes, 1.8% 60 minutes or more (2000)

OAKVILLE (CDP). Covers a land area of 16.076 square miles and a water area of 2.007 square miles. Located at 38.45° N. Lat.; 90.31° W. Long. Elevation is 605 feet.
Population: 35,309 (2000); Race: 98.1% White, 0.4% Black, 0.6% Asian, 0.1% American Indian and Alaska Native, 1.5% Hispanic of any race, 0.5% two or more races (2000); Density: 2,196.4 persons per square mile (2000); Age: 27.2% under 18, 9.6% over 64 (2000); Marriage status: 23.3% never married, 64.9% now married, 5.1% widowed, 6.7% divorced (2000); Foreign born: 2.0% (2000); Ancestry (includes multiple ancestries): 47.8% German, 18.7% Irish, 9.8% Italian, 8.8% English, 6.2% French (except Basque) (2000).
Economy: Employment by occupation: 17.6% management, 24.2% professional, 11.3% services, 31.0% sales, 0.1% farming, 7.6% construction, 8.2% production (2000).
Income: Per capita income: $26,750 (2000); Median household income: $68,248 (2000); Poverty rate: 2.8% (2000).
Education: High school graduation rate: 91.7% (2000); College graduation rate: 32.9% (2000).
Housing: Homeownership rate: 84.7% (2000); Median home value: $148,400 (2000); Median rent: $572 per month (2000); Median age of housing: 20 years (2000).
Transportation: Commute to work: 95.5% car, 0.7% public transportation, 0.6% walk, 2.9% work from home (2000); Travel time to work: 16.7% less than 15 minutes, 34.7% 15 to 30 minutes, 34.0% 30 to 45 minutes, 10.5% 45 to 60 minutes, 4.1% 60 minutes or more (2000)

OLIVETTE (city). Covers a land area of 2.788 square miles and a water area of 0 square miles. Located at 38.67° N. Lat.; 90.37° W. Long. Elevation is 660 feet.
History: Incorporated 1930.
Population: 7,438 (2000); Race: 71.8% White, 22.2% Black, 4.1% Asian, 0.1% American Indian and Alaska Native, 1.4% Hispanic of any race, 1.0% two or more races (2000); Density: 2,667.5 persons per square mile (2000); Age: 24.0% under 18, 17.4% over 64 (2000); Marriage status: 22.0% never married, 60.4% now married, 7.8% widowed, 9.8% divorced (2000); Foreign born: 13.1% (2000); Ancestry (includes multiple ancestries): 30.0% Other groups, 19.7% German, 10.8% Irish, 10.6% Russian, 8.6% English (2000).
Economy: Manufacturing: paper products, pharmaceuticals, cosmetics, glass products, printing and publishing, building materials, furniture; distillery (makes Southern Comfort). Single-family building permits issued: 30 (2001) / 47 (2000); Multi-family building permits issued: 0 (2001) / 0 (2000); Employment by occupation: 18.1% management, 39.0% professional, 10.9% services, 21.1% sales, 0.0% farming, 3.7% construction, 7.2% production (2000).
Income: Per capita income: $32,379 (2000); Median household income: $57,669 (2000); Poverty rate: 4.3% (2000).
Taxes: Total city taxes per capita: $415 (1997); City property taxes per capita: $168 (1997).
Education: High school graduation rate: 94.3% (2000); College graduation rate: 55.1% (2000).
Housing: Homeownership rate: 79.4% (2000); Median home value: $161,600 (2000); Median rent: $595 per month (2000); Median age of housing: 42 years (2000).
Transportation: Commute to work: 92.2% car, 1.8% public transportation, 1.4% walk, 4.2% work from home (2000); Travel time to work: 31.0% less than 15 minutes, 47.9% 15 to 30 minutes, 17.7% 30 to 45 minutes, 1.5% 45 to 60 minutes, 1.8% 60 minutes or more (2000)

OVERLAND (city). Covers a land area of 4.382 square miles and a water area of 0.018 square miles. Located at 38.69° N. Lat.; 90.36° W. Long. Elevation is 641 feet.
History: Incorporated 1939.
Population: 16,838 (2000); Race: 83.7% White, 12.0% Black, 1.2% Asian, 0.2% American Indian and Alaska Native, 1.2% Hispanic of any race, 2.4% two or more races (2000); Density: 3,842.8 persons per square mile (2000); Age: 23.8% under 18, 16.3% over 64 (2000); Marriage status: 28.8% never married, 50.8% now married, 8.8% widowed, 11.6% divorced (2000); Foreign born: 2.5% (2000); Ancestry (includes multiple ancestries): 29.3% German, 21.1% Other groups, 15.5% Irish, 9.9% English, 8.2% United States or American (2000).
Vital Statistics: Birth rate: 113.4 per 10,000 population (1998)
Economy: Manufacturing: machinery, chemicals, printing, signs, processed foods. U.S. military records center. Single-family building permits issued: 0 (2001) / 0 (2000); Multi-family building permits issued: 0 (2001) / 0 (2000); Employment by occupation: 9.4% management, 15.2% professional, 18.2% services, 32.9% sales, 0.2% farming, 10.5% construction, 13.6% production (2000).
Income: Per capita income: $18,266 (2000); Median household income: $34,437 (2000); Poverty rate: 9.7% (2000).
Taxes: Total city taxes per capita: $236 (2000); City property taxes per capita: $28 (2000).
Education: High school graduation rate: 77.9% (2000); College graduation rate: 14.4% (2000).

Housing: Homeownership rate: 74.1% (2000); Median home value: $59,700 (2000); Median rent: $416 per month (2000); Median age of housing: 47 years (2000).
Transportation: Commute to work: 92.0% car, 2.6% public transportation, 2.7% walk, 2.4% work from home (2000); Travel time to work: 34.1% less than 15 minutes, 38.3% 15 to 30 minutes, 18.7% 30 to 45 minutes, 5.4% 45 to 60 minutes, 3.5% 60 minutes or more (2000)
Additional Information Contacts
Overland Chamber of Commerce. 314-423-9913

PAGEDALE (city). Covers a land area of 1.204 square miles and a water area of 0 square miles. Located at 38.67° N. Lat.; 90.31° W. Long. Elevation is 573 feet.
History: Incorporated since 1940.
Population: 3,616 (2000); Race: 4.5% White, 95.5% Black, 0.0% Asian, 0.0% American Indian and Alaska Native, 0.9% Hispanic of any race, 0.0% two or more races (2000); Density: 3,003.8 persons per square mile (2000); Age: 28.2% under 18, 10.7% over 64 (2000); Marriage status: 42.9% never married, 33.7% now married, 8.9% widowed, 14.4% divorced (2000); Foreign born: 0.0% (2000); Ancestry (includes multiple ancestries): 73.3% Other groups, 3.2% United States or American, 1.2% African, 0.9% European, 0.6% French (except Basque) (2000).
Economy: Manufacturing: sheet metal, swimming pool products. Served by Metrolink light railroad. Employment by occupation: 6.3% management, 10.1% professional, 35.7% services, 23.2% sales, 0.3% farming, 5.5% construction, 19.1% production (2000).
Income: Per capita income: $11,005 (2000); Median household income: $23,873 (2000); Poverty rate: 29.5% (2000).
Taxes: Total city taxes per capita: $139 (1997); City property taxes per capita: $58 (1997).
Education: High school graduation rate: 65.3% (2000); College graduation rate: 5.6% (2000).
Housing: Homeownership rate: 70.6% (2000); Median home value: $39,900 (2000); Median rent: $365 per month (2000); Median age of housing: 50 years (2000).
Transportation: Commute to work: 81.6% car, 13.1% public transportation, 1.5% walk, 2.2% work from home (2000); Travel time to work: 17.7% less than 15 minutes, 42.3% 15 to 30 minutes, 27.8% 30 to 45 minutes, 7.1% 45 to 60 minutes, 5.2% 60 minutes or more (2000)

PASADENA HILLS (city). Covers a land area of 0.227 square miles and a water area of 0 square miles. Located at 38.70° N. Lat.; 90.29° W. Long. Elevation is 648 feet.
History: Incorporated 1937.
Population: 1,147 (2000); Race: 32.2% White, 65.8% Black, 0.0% Asian, 0.1% American Indian and Alaska Native, 1.1% Hispanic of any race, 1.6% two or more races (2000); Density: 5,044.0 persons per square mile (2000); Age: 24.3% under 18, 10.3% over 64 (2000); Marriage status: 32.0% never married, 53.4% now married, 5.7% widowed, 9.0% divorced (2000); Foreign born: 1.6% (2000); Ancestry (includes multiple ancestries): 60.9% Other groups, 11.5% German, 8.4% Irish, 6.0% English, 3.2% Italian (2000).
Economy: Employment by occupation: 18.3% management, 30.7% professional, 8.2% services, 27.4% sales, 0.0% farming, 5.5% construction, 10.0% production (2000).
Income: Per capita income: $28,065 (2000); Median household income: $63,438 (2000); Poverty rate: 5.1% (2000).
Taxes: Total city taxes per capita: $101 (1997); City property taxes per capita: $40 (1997).
Education: High school graduation rate: 91.3% (2000); College graduation rate: 46.9% (2000).
Housing: Homeownership rate: 76.1% (2000); Median home value: $129,700 (2000); Median rent: $446 per month (2000); Median age of housing: 59 years (2000).
Transportation: Commute to work: 91.7% car, 5.1% public transportation, 1.0% walk, 1.5% work from home (2000); Travel time to work: 18.6% less than 15 minutes, 52.6% 15 to 30 minutes, 23.1% 30 to 45 minutes, 3.8% 45 to 60 minutes, 2.0% 60 minutes or more (2000)

PASADENA PARK (village). Covers a land area of 0.089 square miles and a water area of 0 square miles. Located at 38.71° N. Lat.; 90.29° W. Long. Elevation is 668 feet.
Population: 489 (2000); Race: 40.3% White, 54.6% Black, 2.7% Asian, 0.6% American Indian and Alaska Native, 0.4% Hispanic of any race, 0.4% two or more races (2000); Density: 5,506.5 persons per square mile (2000); Age: 20.0% under 18, 11.8% over 64 (2000); Marriage status: 33.0% never married, 38.1% now married, 4.3% widowed, 24.6% divorced (2000); Foreign born: 2.3% (2000); Ancestry (includes multiple ancestries): 55.1% Other groups, 13.7% German, 11.6% Irish, 4.6% English, 3.4% French (except Basque) (2000).
Economy: Single-family building permits issued: 1 (2001) / 0 (2000); Multi-family building permits issued: 0 (2001) / 0 (2000); Employment by occupation: 29.6% management, 17.7% professional, 15.5% services, 20.9% sales, 0.0% farming, 5.8% construction, 10.5% production (2000).
Income: Per capita income: $28,274 (2000); Median household income: $44,712 (2000); Poverty rate: 10.3% (2000).
Taxes: Total city taxes per capita: $73 (1997); City property taxes per capita: $20 (1997).
Education: High school graduation rate: 86.6% (2000); College graduation rate: 32.7% (2000).
Housing: Homeownership rate: 91.1% (2000); Median home value: $78,600 (2000); Median rent: $525 per month (2000); Median age of housing: 60+ years (2000).
Safety: Violent crime rate: 0.0 per 10,000 population; Property crime rate: 264.2 per 10,000 population (2001).
Transportation: Commute to work: 93.0% car, 4.4% public transportation, 1.9% walk, 0.7% work from home (2000); Travel time to work: 17.2% less than 15 minutes, 51.9% 15 to 30 minutes, 20.5% 30 to 45 minutes, 7.1% 45 to 60 minutes, 3.4% 60 minutes or more (2000)

PINE LAWN (city). Covers a land area of 0.606 square miles and a water area of 0 square miles. Located at 38.69° N. Lat.; 90.27° W. Long. Elevation is 612 feet.
History: Incorporated 1940.
Population: 4,204 (2000); Race: 2.4% White, 95.7% Black, 0.0% Asian, 0.0% American Indian and Alaska Native, 0.0% Hispanic of any race, 1.5% two or more races (2000); Density: 6,942.5 persons per square mile (2000); Age: 35.2% under 18, 11.3% over 64 (2000); Marriage status: 43.0% never married, 33.6% now married, 11.6% widowed, 11.8% divorced (2000); Foreign born: 0.3% (2000); Ancestry (includes multiple ancestries): 77.5% Other groups, 1.5% African, 1.2% United States or American, 0.5% English, 0.4% German (2000).
Economy: Employment by occupation: 2.5% management, 8.0% professional, 30.4% services, 27.4% sales, 1.1% farming, 4.5% construction, 26.2% production (2000).
Income: Per capita income: $11,908 (2000); Median household income: $21,500 (2000); Poverty rate: 36.9% (2000).
Taxes: Total city taxes per capita: $1,411 (2000); City property taxes per capita: $14 (2000).
Education: High school graduation rate: 62.9% (2000); College graduation rate: 7.1% (2000).
Housing: Homeownership rate: 60.4% (2000); Median home value: $42,300 (2000); Median rent: $350 per month (2000); Median age of housing: 50 years (2000).
Transportation: Commute to work: 82.1% car, 11.8% public transportation, 2.4% walk, 2.6% work from home (2000); Travel time to work: 7.6% less than 15 minutes, 49.0% 15 to 30 minutes, 24.5% 30 to 45 minutes, 12.7% 45 to 60 minutes, 6.1% 60 minutes or more (2000)

RICHMOND HEIGHTS (city). Covers a land area of 2.291 square miles and a water area of 0 square miles. Located at 38.62° N. Lat.; 90.32° W. Long. Elevation is 469 feet.
Population: 9,602 (2000); Race: 81.5% White, 13.7% Black, 2.5% Asian, 0.5% American Indian and Alaska Native, 1.3% Hispanic of any race, 1.8% two or more races (2000); Density: 4,191.5 persons per square mile (2000); Age: 17.3% under 18, 16.3% over 64 (2000); Marriage status: 37.9% never married, 46.2% now married, 7.5% widowed, 8.4% divorced (2000); Foreign born: 4.3% (2000); Ancestry (includes multiple ancestries): 29.5% German, 24.4% Irish, 17.9% Other groups, 12.2% English, 6.3% Italian (2000).
Vital Statistics: Birth rate: 119.8 per 10,000 population (1998)
Economy: Significant commercial and office development spillover from neighboring Clayton to North; light manufacturing. Single-family building permits issued: 2 (2001) / 1 (2000); Multi-family building permits issued: 28 (2001) / 0 (2000); Employment by occupation: 18.0% management, 36.4% professional, 10.0% services, 25.0% sales, 0.2% farming, 4.6% construction, 5.7% production (2000).
Income: Per capita income: $37,217 (2000); Median household income: $50,557 (2000); Poverty rate: 7.3% (2000).
Taxes: Total city taxes per capita: $440 (2000); City property taxes per capita: $180 (2000).
Education: High school graduation rate: 93.3% (2000); College graduation rate: 56.7% (2000).

Housing: Homeownership rate: 57.3% (2000); Median home value: $133,900 (2000); Median rent: $522 per month (2000); Median age of housing: 57 years (2000).
Safety: Violent crime rate: 34.2 per 10,000 population; Property crime rate: 779.4 per 10,000 population (2001).
Transportation: Commute to work: 91.8% car, 2.1% public transportation, 2.4% walk, 3.1% work from home (2000); Travel time to work: 37.8% less than 15 minutes, 49.3% 15 to 30 minutes, 9.4% 30 to 45 minutes, 1.5% 45 to 60 minutes, 2.1% 60 minutes or more (2000)

RIVERVIEW (village). Covers a land area of 0.828 square miles and a water area of 0 square miles. Located at 38.74° N. Lat.; 90.21° W. Long. Elevation is 545 feet.
Population: 3,146 (2000); Race: 62.4% White, 36.4% Black, 0.0% Asian, 0.1% American Indian and Alaska Native, 0.3% Hispanic of any race, 0.9% two or more races (2000); Density: 3,801.0 persons per square mile (2000); Age: 27.4% under 18, 12.0% over 64 (2000); Marriage status: 33.3% never married, 46.4% now married, 6.8% widowed, 13.5% divorced (2000); Foreign born: 1.3% (2000); Ancestry (includes multiple ancestries): 34.3% Other groups, 24.8% German, 13.9% Irish, 7.3% Italian, 7.0% Polish (2000).
Economy: Single-family building permits issued: 0 (2001) / 0 (2000); Multi-family building permits issued: 0 (2001) / 0 (2000); Employment by occupation: 5.3% management, 12.6% professional, 17.7% services, 32.2% sales, 0.0% farming, 12.5% construction, 19.7% production (2000).
Income: Per capita income: $15,237 (2000); Median household income: $30,970 (2000); Poverty rate: 17.2% (2000).
Taxes: Total city taxes per capita: $42 (1997); City property taxes per capita: $18 (1997).
Education: High school graduation rate: 77.1% (2000); College graduation rate: 10.1% (2000).
Housing: Homeownership rate: 60.0% (2000); Median home value: $54,300 (2000); Median rent: $358 per month (2000); Median age of housing: 47 years (2000).
Transportation: Commute to work: 96.6% car, 1.0% public transportation, 0.4% walk, 1.9% work from home (2000); Travel time to work: 19.3% less than 15 minutes, 38.4% 15 to 30 minutes, 29.2% 30 to 45 minutes, 5.1% 45 to 60 minutes, 8.0% 60 minutes or more (2000)

ROCK HILL (city). Covers a land area of 1.090 square miles and a water area of 0 square miles. Located at 38.60° N. Lat.; 90.36° W. Long. Elevation is 530 feet.
History: Incorporated 1929.
Population: 4,765 (2000); Race: 66.3% White, 28.4% Black, 1.3% Asian, 0.2% American Indian and Alaska Native, 0.7% Hispanic of any race, 3.8% two or more races (2000); Density: 4,370.0 persons per square mile (2000); Age: 22.3% under 18, 15.2% over 64 (2000); Marriage status: 30.8% never married, 50.4% now married, 7.3% widowed, 11.5% divorced (2000); Foreign born: 3.5% (2000); Ancestry (includes multiple ancestries): 28.6% Other groups, 26.6% German, 16.4% Irish, 6.7% English, 5.9% Italian (2000).
Economy: Light manufacturing. Single-family building permits issued: 7 (2001) / 5 (2000); Multi-family building permits issued: 26 (2001) / 0 (2000); Employment by occupation: 11.4% management, 28.2% professional, 13.1% services, 31.3% sales, 0.0% farming, 3.3% construction, 12.6% production (2000).
Income: Per capita income: $25,803 (2000); Median household income: $47,869 (2000); Poverty rate: 5.1% (2000).
Taxes: Total city taxes per capita: $217 (2000); City property taxes per capita: $47 (2000).
Education: High school graduation rate: 89.0% (2000); College graduation rate: 40.1% (2000).
Housing: Homeownership rate: 84.9% (2000); Median home value: $100,900 (2000); Median rent: $581 per month (2000); Median age of housing: 47 years (2000).
Safety: Violent crime rate: 4.2 per 10,000 population; Property crime rate: 214.9 per 10,000 population (2001).
Transportation: Commute to work: 91.0% car, 0.9% public transportation, 1.2% walk, 5.9% work from home (2000); Travel time to work: 23.5% less than 15 minutes, 55.9% 15 to 30 minutes, 15.9% 30 to 45 minutes, 3.0% 45 to 60 minutes, 1.7% 60 minutes or more (2000)

SAINT ANN (city). Covers a land area of 3.126 square miles and a water area of 0 square miles. Located at 38.72° N. Lat.; 90.38° W. Long. Elevation is 590 feet.
Population: 13,607 (2000); Race: 83.5% White, 11.1% Black, 2.0% Asian, 0.7% American Indian and Alaska Native, 3.9% Hispanic of any race, 2.0% two or more races (2000); Density: 4,352.8 persons per square mile (2000); Age: 21.4% under 18, 17.7% over 64 (2000); Marriage status: 29.3% never married, 46.6% now married, 8.9% widowed, 15.3% divorced (2000); Foreign born: 5.1% (2000); Ancestry (includes multiple ancestries): 30.1% German, 18.7% Other groups, 15.7% Irish, 9.3% English, 7.7% United States or American (2000).
Vital Statistics: Birth rate: 152.1 per 10,000 population (1998)
Economy: Single-family building permits issued: 31 (2001) / 4 (2000); Multi-family building permits issued: 0 (2001) / 0 (2000); Employment by occupation: 9.6% management, 13.9% professional, 17.7% services, 30.2% sales, 0.0% farming, 11.8% construction, 16.8% production (2000).
Income: Per capita income: $18,318 (2000); Median household income: $32,351 (2000); Poverty rate: 12.8% (2000).
Education: High school graduation rate: 80.2% (2000); College graduation rate: 12.6% (2000).

School District(s)

Pattonville R-III (PK-12)
2000 Enrollment: 6,461 314-213-8500

Four-year College(s)

Lael College and Graduate School (Private, Not-for-profit, Interdenominational)
2001 Enrollment: n/a 314-426-7000

Two-year College(s)

Vatterott College (Private, For-profit)
2001 Enrollment: 465 314-428-5900
2001 Tuition: In-state $8,260; Out-of-state $8,260

Housing: Homeownership rate: 59.4% (2000); Median home value: $63,900 (2000); Median rent: $413 per month (2000); Median age of housing: 43 years (2000).
Safety: Violent crime rate: 84.7 per 10,000 population; Property crime rate: 897.7 per 10,000 population (2001).
Transportation: Commute to work: 93.8% car, 2.1% public transportation, 1.8% walk, 1.6% work from home (2000); Travel time to work: 27.4% less than 15 minutes, 44.3% 15 to 30 minutes, 21.2% 30 to 45 minutes, 3.3% 45 to 60 minutes, 3.7% 60 minutes or more (2000)

SAINT GEORGE (city). Covers a land area of 0.185 square miles and a water area of 0 square miles. Located at 38.53° N. Lat.; 90.31° W. Long. Elevation is 542 feet.
Population: 1,288 (2000); Race: 98.6% White, 0.0% Black, 0.5% Asian, 0.0% American Indian and Alaska Native, 1.1% Hispanic of any race, 0.6% two or more races (2000); Density: 6,949.0 persons per square mile (2000); Age: 14.6% under 18, 31.0% over 64 (2000); Marriage status: 21.9% never married, 43.9% now married, 17.4% widowed, 16.8% divorced (2000); Foreign born: 1.0% (2000); Ancestry (includes multiple ancestries): 41.3% German, 15.0% Irish, 14.3% Italian, 10.4% English, 6.6% United States or American (2000).
Economy: Single-family building permits issued: 0 (2001) / 0 (2000); Multi-family building permits issued: 0 (2001) / 0 (2000); Employment by occupation: 17.2% management, 17.2% professional, 16.0% services, 32.4% sales, 0.0% farming, 6.4% construction, 10.9% production (2000).
Income: Per capita income: $21,924 (2000); Median household income: $33,832 (2000); Poverty rate: 3.1% (2000).
Education: High school graduation rate: 78.8% (2000); College graduation rate: 20.6% (2000).

School District(s)

Hancock Place (PK-12)
2000 Enrollment: 1,699 314-544-1300
Mehlville R-IX (PK-12)
2000 Enrollment: 12,001 314-892-5000

Housing: Homeownership rate: 83.8% (2000); Median home value: $88,500 (2000); Median rent: $409 per month (2000); Median age of housing: 42 years (2000).
Safety: Violent crime rate: 0.0 per 10,000 population; Property crime rate: 246.9 per 10,000 population (2001).
Transportation: Commute to work: 96.1% car, 0.6% public transportation, 0.0% walk, 3.3% work from home (2000); Travel time to work: 21.6% less than 15 minutes, 41.3% 15 to 30 minutes, 29.7% 30 to 45 minutes, 6.7% 45 to 60 minutes, 0.8% 60 minutes or more (2000)

SAINT JOHN (city). Aka Saint Johns. Covers a land area of 1.424 square miles and a water area of 0 square miles. Located at 38.71° N. Lat.; 90.34° W. Long.
Population: 6,871 (2000); Race: 83.0% White, 11.9% Black, 1.0% Asian, 0.4% American Indian and Alaska Native, 4.5% Hispanic of any race, 1.5% two or more races (2000); Density: 4,825.8 persons per square mile (2000);

Age: 25.4% under 18, 15.3% over 64 (2000); Marriage status: 26.1% never married, 54.1% now married, 8.0% widowed, 11.8% divorced (2000); Foreign born: 4.0% (2000); Ancestry (includes multiple ancestries): 25.6% German, 21.5% Other groups, 16.0% Irish, 8.1% United States or American, 7.8% English (2000).
Economy: Single-family building permits issued: 1 (2001) / 0 (2000); Multi-family building permits issued: 0 (2001) / 0 (2000); Employment by occupation: 6.9% management, 16.5% professional, 18.4% services, 31.6% sales, 0.0% farming, 9.9% construction, 16.8% production (2000).
Income: Per capita income: $18,581 (2000); Median household income: $37,754 (2000); Poverty rate: 7.8% (2000).
Education: High school graduation rate: 78.0% (2000); College graduation rate: 14.4% (2000).
Housing: Homeownership rate: 79.2% (2000); Median home value: $57,700 (2000); Median rent: $426 per month (2000); Median age of housing: 49 years (2000).
Safety: Violent crime rate: 31.8 per 10,000 population; Property crime rate: 318.2 per 10,000 population (2001).
Transportation: Commute to work: 93.5% car, 3.0% public transportation, 0.6% walk, 2.3% work from home (2000); Travel time to work: 29.9% less than 15 minutes, 43.2% 15 to 30 minutes, 20.0% 30 to 45 minutes, 4.1% 45 to 60 minutes, 2.8% 60 minutes or more (2000)

SAPPINGTON (CDP). Covers a land area of 2.556 square miles and a water area of 0.058 square miles. Located at 38.52° N. Lat.; 90.37° W. Long. Elevation is 597 feet.
Population: 7,287 (2000); Race: 97.4% White, 0.0% Black, 1.9% Asian, 0.0% American Indian and Alaska Native, 0.6% Hispanic of any race, 0.7% two or more races (2000); Density: 2,850.5 persons per square mile (2000); Age: 18.3% under 18, 26.7% over 64 (2000); Marriage status: 19.8% never married, 59.0% now married, 11.3% widowed, 9.8% divorced (2000); Foreign born: 3.1% (2000); Ancestry (includes multiple ancestries): 44.5% German, 19.2% Irish, 11.0% English, 7.5% Italian, 7.1% French (except Basque) (2000).
Economy: Employment by occupation: 14.4% management, 22.7% professional, 8.8% services, 33.9% sales, 0.4% farming, 9.3% construction, 10.4% production (2000).
Income: Per capita income: $26,727 (2000); Median household income: $44,117 (2000); Poverty rate: 2.9% (2000).
Education: High school graduation rate: 87.8% (2000); College graduation rate: 26.7% (2000).

School District(s)

Lindbergh R-VIII (KG-12)
2000 Enrollment: 5,233 314-729-2480
Housing: Homeownership rate: 70.6% (2000); Median home value: $131,400 (2000); Median rent: $610 per month (2000); Median age of housing: 33 years (2000).
Transportation: Commute to work: 93.9% car, 0.7% public transportation, 0.7% walk, 4.2% work from home (2000); Travel time to work: 22.3% less than 15 minutes, 45.2% 15 to 30 minutes, 28.6% 30 to 45 minutes, 2.9% 45 to 60 minutes, 1.0% 60 minutes or more (2000)
Additional Information Contacts
Crestwood-Sunset Hills Chamber 314-843-8545

SHREWSBURY (city). Covers a land area of 1.427 square miles and a water area of 0 square miles. Located at 38.58° N. Lat.; 90.32° W. Long. Elevation is 545 feet.
History: Kenrick Seminary; majority of the large seminary campus was developed into commercial and residential area in early 1980s.
Population: 6,644 (2000); Race: 95.1% White, 2.1% Black, 2.0% Asian, 0.1% American Indian and Alaska Native, 1.9% Hispanic of any race, 0.1% two or more races (2000); Density: 4,655.4 persons per square mile (2000); Age: 15.4% under 18, 27.1% over 64 (2000); Marriage status: 31.4% never married, 43.8% now married, 16.3% widowed, 8.6% divorced (2000); Foreign born: 4.4% (2000); Ancestry (includes multiple ancestries): 44.3% German, 26.1% Irish, 11.0% English, 6.9% Other groups, 6.6% Italian (2000).
Economy: Manufacturing of ink, drilling rigs. Single-family building permits issued: 2 (2001) / 1 (2000); Multi-family building permits issued: 0 (2001) / 0 (2000); Employment by occupation: 20.7% management, 30.3% professional, 9.9% services, 28.0% sales, 0.0% farming, 4.1% construction, 7.0% production (2000).
Income: Per capita income: $27,479 (2000); Median household income: $40,896 (2000); Poverty rate: 8.7% (2000).
Taxes: Total city taxes per capita: $298 (2000); City property taxes per capita: $114 (2000).
Education: High school graduation rate: 86.4% (2000); College graduation rate: 40.1% (2000).
Housing: Homeownership rate: 60.7% (2000); Median home value: $116,100 (2000); Median rent: $595 per month (2000); Median age of housing: 34 years (2000).
Safety: Violent crime rate: 12.0 per 10,000 population; Property crime rate: 239.3 per 10,000 population (2001).
Transportation: Commute to work: 95.3% car, 1.2% public transportation, 1.0% walk, 2.3% work from home (2000); Travel time to work: 22.1% less than 15 minutes, 58.4% 15 to 30 minutes, 16.1% 30 to 45 minutes, 1.4% 45 to 60 minutes, 2.0% 60 minutes or more (2000)

SPANISH LAKE (CDP). Covers a land area of 7.357 square miles and a water area of 0.165 square miles. Located at 38.78° N. Lat.; 90.21° W. Long. Elevation is 538 feet.
Population: 21,337 (2000); Race: 42.4% White, 54.4% Black, 0.4% Asian, 0.3% American Indian and Alaska Native, 0.9% Hispanic of any race, 1.7% two or more races (2000); Density: 2,900.4 persons per square mile (2000); Age: 30.5% under 18, 10.9% over 64 (2000); Marriage status: 34.9% never married, 46.8% now married, 7.0% widowed, 11.3% divorced (2000); Foreign born: 1.5% (2000); Ancestry (includes multiple ancestries): 51.3% Other groups, 16.8% German, 9.5% Irish, 3.8% Italian, 3.4% United States or American (2000).
Economy: Employment by occupation: 8.3% management, 16.5% professional, 18.4% services, 32.1% sales, 0.1% farming, 7.3% construction, 17.2% production (2000).
Income: Per capita income: $18,976 (2000); Median household income: $37,410 (2000); Poverty rate: 11.7% (2000).
Education: High school graduation rate: 82.2% (2000); College graduation rate: 16.9% (2000).
Housing: Homeownership rate: 55.0% (2000); Median home value: $80,000 (2000); Median rent: $447 per month (2000); Median age of housing: 30 years (2000).
Transportation: Commute to work: 94.8% car, 1.8% public transportation, 1.4% walk, 1.7% work from home (2000); Travel time to work: 15.5% less than 15 minutes, 35.0% 15 to 30 minutes, 34.6% 30 to 45 minutes, 9.4% 45 to 60 minutes, 5.5% 60 minutes or more (2000)

SUNSET HILLS (city). Covers a land area of 9.032 square miles and a water area of 0 square miles. Located at 38.53° N. Lat.; 90.40° W. Long. Elevation is 622 feet.
Population: 8,267 (2000); Race: 95.0% White, 1.1% Black, 2.1% Asian, 0.0% American Indian and Alaska Native, 0.9% Hispanic of any race, 1.2% two or more races (2000); Density: 915.3 persons per square mile (2000); Age: 21.4% under 18, 25.0% over 64 (2000); Marriage status: 17.2% never married, 65.1% now married, 12.5% widowed, 5.3% divorced (2000); Foreign born: 3.4% (2000); Ancestry (includes multiple ancestries): 47.5% German, 16.4% Irish, 10.7% English, 6.9% Italian, 6.7% Other groups (2000).
Economy: Employment by occupation: 22.9% management, 25.7% professional, 10.0% services, 29.8% sales, 0.0% farming, 5.9% construction, 5.7% production (2000).
Income: Per capita income: $40,151 (2000); Median household income: $67,576 (2000); Poverty rate: 3.1% (2000).
Taxes: Total city taxes per capita: $196 (1997); City property taxes per capita: $46 (1997).
Education: High school graduation rate: 88.2% (2000); College graduation rate: 38.8% (2000).

Two-year College(s)

Vatterott College (Private, For-profit)
2001 Enrollment: 651 314-843-4200
2001 Tuition: In-state $8,302; Out-of-state $8,302
Housing: Homeownership rate: 84.5% (2000); Median home value: $217,000 (2000); Median rent: $1,081 per month (2000); Median age of housing: 31 years (2000).
Safety: Violent crime rate: 20.4 per 10,000 population; Property crime rate: 432.8 per 10,000 population (2001).
Transportation: Commute to work: 92.7% car, 0.0% public transportation, 2.3% walk, 4.7% work from home (2000); Travel time to work: 29.1% less than 15 minutes, 45.1% 15 to 30 minutes, 19.0% 30 to 45 minutes, 3.3% 45 to 60 minutes, 3.5% 60 minutes or more (2000)

SYCAMORE HILLS (village). Covers a land area of 0.138 square miles and a water area of 0 square miles. Located at 38.70° N. Lat.; 90.34° W. Long. Elevation is 655 feet.

Population: 722 (2000); Race: 90.5% White, 7.2% Black, 0.0% Asian, 1.9% American Indian and Alaska Native, 0.8% Hispanic of any race, 0.3% two or more races (2000); Density: 5,249.0 persons per square mile (2000); Age: 28.9% under 18, 11.6% over 64 (2000); Marriage status: 29.2% never married, 54.0% now married, 6.8% widowed, 10.0% divorced (2000); Foreign born: 0.4% (2000); Ancestry (includes multiple ancestries): 32.4% German, 21.5% Irish, 15.7% Other groups, 8.5% United States or American, 8.4% English (2000).
Economy: Employment by occupation: 11.2% management, 20.6% professional, 17.2% services, 29.9% sales, 0.0% farming, 9.1% construction, 12.0% production (2000).
Income: Per capita income: $18,761 (2000); Median household income: $41,146 (2000); Poverty rate: 2.4% (2000).
Taxes: Total city taxes per capita: $56 (1997); City property taxes per capita: $31 (1997).
Education: High school graduation rate: 86.5% (2000); College graduation rate: 19.9% (2000).
Housing: Homeownership rate: 87.8% (2000); Median home value: $68,300 (2000); Median rent: $492 per month (2000); Median age of housing: 60+ years (2000).
Transportation: Commute to work: 91.9% car, 1.6% public transportation, 2.6% walk, 3.9% work from home (2000); Travel time to work: 29.5% less than 15 minutes, 43.2% 15 to 30 minutes, 20.8% 30 to 45 minutes, 4.4% 45 to 60 minutes, 2.2% 60 minutes or more (2000)

TOWN AND COUNTRY (city). Covers a land area of 11.883 square miles and a water area of 0 square miles. Located at 38.63° N. Lat.; 90.47° W. Long. Elevation is 590 feet.
History: Site of Missouri Baptist College.
Population: 10,894 (2000); Race: 87.9% White, 2.2% Black, 7.6% Asian, 0.0% American Indian and Alaska Native, 0.3% Hispanic of any race, 2.2% two or more races (2000); Density: 916.8 persons per square mile (2000); Age: 23.0% under 18, 22.1% over 64 (2000); Marriage status: 20.8% never married, 65.8% now married, 9.9% widowed, 3.5% divorced (2000); Foreign born: 9.9% (2000); Ancestry (includes multiple ancestries): 30.1% German, 16.8% Irish, 15.4% English, 12.7% Other groups, 5.3% United States or American (2000).
Economy: Single-family building permits issued: 29 (2001) / 28 (2000); Multi-family building permits issued: 0 (2001) / 0 (2000); Employment by occupation: 26.6% management, 39.5% professional, 5.9% services, 23.4% sales, 0.0% farming, 1.5% construction, 3.1% production (2000).
Income: Per capita income: $69,347 (2000); Median household income: $139,967 (2000); Poverty rate: 2.5% (2000).
Taxes: Total city taxes per capita: $325 (1997); City property taxes per capita: $163 (1997).
Education: High school graduation rate: 92.7% (2000); College graduation rate: 66.2% (2000).
Housing: Homeownership rate: 88.3% (2000); Median home value: $466,700 (2000); Median rent: $872 per month (2000); Median age of housing: 21 years (2000).
Safety: Violent crime rate: 10.9 per 10,000 population; Property crime rate: 259.1 per 10,000 population (2001).
Transportation: Commute to work: 90.8% car, 0.1% public transportation, 2.9% walk, 5.5% work from home (2000); Travel time to work: 25.9% less than 15 minutes, 50.4% 15 to 30 minutes, 18.5% 30 to 45 minutes, 1.8% 45 to 60 minutes, 3.3% 60 minutes or more (2000)

TWIN OAKS (village). Covers a land area of 0.258 square miles and a water area of 0 square miles. Located at 38.56° N. Lat.; 90.50° W. Long. Elevation is 593 feet.
Population: 362 (2000); Race: 96.4% White, 0.0% Black, 3.6% Asian, 0.0% American Indian and Alaska Native, 0.0% Hispanic of any race, 0.0% two or more races (2000); Density: 1,403.8 persons per square mile (2000); Age: 13.1% under 18, 19.3% over 64 (2000); Marriage status: 18.0% never married, 64.0% now married, 6.9% widowed, 11.0% divorced (2000); Foreign born: 4.7% (2000); Ancestry (includes multiple ancestries): 29.3% German, 20.7% Irish, 14.0% English, 8.7% United States or American, 8.4% Other groups (2000).
Economy: Single-family building permits issued: 0 (2001) / 0 (2000); Multi-family building permits issued: 0 (2001) / 0 (2000); Employment by occupation: 18.9% management, 28.1% professional, 14.3% services, 25.8% sales, 0.0% farming, 7.4% construction, 5.5% production (2000).
Income: Per capita income: $33,316 (2000); Median household income: $62,778 (2000); Poverty rate: 1.7% (2000).
Taxes: Total city taxes per capita: $77 (1997); City property taxes per capita: $31 (1997).
Education: High school graduation rate: 86.9% (2000); College graduation rate: 33.3% (2000).
Housing: Homeownership rate: 97.6% (2000); Median home value: $129,200 (2000); Median rent: $400 per month (2000); Median age of housing: 25 years (2000).
Transportation: Commute to work: 92.4% car, 0.0% public transportation, 2.4% walk, 3.8% work from home (2000); Travel time to work: 24.6% less than 15 minutes, 30.5% 15 to 30 minutes, 36.5% 30 to 45 minutes, 5.4% 45 to 60 minutes, 3.0% 60 minutes or more (2000)

UNIVERSITY CITY (city). Covers a land area of 5.882 square miles and a water area of 0 square miles. Located at 38.66° N. Lat.; 90.32° W. Long. Elevation is 530 feet.
History: Washington University between University City and Clayton. Incorporated 1906.
Population: 37,428 (2000); Race: 49.7% White, 44.2% Black, 3.1% Asian, 0.2% American Indian and Alaska Native, 1.7% Hispanic of any race, 2.3% two or more races (2000); Density: 6,363.1 persons per square mile (2000); Age: 22.0% under 18, 13.3% over 64 (2000); Marriage status: 36.2% never married, 45.1% now married, 7.9% widowed, 10.7% divorced (2000); Foreign born: 7.1% (2000); Ancestry (includes multiple ancestries): 44.8% Other groups, 13.2% German, 9.1% Irish, 6.3% English, 3.8% Russian (2000).
Vital Statistics: Birth rate: 142.7 per 10,000 population (1998)
Economy: Manufacturing: textiles, metal fabrication and fabricated metal parts. Unemployment rate: 6.0% (11/2002); Total civilian labor force: 23,102 (11/2002); Single-family building permits issued: 10 (2001) / 13 (2000); Multi-family building permits issued: 152 (2001) / 246 (2000); Employment by occupation: 15.1% management, 36.2% professional, 12.9% services, 24.4% sales, 0.2% farming, 3.2% construction, 8.2% production (2000).
Income: Per capita income: $26,901 (2000); Median household income: $40,902 (2000); Poverty rate: 14.7% (2000).
Taxes: Total city taxes per capita: $218 (2000); City property taxes per capita: $94 (2000).
Education: High school graduation rate: 87.4% (2000); College graduation rate: 45.0% (2000).

School District(s)

University City (PK-12)
2000 Enrollment: 4,366 314-290-4000
Housing: Homeownership rate: 57.8% (2000); Median home value: $104,800 (2000); Median rent: $517 per month (2000); Median age of housing: 51 years (2000).
Safety: Violent crime rate: 38.0 per 10,000 population; Property crime rate: 549.1 per 10,000 population (2001).
Transportation: Commute to work: 86.7% car, 4.9% public transportation, 4.0% walk, 3.1% work from home (2000); Travel time to work: 28.0% less than 15 minutes, 51.6% 15 to 30 minutes, 15.6% 30 to 45 minutes, 2.1% 45 to 60 minutes, 2.6% 60 minutes or more (2000)

UPLANDS PARK (village). Covers a land area of 0.067 square miles and a water area of 0 square miles. Located at 38.69° N. Lat.; 90.28° W. Long. Elevation is 610 feet.
Population: 460 (2000); Race: 2.4% White, 94.9% Black, 0.0% Asian, 0.0% American Indian and Alaska Native, 4.1% Hispanic of any race, 2.2% two or more races (2000); Density: 6,904.3 persons per square mile (2000); Age: 30.2% under 18, 14.0% over 64 (2000); Marriage status: 29.4% never married, 51.4% now married, 7.5% widowed, 11.7% divorced (2000); Foreign born: 0.0% (2000); Ancestry (includes multiple ancestries): 84.8% Other groups, 1.8% European, 0.8% German, 0.6% French (except Basque), 0.6% United States or American (2000).
Economy: Employment by occupation: 11.8% management, 10.4% professional, 26.5% services, 28.4% sales, 0.0% farming, 8.1% construction, 14.7% production (2000).
Income: Per capita income: $17,041 (2000); Median household income: $49,286 (2000); Poverty rate: 4.8% (2000).
Taxes: Total city taxes per capita: $28 (1997); City property taxes per capita: $17 (1997).
Education: High school graduation rate: 83.0% (2000); College graduation rate: 12.5% (2000).
Housing: Homeownership rate: 94.2% (2000); Median home value: $58,400 (2000); Median rent: $313 per month (2000); Median age of housing: 55 years (2000).
Transportation: Commute to work: 90.0% car, 2.9% public transportation, 6.2% walk, 1.0% work from home (2000); Travel time to work: 17.3% less than 15 minutes, 49.5% 15 to 30 minutes, 24.0% 30 to 45 minutes, 2.9% 45 to 60 minutes, 6.3% 60 minutes or more (2000)

VALLEY PARK (city). Covers a land area of 3.023 square miles and a water area of 0.156 square miles. Located at 38.55° N. Lat.; 90.48° W. Long. Elevation is 421 feet.
History: 1993 flooding heavily damaged the city.
Population: 6,518 (2000); Race: 90.4% White, 3.8% Black, 3.3% Asian, 0.0% American Indian and Alaska Native, 1.9% Hispanic of any race, 2.3% two or more races (2000); Density: 2,156.2 persons per square mile (2000); Age: 27.1% under 18, 8.2% over 64 (2000); Marriage status: 27.4% never married, 52.5% now married, 6.5% widowed, 13.6% divorced (2000); Foreign born: 6.2% (2000); Ancestry (includes multiple ancestries): 29.6% German, 17.5% Irish, 14.0% Other groups, 13.4% United States or American, 8.9% English (2000).
Economy: Manufacturing: cotton products; aluminum forging; resins, cement; metal heat treating. Single-family building permits issued: 1 (2001) / 3 (2000); Multi-family building permits issued: 0 (2001) / 0 (2000); Employment by occupation: 18.7% management, 22.1% professional, 11.5% services, 27.8% sales, 0.5% farming, 8.6% construction, 10.8% production (2000).
Income: Per capita income: $20,720 (2000); Median household income: $43,548 (2000); Poverty rate: 10.7% (2000).
Taxes: Total city taxes per capita: $243 (2000); City property taxes per capita: $131 (2000).
Education: High school graduation rate: 85.0% (2000); College graduation rate: 32.6% (2000).

School District(s)

Valley Park (PK-12)
2000 Enrollment: 1,037 636-225-4151

Housing: Homeownership rate: 65.4% (2000); Median home value: $130,000 (2000); Median rent: $556 per month (2000); Median age of housing: 14 years (2000).
Transportation: Commute to work: 92.8% car, 0.6% public transportation, 1.9% walk, 4.1% work from home (2000); Travel time to work: 16.5% less than 15 minutes, 43.9% 15 to 30 minutes, 30.8% 30 to 45 minutes, 6.4% 45 to 60 minutes, 2.4% 60 minutes or more (2000)

VELDA CITY (city). Aka Velda. Covers a land area of 0.164 square miles and a water area of 0 square miles. Located at 38.69° N. Lat.; 90.29° W. Long.
Population: 1,616 (2000); Race: 3.5% White, 94.4% Black, 0.0% Asian, 0.0% American Indian and Alaska Native, 1.2% Hispanic of any race, 2.1% two or more races (2000); Density: 9,872.7 persons per square mile (2000); Age: 26.8% under 18, 12.0% over 64 (2000); Marriage status: 38.7% never married, 37.8% now married, 8.0% widowed, 15.5% divorced (2000); Foreign born: 0.4% (2000); Ancestry (includes multiple ancestries): 75.4% Other groups, 1.0% Italian, 0.8% African, 0.7% German, 0.6% English (2000).
Economy: Single-family building permits issued: 0 (2001) / 0 (2000); Multi-family building permits issued: 0 (2001) / 0 (2000); Employment by occupation: 5.8% management, 11.6% professional, 25.3% services, 27.4% sales, 0.0% farming, 4.7% construction, 25.3% production (2000).
Income: Per capita income: $15,009 (2000); Median household income: $30,000 (2000); Poverty rate: 17.5% (2000).
Taxes: Total city taxes per capita: $102 (1997); City property taxes per capita: $39 (1997).
Education: High school graduation rate: 69.9% (2000); College graduation rate: 8.9% (2000).
Housing: Homeownership rate: 70.1% (2000); Median home value: $46,800 (2000); Median rent: $348 per month (2000); Median age of housing: 50 years (2000).
Transportation: Commute to work: 85.1% car, 12.4% public transportation, 0.3% walk, 1.3% work from home (2000); Travel time to work: 16.6% less than 15 minutes, 43.3% 15 to 30 minutes, 23.4% 30 to 45 minutes, 7.1% 45 to 60 minutes, 9.6% 60 minutes or more (2000)

VELDA VILLAGE HILLS (village). Covers a land area of 0.118 square miles and a water area of 0 square miles. Located at 38.69° N. Lat.; 90.28° W. Long. Elevation is 565 feet.
History: Incorporated since 1940.
Population: 1,090 (2000); Race: 1.1% White, 98.9% Black, 0.0% Asian, 0.0% American Indian and Alaska Native, 0.2% Hispanic of any race, 0.0% two or more races (2000); Density: 9,235.6 persons per square mile (2000); Age: 25.8% under 18, 12.7% over 64 (2000); Marriage status: 36.2% never married, 42.1% now married, 8.6% widowed, 13.1% divorced (2000); Foreign born: 0.1% (2000); Ancestry (includes multiple ancestries): 84.1% Other groups, 2.1% African, 0.6% United States or American, 0.3% West Indian, 0.2% Scottish (2000).
Economy: Employment by occupation: 6.0% management, 13.0% professional, 23.0% services, 28.9% sales, 0.0% farming, 6.7% construction, 22.4% production (2000).
Income: Per capita income: $18,649 (2000); Median household income: $38,173 (2000); Poverty rate: 8.8% (2000).
Taxes: Total city taxes per capita: $19 (1997); City property taxes per capita: $18 (1997).
Education: High school graduation rate: 74.7% (2000); College graduation rate: 6.5% (2000).
Housing: Homeownership rate: 83.4% (2000); Median home value: $48,200 (2000); Median rent: $502 per month (2000); Median age of housing: 52 years (2000).
Transportation: Commute to work: 89.7% car, 8.5% public transportation, 0.5% walk, 1.4% work from home (2000); Travel time to work: 13.9% less than 15 minutes, 43.6% 15 to 30 minutes, 29.9% 30 to 45 minutes, 4.9% 45 to 60 minutes, 7.7% 60 minutes or more (2000)

VINITA PARK (city). Covers a land area of 0.732 square miles and a water area of 0 square miles. Located at 38.69° N. Lat.; 90.33° W. Long. Elevation is 625 feet.
History: Incorporated since 1940.
Population: 1,924 (2000); Race: 33.6% White, 61.5% Black, 0.8% Asian, 0.1% American Indian and Alaska Native, 1.5% Hispanic of any race, 2.8% two or more races (2000); Density: 2,628.7 persons per square mile (2000); Age: 31.5% under 18, 8.4% over 64 (2000); Marriage status: 32.2% never married, 46.6% now married, 7.4% widowed, 13.8% divorced (2000); Foreign born: 5.6% (2000); Ancestry (includes multiple ancestries): 53.9% Other groups, 12.6% German, 7.4% Irish, 3.5% Ethiopian, 3.3% English (2000).
Economy: Manufacturing: food products; printing. Single-family building permits issued: 0 (2001) / 0 (2000); Multi-family building permits issued: 0 (2001) / 0 (2000); Employment by occupation: 5.6% management, 20.3% professional, 19.0% services, 26.2% sales, 0.0% farming, 7.0% construction, 21.8% production (2000).
Income: Per capita income: $15,274 (2000); Median household income: $29,482 (2000); Poverty rate: 16.5% (2000).
Taxes: Total city taxes per capita: $302 (1997); City property taxes per capita: $71 (1997).
Education: High school graduation rate: 77.9% (2000); College graduation rate: 15.7% (2000).
Housing: Homeownership rate: 54.2% (2000); Median home value: $53,500 (2000); Median rent: $405 per month (2000); Median age of housing: 47 years (2000).
Safety: Violent crime rate: 149.8 per 10,000 population; Property crime rate: 490.7 per 10,000 population (2001).
Transportation: Commute to work: 89.8% car, 4.7% public transportation, 3.9% walk, 0.7% work from home (2000); Travel time to work: 22.3% less than 15 minutes, 50.1% 15 to 30 minutes, 23.2% 30 to 45 minutes, 1.9% 45 to 60 minutes, 2.6% 60 minutes or more (2000)

VINITA TERRACE (village). Covers a land area of 0.062 square miles and a water area of 0 square miles. Located at 38.68° N. Lat.; 90.33° W. Long. Elevation is 610 feet.
Population: 292 (2000); Race: 23.4% White, 75.0% Black, 0.8% Asian, 0.0% American Indian and Alaska Native, 0.0% Hispanic of any race, 0.8% two or more races (2000); Density: 4,722.9 persons per square mile (2000); Age: 21.8% under 18, 17.5% over 64 (2000); Marriage status: 16.5% never married, 52.8% now married, 10.8% widowed, 19.8% divorced (2000); Foreign born: 0.4% (2000); Ancestry (includes multiple ancestries): 64.3% Other groups, 7.1% German, 6.0% Irish, 4.4% African, 3.6% Scotch-Irish (2000).
Economy: Employment by occupation: 7.4% management, 27.3% professional, 18.2% services, 25.6% sales, 0.0% farming, 5.8% construction, 15.7% production (2000).
Income: Per capita income: $23,752 (2000); Median household income: $46,250 (2000); Poverty rate: 7.9% (2000).
Taxes: Total city taxes per capita: $3 (1997); City property taxes per capita: $3 (1997).
Education: High school graduation rate: 86.5% (2000); College graduation rate: 33.0% (2000).
Housing: Homeownership rate: 83.0% (2000); Median home value: $61,200 (2000); Median rent: $513 per month (2000); Median age of housing: 56 years (2000).

Transportation: Commute to work: 96.7% car, 1.6% public transportation, 0.0% walk, 1.6% work from home (2000); Travel time to work: 12.4% less than 15 minutes, 57.0% 15 to 30 minutes, 24.0% 30 to 45 minutes, 2.5% 45 to 60 minutes, 4.1% 60 minutes or more (2000)

WARSON WOODS (city). Covers a land area of 0.591 square miles and a water area of 0 square miles. Located at 38.60° N. Lat.; 90.39° W. Long. Elevation is 540 feet.

Population: 1,983 (2000); Race: 98.7% White, 0.6% Black, 0.5% Asian, 0.0% American Indian and Alaska Native, 0.2% Hispanic of any race, 0.2% two or more races (2000); Density: 3,352.6 persons per square mile (2000); Age: 24.6% under 18, 30.7% over 64 (2000); Marriage status: 12.2% never married, 75.0% now married, 9.0% widowed, 3.8% divorced (2000); Foreign born: 1.7% (2000); Ancestry (includes multiple ancestries): 38.7% German, 27.9% Irish, 16.9% English, 7.4% Italian, 4.2% United States or American (2000).

Economy: Single-family building permits issued: 0 (2001) / 0 (2000); Multi-family building permits issued: 0 (2001) / 0 (2000); Employment by occupation: 26.7% management, 33.5% professional, 3.9% services, 30.3% sales, 0.0% farming, 1.3% construction, 4.4% production (2000).

Income: Per capita income: $46,575 (2000); Median household income: $87,330 (2000); Poverty rate: 2.7% (2000).

Taxes: Total city taxes per capita: $416 (1997); City property taxes per capita: $199 (1997).

Education: High school graduation rate: 98.3% (2000); College graduation rate: 70.8% (2000).

Housing: Homeownership rate: 99.2% (2000); Median home value: $251,500 (2000); Median rent: $1,125 per month (2000); Median age of housing: 40 years (2000).

Safety: Violent crime rate: 10.0 per 10,000 population; Property crime rate: 80.2 per 10,000 population (2001).

Transportation: Commute to work: 93.3% car, 0.4% public transportation, 0.6% walk, 5.0% work from home (2000); Travel time to work: 23.9% less than 15 minutes, 56.7% 15 to 30 minutes, 17.0% 30 to 45 minutes, 0.5% 45 to 60 minutes, 1.9% 60 minutes or more (2000)

WEBSTER GROVES (city). Covers a land area of 5.900 square miles and a water area of 0 square miles. Located at 38.58° N. Lat.; 90.35° W. Long. Elevation is 560 feet.

History: Webster Groves had its beginnings in Webster College, a boarding school for boys founded before the Civil War by Artemus Bullard. When the Missouri Pacific Railroad built a station here, they called it Webster. "Groves" was added to the name by the post office, established in 1884. The town was incorporated in 1896 and designated as a city in 1914.

Population: 23,230 (2000); Race: 91.5% White, 6.2% Black, 1.3% Asian, 0.2% American Indian and Alaska Native, 1.8% Hispanic of any race, 0.5% two or more races (2000); Density: 3,937.5 persons per square mile (2000); Age: 25.0% under 18, 17.5% over 64 (2000); Marriage status: 23.5% never married, 58.1% now married, 9.7% widowed, 8.8% divorced (2000); Foreign born: 3.0% (2000); Ancestry (includes multiple ancestries): 39.1% German, 21.2% Irish, 14.7% English, 10.2% Other groups, 5.3% Italian (2000).

Vital Statistics: Birth rate: 115.8 per 10,000 population (1998)

Economy: Single-family building permits issued: 25 (2001) / 22 (2000); Multi-family building permits issued: 84 (2001) / 89 (2000); Employment by occupation: 20.6% management, 34.7% professional, 9.9% services, 25.6% sales, 0.2% farming, 4.8% construction, 4.3% production (2000).

Income: Per capita income: $31,327 (2000); Median household income: $60,524 (2000); Poverty rate: 4.8% (2000).

Taxes: Total city taxes per capita: $316 (2000); City property taxes per capita: $199 (2000).

Education: High school graduation rate: 93.4% (2000); College graduation rate: 56.8% (2000).

School District(s)

Webster Groves (KG-12)
2000 Enrollment: 4,167 314-961-1233

Four-year College(s)

Eden Theological Seminary (Private, Not-for-profit, Reorganized Latter Day Saints Church)
2001 Enrollment: 206 314-961-3627

Housing: Homeownership rate: 80.5% (2000); Median home value: $159,900 (2000); Median rent: $618 per month (2000); Median age of housing: 53 years (2000).

Safety: Violent crime rate: 10.3 per 10,000 population; Property crime rate: 127.9 per 10,000 population (2001).

Transportation: Commute to work: 90.8% car, 1.3% public transportation, 2.4% walk, 5.0% work from home (2000); Travel time to work: 30.6% less than 15 minutes, 53.5% 15 to 30 minutes, 12.5% 30 to 45 minutes, 1.6% 45 to 60 minutes, 1.9% 60 minutes or more (2000)

Additional Information Contacts

Webster Groves Chamber of Commerce 314-962-4142

WELLSTON (city). Covers a land area of 0.900 square miles and a water area of 0 square miles. Located at 38.67° N. Lat.; 90.29° W. Long. Elevation is 520 feet.

History: Industrial base declined significantly in 1970s. Incorporated since 1940.

Population: 2,460 (2000); Race: 5.0% White, 94.8% Black, 0.1% Asian, 0.0% American Indian and Alaska Native, 0.4% Hispanic of any race, 0.0% two or more races (2000); Density: 2,732.6 persons per square mile (2000); Age: 36.7% under 18, 10.2% over 64 (2000); Marriage status: 49.2% never married, 30.2% now married, 9.9% widowed, 10.6% divorced (2000); Foreign born: 0.1% (2000); Ancestry (includes multiple ancestries): 76.5% Other groups, 2.5% German, 1.4% United States or American, 0.9% Irish, 0.9% African (2000).

Economy: Manufacturing: sheet metal fabrication, printing. Single-family building permits issued: 0 (2001) / 0 (2000); Multi-family building permits issued: 0 (2001) / 0 (2000); Employment by occupation: 11.0% management, 10.9% professional, 34.9% services, 20.3% sales, 0.0% farming, 4.4% construction, 18.4% production (2000).

Income: Per capita income: $8,262 (2000); Median household income: $21,596 (2000); Poverty rate: 39.1% (2000).

Taxes: Total city taxes per capita: $196 (1997); City property taxes per capita: $46 (1997).

Education: High school graduation rate: 60.9% (2000); College graduation rate: 5.4% (2000).

Housing: Homeownership rate: 49.5% (2000); Median home value: $29,600 (2000); Median rent: $286 per month (2000); Median age of housing: 51 years (2000).

Transportation: Commute to work: 77.4% car, 19.9% public transportation, 1.0% walk, 0.0% work from home (2000); Travel time to work: 14.5% less than 15 minutes, 42.6% 15 to 30 minutes, 26.8% 30 to 45 minutes, 6.7% 45 to 60 minutes, 9.5% 60 minutes or more (2000)

WESTWOOD (village). Covers a land area of 0.626 square miles and a water area of 0 square miles. Located at 38.64° N. Lat.; 90.43° W. Long. Elevation is 590 feet.

Population: 284 (2000); Race: 84.8% White, 10.9% Black, 1.8% Asian, 0.0% American Indian and Alaska Native, 0.0% Hispanic of any race, 2.5% two or more races (2000); Density: 453.7 persons per square mile (2000); Age: 24.3% under 18, 17.4% over 64 (2000); Marriage status: 10.0% never married, 81.8% now married, 5.5% widowed, 2.7% divorced (2000); Foreign born: 3.3% (2000); Ancestry (includes multiple ancestries): 16.3% German, 14.9% Other groups, 8.0% Russian, 6.5% United States or American, 6.2% Polish (2000).

Economy: Employment by occupation: 33.9% management, 28.2% professional, 1.6% services, 33.1% sales, 0.0% farming, 1.6% construction, 1.6% production (2000).

Income: Per capita income: $80,990 (2000); Median household income: $119,618 (2000); Poverty rate: 0.7% (2000).

Taxes: Total city taxes per capita: $35 (1997); City property taxes per capita: $19 (1997).

Education: High school graduation rate: 95.6% (2000); College graduation rate: 69.8% (2000).

Housing: Homeownership rate: 98.3% (2000); Median home value: $615,700 (2000); Median age of housing: 37 years (2000).

Transportation: Commute to work: 93.3% car, 0.0% public transportation, 1.7% walk, 5.0% work from home (2000); Travel time to work: 36.3% less than 15 minutes, 52.2% 15 to 30 minutes, 11.5% 30 to 45 minutes, 0.0% 45 to 60 minutes, 0.0% 60 minutes or more (2000)

WILBUR PARK (village). Covers a land area of 0.060 square miles and a water area of 0 square miles. Located at 38.55° N. Lat.; 90.30° W. Long. Elevation is 525 feet.

Population: 475 (2000); Race: 89.1% White, 0.0% Black, 8.1% Asian, 0.0% American Indian and Alaska Native, 1.0% Hispanic of any race, 2.8% two or more races (2000); Density: 7,882.2 persons per square mile (2000); Age: 29.2% under 18, 16.9% over 64 (2000); Marriage status: 27.0% never married, 54.0% now married, 11.2% widowed, 7.8% divorced (2000); Foreign born: 13.1% (2000); Ancestry (includes multiple ancestries): 33.1% German, 13.9% Irish, 11.9% English, 11.7% Other groups, 10.1% Italian (2000).

Economy: Employment by occupation: 15.6% management, 24.4% professional, 9.8% services, 26.7% sales, 0.0% farming, 4.4% construction, 19.1% production (2000).
Income: Per capita income: $18,263 (2000); Median household income: $44,167 (2000); Poverty rate: 4.2% (2000).
Taxes: Total city taxes per capita: $54 (1997); City property taxes per capita: $39 (1997).
Education: High school graduation rate: 79.5% (2000); College graduation rate: 26.7% (2000).
Housing: Homeownership rate: 96.0% (2000); Median home value: $91,200 (2000); Median rent: $538 per month (2000); Median age of housing: 57 years (2000).
Transportation: Commute to work: 93.6% car, 0.0% public transportation, 1.4% walk, 5.0% work from home (2000); Travel time to work: 17.4% less than 15 minutes, 54.6% 15 to 30 minutes, 22.7% 30 to 45 minutes, 4.3% 45 to 60 minutes, 1.0% 60 minutes or more (2000)

WILDWOOD (city). Covers a land area of 66.030 square miles and a water area of 0.395 square miles. Located at 38.58° N. Lat.; 90.64° W. Long. Elevation is 758 feet.
Population: 32,884 (2000); Race: 95.1% White, 1.1% Black, 2.0% Asian, 0.1% American Indian and Alaska Native, 1.2% Hispanic of any race, 1.4% two or more races (2000); Density: 498.0 persons per square mile (2000); Age: 33.5% under 18, 5.4% over 64 (2000); Marriage status: 17.3% never married, 75.0% now married, 3.0% widowed, 4.7% divorced (2000); Foreign born: 3.6% (2000); Ancestry (includes multiple ancestries): 37.6% German, 19.8% Irish, 13.7% English, 8.1% Italian, 7.8% Other groups (2000).
Economy: Unemployment rate: 3.2% (11/2002); Total civilian labor force: 16,423 (11/2002); Employment by occupation: 28.5% management, 26.9% professional, 7.6% services, 28.2% sales, 0.2% farming, 4.2% construction, 4.3% production (2000).
Income: Per capita income: $38,485 (2000); Median household income: $94,006 (2000); Poverty rate: 2.2% (2000).
Taxes: Total city taxes per capita: $53 (2000); City property taxes per capita: $0 (2000).
Education: High school graduation rate: 96.6% (2000); College graduation rate: 57.4% (2000).
Housing: Homeownership rate: 90.9% (2000); Median home value: $243,900 (2000); Median rent: $648 per month (2000); Median age of housing: 9 years (2000).
Transportation: Commute to work: 92.1% car, 0.5% public transportation, 0.3% walk, 6.5% work from home (2000); Travel time to work: 17.5% less than 15 minutes, 29.8% 15 to 30 minutes, 31.5% 30 to 45 minutes, 15.5% 45 to 60 minutes, 5.7% 60 minutes or more (2000)

WINCHESTER (city). Covers a land area of 0.246 square miles and a water area of 0 square miles. Located at 38.59° N. Lat.; 90.52° W. Long. Elevation is 625 feet.
Population: 1,651 (2000); Race: 93.6% White, 2.3% Black, 0.9% Asian, 0.8% American Indian and Alaska Native, 4.0% Hispanic of any race, 1.8% two or more races (2000); Density: 6,723.0 persons per square mile (2000); Age: 26.0% under 18, 14.9% over 64 (2000); Marriage status: 28.9% never married, 48.7% now married, 9.0% widowed, 13.4% divorced (2000); Foreign born: 1.3% (2000); Ancestry (includes multiple ancestries): 34.5% German, 20.7% Irish, 13.8% English, 11.9% Other groups, 9.8% United States or American (2000).
Economy: Single-family building permits issued: 0 (2001) / 0 (2000); Multi-family building permits issued: 0 (2001) / 0 (2000); Employment by occupation: 11.3% management, 14.1% professional, 17.9% services, 35.1% sales, 0.2% farming, 13.1% construction, 8.3% production (2000).
Income: Per capita income: $18,920 (2000); Median household income: $47,829 (2000); Poverty rate: 4.0% (2000).
Taxes: Total city taxes per capita: $83 (1997); City property taxes per capita: $16 (1997).
Education: High school graduation rate: 83.6% (2000); College graduation rate: 19.6% (2000).
Housing: Homeownership rate: 80.4% (2000); Median home value: $93,900 (2000); Median rent: $518 per month (2000); Median age of housing: 38 years (2000).
Transportation: Commute to work: 91.4% car, 1.8% public transportation, 2.4% walk, 3.9% work from home (2000); Travel time to work: 26.8% less than 15 minutes, 36.9% 15 to 30 minutes, 26.8% 30 to 45 minutes, 6.6% 45 to 60 minutes, 2.8% 60 minutes or more (2000)

WOODSON TERRACE (city). Covers a land area of 0.784 square miles and a water area of 0 square miles. Located at 38.72° N. Lat.; 90.35° W. Long. Elevation is 635 feet.
Population: 4,189 (2000); Race: 85.1% White, 9.6% Black, 0.7% Asian, 0.0% American Indian and Alaska Native, 4.1% Hispanic of any race, 2.1% two or more races (2000); Density: 5,346.2 persons per square mile (2000); Age: 25.5% under 18, 13.2% over 64 (2000); Marriage status: 26.9% never married, 52.1% now married, 6.5% widowed, 14.5% divorced (2000); Foreign born: 1.7% (2000); Ancestry (includes multiple ancestries): 25.2% German, 21.0% Irish, 17.3% Other groups, 11.8% United States or American, 9.1% English (2000).
Economy: Adjacent to Lambert-Saint Louis Airport. Publishing. Single-family building permits issued: 0 (2001) / 0 (2000); Multi-family building permits issued: 0 (2001) / 0 (2000); Employment by occupation: 11.0% management, 15.3% professional, 16.1% services, 29.8% sales, 0.2% farming, 13.0% construction, 14.6% production (2000).
Income: Per capita income: $18,581 (2000); Median household income: $36,363 (2000); Poverty rate: 7.7% (2000).
Taxes: Total city taxes per capita: $232 (1997); City property taxes per capita: $89 (1997).
Education: High school graduation rate: 80.3% (2000); College graduation rate: 9.3% (2000).
Housing: Homeownership rate: 77.3% (2000); Median home value: $58,800 (2000); Median rent: $466 per month (2000); Median age of housing: 45 years (2000).
Transportation: Commute to work: 93.7% car, 1.8% public transportation, 2.1% walk, 1.5% work from home (2000); Travel time to work: 26.3% less than 15 minutes, 48.1% 15 to 30 minutes, 20.1% 30 to 45 minutes, 3.2% 45 to 60 minutes, 2.2% 60 minutes or more (2000)

Saint Louis Independent City

Located in eastern Missouri, on the Mississippi River. Located in the Central Time Zone. The county government was organized in 1764.

Saint Louis city is part of the St. Louis, MO-IL MSA. The entire metro area includes: Clinton County, IL; Jersey County, IL; Madison County, IL; Monroe County, IL; St. Clair County, IL; Crawford County, MO (part); Franklin County, MO; Jefferson County, MO; Lincoln County, MO; St. Charles County, MO; St. Louis County, MO; Warren County, MO; St. Louis city, MO

Economy: Unemployment rate: 8.4% (11/2002); Total civilian labor force: 157,082 (11/2002); Leading industries: 14.3% health care and social assistance; 10.0% manufacturing; 7.7% finance & insurance (2000); Companies that employ more than 1,000 persons: 25 (2000); Companies that employ more than 100 persons: 418 (2000); Farms: 0 totaling 0 acres (1997); Minority business ownership rate: 20.1% (1997); Women business ownership rate: 26.1% (1997); Retail sales per capita: $6,856 (1997). Single-family building permits issued: 126 (2001) / 162 (2000); Multi-family building permits issued: 52 (2001) / 235 (2000).
Income: Per capita income: $16,108 (2000); Median household income: $27,156 (2000); Poverty rate: 24.6% (2000); Bankruptcy rate: 9.14% (2001).
Housing: Homeownership rate: 46.9% (2000); Median home value: $63,900 (2000); Median rent: $347 per month (2000); Median age of housing: 59 years (2000).
Religion: Five largest groups: 20.2% Catholic Church, 4.4% Southern Baptist Convention, 2.2% Lutheran Church—Missouri Synod, 1.4% The United Methodist Church, 1.3% Evangelical Lutheran Church in America (2000).
Health: Birth rate: 161.3 per 10,000 population (1998); Age adjusted death rate: 124.2 per 10,000 population (1999); Infant mortality rate: 12.5 per 1,000 live births (1998); Age adjusted cancer mortality rate: 254.3 deaths per 100,000 population (1999). Air Quality Index: 64% good, 36% moderate, 0% unhealthy (percent of days in 2000). Number of physicians: n/a (1999); Number of hospital beds: 188.6 per 10,000 population (1999).
Elections: 2000 Presidential election results: 77.4% Gore, 19.9% Bush, 2.1% Nader, 0.3% Buchanan
Physical Characteristics: Covers a land area of 61.924 square miles and a water area of 4.225 square miles. Located at 38.62° N. Lat.; 90.24° W. Long. Elevation is 465 feet.
History: St. Louis owes its beginning to the fur trade, and its growth to its location as a transportation center. The Jesuit Mission of St. Francis Xavier existed for a few years in the early 1700's, but the city dates from 1763 when Pierre Laclede Liguest selected the site for a trading post and named it for

Louis IX, Crusader King of France. Laclede's fur business flourished, attracting new settlers and merchants. For a time pirates made commerce on the Mississippi River dangerous, but in 1788 (called the Year of the Ten Boats), the pirates were driven out by the crews of ten boats which traveled upstream together. This purge, plus the development of steamboat traffic after 1817, shaped St. Louis as a principal trade center. After the Louisiana Purchase brought St. Louis under American rule in 1803, westward-bound immigrants flooded the city.

Population: 348,189 (2000); Race: 43.8% White, 51.0% Black, 2.0% Asian, 0.3% American Indian and Alaska Native, 1.9% Hispanic of any race, 2.1% two or more races (2000); Density: 5,622.9 persons per square mile (2000); Age: 25.7% under 18, 13.7% over 64 (2000); Marriage status: 41.5% never married, 37.0% now married, 9.2% widowed, 12.3% divorced (2000); Foreign born: 5.6% (2000); Ancestry (includes multiple ancestries): 46.3% Other groups, 14.5% German, 8.6% Irish, 3.9% English, 3.6% Italian (2000).
Employment by Occupation: 10.0% management, 19.6% professional, 22.1% services, 26.5% sales, 0.1% farming, 6.2% construction, 15.4% production (2000).
Education: High school graduation rate: 71.3% (2000); College graduation rate: 19.1% (2000).

School District(s)

Saint Louis City (PK-12)
2000 Enrollment: 44,412 314-231-3720

Four-year College(s)

Aquinas Institute of Theology (Private, Not-for-profit, Roman Catholic)
2001 Enrollment: 252 314-977-3882
Concordia Seminary (Private, Not-for-profit, Lutheran Church - Missouri Synod)
2001 Enrollment: 559 314-505-7000
Covenant Theological Seminary (Private, Not-for-profit, The Presbyterian Church in America)
2001 Enrollment: 832 314-434-4044
Deaconess College of Nursing (Private, For-profit)
2001 Enrollment: 243 314-768-3044
2001 Tuition: In-state $9,250; Out-of-state $9,250
Fontbonne College (Private, Not-for-profit, Roman Catholic)
2001 Enrollment: 2,192 314-862-3456
2001 Tuition: In-state $12,596; Out-of-state $12,596
Harris-Stowe State College (Public, Historically black)
2001 Enrollment: 1,921 314-340-3366
Jewish Hospital-College of Nursing and Allied Health (Private, Not-for-profit)
2001 Enrollment: 452 314-454-7055
2001 Tuition: In-state $7,920; Out-of-state $7,920
Kenrick Glennon Seminary (Private, Not-for-profit, Roman Catholic)
2001 Enrollment: 77 314-644-0266
Maryville University of Saint Louis (Private, Not-for-profit)
2001 Enrollment: 3,162 800-627-9855
2001 Tuition: In-state $13,650; Out-of-state $13,650
Missouri Baptist College (Private, Not-for-profit, Southern Baptist)
2001 Enrollment: 3,105 314-434-1115
2001 Tuition: In-state $10,290; Out-of-state $10,290
Missouri Tech (Private, For-profit)
2001 Enrollment: 209 314-569-3600
2001 Tuition: In-state $7,800; Out-of-state $7,800
University of Missouri-Saint Louis (Public)
2001 Enrollment: 14,993 314-516-5000
2001 Tuition: In-state $4,245; Out-of-state $12,690
Saint Louis University-Main Campus (Private, Not-for-profit, Roman Catholic)
2001 Enrollment: 13,521 314-977-2222
2001 Tuition: In-state $19,670; Out-of-state $19,670
Saint Louis College of Pharmacy (Private, Not-for-profit)
2001 Enrollment: 72 314-367-8700
2001 Tuition: In-state $13,650; Out-of-state $13,650
Washington University (Private, Not-for-profit)
2001 Enrollment: 12,187 314-935-5959
2001 Tuition: In-state $25,700; Out-of-state $25,700
Webster University (Private, Not-for-profit)
2001 Enrollment: 15,402 314-968-2660
2001 Tuition: In-state $13,720; Out-of-state $13,720
Saint John's Mercy Medical Center School Clinical Lab Science (Private, Not-for-profit, Roman Catholic)
2001 Enrollment: n/a 314-569-6855
Keller Graduate School of Management Inc (Private, For-profit)
2001 Enrollment: n/a 314-542-4222
Keller Graduate School of Management (Private, For-profit)
2001 Enrollment: 102 314-588-0066
University of Phoenix-Saint Louis Campus (Private, For-profit)
2001 Enrollment: 246 314-298-9755

Two-year College(s)

Hickey College (Private, For-profit)
2001 Enrollment: 408 314-434-2212
2001 Tuition: In-state $9,120; Out-of-state $9,120
Lutheran Medical Center School of Nursing (Private, For-profit)
2001 Enrollment: 56 314-577-5850
2001 Tuition: In-state $7,350; Out-of-state $7,350
Missouri College (Private, For-profit)
2001 Enrollment: 529 314-821-7700
Patricia Stevens College (Private, For-profit)
2001 Enrollment: 164 314-421-0949
2001 Tuition: In-state $11,990; Out-of-state $11,990
Ranken Technical College (Private, Not-for-profit)
2001 Enrollment: 1,384 314-371-0236
2001 Tuition: In-state $8,030; Out-of-state $8,030
Saint John's Mercy Medical Center School of Rad Techn (Private, Not-for-profit, Christian Churches and Churches of Christ)
2001 Enrollment: n/a 314-569-6933
Saint Louis Community College-Florissant Valley (Public)
2001 Enrollment: 6,924 314-595-4200
2001 Tuition: In-state $1,530; Out-of-state $1,950
Saint Louis Community College-Forest Park (Public)
2001 Enrollment: 6,930 314-539-5000
2001 Tuition: In-state $1,530; Out-of-state $1,950

Hospitals: Saint Alexian Hospital (203 beds); Shriners Hospital for Children (80 beds); BJC HealthCare (4,315 beds); Barnes-Jewish Hospital (1,442 beds); Barnes-Jewish Hospital of Saint Louis (1,500 beds); Barnes-Jewish West County Hospital (113 beds); Cardinal Glennon Childrens Hospital (190 beds); Christian Hospital Northeast (678 beds); Department of Veterans Affairs Medical Center; DesPeres Hospital (167 beds); Forest Park Hospital (527 beds); Metropolitan Saint Louis Psychiatric Center (125 beds); Missouri Baptist Medical Center (489 beds); SLUCare (356 beds); SouthPointe Hospital (408 beds); Saint John's Mercy Medical Center (979 beds); Saint Joseph Hospital (269 beds); Saint Louis Children's Hospital (235 beds); Saint Louis Psychiatric Rehabilitation Center (212 beds); Saint Mary's Health Center (622 beds)
Safety: Violent crime rate: 218.8 per 10,000 population; Property crime rate: 1,283.7 per 10,000 population (2001).
Newspapers: Concord Call (1 x week); Saint Louis Chinese Journal (1 x week); Saint Louis Metro Evening Whirl (1 x week); St. Louis Daily Record (5 x week); West County Journal (2 x week); Webster-Kirkwood Journal (2 x week); Press Journal (2 x week); Mid-County Journal (2 x week); Citizen Journal (2 x week); Chesterfield Journal (2 x week); Central West End Journal (1 x week); Saint Louis Jewish Light (1 x week); South County Times (1 x week); North Side Journal (2 x week); North County Journal (2 x week); North County Journal East (2 x week); Maryland Heights/Bridgeton Journal (2 x week); County Star Journal (2 x week); St. Louis Post-Dispatch (7 x week); The Riverfront Times (1 x week); Saint Louis Sentinel (1 x week); Saint Louis Review (1 x week); Saint Louis American (1 x week); Southwest County Journal (2 x week); Southwest City Journal (2 x week); South Side Journal (2 x week); South County Journal (2 x week); South City Journal (1 x week); Oakville-Mehlville Journal (2 x week); Saint Louis Argus (1 x week); The Bulletin (6 x year)
Transportation: Commute to work: 82.5% car, 10.7% public transportation, 4.0% walk, 1.7% work from home (2000); Travel time to work: 25.0% less than 15 minutes, 43.8% 15 to 30 minutes, 19.4% 30 to 45 minutes, 5.7% 45 to 60 minutes, 6.1% 60 minutes or more (2000); Amtrak: Service available.
Airports: Lambert-St Louis International (primary service/large hub); Spirit of St Louis (primary service/large hub); St Louis Downtown (primary service/large hub)

Additional Information Contacts

Chamber of Commerce-Clayton 314-726-3033
Creve Coeur Chamber of Commerce 314-569-3536
Downtown St. Louis Partnership 314-436-6500
Hispanic Chamber of Commerce 314-621-1991
Saint Louis Chamber of Commerce 314-381-3333
St. Louis Association of Realtors 314-576-0033
St. Louis Chamber of Commerce 314-444-1150
St. Louis Convention & Visitors Bureau 847-735-0218
St. Louis Regional Chamber 314-231-5555

Sainte Genevieve County

Located in eastern Missouri; bounded on the northeast by the Mississippi River and the Illinois border; includes part of Clark National Forest. Covers a land area of 502.40 square miles, a water area of 6.50 square miles, and is located in the Central Time Zone. The county government was organized in 1812. County seat is Ste. Genevieve.
Population: 17,842 (2000); Race: 97.9% White, 0.8% Black, 0.0% Asian, 0.3% American Indian and Alaska Native, 0.8% Hispanic of any race, 0.7% two or more races (2000); Density: 35.5 persons per square mile (2000); Age: 26.5% under 18, 14.6% over 64 (2000).
Religion: Five largest groups: 49.6% Catholic Church, 18.4% Southern Baptist Convention, 1.7% The Church of Jesus Christ of Latter-day Saints, 1.2% Lutheran Church—Missouri Synod, 1.0% Presbyterian Church (U.S.A.) (2000).
Economy: Unemployment rate: 4.6% (11/2002); Total civilian labor force: 8,365 (11/2002); Leading industries: 36.2% manufacturing; 13.5% health care and social assistance; 10.9% construction (2000); Companies that employ more than 1,000 persons: 0 (2000); Companies that employ more than 100 persons: 9 (2000); Farms: 631 totaling 168,121 acres (1997); Minority business ownership rate: 0.0% (1997); Women business ownership rate: 23.0% (1997); Retail sales per capita: $4,810 (1997). Single-family building permits issued: 6 (2001) / 9 (2000); Multi-family building permits issued: 0 (2001) / 0 (2000).
Income: Per capita income: $17,283 (2000); Median household income: $39,200 (2000); Poverty rate: 8.2% (2000); Bankruptcy rate: 2.59% (2001).
Taxes: Total county taxes per capita: $131 (2000); County property taxes per capita: $58 (2000).
Education: High school graduation rate: 73.8% (2000); College graduation rate: 8.1% (2000).
Housing: Homeownership rate: 82.3% (2000); Median home value: $83,700 (2000); Median rent: $290 per month (2000); Median age of housing: 26 years (2000).
Health: Birth rate: 106.5 per 10,000 population (1998); Age adjusted death rate: n/a (1999); Age adjusted cancer mortality rate: n/a (1999). Air Quality Index: 50% good, 50% moderate, 0% unhealthy (percent of days in 2000). Number of physicians: 0.6 per 10,000 population (1999); Number of hospital beds: 19.1 per 10,000 population (1999).
Elections: 2000 Presidential election results: 49.2% Gore, 47.9% Bush, 1.7% Nader, 0.6% Buchanan
National and State Parks: Hawn State Park
Additional Information Contacts
Ste. Genevieve County Government Offices 573-883-5589
Ste Genevieve Chamber of Commerce 573-883-3686

Sainte Genevieve County Communities

BLOOMSDALE (city). Covers a land area of 1.612 square miles and a water area of 0 square miles. Located at 38.01° N. Lat.; 90.22° W. Long. Elevation is 506 feet.
History: Bloomsdale was known in the 1830's as La Fourche a Duclos, but was renamed in 1874. Many of the early residents were of French and Creole descent.
Population: 419 (2000); Race: 98.9% White, 0.0% Black, 0.0% Asian, 0.5% American Indian and Alaska Native, 0.0% Hispanic of any race, 0.7% two or more races (2000); Density: 259.9 persons per square mile (2000); Age: 25.9% under 18, 17.6% over 64 (2000); Marriage status: 23.3% never married, 56.2% now married, 13.3% widowed, 7.2% divorced (2000); Foreign born: 0.0% (2000); Ancestry (includes multiple ancestries): 60.4% German, 21.2% French (except Basque), 11.7% United States or American, 11.5% Irish, 6.1% English (2000).
Economy: Employment by occupation: 11.9% management, 21.9% professional, 13.8% services, 21.9% sales, 0.0% farming, 17.6% construction, 12.9% production (2000).
Income: Per capita income: $17,714 (2000); Median household income: $43,125 (2000); Poverty rate: 6.1% (2000).
Taxes: Total city taxes per capita: $3 (1997); City property taxes per capita: $3 (1997).
Education: High school graduation rate: 78.9% (2000); College graduation rate: 10.7% (2000).
Housing: Homeownership rate: 74.4% (2000); Median home value: $97,100 (2000); Median rent: $228 per month (2000); Median age of housing: 37 years (2000).
Transportation: Commute to work: 91.9% car, 0.0% public transportation, 3.3% walk, 4.8% work from home (2000); Travel time to work: 19.0% less than 15 minutes, 40.5% 15 to 30 minutes, 12.5% 30 to 45 minutes, 9.5% 45 to 60 minutes, 18.5% 60 minutes or more (2000)

SAINT MARY (city). Covers a land area of 0.603 square miles and a water area of 0 square miles. Located at 37.87° N. Lat.; 89.94° W. Long. Elevation is 400 feet.
Population: 377 (2000); Race: 94.9% White, 4.3% Black, 0.0% Asian, 0.0% American Indian and Alaska Native, 1.4% Hispanic of any race, 0.0% two or more races (2000); Density: 625.3 persons per square mile (2000); Age: 17.6% under 18, 20.0% over 64 (2000); Marriage status: 20.6% never married, 51.3% now married, 10.4% widowed, 17.7% divorced (2000); Foreign born: 0.5% (2000); Ancestry (includes multiple ancestries): 34.6% German, 17.6% French (except Basque), 10.8% Irish, 10.3% Other groups, 7.3% United States or American (2000).
Economy: Single-family building permits issued: 0 (2001) / 0 (2000); Multi-family building permits issued: 0 (2001) / 0 (2000); Employment by occupation: 10.3% management, 6.0% professional, 27.2% services, 18.5% sales, 0.0% farming, 11.4% construction, 26.6% production (2000).
Income: Per capita income: $16,825 (2000); Median household income: $27,000 (2000); Poverty rate: 13.2% (2000).
Education: High school graduation rate: 67.5% (2000); College graduation rate: 4.9% (2000).
Housing: Homeownership rate: 79.5% (2000); Median home value: $50,000 (2000); Median rent: $231 per month (2000); Median age of housing: 31 years (2000).
Transportation: Commute to work: 96.1% car, 0.0% public transportation, 1.1% walk, 2.8% work from home (2000); Travel time to work: 30.1% less than 15 minutes, 50.6% 15 to 30 minutes, 4.5% 30 to 45 minutes, 1.1% 45 to 60 minutes, 13.6% 60 minutes or more (2000)

SAINTE GENEVIEVE (city). Covers a land area of 4.157 square miles and a water area of 0 square miles. Located at 37.97° N. Lat.; 90.04° W. Long. Elevation is 401 feet.
History: Settlement began in the area of Ste. Genevieve in the early 1700's, when lead deposits were discovered. The region was under Spanish rule from 1762 to 1803, when salt, furs, lead, and grain were being shipped to St. Louis and New Orleans by boat. Annual flooding from the Mississippi River eventually brought about the removal of the community to higher ground, and in 1812 Ste. Genevieve was organized as the seat of government for the Ste. Genevieve District.
Population: 4,476 (2000); Race: 95.2% White, 2.9% Black, 0.0% Asian, 0.0% American Indian and Alaska Native, 1.4% Hispanic of any race, 1.1% two or more races (2000); Density: 1,076.7 persons per square mile (2000); Age: 21.5% under 18, 23.7% over 64 (2000); Marriage status: 23.9% never married, 52.9% now married, 13.2% widowed, 9.9% divorced (2000); Foreign born: 1.1% (2000); Ancestry (includes multiple ancestries): 42.8% German, 16.0% French (except Basque), 9.9% Irish, 9.7% United States or American, 5.6% English (2000).
Economy: Single-family building permits issued: 6 (2001) / n/a (2000); Multi-family building permits issued: 0 (2001) / n/a (2000); Employment by occupation: 11.6% management, 15.9% professional, 13.1% services, 18.1% sales, 0.9% farming, 12.5% construction, 27.8% production (2000).
Income: Per capita income: $17,361 (2000); Median household income: $33,929 (2000); Poverty rate: 9.6% (2000).
Education: High school graduation rate: 70.4% (2000); College graduation rate: 10.0% (2000).

School District(s)

Ste. Genevieve Co. R-II (PK-12)
2000 Enrollment: 2,198 573-883-5720
Housing: Homeownership rate: 67.2% (2000); Median home value: $77,300 (2000); Median rent: $289 per month (2000); Median age of housing: 37 years (2000).
Hospitals: Sainte Genevieve County Memorial Hospital (47 beds)
Safety: Violent crime rate: 37.7 per 10,000 population; Property crime rate: 182.1 per 10,000 population (2001).
Newspapers: Sun Times (7 x week)
Transportation: Commute to work: 91.4% car, 0.0% public transportation, 3.9% walk, 3.4% work from home (2000); Travel time to work: 64.8% less than 15 minutes, 11.0% 15 to 30 minutes, 13.2% 30 to 45 minutes, 2.6% 45 to 60 minutes, 8.3% 60 minutes or more (2000)
Additional Information Contacts
Ste Genevieve Chamber of Commerce 573-883-3686

Saline County

Located in central Missouri; bounded on the north and east by the Missouri River; drained by the Blackwater River. Covers a land area of 755.50 square miles, a water area of 9.00 square miles, and is located in the Central Time Zone. The county government was organized in 1820. County seat is Marshall.

Weather Station: Sweet Springs Elevation: 679 feet

	Jan	Feb	Mar	Apr	May	Jun	Jul	Aug	Sep	Oct	Nov	Dec
High	38	45	56	68	77	85	91	89	81	69	54	42
Low	19	24	34	44	53	63	67	65	56	45	34	24
Precip	1.5	1.8	3.1	4.3	5.0	4.0	3.9	3.9	4.6	3.4	3.2	2.3
Snow	7.2	6.0	3.6	0.7	tr	tr	0.0	0.0	0.0	tr	1.9	4.2

High and Low temperatures in degrees Fahrenheit; Precipitation and Snow in inches

Population: 23,756 (2000); Race: 90.4% White, 4.8% Black, 0.5% Asian, 0.5% American Indian and Alaska Native, 4.2% Hispanic of any race, 2.2% two or more races (2000); Density: 31.4 persons per square mile (2000); Age: 24.4% under 18, 16.2% over 64 (2000).
Religion: Five largest groups: 18.2% Southern Baptist Convention, 8.0% The United Methodist Church, 6.5% Lutheran Church—Missouri Synod, 5.8% Catholic Church, 5.5% Christian Church (Disciples of Christ) (2000).
Economy: Unemployment rate: 4.7% (11/2002); Total civilian labor force: 11,023 (11/2002); Leading industries: 32.1% manufacturing; 17.9% health care and social assistance; 13.4% retail trade (2000); Companies that employ more than 1,000 persons: 0 (2000); Companies that employ more than 100 persons: 11 (2000); Farms: 936 totaling 429,631 acres (1997); Minority business ownership rate: 0.0% (1997); Women business ownership rate: 13.7% (1997); Retail sales per capita: $6,174 (1997). Single-family building permits issued: 17 (2001) / 15 (2000); Multi-family building permits issued: 76 (2001) / 8 (2000).
Income: Per capita income: $16,132 (2000); Median household income: $32,743 (2000); Poverty rate: 13.2% (2000); Bankruptcy rate: 4.00% (2001).
Taxes: Total county taxes per capita: $103 (2000); County property taxes per capita: $32 (2000).
Education: High school graduation rate: 74.0% (2000); College graduation rate: 15.8% (2000).
Housing: Homeownership rate: 69.1% (2000); Median home value: $59,700 (2000); Median rent: $279 per month (2000); Median age of housing: 38 years (2000).
Health: Birth rate: 129.2 per 10,000 population (1998); Age adjusted death rate: 102.9 per 10,000 population (1999); Age adjusted cancer mortality rate: 242.5 deaths per 100,000 population (1999). Number of physicians: 8.4 per 10,000 population (1999); Number of hospital beds: 23.6 per 10,000 population (1999).
Elections: 2000 Presidential election results: 49.0% Gore, 48.9% Bush, 1.4% Nader, 0.4% Buchanan
National and State Parks: Arrow Rock State Historic Site; Marshall Junction State Wildlife Area; Perry State Wildlife Area; Van Meter State Park

Additional Information Contacts
Saline County Government Offices 660-886-3331
Central Missouri Board of Realtors 660-837-3304
Marshall Chamber of Commerce 660-886-3324

Saline County Communities

ARROW ROCK (town). Covers a land area of 0.133 square miles and a water area of 0 square miles. Located at 39.07° N. Lat.; 92.94° W. Long. Elevation is 715 feet.
History: The bluff here was named Pierre a Fleche (French for Arrow Rock) as early as 1723, when Dumont de Montigny mapped the area. William Clark noted it as a good site for a fort when he came through in 1808, and a post was established in 1813. The town that was laid out in 1829 was first called New Philadelphia, but the older name of Arrow Rock was adopted in 1833.
Population: 79 (2000); Race: 97.7% White, 0.0% Black, 0.0% Asian, 2.3% American Indian and Alaska Native, 0.0% Hispanic of any race, 0.0% two or more races (2000); Density: 592.5 persons per square mile (2000); Age: 13.6% under 18, 25.0% over 64 (2000); Marriage status: 21.3% never married, 47.5% now married, 17.5% widowed, 13.8% divorced (2000); Foreign born: 0.0% (2000); Ancestry (includes multiple ancestries): 15.9% United States or American, 13.6% German, 13.6% English, 12.5% Other groups, 8.0% Irish (2000).
Economy: Single-family building permits issued: 0 (2001) / 0 (2000); Multi-family building permits issued: 0 (2001) / 0 (2000); Employment by occupation: 15.7% management, 19.6% professional, 15.7% services, 33.3% sales, 0.0% farming, 15.7% construction, 0.0% production (2000).
Income: Per capita income: $28,344 (2000); Median household income: $45,000 (2000); Poverty rate: 0.0% (2000).
Taxes: Total city taxes per capita: $303 (1997); City property taxes per capita: $15 (1997).
Education: High school graduation rate: 94.4% (2000); College graduation rate: 30.6% (2000).
Housing: Homeownership rate: 81.4% (2000); Median home value: $115,600 (2000); Median rent: $367 per month (2000); Median age of housing: 60+ years (2000).
Transportation: Commute to work: 71.4% car, 0.0% public transportation, 14.3% walk, 14.3% work from home (2000); Travel time to work: 21.4% less than 15 minutes, 38.1% 15 to 30 minutes, 26.2% 30 to 45 minutes, 9.5% 45 to 60 minutes, 4.8% 60 minutes or more (2000)

Additional Information Contacts
Central Missouri Board of Realtors 660-837-3304

BLACKBURN (city). Covers a land area of 0.308 square miles and a water area of 0.014 square miles. Located at 39.10° N. Lat.; 93.48° W. Long. Elevation is 805 feet.
Population: 284 (2000); Race: 98.1% White, 1.1% Black, 0.8% Asian, 0.0% American Indian and Alaska Native, 5.3% Hispanic of any race, 0.0% two or more races (2000); Density: 923.4 persons per square mile (2000); Age: 30.5% under 18, 14.5% over 64 (2000); Marriage status: 17.9% never married, 59.4% now married, 10.6% widowed, 12.1% divorced (2000); Foreign born: 3.1% (2000); Ancestry (includes multiple ancestries): 45.4% German, 16.0% Irish, 16.0% Other groups, 13.4% English, 6.1% United States or American (2000).
Economy: Corn, soybeans; livestock. Employment by occupation: 17.1% management, 15.4% professional, 18.8% services, 17.9% sales, 0.9% farming, 16.2% construction, 13.7% production (2000).
Income: Per capita income: $14,603 (2000); Median household income: $35,313 (2000); Poverty rate: 11.8% (2000).
Taxes: Total city taxes per capita: $357 (1997); City property taxes per capita: $13 (1997).
Education: High school graduation rate: 87.4% (2000); College graduation rate: 10.2% (2000).
Housing: Homeownership rate: 78.8% (2000); Median home value: $36,300 (2000); Median rent: $175 per month (2000); Median age of housing: 53 years (2000).
Transportation: Commute to work: 98.3% car, 0.0% public transportation, 0.0% walk, 1.7% work from home (2000); Travel time to work: 13.8% less than 15 minutes, 49.1% 15 to 30 minutes, 21.6% 30 to 45 minutes, 5.2% 45 to 60 minutes, 10.3% 60 minutes or more (2000)

EMMA (city). Covers a land area of 0.432 square miles and a water area of 0 square miles. Located at 38.97° N. Lat.; 93.49° W. Long. Elevation is 759 feet.
Population: 243 (2000); Race: 97.9% White, 0.0% Black, 0.0% Asian, 0.9% American Indian and Alaska Native, 1.3% Hispanic of any race, 1.3% two or more races (2000); Density: 562.3 persons per square mile (2000); Age: 24.9% under 18, 21.5% over 64 (2000); Marriage status: 12.7% never married, 71.8% now married, 7.2% widowed, 8.3% divorced (2000); Foreign born: 0.0% (2000); Ancestry (includes multiple ancestries): 65.7% German, 8.2% English, 7.7% Irish, 7.3% Other groups, 3.9% United States or American (2000).
Economy: Employment by occupation: 6.7% management, 22.9% professional, 13.3% services, 29.5% sales, 0.0% farming, 8.6% construction, 19.0% production (2000).
Income: Per capita income: $14,994 (2000); Median household income: $34,167 (2000); Poverty rate: 12.4% (2000).
Taxes: Total city taxes per capita: $112 (1997); City property taxes per capita: $112 (1997).
Education: High school graduation rate: 85.4% (2000); College graduation rate: 19.7% (2000).
Housing: Homeownership rate: 89.1% (2000); Median home value: $62,700 (2000); Median rent: $313 per month (2000); Median age of housing: 58 years (2000).
Transportation: Commute to work: 100.0% car, 0.0% public transportation, 0.0% walk, 0.0% work from home (2000); Travel time to work: 65.0% less than 15 minutes, 11.7% 15 to 30 minutes, 14.6% 30 to 45 minutes, 4.9% 45 to 60 minutes, 3.9% 60 minutes or more (2000)

GILLIAM (town). Covers a land area of 0.250 square miles and a water area of 0 square miles. Located at 39.23° N. Lat.; 93.00° W. Long. Elevation is 825 feet.
Population: 229 (2000); Race: 90.4% White, 5.6% Black, 0.0% Asian, 0.0% American Indian and Alaska Native, 1.0% Hispanic of any race, 2.0% two or more races (2000); Density: 915.0 persons per square mile (2000); Age: 26.8% under 18, 22.2% over 64 (2000); Marriage status: 17.4% never married, 48.3% now married, 16.8% widowed, 17.4% divorced (2000); Foreign born: 1.0% (2000); Ancestry (includes multiple ancestries): 31.3% German, 14.1% Irish, 11.6% Other groups, 9.6% United States or American, 4.5% Scottish (2000).
Economy: Limestone quarry. Corn, soybeans, cattle. Employment by occupation: 0.0% management, 9.9% professional, 23.1% services, 14.3% sales, 2.2% farming, 20.9% construction, 29.7% production (2000).
Income: Per capita income: $12,120 (2000); Median household income: $27,813 (2000); Poverty rate: 17.3% (2000).
Taxes: Total city taxes per capita: $19 (1997); City property taxes per capita: $19 (1997).
Education: High school graduation rate: 67.2% (2000); College graduation rate: 1.5% (2000).

School District(s)

Gilliam C-4 (KG-08)
2000 Enrollment: 48 660-784-2225

Housing: Homeownership rate: 77.1% (2000); Median home value: $27,500 (2000); Median rent: $223 per month (2000); Median age of housing: 60+ years (2000).
Transportation: Commute to work: 86.7% car, 0.0% public transportation, 5.6% walk, 3.3% work from home (2000); Travel time to work: 42.5% less than 15 minutes, 43.7% 15 to 30 minutes, 4.6% 30 to 45 minutes, 2.3% 45 to 60 minutes, 6.9% 60 minutes or more (2000)

GRAND PASS (village). Covers a land area of 0.106 square miles and a water area of 0 square miles. Located at 39.20° N. Lat.; 93.44° W. Long. Elevation is 666 feet.
History: Grand Pass was named for the narrow pass between the valleys of Salt Fork Creek and the Missouri River, a route followed by the Santa Fe Trail.
Population: 53 (2000); Race: 95.8% White, 0.0% Black, 0.0% Asian, 0.0% American Indian and Alaska Native, 4.2% Hispanic of any race, 4.2% two or more races (2000); Density: 499.3 persons per square mile (2000); Age: 31.9% under 18, 25.0% over 64 (2000); Marriage status: 21.8% never married, 65.5% now married, 12.7% widowed, 0.0% divorced (2000); Foreign born: 0.0% (2000); Ancestry (includes multiple ancestries): 51.4% German, 20.8% United States or American, 18.1% British, 13.9% Other groups, 11.1% Irish (2000).
Economy: Employment by occupation: 21.7% management, 0.0% professional, 13.0% services, 26.1% sales, 13.0% farming, 0.0% construction, 26.1% production (2000).
Income: Per capita income: $14,089 (2000); Median household income: $40,313 (2000); Poverty rate: 9.7% (2000).
Taxes: Total city taxes per capita: $38 (1997); City property taxes per capita: $19 (1997).
Education: High school graduation rate: 61.4% (2000); College graduation rate: 15.9% (2000).
Housing: Homeownership rate: 92.0% (2000); Median home value: $43,800 (2000); Median age of housing: 60+ years (2000).
Transportation: Commute to work: 100.0% car, 0.0% public transportation, 0.0% walk, 0.0% work from home (2000); Travel time to work: 60.9% less than 15 minutes, 17.4% 15 to 30 minutes, 8.7% 30 to 45 minutes, 13.0% 45 to 60 minutes, 0.0% 60 minutes or more (2000)

MALTA BEND (town). Covers a land area of 0.262 square miles and a water area of 0 square miles. Located at 39.19° N. Lat.; 93.36° W. Long. Elevation is 684 feet.
History: A river steamer captained by Joseph W. Throckmorton, which sank with a cargo of furs near the site of the town, gave its name to Malta Bend. The town was platted in 1867.
Population: 249 (2000); Race: 95.6% White, 1.6% Black, 0.0% Asian, 0.0% American Indian and Alaska Native, 0.4% Hispanic of any race, 2.8% two or more races (2000); Density: 948.8 persons per square mile (2000); Age: 33.5% under 18, 17.1% over 64 (2000); Marriage status: 25.4% never married, 59.1% now married, 4.1% widowed, 11.4% divorced (2000); Foreign born: 0.8% (2000); Ancestry (includes multiple ancestries): 26.3% German, 17.1% Other groups, 12.7% Irish, 8.8% Swedish, 8.4% English (2000).
Economy: Employment by occupation: 7.3% management, 15.6% professional, 27.1% services, 19.8% sales, 0.0% farming, 11.5% construction, 18.8% production (2000).
Income: Per capita income: $14,403 (2000); Median household income: $27,250 (2000); Poverty rate: 11.3% (2000).
Taxes: Total city taxes per capita: $90 (1997); City property taxes per capita: $41 (1997).
Education: High school graduation rate: 70.2% (2000); College graduation rate: 7.5% (2000).

School District(s)

Malta Bend R-V (KG-12)
2000 Enrollment: 160 660-595-2371

Housing: Homeownership rate: 69.9% (2000); Median home value: $35,600 (2000); Median rent: $238 per month (2000); Median age of housing: 50 years (2000).
Transportation: Commute to work: 91.7% car, 1.0% public transportation, 7.3% walk, 0.0% work from home (2000); Travel time to work: 28.1% less than 15 minutes, 39.6% 15 to 30 minutes, 18.8% 30 to 45 minutes, 4.2% 45 to 60 minutes, 9.4% 60 minutes or more (2000)

MARSHALL (city). Covers a land area of 10.146 square miles and a water area of 0.076 square miles. Located at 39.11° N. Lat.; 93.19° W. Long. Elevation is 760 feet.
History: Marshall was settled in 1839 by immigrants from Virginia, Tennessee, and Kentucky, on a site known as Elk's Hill. The town was named for John Marshall, Chief Justice of the United States Supreme Court (1801-1835).
Population: 12,433 (2000); Race: 86.4% White, 6.4% Black, 0.7% Asian, 0.6% American Indian and Alaska Native, 7.3% Hispanic of any race, 2.9% two or more races (2000); Density: 1,225.4 persons per square mile (2000); Age: 24.9% under 18, 15.2% over 64 (2000); Marriage status: 26.8% never married, 53.5% now married, 8.6% widowed, 11.2% divorced (2000); Foreign born: 5.6% (2000); Ancestry (includes multiple ancestries): 20.4% Other groups, 19.8% German, 12.3% United States or American, 10.1% Irish, 9.1% English (2000).
Vital Statistics: Birth rate: 155.2 per 10,000 population (1998)
Economy: Single-family building permits issued: 14 (2001) / 10 (2000); Multi-family building permits issued: 76 (2001) / 8 (2000); Employment by occupation: 9.9% management, 18.8% professional, 19.5% services, 19.1% sales, 1.2% farming, 8.4% construction, 23.2% production (2000).
Income: Per capita income: $16,646 (2000); Median household income: $31,649 (2000); Poverty rate: 15.0% (2000).
Taxes: Total city taxes per capita: $261 (2000); City property taxes per capita: $46 (2000).
Education: High school graduation rate: 72.4% (2000); College graduation rate: 18.5% (2000).

School District(s)

Hardeman R-X (KG-08)
2000 Enrollment: 67 660-837-3400
Marshall (PK-12)
2000 Enrollment: 2,633 660-886-7414

Four-year College(s)

Missouri Valley College (Private, Not-for-profit, Presbyterian Church (USA))
2001 Enrollment: 1,577 660-831-4000
2001 Tuition: In-state $12,000; Out-of-state $12,000

Housing: Homeownership rate: 62.5% (2000); Median home value: $67,500 (2000); Median rent: $299 per month (2000); Median age of housing: 35 years (2000).
Hospitals: Fitzgibbon Memorial Hospital (60 beds)
Safety: Violent crime rate: 4.0 per 10,000 population; Property crime rate: 238.2 per 10,000 population (2001).
Newspapers: The Marshall Democrat-News (5 x week); Messenger (1 x week)
Transportation: Commute to work: 92.5% car, 0.1% public transportation, 4.0% walk, 1.8% work from home (2000); Travel time to work: 75.0% less than 15 minutes, 16.7% 15 to 30 minutes, 4.9% 30 to 45 minutes, 1.2% 45 to 60 minutes, 2.2% 60 minutes or more (2000)
Additional Information Contacts
Marshall Chamber of Commerce 660-886-3324

MIAMI (city). Covers a land area of 0.561 square miles and a water area of 0.071 square miles. Located at 39.32° N. Lat.; 93.22° W. Long. Elevation is 780 feet.
History: Miami was first known as Greenville when it was platted in 1838 on a ridge overlooking the Missouri River valley. Hemp and other produce were shipped from the port at Miami.

Population: 160 (2000); Race: 96.9% White, 1.2% Black, 0.0% Asian, 0.0% American Indian and Alaska Native, 0.0% Hispanic of any race, 1.8% two or more races (2000); Density: 285.2 persons per square mile (2000); Age: 34.4% under 18, 11.7% over 64 (2000); Marriage status: 19.5% never married, 51.3% now married, 8.8% widowed, 20.4% divorced (2000); Foreign born: 1.8% (2000); Ancestry (includes multiple ancestries): 23.9% United States or American, 23.9% Other groups, 23.3% German, 6.7% Irish, 4.3% Norwegian (2000).
Economy: Employment by occupation: 23.9% management, 9.9% professional, 16.9% services, 7.0% sales, 5.6% farming, 4.2% construction, 32.4% production (2000).
Income: Per capita income: $15,055 (2000); Median household income: $27,750 (2000); Poverty rate: 26.1% (2000).
Taxes: Total city taxes per capita: $68 (1997); City property taxes per capita: $34 (1997).
Education: High school graduation rate: 78.0% (2000); College graduation rate: 11.0% (2000).

School District(s)

Miami R-I (KG-08)
2000 Enrollment: 77 660-852-3269

Housing: Homeownership rate: 82.5% (2000); Median home value: $18,800 (2000); Median rent: $108 per month (2000); Median age of housing: 52 years (2000).
Transportation: Commute to work: 97.1% car, 0.0% public transportation, 0.0% walk, 2.9% work from home (2000); Travel time to work: 25.4% less than 15 minutes, 67.2% 15 to 30 minutes, 1.5% 30 to 45 minutes, 0.0% 45 to 60 minutes, 6.0% 60 minutes or more (2000)

MOUNT LEONARD (town). Covers a land area of 0.101 square miles and a water area of 0 square miles. Located at 39.12° N. Lat.; 93.39° W. Long. Elevation is 805 feet.
Population: 123 (2000); Race: 87.3% White, 2.5% Black, 0.0% Asian, 2.5% American Indian and Alaska Native, 0.0% Hispanic of any race, 7.6% two or more races (2000); Density: 1,215.0 persons per square mile (2000); Age: 35.0% under 18, 10.2% over 64 (2000); Marriage status: 26.1% never married, 58.3% now married, 7.0% widowed, 8.7% divorced (2000); Foreign born: 0.0% (2000); Ancestry (includes multiple ancestries): 46.5% German, 27.4% Irish, 22.9% Other groups, 5.1% English, 3.2% United States or American (2000).
Economy: Employment by occupation: 6.4% management, 2.1% professional, 29.8% services, 17.0% sales, 6.4% farming, 17.0% construction, 21.3% production (2000).
Income: Per capita income: $7,405 (2000); Median household income: $20,833 (2000); Poverty rate: 48.4% (2000).
Taxes: Total city taxes per capita: $10 (1997); City property taxes per capita: $10 (1997).
Education: High school graduation rate: 39.3% (2000); College graduation rate: 3.6% (2000).
Housing: Homeownership rate: 70.2% (2000); Median home value: $27,500 (2000); Median rent: $264 per month (2000); Median age of housing: 33 years (2000).
Transportation: Commute to work: 90.9% car, 0.0% public transportation, 0.0% walk, 9.1% work from home (2000); Travel time to work: 0.0% less than 15 minutes, 75.0% 15 to 30 minutes, 20.0% 30 to 45 minutes, 5.0% 45 to 60 minutes, 0.0% 60 minutes or more (2000)

NELSON (city). Covers a land area of 0.331 square miles and a water area of 0 square miles. Located at 38.99° N. Lat.; 93.03° W. Long. Elevation is 675 feet.
Population: 212 (2000); Race: 97.6% White, 0.9% Black, 0.0% Asian, 0.0% American Indian and Alaska Native, 0.0% Hispanic of any race, 1.4% two or more races (2000); Density: 640.5 persons per square mile (2000); Age: 21.3% under 18, 9.0% over 64 (2000); Marriage status: 17.0% never married, 65.9% now married, 2.3% widowed, 14.8% divorced (2000); Foreign born: 0.0% (2000); Ancestry (includes multiple ancestries): 27.0% United States or American, 15.6% German, 13.3% Irish, 10.4% European, 7.1% Other groups (2000).
Economy: Corn, wheat; cattle. Employment by occupation: 3.5% management, 13.0% professional, 21.7% services, 9.6% sales, 2.6% farming, 14.8% construction, 34.8% production (2000).
Income: Per capita income: $12,886 (2000); Median household income: $28,214 (2000); Poverty rate: 11.8% (2000).
Taxes: Total city taxes per capita: $5 (1997); City property taxes per capita: $5 (1997).
Education: High school graduation rate: 68.6% (2000); College graduation rate: 1.3% (2000).
Housing: Homeownership rate: 84.0% (2000); Median home value: $20,500 (2000); Median rent: $213 per month (2000); Median age of housing: 49 years (2000).
Transportation: Commute to work: 100.0% car, 0.0% public transportation, 0.0% walk, 0.0% work from home (2000); Travel time to work: 7.9% less than 15 minutes, 36.8% 15 to 30 minutes, 28.1% 30 to 45 minutes, 14.9% 45 to 60 minutes, 12.3% 60 minutes or more (2000)

SLATER (city). Covers a land area of 1.447 square miles and a water area of 0 square miles. Located at 39.22° N. Lat.; 93.06° W. Long. Elevation is 853 feet.
History: born, wheat, soybeans; cattle; mfg. (flour, apparel, filters, concrete); rock quarry.
Population: 2,083 (2000); Race: 88.4% White, 9.6% Black, 0.0% Asian, 0.8% American Indian and Alaska Native, 1.1% Hispanic of any race, 0.9% two or more races (2000); Density: 1,439.1 persons per square mile (2000); Age: 23.4% under 18, 22.5% over 64 (2000); Marriage status: 22.8% never married, 50.2% now married, 12.9% widowed, 14.1% divorced (2000); Foreign born: 0.4% (2000); Ancestry (includes multiple ancestries): 16.9% German, 15.8% Other groups, 15.1% United States or American, 9.2% Irish, 7.1% English (2000).
Economy: Corn, wheat, soybeans; cattle. Manufacturing includes flour, apparel, filters, concrete. Rock quarry. Single-family building permits issued: 0 (2001) / 2 (2000); Multi-family building permits issued: 0 (2001) / 0 (2000); Employment by occupation: 5.3% management, 10.2% professional, 22.1% services, 16.8% sales, 1.4% farming, 11.1% construction, 33.1% production (2000).
Income: Per capita income: $12,863 (2000); Median household income: $25,270 (2000); Poverty rate: 18.2% (2000).
Taxes: Total city taxes per capita: $192 (1997); City property taxes per capita: $66 (1997).
Education: High school graduation rate: 69.1% (2000); College graduation rate: 10.6% (2000).

School District(s)

Orearville R-IV (KG-08)
2000 Enrollment: 58 660-529-2481
Slater (KG-12)
2000 Enrollment: 409 660-529-2278

Housing: Homeownership rate: 73.2% (2000); Median home value: $32,300 (2000); Median rent: $206 per month (2000); Median age of housing: 49 years (2000).
Safety: Violent crime rate: 19.1 per 10,000 population; Property crime rate: 162.2 per 10,000 population (2001).
Newspapers: Slater Main Street News (1 x week)
Transportation: Commute to work: 91.4% car, 1.6% public transportation, 4.9% walk, 1.2% work from home (2000); Travel time to work: 50.1% less than 15 minutes, 33.0% 15 to 30 minutes, 7.0% 30 to 45 minutes, 1.4% 45 to 60 minutes, 8.5% 60 minutes or more (2000)

SWEET SPRINGS (city). Covers a land area of 1.621 square miles and a water area of 0 square miles. Located at 38.96° N. Lat.; 93.41° W. Long. Elevation is 683 feet.
History: Sweet Springs was settled in 1826 by John Yantes, a Presbyterian minister, and laid out as a town in 1848. A hotel was built in 1877 to accommodate guests coming to enjoy the waters of the springs.
Population: 1,628 (2000); Race: 95.0% White, 1.2% Black, 1.2% Asian, 0.1% American Indian and Alaska Native, 0.7% Hispanic of any race, 2.4% two or more races (2000); Density: 1,004.3 persons per square mile (2000); Age: 26.2% under 18, 20.1% over 64 (2000); Marriage status: 21.5% never married, 56.7% now married, 13.6% widowed, 8.2% divorced (2000); Foreign born: 1.6% (2000); Ancestry (includes multiple ancestries): 34.6% German, 12.6% Irish, 10.9% Other groups, 9.8% English, 8.3% United States or American (2000).
Economy: Single-family building permits issued: 3 (2001) / 3 (2000); Multi-family building permits issued: 0 (2001) / 0 (2000); Employment by occupation: 5.8% management, 12.2% professional, 19.4% services, 25.4% sales, 0.7% farming, 11.9% construction, 24.5% production (2000).
Income: Per capita income: $14,126 (2000); Median household income: $33,819 (2000); Poverty rate: 9.6% (2000).
Taxes: Total city taxes per capita: $106 (1997); City property taxes per capita: $37 (1997).
Education: High school graduation rate: 68.7% (2000); College graduation rate: 10.3% (2000).

School District(s)

Sweet Springs R-VII (PK-12)
2000 Enrollment: 503 660-335-4860

Housing: Homeownership rate: 73.4% (2000); Median home value: $47,300 (2000); Median rent: $252 per month (2000); Median age of housing: 44 years (2000).
Newspapers: Sweet Springs Herald (1 x week)
Transportation: Commute to work: 88.5% car, 1.4% public transportation, 6.6% walk, 2.9% work from home (2000); Travel time to work: 47.6% less than 15 minutes, 17.1% 15 to 30 minutes, 23.1% 30 to 45 minutes, 3.3% 45 to 60 minutes, 8.9% 60 minutes or more (2000)

Schuyler County

Located in northern Missouri; bounded on the west by the Chariton River; drained by the North Fabius River. Covers a land area of 307.90 square miles, a water area of 0.30 square miles, and is located in the Central Time Zone. The county government was organized in 1845. County seat is Lancaster.
Population: 4,170 (2000); Race: 98.8% White, 0.0% Black, 0.0% Asian, 0.5% American Indian and Alaska Native, 0.2% Hispanic of any race, 0.6% two or more races (2000); Density: 13.5 persons per square mile (2000); Age: 24.6% under 18, 19.8% over 64 (2000).
Religion: Five largest groups: 25.0% Southern Baptist Convention, 15.9% Christian Churches and Churches of Christ, 5.2% The United Methodist Church, 2.1% Assemblies of God, 1.6% Old Order Amish Church (2000).
Economy: Unemployment rate: 3.3% (11/2002); Total civilian labor force: 2,186 (11/2002); Leading industries: 34.5% retail trade; 8.8% construction; 6.0% health care and social assistance (2000); Companies that employ more than 1,000 persons: 0 (2000); Companies that employ more than 100 persons: 0 (2000); Farms: 493 totaling 159,543 acres (1997); Minority business ownership rate: 0.0% (1997); Women business ownership rate: 24.9% (1997); Retail sales per capita: $5,147 (1997). Single-family building permits issued: 11 (2001) / 20 (2000); Multi-family building permits issued: 0 (2001) / 0 (2000).
Income: Per capita income: $15,850 (2000); Median household income: $27,385 (2000); Poverty rate: 17.0% (2000); Bankruptcy rate: 3.14% (2001).
Taxes: Total county taxes per capita: $164 (1997); County property taxes per capita: $116 (1997).
Education: High school graduation rate: 81.4% (2000); College graduation rate: 11.6% (2000).
Housing: Homeownership rate: 75.2% (2000); Median home value: $38,500 (2000); Median rent: $212 per month (2000); Median age of housing: 44 years (2000).
Health: Birth rate: 115.1 per 10,000 population (1998); Age adjusted death rate: 104.3 per 10,000 population (1999); Age adjusted cancer mortality rate: 145.0 (Unreliable figure as per CDC) deaths per 100,000 population (1999). Number of physicians: n/a (1999); Number of hospital beds: n/a (1999).
Elections: 2000 Presidential election results: 40.3% Gore, 57.8% Bush, 0.8% Nader, 0.5% Buchanan
Additional Information Contacts
Schuyler County Government Offices 660-457-3842

Schuyler County Communities

COATSVILLE (unincorporated postal area, zip code 63535). Aka Coatesville. Covers a land area of 19.205 square miles and a water area of 0.009 square miles. Located at 40.56° N. Lat.; 92.64° W. Long. Elevation is 992 feet.
Population: 96 (2000); Race: 100.0% White, 0.0% Black, 0.0% Asian, 0.0% American Indian and Alaska Native, 0.0% Hispanic of any race, 0.0% two or more races (2000); Density: 5.0 persons per square mile (2000); Age: 13.9% under 18, 19.4% over 64 (2000); Marriage status: 6.5% never married, 74.2% now married, 16.1% widowed, 3.2% divorced (2000); Foreign born: 0.0% (2000); Ancestry (includes multiple ancestries): 25.9% German, 12.0% Norwegian, 11.1% Scottish, 8.3% Dutch, 7.4% Polish (2000).
Economy: Employment by occupation: 39.7% management, 34.9% professional, 9.5% services, 0.0% sales, 0.0% farming, 11.1% construction, 4.8% production (2000).
Income: Per capita income: $19,119 (2000); Median household income: $40,417 (2000); Poverty rate: 19.4% (2000).
Education: High school graduation rate: 96.6% (2000); College graduation rate: 31.0% (2000).
Housing: Homeownership rate: 100.0% (2000); Median home value: $112,500 (2000); Median age of housing: 60+ years (2000).
Transportation: Commute to work: 90.5% car, 0.0% public transportation, 9.5% walk, 0.0% work from home (2000); Travel time to work: 41.3% less than 15 minutes, 22.2% 15 to 30 minutes, 22.2% 30 to 45 minutes, 4.8% 45 to 60 minutes, 9.5% 60 minutes or more (2000)

DOWNING (city). Covers a land area of 0.665 square miles and a water area of 0 square miles. Located at 40.48° N. Lat.; 92.36° W. Long. Elevation is 873 feet.
Population: 396 (2000); Race: 97.9% White, 0.0% Black, 0.5% Asian, 0.5% American Indian and Alaska Native, 1.1% Hispanic of any race, 1.1% two or more races (2000); Density: 595.4 persons per square mile (2000); Age: 24.5% under 18, 22.4% over 64 (2000); Marriage status: 20.1% never married, 53.9% now married, 13.3% widowed, 12.6% divorced (2000); Foreign born: 0.5% (2000); Ancestry (includes multiple ancestries): 23.7% German, 15.7% Irish, 14.7% United States or American, 12.0% English, 7.7% Other groups (2000).
Economy: Soybeans, corn; hogs, sheep. Employment by occupation: 13.5% management, 9.0% professional, 23.7% services, 21.2% sales, 3.2% farming, 17.9% construction, 11.5% production (2000).
Income: Per capita income: $12,626 (2000); Median household income: $18,864 (2000); Poverty rate: 18.9% (2000).
Taxes: Total city taxes per capita: $60 (1997); City property taxes per capita: $27 (1997).
Education: High school graduation rate: 76.0% (2000); College graduation rate: 10.2% (2000).
Housing: Homeownership rate: 72.0% (2000); Median home value: $27,000 (2000); Median rent: $211 per month (2000); Median age of housing: 60+ years (2000).
Transportation: Commute to work: 98.7% car, 0.0% public transportation, 0.0% walk, 1.3% work from home (2000); Travel time to work: 26.5% less than 15 minutes, 51.0% 15 to 30 minutes, 6.6% 30 to 45 minutes, 13.9% 45 to 60 minutes, 2.0% 60 minutes or more (2000)

GLENWOOD (village). Covers a land area of 0.736 square miles and a water area of 0 square miles. Located at 40.52° N. Lat.; 92.57° W. Long. Elevation is 983 feet.
Population: 203 (2000); Race: 100.0% White, 0.0% Black, 0.0% Asian, 0.0% American Indian and Alaska Native, 0.0% Hispanic of any race, 0.0% two or more races (2000); Density: 275.8 persons per square mile (2000); Age: 26.9% under 18, 16.9% over 64 (2000); Marriage status: 19.9% never married, 65.3% now married, 7.4% widowed, 7.4% divorced (2000); Foreign born: 0.0% (2000); Ancestry (includes multiple ancestries): 27.4% German, 16.0% United States or American, 14.2% Irish, 9.6% Other groups, 8.7% English (2000).
Economy: Employment by occupation: 1.9% management, 19.4% professional, 12.6% services, 15.5% sales, 5.8% farming, 15.5% construction, 29.1% production (2000).
Income: Per capita income: $15,356 (2000); Median household income: $32,500 (2000); Poverty rate: 11.9% (2000).
Taxes: Total city taxes per capita: $20 (1997); City property taxes per capita: $20 (1997).
Education: High school graduation rate: 85.2% (2000); College graduation rate: 4.9% (2000).
Housing: Homeownership rate: 77.6% (2000); Median home value: $36,300 (2000); Median rent: $225 per month (2000); Median age of housing: 60+ years (2000).
Transportation: Commute to work: 96.1% car, 0.0% public transportation, 0.0% walk, 3.9% work from home (2000); Travel time to work: 23.5% less than 15 minutes, 32.7% 15 to 30 minutes, 25.5% 30 to 45 minutes, 10.2% 45 to 60 minutes, 8.2% 60 minutes or more (2000)

GREENTOP (city). Aka Green Top. Covers a land area of 0.819 square miles and a water area of 0 square miles. Located at 40.34° N. Lat.; 92.56° W. Long. Elevation is 993 feet.
Population: 427 (2000); Race: 96.8% White, 0.0% Black, 1.9% Asian, 0.0% American Indian and Alaska Native, 0.0% Hispanic of any race, 1.2% two or more races (2000); Density: 521.4 persons per square mile (2000); Age: 19.4% under 18, 22.8% over 64 (2000); Marriage status: 14.4% never married, 59.8% now married, 13.3% widowed, 12.5% divorced (2000); Foreign born: 1.0% (2000); Ancestry (includes multiple ancestries): 18.0% German, 16.5% United States or American, 10.2% Irish, 8.0% English, 7.8% Other groups (2000).
Economy: Employment by occupation: 6.5% management, 16.2% professional, 14.1% services, 23.8% sales, 1.1% farming, 13.5% construction, 24.9% production (2000).
Income: Per capita income: $15,757 (2000); Median household income: $21,953 (2000); Poverty rate: 17.5% (2000).
Taxes: Total city taxes per capita: $72 (1997); City property taxes per capita: $32 (1997).

Education: High school graduation rate: 70.6% (2000); College graduation rate: 11.0% (2000).
Housing: Homeownership rate: 67.2% (2000); Median home value: $47,300 (2000); Median rent: $213 per month (2000); Median age of housing: 29 years (2000).
Transportation: Commute to work: 96.8% car, 0.0% public transportation, 1.6% walk, 1.1% work from home (2000); Travel time to work: 16.9% less than 15 minutes, 68.9% 15 to 30 minutes, 5.5% 30 to 45 minutes, 3.8% 45 to 60 minutes, 4.9% 60 minutes or more (2000)

LANCASTER (city). Covers a land area of 1.490 square miles and a water area of 0 square miles. Located at 40.52° N. Lat.; 92.52° W. Long. Elevation is 950 feet.
History: Lancaster was the birthplace of writer Rupert Hughes, born in 1872. In 1890 Colonel William P. Hall, who owned a circus, established a business as a horse and mule dealer with a South African trade market.
Population: 737 (2000); Race: 100.0% White, 0.0% Black, 0.0% Asian, 0.0% American Indian and Alaska Native, 0.3% Hispanic of any race, 0.0% two or more races (2000); Density: 494.7 persons per square mile (2000); Age: 24.7% under 18, 24.3% over 64 (2000); Marriage status: 19.6% never married, 61.7% now married, 11.5% widowed, 7.2% divorced (2000); Foreign born: 0.3% (2000); Ancestry (includes multiple ancestries): 21.8% German, 15.4% United States or American, 10.8% Irish, 8.3% English, 5.3% Other groups (2000).
Economy: Employment by occupation: 7.9% management, 18.2% professional, 19.2% services, 25.5% sales, 2.2% farming, 9.4% construction, 17.6% production (2000).
Income: Per capita income: $14,263 (2000); Median household income: $27,202 (2000); Poverty rate: 18.9% (2000).
Taxes: Total city taxes per capita: $161 (1997); City property taxes per capita: $50 (1997).
Education: High school graduation rate: 85.8% (2000); College graduation rate: 18.2% (2000).
Housing: Homeownership rate: 64.0% (2000); Median home value: $47,700 (2000); Median rent: $235 per month (2000); Median age of housing: 44 years (2000).
Newspapers: Lancaster Excelsior (1 x week)
Transportation: Commute to work: 95.2% car, 0.0% public transportation, 2.5% walk, 2.2% work from home (2000); Travel time to work: 48.1% less than 15 minutes, 13.6% 15 to 30 minutes, 23.1% 30 to 45 minutes, 7.1% 45 to 60 minutes, 8.1% 60 minutes or more (2000)

QUEEN CITY (city). Covers a land area of 1.026 square miles and a water area of 0 square miles. Located at 40.40° N. Lat.; 92.56° W. Long. Elevation is 1,003 feet.
History: Queen City was the birthplace of Glenn Frank (1887-1940), who became the president of the University of Wisconsin.
Population: 638 (2000); Race: 98.8% White, 0.0% Black, 0.0% Asian, 0.5% American Indian and Alaska Native, 0.6% Hispanic of any race, 0.8% two or more races (2000); Density: 621.8 persons per square mile (2000); Age: 21.6% under 18, 28.0% over 64 (2000); Marriage status: 14.5% never married, 56.7% now married, 20.2% widowed, 8.7% divorced (2000); Foreign born: 0.0% (2000); Ancestry (includes multiple ancestries): 20.4% United States or American, 10.7% German, 8.5% Other groups, 8.2% English, 5.9% Irish (2000).
Economy: Employment by occupation: 5.7% management, 14.2% professional, 11.7% services, 28.3% sales, 2.0% farming, 11.3% construction, 26.7% production (2000).
Income: Per capita income: $11,928 (2000); Median household income: $20,875 (2000); Poverty rate: 16.4% (2000).
Taxes: Total city taxes per capita: $41 (1997); City property taxes per capita: $38 (1997).
Education: High school graduation rate: 67.7% (2000); College graduation rate: 5.8% (2000).

School District(s)

Schuyler Co. R-I (PK-12)
2000 Enrollment: 776 660-766-2204

Housing: Homeownership rate: 67.6% (2000); Median home value: $31,600 (2000); Median rent: $195 per month (2000); Median age of housing: 39 years (2000).
Transportation: Commute to work: 92.5% car, 0.0% public transportation, 2.9% walk, 2.5% work from home (2000); Travel time to work: 20.4% less than 15 minutes, 45.5% 15 to 30 minutes, 23.8% 30 to 45 minutes, 4.3% 45 to 60 minutes, 6.0% 60 minutes or more (2000)

Scotland County

Located in northeastern Missouri; drained by the North Fabius and North and South Wyaconda Rivers. Covers a land area of 438.50 square miles, a water area of 0.80 square miles, and is located in the Central Time Zone. The county government was organized in 1841. County seat is Memphis.
Population: 4,983 (2000); Race: 99.2% White, 0.0% Black, 0.2% Asian, 0.1% American Indian and Alaska Native, 1.5% Hispanic of any race, 0.3% two or more races (2000); Density: 11.4 persons per square mile (2000); Age: 28.7% under 18, 18.9% over 64 (2000).
Religion: Five largest groups: 17.6% Southern Baptist Convention, 12.4% The United Methodist Church, 11.2% Old Order Mennonite, 8.0% Christian Churches and Churches of Christ, 2.9% Catholic Church (2000).
Economy: Unemployment rate: 3.2% (11/2002); Total civilian labor force: 2,206 (11/2002); Leading industries: 23.4% retail trade; 16.5% manufacturing; 8.9% finance & insurance (2000); Companies that employ more than 1,000 persons: 0 (2000); Companies that employ more than 100 persons: 1 (2000); Farms: 600 totaling 224,606 acres (1997); Minority business ownership rate: 0.0% (1997); Women business ownership rate: 36.8% (1997); Retail sales per capita: $4,981 (1997). Single-family building permits issued: 1 (2001) / 6 (2000); Multi-family building permits issued: 0 (2001) / 0 (2000).
Income: Per capita income: $14,474 (2000); Median household income: $27,409 (2000); Poverty rate: 16.8% (2000); Bankruptcy rate: 4.25% (2001).
Taxes: Total county taxes per capita: $162 (1997); County property taxes per capita: $90 (1997).
Education: High school graduation rate: 76.8% (2000); College graduation rate: 11.2% (2000).
Housing: Homeownership rate: 76.7% (2000); Median home value: $43,300 (2000); Median rent: $193 per month (2000); Median age of housing: 48 years (2000).
Health: Birth rate: 156.5 per 10,000 population (1998); Age adjusted death rate: 114.7 per 10,000 population (1999); Age adjusted cancer mortality rate: 217.2 (Unreliable figure as per CDC) deaths per 100,000 population (1999). Number of physicians: n/a (1999); Number of hospital beds: 64.2 per 10,000 population (1999).
Elections: 2000 Presidential election results: 36.3% Gore, 61.3% Bush, 1.7% Nader, 0.2% Buchanan

Additional Information Contacts

Scotland County Government Offices 660-465-7027

Scotland County Communities

ARBELA (town). Covers a land area of 0.089 square miles and a water area of 0 square miles. Located at 40.46° N. Lat.; 92.01° W. Long. Elevation is 680 feet.
Population: 40 (2000); Race: 84.2% White, 0.0% Black, 15.8% Asian, 0.0% American Indian and Alaska Native, 0.0% Hispanic of any race, 0.0% two or more races (2000); Density: 451.1 persons per square mile (2000); Age: 28.9% under 18, 0.0% over 64 (2000); Marriage status: 24.2% never married, 63.6% now married, 0.0% widowed, 12.1% divorced (2000); Foreign born: 15.8% (2000); Ancestry (includes multiple ancestries): 26.3% Irish, 23.7% Other groups, 15.8% German, 13.2% Swedish, 10.5% Scotch-Irish (2000).
Economy: Employment by occupation: 0.0% management, 0.0% professional, 0.0% services, 41.7% sales, 8.3% farming, 0.0% construction, 50.0% production (2000).
Income: Per capita income: $12,853 (2000); Median household income: $31,250 (2000); Poverty rate: 5.3% (2000).
Taxes: Total city taxes per capita: $24 (1997); City property taxes per capita: $0 (1997).
Education: High school graduation rate: 92.6% (2000); College graduation rate: 0.0% (2000).
Housing: Homeownership rate: 100.0% (2000); Median home value: $21,300 (2000); Median age of housing: 60+ years (2000).
Transportation: Commute to work: 87.5% car, 0.0% public transportation, 12.5% walk, 0.0% work from home (2000); Travel time to work: 20.8% less than 15 minutes, 37.5% 15 to 30 minutes, 25.0% 30 to 45 minutes, 16.7% 45 to 60 minutes, 0.0% 60 minutes or more (2000)

GORIN (unincorporated postal area, zip code 63543). Aka South Gorin. Covers a land area of 41.185 square miles and a water area of 0.030 square miles. Located at 40.45° N. Lat.; 92.14° W. Long. Elevation is 710 feet.
History: The town's post office is officially Gorin. The US Census Bureau recognizes the town as South Gorin.

Population: 412 (2000); Race: 98.8% White, 0.0% Black, 0.5% Asian, 0.7% American Indian and Alaska Native, 0.0% Hispanic of any race, 0.0% two or more races (2000); Density: 10.0 persons per square mile (2000); Age: 33.3% under 18, 14.3% over 64 (2000); Marriage status: 19.4% never married, 59.2% now married, 8.9% widowed, 12.5% divorced (2000); Foreign born: 0.5% (2000); Ancestry (includes multiple ancestries): 27.3% United States or American, 18.1% German, 11.2% Irish, 5.7% Other groups, 2.1% English (2000).
Economy: Employment by occupation: 21.1% management, 2.5% professional, 12.4% services, 15.5% sales, 3.7% farming, 8.1% construction, 36.6% production (2000).
Income: Per capita income: $11,026 (2000); Median household income: $22,250 (2000); Poverty rate: 31.5% (2000).
Education: High school graduation rate: 76.5% (2000); College graduation rate: 6.7% (2000).

School District(s)

Gorin R-III (PK-08)
2000 Enrollment: 58 660-282-3282
Housing: Homeownership rate: 76.9% (2000); Median home value: $26,500 (2000); Median rent: $213 per month (2000); Median age of housing: 60+ years (2000).
Transportation: Commute to work: 76.9% car, 1.3% public transportation, 4.5% walk, 17.3% work from home (2000); Travel time to work: 13.2% less than 15 minutes, 42.6% 15 to 30 minutes, 14.0% 30 to 45 minutes, 4.7% 45 to 60 minutes, 25.6% 60 minutes or more (2000)

GRANGER (village). Covers a land area of 0.157 square miles and a water area of 0 square miles. Located at 40.46° N. Lat.; 91.97° W. Long. Elevation is 760 feet.
Population: 44 (2000); Race: 100.0% White, 0.0% Black, 0.0% Asian, 0.0% American Indian and Alaska Native, 4.3% Hispanic of any race, 0.0% two or more races (2000); Density: 280.5 persons per square mile (2000); Age: 19.1% under 18, 21.3% over 64 (2000); Marriage status: 23.1% never married, 48.7% now married, 15.4% widowed, 12.8% divorced (2000); Foreign born: 0.0% (2000); Ancestry (includes multiple ancestries): 19.1% English, 17.0% German, 14.9% United States or American, 6.4% Other groups, 6.4% Scottish (2000).
Economy: Wood products. Employment by occupation: 11.1% management, 0.0% professional, 5.6% services, 0.0% sales, 11.1% farming, 27.8% construction, 44.4% production (2000).
Income: Per capita income: $12,400 (2000); Median household income: $20,417 (2000); Poverty rate: 14.9% (2000).
Taxes: Total city taxes per capita: $47 (1997); City property taxes per capita: $16 (1997).
Education: High school graduation rate: 74.3% (2000); College graduation rate: 20.0% (2000).
Housing: Homeownership rate: 82.6% (2000); Median home value: $15,000 (2000); Median rent: $175 per month (2000); Median age of housing: 60+ years (2000).
Transportation: Commute to work: 100.0% car, 0.0% public transportation, 0.0% walk, 0.0% work from home (2000); Travel time to work: 22.2% less than 15 minutes, 33.3% 15 to 30 minutes, 11.1% 30 to 45 minutes, 16.7% 45 to 60 minutes, 16.7% 60 minutes or more (2000)

MEMPHIS (city). Covers a land area of 1.566 square miles and a water area of 0 square miles. Located at 40.46° N. Lat.; 92.17° W. Long. Elevation is 801 feet.
History: Settled 1838.
Population: 2,061 (2000); Race: 99.7% White, 0.0% Black, 0.0% Asian, 0.0% American Indian and Alaska Native, 0.3% Hispanic of any race, 0.1% two or more races (2000); Density: 1,316.1 persons per square mile (2000); Age: 22.9% under 18, 28.6% over 64 (2000); Marriage status: 20.9% never married, 53.8% now married, 18.5% widowed, 6.8% divorced (2000); Foreign born: 0.1% (2000); Ancestry (includes multiple ancestries): 22.1% German, 13.2% Irish, 10.8% English, 8.8% United States or American, 6.1% Other groups (2000).
Economy: Livestock: sheep, cattle, hogs. Soybeans and grain (corn). Manufacturing: clothing, beverages. Single-family building permits issued: 1 (2001) / 6 (2000); Multi-family building permits issued: 0 (2001) / 0 (2000); Employment by occupation: 7.8% management, 18.9% professional, 18.5% services, 23.1% sales, 1.7% farming, 8.5% construction, 21.5% production (2000).
Income: Per capita income: $16,220 (2000); Median household income: $24,508 (2000); Poverty rate: 17.6% (2000).
Taxes: Total city taxes per capita: $164 (1997); City property taxes per capita: $37 (1997).
Education: High school graduation rate: 79.6% (2000); College graduation rate: 10.7% (2000).

School District(s)

Scotland Co. R-I (PK-12)
2000 Enrollment: 701 660-465-8531
Housing: Homeownership rate: 71.1% (2000); Median home value: $44,000 (2000); Median rent: $197 per month (2000); Median age of housing: 46 years (2000).
Hospitals: Scotland County Memorial Hospital (40 beds)
Newspapers: Memphis Democrat (1 x week)
Transportation: Commute to work: 96.5% car, 0.0% public transportation, 2.3% walk, 0.5% work from home (2000); Travel time to work: 62.6% less than 15 minutes, 10.8% 15 to 30 minutes, 11.3% 30 to 45 minutes, 7.7% 45 to 60 minutes, 7.6% 60 minutes or more (2000)

RUTLEDGE (town). Covers a land area of 0.129 square miles and a water area of 0 square miles. Located at 40.31° N. Lat.; 92.08° W. Long. Elevation is 770 feet.
History: Amish community nearby.
Population: 103 (2000); Race: 100.0% White, 0.0% Black, 0.0% Asian, 0.0% American Indian and Alaska Native, 0.0% Hispanic of any race, 0.0% two or more races (2000); Density: 797.0 persons per square mile (2000); Age: 21.9% under 18, 30.1% over 64 (2000); Marriage status: 18.6% never married, 55.9% now married, 18.6% widowed, 6.8% divorced (2000); Foreign born: 0.0% (2000); Ancestry (includes multiple ancestries): 15.1% German, 13.7% Other groups, 8.2% Irish, 8.2% United States or American, 8.2% European (2000).
Economy: Employment by occupation: 8.3% management, 0.0% professional, 0.0% services, 29.2% sales, 8.3% farming, 33.3% construction, 20.8% production (2000).
Income: Per capita income: $9,545 (2000); Median household income: $14,063 (2000); Poverty rate: 43.8% (2000).
Taxes: Total city taxes per capita: $151 (1997); City property taxes per capita: $9 (1997).
Education: High school graduation rate: 58.8% (2000); College graduation rate: 3.9% (2000).
Housing: Homeownership rate: 83.3% (2000); Median home value: $32,500 (2000); Median rent: $150 per month (2000); Median age of housing: 60+ years (2000).
Transportation: Commute to work: 75.0% car, 0.0% public transportation, 25.0% walk, 0.0% work from home (2000); Travel time to work: 33.3% less than 15 minutes, 25.0% 15 to 30 minutes, 20.8% 30 to 45 minutes, 8.3% 45 to 60 minutes, 12.5% 60 minutes or more (2000)

SOUTH GORIN (town). Aka Gorin. Covers a land area of 0.201 square miles and a water area of 0 square miles. Located at 40.35° N. Lat.; 92.02° W. Long.
Population: 143 (2000); Race: 100.0% White, 0.0% Black, 0.0% Asian, 0.0% American Indian and Alaska Native, 0.0% Hispanic of any race, 0.0% two or more races (2000); Density: 711.0 persons per square mile (2000); Age: 28.1% under 18, 25.2% over 64 (2000); Marriage status: 11.4% never married, 50.5% now married, 14.3% widowed, 23.8% divorced (2000); Foreign born: 0.0% (2000); Ancestry (includes multiple ancestries): 36.0% United States or American, 20.1% Irish, 11.5% German, 4.3% Other groups, 3.6% Italian (2000).
Economy: Employment by occupation: 8.3% management, 0.0% professional, 6.3% services, 12.5% sales, 0.0% farming, 4.2% construction, 68.8% production (2000).
Income: Per capita income: $16,365 (2000); Median household income: $25,795 (2000); Poverty rate: 19.1% (2000).
Taxes: Total city taxes per capita: $23 (1997); City property taxes per capita: $15 (1997).
Education: High school graduation rate: 72.0% (2000); College graduation rate: 4.0% (2000).
Housing: Homeownership rate: 78.0% (2000); Median home value: $25,300 (2000); Median rent: $222 per month (2000); Median age of housing: 60+ years (2000).
Transportation: Commute to work: 88.9% car, 0.0% public transportation, 11.1% walk, 0.0% work from home (2000); Travel time to work: 6.7% less than 15 minutes, 31.1% 15 to 30 minutes, 17.8% 30 to 45 minutes, 8.9% 45 to 60 minutes, 35.6% 60 minutes or more (2000)

Scott County

Located in southeastern Missouri; bounded on the east by the Mississippi River and the Illinois border. Covers a land area of 421.00 square miles, a water area of 5.00 square miles, and is located in the Central Time Zone. The county government was organized in 1821. County seat is Benton.

Weather Station: Cape Girardeau Municipal Airport Elevation: 334 feet

	Jan	Feb	Mar	Apr	May	Jun	Jul	Aug	Sep	Oct	Nov	Dec
High	40	46	57	69	78	86	90	88	81	70	57	45
Low	23	28	38	47	57	66	70	67	59	47	38	29
Precip	3.2	3.4	4.6	4.5	5.1	3.8	3.5	3.4	3.5	3.3	4.5	4.3
Snow	4.4	4.3	2.1	tr	tr	tr	0.0	0.0	0.0	0.1	0.3	1.8

High and Low temperatures in degrees Fahrenheit; Precipitation and Snow in inches

Population: 40,422 (2000); Race: 88.0% White, 10.5% Black, 0.2% Asian, 0.2% American Indian and Alaska Native, 0.9% Hispanic of any race, 0.8% two or more races (2000); Density: 96.0 persons per square mile (2000); Age: 27.4% under 18, 13.8% over 64 (2000).
Religion: Five largest groups: 23.6% Southern Baptist Convention, 15.8% Catholic Church, 5.4% The United Methodist Church, 2.1% Churches of Christ, 2.0% Assemblies of God (2000).
Economy: Unemployment rate: 4.9% (11/2002); Total civilian labor force: 19,945 (11/2002); Leading industries: 20.2% manufacturing; 16.9% health care and social assistance; 14.1% retail trade (2000); Companies that employ more than 1,000 persons: 0 (2000); Companies that employ more than 100 persons: 17 (2000); Farms: 541 totaling 240,739 acres (1997); Minority business ownership rate: 0.0% (1997); Women business ownership rate: 15.5% (1997); Retail sales per capita: $8,801 (1997). Single-family building permits issued: 62 (2001) / 53 (2000); Multi-family building permits issued: 58 (2001) / 6 (2000).
Income: Per capita income: $15,620 (2000); Median household income: $31,352 (2000); Poverty rate: 16.1% (2000); Bankruptcy rate: 6.39% (2001).
Taxes: Total county taxes per capita: $62 (1997); County property taxes per capita: $26 (1997).
Education: High school graduation rate: 72.9% (2000); College graduation rate: 10.6% (2000).
Housing: Homeownership rate: 69.3% (2000); Median home value: $68,200 (2000); Median rent: $287 per month (2000); Median age of housing: 29 years (2000).
Health: Birth rate: 148.2 per 10,000 population (1998); Age adjusted death rate: 105.3 per 10,000 population (1999); Age adjusted cancer mortality rate: 214.9 deaths per 100,000 population (1999). Number of physicians: 14.1 per 10,000 population (1999); Number of hospital beds: 38.6 per 10,000 population (1999).
Elections: 2000 Presidential election results: 41.1% Gore, 57.3% Bush, 0.7% Nader, 0.6% Buchanan

Additional Information Contacts
Scott County Government Offices........................573-545-3549
Sikeston Area Chamber of Commerce....................573-471-2498
Sikeston Board of Realtors..................................573-472-2411

Scott County Communities

BENTON (city). Covers a land area of 0.414 square miles and a water area of 0 square miles. Located at 37.09° N. Lat.; 89.56° W. Long. Elevation is 440 feet.
History: Benton was platted in 1822 on land owned by Captain William Mayers, and named for Senator Thomas Hart Benton. In 1878 the seat of Scott County, which had been removed from Benton in 1864, was returned to the town.
Population: 732 (2000); Race: 97.0% White, 2.6% Black, 0.0% Asian, 0.3% American Indian and Alaska Native, 0.8% Hispanic of any race, 0.1% two or more races (2000); Density: 1,770.0 persons per square mile (2000); Age: 21.7% under 18, 18.6% over 64 (2000); Marriage status: 21.8% never married, 58.0% now married, 9.0% widowed, 11.2% divorced (2000); Foreign born: 0.0% (2000); Ancestry (includes multiple ancestries): 37.4% German, 17.9% United States or American, 12.0% Irish, 8.7% Other groups, 5.6% French (except Basque) (2000).
Economy: Single-family building permits issued: 0 (2001) / 0 (2000); Multi-family building permits issued: 0 (2001) / 0 (2000); Employment by occupation: 10.3% management, 20.9% professional, 9.7% services, 32.3% sales, 0.0% farming, 11.1% construction, 15.7% production (2000).
Income: Per capita income: $16,161 (2000); Median household income: $33,365 (2000); Poverty rate: 7.5% (2000).
Taxes: Total city taxes per capita: $194 (1997); City property taxes per capita: $46 (1997).
Education: High school graduation rate: 80.7% (2000); College graduation rate: 17.5% (2000).

School District(s)
Kelso C-7 (KG-08)
2000 Enrollment: 148 573-545-3357
Scott Co. R-IV (KG-12)
2000 Enrollment: 1,069..............................573-545-3887

Housing: Homeownership rate: 66.8% (2000); Median home value: $71,700 (2000); Median rent: $343 per month (2000); Median age of housing: 38 years (2000).
Transportation: Commute to work: 94.9% car, 0.0% public transportation, 1.1% walk, 3.4% work from home (2000); Travel time to work: 17.8% less than 15 minutes, 62.1% 15 to 30 minutes, 14.8% 30 to 45 minutes, 4.1% 45 to 60 minutes, 1.2% 60 minutes or more (2000)

BLODGETT (village). Covers a land area of 0.133 square miles and a water area of 0 square miles. Located at 37.00° N. Lat.; 89.52° W. Long. Elevation is 325 feet.
Population: 265 (2000); Race: 100.0% White, 0.0% Black, 0.0% Asian, 0.0% American Indian and Alaska Native, 0.0% Hispanic of any race, 0.0% two or more races (2000); Density: 1,999.5 persons per square mile (2000); Age: 25.7% under 18, 14.9% over 64 (2000); Marriage status: 12.6% never married, 70.3% now married, 10.8% widowed, 6.3% divorced (2000); Foreign born: 0.0% (2000); Ancestry (includes multiple ancestries): 42.8% United States or American, 13.0% Other groups, 11.6% German, 9.1% Irish, 3.3% Dutch (2000).
Economy: Cotton, corn, soybeans. Single-family building permits issued: 0 (2001) / 0 (2000); Multi-family building permits issued: 0 (2001) / 0 (2000); Employment by occupation: 1.5% management, 6.1% professional, 23.5% services, 26.5% sales, 0.0% farming, 11.4% construction, 31.1% production (2000).
Income: Per capita income: $14,674 (2000); Median household income: $33,194 (2000); Poverty rate: 7.4% (2000).
Taxes: Total city taxes per capita: $29 (1997); City property taxes per capita: $10 (1997).
Education: High school graduation rate: 56.9% (2000); College graduation rate: 4.8% (2000).
Housing: Homeownership rate: 74.7% (2000); Median home value: $28,200 (2000); Median rent: $388 per month (2000); Median age of housing: 31 years (2000).
Transportation: Commute to work: 98.4% car, 0.0% public transportation, 0.0% walk, 1.6% work from home (2000); Travel time to work: 10.6% less than 15 minutes, 69.9% 15 to 30 minutes, 14.6% 30 to 45 minutes, 3.3% 45 to 60 minutes, 1.6% 60 minutes or more (2000)

CHAFFEE (city). Covers a land area of 1.774 square miles and a water area of 0.047 square miles. Located at 37.18° N. Lat.; 89.65° W. Long. Elevation is 345 feet.
History: Laid out 1837, incorporated 1906.
Population: 3,044 (2000); Race: 98.7% White, 0.0% Black, 0.3% Asian, 0.4% American Indian and Alaska Native, 0.3% Hispanic of any race, 0.6% two or more races (2000); Density: 1,715.8 persons per square mile (2000); Age: 25.9% under 18, 17.7% over 64 (2000); Marriage status: 18.6% never married, 54.1% now married, 12.3% widowed, 15.0% divorced (2000); Foreign born: 0.5% (2000); Ancestry (includes multiple ancestries): 24.3% German, 15.3% United States or American, 12.4% Irish, 11.8% Other groups, 11.8% English (2000).
Economy: Corn, wheat, soybeans. Manufacturing: apparel. Single-family building permits issued: 4 (2001) / 6 (2000); Multi-family building permits issued: 0 (2001) / 0 (2000); Employment by occupation: 6.9% management, 14.2% professional, 15.5% services, 22.2% sales, 0.0% farming, 13.7% construction, 27.4% production (2000).
Income: Per capita income: $16,554 (2000); Median household income: $27,076 (2000); Poverty rate: 16.2% (2000).
Taxes: Total city taxes per capita: $153 (1997); City property taxes per capita: $37 (1997).
Education: High school graduation rate: 74.1% (2000); College graduation rate: 11.0% (2000).

School District(s)
Chaffee R-II (PK-12)
2000 Enrollment: 620 573-887-3532

Housing: Homeownership rate: 67.8% (2000); Median home value: $50,400 (2000); Median rent: $237 per month (2000); Median age of housing: 42 years (2000).

Safety: Violent crime rate: 52.2 per 10,000 population; Property crime rate: 208.9 per 10,000 population (2001).
Newspapers: Scott County Signal (1 x week)
Transportation: Commute to work: 95.1% car, 0.5% public transportation, 1.8% walk, 1.3% work from home (2000); Travel time to work: 32.0% less than 15 minutes, 43.0% 15 to 30 minutes, 18.9% 30 to 45 minutes, 1.5% 45 to 60 minutes, 4.6% 60 minutes or more (2000)

COMMERCE (village). Covers a land area of 0.320 square miles and a water area of 0 square miles. Located at 37.15° N. Lat.; 89.44° W. Long. Elevation is 345 feet.
History: Heavily damaged in floods of 1993 and 1995.
Population: 110 (2000); Race: 97.8% White, 0.0% Black, 0.0% Asian, 0.0% American Indian and Alaska Native, 4.3% Hispanic of any race, 0.0% two or more races (2000); Density: 344.0 persons per square mile (2000); Age: 24.7% under 18, 7.5% over 64 (2000); Marriage status: 11.0% never married, 64.4% now married, 11.0% widowed, 13.7% divorced (2000); Foreign born: 0.0% (2000); Ancestry (includes multiple ancestries): 17.2% Other groups, 15.1% United States or American, 14.0% Irish, 11.8% German, 6.5% English (2000).
Economy: Single-family building permits issued: 0 (2001) / 0 (2000); Multi-family building permits issued: 0 (2001) / 0 (2000); Employment by occupation: 4.0% management, 6.0% professional, 14.0% services, 30.0% sales, 8.0% farming, 8.0% construction, 30.0% production (2000).
Income: Per capita income: $17,552 (2000); Median household income: $36,667 (2000); Poverty rate: 4.3% (2000).
Taxes: Total city taxes per capita: $17 (1997); City property taxes per capita: $11 (1997).
Education: High school graduation rate: 64.3% (2000); College graduation rate: 12.9% (2000).
Housing: Homeownership rate: 95.0% (2000); Median home value: $47,500 (2000); Median rent: $175 per month (2000); Median age of housing: 27 years (2000).
Transportation: Commute to work: 81.3% car, 0.0% public transportation, 0.0% walk, 6.3% work from home (2000); Travel time to work: 17.8% less than 15 minutes, 35.6% 15 to 30 minutes, 17.8% 30 to 45 minutes, 24.4% 45 to 60 minutes, 4.4% 60 minutes or more (2000)

DIEHLSTADT (village). Covers a land area of 0.076 square miles and a water area of 0 square miles. Located at 36.95° N. Lat.; 89.43° W. Long. Elevation is 328 feet.
Population: 163 (2000); Race: 100.0% White, 0.0% Black, 0.0% Asian, 0.0% American Indian and Alaska Native, 3.2% Hispanic of any race, 0.0% two or more races (2000); Density: 2,149.4 persons per square mile (2000); Age: 27.3% under 18, 5.8% over 64 (2000); Marriage status: 17.5% never married, 53.5% now married, 8.8% widowed, 20.2% divorced (2000); Foreign born: 0.0% (2000); Ancestry (includes multiple ancestries): 29.2% Other groups, 27.3% Irish, 16.9% United States or American, 16.2% German, 3.2% English (2000).
Economy: Employment by occupation: 4.9% management, 7.4% professional, 13.6% services, 24.7% sales, 0.0% farming, 28.4% construction, 21.0% production (2000).
Income: Per capita income: $15,164 (2000); Median household income: $24,375 (2000); Poverty rate: 13.9% (2000).
Taxes: Total city taxes per capita: $7 (1997); City property taxes per capita: $7 (1997).
Education: High school graduation rate: 66.0% (2000); College graduation rate: 0.0% (2000).
Housing: Homeownership rate: 82.3% (2000); Median home value: $29,600 (2000); Median rent: $269 per month (2000); Median age of housing: 30 years (2000).
Transportation: Commute to work: 100.0% car, 0.0% public transportation, 0.0% walk, 0.0% work from home (2000); Travel time to work: 9.3% less than 15 minutes, 72.0% 15 to 30 minutes, 13.3% 30 to 45 minutes, 0.0% 45 to 60 minutes, 5.3% 60 minutes or more (2000)

HAYWOOD CITY (village). Covers a land area of 0.431 square miles and a water area of 0 square miles. Located at 37.01° N. Lat.; 89.60° W. Long. Elevation is 355 feet.
Population: 239 (2000); Race: 5.5% White, 91.7% Black, 0.0% Asian, 0.0% American Indian and Alaska Native, 0.0% Hispanic of any race, 2.8% two or more races (2000); Density: 554.2 persons per square mile (2000); Age: 38.6% under 18, 9.8% over 64 (2000); Marriage status: 33.9% never married, 52.0% now married, 11.1% widowed, 2.9% divorced (2000); Foreign born: 0.0% (2000); Ancestry (includes multiple ancestries): 77.6% Other groups, 3.9% African, 0.8% Scottish, 0.8% French (except Basque) (2000).
Economy: Employment by occupation: 2.1% management, 3.2% professional, 33.7% services, 6.3% sales, 4.2% farming, 8.4% construction, 42.1% production (2000).
Income: Per capita income: $7,553 (2000); Median household income: $14,000 (2000); Poverty rate: 36.5% (2000).
Taxes: Total city taxes per capita: $21 (1997); City property taxes per capita: $21 (1997).
Education: High school graduation rate: 67.4% (2000); College graduation rate: 2.2% (2000).
Housing: Homeownership rate: 78.7% (2000); Median home value: $28,400 (2000); Median rent: $194 per month (2000); Median age of housing: 24 years (2000).
Transportation: Commute to work: 88.6% car, 2.3% public transportation, 0.0% walk, 9.1% work from home (2000); Travel time to work: 5.0% less than 15 minutes, 86.3% 15 to 30 minutes, 0.0% 30 to 45 minutes, 0.0% 45 to 60 minutes, 8.8% 60 minutes or more (2000)

KELSO (village). Covers a land area of 0.319 square miles and a water area of 0 square miles. Located at 37.19° N. Lat.; 89.55° W. Long. Elevation is 440 feet.
Population: 527 (2000); Race: 100.0% White, 0.0% Black, 0.0% Asian, 0.0% American Indian and Alaska Native, 0.0% Hispanic of any race, 0.0% two or more races (2000); Density: 1,653.2 persons per square mile (2000); Age: 26.6% under 18, 15.4% over 64 (2000); Marriage status: 24.1% never married, 63.6% now married, 3.3% widowed, 9.1% divorced (2000); Foreign born: 0.5% (2000); Ancestry (includes multiple ancestries): 52.4% German, 15.2% Irish, 12.2% English, 10.1% United States or American, 3.1% French (except Basque) (2000).
Economy: Feeds. Employment by occupation: 10.9% management, 16.7% professional, 12.5% services, 31.5% sales, 0.0% farming, 14.1% construction, 14.1% production (2000).
Income: Per capita income: $19,099 (2000); Median household income: $45,294 (2000); Poverty rate: 1.6% (2000).
Taxes: Total city taxes per capita: $57 (1997); City property taxes per capita: $30 (1997).
Education: High school graduation rate: 84.9% (2000); College graduation rate: 21.3% (2000).
Housing: Homeownership rate: 86.8% (2000); Median home value: $92,900 (2000); Median rent: $335 per month (2000); Median age of housing: 27 years (2000).
Transportation: Commute to work: 89.4% car, 0.0% public transportation, 7.4% walk, 3.2% work from home (2000); Travel time to work: 42.7% less than 15 minutes, 41.7% 15 to 30 minutes, 12.3% 30 to 45 minutes, 1.3% 45 to 60 minutes, 2.0% 60 minutes or more (2000)

LAMBERT (village). Covers a land area of 0.052 square miles and a water area of 0 square miles. Located at 37.09° N. Lat.; 89.55° W. Long. Elevation is 339 feet.
Population: 49 (2000); Race: 100.0% White, 0.0% Black, 0.0% Asian, 0.0% American Indian and Alaska Native, 0.0% Hispanic of any race, 0.0% two or more races (2000); Density: 942.2 persons per square mile (2000); Age: 6.1% under 18, 9.1% over 64 (2000); Marriage status: 21.2% never married, 69.7% now married, 9.1% widowed, 0.0% divorced (2000); Foreign born: 0.0% (2000); Ancestry (includes multiple ancestries): 15.2% Irish, 6.1% United States or American, 6.1% German (2000).
Economy: Employment by occupation: 16.7% management, 11.1% professional, 0.0% services, 22.2% sales, 0.0% farming, 50.0% construction, 0.0% production (2000).
Income: Per capita income: $16,533 (2000); Median household income: $34,375 (2000); Poverty rate: 6.1% (2000).
Education: High school graduation rate: 60.7% (2000); College graduation rate: 0.0% (2000).
Housing: Homeownership rate: 100.0% (2000); Median home value: $67,000 (2000); Median age of housing: 60+ years (2000).
Transportation: Commute to work: 100.0% car, 0.0% public transportation, 0.0% walk, 0.0% work from home (2000); Travel time to work: 27.8% less than 15 minutes, 55.6% 15 to 30 minutes, 5.6% 30 to 45 minutes, 0.0% 45 to 60 minutes, 11.1% 60 minutes or more (2000)

MINER (city). Covers a land area of 4.100 square miles and a water area of 0.003 square miles. Located at 36.89° N. Lat.; 89.53° W. Long. Elevation is 308 feet.
Population: 1,056 (2000); Race: 91.3% White, 3.9% Black, 0.5% Asian, 1.5% American Indian and Alaska Native, 2.5% Hispanic of any race, 1.8% two or more races (2000); Density: 257.5 persons per square mile (2000); Age: 27.8% under 18, 16.0% over 64 (2000); Marriage status: 14.3% never

married, 65.0% now married, 8.5% widowed, 12.2% divorced (2000); Foreign born: 2.0% (2000); Ancestry (includes multiple ancestries): 19.8% United States or American, 14.3% Other groups, 11.2% German, 8.4% Irish, 7.4% English (2000).
Economy: Residential. Highway service center. Single-family building permits issued: 4 (2001) / 4 (2000); Multi-family building permits issued: 0 (2001) / 0 (2000); Employment by occupation: 11.4% management, 13.8% professional, 17.6% services, 24.9% sales, 0.4% farming, 8.5% construction, 23.4% production (2000).
Income: Per capita income: $17,409 (2000); Median household income: $30,750 (2000); Poverty rate: 18.6% (2000).
Taxes: Total city taxes per capita: $346 (1997); City property taxes per capita: $290 (1997).
Education: High school graduation rate: 69.0% (2000); College graduation rate: 5.3% (2000).
Housing: Homeownership rate: 71.7% (2000); Median home value: $64,600 (2000); Median rent: $270 per month (2000); Median age of housing: 25 years (2000).
Transportation: Commute to work: 92.7% car, 0.0% public transportation, 2.5% walk, 4.3% work from home (2000); Travel time to work: 63.7% less than 15 minutes, 22.3% 15 to 30 minutes, 8.3% 30 to 45 minutes, 1.9% 45 to 60 minutes, 3.8% 60 minutes or more (2000)

MORLEY (city). Covers a land area of 0.740 square miles and a water area of 0 square miles. Located at 37.04° N. Lat.; 89.61° W. Long. Elevation is 343 feet.
Population: 792 (2000); Race: 96.7% White, 1.2% Black, 0.0% Asian, 0.5% American Indian and Alaska Native, 0.0% Hispanic of any race, 1.7% two or more races (2000); Density: 1,070.9 persons per square mile (2000); Age: 27.8% under 18, 15.3% over 64 (2000); Marriage status: 15.0% never married, 58.6% now married, 11.3% widowed, 15.0% divorced (2000); Foreign born: 0.7% (2000); Ancestry (includes multiple ancestries): 18.0% United States or American, 13.6% Irish, 13.1% English, 11.4% German, 9.4% Other groups (2000).
Economy: Manufacturing of motor vehicle parts. Employment by occupation: 9.2% management, 11.8% professional, 13.7% services, 21.3% sales, 1.1% farming, 15.4% construction, 27.5% production (2000).
Income: Per capita income: $12,679 (2000); Median household income: $26,696 (2000); Poverty rate: 15.4% (2000).
Taxes: Total city taxes per capita: $117 (1997); City property taxes per capita: $19 (1997).
Education: High school graduation rate: 67.4% (2000); College graduation rate: 5.4% (2000).
Housing: Homeownership rate: 79.4% (2000); Median home value: $41,500 (2000); Median rent: $255 per month (2000); Median age of housing: 31 years (2000).
Transportation: Commute to work: 93.7% car, 0.6% public transportation, 0.6% walk, 4.6% work from home (2000); Travel time to work: 20.5% less than 15 minutes, 43.7% 15 to 30 minutes, 22.3% 30 to 45 minutes, 7.2% 45 to 60 minutes, 6.3% 60 minutes or more (2000)

ORAN (city). Covers a land area of 1.053 square miles and a water area of 0 square miles. Located at 37.08° N. Lat.; 89.65° W. Long. Elevation is 347 feet.
History: Platted 1869.
Population: 1,264 (2000); Race: 98.3% White, 0.5% Black, 0.0% Asian, 0.5% American Indian and Alaska Native, 2.4% Hispanic of any race, 0.3% two or more races (2000); Density: 1,200.5 persons per square mile (2000); Age: 27.2% under 18, 16.8% over 64 (2000); Marriage status: 18.2% never married, 61.0% now married, 11.5% widowed, 9.3% divorced (2000); Foreign born: 0.3% (2000); Ancestry (includes multiple ancestries): 20.2% United States or American, 17.7% German, 8.4% Irish, 7.9% Other groups, 5.5% French (except Basque) (2000).
Economy: Corn, soybeans; livestock; some manufacturing. Single-family building permits issued: 3 (2001) / 1 (2000); Multi-family building permits issued: 0 (2001) / 0 (2000); Employment by occupation: 8.0% management, 10.6% professional, 15.3% services, 22.0% sales, 0.4% farming, 14.6% construction, 29.1% production (2000).
Income: Per capita income: $13,487 (2000); Median household income: $28,750 (2000); Poverty rate: 14.9% (2000).
Taxes: Total city taxes per capita: $214 (1997); City property taxes per capita: $55 (1997).
Education: High school graduation rate: 69.4% (2000); College graduation rate: 8.7% (2000).

School District(s)

Oran R-III (PK-12)
2000 Enrollment: 389 573-262-2330

Housing: Homeownership rate: 72.0% (2000); Median home value: $48,500 (2000); Median rent: $278 per month (2000); Median age of housing: 38 years (2000).
Transportation: Commute to work: 98.3% car, 0.0% public transportation, 1.1% walk, 0.4% work from home (2000); Travel time to work: 27.7% less than 15 minutes, 27.4% 15 to 30 minutes, 35.8% 30 to 45 minutes, 5.7% 45 to 60 minutes, 3.4% 60 minutes or more (2000)

SCOTT CITY (city). Covers a land area of 4.595 square miles and a water area of 0.036 square miles. Located at 37.21° N. Lat.; 89.52° W. Long. Elevation is 355 feet.
History: Formed by merger of Fornfelt and Illmo.
Population: 4,591 (2000); Race: 98.0% White, 0.5% Black, 0.5% Asian, 0.0% American Indian and Alaska Native, 0.4% Hispanic of any race, 0.8% two or more races (2000); Density: 999.1 persons per square mile (2000); Age: 27.3% under 18, 12.3% over 64 (2000); Marriage status: 21.0% never married, 58.0% now married, 7.4% widowed, 13.6% divorced (2000); Foreign born: 0.7% (2000); Ancestry (includes multiple ancestries): 19.9% German, 18.0% United States or American, 11.4% Irish, 10.9% Other groups, 5.9% English (2000).
Economy: In agricultural area. Melons, corn, soybeans, cotton. Some manufacturing. Railroad junction. Single-family building permits issued: 5 (2001) / 10 (2000); Multi-family building permits issued: 0 (2001) / 0 (2000); Employment by occupation: 7.3% management, 11.6% professional, 16.2% services, 23.5% sales, 0.4% farming, 12.7% construction, 28.3% production (2000).
Income: Per capita income: $15,099 (2000); Median household income: $31,958 (2000); Poverty rate: 12.8% (2000).
Taxes: Total city taxes per capita: $213 (1997); City property taxes per capita: $97 (1997).
Education: High school graduation rate: 78.0% (2000); College graduation rate: 5.5% (2000).

School District(s)

Scott City R-I (PK-12)
2000 Enrollment: 1,087 573-264-2381

Housing: Homeownership rate: 72.8% (2000); Median home value: $64,200 (2000); Median rent: $280 per month (2000); Median age of housing: 34 years (2000).
Transportation: Commute to work: 94.9% car, 0.2% public transportation, 0.5% walk, 3.2% work from home (2000); Travel time to work: 38.5% less than 15 minutes, 40.3% 15 to 30 minutes, 11.8% 30 to 45 minutes, 3.9% 45 to 60 minutes, 5.5% 60 minutes or more (2000)

SIKESTON (city). Covers a land area of 17.935 square miles and a water area of 0.166 square miles. Located at 36.88° N. Lat.; 89.58° W. Long. Elevation is 329 feet.
History: The area of Sikeston was settled during the Spanish period. The town was platted in 1860 by John Sikes, and developed as a lumber center after the Civil War. In the early 1900's, cotton replaced lumber, and later the cultivation of alfalfa, melons, grains, and potatoes was begun.
Population: 16,992 (2000); Race: 75.8% White, 22.2% Black, 0.3% Asian, 0.1% American Indian and Alaska Native, 1.2% Hispanic of any race, 1.1% two or more races (2000); Density: 947.4 persons per square mile (2000); Age: 27.7% under 18, 15.6% over 64 (2000); Marriage status: 24.4% never married, 54.3% now married, 10.1% widowed, 11.1% divorced (2000); Foreign born: 0.6% (2000); Ancestry (includes multiple ancestries): 26.1% Other groups, 17.1% United States or American, 11.8% German, 11.4% Irish, 6.8% English (2000).
Vital Statistics: Birth rate: 174.2 per 10,000 population (1998)
Economy: Single-family building permits issued: 46 (2001) / 32 (2000); Multi-family building permits issued: 58 (2001) / 6 (2000); Employment by occupation: 11.1% management, 14.6% professional, 17.8% services, 27.7% sales, 0.6% farming, 8.6% construction, 19.6% production (2000).
Income: Per capita income: $15,509 (2000); Median household income: $28,589 (2000); Poverty rate: 21.0% (2000).
Taxes: Total city taxes per capita: $401 (2000); City property taxes per capita: $107 (2000).
Education: High school graduation rate: 73.3% (2000); College graduation rate: 14.2% (2000).

School District(s)

Scott Co. Central (PK-12)
2000 Enrollment: 416 573-471-2686

Sikeston R-VI (PK-12)
2000 Enrollment: 4,016 573-472-2581

Housing: Homeownership rate: 56.5% (2000); Median home value: $75,100 (2000); Median rent: $299 per month (2000); Median age of housing: 31 years (2000).
Hospitals: Missouri Delta Medical Center (188 beds)
Safety: Violent crime rate: 80.1 per 10,000 population; Property crime rate: 438.7 per 10,000 population (2001).
Newspapers: Standard Democrat (6 x week)
Transportation: Commute to work: 96.2% car, 1.1% public transportation, 0.7% walk, 1.4% work from home (2000); Travel time to work: 64.8% less than 15 minutes, 19.5% 15 to 30 minutes, 10.8% 30 to 45 minutes, 2.4% 45 to 60 minutes, 2.6% 60 minutes or more (2000)
Airports: Sikeston Memorial Municipal
Additional Information Contacts
Sikeston Area Chamber of Commerce 573-471-2498
Sikeston Board of Realtors 573-472-2411

VANDUSER (village). Covers a land area of 0.132 square miles and a water area of 0 square miles. Located at 36.99° N. Lat.; 89.68° W. Long. Elevation is 313 feet.
Population: 217 (2000); Race: 99.5% White, 0.0% Black, 0.0% Asian, 0.0% American Indian and Alaska Native, 2.0% Hispanic of any race, 0.0% two or more races (2000); Density: 1,643.0 persons per square mile (2000); Age: 26.8% under 18, 15.1% over 64 (2000); Marriage status: 22.9% never married, 49.0% now married, 11.5% widowed, 16.6% divorced (2000); Foreign born: 0.0% (2000); Ancestry (includes multiple ancestries): 31.7% United States or American, 13.2% Irish, 10.2% German, 3.9% Other groups, 2.9% French (except Basque) (2000).
Economy: Single-family building permits issued: 0 (2001) / 0 (2000); Multi-family building permits issued: 0 (2001) / 0 (2000); Employment by occupation: 11.8% management, 8.2% professional, 8.2% services, 27.1% sales, 7.1% farming, 12.9% construction, 24.7% production (2000).
Income: Per capita income: $10,351 (2000); Median household income: $25,417 (2000); Poverty rate: 18.0% (2000).
Taxes: Total city taxes per capita: $13 (1997); City property taxes per capita: $9 (1997).
Education: High school graduation rate: 60.6% (2000); College graduation rate: 4.4% (2000).
Housing: Homeownership rate: 81.8% (2000); Median home value: $27,500 (2000); Median rent: $221 per month (2000); Median age of housing: 40 years (2000).
Transportation: Commute to work: 88.2% car, 0.0% public transportation, 0.0% walk, 5.9% work from home (2000); Travel time to work: 25.0% less than 15 minutes, 48.8% 15 to 30 minutes, 18.8% 30 to 45 minutes, 1.3% 45 to 60 minutes, 6.3% 60 minutes or more (2000)

Shannon County

Located in southern Missouri, in the Ozarks; drained by the Current River; includes part of Clark National Forest. Covers a land area of 1,003.80 square miles, a water area of 0.20 square miles, and is located in the Central Time Zone. The county government was organized in 1841. County seat is Eminence.
Population: 8,324 (2000); Race: 96.3% White, 0.2% Black, 0.0% Asian, 1.7% American Indian and Alaska Native, 0.6% Hispanic of any race, 1.6% two or more races (2000); Density: 8.3 persons per square mile (2000); Age: 26.2% under 18, 14.9% over 64 (2000).
Religion: Five largest groups: 18.6% Southern Baptist Convention, 3.9% The United Methodist Church, 3.5% Christian Churches and Churches of Christ, 2.9% Assemblies of God, 1.9% Church of God of Prophecy (2000).
Economy: Unemployment rate: 7.6% (11/2002); Total civilian labor force: 3,929 (11/2002); Leading industries: 45.7% manufacturing; 16.8% health care and social assistance; 12.9% retail trade (2000); Companies that employ more than 1,000 persons: 0 (2000); Companies that employ more than 100 persons: 3 (2000); Farms: 470 totaling 133,320 acres (1997); Minority business ownership rate: 0.0% (1997); Women business ownership rate: 28.6% (1997); Retail sales per capita: $2,341 (1997). Single-family building permits issued: 1 (2001) / 1 (2000); Multi-family building permits issued: 9 (2001) / 12 (2000).
Income: Per capita income: $11,492 (2000); Median household income: $20,878 (2000); Poverty rate: 26.9% (2000); Bankruptcy rate: 1.69% (2001).
Taxes: Total county taxes per capita: $49 (1997); County property taxes per capita: $28 (1997).
Education: High school graduation rate: 67.6% (2000); College graduation rate: 7.6% (2000).
Housing: Homeownership rate: 79.7% (2000); Median home value: $41,400 (2000); Median rent: $201 per month (2000); Median age of housing: 28 years (2000).
Health: Birth rate: 126.1 per 10,000 population (1998); Age adjusted death rate: 98.8 per 10,000 population (1999); Age adjusted cancer mortality rate: 224.3 deaths per 100,000 population (1999). Number of physicians: 2.4 per 10,000 population (1999); Number of hospital beds: n/a (1999).
Elections: 2000 Presidential election results: 37.8% Gore, 59.4% Bush, 1.3% Nader, 1.0% Buchanan
National and State Parks: Alley Spring State Forest; Alley Spring State Park; Beal State Forest; Blair Creek State Forest; Bloom Creek State Forest; Cardareva State Forest; Cardareva State Forest; Carrs Creek State Forest; Clow State Forest; Flat Rock State Wildlife Area; Hartshorn State Forest; Indian Creek State Forest; Mule Mountain State Forest; Powder Mill State Forest; Rocky Creek State Forest; Round Spring State Park; Shannondale State Forest; Skunk Pond State Wildlife Management Area; Sunklands-Burr Oak State Wildlife Area
Additional Information Contacts
Shannon County Government Offices 573-226-3414
Eminence Chamber of Commerce 573-226-3318
Winona Chamber of Commerce 573-325-4407

Shannon County Communities

BIRCH TREE (city). Covers a land area of 1.326 square miles and a water area of 0 square miles. Located at 36.99° N. Lat.; 91.49° W. Long. Elevation is 991 feet.
History: Birch Tree was named for a large birch that stood on the bank of a creek near the first post office. The town grew around lumber mills.
Population: 634 (2000); Race: 96.2% White, 0.0% Black, 0.0% Asian, 2.1% American Indian and Alaska Native, 0.0% Hispanic of any race, 1.6% two or more races (2000); Density: 478.0 persons per square mile (2000); Age: 28.6% under 18, 16.9% over 64 (2000); Marriage status: 21.7% never married, 52.7% now married, 10.8% widowed, 14.8% divorced (2000); Foreign born: 0.7% (2000); Ancestry (includes multiple ancestries): 20.3% United States or American, 18.5% Other groups, 12.8% German, 11.1% Irish, 4.3% English (2000).
Economy: Single-family building permits issued: 1 (2001) / 1 (2000); Multi-family building permits issued: 0 (2001) / 0 (2000); Employment by occupation: 2.7% management, 10.3% professional, 18.5% services, 12.0% sales, 4.9% farming, 9.2% construction, 42.4% production (2000).
Income: Per capita income: $7,695 (2000); Median household income: $14,236 (2000); Poverty rate: 46.0% (2000).
Taxes: Total city taxes per capita: $146 (1997); City property taxes per capita: $41 (1997).
Education: High school graduation rate: 62.0% (2000); College graduation rate: 4.2% (2000).
Housing: Homeownership rate: 67.4% (2000); Median home value: $32,600 (2000); Median rent: $200 per month (2000); Median age of housing: 32 years (2000).
Transportation: Commute to work: 85.6% car, 3.3% public transportation, 7.2% walk, 1.7% work from home (2000); Travel time to work: 46.6% less than 15 minutes, 35.4% 15 to 30 minutes, 7.9% 30 to 45 minutes, 4.5% 45 to 60 minutes, 5.6% 60 minutes or more (2000)

EMINENCE (city). Covers a land area of 1.887 square miles and a water area of 0 square miles. Located at 37.14° N. Lat.; 91.35° W. Long. Elevation is 677 feet.
History: Eminence developed as the seat of Shannon County, organized in 1841, and as an outfitting point for float trips on the Current River.
Population: 548 (2000); Race: 95.6% White, 0.0% Black, 0.0% Asian, 3.0% American Indian and Alaska Native, 0.0% Hispanic of any race, 1.3% two or more races (2000); Density: 290.4 persons per square mile (2000); Age: 20.7% under 18, 24.5% over 64 (2000); Marriage status: 17.0% never married, 53.4% now married, 16.7% widowed, 12.9% divorced (2000); Foreign born: 0.4% (2000); Ancestry (includes multiple ancestries): 18.4% Irish, 14.0% United States or American, 13.1% Other groups, 12.5% German, 8.5% English (2000).
Economy: Employment by occupation: 6.4% management, 12.9% professional, 12.9% services, 19.9% sales, 0.0% farming, 12.3% construction, 35.7% production (2000).
Income: Per capita income: $10,696 (2000); Median household income: $17,422 (2000); Poverty rate: 31.4% (2000).

Taxes: Total city taxes per capita: $176 (1997); City property taxes per capita: $7 (1997).
Education: High school graduation rate: 63.9% (2000); College graduation rate: 9.5% (2000).

School District(s)

Eminence R-I (PK-12)
2000 Enrollment: 323 573-226-3251
Housing: Homeownership rate: 66.7% (2000); Median home value: $39,100 (2000); Median rent: $182 per month (2000); Median age of housing: 38 years (2000).
Newspapers: Current Wave (1 x week)
Transportation: Commute to work: 91.7% car, 0.0% public transportation, 7.1% walk, 1.2% work from home (2000); Travel time to work: 63.5% less than 15 minutes, 18.0% 15 to 30 minutes, 4.8% 30 to 45 minutes, 4.2% 45 to 60 minutes, 9.6% 60 minutes or more (2000)
Additional Information Contacts
Eminence Chamber of Commerce 573-226-3318

WINONA (city). Covers a land area of 3.768 square miles and a water area of 0 square miles. Located at 37.00° N. Lat.; 91.32° W. Long. Elevation is 920 feet.
Population: 1,290 (2000); Race: 94.6% White, 0.0% Black, 0.0% Asian, 2.3% American Indian and Alaska Native, 0.0% Hispanic of any race, 3.0% two or more races (2000); Density: 342.4 persons per square mile (2000); Age: 30.5% under 18, 13.4% over 64 (2000); Marriage status: 17.1% never married, 57.7% now married, 9.1% widowed, 16.1% divorced (2000); Foreign born: 0.0% (2000); Ancestry (includes multiple ancestries): 23.2% United States or American, 17.0% Other groups, 12.8% Irish, 7.8% German, 3.4% English (2000).
Economy: Fruit; livestock; lumber. Manufacturing: hardware; wood products. Recreation. Surrounded by Mark Twain National Forest. Single-family building permits issued: 0 (2001) / 0 (2000); Multi-family building permits issued: 9 (2001) / 12 (2000); Employment by occupation: 3.0% management, 9.9% professional, 15.0% services, 17.3% sales, 4.4% farming, 9.9% construction, 40.4% production (2000).
Income: Per capita income: $11,564 (2000); Median household income: $18,640 (2000); Poverty rate: 34.7% (2000).
Taxes: Total city taxes per capita: $120 (1997); City property taxes per capita: $7 (1997).
Education: High school graduation rate: 61.8% (2000); College graduation rate: 4.2% (2000).

School District(s)

Winona R-III (KG-12)
2000 Enrollment: 572 573-325-8101
Housing: Homeownership rate: 68.0% (2000); Median home value: $45,800 (2000); Median rent: $204 per month (2000); Median age of housing: 29 years (2000).
Transportation: Commute to work: 95.0% car, 0.0% public transportation, 0.9% walk, 2.6% work from home (2000); Travel time to work: 54.4% less than 15 minutes, 24.2% 15 to 30 minutes, 10.2% 30 to 45 minutes, 2.2% 45 to 60 minutes, 8.9% 60 minutes or more (2000)
Additional Information Contacts
Winona Chamber of Commerce.......................... 573-325-4407

Shelby County

Located in northeastern Missouri; drained by the North and Salt Rivers. Covers a land area of 500.90 square miles, a water area of 1.50 square miles, and is located in the Central Time Zone. The county government was organized in 1835. County seat is Shelbyville.
Population: 6,799 (2000); Race: 98.2% White, 0.7% Black, 0.2% Asian, 0.3% American Indian and Alaska Native, 0.4% Hispanic of any race, 0.4% two or more races (2000); Density: 13.6 persons per square mile (2000); Age: 25.3% under 18, 19.9% over 64 (2000).
Religion: Five largest groups: 23.0% Christian Churches and Churches of Christ, 20.6% Southern Baptist Convention, 10.5% The United Methodist Church, 9.3% Catholic Church, 6.1% Independent, Charismatic Churches (2000).
Economy: Unemployment rate: 4.0% (11/2002); Total civilian labor force: 2,915 (11/2002); Leading industries: 27.5% manufacturing; 16.3% retail trade; 10.2% construction (2000); Companies that employ more than 1,000 persons: 0 (2000); Companies that employ more than 100 persons: 1 (2000); Farms: 644 totaling 272,116 acres (1997); Minority business ownership rate: 0.0% (1997); Women business ownership rate: 0.0% (1997); Retail sales per capita: $4,123 (1997). Single-family building permits issued: 4 (2001) / 0 (2000); Multi-family building permits issued: 0 (2001) / 0 (2000).
Income: Per capita income: $15,632 (2000); Median household income: $29,448 (2000); Poverty rate: 16.3% (2000); Bankruptcy rate: 4.62% (2001).
Taxes: Total county taxes per capita: $123 (2000); County property taxes per capita: $63 (2000).
Education: High school graduation rate: 81.0% (2000); College graduation rate: 12.5% (2000).
Housing: Homeownership rate: 75.1% (2000); Median home value: $44,000 (2000); Median rent: $209 per month (2000); Median age of housing: 43 years (2000).
Health: Birth rate: 91.2 per 10,000 population (1998); Age adjusted death rate: 97.6 per 10,000 population (1999); Age adjusted cancer mortality rate: 203.1 deaths per 100,000 population (1999). Number of physicians: 4.4 per 10,000 population (1999); Number of hospital beds: n/a (1999).
Elections: 2000 Presidential election results: 38.8% Gore, 59.4% Bush, 1.1% Nader, 0.4% Buchanan
Additional Information Contacts
Shelby County Government Offices 573-633-2181

Shelby County Communities

BETHEL (village). Covers a land area of 0.141 square miles and a water area of 0 square miles. Located at 39.87° N. Lat.; 92.02° W. Long. Elevation is 713 feet.
History: Bethel was the location in 1845 of an experiment in communal living led by Dr. William Keil, a Prussian religious zealot and social reformer. Keil brought a group of followers from Pennsylvania and Ohio, and they established a colony that lasted until Keil's death in 1879. Many of the families stayed on in Bethel, joining other families who had settled outside the colony during those years.
Population: 121 (2000); Race: 96.6% White, 0.0% Black, 0.0% Asian, 0.0% American Indian and Alaska Native, 0.0% Hispanic of any race, 3.4% two or more races (2000); Density: 856.5 persons per square mile (2000); Age: 35.6% under 18, 11.9% over 64 (2000); Marriage status: 39.8% never married, 30.7% now married, 13.6% widowed, 15.9% divorced (2000); Foreign born: 0.0% (2000); Ancestry (includes multiple ancestries): 33.9% United States or American, 29.7% German, 6.8% Norwegian, 5.9% Scotch-Irish, 5.9% Dutch (2000).
Economy: Employment by occupation: 5.5% management, 21.8% professional, 12.7% services, 29.1% sales, 0.0% farming, 9.1% construction, 21.8% production (2000).
Income: Per capita income: $13,958 (2000); Median household income: $22,083 (2000); Poverty rate: 6.8% (2000).
Taxes: Total city taxes per capita: $42 (1997); City property taxes per capita: $8 (1997).
Education: High school graduation rate: 94.4% (2000); College graduation rate: 16.9% (2000).
Housing: Homeownership rate: 54.0% (2000); Median home value: $20,600 (2000); Median rent: $208 per month (2000); Median age of housing: 60+ years (2000).
Transportation: Commute to work: 96.2% car, 0.0% public transportation, 3.8% walk, 0.0% work from home (2000); Travel time to work: 50.9% less than 15 minutes, 26.4% 15 to 30 minutes, 15.1% 30 to 45 minutes, 1.9% 45 to 60 minutes, 5.7% 60 minutes or more (2000)

CLARENCE (city). Covers a land area of 1.166 square miles and a water area of 0 square miles. Located at 39.74° N. Lat.; 92.26° W. Long. Elevation is 823 feet.
History: Clarence was platted in 1857 by John Duff, a railroad contractor, and named for one of his children. Clarence grew as a grain and livestock shipping point.
Population: 915 (2000); Race: 98.4% White, 0.6% Black, 0.0% Asian, 0.7% American Indian and Alaska Native, 0.2% Hispanic of any race, 0.2% two or more races (2000); Density: 784.9 persons per square mile (2000); Age: 23.7% under 18, 21.5% over 64 (2000); Marriage status: 16.0% never married, 50.9% now married, 17.2% widowed, 15.9% divorced (2000); Foreign born: 0.5% (2000); Ancestry (includes multiple ancestries): 26.7% German, 14.2% United States or American, 12.0% Irish, 11.3% English, 9.6% Other groups (2000).
Economy: Employment by occupation: 10.4% management, 11.8% professional, 20.0% services, 20.8% sales, 3.3% farming, 7.1% construction, 26.6% production (2000).
Income: Per capita income: $12,970 (2000); Median household income: $21,513 (2000); Poverty rate: 19.0% (2000).

Taxes: Total city taxes per capita: $162 (1997); City property taxes per capita: $39 (1997).
Education: High school graduation rate: 77.6% (2000); College graduation rate: 6.5% (2000).
Housing: Homeownership rate: 74.1% (2000); Median home value: $30,100 (2000); Median rent: $198 per month (2000); Median age of housing: 48 years (2000).
Newspapers: Clarence Courier (1 x week)
Transportation: Commute to work: 91.3% car, 0.3% public transportation, 5.1% walk, 2.5% work from home (2000); Travel time to work: 45.2% less than 15 minutes, 29.1% 15 to 30 minutes, 13.3% 30 to 45 minutes, 2.6% 45 to 60 minutes, 9.8% 60 minutes or more (2000)

EMDEN (unincorporated postal area, zip code 63439). Covers a land area of 26.578 square miles and a water area of 0 square miles. Located at 39.78° N. Lat.; 91.85° W. Long. Elevation is 745 feet.
Population: 199 (2000); Race: 100.0% White, 0.0% Black, 0.0% Asian, 0.0% American Indian and Alaska Native, 0.0% Hispanic of any race, 0.0% two or more races (2000); Density: 7.5 persons per square mile (2000); Age: 36.4% under 18, 10.7% over 64 (2000); Marriage status: 26.9% never married, 66.0% now married, 2.0% widowed, 5.1% divorced (2000); Foreign born: 0.0% (2000); Ancestry (includes multiple ancestries): 39.1% German, 32.4% United States or American, 17.4% Irish, 5.5% Scottish, 3.6% Scotch-Irish (2000).
Economy: Employment by occupation: 14.7% management, 10.8% professional, 6.9% services, 12.7% sales, 0.0% farming, 15.7% construction, 39.2% production (2000).
Income: Per capita income: $11,186 (2000); Median household income: $37,292 (2000); Poverty rate: 30.0% (2000).
Education: High school graduation rate: 73.8% (2000); College graduation rate: 7.8% (2000).
Housing: Homeownership rate: 82.4% (2000); Median home value: $51,000 (2000); Median rent: $195 per month (2000); Median age of housing: 33 years (2000).
Transportation: Commute to work: 81.4% car, 2.0% public transportation, 2.0% walk, 14.7% work from home (2000); Travel time to work: 9.2% less than 15 minutes, 35.6% 15 to 30 minutes, 35.6% 30 to 45 minutes, 2.3% 45 to 60 minutes, 17.2% 60 minutes or more (2000)

HUNNEWELL (city). Covers a land area of 0.634 square miles and a water area of 0 square miles. Located at 39.66° N. Lat.; 91.85° W. Long. Elevation is 753 feet.
Population: 227 (2000); Race: 88.5% White, 8.8% Black, 0.0% Asian, 0.0% American Indian and Alaska Native, 0.4% Hispanic of any race, 2.6% two or more races (2000); Density: 358.3 persons per square mile (2000); Age: 20.3% under 18, 22.0% over 64 (2000); Marriage status: 17.5% never married, 53.4% now married, 10.1% widowed, 19.0% divorced (2000); Foreign born: 0.9% (2000); Ancestry (includes multiple ancestries): 28.6% United States or American, 17.2% Other groups, 13.2% German, 8.8% English, 2.2% Irish (2000).
Economy: Soybeans, corn; cattle, hogs. Employment by occupation: 3.6% management, 10.8% professional, 14.5% services, 14.5% sales, 0.0% farming, 13.3% construction, 43.4% production (2000).
Income: Per capita income: $12,985 (2000); Median household income: $24,861 (2000); Poverty rate: 15.9% (2000).
Taxes: Total city taxes per capita: $31 (1997); City property taxes per capita: $4 (1997).
Education: High school graduation rate: 59.0% (2000); College graduation rate: 1.8% (2000).
Housing: Homeownership rate: 84.5% (2000); Median home value: $24,700 (2000); Median rent: $175 per month (2000); Median age of housing: 30 years (2000).
Transportation: Commute to work: 96.4% car, 0.0% public transportation, 2.4% walk, 0.0% work from home (2000); Travel time to work: 34.9% less than 15 minutes, 26.5% 15 to 30 minutes, 31.3% 30 to 45 minutes, 2.4% 45 to 60 minutes, 4.8% 60 minutes or more (2000)

LENTNER (unincorporated postal area, zip code 63450). Covers a land area of 26.665 square miles and a water area of 0 square miles. Located at 39.65° N. Lat.; 92.14° W. Long. Elevation is 791 feet.
Population: 178 (2000); Race: 100.0% White, 0.0% Black, 0.0% Asian, 0.0% American Indian and Alaska Native, 0.0% Hispanic of any race, 0.0% two or more races (2000); Density: 6.7 persons per square mile (2000); Age: 14.2% under 18, 6.8% over 64 (2000); Marriage status: 18.7% never married, 81.3% now married, 0.0% widowed, 0.0% divorced (2000); Foreign born: 0.0% (2000); Ancestry (includes multiple ancestries): 39.9% German, 30.4% English, 26.4% Irish, 4.7% United States or American, 4.1% Scottish (2000).
Economy: Employment by occupation: 43.8% management, 0.0% professional, 22.9% services, 17.1% sales, 0.0% farming, 3.8% construction, 12.4% production (2000).
Income: Per capita income: $16,878 (2000); Median household income: $41,477 (2000); Poverty rate: 16.9% (2000).
Education: High school graduation rate: 98.2% (2000); College graduation rate: 17.9% (2000).
Housing: Homeownership rate: 62.1% (2000); Median home value: $65,000 (2000); Median rent: $225 per month (2000); Median age of housing: 42 years (2000).
Transportation: Commute to work: 90.5% car, 0.0% public transportation, 0.0% walk, 9.5% work from home (2000); Travel time to work: 26.3% less than 15 minutes, 55.8% 15 to 30 minutes, 6.3% 30 to 45 minutes, 7.4% 45 to 60 minutes, 4.2% 60 minutes or more (2000)

LEONARD (village). Covers a land area of 0.321 square miles and a water area of 0 square miles. Located at 39.89° N. Lat.; 92.18° W. Long. Elevation is 775 feet.
Population: 66 (2000); Race: 100.0% White, 0.0% Black, 0.0% Asian, 0.0% American Indian and Alaska Native, 0.0% Hispanic of any race, 0.0% two or more races (2000); Density: 205.8 persons per square mile (2000); Age: 9.8% under 18, 27.5% over 64 (2000); Marriage status: 18.0% never married, 66.0% now married, 16.0% widowed, 0.0% divorced (2000); Foreign born: 0.0% (2000); Ancestry (includes multiple ancestries): 31.4% United States or American, 17.6% Italian, 13.7% German, 13.7% French (except Basque), 11.8% Scottish (2000).
Economy: Corn, soybeans; cattle, hogs. Employment by occupation: 0.0% management, 25.0% professional, 0.0% services, 25.0% sales, 17.9% farming, 3.6% construction, 28.6% production (2000).
Income: Per capita income: $13,067 (2000); Median household income: $11,250 (2000); Poverty rate: 35.3% (2000).
Taxes: Total city taxes per capita: $56 (1997); City property taxes per capita: $22 (1997).
Education: High school graduation rate: 61.4% (2000); College graduation rate: 6.8% (2000).
Housing: Homeownership rate: 89.3% (2000); Median home value: $23,900 (2000); Median age of housing: 60+ years (2000).
Transportation: Commute to work: 76.9% car, 0.0% public transportation, 0.0% walk, 7.7% work from home (2000); Travel time to work: 33.3% less than 15 minutes, 20.8% 15 to 30 minutes, 45.8% 30 to 45 minutes, 0.0% 45 to 60 minutes, 0.0% 60 minutes or more (2000)

SHELBINA (city). Covers a land area of 2.301 square miles and a water area of 0 square miles. Located at 39.69° N. Lat.; 92.04° W. Long. Elevation is 779 feet.
History: Shelbina was platted in 1857 by Major Josiah Hunt, land commissioner of the Hannibal & St. Joseph Railroad, and developed as an agricultural shipping point.
Population: 1,943 (2000); Race: 97.4% White, 1.1% Black, 0.6% Asian, 0.6% American Indian and Alaska Native, 0.2% Hispanic of any race, 0.4% two or more races (2000); Density: 844.4 persons per square mile (2000); Age: 23.1% under 18, 24.9% over 64 (2000); Marriage status: 19.3% never married, 55.8% now married, 12.2% widowed, 12.6% divorced (2000); Foreign born: 1.7% (2000); Ancestry (includes multiple ancestries): 24.0% German, 15.5% United States or American, 14.5% English, 13.5% Irish, 7.2% Other groups (2000).
Economy: Single-family building permits issued: 4 (2001) / 0 (2000); Multi-family building permits issued: 0 (2001) / 0 (2000); Employment by occupation: 6.4% management, 13.3% professional, 16.3% services, 19.8% sales, 2.4% farming, 9.2% construction, 32.6% production (2000).
Income: Per capita income: $17,645 (2000); Median household income: $25,800 (2000); Poverty rate: 16.8% (2000).
Taxes: Total city taxes per capita: $164 (1997); City property taxes per capita: $37 (1997).
Education: High school graduation rate: 77.0% (2000); College graduation rate: 13.6% (2000).

School District(s)

Shelby Co. R-IV (PK-12)
2000 Enrollment: 853 573-588-4961
Housing: Homeownership rate: 70.4% (2000); Median home value: $49,500 (2000); Median rent: $220 per month (2000); Median age of housing: 44 years (2000).
Newspapers: Shelbina Democrat (1 x week)

Transportation: Commute to work: 90.4% car, 0.0% public transportation, 4.9% walk, 3.7% work from home (2000); Travel time to work: 65.6% less than 15 minutes, 14.8% 15 to 30 minutes, 8.4% 30 to 45 minutes, 4.5% 45 to 60 minutes, 6.6% 60 minutes or more (2000)

SHELBYVILLE (city). Covers a land area of 0.774 square miles and a water area of 0.043 square miles. Located at 39.80° N. Lat.; 92.04° W. Long. Elevation is 768 feet.
History: Shelbyville was organized in 1835 and named for Isaac Shelby, a Revolutionary War soldier and governor of Kentucky.
Population: 682 (2000); Race: 99.4% White, 0.0% Black, 0.0% Asian, 0.0% American Indian and Alaska Native, 1.3% Hispanic of any race, 0.1% two or more races (2000); Density: 881.2 persons per square mile (2000); Age: 26.1% under 18, 18.8% over 64 (2000); Marriage status: 17.3% never married, 57.6% now married, 15.3% widowed, 9.8% divorced (2000); Foreign born: 0.3% (2000); Ancestry (includes multiple ancestries): 20.4% German, 17.5% United States or American, 8.5% English, 6.3% Irish, 3.1% Scotch-Irish (2000).
Economy: Employment by occupation: 6.3% management, 9.7% professional, 14.0% services, 19.3% sales, 1.3% farming, 13.3% construction, 36.0% production (2000).
Income: Per capita income: $13,759 (2000); Median household income: $28,542 (2000); Poverty rate: 16.1% (2000).
Taxes: Total city taxes per capita: $94 (1997); City property taxes per capita: $39 (1997).
Education: High school graduation rate: 81.1% (2000); College graduation rate: 11.7% (2000).

School District(s)

Shelby Co. C-1 (KG-12)
2000 Enrollment: 373 573-633-2410
Housing: Homeownership rate: 75.7% (2000); Median home value: $43,400 (2000); Median rent: $188 per month (2000); Median age of housing: 49 years (2000).
Newspapers: Shelby County Herald (1 x week)
Transportation: Commute to work: 88.3% car, 1.0% public transportation, 2.7% walk, 7.3% work from home (2000); Travel time to work: 50.7% less than 15 minutes, 15.8% 15 to 30 minutes, 17.6% 30 to 45 minutes, 6.5% 45 to 60 minutes, 9.4% 60 minutes or more (2000)

Stoddard County

Located in southeastern Missouri; bounded on the west by the St. Francis River; drained by the Castor River. Covers a land area of 827.10 square miles, a water area of 1.80 square miles, and is located in the Central Time Zone. The county government was organized in 1835. County seat is Bloomfield.

Weather Station: Advance 1 S — Elevation: 357 feet

	Jan	Feb	Mar	Apr	May	Jun	Jul	Aug	Sep	Oct	Nov	Dec
High	41	48	57	68	77	86	90	89	82	71	57	46
Low	23	27	36	44	54	63	67	64	56	44	35	27
Precip	3.2	3.3	4.3	5.1	5.0	3.8	4.1	3.0	3.2	3.4	4.6	3.9
Snow	2.8	3.9	1.4	tr	0.0	0.0	0.0	0.0	0.0	tr	0.4	1.3

High and Low temperatures in degrees Fahrenheit; Precipitation and Snow in inches

Population: 29,705 (2000); Race: 96.9% White, 1.0% Black, 0.3% Asian, 0.2% American Indian and Alaska Native, 0.6% Hispanic of any race, 1.2% two or more races (2000); Density: 35.9 persons per square mile (2000); Age: 23.8% under 18, 17.2% over 64 (2000).
Religion: Five largest groups: 19.0% Southern Baptist Convention, 4.6% The United Methodist Church, 3.3% Churches of Christ, 2.5% Assemblies of God, 2.5% Catholic Church (2000).
Economy: Unemployment rate: 6.0% (11/2002); Total civilian labor force: 12,858 (11/2002); Leading industries: 30.0% manufacturing; 16.0% health care and social assistance; 14.9% retail trade (2000); Companies that employ more than 1,000 persons: 0 (2000); Companies that employ more than 100 persons: 10 (2000); Farms: 941 totaling 448,634 acres (1997); Minority business ownership rate: 0.0% (1997); Women business ownership rate: 22.3% (1997); Retail sales per capita: $8,296 (1997). Single-family building permits issued: 49 (2001) / 33 (2000); Multi-family building permits issued: 10 (2001) / 0 (2000).
Income: Per capita income: $14,656 (2000); Median household income: $26,987 (2000); Poverty rate: 16.5% (2000); Bankruptcy rate: 6.12% (2001).
Taxes: Total county taxes per capita: $45 (2000); County property taxes per capita: $12 (2000).
Education: High school graduation rate: 66.9% (2000); College graduation rate: 10.1% (2000).
Housing: Homeownership rate: 72.3% (2000); Median home value: $57,200 (2000); Median rent: $244 per month (2000); Median age of housing: 30 years (2000).
Health: Birth rate: 116.8 per 10,000 population (1998); Age adjusted death rate: 101.5 per 10,000 population (1999); Age adjusted cancer mortality rate: 263.0 deaths per 100,000 population (1999). Number of physicians: 2.7 per 10,000 population (1999); Number of hospital beds: 16.2 per 10,000 population (1999).
Elections: 2000 Presidential election results: 35.9% Gore, 62.0% Bush, 0.9% Nader, 0.7% Buchanan
National and State Parks: Mingo National Wildlife Refuge; Otter Slough State Wildlife Management Area
Additional Information Contacts
Stoddard County Government Offices 573-568-3339
Dexter Chamber of Commerce. 573-624-7458

Stoddard County Communities

ADVANCE (city). Covers a land area of 0.871 square miles and a water area of 0 square miles. Located at 37.10° N. Lat.; 89.91° W. Long. Elevation is 361 feet.
Population: 1,244 (2000); Race: 98.9% White, 0.0% Black, 0.0% Asian, 0.6% American Indian and Alaska Native, 0.1% Hispanic of any race, 0.6% two or more races (2000); Density: 1,428.8 persons per square mile (2000); Age: 20.6% under 18, 25.9% over 64 (2000); Marriage status: 14.8% never married, 56.3% now married, 19.0% widowed, 9.9% divorced (2000); Foreign born: 0.2% (2000); Ancestry (includes multiple ancestries): 25.2% United States or American, 16.7% German, 10.9% Irish, 6.4% Other groups, 5.9% English (2000).
Economy: Manufactures aluminum doors and windows. Rice, soybeans, corn. Single-family building permits issued: 1 (2001) / 1 (2000); Multi-family building permits issued: 0 (2001) / 0 (2000); Employment by occupation: 6.8% management, 17.8% professional, 11.0% services, 20.6% sales, 1.6% farming, 14.8% construction, 27.4% production (2000).
Income: Per capita income: $15,036 (2000); Median household income: $27,734 (2000); Poverty rate: 12.9% (2000).
Taxes: Total city taxes per capita: $165 (1997); City property taxes per capita: $35 (1997).
Education: High school graduation rate: 62.6% (2000); College graduation rate: 11.7% (2000).

School District(s)

Advance R-IV (KG-12)
2000 Enrollment: 508 573-722-3581
Housing: Homeownership rate: 76.2% (2000); Median home value: $61,200 (2000); Median rent: $215 per month (2000); Median age of housing: 29 years (2000).
Transportation: Commute to work: 92.6% car, 0.2% public transportation, 4.3% walk, 1.6% work from home (2000); Travel time to work: 38.3% less than 15 minutes, 14.2% 15 to 30 minutes, 28.5% 30 to 45 minutes, 11.0% 45 to 60 minutes, 7.9% 60 minutes or more (2000)

BAKER (village). Covers a land area of 0.207 square miles and a water area of 0 square miles. Located at 36.77° N. Lat.; 89.76° W. Long. Elevation is 292 feet.
Population: 5 (2000); Race: 100.0% White, 0.0% Black, 0.0% Asian, 0.0% American Indian and Alaska Native, 0.0% Hispanic of any race, 0.0% two or more races (2000); Density: 24.1 persons per square mile (2000); Age: 0.0% under 18, 100.0% over 64 (2000); Marriage status: 0.0% never married, 0.0% now married, 0.0% widowed, 100.0% divorced (2000); Foreign born: 0.0% (2000); Ancestry (includes multiple ancestries): 100.0% English (2000).
Economy: Employment by occupation: 100.0% management, 0.0% professional, 0.0% services, 0.0% sales, 0.0% farming, 0.0% construction, 0.0% production (2000).
Income: Per capita income: $182,000 (2000); Median household income: $177,361 (2000); Poverty rate: 0.0% (2000).
Education: High school graduation rate: 100.0% (2000); College graduation rate: 100.0% (2000).
Housing: Homeownership rate: 100.0% (2000); Median home value: $275,000 (2000); Median age of housing: 25 years (2000).
Transportation: Commute to work: 100.0% car, 0.0% public transportation, 0.0% walk, 0.0% work from home (2000); Travel time to work: 100.0% less than 15 minutes, 0.0% 15 to 30 minutes, 0.0% 30 to 45 minutes, 0.0% 45 to 60 minutes, 0.0% 60 minutes or more (2000)

BELL CITY (city). Covers a land area of 0.555 square miles and a water area of 0 square miles. Located at 37.02° N. Lat.; 89.81° W. Long. Elevation is 326 feet.
Population: 461 (2000); Race: 99.0% White, 0.6% Black, 0.0% Asian, 0.0% American Indian and Alaska Native, 0.0% Hispanic of any race, 0.4% two or more races (2000); Density: 830.9 persons per square mile (2000); Age: 30.2% under 18, 12.2% over 64 (2000); Marriage status: 19.6% never married, 53.6% now married, 10.2% widowed, 16.6% divorced (2000); Foreign born: 0.6% (2000); Ancestry (includes multiple ancestries): 26.4% United States or American, 13.8% Irish, 10.1% German, 7.4% Other groups, 4.5% English (2000).
Economy: Rice, cotton, soybeans. Single-family building permits issued: 1 (2001) / 0 (2000); Multi-family building permits issued: 0 (2001) / 0 (2000); Employment by occupation: 3.9% management, 6.8% professional, 11.1% services, 20.3% sales, 2.9% farming, 10.6% construction, 44.4% production (2000).
Income: Per capita income: $12,664 (2000); Median household income: $23,125 (2000); Poverty rate: 19.4% (2000).
Taxes: Total city taxes per capita: $80 (1997); City property taxes per capita: $17 (1997).
Education: High school graduation rate: 62.6% (2000); College graduation rate: 3.1% (2000).

School District(s)

Bell City R-II (KG-12)
2000 Enrollment: 286 573-733-4444
Housing: Homeownership rate: 66.8% (2000); Median home value: $28,300 (2000); Median rent: $173 per month (2000); Median age of housing: 30 years (2000).
Transportation: Commute to work: 93.7% car, 0.0% public transportation, 3.4% walk, 1.0% work from home (2000); Travel time to work: 22.0% less than 15 minutes, 30.7% 15 to 30 minutes, 41.0% 30 to 45 minutes, 3.9% 45 to 60 minutes, 2.4% 60 minutes or more (2000)

BERNIE (city). Covers a land area of 1.248 square miles and a water area of 0 square miles. Located at 36.67° N. Lat.; 89.96° W. Long. Elevation is 302 feet.
History: Bernie grew up around a cotton gin.
Population: 1,777 (2000); Race: 97.1% White, 1.5% Black, 0.1% Asian, 0.0% American Indian and Alaska Native, 0.6% Hispanic of any race, 0.9% two or more races (2000); Density: 1,424.3 persons per square mile (2000); Age: 24.6% under 18, 17.2% over 64 (2000); Marriage status: 17.4% never married, 56.7% now married, 11.4% widowed, 14.5% divorced (2000); Foreign born: 0.1% (2000); Ancestry (includes multiple ancestries): 15.7% Other groups, 14.5% United States or American, 13.9% Irish, 11.4% German, 6.4% English (2000).
Economy: Single-family building permits issued: 26 (2001) / 4 (2000); Multi-family building permits issued: 0 (2001) / 0 (2000); Employment by occupation: 5.0% management, 13.0% professional, 16.6% services, 23.2% sales, 3.6% farming, 8.6% construction, 30.0% production (2000).
Income: Per capita income: $13,096 (2000); Median household income: $24,085 (2000); Poverty rate: 20.6% (2000).
Taxes: Total city taxes per capita: $250 (1997); City property taxes per capita: $148 (1997).
Education: High school graduation rate: 62.6% (2000); College graduation rate: 7.0% (2000).

School District(s)

Bernie R-XIII (PK-12)
2000 Enrollment: 583 573-293-5333
Housing: Homeownership rate: 70.7% (2000); Median home value: $39,900 (2000); Median rent: $220 per month (2000); Median age of housing: 36 years (2000).
Transportation: Commute to work: 93.4% car, 0.0% public transportation, 2.2% walk, 2.7% work from home (2000); Travel time to work: 37.9% less than 15 minutes, 37.9% 15 to 30 minutes, 15.2% 30 to 45 minutes, 4.5% 45 to 60 minutes, 4.5% 60 minutes or more (2000)

BLOOMFIELD (city). Covers a land area of 1.397 square miles and a water area of 0 square miles. Located at 36.88° N. Lat.; 89.93° W. Long. Elevation is 497 feet.
History: Bloomfield was platted in 1835, and grew around the lumbering and milling industries, and as the center of a farming, dairying, and poultry region. Bloomfield was a military post for the Union forces during the Civil War, and sustained much damage.
Population: 1,952 (2000); Race: 98.3% White, 0.0% Black, 0.0% Asian, 0.5% American Indian and Alaska Native, 0.1% Hispanic of any race, 1.2% two or more races (2000); Density: 1,396.9 persons per square mile (2000); Age: 24.0% under 18, 17.1% over 64 (2000); Marriage status: 18.4% never married, 58.2% now married, 10.8% widowed, 12.6% divorced (2000); Foreign born: 0.1% (2000); Ancestry (includes multiple ancestries): 26.9% United States or American, 10.5% German, 10.1% Other groups, 9.3% Irish, 6.3% English (2000).
Economy: Single-family building permits issued: 1 (2001) / 1 (2000); Multi-family building permits issued: 0 (2001) / 0 (2000); Employment by occupation: 7.2% management, 15.3% professional, 13.0% services, 24.0% sales, 0.7% farming, 12.4% construction, 27.4% production (2000).
Income: Per capita income: $13,546 (2000); Median household income: $25,426 (2000); Poverty rate: 20.4% (2000).
Taxes: Total city taxes per capita: $100 (1997); City property taxes per capita: $20 (1997).
Education: High school graduation rate: 66.9% (2000); College graduation rate: 9.6% (2000).

School District(s)

Bloomfield R-XIV (PK-12)
2000 Enrollment: 831 573-568-4564
Housing: Homeownership rate: 69.1% (2000); Median home value: $45,000 (2000); Median rent: $211 per month (2000); Median age of housing: 39 years (2000).
Newspapers: The North Stoddard Countian (1 x week)
Transportation: Commute to work: 92.4% car, 0.0% public transportation, 2.6% walk, 4.0% work from home (2000); Travel time to work: 44.0% less than 15 minutes, 29.7% 15 to 30 minutes, 15.2% 30 to 45 minutes, 5.4% 45 to 60 minutes, 5.7% 60 minutes or more (2000)

DEXTER (city). Covers a land area of 6.089 square miles and a water area of 0.129 square miles. Located at 36.79° N. Lat.; 89.96° W. Long. Elevation is 368 feet.
History: Dexter was laid out in 1873 on the peak of Crowley's Ridge. The town grew around a flour mill, cotton gin, shirt factory, and a poultry packing plant.
Population: 7,356 (2000); Race: 96.0% White, 0.1% Black, 1.2% Asian, 0.3% American Indian and Alaska Native, 0.6% Hispanic of any race, 1.8% two or more races (2000); Density: 1,208.0 persons per square mile (2000); Age: 24.1% under 18, 19.9% over 64 (2000); Marriage status: 17.3% never married, 58.8% now married, 11.1% widowed, 12.8% divorced (2000); Foreign born: 1.3% (2000); Ancestry (includes multiple ancestries): 18.9% United States or American, 13.6% German, 12.8% Irish, 10.2% Other groups, 7.0% English (2000).
Economy: Single-family building permits issued: 20 (2001) / 27 (2000); Multi-family building permits issued: 10 (2001) / 0 (2000); Employment by occupation: 10.3% management, 12.2% professional, 22.0% services, 19.1% sales, 1.4% farming, 8.3% construction, 26.9% production (2000).
Income: Per capita income: $15,034 (2000); Median household income: $23,116 (2000); Poverty rate: 18.3% (2000).
Taxes: Total city taxes per capita: $233 (1997); City property taxes per capita: $60 (1997).
Education: High school graduation rate: 65.5% (2000); College graduation rate: 11.2% (2000).

School District(s)

Dexter R-XI (PK-12)
2000 Enrollment: 2,069 573-614-1000
Housing: Homeownership rate: 59.1% (2000); Median home value: $57,500 (2000); Median rent: $255 per month (2000); Median age of housing: 34 years (2000).
Hospitals: Missouri Southern Healthcare (50 beds)
Safety: Violent crime rate: 62.2 per 10,000 population; Property crime rate: 236.5 per 10,000 population (2001).
Newspapers: The Daily Statesman (5 x week)
Transportation: Commute to work: 91.0% car, 0.2% public transportation, 4.7% walk, 2.9% work from home (2000); Travel time to work: 61.5% less than 15 minutes, 17.2% 15 to 30 minutes, 13.4% 30 to 45 minutes, 3.5% 45 to 60 minutes, 4.4% 60 minutes or more (2000)
Additional Information Contacts
Dexter Chamber of Commerce.............................. 573-624-7458

DUDLEY (city). Covers a land area of 0.401 square miles and a water area of 0 square miles. Located at 36.79° N. Lat.; 90.09° W. Long. Elevation is 343 feet.
Population: 289 (2000); Race: 88.8% White, 11.2% Black, 0.0% Asian, 0.0% American Indian and Alaska Native, 0.8% Hispanic of any race, 0.0% two or more races (2000); Density: 721.2 persons per square mile (2000); Age: 26.7% under 18, 15.9% over 64 (2000); Marriage status: 10.8% never

married, 59.1% now married, 10.8% widowed, 19.2% divorced (2000); Foreign born: 0.0% (2000); Ancestry (includes multiple ancestries): 16.3% Other groups, 15.1% United States or American, 13.6% Irish, 5.0% English, 4.7% German (2000).
Economy: Manufacturing: wood cabinets and doors. Employment by occupation: 7.2% management, 2.7% professional, 24.3% services, 16.2% sales, 0.9% farming, 16.2% construction, 32.4% production (2000).
Income: Per capita income: $12,339 (2000); Median household income: $23,542 (2000); Poverty rate: 17.4% (2000).
Taxes: Total city taxes per capita: $157 (1997); City property taxes per capita: $42 (1997).
Education: High school graduation rate: 59.6% (2000); College graduation rate: 2.9% (2000).
Housing: Homeownership rate: 68.1% (2000); Median home value: $50,000 (2000); Median rent: $138 per month (2000); Median age of housing: 23 years (2000).
Transportation: Commute to work: 93.3% car, 0.0% public transportation, 2.9% walk, 1.9% work from home (2000); Travel time to work: 27.2% less than 15 minutes, 35.9% 15 to 30 minutes, 12.6% 30 to 45 minutes, 12.6% 45 to 60 minutes, 11.7% 60 minutes or more (2000)

ESSEX (city). Covers a land area of 0.275 square miles and a water area of 0 square miles. Located at 36.81° N. Lat.; 89.86° W. Long. Elevation is 300 feet.
Population: 524 (2000); Race: 99.8% White, 0.0% Black, 0.0% Asian, 0.0% American Indian and Alaska Native, 0.0% Hispanic of any race, 0.2% two or more races (2000); Density: 1,904.6 persons per square mile (2000); Age: 23.9% under 18, 23.1% over 64 (2000); Marriage status: 14.8% never married, 66.1% now married, 9.4% widowed, 9.6% divorced (2000); Foreign born: 0.0% (2000); Ancestry (includes multiple ancestries): 32.8% United States or American, 15.5% Other groups, 12.6% Irish, 5.2% German, 4.4% English (2000).
Economy: Cotton, rice, soybeans. Single-family building permits issued: 0 (2001) / 0 (2000); Multi-family building permits issued: 0 (2001) / 0 (2000); Employment by occupation: 3.3% management, 9.8% professional, 14.5% services, 23.4% sales, 3.7% farming, 14.5% construction, 30.8% production (2000).
Income: Per capita income: $14,345 (2000); Median household income: $28,036 (2000); Poverty rate: 12.0% (2000).
Taxes: Total city taxes per capita: $104 (1997); City property taxes per capita: $17 (1997).
Education: High school graduation rate: 56.4% (2000); College graduation rate: 5.8% (2000).

School District(s)

Richland R-I (PK-12)
2000 Enrollment: 460 573-283-5332
Housing: Homeownership rate: 76.2% (2000); Median home value: $38,000 (2000); Median rent: $204 per month (2000); Median age of housing: 35 years (2000).
Transportation: Commute to work: 96.2% car, 0.0% public transportation, 1.4% walk, 2.4% work from home (2000); Travel time to work: 38.6% less than 15 minutes, 37.2% 15 to 30 minutes, 15.0% 30 to 45 minutes, 1.9% 45 to 60 minutes, 7.2% 60 minutes or more (2000)

PENERMON (village). Covers a land area of 0.209 square miles and a water area of 0 square miles. Located at 36.78° N. Lat.; 89.82° W. Long. Elevation is 300 feet.
Population: 75 (2000); Race: 3.9% White, 96.1% Black, 0.0% Asian, 0.0% American Indian and Alaska Native, 0.0% Hispanic of any race, 0.0% two or more races (2000); Density: 358.3 persons per square mile (2000); Age: 30.3% under 18, 18.4% over 64 (2000); Marriage status: 30.9% never married, 50.9% now married, 18.2% widowed, 0.0% divorced (2000); Foreign born: 0.0% (2000); Ancestry (includes multiple ancestries): 80.3% Other groups, 3.9% Irish, 3.9% English (2000).
Economy: Employment by occupation: 0.0% management, 8.3% professional, 12.5% services, 25.0% sales, 0.0% farming, 8.3% construction, 45.8% production (2000).
Income: Per capita income: $10,549 (2000); Median household income: $11,875 (2000); Poverty rate: 25.0% (2000).
Taxes: Total city taxes per capita: $72 (1997); City property taxes per capita: $72 (1997).
Education: High school graduation rate: 46.2% (2000); College graduation rate: 0.0% (2000).
Housing: Homeownership rate: 87.5% (2000); Median home value: $25,000 (2000); Median rent: $225 per month (2000); Median age of housing: 31 years (2000).
Transportation: Commute to work: 100.0% car, 0.0% public transportation, 0.0% walk, 0.0% work from home (2000); Travel time to work: 27.3% less than 15 minutes, 50.0% 15 to 30 minutes, 22.7% 30 to 45 minutes, 0.0% 45 to 60 minutes, 0.0% 60 minutes or more (2000)

PUXICO (city). Covers a land area of 0.548 square miles and a water area of 0 square miles. Located at 36.95° N. Lat.; 90.15° W. Long. Elevation is 370 feet.
Population: 1,145 (2000); Race: 96.5% White, 3.0% Black, 0.0% Asian, 0.0% American Indian and Alaska Native, 0.0% Hispanic of any race, 0.5% two or more races (2000); Density: 2,089.4 persons per square mile (2000); Age: 28.2% under 18, 23.3% over 64 (2000); Marriage status: 35.3% never married, 38.9% now married, 15.2% widowed, 10.5% divorced (2000); Foreign born: 0.0% (2000); Ancestry (includes multiple ancestries): 12.5% Other groups, 11.5% German, 10.7% Irish, 9.4% United States or American, 8.3% English (2000).
Economy: Manufacturing of apparel. Mingo National Wildlife Refuge (wetlands) to W. Rice, soybeans, wheat, corn. Employment by occupation: 7.8% management, 13.1% professional, 14.0% services, 18.8% sales, 3.0% farming, 29.4% construction, 14.0% production (2000).
Income: Per capita income: $11,354 (2000); Median household income: $20,900 (2000); Poverty rate: 33.8% (2000).
Taxes: Total city taxes per capita: $47 (1997); City property taxes per capita: $25 (1997).
Education: High school graduation rate: 67.6% (2000); College graduation rate: 12.4% (2000).

School District(s)

Puxico R-VIII (KG-12)
2000 Enrollment: 899 573-222-3762
Housing: Homeownership rate: 66.0% (2000); Median home value: $45,000 (2000); Median rent: $207 per month (2000); Median age of housing: 35 years (2000).
Newspapers: Puxico Press (1 x week)
Transportation: Commute to work: 59.4% car, 0.4% public transportation, 34.2% walk, 4.0% work from home (2000); Travel time to work: 58.6% less than 15 minutes, 14.4% 15 to 30 minutes, 18.6% 30 to 45 minutes, 3.8% 45 to 60 minutes, 4.6% 60 minutes or more (2000)

Stone County

Located in southwestern Missouri, in the Ozarks; bounded on the south by Arkansas; drained by the White and James Rivers; includes part of Mark Twain National Forest. Covers a land area of 463.20 square miles, a water area of 47.70 square miles, and is located in the Central Time Zone. The county government was organized in 1851. County seat is Galena.

Weather Station: Galena 1 SW Elevation: 1,099 feet

	Jan	Feb	Mar	Apr	May	Jun	Jul	Aug	Sep	Oct	Nov	Dec
High	44	50	60	70	76	84	89	89	81	71	58	48
Low	21	25	34	42	52	60	65	63	56	44	33	25
Precip	2.2	2.4	4.1	4.5	4.5	4.6	3.7	3.3	4.8	3.5	4.6	3.4
Snow	3.3	na	1.1	0.1	0.0	0.0	0.0	0.0	0.0	0.0	0.5	1.3

High and Low temperatures in degrees Fahrenheit; Precipitation and Snow in inches

Population: 28,658 (2000); Race: 97.6% White, 0.1% Black, 0.3% Asian, 0.5% American Indian and Alaska Native, 0.7% Hispanic of any race, 1.4% two or more races (2000); Density: 61.9 persons per square mile (2000); Age: 21.4% under 18, 18.9% over 64 (2000).
Religion: Five largest groups: 16.3% Southern Baptist Convention, 4.1% Catholic Church, 3.1% The United Methodist Church, 2.7% Assemblies of God, 1.6% The Church of Jesus Christ of Latter-day Saints (2000).
Economy: Unemployment rate: 7.0% (11/2002); Total civilian labor force: 12,741 (11/2002); Leading industries: 21.9% construction; 17.6% retail trade; 12.3% accommodation & food services (2000); Companies that employ more than 1,000 persons: 0 (2000); Companies that employ more than 100 persons: 5 (2000); Farms: 684 totaling 135,993 acres (1997); Minority business ownership rate: 0.0% (1997); Women business ownership rate: 17.0% (1997); Retail sales per capita: $5,066 (1997). Single-family building permits issued: 18 (2001) / 22 (2000); Multi-family building permits issued: 8 (2001) / 2 (2000).
Income: Per capita income: $18,036 (2000); Median household income: $32,637 (2000); Poverty rate: 12.8% (2000); Bankruptcy rate: 3.77% (2001).
Taxes: Total county taxes per capita: $59 (1997); County property taxes per capita: $30 (1997).
Education: High school graduation rate: 80.4% (2000); College graduation rate: 14.2% (2000).

Housing: Homeownership rate: 81.2% (2000); Median home value: $102,700 (2000); Median rent: $353 per month (2000); Median age of housing: 19 years (2000).
Health: Birth rate: 108.9 per 10,000 population (1998); Age adjusted death rate: 76.3 per 10,000 population (1999); Age adjusted cancer mortality rate: 222.1 deaths per 100,000 population (1999). Number of physicians: 4.2 per 10,000 population (1999); Number of hospital beds: n/a (1999).
Elections: 2000 Presidential election results: 33.4% Gore, 64.1% Bush, 1.5% Nader, 0.7% Buchanan
Additional Information Contacts
Stone County Government Offices 417-357-6127
Cape Fair Chamber... 417-538-2222

Stone County Communities

BLUE EYE (town). Covers a land area of 0.536 square miles and a water area of 0 square miles. Located at 36.50° N. Lat.; 93.39° W. Long. Elevation is 1,295 feet.
Population: 129 (2000); Race: 100.0% White, 0.0% Black, 0.0% Asian, 0.0% American Indian and Alaska Native, 0.0% Hispanic of any race, 0.0% two or more races (2000); Density: 240.5 persons per square mile (2000); Age: 28.3% under 18, 7.1% over 64 (2000); Marriage status: 22.2% never married, 64.2% now married, 7.4% widowed, 6.2% divorced (2000); Foreign born: 0.0% (2000); Ancestry (includes multiple ancestries): 15.9% English, 15.9% United States or American, 6.2% Irish, 5.3% German, 4.4% Other groups (2000).
Economy: Employment by occupation: 6.7% management, 0.0% professional, 23.3% services, 21.7% sales, 3.3% farming, 13.3% construction, 31.7% production (2000).
Income: Per capita income: $14,183 (2000); Median household income: $35,313 (2000); Poverty rate: 23.9% (2000).
Taxes: Total city taxes per capita: $7 (1997); City property taxes per capita: $0 (1997).
Education: High school graduation rate: 78.9% (2000); College graduation rate: 12.7% (2000).

School District(s)

Blue Eye R-V (PK-12)
2000 Enrollment: 710 417-779-5332
Housing: Homeownership rate: 43.8% (2000); Median home value: $63,800 (2000); Median rent: $300 per month (2000); Median age of housing: 30 years (2000).
Transportation: Commute to work: 96.6% car, 0.0% public transportation, 0.0% walk, 3.4% work from home (2000); Travel time to work: 12.5% less than 15 minutes, 33.9% 15 to 30 minutes, 42.9% 30 to 45 minutes, 5.4% 45 to 60 minutes, 5.4% 60 minutes or more (2000)

BRANSON WEST (city). Aka Lakeview. Covers a land area of 1.867 square miles and a water area of 0 square miles. Located at 36.70° N. Lat.; 93.37° W. Long. Elevation is 1,360 feet.
Population: 408 (2000); Race: 97.7% White, 0.0% Black, 0.0% Asian, 0.0% American Indian and Alaska Native, 3.6% Hispanic of any race, 0.7% two or more races (2000); Density: 218.5 persons per square mile (2000); Age: 26.4% under 18, 6.3% over 64 (2000); Marriage status: 25.5% never married, 59.1% now married, 3.5% widowed, 11.9% divorced (2000); Foreign born: 2.0% (2000); Ancestry (includes multiple ancestries): 25.3% German, 17.6% United States or American, 17.4% Other groups, 14.2% Irish, 9.0% English (2000).
Economy: Single-family building permits issued: 2 (2001) / 4 (2000); Multi-family building permits issued: 0 (2001) / 0 (2000); Employment by occupation: 9.0% management, 12.4% professional, 20.9% services, 30.3% sales, 0.0% farming, 19.4% construction, 8.0% production (2000).
Income: Per capita income: $12,326 (2000); Median household income: $31,250 (2000); Poverty rate: 12.2% (2000).
Taxes: Total city taxes per capita: $10,650 (1997); City property taxes per capita: $0 (1997).
Education: High school graduation rate: 78.2% (2000); College graduation rate: 14.0% (2000).
Housing: Homeownership rate: 51.7% (2000); Median home value: $99,100 (2000); Median rent: $558 per month (2000); Median age of housing: 5 years (2000).
Transportation: Commute to work: 88.9% car, 3.0% public transportation, 1.0% walk, 7.0% work from home (2000); Travel time to work: 29.7% less than 15 minutes, 50.8% 15 to 30 minutes, 11.9% 30 to 45 minutes, 5.9% 45 to 60 minutes, 1.6% 60 minutes or more (2000)

CAPE FAIR (unincorporated postal area, zip code 65624). Covers a land area of 2.168 square miles and a water area of 0 square miles. Located at 36.72° N. Lat.; 93.50° W. Long. Elevation is 1,060 feet.
Population: 395 (2000); Race: 88.9% White, 0.0% Black, 11.1% Asian, 0.0% American Indian and Alaska Native, 0.0% Hispanic of any race, 0.0% two or more races (2000); Density: 182.2 persons per square mile (2000); Age: 18.4% under 18, 15.0% over 64 (2000); Marriage status: 21.6% never married, 59.9% now married, 6.9% widowed, 11.6% divorced (2000); Foreign born: 11.1% (2000); Ancestry (includes multiple ancestries): 30.2% German, 23.0% Other groups, 19.8% Irish, 14.3% United States or American, 13.6% English (2000).
Economy: Employment by occupation: 16.5% management, 9.2% professional, 23.9% services, 23.4% sales, 2.3% farming, 8.3% construction, 16.5% production (2000).
Income: Per capita income: $13,973 (2000); Median household income: $27,162 (2000); Poverty rate: 15.9% (2000).
Education: High school graduation rate: 85.1% (2000); College graduation rate: 16.8% (2000).
Housing: Homeownership rate: 80.6% (2000); Median home value: $74,100 (2000); Median rent: $394 per month (2000); Median age of housing: 24 years (2000).
Transportation: Commute to work: 88.5% car, 0.0% public transportation, 5.5% walk, 6.0% work from home (2000); Travel time to work: 17.6% less than 15 minutes, 31.7% 15 to 30 minutes, 27.3% 30 to 45 minutes, 3.9% 45 to 60 minutes, 19.5% 60 minutes or more (2000)
Additional Information Contacts
Cape Fair Chamber.. 417-538-2222

CONEY ISLAND (village). Covers a land area of 0.060 square miles and a water area of 0 square miles. Located at 36.59° N. Lat.; 93.39° W. Long. Elevation is 940 feet.
Population: 94 (2000); Race: 100.0% White, 0.0% Black, 0.0% Asian, 0.0% American Indian and Alaska Native, 0.0% Hispanic of any race, 0.0% two or more races (2000); Density: 1,555.6 persons per square mile (2000); Age: 25.0% under 18, 33.3% over 64 (2000); Marriage status: 6.3% never married, 78.1% now married, 9.4% widowed, 6.3% divorced (2000); Foreign born: 0.0% (2000); Ancestry (includes multiple ancestries): 32.1% Other groups, 27.4% English, 21.4% Irish, 17.9% German, 8.3% United States or American (2000).
Economy: Employment by occupation: 27.3% management, 0.0% professional, 21.2% services, 24.2% sales, 0.0% farming, 6.1% construction, 21.2% production (2000).
Income: Per capita income: $12,204 (2000); Median household income: $27,500 (2000); Poverty rate: 15.5% (2000).
Education: High school graduation rate: 79.4% (2000); College graduation rate: 6.3% (2000).
Housing: Homeownership rate: 76.2% (2000); Median home value: $85,800 (2000); Median rent: $463 per month (2000); Median age of housing: 18 years (2000).
Transportation: Commute to work: 87.9% car, 0.0% public transportation, 0.0% walk, 9.1% work from home (2000); Travel time to work: 3.3% less than 15 minutes, 20.0% 15 to 30 minutes, 23.3% 30 to 45 minutes, 20.0% 45 to 60 minutes, 33.3% 60 minutes or more (2000)

CRANE (city). Covers a land area of 1.471 square miles and a water area of 0 square miles. Located at 36.90° N. Lat.; 93.57° W. Long. Elevation is 1,122 feet.
Population: 1,390 (2000); Race: 96.4% White, 0.0% Black, 0.0% Asian, 0.5% American Indian and Alaska Native, 0.6% Hispanic of any race, 3.1% two or more races (2000); Density: 944.9 persons per square mile (2000); Age: 25.5% under 18, 20.1% over 64 (2000); Marriage status: 18.8% never married, 51.2% now married, 14.0% widowed, 16.0% divorced (2000); Foreign born: 0.4% (2000); Ancestry (includes multiple ancestries): 16.4% United States or American, 12.4% German, 12.2% Irish, 11.3% Other groups, 7.5% English (2000).
Economy: Cattle, poultry; dairying; fruit. Manufacturing: food processing, plastic products. Single-family building permits issued: 4 (2001) / 1 (2000); Multi-family building permits issued: 0 (2001) / 2 (2000); Employment by occupation: 7.0% management, 14.7% professional, 22.3% services, 18.7% sales, 0.6% farming, 17.2% construction, 19.4% production (2000).
Income: Per capita income: $12,120 (2000); Median household income: $20,848 (2000); Poverty rate: 20.8% (2000).
Taxes: Total city taxes per capita: $156 (1997); City property taxes per capita: $38 (1997).

Education: High school graduation rate: 66.0% (2000); College graduation rate: 10.5% (2000).

School District(s)

Crane R-III (PK-12)
2000 Enrollment: 733 417-723-5300

Housing: Homeownership rate: 64.4% (2000); Median home value: $54,800 (2000); Median rent: $230 per month (2000); Median age of housing: 39 years (2000).

Newspapers: The Crane Chronicle/The Stone County Republican (1 x week)

Transportation: Commute to work: 89.7% car, 0.0% public transportation, 3.0% walk, 4.5% work from home (2000); Travel time to work: 33.0% less than 15 minutes, 13.9% 15 to 30 minutes, 16.0% 30 to 45 minutes, 26.5% 45 to 60 minutes, 10.6% 60 minutes or more (2000)

GALENA (city). Covers a land area of 0.684 square miles and a water area of 0 square miles. Located at 36.80° N. Lat.; 93.46° W. Long. Elevation is 985 feet.

Population: 451 (2000); Race: 95.2% White, 0.0% Black, 0.0% Asian, 0.0% American Indian and Alaska Native, 0.0% Hispanic of any race, 4.8% two or more races (2000); Density: 659.7 persons per square mile (2000); Age: 30.3% under 18, 7.9% over 64 (2000); Marriage status: 19.5% never married, 62.3% now married, 4.2% widowed, 14.1% divorced (2000); Foreign born: 0.9% (2000); Ancestry (includes multiple ancestries): 20.0% Other groups, 18.6% Irish, 17.1% German, 14.7% English, 14.3% United States or American (2000).

Economy: Corn, wheat, hay, fruit, vegetables, cattle. Tourism. Manufacturing: medical equipment. Employment by occupation: 10.9% management, 6.4% professional, 26.7% services, 26.2% sales, 0.0% farming, 15.3% construction, 14.4% production (2000).

Income: Per capita income: $9,673 (2000); Median household income: $22,500 (2000); Poverty rate: 30.0% (2000).

Taxes: Total city taxes per capita: $64 (1997); City property taxes per capita: $15 (1997).

Education: High school graduation rate: 83.4% (2000); College graduation rate: 7.6% (2000).

School District(s)

Galena R-II (PK-12)
2000 Enrollment: 525 417-357-6027

Housing: Homeownership rate: 70.7% (2000); Median home value: $58,000 (2000); Median rent: $354 per month (2000); Median age of housing: 40 years (2000).

Transportation: Commute to work: 93.0% car, 0.0% public transportation, 3.5% walk, 2.5% work from home (2000); Travel time to work: 22.4% less than 15 minutes, 14.3% 15 to 30 minutes, 28.6% 30 to 45 minutes, 27.0% 45 to 60 minutes, 7.7% 60 minutes or more (2000)

HURLEY (city). Covers a land area of 0.333 square miles and a water area of 0 square miles. Located at 36.93° N. Lat.; 93.49° W. Long. Elevation is 1,080 feet.

Population: 157 (2000); Race: 94.2% White, 0.0% Black, 0.0% Asian, 1.3% American Indian and Alaska Native, 0.0% Hispanic of any race, 3.2% two or more races (2000); Density: 472.1 persons per square mile (2000); Age: 32.3% under 18, 5.8% over 64 (2000); Marriage status: 16.2% never married, 64.1% now married, 6.8% widowed, 12.8% divorced (2000); Foreign born: 1.3% (2000); Ancestry (includes multiple ancestries): 23.9% German, 21.9% United States or American, 16.1% Irish, 9.0% English, 7.7% Other groups (2000).

Economy: Employment by occupation: 4.7% management, 12.5% professional, 26.6% services, 10.9% sales, 0.0% farming, 23.4% construction, 21.9% production (2000).

Income: Per capita income: $13,644 (2000); Median household income: $30,833 (2000); Poverty rate: 21.9% (2000).

Taxes: Total city taxes per capita: $38 (1997); City property taxes per capita: $19 (1997).

Education: High school graduation rate: 71.6% (2000); College graduation rate: 4.5% (2000).

School District(s)

Hurley R-I (PK-12)
2000 Enrollment: 334 417-369-3271

Housing: Homeownership rate: 65.5% (2000); Median home value: $39,500 (2000); Median rent: $214 per month (2000); Median age of housing: 60+ years (2000).

Transportation: Commute to work: 89.1% car, 0.0% public transportation, 9.4% walk, 1.6% work from home (2000); Travel time to work: 34.9% less than 15 minutes, 25.4% 15 to 30 minutes, 14.3% 30 to 45 minutes, 25.4% 45 to 60 minutes, 0.0% 60 minutes or more (2000)

INDIAN POINT (village). Covers a land area of 2.794 square miles and a water area of 1.064 square miles. Located at 36.63° N. Lat.; 93.34° W. Long. Elevation is 1,045 feet.

Population: 588 (2000); Race: 99.3% White, 0.0% Black, 0.0% Asian, 0.7% American Indian and Alaska Native, 3.5% Hispanic of any race, 0.0% two or more races (2000); Density: 210.5 persons per square mile (2000); Age: 18.2% under 18, 16.3% over 64 (2000); Marriage status: 15.8% never married, 68.9% now married, 6.6% widowed, 8.8% divorced (2000); Foreign born: 2.8% (2000); Ancestry (includes multiple ancestries): 29.3% German, 18.0% Irish, 15.8% English, 11.6% United States or American, 6.4% Other groups (2000).

Economy: Employment by occupation: 20.6% management, 11.3% professional, 20.2% services, 39.9% sales, 0.0% farming, 4.8% construction, 3.2% production (2000).

Income: Per capita income: $18,987 (2000); Median household income: $37,727 (2000); Poverty rate: 5.9% (2000).

Taxes: Total city taxes per capita: $278 (1997); City property taxes per capita: $0 (1997).

Education: High school graduation rate: 88.7% (2000); College graduation rate: 15.3% (2000).

Housing: Homeownership rate: 69.4% (2000); Median home value: $123,100 (2000); Median rent: $495 per month (2000); Median age of housing: 9 years (2000).

Transportation: Commute to work: 89.4% car, 0.0% public transportation, 3.7% walk, 6.9% work from home (2000); Travel time to work: 39.0% less than 15 minutes, 47.4% 15 to 30 minutes, 6.6% 30 to 45 minutes, 3.1% 45 to 60 minutes, 3.9% 60 minutes or more (2000)

KIMBERLING CITY (city). Covers a land area of 3.345 square miles and a water area of 0.476 square miles. Located at 36.64° N. Lat.; 93.42° W. Long. Elevation is 1,050 feet.

Population: 2,253 (2000); Race: 98.7% White, 0.0% Black, 0.3% Asian, 0.0% American Indian and Alaska Native, 1.2% Hispanic of any race, 0.8% two or more races (2000); Density: 673.6 persons per square mile (2000); Age: 16.9% under 18, 32.9% over 64 (2000); Marriage status: 14.4% never married, 66.9% now married, 10.1% widowed, 8.6% divorced (2000); Foreign born: 2.1% (2000); Ancestry (includes multiple ancestries): 27.6% German, 18.0% English, 13.9% Irish, 12.8% United States or American, 6.6% French (except Basque) (2000).

Economy: Single-family building permits issued: 12 (2001) / 17 (2000); Multi-family building permits issued: 8 (2001) / 0 (2000); Employment by occupation: 13.6% management, 18.1% professional, 14.1% services, 39.6% sales, 0.0% farming, 9.1% construction, 5.5% production (2000).

Income: Per capita income: $19,715 (2000); Median household income: $36,727 (2000); Poverty rate: 6.2% (2000).

Education: High school graduation rate: 88.4% (2000); College graduation rate: 20.2% (2000).

Housing: Homeownership rate: 78.8% (2000); Median home value: $116,000 (2000); Median rent: $459 per month (2000); Median age of housing: 20 years (2000).

Transportation: Commute to work: 91.1% car, 0.0% public transportation, 2.6% walk, 6.2% work from home (2000); Travel time to work: 34.5% less than 15 minutes, 31.3% 15 to 30 minutes, 16.1% 30 to 45 minutes, 4.1% 45 to 60 minutes, 14.0% 60 minutes or more (2000)

LAMPE (unincorporated postal area, zip code 65681). Covers a land area of 34.504 square miles and a water area of 0 square miles. Located at 36.56° N. Lat.; 93.46° W. Long. Elevation is 1,313 feet.

Population: 2,261 (2000); Race: 99.4% White, 0.0% Black, 0.0% Asian, 0.0% American Indian and Alaska Native, 0.0% Hispanic of any race, 0.6% two or more races (2000); Density: 65.5 persons per square mile (2000); Age: 21.2% under 18, 16.1% over 64 (2000); Marriage status: 14.8% never married, 72.7% now married, 3.3% widowed, 9.3% divorced (2000); Foreign born: 0.7% (2000); Ancestry (includes multiple ancestries): 15.8% German, 12.9% United States or American, 11.8% Irish, 11.7% English, 8.5% Other groups (2000).

Economy: Employment by occupation: 9.1% management, 10.7% professional, 17.2% services, 32.0% sales, 0.0% farming, 19.9% construction, 11.0% production (2000).

Income: Per capita income: $19,740 (2000); Median household income: $35,288 (2000); Poverty rate: 7.7% (2000).

Education: High school graduation rate: 83.9% (2000); College graduation rate: 12.7% (2000).

Housing: Homeownership rate: 82.8% (2000); Median home value: $109,900 (2000); Median rent: $295 per month (2000); Median age of housing: 22 years (2000).
Transportation: Commute to work: 90.2% car, 0.0% public transportation, 4.1% walk, 5.7% work from home (2000); Travel time to work: 23.0% less than 15 minutes, 29.8% 15 to 30 minutes, 23.4% 30 to 45 minutes, 11.8% 45 to 60 minutes, 12.0% 60 minutes or more (2000)

MCCORD BEND (village). Covers a land area of 0.283 square miles and a water area of 0.029 square miles. Located at 36.78° N. Lat.; 93.50° W. Long. Elevation is 974 feet.
Population: 292 (2000); Race: 95.7% White, 0.0% Black, 0.0% Asian, 2.0% American Indian and Alaska Native, 2.0% Hispanic of any race, 0.7% two or more races (2000); Density: 1,033.0 persons per square mile (2000); Age: 25.5% under 18, 14.9% over 64 (2000); Marriage status: 21.5% never married, 48.1% now married, 11.6% widowed, 18.9% divorced (2000); Foreign born: 0.3% (2000); Ancestry (includes multiple ancestries): 22.5% German, 21.2% Other groups, 16.2% Irish, 13.9% United States or American, 7.3% English (2000).
Economy: Employment by occupation: 3.9% management, 8.6% professional, 32.0% services, 16.4% sales, 0.0% farming, 15.6% construction, 23.4% production (2000).
Income: Per capita income: $11,703 (2000); Median household income: $27,143 (2000); Poverty rate: 25.5% (2000).
Taxes: Total city taxes per capita: $11 (1997); City property taxes per capita: $11 (1997).
Education: High school graduation rate: 62.9% (2000); College graduation rate: 6.1% (2000).
Housing: Homeownership rate: 78.9% (2000); Median home value: $46,700 (2000); Median rent: $305 per month (2000); Median age of housing: 25 years (2000).
Transportation: Commute to work: 98.4% car, 0.0% public transportation, 0.0% walk, 1.6% work from home (2000); Travel time to work: 5.6% less than 15 minutes, 26.2% 15 to 30 minutes, 23.0% 30 to 45 minutes, 22.2% 45 to 60 minutes, 23.0% 60 minutes or more (2000)

PONCE DE LEON (unincorporated postal area, zip code 65728). Covers a land area of 2.967 square miles and a water area of 0 square miles. Located at 36.87° N. Lat.; 93.34° W. Long.
Population: 109 (2000); Race: 100.0% White, 0.0% Black, 0.0% Asian, 0.0% American Indian and Alaska Native, 0.0% Hispanic of any race, 0.0% two or more races (2000); Density: 36.7 persons per square mile (2000); Age: 30.7% under 18, 39.8% over 64 (2000); Marriage status: 0.0% never married, 85.2% now married, 14.8% widowed, 0.0% divorced (2000); Foreign born: 0.0% (2000); Ancestry (includes multiple ancestries): 10.2% United States or American, 9.1% German (2000).
Economy: Employment by occupation: 0.0% management, 47.1% professional, 0.0% services, 52.9% sales, 0.0% farming, 0.0% construction, 0.0% production (2000).
Income: Per capita income: $6,563 (2000); Median household income: $15,714 (2000); Poverty rate: 60.2% (2000).
Education: High school graduation rate: 54.1% (2000); College graduation rate: 0.0% (2000).
Housing: Homeownership rate: 100.0% (2000); Median home value: $65,000 (2000); Median age of housing: 39 years (2000).
Transportation: Commute to work: 100.0% car, 0.0% public transportation, 0.0% walk, 0.0% work from home (2000); Travel time to work: 0.0% less than 15 minutes, 0.0% 15 to 30 minutes, 100.0% 30 to 45 minutes, 0.0% 45 to 60 minutes, 0.0% 60 minutes or more (2000)

REEDS SPRING (city). Covers a land area of 0.632 square miles and a water area of 0 square miles. Located at 36.74° N. Lat.; 93.38° W. Long. Elevation is 1,199 feet.
Population: 465 (2000); Race: 94.6% White, 0.0% Black, 0.0% Asian, 2.4% American Indian and Alaska Native, 3.1% Hispanic of any race, 1.1% two or more races (2000); Density: 735.9 persons per square mile (2000); Age: 23.3% under 18, 16.1% over 64 (2000); Marriage status: 16.8% never married, 62.3% now married, 7.6% widowed, 13.3% divorced (2000); Foreign born: 2.2% (2000); Ancestry (includes multiple ancestries): 20.5% United States or American, 17.4% German, 13.5% Other groups, 11.1% Irish, 5.9% English (2000).
Economy: Tourism. Manufacturing: apparel, concrete products. Employment by occupation: 8.9% management, 9.4% professional, 29.6% services, 22.2% sales, 0.0% farming, 19.2% construction, 10.8% production (2000).
Income: Per capita income: $13,103 (2000); Median household income: $25,982 (2000); Poverty rate: 18.4% (2000).
Taxes: Total city taxes per capita: $90 (1997); City property taxes per capita: $17 (1997).
Education: High school graduation rate: 78.3% (2000); College graduation rate: 10.8% (2000).

School District(s)

Reeds Spring R-IV (PK-12)
2000 Enrollment: 2,047 417-272-8173

Housing: Homeownership rate: 63.1% (2000); Median home value: $69,600 (2000); Median rent: $347 per month (2000); Median age of housing: 24 years (2000).
Transportation: Commute to work: 93.9% car, 0.0% public transportation, 1.5% walk, 3.0% work from home (2000); Travel time to work: 26.2% less than 15 minutes, 37.2% 15 to 30 minutes, 26.7% 30 to 45 minutes, 6.3% 45 to 60 minutes, 3.7% 60 minutes or more (2000)

Sullivan County

Located in northern Missouri; crossed by Locust Creek. Covers a land area of 650.90 square miles, a water area of 0.50 square miles, and is located in the Central Time Zone. The county government was organized in 1845. County seat is Milan.
Population: 7,219 (2000); Race: 95.3% White, 0.2% Black, 0.1% Asian, 0.3% American Indian and Alaska Native, 8.7% Hispanic of any race, 0.5% two or more races (2000); Density: 11.1 persons per square mile (2000); Age: 25.2% under 18, 18.3% over 64 (2000).
Religion: Five largest groups: 20.0% Southern Baptist Convention, 9.5% Christian Churches and Churches of Christ, 6.4% The United Methodist Church, 1.6% Assemblies of God, 1.3% Catholic Church (2000).
Economy: Unemployment rate: 3.4% (11/2002); Total civilian labor force: 3,981 (11/2002); Leading industries: 8.1% health care and social assistance; 7.5% retail trade; 2.8% information (2000); Companies that employ more than 1,000 persons: 0 (2000); Companies that employ more than 100 persons: 2 (2000); Farms: 791 totaling 325,670 acres (1997); Minority business ownership rate: 0.0% (1997); Women business ownership rate: 0.0% (1997); Retail sales per capita: $5,103 (1997). Single-family building permits issued: 3 (2001) / 6 (2000); Multi-family building permits issued: 0 (2001) / 0 (2000).
Income: Per capita income: $13,392 (2000); Median household income: $26,107 (2000); Poverty rate: 16.5% (2000); Bankruptcy rate: 1.87% (2001).
Taxes: Total county taxes per capita: $79 (1997); County property taxes per capita: $21 (1997).
Education: High school graduation rate: 72.4% (2000); College graduation rate: 8.4% (2000).
Housing: Homeownership rate: 71.7% (2000); Median home value: $37,700 (2000); Median rent: $229 per month (2000); Median age of housing: 43 years (2000).
Health: Birth rate: 142.7 per 10,000 population (1998); Age adjusted death rate: 99.7 per 10,000 population (1999); Age adjusted cancer mortality rate: 203.3 deaths per 100,000 population (1999). Number of physicians: 1.4 per 10,000 population (1999); Number of hospital beds: 54.0 per 10,000 population (1999).
Elections: 2000 Presidential election results: 36.8% Gore, 61.3% Bush, 0.9% Nader, 0.8% Buchanan

Additional Information Contacts

Sullivan County Government Offices 660-265-3786
Milan Chamber of Commerce 660-265-5131

Sullivan County Communities

GREEN CASTLE (unincorporated postal area, zip code 63544). Aka Greencastle. Covers a land area of 128.844 square miles and a water area of 0.158 square miles. Located at 40.24° N. Lat.; 92.87° W. Long. Elevation is 1,048 feet.
Population: 872 (2000); Race: 99.0% White, 0.0% Black, 0.0% Asian, 0.0% American Indian and Alaska Native, 0.8% Hispanic of any race, 1.0% two or more races (2000); Density: 6.8 persons per square mile (2000); Age: 23.6% under 18, 18.3% over 64 (2000); Marriage status: 11.8% never married, 69.4% now married, 8.9% widowed, 10.0% divorced (2000); Foreign born: 0.4% (2000); Ancestry (includes multiple ancestries): 22.2% United States or American, 16.9% German, 16.0% Irish, 10.0% Other groups, 8.3% English (2000).
Economy: Employment by occupation: 9.8% management, 13.2% professional, 23.0% services, 17.1% sales, 6.6% farming, 4.5% construction, 25.8% production (2000).

Income: Per capita income: $12,356 (2000); Median household income: $24,306 (2000); Poverty rate: 16.6% (2000).
Education: High school graduation rate: 68.1% (2000); College graduation rate: 8.2% (2000).
Housing: Homeownership rate: 83.0% (2000); Median home value: $24,200 (2000); Median rent: $162 per month (2000); Median age of housing: 44 years (2000).
Transportation: Commute to work: 87.7% car, 0.0% public transportation, 2.8% walk, 8.8% work from home (2000); Travel time to work: 9.7% less than 15 minutes, 57.5% 15 to 30 minutes, 18.9% 30 to 45 minutes, 8.5% 45 to 60 minutes, 5.4% 60 minutes or more (2000)

GREEN CITY (city). Covers a land area of 1.429 square miles and a water area of 0.022 square miles. Located at 40.26° N. Lat.; 92.95° W. Long. Elevation is 1,059 feet.
History: Platted 1880.
Population: 688 (2000); Race: 98.4% White, 0.0% Black, 0.0% Asian, 0.0% American Indian and Alaska Native, 6.5% Hispanic of any race, 0.3% two or more races (2000); Density: 481.4 persons per square mile (2000); Age: 22.6% under 18, 22.5% over 64 (2000); Marriage status: 20.2% never married, 56.2% now married, 13.6% widowed, 10.0% divorced (2000); Foreign born: 2.2% (2000); Ancestry (includes multiple ancestries): 16.4% United States or American, 14.9% German, 12.9% Other groups, 11.7% Irish, 9.7% English (2000).
Economy: Corn, soybeans; sheep, cattle. Employment by occupation: 7.6% management, 11.7% professional, 19.0% services, 19.6% sales, 2.8% farming, 12.7% construction, 26.6% production (2000).
Income: Per capita income: $14,677 (2000); Median household income: $23,125 (2000); Poverty rate: 16.2% (2000).
Taxes: Total city taxes per capita: $125 (1997); City property taxes per capita: $39 (1997).
Education: High school graduation rate: 75.4% (2000); College graduation rate: 12.6% (2000).

School District(s)

Green City R-I (KG-12)
2000 Enrollment: 325 660-874-4127

Housing: Homeownership rate: 73.3% (2000); Median home value: $41,100 (2000); Median rent: $183 per month (2000); Median age of housing: 52 years (2000).
Transportation: Commute to work: 93.1% car, 1.6% public transportation, 0.7% walk, 3.6% work from home (2000); Travel time to work: 28.1% less than 15 minutes, 39.0% 15 to 30 minutes, 19.7% 30 to 45 minutes, 3.1% 45 to 60 minutes, 10.2% 60 minutes or more (2000)

GREENCASTLE (city). Aka Green Castle. Covers a land area of 0.457 square miles and a water area of 0 square miles. Located at 40.26° N. Lat.; 92.88° W. Long.
Population: 308 (2000); Race: 98.0% White, 0.0% Black, 0.0% Asian, 0.0% American Indian and Alaska Native, 1.0% Hispanic of any race, 2.0% two or more races (2000); Density: 673.4 persons per square mile (2000); Age: 28.1% under 18, 18.1% over 64 (2000); Marriage status: 18.9% never married, 56.4% now married, 15.0% widowed, 9.7% divorced (2000); Foreign born: 0.0% (2000); Ancestry (includes multiple ancestries): 15.7% United States or American, 11.7% Irish, 9.4% German, 5.0% Other groups, 5.0% English (2000).
Economy: Employment by occupation: 8.2% management, 11.2% professional, 13.3% services, 11.2% sales, 13.3% farming, 3.1% construction, 39.8% production (2000).
Income: Per capita income: $10,369 (2000); Median household income: $17,500 (2000); Poverty rate: 27.1% (2000).
Taxes: Total city taxes per capita: $40 (1997); City property taxes per capita: $22 (1997).
Education: High school graduation rate: 67.7% (2000); College graduation rate: 3.5% (2000).
Housing: Homeownership rate: 72.5% (2000); Median home value: $17,000 (2000); Median rent: $168 per month (2000); Median age of housing: 50 years (2000).
Transportation: Commute to work: 95.9% car, 0.0% public transportation, 1.0% walk, 1.0% work from home (2000); Travel time to work: 13.4% less than 15 minutes, 58.8% 15 to 30 minutes, 22.7% 30 to 45 minutes, 3.1% 45 to 60 minutes, 2.1% 60 minutes or more (2000)

HARRIS (town). Covers a land area of 0.155 square miles and a water area of 0 square miles. Located at 40.30° N. Lat.; 93.35° W. Long. Elevation is 897 feet.
Population: 105 (2000); Race: 96.3% White, 0.0% Black, 0.0% Asian, 1.9% American Indian and Alaska Native, 0.0% Hispanic of any race, 1.9% two or more races (2000); Density: 676.1 persons per square mile (2000); Age: 44.9% under 18, 14.0% over 64 (2000); Marriage status: 6.6% never married, 68.9% now married, 19.7% widowed, 4.9% divorced (2000); Foreign born: 0.0% (2000); Ancestry (includes multiple ancestries): 45.8% United States or American, 6.5% Other groups, 5.6% English, 4.7% Irish, 2.8% German (2000).
Economy: Employment by occupation: 13.5% management, 5.4% professional, 21.6% services, 10.8% sales, 2.7% farming, 10.8% construction, 35.1% production (2000).
Income: Per capita income: $7,952 (2000); Median household income: $20,500 (2000); Poverty rate: 15.9% (2000).
Taxes: Total city taxes per capita: $257 (1997); City property taxes per capita: $101 (1997).
Education: High school graduation rate: 71.9% (2000); College graduation rate: 5.3% (2000).
Housing: Homeownership rate: 65.0% (2000); Median home value: $15,000 (2000); Median rent: $113 per month (2000); Median age of housing: 60+ years (2000).
Transportation: Commute to work: 100.0% car, 0.0% public transportation, 0.0% walk, 0.0% work from home (2000); Travel time to work: 9.1% less than 15 minutes, 45.5% 15 to 30 minutes, 45.5% 30 to 45 minutes, 0.0% 45 to 60 minutes, 0.0% 60 minutes or more (2000)

HUMPHREYS (village). Covers a land area of 0.256 square miles and a water area of 0 square miles. Located at 40.12° N. Lat.; 93.32° W. Long. Elevation is 928 feet.
Population: 164 (2000); Race: 93.6% White, 0.0% Black, 0.0% Asian, 4.3% American Indian and Alaska Native, 0.0% Hispanic of any race, 2.1% two or more races (2000); Density: 639.5 persons per square mile (2000); Age: 33.2% under 18, 14.4% over 64 (2000); Marriage status: 26.5% never married, 50.0% now married, 16.7% widowed, 6.8% divorced (2000); Foreign born: 0.0% (2000); Ancestry (includes multiple ancestries): 21.4% United States or American, 14.4% Other groups, 10.7% Irish, 8.6% English, 4.8% German (2000).
Economy: Cattle; corn, soybeans. Employment by occupation: 4.5% management, 6.0% professional, 32.8% services, 9.0% sales, 0.0% farming, 20.9% construction, 26.9% production (2000).
Income: Per capita income: $16,207 (2000); Median household income: $25,250 (2000); Poverty rate: 25.1% (2000).
Taxes: Total city taxes per capita: $38 (1997); City property taxes per capita: $38 (1997).
Education: High school graduation rate: 59.8% (2000); College graduation rate: 2.0% (2000).
Housing: Homeownership rate: 75.8% (2000); Median home value: $18,100 (2000); Median rent: $241 per month (2000); Median age of housing: 58 years (2000).
Transportation: Commute to work: 87.3% car, 0.0% public transportation, 12.7% walk, 0.0% work from home (2000); Travel time to work: 19.0% less than 15 minutes, 55.6% 15 to 30 minutes, 11.1% 30 to 45 minutes, 0.0% 45 to 60 minutes, 14.3% 60 minutes or more (2000)

MILAN (city). Covers a land area of 1.833 square miles and a water area of 0 square miles. Located at 40.20° N. Lat.; 93.12° W. Long. Elevation is 969 feet.
History: Laid out 1845.
Population: 1,958 (2000); Race: 89.3% White, 0.6% Black, 0.3% Asian, 0.0% American Indian and Alaska Native, 24.9% Hispanic of any race, 0.6% two or more races (2000); Density: 1,068.4 persons per square mile (2000); Age: 25.9% under 18, 19.3% over 64 (2000); Marriage status: 27.0% never married, 48.5% now married, 13.2% widowed, 11.4% divorced (2000); Foreign born: 17.6% (2000); Ancestry (includes multiple ancestries): 25.3% Other groups, 17.5% United States or American, 9.4% German, 5.9% Irish, 5.0% English (2000).
Economy: Corn, soybeans; sheep, cattle, hogs. Corporate hog farming; poultry processing. Single-family building permits issued: 3 (2001) / 6 (2000); Multi-family building permits issued: 0 (2001) / 0 (2000); Employment by occupation: 6.3% management, 6.9% professional, 18.0% services, 12.2% sales, 2.3% farming, 7.5% construction, 46.9% production (2000).
Income: Per capita income: $10,688 (2000); Median household income: $20,691 (2000); Poverty rate: 22.9% (2000).
Taxes: Total city taxes per capita: $117 (1997); City property taxes per capita: $39 (1997).

Education: High school graduation rate: 56.0% (2000); College graduation rate: 6.9% (2000).

School District(s)

Milan C-2 (PK-12)
2000 Enrollment: 691 660-265-4414

Housing: Homeownership rate: 58.2% (2000); Median home value: $41,600 (2000); Median rent: $262 per month (2000); Median age of housing: 50 years (2000).
Hospitals: Sullivan County Memorial Hospital (39 beds)
Newspapers: The Milan Standard (1 x week)
Transportation: Commute to work: 82.4% car, 0.0% public transportation, 12.0% walk, 2.3% work from home (2000); Travel time to work: 68.9% less than 15 minutes, 14.5% 15 to 30 minutes, 11.6% 30 to 45 minutes, 4.1% 45 to 60 minutes, 0.9% 60 minutes or more (2000)

Additional Information Contacts

Milan Chamber of Commerce 660-265-5131

NEWTOWN (town). Covers a land area of 0.253 square miles and a water area of 0 square miles. Located at 40.37° N. Lat.; 93.33° W. Long. Elevation is 960 feet.
Population: 209 (2000); Race: 99.1% White, 0.0% Black, 0.0% Asian, 0.0% American Indian and Alaska Native, 0.0% Hispanic of any race, 0.9% two or more races (2000); Density: 826.0 persons per square mile (2000); Age: 29.4% under 18, 21.6% over 64 (2000); Marriage status: 23.1% never married, 58.6% now married, 10.1% widowed, 8.3% divorced (2000); Foreign born: 0.0% (2000); Ancestry (includes multiple ancestries): 19.3% United States or American, 19.3% Irish, 16.5% German, 9.2% Other groups, 6.4% English (2000).
Economy: Employment by occupation: 12.9% management, 8.9% professional, 17.8% services, 14.9% sales, 18.8% farming, 13.9% construction, 12.9% production (2000).
Income: Per capita income: $13,561 (2000); Median household income: $21,250 (2000); Poverty rate: 10.6% (2000).
Taxes: Total city taxes per capita: $139 (1997); City property taxes per capita: $123 (1997).
Education: High school graduation rate: 78.2% (2000); College graduation rate: 9.8% (2000).

School District(s)

Newtown-Harris R-III (PK-12)
2000 Enrollment: 130 660-794-2245

Housing: Homeownership rate: 57.8% (2000); Median home value: $26,500 (2000); Median rent: $227 per month (2000); Median age of housing: 60+ years (2000).
Transportation: Commute to work: 81.7% car, 0.0% public transportation, 16.1% walk, 0.0% work from home (2000); Travel time to work: 50.5% less than 15 minutes, 31.2% 15 to 30 minutes, 15.1% 30 to 45 minutes, 3.2% 45 to 60 minutes, 0.0% 60 minutes or more (2000)

OSGOOD (village). Covers a land area of 0.184 square miles and a water area of 0 square miles. Located at 40.19° N. Lat.; 93.34° W. Long. Elevation is 820 feet.
Population: 51 (2000); Race: 100.0% White, 0.0% Black, 0.0% Asian, 0.0% American Indian and Alaska Native, 0.0% Hispanic of any race, 0.0% two or more races (2000); Density: 277.0 persons per square mile (2000); Age: 37.8% under 18, 32.4% over 64 (2000); Marriage status: 4.2% never married, 75.0% now married, 20.8% widowed, 0.0% divorced (2000); Foreign born: 0.0% (2000); Ancestry (includes multiple ancestries): 40.5% United States or American, 18.9% Irish, 18.9% Dutch, 8.1% Other groups, 5.4% German (2000).
Economy: Employment by occupation: 0.0% management, 22.2% professional, 55.6% services, 0.0% sales, 0.0% farming, 0.0% construction, 22.2% production (2000).
Income: Per capita income: $8,889 (2000); Median household income: $14,250 (2000); Poverty rate: 0.0% (2000).
Taxes: Total city taxes per capita: $18 (1997); City property taxes per capita: $18 (1997).
Education: High school graduation rate: 78.3% (2000); College graduation rate: 0.0% (2000).
Housing: Homeownership rate: 85.7% (2000); Median home value: $25,800 (2000); Median rent: $325 per month (2000); Median age of housing: 60+ years (2000).
Transportation: Commute to work: 57.1% car, 0.0% public transportation, 0.0% walk, 42.9% work from home (2000); Travel time to work: 0.0% less than 15 minutes, 0.0% 15 to 30 minutes, 50.0% 30 to 45 minutes, 50.0% 45 to 60 minutes, 0.0% 60 minutes or more (2000)

POLLOCK (village). Covers a land area of 0.167 square miles and a water area of 0 square miles. Located at 40.35° N. Lat.; 93.08° W. Long. Elevation is 990 feet.
Population: 131 (2000); Race: 100.0% White, 0.0% Black, 0.0% Asian, 0.0% American Indian and Alaska Native, 0.0% Hispanic of any race, 0.0% two or more races (2000); Density: 786.8 persons per square mile (2000); Age: 31.0% under 18, 14.7% over 64 (2000); Marriage status: 21.8% never married, 56.4% now married, 7.9% widowed, 13.9% divorced (2000); Foreign born: 0.0% (2000); Ancestry (includes multiple ancestries): 26.4% United States or American, 14.0% German, 10.1% Polish, 3.9% Other groups, 3.9% Dutch (2000).
Economy: Employment by occupation: 13.2% management, 11.3% professional, 7.5% services, 13.2% sales, 5.7% farming, 26.4% construction, 22.6% production (2000).
Income: Per capita income: $10,367 (2000); Median household income: $18,571 (2000); Poverty rate: 35.2% (2000).
Taxes: Total city taxes per capita: $42 (1997); City property taxes per capita: $28 (1997).
Education: High school graduation rate: 65.8% (2000); College graduation rate: 2.7% (2000).
Housing: Homeownership rate: 63.6% (2000); Median home value: $18,100 (2000); Median rent: $175 per month (2000); Median age of housing: 60+ years (2000).
Transportation: Commute to work: 100.0% car, 0.0% public transportation, 0.0% walk, 0.0% work from home (2000); Travel time to work: 15.7% less than 15 minutes, 47.1% 15 to 30 minutes, 9.8% 30 to 45 minutes, 9.8% 45 to 60 minutes, 17.6% 60 minutes or more (2000)

WINIGAN (unincorporated postal area, zip code 63566). Covers a land area of 25.588 square miles and a water area of 0.007 square miles. Located at 40.03° N. Lat.; 92.96° W. Long. Elevation is 993 feet.
Population: 68 (2000); Race: 100.0% White, 0.0% Black, 0.0% Asian, 0.0% American Indian and Alaska Native, 0.0% Hispanic of any race, 0.0% two or more races (2000); Density: 2.7 persons per square mile (2000); Age: 23.3% under 18, 27.4% over 64 (2000); Marriage status: 13.6% never married, 62.7% now married, 16.9% widowed, 6.8% divorced (2000); Foreign born: 2.7% (2000); Ancestry (includes multiple ancestries): 23.3% German, 15.1% Irish, 12.3% Other groups, 8.2% English, 6.8% United States or American (2000).
Economy: Employment by occupation: 27.3% management, 4.5% professional, 6.8% services, 13.6% sales, 4.5% farming, 11.4% construction, 31.8% production (2000).
Income: Per capita income: $14,925 (2000); Median household income: $31,875 (2000); Poverty rate: 24.7% (2000).
Education: High school graduation rate: 88.0% (2000); College graduation rate: 4.0% (2000).
Housing: Homeownership rate: 94.3% (2000); Median home value: <$10,000 (2000); Median age of housing: 54 years (2000).
Transportation: Commute to work: 90.5% car, 0.0% public transportation, 0.0% walk, 9.5% work from home (2000); Travel time to work: 26.3% less than 15 minutes, 39.5% 15 to 30 minutes, 21.1% 30 to 45 minutes, 5.3% 45 to 60 minutes, 7.9% 60 minutes or more (2000)

Taney County

Located in southern Missouri, in the Ozarks; bounded on the south by Arkansas; drained by the White River; includes part of Mark Twain National Forest. Covers a land area of 632.40 square miles, a water area of 19.10 square miles, and is located in the Central Time Zone. The county government was organized in 1837. County seat is Forsyth.

Weather Station: Ozark Beach — Elevation: 698 feet

	Jan	Feb	Mar	Apr	May	Jun	Jul	Aug	Sep	Oct	Nov	Dec
High	45	51	60	71	78	86	91	90	83	72	59	49
Low	20	24	33	41	50	59	64	62	55	43	34	25
Precip	2.3	2.4	4.0	4.0	4.3	4.5	3.5	3.2	4.4	3.1	4.6	3.1
Snow	3.7	2.5	2.2	tr	0.0	0.0	0.0	0.0	0.0	tr	0.7	1.2

High and Low temperatures in degrees Fahrenheit; Precipitation and Snow in inches

Population: 39,703 (2000); Race: 95.9% White, 0.2% Black, 0.7% Asian, 0.8% American Indian and Alaska Native, 1.9% Hispanic of any race, 1.6% two or more races (2000); Density: 62.8 persons per square mile (2000); Age: 22.4% under 18, 16.1% over 64 (2000).

Religion: Five largest groups: 10.6% Southern Baptist Convention, 3.9% Catholic Church, 2.9% Presbyterian Church (U.S.A.), 2.5% Independent, Charismatic Churches, 2.3% The United Methodist Church (2000).
Economy: Unemployment rate: 3.9% (11/2002); Total civilian labor force: 31,612 (11/2002); Leading industries: 26.1% accommodation & food services; 17.4% retail trade; 9.4% real estate & rental & leasing (2000); Companies that employ more than 1,000 persons: 1 (2000); Companies that employ more than 100 persons: 25 (2000); Farms: 459 totaling 158,421 acres (1997); Minority business ownership rate: 4.5% (1997); Women business ownership rate: 20.7% (1997); Retail sales per capita: $13,015 (1997). Single-family building permits issued: 317 (2001) / 229 (2000); Multi-family building permits issued: 94 (2001) / 246 (2000).
Income: Per capita income: $17,267 (2000); Median household income: $30,898 (2000); Poverty rate: 12.4% (2000); Bankruptcy rate: 4.93% (2001).
Taxes: Total county taxes per capita: $368 (2000); County property taxes per capita: $0 (2000).
Education: High school graduation rate: 81.4% (2000); College graduation rate: 14.9% (2000).
Housing: Homeownership rate: 68.9% (2000); Median home value: $93,500 (2000); Median rent: $392 per month (2000); Median age of housing: 17 years (2000).
Health: Birth rate: 130.7 per 10,000 population (1998); Age adjusted death rate: 93.5 per 10,000 population (1999); Age adjusted cancer mortality rate: 189.9 deaths per 100,000 population (1999). Number of physicians: 11.3 per 10,000 population (1999); Number of hospital beds: 28.0 per 10,000 population (1999).
Elections: 2000 Presidential election results: 33.7% Gore, 63.8% Bush, 1.4% Nader, 0.7% Buchanan
National and State Parks: Ruth and Paul Hennings State Forest; Table Rock State Park; Table Rock State Park
Additional Information Contacts
Taney County Government Offices 417-546-7200
Branson Chamber of Commerce 417-334-4136
Branson Lakes Area Chamber 417-339-3999
Hollister Chamber of Commerce 417-334-3050
Tri Lakes Board of Realtors 417-338-4555

Taney County Communities

BRADLEYVILLE (unincorporated postal area, zip code 65614). Covers a land area of 103.911 square miles and a water area of 0 square miles. Located at 36.73° N. Lat.; 92.89° W. Long. Elevation is 843 feet.
Population: 505 (2000); Race: 98.5% White, 0.0% Black, 0.0% Asian, 0.8% American Indian and Alaska Native, 0.0% Hispanic of any race, 0.8% two or more races (2000); Density: 4.9 persons per square mile (2000); Age: 23.5% under 18, 21.1% over 64 (2000); Marriage status: 18.4% never married, 65.9% now married, 6.4% widowed, 9.3% divorced (2000); Foreign born: 0.0% (2000); Ancestry (includes multiple ancestries): 12.7% United States or American, 12.1% English, 10.2% German, 7.4% Irish, 5.3% Other groups (2000).
Economy: Cattle; hay, timber. Charcoal. Employment by occupation: 18.6% management, 14.0% professional, 10.4% services, 19.0% sales, 2.3% farming, 12.2% construction, 23.5% production (2000).
Income: Per capita income: $17,086 (2000); Median household income: $30,341 (2000); Poverty rate: 18.4% (2000).
Education: High school graduation rate: 71.7% (2000); College graduation rate: 9.4% (2000).

School District(s)

Bradleyville R-I (KG-12)
2000 Enrollment: 253 417-796-2288
Housing: Homeownership rate: 83.1% (2000); Median home value: $53,300 (2000); Median rent: $222 per month (2000); Median age of housing: 36 years (2000).
Transportation: Commute to work: 83.6% car, 0.0% public transportation, 4.6% walk, 11.9% work from home (2000); Travel time to work: 28.0% less than 15 minutes, 13.0% 15 to 30 minutes, 14.5% 30 to 45 minutes, 24.9% 45 to 60 minutes, 19.7% 60 minutes or more (2000)

BRANSON (city). Covers a land area of 16.178 square miles and a water area of 0.161 square miles. Located at 36.63° N. Lat.; 93.25° W. Long. Elevation is 722 feet.
History: Branson developed as a resort town on Lake Taneycomo.
Population: 6,050 (2000); Race: 95.5% White, 0.4% Black, 2.2% Asian, 0.4% American Indian and Alaska Native, 2.4% Hispanic of any race, 0.8% two or more races (2000); Density: 374.0 persons per square mile (2000); Age: 18.6% under 18, 20.2% over 64 (2000); Marriage status: 17.8% never married, 58.5% now married, 9.9% widowed, 13.8% divorced (2000); Foreign born: 3.4% (2000); Ancestry (includes multiple ancestries): 18.2% German, 14.3% Other groups, 14.1% English, 11.6% Irish, 10.2% United States or American (2000).
Economy: Single-family building permits issued: 22 (2001) / 28 (2000); Multi-family building permits issued: 0 (2001) / 33 (2000); Employment by occupation: 19.1% management, 16.6% professional, 21.8% services, 32.8% sales, 0.0% farming, 5.9% construction, 3.8% production (2000).
Income: Per capita income: $20,461 (2000); Median household income: $31,997 (2000); Poverty rate: 12.1% (2000).
Taxes: Total city taxes per capita: $2,500 (2000); City property taxes per capita: $234 (2000).
Education: High school graduation rate: 83.3% (2000); College graduation rate: 20.8% (2000).

School District(s)

Branson R-IV (PK-12)
2000 Enrollment: 2,935 417-334-6541
Housing: Homeownership rate: 54.7% (2000); Median home value: $123,900 (2000); Median rent: $448 per month (2000); Median age of housing: 17 years (2000).
Hospitals: Skaggs Community Health Center (111 beds)
Safety: Violent crime rate: 170.9 per 10,000 population; Property crime rate: 1,381.6 per 10,000 population (2001).
Newspapers: Taylor Made News (1 x week)
Transportation: Commute to work: 87.2% car, 0.3% public transportation, 5.3% walk, 4.8% work from home (2000); Travel time to work: 66.0% less than 15 minutes, 23.6% 15 to 30 minutes, 3.7% 30 to 45 minutes, 1.4% 45 to 60 minutes, 5.3% 60 minutes or more (2000)
Additional Information Contacts
Branson Chamber of Commerce 417-334-4136
Branson Lakes Area Chamber 417-339-3999
Tri Lakes Board of Realtors 417-338-4555

BULL CREEK (village). Covers a land area of 0.171 square miles and a water area of 0 square miles. Located at 36.71° N. Lat.; 93.20° W. Long. Elevation is 723 feet.
Population: 225 (2000); Race: 97.6% White, 0.0% Black, 0.0% Asian, 2.4% American Indian and Alaska Native, 1.0% Hispanic of any race, 0.0% two or more races (2000); Density: 1,315.7 persons per square mile (2000); Age: 31.6% under 18, 3.9% over 64 (2000); Marriage status: 23.0% never married, 55.3% now married, 9.9% widowed, 11.8% divorced (2000); Foreign born: 0.0% (2000); Ancestry (includes multiple ancestries): 20.9% United States or American, 18.9% Irish, 16.0% German, 15.5% Other groups, 5.3% French (except Basque) (2000).
Economy: Employment by occupation: 10.5% management, 0.0% professional, 47.6% services, 26.7% sales, 0.0% farming, 6.7% construction, 8.6% production (2000).
Income: Per capita income: $10,411 (2000); Median household income: $21,667 (2000); Poverty rate: 23.8% (2000).
Taxes: Total city taxes per capita: $14 (1997); City property taxes per capita: $0 (1997).
Education: High school graduation rate: 68.0% (2000); College graduation rate: 2.4% (2000).
Housing: Homeownership rate: 71.8% (2000); Median home value: $63,000 (2000); Median rent: $342 per month (2000); Median age of housing: 12 years (2000).
Transportation: Commute to work: 98.1% car, 0.0% public transportation, 0.0% walk, 0.0% work from home (2000); Travel time to work: 24.8% less than 15 minutes, 60.0% 15 to 30 minutes, 4.8% 30 to 45 minutes, 10.5% 45 to 60 minutes, 0.0% 60 minutes or more (2000)

CEDARCREEK (unincorporated postal area, zip code 65627). Covers a land area of 49.865 square miles and a water area of 0.026 square miles. Located at 36.57° N. Lat.; 93.01° W. Long. Elevation is 970 feet.
Population: 507 (2000); Race: 97.6% White, 0.0% Black, 0.0% Asian, 0.0% American Indian and Alaska Native, 0.0% Hispanic of any race, 2.4% two or more races (2000); Density: 10.2 persons per square mile (2000); Age: 19.6% under 18, 7.4% over 64 (2000); Marriage status: 25.3% never married, 55.4% now married, 8.2% widowed, 11.1% divorced (2000); Foreign born: 1.3% (2000); Ancestry (includes multiple ancestries): 18.8% Irish, 14.7% German, 13.6% English, 12.5% Other groups, 8.0% Italian (2000).
Economy: Employment by occupation: 4.7% management, 11.2% professional, 24.4% services, 24.4% sales, 0.0% farming, 9.3% construction, 26.0% production (2000).

Income: Per capita income: $17,966 (2000); Median household income: $37,964 (2000); Poverty rate: 6.2% (2000).
Education: High school graduation rate: 84.8% (2000); College graduation rate: 18.5% (2000).
Housing: Homeownership rate: 82.1% (2000); Median home value: $44,700 (2000); Median rent: $343 per month (2000); Median age of housing: 26 years (2000).
Transportation: Commute to work: 100.0% car, 0.0% public transportation, 0.0% walk, 0.0% work from home (2000); Travel time to work: 16.7% less than 15 minutes, 16.7% 15 to 30 minutes, 13.2% 30 to 45 minutes, 27.1% 45 to 60 minutes, 26.4% 60 minutes or more (2000)

FORSYTH (city). Covers a land area of 2.044 square miles and a water area of 0.008 square miles. Located at 36.68° N. Lat.; 93.11° W. Long. Elevation is 947 feet.
History: Forsyth was once the headquarters of the Bald Knobbers, an organization formed in 1884 as a vigilante group but which became a band of ruffians.
Population: 1,686 (2000); Race: 97.5% White, 0.2% Black, 0.4% Asian, 0.3% American Indian and Alaska Native, 0.7% Hispanic of any race, 0.6% two or more races (2000); Density: 824.9 persons per square mile (2000); Age: 17.1% under 18, 36.2% over 64 (2000); Marriage status: 13.1% never married, 65.8% now married, 13.3% widowed, 7.9% divorced (2000); Foreign born: 0.9% (2000); Ancestry (includes multiple ancestries): 17.8% German, 17.3% English, 12.2% United States or American, 11.7% Irish, 8.3% Other groups (2000).
Economy: Single-family building permits issued: 4 (2001) / 5 (2000); Multi-family building permits issued: 2 (2001) / 2 (2000); Employment by occupation: 14.0% management, 19.6% professional, 16.9% services, 31.7% sales, 1.0% farming, 8.3% construction, 8.6% production (2000).
Income: Per capita income: $21,436 (2000); Median household income: $31,801 (2000); Poverty rate: 9.7% (2000).
Taxes: Total city taxes per capita: $381 (1997); City property taxes per capita: $118 (1997).
Education: High school graduation rate: 79.2% (2000); College graduation rate: 19.5% (2000).

School District(s)

Forsyth R-III (PK-12)
2000 Enrollment: 1,147 417-546-6384
Housing: Homeownership rate: 72.5% (2000); Median home value: $89,700 (2000); Median rent: $345 per month (2000); Median age of housing: 23 years (2000).
Transportation: Commute to work: 90.5% car, 0.0% public transportation, 5.1% walk, 3.9% work from home (2000); Travel time to work: 39.1% less than 15 minutes, 29.4% 15 to 30 minutes, 21.4% 30 to 45 minutes, 4.5% 45 to 60 minutes, 5.7% 60 minutes or more (2000)

HOLLISTER (city). Covers a land area of 3.722 square miles and a water area of 0.057 square miles. Located at 36.62° N. Lat.; 93.21° W. Long. Elevation is 733 feet.
History: Hollister was planned as a resort village on the southern shores of Lake Taneycomo. The town was platted in 1906 by William J. Johnson, a landscape architect. Lake Taneycomo was formed when the White River was dammed.
Population: 3,867 (2000); Race: 95.9% White, 0.4% Black, 0.3% Asian, 0.5% American Indian and Alaska Native, 2.0% Hispanic of any race, 1.1% two or more races (2000); Density: 1,039.0 persons per square mile (2000); Age: 23.7% under 18, 13.2% over 64 (2000); Marriage status: 23.2% never married, 49.6% now married, 12.1% widowed, 15.1% divorced (2000); Foreign born: 2.6% (2000); Ancestry (includes multiple ancestries): 17.6% German, 13.0% Other groups, 12.0% Irish, 11.9% United States or American, 7.0% English (2000).
Economy: Single-family building permits issued: 20 (2001) / 22 (2000); Multi-family building permits issued: 0 (2001) / 0 (2000); Employment by occupation: 6.4% management, 15.1% professional, 27.8% services, 33.2% sales, 0.0% farming, 6.2% construction, 11.2% production (2000).
Income: Per capita income: $12,716 (2000); Median household income: $24,535 (2000); Poverty rate: 13.2% (2000).
Taxes: Total city taxes per capita: $152 (1997); City property taxes per capita: $32 (1997).
Education: High school graduation rate: 81.4% (2000); College graduation rate: 12.0% (2000).

School District(s)

Hollister R-V (PK-12)
2000 Enrollment: 1,181 417-332-0130
Housing: Homeownership rate: 52.2% (2000); Median home value: $74,500 (2000); Median rent: $383 per month (2000); Median age of housing: 14 years (2000).
Newspapers: Branson Tri-Lakes Daily News (5 x week); Marketeer (1 x week)
Transportation: Commute to work: 95.4% car, 0.0% public transportation, 1.6% walk, 1.8% work from home (2000); Travel time to work: 40.6% less than 15 minutes, 44.2% 15 to 30 minutes, 8.3% 30 to 45 minutes, 3.5% 45 to 60 minutes, 3.4% 60 minutes or more (2000)
Additional Information Contacts
Hollister Chamber of Commerce 417-334-3050

KIRBYVILLE (unincorporated postal area, zip code 65679). Covers a land area of 57.116 square miles and a water area of 0 square miles. Located at 36.60° N. Lat.; 93.11° W. Long. Elevation is 1,010 feet.
Population: 2,393 (2000); Race: 95.0% White, 0.9% Black, 1.0% Asian, 1.9% American Indian and Alaska Native, 2.7% Hispanic of any race, 0.9% two or more races (2000); Density: 41.9 persons per square mile (2000); Age: 27.8% under 18, 10.5% over 64 (2000); Marriage status: 19.7% never married, 72.2% now married, 1.4% widowed, 6.8% divorced (2000); Foreign born: 1.5% (2000); Ancestry (includes multiple ancestries): 14.1% Other groups, 13.8% German, 12.9% Irish, 12.5% United States or American, 8.8% English (2000).
Economy: Employment by occupation: 10.9% management, 10.3% professional, 16.4% services, 24.5% sales, 0.0% farming, 20.2% construction, 17.7% production (2000).
Income: Per capita income: $14,470 (2000); Median household income: $36,970 (2000); Poverty rate: 12.1% (2000).
Education: High school graduation rate: 84.2% (2000); College graduation rate: 9.1% (2000).

School District(s)

Kirbyville R-VI (PK-08)
2000 Enrollment: 364 417-337-8913
Housing: Homeownership rate: 66.8% (2000); Median home value: $84,500 (2000); Median rent: $376 per month (2000); Median age of housing: 14 years (2000).
Transportation: Commute to work: 95.2% car, 0.0% public transportation, 1.4% walk, 2.4% work from home (2000); Travel time to work: 21.3% less than 15 minutes, 43.4% 15 to 30 minutes, 28.0% 30 to 45 minutes, 3.1% 45 to 60 minutes, 4.1% 60 minutes or more (2000)

KISSEE MILLS (unincorporated postal area, zip code 65680). Covers a land area of 31.128 square miles and a water area of 0 square miles. Located at 36.66° N. Lat.; 93.01° W. Long. Elevation is 986 feet.
Population: 960 (2000); Race: 97.0% White, 0.0% Black, 0.0% Asian, 0.5% American Indian and Alaska Native, 0.0% Hispanic of any race, 2.5% two or more races (2000); Density: 30.8 persons per square mile (2000); Age: 21.0% under 18, 15.4% over 64 (2000); Marriage status: 12.4% never married, 68.8% now married, 7.2% widowed, 11.5% divorced (2000); Foreign born: 0.6% (2000); Ancestry (includes multiple ancestries): 24.1% German, 19.7% Irish, 15.3% Other groups, 14.5% United States or American, 8.4% English (2000).
Economy: Employment by occupation: 9.2% management, 9.2% professional, 18.2% services, 27.1% sales, 0.0% farming, 19.3% construction, 17.0% production (2000).
Income: Per capita income: $15,242 (2000); Median household income: $22,833 (2000); Poverty rate: 18.4% (2000).
Education: High school graduation rate: 68.9% (2000); College graduation rate: 10.8% (2000).
Housing: Homeownership rate: 87.2% (2000); Median home value: $70,200 (2000); Median rent: $355 per month (2000); Median age of housing: 20 years (2000).
Transportation: Commute to work: 92.3% car, 0.0% public transportation, 1.6% walk, 4.7% work from home (2000); Travel time to work: 15.0% less than 15 minutes, 23.8% 15 to 30 minutes, 30.6% 30 to 45 minutes, 19.4% 45 to 60 minutes, 11.3% 60 minutes or more (2000)

MCCLURG (unincorporated postal area, zip code 65701). Covers a land area of 1.294 square miles and a water area of 0 square miles. Located at 36.79° N. Lat.; 92.77° W. Long. Elevation is 1,121 feet.
Population: 25 (2000); Race: 100.0% White, 0.0% Black, 0.0% Asian, 0.0% American Indian and Alaska Native, 0.0% Hispanic of any race, 0.0% two or more races (2000); Density: 19.3 persons per square mile (2000); Age: 0.0% under 18, 31.8% over 64 (2000); Marriage status: 0.0% never married, 63.6% now married, 18.2% widowed, 18.2% divorced (2000); Foreign born: 0.0%

(2000); Ancestry (includes multiple ancestries): 31.8% German, 27.3% Irish, 27.3% Dutch, 22.7% Polish, 13.6% English (2000).
Economy: Employment by occupation: 33.3% management, 0.0% professional, 22.2% services, 0.0% sales, 0.0% farming, 44.4% construction, 0.0% production (2000).
Income: Per capita income: $14,632 (2000); Median household income: $31,875 (2000); Poverty rate: 9.1% (2000).
Education: High school graduation rate: 38.9% (2000); College graduation rate: 0.0% (2000).
Housing: Homeownership rate: 100.0% (2000); Median home value: $27,500 (2000); Median age of housing: 37 years (2000).
Transportation: Commute to work: 100.0% car, 0.0% public transportation, 0.0% walk, 0.0% work from home (2000); Travel time to work: 0.0% less than 15 minutes, 0.0% 15 to 30 minutes, 33.3% 30 to 45 minutes, 44.4% 45 to 60 minutes, 22.2% 60 minutes or more (2000)

MERRIAM WOODS (village). Covers a land area of 1.412 square miles and a water area of 0 square miles. Located at 36.71° N. Lat.; 93.17° W. Long. Elevation is 939 feet.
Population: 1,142 (2000); Race: 99.5% White, 0.0% Black, 0.0% Asian, 0.4% American Indian and Alaska Native, 0.8% Hispanic of any race, 0.0% two or more races (2000); Density: 809.0 persons per square mile (2000); Age: 26.5% under 18, 20.6% over 64 (2000); Marriage status: 19.3% never married, 53.2% now married, 9.1% widowed, 18.4% divorced (2000); Foreign born: 0.0% (2000); Ancestry (includes multiple ancestries): 21.2% United States or American, 18.6% German, 14.7% Irish, 9.9% English, 8.4% Other groups (2000).
Economy: Single-family building permits issued: 3 (2001) / 0 (2000); Multi-family building permits issued: 0 (2001) / 0 (2000); Employment by occupation: 4.2% management, 9.4% professional, 33.0% services, 30.4% sales, 0.5% farming, 13.2% construction, 9.2% production (2000).
Income: Per capita income: $13,528 (2000); Median household income: $24,132 (2000); Poverty rate: 22.8% (2000).
Taxes: Total city taxes per capita: $27 (1997); City property taxes per capita: $27 (1997).
Education: High school graduation rate: 69.8% (2000); College graduation rate: 5.6% (2000).
Housing: Homeownership rate: 77.4% (2000); Median home value: $61,700 (2000); Median rent: $313 per month (2000); Median age of housing: 20 years (2000).
Transportation: Commute to work: 97.4% car, 0.0% public transportation, 0.0% walk, 1.9% work from home (2000); Travel time to work: 14.6% less than 15 minutes, 50.9% 15 to 30 minutes, 25.3% 30 to 45 minutes, 4.9% 45 to 60 minutes, 4.4% 60 minutes or more (2000)

POWERSITE (unincorporated postal area, zip code 65731). Covers a land area of 2.083 square miles and a water area of 0 square miles. Located at 36.65° N. Lat.; 93.12° W. Long. Elevation is 918 feet.
Population: 346 (2000); Race: 100.0% White, 0.0% Black, 0.0% Asian, 0.0% American Indian and Alaska Native, 0.0% Hispanic of any race, 0.0% two or more races (2000); Density: 166.1 persons per square mile (2000); Age: 24.7% under 18, 11.1% over 64 (2000); Marriage status: 11.2% never married, 81.7% now married, 7.2% widowed, 0.0% divorced (2000); Foreign born: 0.0% (2000); Ancestry (includes multiple ancestries): 16.8% United States or American, 16.8% German, 10.5% English, 8.5% Dutch, 8.2% Irish (2000).
Economy: Employment by occupation: 15.1% management, 5.5% professional, 21.2% services, 15.1% sales, 0.0% farming, 27.4% construction, 15.8% production (2000).
Income: Per capita income: $17,918 (2000); Median household income: $34,688 (2000); Poverty rate: 3.4% (2000).
Education: High school graduation rate: 83.8% (2000); College graduation rate: 10.2% (2000).
Housing: Homeownership rate: 80.3% (2000); Median home value: $107,300 (2000); Median rent: $435 per month (2000); Median age of housing: 23 years (2000).
Transportation: Commute to work: 95.7% car, 0.0% public transportation, 0.0% walk, 4.3% work from home (2000); Travel time to work: 0.0% less than 15 minutes, 57.5% 15 to 30 minutes, 32.1% 30 to 45 minutes, 0.0% 45 to 60 minutes, 10.4% 60 minutes or more (2000)

RIDGEDALE (unincorporated postal area, zip code 65739). Covers a land area of 11.353 square miles and a water area of 0 square miles. Located at 36.53° N. Lat.; 93.28° W. Long. Elevation is 1,388 feet.
Population: 1,072 (2000); Race: 98.1% White, 0.0% Black, 0.0% Asian, 0.0% American Indian and Alaska Native, 7.0% Hispanic of any race, 1.9% two or more races (2000); Density: 94.4 persons per square mile (2000); Age: 20.6% under 18, 13.5% over 64 (2000); Marriage status: 14.7% never married, 66.4% now married, 5.3% widowed, 13.5% divorced (2000); Foreign born: 0.0% (2000); Ancestry (includes multiple ancestries): 13.3% German, 12.9% United States or American, 12.1% English, 10.4% Irish, 9.7% Other groups (2000).
Economy: Employment by occupation: 21.2% management, 11.6% professional, 18.5% services, 27.9% sales, 0.0% farming, 12.5% construction, 8.3% production (2000).
Income: Per capita income: $16,746 (2000); Median household income: $36,959 (2000); Poverty rate: 8.8% (2000).
Education: High school graduation rate: 88.5% (2000); College graduation rate: 19.9% (2000).
Housing: Homeownership rate: 77.5% (2000); Median home value: $123,100 (2000); Median rent: $292 per month (2000); Median age of housing: 17 years (2000).
Transportation: Commute to work: 92.3% car, 0.0% public transportation, 1.2% walk, 6.4% work from home (2000); Travel time to work: 28.7% less than 15 minutes, 51.6% 15 to 30 minutes, 10.8% 30 to 45 minutes, 3.2% 45 to 60 minutes, 5.8% 60 minutes or more (2000)

ROCKAWAY BEACH (city). Covers a land area of 0.556 square miles and a water area of 0.084 square miles. Located at 36.70° N. Lat.; 93.16° W. Long. Elevation is 840 feet.
Population: 577 (2000); Race: 94.6% White, 0.5% Black, 0.0% Asian, 1.3% American Indian and Alaska Native, 1.5% Hispanic of any race, 2.7% two or more races (2000); Density: 1,037.1 persons per square mile (2000); Age: 17.8% under 18, 18.3% over 64 (2000); Marriage status: 9.8% never married, 68.5% now married, 8.5% widowed, 13.2% divorced (2000); Foreign born: 2.0% (2000); Ancestry (includes multiple ancestries): 19.8% German, 16.6% Other groups, 15.4% English, 15.2% United States or American, 11.2% Irish (2000).
Economy: Employment by occupation: 12.7% management, 10.6% professional, 30.4% services, 27.6% sales, 1.4% farming, 9.5% construction, 7.8% production (2000).
Income: Per capita income: $17,589 (2000); Median household income: $33,359 (2000); Poverty rate: 8.7% (2000).
Taxes: Total city taxes per capita: $43 (1997); City property taxes per capita: $12 (1997).
Education: High school graduation rate: 76.9% (2000); College graduation rate: 15.0% (2000).
Housing: Homeownership rate: 76.0% (2000); Median home value: $71,900 (2000); Median rent: $344 per month (2000); Median age of housing: 23 years (2000).
Transportation: Commute to work: 91.4% car, 0.0% public transportation, 6.5% walk, 0.7% work from home (2000); Travel time to work: 18.1% less than 15 minutes, 53.6% 15 to 30 minutes, 18.1% 30 to 45 minutes, 4.0% 45 to 60 minutes, 6.2% 60 minutes or more (2000)

RUETER (unincorporated postal area, zip code 65744). Covers a land area of 34.754 square miles and a water area of 0 square miles. Located at 36.61° N. Lat.; 92.89° W. Long. Elevation is 1,313 feet.
Population: 144 (2000); Race: 95.2% White, 0.0% Black, 0.0% Asian, 1.1% American Indian and Alaska Native, 9.5% Hispanic of any race, 3.7% two or more races (2000); Density: 4.1 persons per square mile (2000); Age: 20.1% under 18, 20.1% over 64 (2000); Marriage status: 19.5% never married, 61.0% now married, 8.5% widowed, 11.0% divorced (2000); Foreign born: 0.0% (2000); Ancestry (includes multiple ancestries): 14.8% German, 12.2% United States or American, 11.1% Other groups, 7.9% Scottish, 7.4% Irish (2000).
Economy: Employment by occupation: 15.2% management, 7.6% professional, 29.3% services, 21.7% sales, 2.2% farming, 17.4% construction, 6.5% production (2000).
Income: Per capita income: $10,749 (2000); Median household income: $32,778 (2000); Poverty rate: 22.8% (2000).
Education: High school graduation rate: 57.7% (2000); College graduation rate: 6.3% (2000).

School District(s)

Mark Twain R-VIII (KG-08)
2000 Enrollment: 52 417-785-4323

Housing: Homeownership rate: 95.9% (2000); Median home value: $88,300 (2000); Median rent: $275 per month (2000); Median age of housing: 24 years (2000).
Transportation: Commute to work: 85.1% car, 1.1% public transportation, 0.0% walk, 10.3% work from home (2000); Travel time to work: 11.5% less

than 15 minutes, 10.3% 15 to 30 minutes, 15.4% 30 to 45 minutes, 28.2% 45 to 60 minutes, 34.6% 60 minutes or more (2000)

TABLE ROCK (village). Covers a land area of 0.209 square miles and a water area of 0 square miles. Located at 36.60° N. Lat.; 93.29° W. Long. Elevation is 900 feet.

Population: 229 (2000); Race: 95.6% White, 0.0% Black, 0.0% Asian, 2.2% American Indian and Alaska Native, 3.1% Hispanic of any race, 2.2% two or more races (2000); Density: 1,094.1 persons per square mile (2000); Age: 18.4% under 18, 7.9% over 64 (2000); Marriage status: 18.2% never married, 64.1% now married, 4.0% widowed, 13.6% divorced (2000); Foreign born: 0.0% (2000); Ancestry (includes multiple ancestries): 28.5% German, 15.4% Irish, 14.9% English, 11.0% Other groups, 7.5% United States or American (2000).
Economy: Single-family building permits issued: 2 (2001) / 3 (2000); Multi-family building permits issued: 0 (2001) / 0 (2000); Employment by occupation: 17.8% management, 25.9% professional, 15.6% services, 27.4% sales, 0.7% farming, 5.9% construction, 6.7% production (2000).
Income: Per capita income: $20,846 (2000); Median household income: $40,000 (2000); Poverty rate: 5.7% (2000).
Taxes: Total city taxes per capita: $102 (1997); City property taxes per capita: $30 (1997).
Education: High school graduation rate: 84.8% (2000); College graduation rate: 14.6% (2000).
Housing: Homeownership rate: 72.2% (2000); Median home value: $130,000 (2000); Median rent: $541 per month (2000); Median age of housing: 11 years (2000).
Transportation: Commute to work: 93.3% car, 3.0% public transportation, 3.7% walk, 0.0% work from home (2000); Travel time to work: 35.6% less than 15 minutes, 51.1% 15 to 30 minutes, 3.0% 30 to 45 minutes, 3.0% 45 to 60 minutes, 7.4% 60 minutes or more (2000)

TANEYVILLE (village). Covers a land area of 0.450 square miles and a water area of 0 square miles. Located at 36.74° N. Lat.; 93.03° W. Long. Elevation is 1,075 feet.

Population: 359 (2000); Race: 95.7% White, 0.0% Black, 0.0% Asian, 0.0% American Indian and Alaska Native, 1.6% Hispanic of any race, 4.3% two or more races (2000); Density: 797.8 persons per square mile (2000); Age: 29.7% under 18, 12.6% over 64 (2000); Marriage status: 26.3% never married, 53.3% now married, 5.6% widowed, 14.7% divorced (2000); Foreign born: 0.5% (2000); Ancestry (includes multiple ancestries): 19.8% Other groups, 16.0% German, 15.8% United States or American, 9.6% Irish, 5.6% English (2000).
Economy: Single-family building permits issued: 0 (2001) / 0 (2000); Multi-family building permits issued: 0 (2001) / 0 (2000); Employment by occupation: 6.3% management, 8.2% professional, 31.4% services, 23.3% sales, 0.0% farming, 14.5% construction, 16.4% production (2000).
Income: Per capita income: $10,220 (2000); Median household income: $23,500 (2000); Poverty rate: 17.4% (2000).
Education: High school graduation rate: 63.8% (2000); College graduation rate: 4.5% (2000).

School District(s)

Taneyville R-II (KG-08)
2000 Enrollment: 197 417-546-5803

Housing: Homeownership rate: 70.5% (2000); Median home value: $55,400 (2000); Median rent: $283 per month (2000); Median age of housing: 28 years (2000).
Transportation: Commute to work: 98.8% car, 0.0% public transportation, 0.0% walk, 1.3% work from home (2000); Travel time to work: 12.0% less than 15 minutes, 31.0% 15 to 30 minutes, 28.5% 30 to 45 minutes, 13.9% 45 to 60 minutes, 14.6% 60 minutes or more (2000)

WALNUT SHADE (unincorporated postal area, zip code 65771). Covers a land area of 40.517 square miles and a water area of 0 square miles. Located at 36.77° N. Lat.; 93.21° W. Long. Elevation is 755 feet.

Population: 896 (2000); Race: 95.3% White, 0.0% Black, 0.9% Asian, 0.4% American Indian and Alaska Native, 1.3% Hispanic of any race, 3.2% two or more races (2000); Density: 22.1 persons per square mile (2000); Age: 27.4% under 18, 8.7% over 64 (2000); Marriage status: 20.6% never married, 65.0% now married, 5.5% widowed, 8.9% divorced (2000); Foreign born: 1.1% (2000); Ancestry (includes multiple ancestries): 16.7% German, 15.8% United States or American, 13.6% English, 12.6% Other groups, 7.0% Irish (2000).
Economy: Employment by occupation: 3.5% management, 21.8% professional, 29.7% services, 19.4% sales, 1.1% farming, 13.1% construction, 11.4% production (2000).
Income: Per capita income: $16,416 (2000); Median household income: $31,250 (2000); Poverty rate: 13.0% (2000).
Education: High school graduation rate: 80.4% (2000); College graduation rate: 17.9% (2000).
Housing: Homeownership rate: 78.8% (2000); Median home value: $95,800 (2000); Median rent: $344 per month (2000); Median age of housing: 18 years (2000).
Transportation: Commute to work: 92.1% car, 0.0% public transportation, 5.0% walk, 2.9% work from home (2000); Travel time to work: 12.8% less than 15 minutes, 49.2% 15 to 30 minutes, 28.2% 30 to 45 minutes, 5.1% 45 to 60 minutes, 4.7% 60 minutes or more (2000)

Texas County

Located in south central Missouri, in the Ozarks; includes part of Mark Twain National Forest. Covers a land area of 1,178.50 square miles, a water area of 0.70 square miles, and is located in the Central Time Zone. The county government was organized in 1845. County seat is Houston.

Weather Station: Licking 4 N Elevation: 1,177 feet

	Jan	Feb	Mar	Apr	May	Jun	Jul	Aug	Sep	Oct	Nov	Dec
High	39	46	56	67	75	83	88	87	79	68	55	44
Low	18	23	33	42	52	60	65	63	56	43	34	24
Precip	2.3	2.5	4.0	4.6	4.8	4.6	3.4	3.4	4.4	3.8	4.4	3.4
Snow	5.7	3.7	3.1	0.1	0.0	0.0	0.0	0.0	0.0	tr	0.8	2.4

High and Low temperatures in degrees Fahrenheit; Precipitation and Snow in inches

Weather Station: Summersville Elevation: 1,177 feet

	Jan	Feb	Mar	Apr	May	Jun	Jul	Aug	Sep	Oct	Nov	Dec
High	42	49	59	69	76	84	89	88	80	70	56	46
Low	22	27	35	44	52	61	66	64	56	45	35	27
Precip	2.0	2.2	4.2	4.0	4.9	4.2	3.6	3.4	4.1	3.5	3.8	3.2
Snow	5.2	3.6	2.8	0.1	0.0	0.0	0.0	0.0	0.0	tr	0.8	1.9

High and Low temperatures in degrees Fahrenheit; Precipitation and Snow in inches

Population: 23,003 (2000); Race: 95.9% White, 0.4% Black, 0.2% Asian, 1.0% American Indian and Alaska Native, 1.1% Hispanic of any race, 2.3% two or more races (2000); Density: 19.5 persons per square mile (2000); Age: 24.9% under 18, 17.9% over 64 (2000).
Religion: Five largest groups: 36.2% Southern Baptist Convention, 6.3% Christian Churches and Churches of Christ, 4.5% National Association of Free Will Baptists, 4.1% The United Methodist Church, 3.0% International Pentecostal Holiness Church (200
Economy: Unemployment rate: 6.6% (11/2002); Total civilian labor force: 9,770 (11/2002); Leading industries: 22.6% manufacturing; 19.5% retail trade; 15.5% transportation & warehousing (2000); Companies that employ more than 1,000 persons: 0 (2000); Companies that employ more than 100 persons: 8 (2000); Farms: 1,478 totaling 429,886 acres (1997); Minority business ownership rate: 0.0% (1997); Women business ownership rate: 15.5% (1997); Retail sales per capita: $6,114 (1997). Single-family building permits issued: 18 (2001) / 9 (2000); Multi-family building permits issued: 0 (2001) / 0 (2000).
Income: Per capita income: $13,799 (2000); Median household income: $24,545 (2000); Poverty rate: 21.4% (2000); Bankruptcy rate: 2.91% (2001).
Taxes: Total county taxes per capita: $43 (2000); County property taxes per capita: $13 (2000).
Education: High school graduation rate: 71.4% (2000); College graduation rate: 10.8% (2000).
Housing: Homeownership rate: 76.6% (2000); Median home value: $61,000 (2000); Median rent: $221 per month (2000); Median age of housing: 27 years (2000).
Health: Birth rate: 122.2 per 10,000 population (1998); Age adjusted death rate: 94.5 per 10,000 population (1999); Age adjusted cancer mortality rate: 239.5 deaths per 100,000 population (1999). Number of physicians: 3.5 per 10,000 population (1999); Number of hospital beds: 28.7 per 10,000 population (1999).
Elections: 2000 Presidential election results: 35.1% Gore, 61.8% Bush, 1.4% Nader, 1.3% Buchanan
National and State Parks: Cabool State Wildlife Management Area; Larson State Wildlife Management Area; Pairlee Freeman Barnes State Wildlife Area; Piney River Narrows State Natural Area; Summersville Towersite State Wildlife Area
Additional Information Contacts
Texas County Government Offices 417-967-2112
Cabool Chamber of Commerce 417-962-3002
Houston Chamber of Commerce 417-967-2220

Ozark Trail Board of Realtors 417-967-2001

Texas County Communities

BUCYRUS (unincorporated postal area, zip code 65444). Covers a land area of 89.086 square miles and a water area of 0 square miles. Located at 37.36° N. Lat.; 92.07° W. Long. Elevation is 1,226 feet.
Population: 1,054 (2000); Race: 98.7% White, 0.0% Black, 0.0% Asian, 0.0% American Indian and Alaska Native, 0.7% Hispanic of any race, 0.9% two or more races (2000); Density: 11.8 persons per square mile (2000); Age: 26.9% under 18, 17.6% over 64 (2000); Marriage status: 21.8% never married, 65.5% now married, 5.5% widowed, 7.1% divorced (2000); Foreign born: 1.1% (2000); Ancestry (includes multiple ancestries): 13.6% United States or American, 11.3% English, 9.8% Other groups, 9.2% German, 6.2% Irish (2000).
Economy: Employment by occupation: 13.0% management, 16.4% professional, 16.4% services, 17.8% sales, 5.0% farming, 15.9% construction, 15.6% production (2000).
Income: Per capita income: $17,562 (2000); Median household income: $25,074 (2000); Poverty rate: 33.2% (2000).
Education: High school graduation rate: 73.8% (2000); College graduation rate: 12.5% (2000).
Housing: Homeownership rate: 86.3% (2000); Median home value: $70,000 (2000); Median rent: $238 per month (2000); Median age of housing: 28 years (2000).
Transportation: Commute to work: 85.5% car, 0.0% public transportation, 4.3% walk, 10.2% work from home (2000); Travel time to work: 30.1% less than 15 minutes, 34.6% 15 to 30 minutes, 11.1% 30 to 45 minutes, 14.0% 45 to 60 minutes, 10.3% 60 minutes or more (2000)

CABOOL (city). Covers a land area of 3.714 square miles and a water area of 0.037 square miles. Located at 37.12° N. Lat.; 92.10° W. Long. Elevation is 1,253 feet.
History: Cabool grew around a poultry industry.
Population: 2,168 (2000); Race: 93.8% White, 0.0% Black, 1.2% Asian, 1.3% American Indian and Alaska Native, 1.1% Hispanic of any race, 3.4% two or more races (2000); Density: 583.7 persons per square mile (2000); Age: 27.7% under 18, 23.4% over 64 (2000); Marriage status: 17.0% never married, 53.1% now married, 16.9% widowed, 13.1% divorced (2000); Foreign born: 1.1% (2000); Ancestry (includes multiple ancestries): 13.6% German, 12.3% United States or American, 11.0% Irish, 10.5% Other groups, 10.2% English (2000).
Economy: Single-family building permits issued: 3 (2001) / 5 (2000); Multi-family building permits issued: 0 (2001) / 0 (2000); Employment by occupation: 7.5% management, 17.0% professional, 18.7% services, 23.7% sales, 1.8% farming, 7.0% construction, 24.3% production (2000).
Income: Per capita income: $13,069 (2000); Median household income: $21,887 (2000); Poverty rate: 22.4% (2000).
Taxes: Total city taxes per capita: $290 (1997); City property taxes per capita: $116 (1997).
Education: High school graduation rate: 66.9% (2000); College graduation rate: 12.7% (2000).

School District(s)

Cabool R-IV (PK-12)
2000 Enrollment: 932 417-962-3153
Housing: Homeownership rate: 59.5% (2000); Median home value: $49,400 (2000); Median rent: $207 per month (2000); Median age of housing: 32 years (2000).
Newspapers: Cabool Enterprise (1 x week)
Transportation: Commute to work: 93.7% car, 0.0% public transportation, 2.0% walk, 2.9% work from home (2000); Travel time to work: 55.6% less than 15 minutes, 22.3% 15 to 30 minutes, 9.3% 30 to 45 minutes, 4.6% 45 to 60 minutes, 8.2% 60 minutes or more (2000)
Additional Information Contacts
Cabool Chamber of Commerce 417-962-3002

ELK CREEK (unincorporated postal area, zip code 65464). Covers a land area of 48.578 square miles and a water area of 0 square miles. Located at 37.19° N. Lat.; 91.91° W. Long. Elevation is 830 feet.
Population: 412 (2000); Race: 91.5% White, 0.0% Black, 0.0% Asian, 6.6% American Indian and Alaska Native, 0.0% Hispanic of any race, 2.0% two or more races (2000); Density: 8.5 persons per square mile (2000); Age: 29.7% under 18, 16.6% over 64 (2000); Marriage status: 23.3% never married, 64.8% now married, 6.3% widowed, 5.5% divorced (2000); Foreign born: 0.0% (2000); Ancestry (includes multiple ancestries): 17.7% German, 13.3% Other groups, 13.1% Irish, 12.4% United States or American, 9.0% English (2000).
Economy: Employment by occupation: 14.1% management, 16.2% professional, 15.1% services, 19.5% sales, 5.9% farming, 4.3% construction, 24.9% production (2000).
Income: Per capita income: $10,843 (2000); Median household income: $21,719 (2000); Poverty rate: 25.3% (2000).
Education: High school graduation rate: 70.1% (2000); College graduation rate: 9.7% (2000).
Housing: Homeownership rate: 88.1% (2000); Median home value: $41,000 (2000); Median rent: $175 per month (2000); Median age of housing: 30 years (2000).
Transportation: Commute to work: 85.4% car, 0.0% public transportation, 3.8% walk, 9.2% work from home (2000); Travel time to work: 20.8% less than 15 minutes, 33.3% 15 to 30 minutes, 25.6% 30 to 45 minutes, 8.9% 45 to 60 minutes, 11.3% 60 minutes or more (2000)

EUNICE (unincorporated postal area, zip code 65468). Covers a land area of 6.498 square miles and a water area of 0 square miles. Located at 37.26° N. Lat.; 91.79° W. Long. Elevation is 1,353 feet.
Population: 35 (2000); Race: 95.0% White, 0.0% Black, 0.0% Asian, 5.0% American Indian and Alaska Native, 0.0% Hispanic of any race, 0.0% two or more races (2000); Density: 5.4 persons per square mile (2000); Age: 10.0% under 18, 15.0% over 64 (2000); Marriage status: 13.9% never married, 61.1% now married, 5.6% widowed, 19.4% divorced (2000); Foreign born: 0.0% (2000); Ancestry (includes multiple ancestries): 27.5% Other groups, 22.5% German, 20.0% Dutch, 5.0% Swedish, 5.0% English (2000).
Economy: Employment by occupation: 0.0% management, 21.1% professional, 0.0% services, 21.1% sales, 0.0% farming, 10.5% construction, 47.4% production (2000).
Income: Per capita income: $15,498 (2000); Median household income: $33,125 (2000); Poverty rate: 5.0% (2000).
Education: High school graduation rate: 80.6% (2000); College graduation rate: 6.5% (2000).
Housing: Homeownership rate: 84.2% (2000); Median home value: $55,000 (2000); Median age of housing: 32 years (2000).
Transportation: Commute to work: 89.5% car, 0.0% public transportation, 0.0% walk, 10.5% work from home (2000); Travel time to work: 11.8% less than 15 minutes, 52.9% 15 to 30 minutes, 0.0% 30 to 45 minutes, 23.5% 45 to 60 minutes, 11.8% 60 minutes or more (2000)

HARTSHORN (unincorporated postal area, zip code 65479). Covers a land area of 64.051 square miles and a water area of 0 square miles. Located at 37.35° N. Lat.; 91.63° W. Long. Elevation is 1,310 feet.
Population: 342 (2000); Race: 99.1% White, 0.3% Black, 0.0% Asian, 0.0% American Indian and Alaska Native, 0.0% Hispanic of any race, 0.6% two or more races (2000); Density: 5.3 persons per square mile (2000); Age: 25.4% under 18, 16.4% over 64 (2000); Marriage status: 15.2% never married, 64.9% now married, 8.3% widowed, 11.6% divorced (2000); Foreign born: 0.0% (2000); Ancestry (includes multiple ancestries): 21.1% United States or American, 12.6% Irish, 12.0% Other groups, 8.5% German, 5.6% French (except Basque) (2000).
Economy: Employment by occupation: 4.0% management, 8.9% professional, 23.4% services, 6.5% sales, 11.3% farming, 11.3% construction, 34.7% production (2000).
Income: Per capita income: $9,320 (2000); Median household income: $17,639 (2000); Poverty rate: 31.6% (2000).
Education: High school graduation rate: 54.1% (2000); College graduation rate: 5.2% (2000).
Housing: Homeownership rate: 95.9% (2000); Median home value: $25,000 (2000); Median rent: $175 per month (2000); Median age of housing: 27 years (2000).
Transportation: Commute to work: 86.3% car, 0.0% public transportation, 0.8% walk, 12.9% work from home (2000); Travel time to work: 17.6% less than 15 minutes, 17.6% 15 to 30 minutes, 35.2% 30 to 45 minutes, 13.0% 45 to 60 minutes, 16.7% 60 minutes or more (2000)

HOUSTON (city). Covers a land area of 3.558 square miles and a water area of 0 square miles. Located at 37.32° N. Lat.; 91.96° W. Long. Elevation is 1,162 feet.
History: Houston was platted in 1846 to serve as the seat of Houston County, both named for General Samuel Houston, president of the Texas Republic. Civil War battles destroyed the town and dispersed the population. After reconstruction, Houston was incorporated in 1872.
Population: 1,992 (2000); Race: 95.5% White, 0.7% Black, 0.4% Asian, 1.0% American Indian and Alaska Native, 1.8% Hispanic of any race, 2.1%

two or more races (2000); Density: 559.8 persons per square mile (2000); Age: 20.6% under 18, 25.7% over 64 (2000); Marriage status: 17.3% never married, 55.5% now married, 14.2% widowed, 13.0% divorced (2000); Foreign born: 0.6% (2000); Ancestry (includes multiple ancestries): 13.1% United States or American, 11.9% Other groups, 10.6% German, 9.0% Irish, 8.0% English (2000).
Economy: Single-family building permits issued: 15 (2001) / 4 (2000); Multi-family building permits issued: 0 (2001) / 0 (2000); Employment by occupation: 12.7% management, 19.4% professional, 16.5% services, 25.2% sales, 1.1% farming, 9.7% construction, 15.4% production (2000).
Income: Per capita income: $14,977 (2000); Median household income: $20,886 (2000); Poverty rate: 26.2% (2000).
Taxes: Total city taxes per capita: $136 (1997); City property taxes per capita: $13 (1997).
Education: High school graduation rate: 70.4% (2000); College graduation rate: 12.3% (2000).

School District(s)

Houston R-I (PK-12)
2000 Enrollment: 1,123 417-967-3024
Housing: Homeownership rate: 60.8% (2000); Median home value: $65,200 (2000); Median rent: $220 per month (2000); Median age of housing: 36 years (2000).
Hospitals: Texas County Memorial Hospital (66 beds)
Newspapers: Houston Herald (1 x week)
Transportation: Commute to work: 86.8% car, 3.5% public transportation, 3.4% walk, 4.5% work from home (2000); Travel time to work: 68.7% less than 15 minutes, 14.0% 15 to 30 minutes, 5.9% 30 to 45 minutes, 4.7% 45 to 60 minutes, 6.7% 60 minutes or more (2000)
Additional Information Contacts
Houston Chamber of Commerce 417-967-2220
Ozark Trail Board of Realtors 417-967-2001

HUGGINS (unincorporated postal area, zip code 65484). Covers a land area of 27.495 square miles and a water area of 0 square miles. Located at 37.36° N. Lat.; 92.20° W. Long. Elevation is 1,492 feet.
Population: 182 (2000); Race: 100.0% White, 0.0% Black, 0.0% Asian, 0.0% American Indian and Alaska Native, 0.0% Hispanic of any race, 0.0% two or more races (2000); Density: 6.6 persons per square mile (2000); Age: 19.9% under 18, 23.7% over 64 (2000); Marriage status: 13.6% never married, 60.8% now married, 9.6% widowed, 16.0% divorced (2000); Foreign born: 0.0% (2000); Ancestry (includes multiple ancestries): 26.3% Irish, 19.2% German, 14.1% Other groups, 8.3% English, 3.2% Scottish (2000).
Economy: Employment by occupation: 41.2% management, 0.0% professional, 5.9% services, 2.9% sales, 11.8% farming, 20.6% construction, 17.6% production (2000).
Income: Per capita income: $16,376 (2000); Median household income: $28,750 (2000); Poverty rate: 24.4% (2000).
Education: High school graduation rate: 68.5% (2000); College graduation rate: 1.6% (2000).
Housing: Homeownership rate: 78.5% (2000); Median age of housing: 35 years (2000).
Transportation: Commute to work: 32.4% car, 0.0% public transportation, 20.6% walk, 47.1% work from home (2000); Travel time to work: 66.7% less than 15 minutes, 11.1% 15 to 30 minutes, 16.7% 30 to 45 minutes, 5.6% 45 to 60 minutes, 0.0% 60 minutes or more (2000)

LICKING (city). Covers a land area of 1.735 square miles and a water area of 0.010 square miles. Located at 37.49° N. Lat.; 91.85° W. Long. Elevation is 1,259 feet.
History: Licking was settled by John Baldridge and Barney Low, who built cabins near a buffalo lick about 1826. The town was surveyed in 1878 and named for the lick.
Population: 1,471 (2000); Race: 98.2% White, 0.0% Black, 0.0% Asian, 0.3% American Indian and Alaska Native, 3.1% Hispanic of any race, 1.2% two or more races (2000); Density: 847.8 persons per square mile (2000); Age: 23.1% under 18, 24.5% over 64 (2000); Marriage status: 17.8% never married, 54.0% now married, 15.1% widowed, 13.1% divorced (2000); Foreign born: 0.5% (2000); Ancestry (includes multiple ancestries): 18.6% United States or American, 14.8% Other groups, 12.9% German, 12.8% Irish, 7.0% English (2000).
Economy: Employment by occupation: 9.6% management, 14.5% professional, 21.2% services, 21.8% sales, 1.5% farming, 9.1% construction, 22.4% production (2000).
Income: Per capita income: $12,802 (2000); Median household income: $17,576 (2000); Poverty rate: 25.5% (2000).
Taxes: Total city taxes per capita: $256 (1997); City property taxes per capita: $138 (1997).
Education: High school graduation rate: 67.3% (2000); College graduation rate: 8.7% (2000).

School District(s)

Licking R-VIII (KG-12)
2000 Enrollment: 856 573-674-2911
Housing: Homeownership rate: 57.5% (2000); Median home value: $55,700 (2000); Median rent: $231 per month (2000); Median age of housing: 29 years (2000).
Newspapers: Licking News (1 x week)
Transportation: Commute to work: 93.8% car, 0.0% public transportation, 3.7% walk, 2.1% work from home (2000); Travel time to work: 62.6% less than 15 minutes, 13.1% 15 to 30 minutes, 10.5% 30 to 45 minutes, 6.1% 45 to 60 minutes, 7.7% 60 minutes or more (2000)

PLATO (unincorporated postal area, zip code 65552). Covers a land area of 128.131 square miles and a water area of 0.127 square miles. Located at 37.54° N. Lat.; 92.17° W. Long. Elevation is 1,120 feet.
Population: 1,430 (2000); Race: 92.5% White, 3.2% Black, 0.0% Asian, 0.0% American Indian and Alaska Native, 1.6% Hispanic of any race, 4.3% two or more races (2000); Density: 11.2 persons per square mile (2000); Age: 24.5% under 18, 14.7% over 64 (2000); Marriage status: 16.5% never married, 68.3% now married, 7.6% widowed, 7.6% divorced (2000); Foreign born: 2.8% (2000); Ancestry (includes multiple ancestries): 17.1% German, 16.2% United States or American, 13.5% Other groups, 12.9% Irish, 12.5% English (2000).
Economy: Employment by occupation: 12.4% management, 9.3% professional, 19.2% services, 29.5% sales, 4.2% farming, 10.4% construction, 14.8% production (2000).
Income: Per capita income: $15,023 (2000); Median household income: $30,125 (2000); Poverty rate: 13.6% (2000).
Education: High school graduation rate: 82.4% (2000); College graduation rate: 9.8% (2000).

School District(s)

Plato R-V (PK-12)
2000 Enrollment: 563 417-458-3333
Housing: Homeownership rate: 82.6% (2000); Median home value: $80,100 (2000); Median rent: $231 per month (2000); Median age of housing: 23 years (2000).
Transportation: Commute to work: 92.6% car, 0.0% public transportation, 0.3% walk, 6.4% work from home (2000); Travel time to work: 6.4% less than 15 minutes, 35.1% 15 to 30 minutes, 35.8% 30 to 45 minutes, 8.1% 45 to 60 minutes, 14.5% 60 minutes or more (2000)

RAYMONDVILLE (town). Covers a land area of 2.947 square miles and a water area of 0 square miles. Located at 37.33° N. Lat.; 91.83° W. Long. Elevation is 1,320 feet.
Population: 442 (2000); Race: 96.3% White, 0.0% Black, 0.0% Asian, 0.0% American Indian and Alaska Native, 0.7% Hispanic of any race, 3.7% two or more races (2000); Density: 150.0 persons per square mile (2000); Age: 28.1% under 18, 15.3% over 64 (2000); Marriage status: 26.5% never married, 50.0% now married, 10.3% widowed, 13.2% divorced (2000); Foreign born: 0.0% (2000); Ancestry (includes multiple ancestries): 39.1% United States or American, 10.2% Other groups, 7.7% Irish, 7.0% English, 6.0% German (2000).
Economy: Single-family building permits issued: 0 (2001) / 0 (2000); Multi-family building permits issued: 0 (2001) / 0 (2000); Employment by occupation: 1.4% management, 9.4% professional, 25.9% services, 15.1% sales, 1.4% farming, 5.8% construction, 41.0% production (2000).
Income: Per capita income: $10,500 (2000); Median household income: $16,806 (2000); Poverty rate: 30.2% (2000).
Taxes: Total city taxes per capita: $12 (1997); City property taxes per capita: $12 (1997).
Education: High school graduation rate: 47.4% (2000); College graduation rate: 4.7% (2000).

School District(s)

Raymondville R-VII (KG-08)
2000 Enrollment: 133 417-457-6237
Housing: Homeownership rate: 78.4% (2000); Median home value: $45,500 (2000); Median rent: $242 per month (2000); Median age of housing: 28 years (2000).
Transportation: Commute to work: 90.4% car, 0.0% public transportation, 0.0% walk, 5.1% work from home (2000); Travel time to work: 28.7% less than 15 minutes, 49.6% 15 to 30 minutes, 10.1% 30 to 45 minutes, 0.8% 45 to 60 minutes, 10.9% 60 minutes or more (2000)

ROBY (unincorporated postal area, zip code 65557). Covers a land area of 6.727 square miles and a water area of 0.008 square miles. Located at 37.50° N. Lat.; 92.09° W. Long. Elevation is 1,395 feet.

Population: 166 (2000); Race: 88.7% White, 0.0% Black, 3.0% Asian, 0.0% American Indian and Alaska Native, 8.3% Hispanic of any race, 0.0% two or more races (2000); Density: 24.7 persons per square mile (2000); Age: 17.3% under 18, 25.6% over 64 (2000); Marriage status: 11.3% never married, 65.2% now married, 17.0% widowed, 6.4% divorced (2000); Foreign born: 3.0% (2000); Ancestry (includes multiple ancestries): 34.5% United States or American, 25.6% Other groups, 10.1% Scotch-Irish, 7.1% German, 5.4% English (2000).

Economy: Employment by occupation: 0.0% management, 10.2% professional, 24.5% services, 30.6% sales, 6.1% farming, 12.2% construction, 16.3% production (2000).

Income: Per capita income: $15,636 (2000); Median household income: $21,964 (2000); Poverty rate: 8.3% (2000).

Education: High school graduation rate: 72.3% (2000); College graduation rate: 9.2% (2000).

Housing: Homeownership rate: 82.4% (2000); Median home value: $60,600 (2000); Median rent: $410 per month (2000); Median age of housing: 25 years (2000).

Transportation: Commute to work: 90.0% car, 0.0% public transportation, 4.0% walk, 6.0% work from home (2000); Travel time to work: 8.5% less than 15 minutes, 36.2% 15 to 30 minutes, 25.5% 30 to 45 minutes, 14.9% 45 to 60 minutes, 14.9% 60 minutes or more (2000)

SOLO (unincorporated postal area, zip code 65564). Covers a land area of 15.238 square miles and a water area of 0 square miles. Located at 37.24° N. Lat.; 91.97° W. Long. Elevation is 1,220 feet.

Population: 175 (2000); Race: 100.0% White, 0.0% Black, 0.0% Asian, 0.0% American Indian and Alaska Native, 0.0% Hispanic of any race, 0.0% two or more races (2000); Density: 11.5 persons per square mile (2000); Age: 23.2% under 18, 7.7% over 64 (2000); Marriage status: 3.9% never married, 78.3% now married, 5.4% widowed, 12.4% divorced (2000); Foreign born: 0.0% (2000); Ancestry (includes multiple ancestries): 23.8% German, 19.0% Irish, 11.3% United States or American, 11.3% French Canadian, 8.3% Scottish (2000).

Economy: Employment by occupation: 48.0% management, 9.3% professional, 6.7% services, 4.0% sales, 0.0% farming, 16.0% construction, 16.0% production (2000).

Income: Per capita income: $27,108 (2000); Median household income: $48,500 (2000); Poverty rate: 6.5% (2000).

Education: High school graduation rate: 92.0% (2000); College graduation rate: 20.0% (2000).

Housing: Homeownership rate: 85.7% (2000); Median home value: $22,500 (2000); Median rent: $250 per month (2000); Median age of housing: 29 years (2000).

Transportation: Commute to work: 73.3% car, 0.0% public transportation, 14.7% walk, 12.0% work from home (2000); Travel time to work: 30.3% less than 15 minutes, 34.8% 15 to 30 minutes, 19.7% 30 to 45 minutes, 7.6% 45 to 60 minutes, 7.6% 60 minutes or more (2000)

SUCCESS (unincorporated postal area, zip code 65570). Covers a land area of 34.279 square miles and a water area of 0 square miles. Located at 37.46° N. Lat.; 92.09° W. Long. Elevation is 1,404 feet.

Population: 525 (2000); Race: 98.2% White, 0.0% Black, 0.0% Asian, 0.0% American Indian and Alaska Native, 0.0% Hispanic of any race, 1.8% two or more races (2000); Density: 15.3 persons per square mile (2000); Age: 22.8% under 18, 13.8% over 64 (2000); Marriage status: 14.5% never married, 69.7% now married, 7.6% widowed, 8.2% divorced (2000); Foreign born: 0.5% (2000); Ancestry (includes multiple ancestries): 21.0% United States or American, 12.6% German, 11.0% Other groups, 9.8% Irish, 8.1% English (2000).

Economy: Employment by occupation: 10.7% management, 13.2% professional, 5.3% services, 18.5% sales, 8.6% farming, 11.9% construction, 31.7% production (2000).

Income: Per capita income: $14,766 (2000); Median household income: $26,250 (2000); Poverty rate: 12.1% (2000).

Education: High school graduation rate: 67.2% (2000); College graduation rate: 12.4% (2000).

School District(s)

Success R-VI (PK-08)
2000 Enrollment: 118 417-967-2597

Housing: Homeownership rate: 85.5% (2000); Median home value: $55,000 (2000); Median rent: $231 per month (2000); Median age of housing: 27 years (2000).

Transportation: Commute to work: 96.3% car, 0.0% public transportation, 1.3% walk, 2.5% work from home (2000); Travel time to work: 15.4% less than 15 minutes, 31.2% 15 to 30 minutes, 34.6% 30 to 45 minutes, 9.0% 45 to 60 minutes, 9.8% 60 minutes or more (2000)

SUMMERSVILLE (city). Covers a land area of 1.113 square miles and a water area of 0 square miles. Located at 37.17° N. Lat.; 91.65° W. Long. Elevation is 1,235 feet.

Population: 544 (2000); Race: 94.9% White, 1.4% Black, 0.0% Asian, 1.7% American Indian and Alaska Native, 0.9% Hispanic of any race, 1.9% two or more races (2000); Density: 489.0 persons per square mile (2000); Age: 30.6% under 18, 26.2% over 64 (2000); Marriage status: 17.0% never married, 60.2% now married, 14.7% widowed, 8.1% divorced (2000); Foreign born: 0.3% (2000); Ancestry (includes multiple ancestries): 15.6% United States or American, 10.7% German, 8.2% Irish, 6.8% Other groups, 4.2% English (2000).

Economy: Employment by occupation: 7.4% management, 14.4% professional, 18.1% services, 20.7% sales, 4.3% farming, 10.6% construction, 24.5% production (2000).

Income: Per capita income: $10,163 (2000); Median household income: $18,359 (2000); Poverty rate: 32.2% (2000).

Taxes: Total city taxes per capita: $28 (1997); City property taxes per capita: $28 (1997).

Education: High school graduation rate: 60.6% (2000); College graduation rate: 10.3% (2000).

School District(s)

Summersville R-II (PK-12)
2000 Enrollment: 588 417-932-4045

Housing: Homeownership rate: 63.0% (2000); Median home value: $42,500 (2000); Median rent: $154 per month (2000); Median age of housing: 28 years (2000).

Transportation: Commute to work: 94.1% car, 0.0% public transportation, 2.2% walk, 1.6% work from home (2000); Travel time to work: 42.1% less than 15 minutes, 23.5% 15 to 30 minutes, 21.3% 30 to 45 minutes, 8.2% 45 to 60 minutes, 4.9% 60 minutes or more (2000)

YUKON (unincorporated postal area, zip code 65589). Covers a land area of 15.418 square miles and a water area of 0 square miles. Located at 37.24° N. Lat.; 91.83° W. Long. Elevation is 1,316 feet.

Population: 272 (2000); Race: 94.9% White, 0.0% Black, 0.0% Asian, 0.0% American Indian and Alaska Native, 0.0% Hispanic of any race, 5.1% two or more races (2000); Density: 17.6 persons per square mile (2000); Age: 30.1% under 18, 8.3% over 64 (2000); Marriage status: 20.8% never married, 67.4% now married, 3.2% widowed, 8.6% divorced (2000); Foreign born: 0.7% (2000); Ancestry (includes multiple ancestries): 17.0% United States or American, 13.8% German, 12.7% Irish, 11.2% Other groups, 5.8% English (2000).

Economy: Employment by occupation: 9.8% management, 22.0% professional, 20.3% services, 13.8% sales, 8.1% farming, 8.9% construction, 17.1% production (2000).

Income: Per capita income: $11,953 (2000); Median household income: $32,188 (2000); Poverty rate: 20.3% (2000).

Education: High school graduation rate: 78.0% (2000); College graduation rate: 11.3% (2000).

Housing: Homeownership rate: 95.7% (2000); Median home value: $48,800 (2000); Median rent: $225 per month (2000); Median age of housing: 28 years (2000).

Transportation: Commute to work: 85.0% car, 0.0% public transportation, 0.0% walk, 15.0% work from home (2000); Travel time to work: 8.8% less than 15 minutes, 70.6% 15 to 30 minutes, 12.7% 30 to 45 minutes, 0.0% 45 to 60 minutes, 7.8% 60 minutes or more (2000)

Vernon County

Located in western Missouri; bounded partly on the north by the Osage River, and on the west by Kansas; drained by the Little Osage and Marmaton Rivers. Covers a land area of 834.00 square miles, a water area of 3.10 square miles, and is located in the Central Time Zone. The county government was organized in 1851. County seat is Nevada.

Weather Station: Nevada Water Plant Elevation: 816 feet

	Jan	Feb	Mar	Apr	May	Jun	Jul	Aug	Sep	Oct	Nov	Dec
High	41	48	59	69	77	86	91	90	82	71	57	46
Low	20	25	35	44	54	63	67	65	57	45	35	25
Precip	1.7	1.9	3.6	4.5	5.3	5.6	3.9	4.1	4.4	4.2	3.5	2.4
Snow	4.9	3.2	2.0	tr	0.0	0.0	0.0	0.0	0.0	tr	0.8	2.5

High and Low temperatures in degrees Fahrenheit; Precipitation and Snow in inches

Population: 20,454 (2000); Race: 97.3% White, 0.4% Black, 0.4% Asian, 0.6% American Indian and Alaska Native, 0.8% Hispanic of any race, 1.0% two or more races (2000); Density: 24.5 persons per square mile (2000); Age: 26.6% under 18, 16.3% over 64 (2000).
Religion: Five largest groups: 22.4% Southern Baptist Convention, 6.2% Christian Churches and Churches of Christ, 5.8% The United Methodist Church, 3.7% Catholic Church, 1.5% Church of the Nazarene (2000).
Economy: Unemployment rate: 4.4% (11/2002); Total civilian labor force: 8,588 (11/2002); Leading industries: 24.6% manufacturing; 19.0% health care and social assistance; 17.2% retail trade (2000); Companies that employ more than 1,000 persons: 0 (2000); Companies that employ more than 100 persons: 10 (2000); Farms: 1,265 totaling 388,549 acres (1997); Minority business ownership rate: 0.0% (1997); Women business ownership rate: 15.8% (1997); Retail sales per capita: $7,454 (1997). Single-family building permits issued: 16 (2001) / 15 (2000); Multi-family building permits issued: 0 (2001) / 0 (2000).
Income: Per capita income: $15,047 (2000); Median household income: $30,021 (2000); Poverty rate: 14.9% (2000); Bankruptcy rate: 3.90% (2001).
Taxes: Total county taxes per capita: $53 (2000); County property taxes per capita: $16 (2000).
Education: High school graduation rate: 76.6% (2000); College graduation rate: 14.2% (2000).
Housing: Homeownership rate: 72.3% (2000); Median home value: $58,500 (2000); Median rent: $258 per month (2000); Median age of housing: 33 years (2000).
Health: Birth rate: 132.0 per 10,000 population (1998); Age adjusted death rate: 103.0 per 10,000 population (1999); Age adjusted cancer mortality rate: 223.9 deaths per 100,000 population (1999). Number of physicians: 10.8 per 10,000 population (1999); Number of hospital beds: 56.2 per 10,000 population (1999).
Elections: 2000 Presidential election results: 37.5% Gore, 59.3% Bush, 1.9% Nader, 0.6% Buchanan

Additional Information Contacts

Vernon County Government Offices 417-448-2500
Five County Board of Realtors.................... 417-667-3311
Nevada Chamber of Commerce.................... 417-667-5300

Vernon County Communities

BRONAUGH (city). Covers a land area of 0.284 square miles and a water area of <.001 square miles. Located at 37.69° N. Lat.; 94.46° W. Long. Elevation is 885 feet.
Population: 245 (2000); Race: 95.6% White, 0.0% Black, 2.0% Asian, 0.0% American Indian and Alaska Native, 0.4% Hispanic of any race, 2.4% two or more races (2000); Density: 863.1 persons per square mile (2000); Age: 30.0% under 18, 13.2% over 64 (2000); Marriage status: 14.5% never married, 68.8% now married, 7.5% widowed, 9.1% divorced (2000); Foreign born: 2.8% (2000); Ancestry (includes multiple ancestries): 19.6% United States or American, 16.0% German, 7.2% Other groups, 6.4% English, 5.6% Irish (2000).
Economy: Agriculture: sorgum, wheat; cattle. Coal in area. Employment by occupation: 10.4% management, 15.2% professional, 15.2% services, 21.6% sales, 4.0% farming, 16.8% construction, 16.8% production (2000).
Income: Per capita income: $13,073 (2000); Median household income: $26,786 (2000); Poverty rate: 7.2% (2000).
Taxes: Total city taxes per capita: $14 (1997); City property taxes per capita: $14 (1997).
Education: High school graduation rate: 89.4% (2000); College graduation rate: 11.3% (2000).

School District(s)

Bronaugh R-VII (PK-12)
2000 Enrollment: 261 417-922-3211

Housing: Homeownership rate: 76.3% (2000); Median home value: $38,900 (2000); Median rent: $223 per month (2000); Median age of housing: 34 years (2000).
Transportation: Commute to work: 97.6% car, 0.0% public transportation, 1.6% walk, 0.8% work from home (2000); Travel time to work: 12.1% less than 15 minutes, 58.9% 15 to 30 minutes, 25.0% 30 to 45 minutes, 3.2% 45 to 60 minutes, 0.8% 60 minutes or more (2000)

DEERFIELD (village). Covers a land area of 0.103 square miles and a water area of 0 square miles. Located at 37.83° N. Lat.; 94.50° W. Long. Elevation is 785 feet.
History: Deerfield was settled by Abram Redfield, who established the Deerfield Pottery here in 1871. Later the town became dependent on the asphalt mines.
Population: 75 (2000); Race: 100.0% White, 0.0% Black, 0.0% Asian, 0.0% American Indian and Alaska Native, 2.3% Hispanic of any race, 0.0% two or more races (2000); Density: 727.6 persons per square mile (2000); Age: 23.3% under 18, 16.3% over 64 (2000); Marriage status: 16.2% never married, 75.0% now married, 2.9% widowed, 5.9% divorced (2000); Foreign born: 0.0% (2000); Ancestry (includes multiple ancestries): 22.1% German, 15.1% English, 14.0% Irish, 4.7% French (except Basque), 4.7% Other groups (2000).
Economy: Employment by occupation: 7.3% management, 7.3% professional, 17.1% services, 22.0% sales, 9.8% farming, 9.8% construction, 26.8% production (2000).
Income: Per capita income: $11,065 (2000); Median household income: $26,667 (2000); Poverty rate: 9.3% (2000).
Taxes: Total city taxes per capita: $45 (1997); City property taxes per capita: $11 (1997).
Education: High school graduation rate: 63.0% (2000); College graduation rate: 3.7% (2000).
Housing: Homeownership rate: 74.3% (2000); Median home value: $46,000 (2000); Median rent: $238 per month (2000); Median age of housing: 48 years (2000).
Transportation: Commute to work: 100.0% car, 0.0% public transportation, 0.0% walk, 0.0% work from home (2000); Travel time to work: 14.6% less than 15 minutes, 70.7% 15 to 30 minutes, 0.0% 30 to 45 minutes, 0.0% 45 to 60 minutes, 14.6% 60 minutes or more (2000)

HARWOOD (village). Covers a land area of 0.103 square miles and a water area of 0 square miles. Located at 37.95° N. Lat.; 94.15° W. Long. Elevation is 840 feet.
Population: 90 (2000); Race: 95.8% White, 0.0% Black, 1.1% Asian, 0.0% American Indian and Alaska Native, 2.1% Hispanic of any race, 0.0% two or more races (2000); Density: 874.4 persons per square mile (2000); Age: 23.2% under 18, 23.2% over 64 (2000); Marriage status: 26.0% never married, 42.9% now married, 14.3% widowed, 16.9% divorced (2000); Foreign born: 7.4% (2000); Ancestry (includes multiple ancestries): 29.5% United States or American, 20.0% Irish, 15.8% German, 8.4% Other groups, 6.3% English (2000).
Economy: Hay, sorghum; cattle. Employment by occupation: 0.0% management, 9.1% professional, 25.0% services, 15.9% sales, 0.0% farming, 9.1% construction, 40.9% production (2000).
Income: Per capita income: $11,028 (2000); Median household income: $21,250 (2000); Poverty rate: 15.8% (2000).
Taxes: Total city taxes per capita: $11 (1997); City property taxes per capita: $11 (1997).
Education: High school graduation rate: 75.4% (2000); College graduation rate: 10.8% (2000).
Housing: Homeownership rate: 95.0% (2000); Median home value: $14,500 (2000); Median rent: $225 per month (2000); Median age of housing: 60+ years (2000).
Transportation: Commute to work: 90.9% car, 0.0% public transportation, 0.0% walk, 9.1% work from home (2000); Travel time to work: 10.0% less than 15 minutes, 27.5% 15 to 30 minutes, 37.5% 30 to 45 minutes, 20.0% 45 to 60 minutes, 5.0% 60 minutes or more (2000)

HORTON (unincorporated postal area, zip code 64751). Covers a land area of 49.617 square miles and a water area of 0.441 square miles. Located at 37.94° N. Lat.; 94.42° W. Long. Elevation is 766 feet.
Population: 265 (2000); Race: 96.8% White, 0.0% Black, 0.0% Asian, 3.2% American Indian and Alaska Native, 0.0% Hispanic of any race, 0.0% two or more races (2000); Density: 5.3 persons per square mile (2000); Age: 29.2% under 18, 39.4% over 64 (2000); Marriage status: 8.6% never married, 68.1% now married, 18.4% widowed, 4.9% divorced (2000); Foreign born: 0.0% (2000); Ancestry (includes multiple ancestries): 20.8% German, 13.4% Other groups, 11.6% United States or American, 10.2% English, 7.4% Swedish (2000).
Economy: Employment by occupation: 21.0% management, 35.5% professional, 16.1% services, 8.1% sales, 0.0% farming, 19.4% construction, 0.0% production (2000).

Income: Per capita income: $12,299 (2000); Median household income: $21,375 (2000); Poverty rate: 8.3% (2000).
Education: High school graduation rate: 74.5% (2000); College graduation rate: 18.3% (2000).
Housing: Homeownership rate: 93.4% (2000); Median home value: $64,000 (2000); Median age of housing: 44 years (2000).
Transportation: Commute to work: 85.5% car, 0.0% public transportation, 0.0% walk, 8.1% work from home (2000); Travel time to work: 15.8% less than 15 minutes, 57.9% 15 to 30 minutes, 19.3% 30 to 45 minutes, 0.0% 45 to 60 minutes, 7.0% 60 minutes or more (2000)

METZ (town). Covers a land area of 0.122 square miles and a water area of 0 square miles. Located at 37.99° N. Lat.; 94.44° W. Long. Elevation is 788 feet.
Population: 67 (2000); Race: 96.4% White, 0.0% Black, 0.0% Asian, 0.0% American Indian and Alaska Native, 0.0% Hispanic of any race, 3.6% two or more races (2000); Density: 548.9 persons per square mile (2000); Age: 16.4% under 18, 43.6% over 64 (2000); Marriage status: 14.0% never married, 40.0% now married, 30.0% widowed, 16.0% divorced (2000); Foreign born: 0.0% (2000); Ancestry (includes multiple ancestries): 12.7% United States or American, 10.9% Other groups, 10.9% Irish, 9.1% German, 5.5% Norwegian (2000).
Economy: Sorghum, hay; cattle. Employment by occupation: 0.0% management, 0.0% professional, 16.7% services, 16.7% sales, 0.0% farming, 16.7% construction, 50.0% production (2000).
Income: Per capita income: $6,940 (2000); Median household income: $9,063 (2000); Poverty rate: 41.8% (2000).
Taxes: Total city taxes per capita: $11 (1997); City property taxes per capita: $11 (1997).
Education: High school graduation rate: 55.8% (2000); College graduation rate: 0.0% (2000).
Housing: Homeownership rate: 78.6% (2000); Median home value: <$10,000 (2000); Median rent: $275 per month (2000); Median age of housing: 60+ years (2000).
Transportation: Commute to work: 100.0% car, 0.0% public transportation, 0.0% walk, 0.0% work from home (2000); Travel time to work: 50.0% less than 15 minutes, 25.0% 15 to 30 minutes, 25.0% 30 to 45 minutes, 0.0% 45 to 60 minutes, 0.0% 60 minutes or more (2000)

MILO (village). Covers a land area of 0.077 square miles and a water area of 0 square miles. Located at 37.75° N. Lat.; 94.30° W. Long. Elevation is 878 feet.
Population: 84 (2000); Race: 100.0% White, 0.0% Black, 0.0% Asian, 0.0% American Indian and Alaska Native, 0.0% Hispanic of any race, 0.0% two or more races (2000); Density: 1,094.3 persons per square mile (2000); Age: 26.9% under 18, 12.8% over 64 (2000); Marriage status: 15.9% never married, 58.7% now married, 14.3% widowed, 11.1% divorced (2000); Foreign born: 0.0% (2000); Ancestry (includes multiple ancestries): 19.2% English, 11.5% United States or American, 10.3% Irish, 6.4% Other groups, 5.1% German (2000).
Economy: Employment by occupation: 9.1% management, 24.2% professional, 6.1% services, 36.4% sales, 6.1% farming, 0.0% construction, 18.2% production (2000).
Income: Per capita income: $11,887 (2000); Median household income: $23,125 (2000); Poverty rate: 15.4% (2000).
Taxes: Total city taxes per capita: $8,150 (1997); City property taxes per capita: $0 (1997).
Education: High school graduation rate: 67.3% (2000); College graduation rate: 6.1% (2000).
Housing: Homeownership rate: 90.3% (2000); Median home value: $28,400 (2000); Median age of housing: 59 years (2000).
Transportation: Commute to work: 100.0% car, 0.0% public transportation, 0.0% walk, 0.0% work from home (2000); Travel time to work: 6.1% less than 15 minutes, 57.6% 15 to 30 minutes, 12.1% 30 to 45 minutes, 9.1% 45 to 60 minutes, 15.2% 60 minutes or more (2000)

MOUNDVILLE (town). Covers a land area of 0.166 square miles and a water area of 0 square miles. Located at 37.76° N. Lat.; 94.45° W. Long. Elevation is 863 feet.
Population: 103 (2000); Race: 97.9% White, 0.0% Black, 0.0% Asian, 2.1% American Indian and Alaska Native, 0.0% Hispanic of any race, 0.0% two or more races (2000); Density: 620.6 persons per square mile (2000); Age: 14.4% under 18, 28.9% over 64 (2000); Marriage status: 4.7% never married, 75.3% now married, 9.4% widowed, 10.6% divorced (2000); Foreign born: 2.1% (2000); Ancestry (includes multiple ancestries): 19.6% United States or American, 17.5% German, 13.4% Other groups, 10.3% Irish, 10.3% English (2000).
Economy: Employment by occupation: 6.5% management, 10.9% professional, 13.0% services, 19.6% sales, 0.0% farming, 15.2% construction, 34.8% production (2000).
Income: Per capita income: $14,051 (2000); Median household income: $25,625 (2000); Poverty rate: 2.1% (2000).
Taxes: Total city taxes per capita: $34 (1997); City property taxes per capita: $7 (1997).
Education: High school graduation rate: 69.1% (2000); College graduation rate: 2.5% (2000).
Housing: Homeownership rate: 75.0% (2000); Median home value: $40,000 (2000); Median rent: $275 per month (2000); Median age of housing: 60+ years (2000).
Transportation: Commute to work: 87.8% car, 0.0% public transportation, 12.2% walk, 0.0% work from home (2000); Travel time to work: 18.4% less than 15 minutes, 53.1% 15 to 30 minutes, 12.2% 30 to 45 minutes, 4.1% 45 to 60 minutes, 12.2% 60 minutes or more (2000)

NEVADA (city). Covers a land area of 8.928 square miles and a water area of 0.060 square miles. Located at 37.84° N. Lat.; 94.35° W. Long. Elevation is 880 feet.
History: Nevada was platted in 1855 and settled by families from Kentucky and Tennessee. It was named for Nevada City, California. During the Civil War, the town was the headquarters of several detachments of Confederate troops. In 1863 it was burned to the ground by Federal militia from Kansas. After the war, the town was reborn as a shipping center for agricultural products.
Population: 8,607 (2000); Race: 96.1% White, 0.7% Black, 0.5% Asian, 0.9% American Indian and Alaska Native, 1.1% Hispanic of any race, 1.5% two or more races (2000); Density: 964.1 persons per square mile (2000); Age: 25.5% under 18, 18.7% over 64 (2000); Marriage status: 24.1% never married, 50.0% now married, 10.8% widowed, 15.2% divorced (2000); Foreign born: 1.0% (2000); Ancestry (includes multiple ancestries): 16.8% German, 16.3% United States or American, 11.5% Other groups, 10.8% Irish, 9.7% English (2000).
Economy: Single-family building permits issued: 16 (2001) / 15 (2000); Multi-family building permits issued: 0 (2001) / 0 (2000); Employment by occupation: 11.4% management, 16.5% professional, 20.8% services, 22.6% sales, 0.1% farming, 9.7% construction, 18.8% production (2000).
Income: Per capita income: $15,118 (2000); Median household income: $25,774 (2000); Poverty rate: 20.0% (2000).
Taxes: Total city taxes per capita: $500 (2000); City property taxes per capita: $102 (2000).
Education: High school graduation rate: 73.2% (2000); College graduation rate: 14.5% (2000).

School District(s)

Nevada R-V (PK-12)
2000 Enrollment: 2,701 417-448-2000

Two-year College(s)

Cottey College (Private, Not-for-profit)
2001 Enrollment: 326 417-667-8181
2001 Tuition: In-state $9,200; Out-of-state $9,200

Housing: Homeownership rate: 57.8% (2000); Median home value: $58,900 (2000); Median rent: $261 per month (2000); Median age of housing: 42 years (2000).
Hospitals: Heartland Behavioral Health Services (162 beds); Nevada Regional Medical Center (97 beds)
Safety: Violent crime rate: 30.0 per 10,000 population; Property crime rate: 606.2 per 10,000 population (2001).
Newspapers: The Nevada Daily Mail and Sunday Herald (5 x week); Nevada News (1 x week)
Transportation: Commute to work: 89.0% car, 0.7% public transportation, 5.6% walk, 3.6% work from home (2000); Travel time to work: 74.7% less than 15 minutes, 11.2% 15 to 30 minutes, 6.4% 30 to 45 minutes, 2.5% 45 to 60 minutes, 5.3% 60 minutes or more (2000)
Additional Information Contacts
Five County Board of Realtors.............................. 417-667-3311
Nevada Chamber of Commerce.............................. 417-667-5300

RICHARDS (town). Covers a land area of 0.274 square miles and a water area of 0 square miles. Located at 37.91° N. Lat.; 94.55° W. Long. Elevation is 833 feet.
Population: 95 (2000); Race: 95.9% White, 2.1% Black, 0.0% Asian, 0.0% American Indian and Alaska Native, 0.0% Hispanic of any race, 2.1% two or more races (2000); Density: 347.1 persons per square mile (2000); Age:

17.5% under 18, 20.6% over 64 (2000); Marriage status: 17.5% never married, 58.8% now married, 10.0% widowed, 13.8% divorced (2000); Foreign born: 0.0% (2000); Ancestry (includes multiple ancestries): 15.5% Other groups, 13.4% Irish, 11.3% English, 9.3% United States or American, 9.3% German (2000).
Economy: Sorghum, wheat, corn, hay; cattle. Employment by occupation: 0.0% management, 5.1% professional, 15.4% services, 35.9% sales, 7.7% farming, 7.7% construction, 28.2% production (2000).
Income: Per capita income: $16,489 (2000); Median household income: $35,938 (2000); Poverty rate: 12.4% (2000).
Taxes: Total city taxes per capita: $9 (1997); City property taxes per capita: $9 (1997).
Education: High school graduation rate: 71.8% (2000); College graduation rate: 2.8% (2000).
Housing: Homeownership rate: 81.6% (2000); Median home value: $22,500 (2000); Median rent: $250 per month (2000); Median age of housing: 60+ years (2000).
Transportation: Commute to work: 100.0% car, 0.0% public transportation, 0.0% walk, 0.0% work from home (2000); Travel time to work: 16.7% less than 15 minutes, 33.3% 15 to 30 minutes, 41.7% 30 to 45 minutes, 0.0% 45 to 60 minutes, 8.3% 60 minutes or more (2000)

SCHELL CITY (city). Covers a land area of 0.630 square miles and a water area of 0 square miles. Located at 38.01° N. Lat.; 94.11° W. Long. Elevation is 747 feet.
Population: 286 (2000); Race: 97.9% White, 0.0% Black, 0.0% Asian, 0.7% American Indian and Alaska Native, 1.0% Hispanic of any race, 1.4% two or more races (2000); Density: 454.3 persons per square mile (2000); Age: 24.0% under 18, 16.1% over 64 (2000); Marriage status: 16.7% never married, 57.9% now married, 6.1% widowed, 19.3% divorced (2000); Foreign born: 0.0% (2000); Ancestry (includes multiple ancestries): 26.0% German, 18.5% Other groups, 17.5% Irish, 10.3% United States or American, 7.2% English (2000).
Economy: Soybeans, wheat, hay; cattle. Employment by occupation: 6.3% management, 8.4% professional, 25.3% services, 16.8% sales, 5.3% farming, 18.9% construction, 18.9% production (2000).
Income: Per capita income: $11,027 (2000); Median household income: $20,500 (2000); Poverty rate: 25.7% (2000).
Taxes: Total city taxes per capita: $16 (1997); City property taxes per capita: $16 (1997).
Education: High school graduation rate: 70.0% (2000); College graduation rate: 6.3% (2000).
Housing: Homeownership rate: 76.9% (2000); Median home value: $21,800 (2000); Median rent: $180 per month (2000); Median age of housing: 40 years (2000).
Transportation: Commute to work: 97.9% car, 0.0% public transportation, 2.1% walk, 0.0% work from home (2000); Travel time to work: 14.9% less than 15 minutes, 28.7% 15 to 30 minutes, 28.7% 30 to 45 minutes, 6.4% 45 to 60 minutes, 21.3% 60 minutes or more (2000)

SHELDON (city). Covers a land area of 0.511 square miles and a water area of 0 square miles. Located at 37.65° N. Lat.; 94.29° W. Long. Elevation is 915 feet.
Population: 529 (2000); Race: 99.6% White, 0.0% Black, 0.0% Asian, 0.4% American Indian and Alaska Native, 0.0% Hispanic of any race, 0.0% two or more races (2000); Density: 1,034.9 persons per square mile (2000); Age: 23.7% under 18, 14.8% over 64 (2000); Marriage status: 17.7% never married, 65.0% now married, 6.0% widowed, 11.3% divorced (2000); Foreign born: 0.6% (2000); Ancestry (includes multiple ancestries): 28.7% United States or American, 15.9% Irish, 15.5% German, 9.7% English, 9.1% Other groups (2000).
Economy: Wheat, sorghum, soybeans; cattle. Employment by occupation: 3.7% management, 15.9% professional, 12.6% services, 23.2% sales, 1.2% farming, 9.3% construction, 34.1% production (2000).
Income: Per capita income: $13,664 (2000); Median household income: $28,125 (2000); Poverty rate: 13.4% (2000).
Taxes: Total city taxes per capita: $100 (1997); City property taxes per capita: $46 (1997).
Education: High school graduation rate: 73.3% (2000); College graduation rate: 8.3% (2000).

School District(s)

Sheldon R-VIII (KG-12)
2000 Enrollment: 180 417-884-5113
Housing: Homeownership rate: 71.3% (2000); Median home value: $31,100 (2000); Median rent: $235 per month (2000); Median age of housing: 44 years (2000).
Transportation: Commute to work: 95.9% car, 0.0% public transportation, 1.2% walk, 1.2% work from home (2000); Travel time to work: 16.2% less than 15 minutes, 56.0% 15 to 30 minutes, 15.4% 30 to 45 minutes, 5.0% 45 to 60 minutes, 7.5% 60 minutes or more (2000)

STOTESBURY (town). Covers a land area of 0.112 square miles and a water area of 0 square miles. Located at 37.97° N. Lat.; 94.56° W. Long. Elevation is 770 feet.
Population: 43 (2000); Race: 100.0% White, 0.0% Black, 0.0% Asian, 0.0% American Indian and Alaska Native, 0.0% Hispanic of any race, 0.0% two or more races (2000); Density: 382.4 persons per square mile (2000); Age: 35.7% under 18, 33.3% over 64 (2000); Marriage status: 39.5% never married, 44.7% now married, 10.5% widowed, 5.3% divorced (2000); Foreign born: 0.0% (2000); Ancestry (includes multiple ancestries): 57.1% United States or American, 31.0% Other groups, 14.3% Irish (2000).
Economy: Employment by occupation: 0.0% management, 0.0% professional, 20.0% services, 0.0% sales, 0.0% farming, 40.0% construction, 40.0% production (2000).
Income: Per capita income: $9,543 (2000); Median household income: $23,438 (2000); Poverty rate: 19.0% (2000).
Taxes: Total city taxes per capita: $295 (1997); City property taxes per capita: $23 (1997).
Education: High school graduation rate: 25.9% (2000); College graduation rate: 0.0% (2000).
Housing: Homeownership rate: 100.0% (2000); Median home value: $21,300 (2000); Median age of housing: 60+ years (2000).
Transportation: Commute to work: 60.0% car, 0.0% public transportation, 0.0% walk, 0.0% work from home (2000); Travel time to work: 0.0% less than 15 minutes, 60.0% 15 to 30 minutes, 0.0% 30 to 45 minutes, 0.0% 45 to 60 minutes, 40.0% 60 minutes or more (2000)

WALKER (city). Covers a land area of 0.311 square miles and a water area of 0 square miles. Located at 37.89° N. Lat.; 94.23° W. Long. Elevation is 852 feet.
Population: 275 (2000); Race: 100.0% White, 0.0% Black, 0.0% Asian, 0.0% American Indian and Alaska Native, 0.0% Hispanic of any race, 0.0% two or more races (2000); Density: 883.7 persons per square mile (2000); Age: 26.7% under 18, 11.4% over 64 (2000); Marriage status: 19.7% never married, 60.6% now married, 10.3% widowed, 9.4% divorced (2000); Foreign born: 1.2% (2000); Ancestry (includes multiple ancestries): 16.5% German, 13.7% Irish, 12.9% Other groups, 12.9% United States or American, 7.5% English (2000).
Economy: Employment by occupation: 10.5% management, 13.5% professional, 17.3% services, 24.8% sales, 0.0% farming, 9.8% construction, 24.1% production (2000).
Income: Per capita income: $16,949 (2000); Median household income: $28,542 (2000); Poverty rate: 12.9% (2000).
Taxes: Total city taxes per capita: $395 (1997); City property taxes per capita: $30 (1997).
Education: High school graduation rate: 78.8% (2000); College graduation rate: 9.6% (2000).

School District(s)

Northeast Vernon Co. R-I (PK-12)
2000 Enrollment: 227 417-465-2221
Housing: Homeownership rate: 76.0% (2000); Median home value: $29,400 (2000); Median rent: $223 per month (2000); Median age of housing: 30 years (2000).
Transportation: Commute to work: 96.9% car, 0.0% public transportation, 3.1% walk, 0.0% work from home (2000); Travel time to work: 31.3% less than 15 minutes, 45.0% 15 to 30 minutes, 9.9% 30 to 45 minutes, 6.9% 45 to 60 minutes, 6.9% 60 minutes or more (2000)

Warren County

Located in east central Missouri; bounded on the south by the Missouri River. Covers a land area of 431.30 square miles, a water area of 6.40 square miles, and is located in the Central Time Zone. The county government was organized in 1833. County seat is Warrenton.

Warren County is part of the St. Louis, MO-IL MSA. The entire metro area includes: Clinton County, IL; Jersey County, IL; Madison County, IL; Monroe County, IL; St. Clair County, IL; Crawford County, MO (pt.)**; Franklin County, MO; Jefferson County, MO; Lincoln County, MO; St. Charles County, MO; St. Louis County, MO; Warren County, MO; St. Louis city, MO

Population: 24,525 (2000); Race: 95.6% White, 2.4% Black, 0.1% Asian, 0.3% American Indian and Alaska Native, 1.4% Hispanic of any race, 1.2% two or more races (2000); Density: 56.9 persons per square mile (2000); Age: 26.8% under 18, 13.0% over 64 (2000).
Religion: Five largest groups: 18.6% Catholic Church, 7.3% United Church of Christ, 6.8% Southern Baptist Convention, 4.8% The Wesleyan Church, 3.2% The United Methodist Church (2000).
Economy: Unemployment rate: 5.2% (11/2002); Total civilian labor force: 13,025 (11/2002); Leading industries: 34.6% manufacturing; 18.2% retail trade; 9.7% construction (2000); Companies that employ more than 1,000 persons: 0 (2000); Companies that employ more than 100 persons: 8 (2000); Farms: 555 totaling 132,520 acres (1997); Minority business ownership rate: 0.0% (1997); Women business ownership rate: 14.4% (1997); Retail sales per capita: $7,973 (1997). Single-family building permits issued: 265 (2001) / 269 (2000); Multi-family building permits issued: 49 (2001) / 70 (2000).
Income: Per capita income: $19,690 (2000); Median household income: $41,016 (2000); Poverty rate: 8.6% (2000); Bankruptcy rate: 5.29% (2001).
Taxes: Total county taxes per capita: $157 (2000); County property taxes per capita: $38 (2000).
Education: High school graduation rate: 79.5% (2000); College graduation rate: 11.1% (2000).
Housing: Homeownership rate: 83.1% (2000); Median home value: $108,600 (2000); Median rent: $372 per month (2000); Median age of housing: 19 years (2000).
Health: Birth rate: 131.7 per 10,000 population (1998); Age adjusted death rate: 81.8 per 10,000 population (1999); Age adjusted cancer mortality rate: 215.0 deaths per 100,000 population (1999). Number of physicians: 1.2 per 10,000 population (1999); Number of hospital beds: n/a (1999).
Elections: 2000 Presidential election results: 42.1% Gore, 55.7% Bush, 1.4% Nader, 0.4% Buchanan
National and State Parks: Daniel Boone Memorial State Forest; Little Lost Creek State Forest; Reifsnider State Forest; Warrenton State Wildlife Area
Additional Information Contacts
Warren County Government Offices 636-456-3331
Marthasville Chamber of Commerce 636-433-5242
Warrenton Chamber of Commerce 636-456-2530

Warren County Communities

INNSBROOK (village). Covers a land area of 8.973 square miles and a water area of 0.658 square miles. Located at 38.76° N. Lat.; 91.05° W. Long. Elevation is 655 feet.
Population: 469 (2000); Race: 98.4% White, 0.9% Black, 0.0% Asian, 0.0% American Indian and Alaska Native, 0.5% Hispanic of any race, 0.2% two or more races (2000); Density: 52.3 persons per square mile (2000); Age: 8.6% under 18, 30.8% over 64 (2000); Marriage status: 7.1% never married, 80.5% now married, 4.6% widowed, 7.9% divorced (2000); Foreign born: 0.9% (2000); Ancestry (includes multiple ancestries): 46.4% German, 21.0% Irish, 17.2% English, 5.4% Italian, 4.9% French (except Basque) (2000).
Economy: Single-family building permits issued: 34 (2001) / 18 (2000); Multi-family building permits issued: 0 (2001) / 0 (2000); Employment by occupation: 14.7% management, 22.1% professional, 3.7% services, 33.1% sales, 0.0% farming, 16.0% construction, 10.4% production (2000).
Income: Per capita income: $40,434 (2000); Median household income: $65,833 (2000); Poverty rate: 1.6% (2000).
Taxes: Total city taxes per capita: $119 (2000); City property taxes per capita: $72 (2000).
Education: High school graduation rate: 92.1% (2000); College graduation rate: 43.9% (2000).
Housing: Homeownership rate: 98.6% (2000); Median home value: $228,300 (2000); Median age of housing: 15 years (2000).
Transportation: Commute to work: 84.4% car, 0.0% public transportation, 0.0% walk, 15.6% work from home (2000); Travel time to work: 5.2% less than 15 minutes, 32.6% 15 to 30 minutes, 27.4% 30 to 45 minutes, 20.0% 45 to 60 minutes, 14.8% 60 minutes or more (2000)

MARTHASVILLE (city). Covers a land area of 0.837 square miles and a water area of 0 square miles. Located at 38.63° N. Lat.; 91.05° W. Long. Elevation is 496 feet.
History: Marthasville was platted in 1817 by John Young. Many of the early residents were of German descent, including Augustus Ferdinand Grabs, whose home housed both the post office and a store in the 1840's.
Population: 837 (2000); Race: 97.6% White, 0.6% Black, 0.0% Asian, 0.5% American Indian and Alaska Native, 0.5% Hispanic of any race, 0.7% two or more races (2000); Density: 999.5 persons per square mile (2000); Age: 28.9% under 18, 9.9% over 64 (2000); Marriage status: 19.2% never married, 64.5% now married, 6.2% widowed, 10.1% divorced (2000); Foreign born: 0.5% (2000); Ancestry (includes multiple ancestries): 50.8% German, 11.6% Irish, 11.1% English, 7.3% United States or American, 4.8% Other groups (2000).
Economy: Employment by occupation: 7.8% management, 13.4% professional, 19.4% services, 16.5% sales, 1.2% farming, 16.9% construction, 24.7% production (2000).
Income: Per capita income: $17,979 (2000); Median household income: $41,141 (2000); Poverty rate: 8.5% (2000).
Taxes: Total city taxes per capita: $135 (1997); City property taxes per capita: $34 (1997).
Education: High school graduation rate: 83.8% (2000); College graduation rate: 12.1% (2000).
Housing: Homeownership rate: 71.7% (2000); Median home value: $79,200 (2000); Median rent: $338 per month (2000); Median age of housing: 17 years (2000).
Newspapers: The Marthasville Record (1 x week)
Transportation: Commute to work: 97.9% car, 0.0% public transportation, 0.0% walk, 2.1% work from home (2000); Travel time to work: 15.7% less than 15 minutes, 50.0% 15 to 30 minutes, 14.3% 30 to 45 minutes, 10.0% 45 to 60 minutes, 10.0% 60 minutes or more (2000)
Additional Information Contacts
Marthasville Chamber of Commerce 636-433-5242

TRUESDALE (city). Aka Truesdail. Covers a land area of 1.101 square miles and a water area of 0 square miles. Located at 38.81° N. Lat.; 91.12° W. Long. Elevation is 863 feet.
History: Sometimes spelled Truesdail.
Population: 397 (2000); Race: 91.4% White, 5.8% Black, 0.0% Asian, 0.6% American Indian and Alaska Native, 3.6% Hispanic of any race, 0.3% two or more races (2000); Density: 360.6 persons per square mile (2000); Age: 33.4% under 18, 11.0% over 64 (2000); Marriage status: 27.1% never married, 52.2% now married, 6.0% widowed, 14.7% divorced (2000); Foreign born: 2.5% (2000); Ancestry (includes multiple ancestries): 25.1% German, 17.7% United States or American, 16.0% Other groups, 13.8% Irish, 7.2% English (2000).
Economy: Employment by occupation: 2.9% management, 3.6% professional, 25.5% services, 10.9% sales, 1.5% farming, 8.8% construction, 46.7% production (2000).
Income: Per capita income: $10,483 (2000); Median household income: $28,359 (2000); Poverty rate: 21.8% (2000).
Taxes: Total city taxes per capita: $403 (1997); City property taxes per capita: $211 (1997).
Education: High school graduation rate: 66.5% (2000); College graduation rate: 1.5% (2000).
Housing: Homeownership rate: 76.6% (2000); Median home value: $70,800 (2000); Median rent: $342 per month (2000); Median age of housing: 23 years (2000).
Transportation: Commute to work: 91.7% car, 0.0% public transportation, 1.5% walk, 1.5% work from home (2000); Travel time to work: 55.0% less than 15 minutes, 23.7% 15 to 30 minutes, 15.3% 30 to 45 minutes, 6.1% 45 to 60 minutes, 0.0% 60 minutes or more (2000)

WARRENTON (city). Covers a land area of 7.329 square miles and a water area of 0.010 square miles. Located at 38.81° N. Lat.; 91.14° W. Long. Elevation is 828 feet.
History: Warrenton was named for General Joseph Warren, Revolutionary patriot killed in the Battle of Bunker Hill. Central Wesleyan College, established by a group of German Methodist ministers in 1852, was moved to Warrenton in 1864.
Population: 5,281 (2000); Race: 93.7% White, 3.5% Black, 0.1% Asian, 0.5% American Indian and Alaska Native, 0.7% Hispanic of any race, 1.7% two or more races (2000); Density: 720.6 persons per square mile (2000); Age: 30.0% under 18, 12.6% over 64 (2000); Marriage status: 23.2% never married, 54.9% now married, 8.0% widowed, 13.9% divorced (2000); Foreign born: 1.6% (2000); Ancestry (includes multiple ancestries): 36.8% German, 13.4% Irish, 13.3% Other groups, 10.8% United States or American, 6.0% English (2000).
Economy: Single-family building permits issued: 45 (2001) / 51 (2000); Multi-family building permits issued: 22 (2001) / 70 (2000); Employment by occupation: 8.2% management, 12.4% professional, 20.1% services, 23.8% sales, 0.3% farming, 14.1% construction, 21.1% production (2000).
Income: Per capita income: $16,431 (2000); Median household income: $34,022 (2000); Poverty rate: 10.6% (2000).

Taxes: Total city taxes per capita: $421 (1997); City property taxes per capita: $45 (1997).
Education: High school graduation rate: 77.6% (2000); College graduation rate: 10.2% (2000).

School District(s)

Warren Co. R-III (PK-12)
2000 Enrollment: 2,596 636-456-6901
Housing: Homeownership rate: 68.4% (2000); Median home value: $91,500 (2000); Median rent: $393 per month (2000); Median age of housing: 24 years (2000).
Newspapers: Warrenton News-Journal (1 x week)
Transportation: Commute to work: 93.8% car, 0.0% public transportation, 3.7% walk, 1.3% work from home (2000); Travel time to work: 41.2% less than 15 minutes, 20.7% 15 to 30 minutes, 20.4% 30 to 45 minutes, 8.5% 45 to 60 minutes, 9.2% 60 minutes or more (2000)
Additional Information Contacts
Warrenton Chamber of Commerce 636-456-2530

WRIGHT CITY (city). Covers a land area of 2.500 square miles and a water area of 0.025 square miles. Located at 38.82° N. Lat.; 91.02° W. Long. Elevation is 727 feet.
Population: 1,532 (2000); Race: 88.2% White, 5.8% Black, 0.0% Asian, 0.7% American Indian and Alaska Native, 7.8% Hispanic of any race, 2.5% two or more races (2000); Density: 612.7 persons per square mile (2000); Age: 28.2% under 18, 12.5% over 64 (2000); Marriage status: 24.5% never married, 53.4% now married, 7.8% widowed, 14.3% divorced (2000); Foreign born: 5.2% (2000); Ancestry (includes multiple ancestries): 28.6% German, 20.2% Other groups, 11.4% Irish, 10.7% United States or American, 5.8% English (2000).
Economy: Manufacturing of furniture. Single-family building permits issued: 11 (2001) / 16 (2000); Multi-family building permits issued: 27 (2001) / 0 (2000); Employment by occupation: 5.6% management, 9.4% professional, 17.0% services, 27.2% sales, 0.4% farming, 13.4% construction, 26.9% production (2000).
Income: Per capita income: $17,153 (2000); Median household income: $30,179 (2000); Poverty rate: 14.6% (2000).
Taxes: Total city taxes per capita: $382 (1997); City property taxes per capita: $145 (1997).
Education: High school graduation rate: 74.8% (2000); College graduation rate: 6.6% (2000).

School District(s)

Wright City R-II (PK-12)
2000 Enrollment: 1,309 636-745-7200
Housing: Homeownership rate: 59.3% (2000); Median home value: $72,700 (2000); Median rent: $277 per month (2000); Median age of housing: 31 years (2000).
Safety: Violent crime rate: 71.4 per 10,000 population; Property crime rate: 889.0 per 10,000 population (2001).
Transportation: Commute to work: 94.0% car, 0.0% public transportation, 2.5% walk, 0.6% work from home (2000); Travel time to work: 31.6% less than 15 minutes, 33.5% 15 to 30 minutes, 18.6% 30 to 45 minutes, 8.5% 45 to 60 minutes, 7.8% 60 minutes or more (2000)

Washington County

Located in southeast central Missouri, in the Ozarks; drained by the Big River; includes part of Clark National Forest. Covers a land area of 759.60 square miles, a water area of 2.90 square miles, and is located in the Central Time Zone. The county government was organized in 1813. County seat is Potosi.
Population: 23,344 (2000); Race: 95.4% White, 2.4% Black, 0.5% Asian, 0.6% American Indian and Alaska Native, 0.8% Hispanic of any race, 1.0% two or more races (2000); Density: 30.7 persons per square mile (2000); Age: 26.6% under 18, 11.7% over 64 (2000).
Religion: Five largest groups: 15.9% Catholic Church, 9.4% Southern Baptist Convention, 7.3% Baptist Missionary Association of America, 2.6% Church of God (Cleveland, Tennessee), 2.4% The United Methodist Church (2000).
Economy: Unemployment rate: 8.6% (11/2002); Total civilian labor force: 9,400 (11/2002); Leading industries: 24.8% manufacturing; 20.1% health care and social assistance; 18.6% retail trade (2000); Companies that employ more than 1,000 persons: 0 (2000); Companies that employ more than 100 persons: 6 (2000); Farms: 499 totaling 126,905 acres (1997); Minority business ownership rate: 0.0% (1997); Women business ownership rate: 18.2% (1997); Retail sales per capita: $4,481 (1997). Single-family building permits issued: 1 (2001) / 1 (2000); Multi-family building permits issued: 0 (2001) / 0 (2000).
Income: Per capita income: $12,934 (2000); Median household income: $27,112 (2000); Poverty rate: 20.8% (2000); Bankruptcy rate: 5.03% (2001).
Taxes: Total county taxes per capita: $93 (2000); County property taxes per capita: $27 (2000).
Education: High school graduation rate: 62.5% (2000); College graduation rate: 7.5% (2000).
Housing: Homeownership rate: 79.9% (2000); Median home value: $57,600 (2000); Median rent: $271 per month (2000); Median age of housing: 25 years (2000).
Health: Birth rate: 141.4 per 10,000 population (1998); Age adjusted death rate: 109.9 per 10,000 population (1999); Age adjusted cancer mortality rate: 237.9 deaths per 100,000 population (1999). Number of physicians: 2.1 per 10,000 population (1999); Number of hospital beds: 18.0 per 10,000 population (1999).
Elections: 2000 Presidential election results: 49.0% Gore, 48.6% Bush, 1.2% Nader, 0.8% Buchanan
National and State Parks: Washington State Park
Additional Information Contacts
Washington County Government Offices 573-438-4901
Potosi Chamber of Commerce 573-438-4517

Washington County Communities

BELGRADE (unincorporated postal area, zip code 63622). Covers a land area of 43.334 square miles and a water area of 0.275 square miles. Located at 37.79° N. Lat.; 90.89° W. Long. Elevation is 888 feet.
Population: 904 (2000); Race: 99.3% White, 0.0% Black, 0.0% Asian, 0.4% American Indian and Alaska Native, 0.6% Hispanic of any race, 0.2% two or more races (2000); Density: 20.9 persons per square mile (2000); Age: 27.3% under 18, 13.8% over 64 (2000); Marriage status: 15.2% never married, 68.3% now married, 9.9% widowed, 6.6% divorced (2000); Foreign born: 0.0% (2000); Ancestry (includes multiple ancestries): 14.5% United States or American, 9.2% English, 7.5% Other groups, 7.4% Irish, 7.1% German (2000).
Economy: Employment by occupation: 6.2% management, 8.3% professional, 14.5% services, 18.7% sales, 0.0% farming, 11.6% construction, 40.7% production (2000).
Income: Per capita income: $13,600 (2000); Median household income: $30,000 (2000); Poverty rate: 13.5% (2000).
Education: High school graduation rate: 64.5% (2000); College graduation rate: 9.0% (2000).
Housing: Homeownership rate: 79.9% (2000); Median home value: $51,100 (2000); Median rent: $298 per month (2000); Median age of housing: 29 years (2000).
Transportation: Commute to work: 94.1% car, 0.0% public transportation, 3.6% walk, 2.4% work from home (2000); Travel time to work: 20.4% less than 15 minutes, 15.8% 15 to 30 minutes, 24.9% 30 to 45 minutes, 18.5% 45 to 60 minutes, 20.4% 60 minutes or more (2000)

CADET (unincorporated postal area, zip code 63630). Covers a land area of 70.449 square miles and a water area of 0.324 square miles. Located at 38.02° N. Lat.; 90.74° W. Long. Elevation is 803 feet.
Population: 4,224 (2000); Race: 98.5% White, 0.3% Black, 0.3% Asian, 0.5% American Indian and Alaska Native, 1.0% Hispanic of any race, 0.3% two or more races (2000); Density: 60.0 persons per square mile (2000); Age: 30.0% under 18, 8.3% over 64 (2000); Marriage status: 26.3% never married, 57.3% now married, 4.8% widowed, 11.6% divorced (2000); Foreign born: 0.8% (2000); Ancestry (includes multiple ancestries): 26.9% French (except Basque), 20.4% United States or American, 17.6% Other groups, 8.7% German, 8.5% Irish (2000).
Economy: Employment by occupation: 3.8% management, 6.5% professional, 19.0% services, 15.9% sales, 0.5% farming, 18.8% construction, 35.6% production (2000).
Income: Per capita income: $10,916 (2000); Median household income: $27,634 (2000); Poverty rate: 24.9% (2000).
Education: High school graduation rate: 53.4% (2000); College graduation rate: 3.3% (2000).

School District(s)

Kingston K-14 (PK-12)
2000 Enrollment: 921 573-438-4982
Housing: Homeownership rate: 85.9% (2000); Median home value: $50,000 (2000); Median rent: $273 per month (2000); Median age of housing: 25 years (2000).

Transportation: Commute to work: 94.6% car, 0.0% public transportation, 2.4% walk, 0.8% work from home (2000); Travel time to work: 23.7% less than 15 minutes, 20.1% 15 to 30 minutes, 12.8% 30 to 45 minutes, 8.5% 45 to 60 minutes, 35.0% 60 minutes or more (2000)

CALEDONIA (village). Covers a land area of 0.139 square miles and a water area of 0 square miles. Located at 37.76° N. Lat.; 90.77° W. Long. Elevation is 915 feet.
History: Caledonia was established in 1819 by Alexander Craighead on the banks of Goose Creek.
Population: 158 (2000); Race: 100.0% White, 0.0% Black, 0.0% Asian, 0.0% American Indian and Alaska Native, 0.0% Hispanic of any race, 0.0% two or more races (2000); Density: 1,133.9 persons per square mile (2000); Age: 26.7% under 18, 10.0% over 64 (2000); Marriage status: 17.5% never married, 62.3% now married, 7.0% widowed, 13.2% divorced (2000); Foreign born: 0.0% (2000); Ancestry (includes multiple ancestries): 21.3% German, 21.3% Irish, 18.7% United States or American, 6.0% French (except Basque), 5.3% English (2000).
Economy: Employment by occupation: 6.6% management, 29.5% professional, 8.2% services, 19.7% sales, 0.0% farming, 16.4% construction, 19.7% production (2000).
Income: Per capita income: $10,685 (2000); Median household income: $20,833 (2000); Poverty rate: 29.3% (2000).
Taxes: Total city taxes per capita: $69 (1997); City property taxes per capita: $7 (1997).
Education: High school graduation rate: 72.0% (2000); College graduation rate: 14.6% (2000).

School District(s)

Valley R-VI (KG-12)
2000 Enrollment: 506 573-779-3515
Housing: Homeownership rate: 68.7% (2000); Median home value: $55,000 (2000); Median rent: $275 per month (2000); Median age of housing: 54 years (2000).
Transportation: Commute to work: 96.7% car, 0.0% public transportation, 3.3% walk, 0.0% work from home (2000); Travel time to work: 14.8% less than 15 minutes, 27.9% 15 to 30 minutes, 27.9% 30 to 45 minutes, 16.4% 45 to 60 minutes, 13.1% 60 minutes or more (2000)

IRONDALE (city). Aka Savoy. Covers a land area of 0.544 square miles and a water area of 0.016 square miles. Located at 37.83° N. Lat.; 90.67° W. Long. Elevation is 810 feet.
Population: 437 (2000); Race: 95.3% White, 0.0% Black, 3.0% Asian, 0.4% American Indian and Alaska Native, 1.7% Hispanic of any race, 0.9% two or more races (2000); Density: 803.8 persons per square mile (2000); Age: 25.2% under 18, 10.1% over 64 (2000); Marriage status: 18.0% never married, 68.3% now married, 6.6% widowed, 7.1% divorced (2000); Foreign born: 3.9% (2000); Ancestry (includes multiple ancestries): 14.2% United States or American, 13.8% German, 13.1% Other groups, 7.8% Irish, 6.3% Dutch (2000).
Economy: Employment by occupation: 8.2% management, 12.8% professional, 20.1% services, 18.7% sales, 0.0% farming, 13.2% construction, 26.9% production (2000).
Income: Per capita income: $11,819 (2000); Median household income: $26,250 (2000); Poverty rate: 23.3% (2000).
Taxes: Total city taxes per capita: $42 (1997); City property taxes per capita: $10 (1997).
Education: High school graduation rate: 71.5% (2000); College graduation rate: 6.7% (2000).
Housing: Homeownership rate: 81.6% (2000); Median home value: $32,300 (2000); Median rent: $289 per month (2000); Median age of housing: 34 years (2000).
Transportation: Commute to work: 89.1% car, 3.8% public transportation, 3.8% walk, 3.3% work from home (2000); Travel time to work: 6.4% less than 15 minutes, 39.7% 15 to 30 minutes, 25.0% 30 to 45 minutes, 6.4% 45 to 60 minutes, 22.5% 60 minutes or more (2000)

MINERAL POINT (town). Covers a land area of 0.255 square miles and a water area of 0 square miles. Located at 37.94° N. Lat.; 90.72° W. Long. Elevation is 880 feet.
History: Former lead-mining district.
Population: 363 (2000); Race: 94.7% White, 1.6% Black, 0.0% Asian, 0.3% American Indian and Alaska Native, 1.6% Hispanic of any race, 3.5% two or more races (2000); Density: 1,425.5 persons per square mile (2000); Age: 32.0% under 18, 6.7% over 64 (2000); Marriage status: 30.5% never married, 47.8% now married, 7.4% widowed, 14.3% divorced (2000); Foreign born: 0.5% (2000); Ancestry (includes multiple ancestries): 17.6% French (except Basque), 14.1% United States or American, 13.1% Other groups, 9.3% Irish, 6.7% German (2000).
Economy: Manufacturing of valves. Missouri State Correctional Center to Northwest. Employment by occupation: 0.0% management, 13.2% professional, 26.4% services, 21.7% sales, 1.6% farming, 10.9% construction, 26.4% production (2000).
Income: Per capita income: $8,365 (2000); Median household income: $15,455 (2000); Poverty rate: 40.4% (2000).
Taxes: Total city taxes per capita: $2 (1997); City property taxes per capita: $2 (1997).
Education: High school graduation rate: 48.2% (2000); College graduation rate: 1.4% (2000).
Housing: Homeownership rate: 58.8% (2000); Median home value: $27,900 (2000); Median rent: $269 per month (2000); Median age of housing: 32 years (2000).
Transportation: Commute to work: 99.2% car, 0.0% public transportation, 0.0% walk, 0.0% work from home (2000); Travel time to work: 31.0% less than 15 minutes, 27.9% 15 to 30 minutes, 7.0% 30 to 45 minutes, 9.3% 45 to 60 minutes, 24.8% 60 minutes or more (2000)

POTOSI (city). Covers a land area of 2.184 square miles and a water area of 0 square miles. Located at 37.93° N. Lat.; 90.78° W. Long. Elevation is 880 feet.
History: Lead deposits were discovered at Potosi about 1773 by Francois Azor, nicknamed Breton for his birthplace in Brittany, France. American and French families settled a town called Mine a Breton in the late 1700's. When Washington County was organized in 1813, two residents of Mine a Breton donated land for a county seat across the creek from their village. The town that was laid out was named for the Mexican silver mining city of San Luis Potosi. In 1826 the two villages were consolidated under the name of Potosi.
Population: 2,662 (2000); Race: 95.9% White, 1.4% Black, 0.2% Asian, 0.0% American Indian and Alaska Native, 0.9% Hispanic of any race, 1.8% two or more races (2000); Density: 1,218.9 persons per square mile (2000); Age: 26.1% under 18, 17.9% over 64 (2000); Marriage status: 23.6% never married, 47.1% now married, 15.8% widowed, 13.6% divorced (2000); Foreign born: 0.7% (2000); Ancestry (includes multiple ancestries): 30.4% United States or American, 17.5% French (except Basque), 10.9% Other groups, 9.4% German, 8.1% Irish (2000).
Economy: Single-family building permits issued: 1 (2001) / 1 (2000); Multi-family building permits issued: 0 (2001) / 0 (2000); Employment by occupation: 9.4% management, 13.4% professional, 22.3% services, 22.3% sales, 2.0% farming, 14.6% construction, 15.9% production (2000).
Income: Per capita income: $12,417 (2000); Median household income: $17,702 (2000); Poverty rate: 31.4% (2000).
Taxes: Total city taxes per capita: $285 (1997); City property taxes per capita: $0 (1997).
Education: High school graduation rate: 60.4% (2000); College graduation rate: 13.0% (2000).

School District(s)

Potosi R-III (PK-12)
2000 Enrollment: 2,436 573-438-5485
Housing: Homeownership rate: 51.8% (2000); Median home value: $59,400 (2000); Median rent: $279 per month (2000); Median age of housing: 38 years (2000).
Hospitals: Washington County Memorial Hospital (42 beds)
Newspapers: The Independent-Journal (1 x week)
Transportation: Commute to work: 89.9% car, 0.0% public transportation, 5.7% walk, 2.1% work from home (2000); Travel time to work: 53.2% less than 15 minutes, 12.1% 15 to 30 minutes, 6.2% 30 to 45 minutes, 8.0% 45 to 60 minutes, 20.6% 60 minutes or more (2000)
Additional Information Contacts
Potosi Chamber of Commerce 573-438-4517

RICHWOODS (unincorporated postal area, zip code 63071). Covers a land area of 63.098 square miles and a water area of 0.280 square miles. Located at 38.13° N. Lat.; 90.83° W. Long. Elevation is 770 feet.
Population: 1,063 (2000); Race: 98.3% White, 0.0% Black, 0.6% Asian, 0.0% American Indian and Alaska Native, 1.2% Hispanic of any race, 1.1% two or more races (2000); Density: 16.8 persons per square mile (2000); Age: 29.8% under 18, 12.9% over 64 (2000); Marriage status: 23.8% never married, 57.2% now married, 8.6% widowed, 10.4% divorced (2000); Foreign born: 0.7% (2000); Ancestry (includes multiple ancestries): 19.5% United States or American, 16.4% German, 14.6% French (except Basque), 11.6% Irish, 9.4% Other groups (2000).

Economy: Employment by occupation: 5.6% management, 5.9% professional, 18.8% services, 15.9% sales, 0.5% farming, 22.2% construction, 31.2% production (2000).
Income: Per capita income: $11,875 (2000); Median household income: $27,109 (2000); Poverty rate: 17.3% (2000).
Education: High school graduation rate: 60.1% (2000); College graduation rate: 4.4% (2000).

School District(s)

Richwoods R-VII (PK-08)
2000 Enrollment: 195 573-678-2257

Housing: Homeownership rate: 79.1% (2000); Median home value: $64,700 (2000); Median rent: $250 per month (2000); Median age of housing: 25 years (2000).
Transportation: Commute to work: 96.8% car, 0.0% public transportation, 0.0% walk, 2.2% work from home (2000); Travel time to work: 11.9% less than 15 minutes, 11.2% 15 to 30 minutes, 16.2% 30 to 45 minutes, 19.3% 45 to 60 minutes, 41.4% 60 minutes or more (2000)

Wayne County

Located in southeastern Missouri, in the Ozarks; drained by the St. Francis and Black Rivers; includes part of Clark National Forest. Covers a land area of 761.00 square miles, a water area of 13.10 square miles, and is located in the Central Time Zone. The county government was organized in 1818. County seat is Greenville.

Weather Station: Clearwater Dam — Elevation: 659 feet

	Jan	Feb	Mar	Apr	May	Jun	Jul	Aug	Sep	Oct	Nov	Dec
High	42	48	58	70	78	86	91	89	81	70	57	46
Low	20	24	33	43	52	61	66	64	56	43	34	24
Precip	3.1	2.9	4.6	4.6	4.6	3.7	3.9	3.6	3.3	3.3	4.8	4.0
Snow	na	na	0.4	0.0	0.0	0.0	0.0	0.0	0.0	tr	0.2	0.4

High and Low temperatures in degrees Fahrenheit; Precipitation and Snow in inches

Population: 13,259 (2000); Race: 97.6% White, 0.1% Black, 0.1% Asian, 0.7% American Indian and Alaska Native, 0.3% Hispanic of any race, 1.4% two or more races (2000); Density: 17.4 persons per square mile (2000); Age: 23.3% under 18, 19.9% over 64 (2000).
Religion: Five largest groups: 22.3% Southern Baptist Convention, 3.5% The United Methodist Church, 2.5% Catholic Church, 2.0% Assemblies of God, 1.7% Church of the Nazarene (2000).
Economy: Unemployment rate: 11.0% (11/2002); Total civilian labor force: 3,542 (11/2002); Leading industries: 27.4% manufacturing; 21.0% retail trade; 12.6% health care and social assistance (2000); Companies that employ more than 1,000 persons: 0 (2000); Companies that employ more than 100 persons: 2 (2000); Farms: 380 totaling 97,664 acres (1997); Minority business ownership rate: 0.0% (1997); Women business ownership rate: 23.6% (1997); Retail sales per capita: $4,472 (1997). Single-family building permits issued: -1 (2001) / -1 (2000); Multi-family building permits issued: -1 (2001) / -1 (2000).
Income: Per capita income: $13,434 (2000); Median household income: $24,007 (2000); Poverty rate: 21.9% (2000); Bankruptcy rate: 4.32% (2001).
Taxes: Total county taxes per capita: $74 (1997); County property taxes per capita: $19 (1997).
Education: High school graduation rate: 59.7% (2000); College graduation rate: 6.8% (2000).
Housing: Homeownership rate: 78.2% (2000); Median home value: $44,700 (2000); Median rent: $230 per month (2000); Median age of housing: 27 years (2000).
Health: Birth rate: 100.3 per 10,000 population (1998); Age adjusted death rate: 100.8 per 10,000 population (1999); Age adjusted cancer mortality rate: 212.3 deaths per 100,000 population (1999). Number of physicians: 3.0 per 10,000 population (1999); Number of hospital beds: n/a (1999).
Elections: 2000 Presidential election results: 40.8% Gore, 57.2% Bush, 0.9% Nader, 0.7% Buchanan
National and State Parks: Coldwater State Forest; Graves Mountain State Forest; Hiram State Wildlife Management Area; Lake Wappapella State Wildlife Management Area; Lake Wappapello State Park; Sam A Baker State Park; Silva State Wildlife Management Area; Yokum School State Wildlife Area
Additional Information Contacts
Wayne County Government Offices 573-224-3011
Piedmont Chamber of Commerce 573-223-4046

Wayne County Communities

CLUBB (unincorporated postal area, zip code 63934). Covers a land area of 0.891 square miles and a water area of 0 square miles. Located at 37.20° N. Lat.; 90.38° W. Long. Elevation is 546 feet.
Population: 93 (2000); Race: 100.0% White, 0.0% Black, 0.0% Asian, 0.0% American Indian and Alaska Native, 0.0% Hispanic of any race, 0.0% two or more races (2000); Density: 104.4 persons per square mile (2000); Age: 33.0% under 18, 6.4% over 64 (2000); Marriage status: 29.7% never married, 60.8% now married, 0.0% widowed, 9.5% divorced (2000); Foreign born: 0.0% (2000); Ancestry (includes multiple ancestries): 11.7% United States or American (2000).
Economy: Employment by occupation: 0.0% management, 0.0% professional, 31.6% services, 0.0% sales, 21.1% farming, 0.0% construction, 47.4% production (2000).
Income: Per capita income: $8,346 (2000); Median household income: $28,438 (2000); Poverty rate: 0.0% (2000).
Education: High school graduation rate: 13.5% (2000); College graduation rate: 0.0% (2000).
Housing: Homeownership rate: 68.8% (2000); Median rent: $275 per month (2000); Median age of housing: 25 years (2000).
Transportation: Commute to work: 74.2% car, 0.0% public transportation, 0.0% walk, 0.0% work from home (2000); Travel time to work: 0.0% less than 15 minutes, 38.7% 15 to 30 minutes, 0.0% 30 to 45 minutes, 0.0% 45 to 60 minutes, 61.3% 60 minutes or more (2000)

GREENVILLE (city). Covers a land area of 0.669 square miles and a water area of 0 square miles. Located at 37.12° N. Lat.; 90.44° W. Long. Elevation is 406 feet.
History: Greenville was established about 1819 on the St. Francis River. A dam constructed to the south at Wappapello created Lake Wappapello, which extended to Greenville and changed the layout of the city.
Population: 451 (2000); Race: 98.5% White, 0.0% Black, 0.0% Asian, 0.4% American Indian and Alaska Native, 0.0% Hispanic of any race, 1.1% two or more races (2000); Density: 674.3 persons per square mile (2000); Age: 20.4% under 18, 26.6% over 64 (2000); Marriage status: 15.5% never married, 62.7% now married, 11.9% widowed, 9.8% divorced (2000); Foreign born: 0.0% (2000); Ancestry (includes multiple ancestries): 26.8% United States or American, 13.8% German, 10.3% Other groups, 9.9% English, 9.0% Irish (2000).
Economy: Employment by occupation: 8.3% management, 20.4% professional, 22.7% services, 17.7% sales, 0.0% farming, 10.5% construction, 20.4% production (2000).
Income: Per capita income: $16,802 (2000); Median household income: $28,214 (2000); Poverty rate: 14.2% (2000).
Taxes: Total city taxes per capita: $190 (1997); City property taxes per capita: $31 (1997).
Education: High school graduation rate: 54.9% (2000); College graduation rate: 9.4% (2000).

School District(s)

Greenville R-II (PK-12)
2000 Enrollment: 868 573-224-3844

Housing: Homeownership rate: 64.0% (2000); Median home value: $46,500 (2000); Median rent: $218 per month (2000); Median age of housing: 32 years (2000).
Transportation: Commute to work: 93.3% car, 0.0% public transportation, 3.9% walk, 2.8% work from home (2000); Travel time to work: 34.5% less than 15 minutes, 14.9% 15 to 30 minutes, 24.7% 30 to 45 minutes, 13.2% 45 to 60 minutes, 12.6% 60 minutes or more (2000)

HIRAM (unincorporated postal area, zip code 63947). Covers a land area of 52.559 square miles and a water area of 0.025 square miles. Located at 37.19° N. Lat.; 90.25° W. Long. Elevation is 505 feet.
Population: 262 (2000); Race: 83.4% White, 0.0% Black, 0.0% Asian, 4.3% American Indian and Alaska Native, 0.0% Hispanic of any race, 12.3% two or more races (2000); Density: 5.0 persons per square mile (2000); Age: 23.5% under 18, 17.6% over 64 (2000); Marriage status: 23.6% never married, 58.4% now married, 8.7% widowed, 9.3% divorced (2000); Foreign born: 0.0% (2000); Ancestry (includes multiple ancestries): 16.6% English, 15.5% Irish, 15.5% Dutch, 13.9% Other groups, 12.8% United States or American (2000).
Economy: Employment by occupation: 19.4% management, 0.0% professional, 25.4% services, 0.0% sales, 0.0% farming, 14.9% construction, 40.3% production (2000).

Income: Per capita income: $8,884 (2000); Median household income: $18,000 (2000); Poverty rate: 14.4% (2000).
Education: High school graduation rate: 58.5% (2000); College graduation rate: 0.0% (2000).
Housing: Homeownership rate: 77.9% (2000); Median home value: $32,500 (2000); Median rent: $225 per month (2000); Median age of housing: 40 years (2000).
Transportation: Commute to work: 83.6% car, 0.0% public transportation, 0.0% walk, 16.4% work from home (2000); Travel time to work: 12.5% less than 15 minutes, 0.0% 15 to 30 minutes, 28.6% 30 to 45 minutes, 21.4% 45 to 60 minutes, 37.5% 60 minutes or more (2000)

LOWNDES (unincorporated postal area, zip code 63951). Covers a land area of 41.890 square miles and a water area of 0.187 square miles. Located at 37.12° N. Lat.; 90.27° W. Long. Elevation is 440 feet.
Population: 394 (2000); Race: 97.9% White, 0.0% Black, 0.0% Asian, 0.0% American Indian and Alaska Native, 0.0% Hispanic of any race, 2.1% two or more races (2000); Density: 9.4 persons per square mile (2000); Age: 14.4% under 18, 22.6% over 64 (2000); Marriage status: 15.4% never married, 79.6% now married, 0.0% widowed, 5.0% divorced (2000); Foreign born: 0.0% (2000); Ancestry (includes multiple ancestries): 23.6% Irish, 15.1% United States or American, 13.6% German, 13.3% English, 9.7% Other groups (2000).
Economy: Employment by occupation: 8.3% management, 12.1% professional, 9.1% services, 11.4% sales, 5.3% farming, 0.0% construction, 53.8% production (2000).
Income: Per capita income: $11,967 (2000); Median household income: $28,077 (2000); Poverty rate: 8.7% (2000).
Education: High school graduation rate: 53.1% (2000); College graduation rate: 3.8% (2000).
Housing: Homeownership rate: 95.4% (2000); Median home value: $33,000 (2000); Median age of housing: 23 years (2000).
Transportation: Commute to work: 91.7% car, 0.0% public transportation, 0.0% walk, 4.5% work from home (2000); Travel time to work: 5.6% less than 15 minutes, 15.9% 15 to 30 minutes, 9.5% 30 to 45 minutes, 17.5% 45 to 60 minutes, 51.6% 60 minutes or more (2000)

MCGEE (unincorporated postal area, zip code 63763). Covers a land area of 15.028 square miles and a water area of 0 square miles. Located at 37.05° N. Lat.; 90.16° W. Long. Elevation is 395 feet.
Population: 138 (2000); Race: 100.0% White, 0.0% Black, 0.0% Asian, 0.0% American Indian and Alaska Native, 0.0% Hispanic of any race, 0.0% two or more races (2000); Density: 9.2 persons per square mile (2000); Age: 19.3% under 18, 25.7% over 64 (2000); Marriage status: 30.7% never married, 42.0% now married, 18.2% widowed, 9.1% divorced (2000); Foreign born: 0.0% (2000); Ancestry (includes multiple ancestries): 56.0% United States or American, 18.3% German, 18.3% Other groups, 11.0% English, 5.5% Dutch (2000).
Economy: Employment by occupation: 0.0% management, 0.0% professional, 25.0% services, 20.8% sales, 20.8% farming, 33.3% construction, 0.0% production (2000).
Income: Per capita income: $7,528 (2000); Median household income: $19,844 (2000); Poverty rate: 11.0% (2000).
Education: High school graduation rate: 49.2% (2000); College graduation rate: 0.0% (2000).
Housing: Homeownership rate: 83.8% (2000); Median home value: $72,500 (2000); Median age of housing: 42 years (2000).
Transportation: Commute to work: 100.0% car, 0.0% public transportation, 0.0% walk, 0.0% work from home (2000); Travel time to work: 41.7% less than 15 minutes, 0.0% 15 to 30 minutes, 25.0% 30 to 45 minutes, 0.0% 45 to 60 minutes, 33.3% 60 minutes or more (2000)

MILL SPRING (village). Covers a land area of 0.210 square miles and a water area of 0 square miles. Located at 37.06° N. Lat.; 90.68° W. Long. Elevation is 435 feet.
Population: 219 (2000); Race: 100.0% White, 0.0% Black, 0.0% Asian, 0.0% American Indian and Alaska Native, 0.0% Hispanic of any race, 0.0% two or more races (2000); Density: 1,041.8 persons per square mile (2000); Age: 26.5% under 18, 19.3% over 64 (2000); Marriage status: 16.3% never married, 47.4% now married, 20.7% widowed, 15.6% divorced (2000); Foreign born: 0.0% (2000); Ancestry (includes multiple ancestries): 32.6% Other groups, 31.5% United States or American, 8.8% German, 6.6% English, 6.1% Irish (2000).
Economy: Employment by occupation: 0.0% management, 0.0% professional, 19.5% services, 14.6% sales, 9.8% farming, 0.0% construction, 56.1% production (2000).
Income: Per capita income: $9,723 (2000); Median household income: $22,750 (2000); Poverty rate: 22.7% (2000).
Taxes: Total city taxes per capita: $21 (1997); City property taxes per capita: $7 (1997).
Education: High school graduation rate: 44.1% (2000); College graduation rate: 0.8% (2000).
Housing: Homeownership rate: 79.2% (2000); Median home value: $17,100 (2000); Median rent: $250 per month (2000); Median age of housing: 45 years (2000).
Transportation: Commute to work: 100.0% car, 0.0% public transportation, 0.0% walk, 0.0% work from home (2000); Travel time to work: 22.0% less than 15 minutes, 29.3% 15 to 30 minutes, 14.6% 30 to 45 minutes, 22.0% 45 to 60 minutes, 12.2% 60 minutes or more (2000)

PATTERSON (unincorporated postal area, zip code 63956). Covers a land area of 68.990 square miles and a water area of 0.194 square miles. Located at 37.20° N. Lat.; 90.52° W. Long. Elevation is 425 feet.
Population: 861 (2000); Race: 96.9% White, 0.0% Black, 0.0% Asian, 0.8% American Indian and Alaska Native, 0.7% Hispanic of any race, 2.3% two or more races (2000); Density: 12.5 persons per square mile (2000); Age: 24.2% under 18, 16.6% over 64 (2000); Marriage status: 21.1% never married, 59.5% now married, 11.4% widowed, 8.0% divorced (2000); Foreign born: 0.0% (2000); Ancestry (includes multiple ancestries): 19.3% Other groups, 17.8% United States or American, 17.3% Irish, 16.0% English, 5.8% German (2000).
Economy: Employment by occupation: 12.0% management, 10.5% professional, 20.7% services, 16.6% sales, 1.5% farming, 16.3% construction, 22.4% production (2000).
Income: Per capita income: $13,091 (2000); Median household income: $28,750 (2000); Poverty rate: 26.3% (2000).
Education: High school graduation rate: 62.2% (2000); College graduation rate: 5.7% (2000).
Housing: Homeownership rate: 77.5% (2000); Median home value: $38,000 (2000); Median rent: $246 per month (2000); Median age of housing: 28 years (2000).
Transportation: Commute to work: 91.6% car, 0.0% public transportation, 1.2% walk, 5.4% work from home (2000); Travel time to work: 15.8% less than 15 minutes, 30.4% 15 to 30 minutes, 12.7% 30 to 45 minutes, 20.6% 45 to 60 minutes, 20.6% 60 minutes or more (2000)

PIEDMONT (city). Covers a land area of 2.085 square miles and a water area of 0 square miles. Located at 37.15° N. Lat.; 90.69° W. Long. Elevation is 502 feet.
Population: 1,992 (2000); Race: 98.0% White, 0.0% Black, 0.5% Asian, 0.2% American Indian and Alaska Native, 0.2% Hispanic of any race, 1.2% two or more races (2000); Density: 955.5 persons per square mile (2000); Age: 25.9% under 18, 23.7% over 64 (2000); Marriage status: 14.9% never married, 55.8% now married, 16.5% widowed, 12.8% divorced (2000); Foreign born: 0.4% (2000); Ancestry (includes multiple ancestries): 21.1% United States or American, 11.4% German, 11.2% Irish, 10.3% Other groups, 8.5% English (2000).
Economy: Agricultural center: cattle and fruit. Lumber mills. Manufacturing: leather products. Clearwater Lake and Dam are West. Employment by occupation: 6.1% management, 12.7% professional, 16.6% services, 28.9% sales, 0.3% farming, 10.5% construction, 24.9% production (2000).
Income: Per capita income: $11,976 (2000); Median household income: $19,490 (2000); Poverty rate: 26.5% (2000).
Taxes: Total city taxes per capita: $184 (1997); City property taxes per capita: $49 (1997).
Education: High school graduation rate: 53.4% (2000); College graduation rate: 7.9% (2000).

School District(s)

Clearwater R-I (PK-12)
2000 Enrollment: 1,204 573-223-7426
Housing: Homeownership rate: 62.9% (2000); Median home value: $45,100 (2000); Median rent: $227 per month (2000); Median age of housing: 34 years (2000).
Newspapers: Wayne County Journal-Banner (1 x week)
Transportation: Commute to work: 94.0% car, 0.9% public transportation, 2.4% walk, 1.7% work from home (2000); Travel time to work: 59.2% less than 15 minutes, 15.0% 15 to 30 minutes, 5.7% 30 to 45 minutes, 5.5% 45 to 60 minutes, 14.6% 60 minutes or more (2000)
Additional Information Contacts
Piedmont Chamber of Commerce 573-223-4046

SHOOK (unincorporated postal area, zip code 63963). Covers a land area of 15.653 square miles and a water area of 0.026 square miles. Located at 37.07° N. Lat.; 90.30° W. Long. Elevation is 405 feet.
Population: 125 (2000); Race: 100.0% White, 0.0% Black, 0.0% Asian, 0.0% American Indian and Alaska Native, 0.0% Hispanic of any race, 0.0% two or more races (2000); Density: 8.0 persons per square mile (2000); Age: 11.6% under 18, 36.1% over 64 (2000); Marriage status: 0.0% never married, 88.5% now married, 11.5% widowed, 0.0% divorced (2000); Foreign born: 0.0% (2000); Ancestry (includes multiple ancestries): 42.2% United States or American, 12.2% English, 7.5% Dutch, 7.5% Irish (2000).
Economy: Employment by occupation: 0.0% management, 0.0% professional, 12.2% services, 12.2% sales, 12.2% farming, 12.2% construction, 51.0% production (2000).
Income: Per capita income: $10,942 (2000); Median household income: $24,375 (2000); Poverty rate: 34.7% (2000).
Education: High school graduation rate: 20.5% (2000); College graduation rate: 0.0% (2000).
Housing: Homeownership rate: 74.6% (2000); Median home value: $60,700 (2000); Median rent: $175 per month (2000); Median age of housing: 33 years (2000).
Transportation: Commute to work: 100.0% car, 0.0% public transportation, 0.0% walk, 0.0% work from home (2000); Travel time to work: 14.0% less than 15 minutes, 0.0% 15 to 30 minutes, 14.0% 30 to 45 minutes, 32.6% 45 to 60 minutes, 39.5% 60 minutes or more (2000)

SILVA (unincorporated postal area, zip code 63964). Covers a land area of 88.960 square miles and a water area of 0.270 square miles. Located at 37.24° N. Lat.; 90.42° W. Long. Elevation is 410 feet.
Population: 1,098 (2000); Race: 95.4% White, 0.5% Black, 0.0% Asian, 2.1% American Indian and Alaska Native, 1.3% Hispanic of any race, 2.0% two or more races (2000); Density: 12.3 persons per square mile (2000); Age: 19.9% under 18, 24.5% over 64 (2000); Marriage status: 12.2% never married, 65.3% now married, 11.8% widowed, 10.8% divorced (2000); Foreign born: 1.1% (2000); Ancestry (includes multiple ancestries): 18.9% German, 18.5% Other groups, 17.0% Irish, 14.1% United States or American, 7.4% English (2000).
Economy: Employment by occupation: 10.5% management, 11.5% professional, 16.7% services, 18.0% sales, 2.3% farming, 12.5% construction, 28.5% production (2000).
Income: Per capita income: $12,514 (2000); Median household income: $20,132 (2000); Poverty rate: 19.2% (2000).
Education: High school graduation rate: 61.2% (2000); College graduation rate: 4.8% (2000).
Housing: Homeownership rate: 85.2% (2000); Median home value: $34,600 (2000); Median rent: $203 per month (2000); Median age of housing: 37 years (2000).
Transportation: Commute to work: 86.6% car, 3.3% public transportation, 1.6% walk, 8.5% work from home (2000); Travel time to work: 26.2% less than 15 minutes, 16.1% 15 to 30 minutes, 22.9% 30 to 45 minutes, 10.8% 45 to 60 minutes, 24.0% 60 minutes or more (2000)

WAPPAPELLO (unincorporated postal area, zip code 63966). Covers a land area of 60.357 square miles and a water area of 4.867 square miles. Located at 36.94° N. Lat.; 90.28° W. Long. Elevation is 350 feet.
Population: 2,437 (2000); Race: 99.3% White, 0.0% Black, 0.2% Asian, 0.0% American Indian and Alaska Native, 0.6% Hispanic of any race, 0.2% two or more races (2000); Density: 40.4 persons per square mile (2000); Age: 23.4% under 18, 19.2% over 64 (2000); Marriage status: 12.7% never married, 60.8% now married, 8.8% widowed, 17.8% divorced (2000); Foreign born: 0.5% (2000); Ancestry (includes multiple ancestries): 20.1% United States or American, 14.5% Irish, 14.1% German, 13.0% Other groups, 5.7% English (2000).
Economy: Employment by occupation: 10.6% management, 13.2% professional, 10.5% services, 22.4% sales, 2.3% farming, 13.7% construction, 27.4% production (2000).
Income: Per capita income: $15,179 (2000); Median household income: $29,653 (2000); Poverty rate: 16.1% (2000).
Education: High school graduation rate: 67.3% (2000); College graduation rate: 7.1% (2000).
Housing: Homeownership rate: 80.2% (2000); Median home value: $70,000 (2000); Median rent: $258 per month (2000); Median age of housing: 22 years (2000).
Transportation: Commute to work: 96.3% car, 0.0% public transportation, 0.0% walk, 3.7% work from home (2000); Travel time to work: 17.4% less than 15 minutes, 20.5% 15 to 30 minutes, 29.8% 30 to 45 minutes, 18.5% 45 to 60 minutes, 13.8% 60 minutes or more (2000)

WILLIAMSVILLE (city). Covers a land area of 0.309 square miles and a water area of 0 square miles. Located at 36.97° N. Lat.; 90.54° W. Long. Elevation is 392 feet.
Population: 379 (2000); Race: 98.2% White, 0.0% Black, 0.0% Asian, 0.5% American Indian and Alaska Native, 0.0% Hispanic of any race, 1.3% two or more races (2000); Density: 1,228.1 persons per square mile (2000); Age: 25.8% under 18, 22.6% over 64 (2000); Marriage status: 13.3% never married, 66.1% now married, 11.3% widowed, 9.3% divorced (2000); Foreign born: 0.0% (2000); Ancestry (includes multiple ancestries): 20.0% Irish, 19.7% United States or American, 15.5% Other groups, 11.6% English, 9.7% German (2000).
Economy: Manufacturing of plastic products; timber. Recreation. Surrounded by Mark Twain National Forest. Employment by occupation: 10.8% management, 11.7% professional, 17.5% services, 17.5% sales, 0.0% farming, 0.0% construction, 42.5% production (2000).
Income: Per capita income: $14,844 (2000); Median household income: $21,111 (2000); Poverty rate: 25.0% (2000).
Taxes: Total city taxes per capita: $19 (1997); City property taxes per capita: $14 (1997).
Education: High school graduation rate: 55.8% (2000); College graduation rate: 4.2% (2000).
Housing: Homeownership rate: 76.1% (2000); Median home value: $29,100 (2000); Median rent: $180 per month (2000); Median age of housing: 42 years (2000).
Transportation: Commute to work: 86.6% car, 0.0% public transportation, 5.0% walk, 4.2% work from home (2000); Travel time to work: 28.1% less than 15 minutes, 13.2% 15 to 30 minutes, 40.4% 30 to 45 minutes, 12.3% 45 to 60 minutes, 6.1% 60 minutes or more (2000)

Webster County

Located in south central Missouri, in the Ozarks; drained by the James and Niangua Rivers. Covers a land area of 593.30 square miles, a water area of 0.40 square miles, and is located in the Central Time Zone. The county government was organized in 1855. County seat is Marshfield.

Webster County is part of the Springfield, MO MSA. The entire metro area includes: Christian County; Greene County; Webster County

Weather Station: Marshfield — Elevation: 1,489 feet

	Jan	Feb	Mar	Apr	May	Jun	Jul	Aug	Sep	Oct	Nov	Dec
High	41	47	57	67	75	83	88	88	79	69	55	45
Low	21	26	35	45	54	63	67	66	58	47	36	26
Precip	2.2	2.1	3.8	4.3	4.7	4.3	3.7	3.1	4.5	3.8	4.2	3.1
Snow	na	3.4	1.3	0.1	0.0	0.0	0.0	0.0	0.0	0.0	0.6	1.4

High and Low temperatures in degrees Fahrenheit; Precipitation and Snow in inches

Population: 31,045 (2000); Race: 96.2% White, 1.0% Black, 0.2% Asian, 0.6% American Indian and Alaska Native, 1.2% Hispanic of any race, 1.6% two or more races (2000); Density: 52.3 persons per square mile (2000); Age: 28.9% under 18, 11.5% over 64 (2000).
Religion: Five largest groups: 25.7% Southern Baptist Convention, 5.7% The United Methodist Church, 3.8% National Association of Free Will Baptists, 2.1% Lutheran Church—Missouri Synod, 2.0% Christian Church (Disciples of Christ) (2000).
Economy: Unemployment rate: 4.6% (11/2002); Total civilian labor force: 15,476 (11/2002); Leading industries: 22.9% manufacturing; 20.7% retail trade; 11.0% accommodation & food services (2000); Companies that employ more than 1,000 persons: 0 (2000); Companies that employ more than 100 persons: 10 (2000); Farms: 1,691 totaling 296,825 acres (1997); Minority business ownership rate: 0.0% (1997); Women business ownership rate: 23.8% (1997); Retail sales per capita: $5,139 (1997). Single-family building permits issued: 53 (2001) / 65 (2000); Multi-family building permits issued: 26 (2001) / 34 (2000).
Income: Per capita income: $14,502 (2000); Median household income: $31,929 (2000); Poverty rate: 14.8% (2000); Bankruptcy rate: 5.32% (2001).
Taxes: Total county taxes per capita: $48 (2000); County property taxes per capita: $19 (2000).
Education: High school graduation rate: 74.8% (2000); College graduation rate: 11.0% (2000).
Housing: Homeownership rate: 78.0% (2000); Median home value: $80,900 (2000); Median rent: $315 per month (2000); Median age of housing: 23 years (2000).

Health: Birth rate: 146.2 per 10,000 population (1998); Age adjusted death rate: 86.9 per 10,000 population (1999); Age adjusted cancer mortality rate: 177.6 deaths per 100,000 population (1999). Number of physicians: 4.2 per 10,000 population (1999); Number of hospital beds: n/a (1999).
Elections: 2000 Presidential election results: 35.1% Gore, 61.9% Bush, 1.4% Nader, 1.2% Buchanan
National and State Parks: Seymour State Wildlife Management Area
Additional Information Contacts
Webster County Government Offices 417-468-2223
Marshfield Chamber of Commerce 417-468-3943
Rogersville Area Chamber of Commerce 417-753-7538

Webster County Communities

DIGGINS (village). Covers a land area of 0.803 square miles and a water area of 0 square miles. Located at 37.17° N. Lat.; 92.85° W. Long. Elevation is 1,651 feet.
Population: 298 (2000); Race: 93.2% White, 0.0% Black, 0.0% Asian, 0.7% American Indian and Alaska Native, 1.1% Hispanic of any race, 6.0% two or more races (2000); Density: 371.0 persons per square mile (2000); Age: 21.4% under 18, 8.2% over 64 (2000); Marriage status: 15.2% never married, 67.4% now married, 5.7% widowed, 11.7% divorced (2000); Foreign born: 0.7% (2000); Ancestry (includes multiple ancestries): 27.0% United States or American, 18.5% Other groups, 11.4% German, 8.5% Irish, 7.1% Dutch (2000).
Economy: Employment by occupation: 14.5% management, 7.2% professional, 17.8% services, 19.7% sales, 1.3% farming, 16.4% construction, 23.0% production (2000).
Income: Per capita income: $15,038 (2000); Median household income: $29,688 (2000); Poverty rate: 11.7% (2000).
Taxes: Total city taxes per capita: $88 (1997); City property taxes per capita: $56 (1997).
Education: High school graduation rate: 76.5% (2000); College graduation rate: 3.4% (2000).
Housing: Homeownership rate: 72.4% (2000); Median home value: $70,000 (2000); Median rent: $332 per month (2000); Median age of housing: 27 years (2000).
Transportation: Commute to work: 96.7% car, 0.0% public transportation, 0.0% walk, 3.3% work from home (2000); Travel time to work: 12.9% less than 15 minutes, 14.3% 15 to 30 minutes, 38.8% 30 to 45 minutes, 25.9% 45 to 60 minutes, 8.2% 60 minutes or more (2000)

ELKLAND (unincorporated postal area, zip code 65644). Covers a land area of 83.490 square miles and a water area of 0.056 square miles. Located at 37.51° N. Lat.; 93.03° W. Long. Elevation is 1,336 feet.
Population: 2,509 (2000); Race: 94.6% White, 0.0% Black, 0.8% Asian, 2.5% American Indian and Alaska Native, 1.4% Hispanic of any race, 1.4% two or more races (2000); Density: 30.1 persons per square mile (2000); Age: 24.2% under 18, 15.7% over 64 (2000); Marriage status: 16.6% never married, 66.6% now married, 7.1% widowed, 9.7% divorced (2000); Foreign born: 0.8% (2000); Ancestry (includes multiple ancestries): 23.0% United States or American, 15.0% German, 12.8% English, 10.1% Other groups, 9.3% Irish (2000).
Economy: Employment by occupation: 9.5% management, 10.2% professional, 9.4% services, 23.1% sales, 0.7% farming, 13.3% construction, 33.7% production (2000).
Income: Per capita income: $16,803 (2000); Median household income: $31,060 (2000); Poverty rate: 11.9% (2000).
Education: High school graduation rate: 73.0% (2000); College graduation rate: 8.0% (2000).
Housing: Homeownership rate: 84.5% (2000); Median home value: $84,100 (2000); Median rent: $264 per month (2000); Median age of housing: 24 years (2000).
Transportation: Commute to work: 89.8% car, 0.0% public transportation, 0.5% walk, 9.7% work from home (2000); Travel time to work: 5.3% less than 15 minutes, 33.3% 15 to 30 minutes, 33.9% 30 to 45 minutes, 15.7% 45 to 60 minutes, 11.8% 60 minutes or more (2000)

FORDLAND (city). Covers a land area of 0.886 square miles and a water area of 0 square miles. Located at 37.15° N. Lat.; 92.94° W. Long. Elevation is 1,608 feet.
History: Fordland became known for W.A. Hagel's Nut Exchange, trading in black walnuts and pecans.
Population: 684 (2000); Race: 95.3% White, 0.0% Black, 0.3% Asian, 0.0% American Indian and Alaska Native, 3.9% Hispanic of any race, 3.6% two or more races (2000); Density: 771.9 persons per square mile (2000); Age: 21.4% under 18, 17.7% over 64 (2000); Marriage status: 19.9% never married, 53.4% now married, 10.7% widowed, 15.9% divorced (2000); Foreign born: 0.9% (2000); Ancestry (includes multiple ancestries): 19.4% Other groups, 12.9% United States or American, 12.5% English, 11.6% Irish, 11.3% German (2000).
Economy: Employment by occupation: 10.9% management, 6.1% professional, 17.0% services, 25.1% sales, 0.6% farming, 15.4% construction, 24.8% production (2000).
Income: Per capita income: $15,676 (2000); Median household income: $31,042 (2000); Poverty rate: 11.4% (2000).
Taxes: Total city taxes per capita: $98 (1997); City property taxes per capita: $42 (1997).
Education: High school graduation rate: 79.4% (2000); College graduation rate: 10.5% (2000).

School District(s)

Fordland R-III (KG-12)
2000 Enrollment: 637 417-738-2296
Housing: Homeownership rate: 71.1% (2000); Median home value: $71,900 (2000); Median rent: $260 per month (2000); Median age of housing: 26 years (2000).
Transportation: Commute to work: 95.7% car, 0.0% public transportation, 1.6% walk, 1.0% work from home (2000); Travel time to work: 22.8% less than 15 minutes, 20.2% 15 to 30 minutes, 46.0% 30 to 45 minutes, 7.9% 45 to 60 minutes, 3.0% 60 minutes or more (2000)

MARSHFIELD (city). Covers a land area of 4.836 square miles and a water area of 0.003 square miles. Located at 37.34° N. Lat.; 92.90° W. Long. Elevation is 1,494 feet.
History: Marshfield was settled in the early 1830's by the Flannagan family. The town was surveyed in 1856 and named for the Massachusetts home of Daniel Webster, for whom Webster County was named. Marshfield developed as a processing and shipping center for the surrounding agricultural area, where tomatoes were a crop of prime importance.
Population: 5,720 (2000); Race: 98.1% White, 0.0% Black, 0.2% Asian, 0.1% American Indian and Alaska Native, 2.5% Hispanic of any race, 1.3% two or more races (2000); Density: 1,182.7 persons per square mile (2000); Age: 27.6% under 18, 16.9% over 64 (2000); Marriage status: 17.5% never married, 58.3% now married, 11.7% widowed, 12.6% divorced (2000); Foreign born: 0.9% (2000); Ancestry (includes multiple ancestries): 17.5% United States or American, 15.7% German, 12.0% English, 11.9% Irish, 11.0% Other groups (2000).
Economy: Single-family building permits issued: 42 (2001) / 50 (2000); Multi-family building permits issued: 26 (2001) / 10 (2000); Employment by occupation: 8.4% management, 11.8% professional, 13.9% services, 26.0% sales, 0.3% farming, 13.5% construction, 26.1% production (2000).
Income: Per capita income: $14,855 (2000); Median household income: $27,753 (2000); Poverty rate: 11.6% (2000).
Taxes: Total city taxes per capita: $229 (1997); City property taxes per capita: $38 (1997).
Education: High school graduation rate: 74.6% (2000); College graduation rate: 13.7% (2000).

School District(s)

Marshfield R-I (PK-12)
2000 Enrollment: 2,798 417-859-2120
Housing: Homeownership rate: 60.1% (2000); Median home value: $78,100 (2000); Median rent: $330 per month (2000); Median age of housing: 25 years (2000).
Newspapers: The Marshfield Mail (1 x week); The Country Mailbox (1 x week)
Transportation: Commute to work: 95.2% car, 2.0% public transportation, 0.6% walk, 0.7% work from home (2000); Travel time to work: 44.9% less than 15 minutes, 16.6% 15 to 30 minutes, 26.9% 30 to 45 minutes, 8.2% 45 to 60 minutes, 3.4% 60 minutes or more (2000)
Additional Information Contacts
Marshfield Chamber of Commerce 417-468-3943

NIANGUA (city). Covers a land area of 0.409 square miles and a water area of 0 square miles. Located at 37.38° N. Lat.; 92.83° W. Long. Elevation is 1,435 feet.
Population: 445 (2000); Race: 96.2% White, 0.0% Black, 0.0% Asian, 2.5% American Indian and Alaska Native, 0.2% Hispanic of any race, 1.3% two or more races (2000); Density: 1,088.6 persons per square mile (2000); Age: 25.5% under 18, 11.6% over 64 (2000); Marriage status: 20.3% never married, 59.6% now married, 7.1% widowed, 13.0% divorced (2000); Foreign born: 0.4% (2000); Ancestry (includes multiple ancestries): 27.1%

United States or American, 18.6% Other groups, 11.0% Irish, 10.5% German, 5.4% English (2000).
Economy: Fruit; dairying; cattle. Employment by occupation: 2.3% management, 5.7% professional, 14.9% services, 21.7% sales, 1.1% farming, 20.0% construction, 34.3% production (2000).
Income: Per capita income: $12,509 (2000); Median household income: $26,000 (2000); Poverty rate: 16.9% (2000).
Taxes: Total city taxes per capita: $29 (1997); City property taxes per capita: $8 (1997).
Education: High school graduation rate: 68.2% (2000); College graduation rate: 6.4% (2000).

School District(s)

Niangua R-V (PK-12)
2000 Enrollment: 349 417-473-6101
Housing: Homeownership rate: 73.4% (2000); Median home value: $39,600 (2000); Median rent: $175 per month (2000); Median age of housing: 40 years (2000).
Transportation: Commute to work: 94.8% car, 0.0% public transportation, 1.7% walk, 2.3% work from home (2000); Travel time to work: 20.8% less than 15 minutes, 32.1% 15 to 30 minutes, 24.4% 30 to 45 minutes, 18.5% 45 to 60 minutes, 4.2% 60 minutes or more (2000)

ROGERSVILLE (city). Covers a land area of 1.144 square miles and a water area of 0 square miles. Located at 37.11° N. Lat.; 93.05° W. Long. Elevation is 1,457 feet.
Population: 1,508 (2000); Race: 95.9% White, 0.0% Black, 0.3% Asian, 2.0% American Indian and Alaska Native, 1.1% Hispanic of any race, 1.6% two or more races (2000); Density: 1,318.4 persons per square mile (2000); Age: 31.6% under 18, 9.4% over 64 (2000); Marriage status: 17.9% never married, 61.7% now married, 6.5% widowed, 13.9% divorced (2000); Foreign born: 0.6% (2000); Ancestry (includes multiple ancestries): 17.7% German, 15.1% United States or American, 14.0% Other groups, 11.9% Irish, 9.6% English (2000).
Economy: Apples; dairying; cattle; light manufacturing. Single-family building permits issued: 11 (2001) / 15 (2000); Multi-family building permits issued: 0 (2001) / 24 (2000); Employment by occupation: 7.1% management, 16.8% professional, 12.5% services, 26.1% sales, 0.0% farming, 14.1% construction, 23.4% production (2000).
Income: Per capita income: $16,173 (2000); Median household income: $30,417 (2000); Poverty rate: 11.5% (2000).
Taxes: Total city taxes per capita: $177 (1997); City property taxes per capita: $58 (1997).
Education: High school graduation rate: 80.9% (2000); College graduation rate: 17.9% (2000).

School District(s)

Greene Co. R-VIII (PK-12)
2000 Enrollment: 1,912 417-753-2891
Housing: Homeownership rate: 66.0% (2000); Median home value: $78,100 (2000); Median rent: $368 per month (2000); Median age of housing: 17 years (2000).
Transportation: Commute to work: 96.7% car, 0.0% public transportation, 2.3% walk, 0.8% work from home (2000); Travel time to work: 20.3% less than 15 minutes, 50.1% 15 to 30 minutes, 25.6% 30 to 45 minutes, 1.5% 45 to 60 minutes, 2.6% 60 minutes or more (2000)
Additional Information Contacts
Rogersville Area Chamber of Commerce 417-753-7538

SEYMOUR (city). Covers a land area of 2.623 square miles and a water area of 0 square miles. Located at 37.14° N. Lat.; 92.76° W. Long. Elevation is 1,653 feet.
History: Seymour was surveyed in 1881 when the railroad announced plans to build a line through the area. The town's early economy was based on the farm products of the surrounding region, processed in a milk condensery, vegetable canneries, and a flour mill.
Population: 1,834 (2000); Race: 95.0% White, 0.7% Black, 1.1% Asian, 0.7% American Indian and Alaska Native, 1.8% Hispanic of any race, 1.5% two or more races (2000); Density: 699.3 persons per square mile (2000); Age: 29.3% under 18, 17.7% over 64 (2000); Marriage status: 17.3% never married, 59.2% now married, 11.2% widowed, 12.2% divorced (2000); Foreign born: 1.2% (2000); Ancestry (includes multiple ancestries): 22.0% United States or American, 12.7% Other groups, 11.4% German, 8.3% English, 7.8% Irish (2000).
Economy: Employment by occupation: 4.9% management, 9.6% professional, 19.6% services, 17.9% sales, 1.3% farming, 13.0% construction, 33.7% production (2000).
Income: Per capita income: $12,486 (2000); Median household income: $25,093 (2000); Poverty rate: 18.1% (2000).
Taxes: Total city taxes per capita: $111 (1997); City property taxes per capita: $29 (1997).
Education: High school graduation rate: 64.7% (2000); College graduation rate: 7.5% (2000).

School District(s)

Seymour R-II (PK-12)
2000 Enrollment: 897 417-935-2287
Housing: Homeownership rate: 68.6% (2000); Median home value: $54,400 (2000); Median rent: $260 per month (2000); Median age of housing: 30 years (2000).
Newspapers: Webster County Citizen (1 x week); Webster County Advertiser (1 x week)
Transportation: Commute to work: 91.9% car, 0.0% public transportation, 3.1% walk, 2.4% work from home (2000); Travel time to work: 35.1% less than 15 minutes, 14.1% 15 to 30 minutes, 19.1% 30 to 45 minutes, 19.3% 45 to 60 minutes, 12.4% 60 minutes or more (2000)

Worth County

Located in northwestern Missouri; bounded on the north by Iowa; drained by the Grand River. Covers a land area of 266.50 square miles, a water area of 0.20 square miles, and is located in the Central Time Zone. The county government was organized in 1861. County seat is Grant City.

Weather Station: Grant City Elevation: 1,128 feet

	Jan	Feb	Mar	Apr	May	Jun	Jul	Aug	Sep	Oct	Nov	Dec
High	33	39	52	65	74	84	88	86	78	66	50	37
Low	14	19	30	41	52	61	65	63	55	43	31	20
Precip	0.8	1.1	2.3	3.2	4.5	4.1	4.6	3.8	4.1	2.9	2.4	1.4
Snow	6.2	5.3	4.0	1.5	0.0	0.0	0.0	0.0	0.0	0.2	2.4	4.2

High and Low temperatures in degrees Fahrenheit; Precipitation and Snow in inches

Population: 2,382 (2000); Race: 98.7% White, 0.1% Black, 0.0% Asian, 0.5% American Indian and Alaska Native, 0.2% Hispanic of any race, 0.7% two or more races (2000); Density: 8.9 persons per square mile (2000); Age: 24.2% under 18, 22.5% over 64 (2000).
Religion: Five largest groups: 35.1% Southern Baptist Convention, 19.5% Christian Churches and Churches of Christ, 11.5% The United Methodist Church, 10.6% Christian Church (Disciples of Christ), 4.7% Assemblies of God (2000).
Economy: Unemployment rate: 4.0% (11/2002); Total civilian labor force: 781 (11/2002); Leading industries: except pub other services; Health car 11.9%; Accommodat 11.9% (2000); Companies that employ more than 1,000 persons: 0 (2000); Companies that employ more than 100 persons: 0 (2000); Farms: 356 totaling 150,155 acres (1997); Minority business ownership rate: 0.0% (1997); Women business ownership rate: 0.0% (1997); Retail sales per capita: $2,623 (1997). Single-family building permits issued: 0 (2001) / 0 (2000); Multi-family building permits issued: 0 (2001) / 0 (2000).
Income: Per capita income: $14,367 (2000); Median household income: $27,471 (2000); Poverty rate: 14.3% (2000); Bankruptcy rate: 3.05% (2001).
Taxes: Total county taxes per capita: $128 (1997); County property taxes per capita: $34 (1997).
Education: High school graduation rate: 80.2% (2000); College graduation rate: 11.3% (2000).
Housing: Homeownership rate: 76.8% (2000); Median home value: $27,200 (2000); Median rent: $174 per month (2000); Median age of housing: 57 years (2000).
Health: Birth rate: 96.6 per 10,000 population (1998); Age adjusted death rate: 81.5 per 10,000 population (1999); Age adjusted cancer mortality rate: n/a (1999). Number of physicians: n/a (1999); Number of hospital beds: n/a (1999).
Elections: 2000 Presidential election results: 40.5% Gore, 56.2% Bush, 1.3% Nader, 0.7% Buchanan
Additional Information Contacts
Worth County Government Offices 660-564-2219

Worth County Communities

ALLENDALE (town). Covers a land area of 0.568 square miles and a water area of 0 square miles. Located at 40.48° N. Lat.; 94.29° W. Long. Elevation is 1,056 feet.
Population: 54 (2000); Race: 100.0% White, 0.0% Black, 0.0% Asian, 0.0% American Indian and Alaska Native, 0.0% Hispanic of any race, 0.0% two or more races (2000); Density: 95.1 persons per square mile (2000); Age: 14.1%

under 18, 28.1% over 64 (2000); Marriage status: 7.3% never married, 65.5% now married, 18.2% widowed, 9.1% divorced (2000); Foreign born: 0.0% (2000); Ancestry (includes multiple ancestries): 18.8% United States or American, 7.8% German, 7.8% Other groups, 7.8% Irish, 6.3% Scottish (2000).
Economy: Employment by occupation: 33.3% management, 6.7% professional, 20.0% services, 13.3% sales, 0.0% farming, 10.0% construction, 16.7% production (2000).
Income: Per capita income: $19,502 (2000); Median household income: $30,833 (2000); Poverty rate: 3.1% (2000).
Taxes: Total city taxes per capita: $52 (1997); City property taxes per capita: $17 (1997).
Education: High school graduation rate: 80.0% (2000); College graduation rate: 14.5% (2000).
Housing: Homeownership rate: 87.9% (2000); Median home value: $31,900 (2000); Median age of housing: 60+ years (2000).
Transportation: Commute to work: 93.3% car, 0.0% public transportation, 6.7% walk, 0.0% work from home (2000); Travel time to work: 40.0% less than 15 minutes, 43.3% 15 to 30 minutes, 16.7% 30 to 45 minutes, 0.0% 45 to 60 minutes, 0.0% 60 minutes or more (2000)

DENVER (village). Covers a land area of 0.383 square miles and a water area of 0 square miles. Located at 40.39° N. Lat.; 94.32° W. Long. Elevation is 898 feet.
Population: 40 (2000); Race: 100.0% White, 0.0% Black, 0.0% Asian, 0.0% American Indian and Alaska Native, 0.0% Hispanic of any race, 0.0% two or more races (2000); Density: 104.4 persons per square mile (2000); Age: 43.3% under 18, 6.7% over 64 (2000); Marriage status: 26.1% never married, 21.7% now married, 8.7% widowed, 43.5% divorced (2000); Foreign born: 0.0% (2000); Ancestry (includes multiple ancestries): 6.7% Scottish, 6.7% Greek, 6.7% German, 6.7% English (2000).
Economy: Employment by occupation: 0.0% management, 0.0% professional, 50.0% services, 0.0% sales, 0.0% farming, 0.0% construction, 50.0% production (2000).
Income: Per capita income: $7,283 (2000); Median household income: $18,750 (2000); Poverty rate: 40.0% (2000).
Taxes: Total city taxes per capita: $20 (1997); City property taxes per capita: $20 (1997).
Education: High school graduation rate: 64.7% (2000); College graduation rate: 0.0% (2000).
Housing: Homeownership rate: 84.6% (2000); Median home value: $12,500 (2000); Median age of housing: 60+ years (2000).
Transportation: Commute to work: 100.0% car, 0.0% public transportation, 0.0% walk, 0.0% work from home (2000); Travel time to work: 0.0% less than 15 minutes, 50.0% 15 to 30 minutes, 50.0% 30 to 45 minutes, 0.0% 45 to 60 minutes, 0.0% 60 minutes or more (2000)

GRANT CITY (town). Covers a land area of 1.259 square miles and a water area of 0 square miles. Located at 40.48° N. Lat.; 94.41° W. Long. Elevation is 1,136 feet.
History: Settled 1864.
Population: 926 (2000); Race: 98.4% White, 0.2% Black, 0.0% Asian, 0.7% American Indian and Alaska Native, 0.4% Hispanic of any race, 0.6% two or more races (2000); Density: 735.2 persons per square mile (2000); Age: 22.4% under 18, 25.4% over 64 (2000); Marriage status: 17.4% never married, 57.2% now married, 13.5% widowed, 11.9% divorced (2000); Foreign born: 0.0% (2000); Ancestry (includes multiple ancestries): 18.5% German, 13.5% Irish, 10.0% English, 8.6% United States or American, 4.9% Other groups (2000).
Economy: Wheat, soybeans; cattle. Manufacturing: apparel. Single-family building permits issued: 0 (2001) / 0 (2000); Multi-family building permits issued: 0 (2001) / 0 (2000); Employment by occupation: 11.1% management, 13.7% professional, 13.7% services, 23.2% sales, 4.9% farming, 13.1% construction, 20.4% production (2000).
Income: Per capita income: $14,009 (2000); Median household income: $23,897 (2000); Poverty rate: 17.2% (2000).
Taxes: Total city taxes per capita: $176 (1997); City property taxes per capita: $7 (1997).
Education: High school graduation rate: 76.1% (2000); College graduation rate: 7.6% (2000).

School District(s)

Worth Co. R-III (KG-12)
2000 Enrollment: 415 660-564-3389

Housing: Homeownership rate: 70.3% (2000); Median home value: $28,600 (2000); Median rent: $174 per month (2000); Median age of housing: 53 years (2000).
Newspapers: The Times-Tribune (1 x week)
Transportation: Commute to work: 92.1% car, 0.5% public transportation, 3.1% walk, 2.1% work from home (2000); Travel time to work: 52.5% less than 15 minutes, 16.1% 15 to 30 minutes, 17.4% 30 to 45 minutes, 4.8% 45 to 60 minutes, 9.1% 60 minutes or more (2000)

IRENA (village). Covers a land area of 1.007 square miles and a water area of 0 square miles. Located at 40.53° N. Lat.; 94.38° W. Long. Elevation is 1,150 feet.
Population: 33 (2000); Race: 100.0% White, 0.0% Black, 0.0% Asian, 0.0% American Indian and Alaska Native, 0.0% Hispanic of any race, 0.0% two or more races (2000); Density: 32.8 persons per square mile (2000); Age: 22.7% under 18, 9.1% over 64 (2000); Marriage status: 15.0% never married, 85.0% now married, 0.0% widowed, 0.0% divorced (2000); Foreign born: 0.0% (2000); Ancestry (includes multiple ancestries): 50.0% United States or American, 36.4% German, 9.1% Irish (2000).
Economy: Employment by occupation: 0.0% management, 18.2% professional, 9.1% services, 36.4% sales, 0.0% farming, 36.4% construction, 0.0% production (2000).
Income: Per capita income: $12,605 (2000); Median household income: $31,875 (2000); Poverty rate: 0.0% (2000).
Education: High school graduation rate: 70.6% (2000); College graduation rate: 11.8% (2000).
Housing: Homeownership rate: 100.0% (2000); Median age of housing: 60 years (2000).
Transportation: Commute to work: 81.8% car, 0.0% public transportation, 0.0% walk, 18.2% work from home (2000); Travel time to work: 33.3% less than 15 minutes, 0.0% 15 to 30 minutes, 22.2% 30 to 45 minutes, 11.1% 45 to 60 minutes, 33.3% 60 minutes or more (2000)

SHERIDAN (town). Covers a land area of 0.194 square miles and a water area of 0 square miles. Located at 40.51° N. Lat.; 94.61° W. Long. Elevation is 1,048 feet.
History: Plotted 1887.
Population: 185 (2000); Race: 100.0% White, 0.0% Black, 0.0% Asian, 0.0% American Indian and Alaska Native, 0.0% Hispanic of any race, 0.0% two or more races (2000); Density: 954.9 persons per square mile (2000); Age: 20.6% under 18, 32.4% over 64 (2000); Marriage status: 16.8% never married, 46.2% now married, 18.9% widowed, 18.2% divorced (2000); Foreign born: 0.0% (2000); Ancestry (includes multiple ancestries): 20.6% German, 11.2% United States or American, 9.4% English, 5.9% Irish, 4.7% Other groups (2000).
Economy: Corn, wheat, soybeans; cattle. Employment by occupation: 10.9% management, 5.5% professional, 21.8% services, 16.4% sales, 14.5% farming, 3.6% construction, 27.3% production (2000).
Income: Per capita income: $12,162 (2000); Median household income: $20,357 (2000); Poverty rate: 13.5% (2000).
Taxes: Total city taxes per capita: $82 (1997); City property taxes per capita: $53 (1997).
Education: High school graduation rate: 64.0% (2000); College graduation rate: 2.4% (2000).
Housing: Homeownership rate: 73.9% (2000); Median home value: $17,500 (2000); Median rent: $150 per month (2000); Median age of housing: 60+ years (2000).
Newspapers: Quad River News (1 x week)
Transportation: Commute to work: 83.6% car, 0.0% public transportation, 10.9% walk, 1.8% work from home (2000); Travel time to work: 40.7% less than 15 minutes, 14.8% 15 to 30 minutes, 31.5% 30 to 45 minutes, 0.0% 45 to 60 minutes, 13.0% 60 minutes or more (2000)

WORTH (town). Covers a land area of 0.248 square miles and a water area of 0 square miles. Located at 40.40° N. Lat.; 94.44° W. Long. Elevation is 923 feet.
Population: 94 (2000); Race: 98.0% White, 0.0% Black, 0.0% Asian, 2.0% American Indian and Alaska Native, 0.0% Hispanic of any race, 0.0% two or more races (2000); Density: 378.8 persons per square mile (2000); Age: 22.5% under 18, 8.8% over 64 (2000); Marriage status: 22.5% never married, 61.8% now married, 2.2% widowed, 13.5% divorced (2000); Foreign born: 0.0% (2000); Ancestry (includes multiple ancestries): 33.3% German, 12.7% United States or American, 12.7% Other groups, 11.8% Irish, 8.8% Scotch-Irish (2000).
Economy: Employment by occupation: 10.2% management, 0.0% professional, 10.2% services, 12.2% sales, 4.1% farming, 16.3% construction, 46.9% production (2000).
Income: Per capita income: $11,261 (2000); Median household income: $28,750 (2000); Poverty rate: 28.4% (2000).

Taxes: Total city taxes per capita: $70 (1997); City property taxes per capita: $70 (1997).
Education: High school graduation rate: 75.4% (2000); College graduation rate: 6.6% (2000).
Housing: Homeownership rate: 89.7% (2000); Median home value: <$10,000 (2000); Median rent: $225 per month (2000); Median age of housing: 60+ years (2000).
Transportation: Commute to work: 95.9% car, 4.1% public transportation, 0.0% walk, 0.0% work from home (2000); Travel time to work: 12.2% less than 15 minutes, 44.9% 15 to 30 minutes, 20.4% 30 to 45 minutes, 22.4% 45 to 60 minutes, 0.0% 60 minutes or more (2000)

Wright County

Located in south central Missouri, in the Ozarks; drained by the Gasconade River; includes part of Mark Twain National Forest. Covers a land area of 682.10 square miles, a water area of 1.10 square miles, and is located in the Central Time Zone. The county government was organized in 1861. County seat is Hartville.

Weather Station: Mansfield Elevation: 1,519 feet

	Jan	Feb	Mar	Apr	May	Jun	Jul	Aug	Sep	Oct	Nov	Dec
High	42	48	58	68	76	84	89	88	80	70	55	46
Low	19	24	32	42	51	59	64	62	55	44	33	24
Precip	2.0	2.4	4.0	4.2	4.5	4.5	3.3	3.1	4.6	3.8	4.5	3.4
Snow	5.8	4.1	2.8	0.3	0.0	0.0	0.0	0.0	0.0	tr	0.7	1.9

High and Low temperatures in degrees Fahrenheit; Precipitation and Snow in inches

Weather Station: Mountain Grove 2 N Elevation: 1,450 feet

	Jan	Feb	Mar	Apr	May	Jun	Jul	Aug	Sep	Oct	Nov	Dec
High	40	47	56	67	75	82	88	87	79	69	55	44
Low	21	26	34	44	53	61	66	64	57	45	35	26
Precip	2.3	2.6	4.3	4.5	4.8	4.2	3.8	3.4	4.3	3.7	4.5	3.6
Snow	5.0	2.9	2.6	0.5	0.0	0.0	0.0	0.0	0.0	tr	1.2	2.0

High and Low temperatures in degrees Fahrenheit; Precipitation and Snow in inches

Population: 17,955 (2000); Race: 97.1% White, 0.4% Black, 0.1% Asian, 0.8% American Indian and Alaska Native, 1.2% Hispanic of any race, 1.3% two or more races (2000); Density: 26.3 persons per square mile (2000); Age: 27.0% under 18, 16.5% over 64 (2000).
Religion: Five largest groups: 29.9% Southern Baptist Convention, 11.8% National Association of Free Will Baptists, 4.5% Assemblies of God, 2.8% The United Methodist Church, 2.2% Church of the Nazarene (2000).
Economy: Unemployment rate: 7.8% (11/2002); Total civilian labor force: 6,282 (11/2002); Leading industries: 25.0% retail trade; 23.0% manufacturing; 12.2% health care and social assistance (2000); Companies that employ more than 1,000 persons: 0 (2000); Companies that employ more than 100 persons: 3 (2000); Farms: 1,331 totaling 312,388 acres (1997); Minority business ownership rate: 0.0% (1997); Women business ownership rate: 35.6% (1997); Retail sales per capita: $6,713 (1997). Single-family building permits issued: 5 (2001) / 15 (2000); Multi-family building permits issued: 0 (2001) / 0 (2000).
Income: Per capita income: $13,135 (2000); Median household income: $24,691 (2000); Poverty rate: 21.7% (2000); Bankruptcy rate: 3.03% (2001).
Taxes: Total county taxes per capita: $38 (1997); County property taxes per capita: $8 (1997).
Education: High school graduation rate: 71.1% (2000); College graduation rate: 9.8% (2000).
Housing: Homeownership rate: 73.1% (2000); Median home value: $57,000 (2000); Median rent: $222 per month (2000); Median age of housing: 28 years (2000).
Health: Birth rate: 144.3 per 10,000 population (1998); Age adjusted death rate: 94.0 per 10,000 population (1999); Age adjusted cancer mortality rate: 225.0 deaths per 100,000 population (1999). Number of physicians: 2.8 per 10,000 population (1999); Number of hospital beds: n/a (1999).
Elections: 2000 Presidential election results: 28.7% Gore, 68.8% Bush, 1.1% Nader, 0.9% Buchanan
National and State Parks: Wilber Allen Memorial State Wildlife Area
Additional Information Contacts
Wright County Government Offices 417-741-6661
Mansfield Area Chamber of Commerce 417-924-3525
Mountain Grove Chamber of Commerce 417-926-4135

Wright County Communities

GRAFF (unincorporated postal area, zip code 65660). Covers a land area of 27.016 square miles and a water area of 0 square miles. Located at 37.33° N. Lat.; 92.27° W. Long. Elevation is 1,325 feet.
Population: 215 (2000); Race: 100.0% White, 0.0% Black, 0.0% Asian, 0.0% American Indian and Alaska Native, 0.0% Hispanic of any race, 0.0% two or more races (2000); Density: 8.0 persons per square mile (2000); Age: 20.7% under 18, 11.5% over 64 (2000); Marriage status: 27.5% never married, 69.5% now married, 3.0% widowed, 0.0% divorced (2000); Foreign born: 0.0% (2000); Ancestry (includes multiple ancestries): 18.5% German, 15.0% Other groups, 12.8% United States or American, 7.9% Irish, 7.9% French (except Basque) (2000).
Economy: Employment by occupation: 9.6% management, 7.7% professional, 7.7% services, 12.5% sales, 14.4% farming, 0.0% construction, 48.1% production (2000).
Income: Per capita income: $8,642 (2000); Median household income: $17,500 (2000); Poverty rate: 27.8% (2000).
Education: High school graduation rate: 63.2% (2000); College graduation rate: 1.3% (2000).
Housing: Homeownership rate: 81.0% (2000); Median home value: $93,300 (2000); Median rent: $225 per month (2000); Median age of housing: 27 years (2000).
Transportation: Commute to work: 74.0% car, 0.0% public transportation, 6.7% walk, 19.2% work from home (2000); Travel time to work: 6.0% less than 15 minutes, 28.6% 15 to 30 minutes, 46.4% 30 to 45 minutes, 2.4% 45 to 60 minutes, 16.7% 60 minutes or more (2000)

GROVESPRING (unincorporated postal area, zip code 65662). Covers a land area of 72.743 square miles and a water area of 0.050 square miles. Located at 37.46° N. Lat.; 92.58° W. Long. Elevation is 1,290 feet.
Population: 1,176 (2000); Race: 98.6% White, 0.6% Black, 0.0% Asian, 0.0% American Indian and Alaska Native, 0.8% Hispanic of any race, 0.8% two or more races (2000); Density: 16.2 persons per square mile (2000); Age: 26.6% under 18, 17.0% over 64 (2000); Marriage status: 21.0% never married, 58.5% now married, 7.5% widowed, 13.0% divorced (2000); Foreign born: 1.1% (2000); Ancestry (includes multiple ancestries): 18.5% United States or American, 14.4% German, 12.8% Irish, 6.0% English, 5.5% Other groups (2000).
Economy: Employment by occupation: 20.1% management, 12.8% professional, 9.5% services, 12.8% sales, 0.7% farming, 12.8% construction, 31.2% production (2000).
Income: Per capita income: $20,990 (2000); Median household income: $29,076 (2000); Poverty rate: 12.8% (2000).
Education: High school graduation rate: 66.7% (2000); College graduation rate: 6.0% (2000).
Housing: Homeownership rate: 81.8% (2000); Median home value: $45,800 (2000); Median rent: $233 per month (2000); Median age of housing: 26 years (2000).
Transportation: Commute to work: 80.2% car, 0.0% public transportation, 4.0% walk, 15.1% work from home (2000); Travel time to work: 9.8% less than 15 minutes, 41.2% 15 to 30 minutes, 28.7% 30 to 45 minutes, 10.2% 45 to 60 minutes, 10.0% 60 minutes or more (2000)

HARTVILLE (city). Covers a land area of 0.623 square miles and a water area of 0.005 square miles. Located at 37.25° N. Lat.; 92.51° W. Long. Elevation is 1,190 feet.
History: Settled 1832. Destroyed during Civil War.
Population: 607 (2000); Race: 98.3% White, 0.0% Black, 0.0% Asian, 1.0% American Indian and Alaska Native, 0.3% Hispanic of any race, 0.7% two or more races (2000); Density: 974.7 persons per square mile (2000); Age: 22.9% under 18, 27.3% over 64 (2000); Marriage status: 19.0% never married, 51.7% now married, 19.8% widowed, 9.6% divorced (2000); Foreign born: 0.3% (2000); Ancestry (includes multiple ancestries): 21.3% United States or American, 11.3% Other groups, 10.6% English, 9.4% Irish, 8.7% German (2000).
Economy: Peaches, apples, hay; dairying; cattle; timber. Manufacturing of livestock feed and fertilizer. Single-family building permits issued: 0 (2001) / 0 (2000); Multi-family building permits issued: 0 (2001) / 0 (2000); Employment by occupation: 19.4% management, 10.5% professional, 16.8% services, 19.4% sales, 6.8% farming, 4.2% construction, 23.0% production (2000).
Income: Per capita income: $11,360 (2000); Median household income: $17,222 (2000); Poverty rate: 24.3% (2000).
Taxes: Total city taxes per capita: $184 (1997); City property taxes per capita: $31 (1997).

Education: High school graduation rate: 56.3% (2000); College graduation rate: 7.0% (2000).

School District(s)

Hartville R-II (PK-12)
2000 Enrollment: 787 417-741-7676

Housing: Homeownership rate: 66.1% (2000); Median home value: $45,200 (2000); Median rent: $202 per month (2000); Median age of housing: 40 years (2000).

Transportation: Commute to work: 94.7% car, 0.0% public transportation, 0.0% walk, 5.3% work from home (2000); Travel time to work: 42.7% less than 15 minutes, 21.9% 15 to 30 minutes, 16.9% 30 to 45 minutes, 7.9% 45 to 60 minutes, 10.7% 60 minutes or more (2000)

MACOMB (unincorporated postal area, zip code 65702). Covers a land area of 35.923 square miles and a water area of 0 square miles. Located at 37.07° N. Lat.; 92.49° W. Long. Elevation is 1,517 feet.

Population: 470 (2000); Race: 91.5% White, 0.0% Black, 0.0% Asian, 0.0% American Indian and Alaska Native, 5.4% Hispanic of any race, 4.9% two or more races (2000); Density: 13.1 persons per square mile (2000); Age: 26.4% under 18, 11.8% over 64 (2000); Marriage status: 19.3% never married, 71.0% now married, 1.8% widowed, 7.9% divorced (2000); Foreign born: 4.7% (2000); Ancestry (includes multiple ancestries): 21.9% United States or American, 10.8% English, 7.5% German, 7.1% Irish, 5.2% Other groups (2000).

Economy: Employment by occupation: 20.4% management, 13.8% professional, 19.3% services, 8.8% sales, 1.1% farming, 11.6% construction, 24.9% production (2000).

Income: Per capita income: $11,256 (2000); Median household income: $23,250 (2000); Poverty rate: 22.8% (2000).

Education: High school graduation rate: 60.9% (2000); College graduation rate: 6.5% (2000).

Housing: Homeownership rate: 73.0% (2000); Median home value: $45,000 (2000); Median rent: $309 per month (2000); Median age of housing: 26 years (2000).

Transportation: Commute to work: 91.2% car, 0.0% public transportation, 0.0% walk, 8.8% work from home (2000); Travel time to work: 27.3% less than 15 minutes, 38.8% 15 to 30 minutes, 13.3% 30 to 45 minutes, 5.5% 45 to 60 minutes, 15.2% 60 minutes or more (2000)

MANSFIELD (city). Covers a land area of 1.570 square miles and a water area of 0 square miles. Located at 37.10° N. Lat.; 92.58° W. Long. Elevation is 1,488 feet.

History: Mansfield was platted in 1884, and prospered as an agricultural center with a cheese plant and creamery.

Population: 1,349 (2000); Race: 95.9% White, 0.0% Black, 0.0% Asian, 1.1% American Indian and Alaska Native, 1.2% Hispanic of any race, 3.0% two or more races (2000); Density: 859.0 persons per square mile (2000); Age: 30.4% under 18, 15.7% over 64 (2000); Marriage status: 16.0% never married, 58.6% now married, 12.1% widowed, 13.3% divorced (2000); Foreign born: 0.4% (2000); Ancestry (includes multiple ancestries): 22.3% United States or American, 12.9% Other groups, 12.8% Irish, 11.5% German, 6.3% English (2000).

Economy: Single-family building permits issued: 1 (2001) / 1 (2000); Multi-family building permits issued: 0 (2001) / 0 (2000); Employment by occupation: 6.9% management, 9.7% professional, 19.9% services, 19.9% sales, 1.4% farming, 14.1% construction, 28.2% production (2000).

Income: Per capita income: $11,303 (2000); Median household income: $21,875 (2000); Poverty rate: 24.2% (2000).

Taxes: Total city taxes per capita: $118 (1997); City property taxes per capita: $46 (1997).

Education: High school graduation rate: 68.1% (2000); College graduation rate: 7.7% (2000).

School District(s)

Mansfield R-IV (PK-12)
2000 Enrollment: 817 417-924-8458

Housing: Homeownership rate: 59.2% (2000); Median home value: $49,100 (2000); Median rent: $200 per month (2000); Median age of housing: 30 years (2000).

Newspapers: The Mansfield Mirror (1 x week)

Transportation: Commute to work: 92.7% car, 0.0% public transportation, 1.4% walk, 5.1% work from home (2000); Travel time to work: 46.1% less than 15 minutes, 26.7% 15 to 30 minutes, 5.6% 30 to 45 minutes, 9.3% 45 to 60 minutes, 12.3% 60 minutes or more (2000)

Additional Information Contacts

Mansfield Area Chamber of Commerce 417-924-3525

MOUNTAIN GROVE (city). Covers a land area of 4.190 square miles and a water area of 0.055 square miles. Located at 37.13° N. Lat.; 92.26° W. Long. Elevation is 1,460 feet.

History: Mountain Grove began as Hickory Springs, where a post office was established in 1851. The Mountain Grove Seminary opened here in 1857. When the railroad was built some distance away in 1883, the town was moved to a new site and renamed Mountain Grove.

Population: 4,574 (2000); Race: 97.9% White, 0.3% Black, 0.0% Asian, 0.9% American Indian and Alaska Native, 1.1% Hispanic of any race, 0.7% two or more races (2000); Density: 1,091.6 persons per square mile (2000); Age: 24.3% under 18, 21.0% over 64 (2000); Marriage status: 17.1% never married, 58.5% now married, 10.7% widowed, 13.7% divorced (2000); Foreign born: 0.6% (2000); Ancestry (includes multiple ancestries): 21.3% United States or American, 12.8% Other groups, 12.2% German, 10.0% Irish, 8.1% English (2000).

Economy: Single-family building permits issued: 4 (2001) / 14 (2000); Multi-family building permits issued: 0 (2001) / 0 (2000); Employment by occupation: 11.0% management, 16.6% professional, 17.5% services, 24.8% sales, 0.5% farming, 9.2% construction, 20.4% production (2000).

Income: Per capita income: $13,508 (2000); Median household income: $21,131 (2000); Poverty rate: 28.2% (2000).

Taxes: Total city taxes per capita: $238 (1997); City property taxes per capita: $0 (1997).

Education: High school graduation rate: 71.1% (2000); College graduation rate: 11.6% (2000).

School District(s)

Manes R-V (KG-08)
2000 Enrollment: 68 417-668-5313

Mountain Grove R-III (PK-12)
2000 Enrollment: 1,698 417-926-3177

Housing: Homeownership rate: 60.2% (2000); Median home value: $59,400 (2000); Median rent: $224 per month (2000); Median age of housing: 32 years (2000).

Newspapers: Mountain Grove News-Journal (1 x week)

Transportation: Commute to work: 97.7% car, 0.3% public transportation, 0.5% walk, 0.7% work from home (2000); Travel time to work: 61.7% less than 15 minutes, 19.2% 15 to 30 minutes, 8.7% 30 to 45 minutes, 0.8% 45 to 60 minutes, 9.6% 60 minutes or more (2000)

Additional Information Contacts

Mountain Grove Chamber of Commerce.................. 417-926-4135

NORWOOD (city). Covers a land area of 1.589 square miles and a water area of 0 square miles. Located at 37.11° N. Lat.; 92.41° W. Long. Elevation is 1,496 feet.

Population: 552 (2000); Race: 95.2% White, 0.0% Black, 0.0% Asian, 1.5% American Indian and Alaska Native, 0.3% Hispanic of any race, 3.3% two or more races (2000); Density: 347.4 persons per square mile (2000); Age: 34.6% under 18, 12.0% over 64 (2000); Marriage status: 21.7% never married, 60.1% now married, 6.3% widowed, 11.9% divorced (2000); Foreign born: 0.0% (2000); Ancestry (includes multiple ancestries): 30.8% United States or American, 12.6% German, 11.1% Irish, 10.6% English, 7.5% Other groups (2000).

Economy: Dairy; cattle, poultry. Employment by occupation: 2.5% management, 19.7% professional, 20.1% services, 9.6% sales, 4.2% farming, 10.0% construction, 33.9% production (2000).

Income: Per capita income: $9,670 (2000); Median household income: $22,614 (2000); Poverty rate: 29.5% (2000).

Education: High school graduation rate: 71.8% (2000); College graduation rate: 5.5% (2000).

School District(s)

Norwood R-I (PK-12)
2000 Enrollment: 482 417-746-4101

Skyline R-II (PK-08)
2000 Enrollment: 128 417-683-4874

Housing: Homeownership rate: 63.7% (2000); Median home value: $36,400 (2000); Median rent: $223 per month (2000); Median age of housing: 29 years (2000).

Transportation: Commute to work: 91.4% car, 1.3% public transportation, 5.2% walk, 2.2% work from home (2000); Travel time to work: 37.4% less than 15 minutes, 26.4% 15 to 30 minutes, 11.0% 30 to 45 minutes, 7.0% 45 to 60 minutes, 18.1% 60 minutes or more (2000)

Wisconsin

The Badger State

WISCONSIN –Metropolitan Areas, Counties, and Central Cities

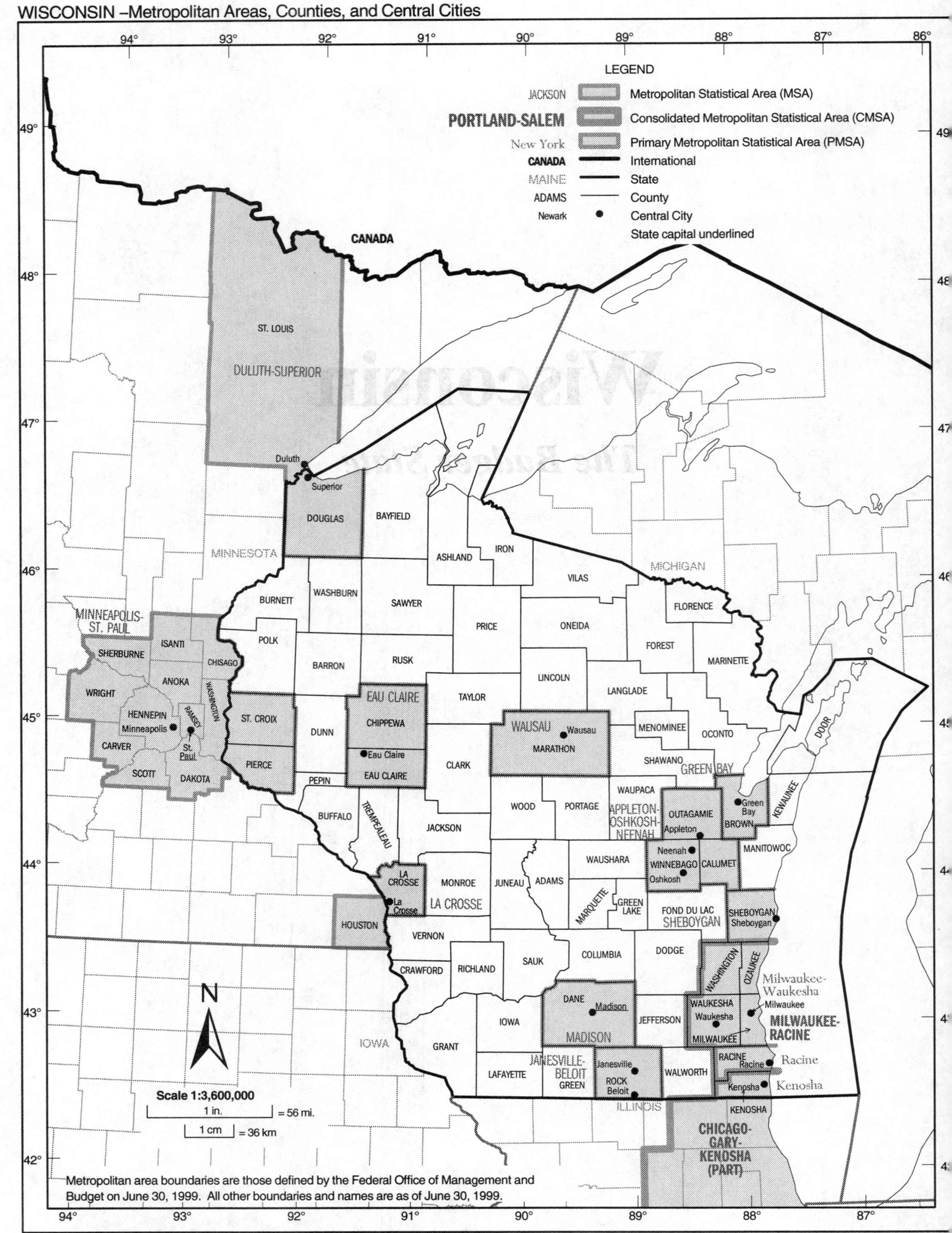

Metropolitan area boundaries are those defined by the Federal Office of Management and Budget on June 30, 1999. All other boundaries and names are as of June 30, 1999.

A

B

CDP = Census Designated Place

E

F

G

H

I

J

K

L

M

N

O

P

Q

R

CDP = Census Designated Place

S

CDP = Census Designated Place

Adams County

Located in central Wisconsin; bounded on the west by the Wisconsin River. Covers a land area of 647.70 square miles, a water area of 40.80 square miles, and is located in the Central Time Zone. The county government was organized in 1848. County seat is Friendship.
Population: 18,643 (2000); Race: 97.4% White, 0.3% Black, 0.5% Asian, 0.5% American Indian and Alaska Native, 1.4% Hispanic of any race, 1.0% two or more races (2000); Density: 28.8 persons per square mile (2000); Age: 20.7% under 18, 21.0% over 64 (2000).
Religion: Five largest groups: 9.7% Catholic Church, 8.1% Evangelical Lutheran Church in America, 3.7% Lutheran Church—Missouri Synod, 1.0% The Church of Jesus Christ of Latter-day Saints, 0.9% Assemblies of God (2000).
Economy: Unemployment rate: 4.8% (11/2002); Total civilian labor force: 8,559 (11/2002); Leading industries: 20.4% manufacturing; 19.6% accommodation & food services; 17.1% health care and social assistance (2000); Companies that employ more than 1,000 persons: 0 (2000); Companies that employ more than 100 persons: 4 (2000); Farms: 360 totaling 121,572 acres (1997); Minority business ownership rate: 0.0% (1997); Women business ownership rate: 13.6% (1997); Retail sales per capita: $3,560 (1997). Single-family building permits issued: 195 (2001) / 236 (2000); Multi-family building permits issued: 18 (2001) / 8 (2000).
Income: Per capita income: $17,777 (2000); Median household income: $33,408 (2000); Poverty rate: 10.4% (2000); Bankruptcy rate: 2.34% (2001).
Taxes: Total county taxes per capita: $425 (1997); County property taxes per capita: $383 (1997).
Education: High school graduation rate: 76.7% (2000); College graduation rate: 10.0% (2000).
Housing: Homeownership rate: 85.4% (2000); Median home value: $83,600 (2000); Median rent: $357 per month (2000); Median age of housing: 22 years (2000).
Health: Birth rate: 90.1 per 10,000 population (1998); Age adjusted death rate: 84.2 per 10,000 population (1999); Age adjusted cancer mortality rate: 210.0 deaths per 100,000 population (1999). Number of physicians: 4.8 per 10,000 population (1999); Number of hospital beds: 31.1 per 10,000 population (1999).
Elections: 2000 Presidential election results: 52.9% Gore, 43.0% Bush, 2.4% Nader, 0.8% Buchanan
National and State Parks: Big Roche A Cri State Fishery Area; Lawrence Creek State Wildlife Area; Leola Marsh State Wildlife Area; Roche a Cri State Park; Upper Neenah Creek State Fishery Area
Additional Information Contacts
Adams County Government Offices 608-339-4200
Friendship Chamber of Commerce 608-339-6997

Adams County Communities

ADAMS (city). Covers a land area of 2.944 square miles and a water area of 0 square miles. Located at 43.95° N. Lat.; 89.81° W. Long. Elevation is 960 feet.
History: Adams was established in the 1850's, shortly after its neighbor of Friendship. It was first called Lower Friendship, when the Wisconsin Central Railroad chose this land for its route.
Population: 1,914 (2000); Race: 95.6% White, 0.6% Black, 0.6% Asian, 0.5% American Indian and Alaska Native, 1.9% Hispanic of any race, 2.3% two or more races (2000); Density: 650.1 persons per square mile (2000); Age: 26.5% under 18, 22.9% over 64 (2000); Marriage status: 21.3% never married, 52.8% now married, 13.3% widowed, 12.6% divorced (2000); Foreign born: 2.0% (2000); Ancestry (includes multiple ancestries): 39.5% German, 13.2% Irish, 11.2% Norwegian, 9.1% Polish, 6.9% English (2000).
Economy: Single-family building permits issued: 5 (2001) / 3 (2000); Multi-family building permits issued: 11 (2001) / 4 (2000); Employment by occupation: 6.7% management, 13.3% professional, 26.5% services, 21.0% sales, 0.3% farming, 9.3% construction, 23.0% production (2000).
Income: Per capita income: $14,744 (2000); Median household income: $26,250 (2000); Poverty rate: 14.6% (2000).
Taxes: Total city taxes per capita: $186 (1997); City property taxes per capita: $174 (1997).
Education: High school graduation rate: 72.2% (2000); College graduation rate: 14.6% (2000).
Housing: Homeownership rate: 59.5% (2000); Median home value: $58,200 (2000); Median rent: $336 per month (2000); Median age of housing: 34 years (2000).
Newspapers: The Friendship Reporter (1 x week); The Adams County Times (1 x week)
Transportation: Commute to work: 89.4% car, 0.6% public transportation, 3.0% walk, 3.5% work from home (2000); Travel time to work: 57.4% less than 15 minutes, 9.5% 15 to 30 minutes, 14.1% 30 to 45 minutes, 11.5% 45 to 60 minutes, 7.5% 60 minutes or more (2000)

ADAMS (town). Covers a land area of 50.502 square miles and a water area of 0.090 square miles. Located at 43.94° N. Lat.; 89.81° W. Long. Elevation is 960 feet.
History: Founded before 1860, incorporated 1926.
Population: 1,267 (2000); Race: 97.2% White, 0.2% Black, 0.0% Asian, 0.9% American Indian and Alaska Native, 1.8% Hispanic of any race, 0.6% two or more races (2000); Density: 25.1 persons per square mile (2000); Age: 20.7% under 18, 15.5% over 64 (2000); Marriage status: 20.3% never married, 59.7% now married, 6.8% widowed, 13.1% divorced (2000); Foreign born: 1.5% (2000); Ancestry (includes multiple ancestries): 45.5% German, 12.4% Irish, 10.3% Norwegian, 8.9% Polish, 7.0% English (2000).
Economy: Manufactures shipping containers, modular housing. Employment by occupation: 10.0% management, 14.1% professional, 14.4% services, 22.3% sales, 2.8% farming, 11.4% construction, 25.0% production (2000).
Income: Per capita income: $18,225 (2000); Median household income: $34,286 (2000); Poverty rate: 9.0% (2000).
Taxes: Total city taxes per capita: $41 (1997); City property taxes per capita: $39 (1997).
Education: High school graduation rate: 71.2% (2000); College graduation rate: 6.1% (2000).
Housing: Homeownership rate: 85.5% (2000); Median home value: $82,600 (2000); Median rent: $340 per month (2000); Median age of housing: 21 years (2000).
Transportation: Commute to work: 92.3% car, 0.6% public transportation, 0.8% walk, 5.5% work from home (2000); Travel time to work: 45.4% less than 15 minutes, 16.7% 15 to 30 minutes, 16.7% 30 to 45 minutes, 12.3% 45 to 60 minutes, 8.9% 60 minutes or more (2000)

ARKDALE (unincorporated postal area, zip code 54613). Covers a land area of 72.113 square miles and a water area of 0.067 square miles. Located at 44.06° N. Lat.; 89.90° W. Long. Elevation is 935 feet.
Population: 1,750 (2000); Race: 98.3% White, 0.4% Black, 0.3% Asian, 0.2% American Indian and Alaska Native, 1.3% Hispanic of any race, 0.1% two or more races (2000); Density: 24.3 persons per square mile (2000); Age: 17.0% under 18, 24.2% over 64 (2000); Marriage status: 17.6% never married, 64.6% now married, 9.0% widowed, 8.7% divorced (2000); Foreign born: 2.2% (2000); Ancestry (includes multiple ancestries): 43.9% German, 16.1% Norwegian, 10.7% Irish, 10.2% Polish, 9.4% English (2000).
Economy: Employment by occupation: 8.6% management, 10.8% professional, 19.6% services, 20.4% sales, 1.6% farming, 10.9% construction, 28.0% production (2000).
Income: Per capita income: $16,314 (2000); Median household income: $30,265 (2000); Poverty rate: 12.2% (2000).
Education: High school graduation rate: 76.8% (2000); College graduation rate: 9.6% (2000).
Housing: Homeownership rate: 86.2% (2000); Median home value: $72,600 (2000); Median rent: $311 per month (2000); Median age of housing: 21 years (2000).
Transportation: Commute to work: 86.8% car, 0.0% public transportation, 4.0% walk, 7.3% work from home (2000); Travel time to work: 23.0% less than 15 minutes, 36.4% 15 to 30 minutes, 19.3% 30 to 45 minutes, 9.3% 45 to 60 minutes, 12.0% 60 minutes or more (2000)

BIG FLATS (town). Covers a land area of 48.099 square miles and a water area of 0.006 square miles. Located at 44.10° N. Lat.; 89.79° W. Long. Elevation is 1,000 feet.
Population: 946 (2000); Race: 96.4% White, 1.3% Black, 0.0% Asian, 0.4% American Indian and Alaska Native, 2.1% Hispanic of any race, 0.9% two or more races (2000); Density: 19.7 persons per square mile (2000); Age: 22.6% under 18, 19.2% over 64 (2000); Marriage status: 17.6% never married, 61.3% now married, 9.2% widowed, 11.9% divorced (2000); Foreign born: 1.9% (2000); Ancestry (includes multiple ancestries): 44.1% German, 10.6% Irish, 9.8% Polish, 9.4% English, 6.7% Other groups (2000).
Economy: Employment by occupation: 5.7% management, 9.5% professional, 21.6% services, 16.5% sales, 1.6% farming, 13.2% construction, 31.9% production (2000).
Income: Per capita income: $14,629 (2000); Median household income: $27,800 (2000); Poverty rate: 13.1% (2000).

Taxes: Total city taxes per capita: $89 (1997); City property taxes per capita: $87 (1997).
Education: High school graduation rate: 71.8% (2000); College graduation rate: 8.2% (2000).
Housing: Homeownership rate: 87.1% (2000); Median home value: $64,500 (2000); Median rent: $319 per month (2000); Median age of housing: 24 years (2000).
Transportation: Commute to work: 93.7% car, 0.0% public transportation, 3.0% walk, 2.7% work from home (2000); Travel time to work: 14.7% less than 15 minutes, 33.9% 15 to 30 minutes, 27.7% 30 to 45 minutes, 10.5% 45 to 60 minutes, 13.3% 60 minutes or more (2000)

COLBURN (town). Covers a land area of 35.919 square miles and a water area of 0 square miles. Located at 44.13° N. Lat.; 89.66° W. Long.
Population: 181 (2000); Race: 96.1% White, 0.0% Black, 0.0% Asian, 2.0% American Indian and Alaska Native, 2.0% Hispanic of any race, 2.0% two or more races (2000); Density: 5.0 persons per square mile (2000); Age: 15.8% under 18, 18.2% over 64 (2000); Marriage status: 15.2% never married, 71.3% now married, 5.1% widowed, 8.4% divorced (2000); Foreign born: 0.0% (2000); Ancestry (includes multiple ancestries): 33.0% German, 23.2% United States or American, 9.9% English, 7.4% Irish, 5.9% French (except Basque) (2000).
Economy: Employment by occupation: 3.2% management, 12.9% professional, 14.0% services, 20.4% sales, 10.8% farming, 15.1% construction, 23.7% production (2000).
Income: Per capita income: $21,440 (2000); Median household income: $35,250 (2000); Poverty rate: 5.9% (2000).
Taxes: Total city taxes per capita: $167 (1997); City property taxes per capita: $167 (1997).
Education: High school graduation rate: 70.5% (2000); College graduation rate: 4.7% (2000).
Housing: Homeownership rate: 76.5% (2000); Median home value: $65,000 (2000); Median rent: $313 per month (2000); Median age of housing: 25 years (2000).
Transportation: Commute to work: 76.3% car, 2.2% public transportation, 3.2% walk, 18.3% work from home (2000); Travel time to work: 18.4% less than 15 minutes, 42.1% 15 to 30 minutes, 28.9% 30 to 45 minutes, 5.3% 45 to 60 minutes, 5.3% 60 minutes or more (2000)

DELL PRAIRIE (town). Covers a land area of 33.336 square miles and a water area of 1.156 square miles. Located at 43.68° N. Lat.; 89.77° W. Long.
Population: 1,415 (2000); Race: 96.9% White, 0.4% Black, 0.1% Asian, 1.1% American Indian and Alaska Native, 0.9% Hispanic of any race, 1.2% two or more races (2000); Density: 42.4 persons per square mile (2000); Age: 23.0% under 18, 13.2% over 64 (2000); Marriage status: 20.8% never married, 61.9% now married, 6.1% widowed, 11.1% divorced (2000); Foreign born: 1.6% (2000); Ancestry (includes multiple ancestries): 40.3% German, 15.3% Norwegian, 13.5% Irish, 9.5% English, 8.6% Polish (2000).
Economy: Single-family building permits issued: 27 (2001) / 27 (2000); Multi-family building permits issued: 3 (2001) / 4 (2000); Employment by occupation: 13.6% management, 11.3% professional, 23.1% services, 23.0% sales, 0.6% farming, 13.9% construction, 14.5% production (2000).
Income: Per capita income: $19,209 (2000); Median household income: $43,750 (2000); Poverty rate: 7.8% (2000).
Taxes: Total city taxes per capita: $84 (1997); City property taxes per capita: $43 (1997).
Education: High school graduation rate: 80.2% (2000); College graduation rate: 14.5% (2000).
Housing: Homeownership rate: 87.5% (2000); Median home value: $96,500 (2000); Median rent: $429 per month (2000); Median age of housing: 19 years (2000).
Transportation: Commute to work: 91.7% car, 0.3% public transportation, 2.3% walk, 3.8% work from home (2000); Travel time to work: 25.4% less than 15 minutes, 39.6% 15 to 30 minutes, 22.4% 30 to 45 minutes, 5.3% 45 to 60 minutes, 7.4% 60 minutes or more (2000)

EASTON (town). Covers a land area of 36.103 square miles and a water area of 0.047 square miles. Located at 43.84° N. Lat.; 89.79° W. Long. Elevation is 916 feet.
Population: 1,194 (2000); Race: 97.0% White, 0.6% Black, 0.4% Asian, 0.3% American Indian and Alaska Native, 2.6% Hispanic of any race, 1.2% two or more races (2000); Density: 33.1 persons per square mile (2000); Age: 25.4% under 18, 15.2% over 64 (2000); Marriage status: 17.2% never married, 60.5% now married, 7.4% widowed, 14.9% divorced (2000); Foreign born: 2.7% (2000); Ancestry (includes multiple ancestries): 44.6% German, 14.7% Polish, 14.1% Irish, 7.8% English, 6.0% Norwegian (2000).
Economy: Employment by occupation: 8.9% management, 7.7% professional, 16.8% services, 21.2% sales, 2.7% farming, 11.0% construction, 31.6% production (2000).
Income: Per capita income: $15,011 (2000); Median household income: $30,469 (2000); Poverty rate: 11.2% (2000).
Taxes: Total city taxes per capita: $1 (1997); City property taxes per capita: $0 (1997).
Education: High school graduation rate: 77.3% (2000); College graduation rate: 5.1% (2000).
Housing: Homeownership rate: 83.8% (2000); Median home value: $66,200 (2000); Median rent: $375 per month (2000); Median age of housing: 24 years (2000).
Transportation: Commute to work: 92.8% car, 1.3% public transportation, 1.7% walk, 1.9% work from home (2000); Travel time to work: 21.3% less than 15 minutes, 31.7% 15 to 30 minutes, 24.8% 30 to 45 minutes, 9.9% 45 to 60 minutes, 12.3% 60 minutes or more (2000)

FRIENDSHIP (village). Covers a land area of 0.886 square miles and a water area of 0.034 square miles. Located at 43.97° N. Lat.; 89.81° W. Long. Elevation is 953 feet.
History: Friendship was founded in 1856 and became a trading center for farmers. When the railroad picked a route a few miles away and the settlment of Lower Friendship grew up around it, there was rivalry instead of friendship between the two Friendships. Lower Friendship later became Adams, the original Friendship became the seat of Adams County, and all was well between the two communities.
Population: 698 (2000); Race: 96.3% White, 0.1% Black, 1.1% Asian, 0.8% American Indian and Alaska Native, 0.7% Hispanic of any race, 1.5% two or more races (2000); Density: 787.4 persons per square mile (2000); Age: 22.5% under 18, 25.4% over 64 (2000); Marriage status: 14.6% never married, 55.7% now married, 16.5% widowed, 13.2% divorced (2000); Foreign born: 1.4% (2000); Ancestry (includes multiple ancestries): 38.1% German, 17.6% Irish, 7.7% English, 7.3% Norwegian, 6.9% Polish (2000).
Economy: Employment by occupation: 14.2% management, 8.8% professional, 28.8% services, 20.8% sales, 1.8% farming, 4.4% construction, 21.2% production (2000).
Income: Per capita income: $14,773 (2000); Median household income: $24,615 (2000); Poverty rate: 23.4% (2000).
Taxes: Total city taxes per capita: $100 (1997); City property taxes per capita: $90 (1997).
Education: High school graduation rate: 71.7% (2000); College graduation rate: 7.2% (2000).

School District(s)

Adams-Friendship Area (PK-12)
2000 Enrollment: 2,055 608-339-3213

Housing: Homeownership rate: 59.1% (2000); Median home value: $64,100 (2000); Median rent: $341 per month (2000); Median age of housing: 39 years (2000).
Hospitals: Adams County Memorial Hospital (29 beds)
Transportation: Commute to work: 87.7% car, 0.0% public transportation, 7.5% walk, 3.8% work from home (2000); Travel time to work: 51.0% less than 15 minutes, 25.5% 15 to 30 minutes, 11.8% 30 to 45 minutes, 9.3% 45 to 60 minutes, 2.5% 60 minutes or more (2000)
Additional Information Contacts
Friendship Chamber of Commerce 608-339-6997

GRAND MARSH (unincorporated postal area, zip code 53936). Covers a land area of 63.916 square miles and a water area of 0.098 square miles. Located at 43.86° N. Lat.; 89.70° W. Long. Elevation is 1,010 feet.
Population: 1,429 (2000); Race: 96.7% White, 0.2% Black, 0.1% Asian, 0.4% American Indian and Alaska Native, 3.0% Hispanic of any race, 1.5% two or more races (2000); Density: 22.4 persons per square mile (2000); Age: 22.2% under 18, 19.5% over 64 (2000); Marriage status: 21.2% never married, 63.8% now married, 5.2% widowed, 9.8% divorced (2000); Foreign born: 1.5% (2000); Ancestry (includes multiple ancestries): 39.1% German, 12.4% Irish, 9.6% English, 9.6% Polish, 8.1% United States or American (2000).
Economy: Employment by occupation: 8.7% management, 10.2% professional, 20.9% services, 15.6% sales, 2.4% farming, 13.2% construction, 29.0% production (2000).
Income: Per capita income: $14,982 (2000); Median household income: $29,471 (2000); Poverty rate: 14.3% (2000).
Education: High school graduation rate: 70.9% (2000); College graduation rate: 6.4% (2000).

Housing: Homeownership rate: 87.6% (2000); Median home value: $76,500 (2000); Median rent: $396 per month (2000); Median age of housing: 24 years (2000).
Transportation: Commute to work: 94.9% car, 0.0% public transportation, 1.6% walk, 2.7% work from home (2000); Travel time to work: 19.1% less than 15 minutes, 36.8% 15 to 30 minutes, 21.1% 30 to 45 minutes, 12.8% 45 to 60 minutes, 10.2% 60 minutes or more (2000)

JACKSON (town). Covers a land area of 34.830 square miles and a water area of 0.957 square miles. Located at 43.77° N. Lat.; 89.64° W. Long.
Population: 926 (2000); Race: 95.6% White, 1.0% Black, 2.5% Asian, 0.0% American Indian and Alaska Native, 1.4% Hispanic of any race, 0.6% two or more races (2000); Density: 26.6 persons per square mile (2000); Age: 19.9% under 18, 20.6% over 64 (2000); Marriage status: 16.7% never married, 68.1% now married, 5.9% widowed, 9.3% divorced (2000); Foreign born: 2.1% (2000); Ancestry (includes multiple ancestries): 38.2% German, 14.4% Irish, 12.0% Polish, 8.8% English, 6.9% Norwegian (2000).
Economy: Employment by occupation: 15.0% management, 10.5% professional, 17.2% services, 22.5% sales, 2.9% farming, 13.5% construction, 18.4% production (2000).
Income: Per capita income: $19,080 (2000); Median household income: $39,338 (2000); Poverty rate: 5.7% (2000).
Taxes: Total city taxes per capita: $87 (1997); City property taxes per capita: $84 (1997).
Education: High school graduation rate: 78.8% (2000); College graduation rate: 9.3% (2000).
Housing: Homeownership rate: 94.2% (2000); Median home value: $97,600 (2000); Median rent: $404 per month (2000); Median age of housing: 23 years (2000).
Transportation: Commute to work: 89.6% car, 0.0% public transportation, 3.0% walk, 7.4% work from home (2000); Travel time to work: 18.4% less than 15 minutes, 35.7% 15 to 30 minutes, 28.8% 30 to 45 minutes, 8.8% 45 to 60 minutes, 8.3% 60 minutes or more (2000)

LEOLA (town). Covers a land area of 37.224 square miles and a water area of 0 square miles. Located at 44.20° N. Lat.; 89.64° W. Long.
Population: 265 (2000); Race: 96.3% White, 0.0% Black, 0.7% Asian, 0.0% American Indian and Alaska Native, 3.3% Hispanic of any race, 0.7% two or more races (2000); Density: 7.1 persons per square mile (2000); Age: 17.8% under 18, 15.6% over 64 (2000); Marriage status: 14.3% never married, 65.8% now married, 10.4% widowed, 9.5% divorced (2000); Foreign born: 2.2% (2000); Ancestry (includes multiple ancestries): 38.3% German, 16.0% Norwegian, 14.5% Polish, 12.6% Irish, 9.7% English (2000).
Economy: Employment by occupation: 11.5% management, 9.8% professional, 13.1% services, 27.0% sales, 9.8% farming, 5.7% construction, 23.0% production (2000).
Income: Per capita income: $15,699 (2000); Median household income: $36,607 (2000); Poverty rate: 10.5% (2000).
Taxes: Total city taxes per capita: $147 (1997); City property taxes per capita: $147 (1997).
Education: High school graduation rate: 78.3% (2000); College graduation rate: 10.1% (2000).
Housing: Homeownership rate: 87.7% (2000); Median home value: $65,000 (2000); Median rent: $325 per month (2000); Median age of housing: 18 years (2000).
Transportation: Commute to work: 76.2% car, 0.0% public transportation, 16.4% walk, 7.4% work from home (2000); Travel time to work: 33.6% less than 15 minutes, 39.8% 15 to 30 minutes, 19.5% 30 to 45 minutes, 7.1% 45 to 60 minutes, 0.0% 60 minutes or more (2000)

LINCOLN (town). Covers a land area of 36.191 square miles and a water area of 0 square miles. Located at 43.94° N. Lat.; 89.66° W. Long.
Population: 311 (2000); Race: 97.2% White, 0.0% Black, 0.0% Asian, 0.3% American Indian and Alaska Native, 5.9% Hispanic of any race, 0.0% two or more races (2000); Density: 8.6 persons per square mile (2000); Age: 20.7% under 18, 18.6% over 64 (2000); Marriage status: 23.6% never married, 60.6% now married, 8.7% widowed, 7.1% divorced (2000); Foreign born: 5.2% (2000); Ancestry (includes multiple ancestries): 43.1% German, 14.1% Irish, 10.7% Polish, 9.7% Norwegian, 9.0% French (except Basque) (2000).
Economy: Single-family building permits issued: 1 (2001) / 0 (2000); Multi-family building permits issued: 0 (2001) / 0 (2000); Employment by occupation: 7.6% management, 10.9% professional, 22.7% services, 24.4% sales, 4.2% farming, 8.4% construction, 21.8% production (2000).
Income: Per capita income: $15,484 (2000); Median household income: $29,107 (2000); Poverty rate: 22.1% (2000).
Taxes: Total city taxes per capita: $159 (1997); City property taxes per capita: $156 (1997).
Education: High school graduation rate: 66.8% (2000); College graduation rate: 6.7% (2000).
Housing: Homeownership rate: 85.2% (2000); Median home value: $54,000 (2000); Median rent: $175 per month (2000); Median age of housing: 23 years (2000).
Transportation: Commute to work: 93.8% car, 0.0% public transportation, 0.0% walk, 6.3% work from home (2000); Travel time to work: 32.4% less than 15 minutes, 41.0% 15 to 30 minutes, 4.8% 30 to 45 minutes, 13.3% 45 to 60 minutes, 8.6% 60 minutes or more (2000)

MONROE (town). Covers a land area of 21.905 square miles and a water area of 16.580 square miles. Located at 44.12° N. Lat.; 89.93° W. Long.
Population: 363 (2000); Race: 99.5% White, 0.0% Black, 0.0% Asian, 0.5% American Indian and Alaska Native, 0.0% Hispanic of any race, 0.0% two or more races (2000); Density: 16.6 persons per square mile (2000); Age: 13.9% under 18, 27.1% over 64 (2000); Marriage status: 11.5% never married, 77.7% now married, 5.4% widowed, 5.4% divorced (2000); Foreign born: 1.3% (2000); Ancestry (includes multiple ancestries): 45.8% German, 16.5% Norwegian, 11.9% English, 10.9% Irish, 10.9% Polish (2000).
Economy: Employment by occupation: 13.0% management, 9.3% professional, 21.6% services, 24.1% sales, 1.2% farming, 11.1% construction, 19.8% production (2000).
Income: Per capita income: $19,970 (2000); Median household income: $34,500 (2000); Poverty rate: 7.3% (2000).
Taxes: Total city taxes per capita: $337 (1997); City property taxes per capita: $334 (1997).
Education: High school graduation rate: 87.8% (2000); College graduation rate: 13.1% (2000).
Housing: Homeownership rate: 91.5% (2000); Median home value: $83,500 (2000); Median rent: $269 per month (2000); Median age of housing: 20 years (2000).
Transportation: Commute to work: 88.9% car, 0.0% public transportation, 4.9% walk, 4.9% work from home (2000); Travel time to work: 15.6% less than 15 minutes, 40.9% 15 to 30 minutes, 26.0% 30 to 45 minutes, 12.3% 45 to 60 minutes, 5.2% 60 minutes or more (2000)

NEW CHESTER (town). Covers a land area of 31.209 square miles and a water area of 0.182 square miles. Located at 43.86° N. Lat.; 89.67° W. Long.
Population: 864 (2000); Race: 96.3% White, 0.3% Black, 0.0% Asian, 0.6% American Indian and Alaska Native, 2.9% Hispanic of any race, 2.1% two or more races (2000); Density: 27.7 persons per square mile (2000); Age: 23.4% under 18, 16.5% over 64 (2000); Marriage status: 23.5% never married, 56.7% now married, 5.8% widowed, 14.1% divorced (2000); Foreign born: 1.2% (2000); Ancestry (includes multiple ancestries): 39.9% German, 13.4% Polish, 13.0% Irish, 8.5% English, 8.4% Norwegian (2000).
Economy: Employment by occupation: 7.2% management, 8.5% professional, 23.6% services, 15.6% sales, 3.7% farming, 13.5% construction, 27.9% production (2000).
Income: Per capita income: $14,727 (2000); Median household income: $28,750 (2000); Poverty rate: 13.3% (2000).
Taxes: Total city taxes per capita: $2 (1997); City property taxes per capita: $1 (1997).
Education: High school graduation rate: 73.7% (2000); College graduation rate: 7.1% (2000).
Housing: Homeownership rate: 88.3% (2000); Median home value: $75,500 (2000); Median rent: $393 per month (2000); Median age of housing: 24 years (2000).
Transportation: Commute to work: 95.6% car, 0.0% public transportation, 2.5% walk, 1.1% work from home (2000); Travel time to work: 16.4% less than 15 minutes, 31.4% 15 to 30 minutes, 28.3% 30 to 45 minutes, 14.7% 45 to 60 minutes, 9.2% 60 minutes or more (2000)

NEW HAVEN (town). Covers a land area of 29.266 square miles and a water area of 1.136 square miles. Located at 43.68° N. Lat.; 89.64° W. Long.
Population: 657 (2000); Race: 99.4% White, 0.0% Black, 0.3% Asian, 0.0% American Indian and Alaska Native, 1.0% Hispanic of any race, 0.3% two or more races (2000); Density: 22.4 persons per square mile (2000); Age: 18.9% under 18, 22.8% over 64 (2000); Marriage status: 17.9% never married, 64.3% now married, 9.0% widowed, 8.8% divorced (2000); Foreign born: 3.7% (2000); Ancestry (includes multiple ancestries): 40.4% German, 18.0% Norwegian, 11.6% Irish, 8.6% Polish, 8.4% English (2000).

Economy: Employment by occupation: 14.8% management, 6.6% professional, 20.5% services, 16.7% sales, 3.8% farming, 13.9% construction, 23.7% production (2000).
Income: Per capita income: $15,624 (2000); Median household income: $35,536 (2000); Poverty rate: 11.3% (2000).
Taxes: Total city taxes per capita: $90 (1997); City property taxes per capita: $89 (1997).
Education: High school graduation rate: 76.0% (2000); College graduation rate: 8.1% (2000).
Housing: Homeownership rate: 88.1% (2000); Median home value: $91,700 (2000); Median rent: $375 per month (2000); Median age of housing: 27 years (2000).
Transportation: Commute to work: 89.4% car, 0.0% public transportation, 0.7% walk, 8.0% work from home (2000); Travel time to work: 18.8% less than 15 minutes, 46.2% 15 to 30 minutes, 17.3% 30 to 45 minutes, 10.5% 45 to 60 minutes, 7.2% 60 minutes or more (2000)

PRESTON (town). Covers a land area of 35.386 square miles and a water area of 0.470 square miles. Located at 44.02° N. Lat.; 89.78° W. Long.
Population: 1,360 (2000); Race: 98.3% White, 0.1% Black, 0.4% Asian, 1.1% American Indian and Alaska Native, 1.1% Hispanic of any race, 0.1% two or more races (2000); Density: 38.4 persons per square mile (2000); Age: 23.6% under 18, 19.7% over 64 (2000); Marriage status: 15.8% never married, 67.1% now married, 5.1% widowed, 12.0% divorced (2000); Foreign born: 2.4% (2000); Ancestry (includes multiple ancestries): 43.5% German, 13.7% Irish, 10.4% Polish, 9.2% Norwegian, 9.2% English (2000).
Economy: Employment by occupation: 10.3% management, 13.5% professional, 18.4% services, 26.0% sales, 1.2% farming, 10.3% construction, 20.3% production (2000).
Income: Per capita income: $19,117 (2000); Median household income: $33,491 (2000); Poverty rate: 9.6% (2000).
Taxes: Total city taxes per capita: $57 (1997); City property taxes per capita: $55 (1997).
Education: High school graduation rate: 76.0% (2000); College graduation rate: 8.0% (2000).
Housing: Homeownership rate: 90.4% (2000); Median home value: $86,500 (2000); Median rent: $396 per month (2000); Median age of housing: 23 years (2000).
Transportation: Commute to work: 93.6% car, 0.0% public transportation, 1.6% walk, 4.1% work from home (2000); Travel time to work: 54.7% less than 15 minutes, 16.7% 15 to 30 minutes, 13.7% 30 to 45 minutes, 9.6% 45 to 60 minutes, 5.2% 60 minutes or more (2000)

QUINCY (town). Covers a land area of 32.812 square miles and a water area of 6.817 square miles. Located at 43.92° N. Lat.; 89.93° W. Long.
Population: 1,181 (2000); Race: 99.7% White, 0.0% Black, 0.0% Asian, 0.0% American Indian and Alaska Native, 0.7% Hispanic of any race, 0.3% two or more races (2000); Density: 36.0 persons per square mile (2000); Age: 14.3% under 18, 33.1% over 64 (2000); Marriage status: 16.7% never married, 63.8% now married, 9.6% widowed, 9.9% divorced (2000); Foreign born: 4.6% (2000); Ancestry (includes multiple ancestries): 39.8% German, 14.3% Irish, 13.0% Polish, 7.4% Norwegian, 7.2% English (2000).
Economy: Employment by occupation: 7.8% management, 9.2% professional, 19.8% services, 28.6% sales, 1.6% farming, 10.1% construction, 22.8% production (2000).
Income: Per capita income: $16,460 (2000); Median household income: $26,533 (2000); Poverty rate: 10.1% (2000).
Taxes: Total city taxes per capita: $133 (1997); City property taxes per capita: $130 (1997).
Education: High school graduation rate: 68.6% (2000); College graduation rate: 4.5% (2000).
Housing: Homeownership rate: 91.0% (2000); Median home value: $70,300 (2000); Median rent: $414 per month (2000); Median age of housing: 21 years (2000).
Transportation: Commute to work: 94.3% car, 1.2% public transportation, 1.2% walk, 2.4% work from home (2000); Travel time to work: 22.2% less than 15 minutes, 37.4% 15 to 30 minutes, 16.4% 30 to 45 minutes, 16.2% 45 to 60 minutes, 7.7% 60 minutes or more (2000)

RICHFIELD (town). Covers a land area of 35.448 square miles and a water area of 0 square miles. Located at 44.01° N. Lat.; 89.64° W. Long.
Population: 144 (2000); Race: 100.0% White, 0.0% Black, 0.0% Asian, 0.0% American Indian and Alaska Native, 0.0% Hispanic of any race, 0.0% two or more races (2000); Density: 4.1 persons per square mile (2000); Age: 15.5% under 18, 16.3% over 64 (2000); Marriage status: 17.0% never married, 66.1% now married, 8.9% widowed, 8.0% divorced (2000); Foreign born: 2.3% (2000); Ancestry (includes multiple ancestries): 38.8% German, 21.7% English, 18.6% Norwegian, 14.7% Polish, 10.9% Irish (2000).
Economy: Employment by occupation: 18.9% management, 5.4% professional, 8.1% services, 18.9% sales, 18.9% farming, 6.8% construction, 23.0% production (2000).
Income: Per capita income: $23,333 (2000); Median household income: $34,792 (2000); Poverty rate: 17.1% (2000).
Taxes: Total city taxes per capita: $218 (1997); City property taxes per capita: $212 (1997).
Education: High school graduation rate: 78.8% (2000); College graduation rate: 1.9% (2000).
Housing: Homeownership rate: 96.1% (2000); Median home value: $62,500 (2000); Median rent: $525 per month (2000); Median age of housing: 22 years (2000).
Transportation: Commute to work: 68.9% car, 0.0% public transportation, 9.5% walk, 21.6% work from home (2000); Travel time to work: 39.7% less than 15 minutes, 25.9% 15 to 30 minutes, 13.8% 30 to 45 minutes, 3.4% 45 to 60 minutes, 17.2% 60 minutes or more (2000)

ROME (town). Covers a land area of 54.256 square miles and a water area of 8.056 square miles. Located at 44.20° N. Lat.; 89.81° W. Long.
Population: 2,656 (2000); Race: 97.8% White, 0.0% Black, 0.8% Asian, 0.2% American Indian and Alaska Native, 0.3% Hispanic of any race, 0.9% two or more races (2000); Density: 49.0 persons per square mile (2000); Age: 17.3% under 18, 24.7% over 64 (2000); Marriage status: 12.4% never married, 71.1% now married, 7.3% widowed, 9.2% divorced (2000); Foreign born: 2.6% (2000); Ancestry (includes multiple ancestries): 52.0% German, 14.9% Polish, 13.2% Irish, 7.2% English, 5.3% Norwegian (2000).
Economy: Single-family building permits issued: 48 (2001) / 56 (2000); Multi-family building permits issued: 4 (2001) / 0 (2000); Employment by occupation: 13.9% management, 14.4% professional, 14.2% services, 21.7% sales, 0.9% farming, 14.1% construction, 20.8% production (2000).
Income: Per capita income: $23,901 (2000); Median household income: $44,000 (2000); Poverty rate: 3.7% (2000).
Taxes: Total city taxes per capita: $440 (2000); City property taxes per capita: $411 (2000).
Education: High school graduation rate: 89.1% (2000); College graduation rate: 17.3% (2000).
Housing: Homeownership rate: 95.3% (2000); Median home value: $115,600 (2000); Median rent: $442 per month (2000); Median age of housing: 15 years (2000).
Transportation: Commute to work: 93.4% car, 0.0% public transportation, 0.5% walk, 5.4% work from home (2000); Travel time to work: 18.9% less than 15 minutes, 50.9% 15 to 30 minutes, 16.8% 30 to 45 minutes, 4.0% 45 to 60 minutes, 9.4% 60 minutes or more (2000)

SPRINGVILLE (town). Covers a land area of 43.901 square miles and a water area of 0.749 square miles. Located at 43.77° N. Lat.; 89.81° W. Long.
Population: 1,167 (2000); Race: 97.6% White, 0.0% Black, 0.3% Asian, 0.2% American Indian and Alaska Native, 2.1% Hispanic of any race, 1.7% two or more races (2000); Density: 26.6 persons per square mile (2000); Age: 21.0% under 18, 19.1% over 64 (2000); Marriage status: 17.6% never married, 65.8% now married, 5.7% widowed, 10.9% divorced (2000); Foreign born: 2.2% (2000); Ancestry (includes multiple ancestries): 39.7% German, 12.7% English, 9.8% Irish, 9.7% Norwegian, 9.3% Polish (2000).
Economy: Employment by occupation: 8.0% management, 8.2% professional, 24.0% services, 20.2% sales, 1.5% farming, 15.6% construction, 22.3% production (2000).
Income: Per capita income: $16,146 (2000); Median household income: $34,531 (2000); Poverty rate: 12.3% (2000).
Taxes: Total city taxes per capita: $67 (1997); City property taxes per capita: $64 (1997).
Education: High school graduation rate: 70.1% (2000); College graduation rate: 5.9% (2000).
Housing: Homeownership rate: 88.3% (2000); Median home value: $83,600 (2000); Median rent: $400 per month (2000); Median age of housing: 21 years (2000).
Transportation: Commute to work: 85.0% car, 1.2% public transportation, 4.1% walk, 7.1% work from home (2000); Travel time to work: 16.1% less than 15 minutes, 38.1% 15 to 30 minutes, 24.6% 30 to 45 minutes, 14.6% 45 to 60 minutes, 6.6% 60 minutes or more (2000)

STRONGS PRAIRIE (town). Covers a land area of 47.415 square miles and a water area of 4.496 square miles. Located at 44.01° N. Lat.; 89.92° W. Long. Elevation is 913 feet.

Population: 1,115 (2000); Race: 99.3% White, 0.0% Black, 0.5% Asian, 0.0% American Indian and Alaska Native, 0.4% Hispanic of any race, 0.0% two or more races (2000); Density: 23.5 persons per square mile (2000); Age: 15.8% under 18, 24.1% over 64 (2000); Marriage status: 17.9% never married, 63.9% now married, 10.4% widowed, 7.7% divorced (2000); Foreign born: 1.8% (2000); Ancestry (includes multiple ancestries): 40.5% German, 19.0% Norwegian, 12.0% Irish, 10.3% English, 9.5% Polish (2000).
Economy: Employment by occupation: 9.6% management, 11.5% professional, 18.2% services, 18.4% sales, 1.7% farming, 11.7% construction, 29.0% production (2000).
Income: Per capita income: $15,583 (2000); Median household income: $30,048 (2000); Poverty rate: 12.7% (2000).
Taxes: Total city taxes per capita: $48 (1997); City property taxes per capita: $47 (1997).
Education: High school graduation rate: 76.5% (2000); College graduation rate: 8.8% (2000).
Housing: Homeownership rate: 85.1% (2000); Median home value: $72,500 (2000); Median rent: $365 per month (2000); Median age of housing: 19 years (2000).
Transportation: Commute to work: 83.9% car, 0.0% public transportation, 4.4% walk, 9.6% work from home (2000); Travel time to work: 31.3% less than 15 minutes, 33.2% 15 to 30 minutes, 12.8% 30 to 45 minutes, 8.8% 45 to 60 minutes, 13.9% 60 minutes or more (2000)

Ashland County

Located in northern Wisconsin; bounded on the north by Lake Superior; includes Apostle Islands, north of Chequamegon Bay; includes part of Chequamegon National Forest. Covers a land area of 1,043.80 square miles, a water area of 1,249.90 square miles, and is located in the Central Time Zone. The county government was organized in 1860. County seat is Ashland.

Weather Station: Mellen 4 NE — Elevation: 1,299 feet

	Jan	Feb	Mar	Apr	May	Jun	Jul	Aug	Sep	Oct	Nov	Dec
High	20	27	37	52	66	74	79	76	67	55	38	25
Low	-2	3	14	28	40	49	55	53	44	34	21	6
Precip	1.6	1.0	2.0	2.3	3.2	3.9	4.2	3.8	3.9	3.2	2.7	1.6
Snow	25.8	13.3	16.6	5.9	0.6	0.0	0.0	0.0	0.1	2.2	14.5	21.9

High and Low temperatures in degrees Fahrenheit; Precipitation and Snow in inches

Population: 16,866 (2000); Race: 87.2% White, 0.3% Black, 0.4% Asian, 10.2% American Indian and Alaska Native, 1.1% Hispanic of any race, 1.6% two or more races (2000); Density: 16.2 persons per square mile (2000); Age: 25.5% under 18, 16.0% over 64 (2000).
Religion: Five largest groups: 36.5% Catholic Church, 12.9% Lutheran Church—Missouri Synod, 6.5% Evangelical Lutheran Church in America, 3.0% Presbyterian Church (U.S.A.), 2.1% United Church of Christ (2000).
Economy: Unemployment rate: 6.9% (11/2002); Total civilian labor force: 8,040 (11/2002); Leading industries: 21.6% manufacturing; 21.2% health care and social assistance; 13.2% retail trade (2000); Companies that employ more than 1,000 persons: 0 (2000); Companies that employ more than 100 persons: 11 (2000); Farms: 186 totaling 46,503 acres (1997); Minority business ownership rate: 0.0% (1997); Women business ownership rate: 15.4% (1997); Retail sales per capita: $9,060 (1997). Single-family building permits issued: 59 (2001) / 41 (2000); Multi-family building permits issued: 2 (2001) / 8 (2000).
Income: Per capita income: $16,069 (2000); Median household income: $31,628 (2000); Poverty rate: 11.9% (2000); Bankruptcy rate: 2.27% (2001).
Taxes: Total county taxes per capita: $196 (1997); County property taxes per capita: $147 (1997).
Education: High school graduation rate: 84.1% (2000); College graduation rate: 16.5% (2000).
Housing: Homeownership rate: 70.6% (2000); Median home value: $60,400 (2000); Median rent: $317 per month (2000); Median age of housing: 41 years (2000).
Health: Birth rate: 123.3 per 10,000 population (1998); Age adjusted death rate: 89.0 per 10,000 population (1999); Age adjusted cancer mortality rate: 170.7 deaths per 100,000 population (1999). Air Quality Index: 100% good, 0% moderate, 0% unhealthy (percent of days in 2000). Number of physicians: 32.0 per 10,000 population (1999); Number of hospital beds: 59.9 per 10,000 population (1999).
Elections: 2000 Presidential election results: 55.2% Gore, 38.5% Bush, 5.6% Nader, 0.2% Buchanan
National and State Parks: Apostle Islands State Forest; Big Bay State Park; Copper Falls State Park
Additional Information Contacts

Ashland County Government Offices 715-682-7000
Ashland Area Chamber of Commerce 715-682-2500
Glidden Chamber of Commerce 715-264-4304
Madeline Island Chamber of Commerce 715-747-2801
Mellen Chamber of Commerce 715-274-2330

Ashland County Communities

AGENDA (town). Covers a land area of 88.649 square miles and a water area of 0.874 square miles. Located at 46.08° N. Lat.; 90.38° W. Long.
Population: 513 (2000); Race: 100.0% White, 0.0% Black, 0.0% Asian, 0.0% American Indian and Alaska Native, 0.0% Hispanic of any race, 0.0% two or more races (2000); Density: 5.8 persons per square mile (2000); Age: 20.0% under 18, 18.4% over 64 (2000); Marriage status: 25.2% never married, 62.1% now married, 6.8% widowed, 5.8% divorced (2000); Foreign born: 0.6% (2000); Ancestry (includes multiple ancestries): 61.4% German, 11.8% Polish, 8.2% Irish, 5.3% United States or American, 4.3% English (2000).
Economy: Single-family building permits issued: 3 (2001) / 1 (2000); Multi-family building permits issued: 0 (2001) / 0 (2000); Employment by occupation: 7.0% management, 13.7% professional, 16.4% services, 16.8% sales, 3.5% farming, 15.2% construction, 27.3% production (2000).
Income: Per capita income: $17,578 (2000); Median household income: $37,857 (2000); Poverty rate: 4.1% (2000).
Taxes: Total city taxes per capita: $46 (1997); City property taxes per capita: $44 (1997).
Education: High school graduation rate: 80.7% (2000); College graduation rate: 8.2% (2000).
Housing: Homeownership rate: 88.7% (2000); Median home value: $78,500 (2000); Median rent: $250 per month (2000); Median age of housing: 38 years (2000).
Transportation: Commute to work: 90.3% car, 1.6% public transportation, 1.6% walk, 6.5% work from home (2000); Travel time to work: 41.6% less than 15 minutes, 35.1% 15 to 30 minutes, 10.0% 30 to 45 minutes, 3.5% 45 to 60 minutes, 10.0% 60 minutes or more (2000)

ASHLAND (city). Covers a land area of 13.400 square miles and a water area of 0.271 square miles. Located at 46.58° N. Lat.; 90.88° W. Long. Elevation is 671 feet.
History: French explorers and missionaries were in this area in the mid-1600's, about 200 years before Asaph Whittlesey built a cabin here in 1854. The first tree Whittlesey felled was a great ash, and he named the place Ashland. The settlement that grew up around Whittlesey's cabin got a boost in the early 1870's when the Wisconsin Central Railroad made Ashland the headquarters for its construction of a line linking Lake Superior with the harbors on Lake Michigan. Mining fever seized Ashland in the 1880's. When both lumbering and mining declined, Ashland turned to other industries such as paper manufacturing and shipping.
Population: 8,620 (2000); Race: 89.8% White, 0.3% Black, 0.5% Asian, 6.7% American Indian and Alaska Native, 1.0% Hispanic of any race, 2.2% two or more races (2000); Density: 643.3 persons per square mile (2000); Age: 22.5% under 18, 17.5% over 64 (2000); Marriage status: 30.4% never married, 49.7% now married, 10.3% widowed, 9.6% divorced (2000); Foreign born: 1.3% (2000); Ancestry (includes multiple ancestries): 29.6% German, 12.3% Norwegian, 12.0% Polish, 11.9% Swedish, 10.9% Irish (2000).
Economy: Single-family building permits issued: 15 (2001) / 7 (2000); Multi-family building permits issued: 2 (2001) / 0 (2000); Employment by occupation: 7.8% management, 22.2% professional, 23.2% services, 24.4% sales, 1.4% farming, 6.6% construction, 14.4% production (2000).
Income: Per capita income: $16,330 (2000); Median household income: $30,853 (2000); Poverty rate: 12.7% (2000).
Taxes: Total city taxes per capita: $224 (2000); City property taxes per capita: $200 (2000).
Education: High school graduation rate: 84.6% (2000); College graduation rate: 20.4% (2000).

School District(s)

Ashland (PK-12)
2000 Enrollment: 2,243 715-682-7080

Four-year College(s)

Northland College (Private, Not-for-profit, United Church of Christ)
2001 Enrollment: 794 715-682-1699
2001 Tuition: In-state $15,500; Out-of-state $15,500
Housing: Homeownership rate: 62.1% (2000); Median home value: $64,000 (2000); Median rent: $345 per month (2000); Median age of housing: 56 years (2000).

Hospitals: Memorial Medical Center (100 beds)
Safety: Violent crime rate: 4.6 per 10,000 population; Property crime rate: 383.6 per 10,000 population (2001).
Newspapers: The Daily Press (6 x week)
Transportation: Commute to work: 83.4% car, 0.2% public transportation, 11.7% walk, 3.0% work from home (2000); Travel time to work: 77.3% less than 15 minutes, 15.4% 15 to 30 minutes, 3.4% 30 to 45 minutes, 0.8% 45 to 60 minutes, 3.1% 60 minutes or more (2000)
Additional Information Contacts
Ashland Area Chamber of Commerce 715-682-2500

ASHLAND (town). Covers a land area of 41.231 square miles and a water area of 0.082 square miles. Located at 46.37° N. Lat.; 90.74° W. Long. Elevation is 671 feet.
History: French explorers visited (17th century) the bay shore; and a French mission was founded (1665) near Ashland by Father Allouez. Settled 1854, the city grew as an iron-mining and lumbering center and as terminus for first railroad in Northern Wisconsin (1877). Incorporated in 1887.
Population: 603 (2000); Race: 95.9% White, 0.7% Black, 0.0% Asian, 2.7% American Indian and Alaska Native, 0.0% Hispanic of any race, 0.7% two or more races (2000); Density: 14.6 persons per square mile (2000); Age: 25.7% under 18, 14.4% over 64 (2000); Marriage status: 24.9% never married, 58.5% now married, 9.0% widowed, 7.5% divorced (2000); Foreign born: 0.3% (2000); Ancestry (includes multiple ancestries): 31.3% German, 30.3% Finnish, 9.4% Swedish, 8.0% Irish, 7.7% Polish (2000).
Economy: Railroad terminus with railroad ship transfer point. Manufacturing includes apparel, consumer goods, construction materials, paper; printing; ironworks, woodworks. Agriculture. Single-family building permits issued: 0 (2001) / 0 (2000); Multi-family building permits issued: 0 (2001) / 0 (2000); Employment by occupation: 12.0% management, 10.6% professional, 11.7% services, 20.8% sales, 4.9% farming, 17.7% construction, 22.3% production (2000).
Income: Per capita income: $15,390 (2000); Median household income: $34,063 (2000); Poverty rate: 12.7% (2000).
Taxes: Total city taxes per capita: $84 (1997); City property taxes per capita: $82 (1997).
Education: High school graduation rate: 87.1% (2000); College graduation rate: 11.8% (2000).
Housing: Homeownership rate: 83.3% (2000); Median home value: $57,000 (2000); Median rent: $250 per month (2000); Median age of housing: 33 years (2000).
Transportation: Commute to work: 90.6% car, 0.0% public transportation, 1.4% walk, 7.2% work from home (2000); Travel time to work: 30.0% less than 15 minutes, 33.5% 15 to 30 minutes, 19.1% 30 to 45 minutes, 7.8% 45 to 60 minutes, 9.7% 60 minutes or more (2000)

BUTTERNUT (village). Covers a land area of 1.601 square miles and a water area of 0 square miles. Located at 46.01° N. Lat.; 90.49° W. Long. Elevation is 1,503 feet.
Population: 407 (2000); Race: 99.5% White, 0.5% Black, 0.0% Asian, 0.0% American Indian and Alaska Native, 0.7% Hispanic of any race, 0.0% two or more races (2000); Density: 254.2 persons per square mile (2000); Age: 27.8% under 18, 19.4% over 64 (2000); Marriage status: 24.6% never married, 51.3% now married, 15.2% widowed, 8.8% divorced (2000); Foreign born: 0.0% (2000); Ancestry (includes multiple ancestries): 60.3% German, 16.9% Polish, 8.8% Irish, 5.0% Swedish, 3.8% Norwegian (2000).
Economy: Lumbering; dairying, poultry raising; woodworking. Single-family building permits issued: 0 (2001) / 0 (2000); Multi-family building permits issued: 0 (2001) / 0 (2000); Employment by occupation: 2.0% management, 15.8% professional, 12.4% services, 15.8% sales, 2.5% farming, 11.4% construction, 40.1% production (2000).
Income: Per capita income: $16,002 (2000); Median household income: $30,446 (2000); Poverty rate: 7.0% (2000).
Taxes: Total city taxes per capita: $46 (1997); City property taxes per capita: $42 (1997).
Education: High school graduation rate: 83.1% (2000); College graduation rate: 8.6% (2000).

School District(s)

Butternut (PK-12)
2000 Enrollment: 233 715-769-3434
Housing: Homeownership rate: 62.9% (2000); Median home value: $48,900 (2000); Median rent: $263 per month (2000); Median age of housing: 50 years (2000).
Transportation: Commute to work: 81.2% car, 1.0% public transportation, 7.9% walk, 4.0% work from home (2000); Travel time to work: 58.2% less than 15 minutes, 23.2% 15 to 30 minutes, 8.2% 30 to 45 minutes, 0.0% 45 to 60 minutes, 10.3% 60 minutes or more (2000)

CHIPPEWA (town). Covers a land area of 124.424 square miles and a water area of 1.092 square miles. Located at 46.03° N. Lat.; 90.70° W. Long.
Population: 433 (2000); Race: 99.5% White, 0.5% Black, 0.0% Asian, 0.0% American Indian and Alaska Native, 0.0% Hispanic of any race, 0.0% two or more races (2000); Density: 3.5 persons per square mile (2000); Age: 25.4% under 18, 18.0% over 64 (2000); Marriage status: 21.1% never married, 69.6% now married, 6.7% widowed, 2.6% divorced (2000); Foreign born: 0.8% (2000); Ancestry (includes multiple ancestries): 53.0% German, 15.9% Polish, 8.5% Irish, 8.0% English, 6.9% Norwegian (2000).
Economy: Single-family building permits issued: 5 (2001) / 0 (2000); Multi-family building permits issued: 0 (2001) / 0 (2000); Employment by occupation: 9.0% management, 10.4% professional, 16.4% services, 20.4% sales, 2.5% farming, 7.0% construction, 34.3% production (2000).
Income: Per capita income: $16,841 (2000); Median household income: $42,159 (2000); Poverty rate: 8.7% (2000).
Taxes: Total city taxes per capita: $65 (2000); City property taxes per capita: $62 (2000).
Education: High school graduation rate: 77.3% (2000); College graduation rate: 8.3% (2000).
Housing: Homeownership rate: 95.5% (2000); Median home value: $76,700 (2000); Median rent: $375 per month (2000); Median age of housing: 32 years (2000).
Transportation: Commute to work: 89.6% car, 1.0% public transportation, 2.0% walk, 6.0% work from home (2000); Travel time to work: 36.5% less than 15 minutes, 41.8% 15 to 30 minutes, 14.3% 30 to 45 minutes, 1.6% 45 to 60 minutes, 5.8% 60 minutes or more (2000)

CLAM LAKE (unincorporated postal area, zip code 54517). Covers a land area of 53.971 square miles and a water area of 3.057 square miles. Located at 46.13° N. Lat.; 90.93° W. Long. Elevation is 1,421 feet.
Population: 133 (2000); Race: 98.5% White, 0.0% Black, 0.0% Asian, 0.0% American Indian and Alaska Native, 0.0% Hispanic of any race, 1.5% two or more races (2000); Density: 2.5 persons per square mile (2000); Age: 10.3% under 18, 36.8% over 64 (2000); Marriage status: 12.9% never married, 69.4% now married, 5.6% widowed, 12.1% divorced (2000); Foreign born: 0.0% (2000); Ancestry (includes multiple ancestries): 37.5% German, 14.0% Irish, 11.8% Norwegian, 10.3% Polish, 8.1% English (2000).
Economy: Employment by occupation: 13.0% management, 3.7% professional, 24.1% services, 24.1% sales, 5.6% farming, 11.1% construction, 18.5% production (2000).
Income: Per capita income: $29,711 (2000); Median household income: $26,875 (2000); Poverty rate: 12.5% (2000).
Education: High school graduation rate: 85.1% (2000); College graduation rate: 13.2% (2000).
Housing: Homeownership rate: 79.1% (2000); Median home value: $92,000 (2000); Median rent: $213 per month (2000); Median age of housing: 36 years (2000).
Transportation: Commute to work: 82.4% car, 0.0% public transportation, 2.0% walk, 11.8% work from home (2000); Travel time to work: 33.3% less than 15 minutes, 20.0% 15 to 30 minutes, 0.0% 30 to 45 minutes, 44.4% 45 to 60 minutes, 2.2% 60 minutes or more (2000)

GINGLES (town). Covers a land area of 38.972 square miles and a water area of 0.005 square miles. Located at 46.54° N. Lat.; 90.84° W. Long.
Population: 640 (2000); Race: 93.9% White, 0.0% Black, 0.0% Asian, 5.6% American Indian and Alaska Native, 0.6% Hispanic of any race, 0.2% two or more races (2000); Density: 16.4 persons per square mile (2000); Age: 29.3% under 18, 7.0% over 64 (2000); Marriage status: 16.7% never married, 71.2% now married, 3.7% widowed, 8.4% divorced (2000); Foreign born: 2.1% (2000); Ancestry (includes multiple ancestries): 23.3% German, 11.6% Finnish, 11.4% Irish, 10.3% Norwegian, 9.1% Polish (2000).
Economy: Single-family building permits issued: 11 (2001) / 7 (2000); Multi-family building permits issued: 0 (2001) / 0 (2000); Employment by occupation: 7.3% management, 19.9% professional, 18.4% services, 23.1% sales, 1.5% farming, 9.9% construction, 19.9% production (2000).
Income: Per capita income: $16,085 (2000); Median household income: $42,188 (2000); Poverty rate: 6.7% (2000).
Taxes: Total city taxes per capita: $88 (1997); City property taxes per capita: $86 (1997).
Education: High school graduation rate: 94.2% (2000); College graduation rate: 21.1% (2000).

Housing: Homeownership rate: 88.3% (2000); Median home value: $78,100 (2000); Median rent: $394 per month (2000); Median age of housing: 25 years (2000).
Transportation: Commute to work: 91.7% car, 0.0% public transportation, 2.1% walk, 5.0% work from home (2000); Travel time to work: 58.8% less than 15 minutes, 31.9% 15 to 30 minutes, 3.8% 30 to 45 minutes, 2.8% 45 to 60 minutes, 2.8% 60 minutes or more (2000)

GLIDDEN (unincorporated postal area, zip code 54527). Covers a land area of 242.789 square miles and a water area of 1.755 square miles. Located at 46.12° N. Lat.; 90.64° W. Long. Elevation is 1,550 feet.
Population: 1,303 (2000); Race: 98.4% White, 0.2% Black, 0.0% Asian, 0.8% American Indian and Alaska Native, 0.4% Hispanic of any race, 0.7% two or more races (2000); Density: 5.4 persons per square mile (2000); Age: 27.6% under 18, 17.7% over 64 (2000); Marriage status: 22.5% never married, 60.2% now married, 7.0% widowed, 10.4% divorced (2000); Foreign born: 0.3% (2000); Ancestry (includes multiple ancestries): 63.1% German, 10.1% Irish, 7.9% Norwegian, 7.0% Polish, 4.2% Swedish (2000).
Economy: In submarginal farm area. Dairy products, lumber, logging. Chequamegon National Forest to West. Employment by occupation: 3.5% management, 12.4% professional, 15.5% services, 13.2% sales, 12.4% farming, 10.7% construction, 32.4% production (2000).
Income: Per capita income: $13,303 (2000); Median household income: $25,417 (2000); Poverty rate: 13.2% (2000).
Education: High school graduation rate: 79.3% (2000); College graduation rate: 7.2% (2000).

School District(s)

Glidden (PK-12)
2000 Enrollment: 275 715-264-2021
Housing: Homeownership rate: 82.0% (2000); Median home value: $40,300 (2000); Median rent: $224 per month (2000); Median age of housing: 39 years (2000).
Newspapers: The Glidden Enterprise (1 x week)
Transportation: Commute to work: 89.7% car, 0.4% public transportation, 5.0% walk, 3.1% work from home (2000); Travel time to work: 39.7% less than 15 minutes, 30.5% 15 to 30 minutes, 11.4% 30 to 45 minutes, 10.6% 45 to 60 minutes, 7.8% 60 minutes or more (2000)
Additional Information Contacts
Glidden Chamber of Commerce. 715-264-4304

GORDON (town). Covers a land area of 104.421 square miles and a water area of 2.561 square miles. Located at 46.20° N. Lat.; 90.72° W. Long.
Population: 357 (2000); Race: 97.0% White, 0.0% Black, 0.0% Asian, 0.3% American Indian and Alaska Native, 0.0% Hispanic of any race, 2.7% two or more races (2000); Density: 3.4 persons per square mile (2000); Age: 26.0% under 18, 17.2% over 64 (2000); Marriage status: 23.3% never married, 58.1% now married, 4.1% widowed, 14.5% divorced (2000); Foreign born: 0.0% (2000); Ancestry (includes multiple ancestries): 60.1% German, 14.2% Irish, 13.7% Norwegian, 8.5% Polish, 6.6% English (2000).
Economy: Single-family building permits issued: 0 (2001) / 1 (2000); Multi-family building permits issued: 0 (2001) / 0 (2000); Employment by occupation: 6.8% management, 10.2% professional, 24.5% services, 23.8% sales, 5.4% farming, 11.6% construction, 17.7% production (2000).
Income: Per capita income: $16,152 (2000); Median household income: $24,583 (2000); Poverty rate: 23.2% (2000).
Taxes: Total city taxes per capita: $54 (1997); City property taxes per capita: $51 (1997).
Education: High school graduation rate: 78.8% (2000); College graduation rate: 12.0% (2000).
Housing: Homeownership rate: 87.5% (2000); Median home value: $53,800 (2000); Median rent: $200 per month (2000); Median age of housing: 31 years (2000).
Transportation: Commute to work: 75.3% car, 0.0% public transportation, 6.2% walk, 14.4% work from home (2000); Travel time to work: 44.8% less than 15 minutes, 15.2% 15 to 30 minutes, 14.4% 30 to 45 minutes, 18.4% 45 to 60 minutes, 7.2% 60 minutes or more (2000)

HIGH BRIDGE (unincorporated postal area, zip code 54846). Covers a land area of 32.626 square miles and a water area of 0.226 square miles. Located at 46.37° N. Lat.; 90.74° W. Long. Elevation is 1,020 feet.
Population: 537 (2000); Race: 95.7% White, 0.8% Black, 0.0% Asian, 2.8% American Indian and Alaska Native, 0.0% Hispanic of any race, 0.8% two or more races (2000); Density: 16.5 persons per square mile (2000); Age: 26.0% under 18, 15.8% over 64 (2000); Marriage status: 23.4% never married, 59.9% now married, 9.2% widowed, 7.5% divorced (2000); Foreign born: 0.4% (2000); Ancestry (includes multiple ancestries): 32.0% German, 26.0% Finnish, 10.3% Swedish, 9.3% Polish, 8.7% Irish (2000).
Economy: Employment by occupation: 13.1% management, 9.8% professional, 11.8% services, 17.6% sales, 3.7% farming, 19.6% construction, 24.5% production (2000).
Income: Per capita income: $14,236 (2000); Median household income: $32,500 (2000); Poverty rate: 14.0% (2000).
Education: High school graduation rate: 85.1% (2000); College graduation rate: 10.8% (2000).
Housing: Homeownership rate: 82.0% (2000); Median home value: $58,000 (2000); Median rent: $250 per month (2000); Median age of housing: 32 years (2000).
Transportation: Commute to work: 89.1% car, 0.0% public transportation, 1.7% walk, 8.4% work from home (2000); Travel time to work: 30.1% less than 15 minutes, 34.2% 15 to 30 minutes, 17.8% 30 to 45 minutes, 8.2% 45 to 60 minutes, 9.6% 60 minutes or more (2000)

JACOBS (town). Covers a land area of 51.065 square miles and a water area of 0.325 square miles. Located at 46.16° N. Lat.; 90.53° W. Long.
Population: 835 (2000); Race: 98.8% White, 0.0% Black, 0.0% Asian, 1.0% American Indian and Alaska Native, 0.6% Hispanic of any race, 0.1% two or more races (2000); Density: 16.4 persons per square mile (2000); Age: 27.1% under 18, 17.9% over 64 (2000); Marriage status: 22.2% never married, 57.9% now married, 8.9% widowed, 11.0% divorced (2000); Foreign born: 0.2% (2000); Ancestry (includes multiple ancestries): 63.7% German, 7.9% Irish, 7.1% Polish, 6.0% Norwegian, 4.0% Other groups (2000).
Economy: Single-family building permits issued: 0 (2001) / 3 (2000); Multi-family building permits issued: 0 (2001) / 0 (2000); Employment by occupation: 2.8% management, 12.0% professional, 12.9% services, 11.4% sales, 13.8% farming, 9.5% construction, 37.5% production (2000).
Income: Per capita income: $13,579 (2000); Median household income: $25,500 (2000); Poverty rate: 11.5% (2000).
Taxes: Total city taxes per capita: $56 (1997); City property taxes per capita: $53 (1997).
Education: High school graduation rate: 80.4% (2000); College graduation rate: 6.1% (2000).
Housing: Homeownership rate: 78.9% (2000); Median home value: $39,200 (2000); Median rent: $216 per month (2000); Median age of housing: 44 years (2000).
Transportation: Commute to work: 93.1% car, 0.6% public transportation, 4.4% walk, 0.6% work from home (2000); Travel time to work: 38.8% less than 15 minutes, 31.5% 15 to 30 minutes, 8.8% 30 to 45 minutes, 12.3% 45 to 60 minutes, 8.5% 60 minutes or more (2000)

LA POINTE (town). Covers a land area of 77.579 square miles and a water area of 0.394 square miles. Located at 46.81° N. Lat.; 90.69° W. Long. Elevation is 610 feet.
History: A French fortified trading post was built here in 1693, evacuated in 1698, and reoccupied 1718—1759. In early-19th century, site of an American Fur Company post. Historical Museum.
Population: 246 (2000); Race: 95.0% White, 0.8% Black, 0.0% Asian, 3.3% American Indian and Alaska Native, 0.0% Hispanic of any race, 0.8% two or more races (2000); Density: 3.2 persons per square mile (2000); Age: 21.3% under 18, 20.0% over 64 (2000); Marriage status: 14.9% never married, 66.7% now married, 9.5% widowed, 9.0% divorced (2000); Foreign born: 0.8% (2000); Ancestry (includes multiple ancestries): 29.6% German, 14.6% Swedish, 13.8% English, 12.5% Norwegian, 10.8% Scottish (2000).
Economy: Fishing; mustard, coffee. Tourism. Single-family building permits issued: 25 (2001) / 22 (2000); Multi-family building permits issued: 0 (2001) / 8 (2000); Employment by occupation: 22.5% management, 15.0% professional, 10.0% services, 18.3% sales, 0.0% farming, 24.2% construction, 10.0% production (2000).
Income: Per capita income: $23,352 (2000); Median household income: $33,500 (2000); Poverty rate: 4.6% (2000).
Taxes: Total city taxes per capita: $4,783 (1997); City property taxes per capita: $4,360 (1997).
Education: High school graduation rate: 87.6% (2000); College graduation rate: 40.0% (2000).
Housing: Homeownership rate: 72.1% (2000); Median home value: $165,000 (2000); Median rent: $275 per month (2000); Median age of housing: 22 years (2000).
Transportation: Commute to work: 81.4% car, 1.7% public transportation, 7.6% walk, 8.5% work from home (2000); Travel time to work: 74.1% less than 15 minutes, 15.7% 15 to 30 minutes, 4.6% 30 to 45 minutes, 2.8% 45 to 60 minutes, 2.8% 60 minutes or more (2000)
Additional Information Contacts

Madeline Island Chamber of Commerce 715-747-2801

MARENGO (town). Covers a land area of 71.331 square miles and a water area of 0.978 square miles. Located at 46.32° N. Lat.; 90.84° W. Long. Elevation is 775 feet.
Population: 362 (2000); Race: 97.0% White, 1.6% Black, 0.0% Asian, 0.5% American Indian and Alaska Native, 0.0% Hispanic of any race, 0.8% two or more races (2000); Density: 5.1 persons per square mile (2000); Age: 30.9% under 18, 14.5% over 64 (2000); Marriage status: 23.3% never married, 65.9% now married, 5.7% widowed, 5.0% divorced (2000); Foreign born: 0.0% (2000); Ancestry (includes multiple ancestries): 34.7% Finnish, 28.2% German, 9.4% Swedish, 6.5% Norwegian, 5.9% Croatian (2000).
Economy: Employment by occupation: 6.4% management, 15.9% professional, 21.7% services, 16.6% sales, 5.1% farming, 7.6% construction, 26.8% production (2000).
Income: Per capita income: $16,487 (2000); Median household income: $33,036 (2000); Poverty rate: 14.0% (2000).
Taxes: Total city taxes per capita: $35 (1997); City property taxes per capita: $35 (1997).
Education: High school graduation rate: 82.9% (2000); College graduation rate: 19.1% (2000).
Housing: Homeownership rate: 90.1% (2000); Median home value: $63,000 (2000); Median rent: $113 per month (2000); Median age of housing: 38 years (2000).
Transportation: Commute to work: 90.3% car, 1.3% public transportation, 1.3% walk, 5.8% work from home (2000); Travel time to work: 24.7% less than 15 minutes, 47.3% 15 to 30 minutes, 20.5% 30 to 45 minutes, 4.8% 45 to 60 minutes, 2.7% 60 minutes or more (2000)

MELLEN (city). Covers a land area of 1.851 square miles and a water area of 0 square miles. Located at 46.32° N. Lat.; 90.65° W. Long. Elevation is 1,250 feet.
History: Mellen was settled in 1886, when the Wisconsin Central Railroad provided access. It was first called Iron City by its prospective residents, who expected a fortune in minerals.
Population: 845 (2000); Race: 95.7% White, 0.0% Black, 0.7% Asian, 1.0% American Indian and Alaska Native, 2.1% Hispanic of any race, 1.6% two or more races (2000); Density: 456.5 persons per square mile (2000); Age: 20.7% under 18, 25.5% over 64 (2000); Marriage status: 23.1% never married, 56.6% now married, 11.1% widowed, 9.2% divorced (2000); Foreign born: 0.9% (2000); Ancestry (includes multiple ancestries): 40.4% German, 11.1% Polish, 9.0% English, 8.1% Finnish, 8.0% Swedish (2000).
Economy: Single-family building permits issued: 0 (2001) / 0 (2000); Multi-family building permits issued: 0 (2001) / 0 (2000); Employment by occupation: 9.9% management, 14.6% professional, 14.6% services, 15.2% sales, 2.3% farming, 4.7% construction, 38.6% production (2000).
Income: Per capita income: $16,297 (2000); Median household income: $31,917 (2000); Poverty rate: 5.9% (2000).
Taxes: Total city taxes per capita: $168 (1997); City property taxes per capita: $160 (1997).
Education: High school graduation rate: 81.5% (2000); College graduation rate: 10.5% (2000).

School District(s)

Mellen (PK-12)
2000 Enrollment: 340 715-274-3601
Housing: Homeownership rate: 71.3% (2000); Median home value: $39,600 (2000); Median rent: $219 per month (2000); Median age of housing: 60+ years (2000).
Newspapers: The Mellen Weekly Record (1 x week)
Transportation: Commute to work: 84.3% car, 0.0% public transportation, 13.9% walk, 1.8% work from home (2000); Travel time to work: 62.0% less than 15 minutes, 7.2% 15 to 30 minutes, 19.0% 30 to 45 minutes, 6.0% 45 to 60 minutes, 5.7% 60 minutes or more (2000)
Additional Information Contacts
Mellen Chamber of Commerce 715-274-2330

MORSE (town). Covers a land area of 102.764 square miles and a water area of 1.618 square miles. Located at 46.30° N. Lat.; 90.64° W. Long. Elevation is 1,510 feet.
Population: 515 (2000); Race: 98.7% White, 0.0% Black, 0.6% Asian, 0.0% American Indian and Alaska Native, 0.4% Hispanic of any race, 0.8% two or more races (2000); Density: 5.0 persons per square mile (2000); Age: 22.5% under 18, 11.3% over 64 (2000); Marriage status: 22.3% never married, 68.1% now married, 5.0% widowed, 4.6% divorced (2000); Foreign born: 0.8% (2000); Ancestry (includes multiple ancestries): 48.4% German, 10.9% Irish, 10.5% Swedish, 9.4% Finnish, 8.4% Polish (2000).
Economy: Single-family building permits issued: 0 (2001) / 0 (2000); Multi-family building permits issued: 0 (2001) / 0 (2000); Employment by occupation: 9.7% management, 12.2% professional, 13.3% services, 16.9% sales, 2.9% farming, 7.6% construction, 37.4% production (2000).
Income: Per capita income: $19,920 (2000); Median household income: $39,000 (2000); Poverty rate: 2.6% (2000).
Taxes: Total city taxes per capita: $43 (1997); City property taxes per capita: $43 (1997).
Education: High school graduation rate: 84.5% (2000); College graduation rate: 13.9% (2000).
Housing: Homeownership rate: 91.2% (2000); Median home value: $75,800 (2000); Median rent: $225 per month (2000); Median age of housing: 28 years (2000).
Transportation: Commute to work: 87.4% car, 0.7% public transportation, 5.2% walk, 6.7% work from home (2000); Travel time to work: 39.0% less than 15 minutes, 21.9% 15 to 30 minutes, 21.9% 30 to 45 minutes, 13.1% 45 to 60 minutes, 4.0% 60 minutes or more (2000)

ODANAH (CDP). Covers a land area of 1.538 square miles and a water area of 0.050 square miles. Located at 46.60° N. Lat.; 90.68° W. Long. Elevation is 610 feet.
Population: 254 (2000); Race: 3.8% White, 0.0% Black, 1.1% Asian, 93.2% American Indian and Alaska Native, 3.8% Hispanic of any race, 1.9% two or more races (2000); Density: 165.2 persons per square mile (2000); Age: 34.5% under 18, 9.1% over 64 (2000); Marriage status: 44.2% never married, 24.3% now married, 10.5% widowed, 21.0% divorced (2000); Foreign born: 1.1% (2000); Ancestry (includes multiple ancestries): 94.3% Other groups, 3.4% German, 3.4% Finnish, 0.8% English, 0.4% French (except Basque) (2000).
Economy: Wild rice. Near Lake Superior. Employment by occupation: 3.4% management, 6.0% professional, 43.1% services, 28.4% sales, 0.0% farming, 11.2% construction, 7.8% production (2000).
Income: Per capita income: $9,950 (2000); Median household income: $25,156 (2000); Poverty rate: 29.7% (2000).
Education: High school graduation rate: 76.9% (2000); College graduation rate: 8.2% (2000).
Housing: Homeownership rate: 58.8% (2000); Median home value: $45,800 (2000); Median rent: $179 per month (2000); Median age of housing: 23 years (2000).
Transportation: Commute to work: 81.6% car, 1.8% public transportation, 4.4% walk, 5.3% work from home (2000); Travel time to work: 75.9% less than 15 minutes, 21.3% 15 to 30 minutes, 0.0% 30 to 45 minutes, 0.0% 45 to 60 minutes, 2.8% 60 minutes or more (2000)

PEEKSVILLE (town). Covers a land area of 36.796 square miles and a water area of 0.106 square miles. Located at 46.12° N. Lat.; 90.51° W. Long. Elevation is 1,538 feet.
Population: 176 (2000); Race: 97.7% White, 1.2% Black, 1.2% Asian, 0.0% American Indian and Alaska Native, 0.0% Hispanic of any race, 0.0% two or more races (2000); Density: 4.8 persons per square mile (2000); Age: 17.4% under 18, 18.0% over 64 (2000); Marriage status: 15.9% never married, 73.5% now married, 4.6% widowed, 6.0% divorced (2000); Foreign born: 2.3% (2000); Ancestry (includes multiple ancestries): 48.8% German, 11.0% Norwegian, 11.0% English, 10.5% Irish, 9.9% Polish (2000).
Economy: Single-family building permits issued: 0 (2001) / 0 (2000); Multi-family building permits issued: 0 (2001) / 0 (2000); Employment by occupation: 8.4% management, 15.7% professional, 16.9% services, 15.7% sales, 1.2% farming, 18.1% construction, 24.1% production (2000).
Income: Per capita income: $20,533 (2000); Median household income: $39,167 (2000); Poverty rate: 4.7% (2000).
Taxes: Total city taxes per capita: $40 (1997); City property taxes per capita: $40 (1997).
Education: High school graduation rate: 76.4% (2000); College graduation rate: 13.0% (2000).
Housing: Homeownership rate: 91.2% (2000); Median home value: $80,000 (2000); Median rent: $425 per month (2000); Median age of housing: 25 years (2000).
Transportation: Commute to work: 97.5% car, 0.0% public transportation, 0.0% walk, 2.5% work from home (2000); Travel time to work: 25.3% less than 15 minutes, 54.4% 15 to 30 minutes, 11.4% 30 to 45 minutes, 2.5% 45 to 60 minutes, 6.3% 60 minutes or more (2000)

SANBORN (town). Covers a land area of 156.405 square miles and a water area of 4.345 square miles. Located at 46.59° N. Lat.; 90.72° W. Long. Elevation is 830 feet.

Population: 1,272 (2000); Race: 12.0% White, 0.0% Black, 1.7% Asian, 83.3% American Indian and Alaska Native, 4.9% Hispanic of any race, 2.8% two or more races (2000); Density: 8.1 persons per square mile (2000); Age: 37.9% under 18, 6.8% over 64 (2000); Marriage status: 41.3% never married, 35.2% now married, 5.9% widowed, 17.6% divorced (2000); Foreign born: 1.1% (2000); Ancestry (includes multiple ancestries): 84.5% Other groups, 5.7% German, 2.7% Polish, 1.5% Norwegian, 1.5% Swedish (2000).
Economy: Employment by occupation: 10.2% management, 12.7% professional, 31.7% services, 23.3% sales, 1.5% farming, 9.3% construction, 11.4% production (2000).
Income: Per capita income: $11,664 (2000); Median household income: $26,711 (2000); Poverty rate: 27.4% (2000).
Taxes: Total city taxes per capita: $3 (1997); City property taxes per capita: $2 (1997).
Education: High school graduation rate: 83.4% (2000); College graduation rate: 12.5% (2000).
Housing: Homeownership rate: 60.0% (2000); Median home value: $49,300 (2000); Median rent: $164 per month (2000); Median age of housing: 19 years (2000).
Transportation: Commute to work: 86.4% car, 2.5% public transportation, 5.2% walk, 2.3% work from home (2000); Travel time to work: 70.8% less than 15 minutes, 21.0% 15 to 30 minutes, 4.1% 30 to 45 minutes, 1.0% 45 to 60 minutes, 3.1% 60 minutes or more (2000)

SHANAGOLDEN (town). Covers a land area of 89.291 square miles and a water area of 0.571 square miles. Located at 46.11° N. Lat.; 90.77° W. Long. Elevation is 1,529 feet.
Population: 150 (2000); Race: 100.0% White, 0.0% Black, 0.0% Asian, 0.0% American Indian and Alaska Native, 0.0% Hispanic of any race, 0.0% two or more races (2000); Density: 1.7 persons per square mile (2000); Age: 26.2% under 18, 23.5% over 64 (2000); Marriage status: 11.4% never married, 76.3% now married, 6.1% widowed, 6.1% divorced (2000); Foreign born: 1.3% (2000); Ancestry (includes multiple ancestries): 51.7% German, 16.8% Irish, 10.1% Norwegian, 10.1% Swedish, 7.4% French (except Basque) (2000).
Economy: Employment by occupation: 0.0% management, 9.8% professional, 7.3% services, 14.6% sales, 22.0% farming, 12.2% construction, 34.1% production (2000).
Income: Per capita income: $17,450 (2000); Median household income: $26,250 (2000); Poverty rate: 4.0% (2000).
Taxes: Total city taxes per capita: $58 (1997); City property taxes per capita: $58 (1997).
Education: High school graduation rate: 80.0% (2000); College graduation rate: 8.6% (2000).
Housing: Homeownership rate: 87.1% (2000); Median home value: $70,000 (2000); Median rent: $275 per month (2000); Median age of housing: 35 years (2000).
Transportation: Commute to work: 95.1% car, 0.0% public transportation, 4.9% walk, 0.0% work from home (2000); Travel time to work: 24.4% less than 15 minutes, 46.3% 15 to 30 minutes, 17.1% 30 to 45 minutes, 12.2% 45 to 60 minutes, 0.0% 60 minutes or more (2000)

WHITE RIVER (town). Covers a land area of 44.044 square miles and a water area of 0.101 square miles. Located at 46.43° N. Lat.; 90.83° W. Long. Elevation is 730 feet.
Population: 892 (2000); Race: 97.4% White, 0.0% Black, 0.0% Asian, 2.1% American Indian and Alaska Native, 0.2% Hispanic of any race, 0.5% two or more races (2000); Density: 20.3 persons per square mile (2000); Age: 41.1% under 18, 6.8% over 64 (2000); Marriage status: 25.9% never married, 64.5% now married, 6.5% widowed, 3.2% divorced (2000); Foreign born: 0.0% (2000); Ancestry (includes multiple ancestries): 36.1% Finnish, 19.1% Swedish, 15.7% German, 9.5% Norwegian, 8.4% English (2000).
Economy: Employment by occupation: 11.2% management, 8.8% professional, 20.0% services, 23.2% sales, 5.9% farming, 17.1% construction, 13.9% production (2000).
Income: Per capita income: $15,667 (2000); Median household income: $38,250 (2000); Poverty rate: 5.6% (2000).
Taxes: Total city taxes per capita: $17 (1997); City property taxes per capita: $15 (1997).
Education: High school graduation rate: 88.0% (2000); College graduation rate: 10.2% (2000).
Housing: Homeownership rate: 91.6% (2000); Median home value: $65,000 (2000); Median rent: $310 per month (2000); Median age of housing: 27 years (2000).
Transportation: Commute to work: 84.3% car, 0.5% public transportation, 2.4% walk, 11.9% work from home (2000); Travel time to work: 21.8% less than 15 minutes, 58.5% 15 to 30 minutes, 8.9% 30 to 45 minutes, 4.0% 45 to 60 minutes, 6.8% 60 minutes or more (2000)

Barron County

Located in northwestern Wisconsin; drained by the Red Cedar and Hay Rivers. Covers a land area of 862.80 square miles, a water area of 27.20 square miles, and is located in the Central Time Zone. The county government was organized in 1859. County seat is Barron.

Weather Station: Cumberland — Elevation: 1,240 feet

	Jan	Feb	Mar	Apr	May	Jun	Jul	Aug	Sep	Oct	Nov	Dec
High	21	28	39	56	70	78	82	80	70	57	39	25
Low	0	6	18	33	45	55	60	57	48	36	23	8
Precip	1.2	0.8	1.8	2.7	3.4	4.5	4.4	4.5	4.2	2.8	2.2	1.1
Snow	13.1	8.0	10.0	3.7	tr	0.0	0.0	0.0	tr	0.6	7.9	10.9

High and Low temperatures in degrees Fahrenheit; Precipitation and Snow in inches

Weather Station: Rice Lake Municipal Airport — Elevation: 1,102 feet

	Jan	Feb	Mar	Apr	May	Jun	Jul	Aug	Sep	Oct	Nov	Dec
High	20	27	39	56	69	77	81	79	69	57	38	25
Low	-1	6	19	32	44	53	58	56	47	36	22	7
Precip	1.1	0.7	1.8	2.7	3.2	4.2	4.0	4.5	4.3	2.7	2.0	1.1
Snow	12.3	6.7	9.3	2.7	tr	0.0	0.0	0.0	tr	0.6	7.0	9.8

High and Low temperatures in degrees Fahrenheit; Precipitation and Snow in inches

Weather Station: Ridgeland 1 NNE — Elevation: 958 feet

	Jan	Feb	Mar	Apr	May	Jun	Jul	Aug	Sep	Oct	Nov	Dec
High	21	28	39	56	69	77	81	79	70	58	40	26
Low	-1	5	18	31	43	53	57	55	46	35	22	7
Precip	1.1	0.8	2.1	2.8	3.5	4.2	3.9	4.9	3.8	2.7	1.9	1.1
Snow	10.9	6.1	9.3	1.7	tr	0.0	0.0	0.0	tr	0.3	5.4	8.5

High and Low temperatures in degrees Fahrenheit; Precipitation and Snow in inches

Population: 44,963 (2000); Race: 97.8% White, 0.2% Black, 0.3% Asian, 0.8% American Indian and Alaska Native, 1.0% Hispanic of any race, 0.6% two or more races (2000); Density: 52.1 persons per square mile (2000); Age: 25.3% under 18, 16.4% over 64 (2000).
Religion: Five largest groups: 20.7% Evangelical Lutheran Church in America, 19.6% Catholic Church, 5.7% Lutheran Church—Missouri Synod, 4.8% The United Methodist Church, 2.0% The Wesleyan Church (2000).
Economy: Unemployment rate: 4.8% (11/2002); Total civilian labor force: 24,048 (11/2002); Leading industries: 35.1% manufacturing; 17.7% retail trade; 12.2% health care and social assistance (2000); Companies that employ more than 1,000 persons: 1 (2000); Companies that employ more than 100 persons: 26 (2000); Farms: 1,384 totaling 325,009 acres (1997); Minority business ownership rate: 0.0% (1997); Women business ownership rate: 15.8% (1997); Retail sales per capita: $10,359 (1997). Single-family building permits issued: 285 (2001) / 253 (2000); Multi-family building permits issued: 48 (2001) / 84 (2000).
Income: Per capita income: $18,091 (2000); Median household income: $37,275 (2000); Poverty rate: 8.8% (2000); Bankruptcy rate: 3.72% (2001).
Taxes: Total county taxes per capita: $239 (2000); County property taxes per capita: $176 (2000).
Education: High school graduation rate: 82.4% (2000); College graduation rate: 14.9% (2000).
Housing: Homeownership rate: 75.9% (2000); Median home value: $78,000 (2000); Median rent: $360 per month (2000); Median age of housing: 32 years (2000).
Health: Birth rate: 105.4 per 10,000 population (1998); Age adjusted death rate: 85.5 per 10,000 population (1999); Age adjusted cancer mortality rate: 208.0 deaths per 100,000 population (1999). Number of physicians: 15.3 per 10,000 population (1999); Number of hospital beds: 60.5 per 10,000 population (1999).
Elections: 2000 Presidential election results: 44.9% Gore, 49.5% Bush, 5.1% Nader, 0.4% Buchanan
National and State Parks: Engle Creek Springs State Public Fishing Area; Grassy Lake State Public Fishery Area; Hickey Creek State Public Fishery Area; Lightning Creek State Wildlife Area; Loon Lake State Wildlife Area; New Auburn State Public Hunting Grounds; Yellow River State Public Fishery Area; Yellow River State Public Fishery Area
Additional Information Contacts
Barron County Government Offices 715-537-6200
Chetek Chamber of Commerce 715-924-3200
Cumberland Chamber of Commerce 715-822-3378
Rice Lake Chamber of Commerce 715-234-2126

Barron County Communities

ALMENA (village). Covers a land area of 1.000 square miles and a water area of 0 square miles. Located at 45.41° N. Lat.; 92.03° W. Long. Elevation is 1,187 feet.
Population: 720 (2000); Race: 96.3% White, 0.0% Black, 0.0% Asian, 2.0% American Indian and Alaska Native, 2.6% Hispanic of any race, 1.7% two or more races (2000); Density: 720.0 persons per square mile (2000); Age: 30.5% under 18, 15.6% over 64 (2000); Marriage status: 24.9% never married, 47.6% now married, 10.6% widowed, 17.0% divorced (2000); Foreign born: 2.3% (2000); Ancestry (includes multiple ancestries): 50.6% German, 18.5% Norwegian, 8.4% Irish, 7.6% Other groups, 6.3% English (2000).
Economy: Single-family building permits issued: 1 (2001) / 3 (2000); Multi-family building permits issued: 2 (2001) / 4 (2000); Employment by occupation: 8.8% management, 8.5% professional, 18.2% services, 19.5% sales, 2.8% farming, 12.3% construction, 29.9% production (2000).
Income: Per capita income: $13,928 (2000); Median household income: $27,917 (2000); Poverty rate: 14.9% (2000).
Taxes: Total city taxes per capita: $134 (1997); City property taxes per capita: $111 (1997).
Education: High school graduation rate: 77.9% (2000); College graduation rate: 9.3% (2000).
Housing: Homeownership rate: 70.9% (2000); Median home value: $52,900 (2000); Median rent: $331 per month (2000); Median age of housing: 33 years (2000).
Transportation: Commute to work: 93.4% car, 0.0% public transportation, 3.5% walk, 2.8% work from home (2000); Travel time to work: 50.8% less than 15 minutes, 26.5% 15 to 30 minutes, 12.0% 30 to 45 minutes, 1.9% 45 to 60 minutes, 8.7% 60 minutes or more (2000)

ALMENA (town). Covers a land area of 30.675 square miles and a water area of 1.909 square miles. Located at 45.42° N. Lat.; 92.09° W. Long. Elevation is 1,187 feet.
Population: 910 (2000); Race: 99.8% White, 0.0% Black, 0.2% Asian, 0.0% American Indian and Alaska Native, 0.0% Hispanic of any race, 0.0% two or more races (2000); Density: 29.7 persons per square mile (2000); Age: 20.2% under 18, 13.7% over 64 (2000); Marriage status: 20.7% never married, 71.0% now married, 3.9% widowed, 4.5% divorced (2000); Foreign born: 0.4% (2000); Ancestry (includes multiple ancestries): 50.3% German, 17.3% Norwegian, 7.3% Swedish, 6.5% Irish, 5.6% English (2000).
Economy: Dairy products; manufactures cheese. Employment by occupation: 18.8% management, 9.6% professional, 14.0% services, 19.4% sales, 3.6% farming, 12.8% construction, 21.6% production (2000).
Income: Per capita income: $21,211 (2000); Median household income: $42,833 (2000); Poverty rate: 6.4% (2000).
Taxes: Total city taxes per capita: $175 (2000); City property taxes per capita: $174 (2000).
Education: High school graduation rate: 80.6% (2000); College graduation rate: 10.7% (2000).
Housing: Homeownership rate: 91.4% (2000); Median home value: $126,000 (2000); Median rent: $446 per month (2000); Median age of housing: 32 years (2000).
Transportation: Commute to work: 82.5% car, 0.4% public transportation, 3.3% walk, 13.1% work from home (2000); Travel time to work: 47.8% less than 15 minutes, 27.0% 15 to 30 minutes, 14.8% 30 to 45 minutes, 3.8% 45 to 60 minutes, 6.5% 60 minutes or more (2000)

ARLAND (town). Covers a land area of 35.343 square miles and a water area of 0 square miles. Located at 45.33° N. Lat.; 91.96° W. Long. Elevation is 1,217 feet.
Population: 670 (2000); Race: 100.0% White, 0.0% Black, 0.0% Asian, 0.0% American Indian and Alaska Native, 0.0% Hispanic of any race, 0.0% two or more races (2000); Density: 19.0 persons per square mile (2000); Age: 28.1% under 18, 11.2% over 64 (2000); Marriage status: 25.1% never married, 64.2% now married, 3.9% widowed, 6.8% divorced (2000); Foreign born: 0.4% (2000); Ancestry (includes multiple ancestries): 41.9% German, 32.5% Norwegian, 11.8% Irish, 5.7% United States or American, 4.7% Swedish (2000).
Economy: Single-family building permits issued: 2 (2001) / 2 (2000); Multi-family building permits issued: 0 (2001) / 0 (2000); Employment by occupation: 19.6% management, 10.9% professional, 12.8% services, 15.4% sales, 8.1% farming, 7.5% construction, 25.7% production (2000).
Income: Per capita income: $13,555 (2000); Median household income: $31,985 (2000); Poverty rate: 12.2% (2000).
Taxes: Total city taxes per capita: $95 (1997); City property taxes per capita: $95 (1997).
Education: High school graduation rate: 71.7% (2000); College graduation rate: 8.8% (2000).
Housing: Homeownership rate: 91.0% (2000); Median home value: $54,000 (2000); Median rent: $242 per month (2000); Median age of housing: 35 years (2000).
Transportation: Commute to work: 72.6% car, 0.0% public transportation, 5.9% walk, 19.8% work from home (2000); Travel time to work: 35.6% less than 15 minutes, 46.5% 15 to 30 minutes, 11.3% 30 to 45 minutes, 1.8% 45 to 60 minutes, 4.9% 60 minutes or more (2000)

BARRON (city). Covers a land area of 2.760 square miles and a water area of 0.084 square miles. Located at 45.40° N. Lat.; 91.84° W. Long. Elevation is 1,115 feet.
History: Barron began in 1878 when a sawmill was built on the Yellow River here. The arrival of the Minneapolis, St. Paul & Sault Ste. Marie Railroad in 1884 led to the founding of another sawmill and a flour mill, which sustained the economy when the timber was gone. A stave mill and wooden ware factory were later established in Barron, to use the hardwood that grew in the area. In 1902 the Barron Cooperative Creamery Company was organized.
Population: 3,248 (2000); Race: 97.0% White, 0.5% Black, 0.6% Asian, 0.0% American Indian and Alaska Native, 0.4% Hispanic of any race, 1.9% two or more races (2000); Density: 1,176.7 persons per square mile (2000); Age: 22.9% under 18, 20.9% over 64 (2000); Marriage status: 22.4% never married, 49.8% now married, 12.0% widowed, 15.7% divorced (2000); Foreign born: 2.4% (2000); Ancestry (includes multiple ancestries): 38.9% German, 25.8% Norwegian, 9.8% Irish, 7.4% English, 5.9% Swedish (2000).
Economy: Single-family building permits issued: 8 (2001) / 4 (2000); Multi-family building permits issued: 14 (2001) / 24 (2000); Employment by occupation: 12.0% management, 16.5% professional, 17.4% services, 19.9% sales, 2.3% farming, 5.3% construction, 26.6% production (2000).
Income: Per capita income: $18,485 (2000); Median household income: $33,281 (2000); Poverty rate: 9.2% (2000).
Taxes: Total city taxes per capita: $137 (1997); City property taxes per capita: $127 (1997).
Education: High school graduation rate: 79.9% (2000); College graduation rate: 17.4% (2000).

School District(s)

Barron Area (PK-12)
2000 Enrollment: 1,546 715-537-5612
Housing: Homeownership rate: 61.9% (2000); Median home value: $70,600 (2000); Median rent: $344 per month (2000); Median age of housing: 37 years (2000).
Hospitals: Barron Memorial Medical Center - Mayo Health System (29 beds)
Safety: Violent crime rate: 12.2 per 10,000 population; Property crime rate: 278.2 per 10,000 population (2001).
Newspapers: Barron News-Shield (1 x week); Barron County Shopper (1 x week)
Transportation: Commute to work: 83.9% car, 0.0% public transportation, 10.8% walk, 5.0% work from home (2000); Travel time to work: 56.3% less than 15 minutes, 31.7% 15 to 30 minutes, 7.1% 30 to 45 minutes, 0.8% 45 to 60 minutes, 4.1% 60 minutes or more (2000)

BARRON (town). Covers a land area of 32.994 square miles and a water area of 0.066 square miles. Located at 45.41° N. Lat.; 91.85° W. Long. Elevation is 1,115 feet.
History: Founded before 1878; incorporated 1887.
Population: 1,014 (2000); Race: 98.7% White, 0.0% Black, 0.0% Asian, 0.0% American Indian and Alaska Native, 1.4% Hispanic of any race, 0.3% two or more races (2000); Density: 30.7 persons per square mile (2000); Age: 24.5% under 18, 14.3% over 64 (2000); Marriage status: 26.0% never married, 61.6% now married, 6.2% widowed, 6.3% divorced (2000); Foreign born: 1.5% (2000); Ancestry (includes multiple ancestries): 40.9% German, 28.0% Norwegian, 8.7% Irish, 7.3% Swedish, 5.0% United States or American (2000).
Economy: Commercial center for farming and dairying area; canning. Manufacturing: apparel, woodworking, machinery, food processing. Has poultry hatcheries and large cooperative creamery. Building stone is quarried nearby. Employment by occupation: 13.3% management, 14.1% professional, 14.8% services, 18.7% sales, 7.5% farming, 8.2% construction, 23.4% production (2000).
Income: Per capita income: $16,776 (2000); Median household income: $46,500 (2000); Poverty rate: 6.3% (2000).

Taxes: Total city taxes per capita: $31 (1997); City property taxes per capita: $31 (1997).
Education: High school graduation rate: 80.2% (2000); College graduation rate: 14.8% (2000).
Housing: Homeownership rate: 85.1% (2000); Median home value: $82,400 (2000); Median rent: $488 per month (2000); Median age of housing: 47 years (2000).
Transportation: Commute to work: 88.7% car, 0.4% public transportation, 1.4% walk, 9.0% work from home (2000); Travel time to work: 63.2% less than 15 minutes, 24.8% 15 to 30 minutes, 3.3% 30 to 45 minutes, 1.9% 45 to 60 minutes, 6.8% 60 minutes or more (2000)

BARRONETT (unincorporated postal area, zip code 54813). Covers a land area of 53.422 square miles and a water area of 1.370 square miles. Located at 45.64° N. Lat.; 92.01° W. Long. Elevation is 1,375 feet.
Population: 643 (2000); Race: 97.3% White, 0.0% Black, 0.0% Asian, 0.6% American Indian and Alaska Native, 0.0% Hispanic of any race, 1.8% two or more races (2000); Density: 12.0 persons per square mile (2000); Age: 28.3% under 18, 12.1% over 64 (2000); Marriage status: 19.2% never married, 65.9% now married, 3.6% widowed, 11.3% divorced (2000); Foreign born: 0.0% (2000); Ancestry (includes multiple ancestries): 36.4% German, 21.5% Norwegian, 12.2% English, 9.0% Irish, 8.8% Swedish (2000).
Economy: Employment by occupation: 20.0% management, 11.6% professional, 14.9% services, 14.0% sales, 3.0% farming, 7.8% construction, 28.7% production (2000).
Income: Per capita income: $20,695 (2000); Median household income: $40,156 (2000); Poverty rate: 3.7% (2000).
Education: High school graduation rate: 80.4% (2000); College graduation rate: 14.5% (2000).
Housing: Homeownership rate: 89.8% (2000); Median home value: $85,800 (2000); Median rent: $371 per month (2000); Median age of housing: 24 years (2000).
Transportation: Commute to work: 83.6% car, 0.0% public transportation, 4.6% walk, 11.5% work from home (2000); Travel time to work: 23.4% less than 15 minutes, 40.9% 15 to 30 minutes, 16.8% 30 to 45 minutes, 8.4% 45 to 60 minutes, 10.5% 60 minutes or more (2000)

BEAR LAKE (town). Covers a land area of 32.875 square miles and a water area of 2.317 square miles. Located at 45.59° N. Lat.; 91.82° W. Long.
Population: 587 (2000); Race: 100.0% White, 0.0% Black, 0.0% Asian, 0.0% American Indian and Alaska Native, 1.2% Hispanic of any race, 0.0% two or more races (2000); Density: 17.9 persons per square mile (2000); Age: 22.5% under 18, 15.2% over 64 (2000); Marriage status: 25.1% never married, 63.4% now married, 4.2% widowed, 7.4% divorced (2000); Foreign born: 0.0% (2000); Ancestry (includes multiple ancestries): 39.2% German, 21.8% Norwegian, 16.7% Czech, 8.9% Irish, 5.4% French (except Basque) (2000).
Economy: Employment by occupation: 23.0% management, 13.3% professional, 7.4% services, 13.9% sales, 3.9% farming, 9.7% construction, 28.8% production (2000).
Income: Per capita income: $18,380 (2000); Median household income: $44,271 (2000); Poverty rate: 5.1% (2000).
Taxes: Total city taxes per capita: $147 (1997); City property taxes per capita: $147 (1997).
Education: High school graduation rate: 82.6% (2000); College graduation rate: 14.4% (2000).
Housing: Homeownership rate: 90.2% (2000); Median home value: $94,400 (2000); Median rent: $313 per month (2000); Median age of housing: 26 years (2000).
Transportation: Commute to work: 86.1% car, 0.0% public transportation, 2.9% walk, 10.0% work from home (2000); Travel time to work: 16.9% less than 15 minutes, 65.1% 15 to 30 minutes, 7.9% 30 to 45 minutes, 1.8% 45 to 60 minutes, 8.3% 60 minutes or more (2000)

CAMERON (village). Covers a land area of 2.411 square miles and a water area of 0.102 square miles. Located at 45.40° N. Lat.; 91.74° W. Long. Elevation is 1,097 feet.
History: Cameron was the site of the Battle of Cameron Dam, waged by John Dietz who demanded reparations when the Chippewa Log and Boom Company's dam flooded his farm in 1904. Dietz held the dam hostage for several years, but was eventually forced to surrender his claims.
Population: 1,546 (2000); Race: 97.6% White, 0.0% Black, 0.5% Asian, 1.0% American Indian and Alaska Native, 2.5% Hispanic of any race, 0.8% two or more races (2000); Density: 641.3 persons per square mile (2000); Age: 28.6% under 18, 12.9% over 64 (2000); Marriage status: 21.8% never married, 59.4% now married, 7.3% widowed, 11.5% divorced (2000); Foreign born: 1.3% (2000); Ancestry (includes multiple ancestries): 35.6% German, 25.2% Norwegian, 11.0% Irish, 8.1% English, 6.3% Other groups (2000).
Economy: Single-family building permits issued: 5 (2001) / 4 (2000); Multi-family building permits issued: 4 (2001) / 10 (2000); Employment by occupation: 8.2% management, 13.1% professional, 17.7% services, 21.2% sales, 1.3% farming, 11.2% construction, 27.2% production (2000).
Income: Per capita income: $16,470 (2000); Median household income: $34,167 (2000); Poverty rate: 10.3% (2000).
Taxes: Total city taxes per capita: $106 (1997); City property taxes per capita: $99 (1997).
Education: High school graduation rate: 83.6% (2000); College graduation rate: 12.0% (2000).

School District(s)

Cameron (PK-12)
2000 Enrollment: 860 715-458-4560

Housing: Homeownership rate: 61.9% (2000); Median home value: $71,300 (2000); Median rent: $366 per month (2000); Median age of housing: 31 years (2000).
Transportation: Commute to work: 96.7% car, 0.0% public transportation, 0.8% walk, 2.5% work from home (2000); Travel time to work: 56.3% less than 15 minutes, 32.0% 15 to 30 minutes, 5.6% 30 to 45 minutes, 2.3% 45 to 60 minutes, 3.7% 60 minutes or more (2000)

CEDAR LAKE (town). Covers a land area of 31.319 square miles and a water area of 4.075 square miles. Located at 45.61° N. Lat.; 91.58° W. Long.
Population: 944 (2000); Race: 100.0% White, 0.0% Black, 0.0% Asian, 0.0% American Indian and Alaska Native, 0.0% Hispanic of any race, 0.0% two or more races (2000); Density: 30.1 persons per square mile (2000); Age: 19.5% under 18, 19.7% over 64 (2000); Marriage status: 16.0% never married, 72.8% now married, 2.9% widowed, 8.3% divorced (2000); Foreign born: 0.0% (2000); Ancestry (includes multiple ancestries): 41.2% German, 21.8% Norwegian, 11.7% Irish, 10.3% English, 8.6% Czech (2000).
Economy: Single-family building permits issued: 23 (2001) / 24 (2000); Multi-family building permits issued: 0 (2001) / 0 (2000); Employment by occupation: 6.7% management, 15.3% professional, 12.9% services, 27.3% sales, 3.3% farming, 12.2% construction, 22.2% production (2000).
Income: Per capita income: $25,087 (2000); Median household income: $40,536 (2000); Poverty rate: 5.0% (2000).
Taxes: Total city taxes per capita: $218 (1997); City property taxes per capita: $215 (1997).
Education: High school graduation rate: 82.8% (2000); College graduation rate: 16.9% (2000).
Housing: Homeownership rate: 92.6% (2000); Median home value: $99,400 (2000); Median rent: $365 per month (2000); Median age of housing: 24 years (2000).
Transportation: Commute to work: 92.5% car, 0.0% public transportation, 1.7% walk, 5.0% work from home (2000); Travel time to work: 24.9% less than 15 minutes, 53.6% 15 to 30 minutes, 13.8% 30 to 45 minutes, 0.9% 45 to 60 minutes, 6.8% 60 minutes or more (2000)

CHETEK (city). Covers a land area of 2.355 square miles and a water area of 0.704 square miles. Located at 45.31° N. Lat.; 91.65° W. Long. Elevation is 1,055 feet.
Population: 2,180 (2000); Race: 98.9% White, 0.2% Black, 0.3% Asian, 0.0% American Indian and Alaska Native, 0.4% Hispanic of any race, 0.5% two or more races (2000); Density: 925.7 persons per square mile (2000); Age: 22.3% under 18, 26.5% over 64 (2000); Marriage status: 16.7% never married, 56.7% now married, 14.9% widowed, 11.8% divorced (2000); Foreign born: 0.6% (2000); Ancestry (includes multiple ancestries): 33.4% German, 23.0% Norwegian, 9.6% Irish, 9.3% Polish, 7.6% English (2000).
Economy: Single-family building permits issued: 7 (2001) / 10 (2000); Multi-family building permits issued: 2 (2001) / 2 (2000); Employment by occupation: 8.2% management, 11.7% professional, 20.3% services, 23.1% sales, 1.7% farming, 9.8% construction, 25.3% production (2000).
Income: Per capita income: $17,922 (2000); Median household income: $31,270 (2000); Poverty rate: 12.4% (2000).
Taxes: Total city taxes per capita: $281 (2000); City property taxes per capita: $267 (2000).
Education: High school graduation rate: 76.7% (2000); College graduation rate: 14.3% (2000).

School District(s)

Chetek (KG-12)
2000 Enrollment: 1,087 715-924-2226

Housing: Homeownership rate: 66.0% (2000); Median home value: $73,200 (2000); Median rent: $358 per month (2000); Median age of housing: 42 years (2000).
Newspapers: Chetek Alert (1 x week)
Transportation: Commute to work: 90.7% car, 0.0% public transportation, 4.3% walk, 4.5% work from home (2000); Travel time to work: 47.2% less than 15 minutes, 33.3% 15 to 30 minutes, 8.1% 30 to 45 minutes, 7.1% 45 to 60 minutes, 4.3% 60 minutes or more (2000)
Additional Information Contacts
Chetek Chamber of Commerce 715-924-3200

CHETEK (town). Covers a land area of 30.446 square miles and a water area of 3.121 square miles. Located at 45.32° N. Lat.; 91.63° W. Long. Elevation is 1,055 feet.
History: Settled 1863, incorporated 1891.
Population: 1,686 (2000); Race: 97.7% White, 0.1% Black, 0.2% Asian, 0.4% American Indian and Alaska Native, 0.9% Hispanic of any race, 1.6% two or more races (2000); Density: 55.4 persons per square mile (2000); Age: 19.9% under 18, 19.9% over 64 (2000); Marriage status: 15.2% never married, 72.8% now married, 5.2% widowed, 6.8% divorced (2000); Foreign born: 1.1% (2000); Ancestry (includes multiple ancestries): 34.0% German, 23.9% Norwegian, 9.0% Polish, 8.8% English, 8.7% Irish (2000).
Economy: In dairying and poultry-raising area. Manufacturing. Summer resort. Single-family building permits issued: 0 (2001) / 0 (2000); Multi-family building permits issued: 0 (2001) / 0 (2000); Employment by occupation: 11.6% management, 16.4% professional, 15.6% services, 25.9% sales, 1.5% farming, 10.0% construction, 19.1% production (2000).
Income: Per capita income: $21,273 (2000); Median household income: $38,125 (2000); Poverty rate: 6.3% (2000).
Taxes: Total city taxes per capita: $239 (1997); City property taxes per capita: $235 (1997).
Education: High school graduation rate: 83.6% (2000); College graduation rate: 11.6% (2000).
Housing: Homeownership rate: 86.8% (2000); Median home value: $106,000 (2000); Median rent: $411 per month (2000); Median age of housing: 27 years (2000).
Transportation: Commute to work: 88.3% car, 0.0% public transportation, 4.0% walk, 7.4% work from home (2000); Travel time to work: 36.9% less than 15 minutes, 33.6% 15 to 30 minutes, 16.1% 30 to 45 minutes, 4.9% 45 to 60 minutes, 8.6% 60 minutes or more (2000)

CLINTON (town). Covers a land area of 35.124 square miles and a water area of 0.295 square miles. Located at 45.42° N. Lat.; 91.97° W. Long.
Population: 920 (2000); Race: 98.1% White, 0.0% Black, 0.0% Asian, 1.4% American Indian and Alaska Native, 0.0% Hispanic of any race, 0.5% two or more races (2000); Density: 26.2 persons per square mile (2000); Age: 28.8% under 18, 13.3% over 64 (2000); Marriage status: 24.3% never married, 67.2% now married, 3.3% widowed, 5.2% divorced (2000); Foreign born: 0.7% (2000); Ancestry (includes multiple ancestries): 46.3% German, 22.4% Norwegian, 10.3% Irish, 8.5% Swedish, 7.4% English (2000).
Economy: Single-family building permits issued: 12 (2001) / 2 (2000); Multi-family building permits issued: 0 (2001) / 0 (2000); Employment by occupation: 21.9% management, 8.0% professional, 15.4% services, 15.6% sales, 7.6% farming, 10.1% construction, 21.5% production (2000).
Income: Per capita income: $15,584 (2000); Median household income: $39,417 (2000); Poverty rate: 10.3% (2000).
Taxes: Total city taxes per capita: $107 (1997); City property taxes per capita: $106 (1997).
Education: High school graduation rate: 66.3% (2000); College graduation rate: 6.4% (2000).
Housing: Homeownership rate: 88.0% (2000); Median home value: $70,000 (2000); Median rent: $367 per month (2000); Median age of housing: 42 years (2000).
Transportation: Commute to work: 73.6% car, 0.0% public transportation, 5.5% walk, 18.9% work from home (2000); Travel time to work: 47.8% less than 15 minutes, 32.8% 15 to 30 minutes, 12.1% 30 to 45 minutes, 3.7% 45 to 60 minutes, 3.7% 60 minutes or more (2000)

COMSTOCK (unincorporated postal area, zip code 54826). Covers a land area of 48.473 square miles and a water area of 1.896 square miles. Located at 45.50° N. Lat.; 92.17° W. Long. Elevation is 1,270 feet.
Population: 799 (2000); Race: 99.2% White, 0.0% Black, 0.2% Asian, 0.0% American Indian and Alaska Native, 0.2% Hispanic of any race, 0.6% two or more races (2000); Density: 16.5 persons per square mile (2000); Age: 21.9% under 18, 13.8% over 64 (2000); Marriage status: 18.4% never married, 65.2% now married, 5.7% widowed, 10.7% divorced (2000); Foreign born: 0.5% (2000); Ancestry (includes multiple ancestries): 44.6% German, 19.6% Norwegian, 8.1% Swedish, 7.9% Irish, 6.3% English (2000).
Economy: Employment by occupation: 18.0% management, 11.7% professional, 12.9% services, 19.0% sales, 3.4% farming, 4.9% construction, 30.0% production (2000).
Income: Per capita income: $17,027 (2000); Median household income: $36,705 (2000); Poverty rate: 13.9% (2000).
Education: High school graduation rate: 85.1% (2000); College graduation rate: 9.6% (2000).
Housing: Homeownership rate: 90.1% (2000); Median home value: $99,600 (2000); Median rent: $369 per month (2000); Median age of housing: 27 years (2000).
Transportation: Commute to work: 77.6% car, 0.0% public transportation, 4.4% walk, 15.5% work from home (2000); Travel time to work: 33.7% less than 15 minutes, 30.5% 15 to 30 minutes, 13.4% 30 to 45 minutes, 8.7% 45 to 60 minutes, 13.7% 60 minutes or more (2000)

CRYSTAL LAKE (town). Covers a land area of 32.728 square miles and a water area of 1.783 square miles. Located at 45.50° N. Lat.; 92.09° W. Long.
Population: 778 (2000); Race: 98.6% White, 0.0% Black, 0.3% Asian, 1.0% American Indian and Alaska Native, 0.3% Hispanic of any race, 0.1% two or more races (2000); Density: 23.8 persons per square mile (2000); Age: 22.8% under 18, 17.5% over 64 (2000); Marriage status: 18.7% never married, 64.4% now married, 5.6% widowed, 11.3% divorced (2000); Foreign born: 0.8% (2000); Ancestry (includes multiple ancestries): 42.3% German, 22.7% Norwegian, 9.5% Italian, 6.8% Swedish, 6.8% Irish (2000).
Economy: Employment by occupation: 12.9% management, 13.1% professional, 16.5% services, 17.1% sales, 1.0% farming, 9.7% construction, 29.7% production (2000).
Income: Per capita income: $16,040 (2000); Median household income: $37,109 (2000); Poverty rate: 11.2% (2000).
Taxes: Total city taxes per capita: $136 (1997); City property taxes per capita: $132 (1997).
Education: High school graduation rate: 79.1% (2000); College graduation rate: 9.0% (2000).
Housing: Homeownership rate: 86.9% (2000); Median home value: $75,000 (2000); Median rent: $338 per month (2000); Median age of housing: 33 years (2000).
Transportation: Commute to work: 85.9% car, 0.0% public transportation, 4.9% walk, 6.5% work from home (2000); Travel time to work: 47.4% less than 15 minutes, 29.4% 15 to 30 minutes, 7.6% 30 to 45 minutes, 4.7% 45 to 60 minutes, 11.0% 60 minutes or more (2000)

CUMBERLAND (city). Covers a land area of 3.396 square miles and a water area of 0.588 square miles. Located at 45.53° N. Lat.; 92.02° W. Long. Elevation is 1,251 feet.
History: Cumberland was founded in the 1870's when the railroad line was built across what was then an island location in Beaver Dam Lake. Many of the early residents were Italian immigrants who came to work in the lumber industry here. The growing of rutabagas became a trademark of early Cumberland, with an annual celebration being held to honor the rutabaga.
Population: 2,280 (2000); Race: 96.4% White, 0.0% Black, 1.1% Asian, 1.4% American Indian and Alaska Native, 0.1% Hispanic of any race, 1.1% two or more races (2000); Density: 671.5 persons per square mile (2000); Age: 22.0% under 18, 24.5% over 64 (2000); Marriage status: 20.2% never married, 55.7% now married, 11.7% widowed, 12.4% divorced (2000); Foreign born: 0.9% (2000); Ancestry (includes multiple ancestries): 34.2% German, 24.7% Norwegian, 14.1% Italian, 10.3% Irish, 9.6% Swedish (2000).
Economy: Single-family building permits issued: 7 (2001) / 5 (2000); Multi-family building permits issued: 8 (2001) / 8 (2000); Employment by occupation: 11.2% management, 15.0% professional, 13.5% services, 25.9% sales, 1.7% farming, 9.3% construction, 23.5% production (2000).
Income: Per capita income: $18,688 (2000); Median household income: $32,661 (2000); Poverty rate: 11.7% (2000).
Taxes: Total city taxes per capita: $238 (1997); City property taxes per capita: $224 (1997).
Education: High school graduation rate: 83.7% (2000); College graduation rate: 17.4% (2000).

School District(s)

Cumberland (PK-12)
2000 Enrollment: 1,239 715-822-5124
Housing: Homeownership rate: 66.4% (2000); Median home value: $78,100 (2000); Median rent: $348 per month (2000); Median age of housing: 41 years (2000).

Hospitals: Cumberland Memorial Hospital (40 beds)
Newspapers: Cumberland Advocate (1 x week)
Transportation: Commute to work: 82.9% car, 0.0% public transportation, 12.1% walk, 4.9% work from home (2000); Travel time to work: 62.0% less than 15 minutes, 25.7% 15 to 30 minutes, 9.1% 30 to 45 minutes, 1.0% 45 to 60 minutes, 2.1% 60 minutes or more (2000)
Additional Information Contacts
Cumberland Chamber of Commerce 715-822-3378

CUMBERLAND (town). Covers a land area of 32.111 square miles and a water area of 0.947 square miles. Located at 45.51° N. Lat.; 91.97° W. Long. Elevation is 1,251 feet.
History: Settled 1874, incorporated 1885.
Population: 942 (2000); Race: 98.2% White, 0.0% Black, 0.0% Asian, 1.1% American Indian and Alaska Native, 0.9% Hispanic of any race, 0.7% two or more races (2000); Density: 29.3 persons per square mile (2000); Age: 27.5% under 18, 15.7% over 64 (2000); Marriage status: 18.8% never married, 68.7% now married, 4.8% widowed, 7.7% divorced (2000); Foreign born: 0.4% (2000); Ancestry (includes multiple ancestries): 46.8% German, 30.5% Norwegian, 15.3% Swedish, 7.9% Italian, 6.7% Irish (2000).
Economy: In dairying and farming area; light manufacturing. Employment by occupation: 18.5% management, 15.5% professional, 8.8% services, 18.0% sales, 4.3% farming, 11.4% construction, 23.6% production (2000).
Income: Per capita income: $18,061 (2000); Median household income: $40,521 (2000); Poverty rate: 8.1% (2000).
Taxes: Total city taxes per capita: $88 (1997); City property taxes per capita: $86 (1997).
Education: High school graduation rate: 84.7% (2000); College graduation rate: 11.7% (2000).
Housing: Homeownership rate: 90.6% (2000); Median home value: $74,800 (2000); Median rent: $394 per month (2000); Median age of housing: 36 years (2000).
Transportation: Commute to work: 89.2% car, 0.0% public transportation, 0.9% walk, 9.5% work from home (2000); Travel time to work: 50.6% less than 15 minutes, 33.3% 15 to 30 minutes, 10.1% 30 to 45 minutes, 1.0% 45 to 60 minutes, 5.0% 60 minutes or more (2000)

DALLAS (village). Covers a land area of 1.455 square miles and a water area of 0.038 square miles. Located at 45.26° N. Lat.; 91.81° W. Long. Elevation is 1,054 feet.
Population: 356 (2000); Race: 93.4% White, 0.0% Black, 0.0% Asian, 2.7% American Indian and Alaska Native, 1.1% Hispanic of any race, 3.5% two or more races (2000); Density: 244.8 persons per square mile (2000); Age: 21.8% under 18, 26.1% over 64 (2000); Marriage status: 17.9% never married, 60.9% now married, 15.7% widowed, 5.4% divorced (2000); Foreign born: 0.3% (2000); Ancestry (includes multiple ancestries): 36.2% Norwegian, 25.0% German, 9.8% English, 7.7% Other groups, 6.1% Polish (2000).
Economy: Single-family building permits issued: 0 (2001) / 1 (2000); Multi-family building permits issued: 0 (2001) / 0 (2000); Employment by occupation: 10.4% management, 5.2% professional, 12.3% services, 26.6% sales, 3.9% farming, 11.0% construction, 30.5% production (2000).
Income: Per capita income: $14,665 (2000); Median household income: $30,833 (2000); Poverty rate: 11.6% (2000).
Taxes: Total city taxes per capita: $16 (1997); City property taxes per capita: $11 (1997).
Education: High school graduation rate: 63.9% (2000); College graduation rate: 3.8% (2000).
Housing: Homeownership rate: 81.9% (2000); Median home value: $48,800 (2000); Median rent: $185 per month (2000); Median age of housing: 50 years (2000).
Transportation: Commute to work: 95.5% car, 0.0% public transportation, 2.6% walk, 1.9% work from home (2000); Travel time to work: 20.5% less than 15 minutes, 48.3% 15 to 30 minutes, 13.2% 30 to 45 minutes, 7.9% 45 to 60 minutes, 9.9% 60 minutes or more (2000)

DALLAS (town). Covers a land area of 33.857 square miles and a water area of 0.006 square miles. Located at 45.25° N. Lat.; 91.85° W. Long. Elevation is 1,054 feet.
Population: 604 (2000); Race: 99.5% White, 0.0% Black, 0.0% Asian, 0.0% American Indian and Alaska Native, 0.0% Hispanic of any race, 0.5% two or more races (2000); Density: 17.8 persons per square mile (2000); Age: 29.1% under 18, 13.6% over 64 (2000); Marriage status: 21.2% never married, 68.2% now married, 3.6% widowed, 7.0% divorced (2000); Foreign born: 0.0% (2000); Ancestry (includes multiple ancestries): 43.4% German, 37.1% Norwegian, 6.3% Irish, 4.0% United States or American, 3.8% Swedish (2000).
Economy: In dairying area. Employment by occupation: 16.4% management, 14.4% professional, 13.7% services, 23.7% sales, 6.0% farming, 9.7% construction, 16.1% production (2000).
Income: Per capita income: $21,069 (2000); Median household income: $40,521 (2000); Poverty rate: 2.9% (2000).
Taxes: Total city taxes per capita: $52 (1997); City property taxes per capita: $52 (1997).
Education: High school graduation rate: 86.6% (2000); College graduation rate: 15.1% (2000).
Housing: Homeownership rate: 84.1% (2000); Median home value: $65,000 (2000); Median rent: $389 per month (2000); Median age of housing: 47 years (2000).
Transportation: Commute to work: 83.8% car, 0.0% public transportation, 4.0% walk, 10.4% work from home (2000); Travel time to work: 38.7% less than 15 minutes, 32.0% 15 to 30 minutes, 17.3% 30 to 45 minutes, 7.1% 45 to 60 minutes, 4.9% 60 minutes or more (2000)

DOVRE (town). Covers a land area of 35.116 square miles and a water area of 0.095 square miles. Located at 45.25° N. Lat.; 91.60° W. Long.
Population: 680 (2000); Race: 100.0% White, 0.0% Black, 0.0% Asian, 0.0% American Indian and Alaska Native, 0.0% Hispanic of any race, 0.0% two or more races (2000); Density: 19.4 persons per square mile (2000); Age: 25.1% under 18, 9.7% over 64 (2000); Marriage status: 25.3% never married, 60.5% now married, 4.4% widowed, 9.8% divorced (2000); Foreign born: 0.7% (2000); Ancestry (includes multiple ancestries): 43.1% German, 26.3% Norwegian, 9.7% Irish, 9.1% English, 8.7% Polish (2000).
Economy: Employment by occupation: 14.9% management, 10.9% professional, 16.0% services, 19.1% sales, 3.7% farming, 12.0% construction, 23.4% production (2000).
Income: Per capita income: $15,624 (2000); Median household income: $36,786 (2000); Poverty rate: 10.6% (2000).
Taxes: Total city taxes per capita: $227 (1997); City property taxes per capita: $227 (1997).
Education: High school graduation rate: 82.8% (2000); College graduation rate: 7.5% (2000).
Housing: Homeownership rate: 85.6% (2000); Median home value: $76,700 (2000); Median rent: $386 per month (2000); Median age of housing: 34 years (2000).
Transportation: Commute to work: 85.1% car, 0.0% public transportation, 4.3% walk, 10.0% work from home (2000); Travel time to work: 32.8% less than 15 minutes, 25.8% 15 to 30 minutes, 20.7% 30 to 45 minutes, 16.2% 45 to 60 minutes, 4.5% 60 minutes or more (2000)

DOYLE (town). Covers a land area of 35.613 square miles and a water area of 0 square miles. Located at 45.51° N. Lat.; 91.61° W. Long.
Population: 498 (2000); Race: 99.6% White, 0.4% Black, 0.0% Asian, 0.0% American Indian and Alaska Native, 0.0% Hispanic of any race, 0.0% two or more races (2000); Density: 14.0 persons per square mile (2000); Age: 33.2% under 18, 13.8% over 64 (2000); Marriage status: 24.0% never married, 63.1% now married, 5.4% widowed, 7.5% divorced (2000); Foreign born: 0.0% (2000); Ancestry (includes multiple ancestries): 38.9% German, 24.5% Norwegian, 11.7% French (except Basque), 11.7% Czech, 6.9% Irish (2000).
Economy: Employment by occupation: 17.6% management, 9.0% professional, 9.7% services, 22.8% sales, 8.6% farming, 10.1% construction, 22.1% production (2000).
Income: Per capita income: $16,014 (2000); Median household income: $40,481 (2000); Poverty rate: 10.1% (2000).
Taxes: Total city taxes per capita: $118 (1997); City property taxes per capita: $118 (1997).
Education: High school graduation rate: 80.3% (2000); College graduation rate: 10.0% (2000).
Housing: Homeownership rate: 90.5% (2000); Median home value: $73,600 (2000); Median rent: $425 per month (2000); Median age of housing: 53 years (2000).
Transportation: Commute to work: 83.0% car, 0.0% public transportation, 2.3% walk, 14.7% work from home (2000); Travel time to work: 27.4% less than 15 minutes, 65.9% 15 to 30 minutes, 5.8% 30 to 45 minutes, 0.4% 45 to 60 minutes, 0.4% 60 minutes or more (2000)

HAUGEN (village). Covers a land area of 0.510 square miles and a water area of 0.006 square miles. Located at 45.60° N. Lat.; 91.77° W. Long. Elevation is 1,229 feet.
Population: 287 (2000); Race: 100.0% White, 0.0% Black, 0.0% Asian, 0.0% American Indian and Alaska Native, 1.1% Hispanic of any race, 0.0%

two or more races (2000); Density: 562.5 persons per square mile (2000); Age: 22.2% under 18, 25.6% over 64 (2000); Marriage status: 20.7% never married, 55.5% now married, 13.7% widowed, 10.1% divorced (2000); Foreign born: 0.0% (2000); Ancestry (includes multiple ancestries): 35.7% German, 20.7% Czech, 15.0% Norwegian, 15.0% French (except Basque), 10.9% Irish (2000).
Economy: Dairying. Single-family building permits issued: 3 (2001) / 1 (2000); Multi-family building permits issued: 0 (2001) / 0 (2000); Employment by occupation: 4.5% management, 14.3% professional, 16.5% services, 26.3% sales, 0.0% farming, 13.5% construction, 24.8% production (2000).
Income: Per capita income: $17,258 (2000); Median household income: $30,714 (2000); Poverty rate: 10.9% (2000).
Taxes: Total city taxes per capita: $29 (1997); City property taxes per capita: $19 (1997).
Education: High school graduation rate: 80.1% (2000); College graduation rate: 7.7% (2000).
Housing: Homeownership rate: 83.7% (2000); Median home value: $60,300 (2000); Median rent: $250 per month (2000); Median age of housing: 46 years (2000).
Transportation: Commute to work: 97.0% car, 0.0% public transportation, 1.5% walk, 1.5% work from home (2000); Travel time to work: 26.7% less than 15 minutes, 45.0% 15 to 30 minutes, 4.6% 30 to 45 minutes, 3.1% 45 to 60 minutes, 20.6% 60 minutes or more (2000)

LAKELAND (town). Covers a land area of 33.037 square miles and a water area of 2.283 square miles. Located at 45.59° N. Lat.; 91.97° W. Long.
Population: 963 (2000); Race: 99.2% White, 0.0% Black, 0.2% Asian, 0.0% American Indian and Alaska Native, 0.2% Hispanic of any race, 0.4% two or more races (2000); Density: 29.1 persons per square mile (2000); Age: 26.9% under 18, 9.5% over 64 (2000); Marriage status: 24.3% never married, 61.2% now married, 4.4% widowed, 10.0% divorced (2000); Foreign born: 0.2% (2000); Ancestry (includes multiple ancestries): 39.4% German, 23.8% Norwegian, 11.5% Swedish, 11.2% English, 8.9% Irish (2000).
Economy: Employment by occupation: 12.9% management, 11.5% professional, 12.1% services, 21.6% sales, 1.8% farming, 8.3% construction, 31.7% production (2000).
Income: Per capita income: $21,152 (2000); Median household income: $42,266 (2000); Poverty rate: 4.1% (2000).
Taxes: Total city taxes per capita: $108 (1997); City property taxes per capita: $106 (1997).
Education: High school graduation rate: 85.1% (2000); College graduation rate: 20.1% (2000).
Housing: Homeownership rate: 89.2% (2000); Median home value: $96,400 (2000); Median rent: $357 per month (2000); Median age of housing: 24 years (2000).
Transportation: Commute to work: 87.3% car, 0.0% public transportation, 4.5% walk, 7.4% work from home (2000); Travel time to work: 41.3% less than 15 minutes, 34.2% 15 to 30 minutes, 14.3% 30 to 45 minutes, 2.4% 45 to 60 minutes, 7.7% 60 minutes or more (2000)

MAPLE GROVE (town). Covers a land area of 35.469 square miles and a water area of 0 square miles. Located at 45.34° N. Lat.; 91.84° W. Long.
Population: 968 (2000); Race: 100.0% White, 0.0% Black, 0.0% Asian, 0.0% American Indian and Alaska Native, 0.0% Hispanic of any race, 0.0% two or more races (2000); Density: 27.3 persons per square mile (2000); Age: 33.2% under 18, 9.1% over 64 (2000); Marriage status: 16.8% never married, 72.4% now married, 3.2% widowed, 7.6% divorced (2000); Foreign born: 0.3% (2000); Ancestry (includes multiple ancestries): 40.1% German, 31.5% Norwegian, 7.4% English, 6.0% Swedish, 5.0% Irish (2000).
Economy: Employment by occupation: 16.5% management, 13.1% professional, 12.0% services, 19.2% sales, 6.8% farming, 9.1% construction, 23.3% production (2000).
Income: Per capita income: $15,707 (2000); Median household income: $44,625 (2000); Poverty rate: 6.7% (2000).
Taxes: Total city taxes per capita: $45 (1997); City property taxes per capita: $45 (1997).
Education: High school graduation rate: 77.0% (2000); College graduation rate: 13.2% (2000).
Housing: Homeownership rate: 91.8% (2000); Median home value: $71,900 (2000); Median rent: $331 per month (2000); Median age of housing: 39 years (2000).
Transportation: Commute to work: 83.7% car, 0.0% public transportation, 1.5% walk, 13.8% work from home (2000); Travel time to work: 39.9% less than 15 minutes, 35.7% 15 to 30 minutes, 11.1% 30 to 45 minutes, 6.4% 45 to 60 minutes, 6.9% 60 minutes or more (2000)

MAPLE PLAIN (town). Covers a land area of 33.292 square miles and a water area of 2.704 square miles. Located at 45.59° N. Lat.; 92.09° W. Long.
Population: 876 (2000); Race: 83.1% White, 0.3% Black, 0.0% Asian, 15.5% American Indian and Alaska Native, 0.0% Hispanic of any race, 0.8% two or more races (2000); Density: 26.3 persons per square mile (2000); Age: 28.7% under 18, 10.3% over 64 (2000); Marriage status: 22.3% never married, 66.4% now married, 3.8% widowed, 7.5% divorced (2000); Foreign born: 0.0% (2000); Ancestry (includes multiple ancestries): 34.7% German, 25.3% Norwegian, 16.6% Other groups, 9.5% English, 9.5% Swedish (2000).
Economy: Employment by occupation: 16.9% management, 20.5% professional, 16.9% services, 16.7% sales, 0.0% farming, 8.3% construction, 20.7% production (2000).
Income: Per capita income: $18,673 (2000); Median household income: $47,333 (2000); Poverty rate: 11.2% (2000).
Taxes: Total city taxes per capita: $323 (1997); City property taxes per capita: $322 (1997).
Education: High school graduation rate: 88.2% (2000); College graduation rate: 22.6% (2000).
Housing: Homeownership rate: 83.9% (2000); Median home value: $156,600 (2000); Median rent: $198 per month (2000); Median age of housing: 25 years (2000).
Transportation: Commute to work: 90.9% car, 0.0% public transportation, 1.2% walk, 7.2% work from home (2000); Travel time to work: 34.9% less than 15 minutes, 30.7% 15 to 30 minutes, 22.2% 30 to 45 minutes, 6.2% 45 to 60 minutes, 5.9% 60 minutes or more (2000)

OAK GROVE (town). Covers a land area of 34.815 square miles and a water area of 0.450 square miles. Located at 45.58° N. Lat.; 91.72° W. Long.
Population: 911 (2000); Race: 98.4% White, 0.0% Black, 0.0% Asian, 1.0% American Indian and Alaska Native, 0.8% Hispanic of any race, 0.5% two or more races (2000); Density: 26.2 persons per square mile (2000); Age: 31.1% under 18, 10.8% over 64 (2000); Marriage status: 23.3% never married, 66.7% now married, 3.8% widowed, 6.2% divorced (2000); Foreign born: 0.2% (2000); Ancestry (includes multiple ancestries): 36.1% German, 17.6% Norwegian, 16.4% Czech, 7.7% United States or American, 7.7% French (except Basque) (2000).
Economy: Employment by occupation: 16.4% management, 11.5% professional, 13.9% services, 21.3% sales, 4.9% farming, 9.6% construction, 22.4% production (2000).
Income: Per capita income: $16,240 (2000); Median household income: $43,088 (2000); Poverty rate: 4.8% (2000).
Taxes: Total city taxes per capita: $78 (1997); City property taxes per capita: $74 (1997).
Education: High school graduation rate: 76.8% (2000); College graduation rate: 8.8% (2000).
Housing: Homeownership rate: 86.2% (2000); Median home value: $85,600 (2000); Median rent: $300 per month (2000); Median age of housing: 39 years (2000).
Transportation: Commute to work: 82.9% car, 0.0% public transportation, 5.0% walk, 11.6% work from home (2000); Travel time to work: 27.7% less than 15 minutes, 57.9% 15 to 30 minutes, 7.4% 30 to 45 minutes, 0.7% 45 to 60 minutes, 6.2% 60 minutes or more (2000)

PRAIRIE FARM (village). Covers a land area of 0.969 square miles and a water area of 0.035 square miles. Located at 45.23° N. Lat.; 91.98° W. Long. Elevation is 1,050 feet.
Population: 508 (2000); Race: 98.3% White, 0.0% Black, 0.0% Asian, 1.0% American Indian and Alaska Native, 3.7% Hispanic of any race, 0.4% two or more races (2000); Density: 524.1 persons per square mile (2000); Age: 21.7% under 18, 22.1% over 64 (2000); Marriage status: 28.3% never married, 46.6% now married, 12.8% widowed, 12.3% divorced (2000); Foreign born: 0.8% (2000); Ancestry (includes multiple ancestries): 46.4% Norwegian, 35.9% German, 9.1% Irish, 7.6% Other groups, 4.7% Swiss (2000).
Economy: Single-family building permits issued: 0 (2001) / 2 (2000); Multi-family building permits issued: 0 (2001) / 0 (2000); Employment by occupation: 4.5% management, 10.6% professional, 18.9% services, 18.2% sales, 4.5% farming, 11.7% construction, 31.4% production (2000).
Income: Per capita income: $15,638 (2000); Median household income: $38,000 (2000); Poverty rate: 7.8% (2000).
Taxes: Total city taxes per capita: $65 (1997); City property taxes per capita: $57 (1997).

Education: High school graduation rate: 71.2% (2000); College graduation rate: 5.8% (2000).

School District(s)

Prairie Farm (PK-12)
2000 Enrollment: 351 715-455-1683

Housing: Homeownership rate: 75.9% (2000); Median home value: $58,800 (2000); Median rent: $285 per month (2000); Median age of housing: 47 years (2000).
Transportation: Commute to work: 93.5% car, 0.0% public transportation, 3.4% walk, 0.8% work from home (2000); Travel time to work: 37.7% less than 15 minutes, 26.2% 15 to 30 minutes, 23.1% 30 to 45 minutes, 5.0% 45 to 60 minutes, 8.1% 60 minutes or more (2000)

PRAIRIE FARM (town). Covers a land area of 34.381 square miles and a water area of 0 square miles. Located at 45.25° N. Lat.; 91.97° W. Long. Elevation is 1,050 feet.
Population: 603 (2000); Race: 99.3% White, 0.7% Black, 0.0% Asian, 0.0% American Indian and Alaska Native, 0.0% Hispanic of any race, 0.0% two or more races (2000); Density: 17.5 persons per square mile (2000); Age: 28.1% under 18, 7.6% over 64 (2000); Marriage status: 25.5% never married, 64.1% now married, 4.1% widowed, 6.2% divorced (2000); Foreign born: 0.0% (2000); Ancestry (includes multiple ancestries): 46.4% German, 38.2% Norwegian, 6.7% Polish, 5.3% Swedish, 4.3% English (2000).
Economy: Dairying. Manufacturing: fabricated metal products. Employment by occupation: 19.7% management, 8.6% professional, 18.1% services, 18.4% sales, 7.0% farming, 9.2% construction, 19.0% production (2000).
Income: Per capita income: $21,295 (2000); Median household income: $45,417 (2000); Poverty rate: 2.7% (2000).
Taxes: Total city taxes per capita: $100 (1997); City property taxes per capita: $100 (1997).
Education: High school graduation rate: 86.6% (2000); College graduation rate: 10.8% (2000).
Housing: Homeownership rate: 85.8% (2000); Median home value: $72,500 (2000); Median rent: $388 per month (2000); Median age of housing: 57 years (2000).
Transportation: Commute to work: 81.0% car, 0.0% public transportation, 2.5% walk, 16.5% work from home (2000); Travel time to work: 30.0% less than 15 minutes, 37.6% 15 to 30 minutes, 18.6% 30 to 45 minutes, 4.9% 45 to 60 minutes, 8.7% 60 minutes or more (2000)

PRAIRIE LAKE (town). Covers a land area of 33.123 square miles and a water area of 1.789 square miles. Located at 45.34° N. Lat.; 91.71° W. Long.
Population: 1,369 (2000); Race: 99.5% White, 0.0% Black, 0.4% Asian, 0.0% American Indian and Alaska Native, 0.6% Hispanic of any race, 0.0% two or more races (2000); Density: 41.3 persons per square mile (2000); Age: 24.2% under 18, 15.8% over 64 (2000); Marriage status: 16.9% never married, 72.3% now married, 3.2% widowed, 7.6% divorced (2000); Foreign born: 0.8% (2000); Ancestry (includes multiple ancestries): 35.6% German, 28.3% Norwegian, 10.2% English, 8.5% Irish, 5.9% Polish (2000).
Economy: Employment by occupation: 11.6% management, 7.9% professional, 10.4% services, 28.7% sales, 2.2% farming, 10.7% construction, 28.5% production (2000).
Income: Per capita income: $17,507 (2000); Median household income: $40,048 (2000); Poverty rate: 8.8% (2000).
Taxes: Total city taxes per capita: $90 (1997); City property taxes per capita: $90 (1997).
Education: High school graduation rate: 81.5% (2000); College graduation rate: 14.6% (2000).
Housing: Homeownership rate: 89.4% (2000); Median home value: $93,300 (2000); Median rent: $415 per month (2000); Median age of housing: 36 years (2000).
Transportation: Commute to work: 89.9% car, 0.0% public transportation, 2.5% walk, 6.9% work from home (2000); Travel time to work: 41.8% less than 15 minutes, 38.9% 15 to 30 minutes, 8.1% 30 to 45 minutes, 4.9% 45 to 60 minutes, 6.3% 60 minutes or more (2000)

RICE LAKE (city). Covers a land area of 8.631 square miles and a water area of 1.033 square miles. Located at 45.49° N. Lat.; 91.73° W. Long. Elevation is 1,140 feet.
History: The city of Rice Lake began as a lumber center, whose wood factories continued to produce products into the 1900's. Both the city and the lake were named for the wild rice that once grew in the marshes along the lake shore. The city developed as a trading center for the surrounding dairy farmers, and for vacationers who came to the lakes in the area.
Population: 8,320 (2000); Race: 98.0% White, 0.2% Black, 0.1% Asian, 0.5% American Indian and Alaska Native, 1.1% Hispanic of any race, 0.3% two or more races (2000); Density: 963.9 persons per square mile (2000); Age: 22.4% under 18, 20.0% over 64 (2000); Marriage status: 23.8% never married, 53.5% now married, 12.2% widowed, 10.5% divorced (2000); Foreign born: 1.4% (2000); Ancestry (includes multiple ancestries): 39.5% German, 22.4% Norwegian, 10.9% Irish, 5.9% English, 5.8% French (except Basque) (2000).
Economy: Single-family building permits issued: 12 (2001) / 20 (2000); Multi-family building permits issued: 10 (2001) / 36 (2000); Employment by occupation: 11.5% management, 13.5% professional, 19.1% services, 25.6% sales, 0.6% farming, 11.1% construction, 18.6% production (2000).
Income: Per capita income: $18,585 (2000); Median household income: $32,808 (2000); Poverty rate: 10.0% (2000).
Taxes: Total city taxes per capita: $369 (1997); City property taxes per capita: $344 (1997).
Education: High school graduation rate: 85.5% (2000); College graduation rate: 16.8% (2000).

School District(s)

Rice Lake Area (PK-12)
2000 Enrollment: 2,703 715-234-9007

Housing: Homeownership rate: 60.9% (2000); Median home value: $71,500 (2000); Median rent: $357 per month (2000); Median age of housing: 37 years (2000).
Hospitals: Lakeview Medical Center of Rice Lake (75 beds)
Safety: Violent crime rate: 25.1 per 10,000 population; Property crime rate: 507.2 per 10,000 population (2001).
Newspapers: Rice Lake Chronotype (1 x week)
Transportation: Commute to work: 91.5% car, 0.7% public transportation, 4.4% walk, 2.5% work from home (2000); Travel time to work: 72.0% less than 15 minutes, 15.9% 15 to 30 minutes, 4.5% 30 to 45 minutes, 1.8% 45 to 60 minutes, 5.8% 60 minutes or more (2000)
Additional Information Contacts
Rice Lake Chamber of Commerce 715-234-2126

RICE LAKE (town). Covers a land area of 26.375 square miles and a water area of 1.235 square miles. Located at 45.50° N. Lat.; 91.72° W. Long. Elevation is 1,140 feet.
History: Has park containing Native American mounds. University of Wisconsin. City grew as a lumbering town. Incorporated 1887.
Population: 3,026 (2000); Race: 96.0% White, 0.7% Black, 0.7% Asian, 0.5% American Indian and Alaska Native, 4.7% Hispanic of any race, 0.7% two or more races (2000); Density: 114.7 persons per square mile (2000); Age: 29.6% under 18, 11.4% over 64 (2000); Marriage status: 22.9% never married, 68.3% now married, 3.6% widowed, 5.2% divorced (2000); Foreign born: 3.1% (2000); Ancestry (includes multiple ancestries): 41.3% German, 19.8% Norwegian, 8.7% Other groups, 8.2% Irish, 5.7% Swedish (2000).
Economy: Commercial center for dairying and cattle-raising area; cheese; light manufacturing. Speedway. Nearby are lake resorts. Hardscrabble Ski Area to East. Employment by occupation: 12.0% management, 19.4% professional, 13.2% services, 29.1% sales, 0.7% farming, 7.1% construction, 18.5% production (2000).
Income: Per capita income: $19,835 (2000); Median household income: $45,649 (2000); Poverty rate: 3.8% (2000).
Taxes: Total city taxes per capita: $44 (1997); City property taxes per capita: $35 (1997).
Education: High school graduation rate: 88.2% (2000); College graduation rate: 25.5% (2000).
Housing: Homeownership rate: 85.7% (2000); Median home value: $113,400 (2000); Median rent: $426 per month (2000); Median age of housing: 23 years (2000).
Transportation: Commute to work: 94.2% car, 0.1% public transportation, 1.2% walk, 4.4% work from home (2000); Travel time to work: 65.0% less than 15 minutes, 23.9% 15 to 30 minutes, 5.1% 30 to 45 minutes, 3.6% 45 to 60 minutes, 2.4% 60 minutes or more (2000)

SIOUX CREEK (town). Covers a land area of 34.922 square miles and a water area of 0.321 square miles. Located at 45.25° N. Lat.; 91.73° W. Long.
Population: 689 (2000); Race: 99.7% White, 0.0% Black, 0.0% Asian, 0.0% American Indian and Alaska Native, 0.4% Hispanic of any race, 0.3% two or more races (2000); Density: 19.7 persons per square mile (2000); Age: 31.7% under 18, 6.8% over 64 (2000); Marriage status: 28.8% never married, 63.1% now married, 3.7% widowed, 4.3% divorced (2000); Foreign born: 0.6% (2000); Ancestry (includes multiple ancestries): 37.6% German, 33.2% Norwegian, 8.5% English, 6.1% Irish, 4.6% Polish (2000).

Economy: Single-family building permits issued: 4 (2001) / 7 (2000); Multi-family building permits issued: 0 (2001) / 0 (2000); Employment by occupation: 19.7% management, 13.2% professional, 16.6% services, 16.6% sales, 4.9% farming, 7.5% construction, 21.3% production (2000).
Income: Per capita income: $14,746 (2000); Median household income: $47,083 (2000); Poverty rate: 5.7% (2000).
Taxes: Total city taxes per capita: $91 (1997); City property taxes per capita: $91 (1997).
Education: High school graduation rate: 85.7% (2000); College graduation rate: 16.2% (2000).
Housing: Homeownership rate: 91.9% (2000); Median home value: $78,300 (2000); Median rent: $400 per month (2000); Median age of housing: 48 years (2000).
Transportation: Commute to work: 80.1% car, 0.0% public transportation, 3.1% walk, 16.2% work from home (2000); Travel time to work: 32.8% less than 15 minutes, 41.6% 15 to 30 minutes, 16.9% 30 to 45 minutes, 6.6% 45 to 60 minutes, 2.2% 60 minutes or more (2000)

STANFOLD (town). Covers a land area of 35.910 square miles and a water area of 0.047 square miles. Located at 45.50° N. Lat.; 91.85° W. Long.
Population: 669 (2000); Race: 96.5% White, 0.0% Black, 0.3% Asian, 0.0% American Indian and Alaska Native, 2.6% Hispanic of any race, 3.2% two or more races (2000); Density: 18.6 persons per square mile (2000); Age: 31.2% under 18, 15.1% over 64 (2000); Marriage status: 21.6% never married, 70.5% now married, 2.5% widowed, 5.5% divorced (2000); Foreign born: 4.1% (2000); Ancestry (includes multiple ancestries): 36.2% German, 20.9% Norwegian, 11.6% Irish, 8.3% Other groups, 7.2% Swedish (2000).
Economy: Employment by occupation: 23.8% management, 10.5% professional, 13.9% services, 24.9% sales, 3.4% farming, 3.1% construction, 20.4% production (2000).
Income: Per capita income: $15,683 (2000); Median household income: $39,000 (2000); Poverty rate: 5.7% (2000).
Taxes: Total city taxes per capita: $104 (1997); City property taxes per capita: $104 (1997).
Education: High school graduation rate: 83.1% (2000); College graduation rate: 13.4% (2000).
Housing: Homeownership rate: 79.4% (2000); Median home value: $82,500 (2000); Median rent: $513 per month (2000); Median age of housing: 57 years (2000).
Transportation: Commute to work: 74.2% car, 0.6% public transportation, 5.5% walk, 19.1% work from home (2000); Travel time to work: 48.7% less than 15 minutes, 42.7% 15 to 30 minutes, 4.7% 30 to 45 minutes, 0.0% 45 to 60 minutes, 3.9% 60 minutes or more (2000)

STANLEY (town). Covers a land area of 31.044 square miles and a water area of 0.575 square miles. Located at 45.41° N. Lat.; 91.73° W. Long.
Population: 2,229 (2000); Race: 99.4% White, 0.0% Black, 0.6% Asian, 0.0% American Indian and Alaska Native, 0.0% Hispanic of any race, 0.0% two or more races (2000); Density: 71.8 persons per square mile (2000); Age: 26.4% under 18, 9.7% over 64 (2000); Marriage status: 21.8% never married, 65.6% now married, 3.2% widowed, 9.3% divorced (2000); Foreign born: 0.8% (2000); Ancestry (includes multiple ancestries): 41.5% German, 22.2% Norwegian, 9.6% Irish, 7.2% Czech, 6.5% Swedish (2000).
Economy: Employment by occupation: 7.8% management, 15.0% professional, 15.5% services, 24.3% sales, 2.0% farming, 11.3% construction, 24.0% production (2000).
Income: Per capita income: $17,598 (2000); Median household income: $41,944 (2000); Poverty rate: 7.7% (2000).
Taxes: Total city taxes per capita: $42 (1997); City property taxes per capita: $38 (1997).
Education: High school graduation rate: 86.6% (2000); College graduation rate: 17.2% (2000).
Housing: Homeownership rate: 90.0% (2000); Median home value: $96,300 (2000); Median rent: $390 per month (2000); Median age of housing: 24 years (2000).
Transportation: Commute to work: 94.2% car, 0.0% public transportation, 1.8% walk, 3.8% work from home (2000); Travel time to work: 48.5% less than 15 minutes, 33.0% 15 to 30 minutes, 5.8% 30 to 45 minutes, 3.9% 45 to 60 minutes, 8.7% 60 minutes or more (2000)

SUMNER (town). Covers a land area of 35.679 square miles and a water area of 0.012 square miles. Located at 45.41° N. Lat.; 91.61° W. Long. Elevation is 1,089 feet.
Population: 598 (2000); Race: 100.0% White, 0.0% Black, 0.0% Asian, 0.0% American Indian and Alaska Native, 0.0% Hispanic of any race, 0.0% two or more races (2000); Density: 16.8 persons per square mile (2000); Age: 26.9% under 18, 12.8% over 64 (2000); Marriage status: 23.5% never married, 60.4% now married, 5.1% widowed, 11.0% divorced (2000); Foreign born: 0.5% (2000); Ancestry (includes multiple ancestries): 43.7% German, 16.0% Norwegian, 10.1% English, 9.5% Irish, 5.7% Polish (2000).
Economy: Employment by occupation: 9.3% management, 10.8% professional, 16.0% services, 25.9% sales, 2.5% farming, 8.6% construction, 26.9% production (2000).
Income: Per capita income: $17,279 (2000); Median household income: $38,333 (2000); Poverty rate: 8.2% (2000).
Taxes: Total city taxes per capita: $55 (1997); City property taxes per capita: $55 (1997).
Education: High school graduation rate: 86.6% (2000); College graduation rate: 12.4% (2000).
Housing: Homeownership rate: 92.3% (2000); Median home value: $75,300 (2000); Median rent: $340 per month (2000); Median age of housing: 29 years (2000).
Transportation: Commute to work: 89.8% car, 0.0% public transportation, 1.5% walk, 6.2% work from home (2000); Travel time to work: 21.4% less than 15 minutes, 65.8% 15 to 30 minutes, 6.9% 30 to 45 minutes, 0.3% 45 to 60 minutes, 5.6% 60 minutes or more (2000)

TURTLE LAKE (village). Covers a land area of 2.798 square miles and a water area of 0.133 square miles. Located at 45.39° N. Lat.; 92.14° W. Long. Elevation is 1,264 feet.
History: Turtle Lake began in 1879 when Stephen F. Richardson built a sawmill here. Later, a cooperative creamery and a pea cannery were established.
Population: 1,065 (2000); Race: 96.4% White, 0.7% Black, 0.7% Asian, 1.6% American Indian and Alaska Native, 0.0% Hispanic of any race, 0.7% two or more races (2000); Density: 380.7 persons per square mile (2000); Age: 26.0% under 18, 18.1% over 64 (2000); Marriage status: 28.4% never married, 44.4% now married, 10.3% widowed, 17.0% divorced (2000); Foreign born: 1.2% (2000); Ancestry (includes multiple ancestries): 47.1% German, 15.4% Norwegian, 7.5% Swedish, 6.1% Irish, 5.6% French (except Basque) (2000).
Economy: Single-family building permits issued: 0 (2001) / 0 (2000); Multi-family building permits issued: 0 (2001) / 0 (2000); Employment by occupation: 8.8% management, 11.6% professional, 26.1% services, 18.7% sales, 1.3% farming, 6.5% construction, 26.9% production (2000).
Income: Per capita income: $16,591 (2000); Median household income: $29,485 (2000); Poverty rate: 16.5% (2000).
Taxes: Total city taxes per capita: $525 (1997); City property taxes per capita: $397 (1997).
Education: High school graduation rate: 78.4% (2000); College graduation rate: 10.8% (2000).

School District(s)

Turtle Lake (PK-12)
2000 Enrollment: 632 715-986-2597

Housing: Homeownership rate: 54.4% (2000); Median home value: $63,200 (2000); Median rent: $368 per month (2000); Median age of housing: 32 years (2000).
Newspapers: Turtle Lake Times (1 x week)
Transportation: Commute to work: 89.8% car, 0.0% public transportation, 7.1% walk, 2.6% work from home (2000); Travel time to work: 58.4% less than 15 minutes, 20.4% 15 to 30 minutes, 12.9% 30 to 45 minutes, 2.2% 45 to 60 minutes, 6.0% 60 minutes or more (2000)

TURTLE LAKE (town). Covers a land area of 35.187 square miles and a water area of 0.433 square miles. Located at 45.34° N. Lat.; 92.09° W. Long. Elevation is 1,264 feet.
Population: 622 (2000); Race: 96.9% White, 0.0% Black, 0.2% Asian, 1.1% American Indian and Alaska Native, 0.3% Hispanic of any race, 1.9% two or more races (2000); Density: 17.7 persons per square mile (2000); Age: 31.0% under 18, 9.3% over 64 (2000); Marriage status: 21.5% never married, 67.1% now married, 3.3% widowed, 8.1% divorced (2000); Foreign born: 0.5% (2000); Ancestry (includes multiple ancestries): 57.9% German, 15.6% Norwegian, 8.1% Irish, 5.5% Polish, 4.2% Dutch (2000).
Economy: Wooded lake-resort area. Some manufacturing. Casino. Employment by occupation: 18.2% management, 11.1% professional, 16.3% services, 10.8% sales, 4.9% farming, 12.9% construction, 25.8% production (2000).
Income: Per capita income: $17,151 (2000); Median household income: $44,375 (2000); Poverty rate: 9.4% (2000).
Taxes: Total city taxes per capita: $188 (1997); City property taxes per capita: $186 (1997).

Education: High school graduation rate: 82.0% (2000); College graduation rate: 6.0% (2000).
Housing: Homeownership rate: 89.4% (2000); Median home value: $62,700 (2000); Median rent: $435 per month (2000); Median age of housing: 50 years (2000).
Transportation: Commute to work: 81.1% car, 0.0% public transportation, 4.7% walk, 13.5% work from home (2000); Travel time to work: 40.4% less than 15 minutes, 30.2% 15 to 30 minutes, 11.6% 30 to 45 minutes, 4.7% 45 to 60 minutes, 13.1% 60 minutes or more (2000)

VANCE CREEK (town). Covers a land area of 35.483 square miles and a water area of 0.034 square miles. Located at 45.24° N. Lat.; 92.08° W. Long.
Population: 747 (2000); Race: 98.7% White, 0.0% Black, 0.9% Asian, 0.4% American Indian and Alaska Native, 0.3% Hispanic of any race, 0.0% two or more races (2000); Density: 21.1 persons per square mile (2000); Age: 28.6% under 18, 13.8% over 64 (2000); Marriage status: 23.8% never married, 63.6% now married, 3.0% widowed, 9.6% divorced (2000); Foreign born: 2.1% (2000); Ancestry (includes multiple ancestries): 31.2% German, 23.8% Norwegian, 10.3% Irish, 7.5% Swedish, 7.5% French (except Basque) (2000).
Economy: Employment by occupation: 17.4% management, 12.2% professional, 11.3% services, 8.7% sales, 5.5% farming, 18.9% construction, 25.9% production (2000).
Income: Per capita income: $14,874 (2000); Median household income: $39,821 (2000); Poverty rate: 17.9% (2000).
Taxes: Total city taxes per capita: $109 (1997); City property taxes per capita: $107 (1997).
Education: High school graduation rate: 84.5% (2000); College graduation rate: 10.0% (2000).
Housing: Homeownership rate: 82.5% (2000); Median home value: $79,000 (2000); Median rent: $406 per month (2000); Median age of housing: 44 years (2000).
Transportation: Commute to work: 84.6% car, 1.2% public transportation, 1.2% walk, 13.0% work from home (2000); Travel time to work: 17.6% less than 15 minutes, 32.2% 15 to 30 minutes, 13.1% 30 to 45 minutes, 13.1% 45 to 60 minutes, 23.9% 60 minutes or more (2000)

Bayfield County

Located in northern Wisconsin, on a peninsula; bounded on the north by Lake Superior, and on the east by Chequamegon Bay; includes part of Chequamegon National Forest. Covers a land area of 1,476.20 square miles, a water area of 565.30 square miles, and is located in the Central Time Zone. The county government was organized in 1845. County seat is Washburn.

Weather Station: Ashland Exp. Farm — Elevation: 649 feet

	Jan	Feb	Mar	Apr	May	Jun	Jul	Aug	Sep	Oct	Nov	Dec
High	22	28	38	52	66	75	80	78	69	57	40	27
Low	1	6	17	28	39	49	55	54	46	35	23	9
Precip	1.3	0.8	1.8	2.1	2.9	3.6	4.1	4.0	3.8	2.6	2.3	1.2
Snow	14.5	8.5	9.7	4.2	tr	0.0	0.0	0.0	0.0	0.3	7.9	12.4

High and Low temperatures in degrees Fahrenheit; Precipitation and Snow in inches

Weather Station: Bayfield 6 N — Elevation: 816 feet

	Jan	Feb	Mar	Apr	May	Jun	Jul	Aug	Sep	Oct	Nov	Dec
High	22	27	37	51	64	73	78	76	66	55	39	27
Low	5	8	18	30	40	49	56	55	47	37	25	12
Precip	1.8	1.0	2.1	2.3	3.3	3.8	4.1	3.9	3.8	2.9	2.8	1.7
Snow	26.3	11.5	13.5	5.4	0.7	0.0	0.0	0.0	tr	0.6	13.4	25.0

High and Low temperatures in degrees Fahrenheit; Precipitation and Snow in inches

Population: 15,013 (2000); Race: 88.9% White, 0.0% Black, 0.4% Asian, 8.9% American Indian and Alaska Native, 0.9% Hispanic of any race, 1.6% two or more races (2000); Density: 10.2 persons per square mile (2000); Age: 24.7% under 18, 16.4% over 64 (2000).
Religion: Five largest groups: 19.5% Catholic Church, 8.9% Evangelical Lutheran Church in America, 2.4% Baptist General Conference, 1.7% United Church of Christ, 1.4% Presbyterian Church (U.S.A.) (2000).
Economy: Unemployment rate: 6.8% (11/2002); Total civilian labor force: 7,691 (11/2002); Leading industries: 23.6% accommodation & food services; 18.7% retail trade; 9.1% manufacturing (2000); Companies that employ more than 1,000 persons: 0 (2000); Companies that employ more than 100 persons: 0 (2000); Farms: 325 totaling 84,222 acres (1997); Minority business ownership rate: 0.0% (1997); Women business ownership rate: 26.5% (1997); Retail sales per capita: $3,359 (1997). Single-family building permits issued: 143 (2001) / 144 (2000); Multi-family building permits issued: 2 (2001) / 2 (2000).
Income: Per capita income: $16,407 (2000); Median household income: $33,390 (2000); Poverty rate: 12.5% (2000); Bankruptcy rate: 1.74% (2001).
Taxes: Total county taxes per capita: $331 (1997); County property taxes per capita: $292 (1997).
Education: High school graduation rate: 86.9% (2000); College graduation rate: 21.6% (2000).
Housing: Homeownership rate: 82.6% (2000); Median home value: $86,100 (2000); Median rent: $313 per month (2000); Median age of housing: 30 years (2000).
Health: Birth rate: 95.3 per 10,000 population (1998); Age adjusted death rate: 85.8 per 10,000 population (1999); Age adjusted cancer mortality rate: 250.0 deaths per 100,000 population (1999). Number of physicians: 8.7 per 10,000 population (1999); Number of hospital beds: n/a (1999).
Elections: 2000 Presidential election results: 53.6% Gore, 39.5% Bush, 6.2% Nader, 0.2% Buchanan
National and State Parks: Apostle Islands National Lakeshore; Flag River State Wildlife Area; Rock Lake National Recreation Trail; Totagatic Lake State Wildlife Managament Area
Additional Information Contacts
Bayfield County Government Offices 715-373-6100
Bayfield Chamber of Commerce 715-779-3335
Cable Area Chamber of Commerce 715-798-3833
Iron River Area Chamber of Commerce 715-372-8558
Madeline Island Chamber of Commerce 715-779-5148
Washburn Area Chamber of Commerce 715-373-5017

Bayfield County Communities

BARKSDALE (town). Covers a land area of 55.245 square miles and a water area of 11.105 square miles. Located at 46.59° N. Lat.; 91.02° W. Long. Elevation is 652 feet.
Population: 801 (2000); Race: 97.7% White, 0.0% Black, 1.0% Asian, 1.0% American Indian and Alaska Native, 0.9% Hispanic of any race, 0.3% two or more races (2000); Density: 14.5 persons per square mile (2000); Age: 29.6% under 18, 13.7% over 64 (2000); Marriage status: 18.7% never married, 69.2% now married, 6.7% widowed, 5.4% divorced (2000); Foreign born: 1.7% (2000); Ancestry (includes multiple ancestries): 31.9% German, 15.4% Norwegian, 10.9% Swedish, 9.6% Polish, 9.6% United States or American (2000).
Economy: Produces chemicals and explosives. Employment by occupation: 8.0% management, 25.2% professional, 18.5% services, 22.3% sales, 1.9% farming, 10.2% construction, 13.9% production (2000).
Income: Per capita income: $19,680 (2000); Median household income: $45,714 (2000); Poverty rate: 2.2% (2000).
Taxes: Total city taxes per capita: $68 (1997); City property taxes per capita: $68 (1997).
Education: High school graduation rate: 89.3% (2000); College graduation rate: 27.6% (2000).
Housing: Homeownership rate: 91.7% (2000); Median home value: $110,400 (2000); Median rent: $409 per month (2000); Median age of housing: 29 years (2000).
Transportation: Commute to work: 86.6% car, 0.8% public transportation, 1.1% walk, 9.7% work from home (2000); Travel time to work: 40.1% less than 15 minutes, 51.5% 15 to 30 minutes, 4.6% 30 to 45 minutes, 0.6% 45 to 60 minutes, 3.1% 60 minutes or more (2000)

BARNES (town). Covers a land area of 117.515 square miles and a water area of 6.727 square miles. Located at 46.33° N. Lat.; 91.50° W. Long.
Population: 610 (2000); Race: 97.7% White, 0.5% Black, 0.0% Asian, 1.5% American Indian and Alaska Native, 0.0% Hispanic of any race, 0.3% two or more races (2000); Density: 5.2 persons per square mile (2000); Age: 19.9% under 18, 24.0% over 64 (2000); Marriage status: 14.7% never married, 70.5% now married, 7.2% widowed, 7.6% divorced (2000); Foreign born: 0.0% (2000); Ancestry (includes multiple ancestries): 33.3% German, 16.1% Irish, 13.2% Swedish, 11.8% English, 10.1% Polish (2000).
Economy: Employment by occupation: 10.2% management, 14.4% professional, 27.4% services, 19.5% sales, 0.9% farming, 13.5% construction, 14.0% production (2000).
Income: Per capita income: $16,405 (2000); Median household income: $28,250 (2000); Poverty rate: 16.1% (2000).
Taxes: Total city taxes per capita: $351 (1997); City property taxes per capita: $337 (1997).

Education: High school graduation rate: 88.2% (2000); College graduation rate: 18.5% (2000).
Housing: Homeownership rate: 87.2% (2000); Median home value: $110,600 (2000); Median rent: $381 per month (2000); Median age of housing: 27 years (2000).
Transportation: Commute to work: 87.2% car, 0.0% public transportation, 10.3% walk, 2.6% work from home (2000); Travel time to work: 38.4% less than 15 minutes, 15.3% 15 to 30 minutes, 24.2% 30 to 45 minutes, 6.8% 45 to 60 minutes, 15.3% 60 minutes or more (2000)

BAYFIELD (city). Covers a land area of 0.869 square miles and a water area of 0.012 square miles. Located at 46.81° N. Lat.; 90.82° W. Long. Elevation is 650 feet.
History: Bayfield was named for Admiral Henry Bayfield of the British Navy, who did surveying here in the early 1820's. The village was settled in 1857 by a group led by Henry M. Rice of St. Paul, when it was a five-day trip on a trail to Superior. When the railroad arrived in 1880, lumbering began.
Population: 611 (2000); Race: 72.5% White, 0.0% Black, 0.3% Asian, 17.7% American Indian and Alaska Native, 0.5% Hispanic of any race, 8.8% two or more races (2000); Density: 703.3 persons per square mile (2000); Age: 22.0% under 18, 18.2% over 64 (2000); Marriage status: 26.4% never married, 50.8% now married, 6.6% widowed, 16.2% divorced (2000); Foreign born: 2.2% (2000); Ancestry (includes multiple ancestries): 25.3% Other groups, 17.7% German, 12.8% English, 12.7% Irish, 11.5% Norwegian (2000).
Economy: Single-family building permits issued: 4 (2001) / 0 (2000); Multi-family building permits issued: 0 (2001) / 0 (2000); Employment by occupation: 14.6% management, 19.3% professional, 20.0% services, 25.1% sales, 1.4% farming, 12.9% construction, 6.8% production (2000).
Income: Per capita income: $18,377 (2000); Median household income: $32,266 (2000); Poverty rate: 11.8% (2000).
Taxes: Total city taxes per capita: $638 (1997); City property taxes per capita: $480 (1997).
Education: High school graduation rate: 88.8% (2000); College graduation rate: 29.5% (2000).

School District(s)

Bayfield (PK-12)
2000 Enrollment: 536 715-779-3201
Housing: Homeownership rate: 65.4% (2000); Median home value: $94,500 (2000); Median rent: $368 per month (2000); Median age of housing: 60+ years (2000).
Safety: Violent crime rate: 48.8 per 10,000 population; Property crime rate: 341.5 per 10,000 population (2001).
Transportation: Commute to work: 66.2% car, 3.5% public transportation, 25.1% walk, 5.2% work from home (2000); Travel time to work: 72.1% less than 15 minutes, 13.6% 15 to 30 minutes, 10.3% 30 to 45 minutes, 1.5% 45 to 60 minutes, 2.6% 60 minutes or more (2000)
Additional Information Contacts
Bayfield Chamber of Commerce 715-779-3335
Madeline Island Chamber of Commerce 715-779-5148

BAYFIELD (town). Covers a land area of 89.073 square miles and a water area of 44.880 square miles. Located at 46.83° N. Lat.; 90.92° W. Long. Elevation is 650 feet.
History: Settled 1856, incorporated 1913.
Population: 625 (2000); Race: 87.5% White, 0.0% Black, 0.0% Asian, 9.4% American Indian and Alaska Native, 0.9% Hispanic of any race, 2.8% two or more races (2000); Density: 7.0 persons per square mile (2000); Age: 25.9% under 18, 12.5% over 64 (2000); Marriage status: 16.4% never married, 67.8% now married, 4.3% widowed, 11.5% divorced (2000); Foreign born: 1.3% (2000); Ancestry (includes multiple ancestries): 32.1% German, 16.0% Norwegian, 13.1% Other groups, 12.6% Swedish, 11.5% English (2000).
Economy: Fishing resort, fruit-growing center: orchard-grown apples and raspberries; tourism. Employment by occupation: 14.7% management, 22.5% professional, 17.6% services, 19.6% sales, 4.9% farming, 12.7% construction, 7.8% production (2000).
Income: Per capita income: $17,890 (2000); Median household income: $39,342 (2000); Poverty rate: 9.1% (2000).
Taxes: Total city taxes per capita: $199 (1997); City property taxes per capita: $171 (1997).
Education: High school graduation rate: 92.7% (2000); College graduation rate: 32.0% (2000).
Housing: Homeownership rate: 90.3% (2000); Median home value: $123,400 (2000); Median rent: $325 per month (2000); Median age of housing: 21 years (2000).
Transportation: Commute to work: 82.6% car, 0.7% public transportation, 5.0% walk, 11.4% work from home (2000); Travel time to work: 51.4% less than 15 minutes, 25.3% 15 to 30 minutes, 18.1% 30 to 45 minutes, 3.6% 45 to 60 minutes, 1.6% 60 minutes or more (2000)

BAYVIEW (town). Covers a land area of 41.481 square miles and a water area of 14.629 square miles. Located at 46.74° N. Lat.; 90.96° W. Long.
Population: 491 (2000); Race: 94.3% White, 0.0% Black, 0.4% Asian, 3.5% American Indian and Alaska Native, 0.0% Hispanic of any race, 1.6% two or more races (2000); Density: 11.8 persons per square mile (2000); Age: 20.9% under 18, 18.3% over 64 (2000); Marriage status: 15.7% never married, 71.8% now married, 3.5% widowed, 9.0% divorced (2000); Foreign born: 2.3% (2000); Ancestry (includes multiple ancestries): 30.4% German, 14.8% Norwegian, 14.6% English, 11.5% Swedish, 10.7% Polish (2000).
Economy: Employment by occupation: 17.2% management, 24.7% professional, 9.2% services, 22.6% sales, 2.9% farming, 14.6% construction, 8.8% production (2000).
Income: Per capita income: $24,083 (2000); Median household income: $46,500 (2000); Poverty rate: 7.6% (2000).
Taxes: Total city taxes per capita: $106 (1997); City property taxes per capita: $106 (1997).
Education: High school graduation rate: 96.2% (2000); College graduation rate: 39.1% (2000).
Housing: Homeownership rate: 93.3% (2000); Median home value: $122,100 (2000); Median rent: $338 per month (2000); Median age of housing: 22 years (2000).
Transportation: Commute to work: 85.2% car, 0.0% public transportation, 4.5% walk, 9.0% work from home (2000); Travel time to work: 44.3% less than 15 minutes, 42.4% 15 to 30 minutes, 8.4% 30 to 45 minutes, 2.5% 45 to 60 minutes, 2.5% 60 minutes or more (2000)

BELL (town). Covers a land area of 59.630 square miles and a water area of 0.796 square miles. Located at 46.80° N. Lat.; 91.10° W. Long.
Population: 230 (2000); Race: 93.1% White, 0.0% Black, 0.0% Asian, 6.9% American Indian and Alaska Native, 0.0% Hispanic of any race, 0.0% two or more races (2000); Density: 3.9 persons per square mile (2000); Age: 13.0% under 18, 19.9% over 64 (2000); Marriage status: 21.6% never married, 56.3% now married, 7.0% widowed, 15.1% divorced (2000); Foreign born: 0.0% (2000); Ancestry (includes multiple ancestries): 41.2% German, 12.0% English, 10.6% French (except Basque), 10.2% Norwegian, 9.7% Other groups (2000).
Economy: Employment by occupation: 16.5% management, 27.8% professional, 7.2% services, 21.6% sales, 4.1% farming, 16.5% construction, 6.2% production (2000).
Income: Per capita income: $18,683 (2000); Median household income: $29,688 (2000); Poverty rate: 17.1% (2000).
Taxes: Total city taxes per capita: $124 (1997); City property taxes per capita: $120 (1997).
Education: High school graduation rate: 92.5% (2000); College graduation rate: 37.4% (2000).
Housing: Homeownership rate: 91.1% (2000); Median home value: $87,500 (2000); Median rent: $275 per month (2000); Median age of housing: 23 years (2000).
Transportation: Commute to work: 93.7% car, 0.0% public transportation, 4.2% walk, 0.0% work from home (2000); Travel time to work: 12.6% less than 15 minutes, 38.9% 15 to 30 minutes, 40.0% 30 to 45 minutes, 5.3% 45 to 60 minutes, 3.2% 60 minutes or more (2000)

CABLE (town). Covers a land area of 69.225 square miles and a water area of 2.182 square miles. Located at 46.20° N. Lat.; 91.26° W. Long. Elevation is 1,370 feet.
History: Cable developed in 1880 around the Omaha Railroad, as it extended its lines northward. For several years during railroad construction, Cable was a trading center for the northland beyond it. After 1900, it became a center for fishermen on the nearby Namekagon River.
Population: 836 (2000); Race: 98.9% White, 0.0% Black, 0.4% Asian, 0.2% American Indian and Alaska Native, 0.2% Hispanic of any race, 0.4% two or more races (2000); Density: 12.1 persons per square mile (2000); Age: 22.3% under 18, 15.5% over 64 (2000); Marriage status: 18.4% never married, 59.7% now married, 6.7% widowed, 15.2% divorced (2000); Foreign born: 0.9% (2000); Ancestry (includes multiple ancestries): 42.2% German, 13.0% Norwegian, 12.3% English, 10.8% Irish, 8.8% Swedish (2000).
Economy: Employment by occupation: 10.9% management, 14.0% professional, 19.1% services, 20.8% sales, 3.1% farming, 18.6% construction, 13.5% production (2000).

Income: Per capita income: $16,985 (2000); Median household income: $31,250 (2000); Poverty rate: 11.8% (2000).
Taxes: Total city taxes per capita: $287 (1997); City property taxes per capita: $253 (1997).
Education: High school graduation rate: 86.4% (2000); College graduation rate: 19.9% (2000).
Housing: Homeownership rate: 81.6% (2000); Median home value: $78,100 (2000); Median rent: $336 per month (2000); Median age of housing: 34 years (2000).
Transportation: Commute to work: 84.5% car, 0.5% public transportation, 9.8% walk, 4.5% work from home (2000); Travel time to work: 44.5% less than 15 minutes, 33.3% 15 to 30 minutes, 12.4% 30 to 45 minutes, 4.5% 45 to 60 minutes, 5.2% 60 minutes or more (2000)
Airports: Cable Union
Additional Information Contacts
Cable Area Chamber of Commerce 715-798-3833

CLOVER (town). Covers a land area of 59.595 square miles and a water area of 0.301 square miles. Located at 46.78° N. Lat.; 91.23° W. Long.
Population: 211 (2000); Race: 100.0% White, 0.0% Black, 0.0% Asian, 0.0% American Indian and Alaska Native, 0.0% Hispanic of any race, 0.0% two or more races (2000); Density: 3.5 persons per square mile (2000); Age: 20.6% under 18, 20.6% over 64 (2000); Marriage status: 15.5% never married, 50.6% now married, 8.9% widowed, 25.0% divorced (2000); Foreign born: 1.4% (2000); Ancestry (includes multiple ancestries): 27.8% German, 12.0% Swedish, 11.0% Irish, 11.0% Finnish, 8.6% English (2000).
Economy: Employment by occupation: 13.8% management, 17.2% professional, 11.5% services, 21.8% sales, 2.3% farming, 12.6% construction, 20.7% production (2000).
Income: Per capita income: $15,355 (2000); Median household income: $27,875 (2000); Poverty rate: 13.6% (2000).
Taxes: Total city taxes per capita: $346 (2000); City property taxes per capita: $341 (2000).
Education: High school graduation rate: 85.5% (2000); College graduation rate: 18.7% (2000).
Housing: Homeownership rate: 91.0% (2000); Median home value: $96,400 (2000); Median rent: $238 per month (2000); Median age of housing: 26 years (2000).
Transportation: Commute to work: 87.4% car, 0.0% public transportation, 5.7% walk, 6.9% work from home (2000); Travel time to work: 46.9% less than 15 minutes, 21.0% 15 to 30 minutes, 7.4% 30 to 45 minutes, 13.6% 45 to 60 minutes, 11.1% 60 minutes or more (2000)

CORNUCOPIA (unincorporated postal area, zip code 54827). Covers a land area of 48.839 square miles and a water area of 0.545 square miles. Located at 46.80° N. Lat.; 91.10° W. Long. Elevation is 630 feet.
Population: 211 (2000); Race: 96.5% White, 0.0% Black, 0.0% Asian, 3.5% American Indian and Alaska Native, 0.0% Hispanic of any race, 0.0% two or more races (2000); Density: 4.3 persons per square mile (2000); Age: 12.9% under 18, 20.4% over 64 (2000); Marriage status: 20.1% never married, 56.0% now married, 7.6% widowed, 16.3% divorced (2000); Foreign born: 0.0% (2000); Ancestry (includes multiple ancestries): 42.8% German, 12.9% English, 11.4% French (except Basque), 10.9% Norwegian, 6.5% Finnish (2000).
Economy: Fishing, resort area. Employment by occupation: 15.4% management, 26.4% professional, 7.7% services, 23.1% sales, 4.4% farming, 16.5% construction, 6.6% production (2000).
Income: Per capita income: $18,928 (2000); Median household income: $29,375 (2000); Poverty rate: 16.4% (2000).
Education: High school graduation rate: 92.1% (2000); College graduation rate: 36.0% (2000).
Housing: Homeownership rate: 90.7% (2000); Median home value: $90,000 (2000); Median rent: $275 per month (2000); Median age of housing: 23 years (2000).
Transportation: Commute to work: 93.3% car, 0.0% public transportation, 4.5% walk, 0.0% work from home (2000); Travel time to work: 12.4% less than 15 minutes, 41.6% 15 to 30 minutes, 37.1% 30 to 45 minutes, 5.6% 45 to 60 minutes, 3.4% 60 minutes or more (2000)

DELTA (town). Covers a land area of 69.552 square miles and a water area of 2.655 square miles. Located at 46.47° N. Lat.; 91.31° W. Long. Elevation is 1,043 feet.
Population: 235 (2000); Race: 95.2% White, 0.0% Black, 1.3% Asian, 3.5% American Indian and Alaska Native, 1.3% Hispanic of any race, 0.0% two or more races (2000); Density: 3.4 persons per square mile (2000); Age: 15.4% under 18, 21.6% over 64 (2000); Marriage status: 6.2% never married, 81.5% now married, 6.2% widowed, 6.2% divorced (2000); Foreign born: 4.4% (2000); Ancestry (includes multiple ancestries): 43.6% German, 16.3% Polish, 10.6% Irish, 8.8% Slovak, 7.0% Norwegian (2000).
Economy: Employment by occupation: 12.2% management, 33.7% professional, 14.3% services, 21.4% sales, 0.0% farming, 13.3% construction, 5.1% production (2000).
Income: Per capita income: $19,697 (2000); Median household income: $37,679 (2000); Poverty rate: 3.6% (2000).
Taxes: Total city taxes per capita: $64 (1997); City property taxes per capita: $60 (1997).
Education: High school graduation rate: 83.0% (2000); College graduation rate: 30.9% (2000).
Housing: Homeownership rate: 97.2% (2000); Median home value: $155,700 (2000); Median age of housing: 25 years (2000).
Transportation: Commute to work: 87.0% car, 0.0% public transportation, 8.7% walk, 4.3% work from home (2000); Travel time to work: 39.8% less than 15 minutes, 15.9% 15 to 30 minutes, 30.7% 30 to 45 minutes, 8.0% 45 to 60 minutes, 5.7% 60 minutes or more (2000)

DRUMMOND (town). Covers a land area of 137.158 square miles and a water area of 6.022 square miles. Located at 46.32° N. Lat.; 91.27° W. Long. Elevation is 1,310 feet.
History: For about 40 years, a lumber mill supported the economy of Drummond. A ranger headquarters for the Chequamegon National Forest was located here.
Population: 541 (2000); Race: 98.6% White, 0.0% Black, 0.0% Asian, 0.4% American Indian and Alaska Native, 1.8% Hispanic of any race, 1.0% two or more races (2000); Density: 3.9 persons per square mile (2000); Age: 21.2% under 18, 27.2% over 64 (2000); Marriage status: 14.0% never married, 66.5% now married, 9.7% widowed, 9.7% divorced (2000); Foreign born: 1.6% (2000); Ancestry (includes multiple ancestries): 30.2% German, 16.7% Norwegian, 10.9% English, 10.5% Irish, 8.7% Swedish (2000).
Economy: Employment by occupation: 13.8% management, 14.3% professional, 22.6% services, 23.5% sales, 0.9% farming, 13.8% construction, 11.1% production (2000).
Income: Per capita income: $16,773 (2000); Median household income: $37,500 (2000); Poverty rate: 12.4% (2000).
Taxes: Total city taxes per capita: $248 (1997); City property taxes per capita: $237 (1997).
Education: High school graduation rate: 88.4% (2000); College graduation rate: 25.3% (2000).

School District(s)

Drummond Area (PK-12)
2000 Enrollment: 582 715-739-6669

Housing: Homeownership rate: 80.3% (2000); Median home value: $85,600 (2000); Median rent: $250 per month (2000); Median age of housing: 31 years (2000).
Transportation: Commute to work: 73.1% car, 0.0% public transportation, 22.6% walk, 3.3% work from home (2000); Travel time to work: 55.1% less than 15 minutes, 20.5% 15 to 30 minutes, 15.1% 30 to 45 minutes, 5.4% 45 to 60 minutes, 3.9% 60 minutes or more (2000)

EILEEN (town). Covers a land area of 35.224 square miles and a water area of 0.077 square miles. Located at 46.56° N. Lat.; 90.98° W. Long.
Population: 640 (2000); Race: 99.2% White, 0.0% Black, 0.0% Asian, 0.8% American Indian and Alaska Native, 0.0% Hispanic of any race, 0.0% two or more races (2000); Density: 18.2 persons per square mile (2000); Age: 23.6% under 18, 15.6% over 64 (2000); Marriage status: 22.5% never married, 64.5% now married, 6.6% widowed, 6.4% divorced (2000); Foreign born: 0.5% (2000); Ancestry (includes multiple ancestries): 27.3% German, 19.8% Swedish, 14.2% Polish, 12.9% Croatian, 10.1% Norwegian (2000).
Economy: Employment by occupation: 15.1% management, 15.1% professional, 14.8% services, 26.2% sales, 2.2% farming, 9.9% construction, 16.7% production (2000).
Income: Per capita income: $19,530 (2000); Median household income: $44,844 (2000); Poverty rate: 8.9% (2000).
Taxes: Total city taxes per capita: $116 (1997); City property taxes per capita: $103 (1997).
Education: High school graduation rate: 88.3% (2000); College graduation rate: 18.5% (2000).
Housing: Homeownership rate: 92.4% (2000); Median home value: $88,400 (2000); Median rent: $325 per month (2000); Median age of housing: 35 years (2000).
Transportation: Commute to work: 88.2% car, 0.0% public transportation, 3.1% walk, 8.1% work from home (2000); Travel time to work: 45.1% less

than 15 minutes, 48.1% 15 to 30 minutes, 3.7% 30 to 45 minutes, 0.0% 45 to 60 minutes, 3.1% 60 minutes or more (2000)

GRANDVIEW (town). Aka Grand View. Covers a land area of 104.299 square miles and a water area of 2.833 square miles. Located at 46.29° N. Lat.; 91.06° W. Long. Elevation is 1,022 feet.
Population: 483 (2000); Race: 96.8% White, 0.0% Black, 0.8% Asian, 1.4% American Indian and Alaska Native, 0.2% Hispanic of any race, 1.0% two or more races (2000); Density: 4.6 persons per square mile (2000); Age: 21.0% under 18, 19.8% over 64 (2000); Marriage status: 24.8% never married, 55.1% now married, 7.3% widowed, 12.9% divorced (2000); Foreign born: 0.8% (2000); Ancestry (includes multiple ancestries): 34.4% German, 21.2% Swedish, 15.0% Norwegian, 10.8% Irish, 9.8% Polish (2000).
Economy: Employment by occupation: 9.0% management, 18.1% professional, 25.6% services, 17.6% sales, 6.0% farming, 10.6% construction, 13.1% production (2000).
Income: Per capita income: $14,052 (2000); Median household income: $25,000 (2000); Poverty rate: 16.8% (2000).
Taxes: Total city taxes per capita: $218 (1997); City property taxes per capita: $199 (1997).
Education: High school graduation rate: 81.9% (2000); College graduation rate: 15.6% (2000).
Housing: Homeownership rate: 84.0% (2000); Median home value: $73,400 (2000); Median rent: $238 per month (2000); Median age of housing: 34 years (2000).
Transportation: Commute to work: 91.5% car, 0.0% public transportation, 3.2% walk, 5.3% work from home (2000); Travel time to work: 16.2% less than 15 minutes, 34.1% 15 to 30 minutes, 38.5% 30 to 45 minutes, 8.4% 45 to 60 minutes, 2.8% 60 minutes or more (2000)

HERBSTER (unincorporated postal area, zip code 54844). Covers a land area of 64.500 square miles and a water area of 0.024 square miles. Located at 46.76° N. Lat.; 91.21° W. Long. Elevation is 614 feet.
Population: 195 (2000); Race: 100.0% White, 0.0% Black, 0.0% Asian, 0.0% American Indian and Alaska Native, 0.0% Hispanic of any race, 0.0% two or more races (2000); Density: 3.0 persons per square mile (2000); Age: 17.3% under 18, 23.2% over 64 (2000); Marriage status: 14.2% never married, 51.6% now married, 9.7% widowed, 24.5% divorced (2000); Foreign born: 1.6% (2000); Ancestry (includes multiple ancestries): 21.6% German, 12.4% Irish, 11.4% Finnish, 9.7% English, 9.2% Swedish (2000).
Economy: Employment by occupation: 13.2% management, 13.2% professional, 13.2% services, 19.7% sales, 2.6% farming, 14.5% construction, 23.7% production (2000).
Income: Per capita income: $15,421 (2000); Median household income: $27,361 (2000); Poverty rate: 11.0% (2000).
Education: High school graduation rate: 84.3% (2000); College graduation rate: 18.3% (2000).
Housing: Homeownership rate: 94.5% (2000); Median home value: $96,400 (2000); Median rent: $308 per month (2000); Median age of housing: 24 years (2000).
Transportation: Commute to work: 85.5% car, 0.0% public transportation, 6.6% walk, 7.9% work from home (2000); Travel time to work: 48.6% less than 15 minutes, 24.3% 15 to 30 minutes, 8.6% 30 to 45 minutes, 8.6% 45 to 60 minutes, 10.0% 60 minutes or more (2000)

HUGHES (town). Covers a land area of 52.000 square miles and a water area of 1.455 square miles. Located at 46.53° N. Lat.; 91.48° W. Long.
Population: 408 (2000); Race: 95.9% White, 0.0% Black, 1.5% Asian, 0.0% American Indian and Alaska Native, 0.0% Hispanic of any race, 2.7% two or more races (2000); Density: 7.8 persons per square mile (2000); Age: 26.4% under 18, 13.3% over 64 (2000); Marriage status: 15.8% never married, 70.9% now married, 4.0% widowed, 9.3% divorced (2000); Foreign born: 2.7% (2000); Ancestry (includes multiple ancestries): 34.9% German, 16.0% Finnish, 15.3% Irish, 12.8% Norwegian, 11.9% Swedish (2000).
Economy: Employment by occupation: 7.9% management, 29.4% professional, 15.8% services, 22.0% sales, 2.3% farming, 13.0% construction, 9.6% production (2000).
Income: Per capita income: $17,373 (2000); Median household income: $37,125 (2000); Poverty rate: 3.1% (2000).
Taxes: Total city taxes per capita: $145 (1997); City property taxes per capita: $134 (1997).
Education: High school graduation rate: 93.0% (2000); College graduation rate: 25.7% (2000).
Housing: Homeownership rate: 91.4% (2000); Median home value: $103,900 (2000); Median rent: $325 per month (2000); Median age of housing: 33 years (2000).
Transportation: Commute to work: 95.5% car, 0.0% public transportation, 0.0% walk, 2.3% work from home (2000); Travel time to work: 38.2% less than 15 minutes, 15.0% 15 to 30 minutes, 17.9% 30 to 45 minutes, 21.4% 45 to 60 minutes, 7.5% 60 minutes or more (2000)

IRON RIVER (town). Covers a land area of 31.430 square miles and a water area of 3.420 square miles. Located at 46.55° N. Lat.; 91.38° W. Long. Elevation is 1,120 feet.
History: Iron River developed around a trading post established in 1887 by John Pettingill to serve the lumbermen. By 1892 there was a sawmill and a hotel in the new settlement. As the lumber industry declined, the area was settled by Scandinavians who began farming, and a canning factory and cooperative creamery were established.
Population: 1,059 (2000); Race: 94.8% White, 0.1% Black, 1.5% Asian, 1.6% American Indian and Alaska Native, 0.7% Hispanic of any race, 1.9% two or more races (2000); Density: 33.7 persons per square mile (2000); Age: 18.8% under 18, 24.8% over 64 (2000); Marriage status: 20.0% never married, 59.1% now married, 9.7% widowed, 11.2% divorced (2000); Foreign born: 1.6% (2000); Ancestry (includes multiple ancestries): 27.7% German, 17.4% Norwegian, 15.9% Swedish, 13.0% Finnish, 11.3% Irish (2000).
Economy: Employment by occupation: 10.0% management, 16.5% professional, 18.7% services, 23.8% sales, 0.6% farming, 12.6% construction, 17.9% production (2000).
Income: Per capita income: $16,449 (2000); Median household income: $28,796 (2000); Poverty rate: 15.4% (2000).
Taxes: Total city taxes per capita: $390 (1997); City property taxes per capita: $377 (1997).
Education: High school graduation rate: 85.9% (2000); College graduation rate: 16.4% (2000).
Housing: Homeownership rate: 83.4% (2000); Median home value: $84,100 (2000); Median rent: $298 per month (2000); Median age of housing: 35 years (2000).
Transportation: Commute to work: 88.6% car, 1.0% public transportation, 6.4% walk, 2.8% work from home (2000); Travel time to work: 35.7% less than 15 minutes, 18.2% 15 to 30 minutes, 17.8% 30 to 45 minutes, 15.9% 45 to 60 minutes, 12.4% 60 minutes or more (2000)
Additional Information Contacts
Iron River Area Chamber of Commerce 715-372-8558

KELLY (town). Covers a land area of 36.673 square miles and a water area of 0 square miles. Located at 46.43° N. Lat.; 90.99° W. Long.
Population: 377 (2000); Race: 95.3% White, 0.0% Black, 0.0% Asian, 4.4% American Indian and Alaska Native, 0.0% Hispanic of any race, 0.3% two or more races (2000); Density: 10.3 persons per square mile (2000); Age: 29.4% under 18, 19.7% over 64 (2000); Marriage status: 15.8% never married, 73.2% now married, 6.5% widowed, 4.5% divorced (2000); Foreign born: 0.0% (2000); Ancestry (includes multiple ancestries): 31.9% German, 19.7% Norwegian, 12.7% Irish, 12.7% Swedish, 12.2% Croatian (2000).
Economy: Employment by occupation: 25.7% management, 12.5% professional, 12.5% services, 19.1% sales, 6.6% farming, 6.6% construction, 17.1% production (2000).
Income: Per capita income: $15,525 (2000); Median household income: $33,125 (2000); Poverty rate: 17.4% (2000).
Taxes: Total city taxes per capita: $50 (1997); City property taxes per capita: $50 (1997).
Education: High school graduation rate: 84.9% (2000); College graduation rate: 13.5% (2000).
Housing: Homeownership rate: 90.2% (2000); Median home value: $65,600 (2000); Median rent: $275 per month (2000); Median age of housing: 34 years (2000).
Transportation: Commute to work: 78.7% car, 0.0% public transportation, 0.0% walk, 21.3% work from home (2000); Travel time to work: 15.3% less than 15 minutes, 65.3% 15 to 30 minutes, 12.7% 30 to 45 minutes, 4.2% 45 to 60 minutes, 2.5% 60 minutes or more (2000)

KEYSTONE (town). Covers a land area of 35.806 square miles and a water area of 0.289 square miles. Located at 46.52° N. Lat.; 91.18° W. Long.
Population: 369 (2000); Race: 95.9% White, 0.0% Black, 0.0% Asian, 4.1% American Indian and Alaska Native, 0.0% Hispanic of any race, 0.0% two or more races (2000); Density: 10.3 persons per square mile (2000); Age: 26.3% under 18, 19.1% over 64 (2000); Marriage status: 14.2% never married, 72.6% now married, 5.2% widowed, 8.0% divorced (2000); Foreign born: 0.0% (2000); Ancestry (includes multiple ancestries): 14.8% German, 14.6% Slovak, 12.2% Irish, 8.1% Finnish, 8.1% English (2000).

Economy: Employment by occupation: 8.8% management, 15.1% professional, 9.3% services, 26.3% sales, 5.9% farming, 6.8% construction, 27.8% production (2000).
Income: Per capita income: $15,638 (2000); Median household income: $40,500 (2000); Poverty rate: 20.0% (2000).
Taxes: Total city taxes per capita: $194 (1997); City property taxes per capita: $180 (1997).
Education: High school graduation rate: 84.1% (2000); College graduation rate: 18.2% (2000).
Housing: Homeownership rate: 86.2% (2000); Median home value: $75,000 (2000); Median rent: $321 per month (2000); Median age of housing: 22 years (2000).
Transportation: Commute to work: 76.6% car, 0.0% public transportation, 19.1% walk, 1.9% work from home (2000); Travel time to work: 35.1% less than 15 minutes, 52.7% 15 to 30 minutes, 5.9% 30 to 45 minutes, 2.4% 45 to 60 minutes, 3.9% 60 minutes or more (2000)

LINCOLN (town). Covers a land area of 35.505 square miles and a water area of 0.354 square miles. Located at 46.35° N. Lat.; 90.98° W. Long.
Population: 293 (2000); Race: 98.2% White, 0.0% Black, 0.0% Asian, 0.0% American Indian and Alaska Native, 1.1% Hispanic of any race, 1.8% two or more races (2000); Density: 8.3 persons per square mile (2000); Age: 17.1% under 18, 18.6% over 64 (2000); Marriage status: 25.6% never married, 60.8% now married, 5.2% widowed, 8.4% divorced (2000); Foreign born: 0.0% (2000); Ancestry (includes multiple ancestries): 28.6% German, 17.9% Swedish, 12.9% Irish, 12.1% Norwegian, 10.7% French (except Basque) (2000).
Economy: Employment by occupation: 5.6% management, 6.3% professional, 19.7% services, 19.7% sales, 6.3% farming, 16.2% construction, 26.1% production (2000).
Income: Per capita income: $13,530 (2000); Median household income: $27,917 (2000); Poverty rate: 6.8% (2000).
Taxes: Total city taxes per capita: $56 (1997); City property taxes per capita: $56 (1997).
Education: High school graduation rate: 81.7% (2000); College graduation rate: 15.5% (2000).
Housing: Homeownership rate: 91.6% (2000); Median home value: $82,500 (2000); Median rent: $325 per month (2000); Median age of housing: 29 years (2000).
Transportation: Commute to work: 81.7% car, 2.1% public transportation, 4.9% walk, 11.3% work from home (2000); Travel time to work: 18.3% less than 15 minutes, 27.8% 15 to 30 minutes, 43.7% 30 to 45 minutes, 7.1% 45 to 60 minutes, 3.2% 60 minutes or more (2000)

MASON (village). Covers a land area of 0.508 square miles and a water area of 0 square miles. Located at 46.43° N. Lat.; 91.06° W. Long. Elevation is 950 feet.
Population: 72 (2000); Race: 100.0% White, 0.0% Black, 0.0% Asian, 0.0% American Indian and Alaska Native, 0.0% Hispanic of any race, 0.0% two or more races (2000); Density: 141.8 persons per square mile (2000); Age: 13.9% under 18, 22.2% over 64 (2000); Marriage status: 6.5% never married, 93.5% now married, 0.0% widowed, 0.0% divorced (2000); Foreign born: 0.0% (2000); Ancestry (includes multiple ancestries): 52.8% United States or American, 19.4% Swedish, 16.7% Norwegian, 8.3% Canadian, 8.3% Scandinavian (2000).
Economy: Employment by occupation: 9.5% management, 0.0% professional, 9.5% services, 28.6% sales, 0.0% farming, 0.0% construction, 52.4% production (2000).
Income: Per capita income: $12,742 (2000); Median household income: $32,917 (2000); Poverty rate: 30.6% (2000).
Taxes: Total city taxes per capita: $54 (1997); City property taxes per capita: $54 (1997).
Education: High school graduation rate: 89.7% (2000); College graduation rate: 17.2% (2000).
Housing: Homeownership rate: 100.0% (2000); Median home value: $41,000 (2000); Median age of housing: 60+ years (2000).
Transportation: Commute to work: 28.6% car, 0.0% public transportation, 38.1% walk, 0.0% work from home (2000); Travel time to work: 85.7% less than 15 minutes, 0.0% 15 to 30 minutes, 14.3% 30 to 45 minutes, 0.0% 45 to 60 minutes, 0.0% 60 minutes or more (2000)

MASON (town). Covers a land area of 35.905 square miles and a water area of 0 square miles. Located at 46.46° N. Lat.; 91.10° W. Long. Elevation is 950 feet.
Population: 326 (2000); Race: 100.0% White, 0.0% Black, 0.0% Asian, 0.0% American Indian and Alaska Native, 0.0% Hispanic of any race, 0.0% two or more races (2000); Density: 9.1 persons per square mile (2000); Age: 34.5% under 18, 6.5% over 64 (2000); Marriage status: 21.9% never married, 56.6% now married, 3.8% widowed, 17.7% divorced (2000); Foreign born: 0.0% (2000); Ancestry (includes multiple ancestries): 31.4% German, 26.6% Swedish, 23.2% Norwegian, 12.7% Irish, 9.9% Polish (2000).
Economy: Lumber. Chequamegon National Forest to North, West and South. Employment by occupation: 11.0% management, 4.1% professional, 12.3% services, 28.1% sales, 15.1% farming, 18.5% construction, 11.0% production (2000).
Income: Per capita income: $13,814 (2000); Median household income: $34,231 (2000); Poverty rate: 9.9% (2000).
Taxes: Total city taxes per capita: $204 (1997); City property taxes per capita: $204 (1997).
Education: High school graduation rate: 89.6% (2000); College graduation rate: 7.2% (2000).
Housing: Homeownership rate: 92.2% (2000); Median home value: $80,000 (2000); Median rent: $413 per month (2000); Median age of housing: 21 years (2000).
Transportation: Commute to work: 86.6% car, 0.0% public transportation, 4.9% walk, 8.5% work from home (2000); Travel time to work: 26.9% less than 15 minutes, 49.2% 15 to 30 minutes, 19.2% 30 to 45 minutes, 3.1% 45 to 60 minutes, 1.5% 60 minutes or more (2000)

NAMAKAGON (town). Covers a land area of 64.971 square miles and a water area of 7.210 square miles. Located at 46.20° N. Lat.; 91.05° W. Long.
Population: 285 (2000); Race: 99.2% White, 0.0% Black, 0.0% Asian, 0.0% American Indian and Alaska Native, 1.6% Hispanic of any race, 0.0% two or more races (2000); Density: 4.4 persons per square mile (2000); Age: 7.8% under 18, 32.2% over 64 (2000); Marriage status: 10.0% never married, 66.4% now married, 8.7% widowed, 14.8% divorced (2000); Foreign born: 0.8% (2000); Ancestry (includes multiple ancestries): 39.6% German, 14.7% Norwegian, 11.4% English, 9.0% United States or American, 7.8% Irish (2000).
Economy: Employment by occupation: 6.8% management, 6.8% professional, 20.5% services, 37.5% sales, 3.4% farming, 12.5% construction, 12.5% production (2000).
Income: Per capita income: $17,576 (2000); Median household income: $20,625 (2000); Poverty rate: 20.8% (2000).
Taxes: Total city taxes per capita: $715 (1997); City property taxes per capita: $517 (1997).
Education: High school graduation rate: 79.2% (2000); College graduation rate: 15.0% (2000).
Housing: Homeownership rate: 86.4% (2000); Median home value: $201,300 (2000); Median rent: $325 per month (2000); Median age of housing: 43 years (2000).
Transportation: Commute to work: 88.4% car, 0.0% public transportation, 7.0% walk, 4.7% work from home (2000); Travel time to work: 31.7% less than 15 minutes, 37.8% 15 to 30 minutes, 3.7% 30 to 45 minutes, 13.4% 45 to 60 minutes, 13.4% 60 minutes or more (2000)

ORIENTA (town). Covers a land area of 54.123 square miles and a water area of 0.198 square miles. Located at 46.73° N. Lat.; 91.46° W. Long.
Population: 101 (2000); Race: 100.0% White, 0.0% Black, 0.0% Asian, 0.0% American Indian and Alaska Native, 0.0% Hispanic of any race, 0.0% two or more races (2000); Density: 1.9 persons per square mile (2000); Age: 14.6% under 18, 21.4% over 64 (2000); Marriage status: 20.5% never married, 53.4% now married, 11.4% widowed, 14.8% divorced (2000); Foreign born: 0.0% (2000); Ancestry (includes multiple ancestries): 38.8% German, 21.4% Swedish, 13.6% Irish, 11.7% Hungarian, 8.7% Norwegian (2000).
Economy: Employment by occupation: 11.9% management, 20.3% professional, 8.5% services, 20.3% sales, 6.8% farming, 16.9% construction, 15.3% production (2000).
Income: Per capita income: $19,775 (2000); Median household income: $33,333 (2000); Poverty rate: 6.8% (2000).
Taxes: Total city taxes per capita: $144 (1997); City property taxes per capita: $144 (1997).
Education: High school graduation rate: 89.4% (2000); College graduation rate: 17.6% (2000).
Housing: Homeownership rate: 100.0% (2000); Median home value: $87,500 (2000); Median age of housing: 21 years (2000).
Transportation: Commute to work: 79.7% car, 0.0% public transportation, 8.5% walk, 11.9% work from home (2000); Travel time to work: 25.0% less than 15 minutes, 19.2% 15 to 30 minutes, 9.6% 30 to 45 minutes, 36.5% 45 to 60 minutes, 9.6% 60 minutes or more (2000)

OULU (town). Covers a land area of 35.472 square miles and a water area of 0 square miles. Located at 46.62° N. Lat.; 91.50° W. Long. Elevation is 998 feet.
Population: 540 (2000); Race: 97.8% White, 0.2% Black, 0.0% Asian, 0.6% American Indian and Alaska Native, 0.4% Hispanic of any race, 1.0% two or more races (2000); Density: 15.2 persons per square mile (2000); Age: 31.2% under 18, 12.4% over 64 (2000); Marriage status: 24.5% never married, 57.4% now married, 9.7% widowed, 8.4% divorced (2000); Foreign born: 0.4% (2000); Ancestry (includes multiple ancestries): 42.4% Finnish, 23.2% German, 10.2% Swedish, 9.2% Norwegian, 8.8% Irish (2000).
Economy: Employment by occupation: 17.3% management, 17.3% professional, 14.7% services, 13.9% sales, 2.6% farming, 18.6% construction, 15.6% production (2000).
Income: Per capita income: $15,017 (2000); Median household income: $35,625 (2000); Poverty rate: 11.4% (2000).
Taxes: Total city taxes per capita: $52 (1997); City property taxes per capita: $52 (1997).
Education: High school graduation rate: 84.0% (2000); College graduation rate: 10.7% (2000).
Housing: Homeownership rate: 86.7% (2000); Median home value: $85,000 (2000); Median rent: $425 per month (2000); Median age of housing: 53 years (2000).
Transportation: Commute to work: 87.7% car, 0.9% public transportation, 0.0% walk, 10.6% work from home (2000); Travel time to work: 25.1% less than 15 minutes, 27.6% 15 to 30 minutes, 13.8% 30 to 45 minutes, 25.1% 45 to 60 minutes, 8.4% 60 minutes or more (2000)

PILSEN (town). Covers a land area of 34.903 square miles and a water area of 0.218 square miles. Located at 46.56° N. Lat.; 91.17° W. Long.
Population: 203 (2000); Race: 100.0% White, 0.0% Black, 0.0% Asian, 0.0% American Indian and Alaska Native, 0.0% Hispanic of any race, 0.0% two or more races (2000); Density: 5.8 persons per square mile (2000); Age: 19.5% under 18, 16.3% over 64 (2000); Marriage status: 17.6% never married, 68.6% now married, 10.1% widowed, 3.8% divorced (2000); Foreign born: 0.0% (2000); Ancestry (includes multiple ancestries): 34.7% German, 16.8% Irish, 11.6% English, 10.5% Czech, 8.9% Slovak (2000).
Economy: Employment by occupation: 15.1% management, 18.3% professional, 0.0% services, 30.1% sales, 2.2% farming, 24.7% construction, 9.7% production (2000).
Income: Per capita income: $17,895 (2000); Median household income: $45,000 (2000); Poverty rate: 2.1% (2000).
Taxes: Total city taxes per capita: $86 (1997); City property taxes per capita: $86 (1997).
Education: High school graduation rate: 93.4% (2000); College graduation rate: 14.7% (2000).
Housing: Homeownership rate: 91.9% (2000); Median home value: $90,000 (2000); Median age of housing: 32 years (2000).
Transportation: Commute to work: 87.5% car, 0.0% public transportation, 6.8% walk, 5.7% work from home (2000); Travel time to work: 28.9% less than 15 minutes, 44.6% 15 to 30 minutes, 10.8% 30 to 45 minutes, 6.0% 45 to 60 minutes, 9.6% 60 minutes or more (2000)

PORT WING (town). Covers a land area of 46.609 square miles and a water area of 0.085 square miles. Located at 46.78° N. Lat.; 91.37° W. Long. Elevation is 660 feet.
Population: 420 (2000); Race: 96.7% White, 0.0% Black, 0.0% Asian, 1.6% American Indian and Alaska Native, 2.1% Hispanic of any race, 0.0% two or more races (2000); Density: 9.0 persons per square mile (2000); Age: 23.3% under 18, 16.7% over 64 (2000); Marriage status: 22.2% never married, 58.4% now married, 9.0% widowed, 10.4% divorced (2000); Foreign born: 1.9% (2000); Ancestry (includes multiple ancestries): 29.5% German, 27.2% Swedish, 20.0% Norwegian, 12.6% Irish, 8.1% Polish (2000).
Economy: Trade center for cooperative-farm area. Chequamegon National Forest to Southeast. Employment by occupation: 13.3% management, 18.6% professional, 13.3% services, 20.7% sales, 4.3% farming, 16.0% construction, 13.8% production (2000).
Income: Per capita income: $17,355 (2000); Median household income: $30,000 (2000); Poverty rate: 18.4% (2000).
Taxes: Total city taxes per capita: $103 (1997); City property taxes per capita: $97 (1997).
Education: High school graduation rate: 93.4% (2000); College graduation rate: 21.5% (2000).

School District(s)

South Shore (PK-12)
2000 Enrollment: 246 715-774-3500

Housing: Homeownership rate: 81.5% (2000); Median home value: $57,800 (2000); Median rent: $275 per month (2000); Median age of housing: 42 years (2000).
Transportation: Commute to work: 82.4% car, 0.0% public transportation, 4.5% walk, 11.9% work from home (2000); Travel time to work: 38.7% less than 15 minutes, 15.5% 15 to 30 minutes, 4.5% 30 to 45 minutes, 19.4% 45 to 60 minutes, 21.9% 60 minutes or more (2000)

RUSSELL (town). Covers a land area of 49.831 square miles and a water area of 50.310 square miles. Located at 46.91° N. Lat.; 90.85° W. Long.
Population: 1,216 (2000); Race: 21.1% White, 0.2% Black, 0.0% Asian, 77.0% American Indian and Alaska Native, 3.6% Hispanic of any race, 1.5% two or more races (2000); Density: 24.4 persons per square mile (2000); Age: 35.1% under 18, 6.5% over 64 (2000); Marriage status: 31.5% never married, 50.5% now married, 6.5% widowed, 11.5% divorced (2000); Foreign born: 0.8% (2000); Ancestry (includes multiple ancestries): 75.5% Other groups, 8.5% German, 4.1% Norwegian, 2.4% Irish, 2.3% English (2000).
Economy: Employment by occupation: 13.6% management, 15.6% professional, 19.8% services, 26.0% sales, 4.3% farming, 14.7% construction, 6.0% production (2000).
Income: Per capita income: $10,387 (2000); Median household income: $25,114 (2000); Poverty rate: 28.6% (2000).
Taxes: Total city taxes per capita: $7 (1997); City property taxes per capita: $6 (1997).
Education: High school graduation rate: 78.1% (2000); College graduation rate: 12.3% (2000).
Housing: Homeownership rate: 60.7% (2000); Median home value: $61,300 (2000); Median rent: $186 per month (2000); Median age of housing: 23 years (2000).
Transportation: Commute to work: 79.1% car, 5.6% public transportation, 3.4% walk, 11.2% work from home (2000); Travel time to work: 56.7% less than 15 minutes, 21.1% 15 to 30 minutes, 4.6% 30 to 45 minutes, 11.9% 45 to 60 minutes, 5.8% 60 minutes or more (2000)

TRIPP (town). Covers a land area of 34.716 square miles and a water area of 0.204 square miles. Located at 46.61° N. Lat.; 91.36° W. Long.
Population: 209 (2000); Race: 93.2% White, 0.0% Black, 0.0% Asian, 4.2% American Indian and Alaska Native, 0.0% Hispanic of any race, 2.6% two or more races (2000); Density: 6.0 persons per square mile (2000); Age: 31.1% under 18, 9.5% over 64 (2000); Marriage status: 23.4% never married, 60.7% now married, 4.8% widowed, 11.0% divorced (2000); Foreign born: 2.1% (2000); Ancestry (includes multiple ancestries): 29.5% Finnish, 28.9% German, 8.9% Irish, 7.9% English, 5.8% Other groups (2000).
Economy: Employment by occupation: 13.4% management, 17.1% professional, 8.5% services, 37.8% sales, 6.1% farming, 13.4% construction, 3.7% production (2000).
Income: Per capita income: $12,653 (2000); Median household income: $35,000 (2000); Poverty rate: 6.3% (2000).
Taxes: Total city taxes per capita: $111 (1997); City property taxes per capita: $111 (1997).
Education: High school graduation rate: 74.2% (2000); College graduation rate: 16.9% (2000).
Housing: Homeownership rate: 90.1% (2000); Median home value: $50,000 (2000); Median rent: $425 per month (2000); Median age of housing: 27 years (2000).
Transportation: Commute to work: 86.3% car, 0.0% public transportation, 0.0% walk, 13.8% work from home (2000); Travel time to work: 33.3% less than 15 minutes, 21.7% 15 to 30 minutes, 21.7% 30 to 45 minutes, 18.8% 45 to 60 minutes, 4.3% 60 minutes or more (2000)

WASHBURN (city). Covers a land area of 3.921 square miles and a water area of 2.244 square miles. Located at 46.67° N. Lat.; 90.89° W. Long. Elevation is 700 feet.
History: Washburn was founded in 1884 by the Chicago, St. Paul, Minnesota & Omaha Railroad, and named for Cadwallader C. Washburn, Wisconsin governor from 1872 to 1874. Coal was shipped from the docks here on a bay of Lake Superior, where lumber mills also operated.
Population: 2,280 (2000); Race: 92.1% White, 0.0% Black, 0.3% Asian, 3.9% American Indian and Alaska Native, 1.2% Hispanic of any race, 2.9% two or more races (2000); Density: 581.5 persons per square mile (2000); Age: 27.2% under 18, 14.9% over 64 (2000); Marriage status: 25.8% never married, 54.9% now married, 7.0% widowed, 12.4% divorced (2000); Foreign born: 1.4% (2000); Ancestry (includes multiple ancestries): 36.2% German, 16.2% Norwegian, 11.0% Swedish, 10.1% Irish, 9.1% French (except Basque) (2000).

Economy: Single-family building permits issued: 6 (2001) / 7 (2000); Multi-family building permits issued: 2 (2001) / 0 (2000); Employment by occupation: 14.3% management, 24.9% professional, 17.8% services, 24.0% sales, 1.0% farming, 7.9% construction, 10.0% production (2000).
Income: Per capita income: $15,331 (2000); Median household income: $33,257 (2000); Poverty rate: 10.3% (2000).
Taxes: Total city taxes per capita: $186 (2000); City property taxes per capita: $163 (2000).
Education: High school graduation rate: 86.6% (2000); College graduation rate: 24.2% (2000).

School District(s)

Washburn (PK-12)
2000 Enrollment: 770 715-373-6187

Housing: Homeownership rate: 72.3% (2000); Median home value: $80,900 (2000); Median rent: $346 per month (2000); Median age of housing: 51 years (2000).
Safety: Violent crime rate: 43.6 per 10,000 population; Property crime rate: 265.7 per 10,000 population (2001).
Newspapers: The County Journal (1 x week)
Transportation: Commute to work: 84.3% car, 1.0% public transportation, 10.1% walk, 3.7% work from home (2000); Travel time to work: 48.3% less than 15 minutes, 44.2% 15 to 30 minutes, 4.3% 30 to 45 minutes, 0.0% 45 to 60 minutes, 3.2% 60 minutes or more (2000)

Additional Information Contacts

Washburn Area Chamber of Commerce 715-373-5017

WASHBURN (town). Covers a land area of 85.009 square miles and a water area of 0.200 square miles. Located at 46.66° N. Lat.; 91.07° W. Long. Elevation is 700 feet.
History: Founded 1884, incorporated 1904.
Population: 541 (2000); Race: 95.9% White, 0.0% Black, 0.2% Asian, 1.7% American Indian and Alaska Native, 0.0% Hispanic of any race, 2.2% two or more races (2000); Density: 6.4 persons per square mile (2000); Age: 24.7% under 18, 8.7% over 64 (2000); Marriage status: 24.8% never married, 62.9% now married, 2.6% widowed, 9.8% divorced (2000); Foreign born: 1.7% (2000); Ancestry (includes multiple ancestries): 39.2% German, 20.3% Swedish, 16.0% Norwegian, 11.9% Polish, 6.7% Irish (2000).
Economy: Commercial center for dairying, lumbering, and fruit-growing area; manufacturing of iron castings. A ranger station; Bayfish State Fish Hatchery to Northeast; agricultural research station 8 miles South; Chaquamegon National Forest to West. Employment by occupation: 10.6% management, 21.6% professional, 16.1% services, 20.2% sales, 5.5% farming, 13.0% construction, 13.0% production (2000).
Income: Per capita income: $17,892 (2000); Median household income: $46,500 (2000); Poverty rate: 4.6% (2000).
Taxes: Total city taxes per capita: $52 (1997); City property taxes per capita: $50 (1997).
Education: High school graduation rate: 89.8% (2000); College graduation rate: 29.3% (2000).
Housing: Homeownership rate: 89.6% (2000); Median home value: $86,000 (2000); Median rent: $313 per month (2000); Median age of housing: 26 years (2000).
Transportation: Commute to work: 89.1% car, 0.0% public transportation, 4.4% walk, 6.5% work from home (2000); Travel time to work: 31.5% less than 15 minutes, 52.1% 15 to 30 minutes, 11.3% 30 to 45 minutes, 1.9% 45 to 60 minutes, 3.1% 60 minutes or more (2000)

Brown County

Located in eastern Wisconsin, partly on the Door Peninsula; bounded on the north by Green Bay of Lake Michigan. Covers a land area of 528.70 square miles, a water area of 86.70 square miles, and is located in the Central Time Zone. The county government was organized in 1818. County seat is Green Bay.

Brown County is part of the Green Bay, WI MSA. The entire metro area includes: Brown County

Weather Station: Green Bay Int'l Airport — Elevation: 685 feet

	Jan	Feb	Mar	Apr	May	Jun	Jul	Aug	Sep	Oct	Nov	Dec
High	23	28	39	54	68	77	81	78	70	57	42	29
Low	7	12	22	34	44	54	59	57	49	38	26	14
Precip	1.2	1.0	2.1	2.5	2.8	3.3	3.4	3.7	3.2	2.3	2.3	1.4
Snow	13.8	8.3	9.5	2.8	0.2	tr	0.0	tr	tr	0.2	5.4	12.0

High and Low temperatures in degrees Fahrenheit; Precipitation and Snow in inches

Population: 226,778 (2000); Race: 91.2% White, 1.2% Black, 2.0% Asian, 2.3% American Indian and Alaska Native, 3.9% Hispanic of any race, 1.3% two or more races (2000); Density: 429.0 persons per square mile (2000); Age: 26.0% under 18, 10.6% over 64 (2000).
Religion: Five largest groups: 52.3% Catholic Church, 6.1% Evangelical Lutheran Church in America, 3.3% Lutheran Church—Missouri Synod, 2.4% Wisconsin Evangelical Lutheran Synod, 1.9% The United Methodist Church (2000).
Economy: Unemployment rate: 4.4% (11/2002); Total civilian labor force: 142,995 (11/2002); Leading industries: 21.6% manufacturing; 12.6% retail trade; 11.1% health care and social assistance (2000); Companies that employ more than 1,000 persons: 15 (2000); Companies that employ more than 100 persons: 201 (2000); Farms: 1,059 totaling 195,966 acres (1997); Minority business ownership rate: 3.0% (1997); Women business ownership rate: 22.9% (1997); Retail sales per capita: $12,000 (1997). Single-family building permits issued: 1,205 (2001) / 1,130 (2000); Multi-family building permits issued: 969 (2001) / 429 (2000).
Income: Per capita income: $21,784 (2000); Median household income: $46,447 (2000); Poverty rate: 6.9% (2000); Bankruptcy rate: 3.82% (2001).
Taxes: Total county taxes per capita: $205 (2000); County property taxes per capita: $202 (2000).
Education: High school graduation rate: 86.3% (2000); College graduation rate: 22.5% (2000).
Housing: Homeownership rate: 65.4% (2000); Median home value: $116,100 (2000); Median rent: $469 per month (2000); Median age of housing: 27 years (2000).
Health: Birth rate: 138.0 per 10,000 population (1998); Age adjusted death rate: 81.0 per 10,000 population (1999); Age adjusted cancer mortality rate: 196.9 deaths per 100,000 population (1999). Air Quality Index: 89% good, 11% moderate, 0% unhealthy (percent of days in 2000). Number of physicians: 19.4 per 10,000 population (1999); Number of hospital beds: 31.7 per 10,000 population (1999).
Elections: 2000 Presidential election results: 45.6% Gore, 50.4% Bush, 3.1% Nader, 0.6% Buchanan
National and State Parks: Green Bay West Shores State Wildlife Area; Heritage Hill State Park; Holland State Wildlife Area; Lost Dauphin State Park; Sensiba State Wildlife Area

Additional Information Contacts

Brown County Government Offices. 920-448-4016
Green Bay Chamber of Commerce 920-437-8704

Brown County Communities

ALLOUEZ (village). Covers a land area of 4.625 square miles and a water area of 0.529 square miles. Located at 44.47° N. Lat.; 88.02° W. Long. Elevation is 600 feet.
Population: 15,443 (2000); Race: 92.0% White, 5.0% Black, 0.7% Asian, 1.5% American Indian and Alaska Native, 1.0% Hispanic of any race, 0.5% two or more races (2000); Density: 3,338.8 persons per square mile (2000); Age: 22.0% under 18, 14.8% over 64 (2000); Marriage status: 18.1% never married, 69.1% now married, 7.3% widowed, 5.4% divorced (2000); Foreign born: 1.5% (2000); Ancestry (includes multiple ancestries): 34.0% German, 12.1% Irish, 10.7% Belgian, 7.3% Polish, 6.4% French (except Basque) (2000).
Vital Statistics: Birth rate: 86.1 per 10,000 population (1998)
Economy: Suburb of Green Bay. Single-family building permits issued: 9 (2001) / 21 (2000); Multi-family building permits issued: 0 (2001) / 4 (2000); Employment by occupation: 17.6% management, 25.4% professional, 10.3% services, 30.6% sales, 0.3% farming, 4.7% construction, 11.2% production (2000).
Income: Per capita income: $25,535 (2000); Median household income: $55,850 (2000); Poverty rate: 3.5% (2000).
Taxes: Total city taxes per capita: $190 (1997); City property taxes per capita: $183 (1997).
Education: High school graduation rate: 89.1% (2000); College graduation rate: 34.0% (2000).
Housing: Homeownership rate: 85.0% (2000); Median home value: $120,000 (2000); Median rent: $524 per month (2000); Median age of housing: 35 years (2000).
Transportation: Commute to work: 95.2% car, 0.8% public transportation, 1.2% walk, 2.3% work from home (2000); Travel time to work: 53.2% less than 15 minutes, 35.7% 15 to 30 minutes, 6.5% 30 to 45 minutes, 1.8% 45 to 60 minutes, 2.8% 60 minutes or more (2000)

ASHWAUBENON (village). Covers a land area of 12.370 square miles and a water area of 0.372 square miles. Located at 44.48° N. Lat.; 88.08° W. Long. Elevation is 590 feet.
Population: 17,634 (2000); Race: 94.7% White, 0.4% Black, 2.2% Asian, 1.3% American Indian and Alaska Native, 1.2% Hispanic of any race, 0.8% two or more races (2000); Density: 1,425.5 persons per square mile (2000); Age: 25.1% under 18, 11.2% over 64 (2000); Marriage status: 26.7% never married, 58.5% now married, 6.2% widowed, 8.7% divorced (2000); Foreign born: 2.6% (2000); Ancestry (includes multiple ancestries): 39.7% German, 11.7% Irish, 10.8% Polish, 7.8% Belgian, 7.2% French (except Basque) (2000).
Vital Statistics: Birth rate: 84.5 per 10,000 population (1998)
Economy: Austin Straubel Airport to West. Single-family building permits issued: 14 (2001) / 15 (2000); Multi-family building permits issued: 0 (2001) / 2 (2000); Employment by occupation: 14.2% management, 20.3% professional, 11.2% services, 32.7% sales, 0.3% farming, 6.5% construction, 14.8% production (2000).
Income: Per capita income: $23,539 (2000); Median household income: $48,353 (2000); Poverty rate: 4.0% (2000).
Taxes: Total city taxes per capita: $699 (2000); City property taxes per capita: $498 (2000).
Education: High school graduation rate: 89.2% (2000); College graduation rate: 25.5% (2000).
Housing: Homeownership rate: 61.1% (2000); Median home value: $121,300 (2000); Median rent: $486 per month (2000); Median age of housing: 25 years (2000).
Safety: Violent crime rate: 4.5 per 10,000 population; Property crime rate: 496.1 per 10,000 population (2001).
Transportation: Commute to work: 96.0% car, 0.8% public transportation, 0.8% walk, 1.8% work from home (2000); Travel time to work: 59.4% less than 15 minutes, 30.9% 15 to 30 minutes, 5.0% 30 to 45 minutes, 2.2% 45 to 60 minutes, 2.5% 60 minutes or more (2000)

BELLEVUE TOWN (CDP). Covers a land area of 14.268 square miles and a water area of 0.053 square miles. Located at 44.46° N. Lat.; 87.96° W. Long. Elevation is 759 feet.
Population: 11,828 (2000); Race: 95.4% White, 0.7% Black, 0.8% Asian, 1.2% American Indian and Alaska Native, 2.0% Hispanic of any race, 1.0% two or more races (2000); Density: 829.0 persons per square mile (2000); Age: 26.7% under 18, 6.8% over 64 (2000); Marriage status: 26.5% never married, 62.0% now married, 3.4% widowed, 8.1% divorced (2000); Foreign born: 2.2% (2000); Ancestry (includes multiple ancestries): 38.8% German, 17.2% Belgian, 11.8% Polish, 8.2% Irish, 7.8% French (except Basque) (2000).
Economy: Employment by occupation: 12.2% management, 17.2% professional, 10.9% services, 29.5% sales, 0.2% farming, 8.7% construction, 21.5% production (2000).
Income: Per capita income: $24,283 (2000); Median household income: $53,672 (2000); Poverty rate: 4.2% (2000).
Education: High school graduation rate: 88.3% (2000); College graduation rate: 22.0% (2000).
Housing: Homeownership rate: 68.4% (2000); Median home value: $142,100 (2000); Median rent: $511 per month (2000); Median age of housing: 11 years (2000).
Transportation: Commute to work: 95.7% car, 0.2% public transportation, 1.2% walk, 2.5% work from home (2000); Travel time to work: 39.9% less than 15 minutes, 47.5% 15 to 30 minutes, 7.6% 30 to 45 minutes, 2.3% 45 to 60 minutes, 2.7% 60 minutes or more (2000)

DE PERE (city). Covers a land area of 10.606 square miles and a water area of 0.714 square miles. Located at 44.44° N. Lat.; 88.06° W. Long. Elevation is 610 feet.
History: Father Claude Allouez established a Jesuit mission called St. Francis Xavier on this site in 1671. The mission continued until the erection of Fort La Baye in 1717. Construction of a dam and locks at the rapids on the Fox River in 1836 attracted land speculators, and the community of De Pere developed. Many mills were built around the dam after 1849, when it was replaced by a stronger structure.
Population: 20,559 (2000); Race: 96.4% White, 0.3% Black, 1.3% Asian, 0.9% American Indian and Alaska Native, 1.2% Hispanic of any race, 0.7% two or more races (2000); Density: 1,938.4 persons per square mile (2000); Age: 24.5% under 18, 11.5% over 64 (2000); Marriage status: 30.3% never married, 56.2% now married, 5.5% widowed, 8.1% divorced (2000); Foreign born: 1.6% (2000); Ancestry (includes multiple ancestries): 42.7% German, 13.7% Irish, 11.2% Dutch, 10.4% Polish, 8.5% Belgian (2000).
Vital Statistics: Birth rate: 149.8 per 10,000 population (1998)
Economy: Single-family building permits issued: 102 (2001) / 129 (2000); Multi-family building permits issued: 291 (2001) / 99 (2000); Employment by occupation: 15.8% management, 21.1% professional, 11.6% services, 30.7% sales, 0.3% farming, 7.4% construction, 13.0% production (2000).
Income: Per capita income: $24,013 (2000); Median household income: $50,282 (2000); Poverty rate: 4.0% (2000).
Taxes: Total city taxes per capita: $257 (2000); City property taxes per capita: $242 (2000).
Education: High school graduation rate: 90.2% (2000); College graduation rate: 30.1% (2000).

School District(s)

Brown Co Cdeb (PK-12)
2000 Enrollment: 139 920-336-5754
De Pere (PK-12)
2000 Enrollment: 2,840 920-337-1032
West De Pere (PK-12)
2000 Enrollment: 1,881 920-337-1393

Four-year College(s)

Saint Norbert College (Private, Not-for-profit, Roman Catholic)
2001 Enrollment: 2,131 920-403-3181
2001 Tuition: In-state $17,757; Out-of-state $17,757
Housing: Homeownership rate: 65.4% (2000); Median home value: $122,100 (2000); Median rent: $540 per month (2000); Median age of housing: 24 years (2000).
Safety: Violent crime rate: 4.8 per 10,000 population; Property crime rate: 197.0 per 10,000 population (2001).
Newspapers: De Pere Journal (1 x week)
Transportation: Commute to work: 87.5% car, 0.7% public transportation, 8.7% walk, 2.4% work from home (2000); Travel time to work: 50.9% less than 15 minutes, 39.8% 15 to 30 minutes, 5.7% 30 to 45 minutes, 1.7% 45 to 60 minutes, 1.9% 60 minutes or more (2000)

DENMARK (village). Covers a land area of 1.482 square miles and a water area of 0 square miles. Located at 44.34° N. Lat.; 87.83° W. Long. Elevation is 880 feet.
History: Denmark was settled in 1848 by Danes who named their new home for their old.
Population: 1,958 (2000); Race: 97.1% White, 0.7% Black, 0.0% Asian, 1.4% American Indian and Alaska Native, 1.0% Hispanic of any race, 0.6% two or more races (2000); Density: 1,321.5 persons per square mile (2000); Age: 26.9% under 18, 15.0% over 64 (2000); Marriage status: 26.3% never married, 54.6% now married, 9.8% widowed, 9.3% divorced (2000); Foreign born: 0.3% (2000); Ancestry (includes multiple ancestries): 47.0% German, 15.8% Polish, 12.5% Czech, 9.7% Irish, 9.3% Danish (2000).
Economy: Single-family building permits issued: 2 (2001) / 4 (2000); Multi-family building permits issued: 16 (2001) / 6 (2000); Employment by occupation: 7.1% management, 13.5% professional, 14.0% services, 28.2% sales, 1.2% farming, 10.4% construction, 25.6% production (2000).
Income: Per capita income: $18,301 (2000); Median household income: $38,894 (2000); Poverty rate: 5.6% (2000).
Taxes: Total city taxes per capita: $132 (1997); City property taxes per capita: $119 (1997).
Education: High school graduation rate: 85.0% (2000); College graduation rate: 11.9% (2000).

School District(s)

Denmark (PK-12)
2000 Enrollment: 1,680 920-863-2176
Housing: Homeownership rate: 63.9% (2000); Median home value: $95,400 (2000); Median rent: $358 per month (2000); Median age of housing: 33 years (2000).
Safety: Violent crime rate: 5.1 per 10,000 population; Property crime rate: 65.9 per 10,000 population (2001).
Newspapers: The Denmark Press (1 x week)
Transportation: Commute to work: 89.2% car, 0.4% public transportation, 6.6% walk, 2.3% work from home (2000); Travel time to work: 32.6% less than 15 minutes, 43.8% 15 to 30 minutes, 19.0% 30 to 45 minutes, 2.0% 45 to 60 minutes, 2.6% 60 minutes or more (2000)

EATON (town). Covers a land area of 24.223 square miles and a water area of 0.075 square miles. Located at 44.45° N. Lat.; 87.83° W. Long.
Population: 1,414 (2000); Race: 98.1% White, 0.1% Black, 0.9% Asian, 0.4% American Indian and Alaska Native, 0.8% Hispanic of any race, 0.0% two or more races (2000); Density: 58.4 persons per square mile (2000); Age: 30.3% under 18, 7.8% over 64 (2000); Marriage status: 22.3% never married, 69.4% now married, 2.8% widowed, 5.5% divorced (2000); Foreign born:

0.5% (2000); Ancestry (includes multiple ancestries): 40.4% German, 30.3% Polish, 25.2% Belgian, 9.8% Czech, 7.5% Dutch (2000).
Economy: Single-family building permits issued: 13 (2001) / 13 (2000); Multi-family building permits issued: 0 (2001) / 0 (2000); Employment by occupation: 16.1% management, 9.2% professional, 11.6% services, 24.0% sales, 3.0% farming, 14.5% construction, 21.6% production (2000).
Income: Per capita income: $20,697 (2000); Median household income: $57,171 (2000); Poverty rate: 5.7% (2000).
Taxes: Total city taxes per capita: $78 (1997); City property taxes per capita: $72 (1997).
Education: High school graduation rate: 85.5% (2000); College graduation rate: 8.5% (2000).
Housing: Homeownership rate: 88.3% (2000); Median home value: $116,100 (2000); Median rent: $375 per month (2000); Median age of housing: 32 years (2000).
Transportation: Commute to work: 89.2% car, 0.3% public transportation, 2.9% walk, 7.3% work from home (2000); Travel time to work: 24.1% less than 15 minutes, 58.3% 15 to 30 minutes, 13.2% 30 to 45 minutes, 1.6% 45 to 60 minutes, 2.7% 60 minutes or more (2000)

GLENMORE (town). Covers a land area of 32.722 square miles and a water area of 0 square miles. Located at 44.37° N. Lat.; 87.94° W. Long. Elevation is 924 feet.
Population: 1,187 (2000); Race: 98.7% White, 0.0% Black, 0.2% Asian, 0.3% American Indian and Alaska Native, 0.9% Hispanic of any race, 0.6% two or more races (2000); Density: 36.3 persons per square mile (2000); Age: 31.3% under 18, 8.7% over 64 (2000); Marriage status: 30.2% never married, 62.7% now married, 4.1% widowed, 2.9% divorced (2000); Foreign born: 0.9% (2000); Ancestry (includes multiple ancestries): 46.0% German, 15.9% Polish, 14.1% Dutch, 13.9% Belgian, 9.6% Irish (2000).
Economy: Single-family building permits issued: 4 (2001) / 7 (2000); Multi-family building permits issued: 0 (2001) / 0 (2000); Employment by occupation: 14.9% management, 9.6% professional, 8.4% services, 25.2% sales, 4.3% farming, 13.8% construction, 23.8% production (2000).
Income: Per capita income: $19,487 (2000); Median household income: $51,466 (2000); Poverty rate: 2.7% (2000).
Taxes: Total city taxes per capita: $205 (1997); City property taxes per capita: $202 (1997).
Education: High school graduation rate: 82.5% (2000); College graduation rate: 11.6% (2000).
Housing: Homeownership rate: 86.6% (2000); Median home value: $117,100 (2000); Median rent: $425 per month (2000); Median age of housing: 30 years (2000).
Transportation: Commute to work: 89.0% car, 0.2% public transportation, 2.8% walk, 7.4% work from home (2000); Travel time to work: 21.9% less than 15 minutes, 58.3% 15 to 30 minutes, 14.2% 30 to 45 minutes, 1.0% 45 to 60 minutes, 4.6% 60 minutes or more (2000)

GREEN BAY (city). Covers a land area of 43.872 square miles and a water area of 10.452 square miles. Located at 44.51° N. Lat.; 88.01° W. Long. Elevation is 594 feet.
History: In the 1600's, Green Bay was known as La Baye by the French, who established a mission as well as a frontier fort and trading post along the Fox River, where it emptied into the long bay off Lake Michigan. Nicholas Perrot was commandant of the region from 1684 to 1700. Several more forts were established and destroyed during the first half of the 18th century. In 1745, Augustin de Langlade settled here, and for the next several decades the Langlade family controlled the trade and commerce of La Baye during the French and British regimes. British fur traders began about 1761 to call the area Green Bay, for the greenish tint seen in the water in the spring. About 1800 the Americans entered the fur trading business with John Jacob Astor's American Fur Company gaining control in the area after the War of 1812. The completion of the Erie Canal led to the opening of lands for settlement, and Green Bay became a farm market center with a flour mill and hotels in the early 1830's. By 1854, when Green Bay was incorporated, lumber had replaced fur as the principal product.
Population: 102,313 (2000); Race: 86.3% White, 1.3% Black, 3.4% Asian, 3.2% American Indian and Alaska Native, 7.3% Hispanic of any race, 2.1% two or more races (2000); Density: 2,332.1 persons per square mile (2000); Age: 25.4% under 18, 11.7% over 64 (2000); Marriage status: 31.3% never married, 50.8% now married, 6.3% widowed, 11.6% divorced (2000); Foreign born: 6.8% (2000); Ancestry (includes multiple ancestries): 35.0% German, 15.8% Other groups, 9.9% Belgian, 9.8% Polish, 9.4% Irish (2000).
Vital Statistics: Birth rate: 175.7 per 10,000 population (1998)
Economy: Unemployment rate: 7.0% (11/2002); Total civilian labor force: 64,630 (11/2002); Single-family building permits issued: 213 (2001) / 187 (2000); Multi-family building permits issued: 182 (2001) / 16 (2000); Employment by occupation: 10.9% management, 15.8% professional, 15.0% services, 28.0% sales, 0.3% farming, 9.1% construction, 20.9% production (2000).
Income: Per capita income: $19,269 (2000); Median household income: $38,820 (2000); Poverty rate: 10.5% (2000).
Taxes: Total city taxes per capita: $341 (2000); City property taxes per capita: $303 (2000).
Education: High school graduation rate: 82.6% (2000); College graduation rate: 19.3% (2000).

School District(s)

Ashwaubenon (PK-12)
2000 Enrollment: 3,200 920-492-2905
Green Bay Area (PK-12)
2000 Enrollment: 20,104 920-448-2101
Howard-Suamico (PK-12)
2000 Enrollment: 4,245 920-662-7878

Four-year College(s)

Bellin College of Nursing (Private, Not-for-profit)
2001 Enrollment: 160 920-433-3560
2001 Tuition: In-state $10,240; Out-of-state $10,240
University of Wisconsin-Green Bay (Public)
2001 Enrollment: 5,851 920-465-2207
2001 Tuition: In-state $2,776; Out-of-state $11,288

Two-year College(s)

Bellin Hospital School of Radiologic Technology (Private, Not-for-profit, United Methodist)
2001 Enrollment: 10 920-433-3497
2001 Tuition: In-state $1,700; Out-of-state $1,700
Northeast Wisconsin Technical College (Public)
2001 Enrollment: 7,607 920-498-5400
2001 Tuition: In-state $1,920; Out-of-state $14,970
Wisconsin College of Cosmetology Inc (Private, For-profit)
2001 Enrollment: 68 920-336-8888
Martins College of Cosmetology (Private, For-profit)
2001 Enrollment: 72 920-684-3028

Housing: Homeownership rate: 56.0% (2000); Median home value: $96,400 (2000); Median rent: $442 per month (2000); Median age of housing: 34 years (2000).
Hospitals: Bellin Memorial Hospital (167 beds); Brown County Mental Health Center (88 beds); Saint Mary's Hospital Medical Center (158 beds); Saint Vincent Hospital (349 beds)
Safety: Violent crime rate: 26.4 per 10,000 population; Property crime rate: 333.8 per 10,000 population (2001).
Newspapers: Green Bay Press-Gazette (7 x week); The Green Bay News-Chronicle (6 x week)
Transportation: Commute to work: 93.2% car, 1.3% public transportation, 2.8% walk, 1.8% work from home (2000); Travel time to work: 45.4% less than 15 minutes, 42.9% 15 to 30 minutes, 6.4% 30 to 45 minutes, 2.5% 45 to 60 minutes, 2.8% 60 minutes or more (2000); Amtrak: Service available.
Airports: Austin Straubel International (primary service/small hub)
Additional Information Contacts
Green Bay Chamber of Commerce 920-437-8704

GREEN BAY (town). Covers a land area of 22.123 square miles and a water area of 8.545 square miles. Located at 44.58° N. Lat.; 87.79° W. Long. Elevation is 594 feet.
History: Jean Nicolet established a trading post on the site in 1634. The permanent settlement, the oldest in the state, dates from 1701. Key to the Fox-Wisconsin water route and an entry to the Midwest, Green Bay became a fur-trading center. It was occupiedsuccessively by the French (1717), the British (1761), and the Americans (1816). With the decline of the fur trade, Green Bay became the trade center of a lumber and farm area. National Railroad Museum here. Incorporated 1854.
Population: 1,772 (2000); Race: 98.1% White, 0.0% Black, 0.2% Asian, 0.1% American Indian and Alaska Native, 0.0% Hispanic of any race, 0.6% two or more races (2000); Density: 80.1 persons per square mile (2000); Age: 25.8% under 18, 9.1% over 64 (2000); Marriage status: 20.7% never married, 69.6% now married, 3.8% widowed, 5.9% divorced (2000); Foreign born: 0.9% (2000); Ancestry (includes multiple ancestries): 39.7% Belgian, 32.7% German, 7.6% French (except Basque), 7.1% Irish, 5.6% Polish (2000).
Economy: Metropolitan area and important Great Lakes harbor, Green Bay is a port of entry, with heavy shipping and a large wholesale and jobbing trade. Manufacturing of food, printing and paper products, sheet metal processing, dairy processing, motor vehicle parts, fabricated metal products, machinery, medical products, lumber, furniture and paints. The city is also the home of

the Green Bay Packers (Lambeau Field stadium) professional football team. Single-family building permits issued: 23 (2001) / 18 (2000); Multi-family building permits issued: 4 (2001) / 0 (2000); Employment by occupation: 13.8% management, 13.0% professional, 11.0% services, 24.6% sales, 2.2% farming, 15.2% construction, 20.1% production (2000).
Income: Per capita income: $22,928 (2000); Median household income: $60,172 (2000); Poverty rate: 3.1% (2000).
Taxes: Total city taxes per capita: $105 (1997); City property taxes per capita: $98 (1997).
Education: High school graduation rate: 89.8% (2000); College graduation rate: 17.5% (2000).
Housing: Homeownership rate: 87.7% (2000); Median home value: $157,400 (2000); Median rent: $513 per month (2000); Median age of housing: 23 years (2000).
Transportation: Commute to work: 92.0% car, 0.0% public transportation, 1.2% walk, 6.5% work from home (2000); Travel time to work: 17.3% less than 15 minutes, 47.0% 15 to 30 minutes, 28.1% 30 to 45 minutes, 3.7% 45 to 60 minutes, 4.0% 60 minutes or more (2000); Amtrak: Service available.

GREENLEAF (unincorporated postal area, zip code 54126). Covers a land area of 76.907 square miles and a water area of 1.395 square miles. Located at 44.29° N. Lat.; 88.05° W. Long. Elevation is 735 feet.
Population: 3,638 (2000); Race: 98.6% White, 0.2% Black, 0.0% Asian, 0.1% American Indian and Alaska Native, 1.4% Hispanic of any race, 0.7% two or more races (2000); Density: 47.3 persons per square mile (2000); Age: 29.7% under 18, 8.0% over 64 (2000); Marriage status: 23.7% never married, 67.7% now married, 3.6% widowed, 5.0% divorced (2000); Foreign born: 1.3% (2000); Ancestry (includes multiple ancestries): 60.1% German, 15.1% Dutch, 11.9% Irish, 7.2% Belgian, 7.0% Polish (2000).
Economy: Employment by occupation: 16.1% management, 11.9% professional, 10.5% services, 20.8% sales, 4.6% farming, 13.4% construction, 22.7% production (2000).
Income: Per capita income: $20,662 (2000); Median household income: $52,639 (2000); Poverty rate: 3.7% (2000).
Education: High school graduation rate: 85.6% (2000); College graduation rate: 13.0% (2000).
Housing: Homeownership rate: 87.8% (2000); Median home value: $119,600 (2000); Median rent: $469 per month (2000); Median age of housing: 34 years (2000).
Transportation: Commute to work: 85.7% car, 0.4% public transportation, 3.4% walk, 9.8% work from home (2000); Travel time to work: 23.9% less than 15 minutes, 46.8% 15 to 30 minutes, 22.3% 30 to 45 minutes, 4.3% 45 to 60 minutes, 2.7% 60 minutes or more (2000)

HOBART (town). Covers a land area of 33.153 square miles and a water area of 0.109 square miles. Located at 44.51° N. Lat.; 88.14° W. Long.
Population: 5,090 (2000); Race: 80.2% White, 0.2% Black, 1.5% Asian, 15.9% American Indian and Alaska Native, 0.8% Hispanic of any race, 1.0% two or more races (2000); Density: 153.5 persons per square mile (2000); Age: 30.9% under 18, 7.5% over 64 (2000); Marriage status: 18.2% never married, 71.2% now married, 5.1% widowed, 5.4% divorced (2000); Foreign born: 2.1% (2000); Ancestry (includes multiple ancestries): 36.5% German, 19.6% Other groups, 11.1% Belgian, 10.2% Polish, 9.5% Dutch (2000).
Economy: Single-family building permits issued: 66 (2001) / 52 (2000); Multi-family building permits issued: 2 (2001) / 6 (2000); Employment by occupation: 19.2% management, 17.3% professional, 11.9% services, 28.6% sales, 1.2% farming, 8.3% construction, 13.4% production (2000).
Income: Per capita income: $29,059 (2000); Median household income: $69,034 (2000); Poverty rate: 6.5% (2000).
Taxes: Total city taxes per capita: $135 (1997); City property taxes per capita: $130 (1997).
Education: High school graduation rate: 88.8% (2000); College graduation rate: 28.7% (2000).
Housing: Homeownership rate: 89.9% (2000); Median home value: $177,700 (2000); Median rent: $337 per month (2000); Median age of housing: 19 years (2000).
Transportation: Commute to work: 92.0% car, 0.8% public transportation, 1.5% walk, 4.4% work from home (2000); Travel time to work: 40.7% less than 15 minutes, 49.2% 15 to 30 minutes, 6.3% 30 to 45 minutes, 2.8% 45 to 60 minutes, 1.0% 60 minutes or more (2000)

HOLLAND (town). Covers a land area of 35.970 square miles and a water area of 0 square miles. Located at 44.27° N. Lat.; 88.12° W. Long. Elevation is 769 feet.
Population: 1,339 (2000); Race: 99.5% White, 0.3% Black, 0.0% Asian, 0.2% American Indian and Alaska Native, 0.6% Hispanic of any race, 0.0% two or more races (2000); Density: 37.2 persons per square mile (2000); Age: 32.0% under 18, 8.1% over 64 (2000); Marriage status: 27.6% never married, 65.3% now married, 3.8% widowed, 3.4% divorced (2000); Foreign born: 0.6% (2000); Ancestry (includes multiple ancestries): 54.9% German, 27.7% Dutch, 14.4% Irish, 6.5% United States or American, 4.6% Polish (2000).
Economy: Single-family building permits issued: 18 (2001) / 11 (2000); Multi-family building permits issued: 0 (2001) / 0 (2000); Employment by occupation: 16.4% management, 11.7% professional, 11.4% services, 19.4% sales, 6.1% farming, 10.9% construction, 24.1% production (2000).
Income: Per capita income: $20,481 (2000); Median household income: $56,406 (2000); Poverty rate: 3.6% (2000).
Taxes: Total city taxes per capita: $172 (1997); City property taxes per capita: $172 (1997).
Education: High school graduation rate: 87.3% (2000); College graduation rate: 9.9% (2000).
Housing: Homeownership rate: 88.7% (2000); Median home value: $125,200 (2000); Median rent: $432 per month (2000); Median age of housing: 31 years (2000).
Transportation: Commute to work: 84.6% car, 1.0% public transportation, 3.7% walk, 10.1% work from home (2000); Travel time to work: 34.1% less than 15 minutes, 37.0% 15 to 30 minutes, 21.3% 30 to 45 minutes, 4.7% 45 to 60 minutes, 3.1% 60 minutes or more (2000)

HOWARD (village). Covers a land area of 17.974 square miles and a water area of 4.969 square miles. Located at 44.56° N. Lat.; 88.08° W. Long. Elevation is 620 feet.
Population: 13,546 (2000); Race: 96.9% White, 0.9% Black, 0.5% Asian, 0.3% American Indian and Alaska Native, 1.4% Hispanic of any race, 1.1% two or more races (2000); Density: 753.7 persons per square mile (2000); Age: 27.8% under 18, 7.6% over 64 (2000); Marriage status: 25.0% never married, 61.1% now married, 4.3% widowed, 9.6% divorced (2000); Foreign born: 1.0% (2000); Ancestry (includes multiple ancestries): 44.8% German, 15.1% Polish, 11.8% Irish, 10.3% Belgian, 7.9% French (except Basque) (2000).
Economy: Railroad junction. Single-family building permits issued: 202 (2001) / 166 (2000); Multi-family building permits issued: 146 (2001) / 58 (2000); Employment by occupation: 12.3% management, 18.2% professional, 10.8% services, 29.8% sales, 0.0% farming, 10.9% construction, 17.9% production (2000).
Income: Per capita income: $21,688 (2000); Median household income: $51,974 (2000); Poverty rate: 4.3% (2000).
Taxes: Total city taxes per capita: $316 (1997); City property taxes per capita: $302 (1997).
Education: High school graduation rate: 91.3% (2000); College graduation rate: 22.8% (2000).
Housing: Homeownership rate: 63.8% (2000); Median home value: $127,100 (2000); Median rent: $551 per month (2000); Median age of housing: 17 years (2000).
Transportation: Commute to work: 96.8% car, 0.2% public transportation, 0.7% walk, 2.1% work from home (2000); Travel time to work: 37.3% less than 15 minutes, 52.6% 15 to 30 minutes, 5.1% 30 to 45 minutes, 2.2% 45 to 60 minutes, 2.8% 60 minutes or more (2000)

HUMBOLDT (town). Covers a land area of 23.949 square miles and a water area of 0 square miles. Located at 44.50° N. Lat.; 87.83° W. Long. Elevation is 810 feet.
Population: 1,338 (2000); Race: 97.3% White, 0.4% Black, 0.0% Asian, 1.0% American Indian and Alaska Native, 1.1% Hispanic of any race, 0.4% two or more races (2000); Density: 55.9 persons per square mile (2000); Age: 27.5% under 18, 8.7% over 64 (2000); Marriage status: 27.2% never married, 63.6% now married, 3.1% widowed, 6.1% divorced (2000); Foreign born: 0.5% (2000); Ancestry (includes multiple ancestries): 41.8% Belgian, 32.1% German, 10.9% Polish, 7.5% French (except Basque), 7.5% Irish (2000).
Economy: Single-family building permits issued: 10 (2001) / 13 (2000); Multi-family building permits issued: 0 (2001) / 0 (2000); Employment by occupation: 10.9% management, 9.0% professional, 11.9% services, 24.6% sales, 3.3% farming, 19.8% construction, 20.5% production (2000).
Income: Per capita income: $19,813 (2000); Median household income: $54,821 (2000); Poverty rate: 2.2% (2000).
Taxes: Total city taxes per capita: $66 (1997); City property taxes per capita: $63 (1997).
Education: High school graduation rate: 83.4% (2000); College graduation rate: 9.9% (2000).
Housing: Homeownership rate: 89.8% (2000); Median home value: $125,200 (2000); Median rent: $411 per month (2000); Median age of housing: 30 years (2000).

Transportation: Commute to work: 88.9% car, 0.0% public transportation, 1.7% walk, 9.5% work from home (2000); Travel time to work: 21.6% less than 15 minutes, 59.0% 15 to 30 minutes, 9.3% 30 to 45 minutes, 1.2% 45 to 60 minutes, 9.0% 60 minutes or more (2000)

LAWRENCE (town). Covers a land area of 15.412 square miles and a water area of 0.646 square miles. Located at 44.40° N. Lat.; 88.14° W. Long.
Population: 1,548 (2000); Race: 98.1% White, 0.8% Black, 0.0% Asian, 0.2% American Indian and Alaska Native, 0.5% Hispanic of any race, 0.8% two or more races (2000); Density: 100.4 persons per square mile (2000); Age: 29.3% under 18, 5.6% over 64 (2000); Marriage status: 16.9% never married, 75.4% now married, 1.9% widowed, 5.7% divorced (2000); Foreign born: 0.8% (2000); Ancestry (includes multiple ancestries): 43.2% German, 21.6% Dutch, 12.9% Irish, 10.2% Belgian, 9.9% Polish (2000).
Economy: Single-family building permits issued: 26 (2001) / 26 (2000); Multi-family building permits issued: 10 (2001) / 10 (2000); Employment by occupation: 17.2% management, 15.5% professional, 8.7% services, 26.6% sales, 1.0% farming, 11.2% construction, 19.7% production (2000).
Income: Per capita income: $29,002 (2000); Median household income: $66,875 (2000); Poverty rate: 1.8% (2000).
Taxes: Total city taxes per capita: $391 (2000); City property taxes per capita: $345 (2000).
Education: High school graduation rate: 92.6% (2000); College graduation rate: 21.0% (2000).
Housing: Homeownership rate: 96.8% (2000); Median home value: $163,300 (2000); Median rent: $661 per month (2000); Median age of housing: 16 years (2000).
Transportation: Commute to work: 91.7% car, 0.0% public transportation, 1.0% walk, 6.8% work from home (2000); Travel time to work: 38.6% less than 15 minutes, 50.4% 15 to 30 minutes, 8.1% 30 to 45 minutes, 1.2% 45 to 60 minutes, 1.6% 60 minutes or more (2000)

LEDGEVIEW (town). Covers a land area of 17.616 square miles and a water area of 0.139 square miles. Located at 44.42° N. Lat.; 87.98° W. Long.
Population: 3,363 (2000); Race: 97.7% White, 0.3% Black, 0.9% Asian, 0.7% American Indian and Alaska Native, 0.6% Hispanic of any race, 0.4% two or more races (2000); Density: 190.9 persons per square mile (2000); Age: 31.9% under 18, 7.1% over 64 (2000); Marriage status: 19.4% never married, 71.0% now married, 4.0% widowed, 5.5% divorced (2000); Foreign born: 2.1% (2000); Ancestry (includes multiple ancestries): 44.5% German, 13.2% Irish, 12.4% Dutch, 10.7% Belgian, 7.7% Polish (2000).
Economy: Single-family building permits issued: 65 (2001) / 35 (2000); Multi-family building permits issued: 104 (2001) / 51 (2000); Employment by occupation: 18.7% management, 26.8% professional, 6.2% services, 23.9% sales, 0.8% farming, 11.6% construction, 11.9% production (2000).
Income: Per capita income: $31,346 (2000); Median household income: $67,188 (2000); Poverty rate: 2.9% (2000).
Education: High school graduation rate: 91.8% (2000); College graduation rate: 40.0% (2000).
Housing: Homeownership rate: 79.2% (2000); Median home value: $185,900 (2000); Median rent: $595 per month (2000); Median age of housing: 5 years (2000).
Transportation: Commute to work: 92.1% car, 0.9% public transportation, 0.4% walk, 6.4% work from home (2000); Travel time to work: 31.9% less than 15 minutes, 52.0% 15 to 30 minutes, 9.4% 30 to 45 minutes, 2.6% 45 to 60 minutes, 4.2% 60 minutes or more (2000)

MORRISON (town). Covers a land area of 35.066 square miles and a water area of 1.395 square miles. Located at 44.28° N. Lat.; 87.94° W. Long. Elevation is 919 feet.
Population: 1,651 (2000); Race: 98.6% White, 0.3% Black, 0.0% Asian, 0.0% American Indian and Alaska Native, 1.1% Hispanic of any race, 0.4% two or more races (2000); Density: 47.1 persons per square mile (2000); Age: 28.4% under 18, 10.2% over 64 (2000); Marriage status: 24.0% never married, 66.8% now married, 4.2% widowed, 5.1% divorced (2000); Foreign born: 1.0% (2000); Ancestry (includes multiple ancestries): 65.3% German, 12.2% Irish, 7.1% Dutch, 5.8% Polish, 5.7% Czech (2000).
Economy: Single-family building permits issued: 7 (2001) / 11 (2000); Multi-family building permits issued: 0 (2001) / 0 (2000); Employment by occupation: 19.0% management, 12.6% professional, 11.6% services, 19.0% sales, 2.9% farming, 12.5% construction, 22.5% production (2000).
Income: Per capita income: $19,841 (2000); Median household income: $55,461 (2000); Poverty rate: 6.2% (2000).
Taxes: Total city taxes per capita: $118 (1997); City property taxes per capita: $113 (1997).
Education: High school graduation rate: 82.3% (2000); College graduation rate: 13.0% (2000).
Housing: Homeownership rate: 90.2% (2000); Median home value: $107,900 (2000); Median rent: $388 per month (2000); Median age of housing: 60+ years (2000).
Transportation: Commute to work: 85.1% car, 0.4% public transportation, 4.5% walk, 8.8% work from home (2000); Travel time to work: 20.0% less than 15 minutes, 46.0% 15 to 30 minutes, 27.2% 30 to 45 minutes, 3.0% 45 to 60 minutes, 3.7% 60 minutes or more (2000)

NEW DENMARK (town). Covers a land area of 34.716 square miles and a water area of 0.121 square miles. Located at 44.37° N. Lat.; 87.83° W. Long.
Population: 1,482 (2000); Race: 99.0% White, 0.0% Black, 0.0% Asian, 0.5% American Indian and Alaska Native, 0.3% Hispanic of any race, 0.5% two or more races (2000); Density: 42.7 persons per square mile (2000); Age: 28.3% under 18, 9.6% over 64 (2000); Marriage status: 21.8% never married, 69.5% now married, 3.3% widowed, 5.4% divorced (2000); Foreign born: 0.7% (2000); Ancestry (includes multiple ancestries): 43.6% German, 15.7% Polish, 12.0% Belgian, 12.0% Czech, 8.5% Irish (2000).
Economy: Single-family building permits issued: 16 (2001) / 13 (2000); Multi-family building permits issued: 0 (2001) / 0 (2000); Employment by occupation: 16.6% management, 15.8% professional, 9.2% services, 22.5% sales, 2.7% farming, 13.7% construction, 19.4% production (2000).
Income: Per capita income: $23,313 (2000); Median household income: $57,891 (2000); Poverty rate: 4.3% (2000).
Taxes: Total city taxes per capita: $105 (1997); City property taxes per capita: $100 (1997).
Education: High school graduation rate: 83.7% (2000); College graduation rate: 16.2% (2000).
Housing: Homeownership rate: 89.4% (2000); Median home value: $121,700 (2000); Median rent: $463 per month (2000); Median age of housing: 36 years (2000).
Transportation: Commute to work: 91.1% car, 0.2% public transportation, 0.7% walk, 7.1% work from home (2000); Travel time to work: 25.4% less than 15 minutes, 48.6% 15 to 30 minutes, 22.4% 30 to 45 minutes, 1.5% 45 to 60 minutes, 2.1% 60 minutes or more (2000)

NEW FRANKEN (unincorporated postal area, zip code 54229). Covers a land area of 43.066 square miles and a water area of 0.011 square miles. Located at 44.56° N. Lat.; 87.81° W. Long. Elevation is 813 feet.
Population: 3,724 (2000); Race: 96.5% White, 1.8% Black, 0.1% Asian, 0.5% American Indian and Alaska Native, 0.8% Hispanic of any race, 0.4% two or more races (2000); Density: 86.5 persons per square mile (2000); Age: 28.0% under 18, 7.4% over 64 (2000); Marriage status: 22.7% never married, 68.1% now married, 2.5% widowed, 6.6% divorced (2000); Foreign born: 0.7% (2000); Ancestry (includes multiple ancestries): 38.8% German, 35.1% Belgian, 9.6% Irish, 9.1% Polish, 6.6% French (except Basque) (2000).
Economy: Employment by occupation: 14.1% management, 13.8% professional, 11.9% services, 27.4% sales, 2.0% farming, 14.8% construction, 16.0% production (2000).
Income: Per capita income: $21,849 (2000); Median household income: $58,198 (2000); Poverty rate: 2.1% (2000).
Education: High school graduation rate: 89.6% (2000); College graduation rate: 15.6% (2000).
Housing: Homeownership rate: 91.3% (2000); Median home value: $143,200 (2000); Median rent: $525 per month (2000); Median age of housing: 18 years (2000).
Transportation: Commute to work: 92.5% car, 0.0% public transportation, 0.7% walk, 6.5% work from home (2000); Travel time to work: 20.9% less than 15 minutes, 54.2% 15 to 30 minutes, 19.2% 30 to 45 minutes, 3.0% 45 to 60 minutes, 2.6% 60 minutes or more (2000)

ONEIDA (CDP). Covers a land area of 5.653 square miles and a water area of 0.056 square miles. Located at 44.49° N. Lat.; 88.18° W. Long. Elevation is 704 feet.
Population: 1,070 (2000); Race: 31.1% White, 1.2% Black, 8.7% Asian, 54.7% American Indian and Alaska Native, 4.3% Hispanic of any race, 2.4% two or more races (2000); Density: 189.3 persons per square mile (2000); Age: 35.6% under 18, 12.4% over 64 (2000); Marriage status: 23.1% never married, 55.2% now married, 13.1% widowed, 8.6% divorced (2000); Foreign born: 5.3% (2000); Ancestry (includes multiple ancestries): 59.4% Other groups, 19.4% German, 6.6% Dutch, 6.4% French (except Basque), 5.6% Irish (2000).

Economy: Employment by occupation: 15.8% management, 12.6% professional, 15.8% services, 21.4% sales, 5.1% farming, 10.0% construction, 19.4% production (2000).
Income: Per capita income: $13,766 (2000); Median household income: $31,588 (2000); Poverty rate: 18.5% (2000).
Education: High school graduation rate: 71.7% (2000); College graduation rate: 13.6% (2000).
Housing: Homeownership rate: 70.9% (2000); Median home value: $102,000 (2000); Median rent: $336 per month (2000); Median age of housing: 26 years (2000).
Transportation: Commute to work: 84.7% car, 5.4% public transportation, 7.9% walk, 1.5% work from home (2000); Travel time to work: 42.7% less than 15 minutes, 45.7% 15 to 30 minutes, 10.6% 30 to 45 minutes, 0.0% 45 to 60 minutes, 1.0% 60 minutes or more (2000)

PITTSFIELD (town). Covers a land area of 32.140 square miles and a water area of 0.023 square miles. Located at 44.62° N. Lat.; 88.18° W. Long. Elevation is 806 feet.
Population: 2,433 (2000); Race: 98.3% White, 0.5% Black, 0.1% Asian, 0.5% American Indian and Alaska Native, 0.4% Hispanic of any race, 0.2% two or more races (2000); Density: 75.7 persons per square mile (2000); Age: 30.7% under 18, 8.0% over 64 (2000); Marriage status: 22.7% never married, 67.4% now married, 5.5% widowed, 4.4% divorced (2000); Foreign born: 0.8% (2000); Ancestry (includes multiple ancestries): 44.9% German, 22.7% Polish, 10.5% Irish, 8.6% Dutch, 7.4% Belgian (2000).
Economy: Single-family building permits issued: 11 (2001) / 31 (2000); Multi-family building permits issued: 0 (2001) / 0 (2000); Employment by occupation: 13.4% management, 13.7% professional, 12.4% services, 23.1% sales, 0.2% farming, 11.0% construction, 26.1% production (2000).
Income: Per capita income: $22,000 (2000); Median household income: $61,250 (2000); Poverty rate: 2.3% (2000).
Taxes: Total city taxes per capita: $43 (1997); City property taxes per capita: $37 (1997).
Education: High school graduation rate: 89.7% (2000); College graduation rate: 16.2% (2000).
Housing: Homeownership rate: 96.9% (2000); Median home value: $143,200 (2000); Median rent: $658 per month (2000); Median age of housing: 24 years (2000).
Transportation: Commute to work: 92.9% car, 0.5% public transportation, 2.0% walk, 4.1% work from home (2000); Travel time to work: 22.8% less than 15 minutes, 53.5% 15 to 30 minutes, 19.1% 30 to 45 minutes, 1.9% 45 to 60 minutes, 2.7% 60 minutes or more (2000)

PULASKI (village). Covers a land area of 2.497 square miles and a water area of 0.039 square miles. Located at 44.66° N. Lat.; 88.23° W. Long. Elevation is 810 feet.
Population: 3,060 (2000); Race: 97.6% White, 0.2% Black, 0.7% Asian, 1.3% American Indian and Alaska Native, 0.8% Hispanic of any race, 0.1% two or more races (2000); Density: 1,225.4 persons per square mile (2000); Age: 27.7% under 18, 13.7% over 64 (2000); Marriage status: 29.3% never married, 50.6% now married, 8.0% widowed, 12.1% divorced (2000); Foreign born: 0.4% (2000); Ancestry (includes multiple ancestries): 40.5% Polish, 37.5% German, 10.8% Irish, 5.0% Other groups, 4.7% Belgian (2000).
Economy: In dairying and farming area. Canning. Manufacturing of machinery. Single-family building permits issued: 15 (2001) / 11 (2000); Multi-family building permits issued: 8 (2001) / 87 (2000); Employment by occupation: 9.7% management, 15.9% professional, 12.7% services, 24.4% sales, 0.4% farming, 10.4% construction, 26.6% production (2000).
Income: Per capita income: $18,711 (2000); Median household income: $43,017 (2000); Poverty rate: 6.9% (2000).
Taxes: Total city taxes per capita: $330 (1997); City property taxes per capita: $309 (1997).
Education: High school graduation rate: 84.1% (2000); College graduation rate: 14.5% (2000).

School District(s)

Pulaski Community (PK-12)
2000 Enrollment: 3,428 920-822-6000

Housing: Homeownership rate: 60.2% (2000); Median home value: $97,000 (2000); Median rent: $444 per month (2000); Median age of housing: 23 years (2000).
Safety: Violent crime rate: 6.5 per 10,000 population; Property crime rate: 107.1 per 10,000 population (2001).
Transportation: Commute to work: 94.7% car, 0.2% public transportation, 3.4% walk, 0.5% work from home (2000); Travel time to work: 37.6% less than 15 minutes, 39.5% 15 to 30 minutes, 19.9% 30 to 45 minutes, 1.5% 45 to 60 minutes, 1.6% 60 minutes or more (2000)

ROCKLAND (town). Covers a land area of 22.308 square miles and a water area of 0.562 square miles. Located at 44.38° N. Lat.; 88.07° W. Long.
Population: 1,522 (2000); Race: 99.2% White, 0.4% Black, 0.0% Asian, 0.4% American Indian and Alaska Native, 0.0% Hispanic of any race, 0.0% two or more races (2000); Density: 68.2 persons per square mile (2000); Age: 32.1% under 18, 7.2% over 64 (2000); Marriage status: 22.3% never married, 72.5% now married, 2.3% widowed, 2.9% divorced (2000); Foreign born: 1.2% (2000); Ancestry (includes multiple ancestries): 45.4% German, 18.2% Dutch, 9.2% Belgian, 8.6% United States or American, 8.0% Polish (2000).
Economy: Single-family building permits issued: 24 (2001) / 24 (2000); Multi-family building permits issued: 0 (2001) / 0 (2000); Employment by occupation: 23.1% management, 19.4% professional, 7.2% services, 21.8% sales, 1.8% farming, 10.8% construction, 15.9% production (2000).
Income: Per capita income: $28,484 (2000); Median household income: $69,583 (2000); Poverty rate: 1.4% (2000).
Taxes: Total city taxes per capita: $120 (1997); City property taxes per capita: $117 (1997).
Education: High school graduation rate: 92.3% (2000); College graduation rate: 28.1% (2000).
Housing: Homeownership rate: 92.4% (2000); Median home value: $184,200 (2000); Median rent: $700 per month (2000); Median age of housing: 16 years (2000).
Transportation: Commute to work: 88.4% car, 0.5% public transportation, 2.5% walk, 6.5% work from home (2000); Travel time to work: 27.4% less than 15 minutes, 60.4% 15 to 30 minutes, 8.1% 30 to 45 minutes, 1.0% 45 to 60 minutes, 3.0% 60 minutes or more (2000)

SCOTT (town). Covers a land area of 19.695 square miles and a water area of 34.574 square miles. Located at 44.58° N. Lat.; 87.87° W. Long.
Population: 3,712 (2000); Race: 95.8% White, 2.2% Black, 0.2% Asian, 0.4% American Indian and Alaska Native, 0.9% Hispanic of any race, 0.7% two or more races (2000); Density: 188.5 persons per square mile (2000); Age: 22.0% under 18, 9.5% over 64 (2000); Marriage status: 33.0% never married, 57.4% now married, 2.5% widowed, 7.1% divorced (2000); Foreign born: 1.1% (2000); Ancestry (includes multiple ancestries): 47.2% German, 21.6% Belgian, 13.8% Irish, 9.4% Polish, 7.1% Dutch (2000).
Economy: Single-family building permits issued: 34 (2001) / 42 (2000); Multi-family building permits issued: 0 (2001) / 0 (2000); Employment by occupation: 13.1% management, 17.6% professional, 13.5% services, 32.7% sales, 0.7% farming, 10.8% construction, 11.5% production (2000).
Income: Per capita income: $21,992 (2000); Median household income: $58,051 (2000); Poverty rate: 2.0% (2000).
Taxes: Total city taxes per capita: $72 (1997); City property taxes per capita: $62 (1997).
Education: High school graduation rate: 90.3% (2000); College graduation rate: 24.3% (2000).
Housing: Homeownership rate: 93.6% (2000); Median home value: $150,600 (2000); Median rent: $603 per month (2000); Median age of housing: 19 years (2000).
Transportation: Commute to work: 89.4% car, 0.0% public transportation, 6.5% walk, 3.7% work from home (2000); Travel time to work: 22.7% less than 15 minutes, 60.0% 15 to 30 minutes, 11.9% 30 to 45 minutes, 2.5% 45 to 60 minutes, 3.0% 60 minutes or more (2000)

SUAMICO (town). Aka Big Suamico. Covers a land area of 36.245 square miles and a water area of 23.061 square miles. Located at 44.63° N. Lat.; 88.07° W. Long. Elevation is 593 feet.
Population: 8,686 (2000); Race: 97.2% White, 0.3% Black, 0.1% Asian, 1.2% American Indian and Alaska Native, 0.5% Hispanic of any race, 1.0% two or more races (2000); Density: 239.6 persons per square mile (2000); Age: 29.1% under 18, 4.6% over 64 (2000); Marriage status: 19.0% never married, 73.5% now married, 1.7% widowed, 5.9% divorced (2000); Foreign born: 0.6% (2000); Ancestry (includes multiple ancestries): 40.2% German, 14.0% Polish, 12.5% Belgian, 11.7% Irish, 7.4% French (except Basque) (2000).
Economy: Single-family building permits issued: 158 (2001) / 168 (2000); Multi-family building permits issued: 0 (2001) / 8 (2000); Employment by occupation: 17.0% management, 16.0% professional, 6.7% services, 26.3% sales, 0.5% farming, 13.4% construction, 20.1% production (2000).
Income: Per capita income: $24,735 (2000); Median household income: $65,189 (2000); Poverty rate: 1.8% (2000).
Taxes: Total city taxes per capita: $186 (2000); City property taxes per capita: $176 (2000).

Education: High school graduation rate: 91.8% (2000); College graduation rate: 21.1% (2000).
Housing: Homeownership rate: 92.3% (2000); Median home value: $157,800 (2000); Median rent: $613 per month (2000); Median age of housing: 11 years (2000).
Transportation: Commute to work: 96.1% car, 0.3% public transportation, 0.7% walk, 2.1% work from home (2000); Travel time to work: 20.2% less than 15 minutes, 64.7% 15 to 30 minutes, 9.6% 30 to 45 minutes, 1.7% 45 to 60 minutes, 3.8% 60 minutes or more (2000)

WRIGHTSTOWN (village). Covers a land area of 2.472 square miles and a water area of 0.245 square miles. Located at 44.32° N. Lat.; 88.16° W. Long. Elevation is 650 feet.
Population: 1,934 (2000); Race: 94.7% White, 0.4% Black, 2.2% Asian, 0.4% American Indian and Alaska Native, 1.3% Hispanic of any race, 1.9% two or more races (2000); Density: 782.3 persons per square mile (2000); Age: 33.2% under 18, 6.0% over 64 (2000); Marriage status: 25.3% never married, 63.1% now married, 4.3% widowed, 7.3% divorced (2000); Foreign born: 3.0% (2000); Ancestry (includes multiple ancestries): 48.7% German, 19.1% Dutch, 8.5% Irish, 7.7% Polish, 7.5% Belgian (2000).
Economy: Single-family building permits issued: 21 (2001) / 21 (2000); Multi-family building permits issued: 8 (2001) / 8 (2000); Employment by occupation: 13.3% management, 14.3% professional, 9.3% services, 26.2% sales, 0.2% farming, 10.6% construction, 26.1% production (2000).
Income: Per capita income: $20,767 (2000); Median household income: $52,885 (2000); Poverty rate: 5.4% (2000).
Taxes: Total city taxes per capita: $283 (1997); City property taxes per capita: $270 (1997).
Education: High school graduation rate: 92.4% (2000); College graduation rate: 20.5% (2000).

School District(s)

Wrightstown Community (KG-12)
2000 Enrollment: 946 920-532-5551
Housing: Homeownership rate: 74.7% (2000); Median home value: $117,000 (2000); Median rent: $499 per month (2000); Median age of housing: 20 years (2000).
Transportation: Commute to work: 93.8% car, 0.0% public transportation, 2.9% walk, 2.4% work from home (2000); Travel time to work: 27.8% less than 15 minutes, 53.5% 15 to 30 minutes, 14.1% 30 to 45 minutes, 2.4% 45 to 60 minutes, 2.2% 60 minutes or more (2000)

WRIGHTSTOWN (town). Covers a land area of 33.525 square miles and a water area of 0.164 square miles. Located at 44.33° N. Lat.; 88.10° W. Long. Elevation is 650 feet.
Population: 2,013 (2000); Race: 98.6% White, 0.0% Black, 0.1% Asian, 0.1% American Indian and Alaska Native, 1.4% Hispanic of any race, 1.0% two or more races (2000); Density: 60.0 persons per square mile (2000); Age: 29.1% under 18, 8.4% over 64 (2000); Marriage status: 21.4% never married, 69.0% now married, 4.9% widowed, 4.7% divorced (2000); Foreign born: 1.3% (2000); Ancestry (includes multiple ancestries): 48.9% German, 21.6% Dutch, 11.9% Irish, 9.6% Belgian, 7.4% Polish (2000).
Economy: In dairying region; cheese spreads. Single-family building permits issued: 14 (2001) / 21 (2000); Multi-family building permits issued: 16 (2001) / 0 (2000); Employment by occupation: 14.7% management, 13.3% professional, 9.4% services, 24.3% sales, 3.2% farming, 12.0% construction, 23.1% production (2000).
Income: Per capita income: $23,256 (2000); Median household income: $54,712 (2000); Poverty rate: 2.7% (2000).
Taxes: Total city taxes per capita: $140 (1997); City property taxes per capita: $126 (1997).
Education: High school graduation rate: 86.3% (2000); College graduation rate: 17.1% (2000).
Housing: Homeownership rate: 85.4% (2000); Median home value: $134,900 (2000); Median rent: $484 per month (2000); Median age of housing: 24 years (2000).
Transportation: Commute to work: 87.7% car, 0.0% public transportation, 2.6% walk, 8.7% work from home (2000); Travel time to work: 25.3% less than 15 minutes, 50.6% 15 to 30 minutes, 19.1% 30 to 45 minutes, 3.7% 45 to 60 minutes, 1.4% 60 minutes or more (2000)

Buffalo County

Located in western Wisconsin; bounded on the northwest by the Chippewa River, on the west and southwest by the Mississippi River, and on the southeast by the Trempealeau River. Covers a land area of 684.50 square miles, a water area of 25.10 square miles, and is located in the Central Time Zone. The county government was organized in 1853. County seat is Alma.

Weather Station: Alma Dam 4 — Elevation: 669 feet

	Jan	Feb	Mar	Apr	May	Jun	Jul	Aug	Sep	Oct	Nov	Dec
High	24	30	41	57	70	79	83	80	72	60	42	29
Low	7	13	24	37	49	58	63	61	52	41	27	14
Precip	1.0	0.7	1.8	3.3	3.9	4.3	5.2	4.7	4.1	2.5	2.3	0.9
Snow	10.8	5.9	7.4	1.3	tr	0.0	0.0	0.0	0.0	tr	3.7	8.4

High and Low temperatures in degrees Fahrenheit; Precipitation and Snow in inches

Population: 13,804 (2000); Race: 98.9% White, 0.2% Black, 0.2% Asian, 0.3% American Indian and Alaska Native, 0.6% Hispanic of any race, 0.3% two or more races (2000); Density: 20.2 persons per square mile (2000); Age: 25.2% under 18, 16.7% over 64 (2000).
Religion: Five largest groups: 26.5% Catholic Church, 22.1% Evangelical Lutheran Church in America, 7.4% Wisconsin Evangelical Lutheran Synod, 7.4% Lutheran Church—Missouri Synod, 3.9% The United Methodist Church (2000).
Economy: Unemployment rate: 3.7% (11/2002); Total civilian labor force: 7,931 (11/2002); Leading industries: 10.9% health care and social assistance; 10.3% accommodation & food services; 8.2% retail trade (2000); Companies that employ more than 1,000 persons: 1 (2000); Companies that employ more than 100 persons: 3 (2000); Farms: 1,000 totaling 308,581 acres (1997); Minority business ownership rate: 0.0% (1997); Women business ownership rate: 25.1% (1997); Retail sales per capita: $3,208 (1997). Single-family building permits issued: 73 (2001) / 69 (2000); Multi-family building permits issued: 18 (2001) / 12 (2000).
Income: Per capita income: $18,123 (2000); Median household income: $37,200 (2000); Poverty rate: 7.5% (2000); Bankruptcy rate: 2.28% (2001).
Taxes: Total county taxes per capita: $240 (1997); County property taxes per capita: $208 (1997).
Education: High school graduation rate: 84.1% (2000); College graduation rate: 14.0% (2000).
Housing: Homeownership rate: 76.5% (2000); Median home value: $78,600 (2000); Median rent: $320 per month (2000); Median age of housing: 44 years (2000).
Health: Birth rate: 105.0 per 10,000 population (1998); Age adjusted death rate: 85.7 per 10,000 population (1999); Age adjusted cancer mortality rate: 226.8 deaths per 100,000 population (1999). Number of physicians: 3.6 per 10,000 population (1999); Number of hospital beds: n/a (1999).
Elections: 2000 Presidential election results: 48.7% Gore, 45.8% Bush, 4.8% Nader, 0.3% Buchanan
National and State Parks: Big Swamp State Public Hunting Grounds; Merrick State Park; Tiffany State Public Hunting Grounds
Additional Information Contacts
Buffalo County Government Offices 608-685-6234

Buffalo County Communities

ALMA (city). Covers a land area of 5.857 square miles and a water area of 1.926 square miles. Located at 44.34° N. Lat.; 91.92° W. Long. Elevation is 687 feet.
Population: 942 (2000); Race: 98.8% White, 0.0% Black, 0.7% Asian, 0.4% American Indian and Alaska Native, 0.6% Hispanic of any race, 0.0% two or more races (2000); Density: 160.8 persons per square mile (2000); Age: 17.4% under 18, 25.6% over 64 (2000); Marriage status: 20.8% never married, 61.1% now married, 7.7% widowed, 10.3% divorced (2000); Foreign born: 1.2% (2000); Ancestry (includes multiple ancestries): 57.0% German, 18.9% Norwegian, 13.3% Swiss, 7.7% Polish, 7.3% Irish (2000).
Economy: Single-family building permits issued: 2 (2001) / 3 (2000); Multi-family building permits issued: 0 (2001) / 0 (2000); Employment by occupation: 11.0% management, 14.3% professional, 20.6% services, 18.8% sales, 4.0% farming, 10.5% construction, 20.8% production (2000).
Income: Per capita income: $21,885 (2000); Median household income: $34,250 (2000); Poverty rate: 8.9% (2000).
Taxes: Total city taxes per capita: $76 (1997); City property taxes per capita: $67 (1997).
Education: High school graduation rate: 86.0% (2000); College graduation rate: 16.3% (2000).

School District(s)

Alma (PK-12)
2000 Enrollment: 409 608-685-4416
Housing: Homeownership rate: 64.7% (2000); Median home value: $72,200 (2000); Median rent: $371 per month (2000); Median age of housing: 46 years (2000).

Transportation: Commute to work: 85.6% car, 0.5% public transportation, 8.9% walk, 4.1% work from home (2000); Travel time to work: 50.0% less than 15 minutes, 16.2% 15 to 30 minutes, 19.8% 30 to 45 minutes, 6.0% 45 to 60 minutes, 8.1% 60 minutes or more (2000)

ALMA (town). Covers a land area of 42.787 square miles and a water area of 0.142 square miles. Located at 44.38° N. Lat.; 91.84° W. Long. Elevation is 687 feet.
History: Lock and Dam No. 4 completed here in 1935. Settled c.1852, incorporated 1885.
Population: 377 (2000); Race: 98.0% White, 0.3% Black, 0.0% Asian, 0.0% American Indian and Alaska Native, 2.6% Hispanic of any race, 1.7% two or more races (2000); Density: 8.8 persons per square mile (2000); Age: 25.6% under 18, 14.2% over 64 (2000); Marriage status: 25.9% never married, 64.3% now married, 4.5% widowed, 5.2% divorced (2000); Foreign born: 0.9% (2000); Ancestry (includes multiple ancestries): 47.3% German, 17.1% Swiss, 15.4% Norwegian, 7.1% Polish, 6.8% Swedish (2000).
Economy: Dairy products, timber. Employment by occupation: 17.5% management, 8.5% professional, 19.5% services, 19.5% sales, 12.0% farming, 5.0% construction, 18.0% production (2000).
Income: Per capita income: $16,044 (2000); Median household income: $40,357 (2000); Poverty rate: 16.2% (2000).
Taxes: Total city taxes per capita: $38 (1997); City property taxes per capita: $34 (1997).
Education: High school graduation rate: 87.1% (2000); College graduation rate: 17.5% (2000).
Housing: Homeownership rate: 89.8% (2000); Median home value: $70,000 (2000); Median rent: $375 per month (2000); Median age of housing: 36 years (2000).
Transportation: Commute to work: 74.6% car, 0.0% public transportation, 8.3% walk, 15.0% work from home (2000); Travel time to work: 43.3% less than 15 minutes, 36.6% 15 to 30 minutes, 6.1% 30 to 45 minutes, 7.3% 45 to 60 minutes, 6.7% 60 minutes or more (2000)

BELVIDERE (town). Covers a land area of 33.153 square miles and a water area of 1.401 square miles. Located at 44.25° N. Lat.; 91.85° W. Long.
Population: 442 (2000); Race: 95.3% White, 0.0% Black, 0.4% Asian, 2.7% American Indian and Alaska Native, 0.4% Hispanic of any race, 1.1% two or more races (2000); Density: 13.3 persons per square mile (2000); Age: 22.0% under 18, 14.2% over 64 (2000); Marriage status: 20.5% never married, 71.6% now married, 3.0% widowed, 4.9% divorced (2000); Foreign born: 0.4% (2000); Ancestry (includes multiple ancestries): 58.2% German, 15.6% Norwegian, 13.6% Polish, 7.8% Irish, 6.2% Swiss (2000).
Economy: Employment by occupation: 32.2% management, 10.2% professional, 6.1% services, 17.1% sales, 7.8% farming, 9.4% construction, 17.1% production (2000).
Income: Per capita income: $20,297 (2000); Median household income: $40,000 (2000); Poverty rate: 10.4% (2000).
Taxes: Total city taxes per capita: $122 (2000); City property taxes per capita: $120 (2000).
Education: High school graduation rate: 86.7% (2000); College graduation rate: 20.8% (2000).
Housing: Homeownership rate: 83.3% (2000); Median home value: $102,800 (2000); Median rent: $375 per month (2000); Median age of housing: 34 years (2000).
Transportation: Commute to work: 79.2% car, 0.0% public transportation, 2.9% walk, 18.0% work from home (2000); Travel time to work: 27.4% less than 15 minutes, 19.4% 15 to 30 minutes, 33.8% 30 to 45 minutes, 9.0% 45 to 60 minutes, 10.4% 60 minutes or more (2000)

BUFFALO (town). Covers a land area of 29.850 square miles and a water area of 4.337 square miles. Located at 44.07° N. Lat.; 91.61° W. Long.
Population: 667 (2000); Race: 99.4% White, 0.0% Black, 0.0% Asian, 0.6% American Indian and Alaska Native, 0.3% Hispanic of any race, 0.0% two or more races (2000); Density: 22.3 persons per square mile (2000); Age: 23.3% under 18, 13.5% over 64 (2000); Marriage status: 22.9% never married, 63.0% now married, 4.8% widowed, 9.3% divorced (2000); Foreign born: 0.3% (2000); Ancestry (includes multiple ancestries): 51.0% German, 29.9% Polish, 10.8% Irish, 7.9% Norwegian, 4.2% English (2000).
Economy: Single-family building permits issued: 8 (2001) / 9 (2000); Multi-family building permits issued: 0 (2001) / 0 (2000); Employment by occupation: 9.2% management, 19.1% professional, 9.7% services, 21.4% sales, 3.8% farming, 11.2% construction, 25.7% production (2000).
Income: Per capita income: $21,431 (2000); Median household income: $44,750 (2000); Poverty rate: 2.2% (2000).
Taxes: Total city taxes per capita: $65 (1997); City property taxes per capita: $59 (1997).
Education: High school graduation rate: 85.1% (2000); College graduation rate: 20.0% (2000).
Housing: Homeownership rate: 88.5% (2000); Median home value: $86,200 (2000); Median rent: $288 per month (2000); Median age of housing: 43 years (2000).
Transportation: Commute to work: 91.9% car, 0.0% public transportation, 0.5% walk, 7.0% work from home (2000); Travel time to work: 24.7% less than 15 minutes, 58.1% 15 to 30 minutes, 10.7% 30 to 45 minutes, 3.4% 45 to 60 minutes, 3.1% 60 minutes or more (2000)

BUFFALO CITY (city). Covers a land area of 2.139 square miles and a water area of 3.909 square miles. Located at 44.23° N. Lat.; 91.86° W. Long. Elevation is 670 feet.
Population: 1,040 (2000); Race: 98.7% White, 0.4% Black, 0.7% Asian, 0.2% American Indian and Alaska Native, 1.7% Hispanic of any race, 0.0% two or more races (2000); Density: 486.2 persons per square mile (2000); Age: 22.6% under 18, 18.3% over 64 (2000); Marriage status: 16.7% never married, 68.4% now married, 5.9% widowed, 9.0% divorced (2000); Foreign born: 0.3% (2000); Ancestry (includes multiple ancestries): 60.8% German, 15.5% Norwegian, 15.2% Polish, 8.8% Irish, 6.4% Swiss (2000).
Economy: Employment by occupation: 11.4% management, 11.3% professional, 14.0% services, 19.6% sales, 1.3% farming, 9.4% construction, 33.0% production (2000).
Income: Per capita income: $18,392 (2000); Median household income: $39,318 (2000); Poverty rate: 3.8% (2000).
Education: High school graduation rate: 82.1% (2000); College graduation rate: 14.7% (2000).
Housing: Homeownership rate: 87.5% (2000); Median home value: $88,800 (2000); Median rent: $294 per month (2000); Median age of housing: 30 years (2000).
Transportation: Commute to work: 95.0% car, 0.0% public transportation, 1.3% walk, 3.2% work from home (2000); Travel time to work: 26.4% less than 15 minutes, 21.3% 15 to 30 minutes, 37.4% 30 to 45 minutes, 7.7% 45 to 60 minutes, 7.3% 60 minutes or more (2000)

CANTON (town). Covers a land area of 35.812 square miles and a water area of 0 square miles. Located at 44.55° N. Lat.; 91.82° W. Long.
Population: 304 (2000); Race: 97.0% White, 0.0% Black, 0.0% Asian, 0.0% American Indian and Alaska Native, 3.7% Hispanic of any race, 0.0% two or more races (2000); Density: 8.5 persons per square mile (2000); Age: 33.4% under 18, 9.7% over 64 (2000); Marriage status: 18.5% never married, 73.1% now married, 3.7% widowed, 4.6% divorced (2000); Foreign born: 1.7% (2000); Ancestry (includes multiple ancestries): 33.8% German, 28.1% Norwegian, 18.4% Austrian, 11.4% United States or American, 9.4% Irish (2000).
Economy: Employment by occupation: 31.7% management, 13.0% professional, 9.3% services, 15.5% sales, 9.3% farming, 4.3% construction, 16.8% production (2000).
Income: Per capita income: $14,749 (2000); Median household income: $38,125 (2000); Poverty rate: 7.4% (2000).
Taxes: Total city taxes per capita: $190 (1997); City property taxes per capita: $190 (1997).
Education: High school graduation rate: 90.9% (2000); College graduation rate: 12.3% (2000).
Housing: Homeownership rate: 68.0% (2000); Median home value: $96,900 (2000); Median rent: $367 per month (2000); Median age of housing: 60+ years (2000).
Transportation: Commute to work: 67.9% car, 0.0% public transportation, 9.0% walk, 21.8% work from home (2000); Travel time to work: 27.9% less than 15 minutes, 36.1% 15 to 30 minutes, 11.5% 30 to 45 minutes, 15.6% 45 to 60 minutes, 9.0% 60 minutes or more (2000)

COCHRANE (village). Covers a land area of 0.721 square miles and a water area of 0 square miles. Located at 44.22° N. Lat.; 91.83° W. Long. Elevation is 680 feet.
Population: 435 (2000); Race: 99.8% White, 0.0% Black, 0.0% Asian, 0.0% American Indian and Alaska Native, 0.5% Hispanic of any race, 0.0% two or more races (2000); Density: 603.4 persons per square mile (2000); Age: 22.9% under 18, 24.7% over 64 (2000); Marriage status: 19.5% never married, 70.2% now married, 8.4% widowed, 1.9% divorced (2000); Foreign born: 0.5% (2000); Ancestry (includes multiple ancestries): 65.8% German, 9.1% Norwegian, 8.6% Polish, 7.7% Irish, 5.9% French (except Basque) (2000).

Economy: In dairy and livestock area; timber. Manufacturing: oat processing, cheese. Single-family building permits issued: 1 (2001) / 0 (2000); Multi-family building permits issued: 0 (2001) / 0 (2000); Employment by occupation: 10.2% management, 14.4% professional, 13.9% services, 23.1% sales, 2.3% farming, 8.8% construction, 27.3% production (2000).
Income: Per capita income: $18,309 (2000); Median household income: $37,019 (2000); Poverty rate: 6.3% (2000).
Taxes: Total city taxes per capita: $60 (1997); City property taxes per capita: $51 (1997).
Education: High school graduation rate: 83.7% (2000); College graduation rate: 13.4% (2000).
Housing: Homeownership rate: 82.0% (2000); Median home value: $70,700 (2000); Median rent: $322 per month (2000); Median age of housing: 60+ years (2000).
Newspapers: Buffalo County Journal (1 x week); Cochrane-Fountain City Recorder (1 x week)
Transportation: Commute to work: 77.3% car, 0.0% public transportation, 14.8% walk, 7.9% work from home (2000); Travel time to work: 38.2% less than 15 minutes, 25.1% 15 to 30 minutes, 24.1% 30 to 45 minutes, 3.0% 45 to 60 minutes, 9.5% 60 minutes or more (2000)

CROSS (town). Covers a land area of 37.678 square miles and a water area of 0.009 square miles. Located at 44.20° N. Lat.; 91.63° W. Long.
Population: 366 (2000); Race: 99.0% White, 0.0% Black, 0.0% Asian, 0.3% American Indian and Alaska Native, 3.3% Hispanic of any race, 0.8% two or more races (2000); Density: 9.7 persons per square mile (2000); Age: 28.5% under 18, 7.6% over 64 (2000); Marriage status: 27.3% never married, 67.7% now married, 1.3% widowed, 3.7% divorced (2000); Foreign born: 0.8% (2000); Ancestry (includes multiple ancestries): 59.8% German, 29.5% Polish, 14.5% Swiss, 13.0% Norwegian, 5.3% Other groups (2000).
Economy: Employment by occupation: 23.8% management, 19.2% professional, 7.5% services, 15.0% sales, 7.1% farming, 15.4% construction, 12.1% production (2000).
Income: Per capita income: $19,625 (2000); Median household income: $50,500 (2000); Poverty rate: 4.1% (2000).
Taxes: Total city taxes per capita: $278 (1997); City property taxes per capita: $278 (1997).
Education: High school graduation rate: 95.9% (2000); College graduation rate: 22.7% (2000).
Housing: Homeownership rate: 83.8% (2000); Median home value: $105,400 (2000); Median rent: $331 per month (2000); Median age of housing: 30 years (2000).
Transportation: Commute to work: 78.3% car, 0.0% public transportation, 3.3% walk, 18.3% work from home (2000); Travel time to work: 13.8% less than 15 minutes, 49.0% 15 to 30 minutes, 27.0% 30 to 45 minutes, 7.1% 45 to 60 minutes, 3.1% 60 minutes or more (2000)

DOVER (town). Covers a land area of 36.210 square miles and a water area of 0 square miles. Located at 44.47° N. Lat.; 91.57° W. Long.
Population: 484 (2000); Race: 100.0% White, 0.0% Black, 0.0% Asian, 0.0% American Indian and Alaska Native, 0.0% Hispanic of any race, 0.0% two or more races (2000); Density: 13.4 persons per square mile (2000); Age: 35.1% under 18, 8.3% over 64 (2000); Marriage status: 24.5% never married, 70.3% now married, 3.2% widowed, 2.0% divorced (2000); Foreign born: 0.0% (2000); Ancestry (includes multiple ancestries): 45.1% Norwegian, 35.6% German, 6.9% Polish, 4.6% Irish, 3.7% United States or American (2000).
Economy: Employment by occupation: 16.7% management, 5.2% professional, 13.9% services, 19.0% sales, 9.1% farming, 10.3% construction, 25.8% production (2000).
Income: Per capita income: $12,821 (2000); Median household income: $40,625 (2000); Poverty rate: 9.0% (2000).
Taxes: Total city taxes per capita: $102 (1997); City property taxes per capita: $102 (1997).
Education: High school graduation rate: 80.2% (2000); College graduation rate: 7.3% (2000).
Housing: Homeownership rate: 89.9% (2000); Median home value: $67,500 (2000); Median rent: $275 per month (2000); Median age of housing: 45 years (2000).
Transportation: Commute to work: 70.4% car, 2.4% public transportation, 6.8% walk, 19.6% work from home (2000); Travel time to work: 22.4% less than 15 minutes, 37.8% 15 to 30 minutes, 28.9% 30 to 45 minutes, 8.0% 45 to 60 minutes, 3.0% 60 minutes or more (2000)

FOUNTAIN CITY (city). Covers a land area of 4.455 square miles and a water area of 1.117 square miles. Located at 44.12° N. Lat.; 91.70° W. Long. Elevation is 663 feet.
Population: 983 (2000); Race: 98.8% White, 0.0% Black, 0.0% Asian, 0.0% American Indian and Alaska Native, 0.0% Hispanic of any race, 1.2% two or more races (2000); Density: 220.6 persons per square mile (2000); Age: 19.0% under 18, 21.2% over 64 (2000); Marriage status: 22.2% never married, 61.4% now married, 7.2% widowed, 9.3% divorced (2000); Foreign born: 0.4% (2000); Ancestry (includes multiple ancestries): 50.1% German, 17.4% Polish, 14.1% Norwegian, 8.6% Swiss, 5.9% Irish (2000).
Economy: Livestock; beer, dairy products. Lock and Dam No. 5 to Northwest, Lock and Dam No. 5A to Southeast. Single-family building permits issued: 1 (2001) / 3 (2000); Multi-family building permits issued: 0 (2001) / 0 (2000); Employment by occupation: 12.8% management, 16.6% professional, 9.6% services, 20.8% sales, 1.4% farming, 8.6% construction, 30.2% production (2000).
Income: Per capita income: $18,396 (2000); Median household income: $31,524 (2000); Poverty rate: 6.8% (2000).
Taxes: Total city taxes per capita: $99 (1997); City property taxes per capita: $87 (1997).
Education: High school graduation rate: 81.4% (2000); College graduation rate: 19.2% (2000).

School District(s)

Cochrane-Fountain City (PK-12)
2000 Enrollment: 782 608-687-7771
Housing: Homeownership rate: 63.3% (2000); Median home value: $80,100 (2000); Median rent: $322 per month (2000); Median age of housing: 60+ years (2000).
Transportation: Commute to work: 88.0% car, 0.0% public transportation, 6.6% walk, 4.8% work from home (2000); Travel time to work: 30.4% less than 15 minutes, 51.7% 15 to 30 minutes, 10.8% 30 to 45 minutes, 1.7% 45 to 60 minutes, 5.5% 60 minutes or more (2000)

GILMANTON (town). Covers a land area of 36.279 square miles and a water area of 0.008 square miles. Located at 44.47° N. Lat.; 91.69° W. Long. Elevation is 786 feet.
Population: 470 (2000); Race: 100.0% White, 0.0% Black, 0.0% Asian, 0.0% American Indian and Alaska Native, 0.0% Hispanic of any race, 0.0% two or more races (2000); Density: 13.0 persons per square mile (2000); Age: 26.3% under 18, 16.5% over 64 (2000); Marriage status: 20.8% never married, 66.7% now married, 5.7% widowed, 6.9% divorced (2000); Foreign born: 0.0% (2000); Ancestry (includes multiple ancestries): 48.2% German, 39.1% Norwegian, 10.6% Swiss, 9.6% English, 4.9% Polish (2000).
Economy: Employment by occupation: 24.9% management, 8.5% professional, 10.9% services, 26.9% sales, 6.0% farming, 2.5% construction, 20.4% production (2000).
Income: Per capita income: $14,769 (2000); Median household income: $30,156 (2000); Poverty rate: 7.3% (2000).
Taxes: Total city taxes per capita: $99 (1997); City property taxes per capita: $94 (1997).
Education: High school graduation rate: 84.9% (2000); College graduation rate: 7.2% (2000).

School District(s)

Gilmanton (PK-12)
2000 Enrollment: 256 715-946-3158
Housing: Homeownership rate: 77.5% (2000); Median home value: $53,000 (2000); Median rent: $354 per month (2000); Median age of housing: 60+ years (2000).
Transportation: Commute to work: 74.9% car, 0.0% public transportation, 6.0% walk, 19.1% work from home (2000); Travel time to work: 28.6% less than 15 minutes, 28.0% 15 to 30 minutes, 25.5% 30 to 45 minutes, 14.3% 45 to 60 minutes, 3.7% 60 minutes or more (2000)

GLENCOE (town). Covers a land area of 44.684 square miles and a water area of 0 square miles. Located at 44.27° N. Lat.; 91.59° W. Long. Elevation is 1,278 feet.
Population: 478 (2000); Race: 100.0% White, 0.0% Black, 0.0% Asian, 0.0% American Indian and Alaska Native, 0.0% Hispanic of any race, 0.0% two or more races (2000); Density: 10.7 persons per square mile (2000); Age: 31.0% under 18, 10.5% over 64 (2000); Marriage status: 21.9% never married, 68.0% now married, 4.2% widowed, 5.9% divorced (2000); Foreign born: 0.0% (2000); Ancestry (includes multiple ancestries): 63.3% German, 34.8% Polish, 14.9% Norwegian, 9.4% Irish, 4.2% Italian (2000).

Economy: Employment by occupation: 30.1% management, 8.9% professional, 11.9% services, 15.6% sales, 5.2% farming, 2.6% construction, 25.7% production (2000).
Income: Per capita income: $15,315 (2000); Median household income: $36,750 (2000); Poverty rate: 5.3% (2000).
Taxes: Total city taxes per capita: $170 (1997); City property taxes per capita: $170 (1997).
Education: High school graduation rate: 84.4% (2000); College graduation rate: 10.6% (2000).
Housing: Homeownership rate: 82.8% (2000); Median home value: $91,400 (2000); Median rent: $317 per month (2000); Median age of housing: 30 years (2000).
Transportation: Commute to work: 72.5% car, 0.8% public transportation, 5.7% walk, 21.0% work from home (2000); Travel time to work: 48.3% less than 15 minutes, 30.0% 15 to 30 minutes, 9.2% 30 to 45 minutes, 5.3% 45 to 60 minutes, 7.2% 60 minutes or more (2000)

LINCOLN (town). Covers a land area of 36.941 square miles and a water area of 0 square miles. Located at 44.34° N. Lat.; 91.74° W. Long.
Population: 187 (2000); Race: 100.0% White, 0.0% Black, 0.0% Asian, 0.0% American Indian and Alaska Native, 0.0% Hispanic of any race, 0.0% two or more races (2000); Density: 5.1 persons per square mile (2000); Age: 21.5% under 18, 20.4% over 64 (2000); Marriage status: 30.3% never married, 54.8% now married, 9.0% widowed, 5.8% divorced (2000); Foreign born: 0.0% (2000); Ancestry (includes multiple ancestries): 73.1% German, 24.7% Swiss, 12.9% Norwegian, 12.4% Polish, 3.2% Other groups (2000).
Economy: Employment by occupation: 27.7% management, 7.9% professional, 9.9% services, 8.9% sales, 5.0% farming, 20.8% construction, 19.8% production (2000).
Income: Per capita income: $17,768 (2000); Median household income: $36,667 (2000); Poverty rate: 6.5% (2000).
Taxes: Total city taxes per capita: $42 (1997); City property taxes per capita: $38 (1997).
Education: High school graduation rate: 78.1% (2000); College graduation rate: 13.1% (2000).
Housing: Homeownership rate: 87.7% (2000); Median home value: $55,000 (2000); Median rent: $325 per month (2000); Median age of housing: 60+ years (2000).
Transportation: Commute to work: 71.3% car, 0.0% public transportation, 5.0% walk, 23.8% work from home (2000); Travel time to work: 19.5% less than 15 minutes, 24.7% 15 to 30 minutes, 23.4% 30 to 45 minutes, 19.5% 45 to 60 minutes, 13.0% 60 minutes or more (2000)

MAXVILLE (town). Covers a land area of 42.027 square miles and a water area of 0.733 square miles. Located at 44.57° N. Lat.; 91.97° W. Long. Elevation is 776 feet.
Population: 325 (2000); Race: 100.0% White, 0.0% Black, 0.0% Asian, 0.0% American Indian and Alaska Native, 0.0% Hispanic of any race, 0.0% two or more races (2000); Density: 7.7 persons per square mile (2000); Age: 34.2% under 18, 7.4% over 64 (2000); Marriage status: 29.5% never married, 58.7% now married, 5.5% widowed, 6.3% divorced (2000); Foreign born: 0.8% (2000); Ancestry (includes multiple ancestries): 51.5% German, 24.5% Norwegian, 16.0% Austrian, 8.3% English, 4.4% French (except Basque) (2000).
Economy: Employment by occupation: 20.8% management, 10.1% professional, 14.0% services, 20.3% sales, 7.7% farming, 11.6% construction, 15.5% production (2000).
Income: Per capita income: $16,168 (2000); Median household income: $42,813 (2000); Poverty rate: 8.3% (2000).
Taxes: Total city taxes per capita: $86 (1997); City property taxes per capita: $86 (1997).
Education: High school graduation rate: 91.3% (2000); College graduation rate: 7.2% (2000).
Housing: Homeownership rate: 73.3% (2000); Median home value: $70,800 (2000); Median rent: $358 per month (2000); Median age of housing: 51 years (2000).
Transportation: Commute to work: 82.7% car, 0.0% public transportation, 3.5% walk, 12.9% work from home (2000); Travel time to work: 37.5% less than 15 minutes, 26.7% 15 to 30 minutes, 12.5% 30 to 45 minutes, 11.4% 45 to 60 minutes, 11.9% 60 minutes or more (2000)

MILTON (town). Covers a land area of 25.046 square miles and a water area of 4.495 square miles. Located at 44.17° N. Lat.; 91.76° W. Long.
Population: 517 (2000); Race: 100.0% White, 0.0% Black, 0.0% Asian, 0.0% American Indian and Alaska Native, 2.0% Hispanic of any race, 0.0% two or more races (2000); Density: 20.6 persons per square mile (2000); Age: 24.3% under 18, 13.9% over 64 (2000); Marriage status: 16.8% never married, 74.3% now married, 4.0% widowed, 5.0% divorced (2000); Foreign born: 0.8% (2000); Ancestry (includes multiple ancestries): 63.6% German, 32.2% Polish, 10.1% Norwegian, 7.8% Swiss, 7.6% Irish (2000).
Economy: Employment by occupation: 11.1% management, 13.7% professional, 10.7% services, 23.2% sales, 3.3% farming, 8.5% construction, 29.5% production (2000).
Income: Per capita income: $22,431 (2000); Median household income: $46,838 (2000); Poverty rate: 5.6% (2000).
Taxes: Total city taxes per capita: $62 (1997); City property taxes per capita: $57 (1997).
Education: High school graduation rate: 88.2% (2000); College graduation rate: 15.0% (2000).
Housing: Homeownership rate: 92.8% (2000); Median home value: $117,600 (2000); Median rent: $363 per month (2000); Median age of housing: 25 years (2000).
Transportation: Commute to work: 88.6% car, 0.0% public transportation, 2.6% walk, 8.9% work from home (2000); Travel time to work: 16.6% less than 15 minutes, 63.2% 15 to 30 minutes, 16.6% 30 to 45 minutes, 3.6% 45 to 60 minutes, 0.0% 60 minutes or more (2000)

MODENA (town). Covers a land area of 36.082 square miles and a water area of 0 square miles. Located at 44.45° N. Lat.; 91.82° W. Long. Elevation is 805 feet.
Population: 318 (2000); Race: 100.0% White, 0.0% Black, 0.0% Asian, 0.0% American Indian and Alaska Native, 0.0% Hispanic of any race, 0.0% two or more races (2000); Density: 8.8 persons per square mile (2000); Age: 25.1% under 18, 15.4% over 64 (2000); Marriage status: 16.9% never married, 65.8% now married, 6.7% widowed, 10.6% divorced (2000); Foreign born: 0.0% (2000); Ancestry (includes multiple ancestries): 50.3% Norwegian, 41.3% German, 7.3% Swiss, 6.1% Austrian, 5.9% Polish (2000).
Economy: Employment by occupation: 20.9% management, 14.0% professional, 5.8% services, 20.9% sales, 2.3% farming, 14.0% construction, 22.1% production (2000).
Income: Per capita income: $16,142 (2000); Median household income: $35,000 (2000); Poverty rate: 5.0% (2000).
Taxes: Total city taxes per capita: $67 (1997); City property taxes per capita: $67 (1997).
Education: High school graduation rate: 81.9% (2000); College graduation rate: 9.2% (2000).
Housing: Homeownership rate: 88.7% (2000); Median home value: $48,300 (2000); Median rent: $375 per month (2000); Median age of housing: 60+ years (2000).
Transportation: Commute to work: 89.3% car, 0.0% public transportation, 4.2% walk, 6.5% work from home (2000); Travel time to work: 21.7% less than 15 minutes, 44.6% 15 to 30 minutes, 12.7% 30 to 45 minutes, 16.6% 45 to 60 minutes, 4.5% 60 minutes or more (2000)

MONDOVI (city). Covers a land area of 3.789 square miles and a water area of 0.030 square miles. Located at 44.56° N. Lat.; 91.67° W. Long. Elevation is 810 feet.
Population: 2,634 (2000); Race: 98.8% White, 0.6% Black, 0.0% Asian, 0.0% American Indian and Alaska Native, 0.2% Hispanic of any race, 0.6% two or more races (2000); Density: 695.2 persons per square mile (2000); Age: 23.7% under 18, 23.0% over 64 (2000); Marriage status: 22.9% never married, 53.2% now married, 12.1% widowed, 11.8% divorced (2000); Foreign born: 0.4% (2000); Ancestry (includes multiple ancestries): 41.0% German, 40.7% Norwegian, 7.1% English, 6.8% Irish, 5.0% Austrian (2000).
Economy: Single-family building permits issued: 2 (2001) / 4 (2000); Multi-family building permits issued: 18 (2001) / 12 (2000); Employment by occupation: 10.8% management, 14.0% professional, 18.9% services, 28.5% sales, 1.3% farming, 10.2% construction, 16.3% production (2000).
Income: Per capita income: $17,023 (2000); Median household income: $31,000 (2000); Poverty rate: 11.2% (2000).
Taxes: Total city taxes per capita: $132 (1997); City property taxes per capita: $125 (1997).
Education: High school graduation rate: 79.4% (2000); College graduation rate: 12.5% (2000).

School District(s)

Mondovi (PK-12)
2000 Enrollment: 1,114 715-926-3684
Housing: Homeownership rate: 63.3% (2000); Median home value: $74,300 (2000); Median rent: $301 per month (2000); Median age of housing: 44 years (2000).
Safety: Violent crime rate: 7.5 per 10,000 population; Property crime rate: 158.3 per 10,000 population (2001).

Newspapers: Mondovi Herald-News (1 x week)
Transportation: Commute to work: 88.1% car, 0.0% public transportation, 7.4% walk, 3.5% work from home (2000); Travel time to work: 47.4% less than 15 minutes, 19.3% 15 to 30 minutes, 22.4% 30 to 45 minutes, 7.0% 45 to 60 minutes, 3.9% 60 minutes or more (2000)

MONDOVI (town). Covers a land area of 32.368 square miles and a water area of 0 square miles. Located at 44.55° N. Lat.; 91.72° W. Long. Elevation is 810 feet.
History: Settled 1855, incorporated 1889.
Population: 449 (2000); Race: 99.8% White, 0.2% Black, 0.0% Asian, 0.0% American Indian and Alaska Native, 0.2% Hispanic of any race, 0.0% two or more races (2000); Density: 13.9 persons per square mile (2000); Age: 27.9% under 18, 8.3% over 64 (2000); Marriage status: 24.0% never married, 64.6% now married, 4.3% widowed, 7.1% divorced (2000); Foreign born: 0.0% (2000); Ancestry (includes multiple ancestries): 41.6% Norwegian, 35.2% German, 11.5% Austrian, 8.8% Irish, 7.1% English (2000).
Economy: Dairy products, poultry hatcheries. Manufacturing: lumber, cabinets. Employment by occupation: 16.5% management, 14.5% professional, 12.9% services, 22.6% sales, 5.6% farming, 11.7% construction, 16.1% production (2000).
Income: Per capita income: $18,672 (2000); Median household income: $39,792 (2000); Poverty rate: 7.7% (2000).
Taxes: Total city taxes per capita: $88 (1997); City property taxes per capita: $88 (1997).
Education: High school graduation rate: 94.4% (2000); College graduation rate: 13.5% (2000).
Housing: Homeownership rate: 88.5% (2000); Median home value: $75,500 (2000); Median rent: $425 per month (2000); Median age of housing: 37 years (2000).
Transportation: Commute to work: 86.9% car, 0.0% public transportation, 4.1% walk, 8.6% work from home (2000); Travel time to work: 48.9% less than 15 minutes, 14.3% 15 to 30 minutes, 22.0% 30 to 45 minutes, 9.9% 45 to 60 minutes, 4.9% 60 minutes or more (2000)

MONTANA (town). Covers a land area of 47.188 square miles and a water area of 0 square miles. Located at 44.37° N. Lat.; 91.61° W. Long. Elevation is 812 feet.
Population: 306 (2000); Race: 98.8% White, 0.0% Black, 1.2% Asian, 0.0% American Indian and Alaska Native, 0.0% Hispanic of any race, 0.0% two or more races (2000); Density: 6.5 persons per square mile (2000); Age: 37.4% under 18, 8.4% over 64 (2000); Marriage status: 26.9% never married, 60.1% now married, 5.8% widowed, 7.2% divorced (2000); Foreign born: 1.5% (2000); Ancestry (includes multiple ancestries): 56.0% German, 35.9% Polish, 12.3% Swiss, 8.1% Norwegian, 4.5% Irish (2000).
Economy: Employment by occupation: 40.4% management, 5.8% professional, 3.8% services, 7.1% sales, 20.5% farming, 5.1% construction, 17.3% production (2000).
Income: Per capita income: $18,708 (2000); Median household income: $34,375 (2000); Poverty rate: 3.3% (2000).
Taxes: Total city taxes per capita: $70 (1997); City property taxes per capita: $70 (1997).
Education: High school graduation rate: 91.8% (2000); College graduation rate: 14.4% (2000).
Housing: Homeownership rate: 77.9% (2000); Median home value: $81,300 (2000); Median rent: $344 per month (2000); Median age of housing: 36 years (2000).
Transportation: Commute to work: 59.0% car, 0.0% public transportation, 11.5% walk, 28.2% work from home (2000); Travel time to work: 48.2% less than 15 minutes, 27.7% 15 to 30 minutes, 8.0% 30 to 45 minutes, 13.4% 45 to 60 minutes, 2.7% 60 minutes or more (2000)

NAPLES (town). Covers a land area of 35.528 square miles and a water area of 0.020 square miles. Located at 44.56° N. Lat.; 91.59° W. Long.
Population: 584 (2000); Race: 99.7% White, 0.0% Black, 0.0% Asian, 0.0% American Indian and Alaska Native, 0.2% Hispanic of any race, 0.3% two or more races (2000); Density: 16.4 persons per square mile (2000); Age: 31.5% under 18, 13.4% over 64 (2000); Marriage status: 21.2% never married, 65.0% now married, 5.0% widowed, 8.8% divorced (2000); Foreign born: 0.0% (2000); Ancestry (includes multiple ancestries): 38.3% German, 34.4% Norwegian, 6.6% Polish, 5.5% English, 5.2% Swedish (2000).
Economy: Employment by occupation: 17.2% management, 9.2% professional, 12.3% services, 28.5% sales, 3.4% farming, 10.1% construction, 19.3% production (2000).
Income: Per capita income: $17,318 (2000); Median household income: $41,484 (2000); Poverty rate: 3.3% (2000).
Taxes: Total city taxes per capita: $68 (1997); City property taxes per capita: $66 (1997).
Education: High school graduation rate: 83.6% (2000); College graduation rate: 12.7% (2000).
Housing: Homeownership rate: 82.2% (2000); Median home value: $109,600 (2000); Median rent: $225 per month (2000); Median age of housing: 47 years (2000).
Transportation: Commute to work: 82.6% car, 0.0% public transportation, 4.7% walk, 12.7% work from home (2000); Travel time to work: 45.2% less than 15 minutes, 20.3% 15 to 30 minutes, 17.1% 30 to 45 minutes, 7.1% 45 to 60 minutes, 10.3% 60 minutes or more (2000)

NELSON (village). Covers a land area of 1.463 square miles and a water area of 0.013 square miles. Located at 44.42° N. Lat.; 92.00° W. Long. Elevation is 690 feet.
History: Nelson was founded in 1844 by James Nelson, an Englishman.
Population: 395 (2000); Race: 97.7% White, 0.0% Black, 1.8% Asian, 0.5% American Indian and Alaska Native, 0.0% Hispanic of any race, 0.0% two or more races (2000); Density: 270.0 persons per square mile (2000); Age: 26.3% under 18, 13.3% over 64 (2000); Marriage status: 27.1% never married, 51.6% now married, 12.3% widowed, 9.0% divorced (2000); Foreign born: 2.6% (2000); Ancestry (includes multiple ancestries): 48.6% German, 32.2% Norwegian, 12.5% Irish, 5.4% Polish, 5.1% Other groups (2000).
Economy: Single-family building permits issued: 3 (2001) / 1 (2000); Multi-family building permits issued: 0 (2001) / 0 (2000); Employment by occupation: 10.5% management, 15.2% professional, 22.5% services, 14.1% sales, 1.6% farming, 7.9% construction, 28.3% production (2000).
Income: Per capita income: $14,958 (2000); Median household income: $30,833 (2000); Poverty rate: 11.3% (2000).
Taxes: Total city taxes per capita: $116 (1997); City property taxes per capita: $103 (1997).
Education: High school graduation rate: 76.6% (2000); College graduation rate: 14.7% (2000).
Housing: Homeownership rate: 71.1% (2000); Median home value: $61,100 (2000); Median rent: $285 per month (2000); Median age of housing: 43 years (2000).
Transportation: Commute to work: 88.4% car, 1.1% public transportation, 8.5% walk, 2.1% work from home (2000); Travel time to work: 52.4% less than 15 minutes, 18.9% 15 to 30 minutes, 10.3% 30 to 45 minutes, 5.9% 45 to 60 minutes, 12.4% 60 minutes or more (2000)

NELSON (town). Covers a land area of 70.658 square miles and a water area of 6.949 square miles. Located at 44.45° N. Lat.; 91.97° W. Long. Elevation is 690 feet.
Population: 586 (2000); Race: 99.5% White, 0.0% Black, 0.0% Asian, 0.5% American Indian and Alaska Native, 0.0% Hispanic of any race, 0.0% two or more races (2000); Density: 8.3 persons per square mile (2000); Age: 21.0% under 18, 15.4% over 64 (2000); Marriage status: 21.8% never married, 66.2% now married, 6.3% widowed, 5.7% divorced (2000); Foreign born: 0.2% (2000); Ancestry (includes multiple ancestries): 51.0% German, 26.8% Norwegian, 9.2% Irish, 6.6% Austrian, 6.5% English (2000).
Economy: Manufacturing: railroad ties, dairy products. Upper Mississippi River Wildlife and Fish Refuge on river. Employment by occupation: 20.5% management, 12.4% professional, 12.7% services, 14.2% sales, 4.8% farming, 8.8% construction, 26.6% production (2000).
Income: Per capita income: $23,633 (2000); Median household income: $44,063 (2000); Poverty rate: 7.6% (2000).
Taxes: Total city taxes per capita: $101 (1997); City property taxes per capita: $99 (1997).
Education: High school graduation rate: 83.8% (2000); College graduation rate: 8.5% (2000).
Housing: Homeownership rate: 81.9% (2000); Median home value: $73,300 (2000); Median rent: $309 per month (2000); Median age of housing: 51 years (2000).
Transportation: Commute to work: 82.5% car, 0.0% public transportation, 2.5% walk, 14.8% work from home (2000); Travel time to work: 25.6% less than 15 minutes, 39.7% 15 to 30 minutes, 14.4% 30 to 45 minutes, 12.3% 45 to 60 minutes, 7.9% 60 minutes or more (2000)

WAUMANDEE (town). Covers a land area of 43.757 square miles and a water area of 0.021 square miles. Located at 44.28° N. Lat.; 91.71° W. Long. Elevation is 770 feet.
Population: 515 (2000); Race: 96.1% White, 2.3% Black, 0.0% Asian, 1.3% American Indian and Alaska Native, 1.5% Hispanic of any race, 0.0% two or more races (2000); Density: 11.8 persons per square mile (2000); Age: 28.7%

under 18, 11.4% over 64 (2000); Marriage status: 30.4% never married, 60.5% now married, 5.0% widowed, 4.1% divorced (2000); Foreign born: 2.4% (2000); Ancestry (includes multiple ancestries): 63.8% German, 32.6% Polish, 7.5% Norwegian, 5.3% Swiss, 4.7% Other groups (2000).
Economy: Employment by occupation: 26.8% management, 12.9% professional, 6.8% services, 18.7% sales, 7.1% farming, 7.7% construction, 20.0% production (2000).
Income: Per capita income: $17,214 (2000); Median household income: $38,375 (2000); Poverty rate: 5.8% (2000).
Taxes: Total city taxes per capita: $201 (1997); City property taxes per capita: $199 (1997).
Education: High school graduation rate: 90.4% (2000); College graduation rate: 12.8% (2000).
Housing: Homeownership rate: 82.8% (2000); Median home value: $81,300 (2000); Median rent: $300 per month (2000); Median age of housing: 39 years (2000).
Transportation: Commute to work: 78.1% car, 1.0% public transportation, 5.8% walk, 15.2% work from home (2000); Travel time to work: 35.4% less than 15 minutes, 20.9% 15 to 30 minutes, 35.4% 30 to 45 minutes, 5.3% 45 to 60 minutes, 3.0% 60 minutes or more (2000)

Burnett County

Located in northwestern Wisconsin; bounded on the west by the St. Croix River and the Minnesota border. Covers a land area of 821.50 square miles, a water area of 58.90 square miles, and is located in the Central Time Zone. The county government was organized in 1856. County seat is Grantsburg.

Weather Station: Danbury — Elevation: 921 feet

	Jan	Feb	Mar	Apr	May	Jun	Jul	Aug	Sep	Oct	Nov	Dec
High	20	28	39	55	69	76	80	78	68	56	38	25
Low	-2	5	18	31	42	52	57	55	46	35	22	6
Precip	1.0	0.8	1.7	2.2	3.3	4.1	4.4	4.4	3.4	2.5	1.9	1.0
Snow	12.1	7.5	8.8	3.1	0.2	0.0	0.0	0.0	tr	0.7	8.2	9.9

High and Low temperatures in degrees Fahrenheit; Precipitation and Snow in inches

Weather Station: Grantsburg — Elevation: 898 feet

	Jan	Feb	Mar	Apr	May	Jun	Jul	Aug	Sep	Oct	Nov	Dec
High	19	27	38	55	69	76	80	78	68	56	39	25
Low	-2	4	17	31	44	53	58	55	46	35	21	5
Precip	1.1	0.8	1.8	2.2	3.5	4.6	4.2	4.5	3.5	2.6	2.0	1.1
Snow	13.5	6.8	8.5	2.3	tr	0.0	0.0	0.0	tr	0.3	na	10.4

High and Low temperatures in degrees Fahrenheit; Precipitation and Snow in inches

Population: 15,674 (2000); Race: 93.3% White, 0.1% Black, 0.3% Asian, 4.4% American Indian and Alaska Native, 0.5% Hispanic of any race, 1.5% two or more races (2000); Density: 19.1 persons per square mile (2000); Age: 22.1% under 18, 20.3% over 64 (2000).
Religion: Five largest groups: 16.5% Evangelical Lutheran Church in America, 9.8% Catholic Church, 3.7% The United Methodist Church, 2.7% Baptist General Conference, 1.4% Lutheran Church—Missouri Synod (2000).
Economy: Unemployment rate: 4.4% (11/2002); Total civilian labor force: 7,119 (11/2002); Leading industries: 29.6% manufacturing; 17.3% health care and social assistance; 15.8% retail trade (2000); Companies that employ more than 1,000 persons: 0 (2000); Companies that employ more than 100 persons: 6 (2000); Farms: 351 totaling 82,742 acres (1997); Minority business ownership rate: 0.0% (1997); Women business ownership rate: 13.1% (1997); Retail sales per capita: $5,311 (1997). Single-family building permits issued: 251 (2001) / 225 (2000). Multi-family building permits issued: 0 (2001) / 0 (2000).
Income: Per capita income: $17,712 (2000); Median household income: $34,218 (2000); Poverty rate: 8.8% (2000); Bankruptcy rate: 3.26% (2001).
Taxes: Total county taxes per capita: $331 (1997); County property taxes per capita: $287 (1997).
Education: High school graduation rate: 82.8% (2000); College graduation rate: 14.0% (2000).
Housing: Homeownership rate: 84.5% (2000); Median home value: $87,500 (2000); Median rent: $322 per month (2000); Median age of housing: 26 years (2000).
Health: Birth rate: 95.7 per 10,000 population (1998); Age adjusted death rate: 89.8 per 10,000 population (1999); Age adjusted cancer mortality rate: 228.6 deaths per 100,000 population (1999). Number of physicians: 5.1 per 10,000 population (1999); Number of hospital beds: 44.7 per 10,000 population (1999).
Elections: 2000 Presidential election results: 44.5% Gore, 48.7% Bush, 6.1% Nader, 0.4% Buchanan

National and State Parks: Amsterdam Sloughs State Public Hunting Grounds; Clam River State Fishery Area; Crex Meadows State Public Hunting Grounds; Crex Meadows State Wildlife Refuge; Culbertson Springs State Fishery Area; Fish Lake State Wildlife Area; Governor Knowles State Forest; Kiezer Lake State Public Hunting Grounds; Spring Brook Springs State Fishery Area
Additional Information Contacts
Burnett County Government Offices 715-349-2173
Grantsburg Chamber of Commerce 715-463-2405

Burnett County Communities

ANDERSON (town). Covers a land area of 62.773 square miles and a water area of 1.201 square miles. Located at 45.68° N. Lat.; 92.74° W. Long.
Population: 372 (2000); Race: 99.3% White, 0.0% Black, 0.0% Asian, 0.0% American Indian and Alaska Native, 0.0% Hispanic of any race, 0.7% two or more races (2000); Density: 5.9 persons per square mile (2000); Age: 22.8% under 18, 15.7% over 64 (2000); Marriage status: 20.6% never married, 61.3% now married, 3.7% widowed, 14.3% divorced (2000); Foreign born: 1.0% (2000); Ancestry (includes multiple ancestries): 43.6% German, 25.7% Swedish, 21.5% Norwegian, 10.4% Irish, 7.7% Polish (2000).
Economy: Employment by occupation: 5.8% management, 5.2% professional, 12.6% services, 14.1% sales, 2.1% farming, 15.2% construction, 45.0% production (2000).
Income: Per capita income: $17,013 (2000); Median household income: $31,818 (2000); Poverty rate: 7.7% (2000).
Taxes: Total city taxes per capita: $75 (2000); City property taxes per capita: $73 (2000).
Education: High school graduation rate: 86.3% (2000); College graduation rate: 8.3% (2000).
Housing: Homeownership rate: 88.9% (2000); Median home value: $59,400 (2000); Median rent: $110 per month (2000); Median age of housing: 27 years (2000).
Transportation: Commute to work: 96.3% car, 0.0% public transportation, 0.5% walk, 3.2% work from home (2000); Travel time to work: 18.0% less than 15 minutes, 25.7% 15 to 30 minutes, 26.8% 30 to 45 minutes, 9.8% 45 to 60 minutes, 19.7% 60 minutes or more (2000)

BLAINE (town). Covers a land area of 68.835 square miles and a water area of 1.434 square miles. Located at 46.11° N. Lat.; 92.15° W. Long.
Population: 224 (2000); Race: 90.8% White, 0.0% Black, 6.6% Asian, 1.5% American Indian and Alaska Native, 1.0% Hispanic of any race, 0.0% two or more races (2000); Density: 3.3 persons per square mile (2000); Age: 21.9% under 18, 28.1% over 64 (2000); Marriage status: 13.7% never married, 73.9% now married, 12.4% widowed, 0.0% divorced (2000); Foreign born: 7.7% (2000); Ancestry (includes multiple ancestries): 32.1% German, 12.2% Swedish, 10.2% Norwegian, 9.2% Irish, 8.7% Italian (2000).
Economy: Single-family building permits issued: 1 (2001) / 1 (2000); Multi-family building permits issued: 0 (2001) / 0 (2000); Employment by occupation: 13.6% management, 13.6% professional, 21.2% services, 21.2% sales, 4.5% farming, 16.7% construction, 9.1% production (2000).
Income: Per capita income: $12,895 (2000); Median household income: $31,250 (2000); Poverty rate: 15.3% (2000).
Taxes: Total city taxes per capita: $89 (1997); City property taxes per capita: $84 (1997).
Education: High school graduation rate: 79.5% (2000); College graduation rate: 8.9% (2000).
Housing: Homeownership rate: 93.8% (2000); Median home value: $92,500 (2000); Median rent: $375 per month (2000); Median age of housing: 26 years (2000).
Transportation: Commute to work: 69.7% car, 0.0% public transportation, 15.2% walk, 15.2% work from home (2000); Travel time to work: 23.2% less than 15 minutes, 23.2% 15 to 30 minutes, 25.0% 30 to 45 minutes, 8.9% 45 to 60 minutes, 19.6% 60 minutes or more (2000)

DANBURY (unincorporated postal area, zip code 54830). Covers a land area of 311.289 square miles and a water area of 13.417 square miles. Located at 46.03° N. Lat.; 92.21° W. Long. Elevation is 947 feet.
History: St. Croix National Scenic Riverway on St. Croix River.
Population: 2,851 (2000); Race: 90.7% White, 0.2% Black, 0.5% Asian, 6.5% American Indian and Alaska Native, 0.3% Hispanic of any race, 1.6% two or more races (2000); Density: 9.2 persons per square mile (2000); Age: 15.0% under 18, 27.4% over 64 (2000); Marriage status: 17.9% never married, 64.7% now married, 7.2% widowed, 10.2% divorced (2000); Foreign born: 1.8% (2000); Ancestry (includes multiple ancestries): 32.3%

German, 11.9% Swedish, 11.6% Norwegian, 10.4% Irish, 10.1% English (2000).
Economy: Employment by occupation: 11.2% management, 16.7% professional, 24.0% services, 21.3% sales, 0.8% farming, 12.3% construction, 13.7% production (2000).
Income: Per capita income: $17,596 (2000); Median household income: $32,219 (2000); Poverty rate: 8.4% (2000).
Education: High school graduation rate: 83.8% (2000); College graduation rate: 16.3% (2000).
Housing: Homeownership rate: 91.0% (2000); Median home value: $97,100 (2000); Median rent: $348 per month (2000); Median age of housing: 24 years (2000).
Transportation: Commute to work: 87.3% car, 0.3% public transportation, 4.3% walk, 7.1% work from home (2000); Travel time to work: 28.6% less than 15 minutes, 30.2% 15 to 30 minutes, 19.0% 30 to 45 minutes, 8.3% 45 to 60 minutes, 13.9% 60 minutes or more (2000)

DANIELS (town). Covers a land area of 33.695 square miles and a water area of 2.092 square miles. Located at 45.75° N. Lat.; 92.47° W. Long.
Population: 665 (2000); Race: 97.7% White, 0.0% Black, 0.6% Asian, 0.4% American Indian and Alaska Native, 0.7% Hispanic of any race, 0.6% two or more races (2000); Density: 19.7 persons per square mile (2000); Age: 20.6% under 18, 20.1% over 64 (2000); Marriage status: 16.0% never married, 65.6% now married, 8.5% widowed, 9.9% divorced (2000); Foreign born: 0.7% (2000); Ancestry (includes multiple ancestries): 35.4% German, 25.8% Swedish, 20.3% Norwegian, 10.7% Irish, 8.3% French (except Basque) (2000).
Economy: Single-family building permits issued: 3 (2001) / 3 (2000); Multi-family building permits issued: 0 (2001) / 0 (2000); Employment by occupation: 8.7% management, 14.6% professional, 13.7% services, 19.3% sales, 5.3% farming, 12.4% construction, 26.1% production (2000).
Income: Per capita income: $19,081 (2000); Median household income: $36,597 (2000); Poverty rate: 8.5% (2000).
Taxes: Total city taxes per capita: $95 (1997); City property taxes per capita: $93 (1997).
Education: High school graduation rate: 79.5% (2000); College graduation rate: 13.2% (2000).
Housing: Homeownership rate: 93.9% (2000); Median home value: $85,000 (2000); Median rent: $281 per month (2000); Median age of housing: 28 years (2000).
Transportation: Commute to work: 88.9% car, 0.0% public transportation, 5.1% walk, 5.4% work from home (2000); Travel time to work: 42.1% less than 15 minutes, 30.6% 15 to 30 minutes, 7.4% 30 to 45 minutes, 2.0% 45 to 60 minutes, 17.8% 60 minutes or more (2000)

DEWEY (town). Covers a land area of 36.311 square miles and a water area of 0.551 square miles. Located at 45.77° N. Lat.; 92.10° W. Long.
Population: 565 (2000); Race: 83.9% White, 0.0% Black, 0.0% Asian, 12.1% American Indian and Alaska Native, 0.4% Hispanic of any race, 4.1% two or more races (2000); Density: 15.6 persons per square mile (2000); Age: 26.2% under 18, 13.1% over 64 (2000); Marriage status: 24.1% never married, 64.4% now married, 3.8% widowed, 7.8% divorced (2000); Foreign born: 0.0% (2000); Ancestry (includes multiple ancestries): 35.3% German, 16.0% Other groups, 11.3% Norwegian, 7.8% English, 7.8% Irish (2000).
Economy: Employment by occupation: 17.8% management, 6.6% professional, 18.7% services, 18.7% sales, 7.5% farming, 12.9% construction, 17.8% production (2000).
Income: Per capita income: $15,399 (2000); Median household income: $28,917 (2000); Poverty rate: 13.1% (2000).
Taxes: Total city taxes per capita: $38 (1997); City property taxes per capita: $36 (1997).
Education: High school graduation rate: 80.3% (2000); College graduation rate: 10.4% (2000).
Housing: Homeownership rate: 86.4% (2000); Median home value: $92,500 (2000); Median rent: $183 per month (2000); Median age of housing: 26 years (2000).
Transportation: Commute to work: 83.3% car, 0.4% public transportation, 1.7% walk, 13.4% work from home (2000); Travel time to work: 29.5% less than 15 minutes, 31.4% 15 to 30 minutes, 15.9% 30 to 45 minutes, 10.6% 45 to 60 minutes, 12.6% 60 minutes or more (2000)

GRANTSBURG (village). Covers a land area of 2.978 square miles and a water area of 0.017 square miles. Located at 45.78° N. Lat.; 92.68° W. Long. Elevation is 940 feet.
History: Grantsburg was founded in 1855 by Canute Anderson, and developed as the seat of Burnett County.
Population: 1,369 (2000); Race: 96.1% White, 0.0% Black, 0.6% Asian, 1.5% American Indian and Alaska Native, 1.2% Hispanic of any race, 0.7% two or more races (2000); Density: 459.8 persons per square mile (2000); Age: 25.9% under 18, 20.9% over 64 (2000); Marriage status: 23.2% never married, 55.6% now married, 10.7% widowed, 10.5% divorced (2000); Foreign born: 2.3% (2000); Ancestry (includes multiple ancestries): 28.1% Swedish, 23.6% German, 18.3% Norwegian, 10.2% Irish, 9.8% English (2000).
Economy: Single-family building permits issued: 9 (2001) / 9 (2000); Multi-family building permits issued: 0 (2001) / 0 (2000); Employment by occupation: 8.7% management, 16.7% professional, 15.6% services, 22.6% sales, 0.8% farming, 9.4% construction, 26.2% production (2000).
Income: Per capita income: $16,875 (2000); Median household income: $34,423 (2000); Poverty rate: 9.7% (2000).
Taxes: Total city taxes per capita: $212 (1997); City property taxes per capita: $192 (1997).
Education: High school graduation rate: 82.4% (2000); College graduation rate: 18.7% (2000).

School District(s)

Grantsburg (PK-12)
2000 Enrollment: 966 715-463-5499
Housing: Homeownership rate: 64.1% (2000); Median home value: $75,800 (2000); Median rent: $316 per month (2000); Median age of housing: 36 years (2000).
Hospitals: Burnett Medical Center (84 beds)
Newspapers: Burnett County Sentinel (1 x week)
Transportation: Commute to work: 85.3% car, 0.0% public transportation, 10.4% walk, 4.0% work from home (2000); Travel time to work: 66.9% less than 15 minutes, 10.6% 15 to 30 minutes, 11.0% 30 to 45 minutes, 3.5% 45 to 60 minutes, 7.9% 60 minutes or more (2000)
Additional Information Contacts
Grantsburg Chamber of Commerce 715-463-2405

GRANTSBURG (town). Covers a land area of 35.649 square miles and a water area of 0.748 square miles. Located at 45.78° N. Lat.; 92.73° W. Long. Elevation is 940 feet.
Population: 967 (2000); Race: 96.8% White, 0.0% Black, 0.0% Asian, 0.9% American Indian and Alaska Native, 0.9% Hispanic of any race, 1.4% two or more races (2000); Density: 27.1 persons per square mile (2000); Age: 28.6% under 18, 9.2% over 64 (2000); Marriage status: 19.7% never married, 64.6% now married, 3.6% widowed, 12.1% divorced (2000); Foreign born: 0.5% (2000); Ancestry (includes multiple ancestries): 35.7% German, 20.2% Norwegian, 18.8% Swedish, 8.9% Irish, 6.7% English (2000).
Economy: Dairy products; poultry. Manufacturing: cheese, plastic products, machinery, wood products. St. Croix National Scenic Riverway to West and North. Single-family building permits issued: 9 (2001) / 7 (2000); Multi-family building permits issued: 0 (2001) / 0 (2000); Employment by occupation: 9.8% management, 13.4% professional, 9.6% services, 23.2% sales, 1.5% farming, 10.5% construction, 32.0% production (2000).
Income: Per capita income: $18,000 (2000); Median household income: $43,264 (2000); Poverty rate: 6.7% (2000).
Taxes: Total city taxes per capita: $34 (1997); City property taxes per capita: $33 (1997).
Education: High school graduation rate: 85.8% (2000); College graduation rate: 12.2% (2000).
Housing: Homeownership rate: 94.5% (2000); Median home value: $77,800 (2000); Median rent: $375 per month (2000); Median age of housing: 23 years (2000).
Transportation: Commute to work: 91.5% car, 0.0% public transportation, 1.7% walk, 5.6% work from home (2000); Travel time to work: 52.4% less than 15 minutes, 13.3% 15 to 30 minutes, 9.0% 30 to 45 minutes, 8.6% 45 to 60 minutes, 16.8% 60 minutes or more (2000)

HERTEL (unincorporated postal area, zip code 54845). Covers a land area of 5.793 square miles and a water area of 0.018 square miles. Located at 45.81° N. Lat.; 92.13° W. Long. Elevation is 1,035 feet.
Population: 131 (2000); Race: 81.1% White, 0.0% Black, 0.0% Asian, 12.6% American Indian and Alaska Native, 0.0% Hispanic of any race, 6.3% two or more races (2000); Density: 22.6 persons per square mile (2000); Age: 14.7% under 18, 21.1% over 64 (2000); Marriage status: 23.3% never married, 51.2% now married, 14.0% widowed, 11.6% divorced (2000); Foreign born: 0.0% (2000); Ancestry (includes multiple ancestries): 38.9% German, 24.2% Other groups, 11.6% Irish, 6.3% European, 6.3% Norwegian (2000).

Economy: Employment by occupation: 0.0% management, 6.8% professional, 27.3% services, 18.2% sales, 13.6% farming, 0.0% construction, 34.1% production (2000).
Income: Per capita income: $11,538 (2000); Median household income: $16,875 (2000); Poverty rate: 21.1% (2000).
Education: High school graduation rate: 85.7% (2000); College graduation rate: 11.4% (2000).
Housing: Homeownership rate: 73.2% (2000); Median home value: $50,000 (2000); Median rent: $438 per month (2000); Median age of housing: 25 years (2000).
Transportation: Commute to work: 93.2% car, 2.3% public transportation, 0.0% walk, 4.5% work from home (2000); Travel time to work: 40.5% less than 15 minutes, 38.1% 15 to 30 minutes, 14.3% 30 to 45 minutes, 2.4% 45 to 60 minutes, 4.8% 60 minutes or more (2000)

JACKSON (town). Covers a land area of 29.133 square miles and a water area of 5.809 square miles. Located at 45.94° N. Lat.; 92.20° W. Long.
Population: 765 (2000); Race: 94.8% White, 1.2% Black, 0.0% Asian, 2.9% American Indian and Alaska Native, 1.2% Hispanic of any race, 1.1% two or more races (2000); Density: 26.3 persons per square mile (2000); Age: 14.5% under 18, 30.9% over 64 (2000); Marriage status: 12.3% never married, 70.5% now married, 6.9% widowed, 10.3% divorced (2000); Foreign born: 2.3% (2000); Ancestry (includes multiple ancestries): 39.0% German, 13.3% Norwegian, 12.7% Swedish, 12.2% Irish, 11.1% English (2000).
Economy: Employment by occupation: 12.4% management, 17.9% professional, 22.1% services, 23.5% sales, 0.0% farming, 11.4% construction, 12.7% production (2000).
Income: Per capita income: $18,844 (2000); Median household income: $35,119 (2000); Poverty rate: 8.5% (2000).
Taxes: Total city taxes per capita: $265 (1997); City property taxes per capita: $261 (1997).
Education: High school graduation rate: 84.9% (2000); College graduation rate: 22.5% (2000).
Housing: Homeownership rate: 100.0% (2000); Median home value: $90,800 (2000); Median age of housing: 19 years (2000).
Transportation: Commute to work: 93.7% car, 0.0% public transportation, 0.0% walk, 6.3% work from home (2000); Travel time to work: 18.5% less than 15 minutes, 47.0% 15 to 30 minutes, 17.1% 30 to 45 minutes, 3.9% 45 to 60 minutes, 13.5% 60 minutes or more (2000)

LA FOLLETTE (town). Covers a land area of 37.056 square miles and a water area of 2.003 square miles. Located at 45.78° N. Lat.; 92.22° W. Long.
Population: 511 (2000); Race: 78.3% White, 1.3% Black, 0.0% Asian, 18.9% American Indian and Alaska Native, 0.9% Hispanic of any race, 1.5% two or more races (2000); Density: 13.8 persons per square mile (2000); Age: 21.9% under 18, 22.6% over 64 (2000); Marriage status: 24.3% never married, 57.1% now married, 11.7% widowed, 6.9% divorced (2000); Foreign born: 0.0% (2000); Ancestry (includes multiple ancestries): 31.4% German, 20.2% Other groups, 13.4% Norwegian, 12.7% Swedish, 11.4% Irish (2000).
Economy: Employment by occupation: 8.0% management, 18.6% professional, 29.8% services, 19.7% sales, 3.2% farming, 6.9% construction, 13.8% production (2000).
Income: Per capita income: $18,129 (2000); Median household income: $30,104 (2000); Poverty rate: 9.2% (2000).
Taxes: Total city taxes per capita: $114 (1997); City property taxes per capita: $108 (1997).
Education: High school graduation rate: 85.2% (2000); College graduation rate: 13.6% (2000).
Housing: Homeownership rate: 73.5% (2000); Median home value: $127,800 (2000); Median rent: $238 per month (2000); Median age of housing: 23 years (2000).
Transportation: Commute to work: 90.6% car, 1.1% public transportation, 1.7% walk, 5.6% work from home (2000); Travel time to work: 21.2% less than 15 minutes, 34.7% 15 to 30 minutes, 22.9% 30 to 45 minutes, 12.9% 45 to 60 minutes, 8.2% 60 minutes or more (2000)

LINCOLN (town). Covers a land area of 34.811 square miles and a water area of 0.371 square miles. Located at 45.86° N. Lat.; 92.47° W. Long.
Population: 286 (2000); Race: 97.2% White, 0.0% Black, 0.0% Asian, 0.0% American Indian and Alaska Native, 0.3% Hispanic of any race, 2.4% two or more races (2000); Density: 8.2 persons per square mile (2000); Age: 23.3% under 18, 7.7% over 64 (2000); Marriage status: 19.8% never married, 65.1% now married, 7.8% widowed, 7.3% divorced (2000); Foreign born: 0.3% (2000); Ancestry (includes multiple ancestries): 34.8% German, 29.3% Swedish, 21.3% Irish, 19.2% Norwegian, 5.6% Polish (2000).
Economy: Employment by occupation: 5.3% management, 17.2% professional, 18.5% services, 24.5% sales, 0.0% farming, 18.5% construction, 15.9% production (2000).
Income: Per capita income: $16,300 (2000); Median household income: $31,786 (2000); Poverty rate: 7.7% (2000).
Taxes: Total city taxes per capita: $77 (1997); City property taxes per capita: $73 (1997).
Education: High school graduation rate: 90.6% (2000); College graduation rate: 7.3% (2000).
Housing: Homeownership rate: 85.6% (2000); Median home value: $68,000 (2000); Median rent: $264 per month (2000); Median age of housing: 24 years (2000).
Transportation: Commute to work: 96.6% car, 0.0% public transportation, 0.0% walk, 3.4% work from home (2000); Travel time to work: 28.0% less than 15 minutes, 47.6% 15 to 30 minutes, 6.3% 30 to 45 minutes, 7.0% 45 to 60 minutes, 11.2% 60 minutes or more (2000)

MEENON (town). Covers a land area of 31.897 square miles and a water area of 1.367 square miles. Located at 45.84° N. Lat.; 92.33° W. Long.
Population: 1,172 (2000); Race: 91.6% White, 0.0% Black, 0.2% Asian, 5.5% American Indian and Alaska Native, 1.7% Hispanic of any race, 2.0% two or more races (2000); Density: 36.7 persons per square mile (2000); Age: 28.0% under 18, 16.1% over 64 (2000); Marriage status: 23.6% never married, 55.3% now married, 5.4% widowed, 15.7% divorced (2000); Foreign born: 0.9% (2000); Ancestry (includes multiple ancestries): 41.8% German, 15.8% Norwegian, 15.2% Irish, 15.0% Swedish, 8.6% Other groups (2000).
Economy: Single-family building permits issued: 9 (2001) / 9 (2000); Multi-family building permits issued: 0 (2001) / 0 (2000); Employment by occupation: 9.3% management, 14.0% professional, 17.1% services, 18.5% sales, 1.0% farming, 20.2% construction, 20.0% production (2000).
Income: Per capita income: $18,067 (2000); Median household income: $37,011 (2000); Poverty rate: 7.0% (2000).
Taxes: Total city taxes per capita: $62 (1997); City property taxes per capita: $58 (1997).
Education: High school graduation rate: 78.8% (2000); College graduation rate: 11.2% (2000).
Housing: Homeownership rate: 91.7% (2000); Median home value: $87,500 (2000); Median rent: $378 per month (2000); Median age of housing: 26 years (2000).
Transportation: Commute to work: 89.9% car, 0.6% public transportation, 1.3% walk, 7.6% work from home (2000); Travel time to work: 48.6% less than 15 minutes, 28.2% 15 to 30 minutes, 9.3% 30 to 45 minutes, 6.8% 45 to 60 minutes, 7.0% 60 minutes or more (2000)

OAKLAND (town). Covers a land area of 25.989 square miles and a water area of 6.940 square miles. Located at 45.94° N. Lat.; 92.34° W. Long. Elevation is 1,004 feet.
Population: 778 (2000); Race: 95.3% White, 0.0% Black, 0.0% Asian, 4.5% American Indian and Alaska Native, 0.0% Hispanic of any race, 0.3% two or more races (2000); Density: 29.9 persons per square mile (2000); Age: 12.6% under 18, 25.6% over 64 (2000); Marriage status: 15.5% never married, 65.8% now married, 4.6% widowed, 14.1% divorced (2000); Foreign born: 0.0% (2000); Ancestry (includes multiple ancestries): 35.5% German, 18.1% Norwegian, 12.0% Swedish, 9.9% English, 8.0% Irish (2000).
Economy: Employment by occupation: 9.0% management, 21.6% professional, 25.1% services, 20.7% sales, 0.0% farming, 8.7% construction, 15.0% production (2000).
Income: Per capita income: $19,773 (2000); Median household income: $35,859 (2000); Poverty rate: 5.4% (2000).
Taxes: Total city taxes per capita: $117 (1997); City property taxes per capita: $110 (1997).
Education: High school graduation rate: 85.5% (2000); College graduation rate: 17.3% (2000).
Housing: Homeownership rate: 91.3% (2000); Median home value: $99,300 (2000); Median rent: $364 per month (2000); Median age of housing: 22 years (2000).
Transportation: Commute to work: 91.5% car, 0.0% public transportation, 3.5% walk, 4.4% work from home (2000); Travel time to work: 40.8% less than 15 minutes, 26.0% 15 to 30 minutes, 13.8% 30 to 45 minutes, 10.2% 45 to 60 minutes, 9.2% 60 minutes or more (2000)

ROOSEVELT (town). Covers a land area of 35.128 square miles and a water area of 0.222 square miles. Located at 45.69° N. Lat.; 92.09° W. Long.

Population: 197 (2000); Race: 92.0% White, 0.0% Black, 0.0% Asian, 3.0% American Indian and Alaska Native, 0.0% Hispanic of any race, 5.0% two or more races (2000); Density: 5.6 persons per square mile (2000); Age: 22.6% under 18, 15.6% over 64 (2000); Marriage status: 20.1% never married, 62.2% now married, 1.2% widowed, 16.5% divorced (2000); Foreign born: 1.0% (2000); Ancestry (includes multiple ancestries): 24.1% German, 14.6% Norwegian, 12.1% Irish, 7.5% English, 6.0% United States or American (2000).
Economy: Employment by occupation: 18.5% management, 14.8% professional, 13.0% services, 18.5% sales, 1.9% farming, 6.5% construction, 26.9% production (2000).
Income: Per capita income: $17,586 (2000); Median household income: $34,500 (2000); Poverty rate: 6.0% (2000).
Taxes: Total city taxes per capita: $60 (1997); City property taxes per capita: $60 (1997).
Education: High school graduation rate: 81.4% (2000); College graduation rate: 7.9% (2000).
Housing: Homeownership rate: 90.8% (2000); Median home value: $77,000 (2000); Median rent: $425 per month (2000); Median age of housing: 25 years (2000).
Transportation: Commute to work: 82.7% car, 0.0% public transportation, 1.9% walk, 15.4% work from home (2000); Travel time to work: 12.5% less than 15 minutes, 42.0% 15 to 30 minutes, 14.8% 30 to 45 minutes, 17.0% 45 to 60 minutes, 13.6% 60 minutes or more (2000)

RUSK (town). Covers a land area of 32.614 square miles and a water area of 2.082 square miles. Located at 45.87° N. Lat.; 92.09° W. Long.
Population: 420 (2000); Race: 98.4% White, 0.0% Black, 0.0% Asian, 0.0% American Indian and Alaska Native, 0.4% Hispanic of any race, 0.0% two or more races (2000); Density: 12.9 persons per square mile (2000); Age: 22.4% under 18, 15.2% over 64 (2000); Marriage status: 14.9% never married, 71.6% now married, 6.6% widowed, 6.9% divorced (2000); Foreign born: 1.6% (2000); Ancestry (includes multiple ancestries): 35.6% German, 20.8% Irish, 11.6% English, 8.1% Norwegian, 6.9% Swedish (2000).
Economy: Employment by occupation: 15.3% management, 18.0% professional, 12.0% services, 20.8% sales, 7.7% farming, 15.3% construction, 10.9% production (2000).
Income: Per capita income: $15,368 (2000); Median household income: $33,750 (2000); Poverty rate: 8.3% (2000).
Taxes: Total city taxes per capita: $87 (1997); City property taxes per capita: $85 (1997).
Education: High school graduation rate: 82.7% (2000); College graduation rate: 13.8% (2000).
Housing: Homeownership rate: 92.4% (2000); Median home value: $97,900 (2000); Median rent: $438 per month (2000); Median age of housing: 20 years (2000).
Transportation: Commute to work: 84.2% car, 0.0% public transportation, 8.5% walk, 7.3% work from home (2000); Travel time to work: 11.0% less than 15 minutes, 48.8% 15 to 30 minutes, 9.8% 30 to 45 minutes, 15.9% 45 to 60 minutes, 14.6% 60 minutes or more (2000)

SAND LAKE (town). Covers a land area of 32.755 square miles and a water area of 3.443 square miles. Located at 45.84° N. Lat.; 92.22° W. Long.
Population: 556 (2000); Race: 75.8% White, 0.0% Black, 1.0% Asian, 21.2% American Indian and Alaska Native, 0.0% Hispanic of any race, 2.0% two or more races (2000); Density: 17.0 persons per square mile (2000); Age: 26.8% under 18, 14.3% over 64 (2000); Marriage status: 26.5% never married, 56.1% now married, 5.1% widowed, 12.3% divorced (2000); Foreign born: 3.9% (2000); Ancestry (includes multiple ancestries): 29.1% German, 19.9% Other groups, 13.2% Swedish, 9.0% Norwegian, 8.6% Irish (2000).
Economy: Single-family building permits issued: 0 (2001) / 0 (2000); Multi-family building permits issued: 0 (2001) / 0 (2000); Employment by occupation: 11.0% management, 9.1% professional, 26.4% services, 20.9% sales, 0.8% farming, 10.6% construction, 21.3% production (2000).
Income: Per capita income: $16,575 (2000); Median household income: $39,583 (2000); Poverty rate: 13.2% (2000).
Taxes: Total city taxes per capita: $208 (1997); City property taxes per capita: $208 (1997).
Education: High school graduation rate: 81.7% (2000); College graduation rate: 9.0% (2000).
Housing: Homeownership rate: 75.7% (2000); Median home value: $119,400 (2000); Median rent: $217 per month (2000); Median age of housing: 21 years (2000).
Transportation: Commute to work: 93.6% car, 0.0% public transportation, 0.0% walk, 5.2% work from home (2000); Travel time to work: 29.2% less than 15 minutes, 27.5% 15 to 30 minutes, 22.9% 30 to 45 minutes, 7.2% 45 to 60 minutes, 13.1% 60 minutes or more (2000)

SCOTT (town). Covers a land area of 27.726 square miles and a water area of 6.478 square miles. Located at 45.93° N. Lat.; 92.11° W. Long.
Population: 590 (2000); Race: 98.5% White, 0.0% Black, 1.2% Asian, 0.3% American Indian and Alaska Native, 0.0% Hispanic of any race, 0.0% two or more races (2000); Density: 21.3 persons per square mile (2000); Age: 11.3% under 18, 32.2% over 64 (2000); Marriage status: 13.3% never married, 68.3% now married, 10.4% widowed, 8.0% divorced (2000); Foreign born: 2.7% (2000); Ancestry (includes multiple ancestries): 34.0% German, 18.9% Norwegian, 12.3% Swedish, 9.3% Irish, 8.9% English (2000).
Economy: Employment by occupation: 20.2% management, 17.7% professional, 16.7% services, 20.7% sales, 4.4% farming, 14.3% construction, 5.9% production (2000).
Income: Per capita income: $18,716 (2000); Median household income: $33,854 (2000); Poverty rate: 6.9% (2000).
Taxes: Total city taxes per capita: $323 (1997); City property taxes per capita: $316 (1997).
Education: High school graduation rate: 88.2% (2000); College graduation rate: 22.5% (2000).
Housing: Homeownership rate: 94.2% (2000); Median home value: $153,000 (2000); Median rent: $375 per month (2000); Median age of housing: 27 years (2000).
Transportation: Commute to work: 86.3% car, 1.5% public transportation, 6.1% walk, 6.1% work from home (2000); Travel time to work: 37.3% less than 15 minutes, 24.9% 15 to 30 minutes, 21.6% 30 to 45 minutes, 9.7% 45 to 60 minutes, 6.5% 60 minutes or more (2000)

SIREN (village). Covers a land area of 1.104 square miles and a water area of 0.022 square miles. Located at 45.78° N. Lat.; 92.38° W. Long. Elevation is 996 feet.
Population: 988 (2000); Race: 95.1% White, 0.0% Black, 0.0% Asian, 2.5% American Indian and Alaska Native, 0.5% Hispanic of any race, 2.4% two or more races (2000); Density: 895.1 persons per square mile (2000); Age: 20.1% under 18, 30.5% over 64 (2000); Marriage status: 25.9% never married, 49.8% now married, 14.1% widowed, 10.2% divorced (2000); Foreign born: 1.7% (2000); Ancestry (includes multiple ancestries): 33.9% German, 20.9% Swedish, 20.2% Norwegian, 14.8% Irish, 8.8% English (2000).
Economy: Single-family building permits issued: 7 (2001) / 5 (2000); Multi-family building permits issued: 0 (2001) / 0 (2000); Employment by occupation: 5.6% management, 14.4% professional, 17.2% services, 22.9% sales, 1.3% farming, 8.2% construction, 30.4% production (2000).
Income: Per capita income: $14,792 (2000); Median household income: $24,342 (2000); Poverty rate: 18.3% (2000).
Taxes: Total city taxes per capita: $86 (1997); City property taxes per capita: $74 (1997).
Education: High school graduation rate: 75.4% (2000); College graduation rate: 11.9% (2000).

School District(s)

Siren (PK-12)
2000 Enrollment: 509 715-349-2290

Housing: Homeownership rate: 60.0% (2000); Median home value: $71,300 (2000); Median rent: $346 per month (2000); Median age of housing: 34 years (2000).
Safety: Violent crime rate: 70.4 per 10,000 population; Property crime rate: 683.4 per 10,000 population (2001).
Transportation: Commute to work: 87.4% car, 0.0% public transportation, 6.8% walk, 4.2% work from home (2000); Travel time to work: 54.9% less than 15 minutes, 19.2% 15 to 30 minutes, 9.4% 30 to 45 minutes, 4.0% 45 to 60 minutes, 12.5% 60 minutes or more (2000)

SIREN (town). Covers a land area of 31.426 square miles and a water area of 4.572 square miles. Located at 45.77° N. Lat.; 92.35° W. Long. Elevation is 996 feet.
Population: 873 (2000); Race: 98.1% White, 0.2% Black, 0.0% Asian, 0.1% American Indian and Alaska Native, 0.2% Hispanic of any race, 1.5% two or more races (2000); Density: 27.8 persons per square mile (2000); Age: 20.3% under 18, 20.9% over 64 (2000); Marriage status: 17.0% never married, 64.3% now married, 7.5% widowed, 11.1% divorced (2000); Foreign born: 0.2% (2000); Ancestry (includes multiple ancestries): 35.8% German, 19.5% Swedish, 16.2% Norwegian, 11.3% Irish, 8.7% English (2000).
Economy: Manufacturing of furniture, fencing. Employment by occupation: 13.1% management, 12.0% professional, 18.6% services, 17.1% sales, 0.9% farming, 13.8% construction, 24.5% production (2000).

Income: Per capita income: $19,434 (2000); Median household income: $36,397 (2000); Poverty rate: 6.1% (2000).
Taxes: Total city taxes per capita: $78 (1997); City property taxes per capita: $76 (1997).
Education: High school graduation rate: 83.3% (2000); College graduation rate: 9.4% (2000).
Housing: Homeownership rate: 89.9% (2000); Median home value: $97,200 (2000); Median rent: $454 per month (2000); Median age of housing: 25 years (2000).
Transportation: Commute to work: 91.2% car, 0.0% public transportation, 2.0% walk, 5.3% work from home (2000); Travel time to work: 47.8% less than 15 minutes, 22.0% 15 to 30 minutes, 12.1% 30 to 45 minutes, 5.6% 45 to 60 minutes, 12.5% 60 minutes or more (2000)

SWISS (town). Covers a land area of 57.442 square miles and a water area of 3.258 square miles. Located at 46.01° N. Lat.; 92.29° W. Long.
Population: 815 (2000); Race: 73.6% White, 0.7% Black, 0.0% Asian, 19.3% American Indian and Alaska Native, 0.0% Hispanic of any race, 4.4% two or more races (2000); Density: 14.2 persons per square mile (2000); Age: 21.8% under 18, 19.8% over 64 (2000); Marriage status: 30.6% never married, 52.9% now married, 5.4% widowed, 11.1% divorced (2000); Foreign born: 1.9% (2000); Ancestry (includes multiple ancestries): 26.4% German, 26.2% Other groups, 14.2% Irish, 11.0% English, 8.4% Swedish (2000).
Economy: Employment by occupation: 7.6% management, 17.2% professional, 23.2% services, 24.2% sales, 1.6% farming, 13.1% construction, 13.1% production (2000).
Income: Per capita income: $16,870 (2000); Median household income: $30,461 (2000); Poverty rate: 10.2% (2000).
Taxes: Total city taxes per capita: $153 (1997); City property taxes per capita: $147 (1997).
Education: High school graduation rate: 82.0% (2000); College graduation rate: 15.4% (2000).
Housing: Homeownership rate: 75.7% (2000); Median home value: $85,900 (2000); Median rent: $334 per month (2000); Median age of housing: 23 years (2000).
Transportation: Commute to work: 83.7% car, 0.0% public transportation, 6.9% walk, 6.9% work from home (2000); Travel time to work: 30.2% less than 15 minutes, 29.1% 15 to 30 minutes, 18.6% 30 to 45 minutes, 8.1% 45 to 60 minutes, 14.0% 60 minutes or more (2000)

TRADE LAKE (town). Covers a land area of 32.538 square miles and a water area of 2.986 square miles. Located at 45.68° N. Lat.; 92.59° W. Long. Elevation is 920 feet.
Population: 871 (2000); Race: 99.6% White, 0.0% Black, 0.0% Asian, 0.0% American Indian and Alaska Native, 0.6% Hispanic of any race, 0.4% two or more races (2000); Density: 26.8 persons per square mile (2000); Age: 23.3% under 18, 18.1% over 64 (2000); Marriage status: 19.6% never married, 64.3% now married, 7.3% widowed, 8.9% divorced (2000); Foreign born: 1.0% (2000); Ancestry (includes multiple ancestries): 33.0% German, 32.2% Swedish, 16.4% Norwegian, 9.9% Irish, 5.8% French (except Basque) (2000).
Economy: Employment by occupation: 16.7% management, 13.6% professional, 11.3% services, 23.6% sales, 0.0% farming, 10.5% construction, 24.4% production (2000).
Income: Per capita income: $19,863 (2000); Median household income: $35,982 (2000); Poverty rate: 8.5% (2000).
Taxes: Total city taxes per capita: $76 (1997); City property taxes per capita: $76 (1997).
Education: High school graduation rate: 83.7% (2000); College graduation rate: 17.1% (2000).
Housing: Homeownership rate: 93.9% (2000); Median home value: $92,500 (2000); Median rent: $758 per month (2000); Median age of housing: 35 years (2000).
Transportation: Commute to work: 85.7% car, 0.0% public transportation, 5.8% walk, 7.4% work from home (2000); Travel time to work: 20.9% less than 15 minutes, 33.4% 15 to 30 minutes, 19.4% 30 to 45 minutes, 4.3% 45 to 60 minutes, 22.0% 60 minutes or more (2000)

UNION (town). Covers a land area of 34.490 square miles and a water area of 3.383 square miles. Located at 45.93° N. Lat.; 92.47° W. Long.
Population: 351 (2000); Race: 99.1% White, 0.0% Black, 0.0% Asian, 0.3% American Indian and Alaska Native, 0.0% Hispanic of any race, 0.6% two or more races (2000); Density: 10.2 persons per square mile (2000); Age: 8.6% under 18, 31.0% over 64 (2000); Marriage status: 10.8% never married, 68.7% now married, 9.6% widowed, 10.8% divorced (2000); Foreign born: 0.0% (2000); Ancestry (includes multiple ancestries): 50.0% German, 13.5% Swedish, 13.2% English, 11.5% Norwegian, 5.2% French (except Basque) (2000).
Economy: Employment by occupation: 15.7% management, 13.9% professional, 24.3% services, 12.2% sales, 0.9% farming, 10.4% construction, 22.6% production (2000).
Income: Per capita income: $18,404 (2000); Median household income: $31,250 (2000); Poverty rate: 8.0% (2000).
Taxes: Total city taxes per capita: $199 (1997); City property taxes per capita: $195 (1997).
Education: High school graduation rate: 82.7% (2000); College graduation rate: 11.5% (2000).
Housing: Homeownership rate: 97.2% (2000); Median home value: $128,200 (2000); Median age of housing: 22 years (2000).
Transportation: Commute to work: 85.8% car, 5.3% public transportation, 4.4% walk, 4.4% work from home (2000); Travel time to work: 18.5% less than 15 minutes, 39.8% 15 to 30 minutes, 24.1% 30 to 45 minutes, 7.4% 45 to 60 minutes, 10.2% 60 minutes or more (2000)

WEBB LAKE (town). Covers a land area of 31.983 square miles and a water area of 4.194 square miles. Located at 46.02° N. Lat.; 92.12° W. Long. Elevation is 1,015 feet.
Population: 381 (2000); Race: 99.3% White, 0.0% Black, 0.0% Asian, 0.7% American Indian and Alaska Native, 0.0% Hispanic of any race, 0.0% two or more races (2000); Density: 11.9 persons per square mile (2000); Age: 16.6% under 18, 29.9% over 64 (2000); Marriage status: 16.3% never married, 63.6% now married, 7.2% widowed, 12.8% divorced (2000); Foreign born: 2.1% (2000); Ancestry (includes multiple ancestries): 25.6% German, 12.3% Irish, 11.4% Swedish, 9.5% Norwegian, 7.8% English (2000).
Economy: Employment by occupation: 12.7% management, 11.2% professional, 28.4% services, 19.4% sales, 0.0% farming, 20.9% construction, 7.5% production (2000).
Income: Per capita income: $17,584 (2000); Median household income: $31,033 (2000); Poverty rate: 5.0% (2000).
Taxes: Total city taxes per capita: $412 (1997); City property taxes per capita: $404 (1997).
Education: High school graduation rate: 86.3% (2000); College graduation rate: 16.4% (2000).
Housing: Homeownership rate: 98.0% (2000); Median home value: $122,900 (2000); Median rent: $275 per month (2000); Median age of housing: 27 years (2000).
Transportation: Commute to work: 88.4% car, 0.0% public transportation, 1.6% walk, 10.1% work from home (2000); Travel time to work: 30.2% less than 15 minutes, 24.1% 15 to 30 minutes, 24.1% 30 to 45 minutes, 7.8% 45 to 60 minutes, 13.8% 60 minutes or more (2000)

WEBSTER (village). Covers a land area of 1.775 square miles and a water area of 0 square miles. Located at 45.87° N. Lat.; 92.36° W. Long. Elevation is 980 feet.
Population: 653 (2000); Race: 91.2% White, 0.0% Black, 0.0% Asian, 6.4% American Indian and Alaska Native, 0.0% Hispanic of any race, 2.4% two or more races (2000); Density: 367.8 persons per square mile (2000); Age: 23.5% under 18, 27.4% over 64 (2000); Marriage status: 15.6% never married, 54.8% now married, 14.7% widowed, 14.9% divorced (2000); Foreign born: 0.3% (2000); Ancestry (includes multiple ancestries): 34.7% German, 15.7% Swedish, 11.1% Irish, 11.0% Norwegian, 10.7% Polish (2000).
Economy: Dairy products, woodworking; manufacturing of brakes and clutches, concrete. St. Croix National Scenic Riverway to West and Northwest. Single-family building permits issued: 2 (2001) / 5 (2000); Multi-family building permits issued: 0 (2001) / 0 (2000); Employment by occupation: 9.9% management, 15.8% professional, 24.9% services, 19.0% sales, 1.8% farming, 16.1% construction, 12.5% production (2000).
Income: Per capita income: $15,411 (2000); Median household income: $29,432 (2000); Poverty rate: 9.9% (2000).
Taxes: Total city taxes per capita: $254 (1997); City property taxes per capita: $233 (1997).
Education: High school graduation rate: 74.9% (2000); College graduation rate: 9.2% (2000).

School District(s)

Webster (PK-12)
2000 Enrollment: 778 715-866-4391

Housing: Homeownership rate: 66.7% (2000); Median home value: $59,500 (2000); Median rent: $272 per month (2000); Median age of housing: 39 years (2000).

Transportation: Commute to work: 79.0% car, 0.0% public transportation, 17.0% walk, 2.6% work from home (2000); Travel time to work: 50.0% less than 15 minutes, 27.7% 15 to 30 minutes, 14.4% 30 to 45 minutes, 1.5% 45 to 60 minutes, 6.4% 60 minutes or more (2000)

WEST MARSHLAND (town). Covers a land area of 69.342 square miles and a water area of 4.072 square miles. Located at 45.87° N. Lat.; 92.63° W. Long.
Population: 331 (2000); Race: 99.3% White, 0.0% Black, 0.0% Asian, 0.7% American Indian and Alaska Native, 0.0% Hispanic of any race, 0.0% two or more races (2000); Density: 4.8 persons per square mile (2000); Age: 26.2% under 18, 5.3% over 64 (2000); Marriage status: 27.1% never married, 61.9% now married, 4.0% widowed, 6.9% divorced (2000); Foreign born: 0.0% (2000); Ancestry (includes multiple ancestries): 35.5% German, 20.3% Norwegian, 17.9% Swedish, 9.6% French (except Basque), 8.3% French Canadian (2000).
Economy: Single-family building permits issued: 12 (2001) / 4 (2000); Multi-family building permits issued: 0 (2001) / 0 (2000); Employment by occupation: 9.7% management, 12.1% professional, 17.0% services, 14.5% sales, 1.2% farming, 15.8% construction, 29.7% production (2000).
Income: Per capita income: $16,552 (2000); Median household income: $40,625 (2000); Poverty rate: 5.6% (2000).
Education: High school graduation rate: 83.6% (2000); College graduation rate: 7.7% (2000).
Housing: Homeownership rate: 87.9% (2000); Median home value: $45,000 (2000); Median age of housing: 19 years (2000).
Transportation: Commute to work: 95.2% car, 0.0% public transportation, 0.0% walk, 3.6% work from home (2000); Travel time to work: 46.5% less than 15 minutes, 23.3% 15 to 30 minutes, 18.9% 30 to 45 minutes, 4.4% 45 to 60 minutes, 6.9% 60 minutes or more (2000)

WOOD RIVER (town). Covers a land area of 34.071 square miles and a water area of 1.615 square miles. Located at 45.76° N. Lat.; 92.57° W. Long.
Population: 974 (2000); Race: 95.6% White, 0.0% Black, 0.0% Asian, 2.0% American Indian and Alaska Native, 0.0% Hispanic of any race, 2.4% two or more races (2000); Density: 28.6 persons per square mile (2000); Age: 24.8% under 18, 14.5% over 64 (2000); Marriage status: 21.5% never married, 66.4% now married, 4.9% widowed, 7.2% divorced (2000); Foreign born: 0.4% (2000); Ancestry (includes multiple ancestries): 29.1% Swedish, 27.3% German, 22.1% Norwegian, 7.8% Irish, 6.6% English (2000).
Economy: Single-family building permits issued: 0 (2001) / 0 (2000); Multi-family building permits issued: 0 (2001) / 0 (2000); Employment by occupation: 10.6% management, 16.1% professional, 15.5% services, 18.9% sales, 2.1% farming, 9.3% construction, 27.6% production (2000).
Income: Per capita income: $20,500 (2000); Median household income: $40,476 (2000); Poverty rate: 6.9% (2000).
Taxes: Total city taxes per capita: $67 (1997); City property taxes per capita: $67 (1997).
Education: High school graduation rate: 87.0% (2000); College graduation rate: 16.1% (2000).
Housing: Homeownership rate: 80.8% (2000); Median home value: $94,200 (2000); Median rent: $336 per month (2000); Median age of housing: 36 years (2000).
Transportation: Commute to work: 87.5% car, 0.0% public transportation, 4.3% walk, 7.4% work from home (2000); Travel time to work: 47.5% less than 15 minutes, 28.4% 15 to 30 minutes, 7.1% 30 to 45 minutes, 6.9% 45 to 60 minutes, 10.1% 60 minutes or more (2000)

Calumet County

Located in eastern Wisconsin; bounded on the west by Lake Winnebago; drained by the Manitowoc River. Covers a land area of 319.80 square miles, a water area of 77.20 square miles, and is located in the Central Time Zone. The county government was organized in 1836. County seat is Chilton.

Calumet County is part of the Appleton-Oshkosh-Neenah, WI MSA. The entire metro area includes: Calumet County; Outagamie County; Winnebago County

Weather Station: Chilton Elevation: 839 feet

	Jan	Feb	Mar	Apr	May	Jun	Jul	Aug	Sep	Oct	Nov	Dec
High	24	29	40	55	69	78	82	80	72	59	43	30
Low	8	13	23	34	45	55	60	58	50	39	28	15
Precip	1.4	1.2	2.2	2.7	3.0	3.7	3.6	3.7	3.6	2.5	2.3	1.6
Snow	12.4	9.5	7.7	2.3	0.3	0.0	0.0	0.0	0.0	0.4	4.5	9.7

High and Low temperatures in degrees Fahrenheit; Precipitation and Snow in inches

Population: 40,631 (2000); Race: 97.0% White, 0.1% Black, 1.7% Asian, 0.3% American Indian and Alaska Native, 1.0% Hispanic of any race, 0.6% two or more races (2000); Density: 127.0 persons per square mile (2000); Age: 28.6% under 18, 10.8% over 64 (2000).
Religion: Five largest groups: 34.0% Catholic Church, 6.3% Lutheran Church—Missouri Synod, 4.0% United Church of Christ, 3.6% Wisconsin Evangelical Lutheran Synod, 1.7% The United Methodist Church (2000).
Economy: Unemployment rate: 4.1% (11/2002); Total civilian labor force: 26,421 (11/2002); Leading industries: 47.2% manufacturing; 12.3% retail trade; 8.3% accommodation & food services (2000); Companies that employ more than 1,000 persons: 2 (2000); Companies that employ more than 100 persons: 17 (2000); Farms: 703 totaling 143,579 acres (1997); Minority business ownership rate: 0.0% (1997); Women business ownership rate: 26.0% (1997); Retail sales per capita: $6,124 (1997). Single-family building permits issued: 452 (2001) / 324 (2000); Multi-family building permits issued: 26 (2001) / 64 (2000).
Income: Per capita income: $21,919 (2000); Median household income: $52,569 (2000); Poverty rate: 3.5% (2000); Bankruptcy rate: 1.42% (2001).
Taxes: Total county taxes per capita: $182 (2000); County property taxes per capita: $179 (2000).
Education: High school graduation rate: 87.3% (2000); College graduation rate: 20.8% (2000).
Housing: Homeownership rate: 80.4% (2000); Median home value: $109,300 (2000); Median rent: $439 per month (2000); Median age of housing: 26 years (2000).
Health: Birth rate: 118.1 per 10,000 population (1998); Age adjusted death rate: 81.5 per 10,000 population (1999); Age adjusted cancer mortality rate: 226.7 deaths per 100,000 population (1999). Number of physicians: 3.0 per 10,000 population (1999); Number of hospital beds: 6.4 per 10,000 population (1999).
Elections: 2000 Presidential election results: 41.1% Gore, 54.3% Bush, 3.3% Nader, 0.7% Buchanan
National and State Parks: Brillion State Wildlife Area; High Cliff State Park
Additional Information Contacts
Calumet County Government Offices 920-849-2361

Calumet County Communities

BRILLION (city). Covers a land area of 2.602 square miles and a water area of 0 square miles. Located at 44.17° N. Lat.; 88.06° W. Long. Elevation is 830 feet.
History: Brillion developed as a trading center for farmers in the surrounding area. Many of the early residents of Brillion were of German ancestry.
Population: 2,937 (2000); Race: 98.7% White, 0.1% Black, 0.3% Asian, 0.0% American Indian and Alaska Native, 1.0% Hispanic of any race, 0.7% two or more races (2000); Density: 1,128.8 persons per square mile (2000); Age: 26.2% under 18, 15.0% over 64 (2000); Marriage status: 21.1% never married, 63.8% now married, 8.3% widowed, 6.8% divorced (2000); Foreign born: 1.3% (2000); Ancestry (includes multiple ancestries): 70.7% German, 7.8% Irish, 4.8% Polish, 4.6% Czech, 3.7% Dutch (2000).
Economy: Single-family building permits issued: 6 (2001) / 10 (2000); Multi-family building permits issued: 2 (2001) / 16 (2000); Employment by occupation: 8.3% management, 16.4% professional, 10.8% services, 20.7% sales, 1.0% farming, 8.7% construction, 34.1% production (2000).
Income: Per capita income: $20,754 (2000); Median household income: $46,633 (2000); Poverty rate: 2.5% (2000).
Taxes: Total city taxes per capita: $322 (1997); City property taxes per capita: $307 (1997).
Education: High school graduation rate: 83.7% (2000); College graduation rate: 15.1% (2000).

School District(s)
Brillion (PK-12)
2000 Enrollment: 861 920-756-2368

Housing: Homeownership rate: 75.3% (2000); Median home value: $86,900 (2000); Median rent: $337 per month (2000); Median age of housing: 36 years (2000).
Newspapers: The Brillion News (1 x week)
Transportation: Commute to work: 86.6% car, 0.0% public transportation, 9.3% walk, 2.5% work from home (2000); Travel time to work: 55.4% less than 15 minutes, 15.0% 15 to 30 minutes, 22.5% 30 to 45 minutes, 4.4% 45 to 60 minutes, 2.6% 60 minutes or more (2000)

BRILLION (town). Covers a land area of 33.280 square miles and a water area of 0.034 square miles. Located at 44.19° N. Lat.; 88.12° W. Long. Elevation is 830 feet.
History: Settled 1850; incorporated 1885 as village, 1944 as city.
Population: 1,438 (2000); Race: 97.7% White, 0.8% Black, 0.2% Asian, 0.4% American Indian and Alaska Native, 0.4% Hispanic of any race, 0.8% two or more races (2000); Density: 43.2 persons per square mile (2000); Age: 30.1% under 18, 8.7% over 64 (2000); Marriage status: 25.7% never married, 64.1% now married, 3.0% widowed, 7.3% divorced (2000); Foreign born: 0.2% (2000); Ancestry (includes multiple ancestries): 61.1% German, 8.5% Irish, 6.7% United States or American, 5.8% French (except Basque), 4.5% Other groups (2000).
Economy: Trade center for agricultural area: oats, clover seeds; dairy. Manufacturing: lawn mowers, fabricated metal products, zinc electroplating. Employment by occupation: 14.6% management, 12.5% professional, 8.8% services, 17.6% sales, 3.7% farming, 12.8% construction, 30.0% production (2000).
Income: Per capita income: $21,927 (2000); Median household income: $52,500 (2000); Poverty rate: 2.6% (2000).
Taxes: Total city taxes per capita: $150 (1997); City property taxes per capita: $138 (1997).
Education: High school graduation rate: 83.4% (2000); College graduation rate: 9.5% (2000).
Housing: Homeownership rate: 88.1% (2000); Median home value: $102,900 (2000); Median rent: $367 per month (2000); Median age of housing: 33 years (2000).
Transportation: Commute to work: 88.6% car, 0.0% public transportation, 2.8% walk, 8.6% work from home (2000); Travel time to work: 41.2% less than 15 minutes, 26.0% 15 to 30 minutes, 24.0% 30 to 45 minutes, 4.5% 45 to 60 minutes, 4.4% 60 minutes or more (2000)

BROTHERTOWN (town). Covers a land area of 36.783 square miles and a water area of 17.670 square miles. Located at 43.97° N. Lat.; 88.25° W. Long. Elevation is 810 feet.
History: Settled 1832 by Brothertown Indians.
Population: 1,404 (2000); Race: 99.0% White, 0.2% Black, 0.0% Asian, 0.0% American Indian and Alaska Native, 0.9% Hispanic of any race, 0.4% two or more races (2000); Density: 38.2 persons per square mile (2000); Age: 27.6% under 18, 10.9% over 64 (2000); Marriage status: 29.2% never married, 61.2% now married, 3.9% widowed, 5.7% divorced (2000); Foreign born: 1.0% (2000); Ancestry (includes multiple ancestries): 75.1% German, 7.1% Irish, 4.8% Polish, 2.5% French (except Basque), 2.1% Dutch (2000).
Economy: In agricultural region. Single-family building permits issued: 9 (2001) / 4 (2000); Multi-family building permits issued: 0 (2001) / 0 (2000); Employment by occupation: 16.0% management, 13.1% professional, 10.8% services, 16.0% sales, 2.2% farming, 14.4% construction, 27.5% production (2000).
Income: Per capita income: $19,816 (2000); Median household income: $49,861 (2000); Poverty rate: 1.6% (2000).
Taxes: Total city taxes per capita: $133 (1997); City property taxes per capita: $126 (1997).
Education: High school graduation rate: 81.9% (2000); College graduation rate: 11.7% (2000).
Housing: Homeownership rate: 86.8% (2000); Median home value: $111,600 (2000); Median rent: $358 per month (2000); Median age of housing: 41 years (2000).
Transportation: Commute to work: 85.9% car, 0.3% public transportation, 2.1% walk, 11.1% work from home (2000); Travel time to work: 28.2% less than 15 minutes, 41.7% 15 to 30 minutes, 16.1% 30 to 45 minutes, 8.5% 45 to 60 minutes, 5.5% 60 minutes or more (2000)

CHARLESTOWN (town). Covers a land area of 31.805 square miles and a water area of 0.044 square miles. Located at 44.01° N. Lat.; 88.10° W. Long.
Population: 789 (2000); Race: 96.8% White, 0.0% Black, 0.0% Asian, 0.0% American Indian and Alaska Native, 0.6% Hispanic of any race, 2.2% two or more races (2000); Density: 24.8 persons per square mile (2000); Age: 26.9% under 18, 13.2% over 64 (2000); Marriage status: 22.4% never married, 65.6% now married, 4.2% widowed, 7.9% divorced (2000); Foreign born: 0.0% (2000); Ancestry (includes multiple ancestries): 76.0% German, 11.3% Irish, 6.4% Other groups, 5.8% French (except Basque), 3.7% Norwegian (2000).
Economy: Employment by occupation: 20.7% management, 11.7% professional, 10.2% services, 15.7% sales, 2.6% farming, 7.4% construction, 31.7% production (2000).
Income: Per capita income: $24,715 (2000); Median household income: $52,300 (2000); Poverty rate: 4.0% (2000).
Taxes: Total city taxes per capita: $67 (1997); City property taxes per capita: $66 (1997).
Education: High school graduation rate: 81.7% (2000); College graduation rate: 14.6% (2000).
Housing: Homeownership rate: 86.9% (2000); Median home value: $114,200 (2000); Median rent: $339 per month (2000); Median age of housing: 40 years (2000).
Transportation: Commute to work: 88.1% car, 1.0% public transportation, 2.9% walk, 5.1% work from home (2000); Travel time to work: 60.1% less than 15 minutes, 18.2% 15 to 30 minutes, 9.2% 30 to 45 minutes, 9.0% 45 to 60 minutes, 3.6% 60 minutes or more (2000)

CHILTON (city). Covers a land area of 3.893 square miles and a water area of 0.017 square miles. Located at 44.03° N. Lat.; 88.15° W. Long. Elevation is 902 feet.
History: Chilton was founded by Moses Stanton, called Elder Stanton, who served as both preacher and doctor to his neighbors. Stanton's wife, a descendant of the Massasoit King Philip who befriended the Pilgrims at Plymouth, was instrumental in gathering the votes that made Chilton the seat of Calumet County in 1856. In the early 1900's, Calumet became a center for the dairy farmers, with a condensery and a cheese factory.
Population: 3,708 (2000); Race: 98.4% White, 0.3% Black, 0.7% Asian, 0.3% American Indian and Alaska Native, 0.1% Hispanic of any race, 0.4% two or more races (2000); Density: 952.4 persons per square mile (2000); Age: 25.0% under 18, 18.7% over 64 (2000); Marriage status: 23.8% never married, 60.8% now married, 8.1% widowed, 7.3% divorced (2000); Foreign born: 0.6% (2000); Ancestry (includes multiple ancestries): 68.2% German, 13.9% Irish, 7.0% French (except Basque), 3.6% United States or American, 3.3% Polish (2000).
Economy: Single-family building permits issued: 4 (2001) / 2 (2000); Multi-family building permits issued: 4 (2001) / 18 (2000); Employment by occupation: 8.1% management, 11.8% professional, 15.0% services, 19.8% sales, 0.4% farming, 7.4% construction, 37.5% production (2000).
Income: Per capita income: $19,778 (2000); Median household income: $38,401 (2000); Poverty rate: 7.4% (2000).
Taxes: Total city taxes per capita: $197 (1997); City property taxes per capita: $179 (1997).
Education: High school graduation rate: 79.5% (2000); College graduation rate: 12.2% (2000).

School District(s)

Chilton (PK-12)
2000 Enrollment: 1,355 920-849-2358
Housing: Homeownership rate: 68.4% (2000); Median home value: $84,900 (2000); Median rent: $416 per month (2000); Median age of housing: 41 years (2000).
Hospitals: Calumet Memorial Hospital (53 beds)
Safety: Violent crime rate: 5.4 per 10,000 population; Property crime rate: 192.8 per 10,000 population (2001).
Newspapers: Chilton Times Journal (1 x week)
Transportation: Commute to work: 90.9% car, 0.0% public transportation, 7.0% walk, 1.5% work from home (2000); Travel time to work: 57.2% less than 15 minutes, 17.8% 15 to 30 minutes, 10.2% 30 to 45 minutes, 9.7% 45 to 60 minutes, 5.0% 60 minutes or more (2000)

CHILTON (town). Covers a land area of 32.513 square miles and a water area of 0 square miles. Located at 44.06° N. Lat.; 88.19° W. Long. Elevation is 902 feet.
History: Settled 1847, incorporated 1877.
Population: 1,130 (2000); Race: 99.7% White, 0.0% Black, 0.0% Asian, 0.2% American Indian and Alaska Native, 0.3% Hispanic of any race, 0.2% two or more races (2000); Density: 34.8 persons per square mile (2000); Age: 28.6% under 18, 9.6% over 64 (2000); Marriage status: 28.0% never married, 64.3% now married, 3.6% widowed, 4.0% divorced (2000); Foreign born: 0.3% (2000); Ancestry (includes multiple ancestries): 69.2% German, 5.0% Irish, 4.8% United States or American, 4.6% Dutch, 3.9% Polish (2000).
Economy: Trade center for dairying and farming area. Manufacturing: malt products, cheese, pet food, machinery. Dairy plants. Single-family building permits issued: 6 (2001) / 0 (2000); Multi-family building permits issued: 0 (2001) / 0 (2000); Employment by occupation: 17.1% management, 8.2% professional, 7.1% services, 24.1% sales, 4.2% farming, 11.4% construction, 27.9% production (2000).
Income: Per capita income: $19,561 (2000); Median household income: $53,603 (2000); Poverty rate: 2.3% (2000).

Taxes: Total city taxes per capita: $79 (1997); City property taxes per capita: $77 (1997).
Education: High school graduation rate: 85.1% (2000); College graduation rate: 9.6% (2000).
Housing: Homeownership rate: 84.5% (2000); Median home value: $119,600 (2000); Median rent: $327 per month (2000); Median age of housing: 60+ years (2000).
Transportation: Commute to work: 82.4% car, 0.5% public transportation, 3.7% walk, 13.4% work from home (2000); Travel time to work: 51.9% less than 15 minutes, 25.7% 15 to 30 minutes, 13.6% 30 to 45 minutes, 6.0% 45 to 60 minutes, 2.8% 60 minutes or more (2000)

FOREST JUNCTION (unincorporated postal area, zip code 54123). Covers a land area of 0.979 square miles and a water area of 0 square miles. Located at 44.20° N. Lat.; 88.15° W. Long. Elevation is 828 feet.
Population: 187 (2000); Race: 97.8% White, 0.0% Black, 0.0% Asian, 0.0% American Indian and Alaska Native, 0.9% Hispanic of any race, 2.2% two or more races (2000); Density: 191.0 persons per square mile (2000); Age: 38.1% under 18, 4.0% over 64 (2000); Marriage status: 14.6% never married, 68.1% now married, 0.0% widowed, 17.4% divorced (2000); Foreign born: 0.0% (2000); Ancestry (includes multiple ancestries): 36.3% German, 10.3% English, 9.9% Polish, 9.4% United States or American, 7.6% French (except Basque) (2000).
Economy: Barley; cheese. Employment by occupation: 7.1% management, 13.4% professional, 12.5% services, 19.6% sales, 0.0% farming, 7.1% construction, 40.2% production (2000).
Income: Per capita income: $17,305 (2000); Median household income: $39,583 (2000); Poverty rate: 6.7% (2000).
Education: High school graduation rate: 83.3% (2000); College graduation rate: 5.6% (2000).
Housing: Homeownership rate: 97.5% (2000); Median home value: $112,500 (2000); Median rent: $375 per month (2000); Median age of housing: 11 years (2000).
Transportation: Commute to work: 95.5% car, 0.0% public transportation, 4.5% walk, 0.0% work from home (2000); Travel time to work: 30.4% less than 15 minutes, 34.8% 15 to 30 minutes, 25.0% 30 to 45 minutes, 1.8% 45 to 60 minutes, 8.0% 60 minutes or more (2000)

HARRISON (town). Covers a land area of 33.515 square miles and a water area of 25.922 square miles. Located at 44.20° N. Lat.; 88.32° W. Long. Elevation is 989 feet.
Population: 5,756 (2000); Race: 98.0% White, 0.4% Black, 0.6% Asian, 0.1% American Indian and Alaska Native, 0.6% Hispanic of any race, 0.8% two or more races (2000); Density: 171.7 persons per square mile (2000); Age: 31.9% under 18, 6.5% over 64 (2000); Marriage status: 18.9% never married, 73.7% now married, 1.2% widowed, 6.1% divorced (2000); Foreign born: 1.6% (2000); Ancestry (includes multiple ancestries): 58.3% German, 15.6% Dutch, 8.7% Polish, 7.1% Irish, 6.6% French (except Basque) (2000).
Economy: Employment by occupation: 15.3% management, 21.7% professional, 6.8% services, 27.2% sales, 1.3% farming, 10.5% construction, 17.2% production (2000).
Income: Per capita income: $24,690 (2000); Median household income: $66,094 (2000); Poverty rate: 1.4% (2000).
Taxes: Total city taxes per capita: $118 (1997); City property taxes per capita: $100 (1997).
Education: High school graduation rate: 93.8% (2000); College graduation rate: 32.1% (2000).
Housing: Homeownership rate: 92.2% (2000); Median home value: $144,000 (2000); Median rent: $667 per month (2000); Median age of housing: 9 years (2000).
Transportation: Commute to work: 94.4% car, 0.0% public transportation, 1.2% walk, 4.2% work from home (2000); Travel time to work: 30.9% less than 15 minutes, 51.9% 15 to 30 minutes, 11.6% 30 to 45 minutes, 2.5% 45 to 60 minutes, 3.1% 60 minutes or more (2000)

HILBERT (village). Covers a land area of 1.108 square miles and a water area of 0 square miles. Located at 44.14° N. Lat.; 88.16° W. Long. Elevation is 839 feet.
Population: 1,089 (2000); Race: 99.3% White, 0.0% Black, 0.0% Asian, 0.0% American Indian and Alaska Native, 1.7% Hispanic of any race, 0.3% two or more races (2000); Density: 982.8 persons per square mile (2000); Age: 26.9% under 18, 12.5% over 64 (2000); Marriage status: 28.5% never married, 55.5% now married, 7.7% widowed, 8.3% divorced (2000); Foreign born: 1.0% (2000); Ancestry (includes multiple ancestries): 66.3% German, 7.9% Irish, 5.3% United States or American, 4.4% Other groups, 3.6% French (except Basque) (2000).
Economy: Manufacturing: cheese, animal feed. Railroad junction. Single-family building permits issued: 5 (2001) / 0 (2000); Multi-family building permits issued: 0 (2001) / 0 (2000); Employment by occupation: 8.8% management, 7.3% professional, 15.3% services, 19.5% sales, 1.9% farming, 14.4% construction, 32.9% production (2000).
Income: Per capita income: $18,872 (2000); Median household income: $42,938 (2000); Poverty rate: 3.7% (2000).
Taxes: Total city taxes per capita: $136 (1997); City property taxes per capita: $114 (1997).
Education: High school graduation rate: 85.7% (2000); College graduation rate: 7.1% (2000).

School District(s)

Hilbert (KG-12)
2000 Enrollment: 543 920-853-3558

Housing: Homeownership rate: 80.6% (2000); Median home value: $84,000 (2000); Median rent: $352 per month (2000); Median age of housing: 29 years (2000).
Transportation: Commute to work: 94.1% car, 0.0% public transportation, 3.9% walk, 0.5% work from home (2000); Travel time to work: 30.3% less than 15 minutes, 35.7% 15 to 30 minutes, 23.2% 30 to 45 minutes, 8.6% 45 to 60 minutes, 2.1% 60 minutes or more (2000)

NEW HOLSTEIN (city). Covers a land area of 2.331 square miles and a water area of 0 square miles. Located at 43.94° N. Lat.; 88.09° W. Long. Elevation is 935 feet.
Population: 3,301 (2000); Race: 99.2% White, 0.0% Black, 0.1% Asian, 0.3% American Indian and Alaska Native, 0.2% Hispanic of any race, 0.3% two or more races (2000); Density: 1,415.9 persons per square mile (2000); Age: 22.8% under 18, 20.2% over 64 (2000); Marriage status: 20.0% never married, 63.2% now married, 6.4% widowed, 10.5% divorced (2000); Foreign born: 1.0% (2000); Ancestry (includes multiple ancestries): 73.2% German, 8.0% Polish, 6.9% Irish, 4.3% English, 4.2% French (except Basque) (2000).
Economy: Single-family building permits issued: 6 (2001) / 6 (2000); Multi-family building permits issued: 10 (2001) / 8 (2000); Employment by occupation: 5.9% management, 12.2% professional, 16.2% services, 24.6% sales, 0.4% farming, 8.9% construction, 31.9% production (2000).
Income: Per capita income: $19,911 (2000); Median household income: $43,180 (2000); Poverty rate: 3.0% (2000).
Taxes: Total city taxes per capita: $227 (1997); City property taxes per capita: $219 (1997).
Education: High school graduation rate: 84.0% (2000); College graduation rate: 13.4% (2000).

School District(s)

New Holstein (PK-12)
2000 Enrollment: 1,283 920-898-3005

Housing: Homeownership rate: 74.6% (2000); Median home value: $85,700 (2000); Median rent: $394 per month (2000); Median age of housing: 37 years (2000).
Safety: Violent crime rate: 3.0 per 10,000 population; Property crime rate: 174.4 per 10,000 population (2001).
Transportation: Commute to work: 82.5% car, 0.3% public transportation, 12.6% walk, 3.5% work from home (2000); Travel time to work: 66.0% less than 15 minutes, 20.9% 15 to 30 minutes, 7.7% 30 to 45 minutes, 2.9% 45 to 60 minutes, 2.5% 60 minutes or more (2000)

NEW HOLSTEIN (town). Covers a land area of 31.918 square miles and a water area of 0.081 square miles. Located at 43.93° N. Lat.; 88.09° W. Long. Elevation is 935 feet.
History: Settled 1849, incorporated 1926.
Population: 1,457 (2000); Race: 99.7% White, 0.0% Black, 0.0% Asian, 0.3% American Indian and Alaska Native, 0.0% Hispanic of any race, 0.0% two or more races (2000); Density: 45.6 persons per square mile (2000); Age: 27.0% under 18, 9.0% over 64 (2000); Marriage status: 26.0% never married, 64.7% now married, 4.3% widowed, 5.0% divorced (2000); Foreign born: 0.5% (2000); Ancestry (includes multiple ancestries): 73.7% German, 7.5% Irish, 4.2% Norwegian, 4.0% English, 3.6% French (except Basque) (2000).
Economy: In dairying and grain-growing area. Manufacturing: construction equipment, machinery, animal feed, engines. Employment by occupation: 15.1% management, 10.9% professional, 11.4% services, 18.0% sales, 2.3% farming, 10.8% construction, 31.5% production (2000).
Income: Per capita income: $21,371 (2000); Median household income: $58,050 (2000); Poverty rate: 6.4% (2000).
Taxes: Total city taxes per capita: $86 (1997); City property taxes per capita: $80 (1997).

Education: High school graduation rate: 84.7% (2000); College graduation rate: 11.5% (2000).
Housing: Homeownership rate: 87.7% (2000); Median home value: $117,900 (2000); Median rent: $352 per month (2000); Median age of housing: 30 years (2000).
Transportation: Commute to work: 89.2% car, 0.2% public transportation, 2.2% walk, 8.3% work from home (2000); Travel time to work: 53.8% less than 15 minutes, 20.4% 15 to 30 minutes, 18.7% 30 to 45 minutes, 6.0% 45 to 60 minutes, 1.1% 60 minutes or more (2000)

POTTER (village). Covers a land area of 0.528 square miles and a water area of 0 square miles. Located at 44.11° N. Lat.; 88.09° W. Long. Elevation is 820 feet.
Population: 223 (2000); Race: 93.3% White, 0.0% Black, 0.0% Asian, 6.7% American Indian and Alaska Native, 0.0% Hispanic of any race, 0.0% two or more races (2000); Density: 422.6 persons per square mile (2000); Age: 30.6% under 18, 12.4% over 64 (2000); Marriage status: 32.2% never married, 51.7% now married, 10.5% widowed, 5.6% divorced (2000); Foreign born: 0.0% (2000); Ancestry (includes multiple ancestries): 71.0% German, 6.7% Other groups, 4.7% United States or American, 3.1% Polish, 1.0% Irish (2000).
Economy: Single-family building permits issued: 0 (2001) / 1 (2000); Multi-family building permits issued: 0 (2001) / 0 (2000); Employment by occupation: 4.5% management, 1.8% professional, 10.8% services, 18.0% sales, 6.3% farming, 22.5% construction, 36.0% production (2000).
Income: Per capita income: $14,519 (2000); Median household income: $43,958 (2000); Poverty rate: 5.7% (2000).
Taxes: Total city taxes per capita: $8 (1997); City property taxes per capita: $4 (1997).
Education: High school graduation rate: 70.3% (2000); College graduation rate: 4.2% (2000).
Housing: Homeownership rate: 68.8% (2000); Median home value: $82,300 (2000); Median rent: $313 per month (2000); Median age of housing: 60+ years (2000).
Transportation: Commute to work: 93.7% car, 1.8% public transportation, 4.5% walk, 0.0% work from home (2000); Travel time to work: 46.8% less than 15 minutes, 27.9% 15 to 30 minutes, 16.2% 30 to 45 minutes, 5.4% 45 to 60 minutes, 3.6% 60 minutes or more (2000)

RANTOUL (town). Covers a land area of 32.438 square miles and a water area of 0.142 square miles. Located at 44.10° N. Lat.; 88.09° W. Long.
Population: 841 (2000); Race: 97.8% White, 0.0% Black, 0.0% Asian, 1.0% American Indian and Alaska Native, 0.5% Hispanic of any race, 1.1% two or more races (2000); Density: 25.9 persons per square mile (2000); Age: 31.8% under 18, 8.8% over 64 (2000); Marriage status: 21.0% never married, 70.8% now married, 3.7% widowed, 4.5% divorced (2000); Foreign born: 0.8% (2000); Ancestry (includes multiple ancestries): 71.5% German, 7.0% Irish, 6.4% United States or American, 3.5% Polish, 3.3% English (2000).
Economy: Employment by occupation: 17.8% management, 6.9% professional, 7.5% services, 23.8% sales, 6.1% farming, 9.4% construction, 28.5% production (2000).
Income: Per capita income: $18,316 (2000); Median household income: $48,000 (2000); Poverty rate: 3.1% (2000).
Taxes: Total city taxes per capita: $105 (1997); City property taxes per capita: $104 (1997).
Education: High school graduation rate: 84.5% (2000); College graduation rate: 7.4% (2000).
Housing: Homeownership rate: 89.1% (2000); Median home value: $101,200 (2000); Median rent: $358 per month (2000); Median age of housing: 60+ years (2000).
Transportation: Commute to work: 80.0% car, 0.0% public transportation, 3.0% walk, 17.1% work from home (2000); Travel time to work: 45.2% less than 15 minutes, 31.6% 15 to 30 minutes, 15.9% 30 to 45 minutes, 2.6% 45 to 60 minutes, 4.6% 60 minutes or more (2000)

SHERWOOD (village). Covers a land area of 2.914 square miles and a water area of 0.009 square miles. Located at 44.17° N. Lat.; 88.27° W. Long. Elevation is 890 feet.
Population: 1,550 (2000); Race: 97.9% White, 0.1% Black, 1.0% Asian, 0.3% American Indian and Alaska Native, 0.9% Hispanic of any race, 0.3% two or more races (2000); Density: 531.9 persons per square mile (2000); Age: 28.7% under 18, 10.4% over 64 (2000); Marriage status: 18.8% never married, 73.5% now married, 3.8% widowed, 3.8% divorced (2000); Foreign born: 1.3% (2000); Ancestry (includes multiple ancestries): 60.8% German, 11.1% Irish, 9.5% Dutch, 6.7% Norwegian, 5.2% Polish (2000).
Economy: Dairying, grain, vegetables, fruit. Single-family building permits issued: 74 (2001) / 51 (2000); Multi-family building permits issued: 0 (2001) / 0 (2000); Employment by occupation: 17.4% management, 22.2% professional, 12.1% services, 25.5% sales, 0.6% farming, 10.0% construction, 12.2% production (2000).
Income: Per capita income: $27,035 (2000); Median household income: $63,913 (2000); Poverty rate: 4.9% (2000).
Taxes: Total city taxes per capita: $445 (1997); City property taxes per capita: $423 (1997).
Education: High school graduation rate: 93.8% (2000); College graduation rate: 35.6% (2000).
Housing: Homeownership rate: 89.1% (2000); Median home value: $160,000 (2000); Median rent: $400 per month (2000); Median age of housing: 11 years (2000).
Transportation: Commute to work: 93.8% car, 0.0% public transportation, 2.4% walk, 3.8% work from home (2000); Travel time to work: 18.6% less than 15 minutes, 55.6% 15 to 30 minutes, 18.6% 30 to 45 minutes, 1.8% 45 to 60 minutes, 5.3% 60 minutes or more (2000)

STOCKBRIDGE (village). Covers a land area of 3.305 square miles and a water area of 0.002 square miles. Located at 44.07° N. Lat.; 88.31° W. Long. Elevation is 830 feet.
Population: 649 (2000); Race: 97.9% White, 0.2% Black, 0.3% Asian, 0.3% American Indian and Alaska Native, 0.0% Hispanic of any race, 1.4% two or more races (2000); Density: 196.4 persons per square mile (2000); Age: 25.8% under 18, 12.4% over 64 (2000); Marriage status: 22.5% never married, 61.6% now married, 7.2% widowed, 8.7% divorced (2000); Foreign born: 0.9% (2000); Ancestry (includes multiple ancestries): 57.2% German, 11.8% Irish, 5.8% Dutch, 4.7% United States or American, 4.6% French (except Basque) (2000).
Economy: Single-family building permits issued: 5 (2001) / 5 (2000); Multi-family building permits issued: 0 (2001) / 2 (2000); Employment by occupation: 16.4% management, 8.9% professional, 9.2% services, 21.3% sales, 0.9% farming, 9.5% construction, 33.9% production (2000).
Income: Per capita income: $21,129 (2000); Median household income: $48,021 (2000); Poverty rate: 2.5% (2000).
Taxes: Total city taxes per capita: $167 (1997); City property taxes per capita: $161 (1997).
Education: High school graduation rate: 84.1% (2000); College graduation rate: 13.6% (2000).

School District(s)

Stockbridge (PK-12)
2000 Enrollment: 265 920-439-1159

Housing: Homeownership rate: 81.4% (2000); Median home value: $93,900 (2000); Median rent: $350 per month (2000); Median age of housing: 35 years (2000).
Transportation: Commute to work: 92.6% car, 0.3% public transportation, 3.3% walk, 3.3% work from home (2000); Travel time to work: 18.1% less than 15 minutes, 34.7% 15 to 30 minutes, 35.0% 30 to 45 minutes, 5.8% 45 to 60 minutes, 6.4% 60 minutes or more (2000)

STOCKBRIDGE (town). Covers a land area of 33.625 square miles and a water area of 33.266 square miles. Located at 44.06° N. Lat.; 88.28° W. Long. Elevation is 830 feet.
History: Settled in 1820s by Stockbridge Indians (Mohicans), after having lost their traditional lands in New England to American settlers. Here, they were able to maintain some of their customs and way of life.
Population: 1,383 (2000); Race: 98.6% White, 0.2% Black, 0.1% Asian, 0.5% American Indian and Alaska Native, 0.6% Hispanic of any race, 0.4% two or more races (2000); Density: 41.1 persons per square mile (2000); Age: 24.5% under 18, 13.9% over 64 (2000); Marriage status: 23.4% never married, 66.6% now married, 5.5% widowed, 4.5% divorced (2000); Foreign born: 0.3% (2000); Ancestry (includes multiple ancestries): 70.9% German, 7.7% Irish, 6.3% Dutch, 3.5% Polish, 3.4% United States or American (2000).
Economy: In dairying and grain-growing area. Manufacturing: transportation equipment, machining. Single-family building permits issued: 15 (2001) / 8 (2000); Multi-family building permits issued: 0 (2001) / 0 (2000); Employment by occupation: 15.2% management, 14.8% professional, 8.9% services, 16.8% sales, 3.4% farming, 11.4% construction, 29.4% production (2000).
Income: Per capita income: $22,392 (2000); Median household income: $55,096 (2000); Poverty rate: 2.4% (2000).
Taxes: Total city taxes per capita: $61 (1997); City property taxes per capita: $60 (1997).

Education: High school graduation rate: 81.7% (2000); College graduation rate: 12.3% (2000).
Housing: Homeownership rate: 90.1% (2000); Median home value: $122,100 (2000); Median rent: $425 per month (2000); Median age of housing: 39 years (2000).
Transportation: Commute to work: 91.6% car, 0.5% public transportation, 2.7% walk, 5.2% work from home (2000); Travel time to work: 27.0% less than 15 minutes, 33.5% 15 to 30 minutes, 27.0% 30 to 45 minutes, 8.2% 45 to 60 minutes, 4.3% 60 minutes or more (2000)

WOODVILLE (town). Covers a land area of 32.901 square miles and a water area of 0 square miles. Located at 44.19° N. Lat.; 88.20° W. Long.
Population: 993 (2000); Race: 98.2% White, 0.0% Black, 0.0% Asian, 1.8% American Indian and Alaska Native, 0.0% Hispanic of any race, 0.0% two or more races (2000); Density: 30.2 persons per square mile (2000); Age: 28.0% under 18, 9.1% over 64 (2000); Marriage status: 23.8% never married, 67.5% now married, 4.2% widowed, 4.6% divorced (2000); Foreign born: 0.2% (2000); Ancestry (includes multiple ancestries): 72.4% German, 12.3% Dutch, 7.6% Irish, 5.0% United States or American, 3.2% English (2000).
Economy: Employment by occupation: 16.8% management, 6.9% professional, 9.9% services, 21.1% sales, 4.3% farming, 12.7% construction, 28.2% production (2000).
Income: Per capita income: $23,411 (2000); Median household income: $52,375 (2000); Poverty rate: 4.5% (2000).
Taxes: Total city taxes per capita: $37 (1997); City property taxes per capita: $35 (1997).
Education: High school graduation rate: 83.1% (2000); College graduation rate: 8.2% (2000).
Housing: Homeownership rate: 91.9% (2000); Median home value: $102,200 (2000); Median rent: $379 per month (2000); Median age of housing: 48 years (2000).
Transportation: Commute to work: 80.9% car, 0.3% public transportation, 3.5% walk, 15.1% work from home (2000); Travel time to work: 33.2% less than 15 minutes, 44.7% 15 to 30 minutes, 15.2% 30 to 45 minutes, 1.8% 45 to 60 minutes, 5.1% 60 minutes or more (2000)

Chippewa County

Located in west central Wisconsin; drained by the Chippewa River; includes Lake Wissota. Covers a land area of 1,010.40 square miles, a water area of 30.90 square miles, and is located in the Central Time Zone. The county government was organized in 1845. County seat is Chippewa Falls.

Chippewa County is part of the Eau Claire, WI MSA. The entire metro area includes: Chippewa County; Eau Claire County

Weather Station: Bloomer — Elevation: 977 feet

	Jan	Feb	Mar	Apr	May	Jun	Jul	Aug	Sep	Oct	Nov	Dec
High	21	28	40	57	70	78	83	80	71	58	40	26
Low	2	8	20	33	45	54	59	56	48	36	23	9
Precip	1.0	0.7	1.8	2.8	3.7	4.4	3.8	5.0	3.8	2.5	2.1	1.0
Snow	12.0	6.1	7.5	1.1	tr	0.0	0.0	0.0	tr	0.3	5.9	9.6

High and Low temperatures in degrees Fahrenheit; Precipitation and Snow in inches

Weather Station: Eau Claire County Airport — Elevation: 889 feet

	Jan	Feb	Mar	Apr	May	Jun	Jul	Aug	Sep	Oct	Nov	Dec
High	21	28	40	57	70	79	83	80	70	58	40	26
Low	2	8	21	33	46	55	60	58	48	37	23	10
Precip	1.0	0.8	1.9	2.9	3.7	4.1	4.0	4.7	3.6	2.4	1.9	1.0
Snow	13.7	7.3	9.3	2.3	tr	tr	tr	tr	tr	0.3	6.5	10.3

High and Low temperatures in degrees Fahrenheit; Precipitation and Snow in inches

Weather Station: Holcombe — Elevation: 1,023 feet

	Jan	Feb	Mar	Apr	May	Jun	Jul	Aug	Sep	Oct	Nov	Dec
High	22	29	40	56	70	78	82	79	71	58	41	27
Low	-0	7	19	33	44	53	58	56	47	37	24	9
Precip	1.0	0.8	1.7	2.6	3.4	4.1	3.6	4.7	4.0	2.5	2.1	1.0
Snow	na	na	na	0.7	tr	0.0	0.0	0.0	0.0	tr	na	na

High and Low temperatures in degrees Fahrenheit; Precipitation and Snow in inches

Weather Station: Stanley — Elevation: 1,089 feet

	Jan	Feb	Mar	Apr	May	Jun	Jul	Aug	Sep	Oct	Nov	Dec
High	21	28	40	56	69	77	81	79	70	57	40	26
Low	2	7	20	32	44	53	58	55	46	35	23	8
Precip	0.9	0.8	1.6	2.7	3.7	4.0	4.1	4.5	3.6	2.4	2.2	1.1
Snow	12.9	7.3	8.3	2.5	tr	0.0	0.0	0.0	tr	0.5	6.5	11.4

High and Low temperatures in degrees Fahrenheit; Precipitation and Snow in inches

Population: 55,195 (2000); Race: 98.0% White, 0.1% Black, 0.8% Asian, 0.3% American Indian and Alaska Native, 0.6% Hispanic of any race, 0.6% two or more races (2000); Density: 54.6 persons per square mile (2000); Age: 26.5% under 18, 14.6% over 64 (2000).
Religion: Five largest groups: 30.0% Catholic Church, 10.0% Evangelical Lutheran Church in America, 3.6% Lutheran Church—Missouri Synod, 2.9% The United Methodist Church, 1.8% Wisconsin Evangelical Lutheran Synod (2000).
Economy: Unemployment rate: 4.7% (11/2002); Total civilian labor force: 31,774 (11/2002); Leading industries: 31.9% manufacturing; 16.3% retail trade; 14.8% health care and social assistance (2000); Companies that employ more than 1,000 persons: 0 (2000); Companies that employ more than 100 persons: 34 (2000); Farms: 1,471 totaling 372,844 acres (1997); Minority business ownership rate: 0.0% (1997); Women business ownership rate: 16.2% (1997); Retail sales per capita: $8,865 (1997). Single-family building permits issued: 451 (2001) / 398 (2000); Multi-family building permits issued: 202 (2001) / 44 (2000).
Income: Per capita income: $18,243 (2000); Median household income: $39,596 (2000); Poverty rate: 8.2% (2000); Bankruptcy rate: 3.85% (2001).
Taxes: Total county taxes per capita: $181 (2000); County property taxes per capita: $121 (2000).
Education: High school graduation rate: 84.3% (2000); College graduation rate: 14.7% (2000).
Housing: Homeownership rate: 75.6% (2000); Median home value: $88,100 (2000); Median rent: $377 per month (2000); Median age of housing: 35 years (2000).
Health: Birth rate: 114.7 per 10,000 population (1998); Age adjusted death rate: 86.0 per 10,000 population (1999); Age adjusted cancer mortality rate: 207.9 deaths per 100,000 population (1999). Number of physicians: 13.2 per 10,000 population (1999); Number of hospital beds: 61.2 per 10,000 population (1999).
Elections: 2000 Presidential election results: 46.2% Gore, 49.0% Bush, 3.7% Nader, 0.4% Buchanan
National and State Parks: Brunet Island State Park; Drywood Creek State Public Hunting Ground; Elk Creek State Public Fishing Area; Hallie State Public Hunting Grounds; Lake Wissota State Park
Additional Information Contacts
Chippewa County Government Offices 715-726-7980
Bloomer Chamber of Commerce 715-568-3339
Cadott Chamber of Commerce 715-289-3338
Chippewa Falls Chamber of Commerce 715-723-0331

Chippewa County Communities

ANSON (town). Covers a land area of 37.429 square miles and a water area of 2.121 square miles. Located at 45.01° N. Lat.; 91.27° W. Long. Elevation is 946 feet.
Population: 1,881 (2000); Race: 99.5% White, 0.0% Black, 0.0% Asian, 0.1% American Indian and Alaska Native, 0.5% Hispanic of any race, 0.3% two or more races (2000); Density: 50.3 persons per square mile (2000); Age: 23.3% under 18, 12.1% over 64 (2000); Marriage status: 22.2% never married, 68.6% now married, 3.2% widowed, 6.0% divorced (2000); Foreign born: 0.4% (2000); Ancestry (includes multiple ancestries): 48.8% German, 20.9% Norwegian, 12.7% Irish, 7.3% French (except Basque), 6.7% Polish (2000).
Economy: Employment by occupation: 13.5% management, 18.3% professional, 12.3% services, 20.7% sales, 2.1% farming, 12.3% construction, 20.7% production (2000).
Income: Per capita income: $20,845 (2000); Median household income: $46,500 (2000); Poverty rate: 3.7% (2000).
Taxes: Total city taxes per capita: $28 (1997); City property taxes per capita: $27 (1997).
Education: High school graduation rate: 86.7% (2000); College graduation rate: 15.8% (2000).
Housing: Homeownership rate: 88.3% (2000); Median home value: $104,000 (2000); Median rent: $411 per month (2000); Median age of housing: 33 years (2000).
Transportation: Commute to work: 88.4% car, 0.3% public transportation, 3.1% walk, 7.7% work from home (2000); Travel time to work: 21.6% less than 15 minutes, 45.7% 15 to 30 minutes, 23.2% 30 to 45 minutes, 5.2% 45 to 60 minutes, 4.4% 60 minutes or more (2000)

ARTHUR (town). Covers a land area of 42.920 square miles and a water area of 0.155 square miles. Located at 45.07° N. Lat.; 91.15° W. Long.

Population: 710 (2000); Race: 99.5% White, 0.1% Black, 0.0% Asian, 0.0% American Indian and Alaska Native, 0.3% Hispanic of any race, 0.4% two or more races (2000); Density: 16.5 persons per square mile (2000); Age: 30.0% under 18, 10.1% over 64 (2000); Marriage status: 23.9% never married, 64.2% now married, 4.6% widowed, 7.3% divorced (2000); Foreign born: 0.3% (2000); Ancestry (includes multiple ancestries): 37.5% German, 15.2% Czech, 11.3% Norwegian, 7.5% French (except Basque), 7.2% United States or American (2000).
Economy: Employment by occupation: 20.3% management, 5.4% professional, 18.2% services, 18.7% sales, 3.3% farming, 16.5% construction, 17.6% production (2000).
Income: Per capita income: $15,570 (2000); Median household income: $40,000 (2000); Poverty rate: 13.4% (2000).
Taxes: Total city taxes per capita: $48 (1997); City property taxes per capita: $47 (1997).
Education: High school graduation rate: 78.7% (2000); College graduation rate: 8.3% (2000).
Housing: Homeownership rate: 87.4% (2000); Median home value: $67,300 (2000); Median rent: $350 per month (2000); Median age of housing: 46 years (2000).
Transportation: Commute to work: 81.3% car, 0.0% public transportation, 3.6% walk, 14.5% work from home (2000); Travel time to work: 30.6% less than 15 minutes, 26.4% 15 to 30 minutes, 30.0% 30 to 45 minutes, 9.1% 45 to 60 minutes, 3.9% 60 minutes or more (2000)

AUBURN (town). Covers a land area of 35.725 square miles and a water area of 0 square miles. Located at 45.16° N. Lat.; 91.61° W. Long.
Population: 580 (2000); Race: 98.2% White, 0.0% Black, 0.0% Asian, 0.0% American Indian and Alaska Native, 0.0% Hispanic of any race, 1.8% two or more races (2000); Density: 16.2 persons per square mile (2000); Age: 22.7% under 18, 14.5% over 64 (2000); Marriage status: 20.4% never married, 69.1% now married, 3.5% widowed, 7.0% divorced (2000); Foreign born: 1.1% (2000); Ancestry (includes multiple ancestries): 52.6% German, 21.8% Norwegian, 6.5% English, 5.0% Polish, 4.6% Irish (2000).
Economy: Dairying; livestock raising. State fishery. Employment by occupation: 18.5% management, 13.4% professional, 12.7% services, 19.7% sales, 2.5% farming, 11.8% construction, 21.3% production (2000).
Income: Per capita income: $17,164 (2000); Median household income: $36,000 (2000); Poverty rate: 8.2% (2000).
Taxes: Total city taxes per capita: $123 (1997); City property taxes per capita: $121 (1997).
Education: High school graduation rate: 82.7% (2000); College graduation rate: 10.7% (2000).
Housing: Homeownership rate: 90.4% (2000); Median home value: $87,000 (2000); Median rent: $363 per month (2000); Median age of housing: 27 years (2000).
Transportation: Commute to work: 81.2% car, 0.0% public transportation, 2.2% walk, 14.6% work from home (2000); Travel time to work: 37.7% less than 15 minutes, 23.1% 15 to 30 minutes, 29.1% 30 to 45 minutes, 7.5% 45 to 60 minutes, 2.6% 60 minutes or more (2000)

BIRCH CREEK (town). Covers a land area of 44.575 square miles and a water area of 2.073 square miles. Located at 45.23° N. Lat.; 91.22° W. Long.
Population: 520 (2000); Race: 100.0% White, 0.0% Black, 0.0% Asian, 0.0% American Indian and Alaska Native, 0.0% Hispanic of any race, 0.0% two or more races (2000); Density: 11.7 persons per square mile (2000); Age: 22.2% under 18, 20.0% over 64 (2000); Marriage status: 17.6% never married, 67.8% now married, 5.9% widowed, 8.8% divorced (2000); Foreign born: 0.4% (2000); Ancestry (includes multiple ancestries): 34.9% German, 15.4% Norwegian, 13.4% Polish, 10.2% United States or American, 9.4% Irish (2000).
Economy: Employment by occupation: 12.3% management, 9.0% professional, 12.3% services, 25.8% sales, 4.9% farming, 11.5% construction, 24.2% production (2000).
Income: Per capita income: $17,475 (2000); Median household income: $39,479 (2000); Poverty rate: 10.4% (2000).
Taxes: Total city taxes per capita: $110 (1997); City property taxes per capita: $105 (1997).
Education: High school graduation rate: 86.7% (2000); College graduation rate: 11.4% (2000).
Housing: Homeownership rate: 92.3% (2000); Median home value: $95,000 (2000); Median rent: $325 per month (2000); Median age of housing: 29 years (2000).
Transportation: Commute to work: 85.1% car, 0.0% public transportation, 2.1% walk, 10.7% work from home (2000); Travel time to work: 22.2% less than 15 minutes, 22.7% 15 to 30 minutes, 20.8% 30 to 45 minutes, 10.2% 45 to 60 minutes, 24.1% 60 minutes or more (2000)

BLOOMER (city). Covers a land area of 2.686 square miles and a water area of 0.060 square miles. Located at 45.10° N. Lat.; 91.49° W. Long. Elevation is 1,011 feet.
History: Bloomer was named for Jacob Bloomer, a merchant from Illinois who built a dam and mill here in 1848. Wheat was the first crop, with the farmers later turning to potatoes. In the 1900's, Bloomer became a dairy center with a creamery and condensery.
Population: 3,347 (2000); Race: 98.8% White, 0.3% Black, 0.0% Asian, 0.1% American Indian and Alaska Native, 0.7% Hispanic of any race, 0.2% two or more races (2000); Density: 1,246.0 persons per square mile (2000); Age: 24.2% under 18, 19.8% over 64 (2000); Marriage status: 19.6% never married, 60.8% now married, 12.7% widowed, 6.9% divorced (2000); Foreign born: 0.4% (2000); Ancestry (includes multiple ancestries): 57.2% German, 16.7% Norwegian, 6.8% Czech, 5.8% Irish, 5.2% English (2000).
Economy: Single-family building permits issued: 11 (2001) / 18 (2000); Multi-family building permits issued: 0 (2001) / 0 (2000); Employment by occupation: 5.3% management, 15.5% professional, 17.9% services, 27.3% sales, 0.4% farming, 13.3% construction, 20.1% production (2000).
Income: Per capita income: $21,288 (2000); Median household income: $38,715 (2000); Poverty rate: 5.4% (2000).
Taxes: Total city taxes per capita: $210 (1997); City property taxes per capita: $201 (1997).
Education: High school graduation rate: 88.3% (2000); College graduation rate: 14.1% (2000).

School District(s)

Bloomer (PK-12)
2000 Enrollment: 1,110 715-568-2800
Housing: Homeownership rate: 70.7% (2000); Median home value: $79,000 (2000); Median rent: $305 per month (2000); Median age of housing: 45 years (2000).
Hospitals: Bloomer Community Memorial Hospital (37 beds)
Safety: Violent crime rate: 8.9 per 10,000 population; Property crime rate: 323.3 per 10,000 population (2001).
Newspapers: The Bloomer Advance (1 x week)
Transportation: Commute to work: 89.3% car, 0.0% public transportation, 5.8% walk, 3.7% work from home (2000); Travel time to work: 47.4% less than 15 minutes, 25.8% 15 to 30 minutes, 21.4% 30 to 45 minutes, 2.4% 45 to 60 minutes, 3.0% 60 minutes or more (2000)
Additional Information Contacts
Bloomer Chamber of Commerce 715-568-3339

BLOOMER (town). Covers a land area of 47.064 square miles and a water area of 0.735 square miles. Located at 45.15° N. Lat.; 91.48° W. Long. Elevation is 1,011 feet.
History: Settled before 1850; incorporated 1920.
Population: 926 (2000); Race: 99.2% White, 0.0% Black, 0.0% Asian, 0.2% American Indian and Alaska Native, 0.2% Hispanic of any race, 0.3% two or more races (2000); Density: 19.7 persons per square mile (2000); Age: 28.3% under 18, 12.1% over 64 (2000); Marriage status: 25.0% never married, 64.1% now married, 3.5% widowed, 7.3% divorced (2000); Foreign born: 0.6% (2000); Ancestry (includes multiple ancestries): 57.3% German, 10.1% Norwegian, 7.9% Irish, 7.4% Polish, 5.8% English (2000).
Economy: Manufacturing: construction materials, polyethelene film, foods. Single-family building permits issued: 9 (2001) / 7 (2000); Multi-family building permits issued: 0 (2001) / 0 (2000); Employment by occupation: 23.7% management, 9.7% professional, 16.5% services, 17.6% sales, 1.5% farming, 11.6% construction, 19.4% production (2000).
Income: Per capita income: $16,243 (2000); Median household income: $40,057 (2000); Poverty rate: 6.4% (2000).
Taxes: Total city taxes per capita: $53 (1997); City property taxes per capita: $47 (1997).
Education: High school graduation rate: 86.1% (2000); College graduation rate: 10.4% (2000).
Housing: Homeownership rate: 87.5% (2000); Median home value: $84,200 (2000); Median rent: $417 per month (2000); Median age of housing: 30 years (2000).
Transportation: Commute to work: 79.1% car, 0.0% public transportation, 2.7% walk, 18.2% work from home (2000); Travel time to work: 38.5% less than 15 minutes, 27.8% 15 to 30 minutes, 24.4% 30 to 45 minutes, 7.2% 45 to 60 minutes, 2.1% 60 minutes or more (2000)

BOYD (village). Covers a land area of 1.850 square miles and a water area of 0 square miles. Located at 44.95° N. Lat.; 91.03° W. Long. Elevation is 1,105 feet.
Population: 680 (2000); Race: 99.3% White, 0.0% Black, 0.0% Asian, 0.7% American Indian and Alaska Native, 0.0% Hispanic of any race, 0.0% two or more races (2000); Density: 367.5 persons per square mile (2000); Age: 27.5% under 18, 16.5% over 64 (2000); Marriage status: 21.2% never married, 62.0% now married, 10.0% widowed, 6.8% divorced (2000); Foreign born: 0.0% (2000); Ancestry (includes multiple ancestries): 51.2% German, 14.9% Norwegian, 14.5% Polish, 8.3% Irish, 5.6% French (except Basque) (2000).
Economy: Manufacturing: wood products. Single-family building permits issued: 0 (2001) / 0 (2000); Multi-family building permits issued: 0 (2001) / 0 (2000); Employment by occupation: 6.1% management, 11.0% professional, 22.6% services, 17.7% sales, 0.6% farming, 12.2% construction, 29.9% production (2000).
Income: Per capita income: $15,738 (2000); Median household income: $37,250 (2000); Poverty rate: 4.7% (2000).
Taxes: Total city taxes per capita: $73 (1997); City property taxes per capita: $65 (1997).
Education: High school graduation rate: 77.5% (2000); College graduation rate: 5.8% (2000).
Housing: Homeownership rate: 79.2% (2000); Median home value: $64,800 (2000); Median rent: $302 per month (2000); Median age of housing: 50 years (2000).
Transportation: Commute to work: 91.4% car, 0.6% public transportation, 1.3% walk, 6.7% work from home (2000); Travel time to work: 23.9% less than 15 minutes, 29.0% 15 to 30 minutes, 36.5% 30 to 45 minutes, 6.8% 45 to 60 minutes, 3.8% 60 minutes or more (2000)

CADOTT (village). Covers a land area of 3.320 square miles and a water area of 0.025 square miles. Located at 44.94° N. Lat.; 91.15° W. Long. Elevation is 979 feet.
History: Annual Rock and Country Music Festival (since 1994).
Population: 1,345 (2000); Race: 99.2% White, 0.0% Black, 0.4% Asian, 0.2% American Indian and Alaska Native, 0.0% Hispanic of any race, 0.2% two or more races (2000); Density: 405.1 persons per square mile (2000); Age: 26.6% under 18, 21.0% over 64 (2000); Marriage status: 21.2% never married, 61.2% now married, 9.4% widowed, 8.1% divorced (2000); Foreign born: 1.1% (2000); Ancestry (includes multiple ancestries): 44.9% German, 17.2% Norwegian, 11.1% Irish, 6.6% Polish, 5.8% French (except Basque) (2000).
Economy: Lumbering, dairying, and stock-raising area. Manufacturing: vinyl profiles, light manufacturing. Single-family building permits issued: 2 (2001) / 4 (2000); Multi-family building permits issued: 0 (2001) / 0 (2000); Employment by occupation: 5.6% management, 17.0% professional, 19.4% services, 21.9% sales, 0.7% farming, 8.8% construction, 26.8% production (2000).
Income: Per capita income: $15,778 (2000); Median household income: $33,295 (2000); Poverty rate: 8.5% (2000).
Taxes: Total city taxes per capita: $153 (1997); City property taxes per capita: $142 (1997).
Education: High school graduation rate: 83.0% (2000); College graduation rate: 14.5% (2000).

School District(s)

Cadott Community (PK-12)
2000 Enrollment: 944 715-289-3795
Housing: Homeownership rate: 66.1% (2000); Median home value: $82,100 (2000); Median rent: $357 per month (2000); Median age of housing: 30 years (2000).
Newspapers: The Cadott Sentinel (1 x week)
Transportation: Commute to work: 90.9% car, 0.0% public transportation, 5.4% walk, 3.4% work from home (2000); Travel time to work: 32.6% less than 15 minutes, 40.8% 15 to 30 minutes, 19.1% 30 to 45 minutes, 4.2% 45 to 60 minutes, 3.3% 60 minutes or more (2000)
Additional Information Contacts
Cadott Chamber of Commerce 715-289-3338

CHIPPEWA FALLS (city). Covers a land area of 10.850 square miles and a water area of 0.532 square miles. Located at 44.93° N. Lat.; 91.39° W. Long. Elevation is 900 feet.
History: Jean Brunet built a sawmill and dam at this point on the Chippewa River in 1836, and soon Chippewa Falls became a bustling lumber town, as well as a trading post and gristmill center. When the lumber declined, the city used the falls to generate hydroelectric power, with the Northern States Power Company's hydro plant.
Population: 12,925 (2000); Race: 98.1% White, 0.0% Black, 0.5% Asian, 0.4% American Indian and Alaska Native, 0.4% Hispanic of any race, 0.7% two or more races (2000); Density: 1,191.2 persons per square mile (2000); Age: 23.7% under 18, 17.7% over 64 (2000); Marriage status: 28.3% never married, 50.0% now married, 9.8% widowed, 11.9% divorced (2000); Foreign born: 0.9% (2000); Ancestry (includes multiple ancestries): 46.1% German, 19.0% Norwegian, 12.8% Irish, 8.2% French (except Basque), 5.9% Polish (2000).
Vital Statistics: Birth rate: 139.3 per 10,000 population (1998)
Economy: Single-family building permits issued: 20 (2001) / 9 (2000); Multi-family building permits issued: 96 (2001) / 34 (2000); Employment by occupation: 10.3% management, 15.5% professional, 14.8% services, 26.2% sales, 0.4% farming, 6.7% construction, 26.2% production (2000).
Income: Per capita income: $18,366 (2000); Median household income: $32,744 (2000); Poverty rate: 10.3% (2000).
Taxes: Total city taxes per capita: $339 (2000); City property taxes per capita: $315 (2000).
Education: High school graduation rate: 84.3% (2000); College graduation rate: 16.4% (2000).

School District(s)

Chippewa Falls Area (PK-12)
2000 Enrollment: 4,438 715-726-2417
Housing: Homeownership rate: 57.7% (2000); Median home value: $81,300 (2000); Median rent: $383 per month (2000); Median age of housing: 45 years (2000).
Hospitals: Saint Joseph's Hospital (193 beds)
Safety: Violent crime rate: 9.2 per 10,000 population; Property crime rate: 288.9 per 10,000 population (2001).
Newspapers: Chippewa Herald (6 x week)
Transportation: Commute to work: 94.0% car, 0.5% public transportation, 2.6% walk, 1.9% work from home (2000); Travel time to work: 50.1% less than 15 minutes, 32.8% 15 to 30 minutes, 11.2% 30 to 45 minutes, 2.0% 45 to 60 minutes, 3.9% 60 minutes or more (2000)
Additional Information Contacts
Chippewa Falls Chamber of Commerce 715-723-0331

CLEVELAND (town). Covers a land area of 54.137 square miles and a water area of 2.225 square miles. Located at 45.16° N. Lat.; 91.29° W. Long.
Population: 900 (2000); Race: 99.0% White, 0.0% Black, 0.0% Asian, 0.2% American Indian and Alaska Native, 0.0% Hispanic of any race, 0.8% two or more races (2000); Density: 16.6 persons per square mile (2000); Age: 32.1% under 18, 8.3% over 64 (2000); Marriage status: 23.8% never married, 63.1% now married, 4.1% widowed, 9.0% divorced (2000); Foreign born: 0.0% (2000); Ancestry (includes multiple ancestries): 37.8% German, 18.2% Norwegian, 9.1% Irish, 7.6% Other groups, 7.4% English (2000).
Economy: Employment by occupation: 15.2% management, 8.6% professional, 17.0% services, 14.0% sales, 7.9% farming, 8.8% construction, 28.5% production (2000).
Income: Per capita income: $13,796 (2000); Median household income: $33,929 (2000); Poverty rate: 10.8% (2000).
Taxes: Total city taxes per capita: $84 (1997); City property taxes per capita: $83 (1997).
Education: High school graduation rate: 80.3% (2000); College graduation rate: 9.5% (2000).
Housing: Homeownership rate: 89.2% (2000); Median home value: $80,700 (2000); Median rent: $350 per month (2000); Median age of housing: 27 years (2000).
Transportation: Commute to work: 84.8% car, 0.5% public transportation, 4.4% walk, 9.7% work from home (2000); Travel time to work: 25.1% less than 15 minutes, 39.1% 15 to 30 minutes, 21.2% 30 to 45 minutes, 10.7% 45 to 60 minutes, 3.8% 60 minutes or more (2000)

COLBURN (town). Covers a land area of 65.045 square miles and a water area of 1.337 square miles. Located at 45.09° N. Lat.; 90.99° W. Long. Elevation is 1,128 feet.
Population: 727 (2000); Race: 98.5% White, 0.0% Black, 0.3% Asian, 0.0% American Indian and Alaska Native, 0.0% Hispanic of any race, 0.5% two or more races (2000); Density: 11.2 persons per square mile (2000); Age: 30.1% under 18, 13.7% over 64 (2000); Marriage status: 21.9% never married, 65.7% now married, 4.1% widowed, 8.3% divorced (2000); Foreign born: 0.7% (2000); Ancestry (includes multiple ancestries): 41.2% German, 20.7% Polish, 16.1% Norwegian, 7.7% Czech, 6.7% Irish (2000).

Economy: Employment by occupation: 27.4% management, 11.9% professional, 17.6% services, 7.7% sales, 3.9% farming, 12.8% construction, 18.8% production (2000).
Income: Per capita income: $17,068 (2000); Median household income: $35,625 (2000); Poverty rate: 10.2% (2000).
Taxes: Total city taxes per capita: $53 (1997); City property taxes per capita: $51 (1997).
Education: High school graduation rate: 83.7% (2000); College graduation rate: 9.0% (2000).
Housing: Homeownership rate: 86.7% (2000); Median home value: $80,000 (2000); Median rent: $194 per month (2000); Median age of housing: 37 years (2000).
Transportation: Commute to work: 69.8% car, 0.0% public transportation, 9.6% walk, 20.1% work from home (2000); Travel time to work: 21.0% less than 15 minutes, 36.7% 15 to 30 minutes, 16.9% 30 to 45 minutes, 11.2% 45 to 60 minutes, 14.2% 60 minutes or more (2000)

COOKS VALLEY (town). Covers a land area of 34.290 square miles and a water area of 0.012 square miles. Located at 45.07° N. Lat.; 91.58° W. Long.
Population: 632 (2000); Race: 100.0% White, 0.0% Black, 0.0% Asian, 0.0% American Indian and Alaska Native, 1.3% Hispanic of any race, 0.0% two or more races (2000); Density: 18.4 persons per square mile (2000); Age: 31.1% under 18, 8.0% over 64 (2000); Marriage status: 27.2% never married, 66.2% now married, 3.3% widowed, 3.3% divorced (2000); Foreign born: 0.9% (2000); Ancestry (includes multiple ancestries): 58.1% German, 11.7% Norwegian, 10.8% Czech, 8.8% Irish, 7.7% Polish (2000).
Economy: Single-family building permits issued: 9 (2001) / 8 (2000); Multi-family building permits issued: 0 (2001) / 0 (2000); Employment by occupation: 19.5% management, 14.6% professional, 13.0% services, 17.3% sales, 2.4% farming, 9.2% construction, 24.1% production (2000).
Income: Per capita income: $14,703 (2000); Median household income: $43,523 (2000); Poverty rate: 5.2% (2000).
Taxes: Total city taxes per capita: $142 (1997); City property taxes per capita: $141 (1997).
Education: High school graduation rate: 88.5% (2000); College graduation rate: 12.2% (2000).
Housing: Homeownership rate: 82.0% (2000); Median home value: $110,000 (2000); Median rent: $395 per month (2000); Median age of housing: 32 years (2000).
Transportation: Commute to work: 76.4% car, 0.0% public transportation, 5.5% walk, 17.0% work from home (2000); Travel time to work: 37.0% less than 15 minutes, 36.0% 15 to 30 minutes, 20.8% 30 to 45 minutes, 5.0% 45 to 60 minutes, 1.3% 60 minutes or more (2000)

CORNELL (city). Covers a land area of 3.831 square miles and a water area of 0.514 square miles. Located at 45.16° N. Lat.; 91.15° W. Long. Elevation is 1,100 feet.
History: Incorporated 1913.
Population: 1,466 (2000); Race: 96.9% White, 0.0% Black, 0.0% Asian, 1.5% American Indian and Alaska Native, 0.6% Hispanic of any race, 1.2% two or more races (2000); Density: 382.6 persons per square mile (2000); Age: 24.4% under 18, 23.5% over 64 (2000); Marriage status: 17.6% never married, 60.1% now married, 11.5% widowed, 10.8% divorced (2000); Foreign born: 1.0% (2000); Ancestry (includes multiple ancestries): 37.1% German, 17.1% Norwegian, 9.6% Irish, 6.8% Polish, 6.3% United States or American (2000).
Economy: Railroad spur terminus. In dairying region. Manufacturing: paper, wood products, construction materials. Single-family building permits issued: 1 (2001) / 2 (2000); Multi-family building permits issued: 0 (2001) / 0 (2000); Employment by occupation: 7.1% management, 15.2% professional, 20.9% services, 21.5% sales, 1.2% farming, 9.4% construction, 24.7% production (2000).
Income: Per capita income: $15,494 (2000); Median household income: $30,690 (2000); Poverty rate: 8.9% (2000).
Taxes: Total city taxes per capita: $133 (1997); City property taxes per capita: $130 (1997).
Education: High school graduation rate: 79.5% (2000); College graduation rate: 10.8% (2000).

School District(s)

Cornell (PK-12)
2000 Enrollment: 578 715-239-6463
Housing: Homeownership rate: 70.7% (2000); Median home value: $55,600 (2000); Median rent: $314 per month (2000); Median age of housing: 51 years (2000).
Newspapers: The Cornell & Lake Holcombe Courier (1 x week)
Transportation: Commute to work: 85.7% car, 0.5% public transportation, 10.0% walk, 2.8% work from home (2000); Travel time to work: 50.7% less than 15 minutes, 10.8% 15 to 30 minutes, 20.2% 30 to 45 minutes, 9.4% 45 to 60 minutes, 8.9% 60 minutes or more (2000)

DELMAR (town). Covers a land area of 42.930 square miles and a water area of 0.022 square miles. Located at 44.97° N. Lat.; 91.00° W. Long.
Population: 941 (2000); Race: 97.7% White, 0.0% Black, 1.0% Asian, 1.2% American Indian and Alaska Native, 0.0% Hispanic of any race, 0.2% two or more races (2000); Density: 21.9 persons per square mile (2000); Age: 30.3% under 18, 13.8% over 64 (2000); Marriage status: 22.7% never married, 64.5% now married, 6.1% widowed, 6.8% divorced (2000); Foreign born: 0.4% (2000); Ancestry (includes multiple ancestries): 54.6% German, 23.7% Polish, 11.8% Norwegian, 8.1% Irish, 4.3% Other groups (2000).
Economy: Single-family building permits issued: 4 (2001) / 0 (2000); Multi-family building permits issued: 0 (2001) / 0 (2000); Employment by occupation: 19.1% management, 10.3% professional, 17.2% services, 17.2% sales, 5.2% farming, 8.4% construction, 22.7% production (2000).
Income: Per capita income: $15,912 (2000); Median household income: $40,278 (2000); Poverty rate: 9.1% (2000).
Taxes: Total city taxes per capita: $63 (1997); City property taxes per capita: $62 (1997).
Education: High school graduation rate: 79.0% (2000); College graduation rate: 10.1% (2000).
Housing: Homeownership rate: 89.7% (2000); Median home value: $81,900 (2000); Median rent: $331 per month (2000); Median age of housing: 51 years (2000).
Transportation: Commute to work: 81.0% car, 0.0% public transportation, 2.4% walk, 16.6% work from home (2000); Travel time to work: 36.6% less than 15 minutes, 26.1% 15 to 30 minutes, 23.8% 30 to 45 minutes, 7.8% 45 to 60 minutes, 5.7% 60 minutes or more (2000)

EAGLE POINT (town). Covers a land area of 61.405 square miles and a water area of 5.160 square miles. Located at 45.02° N. Lat.; 91.35° W. Long. Elevation is 971 feet.
Population: 3,049 (2000); Race: 99.6% White, 0.0% Black, 0.1% Asian, 0.1% American Indian and Alaska Native, 0.0% Hispanic of any race, 0.2% two or more races (2000); Density: 49.7 persons per square mile (2000); Age: 24.2% under 18, 19.8% over 64 (2000); Marriage status: 18.7% never married, 69.5% now married, 7.1% widowed, 4.7% divorced (2000); Foreign born: 0.5% (2000); Ancestry (includes multiple ancestries): 48.1% German, 18.5% Norwegian, 9.8% French (except Basque), 8.1% Irish, 6.7% Polish (2000).
Economy: Employment by occupation: 14.2% management, 16.9% professional, 15.2% services, 20.9% sales, 2.0% farming, 8.3% construction, 22.6% production (2000).
Income: Per capita income: $19,421 (2000); Median household income: $54,250 (2000); Poverty rate: 5.7% (2000).
Taxes: Total city taxes per capita: $83 (1997); City property taxes per capita: $81 (1997).
Education: High school graduation rate: 78.8% (2000); College graduation rate: 12.7% (2000).
Housing: Homeownership rate: 91.1% (2000); Median home value: $122,000 (2000); Median rent: $347 per month (2000); Median age of housing: 26 years (2000).
Transportation: Commute to work: 95.2% car, 0.3% public transportation, 0.9% walk, 3.7% work from home (2000); Travel time to work: 37.1% less than 15 minutes, 45.0% 15 to 30 minutes, 13.3% 30 to 45 minutes, 2.7% 45 to 60 minutes, 2.0% 60 minutes or more (2000)

EDSON (town). Aka Edson Center. Covers a land area of 53.955 square miles and a water area of 0.019 square miles. Located at 44.92° N. Lat.; 91.00° W. Long. Elevation is 1,082 feet.
Population: 966 (2000); Race: 97.5% White, 0.0% Black, 0.0% Asian, 0.2% American Indian and Alaska Native, 1.3% Hispanic of any race, 2.3% two or more races (2000); Density: 17.9 persons per square mile (2000); Age: 36.0% under 18, 7.0% over 64 (2000); Marriage status: 27.6% never married, 62.8% now married, 3.3% widowed, 6.3% divorced (2000); Foreign born: 0.2% (2000); Ancestry (includes multiple ancestries): 56.9% German, 11.6% Polish, 10.8% Norwegian, 9.3% Irish, 4.3% Other groups (2000).
Economy: Employment by occupation: 34.6% management, 9.0% professional, 17.9% services, 11.8% sales, 6.1% farming, 6.6% construction, 14.0% production (2000).
Income: Per capita income: $12,154 (2000); Median household income: $34,722 (2000); Poverty rate: 24.1% (2000).

Taxes: Total city taxes per capita: $54 (1997); City property taxes per capita: $53 (1997).
Education: High school graduation rate: 76.6% (2000); College graduation rate: 5.5% (2000).
Housing: Homeownership rate: 85.3% (2000); Median home value: $65,700 (2000); Median rent: $350 per month (2000); Median age of housing: 57 years (2000).
Transportation: Commute to work: 65.5% car, 0.0% public transportation, 7.3% walk, 26.8% work from home (2000); Travel time to work: 34.1% less than 15 minutes, 24.5% 15 to 30 minutes, 26.9% 30 to 45 minutes, 12.4% 45 to 60 minutes, 2.1% 60 minutes or more (2000)

ESTELLA (town). Covers a land area of 31.536 square miles and a water area of 0.475 square miles. Located at 45.17° N. Lat.; 91.12° W. Long.
Population: 469 (2000); Race: 98.9% White, 0.0% Black, 0.0% Asian, 0.4% American Indian and Alaska Native, 0.0% Hispanic of any race, 0.6% two or more races (2000); Density: 14.9 persons per square mile (2000); Age: 29.2% under 18, 7.9% over 64 (2000); Marriage status: 21.4% never married, 64.7% now married, 7.4% widowed, 6.6% divorced (2000); Foreign born: 0.0% (2000); Ancestry (includes multiple ancestries): 40.9% German, 20.5% Norwegian, 9.0% Polish, 7.7% United States or American, 7.0% Irish (2000).
Economy: Employment by occupation: 10.9% management, 13.5% professional, 11.8% services, 22.3% sales, 0.9% farming, 13.5% construction, 27.1% production (2000).
Income: Per capita income: $14,237 (2000); Median household income: $38,250 (2000); Poverty rate: 7.1% (2000).
Taxes: Total city taxes per capita: $23 (1997); City property taxes per capita: $23 (1997).
Education: High school graduation rate: 84.7% (2000); College graduation rate: 8.1% (2000).
Housing: Homeownership rate: 81.9% (2000); Median home value: $58,300 (2000); Median rent: $294 per month (2000); Median age of housing: 40 years (2000).
Transportation: Commute to work: 92.6% car, 0.0% public transportation, 3.0% walk, 3.5% work from home (2000); Travel time to work: 51.6% less than 15 minutes, 11.2% 15 to 30 minutes, 17.9% 30 to 45 minutes, 15.2% 45 to 60 minutes, 4.0% 60 minutes or more (2000)

GOETZ (town). Covers a land area of 29.898 square miles and a water area of 0 square miles. Located at 44.98° N. Lat.; 91.15° W. Long.
Population: 695 (2000); Race: 99.2% White, 0.3% Black, 0.0% Asian, 0.0% American Indian and Alaska Native, 0.3% Hispanic of any race, 0.5% two or more races (2000); Density: 23.2 persons per square mile (2000); Age: 33.0% under 18, 8.3% over 64 (2000); Marriage status: 22.7% never married, 65.9% now married, 4.3% widowed, 7.1% divorced (2000); Foreign born: 0.9% (2000); Ancestry (includes multiple ancestries): 47.6% German, 19.1% Norwegian, 13.7% Irish, 10.5% United States or American, 8.4% Czech (2000).
Economy: Single-family building permits issued: 1 (2001) / 12 (2000); Multi-family building permits issued: 0 (2001) / 0 (2000); Employment by occupation: 22.4% management, 15.1% professional, 19.7% services, 11.1% sales, 4.3% farming, 10.8% construction, 16.7% production (2000).
Income: Per capita income: $15,871 (2000); Median household income: $39,028 (2000); Poverty rate: 6.4% (2000).
Taxes: Total city taxes per capita: $51 (1997); City property taxes per capita: $49 (1997).
Education: High school graduation rate: 84.1% (2000); College graduation rate: 20.5% (2000).
Housing: Homeownership rate: 85.0% (2000); Median home value: $76,500 (2000); Median rent: $345 per month (2000); Median age of housing: 50 years (2000).
Transportation: Commute to work: 75.2% car, 0.0% public transportation, 5.7% walk, 18.0% work from home (2000); Travel time to work: 32.9% less than 15 minutes, 33.6% 15 to 30 minutes, 13.6% 30 to 45 minutes, 10.3% 45 to 60 minutes, 9.6% 60 minutes or more (2000)

HALLIE (town). Covers a land area of 21.402 square miles and a water area of 0.490 square miles. Located at 44.88° N. Lat.; 91.42° W. Long. Elevation is 900 feet.
Population: 4,703 (2000); Race: 97.1% White, 0.2% Black, 1.5% Asian, 0.2% American Indian and Alaska Native, 0.9% Hispanic of any race, 1.1% two or more races (2000); Density: 219.7 persons per square mile (2000); Age: 29.0% under 18, 9.0% over 64 (2000); Marriage status: 20.9% never married, 68.2% now married, 2.4% widowed, 8.5% divorced (2000); Foreign born: 1.6% (2000); Ancestry (includes multiple ancestries): 46.3% German, 23.3% Norwegian, 11.5% Irish, 6.6% English, 6.4% French (except Basque) (2000).
Economy: Employment by occupation: 9.3% management, 14.4% professional, 16.2% services, 30.4% sales, 0.8% farming, 9.1% construction, 19.7% production (2000).
Income: Per capita income: $17,523 (2000); Median household income: $46,547 (2000); Poverty rate: 6.5% (2000).
Taxes: Total city taxes per capita: $157 (2000); City property taxes per capita: $149 (2000).
Education: High school graduation rate: 87.5% (2000); College graduation rate: 13.9% (2000).
Housing: Homeownership rate: 82.6% (2000); Median home value: $97,400 (2000); Median rent: $458 per month (2000); Median age of housing: 26 years (2000).
Safety: Violent crime rate: 8.4 per 10,000 population; Property crime rate: 367.3 per 10,000 population (2001).
Transportation: Commute to work: 95.0% car, 0.7% public transportation, 1.1% walk, 2.1% work from home (2000); Travel time to work: 37.6% less than 15 minutes, 48.4% 15 to 30 minutes, 8.4% 30 to 45 minutes, 2.1% 45 to 60 minutes, 3.5% 60 minutes or more (2000)

HOLCOMBE (unincorporated postal area, zip code 54745). Covers a land area of 137.333 square miles and a water area of 0.649 square miles. Located at 45.25° N. Lat.; 91.15° W. Long. Elevation is 1,070 feet.
Population: 2,221 (2000); Race: 99.1% White, 0.0% Black, 0.3% Asian, 0.2% American Indian and Alaska Native, 0.5% Hispanic of any race, 0.1% two or more races (2000); Density: 16.2 persons per square mile (2000); Age: 24.9% under 18, 16.0% over 64 (2000); Marriage status: 19.2% never married, 65.4% now married, 6.8% widowed, 8.6% divorced (2000); Foreign born: 1.2% (2000); Ancestry (includes multiple ancestries): 37.1% German, 14.5% Norwegian, 9.8% Polish, 8.7% English, 8.0% Irish (2000).
Economy: Employment by occupation: 10.4% management, 9.8% professional, 12.7% services, 21.7% sales, 4.1% farming, 11.1% construction, 30.2% production (2000).
Income: Per capita income: $15,717 (2000); Median household income: $33,100 (2000); Poverty rate: 11.5% (2000).
Education: High school graduation rate: 81.9% (2000); College graduation rate: 10.2% (2000).

School District(s)

Lake Holcombe (PK-12)
2000 Enrollment: 517 715-595-4241
Housing: Homeownership rate: 89.7% (2000); Median home value: $98,100 (2000); Median rent: $298 per month (2000); Median age of housing: 29 years (2000).
Transportation: Commute to work: 88.8% car, 0.9% public transportation, 3.2% walk, 6.3% work from home (2000); Travel time to work: 28.8% less than 15 minutes, 30.5% 15 to 30 minutes, 15.6% 30 to 45 minutes, 8.8% 45 to 60 minutes, 16.3% 60 minutes or more (2000)

HOWARD (town). Covers a land area of 35.795 square miles and a water area of 0 square miles. Located at 44.97° N. Lat.; 91.59° W. Long. Elevation is 980 feet.
Population: 648 (2000); Race: 99.6% White, 0.3% Black, 0.0% Asian, 0.0% American Indian and Alaska Native, 0.3% Hispanic of any race, 0.1% two or more races (2000); Density: 18.1 persons per square mile (2000); Age: 30.2% under 18, 8.8% over 64 (2000); Marriage status: 23.0% never married, 67.9% now married, 4.4% widowed, 4.6% divorced (2000); Foreign born: 0.0% (2000); Ancestry (includes multiple ancestries): 53.9% German, 25.4% Norwegian, 4.6% Czech, 4.6% French (except Basque), 4.5% Irish (2000).
Economy: Employment by occupation: 12.0% management, 13.4% professional, 13.9% services, 16.9% sales, 3.6% farming, 13.1% construction, 27.0% production (2000).
Income: Per capita income: $15,274 (2000); Median household income: $42,109 (2000); Poverty rate: 8.2% (2000).
Taxes: Total city taxes per capita: $95 (1997); City property taxes per capita: $93 (1997).
Education: High school graduation rate: 86.5% (2000); College graduation rate: 10.0% (2000).
Housing: Homeownership rate: 92.7% (2000); Median home value: $96,900 (2000); Median rent: $188 per month (2000); Median age of housing: 29 years (2000).
Transportation: Commute to work: 87.4% car, 0.0% public transportation, 2.5% walk, 9.6% work from home (2000); Travel time to work: 21.7% less than 15 minutes, 44.1% 15 to 30 minutes, 19.6% 30 to 45 minutes, 7.8% 45 to 60 minutes, 6.8% 60 minutes or more (2000)

JIM FALLS (unincorporated postal area, zip code 54748). Covers a land area of 43.960 square miles and a water area of 0.668 square miles. Located at 45.07° N. Lat.; 91.25° W. Long. Elevation is 956 feet.
Population: 1,233 (2000); Race: 99.8% White, 0.0% Black, 0.0% Asian, 0.0% American Indian and Alaska Native, 0.0% Hispanic of any race, 0.2% two or more races (2000); Density: 28.0 persons per square mile (2000); Age: 26.1% under 18, 13.3% over 64 (2000); Marriage status: 19.1% never married, 69.3% now married, 4.7% widowed, 6.8% divorced (2000); Foreign born: 0.2% (2000); Ancestry (includes multiple ancestries): 47.3% German, 19.3% Norwegian, 10.7% Polish, 10.0% French (except Basque), 8.9% Irish (2000).
Economy: Employment by occupation: 16.3% management, 14.7% professional, 11.3% services, 18.3% sales, 4.9% farming, 10.2% construction, 24.4% production (2000).
Income: Per capita income: $18,173 (2000); Median household income: $42,396 (2000); Poverty rate: 4.1% (2000).
Education: High school graduation rate: 83.4% (2000); College graduation rate: 10.1% (2000).
Housing: Homeownership rate: 83.0% (2000); Median home value: $80,700 (2000); Median rent: $377 per month (2000); Median age of housing: 46 years (2000).
Transportation: Commute to work: 85.0% car, 0.0% public transportation, 4.6% walk, 9.5% work from home (2000); Travel time to work: 19.0% less than 15 minutes, 45.3% 15 to 30 minutes, 23.0% 30 to 45 minutes, 7.8% 45 to 60 minutes, 4.9% 60 minutes or more (2000)

LAFAYETTE (town). Covers a land area of 34.523 square miles and a water area of 4.586 square miles. Located at 44.92° N. Lat.; 91.29° W. Long.
Population: 5,199 (2000); Race: 99.0% White, 0.1% Black, 0.0% Asian, 0.6% American Indian and Alaska Native, 1.2% Hispanic of any race, 0.3% two or more races (2000); Density: 150.6 persons per square mile (2000); Age: 26.6% under 18, 10.1% over 64 (2000); Marriage status: 21.2% never married, 65.1% now married, 5.3% widowed, 8.4% divorced (2000); Foreign born: 1.4% (2000); Ancestry (includes multiple ancestries): 46.5% German, 18.4% Norwegian, 11.0% Irish, 8.2% French (except Basque), 6.3% English (2000).
Economy: Employment by occupation: 11.1% management, 17.3% professional, 14.3% services, 29.5% sales, 0.9% farming, 10.7% construction, 16.1% production (2000).
Income: Per capita income: $23,172 (2000); Median household income: $52,850 (2000); Poverty rate: 4.0% (2000).
Taxes: Total city taxes per capita: $55 (1997); City property taxes per capita: $48 (1997).
Education: High school graduation rate: 90.4% (2000); College graduation rate: 24.4% (2000).
Housing: Homeownership rate: 84.4% (2000); Median home value: $124,400 (2000); Median rent: $450 per month (2000); Median age of housing: 27 years (2000).
Transportation: Commute to work: 96.3% car, 0.0% public transportation, 0.9% walk, 2.4% work from home (2000); Travel time to work: 31.8% less than 15 minutes, 45.1% 15 to 30 minutes, 20.8% 30 to 45 minutes, 0.7% 45 to 60 minutes, 1.6% 60 minutes or more (2000)

LAKE HOLCOMBE (town). Covers a land area of 26.910 square miles and a water area of 3.741 square miles. Located at 45.24° N. Lat.; 91.10° W. Long.
Population: 1,010 (2000); Race: 98.2% White, 0.0% Black, 0.7% Asian, 0.2% American Indian and Alaska Native, 1.1% Hispanic of any race, 0.3% two or more races (2000); Density: 37.5 persons per square mile (2000); Age: 25.8% under 18, 15.2% over 64 (2000); Marriage status: 20.1% never married, 62.1% now married, 7.9% widowed, 9.9% divorced (2000); Foreign born: 1.7% (2000); Ancestry (includes multiple ancestries): 38.1% German, 13.2% Norwegian, 8.7% Irish, 8.4% English, 7.3% Polish (2000).
Economy: Employment by occupation: 6.5% management, 8.7% professional, 14.5% services, 23.4% sales, 3.7% farming, 10.6% construction, 32.7% production (2000).
Income: Per capita income: $15,900 (2000); Median household income: $33,083 (2000); Poverty rate: 10.2% (2000).
Taxes: Total city taxes per capita: $130 (1997); City property taxes per capita: $128 (1997).
Education: High school graduation rate: 81.9% (2000); College graduation rate: 12.6% (2000).
Housing: Homeownership rate: 86.5% (2000); Median home value: $109,200 (2000); Median rent: $310 per month (2000); Median age of housing: 31 years (2000).
Transportation: Commute to work: 92.1% car, 2.0% public transportation, 0.7% walk, 4.8% work from home (2000); Travel time to work: 32.3% less than 15 minutes, 33.6% 15 to 30 minutes, 11.3% 30 to 45 minutes, 7.4% 45 to 60 minutes, 15.4% 60 minutes or more (2000)

LAKE WISSOTA (CDP). Covers a land area of 3.781 square miles and a water area of 0.647 square miles. Located at 44.92° N. Lat.; 91.31° W. Long. Elevation is 926 feet.
Population: 2,458 (2000); Race: 99.8% White, 0.2% Black, 0.0% Asian, 0.0% American Indian and Alaska Native, 0.2% Hispanic of any race, 0.0% two or more races (2000); Density: 650.0 persons per square mile (2000); Age: 25.5% under 18, 12.9% over 64 (2000); Marriage status: 23.8% never married, 58.4% now married, 8.3% widowed, 9.5% divorced (2000); Foreign born: 0.0% (2000); Ancestry (includes multiple ancestries): 43.6% German, 16.0% Norwegian, 12.3% Irish, 12.1% French (except Basque), 4.2% Polish (2000).
Economy: Employment by occupation: 11.8% management, 18.4% professional, 13.7% services, 30.9% sales, 0.9% farming, 11.0% construction, 13.3% production (2000).
Income: Per capita income: $23,851 (2000); Median household income: $48,906 (2000); Poverty rate: 3.0% (2000).
Education: High school graduation rate: 88.9% (2000); College graduation rate: 24.2% (2000).
Housing: Homeownership rate: 82.6% (2000); Median home value: $122,700 (2000); Median rent: $462 per month (2000); Median age of housing: 29 years (2000).
Transportation: Commute to work: 94.5% car, 0.0% public transportation, 1.5% walk, 4.1% work from home (2000); Travel time to work: 38.8% less than 15 minutes, 41.3% 15 to 30 minutes, 18.2% 30 to 45 minutes, 0.0% 45 to 60 minutes, 1.8% 60 minutes or more (2000)

NEW AUBURN (village). Covers a land area of 3.391 square miles and a water area of 0 square miles. Located at 45.20° N. Lat.; 91.56° W. Long. Elevation is 1,100 feet.
Population: 562 (2000); Race: 98.5% White, 0.0% Black, 0.2% Asian, 0.0% American Indian and Alaska Native, 0.3% Hispanic of any race, 1.4% two or more races (2000); Density: 165.8 persons per square mile (2000); Age: 34.2% under 18, 10.3% over 64 (2000); Marriage status: 24.2% never married, 55.9% now married, 8.0% widowed, 11.9% divorced (2000); Foreign born: 0.7% (2000); Ancestry (includes multiple ancestries): 36.8% German, 16.2% Norwegian, 11.3% Irish, 8.2% English, 5.8% French (except Basque) (2000).
Economy: Single-family building permits issued: 2 (2001) / 1 (2000); Multi-family building permits issued: 0 (2001) / 0 (2000); Employment by occupation: 6.3% management, 7.0% professional, 18.1% services, 20.7% sales, 1.5% farming, 11.4% construction, 35.1% production (2000).
Income: Per capita income: $13,444 (2000); Median household income: $30,341 (2000); Poverty rate: 9.9% (2000).
Taxes: Total city taxes per capita: $31 (1997); City property taxes per capita: $22 (1997).
Education: High school graduation rate: 75.4% (2000); College graduation rate: 5.6% (2000).

School District(s)

New Auburn (PK-12)
2000 Enrollment: 346 715-237-2202
Housing: Homeownership rate: 75.6% (2000); Median home value: $62,700 (2000); Median rent: $295 per month (2000); Median age of housing: 38 years (2000).
Transportation: Commute to work: 92.1% car, 0.0% public transportation, 3.8% walk, 3.4% work from home (2000); Travel time to work: 22.3% less than 15 minutes, 34.4% 15 to 30 minutes, 32.4% 30 to 45 minutes, 6.6% 45 to 60 minutes, 4.3% 60 minutes or more (2000)

RUBY (town). Covers a land area of 53.490 square miles and a water area of 0.117 square miles. Located at 45.24° N. Lat.; 90.97° W. Long. Elevation is 1,140 feet.
Population: 446 (2000); Race: 99.5% White, 0.0% Black, 0.0% Asian, 0.5% American Indian and Alaska Native, 0.0% Hispanic of any race, 0.0% two or more races (2000); Density: 8.3 persons per square mile (2000); Age: 32.3% under 18, 11.9% over 64 (2000); Marriage status: 16.5% never married, 72.6% now married, 4.8% widowed, 6.1% divorced (2000); Foreign born: 0.7% (2000); Ancestry (includes multiple ancestries): 38.5% German, 16.1% Norwegian, 7.8% Polish, 6.0% United States or American, 5.7% English (2000).

Economy: Employment by occupation: 15.8% management, 9.6% professional, 15.3% services, 7.9% sales, 5.1% farming, 11.9% construction, 34.5% production (2000).
Income: Per capita income: $12,587 (2000); Median household income: $30,208 (2000); Poverty rate: 16.9% (2000).
Taxes: Total city taxes per capita: $24 (1997); City property taxes per capita: $22 (1997).
Education: High school graduation rate: 73.8% (2000); College graduation rate: 6.3% (2000).
Housing: Homeownership rate: 87.6% (2000); Median home value: $84,000 (2000); Median rent: $171 per month (2000); Median age of housing: 35 years (2000).
Transportation: Commute to work: 80.7% car, 0.0% public transportation, 9.4% walk, 9.9% work from home (2000); Travel time to work: 17.5% less than 15 minutes, 31.2% 15 to 30 minutes, 25.3% 30 to 45 minutes, 14.9% 45 to 60 minutes, 11.0% 60 minutes or more (2000)

SAMPSON (town). Covers a land area of 62.499 square miles and a water area of 5.656 square miles. Located at 45.25° N. Lat.; 91.41° W. Long.
Population: 816 (2000); Race: 99.8% White, 0.0% Black, 0.0% Asian, 0.0% American Indian and Alaska Native, 0.0% Hispanic of any race, 0.2% two or more races (2000); Density: 13.1 persons per square mile (2000); Age: 25.6% under 18, 14.1% over 64 (2000); Marriage status: 22.6% never married, 61.9% now married, 3.7% widowed, 11.8% divorced (2000); Foreign born: 0.0% (2000); Ancestry (includes multiple ancestries): 35.8% German, 20.3% Norwegian, 10.1% English, 9.2% United States or American, 8.1% Irish (2000).
Economy: Employment by occupation: 13.3% management, 11.4% professional, 15.3% services, 15.8% sales, 1.7% farming, 13.9% construction, 28.6% production (2000).
Income: Per capita income: $14,714 (2000); Median household income: $33,021 (2000); Poverty rate: 15.3% (2000).
Taxes: Total city taxes per capita: $220 (1997); City property taxes per capita: $217 (1997).
Education: High school graduation rate: 81.2% (2000); College graduation rate: 12.9% (2000).
Housing: Homeownership rate: 80.4% (2000); Median home value: $111,100 (2000); Median rent: $361 per month (2000); Median age of housing: 27 years (2000).
Transportation: Commute to work: 81.4% car, 0.8% public transportation, 2.8% walk, 13.0% work from home (2000); Travel time to work: 17.2% less than 15 minutes, 27.8% 15 to 30 minutes, 18.8% 30 to 45 minutes, 12.3% 45 to 60 minutes, 23.9% 60 minutes or more (2000)

SIGEL (town). Covers a land area of 35.789 square miles and a water area of 0.067 square miles. Located at 44.90° N. Lat.; 91.17° W. Long.
Population: 825 (2000); Race: 97.5% White, 1.5% Black, 0.0% Asian, 0.5% American Indian and Alaska Native, 0.1% Hispanic of any race, 0.4% two or more races (2000); Density: 23.1 persons per square mile (2000); Age: 27.9% under 18, 16.3% over 64 (2000); Marriage status: 24.1% never married, 62.7% now married, 3.1% widowed, 10.0% divorced (2000); Foreign born: 0.1% (2000); Ancestry (includes multiple ancestries): 40.5% German, 12.0% Norwegian, 7.5% Irish, 7.0% French (except Basque), 4.2% United States or American (2000).
Economy: Single-family building permits issued: 0 (2001) / 0 (2000); Multi-family building permits issued: 0 (2001) / 0 (2000); Employment by occupation: 7.1% management, 15.2% professional, 17.9% services, 15.2% sales, 4.1% farming, 13.6% construction, 26.9% production (2000).
Income: Per capita income: $15,635 (2000); Median household income: $37,639 (2000); Poverty rate: 7.1% (2000).
Taxes: Total city taxes per capita: $60 (1997); City property taxes per capita: $57 (1997).
Education: High school graduation rate: 78.8% (2000); College graduation rate: 8.0% (2000).
Housing: Homeownership rate: 87.9% (2000); Median home value: $84,000 (2000); Median rent: $336 per month (2000); Median age of housing: 27 years (2000).
Transportation: Commute to work: 88.3% car, 0.0% public transportation, 2.2% walk, 7.8% work from home (2000); Travel time to work: 19.7% less than 15 minutes, 42.7% 15 to 30 minutes, 25.2% 30 to 45 minutes, 6.1% 45 to 60 minutes, 6.4% 60 minutes or more (2000)

STANLEY (city). Covers a land area of 3.508 square miles and a water area of 0.050 square miles. Located at 44.96° N. Lat.; 90.93° W. Long. Elevation is 1,100 feet.
History: Stanley grew as a farm trading center, and became the site of a large apiary, with bees producing clover honey.
Population: 1,898 (2000); Race: 98.5% White, 0.2% Black, 1.1% Asian, 0.2% American Indian and Alaska Native, 1.1% Hispanic of any race, 0.0% two or more races (2000); Density: 541.1 persons per square mile (2000); Age: 23.8% under 18, 25.0% over 64 (2000); Marriage status: 23.0% never married, 53.4% now married, 13.6% widowed, 10.0% divorced (2000); Foreign born: 1.7% (2000); Ancestry (includes multiple ancestries): 38.9% German, 17.3% Polish, 15.9% Norwegian, 10.1% Irish, 6.1% Dutch (2000).
Economy: Single-family building permits issued: 7 (2001) / 2 (2000); Multi-family building permits issued: 12 (2001) / 2 (2000); Employment by occupation: 8.9% management, 16.1% professional, 19.0% services, 20.3% sales, 1.6% farming, 9.3% construction, 24.8% production (2000).
Income: Per capita income: $19,421 (2000); Median household income: $27,644 (2000); Poverty rate: 8.0% (2000).
Taxes: Total city taxes per capita: $132 (1997); City property taxes per capita: $121 (1997).
Education: High school graduation rate: 75.9% (2000); College graduation rate: 12.7% (2000).

School District(s)

Stanley-Boyd Area (PK-12)
2000 Enrollment: 1,048 715-644-5357

Housing: Homeownership rate: 69.6% (2000); Median home value: $57,700 (2000); Median rent: $295 per month (2000); Median age of housing: 53 years (2000).
Hospitals: Victory Medical Center (25 beds)
Safety: Violent crime rate: 20.9 per 10,000 population; Property crime rate: 434.1 per 10,000 population (2001).
Newspapers: Stanley Republican (1 x week)
Transportation: Commute to work: 89.1% car, 0.0% public transportation, 6.8% walk, 3.3% work from home (2000); Travel time to work: 42.3% less than 15 minutes, 12.2% 15 to 30 minutes, 24.7% 30 to 45 minutes, 14.7% 45 to 60 minutes, 6.0% 60 minutes or more (2000)

TILDEN (town). Covers a land area of 35.980 square miles and a water area of 0.095 square miles. Located at 44.99° N. Lat.; 91.44° W. Long. Elevation is 955 feet.
Population: 1,185 (2000); Race: 99.8% White, 0.0% Black, 0.2% Asian, 0.0% American Indian and Alaska Native, 0.7% Hispanic of any race, 0.0% two or more races (2000); Density: 32.9 persons per square mile (2000); Age: 29.5% under 18, 9.6% over 64 (2000); Marriage status: 22.6% never married, 67.9% now married, 4.8% widowed, 4.7% divorced (2000); Foreign born: 0.3% (2000); Ancestry (includes multiple ancestries): 60.9% German, 10.9% Norwegian, 8.8% French (except Basque), 7.8% Irish, 5.2% United States or American (2000).
Economy: Employment by occupation: 21.6% management, 13.3% professional, 8.8% services, 24.6% sales, 5.6% farming, 7.0% construction, 19.1% production (2000).
Income: Per capita income: $18,575 (2000); Median household income: $46,477 (2000); Poverty rate: 3.2% (2000).
Taxes: Total city taxes per capita: $70 (1997); City property taxes per capita: $69 (1997).
Education: High school graduation rate: 83.5% (2000); College graduation rate: 12.0% (2000).
Housing: Homeownership rate: 87.4% (2000); Median home value: $106,400 (2000); Median rent: $339 per month (2000); Median age of housing: 28 years (2000).
Transportation: Commute to work: 80.0% car, 0.3% public transportation, 4.3% walk, 14.8% work from home (2000); Travel time to work: 42.1% less than 15 minutes, 39.9% 15 to 30 minutes, 13.5% 30 to 45 minutes, 0.7% 45 to 60 minutes, 3.7% 60 minutes or more (2000)

WHEATON (town). Covers a land area of 54.822 square miles and a water area of 0.443 square miles. Located at 44.90° N. Lat.; 91.55° W. Long.
Population: 2,366 (2000); Race: 97.6% White, 0.0% Black, 1.0% Asian, 0.7% American Indian and Alaska Native, 0.5% Hispanic of any race, 0.5% two or more races (2000); Density: 43.2 persons per square mile (2000); Age: 26.6% under 18, 9.4% over 64 (2000); Marriage status: 21.9% never married, 66.3% now married, 3.1% widowed, 8.7% divorced (2000); Foreign born: 1.3% (2000); Ancestry (includes multiple ancestries): 49.1% German, 23.8% Norwegian, 10.8% Irish, 9.9% English, 7.2% French (except Basque) (2000).
Economy: Employment by occupation: 15.4% management, 17.8% professional, 9.9% services, 20.5% sales, 0.5% farming, 15.1% construction, 20.8% production (2000).
Income: Per capita income: $20,023 (2000); Median household income: $52,692 (2000); Poverty rate: 3.5% (2000).

Taxes: Total city taxes per capita: $68 (1997); City property taxes per capita: $67 (1997).
Education: High school graduation rate: 90.6% (2000); College graduation rate: 21.5% (2000).
Housing: Homeownership rate: 88.2% (2000); Median home value: $104,900 (2000); Median rent: $433 per month (2000); Median age of housing: 26 years (2000).
Transportation: Commute to work: 90.4% car, 0.0% public transportation, 2.6% walk, 6.0% work from home (2000); Travel time to work: 27.0% less than 15 minutes, 58.0% 15 to 30 minutes, 9.8% 30 to 45 minutes, 1.3% 45 to 60 minutes, 3.9% 60 minutes or more (2000)

WOODMOHR (town). Covers a land area of 35.285 square miles and a water area of 0.090 square miles. Located at 45.07° N. Lat.; 91.47° W. Long.
Population: 883 (2000); Race: 99.8% White, 0.2% Black, 0.0% Asian, 0.0% American Indian and Alaska Native, 0.2% Hispanic of any race, 0.0% two or more races (2000); Density: 25.0 persons per square mile (2000); Age: 24.4% under 18, 13.4% over 64 (2000); Marriage status: 23.0% never married, 63.7% now married, 8.0% widowed, 5.4% divorced (2000); Foreign born: 0.7% (2000); Ancestry (includes multiple ancestries): 59.7% German, 14.9% Norwegian, 7.7% Irish, 6.5% French (except Basque), 5.6% United States or American (2000).
Economy: Employment by occupation: 15.9% management, 12.2% professional, 15.0% services, 23.1% sales, 4.8% farming, 9.9% construction, 18.9% production (2000).
Income: Per capita income: $21,045 (2000); Median household income: $47,500 (2000); Poverty rate: 5.6% (2000).
Taxes: Total city taxes per capita: $94 (1997); City property taxes per capita: $92 (1997).
Education: High school graduation rate: 80.8% (2000); College graduation rate: 8.5% (2000).
Housing: Homeownership rate: 90.2% (2000); Median home value: $107,500 (2000); Median rent: $282 per month (2000); Median age of housing: 30 years (2000).
Transportation: Commute to work: 84.0% car, 0.7% public transportation, 3.5% walk, 10.6% work from home (2000); Travel time to work: 48.9% less than 15 minutes, 28.2% 15 to 30 minutes, 18.4% 30 to 45 minutes, 0.8% 45 to 60 minutes, 3.7% 60 minutes or more (2000)

Clark County

Located in central Wisconsin; drained by the Black and Eau Claire Rivers. Covers a land area of 1,215.60 square miles, a water area of 3.40 square miles, and is located in the Central Time Zone. The county government was organized in 1853. County seat is Neillsville.

Weather Station: Neillsville 3 SW — Elevation: 1,033 feet

	Jan	Feb	Mar	Apr	May	Jun	Jul	Aug	Sep	Oct	Nov	Dec
High	23	29	41	56	70	78	82	79	70	58	41	28
Low	2	9	20	32	43	52	56	55	46	35	23	9
Precip	0.9	0.8	1.7	2.7	3.5	4.2	4.6	4.6	4.1	2.4	2.1	1.0
Snow	11.0	7.2	8.7	1.7	tr	0.0	0.0	0.0	0.0	0.3	4.5	9.0

High and Low temperatures in degrees Fahrenheit; Precipitation and Snow in inches

Weather Station: Owen 3 W — Elevation: 1,240 feet

	Jan	Feb	Mar	Apr	May	Jun	Jul	Aug	Sep	Oct	Nov	Dec
High	19	25	36	53	67	75	79	77	68	55	39	25
Low	-1	5	18	32	43	53	57	55	45	34	22	7
Precip	1.0	0.9	1.9	2.5	3.7	4.2	4.3	4.4	4.2	2.6	2.2	1.2
Snow	12.1	8.1	8.9	2.8	tr	0.0	0.0	0.0	tr	0.5	5.7	10.7

High and Low temperatures in degrees Fahrenheit; Precipitation and Snow in inches

Population: 33,557 (2000); Race: 97.9% White, 0.3% Black, 0.2% Asian, 0.5% American Indian and Alaska Native, 0.9% Hispanic of any race, 0.7% two or more races (2000); Density: 27.6 persons per square mile (2000); Age: 29.9% under 18, 16.1% over 64 (2000).
Religion: Five largest groups: 31.7% Catholic Church, 9.4% Lutheran Church—Missouri Synod, 9.3% Evangelical Lutheran Church in America, 3.7% United Church of Christ, 3.3% The United Methodist Church (2000).
Economy: Unemployment rate: 5.4% (11/2002); Total civilian labor force: 15,998 (11/2002); Leading industries: 40.1% manufacturing; 16.4% health care and social assistance; 12.7% retail trade (2000); Companies that employ more than 1,000 persons: 0 (2000); Companies that employ more than 100 persons: 18 (2000); Farms: 1,883 totaling 413,901 acres (1997); Minority business ownership rate: 0.0% (1997); Women business ownership rate: 21.4% (1997); Retail sales per capita: $5,993 (1997). Single-family building permits issued: 98 (2001) / 106 (2000); Multi-family building permits issued: 14 (2001) / 28 (2000).
Income: Per capita income: $15,100 (2000); Median household income: $34,577 (2000); Poverty rate: 12.7% (2000); Bankruptcy rate: 1.61% (2001).
Taxes: Total county taxes per capita: $220 (2000); County property taxes per capita: $216 (2000).
Education: High school graduation rate: 75.4% (2000); College graduation rate: 10.3% (2000).
Housing: Homeownership rate: 81.3% (2000); Median home value: $64,700 (2000); Median rent: $295 per month (2000); Median age of housing: 46 years (2000).
Health: Birth rate: 160.0 per 10,000 population (1998); Age adjusted death rate: 69.5 per 10,000 population (1999); Age adjusted cancer mortality rate: 135.0 deaths per 100,000 population (1999). Number of physicians: 6.3 per 10,000 population (1999); Number of hospital beds: 49.5 per 10,000 population (1999).
Elections: 2000 Presidential election results: 41.9% Gore, 52.7% Bush, 3.7% Nader, 1.1% Buchanan
Additional Information Contacts
Clark County Government Offices. 715-743-5148
Neillsville Chamber of Commerce. 715-743-6444

Clark County Communities

ABBOTSFORD (city). Covers a land area of 3.051 square miles and a water area of 0 square miles. Located at 44.94° N. Lat.; 90.31° W. Long. Elevation is 1,420 feet.
History: Abbotsford began as a logging town, with many of the early residents being of German ancestry. A cheese factory and a milk condensery supported the economy after the timber industry declined.
Population: 1,956 (2000); Race: 99.1% White, 0.0% Black, 0.0% Asian, 0.1% American Indian and Alaska Native, 1.3% Hispanic of any race, 0.7% two or more races (2000); Density: 641.1 persons per square mile (2000); Age: 23.6% under 18, 23.8% over 64 (2000); Marriage status: 23.0% never married, 58.3% now married, 11.1% widowed, 7.7% divorced (2000); Foreign born: 0.6% (2000); Ancestry (includes multiple ancestries): 57.2% German, 11.3% Polish, 10.1% Norwegian, 7.6% Irish, 7.2% United States or American (2000).
Economy: Single-family building permits issued: 3 (2001) / 3 (2000); Multi-family building permits issued: 0 (2001) / 0 (2000); Employment by occupation: 7.1% management, 14.3% professional, 15.9% services, 19.6% sales, 2.3% farming, 8.8% construction, 32.0% production (2000).
Income: Per capita income: $17,133 (2000); Median household income: $36,949 (2000); Poverty rate: 6.7% (2000).
Taxes: Total city taxes per capita: $262 (1997); City property taxes per capita: $245 (1997).
Education: High school graduation rate: 75.9% (2000); College graduation rate: 15.2% (2000).

School District(s)

Abbotsford (PK-12)
2000 Enrollment: 651 715-223-6715
Housing: Homeownership rate: 72.4% (2000); Median home value: $70,300 (2000); Median rent: $303 per month (2000); Median age of housing: 32 years (2000).
Newspapers: Tribune-Phonograph (1 x week); Record-Review (1 x week); Central Wisconsin Shopper (1 x week)
Transportation: Commute to work: 88.6% car, 0.0% public transportation, 7.3% walk, 3.7% work from home (2000); Travel time to work: 57.3% less than 15 minutes, 24.5% 15 to 30 minutes, 10.9% 30 to 45 minutes, 4.5% 45 to 60 minutes, 2.8% 60 minutes or more (2000)

BEAVER (town). Covers a land area of 36.082 square miles and a water area of 0 square miles. Located at 44.81° N. Lat.; 90.50° W. Long.
Population: 854 (2000); Race: 98.0% White, 0.0% Black, 0.0% Asian, 0.0% American Indian and Alaska Native, 0.0% Hispanic of any race, 2.0% two or more races (2000); Density: 23.7 persons per square mile (2000); Age: 42.0% under 18, 6.8% over 64 (2000); Marriage status: 26.1% never married, 68.1% now married, 1.7% widowed, 4.0% divorced (2000); Foreign born: 0.0% (2000); Ancestry (includes multiple ancestries): 52.7% German, 12.8% United States or American, 7.2% Norwegian, 5.9% Irish, 5.8% Polish (2000).
Economy: Employment by occupation: 28.1% management, 10.6% professional, 7.8% services, 12.4% sales, 6.6% farming, 11.9% construction, 22.5% production (2000).
Income: Per capita income: $13,692 (2000); Median household income: $41,458 (2000); Poverty rate: 18.7% (2000).

Taxes: Total city taxes per capita: $67 (1997); City property taxes per capita: $66 (1997).
Education: High school graduation rate: 79.1% (2000); College graduation rate: 10.6% (2000).
Housing: Homeownership rate: 88.0% (2000); Median home value: $70,000 (2000); Median rent: $175 per month (2000); Median age of housing: 51 years (2000).
Transportation: Commute to work: 69.6% car, 0.0% public transportation, 3.9% walk, 25.5% work from home (2000); Travel time to work: 28.6% less than 15 minutes, 34.5% 15 to 30 minutes, 28.6% 30 to 45 minutes, 5.9% 45 to 60 minutes, 2.4% 60 minutes or more (2000)

BUTLER (town). Covers a land area of 35.968 square miles and a water area of 0.006 square miles. Located at 44.80° N. Lat.; 90.87° W. Long.
Population: 88 (2000); Race: 100.0% White, 0.0% Black, 0.0% Asian, 0.0% American Indian and Alaska Native, 0.0% Hispanic of any race, 0.0% two or more races (2000); Density: 2.4 persons per square mile (2000); Age: 7.4% under 18, 29.6% over 64 (2000); Marriage status: 14.8% never married, 59.3% now married, 22.2% widowed, 3.7% divorced (2000); Foreign born: 0.0% (2000); Ancestry (includes multiple ancestries): 44.4% German, 14.8% English, 11.1% Polish, 11.1% Norwegian, 7.4% Irish (2000).
Economy: Employment by occupation: 7.4% management, 7.4% professional, 0.0% services, 22.2% sales, 0.0% farming, 22.2% construction, 40.7% production (2000).
Income: Per capita income: $23,874 (2000); Median household income: $21,250 (2000); Poverty rate: 11.1% (2000).
Taxes: Total city taxes per capita: $43 (1997); City property taxes per capita: $43 (1997).
Education: High school graduation rate: 56.5% (2000); College graduation rate: 0.0% (2000).
Housing: Homeownership rate: 92.3% (2000); Median home value: $55,000 (2000); Median age of housing: 37 years (2000).
Transportation: Commute to work: 85.2% car, 0.0% public transportation, 0.0% walk, 14.8% work from home (2000); Travel time to work: 34.8% less than 15 minutes, 52.2% 15 to 30 minutes, 4.3% 30 to 45 minutes, 8.7% 45 to 60 minutes, 0.0% 60 minutes or more (2000)

CHILI (unincorporated postal area, zip code 54420). Covers a land area of 44.693 square miles and a water area of 0 square miles. Located at 44.61° N. Lat.; 90.36° W. Long. Elevation is 1,235 feet.
Population: 1,287 (2000); Race: 98.6% White, 0.2% Black, 0.9% Asian, 0.0% American Indian and Alaska Native, 0.0% Hispanic of any race, 0.3% two or more races (2000); Density: 28.8 persons per square mile (2000); Age: 29.9% under 18, 10.2% over 64 (2000); Marriage status: 26.4% never married, 66.1% now married, 4.0% widowed, 3.6% divorced (2000); Foreign born: 0.9% (2000); Ancestry (includes multiple ancestries): 59.7% German, 7.8% Irish, 6.1% United States or American, 5.1% English, 5.0% Polish (2000).
Economy: Employment by occupation: 16.0% management, 14.0% professional, 8.8% services, 16.5% sales, 7.8% farming, 14.4% construction, 22.4% production (2000).
Income: Per capita income: $13,776 (2000); Median household income: $37,875 (2000); Poverty rate: 14.8% (2000).
Education: High school graduation rate: 75.1% (2000); College graduation rate: 7.8% (2000).
Housing: Homeownership rate: 87.5% (2000); Median home value: $68,600 (2000); Median rent: $315 per month (2000); Median age of housing: 39 years (2000).
Transportation: Commute to work: 80.0% car, 0.0% public transportation, 8.1% walk, 10.5% work from home (2000); Travel time to work: 23.3% less than 15 minutes, 56.3% 15 to 30 minutes, 11.7% 30 to 45 minutes, 2.0% 45 to 60 minutes, 6.7% 60 minutes or more (2000)

COLBY (city). Covers a land area of 1.482 square miles and a water area of 0 square miles. Located at 44.91° N. Lat.; 90.31° W. Long. Elevation is 1,350 feet.
History: Colby was incorporated in 1891 when the settlements of Colby and Hull united. Colby cheese was named for this area.
Population: 1,616 (2000); Race: 96.2% White, 0.0% Black, 0.1% Asian, 1.0% American Indian and Alaska Native, 3.6% Hispanic of any race, 0.8% two or more races (2000); Density: 1,090.1 persons per square mile (2000); Age: 25.6% under 18, 23.7% over 64 (2000); Marriage status: 18.6% never married, 57.4% now married, 16.7% widowed, 7.4% divorced (2000); Foreign born: 1.7% (2000); Ancestry (includes multiple ancestries): 67.8% German, 7.3% Norwegian, 5.9% Irish, 5.5% Polish, 5.4% English (2000).
Economy: Single-family building permits issued: 8 (2001) / 5 (2000); Multi-family building permits issued: 0 (2001) / 16 (2000); Employment by occupation: 6.6% management, 12.5% professional, 16.3% services, 22.7% sales, 2.9% farming, 8.0% construction, 31.1% production (2000).
Income: Per capita income: $16,137 (2000); Median household income: $34,318 (2000); Poverty rate: 7.0% (2000).
Taxes: Total city taxes per capita: $179 (1997); City property taxes per capita: $159 (1997).
Education: High school graduation rate: 75.0% (2000); College graduation rate: 8.5% (2000).

School District(s)

Colby (PK-12)
2000 Enrollment: 1,111 715-223-2301
Housing: Homeownership rate: 76.6% (2000); Median home value: $72,700 (2000); Median rent: $303 per month (2000); Median age of housing: 37 years (2000).
Transportation: Commute to work: 90.6% car, 0.4% public transportation, 6.5% walk, 2.1% work from home (2000); Travel time to work: 53.7% less than 15 minutes, 25.6% 15 to 30 minutes, 16.4% 30 to 45 minutes, 1.7% 45 to 60 minutes, 2.6% 60 minutes or more (2000)

COLBY (town). Covers a land area of 33.777 square miles and a water area of 0 square miles. Located at 44.90° N. Lat.; 90.36° W. Long. Elevation is 1,350 feet.
Population: 908 (2000); Race: 96.5% White, 1.5% Black, 0.6% Asian, 0.2% American Indian and Alaska Native, 0.3% Hispanic of any race, 0.8% two or more races (2000); Density: 26.9 persons per square mile (2000); Age: 39.0% under 18, 7.5% over 64 (2000); Marriage status: 28.7% never married, 62.3% now married, 4.1% widowed, 4.8% divorced (2000); Foreign born: 0.7% (2000); Ancestry (includes multiple ancestries): 55.9% German, 7.9% Other groups, 7.7% Norwegian, 6.9% Swiss, 5.0% Polish (2000).
Economy: Single-family building permits issued: 1 (2001) / 5 (2000); Multi-family building permits issued: 0 (2001) / 0 (2000); Employment by occupation: 20.9% management, 9.6% professional, 14.8% services, 13.3% sales, 7.2% farming, 7.0% construction, 27.2% production (2000).
Income: Per capita income: $13,591 (2000); Median household income: $41,310 (2000); Poverty rate: 16.3% (2000).
Taxes: Total city taxes per capita: $44 (1997); City property taxes per capita: $43 (1997).
Education: High school graduation rate: 77.9% (2000); College graduation rate: 11.8% (2000).
Housing: Homeownership rate: 83.6% (2000); Median home value: $81,400 (2000); Median rent: $239 per month (2000); Median age of housing: 49 years (2000).
Transportation: Commute to work: 71.5% car, 0.0% public transportation, 3.8% walk, 23.6% work from home (2000); Travel time to work: 50.6% less than 15 minutes, 26.0% 15 to 30 minutes, 19.7% 30 to 45 minutes, 3.8% 45 to 60 minutes, 0.0% 60 minutes or more (2000)

CURTISS (village). Covers a land area of 0.686 square miles and a water area of 0 square miles. Located at 44.95° N. Lat.; 90.43° W. Long. Elevation is 1,365 feet.
Population: 198 (2000); Race: 78.4% White, 0.0% Black, 2.1% Asian, 0.0% American Indian and Alaska Native, 19.6% Hispanic of any race, 0.0% two or more races (2000); Density: 288.8 persons per square mile (2000); Age: 29.9% under 18, 18.6% over 64 (2000); Marriage status: 26.2% never married, 72.3% now married, 1.4% widowed, 0.0% divorced (2000); Foreign born: 17.0% (2000); Ancestry (includes multiple ancestries): 48.5% German, 26.8% Other groups, 8.8% English, 7.7% Norwegian, 6.7% Polish (2000).
Economy: In dairying region. Single-family building permits issued: 1 (2001) / 0 (2000); Multi-family building permits issued: 0 (2001) / 0 (2000); Employment by occupation: 5.8% management, 4.7% professional, 25.6% services, 9.3% sales, 3.5% farming, 5.8% construction, 45.3% production (2000).
Income: Per capita income: $11,061 (2000); Median household income: $29,250 (2000); Poverty rate: 14.4% (2000).
Taxes: Total city taxes per capita: $122 (1997); City property taxes per capita: $110 (1997).
Education: High school graduation rate: 63.5% (2000); College graduation rate: 4.3% (2000).
Housing: Homeownership rate: 89.2% (2000); Median home value: $53,000 (2000); Median rent: $244 per month (2000); Median age of housing: 52 years (2000).
Transportation: Commute to work: 97.7% car, 0.0% public transportation, 0.0% walk, 2.3% work from home (2000); Travel time to work: 46.4% less

than 15 minutes, 45.2% 15 to 30 minutes, 3.6% 30 to 45 minutes, 4.8% 45 to 60 minutes, 0.0% 60 minutes or more (2000)

DEWHURST (town). Covers a land area of 35.407 square miles and a water area of 0.746 square miles. Located at 44.44° N. Lat.; 90.73° W. Long.
Population: 321 (2000); Race: 91.2% White, 0.0% Black, 0.0% Asian, 6.0% American Indian and Alaska Native, 0.6% Hispanic of any race, 2.8% two or more races (2000); Density: 9.1 persons per square mile (2000); Age: 14.8% under 18, 26.4% over 64 (2000); Marriage status: 18.2% never married, 59.4% now married, 9.4% widowed, 12.9% divorced (2000); Foreign born: 3.5% (2000); Ancestry (includes multiple ancestries): 38.7% German, 16.4% Polish, 13.5% Norwegian, 12.3% Irish, 10.1% Other groups (2000).
Economy: Employment by occupation: 8.5% management, 10.6% professional, 18.3% services, 22.5% sales, 0.0% farming, 14.8% construction, 25.4% production (2000).
Income: Per capita income: $20,696 (2000); Median household income: $31,250 (2000); Poverty rate: 6.7% (2000).
Taxes: Total city taxes per capita: $254 (1997); City property taxes per capita: $244 (1997).
Education: High school graduation rate: 77.6% (2000); College graduation rate: 14.4% (2000).
Housing: Homeownership rate: 85.1% (2000); Median home value: $72,200 (2000); Median rent: $388 per month (2000); Median age of housing: 35 years (2000).
Transportation: Commute to work: 94.2% car, 0.0% public transportation, 2.2% walk, 3.6% work from home (2000); Travel time to work: 9.0% less than 15 minutes, 64.7% 15 to 30 minutes, 8.3% 30 to 45 minutes, 6.8% 45 to 60 minutes, 11.3% 60 minutes or more (2000)

DORCHESTER (village). Covers a land area of 1.309 square miles and a water area of 0.016 square miles. Located at 45.00° N. Lat.; 90.33° W. Long. Elevation is 1,425 feet.
Population: 827 (2000); Race: 94.6% White, 0.2% Black, 0.3% Asian, 0.0% American Indian and Alaska Native, 3.7% Hispanic of any race, 2.1% two or more races (2000); Density: 631.7 persons per square mile (2000); Age: 26.5% under 18, 15.7% over 64 (2000); Marriage status: 23.5% never married, 57.5% now married, 6.9% widowed, 12.1% divorced (2000); Foreign born: 2.4% (2000); Ancestry (includes multiple ancestries): 58.7% German, 9.2% Norwegian, 6.8% English, 6.4% Other groups, 5.8% Irish (2000).
Economy: In dairying region: cheese, butter; dairy equipment; manufactured homes, forage boxes; poultry hatchery; stone quarries. Single-family building permits issued: 2 (2001) / 3 (2000); Multi-family building permits issued: 0 (2001) / 8 (2000); Employment by occupation: 6.7% management, 15.7% professional, 12.4% services, 16.9% sales, 4.0% farming, 9.5% construction, 34.8% production (2000).
Income: Per capita income: $15,860 (2000); Median household income: $34,750 (2000); Poverty rate: 10.1% (2000).
Taxes: Total city taxes per capita: $177 (1997); City property taxes per capita: $162 (1997).
Education: High school graduation rate: 72.8% (2000); College graduation rate: 9.2% (2000).
Housing: Homeownership rate: 72.8% (2000); Median home value: $70,700 (2000); Median rent: $327 per month (2000); Median age of housing: 29 years (2000).
Transportation: Commute to work: 88.5% car, 0.0% public transportation, 5.2% walk, 4.3% work from home (2000); Travel time to work: 36.8% less than 15 minutes, 44.1% 15 to 30 minutes, 7.1% 30 to 45 minutes, 7.3% 45 to 60 minutes, 4.7% 60 minutes or more (2000)

EATON (town). Covers a land area of 33.835 square miles and a water area of 0.058 square miles. Located at 44.72° N. Lat.; 90.60° W. Long.
Population: 665 (2000); Race: 99.2% White, 0.0% Black, 0.0% Asian, 0.3% American Indian and Alaska Native, 0.3% Hispanic of any race, 0.3% two or more races (2000); Density: 19.7 persons per square mile (2000); Age: 38.5% under 18, 10.5% over 64 (2000); Marriage status: 28.5% never married, 63.1% now married, 5.4% widowed, 3.1% divorced (2000); Foreign born: 0.6% (2000); Ancestry (includes multiple ancestries): 55.0% German, 9.5% Norwegian, 8.6% Polish, 5.9% Slovene, 5.5% Irish (2000).
Economy: Single-family building permits issued: 7 (2001) / 2 (2000); Multi-family building permits issued: 0 (2001) / 0 (2000); Employment by occupation: 23.8% management, 4.7% professional, 13.6% services, 14.7% sales, 8.0% farming, 12.7% construction, 22.4% production (2000).
Income: Per capita income: $12,250 (2000); Median household income: $37,000 (2000); Poverty rate: 23.2% (2000).
Taxes: Total city taxes per capita: $59 (1997); City property taxes per capita: $58 (1997).
Education: High school graduation rate: 80.6% (2000); College graduation rate: 8.3% (2000).
Housing: Homeownership rate: 89.7% (2000); Median home value: $87,700 (2000); Median rent: $329 per month (2000); Median age of housing: 57 years (2000).
Transportation: Commute to work: 67.9% car, 0.0% public transportation, 8.5% walk, 20.8% work from home (2000); Travel time to work: 47.1% less than 15 minutes, 29.8% 15 to 30 minutes, 15.6% 30 to 45 minutes, 4.5% 45 to 60 minutes, 3.1% 60 minutes or more (2000)

FOSTER (town). Covers a land area of 71.290 square miles and a water area of 0.238 square miles. Located at 44.68° N. Lat.; 90.83° W. Long.
Population: 95 (2000); Race: 96.4% White, 0.0% Black, 0.0% Asian, 0.0% American Indian and Alaska Native, 0.0% Hispanic of any race, 3.6% two or more races (2000); Density: 1.3 persons per square mile (2000); Age: 2.4% under 18, 27.7% over 64 (2000); Marriage status: 18.1% never married, 56.6% now married, 12.0% widowed, 13.3% divorced (2000); Foreign born: 0.0% (2000); Ancestry (includes multiple ancestries): 53.0% German, 9.6% Irish, 9.6% Norwegian, 8.4% Dutch, 8.4% Polish (2000).
Economy: Employment by occupation: 8.5% management, 10.6% professional, 17.0% services, 31.9% sales, 0.0% farming, 6.4% construction, 25.5% production (2000).
Income: Per capita income: $17,039 (2000); Median household income: $28,750 (2000); Poverty rate: 3.6% (2000).
Taxes: Total city taxes per capita: $184 (1997); City property taxes per capita: $172 (1997).
Education: High school graduation rate: 83.1% (2000); College graduation rate: 9.1% (2000).
Housing: Homeownership rate: 91.1% (2000); Median home value: $97,500 (2000); Median rent: $275 per month (2000); Median age of housing: 34 years (2000).
Transportation: Commute to work: 78.7% car, 0.0% public transportation, 8.5% walk, 12.8% work from home (2000); Travel time to work: 24.4% less than 15 minutes, 36.6% 15 to 30 minutes, 17.1% 30 to 45 minutes, 9.8% 45 to 60 minutes, 12.2% 60 minutes or more (2000)

FREMONT (town). Covers a land area of 35.244 square miles and a water area of 0 square miles. Located at 44.62° N. Lat.; 90.37° W. Long.
Population: 1,190 (2000); Race: 99.4% White, 0.0% Black, 0.6% Asian, 0.0% American Indian and Alaska Native, 0.0% Hispanic of any race, 0.0% two or more races (2000); Density: 33.8 persons per square mile (2000); Age: 32.6% under 18, 9.3% over 64 (2000); Marriage status: 27.2% never married, 66.8% now married, 3.1% widowed, 2.9% divorced (2000); Foreign born: 0.6% (2000); Ancestry (includes multiple ancestries): 56.4% German, 6.9% United States or American, 6.9% Irish, 5.2% Polish, 4.3% Norwegian (2000).
Economy: Single-family building permits issued: 11 (2001) / 12 (2000); Multi-family building permits issued: 0 (2001) / 0 (2000); Employment by occupation: 19.7% management, 9.8% professional, 10.6% services, 15.2% sales, 8.9% farming, 13.2% construction, 22.6% production (2000).
Income: Per capita income: $12,068 (2000); Median household income: $35,167 (2000); Poverty rate: 20.7% (2000).
Taxes: Total city taxes per capita: $54 (1997); City property taxes per capita: $52 (1997).
Education: High school graduation rate: 68.4% (2000); College graduation rate: 4.6% (2000).
Housing: Homeownership rate: 85.4% (2000); Median home value: $69,800 (2000); Median rent: $300 per month (2000); Median age of housing: 49 years (2000).
Transportation: Commute to work: 72.6% car, 0.0% public transportation, 8.5% walk, 17.4% work from home (2000); Travel time to work: 24.8% less than 15 minutes, 53.2% 15 to 30 minutes, 12.6% 30 to 45 minutes, 1.9% 45 to 60 minutes, 7.6% 60 minutes or more (2000)

GRANT (town). Covers a land area of 35.760 square miles and a water area of 0 square miles. Located at 44.55° N. Lat.; 90.48° W. Long.
Population: 920 (2000); Race: 98.6% White, 0.0% Black, 0.0% Asian, 0.0% American Indian and Alaska Native, 1.8% Hispanic of any race, 0.0% two or more races (2000); Density: 25.7 persons per square mile (2000); Age: 30.7% under 18, 13.9% over 64 (2000); Marriage status: 24.6% never married, 64.4% now married, 5.1% widowed, 5.9% divorced (2000); Foreign born: 1.4% (2000); Ancestry (includes multiple ancestries): 52.7% German, 7.9% Polish, 6.4% English, 6.0% United States or American, 5.9% Irish (2000).
Economy: Dairy products. Lumber. Manufacturing: cheese, whey products. Single-family building permits issued: 3 (2001) / 5 (2000); Multi-family

building permits issued: 0 (2001) / 0 (2000); Employment by occupation: 17.0% management, 7.5% professional, 13.5% services, 15.4% sales, 3.3% farming, 9.8% construction, 33.6% production (2000).
Income: Per capita income: $16,065 (2000); Median household income: $36,518 (2000); Poverty rate: 13.5% (2000).
Taxes: Total city taxes per capita: $63 (1997); City property taxes per capita: $61 (1997).
Education: High school graduation rate: 76.4% (2000); College graduation rate: 9.8% (2000).
Housing: Homeownership rate: 88.3% (2000); Median home value: $66,900 (2000); Median rent: $313 per month (2000); Median age of housing: 52 years (2000).
Transportation: Commute to work: 84.6% car, 1.2% public transportation, 3.7% walk, 9.6% work from home (2000); Travel time to work: 36.9% less than 15 minutes, 32.5% 15 to 30 minutes, 15.7% 30 to 45 minutes, 6.7% 45 to 60 minutes, 8.2% 60 minutes or more (2000)

GRANTON (village). Covers a land area of 0.565 square miles and a water area of 0 square miles. Located at 44.58° N. Lat.; 90.46° W. Long. Elevation is 1,150 feet.
Population: 406 (2000); Race: 99.6% White, 0.0% Black, 0.0% Asian, 0.0% American Indian and Alaska Native, 0.4% Hispanic of any race, 0.4% two or more races (2000); Density: 718.0 persons per square mile (2000); Age: 34.6% under 18, 12.1% over 64 (2000); Marriage status: 25.4% never married, 62.2% now married, 5.3% widowed, 7.1% divorced (2000); Foreign born: 0.9% (2000); Ancestry (includes multiple ancestries): 59.8% German, 14.7% Irish, 10.5% Norwegian, 8.3% United States or American, 7.6% English (2000).
Economy: Single-family building permits issued: 0 (2001) / 0 (2000); Multi-family building permits issued: 0 (2001) / 0 (2000); Employment by occupation: 3.3% management, 10.4% professional, 9.8% services, 18.0% sales, 7.7% farming, 10.9% construction, 39.9% production (2000).
Income: Per capita income: $12,218 (2000); Median household income: $30,288 (2000); Poverty rate: 14.5% (2000).
Taxes: Total city taxes per capita: $100 (1997); City property taxes per capita: $95 (1997).
Education: High school graduation rate: 81.0% (2000); College graduation rate: 7.9% (2000).

School District(s)

Granton Area (PK-12)
2000 Enrollment: 343 715-238-7292
Housing: Homeownership rate: 74.1% (2000); Median home value: $51,300 (2000); Median rent: $302 per month (2000); Median age of housing: 49 years (2000).
Transportation: Commute to work: 97.8% car, 0.0% public transportation, 0.0% walk, 2.2% work from home (2000); Travel time to work: 27.1% less than 15 minutes, 36.7% 15 to 30 minutes, 28.2% 30 to 45 minutes, 3.4% 45 to 60 minutes, 4.5% 60 minutes or more (2000)

GREEN GROVE (town). Covers a land area of 36.466 square miles and a water area of 0.009 square miles. Located at 44.90° N. Lat.; 90.49° W. Long.
Population: 902 (2000); Race: 97.1% White, 0.0% Black, 2.1% Asian, 0.0% American Indian and Alaska Native, 0.3% Hispanic of any race, 0.4% two or more races (2000); Density: 24.7 persons per square mile (2000); Age: 25.4% under 18, 25.5% over 64 (2000); Marriage status: 18.7% never married, 62.4% now married, 11.2% widowed, 7.7% divorced (2000); Foreign born: 2.9% (2000); Ancestry (includes multiple ancestries): 45.6% German, 6.1% Polish, 4.2% Norwegian, 4.1% United States or American, 3.7% Irish (2000).
Economy: Single-family building permits issued: 3 (2001) / 9 (2000); Multi-family building permits issued: 0 (2001) / 0 (2000); Employment by occupation: 23.1% management, 7.1% professional, 9.5% services, 19.2% sales, 7.4% farming, 7.4% construction, 26.3% production (2000).
Income: Per capita income: $14,067 (2000); Median household income: $37,667 (2000); Poverty rate: 13.1% (2000).
Taxes: Total city taxes per capita: $21 (1997); City property taxes per capita: $20 (1997).
Education: High school graduation rate: 70.0% (2000); College graduation rate: 5.5% (2000).
Housing: Homeownership rate: 84.7% (2000); Median home value: $59,500 (2000); Median rent: $290 per month (2000); Median age of housing: 60+ years (2000).
Transportation: Commute to work: 66.3% car, 0.0% public transportation, 4.3% walk, 27.0% work from home (2000); Travel time to work: 39.9% less than 15 minutes, 33.6% 15 to 30 minutes, 11.8% 30 to 45 minutes, 10.9% 45 to 60 minutes, 3.8% 60 minutes or more (2000)

GREENWOOD (city). Covers a land area of 2.825 square miles and a water area of 0.027 square miles. Located at 44.76° N. Lat.; 90.59° W. Long. Elevation is 1,168 feet.
Population: 1,079 (2000); Race: 98.4% White, 0.3% Black, 0.0% Asian, 0.0% American Indian and Alaska Native, 0.0% Hispanic of any race, 0.5% two or more races (2000); Density: 381.9 persons per square mile (2000); Age: 24.3% under 18, 19.9% over 64 (2000); Marriage status: 22.0% never married, 57.1% now married, 11.8% widowed, 9.1% divorced (2000); Foreign born: 0.7% (2000); Ancestry (includes multiple ancestries): 54.8% German, 13.8% Norwegian, 10.0% Irish, 8.3% Polish, 7.5% United States or American (2000).
Economy: In dairying, lumbering, and farming area. Manufacturing: animal feed; dairy products, especially cheese. Single-family building permits issued: 0 (2001) / 7 (2000); Multi-family building permits issued: 0 (2001) / 0 (2000); Employment by occupation: 7.6% management, 14.0% professional, 17.4% services, 17.4% sales, 1.9% farming, 13.0% construction, 28.7% production (2000).
Income: Per capita income: $18,841 (2000); Median household income: $32,917 (2000); Poverty rate: 9.3% (2000).
Taxes: Total city taxes per capita: $195 (1997); City property taxes per capita: $175 (1997).
Education: High school graduation rate: 76.6% (2000); College graduation rate: 13.5% (2000).

School District(s)

Greenwood (PK-12)
2000 Enrollment: 564 715-267-6101
Housing: Homeownership rate: 70.9% (2000); Median home value: $58,500 (2000); Median rent: $308 per month (2000); Median age of housing: 44 years (2000).
Transportation: Commute to work: 82.1% car, 0.0% public transportation, 12.7% walk, 3.6% work from home (2000); Travel time to work: 54.8% less than 15 minutes, 22.3% 15 to 30 minutes, 13.3% 30 to 45 minutes, 4.8% 45 to 60 minutes, 4.8% 60 minutes or more (2000)

HENDREN (town). Covers a land area of 35.842 square miles and a water area of 0.038 square miles. Located at 44.73° N. Lat.; 90.73° W. Long.
Population: 513 (2000); Race: 99.2% White, 0.0% Black, 0.0% Asian, 0.0% American Indian and Alaska Native, 2.1% Hispanic of any race, 0.0% two or more races (2000); Density: 14.3 persons per square mile (2000); Age: 31.1% under 18, 15.6% over 64 (2000); Marriage status: 21.4% never married, 65.9% now married, 7.8% widowed, 4.9% divorced (2000); Foreign born: 2.7% (2000); Ancestry (includes multiple ancestries): 30.9% German, 17.3% Slovene, 10.5% Polish, 8.9% Irish, 8.4% Norwegian (2000).
Economy: Single-family building permits issued: 0 (2001) / 0 (2000); Multi-family building permits issued: 0 (2001) / 0 (2000); Employment by occupation: 25.7% management, 8.8% professional, 17.3% services, 17.3% sales, 4.0% farming, 6.0% construction, 20.9% production (2000).
Income: Per capita income: $13,318 (2000); Median household income: $27,353 (2000); Poverty rate: 18.6% (2000).
Taxes: Total city taxes per capita: $27 (1997); City property taxes per capita: $25 (1997).
Education: High school graduation rate: 75.9% (2000); College graduation rate: 6.7% (2000).
Housing: Homeownership rate: 89.8% (2000); Median home value: $52,300 (2000); Median rent: $275 per month (2000); Median age of housing: 54 years (2000).
Transportation: Commute to work: 74.7% car, 0.0% public transportation, 5.2% walk, 20.1% work from home (2000); Travel time to work: 27.1% less than 15 minutes, 30.7% 15 to 30 minutes, 18.1% 30 to 45 minutes, 16.6% 45 to 60 minutes, 7.5% 60 minutes or more (2000)

HEWETT (town). Covers a land area of 35.753 square miles and a water area of 0.030 square miles. Located at 44.56° N. Lat.; 90.72° W. Long.
Population: 314 (2000); Race: 100.0% White, 0.0% Black, 0.0% Asian, 0.0% American Indian and Alaska Native, 0.0% Hispanic of any race, 0.0% two or more races (2000); Density: 8.8 persons per square mile (2000); Age: 26.7% under 18, 15.6% over 64 (2000); Marriage status: 17.7% never married, 75.2% now married, 5.3% widowed, 1.9% divorced (2000); Foreign born: 0.0% (2000); Ancestry (includes multiple ancestries): 50.8% German, 13.2% Norwegian, 11.1% Irish, 9.6% Polish, 8.1% English (2000).
Economy: Employment by occupation: 7.3% management, 18.4% professional, 14.5% services, 19.0% sales, 5.6% farming, 6.1% construction, 29.1% production (2000).
Income: Per capita income: $18,039 (2000); Median household income: $46,111 (2000); Poverty rate: 1.2% (2000).

Taxes: Total city taxes per capita: $31 (1997); City property taxes per capita: $28 (1997).
Education: High school graduation rate: 79.6% (2000); College graduation rate: 17.8% (2000).
Housing: Homeownership rate: 92.9% (2000); Median home value: $84,300 (2000); Median rent: $213 per month (2000); Median age of housing: 27 years (2000).
Transportation: Commute to work: 90.3% car, 0.0% public transportation, 1.7% walk, 6.3% work from home (2000); Travel time to work: 35.4% less than 15 minutes, 40.2% 15 to 30 minutes, 11.6% 30 to 45 minutes, 7.3% 45 to 60 minutes, 5.5% 60 minutes or more (2000)

HIXON (town). Covers a land area of 33.349 square miles and a water area of 0.385 square miles. Located at 44.98° N. Lat.; 90.61° W. Long.
Population: 740 (2000); Race: 98.6% White, 0.0% Black, 0.3% Asian, 0.3% American Indian and Alaska Native, 0.3% Hispanic of any race, 0.8% two or more races (2000); Density: 22.2 persons per square mile (2000); Age: 37.1% under 18, 10.7% over 64 (2000); Marriage status: 24.2% never married, 63.2% now married, 6.3% widowed, 6.3% divorced (2000); Foreign born: 1.1% (2000); Ancestry (includes multiple ancestries): 45.2% German, 12.8% Polish, 9.3% Swiss, 7.2% English, 5.6% Dutch (2000).
Economy: Single-family building permits issued: 2 (2001) / 2 (2000); Multi-family building permits issued: 0 (2001) / 0 (2000); Employment by occupation: 19.0% management, 6.9% professional, 12.7% services, 16.0% sales, 2.3% farming, 10.8% construction, 32.4% production (2000).
Income: Per capita income: $12,092 (2000); Median household income: $36,375 (2000); Poverty rate: 12.1% (2000).
Taxes: Total city taxes per capita: $28 (1997); City property taxes per capita: $28 (1997).
Education: High school graduation rate: 67.3% (2000); College graduation rate: 7.4% (2000).
Housing: Homeownership rate: 86.2% (2000); Median home value: $50,000 (2000); Median rent: $330 per month (2000); Median age of housing: 58 years (2000).
Transportation: Commute to work: 70.3% car, 0.0% public transportation, 3.0% walk, 24.4% work from home (2000); Travel time to work: 43.2% less than 15 minutes, 33.2% 15 to 30 minutes, 10.5% 30 to 45 minutes, 7.0% 45 to 60 minutes, 6.1% 60 minutes or more (2000)

HOARD (town). Covers a land area of 35.280 square miles and a water area of 0 square miles. Located at 44.99° N. Lat.; 90.48° W. Long.
Population: 594 (2000); Race: 97.8% White, 0.0% Black, 0.0% Asian, 0.5% American Indian and Alaska Native, 2.0% Hispanic of any race, 0.0% two or more races (2000); Density: 16.8 persons per square mile (2000); Age: 38.6% under 18, 12.6% over 64 (2000); Marriage status: 21.7% never married, 66.0% now married, 5.3% widowed, 7.1% divorced (2000); Foreign born: 1.7% (2000); Ancestry (includes multiple ancestries): 53.6% German, 13.0% Norwegian, 7.2% Swiss, 5.6% Irish, 5.5% Polish (2000).
Economy: Single-family building permits issued: 2 (2001) / 2 (2000); Multi-family building permits issued: 0 (2001) / 0 (2000); Employment by occupation: 28.7% management, 8.8% professional, 10.3% services, 7.3% sales, 3.8% farming, 9.2% construction, 31.8% production (2000).
Income: Per capita income: $12,273 (2000); Median household income: $35,250 (2000); Poverty rate: 14.8% (2000).
Taxes: Total city taxes per capita: $18 (1997); City property taxes per capita: $17 (1997).
Education: High school graduation rate: 73.5% (2000); College graduation rate: 5.5% (2000).
Housing: Homeownership rate: 98.9% (2000); Median home value: $50,500 (2000); Median rent: $325 per month (2000); Median age of housing: 56 years (2000).
Transportation: Commute to work: 63.7% car, 0.0% public transportation, 6.6% walk, 27.0% work from home (2000); Travel time to work: 18.7% less than 15 minutes, 50.3% 15 to 30 minutes, 17.1% 30 to 45 minutes, 4.3% 45 to 60 minutes, 9.6% 60 minutes or more (2000)

HUMBIRD (unincorporated postal area, zip code 54746). Covers a land area of 45.153 square miles and a water area of 0.115 square miles. Located at 44.55° N. Lat.; 90.89° W. Long. Elevation is 1,030 feet.
Population: 685 (2000); Race: 96.6% White, 0.6% Black, 0.0% Asian, 1.7% American Indian and Alaska Native, 0.8% Hispanic of any race, 1.1% two or more races (2000); Density: 15.2 persons per square mile (2000); Age: 24.0% under 18, 10.3% over 64 (2000); Marriage status: 22.3% never married, 66.2% now married, 5.0% widowed, 6.5% divorced (2000); Foreign born: 1.1% (2000); Ancestry (includes multiple ancestries): 32.8% German, 16.8% Irish, 15.8% Norwegian, 12.2% United States or American, 8.0% French (except Basque) (2000).
Economy: In dairying and farming area. Hay, cheese. Employment by occupation: 13.7% management, 14.2% professional, 14.5% services, 14.0% sales, 4.0% farming, 9.1% construction, 30.5% production (2000).
Income: Per capita income: $16,384 (2000); Median household income: $35,288 (2000); Poverty rate: 9.7% (2000).
Education: High school graduation rate: 83.1% (2000); College graduation rate: 10.0% (2000).
Housing: Homeownership rate: 85.1% (2000); Median home value: $46,600 (2000); Median rent: $363 per month (2000); Median age of housing: 33 years (2000).
Transportation: Commute to work: 91.2% car, 0.0% public transportation, 1.7% walk, 5.7% work from home (2000); Travel time to work: 16.3% less than 15 minutes, 43.8% 15 to 30 minutes, 19.3% 30 to 45 minutes, 2.7% 45 to 60 minutes, 17.8% 60 minutes or more (2000)

LEVIS (town). Covers a land area of 35.888 square miles and a water area of 0.294 square miles. Located at 44.47° N. Lat.; 90.64° W. Long.
Population: 504 (2000); Race: 91.8% White, 0.0% Black, 0.0% Asian, 8.2% American Indian and Alaska Native, 0.4% Hispanic of any race, 0.0% two or more races (2000); Density: 14.0 persons per square mile (2000); Age: 26.1% under 18, 11.6% over 64 (2000); Marriage status: 27.9% never married, 62.6% now married, 3.5% widowed, 6.0% divorced (2000); Foreign born: 0.0% (2000); Ancestry (includes multiple ancestries): 45.0% German, 13.1% Irish, 11.0% English, 9.6% Polish, 7.6% Norwegian (2000).
Economy: Employment by occupation: 15.6% management, 7.6% professional, 19.8% services, 15.2% sales, 3.0% farming, 13.1% construction, 25.7% production (2000).
Income: Per capita income: $14,924 (2000); Median household income: $30,521 (2000); Poverty rate: 10.6% (2000).
Taxes: Total city taxes per capita: $70 (1997); City property taxes per capita: $68 (1997).
Education: High school graduation rate: 74.5% (2000); College graduation rate: 6.5% (2000).
Housing: Homeownership rate: 84.3% (2000); Median home value: $80,000 (2000); Median rent: $286 per month (2000); Median age of housing: 36 years (2000).
Transportation: Commute to work: 76.1% car, 0.0% public transportation, 3.0% walk, 19.2% work from home (2000); Travel time to work: 29.1% less than 15 minutes, 41.3% 15 to 30 minutes, 22.8% 30 to 45 minutes, 6.9% 45 to 60 minutes, 0.0% 60 minutes or more (2000)

LONGWOOD (town). Covers a land area of 35.700 square miles and a water area of 0.010 square miles. Located at 44.90° N. Lat.; 90.60° W. Long. Elevation is 1,245 feet.
Population: 698 (2000); Race: 96.2% White, 2.1% Black, 0.3% Asian, 0.0% American Indian and Alaska Native, 1.5% Hispanic of any race, 1.4% two or more races (2000); Density: 19.6 persons per square mile (2000); Age: 33.2% under 18, 14.6% over 64 (2000); Marriage status: 19.4% never married, 67.6% now married, 7.1% widowed, 5.9% divorced (2000); Foreign born: 2.1% (2000); Ancestry (includes multiple ancestries): 49.2% German, 9.5% Polish, 6.0% English, 5.3% Norwegian, 4.7% United States or American (2000).
Economy: Single-family building permits issued: 6 (2001) / 6 (2000); Multi-family building permits issued: 0 (2001) / 0 (2000); Employment by occupation: 25.2% management, 8.5% professional, 10.5% services, 16.3% sales, 4.8% farming, 9.9% construction, 24.8% production (2000).
Income: Per capita income: $13,200 (2000); Median household income: $30,000 (2000); Poverty rate: 17.8% (2000).
Taxes: Total city taxes per capita: $47 (1997); City property taxes per capita: $45 (1997).
Education: High school graduation rate: 74.1% (2000); College graduation rate: 10.5% (2000).
Housing: Homeownership rate: 90.0% (2000); Median home value: $63,200 (2000); Median rent: $244 per month (2000); Median age of housing: 60+ years (2000).
Transportation: Commute to work: 62.2% car, 0.0% public transportation, 7.5% walk, 28.6% work from home (2000); Travel time to work: 33.8% less than 15 minutes, 36.7% 15 to 30 minutes, 8.6% 30 to 45 minutes, 12.9% 45 to 60 minutes, 8.1% 60 minutes or more (2000)

LOYAL (city). Covers a land area of 1.374 square miles and a water area of 0 square miles. Located at 44.73° N. Lat.; 90.49° W. Long. Elevation is 1,250 feet.

Population: 1,308 (2000); Race: 97.8% White, 1.5% Black, 0.0% Asian, 0.0% American Indian and Alaska Native, 0.0% Hispanic of any race, 0.3% two or more races (2000); Density: 951.8 persons per square mile (2000); Age: 27.4% under 18, 20.7% over 64 (2000); Marriage status: 19.3% never married, 62.3% now married, 9.3% widowed, 9.1% divorced (2000); Foreign born: 0.6% (2000); Ancestry (includes multiple ancestries): 53.8% German, 8.5% Norwegian, 7.2% Irish, 5.5% Polish, 5.5% English (2000).
Economy: Single-family building permits issued: 2 (2001) / 0 (2000); Multi-family building permits issued: 2 (2001) / 0 (2000); Employment by occupation: 9.8% management, 10.9% professional, 16.6% services, 23.5% sales, 0.8% farming, 11.7% construction, 26.6% production (2000).
Income: Per capita income: $16,502 (2000); Median household income: $30,647 (2000); Poverty rate: 10.5% (2000).
Taxes: Total city taxes per capita: $175 (1997); City property taxes per capita: $162 (1997).
Education: High school graduation rate: 77.9% (2000); College graduation rate: 8.5% (2000).

School District(s)

Loyal (PK-12)
2000 Enrollment: 666 715-255-8552

Housing: Homeownership rate: 77.2% (2000); Median home value: $58,400 (2000); Median rent: $261 per month (2000); Median age of housing: 42 years (2000).
Newspapers: The Tribune Record-Gleaner (1 x week)
Transportation: Commute to work: 84.5% car, 0.0% public transportation, 8.3% walk, 5.4% work from home (2000); Travel time to work: 43.0% less than 15 minutes, 31.5% 15 to 30 minutes, 20.1% 30 to 45 minutes, 1.9% 45 to 60 minutes, 3.6% 60 minutes or more (2000)

LOYAL (town). Covers a land area of 34.728 square miles and a water area of 0 square miles. Located at 44.74° N. Lat.; 90.48° W. Long. Elevation is 1,250 feet.
History: Incorporated as city in 1948.
Population: 787 (2000); Race: 99.2% White, 0.4% Black, 0.0% Asian, 0.0% American Indian and Alaska Native, 0.4% Hispanic of any race, 0.4% two or more races (2000); Density: 22.7 persons per square mile (2000); Age: 37.1% under 18, 9.1% over 64 (2000); Marriage status: 27.3% never married, 67.4% now married, 1.2% widowed, 4.2% divorced (2000); Foreign born: 1.9% (2000); Ancestry (includes multiple ancestries): 60.8% German, 6.5% Norwegian, 4.4% French (except Basque), 3.8% Irish, 3.7% Swiss (2000).
Economy: In dairying region. Cheese; agricultural machinery. Single-family building permits issued: 0 (2001) / 2 (2000); Multi-family building permits issued: 0 (2001) / 0 (2000); Employment by occupation: 27.3% management, 8.0% professional, 8.6% services, 16.1% sales, 10.5% farming, 9.9% construction, 19.6% production (2000).
Income: Per capita income: $14,023 (2000); Median household income: $45,417 (2000); Poverty rate: 15.8% (2000).
Taxes: Total city taxes per capita: $85 (1997); City property taxes per capita: $84 (1997).
Education: High school graduation rate: 72.3% (2000); College graduation rate: 8.7% (2000).
Housing: Homeownership rate: 83.4% (2000); Median home value: $62,400 (2000); Median rent: $313 per month (2000); Median age of housing: 60+ years (2000).
Transportation: Commute to work: 66.2% car, 0.0% public transportation, 7.0% walk, 24.7% work from home (2000); Travel time to work: 45.6% less than 15 minutes, 29.9% 15 to 30 minutes, 19.6% 30 to 45 minutes, 2.5% 45 to 60 minutes, 2.5% 60 minutes or more (2000)

LYNN (town). Covers a land area of 35.529 square miles and a water area of 0.055 square miles. Located at 44.56° N. Lat.; 90.38° W. Long. Elevation is 1,150 feet.
Population: 834 (2000); Race: 98.8% White, 0.2% Black, 0.5% Asian, 0.0% American Indian and Alaska Native, 0.5% Hispanic of any race, 0.5% two or more races (2000); Density: 23.5 persons per square mile (2000); Age: 39.2% under 18, 10.5% over 64 (2000); Marriage status: 26.6% never married, 63.2% now married, 6.1% widowed, 4.0% divorced (2000); Foreign born: 1.2% (2000); Ancestry (includes multiple ancestries): 60.9% German, 6.5% United States or American, 5.9% Irish, 5.0% Polish, 3.9% Pennsylvania German (2000).
Economy: Single-family building permits issued: 3 (2001) / 3 (2000); Multi-family building permits issued: 0 (2001) / 0 (2000); Employment by occupation: 28.1% management, 12.3% professional, 14.8% services, 13.3% sales, 5.2% farming, 6.8% construction, 19.4% production (2000).
Income: Per capita income: $13,624 (2000); Median household income: $32,396 (2000); Poverty rate: 23.0% (2000).
Taxes: Total city taxes per capita: $92 (1997); City property taxes per capita: $90 (1997).
Education: High school graduation rate: 65.4% (2000); College graduation rate: 9.2% (2000).
Housing: Homeownership rate: 92.2% (2000); Median home value: $56,900 (2000); Median rent: $381 per month (2000); Median age of housing: 29 years (2000).
Transportation: Commute to work: 73.4% car, 0.0% public transportation, 3.1% walk, 21.0% work from home (2000); Travel time to work: 23.0% less than 15 minutes, 50.0% 15 to 30 minutes, 18.3% 30 to 45 minutes, 1.2% 45 to 60 minutes, 7.5% 60 minutes or more (2000)

MAYVILLE (town). Covers a land area of 32.392 square miles and a water area of 0.060 square miles. Located at 44.98° N. Lat.; 90.37° W. Long.
Population: 919 (2000); Race: 97.4% White, 0.0% Black, 0.0% Asian, 1.1% American Indian and Alaska Native, 0.0% Hispanic of any race, 1.5% two or more races (2000); Density: 28.4 persons per square mile (2000); Age: 30.2% under 18, 12.7% over 64 (2000); Marriage status: 25.5% never married, 65.6% now married, 4.2% widowed, 4.8% divorced (2000); Foreign born: 0.7% (2000); Ancestry (includes multiple ancestries): 68.0% German, 8.1% Norwegian, 6.6% English, 4.8% Polish, 4.6% Swiss (2000).
Economy: Single-family building permits issued: 2 (2001) / 3 (2000); Multi-family building permits issued: 0 (2001) / 0 (2000); Employment by occupation: 19.1% management, 9.0% professional, 15.0% services, 21.2% sales, 6.0% farming, 7.9% construction, 21.8% production (2000).
Income: Per capita income: $17,329 (2000); Median household income: $42,813 (2000); Poverty rate: 8.0% (2000).
Taxes: Total city taxes per capita: $47 (1997); City property taxes per capita: $46 (1997).
Education: High school graduation rate: 75.8% (2000); College graduation rate: 9.0% (2000).
Housing: Homeownership rate: 85.9% (2000); Median home value: $71,100 (2000); Median rent: $356 per month (2000); Median age of housing: 60+ years (2000).
Transportation: Commute to work: 77.2% car, 0.4% public transportation, 3.9% walk, 17.6% work from home (2000); Travel time to work: 60.9% less than 15 minutes, 29.0% 15 to 30 minutes, 4.2% 30 to 45 minutes, 2.9% 45 to 60 minutes, 2.9% 60 minutes or more (2000)

MEAD (town). Covers a land area of 35.144 square miles and a water area of 0.542 square miles. Located at 44.79° N. Lat.; 90.73° W. Long.
Population: 290 (2000); Race: 96.3% White, 0.0% Black, 0.0% Asian, 1.7% American Indian and Alaska Native, 0.0% Hispanic of any race, 2.0% two or more races (2000); Density: 8.3 persons per square mile (2000); Age: 24.1% under 18, 17.6% over 64 (2000); Marriage status: 17.4% never married, 69.4% now married, 8.9% widowed, 4.3% divorced (2000); Foreign born: 0.0% (2000); Ancestry (includes multiple ancestries): 54.2% German, 8.8% Norwegian, 8.5% Polish, 6.8% Irish, 6.8% English (2000).
Economy: Employment by occupation: 12.5% management, 13.8% professional, 15.8% services, 13.8% sales, 6.6% farming, 6.6% construction, 30.9% production (2000).
Income: Per capita income: $13,459 (2000); Median household income: $31,875 (2000); Poverty rate: 20.0% (2000).
Taxes: Total city taxes per capita: $189 (1997); City property taxes per capita: $189 (1997).
Education: High school graduation rate: 75.0% (2000); College graduation rate: 7.1% (2000).
Housing: Homeownership rate: 88.9% (2000); Median home value: $94,300 (2000); Median age of housing: 40 years (2000).
Transportation: Commute to work: 82.2% car, 0.0% public transportation, 0.0% walk, 17.8% work from home (2000); Travel time to work: 17.6% less than 15 minutes, 49.6% 15 to 30 minutes, 14.4% 30 to 45 minutes, 12.0% 45 to 60 minutes, 6.4% 60 minutes or more (2000)

MENTOR (town). Covers a land area of 35.703 square miles and a water area of 0.115 square miles. Located at 44.55° N. Lat.; 90.88° W. Long.
Population: 570 (2000); Race: 95.9% White, 0.7% Black, 0.0% Asian, 2.0% American Indian and Alaska Native, 0.9% Hispanic of any race, 1.3% two or more races (2000); Density: 16.0 persons per square mile (2000); Age: 24.2% under 18, 10.0% over 64 (2000); Marriage status: 22.6% never married, 66.1% now married, 4.3% widowed, 7.0% divorced (2000); Foreign born: 1.3% (2000); Ancestry (includes multiple ancestries): 32.9% German, 16.1% Irish, 14.0% Norwegian, 13.9% United States or American, 9.4% French (except Basque) (2000).

Economy: Employment by occupation: 13.4% management, 13.0% professional, 14.1% services, 12.0% sales, 3.9% farming, 10.6% construction, 33.1% production (2000).
Income: Per capita income: $16,661 (2000); Median household income: $36,125 (2000); Poverty rate: 10.8% (2000).
Taxes: Total city taxes per capita: $47 (1997); City property taxes per capita: $43 (1997).
Education: High school graduation rate: 82.2% (2000); College graduation rate: 8.5% (2000).
Housing: Homeownership rate: 85.4% (2000); Median home value: $45,600 (2000); Median rent: $375 per month (2000); Median age of housing: 33 years (2000).
Transportation: Commute to work: 92.0% car, 0.0% public transportation, 2.1% walk, 4.2% work from home (2000); Travel time to work: 17.5% less than 15 minutes, 43.8% 15 to 30 minutes, 17.9% 30 to 45 minutes, 1.5% 45 to 60 minutes, 19.3% 60 minutes or more (2000)

NEILLSVILLE (city). Covers a land area of 2.800 square miles and a water area of 0.028 square miles. Located at 44.56° N. Lat.; 90.59° W. Long. Elevation is 1,030 feet.
History: Neillsville developed as a market center for the surrounding dairy farming region, with a cooperative creamery, milk condensery, and a pea cannery.
Population: 2,731 (2000); Race: 97.6% White, 0.0% Black, 0.7% Asian, 0.8% American Indian and Alaska Native, 0.1% Hispanic of any race, 0.9% two or more races (2000); Density: 975.3 persons per square mile (2000); Age: 25.4% under 18, 23.7% over 64 (2000); Marriage status: 23.9% never married, 55.7% now married, 11.5% widowed, 8.9% divorced (2000); Foreign born: 1.0% (2000); Ancestry (includes multiple ancestries): 54.1% German, 9.1% Irish, 7.5% Norwegian, 7.4% English, 7.1% Polish (2000).
Economy: Single-family building permits issued: 2 (2001) / 2 (2000); Multi-family building permits issued: 0 (2001) / 0 (2000); Employment by occupation: 7.9% management, 22.5% professional, 19.5% services, 18.1% sales, 0.2% farming, 8.8% construction, 23.0% production (2000).
Income: Per capita income: $16,298 (2000); Median household income: $29,969 (2000); Poverty rate: 10.3% (2000).
Taxes: Total city taxes per capita: $218 (1997); City property taxes per capita: $214 (1997).
Education: High school graduation rate: 76.8% (2000); College graduation rate: 18.3% (2000).

School District(s)

Neillsville (PK-12)
2000 Enrollment: 1,254 715-743-3323
Housing: Homeownership rate: 66.1% (2000); Median home value: $59,100 (2000); Median rent: $288 per month (2000); Median age of housing: 60 years (2000).
Hospitals: Memorial Medical Center (28 beds)
Safety: Violent crime rate: 3.6 per 10,000 population; Property crime rate: 243.6 per 10,000 population (2001).
Newspapers: The Shopper (1 x week); The Clark County Press (1 x week)
Transportation: Commute to work: 88.6% car, 0.0% public transportation, 7.8% walk, 3.4% work from home (2000); Travel time to work: 70.6% less than 15 minutes, 12.6% 15 to 30 minutes, 10.2% 30 to 45 minutes, 4.3% 45 to 60 minutes, 2.3% 60 minutes or more (2000)
Additional Information Contacts
Neillsville Chamber of Commerce........................ 715-743-6444

OWEN (city). Covers a land area of 1.832 square miles and a water area of 0.026 square miles. Located at 44.94° N. Lat.; 90.56° W. Long. Elevation is 1,245 feet.
History: Settled c.1890; incorporated as village 1904, as city 1925.
Population: 936 (2000); Race: 96.3% White, 0.9% Black, 0.6% Asian, 1.4% American Indian and Alaska Native, 0.7% Hispanic of any race, 0.0% two or more races (2000); Density: 510.9 persons per square mile (2000); Age: 24.9% under 18, 22.4% over 64 (2000); Marriage status: 23.4% never married, 57.0% now married, 9.7% widowed, 9.9% divorced (2000); Foreign born: 0.7% (2000); Ancestry (includes multiple ancestries): 48.5% German, 9.3% Irish, 8.6% Polish, 8.3% English, 6.9% Norwegian (2000).
Economy: Railroad junction. In dairying, livestock, and lumbering area. Manufacturing: cheese, wooden products, drafting supplies. Single-family building permits issued: 0 (2001) / 1 (2000); Multi-family building permits issued: 0 (2001) / 0 (2000); Employment by occupation: 10.3% management, 11.3% professional, 28.3% services, 16.3% sales, 1.4% farming, 9.9% construction, 22.5% production (2000).
Income: Per capita income: $14,981 (2000); Median household income: $27,368 (2000); Poverty rate: 13.4% (2000).
Taxes: Total city taxes per capita: $204 (1997); City property taxes per capita: $149 (1997).
Education: High school graduation rate: 75.8% (2000); College graduation rate: 9.1% (2000).

School District(s)

Owen-Withee (PK-12)
2000 Enrollment: 620 715-229-2151
Housing: Homeownership rate: 70.9% (2000); Median home value: $47,800 (2000); Median rent: $275 per month (2000); Median age of housing: 52 years (2000).
Hospitals: Clark County Health Care Center (230 beds)
Transportation: Commute to work: 89.3% car, 0.0% public transportation, 2.6% walk, 7.2% work from home (2000); Travel time to work: 52.8% less than 15 minutes, 25.6% 15 to 30 minutes, 11.6% 30 to 45 minutes, 5.0% 45 to 60 minutes, 5.0% 60 minutes or more (2000)

PINE VALLEY (town). Covers a land area of 33.333 square miles and a water area of 0.176 square miles. Located at 44.55° N. Lat.; 90.61° W. Long.
Population: 1,121 (2000); Race: 98.8% White, 0.1% Black, 0.0% Asian, 0.6% American Indian and Alaska Native, 0.6% Hispanic of any race, 0.6% two or more races (2000); Density: 33.6 persons per square mile (2000); Age: 25.0% under 18, 18.6% over 64 (2000); Marriage status: 21.1% never married, 61.6% now married, 8.6% widowed, 8.7% divorced (2000); Foreign born: 1.7% (2000); Ancestry (includes multiple ancestries): 59.7% German, 9.5% Irish, 9.2% English, 8.5% Norwegian, 5.1% United States or American (2000).
Economy: Single-family building permits issued: 10 (2001) / 7 (2000); Multi-family building permits issued: 0 (2001) / 0 (2000); Employment by occupation: 5.6% management, 12.0% professional, 17.5% services, 22.4% sales, 2.3% farming, 10.9% construction, 29.3% production (2000).
Income: Per capita income: $18,736 (2000); Median household income: $37,813 (2000); Poverty rate: 6.1% (2000).
Taxes: Total city taxes per capita: $73 (1997); City property taxes per capita: $72 (1997).
Education: High school graduation rate: 81.7% (2000); College graduation rate: 9.3% (2000).
Housing: Homeownership rate: 88.6% (2000); Median home value: $81,300 (2000); Median rent: $281 per month (2000); Median age of housing: 29 years (2000).
Transportation: Commute to work: 91.5% car, 0.9% public transportation, 1.6% walk, 4.2% work from home (2000); Travel time to work: 60.0% less than 15 minutes, 15.5% 15 to 30 minutes, 12.1% 30 to 45 minutes, 7.2% 45 to 60 minutes, 5.1% 60 minutes or more (2000)

RESEBURG (town). Covers a land area of 35.943 square miles and a water area of 0 square miles. Located at 44.89° N. Lat.; 90.73° W. Long. Elevation is 1,217 feet.
Population: 740 (2000); Race: 98.1% White, 0.0% Black, 0.0% Asian, 0.0% American Indian and Alaska Native, 0.0% Hispanic of any race, 1.9% two or more races (2000); Density: 20.6 persons per square mile (2000); Age: 40.5% under 18, 7.2% over 64 (2000); Marriage status: 32.4% never married, 60.0% now married, 2.4% widowed, 5.3% divorced (2000); Foreign born: 0.2% (2000); Ancestry (includes multiple ancestries): 41.3% German, 26.1% Polish, 7.5% Norwegian, 7.4% Irish, 5.0% Swiss (2000).
Economy: Employment by occupation: 32.2% management, 7.0% professional, 11.9% services, 7.0% sales, 12.2% farming, 8.9% construction, 20.8% production (2000).
Income: Per capita income: $12,377 (2000); Median household income: $34,750 (2000); Poverty rate: 9.4% (2000).
Taxes: Total city taxes per capita: $29 (1997); City property taxes per capita: $27 (1997).
Education: High school graduation rate: 66.9% (2000); College graduation rate: 5.2% (2000).
Housing: Homeownership rate: 88.8% (2000); Median home value: $45,600 (2000); Median rent: $600 per month (2000); Median age of housing: 60+ years (2000).
Transportation: Commute to work: 54.9% car, 0.0% public transportation, 11.1% walk, 28.9% work from home (2000); Travel time to work: 47.5% less than 15 minutes, 20.5% 15 to 30 minutes, 11.0% 30 to 45 minutes, 7.2% 45 to 60 minutes, 13.7% 60 minutes or more (2000)

SEIF (town). Covers a land area of 36.021 square miles and a water area of 0.016 square miles. Located at 44.64° N. Lat.; 90.73° W. Long.
Population: 212 (2000); Race: 100.0% White, 0.0% Black, 0.0% Asian, 0.0% American Indian and Alaska Native, 0.0% Hispanic of any race, 0.0% two or more races (2000); Density: 5.9 persons per square mile (2000); Age:

25.7% under 18, 13.7% over 64 (2000); Marriage status: 17.3% never married, 68.1% now married, 10.5% widowed, 4.2% divorced (2000); Foreign born: 1.6% (2000); Ancestry (includes multiple ancestries): 61.0% German, 16.1% Polish, 14.9% Norwegian, 5.6% United States or American, 3.2% Austrian (2000).
Economy: Employment by occupation: 19.7% management, 12.3% professional, 16.4% services, 4.9% sales, 9.0% farming, 9.0% construction, 28.7% production (2000).
Income: Per capita income: $13,743 (2000); Median household income: $28,333 (2000); Poverty rate: 14.5% (2000).
Taxes: Total city taxes per capita: $116 (1997); City property taxes per capita: $112 (1997).
Education: High school graduation rate: 79.1% (2000); College graduation rate: 10.4% (2000).
Housing: Homeownership rate: 89.0% (2000); Median home value: $81,300 (2000); Median rent: $425 per month (2000); Median age of housing: 30 years (2000).
Transportation: Commute to work: 70.5% car, 0.0% public transportation, 3.3% walk, 26.2% work from home (2000); Travel time to work: 32.2% less than 15 minutes, 38.9% 15 to 30 minutes, 8.9% 30 to 45 minutes, 4.4% 45 to 60 minutes, 15.6% 60 minutes or more (2000)

SHERMAN (town). Covers a land area of 34.969 square miles and a water area of 0 square miles. Located at 44.73° N. Lat.; 90.36° W. Long.
Population: 831 (2000); Race: 95.1% White, 0.4% Black, 0.0% Asian, 0.0% American Indian and Alaska Native, 7.2% Hispanic of any race, 2.1% two or more races (2000); Density: 23.8 persons per square mile (2000); Age: 33.5% under 18, 7.5% over 64 (2000); Marriage status: 25.7% never married, 66.2% now married, 3.4% widowed, 4.8% divorced (2000); Foreign born: 4.6% (2000); Ancestry (includes multiple ancestries): 54.7% German, 9.0% Other groups, 8.6% United States or American, 4.4% Irish, 4.1% Norwegian (2000).
Economy: Employment by occupation: 22.6% management, 14.3% professional, 10.1% services, 16.0% sales, 8.1% farming, 8.4% construction, 20.6% production (2000).
Income: Per capita income: $14,332 (2000); Median household income: $42,344 (2000); Poverty rate: 18.8% (2000).
Taxes: Total city taxes per capita: $69 (1997); City property taxes per capita: $68 (1997).
Education: High school graduation rate: 74.2% (2000); College graduation rate: 11.4% (2000).
Housing: Homeownership rate: 88.2% (2000); Median home value: $76,800 (2000); Median rent: $175 per month (2000); Median age of housing: 43 years (2000).
Transportation: Commute to work: 77.0% car, 0.0% public transportation, 5.2% walk, 13.8% work from home (2000); Travel time to work: 37.2% less than 15 minutes, 43.6% 15 to 30 minutes, 15.5% 30 to 45 minutes, 0.9% 45 to 60 minutes, 2.9% 60 minutes or more (2000)

SHERWOOD (town). Covers a land area of 35.740 square miles and a water area of 0.221 square miles. Located at 44.46° N. Lat.; 90.37° W. Long. Elevation is 1,065 feet.
Population: 252 (2000); Race: 97.8% White, 0.0% Black, 0.0% Asian, 0.0% American Indian and Alaska Native, 0.9% Hispanic of any race, 1.3% two or more races (2000); Density: 7.1 persons per square mile (2000); Age: 22.9% under 18, 24.7% over 64 (2000); Marriage status: 15.7% never married, 70.8% now married, 7.3% widowed, 6.2% divorced (2000); Foreign born: 0.9% (2000); Ancestry (includes multiple ancestries): 58.3% German, 16.6% Norwegian, 12.1% Swedish, 9.4% Polish, 8.1% English (2000).
Economy: Employment by occupation: 15.5% management, 14.6% professional, 11.7% services, 10.7% sales, 10.7% farming, 11.7% construction, 25.2% production (2000).
Income: Per capita income: $16,365 (2000); Median household income: $36,250 (2000); Poverty rate: 4.5% (2000).
Taxes: Total city taxes per capita: $25 (1997); City property taxes per capita: $25 (1997).
Education: High school graduation rate: 74.8% (2000); College graduation rate: 8.2% (2000).
Housing: Homeownership rate: 96.2% (2000); Median home value: $104,200 (2000); Median age of housing: 27 years (2000).
Transportation: Commute to work: 83.5% car, 0.0% public transportation, 1.9% walk, 14.6% work from home (2000); Travel time to work: 14.8% less than 15 minutes, 29.5% 15 to 30 minutes, 38.6% 30 to 45 minutes, 12.5% 45 to 60 minutes, 4.5% 60 minutes or more (2000)

THORP (city). Covers a land area of 1.325 square miles and a water area of 0 square miles. Located at 44.96° N. Lat.; 90.80° W. Long. Elevation is 1,210 feet.
Population: 1,536 (2000); Race: 99.8% White, 0.0% Black, 0.0% Asian, 0.0% American Indian and Alaska Native, 0.6% Hispanic of any race, 0.2% two or more races (2000); Density: 1,158.9 persons per square mile (2000); Age: 23.2% under 18, 27.4% over 64 (2000); Marriage status: 22.2% never married, 56.4% now married, 14.0% widowed, 7.4% divorced (2000); Foreign born: 0.4% (2000); Ancestry (includes multiple ancestries): 44.4% German, 35.9% Polish, 8.4% Irish, 6.8% Norwegian, 4.1% English (2000).
Economy: Single-family building permits issued: 2 (2001) / 3 (2000); Multi-family building permits issued: 12 (2001) / 4 (2000); Employment by occupation: 7.3% management, 18.2% professional, 17.0% services, 18.9% sales, 2.5% farming, 9.5% construction, 26.6% production (2000).
Income: Per capita income: $15,828 (2000); Median household income: $29,102 (2000); Poverty rate: 11.0% (2000).
Taxes: Total city taxes per capita: $125 (1997); City property taxes per capita: $110 (1997).
Education: High school graduation rate: 74.7% (2000); College graduation rate: 14.3% (2000).

School District(s)

Thorp (PK-12)
2000 Enrollment: 610 715-669-5401
Housing: Homeownership rate: 72.5% (2000); Median home value: $64,500 (2000); Median rent: $310 per month (2000); Median age of housing: 43 years (2000).
Newspapers: The Thorp Courier (1 x week)
Transportation: Commute to work: 86.8% car, 0.0% public transportation, 7.6% walk, 3.7% work from home (2000); Travel time to work: 56.8% less than 15 minutes, 20.4% 15 to 30 minutes, 9.0% 30 to 45 minutes, 8.6% 45 to 60 minutes, 5.3% 60 minutes or more (2000)

THORP (town). Covers a land area of 35.168 square miles and a water area of 0 square miles. Located at 44.97° N. Lat.; 90.85° W. Long. Elevation is 1,210 feet.
History: Incorporated as village in 1893, as city in 1948.
Population: 730 (2000); Race: 98.4% White, 0.0% Black, 0.3% Asian, 0.0% American Indian and Alaska Native, 0.3% Hispanic of any race, 1.3% two or more races (2000); Density: 20.8 persons per square mile (2000); Age: 31.1% under 18, 11.0% over 64 (2000); Marriage status: 20.6% never married, 69.4% now married, 4.4% widowed, 5.5% divorced (2000); Foreign born: 0.8% (2000); Ancestry (includes multiple ancestries): 39.5% Polish, 37.1% German, 6.8% Norwegian, 5.9% Irish, 5.0% Other groups (2000).
Economy: In dairying region. Cheese manufacturing. Other manufacturing includes work benches, platform trucks, furniture. Employment by occupation: 25.9% management, 11.7% professional, 12.0% services, 14.7% sales, 7.5% farming, 7.2% construction, 20.9% production (2000).
Income: Per capita income: $16,236 (2000); Median household income: $39,063 (2000); Poverty rate: 8.9% (2000).
Taxes: Total city taxes per capita: $33 (1997); City property taxes per capita: $32 (1997).
Education: High school graduation rate: 75.5% (2000); College graduation rate: 9.0% (2000).
Housing: Homeownership rate: 86.0% (2000); Median home value: $72,000 (2000); Median rent: $275 per month (2000); Median age of housing: 57 years (2000).
Transportation: Commute to work: 69.0% car, 0.0% public transportation, 6.9% walk, 23.1% work from home (2000); Travel time to work: 54.8% less than 15 minutes, 22.8% 15 to 30 minutes, 14.5% 30 to 45 minutes, 4.0% 45 to 60 minutes, 4.0% 60 minutes or more (2000)

UNITY (town). Covers a land area of 34.840 square miles and a water area of 0 square miles. Located at 44.81° N. Lat.; 90.38° W. Long. Elevation is 1,338 feet.
Population: 745 (2000); Race: 100.0% White, 0.0% Black, 0.0% Asian, 0.0% American Indian and Alaska Native, 0.0% Hispanic of any race, 0.0% two or more races (2000); Density: 21.4 persons per square mile (2000); Age: 32.4% under 18, 7.9% over 64 (2000); Marriage status: 22.3% never married, 71.4% now married, 4.5% widowed, 1.8% divorced (2000); Foreign born: 2.0% (2000); Ancestry (includes multiple ancestries): 53.8% German, 8.3% English, 7.5% Irish, 6.6% Norwegian, 6.1% United States or American (2000).
Economy: Single-family building permits issued: 7 (2001) / 3 (2000); Multi-family building permits issued: 0 (2001) / 0 (2000); Employment by

occupation: 25.8% management, 8.5% professional, 9.5% services, 13.7% sales, 5.9% farming, 10.3% construction, 26.3% production (2000).
Income: Per capita income: $13,252 (2000); Median household income: $41,154 (2000); Poverty rate: 15.5% (2000).
Taxes: Total city taxes per capita: $76 (1997); City property taxes per capita: $75 (1997).
Education: High school graduation rate: 78.5% (2000); College graduation rate: 7.5% (2000).
Housing: Homeownership rate: 90.7% (2000); Median home value: $59,700 (2000); Median rent: $338 per month (2000); Median age of housing: 50 years (2000).
Transportation: Commute to work: 72.6% car, 0.5% public transportation, 8.1% walk, 18.0% work from home (2000); Travel time to work: 33.8% less than 15 minutes, 46.8% 15 to 30 minutes, 16.9% 30 to 45 minutes, 2.5% 45 to 60 minutes, 0.0% 60 minutes or more (2000)

WARNER (town). Covers a land area of 34.873 square miles and a water area of 0.129 square miles. Located at 44.81° N. Lat.; 90.60° W. Long.
Population: 627 (2000); Race: 98.7% White, 0.0% Black, 0.3% Asian, 0.0% American Indian and Alaska Native, 0.0% Hispanic of any race, 1.0% two or more races (2000); Density: 18.0 persons per square mile (2000); Age: 34.6% under 18, 12.7% over 64 (2000); Marriage status: 19.9% never married, 66.2% now married, 2.0% widowed, 11.9% divorced (2000); Foreign born: 0.8% (2000); Ancestry (includes multiple ancestries): 51.4% German, 9.5% Norwegian, 7.2% English, 5.9% French (except Basque), 5.5% Irish (2000).
Economy: Employment by occupation: 22.3% management, 6.9% professional, 12.4% services, 14.2% sales, 9.9% farming, 8.0% construction, 26.3% production (2000).
Income: Per capita income: $13,443 (2000); Median household income: $37,273 (2000); Poverty rate: 7.9% (2000).
Taxes: Total city taxes per capita: $44 (1997); City property taxes per capita: $43 (1997).
Education: High school graduation rate: 77.0% (2000); College graduation rate: 9.4% (2000).
Housing: Homeownership rate: 89.4% (2000); Median home value: $55,000 (2000); Median rent: $413 per month (2000); Median age of housing: 60+ years (2000).
Transportation: Commute to work: 69.6% car, 0.0% public transportation, 2.6% walk, 25.3% work from home (2000); Travel time to work: 42.2% less than 15 minutes, 25.5% 15 to 30 minutes, 15.2% 30 to 45 minutes, 6.9% 45 to 60 minutes, 10.3% 60 minutes or more (2000)

WASHBURN (town). Covers a land area of 36.264 square miles and a water area of 0.063 square miles. Located at 44.48° N. Lat.; 90.50° W. Long.
Population: 304 (2000); Race: 97.1% White, 0.0% Black, 0.0% Asian, 0.6% American Indian and Alaska Native, 1.5% Hispanic of any race, 1.8% two or more races (2000); Density: 8.4 persons per square mile (2000); Age: 32.6% under 18, 13.8% over 64 (2000); Marriage status: 17.9% never married, 68.5% now married, 3.2% widowed, 10.4% divorced (2000); Foreign born: 0.6% (2000); Ancestry (includes multiple ancestries): 53.4% German, 15.0% Polish, 12.0% Irish, 7.9% Norwegian, 6.2% English (2000).
Economy: Single-family building permits issued: 0 (2001) / 1 (2000); Multi-family building permits issued: 0 (2001) / 0 (2000); Employment by occupation: 11.4% management, 8.2% professional, 11.4% services, 19.6% sales, 7.6% farming, 8.2% construction, 33.5% production (2000).
Income: Per capita income: $13,479 (2000); Median household income: $36,250 (2000); Poverty rate: 18.8% (2000).
Taxes: Total city taxes per capita: $33 (2000); City property taxes per capita: $30 (2000).
Education: High school graduation rate: 75.5% (2000); College graduation rate: 4.8% (2000).
Housing: Homeownership rate: 90.2% (2000); Median home value: $66,700 (2000); Median rent: $325 per month (2000); Median age of housing: 40 years (2000).
Transportation: Commute to work: 89.2% car, 0.0% public transportation, 0.0% walk, 9.5% work from home (2000); Travel time to work: 24.5% less than 15 minutes, 37.1% 15 to 30 minutes, 30.1% 30 to 45 minutes, 4.9% 45 to 60 minutes, 3.5% 60 minutes or more (2000)

WESTON (town). Covers a land area of 36.143 square miles and a water area of 0.133 square miles. Located at 44.64° N. Lat.; 90.61° W. Long.
Population: 638 (2000); Race: 99.3% White, 0.3% Black, 0.3% Asian, 0.0% American Indian and Alaska Native, 0.7% Hispanic of any race, 0.0% two or more races (2000); Density: 17.7 persons per square mile (2000); Age: 27.0% under 18, 14.7% over 64 (2000); Marriage status: 21.0% never married, 68.7% now married, 4.5% widowed, 5.8% divorced (2000); Foreign born: 1.9% (2000); Ancestry (includes multiple ancestries): 57.8% German, 9.4% Irish, 8.9% United States or American, 6.2% Norwegian, 5.1% Polish (2000).
Economy: Single-family building permits issued: 3 (2001) / 4 (2000); Multi-family building permits issued: 0 (2001) / 0 (2000); Employment by occupation: 21.2% management, 9.1% professional, 15.6% services, 16.2% sales, 7.1% farming, 9.1% construction, 21.8% production (2000).
Income: Per capita income: $15,478 (2000); Median household income: $40,833 (2000); Poverty rate: 17.4% (2000).
Taxes: Total city taxes per capita: $71 (1997); City property taxes per capita: $69 (1997).
Education: High school graduation rate: 78.0% (2000); College graduation rate: 9.2% (2000).
Housing: Homeownership rate: 84.3% (2000); Median home value: $81,000 (2000); Median rent: $263 per month (2000); Median age of housing: 47 years (2000).
Transportation: Commute to work: 77.1% car, 0.0% public transportation, 5.0% walk, 17.3% work from home (2000); Travel time to work: 38.3% less than 15 minutes, 31.9% 15 to 30 minutes, 17.7% 30 to 45 minutes, 4.6% 45 to 60 minutes, 7.4% 60 minutes or more (2000)

WILLARD (unincorporated postal area, zip code 54493). Covers a land area of 101.569 square miles and a water area of 0.286 square miles. Located at 44.73° N. Lat.; 90.79° W. Long. Elevation is 1,179 feet.
Population: 689 (2000); Race: 99.0% White, 0.0% Black, 0.0% Asian, 0.0% American Indian and Alaska Native, 1.5% Hispanic of any race, 0.4% two or more races (2000); Density: 6.8 persons per square mile (2000); Age: 25.0% under 18, 16.3% over 64 (2000); Marriage status: 19.3% never married, 64.9% now married, 9.6% widowed, 6.1% divorced (2000); Foreign born: 2.2% (2000); Ancestry (includes multiple ancestries): 42.0% German, 13.3% Slovene, 11.7% Polish, 11.4% Norwegian, 8.1% Irish (2000).
Economy: Employment by occupation: 19.8% management, 12.2% professional, 17.3% services, 16.3% sales, 2.7% farming, 6.0% construction, 25.7% production (2000).
Income: Per capita income: $14,440 (2000); Median household income: $29,167 (2000); Poverty rate: 14.8% (2000).
Education: High school graduation rate: 79.2% (2000); College graduation rate: 8.1% (2000).
Housing: Homeownership rate: 91.3% (2000); Median home value: $77,900 (2000); Median rent: $292 per month (2000); Median age of housing: 39 years (2000).
Transportation: Commute to work: 79.7% car, 0.0% public transportation, 4.1% walk, 16.3% work from home (2000); Travel time to work: 23.0% less than 15 minutes, 35.9% 15 to 30 minutes, 15.9% 30 to 45 minutes, 14.9% 45 to 60 minutes, 10.4% 60 minutes or more (2000)

WITHEE (village). Covers a land area of 0.838 square miles and a water area of 0 square miles. Located at 44.95° N. Lat.; 90.59° W. Long. Elevation is 1,272 feet.
Population: 508 (2000); Race: 96.5% White, 2.8% Black, 0.0% Asian, 0.0% American Indian and Alaska Native, 0.0% Hispanic of any race, 0.7% two or more races (2000); Density: 606.2 persons per square mile (2000); Age: 18.5% under 18, 27.2% over 64 (2000); Marriage status: 20.5% never married, 58.4% now married, 12.1% widowed, 9.0% divorced (2000); Foreign born: 0.9% (2000); Ancestry (includes multiple ancestries): 45.5% German, 18.1% Polish, 9.9% Norwegian, 9.6% English, 5.2% Irish (2000).
Economy: Single-family building permits issued: 0 (2001) / 2 (2000); Multi-family building permits issued: 0 (2001) / 0 (2000); Employment by occupation: 7.7% management, 11.0% professional, 24.4% services, 18.7% sales, 0.0% farming, 12.4% construction, 25.8% production (2000).
Income: Per capita income: $18,874 (2000); Median household income: $29,625 (2000); Poverty rate: 6.8% (2000).
Taxes: Total city taxes per capita: $118 (1997); City property taxes per capita: $108 (1997).
Education: High school graduation rate: 84.4% (2000); College graduation rate: 11.3% (2000).
Housing: Homeownership rate: 86.1% (2000); Median home value: $46,100 (2000); Median rent: $267 per month (2000); Median age of housing: 54 years (2000).
Newspapers: O-W Enterprise (1 x week)
Transportation: Commute to work: 88.1% car, 0.0% public transportation, 9.0% walk, 3.0% work from home (2000); Travel time to work: 62.1% less than 15 minutes, 27.2% 15 to 30 minutes, 7.2% 30 to 45 minutes, 2.6% 45 to 60 minutes, 1.0% 60 minutes or more (2000)

WITHEE (town). Covers a land area of 35.138 square miles and a water area of 0.019 square miles. Located at 44.98° N. Lat.; 90.73° W. Long. Elevation is 1,272 feet.
Population: 885 (2000); Race: 99.1% White, 0.0% Black, 0.0% Asian, 0.7% American Indian and Alaska Native, 0.2% Hispanic of any race, 0.2% two or more races (2000); Density: 25.2 persons per square mile (2000); Age: 36.8% under 18, 12.5% over 64 (2000); Marriage status: 20.0% never married, 68.7% now married, 3.6% widowed, 7.6% divorced (2000); Foreign born: 0.2% (2000); Ancestry (includes multiple ancestries): 32.9% German, 31.1% Polish, 10.8% United States or American, 6.7% Norwegian, 2.0% Pennsylvania German (2000).
Economy: In dairying and livestock-raising area. Manufacturing: sawmilling, animal feed. Employment by occupation: 31.0% management, 6.6% professional, 14.3% services, 12.2% sales, 5.3% farming, 11.9% construction, 18.8% production (2000).
Income: Per capita income: $13,826 (2000); Median household income: $33,839 (2000); Poverty rate: 15.3% (2000).
Taxes: Total city taxes per capita: $36 (1997); City property taxes per capita: $36 (1997).
Education: High school graduation rate: 66.2% (2000); College graduation rate: 7.1% (2000).
Housing: Homeownership rate: 85.7% (2000); Median home value: $77,300 (2000); Median rent: $200 per month (2000); Median age of housing: 57 years (2000).
Transportation: Commute to work: 59.5% car, 0.0% public transportation, 8.2% walk, 29.7% work from home (2000); Travel time to work: 51.7% less than 15 minutes, 28.5% 15 to 30 minutes, 8.2% 30 to 45 minutes, 4.5% 45 to 60 minutes, 7.1% 60 minutes or more (2000)

WORDEN (town). Covers a land area of 36.123 square miles and a water area of 0 square miles. Located at 44.91° N. Lat.; 90.86° W. Long.
Population: 657 (2000); Race: 100.0% White, 0.0% Black, 0.0% Asian, 0.0% American Indian and Alaska Native, 0.0% Hispanic of any race, 0.0% two or more races (2000); Density: 18.2 persons per square mile (2000); Age: 37.8% under 18, 10.3% over 64 (2000); Marriage status: 28.5% never married, 62.3% now married, 2.3% widowed, 6.9% divorced (2000); Foreign born: 0.0% (2000); Ancestry (includes multiple ancestries): 50.3% German, 18.9% Polish, 11.5% Norwegian, 6.5% French (except Basque), 5.8% Dutch (2000).
Economy: Single-family building permits issued: 2 (2001) / 2 (2000); Multi-family building permits issued: 0 (2001) / 0 (2000); Employment by occupation: 21.9% management, 8.3% professional, 12.0% services, 14.3% sales, 7.0% farming, 15.9% construction, 20.6% production (2000).
Income: Per capita income: $12,381 (2000); Median household income: $37,321 (2000); Poverty rate: 14.6% (2000).
Taxes: Total city taxes per capita: $80 (1997); City property taxes per capita: $78 (1997).
Education: High school graduation rate: 79.1% (2000); College graduation rate: 6.4% (2000).
Housing: Homeownership rate: 93.4% (2000); Median home value: $58,900 (2000); Median rent: $263 per month (2000); Median age of housing: 48 years (2000).
Transportation: Commute to work: 75.7% car, 0.0% public transportation, 3.7% walk, 18.6% work from home (2000); Travel time to work: 56.4% less than 15 minutes, 17.4% 15 to 30 minutes, 8.3% 30 to 45 minutes, 11.6% 45 to 60 minutes, 6.2% 60 minutes or more (2000)

YORK (town). Covers a land area of 36.095 square miles and a water area of 0.004 square miles. Located at 44.63° N. Lat.; 90.49° W. Long.
Population: 853 (2000); Race: 99.8% White, 0.2% Black, 0.0% Asian, 0.0% American Indian and Alaska Native, 0.6% Hispanic of any race, 0.0% two or more races (2000); Density: 23.6 persons per square mile (2000); Age: 31.1% under 18, 9.8% over 64 (2000); Marriage status: 29.7% never married, 59.8% now married, 3.1% widowed, 7.4% divorced (2000); Foreign born: 0.6% (2000); Ancestry (includes multiple ancestries): 59.7% German, 7.7% English, 5.9% Norwegian, 4.2% Irish, 2.9% Swedish (2000).
Economy: Employment by occupation: 23.6% management, 4.2% professional, 13.3% services, 18.8% sales, 5.5% farming, 11.8% construction, 22.8% production (2000).
Income: Per capita income: $14,133 (2000); Median household income: $38,500 (2000); Poverty rate: 12.1% (2000).
Taxes: Total city taxes per capita: $71 (1997); City property taxes per capita: $70 (1997).
Education: High school graduation rate: 76.0% (2000); College graduation rate: 5.1% (2000).
Housing: Homeownership rate: 90.3% (2000); Median home value: $59,300 (2000); Median rent: $325 per month (2000); Median age of housing: 60+ years (2000).
Transportation: Commute to work: 73.1% car, 0.0% public transportation, 5.6% walk, 20.4% work from home (2000); Travel time to work: 39.9% less than 15 minutes, 27.7% 15 to 30 minutes, 23.7% 30 to 45 minutes, 2.5% 45 to 60 minutes, 6.1% 60 minutes or more (2000)

Columbia County

Located in south central Wisconsin; drained by the Wisconsin, Fox, Crawfish, and Baraboo Rivers; includes Mud Lake and Lake Wisconsin. Covers a land area of 773.80 square miles, a water area of 21.90 square miles, and is located in the Central Time Zone. The county government was organized in 1846. County seat is Portage.

Weather Station: Arlington Univ. Farm — Elevation: 1,079 feet

	Jan	Feb	Mar	Apr	May	Jun	Jul	Aug	Sep	Oct	Nov	Dec
High	25	30	42	57	70	79	83	80	73	60	43	30
Low	8	13	24	35	46	55	60	58	50	39	27	15
Precip	1.1	1.1	2.0	3.2	3.3	3.9	3.9	4.2	3.9	2.5	2.4	1.3
Snow	9.7	6.7	5.3	2.2	0.1	0.0	0.0	0.0	0.0	0.3	3.8	8.7

High and Low temperatures in degrees Fahrenheit; Precipitation and Snow in inches

Weather Station: Portage — Elevation: 774 feet

	Jan	Feb	Mar	Apr	May	Jun	Jul	Aug	Sep	Oct	Nov	Dec
High	26	32	43	58	71	80	83	81	73	61	44	31
Low	7	12	23	35	46	55	59	57	49	38	27	14
Precip	1.2	1.2	2.3	3.5	3.5	4.0	4.5	4.3	3.7	2.5	2.4	1.4
Snow	11.0	7.8	5.9	2.0	tr	0.0	0.0	0.0	0.0	0.3	3.5	7.6

High and Low temperatures in degrees Fahrenheit; Precipitation and Snow in inches

Weather Station: Wisconsin Dells — Elevation: 833 feet

	Jan	Feb	Mar	Apr	May	Jun	Jul	Aug	Sep	Oct	Nov	Dec
High	25	31	42	57	70	78	82	79	71	59	43	30
Low	5	10	22	33	45	54	59	57	49	37	25	13
Precip	0.9	1.0	2.1	3.4	3.5	4.1	4.1	4.4	3.6	2.4	2.0	1.2
Snow	11.8	6.8	6.7	2.5	tr	0.0	0.0	0.0	0.0	0.4	4.1	9.0

High and Low temperatures in degrees Fahrenheit; Precipitation and Snow in inches

Population: 52,468 (2000); Race: 97.0% White, 1.0% Black, 0.3% Asian, 0.3% American Indian and Alaska Native, 1.7% Hispanic of any race, 0.9% two or more races (2000); Density: 67.8 persons per square mile (2000); Age: 25.1% under 18, 14.4% over 64 (2000).
Religion: Five largest groups: 26.6% Catholic Church, 9.8% Evangelical Lutheran Church in America, 6.8% Wisconsin Evangelical Lutheran Synod, 6.2% Lutheran Church—Missouri Synod, 5.9% The United Methodist Church (2000).
Economy: Unemployment rate: 5.0% (11/2002); Total civilian labor force: 28,104 (11/2002); Leading industries: 30.3% manufacturing; 15.2% retail trade; 11.4% health care and social assistance (2000); Companies that employ more than 1,000 persons: 0 (2000); Companies that employ more than 100 persons: 35 (2000); Farms: 1,359 totaling 325,723 acres (1997); Minority business ownership rate: 0.0% (1997); Women business ownership rate: 21.4% (1997); Retail sales per capita: $8,083 (1997). Single-family building permits issued: 291 (2001) / 308 (2000); Multi-family building permits issued: 137 (2001) / 73 (2000).
Income: Per capita income: $21,014 (2000); Median household income: $45,064 (2000); Poverty rate: 5.2% (2000); Bankruptcy rate: 4.30% (2001).
Taxes: Total county taxes per capita: $218 (2000); County property taxes per capita: $166 (2000).
Education: High school graduation rate: 86.2% (2000); College graduation rate: 16.7% (2000).
Housing: Homeownership rate: 74.9% (2000); Median home value: $115,000 (2000); Median rent: $437 per month (2000); Median age of housing: 36 years (2000).
Health: Birth rate: 118.2 per 10,000 population (1998); Age adjusted death rate: 90.1 per 10,000 population (1999); Age adjusted cancer mortality rate: 222.3 deaths per 100,000 population (1999). Air Quality Index: 77% good, 23% moderate, 0% unhealthy (percent of days in 2000). Number of physicians: 10.5 per 10,000 population (1999); Number of hospital beds: 36.6 per 10,000 population (1999).
Elections: 2000 Presidential election results: 49.4% Gore, 46.9% Bush, 3.1% Nader, 0.2% Buchanan
National and State Parks: Grassy Lake State Wildlife Area; Jennings Creek State Wildlife Area; Mud Lake State Public Hunting Grounds; Paradise

Marsh State Wildlife Area; Pine Island State Wildlife Area; Springville State Wildlife Area; Swan Lake State Wildlife Area

Additional Information Contacts

Columbia County Government Offices 608-742-2191
Columbus Chamber of Commerce 920-623-3699
Lake Wisconsin Chamber of Commerce 608-635-8070
Portgage Area Chamber of Commerce 608-742-6242
Poynette Chamber of Commerce 608-635-2425
Wisconsin Dells Chamber of Commerce 608-253-4058
Wisconsin Dells Visitors Bureau 608-254-8088

Columbia County Communities

ARLINGTON (village). Covers a land area of 0.663 square miles and a water area of 0 square miles. Located at 43.33° N. Lat.; 89.37° W. Long. Elevation is 1,052 feet.
History: Arlington developed around a pea canning factory. The area around Arlington was settled by many farmers of German ancestry.
Population: 484 (2000); Race: 99.6% White, 0.4% Black, 0.0% Asian, 0.0% American Indian and Alaska Native, 0.0% Hispanic of any race, 0.0% two or more races (2000); Density: 730.1 persons per square mile (2000); Age: 27.7% under 18, 11.1% over 64 (2000); Marriage status: 17.9% never married, 68.4% now married, 5.6% widowed, 8.1% divorced (2000); Foreign born: 1.1% (2000); Ancestry (includes multiple ancestries): 59.0% German, 19.9% Norwegian, 7.4% English, 6.6% Irish, 4.1% Scottish (2000).
Economy: Single-family building permits issued: 5 (2001) / 5 (2000); Multi-family building permits issued: 0 (2001) / 0 (2000); Employment by occupation: 5.7% management, 18.3% professional, 16.1% services, 30.5% sales, 0.4% farming, 11.8% construction, 17.2% production (2000).
Income: Per capita income: $21,270 (2000); Median household income: $51,750 (2000); Poverty rate: 2.6% (2000).
Taxes: Total city taxes per capita: $166 (1997); City property taxes per capita: $158 (1997).
Education: High school graduation rate: 94.7% (2000); College graduation rate: 15.0% (2000).
Housing: Homeownership rate: 78.7% (2000); Median home value: $127,300 (2000); Median rent: $690 per month (2000); Median age of housing: 40 years (2000).
Transportation: Commute to work: 95.7% car, 0.0% public transportation, 2.9% walk, 1.4% work from home (2000); Travel time to work: 25.5% less than 15 minutes, 42.3% 15 to 30 minutes, 21.2% 30 to 45 minutes, 9.5% 45 to 60 minutes, 1.5% 60 minutes or more (2000)

ARLINGTON (town). Covers a land area of 35.219 square miles and a water area of 0.047 square miles. Located at 43.34° N. Lat.; 89.41° W. Long. Elevation is 1,052 feet.
Population: 848 (2000); Race: 99.3% White, 0.0% Black, 0.0% Asian, 0.7% American Indian and Alaska Native, 1.0% Hispanic of any race, 0.0% two or more races (2000); Density: 24.1 persons per square mile (2000); Age: 24.5% under 18, 11.7% over 64 (2000); Marriage status: 15.9% never married, 72.8% now married, 3.4% widowed, 7.9% divorced (2000); Foreign born: 1.0% (2000); Ancestry (includes multiple ancestries): 52.0% German, 16.1% Norwegian, 13.8% Irish, 12.6% English, 5.8% United States or American (2000).
Economy: Manufacturing: food processing. Agricultural research station to South. Employment by occupation: 24.0% management, 12.5% professional, 6.8% services, 25.7% sales, 1.9% farming, 13.2% construction, 15.9% production (2000).
Income: Per capita income: $23,880 (2000); Median household income: $58,750 (2000); Poverty rate: 4.2% (2000).
Taxes: Total city taxes per capita: $169 (1997); City property taxes per capita: $168 (1997).
Education: High school graduation rate: 90.8% (2000); College graduation rate: 22.8% (2000).
Housing: Homeownership rate: 84.5% (2000); Median home value: $144,000 (2000); Median rent: $338 per month (2000); Median age of housing: 29 years (2000).
Transportation: Commute to work: 90.1% car, 0.0% public transportation, 4.1% walk, 5.6% work from home (2000); Travel time to work: 26.8% less than 15 minutes, 37.5% 15 to 30 minutes, 25.7% 30 to 45 minutes, 7.3% 45 to 60 minutes, 2.7% 60 minutes or more (2000)

CALEDONIA (town). Covers a land area of 59.515 square miles and a water area of 4.109 square miles. Located at 43.48° N. Lat.; 89.51° W. Long.
Population: 1,171 (2000); Race: 98.0% White, 0.5% Black, 0.0% Asian, 0.1% American Indian and Alaska Native, 0.4% Hispanic of any race, 0.8% two or more races (2000); Density: 19.7 persons per square mile (2000); Age: 26.1% under 18, 12.4% over 64 (2000); Marriage status: 20.1% never married, 66.6% now married, 4.0% widowed, 9.2% divorced (2000); Foreign born: 0.3% (2000); Ancestry (includes multiple ancestries): 52.9% German, 11.6% English, 10.6% Norwegian, 10.5% Irish, 5.8% Polish (2000).
Economy: Employment by occupation: 17.8% management, 15.5% professional, 17.0% services, 17.8% sales, 1.8% farming, 12.8% construction, 17.3% production (2000).
Income: Per capita income: $23,278 (2000); Median household income: $48,750 (2000); Poverty rate: 6.7% (2000).
Taxes: Total city taxes per capita: $212 (1997); City property taxes per capita: $195 (1997).
Education: High school graduation rate: 91.1% (2000); College graduation rate: 19.9% (2000).
Housing: Homeownership rate: 87.8% (2000); Median home value: $129,100 (2000); Median rent: $345 per month (2000); Median age of housing: 34 years (2000).
Transportation: Commute to work: 87.5% car, 0.0% public transportation, 1.5% walk, 11.0% work from home (2000); Travel time to work: 23.7% less than 15 minutes, 41.2% 15 to 30 minutes, 14.6% 30 to 45 minutes, 11.5% 45 to 60 minutes, 8.9% 60 minutes or more (2000)

CAMBRIA (village). Covers a land area of 1.053 square miles and a water area of 0.038 square miles. Located at 43.54° N. Lat.; 89.11° W. Long. Elevation is 868 feet.
Population: 792 (2000); Race: 94.3% White, 0.0% Black, 0.0% Asian, 1.3% American Indian and Alaska Native, 8.8% Hispanic of any race, 0.3% two or more races (2000); Density: 752.0 persons per square mile (2000); Age: 29.1% under 18, 14.4% over 64 (2000); Marriage status: 23.2% never married, 56.0% now married, 8.4% widowed, 12.4% divorced (2000); Foreign born: 3.9% (2000); Ancestry (includes multiple ancestries): 43.5% German, 11.1% Other groups, 8.9% Dutch, 8.3% Irish, 6.9% Norwegian (2000).
Economy: In agricultural area; makes butter, cheeses. Single-family building permits issued: 0 (2001) / 0 (2000); Multi-family building permits issued: 0 (2001) / 0 (2000); Employment by occupation: 9.2% management, 13.2% professional, 16.1% services, 18.4% sales, 1.1% farming, 12.9% construction, 29.0% production (2000).
Income: Per capita income: $17,070 (2000); Median household income: $38,750 (2000); Poverty rate: 6.6% (2000).
Taxes: Total city taxes per capita: $165 (1997); City property taxes per capita: $159 (1997).
Education: High school graduation rate: 83.2% (2000); College graduation rate: 13.3% (2000).

School District(s)

Cambria-Friesland (PK-12)
2000 Enrollment: 505 920-348-5548

Housing: Homeownership rate: 74.1% (2000); Median home value: $78,900 (2000); Median rent: $333 per month (2000); Median age of housing: 60+ years (2000).
Transportation: Commute to work: 94.8% car, 0.6% public transportation, 4.4% walk, 0.3% work from home (2000); Travel time to work: 30.6% less than 15 minutes, 26.2% 15 to 30 minutes, 23.9% 30 to 45 minutes, 12.0% 45 to 60 minutes, 7.3% 60 minutes or more (2000)

COLUMBUS (city). Covers a land area of 3.989 square miles and a water area of 0.007 square miles. Located at 43.33° N. Lat.; 89.02° W. Long. Elevation is 871 feet.
History: The first settler in Columbus was Major Elbert Dickason, who stopped here in 1838 and returned in 1839 to build a house. Dickason operated a sawmill which later became a grist mill.
Population: 4,479 (2000); Race: 97.3% White, 0.2% Black, 0.1% Asian, 0.4% American Indian and Alaska Native, 1.7% Hispanic of any race, 0.9% two or more races (2000); Density: 1,122.7 persons per square mile (2000); Age: 25.7% under 18, 17.3% over 64 (2000); Marriage status: 22.1% never married, 60.1% now married, 9.1% widowed, 8.7% divorced (2000); Foreign born: 1.7% (2000); Ancestry (includes multiple ancestries): 53.9% German, 14.1% Irish, 11.2% Norwegian, 6.0% English, 4.8% Polish (2000).
Economy: Single-family building permits issued: 18 (2001) / 15 (2000); Multi-family building permits issued: 48 (2001) / 22 (2000); Employment by occupation: 11.3% management, 15.6% professional, 12.6% services, 28.7% sales, 0.5% farming, 7.5% construction, 23.8% production (2000).
Income: Per capita income: $21,435 (2000); Median household income: $42,667 (2000); Poverty rate: 5.4% (2000).

Taxes: Total city taxes per capita: $337 (1997); City property taxes per capita: $323 (1997).
Education: High school graduation rate: 84.6% (2000); College graduation rate: 19.8% (2000).

School District(s)

Columbus (PK-12)
2000 Enrollment: 1,244 920-623-5950
Housing: Homeownership rate: 64.9% (2000); Median home value: $113,000 (2000); Median rent: $453 per month (2000); Median age of housing: 53 years (2000).
Safety: Violent crime rate: 11.1 per 10,000 population; Property crime rate: 221.7 per 10,000 population (2001).
Newspapers: Columbus Journal-Republican (1 x week)
Transportation: Commute to work: 92.6% car, 0.0% public transportation, 4.9% walk, 2.4% work from home (2000); Travel time to work: 42.0% less than 15 minutes, 31.8% 15 to 30 minutes, 15.4% 30 to 45 minutes, 5.5% 45 to 60 minutes, 5.3% 60 minutes or more (2000); Amtrak: Service available.
Additional Information Contacts
Columbus Chamber of Commerce 920-623-3699

COLUMBUS (town). Covers a land area of 31.904 square miles and a water area of 0 square miles. Located at 43.33° N. Lat.; 89.05° W. Long. Elevation is 871 feet.
History: Louis H. Sullivan designed a local bank building (1919). Settled c.1840, incorporated 1874.
Population: 711 (2000); Race: 98.9% White, 0.0% Black, 0.4% Asian, 0.0% American Indian and Alaska Native, 0.8% Hispanic of any race, 0.7% two or more races (2000); Density: 22.3 persons per square mile (2000); Age: 25.3% under 18, 14.5% over 64 (2000); Marriage status: 24.5% never married, 64.1% now married, 8.9% widowed, 2.5% divorced (2000); Foreign born: 1.4% (2000); Ancestry (includes multiple ancestries): 51.4% German, 14.3% Norwegian, 10.3% Irish, 7.1% United States or American, 5.4% Other groups (2000).
Economy: In diversified farming area; dairy products. Manufacturing: printing, machinery, food products, fabricated metal products, rubber products. Employment by occupation: 19.5% management, 12.8% professional, 10.7% services, 20.3% sales, 6.1% farming, 10.7% construction, 19.8% production (2000).
Income: Per capita income: $19,660 (2000); Median household income: $55,682 (2000); Poverty rate: 3.8% (2000).
Taxes: Total city taxes per capita: $138 (1997); City property taxes per capita: $137 (1997).
Education: High school graduation rate: 86.4% (2000); College graduation rate: 14.2% (2000).
Housing: Homeownership rate: 76.5% (2000); Median home value: $109,600 (2000); Median rent: $450 per month (2000); Median age of housing: 60+ years (2000).
Transportation: Commute to work: 79.2% car, 0.8% public transportation, 2.5% walk, 17.5% work from home (2000); Travel time to work: 42.4% less than 15 minutes, 27.5% 15 to 30 minutes, 19.5% 30 to 45 minutes, 7.6% 45 to 60 minutes, 3.0% 60 minutes or more (2000); Amtrak: Service available.

COURTLAND (town). Covers a land area of 35.196 square miles and a water area of 0.146 square miles. Located at 43.49° N. Lat.; 89.06° W. Long.
Population: 463 (2000); Race: 98.1% White, 0.0% Black, 0.0% Asian, 0.4% American Indian and Alaska Native, 1.1% Hispanic of any race, 0.4% two or more races (2000); Density: 13.2 persons per square mile (2000); Age: 23.4% under 18, 16.6% over 64 (2000); Marriage status: 19.2% never married, 66.6% now married, 6.5% widowed, 7.8% divorced (2000); Foreign born: 0.6% (2000); Ancestry (includes multiple ancestries): 45.9% German, 21.5% Dutch, 7.6% English, 7.4% Irish, 5.3% Polish (2000).
Economy: Employment by occupation: 21.5% management, 13.6% professional, 10.9% services, 16.6% sales, 4.9% farming, 13.6% construction, 18.9% production (2000).
Income: Per capita income: $18,355 (2000); Median household income: $42,396 (2000); Poverty rate: 7.2% (2000).
Taxes: Total city taxes per capita: $79 (1997); City property taxes per capita: $78 (1997).
Education: High school graduation rate: 83.0% (2000); College graduation rate: 9.0% (2000).
Housing: Homeownership rate: 84.8% (2000); Median home value: $118,800 (2000); Median rent: $650 per month (2000); Median age of housing: 60+ years (2000).
Transportation: Commute to work: 72.2% car, 0.0% public transportation, 6.8% walk, 20.9% work from home (2000); Travel time to work: 39.9% less than 15 minutes, 27.4% 15 to 30 minutes, 17.3% 30 to 45 minutes, 7.7% 45 to 60 minutes, 7.7% 60 minutes or more (2000)

DEKORRA (town). Covers a land area of 41.142 square miles and a water area of 3.848 square miles. Located at 43.41° N. Lat.; 89.44° W. Long. Elevation is 800 feet.
Population: 2,350 (2000); Race: 97.1% White, 0.1% Black, 0.4% Asian, 1.3% American Indian and Alaska Native, 0.8% Hispanic of any race, 0.8% two or more races (2000); Density: 57.1 persons per square mile (2000); Age: 21.7% under 18, 10.2% over 64 (2000); Marriage status: 17.0% never married, 68.1% now married, 5.4% widowed, 9.5% divorced (2000); Foreign born: 1.6% (2000); Ancestry (includes multiple ancestries): 50.3% German, 14.3% Norwegian, 10.5% Irish, 10.3% English, 5.2% United States or American (2000).
Economy: Employment by occupation: 17.0% management, 13.5% professional, 9.6% services, 23.7% sales, 1.2% farming, 14.7% construction, 20.2% production (2000).
Income: Per capita income: $25,319 (2000); Median household income: $55,737 (2000); Poverty rate: 2.1% (2000).
Taxes: Total city taxes per capita: $114 (1997); City property taxes per capita: $109 (1997).
Education: High school graduation rate: 93.5% (2000); College graduation rate: 19.1% (2000).
Housing: Homeownership rate: 90.9% (2000); Median home value: $138,000 (2000); Median rent: $393 per month (2000); Median age of housing: 31 years (2000).
Transportation: Commute to work: 91.7% car, 0.6% public transportation, 1.1% walk, 6.5% work from home (2000); Travel time to work: 14.7% less than 15 minutes, 24.7% 15 to 30 minutes, 36.8% 30 to 45 minutes, 20.2% 45 to 60 minutes, 3.6% 60 minutes or more (2000)

DOYLESTOWN (village). Covers a land area of 3.931 square miles and a water area of 0.079 square miles. Located at 43.42° N. Lat.; 89.14° W. Long. Elevation is 947 feet.
Population: 328 (2000); Race: 98.1% White, 1.3% Black, 0.0% Asian, 0.0% American Indian and Alaska Native, 8.1% Hispanic of any race, 0.6% two or more races (2000); Density: 83.4 persons per square mile (2000); Age: 29.9% under 18, 13.0% over 64 (2000); Marriage status: 29.1% never married, 51.5% now married, 7.9% widowed, 11.5% divorced (2000); Foreign born: 5.8% (2000); Ancestry (includes multiple ancestries): 43.5% German, 19.5% Irish, 7.5% Other groups, 7.1% Norwegian, 5.2% English (2000).
Economy: In farm area. Hunting and state wildlife area. Single-family building permits issued: 2 (2001) / 2 (2000); Multi-family building permits issued: 0 (2001) / 0 (2000); Employment by occupation: 11.7% management, 6.5% professional, 10.4% services, 20.1% sales, 0.0% farming, 14.3% construction, 37.0% production (2000).
Income: Per capita income: $19,157 (2000); Median household income: $53,125 (2000); Poverty rate: 2.4% (2000).
Taxes: Total city taxes per capita: $55 (1997); City property taxes per capita: $49 (1997).
Education: High school graduation rate: 76.8% (2000); College graduation rate: 9.6% (2000).
Housing: Homeownership rate: 78.1% (2000); Median home value: $78,300 (2000); Median rent: $500 per month (2000); Median age of housing: 60 years (2000).
Transportation: Commute to work: 92.6% car, 0.0% public transportation, 6.0% walk, 1.3% work from home (2000); Travel time to work: 29.3% less than 15 minutes, 28.6% 15 to 30 minutes, 21.1% 30 to 45 minutes, 10.9% 45 to 60 minutes, 10.2% 60 minutes or more (2000)

FALL RIVER (village). Covers a land area of 1.450 square miles and a water area of 0.017 square miles. Located at 43.38° N. Lat.; 89.04° W. Long. Elevation is 858 feet.
Population: 1,097 (2000); Race: 97.9% White, 0.2% Black, 0.2% Asian, 0.0% American Indian and Alaska Native, 0.2% Hispanic of any race, 1.7% two or more races (2000); Density: 756.3 persons per square mile (2000); Age: 30.8% under 18, 10.5% over 64 (2000); Marriage status: 21.2% never married, 61.4% now married, 6.9% widowed, 10.5% divorced (2000); Foreign born: 0.9% (2000); Ancestry (includes multiple ancestries): 55.2% German, 14.3% Irish, 9.1% Norwegian, 6.2% English, 5.1% French (except Basque) (2000).
Economy: Agricultural. Manufacturing: machining, foundry, printing. Single-family building permits issued: 4 (2001) / 4 (2000); Multi-family building permits issued: 0 (2001) / 0 (2000); Employment by occupation: 11.0% management, 12.9% professional, 15.7% services, 21.3% sales, 0.0% farming, 13.0% construction, 26.1% production (2000).

Income: Per capita income: $19,257 (2000); Median household income: $46,597 (2000); Poverty rate: 5.2% (2000).
Taxes: Total city taxes per capita: $181 (1997); City property taxes per capita: $158 (1997).
Education: High school graduation rate: 89.7% (2000); College graduation rate: 17.5% (2000).

School District(s)

Fall River (PK-12)
2000 Enrollment: 439 920-484-3327
Housing: Homeownership rate: 74.4% (2000); Median home value: $112,300 (2000); Median rent: $429 per month (2000); Median age of housing: 25 years (2000).
Transportation: Commute to work: 94.7% car, 0.0% public transportation, 3.9% walk, 1.0% work from home (2000); Travel time to work: 44.6% less than 15 minutes, 15.6% 15 to 30 minutes, 23.2% 30 to 45 minutes, 10.3% 45 to 60 minutes, 6.3% 60 minutes or more (2000)

FORT WINNEBAGO (town). Covers a land area of 33.486 square miles and a water area of 0.477 square miles. Located at 43.61° N. Lat.; 89.41° W. Long.
Population: 855 (2000); Race: 98.9% White, 0.0% Black, 0.0% Asian, 0.2% American Indian and Alaska Native, 0.5% Hispanic of any race, 0.5% two or more races (2000); Density: 25.5 persons per square mile (2000); Age: 24.0% under 18, 12.1% over 64 (2000); Marriage status: 21.7% never married, 68.0% now married, 5.5% widowed, 4.8% divorced (2000); Foreign born: 0.1% (2000); Ancestry (includes multiple ancestries): 51.8% German, 17.9% Irish, 11.8% English, 10.6% Norwegian, 7.9% Polish (2000).
Economy: Employment by occupation: 14.1% management, 7.5% professional, 13.9% services, 27.3% sales, 1.4% farming, 15.0% construction, 20.8% production (2000).
Income: Per capita income: $22,171 (2000); Median household income: $55,673 (2000); Poverty rate: 3.2% (2000).
Taxes: Total city taxes per capita: $47 (1997); City property taxes per capita: $45 (1997).
Education: High school graduation rate: 91.2% (2000); College graduation rate: 13.3% (2000).
Housing: Homeownership rate: 91.4% (2000); Median home value: $118,800 (2000); Median rent: $563 per month (2000); Median age of housing: 32 years (2000).
Transportation: Commute to work: 88.8% car, 0.8% public transportation, 0.0% walk, 9.4% work from home (2000); Travel time to work: 44.3% less than 15 minutes, 24.3% 15 to 30 minutes, 10.3% 30 to 45 minutes, 11.5% 45 to 60 minutes, 9.7% 60 minutes or more (2000)

FOUNTAIN PRAIRIE (town). Covers a land area of 34.740 square miles and a water area of 0.304 square miles. Located at 43.40° N. Lat.; 89.05° W. Long.
Population: 810 (2000); Race: 98.4% White, 1.2% Black, 0.0% Asian, 0.0% American Indian and Alaska Native, 1.0% Hispanic of any race, 0.0% two or more races (2000); Density: 23.3 persons per square mile (2000); Age: 25.9% under 18, 10.3% over 64 (2000); Marriage status: 27.4% never married, 65.6% now married, 3.7% widowed, 3.3% divorced (2000); Foreign born: 1.6% (2000); Ancestry (includes multiple ancestries): 59.6% German, 11.7% Irish, 10.2% Norwegian, 8.1% English, 4.5% French (except Basque) (2000).
Economy: Employment by occupation: 16.2% management, 12.1% professional, 10.9% services, 23.3% sales, 2.8% farming, 8.3% construction, 26.5% production (2000).
Income: Per capita income: $21,985 (2000); Median household income: $51,726 (2000); Poverty rate: 10.0% (2000).
Taxes: Total city taxes per capita: $115 (1997); City property taxes per capita: $113 (1997).
Education: High school graduation rate: 83.0% (2000); College graduation rate: 13.4% (2000).
Housing: Homeownership rate: 83.7% (2000); Median home value: $129,700 (2000); Median rent: $438 per month (2000); Median age of housing: 60+ years (2000).
Transportation: Commute to work: 87.7% car, 0.4% public transportation, 3.3% walk, 8.0% work from home (2000); Travel time to work: 33.2% less than 15 minutes, 30.5% 15 to 30 minutes, 21.2% 30 to 45 minutes, 10.0% 45 to 60 minutes, 5.1% 60 minutes or more (2000)

FRIESLAND (village). Covers a land area of 1.027 square miles and a water area of 0 square miles. Located at 43.58° N. Lat.; 89.06° W. Long. Elevation is 1,010 feet.
Population: 298 (2000); Race: 97.2% White, 0.0% Black, 0.6% Asian, 0.0% American Indian and Alaska Native, 0.0% Hispanic of any race, 2.1% two or more races (2000); Density: 290.1 persons per square mile (2000); Age: 29.4% under 18, 16.9% over 64 (2000); Marriage status: 15.8% never married, 77.3% now married, 6.1% widowed, 0.8% divorced (2000); Foreign born: 1.2% (2000); Ancestry (includes multiple ancestries): 49.4% German, 43.6% Dutch, 5.5% Irish, 5.2% Norwegian, 3.7% United States or American (2000).
Economy: Farming, dairying. Single-family building permits issued: 0 (2001) / 0 (2000); Multi-family building permits issued: 0 (2001) / 0 (2000); Employment by occupation: 9.9% management, 13.0% professional, 12.4% services, 21.7% sales, 1.2% farming, 17.4% construction, 24.2% production (2000).
Income: Per capita income: $17,035 (2000); Median household income: $42,500 (2000); Poverty rate: 1.5% (2000).
Taxes: Total city taxes per capita: $148 (1997); City property taxes per capita: $148 (1997).
Education: High school graduation rate: 82.1% (2000); College graduation rate: 14.2% (2000).
Housing: Homeownership rate: 93.1% (2000); Median home value: $77,000 (2000); Median rent: $175 per month (2000); Median age of housing: 60+ years (2000).
Transportation: Commute to work: 87.4% car, 0.0% public transportation, 4.4% walk, 6.9% work from home (2000); Travel time to work: 45.3% less than 15 minutes, 16.2% 15 to 30 minutes, 24.3% 30 to 45 minutes, 7.4% 45 to 60 minutes, 6.8% 60 minutes or more (2000)

HAMPDEN (town). Covers a land area of 35.666 square miles and a water area of 0.022 square miles. Located at 43.34° N. Lat.; 89.19° W. Long.
Population: 563 (2000); Race: 98.1% White, 0.3% Black, 0.5% Asian, 0.0% American Indian and Alaska Native, 0.3% Hispanic of any race, 0.7% two or more races (2000); Density: 15.8 persons per square mile (2000); Age: 26.2% under 18, 11.9% over 64 (2000); Marriage status: 21.9% never married, 67.5% now married, 4.3% widowed, 6.3% divorced (2000); Foreign born: 0.0% (2000); Ancestry (includes multiple ancestries): 48.6% German, 21.7% Norwegian, 9.8% English, 7.3% Irish, 3.8% United States or American (2000).
Economy: Employment by occupation: 18.6% management, 12.3% professional, 9.9% services, 22.2% sales, 4.5% farming, 11.7% construction, 21.0% production (2000).
Income: Per capita income: $21,406 (2000); Median household income: $51,250 (2000); Poverty rate: 3.2% (2000).
Taxes: Total city taxes per capita: $179 (1997); City property taxes per capita: $178 (1997).
Education: High school graduation rate: 82.2% (2000); College graduation rate: 16.0% (2000).
Housing: Homeownership rate: 79.9% (2000); Median home value: $122,300 (2000); Median rent: $539 per month (2000); Median age of housing: 60+ years (2000).
Transportation: Commute to work: 91.0% car, 0.0% public transportation, 1.8% walk, 6.6% work from home (2000); Travel time to work: 18.6% less than 15 minutes, 37.8% 15 to 30 minutes, 31.4% 30 to 45 minutes, 8.0% 45 to 60 minutes, 4.2% 60 minutes or more (2000)

LAKE WISCONSIN (CDP). Covers a land area of 12.667 square miles and a water area of 8.945 square miles. Located at 43.37° N. Lat.; 89.57° W. Long.
Population: 3,493 (2000); Race: 98.3% White, 0.0% Black, 0.6% Asian, 0.1% American Indian and Alaska Native, 0.1% Hispanic of any race, 1.0% two or more races (2000); Density: 275.8 persons per square mile (2000); Age: 22.8% under 18, 11.5% over 64 (2000); Marriage status: 16.6% never married, 71.6% now married, 4.4% widowed, 7.4% divorced (2000); Foreign born: 1.2% (2000); Ancestry (includes multiple ancestries): 50.4% German, 15.3% Norwegian, 14.9% Irish, 10.3% English, 5.0% Polish (2000).
Economy: Employment by occupation: 16.7% management, 16.6% professional, 12.4% services, 25.9% sales, 0.8% farming, 12.4% construction, 15.2% production (2000).
Income: Per capita income: $26,657 (2000); Median household income: $58,906 (2000); Poverty rate: 1.2% (2000).
Education: High school graduation rate: 93.1% (2000); College graduation rate: 24.1% (2000).
Housing: Homeownership rate: 94.3% (2000); Median home value: $162,100 (2000); Median rent: $393 per month (2000); Median age of housing: 26 years (2000).
Transportation: Commute to work: 91.9% car, 0.0% public transportation, 0.5% walk, 6.9% work from home (2000); Travel time to work: 17.6% less than 15 minutes, 24.6% 15 to 30 minutes, 38.0% 30 to 45 minutes, 15.5% 45 to 60 minutes, 4.3% 60 minutes or more (2000)

LEEDS (town). Covers a land area of 35.514 square miles and a water area of 0.279 square miles. Located at 43.32° N. Lat.; 89.31° W. Long. Elevation is 1,059 feet.
Population: 813 (2000); Race: 98.9% White, 0.4% Black, 0.2% Asian, 0.0% American Indian and Alaska Native, 0.0% Hispanic of any race, 0.5% two or more races (2000); Density: 22.9 persons per square mile (2000); Age: 24.2% under 18, 13.9% over 64 (2000); Marriage status: 23.6% never married, 63.5% now married, 5.4% widowed, 7.5% divorced (2000); Foreign born: 0.2% (2000); Ancestry (includes multiple ancestries): 56.2% German, 21.8% Norwegian, 8.0% Irish, 7.1% English, 3.7% Swiss (2000).
Economy: Employment by occupation: 19.2% management, 12.0% professional, 10.0% services, 27.3% sales, 1.2% farming, 12.0% construction, 18.2% production (2000).
Income: Per capita income: $22,205 (2000); Median household income: $51,750 (2000); Poverty rate: 2.8% (2000).
Taxes: Total city taxes per capita: $92 (1997); City property taxes per capita: $91 (1997).
Education: High school graduation rate: 87.2% (2000); College graduation rate: 14.9% (2000).
Housing: Homeownership rate: 75.2% (2000); Median home value: $115,700 (2000); Median rent: $475 per month (2000); Median age of housing: 50 years (2000).
Transportation: Commute to work: 87.0% car, 0.6% public transportation, 2.5% walk, 8.9% work from home (2000); Travel time to work: 22.6% less than 15 minutes, 32.8% 15 to 30 minutes, 31.7% 30 to 45 minutes, 9.0% 45 to 60 minutes, 3.8% 60 minutes or more (2000)

LEWISTON (town). Covers a land area of 53.960 square miles and a water area of 0.958 square miles. Located at 43.58° N. Lat.; 89.55° W. Long. Elevation is 809 feet.
Population: 1,187 (2000); Race: 98.1% White, 0.6% Black, 0.3% Asian, 0.1% American Indian and Alaska Native, 1.0% Hispanic of any race, 1.0% two or more races (2000); Density: 22.0 persons per square mile (2000); Age: 23.0% under 18, 12.8% over 64 (2000); Marriage status: 21.8% never married, 64.4% now married, 5.2% widowed, 8.6% divorced (2000); Foreign born: 1.0% (2000); Ancestry (includes multiple ancestries): 49.4% German, 13.2% Norwegian, 10.9% Irish, 8.1% English, 7.9% Polish (2000).
Economy: Employment by occupation: 12.7% management, 10.9% professional, 12.1% services, 25.4% sales, 1.2% farming, 14.0% construction, 23.6% production (2000).
Income: Per capita income: $19,644 (2000); Median household income: $45,962 (2000); Poverty rate: 5.3% (2000).
Taxes: Total city taxes per capita: $18 (1997); City property taxes per capita: $11 (1997).
Education: High school graduation rate: 86.1% (2000); College graduation rate: 12.7% (2000).
Housing: Homeownership rate: 89.2% (2000); Median home value: $101,000 (2000); Median rent: $425 per month (2000); Median age of housing: 30 years (2000).
Transportation: Commute to work: 90.7% car, 0.3% public transportation, 0.7% walk, 7.3% work from home (2000); Travel time to work: 32.8% less than 15 minutes, 32.8% 15 to 30 minutes, 16.0% 30 to 45 minutes, 6.6% 45 to 60 minutes, 11.8% 60 minutes or more (2000)

LODI (city). Covers a land area of 1.435 square miles and a water area of 0 square miles. Located at 43.31° N. Lat.; 89.53° W. Long. Elevation is 833 feet.
History: Lodi was settled by Norwegian immigrants who chose the site because of its many springs. The village became a trading center for hogs and horses.
Population: 2,882 (2000); Race: 98.5% White, 0.2% Black, 0.2% Asian, 0.0% American Indian and Alaska Native, 1.5% Hispanic of any race, 0.8% two or more races (2000); Density: 2,008.6 persons per square mile (2000); Age: 27.5% under 18, 15.5% over 64 (2000); Marriage status: 21.1% never married, 60.2% now married, 10.5% widowed, 8.3% divorced (2000); Foreign born: 0.6% (2000); Ancestry (includes multiple ancestries): 47.0% German, 17.6% Norwegian, 14.4% Irish, 11.1% English, 5.1% United States or American (2000).
Economy: Single-family building permits issued: 9 (2001) / 17 (2000); Multi-family building permits issued: 4 (2001) / 0 (2000); Employment by occupation: 14.3% management, 19.3% professional, 13.6% services, 26.1% sales, 0.6% farming, 10.9% construction, 15.3% production (2000).
Income: Per capita income: $23,546 (2000); Median household income: $51,357 (2000); Poverty rate: 2.7% (2000).
Taxes: Total city taxes per capita: $597 (1997); City property taxes per capita: $583 (1997).
Education: High school graduation rate: 90.0% (2000); College graduation rate: 20.7% (2000).

School District(s)

Lodi (PK-12)
2000 Enrollment: 1,585 608-592-3851
Housing: Homeownership rate: 64.5% (2000); Median home value: $129,700 (2000); Median rent: $541 per month (2000); Median age of housing: 30 years (2000).
Safety: Violent crime rate: 6.9 per 10,000 population; Property crime rate: 330.7 per 10,000 population (2001).
Newspapers: The Lodi Shopper (1 x week); The Lodi Enterprise (1 x week)
Transportation: Commute to work: 95.5% car, 0.0% public transportation, 2.9% walk, 1.5% work from home (2000); Travel time to work: 36.7% less than 15 minutes, 20.8% 15 to 30 minutes, 31.8% 30 to 45 minutes, 8.1% 45 to 60 minutes, 2.6% 60 minutes or more (2000)

LODI (town). Covers a land area of 27.055 square miles and a water area of 1.813 square miles. Located at 43.35° N. Lat.; 89.53° W. Long. Elevation is 833 feet.
History: Incorporated as village in 1872, as city in 1941.
Population: 2,791 (2000); Race: 98.9% White, 0.0% Black, 0.3% Asian, 0.0% American Indian and Alaska Native, 0.1% Hispanic of any race, 0.8% two or more races (2000); Density: 103.2 persons per square mile (2000); Age: 23.6% under 18, 11.4% over 64 (2000); Marriage status: 19.3% never married, 69.2% now married, 5.1% widowed, 6.4% divorced (2000); Foreign born: 1.2% (2000); Ancestry (includes multiple ancestries): 48.2% German, 14.8% Norwegian, 13.8% Irish, 10.7% English, 5.9% Polish (2000).
Economy: In diversified farming area. Food processing, machinery and equipment manufacturing. Employment by occupation: 17.0% management, 13.9% professional, 12.5% services, 28.2% sales, 0.0% farming, 11.6% construction, 16.8% production (2000).
Income: Per capita income: $23,900 (2000); Median household income: $56,250 (2000); Poverty rate: 2.7% (2000).
Taxes: Total city taxes per capita: $198 (1997); City property taxes per capita: $175 (1997).
Education: High school graduation rate: 90.0% (2000); College graduation rate: 22.6% (2000).
Housing: Homeownership rate: 91.0% (2000); Median home value: $150,500 (2000); Median rent: $515 per month (2000); Median age of housing: 23 years (2000).
Transportation: Commute to work: 93.2% car, 0.0% public transportation, 0.3% walk, 5.6% work from home (2000); Travel time to work: 18.5% less than 15 minutes, 22.7% 15 to 30 minutes, 36.5% 30 to 45 minutes, 17.2% 45 to 60 minutes, 5.1% 60 minutes or more (2000)

LOWVILLE (town). Covers a land area of 34.256 square miles and a water area of 1.474 square miles. Located at 43.42° N. Lat.; 89.28° W. Long. Elevation is 967 feet.
Population: 987 (2000); Race: 98.6% White, 0.0% Black, 0.0% Asian, 0.7% American Indian and Alaska Native, 0.6% Hispanic of any race, 0.5% two or more races (2000); Density: 28.8 persons per square mile (2000); Age: 24.1% under 18, 12.5% over 64 (2000); Marriage status: 22.2% never married, 68.3% now married, 3.2% widowed, 6.2% divorced (2000); Foreign born: 0.5% (2000); Ancestry (includes multiple ancestries): 49.9% German, 20.5% Norwegian, 11.5% Irish, 9.9% English, 3.6% Polish (2000).
Economy: Employment by occupation: 16.4% management, 12.1% professional, 12.6% services, 25.8% sales, 2.3% farming, 15.3% construction, 15.5% production (2000).
Income: Per capita income: $20,039 (2000); Median household income: $54,519 (2000); Poverty rate: 3.8% (2000).
Taxes: Total city taxes per capita: $59 (1997); City property taxes per capita: $58 (1997).
Education: High school graduation rate: 91.8% (2000); College graduation rate: 17.4% (2000).
Housing: Homeownership rate: 90.7% (2000); Median home value: $125,700 (2000); Median rent: $425 per month (2000); Median age of housing: 29 years (2000).
Transportation: Commute to work: 91.4% car, 0.2% public transportation, 1.5% walk, 6.7% work from home (2000); Travel time to work: 21.1% less than 15 minutes, 30.3% 15 to 30 minutes, 30.3% 30 to 45 minutes, 14.5% 45 to 60 minutes, 3.9% 60 minutes or more (2000)

MARCELLON (town). Covers a land area of 35.496 square miles and a water area of 0.280 square miles. Located at 43.59° N. Lat.; 89.31° W. Long. Elevation is 820 feet.
Population: 1,024 (2000); Race: 99.8% White, 0.0% Black, 0.0% Asian, 0.0% American Indian and Alaska Native, 1.2% Hispanic of any race, 0.2% two or more races (2000); Density: 28.8 persons per square mile (2000); Age: 26.7% under 18, 9.5% over 64 (2000); Marriage status: 20.9% never married, 71.2% now married, 2.8% widowed, 5.2% divorced (2000); Foreign born: 0.5% (2000); Ancestry (includes multiple ancestries): 49.2% German, 16.5% Irish, 12.6% English, 7.6% Norwegian, 5.3% United States or American (2000).
Economy: Employment by occupation: 14.1% management, 9.2% professional, 11.9% services, 25.5% sales, 1.7% farming, 13.9% construction, 23.7% production (2000).
Income: Per capita income: $19,488 (2000); Median household income: $48,333 (2000); Poverty rate: 8.2% (2000).
Taxes: Total city taxes per capita: $34 (1997); City property taxes per capita: $33 (1997).
Education: High school graduation rate: 81.9% (2000); College graduation rate: 13.9% (2000).
Housing: Homeownership rate: 85.1% (2000); Median home value: $114,800 (2000); Median rent: $433 per month (2000); Median age of housing: 33 years (2000).
Transportation: Commute to work: 83.1% car, 0.4% public transportation, 2.6% walk, 12.7% work from home (2000); Travel time to work: 19.0% less than 15 minutes, 43.5% 15 to 30 minutes, 12.7% 30 to 45 minutes, 9.9% 45 to 60 minutes, 15.0% 60 minutes or more (2000)

NEWPORT (town). Covers a land area of 21.472 square miles and a water area of 0.594 square miles. Located at 43.60° N. Lat.; 89.71° W. Long.
Population: 681 (2000); Race: 98.1% White, 0.6% Black, 0.4% Asian, 0.1% American Indian and Alaska Native, 1.4% Hispanic of any race, 0.3% two or more races (2000); Density: 31.7 persons per square mile (2000); Age: 28.7% under 18, 15.0% over 64 (2000); Marriage status: 19.7% never married, 64.1% now married, 6.0% widowed, 10.2% divorced (2000); Foreign born: 2.7% (2000); Ancestry (includes multiple ancestries): 48.6% German, 23.6% Irish, 21.1% Norwegian, 10.9% Polish, 8.0% English (2000).
Economy: Employment by occupation: 15.4% management, 19.3% professional, 16.0% services, 27.0% sales, 0.0% farming, 8.0% construction, 14.3% production (2000).
Income: Per capita income: $19,390 (2000); Median household income: $45,833 (2000); Poverty rate: 5.7% (2000).
Taxes: Total city taxes per capita: $85 (1997); City property taxes per capita: $78 (1997).
Education: High school graduation rate: 83.7% (2000); College graduation rate: 19.5% (2000).
Housing: Homeownership rate: 77.8% (2000); Median home value: $125,300 (2000); Median rent: $375 per month (2000); Median age of housing: 24 years (2000).
Transportation: Commute to work: 94.7% car, 0.0% public transportation, 1.7% walk, 3.7% work from home (2000); Travel time to work: 44.6% less than 15 minutes, 29.7% 15 to 30 minutes, 12.8% 30 to 45 minutes, 5.2% 45 to 60 minutes, 7.6% 60 minutes or more (2000)

OTSEGO (town). Covers a land area of 30.504 square miles and a water area of 0.462 square miles. Located at 43.40° N. Lat.; 89.17° W. Long. Elevation is 950 feet.
Population: 757 (2000); Race: 99.3% White, 0.0% Black, 0.0% Asian, 0.0% American Indian and Alaska Native, 0.9% Hispanic of any race, 0.5% two or more races (2000); Density: 24.8 persons per square mile (2000); Age: 25.7% under 18, 12.1% over 64 (2000); Marriage status: 21.2% never married, 66.6% now married, 4.3% widowed, 7.8% divorced (2000); Foreign born: 1.1% (2000); Ancestry (includes multiple ancestries): 40.3% German, 18.5% Norwegian, 12.3% Irish, 6.7% English, 6.5% United States or American (2000).
Economy: Employment by occupation: 12.2% management, 11.0% professional, 16.7% services, 24.8% sales, 3.6% farming, 17.3% construction, 14.4% production (2000).
Income: Per capita income: $20,620 (2000); Median household income: $52,500 (2000); Poverty rate: 3.6% (2000).
Taxes: Total city taxes per capita: $139 (1997); City property taxes per capita: $138 (1997).
Education: High school graduation rate: 86.2% (2000); College graduation rate: 8.8% (2000).
Housing: Homeownership rate: 87.4% (2000); Median home value: $131,000 (2000); Median rent: $450 per month (2000); Median age of housing: 56 years (2000).
Transportation: Commute to work: 89.0% car, 0.7% public transportation, 0.7% walk, 9.6% work from home (2000); Travel time to work: 22.5% less than 15 minutes, 34.3% 15 to 30 minutes, 21.7% 30 to 45 minutes, 12.6% 45 to 60 minutes, 8.8% 60 minutes or more (2000)

PACIFIC (town). Covers a land area of 20.332 square miles and a water area of 1.266 square miles. Located at 43.51° N. Lat.; 89.40° W. Long.
Population: 2,518 (2000); Race: 99.0% White, 0.2% Black, 0.0% Asian, 0.4% American Indian and Alaska Native, 0.4% Hispanic of any race, 0.4% two or more races (2000); Density: 123.8 persons per square mile (2000); Age: 22.1% under 18, 16.7% over 64 (2000); Marriage status: 17.2% never married, 69.8% now married, 5.9% widowed, 7.2% divorced (2000); Foreign born: 1.0% (2000); Ancestry (includes multiple ancestries): 51.0% German, 13.5% Norwegian, 13.0% English, 11.3% Irish, 5.5% Polish (2000).
Economy: Employment by occupation: 12.9% management, 12.6% professional, 13.1% services, 28.5% sales, 0.3% farming, 10.5% construction, 22.1% production (2000).
Income: Per capita income: $22,489 (2000); Median household income: $49,122 (2000); Poverty rate: 4.9% (2000).
Taxes: Total city taxes per capita: $8 (1997); City property taxes per capita: $0 (1997).
Education: High school graduation rate: 88.4% (2000); College graduation rate: 17.3% (2000).
Housing: Homeownership rate: 89.2% (2000); Median home value: $137,100 (2000); Median rent: $570 per month (2000); Median age of housing: 17 years (2000).
Transportation: Commute to work: 95.8% car, 0.2% public transportation, 1.2% walk, 2.1% work from home (2000); Travel time to work: 33.7% less than 15 minutes, 29.1% 15 to 30 minutes, 17.2% 30 to 45 minutes, 13.3% 45 to 60 minutes, 6.7% 60 minutes or more (2000)

PARDEEVILLE (village). Covers a land area of 2.016 square miles and a water area of 0.277 square miles. Located at 43.53° N. Lat.; 89.29° W. Long. Elevation is 815 feet.
History: Incorporated 1894.
Population: 1,982 (2000); Race: 96.7% White, 0.0% Black, 1.8% Asian, 0.6% American Indian and Alaska Native, 2.3% Hispanic of any race, 0.8% two or more races (2000); Density: 982.9 persons per square mile (2000); Age: 28.2% under 18, 12.9% over 64 (2000); Marriage status: 25.4% never married, 52.0% now married, 9.4% widowed, 13.2% divorced (2000); Foreign born: 0.2% (2000); Ancestry (includes multiple ancestries): 49.7% German, 14.3% Irish, 11.4% Norwegian, 7.6% Other groups, 6.4% English (2000).
Economy: In farm area: livestock; melons; cheese and other dairy products, canned foods; nursery stock. Manufacturing: electronic equipment, molded plastics. Single-family building permits issued: 9 (2001) / 13 (2000); Multi-family building permits issued: 0 (2001) / 0 (2000); Employment by occupation: 8.1% management, 15.1% professional, 13.3% services, 24.3% sales, 0.6% farming, 15.9% construction, 22.7% production (2000).
Income: Per capita income: $21,365 (2000); Median household income: $40,139 (2000); Poverty rate: 3.9% (2000).
Taxes: Total city taxes per capita: $263 (1997); City property taxes per capita: $248 (1997).
Education: High school graduation rate: 88.4% (2000); College graduation rate: 13.5% (2000).

School District(s)

Pardeeville Area (PK-12)
2000 Enrollment: 982 608-429-3666
Housing: Homeownership rate: 65.7% (2000); Median home value: $101,700 (2000); Median rent: $467 per month (2000); Median age of housing: 41 years (2000).
Transportation: Commute to work: 91.6% car, 0.0% public transportation, 3.9% walk, 3.8% work from home (2000); Travel time to work: 28.3% less than 15 minutes, 27.3% 15 to 30 minutes, 25.0% 30 to 45 minutes, 10.6% 45 to 60 minutes, 8.8% 60 minutes or more (2000)

PORTAGE (city). Covers a land area of 8.294 square miles and a water area of 0.727 square miles. Located at 43.54° N. Lat.; 89.46° W. Long. Elevation is 800 feet.
History: Portage was founded in the early 1800's by traders and adventurers who traveled the Fox and Wisconsin Rivers waterway. Furs, wheat, lumber, and railroads brought the city its livelihood in the 1800's. Later Portage

developed as a trading center for the farmers, and the site of some diversified manufacturing.
Population: 9,728 (2000); Race: 92.7% White, 4.4% Black, 0.7% Asian, 0.4% American Indian and Alaska Native, 3.6% Hispanic of any race, 1.0% two or more races (2000); Density: 1,172.9 persons per square mile (2000); Age: 23.3% under 18, 15.0% over 64 (2000); Marriage status: 23.1% never married, 56.3% now married, 9.0% widowed, 11.5% divorced (2000); Foreign born: 1.4% (2000); Ancestry (includes multiple ancestries): 44.2% German, 13.0% Irish, 9.7% English, 8.5% Norwegian, 7.2% Polish (2000).
Economy: Single-family building permits issued: 22 (2001) / 14 (2000); Multi-family building permits issued: 50 (2001) / 14 (2000); Employment by occupation: 10.2% management, 16.3% professional, 14.6% services, 26.2% sales, 0.5% farming, 9.8% construction, 22.4% production (2000).
Income: Per capita income: $18,039 (2000); Median household income: $35,815 (2000); Poverty rate: 7.2% (2000).
Taxes: Total city taxes per capita: $266 (2000); City property taxes per capita: $230 (2000).
Education: High school graduation rate: 82.3% (2000); College graduation rate: 14.8% (2000).

School District(s)

Portage Community (PK-12)
2000 Enrollment: 2,561 608-742-4879
Housing: Homeownership rate: 59.1% (2000); Median home value: $90,600 (2000); Median rent: $424 per month (2000); Median age of housing: 49 years (2000).
Hospitals: Divine Savior Healthcare (73 beds)
Safety: Violent crime rate: 3.1 per 10,000 population; Property crime rate: 511.4 per 10,000 population (2001).
Newspapers: Portage Daily Register (6 x week)
Transportation: Commute to work: 91.2% car, 0.8% public transportation, 5.5% walk, 2.0% work from home (2000); Travel time to work: 57.4% less than 15 minutes, 16.6% 15 to 30 minutes, 12.5% 30 to 45 minutes, 7.9% 45 to 60 minutes, 5.6% 60 minutes or more (2000); Amtrak: Service available.
Additional Information Contacts
Portgage Area Chamber of Commerce 608-742-6242

POYNETTE (village). Covers a land area of 2.412 square miles and a water area of 0.010 square miles. Located at 43.39° N. Lat.; 89.40° W. Long. Elevation is 847 feet.
Population: 2,266 (2000); Race: 97.1% White, 0.2% Black, 0.1% Asian, 0.6% American Indian and Alaska Native, 1.4% Hispanic of any race, 1.1% two or more races (2000); Density: 939.3 persons per square mile (2000); Age: 29.4% under 18, 11.3% over 64 (2000); Marriage status: 24.1% never married, 56.3% now married, 7.2% widowed, 12.4% divorced (2000); Foreign born: 1.4% (2000); Ancestry (includes multiple ancestries): 45.7% German, 17.2% Norwegian, 14.3% Irish, 8.2% English, 4.6% Polish (2000).
Economy: Agriculture. Cannery. Manufacturing: humidifiers; light manufacturing. State environmental center and game farm to Northeast. Single-family building permits issued: 23 (2001) / 18 (2000); Multi-family building permits issued: 0 (2001) / 9 (2000); Employment by occupation: 12.1% management, 15.7% professional, 12.4% services, 26.2% sales, 0.7% farming, 11.8% construction, 21.1% production (2000).
Income: Per capita income: $18,962 (2000); Median household income: $45,000 (2000); Poverty rate: 6.0% (2000).
Taxes: Total city taxes per capita: $217 (1997); City property taxes per capita: $189 (1997).
Education: High school graduation rate: 87.3% (2000); College graduation rate: 18.4% (2000).

School District(s)

Poynette (PK-12)
2000 Enrollment: 1,114 608-635-4347
Housing: Homeownership rate: 63.6% (2000); Median home value: $116,600 (2000); Median rent: $415 per month (2000); Median age of housing: 22 years (2000).
Safety: Violent crime rate: 4.4 per 10,000 population; Property crime rate: 455.7 per 10,000 population (2001).
Newspapers: The Poynette Press (1 x week)
Transportation: Commute to work: 93.4% car, 0.3% public transportation, 3.2% walk, 2.0% work from home (2000); Travel time to work: 25.5% less than 15 minutes, 28.2% 15 to 30 minutes, 29.9% 30 to 45 minutes, 13.2% 45 to 60 minutes, 3.2% 60 minutes or more (2000)
Additional Information Contacts
Lake Wisconsin Chamber of Commerce 608-635-8070
Poynette Chamber of Commerce 608-635-2425

RANDOLPH (town). Covers a land area of 35.124 square miles and a water area of 0.010 square miles. Located at 43.57° N. Lat.; 89.05° W. Long. Elevation is 964 feet.
Population: 699 (2000); Race: 99.7% White, 0.0% Black, 0.3% Asian, 0.0% American Indian and Alaska Native, 0.0% Hispanic of any race, 0.0% two or more races (2000); Density: 19.9 persons per square mile (2000); Age: 33.2% under 18, 12.6% over 64 (2000); Marriage status: 23.8% never married, 71.5% now married, 3.0% widowed, 1.8% divorced (2000); Foreign born: 1.2% (2000); Ancestry (includes multiple ancestries): 48.9% Dutch, 41.3% German, 7.2% English, 6.3% Irish, 2.5% Polish (2000).
Economy: Employment by occupation: 27.8% management, 8.2% professional, 11.3% services, 13.9% sales, 9.3% farming, 11.9% construction, 17.6% production (2000).
Income: Per capita income: $16,670 (2000); Median household income: $41,250 (2000); Poverty rate: 9.6% (2000).
Taxes: Total city taxes per capita: $62 (1997); City property taxes per capita: $62 (1997).
Education: High school graduation rate: 80.9% (2000); College graduation rate: 9.9% (2000).

School District(s)

Randolph (PK-12)
2000 Enrollment: 508 920-326-2427
Housing: Homeownership rate: 79.8% (2000); Median home value: $115,000 (2000); Median rent: $336 per month (2000); Median age of housing: 54 years (2000).
Transportation: Commute to work: 67.3% car, 0.0% public transportation, 4.9% walk, 27.7% work from home (2000); Travel time to work: 50.4% less than 15 minutes, 28.0% 15 to 30 minutes, 11.2% 30 to 45 minutes, 7.2% 45 to 60 minutes, 3.2% 60 minutes or more (2000)

RIO (village). Covers a land area of 1.248 square miles and a water area of 0 square miles. Located at 43.44° N. Lat.; 89.24° W. Long. Elevation is 974 feet.
Population: 938 (2000); Race: 98.4% White, 0.0% Black, 0.0% Asian, 0.0% American Indian and Alaska Native, 1.4% Hispanic of any race, 1.4% two or more races (2000); Density: 751.4 persons per square mile (2000); Age: 26.3% under 18, 16.4% over 64 (2000); Marriage status: 23.9% never married, 60.2% now married, 8.2% widowed, 7.7% divorced (2000); Foreign born: 1.2% (2000); Ancestry (includes multiple ancestries): 46.6% German, 27.4% Norwegian, 12.9% Irish, 9.6% English, 6.9% French (except Basque) (2000).
Economy: In agricultural area: grain, potatoes; dairying. Lime works; light manufacturing. Single-family building permits issued: 1 (2001) / 7 (2000); Multi-family building permits issued: 0 (2001) / 4 (2000); Employment by occupation: 10.7% management, 11.9% professional, 11.3% services, 24.9% sales, 0.8% farming, 10.0% construction, 30.3% production (2000).
Income: Per capita income: $17,668 (2000); Median household income: $42,292 (2000); Poverty rate: 4.9% (2000).
Education: High school graduation rate: 86.8% (2000); College graduation rate: 13.8% (2000).

School District(s)

Rio Community (PK-12)
2000 Enrollment: 571 920-992-3141
Housing: Homeownership rate: 74.0% (2000); Median home value: $93,400 (2000); Median rent: $453 per month (2000); Median age of housing: 60+ years (2000).
Transportation: Commute to work: 90.6% car, 0.0% public transportation, 5.1% walk, 1.3% work from home (2000); Travel time to work: 23.5% less than 15 minutes, 30.8% 15 to 30 minutes, 27.4% 30 to 45 minutes, 11.0% 45 to 60 minutes, 7.3% 60 minutes or more (2000)

SCOTT (town). Covers a land area of 35.820 square miles and a water area of 0 square miles. Located at 43.59° N. Lat.; 89.19° W. Long.
Population: 791 (2000); Race: 93.6% White, 0.4% Black, 0.0% Asian, 0.1% American Indian and Alaska Native, 1.2% Hispanic of any race, 5.3% two or more races (2000); Density: 22.1 persons per square mile (2000); Age: 37.1% under 18, 11.9% over 64 (2000); Marriage status: 22.0% never married, 64.9% now married, 6.2% widowed, 6.9% divorced (2000); Foreign born: 1.2% (2000); Ancestry (includes multiple ancestries): 42.9% German, 10.4% English, 8.7% Dutch, 5.6% Irish, 3.6% Norwegian (2000).
Economy: Employment by occupation: 16.8% management, 11.9% professional, 16.5% services, 13.8% sales, 3.5% farming, 12.5% construction, 24.9% production (2000).
Income: Per capita income: $13,757 (2000); Median household income: $38,839 (2000); Poverty rate: 16.7% (2000).

Taxes: Total city taxes per capita: $46 (1997); City property taxes per capita: $46 (1997).
Education: High school graduation rate: 74.4% (2000); College graduation rate: 10.2% (2000).
Housing: Homeownership rate: 93.8% (2000); Median home value: $105,800 (2000); Median rent: $292 per month (2000); Median age of housing: 50 years (2000).
Transportation: Commute to work: 73.1% car, 0.0% public transportation, 1.4% walk, 19.7% work from home (2000); Travel time to work: 23.5% less than 15 minutes, 20.4% 15 to 30 minutes, 14.5% 30 to 45 minutes, 19.0% 45 to 60 minutes, 22.5% 60 minutes or more (2000)

SPRINGVALE (town). Covers a land area of 41.002 square miles and a water area of 0.049 square miles. Located at 43.50° N. Lat.; 89.19° W. Long.
Population: 550 (2000); Race: 98.0% White, 0.5% Black, 0.0% Asian, 0.0% American Indian and Alaska Native, 0.0% Hispanic of any race, 0.7% two or more races (2000); Density: 13.4 persons per square mile (2000); Age: 29.1% under 18, 8.9% over 64 (2000); Marriage status: 17.7% never married, 71.3% now married, 3.6% widowed, 7.4% divorced (2000); Foreign born: 0.0% (2000); Ancestry (includes multiple ancestries): 51.7% German, 16.9% English, 9.8% Irish, 8.9% Norwegian, 7.3% Dutch (2000).
Economy: Employment by occupation: 16.2% management, 14.0% professional, 7.3% services, 22.9% sales, 1.9% farming, 20.4% construction, 17.2% production (2000).
Income: Per capita income: $19,536 (2000); Median household income: $47,188 (2000); Poverty rate: 2.1% (2000).
Taxes: Total city taxes per capita: $92 (1997); City property taxes per capita: $90 (1997).
Education: High school graduation rate: 86.9% (2000); College graduation rate: 16.6% (2000).
Housing: Homeownership rate: 87.1% (2000); Median home value: $108,300 (2000); Median rent: $419 per month (2000); Median age of housing: 39 years (2000).
Transportation: Commute to work: 81.7% car, 0.0% public transportation, 2.3% walk, 15.4% work from home (2000); Travel time to work: 29.3% less than 15 minutes, 25.1% 15 to 30 minutes, 27.8% 30 to 45 minutes, 9.9% 45 to 60 minutes, 8.0% 60 minutes or more (2000)

WEST POINT (town). Covers a land area of 28.911 square miles and a water area of 3.553 square miles. Located at 43.32° N. Lat.; 89.63° W. Long.
Population: 1,634 (2000); Race: 97.8% White, 0.0% Black, 1.2% Asian, 0.0% American Indian and Alaska Native, 0.0% Hispanic of any race, 1.0% two or more races (2000); Density: 56.5 persons per square mile (2000); Age: 23.6% under 18, 13.4% over 64 (2000); Marriage status: 16.8% never married, 71.0% now married, 4.6% widowed, 7.6% divorced (2000); Foreign born: 1.8% (2000); Ancestry (includes multiple ancestries): 56.8% German, 14.5% Irish, 13.1% English, 11.2% Norwegian, 3.8% French (except Basque) (2000).
Economy: Employment by occupation: 15.9% management, 20.4% professional, 12.4% services, 24.0% sales, 1.0% farming, 14.8% construction, 11.6% production (2000).
Income: Per capita income: $30,750 (2000); Median household income: $55,781 (2000); Poverty rate: 3.8% (2000).
Taxes: Total city taxes per capita: $171 (2000); City property taxes per capita: $127 (2000).
Education: High school graduation rate: 91.2% (2000); College graduation rate: 22.6% (2000).
Housing: Homeownership rate: 93.6% (2000); Median home value: $189,700 (2000); Median rent: $363 per month (2000); Median age of housing: 28 years (2000).
Transportation: Commute to work: 91.1% car, 0.5% public transportation, 0.8% walk, 7.3% work from home (2000); Travel time to work: 32.1% less than 15 minutes, 21.4% 15 to 30 minutes, 28.9% 30 to 45 minutes, 13.6% 45 to 60 minutes, 4.1% 60 minutes or more (2000)

WISCONSIN DELLS (city). Covers a land area of 4.147 square miles and a water area of 0.251 square miles. Located at 43.62° N. Lat.; 89.77° W. Long. Elevation is 912 feet.
History: Wisconsin Dells began in the late 1850's when the Chicago, Milwaukee, St. Paul & Pacific Railroad ran its tracks across the Wisconsin River here. Before 1931, Wisconsin Dells was called Kilbourn. The new name was chosen in the hopes of attracting tourists to the excursion boats that plied the Wisconsin River.
Population: 2,418 (2000); Race: 96.8% White, 0.9% Black, 0.0% Asian, 0.3% American Indian and Alaska Native, 2.9% Hispanic of any race, 1.6% two or more races (2000); Density: 583.1 persons per square mile (2000); Age: 20.8% under 18, 20.1% over 64 (2000); Marriage status: 26.0% never married, 53.9% now married, 9.8% widowed, 10.3% divorced (2000); Foreign born: 5.3% (2000); Ancestry (includes multiple ancestries): 36.8% German, 12.8% Irish, 11.8% Polish, 9.7% Norwegian, 8.6% United States or American (2000).
Economy: Single-family building permits issued: 5 (2001) / 5 (2000); Multi-family building permits issued: 0 (2001) / 0 (2000); Employment by occupation: 15.6% management, 14.5% professional, 20.1% services, 23.9% sales, 0.2% farming, 7.4% construction, 18.3% production (2000).
Income: Per capita income: $23,447 (2000); Median household income: $35,699 (2000); Poverty rate: 7.5% (2000).
Taxes: Total city taxes per capita: $1,009 (1997); City property taxes per capita: $610 (1997).
Education: High school graduation rate: 83.0% (2000); College graduation rate: 17.3% (2000).

School District(s)

Wisconsin Dells (PK-12)
2000 Enrollment: 1,779 608-254-7769

Housing: Homeownership rate: 62.9% (2000); Median home value: $96,300 (2000); Median rent: $365 per month (2000); Median age of housing: 43 years (2000).
Safety: Violent crime rate: 37.0 per 10,000 population; Property crime rate: 1,310.1 per 10,000 population (2001).
Newspapers: Wisconsin Dells Events (2 x week)
Transportation: Commute to work: 86.7% car, 0.0% public transportation, 4.4% walk, 7.6% work from home (2000); Travel time to work: 55.4% less than 15 minutes, 29.0% 15 to 30 minutes, 7.6% 30 to 45 minutes, 2.2% 45 to 60 minutes, 5.8% 60 minutes or more (2000); Amtrak: Service available.

Additional Information Contacts

Wisconsin Dells Chamber of Commerce 608-253-4058
Wisconsin Dells Visitors Bureau 608-254-8088

WYOCENA (village). Covers a land area of 1.433 square miles and a water area of 0.106 square miles. Located at 43.49° N. Lat.; 89.30° W. Long. Elevation is 826 feet.
Population: 668 (2000); Race: 97.7% White, 0.0% Black, 0.0% Asian, 0.3% American Indian and Alaska Native, 1.3% Hispanic of any race, 2.0% two or more races (2000); Density: 466.3 persons per square mile (2000); Age: 14.9% under 18, 29.5% over 64 (2000); Marriage status: 18.7% never married, 69.7% now married, 3.3% widowed, 8.3% divorced (2000); Foreign born: 1.2% (2000); Ancestry (includes multiple ancestries): 25.9% German, 15.8% English, 12.5% Norwegian, 4.3% Irish, 4.3% Polish (2000).
Economy: Single-family building permits issued: 1 (2001) / 5 (2000); Multi-family building permits issued: 10 (2001) / 0 (2000); Employment by occupation: 8.0% management, 14.9% professional, 17.6% services, 18.3% sales, 1.9% farming, 11.8% construction, 27.5% production (2000).
Income: Per capita income: $17,430 (2000); Median household income: $42,857 (2000); Poverty rate: 5.0% (2000).
Taxes: Total city taxes per capita: $84 (1997); City property taxes per capita: $78 (1997).
Education: High school graduation rate: 74.0% (2000); College graduation rate: 12.8% (2000).
Housing: Homeownership rate: 73.1% (2000); Median home value: $98,000 (2000); Median rent: $307 per month (2000); Median age of housing: 32 years (2000).
Transportation: Commute to work: 90.8% car, 3.1% public transportation, 2.3% walk, 3.8% work from home (2000); Travel time to work: 22.0% less than 15 minutes, 26.0% 15 to 30 minutes, 23.6% 30 to 45 minutes, 16.4% 45 to 60 minutes, 12.0% 60 minutes or more (2000)

WYOCENA (town). Covers a land area of 36.233 square miles and a water area of 0.816 square miles. Located at 43.51° N. Lat.; 89.30° W. Long. Elevation is 826 feet.
Population: 1,543 (2000); Race: 99.0% White, 0.0% Black, 0.0% Asian, 0.3% American Indian and Alaska Native, 0.6% Hispanic of any race, 0.6% two or more races (2000); Density: 42.6 persons per square mile (2000); Age: 23.1% under 18, 18.7% over 64 (2000); Marriage status: 18.0% never married, 70.5% now married, 4.7% widowed, 6.9% divorced (2000); Foreign born: 0.1% (2000); Ancestry (includes multiple ancestries): 51.9% German, 14.8% Norwegian, 14.0% English, 12.3% Irish, 5.0% Polish (2000).
Economy: In agricultural area. Employment by occupation: 17.3% management, 13.6% professional, 12.3% services, 21.0% sales, 1.5% farming, 12.1% construction, 22.3% production (2000).
Income: Per capita income: $23,424 (2000); Median household income: $45,150 (2000); Poverty rate: 3.1% (2000).

Taxes: Total city taxes per capita: $42 (1997); City property taxes per capita: $41 (1997).
Education: High school graduation rate: 87.6% (2000); College graduation rate: 15.8% (2000).
Housing: Homeownership rate: 92.2% (2000); Median home value: $139,800 (2000); Median rent: $523 per month (2000); Median age of housing: 32 years (2000).
Transportation: Commute to work: 92.9% car, 0.0% public transportation, 1.2% walk, 5.5% work from home (2000); Travel time to work: 26.1% less than 15 minutes, 28.0% 15 to 30 minutes, 25.1% 30 to 45 minutes, 13.4% 45 to 60 minutes, 7.4% 60 minutes or more (2000)

Crawford County

Located in southwestern Wisconsin; bounded on the west by the Mississippi River and the Iowa border, and on the south by the Wisconsin River; drained by the Kickapoo River. Covers a land area of 572.70 square miles, a water area of 26.50 square miles, and is located in the Central Time Zone. The county government was organized in 1818. County seat is Prairie du Chien.

Weather Station: Lynxville Dam 9 — Elevation: 629 feet

	Jan	Feb	Mar	Apr	May	Jun	Jul	Aug	Sep	Oct	Nov	Dec
High	26	32	44	59	72	80	84	81	73	61	44	31
Low	8	14	26	38	50	59	64	62	54	42	29	16
Precip	1.0	1.0	1.9	3.6	3.8	4.0	4.0	4.3	3.1	2.3	2.3	1.2
Snow	10.2	7.0	4.3	1.2	0.0	0.0	0.0	0.0	0.0	tr	3.7	7.7

High and Low temperatures in degrees Fahrenheit; Precipitation and Snow in inches

Weather Station: Prairie Du Chien — Elevation: 656 feet

	Jan	Feb	Mar	Apr	May	Jun	Jul	Aug	Sep	Oct	Nov	Dec
High	27	34	46	61	73	82	86	83	75	63	46	33
Low	8	15	26	37	49	58	62	61	52	41	28	16
Precip	1.0	1.2	2.0	3.6	3.9	4.2	3.7	4.6	3.2	2.4	2.3	1.3
Snow	13.1	8.0	4.8	1.8	0.0	0.0	0.0	0.0	0.0	0.2	3.5	8.8

High and Low temperatures in degrees Fahrenheit; Precipitation and Snow in inches

Population: 17,243 (2000); Race: 97.1% White, 1.5% Black, 0.3% Asian, 0.4% American Indian and Alaska Native, 0.4% Hispanic of any race, 0.6% two or more races (2000); Density: 30.1 persons per square mile (2000); Age: 26.2% under 18, 15.9% over 64 (2000).
Religion: Five largest groups: 34.1% Catholic Church, 12.7% Evangelical Lutheran Church in America, 4.7% The United Methodist Church, 1.2% Christian Churches and Churches of Christ, 1.0% The Evangelical Free Church of America (2000).
Economy: Unemployment rate: 3.7% (11/2002); Total civilian labor force: 10,739 (11/2002); Leading industries: 35.0% manufacturing; 21.6% retail trade; 17.3% health care and social assistance (2000); Companies that employ more than 1,000 persons: 0 (2000); Companies that employ more than 100 persons: 16 (2000); Farms: 958 totaling 233,481 acres (1997); Minority business ownership rate: 0.0% (1997); Women business ownership rate: 20.0% (1997); Retail sales per capita: $8,086 (1997). Single-family building permits issued: 45 (2001) / 51 (2000); Multi-family building permits issued: 2 (2001) / 6 (2000).
Income: Per capita income: $16,833 (2000); Median household income: $34,135 (2000); Poverty rate: 10.2% (2000); Bankruptcy rate: 3.66% (2001).
Taxes: Total county taxes per capita: $225 (1997); County property taxes per capita: $172 (1997).
Education: High school graduation rate: 81.3% (2000); College graduation rate: 13.2% (2000).
Housing: Homeownership rate: 76.9% (2000); Median home value: $75,100 (2000); Median rent: $325 per month (2000); Median age of housing: 31 years (2000).
Health: Birth rate: 119.5 per 10,000 population (1998); Age adjusted death rate: 92.9 per 10,000 population (1999); Age adjusted cancer mortality rate: 199.1 deaths per 100,000 population (1999). Number of physicians: 8.7 per 10,000 population (1999); Number of hospital beds: 24.9 per 10,000 population (1999).
Elections: 2000 Presidential election results: 54.2% Gore, 40.9% Bush, 4.2% Nader, 0.4% Buchanan
National and State Parks: Kickapoo River State Wildlife Area; Mount Hope Pond State Wildlife Area
Additional Information Contacts
Crawford County Government Offices 608-326-0200
Prairie Du Chien Chamber of Commerce 608-326-8555

Crawford County Communities

BELL CENTER (village). Covers a land area of 5.527 square miles and a water area of 0.039 square miles. Located at 43.29° N. Lat.; 90.83° W. Long. Elevation is 720 feet.
Population: 116 (2000); Race: 100.0% White, 0.0% Black, 0.0% Asian, 0.0% American Indian and Alaska Native, 0.0% Hispanic of any race, 0.0% two or more races (2000); Density: 21.0 persons per square mile (2000); Age: 29.1% under 18, 11.8% over 64 (2000); Marriage status: 20.8% never married, 73.3% now married, 2.0% widowed, 4.0% divorced (2000); Foreign born: 0.0% (2000); Ancestry (includes multiple ancestries): 29.1% German, 21.3% Norwegian, 12.6% English, 8.7% Scottish, 7.9% Irish (2000).
Economy: Stock raising; dairying. Hunting. Snow Bowl Ski Area nearby. Employment by occupation: 13.6% management, 16.9% professional, 8.5% services, 8.5% sales, 6.8% farming, 13.6% construction, 32.2% production (2000).
Income: Per capita income: $23,177 (2000); Median household income: $39,167 (2000); Poverty rate: 19.7% (2000).
Taxes: Total city taxes per capita: $8 (1997); City property taxes per capita: $8 (1997).
Education: High school graduation rate: 72.0% (2000); College graduation rate: 18.3% (2000).
Housing: Homeownership rate: 80.5% (2000); Median home value: $55,000 (2000); Median rent: $408 per month (2000); Median age of housing: 26 years (2000).
Transportation: Commute to work: 96.6% car, 0.0% public transportation, 0.0% walk, 0.0% work from home (2000); Travel time to work: 11.9% less than 15 minutes, 16.9% 15 to 30 minutes, 44.1% 30 to 45 minutes, 13.6% 45 to 60 minutes, 13.6% 60 minutes or more (2000)

BRIDGEPORT (town). Covers a land area of 20.342 square miles and a water area of 2.975 square miles. Located at 43.01° N. Lat.; 91.10° W. Long. Elevation is 768 feet.
Population: 946 (2000); Race: 98.8% White, 0.0% Black, 0.2% Asian, 0.9% American Indian and Alaska Native, 0.1% Hispanic of any race, 0.1% two or more races (2000); Density: 46.5 persons per square mile (2000); Age: 31.5% under 18, 10.1% over 64 (2000); Marriage status: 15.9% never married, 69.5% now married, 7.5% widowed, 7.2% divorced (2000); Foreign born: 0.5% (2000); Ancestry (includes multiple ancestries): 44.8% German, 12.4% Norwegian, 11.2% Irish, 10.8% English, 9.5% Czech (2000).
Economy: Single-family building permits issued: 7 (2001) / 8 (2000); Multi-family building permits issued: 0 (2001) / 0 (2000); Employment by occupation: 12.1% management, 13.7% professional, 14.5% services, 27.1% sales, 1.1% farming, 12.3% construction, 19.2% production (2000).
Income: Per capita income: $21,854 (2000); Median household income: $45,313 (2000); Poverty rate: 3.1% (2000).
Taxes: Total city taxes per capita: $64 (1997); City property taxes per capita: $45 (1997).
Education: High school graduation rate: 91.9% (2000); College graduation rate: 15.1% (2000).
Housing: Homeownership rate: 91.5% (2000); Median home value: $121,500 (2000); Median rent: $375 per month (2000); Median age of housing: 20 years (2000).
Transportation: Commute to work: 93.3% car, 0.0% public transportation, 0.4% walk, 6.2% work from home (2000); Travel time to work: 57.7% less than 15 minutes, 29.7% 15 to 30 minutes, 5.2% 30 to 45 minutes, 1.0% 45 to 60 minutes, 6.4% 60 minutes or more (2000)

CLAYTON (town). Covers a land area of 69.224 square miles and a water area of 0 square miles. Located at 43.37° N. Lat.; 90.74° W. Long.
Population: 956 (2000); Race: 97.5% White, 0.2% Black, 0.0% Asian, 0.8% American Indian and Alaska Native, 2.3% Hispanic of any race, 1.0% two or more races (2000); Density: 13.8 persons per square mile (2000); Age: 25.9% under 18, 14.3% over 64 (2000); Marriage status: 22.3% never married, 61.9% now married, 5.8% widowed, 9.9% divorced (2000); Foreign born: 0.5% (2000); Ancestry (includes multiple ancestries): 38.2% German, 21.7% Irish, 18.4% Norwegian, 9.3% English, 4.5% Dutch (2000).
Economy: Employment by occupation: 12.3% management, 12.8% professional, 13.5% services, 16.9% sales, 5.9% farming, 11.2% construction, 27.4% production (2000).
Income: Per capita income: $13,786 (2000); Median household income: $30,433 (2000); Poverty rate: 18.1% (2000).
Taxes: Total city taxes per capita: $156 (1997); City property taxes per capita: $155 (1997).

Education: High school graduation rate: 82.5% (2000); College graduation rate: 13.2% (2000).
Housing: Homeownership rate: 82.1% (2000); Median home value: $57,100 (2000); Median rent: $283 per month (2000); Median age of housing: 31 years (2000).
Transportation: Commute to work: 78.3% car, 0.0% public transportation, 5.1% walk, 15.9% work from home (2000); Travel time to work: 28.0% less than 15 minutes, 37.4% 15 to 30 minutes, 18.8% 30 to 45 minutes, 8.6% 45 to 60 minutes, 7.2% 60 minutes or more (2000)

EASTMAN (village). Covers a land area of 3.577 square miles and a water area of 0 square miles. Located at 43.16° N. Lat.; 91.01° W. Long. Elevation is 1,224 feet.
Population: 437 (2000); Race: 96.7% White, 0.0% Black, 0.9% Asian, 0.0% American Indian and Alaska Native, 2.3% Hispanic of any race, 0.0% two or more races (2000); Density: 122.2 persons per square mile (2000); Age: 31.8% under 18, 14.7% over 64 (2000); Marriage status: 25.9% never married, 61.2% now married, 8.5% widowed, 4.4% divorced (2000); Foreign born: 0.9% (2000); Ancestry (includes multiple ancestries): 38.1% German, 16.6% Czech, 14.5% Irish, 8.4% Norwegian, 6.3% French (except Basque) (2000).
Economy: Employment by occupation: 7.3% management, 6.3% professional, 16.6% services, 20.5% sales, 2.0% farming, 14.1% construction, 33.2% production (2000).
Income: Per capita income: $12,922 (2000); Median household income: $32,321 (2000); Poverty rate: 10.7% (2000).
Taxes: Total city taxes per capita: $50 (1997); City property taxes per capita: $48 (1997).
Education: High school graduation rate: 77.4% (2000); College graduation rate: 11.3% (2000).
Housing: Homeownership rate: 81.5% (2000); Median home value: $66,300 (2000); Median rent: $280 per month (2000); Median age of housing: 52 years (2000).
Transportation: Commute to work: 84.6% car, 0.0% public transportation, 7.0% walk, 8.5% work from home (2000); Travel time to work: 17.4% less than 15 minutes, 70.1% 15 to 30 minutes, 2.2% 30 to 45 minutes, 3.3% 45 to 60 minutes, 7.1% 60 minutes or more (2000)

EASTMAN (town). Covers a land area of 71.459 square miles and a water area of 1.143 square miles. Located at 43.15° N. Lat.; 90.99° W. Long. Elevation is 1,224 feet.
Population: 790 (2000); Race: 99.6% White, 0.0% Black, 0.0% Asian, 0.4% American Indian and Alaska Native, 0.5% Hispanic of any race, 0.0% two or more races (2000); Density: 11.1 persons per square mile (2000); Age: 28.1% under 18, 11.5% over 64 (2000); Marriage status: 23.7% never married, 62.4% now married, 4.4% widowed, 9.5% divorced (2000); Foreign born: 0.4% (2000); Ancestry (includes multiple ancestries): 41.3% German, 16.0% Czech, 11.4% Norwegian, 9.5% Irish, 8.1% United States or American (2000).
Economy: In livestock and dairy area. Employment by occupation: 16.2% management, 8.8% professional, 10.5% services, 20.0% sales, 4.3% farming, 7.8% construction, 32.5% production (2000).
Income: Per capita income: $16,317 (2000); Median household income: $38,750 (2000); Poverty rate: 10.0% (2000).
Taxes: Total city taxes per capita: $190 (1997); City property taxes per capita: $188 (1997).
Education: High school graduation rate: 85.8% (2000); College graduation rate: 10.9% (2000).
Housing: Homeownership rate: 88.6% (2000); Median home value: $82,700 (2000); Median rent: $400 per month (2000); Median age of housing: 30 years (2000).
Transportation: Commute to work: 78.3% car, 1.9% public transportation, 3.6% walk, 15.8% work from home (2000); Travel time to work: 16.4% less than 15 minutes, 51.0% 15 to 30 minutes, 16.7% 30 to 45 minutes, 5.4% 45 to 60 minutes, 10.5% 60 minutes or more (2000)

FERRYVILLE (village). Covers a land area of 2.466 square miles and a water area of 0 square miles. Located at 43.34° N. Lat.; 91.08° W. Long. Elevation is 634 feet.
Population: 174 (2000); Race: 97.8% White, 0.0% Black, 0.0% Asian, 0.0% American Indian and Alaska Native, 0.0% Hispanic of any race, 2.2% two or more races (2000); Density: 70.5 persons per square mile (2000); Age: 16.3% under 18, 23.6% over 64 (2000); Marriage status: 9.9% never married, 68.9% now married, 15.2% widowed, 6.0% divorced (2000); Foreign born: 0.0% (2000); Ancestry (includes multiple ancestries): 33.7% German, 31.5% Norwegian, 15.2% Irish, 8.4% English, 6.7% Other groups (2000).
Economy: In livestock and dairy area; cheese. Single-family building permits issued: 5 (2001) / 2 (2000); Multi-family building permits issued: 0 (2001) / 0 (2000); Employment by occupation: 26.7% management, 9.3% professional, 16.3% services, 25.6% sales, 0.0% farming, 5.8% construction, 16.3% production (2000).
Income: Per capita income: $20,602 (2000); Median household income: $33,958 (2000); Poverty rate: 4.5% (2000).
Taxes: Total city taxes per capita: $164 (1997); City property taxes per capita: $147 (1997).
Education: High school graduation rate: 77.2% (2000); College graduation rate: 10.3% (2000).
Housing: Homeownership rate: 80.6% (2000); Median home value: $67,500 (2000); Median rent: $194 per month (2000); Median age of housing: 24 years (2000).
Transportation: Commute to work: 71.6% car, 0.0% public transportation, 12.3% walk, 16.0% work from home (2000); Travel time to work: 33.8% less than 15 minutes, 14.7% 15 to 30 minutes, 11.8% 30 to 45 minutes, 27.9% 45 to 60 minutes, 11.8% 60 minutes or more (2000)

FREEMAN (town). Covers a land area of 68.193 square miles and a water area of 9.505 square miles. Located at 43.36° N. Lat.; 91.06° W. Long.
Population: 719 (2000); Race: 97.0% White, 0.7% Black, 0.3% Asian, 0.9% American Indian and Alaska Native, 0.0% Hispanic of any race, 1.1% two or more races (2000); Density: 10.5 persons per square mile (2000); Age: 26.4% under 18, 17.0% over 64 (2000); Marriage status: 22.0% never married, 63.5% now married, 9.0% widowed, 5.5% divorced (2000); Foreign born: 1.5% (2000); Ancestry (includes multiple ancestries): 35.1% Norwegian, 24.5% German, 9.2% English, 8.7% Irish, 3.2% Other groups (2000).
Economy: Single-family building permits issued: 0 (2001) / 6 (2000); Multi-family building permits issued: 0 (2001) / 0 (2000); Employment by occupation: 21.9% management, 9.9% professional, 8.5% services, 25.4% sales, 3.8% farming, 6.7% construction, 23.7% production (2000).
Income: Per capita income: $16,609 (2000); Median household income: $30,500 (2000); Poverty rate: 16.3% (2000).
Taxes: Total city taxes per capita: $174 (2000); City property taxes per capita: $172 (2000).
Education: High school graduation rate: 74.0% (2000); College graduation rate: 12.9% (2000).
Housing: Homeownership rate: 82.0% (2000); Median home value: $74,000 (2000); Median rent: $281 per month (2000); Median age of housing: 30 years (2000).
Transportation: Commute to work: 77.5% car, 0.0% public transportation, 3.2% walk, 18.1% work from home (2000); Travel time to work: 21.1% less than 15 minutes, 24.6% 15 to 30 minutes, 24.6% 30 to 45 minutes, 16.8% 45 to 60 minutes, 12.9% 60 minutes or more (2000)

GAYS MILLS (village). Covers a land area of 4.597 square miles and a water area of 0.026 square miles. Located at 43.31° N. Lat.; 90.84° W. Long. Elevation is 700 feet.
History: Gays Mills was named for John Gay who settled here in 1848. The area became the center of the Kickapoo apple region.
Population: 625 (2000); Race: 98.9% White, 0.0% Black, 0.6% Asian, 0.0% American Indian and Alaska Native, 0.2% Hispanic of any race, 0.5% two or more races (2000); Density: 136.0 persons per square mile (2000); Age: 26.7% under 18, 19.6% over 64 (2000); Marriage status: 21.7% never married, 56.8% now married, 9.7% widowed, 11.8% divorced (2000); Foreign born: 1.8% (2000); Ancestry (includes multiple ancestries): 27.6% German, 23.3% Norwegian, 21.1% Irish, 10.7% English, 4.5% United States or American (2000).
Economy: Single-family building permits issued: 3 (2001) / 1 (2000); Multi-family building permits issued: 0 (2001) / 0 (2000); Employment by occupation: 12.5% management, 15.7% professional, 16.9% services, 20.8% sales, 0.8% farming, 8.2% construction, 25.1% production (2000).
Income: Per capita income: $17,786 (2000); Median household income: $29,250 (2000); Poverty rate: 15.8% (2000).
Taxes: Total city taxes per capita: $134 (1997); City property taxes per capita: $127 (1997).
Education: High school graduation rate: 87.0% (2000); College graduation rate: 13.7% (2000).

School District(s)

North Crawford (PK-12)
2000 Enrollment: 652 608-735-4318
Housing: Homeownership rate: 74.9% (2000); Median home value: $61,600 (2000); Median rent: $258 per month (2000); Median age of housing: 45 years (2000).
Newspapers: Crawford County Independent & Kickapoo Scout (1 x week)

Transportation: Commute to work: 83.7% car, 0.0% public transportation, 11.6% walk, 4.8% work from home (2000); Travel time to work: 36.4% less than 15 minutes, 16.7% 15 to 30 minutes, 26.4% 30 to 45 minutes, 10.0% 45 to 60 minutes, 10.5% 60 minutes or more (2000)

HANEY (town). Covers a land area of 32.678 square miles and a water area of 0.011 square miles. Located at 43.25° N. Lat.; 90.83° W. Long.
Population: 330 (2000); Race: 99.3% White, 0.0% Black, 0.0% Asian, 0.0% American Indian and Alaska Native, 0.7% Hispanic of any race, 0.0% two or more races (2000); Density: 10.1 persons per square mile (2000); Age: 24.4% under 18, 19.7% over 64 (2000); Marriage status: 17.7% never married, 64.6% now married, 9.7% widowed, 8.0% divorced (2000); Foreign born: 0.7% (2000); Ancestry (includes multiple ancestries): 36.3% German, 15.9% Norwegian, 12.9% United States or American, 11.5% Irish, 10.5% English (2000).
Economy: Single-family building permits issued: 4 (2001) / 1 (2000); Multi-family building permits issued: 0 (2001) / 0 (2000); Employment by occupation: 24.2% management, 5.9% professional, 16.3% services, 22.2% sales, 9.2% farming, 6.5% construction, 15.7% production (2000).
Income: Per capita income: $14,877 (2000); Median household income: $29,306 (2000); Poverty rate: 14.1% (2000).
Taxes: Total city taxes per capita: $129 (1997); City property taxes per capita: $127 (1997).
Education: High school graduation rate: 82.5% (2000); College graduation rate: 15.1% (2000).
Housing: Homeownership rate: 79.3% (2000); Median home value: $60,000 (2000); Median rent: $219 per month (2000); Median age of housing: 46 years (2000).
Transportation: Commute to work: 71.2% car, 0.0% public transportation, 9.8% walk, 19.0% work from home (2000); Travel time to work: 29.8% less than 15 minutes, 27.4% 15 to 30 minutes, 20.2% 30 to 45 minutes, 16.9% 45 to 60 minutes, 5.6% 60 minutes or more (2000)

LYNXVILLE (village). Covers a land area of 1.386 square miles and a water area of 0 square miles. Located at 43.24° N. Lat.; 91.05° W. Long. Elevation is 638 feet.
Population: 176 (2000); Race: 100.0% White, 0.0% Black, 0.0% Asian, 0.0% American Indian and Alaska Native, 0.0% Hispanic of any race, 0.0% two or more races (2000); Density: 127.0 persons per square mile (2000); Age: 13.3% under 18, 12.7% over 64 (2000); Marriage status: 25.9% never married, 51.0% now married, 4.1% widowed, 19.0% divorced (2000); Foreign born: 0.0% (2000); Ancestry (includes multiple ancestries): 48.5% German, 15.2% Irish, 10.9% French (except Basque), 10.3% Norwegian, 10.3% English (2000).
Economy: A U.S. fish hatchery is here. Lock and Dam No. 9 to South. Employment by occupation: 13.5% management, 4.1% professional, 18.9% services, 9.5% sales, 4.1% farming, 5.4% construction, 44.6% production (2000).
Income: Per capita income: $14,979 (2000); Median household income: $30,833 (2000); Poverty rate: 6.7% (2000).
Taxes: Total city taxes per capita: $149 (1997); City property taxes per capita: $143 (1997).
Education: High school graduation rate: 85.6% (2000); College graduation rate: 9.1% (2000).
Housing: Homeownership rate: 95.6% (2000); Median home value: $38,800 (2000); Median rent: $325 per month (2000); Median age of housing: 32 years (2000).
Transportation: Commute to work: 87.1% car, 0.0% public transportation, 10.0% walk, 2.9% work from home (2000); Travel time to work: 14.7% less than 15 minutes, 45.6% 15 to 30 minutes, 27.9% 30 to 45 minutes, 2.9% 45 to 60 minutes, 8.8% 60 minutes or more (2000)

MARIETTA (town). Covers a land area of 47.016 square miles and a water area of 1.026 square miles. Located at 43.15° N. Lat.; 90.78° W. Long.
Population: 510 (2000); Race: 99.0% White, 0.0% Black, 0.0% Asian, 0.0% American Indian and Alaska Native, 0.0% Hispanic of any race, 0.6% two or more races (2000); Density: 10.8 persons per square mile (2000); Age: 32.0% under 18, 13.6% over 64 (2000); Marriage status: 24.4% never married, 56.4% now married, 6.7% widowed, 12.5% divorced (2000); Foreign born: 0.4% (2000); Ancestry (includes multiple ancestries): 41.2% German, 23.8% Irish, 11.5% English, 9.8% Norwegian, 4.8% Other groups (2000).
Economy: Single-family building permits issued: 1 (2001) / 1 (2000); Multi-family building permits issued: 0 (2001) / 0 (2000); Employment by occupation: 20.4% management, 9.6% professional, 15.2% services, 16.5% sales, 3.9% farming, 14.8% construction, 19.6% production (2000).
Income: Per capita income: $14,341 (2000); Median household income: $33,906 (2000); Poverty rate: 10.5% (2000).
Taxes: Total city taxes per capita: $135 (1997); City property taxes per capita: $135 (1997).
Education: High school graduation rate: 77.4% (2000); College graduation rate: 13.6% (2000).
Housing: Homeownership rate: 82.4% (2000); Median home value: $61,300 (2000); Median rent: $358 per month (2000); Median age of housing: 26 years (2000).
Transportation: Commute to work: 73.9% car, 0.0% public transportation, 6.5% walk, 19.6% work from home (2000); Travel time to work: 42.2% less than 15 minutes, 23.2% 15 to 30 minutes, 11.4% 30 to 45 minutes, 8.6% 45 to 60 minutes, 14.6% 60 minutes or more (2000)

MOUNT STERLING (village). Covers a land area of 1.418 square miles and a water area of 0 square miles. Located at 43.31° N. Lat.; 90.92° W. Long. Elevation is 1,180 feet.
Population: 215 (2000); Race: 100.0% White, 0.0% Black, 0.0% Asian, 0.0% American Indian and Alaska Native, 0.0% Hispanic of any race, 0.0% two or more races (2000); Density: 151.6 persons per square mile (2000); Age: 22.1% under 18, 24.7% over 64 (2000); Marriage status: 25.0% never married, 57.7% now married, 14.1% widowed, 3.2% divorced (2000); Foreign born: 4.7% (2000); Ancestry (includes multiple ancestries): 51.6% Norwegian, 24.7% German, 11.1% Irish, 9.5% Czech, 5.3% French (except Basque) (2000).
Economy: Hog-raising and dairying area. Goat cheese and milk. Quarry here. Employment by occupation: 7.7% management, 2.6% professional, 9.0% services, 16.7% sales, 2.6% farming, 20.5% construction, 41.0% production (2000).
Income: Per capita income: $13,891 (2000); Median household income: $29,375 (2000); Poverty rate: 11.1% (2000).
Taxes: Total city taxes per capita: $50 (1997); City property taxes per capita: $50 (1997).
Education: High school graduation rate: 80.7% (2000); College graduation rate: 9.3% (2000).
Housing: Homeownership rate: 74.7% (2000); Median home value: $53,000 (2000); Median rent: $240 per month (2000); Median age of housing: 55 years (2000).
Transportation: Commute to work: 97.4% car, 0.0% public transportation, 0.0% walk, 0.0% work from home (2000); Travel time to work: 30.3% less than 15 minutes, 25.0% 15 to 30 minutes, 30.3% 30 to 45 minutes, 9.2% 45 to 60 minutes, 5.3% 60 minutes or more (2000)

PRAIRIE DU CHIEN (city). Covers a land area of 5.594 square miles and a water area of 0.747 square miles. Located at 43.04° N. Lat.; 91.14° W. Long. Elevation is 632 feet.
History: Prairie du Chien was established near the confluence of the Mississippi and Wisconsin Rivers, with the first settlement occurring on St. Friol Island in the Mississippi River. This was a gathering place for traders and trappers in the 1600's and 1700's. The first land claims were filed in 1781 by three French Canadians, and the American Fur Company began operations here in 1817. Fort Shelby and Fort Crawford were erected in 1814 and 1816 to insure American possession of Prairie du Chien. Colonel Zachary Taylor was in command of Fort Crawford in 1829, with Lieutenant Jefferson Davis as one of his assistants.
Population: 6,018 (2000); Race: 94.2% White, 4.0% Black, 0.5% Asian, 0.4% American Indian and Alaska Native, 0.0% Hispanic of any race, 0.9% two or more races (2000); Density: 1,075.9 persons per square mile (2000); Age: 23.7% under 18, 18.5% over 64 (2000); Marriage status: 21.8% never married, 58.4% now married, 10.0% widowed, 9.8% divorced (2000); Foreign born: 0.8% (2000); Ancestry (includes multiple ancestries): 34.5% German, 17.2% Irish, 9.3% Norwegian, 9.1% Czech, 8.0% English (2000).
Economy: Single-family building permits issued: 7 (2001) / 8 (2000); Multi-family building permits issued: 2 (2001) / 6 (2000); Employment by occupation: 5.7% management, 12.5% professional, 24.5% services, 25.2% sales, 0.6% farming, 8.0% construction, 23.5% production (2000).
Income: Per capita income: $17,680 (2000); Median household income: $34,038 (2000); Poverty rate: 8.1% (2000).
Taxes: Total city taxes per capita: $286 (2000); City property taxes per capita: $263 (2000).
Education: High school graduation rate: 81.4% (2000); College graduation rate: 14.6% (2000).

School District(s)

Prairie Du Chien Area (PK-12)
2000 Enrollment: 1,269 608-326-8437

Housing: Homeownership rate: 67.4% (2000); Median home value: $80,500 (2000); Median rent: $353 per month (2000); Median age of housing: 38 years (2000).
Hospitals: Prairie du Chien Memorial Hospital (43 beds)
Newspapers: Courier Press (2 x week)
Transportation: Commute to work: 88.1% car, 1.0% public transportation, 4.6% walk, 4.4% work from home (2000); Travel time to work: 81.8% less than 15 minutes, 10.4% 15 to 30 minutes, 3.2% 30 to 45 minutes, 2.1% 45 to 60 minutes, 2.5% 60 minutes or more (2000)
Additional Information Contacts
Prairie Du Chien Chamber of Commerce 608-326-8555

PRAIRIE DU CHIEN (town). Covers a land area of 33.561 square miles and a water area of 2.768 square miles. Located at 43.07° N. Lat.; 91.10° W. Long. Elevation is 632 feet.
History: City's strategic site on Fox-Wisconsin river route to the Mississippi made it a meeting point for explorers, missionaries, and traders in late 17th cent; Nicolas Perrot erected Fort St. Nicolas here in 1686; French settlers came c.1781, and an American Fur Co. trading post was built here before 1812. In War of 1812, Americans built Fort Shelby (1814), renamed Fort McKay soon after. Fort Crawford (1816; abandoned 1856) was scene of medical (surgery) experiments by Dr. William Beaumont. Inc. 1872.
Population: 1,076 (2000); Race: 98.5% White, 0.2% Black, 0.0% Asian, 0.7% American Indian and Alaska Native, 0.3% Hispanic of any race, 0.7% two or more races (2000); Density: 32.1 persons per square mile (2000); Age: 26.1% under 18, 14.2% over 64 (2000); Marriage status: 22.2% never married, 60.5% now married, 6.0% widowed, 11.3% divorced (2000); Foreign born: 0.7% (2000); Ancestry (includes multiple ancestries): 39.2% German, 11.7% Irish, 10.9% English, 10.0% Norwegian, 9.5% Czech (2000).
Economy: Railroad junction in agricultural area: dairying, grain, farm trade center. Manufacturing of chemicals, electronic products, building materials and lumber. Single-family building permits issued: 5 (2001) / 3 (2000); Multi-family building permits issued: 0 (2001) / 0 (2000); Employment by occupation: 10.5% management, 11.6% professional, 16.7% services, 21.9% sales, 2.7% farming, 6.3% construction, 30.3% production (2000).
Income: Per capita income: $19,762 (2000); Median household income: $34,327 (2000); Poverty rate: 9.4% (2000).
Taxes: Total city taxes per capita: $103 (1997); City property taxes per capita: $84 (1997).
Education: High school graduation rate: 78.0% (2000); College graduation rate: 13.0% (2000).
Housing: Homeownership rate: 82.2% (2000); Median home value: $110,100 (2000); Median rent: $273 per month (2000); Median age of housing: 24 years (2000).
Transportation: Commute to work: 90.8% car, 0.7% public transportation, 1.3% walk, 4.8% work from home (2000); Travel time to work: 63.1% less than 15 minutes, 27.5% 15 to 30 minutes, 4.2% 30 to 45 minutes, 1.9% 45 to 60 minutes, 3.3% 60 minutes or more (2000)

SCOTT (town). Covers a land area of 35.671 square miles and a water area of 0 square miles. Located at 43.25° N. Lat.; 90.71° W. Long.
Population: 503 (2000); Race: 99.2% White, 0.0% Black, 0.4% Asian, 0.0% American Indian and Alaska Native, 0.0% Hispanic of any race, 0.4% two or more races (2000); Density: 14.1 persons per square mile (2000); Age: 25.0% under 18, 7.2% over 64 (2000); Marriage status: 23.9% never married, 64.4% now married, 4.9% widowed, 6.8% divorced (2000); Foreign born: 1.2% (2000); Ancestry (includes multiple ancestries): 37.7% German, 20.8% Irish, 16.7% English, 9.7% Norwegian, 6.8% United States or American (2000).
Economy: Employment by occupation: 15.6% management, 20.0% professional, 12.6% services, 9.3% sales, 3.3% farming, 8.9% construction, 30.4% production (2000).
Income: Per capita income: $15,804 (2000); Median household income: $41,979 (2000); Poverty rate: 8.8% (2000).
Taxes: Total city taxes per capita: $95 (1997); City property taxes per capita: $93 (1997).
Education: High school graduation rate: 84.2% (2000); College graduation rate: 17.3% (2000).
Housing: Homeownership rate: 90.8% (2000); Median home value: $80,000 (2000); Median rent: $325 per month (2000); Median age of housing: 25 years (2000).
Transportation: Commute to work: 80.4% car, 0.0% public transportation, 4.9% walk, 14.7% work from home (2000); Travel time to work: 17.7% less than 15 minutes, 50.4% 15 to 30 minutes, 15.9% 30 to 45 minutes, 5.8% 45 to 60 minutes, 10.2% 60 minutes or more (2000)

SENECA (town). Covers a land area of 58.615 square miles and a water area of 6.902 square miles. Located at 43.25° N. Lat.; 91.00° W. Long. Elevation is 1,260 feet.
Population: 893 (2000); Race: 98.2% White, 0.0% Black, 0.0% Asian, 0.2% American Indian and Alaska Native, 1.4% Hispanic of any race, 0.5% two or more races (2000); Density: 15.2 persons per square mile (2000); Age: 27.9% under 18, 14.8% over 64 (2000); Marriage status: 23.3% never married, 62.8% now married, 6.8% widowed, 7.1% divorced (2000); Foreign born: 0.2% (2000); Ancestry (includes multiple ancestries): 33.3% German, 19.1% Norwegian, 14.7% Irish, 10.7% English, 7.0% Czech (2000).
Economy: Single-family building permits issued: 6 (2001) / 15 (2000); Multi-family building permits issued: 0 (2001) / 0 (2000); Employment by occupation: 15.8% management, 11.1% professional, 17.9% services, 16.9% sales, 5.8% farming, 10.2% construction, 22.3% production (2000).
Income: Per capita income: $16,434 (2000); Median household income: $35,227 (2000); Poverty rate: 6.7% (2000).
Taxes: Total city taxes per capita: $161 (1997); City property taxes per capita: $159 (1997).
Education: High school graduation rate: 78.7% (2000); College graduation rate: 13.3% (2000).

School District(s)

Seneca (PK-12)
2000 Enrollment: 372 608-734-3411
Housing: Homeownership rate: 88.7% (2000); Median home value: $64,100 (2000); Median rent: $320 per month (2000); Median age of housing: 24 years (2000).
Transportation: Commute to work: 73.0% car, 0.5% public transportation, 11.8% walk, 14.7% work from home (2000); Travel time to work: 31.3% less than 15 minutes, 31.0% 15 to 30 minutes, 23.5% 30 to 45 minutes, 5.3% 45 to 60 minutes, 8.9% 60 minutes or more (2000)

SOLDIERS GROVE (village). Covers a land area of 3.561 square miles and a water area of 0 square miles. Located at 43.39° N. Lat.; 90.77° W. Long. Elevation is 740 feet.
History: First called Pine Grove, the name was changed to Soldiers Grove during the Civil War when soldiers camped near the site.
Population: 653 (2000); Race: 98.7% White, 0.0% Black, 0.0% Asian, 0.6% American Indian and Alaska Native, 0.5% Hispanic of any race, 0.6% two or more races (2000); Density: 183.4 persons per square mile (2000); Age: 23.3% under 18, 29.3% over 64 (2000); Marriage status: 14.3% never married, 57.4% now married, 15.6% widowed, 12.7% divorced (2000); Foreign born: 0.0% (2000); Ancestry (includes multiple ancestries): 40.1% Norwegian, 21.7% German, 16.8% Irish, 13.5% English, 6.7% Other groups (2000).
Economy: Single-family building permits issued: 1 (2001) / 0 (2000); Multi-family building permits issued: 0 (2001) / 0 (2000); Employment by occupation: 6.8% management, 15.1% professional, 23.3% services, 15.8% sales, 2.5% farming, 6.1% construction, 30.5% production (2000).
Income: Per capita income: $13,779 (2000); Median household income: $30,078 (2000); Poverty rate: 11.3% (2000).
Taxes: Total city taxes per capita: $216 (1997); City property taxes per capita: $211 (1997).
Education: High school graduation rate: 73.8% (2000); College graduation rate: 11.1% (2000).
Housing: Homeownership rate: 70.6% (2000); Median home value: $45,600 (2000); Median rent: $223 per month (2000); Median age of housing: 43 years (2000).
Transportation: Commute to work: 94.9% car, 0.0% public transportation, 1.1% walk, 1.8% work from home (2000); Travel time to work: 38.7% less than 15 minutes, 21.2% 15 to 30 minutes, 20.1% 30 to 45 minutes, 13.4% 45 to 60 minutes, 6.7% 60 minutes or more (2000)

STEUBEN (village). Covers a land area of 6.192 square miles and a water area of 0 square miles. Located at 43.18° N. Lat.; 90.85° W. Long. Elevation is 675 feet.
Population: 177 (2000); Race: 100.0% White, 0.0% Black, 0.0% Asian, 0.0% American Indian and Alaska Native, 1.0% Hispanic of any race, 0.0% two or more races (2000); Density: 28.6 persons per square mile (2000); Age: 33.8% under 18, 12.1% over 64 (2000); Marriage status: 17.1% never married, 69.9% now married, 3.4% widowed, 9.6% divorced (2000); Foreign born: 0.0% (2000); Ancestry (includes multiple ancestries): 42.0% German, 20.8% Irish, 14.0% English, 10.6% Norwegian, 8.7% Polish (2000).
Economy: Single-family building permits issued: 0 (2001) / 0 (2000); Multi-family building permits issued: 0 (2001) / 0 (2000); Employment by

occupation: 11.3% management, 2.5% professional, 26.3% services, 1.3% sales, 3.8% farming, 20.0% construction, 35.0% production (2000).
Income: Per capita income: $11,657 (2000); Median household income: $41,250 (2000); Poverty rate: 7.2% (2000).
Taxes: Total city taxes per capita: $38 (1997); City property taxes per capita: $32 (1997).
Education: High school graduation rate: 81.1% (2000); College graduation rate: 4.1% (2000).
Housing: Homeownership rate: 79.1% (2000); Median home value: $35,000 (2000); Median rent: $275 per month (2000); Median age of housing: 56 years (2000).
Transportation: Commute to work: 97.2% car, 0.0% public transportation, 0.0% walk, 2.8% work from home (2000); Travel time to work: 13.0% less than 15 minutes, 36.2% 15 to 30 minutes, 31.9% 30 to 45 minutes, 2.9% 45 to 60 minutes, 15.9% 60 minutes or more (2000)

UTICA (town). Covers a land area of 54.105 square miles and a water area of 0 square miles. Located at 43.36° N. Lat.; 90.91° W. Long.
Population: 674 (2000); Race: 100.0% White, 0.0% Black, 0.0% Asian, 0.0% American Indian and Alaska Native, 0.0% Hispanic of any race, 0.0% two or more races (2000); Density: 12.5 persons per square mile (2000); Age: 27.7% under 18, 11.6% over 64 (2000); Marriage status: 27.4% never married, 60.5% now married, 3.1% widowed, 9.0% divorced (2000); Foreign born: 0.1% (2000); Ancestry (includes multiple ancestries): 35.7% Norwegian, 30.2% German, 15.5% Irish, 7.9% English, 3.9% European (2000).
Economy: Single-family building permits issued: 3 (2001) / 3 (2000); Multi-family building permits issued: 0 (2001) / 0 (2000); Employment by occupation: 20.8% management, 7.6% professional, 14.9% services, 21.1% sales, 8.1% farming, 9.2% construction, 18.4% production (2000).
Income: Per capita income: $12,177 (2000); Median household income: $30,000 (2000); Poverty rate: 19.2% (2000).
Taxes: Total city taxes per capita: $161 (1997); City property taxes per capita: $160 (1997).
Education: High school graduation rate: 80.7% (2000); College graduation rate: 12.7% (2000).
Housing: Homeownership rate: 76.8% (2000); Median home value: $66,000 (2000); Median rent: $275 per month (2000); Median age of housing: 60+ years (2000).
Transportation: Commute to work: 76.9% car, 0.0% public transportation, 2.7% walk, 19.0% work from home (2000); Travel time to work: 18.8% less than 15 minutes, 23.5% 15 to 30 minutes, 36.9% 30 to 45 minutes, 6.4% 45 to 60 minutes, 14.4% 60 minutes or more (2000)

WAUZEKA (village). Covers a land area of 4.951 square miles and a water area of 0 square miles. Located at 43.08° N. Lat.; 90.88° W. Long. Elevation is 657 feet.
History: Wauzeka was established at the confluence of the Kickapoo and Wisconsin Rivers. The village grew rapidly during the lumbering years, when it was a transportation center on the railroad, highway, and river. Later its economy was supported by the dairy industry and a wooden cheese box factory.
Population: 768 (2000); Race: 99.7% White, 0.0% Black, 0.0% Asian, 0.0% American Indian and Alaska Native, 1.3% Hispanic of any race, 0.3% two or more races (2000); Density: 155.1 persons per square mile (2000); Age: 34.4% under 18, 11.0% over 64 (2000); Marriage status: 32.5% never married, 53.7% now married, 5.4% widowed, 8.3% divorced (2000); Foreign born: 0.0% (2000); Ancestry (includes multiple ancestries): 42.2% German, 16.1% Irish, 11.6% Czech, 10.5% Norwegian, 8.7% English (2000).
Economy: Single-family building permits issued: 3 (2001) / 3 (2000); Multi-family building permits issued: 0 (2001) / 0 (2000); Employment by occupation: 9.3% management, 13.5% professional, 14.0% services, 16.0% sales, 2.3% farming, 11.8% construction, 33.3% production (2000).
Income: Per capita income: $16,115 (2000); Median household income: $40,556 (2000); Poverty rate: 11.4% (2000).
Taxes: Total city taxes per capita: $153 (1997); City property taxes per capita: $146 (1997).
Education: High school graduation rate: 82.7% (2000); College graduation rate: 7.4% (2000).

School District(s)

Wauzeka-Steuben (PK-12)
2000 Enrollment: 377 608-875-5311

Housing: Homeownership rate: 75.4% (2000); Median home value: $65,500 (2000); Median rent: $308 per month (2000); Median age of housing: 29 years (2000).
Transportation: Commute to work: 87.4% car, 0.5% public transportation, 8.8% walk, 2.8% work from home (2000); Travel time to work: 29.7% less than 15 minutes, 32.6% 15 to 30 minutes, 19.9% 30 to 45 minutes, 4.4% 45 to 60 minutes, 13.4% 60 minutes or more (2000)

WAUZEKA (town). Covers a land area of 42.255 square miles and a water area of 1.358 square miles. Located at 43.08° N. Lat.; 90.93° W. Long. Elevation is 657 feet.
History: Kickapoo Indian Caverns here.
Population: 369 (2000); Race: 100.0% White, 0.0% Black, 0.0% Asian, 0.0% American Indian and Alaska Native, 0.0% Hispanic of any race, 0.0% two or more races (2000); Density: 8.7 persons per square mile (2000); Age: 25.5% under 18, 10.2% over 64 (2000); Marriage status: 22.3% never married, 61.3% now married, 6.3% widowed, 10.0% divorced (2000); Foreign born: 1.9% (2000); Ancestry (includes multiple ancestries): 31.9% German, 18.4% Irish, 16.8% Czech, 15.9% United States or American, 8.2% English (2000).
Economy: Wood products. Employment by occupation: 28.4% management, 14.7% professional, 12.4% services, 8.7% sales, 3.7% farming, 8.7% construction, 23.4% production (2000).
Income: Per capita income: $18,360 (2000); Median household income: $33,750 (2000); Poverty rate: 6.7% (2000).
Taxes: Total city taxes per capita: $362 (1997); City property taxes per capita: $360 (1997).
Education: High school graduation rate: 83.7% (2000); College graduation rate: 11.8% (2000).
Housing: Homeownership rate: 81.7% (2000); Median home value: $86,700 (2000); Median rent: $300 per month (2000); Median age of housing: 37 years (2000).
Transportation: Commute to work: 71.0% car, 0.0% public transportation, 7.8% walk, 20.3% work from home (2000); Travel time to work: 26.6% less than 15 minutes, 41.6% 15 to 30 minutes, 13.3% 30 to 45 minutes, 5.8% 45 to 60 minutes, 12.7% 60 minutes or more (2000)

Dane County

Located in southern Wisconsin; bounded on the northwest by the Wisconsin River; drained by the Yahara and Sugar Rivers; includes the Four Lakes. Covers a land area of 1,201.90 square miles, a water area of 36.40 square miles, and is located in the Central Time Zone. The county government was organized in 1836. County seat is Madison.

Dane County is part of the Madison, WI MSA. The entire metro area includes: Dane County

Weather Station: Arboretum Univ. Wisconsin — Elevation: 862 feet

	Jan	Feb	Mar	Apr	May	Jun	Jul	Aug	Sep	Oct	Nov	Dec
High	27	32	44	57	70	80	84	82	74	62	45	32
Low	6	10	22	33	44	53	58	56	47	36	25	13
Precip	1.3	1.2	2.4	3.9	3.6	4.5	4.5	4.1	3.7	2.7	2.7	1.8
Snow	na	na	na	na	0.0	0.0	0.0	0.0	0.0	tr	na	na

High and Low temperatures in degrees Fahrenheit; Precipitation and Snow in inches

Weather Station: Charmany Farm — Elevation: 908 feet

	Jan	Feb	Mar	Apr	May	Jun	Jul	Aug	Sep	Oct	Nov	Dec
High	25	31	42	56	69	78	82	80	71	60	44	31
Low	7	13	23	35	46	56	60	58	50	38	26	14
Precip	1.1	1.1	2.2	3.6	3.4	4.3	4.1	3.9	3.5	2.5	2.3	1.3
Snow	11.2	6.7	5.0	1.5	tr	0.0	0.0	0.0	0.0	tr	2.3	8.6

High and Low temperatures in degrees Fahrenheit; Precipitation and Snow in inches

Weather Station: Madison Regional Airport — Elevation: 856 feet

	Jan	Feb	Mar	Apr	May	Jun	Jul	Aug	Sep	Oct	Nov	Dec
High	25	31	43	57	70	79	83	80	72	60	44	31
Low	8	13	24	35	45	55	60	58	49	38	27	15
Precip	1.2	1.2	2.3	3.3	3.1	3.8	3.9	4.2	3.3	2.2	2.3	1.7
Snow	12.8	8.3	7.2	3.4	0.1	tr	tr	tr	tr	0.4	4.4	12.0

High and Low temperatures in degrees Fahrenheit; Precipitation and Snow in inches

Population: 426,526 (2000); Race: 89.1% White, 3.9% Black, 3.4% Asian, 0.4% American Indian and Alaska Native, 3.4% Hispanic of any race, 1.8% two or more races (2000); Density: 354.9 persons per square mile (2000); Age: 22.4% under 18, 9.3% over 64 (2000).
Religion: Five largest groups: 27.9% Catholic Church, 11.6% Evangelical Lutheran Church in America, 2.0% The United Methodist Church, 1.3% United Church of Christ, 1.0% Independent, Non-Charismatic Churches (2000).

Economy: Unemployment rate: 2.3% (11/2002); Total civilian labor force: 282,759 (11/2002); Leading industries: 14.3% retail trade; 12.5% manufacturing; 11.4% health care and social assistance (2000); Companies that employ more than 1,000 persons: 11 (2000); Companies that employ more than 100 persons: 366 (2000); Farms: 2,595 totaling 512,971 acres (1997); Minority business ownership rate: 3.7% (1997); Women business ownership rate: 26.7% (1997); Retail sales per capita: $11,515 (1997). Single-family building permits issued: 2,317 (2001) / 1,992 (2000); Multi-family building permits issued: 2,508 (2001) / 1,994 (2000).
Income: Per capita income: $24,985 (2000); Median household income: $49,223 (2000); Poverty rate: 9.4% (2000); Bankruptcy rate: 3.14% (2001).
Taxes: Total county taxes per capita: $246 (2000); County property taxes per capita: $168 (2000).
Education: High school graduation rate: 92.2% (2000); College graduation rate: 40.6% (2000).
Housing: Homeownership rate: 57.6% (2000); Median home value: $146,900 (2000); Median rent: $595 per month (2000); Median age of housing: 28 years (2000).
Health: Birth rate: 120.3 per 10,000 population (1998); Age adjusted death rate: 73.9 per 10,000 population (1999); Infant mortality rate: 7.2 per 1,000 live births (1998); Age adjusted cancer mortality rate: 182.1 deaths per 100,000 population (1999). Air Quality Index: 81% good, 19% moderate, 0% unhealthy (percent of days in 2000). Number of physicians: 50.3 per 10,000 population (1999); Number of hospital beds: 35.4 per 10,000 population (1999).
Elections: 2000 Presidential election results: 61.2% Gore, 32.6% Bush, 5.6% Nader, 0.2% Buchanan
National and State Parks: Cherokee Marsh State Fishery Area; Deansville State Wildlife Area; Dorn Creek Marsh State Fishery Area; Goose Lake State Wildlife Area; Governor Nelson State Park; Lake Kegonsa State Park; Lodi Marsh State Wildlife Area; Mazomanie State Wildlife Area; Waunakee Marsh State Wildlife Management Area
Additional Information Contacts

Dane County Government Offices	608-266-4114
Cambridge Chamber of Commerce	608-423-3780
Cottage Grove Chamber of Commerce	608-839-3165
De Forest Chamber of Commerce	608-846-2922
Greater Madison Convention Bureau	608-255-2537
Madison Chamber of Commerce	608-256-8348
McFarland Chamber of Commerce	608-838-4011
Middleton Chamber of Commerce	608-831-5696
Mt Horeb Chamber of Commerce	608-437-5914
Oregon Chamber of Commerce	608-835-3697
Realtors Association of South Central Wisconsin	608-240-2800
Stoughton Chamber of Commerce	608-873-7912
Sun Prairie Chamber of Commerce	608-837-4547
Verona Chamber of Commerce	608-845-5777
Waunakee Chamber of Commerce	608-849-5977
Wisconsin Realtors Association	608-241-2047

Dane County Communities

ALBION (town). Covers a land area of 35.190 square miles and a water area of 0.616 square miles. Located at 42.88° N. Lat.; 89.05° W. Long. Elevation is 840 feet.
History: Albion was settled in 1841 by English and Norwegian families.
Population: 1,823 (2000); Race: 97.3% White, 0.2% Black, 0.7% Asian, 0.4% American Indian and Alaska Native, 0.6% Hispanic of any race, 1.4% two or more races (2000); Density: 51.8 persons per square mile (2000); Age: 22.1% under 18, 12.7% over 64 (2000); Marriage status: 22.8% never married, 61.6% now married, 6.3% widowed, 9.3% divorced (2000); Foreign born: 0.6% (2000); Ancestry (includes multiple ancestries): 34.1% German, 32.0% Norwegian, 11.2% Irish, 9.9% English, 6.5% Polish (2000).
Economy: Employment by occupation: 11.6% management, 13.6% professional, 15.7% services, 20.2% sales, 2.0% farming, 13.9% construction, 23.1% production (2000).
Income: Per capita income: $24,643 (2000); Median household income: $49,118 (2000); Poverty rate: 5.0% (2000).
Taxes: Total city taxes per capita: $79 (1997); City property taxes per capita: $73 (1997).
Education: High school graduation rate: 85.1% (2000); College graduation rate: 18.2% (2000).
Housing: Homeownership rate: 82.2% (2000); Median home value: $110,300 (2000); Median rent: $516 per month (2000); Median age of housing: 53 years (2000).
Transportation: Commute to work: 94.2% car, 0.0% public transportation, 1.3% walk, 3.7% work from home (2000); Travel time to work: 27.9% less than 15 minutes, 35.8% 15 to 30 minutes, 23.2% 30 to 45 minutes, 7.5% 45 to 60 minutes, 5.6% 60 minutes or more (2000)

BELLEVILLE (village). Covers a land area of 1.158 square miles and a water area of 0.160 square miles. Located at 42.86° N. Lat.; 89.53° W. Long. Elevation is 870 feet.
History: Belleville was named by John Frederick, an early settler, for his former home in Canada. Belleville is French for "beautiful city."
Population: 1,908 (2000); Race: 97.0% White, 0.2% Black, 0.0% Asian, 0.1% American Indian and Alaska Native, 2.7% Hispanic of any race, 2.0% two or more races (2000); Density: 1,648.2 persons per square mile (2000); Age: 28.1% under 18, 12.9% over 64 (2000); Marriage status: 21.0% never married, 62.3% now married, 7.7% widowed, 9.0% divorced (2000); Foreign born: 1.2% (2000); Ancestry (includes multiple ancestries): 39.7% German, 18.3% Norwegian, 15.6% Irish, 15.4% Swiss, 12.9% English (2000).
Economy: Single-family building permits issued: 7 (2001) / 4 (2000); Multi-family building permits issued: 2 (2001) / 30 (2000); Employment by occupation: 15.4% management, 15.1% professional, 12.0% services, 30.2% sales, 1.6% farming, 12.9% construction, 12.8% production (2000).
Income: Per capita income: $21,784 (2000); Median household income: $49,274 (2000); Poverty rate: 5.2% (2000).
Taxes: Total city taxes per capita: $314 (1997); City property taxes per capita: $288 (1997).
Education: High school graduation rate: 90.5% (2000); College graduation rate: 17.6% (2000).

School District(s)

Belleville (PK-12)
2000 Enrollment: 888 608-424-3315
Housing: Homeownership rate: 70.9% (2000); Median home value: $122,400 (2000); Median rent: $515 per month (2000); Median age of housing: 26 years (2000).
Safety: Violent crime rate: 10.4 per 10,000 population; Property crime rate: 109.3 per 10,000 population (2001).
Newspapers: Belleville Recorder (1 x week)
Transportation: Commute to work: 93.9% car, 0.2% public transportation, 2.9% walk, 1.7% work from home (2000); Travel time to work: 22.0% less than 15 minutes, 32.5% 15 to 30 minutes, 36.8% 30 to 45 minutes, 4.6% 45 to 60 minutes, 4.0% 60 minutes or more (2000)

BERRY (town). Covers a land area of 35.852 square miles and a water area of 0.121 square miles. Located at 43.15° N. Lat.; 89.66° W. Long.
Population: 1,084 (2000); Race: 98.9% White, 0.0% Black, 0.8% Asian, 0.0% American Indian and Alaska Native, 1.2% Hispanic of any race, 0.2% two or more races (2000); Density: 30.2 persons per square mile (2000); Age: 23.3% under 18, 11.8% over 64 (2000); Marriage status: 18.6% never married, 72.5% now married, 5.1% widowed, 3.7% divorced (2000); Foreign born: 1.3% (2000); Ancestry (includes multiple ancestries): 61.9% German, 14.3% Norwegian, 10.3% Irish, 10.1% English, 5.5% United States or American (2000).
Economy: Employment by occupation: 14.6% management, 21.3% professional, 10.2% services, 23.8% sales, 1.7% farming, 13.2% construction, 15.2% production (2000).
Income: Per capita income: $27,194 (2000); Median household income: $61,429 (2000); Poverty rate: 1.2% (2000).
Taxes: Total city taxes per capita: $107 (1997); City property taxes per capita: $105 (1997).
Education: High school graduation rate: 90.5% (2000); College graduation rate: 29.9% (2000).
Housing: Homeownership rate: 88.4% (2000); Median home value: $165,600 (2000); Median rent: $622 per month (2000); Median age of housing: 29 years (2000).
Transportation: Commute to work: 88.8% car, 0.0% public transportation, 0.8% walk, 9.8% work from home (2000); Travel time to work: 19.2% less than 15 minutes, 44.7% 15 to 30 minutes, 24.8% 30 to 45 minutes, 6.4% 45 to 60 minutes, 4.9% 60 minutes or more (2000)

BLACK EARTH (village). Covers a land area of 0.663 square miles and a water area of 0 square miles. Located at 43.13° N. Lat.; 89.74° W. Long. Elevation is 818 feet.
History: Black Earth was platted in 1850 on land that had formerly been marsh land. First a grain shipping center, the village later became a rural trading center. One of the earliest farmer cooperatives in Wisconsin, the Patrons' Mercantile Company, was established here.

Population: 1,320 (2000); Race: 96.3% White, 0.0% Black, 1.6% Asian, 0.9% American Indian and Alaska Native, 1.6% Hispanic of any race, 0.9% two or more races (2000); Density: 1,991.6 persons per square mile (2000); Age: 25.4% under 18, 15.3% over 64 (2000); Marriage status: 20.7% never married, 64.6% now married, 5.6% widowed, 9.1% divorced (2000); Foreign born: 0.6% (2000); Ancestry (includes multiple ancestries): 49.6% German, 23.5% Norwegian, 11.5% Irish, 10.4% English, 5.5% United States or American (2000).
Economy: Single-family building permits issued: 2 (2001) / 1 (2000); Multi-family building permits issued: 0 (2001) / 0 (2000); Employment by occupation: 10.9% management, 18.4% professional, 13.1% services, 30.2% sales, 0.1% farming, 13.7% construction, 13.6% production (2000).
Income: Per capita income: $21,363 (2000); Median household income: $51,548 (2000); Poverty rate: 2.2% (2000).
Taxes: Total city taxes per capita: $182 (1997); City property taxes per capita: $179 (1997).
Education: High school graduation rate: 84.9% (2000); College graduation rate: 22.1% (2000).
Housing: Homeownership rate: 78.5% (2000); Median home value: $127,300 (2000); Median rent: $467 per month (2000); Median age of housing: 37 years (2000).
Safety: Violent crime rate: 0.0 per 10,000 population; Property crime rate: 143.0 per 10,000 population (2001).
Newspapers: News-Sickle Arrow (1 x week)
Transportation: Commute to work: 90.4% car, 0.4% public transportation, 4.6% walk, 3.9% work from home (2000); Travel time to work: 30.0% less than 15 minutes, 27.1% 15 to 30 minutes, 31.9% 30 to 45 minutes, 8.7% 45 to 60 minutes, 2.3% 60 minutes or more (2000)

BLACK EARTH (town). Covers a land area of 17.279 square miles and a water area of 0 square miles. Located at 43.14° N. Lat.; 89.76° W. Long. Elevation is 818 feet.
Population: 449 (2000); Race: 99.5% White, 0.5% Black, 0.0% Asian, 0.0% American Indian and Alaska Native, 0.0% Hispanic of any race, 0.0% two or more races (2000); Density: 26.0 persons per square mile (2000); Age: 29.0% under 18, 10.7% over 64 (2000); Marriage status: 18.1% never married, 74.2% now married, 3.4% widowed, 4.3% divorced (2000); Foreign born: 0.9% (2000); Ancestry (includes multiple ancestries): 49.9% German, 24.1% Norwegian, 12.8% Irish, 8.1% English, 7.9% Swiss (2000).
Economy: In agricultural area: cheesemaking. Employment by occupation: 17.4% management, 15.2% professional, 10.3% services, 21.0% sales, 0.0% farming, 23.2% construction, 12.9% production (2000).
Income: Per capita income: $24,351 (2000); Median household income: $61,364 (2000); Poverty rate: 0.0% (2000).
Taxes: Total city taxes per capita: $159 (1997); City property taxes per capita: $156 (1997).
Education: High school graduation rate: 92.1% (2000); College graduation rate: 18.2% (2000).
Housing: Homeownership rate: 81.5% (2000); Median home value: $149,000 (2000); Median rent: $538 per month (2000); Median age of housing: 34 years (2000).
Transportation: Commute to work: 85.1% car, 0.0% public transportation, 2.3% walk, 10.8% work from home (2000); Travel time to work: 31.3% less than 15 minutes, 18.2% 15 to 30 minutes, 34.8% 30 to 45 minutes, 11.6% 45 to 60 minutes, 4.0% 60 minutes or more (2000)

BLOOMING GROVE (town). Covers a land area of 7.499 square miles and a water area of 1.581 square miles. Located at 43.06° N. Lat.; 89.28° W. Long.
Population: 1,768 (2000); Race: 93.4% White, 2.6% Black, 3.3% Asian, 0.0% American Indian and Alaska Native, 2.5% Hispanic of any race, 0.7% two or more races (2000); Density: 235.8 persons per square mile (2000); Age: 24.7% under 18, 7.6% over 64 (2000); Marriage status: 26.2% never married, 56.3% now married, 3.9% widowed, 13.6% divorced (2000); Foreign born: 6.9% (2000); Ancestry (includes multiple ancestries): 39.7% German, 13.2% Norwegian, 9.2% Irish, 9.1% Other groups, 6.2% Polish (2000).
Economy: Employment by occupation: 13.6% management, 16.9% professional, 5.7% services, 34.1% sales, 0.0% farming, 13.1% construction, 16.6% production (2000).
Income: Per capita income: $24,263 (2000); Median household income: $56,328 (2000); Poverty rate: 2.9% (2000).
Taxes: Total city taxes per capita: $168 (1997); City property taxes per capita: $124 (1997).
Education: High school graduation rate: 91.7% (2000); College graduation rate: 23.5% (2000).
Housing: Homeownership rate: 78.5% (2000); Median home value: $123,500 (2000); Median rent: $506 per month (2000); Median age of housing: 31 years (2000).
Transportation: Commute to work: 96.5% car, 1.8% public transportation, 0.9% walk, 0.8% work from home (2000); Travel time to work: 29.9% less than 15 minutes, 53.7% 15 to 30 minutes, 13.7% 30 to 45 minutes, 0.0% 45 to 60 minutes, 2.8% 60 minutes or more (2000)

BLUE MOUNDS (village). Covers a land area of 0.754 square miles and a water area of 0 square miles. Located at 43.01° N. Lat.; 89.83° W. Long. Elevation is 1,261 feet.
Population: 708 (2000); Race: 97.9% White, 0.0% Black, 1.7% Asian, 0.0% American Indian and Alaska Native, 0.3% Hispanic of any race, 0.4% two or more races (2000); Density: 938.4 persons per square mile (2000); Age: 28.0% under 18, 8.9% over 64 (2000); Marriage status: 17.9% never married, 63.7% now married, 4.5% widowed, 13.9% divorced (2000); Foreign born: 1.6% (2000); Ancestry (includes multiple ancestries): 38.7% German, 26.8% Norwegian, 16.4% Irish, 11.7% English, 8.1% Polish (2000).
Economy: Single-family building permits issued: 1 (2001) / 7 (2000); Multi-family building permits issued: 0 (2001) / 0 (2000); Employment by occupation: 10.3% management, 17.3% professional, 13.6% services, 29.9% sales, 0.7% farming, 19.4% construction, 8.9% production (2000).
Income: Per capita income: $25,895 (2000); Median household income: $45,568 (2000); Poverty rate: 4.0% (2000).
Taxes: Total city taxes per capita: $168 (1997); City property taxes per capita: $109 (1997).
Education: High school graduation rate: 88.0% (2000); College graduation rate: 17.2% (2000).
Housing: Homeownership rate: 86.2% (2000); Median home value: $151,000 (2000); Median rent: $440 per month (2000); Median age of housing: 9 years (2000).
Transportation: Commute to work: 92.9% car, 0.0% public transportation, 1.2% walk, 4.5% work from home (2000); Travel time to work: 13.7% less than 15 minutes, 28.7% 15 to 30 minutes, 46.1% 30 to 45 minutes, 7.2% 45 to 60 minutes, 4.2% 60 minutes or more (2000)

BLUE MOUNDS (town). Covers a land area of 33.023 square miles and a water area of 0.008 square miles. Located at 42.99° N. Lat.; 89.78° W. Long. Elevation is 1,261 feet.
Population: 842 (2000); Race: 100.0% White, 0.0% Black, 0.0% Asian, 0.0% American Indian and Alaska Native, 0.0% Hispanic of any race, 0.0% two or more races (2000); Density: 25.5 persons per square mile (2000); Age: 30.8% under 18, 9.6% over 64 (2000); Marriage status: 22.3% never married, 69.7% now married, 2.3% widowed, 5.7% divorced (2000); Foreign born: 1.7% (2000); Ancestry (includes multiple ancestries): 46.3% German, 26.1% Norwegian, 12.9% Irish, 11.3% English, 10.3% Swiss (2000).
Economy: Cheese making. Employment by occupation: 24.9% management, 14.3% professional, 10.9% services, 26.1% sales, 3.1% farming, 13.1% construction, 7.6% production (2000).
Income: Per capita income: $27,696 (2000); Median household income: $61,429 (2000); Poverty rate: 5.0% (2000).
Taxes: Total city taxes per capita: $175 (1997); City property taxes per capita: $171 (1997).
Education: High school graduation rate: 91.9% (2000); College graduation rate: 24.6% (2000).
Housing: Homeownership rate: 90.0% (2000); Median home value: $171,900 (2000); Median rent: $542 per month (2000); Median age of housing: 48 years (2000).
Transportation: Commute to work: 86.8% car, 0.5% public transportation, 0.7% walk, 11.6% work from home (2000); Travel time to work: 21.5% less than 15 minutes, 34.6% 15 to 30 minutes, 29.5% 30 to 45 minutes, 10.5% 45 to 60 minutes, 3.8% 60 minutes or more (2000)

BRISTOL (town). Covers a land area of 34.390 square miles and a water area of 0 square miles. Located at 43.24° N. Lat.; 89.17° W. Long.
Population: 2,698 (2000); Race: 99.5% White, 0.0% Black, 0.3% Asian, 0.0% American Indian and Alaska Native, 0.7% Hispanic of any race, 0.2% two or more races (2000); Density: 78.5 persons per square mile (2000); Age: 31.0% under 18, 4.7% over 64 (2000); Marriage status: 21.2% never married, 70.7% now married, 2.2% widowed, 5.9% divorced (2000); Foreign born: 0.6% (2000); Ancestry (includes multiple ancestries): 52.5% German, 12.7% Norwegian, 12.6% United States or American, 10.2% Irish, 7.4% English (2000).
Economy: Employment by occupation: 15.5% management, 18.8% professional, 11.1% services, 29.2% sales, 1.2% farming, 13.6% construction, 10.7% production (2000).

Income: Per capita income: $26,273 (2000); Median household income: $70,439 (2000); Poverty rate: 2.5% (2000).
Taxes: Total city taxes per capita: $102 (2000); City property taxes per capita: $92 (2000).
Education: High school graduation rate: 94.4% (2000); College graduation rate: 26.2% (2000).
Housing: Homeownership rate: 91.2% (2000); Median home value: $184,400 (2000); Median rent: $504 per month (2000); Median age of housing: 19 years (2000).
Transportation: Commute to work: 90.9% car, 0.0% public transportation, 1.6% walk, 7.3% work from home (2000); Travel time to work: 32.5% less than 15 minutes, 33.9% 15 to 30 minutes, 26.6% 30 to 45 minutes, 5.6% 45 to 60 minutes, 1.4% 60 minutes or more (2000)

BROOKLYN (village). Covers a land area of 1.094 square miles and a water area of 0 square miles. Located at 42.85° N. Lat.; 89.37° W. Long.
Population: 916 (2000); Race: 97.9% White, 0.6% Black, 0.0% Asian, 0.0% American Indian and Alaska Native, 1.2% Hispanic of any race, 1.1% two or more races (2000); Density: 837.4 persons per square mile (2000); Age: 29.3% under 18, 8.3% over 64 (2000); Marriage status: 19.7% never married, 61.8% now married, 4.5% widowed, 14.1% divorced (2000); Foreign born: 0.9% (2000); Ancestry (includes multiple ancestries): 42.6% German, 14.8% Irish, 14.5% Norwegian, 13.9% English, 5.9% United States or American (2000).
Economy: Single-family building permits issued: 19 (2001) / 8 (2000); Multi-family building permits issued: 0 (2001) / 10 (2000); Employment by occupation: 13.9% management, 14.8% professional, 15.4% services, 23.3% sales, 1.7% farming, 16.4% construction, 14.5% production (2000).
Income: Per capita income: $19,480 (2000); Median household income: $48,056 (2000); Poverty rate: 2.9% (2000).
Education: High school graduation rate: 90.3% (2000); College graduation rate: 17.8% (2000).
Housing: Homeownership rate: 77.5% (2000); Median home value: $105,500 (2000); Median rent: $566 per month (2000); Median age of housing: 36 years (2000).
Transportation: Commute to work: 91.1% car, 0.0% public transportation, 1.5% walk, 4.7% work from home (2000); Travel time to work: 19.8% less than 15 minutes, 44.4% 15 to 30 minutes, 28.6% 30 to 45 minutes, 5.4% 45 to 60 minutes, 1.8% 60 minutes or more (2000)

BURKE (town). Covers a land area of 19.487 square miles and a water area of 0 square miles. Located at 43.16° N. Lat.; 89.29° W. Long. Elevation is 895 feet.
Population: 2,990 (2000); Race: 97.2% White, 0.7% Black, 1.4% Asian, 0.0% American Indian and Alaska Native, 0.0% Hispanic of any race, 0.6% two or more races (2000); Density: 153.4 persons per square mile (2000); Age: 23.5% under 18, 9.1% over 64 (2000); Marriage status: 24.6% never married, 68.5% now married, 2.1% widowed, 4.9% divorced (2000); Foreign born: 4.8% (2000); Ancestry (includes multiple ancestries): 56.3% German, 13.7% Irish, 13.7% Norwegian, 11.3% English, 5.7% French (except Basque) (2000).
Economy: Employment by occupation: 18.8% management, 20.6% professional, 9.2% services, 25.7% sales, 0.3% farming, 13.9% construction, 11.5% production (2000).
Income: Per capita income: $28,458 (2000); Median household income: $67,273 (2000); Poverty rate: 2.9% (2000).
Taxes: Total city taxes per capita: $114 (2000); City property taxes per capita: $104 (2000).
Education: High school graduation rate: 92.7% (2000); College graduation rate: 28.8% (2000).
Housing: Homeownership rate: 81.8% (2000); Median home value: $156,900 (2000); Median rent: $687 per month (2000); Median age of housing: 25 years (2000).
Transportation: Commute to work: 94.2% car, 0.0% public transportation, 0.0% walk, 5.8% work from home (2000); Travel time to work: 37.2% less than 15 minutes, 41.1% 15 to 30 minutes, 16.5% 30 to 45 minutes, 2.2% 45 to 60 minutes, 3.0% 60 minutes or more (2000)

CAMBRIDGE (village). Covers a land area of 0.889 square miles and a water area of 0 square miles. Located at 43.00° N. Lat.; 89.01° W. Long.
History: Cambridge was settled by Joseph Keyes in 1847.
Population: 1,101 (2000); Race: 98.6% White, 0.0% Black, 0.4% Asian, 0.0% American Indian and Alaska Native, 1.6% Hispanic of any race, 0.2% two or more races (2000); Density: 1,238.5 persons per square mile (2000); Age: 24.9% under 18, 21.5% over 64 (2000); Marriage status: 19.1% never married, 63.2% now married, 8.7% widowed, 9.0% divorced (2000); Foreign born: 0.9% (2000); Ancestry (includes multiple ancestries): 44.5% German, 26.9% Norwegian, 14.0% Irish, 8.2% English, 4.2% French (except Basque) (2000).
Economy: Single-family building permits issued: 6 (2001) / 7 (2000); Multi-family building permits issued: 4 (2001) / 12 (2000); Employment by occupation: 9.9% management, 24.2% professional, 13.7% services, 33.6% sales, 0.0% farming, 8.7% construction, 9.8% production (2000).
Income: Per capita income: $22,599 (2000); Median household income: $52,039 (2000); Poverty rate: 4.4% (2000).
Taxes: Total city taxes per capita: $344 (1997); City property taxes per capita: $318 (1997).
Education: High school graduation rate: 89.3% (2000); College graduation rate: 28.8% (2000).

School District(s)

Cambridge (PK-12)
2000 Enrollment: 1,027 608-423-4345
Housing: Homeownership rate: 71.5% (2000); Median home value: $128,800 (2000); Median rent: $511 per month (2000); Median age of housing: 27 years (2000).
Newspapers: Cambridge News (1 x week)
Transportation: Commute to work: 94.5% car, 0.0% public transportation, 2.4% walk, 2.8% work from home (2000); Travel time to work: 27.2% less than 15 minutes, 36.2% 15 to 30 minutes, 28.4% 30 to 45 minutes, 4.8% 45 to 60 minutes, 3.4% 60 minutes or more (2000)
Additional Information Contacts
Cambridge Chamber of Commerce 608-423-3780

CHRISTIANA (town). Covers a land area of 35.312 square miles and a water area of 0.140 square miles. Located at 42.99° N. Lat.; 89.09° W. Long.
Population: 1,313 (2000); Race: 97.2% White, 0.0% Black, 0.9% Asian, 0.1% American Indian and Alaska Native, 4.8% Hispanic of any race, 0.9% two or more races (2000); Density: 37.2 persons per square mile (2000); Age: 26.3% under 18, 9.6% over 64 (2000); Marriage status: 22.6% never married, 65.4% now married, 4.2% widowed, 7.7% divorced (2000); Foreign born: 4.5% (2000); Ancestry (includes multiple ancestries): 41.1% German, 37.0% Norwegian, 11.2% Irish, 8.1% English, 6.9% Other groups (2000).
Economy: Employment by occupation: 15.6% management, 19.3% professional, 10.8% services, 28.0% sales, 2.4% farming, 8.3% construction, 15.6% production (2000).
Income: Per capita income: $20,504 (2000); Median household income: $56,042 (2000); Poverty rate: 9.2% (2000).
Taxes: Total city taxes per capita: $142 (1997); City property taxes per capita: $137 (1997).
Education: High school graduation rate: 89.2% (2000); College graduation rate: 21.8% (2000).
Housing: Homeownership rate: 80.4% (2000); Median home value: $147,400 (2000); Median rent: $500 per month (2000); Median age of housing: 54 years (2000).
Transportation: Commute to work: 88.9% car, 0.0% public transportation, 1.4% walk, 9.7% work from home (2000); Travel time to work: 27.1% less than 15 minutes, 41.9% 15 to 30 minutes, 25.0% 30 to 45 minutes, 3.8% 45 to 60 minutes, 2.2% 60 minutes or more (2000)

COTTAGE GROVE (village). Covers a land area of 2.286 square miles and a water area of 0 square miles. Located at 43.08° N. Lat.; 89.20° W. Long. Elevation is 888 feet.
Population: 4,059 (2000); Race: 95.0% White, 1.5% Black, 1.2% Asian, 0.0% American Indian and Alaska Native, 1.5% Hispanic of any race, 2.2% two or more races (2000); Density: 1,775.3 persons per square mile (2000); Age: 32.8% under 18, 6.8% over 64 (2000); Marriage status: 19.7% never married, 68.5% now married, 4.0% widowed, 7.8% divorced (2000); Foreign born: 3.0% (2000); Ancestry (includes multiple ancestries): 49.1% German, 19.2% Norwegian, 12.6% Irish, 7.4% English, 6.7% Other groups (2000).
Economy: Single-family building permits issued: 28 (2001) / 38 (2000); Multi-family building permits issued: 14 (2001) / 45 (2000); Employment by occupation: 14.7% management, 27.0% professional, 8.5% services, 31.8% sales, 0.4% farming, 7.5% construction, 10.1% production (2000).
Income: Per capita income: $25,777 (2000); Median household income: $66,628 (2000); Poverty rate: 3.8% (2000).
Taxes: Total city taxes per capita: $366 (1997); City property taxes per capita: $321 (1997).
Education: High school graduation rate: 94.8% (2000); College graduation rate: 38.2% (2000).
Housing: Homeownership rate: 68.6% (2000); Median home value: $163,600 (2000); Median rent: $755 per month (2000); Median age of housing: 6 years (2000).

Newspapers: The Herald Independant (1 x week)
Transportation: Commute to work: 95.5% car, 0.5% public transportation, 1.2% walk, 2.6% work from home (2000); Travel time to work: 16.5% less than 15 minutes, 63.1% 15 to 30 minutes, 16.5% 30 to 45 minutes, 1.7% 45 to 60 minutes, 2.2% 60 minutes or more (2000)
Additional Information Contacts
Cottage Grove Chamber of Commerce 608-839-3165

COTTAGE GROVE (town). Covers a land area of 33.375 square miles and a water area of 0 square miles. Located at 43.07° N. Lat.; 89.18° W. Long. Elevation is 888 feet.
Population: 3,839 (2000); Race: 98.9% White, 0.0% Black, 0.6% Asian, 0.0% American Indian and Alaska Native, 1.2% Hispanic of any race, 0.3% two or more races (2000); Density: 115.0 persons per square mile (2000); Age: 27.6% under 18, 3.9% over 64 (2000); Marriage status: 18.7% never married, 72.1% now married, 2.5% widowed, 6.8% divorced (2000); Foreign born: 1.4% (2000); Ancestry (includes multiple ancestries): 49.5% German, 22.8% Norwegian, 13.9% Irish, 7.9% Polish, 7.3% English (2000).
Economy: In dairy region. Manufacturing: chemicals, motor vehicle parts. Employment by occupation: 15.7% management, 21.9% professional, 8.3% services, 29.7% sales, 0.3% farming, 13.2% construction, 10.9% production (2000).
Income: Per capita income: $26,602 (2000); Median household income: $71,007 (2000); Poverty rate: 2.4% (2000).
Taxes: Total city taxes per capita: $114 (1997); City property taxes per capita: $102 (1997).
Education: High school graduation rate: 95.0% (2000); College graduation rate: 27.9% (2000).
Housing: Homeownership rate: 91.6% (2000); Median home value: $147,200 (2000); Median rent: $609 per month (2000); Median age of housing: 24 years (2000).
Transportation: Commute to work: 93.1% car, 0.0% public transportation, 1.6% walk, 5.4% work from home (2000); Travel time to work: 22.9% less than 15 minutes, 54.7% 15 to 30 minutes, 17.5% 30 to 45 minutes, 1.3% 45 to 60 minutes, 3.6% 60 minutes or more (2000)

CROSS PLAINS (village). Covers a land area of 1.175 square miles and a water area of 0 square miles. Located at 43.11° N. Lat.; 89.64° W. Long. Elevation is 859 feet.
History: Between 1832 and 1850, many veterans of the War of 1812 settled here on grants given for their military service. The village of Cross Plains was laid out in 1852 by a German baron, Peter L. Mohr, who erected many buildings and named the village Christina, for his wife. The streets were named for his children. When Cross Plains was incorporated, it included both the old Christina and the nearby Foxville.
Population: 3,084 (2000); Race: 98.5% White, 0.4% Black, 0.6% Asian, 0.0% American Indian and Alaska Native, 0.0% Hispanic of any race, 0.4% two or more races (2000); Density: 2,625.0 persons per square mile (2000); Age: 28.4% under 18, 8.4% over 64 (2000); Marriage status: 21.2% never married, 65.8% now married, 3.2% widowed, 9.9% divorced (2000); Foreign born: 1.1% (2000); Ancestry (includes multiple ancestries): 58.0% German, 16.9% Irish, 15.4% Norwegian, 8.7% English, 4.0% United States or American (2000).
Economy: Single-family building permits issued: 33 (2001) / 21 (2000); Multi-family building permits issued: 0 (2001) / 0 (2000); Employment by occupation: 18.0% management, 16.5% professional, 10.7% services, 30.9% sales, 0.6% farming, 11.2% construction, 12.2% production (2000).
Income: Per capita income: $23,894 (2000); Median household income: $56,629 (2000); Poverty rate: 2.6% (2000).
Taxes: Total city taxes per capita: $356 (1997); City property taxes per capita: $341 (1997).
Education: High school graduation rate: 92.9% (2000); College graduation rate: 23.0% (2000).
Housing: Homeownership rate: 66.1% (2000); Median home value: $142,900 (2000); Median rent: $593 per month (2000); Median age of housing: 21 years (2000).
Transportation: Commute to work: 93.1% car, 0.3% public transportation, 3.7% walk, 2.1% work from home (2000); Travel time to work: 35.7% less than 15 minutes, 37.5% 15 to 30 minutes, 20.0% 30 to 45 minutes, 2.8% 45 to 60 minutes, 3.9% 60 minutes or more (2000)

CROSS PLAINS (town). Covers a land area of 35.334 square miles and a water area of 0.035 square miles. Located at 43.09° N. Lat.; 89.66° W. Long. Elevation is 859 feet.
Population: 1,419 (2000); Race: 97.4% White, 1.8% Black, 0.5% Asian, 0.0% American Indian and Alaska Native, 0.5% Hispanic of any race, 0.3% two or more races (2000); Density: 40.2 persons per square mile (2000); Age: 28.1% under 18, 11.5% over 64 (2000); Marriage status: 22.8% never married, 68.3% now married, 3.5% widowed, 5.5% divorced (2000); Foreign born: 1.6% (2000); Ancestry (includes multiple ancestries): 58.5% German, 20.4% Irish, 15.8% Norwegian, 8.9% English, 6.4% Polish (2000).
Economy: In dairy farm area. Manufacturing: butter. Employment by occupation: 23.9% management, 22.9% professional, 11.2% services, 24.4% sales, 1.2% farming, 7.4% construction, 9.1% production (2000).
Income: Per capita income: $30,163 (2000); Median household income: $66,055 (2000); Poverty rate: 1.7% (2000).
Taxes: Total city taxes per capita: $189 (1997); City property taxes per capita: $179 (1997).
Education: High school graduation rate: 89.1% (2000); College graduation rate: 36.6% (2000).
Housing: Homeownership rate: 86.0% (2000); Median home value: $197,400 (2000); Median rent: $600 per month (2000); Median age of housing: 23 years (2000).
Transportation: Commute to work: 85.2% car, 0.0% public transportation, 2.0% walk, 12.6% work from home (2000); Travel time to work: 26.6% less than 15 minutes, 44.9% 15 to 30 minutes, 20.8% 30 to 45 minutes, 4.6% 45 to 60 minutes, 3.1% 60 minutes or more (2000)

DANE (village). Covers a land area of 1.132 square miles and a water area of 0 square miles. Located at 43.25° N. Lat.; 89.50° W. Long. Elevation is 1,070 feet.
Population: 799 (2000); Race: 97.4% White, 1.4% Black, 0.0% Asian, 0.0% American Indian and Alaska Native, 4.0% Hispanic of any race, 0.6% two or more races (2000); Density: 705.6 persons per square mile (2000); Age: 30.2% under 18, 6.7% over 64 (2000); Marriage status: 25.3% never married, 60.5% now married, 4.7% widowed, 9.4% divorced (2000); Foreign born: 0.7% (2000); Ancestry (includes multiple ancestries): 61.2% German, 14.6% Norwegian, 12.8% Irish, 5.2% Other groups, 5.1% English (2000).
Economy: Single-family building permits issued: 6 (2001) / 4 (2000); Multi-family building permits issued: 8 (2001) / 0 (2000); Employment by occupation: 5.7% management, 14.1% professional, 10.7% services, 28.6% sales, 2.3% farming, 21.4% construction, 17.3% production (2000).
Income: Per capita income: $18,533 (2000); Median household income: $51,667 (2000); Poverty rate: 5.4% (2000).
Taxes: Total city taxes per capita: $215 (1997); City property taxes per capita: $200 (1997).
Education: High school graduation rate: 87.9% (2000); College graduation rate: 11.9% (2000).
Housing: Homeownership rate: 67.1% (2000); Median home value: $128,300 (2000); Median rent: $600 per month (2000); Median age of housing: 25 years (2000).
Safety: Violent crime rate: 0.0 per 10,000 population; Property crime rate: 124.2 per 10,000 population (2001).
Transportation: Commute to work: 95.9% car, 0.0% public transportation, 2.1% walk, 2.1% work from home (2000); Travel time to work: 25.2% less than 15 minutes, 40.4% 15 to 30 minutes, 24.8% 30 to 45 minutes, 6.1% 45 to 60 minutes, 3.5% 60 minutes or more (2000)

DANE (town). Covers a land area of 35.095 square miles and a water area of 0.014 square miles. Located at 43.24° N. Lat.; 89.53° W. Long. Elevation is 1,070 feet.
Population: 968 (2000); Race: 97.9% White, 0.2% Black, 0.0% Asian, 0.2% American Indian and Alaska Native, 1.1% Hispanic of any race, 1.7% two or more races (2000); Density: 27.6 persons per square mile (2000); Age: 29.9% under 18, 10.2% over 64 (2000); Marriage status: 20.0% never married, 72.7% now married, 1.7% widowed, 5.6% divorced (2000); Foreign born: 1.8% (2000); Ancestry (includes multiple ancestries): 58.9% German, 10.6% Norwegian, 9.7% Irish, 6.4% English, 4.9% United States or American (2000).
Economy: Manufacturing: plastic products. Employment by occupation: 21.2% management, 16.0% professional, 12.4% services, 19.8% sales, 4.8% farming, 14.3% construction, 11.4% production (2000).
Income: Per capita income: $25,562 (2000); Median household income: $61,250 (2000); Poverty rate: 3.2% (2000).
Taxes: Total city taxes per capita: $97 (1997); City property taxes per capita: $97 (1997).
Education: High school graduation rate: 90.6% (2000); College graduation rate: 20.3% (2000).
Housing: Homeownership rate: 82.0% (2000); Median home value: $157,000 (2000); Median rent: $513 per month (2000); Median age of housing: 34 years (2000).

Transportation: Commute to work: 85.1% car, 0.0% public transportation, 0.3% walk, 14.2% work from home (2000); Travel time to work: 27.2% less than 15 minutes, 39.0% 15 to 30 minutes, 26.8% 30 to 45 minutes, 3.0% 45 to 60 minutes, 4.0% 60 minutes or more (2000)

DE FOREST (village). Covers a land area of 4.831 square miles and a water area of 0.052 square miles. Located at 43.24° N. Lat.; 89.34° W. Long. Elevation is 949 feet.

Population: 7,368 (2000); Race: 95.5% White, 2.3% Black, 0.0% Asian, 0.8% American Indian and Alaska Native, 2.3% Hispanic of any race, 0.9% two or more races (2000); Density: 1,525.3 persons per square mile (2000); Age: 31.2% under 18, 8.3% over 64 (2000); Marriage status: 22.6% never married, 62.7% now married, 5.3% widowed, 9.4% divorced (2000); Foreign born: 1.0% (2000); Ancestry (includes multiple ancestries): 46.4% German, 20.5% Norwegian, 12.5% Irish, 6.5% English, 5.9% Polish (2000).

Economy: In tobacco growing and dairying region. Manufacturing: plastic products. Agricultural research station to North. Single-family building permits issued: 75 (2001) / 45 (2000); Multi-family building permits issued: 34 (2001) / 24 (2000); Employment by occupation: 12.3% management, 17.6% professional, 14.3% services, 28.5% sales, 0.6% farming, 11.3% construction, 15.3% production (2000).

Income: Per capita income: $21,089 (2000); Median household income: $55,369 (2000); Poverty rate: 3.6% (2000).

Taxes: Total city taxes per capita: $419 (2000); City property taxes per capita: $392 (2000).

Education: High school graduation rate: 92.1% (2000); College graduation rate: 24.7% (2000).

School District(s)

De Forest Area (PK-12)
2000 Enrollment: 3,073 608-846-6577

Housing: Homeownership rate: 72.6% (2000); Median home value: $136,700 (2000); Median rent: $598 per month (2000); Median age of housing: 16 years (2000).

Safety: Violent crime rate: 2.7 per 10,000 population; Property crime rate: 218.3 per 10,000 population (2001).

Newspapers: The De Forest Times-Tribune (1 x week)

Transportation: Commute to work: 93.9% car, 0.3% public transportation, 0.7% walk, 4.9% work from home (2000); Travel time to work: 28.9% less than 15 minutes, 37.6% 15 to 30 minutes, 22.0% 30 to 45 minutes, 2.9% 45 to 60 minutes, 8.6% 60 minutes or more (2000)

Additional Information Contacts

De Forest Chamber of Commerce 608-846-2922

DEERFIELD (village). Covers a land area of 1.138 square miles and a water area of 0 square miles. Located at 43.05° N. Lat.; 89.07° W. Long. Elevation is 870 feet.

Population: 1,971 (2000); Race: 94.8% White, 1.6% Black, 0.1% Asian, 0.4% American Indian and Alaska Native, 4.0% Hispanic of any race, 1.1% two or more races (2000); Density: 1,732.6 persons per square mile (2000); Age: 31.5% under 18, 9.2% over 64 (2000); Marriage status: 25.2% never married, 59.4% now married, 5.5% widowed, 9.9% divorced (2000); Foreign born: 3.3% (2000); Ancestry (includes multiple ancestries): 40.4% German, 22.3% Norwegian, 12.4% Irish, 7.5% Other groups, 5.9% English (2000).

Economy: Single-family building permits issued: 1 (2001) / 2 (2000); Multi-family building permits issued: 0 (2001) / 0 (2000); Employment by occupation: 9.5% management, 16.2% professional, 14.0% services, 27.9% sales, 0.2% farming, 11.4% construction, 20.8% production (2000).

Income: Per capita income: $20,209 (2000); Median household income: $50,439 (2000); Poverty rate: 2.4% (2000).

Taxes: Total city taxes per capita: $218 (1997); City property taxes per capita: $198 (1997).

Education: High school graduation rate: 91.2% (2000); College graduation rate: 20.0% (2000).

School District(s)

Deerfield Community (PK-12)
2000 Enrollment: 747 608-764-8261

Housing: Homeownership rate: 70.4% (2000); Median home value: $125,600 (2000); Median rent: $544 per month (2000); Median age of housing: 28 years (2000).

Safety: Violent crime rate: 10.1 per 10,000 population; Property crime rate: 201.5 per 10,000 population (2001).

Newspapers: The Independent (1 x week)

Transportation: Commute to work: 92.1% car, 0.0% public transportation, 4.7% walk, 2.9% work from home (2000); Travel time to work: 24.8% less than 15 minutes, 44.2% 15 to 30 minutes, 23.7% 30 to 45 minutes, 4.0% 45 to 60 minutes, 3.3% 60 minutes or more (2000)

DEERFIELD (town). Covers a land area of 34.320 square miles and a water area of 0.152 square miles. Located at 43.06° N. Lat.; 89.05° W. Long. Elevation is 870 feet.

Population: 1,470 (2000); Race: 95.0% White, 2.6% Black, 0.7% Asian, 0.0% American Indian and Alaska Native, 1.3% Hispanic of any race, 0.4% two or more races (2000); Density: 42.8 persons per square mile (2000); Age: 25.5% under 18, 8.3% over 64 (2000); Marriage status: 21.7% never married, 65.7% now married, 3.1% widowed, 9.5% divorced (2000); Foreign born: 0.8% (2000); Ancestry (includes multiple ancestries): 49.1% German, 26.1% Norwegian, 9.9% English, 9.2% Irish, 5.3% Polish (2000).

Economy: Employment by occupation: 16.9% management, 19.8% professional, 10.6% services, 25.4% sales, 0.5% farming, 12.8% construction, 14.0% production (2000).

Income: Per capita income: $24,763 (2000); Median household income: $63,125 (2000); Poverty rate: 2.2% (2000).

Taxes: Total city taxes per capita: $149 (1997); City property taxes per capita: $141 (1997).

Education: High school graduation rate: 95.4% (2000); College graduation rate: 25.6% (2000).

Housing: Homeownership rate: 91.1% (2000); Median home value: $162,700 (2000); Median rent: $588 per month (2000); Median age of housing: 26 years (2000).

Transportation: Commute to work: 91.8% car, 0.0% public transportation, 1.5% walk, 6.3% work from home (2000); Travel time to work: 15.7% less than 15 minutes, 47.6% 15 to 30 minutes, 25.8% 30 to 45 minutes, 5.7% 45 to 60 minutes, 5.1% 60 minutes or more (2000)

DUNKIRK (town). Covers a land area of 31.910 square miles and a water area of 0.410 square miles. Located at 42.89° N. Lat.; 89.19° W. Long. Elevation is 843 feet.

Population: 2,053 (2000); Race: 99.4% White, 0.0% Black, 0.0% Asian, 0.4% American Indian and Alaska Native, 0.9% Hispanic of any race, 0.3% two or more races (2000); Density: 64.3 persons per square mile (2000); Age: 26.1% under 18, 6.9% over 64 (2000); Marriage status: 20.2% never married, 64.8% now married, 5.9% widowed, 9.1% divorced (2000); Foreign born: 0.3% (2000); Ancestry (includes multiple ancestries): 43.7% Norwegian, 36.9% German, 14.9% Irish, 8.2% English, 3.3% Dutch (2000).

Economy: Employment by occupation: 17.3% management, 15.7% professional, 15.1% services, 22.9% sales, 0.0% farming, 12.8% construction, 16.1% production (2000).

Income: Per capita income: $26,609 (2000); Median household income: $62,426 (2000); Poverty rate: 3.0% (2000).

Taxes: Total city taxes per capita: $51 (1997); City property taxes per capita: $49 (1997).

Education: High school graduation rate: 90.6% (2000); College graduation rate: 24.8% (2000).

Housing: Homeownership rate: 89.2% (2000); Median home value: $141,400 (2000); Median rent: $611 per month (2000); Median age of housing: 32 years (2000).

Transportation: Commute to work: 92.5% car, 0.5% public transportation, 1.8% walk, 4.8% work from home (2000); Travel time to work: 41.9% less than 15 minutes, 29.0% 15 to 30 minutes, 22.4% 30 to 45 minutes, 4.0% 45 to 60 minutes, 2.7% 60 minutes or more (2000)

DUNN (town). Covers a land area of 28.648 square miles and a water area of 5.777 square miles. Located at 42.98° N. Lat.; 89.30° W. Long.

Population: 5,270 (2000); Race: 97.7% White, 0.4% Black, 1.1% Asian, 0.0% American Indian and Alaska Native, 1.3% Hispanic of any race, 0.2% two or more races (2000); Density: 184.0 persons per square mile (2000); Age: 24.7% under 18, 8.6% over 64 (2000); Marriage status: 22.1% never married, 68.2% now married, 2.7% widowed, 7.1% divorced (2000); Foreign born: 1.8% (2000); Ancestry (includes multiple ancestries): 39.2% German, 17.3% Norwegian, 15.5% Irish, 9.4% English, 5.5% United States or American (2000).

Economy: Employment by occupation: 20.5% management, 24.0% professional, 6.5% services, 27.4% sales, 0.4% farming, 10.7% construction, 10.4% production (2000).

Income: Per capita income: $30,881 (2000); Median household income: $66,250 (2000); Poverty rate: 1.7% (2000).

Taxes: Total city taxes per capita: $78 (1997); City property taxes per capita: $68 (1997).

Education: High school graduation rate: 91.9% (2000); College graduation rate: 30.9% (2000).

Housing: Homeownership rate: 88.3% (2000); Median home value: $167,900 (2000); Median rent: $676 per month (2000); Median age of housing: 27 years (2000).
Transportation: Commute to work: 95.3% car, 0.6% public transportation, 0.3% walk, 3.9% work from home (2000); Travel time to work: 23.9% less than 15 minutes, 53.7% 15 to 30 minutes, 18.3% 30 to 45 minutes, 1.9% 45 to 60 minutes, 2.2% 60 minutes or more (2000)

FITCHBURG (city). Covers a land area of 34.820 square miles and a water area of 0.043 square miles. Located at 43.00° N. Lat.; 89.43° W. Long. Elevation is 1,020 feet.
Population: 20,501 (2000); Race: 82.1% White, 9.2% Black, 2.9% Asian, 0.1% American Indian and Alaska Native, 5.4% Hispanic of any race, 2.4% two or more races (2000); Density: 588.8 persons per square mile (2000); Age: 25.0% under 18, 4.3% over 64 (2000); Marriage status: 35.8% never married, 52.3% now married, 2.5% widowed, 9.4% divorced (2000); Foreign born: 8.9% (2000); Ancestry (includes multiple ancestries): 35.8% German, 13.3% Other groups, 13.0% Irish, 11.2% Norwegian, 8.7% English (2000).
Vital Statistics: Birth rate: 65.9 per 10,000 population (1998)
Economy: Mixture of residential and agricultural: dairying; grain, vegetables. Nevin State Fish Hatchery. Manufacturing: tube and wire fabrication. Single-family building permits issued: 63 (2001) / 62 (2000); Multi-family building permits issued: 142 (2001) / 152 (2000); Employment by occupation: 17.2% management, 26.5% professional, 14.5% services, 26.2% sales, 0.3% farming, 5.0% construction, 10.3% production (2000).
Income: Per capita income: $27,317 (2000); Median household income: $50,433 (2000); Poverty rate: 6.4% (2000).
Taxes: Total city taxes per capita: $306 (1997); City property taxes per capita: $291 (1997).
Education: High school graduation rate: 92.0% (2000); College graduation rate: 42.1% (2000).
Housing: Homeownership rate: 45.3% (2000); Median home value: $176,000 (2000); Median rent: $591 per month (2000); Median age of housing: 21 years (2000).
Safety: Violent crime rate: 12.6 per 10,000 population; Property crime rate: 331.8 per 10,000 population (2001).
Newspapers: Fitchburg Star (1 x week)
Transportation: Commute to work: 92.3% car, 2.3% public transportation, 0.8% walk, 3.7% work from home (2000); Travel time to work: 33.3% less than 15 minutes, 51.6% 15 to 30 minutes, 9.9% 30 to 45 minutes, 1.7% 45 to 60 minutes, 3.5% 60 minutes or more (2000)

MADISON (city). Covers a land area of 68.673 square miles and a water area of 16.005 square miles. Located at 43.07° N. Lat.; 89.39° W. Long. Elevation is 863 feet.
History: In 1832, former judge James Duane Doty and his partner, Stevens T. Mason, governor of the newly formed Territory of Wisconsin, purchased land in the Four Lakes region and called it Madison. When the Territorial legislature met to consider the location of a capital, Doty convinced them that his site was right. Before a single building was erected, Madison was named the Territorial capital, site of the state university, and the seat of Dane County. The Peck family built a cabin here in 1837, but it was 1848 before a statehouse was completed. From the first session in 1838, the legislators, with no place to sleep or meet, had been trying to get the capital moved to Milwaukee. Improvements to Madison were slow to come, beginning only after Leonard J. Farwell arrived in 1847 and began to drain marshlands, build streets and sidewalks, and erect a grist and flour mill. When Wisconsin became a state in 1848, the University of Wisconsin was established here. Development in Madison was spurred following the Civil War by the reorganization of the floundering university, and the founding of many factories.
Population: 208,054 (2000); Race: 84.3% White, 5.6% Black, 5.6% Asian, 0.4% American Indian and Alaska Native, 4.2% Hispanic of any race, 2.4% two or more races (2000); Density: 3,029.7 persons per square mile (2000); Age: 17.5% under 18, 9.3% over 64 (2000); Marriage status: 44.3% never married, 42.8% now married, 3.8% widowed, 9.1% divorced (2000); Foreign born: 9.1% (2000); Ancestry (includes multiple ancestries): 35.9% German, 15.9% Other groups, 14.5% Irish, 10.4% Norwegian, 9.8% English (2000).
Vital Statistics: Birth rate: 128.8 per 10,000 population (1998)
Economy: Unemployment rate: 2.4% (11/2002); Total civilian labor force: 139,097 (11/2002); Single-family building permits issued: 843 (2001) / 638 (2000); Multi-family building permits issued: 1,649 (2001) / 1,143 (2000); Employment by occupation: 13.5% management, 33.4% professional, 14.1% services, 25.7% sales, 0.2% farming, 4.4% construction, 8.7% production (2000).
Income: Per capita income: $23,498 (2000); Median household income: $41,941 (2000); Poverty rate: 15.0% (2000).
Taxes: Total city taxes per capita: $502 (2000); City property taxes per capita: $446 (2000).
Education: High school graduation rate: 92.4% (2000); College graduation rate: 48.2% (2000).

School District(s)

Madison Metropolitan (PK-12)
2000 Enrollment: 25,087 608-266-6235
Wi Dept of Health & Family Services (PK-12)
2000 Enrollment: 220 608-266-8740
Wisconsin Dept of Corrections (KG-12)
2000 Enrollment: 1,513 608-266-2473
Wisconsin Dept of Public Instruction (PK-12)
2000 Enrollment: 220 608-266-1771

Four-year College(s)

Edgewood College (Private, Not-for-profit, Roman Catholic)
2001 Enrollment: 2,110 608-663-4861
2001 Tuition: In-state $13,300; Out-of-state $13,300
Herzing College (Private, For-profit)
2001 Enrollment: 605 800-582-1227
2001 Tuition: In-state $7,600; Out-of-state $7,600
University of Wisconsin-Madison (Public)
2001 Enrollment: 40,922 608-262-1234
2001 Tuition: In-state $3,658; Out-of-state $15,454

Two-year College(s)

Madison Area Technical College (Public)
2001 Enrollment: 14,351 608-246-6282
2001 Tuition: In-state $2,105; Out-of-state $14,700
Martin's College of Hair Design (Private, For-profit)
2001 Enrollment: 126 920-426-1555
Scientific College of Beauty and Barbering (Private, For-profit)
2001 Enrollment: 82 608-271-4204
University of Wisconsin Colleges (Public)
2001 Enrollment: 12,249 608-262-1783
2001 Tuition: In-state $2,422; Out-of-state $9,866
Madison Media Institute (Private, For-profit)
2001 Enrollment: 235 608-829-2728
2001 Tuition: In-state $9,360; Out-of-state $9,360

Housing: Homeownership rate: 47.8% (2000); Median home value: $139,300 (2000); Median rent: $602 per month (2000); Median age of housing: 33 years (2000).
Hospitals: Central Wisconsin/Center Developmentally Disabled (540 beds); Mendota Mental Health Institute (394 beds); Meriter Hospital (448 beds); Saint Marys Hospital Medical Center (440 beds); University of Wisconsin Hospital and Clinics (474 beds); William S. Middleton Memorial Veterans Hospital (245 beds)
Safety: Violent crime rate: 33.8 per 10,000 population; Property crime rate: 362.3 per 10,000 population (2001).
Newspapers: Wisconsin State Journal (7 x week); The Capital Times (6 x week); Isthmus (1 x week); The Madison Times (1 x week); Badger Herald (5 x week); Daily Cardinal (5 x week)
Transportation: Commute to work: 75.3% car, 7.2% public transportation, 10.7% walk, 3.1% work from home (2000); Travel time to work: 39.0% less than 15 minutes, 45.7% 15 to 30 minutes, 10.3% 30 to 45 minutes, 2.3% 45 to 60 minutes, 2.7% 60 minutes or more (2000); Amtrak: Service available.
Airports: Dane County Regional-Truax Field (primary service/small hub)
Additional Information Contacts
Greater Madison Convention Bureau 608-255-2537
Madison Chamber of Commerce 608-256-8348
Realtors Association of South Central Wisconsin 608-240-2800
Wisconsin Realtors Association 608-241-2047

MADISON (town). Covers a land area of 3.130 square miles and a water area of 0.459 square miles. Located at 43.04° N. Lat.; 89.40° W. Long. Elevation is 863 feet.
History: Seat of the University of Wisconsin. Among its points of interest are the elaborate capitol, which houses the legislative Library organized by Charles McCarthy; and a Unitarian church designed by Frank Lloyd Wright. Founded in 1836, and chosen (through the efforts of James Duane Doty) territorial capital before it was settled. Incorporated 1856.
Population: 7,005 (2000); Race: 65.4% White, 14.3% Black, 3.0% Asian, 0.9% American Indian and Alaska Native, 21.6% Hispanic of any race, 5.8% two or more races (2000); Density: 2,238.0 persons per square mile (2000); Age: 18.1% under 18, 4.6% over 64 (2000); Marriage status: 49.0% never married, 35.1% now married, 2.8% widowed, 13.0% divorced (2000);

Foreign born: 20.8% (2000); Ancestry (includes multiple ancestries): 35.1% Other groups, 24.7% German, 8.5% Irish, 6.9% Norwegian, 5.3% English (2000).
Economy: Trading and manufacturing center in a fertile agricultural region. Manufacturing includes printing and publishing, dairy products, chemicals, foods and beverages, machinery, lumber, packaging, paper goods, medical and medical research supplies, woodproducts, fabricated metal products, chemicals and chemical supplies and consumer goods. Employment by occupation: 8.5% management, 26.5% professional, 18.0% services, 24.9% sales, 0.5% farming, 7.2% construction, 14.5% production (2000).
Income: Per capita income: $17,738 (2000); Median household income: $29,766 (2000); Poverty rate: 23.8% (2000).
Taxes: Total city taxes per capita: $279 (2000); City property taxes per capita: $264 (2000).
Education: High school graduation rate: 78.1% (2000); College graduation rate: 28.4% (2000).
Housing: Homeownership rate: 25.0% (2000); Median home value: $97,200 (2000); Median rent: $544 per month (2000); Median age of housing: 29 years (2000).
Safety: Violent crime rate: 95.0 per 10,000 population; Property crime rate: 616.6 per 10,000 population (2001).
Transportation: Commute to work: 81.9% car, 12.2% public transportation, 2.6% walk, 1.5% work from home (2000); Travel time to work: 38.9% less than 15 minutes, 40.5% 15 to 30 minutes, 12.8% 30 to 45 minutes, 4.2% 45 to 60 minutes, 3.5% 60 minutes or more (2000); Amtrak: Service available.

MAPLE BLUFF (village). Covers a land area of 0.699 square miles and a water area of 0 square miles. Located at 43.11° N. Lat.; 89.36° W. Long. Elevation is 940 feet.
History: Executive Mansion is here. Incorporated 1930 as Lakewood Bluff; renamed 1931.
Population: 1,358 (2000); Race: 98.4% White, 1.0% Black, 0.2% Asian, 0.0% American Indian and Alaska Native, 0.5% Hispanic of any race, 0.2% two or more races (2000); Density: 1,944.1 persons per square mile (2000); Age: 24.2% under 18, 17.7% over 64 (2000); Marriage status: 18.1% never married, 72.4% now married, 5.5% widowed, 4.0% divorced (2000); Foreign born: 3.9% (2000); Ancestry (includes multiple ancestries): 36.2% German, 17.9% English, 17.4% Irish, 12.3% Norwegian, 4.7% Polish (2000).
Economy: Single-family building permits issued: 2 (2001) / 0 (2000); Multi-family building permits issued: 0 (2001) / 0 (2000); Employment by occupation: 29.6% management, 38.0% professional, 6.6% services, 22.1% sales, 0.4% farming, 1.0% construction, 2.3% production (2000).
Income: Per capita income: $66,380 (2000); Median household income: $111,400 (2000); Poverty rate: 2.5% (2000).
Taxes: Total city taxes per capita: $740 (1997); City property taxes per capita: $723 (1997).
Education: High school graduation rate: 97.8% (2000); College graduation rate: 77.4% (2000).
Housing: Homeownership rate: 95.6% (2000); Median home value: $278,600 (2000); Median rent: $625 per month (2000); Median age of housing: 54 years (2000).
Safety: Violent crime rate: 7.3 per 10,000 population; Property crime rate: 102.3 per 10,000 population (2001).
Transportation: Commute to work: 87.5% car, 0.0% public transportation, 2.4% walk, 7.3% work from home (2000); Travel time to work: 43.6% less than 15 minutes, 40.8% 15 to 30 minutes, 9.5% 30 to 45 minutes, 1.4% 45 to 60 minutes, 4.7% 60 minutes or more (2000)

MARSHALL (village). Covers a land area of 1.700 square miles and a water area of 0.077 square miles. Located at 43.17° N. Lat.; 89.06° W. Long. Elevation is 870 feet.
Population: 3,432 (2000); Race: 92.7% White, 0.9% Black, 0.6% Asian, 2.0% American Indian and Alaska Native, 4.2% Hispanic of any race, 0.7% two or more races (2000); Density: 2,018.3 persons per square mile (2000); Age: 30.4% under 18, 10.3% over 64 (2000); Marriage status: 20.5% never married, 62.8% now married, 6.0% widowed, 10.7% divorced (2000); Foreign born: 2.0% (2000); Ancestry (includes multiple ancestries): 52.1% German, 14.1% Norwegian, 9.4% Other groups, 8.5% Irish, 8.0% English (2000).
Economy: Farm area. Dairy products; feed mill. Manufacturing: construction; pet foods. Single-family building permits issued: 14 (2001) / 19 (2000); Multi-family building permits issued: 8 (2001) / 4 (2000); Employment by occupation: 10.8% management, 13.9% professional, 16.2% services, 24.5% sales, 0.7% farming, 10.9% construction, 23.0% production (2000).
Income: Per capita income: $19,042 (2000); Median household income: $46,141 (2000); Poverty rate: 4.1% (2000).
Taxes: Total city taxes per capita: $220 (1997); City property taxes per capita: $163 (1997).
Education: High school graduation rate: 84.2% (2000); College graduation rate: 15.8% (2000).

School District(s)

Marshall (PK-12)
2000 Enrollment: 1,205 608-655-3466
Housing: Homeownership rate: 75.6% (2000); Median home value: $132,400 (2000); Median rent: $547 per month (2000); Median age of housing: 20 years (2000).
Safety: Violent crime rate: 11.6 per 10,000 population; Property crime rate: 228.6 per 10,000 population (2001).
Transportation: Commute to work: 95.8% car, 0.0% public transportation, 1.2% walk, 2.8% work from home (2000); Travel time to work: 20.0% less than 15 minutes, 44.7% 15 to 30 minutes, 26.4% 30 to 45 minutes, 5.9% 45 to 60 minutes, 3.0% 60 minutes or more (2000)

MAZOMANIE (village). Covers a land area of 1.364 square miles and a water area of 0.008 square miles. Located at 43.17° N. Lat.; 89.79° W. Long. Elevation is 800 feet.
History: Mazomanie was established by three members of the British Temperance Emigration Society who arrived in 1843. Other members of the society followed them.
Population: 1,485 (2000); Race: 95.0% White, 1.8% Black, 0.1% Asian, 0.1% American Indian and Alaska Native, 2.2% Hispanic of any race, 2.0% two or more races (2000); Density: 1,088.6 persons per square mile (2000); Age: 26.5% under 18, 11.7% over 64 (2000); Marriage status: 23.7% never married, 60.8% now married, 5.1% widowed, 10.3% divorced (2000); Foreign born: 2.2% (2000); Ancestry (includes multiple ancestries): 44.8% German, 17.5% Irish, 16.7% English, 14.6% Norwegian, 6.1% Other groups (2000).
Economy: Single-family building permits issued: 3 (2001) / 5 (2000); Multi-family building permits issued: 2 (2001) / 0 (2000); Employment by occupation: 10.0% management, 19.5% professional, 14.1% services, 26.0% sales, 0.6% farming, 15.0% construction, 14.8% production (2000).
Income: Per capita income: $21,634 (2000); Median household income: $49,191 (2000); Poverty rate: 6.1% (2000).
Taxes: Total city taxes per capita: $266 (1997); City property taxes per capita: $254 (1997).
Education: High school graduation rate: 89.1% (2000); College graduation rate: 19.4% (2000).

School District(s)

Wisconsin Heights (PK-12)
2000 Enrollment: 1,195 608-767-2595
Housing: Homeownership rate: 72.4% (2000); Median home value: $116,800 (2000); Median rent: $469 per month (2000); Median age of housing: 43 years (2000).
Safety: Violent crime rate: 13.4 per 10,000 population; Property crime rate: 40.1 per 10,000 population (2001).
Transportation: Commute to work: 92.8% car, 0.0% public transportation, 3.4% walk, 3.3% work from home (2000); Travel time to work: 29.0% less than 15 minutes, 22.3% 15 to 30 minutes, 33.5% 30 to 45 minutes, 11.6% 45 to 60 minutes, 3.5% 60 minutes or more (2000)

MAZOMANIE (town). Covers a land area of 30.163 square miles and a water area of 0.838 square miles. Located at 43.18° N. Lat.; 89.77° W. Long. Elevation is 800 feet.
Population: 1,185 (2000); Race: 95.4% White, 0.0% Black, 0.7% Asian, 0.0% American Indian and Alaska Native, 3.5% Hispanic of any race, 2.1% two or more races (2000); Density: 39.3 persons per square mile (2000); Age: 26.6% under 18, 7.4% over 64 (2000); Marriage status: 18.2% never married, 68.5% now married, 3.7% widowed, 9.6% divorced (2000); Foreign born: 4.5% (2000); Ancestry (includes multiple ancestries): 47.1% German, 16.4% English, 14.9% Irish, 11.2% Norwegian, 9.0% Other groups (2000).
Economy: Lumber; shipping point and trade center for agricultural area. Railroad junction. Timberline Ski Area to West. Employment by occupation: 13.5% management, 18.0% professional, 11.0% services, 26.5% sales, 1.0% farming, 13.7% construction, 16.4% production (2000).
Income: Per capita income: $24,001 (2000); Median household income: $60,298 (2000); Poverty rate: 1.4% (2000).
Taxes: Total city taxes per capita: $84 (1997); City property taxes per capita: $73 (1997).
Education: High school graduation rate: 88.9% (2000); College graduation rate: 23.1% (2000).

Housing: Homeownership rate: 88.0% (2000); Median home value: $144,200 (2000); Median rent: $390 per month (2000); Median age of housing: 26 years (2000).
Transportation: Commute to work: 94.5% car, 0.4% public transportation, 1.5% walk, 2.7% work from home (2000); Travel time to work: 19.9% less than 15 minutes, 23.8% 15 to 30 minutes, 34.7% 30 to 45 minutes, 14.0% 45 to 60 minutes, 7.7% 60 minutes or more (2000)

MCFARLAND (village). Covers a land area of 3.488 square miles and a water area of 0 square miles. Located at 43.01° N. Lat.; 89.29° W. Long. Elevation is 870 feet.
Population: 6,416 (2000); Race: 96.6% White, 0.3% Black, 2.1% Asian, 0.0% American Indian and Alaska Native, 0.9% Hispanic of any race, 0.8% two or more races (2000); Density: 1,839.3 persons per square mile (2000); Age: 28.0% under 18, 8.3% over 64 (2000); Marriage status: 23.1% never married, 62.8% now married, 5.1% widowed, 9.0% divorced (2000); Foreign born: 1.6% (2000); Ancestry (includes multiple ancestries): 45.3% German, 19.6% Norwegian, 16.7% Irish, 11.8% English, 5.7% Polish (2000).
Economy: In dairy and lake-resort region. Manufacturing: telecomunications equipment, metal fabricating, paper products. Single-family building permits issued: 78 (2001) / 75 (2000); Multi-family building permits issued: 23 (2001) / 16 (2000); Employment by occupation: 20.8% management, 21.4% professional, 12.2% services, 29.3% sales, 0.0% farming, 5.6% construction, 10.7% production (2000).
Income: Per capita income: $26,625 (2000); Median household income: $62,969 (2000); Poverty rate: 3.0% (2000).
Taxes: Total city taxes per capita: $292 (1997); City property taxes per capita: $268 (1997).
Education: High school graduation rate: 96.9% (2000); College graduation rate: 35.6% (2000).

School District(s)

Mcfarland (PK-12)
2000 Enrollment: 1,951 608-838-3169

Housing: Homeownership rate: 73.0% (2000); Median home value: $153,400 (2000); Median rent: $571 per month (2000); Median age of housing: 21 years (2000).
Safety: Violent crime rate: 12.4 per 10,000 population; Property crime rate: 182.6 per 10,000 population (2001).
Transportation: Commute to work: 95.8% car, 0.2% public transportation, 1.7% walk, 2.3% work from home (2000); Travel time to work: 32.1% less than 15 minutes, 56.9% 15 to 30 minutes, 7.6% 30 to 45 minutes, 0.0% 45 to 60 minutes, 3.5% 60 minutes or more (2000)
Additional Information Contacts
McFarland Chamber of Commerce 608-838-4011

MEDINA (town). Covers a land area of 33.549 square miles and a water area of 0.285 square miles. Located at 43.15° N. Lat.; 89.06° W. Long.
Population: 1,235 (2000); Race: 96.5% White, 0.0% Black, 0.0% Asian, 0.0% American Indian and Alaska Native, 5.9% Hispanic of any race, 0.4% two or more races (2000); Density: 36.8 persons per square mile (2000); Age: 26.1% under 18, 10.9% over 64 (2000); Marriage status: 19.7% never married, 67.5% now married, 4.7% widowed, 8.0% divorced (2000); Foreign born: 3.7% (2000); Ancestry (includes multiple ancestries): 55.4% German, 15.1% Norwegian, 9.5% Irish, 8.0% English, 5.8% Other groups (2000).
Economy: Employment by occupation: 13.1% management, 19.9% professional, 11.2% services, 27.9% sales, 2.1% farming, 9.1% construction, 16.6% production (2000).
Income: Per capita income: $27,027 (2000); Median household income: $65,250 (2000); Poverty rate: 5.5% (2000).
Taxes: Total city taxes per capita: $137 (1997); City property taxes per capita: $135 (1997).
Education: High school graduation rate: 87.4% (2000); College graduation rate: 19.4% (2000).
Housing: Homeownership rate: 85.5% (2000); Median home value: $169,700 (2000); Median rent: $518 per month (2000); Median age of housing: 29 years (2000).
Transportation: Commute to work: 93.5% car, 0.0% public transportation, 1.6% walk, 4.4% work from home (2000); Travel time to work: 19.9% less than 15 minutes, 44.0% 15 to 30 minutes, 25.5% 30 to 45 minutes, 6.8% 45 to 60 minutes, 3.8% 60 minutes or more (2000)

MIDDLETON (city). Covers a land area of 8.074 square miles and a water area of 0.015 square miles. Located at 43.10° N. Lat.; 89.50° W. Long. Elevation is 940 feet.
History: Middleton was called Peatville, Mendota, and Station, before Middleton became the permanent name. The village was settled by English and German immigrants, and by the 1860's was a milling center as well as a shipping point for grain and stock. It later became a dairying center.
Population: 15,770 (2000); Race: 91.7% White, 1.8% Black, 2.8% Asian, 0.5% American Indian and Alaska Native, 2.8% Hispanic of any race, 1.9% two or more races (2000); Density: 1,953.2 persons per square mile (2000); Age: 23.3% under 18, 10.3% over 64 (2000); Marriage status: 30.8% never married, 52.8% now married, 4.6% widowed, 11.8% divorced (2000); Foreign born: 5.0% (2000); Ancestry (includes multiple ancestries): 45.0% German, 14.4% Irish, 11.6% English, 10.6% Norwegian, 9.5% Other groups (2000).
Vital Statistics: Birth rate: 107.2 per 10,000 population (1998)
Economy: Single-family building permits issued: 76 (2001) / 102 (2000); Multi-family building permits issued: 52 (2001) / 44 (2000); Employment by occupation: 18.5% management, 31.5% professional, 10.4% services, 26.2% sales, 0.2% farming, 5.0% construction, 8.2% production (2000).
Income: Per capita income: $29,464 (2000); Median household income: $50,786 (2000); Poverty rate: 5.0% (2000).
Taxes: Total city taxes per capita: $466 (2000); City property taxes per capita: $412 (2000).
Education: High school graduation rate: 95.0% (2000); College graduation rate: 50.3% (2000).

School District(s)

Middleton-Cross Plains (PK-12)
2000 Enrollment: 5,125 608-828-1500

Housing: Homeownership rate: 51.5% (2000); Median home value: $176,400 (2000); Median rent: $602 per month (2000); Median age of housing: 25 years (2000).
Safety: Violent crime rate: 3.8 per 10,000 population; Property crime rate: 316.7 per 10,000 population (2001).
Newspapers: Middleton Times-Tribune (1 x week); West Side Shopper (1 x week)
Transportation: Commute to work: 89.6% car, 2.9% public transportation, 1.7% walk, 4.7% work from home (2000); Travel time to work: 40.4% less than 15 minutes, 46.8% 15 to 30 minutes, 9.1% 30 to 45 minutes, 1.8% 45 to 60 minutes, 1.9% 60 minutes or more (2000)
Additional Information Contacts
Middleton Chamber of Commerce 608-831-5696

MIDDLETON (town). Covers a land area of 17.686 square miles and a water area of 0 square miles. Located at 43.07° N. Lat.; 89.55° W. Long. Elevation is 940 feet.
History: Incorporated 1905.
Population: 4,594 (2000); Race: 98.4% White, 0.0% Black, 0.0% Asian, 0.9% American Indian and Alaska Native, 0.9% Hispanic of any race, 0.4% two or more races (2000); Density: 259.8 persons per square mile (2000); Age: 29.2% under 18, 7.5% over 64 (2000); Marriage status: 17.6% never married, 75.4% now married, 2.7% widowed, 4.3% divorced (2000); Foreign born: 1.8% (2000); Ancestry (includes multiple ancestries): 50.1% German, 15.2% Irish, 12.3% English, 11.4% Norwegian, 8.5% Polish (2000).
Economy: In farming and dairying area. Manufacturing; brewery, furniture, textiles, transportation equipment, medical instruments, household furnishings; food and beverage processing, genetic engineering. Morey Airport to Northwest. Employment by occupation: 23.2% management, 31.0% professional, 8.0% services, 25.8% sales, 0.2% farming, 4.6% construction, 7.3% production (2000).
Income: Per capita income: $46,214 (2000); Median household income: $93,008 (2000); Poverty rate: 0.7% (2000).
Taxes: Total city taxes per capita: $170 (1997); City property taxes per capita: $147 (1997).
Education: High school graduation rate: 97.4% (2000); College graduation rate: 55.8% (2000).
Housing: Homeownership rate: 87.8% (2000); Median home value: $246,700 (2000); Median rent: $772 per month (2000); Median age of housing: 15 years (2000).
Transportation: Commute to work: 92.5% car, 1.3% public transportation, 0.3% walk, 6.0% work from home (2000); Travel time to work: 33.1% less than 15 minutes, 49.0% 15 to 30 minutes, 14.9% 30 to 45 minutes, 0.5% 45 to 60 minutes, 2.5% 60 minutes or more (2000)

MONONA (city). Covers a land area of 3.358 square miles and a water area of 0.064 square miles. Located at 43.05° N. Lat.; 89.33° W. Long. Elevation is 880 feet.
History: Incorporated 1938.
Population: 8,018 (2000); Race: 93.5% White, 2.9% Black, 0.0% Asian, 0.5% American Indian and Alaska Native, 2.9% Hispanic of any race, 1.3% two or more races (2000); Density: 2,387.5 persons per square mile (2000);

Age: 20.7% under 18, 17.5% over 64 (2000); Marriage status: 27.8% never married, 51.9% now married, 7.0% widowed, 13.3% divorced (2000); Foreign born: 2.9% (2000); Ancestry (includes multiple ancestries): 42.5% German, 16.9% Irish, 16.3% Norwegian, 11.8% English, 7.2% Other groups (2000).
Economy: In dairy region. Manufacturing: wood products. Single-family building permits issued: 4 (2001) / 5 (2000); Multi-family building permits issued: 0 (2001) / 24 (2000); Employment by occupation: 14.9% management, 26.2% professional, 12.2% services, 29.4% sales, 0.1% farming, 6.8% construction, 10.4% production (2000).
Income: Per capita income: $26,072 (2000); Median household income: $48,034 (2000); Poverty rate: 5.7% (2000).
Taxes: Total city taxes per capita: $405 (1997); City property taxes per capita: $386 (1997).
Education: High school graduation rate: 94.1% (2000); College graduation rate: 36.2% (2000).

School District(s)

Monona Grove (PK-12)
2000 Enrollment: 2,702 608-221-7660
Housing: Homeownership rate: 60.2% (2000); Median home value: $137,300 (2000); Median rent: $544 per month (2000); Median age of housing: 41 years (2000).
Safety: Violent crime rate: 12.4 per 10,000 population; Property crime rate: 495.4 per 10,000 population (2001).
Newspapers: McFarland Community Life (1 x week); The Herald-Independent (1 x week)
Transportation: Commute to work: 91.4% car, 2.2% public transportation, 1.6% walk, 3.9% work from home (2000); Travel time to work: 36.7% less than 15 minutes, 50.2% 15 to 30 minutes, 7.8% 30 to 45 minutes, 1.0% 45 to 60 minutes, 4.4% 60 minutes or more (2000); Amtrak: Service available.

MONTROSE (town). Covers a land area of 34.312 square miles and a water area of 0.233 square miles. Located at 42.90° N. Lat.; 89.54° W. Long. Elevation is 985 feet.
Population: 1,134 (2000); Race: 97.6% White, 0.5% Black, 0.0% Asian, 0.0% American Indian and Alaska Native, 0.8% Hispanic of any race, 1.9% two or more races (2000); Density: 33.0 persons per square mile (2000); Age: 26.3% under 18, 8.7% over 64 (2000); Marriage status: 19.9% never married, 71.1% now married, 2.3% widowed, 6.7% divorced (2000); Foreign born: 0.7% (2000); Ancestry (includes multiple ancestries): 45.4% German, 18.4% Swiss, 15.9% Irish, 14.4% Norwegian, 10.9% English (2000).
Economy: Employment by occupation: 24.9% management, 19.5% professional, 9.1% services, 23.8% sales, 2.5% farming, 9.8% construction, 10.2% production (2000).
Income: Per capita income: $24,364 (2000); Median household income: $59,821 (2000); Poverty rate: 1.6% (2000).
Taxes: Total city taxes per capita: $241 (1997); City property taxes per capita: $234 (1997).
Education: High school graduation rate: 94.1% (2000); College graduation rate: 27.4% (2000).
Housing: Homeownership rate: 83.1% (2000); Median home value: $144,100 (2000); Median rent: $510 per month (2000); Median age of housing: 34 years (2000).
Transportation: Commute to work: 84.1% car, 0.0% public transportation, 3.5% walk, 11.4% work from home (2000); Travel time to work: 27.9% less than 15 minutes, 34.8% 15 to 30 minutes, 30.6% 30 to 45 minutes, 2.1% 45 to 60 minutes, 4.6% 60 minutes or more (2000)

MOUNT HOREB (village). Covers a land area of 2.913 square miles and a water area of 0 square miles. Located at 43.00° N. Lat.; 89.73° W. Long. Elevation is 1,240 feet.
History: Settled 1860 by Norwegians and Swiss; incorporated 1899.
Population: 5,860 (2000); Race: 98.3% White, 0.1% Black, 0.7% Asian, 0.1% American Indian and Alaska Native, 0.9% Hispanic of any race, 0.5% two or more races (2000); Density: 2,011.5 persons per square mile (2000); Age: 28.5% under 18, 13.1% over 64 (2000); Marriage status: 20.9% never married, 65.4% now married, 5.1% widowed, 8.6% divorced (2000); Foreign born: 1.5% (2000); Ancestry (includes multiple ancestries): 45.7% German, 26.8% Norwegian, 17.2% Irish, 10.0% English, 6.9% Swiss (2000).
Economy: In dairying and farming area; processes dairy products, feed. Manufacturing: plastic injection molding. Single-family building permits issued: 29 (2001) / 45 (2000); Multi-family building permits issued: 0 (2001) / 23 (2000); Employment by occupation: 15.6% management, 18.4% professional, 13.1% services, 30.7% sales, 0.2% farming, 11.7% construction, 10.3% production (2000).
Income: Per capita income: $23,359 (2000); Median household income: $55,513 (2000); Poverty rate: 3.1% (2000).
Taxes: Total city taxes per capita: $379 (1997); City property taxes per capita: $365 (1997).
Education: High school graduation rate: 92.2% (2000); College graduation rate: 27.5% (2000).

School District(s)

Mount Horeb Area (PK-12)
2000 Enrollment: 1,979 608-437-5595
Housing: Homeownership rate: 63.4% (2000); Median home value: $145,700 (2000); Median rent: $558 per month (2000); Median age of housing: 21 years (2000).
Safety: Violent crime rate: 16.9 per 10,000 population; Property crime rate: 294.8 per 10,000 population (2001).
Newspapers: Town and Country Shopping News (1 x week); Mount Horeb Mail (1 x week)
Transportation: Commute to work: 91.3% car, 0.2% public transportation, 3.8% walk, 4.1% work from home (2000); Travel time to work: 26.5% less than 15 minutes, 36.7% 15 to 30 minutes, 26.9% 30 to 45 minutes, 7.0% 45 to 60 minutes, 2.9% 60 minutes or more (2000)
Additional Information Contacts
Mt Horeb Chamber of Commerce 608-437-5914

OREGON (village). Covers a land area of 3.065 square miles and a water area of 0 square miles. Located at 42.92° N. Lat.; 89.38° W. Long. Elevation is 949 feet.
History: Oregon was settled in 1842 and platted in 1856. The village became an agricultural trading center, with tobacco as a primary product. John Muir once taught in a rural school near Oregon.
Population: 7,514 (2000); Race: 97.2% White, 0.6% Black, 0.4% Asian, 0.3% American Indian and Alaska Native, 0.5% Hispanic of any race, 1.2% two or more races (2000); Density: 2,451.2 persons per square mile (2000); Age: 30.7% under 18, 9.3% over 64 (2000); Marriage status: 19.4% never married, 66.2% now married, 4.2% widowed, 10.2% divorced (2000); Foreign born: 2.2% (2000); Ancestry (includes multiple ancestries): 46.7% German, 19.2% Irish, 14.3% Norwegian, 11.0% English, 5.0% Polish (2000).
Economy: Single-family building permits issued: 45 (2001) / 36 (2000); Multi-family building permits issued: 65 (2001) / 22 (2000); Employment by occupation: 17.3% management, 25.0% professional, 12.6% services, 29.0% sales, 0.2% farming, 7.7% construction, 8.2% production (2000).
Income: Per capita income: $23,650 (2000); Median household income: $56,584 (2000); Poverty rate: 3.3% (2000).
Taxes: Total city taxes per capita: $279 (2000); City property taxes per capita: $256 (2000).
Education: High school graduation rate: 93.6% (2000); College graduation rate: 40.2% (2000).

School District(s)

Oregon (PK-12)
2000 Enrollment: 3,430 608-835-4003
Housing: Homeownership rate: 71.9% (2000); Median home value: $146,000 (2000); Median rent: $570 per month (2000); Median age of housing: 18 years (2000).
Safety: Violent crime rate: 5.3 per 10,000 population; Property crime rate: 277.5 per 10,000 population (2001).
Newspapers: Oregon Observer (1 x week); The Great Dane Shopping News (1 x week)
Transportation: Commute to work: 96.5% car, 0.0% public transportation, 1.5% walk, 2.0% work from home (2000); Travel time to work: 21.7% less than 15 minutes, 57.3% 15 to 30 minutes, 15.0% 30 to 45 minutes, 2.2% 45 to 60 minutes, 3.8% 60 minutes or more (2000)
Additional Information Contacts
Oregon Chamber of Commerce 608-835-3697

OREGON (town). Covers a land area of 32.148 square miles and a water area of 0.131 square miles. Located at 42.90° N. Lat.; 89.43° W. Long. Elevation is 949 feet.
History: Settled 1842, incorporated 1883.
Population: 3,148 (2000); Race: 98.4% White, 0.3% Black, 0.2% Asian, 0.2% American Indian and Alaska Native, 0.6% Hispanic of any race, 0.8% two or more races (2000); Density: 97.9 persons per square mile (2000); Age: 32.0% under 18, 5.0% over 64 (2000); Marriage status: 18.3% never married, 73.5% now married, 2.9% widowed, 5.3% divorced (2000); Foreign born: 1.7% (2000); Ancestry (includes multiple ancestries): 47.4% German, 15.5% Irish, 14.5% Norwegian, 11.2% English, 5.9% Swiss (2000).
Economy: In dairying and farming area: hogs; tobacco; creamery. Light manufacturing. Employment by occupation: 17.2% management, 31.1%

professional, 10.5% services, 23.0% sales, 0.1% farming, 10.2% construction, 7.9% production (2000).
Income: Per capita income: $28,218 (2000); Median household income: $72,250 (2000); Poverty rate: 0.4% (2000).
Taxes: Total city taxes per capita: $152 (1997); City property taxes per capita: $142 (1997).
Education: High school graduation rate: 95.8% (2000); College graduation rate: 43.3% (2000).
Housing: Homeownership rate: 93.3% (2000); Median home value: $183,200 (2000); Median rent: $807 per month (2000); Median age of housing: 20 years (2000).
Transportation: Commute to work: 90.4% car, 0.0% public transportation, 0.3% walk, 8.9% work from home (2000); Travel time to work: 22.5% less than 15 minutes, 52.2% 15 to 30 minutes, 20.0% 30 to 45 minutes, 2.8% 45 to 60 minutes, 2.5% 60 minutes or more (2000)

PERRY (town). Covers a land area of 36.137 square miles and a water area of 0 square miles. Located at 42.89° N. Lat.; 89.79° W. Long.
Population: 670 (2000); Race: 96.7% White, 0.3% Black, 0.3% Asian, 0.0% American Indian and Alaska Native, 0.6% Hispanic of any race, 1.1% two or more races (2000); Density: 18.5 persons per square mile (2000); Age: 26.7% under 18, 10.7% over 64 (2000); Marriage status: 19.9% never married, 70.3% now married, 1.7% widowed, 8.1% divorced (2000); Foreign born: 1.0% (2000); Ancestry (includes multiple ancestries): 39.0% German, 29.0% Norwegian, 15.0% Irish, 10.7% Swiss, 9.0% English (2000).
Economy: Employment by occupation: 19.8% management, 18.0% professional, 6.0% services, 23.8% sales, 1.8% farming, 14.5% construction, 16.0% production (2000).
Income: Per capita income: $22,596 (2000); Median household income: $57,125 (2000); Poverty rate: 6.2% (2000).
Taxes: Total city taxes per capita: $155 (1997); City property taxes per capita: $149 (1997).
Education: High school graduation rate: 88.6% (2000); College graduation rate: 26.3% (2000).
Housing: Homeownership rate: 91.6% (2000); Median home value: $117,500 (2000); Median rent: $450 per month (2000); Median age of housing: 60+ years (2000).
Transportation: Commute to work: 94.1% car, 0.0% public transportation, 0.0% walk, 5.1% work from home (2000); Travel time to work: 11.0% less than 15 minutes, 23.6% 15 to 30 minutes, 44.0% 30 to 45 minutes, 17.2% 45 to 60 minutes, 4.3% 60 minutes or more (2000)

PLEASANT SPRINGS (town). Covers a land area of 33.363 square miles and a water area of 2.229 square miles. Located at 42.97° N. Lat.; 89.21° W. Long.
Population: 3,053 (2000); Race: 97.8% White, 0.4% Black, 1.1% Asian, 0.1% American Indian and Alaska Native, 0.0% Hispanic of any race, 0.5% two or more races (2000); Density: 91.5 persons per square mile (2000); Age: 26.6% under 18, 10.4% over 64 (2000); Marriage status: 20.0% never married, 69.7% now married, 3.7% widowed, 6.5% divorced (2000); Foreign born: 1.2% (2000); Ancestry (includes multiple ancestries): 43.9% German, 30.5% Norwegian, 14.2% Irish, 8.5% English, 4.7% Polish (2000).
Economy: Employment by occupation: 14.4% management, 25.6% professional, 13.0% services, 25.4% sales, 0.9% farming, 10.4% construction, 10.3% production (2000).
Income: Per capita income: $28,938 (2000); Median household income: $68,958 (2000); Poverty rate: 4.1% (2000).
Taxes: Total city taxes per capita: $98 (1997); City property taxes per capita: $96 (1997).
Education: High school graduation rate: 92.0% (2000); College graduation rate: 30.1% (2000).
Housing: Homeownership rate: 91.1% (2000); Median home value: $165,300 (2000); Median rent: $448 per month (2000); Median age of housing: 29 years (2000).
Transportation: Commute to work: 92.4% car, 0.0% public transportation, 1.4% walk, 6.1% work from home (2000); Travel time to work: 26.3% less than 15 minutes, 50.1% 15 to 30 minutes, 19.3% 30 to 45 minutes, 1.9% 45 to 60 minutes, 2.4% 60 minutes or more (2000)

PRIMROSE (town). Covers a land area of 35.835 square miles and a water area of 0 square miles. Located at 42.90° N. Lat.; 89.65° W. Long. Elevation is 1,002 feet.
Population: 682 (2000); Race: 97.7% White, 0.6% Black, 0.0% Asian, 0.8% American Indian and Alaska Native, 0.0% Hispanic of any race, 0.9% two or more races (2000); Density: 19.0 persons per square mile (2000); Age: 23.7% under 18, 10.5% over 64 (2000); Marriage status: 23.5% never married, 65.6% now married, 4.0% widowed, 6.9% divorced (2000); Foreign born: 1.8% (2000); Ancestry (includes multiple ancestries): 38.8% German, 32.4% Norwegian, 18.2% Swiss, 15.1% English, 8.9% Irish (2000).
Economy: Employment by occupation: 24.2% management, 17.3% professional, 10.4% services, 27.9% sales, 1.3% farming, 8.2% construction, 10.6% production (2000).
Income: Per capita income: $23,935 (2000); Median household income: $51,964 (2000); Poverty rate: 4.4% (2000).
Taxes: Total city taxes per capita: $165 (1997); City property taxes per capita: $163 (1997).
Education: High school graduation rate: 88.0% (2000); College graduation rate: 20.4% (2000).
Housing: Homeownership rate: 83.5% (2000); Median home value: $158,300 (2000); Median rent: $608 per month (2000); Median age of housing: 36 years (2000).
Transportation: Commute to work: 81.8% car, 0.0% public transportation, 3.6% walk, 14.6% work from home (2000); Travel time to work: 16.1% less than 15 minutes, 39.4% 15 to 30 minutes, 33.5% 30 to 45 minutes, 8.7% 45 to 60 minutes, 2.3% 60 minutes or more (2000)

ROCKDALE (village). Covers a land area of 0.234 square miles and a water area of 0.009 square miles. Located at 42.97° N. Lat.; 89.03° W. Long. Elevation is 830 feet.
Population: 214 (2000); Race: 98.3% White, 0.0% Black, 0.0% Asian, 0.0% American Indian and Alaska Native, 0.0% Hispanic of any race, 1.7% two or more races (2000); Density: 914.7 persons per square mile (2000); Age: 29.0% under 18, 9.7% over 64 (2000); Marriage status: 30.6% never married, 51.4% now married, 3.8% widowed, 14.2% divorced (2000); Foreign born: 1.3% (2000); Ancestry (includes multiple ancestries): 53.4% German, 34.9% Norwegian, 14.3% English, 13.4% Irish, 9.2% French (except Basque) (2000).
Economy: In dairying and tobacco-growing region. Single-family building permits issued: 0 (2001) / 0 (2000); Multi-family building permits issued: 0 (2001) / 0 (2000); Employment by occupation: 13.8% management, 22.0% professional, 13.8% services, 22.8% sales, 0.0% farming, 10.6% construction, 17.1% production (2000).
Income: Per capita income: $19,416 (2000); Median household income: $37,500 (2000); Poverty rate: 8.8% (2000).
Taxes: Total city taxes per capita: $17 (1997); City property taxes per capita: $13 (1997).
Education: High school graduation rate: 87.7% (2000); College graduation rate: 30.3% (2000).
Housing: Homeownership rate: 65.3% (2000); Median home value: $119,400 (2000); Median rent: $480 per month (2000); Median age of housing: 60+ years (2000).
Transportation: Commute to work: 92.7% car, 0.0% public transportation, 3.3% walk, 4.1% work from home (2000); Travel time to work: 40.7% less than 15 minutes, 24.6% 15 to 30 minutes, 28.8% 30 to 45 minutes, 1.7% 45 to 60 minutes, 4.2% 60 minutes or more (2000)

ROXBURY (town). Covers a land area of 34.597 square miles and a water area of 1.311 square miles. Located at 43.25° N. Lat.; 89.66° W. Long. Elevation is 868 feet.
Population: 1,700 (2000); Race: 99.0% White, 0.0% Black, 0.5% Asian, 0.2% American Indian and Alaska Native, 0.9% Hispanic of any race, 0.1% two or more races (2000); Density: 49.1 persons per square mile (2000); Age: 29.4% under 18, 9.0% over 64 (2000); Marriage status: 17.1% never married, 73.4% now married, 4.0% widowed, 5.5% divorced (2000); Foreign born: 0.8% (2000); Ancestry (includes multiple ancestries): 69.4% German, 10.1% Irish, 8.0% Norwegian, 6.4% English, 4.5% Polish (2000).
Economy: Employment by occupation: 21.6% management, 19.7% professional, 11.8% services, 22.9% sales, 1.3% farming, 10.8% construction, 12.0% production (2000).
Income: Per capita income: $24,708 (2000); Median household income: $60,463 (2000); Poverty rate: 5.4% (2000).
Taxes: Total city taxes per capita: $64 (1997); City property taxes per capita: $61 (1997).
Education: High school graduation rate: 87.8% (2000); College graduation rate: 22.1% (2000).
Housing: Homeownership rate: 86.7% (2000); Median home value: $160,500 (2000); Median rent: $525 per month (2000); Median age of housing: 28 years (2000).
Transportation: Commute to work: 87.9% car, 0.5% public transportation, 1.8% walk, 9.1% work from home (2000); Travel time to work: 32.1% less than 15 minutes, 27.0% 15 to 30 minutes, 27.8% 30 to 45 minutes, 9.1% 45 to 60 minutes, 4.0% 60 minutes or more (2000)

RUTLAND (town). Covers a land area of 35.269 square miles and a water area of 0.137 square miles. Located at 42.88° N. Lat.; 89.31° W. Long. Elevation is 940 feet.
Population: 1,887 (2000); Race: 97.1% White, 0.2% Black, 0.0% Asian, 1.6% American Indian and Alaska Native, 1.4% Hispanic of any race, 1.1% two or more races (2000); Density: 53.5 persons per square mile (2000); Age: 26.0% under 18, 7.7% over 64 (2000); Marriage status: 19.5% never married, 69.3% now married, 3.5% widowed, 7.8% divorced (2000); Foreign born: 2.6% (2000); Ancestry (includes multiple ancestries): 40.7% German, 22.1% Norwegian, 13.4% English, 10.6% Irish, 5.9% United States or American (2000).
Economy: Employment by occupation: 19.5% management, 22.9% professional, 12.0% services, 21.9% sales, 1.2% farming, 15.3% construction, 7.1% production (2000).
Income: Per capita income: $27,695 (2000); Median household income: $64,740 (2000); Poverty rate: 1.3% (2000).
Taxes: Total city taxes per capita: $133 (1997); City property taxes per capita: $131 (1997).
Education: High school graduation rate: 92.3% (2000); College graduation rate: 25.2% (2000).
Housing: Homeownership rate: 91.6% (2000); Median home value: $159,200 (2000); Median rent: $559 per month (2000); Median age of housing: 27 years (2000).
Transportation: Commute to work: 93.5% car, 0.0% public transportation, 0.9% walk, 5.0% work from home (2000); Travel time to work: 18.3% less than 15 minutes, 51.8% 15 to 30 minutes, 22.3% 30 to 45 minutes, 3.3% 45 to 60 minutes, 4.3% 60 minutes or more (2000)

SHOREWOOD HILLS (village). Covers a land area of 0.809 square miles and a water area of 0 square miles. Located at 43.07° N. Lat.; 89.44° W. Long. Elevation is 950 feet.
History: At West end of University of Wisconsin campus. Incorporated 1927.
Population: 1,732 (2000); Race: 94.0% White, 2.0% Black, 2.1% Asian, 0.8% American Indian and Alaska Native, 0.3% Hispanic of any race, 1.1% two or more races (2000); Density: 2,139.8 persons per square mile (2000); Age: 26.9% under 18, 16.5% over 64 (2000); Marriage status: 16.4% never married, 66.8% now married, 4.4% widowed, 12.3% divorced (2000); Foreign born: 7.5% (2000); Ancestry (includes multiple ancestries): 31.2% German, 25.4% English, 13.5% Irish, 11.5% Other groups, 7.2% Norwegian (2000).
Economy: Single-family building permits issued: 1 (2001) / 1 (2000); Multi-family building permits issued: 0 (2001) / 0 (2000); Employment by occupation: 16.9% management, 66.7% professional, 1.9% services, 9.3% sales, 0.0% farming, 2.3% construction, 2.9% production (2000).
Income: Per capita income: $57,328 (2000); Median household income: $122,879 (2000); Poverty rate: 2.7% (2000).
Taxes: Total city taxes per capita: $847 (1997); City property taxes per capita: $816 (1997).
Education: High school graduation rate: 99.5% (2000); College graduation rate: 81.8% (2000).
Housing: Homeownership rate: 93.7% (2000); Median home value: $311,300 (2000); Median rent: $641 per month (2000); Median age of housing: 56 years (2000).
Safety: Violent crime rate: 0.0 per 10,000 population; Property crime rate: 223.6 per 10,000 population (2001).
Transportation: Commute to work: 72.0% car, 6.9% public transportation, 6.0% walk, 7.7% work from home (2000); Travel time to work: 50.1% less than 15 minutes, 38.8% 15 to 30 minutes, 3.5% 30 to 45 minutes, 3.8% 45 to 60 minutes, 3.9% 60 minutes or more (2000)

SPRINGDALE (town). Covers a land area of 35.277 square miles and a water area of 0 square miles. Located at 42.97° N. Lat.; 89.65° W. Long.
Population: 1,530 (2000); Race: 96.9% White, 0.8% Black, 0.7% Asian, 0.0% American Indian and Alaska Native, 1.0% Hispanic of any race, 1.1% two or more races (2000); Density: 43.4 persons per square mile (2000); Age: 27.9% under 18, 9.1% over 64 (2000); Marriage status: 19.1% never married, 70.4% now married, 2.4% widowed, 8.1% divorced (2000); Foreign born: 1.6% (2000); Ancestry (includes multiple ancestries): 44.3% German, 17.9% Norwegian, 16.6% Irish, 11.7% English, 8.3% Swiss (2000).
Economy: Employment by occupation: 19.0% management, 25.9% professional, 8.7% services, 23.3% sales, 0.4% farming, 12.7% construction, 10.0% production (2000).
Income: Per capita income: $27,138 (2000); Median household income: $65,655 (2000); Poverty rate: 1.9% (2000).
Taxes: Total city taxes per capita: $162 (1997); City property taxes per capita: $152 (1997).
Education: High school graduation rate: 93.9% (2000); College graduation rate: 31.5% (2000).
Housing: Homeownership rate: 86.7% (2000); Median home value: $181,600 (2000); Median rent: $586 per month (2000); Median age of housing: 26 years (2000).
Transportation: Commute to work: 91.2% car, 0.7% public transportation, 0.7% walk, 6.6% work from home (2000); Travel time to work: 23.9% less than 15 minutes, 47.1% 15 to 30 minutes, 23.2% 30 to 45 minutes, 4.1% 45 to 60 minutes, 1.7% 60 minutes or more (2000)

SPRINGFIELD (town). Covers a land area of 36.205 square miles and a water area of 0.178 square miles. Located at 43.16° N. Lat.; 89.54° W. Long.
Population: 2,762 (2000); Race: 98.8% White, 0.0% Black, 0.5% Asian, 0.0% American Indian and Alaska Native, 0.7% Hispanic of any race, 0.1% two or more races (2000); Density: 76.3 persons per square mile (2000); Age: 30.8% under 18, 7.1% over 64 (2000); Marriage status: 19.5% never married, 72.8% now married, 0.8% widowed, 6.9% divorced (2000); Foreign born: 2.2% (2000); Ancestry (includes multiple ancestries): 63.0% German, 9.8% English, 9.1% Norwegian, 7.7% Irish, 4.5% United States or American (2000).
Economy: Employment by occupation: 22.2% management, 21.0% professional, 9.7% services, 23.4% sales, 2.4% farming, 11.6% construction, 9.8% production (2000).
Income: Per capita income: $26,946 (2000); Median household income: $68,663 (2000); Poverty rate: 3.8% (2000).
Taxes: Total city taxes per capita: $134 (1997); City property taxes per capita: $124 (1997).
Education: High school graduation rate: 91.7% (2000); College graduation rate: 31.1% (2000).
Housing: Homeownership rate: 87.3% (2000); Median home value: $194,500 (2000); Median rent: $441 per month (2000); Median age of housing: 25 years (2000).
Transportation: Commute to work: 88.3% car, 0.0% public transportation, 2.4% walk, 7.1% work from home (2000); Travel time to work: 33.7% less than 15 minutes, 50.7% 15 to 30 minutes, 14.5% 30 to 45 minutes, 0.1% 45 to 60 minutes, 1.0% 60 minutes or more (2000)

STOUGHTON (city). Covers a land area of 3.964 square miles and a water area of 0.144 square miles. Located at 42.92° N. Lat.; 89.22° W. Long. Elevation is 900 feet.
History: Stoughton was named for Luke Stoughton, who acquired land here from Daniel Webster in 1847. After T.G. Mandt founded the T.G. Mandt Wagon Company in 1865, Stoughton became known as the Wagon City. Many Norwegian immigrants came to Stoughton in the 1870's.
Population: 12,354 (2000); Race: 95.9% White, 0.8% Black, 1.1% Asian, 0.4% American Indian and Alaska Native, 1.1% Hispanic of any race, 1.4% two or more races (2000); Density: 3,116.6 persons per square mile (2000); Age: 28.5% under 18, 14.6% over 64 (2000); Marriage status: 20.5% never married, 62.1% now married, 6.9% widowed, 10.5% divorced (2000); Foreign born: 1.6% (2000); Ancestry (includes multiple ancestries): 38.6% German, 29.6% Norwegian, 14.2% Irish, 9.7% English, 5.3% Other groups (2000).
Economy: Single-family building permits issued: 50 (2001) / 44 (2000); Multi-family building permits issued: 18 (2001) / 28 (2000); Employment by occupation: 14.5% management, 19.4% professional, 14.1% services, 27.4% sales, 0.0% farming, 9.4% construction, 15.2% production (2000).
Income: Per capita income: $21,037 (2000); Median household income: $47,633 (2000); Poverty rate: 5.0% (2000).
Taxes: Total city taxes per capita: $242 (1997); City property taxes per capita: $221 (1997).
Education: High school graduation rate: 88.5% (2000); College graduation rate: 27.7% (2000).

School District(s)

Stoughton Area (PK-12)
2000 Enrollment: 3,657 608-877-5001
Housing: Homeownership rate: 64.8% (2000); Median home value: $131,600 (2000); Median rent: $561 per month (2000); Median age of housing: 26 years (2000).
Hospitals: Stoughton Hospital Association (69 beds)
Safety: Violent crime rate: 4.8 per 10,000 population; Property crime rate: 221.8 per 10,000 population (2001).
Newspapers: Stoughton Courier-Hub (1 x week)
Transportation: Commute to work: 90.4% car, 1.4% public transportation, 3.5% walk, 3.9% work from home (2000); Travel time to work: 34.7% less

than 15 minutes, 33.3% 15 to 30 minutes, 26.2% 30 to 45 minutes, 3.1% 45 to 60 minutes, 2.6% 60 minutes or more (2000)
Additional Information Contacts
Stoughton Chamber of Commerce 608-873-7912

SUN PRAIRIE (city). Covers a land area of 9.546 square miles and a water area of 0 square miles. Located at 43.18° N. Lat.; 89.23° W. Long. Elevation is 951 feet.
History: Sun Prairie was named in 1837 by a group passing this way from Milwaukee to Madison, who had endured nine days of rain and were pleased to have sunshine here. One of the party, Charles H. Bird, became the first settler in Sun Prairie. Artist Georgia O'Keeffe was born in Sun Prairie.
Population: 20,369 (2000); Race: 92.7% White, 2.5% Black, 1.5% Asian, 0.4% American Indian and Alaska Native, 3.6% Hispanic of any race, 1.0% two or more races (2000); Density: 2,133.7 persons per square mile (2000); Age: 28.8% under 18, 9.0% over 64 (2000); Marriage status: 26.1% never married, 59.9% now married, 4.8% widowed, 9.2% divorced (2000); Foreign born: 3.7% (2000); Ancestry (includes multiple ancestries): 46.0% German, 13.5% Irish, 13.5% Norwegian, 9.0% Other groups, 8.4% English (2000).
Vital Statistics: Birth rate: 156.6 per 10,000 population (1998)
Economy: Single-family building permits issued: 264 (2001) / 155 (2000); Multi-family building permits issued: 252 (2001) / 222 (2000); Employment by occupation: 17.4% management, 22.5% professional, 10.1% services, 29.8% sales, 0.2% farming, 7.2% construction, 12.9% production (2000).
Income: Per capita income: $23,277 (2000); Median household income: $51,345 (2000); Poverty rate: 4.4% (2000).
Taxes: Total city taxes per capita: $337 (1997); City property taxes per capita: $321 (1997).
Education: High school graduation rate: 90.9% (2000); College graduation rate: 34.4% (2000).

School District(s)

Sun Prairie Area (PK-12)
2000 Enrollment: 4,776 608-834-6501
Housing: Homeownership rate: 60.9% (2000); Median home value: $143,400 (2000); Median rent: $606 per month (2000); Median age of housing: 21 years (2000).
Safety: Violent crime rate: 11.7 per 10,000 population; Property crime rate: 319.3 per 10,000 population (2001).
Newspapers: The Star (1 x week); The Advertiser (1 x week)
Transportation: Commute to work: 95.2% car, 0.3% public transportation, 1.4% walk, 2.7% work from home (2000); Travel time to work: 38.0% less than 15 minutes, 36.3% 15 to 30 minutes, 18.5% 30 to 45 minutes, 3.9% 45 to 60 minutes, 3.3% 60 minutes or more (2000)
Additional Information Contacts
Sun Prairie Chamber of Commerce 608-837-4547

SUN PRAIRIE (town). Covers a land area of 31.367 square miles and a water area of 0 square miles. Located at 43.15° N. Lat.; 89.19° W. Long. Elevation is 951 feet.
History: Georgia O'Keeffe born here. Settled c.1837, incorporated 1868.
Population: 2,308 (2000); Race: 96.6% White, 0.2% Black, 0.0% Asian, 0.3% American Indian and Alaska Native, 2.7% Hispanic of any race, 1.0% two or more races (2000); Density: 73.6 persons per square mile (2000); Age: 23.8% under 18, 10.3% over 64 (2000); Marriage status: 17.9% never married, 72.1% now married, 2.5% widowed, 7.5% divorced (2000); Foreign born: 2.4% (2000); Ancestry (includes multiple ancestries): 50.0% German, 16.1% Irish, 14.4% Norwegian, 7.8% English, 6.4% Other groups (2000).
Economy: In farm area; porcelain manufacturing; canned foods, dairy products, wood and laminated materials. Employment by occupation: 14.4% management, 17.2% professional, 6.4% services, 27.8% sales, 0.6% farming, 17.3% construction, 16.3% production (2000).
Income: Per capita income: $24,954 (2000); Median household income: $60,938 (2000); Poverty rate: 1.5% (2000).
Taxes: Total city taxes per capita: $141 (1997); City property taxes per capita: $127 (1997).
Education: High school graduation rate: 87.5% (2000); College graduation rate: 17.2% (2000).
Housing: Homeownership rate: 79.8% (2000); Median home value: $161,700 (2000); Median rent: $711 per month (2000); Median age of housing: 28 years (2000).
Transportation: Commute to work: 93.4% car, 0.0% public transportation, 1.7% walk, 4.5% work from home (2000); Travel time to work: 23.9% less than 15 minutes, 50.3% 15 to 30 minutes, 21.1% 30 to 45 minutes, 2.1% 45 to 60 minutes, 2.7% 60 minutes or more (2000)

VERMONT (town). Covers a land area of 35.772 square miles and a water area of 0 square miles. Located at 43.08° N. Lat.; 89.77° W. Long.
Population: 839 (2000); Race: 98.8% White, 0.0% Black, 0.6% Asian, 0.2% American Indian and Alaska Native, 0.0% Hispanic of any race, 0.4% two or more races (2000); Density: 23.5 persons per square mile (2000); Age: 27.2% under 18, 10.4% over 64 (2000); Marriage status: 14.2% never married, 77.1% now married, 2.6% widowed, 6.1% divorced (2000); Foreign born: 1.1% (2000); Ancestry (includes multiple ancestries): 45.4% German, 27.0% Norwegian, 15.3% Irish, 9.5% English, 7.2% Swiss (2000).
Economy: Employment by occupation: 17.4% management, 30.2% professional, 11.5% services, 17.8% sales, 0.2% farming, 15.0% construction, 7.8% production (2000).
Income: Per capita income: $26,549 (2000); Median household income: $65,208 (2000); Poverty rate: 2.8% (2000).
Taxes: Total city taxes per capita: $211 (1997); City property taxes per capita: $201 (1997).
Education: High school graduation rate: 93.5% (2000); College graduation rate: 41.9% (2000).
Housing: Homeownership rate: 88.1% (2000); Median home value: $163,500 (2000); Median rent: $438 per month (2000); Median age of housing: 26 years (2000).
Transportation: Commute to work: 88.6% car, 0.4% public transportation, 1.8% walk, 9.2% work from home (2000); Travel time to work: 21.9% less than 15 minutes, 31.3% 15 to 30 minutes, 30.8% 30 to 45 minutes, 9.6% 45 to 60 minutes, 6.3% 60 minutes or more (2000)

VERONA (city). Covers a land area of 3.270 square miles and a water area of 0 square miles. Located at 42.99° N. Lat.; 89.53° W. Long. Elevation is 980 feet.
Population: 7,052 (2000); Race: 96.2% White, 0.9% Black, 1.8% Asian, 0.1% American Indian and Alaska Native, 1.2% Hispanic of any race, 0.9% two or more races (2000); Density: 2,156.3 persons per square mile (2000); Age: 31.6% under 18, 10.0% over 64 (2000); Marriage status: 21.3% never married, 63.9% now married, 5.4% widowed, 9.4% divorced (2000); Foreign born: 3.1% (2000); Ancestry (includes multiple ancestries): 40.9% German, 17.5% Norwegian, 16.7% Irish, 11.6% English, 4.4% Other groups (2000).
Economy: Single-family building permits issued: 157 (2001) / 158 (2000); Multi-family building permits issued: 223 (2001) / 164 (2000); Employment by occupation: 20.3% management, 25.6% professional, 10.1% services, 30.2% sales, 0.2% farming, 8.4% construction, 5.2% production (2000).
Income: Per capita income: $26,433 (2000); Median household income: $65,367 (2000); Poverty rate: 3.7% (2000).
Taxes: Total city taxes per capita: $403 (2000); City property taxes per capita: $375 (2000).
Education: High school graduation rate: 94.5% (2000); College graduation rate: 39.8% (2000).

School District(s)

Verona Area (PK-12)
2000 Enrollment: 4,222 608-845-4310
Housing: Homeownership rate: 72.6% (2000); Median home value: $161,500 (2000); Median rent: $577 per month (2000); Median age of housing: 18 years (2000).
Safety: Violent crime rate: 35.2 per 10,000 population; Property crime rate: 202.8 per 10,000 population (2001).
Newspapers: The Verona Press (1 x week)
Transportation: Commute to work: 92.1% car, 0.2% public transportation, 2.7% walk, 4.8% work from home (2000); Travel time to work: 31.7% less than 15 minutes, 53.5% 15 to 30 minutes, 11.0% 30 to 45 minutes, 1.4% 45 to 60 minutes, 2.4% 60 minutes or more (2000)
Additional Information Contacts
Verona Chamber of Commerce 608-845-5777

VERONA (town). Covers a land area of 29.315 square miles and a water area of 0.039 square miles. Located at 42.98° N. Lat.; 89.54° W. Long. Elevation is 980 feet.
Population: 2,153 (2000); Race: 98.0% White, 0.9% Black, 0.0% Asian, 0.0% American Indian and Alaska Native, 0.4% Hispanic of any race, 0.6% two or more races (2000); Density: 73.4 persons per square mile (2000); Age: 24.8% under 18, 13.9% over 64 (2000); Marriage status: 26.3% never married, 61.8% now married, 4.3% widowed, 7.6% divorced (2000); Foreign born: 0.5% (2000); Ancestry (includes multiple ancestries): 50.1% German, 13.5% Norwegian, 10.4% Irish, 9.7% English, 7.0% Swiss (2000).
Economy: In dairying region. Manufacturing: diffusers, registers; post frame buildings, molded plastic parts, printing. Agricultural research station to North. Employment by occupation: 14.6% management, 28.4% professional,

6.9% services, 30.1% sales, 0.7% farming, 8.7% construction, 10.6% production (2000).
Income: Per capita income: $31,405 (2000); Median household income: $69,519 (2000); Poverty rate: 2.2% (2000).
Taxes: Total city taxes per capita: $189 (1997); City property taxes per capita: $179 (1997).
Education: High school graduation rate: 93.5% (2000); College graduation rate: 38.2% (2000).
Housing: Homeownership rate: 82.4% (2000); Median home value: $192,400 (2000); Median rent: $600 per month (2000); Median age of housing: 27 years (2000).
Transportation: Commute to work: 93.9% car, 0.3% public transportation, 0.1% walk, 5.7% work from home (2000); Travel time to work: 42.2% less than 15 minutes, 36.1% 15 to 30 minutes, 17.6% 30 to 45 minutes, 0.6% 45 to 60 minutes, 3.5% 60 minutes or more (2000)

VIENNA (town). Covers a land area of 35.557 square miles and a water area of 0.020 square miles. Located at 43.24° N. Lat.; 89.41° W. Long.
Population: 1,294 (2000); Race: 98.9% White, 0.2% Black, 0.0% Asian, 0.3% American Indian and Alaska Native, 0.5% Hispanic of any race, 0.7% two or more races (2000); Density: 36.4 persons per square mile (2000); Age: 28.0% under 18, 7.3% over 64 (2000); Marriage status: 22.7% never married, 69.9% now married, 2.5% widowed, 4.8% divorced (2000); Foreign born: 1.2% (2000); Ancestry (includes multiple ancestries): 57.3% German, 21.6% Norwegian, 15.1% Irish, 7.3% English, 4.1% French (except Basque) (2000).
Economy: Employment by occupation: 17.8% management, 15.4% professional, 10.2% services, 25.6% sales, 3.4% farming, 14.2% construction, 13.5% production (2000).
Income: Per capita income: $24,783 (2000); Median household income: $60,000 (2000); Poverty rate: 3.3% (2000).
Taxes: Total city taxes per capita: $236 (2000); City property taxes per capita: $230 (2000).
Education: High school graduation rate: 92.6% (2000); College graduation rate: 17.2% (2000).
Housing: Homeownership rate: 84.7% (2000); Median home value: $157,200 (2000); Median rent: $622 per month (2000); Median age of housing: 31 years (2000).
Transportation: Commute to work: 86.9% car, 0.6% public transportation, 2.4% walk, 10.0% work from home (2000); Travel time to work: 38.0% less than 15 minutes, 36.1% 15 to 30 minutes, 21.4% 30 to 45 minutes, 1.1% 45 to 60 minutes, 3.4% 60 minutes or more (2000)

WAUNAKEE (village). Covers a land area of 5.957 square miles and a water area of 0 square miles. Located at 43.18° N. Lat.; 89.45° W. Long. Elevation is 925 feet.
Population: 8,995 (2000); Race: 98.4% White, 0.1% Black, 0.7% Asian, 0.0% American Indian and Alaska Native, 0.7% Hispanic of any race, 0.7% two or more races (2000); Density: 1,509.9 persons per square mile (2000); Age: 31.3% under 18, 9.3% over 64 (2000); Marriage status: 22.3% never married, 66.4% now married, 3.8% widowed, 7.5% divorced (2000); Foreign born: 1.8% (2000); Ancestry (includes multiple ancestries): 50.2% German, 15.6% Irish, 13.1% Norwegian, 7.2% English, 5.1% United States or American (2000).
Economy: In farming and dairying area; dairy products. Manufacturing includes dairy equipment, gear reducers, pharmaceutical products; printing. Single-family building permits issued: 114 (2001) / 99 (2000); Multi-family building permits issued: 2 (2001) / 4 (2000); Employment by occupation: 16.9% management, 22.8% professional, 10.9% services, 30.2% sales, 0.4% farming, 7.9% construction, 10.9% production (2000).
Income: Per capita income: $25,952 (2000); Median household income: $59,225 (2000); Poverty rate: 1.7% (2000).
Taxes: Total city taxes per capita: $270 (1997); City property taxes per capita: $238 (1997).
Education: High school graduation rate: 92.2% (2000); College graduation rate: 32.3% (2000).

School District(s)

Waunakee Community (PK-12)
2000 Enrollment: 2,836 608-849-2000

Housing: Homeownership rate: 67.0% (2000); Median home value: $175,300 (2000); Median rent: $665 per month (2000); Median age of housing: 14 years (2000).
Safety: Violent crime rate: 2.2 per 10,000 population; Property crime rate: 103.8 per 10,000 population (2001).
Newspapers: The Waunakee Tribune (1 x week)
Transportation: Commute to work: 91.7% car, 0.2% public transportation, 3.4% walk, 4.0% work from home (2000); Travel time to work: 28.7% less than 15 minutes, 52.0% 15 to 30 minutes, 15.2% 30 to 45 minutes, 1.9% 45 to 60 minutes, 2.2% 60 minutes or more (2000)

Additional Information Contacts

Waunakee Chamber of Commerce. 608-849-5977

WESTPORT (town). Covers a land area of 22.231 square miles and a water area of 5.006 square miles. Located at 43.15° N. Lat.; 89.42° W. Long.
Population: 3,586 (2000); Race: 97.7% White, 0.4% Black, 0.2% Asian, 0.0% American Indian and Alaska Native, 3.2% Hispanic of any race, 0.4% two or more races (2000); Density: 161.3 persons per square mile (2000); Age: 23.0% under 18, 15.3% over 64 (2000); Marriage status: 19.8% never married, 64.1% now married, 5.9% widowed, 10.1% divorced (2000); Foreign born: 1.4% (2000); Ancestry (includes multiple ancestries): 52.5% German, 18.2% Irish, 12.4% Norwegian, 9.8% English, 6.1% United States or American (2000).
Economy: Employment by occupation: 21.4% management, 26.5% professional, 4.5% services, 28.4% sales, 0.5% farming, 9.2% construction, 9.5% production (2000).
Income: Per capita income: $40,268 (2000); Median household income: $64,750 (2000); Poverty rate: 3.0% (2000).
Taxes: Total city taxes per capita: $200 (2000); City property taxes per capita: $158 (2000).
Education: High school graduation rate: 94.8% (2000); College graduation rate: 38.2% (2000).
Housing: Homeownership rate: 78.3% (2000); Median home value: $195,100 (2000); Median rent: $660 per month (2000); Median age of housing: 14 years (2000).
Transportation: Commute to work: 91.3% car, 0.5% public transportation, 1.1% walk, 6.7% work from home (2000); Travel time to work: 23.2% less than 15 minutes, 56.8% 15 to 30 minutes, 15.3% 30 to 45 minutes, 3.0% 45 to 60 minutes, 1.6% 60 minutes or more (2000)

WINDSOR (town). Covers a land area of 30.732 square miles and a water area of 0.104 square miles. Located at 43.23° N. Lat.; 89.33° W. Long. Elevation is 902 feet.
Population: 5,286 (2000); Race: 96.6% White, 1.2% Black, 1.1% Asian, 0.0% American Indian and Alaska Native, 0.7% Hispanic of any race, 0.8% two or more races (2000); Density: 172.0 persons per square mile (2000); Age: 28.4% under 18, 6.0% over 64 (2000); Marriage status: 19.8% never married, 72.8% now married, 1.6% widowed, 5.8% divorced (2000); Foreign born: 1.5% (2000); Ancestry (includes multiple ancestries): 49.0% German, 18.2% Norwegian, 15.3% Irish, 11.6% English, 4.6% United States or American (2000).
Economy: Employment by occupation: 21.8% management, 23.8% professional, 8.4% services, 27.8% sales, 1.2% farming, 7.6% construction, 9.5% production (2000).
Income: Per capita income: $29,266 (2000); Median household income: $67,610 (2000); Poverty rate: 0.5% (2000).
Taxes: Total city taxes per capita: $191 (2000); City property taxes per capita: $177 (2000).
Education: High school graduation rate: 94.7% (2000); College graduation rate: 31.7% (2000).
Housing: Homeownership rate: 80.5% (2000); Median home value: $155,700 (2000); Median rent: $609 per month (2000); Median age of housing: 24 years (2000).
Transportation: Commute to work: 90.0% car, 0.2% public transportation, 0.8% walk, 8.7% work from home (2000); Travel time to work: 31.2% less than 15 minutes, 37.9% 15 to 30 minutes, 21.3% 30 to 45 minutes, 2.3% 45 to 60 minutes, 7.2% 60 minutes or more (2000)

YORK (town). Covers a land area of 35.879 square miles and a water area of 0.021 square miles. Located at 43.24° N. Lat.; 89.07° W. Long.
Population: 703 (2000); Race: 98.8% White, 0.0% Black, 1.2% Asian, 0.0% American Indian and Alaska Native, 0.3% Hispanic of any race, 0.0% two or more races (2000); Density: 19.6 persons per square mile (2000); Age: 29.4% under 18, 13.5% over 64 (2000); Marriage status: 19.2% never married, 70.5% now married, 3.0% widowed, 7.2% divorced (2000); Foreign born: 2.0% (2000); Ancestry (includes multiple ancestries): 55.0% German, 12.1% Norwegian, 9.9% Irish, 5.6% United States or American, 5.5% English (2000).
Economy: Employment by occupation: 19.5% management, 12.8% professional, 5.5% services, 18.3% sales, 5.8% farming, 16.3% construction, 21.8% production (2000).
Income: Per capita income: $21,805 (2000); Median household income: $52,019 (2000); Poverty rate: 7.7% (2000).

Taxes: Total city taxes per capita: $190 (1997); City property taxes per capita: $188 (1997).
Education: High school graduation rate: 85.9% (2000); College graduation rate: 15.6% (2000).
Housing: Homeownership rate: 83.2% (2000); Median home value: $151,900 (2000); Median rent: $620 per month (2000); Median age of housing: 53 years (2000).
Transportation: Commute to work: 82.7% car, 0.0% public transportation, 5.3% walk, 12.0% work from home (2000); Travel time to work: 24.3% less than 15 minutes, 44.5% 15 to 30 minutes, 25.9% 30 to 45 minutes, 3.0% 45 to 60 minutes, 2.3% 60 minutes or more (2000)

Dodge County

Located in south central Wisconsin; drained by Rock River and its tributaries; includes Beaverdam, Fox, and Sinissippi Lakes. Covers a land area of 882.30 square miles, a water area of 24.70 square miles, and is located in the Central Time Zone. The county government was organized in 1836. County seat is Juneau.

Weather Station: Beaver Dam — Elevation: 839 feet

	Jan	Feb	Mar	Apr	May	Jun	Jul	Aug	Sep	Oct	Nov	Dec
High	26	31	43	57	70	79	83	80	73	61	44	31
Low	9	14	25	36	46	56	60	58	50	39	28	16
Precip	1.3	1.2	2.2	3.4	3.1	3.9	4.2	3.7	3.8	2.6	2.3	1.7
Snow	10.7	7.3	5.8	1.5	tr	0.0	0.0	0.0	0.0	0.2	2.5	10.1

High and Low temperatures in degrees Fahrenheit; Precipitation and Snow in inches

Weather Station: Horicon — Elevation: 879 feet

	Jan	Feb	Mar	Apr	May	Jun	Jul	Aug	Sep	Oct	Nov	Dec
High	25	30	42	56	69	78	82	80	72	60	44	31
Low	7	12	23	35	46	55	60	57	49	38	27	14
Precip	1.2	1.1	2.1	3.3	3.0	3.9	4.3	4.1	3.8	2.7	2.1	1.5
Snow	11.8	6.8	5.5	1.7	0.2	0.0	0.0	0.0	0.0	0.1	2.5	9.1

High and Low temperatures in degrees Fahrenheit; Precipitation and Snow in inches

Population: 85,897 (2000); Race: 95.1% White, 2.5% Black, 0.3% Asian, 0.5% American Indian and Alaska Native, 2.3% Hispanic of any race, 0.7% two or more races (2000); Density: 97.4 persons per square mile (2000); Age: 24.8% under 18, 14.0% over 64 (2000).
Religion: Five largest groups: 19.5% Catholic Church, 11.9% Wisconsin Evangelical Lutheran Synod, 8.7% Evangelical Lutheran Church in America, 7.6% Lutheran Church—Missouri Synod, 3.4% Reformed Church in America (2000).
Economy: Unemployment rate: 4.6% (11/2002); Total civilian labor force: 47,501 (11/2002); Leading industries: 43.9% manufacturing; 11.5% health care and social assistance; 11.2% retail trade (2000); Companies that employ more than 1,000 persons: 2 (2000); Companies that employ more than 100 persons: 52 (2000); Farms: 1,807 totaling 391,959 acres (1997); Minority business ownership rate: 0.0% (1997); Women business ownership rate: 22.2% (1997); Retail sales per capita: $6,609 (1997). Single-family building permits issued: 308 (2001) / 320 (2000); Multi-family building permits issued: 40 (2001) / 64 (2000).
Income: Per capita income: $19,574 (2000); Median household income: $45,190 (2000); Poverty rate: 5.3% (2000); Bankruptcy rate: 3.16% (2001).
Taxes: Total county taxes per capita: $259 (2000); County property taxes per capita: $216 (2000).
Education: High school graduation rate: 82.3% (2000); College graduation rate: 13.2% (2000).
Housing: Homeownership rate: 73.5% (2000); Median home value: $105,800 (2000); Median rent: $453 per month (2000); Median age of housing: 40 years (2000).
Health: Birth rate: 109.8 per 10,000 population (1998); Age adjusted death rate: 91.5 per 10,000 population (1999); Age adjusted cancer mortality rate: 215.9 deaths per 100,000 population (1999). Air Quality Index: 84% good, 16% moderate, 0% unhealthy (percent of days in 2000). Number of physicians: 9.8 per 10,000 population (1999); Number of hospital beds: 30.4 per 10,000 population (1999).
Elections: 2000 Presidential election results: 38.7% Gore, 57.5% Bush, 2.9% Nader, 0.4% Buchanan
National and State Parks: Beaver Dam Lake State Wildlife Area; Horicon Marsh State Public Hunting Grounds; Horicon National Wildlife Refuge; Shaw Marsh State Wildlife Area
Additional Information Contacts
Dodge County Government Offices 920-386-4411
Beaver Dam Area Chamber of Commerce 262-887-8879
Dodge County Board of Realtors 262-887-7909
Fox Lake Chamber of Commerce 920-928-3777
Horicon Chamber of Commerce 920-485-3200
Mayville Chamber of Commerce 920-387-5776
Randolph Chamber of Commerce 920-326-4769
Waupun Chamber of Commerce 920-324-3491

Dodge County Communities

ASHIPPUN (town). Covers a land area of 35.642 square miles and a water area of 0.085 square miles. Located at 43.24° N. Lat.; 88.48° W. Long. Elevation is 858 feet.
Population: 2,308 (2000); Race: 98.9% White, 0.0% Black, 0.2% Asian, 0.3% American Indian and Alaska Native, 1.6% Hispanic of any race, 0.3% two or more races (2000); Density: 64.8 persons per square mile (2000); Age: 25.8% under 18, 9.4% over 64 (2000); Marriage status: 19.8% never married, 68.4% now married, 3.8% widowed, 8.0% divorced (2000); Foreign born: 0.9% (2000); Ancestry (includes multiple ancestries): 59.2% German, 10.5% Irish, 7.0% Norwegian, 6.8% Polish, 6.8% English (2000).
Economy: Employment by occupation: 11.7% management, 11.5% professional, 14.4% services, 25.0% sales, 3.2% farming, 14.2% construction, 20.1% production (2000).
Income: Per capita income: $22,698 (2000); Median household income: $55,982 (2000); Poverty rate: 2.1% (2000).
Taxes: Total city taxes per capita: $168 (1997); City property taxes per capita: $160 (1997).
Education: High school graduation rate: 86.6% (2000); College graduation rate: 12.8% (2000).
Housing: Homeownership rate: 79.4% (2000); Median home value: $140,000 (2000); Median rent: $601 per month (2000); Median age of housing: 33 years (2000).
Transportation: Commute to work: 94.5% car, 0.0% public transportation, 1.6% walk, 3.5% work from home (2000); Travel time to work: 13.8% less than 15 minutes, 45.1% 15 to 30 minutes, 24.6% 30 to 45 minutes, 11.1% 45 to 60 minutes, 5.4% 60 minutes or more (2000)

BEAVER DAM (city). Covers a land area of 5.222 square miles and a water area of 1.338 square miles. Located at 43.46° N. Lat.; 88.83° W. Long. Elevation is 879 feet.
History: Beaver Dam, settled in the early 1840's, developed as a trading and manufacturing center. It was named for the nearby lake which offered good fishing.
Population: 15,169 (2000); Race: 95.5% White, 0.6% Black, 0.4% Asian, 1.0% American Indian and Alaska Native, 3.4% Hispanic of any race, 1.1% two or more races (2000); Density: 2,904.6 persons per square mile (2000); Age: 24.9% under 18, 16.5% over 64 (2000); Marriage status: 24.0% never married, 54.5% now married, 9.2% widowed, 12.2% divorced (2000); Foreign born: 2.8% (2000); Ancestry (includes multiple ancestries): 55.0% German, 11.3% Irish, 8.2% Polish, 7.8% Other groups, 6.0% English (2000).
Vital Statistics: Birth rate: 146.4 per 10,000 population (1998)
Economy: Single-family building permits issued: 11 (2001) / 14 (2000); Multi-family building permits issued: 8 (2001) / 10 (2000); Employment by occupation: 8.7% management, 15.7% professional, 18.1% services, 21.7% sales, 0.9% farming, 6.4% construction, 28.6% production (2000).
Income: Per capita income: $19,592 (2000); Median household income: $37,873 (2000); Poverty rate: 7.0% (2000).
Taxes: Total city taxes per capita: $309 (1997); City property taxes per capita: $290 (1997).
Education: High school graduation rate: 82.8% (2000); College graduation rate: 16.0% (2000).

School District(s)

Beaver Dam (PK-12)
2000 Enrollment: 3,432 920-885-7300

Housing: Homeownership rate: 60.9% (2000); Median home value: $91,400 (2000); Median rent: $461 per month (2000); Median age of housing: 46 years (2000).
Hospitals: Beaver Dam Community Hospital (125 beds)
Safety: Violent crime rate: 6.5 per 10,000 population; Property crime rate: 408.5 per 10,000 population (2001).
Newspapers: Daily Citizen (6 x week); Tri-County (1 x week); Monday Mini (1 x week)
Transportation: Commute to work: 92.5% car, 1.6% public transportation, 3.3% walk, 1.8% work from home (2000); Travel time to work: 54.1% less than 15 minutes, 26.2% 15 to 30 minutes, 12.6% 30 to 45 minutes, 3.6% 45 to 60 minutes, 3.5% 60 minutes or more (2000)

Additional Information Contacts
Beaver Dam Area Chamber of Commerce. 262-887-8879
Dodge County Board of Realtors 262-887-7909

BEAVER DAM (town). Covers a land area of 34.261 square miles and a water area of 2.763 square miles. Located at 43.44° N. Lat.; 88.82° W. Long. Elevation is 879 feet.
History: Incorporated 1856.
Population: 3,440 (2000); Race: 97.5% White, 0.0% Black, 0.0% Asian, 0.1% American Indian and Alaska Native, 3.2% Hispanic of any race, 0.6% two or more races (2000); Density: 100.4 persons per square mile (2000); Age: 27.5% under 18, 11.9% over 64 (2000); Marriage status: 21.6% never married, 67.8% now married, 3.0% widowed, 7.6% divorced (2000); Foreign born: 1.8% (2000); Ancestry (includes multiple ancestries): 55.4% German, 11.6% Irish, 6.7% Polish, 5.5% United States or American, 5.5% English (2000).
Economy: Railroad junction in a productive farm and dairy area. There is a foundry here. Manufacturing: food processing, metal fabrication, machinery, printing, metal products. Single-family building permits issued: 36 (2001) / 36 (2000); Multi-family building permits issued: 0 (2001) / 0 (2000); Employment by occupation: 11.4% management, 14.8% professional, 11.5% services, 22.9% sales, 1.7% farming, 10.2% construction, 27.5% production (2000).
Income: Per capita income: $21,541 (2000); Median household income: $49,964 (2000); Poverty rate: 6.0% (2000).
Taxes: Total city taxes per capita: $67 (1997); City property taxes per capita: $44 (1997).
Education: High school graduation rate: 86.2% (2000); College graduation rate: 16.6% (2000).
Housing: Homeownership rate: 91.9% (2000); Median home value: $154,000 (2000); Median rent: $463 per month (2000); Median age of housing: 26 years (2000).
Transportation: Commute to work: 93.3% car, 0.3% public transportation, 1.9% walk, 4.5% work from home (2000); Travel time to work: 51.2% less than 15 minutes, 27.6% 15 to 30 minutes, 9.5% 30 to 45 minutes, 5.6% 45 to 60 minutes, 6.0% 60 minutes or more (2000)

BROWNSVILLE (village). Covers a land area of 0.388 square miles and a water area of 0 square miles. Located at 43.61° N. Lat.; 88.49° W. Long. Elevation is 1,000 feet.
Population: 570 (2000); Race: 99.1% White, 0.2% Black, 0.0% Asian, 0.0% American Indian and Alaska Native, 1.2% Hispanic of any race, 0.0% two or more races (2000); Density: 1,467.3 persons per square mile (2000); Age: 26.7% under 18, 12.8% over 64 (2000); Marriage status: 19.8% never married, 72.8% now married, 4.5% widowed, 2.9% divorced (2000); Foreign born: 1.6% (2000); Ancestry (includes multiple ancestries): 67.4% German, 11.1% Irish, 8.2% English, 7.7% Norwegian, 6.3% Polish (2000).
Economy: Dairying; general farming. Horicon National Wildlife Refuge to West. Single-family building permits issued: 0 (2001) / 1 (2000); Multi-family building permits issued: 0 (2001) / 0 (2000); Employment by occupation: 11.3% management, 24.1% professional, 11.6% services, 16.9% sales, 0.0% farming, 8.8% construction, 27.3% production (2000).
Income: Per capita income: $22,452 (2000); Median household income: $62,679 (2000); Poverty rate: 0.0% (2000).
Taxes: Total city taxes per capita: $378 (1997); City property taxes per capita: $367 (1997).
Education: High school graduation rate: 93.2% (2000); College graduation rate: 20.7% (2000).
Housing: Homeownership rate: 81.7% (2000); Median home value: $124,000 (2000); Median rent: $508 per month (2000); Median age of housing: 30 years (2000).
Transportation: Commute to work: 95.5% car, 0.0% public transportation, 2.5% walk, 1.9% work from home (2000); Travel time to work: 45.8% less than 15 minutes, 39.3% 15 to 30 minutes, 7.5% 30 to 45 minutes, 3.2% 45 to 60 minutes, 4.2% 60 minutes or more (2000)

BURNETT (town). Covers a land area of 36.191 square miles and a water area of 0.266 square miles. Located at 43.50° N. Lat.; 88.71° W. Long. Elevation is 875 feet.
Population: 919 (2000); Race: 98.6% White, 0.0% Black, 0.0% Asian, 0.0% American Indian and Alaska Native, 0.3% Hispanic of any race, 1.1% two or more races (2000); Density: 25.4 persons per square mile (2000); Age: 27.1% under 18, 12.2% over 64 (2000); Marriage status: 20.0% never married, 67.1% now married, 4.8% widowed, 8.0% divorced (2000); Foreign born: 1.2% (2000); Ancestry (includes multiple ancestries): 63.4% German, 6.8% Norwegian, 6.8% Dutch, 6.7% Polish, 5.4% English (2000).
Economy: Single-family building permits issued: 5 (2001) / 5 (2000); Multi-family building permits issued: 0 (2001) / 0 (2000); Employment by occupation: 12.5% management, 12.5% professional, 10.0% services, 19.1% sales, 4.0% farming, 11.6% construction, 30.3% production (2000).
Income: Per capita income: $22,043 (2000); Median household income: $55,000 (2000); Poverty rate: 5.8% (2000).
Taxes: Total city taxes per capita: $144 (1997); City property taxes per capita: $140 (1997).
Education: High school graduation rate: 83.4% (2000); College graduation rate: 11.0% (2000).
Housing: Homeownership rate: 87.4% (2000); Median home value: $109,400 (2000); Median rent: $250 per month (2000); Median age of housing: 60+ years (2000).
Transportation: Commute to work: 87.7% car, 0.0% public transportation, 2.7% walk, 9.6% work from home (2000); Travel time to work: 42.4% less than 15 minutes, 43.3% 15 to 30 minutes, 7.5% 30 to 45 minutes, 4.1% 45 to 60 minutes, 2.8% 60 minutes or more (2000)

CALAMUS (town). Covers a land area of 36.083 square miles and a water area of 0.469 square miles. Located at 43.42° N. Lat.; 88.94° W. Long.
Population: 1,005 (2000); Race: 99.3% White, 0.0% Black, 0.0% Asian, 0.2% American Indian and Alaska Native, 0.5% Hispanic of any race, 0.0% two or more races (2000); Density: 27.9 persons per square mile (2000); Age: 24.3% under 18, 11.3% over 64 (2000); Marriage status: 26.1% never married, 63.4% now married, 3.6% widowed, 6.9% divorced (2000); Foreign born: 1.5% (2000); Ancestry (includes multiple ancestries): 62.3% German, 9.1% Irish, 6.9% English, 6.6% Polish, 5.9% Norwegian (2000).
Economy: Employment by occupation: 18.6% management, 12.9% professional, 8.4% services, 24.7% sales, 3.8% farming, 8.8% construction, 22.8% production (2000).
Income: Per capita income: $19,818 (2000); Median household income: $50,000 (2000); Poverty rate: 7.8% (2000).
Taxes: Total city taxes per capita: $88 (1997); City property taxes per capita: $76 (1997).
Education: High school graduation rate: 85.0% (2000); College graduation rate: 11.7% (2000).
Housing: Homeownership rate: 86.7% (2000); Median home value: $119,600 (2000); Median rent: $433 per month (2000); Median age of housing: 44 years (2000).
Transportation: Commute to work: 87.7% car, 0.0% public transportation, 3.3% walk, 8.6% work from home (2000); Travel time to work: 39.8% less than 15 minutes, 35.2% 15 to 30 minutes, 14.8% 30 to 45 minutes, 3.5% 45 to 60 minutes, 6.7% 60 minutes or more (2000)

CHESTER (town). Covers a land area of 33.196 square miles and a water area of 1.220 square miles. Located at 43.60° N. Lat.; 88.72° W. Long.
Population: 960 (2000); Race: 87.8% White, 8.8% Black, 0.0% Asian, 0.5% American Indian and Alaska Native, 5.5% Hispanic of any race, 0.8% two or more races (2000); Density: 28.9 persons per square mile (2000); Age: 21.3% under 18, 10.3% over 64 (2000); Marriage status: 17.9% never married, 68.4% now married, 5.7% widowed, 8.0% divorced (2000); Foreign born: 1.0% (2000); Ancestry (includes multiple ancestries): 42.3% German, 24.6% Dutch, 12.9% Other groups, 7.2% Irish, 6.1% English (2000).
Economy: Single-family building permits issued: 2 (2001) / 2 (2000); Multi-family building permits issued: 0 (2001) / 0 (2000); Employment by occupation: 17.8% management, 12.0% professional, 12.0% services, 15.5% sales, 2.3% farming, 7.9% construction, 32.6% production (2000).
Income: Per capita income: $20,915 (2000); Median household income: $49,688 (2000); Poverty rate: 3.0% (2000).
Taxes: Total city taxes per capita: $33 (1997); City property taxes per capita: $27 (1997).
Education: High school graduation rate: 79.5% (2000); College graduation rate: 6.7% (2000).
Housing: Homeownership rate: 92.1% (2000); Median home value: $110,300 (2000); Median rent: $417 per month (2000); Median age of housing: 44 years (2000).
Transportation: Commute to work: 88.5% car, 0.5% public transportation, 4.3% walk, 6.6% work from home (2000); Travel time to work: 39.1% less than 15 minutes, 43.2% 15 to 30 minutes, 12.0% 30 to 45 minutes, 1.1% 45 to 60 minutes, 4.6% 60 minutes or more (2000)

CLYMAN (village). Covers a land area of 0.242 square miles and a water area of 0 square miles. Located at 43.31° N. Lat.; 88.72° W. Long. Elevation is 906 feet.
Population: 388 (2000); Race: 93.8% White, 0.0% Black, 0.5% Asian, 2.0% American Indian and Alaska Native, 4.2% Hispanic of any race, 1.7% two or

more races (2000); Density: 1,605.2 persons per square mile (2000); Age: 31.3% under 18, 11.1% over 64 (2000); Marriage status: 21.9% never married, 57.1% now married, 5.6% widowed, 15.3% divorced (2000); Foreign born: 2.0% (2000); Ancestry (includes multiple ancestries): 60.1% German, 11.6% Irish, 8.4% Other groups, 4.7% Polish, 3.4% Norwegian (2000).
Economy: Single-family building permits issued: 0 (2001) / 0 (2000); Multi-family building permits issued: 0 (2001) / 0 (2000); Employment by occupation: 6.0% management, 5.5% professional, 8.0% services, 22.4% sales, 0.5% farming, 10.9% construction, 46.8% production (2000).
Income: Per capita income: $16,346 (2000); Median household income: $40,000 (2000); Poverty rate: 6.4% (2000).
Taxes: Total city taxes per capita: $206 (1997); City property taxes per capita: $201 (1997).
Education: High school graduation rate: 77.4% (2000); College graduation rate: 4.4% (2000).
Housing: Homeownership rate: 69.0% (2000); Median home value: $96,400 (2000); Median rent: $494 per month (2000); Median age of housing: 33 years (2000).
Transportation: Commute to work: 95.9% car, 0.0% public transportation, 2.1% walk, 2.1% work from home (2000); Travel time to work: 24.2% less than 15 minutes, 39.5% 15 to 30 minutes, 17.9% 30 to 45 minutes, 11.1% 45 to 60 minutes, 7.4% 60 minutes or more (2000)

CLYMAN (town). Covers a land area of 35.399 square miles and a water area of 0.025 square miles. Located at 43.33° N. Lat.; 88.72° W. Long. Elevation is 906 feet.
Population: 849 (2000); Race: 98.4% White, 0.0% Black, 0.0% Asian, 0.7% American Indian and Alaska Native, 0.4% Hispanic of any race, 0.7% two or more races (2000); Density: 24.0 persons per square mile (2000); Age: 26.5% under 18, 10.4% over 64 (2000); Marriage status: 24.5% never married, 65.5% now married, 5.9% widowed, 4.1% divorced (2000); Foreign born: 1.2% (2000); Ancestry (includes multiple ancestries): 62.8% German, 11.1% Polish, 7.2% Irish, 6.2% English, 3.6% French (except Basque) (2000).
Economy: In dairying region. Railroad junction. Manufacturing: vegetable processing, California olives, cherries. Employment by occupation: 17.2% management, 9.1% professional, 15.7% services, 22.9% sales, 2.3% farming, 12.9% construction, 19.9% production (2000).
Income: Per capita income: $20,102 (2000); Median household income: $48,462 (2000); Poverty rate: 4.8% (2000).
Taxes: Total city taxes per capita: $99 (1997); City property taxes per capita: $98 (1997).
Education: High school graduation rate: 83.1% (2000); College graduation rate: 14.0% (2000).
Housing: Homeownership rate: 82.6% (2000); Median home value: $116,100 (2000); Median rent: $431 per month (2000); Median age of housing: 60+ years (2000).
Transportation: Commute to work: 80.2% car, 0.2% public transportation, 4.5% walk, 14.5% work from home (2000); Travel time to work: 30.8% less than 15 minutes, 35.3% 15 to 30 minutes, 17.2% 30 to 45 minutes, 7.5% 45 to 60 minutes, 9.2% 60 minutes or more (2000)

ELBA (town). Covers a land area of 35.435 square miles and a water area of 0.050 square miles. Located at 43.32° N. Lat.; 88.95° W. Long.
Population: 1,086 (2000); Race: 97.8% White, 0.0% Black, 0.4% Asian, 0.0% American Indian and Alaska Native, 0.6% Hispanic of any race, 0.7% two or more races (2000); Density: 30.6 persons per square mile (2000); Age: 25.9% under 18, 10.7% over 64 (2000); Marriage status: 21.0% never married, 64.5% now married, 5.3% widowed, 9.2% divorced (2000); Foreign born: 0.6% (2000); Ancestry (includes multiple ancestries): 62.4% German, 11.6% Irish, 10.0% Norwegian, 6.9% English, 6.2% Polish (2000).
Economy: Single-family building permits issued: 6 (2001) / 2 (2000); Multi-family building permits issued: 0 (2001) / 0 (2000); Employment by occupation: 17.1% management, 12.4% professional, 10.8% services, 23.8% sales, 2.9% farming, 12.9% construction, 20.1% production (2000).
Income: Per capita income: $22,055 (2000); Median household income: $57,132 (2000); Poverty rate: 3.6% (2000).
Taxes: Total city taxes per capita: $133 (1997); City property taxes per capita: $128 (1997).
Education: High school graduation rate: 85.8% (2000); College graduation rate: 16.3% (2000).
Housing: Homeownership rate: 82.3% (2000); Median home value: $153,200 (2000); Median rent: $475 per month (2000); Median age of housing: 45 years (2000).
Transportation: Commute to work: 87.4% car, 0.0% public transportation, 1.6% walk, 10.9% work from home (2000); Travel time to work: 39.8% less than 15 minutes, 21.3% 15 to 30 minutes, 20.4% 30 to 45 minutes, 10.8% 45 to 60 minutes, 7.7% 60 minutes or more (2000)

EMMET (town). Covers a land area of 31.735 square miles and a water area of 0 square miles. Located at 43.25° N. Lat.; 88.71° W. Long.
Population: 1,221 (2000); Race: 97.9% White, 0.2% Black, 0.4% Asian, 0.0% American Indian and Alaska Native, 1.5% Hispanic of any race, 0.3% two or more races (2000); Density: 38.5 persons per square mile (2000); Age: 29.8% under 18, 8.3% over 64 (2000); Marriage status: 20.7% never married, 69.6% now married, 3.3% widowed, 6.4% divorced (2000); Foreign born: 1.9% (2000); Ancestry (includes multiple ancestries): 69.1% German, 9.0% Irish, 7.5% English, 4.9% Polish, 3.9% Other groups (2000).
Economy: Single-family building permits issued: 6 (2001) / 6 (2000); Multi-family building permits issued: 0 (2001) / 0 (2000); Employment by occupation: 11.2% management, 12.7% professional, 8.9% services, 23.5% sales, 2.7% farming, 13.7% construction, 27.3% production (2000).
Income: Per capita income: $18,904 (2000); Median household income: $51,154 (2000); Poverty rate: 2.3% (2000).
Taxes: Total city taxes per capita: $169 (1997); City property taxes per capita: $165 (1997).
Education: High school graduation rate: 87.8% (2000); College graduation rate: 12.7% (2000).
Housing: Homeownership rate: 78.8% (2000); Median home value: $142,500 (2000); Median rent: $528 per month (2000); Median age of housing: 47 years (2000).
Transportation: Commute to work: 88.5% car, 0.0% public transportation, 2.7% walk, 8.3% work from home (2000); Travel time to work: 42.9% less than 15 minutes, 31.8% 15 to 30 minutes, 11.8% 30 to 45 minutes, 6.5% 45 to 60 minutes, 7.0% 60 minutes or more (2000)

FOX LAKE (city). Covers a land area of 1.403 square miles and a water area of 0.105 square miles. Located at 43.56° N. Lat.; 88.91° W. Long. Elevation is 920 feet.
Population: 1,454 (2000); Race: 97.1% White, 0.8% Black, 0.0% Asian, 0.3% American Indian and Alaska Native, 3.0% Hispanic of any race, 1.5% two or more races (2000); Density: 1,036.1 persons per square mile (2000); Age: 24.8% under 18, 17.7% over 64 (2000); Marriage status: 22.5% never married, 56.6% now married, 10.7% widowed, 10.2% divorced (2000); Foreign born: 1.3% (2000); Ancestry (includes multiple ancestries): 54.6% German, 13.7% Irish, 8.6% Polish, 7.4% Norwegian, 6.7% Other groups (2000).
Economy: Single-family building permits issued: 12 (2001) / 7 (2000); Multi-family building permits issued: 0 (2001) / 0 (2000); Employment by occupation: 7.5% management, 10.8% professional, 11.9% services, 24.2% sales, 1.2% farming, 13.4% construction, 31.1% production (2000).
Income: Per capita income: $17,753 (2000); Median household income: $36,607 (2000); Poverty rate: 7.7% (2000).
Taxes: Total city taxes per capita: $357 (1997); City property taxes per capita: $345 (1997).
Education: High school graduation rate: 78.1% (2000); College graduation rate: 8.2% (2000).
Housing: Homeownership rate: 69.6% (2000); Median home value: $82,300 (2000); Median rent: $409 per month (2000); Median age of housing: 48 years (2000).
Safety: Violent crime rate: 6.8 per 10,000 population; Property crime rate: 368.9 per 10,000 population (2001).
Newspapers: Fox Lake Representative (1 x week)
Transportation: Commute to work: 94.1% car, 0.0% public transportation, 4.0% walk, 0.3% work from home (2000); Travel time to work: 32.6% less than 15 minutes, 32.1% 15 to 30 minutes, 20.9% 30 to 45 minutes, 7.0% 45 to 60 minutes, 7.4% 60 minutes or more (2000)
Additional Information Contacts
Fox Lake Chamber of Commerce 920-928-3777

FOX LAKE (town). Covers a land area of 32.254 square miles and a water area of 5.957 square miles. Located at 43.57° N. Lat.; 88.93° W. Long. Elevation is 920 feet.
History: Settled 1838, incorporated as village in 1893, as city in 1930.
Population: 2,402 (2000); Race: 73.4% White, 23.3% Black, 0.0% Asian, 2.0% American Indian and Alaska Native, 4.7% Hispanic of any race, 0.4% two or more races (2000); Density: 74.5 persons per square mile (2000); Age: 8.8% under 18, 8.9% over 64 (2000); Marriage status: 8.8% never married, 83.4% now married, 4.0% widowed, 3.8% divorced (2000); Foreign born: 0.6% (2000); Ancestry (includes multiple ancestries): 24.1% German, 5.9% Dutch, 4.9% Polish, 4.0% Irish, 2.7% Norwegian (2000).

Economy: In dairying region. Manufacturing: printed circuit boards, gun cases. Single-family building permits issued: 9 (2001) / 7 (2000); Multi-family building permits issued: 0 (2001) / 0 (2000); Employment by occupation: 15.3% management, 11.4% professional, 16.3% services, 18.0% sales, 3.2% farming, 12.1% construction, 23.6% production (2000).
Income: Per capita income: $17,227 (2000); Median household income: $52,721 (2000); Poverty rate: 5.4% (2000).
Taxes: Total city taxes per capita: $132 (1997); City property taxes per capita: $127 (1997).
Education: High school graduation rate: 79.0% (2000); College graduation rate: 7.7% (2000).
Housing: Homeownership rate: 86.2% (2000); Median home value: $145,500 (2000); Median rent: $450 per month (2000); Median age of housing: 43 years (2000).
Transportation: Commute to work: 92.8% car, 0.0% public transportation, 0.3% walk, 6.8% work from home (2000); Travel time to work: 28.6% less than 15 minutes, 38.6% 15 to 30 minutes, 17.8% 30 to 45 minutes, 7.7% 45 to 60 minutes, 7.3% 60 minutes or more (2000)

HERMAN (town). Covers a land area of 36.408 square miles and a water area of 0 square miles. Located at 43.42° N. Lat.; 88.47° W. Long.
Population: 1,207 (2000); Race: 98.4% White, 0.0% Black, 0.0% Asian, 0.0% American Indian and Alaska Native, 1.6% Hispanic of any race, 0.9% two or more races (2000); Density: 33.2 persons per square mile (2000); Age: 28.4% under 18, 11.4% over 64 (2000); Marriage status: 28.9% never married, 62.9% now married, 4.2% widowed, 4.0% divorced (2000); Foreign born: 0.5% (2000); Ancestry (includes multiple ancestries): 73.1% German, 5.3% United States or American, 4.3% Irish, 3.6% Polish, 3.0% English (2000).
Economy: Single-family building permits issued: 5 (2001) / 5 (2000); Multi-family building permits issued: 0 (2001) / 0 (2000); Employment by occupation: 15.7% management, 12.9% professional, 7.4% services, 18.5% sales, 2.2% farming, 13.6% construction, 29.6% production (2000).
Income: Per capita income: $18,401 (2000); Median household income: $49,938 (2000); Poverty rate: 4.6% (2000).
Taxes: Total city taxes per capita: $58 (1997); City property taxes per capita: $56 (1997).
Education: High school graduation rate: 82.0% (2000); College graduation rate: 12.6% (2000).
Housing: Homeownership rate: 78.8% (2000); Median home value: $127,600 (2000); Median rent: $477 per month (2000); Median age of housing: 60+ years (2000).
Transportation: Commute to work: 80.9% car, 0.3% public transportation, 4.5% walk, 14.0% work from home (2000); Travel time to work: 33.0% less than 15 minutes, 36.0% 15 to 30 minutes, 12.7% 30 to 45 minutes, 9.6% 45 to 60 minutes, 8.7% 60 minutes or more (2000)

HORICON (city). Covers a land area of 3.350 square miles and a water area of 0.039 square miles. Located at 43.44° N. Lat.; 88.63° W. Long. Elevation is 884 feet.
History: Incorporated 1897.
Population: 3,775 (2000); Race: 97.7% White, 0.5% Black, 0.2% Asian, 0.5% American Indian and Alaska Native, 2.7% Hispanic of any race, 0.3% two or more races (2000); Density: 1,126.8 persons per square mile (2000); Age: 25.8% under 18, 12.8% over 64 (2000); Marriage status: 25.8% never married, 61.7% now married, 7.1% widowed, 5.4% divorced (2000); Foreign born: 1.8% (2000); Ancestry (includes multiple ancestries): 63.0% German, 7.9% Irish, 6.2% English, 5.3% Polish, 5.0% Norwegian (2000).
Economy: In farm area. Agriculture: dairy; livestock, poultry; grain. Manufacturing: plastics, machinery, furniture, wood, iron and steel products, foods. Railroad junction. Horicon National Wildlife Refuge to North. Single-family building permits issued: 4 (2001) / 5 (2000); Multi-family building permits issued: 0 (2001) / 2 (2000); Employment by occupation: 8.6% management, 11.9% professional, 16.5% services, 22.3% sales, 0.6% farming, 5.9% construction, 34.2% production (2000).
Income: Per capita income: $21,690 (2000); Median household income: $50,577 (2000); Poverty rate: 2.1% (2000).
Taxes: Total city taxes per capita: $297 (1997); City property taxes per capita: $287 (1997).
Education: High school graduation rate: 88.4% (2000); College graduation rate: 14.8% (2000).

School District(s)

Horicon (PK-12)
2000 Enrollment: 1,067 920-485-2898

Housing: Homeownership rate: 72.1% (2000); Median home value: $94,100 (2000); Median rent: $464 per month (2000); Median age of housing: 41 years (2000).
Safety: Violent crime rate: 13.2 per 10,000 population; Property crime rate: 226.2 per 10,000 population (2001).
Newspapers: Horicon Reporter (1 x week)
Transportation: Commute to work: 89.1% car, 0.0% public transportation, 7.3% walk, 1.4% work from home (2000); Travel time to work: 58.1% less than 15 minutes, 23.6% 15 to 30 minutes, 7.9% 30 to 45 minutes, 4.8% 45 to 60 minutes, 5.7% 60 minutes or more (2000)
Additional Information Contacts
Horicon Chamber of Commerce 920-485-3200

HUBBARD (town). Covers a land area of 31.729 square miles and a water area of 1.656 square miles. Located at 43.41° N. Lat.; 88.58° W. Long.
Population: 1,643 (2000); Race: 99.6% White, 0.0% Black, 0.0% Asian, 0.2% American Indian and Alaska Native, 0.0% Hispanic of any race, 0.1% two or more races (2000); Density: 51.8 persons per square mile (2000); Age: 24.0% under 18, 12.9% over 64 (2000); Marriage status: 18.6% never married, 69.7% now married, 4.8% widowed, 6.9% divorced (2000); Foreign born: 0.7% (2000); Ancestry (includes multiple ancestries): 67.5% German, 8.6% Irish, 4.7% Polish, 4.1% French (except Basque), 3.8% English (2000).
Economy: Single-family building permits issued: 13 (2001) / 13 (2000); Multi-family building permits issued: 0 (2001) / 0 (2000); Employment by occupation: 13.1% management, 13.4% professional, 11.7% services, 21.0% sales, 0.7% farming, 14.2% construction, 25.9% production (2000).
Income: Per capita income: $23,142 (2000); Median household income: $51,250 (2000); Poverty rate: 5.9% (2000).
Taxes: Total city taxes per capita: $154 (1997); City property taxes per capita: $146 (1997).
Education: High school graduation rate: 78.5% (2000); College graduation rate: 11.7% (2000).
Housing: Homeownership rate: 91.8% (2000); Median home value: $147,300 (2000); Median rent: $572 per month (2000); Median age of housing: 34 years (2000).
Transportation: Commute to work: 92.1% car, 0.0% public transportation, 2.0% walk, 4.9% work from home (2000); Travel time to work: 45.7% less than 15 minutes, 25.9% 15 to 30 minutes, 11.6% 30 to 45 minutes, 9.0% 45 to 60 minutes, 7.7% 60 minutes or more (2000)

HUSTISFORD (village). Covers a land area of 0.809 square miles and a water area of 0.164 square miles. Located at 43.34° N. Lat.; 88.60° W. Long. Elevation is 867 feet.
Population: 1,135 (2000); Race: 99.6% White, 0.0% Black, 0.0% Asian, 0.0% American Indian and Alaska Native, 0.4% Hispanic of any race, 0.2% two or more races (2000); Density: 1,402.6 persons per square mile (2000); Age: 27.1% under 18, 16.3% over 64 (2000); Marriage status: 21.0% never married, 58.2% now married, 9.8% widowed, 11.0% divorced (2000); Foreign born: 1.0% (2000); Ancestry (includes multiple ancestries): 59.1% German, 9.3% Irish, 6.0% Polish, 5.9% United States or American, 3.9% Norwegian (2000).
Economy: Single-family building permits issued: 2 (2001) / 6 (2000); Multi-family building permits issued: 0 (2001) / 0 (2000); Employment by occupation: 6.6% management, 15.0% professional, 12.1% services, 21.8% sales, 0.0% farming, 12.1% construction, 32.4% production (2000).
Income: Per capita income: $20,599 (2000); Median household income: $40,929 (2000); Poverty rate: 2.7% (2000).
Taxes: Total city taxes per capita: $239 (1997); City property taxes per capita: $225 (1997).
Education: High school graduation rate: 80.5% (2000); College graduation rate: 13.3% (2000).

School District(s)

Hustisford (PK-12)
2000 Enrollment: 435 920-349-3261

Housing: Homeownership rate: 54.7% (2000); Median home value: $108,700 (2000); Median rent: $445 per month (2000); Median age of housing: 49 years (2000).
Transportation: Commute to work: 91.4% car, 0.5% public transportation, 5.7% walk, 2.4% work from home (2000); Travel time to work: 36.6% less than 15 minutes, 35.8% 15 to 30 minutes, 11.9% 30 to 45 minutes, 11.1% 45 to 60 minutes, 4.7% 60 minutes or more (2000)

HUSTISFORD (town). Covers a land area of 33.735 square miles and a water area of 1.198 square miles. Located at 43.33° N. Lat.; 88.59° W. Long. Elevation is 867 feet.

Population: 1,379 (2000); Race: 99.5% White, 0.0% Black, 0.1% Asian, 0.3% American Indian and Alaska Native, 1.2% Hispanic of any race, 0.0% two or more races (2000); Density: 40.9 persons per square mile (2000); Age: 22.7% under 18, 13.5% over 64 (2000); Marriage status: 20.8% never married, 68.4% now married, 4.1% widowed, 6.7% divorced (2000); Foreign born: 0.6% (2000); Ancestry (includes multiple ancestries): 64.2% German, 8.7% Irish, 4.9% United States or American, 4.3% English, 3.4% Other groups (2000).
Economy: Here dammed to form Sinissippi Lake to North. Dairy products. Manufacturing: air compressors, hardware. Single-family building permits issued: 6 (2001) / 1 (2000); Multi-family building permits issued: 0 (2001) / 0 (2000); Employment by occupation: 19.4% management, 10.6% professional, 8.8% services, 25.8% sales, 0.5% farming, 9.5% construction, 25.4% production (2000).
Income: Per capita income: $23,965 (2000); Median household income: $60,086 (2000); Poverty rate: 5.5% (2000).
Taxes: Total city taxes per capita: $126 (1997); City property taxes per capita: $114 (1997).
Education: High school graduation rate: 87.3% (2000); College graduation rate: 12.2% (2000).
Housing: Homeownership rate: 86.5% (2000); Median home value: $130,600 (2000); Median rent: $525 per month (2000); Median age of housing: 33 years (2000).
Transportation: Commute to work: 89.7% car, 0.0% public transportation, 3.0% walk, 7.1% work from home (2000); Travel time to work: 17.7% less than 15 minutes, 39.4% 15 to 30 minutes, 18.1% 30 to 45 minutes, 13.2% 45 to 60 minutes, 11.7% 60 minutes or more (2000)

IRON RIDGE (village). Covers a land area of 0.712 square miles and a water area of 0 square miles. Located at 43.39° N. Lat.; 88.53° W. Long. Elevation is 950 feet.
Population: 998 (2000); Race: 98.6% White, 0.0% Black, 0.0% Asian, 1.0% American Indian and Alaska Native, 0.1% Hispanic of any race, 0.4% two or more races (2000); Density: 1,402.6 persons per square mile (2000); Age: 35.5% under 18, 7.8% over 64 (2000); Marriage status: 24.3% never married, 63.7% now married, 6.0% widowed, 6.0% divorced (2000); Foreign born: 1.0% (2000); Ancestry (includes multiple ancestries): 69.8% German, 8.3% Irish, 5.3% English, 5.0% Polish, 4.6% Norwegian (2000).
Economy: In dairying region. Manufacturing: custom tools. Railroad junction. Single-family building permits issued: 1 (2001) / 1 (2000); Multi-family building permits issued: 2 (2001) / 0 (2000); Employment by occupation: 7.2% management, 8.7% professional, 17.5% services, 21.5% sales, 0.4% farming, 8.0% construction, 36.8% production (2000).
Income: Per capita income: $16,214 (2000); Median household income: $42,083 (2000); Poverty rate: 3.4% (2000).
Taxes: Total city taxes per capita: $243 (1997); City property taxes per capita: $208 (1997).
Education: High school graduation rate: 77.5% (2000); College graduation rate: 6.2% (2000).
Housing: Homeownership rate: 78.5% (2000); Median home value: $113,000 (2000); Median rent: $488 per month (2000); Median age of housing: 24 years (2000).
Safety: Violent crime rate: 0.0 per 10,000 population; Property crime rate: 209.0 per 10,000 population (2001).
Transportation: Commute to work: 94.0% car, 0.0% public transportation, 2.8% walk, 2.0% work from home (2000); Travel time to work: 31.4% less than 15 minutes, 35.2% 15 to 30 minutes, 12.2% 30 to 45 minutes, 15.3% 45 to 60 minutes, 5.9% 60 minutes or more (2000)

JUNEAU (city). Covers a land area of 1.551 square miles and a water area of 0.013 square miles. Located at 43.40° N. Lat.; 88.70° W. Long. Elevation is 910 feet.
History: Incorporated 1887.
Population: 2,485 (2000); Race: 97.3% White, 0.2% Black, 0.2% Asian, 0.1% American Indian and Alaska Native, 2.2% Hispanic of any race, 0.7% two or more races (2000); Density: 1,602.5 persons per square mile (2000); Age: 20.3% under 18, 20.9% over 64 (2000); Marriage status: 21.9% never married, 63.0% now married, 7.1% widowed, 8.0% divorced (2000); Foreign born: 1.1% (2000); Ancestry (includes multiple ancestries): 48.9% German, 7.6% Irish, 5.3% Polish, 4.6% Other groups, 4.5% United States or American (2000).
Economy: In dairying region. Manufacturing: porcelain products, machinery; food and dairy processing. Single-family building permits issued: 4 (2001) / 4 (2000); Multi-family building permits issued: 0 (2001) / 0 (2000); Employment by occupation: 6.1% management, 13.5% professional, 15.5% services, 21.9% sales, 1.6% farming, 10.7% construction, 30.7% production (2000).
Income: Per capita income: $17,286 (2000); Median household income: $42,162 (2000); Poverty rate: 5.9% (2000).
Taxes: Total city taxes per capita: $248 (1997); City property taxes per capita: $240 (1997).
Education: High school graduation rate: 78.6% (2000); College graduation rate: 10.3% (2000).

School District(s)

Dodgeland (PK-12)
2000 Enrollment: 780 920-386-4404
Housing: Homeownership rate: 65.7% (2000); Median home value: $92,900 (2000); Median rent: $416 per month (2000); Median age of housing: 45 years (2000).
Safety: Violent crime rate: 0.0 per 10,000 population; Property crime rate: 231.7 per 10,000 population (2001).
Newspapers: Dodge County Independent News (1 x week)
Transportation: Commute to work: 91.2% car, 0.3% public transportation, 5.5% walk, 2.2% work from home (2000); Travel time to work: 45.7% less than 15 minutes, 35.2% 15 to 30 minutes, 10.6% 30 to 45 minutes, 3.1% 45 to 60 minutes, 5.4% 60 minutes or more (2000)
Airports: Dodge County

KEKOSKEE (village). Covers a land area of 0.235 square miles and a water area of 0.009 square miles. Located at 43.52° N. Lat.; 88.56° W. Long. Elevation is 909 feet.
Population: 169 (2000); Race: 96.8% White, 0.0% Black, 3.2% Asian, 0.0% American Indian and Alaska Native, 0.0% Hispanic of any race, 0.0% two or more races (2000); Density: 719.9 persons per square mile (2000); Age: 18.7% under 18, 19.3% over 64 (2000); Marriage status: 25.3% never married, 62.7% now married, 7.0% widowed, 5.1% divorced (2000); Foreign born: 3.2% (2000); Ancestry (includes multiple ancestries): 62.0% German, 11.2% Other groups, 10.2% United States or American, 8.0% Polish, 3.2% Irish (2000).
Economy: Single-family building permits issued: 1 (2001) / 0 (2000); Multi-family building permits issued: 0 (2001) / 0 (2000); Employment by occupation: 7.7% management, 13.2% professional, 4.4% services, 11.0% sales, 2.2% farming, 11.0% construction, 50.5% production (2000).
Income: Per capita income: $18,822 (2000); Median household income: $38,750 (2000); Poverty rate: 1.1% (2000).
Taxes: Total city taxes per capita: $14 (1997); City property taxes per capita: $14 (1997).
Education: High school graduation rate: 68.6% (2000); College graduation rate: 9.3% (2000).
Housing: Homeownership rate: 88.9% (2000); Median home value: $85,600 (2000); Median rent: $375 per month (2000); Median age of housing: 60+ years (2000).
Transportation: Commute to work: 93.4% car, 0.0% public transportation, 2.2% walk, 2.2% work from home (2000); Travel time to work: 55.1% less than 15 minutes, 23.6% 15 to 30 minutes, 10.1% 30 to 45 minutes, 3.4% 45 to 60 minutes, 7.9% 60 minutes or more (2000)

LEBANON (town). Covers a land area of 35.818 square miles and a water area of 0.192 square miles. Located at 43.24° N. Lat.; 88.58° W. Long. Elevation is 900 feet.
Population: 1,664 (2000); Race: 98.4% White, 0.8% Black, 0.0% Asian, 0.7% American Indian and Alaska Native, 0.4% Hispanic of any race, 0.1% two or more races (2000); Density: 46.5 persons per square mile (2000); Age: 26.1% under 18, 14.7% over 64 (2000); Marriage status: 22.8% never married, 66.1% now married, 4.3% widowed, 6.8% divorced (2000); Foreign born: 0.5% (2000); Ancestry (includes multiple ancestries): 59.9% German, 8.6% Irish, 6.2% English, 5.5% Norwegian, 5.3% Polish (2000).
Economy: Employment by occupation: 16.8% management, 10.7% professional, 15.4% services, 21.3% sales, 1.7% farming, 9.6% construction, 24.6% production (2000).
Income: Per capita income: $19,063 (2000); Median household income: $45,897 (2000); Poverty rate: 5.6% (2000).
Taxes: Total city taxes per capita: $101 (1997); City property taxes per capita: $99 (1997).
Education: High school graduation rate: 80.3% (2000); College graduation rate: 10.5% (2000).
Housing: Homeownership rate: 83.0% (2000); Median home value: $130,600 (2000); Median rent: $507 per month (2000); Median age of housing: 36 years (2000).
Transportation: Commute to work: 89.0% car, 0.2% public transportation, 2.8% walk, 7.0% work from home (2000); Travel time to work: 23.1% less

than 15 minutes, 47.8% 15 to 30 minutes, 13.9% 30 to 45 minutes, 7.2% 45 to 60 minutes, 7.9% 60 minutes or more (2000)

LEROY (town). Covers a land area of 36.556 square miles and a water area of 0.825 square miles. Located at 43.59° N. Lat.; 88.57° W. Long.
Population: 1,116 (2000); Race: 99.4% White, 0.1% Black, 0.2% Asian, 0.2% American Indian and Alaska Native, 0.7% Hispanic of any race, 0.2% two or more races (2000); Density: 30.5 persons per square mile (2000); Age: 28.0% under 18, 11.8% over 64 (2000); Marriage status: 26.2% never married, 64.1% now married, 6.7% widowed, 3.0% divorced (2000); Foreign born: 0.9% (2000); Ancestry (includes multiple ancestries): 71.9% German, 5.6% Polish, 5.2% Irish, 5.2% United States or American, 3.8% English (2000).
Economy: Employment by occupation: 15.3% management, 12.3% professional, 11.3% services, 15.3% sales, 4.2% farming, 9.5% construction, 32.1% production (2000).
Income: Per capita income: $18,714 (2000); Median household income: $53,333 (2000); Poverty rate: 3.9% (2000).
Taxes: Total city taxes per capita: $134 (1997); City property taxes per capita: $131 (1997).
Education: High school graduation rate: 81.1% (2000); College graduation rate: 7.8% (2000).
Housing: Homeownership rate: 87.3% (2000); Median home value: $111,700 (2000); Median rent: $413 per month (2000); Median age of housing: 60+ years (2000).
Transportation: Commute to work: 84.9% car, 0.3% public transportation, 1.4% walk, 13.4% work from home (2000); Travel time to work: 43.7% less than 15 minutes, 37.1% 15 to 30 minutes, 11.4% 30 to 45 minutes, 3.1% 45 to 60 minutes, 4.7% 60 minutes or more (2000)

LOMIRA (village). Covers a land area of 1.944 square miles and a water area of 0 square miles. Located at 43.59° N. Lat.; 88.44° W. Long. Elevation is 1,039 feet.
History: Lomira was founded in 1849 and named Elmira for the young daughter of a pioneer. The name was twisted through usage into Lomira.
Population: 2,233 (2000); Race: 97.6% White, 0.5% Black, 0.5% Asian, 0.0% American Indian and Alaska Native, 2.2% Hispanic of any race, 0.7% two or more races (2000); Density: 1,148.8 persons per square mile (2000); Age: 28.7% under 18, 12.4% over 64 (2000); Marriage status: 25.6% never married, 60.0% now married, 6.0% widowed, 8.4% divorced (2000); Foreign born: 1.6% (2000); Ancestry (includes multiple ancestries): 65.0% German, 10.2% Irish, 5.7% French (except Basque), 4.6% Italian, 4.5% English (2000).
Economy: Single-family building permits issued: 7 (2001) / 23 (2000); Multi-family building permits issued: 0 (2001) / 8 (2000); Employment by occupation: 8.5% management, 13.1% professional, 10.6% services, 19.9% sales, 0.9% farming, 12.9% construction, 34.2% production (2000).
Income: Per capita income: $20,256 (2000); Median household income: $46,522 (2000); Poverty rate: 3.9% (2000).
Taxes: Total city taxes per capita: $135 (1997); City property taxes per capita: $114 (1997).
Education: High school graduation rate: 84.0% (2000); College graduation rate: 12.2% (2000).

School District(s)

Lomira (PK-12)
2000 Enrollment: 1,099 920-269-4396
Housing: Homeownership rate: 59.9% (2000); Median home value: $117,300 (2000); Median rent: $485 per month (2000); Median age of housing: 20 years (2000).
Transportation: Commute to work: 93.8% car, 0.1% public transportation, 3.5% walk, 2.5% work from home (2000); Travel time to work: 43.3% less than 15 minutes, 35.4% 15 to 30 minutes, 12.2% 30 to 45 minutes, 4.0% 45 to 60 minutes, 5.0% 60 minutes or more (2000)

LOMIRA (town). Covers a land area of 34.374 square miles and a water area of 0 square miles. Located at 43.57° N. Lat.; 88.44° W. Long. Elevation is 1,039 feet.
Population: 1,228 (2000); Race: 98.4% White, 0.2% Black, 0.0% Asian, 0.8% American Indian and Alaska Native, 0.0% Hispanic of any race, 0.0% two or more races (2000); Density: 35.7 persons per square mile (2000); Age: 30.2% under 18, 9.3% over 64 (2000); Marriage status: 23.9% never married, 65.5% now married, 5.9% widowed, 4.6% divorced (2000); Foreign born: 1.5% (2000); Ancestry (includes multiple ancestries): 75.7% German, 8.1% Irish, 3.9% Polish, 3.6% Italian, 3.3% United States or American (2000).
Economy: In dairying region. Light manufacturing. Employment by occupation: 14.5% management, 14.8% professional, 9.5% services, 18.7% sales, 5.1% farming, 11.1% construction, 26.3% production (2000).
Income: Per capita income: $21,548 (2000); Median household income: $51,071 (2000); Poverty rate: 5.1% (2000).
Taxes: Total city taxes per capita: $129 (1997); City property taxes per capita: $119 (1997).
Education: High school graduation rate: 86.0% (2000); College graduation rate: 11.4% (2000).
Housing: Homeownership rate: 85.3% (2000); Median home value: $131,400 (2000); Median rent: $471 per month (2000); Median age of housing: 57 years (2000).
Transportation: Commute to work: 84.8% car, 0.4% public transportation, 3.4% walk, 11.0% work from home (2000); Travel time to work: 47.0% less than 15 minutes, 35.0% 15 to 30 minutes, 11.0% 30 to 45 minutes, 3.9% 45 to 60 minutes, 3.1% 60 minutes or more (2000)

LOWELL (village). Covers a land area of 0.994 square miles and a water area of 0.033 square miles. Located at 43.33° N. Lat.; 88.82° W. Long. Elevation is 830 feet.
Population: 366 (2000); Race: 96.1% White, 0.8% Black, 0.0% Asian, 1.5% American Indian and Alaska Native, 1.0% Hispanic of any race, 1.0% two or more races (2000); Density: 368.1 persons per square mile (2000); Age: 33.2% under 18, 8.2% over 64 (2000); Marriage status: 13.2% never married, 71.8% now married, 9.0% widowed, 6.0% divorced (2000); Foreign born: 0.0% (2000); Ancestry (includes multiple ancestries): 63.4% German, 13.1% Other groups, 8.2% Irish, 6.2% Dutch, 5.4% United States or American (2000).
Economy: Single-family building permits issued: 5 (2001) / 0 (2000); Multi-family building permits issued: 0 (2001) / 0 (2000); Employment by occupation: 10.8% management, 7.8% professional, 15.7% services, 10.2% sales, 2.4% farming, 10.8% construction, 42.2% production (2000).
Income: Per capita income: $14,393 (2000); Median household income: $43,594 (2000); Poverty rate: 9.5% (2000).
Taxes: Total city taxes per capita: $72 (1997); City property taxes per capita: $62 (1997).
Education: High school graduation rate: 71.1% (2000); College graduation rate: 3.3% (2000).
Housing: Homeownership rate: 69.3% (2000); Median home value: $86,000 (2000); Median rent: $390 per month (2000); Median age of housing: 60+ years (2000).
Transportation: Commute to work: 89.7% car, 0.0% public transportation, 3.0% walk, 7.3% work from home (2000); Travel time to work: 10.5% less than 15 minutes, 54.9% 15 to 30 minutes, 19.0% 30 to 45 minutes, 10.5% 45 to 60 minutes, 5.2% 60 minutes or more (2000)

LOWELL (town). Covers a land area of 51.445 square miles and a water area of 0.446 square miles. Located at 43.32° N. Lat.; 88.82° W. Long. Elevation is 830 feet.
Population: 1,169 (2000); Race: 97.6% White, 0.4% Black, 0.3% Asian, 0.0% American Indian and Alaska Native, 2.4% Hispanic of any race, 0.3% two or more races (2000); Density: 22.7 persons per square mile (2000); Age: 23.0% under 18, 9.1% over 64 (2000); Marriage status: 27.0% never married, 60.5% now married, 3.5% widowed, 9.1% divorced (2000); Foreign born: 2.8% (2000); Ancestry (includes multiple ancestries): 66.0% German, 7.7% Irish, 5.5% English, 4.4% Norwegian, 4.4% United States or American (2000).
Economy: In dairying region. Cheese. Single-family building permits issued: 5 (2001) / 10 (2000); Multi-family building permits issued: 0 (2001) / 0 (2000); Employment by occupation: 14.4% management, 7.4% professional, 10.8% services, 19.4% sales, 2.7% farming, 15.4% construction, 29.9% production (2000).
Income: Per capita income: $19,729 (2000); Median household income: $47,833 (2000); Poverty rate: 6.8% (2000).
Taxes: Total city taxes per capita: $130 (1997); City property taxes per capita: $128 (1997).
Education: High school graduation rate: 82.3% (2000); College graduation rate: 9.6% (2000).
Housing: Homeownership rate: 77.7% (2000); Median home value: $111,900 (2000); Median rent: $424 per month (2000); Median age of housing: 59 years (2000).
Transportation: Commute to work: 88.1% car, 0.0% public transportation, 1.9% walk, 9.1% work from home (2000); Travel time to work: 24.5% less than 15 minutes, 44.7% 15 to 30 minutes, 13.2% 30 to 45 minutes, 6.9% 45 to 60 minutes, 10.7% 60 minutes or more (2000)

MAYVILLE (city). Covers a land area of 3.113 square miles and a water area of 0.001 square miles. Located at 43.49° N. Lat.; 88.54° W. Long. Elevation is 950 feet.
History: Settled c.1844, Incorporated 1885.
Population: 4,902 (2000); Race: 98.2% White, 0.0% Black, 0.6% Asian, 0.0% American Indian and Alaska Native, 1.6% Hispanic of any race, 0.8% two or more races (2000); Density: 1,574.4 persons per square mile (2000); Age: 25.8% under 18, 17.4% over 64 (2000); Marriage status: 22.5% never married, 57.2% now married, 9.8% widowed, 10.5% divorced (2000); Foreign born: 1.7% (2000); Ancestry (includes multiple ancestries): 67.3% German, 6.6% United States or American, 5.7% Polish, 5.1% Irish, 4.4% English (2000).
Economy: In farming, dairying and resort area. Manufacturing includes metal products, dairy products, canned foods, cheese, maple syrup, cable and hose reels, work platforms, tool and die, furniture, fabricated metal products, paper goods, sheet metal fabricating and printing. Railroad spur terminus. Employment by occupation: 12.0% management, 13.5% professional, 11.9% services, 20.2% sales, 0.2% farming, 7.6% construction, 34.6% production (2000).
Income: Per capita income: $19,644 (2000); Median household income: $42,393 (2000); Poverty rate: 5.7% (2000).
Taxes: Total city taxes per capita: $293 (1997); City property taxes per capita: $275 (1997).
Education: High school graduation rate: 82.2% (2000); College graduation rate: 12.4% (2000).

School District(s)

Herman #22 (PK-08)
2000 Enrollment: 108 920-387-3902
Mayville (PK-12)
2000 Enrollment: 1,247 920-387-7963

Housing: Homeownership rate: 68.9% (2000); Median home value: $102,100 (2000); Median rent: $435 per month (2000); Median age of housing: 41 years (2000).
Safety: Violent crime rate: 36.5 per 10,000 population; Property crime rate: 145.8 per 10,000 population (2001).
Newspapers: Wisconsin Free Press-Mayville News (1 x week)
Transportation: Commute to work: 94.0% car, 0.0% public transportation, 4.3% walk, 1.2% work from home (2000); Travel time to work: 58.4% less than 15 minutes, 20.5% 15 to 30 minutes, 11.5% 30 to 45 minutes, 4.5% 45 to 60 minutes, 5.1% 60 minutes or more (2000)
Additional Information Contacts
Mayville Chamber of Commerce 920-387-5776

NEOSHO (village). Covers a land area of 0.598 square miles and a water area of 0.034 square miles. Located at 43.31° N. Lat.; 88.51° W. Long. Elevation is 883 feet.
Population: 593 (2000); Race: 98.6% White, 0.0% Black, 0.0% Asian, 0.0% American Indian and Alaska Native, 0.0% Hispanic of any race, 1.4% two or more races (2000); Density: 991.4 persons per square mile (2000); Age: 30.3% under 18, 8.3% over 64 (2000); Marriage status: 22.5% never married, 62.8% now married, 6.2% widowed, 8.5% divorced (2000); Foreign born: 0.3% (2000); Ancestry (includes multiple ancestries): 62.9% German, 13.2% Irish, 11.6% Polish, 3.9% United States or American, 3.7% Swiss (2000).
Economy: Dairying region. Single-family building permits issued: 3 (2001) / 2 (2000); Multi-family building permits issued: 0 (2001) / 0 (2000); Employment by occupation: 6.8% management, 8.8% professional, 6.5% services, 28.9% sales, 1.2% farming, 12.7% construction, 35.1% production (2000).
Income: Per capita income: $19,134 (2000); Median household income: $50,167 (2000); Poverty rate: 1.8% (2000).
Taxes: Total city taxes per capita: $147 (1997); City property taxes per capita: $135 (1997).
Education: High school graduation rate: 82.3% (2000); College graduation rate: 9.0% (2000).

School District(s)

Neosho J3 (KG-08)
2000 Enrollment: 186 920-625-3531

Housing: Homeownership rate: 76.0% (2000); Median home value: $118,600 (2000); Median rent: $421 per month (2000); Median age of housing: 34 years (2000).
Transportation: Commute to work: 96.4% car, 0.0% public transportation, 0.6% walk, 2.1% work from home (2000); Travel time to work: 27.6% less than 15 minutes, 27.6% 15 to 30 minutes, 18.0% 30 to 45 minutes, 17.3% 45 to 60 minutes, 9.6% 60 minutes or more (2000)

OAK GROVE (town). Covers a land area of 34.093 square miles and a water area of 0.112 square miles. Located at 43.43° N. Lat.; 88.70° W. Long. Elevation is 861 feet.
Population: 1,126 (2000); Race: 98.0% White, 0.7% Black, 0.7% Asian, 0.0% American Indian and Alaska Native, 0.6% Hispanic of any race, 0.7% two or more races (2000); Density: 33.0 persons per square mile (2000); Age: 27.5% under 18, 12.0% over 64 (2000); Marriage status: 24.5% never married, 66.5% now married, 3.7% widowed, 5.2% divorced (2000); Foreign born: 0.9% (2000); Ancestry (includes multiple ancestries): 61.8% German, 7.7% English, 6.6% Other groups, 5.6% Irish, 3.2% Norwegian (2000).
Economy: Employment by occupation: 13.4% management, 11.3% professional, 9.3% services, 21.5% sales, 5.1% farming, 11.0% construction, 28.5% production (2000).
Income: Per capita income: $20,277 (2000); Median household income: $53,068 (2000); Poverty rate: 7.4% (2000).
Taxes: Total city taxes per capita: $89 (1997); City property taxes per capita: $87 (1997).
Education: High school graduation rate: 85.5% (2000); College graduation rate: 11.1% (2000).
Housing: Homeownership rate: 83.6% (2000); Median home value: $106,500 (2000); Median rent: $385 per month (2000); Median age of housing: 58 years (2000).
Transportation: Commute to work: 85.6% car, 0.0% public transportation, 4.9% walk, 8.0% work from home (2000); Travel time to work: 44.7% less than 15 minutes, 35.8% 15 to 30 minutes, 8.2% 30 to 45 minutes, 5.5% 45 to 60 minutes, 5.8% 60 minutes or more (2000)

PORTLAND (town). Covers a land area of 35.329 square miles and a water area of 0.356 square miles. Located at 43.22° N. Lat.; 88.95° W. Long.
Population: 1,106 (2000); Race: 94.3% White, 2.2% Black, 0.0% Asian, 1.8% American Indian and Alaska Native, 2.3% Hispanic of any race, 0.2% two or more races (2000); Density: 31.3 persons per square mile (2000); Age: 28.6% under 18, 9.7% over 64 (2000); Marriage status: 20.6% never married, 66.0% now married, 4.7% widowed, 8.7% divorced (2000); Foreign born: 1.5% (2000); Ancestry (includes multiple ancestries): 53.6% German, 11.8% Irish, 7.8% Other groups, 5.8% United States or American, 5.2% Norwegian (2000).
Economy: Single-family building permits issued: 6 (2001) / 6 (2000); Multi-family building permits issued: 0 (2001) / 0 (2000); Employment by occupation: 10.8% management, 13.9% professional, 8.0% services, 20.8% sales, 4.8% farming, 10.4% construction, 31.3% production (2000).
Income: Per capita income: $19,070 (2000); Median household income: $49,881 (2000); Poverty rate: 5.7% (2000).
Taxes: Total city taxes per capita: $111 (1997); City property taxes per capita: $109 (1997).
Education: High school graduation rate: 83.8% (2000); College graduation rate: 10.1% (2000).
Housing: Homeownership rate: 87.2% (2000); Median home value: $135,500 (2000); Median rent: $463 per month (2000); Median age of housing: 37 years (2000).
Transportation: Commute to work: 90.7% car, 0.3% public transportation, 1.5% walk, 6.5% work from home (2000); Travel time to work: 32.4% less than 15 minutes, 33.3% 15 to 30 minutes, 20.8% 30 to 45 minutes, 9.1% 45 to 60 minutes, 4.4% 60 minutes or more (2000)

RANDOLPH (village). Covers a land area of 1.068 square miles and a water area of 0 square miles. Located at 43.54° N. Lat.; 89.00° W. Long.
History: Settled 1844; plotted 1857; incorporated 1870.
Population: 1,869 (2000); Race: 98.5% White, 0.0% Black, 0.0% Asian, 0.3% American Indian and Alaska Native, 1.0% Hispanic of any race, 1.0% two or more races (2000); Density: 1,750.3 persons per square mile (2000); Age: 26.4% under 18, 20.3% over 64 (2000); Marriage status: 22.2% never married, 60.2% now married, 9.6% widowed, 8.0% divorced (2000); Foreign born: 1.1% (2000); Ancestry (includes multiple ancestries): 36.6% German, 33.5% Dutch, 6.7% English, 6.4% Irish, 4.6% Polish (2000).
Economy: Railroad junction in dairy and livestock region; seed warehouses. Manufacturing: can and bottle handling equipment, light manufacturing. Single-family building permits issued: 0 (2001) / 1 (2000); Multi-family building permits issued: 0 (2001) / 2 (2000); Employment by occupation: 9.2% management, 14.0% professional, 16.6% services, 21.1% sales, 0.8% farming, 13.4% construction, 24.8% production (2000).
Income: Per capita income: $18,517 (2000); Median household income: $39,620 (2000); Poverty rate: 7.2% (2000).
Taxes: Total city taxes per capita: $274 (2000); City property taxes per capita: $266 (2000).

Education: High school graduation rate: 81.4% (2000); College graduation rate: 13.3% (2000).
Housing: Homeownership rate: 70.6% (2000); Median home value: $88,400 (2000); Median rent: $385 per month (2000); Median age of housing: 52 years (2000).
Transportation: Commute to work: 89.4% car, 0.0% public transportation, 6.3% walk, 3.0% work from home (2000); Travel time to work: 43.8% less than 15 minutes, 34.1% 15 to 30 minutes, 12.4% 30 to 45 minutes, 6.0% 45 to 60 minutes, 3.7% 60 minutes or more (2000)
Additional Information Contacts
Randolph Chamber of Commerce 920-326-4769

REESEVILLE (village). Covers a land area of 0.607 square miles and a water area of 0 square miles. Located at 43.30° N. Lat.; 88.84° W. Long. Elevation is 856 feet.
Population: 703 (2000); Race: 98.5% White, 0.0% Black, 0.0% Asian, 0.0% American Indian and Alaska Native, 0.4% Hispanic of any race, 1.1% two or more races (2000); Density: 1,158.8 persons per square mile (2000); Age: 29.1% under 18, 12.7% over 64 (2000); Marriage status: 23.9% never married, 58.7% now married, 7.8% widowed, 9.6% divorced (2000); Foreign born: 0.7% (2000); Ancestry (includes multiple ancestries): 54.3% German, 11.4% Irish, 6.6% United States or American, 5.3% Polish, 4.2% Swiss (2000).
Economy: In dairying region. Single-family building permits issued: 2 (2001) / 2 (2000); Multi-family building permits issued: 0 (2001) / 0 (2000); Employment by occupation: 9.9% management, 13.5% professional, 14.4% services, 12.6% sales, 0.0% farming, 14.1% construction, 35.6% production (2000).
Income: Per capita income: $16,036 (2000); Median household income: $37,120 (2000); Poverty rate: 9.9% (2000).
Taxes: Total city taxes per capita: $127 (1997); City property taxes per capita: $113 (1997).
Education: High school graduation rate: 76.2% (2000); College graduation rate: 11.8% (2000).
Housing: Homeownership rate: 72.5% (2000); Median home value: $86,300 (2000); Median rent: $438 per month (2000); Median age of housing: 42 years (2000).
Transportation: Commute to work: 88.3% car, 0.0% public transportation, 6.9% walk, 4.2% work from home (2000); Travel time to work: 17.0% less than 15 minutes, 47.2% 15 to 30 minutes, 16.4% 30 to 45 minutes, 6.9% 45 to 60 minutes, 12.6% 60 minutes or more (2000)

RUBICON (town). Covers a land area of 34.534 square miles and a water area of 0.410 square miles. Located at 43.33° N. Lat.; 88.46° W. Long. Elevation is 1,013 feet.
Population: 2,005 (2000); Race: 98.1% White, 0.0% Black, 0.0% Asian, 0.2% American Indian and Alaska Native, 1.3% Hispanic of any race, 1.6% two or more races (2000); Density: 58.1 persons per square mile (2000); Age: 30.0% under 18, 9.2% over 64 (2000); Marriage status: 25.8% never married, 65.2% now married, 3.4% widowed, 5.6% divorced (2000); Foreign born: 1.0% (2000); Ancestry (includes multiple ancestries): 67.4% German, 11.0% Irish, 7.5% Polish, 4.1% Norwegian, 3.7% United States or American (2000).
Economy: Employment by occupation: 14.1% management, 10.1% professional, 11.6% services, 19.8% sales, 1.2% farming, 13.8% construction, 29.4% production (2000).
Income: Per capita income: $20,964 (2000); Median household income: $54,583 (2000); Poverty rate: 3.9% (2000).
Taxes: Total city taxes per capita: $57 (1997); City property taxes per capita: $57 (1997).
Education: High school graduation rate: 84.9% (2000); College graduation rate: 11.5% (2000).

School District(s)

Rubicon J6 (KG-08)
2000 Enrollment: 146 262-673-2920
Housing: Homeownership rate: 85.9% (2000); Median home value: $147,600 (2000); Median rent: $511 per month (2000); Median age of housing: 30 years (2000).
Transportation: Commute to work: 92.3% car, 0.3% public transportation, 1.8% walk, 5.6% work from home (2000); Travel time to work: 38.5% less than 15 minutes, 24.2% 15 to 30 minutes, 18.8% 30 to 45 minutes, 12.5% 45 to 60 minutes, 6.0% 60 minutes or more (2000)

SHIELDS (town). Covers a land area of 26.508 square miles and a water area of 0.450 square miles. Located at 43.23° N. Lat.; 88.81° W. Long.
Population: 554 (2000); Race: 98.4% White, 0.4% Black, 0.0% Asian, 0.0% American Indian and Alaska Native, 1.6% Hispanic of any race, 0.7% two or more races (2000); Density: 20.9 persons per square mile (2000); Age: 26.7% under 18, 10.3% over 64 (2000); Marriage status: 25.0% never married, 63.0% now married, 6.1% widowed, 5.9% divorced (2000); Foreign born: 0.0% (2000); Ancestry (includes multiple ancestries): 64.4% German, 16.7% Irish, 7.3% English, 5.3% United States or American, 3.9% Other groups (2000).
Economy: Employment by occupation: 11.3% management, 14.7% professional, 13.4% services, 25.0% sales, 3.4% farming, 6.9% construction, 25.3% production (2000).
Income: Per capita income: $21,218 (2000); Median household income: $50,000 (2000); Poverty rate: 1.6% (2000).
Taxes: Total city taxes per capita: $78 (1997); City property taxes per capita: $76 (1997).
Education: High school graduation rate: 81.4% (2000); College graduation rate: 14.5% (2000).
Housing: Homeownership rate: 86.4% (2000); Median home value: $128,600 (2000); Median rent: $531 per month (2000); Median age of housing: 60+ years (2000).
Transportation: Commute to work: 88.4% car, 0.0% public transportation, 0.3% walk, 10.6% work from home (2000); Travel time to work: 28.0% less than 15 minutes, 38.1% 15 to 30 minutes, 18.2% 30 to 45 minutes, 8.4% 45 to 60 minutes, 7.3% 60 minutes or more (2000)

THERESA (village). Covers a land area of 0.748 square miles and a water area of 0.022 square miles. Located at 43.51° N. Lat.; 88.45° W. Long. Elevation is 960 feet.
Population: 1,252 (2000); Race: 98.9% White, 0.0% Black, 0.0% Asian, 0.0% American Indian and Alaska Native, 1.6% Hispanic of any race, 0.8% two or more races (2000); Density: 1,672.8 persons per square mile (2000); Age: 26.7% under 18, 14.7% over 64 (2000); Marriage status: 23.7% never married, 63.8% now married, 6.3% widowed, 6.2% divorced (2000); Foreign born: 1.0% (2000); Ancestry (includes multiple ancestries): 58.8% German, 12.6% Irish, 11.3% Polish, 4.7% Norwegian, 4.0% English (2000).
Economy: Single-family building permits issued: 6 (2001) / 1 (2000); Multi-family building permits issued: 0 (2001) / 0 (2000); Employment by occupation: 7.8% management, 10.7% professional, 12.9% services, 20.0% sales, 0.3% farming, 11.3% construction, 36.9% production (2000).
Income: Per capita income: $17,906 (2000); Median household income: $44,200 (2000); Poverty rate: 3.6% (2000).
Taxes: Total city taxes per capita: $437 (1997); City property taxes per capita: $296 (1997).
Education: High school graduation rate: 79.8% (2000); College graduation rate: 7.5% (2000).
Housing: Homeownership rate: 80.9% (2000); Median home value: $101,700 (2000); Median rent: $486 per month (2000); Median age of housing: 21 years (2000).
Safety: Violent crime rate: 0.0 per 10,000 population; Property crime rate: 420.3 per 10,000 population (2001).
Transportation: Commute to work: 93.0% car, 0.0% public transportation, 3.6% walk, 3.4% work from home (2000); Travel time to work: 27.4% less than 15 minutes, 36.5% 15 to 30 minutes, 19.0% 30 to 45 minutes, 10.9% 45 to 60 minutes, 6.1% 60 minutes or more (2000)

THERESA (town). Covers a land area of 35.156 square miles and a water area of 0.476 square miles. Located at 43.50° N. Lat.; 88.45° W. Long. Elevation is 960 feet.
History: Theresa was founded by Solomon Juneau, who named it for his daughter. Many of Theresa's early residents were of German descent.
Population: 1,080 (2000); Race: 97.5% White, 0.8% Black, 0.8% Asian, 0.6% American Indian and Alaska Native, 0.0% Hispanic of any race, 0.5% two or more races (2000); Density: 30.7 persons per square mile (2000); Age: 27.5% under 18, 9.2% over 64 (2000); Marriage status: 20.2% never married, 72.2% now married, 4.7% widowed, 2.9% divorced (2000); Foreign born: 1.1% (2000); Ancestry (includes multiple ancestries): 65.8% German, 6.0% Norwegian, 5.7% Irish, 3.6% United States or American, 2.6% Polish (2000).
Economy: Cheese. Hunting. Horicon Marsh State Wildlife Area to West. Single-family building permits issued: 5 (2001) / 1 (2000); Multi-family building permits issued: 0 (2001) / 0 (2000); Employment by occupation: 16.0% management, 12.2% professional, 10.1% services, 18.1% sales, 5.9% farming, 10.7% construction, 27.0% production (2000).
Income: Per capita income: $20,451 (2000); Median household income: $55,417 (2000); Poverty rate: 2.2% (2000).
Taxes: Total city taxes per capita: $157 (1997); City property taxes per capita: $155 (1997).
Education: High school graduation rate: 81.0% (2000); College graduation rate: 10.6% (2000).

Housing: Homeownership rate: 87.9% (2000); Median home value: $119,900 (2000); Median rent: $418 per month (2000); Median age of housing: 60+ years (2000).
Transportation: Commute to work: 85.2% car, 0.0% public transportation, 1.9% walk, 12.4% work from home (2000); Travel time to work: 42.5% less than 15 minutes, 34.5% 15 to 30 minutes, 12.7% 30 to 45 minutes, 6.5% 45 to 60 minutes, 3.8% 60 minutes or more (2000)

TRENTON (town). Covers a land area of 53.862 square miles and a water area of 0.521 square miles. Located at 43.56° N. Lat.; 88.83° W. Long.
Population: 1,301 (2000); Race: 99.2% White, 0.0% Black, 0.2% Asian, 0.0% American Indian and Alaska Native, 0.6% Hispanic of any race, 0.6% two or more races (2000); Density: 24.2 persons per square mile (2000); Age: 27.9% under 18, 9.7% over 64 (2000); Marriage status: 24.0% never married, 69.6% now married, 2.6% widowed, 3.8% divorced (2000); Foreign born: 1.0% (2000); Ancestry (includes multiple ancestries): 59.4% German, 22.1% Dutch, 6.2% Irish, 4.4% Polish, 4.3% English (2000).
Economy: Employment by occupation: 23.1% management, 16.6% professional, 10.1% services, 18.5% sales, 3.4% farming, 11.4% construction, 16.8% production (2000).
Income: Per capita income: $19,374 (2000); Median household income: $50,820 (2000); Poverty rate: 4.4% (2000).
Taxes: Total city taxes per capita: $122 (1997); City property taxes per capita: $121 (1997).
Education: High school graduation rate: 84.8% (2000); College graduation rate: 14.2% (2000).
Housing: Homeownership rate: 83.3% (2000); Median home value: $131,700 (2000); Median rent: $385 per month (2000); Median age of housing: 49 years (2000).
Transportation: Commute to work: 77.5% car, 0.0% public transportation, 3.9% walk, 17.5% work from home (2000); Travel time to work: 46.1% less than 15 minutes, 36.4% 15 to 30 minutes, 7.5% 30 to 45 minutes, 4.6% 45 to 60 minutes, 5.4% 60 minutes or more (2000)

WAUPUN (city). Covers a land area of 3.688 square miles and a water area of 0 square miles. Located at 43.63° N. Lat.; 88.73° W. Long.
History: On route of first US auto race. Settled 1838, incorporated 1878.
Population: 10,718 (2000); Race: 85.7% White, 12.0% Black, 0.3% Asian, 1.0% American Indian and Alaska Native, 2.7% Hispanic of any race, 0.4% two or more races (2000); Density: 2,906.3 persons per square mile (2000); Age: 20.0% under 18, 13.5% over 64 (2000); Marriage status: 14.2% never married, 72.4% now married, 7.7% widowed, 5.7% divorced (2000); Foreign born: 1.2% (2000); Ancestry (includes multiple ancestries): 34.2% German, 20.1% Dutch, 5.6% Irish, 4.9% English, 3.9% Polish (2000).
Economy: In farm and dairy region. Manufacturing of cheese, dairy products; power cords and cables, fasteners, chemicals. The state prison and a state hospital are here. Horicon National Wildlife Refuge. Single-family building permits issued: 10 (2001) / 17 (2000); Multi-family building permits issued: 0 (2001) / 8 (2000); Employment by occupation: 8.5% management, 17.1% professional, 20.5% services, 21.7% sales, 0.7% farming, 5.4% construction, 26.2% production (2000).
Income: Per capita income: $16,947 (2000); Median household income: $40,597 (2000); Poverty rate: 5.5% (2000).
Taxes: Total city taxes per capita: $147 (1997); City property taxes per capita: $139 (1997).
Education: High school graduation rate: 79.3% (2000); College graduation rate: 12.8% (2000).
Housing: Homeownership rate: 68.5% (2000); Median home value: $88,600 (2000); Median rent: $402 per month (2000); Median age of housing: 44 years (2000).
Hospitals: Waupun Memorial Hospital (70 beds)
Safety: Violent crime rate: 3.7 per 10,000 population; Property crime rate: 248.3 per 10,000 population (2001).
Newspapers: The Citizen Neighbors (1 x week); Monday Marketeer (1 x week)
Transportation: Commute to work: 92.1% car, 0.1% public transportation, 4.1% walk, 2.3% work from home (2000); Travel time to work: 55.3% less than 15 minutes, 26.6% 15 to 30 minutes, 10.3% 30 to 45 minutes, 4.2% 45 to 60 minutes, 3.7% 60 minutes or more (2000)
Additional Information Contacts
Waupun Chamber of Commerce 920-324-3491

WESTFORD (town). Covers a land area of 30.168 square miles and a water area of 4.633 square miles. Located at 43.51° N. Lat.; 88.95° W. Long.
Population: 1,400 (2000); Race: 96.8% White, 0.0% Black, 0.4% Asian, 0.8% American Indian and Alaska Native, 2.1% Hispanic of any race, 0.1% two or more races (2000); Density: 46.4 persons per square mile (2000); Age: 22.0% under 18, 16.4% over 64 (2000); Marriage status: 19.8% never married, 66.9% now married, 5.6% widowed, 7.7% divorced (2000); Foreign born: 1.6% (2000); Ancestry (includes multiple ancestries): 56.4% German, 11.3% Irish, 8.7% Dutch, 8.6% Polish, 7.2% English (2000).
Economy: Single-family building permits issued: 7 (2001) / 4 (2000); Multi-family building permits issued: 0 (2001) / 0 (2000); Employment by occupation: 14.6% management, 11.5% professional, 10.4% services, 22.0% sales, 0.3% farming, 9.0% construction, 32.2% production (2000).
Income: Per capita income: $22,582 (2000); Median household income: $48,516 (2000); Poverty rate: 2.8% (2000).
Taxes: Total city taxes per capita: $71 (1997); City property taxes per capita: $70 (1997).
Education: High school graduation rate: 81.1% (2000); College graduation rate: 10.0% (2000).
Housing: Homeownership rate: 90.5% (2000); Median home value: $125,100 (2000); Median rent: $279 per month (2000); Median age of housing: 32 years (2000).
Transportation: Commute to work: 88.1% car, 0.0% public transportation, 1.6% walk, 8.7% work from home (2000); Travel time to work: 21.8% less than 15 minutes, 43.6% 15 to 30 minutes, 16.1% 30 to 45 minutes, 12.2% 45 to 60 minutes, 6.3% 60 minutes or more (2000)

WILLIAMSTOWN (town). Covers a land area of 32.893 square miles and a water area of 0.675 square miles. Located at 43.50° N. Lat.; 88.56° W. Long.
Population: 646 (2000); Race: 98.9% White, 0.0% Black, 0.0% Asian, 0.0% American Indian and Alaska Native, 0.5% Hispanic of any race, 1.1% two or more races (2000); Density: 19.6 persons per square mile (2000); Age: 24.0% under 18, 12.1% over 64 (2000); Marriage status: 23.1% never married, 66.0% now married, 6.2% widowed, 4.7% divorced (2000); Foreign born: 0.9% (2000); Ancestry (includes multiple ancestries): 67.3% German, 7.3% Polish, 6.8% Irish, 5.0% English, 4.2% United States or American (2000).
Economy: Single-family building permits issued: 2 (2001) / 2 (2000); Multi-family building permits issued: 0 (2001) / 0 (2000); Employment by occupation: 13.6% management, 16.2% professional, 8.1% services, 21.7% sales, 1.0% farming, 10.5% construction, 28.8% production (2000).
Income: Per capita income: $25,167 (2000); Median household income: $62,969 (2000); Poverty rate: 1.9% (2000).
Taxes: Total city taxes per capita: $158 (1997); City property taxes per capita: $155 (1997).
Education: High school graduation rate: 86.9% (2000); College graduation rate: 12.6% (2000).
Housing: Homeownership rate: 80.5% (2000); Median home value: $151,600 (2000); Median rent: $450 per month (2000); Median age of housing: 44 years (2000).
Transportation: Commute to work: 90.3% car, 0.0% public transportation, 2.7% walk, 6.5% work from home (2000); Travel time to work: 58.2% less than 15 minutes, 20.5% 15 to 30 minutes, 13.3% 30 to 45 minutes, 4.6% 45 to 60 minutes, 3.5% 60 minutes or more (2000)

Door County

Located in northeastern Wisconsin, on the Door Peninsula; bounded on the east by Lake Michigan, and on the west by Green Bay; includes Washington and Chambers Islands. Covers a land area of 482.70 square miles, a water area of 1,887.10 square miles, and is located in the Central Time Zone. The county government was organized in 1851. County seat is Sturgeon Bay.

Weather Station: Sturgeon Bay Exp. Farm Elevation: 652 feet

	Jan	Feb	Mar	Apr	May	Jun	Jul	Aug	Sep	Oct	Nov	Dec
High	25	29	38	52	65	74	79	78	69	57	42	31
Low	9	13	22	33	43	52	59	58	50	40	29	18
Precip	1.8	1.1	2.1	2.7	3.0	3.4	3.4	3.5	3.5	2.8	2.5	1.7
Snow	15.5	7.9	7.9	2.2	tr	0.0	0.0	0.0	tr	tr	3.2	10.7

High and Low temperatures in degrees Fahrenheit; Precipitation and Snow in inches

Weather Station: Washington Island Elevation: 610 feet

	Jan	Feb	Mar	Apr	May	Jun	Jul	Aug	Sep	Oct	Nov	Dec
High	25	29	37	48	61	70	76	75	67	55	42	31
Low	10	12	21	31	40	50	57	57	50	40	30	19
Precip	1.6	0.8	1.6	2.2	2.7	3.1	3.0	3.2	3.4	2.9	2.4	1.5
Snow	15.5	8.4	9.8	2.8	0.2	0.0	0.0	0.0	0.0	0.1	4.0	11.6

High and Low temperatures in degrees Fahrenheit; Precipitation and Snow in inches

Population: 27,961 (2000); Race: 97.6% White, 0.1% Black, 0.4% Asian, 0.7% American Indian and Alaska Native, 0.8% Hispanic of any race, 0.8% two or more races (2000); Density: 57.9 persons per square mile (2000); Age: 22.0% under 18, 18.7% over 64 (2000).
Religion: Five largest groups: 36.7% Catholic Church, 10.7% Evangelical Lutheran Church in America, 9.9% Wisconsin Evangelical Lutheran Synod, 3.1% Moravian Church in America—Northern Province, 2.7% The United Methodist Church (2000).
Economy: Unemployment rate: 5.5% (11/2002); Total civilian labor force: 15,817 (11/2002); Leading industries: 22.3% manufacturing; 19.2% accommodation & food services; 16.0% retail trade (2000); Companies that employ more than 1,000 persons: 0 (2000); Companies that employ more than 100 persons: 16 (2000); Farms: 702 totaling 121,879 acres (1997); Minority business ownership rate: 0.0% (1997); Women business ownership rate: 28.7% (1997); Retail sales per capita: $9,623 (1997). Single-family building permits issued: 336 (2001) / 327 (2000); Multi-family building permits issued: 176 (2001) / 131 (2000).
Income: Per capita income: $21,356 (2000); Median household income: $38,813 (2000); Poverty rate: 6.4% (2000); Bankruptcy rate: 2.27% (2001).
Taxes: Total county taxes per capita: $412 (1997); County property taxes per capita: $329 (1997).
Education: High school graduation rate: 87.8% (2000); College graduation rate: 21.4% (2000).
Housing: Homeownership rate: 79.3% (2000); Median home value: $120,800 (2000); Median rent: $388 per month (2000); Median age of housing: 29 years (2000).
Health: Birth rate: 85.5 per 10,000 population (1998); Age adjusted death rate: 82.1 per 10,000 population (1999); Age adjusted cancer mortality rate: 191.9 deaths per 100,000 population (1999). Air Quality Index: 78% good, 22% moderate, 1% unhealthy (percent of days in 2000). Number of physicians: 14.7 per 10,000 population (1999); Number of hospital beds: 27.5 per 10,000 population (1999).
Elections: 2000 Presidential election results: 43.1% Gore, 51.3% Bush, 4.7% Nader, 0.4% Buchanan
National and State Parks: Ahnapee State Trail; Gardner Swamp State Wildlife Area; Gravel Island National Wildlife Refuge; Green Bay National Wildlife Refuge; Mud Lake State Wildlife Area; Newport State Park; Peninsula State Park; Potawatomi State Park; Rock Island State Park; Schuyler Creek State Fishery Area
Additional Information Contacts
Door County Government Offices 920-746-2200
Door County Board of Realtors 920-743-9651
Sturgeon Bay Chamber of Commerce 920-743-4456

Door County Communities

BAILEYS HARBOR (town). Covers a land area of 29.525 square miles and a water area of 39.236 square miles. Located at 45.06° N. Lat.; 87.12° W. Long. Elevation is 595 feet.
Population: 1,003 (2000); Race: 97.6% White, 0.0% Black, 0.0% Asian, 0.6% American Indian and Alaska Native, 2.9% Hispanic of any race, 1.6% two or more races (2000); Density: 34.0 persons per square mile (2000); Age: 16.0% under 18, 20.5% over 64 (2000); Marriage status: 17.6% never married, 65.4% now married, 7.0% widowed, 10.0% divorced (2000); Foreign born: 1.7% (2000); Ancestry (includes multiple ancestries): 45.5% German, 12.8% Irish, 10.2% English, 10.0% Swedish, 9.2% Polish (2000).
Economy: In resort and fishing area. Lumber. Employment by occupation: 10.7% management, 14.6% professional, 22.4% services, 26.6% sales, 1.7% farming, 14.6% construction, 9.4% production (2000).
Income: Per capita income: $23,835 (2000); Median household income: $41,350 (2000); Poverty rate: 4.5% (2000).
Taxes: Total city taxes per capita: $624 (2000); City property taxes per capita: $615 (2000).
Education: High school graduation rate: 91.6% (2000); College graduation rate: 30.1% (2000).
Housing: Homeownership rate: 83.4% (2000); Median home value: $164,600 (2000); Median rent: $496 per month (2000); Median age of housing: 29 years (2000).
Transportation: Commute to work: 90.1% car, 0.0% public transportation, 1.8% walk, 6.9% work from home (2000); Travel time to work: 41.8% less than 15 minutes, 38.2% 15 to 30 minutes, 14.1% 30 to 45 minutes, 1.1% 45 to 60 minutes, 4.9% 60 minutes or more (2000)

BRUSSELS (town). Covers a land area of 36.145 square miles and a water area of 0 square miles. Located at 44.73° N. Lat.; 87.57° W. Long. Elevation is 754 feet.
History: Brussels was settled in 1854 by Belgians, many of whom acquired large farms.
Population: 1,112 (2000); Race: 98.9% White, 0.4% Black, 0.2% Asian, 0.0% American Indian and Alaska Native, 0.2% Hispanic of any race, 0.5% two or more races (2000); Density: 30.8 persons per square mile (2000); Age: 27.1% under 18, 9.8% over 64 (2000); Marriage status: 23.9% never married, 62.4% now married, 7.4% widowed, 6.3% divorced (2000); Foreign born: 0.8% (2000); Ancestry (includes multiple ancestries): 47.8% Belgian, 42.0% German, 6.2% Irish, 4.6% Polish, 4.6% Norwegian (2000).
Economy: Single-family building permits issued: 8 (2001) / 9 (2000); Multi-family building permits issued: 0 (2001) / 0 (2000); Employment by occupation: 20.2% management, 11.9% professional, 11.1% services, 18.9% sales, 1.1% farming, 13.5% construction, 23.3% production (2000).
Income: Per capita income: $16,871 (2000); Median household income: $42,212 (2000); Poverty rate: 6.5% (2000).
Taxes: Total city taxes per capita: $38 (1997); City property taxes per capita: $36 (1997).
Education: High school graduation rate: 85.7% (2000); College graduation rate: 12.4% (2000).

School District(s)

Southern Door (PK-12)
2000 Enrollment: 1,327 920-825-7311
Housing: Homeownership rate: 86.1% (2000); Median home value: $94,800 (2000); Median rent: $393 per month (2000); Median age of housing: 48 years (2000).
Transportation: Commute to work: 83.8% car, 0.0% public transportation, 2.6% walk, 13.6% work from home (2000); Travel time to work: 18.6% less than 15 minutes, 45.1% 15 to 30 minutes, 20.1% 30 to 45 minutes, 12.0% 45 to 60 minutes, 4.1% 60 minutes or more (2000)

CLAY BANKS (town). Covers a land area of 14.885 square miles and a water area of 32.201 square miles. Located at 44.72° N. Lat.; 87.36° W. Long.
Population: 410 (2000); Race: 99.2% White, 0.0% Black, 0.0% Asian, 0.0% American Indian and Alaska Native, 0.0% Hispanic of any race, 0.8% two or more races (2000); Density: 27.5 persons per square mile (2000); Age: 25.4% under 18, 19.6% over 64 (2000); Marriage status: 15.1% never married, 64.9% now married, 13.0% widowed, 7.0% divorced (2000); Foreign born: 0.5% (2000); Ancestry (includes multiple ancestries): 46.3% German, 20.4% Norwegian, 14.9% Belgian, 7.9% Irish, 5.5% English (2000).
Economy: Employment by occupation: 15.3% management, 20.3% professional, 10.2% services, 21.5% sales, 2.3% farming, 11.9% construction, 18.6% production (2000).
Income: Per capita income: $19,027 (2000); Median household income: $42,708 (2000); Poverty rate: 8.2% (2000).
Taxes: Total city taxes per capita: $102 (1997); City property taxes per capita: $102 (1997).
Education: High school graduation rate: 88.7% (2000); College graduation rate: 22.0% (2000).
Housing: Homeownership rate: 89.3% (2000); Median home value: $125,000 (2000); Median rent: $375 per month (2000); Median age of housing: 38 years (2000).
Transportation: Commute to work: 88.9% car, 0.0% public transportation, 0.0% walk, 11.1% work from home (2000); Travel time to work: 27.6% less than 15 minutes, 62.5% 15 to 30 minutes, 2.6% 30 to 45 minutes, 5.9% 45 to 60 minutes, 1.3% 60 minutes or more (2000)

EGG HARBOR (village). Covers a land area of 1.930 square miles and a water area of 0 square miles. Located at 45.04° N. Lat.; 87.29° W. Long. Elevation is 600 feet.
Population: 250 (2000); Race: 95.2% White, 0.0% Black, 0.0% Asian, 4.8% American Indian and Alaska Native, 0.0% Hispanic of any race, 0.0% two or more races (2000); Density: 129.6 persons per square mile (2000); Age: 9.6% under 18, 39.9% over 64 (2000); Marriage status: 16.2% never married, 64.9% now married, 14.1% widowed, 4.7% divorced (2000); Foreign born: 1.9% (2000); Ancestry (includes multiple ancestries): 49.0% German, 15.9% Irish, 12.0% English, 8.2% Dutch, 8.2% United States or American (2000).
Economy: Single-family building permits issued: 9 (2001) / 9 (2000); Multi-family building permits issued: 11 (2001) / 8 (2000); Employment by occupation: 17.6% management, 16.7% professional, 5.6% services, 34.3% sales, 0.0% farming, 18.5% construction, 7.4% production (2000).

Income: Per capita income: $41,977 (2000); Median household income: $41,667 (2000); Poverty rate: 2.9% (2000).
Taxes: Total city taxes per capita: $1,235 (1997); City property taxes per capita: $1,205 (1997).
Education: High school graduation rate: 92.2% (2000); College graduation rate: 41.7% (2000).
Housing: Homeownership rate: 82.1% (2000); Median home value: $262,500 (2000); Median rent: $583 per month (2000); Median age of housing: 17 years (2000).
Transportation: Commute to work: 75.5% car, 0.0% public transportation, 16.0% walk, 8.5% work from home (2000); Travel time to work: 56.7% less than 15 minutes, 41.2% 15 to 30 minutes, 0.0% 30 to 45 minutes, 0.0% 45 to 60 minutes, 2.1% 60 minutes or more (2000)

EGG HARBOR (town). Covers a land area of 36.558 square miles and a water area of 66.355 square miles. Located at 45.00° N. Lat.; 87.31° W. Long. Elevation is 600 feet.
History: Egg Harbor received its name in 1825 when several boatloads of Green Bay residents came here on a pleasure excursion. Somehow they began throwing eggs at each other between the boats, and continued the egg throwing on the shore, where they named the place Egg Harbor.
Population: 1,194 (2000); Race: 96.3% White, 0.5% Black, 0.2% Asian, 1.5% American Indian and Alaska Native, 0.2% Hispanic of any race, 1.5% two or more races (2000); Density: 32.7 persons per square mile (2000); Age: 23.0% under 18, 14.5% over 64 (2000); Marriage status: 19.6% never married, 67.4% now married, 5.7% widowed, 7.3% divorced (2000); Foreign born: 1.5% (2000); Ancestry (includes multiple ancestries): 52.4% German, 12.4% Irish, 7.9% English, 7.5% Norwegian, 6.3% Other groups (2000).
Economy: Single-family building permits issued: 42 (2001) / 29 (2000); Multi-family building permits issued: 25 (2001) / 0 (2000); Employment by occupation: 15.3% management, 7.9% professional, 21.1% services, 22.2% sales, 4.3% farming, 14.8% construction, 14.5% production (2000).
Income: Per capita income: $24,329 (2000); Median household income: $43,098 (2000); Poverty rate: 8.5% (2000).
Taxes: Total city taxes per capita: $155 (1997); City property taxes per capita: $148 (1997).
Education: High school graduation rate: 86.5% (2000); College graduation rate: 21.3% (2000).
Housing: Homeownership rate: 87.8% (2000); Median home value: $165,400 (2000); Median rent: $392 per month (2000); Median age of housing: 20 years (2000).
Transportation: Commute to work: 83.3% car, 0.6% public transportation, 2.7% walk, 12.7% work from home (2000); Travel time to work: 32.8% less than 15 minutes, 49.5% 15 to 30 minutes, 10.1% 30 to 45 minutes, 1.5% 45 to 60 minutes, 6.1% 60 minutes or more (2000)

ELLISON BAY (unincorporated postal area, zip code 54210). Covers a land area of 27.652 square miles and a water area of 0.449 square miles. Located at 45.27° N. Lat.; 87.04° W. Long. Elevation is 592 feet.
History: Maritime Museum Newport State Park to East.
Population: 1,022 (2000); Race: 99.3% White, 0.0% Black, 0.0% Asian, 0.0% American Indian and Alaska Native, 1.5% Hispanic of any race, 0.2% two or more races (2000); Density: 37.0 persons per square mile (2000); Age: 20.1% under 18, 23.3% over 64 (2000); Marriage status: 13.1% never married, 70.0% now married, 9.3% widowed, 7.6% divorced (2000); Foreign born: 2.3% (2000); Ancestry (includes multiple ancestries): 40.0% German, 20.9% Swedish, 10.6% Norwegian, 8.9% Irish, 7.7% Polish (2000).
Economy: Employment by occupation: 15.4% management, 12.6% professional, 15.9% services, 30.3% sales, 2.8% farming, 17.0% construction, 6.1% production (2000).
Income: Per capita income: $23,749 (2000); Median household income: $42,128 (2000); Poverty rate: 4.4% (2000).
Education: High school graduation rate: 92.1% (2000); College graduation rate: 32.8% (2000).
Housing: Homeownership rate: 86.9% (2000); Median home value: $158,200 (2000); Median rent: $430 per month (2000); Median age of housing: 22 years (2000).
Transportation: Commute to work: 84.0% car, 1.4% public transportation, 3.1% walk, 11.5% work from home (2000); Travel time to work: 46.5% less than 15 minutes, 38.1% 15 to 30 minutes, 7.0% 30 to 45 minutes, 3.2% 45 to 60 minutes, 5.1% 60 minutes or more (2000)

EPHRAIM (village). Covers a land area of 3.898 square miles and a water area of 0 square miles. Located at 45.15° N. Lat.; 87.17° W. Long. Elevation is 600 feet.
History: Ephraim was founded in 1853 on Eagle Harbor by a colony of Moravians, who had fled from an earlier settlement near Green Bay when they began to distrust their leader there. The good harbor at Ephraim helped it to become a resort village, with a yacht club and an annual regatta.
Population: 353 (2000); Race: 100.0% White, 0.0% Black, 0.0% Asian, 0.0% American Indian and Alaska Native, 0.0% Hispanic of any race, 0.0% two or more races (2000); Density: 90.6 persons per square mile (2000); Age: 17.3% under 18, 28.5% over 64 (2000); Marriage status: 15.1% never married, 71.8% now married, 7.4% widowed, 5.6% divorced (2000); Foreign born: 2.1% (2000); Ancestry (includes multiple ancestries): 42.1% German, 17.3% English, 13.6% Norwegian, 12.1% Swedish, 11.5% Irish (2000).
Economy: Single-family building permits issued: 1 (2001) / 0 (2000); Multi-family building permits issued: 0 (2001) / 0 (2000); Employment by occupation: 30.5% management, 14.3% professional, 23.4% services, 19.5% sales, 0.0% farming, 7.8% construction, 4.5% production (2000).
Income: Per capita income: $30,579 (2000); Median household income: $52,500 (2000); Poverty rate: 5.2% (2000).
Taxes: Total city taxes per capita: $2,976 (1997); City property taxes per capita: $2,915 (1997).
Education: High school graduation rate: 96.6% (2000); College graduation rate: 47.5% (2000).
Housing: Homeownership rate: 88.3% (2000); Median home value: $225,000 (2000); Median rent: $431 per month (2000); Median age of housing: 28 years (2000).
Transportation: Commute to work: 68.7% car, 2.0% public transportation, 10.2% walk, 17.0% work from home (2000); Travel time to work: 80.3% less than 15 minutes, 12.3% 15 to 30 minutes, 2.5% 30 to 45 minutes, 2.5% 45 to 60 minutes, 2.5% 60 minutes or more (2000)

FISH CREEK (unincorporated postal area, zip code 54212). Covers a land area of 35.387 square miles and a water area of 0.563 square miles. Located at 45.14° N. Lat.; 87.24° W. Long. Elevation is 583 feet.
History: Fish Creek was settled in 1844 by Increase Claflin, a horse breeder and trader. It became a fishing village, a farming town, and later a resort center.
Population: 1,120 (2000); Race: 97.8% White, 0.0% Black, 0.4% Asian, 0.7% American Indian and Alaska Native, 0.5% Hispanic of any race, 0.8% two or more races (2000); Density: 31.7 persons per square mile (2000); Age: 16.6% under 18, 18.9% over 64 (2000); Marriage status: 19.4% never married, 68.5% now married, 5.2% widowed, 7.0% divorced (2000); Foreign born: 1.7% (2000); Ancestry (includes multiple ancestries): 49.6% German, 14.4% English, 13.4% Irish, 9.3% Polish, 8.1% Swedish (2000).
Economy: Employment by occupation: 17.0% management, 18.5% professional, 19.9% services, 24.2% sales, 1.4% farming, 11.1% construction, 7.9% production (2000).
Income: Per capita income: $29,373 (2000); Median household income: $47,667 (2000); Poverty rate: 7.6% (2000).
Education: High school graduation rate: 95.4% (2000); College graduation rate: 38.6% (2000).

School District(s)

Gibraltar Area (PK-12)
2000 Enrollment: 693 920-868-3284
Housing: Homeownership rate: 85.9% (2000); Median home value: $210,800 (2000); Median rent: $438 per month (2000); Median age of housing: 23 years (2000).
Transportation: Commute to work: 83.6% car, 0.4% public transportation, 3.5% walk, 11.9% work from home (2000); Travel time to work: 58.6% less than 15 minutes, 21.1% 15 to 30 minutes, 16.2% 30 to 45 minutes, 0.8% 45 to 60 minutes, 3.2% 60 minutes or more (2000)

FORESTVILLE (village). Covers a land area of 0.521 square miles and a water area of 0 square miles. Located at 44.68° N. Lat.; 87.48° W. Long. Elevation is 633 feet.
Population: 429 (2000); Race: 97.9% White, 1.6% Black, 0.0% Asian, 0.0% American Indian and Alaska Native, 0.0% Hispanic of any race, 0.5% two or more races (2000); Density: 823.7 persons per square mile (2000); Age: 23.2% under 18, 17.0% over 64 (2000); Marriage status: 23.8% never married, 55.7% now married, 9.2% widowed, 11.2% divorced (2000); Foreign born: 0.0% (2000); Ancestry (includes multiple ancestries): 54.9% German, 18.6% Belgian, 6.4% Czech, 5.3% Norwegian, 5.3% Polish (2000).
Economy: Single-family building permits issued: 1 (2001) / 1 (2000); Multi-family building permits issued: 0 (2001) / 0 (2000); Employment by occupation: 5.4% management, 11.2% professional, 10.3% services, 27.2% sales, 0.9% farming, 16.5% construction, 28.6% production (2000).
Income: Per capita income: $16,521 (2000); Median household income: $39,167 (2000); Poverty rate: 7.4% (2000).

Taxes: Total city taxes per capita: $45 (1997); City property taxes per capita: $41 (1997).
Education: High school graduation rate: 86.2% (2000); College graduation rate: 6.7% (2000).
Housing: Homeownership rate: 74.7% (2000); Median home value: $79,300 (2000); Median rent: $377 per month (2000); Median age of housing: 37 years (2000).
Transportation: Commute to work: 91.5% car, 0.9% public transportation, 1.8% walk, 4.9% work from home (2000); Travel time to work: 25.8% less than 15 minutes, 57.7% 15 to 30 minutes, 8.0% 30 to 45 minutes, 6.6% 45 to 60 minutes, 1.9% 60 minutes or more (2000)

FORESTVILLE (town). Covers a land area of 35.387 square miles and a water area of 0.144 square miles. Located at 44.71° N. Lat.; 87.46° W. Long. Elevation is 633 feet.
Population: 1,086 (2000); Race: 96.4% White, 0.1% Black, 0.0% Asian, 0.5% American Indian and Alaska Native, 0.6% Hispanic of any race, 3.0% two or more races (2000); Density: 30.7 persons per square mile (2000); Age: 28.5% under 18, 11.6% over 64 (2000); Marriage status: 24.3% never married, 64.2% now married, 4.7% widowed, 6.8% divorced (2000); Foreign born: 0.5% (2000); Ancestry (includes multiple ancestries): 50.4% German, 26.4% Belgian, 9.0% Norwegian, 6.4% Irish, 5.4% Polish (2000).
Economy: In dairying and fruit-growing area. Manufacturing: dehydrated cherries, cranberries. Single-family building permits issued: 10 (2001) / 7 (2000); Multi-family building permits issued: 0 (2001) / 0 (2000); Employment by occupation: 13.2% management, 11.4% professional, 10.6% services, 17.1% sales, 2.7% farming, 15.2% construction, 29.8% production (2000).
Income: Per capita income: $19,174 (2000); Median household income: $46,818 (2000); Poverty rate: 4.5% (2000).
Taxes: Total city taxes per capita: $41 (1997); City property taxes per capita: $39 (1997).
Education: High school graduation rate: 84.3% (2000); College graduation rate: 13.1% (2000).
Housing: Homeownership rate: 86.7% (2000); Median home value: $92,500 (2000); Median rent: $330 per month (2000); Median age of housing: 48 years (2000).
Transportation: Commute to work: 90.1% car, 1.2% public transportation, 1.3% walk, 6.2% work from home (2000); Travel time to work: 27.6% less than 15 minutes, 53.0% 15 to 30 minutes, 6.3% 30 to 45 minutes, 5.6% 45 to 60 minutes, 7.5% 60 minutes or more (2000)

GARDNER (town). Covers a land area of 34.291 square miles and a water area of 79.241 square miles. Located at 44.81° N. Lat.; 87.58° W. Long.
Population: 1,197 (2000); Race: 96.7% White, 0.9% Black, 0.5% Asian, 1.6% American Indian and Alaska Native, 1.2% Hispanic of any race, 0.0% two or more races (2000); Density: 34.9 persons per square mile (2000); Age: 19.7% under 18, 16.6% over 64 (2000); Marriage status: 18.7% never married, 64.8% now married, 6.6% widowed, 9.9% divorced (2000); Foreign born: 1.4% (2000); Ancestry (includes multiple ancestries): 41.1% German, 21.1% Belgian, 8.5% Polish, 7.9% Irish, 5.4% Other groups (2000).
Economy: Single-family building permits issued: 15 (2001) / 14 (2000); Multi-family building permits issued: 0 (2001) / 0 (2000); Employment by occupation: 11.5% management, 10.5% professional, 12.7% services, 22.2% sales, 3.0% farming, 17.4% construction, 22.6% production (2000).
Income: Per capita income: $21,181 (2000); Median household income: $39,063 (2000); Poverty rate: 6.4% (2000).
Taxes: Total city taxes per capita: $255 (1997); City property taxes per capita: $246 (1997).
Education: High school graduation rate: 83.0% (2000); College graduation rate: 9.8% (2000).
Housing: Homeownership rate: 90.9% (2000); Median home value: $122,200 (2000); Median rent: $339 per month (2000); Median age of housing: 29 years (2000).
Transportation: Commute to work: 87.5% car, 0.3% public transportation, 1.9% walk, 8.9% work from home (2000); Travel time to work: 17.7% less than 15 minutes, 48.5% 15 to 30 minutes, 16.2% 30 to 45 minutes, 7.9% 45 to 60 minutes, 9.6% 60 minutes or more (2000)

GIBRALTAR (town). Covers a land area of 33.847 square miles and a water area of 117.591 square miles. Located at 45.13° N. Lat.; 87.24° W. Long.
Population: 1,063 (2000); Race: 97.5% White, 0.0% Black, 0.4% Asian, 0.9% American Indian and Alaska Native, 0.6% Hispanic of any race, 0.8% two or more races (2000); Density: 31.4 persons per square mile (2000); Age: 16.4% under 18, 19.2% over 64 (2000); Marriage status: 20.5% never married, 67.3% now married, 5.6% widowed, 6.6% divorced (2000); Foreign born: 1.6% (2000); Ancestry (includes multiple ancestries): 49.9% German, 17.5% English, 12.5% Irish, 9.9% Polish, 7.7% Norwegian (2000).
Economy: Employment by occupation: 16.2% management, 19.0% professional, 19.2% services, 23.5% sales, 1.5% farming, 11.3% construction, 9.3% production (2000).
Income: Per capita income: $29,755 (2000); Median household income: $47,604 (2000); Poverty rate: 4.2% (2000).
Education: High school graduation rate: 94.8% (2000); College graduation rate: 38.3% (2000).
Housing: Homeownership rate: 87.0% (2000); Median home value: $209,100 (2000); Median rent: $431 per month (2000); Median age of housing: 20 years (2000).
Transportation: Commute to work: 85.7% car, 0.4% public transportation, 1.7% walk, 11.7% work from home (2000); Travel time to work: 56.5% less than 15 minutes, 21.5% 15 to 30 minutes, 17.1% 30 to 45 minutes, 1.3% 45 to 60 minutes, 3.6% 60 minutes or more (2000)

JACKSONPORT (town). Covers a land area of 29.039 square miles and a water area of 29.257 square miles. Located at 44.97° N. Lat.; 87.21° W. Long. Elevation is 593 feet.
History: Jacksonport was once a prosperous lake-port lumber town. When the timber was depleted, the community turned to fishing.
Population: 738 (2000); Race: 98.6% White, 0.5% Black, 0.0% Asian, 0.0% American Indian and Alaska Native, 0.0% Hispanic of any race, 0.8% two or more races (2000); Density: 25.4 persons per square mile (2000); Age: 22.0% under 18, 18.2% over 64 (2000); Marriage status: 18.8% never married, 68.4% now married, 6.7% widowed, 6.2% divorced (2000); Foreign born: 0.7% (2000); Ancestry (includes multiple ancestries): 53.4% German, 11.7% Irish, 11.3% Norwegian, 9.9% French (except Basque), 7.1% English (2000).
Economy: Employment by occupation: 13.6% management, 14.1% professional, 17.1% services, 21.4% sales, 3.3% farming, 17.3% construction, 13.3% production (2000).
Income: Per capita income: $20,493 (2000); Median household income: $42,404 (2000); Poverty rate: 3.4% (2000).
Taxes: Total city taxes per capita: $198 (1997); City property taxes per capita: $197 (1997).
Education: High school graduation rate: 88.2% (2000); College graduation rate: 24.3% (2000).
Housing: Homeownership rate: 89.5% (2000); Median home value: $156,800 (2000); Median rent: $395 per month (2000); Median age of housing: 41 years (2000).
Transportation: Commute to work: 85.4% car, 0.0% public transportation, 3.8% walk, 10.0% work from home (2000); Travel time to work: 28.8% less than 15 minutes, 49.0% 15 to 30 minutes, 16.8% 30 to 45 minutes, 2.6% 45 to 60 minutes, 2.8% 60 minutes or more (2000)

LIBERTY GROVE (town). Covers a land area of 53.578 square miles and a water area of 135.887 square miles. Located at 45.21° N. Lat.; 87.06° W. Long.
Population: 1,858 (2000); Race: 99.4% White, 0.0% Black, 0.0% Asian, 0.0% American Indian and Alaska Native, 1.1% Hispanic of any race, 0.4% two or more races (2000); Density: 34.7 persons per square mile (2000); Age: 18.8% under 18, 23.3% over 64 (2000); Marriage status: 13.3% never married, 70.8% now married, 9.2% widowed, 6.6% divorced (2000); Foreign born: 2.5% (2000); Ancestry (includes multiple ancestries): 43.7% German, 20.1% Swedish, 13.1% Norwegian, 9.6% English, 8.8% Irish (2000).
Economy: Employment by occupation: 14.1% management, 15.7% professional, 17.2% services, 29.4% sales, 1.8% farming, 15.9% construction, 6.0% production (2000).
Income: Per capita income: $24,555 (2000); Median household income: $43,472 (2000); Poverty rate: 4.0% (2000).
Taxes: Total city taxes per capita: $312 (1997); City property taxes per capita: $309 (1997).
Education: High school graduation rate: 91.6% (2000); College graduation rate: 35.8% (2000).
Housing: Homeownership rate: 87.8% (2000); Median home value: $167,200 (2000); Median rent: $428 per month (2000); Median age of housing: 22 years (2000).
Transportation: Commute to work: 85.3% car, 0.7% public transportation, 1.6% walk, 12.4% work from home (2000); Travel time to work: 57.0% less than 15 minutes, 30.7% 15 to 30 minutes, 5.1% 30 to 45 minutes, 3.3% 45 to 60 minutes, 3.9% 60 minutes or more (2000)

NASEWAUPEE (town). Covers a land area of 43.068 square miles and a water area of 28.056 square miles. Located at 44.84° N. Lat.; 87.46° W. Long.
Population: 1,873 (2000); Race: 97.0% White, 0.0% Black, 0.2% Asian, 1.6% American Indian and Alaska Native, 0.6% Hispanic of any race, 1.2% two or more races (2000); Density: 43.5 persons per square mile (2000); Age: 21.8% under 18, 15.6% over 64 (2000); Marriage status: 20.5% never married, 66.6% now married, 6.2% widowed, 6.6% divorced (2000); Foreign born: 0.6% (2000); Ancestry (includes multiple ancestries): 46.7% German, 17.6% Belgian, 10.5% Norwegian, 10.4% Irish, 6.4% English (2000).
Economy: Single-family building permits issued: 19 (2001) / 16 (2000); Multi-family building permits issued: 0 (2001) / 0 (2000); Employment by occupation: 12.7% management, 13.2% professional, 17.5% services, 19.4% sales, 0.9% farming, 12.6% construction, 23.7% production (2000).
Income: Per capita income: $20,815 (2000); Median household income: $43,292 (2000); Poverty rate: 3.4% (2000).
Taxes: Total city taxes per capita: $147 (1997); City property taxes per capita: $137 (1997).
Education: High school graduation rate: 86.1% (2000); College graduation rate: 16.9% (2000).
Housing: Homeownership rate: 88.9% (2000); Median home value: $125,400 (2000); Median rent: $360 per month (2000); Median age of housing: 34 years (2000).
Transportation: Commute to work: 89.6% car, 0.7% public transportation, 2.5% walk, 6.6% work from home (2000); Travel time to work: 45.0% less than 15 minutes, 34.9% 15 to 30 minutes, 6.6% 30 to 45 minutes, 5.6% 45 to 60 minutes, 7.9% 60 minutes or more (2000)

SEVASTOPOL (town). Covers a land area of 51.854 square miles and a water area of 38.734 square miles. Located at 44.89° N. Lat.; 87.30° W. Long.
Population: 2,667 (2000); Race: 97.8% White, 0.0% Black, 0.2% Asian, 0.1% American Indian and Alaska Native, 1.8% Hispanic of any race, 0.4% two or more races (2000); Density: 51.4 persons per square mile (2000); Age: 22.5% under 18, 17.3% over 64 (2000); Marriage status: 17.3% never married, 69.1% now married, 7.4% widowed, 6.3% divorced (2000); Foreign born: 1.6% (2000); Ancestry (includes multiple ancestries): 52.7% German, 14.6% Irish, 9.6% Belgian, 7.0% Norwegian, 6.6% English (2000).
Economy: Employment by occupation: 17.5% management, 12.8% professional, 12.0% services, 24.4% sales, 2.6% farming, 12.4% construction, 18.2% production (2000).
Income: Per capita income: $24,150 (2000); Median household income: $47,227 (2000); Poverty rate: 7.3% (2000).
Taxes: Total city taxes per capita: $111 (1997); City property taxes per capita: $108 (1997).
Education: High school graduation rate: 91.0% (2000); College graduation rate: 22.7% (2000).
Housing: Homeownership rate: 87.6% (2000); Median home value: $156,800 (2000); Median rent: $440 per month (2000); Median age of housing: 30 years (2000).
Transportation: Commute to work: 86.1% car, 0.4% public transportation, 2.9% walk, 9.5% work from home (2000); Travel time to work: 52.3% less than 15 minutes, 35.2% 15 to 30 minutes, 5.6% 30 to 45 minutes, 2.1% 45 to 60 minutes, 4.8% 60 minutes or more (2000)

SISTER BAY (village). Covers a land area of 2.591 square miles and a water area of 0.455 square miles. Located at 45.18° N. Lat.; 87.12° W. Long. Elevation is 587 feet.
History: The hillside village of Sister Bay was established in the shadow of the Sister Bluffs, with the Sister Islands offshore serving as a breeding ground for herring gulls and terns.
Population: 886 (2000); Race: 97.4% White, 0.0% Black, 0.0% Asian, 1.1% American Indian and Alaska Native, 2.0% Hispanic of any race, 0.9% two or more races (2000); Density: 341.9 persons per square mile (2000); Age: 11.0% under 18, 47.2% over 64 (2000); Marriage status: 17.0% never married, 55.8% now married, 22.5% widowed, 4.7% divorced (2000); Foreign born: 3.7% (2000); Ancestry (includes multiple ancestries): 42.0% German, 18.2% Swedish, 11.4% Norwegian, 10.8% Irish, 9.3% English (2000).
Economy: Single-family building permits issued: 1 (2001) / 11 (2000); Multi-family building permits issued: 2 (2001) / 5 (2000); Employment by occupation: 16.6% management, 10.5% professional, 23.6% services, 28.7% sales, 0.0% farming, 13.7% construction, 7.0% production (2000).
Income: Per capita income: $25,029 (2000); Median household income: $33,224 (2000); Poverty rate: 3.5% (2000).
Taxes: Total city taxes per capita: $1,069 (1997); City property taxes per capita: $1,056 (1997).
Education: High school graduation rate: 87.5% (2000); College graduation rate: 30.5% (2000).
Housing: Homeownership rate: 60.1% (2000); Median home value: $190,800 (2000); Median rent: $589 per month (2000); Median age of housing: 17 years (2000).
Newspapers: Door Reminder (1 x week)
Transportation: Commute to work: 80.0% car, 0.0% public transportation, 10.5% walk, 9.5% work from home (2000); Travel time to work: 73.6% less than 15 minutes, 21.4% 15 to 30 minutes, 3.3% 30 to 45 minutes, 0.4% 45 to 60 minutes, 1.4% 60 minutes or more (2000)

STURGEON BAY (city). Covers a land area of 9.616 square miles and a water area of 1.691 square miles. Located at 44.83° N. Lat.; 87.37° W. Long. Elevation is 588 feet.
History: Father Jacques Marquette recorded stopping at Sturgeon Bay in 1673. In the early 1850's, Crandall and Bradley's sawmill here was a wilderness outpost, cut off during the winter by the frozen bay. A particularly early freeze in 1857 deprived the sawmill employees of their winter rations. Facing starvation, the men cut a path through frozen swamps and forests to Egg Harbor, where supplies were available. The route they cut later became part of the state highway system.
Population: 9,437 (2000); Race: 97.3% White, 0.0% Black, 0.8% Asian, 0.9% American Indian and Alaska Native, 0.7% Hispanic of any race, 0.9% two or more races (2000); Density: 981.4 persons per square mile (2000); Age: 23.4% under 18, 18.7% over 64 (2000); Marriage status: 24.5% never married, 53.3% now married, 9.7% widowed, 12.5% divorced (2000); Foreign born: 1.6% (2000); Ancestry (includes multiple ancestries): 45.9% German, 10.6% Norwegian, 10.6% Irish, 10.1% Belgian, 7.3% English (2000).
Economy: Single-family building permits issued: 30 (2001) / 34 (2000); Multi-family building permits issued: 118 (2001) / 18 (2000); Employment by occupation: 10.4% management, 15.9% professional, 15.8% services, 25.3% sales, 1.7% farming, 11.1% construction, 19.7% production (2000).
Income: Per capita income: $18,899 (2000); Median household income: $31,935 (2000); Poverty rate: 7.7% (2000).
Taxes: Total city taxes per capita: $425 (2000); City property taxes per capita: $383 (2000).
Education: High school graduation rate: 86.0% (2000); College graduation rate: 17.1% (2000).

School District(s)

Sevastopol (PK-12)
2000 Enrollment: 669 920-743-6282
Sturgeon Bay (PK-12)
2000 Enrollment: 1,440 920-746-2801

Housing: Homeownership rate: 67.4% (2000); Median home value: $89,700 (2000); Median rent: $367 per month (2000); Median age of housing: 34 years (2000).
Hospitals: Door County Memorial Hospital (89 beds)
Safety: Violent crime rate: 14.7 per 10,000 population; Property crime rate: 299.9 per 10,000 population (2001).
Newspapers: Door County Advocate (2 x week)
Transportation: Commute to work: 87.2% car, 1.3% public transportation, 6.3% walk, 3.6% work from home (2000); Travel time to work: 75.1% less than 15 minutes, 14.9% 15 to 30 minutes, 5.5% 30 to 45 minutes, 1.8% 45 to 60 minutes, 2.8% 60 minutes or more (2000)
Additional Information Contacts
Door County Board of Realtors 920-743-9651
Sturgeon Bay Chamber of Commerce 920-743-4456

STURGEON BAY (town). Covers a land area of 19.321 square miles and a water area of 15.860 square miles. Located at 44.81° N. Lat.; 87.31° W. Long. Elevation is 588 feet.
Population: 865 (2000); Race: 97.0% White, 0.3% Black, 0.5% Asian, 1.4% American Indian and Alaska Native, 0.8% Hispanic of any race, 0.8% two or more races (2000); Density: 44.8 persons per square mile (2000); Age: 17.8% under 18, 16.4% over 64 (2000); Marriage status: 19.6% never married, 70.9% now married, 3.4% widowed, 6.0% divorced (2000); Foreign born: 1.0% (2000); Ancestry (includes multiple ancestries): 49.8% German, 11.8% Irish, 11.4% Norwegian, 10.4% Belgian, 8.5% English (2000).
Economy: Employment by occupation: 10.9% management, 18.2% professional, 12.0% services, 27.4% sales, 1.1% farming, 13.3% construction, 17.1% production (2000).
Income: Per capita income: $22,397 (2000); Median household income: $42,434 (2000); Poverty rate: 8.6% (2000).

Taxes: Total city taxes per capita: $40 (1997); City property taxes per capita: $40 (1997).
Education: High school graduation rate: 89.3% (2000); College graduation rate: 18.4% (2000).
Housing: Homeownership rate: 90.3% (2000); Median home value: $133,900 (2000); Median rent: $375 per month (2000); Median age of housing: 28 years (2000).
Transportation: Commute to work: 90.0% car, 0.4% public transportation, 2.2% walk, 6.5% work from home (2000); Travel time to work: 52.7% less than 15 minutes, 33.6% 15 to 30 minutes, 8.4% 30 to 45 minutes, 2.8% 45 to 60 minutes, 2.6% 60 minutes or more (2000)

UNION (town). Covers a land area of 21.175 square miles and a water area of 14.732 square miles. Located at 44.71° N. Lat.; 87.69° W. Long.
Population: 880 (2000); Race: 99.8% White, 0.0% Black, 0.0% Asian, 0.0% American Indian and Alaska Native, 0.0% Hispanic of any race, 0.2% two or more races (2000); Density: 41.6 persons per square mile (2000); Age: 28.0% under 18, 11.0% over 64 (2000); Marriage status: 17.8% never married, 71.6% now married, 5.8% widowed, 4.7% divorced (2000); Foreign born: 0.8% (2000); Ancestry (includes multiple ancestries): 52.5% Belgian, 24.9% German, 4.7% Irish, 3.7% Norwegian, 3.2% Dutch (2000).
Economy: Single-family building permits issued: 13 (2001) / 15 (2000); Multi-family building permits issued: 0 (2001) / 0 (2000); Employment by occupation: 14.9% management, 14.9% professional, 14.7% services, 15.9% sales, 2.6% farming, 13.4% construction, 23.7% production (2000).
Income: Per capita income: $19,372 (2000); Median household income: $47,604 (2000); Poverty rate: 5.1% (2000).
Taxes: Total city taxes per capita: $120 (1997); City property taxes per capita: $119 (1997).
Education: High school graduation rate: 82.6% (2000); College graduation rate: 13.4% (2000).
Housing: Homeownership rate: 82.1% (2000); Median home value: $124,100 (2000); Median rent: $350 per month (2000); Median age of housing: 42 years (2000).
Transportation: Commute to work: 86.8% car, 1.1% public transportation, 1.9% walk, 9.7% work from home (2000); Travel time to work: 18.9% less than 15 minutes, 31.2% 15 to 30 minutes, 32.4% 30 to 45 minutes, 10.6% 45 to 60 minutes, 7.0% 60 minutes or more (2000)

WASHINGTON (town). Covers a land area of 25.491 square miles and a water area of 99.994 square miles. Located at 45.36° N. Lat.; 86.89° W. Long. Elevation is 630 feet.
Population: 660 (2000); Race: 99.5% White, 0.0% Black, 0.5% Asian, 0.0% American Indian and Alaska Native, 0.0% Hispanic of any race, 0.0% two or more races (2000); Density: 25.9 persons per square mile (2000); Age: 25.7% under 18, 20.7% over 64 (2000); Marriage status: 16.0% never married, 64.4% now married, 10.2% widowed, 9.4% divorced (2000); Foreign born: 2.9% (2000); Ancestry (includes multiple ancestries): 39.4% German, 22.0% Norwegian, 17.8% English, 16.3% Danish, 13.5% Irish (2000).
Economy: Employment by occupation: 12.2% management, 12.6% professional, 18.5% services, 15.0% sales, 2.8% farming, 26.4% construction, 12.6% production (2000).
Income: Per capita income: $17,065 (2000); Median household income: $31,146 (2000); Poverty rate: 10.5% (2000).
Taxes: Total city taxes per capita: $1,005 (2000); City property taxes per capita: $998 (2000).
Education: High school graduation rate: 90.0% (2000); College graduation rate: 29.3% (2000).
Housing: Homeownership rate: 83.4% (2000); Median home value: $134,400 (2000); Median rent: $339 per month (2000); Median age of housing: 37 years (2000).
Transportation: Commute to work: 79.7% car, 0.0% public transportation, 8.9% walk, 9.3% work from home (2000); Travel time to work: 84.3% less than 15 minutes, 9.0% 15 to 30 minutes, 2.7% 30 to 45 minutes, 0.0% 45 to 60 minutes, 4.0% 60 minutes or more (2000)

Douglas County

Located in northwestern Wisconsin; bounded on the west by Minnesota, and on the north by the St. Louis River, Lake Superior, and the Minnesota border; drained by the St. Croix, Eau Claire, and Black Rivers. Covers a land area of 1,309.10 square miles, a water area of 170.80 square miles, and is located in the Central Time Zone. The county government was organized in 1854. County seat is Superior.

Douglas County is part of the Duluth-Superior, MN-WI MSA. The entire metro area includes: St. Louis County, MN; Douglas County, WI

Weather Station: Foxboro — Elevation: 931 feet

	Jan	Feb	Mar	Apr	May	Jun	Jul	Aug	Sep	Oct	Nov	Dec
High	20	27	37	52	66	75	80	77	68	56	38	25
Low	-3	3	15	27	36	45	53	52	44	33	20	4
Precip	1.0	0.7	1.4	2.1	3.3	4.2	4.5	4.2	3.9	2.7	2.1	0.9
Snow	na	na	na	na	na	na	na	na	na	na	na	na

High and Low temperatures in degrees Fahrenheit; Precipitation and Snow in inches

Weather Station: Gordon — Elevation: 1,040 feet

	Jan	Feb	Mar	Apr	May	Jun	Jul	Aug	Sep	Oct	Nov	Dec
High	19	27	38	54	68	77	81	78	68	55	37	24
Low	-6	0	14	27	39	49	54	51	43	32	18	3
Precip	1.1	0.8	1.7	2.2	3.4	3.8	4.9	4.4	3.9	2.7	1.9	1.0
Snow	13.2	7.7	9.5	3.7	0.2	0.0	0.0	0.0	tr	0.8	9.1	11.4

High and Low temperatures in degrees Fahrenheit; Precipitation and Snow in inches

Weather Station: Solon Springs — Elevation: 1,079 feet

	Jan	Feb	Mar	Apr	May	Jun	Jul	Aug	Sep	Oct	Nov	Dec
High	20	27	38	54	69	78	82	79	69	56	37	24
Low	-4	2	15	28	39	49	54	52	43	33	20	4
Precip	1.0	0.8	1.7	2.2	3.2	3.9	4.8	4.2	3.6	2.7	2.0	1.0
Snow	13.0	8.2	9.0	3.7	0.2	0.0	0.0	0.0	0.0	0.6	8.8	11.1

High and Low temperatures in degrees Fahrenheit; Precipitation and Snow in inches

Weather Station: Superior — Elevation: 629 feet

	Jan	Feb	Mar	Apr	May	Jun	Jul	Aug	Sep	Oct	Nov	Dec
High	20	26	35	47	58	68	76	74	66	54	38	25
Low	1	7	19	30	40	48	56	56	47	36	23	8
Precip	1.0	0.7	1.9	2.2	3.2	4.0	4.3	4.0	4.2	2.5	2.0	0.9
Snow	13.9	7.5	8.3	2.3	tr	0.0	0.0	0.0	0.0	0.3	7.7	10.9

High and Low temperatures in degrees Fahrenheit; Precipitation and Snow in inches

Population: 43,287 (2000); Race: 95.4% White, 0.5% Black, 0.7% Asian, 1.8% American Indian and Alaska Native, 0.6% Hispanic of any race, 1.5% two or more races (2000); Density: 33.1 persons per square mile (2000); Age: 23.6% under 18, 14.5% over 64 (2000).
Religion: Five largest groups: 24.4% Catholic Church, 10.3% Evangelical Lutheran Church in America, 3.3% The Salvation Army, 2.5% The Wesleyan Church, 1.8% Presbyterian Church (U.S.A.) (2000).
Economy: Unemployment rate: 4.2% (11/2002); Total civilian labor force: 23,231 (11/2002); Leading industries: 17.1% retail trade; 14.0% health care and social assistance; 13.4% accommodation & food services (2000); Companies that employ more than 1,000 persons: 0 (2000); Companies that employ more than 100 persons: 21 (2000); Farms: 267 totaling 70,806 acres (1997); Minority business ownership rate: 0.0% (1997); Women business ownership rate: 21.8% (1997); Retail sales per capita: $7,754 (1997). Single-family building permits issued: 213 (2001) / 224 (2000); Multi-family building permits issued: 10 (2001) / 27 (2000).
Income: Per capita income: $17,638 (2000); Median household income: $35,226 (2000); Poverty rate: 11.0% (2000); Bankruptcy rate: 4.13% (2001).
Taxes: Total county taxes per capita: $203 (1997); County property taxes per capita: $154 (1997).
Education: High school graduation rate: 85.9% (2000); College graduation rate: 18.3% (2000).
Housing: Homeownership rate: 71.5% (2000); Median home value: $69,900 (2000); Median rent: $351 per month (2000); Median age of housing: 44 years (2000).
Health: Birth rate: 116.2 per 10,000 population (1998); Age adjusted death rate: 98.5 per 10,000 population (1999); Age adjusted cancer mortality rate: 275.6 deaths per 100,000 population (1999). Air Quality Index: 100% good, 0% moderate, 0% unhealthy (percent of days in 2000). Number of physicians: 5.5 per 10,000 population (1999); Number of hospital beds: 8.8 per 10,000 population (1999).
Elections: 2000 Presidential election results: 62.6% Gore, 31.9% Bush, 4.5% Nader, 0.5% Buchanan
National and State Parks: Brule River State Forest; Brule River State Forest Annex; Brule River State Forest Waterfowl Management Area; Douglas County State Wildlife Area; Lucius Woods State Park; Pattison State Park
Additional Information Contacts
Douglas County Government Offices 715-395-1341
Superior Chamber of Commerce 715-394-7716

Douglas County Communities

AMNICON (town). Covers a land area of 39.077 square miles and a water area of 0.016 square miles. Located at 46.58° N. Lat.; 91.87° W. Long.
Population: 1,074 (2000); Race: 97.2% White, 0.8% Black, 0.3% Asian, 0.8% American Indian and Alaska Native, 0.2% Hispanic of any race, 1.0% two or more races (2000); Density: 27.5 persons per square mile (2000); Age: 31.7% under 18, 8.6% over 64 (2000); Marriage status: 24.8% never married, 64.6% now married, 4.4% widowed, 6.2% divorced (2000); Foreign born: 0.6% (2000); Ancestry (includes multiple ancestries): 32.5% German, 14.5% Swedish, 12.9% Norwegian, 11.7% Irish, 10.7% Finnish (2000).
Economy: Employment by occupation: 8.6% management, 17.2% professional, 18.6% services, 23.8% sales, 1.2% farming, 13.4% construction, 17.2% production (2000).
Income: Per capita income: $16,968 (2000); Median household income: $48,654 (2000); Poverty rate: 4.8% (2000).
Taxes: Total city taxes per capita: $26 (2000); City property taxes per capita: $25 (2000).
Education: High school graduation rate: 89.3% (2000); College graduation rate: 20.4% (2000).
Housing: Homeownership rate: 90.2% (2000); Median home value: $78,500 (2000); Median rent: $413 per month (2000); Median age of housing: 29 years (2000).
Transportation: Commute to work: 94.4% car, 0.6% public transportation, 0.0% walk, 3.7% work from home (2000); Travel time to work: 11.6% less than 15 minutes, 43.7% 15 to 30 minutes, 36.1% 30 to 45 minutes, 5.2% 45 to 60 minutes, 3.4% 60 minutes or more (2000)

BENNETT (town). Covers a land area of 47.525 square miles and a water area of 0.774 square miles. Located at 46.45° N. Lat.; 91.80° W. Long. Elevation is 1,200 feet.
Population: 622 (2000); Race: 97.3% White, 0.0% Black, 0.2% Asian, 1.8% American Indian and Alaska Native, 0.0% Hispanic of any race, 0.8% two or more races (2000); Density: 13.1 persons per square mile (2000); Age: 27.2% under 18, 10.6% over 64 (2000); Marriage status: 16.8% never married, 73.1% now married, 2.9% widowed, 7.2% divorced (2000); Foreign born: 1.1% (2000); Ancestry (includes multiple ancestries): 24.1% German, 19.5% Swedish, 14.2% Norwegian, 10.9% Irish, 10.7% Finnish (2000).
Economy: Employment by occupation: 7.1% management, 19.2% professional, 17.5% services, 16.5% sales, 2.7% farming, 11.4% construction, 25.6% production (2000).
Income: Per capita income: $18,335 (2000); Median household income: $40,313 (2000); Poverty rate: 7.7% (2000).
Taxes: Total city taxes per capita: $79 (1997); City property taxes per capita: $79 (1997).
Education: High school graduation rate: 86.5% (2000); College graduation rate: 19.5% (2000).
Housing: Homeownership rate: 96.6% (2000); Median home value: $104,200 (2000); Median rent: $375 per month (2000); Median age of housing: 34 years (2000).
Transportation: Commute to work: 96.9% car, 0.0% public transportation, 0.0% walk, 3.1% work from home (2000); Travel time to work: 15.5% less than 15 minutes, 23.7% 15 to 30 minutes, 34.6% 30 to 45 minutes, 21.2% 45 to 60 minutes, 4.9% 60 minutes or more (2000)

BRULE (town). Covers a land area of 55.708 square miles and a water area of 0.176 square miles. Located at 46.56° N. Lat.; 91.59° W. Long. Elevation is 985 feet.
History: Brule was the location of President Calvin Coolidge's summer White House in 1928, when he spent 88 days along the Bois Brule River, and pronounced the fishing to be excellent.
Population: 591 (2000); Race: 98.3% White, 0.0% Black, 0.0% Asian, 1.7% American Indian and Alaska Native, 2.3% Hispanic of any race, 0.0% two or more races (2000); Density: 10.6 persons per square mile (2000); Age: 29.8% under 18, 11.7% over 64 (2000); Marriage status: 19.3% never married, 63.7% now married, 5.3% widowed, 11.7% divorced (2000); Foreign born: 0.5% (2000); Ancestry (includes multiple ancestries): 36.0% Finnish, 20.4% German, 12.2% Irish, 11.7% Swedish, 11.0% Norwegian (2000).
Economy: Employment by occupation: 8.1% management, 19.2% professional, 14.6% services, 18.1% sales, 2.3% farming, 21.9% construction, 15.8% production (2000).
Income: Per capita income: $14,620 (2000); Median household income: $35,972 (2000); Poverty rate: 12.4% (2000).
Taxes: Total city taxes per capita: $86 (1997); City property taxes per capita: $82 (1997).
Education: High school graduation rate: 85.5% (2000); College graduation rate: 14.7% (2000).
Housing: Homeownership rate: 80.6% (2000); Median home value: $70,300 (2000); Median rent: $331 per month (2000); Median age of housing: 30 years (2000).
Transportation: Commute to work: 92.7% car, 0.0% public transportation, 1.5% walk, 4.6% work from home (2000); Travel time to work: 16.5% less than 15 minutes, 20.2% 15 to 30 minutes, 31.9% 30 to 45 minutes, 25.4% 45 to 60 minutes, 6.0% 60 minutes or more (2000)

CLOVERLAND (town). Covers a land area of 46.192 square miles and a water area of 0 square miles. Located at 46.70° N. Lat.; 91.62° W. Long. Elevation is 804 feet.
Population: 247 (2000); Race: 95.0% White, 0.0% Black, 0.0% Asian, 0.8% American Indian and Alaska Native, 0.4% Hispanic of any race, 4.1% two or more races (2000); Density: 5.3 persons per square mile (2000); Age: 27.4% under 18, 19.5% over 64 (2000); Marriage status: 20.7% never married, 70.7% now married, 3.7% widowed, 4.8% divorced (2000); Foreign born: 1.2% (2000); Ancestry (includes multiple ancestries): 34.0% German, 19.9% Finnish, 10.8% Swedish, 10.0% Polish, 7.9% Norwegian (2000).
Economy: Employment by occupation: 7.5% management, 8.5% professional, 18.9% services, 22.6% sales, 1.9% farming, 14.2% construction, 26.4% production (2000).
Income: Per capita income: $16,220 (2000); Median household income: $35,000 (2000); Poverty rate: 7.5% (2000).
Taxes: Total city taxes per capita: $109 (1997); City property taxes per capita: $109 (1997).
Education: High school graduation rate: 83.9% (2000); College graduation rate: 13.5% (2000).
Housing: Homeownership rate: 92.0% (2000); Median home value: $56,700 (2000); Median rent: $225 per month (2000); Median age of housing: 40 years (2000).
Transportation: Commute to work: 81.1% car, 0.0% public transportation, 1.9% walk, 17.0% work from home (2000); Travel time to work: 15.9% less than 15 minutes, 21.6% 15 to 30 minutes, 30.7% 30 to 45 minutes, 27.3% 45 to 60 minutes, 4.5% 60 minutes or more (2000)

DAIRYLAND (town). Covers a land area of 140.209 square miles and a water area of 0.601 square miles. Located at 46.23° N. Lat.; 92.18° W. Long. Elevation is 1,122 feet.
Population: 186 (2000); Race: 99.0% White, 0.0% Black, 0.0% Asian, 0.0% American Indian and Alaska Native, 0.0% Hispanic of any race, 1.0% two or more races (2000); Density: 1.3 persons per square mile (2000); Age: 10.8% under 18, 24.1% over 64 (2000); Marriage status: 17.8% never married, 64.9% now married, 9.7% widowed, 7.6% divorced (2000); Foreign born: 0.0% (2000); Ancestry (includes multiple ancestries): 32.5% German, 14.8% Swedish, 12.8% Norwegian, 10.3% United States or American, 7.9% Irish (2000).
Economy: Employment by occupation: 8.4% management, 20.0% professional, 23.2% services, 14.7% sales, 0.0% farming, 9.5% construction, 24.2% production (2000).
Income: Per capita income: $18,155 (2000); Median household income: $35,313 (2000); Poverty rate: 9.0% (2000).
Taxes: Total city taxes per capita: $42 (1997); City property taxes per capita: $38 (1997).
Education: High school graduation rate: 74.3% (2000); College graduation rate: 12.0% (2000).
Housing: Homeownership rate: 93.9% (2000); Median home value: $22,500 (2000); Median age of housing: 27 years (2000).
Transportation: Commute to work: 88.8% car, 0.0% public transportation, 3.4% walk, 5.6% work from home (2000); Travel time to work: 11.9% less than 15 minutes, 28.6% 15 to 30 minutes, 27.4% 30 to 45 minutes, 10.7% 45 to 60 minutes, 21.4% 60 minutes or more (2000)

FOXBORO (unincorporated postal area, zip code 54836). Covers a land area of 163.279 square miles and a water area of 0.355 square miles. Located at 46.45° N. Lat.; 92.21° W. Long. Elevation is 925 feet.
Population: 1,032 (2000); Race: 97.6% White, 0.0% Black, 0.8% Asian, 0.1% American Indian and Alaska Native, 0.2% Hispanic of any race, 1.5% two or more races (2000); Density: 6.3 persons per square mile (2000); Age: 27.0% under 18, 11.0% over 64 (2000); Marriage status: 20.0% never married, 70.2% now married, 5.3% widowed, 4.6% divorced (2000); Foreign born: 1.1% (2000); Ancestry (includes multiple ancestries): 29.7% German, 15.0% Norwegian, 14.6% Swedish, 11.7% Polish, 10.6% Irish (2000).

Economy: Employment by occupation: 7.8% management, 20.3% professional, 11.3% services, 22.9% sales, 0.7% farming, 16.5% construction, 20.5% production (2000).
Income: Per capita income: $17,652 (2000); Median household income: $44,423 (2000); Poverty rate: 6.4% (2000).
Education: High school graduation rate: 82.5% (2000); College graduation rate: 12.3% (2000).
Housing: Homeownership rate: 92.5% (2000); Median home value: $87,100 (2000); Median rent: $163 per month (2000); Median age of housing: 28 years (2000).
Transportation: Commute to work: 94.9% car, 0.4% public transportation, 2.2% walk, 1.8% work from home (2000); Travel time to work: 6.6% less than 15 minutes, 26.0% 15 to 30 minutes, 41.8% 30 to 45 minutes, 16.7% 45 to 60 minutes, 9.0% 60 minutes or more (2000)

GORDON (town). Covers a land area of 151.756 square miles and a water area of 5.644 square miles. Located at 46.28° N. Lat.; 91.78° W. Long. Elevation is 1,035 feet.
History: St. Croix National Scenic Riverway to West, below dam.
Population: 645 (2000); Race: 93.1% White, 0.4% Black, 0.0% Asian, 3.3% American Indian and Alaska Native, 0.0% Hispanic of any race, 3.3% two or more races (2000); Density: 4.3 persons per square mile (2000); Age: 17.8% under 18, 17.1% over 64 (2000); Marriage status: 15.9% never married, 62.9% now married, 11.1% widowed, 10.0% divorced (2000); Foreign born: 0.9% (2000); Ancestry (includes multiple ancestries): 26.2% German, 19.8% Norwegian, 12.9% Irish, 10.5% Swedish, 6.7% Polish (2000).
Economy: Employment by occupation: 10.2% management, 14.0% professional, 23.7% services, 12.6% sales, 0.9% farming, 18.6% construction, 20.0% production (2000).
Income: Per capita income: $18,065 (2000); Median household income: $34,412 (2000); Poverty rate: 8.0% (2000).
Taxes: Total city taxes per capita: $147 (1997); City property taxes per capita: $142 (1997).
Education: High school graduation rate: 91.2% (2000); College graduation rate: 13.0% (2000).
Housing: Homeownership rate: 84.9% (2000); Median home value: $73,300 (2000); Median rent: $425 per month (2000); Median age of housing: 27 years (2000).
Transportation: Commute to work: 89.7% car, 0.0% public transportation, 2.3% walk, 5.1% work from home (2000); Travel time to work: 23.6% less than 15 minutes, 27.1% 15 to 30 minutes, 16.3% 30 to 45 minutes, 23.6% 45 to 60 minutes, 9.4% 60 minutes or more (2000)

HAWTHORNE (town). Covers a land area of 45.613 square miles and a water area of 0.543 square miles. Located at 46.51° N. Lat.; 91.83° W. Long. Elevation is 1,160 feet.
Population: 1,045 (2000); Race: 95.9% White, 0.6% Black, 0.0% Asian, 2.8% American Indian and Alaska Native, 0.0% Hispanic of any race, 0.8% two or more races (2000); Density: 22.9 persons per square mile (2000); Age: 26.7% under 18, 17.4% over 64 (2000); Marriage status: 18.1% never married, 63.2% now married, 12.0% widowed, 6.7% divorced (2000); Foreign born: 0.4% (2000); Ancestry (includes multiple ancestries): 22.7% Swedish, 20.3% German, 16.6% Norwegian, 8.9% Finnish, 8.4% Irish (2000).
Economy: Employment by occupation: 10.2% management, 17.1% professional, 15.6% services, 21.8% sales, 1.1% farming, 14.2% construction, 20.0% production (2000).
Income: Per capita income: $16,855 (2000); Median household income: $44,856 (2000); Poverty rate: 7.0% (2000).
Taxes: Total city taxes per capita: $5 (1997); City property taxes per capita: $4 (1997).
Education: High school graduation rate: 77.4% (2000); College graduation rate: 13.7% (2000).
Housing: Homeownership rate: 96.0% (2000); Median home value: $76,400 (2000); Median rent: $475 per month (2000); Median age of housing: 26 years (2000).
Transportation: Commute to work: 92.7% car, 0.0% public transportation, 1.4% walk, 4.1% work from home (2000); Travel time to work: 12.4% less than 15 minutes, 29.1% 15 to 30 minutes, 42.0% 30 to 45 minutes, 12.9% 45 to 60 minutes, 3.6% 60 minutes or more (2000)

HIGHLAND (town). Covers a land area of 76.502 square miles and a water area of 1.556 square miles. Located at 46.42° N. Lat.; 91.60° W. Long.
Population: 245 (2000); Race: 98.3% White, 0.0% Black, 0.9% Asian, 0.0% American Indian and Alaska Native, 0.0% Hispanic of any race, 0.9% two or more races (2000); Density: 3.2 persons per square mile (2000); Age: 12.5% under 18, 34.5% over 64 (2000); Marriage status: 11.8% never married, 75.9% now married, 10.3% widowed, 2.0% divorced (2000); Foreign born: 1.7% (2000); Ancestry (includes multiple ancestries): 29.7% German, 21.1% Swedish, 18.5% Norwegian, 9.9% Polish, 7.8% Irish (2000).
Economy: Employment by occupation: 13.1% management, 28.6% professional, 8.3% services, 14.3% sales, 2.4% farming, 11.9% construction, 21.4% production (2000).
Income: Per capita income: $20,163 (2000); Median household income: $41,071 (2000); Poverty rate: 11.2% (2000).
Taxes: Total city taxes per capita: $223 (1997); City property taxes per capita: $219 (1997).
Education: High school graduation rate: 83.5% (2000); College graduation rate: 15.5% (2000).
Housing: Homeownership rate: 90.2% (2000); Median home value: $97,300 (2000); Median age of housing: 21 years (2000).
Transportation: Commute to work: 85.7% car, 3.6% public transportation, 0.0% walk, 10.7% work from home (2000); Travel time to work: 24.0% less than 15 minutes, 12.0% 15 to 30 minutes, 26.7% 30 to 45 minutes, 20.0% 45 to 60 minutes, 17.3% 60 minutes or more (2000)

LAKE NEBAGAMON (village). Covers a land area of 12.656 square miles and a water area of 1.690 square miles. Located at 46.51° N. Lat.; 91.70° W. Long. Elevation is 1,150 feet.
History: Was lumbering center in late 1800s.
Population: 1,015 (2000); Race: 97.8% White, 0.6% Black, 0.9% Asian, 0.4% American Indian and Alaska Native, 0.2% Hispanic of any race, 0.4% two or more races (2000); Density: 80.2 persons per square mile (2000); Age: 24.8% under 18, 15.7% over 64 (2000); Marriage status: 15.2% never married, 68.0% now married, 6.3% widowed, 10.5% divorced (2000); Foreign born: 1.3% (2000); Ancestry (includes multiple ancestries): 24.7% German, 19.2% Swedish, 13.6% Irish, 12.1% Norwegian, 9.0% English (2000).
Economy: Single-family building permits issued: 14 (2001) / 14 (2000); Multi-family building permits issued: 0 (2001) / 0 (2000); Employment by occupation: 16.1% management, 25.2% professional, 13.4% services, 21.5% sales, 1.0% farming, 10.3% construction, 12.4% production (2000).
Income: Per capita income: $23,665 (2000); Median household income: $48,333 (2000); Poverty rate: 5.1% (2000).
Taxes: Total city taxes per capita: $220 (1997); City property taxes per capita: $215 (1997).
Education: High school graduation rate: 91.4% (2000); College graduation rate: 31.0% (2000).
Housing: Homeownership rate: 79.8% (2000); Median home value: $115,200 (2000); Median rent: $374 per month (2000); Median age of housing: 31 years (2000).
Transportation: Commute to work: 91.2% car, 0.0% public transportation, 3.8% walk, 3.5% work from home (2000); Travel time to work: 21.6% less than 15 minutes, 13.9% 15 to 30 minutes, 35.7% 30 to 45 minutes, 22.3% 45 to 60 minutes, 6.5% 60 minutes or more (2000)

LAKESIDE (town). Covers a land area of 39.863 square miles and a water area of 0.032 square miles. Located at 46.64° N. Lat.; 91.85° W. Long.
Population: 609 (2000); Race: 97.3% White, 0.0% Black, 0.0% Asian, 1.1% American Indian and Alaska Native, 1.0% Hispanic of any race, 1.3% two or more races (2000); Density: 15.3 persons per square mile (2000); Age: 26.4% under 18, 10.4% over 64 (2000); Marriage status: 25.5% never married, 62.0% now married, 6.3% widowed, 6.1% divorced (2000); Foreign born: 1.0% (2000); Ancestry (includes multiple ancestries): 26.8% Finnish, 22.9% German, 19.6% Swedish, 13.0% Norwegian, 8.3% Irish (2000).
Economy: Employment by occupation: 9.6% management, 26.8% professional, 12.5% services, 20.7% sales, 2.5% farming, 12.9% construction, 15.0% production (2000).
Income: Per capita income: $17,309 (2000); Median household income: $42,125 (2000); Poverty rate: 8.2% (2000).
Taxes: Total city taxes per capita: $68 (1997); City property taxes per capita: $68 (1997).
Education: High school graduation rate: 89.7% (2000); College graduation rate: 22.1% (2000).
Housing: Homeownership rate: 93.3% (2000); Median home value: $69,100 (2000); Median rent: $275 per month (2000); Median age of housing: 35 years (2000).
Transportation: Commute to work: 95.4% car, 0.0% public transportation, 0.0% walk, 3.9% work from home (2000); Travel time to work: 5.6% less than 15 minutes, 40.9% 15 to 30 minutes, 42.8% 30 to 45 minutes, 5.2% 45 to 60 minutes, 5.6% 60 minutes or more (2000)

MAPLE (town). Covers a land area of 32.089 square miles and a water area of 0 square miles. Located at 46.60° N. Lat.; 91.70° W. Long. Elevation is 1,099 feet.
Population: 649 (2000); Race: 95.9% White, 0.0% Black, 0.3% Asian, 1.7% American Indian and Alaska Native, 0.6% Hispanic of any race, 1.5% two or more races (2000); Density: 20.2 persons per square mile (2000); Age: 23.8% under 18, 13.1% over 64 (2000); Marriage status: 18.5% never married, 64.2% now married, 8.5% widowed, 8.9% divorced (2000); Foreign born: 1.5% (2000); Ancestry (includes multiple ancestries): 42.1% Finnish, 19.9% German, 17.6% Swedish, 9.0% Norwegian, 6.8% Other groups (2000).
Economy: Employment by occupation: 5.5% management, 22.0% professional, 15.1% services, 20.3% sales, 2.1% farming, 13.4% construction, 21.6% production (2000).
Income: Per capita income: $16,828 (2000); Median household income: $35,781 (2000); Poverty rate: 4.7% (2000).
Taxes: Total city taxes per capita: $40 (1997); City property taxes per capita: $40 (1997).
Education: High school graduation rate: 77.8% (2000); College graduation rate: 11.0% (2000).

School District(s)

Maple (PK-12)
2000 Enrollment: 1,388 715-363-2431
Housing: Homeownership rate: 90.0% (2000); Median home value: $62,100 (2000); Median rent: $367 per month (2000); Median age of housing: 35 years (2000).
Transportation: Commute to work: 92.4% car, 0.0% public transportation, 3.1% walk, 3.8% work from home (2000); Travel time to work: 21.6% less than 15 minutes, 18.7% 15 to 30 minutes, 42.8% 30 to 45 minutes, 12.9% 45 to 60 minutes, 4.0% 60 minutes or more (2000)

OAKLAND (town). Covers a land area of 63.916 square miles and a water area of 1.050 square miles. Located at 46.51° N. Lat.; 91.99° W. Long.
Population: 1,144 (2000); Race: 99.2% White, 0.0% Black, 0.0% Asian, 0.3% American Indian and Alaska Native, 0.6% Hispanic of any race, 0.5% two or more races (2000); Density: 17.9 persons per square mile (2000); Age: 23.2% under 18, 8.6% over 64 (2000); Marriage status: 23.7% never married, 63.5% now married, 4.1% widowed, 8.6% divorced (2000); Foreign born: 0.9% (2000); Ancestry (includes multiple ancestries): 20.9% German, 17.4% Norwegian, 14.2% Swedish, 10.1% Polish, 9.3% Irish (2000).
Economy: Employment by occupation: 8.4% management, 19.4% professional, 12.5% services, 30.0% sales, 0.3% farming, 10.8% construction, 18.5% production (2000).
Income: Per capita income: $18,489 (2000); Median household income: $46,528 (2000); Poverty rate: 5.4% (2000).
Taxes: Total city taxes per capita: $27 (1997); City property taxes per capita: $26 (1997).
Education: High school graduation rate: 89.0% (2000); College graduation rate: 19.0% (2000).
Housing: Homeownership rate: 95.0% (2000); Median home value: $88,900 (2000); Median rent: $363 per month (2000); Median age of housing: 30 years (2000).
Transportation: Commute to work: 95.8% car, 0.0% public transportation, 1.2% walk, 2.1% work from home (2000); Travel time to work: 2.5% less than 15 minutes, 27.6% 15 to 30 minutes, 52.0% 30 to 45 minutes, 10.9% 45 to 60 minutes, 7.1% 60 minutes or more (2000)

OLIVER (village). Covers a land area of 2.047 square miles and a water area of 0.017 square miles. Located at 46.65° N. Lat.; 92.19° W. Long. Elevation is 649 feet.
Population: 358 (2000); Race: 98.8% White, 0.0% Black, 0.0% Asian, 1.2% American Indian and Alaska Native, 0.0% Hispanic of any race, 0.0% two or more races (2000); Density: 174.9 persons per square mile (2000); Age: 27.6% under 18, 14.7% over 64 (2000); Marriage status: 19.2% never married, 64.9% now married, 4.1% widowed, 11.8% divorced (2000); Foreign born: 0.0% (2000); Ancestry (includes multiple ancestries): 24.0% German, 13.2% Irish, 12.3% Polish, 7.9% United States or American, 7.6% French (except Basque) (2000).
Economy: Railroad terminus. Grain growing. Mont Du Lac Ski Area to Southwest. Employment by occupation: 5.2% management, 9.9% professional, 17.4% services, 36.0% sales, 0.0% farming, 11.6% construction, 19.8% production (2000).
Income: Per capita income: $19,527 (2000); Median household income: $41,750 (2000); Poverty rate: 8.3% (2000).
Taxes: Total city taxes per capita: $131 (2000); City property taxes per capita: $126 (2000).
Education: High school graduation rate: 80.1% (2000); College graduation rate: 9.5% (2000).
Housing: Homeownership rate: 84.8% (2000); Median home value: $79,100 (2000); Median rent: $385 per month (2000); Median age of housing: 26 years (2000).
Transportation: Commute to work: 89.5% car, 0.0% public transportation, 4.3% walk, 3.7% work from home (2000); Travel time to work: 19.2% less than 15 minutes, 49.4% 15 to 30 minutes, 20.5% 30 to 45 minutes, 1.3% 45 to 60 minutes, 9.6% 60 minutes or more (2000)

PARKLAND (town). Covers a land area of 35.504 square miles and a water area of 0 square miles. Located at 46.63° N. Lat.; 91.98° W. Long. Elevation is 693 feet.
Population: 1,240 (2000); Race: 97.6% White, 0.2% Black, 0.3% Asian, 0.7% American Indian and Alaska Native, 0.6% Hispanic of any race, 1.2% two or more races (2000); Density: 34.9 persons per square mile (2000); Age: 27.5% under 18, 12.6% over 64 (2000); Marriage status: 18.3% never married, 68.0% now married, 4.3% widowed, 9.3% divorced (2000); Foreign born: 0.8% (2000); Ancestry (includes multiple ancestries): 26.0% German, 18.7% Norwegian, 18.5% Swedish, 11.4% Finnish, 11.3% Irish (2000).
Economy: Employment by occupation: 6.6% management, 15.4% professional, 16.5% services, 22.6% sales, 1.3% farming, 17.1% construction, 20.5% production (2000).
Income: Per capita income: $17,090 (2000); Median household income: $40,804 (2000); Poverty rate: 4.7% (2000).
Taxes: Total city taxes per capita: $31 (1997); City property taxes per capita: $26 (1997).
Education: High school graduation rate: 85.1% (2000); College graduation rate: 12.1% (2000).
Housing: Homeownership rate: 94.5% (2000); Median home value: $68,000 (2000); Median rent: $390 per month (2000); Median age of housing: 41 years (2000).
Transportation: Commute to work: 92.3% car, 0.8% public transportation, 1.8% walk, 3.9% work from home (2000); Travel time to work: 15.1% less than 15 minutes, 58.9% 15 to 30 minutes, 17.6% 30 to 45 minutes, 4.0% 45 to 60 minutes, 4.5% 60 minutes or more (2000)

POPLAR (village). Covers a land area of 11.922 square miles and a water area of 0.013 square miles. Located at 46.58° N. Lat.; 91.79° W. Long. Elevation is 985 feet.
Population: 552 (2000); Race: 97.0% White, 1.1% Black, 0.0% Asian, 1.9% American Indian and Alaska Native, 1.9% Hispanic of any race, 0.0% two or more races (2000); Density: 46.3 persons per square mile (2000); Age: 30.4% under 18, 12.3% over 64 (2000); Marriage status: 16.5% never married, 68.4% now married, 5.3% widowed, 9.7% divorced (2000); Foreign born: 0.0% (2000); Ancestry (includes multiple ancestries): 25.0% Swedish, 23.7% German, 16.3% Irish, 14.8% Norwegian, 12.0% Finnish (2000).
Economy: Food processing. Single-family building permits issued: 3 (2001) / 3 (2000); Multi-family building permits issued: 0 (2001) / 0 (2000); Employment by occupation: 8.6% management, 15.9% professional, 17.2% services, 28.6% sales, 2.8% farming, 10.0% construction, 16.9% production (2000).
Income: Per capita income: $18,218 (2000); Median household income: $41,406 (2000); Poverty rate: 8.7% (2000).
Taxes: Total city taxes per capita: $34 (1997); City property taxes per capita: $34 (1997).
Education: High school graduation rate: 86.9% (2000); College graduation rate: 21.4% (2000).
Housing: Homeownership rate: 83.5% (2000); Median home value: $69,300 (2000); Median rent: $390 per month (2000); Median age of housing: 33 years (2000).
Transportation: Commute to work: 88.6% car, 0.3% public transportation, 2.8% walk, 7.6% work from home (2000); Travel time to work: 33.2% less than 15 minutes, 22.8% 15 to 30 minutes, 28.4% 30 to 45 minutes, 12.3% 45 to 60 minutes, 3.4% 60 minutes or more (2000)

SOLON SPRINGS (village). Covers a land area of 1.599 square miles and a water area of 0.702 square miles. Located at 46.35° N. Lat.; 91.81° W. Long. Elevation is 1,083 feet.
History: Solon Springs grew up along the route of the trail from Lake Superior to the Mississippi River, traveled for two centuries by traders, priests, and soldiers. The village of Solon Springs developed as a tourist center, with Lake St. Croix as the attraction.
Population: 576 (2000); Race: 94.6% White, 0.0% Black, 0.7% Asian, 1.9% American Indian and Alaska Native, 1.2% Hispanic of any race, 1.6% two or more races (2000); Density: 360.3 persons per square mile (2000); Age:

25.3% under 18, 18.4% over 64 (2000); Marriage status: 23.0% never married, 53.8% now married, 13.3% widowed, 9.8% divorced (2000); Foreign born: 2.3% (2000); Ancestry (includes multiple ancestries): 29.2% German, 14.5% Norwegian, 12.9% Irish, 9.1% Swedish, 8.7% English (2000).
Economy: Single-family building permits issued: 1 (2001) / 2 (2000); Multi-family building permits issued: 0 (2001) / 0 (2000); Employment by occupation: 10.3% management, 12.3% professional, 20.2% services, 24.1% sales, 2.0% farming, 15.4% construction, 15.8% production (2000).
Income: Per capita income: $16,807 (2000); Median household income: $30,250 (2000); Poverty rate: 10.6% (2000).
Taxes: Total city taxes per capita: $90 (1997); City property taxes per capita: $84 (1997).
Education: High school graduation rate: 86.3% (2000); College graduation rate: 12.4% (2000).

School District(s)

Solon Springs (PK-12)
2000 Enrollment: 400 715-378-2263
Housing: Homeownership rate: 74.5% (2000); Median home value: $66,800 (2000); Median rent: $365 per month (2000); Median age of housing: 40 years (2000).
Transportation: Commute to work: 83.8% car, 0.0% public transportation, 8.1% walk, 4.5% work from home (2000); Travel time to work: 44.1% less than 15 minutes, 19.1% 15 to 30 minutes, 12.3% 30 to 45 minutes, 16.1% 45 to 60 minutes, 8.5% 60 minutes or more (2000)

SOLON SPRINGS (town). Covers a land area of 83.017 square miles and a water area of 1.481 square miles. Located at 46.35° N. Lat.; 91.80° W. Long. Elevation is 1,083 feet.
Population: 807 (2000); Race: 96.7% White, 0.6% Black, 0.0% Asian, 1.1% American Indian and Alaska Native, 0.5% Hispanic of any race, 1.6% two or more races (2000); Density: 9.7 persons per square mile (2000); Age: 23.5% under 18, 17.9% over 64 (2000); Marriage status: 20.5% never married, 65.3% now married, 5.0% widowed, 9.1% divorced (2000); Foreign born: 2.1% (2000); Ancestry (includes multiple ancestries): 26.6% German, 13.5% Irish, 12.3% Norwegian, 10.7% Swedish, 9.4% English (2000).
Economy: In timber area. Nearby is the county bird sanctuary, state hunting grounds. Employment by occupation: 12.8% management, 12.8% professional, 20.5% services, 28.7% sales, 0.5% farming, 11.2% construction, 13.6% production (2000).
Income: Per capita income: $19,561 (2000); Median household income: $42,300 (2000); Poverty rate: 9.0% (2000).
Taxes: Total city taxes per capita: $112 (1997); City property taxes per capita: $109 (1997).
Education: High school graduation rate: 86.7% (2000); College graduation rate: 17.8% (2000).
Housing: Homeownership rate: 89.8% (2000); Median home value: $100,700 (2000); Median rent: $300 per month (2000); Median age of housing: 27 years (2000).
Transportation: Commute to work: 92.8% car, 0.8% public transportation, 1.1% walk, 4.4% work from home (2000); Travel time to work: 27.1% less than 15 minutes, 16.4% 15 to 30 minutes, 30.0% 30 to 45 minutes, 19.3% 45 to 60 minutes, 7.2% 60 minutes or more (2000)

SOUTH RANGE (unincorporated postal area, zip code 54874). Covers a land area of 141.183 square miles and a water area of 0.713 square miles. Located at 46.58° N. Lat.; 91.95° W. Long. Elevation is 763 feet.
Population: 3,299 (2000); Race: 97.6% White, 0.1% Black, 0.2% Asian, 1.1% American Indian and Alaska Native, 0.3% Hispanic of any race, 1.0% two or more races (2000); Density: 23.4 persons per square mile (2000); Age: 26.6% under 18, 9.7% over 64 (2000); Marriage status: 22.6% never married, 64.8% now married, 4.4% widowed, 8.3% divorced (2000); Foreign born: 0.9% (2000); Ancestry (includes multiple ancestries): 26.8% German, 17.2% Norwegian, 16.3% Swedish, 10.9% Finnish, 9.9% Irish (2000).
Economy: Employment by occupation: 8.0% management, 18.5% professional, 15.5% services, 24.6% sales, 1.0% farming, 13.7% construction, 18.7% production (2000).
Income: Per capita income: $17,452 (2000); Median household income: $43,553 (2000); Poverty rate: 5.2% (2000).
Education: High school graduation rate: 86.3% (2000); College graduation rate: 17.0% (2000).
Housing: Homeownership rate: 94.1% (2000); Median home value: $71,700 (2000); Median rent: $383 per month (2000); Median age of housing: 33 years (2000).
Transportation: Commute to work: 94.2% car, 0.5% public transportation, 0.7% walk, 3.3% work from home (2000); Travel time to work: 8.4% less than 15 minutes, 44.6% 15 to 30 minutes, 34.8% 30 to 45 minutes, 7.1% 45 to 60 minutes, 5.1% 60 minutes or more (2000)

SUMMIT (town). Covers a land area of 146.607 square miles and a water area of 0.964 square miles. Located at 46.45° N. Lat.; 92.19° W. Long.
Population: 1,042 (2000); Race: 97.2% White, 0.0% Black, 0.9% Asian, 0.3% American Indian and Alaska Native, 0.0% Hispanic of any race, 1.6% two or more races (2000); Density: 7.1 persons per square mile (2000); Age: 24.1% under 18, 11.6% over 64 (2000); Marriage status: 20.4% never married, 67.9% now married, 4.9% widowed, 6.9% divorced (2000); Foreign born: 1.2% (2000); Ancestry (includes multiple ancestries): 25.6% German, 13.8% Swedish, 12.7% Norwegian, 12.5% Polish, 9.9% Irish (2000).
Economy: Employment by occupation: 8.6% management, 21.0% professional, 11.8% services, 17.3% sales, 0.8% farming, 20.6% construction, 19.9% production (2000).
Income: Per capita income: $18,275 (2000); Median household income: $42,386 (2000); Poverty rate: 7.0% (2000).
Taxes: Total city taxes per capita: $24 (1997); City property taxes per capita: $21 (1997).
Education: High school graduation rate: 83.7% (2000); College graduation rate: 13.7% (2000).
Housing: Homeownership rate: 95.0% (2000); Median home value: $81,400 (2000); Median rent: $138 per month (2000); Median age of housing: 32 years (2000).
Transportation: Commute to work: 96.1% car, 0.9% public transportation, 0.7% walk, 1.1% work from home (2000); Travel time to work: 6.8% less than 15 minutes, 20.4% 15 to 30 minutes, 45.1% 30 to 45 minutes, 18.5% 45 to 60 minutes, 9.2% 60 minutes or more (2000)

SUPERIOR (city). Covers a land area of 36.940 square miles and a water area of 18.493 square miles. Located at 46.70° N. Lat.; 92.08° W. Long. Elevation is 642 feet.
History: A North West Fur Company post was established in 1787 at the southwestern tip of Lake Superior, followed by an American Fur Company post in 1816. The settlement of Superior grew up here in the early 1850's, but the first rush of people left with the economic depression of 1857. Not until the 1880's, when the Northern Pacific Railroad reached Superior, did the town revive. In 1883 iron ore was discovered in the Gogebic Range and the next year in the Vermillion Range, and Superior began its role as an outlet for the iron ranges. After receiving a village charter in 1887, Superior became a city in 1889. Many of the people who came to Superior in the 1880's and 1890's were of Finnish and Scandinavian heritage.
Population: 27,368 (2000); Race: 94.5% White, 0.5% Black, 0.9% Asian, 2.1% American Indian and Alaska Native, 0.7% Hispanic of any race, 1.7% two or more races (2000); Density: 740.9 persons per square mile (2000); Age: 22.7% under 18, 15.0% over 64 (2000); Marriage status: 30.8% never married, 48.2% now married, 7.9% widowed, 13.0% divorced (2000); Foreign born: 2.0% (2000); Ancestry (includes multiple ancestries): 20.7% German, 15.2% Swedish, 15.2% Norwegian, 13.2% Irish, 9.3% Polish (2000).
Economy: Unemployment rate: 4.1% (11/2002); Total civilian labor force: 14,763 (11/2002); Single-family building permits issued: 44 (2001) / 28 (2000); Multi-family building permits issued: 10 (2001) / 27 (2000); Employment by occupation: 9.1% management, 16.6% professional, 20.1% services, 30.4% sales, 0.4% farming, 8.2% construction, 15.1% production (2000).
Income: Per capita income: $17,253 (2000); Median household income: $31,921 (2000); Poverty rate: 13.4% (2000).
Taxes: Total city taxes per capita: $352 (2000); City property taxes per capita: $294 (2000).
Education: High school graduation rate: 85.9% (2000); College graduation rate: 19.2% (2000).

School District(s)

Superior (PK-12)
2000 Enrollment: 5,170 715-394-8710

Four-year College(s)

University of Wisconsin-Superior (Public)
2001 Enrollment: 2,842 715-394-8101
2001 Tuition: In-state $2,776; Out-of-state $11,288
Housing: Homeownership rate: 61.8% (2000); Median home value: $65,900 (2000); Median rent: $349 per month (2000); Median age of housing: 55 years (2000).
Hospitals: Saint Mary's Hospital of Superior (162 beds)
Safety: Violent crime rate: 23.2 per 10,000 population; Property crime rate: 583.8 per 10,000 population (2001).
Newspapers: The Daily Telegram (6 x week)

Transportation: Commute to work: 89.9% car, 2.0% public transportation, 5.7% walk, 1.6% work from home (2000); Travel time to work: 56.6% less than 15 minutes, 34.7% 15 to 30 minutes, 4.8% 30 to 45 minutes, 0.9% 45 to 60 minutes, 3.0% 60 minutes or more (2000)

Additional Information Contacts

Superior Chamber of Commerce 715-394-7716

SUPERIOR (village). Covers a land area of 1.235 square miles and a water area of 0.008 square miles. Located at 46.65° N. Lat.; 92.10° W. Long. Elevation is 642 feet.

Population: 500 (2000); Race: 95.6% White, 0.4% Black, 0.9% Asian, 1.3% American Indian and Alaska Native, 0.0% Hispanic of any race, 1.8% two or more races (2000); Density: 404.7 persons per square mile (2000); Age: 17.0% under 18, 18.1% over 64 (2000); Marriage status: 14.7% never married, 70.4% now married, 6.2% widowed, 8.8% divorced (2000); Foreign born: 1.3% (2000); Ancestry (includes multiple ancestries): 24.8% German, 15.5% Swedish, 15.3% Norwegian, 15.0% Polish, 10.8% Irish (2000).
Economy: Single-family building permits issued: 8 (2001) / 8 (2000); Multi-family building permits issued: 0 (2001) / 0 (2000); Employment by occupation: 8.8% management, 13.7% professional, 16.1% services, 30.9% sales, 0.0% farming, 13.3% construction, 17.3% production (2000).
Income: Per capita income: $20,328 (2000); Median household income: $42,778 (2000); Poverty rate: 3.8% (2000).
Taxes: Total city taxes per capita: $62 (1997); City property taxes per capita: $58 (1997).
Education: High school graduation rate: 84.3% (2000); College graduation rate: 11.8% (2000).
Housing: Homeownership rate: 84.2% (2000); Median home value: $77,900 (2000); Median rent: $308 per month (2000); Median age of housing: 31 years (2000).
Transportation: Commute to work: 92.8% car, 2.0% public transportation, 1.6% walk, 3.6% work from home (2000); Travel time to work: 48.3% less than 15 minutes, 33.3% 15 to 30 minutes, 16.7% 30 to 45 minutes, 0.0% 45 to 60 minutes, 1.7% 60 minutes or more (2000)

SUPERIOR (town). Covers a land area of 106.197 square miles and a water area of 1.557 square miles. Located at 46.59° N. Lat.; 92.13° W. Long. Elevation is 642 feet.

History: The area was visited by the French explorers Radisson (1661) and Duluth (1679). The city grew after iron ore was discovered (1880s) in the Gogebic range. The University of Wisconsin at Superior is here. Incorporated 1883.
Population: 2,058 (2000); Race: 97.9% White, 0.0% Black, 0.0% Asian, 1.3% American Indian and Alaska Native, 0.8% Hispanic of any race, 0.8% two or more races (2000); Density: 19.4 persons per square mile (2000); Age: 26.8% under 18, 9.7% over 64 (2000); Marriage status: 19.1% never married, 70.9% now married, 3.2% widowed, 6.8% divorced (2000); Foreign born: 0.5% (2000); Ancestry (includes multiple ancestries): 28.0% German, 20.5% Norwegian, 16.3% Swedish, 11.2% Irish, 8.5% Polish (2000).
Economy: Port of entry with many railroad lines. The natural harbor, shared with Duluth, Minnesota, has some of the nation's largest coal and ore docks. Copper, limestone and grain are also shipped. Superior has shipyards, flour milling and an oil refinery. Manufacturing includes lumber, machinery, hand tools and railroad-track materials. Tourists are attracted to the surrounding scenic features. Employment by occupation: 12.2% management, 19.4% professional, 12.2% services, 24.3% sales, 0.4% farming, 12.8% construction, 18.7% production (2000).
Income: Per capita income: $18,775 (2000); Median household income: $48,833 (2000); Poverty rate: 6.9% (2000).
Taxes: Total city taxes per capita: $2 (1997); City property taxes per capita: $0 (1997).
Education: High school graduation rate: 86.7% (2000); College graduation rate: 16.3% (2000).
Housing: Homeownership rate: 91.1% (2000); Median home value: $86,800 (2000); Median rent: $386 per month (2000); Median age of housing: 29 years (2000).
Transportation: Commute to work: 94.1% car, 0.9% public transportation, 1.3% walk, 2.6% work from home (2000); Travel time to work: 10.1% less than 15 minutes, 51.3% 15 to 30 minutes, 30.8% 30 to 45 minutes, 5.8% 45 to 60 minutes, 2.0% 60 minutes or more (2000)

WASCOTT (town). Covers a land area of 132.958 square miles and a water area of 8.156 square miles. Located at 46.19° N. Lat.; 91.85° W. Long. Elevation is 1,090 feet.

Population: 714 (2000); Race: 94.7% White, 2.4% Black, 0.3% Asian, 1.5% American Indian and Alaska Native, 0.3% Hispanic of any race, 1.1% two or more races (2000); Density: 5.4 persons per square mile (2000); Age: 16.1% under 18, 21.0% over 64 (2000); Marriage status: 12.1% never married, 68.8% now married, 11.1% widowed, 8.0% divorced (2000); Foreign born: 1.8% (2000); Ancestry (includes multiple ancestries): 30.0% German, 17.5% Norwegian, 14.0% Irish, 12.8% Swedish, 10.0% Polish (2000).
Economy: Employment by occupation: 17.2% management, 20.9% professional, 13.9% services, 20.9% sales, 0.7% farming, 13.9% construction, 12.5% production (2000).
Income: Per capita income: $18,165 (2000); Median household income: $40,714 (2000); Poverty rate: 8.6% (2000).
Taxes: Total city taxes per capita: $334 (1997); City property taxes per capita: $328 (1997).
Education: High school graduation rate: 85.8% (2000); College graduation rate: 19.5% (2000).
Housing: Homeownership rate: 95.1% (2000); Median home value: $120,500 (2000); Median rent: $308 per month (2000); Median age of housing: 23 years (2000).
Transportation: Commute to work: 92.8% car, 0.8% public transportation, 1.5% walk, 4.9% work from home (2000); Travel time to work: 21.8% less than 15 minutes, 22.2% 15 to 30 minutes, 9.5% 30 to 45 minutes, 22.6% 45 to 60 minutes, 23.8% 60 minutes or more (2000)

Dunn County

Located in western Wisconsin; drained by the Red Cedar and Chippewa Rivers. Covers a land area of 852.00 square miles, a water area of 11.90 square miles, and is located in the Central Time Zone. The county government was organized in 1854. County seat is Menomonie.

Weather Station: Menomonie Elevation: 777 feet

	Jan	Feb	Mar	Apr	May	Jun	Jul	Aug	Sep	Oct	Nov	Dec
High	24	31	42	59	71	79	84	81	72	60	42	28
Low	4	10	21	34	45	55	60	57	49	37	25	11
Precip	0.8	0.6	1.7	2.6	3.6	4.4	4.1	4.1	3.7	2.3	1.9	0.9
Snow	12.3	6.7	8.3	1.1	tr	0.0	0.0	tr	tr	tr	5.0	7.9

High and Low temperatures in degrees Fahrenheit; Precipitation and Snow in inches

Population: 39,858 (2000); Race: 96.2% White, 0.2% Black, 1.8% Asian, 0.4% American Indian and Alaska Native, 1.0% Hispanic of any race, 1.0% two or more races (2000); Density: 46.8 persons per square mile (2000); Age: 23.3% under 18, 11.2% over 64 (2000).
Religion: Five largest groups: 22.3% Evangelical Lutheran Church in America, 11.5% Catholic Church, 4.5% The United Methodist Church, 3.6% Wisconsin Evangelical Lutheran Synod, 1.7% Lutheran Church—Missouri Synod (2000).
Economy: Unemployment rate: 3.3% (11/2002); Total civilian labor force: 23,680 (11/2002); Leading industries: 19.8% manufacturing; 14.3% health care and social assistance; 14.2% retail trade (2000); Companies that employ more than 1,000 persons: 1 (2000); Companies that employ more than 100 persons: 18 (2000); Farms: 1,397 totaling 368,618 acres (1997); Minority business ownership rate: 0.0% (1997); Women business ownership rate: 19.6% (1997); Retail sales per capita: $8,370 (1997). Single-family building permits issued: 207 (2001) / 219 (2000); Multi-family building permits issued: 105 (2001) / 86 (2000).
Income: Per capita income: $17,520 (2000); Median household income: $38,753 (2000); Poverty rate: 12.9% (2000); Bankruptcy rate: 2.85% (2001).
Taxes: Total county taxes per capita: $295 (2000); County property taxes per capita: $249 (2000).
Education: High school graduation rate: 86.6% (2000); College graduation rate: 21.1% (2000).
Housing: Homeownership rate: 69.0% (2000); Median home value: $92,900 (2000); Median rent: $389 per month (2000); Median age of housing: 29 years (2000).
Health: Birth rate: 118.7 per 10,000 population (1998); Age adjusted death rate: 76.1 per 10,000 population (1999); Age adjusted cancer mortality rate: 154.2 deaths per 100,000 population (1999). Number of physicians: 7.3 per 10,000 population (1999); Number of hospital beds: 10.8 per 10,000 population (1999).
Elections: 2000 Presidential election results: 47.5% Gore, 46.1% Bush, 5.7% Nader, 0.1% Buchanan
National and State Parks: Big Beaver Creek State Public Hunting Ground; Bolen Creek State Public Hunting Grounds; Chimney Rock State Wetlands Area; Dunnville State Public Hunting Grounds; Eau Galle River State Public Hunting Grounds; Elk Creek State Public Fishing Area; Hay Creek State Public Hunting Grounds; Muddy Creek State Public Hunting Grounds; Otter Creek State Fishery Area; Otter Creek State Public Hunting Grounds

Additional Information Contacts
Dunn County Government Offices. 715-232-1677
Menomonie Chamber of Commerce 715-235-9087

Dunn County Communities

BOYCEVILLE (village). Covers a land area of 3.877 square miles and a water area of 0 square miles. Located at 45.04° N. Lat.; 92.04° W. Long. Elevation is 948 feet.
Population: 1,043 (2000); Race: 98.8% White, 0.0% Black, 0.4% Asian, 0.3% American Indian and Alaska Native, 0.8% Hispanic of any race, 0.5% two or more races (2000); Density: 269.0 persons per square mile (2000); Age: 29.2% under 18, 14.8% over 64 (2000); Marriage status: 27.3% never married, 51.2% now married, 8.1% widowed, 13.4% divorced (2000); Foreign born: 0.2% (2000); Ancestry (includes multiple ancestries): 37.1% German, 26.9% Norwegian, 6.0% Irish, 5.1% Other groups, 4.9% United States or American (2000).
Economy: In dairy and grain area. Manufacturing: fabrics, dairy food ingredients. Single-family building permits issued: 2 (2001) / 3 (2000); Multi-family building permits issued: 2 (2001) / 2 (2000); Employment by occupation: 8.2% management, 11.0% professional, 14.9% services, 20.3% sales, 0.4% farming, 10.8% construction, 34.5% production (2000).
Income: Per capita income: $14,674 (2000); Median household income: $31,250 (2000); Poverty rate: 13.8% (2000).
Taxes: Total city taxes per capita: $87 (1997); City property taxes per capita: $75 (1997).
Education: High school graduation rate: 79.9% (2000); College graduation rate: 10.1% (2000).

School District(s)
Boyceville Community (PK-12)
2000 Enrollment: 951 715-643-4311
Housing: Homeownership rate: 71.1% (2000); Median home value: $69,100 (2000); Median rent: $330 per month (2000); Median age of housing: 32 years (2000).
Transportation: Commute to work: 91.6% car, 0.0% public transportation, 3.3% walk, 3.5% work from home (2000); Travel time to work: 24.9% less than 15 minutes, 33.1% 15 to 30 minutes, 21.7% 30 to 45 minutes, 11.9% 45 to 60 minutes, 8.4% 60 minutes or more (2000)

COLFAX (village). Covers a land area of 1.390 square miles and a water area of 0.030 square miles. Located at 44.99° N. Lat.; 91.72° W. Long. Elevation is 942 feet.
Population: 1,136 (2000); Race: 97.5% White, 0.4% Black, 0.0% Asian, 0.9% American Indian and Alaska Native, 1.8% Hispanic of any race, 0.6% two or more races (2000); Density: 817.0 persons per square mile (2000); Age: 24.3% under 18, 23.7% over 64 (2000); Marriage status: 22.5% never married, 58.0% now married, 9.7% widowed, 9.7% divorced (2000); Foreign born: 0.6% (2000); Ancestry (includes multiple ancestries): 42.2% Norwegian, 35.8% German, 6.0% Other groups, 5.1% Irish, 4.3% English (2000).
Economy: Single-family building permits issued: 0 (2001) / 1 (2000); Multi-family building permits issued: 0 (2001) / 0 (2000); Employment by occupation: 6.7% management, 15.6% professional, 19.7% services, 19.6% sales, 1.6% farming, 12.5% construction, 24.3% production (2000).
Income: Per capita income: $15,040 (2000); Median household income: $31,118 (2000); Poverty rate: 5.4% (2000).
Taxes: Total city taxes per capita: $302 (2000); City property taxes per capita: $290 (2000).
Education: High school graduation rate: 77.3% (2000); College graduation rate: 15.2% (2000).

School District(s)
Colfax (PK-12)
2000 Enrollment: 895 715-962-3773
Housing: Homeownership rate: 71.0% (2000); Median home value: $65,700 (2000); Median rent: $383 per month (2000); Median age of housing: 45 years (2000).
Newspapers: The Colfax Messenger (1 x week)
Transportation: Commute to work: 85.8% car, 0.4% public transportation, 8.3% walk, 3.5% work from home (2000); Travel time to work: 39.4% less than 15 minutes, 31.2% 15 to 30 minutes, 21.4% 30 to 45 minutes, 2.9% 45 to 60 minutes, 5.2% 60 minutes or more (2000)

COLFAX (town). Covers a land area of 34.238 square miles and a water area of 0.319 square miles. Located at 44.99° N. Lat.; 91.70° W. Long. Elevation is 942 feet.
Population: 909 (2000); Race: 99.8% White, 0.0% Black, 0.0% Asian, 0.2% American Indian and Alaska Native, 0.0% Hispanic of any race, 0.0% two or more races (2000); Density: 26.5 persons per square mile (2000); Age: 30.1% under 18, 6.8% over 64 (2000); Marriage status: 21.4% never married, 66.7% now married, 2.6% widowed, 9.4% divorced (2000); Foreign born: 0.0% (2000); Ancestry (includes multiple ancestries): 43.0% German, 38.1% Norwegian, 7.0% Irish, 6.2% English, 5.1% French Canadian (2000).
Economy: Dairying. Manufacturing: malted milk products, wood products. Deepwood Ski Area to West. Employment by occupation: 12.7% management, 11.5% professional, 15.5% services, 14.9% sales, 3.2% farming, 17.1% construction, 25.2% production (2000).
Income: Per capita income: $17,364 (2000); Median household income: $46,111 (2000); Poverty rate: 6.1% (2000).
Taxes: Total city taxes per capita: $77 (1997); City property taxes per capita: $75 (1997).
Education: High school graduation rate: 90.4% (2000); College graduation rate: 12.8% (2000).
Housing: Homeownership rate: 87.9% (2000); Median home value: $95,000 (2000); Median rent: $364 per month (2000); Median age of housing: 26 years (2000).
Transportation: Commute to work: 90.2% car, 0.6% public transportation, 1.6% walk, 7.2% work from home (2000); Travel time to work: 23.8% less than 15 minutes, 45.8% 15 to 30 minutes, 20.0% 30 to 45 minutes, 2.4% 45 to 60 minutes, 7.9% 60 minutes or more (2000)

DOWNING (village). Covers a land area of 2.975 square miles and a water area of 0 square miles. Located at 45.04° N. Lat.; 92.12° W. Long. Elevation is 983 feet.
Population: 257 (2000); Race: 94.0% White, 0.0% Black, 0.0% Asian, 0.0% American Indian and Alaska Native, 4.6% Hispanic of any race, 1.4% two or more races (2000); Density: 86.4 persons per square mile (2000); Age: 22.0% under 18, 17.4% over 64 (2000); Marriage status: 23.5% never married, 61.3% now married, 4.8% widowed, 10.4% divorced (2000); Foreign born: 4.6% (2000); Ancestry (includes multiple ancestries): 50.4% German, 32.6% Norwegian, 7.4% Other groups, 7.4% English, 6.4% Irish (2000).
Economy: Dairying. Single-family building permits issued: 0 (2001) / 2 (2000); Multi-family building permits issued: 0 (2001) / 0 (2000); Employment by occupation: 5.9% management, 4.4% professional, 15.4% services, 27.2% sales, 8.1% farming, 20.6% construction, 18.4% production (2000).
Income: Per capita income: $17,927 (2000); Median household income: $41,375 (2000); Poverty rate: 5.7% (2000).
Taxes: Total city taxes per capita: $8 (1997); City property taxes per capita: $4 (1997).
Education: High school graduation rate: 78.7% (2000); College graduation rate: 5.6% (2000).
Housing: Homeownership rate: 80.8% (2000); Median home value: $74,100 (2000); Median rent: $318 per month (2000); Median age of housing: 60+ years (2000).
Transportation: Commute to work: 82.7% car, 0.0% public transportation, 3.8% walk, 13.5% work from home (2000); Travel time to work: 33.0% less than 15 minutes, 29.6% 15 to 30 minutes, 8.7% 30 to 45 minutes, 7.0% 45 to 60 minutes, 21.7% 60 minutes or more (2000)

DUNN (town). Covers a land area of 55.706 square miles and a water area of 1.358 square miles. Located at 44.75° N. Lat.; 91.92° W. Long.
Population: 1,492 (2000); Race: 98.3% White, 0.1% Black, 0.9% Asian, 0.0% American Indian and Alaska Native, 0.0% Hispanic of any race, 0.7% two or more races (2000); Density: 26.8 persons per square mile (2000); Age: 29.2% under 18, 9.2% over 64 (2000); Marriage status: 22.3% never married, 65.8% now married, 3.3% widowed, 8.6% divorced (2000); Foreign born: 1.2% (2000); Ancestry (includes multiple ancestries): 44.6% German, 21.4% Norwegian, 8.0% United States or American, 5.7% Irish, 5.2% English (2000).
Economy: Single-family building permits issued: 14 (2001) / 9 (2000); Multi-family building permits issued: 0 (2001) / 0 (2000); Employment by occupation: 15.3% management, 11.6% professional, 13.8% services, 22.0% sales, 3.0% farming, 14.3% construction, 20.0% production (2000).
Income: Per capita income: $16,429 (2000); Median household income: $45,043 (2000); Poverty rate: 10.5% (2000).
Taxes: Total city taxes per capita: $78 (1997); City property taxes per capita: $71 (1997).
Education: High school graduation rate: 85.4% (2000); College graduation rate: 15.4% (2000).

Housing: Homeownership rate: 81.6% (2000); Median home value: $97,400 (2000); Median rent: $367 per month (2000); Median age of housing: 28 years (2000).
Transportation: Commute to work: 85.5% car, 0.0% public transportation, 3.2% walk, 10.5% work from home (2000); Travel time to work: 25.8% less than 15 minutes, 44.1% 15 to 30 minutes, 14.9% 30 to 45 minutes, 7.7% 45 to 60 minutes, 7.5% 60 minutes or more (2000)

EAU GALLE (town). Covers a land area of 47.365 square miles and a water area of 0.580 square miles. Located at 44.72° N. Lat.; 92.05° W. Long. Elevation is 780 feet.
Population: 797 (2000); Race: 99.5% White, 0.0% Black, 0.3% Asian, 0.0% American Indian and Alaska Native, 0.0% Hispanic of any race, 0.0% two or more races (2000); Density: 16.8 persons per square mile (2000); Age: 25.3% under 18, 15.3% over 64 (2000); Marriage status: 24.8% never married, 62.1% now married, 5.3% widowed, 7.8% divorced (2000); Foreign born: 0.3% (2000); Ancestry (includes multiple ancestries): 50.4% German, 10.5% Irish, 10.4% Austrian, 8.0% Norwegian, 7.5% English (2000).
Economy: Single-family building permits issued: 4 (2001) / 3 (2000); Multi-family building permits issued: 0 (2001) / 0 (2000); Employment by occupation: 19.4% management, 10.2% professional, 14.6% services, 13.1% sales, 6.3% farming, 7.5% construction, 28.9% production (2000).
Income: Per capita income: $17,103 (2000); Median household income: $39,167 (2000); Poverty rate: 9.0% (2000).
Taxes: Total city taxes per capita: $114 (1997); City property taxes per capita: $112 (1997).
Education: High school graduation rate: 87.6% (2000); College graduation rate: 9.2% (2000).
Housing: Homeownership rate: 83.9% (2000); Median home value: $78,900 (2000); Median rent: $339 per month (2000); Median age of housing: 46 years (2000).
Transportation: Commute to work: 81.8% car, 0.0% public transportation, 7.0% walk, 11.2% work from home (2000); Travel time to work: 32.5% less than 15 minutes, 32.2% 15 to 30 minutes, 21.6% 30 to 45 minutes, 7.9% 45 to 60 minutes, 5.7% 60 minutes or more (2000)

ELK MOUND (village). Covers a land area of 2.273 square miles and a water area of 0 square miles. Located at 44.87° N. Lat.; 91.69° W. Long. Elevation is 930 feet.
Population: 785 (2000); Race: 97.1% White, 0.0% Black, 1.6% Asian, 0.3% American Indian and Alaska Native, 0.0% Hispanic of any race, 1.1% two or more races (2000); Density: 345.3 persons per square mile (2000); Age: 27.3% under 18, 8.4% over 64 (2000); Marriage status: 23.9% never married, 59.5% now married, 2.9% widowed, 13.7% divorced (2000); Foreign born: 1.6% (2000); Ancestry (includes multiple ancestries): 42.7% German, 32.8% Norwegian, 12.3% Irish, 7.2% English, 6.5% French (except Basque) (2000).
Economy: Single-family building permits issued: 4 (2001) / 4 (2000); Multi-family building permits issued: 8 (2001) / 0 (2000); Employment by occupation: 11.2% management, 9.7% professional, 17.6% services, 30.3% sales, 1.8% farming, 7.5% construction, 22.0% production (2000).
Income: Per capita income: $16,156 (2000); Median household income: $36,513 (2000); Poverty rate: 6.4% (2000).
Taxes: Total city taxes per capita: $78 (1997); City property taxes per capita: $69 (1997).
Education: High school graduation rate: 88.0% (2000); College graduation rate: 12.8% (2000).

School District(s)

Elk Mound Area (PK-12)
2000 Enrollment: 868 715-879-5066

Housing: Homeownership rate: 68.6% (2000); Median home value: $78,200 (2000); Median rent: $400 per month (2000); Median age of housing: 27 years (2000).
Safety: Violent crime rate: 0.0 per 10,000 population; Property crime rate: 12.6 per 10,000 population (2001).
Transportation: Commute to work: 94.3% car, 0.4% public transportation, 1.5% walk, 2.4% work from home (2000); Travel time to work: 25.6% less than 15 minutes, 58.4% 15 to 30 minutes, 11.5% 30 to 45 minutes, 1.4% 45 to 60 minutes, 3.2% 60 minutes or more (2000)

ELK MOUND (town). Covers a land area of 33.696 square miles and a water area of 0.023 square miles. Located at 44.90° N. Lat.; 91.70° W. Long. Elevation is 930 feet.
Population: 1,121 (2000); Race: 95.8% White, 0.0% Black, 3.2% Asian, 0.6% American Indian and Alaska Native, 0.6% Hispanic of any race, 0.3% two or more races (2000); Density: 33.3 persons per square mile (2000); Age: 34.7% under 18, 5.8% over 64 (2000); Marriage status: 24.9% never married, 65.6% now married, 2.9% widowed, 6.6% divorced (2000); Foreign born: 2.2% (2000); Ancestry (includes multiple ancestries): 50.5% German, 39.3% Norwegian, 6.6% Other groups, 6.6% Polish, 6.2% Irish (2000).
Economy: Manufacturing: trailers. Hoffman Hills State Recreational Area to Northwest. Single-family building permits issued: 39 (2001) / 57 (2000); Multi-family building permits issued: 10 (2001) / 30 (2000); Employment by occupation: 14.0% management, 14.5% professional, 14.0% services, 21.6% sales, 4.0% farming, 10.8% construction, 21.1% production (2000).
Income: Per capita income: $17,138 (2000); Median household income: $48,594 (2000); Poverty rate: 8.1% (2000).
Taxes: Total city taxes per capita: $102 (1997); City property taxes per capita: $90 (1997).
Education: High school graduation rate: 92.7% (2000); College graduation rate: 21.2% (2000).
Housing: Homeownership rate: 88.0% (2000); Median home value: $112,500 (2000); Median rent: $531 per month (2000); Median age of housing: 22 years (2000).
Transportation: Commute to work: 87.2% car, 0.5% public transportation, 1.6% walk, 9.9% work from home (2000); Travel time to work: 19.6% less than 15 minutes, 55.2% 15 to 30 minutes, 18.3% 30 to 45 minutes, 2.9% 45 to 60 minutes, 4.0% 60 minutes or more (2000)

GRANT (town). Covers a land area of 36.857 square miles and a water area of 0.484 square miles. Located at 45.07° N. Lat.; 91.71° W. Long.
Population: 426 (2000); Race: 100.0% White, 0.0% Black, 0.0% Asian, 0.0% American Indian and Alaska Native, 0.0% Hispanic of any race, 0.0% two or more races (2000); Density: 11.6 persons per square mile (2000); Age: 25.9% under 18, 10.6% over 64 (2000); Marriage status: 25.6% never married, 65.3% now married, 4.7% widowed, 4.4% divorced (2000); Foreign born: 0.7% (2000); Ancestry (includes multiple ancestries): 42.5% German, 40.4% Norwegian, 6.9% Irish, 5.1% English, 3.9% Swedish (2000).
Economy: Employment by occupation: 21.7% management, 17.6% professional, 15.7% services, 15.7% sales, 7.9% farming, 7.5% construction, 13.9% production (2000).
Income: Per capita income: $15,669 (2000); Median household income: $38,409 (2000); Poverty rate: 9.9% (2000).
Taxes: Total city taxes per capita: $94 (1997); City property taxes per capita: $94 (1997).
Education: High school graduation rate: 85.7% (2000); College graduation rate: 23.3% (2000).
Housing: Homeownership rate: 84.4% (2000); Median home value: $48,100 (2000); Median rent: $275 per month (2000); Median age of housing: 54 years (2000).
Transportation: Commute to work: 70.2% car, 0.4% public transportation, 3.4% walk, 26.0% work from home (2000); Travel time to work: 28.9% less than 15 minutes, 17.5% 15 to 30 minutes, 28.9% 30 to 45 minutes, 17.0% 45 to 60 minutes, 7.7% 60 minutes or more (2000)

HAY RIVER (town). Covers a land area of 36.070 square miles and a water area of 0 square miles. Located at 45.08° N. Lat.; 91.94° W. Long.
Population: 546 (2000); Race: 97.5% White, 0.0% Black, 0.2% Asian, 0.0% American Indian and Alaska Native, 1.4% Hispanic of any race, 0.9% two or more races (2000); Density: 15.1 persons per square mile (2000); Age: 29.0% under 18, 12.0% over 64 (2000); Marriage status: 19.9% never married, 68.1% now married, 3.1% widowed, 9.0% divorced (2000); Foreign born: 0.9% (2000); Ancestry (includes multiple ancestries): 37.9% German, 32.4% Norwegian, 8.3% Irish, 6.4% English, 4.6% United States or American (2000).
Economy: Employment by occupation: 11.8% management, 13.6% professional, 14.3% services, 17.9% sales, 3.9% farming, 16.4% construction, 22.1% production (2000).
Income: Per capita income: $19,272 (2000); Median household income: $41,458 (2000); Poverty rate: 6.2% (2000).
Taxes: Total city taxes per capita: $85 (1997); City property taxes per capita: $85 (1997).
Education: High school graduation rate: 80.2% (2000); College graduation rate: 23.2% (2000).
Housing: Homeownership rate: 89.1% (2000); Median home value: $98,300 (2000); Median rent: $289 per month (2000); Median age of housing: 34 years (2000).
Transportation: Commute to work: 85.0% car, 0.0% public transportation, 3.2% walk, 10.0% work from home (2000); Travel time to work: 23.0% less than 15 minutes, 45.2% 15 to 30 minutes, 15.5% 30 to 45 minutes, 4.0% 45 to 60 minutes, 12.3% 60 minutes or more (2000)

KNAPP (village). Covers a land area of 1.582 square miles and a water area of 0 square miles. Located at 44.95° N. Lat.; 92.08° W. Long. Elevation is 940 feet.
Population: 421 (2000); Race: 99.2% White, 0.5% Black, 0.0% Asian, 0.0% American Indian and Alaska Native, 0.0% Hispanic of any race, 0.3% two or more races (2000); Density: 266.1 persons per square mile (2000); Age: 22.2% under 18, 16.4% over 64 (2000); Marriage status: 25.5% never married, 58.3% now married, 9.0% widowed, 7.2% divorced (2000); Foreign born: 0.0% (2000); Ancestry (includes multiple ancestries): 40.3% German, 23.4% Norwegian, 8.3% Irish, 8.1% United States or American, 4.8% English (2000).
Economy: In dairying area. Creamery; cheese. Single-family building permits issued: 2 (2001) / 2 (2000); Multi-family building permits issued: 0 (2001) / 0 (2000); Employment by occupation: 4.5% management, 7.2% professional, 16.2% services, 25.2% sales, 0.9% farming, 10.8% construction, 35.1% production (2000).
Income: Per capita income: $22,636 (2000); Median household income: $38,472 (2000); Poverty rate: 8.1% (2000).
Taxes: Total city taxes per capita: $191 (1997); City property taxes per capita: $149 (1997).
Education: High school graduation rate: 85.1% (2000); College graduation rate: 6.5% (2000).
Housing: Homeownership rate: 77.3% (2000); Median home value: $66,600 (2000); Median rent: $300 per month (2000); Median age of housing: 29 years (2000).
Transportation: Commute to work: 96.4% car, 0.0% public transportation, 0.0% walk, 3.6% work from home (2000); Travel time to work: 22.6% less than 15 minutes, 48.6% 15 to 30 minutes, 13.2% 30 to 45 minutes, 6.6% 45 to 60 minutes, 9.0% 60 minutes or more (2000)

LUCAS (town). Covers a land area of 35.742 square miles and a water area of 0 square miles. Located at 44.91° N. Lat.; 92.06° W. Long.
Population: 658 (2000); Race: 98.8% White, 0.0% Black, 0.0% Asian, 0.0% American Indian and Alaska Native, 1.3% Hispanic of any race, 0.6% two or more races (2000); Density: 18.4 persons per square mile (2000); Age: 26.6% under 18, 10.0% over 64 (2000); Marriage status: 24.0% never married, 64.1% now married, 3.5% widowed, 8.3% divorced (2000); Foreign born: 0.3% (2000); Ancestry (includes multiple ancestries): 54.0% German, 28.6% Norwegian, 9.7% English, 7.5% Irish, 5.4% United States or American (2000).
Economy: Employment by occupation: 16.9% management, 12.9% professional, 10.3% services, 15.3% sales, 3.7% farming, 11.6% construction, 29.3% production (2000).
Income: Per capita income: $21,646 (2000); Median household income: $43,750 (2000); Poverty rate: 9.7% (2000).
Taxes: Total city taxes per capita: $93 (1997); City property taxes per capita: $87 (1997).
Education: High school graduation rate: 87.9% (2000); College graduation rate: 15.5% (2000).
Housing: Homeownership rate: 82.7% (2000); Median home value: $92,100 (2000); Median rent: $384 per month (2000); Median age of housing: 32 years (2000).
Transportation: Commute to work: 80.3% car, 0.0% public transportation, 6.4% walk, 11.7% work from home (2000); Travel time to work: 32.0% less than 15 minutes, 44.1% 15 to 30 minutes, 8.8% 30 to 45 minutes, 5.4% 45 to 60 minutes, 9.7% 60 minutes or more (2000)

MENOMONIE (city). Covers a land area of 12.869 square miles and a water area of 1.738 square miles. Located at 44.87° N. Lat.; 91.91° W. Long. Elevation is 877 feet.
History: Menomonie was established on the Red Cedar River as a sawmill site. Platted in 1859, by the 1870's Menomonie was headquarters of one of the largest lumber corporations in Wisconsin. When the timber supply was exhausted, a power plant on the Red Cedar River provided a source of revenue. In 1903, James H. Stout founded Stout Institute here as a vocational training college.
Population: 14,937 (2000); Race: 94.5% White, 0.3% Black, 2.0% Asian, 0.6% American Indian and Alaska Native, 1.6% Hispanic of any race, 1.6% two or more races (2000); Density: 1,160.7 persons per square mile (2000); Age: 15.3% under 18, 11.0% over 64 (2000); Marriage status: 48.4% never married, 39.9% now married, 4.8% widowed, 7.0% divorced (2000); Foreign born: 3.3% (2000); Ancestry (includes multiple ancestries): 40.9% German, 19.3% Norwegian, 8.8% Irish, 6.7% Other groups, 5.2% English (2000).
Vital Statistics: Birth rate: 103.1 per 10,000 population (1998)
Economy: Single-family building permits issued: 18 (2001) / 16 (2000); Multi-family building permits issued: 67 (2001) / 50 (2000); Employment by occupation: 6.6% management, 18.9% professional, 23.8% services, 25.0% sales, 1.1% farming, 5.6% construction, 19.1% production (2000).
Income: Per capita income: $15,994 (2000); Median household income: $31,103 (2000); Poverty rate: 23.5% (2000).
Taxes: Total city taxes per capita: $346 (2000); City property taxes per capita: $324 (2000).
Education: High school graduation rate: 87.7% (2000); College graduation rate: 29.1% (2000).

School District(s)

Menomonie Area (PK-12)
2000 Enrollment: 3,366 715-232-1642

Four-year College(s)

University of Wisconsin-Stout (Public)
2001 Enrollment: 8,052 715-232-1431
2001 Tuition: In-state $2,916; Out-of-state $11,440

Housing: Homeownership rate: 43.7% (2000); Median home value: $94,200 (2000); Median rent: $395 per month (2000); Median age of housing: 28 years (2000).
Hospitals: Myrtle Werth Hospital-Mayo Health System (63 beds)
Safety: Violent crime rate: 6.0 per 10,000 population; Property crime rate: 401.5 per 10,000 population (2001).
Newspapers: Dunn County Shopper (1 x week); Dunn County Reminder (1 x week); Dunn County News (2 x week)
Transportation: Commute to work: 80.7% car, 0.4% public transportation, 14.5% walk, 3.2% work from home (2000); Travel time to work: 61.3% less than 15 minutes, 21.1% 15 to 30 minutes, 10.0% 30 to 45 minutes, 3.0% 45 to 60 minutes, 4.6% 60 minutes or more (2000)
Additional Information Contacts
Menomonie Chamber of Commerce 715-235-9087

MENOMONIE (town). Covers a land area of 41.813 square miles and a water area of 0.206 square miles. Located at 44.88° N. Lat.; 91.96° W. Long. Elevation is 877 feet.
History: Once a lumber town. The University of Wisconsin-Stout campus is here. The ornate civic center building was erected (1890s) by a lumber baron. Plotted 1859, Incorporated 1882.
Population: 3,174 (2000); Race: 90.5% White, 0.2% Black, 8.8% Asian, 0.1% American Indian and Alaska Native, 1.0% Hispanic of any race, 0.4% two or more races (2000); Density: 75.9 persons per square mile (2000); Age: 29.4% under 18, 10.8% over 64 (2000); Marriage status: 23.0% never married, 68.8% now married, 3.2% widowed, 5.0% divorced (2000); Foreign born: 4.2% (2000); Ancestry (includes multiple ancestries): 48.5% German, 27.5% Norwegian, 10.2% Other groups, 9.7% Irish, 6.8% English (2000).
Economy: Trade center in an area of poultry and dairy farms. Manufacturing of fabricated metal products, foods and machinery. Employment by occupation: 17.9% management, 21.8% professional, 10.9% services, 16.6% sales, 0.8% farming, 11.1% construction, 20.9% production (2000).
Income: Per capita income: $20,814 (2000); Median household income: $43,547 (2000); Poverty rate: 8.1% (2000).
Taxes: Total city taxes per capita: $56 (1997); City property taxes per capita: $41 (1997).
Education: High school graduation rate: 88.0% (2000); College graduation rate: 25.5% (2000).
Housing: Homeownership rate: 89.0% (2000); Median home value: $116,700 (2000); Median rent: $352 per month (2000); Median age of housing: 24 years (2000).
Transportation: Commute to work: 87.5% car, 0.1% public transportation, 1.3% walk, 9.4% work from home (2000); Travel time to work: 45.1% less than 15 minutes, 29.7% 15 to 30 minutes, 15.3% 30 to 45 minutes, 3.6% 45 to 60 minutes, 6.4% 60 minutes or more (2000)

NEW HAVEN (town). Covers a land area of 36.389 square miles and a water area of 0 square miles. Located at 45.15° N. Lat.; 92.11° W. Long.
Population: 656 (2000); Race: 98.4% White, 0.0% Black, 0.0% Asian, 0.9% American Indian and Alaska Native, 0.0% Hispanic of any race, 0.7% two or more races (2000); Density: 18.0 persons per square mile (2000); Age: 28.9% under 18, 13.0% over 64 (2000); Marriage status: 22.8% never married, 62.8% now married, 8.0% widowed, 6.3% divorced (2000); Foreign born: 0.3% (2000); Ancestry (includes multiple ancestries): 40.2% German, 33.1% Norwegian, 11.7% Irish, 9.1% Swedish, 7.1% English (2000).
Economy: Employment by occupation: 17.7% management, 10.5% professional, 12.0% services, 15.3% sales, 3.6% farming, 12.0% construction, 28.8% production (2000).

Income: Per capita income: $19,019 (2000); Median household income: $40,938 (2000); Poverty rate: 5.0% (2000).
Taxes: Total city taxes per capita: $80 (1997); City property taxes per capita: $79 (1997).
Education: High school graduation rate: 79.3% (2000); College graduation rate: 12.1% (2000).
Housing: Homeownership rate: 90.3% (2000); Median home value: $70,000 (2000); Median rent: $175 per month (2000); Median age of housing: 57 years (2000).
Transportation: Commute to work: 84.8% car, 0.0% public transportation, 0.6% walk, 14.6% work from home (2000); Travel time to work: 11.7% less than 15 minutes, 21.7% 15 to 30 minutes, 37.0% 30 to 45 minutes, 10.7% 45 to 60 minutes, 18.9% 60 minutes or more (2000)

OTTER CREEK (town). Covers a land area of 36.923 square miles and a water area of 0 square miles. Located at 45.07° N. Lat.; 91.83° W. Long.
Population: 474 (2000); Race: 98.1% White, 0.0% Black, 1.4% Asian, 0.5% American Indian and Alaska Native, 0.0% Hispanic of any race, 0.0% two or more races (2000); Density: 12.8 persons per square mile (2000); Age: 31.5% under 18, 6.5% over 64 (2000); Marriage status: 23.2% never married, 66.9% now married, 3.4% widowed, 6.5% divorced (2000); Foreign born: 1.9% (2000); Ancestry (includes multiple ancestries): 40.5% German, 22.9% Norwegian, 11.1% English, 10.2% Irish, 3.9% Other groups (2000).
Economy: Employment by occupation: 12.6% management, 18.2% professional, 13.1% services, 17.2% sales, 8.1% farming, 9.1% construction, 21.7% production (2000).
Income: Per capita income: $16,799 (2000); Median household income: $41,000 (2000); Poverty rate: 1.9% (2000).
Taxes: Total city taxes per capita: $136 (1997); City property taxes per capita: $134 (1997).
Education: High school graduation rate: 87.5% (2000); College graduation rate: 22.9% (2000).
Housing: Homeownership rate: 90.8% (2000); Median home value: $110,000 (2000); Median rent: $213 per month (2000); Median age of housing: 18 years (2000).
Transportation: Commute to work: 89.6% car, 0.0% public transportation, 0.0% walk, 9.3% work from home (2000); Travel time to work: 6.9% less than 15 minutes, 42.9% 15 to 30 minutes, 25.1% 30 to 45 minutes, 12.0% 45 to 60 minutes, 13.1% 60 minutes or more (2000)

PERU (town). Covers a land area of 18.720 square miles and a water area of 0.881 square miles. Located at 44.71° N. Lat.; 91.81° W. Long.
Population: 247 (2000); Race: 97.9% White, 0.0% Black, 0.0% Asian, 0.0% American Indian and Alaska Native, 0.0% Hispanic of any race, 1.7% two or more races (2000); Density: 13.2 persons per square mile (2000); Age: 32.5% under 18, 13.8% over 64 (2000); Marriage status: 18.4% never married, 75.9% now married, 4.0% widowed, 1.7% divorced (2000); Foreign born: 1.3% (2000); Ancestry (includes multiple ancestries): 33.8% Norwegian, 27.1% German, 22.1% Austrian, 10.0% Irish, 9.2% United States or American (2000).
Economy: Employment by occupation: 14.0% management, 11.4% professional, 11.4% services, 19.3% sales, 4.4% farming, 14.0% construction, 25.4% production (2000).
Income: Per capita income: $14,774 (2000); Median household income: $34,375 (2000); Poverty rate: 10.8% (2000).
Taxes: Total city taxes per capita: $64 (1997); City property taxes per capita: $64 (1997).
Education: High school graduation rate: 81.1% (2000); College graduation rate: 13.5% (2000).
Housing: Homeownership rate: 89.9% (2000); Median home value: $75,000 (2000); Median rent: $238 per month (2000); Median age of housing: 33 years (2000).
Transportation: Commute to work: 84.2% car, 0.0% public transportation, 6.1% walk, 9.6% work from home (2000); Travel time to work: 11.7% less than 15 minutes, 26.2% 15 to 30 minutes, 53.4% 30 to 45 minutes, 6.8% 45 to 60 minutes, 1.9% 60 minutes or more (2000)

RED CEDAR (town). Covers a land area of 39.764 square miles and a water area of 0.937 square miles. Located at 44.89° N. Lat.; 91.84° W. Long. Elevation is 758 feet.
Population: 1,673 (2000); Race: 98.2% White, 0.0% Black, 0.7% Asian, 0.0% American Indian and Alaska Native, 0.5% Hispanic of any race, 0.5% two or more races (2000); Density: 42.1 persons per square mile (2000); Age: 28.0% under 18, 10.0% over 64 (2000); Marriage status: 23.9% never married, 66.1% now married, 3.1% widowed, 6.9% divorced (2000); Foreign born: 2.1% (2000); Ancestry (includes multiple ancestries): 49.4% German, 26.0% Norwegian, 9.3% Irish, 7.5% English, 5.3% Polish (2000).
Economy: Employment by occupation: 14.9% management, 15.3% professional, 12.1% services, 27.3% sales, 3.3% farming, 7.9% construction, 19.1% production (2000).
Income: Per capita income: $21,067 (2000); Median household income: $50,972 (2000); Poverty rate: 3.5% (2000).
Taxes: Total city taxes per capita: $63 (1997); City property taxes per capita: $61 (1997).
Education: High school graduation rate: 88.0% (2000); College graduation rate: 24.0% (2000).
Housing: Homeownership rate: 87.4% (2000); Median home value: $108,000 (2000); Median rent: $540 per month (2000); Median age of housing: 23 years (2000).
Transportation: Commute to work: 86.6% car, 0.0% public transportation, 3.7% walk, 8.8% work from home (2000); Travel time to work: 46.7% less than 15 minutes, 30.1% 15 to 30 minutes, 13.4% 30 to 45 minutes, 3.6% 45 to 60 minutes, 6.2% 60 minutes or more (2000)

RIDGELAND (village). Covers a land area of 0.424 square miles and a water area of 0 square miles. Located at 45.20° N. Lat.; 91.89° W. Long. Elevation is 1,090 feet.
Population: 265 (2000); Race: 97.6% White, 0.0% Black, 0.0% Asian, 0.0% American Indian and Alaska Native, 0.4% Hispanic of any race, 2.0% two or more races (2000); Density: 625.0 persons per square mile (2000); Age: 25.1% under 18, 29.1% over 64 (2000); Marriage status: 14.0% never married, 56.5% now married, 15.5% widowed, 14.0% divorced (2000); Foreign born: 0.0% (2000); Ancestry (includes multiple ancestries): 46.6% German, 42.2% Norwegian, 8.0% Irish, 6.0% English, 4.4% French (except Basque) (2000).
Economy: In dairying area. Manufacturing of recycling equipment. Hunting and state fishery. Single-family building permits issued: 5 (2001) / 0 (2000); Multi-family building permits issued: 0 (2001) / 0 (2000); Employment by occupation: 3.8% management, 13.3% professional, 11.4% services, 25.7% sales, 5.7% farming, 11.4% construction, 28.6% production (2000).
Income: Per capita income: $13,257 (2000); Median household income: $25,000 (2000); Poverty rate: 15.8% (2000).
Taxes: Total city taxes per capita: $76 (1997); City property taxes per capita: $64 (1997).
Education: High school graduation rate: 75.6% (2000); College graduation rate: 6.8% (2000).
Housing: Homeownership rate: 69.4% (2000); Median home value: $46,400 (2000); Median rent: $315 per month (2000); Median age of housing: 48 years (2000).
Transportation: Commute to work: 92.2% car, 0.0% public transportation, 7.8% walk, 0.0% work from home (2000); Travel time to work: 33.0% less than 15 minutes, 33.0% 15 to 30 minutes, 27.2% 30 to 45 minutes, 2.9% 45 to 60 minutes, 3.9% 60 minutes or more (2000)

ROCK CREEK (town). Covers a land area of 30.806 square miles and a water area of 0.777 square miles. Located at 44.72° N. Lat.; 91.70° W. Long.
Population: 793 (2000); Race: 97.7% White, 0.0% Black, 0.7% Asian, 0.2% American Indian and Alaska Native, 0.8% Hispanic of any race, 1.3% two or more races (2000); Density: 25.7 persons per square mile (2000); Age: 27.7% under 18, 7.6% over 64 (2000); Marriage status: 29.7% never married, 62.2% now married, 4.2% widowed, 3.9% divorced (2000); Foreign born: 1.3% (2000); Ancestry (includes multiple ancestries): 42.0% German, 24.3% Norwegian, 7.7% Irish, 7.6% English, 7.5% United States or American (2000).
Economy: Employment by occupation: 15.1% management, 10.3% professional, 9.9% services, 19.7% sales, 5.5% farming, 12.4% construction, 27.1% production (2000).
Income: Per capita income: $16,735 (2000); Median household income: $43,906 (2000); Poverty rate: 7.7% (2000).
Taxes: Total city taxes per capita: $46 (1997); City property taxes per capita: $44 (1997).
Education: High school graduation rate: 84.9% (2000); College graduation rate: 8.6% (2000).
Housing: Homeownership rate: 85.7% (2000); Median home value: $90,700 (2000); Median rent: $436 per month (2000); Median age of housing: 31 years (2000).
Transportation: Commute to work: 84.2% car, 0.0% public transportation, 3.9% walk, 10.4% work from home (2000); Travel time to work: 11.4% less than 15 minutes, 48.3% 15 to 30 minutes, 26.1% 30 to 45 minutes, 9.4% 45 to 60 minutes, 4.8% 60 minutes or more (2000)

SAND CREEK (town). Covers a land area of 35.747 square miles and a water area of 0.405 square miles. Located at 45.16° N. Lat.; 91.71° W. Long. Elevation is 1,000 feet.
Population: 586 (2000); Race: 99.3% White, 0.0% Black, 0.0% Asian, 0.3% American Indian and Alaska Native, 0.0% Hispanic of any race, 0.3% two or more races (2000); Density: 16.4 persons per square mile (2000); Age: 25.0% under 18, 13.9% over 64 (2000); Marriage status: 21.6% never married, 64.5% now married, 6.7% widowed, 7.1% divorced (2000); Foreign born: 0.0% (2000); Ancestry (includes multiple ancestries): 46.0% Norwegian, 35.1% German, 10.1% Irish, 7.3% English, 5.2% Polish (2000).
Economy: Single-family building permits issued: 4 (2001) / 2 (2000); Multi-family building permits issued: 0 (2001) / 0 (2000); Employment by occupation: 17.4% management, 12.6% professional, 14.7% services, 17.7% sales, 6.9% farming, 13.8% construction, 16.8% production (2000).
Income: Per capita income: $16,937 (2000); Median household income: $40,197 (2000); Poverty rate: 8.2% (2000).
Taxes: Total city taxes per capita: $133 (1997); City property taxes per capita: $133 (1997).
Education: High school graduation rate: 86.0% (2000); College graduation rate: 18.9% (2000).
Housing: Homeownership rate: 81.8% (2000); Median home value: $63,900 (2000); Median rent: $317 per month (2000); Median age of housing: 52 years (2000).
Transportation: Commute to work: 75.7% car, 0.0% public transportation, 11.7% walk, 10.5% work from home (2000); Travel time to work: 24.5% less than 15 minutes, 32.2% 15 to 30 minutes, 22.1% 30 to 45 minutes, 15.8% 45 to 60 minutes, 5.4% 60 minutes or more (2000)

SHERIDAN (town). Covers a land area of 36.091 square miles and a water area of 0.006 square miles. Located at 45.16° N. Lat.; 91.97° W. Long.
Population: 483 (2000); Race: 98.5% White, 0.0% Black, 0.0% Asian, 0.4% American Indian and Alaska Native, 1.1% Hispanic of any race, 1.1% two or more races (2000); Density: 13.4 persons per square mile (2000); Age: 26.2% under 18, 8.7% over 64 (2000); Marriage status: 21.1% never married, 67.5% now married, 2.9% widowed, 8.4% divorced (2000); Foreign born: 0.6% (2000); Ancestry (includes multiple ancestries): 46.2% German, 40.0% Norwegian, 6.0% English, 5.7% Irish, 3.6% United States or American (2000).
Economy: Employment by occupation: 24.9% management, 16.2% professional, 5.1% services, 15.4% sales, 5.1% farming, 7.1% construction, 26.1% production (2000).
Income: Per capita income: $16,550 (2000); Median household income: $44,167 (2000); Poverty rate: 7.5% (2000).
Taxes: Total city taxes per capita: $103 (1997); City property taxes per capita: $103 (1997).
Education: High school graduation rate: 89.9% (2000); College graduation rate: 16.7% (2000).
Housing: Homeownership rate: 88.2% (2000); Median home value: $86,700 (2000); Median rent: $363 per month (2000); Median age of housing: 42 years (2000).
Transportation: Commute to work: 79.1% car, 0.0% public transportation, 5.2% walk, 14.5% work from home (2000); Travel time to work: 23.0% less than 15 minutes, 16.9% 15 to 30 minutes, 34.7% 30 to 45 minutes, 9.9% 45 to 60 minutes, 15.5% 60 minutes or more (2000)

SHERMAN (town). Covers a land area of 35.277 square miles and a water area of 0.096 square miles. Located at 44.98° N. Lat.; 91.95° W. Long.
Population: 748 (2000); Race: 96.7% White, 0.5% Black, 0.4% Asian, 0.3% American Indian and Alaska Native, 0.7% Hispanic of any race, 1.7% two or more races (2000); Density: 21.2 persons per square mile (2000); Age: 23.3% under 18, 13.2% over 64 (2000); Marriage status: 20.8% never married, 69.6% now married, 3.0% widowed, 6.6% divorced (2000); Foreign born: 0.9% (2000); Ancestry (includes multiple ancestries): 41.3% German, 23.4% Norwegian, 12.4% Irish, 9.3% English, 7.5% Swedish (2000).
Economy: Employment by occupation: 16.4% management, 13.9% professional, 13.6% services, 21.2% sales, 2.3% farming, 12.9% construction, 19.6% production (2000).
Income: Per capita income: $19,467 (2000); Median household income: $45,795 (2000); Poverty rate: 8.4% (2000).
Taxes: Total city taxes per capita: $102 (1997); City property taxes per capita: $101 (1997).
Education: High school graduation rate: 90.0% (2000); College graduation rate: 21.2% (2000).
Housing: Homeownership rate: 85.5% (2000); Median home value: $106,500 (2000); Median rent: $325 per month (2000); Median age of housing: 32 years (2000).
Transportation: Commute to work: 88.7% car, 0.0% public transportation, 3.1% walk, 6.9% work from home (2000); Travel time to work: 28.2% less than 15 minutes, 42.9% 15 to 30 minutes, 15.0% 30 to 45 minutes, 5.6% 45 to 60 minutes, 8.4% 60 minutes or more (2000)

SPRING BROOK (town). Covers a land area of 60.780 square miles and a water area of 1.353 square miles. Located at 44.80° N. Lat.; 91.74° W. Long.
Population: 1,320 (2000); Race: 98.0% White, 0.0% Black, 0.5% Asian, 0.4% American Indian and Alaska Native, 0.8% Hispanic of any race, 0.7% two or more races (2000); Density: 21.7 persons per square mile (2000); Age: 29.7% under 18, 9.4% over 64 (2000); Marriage status: 22.0% never married, 67.9% now married, 2.8% widowed, 7.4% divorced (2000); Foreign born: 1.2% (2000); Ancestry (includes multiple ancestries): 44.3% German, 30.7% Norwegian, 6.9% English, 6.1% United States or American, 5.4% Irish (2000).
Economy: Employment by occupation: 14.6% management, 16.6% professional, 11.9% services, 24.3% sales, 6.5% farming, 9.6% construction, 16.6% production (2000).
Income: Per capita income: $19,936 (2000); Median household income: $46,600 (2000); Poverty rate: 3.1% (2000).
Taxes: Total city taxes per capita: $85 (1997); City property taxes per capita: $84 (1997).
Education: High school graduation rate: 90.9% (2000); College graduation rate: 17.1% (2000).
Housing: Homeownership rate: 84.3% (2000); Median home value: $91,000 (2000); Median rent: $412 per month (2000); Median age of housing: 35 years (2000).
Transportation: Commute to work: 86.4% car, 0.0% public transportation, 4.2% walk, 9.0% work from home (2000); Travel time to work: 22.9% less than 15 minutes, 54.1% 15 to 30 minutes, 16.9% 30 to 45 minutes, 3.8% 45 to 60 minutes, 2.4% 60 minutes or more (2000)

STANTON (town). Covers a land area of 33.861 square miles and a water area of 0 square miles. Located at 44.96° N. Lat.; 92.08° W. Long.
Population: 715 (2000); Race: 98.3% White, 0.0% Black, 0.0% Asian, 0.0% American Indian and Alaska Native, 4.0% Hispanic of any race, 1.4% two or more races (2000); Density: 21.1 persons per square mile (2000); Age: 34.0% under 18, 8.1% over 64 (2000); Marriage status: 23.6% never married, 64.0% now married, 3.4% widowed, 9.0% divorced (2000); Foreign born: 0.6% (2000); Ancestry (includes multiple ancestries): 37.1% German, 21.2% Norwegian, 10.5% Irish, 8.1% Other groups, 7.0% English (2000).
Economy: Employment by occupation: 19.7% management, 8.7% professional, 14.2% services, 18.0% sales, 5.2% farming, 12.6% construction, 21.6% production (2000).
Income: Per capita income: $15,398 (2000); Median household income: $45,781 (2000); Poverty rate: 10.7% (2000).
Taxes: Total city taxes per capita: $161 (1997); City property taxes per capita: $159 (1997).
Education: High school graduation rate: 86.3% (2000); College graduation rate: 13.7% (2000).
Housing: Homeownership rate: 86.0% (2000); Median home value: $100,000 (2000); Median rent: $325 per month (2000); Median age of housing: 30 years (2000).
Transportation: Commute to work: 86.4% car, 1.1% public transportation, 3.3% walk, 8.6% work from home (2000); Travel time to work: 25.2% less than 15 minutes, 41.6% 15 to 30 minutes, 12.5% 30 to 45 minutes, 11.2% 45 to 60 minutes, 9.4% 60 minutes or more (2000)

TAINTER (town). Covers a land area of 32.998 square miles and a water area of 2.683 square miles. Located at 44.99° N. Lat.; 91.84° W. Long.
Population: 2,116 (2000); Race: 97.9% White, 0.1% Black, 1.1% Asian, 0.1% American Indian and Alaska Native, 0.0% Hispanic of any race, 0.6% two or more races (2000); Density: 64.1 persons per square mile (2000); Age: 25.6% under 18, 11.1% over 64 (2000); Marriage status: 20.9% never married, 66.6% now married, 3.3% widowed, 9.2% divorced (2000); Foreign born: 1.5% (2000); Ancestry (includes multiple ancestries): 48.0% German, 25.4% Norwegian, 11.9% Irish, 7.0% English, 4.8% Polish (2000).
Economy: Employment by occupation: 12.3% management, 22.5% professional, 13.9% services, 21.2% sales, 1.1% farming, 9.8% construction, 19.1% production (2000).
Income: Per capita income: $22,916 (2000); Median household income: $50,741 (2000); Poverty rate: 5.9% (2000).

Taxes: Total city taxes per capita: $111 (1997); City property taxes per capita: $105 (1997).
Education: High school graduation rate: 89.4% (2000); College graduation rate: 27.1% (2000).
Housing: Homeownership rate: 84.9% (2000); Median home value: $118,300 (2000); Median rent: $463 per month (2000); Median age of housing: 25 years (2000).
Transportation: Commute to work: 93.8% car, 0.4% public transportation, 1.2% walk, 4.4% work from home (2000); Travel time to work: 25.1% less than 15 minutes, 45.9% 15 to 30 minutes, 15.3% 30 to 45 minutes, 6.6% 45 to 60 minutes, 7.1% 60 minutes or more (2000)

TAINTER LAKE (CDP). Covers a land area of 18.622 square miles and a water area of 2.841 square miles. Located at 44.97° N. Lat.; 91.84° W. Long.
Population: 2,089 (2000); Race: 97.8% White, 0.1% Black, 1.2% Asian, 0.1% American Indian and Alaska Native, 0.0% Hispanic of any race, 0.6% two or more races (2000); Density: 112.2 persons per square mile (2000); Age: 23.0% under 18, 12.1% over 64 (2000); Marriage status: 19.0% never married, 68.9% now married, 3.5% widowed, 8.6% divorced (2000); Foreign born: 1.6% (2000); Ancestry (includes multiple ancestries): 48.3% German, 26.6% Norwegian, 11.5% Irish, 8.1% English, 5.6% Polish (2000).
Economy: Employment by occupation: 13.0% management, 23.5% professional, 13.6% services, 22.3% sales, 0.6% farming, 8.4% construction, 18.5% production (2000).
Income: Per capita income: $25,292 (2000); Median household income: $54,265 (2000); Poverty rate: 5.7% (2000).
Education: High school graduation rate: 89.0% (2000); College graduation rate: 29.7% (2000).
Housing: Homeownership rate: 85.5% (2000); Median home value: $121,400 (2000); Median rent: $478 per month (2000); Median age of housing: 25 years (2000).
Transportation: Commute to work: 95.5% car, 0.4% public transportation, 1.0% walk, 2.9% work from home (2000); Travel time to work: 26.9% less than 15 minutes, 43.2% 15 to 30 minutes, 15.4% 30 to 45 minutes, 5.2% 45 to 60 minutes, 9.3% 60 minutes or more (2000)

TIFFANY (town). Covers a land area of 29.933 square miles and a water area of 0.009 square miles. Located at 45.08° N. Lat.; 92.07° W. Long.
Population: 633 (2000); Race: 99.3% White, 0.0% Black, 0.0% Asian, 0.3% American Indian and Alaska Native, 1.2% Hispanic of any race, 0.3% two or more races (2000); Density: 21.1 persons per square mile (2000); Age: 26.6% under 18, 10.9% over 64 (2000); Marriage status: 26.2% never married, 59.3% now married, 6.3% widowed, 8.2% divorced (2000); Foreign born: 0.0% (2000); Ancestry (includes multiple ancestries): 37.7% German, 26.7% Norwegian, 9.4% Slovak, 8.2% Irish, 7.1% English (2000).
Economy: Employment by occupation: 18.3% management, 16.5% professional, 10.2% services, 18.0% sales, 2.2% farming, 11.5% construction, 23.3% production (2000).
Income: Per capita income: $18,203 (2000); Median household income: $38,750 (2000); Poverty rate: 10.4% (2000).
Taxes: Total city taxes per capita: $92 (1997); City property taxes per capita: $87 (1997).
Education: High school graduation rate: 90.4% (2000); College graduation rate: 14.4% (2000).
Housing: Homeownership rate: 87.2% (2000); Median home value: $97,500 (2000); Median rent: $306 per month (2000); Median age of housing: 29 years (2000).
Transportation: Commute to work: 87.1% car, 0.0% public transportation, 3.2% walk, 9.6% work from home (2000); Travel time to work: 27.4% less than 15 minutes, 28.5% 15 to 30 minutes, 28.1% 30 to 45 minutes, 5.0% 45 to 60 minutes, 11.0% 60 minutes or more (2000)

WESTON (town). Covers a land area of 41.509 square miles and a water area of 0 square miles. Located at 44.80° N. Lat.; 92.06° W. Long. Elevation is 860 feet.
Population: 630 (2000); Race: 99.1% White, 0.0% Black, 0.4% Asian, 0.0% American Indian and Alaska Native, 0.0% Hispanic of any race, 0.4% two or more races (2000); Density: 15.2 persons per square mile (2000); Age: 33.9% under 18, 8.3% over 64 (2000); Marriage status: 19.3% never married, 67.0% now married, 3.9% widowed, 9.9% divorced (2000); Foreign born: 0.4% (2000); Ancestry (includes multiple ancestries): 50.4% German, 20.0% Norwegian, 8.0% United States or American, 7.1% Swedish, 6.1% Irish (2000).
Economy: Employment by occupation: 20.2% management, 9.8% professional, 7.6% services, 17.4% sales, 7.3% farming, 12.6% construction, 25.2% production (2000).
Income: Per capita income: $16,125 (2000); Median household income: $46,042 (2000); Poverty rate: 9.8% (2000).
Taxes: Total city taxes per capita: $129 (1997); City property taxes per capita: $124 (1997).
Education: High school graduation rate: 84.6% (2000); College graduation rate: 13.7% (2000).
Housing: Homeownership rate: 85.8% (2000); Median home value: $78,300 (2000); Median rent: $263 per month (2000); Median age of housing: 60 years (2000).
Transportation: Commute to work: 78.6% car, 0.6% public transportation, 4.2% walk, 16.0% work from home (2000); Travel time to work: 28.1% less than 15 minutes, 36.1% 15 to 30 minutes, 21.3% 30 to 45 minutes, 6.5% 45 to 60 minutes, 8.0% 60 minutes or more (2000)

WHEELER (village). Covers a land area of 0.820 square miles and a water area of 0 square miles. Located at 45.04° N. Lat.; 91.90° W. Long. Elevation is 938 feet.
Population: 317 (2000); Race: 97.7% White, 0.0% Black, 0.0% Asian, 2.3% American Indian and Alaska Native, 0.0% Hispanic of any race, 0.0% two or more races (2000); Density: 386.8 persons per square mile (2000); Age: 22.1% under 18, 14.4% over 64 (2000); Marriage status: 23.6% never married, 45.9% now married, 12.0% widowed, 18.6% divorced (2000); Foreign born: 0.7% (2000); Ancestry (includes multiple ancestries): 33.2% Norwegian, 27.2% German, 12.1% Irish, 8.7% English, 5.7% French (except Basque) (2000).
Economy: In dairying area. Deepwood Ski Area to East. Single-family building permits issued: 2 (2001) / 2 (2000); Multi-family building permits issued: 0 (2001) / 0 (2000); Employment by occupation: 7.0% management, 2.1% professional, 16.1% services, 24.5% sales, 1.4% farming, 14.0% construction, 35.0% production (2000).
Income: Per capita income: $20,883 (2000); Median household income: $25,938 (2000); Poverty rate: 15.6% (2000).
Taxes: Total city taxes per capita: $82 (1997); City property taxes per capita: $66 (1997).
Education: High school graduation rate: 70.6% (2000); College graduation rate: 8.3% (2000).
Housing: Homeownership rate: 57.3% (2000); Median home value: $53,300 (2000); Median rent: $317 per month (2000); Median age of housing: 45 years (2000).
Transportation: Commute to work: 95.8% car, 0.0% public transportation, 2.1% walk, 2.1% work from home (2000); Travel time to work: 16.3% less than 15 minutes, 36.2% 15 to 30 minutes, 17.0% 30 to 45 minutes, 9.2% 45 to 60 minutes, 21.3% 60 minutes or more (2000)

WILSON (town). Covers a land area of 35.531 square miles and a water area of 0 square miles. Located at 45.17° N. Lat.; 91.84° W. Long.
Population: 500 (2000); Race: 97.2% White, 0.6% Black, 0.0% Asian, 0.2% American Indian and Alaska Native, 0.6% Hispanic of any race, 1.6% two or more races (2000); Density: 14.1 persons per square mile (2000); Age: 28.9% under 18, 12.8% over 64 (2000); Marriage status: 20.7% never married, 67.0% now married, 3.8% widowed, 8.4% divorced (2000); Foreign born: 0.6% (2000); Ancestry (includes multiple ancestries): 44.7% German, 36.5% Norwegian, 13.2% Irish, 5.6% Other groups, 5.6% English (2000).
Economy: Employment by occupation: 18.8% management, 10.8% professional, 10.4% services, 12.8% sales, 6.4% farming, 15.2% construction, 25.6% production (2000).
Income: Per capita income: $14,319 (2000); Median household income: $33,750 (2000); Poverty rate: 11.4% (2000).
Taxes: Total city taxes per capita: $92 (1997); City property taxes per capita: $89 (1997).
Education: High school graduation rate: 81.4% (2000); College graduation rate: 10.6% (2000).
Housing: Homeownership rate: 81.7% (2000); Median home value: $67,500 (2000); Median rent: $438 per month (2000); Median age of housing: 28 years (2000).
Transportation: Commute to work: 85.1% car, 0.0% public transportation, 4.8% walk, 9.3% work from home (2000); Travel time to work: 35.1% less than 15 minutes, 23.1% 15 to 30 minutes, 18.7% 30 to 45 minutes, 8.9% 45 to 60 minutes, 14.2% 60 minutes or more (2000)

Eau Claire County

Located in west central Wisconsin; drained by the Chippewa and Eau Claire Rivers. Covers a land area of 637.60 square miles, a water area of 7.60 square miles, and is located in the Central Time Zone. The county government was organized in 1856. County seat is Eau Claire.

Eau Claire County is part of the Eau Claire, WI MSA. The entire metro area includes: Chippewa County; Eau Claire County

Weather Station: Fairchild Ranger Station Elevation: 1,079 feet

	Jan	Feb	Mar	Apr	May	Jun	Jul	Aug	Sep	Oct	Nov	Dec
High	19	27	39	55	68	77	81	79	70	57	41	na
Low	na	7	20	34	45	54	59	56	47	36	24	9
Precip	1.1	0.8	2.0	2.9	3.7	4.2	4.4	4.4	4.4	2.7	2.2	1.2
Snow	11.4	7.3	8.6	2.7	tr	0.0	0.0	0.0	tr	0.5	5.3	10.4

High and Low temperatures in degrees Fahrenheit; Precipitation and Snow in inches

Population: 93,142 (2000); Race: 95.0% White, 0.5% Black, 2.5% Asian, 0.6% American Indian and Alaska Native, 0.9% Hispanic of any race, 1.1% two or more races (2000); Density: 146.1 persons per square mile (2000); Age: 23.4% under 18, 12.2% over 64 (2000).
Religion: Five largest groups: 19.5% Catholic Church, 16.4% Evangelical Lutheran Church in America, 8.3% Lutheran Church—Missouri Synod, 3.1% The United Methodist Church, 1.6% Baptist General Conference (2000).
Economy: Unemployment rate: 3.8% (11/2002); Total civilian labor force: 53,995 (11/2002); Leading industries: 17.0% retail trade; 16.5% health care and social assistance; 14.5% manufacturing (2000); Companies that employ more than 1,000 persons: 2 (2000); Companies that employ more than 100 persons: 77 (2000); Farms: 927 totaling 191,367 acres (1997); Minority business ownership rate: 3.8% (1997); Women business ownership rate: 24.8% (1997); Retail sales per capita: $11,621 (1997). Single-family building permits issued: 413 (2001) / 441 (2000); Multi-family building permits issued: 356 (2001) / 290 (2000).
Income: Per capita income: $19,250 (2000); Median household income: $39,219 (2000); Poverty rate: 10.9% (2000); Bankruptcy rate: 3.20% (2001).
Taxes: Total county taxes per capita: $128 (2000); County property taxes per capita: $123 (2000).
Education: High school graduation rate: 88.9% (2000); College graduation rate: 27.0% (2000).
Housing: Homeownership rate: 65.0% (2000); Median home value: $96,300 (2000); Median rent: $412 per month (2000); Median age of housing: 30 years (2000).
Health: Birth rate: 113.9 per 10,000 population (1998); Age adjusted death rate: 78.1 per 10,000 population (1999); Age adjusted cancer mortality rate: 190.5 deaths per 100,000 population (1999). Number of physicians: 34.8 per 10,000 population (1999); Number of hospital beds: 39.1 per 10,000 population (1999).
Elections: 2000 Presidential election results: 50.3% Gore, 43.7% Bush, 5.1% Nader, 0.2% Buchanan
National and State Parks: Augusta State Wildlife Area
Additional Information Contacts
Eau Claire County Government Offices 715-839-4801
Eau Claire Area Convention & Visitors Bureau 715-831-2345
Eau Claire Chamber of Commerce 715-834-1204
Realtors Association of The Chippewa Valley 715-835-0923

Eau Claire County Communities

ALTOONA (city). Covers a land area of 4.088 square miles and a water area of 0.211 square miles. Located at 44.80° N. Lat.; 91.44° W. Long. Elevation is 890 feet.
History: Settled 1882, incorporated 1887.
Population: 6,698 (2000); Race: 95.9% White, 0.6% Black, 1.8% Asian, 0.5% American Indian and Alaska Native, 0.2% Hispanic of any race, 1.1% two or more races (2000); Density: 1,638.6 persons per square mile (2000); Age: 25.0% under 18, 16.1% over 64 (2000); Marriage status: 24.6% never married, 54.0% now married, 9.5% widowed, 11.8% divorced (2000); Foreign born: 2.2% (2000); Ancestry (includes multiple ancestries): 44.0% German, 26.4% Norwegian, 9.7% Irish, 7.1% English, 6.2% Polish (2000).
Economy: In manufacturing and services area. Light manufacturing. Single-family building permits issued: 6 (2001) / 6 (2000); Multi-family building permits issued: 26 (2001) / 2 (2000); Employment by occupation: 12.2% management, 21.4% professional, 12.7% services, 29.8% sales, 0.7% farming, 8.4% construction, 14.8% production (2000).
Income: Per capita income: $21,236 (2000); Median household income: $40,394 (2000); Poverty rate: 5.2% (2000).
Taxes: Total city taxes per capita: $388 (1997); City property taxes per capita: $360 (1997).
Education: High school graduation rate: 89.5% (2000); College graduation rate: 26.9% (2000).

School District(s)

Altoona (PK-12)
2000 Enrollment: 1,416 715-839-6032
Housing: Homeownership rate: 61.6% (2000); Median home value: $98,400 (2000); Median rent: $444 per month (2000); Median age of housing: 22 years (2000).
Safety: Violent crime rate: 5.9 per 10,000 population; Property crime rate: 222.4 per 10,000 population (2001).
Transportation: Commute to work: 94.8% car, 0.9% public transportation, 1.3% walk, 2.3% work from home (2000); Travel time to work: 52.4% less than 15 minutes, 34.1% 15 to 30 minutes, 6.9% 30 to 45 minutes, 1.6% 45 to 60 minutes, 5.1% 60 minutes or more (2000)

AUGUSTA (city). Covers a land area of 2.024 square miles and a water area of 0 square miles. Located at 44.68° N. Lat.; 91.12° W. Long. Elevation is 960 feet.
History: Incorporated 1885.
Population: 1,460 (2000); Race: 95.8% White, 0.0% Black, 1.0% Asian, 1.7% American Indian and Alaska Native, 2.5% Hispanic of any race, 1.4% two or more races (2000); Density: 721.5 persons per square mile (2000); Age: 24.4% under 18, 23.7% over 64 (2000); Marriage status: 22.2% never married, 53.6% now married, 13.6% widowed, 10.6% divorced (2000); Foreign born: 1.2% (2000); Ancestry (includes multiple ancestries): 45.4% German, 14.6% Norwegian, 12.4% Irish, 8.7% Other groups, 8.5% English (2000).
Economy: In dairying, stock-raising, and farming area: grain, cranberries; creameries, feed mill, cannery. Manufacturing: fabricated metal products, foods, wire harnesses. Single-family building permits issued: 2 (2001) / 4 (2000); Multi-family building permits issued: 0 (2001) / 0 (2000); Employment by occupation: 9.1% management, 7.7% professional, 23.0% services, 22.3% sales, 1.8% farming, 7.2% construction, 28.9% production (2000).
Income: Per capita income: $15,469 (2000); Median household income: $28,478 (2000); Poverty rate: 11.0% (2000).
Taxes: Total city taxes per capita: $147 (1997); City property taxes per capita: $141 (1997).
Education: High school graduation rate: 78.9% (2000); College graduation rate: 9.0% (2000).

School District(s)

Augusta (PK-12)
2000 Enrollment: 691 715-286-3300
Housing: Homeownership rate: 73.1% (2000); Median home value: $61,200 (2000); Median rent: $328 per month (2000); Median age of housing: 58 years (2000).
Newspapers: Augusta Area Times (1 x week)
Transportation: Commute to work: 84.2% car, 1.2% public transportation, 8.3% walk, 4.0% work from home (2000); Travel time to work: 47.1% less than 15 minutes, 15.9% 15 to 30 minutes, 27.2% 30 to 45 minutes, 5.5% 45 to 60 minutes, 4.3% 60 minutes or more (2000)

BRIDGE CREEK (town). Covers a land area of 102.432 square miles and a water area of 1.836 square miles. Located at 44.68° N. Lat.; 91.06° W. Long.
Population: 1,844 (2000); Race: 98.6% White, 0.1% Black, 0.3% Asian, 0.0% American Indian and Alaska Native, 0.3% Hispanic of any race, 1.0% two or more races (2000); Density: 18.0 persons per square mile (2000); Age: 38.5% under 18, 8.5% over 64 (2000); Marriage status: 24.8% never married, 66.2% now married, 2.7% widowed, 6.4% divorced (2000); Foreign born: 0.9% (2000); Ancestry (includes multiple ancestries): 44.5% German, 14.9% Norwegian, 7.1% United States or American, 5.3% English, 4.5% Irish (2000).
Economy: Employment by occupation: 20.8% management, 10.3% professional, 14.5% services, 20.1% sales, 2.0% farming, 12.6% construction, 19.8% production (2000).
Income: Per capita income: $11,793 (2000); Median household income: $34,348 (2000); Poverty rate: 27.4% (2000).
Taxes: Total city taxes per capita: $129 (1997); City property taxes per capita: $128 (1997).
Education: High school graduation rate: 68.1% (2000); College graduation rate: 11.8% (2000).

Housing: Homeownership rate: 90.8% (2000); Median home value: $93,100 (2000); Median rent: $275 per month (2000); Median age of housing: 34 years (2000).
Transportation: Commute to work: 71.2% car, 0.6% public transportation, 8.7% walk, 18.7% work from home (2000); Travel time to work: 35.8% less than 15 minutes, 21.6% 15 to 30 minutes, 25.5% 30 to 45 minutes, 7.9% 45 to 60 minutes, 9.2% 60 minutes or more (2000)

BRUNSWICK (town). Covers a land area of 36.579 square miles and a water area of 0.782 square miles. Located at 44.73° N. Lat.; 91.57° W. Long.
Population: 1,598 (2000); Race: 97.6% White, 0.0% Black, 0.6% Asian, 0.6% American Indian and Alaska Native, 1.1% Hispanic of any race, 0.3% two or more races (2000); Density: 43.7 persons per square mile (2000); Age: 23.4% under 18, 13.4% over 64 (2000); Marriage status: 21.0% never married, 65.7% now married, 4.2% widowed, 9.1% divorced (2000); Foreign born: 1.2% (2000); Ancestry (includes multiple ancestries): 42.1% German, 27.9% Norwegian, 7.7% English, 7.1% Irish, 5.7% Polish (2000).
Economy: Employment by occupation: 10.7% management, 17.8% professional, 12.4% services, 22.8% sales, 0.8% farming, 11.9% construction, 23.6% production (2000).
Income: Per capita income: $21,774 (2000); Median household income: $46,458 (2000); Poverty rate: 4.0% (2000).
Taxes: Total city taxes per capita: $30 (1997); City property taxes per capita: $22 (1997).
Education: High school graduation rate: 85.0% (2000); College graduation rate: 19.2% (2000).
Housing: Homeownership rate: 92.5% (2000); Median home value: $117,000 (2000); Median rent: $380 per month (2000); Median age of housing: 27 years (2000).
Transportation: Commute to work: 91.6% car, 1.3% public transportation, 2.6% walk, 4.5% work from home (2000); Travel time to work: 23.9% less than 15 minutes, 55.1% 15 to 30 minutes, 14.4% 30 to 45 minutes, 2.6% 45 to 60 minutes, 4.1% 60 minutes or more (2000)

CLEAR CREEK (town). Covers a land area of 35.943 square miles and a water area of 0 square miles. Located at 44.64° N. Lat.; 91.34° W. Long.
Population: 712 (2000); Race: 99.1% White, 0.6% Black, 0.0% Asian, 0.0% American Indian and Alaska Native, 0.3% Hispanic of any race, 0.0% two or more races (2000); Density: 19.8 persons per square mile (2000); Age: 26.3% under 18, 12.7% over 64 (2000); Marriage status: 21.7% never married, 67.2% now married, 3.5% widowed, 7.7% divorced (2000); Foreign born: 0.3% (2000); Ancestry (includes multiple ancestries): 46.5% German, 35.4% Norwegian, 11.5% Irish, 6.3% Polish, 5.8% English (2000).
Economy: Employment by occupation: 20.8% management, 14.3% professional, 10.7% services, 16.9% sales, 2.6% farming, 16.4% construction, 18.2% production (2000).
Income: Per capita income: $17,360 (2000); Median household income: $44,833 (2000); Poverty rate: 7.6% (2000).
Taxes: Total city taxes per capita: $101 (1997); City property taxes per capita: $99 (1997).
Education: High school graduation rate: 87.7% (2000); College graduation rate: 12.3% (2000).
Housing: Homeownership rate: 85.8% (2000); Median home value: $80,600 (2000); Median rent: $369 per month (2000); Median age of housing: 50 years (2000).
Transportation: Commute to work: 80.8% car, 0.0% public transportation, 1.8% walk, 16.3% work from home (2000); Travel time to work: 17.2% less than 15 minutes, 46.7% 15 to 30 minutes, 26.3% 30 to 45 minutes, 4.7% 45 to 60 minutes, 5.0% 60 minutes or more (2000)

DRAMMEN (town). Covers a land area of 35.931 square miles and a water area of <.001 square miles. Located at 44.64° N. Lat.; 91.59° W. Long.
Population: 800 (2000); Race: 99.6% White, 0.0% Black, 0.0% Asian, 0.0% American Indian and Alaska Native, 1.6% Hispanic of any race, 0.4% two or more races (2000); Density: 22.3 persons per square mile (2000); Age: 27.6% under 18, 12.0% over 64 (2000); Marriage status: 19.3% never married, 68.4% now married, 4.7% widowed, 7.6% divorced (2000); Foreign born: 0.8% (2000); Ancestry (includes multiple ancestries): 37.4% German, 35.9% Norwegian, 9.4% Irish, 7.9% English, 5.7% Austrian (2000).
Economy: Employment by occupation: 9.1% management, 23.6% professional, 8.4% services, 26.7% sales, 1.2% farming, 12.7% construction, 18.3% production (2000).
Income: Per capita income: $19,939 (2000); Median household income: $46,827 (2000); Poverty rate: 5.4% (2000).
Education: High school graduation rate: 86.1% (2000); College graduation rate: 18.9% (2000).
Housing: Homeownership rate: 88.4% (2000); Median home value: $98,800 (2000); Median rent: $363 per month (2000); Median age of housing: 35 years (2000).
Transportation: Commute to work: 93.5% car, 0.0% public transportation, 0.7% walk, 5.3% work from home (2000); Travel time to work: 12.2% less than 15 minutes, 58.2% 15 to 30 minutes, 18.6% 30 to 45 minutes, 4.3% 45 to 60 minutes, 6.6% 60 minutes or more (2000)

EAU CLAIRE (city). Covers a land area of 30.280 square miles and a water area of 2.085 square miles. Located at 44.81° N. Lat.; 91.49° W. Long. Elevation is 850 feet.
History: The first claims were staked here in the 1840's by Jeremiah Thomas and Stephen S. McCann, though logging had been going on for some years before that. Eau Claire County was organized in 1856, and more settlers arrived. The white pine that grew here was the basis for Eau Claire's timber economy, with many sawmills operating along the Eau Claire and Chippewa Rivers. When logging declined, paper and pulp mills replaced the sawmills, and wood product factories developed.
Population: 61,704 (2000); Race: 93.5% White, 0.6% Black, 3.6% Asian, 0.8% American Indian and Alaska Native, 0.9% Hispanic of any race, 1.2% two or more races (2000); Density: 2,037.8 persons per square mile (2000); Age: 21.5% under 18, 11.9% over 64 (2000); Marriage status: 39.4% never married, 46.3% now married, 5.7% widowed, 8.6% divorced (2000); Foreign born: 2.7% (2000); Ancestry (includes multiple ancestries): 41.7% German, 25.0% Norwegian, 11.9% Irish, 7.2% Other groups, 6.8% English (2000).
Vital Statistics: Birth rate: 110.2 per 10,000 population (1998)
Economy: Unemployment rate: 4.2% (11/2002); Total civilian labor force: 36,178 (11/2002); Single-family building permits issued: 169 (2001) / 188 (2000); Multi-family building permits issued: 328 (2001) / 284 (2000); Employment by occupation: 9.7% management, 20.5% professional, 18.2% services, 29.9% sales, 0.3% farming, 6.6% construction, 14.7% production (2000).
Income: Per capita income: $18,230 (2000); Median household income: $36,399 (2000); Poverty rate: 13.6% (2000).
Taxes: Total city taxes per capita: $302 (2000); City property taxes per capita: $260 (2000).
Education: High school graduation rate: 90.3% (2000); College graduation rate: 28.9% (2000).

School District(s)

Eau Claire Area (PK-12)
2000 Enrollment: 11,268 715-833-3465

Four-year College(s)

Immanuel Lutheran College (Private, Not-for-profit, Multiple Protestant Denomination)
2001 Enrollment: n/a 715-836-6621
2001 Tuition: In-state $2,700; Out-of-state $2,700
University of Wisconsin-Eau Claire (Public)
2001 Enrollment: 10,802 715-836-2637
2001 Tuition: In-state $2,876; Out-of-state $11,388

Two-year College(s)

Professional Hair Design Academy (Private, For-profit)
2001 Enrollment: 80 715-835-3375
Chippewa Valley Technical College (Public)
2001 Enrollment: 4,582 715-833-6200
2001 Tuition: In-state $2,176; Out-of-state $17,000

Housing: Homeownership rate: 57.4% (2000); Median home value: $92,800 (2000); Median rent: $412 per month (2000); Median age of housing: 33 years (2000).
Hospitals: Sacred Heart Hospital (344 beds)
Safety: Violent crime rate: 22.7 per 10,000 population; Property crime rate: 429.0 per 10,000 population (2001).
Newspapers: Leader-Telegram (7 x week)
Transportation: Commute to work: 87.9% car, 1.7% public transportation, 6.7% walk, 2.4% work from home (2000); Travel time to work: 57.6% less than 15 minutes, 32.7% 15 to 30 minutes, 5.4% 30 to 45 minutes, 1.5% 45 to 60 minutes, 2.8% 60 minutes or more (2000); Amtrak: Service available.
Airports: Chippewa Valley Regional (primary service)

Additional Information Contacts

Eau Claire Area Convention & Visitors Bureau 715-831-2345
Eau Claire Chamber of Commerce 715-834-1204
Realtors Association of The Chippewa Valley 715-835-0923

FAIRCHILD (village). Covers a land area of 1.456 square miles and a water area of 0.025 square miles. Located at 44.60° N. Lat.; 90.96° W. Long. Elevation is 1,080 feet.

Population: 564 (2000); Race: 99.3% White, 0.0% Black, 0.0% Asian, 0.4% American Indian and Alaska Native, 1.7% Hispanic of any race, 0.4% two or more races (2000); Density: 387.4 persons per square mile (2000); Age: 26.0% under 18, 22.1% over 64 (2000); Marriage status: 18.8% never married, 58.9% now married, 10.7% widowed, 11.6% divorced (2000); Foreign born: 1.3% (2000); Ancestry (includes multiple ancestries): 45.0% German, 23.2% Norwegian, 7.6% Irish, 6.5% Polish, 6.1% English (2000).
Economy: Employment by occupation: 7.4% management, 7.9% professional, 20.1% services, 22.8% sales, 3.2% farming, 9.0% construction, 29.6% production (2000).
Income: Per capita income: $12,729 (2000); Median household income: $23,625 (2000); Poverty rate: 18.0% (2000).
Taxes: Total city taxes per capita: $127 (1997); City property taxes per capita: $125 (1997).
Education: High school graduation rate: 60.0% (2000); College graduation rate: 3.6% (2000).
Housing: Homeownership rate: 72.8% (2000); Median home value: $43,900 (2000); Median rent: $294 per month (2000); Median age of housing: 50 years (2000).
Transportation: Commute to work: 89.9% car, 1.1% public transportation, 6.9% walk, 2.1% work from home (2000); Travel time to work: 31.9% less than 15 minutes, 31.9% 15 to 30 minutes, 18.4% 30 to 45 minutes, 4.3% 45 to 60 minutes, 13.5% 60 minutes or more (2000)

FAIRCHILD (town). Covers a land area of 34.495 square miles and a water area of 0.033 square miles. Located at 44.62° N. Lat.; 91.00° W. Long. Elevation is 1,080 feet.
Population: 351 (2000); Race: 94.8% White, 0.0% Black, 0.0% Asian, 0.0% American Indian and Alaska Native, 1.4% Hispanic of any race, 3.8% two or more races (2000); Density: 10.2 persons per square mile (2000); Age: 30.7% under 18, 14.0% over 64 (2000); Marriage status: 26.4% never married, 59.0% now married, 3.7% widowed, 11.0% divorced (2000); Foreign born: 1.4% (2000); Ancestry (includes multiple ancestries): 41.1% German, 9.9% Norwegian, 9.3% Irish, 9.0% United States or American, 5.5% English (2000).
Economy: In hilly stock-raising region. East terminus of Buffalo River State Trail. Employment by occupation: 18.9% management, 13.3% professional, 23.8% services, 14.7% sales, 1.4% farming, 8.4% construction, 19.6% production (2000).
Income: Per capita income: $11,163 (2000); Median household income: $30,625 (2000); Poverty rate: 21.6% (2000).
Taxes: Total city taxes per capita: $90 (1997); City property taxes per capita: $90 (1997).
Education: High school graduation rate: 66.7% (2000); College graduation rate: 5.0% (2000).
Housing: Homeownership rate: 96.7% (2000); Median home value: $77,000 (2000); Median rent: $175 per month (2000); Median age of housing: 32 years (2000).
Transportation: Commute to work: 80.0% car, 0.0% public transportation, 2.9% walk, 17.1% work from home (2000); Travel time to work: 34.5% less than 15 minutes, 24.1% 15 to 30 minutes, 15.5% 30 to 45 minutes, 8.6% 45 to 60 minutes, 17.2% 60 minutes or more (2000)

FALL CREEK (village). Covers a land area of 1.572 square miles and a water area of 0.030 square miles. Located at 44.76° N. Lat.; 91.27° W. Long. Elevation is 935 feet.
Population: 1,236 (2000); Race: 99.1% White, 0.0% Black, 0.0% Asian, 0.5% American Indian and Alaska Native, 0.2% Hispanic of any race, 0.2% two or more races (2000); Density: 786.1 persons per square mile (2000); Age: 27.5% under 18, 20.6% over 64 (2000); Marriage status: 18.8% never married, 60.9% now married, 13.1% widowed, 7.3% divorced (2000); Foreign born: 0.5% (2000); Ancestry (includes multiple ancestries): 61.6% German, 20.3% Norwegian, 4.8% English, 4.5% Irish, 4.0% Swedish (2000).
Economy: Dairying, stock raising. Single-family building permits issued: 5 (2001) / 13 (2000); Multi-family building permits issued: 2 (2001) / 0 (2000); Employment by occupation: 11.5% management, 16.2% professional, 15.7% services, 26.7% sales, 0.0% farming, 11.0% construction, 18.9% production (2000).
Income: Per capita income: $17,566 (2000); Median household income: $40,284 (2000); Poverty rate: 7.7% (2000).
Taxes: Total city taxes per capita: $103 (1997); City property taxes per capita: $95 (1997).
Education: High school graduation rate: 81.0% (2000); College graduation rate: 15.1% (2000).

School District(s)

Fall Creek (PK-12)
2000 Enrollment: 861 715-877-2123

Housing: Homeownership rate: 73.4% (2000); Median home value: $83,600 (2000); Median rent: $373 per month (2000); Median age of housing: 39 years (2000).
Transportation: Commute to work: 87.9% car, 0.0% public transportation, 8.6% walk, 3.5% work from home (2000); Travel time to work: 26.6% less than 15 minutes, 54.5% 15 to 30 minutes, 14.2% 30 to 45 minutes, 2.3% 45 to 60 minutes, 2.5% 60 minutes or more (2000)

LINCOLN (town). Covers a land area of 58.240 square miles and a water area of 0.490 square miles. Located at 44.75° N. Lat.; 91.23° W. Long.
Population: 1,080 (2000); Race: 99.2% White, 0.0% Black, 0.0% Asian, 0.0% American Indian and Alaska Native, 0.0% Hispanic of any race, 0.8% two or more races (2000); Density: 18.5 persons per square mile (2000); Age: 30.5% under 18, 8.7% over 64 (2000); Marriage status: 18.7% never married, 69.8% now married, 4.4% widowed, 7.1% divorced (2000); Foreign born: 0.6% (2000); Ancestry (includes multiple ancestries): 60.8% German, 15.4% Norwegian, 6.3% Irish, 5.6% United States or American, 5.1% English (2000).
Economy: Employment by occupation: 24.9% management, 11.3% professional, 10.4% services, 21.7% sales, 4.4% farming, 9.8% construction, 17.5% production (2000).
Income: Per capita income: $20,678 (2000); Median household income: $48,542 (2000); Poverty rate: 3.3% (2000).
Taxes: Total city taxes per capita: $101 (1997); City property taxes per capita: $100 (1997).
Education: High school graduation rate: 85.5% (2000); College graduation rate: 18.4% (2000).
Housing: Homeownership rate: 89.2% (2000); Median home value: $90,700 (2000); Median rent: $288 per month (2000); Median age of housing: 38 years (2000).
Transportation: Commute to work: 75.2% car, 1.0% public transportation, 6.4% walk, 16.5% work from home (2000); Travel time to work: 31.0% less than 15 minutes, 38.3% 15 to 30 minutes, 22.5% 30 to 45 minutes, 2.5% 45 to 60 minutes, 5.8% 60 minutes or more (2000)

LUDINGTON (town). Covers a land area of 45.771 square miles and a water area of 0.182 square miles. Located at 44.79° N. Lat.; 91.17° W. Long. Elevation is 1,100 feet.
Population: 998 (2000); Race: 99.3% White, 0.0% Black, 0.0% Asian, 0.2% American Indian and Alaska Native, 0.3% Hispanic of any race, 0.2% two or more races (2000); Density: 21.8 persons per square mile (2000); Age: 25.7% under 18, 10.8% over 64 (2000); Marriage status: 21.3% never married, 69.6% now married, 3.4% widowed, 5.7% divorced (2000); Foreign born: 0.3% (2000); Ancestry (includes multiple ancestries): 52.6% German, 15.4% Norwegian, 10.3% United States or American, 9.4% Irish, 5.7% French (except Basque) (2000).
Economy: Employment by occupation: 20.2% management, 11.0% professional, 14.9% services, 13.1% sales, 2.8% farming, 14.2% construction, 23.9% production (2000).
Income: Per capita income: $16,291 (2000); Median household income: $42,396 (2000); Poverty rate: 4.9% (2000).
Taxes: Total city taxes per capita: $33 (1997); City property taxes per capita: $31 (1997).
Education: High school graduation rate: 80.0% (2000); College graduation rate: 11.2% (2000).
Housing: Homeownership rate: 91.5% (2000); Median home value: $70,000 (2000); Median rent: $375 per month (2000); Median age of housing: 33 years (2000).
Transportation: Commute to work: 86.9% car, 1.1% public transportation, 1.1% walk, 10.7% work from home (2000); Travel time to work: 11.5% less than 15 minutes, 41.4% 15 to 30 minutes, 39.3% 30 to 45 minutes, 3.3% 45 to 60 minutes, 4.4% 60 minutes or more (2000)

OTTER CREEK (town). Covers a land area of 35.573 square miles and a water area of 0 square miles. Located at 44.65° N. Lat.; 91.22° W. Long.
Population: 531 (2000); Race: 99.5% White, 0.2% Black, 0.0% Asian, 0.4% American Indian and Alaska Native, 0.0% Hispanic of any race, 0.0% two or more races (2000); Density: 14.9 persons per square mile (2000); Age: 31.2% under 18, 7.4% over 64 (2000); Marriage status: 26.9% never married, 64.3% now married, 2.9% widowed, 5.9% divorced (2000); Foreign born: 0.0% (2000); Ancestry (includes multiple ancestries): 57.8% German, 23.9% Norwegian, 8.0% Irish, 6.2% English, 6.0% Polish (2000).

Economy: Employment by occupation: 24.0% management, 9.6% professional, 8.0% services, 22.4% sales, 7.3% farming, 13.7% construction, 15.0% production (2000).
Income: Per capita income: $17,609 (2000); Median household income: $45,893 (2000); Poverty rate: 4.2% (2000).
Taxes: Total city taxes per capita: $73 (1997); City property taxes per capita: $73 (1997).
Education: High school graduation rate: 88.0% (2000); College graduation rate: 12.9% (2000).
Housing: Homeownership rate: 81.9% (2000); Median home value: $87,200 (2000); Median rent: $400 per month (2000); Median age of housing: 60+ years (2000).
Transportation: Commute to work: 71.8% car, 0.6% public transportation, 6.5% walk, 21.1% work from home (2000); Travel time to work: 46.5% less than 15 minutes, 24.3% 15 to 30 minutes, 23.5% 30 to 45 minutes, 3.7% 45 to 60 minutes, 2.1% 60 minutes or more (2000)

PLEASANT VALLEY (town). Covers a land area of 54.215 square miles and a water area of 0 square miles. Located at 44.67° N. Lat.; 91.46° W. Long.
Population: 2,681 (2000); Race: 98.6% White, 0.0% Black, 0.1% Asian, 0.0% American Indian and Alaska Native, 1.4% Hispanic of any race, 0.7% two or more races (2000); Density: 49.5 persons per square mile (2000); Age: 29.5% under 18, 7.5% over 64 (2000); Marriage status: 19.2% never married, 72.5% now married, 3.4% widowed, 4.8% divorced (2000); Foreign born: 0.5% (2000); Ancestry (includes multiple ancestries): 49.0% German, 34.4% Norwegian, 11.5% English, 9.9% Irish, 7.5% Polish (2000).
Economy: Employment by occupation: 14.9% management, 25.5% professional, 8.9% services, 24.6% sales, 1.2% farming, 11.0% construction, 13.8% production (2000).
Income: Per capita income: $23,539 (2000); Median household income: $61,645 (2000); Poverty rate: 2.0% (2000).
Taxes: Total city taxes per capita: $94 (1997); City property taxes per capita: $91 (1997).
Education: High school graduation rate: 92.0% (2000); College graduation rate: 30.3% (2000).
Housing: Homeownership rate: 93.5% (2000); Median home value: $146,100 (2000); Median rent: $398 per month (2000); Median age of housing: 23 years (2000).
Transportation: Commute to work: 92.5% car, 0.3% public transportation, 2.3% walk, 5.0% work from home (2000); Travel time to work: 18.5% less than 15 minutes, 58.4% 15 to 30 minutes, 18.9% 30 to 45 minutes, 1.6% 45 to 60 minutes, 2.7% 60 minutes or more (2000)

SEYMOUR (town). Covers a land area of 31.159 square miles and a water area of 1.073 square miles. Located at 44.83° N. Lat.; 91.37° W. Long.
Population: 2,978 (2000); Race: 98.8% White, 0.7% Black, 0.0% Asian, 0.0% American Indian and Alaska Native, 0.6% Hispanic of any race, 0.4% two or more races (2000); Density: 95.6 persons per square mile (2000); Age: 26.1% under 18, 11.8% over 64 (2000); Marriage status: 21.6% never married, 66.0% now married, 4.0% widowed, 8.4% divorced (2000); Foreign born: 0.2% (2000); Ancestry (includes multiple ancestries): 48.3% German, 20.5% Norwegian, 14.8% Irish, 8.3% English, 5.4% French (except Basque) (2000).
Economy: Single-family building permits issued: 21 (2001) / 18 (2000); Multi-family building permits issued: 0 (2001) / 0 (2000); Employment by occupation: 11.9% management, 21.1% professional, 12.2% services, 27.3% sales, 0.0% farming, 10.6% construction, 16.8% production (2000).
Income: Per capita income: $20,263 (2000); Median household income: $48,365 (2000); Poverty rate: 3.7% (2000).
Taxes: Total city taxes per capita: $62 (1997); City property taxes per capita: $54 (1997).
Education: High school graduation rate: 89.3% (2000); College graduation rate: 22.0% (2000).
Housing: Homeownership rate: 91.1% (2000); Median home value: $111,300 (2000); Median rent: $468 per month (2000); Median age of housing: 28 years (2000).
Transportation: Commute to work: 92.8% car, 0.0% public transportation, 2.5% walk, 3.3% work from home (2000); Travel time to work: 27.2% less than 15 minutes, 56.0% 15 to 30 minutes, 7.6% 30 to 45 minutes, 3.0% 45 to 60 minutes, 6.2% 60 minutes or more (2000)

UNION (town). Covers a land area of 27.938 square miles and a water area of 0.476 square miles. Located at 44.82° N. Lat.; 91.58° W. Long. Elevation is 915 feet.
Population: 2,402 (2000); Race: 93.4% White, 0.0% Black, 4.5% Asian, 1.1% American Indian and Alaska Native, 1.3% Hispanic of any race, 0.1% two or more races (2000); Density: 86.0 persons per square mile (2000); Age: 28.0% under 18, 11.4% over 64 (2000); Marriage status: 20.9% never married, 66.5% now married, 3.5% widowed, 9.1% divorced (2000); Foreign born: 1.7% (2000); Ancestry (includes multiple ancestries): 40.8% German, 31.6% Norwegian, 8.1% Irish, 7.1% Other groups, 6.2% Polish (2000).
Economy: Single-family building permits issued: 23 (2001) / 26 (2000); Multi-family building permits issued: 0 (2001) / 2 (2000); Employment by occupation: 12.9% management, 14.2% professional, 13.1% services, 26.6% sales, 1.0% farming, 11.0% construction, 21.2% production (2000).
Income: Per capita income: $20,518 (2000); Median household income: $52,333 (2000); Poverty rate: 5.4% (2000).
Taxes: Total city taxes per capita: $94 (1997); City property taxes per capita: $83 (1997).
Education: High school graduation rate: 89.2% (2000); College graduation rate: 22.2% (2000).
Housing: Homeownership rate: 85.8% (2000); Median home value: $111,100 (2000); Median rent: $525 per month (2000); Median age of housing: 30 years (2000).
Transportation: Commute to work: 92.5% car, 0.7% public transportation, 1.2% walk, 4.8% work from home (2000); Travel time to work: 43.8% less than 15 minutes, 42.9% 15 to 30 minutes, 8.2% 30 to 45 minutes, 0.9% 45 to 60 minutes, 4.2% 60 minutes or more (2000)

WASHINGTON (town). Covers a land area of 56.059 square miles and a water area of 0.470 square miles. Located at 44.77° N. Lat.; 91.42° W. Long.
Population: 6,995 (2000); Race: 96.1% White, 0.4% Black, 1.5% Asian, 0.3% American Indian and Alaska Native, 1.0% Hispanic of any race, 0.9% two or more races (2000); Density: 124.8 persons per square mile (2000); Age: 26.8% under 18, 10.4% over 64 (2000); Marriage status: 20.6% never married, 68.5% now married, 4.3% widowed, 6.6% divorced (2000); Foreign born: 2.5% (2000); Ancestry (includes multiple ancestries): 46.2% German, 23.3% Norwegian, 13.3% Irish, 9.2% English, 6.5% Polish (2000).
Economy: Employment by occupation: 12.2% management, 26.0% professional, 10.7% services, 25.6% sales, 0.4% farming, 9.5% construction, 15.7% production (2000).
Income: Per capita income: $27,026 (2000); Median household income: $55,570 (2000); Poverty rate: 4.1% (2000).
Taxes: Total city taxes per capita: $100 (1997); City property taxes per capita: $95 (1997).
Education: High school graduation rate: 91.6% (2000); College graduation rate: 34.7% (2000).
Housing: Homeownership rate: 80.6% (2000); Median home value: $128,200 (2000); Median rent: $428 per month (2000); Median age of housing: 25 years (2000).
Transportation: Commute to work: 93.0% car, 1.7% public transportation, 2.7% walk, 2.5% work from home (2000); Travel time to work: 41.0% less than 15 minutes, 46.0% 15 to 30 minutes, 6.1% 30 to 45 minutes, 3.2% 45 to 60 minutes, 3.7% 60 minutes or more (2000)

WILSON (town). Covers a land area of 47.674 square miles and a water area of 0.037 square miles. Located at 44.83° N. Lat.; 91.00° W. Long. Elevation is 980 feet.
Population: 420 (2000); Race: 97.3% White, 0.0% Black, 0.7% Asian, 0.5% American Indian and Alaska Native, 1.6% Hispanic of any race, 1.6% two or more races (2000); Density: 8.8 persons per square mile (2000); Age: 28.8% under 18, 12.8% over 64 (2000); Marriage status: 20.7% never married, 68.3% now married, 4.3% widowed, 6.7% divorced (2000); Foreign born: 1.1% (2000); Ancestry (includes multiple ancestries): 47.7% German, 12.1% Norwegian, 11.6% United States or American, 10.0% Irish, 8.4% Polish (2000).
Economy: Employment by occupation: 7.7% management, 15.9% professional, 11.8% services, 20.0% sales, 6.2% farming, 13.3% construction, 25.1% production (2000).
Income: Per capita income: $14,970 (2000); Median household income: $36,563 (2000); Poverty rate: 12.2% (2000).
Taxes: Total city taxes per capita: $25 (1997); City property taxes per capita: $23 (1997).
Education: High school graduation rate: 65.1% (2000); College graduation rate: 6.6% (2000).
Housing: Homeownership rate: 90.6% (2000); Median home value: $77,500 (2000); Median rent: $288 per month (2000); Median age of housing: 36 years (2000).

Transportation: Commute to work: 86.5% car, 0.0% public transportation, 1.0% walk, 12.5% work from home (2000); Travel time to work: 16.1% less than 15 minutes, 29.2% 15 to 30 minutes, 31.5% 30 to 45 minutes, 13.7% 45 to 60 minutes, 9.5% 60 minutes or more (2000)

Florence County

Located in northeastern Wisconsin; bounded on the north by the Brule River and the Michigan border, and on the east by the Menominee River and the Michigan border; includes part of Nicolet National Forest. Covers a land area of 488.00 square miles, a water area of 9.40 square miles, and is located in the Central Time Zone. The county government was organized in 1882. County seat is Florence.

Population: 5,088 (2000); Race: 99.3% White, 0.3% Black, 0.1% Asian, 0.2% American Indian and Alaska Native, 0.1% Hispanic of any race, 0.2% two or more races (2000); Density: 10.4 persons per square mile (2000); Age: 23.0% under 18, 17.6% over 64 (2000).

Religion: Five largest groups: 23.4% Catholic Church, 3.3% Wisconsin Evangelical Lutheran Synod, 2.3% Pentecostal Church of God, 1.9% Baptist General Conference, 1.7% Evangelical Lutheran Church in America (2000).

Economy: Unemployment rate: 8.7% (11/2002); Total civilian labor force: 1,927 (11/2002); Leading industries: 34.9% manufacturing; 14.4% retail trade; except pub other services (2000); Companies that employ more than 1,000 persons: 0 (2000); Companies that employ more than 100 persons: 1 (2000); Farms: 86 totaling 19,371 acres (1997); Minority business ownership rate: 0.0% (1997); Women business ownership rate: 0.0% (1997); Retail sales per capita: $2,882 (1997). Single-family building permits issued: 0 (2001) / 0 (2000); Multi-family building permits issued: 0 (2001) / 0 (2000).

Income: Per capita income: $18,328 (2000); Median household income: $34,750 (2000); Poverty rate: 9.1% (2000); Bankruptcy rate: 2.12% (2001).

Taxes: Total county taxes per capita: $346 (1997); County property taxes per capita: $339 (1997).

Education: High school graduation rate: 83.7% (2000); College graduation rate: 12.4% (2000).

Housing: Homeownership rate: 85.6% (2000); Median home value: $82,200 (2000); Median rent: $323 per month (2000); Median age of housing: 28 years (2000).

Health: Birth rate: 88.4 per 10,000 population (1998); Age adjusted death rate: 80.9 per 10,000 population (1999); Age adjusted cancer mortality rate: 219.3 (Unreliable figure as per CDC) deaths per 100,000 population (1999). Air Quality Index: 86% good, 14% moderate, 0% unhealthy (percent of days in 2000). Number of physicians: 3.9 per 10,000 population (1999); Number of hospital beds: n/a (1999).

Elections: 2000 Presidential election results: 33.9% Gore, 63.5% Bush, 2.0% Nader, 0.3% Buchanan

Additional Information Contacts

Florence County Government Offices 715-528-3201

Florence County Communities

AURORA (town). Covers a land area of 37.961 square miles and a water area of 0.408 square miles. Located at 45.75° N. Lat.; 88.10° W. Long. Elevation is 1,072 feet.

Population: 1,186 (2000); Race: 99.4% White, 0.2% Black, 0.0% Asian, 0.4% American Indian and Alaska Native, 0.3% Hispanic of any race, 0.0% two or more races (2000); Density: 31.2 persons per square mile (2000); Age: 25.1% under 18, 15.2% over 64 (2000); Marriage status: 20.3% never married, 62.9% now married, 6.8% widowed, 10.0% divorced (2000); Foreign born: 0.8% (2000); Ancestry (includes multiple ancestries): 29.5% German, 19.8% Swedish, 11.1% French (except Basque), 10.4% Irish, 10.3% English (2000).

Economy: Employment by occupation: 5.5% management, 11.3% professional, 16.0% services, 27.2% sales, 2.3% farming, 17.1% construction, 20.6% production (2000).

Income: Per capita income: $19,226 (2000); Median household income: $34,107 (2000); Poverty rate: 7.2% (2000).

Taxes: Total city taxes per capita: $32 (1997); City property taxes per capita: $30 (1997).

Education: High school graduation rate: 87.6% (2000); College graduation rate: 10.3% (2000).

Housing: Homeownership rate: 84.2% (2000); Median home value: $80,300 (2000); Median rent: $348 per month (2000); Median age of housing: 32 years (2000).

Transportation: Commute to work: 96.2% car, 0.0% public transportation, 1.4% walk, 2.3% work from home (2000); Travel time to work: 47.8% less than 15 minutes, 42.6% 15 to 30 minutes, 3.5% 30 to 45 minutes, 1.8% 45 to 60 minutes, 4.2% 60 minutes or more (2000)

COMMONWEALTH (town). Covers a land area of 42.329 square miles and a water area of 0.610 square miles. Located at 45.87° N. Lat.; 88.27° W. Long. Elevation is 1,360 feet.

Population: 419 (2000); Race: 100.0% White, 0.0% Black, 0.0% Asian, 0.0% American Indian and Alaska Native, 0.0% Hispanic of any race, 0.0% two or more races (2000); Density: 9.9 persons per square mile (2000); Age: 24.5% under 18, 13.4% over 64 (2000); Marriage status: 24.3% never married, 60.0% now married, 6.9% widowed, 8.9% divorced (2000); Foreign born: 0.0% (2000); Ancestry (includes multiple ancestries): 36.2% German, 13.9% Polish, 13.6% Italian, 12.0% Swedish, 11.8% French (except Basque) (2000).

Economy: Employment by occupation: 17.0% management, 16.5% professional, 16.5% services, 17.4% sales, 2.6% farming, 9.1% construction, 20.9% production (2000).

Income: Per capita income: $19,137 (2000); Median household income: $38,015 (2000); Poverty rate: 6.4% (2000).

Taxes: Total city taxes per capita: $26 (1997); City property taxes per capita: $24 (1997).

Education: High school graduation rate: 85.0% (2000); College graduation rate: 17.5% (2000).

Housing: Homeownership rate: 91.7% (2000); Median home value: $82,700 (2000); Median rent: $438 per month (2000); Median age of housing: 29 years (2000).

Transportation: Commute to work: 94.2% car, 0.0% public transportation, 1.3% walk, 3.6% work from home (2000); Travel time to work: 43.1% less than 15 minutes, 38.9% 15 to 30 minutes, 11.6% 30 to 45 minutes, 4.2% 45 to 60 minutes, 2.3% 60 minutes or more (2000)

FENCE (town). Covers a land area of 89.443 square miles and a water area of 0.592 square miles. Located at 45.75° N. Lat.; 88.51° W. Long. Elevation is 1,548 feet.

Population: 231 (2000); Race: 97.9% White, 0.0% Black, 0.9% Asian, 1.3% American Indian and Alaska Native, 0.9% Hispanic of any race, 0.0% two or more races (2000); Density: 2.6 persons per square mile (2000); Age: 22.2% under 18, 17.5% over 64 (2000); Marriage status: 19.3% never married, 63.6% now married, 4.8% widowed, 12.3% divorced (2000); Foreign born: 0.9% (2000); Ancestry (includes multiple ancestries): 35.0% German, 14.5% Irish, 13.2% Polish, 9.4% Swedish, 9.0% United States or American (2000).

Economy: Employment by occupation: 5.9% management, 8.9% professional, 8.9% services, 8.9% sales, 9.9% farming, 13.9% construction, 43.6% production (2000).

Income: Per capita income: $15,169 (2000); Median household income: $30,278 (2000); Poverty rate: 13.3% (2000).

Taxes: Total city taxes per capita: $47 (1997); City property taxes per capita: $47 (1997).

Education: High school graduation rate: 67.9% (2000); College graduation rate: 5.5% (2000).

Housing: Homeownership rate: 91.9% (2000); Median home value: $56,900 (2000); Median rent: $225 per month (2000); Median age of housing: 26 years (2000).

Transportation: Commute to work: 85.3% car, 0.0% public transportation, 6.3% walk, 8.4% work from home (2000); Travel time to work: 20.7% less than 15 minutes, 35.6% 15 to 30 minutes, 37.9% 30 to 45 minutes, 5.7% 45 to 60 minutes, 0.0% 60 minutes or more (2000)

FERN (town). Covers a land area of 33.996 square miles and a water area of 1.168 square miles. Located at 45.86° N. Lat.; 88.34° W. Long. Elevation is 1,380 feet.

Population: 153 (2000); Race: 100.0% White, 0.0% Black, 0.0% Asian, 0.0% American Indian and Alaska Native, 0.0% Hispanic of any race, 0.0% two or more races (2000); Density: 4.5 persons per square mile (2000); Age: 31.0% under 18, 17.1% over 64 (2000); Marriage status: 15.0% never married, 65.4% now married, 9.4% widowed, 10.2% divorced (2000); Foreign born: 0.0% (2000); Ancestry (includes multiple ancestries): 38.0% German, 17.1% Polish, 8.9% Swedish, 7.6% French Canadian, 7.6% Italian (2000).

Economy: Employment by occupation: 12.9% management, 7.1% professional, 17.1% services, 28.6% sales, 7.1% farming, 8.6% construction, 18.6% production (2000).

Income: Per capita income: $16,746 (2000); Median household income: $37,708 (2000); Poverty rate: 10.1% (2000).

Taxes: Total city taxes per capita: $164 (1997); City property taxes per capita: $164 (1997).

Education: High school graduation rate: 88.1% (2000); College graduation rate: 14.7% (2000).
Housing: Homeownership rate: 95.6% (2000); Median home value: $95,000 (2000); Median rent: $225 per month (2000); Median age of housing: 26 years (2000).
Transportation: Commute to work: 91.4% car, 0.0% public transportation, 2.9% walk, 5.7% work from home (2000); Travel time to work: 25.8% less than 15 minutes, 30.3% 15 to 30 minutes, 27.3% 30 to 45 minutes, 10.6% 45 to 60 minutes, 6.1% 60 minutes or more (2000)

FLORENCE (town). Covers a land area of 153.642 square miles and a water area of 4.046 square miles. Located at 45.90° N. Lat.; 88.27° W. Long. Elevation is 1,296 feet.
Population: 2,319 (2000); Race: 99.3% White, 0.5% Black, 0.0% Asian, 0.0% American Indian and Alaska Native, 0.0% Hispanic of any race, 0.2% two or more races (2000); Density: 15.1 persons per square mile (2000); Age: 21.4% under 18, 20.9% over 64 (2000); Marriage status: 16.4% never married, 62.1% now married, 9.8% widowed, 11.6% divorced (2000); Foreign born: 0.6% (2000); Ancestry (includes multiple ancestries): 28.5% German, 12.2% Swedish, 11.6% French (except Basque), 10.8% Irish, 10.7% Polish (2000).
Economy: Lumbering. Employment by occupation: 9.1% management, 20.5% professional, 20.5% services, 15.2% sales, 0.6% farming, 13.0% construction, 21.1% production (2000).
Income: Per capita income: $18,131 (2000); Median household income: $35,640 (2000); Poverty rate: 9.7% (2000).
Taxes: Total city taxes per capita: $204 (2000); City property taxes per capita: $197 (2000).
Education: High school graduation rate: 84.9% (2000); College graduation rate: 14.9% (2000).

School District(s)

Florence (PK-12)
2000 Enrollment: 870 715-528-3217
Housing: Homeownership rate: 82.4% (2000); Median home value: $91,800 (2000); Median rent: $308 per month (2000); Median age of housing: 29 years (2000).
Newspapers: Florence Mining News (1 x week)
Transportation: Commute to work: 95.9% car, 0.0% public transportation, 2.1% walk, 1.8% work from home (2000); Travel time to work: 36.7% less than 15 minutes, 43.4% 15 to 30 minutes, 15.7% 30 to 45 minutes, 1.5% 45 to 60 minutes, 2.7% 60 minutes or more (2000)

HOMESTEAD (town). Covers a land area of 53.856 square miles and a water area of 0.465 square miles. Located at 45.76° N. Lat.; 88.27° W. Long.
Population: 378 (2000); Race: 98.7% White, 0.0% Black, 0.5% Asian, 0.8% American Indian and Alaska Native, 0.0% Hispanic of any race, 0.0% two or more races (2000); Density: 7.0 persons per square mile (2000); Age: 22.5% under 18, 11.8% over 64 (2000); Marriage status: 19.3% never married, 63.9% now married, 2.8% widowed, 13.9% divorced (2000); Foreign born: 0.5% (2000); Ancestry (includes multiple ancestries): 30.9% German, 23.3% Swedish, 10.5% Norwegian, 9.2% Irish, 8.9% English (2000).
Economy: Employment by occupation: 11.0% management, 15.4% professional, 18.1% services, 20.3% sales, 1.1% farming, 11.0% construction, 23.1% production (2000).
Income: Per capita income: $21,491 (2000); Median household income: $31,944 (2000); Poverty rate: 4.2% (2000).
Taxes: Total city taxes per capita: $73 (1997); City property taxes per capita: $73 (1997).
Education: High school graduation rate: 82.0% (2000); College graduation rate: 11.9% (2000).
Housing: Homeownership rate: 96.4% (2000); Median home value: $67,500 (2000); Median rent: $325 per month (2000); Median age of housing: 22 years (2000).
Transportation: Commute to work: 92.2% car, 0.0% public transportation, 3.4% walk, 3.4% work from home (2000); Travel time to work: 19.1% less than 15 minutes, 57.8% 15 to 30 minutes, 16.2% 30 to 45 minutes, 3.5% 45 to 60 minutes, 3.5% 60 minutes or more (2000)

LONG LAKE (town). Covers a land area of 33.986 square miles and a water area of 1.853 square miles. Located at 45.85° N. Lat.; 88.62° W. Long. Elevation is 1,550 feet.
Population: 197 (2000); Race: 97.8% White, 0.0% Black, 0.0% Asian, 0.0% American Indian and Alaska Native, 0.0% Hispanic of any race, 2.2% two or more races (2000); Density: 5.8 persons per square mile (2000); Age: 16.3% under 18, 18.5% over 64 (2000); Marriage status: 8.6% never married, 75.0% now married, 7.9% widowed, 8.6% divorced (2000); Foreign born: 0.0% (2000); Ancestry (includes multiple ancestries): 36.5% German, 16.3% English, 15.7% Irish, 11.8% Polish, 11.2% French (except Basque) (2000).
Economy: Employment by occupation: 7.8% management, 3.9% professional, 27.5% services, 29.4% sales, 0.0% farming, 3.9% construction, 27.5% production (2000).
Income: Per capita income: $15,818 (2000); Median household income: $27,500 (2000); Poverty rate: 18.5% (2000).
Taxes: Total city taxes per capita: $85 (1997); City property taxes per capita: $81 (1997).
Education: High school graduation rate: 81.1% (2000); College graduation rate: 1.4% (2000).
Housing: Homeownership rate: 80.7% (2000); Median home value: $63,600 (2000); Median rent: $300 per month (2000); Median age of housing: 19 years (2000).
Transportation: Commute to work: 72.5% car, 0.0% public transportation, 15.7% walk, 9.8% work from home (2000); Travel time to work: 52.2% less than 15 minutes, 4.3% 15 to 30 minutes, 21.7% 30 to 45 minutes, 15.2% 45 to 60 minutes, 6.5% 60 minutes or more (2000)

TIPLER (town). Covers a land area of 42.821 square miles and a water area of 0.288 square miles. Located at 45.95° N. Lat.; 88.61° W. Long. Elevation is 1,537 feet.
Population: 205 (2000); Race: 100.0% White, 0.0% Black, 0.0% Asian, 0.0% American Indian and Alaska Native, 0.0% Hispanic of any race, 0.0% two or more races (2000); Density: 4.8 persons per square mile (2000); Age: 28.4% under 18, 11.5% over 64 (2000); Marriage status: 15.2% never married, 63.0% now married, 7.2% widowed, 14.5% divorced (2000); Foreign born: 0.0% (2000); Ancestry (includes multiple ancestries): 27.9% German, 26.8% Irish, 20.8% French (except Basque), 8.7% United States or American, 7.1% English (2000).
Economy: Employment by occupation: 10.0% management, 2.5% professional, 17.5% services, 25.0% sales, 3.8% farming, 10.0% construction, 31.3% production (2000).
Income: Per capita income: $14,406 (2000); Median household income: $31,250 (2000); Poverty rate: 16.0% (2000).
Taxes: Total city taxes per capita: $35 (1997); City property taxes per capita: $30 (1997).
Education: High school graduation rate: 63.3% (2000); College graduation rate: 1.7% (2000).
Housing: Homeownership rate: 86.3% (2000); Median home value: $63,300 (2000); Median rent: $308 per month (2000); Median age of housing: 29 years (2000).
Transportation: Commute to work: 97.5% car, 0.0% public transportation, 0.0% walk, 2.5% work from home (2000); Travel time to work: 30.8% less than 15 minutes, 23.1% 15 to 30 minutes, 19.2% 30 to 45 minutes, 12.8% 45 to 60 minutes, 14.1% 60 minutes or more (2000)

Fond du Lac County

Located in eastern Wisconsin; drained by the Milwaukee, Rock, Sheboygan, and Fond du Lac Rivers; includes part of Lake Winnebago. Covers a land area of 722.90 square miles, a water area of 42.90 square miles, and is located in the Central Time Zone. The county government was organized in 1836. County seat is Fond du Lac.

Weather Station: Fond Du Lac — Elevation: 757 feet

	Jan	Feb	Mar	Apr	May	Jun	Jul	Aug	Sep	Oct	Nov	Dec
High	24	29	40	54	68	77	82	79	71	58	43	30
Low	9	13	24	36	48	57	62	60	52	41	28	16
Precip	1.1	0.9	1.8	2.7	2.9	3.3	3.5	4.1	3.5	2.5	2.0	1.4
Snow	11.1	7.4	7.0	1.8	0.1	0.0	0.0	0.0	0.0	0.1	3.3	9.4

High and Low temperatures in degrees Fahrenheit; Precipitation and Snow in inches

Population: 97,296 (2000); Race: 96.1% White, 1.0% Black, 0.6% Asian, 0.6% American Indian and Alaska Native, 2.1% Hispanic of any race, 0.8% two or more races (2000); Density: 134.6 persons per square mile (2000); Age: 25.2% under 18, 14.3% over 64 (2000).
Religion: Five largest groups: 35.9% Catholic Church, 8.0% Wisconsin Evangelical Lutheran Synod, 5.6% Evangelical Lutheran Church in America, 4.2% United Church of Christ, 3.2% Lutheran Church—Missouri Synod (2000).
Economy: Unemployment rate: 3.9% (11/2002); Total civilian labor force: 57,156 (11/2002); Leading industries: 26.9% manufacturing; 13.9% retail trade; 10.6% health care and social assistance (2000); Companies that employ more than 1,000 persons: 4 (2000); Companies that employ more than 100 persons: 81 (2000); Farms: 1,488 totaling 324,893 acres (1997); Minority

business ownership rate: 2.1% (1997); Women business ownership rate: 25.6% (1997); Retail sales per capita: $9,442 (1997). Single-family building permits issued: 328 (2001) / 347 (2000); Multi-family building permits issued: 237 (2001) / 68 (2000).
Income: Per capita income: $20,022 (2000); Median household income: $45,578 (2000); Poverty rate: 5.8% (2000); Bankruptcy rate: 4.35% (2001).
Taxes: Total county taxes per capita: $169 (2000); County property taxes per capita: $165 (2000).
Education: High school graduation rate: 84.2% (2000); College graduation rate: 16.9% (2000).
Housing: Homeownership rate: 73.0% (2000); Median home value: $101,000 (2000); Median rent: $441 per month (2000); Median age of housing: 39 years (2000).
Health: Birth rate: 117.2 per 10,000 population (1998); Age adjusted death rate: 79.6 per 10,000 population (1999); Age adjusted cancer mortality rate: 195.6 deaths per 100,000 population (1999). Air Quality Index: 76% good, 24% moderate, 0% unhealthy (percent of days in 2000). Number of physicians: 14.6 per 10,000 population (1999); Number of hospital beds: 19.1 per 10,000 population (1999).
Elections: 2000 Presidential election results: 39.0% Gore, 57.0% Bush, 3.0% Nader, 0.6% Buchanan
National and State Parks: Eldorado State Public Hunting Grounds; Mullet River State Wildlife Area; Saint Cloud State Wildlife Areas
Additional Information Contacts
Fond du Lac County Government Offices 920-929-3155
Fond du Lac Association of Commerce 920-921-9500
Green Lake County Ripon Area Board of Realtors 920-748-7007
Ripon Chamber of Commerce 920-748-6764

Fond du Lac County Communities

ALTO (town). Covers a land area of 36.302 square miles and a water area of 0 square miles. Located at 43.69° N. Lat.; 88.83° W. Long. Elevation is 950 feet.
Population: 1,103 (2000); Race: 99.2% White, 0.5% Black, 0.2% Asian, 0.0% American Indian and Alaska Native, 1.2% Hispanic of any race, 0.0% two or more races (2000); Density: 30.4 persons per square mile (2000); Age: 32.5% under 18, 10.9% over 64 (2000); Marriage status: 23.1% never married, 71.4% now married, 2.0% widowed, 3.5% divorced (2000); Foreign born: 0.4% (2000); Ancestry (includes multiple ancestries): 51.3% Dutch, 38.3% German, 5.4% United States or American, 5.0% Norwegian, 4.3% English (2000).
Economy: Single-family building permits issued: 1 (2001) / 3 (2000); Multi-family building permits issued: 0 (2001) / 0 (2000); Employment by occupation: 17.2% management, 10.5% professional, 12.4% services, 21.2% sales, 6.4% farming, 8.5% construction, 23.7% production (2000).
Income: Per capita income: $17,872 (2000); Median household income: $53,235 (2000); Poverty rate: 2.3% (2000).
Taxes: Total city taxes per capita: $118 (1997); City property taxes per capita: $116 (1997).
Education: High school graduation rate: 81.4% (2000); College graduation rate: 9.2% (2000).
Housing: Homeownership rate: 90.4% (2000); Median home value: $102,700 (2000); Median rent: $383 per month (2000); Median age of housing: 60+ years (2000).
Transportation: Commute to work: 82.9% car, 0.0% public transportation, 6.3% walk, 10.8% work from home (2000); Travel time to work: 54.1% less than 15 minutes, 29.1% 15 to 30 minutes, 11.1% 30 to 45 minutes, 2.6% 45 to 60 minutes, 3.0% 60 minutes or more (2000)

ASHFORD (town). Covers a land area of 35.771 square miles and a water area of 0.069 square miles. Located at 43.57° N. Lat.; 88.33° W. Long. Elevation is 1,050 feet.
Population: 1,773 (2000); Race: 97.8% White, 0.0% Black, 0.2% Asian, 0.8% American Indian and Alaska Native, 1.1% Hispanic of any race, 0.9% two or more races (2000); Density: 49.6 persons per square mile (2000); Age: 24.4% under 18, 10.3% over 64 (2000); Marriage status: 25.9% never married, 62.2% now married, 3.7% widowed, 8.2% divorced (2000); Foreign born: 1.5% (2000); Ancestry (includes multiple ancestries): 68.5% German, 9.3% Irish, 4.5% English, 4.5% Polish, 4.0% United States or American (2000).
Economy: Single-family building permits issued: 7 (2001) / 13 (2000); Multi-family building permits issued: 0 (2001) / 0 (2000); Employment by occupation: 13.8% management, 10.0% professional, 10.7% services, 18.3% sales, 1.8% farming, 14.7% construction, 30.7% production (2000).
Income: Per capita income: $21,777 (2000); Median household income: $50,708 (2000); Poverty rate: 3.0% (2000).
Taxes: Total city taxes per capita: $71 (1997); City property taxes per capita: $59 (1997).
Education: High school graduation rate: 81.4% (2000); College graduation rate: 9.7% (2000).
Housing: Homeownership rate: 86.4% (2000); Median home value: $132,300 (2000); Median rent: $423 per month (2000); Median age of housing: 34 years (2000).
Transportation: Commute to work: 91.0% car, 0.2% public transportation, 2.8% walk, 5.1% work from home (2000); Travel time to work: 29.8% less than 15 minutes, 34.6% 15 to 30 minutes, 21.5% 30 to 45 minutes, 8.3% 45 to 60 minutes, 5.9% 60 minutes or more (2000)

AUBURN (town). Covers a land area of 35.179 square miles and a water area of 0.574 square miles. Located at 43.58° N. Lat.; 88.21° W. Long.
Population: 2,075 (2000); Race: 96.0% White, 0.0% Black, 0.0% Asian, 2.1% American Indian and Alaska Native, 0.3% Hispanic of any race, 1.6% two or more races (2000); Density: 59.0 persons per square mile (2000); Age: 27.0% under 18, 9.2% over 64 (2000); Marriage status: 21.8% never married, 69.1% now married, 3.0% widowed, 6.1% divorced (2000); Foreign born: 0.7% (2000); Ancestry (includes multiple ancestries): 71.0% German, 8.8% Irish, 6.2% Polish, 5.3% United States or American, 4.5% Other groups (2000).
Economy: Single-family building permits issued: 20 (2001) / 14 (2000); Multi-family building permits issued: 0 (2001) / 0 (2000); Employment by occupation: 10.3% management, 13.1% professional, 11.4% services, 21.2% sales, 1.2% farming, 11.9% construction, 31.0% production (2000).
Income: Per capita income: $21,013 (2000); Median household income: $57,986 (2000); Poverty rate: 1.3% (2000).
Taxes: Total city taxes per capita: $97 (1997); City property taxes per capita: $90 (1997).
Education: High school graduation rate: 84.8% (2000); College graduation rate: 9.2% (2000).
Housing: Homeownership rate: 90.8% (2000); Median home value: $145,200 (2000); Median rent: $488 per month (2000); Median age of housing: 27 years (2000).
Transportation: Commute to work: 91.9% car, 0.0% public transportation, 1.3% walk, 5.9% work from home (2000); Travel time to work: 23.4% less than 15 minutes, 41.2% 15 to 30 minutes, 18.9% 30 to 45 minutes, 10.1% 45 to 60 minutes, 6.4% 60 minutes or more (2000)

BRANDON (village). Covers a land area of 0.782 square miles and a water area of 0 square miles. Located at 43.73° N. Lat.; 88.78° W. Long. Elevation is 999 feet.
Population: 912 (2000); Race: 96.8% White, 1.0% Black, 0.2% Asian, 0.3% American Indian and Alaska Native, 1.0% Hispanic of any race, 0.7% two or more races (2000); Density: 1,165.9 persons per square mile (2000); Age: 28.4% under 18, 14.6% over 64 (2000); Marriage status: 21.8% never married, 65.2% now married, 6.6% widowed, 6.4% divorced (2000); Foreign born: 1.3% (2000); Ancestry (includes multiple ancestries): 46.5% German, 24.4% Dutch, 7.8% English, 7.5% Irish, 5.5% United States or American (2000).
Economy: Railroad junction in agricultural area: dairy products; meat processing. Single-family building permits issued: 1 (2001) / 3 (2000); Multi-family building permits issued: 0 (2001) / 0 (2000); Employment by occupation: 9.2% management, 11.6% professional, 20.8% services, 19.4% sales, 1.2% farming, 9.8% construction, 27.9% production (2000).
Income: Per capita income: $17,437 (2000); Median household income: $43,542 (2000); Poverty rate: 5.3% (2000).
Taxes: Total city taxes per capita: $109 (1997); City property taxes per capita: $107 (1997).
Education: High school graduation rate: 84.5% (2000); College graduation rate: 15.3% (2000).
Housing: Homeownership rate: 77.2% (2000); Median home value: $81,200 (2000); Median rent: $317 per month (2000); Median age of housing: 60+ years (2000).
Transportation: Commute to work: 90.2% car, 1.0% public transportation, 4.5% walk, 3.1% work from home (2000); Travel time to work: 31.8% less than 15 minutes, 34.5% 15 to 30 minutes, 23.2% 30 to 45 minutes, 6.5% 45 to 60 minutes, 4.0% 60 minutes or more (2000)

BYRON (town). Covers a land area of 36.318 square miles and a water area of 0 square miles. Located at 43.68° N. Lat.; 88.45° W. Long. Elevation is 1,060 feet.

Population: 1,550 (2000); Race: 99.5% White, 0.0% Black, 0.1% Asian, 0.2% American Indian and Alaska Native, 2.7% Hispanic of any race, 0.1% two or more races (2000); Density: 42.7 persons per square mile (2000); Age: 25.9% under 18, 11.2% over 64 (2000); Marriage status: 26.6% never married, 62.3% now married, 5.6% widowed, 5.5% divorced (2000); Foreign born: 1.5% (2000); Ancestry (includes multiple ancestries): 57.8% German, 10.7% Irish, 7.1% English, 5.6% Polish, 5.3% Other groups (2000).
Economy: Single-family building permits issued: 10 (2001) / 7 (2000); Multi-family building permits issued: 0 (2001) / 0 (2000); Employment by occupation: 13.9% management, 10.8% professional, 11.6% services, 24.5% sales, 2.1% farming, 12.7% construction, 24.3% production (2000).
Income: Per capita income: $22,593 (2000); Median household income: $56,667 (2000); Poverty rate: 4.9% (2000).
Taxes: Total city taxes per capita: $47 (1997); City property taxes per capita: $44 (1997).
Education: High school graduation rate: 88.2% (2000); College graduation rate: 13.2% (2000).
Housing: Homeownership rate: 88.5% (2000); Median home value: $126,000 (2000); Median rent: $445 per month (2000); Median age of housing: 37 years (2000).
Transportation: Commute to work: 88.6% car, 0.2% public transportation, 4.1% walk, 6.6% work from home (2000); Travel time to work: 37.6% less than 15 minutes, 46.8% 15 to 30 minutes, 8.5% 30 to 45 minutes, 3.7% 45 to 60 minutes, 3.4% 60 minutes or more (2000)

CALUMET (town). Covers a land area of 30.179 square miles and a water area of 13.908 square miles. Located at 43.91° N. Lat.; 88.27° W. Long.
Population: 1,514 (2000); Race: 98.4% White, 0.0% Black, 0.0% Asian, 1.0% American Indian and Alaska Native, 1.3% Hispanic of any race, 0.6% two or more races (2000); Density: 50.2 persons per square mile (2000); Age: 23.1% under 18, 14.9% over 64 (2000); Marriage status: 26.5% never married, 62.7% now married, 5.0% widowed, 5.8% divorced (2000); Foreign born: 0.7% (2000); Ancestry (includes multiple ancestries): 70.7% German, 6.6% Irish, 4.2% English, 4.2% United States or American, 3.6% Other groups (2000).
Economy: Single-family building permits issued: 7 (2001) / 7 (2000); Multi-family building permits issued: 0 (2001) / 0 (2000); Employment by occupation: 16.8% management, 10.5% professional, 11.1% services, 18.1% sales, 2.1% farming, 11.6% construction, 29.7% production (2000).
Income: Per capita income: $19,707 (2000); Median household income: $45,789 (2000); Poverty rate: 5.4% (2000).
Taxes: Total city taxes per capita: $77 (1997); City property taxes per capita: $74 (1997).
Education: High school graduation rate: 79.8% (2000); College graduation rate: 11.7% (2000).
Housing: Homeownership rate: 85.8% (2000); Median home value: $117,500 (2000); Median rent: $388 per month (2000); Median age of housing: 53 years (2000).
Transportation: Commute to work: 83.9% car, 2.1% public transportation, 3.8% walk, 10.2% work from home (2000); Travel time to work: 26.6% less than 15 minutes, 47.3% 15 to 30 minutes, 17.4% 30 to 45 minutes, 3.2% 45 to 60 minutes, 5.5% 60 minutes or more (2000)

CAMPBELLSPORT (village). Covers a land area of 1.165 square miles and a water area of 0.002 square miles. Located at 43.59° N. Lat.; 88.28° W. Long. Elevation is 1,050 feet.
History: Incorporated 1902.
Population: 1,913 (2000); Race: 98.6% White, 0.1% Black, 0.0% Asian, 0.5% American Indian and Alaska Native, 0.1% Hispanic of any race, 0.7% two or more races (2000); Density: 1,642.0 persons per square mile (2000); Age: 22.0% under 18, 24.1% over 64 (2000); Marriage status: 23.7% never married, 62.8% now married, 8.2% widowed, 5.3% divorced (2000); Foreign born: 0.3% (2000); Ancestry (includes multiple ancestries): 63.1% German, 14.8% Irish, 4.8% Polish, 4.2% United States or American, 3.6% Other groups (2000).
Economy: In farm area: dairy products; grain. Manufacturing: construction materials. Single-family building permits issued: 5 (2001) / 4 (2000); Multi-family building permits issued: 0 (2001) / 4 (2000); Employment by occupation: 9.4% management, 12.4% professional, 14.7% services, 23.9% sales, 1.0% farming, 11.4% construction, 27.3% production (2000).
Income: Per capita income: $18,622 (2000); Median household income: $44,740 (2000); Poverty rate: 7.8% (2000).
Taxes: Total city taxes per capita: $197 (1997); City property taxes per capita: $180 (1997).
Education: High school graduation rate: 78.1% (2000); College graduation rate: 15.9% (2000).

School District(s)

Campbellsport (PK-12)
2000 Enrollment: 1,495 920-533-8381

Housing: Homeownership rate: 68.8% (2000); Median home value: $111,700 (2000); Median rent: $408 per month (2000); Median age of housing: 37 years (2000).
Safety: Violent crime rate: 0.0 per 10,000 population; Property crime rate: 109.0 per 10,000 population (2001).
Newspapers: Campbellsport News (1 x week)
Transportation: Commute to work: 91.3% car, 0.2% public transportation, 6.0% walk, 2.0% work from home (2000); Travel time to work: 33.6% less than 15 minutes, 37.3% 15 to 30 minutes, 16.5% 30 to 45 minutes, 8.3% 45 to 60 minutes, 4.3% 60 minutes or more (2000)

EDEN (village). Covers a land area of 0.520 square miles and a water area of 0 square miles. Located at 43.69° N. Lat.; 88.36° W. Long. Elevation is 1,030 feet.
History: Eden was settled by Britishers around 1845, and jokingly called Eden because one of the early residents was named Adam.
Population: 687 (2000); Race: 97.6% White, 0.0% Black, 0.0% Asian, 0.3% American Indian and Alaska Native, 2.9% Hispanic of any race, 1.2% two or more races (2000); Density: 1,321.2 persons per square mile (2000); Age: 32.4% under 18, 12.6% over 64 (2000); Marriage status: 19.3% never married, 61.6% now married, 6.2% widowed, 12.9% divorced (2000); Foreign born: 1.5% (2000); Ancestry (includes multiple ancestries): 63.4% German, 22.9% Irish, 6.6% Other groups, 6.2% Polish, 4.4% Italian (2000).
Economy: Employment by occupation: 3.2% management, 9.3% professional, 13.0% services, 26.1% sales, 2.3% farming, 12.8% construction, 33.3% production (2000).
Income: Per capita income: $19,614 (2000); Median household income: $41,579 (2000); Poverty rate: 4.2% (2000).
Taxes: Total city taxes per capita: $49 (1997); City property taxes per capita: $16 (1997).
Education: High school graduation rate: 78.2% (2000); College graduation rate: 5.9% (2000).
Housing: Homeownership rate: 85.0% (2000); Median home value: $98,600 (2000); Median rent: $425 per month (2000); Median age of housing: 24 years (2000).
Transportation: Commute to work: 93.9% car, 0.0% public transportation, 3.2% walk, 2.9% work from home (2000); Travel time to work: 29.1% less than 15 minutes, 54.7% 15 to 30 minutes, 11.1% 30 to 45 minutes, 1.2% 45 to 60 minutes, 3.9% 60 minutes or more (2000)

EDEN (town). Covers a land area of 36.002 square miles and a water area of 0.045 square miles. Located at 43.67° N. Lat.; 88.34° W. Long. Elevation is 1,030 feet.
Population: 979 (2000); Race: 98.2% White, 0.3% Black, 0.0% Asian, 0.2% American Indian and Alaska Native, 1.5% Hispanic of any race, 1.1% two or more races (2000); Density: 27.2 persons per square mile (2000); Age: 24.9% under 18, 11.5% over 64 (2000); Marriage status: 30.2% never married, 61.8% now married, 3.7% widowed, 4.3% divorced (2000); Foreign born: 0.6% (2000); Ancestry (includes multiple ancestries): 64.6% German, 14.9% Irish, 6.7% English, 5.3% United States or American, 3.4% Polish (2000).
Economy: In farm area; canned vegetables. Single-family building permits issued: 4 (2001) / 2 (2000); Multi-family building permits issued: 0 (2001) / 0 (2000); Employment by occupation: 19.0% management, 10.8% professional, 9.8% services, 22.7% sales, 4.7% farming, 15.1% construction, 17.9% production (2000).
Income: Per capita income: $20,131 (2000); Median household income: $52,417 (2000); Poverty rate: 2.1% (2000).
Taxes: Total city taxes per capita: $112 (1997); City property taxes per capita: $110 (1997).
Education: High school graduation rate: 83.9% (2000); College graduation rate: 9.7% (2000).
Housing: Homeownership rate: 83.8% (2000); Median home value: $129,200 (2000); Median rent: $369 per month (2000); Median age of housing: 44 years (2000).
Transportation: Commute to work: 81.2% car, 0.3% public transportation, 7.0% walk, 10.3% work from home (2000); Travel time to work: 37.3% less than 15 minutes, 37.3% 15 to 30 minutes, 15.3% 30 to 45 minutes, 6.2% 45 to 60 minutes, 3.8% 60 minutes or more (2000)

ELDORADO (town). Covers a land area of 35.770 square miles and a water area of 0.470 square miles. Located at 43.85° N. Lat.; 88.58° W. Long. Elevation is 880 feet.
Population: 1,447 (2000); Race: 100.0% White, 0.0% Black, 0.0% Asian, 0.0% American Indian and Alaska Native, 0.7% Hispanic of any race, 0.0% two or more races (2000); Density: 40.5 persons per square mile (2000); Age: 26.2% under 18, 10.5% over 64 (2000); Marriage status: 22.1% never married, 70.4% now married, 3.2% widowed, 4.2% divorced (2000); Foreign born: 0.1% (2000); Ancestry (includes multiple ancestries): 63.9% German, 8.0% Irish, 5.2% English, 5.1% United States or American, 4.0% Polish (2000).
Economy: Single-family building permits issued: 8 (2001) / 6 (2000); Multi-family building permits issued: 0 (2001) / 0 (2000); Employment by occupation: 14.4% management, 10.6% professional, 10.5% services, 25.0% sales, 1.6% farming, 11.7% construction, 26.2% production (2000).
Income: Per capita income: $22,239 (2000); Median household income: $54,706 (2000); Poverty rate: 2.7% (2000).
Taxes: Total city taxes per capita: $87 (1997); City property taxes per capita: $84 (1997).
Education: High school graduation rate: 85.6% (2000); College graduation rate: 10.0% (2000).
Housing: Homeownership rate: 88.9% (2000); Median home value: $116,200 (2000); Median rent: $400 per month (2000); Median age of housing: 37 years (2000).
Transportation: Commute to work: 88.0% car, 0.2% public transportation, 2.5% walk, 8.7% work from home (2000); Travel time to work: 18.1% less than 15 minutes, 58.6% 15 to 30 minutes, 14.5% 30 to 45 minutes, 2.5% 45 to 60 minutes, 6.3% 60 minutes or more (2000)

EMPIRE (town). Covers a land area of 29.015 square miles and a water area of 0.127 square miles. Located at 43.75° N. Lat.; 88.36° W. Long.
Population: 2,620 (2000); Race: 98.3% White, 0.0% Black, 0.3% Asian, 0.8% American Indian and Alaska Native, 0.2% Hispanic of any race, 0.6% two or more races (2000); Density: 90.3 persons per square mile (2000); Age: 28.4% under 18, 10.2% over 64 (2000); Marriage status: 18.2% never married, 73.3% now married, 3.1% widowed, 5.5% divorced (2000); Foreign born: 0.9% (2000); Ancestry (includes multiple ancestries): 63.3% German, 14.7% Irish, 7.1% English, 5.7% Polish, 5.3% French (except Basque) (2000).
Economy: Single-family building permits issued: 18 (2001) / 17 (2000); Multi-family building permits issued: 0 (2001) / 0 (2000); Employment by occupation: 17.6% management, 24.1% professional, 10.8% services, 17.6% sales, 2.5% farming, 10.6% construction, 16.7% production (2000).
Income: Per capita income: $27,174 (2000); Median household income: $67,330 (2000); Poverty rate: 1.5% (2000).
Taxes: Total city taxes per capita: $88 (1997); City property taxes per capita: $84 (1997).
Education: High school graduation rate: 92.6% (2000); College graduation rate: 30.9% (2000).
Housing: Homeownership rate: 96.0% (2000); Median home value: $157,900 (2000); Median rent: $530 per month (2000); Median age of housing: 26 years (2000).
Transportation: Commute to work: 93.9% car, 0.0% public transportation, 1.4% walk, 4.4% work from home (2000); Travel time to work: 38.9% less than 15 minutes, 44.7% 15 to 30 minutes, 8.6% 30 to 45 minutes, 4.9% 45 to 60 minutes, 2.9% 60 minutes or more (2000)

FAIRWATER (village). Aka Fair Water. Covers a land area of 0.743 square miles and a water area of 0 square miles. Located at 43.74° N. Lat.; 88.86° W. Long. Elevation is 970 feet.
Population: 350 (2000); Race: 98.8% White, 0.0% Black, 0.0% Asian, 0.0% American Indian and Alaska Native, 0.0% Hispanic of any race, 1.2% two or more races (2000); Density: 470.8 persons per square mile (2000); Age: 23.9% under 18, 15.7% over 64 (2000); Marriage status: 21.7% never married, 71.7% now married, 4.4% widowed, 2.2% divorced (2000); Foreign born: 0.6% (2000); Ancestry (includes multiple ancestries): 59.8% German, 11.2% Dutch, 6.0% Polish, 5.4% English, 3.6% French (except Basque) (2000).
Economy: In farm area. Manufacturing: frozen vegetables. Single-family building permits issued: 0 (2001) / 5 (2000); Multi-family building permits issued: 0 (2001) / 0 (2000); Employment by occupation: 4.4% management, 16.4% professional, 12.6% services, 21.3% sales, 2.2% farming, 12.6% construction, 30.6% production (2000).
Income: Per capita income: $19,281 (2000); Median household income: $42,292 (2000); Poverty rate: 3.6% (2000).
Taxes: Total city taxes per capita: $131 (1997); City property taxes per capita: $124 (1997).
Education: High school graduation rate: 78.2% (2000); College graduation rate: 14.4% (2000).
Housing: Homeownership rate: 80.7% (2000); Median home value: $73,300 (2000); Median rent: $367 per month (2000); Median age of housing: 52 years (2000).
Transportation: Commute to work: 91.1% car, 0.0% public transportation, 5.6% walk, 2.2% work from home (2000); Travel time to work: 30.3% less than 15 minutes, 46.9% 15 to 30 minutes, 13.7% 30 to 45 minutes, 5.7% 45 to 60 minutes, 3.4% 60 minutes or more (2000)

FOND DU LAC (city). Covers a land area of 16.872 square miles and a water area of 1.331 square miles. Located at 43.77° N. Lat.; 88.44° W. Long. Elevation is 760 feet.
History: Fond du Lac began as a French trading post in 1785. Settlers came in the mid-1830's, and a sawmill and gristmill were soon built. After a slow start, the lumber industry brought prosperity to Fond du Lac in the 1860's and 1870's. After considerable difficulty, a rail line was completed from Chicago in 1859, but the first train that came through was derailed by an ox stuck between the ties on a trestle.
Population: 42,203 (2000); Race: 93.5% White, 2.1% Black, 0.9% Asian, 0.7% American Indian and Alaska Native, 3.2% Hispanic of any race, 1.0% two or more races (2000); Density: 2,501.3 persons per square mile (2000); Age: 24.1% under 18, 15.4% over 64 (2000); Marriage status: 26.5% never married, 56.3% now married, 7.4% widowed, 9.7% divorced (2000); Foreign born: 3.3% (2000); Ancestry (includes multiple ancestries): 54.3% German, 11.2% Irish, 7.4% Other groups, 6.1% Polish, 5.7% English (2000).
Vital Statistics: Birth rate: 138.4 per 10,000 population (1998)
Economy: Unemployment rate: 5.0% (11/2002); Total civilian labor force: 23,837 (11/2002); Single-family building permits issued: 87 (2001) / 93 (2000); Multi-family building permits issued: 162 (2001) / 60 (2000); Employment by occupation: 9.9% management, 15.7% professional, 16.9% services, 24.6% sales, 0.6% farming, 7.4% construction, 24.9% production (2000).
Income: Per capita income: $18,996 (2000); Median household income: $41,113 (2000); Poverty rate: 7.5% (2000).
Taxes: Total city taxes per capita: $348 (2000); City property taxes per capita: $318 (2000).
Education: High school graduation rate: 83.9% (2000); College graduation rate: 19.0% (2000).

School District(s)

Fond Du Lac (PK-12)
2000 Enrollment: 7,241 920-929-2760

Four-year College(s)

Marian College of Fond Du Lac (Private, Not-for-profit, Roman Catholic)
2001 Enrollment: 2,559 920-923-7600
2001 Tuition: In-state $13,230; Out-of-state $13,230

Two-year College(s)

Moraine Park Technical College (Public)
2001 Enrollment: 7,596 920-922-8611
2001 Tuition: In-state $1,920; Out-of-state $16,908

Housing: Homeownership rate: 62.0% (2000); Median home value: $91,200 (2000); Median rent: $459 per month (2000); Median age of housing: 41 years (2000).
Hospitals: Fond Du Lac County Community Program - Acute Psychiatric (25 beds)
Safety: Violent crime rate: 15.8 per 10,000 population; Property crime rate: 380.0 per 10,000 population (2001).
Newspapers: The Reporter (6 x week)
Transportation: Commute to work: 92.9% car, 1.0% public transportation, 3.3% walk, 1.3% work from home (2000); Travel time to work: 60.6% less than 15 minutes, 22.8% 15 to 30 minutes, 9.4% 30 to 45 minutes, 3.7% 45 to 60 minutes, 3.5% 60 minutes or more (2000); Amtrak: Service available.

Additional Information Contacts

Fond du Lac Association of Commerce 920-921-9500

FOND DU LAC (town). Covers a land area of 19.852 square miles and a water area of 1.076 square miles. Located at 43.75° N. Lat.; 88.44° W. Long. Elevation is 760 feet.
History: A French fur-trading post in the late 18th century, it later grew into a lumbering town. After the arrival of the railroad, it became an industrial city. University of Wisconsin, Fond du Lac campus here. Incorporated 1852.
Population: 2,027 (2000); Race: 99.6% White, 0.0% Black, 0.0% Asian, 0.0% American Indian and Alaska Native, 1.0% Hispanic of any race, 0.1% two or more races (2000); Density: 102.1 persons per square mile (2000);

Age: 25.2% under 18, 13.8% over 64 (2000); Marriage status: 21.0% never married, 66.5% now married, 2.8% widowed, 9.7% divorced (2000); Foreign born: 1.0% (2000); Ancestry (includes multiple ancestries): 59.0% German, 14.9% Irish, 7.7% United States or American, 6.7% English, 6.3% French (except Basque) (2000).
Economy: In a resort region. Railroad junction. Highly diversified manufacturing. The city's economy is based on dairy farming and the manufacture of machine tools, leather goods, engines and auto parts. Single-family building permits issued: 22 (2001) / 36 (2000); Multi-family building permits issued: 0 (2001) / 2 (2000); Employment by occupation: 20.4% management, 14.1% professional, 12.2% services, 18.9% sales, 1.6% farming, 11.0% construction, 21.8% production (2000).
Income: Per capita income: $29,070 (2000); Median household income: $58,281 (2000); Poverty rate: 4.1% (2000).
Taxes: Total city taxes per capita: $39 (1997); City property taxes per capita: $30 (1997).
Education: High school graduation rate: 89.6% (2000); College graduation rate: 18.3% (2000).
Housing: Homeownership rate: 81.2% (2000); Median home value: $142,100 (2000); Median rent: $421 per month (2000); Median age of housing: 34 years (2000).
Transportation: Commute to work: 95.1% car, 0.0% public transportation, 0.4% walk, 3.0% work from home (2000); Travel time to work: 52.7% less than 15 minutes, 31.3% 15 to 30 minutes, 9.5% 30 to 45 minutes, 1.5% 45 to 60 minutes, 5.0% 60 minutes or more (2000); Amtrak: Service available.

FOREST (town). Covers a land area of 35.246 square miles and a water area of 0.868 square miles. Located at 43.76° N. Lat.; 88.22° W. Long.
Population: 1,108 (2000); Race: 99.4% White, 0.0% Black, 0.0% Asian, 0.0% American Indian and Alaska Native, 0.8% Hispanic of any race, 0.2% two or more races (2000); Density: 31.4 persons per square mile (2000); Age: 27.9% under 18, 12.0% over 64 (2000); Marriage status: 23.6% never married, 67.2% now married, 5.0% widowed, 4.1% divorced (2000); Foreign born: 1.1% (2000); Ancestry (includes multiple ancestries): 72.8% German, 12.2% Irish, 6.4% United States or American, 4.6% Polish, 2.8% French (except Basque) (2000).
Economy: Single-family building permits issued: 5 (2001) / 8 (2000); Multi-family building permits issued: 0 (2001) / 0 (2000); Employment by occupation: 19.4% management, 9.5% professional, 10.7% services, 18.0% sales, 6.3% farming, 12.8% construction, 23.3% production (2000).
Income: Per capita income: $19,848 (2000); Median household income: $49,583 (2000); Poverty rate: 3.3% (2000).
Taxes: Total city taxes per capita: $54 (1997); City property taxes per capita: $52 (1997).
Education: High school graduation rate: 83.3% (2000); College graduation rate: 11.4% (2000).
Housing: Homeownership rate: 88.3% (2000); Median home value: $120,600 (2000); Median rent: $363 per month (2000); Median age of housing: 54 years (2000).
Transportation: Commute to work: 82.4% car, 0.0% public transportation, 4.4% walk, 12.5% work from home (2000); Travel time to work: 29.3% less than 15 minutes, 42.7% 15 to 30 minutes, 16.8% 30 to 45 minutes, 5.4% 45 to 60 minutes, 5.7% 60 minutes or more (2000)

FRIENDSHIP (town). Covers a land area of 17.023 square miles and a water area of 17.414 square miles. Located at 43.84° N. Lat.; 88.48° W. Long.
Population: 2,406 (2000); Race: 98.1% White, 0.0% Black, 0.2% Asian, 0.0% American Indian and Alaska Native, 0.2% Hispanic of any race, 1.7% two or more races (2000); Density: 141.3 persons per square mile (2000); Age: 22.0% under 18, 14.0% over 64 (2000); Marriage status: 19.4% never married, 66.4% now married, 5.4% widowed, 8.8% divorced (2000); Foreign born: 0.7% (2000); Ancestry (includes multiple ancestries): 63.5% German, 7.3% English, 7.3% Irish, 5.6% French (except Basque), 5.4% Polish (2000).
Economy: Single-family building permits issued: 18 (2001) / 10 (2000); Multi-family building permits issued: 0 (2001) / 0 (2000); Employment by occupation: 9.6% management, 13.8% professional, 15.4% services, 19.2% sales, 0.5% farming, 12.7% construction, 28.7% production (2000).
Income: Per capita income: $22,751 (2000); Median household income: $46,953 (2000); Poverty rate: 2.7% (2000).
Taxes: Total city taxes per capita: $49 (1997); City property taxes per capita: $13 (1997).
Education: High school graduation rate: 87.5% (2000); College graduation rate: 14.6% (2000).
Housing: Homeownership rate: 88.9% (2000); Median home value: $118,400 (2000); Median rent: $424 per month (2000); Median age of housing: 30 years (2000).
Transportation: Commute to work: 94.7% car, 0.0% public transportation, 2.6% walk, 2.7% work from home (2000); Travel time to work: 28.4% less than 15 minutes, 52.2% 15 to 30 minutes, 12.5% 30 to 45 minutes, 3.1% 45 to 60 minutes, 3.9% 60 minutes or more (2000)

LAMARTINE (town). Covers a land area of 36.499 square miles and a water area of 0.066 square miles. Located at 43.76° N. Lat.; 88.57° W. Long. Elevation is 870 feet.
Population: 1,616 (2000); Race: 98.4% White, 0.6% Black, 0.0% Asian, 0.1% American Indian and Alaska Native, 1.4% Hispanic of any race, 0.8% two or more races (2000); Density: 44.3 persons per square mile (2000); Age: 26.2% under 18, 9.8% over 64 (2000); Marriage status: 24.7% never married, 65.6% now married, 3.8% widowed, 5.9% divorced (2000); Foreign born: 0.6% (2000); Ancestry (includes multiple ancestries): 68.0% German, 10.6% Irish, 8.0% English, 4.9% Dutch, 4.5% Other groups (2000).
Economy: Single-family building permits issued: 8 (2001) / 14 (2000); Multi-family building permits issued: 0 (2001) / 0 (2000); Employment by occupation: 12.5% management, 9.8% professional, 14.3% services, 22.3% sales, 1.1% farming, 13.8% construction, 26.3% production (2000).
Income: Per capita income: $25,202 (2000); Median household income: $54,400 (2000); Poverty rate: 3.3% (2000).
Taxes: Total city taxes per capita: $94 (1997); City property taxes per capita: $92 (1997).
Education: High school graduation rate: 84.8% (2000); College graduation rate: 10.0% (2000).
Housing: Homeownership rate: 86.7% (2000); Median home value: $124,300 (2000); Median rent: $382 per month (2000); Median age of housing: 36 years (2000).
Transportation: Commute to work: 91.4% car, 0.2% public transportation, 2.2% walk, 5.0% work from home (2000); Travel time to work: 31.7% less than 15 minutes, 47.9% 15 to 30 minutes, 11.2% 30 to 45 minutes, 3.8% 45 to 60 minutes, 5.5% 60 minutes or more (2000)

MALONE (unincorporated postal area, zip code 53049). Covers a land area of 39.017 square miles and a water area of 0.013 square miles. Located at 43.88° N. Lat.; 88.28° W. Long. Elevation is 975 feet.
Population: 2,403 (2000); Race: 99.5% White, 0.0% Black, 0.0% Asian, 0.2% American Indian and Alaska Native, 0.5% Hispanic of any race, 0.3% two or more races (2000); Density: 61.6 persons per square mile (2000); Age: 25.3% under 18, 13.8% over 64 (2000); Marriage status: 25.8% never married, 62.5% now married, 5.9% widowed, 5.8% divorced (2000); Foreign born: 0.3% (2000); Ancestry (includes multiple ancestries): 69.1% German, 8.3% Irish, 4.7% English, 3.8% Swedish, 3.6% Polish (2000).
Economy: Employment by occupation: 16.8% management, 10.2% professional, 16.0% services, 16.0% sales, 2.7% farming, 15.1% construction, 23.3% production (2000).
Income: Per capita income: $19,925 (2000); Median household income: $49,410 (2000); Poverty rate: 3.4% (2000).
Education: High school graduation rate: 80.9% (2000); College graduation rate: 14.5% (2000).
Housing: Homeownership rate: 86.2% (2000); Median home value: $126,300 (2000); Median rent: $373 per month (2000); Median age of housing: 47 years (2000).
Transportation: Commute to work: 89.3% car, 1.2% public transportation, 2.4% walk, 6.8% work from home (2000); Travel time to work: 25.6% less than 15 minutes, 49.3% 15 to 30 minutes, 14.7% 30 to 45 minutes, 6.5% 45 to 60 minutes, 3.8% 60 minutes or more (2000)

MARSHFIELD (town). Covers a land area of 34.123 square miles and a water area of 0.204 square miles. Located at 43.83° N. Lat.; 88.23° W. Long.
Population: 1,118 (2000); Race: 99.4% White, 0.5% Black, 0.0% Asian, 0.1% American Indian and Alaska Native, 0.1% Hispanic of any race, 0.0% two or more races (2000); Density: 32.8 persons per square mile (2000); Age: 24.8% under 18, 14.7% over 64 (2000); Marriage status: 24.5% never married, 68.6% now married, 4.3% widowed, 2.6% divorced (2000); Foreign born: 0.7% (2000); Ancestry (includes multiple ancestries): 75.2% German, 8.4% Irish, 6.1% United States or American, 2.7% English, 2.6% Polish (2000).
Economy: Single-family building permits issued: 0 (2001) / 9 (2000); Multi-family building permits issued: 0 (2001) / 0 (2000); Employment by occupation: 18.7% management, 14.2% professional, 13.7% services, 18.1% sales, 3.5% farming, 14.5% construction, 17.3% production (2000).

Income: Per capita income: $21,467 (2000); Median household income: $56,250 (2000); Poverty rate: 6.3% (2000).
Taxes: Total city taxes per capita: $88 (1997); City property taxes per capita: $86 (1997).
Education: High school graduation rate: 84.7% (2000); College graduation rate: 11.2% (2000).
Housing: Homeownership rate: 91.0% (2000); Median home value: $114,200 (2000); Median rent: $230 per month (2000); Median age of housing: 49 years (2000).
Transportation: Commute to work: 81.6% car, 0.3% public transportation, 6.0% walk, 11.8% work from home (2000); Travel time to work: 26.8% less than 15 minutes, 38.9% 15 to 30 minutes, 24.3% 30 to 45 minutes, 4.9% 45 to 60 minutes, 5.1% 60 minutes or more (2000)

METOMEN (town). Covers a land area of 34.636 square miles and a water area of 0 square miles. Located at 43.76° N. Lat.; 88.82° W. Long.
Population: 709 (2000); Race: 99.6% White, 0.0% Black, 0.0% Asian, 0.0% American Indian and Alaska Native, 0.0% Hispanic of any race, 0.4% two or more races (2000); Density: 20.5 persons per square mile (2000); Age: 30.6% under 18, 10.8% over 64 (2000); Marriage status: 22.4% never married, 68.4% now married, 4.7% widowed, 4.5% divorced (2000); Foreign born: 0.3% (2000); Ancestry (includes multiple ancestries): 55.0% German, 19.6% Dutch, 10.2% Polish, 8.8% English, 5.7% Irish (2000).
Economy: Single-family building permits issued: 6 (2001) / 2 (2000); Multi-family building permits issued: 0 (2001) / 0 (2000); Employment by occupation: 19.4% management, 13.9% professional, 12.6% services, 17.6% sales, 5.0% farming, 6.8% construction, 24.7% production (2000).
Income: Per capita income: $17,776 (2000); Median household income: $44,722 (2000); Poverty rate: 5.3% (2000).
Taxes: Total city taxes per capita: $153 (1997); City property taxes per capita: $151 (1997).
Education: High school graduation rate: 82.3% (2000); College graduation rate: 14.1% (2000).
Housing: Homeownership rate: 87.9% (2000); Median home value: $108,500 (2000); Median rent: $463 per month (2000); Median age of housing: 60+ years (2000).
Transportation: Commute to work: 79.7% car, 0.0% public transportation, 3.2% walk, 17.1% work from home (2000); Travel time to work: 46.8% less than 15 minutes, 31.3% 15 to 30 minutes, 10.3% 30 to 45 minutes, 4.8% 45 to 60 minutes, 6.8% 60 minutes or more (2000)

MOUNT CALVARY (village). Covers a land area of 1.060 square miles and a water area of 0 square miles. Located at 43.82° N. Lat.; 88.24° W. Long. Elevation is 960 feet.
Population: 956 (2000); Race: 85.1% White, 0.0% Black, 7.3% Asian, 0.0% American Indian and Alaska Native, 8.5% Hispanic of any race, 0.1% two or more races (2000); Density: 902.0 persons per square mile (2000); Age: 33.5% under 18, 27.6% over 64 (2000); Marriage status: 25.2% never married, 68.1% now married, 4.2% widowed, 2.5% divorced (2000); Foreign born: 0.7% (2000); Ancestry (includes multiple ancestries): 38.2% German, 9.1% Other groups, 4.3% Irish, 2.7% United States or American, 1.4% French Canadian (2000).
Economy: In dairying region. Single-family building permits issued: 2 (2001) / 1 (2000); Multi-family building permits issued: 0 (2001) / 0 (2000); Employment by occupation: 11.7% management, 10.4% professional, 15.3% services, 22.5% sales, 0.7% farming, 24.1% construction, 15.3% production (2000).
Income: Per capita income: $13,631 (2000); Median household income: $50,104 (2000); Poverty rate: 35.6% (2000).
Education: High school graduation rate: 66.6% (2000); College graduation rate: 20.1% (2000).
Housing: Homeownership rate: 78.6% (2000); Median home value: $94,100 (2000); Median rent: $360 per month (2000); Median age of housing: 60+ years (2000).
Transportation: Commute to work: 91.5% car, 0.0% public transportation, 5.6% walk, 2.3% work from home (2000); Travel time to work: 29.2% less than 15 minutes, 36.2% 15 to 30 minutes, 26.2% 30 to 45 minutes, 3.4% 45 to 60 minutes, 5.0% 60 minutes or more (2000)

NORTH FOND DU LAC (village). Covers a land area of 1.909 square miles and a water area of 0.002 square miles. Located at 43.81° N. Lat.; 88.48° W. Long. Elevation is 760 feet.
History: North Fond du Lac began as a farming community, but became a railroad center when the Soo Line and Chicago & North Western Railway located their shops here in the early 1900's.
Population: 4,557 (2000); Race: 97.4% White, 0.0% Black, 0.9% Asian, 0.8% American Indian and Alaska Native, 0.7% Hispanic of any race, 0.4% two or more races (2000); Density: 2,387.6 persons per square mile (2000); Age: 27.6% under 18, 11.4% over 64 (2000); Marriage status: 22.6% never married, 61.5% now married, 7.9% widowed, 8.0% divorced (2000); Foreign born: 1.0% (2000); Ancestry (includes multiple ancestries): 60.2% German, 12.3% Irish, 7.6% English, 6.7% Polish, 5.5% United States or American (2000).
Economy: Single-family building permits issued: 14 (2001) / 13 (2000); Multi-family building permits issued: 63 (2001) / 0 (2000); Employment by occupation: 10.2% management, 11.6% professional, 16.3% services, 20.4% sales, 0.4% farming, 6.7% construction, 34.4% production (2000).
Income: Per capita income: $17,492 (2000); Median household income: $44,327 (2000); Poverty rate: 6.9% (2000).
Taxes: Total city taxes per capita: $176 (1997); City property taxes per capita: $141 (1997).
Education: High school graduation rate: 85.8% (2000); College graduation rate: 11.5% (2000).

School District(s)

North Fond Du Lac (PK-12)
2000 Enrollment: 1,252 920-929-3750
Housing: Homeownership rate: 82.4% (2000); Median home value: $85,600 (2000); Median rent: $385 per month (2000); Median age of housing: 30 years (2000).
Safety: Violent crime rate: 8.7 per 10,000 population; Property crime rate: 320.3 per 10,000 population (2001).
Transportation: Commute to work: 97.0% car, 0.0% public transportation, 0.1% walk, 1.1% work from home (2000); Travel time to work: 42.9% less than 15 minutes, 37.8% 15 to 30 minutes, 10.1% 30 to 45 minutes, 2.7% 45 to 60 minutes, 6.7% 60 minutes or more (2000)

OAKFIELD (village). Covers a land area of 0.964 square miles and a water area of 0 square miles. Located at 43.68° N. Lat.; 88.54° W. Long. Elevation is 894 feet.
Population: 1,012 (2000); Race: 98.4% White, 0.0% Black, 0.6% Asian, 0.0% American Indian and Alaska Native, 2.5% Hispanic of any race, 0.0% two or more races (2000); Density: 1,049.9 persons per square mile (2000); Age: 28.1% under 18, 11.8% over 64 (2000); Marriage status: 22.0% never married, 63.7% now married, 8.3% widowed, 6.0% divorced (2000); Foreign born: 0.7% (2000); Ancestry (includes multiple ancestries): 62.3% German, 11.2% Irish, 6.2% English, 5.8% Polish, 4.0% Other groups (2000).
Economy: Single-family building permits issued: 5 (2001) / 6 (2000); Multi-family building permits issued: 0 (2001) / 0 (2000); Employment by occupation: 12.5% management, 11.6% professional, 13.1% services, 25.9% sales, 0.4% farming, 11.7% construction, 24.8% production (2000).
Income: Per capita income: $21,131 (2000); Median household income: $51,053 (2000); Poverty rate: 1.9% (2000).
Taxes: Total city taxes per capita: $184 (1997); City property taxes per capita: $140 (1997).
Education: High school graduation rate: 89.8% (2000); College graduation rate: 14.6% (2000).

School District(s)

Oakfield (PK-12)
2000 Enrollment: 659 920-583-3146
Housing: Homeownership rate: 78.2% (2000); Median home value: $115,100 (2000); Median rent: $430 per month (2000); Median age of housing: 40 years (2000).
Transportation: Commute to work: 96.0% car, 0.0% public transportation, 1.9% walk, 1.7% work from home (2000); Travel time to work: 30.1% less than 15 minutes, 53.5% 15 to 30 minutes, 8.6% 30 to 45 minutes, 4.1% 45 to 60 minutes, 3.7% 60 minutes or more (2000)

OAKFIELD (town). Covers a land area of 35.746 square miles and a water area of 0.054 square miles. Located at 43.67° N. Lat.; 88.58° W. Long. Elevation is 894 feet.
Population: 767 (2000); Race: 99.1% White, 0.0% Black, 0.1% Asian, 0.0% American Indian and Alaska Native, 0.6% Hispanic of any race, 0.5% two or more races (2000); Density: 21.5 persons per square mile (2000); Age: 32.5% under 18, 7.4% over 64 (2000); Marriage status: 24.0% never married, 67.2% now married, 3.3% widowed, 5.5% divorced (2000); Foreign born: 0.1% (2000); Ancestry (includes multiple ancestries): 59.9% German, 7.9% United States or American, 6.8% Dutch, 6.6% Irish, 5.8% English (2000).
Economy: Railroad spur terminus. In dairy and farm region. Manufacturing: limestone products. Horicon National Wildlife Refuge to Southwest. Single-family building permits issued: 3 (2001) / 1 (2000); Multi-family building permits issued: 0 (2001) / 0 (2000); Employment by occupation:

12.2% management, 7.7% professional, 14.0% services, 19.6% sales, 3.4% farming, 16.5% construction, 26.6% production (2000).
Income: Per capita income: $18,615 (2000); Median household income: $51,917 (2000); Poverty rate: 2.1% (2000).
Taxes: Total city taxes per capita: $86 (1997); City property taxes per capita: $83 (1997).
Education: High school graduation rate: 93.4% (2000); College graduation rate: 11.7% (2000).
Housing: Homeownership rate: 88.1% (2000); Median home value: $121,000 (2000); Median rent: $469 per month (2000); Median age of housing: 50 years (2000).
Transportation: Commute to work: 86.1% car, 0.0% public transportation, 2.6% walk, 10.7% work from home (2000); Travel time to work: 23.6% less than 15 minutes, 54.0% 15 to 30 minutes, 14.3% 30 to 45 minutes, 3.6% 45 to 60 minutes, 4.4% 60 minutes or more (2000)

OSCEOLA (town). Covers a land area of 35.127 square miles and a water area of 1.229 square miles. Located at 43.66° N. Lat.; 88.19° W. Long.
Population: 1,802 (2000); Race: 98.5% White, 0.0% Black, 0.0% Asian, 0.5% American Indian and Alaska Native, 1.4% Hispanic of any race, 0.2% two or more races (2000); Density: 51.3 persons per square mile (2000); Age: 24.4% under 18, 12.6% over 64 (2000); Marriage status: 22.0% never married, 65.0% now married, 4.3% widowed, 8.7% divorced (2000); Foreign born: 1.9% (2000); Ancestry (includes multiple ancestries): 59.5% German, 14.0% Irish, 6.3% Polish, 5.5% United States or American, 3.0% English (2000).
Economy: Single-family building permits issued: 11 (2001) / 14 (2000); Multi-family building permits issued: 0 (2001) / 0 (2000); Employment by occupation: 12.1% management, 12.9% professional, 10.5% services, 21.1% sales, 3.1% farming, 10.7% construction, 29.6% production (2000).
Income: Per capita income: $20,568 (2000); Median household income: $47,672 (2000); Poverty rate: 4.0% (2000).
Taxes: Total city taxes per capita: $88 (1997); City property taxes per capita: $84 (1997).
Education: High school graduation rate: 82.6% (2000); College graduation rate: 11.2% (2000).
Housing: Homeownership rate: 81.9% (2000); Median home value: $138,400 (2000); Median rent: $496 per month (2000); Median age of housing: 33 years (2000).
Transportation: Commute to work: 87.3% car, 0.0% public transportation, 4.6% walk, 7.5% work from home (2000); Travel time to work: 28.6% less than 15 minutes, 35.5% 15 to 30 minutes, 22.7% 30 to 45 minutes, 8.4% 45 to 60 minutes, 4.7% 60 minutes or more (2000)

RIPON (city). Covers a land area of 4.234 square miles and a water area of 0.024 square miles. Located at 43.84° N. Lat.; 88.84° W. Long. Elevation is 943 feet.
History: The first settlers in Ripon were members of a stock company called the Wisconsin Phalanx, followers of Francois Charles Marie Fourier, early 19th-century socialist. In 1844 they named their settlement Ceresco, for Ceres, Roman goddess of agriculture. The Phalanx disbanded by mutual consent in 1850, and the settlement of Ceresco was absorbed by a nearby community named Ripon. Ripon was a stronghold of abolitionists during the Civil War.
Population: 6,828 (2000); Race: 97.9% White, 0.4% Black, 0.4% Asian, 0.4% American Indian and Alaska Native, 1.5% Hispanic of any race, 0.8% two or more races (2000); Density: 1,612.8 persons per square mile (2000); Age: 22.7% under 18, 19.5% over 64 (2000); Marriage status: 21.5% never married, 57.7% now married, 12.2% widowed, 8.6% divorced (2000); Foreign born: 1.8% (2000); Ancestry (includes multiple ancestries): 54.2% German, 10.0% English, 7.7% Irish, 7.5% Polish, 7.0% Norwegian (2000).
Economy: Single-family building permits issued: 9 (2001) / 9 (2000); Multi-family building permits issued: 2 (2001) / 0 (2000); Employment by occupation: 10.0% management, 18.2% professional, 15.2% services, 20.8% sales, 0.0% farming, 8.4% construction, 27.3% production (2000).
Income: Per capita income: $20,313 (2000); Median household income: $37,399 (2000); Poverty rate: 6.4% (2000).
Taxes: Total city taxes per capita: $224 (1997); City property taxes per capita: $210 (1997).
Education: High school graduation rate: 82.7% (2000); College graduation rate: 19.6% (2000).

School District(s)

Ripon (PK-12)
2000 Enrollment: 1,669 920-748-4600

Four-year College(s)

Ripon College (Private, Not-for-profit)
2001 Enrollment: 903 920-748-8115
2001 Tuition: In-state $19,260; Out-of-state $19,260
Housing: Homeownership rate: 64.8% (2000); Median home value: $89,500 (2000); Median rent: $381 per month (2000); Median age of housing: 45 years (2000).
Hospitals: Ripon Medical Center (40 beds)
Safety: Violent crime rate: 2.9 per 10,000 population; Property crime rate: 319.9 per 10,000 population (2001).
Newspapers: The Ripon Commonwealth-Press (1 x week)
Transportation: Commute to work: 89.7% car, 0.0% public transportation, 7.3% walk, 1.8% work from home (2000); Travel time to work: 62.8% less than 15 minutes, 21.0% 15 to 30 minutes, 13.1% 30 to 45 minutes, 1.6% 45 to 60 minutes, 1.5% 60 minutes or more (2000)
Additional Information Contacts
Green Lake County Ripon Area Board of Realtors 920-748-7007
Ripon Chamber of Commerce 920-748-6764

RIPON (town). Covers a land area of 31.808 square miles and a water area of 0.146 square miles. Located at 43.86° N. Lat.; 88.83° W. Long. Elevation is 943 feet.
History: Seat of Ripon College. One of the meetings leading to formation of Republican Party was held here in 1854. Carrie Chapman Catt was born here. Settled 1844 as Ceresco by Socialist Fourierists; Incorporated as Ripon in 1858.
Population: 2,001 (2000); Race: 94.9% White, 0.6% Black, 0.6% Asian, 0.4% American Indian and Alaska Native, 5.0% Hispanic of any race, 1.6% two or more races (2000); Density: 62.9 persons per square mile (2000); Age: 20.9% under 18, 6.8% over 64 (2000); Marriage status: 41.5% never married, 52.3% now married, 2.2% widowed, 4.0% divorced (2000); Foreign born: 2.1% (2000); Ancestry (includes multiple ancestries): 51.7% German, 10.5% Irish, 9.7% Polish, 8.3% Other groups, 8.0% English (2000).
Economy: Railroad junction in agricultural area. Manufacturing includes iron castings, travel bags, prepared foods, coin-operated washing machines and dryers, printing and publishing. Seat of Ripon College. Single-family building permits issued: 7 (2001) / 4 (2000); Multi-family building permits issued: 0 (2001) / 0 (2000); Employment by occupation: 11.4% management, 14.4% professional, 17.1% services, 26.2% sales, 0.9% farming, 6.9% construction, 23.1% production (2000).
Income: Per capita income: $15,591 (2000); Median household income: $49,323 (2000); Poverty rate: 8.8% (2000).
Taxes: Total city taxes per capita: $90 (1997); City property taxes per capita: $86 (1997).
Education: High school graduation rate: 88.3% (2000); College graduation rate: 13.0% (2000).
Housing: Homeownership rate: 85.8% (2000); Median home value: $110,000 (2000); Median rent: $367 per month (2000); Median age of housing: 35 years (2000).
Transportation: Commute to work: 72.6% car, 0.0% public transportation, 21.6% walk, 5.5% work from home (2000); Travel time to work: 64.0% less than 15 minutes, 19.2% 15 to 30 minutes, 12.4% 30 to 45 minutes, 3.1% 45 to 60 minutes, 1.4% 60 minutes or more (2000)

ROSENDALE (village). Covers a land area of 1.120 square miles and a water area of 0 square miles. Located at 43.81° N. Lat.; 88.67° W. Long. Elevation is 900 feet.
Population: 923 (2000); Race: 99.6% White, 0.0% Black, 0.2% Asian, 0.0% American Indian and Alaska Native, 0.5% Hispanic of any race, 0.2% two or more races (2000); Density: 824.3 persons per square mile (2000); Age: 29.8% under 18, 7.9% over 64 (2000); Marriage status: 23.8% never married, 66.7% now married, 4.3% widowed, 5.3% divorced (2000); Foreign born: 0.4% (2000); Ancestry (includes multiple ancestries): 56.0% German, 12.1% Irish, 8.7% United States or American, 6.5% Norwegian, 6.3% English (2000).
Economy: Single-family building permits issued: 5 (2001) / 6 (2000); Multi-family building permits issued: 8 (2001) / 0 (2000); Employment by occupation: 9.8% management, 11.5% professional, 13.5% services, 24.8% sales, 1.5% farming, 8.9% construction, 30.0% production (2000).
Income: Per capita income: $18,653 (2000); Median household income: $52,448 (2000); Poverty rate: 2.3% (2000).
Taxes: Total city taxes per capita: $103 (1997); City property taxes per capita: $100 (1997).
Education: High school graduation rate: 91.2% (2000); College graduation rate: 16.4% (2000).

School District(s)

Rosendale-Brandon (PK-12)
2000 Enrollment: 1,028 920-872-2851

Housing: Homeownership rate: 85.9% (2000); Median home value: $111,800 (2000); Median rent: $442 per month (2000); Median age of housing: 26 years (2000).
Transportation: Commute to work: 91.6% car, 0.0% public transportation, 4.3% walk, 3.0% work from home (2000); Travel time to work: 18.9% less than 15 minutes, 60.4% 15 to 30 minutes, 13.1% 30 to 45 minutes, 3.5% 45 to 60 minutes, 4.1% 60 minutes or more (2000)

ROSENDALE (town). Covers a land area of 35.618 square miles and a water area of 0.035 square miles. Located at 43.85° N. Lat.; 88.71° W. Long. Elevation is 900 feet.
Population: 783 (2000); Race: 100.0% White, 0.0% Black, 0.0% Asian, 0.0% American Indian and Alaska Native, 0.0% Hispanic of any race, 0.0% two or more races (2000); Density: 22.0 persons per square mile (2000); Age: 26.5% under 18, 14.4% over 64 (2000); Marriage status: 20.2% never married, 67.9% now married, 5.7% widowed, 6.2% divorced (2000); Foreign born: 0.2% (2000); Ancestry (includes multiple ancestries): 58.3% German, 10.0% English, 8.1% Polish, 5.9% Irish, 5.7% United States or American (2000).
Economy: In farm area. Single-family building permits issued: 5 (2001) / 2 (2000); Multi-family building permits issued: 0 (2001) / 0 (2000); Employment by occupation: 15.5% management, 9.5% professional, 12.0% services, 19.8% sales, 3.4% farming, 12.7% construction, 27.0% production (2000).
Income: Per capita income: $20,404 (2000); Median household income: $50,272 (2000); Poverty rate: 3.3% (2000).
Taxes: Total city taxes per capita: $105 (1997); City property taxes per capita: $102 (1997).
Education: High school graduation rate: 84.4% (2000); College graduation rate: 14.3% (2000).
Housing: Homeownership rate: 85.4% (2000); Median home value: $115,800 (2000); Median rent: $500 per month (2000); Median age of housing: 45 years (2000).
Transportation: Commute to work: 92.0% car, 0.0% public transportation, 2.8% walk, 4.9% work from home (2000); Travel time to work: 24.9% less than 15 minutes, 47.3% 15 to 30 minutes, 18.5% 30 to 45 minutes, 4.4% 45 to 60 minutes, 4.9% 60 minutes or more (2000)

SAINT CLOUD (village). Covers a land area of 0.931 square miles and a water area of 0 square miles. Located at 43.82° N. Lat.; 88.16° W. Long. Elevation is 930 feet.
Population: 497 (2000); Race: 99.4% White, 0.0% Black, 0.2% Asian, 0.4% American Indian and Alaska Native, 0.6% Hispanic of any race, 0.0% two or more races (2000); Density: 533.9 persons per square mile (2000); Age: 27.2% under 18, 13.5% over 64 (2000); Marriage status: 28.4% never married, 60.7% now married, 6.7% widowed, 4.1% divorced (2000); Foreign born: 0.6% (2000); Ancestry (includes multiple ancestries): 76.3% German, 5.8% French (except Basque), 4.2% United States or American, 4.0% Irish, 4.0% Swedish (2000).
Economy: Single-family building permits issued: 1 (2001) / 4 (2000); Multi-family building permits issued: 0 (2001) / 0 (2000); Employment by occupation: 9.0% management, 15.4% professional, 19.4% services, 18.6% sales, 1.4% farming, 17.6% construction, 18.6% production (2000).
Income: Per capita income: $20,539 (2000); Median household income: $51,964 (2000); Poverty rate: 4.5% (2000).
Education: High school graduation rate: 82.6% (2000); College graduation rate: 10.6% (2000).
Housing: Homeownership rate: 83.7% (2000); Median home value: $86,700 (2000); Median rent: $375 per month (2000); Median age of housing: 50 years (2000).
Transportation: Commute to work: 89.5% car, 0.0% public transportation, 7.9% walk, 2.5% work from home (2000); Travel time to work: 26.3% less than 15 minutes, 40.0% 15 to 30 minutes, 21.5% 30 to 45 minutes, 3.0% 45 to 60 minutes, 9.3% 60 minutes or more (2000)

SPRINGVALE (town). Covers a land area of 35.978 square miles and a water area of 0 square miles. Located at 43.76° N. Lat.; 88.70° W. Long.
Population: 727 (2000); Race: 99.9% White, 0.0% Black, 0.0% Asian, 0.1% American Indian and Alaska Native, 0.6% Hispanic of any race, 0.0% two or more races (2000); Density: 20.2 persons per square mile (2000); Age: 27.6% under 18, 12.8% over 64 (2000); Marriage status: 22.6% never married, 65.0% now married, 5.7% widowed, 6.6% divorced (2000); Foreign born: 0.0% (2000); Ancestry (includes multiple ancestries): 52.2% German, 14.2% Dutch, 9.1% English, 7.8% Irish, 7.0% United States or American (2000).
Economy: Single-family building permits issued: 2 (2001) / 2 (2000); Multi-family building permits issued: 0 (2001) / 0 (2000); Employment by occupation: 15.7% management, 9.3% professional, 9.3% services, 19.8% sales, 3.1% farming, 11.8% construction, 31.1% production (2000).
Income: Per capita income: $19,369 (2000); Median household income: $47,604 (2000); Poverty rate: 4.5% (2000).
Taxes: Total city taxes per capita: $125 (1997); City property taxes per capita: $123 (1997).
Education: High school graduation rate: 80.5% (2000); College graduation rate: 15.4% (2000).
Housing: Homeownership rate: 83.6% (2000); Median home value: $114,400 (2000); Median rent: $442 per month (2000); Median age of housing: 37 years (2000).
Transportation: Commute to work: 86.4% car, 0.0% public transportation, 2.6% walk, 11.0% work from home (2000); Travel time to work: 30.3% less than 15 minutes, 46.2% 15 to 30 minutes, 14.1% 30 to 45 minutes, 3.8% 45 to 60 minutes, 5.6% 60 minutes or more (2000)

TAYCHEEDAH (town). Covers a land area of 29.995 square miles and a water area of 5.249 square miles. Located at 43.83° N. Lat.; 88.35° W. Long. Elevation is 755 feet.
History: Taycheedah was founded in 1839 by Francis D. McCarty, who hoped to build an industrial and commercial city here, where several travel routes converged. After the Civil War, trade moved from Taycheedah to Fond du Lac.
Population: 3,666 (2000); Race: 100.0% White, 0.0% Black, 0.0% Asian, 0.0% American Indian and Alaska Native, 0.0% Hispanic of any race, 0.0% two or more races (2000); Density: 122.2 persons per square mile (2000); Age: 27.5% under 18, 12.2% over 64 (2000); Marriage status: 19.7% never married, 71.0% now married, 4.9% widowed, 4.4% divorced (2000); Foreign born: 0.6% (2000); Ancestry (includes multiple ancestries): 65.5% German, 14.3% Irish, 7.1% English, 3.9% Polish, 3.8% Italian (2000).
Economy: Single-family building permits issued: 30 (2001) / 23 (2000); Multi-family building permits issued: 0 (2001) / 2 (2000); Employment by occupation: 15.3% management, 18.8% professional, 13.0% services, 21.6% sales, 2.0% farming, 12.2% construction, 17.2% production (2000).
Income: Per capita income: $23,423 (2000); Median household income: $59,231 (2000); Poverty rate: 2.6% (2000).
Taxes: Total city taxes per capita: $59 (1997); City property taxes per capita: $51 (1997).
Education: High school graduation rate: 86.4% (2000); College graduation rate: 23.5% (2000).
Housing: Homeownership rate: 91.9% (2000); Median home value: $144,200 (2000); Median rent: $565 per month (2000); Median age of housing: 27 years (2000).
Transportation: Commute to work: 93.3% car, 0.0% public transportation, 1.9% walk, 4.6% work from home (2000); Travel time to work: 20.5% less than 15 minutes, 56.9% 15 to 30 minutes, 13.6% 30 to 45 minutes, 5.3% 45 to 60 minutes, 3.8% 60 minutes or more (2000)

VAN DYNE (unincorporated postal area, zip code 54979). Aka Vandyne. Covers a land area of 24.180 square miles and a water area of 0 square miles. Located at 43.87° N. Lat.; 88.52° W. Long. Elevation is 790 feet.
History: Van Dyne was named for an early Dutch settler during the 1860's.
Population: 1,375 (2000); Race: 99.4% White, 0.0% Black, 0.0% Asian, 0.0% American Indian and Alaska Native, 0.1% Hispanic of any race, 0.6% two or more races (2000); Density: 56.9 persons per square mile (2000); Age: 25.9% under 18, 11.8% over 64 (2000); Marriage status: 23.7% never married, 68.2% now married, 4.1% widowed, 4.0% divorced (2000); Foreign born: 0.0% (2000); Ancestry (includes multiple ancestries): 66.8% German, 6.4% English, 5.2% United States or American, 5.2% French (except Basque), 5.0% Polish (2000).
Economy: Employment by occupation: 10.9% management, 10.6% professional, 13.7% services, 22.0% sales, 1.8% farming, 11.3% construction, 29.8% production (2000).
Income: Per capita income: $19,338 (2000); Median household income: $53,681 (2000); Poverty rate: 2.7% (2000).
Education: High school graduation rate: 84.4% (2000); College graduation rate: 11.4% (2000).
Housing: Homeownership rate: 87.1% (2000); Median home value: $113,900 (2000); Median rent: $442 per month (2000); Median age of housing: 42 years (2000).
Transportation: Commute to work: 88.5% car, 0.3% public transportation, 3.1% walk, 8.1% work from home (2000); Travel time to work: 23.4% less

than 15 minutes, 59.4% 15 to 30 minutes, 11.1% 30 to 45 minutes, 2.2% 45 to 60 minutes, 3.9% 60 minutes or more (2000)

WAUPUN (town). Covers a land area of 34.978 square miles and a water area of 0 square miles. Located at 43.65° N. Lat.; 88.70° W. Long. Elevation is 904 feet.

Population: 1,385 (2000); Race: 98.2% White, 1.4% Black, 0.4% Asian, 0.0% American Indian and Alaska Native, 0.0% Hispanic of any race, 0.0% two or more races (2000); Density: 39.6 persons per square mile (2000); Age: 28.3% under 18, 11.4% over 64 (2000); Marriage status: 20.1% never married, 71.9% now married, 3.7% widowed, 4.3% divorced (2000); Foreign born: 0.8% (2000); Ancestry (includes multiple ancestries): 43.8% German, 32.6% Dutch, 6.7% Irish, 6.4% United States or American, 6.0% English (2000).

Economy: Single-family building permits issued: 5 (2001) / 7 (2000); Multi-family building permits issued: 0 (2001) / 0 (2000); Employment by occupation: 14.0% management, 14.7% professional, 14.6% services, 23.2% sales, 3.1% farming, 10.4% construction, 20.0% production (2000).

Income: Per capita income: $20,641 (2000); Median household income: $55,071 (2000); Poverty rate: 2.1% (2000).

Taxes: Total city taxes per capita: $41 (1997); City property taxes per capita: $39 (1997).

Education: High school graduation rate: 80.7% (2000); College graduation rate: 13.7% (2000).

School District(s)

Waupun (PK-12)
2000 Enrollment: 2,389 920-324-9341

Housing: Homeownership rate: 90.8% (2000); Median home value: $128,700 (2000); Median rent: $296 per month (2000); Median age of housing: 35 years (2000).

Transportation: Commute to work: 88.0% car, 0.0% public transportation, 3.8% walk, 8.3% work from home (2000); Travel time to work: 51.7% less than 15 minutes, 32.1% 15 to 30 minutes, 10.9% 30 to 45 minutes, 2.1% 45 to 60 minutes, 3.1% 60 minutes or more (2000)

Forest County

Located in northeastern Wisconsin; bounded on the north by the Brule River and the Michigan border; includes Sugarbush Hill, the highest point in the state (1,951 ft), and most of Nicolet National Forest. Covers a land area of 1,014.10 square miles, a water area of 32.30 square miles, and is located in the Central Time Zone. The county government was organized in 1885. County seat is Crandon.

Weather Station: Laona 6 SW — Elevation: 1,522 feet

	Jan	Feb	Mar	Apr	May	Jun	Jul	Aug	Sep	Oct	Nov	Dec
High	21	27	37	53	66	73	76	73	64	54	37	25
Low	3	7	17	29	40	49	55	53	45	35	22	9
Precip	1.3	0.9	2.0	2.6	3.4	3.7	3.6	3.6	3.8	2.8	2.3	1.5
Snow	16.8	9.8	12.5	6.0	0.8	0.0	0.0	0.0	tr	1.9	9.2	15.7

High and Low temperatures in degrees Fahrenheit; Precipitation and Snow in inches

Population: 10,024 (2000); Race: 86.1% White, 0.9% Black, 0.4% Asian, 10.9% American Indian and Alaska Native, 1.6% Hispanic of any race, 1.3% two or more races (2000); Density: 9.9 persons per square mile (2000); Age: 25.4% under 18, 19.3% over 64 (2000).

Religion: Five largest groups: 26.4% Catholic Church, 5.0% Wisconsin Evangelical Lutheran Synod, 4.5% Lutheran Church—Missouri Synod, 2.0% The United Methodist Church, 1.5% Church of God (Cleveland, Tennessee) (2000).

Economy: Unemployment rate: 5.5% (11/2002); Total civilian labor force: 4,947 (11/2002); Leading industries: 17.7% manufacturing; 13.5% retail trade; 11.4% health care and social assistance (2000); Companies that employ more than 1,000 persons: 0 (2000); Companies that employ more than 100 persons: 4 (2000); Farms: 111 totaling 26,150 acres (1997); Minority business ownership rate: 0.0% (1997); Women business ownership rate: 20.1% (1997); Retail sales per capita: $5,332 (1997). Single-family building permits issued: 101 (2001) / 96 (2000); Multi-family building permits issued: 0 (2001) / 0 (2000).

Income: Per capita income: $16,451 (2000); Median household income: $32,023 (2000); Poverty rate: 13.1% (2000); Bankruptcy rate: 3.77% (2001).

Taxes: Total county taxes per capita: $195 (1997); County property taxes per capita: $161 (1997).

Education: High school graduation rate: 78.5% (2000); College graduation rate: 10.0% (2000).

Housing: Homeownership rate: 78.9% (2000); Median home value: $77,400 (2000); Median rent: $256 per month (2000); Median age of housing: 29 years (2000).

Health: Birth rate: 92.8 per 10,000 population (1998); Age adjusted death rate: 92.3 per 10,000 population (1999); Age adjusted cancer mortality rate: 215.6 deaths per 100,000 population (1999). Number of physicians: 3.0 per 10,000 population (1999); Number of hospital beds: n/a (1999).

Elections: 2000 Presidential election results: 45.8% Gore, 51.0% Bush, 2.7% Nader, 0.3% Buchanan

National and State Parks: Bog Brook State Wildlife Area; Little Rice State Wildlife Area; Nicolet National Forest

Additional Information Contacts

Forest County Government Offices 715-478-2422
Crandon Chamber of Commerce 715-478-3450
Laona Chamber of Commerce 715-674-3007

Forest County Communities

ALVIN (town). Covers a land area of 114.979 square miles and a water area of 1.012 square miles. Located at 45.96° N. Lat.; 88.82° W. Long. Elevation is 1,670 feet.

Population: 186 (2000); Race: 100.0% White, 0.0% Black, 0.0% Asian, 0.0% American Indian and Alaska Native, 0.0% Hispanic of any race, 0.0% two or more races (2000); Density: 1.6 persons per square mile (2000); Age: 4.4% under 18, 39.9% over 64 (2000); Marriage status: 13.9% never married, 72.2% now married, 6.0% widowed, 7.9% divorced (2000); Foreign born: 0.0% (2000); Ancestry (includes multiple ancestries): 28.5% German, 17.1% English, 12.0% Irish, 3.2% Polish, 3.2% Dutch (2000).

Economy: Single-family building permits issued: 16 (2001) / 10 (2000); Multi-family building permits issued: 0 (2001) / 0 (2000); Employment by occupation: 5.4% management, 0.0% professional, 13.5% services, 18.9% sales, 0.0% farming, 40.5% construction, 21.6% production (2000).

Income: Per capita income: $15,643 (2000); Median household income: $26,500 (2000); Poverty rate: 13.9% (2000).

Taxes: Total city taxes per capita: $6 (1997); City property taxes per capita: $0 (1997).

Education: High school graduation rate: 61.0% (2000); College graduation rate: 3.4% (2000).

Housing: Homeownership rate: 98.8% (2000); Median home value: $84,400 (2000); Median age of housing: 24 years (2000).

Transportation: Commute to work: 81.1% car, 0.0% public transportation, 10.8% walk, 0.0% work from home (2000); Travel time to work: 10.8% less than 15 minutes, 45.9% 15 to 30 minutes, 8.1% 30 to 45 minutes, 16.2% 45 to 60 minutes, 18.9% 60 minutes or more (2000)

ARGONNE (town). Aka North Crandon. Covers a land area of 108.236 square miles and a water area of 0.072 square miles. Located at 45.73° N. Lat.; 88.85° W. Long. Elevation is 1,641 feet.

Population: 532 (2000); Race: 94.8% White, 0.0% Black, 0.0% Asian, 4.5% American Indian and Alaska Native, 0.0% Hispanic of any race, 0.7% two or more races (2000); Density: 4.9 persons per square mile (2000); Age: 26.3% under 18, 12.5% over 64 (2000); Marriage status: 29.2% never married, 52.9% now married, 6.0% widowed, 11.9% divorced (2000); Foreign born: 0.0% (2000); Ancestry (includes multiple ancestries): 29.5% German, 20.9% Irish, 12.1% Polish, 7.0% Other groups, 5.9% French (except Basque) (2000).

Economy: Employment by occupation: 8.7% management, 11.6% professional, 21.7% services, 18.1% sales, 5.1% farming, 13.7% construction, 21.3% production (2000).

Income: Per capita income: $18,169 (2000); Median household income: $40,909 (2000); Poverty rate: 10.1% (2000).

Taxes: Total city taxes per capita: $19 (1997); City property taxes per capita: $19 (1997).

Education: High school graduation rate: 85.1% (2000); College graduation rate: 10.7% (2000).

Housing: Homeownership rate: 93.0% (2000); Median home value: $66,700 (2000); Median rent: $271 per month (2000); Median age of housing: 37 years (2000).

Transportation: Commute to work: 89.1% car, 0.0% public transportation, 3.7% walk, 6.4% work from home (2000); Travel time to work: 36.8% less than 15 minutes, 31.6% 15 to 30 minutes, 3.2% 30 to 45 minutes, 16.4% 45 to 60 minutes, 12.0% 60 minutes or more (2000)

ARMSTRONG CREEK (town). Covers a land area of 47.987 square miles and a water area of 0.655 square miles. Located at 45.66° N. Lat.; 88.48° W. Long. Elevation is 1,516 feet.

Population: 463 (2000); Race: 100.0% White, 0.0% Black, 0.0% Asian, 0.0% American Indian and Alaska Native, 1.2% Hispanic of any race, 0.0% two or more races (2000); Density: 9.6 persons per square mile (2000); Age: 24.7% under 18, 24.3% over 64 (2000); Marriage status: 19.6% never married, 59.1% now married, 12.9% widowed, 8.4% divorced (2000); Foreign born: 4.4% (2000); Ancestry (includes multiple ancestries): 53.1% Polish, 25.6% German, 9.3% Irish, 4.6% English, 4.0% Swedish (2000).
Economy: Employment by occupation: 10.1% management, 8.8% professional, 14.5% services, 13.2% sales, 4.8% farming, 13.7% construction, 34.8% production (2000).
Income: Per capita income: $18,266 (2000); Median household income: $27,500 (2000); Poverty rate: 9.7% (2000).
Taxes: Total city taxes per capita: $25 (1997); City property taxes per capita: $24 (1997).
Education: High school graduation rate: 74.2% (2000); College graduation rate: 8.4% (2000).
Housing: Homeownership rate: 91.7% (2000); Median home value: $61,500 (2000); Median rent: $325 per month (2000); Median age of housing: 36 years (2000).
Transportation: Commute to work: 85.0% car, 0.0% public transportation, 5.6% walk, 6.5% work from home (2000); Travel time to work: 33.5% less than 15 minutes, 25.0% 15 to 30 minutes, 14.5% 30 to 45 minutes, 12.5% 45 to 60 minutes, 14.5% 60 minutes or more (2000)

BLACKWELL (town). Covers a land area of 65.998 square miles and a water area of 0.371 square miles. Located at 45.53° N. Lat.; 88.54° W. Long. Elevation is 1,480 feet.
Population: 347 (2000); Race: 63.9% White, 21.8% Black, 0.0% Asian, 9.5% American Indian and Alaska Native, 4.0% Hispanic of any race, 0.9% two or more races (2000); Density: 5.3 persons per square mile (2000); Age: 23.8% under 18, 26.4% over 64 (2000); Marriage status: 51.2% never married, 28.1% now married, 17.3% widowed, 3.4% divorced (2000); Foreign born: 0.0% (2000); Ancestry (includes multiple ancestries): 38.4% German, 36.4% Other groups, 9.7% Polish, 8.9% Irish, 4.6% Swedish (2000).
Economy: Employment by occupation: 3.5% management, 1.8% professional, 9.6% services, 38.6% sales, 4.4% farming, 35.1% construction, 7.0% production (2000).
Income: Per capita income: $9,089 (2000); Median household income: $28,750 (2000); Poverty rate: 62.9% (2000).
Education: High school graduation rate: 50.0% (2000); College graduation rate: 3.8% (2000).
Housing: Homeownership rate: 81.0% (2000); Median home value: $45,000 (2000); Median rent: $375 per month (2000); Median age of housing: 37 years (2000).
Transportation: Commute to work: 37.7% car, 0.0% public transportation, 58.8% walk, 3.5% work from home (2000); Travel time to work: 74.5% less than 15 minutes, 12.7% 15 to 30 minutes, 4.5% 30 to 45 minutes, 1.8% 45 to 60 minutes, 6.4% 60 minutes or more (2000)

CASWELL (town). Covers a land area of 47.740 square miles and a water area of 0.171 square miles. Located at 45.65° N. Lat.; 88.67° W. Long.
Population: 102 (2000); Race: 76.2% White, 5.7% Black, 0.0% Asian, 4.8% American Indian and Alaska Native, 11.4% Hispanic of any race, 1.9% two or more races (2000); Density: 2.1 persons per square mile (2000); Age: 27.6% under 18, 14.3% over 64 (2000); Marriage status: 22.2% never married, 67.9% now married, 6.2% widowed, 3.7% divorced (2000); Foreign born: 3.8% (2000); Ancestry (includes multiple ancestries): 35.2% German, 21.0% Other groups, 12.4% United States or American, 8.6% Norwegian, 7.6% Danish (2000).
Economy: Single-family building permits issued: 1 (2001) / 1 (2000); Multi-family building permits issued: 0 (2001) / 0 (2000); Employment by occupation: 0.0% management, 4.3% professional, 10.6% services, 21.3% sales, 4.3% farming, 2.1% construction, 57.4% production (2000).
Income: Per capita income: $15,560 (2000); Median household income: $37,750 (2000); Poverty rate: 22.5% (2000).
Taxes: Total city taxes per capita: $49 (1997); City property taxes per capita: $49 (1997).
Education: High school graduation rate: 82.9% (2000); College graduation rate: 6.6% (2000).
Housing: Homeownership rate: 82.9% (2000); Median home value: $86,300 (2000); Median rent: $200 per month (2000); Median age of housing: 39 years (2000).
Transportation: Commute to work: 81.0% car, 0.0% public transportation, 19.0% walk, 0.0% work from home (2000); Travel time to work: 31.0% less than 15 minutes, 40.5% 15 to 30 minutes, 7.1% 30 to 45 minutes, 7.1% 45 to 60 minutes, 14.3% 60 minutes or more (2000)

CRANDON (city). Covers a land area of 5.219 square miles and a water area of 0.951 square miles. Located at 45.57° N. Lat.; 88.90° W. Long. Elevation is 1,630 feet.
History: Crandon, built around several lakes, was named for F.P. Crandon, a railroad official. Lumber was the basis of Crandon's economy, which also had a furniture factory and a creamery in the early 1900's.
Population: 1,961 (2000); Race: 90.9% White, 0.0% Black, 0.0% Asian, 7.6% American Indian and Alaska Native, 1.0% Hispanic of any race, 1.5% two or more races (2000); Density: 375.8 persons per square mile (2000); Age: 26.5% under 18, 20.6% over 64 (2000); Marriage status: 23.2% never married, 52.2% now married, 13.3% widowed, 11.3% divorced (2000); Foreign born: 0.9% (2000); Ancestry (includes multiple ancestries): 34.2% German, 15.3% Irish, 9.5% English, 9.4% Other groups, 9.0% Polish (2000).
Economy: Employment by occupation: 8.0% management, 16.6% professional, 22.6% services, 23.8% sales, 3.0% farming, 8.3% construction, 17.8% production (2000).
Income: Per capita income: $14,757 (2000); Median household income: $27,125 (2000); Poverty rate: 14.4% (2000).
Taxes: Total city taxes per capita: $183 (1997); City property taxes per capita: $151 (1997).
Education: High school graduation rate: 75.7% (2000); College graduation rate: 10.7% (2000).

School District(s)

Crandon (PK-12)
2000 Enrollment: 1,074 715-478-3339
Housing: Homeownership rate: 62.9% (2000); Median home value: $72,000 (2000); Median rent: $273 per month (2000); Median age of housing: 36 years (2000).
Safety: Violent crime rate: 15.2 per 10,000 population; Property crime rate: 313.9 per 10,000 population (2001).
Newspapers: Forest Republican (1 x week)
Transportation: Commute to work: 85.8% car, 0.4% public transportation, 7.4% walk, 5.3% work from home (2000); Travel time to work: 66.1% less than 15 minutes, 12.2% 15 to 30 minutes, 14.9% 30 to 45 minutes, 3.0% 45 to 60 minutes, 3.8% 60 minutes or more (2000)
Additional Information Contacts
Crandon Chamber of Commerce 715-478-3450

CRANDON (town). Covers a land area of 33.792 square miles and a water area of 1.994 square miles. Located at 45.59° N. Lat.; 88.99° W. Long. Elevation is 1,630 feet.
History: Incorporated 1898.
Population: 614 (2000); Race: 97.2% White, 0.0% Black, 0.3% Asian, 0.8% American Indian and Alaska Native, 0.0% Hispanic of any race, 1.7% two or more races (2000); Density: 18.2 persons per square mile (2000); Age: 25.8% under 18, 14.0% over 64 (2000); Marriage status: 18.6% never married, 64.1% now married, 8.2% widowed, 9.1% divorced (2000); Foreign born: 1.3% (2000); Ancestry (includes multiple ancestries): 39.3% German, 14.6% Irish, 13.0% English, 10.8% Polish, 7.7% United States or American (2000).
Economy: Resort in wooded-lake, lumbering, dairying, and potato-growing region. Manufacturing: wood products, cutlery, pulp; sawmilling, woodworking. Indian Reservation to Southwest is proposed site for large zinc and copper mine. Employment by occupation: 8.6% management, 12.5% professional, 12.9% services, 21.8% sales, 8.2% farming, 14.6% construction, 21.4% production (2000).
Income: Per capita income: $14,933 (2000); Median household income: $33,375 (2000); Poverty rate: 11.1% (2000).
Taxes: Total city taxes per capita: $51 (1997); City property taxes per capita: $51 (1997).
Education: High school graduation rate: 72.5% (2000); College graduation rate: 8.3% (2000).
Housing: Homeownership rate: 90.9% (2000); Median home value: $59,200 (2000); Median rent: $325 per month (2000); Median age of housing: 25 years (2000).
Transportation: Commute to work: 92.7% car, 0.0% public transportation, 0.0% walk, 7.3% work from home (2000); Travel time to work: 46.7% less than 15 minutes, 18.0% 15 to 30 minutes, 14.9% 30 to 45 minutes, 6.3% 45 to 60 minutes, 14.1% 60 minutes or more (2000)

FREEDOM (town). Covers a land area of 34.064 square miles and a water area of 2.028 square miles. Located at 45.43° N. Lat.; 88.75° W. Long.
Population: 376 (2000); Race: 97.9% White, 0.0% Black, 0.5% Asian, 0.5% American Indian and Alaska Native, 1.6% Hispanic of any race, 0.5% two or more races (2000); Density: 11.0 persons per square mile (2000); Age: 17.6% under 18, 20.5% over 64 (2000); Marriage status: 16.5% never married,

72.9% now married, 6.5% widowed, 4.0% divorced (2000); Foreign born: 1.1% (2000); Ancestry (includes multiple ancestries): 57.2% German, 16.5% Irish, 12.8% Polish, 12.0% United States or American, 5.3% French (except Basque) (2000).
Economy: Employment by occupation: 9.9% management, 8.7% professional, 16.9% services, 14.5% sales, 3.5% farming, 17.4% construction, 29.1% production (2000).
Income: Per capita income: $17,280 (2000); Median household income: $35,313 (2000); Poverty rate: 5.6% (2000).
Taxes: Total city taxes per capita: $168 (1997); City property taxes per capita: $168 (1997).
Education: High school graduation rate: 81.1% (2000); College graduation rate: 11.5% (2000).
Housing: Homeownership rate: 90.0% (2000); Median home value: $91,100 (2000); Median rent: $225 per month (2000); Median age of housing: 31 years (2000).
Transportation: Commute to work: 82.4% car, 1.2% public transportation, 5.5% walk, 8.5% work from home (2000); Travel time to work: 21.2% less than 15 minutes, 29.8% 15 to 30 minutes, 26.5% 30 to 45 minutes, 9.9% 45 to 60 minutes, 12.6% 60 minutes or more (2000)

HILES (town). Covers a land area of 131.443 square miles and a water area of 9.518 square miles. Located at 45.82° N. Lat.; 88.99° W. Long. Elevation is 1,670 feet.
Population: 404 (2000); Race: 95.1% White, 0.0% Black, 0.0% Asian, 4.9% American Indian and Alaska Native, 0.0% Hispanic of any race, 0.0% two or more races (2000); Density: 3.1 persons per square mile (2000); Age: 13.5% under 18, 35.8% over 64 (2000); Marriage status: 12.4% never married, 75.7% now married, 4.9% widowed, 6.9% divorced (2000); Foreign born: 0.5% (2000); Ancestry (includes multiple ancestries): 47.2% German, 8.5% Polish, 7.5% Norwegian, 6.5% English, 6.2% Irish (2000).
Economy: Employment by occupation: 12.2% management, 10.4% professional, 20.0% services, 15.7% sales, 1.7% farming, 9.6% construction, 30.4% production (2000).
Income: Per capita income: $17,830 (2000); Median household income: $26,806 (2000); Poverty rate: 11.9% (2000).
Taxes: Total city taxes per capita: $127 (1997); City property taxes per capita: $124 (1997).
Education: High school graduation rate: 80.2% (2000); College graduation rate: 16.5% (2000).
Housing: Homeownership rate: 94.0% (2000); Median home value: $87,000 (2000); Median rent: $142 per month (2000); Median age of housing: 29 years (2000).
Transportation: Commute to work: 84.3% car, 1.7% public transportation, 4.3% walk, 9.6% work from home (2000); Travel time to work: 26.0% less than 15 minutes, 34.6% 15 to 30 minutes, 8.7% 30 to 45 minutes, 4.8% 45 to 60 minutes, 26.0% 60 minutes or more (2000)

LAONA (town). Aka Snyders. Covers a land area of 103.391 square miles and a water area of 4.149 square miles. Located at 45.55° N. Lat.; 88.68° W. Long. Elevation is 1,580 feet.
History: Laona, which developed as a lumbering and recreation area, was named for the daughter of a local businessman. The village was built largely by the Connor Lumber and Land Company, which operated a sawmill, planing mill, and factories producing flooring and lawn furniture.
Population: 1,367 (2000); Race: 97.2% White, 0.2% Black, 0.0% Asian, 1.4% American Indian and Alaska Native, 0.5% Hispanic of any race, 1.1% two or more races (2000); Density: 13.2 persons per square mile (2000); Age: 26.3% under 18, 18.3% over 64 (2000); Marriage status: 20.4% never married, 61.1% now married, 10.0% widowed, 8.5% divorced (2000); Foreign born: 0.7% (2000); Ancestry (includes multiple ancestries): 39.3% German, 17.8% Polish, 12.7% Irish, 8.0% French Canadian, 7.2% French (except Basque) (2000).
Economy: Employment by occupation: 10.2% management, 12.3% professional, 18.8% services, 20.0% sales, 5.2% farming, 8.4% construction, 25.0% production (2000).
Income: Per capita income: $15,652 (2000); Median household income: $31,852 (2000); Poverty rate: 11.2% (2000).
Taxes: Total city taxes per capita: $32 (1997); City property taxes per capita: $27 (1997).
Education: High school graduation rate: 84.5% (2000); College graduation rate: 10.5% (2000).

School District(s)

Laona (PK-12)
2000 Enrollment: 318 715-674-2143

Housing: Homeownership rate: 76.4% (2000); Median home value: $67,200 (2000); Median rent: $256 per month (2000); Median age of housing: 35 years (2000).
Transportation: Commute to work: 89.6% car, 1.3% public transportation, 4.5% walk, 3.5% work from home (2000); Travel time to work: 51.0% less than 15 minutes, 28.4% 15 to 30 minutes, 5.8% 30 to 45 minutes, 7.5% 45 to 60 minutes, 7.2% 60 minutes or more (2000)
Additional Information Contacts
Laona Chamber of Commerce 715-674-3007

LINCOLN (town). Covers a land area of 58.121 square miles and a water area of 4.803 square miles. Located at 45.53° N. Lat.; 88.85° W. Long.
Population: 1,005 (2000); Race: 69.7% White, 0.0% Black, 0.6% Asian, 28.2% American Indian and Alaska Native, 4.6% Hispanic of any race, 1.3% two or more races (2000); Density: 17.3 persons per square mile (2000); Age: 26.4% under 18, 16.7% over 64 (2000); Marriage status: 21.2% never married, 63.9% now married, 5.6% widowed, 9.4% divorced (2000); Foreign born: 0.9% (2000); Ancestry (includes multiple ancestries): 32.5% German, 30.3% Other groups, 9.1% Irish, 9.0% Polish, 6.9% English (2000).
Economy: Single-family building permits issued: 10 (2001) / 10 (2000); Multi-family building permits issued: 0 (2001) / 0 (2000); Employment by occupation: 9.0% management, 14.4% professional, 23.5% services, 19.6% sales, 4.4% farming, 10.6% construction, 18.6% production (2000).
Income: Per capita income: $21,602 (2000); Median household income: $44,917 (2000); Poverty rate: 7.7% (2000).
Taxes: Total city taxes per capita: $126 (1997); City property taxes per capita: $121 (1997).
Education: High school graduation rate: 80.5% (2000); College graduation rate: 13.4% (2000).
Housing: Homeownership rate: 83.6% (2000); Median home value: $100,000 (2000); Median rent: $275 per month (2000); Median age of housing: 16 years (2000).
Transportation: Commute to work: 90.6% car, 0.5% public transportation, 1.8% walk, 6.5% work from home (2000); Travel time to work: 52.1% less than 15 minutes, 23.4% 15 to 30 minutes, 13.1% 30 to 45 minutes, 3.3% 45 to 60 minutes, 8.1% 60 minutes or more (2000)

NASHVILLE (town). Covers a land area of 67.167 square miles and a water area of 5.183 square miles. Located at 45.45° N. Lat.; 88.91° W. Long. Elevation is 1,700 feet.
Population: 1,157 (2000); Race: 68.6% White, 0.0% Black, 1.4% Asian, 27.8% American Indian and Alaska Native, 1.6% Hispanic of any race, 1.7% two or more races (2000); Density: 17.2 persons per square mile (2000); Age: 27.3% under 18, 16.6% over 64 (2000); Marriage status: 19.2% never married, 66.7% now married, 5.0% widowed, 9.1% divorced (2000); Foreign born: 1.8% (2000); Ancestry (includes multiple ancestries): 32.8% Other groups, 29.4% German, 8.8% Polish, 8.3% Irish, 4.8% English (2000).
Economy: Single-family building permits issued: 18 (2001) / 18 (2000); Multi-family building permits issued: 0 (2001) / 0 (2000); Employment by occupation: 11.4% management, 8.1% professional, 25.3% services, 20.1% sales, 5.7% farming, 7.2% construction, 22.3% production (2000).
Income: Per capita income: $16,013 (2000); Median household income: $29,750 (2000); Poverty rate: 16.8% (2000).
Taxes: Total city taxes per capita: $126 (1997); City property taxes per capita: $119 (1997).
Education: High school graduation rate: 81.3% (2000); College graduation rate: 8.5% (2000).
Housing: Homeownership rate: 72.0% (2000); Median home value: $103,100 (2000); Median rent: $188 per month (2000); Median age of housing: 26 years (2000).
Transportation: Commute to work: 86.5% car, 0.4% public transportation, 4.9% walk, 7.7% work from home (2000); Travel time to work: 56.2% less than 15 minutes, 15.3% 15 to 30 minutes, 16.7% 30 to 45 minutes, 3.3% 45 to 60 minutes, 8.4% 60 minutes or more (2000)

POPPLE RIVER (town). Covers a land area of 50.087 square miles and a water area of 0.386 square miles. Located at 45.83° N. Lat.; 88.72° W. Long. Elevation is 1,523 feet.
Population: 79 (2000); Race: 100.0% White, 0.0% Black, 0.0% Asian, 0.0% American Indian and Alaska Native, 0.0% Hispanic of any race, 0.0% two or more races (2000); Density: 1.6 persons per square mile (2000); Age: 18.2% under 18, 23.6% over 64 (2000); Marriage status: 16.3% never married, 65.3% now married, 14.3% widowed, 4.1% divorced (2000); Foreign born: 0.0% (2000); Ancestry (includes multiple ancestries): 61.8% German, 29.1% Irish, 12.7% French Canadian, 10.9% French (except Basque), 7.3% Belgian (2000).

Economy: Employment by occupation: 9.1% management, 0.0% professional, 27.3% services, 31.8% sales, 4.5% farming, 9.1% construction, 18.2% production (2000).
Income: Per capita income: $13,865 (2000); Median household income: $30,000 (2000); Poverty rate: 3.6% (2000).
Education: High school graduation rate: 90.5% (2000); College graduation rate: 0.0% (2000).
Housing: Homeownership rate: 93.1% (2000); Median home value: $62,500 (2000); Median rent: $225 per month (2000); Median age of housing: 16 years (2000).
Transportation: Commute to work: 100.0% car, 0.0% public transportation, 0.0% walk, 0.0% work from home (2000); Travel time to work: 18.2% less than 15 minutes, 40.9% 15 to 30 minutes, 31.8% 30 to 45 minutes, 0.0% 45 to 60 minutes, 9.1% 60 minutes or more (2000)

ROSS (town). Covers a land area of 38.493 square miles and a water area of 0.102 square miles. Located at 45.74° N. Lat.; 88.71° W. Long.
Population: 167 (2000); Race: 100.0% White, 0.0% Black, 0.0% Asian, 0.0% American Indian and Alaska Native, 0.0% Hispanic of any race, 0.0% two or more races (2000); Density: 4.3 persons per square mile (2000); Age: 13.1% under 18, 34.0% over 64 (2000); Marriage status: 18.0% never married, 73.2% now married, 4.9% widowed, 3.8% divorced (2000); Foreign born: 0.0% (2000); Ancestry (includes multiple ancestries): 57.3% German, 15.0% Polish, 13.6% Irish, 6.8% French Canadian, 5.8% Swedish (2000).
Economy: Single-family building permits issued: 6 (2001) / 0 (2000); Multi-family building permits issued: 0 (2001) / 0 (2000); Employment by occupation: 2.2% management, 3.3% professional, 29.7% services, 12.1% sales, 4.4% farming, 8.8% construction, 39.6% production (2000).
Income: Per capita income: $17,361 (2000); Median household income: $28,750 (2000); Poverty rate: 6.3% (2000).
Taxes: Total city taxes per capita: $40 (1997); City property taxes per capita: $40 (1997).
Education: High school graduation rate: 68.4% (2000); College graduation rate: 2.0% (2000).
Housing: Homeownership rate: 89.9% (2000); Median home value: $42,500 (2000); Median rent: $275 per month (2000); Median age of housing: 34 years (2000).
Transportation: Commute to work: 94.2% car, 0.0% public transportation, 0.0% walk, 0.0% work from home (2000); Travel time to work: 24.4% less than 15 minutes, 26.7% 15 to 30 minutes, 36.0% 30 to 45 minutes, 5.8% 45 to 60 minutes, 7.0% 60 minutes or more (2000)

WABENO (town). Covers a land area of 107.336 square miles and a water area of 0.948 square miles. Located at 45.44° N. Lat.; 88.57° W. Long. Elevation is 1,540 feet.
Population: 1,264 (2000); Race: 78.3% White, 0.2% Black, 0.7% Asian, 16.7% American Indian and Alaska Native, 2.5% Hispanic of any race, 2.9% two or more races (2000); Density: 11.8 persons per square mile (2000); Age: 31.4% under 18, 14.1% over 64 (2000); Marriage status: 25.0% never married, 56.5% now married, 6.9% widowed, 11.6% divorced (2000); Foreign born: 1.0% (2000); Ancestry (includes multiple ancestries): 41.1% German, 22.3% Other groups, 11.3% Irish, 7.8% Polish, 7.2% French (except Basque) (2000).
Economy: Railroad terminus. Sawmilling; lumber; sport fishing, hunting. In Nicolet National Forest. Single-family building permits issued: 5 (2001) / 7 (2000); Multi-family building permits issued: 0 (2001) / 0 (2000); Employment by occupation: 7.7% management, 13.6% professional, 27.3% services, 15.5% sales, 3.3% farming, 14.0% construction, 18.6% production (2000).
Income: Per capita income: $16,809 (2000); Median household income: $37,768 (2000); Poverty rate: 11.1% (2000).
Taxes: Total city taxes per capita: $77 (2000); City property taxes per capita: $74 (2000).
Education: High school graduation rate: 82.0% (2000); College graduation rate: 10.1% (2000).

School District(s)

Wabeno Area (PK-12)
2000 Enrollment: 643 715-473-2592

Housing: Homeownership rate: 76.3% (2000); Median home value: $63,800 (2000); Median rent: $258 per month (2000); Median age of housing: 38 years (2000).
Transportation: Commute to work: 90.1% car, 0.0% public transportation, 3.0% walk, 5.9% work from home (2000); Travel time to work: 54.5% less than 15 minutes, 25.8% 15 to 30 minutes, 8.0% 30 to 45 minutes, 3.4% 45 to 60 minutes, 8.4% 60 minutes or more (2000)

Grant County

Located in southwestern Wisconsin; bounded on the south by Illinois, on the north by the Wisconsin River, and on the west by the Mississippi River and the Iowa border; drained by the Platte and Blue Rivers. Covers a land area of 1,147.80 square miles, a water area of 35.50 square miles, and is located in the Central Time Zone. The county government was organized in 1836. County seat is Lancaster.

Weather Station: Lancaster 4 WSW — Elevation: 1,040 feet

	Jan	Feb	Mar	Apr	May	Jun	Jul	Aug	Sep	Oct	Nov	Dec
High	24	31	42	57	69	79	82	80	72	60	43	30
Low	7	13	25	36	47	57	61	59	51	39	27	14
Precip	0.8	1.0	2.2	3.3	3.7	4.5	4.3	4.6	3.4	2.5	2.5	1.2
Snow	10.8	7.2	6.3	2.6	0.2	0.0	0.0	0.0	0.0	0.3	4.2	8.9

High and Low temperatures in degrees Fahrenheit; Precipitation and Snow in inches

Weather Station: Platteville — Elevation: 1,003 feet

	Jan	Feb	Mar	Apr	May	Jun	Jul	Aug	Sep	Oct	Nov	Dec
High	25	32	44	59	71	80	83	81	73	61	44	31
Low	8	14	25	36	47	57	61	60	51	40	27	15
Precip	1.1	1.3	2.2	3.5	4.0	4.8	4.5	4.4	3.6	2.6	2.4	1.4
Snow	11.0	7.5	5.6	2.2	0.1	0.0	0.0	0.0	tr	0.3	3.3	9.6

High and Low temperatures in degrees Fahrenheit; Precipitation and Snow in inches

Population: 49,597 (2000); Race: 98.1% White, 0.5% Black, 0.4% Asian, 0.3% American Indian and Alaska Native, 0.6% Hispanic of any race, 0.5% two or more races (2000); Density: 43.2 persons per square mile (2000); Age: 23.6% under 18, 15.3% over 64 (2000).
Religion: Five largest groups: 56.2% Catholic Church, 7.5% Evangelical Lutheran Church in America, 7.2% The United Methodist Church, 1.7% United Church of Christ, 0.8% New Testament Association of Independent Baptist Churches and other Fundamental
Economy: Unemployment rate: 4.2% (11/2002); Total civilian labor force: 25,308 (11/2002); Leading industries: 22.9% manufacturing; 16.6% retail trade; 13.8% health care and social assistance (2000); Companies that employ more than 1,000 persons: 0 (2000); Companies that employ more than 100 persons: 20 (2000); Farms: 2,238 totaling 599,617 acres (1997); Minority business ownership rate: 0.0% (1997); Women business ownership rate: 15.0% (1997); Retail sales per capita: $7,254 (1997). Single-family building permits issued: 127 (2001) / 143 (2000); Multi-family building permits issued: 12 (2001) / 16 (2000).
Income: Per capita income: $16,764 (2000); Median household income: $36,268 (2000); Poverty rate: 11.2% (2000); Bankruptcy rate: 2.35% (2001).
Taxes: Total county taxes per capita: $135 (2000); County property taxes per capita: $132 (2000).
Education: High school graduation rate: 83.5% (2000); College graduation rate: 17.2% (2000).
Housing: Homeownership rate: 72.4% (2000); Median home value: $78,000 (2000); Median rent: $332 per month (2000); Median age of housing: 40 years (2000).
Health: Birth rate: 102.2 per 10,000 population (1998); Age adjusted death rate: 84.4 per 10,000 population (1999); Age adjusted cancer mortality rate: 195.6 deaths per 100,000 population (1999). Number of physicians: 8.3 per 10,000 population (1999); Number of hospital beds: 57.7 per 10,000 population (1999).
Elections: 2000 Presidential election results: 48.7% Gore, 46.6% Bush, 3.9% Nader, 0.3% Buchanan
National and State Parks: Nelson Dewey State Park; Wyalusing State Park
Additional Information Contacts
Grant County Government Offices 608-723-2675
Boscobel Chamber of Commerce. 608-375-2672
Fennimore Chamber of Commerce 608-822-3599
Lancaster Chamber of Commerce 608-723-2820
Platteville Chamber of Commerce 608-348-8888
Realtors Association of Southwest Wisconsin. 608-822-4444

Grant County Communities

BAGLEY (village). Covers a land area of 0.750 square miles and a water area of 0.040 square miles. Located at 42.90° N. Lat.; 91.10° W. Long. Elevation is 630 feet.
Population: 339 (2000); Race: 92.8% White, 1.5% Black, 0.0% Asian, 0.0% American Indian and Alaska Native, 2.1% Hispanic of any race, 4.2% two or more races (2000); Density: 451.7 persons per square mile (2000); Age: 16.0% under 18, 22.3% over 64 (2000); Marriage status: 17.5% never

married, 62.5% now married, 8.9% widowed, 11.0% divorced (2000); Foreign born: 1.5% (2000); Ancestry (includes multiple ancestries): 38.0% German, 22.6% English, 11.1% Irish, 8.1% United States or American, 7.8% Other groups (2000).
Economy: In livestock and dairy region. Logs, lumber. Employment by occupation: 7.9% management, 12.5% professional, 23.0% services, 21.1% sales, 0.7% farming, 13.8% construction, 21.1% production (2000).
Income: Per capita income: $15,685 (2000); Median household income: $26,944 (2000); Poverty rate: 11.1% (2000).
Taxes: Total city taxes per capita: $29 (1997); City property taxes per capita: $3 (1997).
Education: High school graduation rate: 77.7% (2000); College graduation rate: 8.7% (2000).
Housing: Homeownership rate: 92.3% (2000); Median home value: $48,300 (2000); Median rent: $288 per month (2000); Median age of housing: 29 years (2000).
Transportation: Commute to work: 84.9% car, 0.0% public transportation, 8.6% walk, 6.6% work from home (2000); Travel time to work: 14.1% less than 15 minutes, 52.1% 15 to 30 minutes, 21.1% 30 to 45 minutes, 4.2% 45 to 60 minutes, 8.5% 60 minutes or more (2000)

BEETOWN (town). Covers a land area of 48.411 square miles and a water area of 0 square miles. Located at 42.80° N. Lat.; 90.86° W. Long. Elevation is 800 feet.
Population: 734 (2000); Race: 99.7% White, 0.0% Black, 0.0% Asian, 0.0% American Indian and Alaska Native, 0.0% Hispanic of any race, 0.3% two or more races (2000); Density: 15.2 persons per square mile (2000); Age: 29.3% under 18, 11.2% over 64 (2000); Marriage status: 22.6% never married, 66.2% now married, 4.1% widowed, 7.1% divorced (2000); Foreign born: 0.3% (2000); Ancestry (includes multiple ancestries): 51.4% German, 14.1% English, 10.3% Irish, 9.7% United States or American, 4.1% Other groups (2000).
Economy: Employment by occupation: 27.3% management, 8.3% professional, 15.9% services, 18.8% sales, 7.4% farming, 8.3% construction, 14.0% production (2000).
Income: Per capita income: $14,412 (2000); Median household income: $34,750 (2000); Poverty rate: 14.5% (2000).
Taxes: Total city taxes per capita: $159 (1997); City property taxes per capita: $158 (1997).
Education: High school graduation rate: 82.0% (2000); College graduation rate: 6.1% (2000).
Housing: Homeownership rate: 77.0% (2000); Median home value: $71,700 (2000); Median rent: $242 per month (2000); Median age of housing: 50 years (2000).
Transportation: Commute to work: 73.4% car, 0.0% public transportation, 2.4% walk, 23.4% work from home (2000); Travel time to work: 32.5% less than 15 minutes, 41.0% 15 to 30 minutes, 14.8% 30 to 45 minutes, 7.3% 45 to 60 minutes, 4.4% 60 minutes or more (2000)

BLOOMINGTON (village). Covers a land area of 1.295 square miles and a water area of 0 square miles. Located at 42.88° N. Lat.; 90.92° W. Long. Elevation is 960 feet.
Population: 701 (2000); Race: 100.0% White, 0.0% Black, 0.0% Asian, 0.0% American Indian and Alaska Native, 0.0% Hispanic of any race, 0.0% two or more races (2000); Density: 541.2 persons per square mile (2000); Age: 24.2% under 18, 22.0% over 64 (2000); Marriage status: 17.9% never married, 65.5% now married, 9.6% widowed, 7.0% divorced (2000); Foreign born: 0.1% (2000); Ancestry (includes multiple ancestries): 52.0% German, 13.6% English, 11.3% Irish, 7.1% Norwegian, 5.3% United States or American (2000).
Economy: Single-family building permits issued: 0 (2001) / 2 (2000); Multi-family building permits issued: 0 (2001) / 0 (2000); Employment by occupation: 9.6% management, 7.9% professional, 10.4% services, 26.1% sales, 2.2% farming, 15.4% construction, 28.4% production (2000).
Income: Per capita income: $17,960 (2000); Median household income: $34,750 (2000); Poverty rate: 4.6% (2000).
Taxes: Total city taxes per capita: $60 (1997); City property taxes per capita: $49 (1997).
Education: High school graduation rate: 83.0% (2000); College graduation rate: 7.6% (2000).
Housing: Homeownership rate: 86.6% (2000); Median home value: $53,300 (2000); Median rent: $283 per month (2000); Median age of housing: 56 years (2000).
Transportation: Commute to work: 84.6% car, 1.1% public transportation, 9.0% walk, 3.4% work from home (2000); Travel time to work: 32.3% less than 15 minutes, 43.3% 15 to 30 minutes, 13.7% 30 to 45 minutes, 3.2% 45 to 60 minutes, 7.6% 60 minutes or more (2000)

BLOOMINGTON (town). Covers a land area of 36.365 square miles and a water area of 3.500 square miles. Located at 42.87° N. Lat.; 90.99° W. Long. Elevation is 960 feet.
Population: 399 (2000); Race: 100.0% White, 0.0% Black, 0.0% Asian, 0.0% American Indian and Alaska Native, 0.0% Hispanic of any race, 0.0% two or more races (2000); Density: 11.0 persons per square mile (2000); Age: 37.6% under 18, 7.8% over 64 (2000); Marriage status: 29.0% never married, 57.2% now married, 6.7% widowed, 7.1% divorced (2000); Foreign born: 0.0% (2000); Ancestry (includes multiple ancestries): 58.1% German, 24.7% English, 12.7% Irish, 5.4% Czech, 3.5% United States or American (2000).
Economy: In farm area; meat processing. Employment by occupation: 27.7% management, 5.3% professional, 13.1% services, 18.9% sales, 8.7% farming, 11.7% construction, 14.6% production (2000).
Income: Per capita income: $11,622 (2000); Median household income: $27,679 (2000); Poverty rate: 20.5% (2000).
Taxes: Total city taxes per capita: $332 (1997); City property taxes per capita: $332 (1997).
Education: High school graduation rate: 89.7% (2000); College graduation rate: 12.1% (2000).
Housing: Homeownership rate: 69.9% (2000); Median home value: $66,300 (2000); Median rent: $293 per month (2000); Median age of housing: 49 years (2000).
Transportation: Commute to work: 72.1% car, 0.0% public transportation, 0.0% walk, 23.4% work from home (2000); Travel time to work: 28.6% less than 15 minutes, 39.6% 15 to 30 minutes, 27.3% 30 to 45 minutes, 2.6% 45 to 60 minutes, 1.9% 60 minutes or more (2000)

BLUE RIVER (village). Covers a land area of 0.743 square miles and a water area of 0 square miles. Located at 43.18° N. Lat.; 90.57° W. Long. Elevation is 676 feet.
Population: 429 (2000); Race: 98.4% White, 0.7% Black, 0.0% Asian, 0.9% American Indian and Alaska Native, 0.0% Hispanic of any race, 0.0% two or more races (2000); Density: 577.8 persons per square mile (2000); Age: 24.9% under 18, 16.8% over 64 (2000); Marriage status: 27.7% never married, 46.0% now married, 15.3% widowed, 11.0% divorced (2000); Foreign born: 0.7% (2000); Ancestry (includes multiple ancestries): 29.7% German, 18.9% Irish, 11.5% Norwegian, 10.8% English, 3.7% Czech (2000).
Economy: Makes cheese. Manufacturing: cattle butchering; lumber. Single-family building permits issued: 0 (2001) / 3 (2000); Multi-family building permits issued: 0 (2001) / 0 (2000); Employment by occupation: 7.9% management, 13.3% professional, 17.7% services, 14.3% sales, 3.4% farming, 12.3% construction, 31.0% production (2000).
Income: Per capita income: $16,548 (2000); Median household income: $34,250 (2000); Poverty rate: 8.6% (2000).
Taxes: Total city taxes per capita: $140 (2000); City property taxes per capita: $133 (2000).
Education: High school graduation rate: 76.3% (2000); College graduation rate: 13.7% (2000).
Housing: Homeownership rate: 73.5% (2000); Median home value: $64,100 (2000); Median rent: $367 per month (2000); Median age of housing: 53 years (2000).
Transportation: Commute to work: 89.1% car, 0.0% public transportation, 6.5% walk, 2.0% work from home (2000); Travel time to work: 40.1% less than 15 minutes, 32.5% 15 to 30 minutes, 14.2% 30 to 45 minutes, 5.1% 45 to 60 minutes, 8.1% 60 minutes or more (2000)

BOSCOBEL (city). Covers a land area of 2.851 square miles and a water area of 0.047 square miles. Located at 43.13° N. Lat.; 90.70° W. Long. Elevation is 672 feet.
History: Boscobel developed as a shipping center on the Wisconsin River, serving both travelers who came to Boscobel by stagecoach and continued on by river steamer, and freight and farm produce. It was in Boscobel in 1899 that the organization known as the Gideons was founded by two travelers, forced to share a room, who thought of the idea of placing Bibles in hotel rooms.
Population: 3,047 (2000); Race: 94.5% White, 4.0% Black, 0.1% Asian, 0.3% American Indian and Alaska Native, 1.6% Hispanic of any race, 0.2% two or more races (2000); Density: 1,068.6 persons per square mile (2000); Age: 24.6% under 18, 17.0% over 64 (2000); Marriage status: 23.8% never married, 57.5% now married, 9.3% widowed, 9.3% divorced (2000); Foreign born: 0.8% (2000); Ancestry (includes multiple ancestries): 37.9% German, 17.8% Irish, 10.6% Norwegian, 10.3% English, 4.7% Czech (2000).

Economy: Single-family building permits issued: 6 (2001) / 16 (2000); Multi-family building permits issued: 0 (2001) / 4 (2000); Employment by occupation: 6.4% management, 15.6% professional, 20.6% services, 19.6% sales, 1.1% farming, 6.9% construction, 29.8% production (2000).
Income: Per capita income: $15,432 (2000); Median household income: $32,698 (2000); Poverty rate: 9.6% (2000).
Taxes: Total city taxes per capita: $129 (1997); City property taxes per capita: $117 (1997).
Education: High school graduation rate: 75.4% (2000); College graduation rate: 11.9% (2000).

School District(s)

Boscobel Area (PK-12)
2000 Enrollment: 1,006 608-375-4164
Housing: Homeownership rate: 67.8% (2000); Median home value: $70,200 (2000); Median rent: $296 per month (2000); Median age of housing: 41 years (2000).
Hospitals: Boscobel Area Health Care (123 beds)
Newspapers: The Boscobel Dial (1 x week)
Transportation: Commute to work: 89.9% car, 0.0% public transportation, 5.7% walk, 1.8% work from home (2000); Travel time to work: 59.7% less than 15 minutes, 16.4% 15 to 30 minutes, 11.5% 30 to 45 minutes, 5.5% 45 to 60 minutes, 6.9% 60 minutes or more (2000)
Additional Information Contacts
Boscobel Chamber of Commerce........................ 608-375-2672

BOSCOBEL (town). Covers a land area of 6.834 square miles and a water area of 0.468 square miles. Located at 43.13° N. Lat.; 90.69° W. Long. Elevation is 672 feet.
History: Gideons Bible Society founded here, 1898. Incorporated 1873.
Population: 433 (2000); Race: 100.0% White, 0.0% Black, 0.0% Asian, 0.0% American Indian and Alaska Native, 0.7% Hispanic of any race, 0.0% two or more races (2000); Density: 63.4 persons per square mile (2000); Age: 15.1% under 18, 24.5% over 64 (2000); Marriage status: 16.3% never married, 64.6% now married, 9.4% widowed, 9.7% divorced (2000); Foreign born: 1.2% (2000); Ancestry (includes multiple ancestries): 32.1% German, 22.5% Irish, 14.4% English, 10.3% Norwegian, 9.4% United States or American (2000).
Economy: Manufacturing: electrical products; dairy products, feed. Bull Run Ski Area to Southwest. Employment by occupation: 6.7% management, 9.0% professional, 16.3% services, 15.7% sales, 1.1% farming, 14.0% construction, 37.1% production (2000).
Income: Per capita income: $18,964 (2000); Median household income: $32,841 (2000); Poverty rate: 8.1% (2000).
Taxes: Total city taxes per capita: $30 (1997); City property taxes per capita: $28 (1997).
Education: High school graduation rate: 77.8% (2000); College graduation rate: 9.8% (2000).
Housing: Homeownership rate: 79.6% (2000); Median home value: $67,800 (2000); Median rent: $234 per month (2000); Median age of housing: 31 years (2000).
Transportation: Commute to work: 90.2% car, 0.0% public transportation, 1.7% walk, 5.2% work from home (2000); Travel time to work: 58.8% less than 15 minutes, 9.7% 15 to 30 minutes, 12.7% 30 to 45 minutes, 9.1% 45 to 60 minutes, 9.7% 60 minutes or more (2000)

CASSVILLE (village). Covers a land area of 1.079 square miles and a water area of 0.011 square miles. Located at 42.71° N. Lat.; 90.98° W. Long. Elevation is 621 feet.
History: Cassville was settled in 1831 by Glendower Price, who opened a general store. The village was platted in 1836 by land speculators, who planned for it to be the future state capital. When that failed to happen, the village became a lead and wheat shipping port, and later a farmers' trade center.
Population: 1,085 (2000); Race: 98.4% White, 0.0% Black, 0.0% Asian, 1.0% American Indian and Alaska Native, 0.5% Hispanic of any race, 0.4% two or more races (2000); Density: 1,005.1 persons per square mile (2000); Age: 24.5% under 18, 24.6% over 64 (2000); Marriage status: 22.0% never married, 56.2% now married, 12.7% widowed, 9.1% divorced (2000); Foreign born: 1.4% (2000); Ancestry (includes multiple ancestries): 61.3% German, 17.3% Irish, 9.6% English, 4.0% United States or American, 3.5% Norwegian (2000).
Economy: Single-family building permits issued: 0 (2001) / 0 (2000); Multi-family building permits issued: 0 (2001) / 0 (2000); Employment by occupation: 10.2% management, 11.8% professional, 13.9% services, 18.5% sales, 0.5% farming, 8.6% construction, 36.6% production (2000).
Income: Per capita income: $16,010 (2000); Median household income: $28,179 (2000); Poverty rate: 14.6% (2000).
Taxes: Total city taxes per capita: $188 (1997); City property taxes per capita: $175 (1997).
Education: High school graduation rate: 75.7% (2000); College graduation rate: 7.3% (2000).

School District(s)

Cassville (PK-12)
2000 Enrollment: 363 608-725-5116
Housing: Homeownership rate: 73.9% (2000); Median home value: $58,600 (2000); Median rent: $253 per month (2000); Median age of housing: 51 years (2000).
Transportation: Commute to work: 89.5% car, 0.0% public transportation, 9.1% walk, 0.9% work from home (2000); Travel time to work: 47.0% less than 15 minutes, 10.6% 15 to 30 minutes, 19.9% 30 to 45 minutes, 13.7% 45 to 60 minutes, 8.7% 60 minutes or more (2000)

CASSVILLE (town). Covers a land area of 33.448 square miles and a water area of 2.913 square miles. Located at 42.73° N. Lat.; 90.96° W. Long. Elevation is 621 feet.
History: Stonefield State Historical Site in Northwest.
Population: 487 (2000); Race: 99.6% White, 0.4% Black, 0.0% Asian, 0.0% American Indian and Alaska Native, 0.0% Hispanic of any race, 0.0% two or more races (2000); Density: 14.6 persons per square mile (2000); Age: 27.4% under 18, 12.8% over 64 (2000); Marriage status: 18.6% never married, 69.1% now married, 7.2% widowed, 5.2% divorced (2000); Foreign born: 0.4% (2000); Ancestry (includes multiple ancestries): 59.4% German, 11.6% Irish, 10.0% United States or American, 6.7% English, 3.1% French (except Basque) (2000).
Economy: In agricultural area. Manufacturing: speaker cones. Employment by occupation: 31.3% management, 8.6% professional, 11.5% services, 13.2% sales, 4.1% farming, 7.4% construction, 23.9% production (2000).
Income: Per capita income: $15,492 (2000); Median household income: $35,104 (2000); Poverty rate: 16.8% (2000).
Taxes: Total city taxes per capita: $136 (1997); City property taxes per capita: $134 (1997).
Education: High school graduation rate: 80.8% (2000); College graduation rate: 5.8% (2000).
Housing: Homeownership rate: 86.4% (2000); Median home value: $70,600 (2000); Median rent: $294 per month (2000); Median age of housing: 27 years (2000).
Transportation: Commute to work: 71.1% car, 0.0% public transportation, 7.2% walk, 20.0% work from home (2000); Travel time to work: 48.4% less than 15 minutes, 13.3% 15 to 30 minutes, 17.6% 30 to 45 minutes, 6.4% 45 to 60 minutes, 14.4% 60 minutes or more (2000)

CASTLE ROCK (town). Covers a land area of 35.792 square miles and a water area of 0 square miles. Located at 43.07° N. Lat.; 90.49° W. Long.
Population: 314 (2000); Race: 100.0% White, 0.0% Black, 0.0% Asian, 0.0% American Indian and Alaska Native, 0.0% Hispanic of any race, 0.0% two or more races (2000); Density: 8.8 persons per square mile (2000); Age: 20.9% under 18, 15.6% over 64 (2000); Marriage status: 27.4% never married, 59.8% now married, 8.5% widowed, 4.2% divorced (2000); Foreign born: 0.7% (2000); Ancestry (includes multiple ancestries): 33.4% German, 27.5% Czech, 15.2% Irish, 8.9% United States or American, 8.3% Norwegian (2000).
Economy: Employment by occupation: 25.3% management, 14.7% professional, 8.8% services, 19.4% sales, 7.6% farming, 11.8% construction, 12.4% production (2000).
Income: Per capita income: $16,201 (2000); Median household income: $40,000 (2000); Poverty rate: 3.0% (2000).
Taxes: Total city taxes per capita: $229 (1997); City property taxes per capita: $226 (1997).
Education: High school graduation rate: 84.2% (2000); College graduation rate: 18.1% (2000).
Housing: Homeownership rate: 77.7% (2000); Median home value: $97,500 (2000); Median rent: $313 per month (2000); Median age of housing: 60+ years (2000).
Transportation: Commute to work: 70.8% car, 0.0% public transportation, 5.4% walk, 21.4% work from home (2000); Travel time to work: 26.5% less than 15 minutes, 21.2% 15 to 30 minutes, 30.3% 30 to 45 minutes, 10.6% 45 to 60 minutes, 11.4% 60 minutes or more (2000)

CLIFTON (town). Covers a land area of 35.723 square miles and a water area of 0.011 square miles. Located at 42.91° N. Lat.; 90.50° W. Long.

Population: 304 (2000); Race: 100.0% White, 0.0% Black, 0.0% Asian, 0.0% American Indian and Alaska Native, 0.0% Hispanic of any race, 0.0% two or more races (2000); Density: 8.5 persons per square mile (2000); Age: 29.5% under 18, 9.1% over 64 (2000); Marriage status: 21.6% never married, 69.9% now married, 3.8% widowed, 4.7% divorced (2000); Foreign born: 0.0% (2000); Ancestry (includes multiple ancestries): 38.3% German, 16.8% English, 8.7% Norwegian, 6.7% Irish, 6.7% Swiss (2000).
Economy: Employment by occupation: 34.1% management, 13.2% professional, 4.2% services, 12.6% sales, 5.4% farming, 16.2% construction, 14.4% production (2000).
Income: Per capita income: $16,978 (2000); Median household income: $45,625 (2000); Poverty rate: 17.2% (2000).
Taxes: Total city taxes per capita: $275 (1997); City property taxes per capita: $275 (1997).
Education: High school graduation rate: 83.6% (2000); College graduation rate: 20.8% (2000).
Housing: Homeownership rate: 81.7% (2000); Median home value: $87,500 (2000); Median rent: $188 per month (2000); Median age of housing: 41 years (2000).
Transportation: Commute to work: 69.1% car, 0.0% public transportation, 4.3% walk, 23.5% work from home (2000); Travel time to work: 38.7% less than 15 minutes, 36.3% 15 to 30 minutes, 19.4% 30 to 45 minutes, 4.0% 45 to 60 minutes, 1.6% 60 minutes or more (2000)

CUBA CITY (city). Covers a land area of 1.080 square miles and a water area of 0 square miles. Located at 42.60° N. Lat.; 90.43° W. Long. Elevation is 1,012 feet.
History: Incorporated 1925.
Population: 2,156 (2000); Race: 99.3% White, 0.0% Black, 0.5% Asian, 0.0% American Indian and Alaska Native, 1.6% Hispanic of any race, 0.2% two or more races (2000); Density: 1,997.1 persons per square mile (2000); Age: 23.4% under 18, 22.9% over 64 (2000); Marriage status: 19.5% never married, 65.4% now married, 9.5% widowed, 5.6% divorced (2000); Foreign born: 0.7% (2000); Ancestry (includes multiple ancestries): 46.5% German, 15.7% Irish, 11.6% English, 8.5% United States or American, 4.4% Other groups (2000).
Economy: In agricultural area: livestock; corn, alfalfa; processes dairy and farm products. Single-family building permits issued: 9 (2001) / 7 (2000); Multi-family building permits issued: 0 (2001) / 0 (2000); Employment by occupation: 11.0% management, 15.0% professional, 16.2% services, 25.9% sales, 1.9% farming, 10.6% construction, 19.4% production (2000).
Income: Per capita income: $19,375 (2000); Median household income: $38,750 (2000); Poverty rate: 8.8% (2000).
Taxes: Total city taxes per capita: $105 (1997); City property taxes per capita: $96 (1997).
Education: High school graduation rate: 80.0% (2000); College graduation rate: 13.4% (2000).

School District(s)

Cuba City (PK-12)
2000 Enrollment: 789 608-744-2847
Housing: Homeownership rate: 75.0% (2000); Median home value: $78,900 (2000); Median rent: $324 per month (2000); Median age of housing: 42 years (2000).
Safety: Violent crime rate: 9.2 per 10,000 population; Property crime rate: 234.9 per 10,000 population (2001).
Newspapers: Tri-County Press (1 x week)
Transportation: Commute to work: 89.1% car, 0.3% public transportation, 7.8% walk, 2.5% work from home (2000); Travel time to work: 46.5% less than 15 minutes, 29.6% 15 to 30 minutes, 17.0% 30 to 45 minutes, 2.5% 45 to 60 minutes, 4.5% 60 minutes or more (2000)

DICKEYVILLE (village). Covers a land area of 0.871 square miles and a water area of 0 square miles. Located at 42.62° N. Lat.; 90.59° W. Long. Elevation is 957 feet.
History: An elaborately constructed shrine of Christ and His Mother is here.
Population: 1,043 (2000); Race: 99.0% White, 0.0% Black, 0.0% Asian, 0.3% American Indian and Alaska Native, 0.2% Hispanic of any race, 0.7% two or more races (2000); Density: 1,197.3 persons per square mile (2000); Age: 24.9% under 18, 15.3% over 64 (2000); Marriage status: 22.7% never married, 65.3% now married, 6.6% widowed, 5.5% divorced (2000); Foreign born: 0.7% (2000); Ancestry (includes multiple ancestries): 64.1% German, 15.4% Irish, 8.6% English, 3.8% United States or American, 3.8% Dutch (2000).
Economy: In agricultural area. Manufacturing: concrete. Single-family building permits issued: 7 (2001) / 3 (2000); Multi-family building permits issued: 0 (2001) / 0 (2000); Employment by occupation: 11.0% management, 8.4% professional, 18.0% services, 30.3% sales, 0.4% farming, 8.2% construction, 23.6% production (2000).
Income: Per capita income: $19,989 (2000); Median household income: $41,089 (2000); Poverty rate: 3.2% (2000).
Taxes: Total city taxes per capita: $163 (1997); City property taxes per capita: $154 (1997).
Education: High school graduation rate: 83.7% (2000); College graduation rate: 9.9% (2000).
Housing: Homeownership rate: 71.7% (2000); Median home value: $89,800 (2000); Median rent: $304 per month (2000); Median age of housing: 34 years (2000).
Transportation: Commute to work: 93.7% car, 0.0% public transportation, 2.2% walk, 4.2% work from home (2000); Travel time to work: 26.3% less than 15 minutes, 63.7% 15 to 30 minutes, 7.6% 30 to 45 minutes, 1.7% 45 to 60 minutes, 0.8% 60 minutes or more (2000)

ELLENBORO (town). Covers a land area of 36.151 square miles and a water area of 0 square miles. Located at 42.80° N. Lat.; 90.60° W. Long. Elevation is 740 feet.
Population: 608 (2000); Race: 99.6% White, 0.0% Black, 0.0% Asian, 0.0% American Indian and Alaska Native, 0.4% Hispanic of any race, 0.4% two or more races (2000); Density: 16.8 persons per square mile (2000); Age: 31.2% under 18, 8.8% over 64 (2000); Marriage status: 29.1% never married, 58.7% now married, 3.7% widowed, 8.4% divorced (2000); Foreign born: 0.5% (2000); Ancestry (includes multiple ancestries): 44.4% German, 19.3% English, 11.4% Irish, 6.3% Other groups, 4.9% United States or American (2000).
Economy: Employment by occupation: 16.1% management, 14.0% professional, 12.4% services, 18.6% sales, 6.5% farming, 9.9% construction, 22.4% production (2000).
Income: Per capita income: $16,892 (2000); Median household income: $42,917 (2000); Poverty rate: 7.1% (2000).
Taxes: Total city taxes per capita: $216 (1997); City property taxes per capita: $214 (1997).
Education: High school graduation rate: 81.6% (2000); College graduation rate: 15.7% (2000).
Housing: Homeownership rate: 79.7% (2000); Median home value: $77,500 (2000); Median rent: $282 per month (2000); Median age of housing: 33 years (2000).
Transportation: Commute to work: 80.3% car, 0.0% public transportation, 9.5% walk, 9.5% work from home (2000); Travel time to work: 39.3% less than 15 minutes, 33.0% 15 to 30 minutes, 15.1% 30 to 45 minutes, 9.1% 45 to 60 minutes, 3.5% 60 minutes or more (2000)

FENNIMORE (city). Covers a land area of 1.482 square miles and a water area of 0 square miles. Located at 42.98° N. Lat.; 90.65° W. Long. Elevation is 1,200 feet.
Population: 2,387 (2000); Race: 99.1% White, 0.1% Black, 0.5% Asian, 0.3% American Indian and Alaska Native, 0.6% Hispanic of any race, 0.0% two or more races (2000); Density: 1,610.5 persons per square mile (2000); Age: 23.1% under 18, 21.9% over 64 (2000); Marriage status: 21.3% never married, 58.0% now married, 11.3% widowed, 9.4% divorced (2000); Foreign born: 1.0% (2000); Ancestry (includes multiple ancestries): 45.4% German, 18.1% English, 16.5% Irish, 15.0% Norwegian, 3.9% United States or American (2000).
Economy: Single-family building permits issued: 4 (2001) / 3 (2000); Multi-family building permits issued: 0 (2001) / 4 (2000); Employment by occupation: 10.7% management, 14.4% professional, 15.6% services, 23.8% sales, 3.6% farming, 8.1% construction, 23.8% production (2000).
Income: Per capita income: $18,701 (2000); Median household income: $34,453 (2000); Poverty rate: 7.9% (2000).
Taxes: Total city taxes per capita: $176 (1997); City property taxes per capita: $164 (1997).
Education: High school graduation rate: 83.9% (2000); College graduation rate: 17.4% (2000).

School District(s)

Fennimore Community (PK-12)
2000 Enrollment: 879 608-822-3243

Two-year College(s)

Southwest Wisconsin Technical College (Public)
2001 Enrollment: 2,003 608-822-3262
2001 Tuition: In-state $2,304; Out-of-state $17,986
Housing: Homeownership rate: 70.6% (2000); Median home value: $73,500 (2000); Median rent: $352 per month (2000); Median age of housing: 41 years (2000).

Safety: Violent crime rate: 8.3 per 10,000 population; Property crime rate: 124.8 per 10,000 population (2001).
Newspapers: Fennimore Times (1 x week)
Transportation: Commute to work: 89.9% car, 0.2% public transportation, 4.4% walk, 4.5% work from home (2000); Travel time to work: 58.9% less than 15 minutes, 22.2% 15 to 30 minutes, 14.0% 30 to 45 minutes, 2.1% 45 to 60 minutes, 2.8% 60 minutes or more (2000)
Additional Information Contacts
Fennimore Chamber of Commerce 608-822-3599
Realtors Association of Southwest Wisconsin 608-822-4444

FENNIMORE (town). Covers a land area of 34.759 square miles and a water area of 0 square miles. Located at 42.98° N. Lat.; 90.60° W. Long. Elevation is 1,200 feet.
History: Incorporated 1919.
Population: 599 (2000); Race: 100.0% White, 0.0% Black, 0.0% Asian, 0.0% American Indian and Alaska Native, 0.0% Hispanic of any race, 0.0% two or more races (2000); Density: 17.2 persons per square mile (2000); Age: 30.3% under 18, 9.6% over 64 (2000); Marriage status: 28.3% never married, 59.5% now married, 5.2% widowed, 7.1% divorced (2000); Foreign born: 0.3% (2000); Ancestry (includes multiple ancestries): 49.2% German, 15.7% English, 12.1% Norwegian, 10.8% Irish, 5.5% Pennsylvania German (2000).
Economy: In farm area: livestock, poultry; grain; dairy products, feed. Manufacturing: cheese. Has headquarters of a U.S. soil conservation project. Employment by occupation: 17.7% management, 13.5% professional, 15.9% services, 19.5% sales, 4.5% farming, 9.9% construction, 19.2% production (2000).
Income: Per capita income: $13,360 (2000); Median household income: $36,400 (2000); Poverty rate: 17.2% (2000).
Taxes: Total city taxes per capita: $88 (1997); City property taxes per capita: $86 (1997).
Education: High school graduation rate: 81.0% (2000); College graduation rate: 10.3% (2000).
Housing: Homeownership rate: 81.1% (2000); Median home value: $63,600 (2000); Median rent: $375 per month (2000); Median age of housing: 52 years (2000).
Transportation: Commute to work: 80.1% car, 0.0% public transportation, 3.7% walk, 13.8% work from home (2000); Travel time to work: 43.1% less than 15 minutes, 23.8% 15 to 30 minutes, 19.6% 30 to 45 minutes, 7.8% 45 to 60 minutes, 5.7% 60 minutes or more (2000)

GLEN HAVEN (town). Covers a land area of 34.258 square miles and a water area of 1.121 square miles. Located at 42.81° N. Lat.; 91.00° W. Long. Elevation is 660 feet.
Population: 490 (2000); Race: 100.0% White, 0.0% Black, 0.0% Asian, 0.0% American Indian and Alaska Native, 0.0% Hispanic of any race, 0.0% two or more races (2000); Density: 14.3 persons per square mile (2000); Age: 24.2% under 18, 19.0% over 64 (2000); Marriage status: 19.5% never married, 65.1% now married, 9.6% widowed, 5.7% divorced (2000); Foreign born: 0.0% (2000); Ancestry (includes multiple ancestries): 53.3% German, 8.1% Irish, 7.2% English, 4.1% United States or American, 3.7% Norwegian (2000).
Economy: Employment by occupation: 22.6% management, 9.5% professional, 11.8% services, 19.0% sales, 10.0% farming, 5.0% construction, 22.2% production (2000).
Income: Per capita income: $14,077 (2000); Median household income: $28,929 (2000); Poverty rate: 15.5% (2000).
Taxes: Total city taxes per capita: $331 (2000); City property taxes per capita: $329 (2000).
Education: High school graduation rate: 79.6% (2000); College graduation rate: 10.9% (2000).
Housing: Homeownership rate: 76.2% (2000); Median home value: $45,000 (2000); Median rent: $314 per month (2000); Median age of housing: 60+ years (2000).
Transportation: Commute to work: 70.9% car, 0.9% public transportation, 8.2% walk, 20.0% work from home (2000); Travel time to work: 34.7% less than 15 minutes, 28.4% 15 to 30 minutes, 30.1% 30 to 45 minutes, 5.1% 45 to 60 minutes, 1.7% 60 minutes or more (2000)

HARRISON (town). Covers a land area of 36.132 square miles and a water area of 0 square miles. Located at 42.72° N. Lat.; 90.62° W. Long.
Population: 497 (2000); Race: 99.6% White, 0.0% Black, 0.4% Asian, 0.0% American Indian and Alaska Native, 0.0% Hispanic of any race, 0.0% two or more races (2000); Density: 13.8 persons per square mile (2000); Age: 27.3% under 18, 8.8% over 64 (2000); Marriage status: 22.0% never married, 73.9% now married, 1.6% widowed, 2.5% divorced (2000); Foreign born: 0.7% (2000); Ancestry (includes multiple ancestries): 55.4% German, 14.7% Irish, 11.5% English, 5.1% United States or American, 3.7% Norwegian (2000).
Economy: Employment by occupation: 16.3% management, 11.6% professional, 17.2% services, 21.6% sales, 5.3% farming, 8.8% construction, 19.4% production (2000).
Income: Per capita income: $16,647 (2000); Median household income: $45,375 (2000); Poverty rate: 6.9% (2000).
Taxes: Total city taxes per capita: $171 (2000); City property taxes per capita: $169 (2000).
Education: High school graduation rate: 87.9% (2000); College graduation rate: 17.4% (2000).
Housing: Homeownership rate: 84.7% (2000); Median home value: $85,000 (2000); Median rent: $345 per month (2000); Median age of housing: 54 years (2000).
Transportation: Commute to work: 79.9% car, 0.0% public transportation, 0.9% walk, 17.9% work from home (2000); Travel time to work: 23.4% less than 15 minutes, 37.9% 15 to 30 minutes, 22.2% 30 to 45 minutes, 8.8% 45 to 60 minutes, 7.7% 60 minutes or more (2000)

HAZEL GREEN (village). Covers a land area of 1.256 square miles and a water area of 0 square miles. Located at 42.53° N. Lat.; 90.43° W. Long. Elevation is 960 feet.
History: First called Hardscrabble, the mining town that became Hazel Green was established when lead was found here in 1824. When the lead was gone, the miners turned to wheat farming, and later to corn and stock raising.
Population: 1,183 (2000); Race: 99.3% White, 0.0% Black, 0.2% Asian, 0.0% American Indian and Alaska Native, 0.3% Hispanic of any race, 0.6% two or more races (2000); Density: 941.8 persons per square mile (2000); Age: 26.2% under 18, 13.9% over 64 (2000); Marriage status: 22.6% never married, 62.0% now married, 7.1% widowed, 8.4% divorced (2000); Foreign born: 0.4% (2000); Ancestry (includes multiple ancestries): 49.5% German, 16.1% Irish, 16.1% English, 8.3% United States or American, 3.7% Dutch (2000).
Economy: Single-family building permits issued: 2 (2001) / 7 (2000); Multi-family building permits issued: 0 (2001) / 0 (2000); Employment by occupation: 7.3% management, 13.9% professional, 17.7% services, 26.4% sales, 0.9% farming, 14.2% construction, 19.5% production (2000).
Income: Per capita income: $18,052 (2000); Median household income: $39,643 (2000); Poverty rate: 10.7% (2000).
Taxes: Total city taxes per capita: $92 (1997); City property taxes per capita: $85 (1997).
Education: High school graduation rate: 87.5% (2000); College graduation rate: 15.7% (2000).

School District(s)

Southwestern Wisconsin (PK-12)
2000 Enrollment: 617 608-854-2261
Housing: Homeownership rate: 72.8% (2000); Median home value: $73,700 (2000); Median rent: $341 per month (2000); Median age of housing: 37 years (2000).
Safety: Violent crime rate: 16.8 per 10,000 population; Property crime rate: 134.3 per 10,000 population (2001).
Transportation: Commute to work: 94.2% car, 0.0% public transportation, 3.1% walk, 2.7% work from home (2000); Travel time to work: 28.6% less than 15 minutes, 53.0% 15 to 30 minutes, 14.0% 30 to 45 minutes, 2.7% 45 to 60 minutes, 1.8% 60 minutes or more (2000)

HAZEL GREEN (town). Covers a land area of 35.186 square miles and a water area of 0 square miles. Located at 42.55° N. Lat.; 90.48° W. Long. Elevation is 960 feet.
Population: 1,043 (2000); Race: 98.6% White, 0.5% Black, 0.0% Asian, 0.0% American Indian and Alaska Native, 0.0% Hispanic of any race, 0.9% two or more races (2000); Density: 29.6 persons per square mile (2000); Age: 26.6% under 18, 24.3% over 64 (2000); Marriage status: 39.3% never married, 54.1% now married, 2.2% widowed, 4.4% divorced (2000); Foreign born: 0.6% (2000); Ancestry (includes multiple ancestries): 56.1% German, 17.5% Irish, 10.2% United States or American, 10.0% English, 3.4% Norwegian (2000).
Economy: In livestock area. Formerly an important lead-mining center. Single-family building permits issued: 13 (2001) / 4 (2000); Multi-family building permits issued: 0 (2001) / 0 (2000); Employment by occupation: 20.8% management, 18.1% professional, 12.2% services, 17.6% sales, 8.4% farming, 8.8% construction, 14.0% production (2000).
Income: Per capita income: $17,128 (2000); Median household income: $42,083 (2000); Poverty rate: 16.2% (2000).
Taxes: Total city taxes per capita: $142 (1997); City property taxes per capita: $141 (1997).

Education: High school graduation rate: 87.0% (2000); College graduation rate: 34.4% (2000).
Housing: Homeownership rate: 74.7% (2000); Median home value: $93,300 (2000); Median rent: $367 per month (2000); Median age of housing: 45 years (2000).
Transportation: Commute to work: 73.5% car, 0.0% public transportation, 8.5% walk, 18.0% work from home (2000); Travel time to work: 45.5% less than 15 minutes, 37.5% 15 to 30 minutes, 9.9% 30 to 45 minutes, 3.3% 45 to 60 minutes, 3.8% 60 minutes or more (2000)

HICKORY GROVE (town). Covers a land area of 36.351 square miles and a water area of 0 square miles. Located at 43.06° N. Lat.; 90.59° W. Long. Elevation is 1,106 feet.
Population: 443 (2000); Race: 96.7% White, 0.0% Black, 0.5% Asian, 0.0% American Indian and Alaska Native, 2.9% Hispanic of any race, 0.0% two or more races (2000); Density: 12.2 persons per square mile (2000); Age: 32.8% under 18, 11.6% over 64 (2000); Marriage status: 29.2% never married, 66.0% now married, 1.3% widowed, 3.5% divorced (2000); Foreign born: 3.3% (2000); Ancestry (includes multiple ancestries): 57.7% German, 17.1% English, 15.2% Norwegian, 12.8% Irish, 6.2% Czech (2000).
Economy: Employment by occupation: 27.9% management, 8.2% professional, 9.6% services, 18.8% sales, 6.3% farming, 13.9% construction, 15.4% production (2000).
Income: Per capita income: $13,903 (2000); Median household income: $36,250 (2000); Poverty rate: 13.2% (2000).
Taxes: Total city taxes per capita: $177 (1997); City property taxes per capita: $174 (1997).
Education: High school graduation rate: 77.6% (2000); College graduation rate: 8.1% (2000).
Housing: Homeownership rate: 77.0% (2000); Median home value: $83,000 (2000); Median rent: $275 per month (2000); Median age of housing: 46 years (2000).
Transportation: Commute to work: 82.0% car, 0.0% public transportation, 6.3% walk, 11.7% work from home (2000); Travel time to work: 37.4% less than 15 minutes, 37.4% 15 to 30 minutes, 15.9% 30 to 45 minutes, 2.2% 45 to 60 minutes, 7.1% 60 minutes or more (2000)

JAMESTOWN (town). Covers a land area of 30.071 square miles and a water area of 2.618 square miles. Located at 42.56° N. Lat.; 90.60° W. Long. Elevation is 923 feet.
Population: 2,077 (2000); Race: 98.9% White, 0.7% Black, 0.0% Asian, 0.0% American Indian and Alaska Native, 0.5% Hispanic of any race, 0.2% two or more races (2000); Density: 69.1 persons per square mile (2000); Age: 25.9% under 18, 11.8% over 64 (2000); Marriage status: 24.7% never married, 65.4% now married, 4.6% widowed, 5.3% divorced (2000); Foreign born: 0.1% (2000); Ancestry (includes multiple ancestries): 65.5% German, 14.0% Irish, 6.8% United States or American, 6.0% English, 3.7% Dutch (2000).
Economy: Employment by occupation: 11.8% management, 12.5% professional, 17.0% services, 25.5% sales, 2.3% farming, 10.7% construction, 20.1% production (2000).
Income: Per capita income: $18,733 (2000); Median household income: $45,625 (2000); Poverty rate: 2.3% (2000).
Taxes: Total city taxes per capita: $9 (1997); City property taxes per capita: $6 (1997).
Education: High school graduation rate: 83.7% (2000); College graduation rate: 12.9% (2000).
Housing: Homeownership rate: 89.7% (2000); Median home value: $98,800 (2000); Median rent: $363 per month (2000); Median age of housing: 29 years (2000).
Transportation: Commute to work: 87.6% car, 0.6% public transportation, 3.0% walk, 7.9% work from home (2000); Travel time to work: 39.8% less than 15 minutes, 49.9% 15 to 30 minutes, 6.3% 30 to 45 minutes, 1.1% 45 to 60 minutes, 2.8% 60 minutes or more (2000)

LANCASTER (city). Covers a land area of 2.824 square miles and a water area of 0 square miles. Located at 42.84° N. Lat.; 90.71° W. Long. Elevation is 1,100 feet.
History: Settled before 1840, incorporated 1878.
Population: 4,070 (2000); Race: 98.9% White, 0.1% Black, 0.1% Asian, 0.0% American Indian and Alaska Native, 0.5% Hispanic of any race, 0.4% two or more races (2000); Density: 1,441.1 persons per square mile (2000); Age: 23.6% under 18, 20.6% over 64 (2000); Marriage status: 21.0% never married, 60.3% now married, 10.9% widowed, 7.7% divorced (2000); Foreign born: 0.2% (2000); Ancestry (includes multiple ancestries): 48.0% German, 14.3% Irish, 13.6% English, 6.4% Norwegian, 5.9% United States or American (2000).
Economy: In livestock and dairying area. Dairy products. Manufacturing: canned foods, beverages, veterinary remedies, feed, timber; ships, transportation equipment, flexible packaging. Agricultural research station. Single-family building permits issued: 6 (2001) / 5 (2000); Multi-family building permits issued: 0 (2001) / 0 (2000); Employment by occupation: 11.8% management, 16.8% professional, 18.5% services, 25.8% sales, 0.5% farming, 10.5% construction, 16.0% production (2000).
Income: Per capita income: $17,797 (2000); Median household income: $32,723 (2000); Poverty rate: 8.9% (2000).
Taxes: Total city taxes per capita: $236 (2000); City property taxes per capita: $219 (2000).
Education: High school graduation rate: 84.5% (2000); College graduation rate: 19.0% (2000).

School District(s)

Lancaster Community (PK-12)
2000 Enrollment: 1,155 608-723-2175

Housing: Homeownership rate: 69.7% (2000); Median home value: $78,900 (2000); Median rent: $298 per month (2000); Median age of housing: 51 years (2000).
Hospitals: Grant Regional Health Center (35 beds)
Safety: Violent crime rate: 14.6 per 10,000 population; Property crime rate: 158.6 per 10,000 population (2001).
Newspapers: Grant County Herald Independent (1x week)
Transportation: Commute to work: 86.3% car, 0.6% public transportation, 7.2% walk, 4.2% work from home (2000); Travel time to work: 59.8% less than 15 minutes, 16.0% 15 to 30 minutes, 12.8% 30 to 45 minutes, 6.4% 45 to 60 minutes, 5.0% 60 minutes or more (2000)
Airports: Lancaster Municipal
Additional Information Contacts
Lancaster Chamber of Commerce 608-723-2820

LIBERTY (town). Covers a land area of 36.491 square miles and a water area of 0 square miles. Located at 42.89° N. Lat.; 90.60° W. Long.
Population: 552 (2000); Race: 100.0% White, 0.0% Black, 0.0% Asian, 0.0% American Indian and Alaska Native, 0.0% Hispanic of any race, 0.0% two or more races (2000); Density: 15.1 persons per square mile (2000); Age: 31.9% under 18, 9.1% over 64 (2000); Marriage status: 20.9% never married, 70.5% now married, 3.2% widowed, 5.4% divorced (2000); Foreign born: 0.5% (2000); Ancestry (includes multiple ancestries): 54.5% German, 15.8% Irish, 14.7% English, 7.0% Norwegian, 3.9% Swiss (2000).
Economy: Employment by occupation: 23.2% management, 11.0% professional, 11.0% services, 20.7% sales, 1.3% farming, 11.3% construction, 21.6% production (2000).
Income: Per capita income: $15,560 (2000); Median household income: $37,000 (2000); Poverty rate: 16.3% (2000).
Taxes: Total city taxes per capita: $163 (1997); City property taxes per capita: $163 (1997).
Education: High school graduation rate: 92.8% (2000); College graduation rate: 18.9% (2000).
Housing: Homeownership rate: 84.4% (2000); Median home value: $71,300 (2000); Median rent: $288 per month (2000); Median age of housing: 51 years (2000).
Transportation: Commute to work: 82.2% car, 0.0% public transportation, 4.6% walk, 13.2% work from home (2000); Travel time to work: 50.8% less than 15 minutes, 29.9% 15 to 30 minutes, 14.8% 30 to 45 minutes, 2.3% 45 to 60 minutes, 2.3% 60 minutes or more (2000)

LIMA (town). Covers a land area of 36.549 square miles and a water area of 0.010 square miles. Located at 42.82° N. Lat.; 90.48° W. Long.
Population: 721 (2000); Race: 98.8% White, 0.0% Black, 1.2% Asian, 0.0% American Indian and Alaska Native, 0.0% Hispanic of any race, 0.0% two or more races (2000); Density: 19.7 persons per square mile (2000); Age: 31.7% under 18, 7.6% over 64 (2000); Marriage status: 23.4% never married, 66.9% now married, 4.0% widowed, 5.8% divorced (2000); Foreign born: 1.9% (2000); Ancestry (includes multiple ancestries): 43.9% German, 15.7% English, 12.7% Irish, 8.6% United States or American, 5.3% Swiss (2000).
Economy: Employment by occupation: 28.2% management, 15.8% professional, 13.6% services, 19.1% sales, 4.0% farming, 7.4% construction, 11.9% production (2000).
Income: Per capita income: $15,187 (2000); Median household income: $39,464 (2000); Poverty rate: 13.6% (2000).
Taxes: Total city taxes per capita: $133 (1997); City property taxes per capita: $132 (1997).

Education: High school graduation rate: 87.4% (2000); College graduation rate: 19.0% (2000).
Housing: Homeownership rate: 76.3% (2000); Median home value: $96,100 (2000); Median rent: $381 per month (2000); Median age of housing: 56 years (2000).
Transportation: Commute to work: 75.2% car, 0.5% public transportation, 2.2% walk, 21.5% work from home (2000); Travel time to work: 37.5% less than 15 minutes, 33.1% 15 to 30 minutes, 15.8% 30 to 45 minutes, 7.9% 45 to 60 minutes, 5.7% 60 minutes or more (2000)

LITTLE GRANT (town). Covers a land area of 36.007 square miles and a water area of 0 square miles. Located at 42.90° N. Lat.; 90.83° W. Long.
Population: 257 (2000); Race: 100.0% White, 0.0% Black, 0.0% Asian, 0.0% American Indian and Alaska Native, 0.0% Hispanic of any race, 0.0% two or more races (2000); Density: 7.1 persons per square mile (2000); Age: 25.8% under 18, 10.9% over 64 (2000); Marriage status: 22.6% never married, 62.5% now married, 7.2% widowed, 7.7% divorced (2000); Foreign born: 0.8% (2000); Ancestry (includes multiple ancestries): 50.8% German, 23.4% English, 10.2% Irish, 5.9% United States or American, 5.5% Swiss (2000).
Economy: Employment by occupation: 50.3% management, 5.0% professional, 11.8% services, 9.9% sales, 3.1% farming, 5.6% construction, 14.3% production (2000).
Income: Per capita income: $16,239 (2000); Median household income: $35,833 (2000); Poverty rate: 12.9% (2000).
Taxes: Total city taxes per capita: $243 (1997); City property taxes per capita: $243 (1997).
Education: High school graduation rate: 85.4% (2000); College graduation rate: 11.7% (2000).
Housing: Homeownership rate: 87.8% (2000); Median home value: $92,500 (2000); Median age of housing: 60+ years (2000).
Transportation: Commute to work: 64.6% car, 0.0% public transportation, 2.5% walk, 32.9% work from home (2000); Travel time to work: 26.4% less than 15 minutes, 33.0% 15 to 30 minutes, 24.5% 30 to 45 minutes, 15.1% 45 to 60 minutes, 0.9% 60 minutes or more (2000)

LIVINGSTON (village). Covers a land area of 1.027 square miles and a water area of 0 square miles. Located at 42.90° N. Lat.; 90.43° W. Long. Elevation is 1,164 feet.
Population: 597 (2000); Race: 99.8% White, 0.0% Black, 0.0% Asian, 0.0% American Indian and Alaska Native, 1.3% Hispanic of any race, 0.2% two or more races (2000); Density: 581.5 persons per square mile (2000); Age: 25.4% under 18, 17.3% over 64 (2000); Marriage status: 25.1% never married, 57.7% now married, 9.8% widowed, 7.4% divorced (2000); Foreign born: 1.1% (2000); Ancestry (includes multiple ancestries): 51.3% German, 20.4% Irish, 19.5% English, 16.6% Norwegian, 4.2% Czech (2000).
Economy: Single-family building permits issued: 1 (2001) / 1 (2000); Multi-family building permits issued: 0 (2001) / 0 (2000); Employment by occupation: 8.2% management, 6.3% professional, 18.2% services, 27.7% sales, 3.5% farming, 12.9% construction, 23.3% production (2000).
Income: Per capita income: $16,647 (2000); Median household income: $35,417 (2000); Poverty rate: 5.4% (2000).
Taxes: Total city taxes per capita: $95 (1997); City property taxes per capita: $92 (1997).
Education: High school graduation rate: 87.9% (2000); College graduation rate: 8.9% (2000).

School District(s)

Iowa-Grant (PK-12)
2000 Enrollment: 1,016 608-943-6311
Housing: Homeownership rate: 76.6% (2000); Median home value: $68,400 (2000); Median rent: $311 per month (2000); Median age of housing: 50 years (2000).
Transportation: Commute to work: 91.8% car, 0.0% public transportation, 7.0% walk, 1.3% work from home (2000); Travel time to work: 30.8% less than 15 minutes, 42.6% 15 to 30 minutes, 14.1% 30 to 45 minutes, 4.8% 45 to 60 minutes, 7.7% 60 minutes or more (2000)

MARION (town). Covers a land area of 35.435 square miles and a water area of 0.293 square miles. Located at 43.07° N. Lat.; 90.72° W. Long.
Population: 517 (2000); Race: 98.6% White, 0.0% Black, 0.0% Asian, 0.0% American Indian and Alaska Native, 2.3% Hispanic of any race, 0.6% two or more races (2000); Density: 14.6 persons per square mile (2000); Age: 29.5% under 18, 13.8% over 64 (2000); Marriage status: 25.5% never married, 67.6% now married, 1.4% widowed, 5.5% divorced (2000); Foreign born: 1.0% (2000); Ancestry (includes multiple ancestries): 45.4% German, 13.6% Irish, 12.4% English, 7.2% Norwegian, 6.8% Czech (2000).
Economy: Employment by occupation: 13.9% management, 6.0% professional, 17.1% services, 15.1% sales, 1.6% farming, 15.5% construction, 30.7% production (2000).
Income: Per capita income: $12,942 (2000); Median household income: $33,750 (2000); Poverty rate: 8.5% (2000).
Taxes: Total city taxes per capita: $141 (1997); City property taxes per capita: $139 (1997).
Education: High school graduation rate: 77.9% (2000); College graduation rate: 6.9% (2000).
Housing: Homeownership rate: 82.4% (2000); Median home value: $96,300 (2000); Median rent: $431 per month (2000); Median age of housing: 27 years (2000).
Transportation: Commute to work: 82.1% car, 0.0% public transportation, 5.3% walk, 11.4% work from home (2000); Travel time to work: 52.3% less than 15 minutes, 24.8% 15 to 30 minutes, 10.1% 30 to 45 minutes, 7.8% 45 to 60 minutes, 5.0% 60 minutes or more (2000)

MILLVILLE (town). Covers a land area of 20.980 square miles and a water area of 0.752 square miles. Located at 43.01° N. Lat.; 90.93° W. Long. Elevation is 680 feet.
Population: 147 (2000); Race: 100.0% White, 0.0% Black, 0.0% Asian, 0.0% American Indian and Alaska Native, 1.3% Hispanic of any race, 0.0% two or more races (2000); Density: 7.0 persons per square mile (2000); Age: 16.1% under 18, 17.4% over 64 (2000); Marriage status: 14.0% never married, 72.9% now married, 2.3% widowed, 10.9% divorced (2000); Foreign born: 0.0% (2000); Ancestry (includes multiple ancestries): 38.3% German, 10.7% English, 8.7% United States or American, 6.0% Dutch, 6.0% Other groups (2000).
Economy: Employment by occupation: 17.7% management, 14.6% professional, 8.3% services, 12.5% sales, 6.3% farming, 17.7% construction, 22.9% production (2000).
Income: Per capita income: $20,618 (2000); Median household income: $43,750 (2000); Poverty rate: 1.3% (2000).
Taxes: Total city taxes per capita: $88 (1997); City property taxes per capita: $88 (1997).
Education: High school graduation rate: 79.6% (2000); College graduation rate: 8.0% (2000).
Housing: Homeownership rate: 84.4% (2000); Median home value: $75,000 (2000); Median rent: $275 per month (2000); Median age of housing: 31 years (2000).
Transportation: Commute to work: 90.4% car, 0.0% public transportation, 0.0% walk, 9.6% work from home (2000); Travel time to work: 10.6% less than 15 minutes, 60.0% 15 to 30 minutes, 22.4% 30 to 45 minutes, 0.0% 45 to 60 minutes, 7.1% 60 minutes or more (2000)

MONTFORT (village). Covers a land area of 0.530 square miles and a water area of 0 square miles. Located at 42.97° N. Lat.; 90.43° W. Long. Elevation is 1,150 feet.
History: The chance discovery of lead crystals here in 1827 led to Montfort's development as a mining town. When the lead mines closed, the community became the center of a farming area.
Population: 663 (2000); Race: 99.1% White, 0.0% Black, 0.0% Asian, 0.0% American Indian and Alaska Native, 0.0% Hispanic of any race, 0.9% two or more races (2000); Density: 1,252.1 persons per square mile (2000); Age: 29.3% under 18, 15.0% over 64 (2000); Marriage status: 25.1% never married, 57.3% now married, 6.8% widowed, 10.8% divorced (2000); Foreign born: 0.0% (2000); Ancestry (includes multiple ancestries): 47.0% German, 16.9% Irish, 13.6% Czech, 13.0% Norwegian, 12.1% English (2000).
Economy: Single-family building permits issued: 1 (2001) / 6 (2000); Multi-family building permits issued: 2 (2001) / 0 (2000); Employment by occupation: 8.8% management, 15.0% professional, 17.4% services, 28.2% sales, 3.5% farming, 8.8% construction, 18.2% production (2000).
Income: Per capita income: $16,126 (2000); Median household income: $37,500 (2000); Poverty rate: 5.7% (2000).
Taxes: Total city taxes per capita: $74 (1997); City property taxes per capita: $71 (1997).
Education: High school graduation rate: 87.8% (2000); College graduation rate: 17.3% (2000).
Housing: Homeownership rate: 83.3% (2000); Median home value: $68,200 (2000); Median rent: $308 per month (2000); Median age of housing: 58 years (2000).
Transportation: Commute to work: 98.2% car, 0.0% public transportation, 1.8% walk, 0.0% work from home (2000); Travel time to work: 36.2% less

than 15 minutes, 40.0% 15 to 30 minutes, 13.2% 30 to 45 minutes, 3.5% 45 to 60 minutes, 7.1% 60 minutes or more (2000)

MOUNT HOPE (village). Covers a land area of 0.319 square miles and a water area of 0 square miles. Located at 42.96° N. Lat.; 90.85° W. Long. Elevation is 1,100 feet.
Population: 186 (2000); Race: 100.0% White, 0.0% Black, 0.0% Asian, 0.0% American Indian and Alaska Native, 0.0% Hispanic of any race, 0.0% two or more races (2000); Density: 583.9 persons per square mile (2000); Age: 24.5% under 18, 9.6% over 64 (2000); Marriage status: 30.5% never married, 53.1% now married, 7.9% widowed, 8.5% divorced (2000); Foreign born: 0.0% (2000); Ancestry (includes multiple ancestries): 37.5% German, 23.6% English, 14.9% Norwegian, 14.4% Irish, 10.1% Polish (2000).
Economy: Employment by occupation: 3.1% management, 12.6% professional, 19.7% services, 15.7% sales, 10.2% farming, 15.0% construction, 23.6% production (2000).
Income: Per capita income: $15,141 (2000); Median household income: $37,813 (2000); Poverty rate: 1.4% (2000).
Taxes: Total city taxes per capita: $29 (1997); City property taxes per capita: $23 (1997).
Education: High school graduation rate: 87.6% (2000); College graduation rate: 6.6% (2000).
Housing: Homeownership rate: 82.1% (2000); Median home value: $50,600 (2000); Median rent: $208 per month (2000); Median age of housing: 35 years (2000).
Transportation: Commute to work: 96.0% car, 0.0% public transportation, 2.4% walk, 1.6% work from home (2000); Travel time to work: 16.3% less than 15 minutes, 52.8% 15 to 30 minutes, 20.3% 30 to 45 minutes, 6.5% 45 to 60 minutes, 4.1% 60 minutes or more (2000)

MOUNT HOPE (town). Covers a land area of 29.901 square miles and a water area of 0 square miles. Located at 42.98° N. Lat.; 90.83° W. Long. Elevation is 1,100 feet.
Population: 225 (2000); Race: 100.0% White, 0.0% Black, 0.0% Asian, 0.0% American Indian and Alaska Native, 0.0% Hispanic of any race, 0.0% two or more races (2000); Density: 7.5 persons per square mile (2000); Age: 21.6% under 18, 13.6% over 64 (2000); Marriage status: 20.3% never married, 70.1% now married, 4.6% widowed, 5.1% divorced (2000); Foreign born: 0.0% (2000); Ancestry (includes multiple ancestries): 59.7% German, 21.2% Irish, 13.6% English, 5.1% Czech, 5.1% Dutch (2000).
Economy: Livestock and dairy region. Employment by occupation: 29.8% management, 9.2% professional, 13.7% services, 19.1% sales, 6.9% farming, 1.5% construction, 19.8% production (2000).
Income: Per capita income: $18,442 (2000); Median household income: $35,000 (2000); Poverty rate: 9.7% (2000).
Taxes: Total city taxes per capita: $211 (1997); City property taxes per capita: $211 (1997).
Education: High school graduation rate: 89.2% (2000); College graduation rate: 7.8% (2000).
Housing: Homeownership rate: 84.6% (2000); Median home value: $70,000 (2000); Median age of housing: 45 years (2000).
Transportation: Commute to work: 68.0% car, 0.0% public transportation, 6.4% walk, 25.6% work from home (2000); Travel time to work: 24.7% less than 15 minutes, 54.8% 15 to 30 minutes, 18.3% 30 to 45 minutes, 0.0% 45 to 60 minutes, 2.2% 60 minutes or more (2000)

MOUNT IDA (town). Covers a land area of 36.292 square miles and a water area of 0 square miles. Located at 42.98° N. Lat.; 90.72° W. Long. Elevation is 1,220 feet.
Population: 523 (2000); Race: 100.0% White, 0.0% Black, 0.0% Asian, 0.0% American Indian and Alaska Native, 0.6% Hispanic of any race, 0.0% two or more races (2000); Density: 14.4 persons per square mile (2000); Age: 26.0% under 18, 11.3% over 64 (2000); Marriage status: 23.2% never married, 67.2% now married, 3.6% widowed, 6.1% divorced (2000); Foreign born: 0.0% (2000); Ancestry (includes multiple ancestries): 47.3% German, 19.9% Irish, 14.8% English, 9.2% United States or American, 9.0% Norwegian (2000).
Economy: Employment by occupation: 24.1% management, 12.2% professional, 9.9% services, 18.0% sales, 5.1% farming, 12.9% construction, 17.7% production (2000).
Income: Per capita income: $18,700 (2000); Median household income: $41,250 (2000); Poverty rate: 13.3% (2000).
Taxes: Total city taxes per capita: $111 (1997); City property taxes per capita: $109 (1997).
Education: High school graduation rate: 90.1% (2000); College graduation rate: 13.9% (2000).
Housing: Homeownership rate: 78.8% (2000); Median home value: $87,100 (2000); Median rent: $525 per month (2000); Median age of housing: 37 years (2000).
Transportation: Commute to work: 76.2% car, 0.0% public transportation, 4.8% walk, 19.0% work from home (2000); Travel time to work: 29.4% less than 15 minutes, 41.6% 15 to 30 minutes, 11.8% 30 to 45 minutes, 10.5% 45 to 60 minutes, 6.7% 60 minutes or more (2000)

MUSCODA (village). Covers a land area of 1.359 square miles and a water area of 0 square miles. Located at 43.18° N. Lat.; 90.44° W. Long. Elevation is 680 feet.
Population: 1,453 (2000); Race: 98.8% White, 0.6% Black, 0.0% Asian, 0.0% American Indian and Alaska Native, 1.4% Hispanic of any race, 0.5% two or more races (2000); Density: 1,069.1 persons per square mile (2000); Age: 24.8% under 18, 19.3% over 64 (2000); Marriage status: 25.3% never married, 58.0% now married, 8.4% widowed, 8.4% divorced (2000); Foreign born: 1.7% (2000); Ancestry (includes multiple ancestries): 42.3% German, 16.1% Irish, 10.4% Norwegian, 10.2% English, 9.1% Czech (2000).
Economy: Single-family building permits issued: 1 (2001) / 6 (2000); Multi-family building permits issued: 0 (2001) / 0 (2000); Employment by occupation: 5.1% management, 10.4% professional, 16.7% services, 20.5% sales, 1.8% farming, 9.1% construction, 36.4% production (2000).
Income: Per capita income: $15,390 (2000); Median household income: $30,903 (2000); Poverty rate: 10.2% (2000).
Taxes: Total city taxes per capita: $291 (1997); City property taxes per capita: $267 (1997).
Education: High school graduation rate: 80.5% (2000); College graduation rate: 10.8% (2000).

School District(s)

Riverdale (PK-12)
2000 Enrollment: 911 608-739-3832
Housing: Homeownership rate: 71.8% (2000); Median home value: $60,200 (2000); Median rent: $332 per month (2000); Median age of housing: 45 years (2000).
Newspapers: Progressive (1 x week)
Transportation: Commute to work: 90.0% car, 0.0% public transportation, 5.5% walk, 2.2% work from home (2000); Travel time to work: 35.6% less than 15 minutes, 33.3% 15 to 30 minutes, 15.2% 30 to 45 minutes, 5.0% 45 to 60 minutes, 10.8% 60 minutes or more (2000)

MUSCODA (town). Covers a land area of 33.490 square miles and a water area of 1.107 square miles. Located at 43.17° N. Lat.; 90.47° W. Long. Elevation is 680 feet.
Population: 674 (2000); Race: 95.9% White, 0.3% Black, 0.3% Asian, 1.7% American Indian and Alaska Native, 0.6% Hispanic of any race, 1.1% two or more races (2000); Density: 20.1 persons per square mile (2000); Age: 24.5% under 18, 13.0% over 64 (2000); Marriage status: 29.8% never married, 54.6% now married, 4.8% widowed, 10.8% divorced (2000); Foreign born: 1.1% (2000); Ancestry (includes multiple ancestries): 42.0% German, 14.4% Irish, 9.7% Czech, 9.2% Norwegian, 6.6% English (2000).
Economy: In livestock and dairy region. Manufacturing: lumber, cheese, whey protein. Employment by occupation: 10.8% management, 13.3% professional, 11.1% services, 14.9% sales, 2.5% farming, 6.0% construction, 41.3% production (2000).
Income: Per capita income: $17,175 (2000); Median household income: $34,750 (2000); Poverty rate: 10.3% (2000).
Taxes: Total city taxes per capita: $21 (1997); City property taxes per capita: $21 (1997).
Education: High school graduation rate: 73.0% (2000); College graduation rate: 8.9% (2000).
Housing: Homeownership rate: 82.1% (2000); Median home value: $63,100 (2000); Median rent: $250 per month (2000); Median age of housing: 28 years (2000).
Transportation: Commute to work: 92.0% car, 0.0% public transportation, 1.0% walk, 6.4% work from home (2000); Travel time to work: 34.6% less than 15 minutes, 33.9% 15 to 30 minutes, 8.9% 30 to 45 minutes, 10.3% 45 to 60 minutes, 12.3% 60 minutes or more (2000)

NORTH LANCASTER (town). Covers a land area of 36.020 square miles and a water area of 0.011 square miles. Located at 42.90° N. Lat.; 90.72° W. Long.
Population: 515 (2000); Race: 99.6% White, 0.0% Black, 0.0% Asian, 0.0% American Indian and Alaska Native, 0.2% Hispanic of any race, 0.4% two or more races (2000); Density: 14.3 persons per square mile (2000); Age: 36.8% under 18, 7.9% over 64 (2000); Marriage status: 23.5% never married, 66.4% now married, 3.1% widowed, 7.0% divorced (2000); Foreign born: 0.0%

(2000); Ancestry (includes multiple ancestries): 55.6% German, 16.5% Irish, 11.0% English, 8.9% United States or American, 6.0% Norwegian (2000).
Economy: Employment by occupation: 32.3% management, 10.0% professional, 10.0% services, 17.6% sales, 4.7% farming, 8.6% construction, 16.8% production (2000).
Income: Per capita income: $17,038 (2000); Median household income: $41,528 (2000); Poverty rate: 10.6% (2000).
Taxes: Total city taxes per capita: $106 (1997); City property taxes per capita: $104 (1997).
Education: High school graduation rate: 95.8% (2000); College graduation rate: 14.4% (2000).
Housing: Homeownership rate: 81.3% (2000); Median home value: $88,800 (2000); Median rent: $275 per month (2000); Median age of housing: 50 years (2000).
Transportation: Commute to work: 68.8% car, 1.1% public transportation, 8.7% walk, 17.0% work from home (2000); Travel time to work: 55.5% less than 15 minutes, 26.2% 15 to 30 minutes, 4.8% 30 to 45 minutes, 7.9% 45 to 60 minutes, 5.7% 60 minutes or more (2000)

PARIS (town). Covers a land area of 35.123 square miles and a water area of 0.413 square miles. Located at 42.65° N. Lat.; 90.61° W. Long.
Population: 754 (2000); Race: 99.6% White, 0.0% Black, 0.0% Asian, 0.0% American Indian and Alaska Native, 0.0% Hispanic of any race, 0.4% two or more races (2000); Density: 21.5 persons per square mile (2000); Age: 27.8% under 18, 8.9% over 64 (2000); Marriage status: 23.0% never married, 66.0% now married, 4.5% widowed, 6.4% divorced (2000); Foreign born: 0.4% (2000); Ancestry (includes multiple ancestries): 63.7% German, 10.6% Irish, 4.1% English, 3.8% Norwegian, 3.7% United States or American (2000).
Economy: Employment by occupation: 21.2% management, 16.3% professional, 11.9% services, 17.5% sales, 2.9% farming, 11.4% construction, 18.7% production (2000).
Income: Per capita income: $19,199 (2000); Median household income: $41,111 (2000); Poverty rate: 10.9% (2000).
Taxes: Total city taxes per capita: $131 (1997); City property taxes per capita: $130 (1997).
Education: High school graduation rate: 87.0% (2000); College graduation rate: 14.5% (2000).
Housing: Homeownership rate: 86.8% (2000); Median home value: $100,500 (2000); Median rent: $325 per month (2000); Median age of housing: 33 years (2000).
Transportation: Commute to work: 83.5% car, 0.0% public transportation, 2.5% walk, 14.1% work from home (2000); Travel time to work: 24.4% less than 15 minutes, 46.0% 15 to 30 minutes, 19.5% 30 to 45 minutes, 3.7% 45 to 60 minutes, 6.3% 60 minutes or more (2000)

PATCH GROVE (village). Covers a land area of 0.392 square miles and a water area of 0 square miles. Located at 42.93° N. Lat.; 90.97° W. Long. Elevation is 1,060 feet.
Population: 166 (2000); Race: 100.0% White, 0.0% Black, 0.0% Asian, 0.0% American Indian and Alaska Native, 0.0% Hispanic of any race, 0.0% two or more races (2000); Density: 423.7 persons per square mile (2000); Age: 30.1% under 18, 19.5% over 64 (2000); Marriage status: 20.2% never married, 68.1% now married, 8.5% widowed, 3.2% divorced (2000); Foreign born: 0.0% (2000); Ancestry (includes multiple ancestries): 66.7% German, 23.6% Irish, 19.5% United States or American, 7.3% French (except Basque), 6.5% Polish (2000).
Economy: Single-family building permits issued: 1 (2001) / 1 (2000); Multi-family building permits issued: 0 (2001) / 0 (2000); Employment by occupation: 14.3% management, 23.2% professional, 5.4% services, 16.1% sales, 5.4% farming, 12.5% construction, 23.2% production (2000).
Income: Per capita income: $13,189 (2000); Median household income: $25,625 (2000); Poverty rate: 13.0% (2000).
Taxes: Total city taxes per capita: $50 (1997); City property taxes per capita: $35 (1997).
Education: High school graduation rate: 86.7% (2000); College graduation rate: 10.7% (2000).

School District(s)

River Ridge (PK-12)
2000 Enrollment: 667 608-994-2718

Housing: Homeownership rate: 90.4% (2000); Median home value: $59,200 (2000); Median rent: $225 per month (2000); Median age of housing: 47 years (2000).
Transportation: Commute to work: 83.9% car, 0.0% public transportation, 8.9% walk, 7.1% work from home (2000); Travel time to work: 30.8% less than 15 minutes, 40.4% 15 to 30 minutes, 19.2% 30 to 45 minutes, 0.0% 45 to 60 minutes, 9.6% 60 minutes or more (2000)

PATCH GROVE (town). Covers a land area of 32.874 square miles and a water area of 0 square miles. Located at 42.95° N. Lat.; 90.95° W. Long. Elevation is 1,060 feet.
Population: 390 (2000); Race: 99.6% White, 0.0% Black, 0.0% Asian, 0.0% American Indian and Alaska Native, 0.0% Hispanic of any race, 0.4% two or more races (2000); Density: 11.9 persons per square mile (2000); Age: 29.7% under 18, 11.1% over 64 (2000); Marriage status: 26.5% never married, 65.5% now married, 4.1% widowed, 3.9% divorced (2000); Foreign born: 0.0% (2000); Ancestry (includes multiple ancestries): 49.8% German, 17.5% Irish, 16.4% English, 10.3% United States or American, 9.6% Czech (2000).
Economy: Single-family building permits issued: 3 (2001) / 0 (2000); Multi-family building permits issued: 0 (2001) / 0 (2000); Employment by occupation: 29.7% management, 7.8% professional, 15.1% services, 13.8% sales, 9.5% farming, 11.2% construction, 12.9% production (2000).
Income: Per capita income: $16,527 (2000); Median household income: $38,281 (2000); Poverty rate: 10.9% (2000).
Taxes: Total city taxes per capita: $216 (1997); City property taxes per capita: $216 (1997).
Education: High school graduation rate: 87.0% (2000); College graduation rate: 10.4% (2000).
Housing: Homeownership rate: 75.0% (2000); Median home value: $76,300 (2000); Median rent: $250 per month (2000); Median age of housing: 36 years (2000).
Transportation: Commute to work: 70.6% car, 0.0% public transportation, 4.4% walk, 24.1% work from home (2000); Travel time to work: 35.8% less than 15 minutes, 45.1% 15 to 30 minutes, 11.6% 30 to 45 minutes, 3.5% 45 to 60 minutes, 4.0% 60 minutes or more (2000)

PLATTEVILLE (city). Covers a land area of 4.203 square miles and a water area of 0 square miles. Located at 42.73° N. Lat.; 90.47° W. Long. Elevation is 994 feet.
History: Platteville was founded in 1827 by Major John H. Rountree, and developed as the center of the southwestern Wisconsin mining area. The Wisconsin Institute of Technology, specializing in training for mining engineers and foremen, was established here in 1907.
Population: 9,989 (2000); Race: 95.7% White, 1.0% Black, 1.3% Asian, 0.8% American Indian and Alaska Native, 0.9% Hispanic of any race, 1.0% two or more races (2000); Density: 2,376.4 persons per square mile (2000); Age: 14.2% under 18, 12.3% over 64 (2000); Marriage status: 51.3% never married, 37.9% now married, 5.4% widowed, 5.4% divorced (2000); Foreign born: 2.2% (2000); Ancestry (includes multiple ancestries): 49.6% German, 13.7% Irish, 12.2% English, 8.9% Norwegian, 5.7% Polish (2000).
Economy: Single-family building permits issued: 13 (2001) / 14 (2000); Multi-family building permits issued: 10 (2001) / 8 (2000); Employment by occupation: 11.4% management, 25.6% professional, 18.3% services, 25.0% sales, 2.9% farming, 5.4% construction, 11.3% production (2000).
Income: Per capita income: $15,858 (2000); Median household income: $35,742 (2000); Poverty rate: 19.4% (2000).
Taxes: Total city taxes per capita: $151 (1997); City property taxes per capita: $143 (1997).
Education: High school graduation rate: 87.9% (2000); College graduation rate: 34.5% (2000).

School District(s)

Platteville (PK-12)
2000 Enrollment: 1,664 608-342-4400

Four-year College(s)

University of Wisconsin-Platteville (Public)
2001 Enrollment: 5,600 608-342-1421
2001 Tuition: In-state $2,776; Out-of-state $11,288

Housing: Homeownership rate: 51.6% (2000); Median home value: $88,100 (2000); Median rent: $379 per month (2000); Median age of housing: 37 years (2000).
Hospitals: Southwest Health Center (155 beds); Southwest Health Center (145 beds)
Safety: Violent crime rate: 21.9 per 10,000 population; Property crime rate: 347.9 per 10,000 population (2001).
Newspapers: Platteville Journal (2 x week)
Transportation: Commute to work: 79.7% car, 0.5% public transportation, 14.6% walk, 3.2% work from home (2000); Travel time to work: 62.2% less than 15 minutes, 16.4% 15 to 30 minutes, 13.7% 30 to 45 minutes, 4.3% 45 to 60 minutes, 3.3% 60 minutes or more (2000)

Additional Information Contacts

Platteville Chamber of Commerce 608-348-8888

PLATTEVILLE (town). Covers a land area of 32.108 square miles and a water area of 0 square miles. Located at 42.72° N. Lat.; 90.48° W. Long. Elevation is 994 feet.
History: Mining Museum. Seat of University of Wisconsin, Platteville. Wisconsin's early territorial capitol building (1836), now restored in First Capitol State Park to Northeast. Founded 1827, incorporated 1876.
Population: 1,343 (2000); Race: 97.0% White, 0.0% Black, 0.4% Asian, 1.8% American Indian and Alaska Native, 0.3% Hispanic of any race, 0.7% two or more races (2000); Density: 41.8 persons per square mile (2000); Age: 27.6% under 18, 11.4% over 64 (2000); Marriage status: 23.4% never married, 66.7% now married, 3.0% widowed, 6.9% divorced (2000); Foreign born: 1.0% (2000); Ancestry (includes multiple ancestries): 48.6% German, 16.8% Irish, 14.2% English, 7.5% Norwegian, 6.9% United States or American (2000).
Economy: Trade center for dairying, farming; cheese. Manufacturing: fluorescent and mercury ballasts for lighting, masks. Employment by occupation: 14.4% management, 19.2% professional, 18.5% services, 21.8% sales, 1.9% farming, 8.1% construction, 16.1% production (2000).
Income: Per capita income: $18,886 (2000); Median household income: $43,553 (2000); Poverty rate: 12.2% (2000).
Taxes: Total city taxes per capita: $7 (1997); City property taxes per capita: $2 (1997).
Education: High school graduation rate: 87.9% (2000); College graduation rate: 27.5% (2000).
Housing: Homeownership rate: 81.6% (2000); Median home value: $116,100 (2000); Median rent: $351 per month (2000); Median age of housing: 27 years (2000).
Transportation: Commute to work: 87.9% car, 0.0% public transportation, 3.7% walk, 7.8% work from home (2000); Travel time to work: 56.2% less than 15 minutes, 20.8% 15 to 30 minutes, 11.9% 30 to 45 minutes, 6.6% 45 to 60 minutes, 4.4% 60 minutes or more (2000)

POTOSI (village). Covers a land area of 1.645 square miles and a water area of 0.009 square miles. Located at 42.68° N. Lat.; 90.72° W. Long. Elevation is 800 feet.
Population: 711 (2000); Race: 99.2% White, 0.0% Black, 0.0% Asian, 0.0% American Indian and Alaska Native, 0.0% Hispanic of any race, 0.8% two or more races (2000); Density: 432.1 persons per square mile (2000); Age: 25.5% under 18, 17.2% over 64 (2000); Marriage status: 21.1% never married, 61.9% now married, 10.4% widowed, 6.5% divorced (2000); Foreign born: 0.6% (2000); Ancestry (includes multiple ancestries): 57.4% German, 15.3% Irish, 8.2% United States or American, 7.0% English, 3.2% Norwegian (2000).
Economy: Single-family building permits issued: 5 (2001) / 9 (2000); Multi-family building permits issued: 0 (2001) / 0 (2000); Employment by occupation: 7.1% management, 14.9% professional, 12.2% services, 21.2% sales, 0.8% farming, 20.1% construction, 23.6% production (2000).
Income: Per capita income: $17,189 (2000); Median household income: $35,294 (2000); Poverty rate: 7.3% (2000).
Taxes: Total city taxes per capita: $95 (1997); City property taxes per capita: $83 (1997).
Education: High school graduation rate: 82.2% (2000); College graduation rate: 10.4% (2000).

School District(s)

Potosi (PK-12)
2000 Enrollment: 427 608-763-2162
Housing: Homeownership rate: 76.2% (2000); Median home value: $72,600 (2000); Median rent: $272 per month (2000); Median age of housing: 45 years (2000).
Transportation: Commute to work: 95.6% car, 0.0% public transportation, 0.8% walk, 3.6% work from home (2000); Travel time to work: 12.8% less than 15 minutes, 52.3% 15 to 30 minutes, 26.1% 30 to 45 minutes, 4.8% 45 to 60 minutes, 4.0% 60 minutes or more (2000)

POTOSI (town). Covers a land area of 46.452 square miles and a water area of 11.223 square miles. Located at 42.70° N. Lat.; 90.71° W. Long. Elevation is 800 feet.
History: Site of St. John Mine, the nation's oldest lead mine, now a museum.
Population: 831 (2000); Race: 100.0% White, 0.0% Black, 0.0% Asian, 0.0% American Indian and Alaska Native, 0.0% Hispanic of any race, 0.0% two or more races (2000); Density: 17.9 persons per square mile (2000); Age: 29.1% under 18, 8.6% over 64 (2000); Marriage status: 22.9% never married, 65.5% now married, 4.3% widowed, 7.2% divorced (2000); Foreign born: 0.0% (2000); Ancestry (includes multiple ancestries): 60.3% German, 11.0% English, 9.8% Irish, 7.1% United States or American, 4.3% Norwegian (2000).
Economy: In agricultural region. Manufacturing: machinery. Smoked fish. Employment by occupation: 14.1% management, 10.3% professional, 12.6% services, 18.5% sales, 3.2% farming, 10.1% construction, 31.2% production (2000).
Income: Per capita income: $16,379 (2000); Median household income: $42,697 (2000); Poverty rate: 3.9% (2000).
Taxes: Total city taxes per capita: $210 (1997); City property taxes per capita: $209 (1997).
Education: High school graduation rate: 88.0% (2000); College graduation rate: 10.9% (2000).
Housing: Homeownership rate: 80.8% (2000); Median home value: $80,400 (2000); Median rent: $283 per month (2000); Median age of housing: 41 years (2000).
Transportation: Commute to work: 86.2% car, 0.0% public transportation, 2.8% walk, 11.1% work from home (2000); Travel time to work: 23.9% less than 15 minutes, 40.0% 15 to 30 minutes, 22.5% 30 to 45 minutes, 7.7% 45 to 60 minutes, 6.0% 60 minutes or more (2000)

SMELSER (town). Covers a land area of 35.115 square miles and a water area of 0 square miles. Located at 42.64° N. Lat.; 90.49° W. Long.
Population: 756 (2000); Race: 99.9% White, 0.0% Black, 0.0% Asian, 0.0% American Indian and Alaska Native, 0.1% Hispanic of any race, 0.1% two or more races (2000); Density: 21.5 persons per square mile (2000); Age: 29.2% under 18, 11.2% over 64 (2000); Marriage status: 22.0% never married, 68.1% now married, 6.1% widowed, 3.8% divorced (2000); Foreign born: 0.5% (2000); Ancestry (includes multiple ancestries): 60.4% German, 13.3% Irish, 10.3% English, 8.0% United States or American, 7.5% Norwegian (2000).
Economy: Employment by occupation: 16.8% management, 12.7% professional, 13.5% services, 24.3% sales, 4.3% farming, 11.3% construction, 17.1% production (2000).
Income: Per capita income: $15,652 (2000); Median household income: $41,429 (2000); Poverty rate: 5.2% (2000).
Taxes: Total city taxes per capita: $90 (1997); City property taxes per capita: $88 (1997).
Education: High school graduation rate: 84.9% (2000); College graduation rate: 16.3% (2000).
Housing: Homeownership rate: 83.8% (2000); Median home value: $83,400 (2000); Median rent: $331 per month (2000); Median age of housing: 32 years (2000).
Transportation: Commute to work: 85.4% car, 0.0% public transportation, 3.0% walk, 10.7% work from home (2000); Travel time to work: 41.9% less than 15 minutes, 35.0% 15 to 30 minutes, 14.7% 30 to 45 minutes, 4.7% 45 to 60 minutes, 3.6% 60 minutes or more (2000)

SOUTH LANCASTER (town). Covers a land area of 33.992 square miles and a water area of 0 square miles. Located at 42.80° N. Lat.; 90.73° W. Long.
Population: 808 (2000); Race: 99.2% White, 0.0% Black, 0.4% Asian, 0.0% American Indian and Alaska Native, 0.0% Hispanic of any race, 0.4% two or more races (2000); Density: 23.8 persons per square mile (2000); Age: 23.3% under 18, 21.2% over 64 (2000); Marriage status: 20.8% never married, 68.6% now married, 6.8% widowed, 3.7% divorced (2000); Foreign born: 0.6% (2000); Ancestry (includes multiple ancestries): 41.0% German, 13.9% English, 9.9% Irish, 9.3% United States or American, 4.6% Other groups (2000).
Economy: Employment by occupation: 22.5% management, 10.5% professional, 15.3% services, 12.9% sales, 6.7% farming, 9.1% construction, 23.1% production (2000).
Income: Per capita income: $18,698 (2000); Median household income: $36,250 (2000); Poverty rate: 5.0% (2000).
Taxes: Total city taxes per capita: $57 (1997); City property taxes per capita: $55 (1997).
Education: High school graduation rate: 76.8% (2000); College graduation rate: 14.6% (2000).
Housing: Homeownership rate: 75.3% (2000); Median home value: $76,800 (2000); Median rent: $321 per month (2000); Median age of housing: 41 years (2000).
Transportation: Commute to work: 80.7% car, 0.0% public transportation, 5.7% walk, 11.7% work from home (2000); Travel time to work: 51.1% less than 15 minutes, 22.5% 15 to 30 minutes, 13.5% 30 to 45 minutes, 7.7% 45 to 60 minutes, 5.2% 60 minutes or more (2000)

STITZER (unincorporated postal area, zip code 53825). Covers a land area of 27.408 square miles and a water area of 0 square miles. Located at 42.92° N. Lat.; 90.56° W. Long. Elevation is 1,191 feet.
Population: 407 (2000); Race: 100.0% White, 0.0% Black, 0.0% Asian, 0.0% American Indian and Alaska Native, 0.0% Hispanic of any race, 0.0% two or more races (2000); Density: 14.8 persons per square mile (2000); Age: 35.3% under 18, 8.8% over 64 (2000); Marriage status: 23.4% never married, 65.8% now married, 4.9% widowed, 5.9% divorced (2000); Foreign born: 0.7% (2000); Ancestry (includes multiple ancestries): 57.5% German, 15.5% Irish, 12.2% English, 8.3% Norwegian, 3.9% United States or American (2000).
Economy: Employment by occupation: 25.4% management, 12.9% professional, 14.3% services, 16.1% sales, 1.8% farming, 6.7% construction, 22.8% production (2000).
Income: Per capita income: $14,164 (2000); Median household income: $35,556 (2000); Poverty rate: 19.9% (2000).
Education: High school graduation rate: 91.2% (2000); College graduation rate: 17.9% (2000).
Housing: Homeownership rate: 78.5% (2000); Median home value: $70,000 (2000); Median rent: $250 per month (2000); Median age of housing: 56 years (2000).
Transportation: Commute to work: 81.4% car, 0.0% public transportation, 5.4% walk, 13.2% work from home (2000); Travel time to work: 45.2% less than 15 minutes, 32.2% 15 to 30 minutes, 19.2% 30 to 45 minutes, 1.1% 45 to 60 minutes, 2.3% 60 minutes or more (2000)

TENNYSON (village). Covers a land area of 0.421 square miles and a water area of 0 square miles. Located at 42.68° N. Lat.; 90.68° W. Long. Elevation is 835 feet.
Population: 370 (2000); Race: 100.0% White, 0.0% Black, 0.0% Asian, 0.0% American Indian and Alaska Native, 0.0% Hispanic of any race, 0.0% two or more races (2000); Density: 878.7 persons per square mile (2000); Age: 22.5% under 18, 17.6% over 64 (2000); Marriage status: 22.0% never married, 62.3% now married, 9.3% widowed, 6.3% divorced (2000); Foreign born: 0.0% (2000); Ancestry (includes multiple ancestries): 75.4% German, 16.1% Irish, 9.1% English, 3.3% Dutch, 3.3% United States or American (2000).
Economy: Single-family building permits issued: 0 (2001) / 2 (2000); Multi-family building permits issued: 0 (2001) / 0 (2000); Employment by occupation: 11.1% management, 13.9% professional, 9.4% services, 27.2% sales, 1.1% farming, 12.8% construction, 24.4% production (2000).
Income: Per capita income: $17,065 (2000); Median household income: $35,000 (2000); Poverty rate: 4.0% (2000).
Taxes: Total city taxes per capita: $19 (1997); City property taxes per capita: $13 (1997).
Education: High school graduation rate: 83.6% (2000); College graduation rate: 12.5% (2000).
Housing: Homeownership rate: 81.9% (2000); Median home value: $72,400 (2000); Median rent: $300 per month (2000); Median age of housing: 40 years (2000).
Transportation: Commute to work: 96.2% car, 0.0% public transportation, 1.6% walk, 1.1% work from home (2000); Travel time to work: 21.1% less than 15 minutes, 50.6% 15 to 30 minutes, 22.2% 30 to 45 minutes, 1.1% 45 to 60 minutes, 5.0% 60 minutes or more (2000)

WATERLOO (town). Covers a land area of 38.173 square miles and a water area of 6.418 square miles. Located at 42.72° N. Lat.; 90.83° W. Long.
Population: 557 (2000); Race: 98.7% White, 0.0% Black, 0.0% Asian, 0.9% American Indian and Alaska Native, 0.4% Hispanic of any race, 0.4% two or more races (2000); Density: 14.6 persons per square mile (2000); Age: 26.4% under 18, 9.9% over 64 (2000); Marriage status: 20.4% never married, 71.1% now married, 4.5% widowed, 4.0% divorced (2000); Foreign born: 0.0% (2000); Ancestry (includes multiple ancestries): 59.4% German, 13.0% Irish, 7.6% United States or American, 6.3% English, 3.8% Norwegian (2000).
Economy: Employment by occupation: 23.1% management, 6.9% professional, 12.8% services, 11.0% sales, 2.1% farming, 11.7% construction, 32.4% production (2000).
Income: Per capita income: $17,579 (2000); Median household income: $36,932 (2000); Poverty rate: 15.3% (2000).
Taxes: Total city taxes per capita: $143 (1997); City property taxes per capita: $141 (1997).
Education: High school graduation rate: 78.4% (2000); College graduation rate: 5.7% (2000).
Housing: Homeownership rate: 89.8% (2000); Median home value: $76,400 (2000); Median rent: $308 per month (2000); Median age of housing: 39 years (2000).
Transportation: Commute to work: 77.5% car, 0.0% public transportation, 2.8% walk, 19.7% work from home (2000); Travel time to work: 23.7% less than 15 minutes, 36.8% 15 to 30 minutes, 23.2% 30 to 45 minutes, 9.6% 45 to 60 minutes, 6.6% 60 minutes or more (2000)

WATTERSTOWN (town). Covers a land area of 27.739 square miles and a water area of 1.038 square miles. Located at 43.16° N. Lat.; 90.59° W. Long.
Population: 362 (2000); Race: 100.0% White, 0.0% Black, 0.0% Asian, 0.0% American Indian and Alaska Native, 0.0% Hispanic of any race, 0.0% two or more races (2000); Density: 13.1 persons per square mile (2000); Age: 31.2% under 18, 13.2% over 64 (2000); Marriage status: 20.6% never married, 62.9% now married, 9.3% widowed, 7.2% divorced (2000); Foreign born: 1.5% (2000); Ancestry (includes multiple ancestries): 35.5% German, 16.2% Norwegian, 10.9% Irish, 10.7% English, 8.6% Czech (2000).
Economy: Employment by occupation: 25.7% management, 13.2% professional, 7.2% services, 12.0% sales, 4.2% farming, 13.2% construction, 24.6% production (2000).
Income: Per capita income: $15,726 (2000); Median household income: $41,806 (2000); Poverty rate: 14.3% (2000).
Taxes: Total city taxes per capita: $134 (1997); City property taxes per capita: $134 (1997).
Education: High school graduation rate: 74.3% (2000); College graduation rate: 15.4% (2000).
Housing: Homeownership rate: 93.5% (2000); Median home value: $92,900 (2000); Median rent: $325 per month (2000); Median age of housing: 27 years (2000).
Transportation: Commute to work: 82.4% car, 0.0% public transportation, 3.6% walk, 13.9% work from home (2000); Travel time to work: 47.9% less than 15 minutes, 30.3% 15 to 30 minutes, 16.2% 30 to 45 minutes, 1.4% 45 to 60 minutes, 4.2% 60 minutes or more (2000)

WINGVILLE (town). Covers a land area of 35.456 square miles and a water area of 0.010 square miles. Located at 42.99° N. Lat.; 90.49° W. Long.
Population: 394 (2000); Race: 98.8% White, 1.2% Black, 0.0% Asian, 0.0% American Indian and Alaska Native, 0.0% Hispanic of any race, 0.0% two or more races (2000); Density: 11.1 persons per square mile (2000); Age: 37.0% under 18, 7.4% over 64 (2000); Marriage status: 27.5% never married, 66.9% now married, 2.5% widowed, 3.2% divorced (2000); Foreign born: 0.7% (2000); Ancestry (includes multiple ancestries): 46.2% German, 14.8% English, 8.4% Norwegian, 5.2% United States or American, 5.2% Irish (2000).
Economy: Employment by occupation: 37.3% management, 3.5% professional, 11.4% services, 24.9% sales, 2.5% farming, 6.0% construction, 14.4% production (2000).
Income: Per capita income: $12,733 (2000); Median household income: $30,893 (2000); Poverty rate: 17.3% (2000).
Taxes: Total city taxes per capita: $286 (1997); City property taxes per capita: $286 (1997).
Education: High school graduation rate: 83.6% (2000); College graduation rate: 15.1% (2000).
Housing: Homeownership rate: 77.3% (2000); Median home value: $65,000 (2000); Median rent: $367 per month (2000); Median age of housing: 38 years (2000).
Transportation: Commute to work: 73.1% car, 0.0% public transportation, 2.5% walk, 22.4% work from home (2000); Travel time to work: 26.3% less than 15 minutes, 34.0% 15 to 30 minutes, 25.0% 30 to 45 minutes, 6.4% 45 to 60 minutes, 8.3% 60 minutes or more (2000)

WOODMAN (village). Covers a land area of 0.236 square miles and a water area of 0 square miles. Located at 43.09° N. Lat.; 90.80° W. Long. Elevation is 650 feet.
Population: 96 (2000); Race: 100.0% White, 0.0% Black, 0.0% Asian, 0.0% American Indian and Alaska Native, 0.0% Hispanic of any race, 0.0% two or more races (2000); Density: 407.6 persons per square mile (2000); Age: 11.8% under 18, 22.5% over 64 (2000); Marriage status: 22.3% never married, 50.0% now married, 10.6% widowed, 17.0% divorced (2000); Foreign born: 0.0% (2000); Ancestry (includes multiple ancestries): 48.0% German, 30.4% English, 19.6% Irish, 7.8% United States or American, 5.9% Norwegian (2000).
Economy: Employment by occupation: 0.0% management, 5.9% professional, 23.5% services, 17.6% sales, 0.0% farming, 11.8% construction, 41.2% production (2000).

Income: Per capita income: $16,363 (2000); Median household income: $27,500 (2000); Poverty rate: 8.8% (2000).
Taxes: Total city taxes per capita: $17 (1997); City property taxes per capita: $8 (1997).
Education: High school graduation rate: 70.0% (2000); College graduation rate: 6.3% (2000).
Housing: Homeownership rate: 74.5% (2000); Median home value: $47,500 (2000); Median rent: $300 per month (2000); Median age of housing: 60+ years (2000).
Transportation: Commute to work: 100.0% car, 0.0% public transportation, 0.0% walk, 0.0% work from home (2000); Travel time to work: 31.4% less than 15 minutes, 27.5% 15 to 30 minutes, 15.7% 30 to 45 minutes, 7.8% 45 to 60 minutes, 17.6% 60 minutes or more (2000)

WOODMAN (town). Covers a land area of 26.723 square miles and a water area of 0.772 square miles. Located at 43.06° N. Lat.; 90.82° W. Long. Elevation is 650 feet.
Population: 194 (2000); Race: 100.0% White, 0.0% Black, 0.0% Asian, 0.0% American Indian and Alaska Native, 0.0% Hispanic of any race, 0.0% two or more races (2000); Density: 7.3 persons per square mile (2000); Age: 29.2% under 18, 13.5% over 64 (2000); Marriage status: 27.6% never married, 64.7% now married, 4.5% widowed, 3.2% divorced (2000); Foreign born: 0.0% (2000); Ancestry (includes multiple ancestries): 35.9% German, 11.5% Irish, 8.3% Norwegian, 5.7% English, 5.7% United States or American (2000).
Economy: In farm area. Bull Run Ski Area to Northeast. Employment by occupation: 14.3% management, 16.3% professional, 25.5% services, 11.2% sales, 2.0% farming, 5.1% construction, 25.5% production (2000).
Income: Per capita income: $13,024 (2000); Median household income: $33,333 (2000); Poverty rate: 21.5% (2000).
Taxes: Total city taxes per capita: $142 (1997); City property taxes per capita: $142 (1997).
Education: High school graduation rate: 89.2% (2000); College graduation rate: 20.7% (2000).
Housing: Homeownership rate: 63.6% (2000); Median home value: $92,500 (2000); Median rent: $250 per month (2000); Median age of housing: 60 years (2000).
Transportation: Commute to work: 83.7% car, 0.0% public transportation, 0.0% walk, 16.3% work from home (2000); Travel time to work: 11.0% less than 15 minutes, 52.4% 15 to 30 minutes, 20.7% 30 to 45 minutes, 7.3% 45 to 60 minutes, 8.5% 60 minutes or more (2000)

WYALUSING (town). Covers a land area of 39.897 square miles and a water area of 2.670 square miles. Located at 42.94° N. Lat.; 91.09° W. Long. Elevation is 650 feet.
Population: 370 (2000); Race: 99.4% White, 0.0% Black, 0.0% Asian, 0.0% American Indian and Alaska Native, 1.2% Hispanic of any race, 0.0% two or more races (2000); Density: 9.3 persons per square mile (2000); Age: 25.2% under 18, 20.4% over 64 (2000); Marriage status: 15.6% never married, 70.0% now married, 9.5% widowed, 4.9% divorced (2000); Foreign born: 1.5% (2000); Ancestry (includes multiple ancestries): 50.2% German, 17.9% English, 10.6% Irish, 5.8% Scottish, 5.2% French (except Basque) (2000).
Economy: Single-family building permits issued: 5 (2001) / 5 (2000); Multi-family building permits issued: 0 (2001) / 0 (2000); Employment by occupation: 29.3% management, 7.5% professional, 20.1% services, 17.8% sales, 1.7% farming, 8.0% construction, 15.5% production (2000).
Income: Per capita income: $14,602 (2000); Median household income: $29,038 (2000); Poverty rate: 8.8% (2000).
Taxes: Total city taxes per capita: $83 (1997); City property taxes per capita: $80 (1997).
Education: High school graduation rate: 85.0% (2000); College graduation rate: 13.3% (2000).
Housing: Homeownership rate: 86.9% (2000); Median home value: $84,000 (2000); Median rent: $250 per month (2000); Median age of housing: 38 years (2000).
Transportation: Commute to work: 81.6% car, 0.0% public transportation, 2.9% walk, 15.5% work from home (2000); Travel time to work: 19.0% less than 15 minutes, 59.9% 15 to 30 minutes, 11.6% 30 to 45 minutes, 4.8% 45 to 60 minutes, 4.8% 60 minutes or more (2000)

Green County

Located in southern Wisconsin; hilly area, bounded on the south by Illinois; drained by the Sugar and Pecatonica Rivers. Covers a land area of 584.00 square miles, a water area of 0.60 square miles, and is located in the Central Time Zone. The county government was organized in 1836. County seat is Monroe.

Weather Station: Brodhead — Elevation: 787 feet

	Jan	Feb	Mar	Apr	May	Jun	Jul	Aug	Sep	Oct	Nov	Dec
High	26	32	43	58	70	80	84	81	74	61	45	32
Low	7	12	23	35	46	55	60	57	48	37	26	14
Precip	1.3	1.3	2.3	3.5	3.6	4.5	3.9	4.2	3.6	2.8	2.4	1.8
Snow	10.5	6.2	5.2	1.4	tr	0.0	0.0	0.0	0.0	tr	2.1	8.0

High and Low temperatures in degrees Fahrenheit; Precipitation and Snow in inches

Weather Station: Dalton — Elevation: 859 feet

	Jan	Feb	Mar	Apr	May	Jun	Jul	Aug	Sep	Oct	Nov	Dec
High	26	32	43	58	71	80	83	81	73	60	44	31
Low	8	13	23	35	46	55	60	58	50	39	27	14
Precip	1.3	1.1	2.3	3.1	3.6	4.0	4.2	3.8	3.7	2.4	2.4	1.4
Snow	12.5	7.8	8.3	2.9	0.1	0.0	0.0	0.0	tr	0.5	4.6	10.2

High and Low temperatures in degrees Fahrenheit; Precipitation and Snow in inches

Population: 33,647 (2000); Race: 98.3% White, 0.2% Black, 0.2% Asian, 0.4% American Indian and Alaska Native, 0.8% Hispanic of any race, 0.7% two or more races (2000); Density: 57.6 persons per square mile (2000); Age: 26.5% under 18, 14.7% over 64 (2000).
Religion: Five largest groups: 12.7% Catholic Church, 12.5% United Church of Christ, 10.6% Evangelical Lutheran Church in America, 7.1% The United Methodist Church, 1.2% New Testament Association of Independent Baptist Churches and other Fundamenta
Economy: Unemployment rate: 3.8% (11/2002); Total civilian labor force: 19,351 (11/2002); Leading industries: 25.3% manufacturing; 24.5% retail trade; 14.8% health care and social assistance (2000); Companies that employ more than 1,000 persons: 0 (2000); Companies that employ more than 100 persons: 24 (2000); Farms: 1,295 totaling 304,963 acres (1997); Minority business ownership rate: 0.0% (1997); Women business ownership rate: 26.5% (1997); Retail sales per capita: $17,305 (1997). Single-family building permits issued: 195 (2001) / 175 (2000); Multi-family building permits issued: 2 (2001) / 36 (2000).
Income: Per capita income: $20,795 (2000); Median household income: $43,228 (2000); Poverty rate: 5.1% (2000); Bankruptcy rate: 3.58% (2001).
Taxes: Total county taxes per capita: $211 (2000); County property taxes per capita: $203 (2000).
Education: High school graduation rate: 84.1% (2000); College graduation rate: 16.7% (2000).
Housing: Homeownership rate: 73.7% (2000); Median home value: $97,700 (2000); Median rent: $392 per month (2000); Median age of housing: 39 years (2000).
Health: Birth rate: 112.9 per 10,000 population (1998); Age adjusted death rate: 80.0 per 10,000 population (1999); Age adjusted cancer mortality rate: 173.3 deaths per 100,000 population (1999). Air Quality Index: 70% good, 30% moderate, 0% unhealthy (percent of days in 2000). Number of physicians: 21.4 per 10,000 population (1999); Number of hospital beds: 34.8 per 10,000 population (1999).
Elections: 2000 Presidential election results: 51.5% Gore, 44.5% Bush, 3.2% Nader, 0.2% Buchanan
National and State Parks: New Glarus Woods State Park
Additional Information Contacts
Green County Government Offices 608-328-9430
Brodhead Chamber of Commerce 608-897-8411
Monroe Chamber of Commerce. 608-325-7648
New Glarus Community Partners. 608-527-4990

Green County Communities

ADAMS (town). Covers a land area of 36.182 square miles and a water area of 0 square miles. Located at 42.72° N. Lat.; 89.76° W. Long.
Population: 464 (2000); Race: 99.4% White, 0.0% Black, 0.0% Asian, 0.0% American Indian and Alaska Native, 0.4% Hispanic of any race, 0.6% two or more races (2000); Density: 12.8 persons per square mile (2000); Age: 25.8% under 18, 9.7% over 64 (2000); Marriage status: 25.0% never married, 64.9% now married, 2.4% widowed, 7.7% divorced (2000); Foreign born: 0.0% (2000); Ancestry (includes multiple ancestries): 42.4% German, 24.6% Norwegian, 21.6% Swiss, 16.3% Irish, 9.3% English (2000).
Economy: Employment by occupation: 23.4% management, 9.0% professional, 9.7% services, 19.3% sales, 7.9% farming, 9.3% construction, 21.4% production (2000).
Income: Per capita income: $20,826 (2000); Median household income: $46,731 (2000); Poverty rate: 8.7% (2000).

Taxes: Total city taxes per capita: $116 (1997); City property taxes per capita: $116 (1997).
Education: High school graduation rate: 85.5% (2000); College graduation rate: 8.7% (2000).
Housing: Homeownership rate: 79.1% (2000); Median home value: $107,100 (2000); Median rent: $367 per month (2000); Median age of housing: 60+ years (2000).
Transportation: Commute to work: 76.9% car, 0.0% public transportation, 3.4% walk, 19.7% work from home (2000); Travel time to work: 16.3% less than 15 minutes, 44.6% 15 to 30 minutes, 12.9% 30 to 45 minutes, 9.9% 45 to 60 minutes, 16.3% 60 minutes or more (2000)

ALBANY (village). Covers a land area of 1.274 square miles and a water area of 0.028 square miles. Located at 42.70° N. Lat.; 89.43° W. Long. Elevation is 810 feet.
Population: 1,191 (2000); Race: 97.9% White, 0.3% Black, 0.0% Asian, 0.2% American Indian and Alaska Native, 0.3% Hispanic of any race, 1.5% two or more races (2000); Density: 934.9 persons per square mile (2000); Age: 27.9% under 18, 12.1% over 64 (2000); Marriage status: 25.0% never married, 54.9% now married, 8.4% widowed, 11.7% divorced (2000); Foreign born: 0.9% (2000); Ancestry (includes multiple ancestries): 37.7% German, 19.8% Norwegian, 14.7% Irish, 14.3% Swiss, 12.3% English (2000).
Economy: Single-family building permits issued: 0 (2001) / 1 (2000); Multi-family building permits issued: 0 (2001) / 0 (2000); Employment by occupation: 7.4% management, 8.8% professional, 12.3% services, 25.1% sales, 2.9% farming, 12.3% construction, 31.1% production (2000).
Income: Per capita income: $19,186 (2000); Median household income: $40,109 (2000); Poverty rate: 3.5% (2000).
Taxes: Total city taxes per capita: $148 (1997); City property taxes per capita: $137 (1997).
Education: High school graduation rate: 83.2% (2000); College graduation rate: 9.2% (2000).

School District(s)

Albany (PK-12)
2000 Enrollment: 460 608-862-3225
Housing: Homeownership rate: 66.5% (2000); Median home value: $82,900 (2000); Median rent: $375 per month (2000); Median age of housing: 46 years (2000).
Transportation: Commute to work: 92.9% car, 0.2% public transportation, 4.3% walk, 2.4% work from home (2000); Travel time to work: 18.9% less than 15 minutes, 39.5% 15 to 30 minutes, 17.2% 30 to 45 minutes, 17.2% 45 to 60 minutes, 7.3% 60 minutes or more (2000)

ALBANY (town). Covers a land area of 34.164 square miles and a water area of 0.158 square miles. Located at 42.71° N. Lat.; 89.43° W. Long. Elevation is 810 feet.
Population: 775 (2000); Race: 98.9% White, 0.0% Black, 0.0% Asian, 0.0% American Indian and Alaska Native, 0.7% Hispanic of any race, 0.4% two or more races (2000); Density: 22.7 persons per square mile (2000); Age: 25.0% under 18, 10.0% over 64 (2000); Marriage status: 19.4% never married, 71.9% now married, 4.3% widowed, 4.3% divorced (2000); Foreign born: 1.2% (2000); Ancestry (includes multiple ancestries): 42.8% German, 18.2% Swiss, 15.3% Norwegian, 11.6% Irish, 9.1% English (2000).
Economy: In agricultural area. Manufactures cheese, electric heating elements. Employment by occupation: 19.5% management, 8.6% professional, 9.1% services, 22.3% sales, 3.5% farming, 16.3% construction, 20.7% production (2000).
Income: Per capita income: $21,610 (2000); Median household income: $52,083 (2000); Poverty rate: 3.2% (2000).
Taxes: Total city taxes per capita: $102 (1997); City property taxes per capita: $102 (1997).
Education: High school graduation rate: 85.1% (2000); College graduation rate: 14.1% (2000).
Housing: Homeownership rate: 86.7% (2000); Median home value: $117,000 (2000); Median rent: $330 per month (2000); Median age of housing: 27 years (2000).
Transportation: Commute to work: 86.1% car, 0.0% public transportation, 1.9% walk, 11.6% work from home (2000); Travel time to work: 26.2% less than 15 minutes, 27.5% 15 to 30 minutes, 29.1% 30 to 45 minutes, 12.0% 45 to 60 minutes, 5.1% 60 minutes or more (2000)

BRODHEAD (city). Covers a land area of 1.626 square miles and a water area of 0 square miles. Located at 42.61° N. Lat.; 89.37° W. Long. Elevation is 798 feet.
History: Incorporated 1891.
Population: 3,180 (2000); Race: 99.5% White, 0.0% Black, 0.0% Asian, 0.5% American Indian and Alaska Native, 0.4% Hispanic of any race, 0.0% two or more races (2000); Density: 1,956.1 persons per square mile (2000); Age: 26.4% under 18, 16.8% over 64 (2000); Marriage status: 20.0% never married, 56.8% now married, 9.9% widowed, 13.3% divorced (2000); Foreign born: 0.9% (2000); Ancestry (includes multiple ancestries): 39.9% German, 18.7% Norwegian, 14.3% Irish, 11.0% Swiss, 11.0% United States or American (2000).
Economy: In dairying area. Manufacturing: agricultural and transportation equipment. Single-family building permits issued: 1 (2001) / 4 (2000); Multi-family building permits issued: 0 (2001) / 0 (2000); Employment by occupation: 3.6% management, 14.5% professional, 14.4% services, 23.8% sales, 1.9% farming, 10.2% construction, 31.5% production (2000).
Income: Per capita income: $17,455 (2000); Median household income: $36,506 (2000); Poverty rate: 7.3% (2000).
Taxes: Total city taxes per capita: $258 (1997); City property taxes per capita: $243 (1997).
Education: High school graduation rate: 77.4% (2000); College graduation rate: 13.2% (2000).

School District(s)

Brodhead (PK-12)
2000 Enrollment: 1,256 608-897-2141
Housing: Homeownership rate: 73.1% (2000); Median home value: $82,900 (2000); Median rent: $365 per month (2000); Median age of housing: 49 years (2000).
Safety: Violent crime rate: 6.2 per 10,000 population; Property crime rate: 81.2 per 10,000 population (2001).
Newspapers: Independent-Register (1 x week)
Transportation: Commute to work: 95.9% car, 0.0% public transportation, 1.7% walk, 1.7% work from home (2000); Travel time to work: 41.0% less than 15 minutes, 25.2% 15 to 30 minutes, 21.0% 30 to 45 minutes, 7.4% 45 to 60 minutes, 5.4% 60 minutes or more (2000)
Additional Information Contacts
Brodhead Chamber of Commerce 608-897-8411

BROOKLYN (town). Covers a land area of 35.474 square miles and a water area of 0.012 square miles. Located at 42.80° N. Lat.; 89.43° W. Long. Elevation is 980 feet.
Population: 944 (2000); Race: 98.5% White, 0.4% Black, 0.4% Asian, 0.0% American Indian and Alaska Native, 0.2% Hispanic of any race, 0.6% two or more races (2000); Density: 26.6 persons per square mile (2000); Age: 28.4% under 18, 8.4% over 64 (2000); Marriage status: 20.5% never married, 70.1% now married, 3.0% widowed, 6.3% divorced (2000); Foreign born: 0.2% (2000); Ancestry (includes multiple ancestries): 46.0% German, 16.3% Swiss, 15.5% Irish, 12.7% Norwegian, 11.9% English (2000).
Economy: Employment by occupation: 20.1% management, 19.2% professional, 7.7% services, 20.3% sales, 2.3% farming, 14.5% construction, 15.9% production (2000).
Income: Per capita income: $21,458 (2000); Median household income: $53,333 (2000); Poverty rate: 2.7% (2000).
Taxes: Total city taxes per capita: $167 (1997); City property taxes per capita: $164 (1997).
Education: High school graduation rate: 89.1% (2000); College graduation rate: 19.5% (2000).
Housing: Homeownership rate: 91.2% (2000); Median home value: $147,900 (2000); Median rent: $413 per month (2000); Median age of housing: 28 years (2000).
Transportation: Commute to work: 89.8% car, 0.0% public transportation, 2.0% walk, 6.3% work from home (2000); Travel time to work: 16.1% less than 15 minutes, 27.0% 15 to 30 minutes, 42.3% 30 to 45 minutes, 7.1% 45 to 60 minutes, 7.6% 60 minutes or more (2000)

BROWNTOWN (village). Covers a land area of 1.055 square miles and a water area of 0 square miles. Located at 42.57° N. Lat.; 89.79° W. Long. Elevation is 850 feet.
Population: 252 (2000); Race: 99.3% White, 0.7% Black, 0.0% Asian, 0.0% American Indian and Alaska Native, 0.0% Hispanic of any race, 0.0% two or more races (2000); Density: 238.9 persons per square mile (2000); Age: 27.4% under 18, 17.8% over 64 (2000); Marriage status: 19.6% never married, 62.7% now married, 4.8% widowed, 12.9% divorced (2000); Foreign born: 0.0% (2000); Ancestry (includes multiple ancestries): 44.8% German, 15.9% Irish, 15.9% Norwegian, 10.0% Swiss, 7.4% English (2000).
Economy: Dairy products (cheese). Manufacturing: iron castings. Hunting and recreation area nearby. Single-family building permits issued: 2 (2001) / 0 (2000); Multi-family building permits issued: 0 (2001) / 0 (2000); Employment by occupation: 6.4% management, 7.1% professional, 20.7%

services, 25.7% sales, 0.0% farming, 7.1% construction, 32.9% production (2000).
Income: Per capita income: $14,876 (2000); Median household income: $36,500 (2000); Poverty rate: 5.6% (2000).
Taxes: Total city taxes per capita: $85 (1997); City property taxes per capita: $81 (1997).
Education: High school graduation rate: 78.0% (2000); College graduation rate: 9.1% (2000).
Housing: Homeownership rate: 91.6% (2000); Median home value: $58,900 (2000); Median rent: $392 per month (2000); Median age of housing: 53 years (2000).
Transportation: Commute to work: 93.5% car, 0.0% public transportation, 5.1% walk, 1.4% work from home (2000); Travel time to work: 32.4% less than 15 minutes, 54.4% 15 to 30 minutes, 3.7% 30 to 45 minutes, 0.0% 45 to 60 minutes, 9.6% 60 minutes or more (2000)

CADIZ (town). Covers a land area of 36.419 square miles and a water area of 0.144 square miles. Located at 42.55° N. Lat.; 89.77° W. Long.
Population: 863 (2000); Race: 97.6% White, 0.7% Black, 0.0% Asian, 0.0% American Indian and Alaska Native, 0.0% Hispanic of any race, 1.7% two or more races (2000); Density: 23.7 persons per square mile (2000); Age: 27.8% under 18, 11.5% over 64 (2000); Marriage status: 22.7% never married, 66.0% now married, 4.1% widowed, 7.2% divorced (2000); Foreign born: 0.2% (2000); Ancestry (includes multiple ancestries): 35.1% German, 20.5% Swiss, 17.6% Norwegian, 12.9% Irish, 11.8% English (2000).
Economy: Employment by occupation: 20.7% management, 9.0% professional, 7.9% services, 25.1% sales, 5.5% farming, 12.3% construction, 19.4% production (2000).
Income: Per capita income: $16,070 (2000); Median household income: $37,500 (2000); Poverty rate: 6.1% (2000).
Taxes: Total city taxes per capita: $114 (1997); City property taxes per capita: $109 (1997).
Education: High school graduation rate: 87.6% (2000); College graduation rate: 9.4% (2000).
Housing: Homeownership rate: 77.3% (2000); Median home value: $102,100 (2000); Median rent: $350 per month (2000); Median age of housing: 56 years (2000).
Transportation: Commute to work: 78.3% car, 0.4% public transportation, 3.5% walk, 17.0% work from home (2000); Travel time to work: 34.4% less than 15 minutes, 45.1% 15 to 30 minutes, 6.1% 30 to 45 minutes, 4.8% 45 to 60 minutes, 9.6% 60 minutes or more (2000)

CLARNO (town). Covers a land area of 36.530 square miles and a water area of 0 square miles. Located at 42.54° N. Lat.; 89.65° W. Long. Elevation is 909 feet.
Population: 1,079 (2000); Race: 99.1% White, 0.0% Black, 0.4% Asian, 0.0% American Indian and Alaska Native, 0.2% Hispanic of any race, 0.5% two or more races (2000); Density: 29.5 persons per square mile (2000); Age: 26.4% under 18, 11.8% over 64 (2000); Marriage status: 21.7% never married, 66.1% now married, 5.5% widowed, 6.7% divorced (2000); Foreign born: 0.9% (2000); Ancestry (includes multiple ancestries): 46.5% German, 34.0% Swiss, 13.3% Norwegian, 10.7% Irish, 8.1% English (2000).
Economy: Employment by occupation: 22.2% management, 9.7% professional, 12.1% services, 24.1% sales, 4.8% farming, 5.7% construction, 21.6% production (2000).
Income: Per capita income: $20,500 (2000); Median household income: $47,167 (2000); Poverty rate: 7.0% (2000).
Taxes: Total city taxes per capita: $152 (1997); City property taxes per capita: $149 (1997).
Education: High school graduation rate: 82.2% (2000); College graduation rate: 10.5% (2000).
Housing: Homeownership rate: 74.9% (2000); Median home value: $120,000 (2000); Median rent: $346 per month (2000); Median age of housing: 45 years (2000).
Transportation: Commute to work: 76.6% car, 0.0% public transportation, 4.2% walk, 16.5% work from home (2000); Travel time to work: 60.6% less than 15 minutes, 23.0% 15 to 30 minutes, 5.4% 30 to 45 minutes, 6.5% 45 to 60 minutes, 4.5% 60 minutes or more (2000)

DECATUR (town). Covers a land area of 34.190 square miles and a water area of 0.194 square miles. Located at 42.64° N. Lat.; 89.42° W. Long.
Population: 1,688 (2000); Race: 98.2% White, 0.2% Black, 0.2% Asian, 0.4% American Indian and Alaska Native, 1.8% Hispanic of any race, 0.1% two or more races (2000); Density: 49.4 persons per square mile (2000); Age: 29.2% under 18, 10.6% over 64 (2000); Marriage status: 19.7% never married, 72.7% now married, 2.3% widowed, 5.3% divorced (2000); Foreign born: 0.8% (2000); Ancestry (includes multiple ancestries): 42.0% German, 16.6% Norwegian, 16.2% Swiss, 10.4% English, 9.4% Irish (2000).
Economy: Employment by occupation: 13.6% management, 16.0% professional, 9.2% services, 22.1% sales, 3.1% farming, 10.1% construction, 26.0% production (2000).
Income: Per capita income: $19,482 (2000); Median household income: $50,809 (2000); Poverty rate: 5.1% (2000).
Taxes: Total city taxes per capita: $77 (1997); City property taxes per capita: $69 (1997).
Education: High school graduation rate: 87.3% (2000); College graduation rate: 15.0% (2000).
Housing: Homeownership rate: 89.9% (2000); Median home value: $133,800 (2000); Median rent: $394 per month (2000); Median age of housing: 22 years (2000).
Transportation: Commute to work: 89.5% car, 0.0% public transportation, 0.5% walk, 9.0% work from home (2000); Travel time to work: 31.0% less than 15 minutes, 26.4% 15 to 30 minutes, 25.8% 30 to 45 minutes, 12.3% 45 to 60 minutes, 4.6% 60 minutes or more (2000)

EXETER (town). Covers a land area of 35.142 square miles and a water area of 0 square miles. Located at 42.81° N. Lat.; 89.54° W. Long. Elevation is 880 feet.
Population: 1,261 (2000); Race: 99.0% White, 0.0% Black, 0.3% Asian, 0.3% American Indian and Alaska Native, 0.3% Hispanic of any race, 0.3% two or more races (2000); Density: 35.9 persons per square mile (2000); Age: 25.9% under 18, 7.7% over 64 (2000); Marriage status: 20.0% never married, 70.2% now married, 2.2% widowed, 7.7% divorced (2000); Foreign born: 1.4% (2000); Ancestry (includes multiple ancestries): 43.2% German, 21.2% Swiss, 21.0% Norwegian, 12.2% Irish, 9.4% English (2000).
Economy: Employment by occupation: 18.8% management, 19.0% professional, 10.1% services, 24.6% sales, 2.4% farming, 12.7% construction, 12.5% production (2000).
Income: Per capita income: $22,838 (2000); Median household income: $58,824 (2000); Poverty rate: 2.6% (2000).
Education: High school graduation rate: 90.1% (2000); College graduation rate: 25.1% (2000).
Housing: Homeownership rate: 84.2% (2000); Median home value: $160,400 (2000); Median rent: $563 per month (2000); Median age of housing: 15 years (2000).
Transportation: Commute to work: 89.2% car, 0.3% public transportation, 1.9% walk, 8.1% work from home (2000); Travel time to work: 23.8% less than 15 minutes, 25.9% 15 to 30 minutes, 39.4% 30 to 45 minutes, 7.7% 45 to 60 minutes, 3.2% 60 minutes or more (2000)

JEFFERSON (town). Covers a land area of 38.750 square miles and a water area of 0.010 square miles. Located at 42.56° N. Lat.; 89.53° W. Long.
Population: 1,212 (2000); Race: 99.0% White, 0.4% Black, 0.0% Asian, 0.3% American Indian and Alaska Native, 0.0% Hispanic of any race, 0.3% two or more races (2000); Density: 31.3 persons per square mile (2000); Age: 29.2% under 18, 11.9% over 64 (2000); Marriage status: 22.4% never married, 67.3% now married, 4.8% widowed, 5.5% divorced (2000); Foreign born: 0.7% (2000); Ancestry (includes multiple ancestries): 42.1% German, 23.6% Swiss, 12.5% Norwegian, 9.4% Irish, 6.4% English (2000).
Economy: Employment by occupation: 15.5% management, 9.1% professional, 16.6% services, 23.7% sales, 4.5% farming, 11.0% construction, 19.5% production (2000).
Income: Per capita income: $22,156 (2000); Median household income: $43,393 (2000); Poverty rate: 4.1% (2000).
Taxes: Total city taxes per capita: $66 (1997); City property taxes per capita: $64 (1997).
Education: High school graduation rate: 83.8% (2000); College graduation rate: 7.6% (2000).
Housing: Homeownership rate: 82.4% (2000); Median home value: $89,100 (2000); Median rent: $343 per month (2000); Median age of housing: 57 years (2000).
Transportation: Commute to work: 78.7% car, 0.0% public transportation, 3.6% walk, 17.4% work from home (2000); Travel time to work: 45.5% less than 15 minutes, 34.2% 15 to 30 minutes, 9.2% 30 to 45 minutes, 6.3% 45 to 60 minutes, 4.8% 60 minutes or more (2000)

JORDAN (town). Covers a land area of 36.002 square miles and a water area of 0.008 square miles. Located at 42.64° N. Lat.; 89.78° W. Long.
Population: 577 (2000); Race: 99.3% White, 0.0% Black, 0.4% Asian, 0.0% American Indian and Alaska Native, 1.1% Hispanic of any race, 0.4% two or more races (2000); Density: 16.0 persons per square mile (2000); Age: 30.6% under 18, 8.5% over 64 (2000); Marriage status: 23.6% never married, 68.2%

now married, 4.2% widowed, 4.0% divorced (2000); Foreign born: 2.1% (2000); Ancestry (includes multiple ancestries): 50.7% German, 28.3% Swiss, 18.9% Irish, 10.0% Norwegian, 9.3% English (2000).
Economy: Employment by occupation: 19.1% management, 9.5% professional, 13.5% services, 20.6% sales, 2.8% farming, 12.9% construction, 21.5% production (2000).
Income: Per capita income: $25,046 (2000); Median household income: $46,458 (2000); Poverty rate: 1.4% (2000).
Taxes: Total city taxes per capita: $169 (1997); City property taxes per capita: $169 (1997).
Education: High school graduation rate: 82.5% (2000); College graduation rate: 16.7% (2000).
Housing: Homeownership rate: 82.3% (2000); Median home value: $97,500 (2000); Median rent: $413 per month (2000); Median age of housing: 60+ years (2000).
Transportation: Commute to work: 76.8% car, 0.0% public transportation, 9.8% walk, 12.8% work from home (2000); Travel time to work: 39.3% less than 15 minutes, 44.6% 15 to 30 minutes, 5.6% 30 to 45 minutes, 3.2% 45 to 60 minutes, 7.4% 60 minutes or more (2000)

JUDA (unincorporated postal area, zip code 53550). Covers a land area of 47.617 square miles and a water area of 0.010 square miles. Located at 42.56° N. Lat.; 89.49° W. Long. Elevation is 830 feet.
Population: 1,244 (2000); Race: 98.9% White, 0.2% Black, 0.0% Asian, 0.2% American Indian and Alaska Native, 0.7% Hispanic of any race, 0.6% two or more races (2000); Density: 26.1 persons per square mile (2000); Age: 30.2% under 18, 10.6% over 64 (2000); Marriage status: 21.5% never married, 70.1% now married, 2.9% widowed, 5.4% divorced (2000); Foreign born: 1.1% (2000); Ancestry (includes multiple ancestries): 43.5% German, 23.6% Swiss, 11.4% Norwegian, 8.1% English, 7.6% Irish (2000).
Economy: In livestock, dairy, and grain region. Manufacturing: cheese, whey products; meat processing. Employment by occupation: 18.8% management, 6.5% professional, 13.9% services, 24.3% sales, 5.6% farming, 12.6% construction, 18.4% production (2000).
Income: Per capita income: $20,452 (2000); Median household income: $43,421 (2000); Poverty rate: 6.4% (2000).
Education: High school graduation rate: 83.0% (2000); College graduation rate: 7.1% (2000).

School District(s)

Juda (PK-12)
2000 Enrollment: 335 608-934-5251
Housing: Homeownership rate: 76.9% (2000); Median home value: $87,100 (2000); Median rent: $394 per month (2000); Median age of housing: 60+ years (2000).
Transportation: Commute to work: 74.3% car, 0.0% public transportation, 4.8% walk, 20.6% work from home (2000); Travel time to work: 39.4% less than 15 minutes, 38.2% 15 to 30 minutes, 11.4% 30 to 45 minutes, 6.6% 45 to 60 minutes, 4.4% 60 minutes or more (2000)

MONROE (city). Covers a land area of 4.340 square miles and a water area of 0 square miles. Located at 42.59° N. Lat.; 89.64° W. Long. Elevation is 1,099 feet.
History: Monroe earned a reputation as the Swiss cheese capital of the United States for its manufacture of Swiss and Limburger cheeses. Though Monroe was named the seat of Green County in 1839, it began to grow only after the coming of the Milwaukee & Mississippi Railroad in 1857. The success of the cheese industry at New Glarus attracted more immigrants from Switzerland, and by 1875 there were 75 cheese factories in Green County, most of the product marketed through Monroe.
Population: 10,843 (2000); Race: 97.6% White, 0.3% Black, 0.1% Asian, 0.5% American Indian and Alaska Native, 1.4% Hispanic of any race, 1.1% two or more races (2000); Density: 2,498.5 persons per square mile (2000); Age: 24.6% under 18, 18.7% over 64 (2000); Marriage status: 22.8% never married, 56.4% now married, 10.0% widowed, 10.9% divorced (2000); Foreign born: 1.6% (2000); Ancestry (includes multiple ancestries): 40.7% German, 23.9% Swiss, 15.2% Norwegian, 11.1% Irish, 9.0% English (2000).
Vital Statistics: Birth rate: 131.9 per 10,000 population (1998)
Economy: Single-family building permits issued: 8 (2001) / 8 (2000); Multi-family building permits issued: 0 (2001) / 14 (2000); Employment by occupation: 9.5% management, 16.3% professional, 14.2% services, 26.3% sales, 0.9% farming, 9.2% construction, 23.6% production (2000).
Income: Per capita income: $21,657 (2000); Median household income: $36,922 (2000); Poverty rate: 5.4% (2000).
Taxes: Total city taxes per capita: $338 (1997); City property taxes per capita: $317 (1997).
Education: High school graduation rate: 81.5% (2000); College graduation rate: 17.6% (2000).

School District(s)

Monroe (PK-12)
2000 Enrollment: 2,759 608-328-9171
Housing: Homeownership rate: 63.4% (2000); Median home value: $90,100 (2000); Median rent: $385 per month (2000); Median age of housing: 39 years (2000).
Hospitals: Monroe Clinic (221 beds)
Safety: Violent crime rate: 4.6 per 10,000 population; Property crime rate: 242.7 per 10,000 population (2001).
Newspapers: Monroe Times (6 x week)
Transportation: Commute to work: 89.5% car, 0.4% public transportation, 6.9% walk, 2.4% work from home (2000); Travel time to work: 69.3% less than 15 minutes, 14.0% 15 to 30 minutes, 5.9% 30 to 45 minutes, 5.1% 45 to 60 minutes, 5.7% 60 minutes or more (2000)
Additional Information Contacts
Monroe Chamber of Commerce.......................... 608-325-7648

MONROE (town). Covers a land area of 33.041 square miles and a water area of 0.007 square miles. Located at 42.64° N. Lat.; 89.65° W. Long. Elevation is 1,099 feet.
History: Inhabitants mostly of Swiss descent; annual cheese fair is held. Incorporated as village c.1859, as city in 1882.
Population: 1,142 (2000); Race: 99.7% White, 0.3% Black, 0.0% Asian, 0.0% American Indian and Alaska Native, 0.3% Hispanic of any race, 0.0% two or more races (2000); Density: 34.6 persons per square mile (2000); Age: 25.1% under 18, 18.5% over 64 (2000); Marriage status: 21.8% never married, 68.9% now married, 4.7% widowed, 4.5% divorced (2000); Foreign born: 1.8% (2000); Ancestry (includes multiple ancestries): 31.1% German, 30.5% Swiss, 14.3% Norwegian, 13.8% Irish, 13.6% English (2000).
Economy: Dairying region. One of state's leading cheese-producing centers. Manufacturing: food and beverages, electronic equipment, wood products. Brownstone-Cadiz State Recreation Area (former Cadiz Springs State Park) to West. Employment by occupation: 15.8% management, 14.4% professional, 14.6% services, 20.6% sales, 2.8% farming, 11.6% construction, 20.3% production (2000).
Income: Per capita income: $20,204 (2000); Median household income: $55,625 (2000); Poverty rate: 3.3% (2000).
Taxes: Total city taxes per capita: $80 (1997); City property taxes per capita: $77 (1997).
Education: High school graduation rate: 80.1% (2000); College graduation rate: 18.9% (2000).
Housing: Homeownership rate: 84.2% (2000); Median home value: $136,800 (2000); Median rent: $506 per month (2000); Median age of housing: 27 years (2000).
Transportation: Commute to work: 89.0% car, 1.0% public transportation, 2.7% walk, 7.4% work from home (2000); Travel time to work: 71.7% less than 15 minutes, 14.2% 15 to 30 minutes, 4.3% 30 to 45 minutes, 4.3% 45 to 60 minutes, 5.5% 60 minutes or more (2000)

MONTICELLO (village). Covers a land area of 1.165 square miles and a water area of 0.012 square miles. Located at 42.74° N. Lat.; 89.59° W. Long. Elevation is 847 feet.
Population: 1,146 (2000); Race: 99.2% White, 0.0% Black, 0.1% Asian, 0.0% American Indian and Alaska Native, 0.7% Hispanic of any race, 0.7% two or more races (2000); Density: 983.7 persons per square mile (2000); Age: 25.4% under 18, 16.0% over 64 (2000); Marriage status: 20.4% never married, 58.0% now married, 9.8% widowed, 11.9% divorced (2000); Foreign born: 0.6% (2000); Ancestry (includes multiple ancestries): 35.9% Swiss, 34.8% German, 22.2% Norwegian, 6.9% Irish, 6.5% English (2000).
Economy: In agricultural area. Manufacturing cooperative: feed, cheese, wire garment hangers. Single-family building permits issued: 1 (2001) / 3 (2000); Multi-family building permits issued: 0 (2001) / 4 (2000); Employment by occupation: 10.7% management, 9.5% professional, 16.6% services, 24.7% sales, 1.6% farming, 8.7% construction, 28.1% production (2000).
Income: Per capita income: $21,772 (2000); Median household income: $44,087 (2000); Poverty rate: 5.8% (2000).
Taxes: Total city taxes per capita: $136 (1997); City property taxes per capita: $109 (1997).
Education: High school graduation rate: 83.7% (2000); College graduation rate: 16.1% (2000).

School District(s)

Monticello (PK-12)
2000 Enrollment: 437 608-938-4194

Housing: Homeownership rate: 72.1% (2000); Median home value: $91,100 (2000); Median rent: $420 per month (2000); Median age of housing: 42 years (2000).
Transportation: Commute to work: 89.7% car, 0.0% public transportation, 6.8% walk, 3.2% work from home (2000); Travel time to work: 39.6% less than 15 minutes, 25.7% 15 to 30 minutes, 17.4% 30 to 45 minutes, 15.3% 45 to 60 minutes, 2.0% 60 minutes or more (2000)

MOUNT PLEASANT (town). Covers a land area of 34.288 square miles and a water area of 0.003 square miles. Located at 42.72° N. Lat.; 89.55° W. Long.
Population: 547 (2000); Race: 99.4% White, 0.0% Black, 0.0% Asian, 0.0% American Indian and Alaska Native, 0.0% Hispanic of any race, 0.6% two or more races (2000); Density: 16.0 persons per square mile (2000); Age: 31.4% under 18, 8.2% over 64 (2000); Marriage status: 19.5% never married, 72.9% now married, 3.7% widowed, 3.9% divorced (2000); Foreign born: 0.9% (2000); Ancestry (includes multiple ancestries): 37.7% German, 36.0% Swiss, 17.9% Norwegian, 10.8% Irish, 9.0% English (2000).
Economy: Employment by occupation: 18.7% management, 16.3% professional, 6.5% services, 20.1% sales, 5.4% farming, 7.6% construction, 25.5% production (2000).
Income: Per capita income: $23,405 (2000); Median household income: $57,656 (2000); Poverty rate: 3.8% (2000).
Taxes: Total city taxes per capita: $117 (1997); City property taxes per capita: $117 (1997).
Education: High school graduation rate: 89.2% (2000); College graduation rate: 16.2% (2000).
Housing: Homeownership rate: 77.8% (2000); Median home value: $125,000 (2000); Median rent: $350 per month (2000); Median age of housing: 60+ years (2000).
Transportation: Commute to work: 77.8% car, 1.1% public transportation, 7.6% walk, 12.2% work from home (2000); Travel time to work: 35.8% less than 15 minutes, 29.9% 15 to 30 minutes, 15.1% 30 to 45 minutes, 13.0% 45 to 60 minutes, 6.2% 60 minutes or more (2000)

NEW GLARUS (village). Covers a land area of 1.437 square miles and a water area of 0 square miles. Located at 42.81° N. Lat.; 89.63° W. Long. Elevation is 900 feet.
History: New Glarus was founded by a group of Swiss immigrants who arrived in 1845, following two men who had been sent by a Swiss emigration society to locate and purchase land for a colony.
Population: 2,111 (2000); Race: 96.1% White, 0.3% Black, 0.7% Asian, 1.5% American Indian and Alaska Native, 1.1% Hispanic of any race, 0.5% two or more races (2000); Density: 1,469.2 persons per square mile (2000); Age: 24.1% under 18, 22.1% over 64 (2000); Marriage status: 18.0% never married, 57.7% now married, 15.3% widowed, 9.0% divorced (2000); Foreign born: 2.6% (2000); Ancestry (includes multiple ancestries): 35.5% Swiss, 33.8% German, 20.5% Norwegian, 8.7% English, 8.5% Irish (2000).
Economy: Single-family building permits issued: 2 (2001) / 2 (2000); Multi-family building permits issued: 0 (2001) / 0 (2000); Employment by occupation: 15.4% management, 18.9% professional, 13.9% services, 21.4% sales, 0.9% farming, 12.6% construction, 16.9% production (2000).
Income: Per capita income: $21,392 (2000); Median household income: $45,000 (2000); Poverty rate: 6.6% (2000).
Taxes: Total city taxes per capita: $241 (1997); City property taxes per capita: $227 (1997).
Education: High school graduation rate: 88.4% (2000); College graduation rate: 22.1% (2000).

School District(s)

New Glarus (PK-12)
2000 Enrollment: 735 608-527-2810
Housing: Homeownership rate: 73.7% (2000); Median home value: $113,800 (2000); Median rent: $439 per month (2000); Median age of housing: 38 years (2000).
Safety: Violent crime rate: 9.4 per 10,000 population; Property crime rate: 310.4 per 10,000 population (2001).
Newspapers: Post Messenger (1 x week); Sugar River Shopper (1 x week)
Transportation: Commute to work: 88.8% car, 0.0% public transportation, 6.7% walk, 3.1% work from home (2000); Travel time to work: 39.8% less than 15 minutes, 19.3% 15 to 30 minutes, 24.8% 30 to 45 minutes, 13.7% 45 to 60 minutes, 2.4% 60 minutes or more (2000)
Additional Information Contacts
New Glarus Community Partners. 608-527-4990

NEW GLARUS (town). Covers a land area of 34.696 square miles and a water area of 0 square miles. Located at 42.81° N. Lat.; 89.65° W. Long. Elevation is 900 feet.
History: Swiss historical village. Founded by Swiss in 1845, incorporated 1901.
Population: 943 (2000); Race: 98.7% White, 0.2% Black, 0.3% Asian, 0.0% American Indian and Alaska Native, 0.0% Hispanic of any race, 0.7% two or more races (2000); Density: 27.2 persons per square mile (2000); Age: 30.9% under 18, 6.6% over 64 (2000); Marriage status: 17.0% never married, 73.2% now married, 4.4% widowed, 5.4% divorced (2000); Foreign born: 1.5% (2000); Ancestry (includes multiple ancestries): 31.3% German, 26.7% Swiss, 26.5% Norwegian, 10.8% Irish, 7.9% English (2000).
Economy: In dairying region. Manufacturing of meat products. Cheese center. Makes Swiss embroidery. Annual Swiss festival held here. Northern terminus of Sugar River State Trail. Employment by occupation: 18.8% management, 27.1% professional, 11.8% services, 22.5% sales, 3.8% farming, 8.4% construction, 7.7% production (2000).
Income: Per capita income: $23,297 (2000); Median household income: $63,667 (2000); Poverty rate: 3.6% (2000).
Taxes: Total city taxes per capita: $165 (1997); City property taxes per capita: $155 (1997).
Education: High school graduation rate: 93.9% (2000); College graduation rate: 35.7% (2000).
Housing: Homeownership rate: 88.5% (2000); Median home value: $201,300 (2000); Median rent: $563 per month (2000); Median age of housing: 21 years (2000).
Transportation: Commute to work: 82.2% car, 0.4% public transportation, 3.7% walk, 13.6% work from home (2000); Travel time to work: 33.0% less than 15 minutes, 18.3% 15 to 30 minutes, 33.4% 30 to 45 minutes, 7.2% 45 to 60 minutes, 8.1% 60 minutes or more (2000)

SPRING GROVE (town). Covers a land area of 39.823 square miles and a water area of 0 square miles. Located at 42.54° N. Lat.; 89.42° W. Long.
Population: 861 (2000); Race: 98.5% White, 0.0% Black, 0.0% Asian, 0.7% American Indian and Alaska Native, 1.3% Hispanic of any race, 0.7% two or more races (2000); Density: 21.6 persons per square mile (2000); Age: 30.8% under 18, 7.1% over 64 (2000); Marriage status: 22.9% never married, 68.4% now married, 4.4% widowed, 4.2% divorced (2000); Foreign born: 2.4% (2000); Ancestry (includes multiple ancestries): 38.7% German, 19.5% Swiss, 12.0% Norwegian, 10.1% Irish, 7.7% English (2000).
Economy: Employment by occupation: 18.6% management, 9.1% professional, 10.8% services, 18.6% sales, 6.6% farming, 13.8% construction, 22.5% production (2000).
Income: Per capita income: $16,975 (2000); Median household income: $45,515 (2000); Poverty rate: 4.7% (2000).
Taxes: Total city taxes per capita: $101 (1997); City property taxes per capita: $100 (1997).
Education: High school graduation rate: 85.0% (2000); College graduation rate: 9.9% (2000).
Housing: Homeownership rate: 85.6% (2000); Median home value: $118,000 (2000); Median rent: $375 per month (2000); Median age of housing: 46 years (2000).
Transportation: Commute to work: 78.0% car, 0.0% public transportation, 1.9% walk, 19.6% work from home (2000); Travel time to work: 39.3% less than 15 minutes, 27.6% 15 to 30 minutes, 17.0% 30 to 45 minutes, 9.0% 45 to 60 minutes, 7.2% 60 minutes or more (2000)

SYLVESTER (town). Covers a land area of 35.919 square miles and a water area of 0 square miles. Located at 42.63° N. Lat.; 89.54° W. Long.
Population: 809 (2000); Race: 99.3% White, 0.0% Black, 0.5% Asian, 0.0% American Indian and Alaska Native, 0.1% Hispanic of any race, 0.1% two or more races (2000); Density: 22.5 persons per square mile (2000); Age: 28.1% under 18, 10.3% over 64 (2000); Marriage status: 13.6% never married, 79.1% now married, 2.7% widowed, 4.5% divorced (2000); Foreign born: 1.8% (2000); Ancestry (includes multiple ancestries): 43.9% German, 24.5% Swiss, 16.4% Norwegian, 9.4% Irish, 5.2% English (2000).
Economy: Employment by occupation: 17.4% management, 15.5% professional, 10.0% services, 27.8% sales, 3.7% farming, 11.4% construction, 14.2% production (2000).
Income: Per capita income: $23,871 (2000); Median household income: $52,917 (2000); Poverty rate: 3.7% (2000).
Taxes: Total city taxes per capita: $55 (1997); City property taxes per capita: $55 (1997).

Education: High school graduation rate: 91.0% (2000); College graduation rate: 16.4% (2000).
Housing: Homeownership rate: 87.4% (2000); Median home value: $147,100 (2000); Median rent: $433 per month (2000); Median age of housing: 32 years (2000).
Transportation: Commute to work: 86.8% car, 0.0% public transportation, 2.8% walk, 10.4% work from home (2000); Travel time to work: 49.1% less than 15 minutes, 31.5% 15 to 30 minutes, 5.8% 30 to 45 minutes, 6.8% 45 to 60 minutes, 6.8% 60 minutes or more (2000)

WASHINGTON (town). Covers a land area of 35.830 square miles and a water area of 0 square miles. Located at 42.72° N. Lat.; 89.65° W. Long.
Population: 627 (2000); Race: 98.4% White, 0.0% Black, 0.0% Asian, 0.0% American Indian and Alaska Native, 1.0% Hispanic of any race, 1.6% two or more races (2000); Density: 17.5 persons per square mile (2000); Age: 27.4% under 18, 10.8% over 64 (2000); Marriage status: 19.5% never married, 71.4% now married, 2.9% widowed, 6.2% divorced (2000); Foreign born: 1.0% (2000); Ancestry (includes multiple ancestries): 43.1% Swiss, 34.8% German, 18.7% Norwegian, 8.5% English, 5.9% Irish (2000).
Economy: Employment by occupation: 19.6% management, 9.3% professional, 10.9% services, 21.8% sales, 7.7% farming, 8.2% construction, 22.5% production (2000).
Income: Per capita income: $21,424 (2000); Median household income: $50,000 (2000); Poverty rate: 3.9% (2000).
Taxes: Total city taxes per capita: $71 (1997); City property taxes per capita: $71 (1997).
Education: High school graduation rate: 86.7% (2000); College graduation rate: 10.1% (2000).
Housing: Homeownership rate: 74.2% (2000); Median home value: $127,900 (2000); Median rent: $528 per month (2000); Median age of housing: 38 years (2000).
Transportation: Commute to work: 74.3% car, 0.8% public transportation, 7.5% walk, 15.8% work from home (2000); Travel time to work: 42.9% less than 15 minutes, 28.6% 15 to 30 minutes, 9.2% 30 to 45 minutes, 11.1% 45 to 60 minutes, 8.3% 60 minutes or more (2000)

YORK (town). Covers a land area of 35.971 square miles and a water area of 0 square miles. Located at 42.81° N. Lat.; 89.76° W. Long.
Population: 605 (2000); Race: 99.0% White, 0.3% Black, 0.0% Asian, 0.6% American Indian and Alaska Native, 0.3% Hispanic of any race, 0.0% two or more races (2000); Density: 16.8 persons per square mile (2000); Age: 29.9% under 18, 7.6% over 64 (2000); Marriage status: 19.9% never married, 73.3% now married, 1.2% widowed, 5.6% divorced (2000); Foreign born: 1.4% (2000); Ancestry (includes multiple ancestries): 42.0% German, 35.8% Norwegian, 18.6% Swiss, 13.8% English, 12.6% Irish (2000).
Economy: Employment by occupation: 23.4% management, 22.4% professional, 7.9% services, 18.3% sales, 4.6% farming, 10.9% construction, 12.5% production (2000).
Income: Per capita income: $20,622 (2000); Median household income: $50,833 (2000); Poverty rate: 1.9% (2000).
Taxes: Total city taxes per capita: $122 (1997); City property taxes per capita: $118 (1997).
Education: High school graduation rate: 95.2% (2000); College graduation rate: 31.7% (2000).
Housing: Homeownership rate: 91.0% (2000); Median home value: $158,300 (2000); Median rent: $608 per month (2000); Median age of housing: 39 years (2000).
Transportation: Commute to work: 79.8% car, 0.0% public transportation, 3.1% walk, 17.1% work from home (2000); Travel time to work: 21.9% less than 15 minutes, 18.8% 15 to 30 minutes, 31.5% 30 to 45 minutes, 21.9% 45 to 60 minutes, 5.9% 60 minutes or more (2000)

Green Lake County

Located in central Wisconsin; crossed by the Fox and Grand Rivers; includes Green Lake and Lake Puckaway. Covers a land area of 354.30 square miles, a water area of 26.20 square miles, and is located in the Central Time Zone. The county government was organized in 1858. County seat is Green Lake.

Weather Station: Dalton Elevation: 859 feet

	Jan	Feb	Mar	Apr	May	Jun	Jul	Aug	Sep	Oct	Nov	Dec
High	26	32	43	58	71	80	83	81	73	60	44	31
Low	8	13	23	35	46	55	60	58	50	39	27	14
Precip	1.3	1.1	2.3	3.1	3.6	4.0	4.2	3.8	3.7	2.4	2.4	1.4
Snow	12.5	7.8	8.3	2.9	0.1	0.0	0.0	0.0	tr	0.5	4.6	10.2

High and Low temperatures in degrees Fahrenheit; Precipitation and Snow in inches

Population: 19,105 (2000); Race: 97.8% White, 0.3% Black, 0.1% Asian, 0.1% American Indian and Alaska Native, 2.1% Hispanic of any race, 0.5% two or more races (2000); Density: 53.9 persons per square mile (2000); Age: 24.0% under 18, 18.8% over 64 (2000).
Religion: Five largest groups: 38.2% Catholic Church, 16.0% Wisconsin Evangelical Lutheran Synod, 6.1% Lutheran Church—Missouri Synod, 5.4% Evangelical Lutheran Church in America, 5.3% The United Methodist Church (2000).
Economy: Unemployment rate: 5.4% (11/2002); Total civilian labor force: 11,106 (11/2002); Leading industries: 27.6% manufacturing; 17.8% retail trade; 14.3% health care and social assistance (2000); Companies that employ more than 1,000 persons: 0 (2000); Companies that employ more than 100 persons: 12 (2000); Farms: 584 totaling 134,271 acres (1997); Minority business ownership rate: 0.0% (1997); Women business ownership rate: 17.9% (1997); Retail sales per capita: $8,332 (1997). Single-family building permits issued: 84 (2001) / 69 (2000); Multi-family building permits issued: 10 (2001) / 13 (2000).
Income: Per capita income: $19,024 (2000); Median household income: $39,462 (2000); Poverty rate: 7.0% (2000); Bankruptcy rate: 3.23% (2001).
Taxes: Total county taxes per capita: $330 (1997); County property taxes per capita: $322 (1997).
Education: High school graduation rate: 81.9% (2000); College graduation rate: 14.5% (2000).
Housing: Homeownership rate: 77.2% (2000); Median home value: $90,100 (2000); Median rent: $381 per month (2000); Median age of housing: 40 years (2000).
Health: Birth rate: 119.9 per 10,000 population (1998); Age adjusted death rate: 82.8 per 10,000 population (1999); Age adjusted cancer mortality rate: 226.3 deaths per 100,000 population (1999). Number of physicians: 12.6 per 10,000 population (1999); Number of hospital beds: 86.4 per 10,000 population (1999).
Elections: 2000 Presidential election results: 36.3% Gore, 59.9% Bush, 3.1% Nader, 0.5% Buchanan
National and State Parks: Grand River Marsh State Public Hunting Grounds; Rogers Memorial State Habitat Preserve; White River Marsh State Wildlife Area
Additional Information Contacts
Green Lake County Government Offices. 920-294-4005
Berlin Chamber of Commerce 920-361-3636
Green Lake Chamber of Commerce. 920-294-3231
Princeton Chamber of Commerce 920-295-3877

Green Lake County Communities

BERLIN (city). Covers a land area of 5.978 square miles and a water area of 0.327 square miles. Located at 43.97° N. Lat.; 88.94° W. Long. Elevation is 764 feet.
Population: 5,305 (2000); Race: 96.1% White, 0.1% Black, 0.0% Asian, 0.2% American Indian and Alaska Native, 5.0% Hispanic of any race, 0.4% two or more races (2000); Density: 887.4 persons per square mile (2000); Age: 24.8% under 18, 17.8% over 64 (2000); Marriage status: 21.8% never married, 59.9% now married, 9.1% widowed, 9.2% divorced (2000); Foreign born: 3.3% (2000); Ancestry (includes multiple ancestries): 46.7% German, 15.9% Polish, 9.7% Irish, 7.2% Other groups, 6.4% English (2000).
Economy: Single-family building permits issued: 11 (2001) / 5 (2000); Multi-family building permits issued: 2 (2001) / 7 (2000); Employment by occupation: 6.6% management, 14.2% professional, 13.9% services, 27.4% sales, 0.8% farming, 8.6% construction, 28.5% production (2000).
Income: Per capita income: $17,667 (2000); Median household income: $36,896 (2000); Poverty rate: 7.0% (2000).
Taxes: Total city taxes per capita: $239 (1997); City property taxes per capita: $227 (1997).
Education: High school graduation rate: 81.3% (2000); College graduation rate: 15.8% (2000).

School District(s)

Berlin Area (PK-12)
2000 Enrollment: 1,790 920-361-2004
Housing: Homeownership rate: 68.5% (2000); Median home value: $77,000 (2000); Median rent: $394 per month (2000); Median age of housing: 49 years (2000).
Hospitals: Berlin Memorial Hospital (61 beds)
Safety: Violent crime rate: 13.1 per 10,000 population; Property crime rate: 325.7 per 10,000 population (2001).
Newspapers: Markesan Regional Reporter (1 x week); Princeton Times-Republic (1 x week); Omro Herald (1 x week); Green Lake County

Reporter (1 x week); Buyers Guide (1 x week); The Billboard Shopper (1 x week); Berlin Journal (1 x week)
Transportation: Commute to work: 87.9% car, 0.6% public transportation, 9.4% walk, 1.9% work from home (2000); Travel time to work: 51.4% less than 15 minutes, 25.5% 15 to 30 minutes, 16.2% 30 to 45 minutes, 3.8% 45 to 60 minutes, 3.1% 60 minutes or more (2000)
Additional Information Contacts
Berlin Chamber of Commerce 920-361-3636

BERLIN (town). Covers a land area of 29.650 square miles and a water area of 0.317 square miles. Located at 43.94° N. Lat.; 88.94° W. Long. Elevation is 764 feet.
Population: 1,145 (2000); Race: 100.0% White, 0.0% Black, 0.0% Asian, 0.0% American Indian and Alaska Native, 0.1% Hispanic of any race, 0.0% two or more races (2000); Density: 38.6 persons per square mile (2000); Age: 28.0% under 18, 16.0% over 64 (2000); Marriage status: 21.7% never married, 69.5% now married, 4.7% widowed, 4.1% divorced (2000); Foreign born: 0.4% (2000); Ancestry (includes multiple ancestries): 54.6% German, 24.0% Polish, 8.3% Irish, 6.3% Norwegian, 5.2% English (2000).
Economy: Employment by occupation: 10.9% management, 15.7% professional, 13.7% services, 23.3% sales, 2.7% farming, 10.7% construction, 22.9% production (2000).
Income: Per capita income: $18,767 (2000); Median household income: $44,659 (2000); Poverty rate: 5.9% (2000).
Taxes: Total city taxes per capita: $2 (1997); City property taxes per capita: $0 (1997).
Education: High school graduation rate: 82.5% (2000); College graduation rate: 14.7% (2000).
Housing: Homeownership rate: 87.4% (2000); Median home value: $115,300 (2000); Median rent: $363 per month (2000); Median age of housing: 29 years (2000).
Transportation: Commute to work: 87.8% car, 0.3% public transportation, 3.1% walk, 8.0% work from home (2000); Travel time to work: 49.5% less than 15 minutes, 25.9% 15 to 30 minutes, 18.1% 30 to 45 minutes, 3.4% 45 to 60 minutes, 3.2% 60 minutes or more (2000)

BROOKLYN (town). Covers a land area of 35.435 square miles and a water area of 11.813 square miles. Located at 43.84° N. Lat.; 88.97° W. Long.
Population: 1,904 (2000); Race: 98.4% White, 0.0% Black, 0.8% Asian, 0.0% American Indian and Alaska Native, 0.8% Hispanic of any race, 0.3% two or more races (2000); Density: 53.7 persons per square mile (2000); Age: 23.3% under 18, 16.6% over 64 (2000); Marriage status: 18.4% never married, 70.0% now married, 3.0% widowed, 8.7% divorced (2000); Foreign born: 1.3% (2000); Ancestry (includes multiple ancestries): 56.8% German, 10.3% Polish, 10.2% Irish, 9.6% English, 4.7% Norwegian (2000).
Economy: Employment by occupation: 11.3% management, 18.0% professional, 11.4% services, 25.2% sales, 0.5% farming, 13.7% construction, 19.9% production (2000).
Income: Per capita income: $24,174 (2000); Median household income: $51,250 (2000); Poverty rate: 3.5% (2000).
Taxes: Total city taxes per capita: $124 (1997); City property taxes per capita: $103 (1997).
Education: High school graduation rate: 86.7% (2000); College graduation rate: 23.5% (2000).
Housing: Homeownership rate: 87.2% (2000); Median home value: $136,800 (2000); Median rent: $383 per month (2000); Median age of housing: 24 years (2000).
Transportation: Commute to work: 93.5% car, 0.0% public transportation, 1.1% walk, 5.4% work from home (2000); Travel time to work: 39.7% less than 15 minutes, 30.8% 15 to 30 minutes, 16.8% 30 to 45 minutes, 10.1% 45 to 60 minutes, 2.6% 60 minutes or more (2000)

DALTON (unincorporated postal area, zip code 53926). Covers a land area of 52.045 square miles and a water area of 0.149 square miles. Located at 43.66° N. Lat.; 89.19° W. Long. Elevation is 861 feet.
Population: 1,377 (2000); Race: 98.0% White, 0.2% Black, 0.0% Asian, 0.1% American Indian and Alaska Native, 0.4% Hispanic of any race, 1.5% two or more races (2000); Density: 26.5 persons per square mile (2000); Age: 34.0% under 18, 13.1% over 64 (2000); Marriage status: 25.3% never married, 61.4% now married, 7.7% widowed, 5.6% divorced (2000); Foreign born: 0.5% (2000); Ancestry (includes multiple ancestries): 42.5% German, 8.9% Irish, 7.7% United States or American, 6.0% English, 4.6% Norwegian (2000).
Economy: Employment by occupation: 11.2% management, 8.6% professional, 18.2% services, 15.3% sales, 3.9% farming, 15.0% construction, 27.9% production (2000).
Income: Per capita income: $13,727 (2000); Median household income: $37,009 (2000); Poverty rate: 13.1% (2000).
Education: High school graduation rate: 70.5% (2000); College graduation rate: 6.9% (2000).
Housing: Homeownership rate: 83.1% (2000); Median home value: $78,500 (2000); Median rent: $366 per month (2000); Median age of housing: 47 years (2000).
Transportation: Commute to work: 78.5% car, 0.5% public transportation, 3.8% walk, 15.9% work from home (2000); Travel time to work: 19.8% less than 15 minutes, 30.4% 15 to 30 minutes, 26.3% 30 to 45 minutes, 11.0% 45 to 60 minutes, 12.5% 60 minutes or more (2000)

GREEN LAKE (city). Covers a land area of 1.397 square miles and a water area of 0.227 square miles. Located at 43.84° N. Lat.; 88.95° W. Long. Elevation is 828 feet.
Population: 1,100 (2000); Race: 98.6% White, 0.7% Black, 0.0% Asian, 0.3% American Indian and Alaska Native, 0.0% Hispanic of any race, 0.5% two or more races (2000); Density: 787.2 persons per square mile (2000); Age: 17.2% under 18, 23.4% over 64 (2000); Marriage status: 20.3% never married, 57.6% now married, 12.1% widowed, 9.9% divorced (2000); Foreign born: 1.4% (2000); Ancestry (includes multiple ancestries): 50.8% German, 14.6% Irish, 13.9% Polish, 12.0% English, 6.1% French (except Basque) (2000).
Economy: Single-family building permits issued: 5 (2001) / 3 (2000); Multi-family building permits issued: 8 (2001) / 6 (2000); Employment by occupation: 11.5% management, 17.2% professional, 14.0% services, 30.6% sales, 1.2% farming, 6.1% construction, 19.4% production (2000).
Income: Per capita income: $20,444 (2000); Median household income: $35,435 (2000); Poverty rate: 5.9% (2000).
Taxes: Total city taxes per capita: $794 (1997); City property taxes per capita: $608 (1997).
Education: High school graduation rate: 87.3% (2000); College graduation rate: 23.6% (2000).

School District(s)

Green Lake (KG-12)
2000 Enrollment: 357 920-294-6411
Housing: Homeownership rate: 67.2% (2000); Median home value: $103,700 (2000); Median rent: $395 per month (2000); Median age of housing: 35 years (2000).
Transportation: Commute to work: 87.5% car, 0.0% public transportation, 9.2% walk, 3.3% work from home (2000); Travel time to work: 50.0% less than 15 minutes, 29.7% 15 to 30 minutes, 9.7% 30 to 45 minutes, 4.2% 45 to 60 minutes, 6.4% 60 minutes or more (2000)
Additional Information Contacts
Green Lake Chamber of Commerce 920-294-3231

GREEN LAKE (town). Covers a land area of 47.228 square miles and a water area of 1.343 square miles. Located at 43.78° N. Lat.; 88.96° W. Long. Elevation is 828 feet.
Population: 1,258 (2000); Race: 99.5% White, 0.5% Black, 0.0% Asian, 0.0% American Indian and Alaska Native, 0.2% Hispanic of any race, 0.0% two or more races (2000); Density: 26.6 persons per square mile (2000); Age: 17.6% under 18, 24.7% over 64 (2000); Marriage status: 18.3% never married, 66.3% now married, 8.0% widowed, 7.4% divorced (2000); Foreign born: 0.6% (2000); Ancestry (includes multiple ancestries): 55.5% German, 8.7% Irish, 8.4% English, 8.1% Polish, 5.9% United States or American (2000).
Economy: Boats, textiles; summer resort. Employment by occupation: 19.5% management, 11.7% professional, 12.9% services, 21.0% sales, 4.3% farming, 12.6% construction, 18.1% production (2000).
Income: Per capita income: $23,659 (2000); Median household income: $42,574 (2000); Poverty rate: 3.8% (2000).
Taxes: Total city taxes per capita: $240 (1997); City property taxes per capita: $228 (1997).
Education: High school graduation rate: 86.2% (2000); College graduation rate: 16.7% (2000).
Housing: Homeownership rate: 86.4% (2000); Median home value: $124,500 (2000); Median rent: $406 per month (2000); Median age of housing: 31 years (2000).
Transportation: Commute to work: 82.3% car, 0.5% public transportation, 3.7% walk, 13.4% work from home (2000); Travel time to work: 35.8% less than 15 minutes, 37.4% 15 to 30 minutes, 16.8% 30 to 45 minutes, 3.9% 45 to 60 minutes, 6.2% 60 minutes or more (2000)

KINGSTON (village). Covers a land area of 1.354 square miles and a water area of 0.173 square miles. Located at 43.69° N. Lat.; 89.12° W. Long. Elevation is 800 feet.
Population: 288 (2000); Race: 100.0% White, 0.0% Black, 0.0% Asian, 0.0% American Indian and Alaska Native, 1.2% Hispanic of any race, 0.0% two or more races (2000); Density: 212.7 persons per square mile (2000); Age: 22.0% under 18, 20.0% over 64 (2000); Marriage status: 22.0% never married, 55.1% now married, 11.2% widowed, 11.7% divorced (2000); Foreign born: 0.0% (2000); Ancestry (includes multiple ancestries): 52.9% German, 14.5% Irish, 13.7% English, 12.9% Polish, 7.1% United States or American (2000).
Economy: Single-family building permits issued: 4 (2001) / 1 (2000); Multi-family building permits issued: 0 (2001) / 0 (2000); Employment by occupation: 13.2% management, 5.8% professional, 28.9% services, 11.6% sales, 0.0% farming, 10.7% construction, 29.8% production (2000).
Income: Per capita income: $18,770 (2000); Median household income: $36,250 (2000); Poverty rate: 5.1% (2000).
Taxes: Total city taxes per capita: $133 (1997); City property taxes per capita: $130 (1997).
Education: High school graduation rate: 82.9% (2000); College graduation rate: 9.6% (2000).
Housing: Homeownership rate: 85.0% (2000); Median home value: $80,000 (2000); Median rent: $294 per month (2000); Median age of housing: 60+ years (2000).
Transportation: Commute to work: 90.1% car, 0.0% public transportation, 5.0% walk, 5.0% work from home (2000); Travel time to work: 36.5% less than 15 minutes, 30.4% 15 to 30 minutes, 17.4% 30 to 45 minutes, 5.2% 45 to 60 minutes, 10.4% 60 minutes or more (2000)

KINGSTON (town). Covers a land area of 28.834 square miles and a water area of 0.584 square miles. Located at 43.66° N. Lat.; 89.19° W. Long. Elevation is 800 feet.
Population: 900 (2000); Race: 97.9% White, 0.2% Black, 0.0% Asian, 0.0% American Indian and Alaska Native, 0.6% Hispanic of any race, 1.9% two or more races (2000); Density: 31.2 persons per square mile (2000); Age: 35.1% under 18, 12.1% over 64 (2000); Marriage status: 27.3% never married, 62.2% now married, 6.7% widowed, 3.8% divorced (2000); Foreign born: 0.7% (2000); Ancestry (includes multiple ancestries): 45.4% German, 9.7% United States or American, 6.7% Irish, 5.7% English, 3.8% Other groups (2000).
Economy: Employment by occupation: 12.2% management, 10.2% professional, 13.4% services, 14.7% sales, 5.0% farming, 15.9% construction, 28.6% production (2000).
Income: Per capita income: $13,581 (2000); Median household income: $39,345 (2000); Poverty rate: 13.6% (2000).
Taxes: Total city taxes per capita: $54 (1997); City property taxes per capita: $51 (1997).
Education: High school graduation rate: 67.9% (2000); College graduation rate: 8.8% (2000).
Housing: Homeownership rate: 82.1% (2000); Median home value: $77,800 (2000); Median rent: $367 per month (2000); Median age of housing: 41 years (2000).
Transportation: Commute to work: 73.6% car, 0.7% public transportation, 7.4% walk, 16.4% work from home (2000); Travel time to work: 18.3% less than 15 minutes, 31.0% 15 to 30 minutes, 32.4% 30 to 45 minutes, 8.3% 45 to 60 minutes, 10.0% 60 minutes or more (2000)

MACKFORD (town). Covers a land area of 33.571 square miles and a water area of 0.699 square miles. Located at 43.68° N. Lat.; 88.94° W. Long.
Population: 585 (2000); Race: 99.1% White, 0.0% Black, 0.0% Asian, 0.0% American Indian and Alaska Native, 0.4% Hispanic of any race, 0.9% two or more races (2000); Density: 17.4 persons per square mile (2000); Age: 22.9% under 18, 10.6% over 64 (2000); Marriage status: 19.0% never married, 71.0% now married, 2.7% widowed, 7.3% divorced (2000); Foreign born: 0.7% (2000); Ancestry (includes multiple ancestries): 63.0% German, 10.3% Dutch, 10.1% English, 9.9% Polish, 8.1% United States or American (2000).
Economy: Employment by occupation: 22.8% management, 7.5% professional, 8.8% services, 19.5% sales, 7.2% farming, 12.7% construction, 21.5% production (2000).
Income: Per capita income: $20,351 (2000); Median household income: $44,688 (2000); Poverty rate: 7.0% (2000).
Taxes: Total city taxes per capita: $140 (1997); City property taxes per capita: $139 (1997).
Education: High school graduation rate: 80.4% (2000); College graduation rate: 5.8% (2000).
Housing: Homeownership rate: 71.6% (2000); Median home value: $87,000 (2000); Median rent: $325 per month (2000); Median age of housing: 60+ years (2000).
Transportation: Commute to work: 76.2% car, 0.0% public transportation, 7.2% walk, 15.6% work from home (2000); Travel time to work: 44.0% less than 15 minutes, 29.0% 15 to 30 minutes, 13.1% 30 to 45 minutes, 5.4% 45 to 60 minutes, 8.5% 60 minutes or more (2000)

MANCHESTER (town). Covers a land area of 34.895 square miles and a water area of 0.485 square miles. Located at 43.67° N. Lat.; 89.06° W. Long. Elevation is 880 feet.
Population: 848 (2000); Race: 99.5% White, 0.0% Black, 0.0% Asian, 0.0% American Indian and Alaska Native, 0.2% Hispanic of any race, 0.0% two or more races (2000); Density: 24.3 persons per square mile (2000); Age: 33.9% under 18, 11.1% over 64 (2000); Marriage status: 23.0% never married, 67.8% now married, 4.2% widowed, 5.0% divorced (2000); Foreign born: 0.2% (2000); Ancestry (includes multiple ancestries): 57.9% German, 7.8% Dutch, 5.9% Polish, 5.5% Irish, 4.7% English (2000).
Economy: Employment by occupation: 11.4% management, 10.4% professional, 18.2% services, 16.3% sales, 3.9% farming, 14.3% construction, 25.5% production (2000).
Income: Per capita income: $15,771 (2000); Median household income: $42,375 (2000); Poverty rate: 12.0% (2000).
Taxes: Total city taxes per capita: $172 (1997); City property taxes per capita: $170 (1997).
Education: High school graduation rate: 76.2% (2000); College graduation rate: 8.6% (2000).
Housing: Homeownership rate: 75.8% (2000); Median home value: $88,600 (2000); Median rent: $323 per month (2000); Median age of housing: 55 years (2000).
Transportation: Commute to work: 83.3% car, 0.0% public transportation, 5.1% walk, 9.5% work from home (2000); Travel time to work: 38.1% less than 15 minutes, 35.4% 15 to 30 minutes, 17.2% 30 to 45 minutes, 5.9% 45 to 60 minutes, 3.5% 60 minutes or more (2000)

MARKESAN (city). Covers a land area of 2.358 square miles and a water area of 0 square miles. Located at 43.70° N. Lat.; 88.98° W. Long. Elevation is 847 feet.
Population: 1,396 (2000); Race: 98.4% White, 0.0% Black, 0.0% Asian, 0.0% American Indian and Alaska Native, 3.4% Hispanic of any race, 0.4% two or more races (2000); Density: 592.0 persons per square mile (2000); Age: 25.3% under 18, 20.5% over 64 (2000); Marriage status: 20.4% never married, 61.5% now married, 10.5% widowed, 7.7% divorced (2000); Foreign born: 3.4% (2000); Ancestry (includes multiple ancestries): 59.8% German, 7.5% Polish, 6.8% English, 6.5% Irish, 5.2% Dutch (2000).
Economy: In farming, dairying, and livestock-raising region. Manufacturing: canned vegetables, fabricated metal products. Railroad terminus. Single-family building permits issued: 0 (2001) / 2 (2000); Multi-family building permits issued: 0 (2001) / 0 (2000); Employment by occupation: 11.1% management, 16.7% professional, 15.3% services, 19.8% sales, 2.7% farming, 8.7% construction, 25.7% production (2000).
Income: Per capita income: $18,774 (2000); Median household income: $38,472 (2000); Poverty rate: 4.0% (2000).
Taxes: Total city taxes per capita: $176 (1997); City property taxes per capita: $167 (1997).
Education: High school graduation rate: 82.1% (2000); College graduation rate: 13.5% (2000).

School District(s)

Markesan (PK-12)
2000 Enrollment: 990 920-398-2373
Housing: Homeownership rate: 68.7% (2000); Median home value: $79,700 (2000); Median rent: $347 per month (2000); Median age of housing: 47 years (2000).
Safety: Violent crime rate: 28.4 per 10,000 population; Property crime rate: 305.8 per 10,000 population (2001).
Newspapers: Neighbors (1 x week)
Transportation: Commute to work: 89.9% car, 0.0% public transportation, 6.3% walk, 3.8% work from home (2000); Travel time to work: 50.5% less than 15 minutes, 20.5% 15 to 30 minutes, 15.9% 30 to 45 minutes, 5.5% 45 to 60 minutes, 7.6% 60 minutes or more (2000)

MARQUETTE (village). Covers a land area of 0.369 square miles and a water area of 0 square miles. Located at 43.74° N. Lat.; 89.14° W. Long. Elevation is 800 feet.
Population: 169 (2000); Race: 97.5% White, 0.0% Black, 0.0% Asian, 0.0% American Indian and Alaska Native, 0.0% Hispanic of any race, 2.5% two or

more races (2000); Density: 457.6 persons per square mile (2000); Age: 15.0% under 18, 36.9% over 64 (2000); Marriage status: 18.9% never married, 66.2% now married, 6.8% widowed, 8.1% divorced (2000); Foreign born: 0.0% (2000); Ancestry (includes multiple ancestries): 53.1% German, 18.8% English, 8.1% Polish, 7.5% Other groups, 6.9% Irish (2000).
Economy: Single-family building permits issued: 2 (2001) / 0 (2000); Multi-family building permits issued: 0 (2001) / 0 (2000); Employment by occupation: 17.6% management, 2.7% professional, 24.3% services, 16.2% sales, 2.7% farming, 16.2% construction, 20.3% production (2000).
Income: Per capita income: $17,053 (2000); Median household income: $36,667 (2000); Poverty rate: 4.5% (2000).
Taxes: Total city taxes per capita: $99 (1997); City property taxes per capita: $88 (1997).
Education: High school graduation rate: 76.2% (2000); College graduation rate: 3.1% (2000).
Housing: Homeownership rate: 85.9% (2000); Median home value: $67,900 (2000); Median rent: $400 per month (2000); Median age of housing: 42 years (2000).
Transportation: Commute to work: 74.0% car, 0.0% public transportation, 6.8% walk, 15.1% work from home (2000); Travel time to work: 22.6% less than 15 minutes, 40.3% 15 to 30 minutes, 27.4% 30 to 45 minutes, 3.2% 45 to 60 minutes, 6.5% 60 minutes or more (2000)

MARQUETTE (town). Covers a land area of 30.765 square miles and a water area of 9.862 square miles. Located at 43.74° N. Lat.; 89.14° W. Long. Elevation is 800 feet.
Population: 481 (2000); Race: 97.7% White, 2.3% Black, 0.0% Asian, 0.0% American Indian and Alaska Native, 0.0% Hispanic of any race, 0.0% two or more races (2000); Density: 15.6 persons per square mile (2000); Age: 25.4% under 18, 15.8% over 64 (2000); Marriage status: 22.1% never married, 58.3% now married, 9.9% widowed, 9.6% divorced (2000); Foreign born: 1.7% (2000); Ancestry (includes multiple ancestries): 58.5% German, 9.0% Irish, 8.3% Norwegian, 8.3% Polish, 6.9% English (2000).
Economy: Employment by occupation: 14.0% management, 7.0% professional, 18.3% services, 23.6% sales, 1.7% farming, 17.0% construction, 18.3% production (2000).
Income: Per capita income: $17,537 (2000); Median household income: $39,018 (2000); Poverty rate: 5.7% (2000).
Taxes: Total city taxes per capita: $47 (1997); City property taxes per capita: $28 (1997).
Education: High school graduation rate: 84.4% (2000); College graduation rate: 12.5% (2000).
Housing: Homeownership rate: 83.9% (2000); Median home value: $100,800 (2000); Median rent: $436 per month (2000); Median age of housing: 31 years (2000).
Transportation: Commute to work: 81.7% car, 0.0% public transportation, 2.2% walk, 16.2% work from home (2000); Travel time to work: 19.3% less than 15 minutes, 34.4% 15 to 30 minutes, 22.9% 30 to 45 minutes, 6.8% 45 to 60 minutes, 16.7% 60 minutes or more (2000)

PRINCETON (city). Covers a land area of 1.629 square miles and a water area of 0 square miles. Located at 43.85° N. Lat.; 89.13° W. Long. Elevation is 770 feet.
History: Princeton was settled by Royal C. Treat, who filed a claim here in 1848 and laid out the city along the Fox River in 1849.
Population: 1,504 (2000); Race: 98.4% White, 1.1% Black, 0.0% Asian, 0.2% American Indian and Alaska Native, 0.4% Hispanic of any race, 0.3% two or more races (2000); Density: 923.5 persons per square mile (2000); Age: 20.3% under 18, 29.5% over 64 (2000); Marriage status: 21.2% never married, 57.4% now married, 14.1% widowed, 7.3% divorced (2000); Foreign born: 0.5% (2000); Ancestry (includes multiple ancestries): 46.3% German, 21.4% Polish, 7.9% English, 7.0% Irish, 4.7% Norwegian (2000).
Economy: Single-family building permits issued: 0 (2001) / 2 (2000); Multi-family building permits issued: 0 (2001) / 0 (2000); Employment by occupation: 8.3% management, 9.7% professional, 18.3% services, 22.0% sales, 0.8% farming, 12.8% construction, 28.2% production (2000).
Income: Per capita income: $18,047 (2000); Median household income: $32,679 (2000); Poverty rate: 12.9% (2000).
Taxes: Total city taxes per capita: $176 (1997); City property taxes per capita: $165 (1997).
Education: High school graduation rate: 77.7% (2000); College graduation rate: 7.5% (2000).

School District(s)

Princeton (KG-12)
2000 Enrollment: 481 920-295-6571

Housing: Homeownership rate: 74.8% (2000); Median home value: $70,500 (2000); Median rent: $366 per month (2000); Median age of housing: 58 years (2000).
Safety: Violent crime rate: 13.2 per 10,000 population; Property crime rate: 264.0 per 10,000 population (2001).
Transportation: Commute to work: 88.2% car, 0.0% public transportation, 3.9% walk, 7.1% work from home (2000); Travel time to work: 35.9% less than 15 minutes, 34.5% 15 to 30 minutes, 17.3% 30 to 45 minutes, 3.8% 45 to 60 minutes, 8.5% 60 minutes or more (2000)

Additional Information Contacts

Princeton Chamber of Commerce 920-295-3877

PRINCETON (town). Covers a land area of 35.335 square miles and a water area of 0.295 square miles. Located at 43.82° N. Lat.; 89.11° W. Long. Elevation is 770 feet.
Population: 1,540 (2000); Race: 97.8% White, 0.2% Black, 0.1% Asian, 0.5% American Indian and Alaska Native, 1.8% Hispanic of any race, 0.7% two or more races (2000); Density: 43.6 persons per square mile (2000); Age: 21.7% under 18, 20.0% over 64 (2000); Marriage status: 17.5% never married, 64.5% now married, 8.8% widowed, 9.2% divorced (2000); Foreign born: 1.2% (2000); Ancestry (includes multiple ancestries): 49.7% German, 22.1% Polish, 9.4% Irish, 8.8% English, 4.1% Other groups (2000).
Economy: Employment by occupation: 12.4% management, 10.4% professional, 15.8% services, 21.9% sales, 2.3% farming, 15.2% construction, 22.1% production (2000).
Income: Per capita income: $20,003 (2000); Median household income: $37,340 (2000); Poverty rate: 8.2% (2000).
Taxes: Total city taxes per capita: $101 (1997); City property taxes per capita: $98 (1997).
Education: High school graduation rate: 84.5% (2000); College graduation rate: 12.0% (2000).
Housing: Homeownership rate: 85.6% (2000); Median home value: $125,000 (2000); Median rent: $408 per month (2000); Median age of housing: 31 years (2000).
Transportation: Commute to work: 91.9% car, 0.0% public transportation, 3.0% walk, 5.1% work from home (2000); Travel time to work: 32.4% less than 15 minutes, 33.0% 15 to 30 minutes, 13.1% 30 to 45 minutes, 11.3% 45 to 60 minutes, 10.2% 60 minutes or more (2000)

SAINT MARIE (town). Covers a land area of 33.497 square miles and a water area of 0.020 square miles. Located at 43.89° N. Lat.; 89.09° W. Long.
Population: 341 (2000); Race: 93.8% White, 0.0% Black, 0.0% Asian, 0.0% American Indian and Alaska Native, 6.2% Hispanic of any race, 0.0% two or more races (2000); Density: 10.2 persons per square mile (2000); Age: 17.2% under 18, 15.3% over 64 (2000); Marriage status: 22.8% never married, 66.9% now married, 5.1% widowed, 5.1% divorced (2000); Foreign born: 7.9% (2000); Ancestry (includes multiple ancestries): 45.2% German, 17.5% Polish, 12.7% Other groups, 5.4% English, 4.8% Irish (2000).
Economy: Employment by occupation: 9.8% management, 13.8% professional, 9.8% services, 17.2% sales, 2.3% farming, 9.8% construction, 37.4% production (2000).
Income: Per capita income: $17,998 (2000); Median household income: $40,417 (2000); Poverty rate: 2.0% (2000).
Education: High school graduation rate: 77.1% (2000); College graduation rate: 7.5% (2000).
Housing: Homeownership rate: 92.0% (2000); Median home value: $96,700 (2000); Median rent: $388 per month (2000); Median age of housing: 20 years (2000).
Transportation: Commute to work: 85.9% car, 0.0% public transportation, 1.2% walk, 12.9% work from home (2000); Travel time to work: 18.2% less than 15 minutes, 43.2% 15 to 30 minutes, 26.4% 30 to 45 minutes, 4.7% 45 to 60 minutes, 7.4% 60 minutes or more (2000)

SENECA (town). Covers a land area of 32.743 square miles and a water area of 0.070 square miles. Located at 43.96° N. Lat.; 89.08° W. Long.
Population: 424 (2000); Race: 96.5% White, 0.0% Black, 0.0% Asian, 0.2% American Indian and Alaska Native, 0.0% Hispanic of any race, 3.2% two or more races (2000); Density: 12.9 persons per square mile (2000); Age: 24.6% under 18, 12.3% over 64 (2000); Marriage status: 23.2% never married, 66.2% now married, 6.8% widowed, 3.8% divorced (2000); Foreign born: 0.0% (2000); Ancestry (includes multiple ancestries): 48.0% German, 31.6% Polish, 7.0% United States or American, 3.9% English, 3.7% Norwegian (2000).
Economy: Employment by occupation: 12.9% management, 10.4% professional, 14.1% services, 18.1% sales, 2.0% farming, 12.4% construction, 30.1% production (2000).

Income: Per capita income: $17,839 (2000); Median household income: $48,594 (2000); Poverty rate: 4.2% (2000).
Taxes: Total city taxes per capita: $19 (1997); City property taxes per capita: $16 (1997).
Education: High school graduation rate: 81.7% (2000); College graduation rate: 8.7% (2000).
Housing: Homeownership rate: 91.5% (2000); Median home value: $96,700 (2000); Median rent: $438 per month (2000); Median age of housing: 29 years (2000).
Transportation: Commute to work: 86.6% car, 0.8% public transportation, 0.0% walk, 12.6% work from home (2000); Travel time to work: 29.6% less than 15 minutes, 32.4% 15 to 30 minutes, 13.0% 30 to 45 minutes, 17.1% 45 to 60 minutes, 7.9% 60 minutes or more (2000)

Iowa County

Located in southern Wisconsin; bounded on the north by the Wisconsin River; drained by the Pecatonica and Blue Rivers. Covers a land area of 762.70 square miles, a water area of 5.40 square miles, and is located in the Central Time Zone. The county government was organized in 1829. County seat is Dodgeville.

Weather Station: Dodgeville Elevation: 1,108 feet

	Jan	Feb	Mar	Apr	May	Jun	Jul	Aug	Sep	Oct	Nov	Dec
High	25	30	42	57	69	78	82	79	71	59	42	30
Low	7	12	23	35	46	55	60	58	49	37	26	14
Precip	1.3	1.4	2.7	3.6	3.4	4.3	4.5	4.8	3.7	2.4	2.5	1.5
Snow	10.4	7.2	6.2	2.4	tr	0.0	0.0	0.0	0.0	0.5	4.6	9.9

High and Low temperatures in degrees Fahrenheit; Precipitation and Snow in inches

Population: 22,780 (2000); Race: 98.7% White, 0.1% Black, 0.2% Asian, 0.4% American Indian and Alaska Native, 0.3% Hispanic of any race, 0.6% two or more races (2000); Density: 29.9 persons per square mile (2000); Age: 27.1% under 18, 13.4% over 64 (2000).
Religion: Five largest groups: 32.6% Catholic Church, 10.9% Evangelical Lutheran Church in America, 6.2% The United Methodist Church, 3.0% United Church of Christ, 0.6% Lutheran Church—Missouri Synod (2000).
Economy: Unemployment rate: 3.0% (11/2002); Total civilian labor force: 16,497 (11/2002); Leading industries: 50.0% retail trade; 13.4% manufacturing; 7.8% health care and social assistance (2000); Companies that employ more than 1,000 persons: 1 (2000); Companies that employ more than 100 persons: 9 (2000); Farms: 1,394 totaling 366,709 acres (1997); Minority business ownership rate: 0.0% (1997); Women business ownership rate: 19.2% (1997); Retail sales per capita: $54,744 (1997). Single-family building permits issued: 164 (2001) / 134 (2000); Multi-family building permits issued: 82 (2001) / 64 (2000).
Income: Per capita income: $19,497 (2000); Median household income: $42,518 (2000); Poverty rate: 7.3% (2000); Bankruptcy rate: 3.21% (2001).
Taxes: Total county taxes per capita: $280 (1997); County property taxes per capita: $226 (1997).
Education: High school graduation rate: 88.5% (2000); College graduation rate: 18.5% (2000).
Housing: Homeownership rate: 75.8% (2000); Median home value: $91,800 (2000); Median rent: $407 per month (2000); Median age of housing: 41 years (2000).
Health: Birth rate: 127.3 per 10,000 population (1998); Age adjusted death rate: 77.5 per 10,000 population (1999); Age adjusted cancer mortality rate: 199.3 deaths per 100,000 population (1999). Number of physicians: 6.1 per 10,000 population (1999); Number of hospital beds: 36.9 per 10,000 population (1999).
Elections: 2000 Presidential election results: 55.4% Gore, 40.0% Bush, 4.1% Nader, 0.2% Buchanan
National and State Parks: Blue Mounds State Park; Governor Dodge State Park; Tower Hill State Park
Additional Information Contacts
Iowa County Government Offices 608-935-5445
Dodgeville Chamber of Commerce 608-935-9200
Mineral Point Chamber of Commerce 608-987-3201

Iowa County Communities

ARENA (village). Covers a land area of 1.090 square miles and a water area of 0.005 square miles. Located at 43.16° N. Lat.; 89.90° W. Long. Elevation is 735 feet.
History: There was a village of Arena in a nearby location, but when the railroad extended its line through the present site, the inhabitants of old Arena moved to the new Arena. Arena became a shipping center for beef cattle and wheat.
Population: 685 (2000); Race: 99.7% White, 0.0% Black, 0.0% Asian, 0.2% American Indian and Alaska Native, 0.8% Hispanic of any race, 0.2% two or more races (2000); Density: 628.5 persons per square mile (2000); Age: 30.3% under 18, 8.7% over 64 (2000); Marriage status: 22.7% never married, 62.3% now married, 7.2% widowed, 7.8% divorced (2000); Foreign born: 1.0% (2000); Ancestry (includes multiple ancestries): 32.1% German, 22.3% United States or American, 19.9% Norwegian, 13.6% Irish, 7.2% English (2000).
Economy: Single-family building permits issued: 3 (2001) / 7 (2000); Multi-family building permits issued: 9 (2001) / 6 (2000); Employment by occupation: 7.0% management, 8.1% professional, 17.0% services, 24.5% sales, 0.6% farming, 18.9% construction, 24.0% production (2000).
Income: Per capita income: $20,765 (2000); Median household income: $45,870 (2000); Poverty rate: 3.7% (2000).
Taxes: Total city taxes per capita: $137 (1997); City property taxes per capita: $128 (1997).
Education: High school graduation rate: 84.7% (2000); College graduation rate: 12.2% (2000).
Housing: Homeownership rate: 71.7% (2000); Median home value: $105,100 (2000); Median rent: $438 per month (2000); Median age of housing: 24 years (2000).
Transportation: Commute to work: 93.8% car, 0.0% public transportation, 2.3% walk, 2.5% work from home (2000); Travel time to work: 22.0% less than 15 minutes, 19.9% 15 to 30 minutes, 25.7% 30 to 45 minutes, 19.4% 45 to 60 minutes, 13.0% 60 minutes or more (2000)

ARENA (town). Covers a land area of 78.041 square miles and a water area of 1.464 square miles. Located at 43.14° N. Lat.; 89.93° W. Long. Elevation is 735 feet.
Population: 1,444 (2000); Race: 99.2% White, 0.0% Black, 0.0% Asian, 0.3% American Indian and Alaska Native, 0.5% Hispanic of any race, 0.5% two or more races (2000); Density: 18.5 persons per square mile (2000); Age: 25.2% under 18, 10.0% over 64 (2000); Marriage status: 21.1% never married, 68.5% now married, 3.8% widowed, 6.6% divorced (2000); Foreign born: 0.8% (2000); Ancestry (includes multiple ancestries): 35.5% German, 17.6% Norwegian, 13.5% English, 11.6% United States or American, 7.4% Irish (2000).
Economy: Employment by occupation: 15.5% management, 11.7% professional, 12.8% services, 25.6% sales, 2.2% farming, 15.8% construction, 16.5% production (2000).
Income: Per capita income: $20,060 (2000); Median household income: $51,042 (2000); Poverty rate: 6.7% (2000).
Taxes: Total city taxes per capita: $115 (1997); City property taxes per capita: $113 (1997).
Education: High school graduation rate: 82.5% (2000); College graduation rate: 15.6% (2000).
Housing: Homeownership rate: 83.4% (2000); Median home value: $122,700 (2000); Median rent: $425 per month (2000); Median age of housing: 27 years (2000).
Transportation: Commute to work: 90.1% car, 0.2% public transportation, 1.7% walk, 7.8% work from home (2000); Travel time to work: 21.8% less than 15 minutes, 24.0% 15 to 30 minutes, 28.8% 30 to 45 minutes, 20.6% 45 to 60 minutes, 4.7% 60 minutes or more (2000)

AVOCA (village). Covers a land area of 2.270 square miles and a water area of 0.127 square miles. Located at 43.18° N. Lat.; 90.32° W. Long. Elevation is 698 feet.
Population: 608 (2000); Race: 99.3% White, 0.0% Black, 0.0% Asian, 0.3% American Indian and Alaska Native, 0.0% Hispanic of any race, 0.3% two or more races (2000); Density: 267.8 persons per square mile (2000); Age: 24.1% under 18, 17.1% over 64 (2000); Marriage status: 26.3% never married, 42.6% now married, 8.8% widowed, 22.3% divorced (2000); Foreign born: 0.0% (2000); Ancestry (includes multiple ancestries): 41.1% German, 11.5% Irish, 11.3% Norwegian, 10.0% English, 4.8% Czech (2000).
Economy: Single-family building permits issued: 8 (2001) / 0 (2000); Multi-family building permits issued: 0 (2001) / 0 (2000); Employment by occupation: 5.2% management, 7.0% professional, 12.9% services, 24.7% sales, 1.1% farming, 14.0% construction, 35.1% production (2000).
Income: Per capita income: $16,758 (2000); Median household income: $28,625 (2000); Poverty rate: 17.3% (2000).
Taxes: Total city taxes per capita: $124 (1997); City property taxes per capita: $114 (1997).
Education: High school graduation rate: 78.5% (2000); College graduation rate: 3.7% (2000).

Housing: Homeownership rate: 77.9% (2000); Median home value: $48,900 (2000); Median rent: $318 per month (2000); Median age of housing: 38 years (2000).
Transportation: Commute to work: 97.7% car, 0.0% public transportation, 0.0% walk, 0.8% work from home (2000); Travel time to work: 16.0% less than 15 minutes, 29.4% 15 to 30 minutes, 21.4% 30 to 45 minutes, 6.1% 45 to 60 minutes, 27.1% 60 minutes or more (2000)

BARNEVELD (village). Covers a land area of 1.350 square miles and a water area of 0 square miles. Located at 43.01° N. Lat.; 89.89° W. Long. Elevation is 1,220 feet.
Population: 1,088 (2000); Race: 99.6% White, 0.0% Black, 0.0% Asian, 0.4% American Indian and Alaska Native, 0.2% Hispanic of any race, 0.0% two or more races (2000); Density: 805.7 persons per square mile (2000); Age: 29.1% under 18, 8.2% over 64 (2000); Marriage status: 23.2% never married, 60.8% now married, 7.0% widowed, 8.9% divorced (2000); Foreign born: 0.4% (2000); Ancestry (includes multiple ancestries): 33.3% Norwegian, 29.2% German, 19.6% Irish, 12.3% English, 7.0% Swiss (2000).
Economy: Single-family building permits issued: 4 (2001) / 4 (2000); Multi-family building permits issued: 0 (2001) / 0 (2000); Employment by occupation: 15.2% management, 15.9% professional, 11.4% services, 27.2% sales, 0.3% farming, 13.9% construction, 16.0% production (2000).
Income: Per capita income: $22,009 (2000); Median household income: $55,350 (2000); Poverty rate: 7.5% (2000).
Taxes: Total city taxes per capita: $251 (1997); City property taxes per capita: $236 (1997).
Education: High school graduation rate: 92.0% (2000); College graduation rate: 20.5% (2000).

School District(s)

Barneveld (PK-12)
2000 Enrollment: 438 608-924-4711

Housing: Homeownership rate: 76.8% (2000); Median home value: $117,600 (2000); Median rent: $461 per month (2000); Median age of housing: 14 years (2000).
Transportation: Commute to work: 95.3% car, 0.0% public transportation, 2.9% walk, 1.8% work from home (2000); Travel time to work: 23.1% less than 15 minutes, 25.8% 15 to 30 minutes, 35.5% 30 to 45 minutes, 12.1% 45 to 60 minutes, 3.5% 60 minutes or more (2000)

BRIGHAM (town). Covers a land area of 64.068 square miles and a water area of 0.024 square miles. Located at 43.00° N. Lat.; 89.90° W. Long.
Population: 908 (2000); Race: 98.5% White, 0.0% Black, 0.0% Asian, 0.2% American Indian and Alaska Native, 0.7% Hispanic of any race, 1.0% two or more races (2000); Density: 14.2 persons per square mile (2000); Age: 27.4% under 18, 10.7% over 64 (2000); Marriage status: 20.5% never married, 67.6% now married, 5.0% widowed, 6.8% divorced (2000); Foreign born: 0.5% (2000); Ancestry (includes multiple ancestries): 33.4% German, 28.2% Norwegian, 17.2% Irish, 10.4% English, 9.0% United States or American (2000).
Economy: Employment by occupation: 24.1% management, 19.7% professional, 12.2% services, 19.9% sales, 5.3% farming, 10.3% construction, 8.5% production (2000).
Income: Per capita income: $23,469 (2000); Median household income: $57,500 (2000); Poverty rate: 5.5% (2000).
Taxes: Total city taxes per capita: $228 (1997); City property taxes per capita: $224 (1997).
Education: High school graduation rate: 92.3% (2000); College graduation rate: 27.2% (2000).
Housing: Homeownership rate: 84.2% (2000); Median home value: $142,000 (2000); Median rent: $450 per month (2000); Median age of housing: 40 years (2000).
Transportation: Commute to work: 78.4% car, 0.0% public transportation, 8.1% walk, 12.8% work from home (2000); Travel time to work: 26.3% less than 15 minutes, 33.1% 15 to 30 minutes, 25.6% 30 to 45 minutes, 11.7% 45 to 60 minutes, 3.4% 60 minutes or more (2000)

CLYDE (town). Covers a land area of 34.144 square miles and a water area of 0.499 square miles. Located at 43.13° N. Lat.; 90.22° W. Long. Elevation is 734 feet.
Population: 322 (2000); Race: 96.2% White, 0.0% Black, 3.8% Asian, 0.0% American Indian and Alaska Native, 2.4% Hispanic of any race, 0.0% two or more races (2000); Density: 9.4 persons per square mile (2000); Age: 22.0% under 18, 17.4% over 64 (2000); Marriage status: 28.6% never married, 58.9% now married, 4.4% widowed, 8.1% divorced (2000); Foreign born: 6.6% (2000); Ancestry (includes multiple ancestries): 38.7% German, 18.8% English, 15.3% Irish, 12.5% Norwegian, 7.0% Other groups (2000).
Economy: Employment by occupation: 21.9% management, 12.4% professional, 10.1% services, 23.1% sales, 4.7% farming, 13.0% construction, 14.8% production (2000).
Income: Per capita income: $27,920 (2000); Median household income: $50,625 (2000); Poverty rate: 6.0% (2000).
Taxes: Total city taxes per capita: $232 (1997); City property taxes per capita: $232 (1997).
Education: High school graduation rate: 88.6% (2000); College graduation rate: 32.2% (2000).
Housing: Homeownership rate: 82.5% (2000); Median home value: $87,500 (2000); Median rent: $125 per month (2000); Median age of housing: 60+ years (2000).
Transportation: Commute to work: 79.9% car, 0.0% public transportation, 1.8% walk, 15.4% work from home (2000); Travel time to work: 16.8% less than 15 minutes, 42.7% 15 to 30 minutes, 14.7% 30 to 45 minutes, 7.7% 45 to 60 minutes, 18.2% 60 minutes or more (2000)

COBB (village). Covers a land area of 0.899 square miles and a water area of 0 square miles. Located at 42.96° N. Lat.; 90.33° W. Long. Elevation is 1,165 feet.
Population: 442 (2000); Race: 98.5% White, 0.0% Black, 0.0% Asian, 0.0% American Indian and Alaska Native, 1.7% Hispanic of any race, 1.5% two or more races (2000); Density: 491.7 persons per square mile (2000); Age: 27.0% under 18, 18.6% over 64 (2000); Marriage status: 21.0% never married, 62.9% now married, 8.1% widowed, 8.1% divorced (2000); Foreign born: 0.0% (2000); Ancestry (includes multiple ancestries): 49.6% German, 22.0% English, 16.3% Norwegian, 8.2% Irish, 7.5% Czech (2000).
Economy: Single-family building permits issued: 1 (2001) / 2 (2000); Multi-family building permits issued: 0 (2001) / 0 (2000); Employment by occupation: 18.8% management, 13.1% professional, 6.9% services, 35.9% sales, 0.8% farming, 9.8% construction, 14.7% production (2000).
Income: Per capita income: $18,815 (2000); Median household income: $34,531 (2000); Poverty rate: 4.2% (2000).
Taxes: Total city taxes per capita: $170 (1997); City property taxes per capita: $168 (1997).
Education: High school graduation rate: 90.7% (2000); College graduation rate: 15.8% (2000).
Housing: Homeownership rate: 88.5% (2000); Median home value: $81,200 (2000); Median rent: $350 per month (2000); Median age of housing: 42 years (2000).
Transportation: Commute to work: 92.0% car, 0.0% public transportation, 2.5% walk, 5.5% work from home (2000); Travel time to work: 46.0% less than 15 minutes, 37.9% 15 to 30 minutes, 2.2% 30 to 45 minutes, 3.1% 45 to 60 minutes, 10.7% 60 minutes or more (2000)

DODGEVILLE (city). Covers a land area of 3.581 square miles and a water area of 0 square miles. Located at 42.96° N. Lat.; 90.13° W. Long. Elevation is 1,222 feet.
History: Dodgeville was named for Governor Henry Dodge (1782-1867), who came to Wisconsin in 1827 after being implicated in the Aaron Burr conspiracy and indicted for treason by a grand jury. Dodge became the Territorial governor in 1836, and later served as the first governor when Wisconsin became a state. Dodge had a home near Dodgeville, which in the late 1820's had a lead furnace. After 1900, Dodgeville became a retail and shipping center for a dairy district, and a pea-growing region.
Population: 4,220 (2000); Race: 99.0% White, 0.0% Black, 0.0% Asian, 0.0% American Indian and Alaska Native, 0.0% Hispanic of any race, 1.0% two or more races (2000); Density: 1,178.5 persons per square mile (2000); Age: 26.0% under 18, 16.6% over 64 (2000); Marriage status: 23.8% never married, 57.3% now married, 7.4% widowed, 11.5% divorced (2000); Foreign born: 0.0% (2000); Ancestry (includes multiple ancestries): 39.5% German, 22.3% English, 19.1% Norwegian, 18.0% Irish, 7.0% United States or American (2000).
Economy: Single-family building permits issued: 20 (2001) / 20 (2000); Multi-family building permits issued: 73 (2001) / 52 (2000); Employment by occupation: 8.2% management, 20.0% professional, 17.4% services, 30.8% sales, 0.4% farming, 6.2% construction, 17.0% production (2000).
Income: Per capita income: $20,962 (2000); Median household income: $41,615 (2000); Poverty rate: 5.3% (2000).
Taxes: Total city taxes per capita: $54 (1997); City property taxes per capita: $38 (1997).
Education: High school graduation rate: 90.3% (2000); College graduation rate: 22.0% (2000).

School District(s)

Dodgeville (PK-12)
2000 Enrollment: 1,249 608-935-3307

Housing: Homeownership rate: 67.2% (2000); Median home value: $88,200 (2000); Median rent: $506 per month (2000); Median age of housing: 38 years (2000).
Hospitals: Upland Hills Health (40 beds)
Safety: Violent crime rate: 11.8 per 10,000 population; Property crime rate: 277.6 per 10,000 population (2001).
Newspapers: The Dodgeville Chronicle (1 x week)
Transportation: Commute to work: 94.1% car, 0.3% public transportation, 2.1% walk, 3.6% work from home (2000); Travel time to work: 70.0% less than 15 minutes, 9.7% 15 to 30 minutes, 6.8% 30 to 45 minutes, 6.5% 45 to 60 minutes, 7.0% 60 minutes or more (2000)
Additional Information Contacts
Dodgeville Chamber of Commerce 608-935-9200

DODGEVILLE (town). Covers a land area of 89.864 square miles and a water area of 0.404 square miles. Located at 42.98° N. Lat.; 90.11° W. Long. Elevation is 1,222 feet.
Population: 1,407 (2000); Race: 99.7% White, 0.0% Black, 0.0% Asian, 0.0% American Indian and Alaska Native, 0.2% Hispanic of any race, 0.3% two or more races (2000); Density: 15.7 persons per square mile (2000); Age: 28.4% under 18, 12.8% over 64 (2000); Marriage status: 18.9% never married, 69.0% now married, 5.1% widowed, 7.1% divorced (2000); Foreign born: 0.8% (2000); Ancestry (includes multiple ancestries): 43.8% German, 24.9% Norwegian, 18.5% English, 17.3% Irish, 4.1% Swiss (2000).
Economy: Employment by occupation: 18.6% management, 21.4% professional, 10.0% services, 22.1% sales, 1.6% farming, 10.8% construction, 15.5% production (2000).
Income: Per capita income: $22,521 (2000); Median household income: $49,327 (2000); Poverty rate: 4.9% (2000).
Taxes: Total city taxes per capita: $162 (1997); City property taxes per capita: $155 (1997).
Education: High school graduation rate: 90.5% (2000); College graduation rate: 21.5% (2000).
Housing: Homeownership rate: 83.9% (2000); Median home value: $134,500 (2000); Median rent: $502 per month (2000); Median age of housing: 26 years (2000).
Transportation: Commute to work: 83.1% car, 0.2% public transportation, 2.4% walk, 13.2% work from home (2000); Travel time to work: 50.5% less than 15 minutes, 24.8% 15 to 30 minutes, 8.6% 30 to 45 minutes, 8.1% 45 to 60 minutes, 7.9% 60 minutes or more (2000)

EDEN (town). Covers a land area of 35.190 square miles and a water area of 0.116 square miles. Located at 42.97° N. Lat.; 90.33° W. Long.
Population: 397 (2000); Race: 97.9% White, 0.0% Black, 0.0% Asian, 0.0% American Indian and Alaska Native, 0.0% Hispanic of any race, 2.1% two or more races (2000); Density: 11.3 persons per square mile (2000); Age: 32.0% under 18, 10.4% over 64 (2000); Marriage status: 23.8% never married, 71.5% now married, 0.7% widowed, 4.0% divorced (2000); Foreign born: 0.0% (2000); Ancestry (includes multiple ancestries): 50.1% German, 18.4% English, 12.0% Irish, 11.7% Czech, 9.3% Norwegian (2000).
Economy: Employment by occupation: 29.3% management, 7.3% professional, 6.3% services, 18.5% sales, 12.7% farming, 16.6% construction, 9.3% production (2000).
Income: Per capita income: $18,084 (2000); Median household income: $42,813 (2000); Poverty rate: 8.8% (2000).
Taxes: Total city taxes per capita: $145 (1997); City property taxes per capita: $142 (1997).
Education: High school graduation rate: 93.7% (2000); College graduation rate: 15.2% (2000).
Housing: Homeownership rate: 65.2% (2000); Median home value: $122,500 (2000); Median rent: $375 per month (2000); Median age of housing: 41 years (2000).
Transportation: Commute to work: 63.4% car, 0.0% public transportation, 12.9% walk, 23.3% work from home (2000); Travel time to work: 45.2% less than 15 minutes, 40.6% 15 to 30 minutes, 5.2% 30 to 45 minutes, 2.6% 45 to 60 minutes, 6.5% 60 minutes or more (2000)

HIGHLAND (village). Covers a land area of 1.131 square miles and a water area of 0 square miles. Located at 43.04° N. Lat.; 90.37° W. Long. Elevation is 1,192 feet.
Population: 855 (2000); Race: 99.8% White, 0.0% Black, 0.0% Asian, 0.0% American Indian and Alaska Native, 0.1% Hispanic of any race, 0.1% two or more races (2000); Density: 756.0 persons per square mile (2000); Age: 24.5% under 18, 17.3% over 64 (2000); Marriage status: 25.7% never married, 58.2% now married, 9.9% widowed, 6.1% divorced (2000); Foreign born: 0.3% (2000); Ancestry (includes multiple ancestries): 52.5% German, 22.4% Irish, 12.9% Czech, 7.8% Norwegian, 7.1% English (2000).
Economy: Single-family building permits issued: 5 (2001) / 3 (2000); Multi-family building permits issued: 0 (2001) / 0 (2000); Employment by occupation: 10.8% management, 12.2% professional, 12.8% services, 31.0% sales, 0.0% farming, 16.5% construction, 16.7% production (2000).
Income: Per capita income: $16,176 (2000); Median household income: $37,228 (2000); Poverty rate: 7.2% (2000).
Taxes: Total city taxes per capita: $162 (1997); City property taxes per capita: $158 (1997).
Education: High school graduation rate: 85.9% (2000); College graduation rate: 10.5% (2000).

School District(s)

Highland (PK-12)
2000 Enrollment: 378 608-929-4525
Housing: Homeownership rate: 79.4% (2000); Median home value: $77,200 (2000); Median rent: $317 per month (2000); Median age of housing: 51 years (2000).
Transportation: Commute to work: 95.2% car, 0.4% public transportation, 2.5% walk, 1.4% work from home (2000); Travel time to work: 30.2% less than 15 minutes, 34.0% 15 to 30 minutes, 18.2% 30 to 45 minutes, 5.0% 45 to 60 minutes, 12.6% 60 minutes or more (2000)

HIGHLAND (town). Covers a land area of 64.651 square miles and a water area of 0.214 square miles. Located at 43.04° N. Lat.; 90.33° W. Long. Elevation is 1,192 feet.
Population: 797 (2000); Race: 98.3% White, 0.3% Black, 0.4% Asian, 0.3% American Indian and Alaska Native, 0.3% Hispanic of any race, 0.8% two or more races (2000); Density: 12.3 persons per square mile (2000); Age: 27.3% under 18, 13.6% over 64 (2000); Marriage status: 26.6% never married, 64.2% now married, 4.2% widowed, 5.0% divorced (2000); Foreign born: 1.4% (2000); Ancestry (includes multiple ancestries): 49.7% German, 18.3% Norwegian, 18.2% Irish, 12.3% Czech, 10.1% English (2000).
Economy: Employment by occupation: 23.8% management, 11.0% professional, 11.2% services, 18.1% sales, 8.7% farming, 12.6% construction, 14.6% production (2000).
Income: Per capita income: $17,361 (2000); Median household income: $37,868 (2000); Poverty rate: 6.8% (2000).
Taxes: Total city taxes per capita: $233 (1997); City property taxes per capita: $232 (1997).
Education: High school graduation rate: 86.7% (2000); College graduation rate: 12.4% (2000).
Housing: Homeownership rate: 87.3% (2000); Median home value: $105,100 (2000); Median rent: $400 per month (2000); Median age of housing: 51 years (2000).
Transportation: Commute to work: 76.3% car, 0.0% public transportation, 6.9% walk, 16.8% work from home (2000); Travel time to work: 33.4% less than 15 minutes, 29.3% 15 to 30 minutes, 20.7% 30 to 45 minutes, 3.6% 45 to 60 minutes, 13.0% 60 minutes or more (2000)

HOLLANDALE (village). Covers a land area of 0.691 square miles and a water area of 0 square miles. Located at 42.87° N. Lat.; 89.93° W. Long. Elevation is 862 feet.
Population: 283 (2000); Race: 100.0% White, 0.0% Black, 0.0% Asian, 0.0% American Indian and Alaska Native, 0.0% Hispanic of any race, 0.0% two or more races (2000); Density: 409.4 persons per square mile (2000); Age: 19.1% under 18, 27.0% over 64 (2000); Marriage status: 21.5% never married, 54.2% now married, 18.2% widowed, 6.1% divorced (2000); Foreign born: 1.2% (2000); Ancestry (includes multiple ancestries): 51.2% Norwegian, 20.3% English, 18.8% Irish, 14.5% German, 13.3% Swiss (2000).
Economy: Single-family building permits issued: 2 (2001) / 0 (2000); Multi-family building permits issued: 0 (2001) / 0 (2000); Employment by occupation: 8.6% management, 6.0% professional, 8.6% services, 39.7% sales, 1.7% farming, 16.4% construction, 19.0% production (2000).
Income: Per capita income: $21,141 (2000); Median household income: $35,938 (2000); Poverty rate: 3.5% (2000).
Taxes: Total city taxes per capita: $81 (1997); City property taxes per capita: $74 (1997).
Education: High school graduation rate: 83.5% (2000); College graduation rate: 8.0% (2000).
Housing: Homeownership rate: 79.2% (2000); Median home value: $70,300 (2000); Median rent: $270 per month (2000); Median age of housing: 55 years (2000).
Transportation: Commute to work: 89.2% car, 0.0% public transportation, 3.6% walk, 7.2% work from home (2000); Travel time to work: 7.8% less

than 15 minutes, 27.2% 15 to 30 minutes, 32.0% 30 to 45 minutes, 28.2% 45 to 60 minutes, 4.9% 60 minutes or more (2000)

LINDEN (village). Covers a land area of 0.772 square miles and a water area of 0 square miles. Located at 42.91° N. Lat.; 90.27° W. Long. Elevation is 1,101 feet.
Population: 615 (2000); Race: 99.3% White, 0.0% Black, 0.0% Asian, 0.0% American Indian and Alaska Native, 0.0% Hispanic of any race, 0.7% two or more races (2000); Density: 796.2 persons per square mile (2000); Age: 30.5% under 18, 10.4% over 64 (2000); Marriage status: 24.0% never married, 55.5% now married, 7.4% widowed, 13.1% divorced (2000); Foreign born: 0.0% (2000); Ancestry (includes multiple ancestries): 32.5% English, 28.9% German, 9.8% Irish, 9.3% Norwegian, 4.4% United States or American (2000).
Economy: Single-family building permits issued: 1 (2001) / 1 (2000); Multi-family building permits issued: 0 (2001) / 0 (2000); Employment by occupation: 10.8% management, 9.7% professional, 18.1% services, 23.5% sales, 2.5% farming, 18.1% construction, 17.3% production (2000).
Income: Per capita income: $16,331 (2000); Median household income: $35,833 (2000); Poverty rate: 8.8% (2000).
Taxes: Total city taxes per capita: $105 (1997); City property taxes per capita: $96 (1997).
Education: High school graduation rate: 82.2% (2000); College graduation rate: 5.3% (2000).
Housing: Homeownership rate: 77.5% (2000); Median home value: $70,600 (2000); Median rent: $342 per month (2000); Median age of housing: 56 years (2000).
Transportation: Commute to work: 94.9% car, 1.8% public transportation, 1.8% walk, 1.5% work from home (2000); Travel time to work: 27.1% less than 15 minutes, 39.8% 15 to 30 minutes, 9.7% 30 to 45 minutes, 7.8% 45 to 60 minutes, 15.6% 60 minutes or more (2000)

LINDEN (town). Covers a land area of 60.660 square miles and a water area of 0.008 square miles. Located at 42.92° N. Lat.; 90.26° W. Long. Elevation is 1,101 feet.
Population: 873 (2000); Race: 98.5% White, 0.5% Black, 0.0% Asian, 0.6% American Indian and Alaska Native, 0.0% Hispanic of any race, 0.5% two or more races (2000); Density: 14.4 persons per square mile (2000); Age: 28.0% under 18, 17.5% over 64 (2000); Marriage status: 18.3% never married, 69.8% now married, 4.9% widowed, 7.1% divorced (2000); Foreign born: 0.2% (2000); Ancestry (includes multiple ancestries): 37.7% German, 21.7% English, 18.4% Norwegian, 11.6% Irish, 5.0% United States or American (2000).
Economy: Employment by occupation: 22.6% management, 12.1% professional, 8.1% services, 23.0% sales, 5.6% farming, 9.3% construction, 19.3% production (2000).
Income: Per capita income: $15,446 (2000); Median household income: $36,726 (2000); Poverty rate: 13.3% (2000).
Taxes: Total city taxes per capita: $193 (1997); City property taxes per capita: $193 (1997).
Education: High school graduation rate: 84.6% (2000); College graduation rate: 13.3% (2000).
Housing: Homeownership rate: 76.8% (2000); Median home value: $106,300 (2000); Median rent: $422 per month (2000); Median age of housing: 52 years (2000).
Transportation: Commute to work: 78.7% car, 0.5% public transportation, 2.1% walk, 18.7% work from home (2000); Travel time to work: 43.9% less than 15 minutes, 32.6% 15 to 30 minutes, 8.4% 30 to 45 minutes, 6.1% 45 to 60 minutes, 9.0% 60 minutes or more (2000)

MIFFLIN (town). Covers a land area of 50.681 square miles and a water area of 0 square miles. Located at 42.87° N. Lat.; 90.35° W. Long. Elevation is 955 feet.
Population: 617 (2000); Race: 100.0% White, 0.0% Black, 0.0% Asian, 0.0% American Indian and Alaska Native, 0.0% Hispanic of any race, 0.0% two or more races (2000); Density: 12.2 persons per square mile (2000); Age: 35.1% under 18, 6.5% over 64 (2000); Marriage status: 23.9% never married, 67.6% now married, 4.0% widowed, 4.4% divorced (2000); Foreign born: 0.3% (2000); Ancestry (includes multiple ancestries): 43.0% German, 21.9% English, 11.0% Irish, 8.8% Norwegian, 6.3% United States or American (2000).
Economy: Employment by occupation: 28.9% management, 12.2% professional, 5.5% services, 25.9% sales, 9.0% farming, 7.9% construction, 10.5% production (2000).
Income: Per capita income: $15,129 (2000); Median household income: $42,083 (2000); Poverty rate: 11.5% (2000).
Taxes: Total city taxes per capita: $184 (1997); City property taxes per capita: $184 (1997).
Education: High school graduation rate: 92.0% (2000); College graduation rate: 19.2% (2000).
Housing: Homeownership rate: 78.7% (2000); Median home value: $73,100 (2000); Median rent: $263 per month (2000); Median age of housing: 60+ years (2000).
Transportation: Commute to work: 68.9% car, 0.0% public transportation, 12.3% walk, 18.8% work from home (2000); Travel time to work: 32.9% less than 15 minutes, 38.6% 15 to 30 minutes, 20.2% 30 to 45 minutes, 1.4% 45 to 60 minutes, 6.9% 60 minutes or more (2000)

MINERAL POINT (city). Covers a land area of 3.014 square miles and a water area of 0 square miles. Located at 42.86° N. Lat.; 90.18° W. Long. Elevation is 1,135 feet.
History: Lead was discovered in Mineral Point Hill in 1828 by prospector Nat Morris. The community that grew up here was settled by many Cornish miners after 1832. Its early name of Shake Rag came from the custom of the miners' wives of waving dishcloths to summon the men home at dinnertime. From lead mining, Mineral Point turned to zinc, and then to shipping and dairy industries.
Population: 2,617 (2000); Race: 98.8% White, 0.2% Black, 0.2% Asian, 0.0% American Indian and Alaska Native, 0.2% Hispanic of any race, 0.5% two or more races (2000); Density: 868.1 persons per square mile (2000); Age: 23.0% under 18, 18.8% over 64 (2000); Marriage status: 22.1% never married, 58.9% now married, 8.8% widowed, 10.2% divorced (2000); Foreign born: 0.9% (2000); Ancestry (includes multiple ancestries): 42.1% German, 23.0% English, 22.7% Irish, 10.3% Norwegian, 6.8% United States or American (2000).
Economy: Single-family building permits issued: 6 (2001) / 6 (2000); Multi-family building permits issued: 0 (2001) / 2 (2000); Employment by occupation: 9.8% management, 20.1% professional, 13.9% services, 25.6% sales, 0.6% farming, 9.6% construction, 20.5% production (2000).
Income: Per capita income: $21,097 (2000); Median household income: $43,182 (2000); Poverty rate: 4.9% (2000).
Taxes: Total city taxes per capita: $210 (1997); City property taxes per capita: $203 (1997).
Education: High school graduation rate: 87.8% (2000); College graduation rate: 23.4% (2000).

School District(s)

Mineral Point (PK-12)
2000 Enrollment: 871 608-987-3924
Housing: Homeownership rate: 69.4% (2000); Median home value: $90,300 (2000); Median rent: $369 per month (2000); Median age of housing: 60+ years (2000).
Safety: Violent crime rate: 0.0 per 10,000 population; Property crime rate: 364.2 per 10,000 population (2001).
Newspapers: Democrat Tribune (1 x week)
Transportation: Commute to work: 90.9% car, 0.0% public transportation, 5.8% walk, 2.2% work from home (2000); Travel time to work: 42.8% less than 15 minutes, 30.7% 15 to 30 minutes, 8.8% 30 to 45 minutes, 8.1% 45 to 60 minutes, 9.6% 60 minutes or more (2000)
Additional Information Contacts
Mineral Point Chamber of Commerce 608-987-3201

MINERAL POINT (town). Covers a land area of 59.032 square miles and a water area of 0.094 square miles. Located at 42.86° N. Lat.; 90.15° W. Long. Elevation is 1,135 feet.
Population: 867 (2000); Race: 95.4% White, 0.0% Black, 0.0% Asian, 3.8% American Indian and Alaska Native, 0.5% Hispanic of any race, 0.8% two or more races (2000); Density: 14.7 persons per square mile (2000); Age: 32.1% under 18, 6.6% over 64 (2000); Marriage status: 24.9% never married, 67.2% now married, 1.7% widowed, 6.1% divorced (2000); Foreign born: 0.8% (2000); Ancestry (includes multiple ancestries): 45.3% German, 20.1% Irish, 19.4% English, 14.8% Norwegian, 7.2% United States or American (2000).
Economy: Employment by occupation: 24.4% management, 15.1% professional, 14.1% services, 18.5% sales, 3.3% farming, 9.0% construction, 15.5% production (2000).
Income: Per capita income: $17,337 (2000); Median household income: $42,171 (2000); Poverty rate: 8.5% (2000).
Taxes: Total city taxes per capita: $124 (1997); City property taxes per capita: $120 (1997).
Education: High school graduation rate: 94.6% (2000); College graduation rate: 22.9% (2000).

Housing: Homeownership rate: 73.0% (2000); Median home value: $135,300 (2000); Median rent: $469 per month (2000); Median age of housing: 36 years (2000).
Transportation: Commute to work: 76.3% car, 0.0% public transportation, 6.0% walk, 15.7% work from home (2000); Travel time to work: 44.6% less than 15 minutes, 34.0% 15 to 30 minutes, 7.5% 30 to 45 minutes, 8.7% 45 to 60 minutes, 5.2% 60 minutes or more (2000)

MOSCOW (town). Covers a land area of 41.348 square miles and a water area of 0.007 square miles. Located at 42.88° N. Lat.; 89.89° W. Long. Elevation is 850 feet.
Population: 594 (2000); Race: 98.6% White, 0.0% Black, 0.0% Asian, 0.0% American Indian and Alaska Native, 0.3% Hispanic of any race, 1.0% two or more races (2000); Density: 14.4 persons per square mile (2000); Age: 29.2% under 18, 6.8% over 64 (2000); Marriage status: 25.6% never married, 65.0% now married, 1.8% widowed, 7.6% divorced (2000); Foreign born: 0.3% (2000); Ancestry (includes multiple ancestries): 39.0% Norwegian, 24.4% German, 13.4% Irish, 13.2% United States or American, 12.5% Swiss (2000).
Economy: Employment by occupation: 27.4% management, 17.1% professional, 11.8% services, 18.9% sales, 4.1% farming, 7.7% construction, 13.0% production (2000).
Income: Per capita income: $17,515 (2000); Median household income: $45,000 (2000); Poverty rate: 6.2% (2000).
Taxes: Total city taxes per capita: $263 (2000); City property taxes per capita: $261 (2000).
Education: High school graduation rate: 93.5% (2000); College graduation rate: 16.9% (2000).
Housing: Homeownership rate: 80.0% (2000); Median home value: $115,600 (2000); Median rent: $431 per month (2000); Median age of housing: 60+ years (2000).
Transportation: Commute to work: 79.2% car, 0.0% public transportation, 4.2% walk, 16.6% work from home (2000); Travel time to work: 18.1% less than 15 minutes, 28.1% 15 to 30 minutes, 24.2% 30 to 45 minutes, 12.8% 45 to 60 minutes, 16.7% 60 minutes or more (2000)

PULASKI (town). Covers a land area of 43.296 square miles and a water area of 1.346 square miles. Located at 43.16° N. Lat.; 90.34° W. Long.
Population: 381 (2000); Race: 96.8% White, 0.0% Black, 0.0% Asian, 3.2% American Indian and Alaska Native, 0.0% Hispanic of any race, 0.0% two or more races (2000); Density: 8.8 persons per square mile (2000); Age: 32.6% under 18, 8.1% over 64 (2000); Marriage status: 28.6% never married, 61.1% now married, 4.0% widowed, 6.3% divorced (2000); Foreign born: 0.5% (2000); Ancestry (includes multiple ancestries): 48.9% German, 16.5% Czech, 12.1% Irish, 9.9% Norwegian, 7.2% English (2000).
Economy: Employment by occupation: 25.7% management, 9.9% professional, 11.3% services, 17.6% sales, 5.9% farming, 9.5% construction, 20.3% production (2000).
Income: Per capita income: $15,561 (2000); Median household income: $43,036 (2000); Poverty rate: 9.2% (2000).
Taxes: Total city taxes per capita: $138 (1997); City property taxes per capita: $138 (1997).
Education: High school graduation rate: 86.0% (2000); College graduation rate: 12.8% (2000).
Housing: Homeownership rate: 71.5% (2000); Median home value: $78,800 (2000); Median rent: $431 per month (2000); Median age of housing: 52 years (2000).
Transportation: Commute to work: 73.7% car, 0.0% public transportation, 8.9% walk, 17.4% work from home (2000); Travel time to work: 30.3% less than 15 minutes, 28.6% 15 to 30 minutes, 30.3% 30 to 45 minutes, 3.8% 45 to 60 minutes, 7.0% 60 minutes or more (2000)

REWEY (village). Covers a land area of 0.496 square miles and a water area of 0 square miles. Located at 42.84° N. Lat.; 90.39° W. Long. Elevation is 1,140 feet.
Population: 311 (2000); Race: 96.4% White, 0.0% Black, 0.0% Asian, 0.0% American Indian and Alaska Native, 4.6% Hispanic of any race, 3.6% two or more races (2000); Density: 626.8 persons per square mile (2000); Age: 31.3% under 18, 14.9% over 64 (2000); Marriage status: 30.5% never married, 46.2% now married, 9.0% widowed, 14.3% divorced (2000); Foreign born: 1.1% (2000); Ancestry (includes multiple ancestries): 52.0% German, 26.3% English, 13.5% Irish, 7.5% Welsh, 7.1% United States or American (2000).
Economy: Single-family building permits issued: 0 (2001) / 0 (2000); Multi-family building permits issued: 0 (2001) / 0 (2000); Employment by occupation: 11.8% management, 13.4% professional, 11.8% services, 27.6% sales, 3.9% farming, 15.0% construction, 16.5% production (2000).
Income: Per capita income: $12,298 (2000); Median household income: $24,643 (2000); Poverty rate: 10.6% (2000).
Taxes: Total city taxes per capita: $83 (1997); City property taxes per capita: $78 (1997).
Education: High school graduation rate: 81.9% (2000); College graduation rate: 15.1% (2000).
Housing: Homeownership rate: 69.9% (2000); Median home value: $51,400 (2000); Median rent: $300 per month (2000); Median age of housing: 60+ years (2000).
Transportation: Commute to work: 89.0% car, 0.0% public transportation, 5.5% walk, 3.1% work from home (2000); Travel time to work: 23.6% less than 15 minutes, 47.2% 15 to 30 minutes, 16.3% 30 to 45 minutes, 6.5% 45 to 60 minutes, 6.5% 60 minutes or more (2000)

RIDGEWAY (village). Covers a land area of 1.264 square miles and a water area of 0 square miles. Located at 42.99° N. Lat.; 89.99° W. Long. Elevation is 1,170 feet.
Population: 689 (2000); Race: 95.0% White, 0.0% Black, 5.0% Asian, 0.0% American Indian and Alaska Native, 0.4% Hispanic of any race, 0.0% two or more races (2000); Density: 545.0 persons per square mile (2000); Age: 26.7% under 18, 8.9% over 64 (2000); Marriage status: 26.7% never married, 52.1% now married, 6.5% widowed, 14.7% divorced (2000); Foreign born: 1.9% (2000); Ancestry (includes multiple ancestries): 31.1% German, 26.8% Irish, 24.1% Norwegian, 9.1% Other groups, 6.9% English (2000).
Economy: Single-family building permits issued: 1 (2001) / 1 (2000); Multi-family building permits issued: 0 (2001) / 0 (2000); Employment by occupation: 5.6% management, 7.6% professional, 11.5% services, 30.3% sales, 1.0% farming, 15.8% construction, 28.2% production (2000).
Income: Per capita income: $17,887 (2000); Median household income: $41,548 (2000); Poverty rate: 10.8% (2000).
Taxes: Total city taxes per capita: $75 (1997); City property taxes per capita: $67 (1997).
Education: High school graduation rate: 82.0% (2000); College graduation rate: 10.6% (2000).
Housing: Homeownership rate: 77.7% (2000); Median home value: $88,000 (2000); Median rent: $396 per month (2000); Median age of housing: 39 years (2000).
Transportation: Commute to work: 94.1% car, 0.5% public transportation, 2.1% walk, 3.4% work from home (2000); Travel time to work: 26.4% less than 15 minutes, 27.7% 15 to 30 minutes, 23.5% 30 to 45 minutes, 19.7% 45 to 60 minutes, 2.7% 60 minutes or more (2000)

RIDGEWAY (town). Covers a land area of 42.694 square miles and a water area of 0.027 square miles. Located at 42.99° N. Lat.; 89.98° W. Long. Elevation is 1,170 feet.
Population: 581 (2000); Race: 99.7% White, 0.0% Black, 0.0% Asian, 0.0% American Indian and Alaska Native, 0.0% Hispanic of any race, 0.3% two or more races (2000); Density: 13.6 persons per square mile (2000); Age: 28.8% under 18, 8.8% over 64 (2000); Marriage status: 21.8% never married, 67.8% now married, 4.2% widowed, 6.2% divorced (2000); Foreign born: 0.0% (2000); Ancestry (includes multiple ancestries): 40.2% German, 28.8% Norwegian, 24.6% Irish, 11.4% English, 4.9% United States or American (2000).
Economy: Employment by occupation: 22.4% management, 14.6% professional, 10.6% services, 23.6% sales, 3.1% farming, 7.1% construction, 18.6% production (2000).
Income: Per capita income: $18,419 (2000); Median household income: $50,938 (2000); Poverty rate: 11.2% (2000).
Taxes: Total city taxes per capita: $259 (1997); City property taxes per capita: $256 (1997).
Education: High school graduation rate: 91.0% (2000); College graduation rate: 16.3% (2000).
Housing: Homeownership rate: 87.4% (2000); Median home value: $153,400 (2000); Median rent: $425 per month (2000); Median age of housing: 43 years (2000).
Transportation: Commute to work: 81.4% car, 0.9% public transportation, 1.3% walk, 16.4% work from home (2000); Travel time to work: 24.1% less than 15 minutes, 33.1% 15 to 30 minutes, 10.5% 30 to 45 minutes, 22.9% 45 to 60 minutes, 9.4% 60 minutes or more (2000)

WALDWICK (town). Covers a land area of 41.944 square miles and a water area of 0 square miles. Located at 42.86° N. Lat.; 90.01° W. Long. Elevation is 1,080 feet.
Population: 500 (2000); Race: 100.0% White, 0.0% Black, 0.0% Asian, 0.0% American Indian and Alaska Native, 0.0% Hispanic of any race, 0.0% two or more races (2000); Density: 11.9 persons per square mile (2000); Age:

28.5% under 18, 15.3% over 64 (2000); Marriage status: 20.9% never married, 69.7% now married, 4.5% widowed, 5.0% divorced (2000); Foreign born: 0.4% (2000); Ancestry (includes multiple ancestries): 39.6% German, 23.8% Norwegian, 22.1% English, 18.9% Irish, 9.4% Swiss (2000).
Economy: Employment by occupation: 23.8% management, 10.9% professional, 5.9% services, 28.7% sales, 6.9% farming, 8.9% construction, 14.9% production (2000).
Income: Per capita income: $15,446 (2000); Median household income: $39,271 (2000); Poverty rate: 13.6% (2000).
Taxes: Total city taxes per capita: $136 (1997); City property taxes per capita: $136 (1997).
Education: High school graduation rate: 93.9% (2000); College graduation rate: 10.5% (2000).
Housing: Homeownership rate: 82.7% (2000); Median home value: $80,000 (2000); Median rent: $375 per month (2000); Median age of housing: 52 years (2000).
Transportation: Commute to work: 70.8% car, 0.0% public transportation, 4.3% walk, 23.3% work from home (2000); Travel time to work: 20.3% less than 15 minutes, 48.1% 15 to 30 minutes, 15.6% 30 to 45 minutes, 10.0% 45 to 60 minutes, 6.1% 60 minutes or more (2000)

WYOMING (town). Covers a land area of 39.759 square miles and a water area of 1.078 square miles. Located at 43.11° N. Lat.; 90.10° W. Long. Elevation is 738 feet.
Population: 364 (2000); Race: 98.8% White, 0.0% Black, 0.0% Asian, 1.2% American Indian and Alaska Native, 0.3% Hispanic of any race, 0.0% two or more races (2000); Density: 9.2 persons per square mile (2000); Age: 21.3% under 18, 7.4% over 64 (2000); Marriage status: 16.9% never married, 76.6% now married, 0.8% widowed, 5.7% divorced (2000); Foreign born: 0.6% (2000); Ancestry (includes multiple ancestries): 30.9% German, 20.7% Norwegian, 17.3% Irish, 14.2% English, 8.6% United States or American (2000).
Economy: Employment by occupation: 18.5% management, 27.2% professional, 9.2% services, 15.4% sales, 0.0% farming, 10.8% construction, 19.0% production (2000).
Income: Per capita income: $23,253 (2000); Median household income: $48,438 (2000); Poverty rate: 9.7% (2000).
Taxes: Total city taxes per capita: $278 (1997); City property taxes per capita: $262 (1997).
Education: High school graduation rate: 93.9% (2000); College graduation rate: 41.2% (2000).
Housing: Homeownership rate: 72.6% (2000); Median home value: $123,200 (2000); Median rent: $492 per month (2000); Median age of housing: 44 years (2000).
Transportation: Commute to work: 87.4% car, 0.0% public transportation, 1.0% walk, 11.5% work from home (2000); Travel time to work: 26.6% less than 15 minutes, 33.7% 15 to 30 minutes, 6.5% 30 to 45 minutes, 16.0% 45 to 60 minutes, 17.2% 60 minutes or more (2000)

Iron County

Located in northern Wisconsin; bounded partly on the north by Lake Superior, the Montreal River, and the Michigan border; includes the Gogebic Range, and many lakes. Covers a land area of 757.20 square miles, a water area of 162.00 square miles, and is located in the Central Time Zone. The county government was organized in 1893. County seat is Hurley.

Weather Station: Gurney Elevation: 967 feet

	Jan	Feb	Mar	Apr	May	Jun	Jul	Aug	Sep	Oct	Nov	Dec
High	22	28	38	51	65	74	78	76	67	56	39	27
Low	2	6	17	29	40	49	55	54	46	36	24	10
Precip	1.8	1.1	2.0	2.1	3.0	4.0	4.1	4.2	4.2	3.5	2.8	1.8
Snow	35.4	20.0	21.3	7.8	1.2	0.0	0.0	0.0	0.2	1.9	20.1	30.8

High and Low temperatures in degrees Fahrenheit; Precipitation and Snow in inches

Population: 6,861 (2000); Race: 98.4% White, 0.1% Black, 0.3% Asian, 0.3% American Indian and Alaska Native, 0.2% Hispanic of any race, 0.9% two or more races (2000); Density: 9.1 persons per square mile (2000); Age: 19.4% under 18, 23.2% over 64 (2000).
Religion: Five largest groups: 28.1% Catholic Church, 2.9% Wisconsin Evangelical Lutheran Synod, 2.4% Lutheran Church—Missouri Synod, 1.6% The United Methodist Church, 1.1% Presbyterian Church (U.S.A.) (2000).
Economy: Unemployment rate: 8.6% (11/2002); Total civilian labor force: 3,518 (11/2002); Leading industries: 19.1% retail trade; 18.5% manufacturing; 15.4% health care and social assistance (2000); Companies that employ more than 1,000 persons: 0 (2000); Companies that employ more than 100 persons: 3 (2000); Farms: 38 totaling 9,633 acres (1997); Minority business ownership rate: 0.0% (1997); Women business ownership rate: 0.0% (1997); Retail sales per capita: $7,675 (1997). Single-family building permits issued: 67 (2001) / 73 (2000); Multi-family building permits issued: 0 (2001) / 0 (2000).
Income: Per capita income: $17,371 (2000); Median household income: $29,580 (2000); Poverty rate: 11.1% (2000); Bankruptcy rate: 1.73% (2001).
Taxes: Total county taxes per capita: $245 (1997); County property taxes per capita: $193 (1997).
Education: High school graduation rate: 83.7% (2000); College graduation rate: 13.2% (2000).
Housing: Homeownership rate: 80.7% (2000); Median home value: $58,900 (2000); Median rent: $251 per month (2000); Median age of housing: 39 years (2000).
Health: Birth rate: 56.8 per 10,000 population (1998); Age adjusted death rate: 73.0 per 10,000 population (1999); Age adjusted cancer mortality rate: 141.9 (Unreliable figure as per CDC) deaths per 100,000 population (1999). Number of physicians: 8.7 per 10,000 population (1999); Number of hospital beds: n/a (1999).
Elections: 2000 Presidential election results: 46.2% Gore, 49.4% Bush, 3.8% Nader, 0.1% Buchanan
National and State Parks: Big Island State Wildlife Area; Boot Lake State Wildlife Area; Hay Creek Hoffman Lake State Wildlife Area; Hay Creek-Hoffman Lake State Wildlife Area; Underwood State Wildlife Area
Additional Information Contacts
Iron County Government Offices 715-561-3375
Hurley Chamber of Commerce 715-561-4334
Mercer Chamber of Commerce 715-476-2389

Iron County Communities

ANDERSON (town). Covers a land area of 83.185 square miles and a water area of 0.424 square miles. Located at 46.36° N. Lat.; 90.44° W. Long.
Population: 61 (2000); Race: 100.0% White, 0.0% Black, 0.0% Asian, 0.0% American Indian and Alaska Native, 0.0% Hispanic of any race, 0.0% two or more races (2000); Density: 0.7 persons per square mile (2000); Age: 10.9% under 18, 30.4% over 64 (2000); Marriage status: 19.5% never married, 43.9% now married, 19.5% widowed, 17.1% divorced (2000); Foreign born: 6.5% (2000); Ancestry (includes multiple ancestries): 26.1% Finnish, 19.6% German, 15.2% Italian, 13.0% Swedish, 10.9% Irish (2000).
Economy: Employment by occupation: 12.0% management, 12.0% professional, 32.0% services, 8.0% sales, 0.0% farming, 16.0% construction, 20.0% production (2000).
Income: Per capita income: $17,611 (2000); Median household income: $15,417 (2000); Poverty rate: 10.9% (2000).
Taxes: Total city taxes per capita: $461 (1997); City property taxes per capita: $316 (1997).
Education: High school graduation rate: 71.1% (2000); College graduation rate: 7.9% (2000).
Housing: Homeownership rate: 83.3% (2000); Median home value: $20,000 (2000); Median rent: $325 per month (2000); Median age of housing: 26 years (2000).
Transportation: Commute to work: 80.0% car, 0.0% public transportation, 12.0% walk, 8.0% work from home (2000); Travel time to work: 21.7% less than 15 minutes, 26.1% 15 to 30 minutes, 47.8% 30 to 45 minutes, 4.3% 45 to 60 minutes, 0.0% 60 minutes or more (2000)

CAREY (town). Covers a land area of 41.552 square miles and a water area of 1.467 square miles. Located at 46.34° N. Lat.; 90.22° W. Long.
Population: 191 (2000); Race: 100.0% White, 0.0% Black, 0.0% Asian, 0.0% American Indian and Alaska Native, 3.0% Hispanic of any race, 0.0% two or more races (2000); Density: 4.6 persons per square mile (2000); Age: 20.3% under 18, 26.4% over 64 (2000); Marriage status: 22.8% never married, 67.7% now married, 7.8% widowed, 1.8% divorced (2000); Foreign born: 0.0% (2000); Ancestry (includes multiple ancestries): 27.9% German, 24.4% Finnish, 17.8% English, 17.3% Italian, 14.2% Irish (2000).
Economy: Employment by occupation: 9.9% management, 14.8% professional, 25.9% services, 22.2% sales, 0.0% farming, 12.3% construction, 14.8% production (2000).
Income: Per capita income: $24,918 (2000); Median household income: $35,625 (2000); Poverty rate: 3.6% (2000).
Taxes: Total city taxes per capita: $94 (1997); City property taxes per capita: $94 (1997).
Education: High school graduation rate: 83.8% (2000); College graduation rate: 12.7% (2000).

Housing: Homeownership rate: 93.6% (2000); Median home value: $52,500 (2000); Median age of housing: 45 years (2000).
Transportation: Commute to work: 95.1% car, 0.0% public transportation, 0.0% walk, 4.9% work from home (2000); Travel time to work: 63.6% less than 15 minutes, 22.1% 15 to 30 minutes, 3.9% 30 to 45 minutes, 7.8% 45 to 60 minutes, 2.6% 60 minutes or more (2000)

GURNEY (town). Covers a land area of 36.999 square miles and a water area of 0 square miles. Located at 46.47° N. Lat.; 90.49° W. Long. Elevation is 1,094 feet.
Population: 158 (2000); Race: 100.0% White, 0.0% Black, 0.0% Asian, 0.0% American Indian and Alaska Native, 0.0% Hispanic of any race, 0.0% two or more races (2000); Density: 4.3 persons per square mile (2000); Age: 27.2% under 18, 13.0% over 64 (2000); Marriage status: 7.3% never married, 91.1% now married, 1.6% widowed, 0.0% divorced (2000); Foreign born: 0.0% (2000); Ancestry (includes multiple ancestries): 21.6% German, 11.1% Finnish, 10.5% French (except Basque), 9.9% English, 8.0% French Canadian (2000).
Economy: Employment by occupation: 12.3% management, 12.3% professional, 12.3% services, 20.0% sales, 6.2% farming, 15.4% construction, 21.5% production (2000).
Income: Per capita income: $15,022 (2000); Median household income: $35,417 (2000); Poverty rate: 9.9% (2000).
Taxes: Total city taxes per capita: $51 (1997); City property taxes per capita: $51 (1997).
Education: High school graduation rate: 88.8% (2000); College graduation rate: 13.8% (2000).
Housing: Homeownership rate: 96.7% (2000); Median home value: $72,500 (2000); Median age of housing: 24 years (2000).
Transportation: Commute to work: 92.3% car, 0.0% public transportation, 1.5% walk, 1.5% work from home (2000); Travel time to work: 6.3% less than 15 minutes, 43.8% 15 to 30 minutes, 39.1% 30 to 45 minutes, 0.0% 45 to 60 minutes, 10.9% 60 minutes or more (2000)

HURLEY (city). Covers a land area of 3.149 square miles and a water area of 0.162 square miles. Located at 46.45° N. Lat.; 90.19° W. Long. Elevation is 1,480 feet.
History: Hurley began in 1884 as a lumber town, soon attracting thousands of men working on the Gogebic Range in the ore mines. Soon after 1900 the mining activity in Hurley declined, and it was left with its reputation for rowdiness and crime. In 1938, 80 of the 115 businesses in town were taverns.
Population: 1,818 (2000); Race: 96.9% White, 0.0% Black, 0.3% Asian, 0.6% American Indian and Alaska Native, 0.3% Hispanic of any race, 2.3% two or more races (2000); Density: 577.3 persons per square mile (2000); Age: 18.3% under 18, 26.2% over 64 (2000); Marriage status: 26.9% never married, 46.7% now married, 14.5% widowed, 11.9% divorced (2000); Foreign born: 1.4% (2000); Ancestry (includes multiple ancestries): 28.8% Italian, 22.9% Finnish, 14.5% German, 11.5% Polish, 8.3% Swedish (2000).
Economy: Single-family building permits issued: 0 (2001) / 1 (2000); Multi-family building permits issued: 0 (2001) / 0 (2000); Employment by occupation: 9.0% management, 11.5% professional, 24.4% services, 18.8% sales, 1.0% farming, 11.6% construction, 23.5% production (2000).
Income: Per capita income: $14,554 (2000); Median household income: $24,821 (2000); Poverty rate: 14.7% (2000).
Taxes: Total city taxes per capita: $316 (1997); City property taxes per capita: $269 (1997).
Education: High school graduation rate: 81.9% (2000); College graduation rate: 11.0% (2000).

School District(s)

Hurley (PK-12)
2000 Enrollment: 771 715-561-4900
Housing: Homeownership rate: 64.2% (2000); Median home value: $37,100 (2000); Median rent: $257 per month (2000); Median age of housing: 54 years (2000).
Safety: Violent crime rate: 21.8 per 10,000 population; Property crime rate: 382.3 per 10,000 population (2001).
Newspapers: Iron County Miner (1 x week)
Transportation: Commute to work: 89.3% car, 0.4% public transportation, 6.0% walk, 3.7% work from home (2000); Travel time to work: 66.4% less than 15 minutes, 20.7% 15 to 30 minutes, 8.0% 30 to 45 minutes, 2.4% 45 to 60 minutes, 2.5% 60 minutes or more (2000)
Additional Information Contacts
Hurley Chamber of Commerce 715-561-4334

IRON BELT (unincorporated postal area, zip code 54536). Covers a land area of 48.665 square miles and a water area of 0.452 square miles. Located at 46.34° N. Lat.; 90.33° W. Long. Elevation is 1,570 feet.
Population: 269 (2000); Race: 100.0% White, 0.0% Black, 0.0% Asian, 0.0% American Indian and Alaska Native, 0.0% Hispanic of any race, 0.0% two or more races (2000); Density: 5.5 persons per square mile (2000); Age: 21.1% under 18, 14.2% over 64 (2000); Marriage status: 22.5% never married, 54.9% now married, 8.0% widowed, 14.6% divorced (2000); Foreign born: 2.0% (2000); Ancestry (includes multiple ancestries): 39.3% Finnish, 35.6% Italian, 8.9% German, 8.5% Irish, 7.7% Swedish (2000).
Economy: Manufacturing: paving products. Employment by occupation: 9.5% management, 18.1% professional, 17.1% services, 13.3% sales, 3.8% farming, 13.3% construction, 24.8% production (2000).
Income: Per capita income: $14,934 (2000); Median household income: $30,000 (2000); Poverty rate: 7.8% (2000).
Education: High school graduation rate: 86.2% (2000); College graduation rate: 13.3% (2000).
Housing: Homeownership rate: 78.4% (2000); Median home value: $36,500 (2000); Median rent: $175 per month (2000); Median age of housing: 47 years (2000).
Transportation: Commute to work: 77.3% car, 2.1% public transportation, 4.1% walk, 16.5% work from home (2000); Travel time to work: 17.3% less than 15 minutes, 56.8% 15 to 30 minutes, 11.1% 30 to 45 minutes, 9.9% 45 to 60 minutes, 4.9% 60 minutes or more (2000)

KIMBALL (town). Covers a land area of 37.093 square miles and a water area of 0.021 square miles. Located at 46.48° N. Lat.; 90.26° W. Long. Elevation is 1,260 feet.
Population: 540 (2000); Race: 98.5% White, 0.0% Black, 0.0% Asian, 0.4% American Indian and Alaska Native, 0.0% Hispanic of any race, 1.1% two or more races (2000); Density: 14.6 persons per square mile (2000); Age: 21.9% under 18, 15.9% over 64 (2000); Marriage status: 24.3% never married, 61.2% now married, 9.8% widowed, 4.7% divorced (2000); Foreign born: 4.5% (2000); Ancestry (includes multiple ancestries): 35.0% Finnish, 19.1% German, 18.5% Italian, 11.2% Polish, 6.9% French (except Basque) (2000).
Economy: Employment by occupation: 10.4% management, 20.1% professional, 20.1% services, 22.5% sales, 0.8% farming, 10.4% construction, 15.7% production (2000).
Income: Per capita income: $19,100 (2000); Median household income: $33,750 (2000); Poverty rate: 8.1% (2000).
Taxes: Total city taxes per capita: $112 (1997); City property taxes per capita: $110 (1997).
Education: High school graduation rate: 81.4% (2000); College graduation rate: 16.7% (2000).
Housing: Homeownership rate: 93.7% (2000); Median home value: $61,900 (2000); Median rent: $238 per month (2000); Median age of housing: 30 years (2000).
Transportation: Commute to work: 89.8% car, 0.0% public transportation, 6.1% walk, 4.1% work from home (2000); Travel time to work: 47.4% less than 15 minutes, 41.0% 15 to 30 minutes, 1.7% 30 to 45 minutes, 5.1% 45 to 60 minutes, 4.7% 60 minutes or more (2000)

KNIGHT (town). Covers a land area of 94.080 square miles and a water area of 0.999 square miles. Located at 46.27° N. Lat.; 90.34° W. Long.
Population: 284 (2000); Race: 100.0% White, 0.0% Black, 0.0% Asian, 0.0% American Indian and Alaska Native, 0.0% Hispanic of any race, 0.0% two or more races (2000); Density: 3.0 persons per square mile (2000); Age: 20.5% under 18, 15.7% over 64 (2000); Marriage status: 22.9% never married, 55.8% now married, 7.4% widowed, 13.9% divorced (2000); Foreign born: 1.9% (2000); Ancestry (includes multiple ancestries): 36.9% Finnish, 34.7% Italian, 13.4% German, 8.2% Swedish, 6.7% Irish (2000).
Economy: Employment by occupation: 8.4% management, 15.1% professional, 15.1% services, 17.6% sales, 3.4% farming, 13.4% construction, 26.9% production (2000).
Income: Per capita income: $15,278 (2000); Median household income: $32,969 (2000); Poverty rate: 7.3% (2000).
Taxes: Total city taxes per capita: $60 (2000); City property taxes per capita: $56 (2000).
Education: High school graduation rate: 85.4% (2000); College graduation rate: 13.6% (2000).
Housing: Homeownership rate: 80.0% (2000); Median home value: $37,000 (2000); Median rent: $175 per month (2000); Median age of housing: 44 years (2000).
Transportation: Commute to work: 80.2% car, 1.8% public transportation, 3.6% walk, 14.4% work from home (2000); Travel time to work: 16.8% less

than 15 minutes, 57.9% 15 to 30 minutes, 12.6% 30 to 45 minutes, 8.4% 45 to 60 minutes, 4.2% 60 minutes or more (2000)

MERCER (town). Covers a land area of 168.041 square miles and a water area of 16.718 square miles. Located at 46.16° N. Lat.; 90.10° W. Long. Elevation is 1,600 feet.

Population: 1,732 (2000); Race: 99.4% White, 0.2% Black, 0.0% Asian, 0.2% American Indian and Alaska Native, 0.1% Hispanic of any race, 0.2% two or more races (2000); Density: 10.3 persons per square mile (2000); Age: 17.7% under 18, 24.4% over 64 (2000); Marriage status: 16.9% never married, 62.3% now married, 10.2% widowed, 10.7% divorced (2000); Foreign born: 1.7% (2000); Ancestry (includes multiple ancestries): 43.7% German, 13.8% Irish, 11.2% Polish, 9.7% English, 5.5% French (except Basque) (2000).

Economy: In wooded lake region; fishing. Manufacturing: forest products. Nearby is a fish hatchery. Employment by occupation: 7.4% management, 14.6% professional, 17.2% services, 22.5% sales, 1.1% farming, 19.8% construction, 17.4% production (2000).

Income: Per capita income: $19,087 (2000); Median household income: $31,413 (2000); Poverty rate: 13.5% (2000).

Taxes: Total city taxes per capita: $398 (2000); City property taxes per capita: $389 (2000).

Education: High school graduation rate: 84.3% (2000); College graduation rate: 14.1% (2000).

School District(s)

Mercer (KG-12)
2000 Enrollment: 232 715-476-2154

Housing: Homeownership rate: 81.3% (2000); Median home value: $114,700 (2000); Median rent: $270 per month (2000); Median age of housing: 30 years (2000).

Transportation: Commute to work: 87.6% car, 0.4% public transportation, 3.8% walk, 7.8% work from home (2000); Travel time to work: 41.7% less than 15 minutes, 25.8% 15 to 30 minutes, 20.3% 30 to 45 minutes, 4.7% 45 to 60 minutes, 7.4% 60 minutes or more (2000)

Additional Information Contacts

Mercer Chamber of Commerce 715-476-2389

MONTREAL (city). Covers a land area of 2.241 square miles and a water area of 0.010 square miles. Located at 46.42° N. Lat.; 90.23° W. Long. Elevation is 1,580 feet.

History: Montreal grew around the operations of the Montreal Mining Company, producing iron ore.

Population: 838 (2000); Race: 98.7% White, 0.0% Black, 1.0% Asian, 0.0% American Indian and Alaska Native, 0.0% Hispanic of any race, 0.2% two or more races (2000); Density: 373.9 persons per square mile (2000); Age: 25.2% under 18, 17.9% over 64 (2000); Marriage status: 19.4% never married, 57.8% now married, 8.6% widowed, 14.2% divorced (2000); Foreign born: 2.0% (2000); Ancestry (includes multiple ancestries): 31.5% Italian, 19.4% Polish, 19.0% Finnish, 18.1% German, 8.3% English (2000).

Economy: Single-family building permits issued: 0 (2001) / 0 (2000); Multi-family building permits issued: 0 (2001) / 0 (2000); Employment by occupation: 9.5% management, 19.0% professional, 15.2% services, 22.4% sales, 1.0% farming, 12.9% construction, 20.1% production (2000).

Income: Per capita income: $17,097 (2000); Median household income: $29,219 (2000); Poverty rate: 7.6% (2000).

Taxes: Total city taxes per capita: $93 (1997); City property taxes per capita: $89 (1997).

Education: High school graduation rate: 84.4% (2000); College graduation rate: 15.5% (2000).

Housing: Homeownership rate: 83.5% (2000); Median home value: $41,000 (2000); Median rent: $226 per month (2000); Median age of housing: 60+ years (2000).

Transportation: Commute to work: 94.8% car, 0.5% public transportation, 1.0% walk, 3.7% work from home (2000); Travel time to work: 54.7% less than 15 minutes, 28.7% 15 to 30 minutes, 7.3% 30 to 45 minutes, 4.6% 45 to 60 minutes, 4.6% 60 minutes or more (2000)

OMA (town). Covers a land area of 74.714 square miles and a water area of 3.035 square miles. Located at 46.28° N. Lat.; 90.05° W. Long.

Population: 355 (2000); Race: 97.2% White, 0.0% Black, 0.6% Asian, 1.5% American Indian and Alaska Native, 0.6% Hispanic of any race, 0.6% two or more races (2000); Density: 4.8 persons per square mile (2000); Age: 20.4% under 18, 12.1% over 64 (2000); Marriage status: 10.6% never married, 72.2% now married, 8.7% widowed, 8.4% divorced (2000); Foreign born: 1.2% (2000); Ancestry (includes multiple ancestries): 27.9% German, 22.3% Finnish, 18.6% Italian, 15.2% Irish, 12.4% Polish (2000).

Economy: Employment by occupation: 11.3% management, 14.8% professional, 21.8% services, 30.3% sales, 2.1% farming, 8.5% construction, 11.3% production (2000).

Income: Per capita income: $16,146 (2000); Median household income: $30,917 (2000); Poverty rate: 16.1% (2000).

Education: High school graduation rate: 84.7% (2000); College graduation rate: 15.3% (2000).

Housing: Homeownership rate: 91.0% (2000); Median home value: $122,500 (2000); Median age of housing: 29 years (2000).

Transportation: Commute to work: 87.1% car, 2.1% public transportation, 1.4% walk, 9.3% work from home (2000); Travel time to work: 38.6% less than 15 minutes, 41.7% 15 to 30 minutes, 6.3% 30 to 45 minutes, 7.1% 45 to 60 minutes, 6.3% 60 minutes or more (2000)

PENCE (town). Covers a land area of 32.164 square miles and a water area of 3.937 square miles. Located at 46.37° N. Lat.; 90.25° W. Long. Elevation is 1,630 feet.

Population: 198 (2000); Race: 100.0% White, 0.0% Black, 0.0% Asian, 0.0% American Indian and Alaska Native, 0.0% Hispanic of any race, 0.0% two or more races (2000); Density: 6.2 persons per square mile (2000); Age: 23.2% under 18, 30.3% over 64 (2000); Marriage status: 19.6% never married, 58.3% now married, 12.5% widowed, 9.5% divorced (2000); Foreign born: 0.0% (2000); Ancestry (includes multiple ancestries): 44.4% Italian, 19.2% Finnish, 16.7% Polish, 13.6% German, 7.6% Irish (2000).

Economy: Employment by occupation: 0.0% management, 15.1% professional, 31.5% services, 19.2% sales, 0.0% farming, 12.3% construction, 21.9% production (2000).

Income: Per capita income: $14,070 (2000); Median household income: $31,250 (2000); Poverty rate: 2.1% (2000).

Taxes: Total city taxes per capita: $50 (1997); City property taxes per capita: $50 (1997).

Education: High school graduation rate: 86.6% (2000); College graduation rate: 5.6% (2000).

Housing: Homeownership rate: 97.6% (2000); Median home value: $36,600 (2000); Median age of housing: 60 years (2000).

Transportation: Commute to work: 91.8% car, 0.0% public transportation, 5.5% walk, 2.7% work from home (2000); Travel time to work: 52.1% less than 15 minutes, 33.8% 15 to 30 minutes, 0.0% 30 to 45 minutes, 0.0% 45 to 60 minutes, 14.1% 60 minutes or more (2000)

SAXON (town). Covers a land area of 66.068 square miles and a water area of 0.064 square miles. Located at 46.49° N. Lat.; 90.41° W. Long. Elevation is 1,115 feet.

Population: 350 (2000); Race: 97.4% White, 0.0% Black, 1.7% Asian, 0.0% American Indian and Alaska Native, 0.0% Hispanic of any race, 0.9% two or more races (2000); Density: 5.3 persons per square mile (2000); Age: 23.5% under 18, 17.2% over 64 (2000); Marriage status: 21.3% never married, 65.3% now married, 7.9% widowed, 5.4% divorced (2000); Foreign born: 1.5% (2000); Ancestry (includes multiple ancestries): 19.8% Finnish, 16.0% German, 15.4% Swedish, 12.8% Italian, 8.4% French (except Basque) (2000).

Economy: Trade center in submarginal farm area. Fishing, skiing. Whitecap Mt. Ski Area to South. Employment by occupation: 7.9% management, 12.2% professional, 10.1% services, 29.5% sales, 5.8% farming, 17.3% construction, 17.3% production (2000).

Income: Per capita income: $16,705 (2000); Median household income: $27,212 (2000); Poverty rate: 9.9% (2000).

Taxes: Total city taxes per capita: $120 (1997); City property taxes per capita: $120 (1997).

Education: High school graduation rate: 78.7% (2000); College graduation rate: 6.3% (2000).

Housing: Homeownership rate: 94.4% (2000); Median home value: $45,000 (2000); Median rent: $125 per month (2000); Median age of housing: 32 years (2000).

Transportation: Commute to work: 91.2% car, 0.0% public transportation, 1.5% walk, 7.3% work from home (2000); Travel time to work: 13.4% less than 15 minutes, 57.5% 15 to 30 minutes, 18.1% 30 to 45 minutes, 6.3% 45 to 60 minutes, 4.7% 60 minutes or more (2000)

SHERMAN (town). Covers a land area of 117.944 square miles and a water area of 18.626 square miles. Located at 46.02° N. Lat.; 90.10° W. Long.

Population: 336 (2000); Race: 97.9% White, 0.0% Black, 0.7% Asian, 0.7% American Indian and Alaska Native, 0.0% Hispanic of any race, 0.7% two or more races (2000); Density: 2.8 persons per square mile (2000); Age: 1.7% under 18, 51.2% over 64 (2000); Marriage status: 8.5% never married, 73.6%

now married, 10.9% widowed, 7.0% divorced (2000); Foreign born: 2.1% (2000); Ancestry (includes multiple ancestries): 39.1% German, 13.5% Polish, 13.1% English, 7.3% Norwegian, 7.3% Irish (2000).
Economy: Employment by occupation: 12.8% management, 17.9% professional, 14.1% services, 15.4% sales, 2.6% farming, 14.1% construction, 23.1% production (2000).
Income: Per capita income: $24,336 (2000); Median household income: $34,375 (2000); Poverty rate: 3.5% (2000).
Taxes: Total city taxes per capita: $96 (1997); City property taxes per capita: $92 (1997).
Education: High school graduation rate: 90.7% (2000); College graduation rate: 16.7% (2000).
Housing: Homeownership rate: 94.8% (2000); Median home value: $148,600 (2000); Median rent: $1,125 per month (2000); Median age of housing: 29 years (2000).
Transportation: Commute to work: 79.5% car, 0.0% public transportation, 9.0% walk, 9.0% work from home (2000); Travel time to work: 35.2% less than 15 minutes, 35.2% 15 to 30 minutes, 14.1% 30 to 45 minutes, 7.0% 45 to 60 minutes, 8.5% 60 minutes or more (2000)

UPSON (unincorporated postal area, zip code 54565). Covers a land area of 84.689 square miles and a water area of 0.430 square miles. Located at 46.30° N. Lat.; 90.43° W. Long. Elevation is 1,497 feet.
Population: 50 (2000); Race: 100.0% White, 0.0% Black, 0.0% Asian, 0.0% American Indian and Alaska Native, 0.0% Hispanic of any race, 0.0% two or more races (2000); Density: 0.6 persons per square mile (2000); Age: 13.5% under 18, 43.2% over 64 (2000); Marriage status: 12.5% never married, 50.0% now married, 25.0% widowed, 12.5% divorced (2000); Foreign born: 8.1% (2000); Ancestry (includes multiple ancestries): 37.8% Finnish, 24.3% Italian, 24.3% German, 8.1% Russian, 8.1% Norwegian (2000).
Economy: Employment by occupation: 0.0% management, 0.0% professional, 12.5% services, 37.5% sales, 0.0% farming, 18.8% construction, 31.3% production (2000).
Income: Per capita income: $14,705 (2000); Median household income: $16,250 (2000); Poverty rate: 13.5% (2000).
Education: High school graduation rate: 82.8% (2000); College graduation rate: 0.0% (2000).
Housing: Homeownership rate: 90.5% (2000); Median home value: $22,500 (2000); Median rent: $325 per month (2000); Median age of housing: 44 years (2000).
Transportation: Commute to work: 87.5% car, 0.0% public transportation, 0.0% walk, 12.5% work from home (2000); Travel time to work: 0.0% less than 15 minutes, 50.0% 15 to 30 minutes, 50.0% 30 to 45 minutes, 0.0% 45 to 60 minutes, 0.0% 60 minutes or more (2000)

Jackson County

Located in west central Wisconsin; crossed by the Black, Buffalo, and Trempealeau Rivers. Covers a land area of 987.30 square miles, a water area of 12.80 square miles, and is located in the Central Time Zone. The county government was organized in 1853. County seat is Black River Falls.

Weather Station: Mather 3 NW — Elevation: 967 feet

	Jan	Feb	Mar	Apr	May	Jun	Jul	Aug	Sep	Oct	Nov	Dec
High	23	29	40	55	68	77	81	79	70	58	42	28
Low	3	8	20	32	43	53	57	55	46	35	24	10
Precip	1.1	0.8	2.0	3.0	3.6	4.0	4.6	4.6	3.8	2.4	2.4	1.3
Snow	14.0	8.2	8.8	2.1	tr	0.0	0.0	0.0	0.0	0.4	5.5	10.3

High and Low temperatures in degrees Fahrenheit; Precipitation and Snow in inches

Population: 19,100 (2000); Race: 89.4% White, 2.3% Black, 0.5% Asian, 5.7% American Indian and Alaska Native, 1.8% Hispanic of any race, 1.1% two or more races (2000); Density: 19.3 persons per square mile (2000); Age: 24.1% under 18, 15.0% over 64 (2000).
Religion: Five largest groups: 20.9% Evangelical Lutheran Church in America, 8.4% Catholic Church, 6.9% The United Methodist Church, 2.7% Lutheran Church—Missouri Synod, 1.5% Assemblies of God (2000).
Economy: Unemployment rate: 3.9% (11/2002); Total civilian labor force: 11,970 (11/2002); Leading industries: 19.2% manufacturing; 16.1% retail trade; 13.3% construction (2000); Companies that employ more than 1,000 persons: 0 (2000); Companies that employ more than 100 persons: 8 (2000); Farms: 774 totaling 243,923 acres (1997); Minority business ownership rate: 0.0% (1997); Women business ownership rate: 32.3% (1997); Retail sales per capita: $7,075 (1997). Single-family building permits issued: 97 (2001) / 85 (2000); Multi-family building permits issued: 6 (2001) / 4 (2000).
Income: Per capita income: $17,604 (2000); Median household income: $37,015 (2000); Poverty rate: 9.6% (2000); Bankruptcy rate: 3.39% (2001).
Taxes: Total county taxes per capita: $300 (2000); County property taxes per capita: $254 (2000).
Education: High school graduation rate: 79.0% (2000); College graduation rate: 11.3% (2000).
Housing: Homeownership rate: 75.0% (2000); Median home value: $76,800 (2000); Median rent: $321 per month (2000); Median age of housing: 33 years (2000).
Health: Birth rate: 103.1 per 10,000 population (1998); Age adjusted death rate: 87.3 per 10,000 population (1999); Age adjusted cancer mortality rate: 216.7 deaths per 100,000 population (1999). Number of physicians: 8.4 per 10,000 population (1999); Number of hospital beds: 13.1 per 10,000 population (1999).
Elections: 2000 Presidential election results: 52.0% Gore, 43.6% Bush, 3.5% Nader, 0.3% Buchanan
National and State Parks: Black River State Forest; Lowe Creek State Wildlife Area; Meadow Valley State Wildlife Management Area; Trump Lake State Fishery Area; West Taylor State Wildlife Area
Additional Information Contacts
Jackson County Government Offices 715-284-0201
Black River Fls Chamber of Commerce 715-284-4658

Jackson County Communities

ADAMS (town). Covers a land area of 36.005 square miles and a water area of 1.037 square miles. Located at 44.36° N. Lat.; 90.80° W. Long.
Population: 1,208 (2000); Race: 95.6% White, 0.4% Black, 0.1% Asian, 3.7% American Indian and Alaska Native, 0.7% Hispanic of any race, 0.2% two or more races (2000); Density: 33.6 persons per square mile (2000); Age: 22.0% under 18, 16.2% over 64 (2000); Marriage status: 23.1% never married, 62.7% now married, 7.2% widowed, 7.0% divorced (2000); Foreign born: 0.8% (2000); Ancestry (includes multiple ancestries): 37.5% German, 33.5% Norwegian, 11.2% English, 10.6% Irish, 5.6% Polish (2000).
Economy: Employment by occupation: 9.8% management, 17.6% professional, 21.8% services, 22.2% sales, 1.2% farming, 9.5% construction, 17.9% production (2000).
Income: Per capita income: $19,729 (2000); Median household income: $44,191 (2000); Poverty rate: 4.8% (2000).
Taxes: Total city taxes per capita: $151 (1997); City property taxes per capita: $150 (1997).
Education: High school graduation rate: 84.0% (2000); College graduation rate: 12.9% (2000).
Housing: Homeownership rate: 88.1% (2000); Median home value: $91,400 (2000); Median rent: $375 per month (2000); Median age of housing: 30 years (2000).
Transportation: Commute to work: 94.3% car, 0.0% public transportation, 0.9% walk, 3.9% work from home (2000); Travel time to work: 61.9% less than 15 minutes, 21.9% 15 to 30 minutes, 4.2% 30 to 45 minutes, 5.7% 45 to 60 minutes, 6.2% 60 minutes or more (2000)

ALBION (town). Covers a land area of 45.567 square miles and a water area of 0.204 square miles. Located at 44.28° N. Lat.; 90.95° W. Long.
Population: 1,093 (2000); Race: 95.1% White, 0.0% Black, 0.0% Asian, 2.7% American Indian and Alaska Native, 0.2% Hispanic of any race, 2.1% two or more races (2000); Density: 24.0 persons per square mile (2000); Age: 30.6% under 18, 9.0% over 64 (2000); Marriage status: 18.9% never married, 70.5% now married, 3.3% widowed, 7.2% divorced (2000); Foreign born: 1.8% (2000); Ancestry (includes multiple ancestries): 39.7% German, 35.8% Norwegian, 11.5% Irish, 7.9% English, 6.7% Polish (2000).
Economy: Employment by occupation: 11.1% management, 16.9% professional, 20.0% services, 22.1% sales, 1.4% farming, 11.2% construction, 17.2% production (2000).
Income: Per capita income: $18,570 (2000); Median household income: $45,284 (2000); Poverty rate: 8.8% (2000).
Taxes: Total city taxes per capita: $50 (1997); City property taxes per capita: $47 (1997).
Education: High school graduation rate: 84.2% (2000); College graduation rate: 15.5% (2000).
Housing: Homeownership rate: 86.7% (2000); Median home value: $90,500 (2000); Median rent: $419 per month (2000); Median age of housing: 26 years (2000).
Transportation: Commute to work: 90.1% car, 0.7% public transportation, 1.8% walk, 6.7% work from home (2000); Travel time to work: 50.8% less

than 15 minutes, 34.2% 15 to 30 minutes, 7.2% 30 to 45 minutes, 4.0% 45 to 60 minutes, 3.8% 60 minutes or more (2000)

ALMA (town). Covers a land area of 57.939 square miles and a water area of 0.027 square miles. Located at 44.43° N. Lat.; 90.86° W. Long.
Population: 983 (2000); Race: 89.6% White, 1.1% Black, 0.9% Asian, 1.4% American Indian and Alaska Native, 7.6% Hispanic of any race, 0.2% two or more races (2000); Density: 17.0 persons per square mile (2000); Age: 27.4% under 18, 10.2% over 64 (2000); Marriage status: 19.5% never married, 67.3% now married, 5.4% widowed, 7.8% divorced (2000); Foreign born: 6.8% (2000); Ancestry (includes multiple ancestries): 46.5% German, 29.6% Norwegian, 10.8% Other groups, 10.8% Irish, 6.5% English (2000).
Economy: In dairying region; construction; manufactures cheese. Single-family building permits issued: 7 (2001) / 4 (2000); Multi-family building permits issued: 0 (2001) / 0 (2000); Employment by occupation: 15.2% management, 10.9% professional, 16.7% services, 21.1% sales, 6.2% farming, 11.3% construction, 18.7% production (2000).
Income: Per capita income: $15,602 (2000); Median household income: $38,000 (2000); Poverty rate: 8.1% (2000).
Taxes: Total city taxes per capita: $93 (1997); City property taxes per capita: $92 (1997).
Education: High school graduation rate: 81.5% (2000); College graduation rate: 8.4% (2000).
Housing: Homeownership rate: 88.0% (2000); Median home value: $84,200 (2000); Median rent: $460 per month (2000); Median age of housing: 28 years (2000).
Transportation: Commute to work: 78.2% car, 0.6% public transportation, 12.1% walk, 8.1% work from home (2000); Travel time to work: 43.1% less than 15 minutes, 40.1% 15 to 30 minutes, 7.2% 30 to 45 minutes, 3.4% 45 to 60 minutes, 6.2% 60 minutes or more (2000)

ALMA CENTER (village). Covers a land area of 1.008 square miles and a water area of 0 square miles. Located at 44.43° N. Lat.; 90.91° W. Long. Elevation is 680 feet.
Population: 446 (2000); Race: 98.3% White, 0.0% Black, 0.0% Asian, 0.5% American Indian and Alaska Native, 1.2% Hispanic of any race, 0.0% two or more races (2000); Density: 442.5 persons per square mile (2000); Age: 23.3% under 18, 23.6% over 64 (2000); Marriage status: 17.3% never married, 61.7% now married, 12.7% widowed, 8.3% divorced (2000); Foreign born: 1.7% (2000); Ancestry (includes multiple ancestries): 49.9% German, 30.7% Norwegian, 9.1% Irish, 8.1% English, 7.6% Czech (2000).
Economy: Single-family building permits issued: 1 (2001) / 3 (2000); Multi-family building permits issued: 0 (2001) / 0 (2000); Employment by occupation: 4.0% management, 14.4% professional, 16.3% services, 17.8% sales, 2.5% farming, 12.9% construction, 32.2% production (2000).
Income: Per capita income: $16,142 (2000); Median household income: $27,404 (2000); Poverty rate: 9.8% (2000).
Taxes: Total city taxes per capita: $65 (1997); City property taxes per capita: $56 (1997).
Education: High school graduation rate: 83.9% (2000); College graduation rate: 10.0% (2000).

School District(s)

Alma Center (PK-12)
2000 Enrollment: 622 715-964-8271

Housing: Homeownership rate: 73.7% (2000); Median home value: $66,300 (2000); Median rent: $305 per month (2000); Median age of housing: 60+ years (2000).
Transportation: Commute to work: 95.8% car, 0.0% public transportation, 3.2% walk, 1.1% work from home (2000); Travel time to work: 30.3% less than 15 minutes, 48.4% 15 to 30 minutes, 7.4% 30 to 45 minutes, 5.3% 45 to 60 minutes, 8.5% 60 minutes or more (2000)

BEAR BLUFF (town). Covers a land area of 53.049 square miles and a water area of 3.022 square miles. Located at 44.19° N. Lat.; 90.37° W. Long.
Population: 128 (2000); Race: 100.0% White, 0.0% Black, 0.0% Asian, 0.0% American Indian and Alaska Native, 0.0% Hispanic of any race, 0.0% two or more races (2000); Density: 2.4 persons per square mile (2000); Age: 33.3% under 18, 6.7% over 64 (2000); Marriage status: 20.8% never married, 65.3% now married, 3.0% widowed, 10.9% divorced (2000); Foreign born: 0.0% (2000); Ancestry (includes multiple ancestries): 25.2% United States or American, 21.5% English, 19.3% German, 17.8% Irish, 5.9% Italian (2000).
Economy: Employment by occupation: 20.4% management, 7.4% professional, 14.8% services, 20.4% sales, 9.3% farming, 24.1% construction, 3.7% production (2000).
Income: Per capita income: $26,170 (2000); Median household income: $35,156 (2000); Poverty rate: 21.4% (2000).
Taxes: Total city taxes per capita: $138 (1997); City property taxes per capita: $138 (1997).
Education: High school graduation rate: 72.6% (2000); College graduation rate: 6.0% (2000).
Housing: Homeownership rate: 66.7% (2000); Median rent: $613 per month (2000); Median age of housing: 18 years (2000).
Transportation: Commute to work: 66.7% car, 0.0% public transportation, 7.4% walk, 25.9% work from home (2000); Travel time to work: 52.5% less than 15 minutes, 17.5% 15 to 30 minutes, 20.0% 30 to 45 minutes, 10.0% 45 to 60 minutes, 0.0% 60 minutes or more (2000)

BLACK RIVER FALLS (city). Covers a land area of 3.156 square miles and a water area of 0.096 square miles. Located at 44.29° N. Lat.; 90.84° W. Long. Elevation is 796 feet.
History: A sawmill was built at this location on the Black River in 1819, one of the first mills in Wisconsin. The settlement of Black River Falls grew up around the mill.
Population: 3,618 (2000); Race: 94.1% White, 0.0% Black, 0.4% Asian, 3.7% American Indian and Alaska Native, 0.9% Hispanic of any race, 1.5% two or more races (2000); Density: 1,146.4 persons per square mile (2000); Age: 20.9% under 18, 26.0% over 64 (2000); Marriage status: 21.4% never married, 54.0% now married, 14.0% widowed, 10.6% divorced (2000); Foreign born: 1.5% (2000); Ancestry (includes multiple ancestries): 41.2% German, 32.9% Norwegian, 11.2% Irish, 6.5% English, 4.1% Other groups (2000).
Economy: Single-family building permits issued: 1 (2001) / 4 (2000); Multi-family building permits issued: 2 (2001) / 0 (2000); Employment by occupation: 7.6% management, 18.8% professional, 23.6% services, 22.7% sales, 1.5% farming, 11.1% construction, 14.7% production (2000).
Income: Per capita income: $21,532 (2000); Median household income: $33,555 (2000); Poverty rate: 7.7% (2000).
Taxes: Total city taxes per capita: $210 (1997); City property taxes per capita: $202 (1997).
Education: High school graduation rate: 80.4% (2000); College graduation rate: 17.0% (2000).

School District(s)

Black River Falls (PK-12)
2000 Enrollment: 2,003 715-284-4357

Housing: Homeownership rate: 59.9% (2000); Median home value: $78,500 (2000); Median rent: $323 per month (2000); Median age of housing: 41 years (2000).
Hospitals: Black River Memorial Hospital (51 beds)
Safety: Violent crime rate: 8.0 per 10,000 population; Property crime rate: 333.2 per 10,000 population (2001).
Newspapers: The Black River Shopper (1 x week); Banner Journal (1 x week)
Transportation: Commute to work: 89.3% car, 1.8% public transportation, 3.2% walk, 4.6% work from home (2000); Travel time to work: 71.4% less than 15 minutes, 14.9% 15 to 30 minutes, 4.9% 30 to 45 minutes, 4.9% 45 to 60 minutes, 4.0% 60 minutes or more (2000)
Additional Information Contacts
Black River Fls Chamber of Commerce 715-284-4658

BROCKWAY (town). Covers a land area of 47.690 square miles and a water area of 0.772 square miles. Located at 44.30° N. Lat.; 90.79° W. Long. Elevation is 838 feet.
Population: 2,580 (2000); Race: 63.3% White, 15.0% Black, 1.7% Asian, 17.0% American Indian and Alaska Native, 3.2% Hispanic of any race, 1.9% two or more races (2000); Density: 54.1 persons per square mile (2000); Age: 18.0% under 18, 7.2% over 64 (2000); Marriage status: 14.0% never married, 70.8% now married, 5.8% widowed, 9.3% divorced (2000); Foreign born: 2.2% (2000); Ancestry (includes multiple ancestries): 19.4% Other groups, 17.5% German, 11.9% Norwegian, 4.2% Irish, 3.4% Polish (2000).
Economy: Employment by occupation: 7.1% management, 11.5% professional, 25.2% services, 19.0% sales, 2.2% farming, 11.8% construction, 23.3% production (2000).
Income: Per capita income: $14,709 (2000); Median household income: $34,519 (2000); Poverty rate: 16.9% (2000).
Taxes: Total city taxes per capita: $51 (1997); City property taxes per capita: $31 (1997).
Education: High school graduation rate: 67.4% (2000); College graduation rate: 4.1% (2000).
Housing: Homeownership rate: 59.1% (2000); Median home value: $81,400 (2000); Median rent: $350 per month (2000); Median age of housing: 21 years (2000).

Transportation: Commute to work: 91.2% car, 0.7% public transportation, 3.3% walk, 2.8% work from home (2000); Travel time to work: 67.7% less than 15 minutes, 18.5% 15 to 30 minutes, 6.0% 30 to 45 minutes, 3.0% 45 to 60 minutes, 4.8% 60 minutes or more (2000)

CITY POINT (town). Covers a land area of 89.096 square miles and a water area of 1.136 square miles. Located at 44.36° N. Lat.; 90.40° W. Long. Elevation is 965 feet.
Population: 189 (2000); Race: 97.7% White, 1.1% Black, 0.0% Asian, 0.0% American Indian and Alaska Native, 0.0% Hispanic of any race, 1.1% two or more races (2000); Density: 2.1 persons per square mile (2000); Age: 17.7% under 18, 26.3% over 64 (2000); Marriage status: 22.5% never married, 59.6% now married, 10.6% widowed, 7.3% divorced (2000); Foreign born: 0.0% (2000); Ancestry (includes multiple ancestries): 40.0% German, 34.9% Polish, 17.1% Norwegian, 9.7% Irish, 6.9% English (2000).
Economy: Employment by occupation: 14.5% management, 11.6% professional, 2.9% services, 34.8% sales, 0.0% farming, 13.0% construction, 23.2% production (2000).
Income: Per capita income: $16,911 (2000); Median household income: $33,750 (2000); Poverty rate: 6.9% (2000).
Taxes: Total city taxes per capita: $404 (1997); City property taxes per capita: $399 (1997).
Education: High school graduation rate: 63.2% (2000); College graduation rate: 13.5% (2000).
Housing: Homeownership rate: 79.2% (2000); Median home value: $86,300 (2000); Median rent: $275 per month (2000); Median age of housing: 19 years (2000).
Transportation: Commute to work: 97.0% car, 0.0% public transportation, 3.0% walk, 0.0% work from home (2000); Travel time to work: 30.3% less than 15 minutes, 6.1% 15 to 30 minutes, 36.4% 30 to 45 minutes, 16.7% 45 to 60 minutes, 10.6% 60 minutes or more (2000)

CLEVELAND (town). Covers a land area of 35.864 square miles and a water area of 0 square miles. Located at 44.57° N. Lat.; 90.97° W. Long.
Population: 438 (2000); Race: 94.9% White, 0.0% Black, 0.0% Asian, 3.0% American Indian and Alaska Native, 1.2% Hispanic of any race, 0.9% two or more races (2000); Density: 12.2 persons per square mile (2000); Age: 26.9% under 18, 16.0% over 64 (2000); Marriage status: 21.5% never married, 59.9% now married, 9.1% widowed, 9.4% divorced (2000); Foreign born: 2.8% (2000); Ancestry (includes multiple ancestries): 44.0% German, 19.4% Norwegian, 12.5% Irish, 10.6% Polish, 10.0% Other groups (2000).
Economy: Single-family building permits issued: 0 (2001) / 3 (2000); Multi-family building permits issued: 0 (2001) / 0 (2000); Employment by occupation: 15.8% management, 12.3% professional, 16.7% services, 23.2% sales, 3.9% farming, 6.6% construction, 21.5% production (2000).
Income: Per capita income: $18,767 (2000); Median household income: $43,125 (2000); Poverty rate: 5.4% (2000).
Taxes: Total city taxes per capita: $90 (1997); City property taxes per capita: $88 (1997).
Education: High school graduation rate: 76.9% (2000); College graduation rate: 15.0% (2000).
Housing: Homeownership rate: 81.5% (2000); Median home value: $69,500 (2000); Median rent: $263 per month (2000); Median age of housing: 38 years (2000).
Transportation: Commute to work: 81.5% car, 0.0% public transportation, 0.0% walk, 18.5% work from home (2000); Travel time to work: 15.9% less than 15 minutes, 26.1% 15 to 30 minutes, 33.0% 30 to 45 minutes, 12.5% 45 to 60 minutes, 12.5% 60 minutes or more (2000)

CURRAN (town). Covers a land area of 36.207 square miles and a water area of 0 square miles. Located at 44.38° N. Lat.; 91.08° W. Long.
Population: 366 (2000); Race: 100.0% White, 0.0% Black, 0.0% Asian, 0.0% American Indian and Alaska Native, 0.0% Hispanic of any race, 0.0% two or more races (2000); Density: 10.1 persons per square mile (2000); Age: 29.3% under 18, 9.5% over 64 (2000); Marriage status: 22.6% never married, 68.6% now married, 2.9% widowed, 5.8% divorced (2000); Foreign born: 0.0% (2000); Ancestry (includes multiple ancestries): 49.2% Norwegian, 24.0% German, 7.5% Swedish, 4.5% United States or American, 3.9% Danish (2000).
Economy: Employment by occupation: 19.2% management, 14.1% professional, 13.1% services, 17.2% sales, 9.1% farming, 7.1% construction, 20.2% production (2000).
Income: Per capita income: $16,119 (2000); Median household income: $41,750 (2000); Poverty rate: 8.9% (2000).
Taxes: Total city taxes per capita: $186 (1997); City property taxes per capita: $186 (1997).
Education: High school graduation rate: 83.0% (2000); College graduation rate: 19.1% (2000).
Housing: Homeownership rate: 75.0% (2000); Median home value: $70,800 (2000); Median rent: $333 per month (2000); Median age of housing: 60+ years (2000).
Transportation: Commute to work: 77.7% car, 3.1% public transportation, 2.1% walk, 17.1% work from home (2000); Travel time to work: 26.9% less than 15 minutes, 45.0% 15 to 30 minutes, 18.8% 30 to 45 minutes, 5.0% 45 to 60 minutes, 4.4% 60 minutes or more (2000)

FRANKLIN (town). Covers a land area of 36.612 square miles and a water area of 0 square miles. Located at 44.21° N. Lat.; 91.08° W. Long. Elevation is 890 feet.
Population: 325 (2000); Race: 100.0% White, 0.0% Black, 0.0% Asian, 0.0% American Indian and Alaska Native, 0.0% Hispanic of any race, 0.0% two or more races (2000); Density: 8.9 persons per square mile (2000); Age: 23.7% under 18, 11.6% over 64 (2000); Marriage status: 29.8% never married, 55.0% now married, 4.3% widowed, 10.9% divorced (2000); Foreign born: 0.5% (2000); Ancestry (includes multiple ancestries): 60.9% Norwegian, 35.6% German, 10.6% Irish, 5.8% Italian, 5.1% Polish (2000).
Economy: Employment by occupation: 16.7% management, 6.4% professional, 14.8% services, 20.7% sales, 10.8% farming, 5.9% construction, 24.6% production (2000).
Income: Per capita income: $18,891 (2000); Median household income: $41,250 (2000); Poverty rate: 12.6% (2000).
Taxes: Total city taxes per capita: $101 (1997); City property taxes per capita: $101 (1997).
Education: High school graduation rate: 77.4% (2000); College graduation rate: 11.7% (2000).
Housing: Homeownership rate: 91.8% (2000); Median home value: $86,300 (2000); Median rent: $275 per month (2000); Median age of housing: 39 years (2000).
Transportation: Commute to work: 87.7% car, 0.0% public transportation, 0.0% walk, 9.9% work from home (2000); Travel time to work: 9.3% less than 15 minutes, 44.3% 15 to 30 minutes, 30.1% 30 to 45 minutes, 10.4% 45 to 60 minutes, 6.0% 60 minutes or more (2000)

GARDEN VALLEY (town). Covers a land area of 36.206 square miles and a water area of 0 square miles. Located at 44.46° N. Lat.; 90.97° W. Long.
Population: 406 (2000); Race: 100.0% White, 0.0% Black, 0.0% Asian, 0.0% American Indian and Alaska Native, 5.6% Hispanic of any race, 0.0% two or more races (2000); Density: 11.2 persons per square mile (2000); Age: 32.1% under 18, 7.0% over 64 (2000); Marriage status: 28.6% never married, 64.9% now married, 2.8% widowed, 3.7% divorced (2000); Foreign born: 5.9% (2000); Ancestry (includes multiple ancestries): 40.4% German, 26.4% Norwegian, 9.5% United States or American, 7.2% Irish, 7.0% English (2000).
Economy: Employment by occupation: 17.5% management, 10.9% professional, 18.3% services, 18.8% sales, 5.7% farming, 8.7% construction, 20.1% production (2000).
Income: Per capita income: $18,191 (2000); Median household income: $40,417 (2000); Poverty rate: 9.0% (2000).
Taxes: Total city taxes per capita: $171 (1997); City property taxes per capita: $171 (1997).
Education: High school graduation rate: 90.4% (2000); College graduation rate: 12.6% (2000).
Housing: Homeownership rate: 85.8% (2000); Median home value: $65,000 (2000); Median rent: $275 per month (2000); Median age of housing: 60+ years (2000).
Transportation: Commute to work: 79.6% car, 0.0% public transportation, 2.2% walk, 15.1% work from home (2000); Travel time to work: 26.2% less than 15 minutes, 37.2% 15 to 30 minutes, 26.2% 30 to 45 minutes, 3.1% 45 to 60 minutes, 7.3% 60 minutes or more (2000)

GARFIELD (town). Covers a land area of 35.954 square miles and a water area of 0.009 square miles. Located at 44.55° N. Lat.; 91.11° W. Long.
Population: 529 (2000); Race: 90.0% White, 0.0% Black, 0.9% Asian, 2.4% American Indian and Alaska Native, 6.3% Hispanic of any race, 0.0% two or more races (2000); Density: 14.7 persons per square mile (2000); Age: 27.6% under 18, 6.5% over 64 (2000); Marriage status: 23.6% never married, 65.5% now married, 2.2% widowed, 8.7% divorced (2000); Foreign born: 7.2% (2000); Ancestry (includes multiple ancestries): 38.0% Norwegian, 34.5% German, 10.2% Other groups, 6.9% United States or American, 5.8% Polish (2000).

Economy: Single-family building permits issued: 4 (2001) / 4 (2000); Multi-family building permits issued: 0 (2001) / 0 (2000); Employment by occupation: 7.0% management, 12.2% professional, 23.2% services, 25.0% sales, 4.9% farming, 8.2% construction, 19.5% production (2000).
Income: Per capita income: $16,869 (2000); Median household income: $43,125 (2000); Poverty rate: 9.9% (2000).
Taxes: Total city taxes per capita: $113 (1997); City property taxes per capita: $111 (1997).
Education: High school graduation rate: 73.8% (2000); College graduation rate: 14.7% (2000).
Housing: Homeownership rate: 85.8% (2000); Median home value: $98,800 (2000); Median rent: $263 per month (2000); Median age of housing: 25 years (2000).
Transportation: Commute to work: 81.9% car, 0.0% public transportation, 1.5% walk, 6.7% work from home (2000); Travel time to work: 22.4% less than 15 minutes, 37.5% 15 to 30 minutes, 27.6% 30 to 45 minutes, 8.9% 45 to 60 minutes, 3.6% 60 minutes or more (2000)

HIXTON (village). Covers a land area of 1.071 square miles and a water area of 0 square miles. Located at 44.38° N. Lat.; 91.01° W. Long. Elevation is 930 feet.
Population: 446 (2000); Race: 97.9% White, 0.0% Black, 0.0% Asian, 2.1% American Indian and Alaska Native, 0.0% Hispanic of any race, 0.0% two or more races (2000); Density: 416.4 persons per square mile (2000); Age: 21.4% under 18, 23.7% over 64 (2000); Marriage status: 21.1% never married, 62.1% now married, 10.4% widowed, 6.4% divorced (2000); Foreign born: 0.0% (2000); Ancestry (includes multiple ancestries): 40.6% German, 38.5% Norwegian, 7.8% Irish, 6.9% English, 6.5% Other groups (2000).
Economy: Single-family building permits issued: 0 (2001) / 0 (2000); Multi-family building permits issued: 0 (2001) / 0 (2000); Employment by occupation: 7.7% management, 9.0% professional, 21.2% services, 19.8% sales, 1.8% farming, 7.7% construction, 32.9% production (2000).
Income: Per capita income: $16,314 (2000); Median household income: $28,839 (2000); Poverty rate: 8.3% (2000).
Taxes: Total city taxes per capita: $64 (1997); City property taxes per capita: $55 (1997).
Education: High school graduation rate: 72.4% (2000); College graduation rate: 5.8% (2000).
Housing: Homeownership rate: 70.1% (2000); Median home value: $66,500 (2000); Median rent: $320 per month (2000); Median age of housing: 38 years (2000).
Transportation: Commute to work: 86.0% car, 0.0% public transportation, 9.3% walk, 2.3% work from home (2000); Travel time to work: 32.1% less than 15 minutes, 48.8% 15 to 30 minutes, 8.6% 30 to 45 minutes, 8.6% 45 to 60 minutes, 1.9% 60 minutes or more (2000)

HIXTON (town). Covers a land area of 34.888 square miles and a water area of 0.024 square miles. Located at 44.38° N. Lat.; 90.99° W. Long. Elevation is 930 feet.
Population: 611 (2000); Race: 93.5% White, 0.0% Black, 0.0% Asian, 2.5% American Indian and Alaska Native, 0.7% Hispanic of any race, 3.5% two or more races (2000); Density: 17.5 persons per square mile (2000); Age: 28.5% under 18, 10.1% over 64 (2000); Marriage status: 23.1% never married, 62.7% now married, 2.7% widowed, 11.5% divorced (2000); Foreign born: 0.5% (2000); Ancestry (includes multiple ancestries): 35.4% Norwegian, 32.8% German, 11.6% Irish, 6.3% Other groups, 5.5% English (2000).
Economy: In dairying region. Timber. Single-family building permits issued: 5 (2001) / 3 (2000); Multi-family building permits issued: 0 (2001) / 0 (2000); Employment by occupation: 13.0% management, 6.9% professional, 17.5% services, 17.5% sales, 7.9% farming, 13.0% construction, 24.2% production (2000).
Income: Per capita income: $15,866 (2000); Median household income: $38,056 (2000); Poverty rate: 6.3% (2000).
Taxes: Total city taxes per capita: $128 (1997); City property taxes per capita: $128 (1997).
Education: High school graduation rate: 78.1% (2000); College graduation rate: 5.9% (2000).
Housing: Homeownership rate: 83.9% (2000); Median home value: $91,500 (2000); Median rent: $325 per month (2000); Median age of housing: 26 years (2000).
Transportation: Commute to work: 88.1% car, 1.5% public transportation, 1.8% walk, 7.5% work from home (2000); Travel time to work: 24.5% less than 15 minutes, 54.5% 15 to 30 minutes, 12.3% 30 to 45 minutes, 2.9% 45 to 60 minutes, 5.8% 60 minutes or more (2000)

IRVING (town). Covers a land area of 43.896 square miles and a water area of 0.519 square miles. Located at 44.19° N. Lat.; 90.96° W. Long. Elevation is 745 feet.
Population: 602 (2000); Race: 97.9% White, 0.0% Black, 0.0% Asian, 1.7% American Indian and Alaska Native, 0.0% Hispanic of any race, 0.3% two or more races (2000); Density: 13.7 persons per square mile (2000); Age: 26.3% under 18, 11.8% over 64 (2000); Marriage status: 21.7% never married, 62.2% now married, 4.2% widowed, 11.9% divorced (2000); Foreign born: 0.7% (2000); Ancestry (includes multiple ancestries): 42.5% German, 41.6% Norwegian, 12.9% Irish, 6.6% Polish, 5.6% Other groups (2000).
Economy: Employment by occupation: 21.2% management, 13.3% professional, 7.6% services, 19.0% sales, 8.5% farming, 12.0% construction, 18.4% production (2000).
Income: Per capita income: $15,287 (2000); Median household income: $37,625 (2000); Poverty rate: 12.9% (2000).
Taxes: Total city taxes per capita: $201 (1997); City property taxes per capita: $201 (1997).
Education: High school graduation rate: 84.7% (2000); College graduation rate: 9.5% (2000).
Housing: Homeownership rate: 77.8% (2000); Median home value: $90,000 (2000); Median rent: $269 per month (2000); Median age of housing: 44 years (2000).
Transportation: Commute to work: 85.6% car, 0.0% public transportation, 0.6% walk, 12.5% work from home (2000); Travel time to work: 24.8% less than 15 minutes, 49.3% 15 to 30 minutes, 8.8% 30 to 45 minutes, 11.7% 45 to 60 minutes, 5.5% 60 minutes or more (2000)

KNAPP (town). Covers a land area of 69.128 square miles and a water area of 2.420 square miles. Located at 44.22° N. Lat.; 90.50° W. Long.
Population: 275 (2000); Race: 98.3% White, 0.0% Black, 0.0% Asian, 0.0% American Indian and Alaska Native, 0.0% Hispanic of any race, 1.7% two or more races (2000); Density: 4.0 persons per square mile (2000); Age: 21.2% under 18, 12.9% over 64 (2000); Marriage status: 21.9% never married, 69.7% now married, 2.0% widowed, 6.4% divorced (2000); Foreign born: 0.7% (2000); Ancestry (includes multiple ancestries): 42.7% German, 14.2% Irish, 13.9% Norwegian, 10.3% English, 5.0% Swedish (2000).
Economy: Employment by occupation: 7.5% management, 6.0% professional, 16.4% services, 9.7% sales, 18.7% farming, 6.0% construction, 35.8% production (2000).
Income: Per capita income: $19,212 (2000); Median household income: $40,446 (2000); Poverty rate: 7.0% (2000).
Taxes: Total city taxes per capita: $61 (1997); City property taxes per capita: $61 (1997).
Education: High school graduation rate: 79.9% (2000); College graduation rate: 8.1% (2000).
Housing: Homeownership rate: 79.3% (2000); Median home value: $80,600 (2000); Median rent: $275 per month (2000); Median age of housing: 23 years (2000).
Transportation: Commute to work: 90.1% car, 1.5% public transportation, 3.1% walk, 5.3% work from home (2000); Travel time to work: 37.9% less than 15 minutes, 21.8% 15 to 30 minutes, 25.0% 30 to 45 minutes, 11.3% 45 to 60 minutes, 4.0% 60 minutes or more (2000)

KOMENSKY (town). Covers a land area of 58.938 square miles and a water area of 0.541 square miles. Located at 44.36° N. Lat.; 90.70° W. Long.
Population: 462 (2000); Race: 24.1% White, 8.7% Black, 3.2% Asian, 58.2% American Indian and Alaska Native, 6.8% Hispanic of any race, 2.3% two or more races (2000); Density: 7.8 persons per square mile (2000); Age: 29.6% under 18, 4.1% over 64 (2000); Marriage status: 34.5% never married, 56.8% now married, 2.3% widowed, 6.5% divorced (2000); Foreign born: 2.3% (2000); Ancestry (includes multiple ancestries): 64.0% Other groups, 8.7% German, 4.5% Norwegian, 4.3% Danish, 3.2% Irish (2000).
Economy: Employment by occupation: 11.3% management, 10.5% professional, 19.4% services, 35.5% sales, 1.6% farming, 9.7% construction, 12.1% production (2000).
Income: Per capita income: $10,062 (2000); Median household income: $37,188 (2000); Poverty rate: 18.9% (2000).
Education: High school graduation rate: 78.4% (2000); College graduation rate: 6.5% (2000).
Housing: Homeownership rate: 66.0% (2000); Median home value: $65,000 (2000); Median rent: $182 per month (2000); Median age of housing: 22 years (2000).
Transportation: Commute to work: 86.7% car, 0.0% public transportation, 0.0% walk, 1.7% work from home (2000); Travel time to work: 72.0% less

than 15 minutes, 25.4% 15 to 30 minutes, 0.0% 30 to 45 minutes, 0.0% 45 to 60 minutes, 2.5% 60 minutes or more (2000)

MANCHESTER (town). Covers a land area of 64.246 square miles and a water area of 0.187 square miles. Located at 44.20° N. Lat.; 90.78° W. Long.

Population: 680 (2000); Race: 91.5% White, 0.0% Black, 0.0% Asian, 7.7% American Indian and Alaska Native, 1.6% Hispanic of any race, 0.7% two or more races (2000); Density: 10.6 persons per square mile (2000); Age: 24.8% under 18, 11.1% over 64 (2000); Marriage status: 18.7% never married, 66.4% now married, 6.3% widowed, 8.6% divorced (2000); Foreign born: 1.2% (2000); Ancestry (includes multiple ancestries): 41.8% German, 22.2% Norwegian, 12.7% Irish, 11.1% English, 10.1% Other groups (2000).
Economy: Employment by occupation: 10.5% management, 15.5% professional, 14.9% services, 27.5% sales, 5.0% farming, 11.7% construction, 14.9% production (2000).
Income: Per capita income: $18,184 (2000); Median household income: $40,625 (2000); Poverty rate: 5.0% (2000).
Taxes: Total city taxes per capita: $28 (1997); City property taxes per capita: $28 (1997).
Education: High school graduation rate: 81.4% (2000); College graduation rate: 11.4% (2000).
Housing: Homeownership rate: 92.0% (2000); Median home value: $80,000 (2000); Median rent: $238 per month (2000); Median age of housing: 24 years (2000).
Transportation: Commute to work: 97.9% car, 0.0% public transportation, 0.6% walk, 1.5% work from home (2000); Travel time to work: 20.1% less than 15 minutes, 49.2% 15 to 30 minutes, 14.6% 30 to 45 minutes, 9.1% 45 to 60 minutes, 7.0% 60 minutes or more (2000)

MELROSE (village). Covers a land area of 0.789 square miles and a water area of 0.030 square miles. Located at 44.13° N. Lat.; 90.99° W. Long. Elevation is 790 feet.

Population: 529 (2000); Race: 99.4% White, 0.0% Black, 0.2% Asian, 0.0% American Indian and Alaska Native, 0.0% Hispanic of any race, 0.4% two or more races (2000); Density: 670.1 persons per square mile (2000); Age: 24.1% under 18, 25.1% over 64 (2000); Marriage status: 19.3% never married, 58.2% now married, 15.8% widowed, 6.7% divorced (2000); Foreign born: 0.6% (2000); Ancestry (includes multiple ancestries): 49.2% German, 38.8% Norwegian, 16.7% Irish, 8.6% English, 4.9% French (except Basque) (2000).
Economy: Single-family building permits issued: 1 (2001) / 1 (2000); Multi-family building permits issued: 0 (2001) / 0 (2000); Employment by occupation: 6.0% management, 15.1% professional, 18.1% services, 23.0% sales, 1.1% farming, 15.1% construction, 21.5% production (2000).
Income: Per capita income: $18,765 (2000); Median household income: $37,955 (2000); Poverty rate: 3.4% (2000).
Taxes: Total city taxes per capita: $77 (1997); City property taxes per capita: $70 (1997).
Education: High school graduation rate: 85.6% (2000); College graduation rate: 11.1% (2000).

School District(s)

Melrose-Mindoro (PK-12)
2000 Enrollment: 729 608-488-2201

Housing: Homeownership rate: 77.7% (2000); Median home value: $66,500 (2000); Median rent: $306 per month (2000); Median age of housing: 57 years (2000).
Newspapers: The Chronicle (1 x week)
Transportation: Commute to work: 78.1% car, 0.8% public transportation, 16.2% walk, 4.9% work from home (2000); Travel time to work: 34.5% less than 15 minutes, 19.8% 15 to 30 minutes, 24.2% 30 to 45 minutes, 14.7% 45 to 60 minutes, 6.7% 60 minutes or more (2000)

MELROSE (town). Covers a land area of 26.869 square miles and a water area of 0.650 square miles. Located at 44.11° N. Lat.; 91.00° W. Long. Elevation is 790 feet.

Population: 402 (2000); Race: 99.5% White, 0.0% Black, 0.0% Asian, 0.0% American Indian and Alaska Native, 0.0% Hispanic of any race, 0.5% two or more races (2000); Density: 15.0 persons per square mile (2000); Age: 29.3% under 18, 10.7% over 64 (2000); Marriage status: 18.1% never married, 69.9% now married, 1.3% widowed, 10.7% divorced (2000); Foreign born: 0.0% (2000); Ancestry (includes multiple ancestries): 59.0% German, 42.4% Norwegian, 7.9% Italian, 5.5% English, 5.0% Irish (2000).
Economy: Creamery; feeds. Single-family building permits issued: 5 (2001) / 3 (2000); Multi-family building permits issued: 0 (2001) / 0 (2000); Employment by occupation: 33.8% management, 10.6% professional, 11.1% services, 14.4% sales, 8.3% farming, 9.3% construction, 12.5% production (2000).
Income: Per capita income: $16,861 (2000); Median household income: $34,375 (2000); Poverty rate: 12.7% (2000).
Taxes: Total city taxes per capita: $157 (1997); City property taxes per capita: $154 (1997).
Education: High school graduation rate: 88.3% (2000); College graduation rate: 11.0% (2000).
Housing: Homeownership rate: 82.9% (2000); Median home value: $86,300 (2000); Median rent: $300 per month (2000); Median age of housing: 30 years (2000).
Transportation: Commute to work: 59.4% car, 0.0% public transportation, 2.8% walk, 35.4% work from home (2000); Travel time to work: 27.0% less than 15 minutes, 15.3% 15 to 30 minutes, 39.4% 30 to 45 minutes, 10.2% 45 to 60 minutes, 8.0% 60 minutes or more (2000)

MERRILLAN (village). Covers a land area of 1.260 square miles and a water area of 0.070 square miles. Located at 44.45° N. Lat.; 90.83° W. Long. Elevation is 937 feet.

Population: 585 (2000); Race: 92.4% White, 0.0% Black, 0.3% Asian, 4.3% American Indian and Alaska Native, 2.6% Hispanic of any race, 0.7% two or more races (2000); Density: 464.2 persons per square mile (2000); Age: 22.2% under 18, 18.9% over 64 (2000); Marriage status: 24.4% never married, 50.8% now married, 9.5% widowed, 15.3% divorced (2000); Foreign born: 3.3% (2000); Ancestry (includes multiple ancestries): 39.7% German, 14.7% Norwegian, 11.1% English, 9.8% Other groups, 9.1% Irish (2000).
Economy: Railroad junction. In dairying region. Bruce Mound Ski Area to East. Single-family building permits issued: 1 (2001) / 1 (2000); Multi-family building permits issued: 4 (2001) / 4 (2000); Employment by occupation: 5.7% management, 12.5% professional, 21.6% services, 26.1% sales, 0.0% farming, 9.8% construction, 24.2% production (2000).
Income: Per capita income: $18,811 (2000); Median household income: $28,917 (2000); Poverty rate: 13.7% (2000).
Taxes: Total city taxes per capita: $27 (1997); City property taxes per capita: $19 (1997).
Education: High school graduation rate: 78.7% (2000); College graduation rate: 12.1% (2000).
Housing: Homeownership rate: 70.8% (2000); Median home value: $59,500 (2000); Median rent: $252 per month (2000); Median age of housing: 50 years (2000).
Transportation: Commute to work: 90.4% car, 0.0% public transportation, 1.5% walk, 5.4% work from home (2000); Travel time to work: 13.8% less than 15 minutes, 60.7% 15 to 30 minutes, 12.6% 30 to 45 minutes, 7.7% 45 to 60 minutes, 5.3% 60 minutes or more (2000)

MILLSTON (town). Covers a land area of 70.939 square miles and a water area of 1.465 square miles. Located at 44.20° N. Lat.; 90.63° W. Long. Elevation is 920 feet.

Population: 136 (2000); Race: 93.9% White, 0.0% Black, 0.0% Asian, 6.1% American Indian and Alaska Native, 0.0% Hispanic of any race, 0.0% two or more races (2000); Density: 1.9 persons per square mile (2000); Age: 25.9% under 18, 27.9% over 64 (2000); Marriage status: 13.9% never married, 55.7% now married, 12.2% widowed, 18.3% divorced (2000); Foreign born: 0.0% (2000); Ancestry (includes multiple ancestries): 40.8% German, 26.5% Norwegian, 15.0% United States or American, 9.5% Irish, 6.1% Other groups (2000).
Economy: Employment by occupation: 12.5% management, 4.2% professional, 35.4% services, 6.3% sales, 6.3% farming, 6.3% construction, 29.2% production (2000).
Income: Per capita income: $18,914 (2000); Median household income: $27,500 (2000); Poverty rate: 0.0% (2000).
Education: High school graduation rate: 71.0% (2000); College graduation rate: 4.7% (2000).
Housing: Homeownership rate: 76.9% (2000); Median home value: $67,500 (2000); Median rent: $405 per month (2000); Median age of housing: 32 years (2000).
Transportation: Commute to work: 56.3% car, 0.0% public transportation, 39.6% walk, 4.2% work from home (2000); Travel time to work: 41.3% less than 15 minutes, 34.8% 15 to 30 minutes, 23.9% 30 to 45 minutes, 0.0% 45 to 60 minutes, 0.0% 60 minutes or more (2000)

NORTH BEND (town). Covers a land area of 27.785 square miles and a water area of 0.519 square miles. Located at 44.11° N. Lat.; 91.11° W. Long. Elevation is 720 feet.

Population: 397 (2000); Race: 100.0% White, 0.0% Black, 0.0% Asian, 0.0% American Indian and Alaska Native, 0.6% Hispanic of any race, 0.0% two or more races (2000); Density: 14.3 persons per square mile (2000); Age: 20.9% under 18, 12.1% over 64 (2000); Marriage status: 20.9% never married, 61.8% now married, 5.6% widowed, 11.6% divorced (2000); Foreign born: 1.1% (2000); Ancestry (includes multiple ancestries): 49.6% German, 35.5% Norwegian, 13.8% Irish, 8.3% Polish, 7.4% Scottish (2000).
Economy: Single-family building permits issued: 2 (2001) / 2 (2000); Multi-family building permits issued: 0 (2001) / 0 (2000); Employment by occupation: 7.9% management, 14.3% professional, 14.3% services, 22.7% sales, 2.0% farming, 17.7% construction, 21.2% production (2000).
Income: Per capita income: $19,341 (2000); Median household income: $39,018 (2000); Poverty rate: 3.0% (2000).
Taxes: Total city taxes per capita: $100 (1997); City property taxes per capita: $95 (1997).
Education: High school graduation rate: 86.2% (2000); College graduation rate: 17.6% (2000).
Housing: Homeownership rate: 84.7% (2000); Median home value: $81,700 (2000); Median rent: $342 per month (2000); Median age of housing: 60+ years (2000).
Transportation: Commute to work: 90.0% car, 0.0% public transportation, 4.0% walk, 6.0% work from home (2000); Travel time to work: 17.0% less than 15 minutes, 17.0% 15 to 30 minutes, 52.1% 30 to 45 minutes, 6.4% 45 to 60 minutes, 7.4% 60 minutes or more (2000)

NORTHFIELD (town). Covers a land area of 35.953 square miles and a water area of 0.042 square miles. Located at 44.46° N. Lat.; 91.10° W. Long. Elevation is 950 feet.
Population: 586 (2000); Race: 100.0% White, 0.0% Black, 0.0% Asian, 0.0% American Indian and Alaska Native, 0.0% Hispanic of any race, 0.0% two or more races (2000); Density: 16.3 persons per square mile (2000); Age: 16.8% under 18, 22.5% over 64 (2000); Marriage status: 20.7% never married, 68.8% now married, 4.6% widowed, 6.0% divorced (2000); Foreign born: 1.2% (2000); Ancestry (includes multiple ancestries): 54.8% Norwegian, 28.5% German, 7.2% Polish, 7.0% English, 6.5% Irish (2000).
Economy: Employment by occupation: 16.9% management, 7.2% professional, 15.9% services, 18.3% sales, 6.9% farming, 13.1% construction, 21.7% production (2000).
Income: Per capita income: $15,356 (2000); Median household income: $35,250 (2000); Poverty rate: 10.0% (2000).
Taxes: Total city taxes per capita: $69 (1997); City property taxes per capita: $68 (1997).
Education: High school graduation rate: 76.7% (2000); College graduation rate: 7.7% (2000).
Housing: Homeownership rate: 91.5% (2000); Median home value: $55,000 (2000); Median rent: $313 per month (2000); Median age of housing: 60+ years (2000).
Transportation: Commute to work: 83.2% car, 2.5% public transportation, 0.7% walk, 13.7% work from home (2000); Travel time to work: 20.3% less than 15 minutes, 48.4% 15 to 30 minutes, 18.3% 30 to 45 minutes, 2.4% 45 to 60 minutes, 10.6% 60 minutes or more (2000)

SPRINGFIELD (town). Covers a land area of 36.477 square miles and a water area of 0.020 square miles. Located at 44.28° N. Lat.; 91.10° W. Long.
Population: 567 (2000); Race: 95.7% White, 0.0% Black, 0.0% Asian, 2.8% American Indian and Alaska Native, 0.0% Hispanic of any race, 1.5% two or more races (2000); Density: 15.5 persons per square mile (2000); Age: 34.8% under 18, 9.3% over 64 (2000); Marriage status: 20.1% never married, 68.9% now married, 3.6% widowed, 7.5% divorced (2000); Foreign born: 2.0% (2000); Ancestry (includes multiple ancestries): 31.9% Norwegian, 26.9% German, 15.4% Polish, 8.1% Irish, 6.9% English (2000).
Economy: Employment by occupation: 16.8% management, 6.6% professional, 15.6% services, 18.0% sales, 6.6% farming, 12.5% construction, 23.8% production (2000).
Income: Per capita income: $16,075 (2000); Median household income: $40,179 (2000); Poverty rate: 9.5% (2000).
Taxes: Total city taxes per capita: $141 (1997); City property taxes per capita: $141 (1997).
Education: High school graduation rate: 84.3% (2000); College graduation rate: 9.2% (2000).
Housing: Homeownership rate: 90.1% (2000); Median home value: $81,000 (2000); Median rent: $375 per month (2000); Median age of housing: 60+ years (2000).
Transportation: Commute to work: 83.4% car, 0.0% public transportation, 2.8% walk, 13.0% work from home (2000); Travel time to work: 28.6% less than 15 minutes, 40.0% 15 to 30 minutes, 17.3% 30 to 45 minutes, 7.7% 45 to 60 minutes, 6.4% 60 minutes or more (2000)

TAYLOR (village). Covers a land area of 0.726 square miles and a water area of 0 square miles. Located at 44.32° N. Lat.; 91.12° W. Long. Elevation is 890 feet.
Population: 513 (2000); Race: 98.0% White, 0.0% Black, 0.0% Asian, 0.8% American Indian and Alaska Native, 1.2% Hispanic of any race, 1.2% two or more races (2000); Density: 706.6 persons per square mile (2000); Age: 32.3% under 18, 12.2% over 64 (2000); Marriage status: 20.2% never married, 55.4% now married, 7.5% widowed, 16.9% divorced (2000); Foreign born: 0.0% (2000); Ancestry (includes multiple ancestries): 44.2% Norwegian, 18.3% German, 10.6% Irish, 9.8% Polish, 8.4% English (2000).
Economy: In dairying region. Single-family building permits issued: 1 (2001) / 1 (2000); Multi-family building permits issued: 0 (2001) / 0 (2000); Employment by occupation: 8.4% management, 4.5% professional, 25.2% services, 20.3% sales, 3.0% farming, 7.4% construction, 31.2% production (2000).
Income: Per capita income: $11,091 (2000); Median household income: $25,833 (2000); Poverty rate: 20.5% (2000).
Taxes: Total city taxes per capita: $135 (1997); City property taxes per capita: $116 (1997).
Education: High school graduation rate: 73.0% (2000); College graduation rate: 3.8% (2000).
Housing: Homeownership rate: 58.2% (2000); Median home value: $45,300 (2000); Median rent: $288 per month (2000); Median age of housing: 32 years (2000).
Transportation: Commute to work: 88.4% car, 0.0% public transportation, 9.0% walk, 2.5% work from home (2000); Travel time to work: 26.8% less than 15 minutes, 30.9% 15 to 30 minutes, 28.4% 30 to 45 minutes, 3.1% 45 to 60 minutes, 10.8% 60 minutes or more (2000)

Jefferson County

Located in southern Wisconsin; drained by the Rock, Bark, and Crawfish Rivers. Covers a land area of 557.00 square miles, a water area of 25.70 square miles, and is located in the Central Time Zone. The county government was organized in 1836. County seat is Jefferson.

Weather Station: Fort Atkinson — Elevation: 797 feet

	Jan	Feb	Mar	Apr	May	Jun	Jul	Aug	Sep	Oct	Nov	Dec
High	26	31	43	57	70	80	83	81	73	61	45	32
Low	8	13	25	36	46	56	61	58	50	38	28	15
Precip	1.4	1.3	2.1	3.4	3.2	3.7	4.0	4.0	3.5	2.6	2.5	1.7
Snow	12.4	6.7	5.4	1.9	0.2	0.0	0.0	0.0	0.0	tr	2.8	8.7

High and Low temperatures in degrees Fahrenheit; Precipitation and Snow in inches

Weather Station: Lake Mills — Elevation: 849 feet

	Jan	Feb	Mar	Apr	May	Jun	Jul	Aug	Sep	Oct	Nov	Dec
High	27	32	44	59	72	81	85	82	74	62	45	32
Low	9	14	24	36	47	56	61	59	51	40	28	16
Precip	1.4	1.2	2.3	3.3	3.2	3.9	4.2	4.5	3.7	2.5	2.4	1.7
Snow	10.9	7.3	5.4	2.0	0.1	0.0	0.0	0.0	0.0	tr	3.2	9.8

High and Low temperatures in degrees Fahrenheit; Precipitation and Snow in inches

Weather Station: Watertown — Elevation: 823 feet

	Jan	Feb	Mar	Apr	May	Jun	Jul	Aug	Sep	Oct	Nov	Dec
High	26	31	42	57	70	80	83	81	73	61	44	31
Low	8	14	25	36	47	56	61	59	51	40	29	16
Precip	1.3	1.2	2.1	3.1	3.0	4.2	4.4	4.4	3.8	2.6	2.4	1.7
Snow	12.4	7.4	5.3	1.8	0.2	0.0	0.0	0.0	tr	0.1	2.8	9.0

High and Low temperatures in degrees Fahrenheit; Precipitation and Snow in inches

Weather Station: Whitewater — Elevation: 872 feet

	Jan	Feb	Mar	Apr	May	Jun	Jul	Aug	Sep	Oct	Nov	Dec
High	26	32	44	58	71	80	83	81	74	62	45	32
Low	9	14	25	35	46	55	60	58	50	39	28	16
Precip	1.2	1.1	2.0	3.4	3.2	3.7	4.0	4.5	3.5	2.7	2.5	1.6
Snow	9.7	6.1	4.2	1.3	tr	0.0	0.0	0.0	0.0	tr	1.6	7.6

High and Low temperatures in degrees Fahrenheit; Precipitation and Snow in inches

Population: 74,021 (2000); Race: 96.5% White, 0.3% Black, 0.3% Asian, 0.3% American Indian and Alaska Native, 4.0% Hispanic of any race, 1.2% two or more races (2000); Density: 132.9 persons per square mile (2000); Age: 25.3% under 18, 12.6% over 64 (2000).
Religion: Five largest groups: 29.0% Catholic Church, 22.4% Wisconsin Evangelical Lutheran Synod, 10.6% Evangelical Lutheran Church in

America, 4.1% The United Methodist Church, 2.4% United Church of Christ (2000).
Economy: Unemployment rate: 3.7% (11/2002); Total civilian labor force: 43,489 (11/2002); Leading industries: 37.6% manufacturing; 11.9% retail trade; 10.4% health care and social assistance (2000); Companies that employ more than 1,000 persons: 0 (2000); Companies that employ more than 100 persons: 62 (2000); Farms: 1,240 totaling 242,301 acres (1997); Minority business ownership rate: 0.0% (1997); Women business ownership rate: 22.4% (1997); Retail sales per capita: $7,750 (1997). Single-family building permits issued: 388 (2001) / 406 (2000); Multi-family building permits issued: 176 (2001) / 171 (2000).
Income: Per capita income: $21,236 (2000); Median household income: $46,901 (2000); Poverty rate: 5.7% (2000); Bankruptcy rate: 3.44% (2001).
Taxes: Total county taxes per capita: $225 (2000); County property taxes per capita: $172 (2000).
Education: High school graduation rate: 84.7% (2000); College graduation rate: 17.4% (2000).
Housing: Homeownership rate: 71.7% (2000); Median home value: $123,800 (2000); Median rent: $495 per month (2000); Median age of housing: 37 years (2000).
Health: Birth rate: 120.6 per 10,000 population (1998); Age adjusted death rate: 81.3 per 10,000 population (1999); Age adjusted cancer mortality rate: 202.4 deaths per 100,000 population (1999). Air Quality Index: 68% good, 32% moderate, 0% unhealthy (percent of days in 2000). Number of physicians: 7.8 per 10,000 population (1999); Number of hospital beds: 13.8 per 10,000 population (1999).
Elections: 2000 Presidential election results: 42.1% Gore, 53.2% Bush, 3.8% Nader, 0.4% Buchanan
National and State Parks: Aztalan State Park
Additional Information Contacts
Jefferson County Government Offices 920-674-7101
Fort Atkinson Chamber of Commerce 920-563-3210
Jefferson Chamber of Commerce 920-674-4511
Jefferson County Board of Realtors 920-674-5135
Lake Mills Chamber of Commerce 920-648-3585
Palmyra Area Chamber of Commerce 262-495-2611
Watertown Chamber of Commerce 920-261-6320

Jefferson County Communities

AZTALAN (town). Covers a land area of 24.456 square miles and a water area of 0.622 square miles. Located at 43.05° N. Lat.; 88.83° W. Long. Elevation is 850 feet.
Population: 1,447 (2000); Race: 98.4% White, 0.0% Black, 0.2% Asian, 0.0% American Indian and Alaska Native, 1.4% Hispanic of any race, 0.5% two or more races (2000); Density: 59.2 persons per square mile (2000); Age: 25.4% under 18, 11.9% over 64 (2000); Marriage status: 20.6% never married, 67.9% now married, 5.2% widowed, 6.3% divorced (2000); Foreign born: 0.8% (2000); Ancestry (includes multiple ancestries): 59.5% German, 13.4% Irish, 10.2% Norwegian, 6.0% English, 5.8% United States or American (2000).
Economy: Employment by occupation: 14.1% management, 14.1% professional, 9.8% services, 22.7% sales, 0.6% farming, 14.3% construction, 24.3% production (2000).
Income: Per capita income: $23,193 (2000); Median household income: $55,048 (2000); Poverty rate: 2.2% (2000).
Taxes: Total city taxes per capita: $83 (1997); City property taxes per capita: $76 (1997).
Education: High school graduation rate: 85.5% (2000); College graduation rate: 16.9% (2000).
Housing: Homeownership rate: 89.8% (2000); Median home value: $137,400 (2000); Median rent: $531 per month (2000); Median age of housing: 32 years (2000).
Transportation: Commute to work: 90.4% car, 0.2% public transportation, 1.3% walk, 6.6% work from home (2000); Travel time to work: 42.8% less than 15 minutes, 28.0% 15 to 30 minutes, 19.7% 30 to 45 minutes, 5.8% 45 to 60 minutes, 3.7% 60 minutes or more (2000)

COLD SPRING (town). Covers a land area of 23.451 square miles and a water area of 0.052 square miles. Located at 42.86° N. Lat.; 88.72° W. Long. Elevation is 810 feet.
Population: 766 (2000); Race: 97.9% White, 0.1% Black, 1.1% Asian, 0.9% American Indian and Alaska Native, 2.0% Hispanic of any race, 0.0% two or more races (2000); Density: 32.7 persons per square mile (2000); Age: 24.6% under 18, 7.4% over 64 (2000); Marriage status: 22.5% never married, 65.6% now married, 3.7% widowed, 8.3% divorced (2000); Foreign born: 2.7% (2000); Ancestry (includes multiple ancestries): 49.0% German, 12.8% English, 10.6% Irish, 9.3% Polish, 9.2% United States or American (2000).
Economy: Employment by occupation: 18.5% management, 17.0% professional, 10.5% services, 27.0% sales, 0.9% farming, 6.4% construction, 19.7% production (2000).
Income: Per capita income: $22,335 (2000); Median household income: $60,789 (2000); Poverty rate: 3.8% (2000).
Taxes: Total city taxes per capita: $65 (1997); City property taxes per capita: $64 (1997).
Education: High school graduation rate: 85.4% (2000); College graduation rate: 18.8% (2000).
Housing: Homeownership rate: 85.3% (2000); Median home value: $153,900 (2000); Median rent: $513 per month (2000); Median age of housing: 37 years (2000).
Transportation: Commute to work: 89.1% car, 0.0% public transportation, 3.2% walk, 7.7% work from home (2000); Travel time to work: 54.7% less than 15 minutes, 24.7% 15 to 30 minutes, 9.1% 30 to 45 minutes, 3.7% 45 to 60 minutes, 7.9% 60 minutes or more (2000)

CONCORD (town). Covers a land area of 36.015 square miles and a water area of 0.555 square miles. Located at 43.06° N. Lat.; 88.58° W. Long. Elevation is 852 feet.
Population: 2,023 (2000); Race: 99.4% White, 0.0% Black, 0.0% Asian, 0.0% American Indian and Alaska Native, 0.6% Hispanic of any race, 0.4% two or more races (2000); Density: 56.2 persons per square mile (2000); Age: 24.3% under 18, 11.3% over 64 (2000); Marriage status: 20.3% never married, 65.7% now married, 5.5% widowed, 8.6% divorced (2000); Foreign born: 1.2% (2000); Ancestry (includes multiple ancestries): 62.6% German, 11.8% Irish, 11.7% Polish, 7.2% Norwegian, 6.2% English (2000).
Economy: Employment by occupation: 13.0% management, 13.6% professional, 11.6% services, 24.8% sales, 1.4% farming, 13.6% construction, 21.8% production (2000).
Income: Per capita income: $21,813 (2000); Median household income: $52,885 (2000); Poverty rate: 4.9% (2000).
Taxes: Total city taxes per capita: $50 (1997); City property taxes per capita: $29 (1997).
Education: High school graduation rate: 80.4% (2000); College graduation rate: 12.0% (2000).
Housing: Homeownership rate: 90.8% (2000); Median home value: $160,900 (2000); Median rent: $419 per month (2000); Median age of housing: 26 years (2000).
Transportation: Commute to work: 90.0% car, 0.2% public transportation, 2.1% walk, 6.6% work from home (2000); Travel time to work: 18.1% less than 15 minutes, 44.2% 15 to 30 minutes, 23.8% 30 to 45 minutes, 7.0% 45 to 60 minutes, 6.9% 60 minutes or more (2000)

FARMINGTON (town). Covers a land area of 35.813 square miles and a water area of 0.102 square miles. Located at 43.06° N. Lat.; 88.73° W. Long. Elevation is 872 feet.
Population: 1,498 (2000); Race: 98.0% White, 0.2% Black, 0.6% Asian, 0.0% American Indian and Alaska Native, 1.7% Hispanic of any race, 0.7% two or more races (2000); Density: 41.8 persons per square mile (2000); Age: 25.2% under 18, 10.5% over 64 (2000); Marriage status: 19.7% never married, 69.7% now married, 5.6% widowed, 5.0% divorced (2000); Foreign born: 1.2% (2000); Ancestry (includes multiple ancestries): 60.1% German, 9.4% Irish, 7.5% English, 6.1% Norwegian, 6.0% Polish (2000).
Economy: Employment by occupation: 14.5% management, 12.6% professional, 15.1% services, 18.9% sales, 1.0% farming, 14.1% construction, 23.8% production (2000).
Income: Per capita income: $20,077 (2000); Median household income: $46,875 (2000); Poverty rate: 4.3% (2000).
Taxes: Total city taxes per capita: $32 (1997); City property taxes per capita: $31 (1997).
Education: High school graduation rate: 86.6% (2000); College graduation rate: 15.3% (2000).
Housing: Homeownership rate: 86.2% (2000); Median home value: $149,000 (2000); Median rent: $495 per month (2000); Median age of housing: 48 years (2000).
Transportation: Commute to work: 90.9% car, 0.0% public transportation, 1.1% walk, 7.8% work from home (2000); Travel time to work: 28.8% less than 15 minutes, 39.4% 15 to 30 minutes, 18.8% 30 to 45 minutes, 9.4% 45 to 60 minutes, 3.5% 60 minutes or more (2000)

FORT ATKINSON (city). Covers a land area of 5.393 square miles and a water area of 0.095 square miles. Located at 42.92° N. Lat.; 88.84° W. Long. Elevation is 790 feet.
History: In 1832 General Henry Atkinson set up a stockade with two blockhouses at the confluence of the Rock and Bark Rivers. When Dwight Foster built a house here in 1836, the fort had been demolished, but the community that grew up around it was named Fort Atkinson.
Population: 11,621 (2000); Race: 95.6% White, 0.6% Black, 0.7% Asian, 0.1% American Indian and Alaska Native, 4.5% Hispanic of any race, 1.8% two or more races (2000); Density: 2,154.8 persons per square mile (2000); Age: 24.8% under 18, 14.2% over 64 (2000); Marriage status: 24.4% never married, 58.3% now married, 7.3% widowed, 10.0% divorced (2000); Foreign born: 4.2% (2000); Ancestry (includes multiple ancestries): 50.0% German, 11.1% Irish, 10.0% English, 8.2% Norwegian, 6.7% Other groups (2000).
Vital Statistics: Birth rate: 123.1 per 10,000 population (1998)
Economy: Single-family building permits issued: 19 (2001) / 23 (2000); Multi-family building permits issued: 94 (2001) / 50 (2000); Employment by occupation: 10.0% management, 16.0% professional, 15.0% services, 25.2% sales, 0.6% farming, 7.0% construction, 26.3% production (2000).
Income: Per capita income: $21,008 (2000); Median household income: $43,807 (2000); Poverty rate: 5.3% (2000).
Taxes: Total city taxes per capita: $274 (1997); City property taxes per capita: $261 (1997).
Education: High school graduation rate: 87.1% (2000); College graduation rate: 19.9% (2000).

School District(s)

Fort Atkinson (PK-12)
2000 Enrollment: 2,650 920-563-7807
Housing: Homeownership rate: 63.5% (2000); Median home value: $111,200 (2000); Median rent: $478 per month (2000); Median age of housing: 39 years (2000).
Hospitals: Fort Atkinson Memorial Health Services (82 beds)
Safety: Violent crime rate: 4.3 per 10,000 population; Property crime rate: 374.2 per 10,000 population (2001).
Newspapers: Daily Jefferson County Union (5 x week)
Transportation: Commute to work: 92.4% car, 1.1% public transportation, 3.1% walk, 2.3% work from home (2000); Travel time to work: 58.6% less than 15 minutes, 24.6% 15 to 30 minutes, 8.8% 30 to 45 minutes, 4.8% 45 to 60 minutes, 3.3% 60 minutes or more (2000)
Additional Information Contacts
Fort Atkinson Chamber of Commerce 920-563-3210

HEBRON (town). Covers a land area of 28.845 square miles and a water area of 0.097 square miles. Located at 42.94° N. Lat.; 88.69° W. Long. Elevation is 840 feet.
Population: 1,135 (2000); Race: 97.2% White, 0.0% Black, 0.0% Asian, 0.9% American Indian and Alaska Native, 4.5% Hispanic of any race, 0.3% two or more races (2000); Density: 39.3 persons per square mile (2000); Age: 26.2% under 18, 9.0% over 64 (2000); Marriage status: 25.5% never married, 59.1% now married, 6.2% widowed, 9.3% divorced (2000); Foreign born: 0.8% (2000); Ancestry (includes multiple ancestries): 55.7% German, 9.5% English, 8.9% Irish, 6.3% Norwegian, 5.6% United States or American (2000).
Economy: Employment by occupation: 10.7% management, 12.7% professional, 16.4% services, 19.1% sales, 3.9% farming, 14.0% construction, 23.1% production (2000).
Income: Per capita income: $20,516 (2000); Median household income: $53,929 (2000); Poverty rate: 3.5% (2000).
Taxes: Total city taxes per capita: $68 (1997); City property taxes per capita: $67 (1997).
Education: High school graduation rate: 88.7% (2000); College graduation rate: 15.2% (2000).
Housing: Homeownership rate: 87.1% (2000); Median home value: $123,600 (2000); Median rent: $520 per month (2000); Median age of housing: 51 years (2000).
Transportation: Commute to work: 91.4% car, 0.8% public transportation, 1.8% walk, 6.0% work from home (2000); Travel time to work: 33.3% less than 15 minutes, 44.1% 15 to 30 minutes, 10.4% 30 to 45 minutes, 6.6% 45 to 60 minutes, 5.6% 60 minutes or more (2000)

HELENVILLE (CDP). Covers a land area of 0.517 square miles and a water area of 0 square miles. Located at 43.02° N. Lat.; 88.69° W. Long. Elevation is 845 feet.
Population: 225 (2000); Race: 100.0% White, 0.0% Black, 0.0% Asian, 0.0% American Indian and Alaska Native, 0.0% Hispanic of any race, 0.0% two or more races (2000); Density: 435.2 persons per square mile (2000); Age: 46.2% under 18, 6.5% over 64 (2000); Marriage status: 21.8% never married, 67.7% now married, 1.6% widowed, 8.9% divorced (2000); Foreign born: 0.0% (2000); Ancestry (includes multiple ancestries): 66.8% German, 15.1% English, 9.0% Scotch-Irish, 8.5% Irish, 2.5% Italian (2000).
Economy: Employment by occupation: 11.0% management, 4.1% professional, 11.0% services, 9.6% sales, 0.0% farming, 24.7% construction, 39.7% production (2000).
Income: Per capita income: $14,334 (2000); Median household income: $50,089 (2000); Poverty rate: 4.6% (2000).
Education: High school graduation rate: 85.0% (2000); College graduation rate: 0.0% (2000).
Housing: Homeownership rate: 79.3% (2000); Median home value: $109,100 (2000); Median rent: $325 per month (2000); Median age of housing: 49 years (2000).
Transportation: Commute to work: 97.3% car, 0.0% public transportation, 0.0% walk, 2.7% work from home (2000); Travel time to work: 15.5% less than 15 minutes, 43.7% 15 to 30 minutes, 23.9% 30 to 45 minutes, 15.5% 45 to 60 minutes, 1.4% 60 minutes or more (2000)

IXONIA (town). Covers a land area of 35.940 square miles and a water area of 0.598 square miles. Located at 43.15° N. Lat.; 88.59° W. Long. Elevation is 870 feet.
Population: 2,902 (2000); Race: 97.3% White, 0.0% Black, 1.4% Asian, 0.7% American Indian and Alaska Native, 0.9% Hispanic of any race, 0.6% two or more races (2000); Density: 80.7 persons per square mile (2000); Age: 25.7% under 18, 9.5% over 64 (2000); Marriage status: 21.2% never married, 67.7% now married, 4.1% widowed, 7.0% divorced (2000); Foreign born: 2.0% (2000); Ancestry (includes multiple ancestries): 61.9% German, 9.0% Irish, 9.0% Polish, 5.6% Norwegian, 5.3% Other groups (2000).
Economy: Dairying, wheat. Transitional urban area. Manufacturing: tool and die, metal products, feeds, furniture. Employment by occupation: 14.4% management, 17.2% professional, 11.2% services, 25.4% sales, 0.9% farming, 12.3% construction, 18.6% production (2000).
Income: Per capita income: $23,979 (2000); Median household income: $58,629 (2000); Poverty rate: 1.5% (2000).
Taxes: Total city taxes per capita: $146 (1997); City property taxes per capita: $136 (1997).
Education: High school graduation rate: 89.1% (2000); College graduation rate: 17.2% (2000).
Housing: Homeownership rate: 83.1% (2000); Median home value: $151,100 (2000); Median rent: $511 per month (2000); Median age of housing: 33 years (2000).
Transportation: Commute to work: 89.9% car, 0.4% public transportation, 3.9% walk, 5.2% work from home (2000); Travel time to work: 33.6% less than 15 minutes, 35.7% 15 to 30 minutes, 15.0% 30 to 45 minutes, 13.1% 45 to 60 minutes, 2.6% 60 minutes or more (2000)

JEFFERSON (city). Covers a land area of 4.458 square miles and a water area of 0.198 square miles. Located at 43.00° N. Lat.; 88.80° W. Long. Elevation is 820 feet.
History: Jefferson was settled in the mid-1830's, but grew slowly despite the arrival of German immigrants in the 1840's. A chair factory was established in 1856, a woolen mill in 1866, and a shoe factory in 1868.
Population: 7,338 (2000); Race: 95.3% White, 0.0% Black, 0.0% Asian, 0.5% American Indian and Alaska Native, 6.8% Hispanic of any race, 1.1% two or more races (2000); Density: 1,645.9 persons per square mile (2000); Age: 23.2% under 18, 15.9% over 64 (2000); Marriage status: 25.8% never married, 54.6% now married, 9.4% widowed, 10.1% divorced (2000); Foreign born: 3.7% (2000); Ancestry (includes multiple ancestries): 53.6% German, 10.5% Irish, 8.3% Other groups, 8.3% Norwegian, 5.6% United States or American (2000).
Economy: Single-family building permits issued: 24 (2001) / 22 (2000); Multi-family building permits issued: 4 (2001) / 2 (2000); Employment by occupation: 8.0% management, 11.9% professional, 16.7% services, 23.3% sales, 0.4% farming, 7.2% construction, 32.5% production (2000).
Income: Per capita income: $19,124 (2000); Median household income: $40,962 (2000); Poverty rate: 8.3% (2000).
Taxes: Total city taxes per capita: $307 (1997); City property taxes per capita: $285 (1997).
Education: High school graduation rate: 78.3% (2000); College graduation rate: 12.9% (2000).

School District(s)

Jefferson (PK-12)
2000 Enrollment: 1,726 920-675-1000

Housing: Homeownership rate: 60.8% (2000); Median home value: $112,800 (2000); Median rent: $494 per month (2000); Median age of housing: 37 years (2000).
Safety: Violent crime rate: 10.8 per 10,000 population; Property crime rate: 406.0 per 10,000 population (2001).
Newspapers: Jefferson County Advertiser (3 x week)
Transportation: Commute to work: 91.5% car, 1.1% public transportation, 4.2% walk, 2.1% work from home (2000); Travel time to work: 49.0% less than 15 minutes, 29.8% 15 to 30 minutes, 10.8% 30 to 45 minutes, 5.8% 45 to 60 minutes, 4.6% 60 minutes or more (2000)
Additional Information Contacts
Jefferson Chamber of Commerce. 920-674-4511
Jefferson County Board of Realtors 920-674-5135

JEFFERSON (town). Covers a land area of 43.506 square miles and a water area of 0.458 square miles. Located at 42.99° N. Lat.; 88.77° W. Long. Elevation is 820 feet.
History: Glacial Drumlin State Trail passes to North. Settled c.1836, incorporated 1878.
Population: 2,265 (2000); Race: 98.3% White, 0.0% Black, 0.0% Asian, 0.2% American Indian and Alaska Native, 0.6% Hispanic of any race, 1.2% two or more races (2000); Density: 52.1 persons per square mile (2000); Age: 20.0% under 18, 14.2% over 64 (2000); Marriage status: 25.7% never married, 64.1% now married, 3.6% widowed, 6.6% divorced (2000); Foreign born: 0.8% (2000); Ancestry (includes multiple ancestries): 56.1% German, 9.5% Irish, 8.2% English, 5.9% Polish, 4.8% Norwegian (2000).
Economy: In dairying and farming region. Manufacturing: furniture, shoes, textiles, wood products, food and meat products, vegetable processing; printing. Employment by occupation: 11.1% management, 11.8% professional, 12.3% services, 20.0% sales, 1.6% farming, 16.6% construction, 26.6% production (2000).
Income: Per capita income: $23,327 (2000); Median household income: $52,813 (2000); Poverty rate: 2.2% (2000).
Taxes: Total city taxes per capita: $58 (1997); City property taxes per capita: $57 (1997).
Education: High school graduation rate: 79.4% (2000); College graduation rate: 12.4% (2000).
Housing: Homeownership rate: 82.1% (2000); Median home value: $128,100 (2000); Median rent: $445 per month (2000); Median age of housing: 47 years (2000).
Transportation: Commute to work: 92.7% car, 0.8% public transportation, 1.6% walk, 4.5% work from home (2000); Travel time to work: 41.5% less than 15 minutes, 34.5% 15 to 30 minutes, 13.3% 30 to 45 minutes, 6.0% 45 to 60 minutes, 4.7% 60 minutes or more (2000)

JOHNSON CREEK (village). Covers a land area of 2.151 square miles and a water area of 0 square miles. Located at 43.07° N. Lat.; 88.77° W. Long. Elevation is 812 feet.
History: Johnson Creek developed as a shipping center for dairy produce, with the establishment of the H.C. Christians Company offices and plant producing butter and eggs.
Population: 1,581 (2000); Race: 92.8% White, 0.5% Black, 0.6% Asian, 0.8% American Indian and Alaska Native, 5.1% Hispanic of any race, 1.4% two or more races (2000); Density: 735.2 persons per square mile (2000); Age: 27.7% under 18, 8.9% over 64 (2000); Marriage status: 26.4% never married, 56.7% now married, 5.8% widowed, 11.2% divorced (2000); Foreign born: 1.5% (2000); Ancestry (includes multiple ancestries): 56.7% German, 10.0% Irish, 9.4% Other groups, 7.5% English, 6.2% Norwegian (2000).
Economy: Single-family building permits issued: 6 (2001) / 6 (2000); Multi-family building permits issued: 0 (2001) / 16 (2000); Employment by occupation: 8.9% management, 14.9% professional, 10.3% services, 22.9% sales, 0.4% farming, 7.3% construction, 35.4% production (2000).
Income: Per capita income: $19,671 (2000); Median household income: $45,694 (2000); Poverty rate: 4.3% (2000).
Taxes: Total city taxes per capita: $182 (1997); City property taxes per capita: $127 (1997).
Education: High school graduation rate: 85.5% (2000); College graduation rate: 16.3% (2000).

School District(s)

Johnson Creek (PK-12)
2000 Enrollment: 610 920-699-2811

Housing: Homeownership rate: 67.3% (2000); Median home value: $122,200 (2000); Median rent: $583 per month (2000); Median age of housing: 25 years (2000).
Transportation: Commute to work: 93.3% car, 0.0% public transportation, 4.7% walk, 2.0% work from home (2000); Travel time to work: 38.6% less than 15 minutes, 31.5% 15 to 30 minutes, 16.8% 30 to 45 minutes, 7.9% 45 to 60 minutes, 5.1% 60 minutes or more (2000)

KOSHKONONG (town). Covers a land area of 42.063 square miles and a water area of 0.943 square miles. Located at 42.90° N. Lat.; 88.84° W. Long. Elevation is 820 feet.
Population: 3,395 (2000); Race: 99.1% White, 0.0% Black, 0.3% Asian, 0.0% American Indian and Alaska Native, 0.9% Hispanic of any race, 0.4% two or more races (2000); Density: 80.7 persons per square mile (2000); Age: 26.4% under 18, 12.4% over 64 (2000); Marriage status: 22.6% never married, 67.6% now married, 2.8% widowed, 6.9% divorced (2000); Foreign born: 1.3% (2000); Ancestry (includes multiple ancestries): 54.0% German, 10.9% Irish, 10.9% Norwegian, 8.5% English, 8.0% Polish (2000).
Economy: Employment by occupation: 11.3% management, 17.0% professional, 14.8% services, 22.1% sales, 2.3% farming, 9.6% construction, 23.0% production (2000).
Income: Per capita income: $24,100 (2000); Median household income: $60,000 (2000); Poverty rate: 3.3% (2000).
Taxes: Total city taxes per capita: $43 (1997); City property taxes per capita: $39 (1997).
Education: High school graduation rate: 87.3% (2000); College graduation rate: 20.4% (2000).
Housing: Homeownership rate: 87.2% (2000); Median home value: $146,100 (2000); Median rent: $618 per month (2000); Median age of housing: 30 years (2000).
Transportation: Commute to work: 94.8% car, 0.3% public transportation, 2.3% walk, 2.6% work from home (2000); Travel time to work: 51.7% less than 15 minutes, 29.7% 15 to 30 minutes, 7.6% 30 to 45 minutes, 3.9% 45 to 60 minutes, 7.1% 60 minutes or more (2000)

LAKE KOSHKONONG (CDP). Covers a land area of 14.306 square miles and a water area of 15.574 square miles. Located at 42.86° N. Lat.; 88.94° W. Long.
Population: 1,219 (2000); Race: 97.7% White, 0.0% Black, 0.9% Asian, 0.1% American Indian and Alaska Native, 0.9% Hispanic of any race, 1.3% two or more races (2000); Density: 85.2 persons per square mile (2000); Age: 23.2% under 18, 12.5% over 64 (2000); Marriage status: 23.6% never married, 62.8% now married, 5.2% widowed, 8.3% divorced (2000); Foreign born: 0.5% (2000); Ancestry (includes multiple ancestries): 55.6% German, 14.1% Irish, 12.7% Norwegian, 7.7% English, 5.1% French (except Basque) (2000).
Economy: Employment by occupation: 9.5% management, 14.3% professional, 12.5% services, 26.1% sales, 0.7% farming, 9.5% construction, 27.3% production (2000).
Income: Per capita income: $23,801 (2000); Median household income: $54,412 (2000); Poverty rate: 5.1% (2000).
Education: High school graduation rate: 88.5% (2000); College graduation rate: 19.6% (2000).
Housing: Homeownership rate: 85.8% (2000); Median home value: $136,000 (2000); Median rent: $556 per month (2000); Median age of housing: 44 years (2000).
Transportation: Commute to work: 94.5% car, 0.6% public transportation, 2.3% walk, 2.6% work from home (2000); Travel time to work: 28.3% less than 15 minutes, 40.1% 15 to 30 minutes, 17.8% 30 to 45 minutes, 4.5% 45 to 60 minutes, 9.3% 60 minutes or more (2000)

LAKE LAC LA BELLE (CDP). Covers a land area of 0.951 square miles and a water area of 0 square miles. Located at 43.13° N. Lat.; 88.54° W. Long.
Population: 833 (2000); Race: 96.1% White, 0.0% Black, 1.0% Asian, 1.2% American Indian and Alaska Native, 1.6% Hispanic of any race, 1.7% two or more races (2000); Density: 876.1 persons per square mile (2000); Age: 26.0% under 18, 8.5% over 64 (2000); Marriage status: 19.8% never married, 71.7% now married, 4.0% widowed, 4.5% divorced (2000); Foreign born: 1.5% (2000); Ancestry (includes multiple ancestries): 53.6% German, 16.0% Irish, 14.6% Polish, 9.5% Other groups, 6.6% Norwegian (2000).
Economy: Employment by occupation: 15.4% management, 18.2% professional, 7.9% services, 27.1% sales, 0.8% farming, 12.7% construction, 17.7% production (2000).
Income: Per capita income: $25,461 (2000); Median household income: $67,917 (2000); Poverty rate: 0.5% (2000).

Education: High school graduation rate: 93.5% (2000); College graduation rate: 22.4% (2000).
Housing: Homeownership rate: 94.5% (2000); Median home value: $156,700 (2000); Median rent: $683 per month (2000); Median age of housing: 31 years (2000).
Transportation: Commute to work: 93.8% car, 0.0% public transportation, 0.8% walk, 4.1% work from home (2000); Travel time to work: 33.3% less than 15 minutes, 29.8% 15 to 30 minutes, 20.5% 30 to 45 minutes, 14.7% 45 to 60 minutes, 1.7% 60 minutes or more (2000)

LAKE MILLS (city). Covers a land area of 3.421 square miles and a water area of 0.396 square miles. Located at 43.08° N. Lat.; 88.90° W. Long. Elevation is 835 feet.
History: Aztalan State Park to east contains remains of 12th century Indian village, rare platform mounds and a Museum with ancient Indian relics. Glacial Drumlin State Trail passes east-west to south. Settled c. 1836, Incorporated 1905.
Population: 4,843 (2000); Race: 98.8% White, 0.0% Black, 0.3% Asian, 0.0% American Indian and Alaska Native, 1.1% Hispanic of any race, 0.9% two or more races (2000); Density: 1,415.6 persons per square mile (2000); Age: 27.3% under 18, 14.4% over 64 (2000); Marriage status: 22.5% never married, 59.7% now married, 8.9% widowed, 9.0% divorced (2000); Foreign born: 2.0% (2000); Ancestry (includes multiple ancestries): 60.8% German, 11.6% Norwegian, 9.2% Irish, 9.2% English, 5.8% Polish (2000).
Economy: In dairying, farming and resort region. Manufacturing includes dairy equipment, food processing and refrigation equipment, magnetic switches, liquid crystal displays, metal components; food processing. Single-family building permits issued: 15 (2001) / 22 (2000); Multi-family building permits issued: 2 (2001) / 2 (2000); Employment by occupation: 12.9% management, 21.0% professional, 13.5% services, 22.2% sales, 0.1% farming, 6.8% construction, 23.5% production (2000).
Income: Per capita income: $21,929 (2000); Median household income: $44,132 (2000); Poverty rate: 7.3% (2000).
Taxes: Total city taxes per capita: $332 (1997); City property taxes per capita: $304 (1997).
Education: High school graduation rate: 88.5% (2000); College graduation rate: 26.8% (2000).

School District(s)

Lake Mills Area (PK-12)
2000 Enrollment: 1,287 920-648-2215
Housing: Homeownership rate: 68.4% (2000); Median home value: $129,100 (2000); Median rent: $505 per month (2000); Median age of housing: 39 years (2000).
Safety: Violent crime rate: 8.2 per 10,000 population; Property crime rate: 190.7 per 10,000 population (2001).
Newspapers: The Lake Mills Leader (1 x week)
Transportation: Commute to work: 91.0% car, 0.6% public transportation, 4.2% walk, 3.3% work from home (2000); Travel time to work: 40.5% less than 15 minutes, 24.0% 15 to 30 minutes, 21.4% 30 to 45 minutes, 8.5% 45 to 60 minutes, 5.5% 60 minutes or more (2000)
Additional Information Contacts
Lake Mills Chamber of Commerce 920-648-3585

LAKE MILLS (town). Covers a land area of 30.977 square miles and a water area of 2.107 square miles. Located at 43.07° N. Lat.; 88.95° W. Long. Elevation is 835 feet.
Population: 1,936 (2000); Race: 97.9% White, 0.0% Black, 0.1% Asian, 0.1% American Indian and Alaska Native, 2.6% Hispanic of any race, 0.5% two or more races (2000); Density: 62.5 persons per square mile (2000); Age: 24.9% under 18, 14.6% over 64 (2000); Marriage status: 20.0% never married, 68.8% now married, 4.5% widowed, 6.8% divorced (2000); Foreign born: 2.0% (2000); Ancestry (includes multiple ancestries): 59.2% German, 9.1% English, 8.6% Irish, 8.5% Norwegian, 4.7% Swedish (2000).
Economy: Employment by occupation: 20.6% management, 18.3% professional, 9.3% services, 20.5% sales, 2.9% farming, 7.2% construction, 21.2% production (2000).
Income: Per capita income: $24,105 (2000); Median household income: $55,278 (2000); Poverty rate: 3.4% (2000).
Taxes: Total city taxes per capita: $157 (1997); City property taxes per capita: $148 (1997).
Education: High school graduation rate: 91.8% (2000); College graduation rate: 28.4% (2000).
Housing: Homeownership rate: 88.8% (2000); Median home value: $179,200 (2000); Median rent: $538 per month (2000); Median age of housing: 26 years (2000).
Transportation: Commute to work: 85.9% car, 0.9% public transportation, 4.4% walk, 8.0% work from home (2000); Travel time to work: 39.1% less than 15 minutes, 26.6% 15 to 30 minutes, 20.5% 30 to 45 minutes, 9.4% 45 to 60 minutes, 4.4% 60 minutes or more (2000)

LAKE RIPLEY (CDP). Covers a land area of 1.930 square miles and a water area of 0.643 square miles. Located at 43.00° N. Lat.; 88.98° W. Long.
Population: 1,603 (2000); Race: 98.0% White, 0.0% Black, 0.0% Asian, 0.0% American Indian and Alaska Native, 1.9% Hispanic of any race, 1.2% two or more races (2000); Density: 830.7 persons per square mile (2000); Age: 24.7% under 18, 12.7% over 64 (2000); Marriage status: 24.6% never married, 58.5% now married, 5.4% widowed, 11.6% divorced (2000); Foreign born: 1.8% (2000); Ancestry (includes multiple ancestries): 48.0% German, 21.0% Norwegian, 14.4% Irish, 8.1% English, 6.2% Polish (2000).
Economy: Employment by occupation: 16.8% management, 22.4% professional, 9.1% services, 26.2% sales, 0.4% farming, 9.1% construction, 15.9% production (2000).
Income: Per capita income: $25,692 (2000); Median household income: $51,420 (2000); Poverty rate: 6.6% (2000).
Education: High school graduation rate: 94.8% (2000); College graduation rate: 34.6% (2000).
Housing: Homeownership rate: 85.3% (2000); Median home value: $160,600 (2000); Median rent: $613 per month (2000); Median age of housing: 30 years (2000).
Transportation: Commute to work: 95.8% car, 0.0% public transportation, 1.2% walk, 2.0% work from home (2000); Travel time to work: 28.9% less than 15 minutes, 30.7% 15 to 30 minutes, 31.5% 30 to 45 minutes, 6.3% 45 to 60 minutes, 2.6% 60 minutes or more (2000)

MILFORD (town). Covers a land area of 33.858 square miles and a water area of 1.188 square miles. Located at 43.14° N. Lat.; 88.83° W. Long. Elevation is 811 feet.
Population: 1,055 (2000); Race: 97.3% White, 0.9% Black, 0.0% Asian, 1.1% American Indian and Alaska Native, 1.6% Hispanic of any race, 0.4% two or more races (2000); Density: 31.2 persons per square mile (2000); Age: 25.3% under 18, 16.0% over 64 (2000); Marriage status: 21.6% never married, 67.1% now married, 4.8% widowed, 6.5% divorced (2000); Foreign born: 1.6% (2000); Ancestry (includes multiple ancestries): 62.1% German, 8.0% Irish, 6.2% English, 4.5% Polish, 4.4% Other groups (2000).
Economy: Employment by occupation: 13.4% management, 12.7% professional, 11.4% services, 22.9% sales, 3.1% farming, 12.1% construction, 24.4% production (2000).
Income: Per capita income: $22,953 (2000); Median household income: $47,619 (2000); Poverty rate: 4.1% (2000).
Taxes: Total city taxes per capita: $159 (1997); City property taxes per capita: $154 (1997).
Education: High school graduation rate: 85.1% (2000); College graduation rate: 15.9% (2000).
Housing: Homeownership rate: 85.6% (2000); Median home value: $116,800 (2000); Median rent: $463 per month (2000); Median age of housing: 60+ years (2000).
Transportation: Commute to work: 86.3% car, 0.4% public transportation, 1.1% walk, 11.1% work from home (2000); Travel time to work: 33.1% less than 15 minutes, 34.6% 15 to 30 minutes, 22.4% 30 to 45 minutes, 5.9% 45 to 60 minutes, 4.0% 60 minutes or more (2000)

OAKLAND (town). Covers a land area of 34.875 square miles and a water area of 1.263 square miles. Located at 42.98° N. Lat.; 88.96° W. Long. Elevation is 875 feet.
Population: 3,135 (2000); Race: 98.3% White, 0.0% Black, 0.0% Asian, 0.0% American Indian and Alaska Native, 1.5% Hispanic of any race, 1.1% two or more races (2000); Density: 89.9 persons per square mile (2000); Age: 25.9% under 18, 11.8% over 64 (2000); Marriage status: 24.5% never married, 60.6% now married, 5.5% widowed, 9.4% divorced (2000); Foreign born: 1.0% (2000); Ancestry (includes multiple ancestries): 50.6% German, 20.3% Norwegian, 11.8% Irish, 7.6% English, 5.9% Polish (2000).
Economy: Employment by occupation: 14.8% management, 19.2% professional, 11.7% services, 24.4% sales, 0.7% farming, 9.9% construction, 19.2% production (2000).
Income: Per capita income: $24,622 (2000); Median household income: $54,412 (2000); Poverty rate: 5.4% (2000).
Taxes: Total city taxes per capita: $106 (1997); City property taxes per capita: $74 (1997).
Education: High school graduation rate: 93.0% (2000); College graduation rate: 28.3% (2000).

Housing: Homeownership rate: 87.2% (2000); Median home value: $161,700 (2000); Median rent: $588 per month (2000); Median age of housing: 27 years (2000).
Transportation: Commute to work: 94.7% car, 0.0% public transportation, 0.8% walk, 3.8% work from home (2000); Travel time to work: 32.9% less than 15 minutes, 31.2% 15 to 30 minutes, 25.7% 30 to 45 minutes, 6.0% 45 to 60 minutes, 4.2% 60 minutes or more (2000)

PALMYRA (village). Covers a land area of 1.214 square miles and a water area of 0.036 square miles. Located at 42.87° N. Lat.; 88.58° W. Long. Elevation is 848 feet.
Population: 1,766 (2000); Race: 95.1% White, 0.0% Black, 0.0% Asian, 0.6% American Indian and Alaska Native, 6.5% Hispanic of any race, 1.4% two or more races (2000); Density: 1,454.6 persons per square mile (2000); Age: 26.7% under 18, 12.3% over 64 (2000); Marriage status: 25.1% never married, 56.7% now married, 5.8% widowed, 12.3% divorced (2000); Foreign born: 2.1% (2000); Ancestry (includes multiple ancestries): 46.9% German, 10.5% Irish, 8.1% Polish, 8.1% English, 7.8% Other groups (2000).
Economy: Single-family building permits issued: 8 (2001) / 8 (2000); Multi-family building permits issued: 0 (2001) / 0 (2000); Employment by occupation: 7.2% management, 14.4% professional, 13.8% services, 15.9% sales, 1.6% farming, 12.8% construction, 34.3% production (2000).
Income: Per capita income: $19,849 (2000); Median household income: $45,521 (2000); Poverty rate: 5.4% (2000).
Taxes: Total city taxes per capita: $195 (1997); City property taxes per capita: $185 (1997).
Education: High school graduation rate: 82.0% (2000); College graduation rate: 9.4% (2000).

School District(s)

Palmyra-Eagle Area (PK-12)
2000 Enrollment: 1,188 262-495-7100

Housing: Homeownership rate: 67.5% (2000); Median home value: $112,300 (2000); Median rent: $491 per month (2000); Median age of housing: 38 years (2000).
Safety: Violent crime rate: 5.6 per 10,000 population; Property crime rate: 365.4 per 10,000 population (2001).
Newspapers: Palmyra Enterprise (1 x week)
Transportation: Commute to work: 93.2% car, 0.2% public transportation, 3.8% walk, 1.5% work from home (2000); Travel time to work: 26.8% less than 15 minutes, 24.4% 15 to 30 minutes, 27.8% 30 to 45 minutes, 11.5% 45 to 60 minutes, 9.5% 60 minutes or more (2000)

Additional Information Contacts

Palmyra Area Chamber of Commerce 262-495-2611

PALMYRA (town). Covers a land area of 34.790 square miles and a water area of 0.378 square miles. Located at 42.87° N. Lat.; 88.59° W. Long. Elevation is 848 feet.
Population: 1,145 (2000); Race: 96.5% White, 0.1% Black, 0.2% Asian, 0.0% American Indian and Alaska Native, 7.1% Hispanic of any race, 1.5% two or more races (2000); Density: 32.9 persons per square mile (2000); Age: 20.4% under 18, 14.1% over 64 (2000); Marriage status: 21.9% never married, 65.3% now married, 6.3% widowed, 6.5% divorced (2000); Foreign born: 3.7% (2000); Ancestry (includes multiple ancestries): 48.6% German, 12.3% English, 10.6% Polish, 10.1% Irish, 7.5% Other groups (2000).
Economy: In agricultural and resort region. Manufacturing: food supplements. Employment by occupation: 13.4% management, 18.5% professional, 10.6% services, 24.0% sales, 3.0% farming, 13.4% construction, 17.1% production (2000).
Income: Per capita income: $22,244 (2000); Median household income: $50,375 (2000); Poverty rate: 4.9% (2000).
Taxes: Total city taxes per capita: $162 (1997); City property taxes per capita: $158 (1997).
Education: High school graduation rate: 87.5% (2000); College graduation rate: 22.1% (2000).
Housing: Homeownership rate: 82.6% (2000); Median home value: $164,400 (2000); Median rent: $550 per month (2000); Median age of housing: 40 years (2000).
Transportation: Commute to work: 88.7% car, 0.5% public transportation, 2.1% walk, 7.6% work from home (2000); Travel time to work: 27.1% less than 15 minutes, 28.5% 15 to 30 minutes, 22.6% 30 to 45 minutes, 14.6% 45 to 60 minutes, 7.2% 60 minutes or more (2000)

SULLIVAN (village). Covers a land area of 1.120 square miles and a water area of 0 square miles. Located at 43.01° N. Lat.; 88.58° W. Long. Elevation is 860 feet.
Population: 688 (2000); Race: 99.3% White, 0.0% Black, 0.0% Asian, 0.3% American Indian and Alaska Native, 0.0% Hispanic of any race, 0.4% two or more races (2000); Density: 614.2 persons per square mile (2000); Age: 19.3% under 18, 11.6% over 64 (2000); Marriage status: 23.4% never married, 59.1% now married, 7.5% widowed, 9.9% divorced (2000); Foreign born: 2.7% (2000); Ancestry (includes multiple ancestries): 53.7% German, 10.8% Polish, 8.9% Irish, 8.1% Norwegian, 7.5% English (2000).
Economy: Single-family building permits issued: 0 (2001) / 0 (2000); Multi-family building permits issued: 0 (2001) / 0 (2000); Employment by occupation: 9.7% management, 15.4% professional, 14.3% services, 28.0% sales, 0.5% farming, 9.2% construction, 23.0% production (2000).
Income: Per capita income: $24,621 (2000); Median household income: $43,229 (2000); Poverty rate: 1.8% (2000).
Taxes: Total city taxes per capita: $281 (1997); City property taxes per capita: $261 (1997).
Education: High school graduation rate: 82.1% (2000); College graduation rate: 11.9% (2000).
Housing: Homeownership rate: 54.6% (2000); Median home value: $131,000 (2000); Median rent: $574 per month (2000); Median age of housing: 27 years (2000).
Transportation: Commute to work: 92.5% car, 0.0% public transportation, 1.9% walk, 4.0% work from home (2000); Travel time to work: 15.8% less than 15 minutes, 38.2% 15 to 30 minutes, 29.9% 30 to 45 minutes, 10.2% 45 to 60 minutes, 5.8% 60 minutes or more (2000)

SULLIVAN (town). Covers a land area of 34.669 square miles and a water area of 0.852 square miles. Located at 42.96° N. Lat.; 88.60° W. Long. Elevation is 860 feet.
Population: 2,124 (2000); Race: 99.0% White, 0.2% Black, 0.0% Asian, 0.0% American Indian and Alaska Native, 1.8% Hispanic of any race, 0.5% two or more races (2000); Density: 61.3 persons per square mile (2000); Age: 25.0% under 18, 10.6% over 64 (2000); Marriage status: 21.3% never married, 64.9% now married, 4.9% widowed, 8.9% divorced (2000); Foreign born: 1.1% (2000); Ancestry (includes multiple ancestries): 57.5% German, 12.4% Polish, 11.9% Irish, 9.3% English, 5.5% Norwegian (2000).
Economy: In dairying region. Manufacturing of machinery. Employment by occupation: 11.9% management, 9.3% professional, 12.0% services, 23.4% sales, 0.8% farming, 13.7% construction, 28.9% production (2000).
Income: Per capita income: $22,753 (2000); Median household income: $50,492 (2000); Poverty rate: 5.1% (2000).
Taxes: Total city taxes per capita: $85 (1997); City property taxes per capita: $63 (1997).
Education: High school graduation rate: 84.2% (2000); College graduation rate: 11.2% (2000).
Housing: Homeownership rate: 86.2% (2000); Median home value: $143,100 (2000); Median rent: $502 per month (2000); Median age of housing: 26 years (2000).
Transportation: Commute to work: 92.6% car, 0.3% public transportation, 2.0% walk, 4.1% work from home (2000); Travel time to work: 13.7% less than 15 minutes, 37.3% 15 to 30 minutes, 28.4% 30 to 45 minutes, 11.9% 45 to 60 minutes, 8.7% 60 minutes or more (2000)

SUMNER (town). Covers a land area of 16.276 square miles and a water area of 15.010 square miles. Located at 42.90° N. Lat.; 88.96° W. Long.
Population: 904 (2000); Race: 99.4% White, 0.0% Black, 0.0% Asian, 0.1% American Indian and Alaska Native, 1.4% Hispanic of any race, 0.5% two or more races (2000); Density: 55.5 persons per square mile (2000); Age: 18.2% under 18, 15.4% over 64 (2000); Marriage status: 23.0% never married, 61.0% now married, 7.5% widowed, 8.6% divorced (2000); Foreign born: 1.2% (2000); Ancestry (includes multiple ancestries): 51.9% German, 18.6% Norwegian, 12.2% Irish, 10.4% English, 3.5% Other groups (2000).
Economy: Employment by occupation: 7.6% management, 8.7% professional, 12.2% services, 26.4% sales, 0.6% farming, 14.0% construction, 30.5% production (2000).
Income: Per capita income: $25,416 (2000); Median household income: $51,250 (2000); Poverty rate: 3.5% (2000).
Taxes: Total city taxes per capita: $114 (1997); City property taxes per capita: $111 (1997).
Education: High school graduation rate: 84.1% (2000); College graduation rate: 10.5% (2000).
Housing: Homeownership rate: 85.9% (2000); Median home value: $112,700 (2000); Median rent: $450 per month (2000); Median age of housing: 48 years (2000).
Transportation: Commute to work: 94.4% car, 0.7% public transportation, 0.9% walk, 3.9% work from home (2000); Travel time to work: 22.4% less

than 15 minutes, 37.3% 15 to 30 minutes, 21.5% 30 to 45 minutes, 9.7% 45 to 60 minutes, 9.1% 60 minutes or more (2000)

WATERLOO (city). Covers a land area of 3.907 square miles and a water area of 0.024 square miles. Located at 43.18° N. Lat.; 88.99° W. Long. Elevation is 819 feet.
Population: 3,259 (2000); Race: 91.9% White, 3.0% Black, 0.0% Asian, 0.7% American Indian and Alaska Native, 6.6% Hispanic of any race, 0.3% two or more races (2000); Density: 834.1 persons per square mile (2000); Age: 27.0% under 18, 11.3% over 64 (2000); Marriage status: 25.2% never married, 60.3% now married, 5.9% widowed, 8.5% divorced (2000); Foreign born: 1.4% (2000); Ancestry (includes multiple ancestries): 57.4% German, 14.5% Norwegian, 10.4% Irish, 7.9% English, 6.9% Other groups (2000).
Economy: Single-family building permits issued: 17 (2001) / 7 (2000); Multi-family building permits issued: 2 (2001) / 2 (2000); Employment by occupation: 10.5% management, 18.5% professional, 17.1% services, 22.3% sales, 1.1% farming, 7.2% construction, 23.3% production (2000).
Income: Per capita income: $22,099 (2000); Median household income: $49,221 (2000); Poverty rate: 5.1% (2000).
Taxes: Total city taxes per capita: $220 (1997); City property taxes per capita: $196 (1997).
Education: High school graduation rate: 83.0% (2000); College graduation rate: 16.0% (2000).

School District(s)

Waterloo (PK-12)
2000 Enrollment: 905 920-478-3633

Housing: Homeownership rate: 72.2% (2000); Median home value: $119,000 (2000); Median rent: $540 per month (2000); Median age of housing: 33 years (2000).
Safety: Violent crime rate: 15.2 per 10,000 population; Property crime rate: 231.6 per 10,000 population (2001).
Transportation: Commute to work: 89.7% car, 0.0% public transportation, 7.2% walk, 2.8% work from home (2000); Travel time to work: 45.2% less than 15 minutes, 24.5% 15 to 30 minutes, 20.6% 30 to 45 minutes, 4.2% 45 to 60 minutes, 5.6% 60 minutes or more (2000)

WATERLOO (town). Covers a land area of 32.318 square miles and a water area of 0 square miles. Located at 43.15° N. Lat.; 88.95° W. Long. Elevation is 819 feet.
History: Incorporated 1859.
Population: 832 (2000); Race: 98.2% White, 0.1% Black, 0.0% Asian, 0.0% American Indian and Alaska Native, 3.7% Hispanic of any race, 0.6% two or more races (2000); Density: 25.7 persons per square mile (2000); Age: 26.3% under 18, 10.8% over 64 (2000); Marriage status: 23.6% never married, 67.5% now married, 4.3% widowed, 4.6% divorced (2000); Foreign born: 2.4% (2000); Ancestry (includes multiple ancestries): 57.1% German, 11.0% Irish, 9.9% Norwegian, 7.0% English, 5.0% Dutch (2000).
Economy: In dairying region. Manufacturing includes printing and publishing; wooden pallets, bicycles, pickles. Employment by occupation: 16.5% management, 14.9% professional, 7.9% services, 18.9% sales, 3.1% farming, 13.6% construction, 25.1% production (2000).
Income: Per capita income: $25,950 (2000); Median household income: $57,778 (2000); Poverty rate: 4.0% (2000).
Taxes: Total city taxes per capita: $99 (1997); City property taxes per capita: $97 (1997).
Education: High school graduation rate: 85.1% (2000); College graduation rate: 19.5% (2000).
Housing: Homeownership rate: 88.7% (2000); Median home value: $138,100 (2000); Median rent: $525 per month (2000); Median age of housing: 47 years (2000).
Transportation: Commute to work: 89.0% car, 0.2% public transportation, 2.7% walk, 7.9% work from home (2000); Travel time to work: 37.3% less than 15 minutes, 24.9% 15 to 30 minutes, 25.9% 30 to 45 minutes, 6.8% 45 to 60 minutes, 5.1% 60 minutes or more (2000)

WATERTOWN (city). Covers a land area of 10.940 square miles and a water area of 0.387 square miles. Located at 43.19° N. Lat.; 88.72° W. Long. Elevation is 823 feet.
History: Watertown was settled about 1836 by New Englanders who, attracted by the water power, established sawmills and factories making wagons, carriages, and barrels. The 1840's brought German immigrants, including political refugees and university students. Watertown claims the first kindergarten in America, started in 1856 by a Mrs. Schurz, one of the German settlers.
Population: 21,598 (2000); Race: 95.9% White, 0.3% Black, 0.5% Asian, 0.4% American Indian and Alaska Native, 5.0% Hispanic of any race, 1.7% two or more races (2000); Density: 1,974.1 persons per square mile (2000); Age: 25.9% under 18, 14.7% over 64 (2000); Marriage status: 23.8% never married, 59.9% now married, 8.1% widowed, 8.3% divorced (2000); Foreign born: 3.2% (2000); Ancestry (includes multiple ancestries): 56.7% German, 9.1% Irish, 7.6% Other groups, 5.3% Polish, 4.8% English (2000).
Vital Statistics: Birth rate: 141.2 per 10,000 population (1998)
Economy: Single-family building permits issued: 121 (2001) / 152 (2000); Multi-family building permits issued: 70 (2001) / 97 (2000); Employment by occupation: 8.4% management, 16.1% professional, 15.4% services, 24.9% sales, 0.5% farming, 7.9% construction, 26.8% production (2000).
Income: Per capita income: $18,977 (2000); Median household income: $42,562 (2000); Poverty rate: 6.7% (2000).
Taxes: Total city taxes per capita: $277 (2000); City property taxes per capita: $240 (2000).
Education: High school graduation rate: 81.9% (2000); College graduation rate: 16.2% (2000).

School District(s)

Watertown (PK-12)
2000 Enrollment: 3,725 920-262-1460

Four-year College(s)

Maranatha Baptist Bible College Inc (Private, Not-for-profit, Baptist)
2001 Enrollment: 776 920-261-9300
2001 Tuition: In-state $6,400; Out-of-state $6,400

Housing: Homeownership rate: 63.7% (2000); Median home value: $110,200 (2000); Median rent: $494 per month (2000); Median age of housing: 39 years (2000).
Hospitals: Watertown Memorial Hospital (95 beds)
Safety: Violent crime rate: 16.1 per 10,000 population; Property crime rate: 291.0 per 10,000 population (2001).
Newspapers: Watertown Daily Times (6 x week)
Transportation: Commute to work: 91.5% car, 1.6% public transportation, 4.7% walk, 1.5% work from home (2000); Travel time to work: 54.1% less than 15 minutes, 23.0% 15 to 30 minutes, 11.7% 30 to 45 minutes, 7.1% 45 to 60 minutes, 4.1% 60 minutes or more (2000)
Additional Information Contacts
Watertown Chamber of Commerce 920-261-6320

WATERTOWN (town). Covers a land area of 38.368 square miles and a water area of 0.535 square miles. Located at 43.15° N. Lat.; 88.73° W. Long. Elevation is 823 feet.
Population: 1,876 (2000); Race: 97.8% White, 0.0% Black, 0.3% Asian, 0.8% American Indian and Alaska Native, 0.7% Hispanic of any race, 0.4% two or more races (2000); Density: 48.9 persons per square mile (2000); Age: 26.7% under 18, 9.8% over 64 (2000); Marriage status: 19.2% never married, 71.4% now married, 4.0% widowed, 5.4% divorced (2000); Foreign born: 1.6% (2000); Ancestry (includes multiple ancestries): 59.6% German, 11.8% Irish, 6.9% English, 4.4% United States or American, 4.3% Norwegian (2000).
Economy: Employment by occupation: 13.0% management, 13.6% professional, 11.8% services, 22.0% sales, 1.8% farming, 14.4% construction, 23.3% production (2000).
Income: Per capita income: $21,298 (2000); Median household income: $52,667 (2000); Poverty rate: 2.7% (2000).
Taxes: Total city taxes per capita: $29 (1997); City property taxes per capita: $21 (1997).
Education: High school graduation rate: 88.7% (2000); College graduation rate: 15.9% (2000).
Housing: Homeownership rate: 88.7% (2000); Median home value: $138,500 (2000); Median rent: $621 per month (2000); Median age of housing: 37 years (2000).
Transportation: Commute to work: 90.8% car, 0.2% public transportation, 0.8% walk, 7.0% work from home (2000); Travel time to work: 39.0% less than 15 minutes, 35.2% 15 to 30 minutes, 14.5% 30 to 45 minutes, 6.8% 45 to 60 minutes, 4.5% 60 minutes or more (2000)

Juneau County

Located in central Wisconsin; bounded on the east by the Wisconsin River; drained by the Yellow, Lemonweir, and Baraboo Rivers; includes the Dells of the Wisconsin in the southeast. Covers a land area of 767.60 square miles, a water area of 36.50 square miles, and is located in the Central Time Zone. The county government was organized in 1856. County seat is Mauston.

Weather Station: Mauston 1 SE										Elevation: 862 feet		
	Jan	Feb	Mar	Apr	May	Jun	Jul	Aug	Sep	Oct	Nov	Dec
High	26	32	43	58	71	79	83	80	72	60	44	31
Low	4	10	21	34	45	54	59	56	48	36	25	13
Precip	1.1	1.0	2.0	3.4	3.6	3.7	4.0	4.2	4.0	2.4	2.4	1.2
Snow	13.5	8.9	8.3	2.8	tr	0.0	0.0	0.0	0.0	0.4	5.2	10.4

High and Low temperatures in degrees Fahrenheit; Precipitation and Snow in inches

Weather Station: Necedah										Elevation: 921 feet		
	Jan	Feb	Mar	Apr	May	Jun	Jul	Aug	Sep	Oct	Nov	Dec
High	25	32	43	59	72	81	85	82	73	61	43	30
Low	4	10	21	33	44	54	59	56	48	37	25	12
Precip	1.0	0.9	2.0	3.0	3.6	3.5	4.2	4.6	3.8	2.3	2.2	1.2
Snow	8.1	5.3	4.9	1.7	tr	0.0	0.0	0.0	0.0	0.3	3.3	7.7

High and Low temperatures in degrees Fahrenheit; Precipitation and Snow in inches

Population: 24,316 (2000); Race: 96.8% White, 0.3% Black, 0.4% Asian, 1.3% American Indian and Alaska Native, 1.3% Hispanic of any race, 0.9% two or more races (2000); Density: 31.7 persons per square mile (2000); Age: 25.5% under 18, 16.8% over 64 (2000).
Religion: Five largest groups: 24.3% Catholic Church, 11.7% Evangelical Lutheran Church in America, 7.7% Wisconsin Evangelical Lutheran Synod, 4.4% The United Methodist Church, 2.3% New Testament Association of Independent Baptist Churches and othe
Economy: Unemployment rate: 8.0% (11/2002); Total civilian labor force: 10,098 (11/2002); Leading industries: 34.3% manufacturing; 20.4% accommodation & food services; 12.7% retail trade (2000); Companies that employ more than 1,000 persons: 0 (2000); Companies that employ more than 100 persons: 17 (2000); Farms: 654 totaling 169,188 acres (1997); Minority business ownership rate: 0.0% (1997); Women business ownership rate: 11.1% (1997); Retail sales per capita: $7,133 (1997). Single-family building permits issued: 183 (2001) / 143 (2000); Multi-family building permits issued: 48 (2001) / 44 (2000).
Income: Per capita income: $17,892 (2000); Median household income: $35,335 (2000); Poverty rate: 10.1% (2000); Bankruptcy rate: 4.22% (2001).
Taxes: Total county taxes per capita: $205 (1997); County property taxes per capita: $161 (1997).
Education: High school graduation rate: 78.5% (2000); College graduation rate: 10.0% (2000).
Housing: Homeownership rate: 76.9% (2000); Median home value: $71,200 (2000); Median rent: $346 per month (2000); Median age of housing: 28 years (2000).
Health: Birth rate: 114.3 per 10,000 population (1998); Age adjusted death rate: 95.5 per 10,000 population (1999); Age adjusted cancer mortality rate: 295.4 deaths per 100,000 population (1999). Number of physicians: 7.0 per 10,000 population (1999); Number of hospital beds: 39.9 per 10,000 population (1999).
Elections: 2000 Presidential election results: 47.1% Gore, 48.1% Bush, 2.9% Nader, 1.3% Buchanan
National and State Parks: Buckhorn State Park; Buckhorn State Wildlife Area; Meadow Valley State Wildlife Area; Necedah National Wildlife Refuge; Rocky Arbor State Park
Additional Information Contacts
Juneau County Government Offices 608-847-9300
Mauston Area Chamber of Commerce. 608-847-4142
New Lisbon Chamber of Commerce 608-562-3555

Juneau County Communities

ARMENIA (town). Covers a land area of 65.999 square miles and a water area of 11.692 square miles. Located at 44.17° N. Lat.; 90.01° W. Long.
Population: 707 (2000); Race: 88.9% White, 0.0% Black, 0.0% Asian, 1.3% American Indian and Alaska Native, 9.5% Hispanic of any race, 1.5% two or more races (2000); Density: 10.7 persons per square mile (2000); Age: 21.8% under 18, 15.3% over 64 (2000); Marriage status: 19.2% never married, 62.6% now married, 3.2% widowed, 15.0% divorced (2000); Foreign born: 7.3% (2000); Ancestry (includes multiple ancestries): 47.7% German, 12.8% Other groups, 12.1% Irish, 9.8% Polish, 8.5% Norwegian (2000).
Economy: Single-family building permits issued: 15 (2001) / 2 (2000); Multi-family building permits issued: 0 (2001) / 0 (2000); Employment by occupation: 11.1% management, 12.1% professional, 23.2% services, 15.9% sales, 3.5% farming, 10.0% construction, 24.2% production (2000).
Income: Per capita income: $19,539 (2000); Median household income: $35,568 (2000); Poverty rate: 11.2% (2000).
Taxes: Total city taxes per capita: $161 (1997); City property taxes per capita: $158 (1997).
Education: High school graduation rate: 75.1% (2000); College graduation rate: 9.0% (2000).
Housing: Homeownership rate: 89.5% (2000); Median home value: $68,800 (2000); Median rent: $292 per month (2000); Median age of housing: 23 years (2000).
Transportation: Commute to work: 92.0% car, 0.0% public transportation, 2.4% walk, 3.5% work from home (2000); Travel time to work: 19.9% less than 15 minutes, 32.2% 15 to 30 minutes, 31.2% 30 to 45 minutes, 6.9% 45 to 60 minutes, 9.8% 60 minutes or more (2000)

CAMP DOUGLAS (village). Covers a land area of 0.952 square miles and a water area of 0 square miles. Located at 43.92° N. Lat.; 90.27° W. Long. Elevation is 933 feet.
Population: 592 (2000); Race: 99.3% White, 0.4% Black, 0.0% Asian, 0.0% American Indian and Alaska Native, 1.1% Hispanic of any race, 0.4% two or more races (2000); Density: 621.9 persons per square mile (2000); Age: 28.4% under 18, 15.6% over 64 (2000); Marriage status: 16.4% never married, 59.4% now married, 11.5% widowed, 12.7% divorced (2000); Foreign born: 0.7% (2000); Ancestry (includes multiple ancestries): 43.1% German, 16.8% Norwegian, 14.2% Irish, 8.6% Polish, 7.7% English (2000).
Economy: Wood products. US Camp Williams military reservation is here. Single-family building permits issued: 4 (2001) / 2 (2000); Multi-family building permits issued: 0 (2001) / 0 (2000); Employment by occupation: 7.3% management, 10.7% professional, 20.6% services, 27.5% sales, 0.0% farming, 12.6% construction, 21.4% production (2000).
Income: Per capita income: $17,919 (2000); Median household income: $39,583 (2000); Poverty rate: 2.8% (2000).
Taxes: Total city taxes per capita: $135 (1997); City property taxes per capita: $125 (1997).
Education: High school graduation rate: 82.8% (2000); College graduation rate: 4.0% (2000).
Housing: Homeownership rate: 78.2% (2000); Median home value: $63,800 (2000); Median rent: $311 per month (2000); Median age of housing: 41 years (2000).
Transportation: Commute to work: 92.5% car, 0.0% public transportation, 4.9% walk, 2.6% work from home (2000); Travel time to work: 37.3% less than 15 minutes, 44.6% 15 to 30 minutes, 9.2% 30 to 45 minutes, 5.8% 45 to 60 minutes, 3.1% 60 minutes or more (2000)
Airports: Volk Field

CLEARFIELD (town). Covers a land area of 35.832 square miles and a water area of 0 square miles. Located at 43.92° N. Lat.; 90.14° W. Long.
Population: 737 (2000); Race: 96.5% White, 0.0% Black, 0.8% Asian, 0.1% American Indian and Alaska Native, 0.3% Hispanic of any race, 2.5% two or more races (2000); Density: 20.6 persons per square mile (2000); Age: 22.4% under 18, 16.7% over 64 (2000); Marriage status: 14.0% never married, 67.0% now married, 8.9% widowed, 10.1% divorced (2000); Foreign born: 1.5% (2000); Ancestry (includes multiple ancestries): 33.8% German, 10.8% Norwegian, 9.3% Irish, 8.7% English, 8.0% Polish (2000).
Economy: Single-family building permits issued: 8 (2001) / 3 (2000); Multi-family building permits issued: 0 (2001) / 0 (2000); Employment by occupation: 12.0% management, 6.5% professional, 15.9% services, 23.3% sales, 1.3% farming, 8.4% construction, 32.7% production (2000).
Income: Per capita income: $17,445 (2000); Median household income: $35,781 (2000); Poverty rate: 13.5% (2000).
Taxes: Total city taxes per capita: $103 (1997); City property taxes per capita: $99 (1997).
Education: High school graduation rate: 72.6% (2000); College graduation rate: 4.8% (2000).
Housing: Homeownership rate: 85.5% (2000); Median home value: $79,600 (2000); Median rent: $319 per month (2000); Median age of housing: 24 years (2000).
Transportation: Commute to work: 91.9% car, 0.0% public transportation, 0.0% walk, 7.1% work from home (2000); Travel time to work: 32.8% less than 15 minutes, 41.1% 15 to 30 minutes, 15.3% 30 to 45 minutes, 4.5% 45 to 60 minutes, 6.3% 60 minutes or more (2000)

CUTLER (town). Covers a land area of 52.169 square miles and a water area of 1.865 square miles. Located at 44.04° N. Lat.; 90.27° W. Long. Elevation is 925 feet.
Population: 282 (2000); Race: 100.0% White, 0.0% Black, 0.0% Asian, 0.0% American Indian and Alaska Native, 0.0% Hispanic of any race, 0.0% two or more races (2000); Density: 5.4 persons per square mile (2000); Age: 21.6% under 18, 19.7% over 64 (2000); Marriage status: 13.8% never married, 71.4% now married, 11.4% widowed, 3.3% divorced (2000); Foreign born: 0.0% (2000); Ancestry (includes multiple ancestries): 44.8%

German, 8.9% French (except Basque), 8.5% Norwegian, 8.5% English, 7.3% Czech (2000).
Economy: Single-family building permits issued: 4 (2001) / 4 (2000); Multi-family building permits issued: 0 (2001) / 0 (2000); Employment by occupation: 18.6% management, 13.2% professional, 12.4% services, 20.9% sales, 4.7% farming, 12.4% construction, 17.8% production (2000).
Income: Per capita income: $17,591 (2000); Median household income: $37,813 (2000); Poverty rate: 1.5% (2000).
Taxes: Total city taxes per capita: $84 (1997); City property taxes per capita: $84 (1997).
Education: High school graduation rate: 80.1% (2000); College graduation rate: 3.8% (2000).
Housing: Homeownership rate: 86.2% (2000); Median home value: $90,000 (2000); Median age of housing: 27 years (2000).
Transportation: Commute to work: 95.5% car, 0.0% public transportation, 0.0% walk, 3.0% work from home (2000); Travel time to work: 17.7% less than 15 minutes, 48.5% 15 to 30 minutes, 20.0% 30 to 45 minutes, 8.5% 45 to 60 minutes, 5.4% 60 minutes or more (2000)

ELROY (city). Covers a land area of 1.917 square miles and a water area of 0 square miles. Located at 43.74° N. Lat.; 90.27° W. Long. Elevation is 959 feet.
History: Settled 1854, incorporated 1885.
Population: 1,578 (2000); Race: 98.5% White, 0.0% Black, 0.3% Asian, 0.7% American Indian and Alaska Native, 0.3% Hispanic of any race, 0.6% two or more races (2000); Density: 823.0 persons per square mile (2000); Age: 26.1% under 18, 20.9% over 64 (2000); Marriage status: 24.1% never married, 54.2% now married, 12.7% widowed, 9.1% divorced (2000); Foreign born: 0.4% (2000); Ancestry (includes multiple ancestries): 42.5% German, 13.8% Norwegian, 12.5% Irish, 9.4% English, 5.5% United States or American (2000).
Economy: In timber and farm area: dairy products; poultry, livestock. Light manufacturing. East terminus of La Crosse State Trail. Single-family building permits issued: 1 (2001) / 1 (2000); Multi-family building permits issued: 2 (2001) / 0 (2000); Employment by occupation: 7.8% management, 10.9% professional, 17.3% services, 20.2% sales, 0.4% farming, 9.4% construction, 33.9% production (2000).
Income: Per capita income: $15,529 (2000); Median household income: $31,859 (2000); Poverty rate: 14.2% (2000).
Taxes: Total city taxes per capita: $181 (1997); City property taxes per capita: $175 (1997).
Education: High school graduation rate: 80.9% (2000); College graduation rate: 12.3% (2000).

School District(s)

Royall (PK-12)
2000 Enrollment: 731 608-462-2600
Housing: Homeownership rate: 63.3% (2000); Median home value: $58,300 (2000); Median rent: $355 per month (2000); Median age of housing: 57 years (2000).
Safety: Violent crime rate: 44.1 per 10,000 population; Property crime rate: 214.0 per 10,000 population (2001).
Transportation: Commute to work: 84.3% car, 0.4% public transportation, 12.3% walk, 2.0% work from home (2000); Travel time to work: 52.1% less than 15 minutes, 30.0% 15 to 30 minutes, 12.4% 30 to 45 minutes, 4.0% 45 to 60 minutes, 1.6% 60 minutes or more (2000)

FINLEY (town). Covers a land area of 38.279 square miles and a water area of 0.303 square miles. Located at 44.19° N. Lat.; 90.16° W. Long. Elevation is 952 feet.
Population: 84 (2000); Race: 96.8% White, 0.0% Black, 0.0% Asian, 0.0% American Indian and Alaska Native, 0.0% Hispanic of any race, 0.0% two or more races (2000); Density: 2.2 persons per square mile (2000); Age: 25.3% under 18, 16.8% over 64 (2000); Marriage status: 18.4% never married, 64.5% now married, 3.9% widowed, 13.2% divorced (2000); Foreign born: 0.0% (2000); Ancestry (includes multiple ancestries): 56.8% German, 14.7% Polish, 11.6% Irish, 2.1% Norwegian, 2.1% Lithuanian (2000).
Economy: Employment by occupation: 30.6% management, 5.6% professional, 16.7% services, 5.6% sales, 22.2% farming, 2.8% construction, 16.7% production (2000).
Income: Per capita income: $13,715 (2000); Median household income: $31,250 (2000); Poverty rate: 8.4% (2000).
Taxes: Total city taxes per capita: $42 (1997); City property taxes per capita: $42 (1997).
Education: High school graduation rate: 67.6% (2000); College graduation rate: 8.5% (2000).
Housing: Homeownership rate: 80.0% (2000); Median home value: $41,000 (2000); Median rent: $275 per month (2000); Median age of housing: 24 years (2000).
Transportation: Commute to work: 72.2% car, 0.0% public transportation, 5.6% walk, 22.2% work from home (2000); Travel time to work: 39.3% less than 15 minutes, 10.7% 15 to 30 minutes, 7.1% 30 to 45 minutes, 28.6% 45 to 60 minutes, 14.3% 60 minutes or more (2000)

FOUNTAIN (town). Covers a land area of 30.841 square miles and a water area of 0 square miles. Located at 43.86° N. Lat.; 90.26° W. Long.
Population: 582 (2000); Race: 99.6% White, 0.0% Black, 0.4% Asian, 0.0% American Indian and Alaska Native, 0.0% Hispanic of any race, 0.0% two or more races (2000); Density: 18.9 persons per square mile (2000); Age: 20.1% under 18, 20.3% over 64 (2000); Marriage status: 14.2% never married, 67.7% now married, 12.9% widowed, 5.2% divorced (2000); Foreign born: 1.8% (2000); Ancestry (includes multiple ancestries): 37.7% German, 22.2% Norwegian, 12.5% Irish, 10.7% English, 7.5% Polish (2000).
Economy: Single-family building permits issued: 9 (2001) / 4 (2000); Multi-family building permits issued: 0 (2001) / 0 (2000); Employment by occupation: 21.8% management, 12.5% professional, 13.7% services, 17.3% sales, 0.0% farming, 9.2% construction, 25.5% production (2000).
Income: Per capita income: $17,350 (2000); Median household income: $47,500 (2000); Poverty rate: 11.7% (2000).
Taxes: Total city taxes per capita: $107 (1997); City property taxes per capita: $105 (1997).
Education: High school graduation rate: 80.2% (2000); College graduation rate: 12.3% (2000).
Housing: Homeownership rate: 82.6% (2000); Median home value: $76,300 (2000); Median rent: $330 per month (2000); Median age of housing: 30 years (2000).
Transportation: Commute to work: 82.0% car, 0.0% public transportation, 1.5% walk, 14.6% work from home (2000); Travel time to work: 26.8% less than 15 minutes, 39.0% 15 to 30 minutes, 18.9% 30 to 45 minutes, 10.5% 45 to 60 minutes, 4.8% 60 minutes or more (2000)

GERMANTOWN (town). Covers a land area of 33.214 square miles and a water area of 11.776 square miles. Located at 43.91° N. Lat.; 90.03° W. Long.
Population: 1,174 (2000); Race: 96.2% White, 0.4% Black, 0.2% Asian, 2.0% American Indian and Alaska Native, 0.7% Hispanic of any race, 1.0% two or more races (2000); Density: 35.3 persons per square mile (2000); Age: 18.1% under 18, 23.0% over 64 (2000); Marriage status: 12.3% never married, 68.5% now married, 6.9% widowed, 12.4% divorced (2000); Foreign born: 3.2% (2000); Ancestry (includes multiple ancestries): 35.6% German, 12.1% Polish, 11.2% Irish, 10.1% Norwegian, 6.7% English (2000).
Economy: Single-family building permits issued: 21 (2001) / 16 (2000); Multi-family building permits issued: 0 (2001) / 4 (2000); Employment by occupation: 7.9% management, 8.1% professional, 17.9% services, 24.7% sales, 1.3% farming, 13.9% construction, 26.2% production (2000).
Income: Per capita income: $17,815 (2000); Median household income: $31,204 (2000); Poverty rate: 12.0% (2000).
Taxes: Total city taxes per capita: $343 (1997); City property taxes per capita: $331 (1997).
Education: High school graduation rate: 71.6% (2000); College graduation rate: 9.7% (2000).
Housing: Homeownership rate: 90.4% (2000); Median home value: $94,600 (2000); Median rent: $326 per month (2000); Median age of housing: 17 years (2000).
Transportation: Commute to work: 94.8% car, 0.0% public transportation, 3.2% walk, 1.9% work from home (2000); Travel time to work: 25.4% less than 15 minutes, 41.7% 15 to 30 minutes, 19.7% 30 to 45 minutes, 4.2% 45 to 60 minutes, 9.0% 60 minutes or more (2000)

HUSTLER (village). Covers a land area of 0.622 square miles and a water area of 0 square miles. Located at 43.87° N. Lat.; 90.27° W. Long. Elevation is 929 feet.
Population: 113 (2000); Race: 100.0% White, 0.0% Black, 0.0% Asian, 0.0% American Indian and Alaska Native, 0.0% Hispanic of any race, 0.0% two or more races (2000); Density: 181.7 persons per square mile (2000); Age: 19.4% under 18, 43.5% over 64 (2000); Marriage status: 14.1% never married, 48.9% now married, 32.6% widowed, 4.3% divorced (2000); Foreign born: 2.8% (2000); Ancestry (includes multiple ancestries): 56.5% German, 16.7% English, 13.9% Norwegian, 12.0% French (except Basque), 10.2% Irish (2000).
Economy: In farming area. Butter and cheese. Single-family building permits issued: 1 (2001) / 0 (2000); Multi-family building permits issued: 0 (2001) / 0

(2000); Employment by occupation: 4.8% management, 33.3% professional, 0.0% services, 28.6% sales, 0.0% farming, 9.5% construction, 23.8% production (2000).
Income: Per capita income: $15,839 (2000); Median household income: $21,250 (2000); Poverty rate: 5.4% (2000).
Taxes: Total city taxes per capita: $71 (1997); City property taxes per capita: $59 (1997).
Education: High school graduation rate: 61.2% (2000); College graduation rate: 10.6% (2000).
Housing: Homeownership rate: 73.9% (2000); Median home value: $59,000 (2000); Median rent: $130 per month (2000); Median age of housing: 32 years (2000).
Transportation: Commute to work: 90.5% car, 0.0% public transportation, 9.5% walk, 0.0% work from home (2000); Travel time to work: 71.4% less than 15 minutes, 23.8% 15 to 30 minutes, 4.8% 30 to 45 minutes, 0.0% 45 to 60 minutes, 0.0% 60 minutes or more (2000)

KILDARE (town). Covers a land area of 27.770 square miles and a water area of 0.460 square miles. Located at 43.73° N. Lat.; 89.88° W. Long.
Population: 557 (2000); Race: 95.4% White, 0.4% Black, 0.4% Asian, 0.7% American Indian and Alaska Native, 2.2% Hispanic of any race, 3.1% two or more races (2000); Density: 20.1 persons per square mile (2000); Age: 19.6% under 18, 15.2% over 64 (2000); Marriage status: 24.3% never married, 58.8% now married, 5.2% widowed, 11.7% divorced (2000); Foreign born: 3.7% (2000); Ancestry (includes multiple ancestries): 40.3% German, 17.4% Irish, 12.9% Polish, 7.6% Other groups, 7.6% English (2000).
Economy: Single-family building permits issued: 9 (2001) / 4 (2000); Multi-family building permits issued: 0 (2001) / 0 (2000); Employment by occupation: 7.2% management, 10.9% professional, 17.7% services, 21.5% sales, 1.5% farming, 18.9% construction, 22.3% production (2000).
Income: Per capita income: $17,052 (2000); Median household income: $34,464 (2000); Poverty rate: 3.9% (2000).
Taxes: Total city taxes per capita: $66 (1997); City property taxes per capita: $63 (1997).
Education: High school graduation rate: 71.9% (2000); College graduation rate: 6.9% (2000).
Housing: Homeownership rate: 81.1% (2000); Median home value: $86,700 (2000); Median rent: $350 per month (2000); Median age of housing: 26 years (2000).
Transportation: Commute to work: 90.2% car, 0.0% public transportation, 1.6% walk, 8.2% work from home (2000); Travel time to work: 17.9% less than 15 minutes, 51.3% 15 to 30 minutes, 17.5% 30 to 45 minutes, 5.1% 45 to 60 minutes, 8.1% 60 minutes or more (2000)

KINGSTON (town). Covers a land area of 54.572 square miles and a water area of 2.512 square miles. Located at 44.17° N. Lat.; 90.25° W. Long.
Population: 58 (2000); Race: 100.0% White, 0.0% Black, 0.0% Asian, 0.0% American Indian and Alaska Native, 2.6% Hispanic of any race, 0.0% two or more races (2000); Density: 1.1 persons per square mile (2000); Age: 35.9% under 18, 5.1% over 64 (2000); Marriage status: 19.7% never married, 70.5% now married, 0.0% widowed, 9.8% divorced (2000); Foreign born: 0.0% (2000); Ancestry (includes multiple ancestries): 32.1% German, 25.6% English, 23.1% Serbian, 7.7% Norwegian, 7.7% Irish (2000).
Economy: Employment by occupation: 17.9% management, 0.0% professional, 7.1% services, 14.3% sales, 21.4% farming, 17.9% construction, 21.4% production (2000).
Income: Per capita income: $11,554 (2000); Median household income: $33,125 (2000); Poverty rate: 7.7% (2000).
Education: High school graduation rate: 68.2% (2000); College graduation rate: 0.0% (2000).
Housing: Homeownership rate: 59.1% (2000); Median home value: $68,800 (2000); Median rent: $425 per month (2000); Median age of housing: 23 years (2000).
Transportation: Commute to work: 92.9% car, 0.0% public transportation, 0.0% walk, 0.0% work from home (2000); Travel time to work: 57.1% less than 15 minutes, 14.3% 15 to 30 minutes, 7.1% 30 to 45 minutes, 0.0% 45 to 60 minutes, 21.4% 60 minutes or more (2000)

LEMONWEIR (town). Covers a land area of 42.628 square miles and a water area of 0.048 square miles. Located at 43.78° N. Lat.; 90.01° W. Long. Elevation is 863 feet.
Population: 1,763 (2000); Race: 97.5% White, 0.3% Black, 0.3% Asian, 0.8% American Indian and Alaska Native, 0.3% Hispanic of any race, 1.0% two or more races (2000); Density: 41.4 persons per square mile (2000); Age: 29.0% under 18, 13.4% over 64 (2000); Marriage status: 24.4% never married, 61.1% now married, 3.2% widowed, 11.2% divorced (2000); Foreign born: 1.2% (2000); Ancestry (includes multiple ancestries): 45.9% German, 19.2% Irish, 11.6% English, 10.6% Norwegian, 10.1% Polish (2000).
Economy: Single-family building permits issued: 16 (2001) / 15 (2000); Multi-family building permits issued: 0 (2001) / 0 (2000); Employment by occupation: 9.7% management, 7.5% professional, 21.1% services, 27.6% sales, 2.6% farming, 10.7% construction, 20.8% production (2000).
Income: Per capita income: $16,815 (2000); Median household income: $39,271 (2000); Poverty rate: 10.0% (2000).
Taxes: Total city taxes per capita: $46 (1997); City property taxes per capita: $37 (1997).
Education: High school graduation rate: 77.5% (2000); College graduation rate: 10.1% (2000).
Housing: Homeownership rate: 84.3% (2000); Median home value: $89,500 (2000); Median rent: $383 per month (2000); Median age of housing: 22 years (2000).
Transportation: Commute to work: 90.9% car, 0.2% public transportation, 2.3% walk, 6.1% work from home (2000); Travel time to work: 49.1% less than 15 minutes, 27.2% 15 to 30 minutes, 17.1% 30 to 45 minutes, 2.5% 45 to 60 minutes, 4.2% 60 minutes or more (2000)

LINDINA (town). Covers a land area of 33.107 square miles and a water area of 0 square miles. Located at 43.78° N. Lat.; 90.13° W. Long. Elevation is 925 feet.
Population: 730 (2000); Race: 99.3% White, 0.3% Black, 0.4% Asian, 0.0% American Indian and Alaska Native, 1.0% Hispanic of any race, 0.0% two or more races (2000); Density: 22.0 persons per square mile (2000); Age: 29.5% under 18, 14.1% over 64 (2000); Marriage status: 20.6% never married, 65.0% now married, 5.3% widowed, 9.0% divorced (2000); Foreign born: 1.6% (2000); Ancestry (includes multiple ancestries): 46.3% German, 13.3% Irish, 9.7% English, 8.8% Norwegian, 7.9% Polish (2000).
Economy: Single-family building permits issued: 1 (2001) / 2 (2000); Multi-family building permits issued: 0 (2001) / 0 (2000); Employment by occupation: 11.0% management, 12.9% professional, 19.1% services, 25.0% sales, 1.6% farming, 15.1% construction, 15.3% production (2000).
Income: Per capita income: $16,047 (2000); Median household income: $41,250 (2000); Poverty rate: 7.3% (2000).
Taxes: Total city taxes per capita: $83 (1997); City property taxes per capita: $83 (1997).
Education: High school graduation rate: 82.8% (2000); College graduation rate: 13.5% (2000).
Housing: Homeownership rate: 78.1% (2000); Median home value: $76,900 (2000); Median rent: $381 per month (2000); Median age of housing: 40 years (2000).
Transportation: Commute to work: 87.1% car, 0.0% public transportation, 5.4% walk, 7.0% work from home (2000); Travel time to work: 44.7% less than 15 minutes, 26.2% 15 to 30 minutes, 19.0% 30 to 45 minutes, 5.8% 45 to 60 minutes, 4.3% 60 minutes or more (2000)

LISBON (town). Covers a land area of 28.245 square miles and a water area of 0.054 square miles. Located at 43.85° N. Lat.; 90.14° W. Long.
History: Incorporated 1889.
Population: 1,020 (2000); Race: 95.2% White, 0.2% Black, 4.3% Asian, 0.0% American Indian and Alaska Native, 1.4% Hispanic of any race, 0.4% two or more races (2000); Density: 36.1 persons per square mile (2000); Age: 24.5% under 18, 14.8% over 64 (2000); Marriage status: 19.7% never married, 63.3% now married, 8.2% widowed, 8.8% divorced (2000); Foreign born: 2.5% (2000); Ancestry (includes multiple ancestries): 50.6% German, 12.1% Norwegian, 11.3% English, 9.6% Irish, 6.3% Other groups (2000).
Economy: Railroad junction. In dairying and farming region. Manufacturing: furniture, machinery. Necedah National Wildlife Refuge to North. Single-family building permits issued: 2 (2001) / 5 (2000); Multi-family building permits issued: 0 (2001) / 0 (2000); Employment by occupation: 14.9% management, 14.1% professional, 13.7% services, 19.0% sales, 3.0% farming, 9.7% construction, 25.5% production (2000).
Income: Per capita income: $18,231 (2000); Median household income: $41,354 (2000); Poverty rate: 8.9% (2000).
Taxes: Total city taxes per capita: $22 (1997); City property taxes per capita: $17 (1997).
Education: High school graduation rate: 80.8% (2000); College graduation rate: 14.9% (2000).
Housing: Homeownership rate: 94.5% (2000); Median home value: $88,200 (2000); Median rent: $410 per month (2000); Median age of housing: 25 years (2000).
Transportation: Commute to work: 89.3% car, 0.0% public transportation, 4.7% walk, 6.0% work from home (2000); Travel time to work: 49.3% less

than 15 minutes, 26.0% 15 to 30 minutes, 15.9% 30 to 45 minutes, 4.1% 45 to 60 minutes, 4.6% 60 minutes or more (2000)

LYNDON (town). Covers a land area of 28.344 square miles and a water area of 1.301 square miles. Located at 43.67° N. Lat.; 89.85° W. Long.
Population: 1,217 (2000); Race: 80.6% White, 1.6% Black, 1.2% Asian, 14.5% American Indian and Alaska Native, 0.9% Hispanic of any race, 1.9% two or more races (2000); Density: 42.9 persons per square mile (2000); Age: 29.9% under 18, 8.4% over 64 (2000); Marriage status: 24.7% never married, 58.9% now married, 5.7% widowed, 10.7% divorced (2000); Foreign born: 2.5% (2000); Ancestry (includes multiple ancestries): 31.9% German, 17.7% Other groups, 15.0% Irish, 9.3% Norwegian, 8.3% United States or American (2000).
Economy: Lumber. Manufacturing: wood products. Single-family building permits issued: 15 (2001) / 15 (2000); Multi-family building permits issued: 0 (2001) / 0 (2000); Employment by occupation: 16.1% management, 7.6% professional, 18.2% services, 28.3% sales, 0.3% farming, 11.5% construction, 17.9% production (2000).
Income: Per capita income: $17,014 (2000); Median household income: $42,639 (2000); Poverty rate: 5.1% (2000).
Taxes: Total city taxes per capita: $37 (1997); City property taxes per capita: $28 (1997).
Education: High school graduation rate: 80.4% (2000); College graduation rate: 9.0% (2000).
Housing: Homeownership rate: 78.5% (2000); Median home value: $113,900 (2000); Median rent: $318 per month (2000); Median age of housing: 17 years (2000).
Transportation: Commute to work: 89.9% car, 0.2% public transportation, 3.3% walk, 5.7% work from home (2000); Travel time to work: 30.8% less than 15 minutes, 38.8% 15 to 30 minutes, 15.4% 30 to 45 minutes, 4.5% 45 to 60 minutes, 10.6% 60 minutes or more (2000)

LYNDON STATION (village). Aka Lyndon. Covers a land area of 1.993 square miles and a water area of 0 square miles. Located at 43.71° N. Lat.; 89.89° W. Long. Elevation is 910 feet.
Population: 458 (2000); Race: 95.5% White, 0.8% Black, 0.8% Asian, 1.8% American Indian and Alaska Native, 1.2% Hispanic of any race, 0.6% two or more races (2000); Density: 229.8 persons per square mile (2000); Age: 22.9% under 18, 24.3% over 64 (2000); Marriage status: 20.1% never married, 43.4% now married, 15.0% widowed, 21.6% divorced (2000); Foreign born: 1.2% (2000); Ancestry (includes multiple ancestries): 41.5% German, 26.0% Irish, 7.0% Other groups, 5.3% United States or American, 4.9% English (2000).
Economy: Single-family building permits issued: 2 (2001) / 3 (2000); Multi-family building permits issued: 0 (2001) / 0 (2000); Employment by occupation: 10.7% management, 8.0% professional, 24.1% services, 21.4% sales, 1.3% farming, 9.8% construction, 24.6% production (2000).
Income: Per capita income: $16,127 (2000); Median household income: $27,059 (2000); Poverty rate: 9.7% (2000).
Taxes: Total city taxes per capita: $168 (1997); City property taxes per capita: $156 (1997).
Education: High school graduation rate: 67.8% (2000); College graduation rate: 5.8% (2000).
Housing: Homeownership rate: 66.8% (2000); Median home value: $62,200 (2000); Median rent: $318 per month (2000); Median age of housing: 33 years (2000).
Transportation: Commute to work: 96.8% car, 0.0% public transportation, 3.2% walk, 0.0% work from home (2000); Travel time to work: 30.9% less than 15 minutes, 44.7% 15 to 30 minutes, 13.8% 30 to 45 minutes, 1.4% 45 to 60 minutes, 9.2% 60 minutes or more (2000)

MARION (town). Covers a land area of 23.485 square miles and a water area of 0.941 square miles. Located at 43.82° N. Lat.; 89.94° W. Long.
Population: 433 (2000); Race: 98.1% White, 0.0% Black, 0.0% Asian, 0.9% American Indian and Alaska Native, 0.9% Hispanic of any race, 0.9% two or more races (2000); Density: 18.4 persons per square mile (2000); Age: 20.9% under 18, 13.9% over 64 (2000); Marriage status: 23.4% never married, 60.6% now married, 5.4% widowed, 10.6% divorced (2000); Foreign born: 1.9% (2000); Ancestry (includes multiple ancestries): 35.1% German, 23.3% Polish, 15.8% Irish, 6.8% Czech, 6.8% English (2000).
Economy: Single-family building permits issued: 2 (2001) / 5 (2000); Multi-family building permits issued: 0 (2001) / 0 (2000); Employment by occupation: 15.7% management, 15.7% professional, 13.9% services, 21.8% sales, 3.7% farming, 9.3% construction, 19.9% production (2000).
Income: Per capita income: $20,764 (2000); Median household income: $41,058 (2000); Poverty rate: 4.5% (2000).
Taxes: Total city taxes per capita: $57 (1997); City property taxes per capita: $52 (1997).
Education: High school graduation rate: 72.3% (2000); College graduation rate: 10.1% (2000).
Housing: Homeownership rate: 84.2% (2000); Median home value: $76,000 (2000); Median rent: $381 per month (2000); Median age of housing: 23 years (2000).
Transportation: Commute to work: 93.5% car, 0.0% public transportation, 1.9% walk, 3.7% work from home (2000); Travel time to work: 27.1% less than 15 minutes, 46.4% 15 to 30 minutes, 16.4% 30 to 45 minutes, 1.9% 45 to 60 minutes, 8.2% 60 minutes or more (2000)

MAUSTON (city). Covers a land area of 3.657 square miles and a water area of 0.438 square miles. Located at 43.79° N. Lat.; 90.07° W. Long. Elevation is 883 feet.
History: Mauston grew up in 1840 around the sawmill established by General M.M. Maughs along the Lemonweir River.
Population: 3,740 (2000); Race: 97.1% White, 0.5% Black, 0.0% Asian, 0.9% American Indian and Alaska Native, 2.8% Hispanic of any race, 1.3% two or more races (2000); Density: 1,022.6 persons per square mile (2000); Age: 24.4% under 18, 20.3% over 64 (2000); Marriage status: 23.1% never married, 51.9% now married, 11.9% widowed, 13.1% divorced (2000); Foreign born: 1.4% (2000); Ancestry (includes multiple ancestries): 42.5% German, 17.5% Irish, 14.1% Norwegian, 11.8% English, 6.9% Other groups (2000).
Economy: Single-family building permits issued: 8 (2001) / 10 (2000); Multi-family building permits issued: 46 (2001) / 40 (2000); Employment by occupation: 9.2% management, 12.6% professional, 21.3% services, 21.7% sales, 0.0% farming, 6.2% construction, 29.0% production (2000).
Income: Per capita income: $21,640 (2000); Median household income: $32,341 (2000); Poverty rate: 11.9% (2000).
Taxes: Total city taxes per capita: $265 (2000); City property taxes per capita: $241 (2000).
Education: High school graduation rate: 80.9% (2000); College graduation rate: 12.6% (2000).

School District(s)

Mauston (PK-12)
2000 Enrollment: 1,636 608-847-5451

Housing: Homeownership rate: 62.6% (2000); Median home value: $61,500 (2000); Median rent: $363 per month (2000); Median age of housing: 45 years (2000).
Hospitals: Hess Memorial Hospital (100 beds)
Safety: Violent crime rate: 10.6 per 10,000 population; Property crime rate: 448.6 per 10,000 population (2001).
Newspapers: Juneau County Star-Times (2 x week); Buyers Guide Shopper (1 x week)
Transportation: Commute to work: 93.4% car, 0.0% public transportation, 2.9% walk, 1.8% work from home (2000); Travel time to work: 55.1% less than 15 minutes, 22.9% 15 to 30 minutes, 12.1% 30 to 45 minutes, 5.4% 45 to 60 minutes, 4.5% 60 minutes or more (2000)
Additional Information Contacts
Mauston Area Chamber of Commerce. 608-847-4142

NECEDAH (village). Covers a land area of 2.664 square miles and a water area of 0.317 square miles. Located at 44.02° N. Lat.; 90.07° W. Long. Elevation is 920 feet.
Population: 888 (2000); Race: 98.4% White, 0.7% Black, 0.2% Asian, 0.0% American Indian and Alaska Native, 1.3% Hispanic of any race, 0.8% two or more races (2000); Density: 333.3 persons per square mile (2000); Age: 31.6% under 18, 13.2% over 64 (2000); Marriage status: 20.2% never married, 57.3% now married, 9.3% widowed, 13.1% divorced (2000); Foreign born: 1.0% (2000); Ancestry (includes multiple ancestries): 41.3% German, 14.1% Irish, 12.1% Polish, 7.5% English, 6.7% Italian (2000).
Economy: Single-family building permits issued: 0 (2001) / 2 (2000); Multi-family building permits issued: 0 (2001) / 0 (2000); Employment by occupation: 3.1% management, 12.3% professional, 22.3% services, 20.3% sales, 1.3% farming, 11.3% construction, 29.5% production (2000).
Income: Per capita income: $14,766 (2000); Median household income: $32,135 (2000); Poverty rate: 13.1% (2000).
Taxes: Total city taxes per capita: $328 (1997); City property taxes per capita: $316 (1997).
Education: High school graduation rate: 80.0% (2000); College graduation rate: 10.2% (2000).

School District(s)

Necedah Area (PK-12)
2000 Enrollment: 751 608-565-2256

Housing: Homeownership rate: 63.6% (2000); Median home value: $68,600 (2000); Median rent: $374 per month (2000); Median age of housing: 37 years (2000).
Transportation: Commute to work: 96.1% car, 0.0% public transportation, 0.0% walk, 3.4% work from home (2000); Travel time to work: 39.5% less than 15 minutes, 29.6% 15 to 30 minutes, 16.1% 30 to 45 minutes, 6.5% 45 to 60 minutes, 8.3% 60 minutes or more (2000)

NECEDAH (town). Covers a land area of 78.309 square miles and a water area of 4.560 square miles. Located at 44.05° N. Lat.; 90.09° W. Long. Elevation is 920 feet.
Population: 2,156 (2000); Race: 98.4% White, 0.1% Black, 0.2% Asian, 0.2% American Indian and Alaska Native, 1.0% Hispanic of any race, 0.9% two or more races (2000); Density: 27.5 persons per square mile (2000); Age: 29.5% under 18, 14.4% over 64 (2000); Marriage status: 21.8% never married, 63.0% now married, 6.0% widowed, 9.3% divorced (2000); Foreign born: 1.8% (2000); Ancestry (includes multiple ancestries): 36.3% German, 13.0% Irish, 11.9% Polish, 6.3% French (except Basque), 5.3% Other groups (2000).
Economy: Railroad junction. Wood products. Dairy products. Manufacturing: machinery, wood products, fabricated metal products. Necedah National Wildlife Refuge to Northwest; Petenwell Dam to Northeast. Single-family building permits issued: 31 (2001) / 21 (2000); Multi-family building permits issued: 0 (2001) / 0 (2000); Employment by occupation: 9.8% management, 10.9% professional, 16.1% services, 21.6% sales, 0.9% farming, 11.0% construction, 29.6% production (2000).
Income: Per capita income: $15,013 (2000); Median household income: $34,281 (2000); Poverty rate: 10.7% (2000).
Taxes: Total city taxes per capita: $38 (1997); City property taxes per capita: $36 (1997).
Education: High school graduation rate: 78.7% (2000); College graduation rate: 7.6% (2000).
Housing: Homeownership rate: 86.6% (2000); Median home value: $82,900 (2000); Median rent: $373 per month (2000); Median age of housing: 22 years (2000).
Transportation: Commute to work: 92.7% car, 0.1% public transportation, 3.1% walk, 2.9% work from home (2000); Travel time to work: 36.3% less than 15 minutes, 32.7% 15 to 30 minutes, 18.5% 30 to 45 minutes, 6.9% 45 to 60 minutes, 5.6% 60 minutes or more (2000)

NEW LISBON (city). Covers a land area of 2.666 square miles and a water area of 0.188 square miles. Located at 43.87° N. Lat.; 90.16° W. Long. Elevation is 891 feet.
Population: 1,436 (2000); Race: 98.1% White, 0.1% Black, 0.2% Asian, 0.9% American Indian and Alaska Native, 0.6% Hispanic of any race, 0.7% two or more races (2000); Density: 538.6 persons per square mile (2000); Age: 22.9% under 18, 16.5% over 64 (2000); Marriage status: 21.6% never married, 56.4% now married, 10.0% widowed, 12.0% divorced (2000); Foreign born: 0.6% (2000); Ancestry (includes multiple ancestries): 44.7% German, 13.2% Norwegian, 12.2% English, 12.2% Irish, 6.2% Polish (2000).
Economy: Single-family building permits issued: 3 (2001) / 4 (2000); Multi-family building permits issued: 0 (2001) / 0 (2000); Employment by occupation: 4.9% management, 16.2% professional, 19.1% services, 25.5% sales, 1.4% farming, 7.9% construction, 25.0% production (2000).
Income: Per capita income: $19,165 (2000); Median household income: $34,479 (2000); Poverty rate: 10.6% (2000).
Taxes: Total city taxes per capita: $155 (1997); City property taxes per capita: $139 (1997).
Education: High school graduation rate: 81.0% (2000); College graduation rate: 10.4% (2000).

School District(s)

New Lisbon (PK-12)
2000 Enrollment: 714 608-562-3700
Housing: Homeownership rate: 71.6% (2000); Median home value: $62,700 (2000); Median rent: $317 per month (2000); Median age of housing: 41 years (2000).
Safety: Violent crime rate: 6.9 per 10,000 population; Property crime rate: 325.0 per 10,000 population (2001).
Transportation: Commute to work: 89.5% car, 0.3% public transportation, 7.8% walk, 1.4% work from home (2000); Travel time to work: 48.5% less than 15 minutes, 29.6% 15 to 30 minutes, 12.5% 30 to 45 minutes, 4.7% 45 to 60 minutes, 4.7% 60 minutes or more (2000)
Additional Information Contacts
New Lisbon Chamber of Commerce 608-562-3555

ORANGE (town). Covers a land area of 35.129 square miles and a water area of 0.014 square miles. Located at 43.92° N. Lat.; 90.25° W. Long.
Population: 549 (2000); Race: 100.0% White, 0.0% Black, 0.0% Asian, 0.0% American Indian and Alaska Native, 0.0% Hispanic of any race, 0.0% two or more races (2000); Density: 15.6 persons per square mile (2000); Age: 28.2% under 18, 17.1% over 64 (2000); Marriage status: 18.4% never married, 62.0% now married, 7.9% widowed, 11.8% divorced (2000); Foreign born: 0.2% (2000); Ancestry (includes multiple ancestries): 42.1% German, 13.3% Irish, 9.4% English, 9.4% Norwegian, 8.7% Danish (2000).
Economy: Single-family building permits issued: 5 (2001) / 4 (2000); Multi-family building permits issued: 0 (2001) / 0 (2000); Employment by occupation: 16.7% management, 8.7% professional, 17.5% services, 20.2% sales, 0.0% farming, 5.6% construction, 31.3% production (2000).
Income: Per capita income: $17,788 (2000); Median household income: $35,909 (2000); Poverty rate: 15.2% (2000).
Taxes: Total city taxes per capita: $45 (1997); City property taxes per capita: $44 (1997).
Education: High school graduation rate: 76.4% (2000); College graduation rate: 5.7% (2000).
Housing: Homeownership rate: 79.9% (2000); Median home value: $73,500 (2000); Median rent: $306 per month (2000); Median age of housing: 33 years (2000).
Transportation: Commute to work: 85.3% car, 0.0% public transportation, 3.6% walk, 9.6% work from home (2000); Travel time to work: 31.3% less than 15 minutes, 44.5% 15 to 30 minutes, 20.7% 30 to 45 minutes, 0.9% 45 to 60 minutes, 2.6% 60 minutes or more (2000)

PLYMOUTH (town). Covers a land area of 34.562 square miles and a water area of 0.025 square miles. Located at 43.76° N. Lat.; 90.25° W. Long.
Population: 639 (2000); Race: 100.0% White, 0.0% Black, 0.0% Asian, 0.0% American Indian and Alaska Native, 0.5% Hispanic of any race, 0.0% two or more races (2000); Density: 18.5 persons per square mile (2000); Age: 23.7% under 18, 15.4% over 64 (2000); Marriage status: 20.7% never married, 65.3% now married, 6.8% widowed, 7.2% divorced (2000); Foreign born: 0.5% (2000); Ancestry (includes multiple ancestries): 50.5% German, 17.6% Irish, 13.8% Norwegian, 9.1% English, 6.6% Polish (2000).
Economy: Single-family building permits issued: 5 (2001) / 4 (2000); Multi-family building permits issued: 0 (2001) / 0 (2000); Employment by occupation: 20.5% management, 11.9% professional, 11.3% services, 18.0% sales, 4.6% farming, 8.3% construction, 25.4% production (2000).
Income: Per capita income: $21,996 (2000); Median household income: $44,271 (2000); Poverty rate: 8.2% (2000).
Taxes: Total city taxes per capita: $185 (1997); City property taxes per capita: $185 (1997).
Education: High school graduation rate: 84.1% (2000); College graduation rate: 16.1% (2000).
Housing: Homeownership rate: 91.5% (2000); Median home value: $91,400 (2000); Median rent: $275 per month (2000); Median age of housing: 42 years (2000).
Transportation: Commute to work: 82.9% car, 2.2% public transportation, 5.3% walk, 9.7% work from home (2000); Travel time to work: 38.3% less than 15 minutes, 44.1% 15 to 30 minutes, 6.6% 30 to 45 minutes, 4.1% 45 to 60 minutes, 6.9% 60 minutes or more (2000)

SEVEN MILE CREEK (town). Covers a land area of 36.370 square miles and a water area of 0.004 square miles. Located at 43.68° N. Lat.; 90.01° W. Long.
Population: 369 (2000); Race: 99.7% White, 0.0% Black, 0.0% Asian, 0.0% American Indian and Alaska Native, 0.9% Hispanic of any race, 0.0% two or more races (2000); Density: 10.1 persons per square mile (2000); Age: 25.8% under 18, 12.3% over 64 (2000); Marriage status: 26.6% never married, 50.2% now married, 7.2% widowed, 16.0% divorced (2000); Foreign born: 2.2% (2000); Ancestry (includes multiple ancestries): 39.7% German, 11.4% Irish, 7.1% Norwegian, 5.2% Swedish, 4.6% English (2000).
Economy: Single-family building permits issued: 10 (2001) / 10 (2000); Multi-family building permits issued: 0 (2001) / 0 (2000); Employment by occupation: 7.0% management, 8.3% professional, 13.4% services, 19.1% sales, 5.7% farming, 9.6% construction, 36.9% production (2000).
Income: Per capita income: $16,939 (2000); Median household income: $36,731 (2000); Poverty rate: 16.0% (2000).
Taxes: Total city taxes per capita: $160 (2000); City property taxes per capita: $157 (2000).
Education: High school graduation rate: 82.4% (2000); College graduation rate: 5.1% (2000).

Housing: Homeownership rate: 82.9% (2000); Median home value: $84,000 (2000); Median rent: $325 per month (2000); Median age of housing: 38 years (2000).
Transportation: Commute to work: 82.7% car, 0.0% public transportation, 5.1% walk, 10.9% work from home (2000); Travel time to work: 18.0% less than 15 minutes, 45.3% 15 to 30 minutes, 19.4% 30 to 45 minutes, 10.1% 45 to 60 minutes, 7.2% 60 minutes or more (2000)

SUMMIT (town). Covers a land area of 36.919 square miles and a water area of 0.013 square miles. Located at 43.68° N. Lat.; 90.13° W. Long.
Population: 623 (2000); Race: 98.5% White, 0.3% Black, 0.2% Asian, 0.0% American Indian and Alaska Native, 0.3% Hispanic of any race, 1.1% two or more races (2000); Density: 16.9 persons per square mile (2000); Age: 30.6% under 18, 12.0% over 64 (2000); Marriage status: 19.6% never married, 66.8% now married, 5.1% widowed, 8.5% divorced (2000); Foreign born: 0.8% (2000); Ancestry (includes multiple ancestries): 49.5% German, 14.0% Irish, 12.8% English, 8.6% United States or American, 6.6% Norwegian (2000).
Economy: Single-family building permits issued: 9 (2001) / 6 (2000); Multi-family building permits issued: 0 (2001) / 0 (2000); Employment by occupation: 23.9% management, 7.9% professional, 11.5% services, 19.7% sales, 4.2% farming, 7.9% construction, 24.8% production (2000).
Income: Per capita income: $15,584 (2000); Median household income: $35,536 (2000); Poverty rate: 11.6% (2000).
Taxes: Total city taxes per capita: $161 (1997); City property taxes per capita: $158 (1997).
Education: High school graduation rate: 82.9% (2000); College graduation rate: 6.9% (2000).
Housing: Homeownership rate: 88.4% (2000); Median home value: $74,400 (2000); Median rent: $225 per month (2000); Median age of housing: 36 years (2000).
Transportation: Commute to work: 73.8% car, 1.5% public transportation, 4.5% walk, 18.7% work from home (2000); Travel time to work: 29.6% less than 15 minutes, 37.0% 15 to 30 minutes, 23.0% 30 to 45 minutes, 5.6% 45 to 60 minutes, 4.8% 60 minutes or more (2000)

UNION CENTER (village). Covers a land area of 0.801 square miles and a water area of 0 square miles. Located at 43.68° N. Lat.; 90.26° W. Long. Elevation is 922 feet.
Population: 214 (2000); Race: 100.0% White, 0.0% Black, 0.0% Asian, 0.0% American Indian and Alaska Native, 2.2% Hispanic of any race, 0.0% two or more races (2000); Density: 267.1 persons per square mile (2000); Age: 19.7% under 18, 15.3% over 64 (2000); Marriage status: 21.9% never married, 55.1% now married, 6.1% widowed, 16.8% divorced (2000); Foreign born: 0.4% (2000); Ancestry (includes multiple ancestries): 45.9% German, 23.6% Irish, 17.0% Czech, 10.9% English, 7.4% Norwegian (2000).
Economy: In dairying region. Manufacturing of machinery. Single-family building permits issued: 0 (2001) / 1 (2000); Multi-family building permits issued: 0 (2001) / 0 (2000); Employment by occupation: 6.1% management, 7.9% professional, 11.4% services, 18.4% sales, 0.0% farming, 15.8% construction, 40.4% production (2000).
Income: Per capita income: $17,121 (2000); Median household income: $34,063 (2000); Poverty rate: 8.3% (2000).
Taxes: Total city taxes per capita: $273 (1997); City property taxes per capita: $263 (1997).
Education: High school graduation rate: 75.8% (2000); College graduation rate: 6.7% (2000).
Housing: Homeownership rate: 65.3% (2000); Median home value: $65,400 (2000); Median rent: $325 per month (2000); Median age of housing: 36 years (2000).
Transportation: Commute to work: 87.7% car, 0.0% public transportation, 7.0% walk, 5.3% work from home (2000); Travel time to work: 60.2% less than 15 minutes, 7.4% 15 to 30 minutes, 25.0% 30 to 45 minutes, 3.7% 45 to 60 minutes, 3.7% 60 minutes or more (2000)

WONEWOC (village). Covers a land area of 1.038 square miles and a water area of 0 square miles. Located at 43.65° N. Lat.; 90.22° W. Long. Elevation is 938 feet.
Population: 834 (2000); Race: 98.4% White, 0.0% Black, 0.0% Asian, 0.7% American Indian and Alaska Native, 2.2% Hispanic of any race, 0.0% two or more races (2000); Density: 803.3 persons per square mile (2000); Age: 23.0% under 18, 20.7% over 64 (2000); Marriage status: 22.9% never married, 51.7% now married, 14.2% widowed, 11.3% divorced (2000); Foreign born: 1.2% (2000); Ancestry (includes multiple ancestries): 49.9% German, 10.7% Irish, 8.6% English, 6.0% French (except Basque), 5.9% United States or American (2000).
Economy: Single-family building permits issued: 2 (2001) / 0 (2000); Multi-family building permits issued: 0 (2001) / 0 (2000); Employment by occupation: 6.6% management, 15.2% professional, 19.0% services, 14.2% sales, 1.5% farming, 9.1% construction, 34.3% production (2000).
Income: Per capita income: $18,957 (2000); Median household income: $28,393 (2000); Poverty rate: 9.6% (2000).
Taxes: Total city taxes per capita: $83 (1997); City property taxes per capita: $70 (1997).
Education: High school graduation rate: 75.4% (2000); College graduation rate: 11.8% (2000).

School District(s)

Wonewoc-Union Center (PK-12)
2000 Enrollment: 429 608-464-3165

Housing: Homeownership rate: 68.5% (2000); Median home value: $64,100 (2000); Median rent: $318 per month (2000); Median age of housing: 60+ years (2000).
Transportation: Commute to work: 84.3% car, 0.5% public transportation, 9.4% walk, 5.3% work from home (2000); Travel time to work: 36.2% less than 15 minutes, 37.3% 15 to 30 minutes, 12.1% 30 to 45 minutes, 8.8% 45 to 60 minutes, 5.6% 60 minutes or more (2000)

WONEWOC (town). Covers a land area of 35.520 square miles and a water area of 0.017 square miles. Located at 43.68° N. Lat.; 90.25° W. Long. Elevation is 938 feet.
Population: 783 (2000); Race: 100.0% White, 0.0% Black, 0.0% Asian, 0.0% American Indian and Alaska Native, 0.3% Hispanic of any race, 0.0% two or more races (2000); Density: 22.0 persons per square mile (2000); Age: 25.6% under 18, 17.7% over 64 (2000); Marriage status: 20.6% never married, 67.7% now married, 8.4% widowed, 3.3% divorced (2000); Foreign born: 0.0% (2000); Ancestry (includes multiple ancestries): 50.3% German, 14.8% English, 12.1% Irish, 10.8% Norwegian, 6.6% United States or American (2000).
Economy: In agricultural area: poultry, fruit. Manufacturing of batteries, wood products. Employment by occupation: 15.9% management, 10.9% professional, 13.0% services, 20.7% sales, 2.1% farming, 9.0% construction, 28.4% production (2000).
Income: Per capita income: $18,666 (2000); Median household income: $37,875 (2000); Poverty rate: 4.5% (2000).
Taxes: Total city taxes per capita: $181 (1997); City property taxes per capita: $180 (1997).
Education: High school graduation rate: 78.6% (2000); College graduation rate: 8.0% (2000).
Housing: Homeownership rate: 82.6% (2000); Median home value: $74,000 (2000); Median rent: $288 per month (2000); Median age of housing: 39 years (2000).
Transportation: Commute to work: 81.4% car, 0.0% public transportation, 6.6% walk, 10.1% work from home (2000); Travel time to work: 49.4% less than 15 minutes, 26.5% 15 to 30 minutes, 13.1% 30 to 45 minutes, 7.9% 45 to 60 minutes, 3.0% 60 minutes or more (2000)

Kenosha County

Located in southeastern Wisconsin; bounded on the east by Lake Michigan, and on the south by Illinois; drained by the Des Plaines and Fox Rivers. Covers a land area of 272.80 square miles, a water area of 481.50 square miles, and is located in the Central Time Zone. The county government was organized in 1850. County seat is Kenosha.

Kenosha County is part of the Kenosha, WI PMSA. The entire metro area includes: Kenosha County

Weather Station: Kenosha Elevation: 597 feet

	Jan	Feb	Mar	Apr	May	Jun	Jul	Aug	Sep	Oct	Nov	Dec
High	29	33	42	52	62	73	79	78	71	59	46	34
Low	13	18	27	36	45	55	62	61	53	42	31	19
Precip	1.6	1.2	2.3	3.8	3.3	3.5	3.6	4.1	3.7	2.5	2.7	2.1
Snow	12.4	9.0	6.0	1.5	tr	0.0	0.0	0.0	0.0	tr	1.4	7.1

High and Low temperatures in degrees Fahrenheit; Precipitation and Snow in inches

Population: 149,577 (2000); Race: 88.5% White, 4.8% Black, 0.9% Asian, 0.4% American Indian and Alaska Native, 7.0% Hispanic of any race, 2.0% two or more races (2000); Density: 548.2 persons per square mile (2000); Age: 27.0% under 18, 11.5% over 64 (2000).
Religion: Five largest groups: 29.6% Catholic Church, 5.5% Evangelical Lutheran Church in America, 2.1% Wisconsin Evangelical Lutheran Synod, 1.5% Muslim estimate, 1.4% The United Methodist Church (2000).

Economy: Unemployment rate: 4.8% (11/2002); Total civilian labor force: 85,194 (11/2002); Leading industries: 24.5% manufacturing; 14.1% retail trade; 13.3% health care and social assistance (2000); Companies that employ more than 1,000 persons: 2 (2000); Companies that employ more than 100 persons: 81 (2000); Farms: 388 totaling 84,744 acres (1997); Minority business ownership rate: 5.5% (1997); Women business ownership rate: 23.9% (1997); Retail sales per capita: $7,502 (1997). Single-family building permits issued: 732 (2001) / 626 (2000); Multi-family building permits issued: 321 (2001) / 388 (2000).
Income: Per capita income: $21,207 (2000); Median household income: $46,970 (2000); Poverty rate: 7.5% (2000); Bankruptcy rate: 5.41% (2001).
Taxes: Total county taxes per capita: $284 (2000); County property taxes per capita: $231 (2000).
Education: High school graduation rate: 83.5% (2000); College graduation rate: 19.2% (2000).
Housing: Homeownership rate: 69.1% (2000); Median home value: $120,900 (2000); Median rent: $531 per month (2000); Median age of housing: 36 years (2000).
Health: Birth rate: 139.0 per 10,000 population (1998); Age adjusted death rate: 86.3 per 10,000 population (1999); Age adjusted cancer mortality rate: 208.9 deaths per 100,000 population (1999). Air Quality Index: 55% good, 43% moderate, 2% unhealthy (percent of days in 2000). Number of physicians: 13.2 per 10,000 population (1999); Number of hospital beds: 23.3 per 10,000 population (1999).
Elections: 2000 Presidential election results: 50.9% Gore, 45.4% Bush, 2.9% Nader, 0.4% Buchanan

Additional Information Contacts

Kenosha County Government Offices 262-653-2552
Kenosha Area Convention Bureau 262-654-7307
Kenosha Chamber of Commerce 262-654-1234
Kenosha Realtors Association 262-942-0592
Twin Lakes Chamber of Commerce 262-877-2220

Kenosha County Communities

BRIGHTON (town). Covers a land area of 35.785 square miles and a water area of 0.185 square miles. Located at 42.61° N. Lat.; 88.12° W. Long. Elevation is 810 feet.
Population: 1,450 (2000); Race: 97.4% White, 0.0% Black, 0.3% Asian, 0.2% American Indian and Alaska Native, 2.1% Hispanic of any race, 1.1% two or more races (2000); Density: 40.5 persons per square mile (2000); Age: 26.1% under 18, 9.1% over 64 (2000); Marriage status: 22.6% never married, 65.9% now married, 3.7% widowed, 7.8% divorced (2000); Foreign born: 0.9% (2000); Ancestry (includes multiple ancestries): 45.2% German, 14.9% Irish, 9.0% English, 8.7% Polish, 6.4% French (except Basque) (2000).
Economy: Single-family building permits issued: 6 (2001) / 12 (2000); Multi-family building permits issued: 0 (2001) / 0 (2000); Employment by occupation: 16.9% management, 13.2% professional, 8.6% services, 27.8% sales, 0.6% farming, 16.7% construction, 16.1% production (2000).
Income: Per capita income: $26,518 (2000); Median household income: $70,078 (2000); Poverty rate: 1.9% (2000).
Education: High school graduation rate: 90.5% (2000); College graduation rate: 20.5% (2000).
Housing: Homeownership rate: 91.3% (2000); Median home value: $173,500 (2000); Median rent: $575 per month (2000); Median age of housing: 28 years (2000).
Transportation: Commute to work: 86.1% car, 1.1% public transportation, 1.7% walk, 9.5% work from home (2000); Travel time to work: 23.2% less than 15 minutes, 32.2% 15 to 30 minutes, 22.2% 30 to 45 minutes, 10.8% 45 to 60 minutes, 11.6% 60 minutes or more (2000)

BRISTOL (town). Covers a land area of 34.703 square miles and a water area of 0.339 square miles. Located at 42.54° N. Lat.; 88.01° W. Long. Elevation is 770 feet.
History: Bristol was established in 1838 by settlers from Vermont and Connecticut. Originally three miles east, it was moved in the 1850's when the railroad arrived in the area. Circus owner P.T. Barnum, whose sister lived near Bristol, was a frequent visitor here.
Population: 4,538 (2000); Race: 98.4% White, 0.0% Black, 0.0% Asian, 0.0% American Indian and Alaska Native, 2.4% Hispanic of any race, 0.8% two or more races (2000); Density: 130.8 persons per square mile (2000); Age: 26.0% under 18, 12.3% over 64 (2000); Marriage status: 20.1% never married, 63.7% now married, 5.9% widowed, 10.3% divorced (2000); Foreign born: 3.1% (2000); Ancestry (includes multiple ancestries): 39.8% German, 15.9% Irish, 12.2% Polish, 9.5% English, 5.8% United States or American (2000).
Economy: Single-family building permits issued: 17 (2001) / 19 (2000); Multi-family building permits issued: 0 (2001) / 12 (2000); Employment by occupation: 16.0% management, 14.0% professional, 10.8% services, 29.8% sales, 0.3% farming, 13.8% construction, 15.4% production (2000).
Income: Per capita income: $24,454 (2000); Median household income: $54,661 (2000); Poverty rate: 2.2% (2000).
Taxes: Total city taxes per capita: $226 (2000); City property taxes per capita: $190 (2000).
Education: High school graduation rate: 84.9% (2000); College graduation rate: 18.2% (2000).

School District(s)

Bristol #1 (PK-08)
2000 Enrollment: 550 262-857-2334

Housing: Homeownership rate: 83.7% (2000); Median home value: $156,400 (2000); Median rent: $584 per month (2000); Median age of housing: 26 years (2000).
Transportation: Commute to work: 92.9% car, 0.7% public transportation, 1.4% walk, 4.7% work from home (2000); Travel time to work: 23.5% less than 15 minutes, 34.4% 15 to 30 minutes, 21.5% 30 to 45 minutes, 11.9% 45 to 60 minutes, 8.8% 60 minutes or more (2000)

CAMP LAKE (CDP). Covers a land area of 4.496 square miles and a water area of 0.941 square miles. Located at 42.52° N. Lat.; 88.13° W. Long. Elevation is 750 feet.
Population: 3,255 (2000); Race: 98.6% White, 0.1% Black, 0.1% Asian, 0.2% American Indian and Alaska Native, 1.7% Hispanic of any race, 0.7% two or more races (2000); Density: 724.0 persons per square mile (2000); Age: 32.2% under 18, 7.9% over 64 (2000); Marriage status: 21.5% never married, 66.2% now married, 4.2% widowed, 8.0% divorced (2000); Foreign born: 2.7% (2000); Ancestry (includes multiple ancestries): 41.4% German, 17.9% Irish, 13.2% Polish, 7.1% Italian, 5.0% Other groups (2000).
Economy: Employment by occupation: 10.4% management, 9.2% professional, 13.9% services, 28.1% sales, 0.1% farming, 15.3% construction, 23.0% production (2000).
Income: Per capita income: $17,863 (2000); Median household income: $42,986 (2000); Poverty rate: 9.8% (2000).
Education: High school graduation rate: 82.5% (2000); College graduation rate: 9.3% (2000).
Housing: Homeownership rate: 85.5% (2000); Median home value: $119,800 (2000); Median rent: $625 per month (2000); Median age of housing: 41 years (2000).
Transportation: Commute to work: 96.3% car, 1.1% public transportation, 0.2% walk, 2.0% work from home (2000); Travel time to work: 18.9% less than 15 minutes, 27.6% 15 to 30 minutes, 22.3% 30 to 45 minutes, 18.4% 45 to 60 minutes, 12.8% 60 minutes or more (2000)

KENOSHA (city). Covers a land area of 23.808 square miles and a water area of 0.154 square miles. Located at 42.58° N. Lat.; 87.84° W. Long. Elevation is 620 feet.
History: Kenosha was selected as a town site by John Bullen, Jr., of the Western Emigration Company, which sent out eight families from New York in 1835 to settle the area called Pike Creek. Wheat farming was the principal occupation, but growth was retarded by the lack of an adequate harbor. The name was soon changed to Southport, and in 1842 a resident, at his own expense, built a wharf that enabled boats to dock here. The first free public school in Wisconsin was opened in Southport in 1849. In 1850 Southport was incorporated as the city of Kenosha, and became the seat of the newly created Kenosha County. The decade of the 1890's marked the beginning of large-scale manufacturing in Kenosha, with the coming of the Chicago Brass Company, the expansion of the Simmons Company from a small cheese box factory to the Northwestern Wire Mattress Company, and the founding of the Chicago and Rockford Hosiery Company. After 1900, many European immigrants came to Kenosha to work in the factories.
Population: 90,352 (2000); Race: 83.8% White, 7.4% Black, 0.9% Asian, 0.4% American Indian and Alaska Native, 9.6% Hispanic of any race, 2.4% two or more races (2000); Density: 3,795.1 persons per square mile (2000); Age: 27.1% under 18, 12.2% over 64 (2000); Marriage status: 28.3% never married, 53.5% now married, 6.9% widowed, 11.4% divorced (2000); Foreign born: 5.9% (2000); Ancestry (includes multiple ancestries): 31.5% German, 19.2% Other groups, 11.9% Italian, 11.5% Irish, 8.5% Polish (2000).
Vital Statistics: Birth rate: 177.5 per 10,000 population (1998)
Economy: Unemployment rate: 6.0% (11/2002); Total civilian labor force: 50,412 (11/2002); Single-family building permits issued: 209 (2001) / 233

(2000); Multi-family building permits issued: 266 (2001) / 289 (2000); Employment by occupation: 10.5% management, 18.0% professional, 15.9% services, 26.7% sales, 0.1% farming, 7.5% construction, 21.3% production (2000).
Income: Per capita income: $19,578 (2000); Median household income: $41,902 (2000); Poverty rate: 9.5% (2000).
Taxes: Total city taxes per capita: $364 (2000); City property taxes per capita: $339 (2000).
Education: High school graduation rate: 81.8% (2000); College graduation rate: 18.2% (2000).

School District(s)

Kenosha (PK-12)
2000 Enrollment: 20,099 262-653-6320
Paris J1 (KG-08)
2000 Enrollment: 212 262-859-2350

Four-year College(s)

Carthage College (Private, Not-for-profit, Evangelical Lutheran Church)
2001 Enrollment: 2,345 262-551-8500
2001 Tuition: In-state $18,205; Out-of-state $18,205
University of Wisconsin-Parkside (Public)
2001 Enrollment: 4,964 262-595-2573
2001 Tuition: In-state $2,776; Out-of-state $11,288

Two-year College(s)

Gateway Technical College (Public)
2001 Enrollment: 6,247 262-564-2200
2001 Tuition: In-state $2,048; Out-of-state $15,456

Housing: Homeownership rate: 62.2% (2000); Median home value: $108,000 (2000); Median rent: $516 per month (2000); Median age of housing: 40 years (2000).
Hospitals: Aurora Medical Center; Kenosha Hospital and Medical Center (315 beds)
Safety: Violent crime rate: 60.1 per 10,000 population; Property crime rate: 289.6 per 10,000 population (2001).
Newspapers: Kenosha News (7 x week)
Transportation: Commute to work: 92.8% car, 1.5% public transportation, 2.8% walk, 1.8% work from home (2000); Travel time to work: 39.5% less than 15 minutes, 30.2% 15 to 30 minutes, 15.0% 30 to 45 minutes, 8.3% 45 to 60 minutes, 7.1% 60 minutes or more (2000)
Airports: Kenosha Regional
Additional Information Contacts
Kenosha Area Convention Bureau 262-654-7307
Kenosha Chamber of Commerce 262-654-1234
Kenosha Realtors Association 262-942-0592

LAKE SHANGRILA (CDP). Covers a land area of 0.726 square miles and a water area of 0.239 square miles. Located at 42.50° N. Lat.; 88.07° W. Long.
Population: 805 (2000); Race: 94.4% White, 0.9% Black, 0.0% Asian, 0.0% American Indian and Alaska Native, 2.6% Hispanic of any race, 2.0% two or more races (2000); Density: 1,108.4 persons per square mile (2000); Age: 25.9% under 18, 10.7% over 64 (2000); Marriage status: 21.9% never married, 56.5% now married, 5.5% widowed, 16.1% divorced (2000); Foreign born: 3.6% (2000); Ancestry (includes multiple ancestries): 32.5% German, 15.6% Italian, 10.2% Polish, 9.4% Irish, 8.4% Norwegian (2000).
Economy: Employment by occupation: 17.8% management, 9.4% professional, 3.7% services, 33.1% sales, 0.0% farming, 17.8% construction, 18.2% production (2000).
Income: Per capita income: $24,606 (2000); Median household income: $65,977 (2000); Poverty rate: 7.5% (2000).
Education: High school graduation rate: 80.4% (2000); College graduation rate: 18.9% (2000).
Housing: Homeownership rate: 85.5% (2000); Median home value: $147,000 (2000); Median rent: $721 per month (2000); Median age of housing: 35 years (2000).
Transportation: Commute to work: 89.9% car, 1.8% public transportation, 0.9% walk, 4.2% work from home (2000); Travel time to work: 19.5% less than 15 minutes, 26.8% 15 to 30 minutes, 26.3% 30 to 45 minutes, 18.5% 45 to 60 minutes, 8.9% 60 minutes or more (2000)

PADDOCK LAKE (village). Covers a land area of 1.956 square miles and a water area of 0.244 square miles. Located at 42.57° N. Lat.; 88.10° W. Long. Elevation is 820 feet.
Population: 3,012 (2000); Race: 96.6% White, 0.7% Black, 0.1% Asian, 0.0% American Indian and Alaska Native, 4.7% Hispanic of any race, 1.3% two or more races (2000); Density: 1,539.9 persons per square mile (2000); Age: 29.0% under 18, 9.1% over 64 (2000); Marriage status: 26.8% never married, 61.4% now married, 5.2% widowed, 6.5% divorced (2000); Foreign born: 1.2% (2000); Ancestry (includes multiple ancestries): 44.1% German, 19.8% Irish, 11.3% Polish, 10.9% Italian, 10.2% English (2000).
Economy: Recreation area; small lakes to Southwest. Bong St. Recreation Area to North. Dairying, livestock, soybeans. Single-family building permits issued: 17 (2001) / 21 (2000); Multi-family building permits issued: 0 (2001) / 0 (2000); Employment by occupation: 7.2% management, 17.1% professional, 10.2% services, 29.5% sales, 0.5% farming, 16.6% construction, 18.9% production (2000).
Income: Per capita income: $20,621 (2000); Median household income: $53,382 (2000); Poverty rate: 1.5% (2000).
Taxes: Total city taxes per capita: $220 (1997); City property taxes per capita: $208 (1997).
Education: High school graduation rate: 80.8% (2000); College graduation rate: 14.1% (2000).
Housing: Homeownership rate: 82.5% (2000); Median home value: $112,600 (2000); Median rent: $602 per month (2000); Median age of housing: 34 years (2000).
Transportation: Commute to work: 95.7% car, 1.5% public transportation, 0.7% walk, 2.2% work from home (2000); Travel time to work: 20.7% less than 15 minutes, 31.6% 15 to 30 minutes, 25.1% 30 to 45 minutes, 10.5% 45 to 60 minutes, 12.0% 60 minutes or more (2000)

PARIS (town). Covers a land area of 36.475 square miles and a water area of 0.002 square miles. Located at 42.61° N. Lat.; 88.01° W. Long. Elevation is 755 feet.
Population: 1,473 (2000); Race: 95.7% White, 0.1% Black, 0.5% Asian, 0.3% American Indian and Alaska Native, 1.4% Hispanic of any race, 2.4% two or more races (2000); Density: 40.4 persons per square mile (2000); Age: 25.1% under 18, 14.5% over 64 (2000); Marriage status: 21.5% never married, 65.7% now married, 4.5% widowed, 8.3% divorced (2000); Foreign born: 2.0% (2000); Ancestry (includes multiple ancestries): 50.1% German, 15.6% Irish, 10.6% Polish, 9.6% English, 9.3% Italian (2000).
Economy: Single-family building permits issued: 6 (2001) / 9 (2000); Multi-family building permits issued: 0 (2001) / 0 (2000); Employment by occupation: 18.4% management, 9.7% professional, 11.4% services, 26.9% sales, 2.2% farming, 16.0% construction, 15.4% production (2000).
Income: Per capita income: $23,458 (2000); Median household income: $54,375 (2000); Poverty rate: 3.6% (2000).
Taxes: Total city taxes per capita: $12 (1997); City property taxes per capita: $0 (1997).
Education: High school graduation rate: 86.3% (2000); College graduation rate: 15.0% (2000).
Housing: Homeownership rate: 81.4% (2000); Median home value: $157,300 (2000); Median rent: $506 per month (2000); Median age of housing: 42 years (2000).
Transportation: Commute to work: 90.9% car, 0.7% public transportation, 1.3% walk, 6.4% work from home (2000); Travel time to work: 27.4% less than 15 minutes, 39.3% 15 to 30 minutes, 21.0% 30 to 45 minutes, 7.3% 45 to 60 minutes, 5.1% 60 minutes or more (2000)

PLEASANT PRAIRIE (village). Covers a land area of 33.453 square miles and a water area of 0.126 square miles. Located at 42.53° N. Lat.; 87.87° W. Long. Elevation is 700 feet.
Population: 16,136 (2000); Race: 94.4% White, 0.6% Black, 1.6% Asian, 0.6% American Indian and Alaska Native, 3.1% Hispanic of any race, 2.1% two or more races (2000); Density: 482.3 persons per square mile (2000); Age: 27.2% under 18, 11.2% over 64 (2000); Marriage status: 20.7% never married, 66.5% now married, 5.3% widowed, 7.5% divorced (2000); Foreign born: 4.3% (2000); Ancestry (includes multiple ancestries): 36.1% German, 14.0% Irish, 10.5% Italian, 9.8% Polish, 9.3% Other groups (2000).
Vital Statistics: Birth rate: 49.6 per 10,000 population (1998)
Economy: Manufacturing: primary metals, metal products. Single-family building permits issued: 245 (2001) / 129 (2000); Multi-family building permits issued: 23 (2001) / 57 (2000); Employment by occupation: 13.1% management, 20.6% professional, 12.9% services, 26.2% sales, 0.0% farming, 10.4% construction, 16.9% production (2000).
Income: Per capita income: $26,087 (2000); Median household income: $62,856 (2000); Poverty rate: 3.2% (2000).
Taxes: Total city taxes per capita: $657 (2000); City property taxes per capita: $599 (2000).
Education: High school graduation rate: 87.1% (2000); College graduation rate: 27.2% (2000).
Housing: Homeownership rate: 82.1% (2000); Median home value: $159,800 (2000); Median rent: $790 per month (2000); Median age of housing: 24 years (2000).

Safety: Violent crime rate: 3.1 per 10,000 population; Property crime rate: 324.3 per 10,000 population (2001).
Transportation: Commute to work: 96.0% car, 0.8% public transportation, 0.5% walk, 2.3% work from home (2000); Travel time to work: 29.0% less than 15 minutes, 33.4% 15 to 30 minutes, 19.9% 30 to 45 minutes, 9.2% 45 to 60 minutes, 8.5% 60 minutes or more (2000)

POWERS LAKE (CDP). Covers a land area of 1.914 square miles and a water area of 0.854 square miles. Located at 42.53° N. Lat.; 88.29° W. Long. Elevation is 860 feet.
Population: 1,500 (2000); Race: 96.6% White, 0.0% Black, 0.0% Asian, 0.5% American Indian and Alaska Native, 1.3% Hispanic of any race, 1.7% two or more races (2000); Density: 783.6 persons per square mile (2000); Age: 27.4% under 18, 11.8% over 64 (2000); Marriage status: 23.5% never married, 60.8% now married, 6.6% widowed, 9.1% divorced (2000); Foreign born: 2.4% (2000); Ancestry (includes multiple ancestries): 42.6% German, 20.2% Irish, 11.6% Polish, 8.0% Italian, 7.5% English (2000).
Economy: Employment by occupation: 11.5% management, 13.1% professional, 14.7% services, 28.2% sales, 1.0% farming, 9.8% construction, 21.6% production (2000).
Income: Per capita income: $22,766 (2000); Median household income: $53,403 (2000); Poverty rate: 7.4% (2000).
Education: High school graduation rate: 87.1% (2000); College graduation rate: 14.3% (2000).
Housing: Homeownership rate: 80.8% (2000); Median home value: $145,300 (2000); Median rent: $656 per month (2000); Median age of housing: 40 years (2000).
Transportation: Commute to work: 95.7% car, 0.5% public transportation, 0.7% walk, 2.0% work from home (2000); Travel time to work: 18.3% less than 15 minutes, 29.6% 15 to 30 minutes, 18.6% 30 to 45 minutes, 10.2% 45 to 60 minutes, 23.3% 60 minutes or more (2000)

RANDALL (town). Covers a land area of 15.890 square miles and a water area of 0.651 square miles. Located at 42.53° N. Lat.; 88.27° W. Long.
Population: 2,929 (2000); Race: 97.5% White, 0.0% Black, 0.1% Asian, 0.3% American Indian and Alaska Native, 1.4% Hispanic of any race, 1.7% two or more races (2000); Density: 184.3 persons per square mile (2000); Age: 28.7% under 18, 8.7% over 64 (2000); Marriage status: 24.0% never married, 67.7% now married, 3.7% widowed, 4.7% divorced (2000); Foreign born: 1.8% (2000); Ancestry (includes multiple ancestries): 44.2% German, 18.9% Irish, 14.7% Polish, 10.5% Italian, 9.2% English (2000).
Economy: Single-family building permits issued: 42 (2001) / 36 (2000); Multi-family building permits issued: 0 (2001) / 0 (2000); Employment by occupation: 12.8% management, 15.6% professional, 13.3% services, 25.9% sales, 0.5% farming, 14.6% construction, 17.3% production (2000).
Income: Per capita income: $22,000 (2000); Median household income: $63,063 (2000); Poverty rate: 3.9% (2000).
Taxes: Total city taxes per capita: $133 (1997); City property taxes per capita: $120 (1997).
Education: High school graduation rate: 92.1% (2000); College graduation rate: 19.1% (2000).
Housing: Homeownership rate: 85.7% (2000); Median home value: $164,000 (2000); Median rent: $557 per month (2000); Median age of housing: 30 years (2000).
Transportation: Commute to work: 96.2% car, 0.8% public transportation, 1.5% walk, 1.3% work from home (2000); Travel time to work: 23.6% less than 15 minutes, 27.5% 15 to 30 minutes, 17.8% 30 to 45 minutes, 13.9% 45 to 60 minutes, 17.3% 60 minutes or more (2000)

SALEM (town). Covers a land area of 29.688 square miles and a water area of 2.697 square miles. Located at 42.52° N. Lat.; 88.13° W. Long. Elevation is 780 feet.
Population: 9,871 (2000); Race: 97.9% White, 0.2% Black, 0.2% Asian, 0.2% American Indian and Alaska Native, 2.1% Hispanic of any race, 1.2% two or more races (2000); Density: 332.5 persons per square mile (2000); Age: 29.8% under 18, 7.8% over 64 (2000); Marriage status: 23.1% never married, 63.0% now married, 4.3% widowed, 9.7% divorced (2000); Foreign born: 2.3% (2000); Ancestry (includes multiple ancestries): 39.7% German, 15.9% Irish, 12.3% Polish, 8.2% English, 7.7% Italian (2000).
Economy: Lakes district; recreation. Wheat, soybeans. Single-family building permits issued: 97 (2001) / 88 (2000); Multi-family building permits issued: 30 (2001) / 18 (2000); Employment by occupation: 13.1% management, 12.6% professional, 12.2% services, 29.6% sales, 0.6% farming, 15.4% construction, 16.5% production (2000).
Income: Per capita income: $22,814 (2000); Median household income: $54,392 (2000); Poverty rate: 6.8% (2000).
Taxes: Total city taxes per capita: $156 (2000); City property taxes per capita: $130 (2000).
Education: High school graduation rate: 85.5% (2000); College graduation rate: 15.2% (2000).

School District(s)

Central/Westosha UHS (09-12)
2000 Enrollment: 1,135 262-843-4211
Salem J2 (KG-08)
2000 Enrollment: 1,075 262-843-2356

Housing: Homeownership rate: 83.2% (2000); Median home value: $137,300 (2000); Median rent: $563 per month (2000); Median age of housing: 35 years (2000).
Transportation: Commute to work: 94.9% car, 1.0% public transportation, 0.7% walk, 2.4% work from home (2000); Travel time to work: 21.8% less than 15 minutes, 26.5% 15 to 30 minutes, 23.9% 30 to 45 minutes, 14.8% 45 to 60 minutes, 12.9% 60 minutes or more (2000)

SILVER LAKE (village). Covers a land area of 1.528 square miles and a water area of 0 square miles. Located at 42.54° N. Lat.; 88.16° W. Long. Elevation is 750 feet.
Population: 2,341 (2000); Race: 96.1% White, 0.1% Black, 0.2% Asian, 0.7% American Indian and Alaska Native, 2.2% Hispanic of any race, 1.4% two or more races (2000); Density: 1,532.4 persons per square mile (2000); Age: 29.7% under 18, 10.2% over 64 (2000); Marriage status: 22.2% never married, 58.4% now married, 6.9% widowed, 12.5% divorced (2000); Foreign born: 2.8% (2000); Ancestry (includes multiple ancestries): 45.9% German, 14.0% Irish, 11.2% Polish, 7.6% Italian, 7.1% Other groups (2000).
Economy: Manufacturing of underwater weed cutters. Small lakes in area; recreation. Single-family building permits issued: 12 (2001) / 5 (2000); Multi-family building permits issued: 0 (2001) / 0 (2000); Employment by occupation: 10.7% management, 13.2% professional, 13.3% services, 24.3% sales, 0.2% farming, 15.1% construction, 23.2% production (2000).
Income: Per capita income: $20,757 (2000); Median household income: $50,431 (2000); Poverty rate: 4.9% (2000).
Taxes: Total city taxes per capita: $255 (1997); City property taxes per capita: $239 (1997).
Education: High school graduation rate: 85.3% (2000); College graduation rate: 14.7% (2000).

School District(s)

Silver Lake J1 (KG-08)
2000 Enrollment: 603 262-889-4384

Housing: Homeownership rate: 77.6% (2000); Median home value: $117,500 (2000); Median rent: $561 per month (2000); Median age of housing: 28 years (2000).
Safety: Violent crime rate: 4.2 per 10,000 population; Property crime rate: 229.0 per 10,000 population (2001).
Transportation: Commute to work: 95.2% car, 0.6% public transportation, 1.0% walk, 2.1% work from home (2000); Travel time to work: 22.8% less than 15 minutes, 31.2% 15 to 30 minutes, 21.1% 30 to 45 minutes, 11.6% 45 to 60 minutes, 13.3% 60 minutes or more (2000)

SOMERS (town). Covers a land area of 30.510 square miles and a water area of 0.019 square miles. Located at 42.62° N. Lat.; 87.87° W. Long. Elevation is 700 feet.
History: University of Wisconsin (Parkside Campus) to East.
Population: 9,059 (2000); Race: 90.9% White, 3.3% Black, 1.9% Asian, 0.7% American Indian and Alaska Native, 5.1% Hispanic of any race, 1.3% two or more races (2000); Density: 296.9 persons per square mile (2000); Age: 20.7% under 18, 10.9% over 64 (2000); Marriage status: 27.2% never married, 57.3% now married, 5.7% widowed, 9.8% divorced (2000); Foreign born: 3.9% (2000); Ancestry (includes multiple ancestries): 37.0% German, 11.4% Italian, 10.8% Other groups, 10.5% Irish, 9.7% English (2000).
Economy: Kenosha Airport to South. Single-family building permits issued: 18 (2001) / 20 (2000); Multi-family building permits issued: 2 (2001) / 12 (2000); Employment by occupation: 12.1% management, 18.1% professional, 13.1% services, 27.4% sales, 0.2% farming, 9.6% construction, 19.4% production (2000).
Income: Per capita income: $23,837 (2000); Median household income: $49,608 (2000); Poverty rate: 5.6% (2000).
Taxes: Total city taxes per capita: $119 (2000); City property taxes per capita: $96 (2000).
Education: High school graduation rate: 84.7% (2000); College graduation rate: 25.2% (2000).
Housing: Homeownership rate: 70.6% (2000); Median home value: $151,700 (2000); Median rent: $555 per month (2000); Median age of housing: 30 years (2000).

Transportation: Commute to work: 93.0% car, 0.3% public transportation, 2.8% walk, 3.5% work from home (2000); Travel time to work: 35.6% less than 15 minutes, 40.9% 15 to 30 minutes, 11.6% 30 to 45 minutes, 6.6% 45 to 60 minutes, 5.3% 60 minutes or more (2000)

TREVOR (unincorporated postal area, zip code 53179). Covers a land area of 10.255 square miles and a water area of 1.254 square miles. Located at 42.51° N. Lat.; 88.13° W. Long. Elevation is 776 feet.
Population: 5,011 (2000); Race: 97.6% White, 0.2% Black, 0.0% Asian, 0.4% American Indian and Alaska Native, 3.4% Hispanic of any race, 1.4% two or more races (2000); Density: 488.7 persons per square mile (2000); Age: 31.5% under 18, 8.1% over 64 (2000); Marriage status: 21.1% never married, 63.7% now married, 4.6% widowed, 10.6% divorced (2000); Foreign born: 2.2% (2000); Ancestry (includes multiple ancestries): 38.1% German, 17.8% Irish, 12.8% Polish, 8.4% Italian, 6.3% English (2000).
Economy: Recreation. Manufacturing of cork and rubber products. Employment by occupation: 11.9% management, 10.9% professional, 15.9% services, 26.8% sales, 0.0% farming, 16.8% construction, 17.6% production (2000).
Income: Per capita income: $19,880 (2000); Median household income: $47,778 (2000); Poverty rate: 8.7% (2000).
Education: High school graduation rate: 81.9% (2000); College graduation rate: 12.1% (2000).

School District(s)

Trevor Grade (PK-08)
2000 Enrollment: 366 262-862-2356

Housing: Homeownership rate: 85.4% (2000); Median home value: $123,400 (2000); Median rent: $564 per month (2000); Median age of housing: 40 years (2000).
Transportation: Commute to work: 95.6% car, 1.0% public transportation, 0.3% walk, 1.8% work from home (2000); Travel time to work: 22.7% less than 15 minutes, 26.2% 15 to 30 minutes, 24.8% 30 to 45 minutes, 14.1% 45 to 60 minutes, 12.3% 60 minutes or more (2000)

TWIN LAKES (village). Covers a land area of 5.402 square miles and a water area of 1.537 square miles. Located at 42.52° N. Lat.; 88.26° W. Long. Elevation is 810 feet.
Population: 5,124 (2000); Race: 98.2% White, 0.0% Black, 1.0% Asian, 0.0% American Indian and Alaska Native, 1.5% Hispanic of any race, 0.5% two or more races (2000); Density: 948.5 persons per square mile (2000); Age: 26.5% under 18, 13.9% over 64 (2000); Marriage status: 19.0% never married, 62.4% now married, 6.9% widowed, 11.7% divorced (2000); Foreign born: 3.4% (2000); Ancestry (includes multiple ancestries): 37.4% German, 18.6% Irish, 16.8% Polish, 7.4% English, 7.3% Italian (2000).
Economy: Farm and recreation area; light manufacturing. Single-family building permits issued: 48 (2001) / 30 (2000); Multi-family building permits issued: 0 (2001) / 0 (2000); Employment by occupation: 13.9% management, 16.1% professional, 9.2% services, 28.0% sales, 0.0% farming, 12.4% construction, 20.3% production (2000).
Income: Per capita income: $22,226 (2000); Median household income: $46,601 (2000); Poverty rate: 6.6% (2000).
Taxes: Total city taxes per capita: $361 (1997); City property taxes per capita: $344 (1997).
Education: High school graduation rate: 87.9% (2000); College graduation rate: 19.6% (2000).

School District(s)

Twin Lakes #4 (KG-08)
2000 Enrollment: 399 262-877-2148

Housing: Homeownership rate: 73.5% (2000); Median home value: $125,900 (2000); Median rent: $563 per month (2000); Median age of housing: 28 years (2000).
Safety: Violent crime rate: 5.8 per 10,000 population; Property crime rate: 240.3 per 10,000 population (2001).
Transportation: Commute to work: 95.1% car, 0.9% public transportation, 0.3% walk, 3.6% work from home (2000); Travel time to work: 23.8% less than 15 minutes, 26.9% 15 to 30 minutes, 19.3% 30 to 45 minutes, 12.4% 45 to 60 minutes, 17.6% 60 minutes or more (2000)
Additional Information Contacts
Twin Lakes Chamber of Commerce 262-877-2220

WHEATLAND (town). Covers a land area of 23.551 square miles and a water area of 0.467 square miles. Located at 42.57° N. Lat.; 88.22° W. Long. Elevation is 763 feet.
Population: 3,292 (2000); Race: 96.9% White, 0.6% Black, 0.1% Asian, 0.0% American Indian and Alaska Native, 2.2% Hispanic of any race, 1.4% two or more races (2000); Density: 139.8 persons per square mile (2000); Age: 27.3% under 18, 9.3% over 64 (2000); Marriage status: 26.9% never married, 58.2% now married, 4.8% widowed, 10.1% divorced (2000); Foreign born: 1.5% (2000); Ancestry (includes multiple ancestries): 47.8% German, 16.1% Irish, 10.1% Polish, 8.9% English, 7.3% United States or American (2000).
Economy: Single-family building permits issued: 15 (2001) / 24 (2000); Multi-family building permits issued: 0 (2001) / 0 (2000); Employment by occupation: 11.9% management, 11.4% professional, 15.5% services, 24.6% sales, 0.0% farming, 15.2% construction, 21.4% production (2000).
Income: Per capita income: $21,299 (2000); Median household income: $52,386 (2000); Poverty rate: 5.3% (2000).
Taxes: Total city taxes per capita: $82 (1997); City property taxes per capita: $64 (1997).
Education: High school graduation rate: 82.3% (2000); College graduation rate: 11.6% (2000).
Housing: Homeownership rate: 84.5% (2000); Median home value: $138,300 (2000); Median rent: $613 per month (2000); Median age of housing: 35 years (2000).
Transportation: Commute to work: 95.1% car, 0.2% public transportation, 0.7% walk, 3.0% work from home (2000); Travel time to work: 22.6% less than 15 minutes, 34.7% 15 to 30 minutes, 19.6% 30 to 45 minutes, 8.3% 45 to 60 minutes, 14.8% 60 minutes or more (2000)

Kewaunee County

Located in eastern Wisconsin, at the base of the Door Peninsula; bounded on the east by Lake Michigan, and on the northwest by Green Bay. Covers a land area of 342.60 square miles, a water area of 741.90 square miles, and is located in the Central Time Zone. The county government was organized in 1852. County seat is Kewaunee.
Population: 20,187 (2000); Race: 98.5% White, 0.0% Black, 0.2% Asian, 0.2% American Indian and Alaska Native, 0.9% Hispanic of any race, 0.6% two or more races (2000); Density: 58.9 persons per square mile (2000); Age: 25.7% under 18, 15.3% over 64 (2000).
Religion: Five largest groups: 57.4% Catholic Church, 9.8% Wisconsin Evangelical Lutheran Synod, 6.0% Lutheran Church—Missouri Synod, 1.5% Evangelical Lutheran Church in America, 1.2% National Association of Congregational Christian Churches (2000
Economy: Unemployment rate: 5.3% (11/2002); Total civilian labor force: 10,597 (11/2002); Leading industries: 42.6% manufacturing; 11.9% retail trade; 9.8% construction (2000); Companies that employ more than 1,000 persons: 0 (2000); Companies that employ more than 100 persons: 7 (2000); Farms: 795 totaling 161,268 acres (1997); Minority business ownership rate: 0.0% (1997); Women business ownership rate: 15.1% (1997); Retail sales per capita: $5,776 (1997). Single-family building permits issued: 104 (2001) / 114 (2000); Multi-family building permits issued: 4 (2001) / 17 (2000).
Income: Per capita income: $18,456 (2000); Median household income: $43,824 (2000); Poverty rate: 5.8% (2000); Bankruptcy rate: 2.69% (2001).
Taxes: Total county taxes per capita: $233 (2000); County property taxes per capita: $230 (2000).
Education: High school graduation rate: 84.0% (2000); College graduation rate: 11.4% (2000).
Housing: Homeownership rate: 81.9% (2000); Median home value: $92,100 (2000); Median rent: $355 per month (2000); Median age of housing: 42 years (2000).
Health: Birth rate: 109.0 per 10,000 population (1998); Age adjusted death rate: 82.2 per 10,000 population (1999); Age adjusted cancer mortality rate: 230.6 deaths per 100,000 population (1999). Air Quality Index: 76% good, 24% moderate, 0% unhealthy (percent of days in 2000). Number of physicians: 4.5 per 10,000 population (1999); Number of hospital beds: 7.9 per 10,000 population (1999).
Elections: 2000 Presidential election results: 46.3% Gore, 48.4% Bush, 3.9% Nader, 1.1% Buchanan
National and State Parks: Kewaunee River State Public Fishery Area; Kewaunee State Public Hunting Grounds; Little Scarboro State Public Fishery Area; Little Scarboro State Public Hunting Grounds
Additional Information Contacts
Kewaunee County Government Offices.................... 920-388-7133
Algoma Chamber of Commerce.......................... 920-487-2041
Kewaunee Chamber of Commerce........................ 920-388-4822

Kewaunee County Communities

AHNAPEE (town). Covers a land area of 30.974 square miles and a wate area of 0.188 square miles. Located at 44.63° N. Lat.; 87.46° W. Long.

Population: 977 (2000); Race: 98.1% White, 0.0% Black, 0.0% Asian, 0.6% American Indian and Alaska Native, 3.0% Hispanic of any race, 1.3% two or more races (2000); Density: 31.5 persons per square mile (2000); Age: 24.6% under 18, 14.3% over 64 (2000); Marriage status: 24.5% never married, 62.2% now married, 4.9% widowed, 8.4% divorced (2000); Foreign born: 2.4% (2000); Ancestry (includes multiple ancestries): 50.1% German, 21.3% Belgian, 10.0% Czech, 6.0% Irish, 5.6% Norwegian (2000).
Economy: Single-family building permits issued: 8 (2001) / 9 (2000); Multi-family building permits issued: 0 (2001) / 0 (2000); Employment by occupation: 10.4% management, 10.0% professional, 7.9% services, 18.1% sales, 5.4% farming, 13.2% construction, 35.1% production (2000).
Income: Per capita income: $20,385 (2000); Median household income: $47,500 (2000); Poverty rate: 3.2% (2000).
Taxes: Total city taxes per capita: $87 (1997); City property taxes per capita: $85 (1997).
Education: High school graduation rate: 86.5% (2000); College graduation rate: 9.0% (2000).
Housing: Homeownership rate: 88.3% (2000); Median home value: $94,800 (2000); Median rent: $355 per month (2000); Median age of housing: 40 years (2000).
Transportation: Commute to work: 89.9% car, 0.4% public transportation, 4.3% walk, 5.1% work from home (2000); Travel time to work: 63.2% less than 15 minutes, 16.6% 15 to 30 minutes, 8.0% 30 to 45 minutes, 8.0% 45 to 60 minutes, 4.2% 60 minutes or more (2000)

ALGOMA (city). Covers a land area of 2.442 square miles and a water area of 0.039 square miles. Located at 44.60° N. Lat.; 87.44° W. Long. Elevation is 600 feet.
History: The name of Algoma is of Indian origin meaning "sandy place." The town developed in the 1850's around a sawmill.
Population: 3,357 (2000); Race: 95.6% White, 0.0% Black, 0.9% Asian, 0.4% American Indian and Alaska Native, 2.0% Hispanic of any race, 1.1% two or more races (2000); Density: 1,374.9 persons per square mile (2000); Age: 21.1% under 18, 21.9% over 64 (2000); Marriage status: 23.2% never married, 55.7% now married, 13.3% widowed, 7.9% divorced (2000); Foreign born: 1.3% (2000); Ancestry (includes multiple ancestries): 44.1% German, 16.8% Belgian, 8.1% Irish, 7.3% Polish, 6.7% Other groups (2000).
Economy: Single-family building permits issued: 1 (2001) / 6 (2000); Multi-family building permits issued: 0 (2001) / 2 (2000); Employment by occupation: 10.7% management, 13.4% professional, 12.8% services, 22.0% sales, 1.0% farming, 9.0% construction, 31.2% production (2000).
Income: Per capita income: $18,043 (2000); Median household income: $35,029 (2000); Poverty rate: 5.2% (2000).
Taxes: Total city taxes per capita: $260 (2000); City property taxes per capita: $239 (2000).
Education: High school graduation rate: 80.8% (2000); College graduation rate: 14.5% (2000).

School District(s)

Algoma (PK-12)
2000 Enrollment: 706 920-487-7001
Housing: Homeownership rate: 73.1% (2000); Median home value: $73,600 (2000); Median rent: $306 per month (2000); Median age of housing: 46 years (2000).
Safety: Violent crime rate: 17.7 per 10,000 population; Property crime rate: 186.3 per 10,000 population (2001).
Newspapers: Algoma Record-Herald (1 x week)
Transportation: Commute to work: 90.9% car, 0.3% public transportation, 6.2% walk, 2.1% work from home (2000); Travel time to work: 60.2% less than 15 minutes, 19.2% 15 to 30 minutes, 8.5% 30 to 45 minutes, 7.9% 45 to 60 minutes, 4.2% 60 minutes or more (2000)
Additional Information Contacts
Algoma Chamber of Commerce. 920-487-2041

CARLTON (town). Covers a land area of 35.632 square miles and a water area of 0 square miles. Located at 44.37° N. Lat.; 87.57° W. Long.
Population: 1,000 (2000); Race: 99.8% White, 0.0% Black, 0.0% Asian, 0.0% American Indian and Alaska Native, 0.0% Hispanic of any race, 0.2% two or more races (2000); Density: 28.1 persons per square mile (2000); Age: 23.2% under 18, 13.1% over 64 (2000); Marriage status: 28.3% never married, 61.6% now married, 6.1% widowed, 4.1% divorced (2000); Foreign born: 0.5% (2000); Ancestry (includes multiple ancestries): 47.7% German, 29.4% Czech, 17.4% Polish, 13.1% Belgian, 6.8% Irish (2000).
Economy: Single-family building permits issued: 6 (2001) / 10 (2000); Multi-family building permits issued: 0 (2001) / 0 (2000); Employment by occupation: 18.4% management, 9.4% professional, 11.6% services, 15.2% sales, 4.0% farming, 14.1% construction, 27.3% production (2000).
Income: Per capita income: $20,660 (2000); Median household income: $50,227 (2000); Poverty rate: 3.0% (2000).
Taxes: Total city taxes per capita: $4 (1997); City property taxes per capita: $0 (1997).
Education: High school graduation rate: 83.0% (2000); College graduation rate: 7.9% (2000).
Housing: Homeownership rate: 91.6% (2000); Median home value: $94,300 (2000); Median rent: $335 per month (2000); Median age of housing: 49 years (2000).
Transportation: Commute to work: 81.0% car, 0.0% public transportation, 4.0% walk, 14.7% work from home (2000); Travel time to work: 26.4% less than 15 minutes, 32.4% 15 to 30 minutes, 28.3% 30 to 45 minutes, 7.6% 45 to 60 minutes, 5.3% 60 minutes or more (2000)

CASCO (village). Covers a land area of 0.560 square miles and a water area of 0.006 square miles. Located at 44.55° N. Lat.; 87.62° W. Long. Elevation is 720 feet.
Population: 572 (2000); Race: 98.3% White, 0.0% Black, 0.0% Asian, 1.2% American Indian and Alaska Native, 0.0% Hispanic of any race, 0.5% two or more races (2000); Density: 1,022.1 persons per square mile (2000); Age: 27.9% under 18, 14.4% over 64 (2000); Marriage status: 22.3% never married, 66.8% now married, 7.6% widowed, 3.3% divorced (2000); Foreign born: 0.0% (2000); Ancestry (includes multiple ancestries): 46.4% Belgian, 38.9% German, 13.0% Czech, 7.1% Polish, 4.8% Norwegian (2000).
Economy: Single-family building permits issued: 3 (2001) / 0 (2000); Multi-family building permits issued: 0 (2001) / 0 (2000); Employment by occupation: 8.2% management, 12.6% professional, 14.7% services, 24.6% sales, 1.4% farming, 17.7% construction, 20.8% production (2000).
Income: Per capita income: $18,168 (2000); Median household income: $44,583 (2000); Poverty rate: 4.0% (2000).
Taxes: Total city taxes per capita: $57 (1997); City property taxes per capita: $52 (1997).
Education: High school graduation rate: 86.1% (2000); College graduation rate: 13.3% (2000).
Housing: Homeownership rate: 73.6% (2000); Median home value: $90,400 (2000); Median rent: $317 per month (2000); Median age of housing: 48 years (2000).
Transportation: Commute to work: 93.5% car, 0.0% public transportation, 2.1% walk, 4.5% work from home (2000); Travel time to work: 24.4% less than 15 minutes, 27.2% 15 to 30 minutes, 32.3% 30 to 45 minutes, 14.7% 45 to 60 minutes, 1.4% 60 minutes or more (2000)

CASCO (town). Covers a land area of 35.715 square miles and a water area of 0.002 square miles. Located at 44.53° N. Lat.; 87.59° W. Long. Elevation is 720 feet.
Population: 1,153 (2000); Race: 99.6% White, 0.0% Black, 0.0% Asian, 0.0% American Indian and Alaska Native, 1.2% Hispanic of any race, 0.3% two or more races (2000); Density: 32.3 persons per square mile (2000); Age: 26.6% under 18, 12.9% over 64 (2000); Marriage status: 26.9% never married, 62.1% now married, 5.0% widowed, 6.1% divorced (2000); Foreign born: 0.4% (2000); Ancestry (includes multiple ancestries): 47.2% German, 30.1% Belgian, 15.2% Czech, 5.5% Polish, 5.1% French (except Basque) (2000).
Economy: In dairying and farming area. Railroad junction to Southwest. Fruit (cherries, apples, strawberries, pears, plums). Single-family building permits issued: 6 (2001) / 5 (2000); Multi-family building permits issued: 0 (2001) / 0 (2000); Employment by occupation: 19.9% management, 11.1% professional, 8.8% services, 16.6% sales, 5.1% farming, 15.1% construction, 23.5% production (2000).
Income: Per capita income: $17,605 (2000); Median household income: $46,250 (2000); Poverty rate: 4.1% (2000).
Taxes: Total city taxes per capita: $125 (1997); City property taxes per capita: $120 (1997).
Education: High school graduation rate: 86.1% (2000); College graduation rate: 10.7% (2000).
Housing: Homeownership rate: 89.4% (2000); Median home value: $106,000 (2000); Median rent: $463 per month (2000); Median age of housing: 35 years (2000).
Transportation: Commute to work: 85.2% car, 0.5% public transportation, 3.7% walk, 10.3% work from home (2000); Travel time to work: 33.1% less than 15 minutes, 24.1% 15 to 30 minutes, 26.9% 30 to 45 minutes, 11.5% 45 to 60 minutes, 4.4% 60 minutes or more (2000)

FRANKLIN (town). Covers a land area of 35.478 square miles and a water area of 0.688 square miles. Located at 44.36° N. Lat.; 87.71° W. Long.

Population: 997 (2000); Race: 99.4% White, 0.0% Black, 0.4% Asian, 0.2% American Indian and Alaska Native, 0.0% Hispanic of any race, 0.0% two or more races (2000); Density: 28.1 persons per square mile (2000); Age: 29.9% under 18, 9.7% over 64 (2000); Marriage status: 26.8% never married, 62.9% now married, 4.8% widowed, 5.5% divorced (2000); Foreign born: 0.4% (2000); Ancestry (includes multiple ancestries): 45.8% German, 35.2% Czech, 12.0% Belgian, 11.2% Polish, 6.8% Dutch (2000).
Economy: Single-family building permits issued: 15 (2001) / 10 (2000); Multi-family building permits issued: 0 (2001) / 0 (2000); Employment by occupation: 19.2% management, 7.6% professional, 9.5% services, 18.3% sales, 6.9% farming, 11.6% construction, 27.1% production (2000).
Income: Per capita income: $19,401 (2000); Median household income: $52,019 (2000); Poverty rate: 2.4% (2000).
Taxes: Total city taxes per capita: $84 (1997); City property taxes per capita: $82 (1997).
Education: High school graduation rate: 84.6% (2000); College graduation rate: 8.4% (2000).
Housing: Homeownership rate: 91.3% (2000); Median home value: $106,000 (2000); Median rent: $338 per month (2000); Median age of housing: 42 years (2000).
Transportation: Commute to work: 85.9% car, 0.2% public transportation, 2.5% walk, 9.9% work from home (2000); Travel time to work: 24.3% less than 15 minutes, 34.1% 15 to 30 minutes, 34.4% 30 to 45 minutes, 4.5% 45 to 60 minutes, 2.7% 60 minutes or more (2000)

KEWAUNEE (city). Covers a land area of 3.474 square miles and a water area of 0.742 square miles. Located at 44.45° N. Lat.; 87.50° W. Long. Elevation is 700 feet.
History: Jean Nicolet passed through this area in 1634, but the first settlement was in 1795, when Jacques Vieau established a North West Fur Company trading post. Rumors of gold brought land speculators in 1836, and Kewaunee (Indian, "prairie hen") was established. Lumbering began after 1840, but declined as the timber disappeared in the 1850's.
Population: 2,806 (2000); Race: 98.5% White, 0.0% Black, 0.0% Asian, 0.1% American Indian and Alaska Native, 0.3% Hispanic of any race, 1.4% two or more races (2000); Density: 807.7 persons per square mile (2000); Age: 22.6% under 18, 22.3% over 64 (2000); Marriage status: 21.7% never married, 58.0% now married, 11.1% widowed, 9.2% divorced (2000); Foreign born: 1.0% (2000); Ancestry (includes multiple ancestries): 44.4% German, 22.4% Czech, 16.1% Belgian, 14.0% Polish, 6.9% Irish (2000).
Economy: Single-family building permits issued: 0 (2001) / 11 (2000); Multi-family building permits issued: 0 (2001) / 5 (2000); Employment by occupation: 8.9% management, 20.1% professional, 13.9% services, 19.5% sales, 2.7% farming, 8.4% construction, 26.5% production (2000).
Income: Per capita income: $17,384 (2000); Median household income: $36,420 (2000); Poverty rate: 10.5% (2000).
Taxes: Total city taxes per capita: $272 (1997); City property taxes per capita: $255 (1997).
Education: High school graduation rate: 81.5% (2000); College graduation rate: 15.0% (2000).

School District(s)

Kewaunee (PK-12)
2000 Enrollment: 1,154 920-388-3230
Housing: Homeownership rate: 76.7% (2000); Median home value: $80,100 (2000); Median rent: $342 per month (2000); Median age of housing: 50 years (2000).
Safety: Violent crime rate: 3.5 per 10,000 population; Property crime rate: 173.4 per 10,000 population (2001).
Newspapers: Kewaunee Enterprise (1 x week)
Transportation: Commute to work: 92.2% car, 0.0% public transportation, 3.4% walk, 4.2% work from home (2000); Travel time to work: 50.7% less than 15 minutes, 17.8% 15 to 30 minutes, 16.0% 30 to 45 minutes, 10.7% 45 to 60 minutes, 4.7% 60 minutes or more (2000)
Additional Information Contacts
Kewaunee Chamber of Commerce.................................... 920-388-4822

LINCOLN (town). Covers a land area of 35.689 square miles and a water area of 0 square miles. Located at 44.63° N. Lat.; 87.58° W. Long. Elevation is 842 feet.
Population: 957 (2000); Race: 98.1% White, 0.0% Black, 0.4% Asian, 0.0% American Indian and Alaska Native, 1.2% Hispanic of any race, 0.3% two or more races (2000); Density: 26.8 persons per square mile (2000); Age: 27.6% under 18, 13.9% over 64 (2000); Marriage status: 23.0% never married, 65.0% now married, 4.7% widowed, 7.3% divorced (2000); Foreign born: 1.8% (2000); Ancestry (includes multiple ancestries): 40.8% Belgian, 31.9% German, 10.6% United States or American, 8.7% Czech, 6.3% Polish (2000).
Economy: Single-family building permits issued: 9 (2001) / 8 (2000); Multi-family building permits issued: 0 (2001) / 0 (2000); Employment by occupation: 19.1% management, 10.1% professional, 7.0% services, 13.5% sales, 7.8% farming, 12.7% construction, 29.8% production (2000).
Income: Per capita income: $16,183 (2000); Median household income: $42,188 (2000); Poverty rate: 8.9% (2000).
Taxes: Total city taxes per capita: $77 (1997); City property taxes per capita: $75 (1997).
Education: High school graduation rate: 81.3% (2000); College graduation rate: 8.4% (2000).
Housing: Homeownership rate: 88.1% (2000); Median home value: $88,300 (2000); Median rent: $379 per month (2000); Median age of housing: 56 years (2000).
Transportation: Commute to work: 80.0% car, 0.8% public transportation, 7.1% walk, 11.5% work from home (2000); Travel time to work: 24.8% less than 15 minutes, 28.7% 15 to 30 minutes, 25.3% 30 to 45 minutes, 13.0% 45 to 60 minutes, 8.2% 60 minutes or more (2000)

LUXEMBURG (village). Covers a land area of 2.068 square miles and a water area of 0 square miles. Located at 44.53° N. Lat.; 87.70° W. Long. Elevation is 810 feet.
Population: 1,935 (2000); Race: 99.3% White, 0.2% Black, 0.4% Asian, 0.0% American Indian and Alaska Native, 0.0% Hispanic of any race, 0.1% two or more races (2000); Density: 935.7 persons per square mile (2000); Age: 28.5% under 18, 15.7% over 64 (2000); Marriage status: 22.1% never married, 61.3% now married, 9.2% widowed, 7.5% divorced (2000); Foreign born: 0.8% (2000); Ancestry (includes multiple ancestries): 40.4% Belgian, 40.4% German, 12.9% Czech, 7.2% Polish, 4.6% French (except Basque) (2000).
Economy: Single-family building permits issued: 24 (2001) / 20 (2000); Multi-family building permits issued: 4 (2001) / 8 (2000); Employment by occupation: 12.9% management, 11.9% professional, 13.8% services, 25.4% sales, 1.7% farming, 16.4% construction, 18.0% production (2000).
Income: Per capita income: $17,856 (2000); Median household income: $45,000 (2000); Poverty rate: 5.6% (2000).
Taxes: Total city taxes per capita: $120 (1997); City property taxes per capita: $101 (1997).
Education: High school graduation rate: 82.9% (2000); College graduation rate: 10.1% (2000).

School District(s)

Luxemburg-Casco (PK-12)
2000 Enrollment: 1,853 920-845-2391
Housing: Homeownership rate: 72.7% (2000); Median home value: $109,800 (2000); Median rent: $498 per month (2000); Median age of housing: 18 years (2000).
Safety: Violent crime rate: 5.1 per 10,000 population; Property crime rate: 51.3 per 10,000 population (2001).
Newspapers: Luxemburg News (1 x week)
Transportation: Commute to work: 89.7% car, 0.9% public transportation, 3.5% walk, 5.9% work from home (2000); Travel time to work: 29.6% less than 15 minutes, 31.2% 15 to 30 minutes, 30.6% 30 to 45 minutes, 5.2% 45 to 60 minutes, 3.4% 60 minutes or more (2000)

LUXEMBURG (town). Covers a land area of 34.186 square miles and a water area of 0 square miles. Located at 44.54° N. Lat.; 87.69° W. Long. Elevation is 810 feet.
Population: 1,402 (2000); Race: 99.1% White, 0.0% Black, 0.2% Asian, 0.0% American Indian and Alaska Native, 0.6% Hispanic of any race, 0.2% two or more races (2000); Density: 41.0 persons per square mile (2000); Age: 31.8% under 18, 5.5% over 64 (2000); Marriage status: 24.5% never married, 68.4% now married, 3.4% widowed, 3.7% divorced (2000); Foreign born: 0.8% (2000); Ancestry (includes multiple ancestries): 48.9% German, 44.9% Belgian, 13.9% Czech, 10.5% Polish, 4.9% Dutch (2000).
Economy: Dairying. Manufacturing: wood cabinets, cheese, plastic bottles. Railroad junction to East. Speedway here. Single-family building permits issued: 0 (2001) / 0 (2000); Multi-family building permits issued: 0 (2001) / 0 (2000); Employment by occupation: 18.2% management, 9.2% professional, 12.8% services, 19.9% sales, 3.9% farming, 14.5% construction, 21.6% production (2000).
Income: Per capita income: $19,322 (2000); Median household income: $54,875 (2000); Poverty rate: 0.9% (2000).
Taxes: Total city taxes per capita: $106 (1997); City property taxes per capita: $104 (1997).
Education: High school graduation rate: 89.4% (2000); College graduation rate: 7.0% (2000).

Housing: Homeownership rate: 87.7% (2000); Median home value: $118,100 (2000); Median rent: $375 per month (2000); Median age of housing: 29 years (2000).
Transportation: Commute to work: 86.3% car, 0.6% public transportation, 5.0% walk, 7.1% work from home (2000); Travel time to work: 32.5% less than 15 minutes, 26.7% 15 to 30 minutes, 31.4% 30 to 45 minutes, 5.2% 45 to 60 minutes, 4.2% 60 minutes or more (2000)

MONTPELIER (town). Covers a land area of 36.182 square miles and a water area of 0.008 square miles. Located at 44.45° N. Lat.; 87.70° W. Long.
Population: 1,371 (2000); Race: 99.3% White, 0.0% Black, 0.0% Asian, 0.4% American Indian and Alaska Native, 0.2% Hispanic of any race, 0.0% two or more races (2000); Density: 37.9 persons per square mile (2000); Age: 24.6% under 18, 12.6% over 64 (2000); Marriage status: 24.9% never married, 64.2% now married, 6.2% widowed, 4.7% divorced (2000); Foreign born: 0.4% (2000); Ancestry (includes multiple ancestries): 46.6% German, 22.9% Czech, 21.2% Belgian, 8.5% Polish, 4.5% Dutch (2000).
Economy: Single-family building permits issued: 7 (2001) / 7 (2000); Multi-family building permits issued: 0 (2001) / 0 (2000); Employment by occupation: 16.1% management, 11.0% professional, 9.5% services, 22.4% sales, 5.0% farming, 13.1% construction, 22.9% production (2000).
Income: Per capita income: $19,812 (2000); Median household income: $51,000 (2000); Poverty rate: 3.8% (2000).
Taxes: Total city taxes per capita: $28 (1997); City property taxes per capita: $27 (1997).
Education: High school graduation rate: 86.4% (2000); College graduation rate: 9.9% (2000).
Housing: Homeownership rate: 85.7% (2000); Median home value: $111,000 (2000); Median rent: $334 per month (2000); Median age of housing: 37 years (2000).
Transportation: Commute to work: 83.3% car, 0.3% public transportation, 1.9% walk, 14.0% work from home (2000); Travel time to work: 23.7% less than 15 minutes, 37.5% 15 to 30 minutes, 32.6% 30 to 45 minutes, 3.7% 45 to 60 minutes, 2.5% 60 minutes or more (2000)

PIERCE (town). Covers a land area of 18.583 square miles and a water area of 3.182 square miles. Located at 44.53° N. Lat.; 87.49° W. Long.
Population: 897 (2000); Race: 99.4% White, 0.0% Black, 0.0% Asian, 0.2% American Indian and Alaska Native, 1.1% Hispanic of any race, 0.1% two or more races (2000); Density: 48.3 persons per square mile (2000); Age: 27.4% under 18, 10.5% over 64 (2000); Marriage status: 22.8% never married, 63.0% now married, 5.3% widowed, 8.9% divorced (2000); Foreign born: 1.3% (2000); Ancestry (includes multiple ancestries): 46.8% German, 14.8% Belgian, 12.8% Czech, 9.9% Irish, 8.9% Polish (2000).
Economy: Single-family building permits issued: 4 (2001) / 1 (2000); Multi-family building permits issued: 0 (2001) / 0 (2000); Employment by occupation: 16.7% management, 10.2% professional, 14.0% services, 18.6% sales, 4.3% farming, 14.3% construction, 21.9% production (2000).
Income: Per capita income: $18,384 (2000); Median household income: $43,000 (2000); Poverty rate: 15.2% (2000).
Taxes: Total city taxes per capita: $98 (1997); City property taxes per capita: $90 (1997).
Education: High school graduation rate: 87.2% (2000); College graduation rate: 16.5% (2000).
Housing: Homeownership rate: 90.0% (2000); Median home value: $99,500 (2000); Median rent: $431 per month (2000); Median age of housing: 34 years (2000).
Transportation: Commute to work: 88.7% car, 0.0% public transportation, 3.2% walk, 8.0% work from home (2000); Travel time to work: 49.0% less than 15 minutes, 15.5% 15 to 30 minutes, 17.0% 30 to 45 minutes, 10.5% 45 to 60 minutes, 8.0% 60 minutes or more (2000)

RED RIVER (town). Covers a land area of 34.747 square miles and a water area of 1.377 square miles. Located at 44.63° N. Lat.; 87.72° W. Long.
Population: 1,476 (2000); Race: 99.9% White, 0.0% Black, 0.0% Asian, 0.0% American Indian and Alaska Native, 1.2% Hispanic of any race, 0.0% two or more races (2000); Density: 42.5 persons per square mile (2000); Age: 26.3% under 18, 13.7% over 64 (2000); Marriage status: 24.5% never married, 64.7% now married, 4.9% widowed, 5.9% divorced (2000); Foreign born: 0.5% (2000); Ancestry (includes multiple ancestries): 55.8% Belgian, 21.8% German, 6.1% Irish, 5.8% Polish, 5.5% French (except Basque) (2000).
Economy: Single-family building permits issued: 12 (2001) / 15 (2000); Multi-family building permits issued: 0 (2001) / 0 (2000); Employment by occupation: 15.8% management, 9.0% professional, 12.7% services, 22.1% sales, 2.6% farming, 14.1% construction, 23.8% production (2000).
Income: Per capita income: $19,673 (2000); Median household income: $47,833 (2000); Poverty rate: 6.1% (2000).
Taxes: Total city taxes per capita: $79 (1997); City property taxes per capita: $76 (1997).
Education: High school graduation rate: 85.3% (2000); College graduation rate: 8.6% (2000).
Housing: Homeownership rate: 85.2% (2000); Median home value: $122,200 (2000); Median rent: $438 per month (2000); Median age of housing: 30 years (2000).
Transportation: Commute to work: 84.7% car, 0.0% public transportation, 5.9% walk, 8.7% work from home (2000); Travel time to work: 26.8% less than 15 minutes, 31.7% 15 to 30 minutes, 34.0% 30 to 45 minutes, 4.7% 45 to 60 minutes, 2.8% 60 minutes or more (2000)

WEST KEWAUNEE (town). Covers a land area of 36.910 square miles and a water area of 0.108 square miles. Located at 44.45° N. Lat.; 87.56° W. Long.
Population: 1,287 (2000); Race: 98.9% White, 0.0% Black, 0.0% Asian, 0.0% American Indian and Alaska Native, 1.4% Hispanic of any race, 0.4% two or more races (2000); Density: 34.9 persons per square mile (2000); Age: 29.5% under 18, 11.6% over 64 (2000); Marriage status: 23.5% never married, 65.3% now married, 6.4% widowed, 4.8% divorced (2000); Foreign born: 1.1% (2000); Ancestry (includes multiple ancestries): 45.8% German, 24.5% Czech, 15.4% Polish, 14.8% Belgian, 6.7% Irish (2000).
Economy: Single-family building permits issued: 9 (2001) / 12 (2000); Multi-family building permits issued: 0 (2001) / 2 (2000); Employment by occupation: 15.3% management, 13.6% professional, 8.1% services, 15.6% sales, 3.1% farming, 12.9% construction, 31.5% production (2000).
Income: Per capita income: $17,621 (2000); Median household income: $47,059 (2000); Poverty rate: 6.1% (2000).
Taxes: Total city taxes per capita: $33 (1997); City property taxes per capita: $30 (1997).
Education: High school graduation rate: 86.2% (2000); College graduation rate: 10.8% (2000).
Housing: Homeownership rate: 91.2% (2000); Median home value: $98,100 (2000); Median rent: $267 per month (2000); Median age of housing: 41 years (2000).
Transportation: Commute to work: 87.4% car, 0.0% public transportation, 3.0% walk, 9.0% work from home (2000); Travel time to work: 36.8% less than 15 minutes, 24.8% 15 to 30 minutes, 24.7% 30 to 45 minutes, 9.3% 45 to 60 minutes, 4.4% 60 minutes or more (2000)

La Crosse County

Located in western Wisconsin; drained by the La Crosse and Black Rivers. Covers a land area of 452.70 square miles, a water area of 27.20 square miles, and is located in the Central Time Zone. The county government was organized in 1851. County seat is La Crosse.

La Crosse County is part of the La Crosse, WI-MN MSA. The entire metro area includes: Houston County, MN; La Crosse County, WI

Weather Station: La Crosse Municipal Airport Elevation: 649 feet

	Jan	Feb	Mar	Apr	May	Jun	Jul	Aug	Sep	Oct	Nov	Dec
High	24	31	43	58	71	80	84	82	73	60	43	29
Low	6	12	24	37	49	58	63	61	52	40	28	14
Precip	1.2	1.0	2.0	3.4	3.4	3.8	4.3	4.2	3.5	2.2	2.1	1.2
Snow	13.0	8.0	7.2	2.0	tr	tr	0.0	tr	tr	0.2	4.5	9.1

High and Low temperatures in degrees Fahrenheit; Precipitation and Snow in inches

Population: 107,120 (2000); Race: 94.3% White, 0.9% Black, 2.7% Asian, 0.6% American Indian and Alaska Native, 0.8% Hispanic of any race, 1.2% two or more races (2000); Density: 236.6 persons per square mile (2000); Age: 23.6% under 18, 12.6% over 64 (2000).
Religion: Five largest groups: 29.4% Catholic Church, 16.1% Evangelical Lutheran Church in America, 7.4% Wisconsin Evangelical Lutheran Synod, 2.1% The United Methodist Church, 1.4% The Evangelical Free Church of America (2000).
Economy: Unemployment rate: 3.5% (11/2002); Total civilian labor force: 64,349 (11/2002); Leading industries: 19.5% health care and social assistance; 16.3% manufacturing; 15.8% retail trade (2000); Companies that employ more than 1,000 persons: 4 (2000); Companies that employ more than 100 persons: 97 (2000); Farms: 759 totaling 169,543 acres (1997); Minority business ownership rate: 2.3% (1997); Women business ownership rate: 26.4% (1997); Retail sales per capita: $14,230 (1997). Single-family

building permits issued: 433 (2001) / 401 (2000); Multi-family building permits issued: 145 (2001) / 170 (2000).
Income: Per capita income: $19,800 (2000); Median household income: $39,472 (2000); Poverty rate: 10.7% (2000); Bankruptcy rate: 3.55% (2001).
Taxes: Total county taxes per capita: $190 (2000); County property taxes per capita: $115 (2000).
Education: High school graduation rate: 89.7% (2000); College graduation rate: 25.4% (2000).
Housing: Homeownership rate: 65.1% (2000); Median home value: $96,900 (2000); Median rent: $400 per month (2000); Median age of housing: 31 years (2000).
Health: Birth rate: 118.4 per 10,000 population (1998); Age adjusted death rate: 86.7 per 10,000 population (1999); Age adjusted cancer mortality rate: 205.6 deaths per 100,000 population (1999). Number of physicians: 42.6 per 10,000 population (1999); Number of hospital beds: 44.5 per 10,000 population (1999).
Elections: 2000 Presidential election results: 51.2% Gore, 43.8% Bush, 4.1% Nader, 0.3% Buchanan
National and State Parks: Van Loon State Public Hunting Grounds
Additional Information Contacts
La Crosse County Government Offices 608-785-9581
Greater La Crosse Area Chamber 608-784-4880
La Crosse Area Realtors Association. 608-785-7744
La Crosse Convention & Visitors Bureau 608-782-2366

La Crosse County Communities

BANGOR (village). Covers a land area of 1.064 square miles and a water area of 0 square miles. Located at 43.89° N. Lat.; 90.99° W. Long. Elevation is 745 feet.
Population: 1,400 (2000); Race: 96.9% White, 0.4% Black, 0.6% Asian, 0.9% American Indian and Alaska Native, 0.0% Hispanic of any race, 0.9% two or more races (2000); Density: 1,315.4 persons per square mile (2000); Age: 27.8% under 18, 16.8% over 64 (2000); Marriage status: 20.2% never married, 66.3% now married, 7.1% widowed, 6.4% divorced (2000); Foreign born: 1.3% (2000); Ancestry (includes multiple ancestries): 48.3% German, 23.3% Norwegian, 8.2% Irish, 6.1% United States or American, 4.6% Polish (2000).
Economy: Single-family building permits issued: 8 (2001) / 8 (2000); Multi-family building permits issued: 0 (2001) / 0 (2000); Employment by occupation: 9.7% management, 14.2% professional, 12.5% services, 28.9% sales, 0.4% farming, 14.5% construction, 19.7% production (2000).
Income: Per capita income: $17,648 (2000); Median household income: $42,102 (2000); Poverty rate: 6.3% (2000).
Taxes: Total city taxes per capita: $70 (1997); City property taxes per capita: $53 (1997).
Education: High school graduation rate: 84.8% (2000); College graduation rate: 13.7% (2000).

School District(s)

Bangor (KG-12)
2000 Enrollment: 676 608-486-5202
Housing: Homeownership rate: 75.6% (2000); Median home value: $90,600 (2000); Median rent: $365 per month (2000); Median age of housing: 31 years (2000).
Transportation: Commute to work: 92.8% car, 0.0% public transportation, 4.7% walk, 2.1% work from home (2000); Travel time to work: 38.9% less than 15 minutes, 36.4% 15 to 30 minutes, 18.3% 30 to 45 minutes, 3.6% 45 to 60 minutes, 2.8% 60 minutes or more (2000)

BANGOR (town). Covers a land area of 35.035 square miles and a water area of 0 square miles. Located at 43.85° N. Lat.; 90.95° W. Long. Elevation is 745 feet.
Population: 583 (2000); Race: 98.0% White, 0.0% Black, 1.6% Asian, 0.4% American Indian and Alaska Native, 0.7% Hispanic of any race, 0.0% two or more races (2000); Density: 16.6 persons per square mile (2000); Age: 29.8% under 18, 11.5% over 64 (2000); Marriage status: 22.3% never married, 68.1% now married, 3.6% widowed, 5.9% divorced (2000); Foreign born: 0.9% (2000); Ancestry (includes multiple ancestries): 47.7% German, 24.5% Norwegian, 6.9% United States or American, 5.9% English, 5.9% Irish (2000).
Economy: Butter, cheese; ships livestock. Manufacturing: wood products, lumber. Employment by occupation: 19.8% management, 16.8% professional, 16.5% services, 15.5% sales, 4.0% farming, 12.9% construction, 14.5% production (2000).
Income: Per capita income: $17,800 (2000); Median household income: $44,219 (2000); Poverty rate: 3.9% (2000).
Taxes: Total city taxes per capita: $101 (2000); City property taxes per capita: $99 (2000).
Education: High school graduation rate: 90.6% (2000); College graduation rate: 17.7% (2000).
Housing: Homeownership rate: 79.0% (2000); Median home value: $87,000 (2000); Median rent: $257 per month (2000); Median age of housing: 30 years (2000).
Transportation: Commute to work: 83.2% car, 1.3% public transportation, 3.7% walk, 10.1% work from home (2000); Travel time to work: 24.7% less than 15 minutes, 38.6% 15 to 30 minutes, 24.0% 30 to 45 minutes, 3.0% 45 to 60 minutes, 9.7% 60 minutes or more (2000)

BARRE (town). Covers a land area of 20.667 square miles and a water area of 0.002 square miles. Located at 43.83° N. Lat.; 91.10° W. Long.
Population: 1,014 (2000); Race: 96.8% White, 0.6% Black, 0.2% Asian, 1.3% American Indian and Alaska Native, 0.9% Hispanic of any race, 1.1% two or more races (2000); Density: 49.1 persons per square mile (2000); Age: 32.5% under 18, 5.4% over 64 (2000); Marriage status: 22.9% never married, 68.1% now married, 1.8% widowed, 7.2% divorced (2000); Foreign born: 0.8% (2000); Ancestry (includes multiple ancestries): 53.0% German, 26.9% Norwegian, 14.5% Irish, 4.5% English, 3.8% United States or American (2000).
Economy: Employment by occupation: 16.2% management, 17.3% professional, 9.8% services, 25.1% sales, 0.7% farming, 8.8% construction, 22.2% production (2000).
Income: Per capita income: $21,609 (2000); Median household income: $49,474 (2000); Poverty rate: 2.9% (2000).
Taxes: Total city taxes per capita: $63 (1997); City property taxes per capita: $53 (1997).
Education: High school graduation rate: 91.9% (2000); College graduation rate: 21.0% (2000).
Housing: Homeownership rate: 84.0% (2000); Median home value: $124,300 (2000); Median rent: $343 per month (2000); Median age of housing: 26 years (2000).
Transportation: Commute to work: 93.1% car, 0.5% public transportation, 2.4% walk, 2.6% work from home (2000); Travel time to work: 22.3% less than 15 minutes, 61.0% 15 to 30 minutes, 12.4% 30 to 45 minutes, 2.5% 45 to 60 minutes, 1.9% 60 minutes or more (2000)

BRICE PRAIRIE (CDP). Covers a land area of 4.533 square miles and a water area of 0 square miles. Located at 43.94° N. Lat.; 91.31° W. Long.
Population: 1,804 (2000); Race: 97.6% White, 2.0% Black, 0.5% Asian, 0.0% American Indian and Alaska Native, 0.0% Hispanic of any race, 0.0% two or more races (2000); Density: 398.0 persons per square mile (2000); Age: 28.9% under 18, 7.0% over 64 (2000); Marriage status: 17.4% never married, 71.3% now married, 3.9% widowed, 7.4% divorced (2000); Foreign born: 0.5% (2000); Ancestry (includes multiple ancestries): 53.5% German, 21.4% Norwegian, 13.3% Irish, 8.2% United States or American, 7.2% English (2000).
Economy: Employment by occupation: 7.8% management, 20.3% professional, 17.4% services, 22.5% sales, 0.5% farming, 10.6% construction, 20.9% production (2000).
Income: Per capita income: $19,295 (2000); Median household income: $49,303 (2000); Poverty rate: 3.8% (2000).
Education: High school graduation rate: 92.7% (2000); College graduation rate: 19.6% (2000).
Housing: Homeownership rate: 88.1% (2000); Median home value: $106,300 (2000); Median rent: $492 per month (2000); Median age of housing: 25 years (2000).
Transportation: Commute to work: 94.8% car, 0.0% public transportation, 0.0% walk, 4.1% work from home (2000); Travel time to work: 23.9% less than 15 minutes, 66.2% 15 to 30 minutes, 7.0% 30 to 45 minutes, 1.5% 45 to 60 minutes, 1.4% 60 minutes or more (2000)

BURNS (town). Covers a land area of 48.334 square miles and a water area of 0.023 square miles. Located at 43.95° N. Lat.; 90.96° W. Long. Elevation is 780 feet.
Population: 979 (2000); Race: 98.9% White, 0.2% Black, 0.0% Asian, 0.0% American Indian and Alaska Native, 0.4% Hispanic of any race, 0.9% two or more races (2000); Density: 20.3 persons per square mile (2000); Age: 28.2% under 18, 11.6% over 64 (2000); Marriage status: 26.3% never married, 62.0% now married, 4.2% widowed, 7.5% divorced (2000); Foreign born: 0.0% (2000); Ancestry (includes multiple ancestries): 56.0% German, 29.0% Norwegian, 6.0% Irish, 4.5% Polish, 4.4% English (2000).

Economy: Employment by occupation: 16.2% management, 10.7% professional, 9.9% services, 21.0% sales, 5.3% farming, 8.4% construction, 28.6% production (2000).
Income: Per capita income: $16,947 (2000); Median household income: $41,620 (2000); Poverty rate: 6.3% (2000).
Taxes: Total city taxes per capita: $124 (1997); City property taxes per capita: $120 (1997).
Education: High school graduation rate: 81.6% (2000); College graduation rate: 11.3% (2000).
Housing: Homeownership rate: 88.0% (2000); Median home value: $90,600 (2000); Median rent: $354 per month (2000); Median age of housing: 28 years (2000).
Transportation: Commute to work: 86.5% car, 0.0% public transportation, 3.3% walk, 10.2% work from home (2000); Travel time to work: 27.0% less than 15 minutes, 36.6% 15 to 30 minutes, 31.3% 30 to 45 minutes, 4.7% 45 to 60 minutes, 0.4% 60 minutes or more (2000)

CAMPBELL (town). Covers a land area of 3.842 square miles and a water area of 8.728 square miles. Located at 43.85° N. Lat.; 91.26° W. Long.
Population: 4,410 (2000); Race: 96.3% White, 0.0% Black, 2.1% Asian, 0.4% American Indian and Alaska Native, 0.0% Hispanic of any race, 1.3% two or more races (2000); Density: 1,148.0 persons per square mile (2000); Age: 23.4% under 18, 11.5% over 64 (2000); Marriage status: 26.6% never married, 60.1% now married, 4.3% widowed, 9.0% divorced (2000); Foreign born: 2.2% (2000); Ancestry (includes multiple ancestries): 48.0% German, 24.4% Norwegian, 14.8% Irish, 5.7% English, 5.1% Polish (2000).
Economy: Employment by occupation: 8.9% management, 21.7% professional, 15.4% services, 23.4% sales, 0.4% farming, 8.0% construction, 22.2% production (2000).
Income: Per capita income: $20,741 (2000); Median household income: $44,736 (2000); Poverty rate: 5.1% (2000).
Taxes: Total city taxes per capita: $111 (2000); City property taxes per capita: $95 (2000).
Education: High school graduation rate: 87.8% (2000); College graduation rate: 18.9% (2000).
Housing: Homeownership rate: 77.1% (2000); Median home value: $94,600 (2000); Median rent: $402 per month (2000); Median age of housing: 29 years (2000).
Safety: Violent crime rate: 6.8 per 10,000 population; Property crime rate: 173.4 per 10,000 population (2001).
Transportation: Commute to work: 96.4% car, 0.8% public transportation, 0.8% walk, 1.6% work from home (2000); Travel time to work: 48.0% less than 15 minutes, 41.4% 15 to 30 minutes, 5.7% 30 to 45 minutes, 2.4% 45 to 60 minutes, 2.5% 60 minutes or more (2000)

FARMINGTON (town). Covers a land area of 75.414 square miles and a water area of 0.170 square miles. Located at 44.02° N. Lat.; 91.10° W. Long.
Population: 1,733 (2000); Race: 96.7% White, 0.1% Black, 0.6% Asian, 0.5% American Indian and Alaska Native, 1.8% Hispanic of any race, 1.6% two or more races (2000); Density: 23.0 persons per square mile (2000); Age: 25.2% under 18, 11.2% over 64 (2000); Marriage status: 19.7% never married, 67.2% now married, 5.3% widowed, 7.8% divorced (2000); Foreign born: 1.0% (2000); Ancestry (includes multiple ancestries): 46.5% German, 36.9% Norwegian, 8.6% Irish, 6.2% English, 5.0% Other groups (2000).
Economy: Employment by occupation: 16.5% management, 9.0% professional, 13.8% services, 20.7% sales, 1.4% farming, 13.6% construction, 25.1% production (2000).
Income: Per capita income: $18,096 (2000); Median household income: $41,477 (2000); Poverty rate: 6.9% (2000).
Taxes: Total city taxes per capita: $75 (1997); City property taxes per capita: $72 (1997).
Education: High school graduation rate: 86.3% (2000); College graduation rate: 10.8% (2000).
Housing: Homeownership rate: 85.6% (2000); Median home value: $84,500 (2000); Median rent: $368 per month (2000); Median age of housing: 37 years (2000).
Transportation: Commute to work: 90.5% car, 0.8% public transportation, 1.8% walk, 6.5% work from home (2000); Travel time to work: 11.2% less than 15 minutes, 36.5% 15 to 30 minutes, 34.7% 30 to 45 minutes, 11.0% 45 to 60 minutes, 6.6% 60 minutes or more (2000)

FRENCH ISLAND (CDP). Covers a land area of 1.998 square miles and a water area of 0.385 square miles. Located at 43.85° N. Lat.; 91.26° W. Long.
Population: 4,410 (2000); Race: 96.3% White, 0.0% Black, 2.1% Asian, 0.4% American Indian and Alaska Native, 0.0% Hispanic of any race, 1.3% two or more races (2000); Density: 2,207.6 persons per square mile (2000); Age: 23.4% under 18, 11.5% over 64 (2000); Marriage status: 26.6% never married, 60.1% now married, 4.3% widowed, 9.0% divorced (2000); Foreign born: 2.2% (2000); Ancestry (includes multiple ancestries): 48.0% German, 24.4% Norwegian, 14.8% Irish, 5.7% English, 5.1% Polish (2000).
Economy: Employment by occupation: 8.9% management, 21.7% professional, 15.4% services, 23.4% sales, 0.4% farming, 8.0% construction, 22.2% production (2000).
Income: Per capita income: $20,741 (2000); Median household income: $44,736 (2000); Poverty rate: 5.1% (2000).
Education: High school graduation rate: 87.8% (2000); College graduation rate: 18.9% (2000).
Housing: Homeownership rate: 77.1% (2000); Median home value: $94,600 (2000); Median rent: $402 per month (2000); Median age of housing: 29 years (2000).
Transportation: Commute to work: 96.4% car, 0.8% public transportation, 0.8% walk, 1.6% work from home (2000); Travel time to work: 48.0% less than 15 minutes, 41.4% 15 to 30 minutes, 5.7% 30 to 45 minutes, 2.4% 45 to 60 minutes, 2.5% 60 minutes or more (2000)

GREENFIELD (town). Covers a land area of 30.082 square miles and a water area of 0 square miles. Located at 43.77° N. Lat.; 91.06° W. Long.
Population: 1,538 (2000); Race: 99.0% White, 0.4% Black, 0.0% Asian, 0.5% American Indian and Alaska Native, 0.5% Hispanic of any race, 0.2% two or more races (2000); Density: 51.1 persons per square mile (2000); Age: 30.6% under 18, 9.1% over 64 (2000); Marriage status: 21.5% never married, 70.6% now married, 2.1% widowed, 5.8% divorced (2000); Foreign born: 0.0% (2000); Ancestry (includes multiple ancestries): 55.9% German, 31.1% Norwegian, 10.1% Irish, 5.9% English, 4.3% United States or American (2000).
Economy: Employment by occupation: 19.0% management, 15.5% professional, 14.0% services, 24.1% sales, 0.5% farming, 9.7% construction, 17.2% production (2000).
Income: Per capita income: $20,501 (2000); Median household income: $49,653 (2000); Poverty rate: 4.6% (2000).
Taxes: Total city taxes per capita: $16 (1997); City property taxes per capita: $8 (1997).
Education: High school graduation rate: 89.1% (2000); College graduation rate: 23.8% (2000).
Housing: Homeownership rate: 89.6% (2000); Median home value: $128,200 (2000); Median rent: $373 per month (2000); Median age of housing: 25 years (2000).
Transportation: Commute to work: 87.9% car, 0.4% public transportation, 3.9% walk, 7.4% work from home (2000); Travel time to work: 22.8% less than 15 minutes, 58.5% 15 to 30 minutes, 12.8% 30 to 45 minutes, 0.4% 45 to 60 minutes, 5.5% 60 minutes or more (2000)

HAMILTON (town). Covers a land area of 50.068 square miles and a water area of 1.043 square miles. Located at 43.91° N. Lat.; 91.09° W. Long.
Population: 2,301 (2000); Race: 99.0% White, 0.2% Black, 0.4% Asian, 0.4% American Indian and Alaska Native, 0.3% Hispanic of any race, 0.0% two or more races (2000); Density: 46.0 persons per square mile (2000); Age: 29.8% under 18, 12.6% over 64 (2000); Marriage status: 18.8% never married, 75.6% now married, 2.2% widowed, 3.4% divorced (2000); Foreign born: 1.3% (2000); Ancestry (includes multiple ancestries): 46.5% German, 27.6% Norwegian, 9.2% Irish, 5.6% English, 3.9% United States or American (2000).
Economy: Employment by occupation: 17.2% management, 20.8% professional, 13.6% services, 24.1% sales, 1.4% farming, 8.7% construction, 14.2% production (2000).
Income: Per capita income: $20,142 (2000); Median household income: $57,955 (2000); Poverty rate: 2.1% (2000).
Taxes: Total city taxes per capita: $135 (1997); City property taxes per capita: $132 (1997).
Education: High school graduation rate: 91.2% (2000); College graduation rate: 27.9% (2000).
Housing: Homeownership rate: 90.5% (2000); Median home value: $123,800 (2000); Median rent: $421 per month (2000); Median age of housing: 24 years (2000).
Transportation: Commute to work: 93.8% car, 0.0% public transportation, 0.3% walk, 5.6% work from home (2000); Travel time to work: 29.1% less than 15 minutes, 51.3% 15 to 30 minutes, 14.8% 30 to 45 minutes, 2.7% 45 to 60 minutes, 2.1% 60 minutes or more (2000)

HOLLAND (town). Covers a land area of 42.513 square miles and a water area of 3.128 square miles. Located at 43.98° N. Lat.; 91.29° W. Long.
Population: 3,042 (2000); Race: 96.8% White, 0.0% Black, 1.5% Asian, 0.4% American Indian and Alaska Native, 1.2% Hispanic of any race, 0.7% two or more races (2000); Density: 71.6 persons per square mile (2000); Age: 31.3% under 18, 5.8% over 64 (2000); Marriage status: 21.5% never married, 69.5% now married, 2.3% widowed, 6.7% divorced (2000); Foreign born: 1.5% (2000); Ancestry (includes multiple ancestries): 47.8% German, 29.2% Norwegian, 13.4% Irish, 7.4% English, 6.3% Polish (2000).
Economy: Employment by occupation: 14.3% management, 17.1% professional, 13.2% services, 27.8% sales, 0.2% farming, 10.1% construction, 17.3% production (2000).
Income: Per capita income: $20,126 (2000); Median household income: $55,846 (2000); Poverty rate: 4.2% (2000).
Taxes: Total city taxes per capita: $62 (1997); City property taxes per capita: $53 (1997).
Education: High school graduation rate: 90.1% (2000); College graduation rate: 22.7% (2000).
Housing: Homeownership rate: 93.7% (2000); Median home value: $123,400 (2000); Median rent: $572 per month (2000); Median age of housing: 17 years (2000).
Transportation: Commute to work: 95.3% car, 0.2% public transportation, 0.5% walk, 4.1% work from home (2000); Travel time to work: 23.1% less than 15 minutes, 45.4% 15 to 30 minutes, 25.6% 30 to 45 minutes, 2.6% 45 to 60 minutes, 3.3% 60 minutes or more (2000)

HOLMEN (village). Covers a land area of 3.188 square miles and a water area of 0 square miles. Located at 43.95° N. Lat.; 91.25° W. Long. Elevation is 718 feet.
Population: 6,200 (2000); Race: 94.3% White, 0.0% Black, 2.3% Asian, 0.4% American Indian and Alaska Native, 1.9% Hispanic of any race, 1.2% two or more races (2000); Density: 1,944.9 persons per square mile (2000); Age: 31.9% under 18, 7.3% over 64 (2000); Marriage status: 23.7% never married, 62.6% now married, 4.2% widowed, 9.5% divorced (2000); Foreign born: 3.1% (2000); Ancestry (includes multiple ancestries): 47.6% German, 30.1% Norwegian, 17.2% Irish, 7.5% English, 6.1% Other groups (2000).
Economy: In farm and dairy region. Manufacturing: custom casework, silk screening, feather processing, concrete products. Single-family building permits issued: 69 (2001) / 84 (2000); Multi-family building permits issued: 35 (2001) / 24 (2000); Employment by occupation: 8.8% management, 16.6% professional, 15.0% services, 24.8% sales, 0.1% farming, 9.8% construction, 25.0% production (2000).
Income: Per capita income: $17,002 (2000); Median household income: $42,021 (2000); Poverty rate: 7.8% (2000).
Taxes: Total city taxes per capita: $175 (1997); City property taxes per capita: $138 (1997).
Education: High school graduation rate: 91.6% (2000); College graduation rate: 20.9% (2000).

School District(s)

Holmen (PK-12)
2000 Enrollment: 2,976 608-526-6610

Housing: Homeownership rate: 80.3% (2000); Median home value: $106,700 (2000); Median rent: $473 per month (2000); Median age of housing: 13 years (2000).
Safety: Violent crime rate: 3.2 per 10,000 population; Property crime rate: 381.2 per 10,000 population (2001).
Transportation: Commute to work: 97.6% car, 0.0% public transportation, 0.7% walk, 1.7% work from home (2000); Travel time to work: 36.4% less than 15 minutes, 47.0% 15 to 30 minutes, 11.7% 30 to 45 minutes, 2.1% 45 to 60 minutes, 2.8% 60 minutes or more (2000)

LA CROSSE (city). Covers a land area of 20.136 square miles and a water area of 2.024 square miles. Located at 43.81° N. Lat.; 91.23° W. Long. Elevation is 669 feet.
History: La Crosse started as a trading post, called Prairie la Crosse by the French for a game they saw the Indians playing that reminded them of the French game of lacrosse. Nathan Myrick built the trading post in 1842, and settlers followed in the 1850's, building sawmills and grist mills. Many of these early settlers were from Germany and Norway, artisans and professional people forced to leave their homelands by the revolutions of 1848. In 1856 La Crosse received a city charter, and the "Prairie" was dropped from the name. After the Civil War, La Crosse became an important center for men and supplies heading west. A railroad bridge built in 1876 allowed trains to cross the Mississippi, and made La Crosse the most important distribution point between St. Louis and St. Paul. A flourishing lumber business in the 1880's and 1890's was replaced by breweries, furniture factories, woolen mills, and other diversified industry after 1900.
Population: 51,818 (2000); Race: 91.9% White, 1.6% Black, 3.8% Asian, 0.9% American Indian and Alaska Native, 0.8% Hispanic of any race, 1.5% two or more races (2000); Density: 2,573.4 persons per square mile (2000); Age: 18.9% under 18, 15.0% over 64 (2000); Marriage status: 43.1% never married, 40.4% now married, 7.4% widowed, 9.1% divorced (2000); Foreign born: 3.3% (2000); Ancestry (includes multiple ancestries): 41.9% German, 20.5% Norwegian, 14.2% Irish, 8.1% Other groups, 5.6% English (2000).
Vital Statistics: Birth rate: 116.4 per 10,000 population (1998)
Economy: Unemployment rate: 4.6% (11/2002); Total civilian labor force: 29,792 (11/2002); Single-family building permits issued: 40 (2001) / 29 (2000); Multi-family building permits issued: 48 (2001) / 73 (2000); Employment by occupation: 8.1% management, 19.8% professional, 20.4% services, 29.1% sales, 0.2% farming, 6.6% construction, 15.9% production (2000).
Income: Per capita income: $17,650 (2000); Median household income: $31,103 (2000); Poverty rate: 17.2% (2000).
Taxes: Total city taxes per capita: $418 (2000); City property taxes per capita: $377 (2000).
Education: High school graduation rate: 87.8% (2000); College graduation rate: 24.1% (2000).

School District(s)

La Crosse (PK-12)
2000 Enrollment: 7,775 608-789-7628

Four-year College(s)

Viterbo University (Private, Not-for-profit, Roman Catholic)
2001 Enrollment: 2,623 608-796-3000
2001 Tuition: In-state $13,350; Out-of-state $13,350
University of Wisconsin-La Crosse (Public)
2001 Enrollment: 9,650 608-785-8000
2001 Tuition: In-state $2,776; Out-of-state $11,288

Two-year College(s)

Western Wisconsin Technical College (Public)
2001 Enrollment: 5,272 608-785-9200
2001 Tuition: In-state $1,920; Out-of-state $13,068

Housing: Homeownership rate: 50.7% (2000); Median home value: $85,100 (2000); Median rent: $386 per month (2000); Median age of housing: 45 years (2000).
Hospitals: Franciscan Skemp Medical Center (350 beds); Gundersen Lutheran (380 beds)
Safety: Violent crime rate: 19.0 per 10,000 population; Property crime rate: 382.1 per 10,000 population (2001).
Newspapers: The Buyer Express (1 x week); La Crosse Tribune (7 x week); Times Review (1 x week)
Transportation: Commute to work: 84.6% car, 2.4% public transportation, 9.1% walk, 2.3% work from home (2000); Travel time to work: 57.2% less than 15 minutes, 32.6% 15 to 30 minutes, 5.8% 30 to 45 minutes, 1.5% 45 to 60 minutes, 2.9% 60 minutes or more (2000); Amtrak: Service available.
Airports: La Crosse Municipal (primary service)
Additional Information Contacts
Greater La Crosse Area Chamber 608-784-4880
La Crosse Area Realtors Association 608-785-7744
La Crosse Convention & Visitors Bureau 608-782-2366

MEDARY (town). Covers a land area of 11.709 square miles and a water area of 0.017 square miles. Located at 43.85° N. Lat.; 91.18° W. Long. Elevation is 700 feet.
Population: 1,463 (2000); Race: 97.1% White, 0.0% Black, 1.0% Asian, 0.3% American Indian and Alaska Native, 0.0% Hispanic of any race, 1.6% two or more races (2000); Density: 124.9 persons per square mile (2000); Age: 27.7% under 18, 6.6% over 64 (2000); Marriage status: 24.8% never married, 64.1% now married, 4.6% widowed, 6.5% divorced (2000); Foreign born: 1.4% (2000); Ancestry (includes multiple ancestries): 55.1% German, 21.8% Norwegian, 9.7% Irish, 9.3% Polish, 5.9% English (2000).
Economy: Employment by occupation: 11.0% management, 24.3% professional, 12.8% services, 29.6% sales, 0.0% farming, 9.9% construction, 12.4% production (2000).
Income: Per capita income: $25,395 (2000); Median household income: $57,431 (2000); Poverty rate: 3.6% (2000).
Taxes: Total city taxes per capita: $4 (1997); City property taxes per capita: $0 (1997).
Education: High school graduation rate: 94.7% (2000); College graduation rate: 36.3% (2000).

Housing: Homeownership rate: 89.0% (2000); Median home value: $128,500 (2000); Median rent: $475 per month (2000); Median age of housing: 26 years (2000).
Transportation: Commute to work: 93.6% car, 0.4% public transportation, 0.9% walk, 4.9% work from home (2000); Travel time to work: 41.2% less than 15 minutes, 46.1% 15 to 30 minutes, 6.2% 30 to 45 minutes, 3.5% 45 to 60 minutes, 3.0% 60 minutes or more (2000)

MINDORO (unincorporated postal area, zip code 54644). Covers a land area of 50.234 square miles and a water area of <.001 square miles. Located at 44.02° N. Lat.; 91.06° W. Long. Elevation is 786 feet.
Population: 1,257 (2000); Race: 96.3% White, 0.1% Black, 1.1% Asian, 0.3% American Indian and Alaska Native, 1.9% Hispanic of any race, 1.7% two or more races (2000); Density: 25.0 persons per square mile (2000); Age: 27.4% under 18, 9.1% over 64 (2000); Marriage status: 21.9% never married, 64.7% now married, 6.9% widowed, 6.4% divorced (2000); Foreign born: 1.4% (2000); Ancestry (includes multiple ancestries): 48.8% German, 34.3% Norwegian, 9.7% Irish, 5.8% Polish, 4.9% Other groups (2000).
Economy: Employment by occupation: 12.6% management, 12.5% professional, 13.0% services, 20.7% sales, 1.9% farming, 13.6% construction, 25.8% production (2000).
Income: Per capita income: $16,598 (2000); Median household income: $39,286 (2000); Poverty rate: 9.8% (2000).
Education: High school graduation rate: 85.7% (2000); College graduation rate: 10.9% (2000).
Housing: Homeownership rate: 83.7% (2000); Median home value: $84,800 (2000); Median rent: $370 per month (2000); Median age of housing: 32 years (2000).
Transportation: Commute to work: 88.8% car, 1.1% public transportation, 2.6% walk, 6.7% work from home (2000); Travel time to work: 17.8% less than 15 minutes, 35.6% 15 to 30 minutes, 31.3% 30 to 45 minutes, 9.4% 45 to 60 minutes, 5.8% 60 minutes or more (2000)

ONALASKA (city). Covers a land area of 9.095 square miles and a water area of 0.582 square miles. Located at 43.88° N. Lat.; 91.21° W. Long. Elevation is 716 feet.
Population: 14,839 (2000); Race: 94.6% White, 0.3% Black, 3.0% Asian, 0.1% American Indian and Alaska Native, 1.3% Hispanic of any race, 1.6% two or more races (2000); Density: 1,631.6 persons per square mile (2000); Age: 25.9% under 18, 11.2% over 64 (2000); Marriage status: 26.8% never married, 59.1% now married, 5.0% widowed, 9.0% divorced (2000); Foreign born: 2.6% (2000); Ancestry (includes multiple ancestries): 46.2% German, 22.9% Norwegian, 14.2% Irish, 8.0% English, 7.8% Other groups (2000).
Vital Statistics: Birth rate: 138.8 per 10,000 population (1998)
Economy: Single-family building permits issued: 121 (2001) / 76 (2000); Multi-family building permits issued: 20 (2001) / 40 (2000); Employment by occupation: 13.7% management, 23.1% professional, 12.9% services, 29.6% sales, 0.1% farming, 6.4% construction, 14.1% production (2000).
Income: Per capita income: $24,066 (2000); Median household income: $47,800 (2000); Poverty rate: 6.2% (2000).
Taxes: Total city taxes per capita: $426 (2000); City property taxes per capita: $405 (2000).
Education: High school graduation rate: 94.0% (2000); College graduation rate: 31.3% (2000).

School District(s)

Onalaska (PK-12)
2000 Enrollment: 2,762 608-781-9704
Housing: Homeownership rate: 68.3% (2000); Median home value: $114,400 (2000); Median rent: $458 per month (2000); Median age of housing: 21 years (2000).
Safety: Violent crime rate: 12.0 per 10,000 population; Property crime rate: 392.8 per 10,000 population (2001).
Newspapers: Holmen Courier (1 x week); Onalaska Community Life (1 x week)
Transportation: Commute to work: 97.1% car, 0.2% public transportation, 0.5% walk, 1.5% work from home (2000); Travel time to work: 45.1% less than 15 minutes, 45.0% 15 to 30 minutes, 5.6% 30 to 45 minutes, 1.7% 45 to 60 minutes, 2.6% 60 minutes or more (2000)

ONALASKA (town). Covers a land area of 37.002 square miles and a water area of 7.896 square miles. Located at 43.93° N. Lat.; 91.25° W. Long. Elevation is 716 feet.
History: Hamlin Garland born nearby. Settled 1854, incorporated 1887.
Population: 5,210 (2000); Race: 97.4% White, 0.7% Black, 1.3% Asian, 0.0% American Indian and Alaska Native, 0.6% Hispanic of any race, 0.4% two or more races (2000); Density: 140.8 persons per square mile (2000); Age: 29.6% under 18, 5.7% over 64 (2000); Marriage status: 20.2% never married, 71.8% now married, 2.0% widowed, 5.9% divorced (2000); Foreign born: 0.9% (2000); Ancestry (includes multiple ancestries): 47.4% German, 24.1% Norwegian, 14.4% Irish, 6.0% English, 5.9% United States or American (2000).
Economy: In farm and dairy area. Dairy products. Manufacturing: consumer goods, printing, printed circuit boards, machinery. Summer resort. Lock and Dam No. 7 and La Crosse Airport to East. Interstate 90 bridge to Minnesota. Employment by occupation: 9.9% management, 19.2% professional, 15.8% services, 25.9% sales, 0.4% farming, 9.9% construction, 19.0% production (2000).
Income: Per capita income: $19,887 (2000); Median household income: $54,075 (2000); Poverty rate: 3.8% (2000).
Taxes: Total city taxes per capita: $37 (1997); City property taxes per capita: $33 (1997).
Education: High school graduation rate: 92.2% (2000); College graduation rate: 27.7% (2000).
Housing: Homeownership rate: 90.7% (2000); Median home value: $111,100 (2000); Median rent: $442 per month (2000); Median age of housing: 25 years (2000).
Transportation: Commute to work: 92.3% car, 0.0% public transportation, 0.8% walk, 6.5% work from home (2000); Travel time to work: 31.1% less than 15 minutes, 54.5% 15 to 30 minutes, 11.1% 30 to 45 minutes, 1.7% 45 to 60 minutes, 1.7% 60 minutes or more (2000)

ROCKLAND (village). Covers a land area of 0.543 square miles and a water area of 0 square miles. Located at 43.90° N. Lat.; 90.91° W. Long. Elevation is 752 feet.
Population: 628 (2000); Race: 98.5% White, 0.3% Black, 0.0% Asian, 0.0% American Indian and Alaska Native, 0.3% Hispanic of any race, 1.0% two or more races (2000); Density: 1,156.4 persons per square mile (2000); Age: 28.8% under 18, 8.6% over 64 (2000); Marriage status: 32.4% never married, 57.3% now married, 3.3% widowed, 6.9% divorced (2000); Foreign born: 0.4% (2000); Ancestry (includes multiple ancestries): 45.0% German, 32.6% Norwegian, 9.1% Irish, 3.3% Italian, 3.1% Czech (2000).
Economy: In dairy and livestock area. Manufacturing of lumber. Single-family building permits issued: 3 (2001) / 8 (2000); Multi-family building permits issued: 0 (2001) / 0 (2000); Employment by occupation: 8.9% management, 9.5% professional, 12.5% services, 35.7% sales, 0.0% farming, 3.6% construction, 29.8% production (2000).
Income: Per capita income: $17,914 (2000); Median household income: $46,429 (2000); Poverty rate: 8.6% (2000).
Taxes: Total city taxes per capita: $48 (1997); City property taxes per capita: $43 (1997).
Education: High school graduation rate: 78.6% (2000); College graduation rate: 8.7% (2000).
Housing: Homeownership rate: 79.3% (2000); Median home value: $79,100 (2000); Median rent: $398 per month (2000); Median age of housing: 23 years (2000).
Transportation: Commute to work: 98.0% car, 0.0% public transportation, 0.0% walk, 1.4% work from home (2000); Travel time to work: 19.7% less than 15 minutes, 32.1% 15 to 30 minutes, 37.9% 30 to 45 minutes, 4.6% 45 to 60 minutes, 5.8% 60 minutes or more (2000)

SHELBY (town). Covers a land area of 25.578 square miles and a water area of 3.552 square miles. Located at 43.77° N. Lat.; 91.19° W. Long. Elevation is 694 feet.
Population: 4,687 (2000); Race: 97.5% White, 0.4% Black, 1.0% Asian, 0.4% American Indian and Alaska Native, 0.0% Hispanic of any race, 0.8% two or more races (2000); Density: 183.2 persons per square mile (2000); Age: 26.7% under 18, 13.0% over 64 (2000); Marriage status: 16.7% never married, 73.2% now married, 4.2% widowed, 6.0% divorced (2000); Foreign born: 2.5% (2000); Ancestry (includes multiple ancestries): 51.5% German, 19.8% Norwegian, 13.6% Irish, 8.9% English, 5.0% Polish (2000).
Economy: Employment by occupation: 13.3% management, 38.3% professional, 10.2% services, 22.7% sales, 0.3% farming, 6.0% construction, 9.1% production (2000).
Income: Per capita income: $32,899 (2000); Median household income: $64,890 (2000); Poverty rate: 1.1% (2000).
Taxes: Total city taxes per capita: $196 (2000); City property taxes per capita: $185 (2000).
Education: High school graduation rate: 95.0% (2000); College graduation rate: 45.8% (2000).
Housing: Homeownership rate: 94.2% (2000); Median home value: $129,500 (2000); Median rent: $385 per month (2000); Median age of housing: 28 years (2000).

Transportation: Commute to work: 92.7% car, 0.5% public transportation, 1.0% walk, 4.2% work from home (2000); Travel time to work: 45.8% less than 15 minutes, 44.1% 15 to 30 minutes, 6.9% 30 to 45 minutes, 1.2% 45 to 60 minutes, 2.0% 60 minutes or more (2000)

WASHINGTON (town). Covers a land area of 36.101 square miles and a water area of 0 square miles. Located at 43.76° N. Lat.; 90.98° W. Long.
Population: 738 (2000); Race: 99.3% White, 0.0% Black, 0.3% Asian, 0.4% American Indian and Alaska Native, 0.7% Hispanic of any race, 0.0% two or more races (2000); Density: 20.4 persons per square mile (2000); Age: 25.3% under 18, 22.8% over 64 (2000); Marriage status: 33.1% never married, 60.7% now married, 4.0% widowed, 2.2% divorced (2000); Foreign born: 0.4% (2000); Ancestry (includes multiple ancestries): 55.8% German, 24.3% Norwegian, 12.4% Irish, 11.0% Czech, 5.3% English (2000).
Economy: Employment by occupation: 25.3% management, 19.9% professional, 14.5% services, 14.2% sales, 2.3% farming, 9.1% construction, 14.8% production (2000).
Income: Per capita income: $16,424 (2000); Median household income: $42,143 (2000); Poverty rate: 8.7% (2000).
Taxes: Total city taxes per capita: $59 (1997); City property taxes per capita: $57 (1997).
Education: High school graduation rate: 86.9% (2000); College graduation rate: 22.1% (2000).
Housing: Homeownership rate: 83.3% (2000); Median home value: $82,500 (2000); Median rent: $460 per month (2000); Median age of housing: 49 years (2000).
Transportation: Commute to work: 76.5% car, 0.0% public transportation, 4.1% walk, 19.5% work from home (2000); Travel time to work: 18.8% less than 15 minutes, 47.7% 15 to 30 minutes, 26.4% 30 to 45 minutes, 2.5% 45 to 60 minutes, 4.7% 60 minutes or more (2000)

WEST SALEM (village). Covers a land area of 2.375 square miles and a water area of 0.010 square miles. Located at 43.90° N. Lat.; 91.08° W. Long. Elevation is 742 feet.
History: West Salem was founded in 1858 and soon attracted Norwegian and German immigrants. Developing as a farm trade center, West Salem had a cooperative creamery established in 1891. Author Hamlin Garland lived in West Salem.
Population: 4,540 (2000); Race: 99.0% White, 0.0% Black, 0.3% Asian, 0.6% American Indian and Alaska Native, 0.0% Hispanic of any race, 0.1% two or more races (2000); Density: 1,911.2 persons per square mile (2000); Age: 29.4% under 18, 13.1% over 64 (2000); Marriage status: 19.7% never married, 63.7% now married, 7.1% widowed, 9.5% divorced (2000); Foreign born: 0.7% (2000); Ancestry (includes multiple ancestries): 55.5% German, 28.3% Norwegian, 10.3% Irish, 6.4% English, 3.3% Polish (2000).
Economy: Single-family building permits issued: 0 (2001) / 18 (2000); Multi-family building permits issued: 18 (2001) / 15 (2000); Employment by occupation: 11.6% management, 17.9% professional, 15.6% services, 23.3% sales, 0.0% farming, 9.0% construction, 22.6% production (2000).
Income: Per capita income: $19,904 (2000); Median household income: $43,449 (2000); Poverty rate: 3.5% (2000).
Taxes: Total city taxes per capita: $110 (1997); City property taxes per capita: $87 (1997).
Education: High school graduation rate: 88.7% (2000); College graduation rate: 21.9% (2000).

School District(s)

West Salem (PK-12)
2000 Enrollment: 1,562 608-786-0700
Housing: Homeownership rate: 73.8% (2000); Median home value: $102,500 (2000); Median rent: $437 per month (2000); Median age of housing: 24 years (2000).
Safety: Violent crime rate: 13.1 per 10,000 population; Property crime rate: 336.8 per 10,000 population (2001).
Newspapers: Economy Shopper (1 x week); Coulee News (1 x week)
Transportation: Commute to work: 93.3% car, 0.2% public transportation, 3.5% walk, 2.1% work from home (2000); Travel time to work: 34.1% less than 15 minutes, 49.2% 15 to 30 minutes, 10.5% 30 to 45 minutes, 2.5% 45 to 60 minutes, 3.8% 60 minutes or more (2000)

Lafayette County

Located in southern Wisconsin; bounded on the south by Illinois; drained by the Pecatonica and Galena Rivers. Covers a land area of 633.60 square miles, a water area of 1.00 square miles, and is located in the Central Time Zone. The county government was organized in 1846. County seat is Darlington.

Weather Station: Darlington Elevation: 928 feet

	Jan	Feb	Mar	Apr	May	Jun	Jul	Aug	Sep	Oct	Nov	Dec
High	26	32	44	58	71	79	83	81	73	61	45	31
Low	7	13	24	35	46	56	61	58	49	38	26	14
Precip	1.2	1.3	2.4	3.4	3.5	4.6	4.2	4.3	3.8	2.3	2.4	1.6
Snow	9.9	7.4	6.3	2.9	0.2	0.0	0.0	0.0	0.0	0.4	3.0	8.1

High and Low temperatures in degrees Fahrenheit; Precipitation and Snow in inches

Population: 16,137 (2000); Race: 99.2% White, 0.0% Black, 0.2% Asian, 0.1% American Indian and Alaska Native, 0.5% Hispanic of any race, 0.3% two or more races (2000); Density: 25.5 persons per square mile (2000); Age: 27.2% under 18, 15.8% over 64 (2000).
Religion: Five largest groups: 44.4% Catholic Church, 17.2% Evangelical Lutheran Church in America, 9.3% The United Methodist Church, 2.2% United Church of Christ, 1.1% Primitive Methodist Church in the USA (2000).
Economy: Unemployment rate: 5.9% (11/2002); Total civilian labor force: 7,534 (11/2002); Leading industries: 23.9% manufacturing; 19.6% retail trade; 19.6% transportation & warehousing (2000); Companies that employ more than 1,000 persons: 0 (2000); Companies that employ more than 100 persons: 3 (2000); Farms: 1,127 totaling 338,376 acres (1997); Minority business ownership rate: 0.0% (1997); Women business ownership rate: 20.1% (1997); Retail sales per capita: $5,806 (1997). Single-family building permits issued: 55 (2001) / 61 (2000); Multi-family building permits issued: 15 (2001) / 0 (2000).
Income: Per capita income: $16,811 (2000); Median household income: $37,220 (2000); Poverty rate: 9.1% (2000); Bankruptcy rate: 2.05% (2001).
Taxes: Total county taxes per capita: $307 (1997); County property taxes per capita: $305 (1997).
Education: High school graduation rate: 85.5% (2000); College graduation rate: 13.3% (2000).
Housing: Homeownership rate: 77.4% (2000); Median home value: $74,600 (2000); Median rent: $317 per month (2000); Median age of housing: 53 years (2000).
Health: Birth rate: 109.7 per 10,000 population (1998); Age adjusted death rate: 80.1 per 10,000 population (1999); Age adjusted cancer mortality rate: 225.1 deaths per 100,000 population (1999). Number of physicians: 5.0 per 10,000 population (1999); Number of hospital beds: 17.4 per 10,000 population (1999).
Elections: 2000 Presidential election results: 51.1% Gore, 45.9% Bush, 2.6% Nader, 0.2% Buchanan
National and State Parks: First Capitol State Park
Additional Information Contacts
Lafayette County Government Offices 608-776-4850

Lafayette County Communities

ARGYLE (village). Covers a land area of 0.605 square miles and a water area of 0 square miles. Located at 42.70° N. Lat.; 89.86° W. Long. Elevation is 810 feet.
Population: 823 (2000); Race: 99.4% White, 0.0% Black, 0.0% Asian, 0.0% American Indian and Alaska Native, 0.8% Hispanic of any race, 0.6% two or more races (2000); Density: 1,361.0 persons per square mile (2000); Age: 24.6% under 18, 20.3% over 64 (2000); Marriage status: 25.3% never married, 55.4% now married, 10.5% widowed, 8.7% divorced (2000); Foreign born: 0.2% (2000); Ancestry (includes multiple ancestries): 38.5% Norwegian, 27.2% German, 24.8% Swiss, 17.1% Irish, 12.0% English (2000).
Economy: Single-family building permits issued: 0 (2001) / 0 (2000); Multi-family building permits issued: 0 (2001) / 0 (2000); Employment by occupation: 11.3% management, 14.9% professional, 15.8% services, 17.6% sales, 2.7% farming, 8.4% construction, 29.3% production (2000).
Income: Per capita income: $15,974 (2000); Median household income: $36,103 (2000); Poverty rate: 8.7% (2000).
Taxes: Total city taxes per capita: $118 (1997); City property taxes per capita: $107 (1997).
Education: High school graduation rate: 82.1% (2000); College graduation rate: 8.7% (2000).

School District(s)

Argyle (PK-12)
2000 Enrollment: 373 608-543-3318
Housing: Homeownership rate: 75.3% (2000); Median home value: $77,400 (2000); Median rent: $319 per month (2000); Median age of housing: 60+ years (2000).
Transportation: Commute to work: 83.8% car, 0.9% public transportation, 10.3% walk, 4.1% work from home (2000); Travel time to work: 37.3% less

than 15 minutes, 39.4% 15 to 30 minutes, 10.9% 30 to 45 minutes, 6.2% 45 to 60 minutes, 6.2% 60 minutes or more (2000)

ARGYLE (town). Covers a land area of 35.610 square miles and a water area of 0.054 square miles. Located at 42.73° N. Lat.; 89.90° W. Long. Elevation is 810 feet.
Population: 479 (2000); Race: 97.5% White, 0.0% Black, 0.0% Asian, 0.4% American Indian and Alaska Native, 0.6% Hispanic of any race, 1.9% two or more races (2000); Density: 13.5 persons per square mile (2000); Age: 30.0% under 18, 18.4% over 64 (2000); Marriage status: 16.7% never married, 69.4% now married, 4.4% widowed, 9.4% divorced (2000); Foreign born: 0.8% (2000); Ancestry (includes multiple ancestries): 29.8% Norwegian, 25.5% German, 20.3% Swiss, 17.2% Irish, 10.6% English (2000).
Economy: In agricultural area: cheese, sorghum. Manufacturing: water pumps, food processing. Employment by occupation: 25.9% management, 10.7% professional, 8.2% services, 18.5% sales, 7.0% farming, 5.8% construction, 23.9% production (2000).
Income: Per capita income: $17,609 (2000); Median household income: $39,519 (2000); Poverty rate: 12.5% (2000).
Taxes: Total city taxes per capita: $193 (1997); City property taxes per capita: $193 (1997).
Education: High school graduation rate: 83.2% (2000); College graduation rate: 14.1% (2000).
Housing: Homeownership rate: 85.0% (2000); Median home value: $113,900 (2000); Median rent: $338 per month (2000); Median age of housing: 52 years (2000).
Transportation: Commute to work: 73.7% car, 0.0% public transportation, 4.5% walk, 21.8% work from home (2000); Travel time to work: 44.7% less than 15 minutes, 20.0% 15 to 30 minutes, 10.5% 30 to 45 minutes, 12.1% 45 to 60 minutes, 12.6% 60 minutes or more (2000)

BELMONT (village). Covers a land area of 0.576 square miles and a water area of 0 square miles. Located at 42.73° N. Lat.; 90.33° W. Long. Elevation is 1,060 feet.
Population: 871 (2000); Race: 100.0% White, 0.0% Black, 0.0% Asian, 0.0% American Indian and Alaska Native, 0.0% Hispanic of any race, 0.0% two or more races (2000); Density: 1,511.6 persons per square mile (2000); Age: 21.4% under 18, 20.8% over 64 (2000); Marriage status: 25.2% never married, 57.4% now married, 10.1% widowed, 7.3% divorced (2000); Foreign born: 0.8% (2000); Ancestry (includes multiple ancestries): 55.4% German, 17.6% Irish, 17.6% English, 9.4% Norwegian, 7.1% United States or American (2000).
Economy: Single-family building permits issued: 2 (2001) / 3 (2000); Multi-family building permits issued: 15 (2001) / 0 (2000); Employment by occupation: 10.0% management, 14.4% professional, 15.2% services, 25.2% sales, 4.5% farming, 8.3% construction, 22.4% production (2000).
Income: Per capita income: $17,763 (2000); Median household income: $34,853 (2000); Poverty rate: 5.4% (2000).
Taxes: Total city taxes per capita: $86 (1997); City property taxes per capita: $75 (1997).
Education: High school graduation rate: 88.1% (2000); College graduation rate: 16.6% (2000).

School District(s)

Belmont Community (PK-12)
2000 Enrollment: 395 608-762-5131
Housing: Homeownership rate: 75.2% (2000); Median home value: $78,300 (2000); Median rent: $310 per month (2000); Median age of housing: 32 years (2000).
Transportation: Commute to work: 90.8% car, 0.0% public transportation, 4.8% walk, 4.0% work from home (2000); Travel time to work: 46.5% less than 15 minutes, 27.2% 15 to 30 minutes, 16.5% 30 to 45 minutes, 6.7% 45 to 60 minutes, 3.0% 60 minutes or more (2000)

BELMONT (town). Covers a land area of 41.247 square miles and a water area of 0.128 square miles. Located at 42.75° N. Lat.; 90.36° W. Long. Elevation is 1,060 feet.
Population: 676 (2000); Race: 99.7% White, 0.0% Black, 0.0% Asian, 0.0% American Indian and Alaska Native, 0.0% Hispanic of any race, 0.3% two or more races (2000); Density: 16.4 persons per square mile (2000); Age: 31.6% under 18, 10.0% over 64 (2000); Marriage status: 30.4% never married, 56.2% now married, 4.8% widowed, 8.6% divorced (2000); Foreign born: 0.3% (2000); Ancestry (includes multiple ancestries): 47.3% German, 18.0% Irish, 17.7% English, 8.5% United States or American, 6.8% Norwegian (2000).
Economy: Makes cheese. Single-family building permits issued: 0 (2001) / 0 (2000); Multi-family building permits issued: 0 (2001) / 0 (2000); Employment by occupation: 19.1% management, 11.6% professional, 13.3% services, 23.4% sales, 5.5% farming, 6.1% construction, 21.1% production (2000).
Income: Per capita income: $16,879 (2000); Median household income: $39,196 (2000); Poverty rate: 7.4% (2000).
Taxes: Total city taxes per capita: $115 (1997); City property taxes per capita: $106 (1997).
Education: High school graduation rate: 85.9% (2000); College graduation rate: 16.6% (2000).
Housing: Homeownership rate: 77.2% (2000); Median home value: $99,700 (2000); Median rent: $394 per month (2000); Median age of housing: 30 years (2000).
Transportation: Commute to work: 80.8% car, 0.9% public transportation, 4.1% walk, 13.6% work from home (2000); Travel time to work: 38.2% less than 15 minutes, 27.6% 15 to 30 minutes, 23.9% 30 to 45 minutes, 5.1% 45 to 60 minutes, 5.1% 60 minutes or more (2000)

BENTON (village). Covers a land area of 0.834 square miles and a water area of 0 square miles. Located at 42.57° N. Lat.; 90.38° W. Long. Elevation is 932 feet.
History: Lead was discovered here in the 1820's, and a village soon sprang up. It was named Benton for Thomas H. Benton, U.S. senator from Missouri. One of the earliest flour mills in the area was built here in 1827.
Population: 976 (2000); Race: 99.7% White, 0.0% Black, 0.0% Asian, 0.0% American Indian and Alaska Native, 0.0% Hispanic of any race, 0.0% two or more races (2000); Density: 1,170.2 persons per square mile (2000); Age: 25.9% under 18, 13.7% over 64 (2000); Marriage status: 19.1% never married, 58.3% now married, 11.2% widowed, 11.3% divorced (2000); Foreign born: 0.0% (2000); Ancestry (includes multiple ancestries): 37.3% German, 23.4% English, 18.7% Irish, 7.2% United States or American, 5.3% Norwegian (2000).
Economy: Single-family building permits issued: 8 (2001) / 4 (2000); Multi-family building permits issued: 0 (2001) / 0 (2000); Employment by occupation: 11.2% management, 12.8% professional, 18.1% services, 19.6% sales, 2.1% farming, 7.2% construction, 29.1% production (2000).
Income: Per capita income: $15,702 (2000); Median household income: $30,313 (2000); Poverty rate: 7.5% (2000).
Taxes: Total city taxes per capita: $97 (1997); City property taxes per capita: $90 (1997).
Education: High school graduation rate: 83.7% (2000); College graduation rate: 15.2% (2000).

School District(s)

Benton (PK-12)
2000 Enrollment: 299 608-759-4002
Housing: Homeownership rate: 81.2% (2000); Median home value: $64,500 (2000); Median rent: $310 per month (2000); Median age of housing: 60+ years (2000).
Safety: Violent crime rate: 0.0 per 10,000 population; Property crime rate: 20.3 per 10,000 population (2001).
Transportation: Commute to work: 89.8% car, 0.0% public transportation, 9.1% walk, 0.6% work from home (2000); Travel time to work: 28.9% less than 15 minutes, 41.5% 15 to 30 minutes, 19.5% 30 to 45 minutes, 3.0% 45 to 60 minutes, 7.1% 60 minutes or more (2000)

BENTON (town). Covers a land area of 28.029 square miles and a water area of 0 square miles. Located at 42.56° N. Lat.; 90.39° W. Long. Elevation is 932 feet.
Population: 469 (2000); Race: 100.0% White, 0.0% Black, 0.0% Asian, 0.0% American Indian and Alaska Native, 0.0% Hispanic of any race, 0.0% two or more races (2000); Density: 16.7 persons per square mile (2000); Age: 34.6% under 18, 7.2% over 64 (2000); Marriage status: 25.3% never married, 66.8% now married, 2.2% widowed, 5.8% divorced (2000); Foreign born: 1.6% (2000); Ancestry (includes multiple ancestries): 37.0% German, 13.5% English, 12.3% Irish, 9.9% United States or American, 6.2% Norwegian (2000).
Economy: In dairy and livestock area. Formerly a lead and zinc mining center. Single-family building permits issued: 3 (2001) / 5 (2000); Multi-family building permits issued: 0 (2001) / 0 (2000); Employment by occupation: 24.1% management, 11.9% professional, 11.9% services, 14.6% sales, 3.1% farming, 5.0% construction, 29.5% production (2000).
Income: Per capita income: $16,621 (2000); Median household income: $38,077 (2000); Poverty rate: 11.9% (2000).
Taxes: Total city taxes per capita: $104 (1997); City property taxes per capita: $104 (1997).
Education: High school graduation rate: 85.8% (2000); College graduation rate: 13.6% (2000).

Housing: Homeownership rate: 86.2% (2000); Median home value: $79,800 (2000); Median rent: $342 per month (2000); Median age of housing: 44 years (2000).
Transportation: Commute to work: 75.7% car, 0.0% public transportation, 5.0% walk, 17.4% work from home (2000); Travel time to work: 31.3% less than 15 minutes, 26.6% 15 to 30 minutes, 22.4% 30 to 45 minutes, 12.1% 45 to 60 minutes, 7.5% 60 minutes or more (2000)

BLANCHARD (town). Covers a land area of 17.511 square miles and a water area of 0.022 square miles. Located at 42.79° N. Lat.; 89.88° W. Long.
Population: 261 (2000); Race: 100.0% White, 0.0% Black, 0.0% Asian, 0.0% American Indian and Alaska Native, 0.8% Hispanic of any race, 0.0% two or more races (2000); Density: 14.9 persons per square mile (2000); Age: 22.5% under 18, 15.1% over 64 (2000); Marriage status: 15.5% never married, 77.3% now married, 1.9% widowed, 5.3% divorced (2000); Foreign born: 0.8% (2000); Ancestry (includes multiple ancestries): 47.3% Norwegian, 29.5% German, 12.8% Swiss, 12.8% English, 10.1% Irish (2000).
Economy: Cheese factories. Employment by occupation: 21.7% management, 7.9% professional, 4.6% services, 32.9% sales, 7.2% farming, 1.3% construction, 24.3% production (2000).
Income: Per capita income: $20,160 (2000); Median household income: $48,068 (2000); Poverty rate: 3.1% (2000).
Taxes: Total city taxes per capita: $149 (1997); City property taxes per capita: $149 (1997).
Education: High school graduation rate: 88.7% (2000); College graduation rate: 11.3% (2000).
Housing: Homeownership rate: 83.8% (2000); Median home value: $121,900 (2000); Median rent: $1,150 per month (2000); Median age of housing: 30 years (2000).
Transportation: Commute to work: 76.9% car, 0.0% public transportation, 1.4% walk, 21.8% work from home (2000); Travel time to work: 17.4% less than 15 minutes, 20.9% 15 to 30 minutes, 21.7% 30 to 45 minutes, 26.1% 45 to 60 minutes, 13.9% 60 minutes or more (2000)

BLANCHARDVILLE (village). Covers a land area of 0.439 square miles and a water area of 0 square miles. Located at 42.81° N. Lat.; 89.86° W. Long. Elevation is 833 feet.
Population: 806 (2000); Race: 98.9% White, 0.0% Black, 0.0% Asian, 1.1% American Indian and Alaska Native, 0.5% Hispanic of any race, 0.0% two or more races (2000); Density: 1,837.4 persons per square mile (2000); Age: 26.8% under 18, 15.4% over 64 (2000); Marriage status: 26.5% never married, 54.5% now married, 8.3% widowed, 10.7% divorced (2000); Foreign born: 0.4% (2000); Ancestry (includes multiple ancestries): 40.6% Norwegian, 27.0% German, 19.4% Irish, 14.9% Swiss, 7.4% English (2000).
Economy: Single-family building permits issued: 0 (2001) / 3 (2000); Multi-family building permits issued: 0 (2001) / 0 (2000); Employment by occupation: 12.5% management, 12.5% professional, 13.2% services, 27.3% sales, 1.2% farming, 13.4% construction, 19.9% production (2000).
Income: Per capita income: $18,104 (2000); Median household income: $40,313 (2000); Poverty rate: 9.8% (2000).
Taxes: Total city taxes per capita: $111 (1997); City property taxes per capita: $105 (1997).
Education: High school graduation rate: 84.7% (2000); College graduation rate: 15.9% (2000).

School District(s)

Pecatonica Area (PK-12)
2000 Enrollment: 514 608-523-4248
Housing: Homeownership rate: 77.2% (2000); Median home value: $78,800 (2000); Median rent: $237 per month (2000); Median age of housing: 60+ years (2000).
Safety: Violent crime rate: 0.0 per 10,000 population; Property crime rate: 73.9 per 10,000 population (2001).
Newspapers: Pecatonica Valley Leader (1 x week)
Transportation: Commute to work: 88.1% car, 0.5% public transportation, 7.5% walk, 3.4% work from home (2000); Travel time to work: 23.9% less than 15 minutes, 14.8% 15 to 30 minutes, 34.7% 30 to 45 minutes, 18.6% 45 to 60 minutes, 8.0% 60 minutes or more (2000)

DARLINGTON (city). Covers a land area of 1.305 square miles and a water area of 0 square miles. Located at 42.68° N. Lat.; 90.11° W. Long. Elevation is 817 feet.
Population: 2,418 (2000); Race: 99.5% White, 0.0% Black, 0.0% Asian, 0.1% American Indian and Alaska Native, 0.8% Hispanic of any race, 0.0% two or more races (2000); Density: 1,852.8 persons per square mile (2000); Age: 24.6% under 18, 23.0% over 64 (2000); Marriage status: 23.1% never married, 58.7% now married, 11.1% widowed, 7.2% divorced (2000); Foreign born: 1.2% (2000); Ancestry (includes multiple ancestries): 36.9% German, 24.7% Irish, 23.5% English, 17.8% Norwegian, 6.6% Swiss (2000).
Economy: Single-family building permits issued: 1 (2001) / 2 (2000); Multi-family building permits issued: 0 (2001) / 0 (2000); Employment by occupation: 11.2% management, 13.7% professional, 16.2% services, 24.3% sales, 2.4% farming, 10.1% construction, 22.0% production (2000).
Income: Per capita income: $17,403 (2000); Median household income: $34,539 (2000); Poverty rate: 9.9% (2000).
Taxes: Total city taxes per capita: $222 (1997); City property taxes per capita: $202 (1997).
Education: High school graduation rate: 88.0% (2000); College graduation rate: 15.9% (2000).

School District(s)

Darlington Community (PK-12)
2000 Enrollment: 892 608-776-2006
Housing: Homeownership rate: 73.9% (2000); Median home value: $67,000 (2000); Median rent: $313 per month (2000); Median age of housing: 52 years (2000).
Hospitals: Memorial Hospital of Lafayette County (28 beds)
Safety: Violent crime rate: 8.2 per 10,000 population; Property crime rate: 176.6 per 10,000 population (2001).
Newspapers: Republican-Journal (1 x week)
Transportation: Commute to work: 89.6% car, 0.7% public transportation, 6.5% walk, 2.1% work from home (2000); Travel time to work: 60.4% less than 15 minutes, 11.7% 15 to 30 minutes, 18.0% 30 to 45 minutes, 4.6% 45 to 60 minutes, 5.3% 60 minutes or more (2000)

DARLINGTON (town). Covers a land area of 46.261 square miles and a water area of 0 square miles. Located at 42.66° N. Lat.; 90.12° W. Long. Elevation is 817 feet.
History: Incorporated 1877.
Population: 757 (2000); Race: 97.9% White, 0.0% Black, 0.0% Asian, 1.0% American Indian and Alaska Native, 0.6% Hispanic of any race, 1.1% two or more races (2000); Density: 16.4 persons per square mile (2000); Age: 30.8% under 18, 14.2% over 64 (2000); Marriage status: 21.8% never married, 63.7% now married, 7.3% widowed, 7.2% divorced (2000); Foreign born: 0.3% (2000); Ancestry (includes multiple ancestries): 33.5% German, 23.1% Irish, 21.8% English, 18.0% Norwegian, 10.9% Swiss (2000).
Economy: Dairying; feed, cheese. Manufacturing: concrete. Employment by occupation: 21.7% management, 8.0% professional, 7.3% services, 25.1% sales, 7.3% farming, 12.8% construction, 17.7% production (2000).
Income: Per capita income: $16,614 (2000); Median household income: $38,750 (2000); Poverty rate: 5.1% (2000).
Taxes: Total city taxes per capita: $127 (1997); City property taxes per capita: $126 (1997).
Education: High school graduation rate: 89.6% (2000); College graduation rate: 12.2% (2000).
Housing: Homeownership rate: 74.6% (2000); Median home value: $87,200 (2000); Median rent: $341 per month (2000); Median age of housing: 46 years (2000).
Transportation: Commute to work: 81.3% car, 0.0% public transportation, 4.5% walk, 13.6% work from home (2000); Travel time to work: 49.3% less than 15 minutes, 18.6% 15 to 30 minutes, 17.5% 30 to 45 minutes, 4.4% 45 to 60 minutes, 10.2% 60 minutes or more (2000)

ELK GROVE (town). Covers a land area of 36.257 square miles and a water area of 0 square miles. Located at 42.67° N. Lat.; 90.36° W. Long. Elevation is 1,010 feet.
Population: 463 (2000); Race: 100.0% White, 0.0% Black, 0.0% Asian, 0.0% American Indian and Alaska Native, 0.0% Hispanic of any race, 0.0% two or more races (2000); Density: 12.8 persons per square mile (2000); Age: 37.3% under 18, 7.3% over 64 (2000); Marriage status: 32.4% never married, 54.2% now married, 6.9% widowed, 6.5% divorced (2000); Foreign born: 0.7% (2000); Ancestry (includes multiple ancestries): 45.2% German, 14.2% English, 12.4% Irish, 5.8% United States or American, 2.4% Norwegian (2000).
Economy: Employment by occupation: 27.3% management, 6.7% professional, 12.2% services, 20.2% sales, 11.8% farming, 2.9% construction, 18.9% production (2000).
Income: Per capita income: $13,519 (2000); Median household income: $36,607 (2000); Poverty rate: 19.8% (2000).
Taxes: Total city taxes per capita: $172 (1997); City property taxes per capita: $172 (1997).
Education: High school graduation rate: 79.4% (2000); College graduation rate: 10.9% (2000).

Housing: Homeownership rate: 73.2% (2000); Median home value: $97,500 (2000); Median rent: $394 per month (2000); Median age of housing: 60+ years (2000).
Transportation: Commute to work: 68.6% car, 0.0% public transportation, 5.5% walk, 25.0% work from home (2000); Travel time to work: 41.8% less than 15 minutes, 33.9% 15 to 30 minutes, 10.7% 30 to 45 minutes, 5.1% 45 to 60 minutes, 8.5% 60 minutes or more (2000)

FAYETTE (town). Covers a land area of 35.219 square miles and a water area of 0.716 square miles. Located at 42.77° N. Lat.; 89.99° W. Long. Elevation is 1,040 feet.
Population: 366 (2000); Race: 100.0% White, 0.0% Black, 0.0% Asian, 0.0% American Indian and Alaska Native, 0.0% Hispanic of any race, 0.0% two or more races (2000); Density: 10.4 persons per square mile (2000); Age: 27.5% under 18, 16.9% over 64 (2000); Marriage status: 24.2% never married, 64.2% now married, 7.2% widowed, 4.5% divorced (2000); Foreign born: 0.0% (2000); Ancestry (includes multiple ancestries): 33.8% Norwegian, 24.1% German, 14.9% Swiss, 14.0% Irish, 13.5% English (2000).
Economy: Employment by occupation: 29.2% management, 10.7% professional, 13.1% services, 8.9% sales, 3.6% farming, 12.5% construction, 22.0% production (2000).
Income: Per capita income: $16,566 (2000); Median household income: $36,250 (2000); Poverty rate: 9.7% (2000).
Taxes: Total city taxes per capita: $129 (1997); City property taxes per capita: $129 (1997).
Education: High school graduation rate: 87.6% (2000); College graduation rate: 10.7% (2000).
Housing: Homeownership rate: 86.0% (2000); Median home value: $88,000 (2000); Median rent: $375 per month (2000); Median age of housing: 43 years (2000).
Transportation: Commute to work: 76.2% car, 1.2% public transportation, 3.7% walk, 18.9% work from home (2000); Travel time to work: 25.6% less than 15 minutes, 39.1% 15 to 30 minutes, 17.3% 30 to 45 minutes, 9.8% 45 to 60 minutes, 8.3% 60 minutes or more (2000)

GRATIOT (village). Covers a land area of 0.583 square miles and a water area of 0 square miles. Located at 42.57° N. Lat.; 90.02° W. Long. Elevation is 840 feet.
History: Gratiot was named for Henry Gratiot, a miner who came to the area in 1816 from the southern states.
Population: 252 (2000); Race: 99.2% White, 0.0% Black, 0.8% Asian, 0.0% American Indian and Alaska Native, 0.0% Hispanic of any race, 0.0% two or more races (2000); Density: 432.6 persons per square mile (2000); Age: 29.5% under 18, 15.5% over 64 (2000); Marriage status: 24.3% never married, 57.9% now married, 5.4% widowed, 12.4% divorced (2000); Foreign born: 1.5% (2000); Ancestry (includes multiple ancestries): 29.9% German, 21.2% Irish, 17.4% Norwegian, 13.6% Swiss, 9.8% English (2000).
Economy: Employment by occupation: 12.2% management, 7.5% professional, 20.4% services, 15.0% sales, 4.1% farming, 9.5% construction, 31.3% production (2000).
Income: Per capita income: $16,902 (2000); Median household income: $41,944 (2000); Poverty rate: 9.2% (2000).
Taxes: Total city taxes per capita: $173 (1997); City property taxes per capita: $164 (1997).
Education: High school graduation rate: 76.2% (2000); College graduation rate: 6.5% (2000).
Housing: Homeownership rate: 80.6% (2000); Median home value: $58,800 (2000); Median rent: $345 per month (2000); Median age of housing: 60+ years (2000).
Transportation: Commute to work: 85.5% car, 0.0% public transportation, 6.9% walk, 4.1% work from home (2000); Travel time to work: 24.5% less than 15 minutes, 38.1% 15 to 30 minutes, 18.0% 30 to 45 minutes, 3.6% 45 to 60 minutes, 15.8% 60 minutes or more (2000)

GRATIOT (town). Covers a land area of 54.316 square miles and a water area of 0 square miles. Located at 42.56° N. Lat.; 90.04° W. Long. Elevation is 840 feet.
Population: 653 (2000); Race: 100.0% White, 0.0% Black, 0.0% Asian, 0.0% American Indian and Alaska Native, 0.0% Hispanic of any race, 0.0% two or more races (2000); Density: 12.0 persons per square mile (2000); Age: 25.3% under 18, 13.6% over 64 (2000); Marriage status: 26.0% never married, 61.1% now married, 3.6% widowed, 9.2% divorced (2000); Foreign born: 0.6% (2000); Ancestry (includes multiple ancestries): 46.3% German, 18.1% Irish, 16.5% Norwegian, 13.0% English, 10.2% Swiss (2000).
Economy: In livestock and dairy area. Employment by occupation: 23.1% management, 12.4% professional, 9.7% services, 17.7% sales, 9.7% farming, 8.6% construction, 18.8% production (2000).
Income: Per capita income: $17,987 (2000); Median household income: $46,583 (2000); Poverty rate: 6.2% (2000).
Taxes: Total city taxes per capita: $192 (1997); City property taxes per capita: $192 (1997).
Education: High school graduation rate: 88.3% (2000); College graduation rate: 13.3% (2000).
Housing: Homeownership rate: 77.5% (2000); Median home value: $75,300 (2000); Median rent: $300 per month (2000); Median age of housing: 54 years (2000).
Transportation: Commute to work: 81.9% car, 1.6% public transportation, 6.2% walk, 10.3% work from home (2000); Travel time to work: 37.0% less than 15 minutes, 27.4% 15 to 30 minutes, 23.2% 30 to 45 minutes, 7.5% 45 to 60 minutes, 4.8% 60 minutes or more (2000)

KENDALL (town). Covers a land area of 42.585 square miles and a water area of 0.014 square miles. Located at 42.75° N. Lat.; 90.23° W. Long.
Population: 320 (2000); Race: 99.7% White, 0.3% Black, 0.0% Asian, 0.0% American Indian and Alaska Native, 0.0% Hispanic of any race, 0.0% two or more races (2000); Density: 7.5 persons per square mile (2000); Age: 30.4% under 18, 7.6% over 64 (2000); Marriage status: 25.5% never married, 69.9% now married, 1.7% widowed, 2.9% divorced (2000); Foreign born: 0.6% (2000); Ancestry (includes multiple ancestries): 60.8% German, 25.9% Irish, 13.3% English, 6.3% French (except Basque), 4.1% Swiss (2000).
Economy: Employment by occupation: 23.5% management, 17.5% professional, 9.8% services, 20.8% sales, 7.7% farming, 6.0% construction, 14.8% production (2000).
Income: Per capita income: $15,466 (2000); Median household income: $40,714 (2000); Poverty rate: 1.3% (2000).
Taxes: Total city taxes per capita: $226 (1997); City property taxes per capita: $226 (1997).
Education: High school graduation rate: 92.4% (2000); College graduation rate: 21.2% (2000).
Housing: Homeownership rate: 67.6% (2000); Median home value: $102,500 (2000); Median rent: $383 per month (2000); Median age of housing: 55 years (2000).
Transportation: Commute to work: 75.4% car, 1.6% public transportation, 0.5% walk, 20.8% work from home (2000); Travel time to work: 22.1% less than 15 minutes, 49.7% 15 to 30 minutes, 17.9% 30 to 45 minutes, 6.9% 45 to 60 minutes, 3.4% 60 minutes or more (2000)

LAMONT (town). Covers a land area of 19.907 square miles and a water area of 0 square miles. Located at 42.70° N. Lat.; 90.00° W. Long. Elevation is 1,071 feet.
Population: 267 (2000); Race: 99.3% White, 0.0% Black, 0.0% Asian, 0.0% American Indian and Alaska Native, 1.1% Hispanic of any race, 0.7% two or more races (2000); Density: 13.4 persons per square mile (2000); Age: 22.9% under 18, 10.4% over 64 (2000); Marriage status: 28.0% never married, 62.9% now married, 5.6% widowed, 3.4% divorced (2000); Foreign born: 0.0% (2000); Ancestry (includes multiple ancestries): 30.7% Norwegian, 27.5% German, 14.6% English, 13.2% Irish, 11.4% Swiss (2000).
Economy: Employment by occupation: 32.7% management, 11.3% professional, 10.7% services, 11.3% sales, 7.3% farming, 12.0% construction, 14.7% production (2000).
Income: Per capita income: $15,355 (2000); Median household income: $40,156 (2000); Poverty rate: 10.4% (2000).
Taxes: Total city taxes per capita: $265 (1997); City property taxes per capita: $265 (1997).
Education: High school graduation rate: 81.8% (2000); College graduation rate: 9.9% (2000).
Housing: Homeownership rate: 82.5% (2000); Median home value: $53,300 (2000); Median rent: $294 per month (2000); Median age of housing: 60+ years (2000).
Transportation: Commute to work: 76.7% car, 0.0% public transportation, 0.0% walk, 23.3% work from home (2000); Travel time to work: 23.5% less than 15 minutes, 40.9% 15 to 30 minutes, 20.9% 30 to 45 minutes, 7.8% 45 to 60 minutes, 7.0% 60 minutes or more (2000)

MONTICELLO (town). Covers a land area of 19.636 square miles and a water area of 0 square miles. Located at 42.53° N. Lat.; 90.12° W. Long.
Population: 148 (2000); Race: 100.0% White, 0.0% Black, 0.0% Asian, 0.0% American Indian and Alaska Native, 0.0% Hispanic of any race, 0.0% two or more races (2000); Density: 7.5 persons per square mile (2000); Age: 25.3% under 18, 10.7% over 64 (2000); Marriage status: 33.1% never

married, 59.1% now married, 3.1% widowed, 4.7% divorced (2000); Foreign born: 0.0% (2000); Ancestry (includes multiple ancestries): 26.0% English, 24.0% German, 12.0% Irish, 10.7% Norwegian, 9.3% Swiss (2000).
Economy: Employment by occupation: 32.2% management, 9.2% professional, 13.8% services, 18.4% sales, 10.3% farming, 5.7% construction, 10.3% production (2000).
Income: Per capita income: $13,120 (2000); Median household income: $35,000 (2000); Poverty rate: 22.0% (2000).
Taxes: Total city taxes per capita: $238 (1997); City property taxes per capita: $238 (1997).
Education: High school graduation rate: 89.2% (2000); College graduation rate: 5.4% (2000).
Housing: Homeownership rate: 76.0% (2000); Median home value: $87,500 (2000); Median rent: $158 per month (2000); Median age of housing: 60+ years (2000).
Transportation: Commute to work: 75.9% car, 0.0% public transportation, 2.3% walk, 21.8% work from home (2000); Travel time to work: 42.6% less than 15 minutes, 26.5% 15 to 30 minutes, 13.2% 30 to 45 minutes, 7.4% 45 to 60 minutes, 10.3% 60 minutes or more (2000)

NEW DIGGINGS (town). Covers a land area of 25.335 square miles and a water area of 0 square miles. Located at 42.56° N. Lat.; 90.33° W. Long. Elevation is 800 feet.
Population: 473 (2000); Race: 98.6% White, 0.0% Black, 1.4% Asian, 0.0% American Indian and Alaska Native, 0.0% Hispanic of any race, 0.0% two or more races (2000); Density: 18.7 persons per square mile (2000); Age: 28.3% under 18, 11.6% over 64 (2000); Marriage status: 20.8% never married, 65.9% now married, 6.8% widowed, 6.5% divorced (2000); Foreign born: 2.7% (2000); Ancestry (includes multiple ancestries): 48.1% German, 24.5% English, 14.1% Irish, 11.6% United States or American, 3.2% Norwegian (2000).
Economy: Employment by occupation: 18.3% management, 5.7% professional, 10.5% services, 19.2% sales, 2.6% farming, 17.0% construction, 26.6% production (2000).
Income: Per capita income: $17,122 (2000); Median household income: $41,250 (2000); Poverty rate: 6.4% (2000).
Taxes: Total city taxes per capita: $68 (1997); City property taxes per capita: $66 (1997).
Education: High school graduation rate: 82.0% (2000); College graduation rate: 9.2% (2000).
Housing: Homeownership rate: 83.7% (2000); Median home value: $74,700 (2000); Median rent: $313 per month (2000); Median age of housing: 55 years (2000).
Transportation: Commute to work: 81.8% car, 0.0% public transportation, 4.0% walk, 14.2% work from home (2000); Travel time to work: 16.6% less than 15 minutes, 36.3% 15 to 30 minutes, 32.1% 30 to 45 minutes, 8.3% 45 to 60 minutes, 6.7% 60 minutes or more (2000)

SEYMOUR (town). Covers a land area of 36.125 square miles and a water area of 0 square miles. Located at 42.65° N. Lat.; 90.24° W. Long.
Population: 363 (2000); Race: 99.5% White, 0.0% Black, 0.0% Asian, 0.5% American Indian and Alaska Native, 0.0% Hispanic of any race, 0.0% two or more races (2000); Density: 10.0 persons per square mile (2000); Age: 39.9% under 18, 8.1% over 64 (2000); Marriage status: 22.3% never married, 68.7% now married, 1.5% widowed, 7.5% divorced (2000); Foreign born: 0.0% (2000); Ancestry (includes multiple ancestries): 35.8% German, 21.7% Irish, 17.0% English, 10.4% Norwegian, 8.4% United States or American (2000).
Economy: Employment by occupation: 32.8% management, 9.7% professional, 8.2% services, 22.1% sales, 9.7% farming, 2.6% construction, 14.9% production (2000).
Income: Per capita income: $13,390 (2000); Median household income: $40,000 (2000); Poverty rate: 14.1% (2000).
Taxes: Total city taxes per capita: $190 (1997); City property taxes per capita: $190 (1997).
Education: High school graduation rate: 88.2% (2000); College graduation rate: 12.7% (2000).
Housing: Homeownership rate: 68.5% (2000); Median home value: $105,800 (2000); Median rent: $475 per month (2000); Median age of housing: 60+ years (2000).
Transportation: Commute to work: 68.4% car, 0.0% public transportation, 2.1% walk, 28.5% work from home (2000); Travel time to work: 46.4% less than 15 minutes, 28.3% 15 to 30 minutes, 13.8% 30 to 45 minutes, 11.6% 45 to 60 minutes, 0.0% 60 minutes or more (2000)

SHULLSBURG (city). Covers a land area of 1.109 square miles and a water area of 0 square miles. Located at 42.57° N. Lat.; 90.23° W. Long. Elevation is 1,021 feet.
History: Shullsburg was named for Jesse Shull, a fur trader who settled near the site of the present city. For a time after Lafayette County was formed in 1847, Shullsburg served as the county seat. Lead mining began in the area in the mid-1820's.
Population: 1,246 (2000); Race: 98.8% White, 0.2% Black, 1.0% Asian, 0.1% American Indian and Alaska Native, 0.0% Hispanic of any race, 0.0% two or more races (2000); Density: 1,123.6 persons per square mile (2000); Age: 23.5% under 18, 19.6% over 64 (2000); Marriage status: 22.7% never married, 57.3% now married, 10.8% widowed, 9.2% divorced (2000); Foreign born: 1.3% (2000); Ancestry (includes multiple ancestries): 37.1% German, 24.3% Irish, 20.0% English, 7.7% United States or American, 5.3% Norwegian (2000).
Economy: Single-family building permits issued: 1 (2001) / 0 (2000); Multi-family building permits issued: 0 (2001) / 0 (2000); Employment by occupation: 9.3% management, 11.2% professional, 13.4% services, 23.8% sales, 1.6% farming, 9.0% construction, 31.8% production (2000).
Income: Per capita income: $16,902 (2000); Median household income: $32,333 (2000); Poverty rate: 9.9% (2000).
Taxes: Total city taxes per capita: $57 (1997); City property taxes per capita: $47 (1997).
Education: High school graduation rate: 81.9% (2000); College graduation rate: 11.0% (2000).

School District(s)

Shullsburg (PK-12)
2000 Enrollment: 431 608-965-4427
Housing: Homeownership rate: 79.7% (2000); Median home value: $60,700 (2000); Median rent: $255 per month (2000); Median age of housing: 56 years (2000).
Transportation: Commute to work: 88.9% car, 0.2% public transportation, 7.0% walk, 3.7% work from home (2000); Travel time to work: 38.8% less than 15 minutes, 26.0% 15 to 30 minutes, 19.5% 30 to 45 minutes, 11.1% 45 to 60 minutes, 4.6% 60 minutes or more (2000)

SHULLSBURG (town). Covers a land area of 34.963 square miles and a water area of 0 square miles. Located at 42.58° N. Lat.; 90.23° W. Long. Elevation is 1,021 feet.
History: Incorporated 1889.
Population: 364 (2000); Race: 97.8% White, 0.0% Black, 2.2% Asian, 0.0% American Indian and Alaska Native, 0.0% Hispanic of any race, 0.0% two or more races (2000); Density: 10.4 persons per square mile (2000); Age: 25.4% under 18, 19.1% over 64 (2000); Marriage status: 30.7% never married, 59.5% now married, 5.1% widowed, 4.7% divorced (2000); Foreign born: 1.7% (2000); Ancestry (includes multiple ancestries): 39.2% German, 24.9% Irish, 15.2% English, 6.1% United States or American, 5.5% Swiss (2000).
Economy: In dairy-farming area; cheese. Single-family building permits issued: 0 (2001) / 2 (2000); Multi-family building permits issued: 0 (2001) / 0 (2000); Employment by occupation: 27.1% management, 6.9% professional, 17.6% services, 13.3% sales, 10.6% farming, 5.3% construction, 19.1% production (2000).
Income: Per capita income: $15,096 (2000); Median household income: $30,682 (2000); Poverty rate: 10.8% (2000).
Taxes: Total city taxes per capita: $158 (1997); City property taxes per capita: $158 (1997).
Education: High school graduation rate: 86.7% (2000); College graduation rate: 8.0% (2000).
Housing: Homeownership rate: 71.2% (2000); Median home value: $90,700 (2000); Median rent: $260 per month (2000); Median age of housing: 37 years (2000).
Transportation: Commute to work: 68.1% car, 0.0% public transportation, 6.9% walk, 25.0% work from home (2000); Travel time to work: 39.7% less than 15 minutes, 29.8% 15 to 30 minutes, 20.6% 30 to 45 minutes, 5.0% 45 to 60 minutes, 5.0% 60 minutes or more (2000)

SOUTH WAYNE (village). Covers a land area of 0.790 square miles and a water area of 0 square miles. Located at 42.56° N. Lat.; 89.87° W. Long. Elevation is 803 feet.
Population: 484 (2000); Race: 100.0% White, 0.0% Black, 0.0% Asian, 0.0% American Indian and Alaska Native, 0.0% Hispanic of any race, 0.0% two or more races (2000); Density: 612.5 persons per square mile (2000); Age: 25.1% under 18, 22.8% over 64 (2000); Marriage status: 23.9% never married, 52.6% now married, 12.5% widowed, 11.1% divorced (2000);

Foreign born: 0.5% (2000); Ancestry (includes multiple ancestries): 33.3% Norwegian, 30.8% German, 16.0% Swiss, 9.1% Irish, 5.0% English (2000).
Economy: Single-family building permits issued: 0 (2001) / 1 (2000); Multi-family building permits issued: 0 (2001) / 0 (2000); Employment by occupation: 11.2% management, 13.5% professional, 15.8% services, 22.3% sales, 2.3% farming, 15.8% construction, 19.1% production (2000).
Income: Per capita income: $15,631 (2000); Median household income: $30,909 (2000); Poverty rate: 9.0% (2000).
Taxes: Total city taxes per capita: $130 (1997); City property taxes per capita: $116 (1997).
Education: High school graduation rate: 80.7% (2000); College graduation rate: 8.3% (2000).

School District(s)

Black Hawk (PK-12)
2000 Enrollment: 609 608-439-5400

Housing: Homeownership rate: 73.0% (2000); Median home value: $67,800 (2000); Median rent: $319 per month (2000); Median age of housing: 49 years (2000).
Transportation: Commute to work: 91.1% car, 0.0% public transportation, 7.0% walk, 1.9% work from home (2000); Travel time to work: 28.7% less than 15 minutes, 57.4% 15 to 30 minutes, 3.3% 30 to 45 minutes, 1.0% 45 to 60 minutes, 9.6% 60 minutes or more (2000)

WAYNE (town). Covers a land area of 36.730 square miles and a water area of 0.035 square miles. Located at 42.56° N. Lat.; 89.89° W. Long.
Population: 496 (2000); Race: 97.9% White, 0.0% Black, 0.0% Asian, 0.0% American Indian and Alaska Native, 2.9% Hispanic of any race, 2.1% two or more races (2000); Density: 13.5 persons per square mile (2000); Age: 29.6% under 18, 6.6% over 64 (2000); Marriage status: 24.5% never married, 63.9% now married, 3.5% widowed, 8.1% divorced (2000); Foreign born: 0.9% (2000); Ancestry (includes multiple ancestries): 46.4% German, 25.2% Norwegian, 14.5% Swiss, 12.7% English, 10.4% Irish (2000).
Economy: In dairy-farming area; cheese. Employment by occupation: 22.3% management, 8.8% professional, 6.3% services, 21.1% sales, 7.2% farming, 6.9% construction, 27.4% production (2000).
Income: Per capita income: $19,621 (2000); Median household income: $44,821 (2000); Poverty rate: 8.9% (2000).
Taxes: Total city taxes per capita: $329 (1997); City property taxes per capita: $329 (1997).
Education: High school graduation rate: 83.5% (2000); College graduation rate: 9.9% (2000).
Housing: Homeownership rate: 74.6% (2000); Median home value: $68,800 (2000); Median rent: $363 per month (2000); Median age of housing: 58 years (2000).
Transportation: Commute to work: 76.0% car, 0.0% public transportation, 2.9% walk, 21.1% work from home (2000); Travel time to work: 21.1% less than 15 minutes, 58.3% 15 to 30 minutes, 12.1% 30 to 45 minutes, 0.8% 45 to 60 minutes, 7.7% 60 minutes or more (2000)

WHITE OAK SPRINGS (town). Covers a land area of 16.494 square miles and a water area of 0 square miles. Located at 42.53° N. Lat.; 90.26° W. Long.
Population: 97 (2000); Race: 100.0% White, 0.0% Black, 0.0% Asian, 0.0% American Indian and Alaska Native, 0.0% Hispanic of any race, 0.0% two or more races (2000); Density: 5.9 persons per square mile (2000); Age: 35.3% under 18, 9.0% over 64 (2000); Marriage status: 24.2% never married, 62.6% now married, 7.1% widowed, 6.1% divorced (2000); Foreign born: 0.0% (2000); Ancestry (includes multiple ancestries): 33.8% English, 31.6% German, 13.5% Irish, 6.0% Swiss, 3.8% French (except Basque) (2000).
Economy: Employment by occupation: 24.0% management, 14.7% professional, 18.7% services, 13.3% sales, 8.0% farming, 5.3% construction, 16.0% production (2000).
Income: Per capita income: $14,362 (2000); Median household income: $41,000 (2000); Poverty rate: 4.5% (2000).
Taxes: Total city taxes per capita: $248 (1997); City property taxes per capita: $248 (1997).
Education: High school graduation rate: 74.1% (2000); College graduation rate: 16.0% (2000).
Housing: Homeownership rate: 50.0% (2000); Median home value: $77,500 (2000); Median rent: $413 per month (2000); Median age of housing: 60+ years (2000).
Transportation: Commute to work: 77.5% car, 0.0% public transportation, 2.8% walk, 19.7% work from home (2000); Travel time to work: 33.3% less than 15 minutes, 22.8% 15 to 30 minutes, 24.6% 30 to 45 minutes, 10.5% 45 to 60 minutes, 8.8% 60 minutes or more (2000)

WILLOW SPRINGS (town). Covers a land area of 48.258 square miles and a water area of 0 square miles. Located at 42.75° N. Lat.; 90.13° W. Long.
Population: 632 (2000); Race: 95.6% White, 0.0% Black, 0.0% Asian, 0.0% American Indian and Alaska Native, 2.6% Hispanic of any race, 1.8% two or more races (2000); Density: 13.1 persons per square mile (2000); Age: 28.2% under 18, 10.9% over 64 (2000); Marriage status: 20.6% never married, 70.5% now married, 6.1% widowed, 2.8% divorced (2000); Foreign born: 1.2% (2000); Ancestry (includes multiple ancestries): 40.1% German, 22.6% Irish, 16.0% English, 14.9% Norwegian, 10.3% Swiss (2000).
Economy: Employment by occupation: 22.3% management, 12.2% professional, 8.0% services, 21.0% sales, 10.4% farming, 10.4% construction, 15.7% production (2000).
Income: Per capita income: $16,458 (2000); Median household income: $41,094 (2000); Poverty rate: 12.1% (2000).
Taxes: Total city taxes per capita: $220 (1997); City property taxes per capita: $220 (1997).
Education: High school graduation rate: 85.2% (2000); College graduation rate: 19.6% (2000).
Housing: Homeownership rate: 81.2% (2000); Median home value: $85,000 (2000); Median rent: $404 per month (2000); Median age of housing: 47 years (2000).
Transportation: Commute to work: 74.2% car, 2.2% public transportation, 5.4% walk, 18.3% work from home (2000); Travel time to work: 40.8% less than 15 minutes, 30.9% 15 to 30 minutes, 15.1% 30 to 45 minutes, 5.3% 45 to 60 minutes, 7.9% 60 minutes or more (2000)

WIOTA (town). Covers a land area of 52.770 square miles and a water area of 0.027 square miles. Located at 42.63° N. Lat.; 89.92° W. Long. Elevation is 1,000 feet.
Population: 900 (2000); Race: 99.6% White, 0.0% Black, 0.0% Asian, 0.0% American Indian and Alaska Native, 0.2% Hispanic of any race, 0.4% two or more races (2000); Density: 17.1 persons per square mile (2000); Age: 27.2% under 18, 14.3% over 64 (2000); Marriage status: 23.4% never married, 62.6% now married, 5.4% widowed, 8.6% divorced (2000); Foreign born: 0.0% (2000); Ancestry (includes multiple ancestries): 39.5% Norwegian, 33.0% German, 23.6% Swiss, 14.9% Irish, 6.5% English (2000).
Economy: Employment by occupation: 27.2% management, 14.6% professional, 9.1% services, 15.9% sales, 9.1% farming, 7.6% construction, 16.5% production (2000).
Income: Per capita income: $18,176 (2000); Median household income: $40,000 (2000); Poverty rate: 6.3% (2000).
Taxes: Total city taxes per capita: $163 (1997); City property taxes per capita: $162 (1997).
Education: High school graduation rate: 89.4% (2000); College graduation rate: 12.7% (2000).
Housing: Homeownership rate: 81.8% (2000); Median home value: $74,100 (2000); Median rent: $332 per month (2000); Median age of housing: 60+ years (2000).
Transportation: Commute to work: 75.6% car, 0.9% public transportation, 2.2% walk, 18.5% work from home (2000); Travel time to work: 30.2% less than 15 minutes, 40.9% 15 to 30 minutes, 14.2% 30 to 45 minutes, 5.1% 45 to 60 minutes, 9.6% 60 minutes or more (2000)

Langlade County

Located in northeastern Wisconsin; drained by the Wolf and Eau Claire Rivers; includes part of Nicolet National Forest, and several lakes. Covers a land area of 872.70 square miles, a water area of 15.20 square miles, and is located in the Central Time Zone. The county government was organized in 1879. County seat is Antigo.

Weather Station: Antigo — Elevation: 1,519 feet

	Jan	Feb	Mar	Apr	May	Jun	Jul	Aug	Sep	Oct	Nov	Dec
High	21	26	37	53	67	75	79	77	68	56	39	25
Low	0	5	16	31	41	50	55	53	45	35	23	8
Precip	0.9	0.8	1.7	2.5	3.0	3.6	3.9	4.2	4.2	2.7	2.1	1.2
Snow	13.6	8.9	9.8	4.0	0.5	0.0	0.0	0.0	tr	1.0	7.6	14.2

High and Low temperatures in degrees Fahrenheit; Precipitation and Snow in inches

Population: 20,740 (2000); Race: 97.5% White, 0.1% Black, 0.5% Asian, 0.9% American Indian and Alaska Native, 0.6% Hispanic of any race, 0.9% two or more races (2000); Density: 23.8 persons per square mile (2000); Age: 24.3% under 18, 19.0% over 64 (2000).

Religion: Five largest groups: 41.0% Catholic Church, 13.5% Lutheran Church—Missouri Synod, 4.8% Evangelical Lutheran Church in America, 2.1% United Church of Christ, 2.0% The United Methodist Church (2000).
Economy: Unemployment rate: 7.6% (11/2002); Total civilian labor force: 9,688 (11/2002); Leading industries: 25.5% manufacturing; 18.5% retail trade; 12.7% health care and social assistance (2000); Companies that employ more than 1,000 persons: 0 (2000); Companies that employ more than 100 persons: 10 (2000); Farms: 453 totaling 123,892 acres (1997); Minority business ownership rate: 0.0% (1997); Women business ownership rate: 15.6% (1997); Retail sales per capita: $12,440 (1997). Single-family building permits issued: 154 (2001) / 153 (2000); Multi-family building permits issued: 12 (2001) / 0 (2000).
Income: Per capita income: $16,960 (2000); Median household income: $33,168 (2000); Poverty rate: 10.1% (2000); Bankruptcy rate: 3.03% (2001).
Taxes: Total county taxes per capita: $260 (1997); County property taxes per capita: $212 (1997).
Education: High school graduation rate: 80.9% (2000); College graduation rate: 11.7% (2000).
Housing: Homeownership rate: 78.7% (2000); Median home value: $68,600 (2000); Median rent: $340 per month (2000); Median age of housing: 36 years (2000).
Health: Birth rate: 96.4 per 10,000 population (1998); Age adjusted death rate: 82.2 per 10,000 population (1999); Age adjusted cancer mortality rate: 197.3 deaths per 100,000 population (1999). Number of physicians: 11.1 per 10,000 population (1999); Number of hospital beds: 20.7 per 10,000 population (1999).
Elections: 2000 Presidential election results: 43.2% Gore, 52.7% Bush, 2.7% Nader, 0.9% Buchanan
National and State Parks: Ackley State Wildlife Areas; Clubhouse Springpond State Fishery Area; Demlow Lake State Fishery Area; Deneault Springs State Fishery Area; Evergreen River State Fishery Area; Lily Springs State Fishery Area; Peters Marsh State Wildlife Area; Rabe Lake State Fishery Area; Upper Wolf River State Fishery Area; Wolf River State Fishery Area; Woods Flowage State Fishery Area
Additional Information Contacts
Langlade County Government Offices. 715-627-6200
Antigo Chamber of Commerce 715-623-4134

Langlade County Communities

ACKLEY (town). Covers a land area of 70.844 square miles and a water area of 0.076 square miles. Located at 45.15° N. Lat.; 89.25° W. Long.
Population: 510 (2000); Race: 99.2% White, 0.0% Black, 0.0% Asian, 0.2% American Indian and Alaska Native, 0.0% Hispanic of any race, 0.6% two or more races (2000); Density: 7.2 persons per square mile (2000); Age: 23.0% under 18, 14.0% over 64 (2000); Marriage status: 21.0% never married, 66.8% now married, 6.1% widowed, 6.1% divorced (2000); Foreign born: 1.0% (2000); Ancestry (includes multiple ancestries): 54.4% German, 16.0% Polish, 10.3% Irish, 6.8% Czech, 4.9% French (except Basque) (2000).
Economy: Employment by occupation: 19.0% management, 8.2% professional, 8.2% services, 23.7% sales, 5.0% farming, 8.6% construction, 27.2% production (2000).
Income: Per capita income: $18,113 (2000); Median household income: $42,000 (2000); Poverty rate: 4.7% (2000).
Taxes: Total city taxes per capita: $59 (1997); City property taxes per capita: $59 (1997).
Education: High school graduation rate: 84.9% (2000); College graduation rate: 9.6% (2000).
Housing: Homeownership rate: 92.6% (2000); Median home value: $75,800 (2000); Median rent: $250 per month (2000); Median age of housing: 55 years (2000).
Transportation: Commute to work: 88.1% car, 0.4% public transportation, 2.2% walk, 7.9% work from home (2000); Travel time to work: 55.5% less than 15 minutes, 17.2% 15 to 30 minutes, 10.2% 30 to 45 minutes, 8.2% 45 to 60 minutes, 9.0% 60 minutes or more (2000)

AINSWORTH (town). Covers a land area of 69.478 square miles and a water area of 2.457 square miles. Located at 45.38° N. Lat.; 88.97° W. Long.
Population: 571 (2000); Race: 97.2% White, 0.0% Black, 1.7% Asian, 0.3% American Indian and Alaska Native, 0.0% Hispanic of any race, 0.7% two or more races (2000); Density: 8.2 persons per square mile (2000); Age: 17.8% under 18, 20.2% over 64 (2000); Marriage status: 16.6% never married, 62.3% now married, 8.6% widowed, 12.5% divorced (2000); Foreign born: 1.4% (2000); Ancestry (includes multiple ancestries): 41.4% German, 13.1% Polish, 8.2% English, 8.0% Irish, 7.0% Norwegian (2000).
Economy: Employment by occupation: 11.3% management, 3.8% professional, 20.0% services, 18.3% sales, 4.2% farming, 24.2% construction, 18.3% production (2000).
Income: Per capita income: $14,162 (2000); Median household income: $27,727 (2000); Poverty rate: 10.6% (2000).
Taxes: Total city taxes per capita: $40 (1997); City property taxes per capita: $38 (1997).
Education: High school graduation rate: 67.3% (2000); College graduation rate: 2.9% (2000).
Housing: Homeownership rate: 88.1% (2000); Median home value: $71,200 (2000); Median rent: $338 per month (2000); Median age of housing: 26 years (2000).
Transportation: Commute to work: 85.8% car, 0.4% public transportation, 6.9% walk, 6.0% work from home (2000); Travel time to work: 18.8% less than 15 minutes, 24.8% 15 to 30 minutes, 32.6% 30 to 45 minutes, 4.1% 45 to 60 minutes, 19.7% 60 minutes or more (2000)

ANTIGO (city). Covers a land area of 6.443 square miles and a water area of 0.045 square miles. Located at 45.14° N. Lat.; 89.15° W. Long. Elevation is 1,500 feet.
History: Antigo was founded after the Civil War by Francis Augustine Deleglise, a Swiss immigrant. First built around sawmills, the city later produced heel planks, shoe lasts, and other wood products. A Kraft-Phoenix processed-cheese factory was founded here.
Population: 8,560 (2000); Race: 96.7% White, 0.1% Black, 0.6% Asian, 1.6% American Indian and Alaska Native, 0.5% Hispanic of any race, 0.9% two or more races (2000); Density: 1,328.7 persons per square mile (2000); Age: 24.2% under 18, 21.4% over 64 (2000); Marriage status: 20.6% never married, 57.6% now married, 10.2% widowed, 11.6% divorced (2000); Foreign born: 0.9% (2000); Ancestry (includes multiple ancestries): 45.0% German, 11.1% Polish, 10.9% Irish, 6.5% Other groups, 6.3% English (2000).
Economy: Single-family building permits issued: 10 (2001) / 15 (2000); Multi-family building permits issued: 0 (2001) / 0 (2000); Employment by occupation: 8.9% management, 12.1% professional, 18.2% services, 26.0% sales, 2.7% farming, 7.7% construction, 24.4% production (2000).
Income: Per capita income: $16,592 (2000); Median household income: $29,548 (2000); Poverty rate: 13.2% (2000).
Taxes: Total city taxes per capita: $273 (2000); City property taxes per capita: $251 (2000).
Education: High school graduation rate: 83.3% (2000); College graduation rate: 14.4% (2000).

School District(s)

Antigo (PK-12)
2000 Enrollment: 3,029 715-627-4355
Housing: Homeownership rate: 66.8% (2000); Median home value: $56,700 (2000); Median rent: $341 per month (2000); Median age of housing: 53 years (2000).
Hospitals: Langlade Memorial Hospital (49 beds)
Safety: Violent crime rate: 46.4 per 10,000 population; Property crime rate: 515.0 per 10,000 population (2001).
Newspapers: Antigo Daily Journal (6 x week); Journal Express (1 x week)
Transportation: Commute to work: 92.6% car, 0.1% public transportation, 4.7% walk, 1.3% work from home (2000); Travel time to work: 72.4% less than 15 minutes, 10.7% 15 to 30 minutes, 4.8% 30 to 45 minutes, 8.1% 45 to 60 minutes, 4.0% 60 minutes or more (2000)
Additional Information Contacts
Antigo Chamber of Commerce 715-623-4134

ANTIGO (town). Covers a land area of 31.071 square miles and a water area of 0.014 square miles. Located at 45.16° N. Lat.; 89.12° W. Long. Elevation is 1,500 feet.
History: Settled 1876, incorporated 1885.
Population: 1,487 (2000); Race: 96.5% White, 0.8% Black, 1.7% Asian, 0.1% American Indian and Alaska Native, 1.2% Hispanic of any race, 0.3% two or more races (2000); Density: 47.9 persons per square mile (2000); Age: 26.5% under 18, 15.9% over 64 (2000); Marriage status: 20.8% never married, 66.6% now married, 5.3% widowed, 7.3% divorced (2000); Foreign born: 1.1% (2000); Ancestry (includes multiple ancestries): 54.3% German, 11.3% Polish, 10.3% Irish, 8.7% Czech, 5.4% English (2000).
Economy: In potato growing area. Manufactures food and dairy products, sand and gravel quarrying, transformers, lumber, plastic products, wood products, shoes. Employment by occupation: 15.3% management, 11.5% professional, 10.8% services, 24.3% sales, 4.4% farming, 10.0% construction, 23.7% production (2000).

Income: Per capita income: $18,445 (2000); Median household income: $43,849 (2000); Poverty rate: 10.5% (2000).
Taxes: Total city taxes per capita: $39 (1997); City property taxes per capita: $37 (1997).
Education: High school graduation rate: 83.5% (2000); College graduation rate: 10.3% (2000).
Housing: Homeownership rate: 86.0% (2000); Median home value: $85,700 (2000); Median rent: $365 per month (2000); Median age of housing: 38 years (2000).
Transportation: Commute to work: 90.6% car, 0.0% public transportation, 4.3% walk, 5.1% work from home (2000); Travel time to work: 67.6% less than 15 minutes, 19.2% 15 to 30 minutes, 3.9% 30 to 45 minutes, 3.9% 45 to 60 minutes, 5.4% 60 minutes or more (2000)

BRYANT (unincorporated postal area, zip code 54418). Covers a land area of 151.641 square miles and a water area of 0.681 square miles. Located at 45.22° N. Lat.; 88.96° W. Long. Elevation is 1,586 feet.
Population: 1,288 (2000); Race: 98.8% White, 0.2% Black, 0.0% Asian, 0.4% American Indian and Alaska Native, 0.0% Hispanic of any race, 0.3% two or more races (2000); Density: 8.5 persons per square mile (2000); Age: 30.1% under 18, 12.5% over 64 (2000); Marriage status: 22.2% never married, 64.7% now married, 6.1% widowed, 6.9% divorced (2000); Foreign born: 0.8% (2000); Ancestry (includes multiple ancestries): 47.1% German, 8.4% Polish, 7.8% Irish, 7.8% Czech, 7.3% English (2000).
Economy: Employment by occupation: 17.3% management, 10.9% professional, 14.3% services, 20.5% sales, 8.0% farming, 7.8% construction, 21.2% production (2000).
Income: Per capita income: $16,516 (2000); Median household income: $39,625 (2000); Poverty rate: 7.6% (2000).
Education: High school graduation rate: 78.0% (2000); College graduation rate: 12.1% (2000).
Housing: Homeownership rate: 84.9% (2000); Median home value: $84,700 (2000); Median rent: $305 per month (2000); Median age of housing: 33 years (2000).
Transportation: Commute to work: 86.8% car, 0.3% public transportation, 4.8% walk, 7.8% work from home (2000); Travel time to work: 31.3% less than 15 minutes, 50.9% 15 to 30 minutes, 7.4% 30 to 45 minutes, 4.2% 45 to 60 minutes, 6.2% 60 minutes or more (2000)

DEERBROOK (unincorporated postal area, zip code 54424). Covers a land area of 170.333 square miles and a water area of 2.239 square miles. Located at 45.28° N. Lat.; 89.20° W. Long. Elevation is 1,530 feet.
Population: 1,729 (2000); Race: 99.2% White, 0.0% Black, 0.0% Asian, 0.0% American Indian and Alaska Native, 0.3% Hispanic of any race, 0.8% two or more races (2000); Density: 10.2 persons per square mile (2000); Age: 23.0% under 18, 17.2% over 64 (2000); Marriage status: 17.5% never married, 71.2% now married, 4.8% widowed, 6.6% divorced (2000); Foreign born: 1.0% (2000); Ancestry (includes multiple ancestries): 51.2% German, 10.4% Polish, 10.3% Czech, 8.6% Irish, 5.9% Norwegian (2000).
Economy: Employment by occupation: 10.6% management, 9.9% professional, 15.5% services, 22.1% sales, 3.3% farming, 15.2% construction, 23.4% production (2000).
Income: Per capita income: $17,718 (2000); Median household income: $37,917 (2000); Poverty rate: 4.4% (2000).
Education: High school graduation rate: 79.0% (2000); College graduation rate: 9.8% (2000).
Housing: Homeownership rate: 92.4% (2000); Median home value: $85,800 (2000); Median rent: $294 per month (2000); Median age of housing: 33 years (2000).
Transportation: Commute to work: 90.4% car, 0.0% public transportation, 1.3% walk, 7.1% work from home (2000); Travel time to work: 24.3% less than 15 minutes, 49.0% 15 to 30 minutes, 8.9% 30 to 45 minutes, 10.0% 45 to 60 minutes, 7.8% 60 minutes or more (2000)

ELCHO (town). Covers a land area of 71.371 square miles and a water area of 3.878 square miles. Located at 45.43° N. Lat.; 89.16° W. Long. Elevation is 1,635 feet.
Population: 1,317 (2000); Race: 99.8% White, 0.2% Black, 0.0% Asian, 0.0% American Indian and Alaska Native, 0.7% Hispanic of any race, 0.1% two or more races (2000); Density: 18.5 persons per square mile (2000); Age: 16.6% under 18, 28.1% over 64 (2000); Marriage status: 15.2% never married, 65.1% now married, 9.9% widowed, 9.8% divorced (2000); Foreign born: 1.1% (2000); Ancestry (includes multiple ancestries): 42.4% German, 11.4% Irish, 10.9% Polish, 6.0% English, 5.8% Norwegian (2000).
Economy: In wooded lake region. Resort. Employment by occupation: 11.6% management, 15.0% professional, 19.1% services, 16.6% sales, 0.6% farming, 17.5% construction, 19.7% production (2000).
Income: Per capita income: $17,016 (2000); Median household income: $29,010 (2000); Poverty rate: 9.0% (2000).
Taxes: Total city taxes per capita: $125 (1997); City property taxes per capita: $117 (1997).
Education: High school graduation rate: 81.3% (2000); College graduation rate: 10.9% (2000).

School District(s)

Elcho (PK-12)
2000 Enrollment: 417 715-275-3205

Housing: Homeownership rate: 85.5% (2000); Median home value: $95,300 (2000); Median rent: $341 per month (2000); Median age of housing: 33 years (2000).
Transportation: Commute to work: 86.0% car, 0.4% public transportation, 6.4% walk, 6.0% work from home (2000); Travel time to work: 35.7% less than 15 minutes, 22.9% 15 to 30 minutes, 31.0% 30 to 45 minutes, 4.0% 45 to 60 minutes, 6.4% 60 minutes or more (2000)

ELTON (unincorporated postal area, zip code 54430). Covers a land area of 7.435 square miles and a water area of 0.167 square miles. Located at 45.13° N. Lat.; 88.88° W. Long. Elevation is 1,390 feet.
Population: 117 (2000); Race: 100.0% White, 0.0% Black, 0.0% Asian, 0.0% American Indian and Alaska Native, 0.0% Hispanic of any race, 0.0% two or more races (2000); Density: 15.7 persons per square mile (2000); Age: 27.4% under 18, 15.3% over 64 (2000); Marriage status: 20.0% never married, 73.0% now married, 5.0% widowed, 2.0% divorced (2000); Foreign born: 0.0% (2000); Ancestry (includes multiple ancestries): 37.9% German, 16.9% Irish, 10.5% French (except Basque), 10.5% United States or American, 7.3% Polish (2000).
Economy: Employment by occupation: 3.8% management, 30.2% professional, 3.8% services, 24.5% sales, 3.8% farming, 13.2% construction, 20.8% production (2000).
Income: Per capita income: $10,030 (2000); Median household income: $27,917 (2000); Poverty rate: 6.6% (2000).
Education: High school graduation rate: 80.0% (2000); College graduation rate: 10.6% (2000).
Housing: Homeownership rate: 93.3% (2000); Median home value: $65,000 (2000); Median age of housing: 22 years (2000).
Transportation: Commute to work: 94.3% car, 0.0% public transportation, 0.0% walk, 5.7% work from home (2000); Travel time to work: 14.0% less than 15 minutes, 60.0% 15 to 30 minutes, 8.0% 30 to 45 minutes, 4.0% 45 to 60 minutes, 14.0% 60 minutes or more (2000)

EVERGREEN (town). Covers a land area of 35.844 square miles and a water area of 0.409 square miles. Located at 45.15° N. Lat.; 88.87° W. Long.
Population: 468 (2000); Race: 100.0% White, 0.0% Black, 0.0% Asian, 0.0% American Indian and Alaska Native, 0.0% Hispanic of any race, 0.0% two or more races (2000); Density: 13.1 persons per square mile (2000); Age: 27.0% under 18, 15.1% over 64 (2000); Marriage status: 17.3% never married, 62.5% now married, 9.3% widowed, 11.0% divorced (2000); Foreign born: 1.1% (2000); Ancestry (includes multiple ancestries): 37.6% German, 15.9% Irish, 9.6% English, 8.1% French (except Basque), 6.8% Norwegian (2000).
Economy: Employment by occupation: 12.5% management, 12.5% professional, 8.3% services, 12.5% sales, 13.0% farming, 12.5% construction, 28.7% production (2000).
Income: Per capita income: $16,519 (2000); Median household income: $30,536 (2000); Poverty rate: 6.0% (2000).
Taxes: Total city taxes per capita: $35 (1997); City property taxes per capita: $35 (1997).
Education: High school graduation rate: 70.8% (2000); College graduation rate: 6.8% (2000).
Housing: Homeownership rate: 89.0% (2000); Median home value: $56,700 (2000); Median rent: $245 per month (2000); Median age of housing: 26 years (2000).
Transportation: Commute to work: 86.0% car, 0.0% public transportation, 1.9% walk, 11.2% work from home (2000); Travel time to work: 19.5% less than 15 minutes, 45.8% 15 to 30 minutes, 17.4% 30 to 45 minutes, 5.3% 45 to 60 minutes, 12.1% 60 minutes or more (2000)

LANGLADE (town). Covers a land area of 71.516 square miles and a water area of 0.969 square miles. Located at 45.30° N. Lat.; 88.85° W. Long. Elevation is 1,257 feet.

History: Langlade was named for Charles Michel de Langlade (1729-1800), a fur trader. Langlade helped to organize and lead the northwest tribes against the British during the French and Indian War. During the Revolution, Langlade worked for the British against the American colonies.
Population: 472 (2000); Race: 98.4% White, 0.0% Black, 0.0% Asian, 1.2% American Indian and Alaska Native, 0.0% Hispanic of any race, 0.4% two or more races (2000); Density: 6.6 persons per square mile (2000); Age: 19.6% under 18, 21.6% over 64 (2000); Marriage status: 16.1% never married, 62.1% now married, 9.0% widowed, 12.8% divorced (2000); Foreign born: 2.0% (2000); Ancestry (includes multiple ancestries): 50.2% German, 11.5% Irish, 9.5% Polish, 7.9% English, 7.1% United States or American (2000).
Economy: Sawmilling. Manufacturing: machinery, wood products. Langlade Fish Hatchery to North. Nicolet National Forest to East. Single-family building permits issued: 6 (2001) / 7 (2000); Multi-family building permits issued: 0 (2001) / 0 (2000); Employment by occupation: 7.4% management, 10.1% professional, 17.5% services, 14.7% sales, 3.7% farming, 24.0% construction, 22.6% production (2000).
Income: Per capita income: $14,418 (2000); Median household income: $27,054 (2000); Poverty rate: 13.8% (2000).
Taxes: Total city taxes per capita: $5 (1997); City property taxes per capita: $2 (1997).
Education: High school graduation rate: 73.7% (2000); College graduation rate: 7.4% (2000).
Housing: Homeownership rate: 86.5% (2000); Median home value: $78,900 (2000); Median rent: $275 per month (2000); Median age of housing: 24 years (2000).
Transportation: Commute to work: 91.9% car, 0.5% public transportation, 2.4% walk, 5.3% work from home (2000); Travel time to work: 25.3% less than 15 minutes, 27.3% 15 to 30 minutes, 25.8% 30 to 45 minutes, 12.1% 45 to 60 minutes, 9.6% 60 minutes or more (2000)

NEVA (town). Covers a land area of 37.431 square miles and a water area of 0.281 square miles. Located at 45.24° N. Lat.; 89.12° W. Long. Elevation is 1,575 feet.
Population: 994 (2000); Race: 98.8% White, 0.0% Black, 0.0% Asian, 0.0% American Indian and Alaska Native, 0.5% Hispanic of any race, 0.8% two or more races (2000); Density: 26.6 persons per square mile (2000); Age: 30.0% under 18, 14.4% over 64 (2000); Marriage status: 22.9% never married, 69.1% now married, 3.5% widowed, 4.5% divorced (2000); Foreign born: 0.4% (2000); Ancestry (includes multiple ancestries): 46.2% German, 12.8% Czech, 9.2% Polish, 8.4% United States or American, 7.2% Irish (2000).
Economy: Employment by occupation: 14.5% management, 7.6% professional, 14.9% services, 27.8% sales, 3.3% farming, 11.8% construction, 20.0% production (2000).
Income: Per capita income: $16,503 (2000); Median household income: $40,368 (2000); Poverty rate: 5.4% (2000).
Taxes: Total city taxes per capita: $49 (1997); City property taxes per capita: $48 (1997).
Education: High school graduation rate: 79.1% (2000); College graduation rate: 7.1% (2000).
Housing: Homeownership rate: 89.2% (2000); Median home value: $81,100 (2000); Median rent: $294 per month (2000); Median age of housing: 35 years (2000).
Transportation: Commute to work: 94.8% car, 0.0% public transportation, 0.2% walk, 5.0% work from home (2000); Travel time to work: 33.4% less than 15 minutes, 46.7% 15 to 30 minutes, 4.7% 30 to 45 minutes, 10.0% 45 to 60 minutes, 5.2% 60 minutes or more (2000)

NORWOOD (town). Covers a land area of 35.748 square miles and a water area of 0.381 square miles. Located at 45.07° N. Lat.; 89.03° W. Long.
Population: 918 (2000); Race: 97.4% White, 0.0% Black, 0.0% Asian, 0.8% American Indian and Alaska Native, 0.0% Hispanic of any race, 1.8% two or more races (2000); Density: 25.7 persons per square mile (2000); Age: 30.0% under 18, 12.2% over 64 (2000); Marriage status: 22.3% never married, 65.5% now married, 6.3% widowed, 5.9% divorced (2000); Foreign born: 0.3% (2000); Ancestry (includes multiple ancestries): 54.9% German, 15.6% Polish, 9.1% Dutch, 6.4% English, 6.4% Other groups (2000).
Economy: Employment by occupation: 13.2% management, 9.3% professional, 13.6% services, 24.1% sales, 4.7% farming, 11.8% construction, 23.3% production (2000).
Income: Per capita income: $17,893 (2000); Median household income: $45,000 (2000); Poverty rate: 6.7% (2000).
Taxes: Total city taxes per capita: $92 (1997); City property taxes per capita: $91 (1997).
Education: High school graduation rate: 81.7% (2000); College graduation rate: 10.7% (2000).
Housing: Homeownership rate: 88.9% (2000); Median home value: $77,400 (2000); Median rent: $344 per month (2000); Median age of housing: 24 years (2000).
Transportation: Commute to work: 83.7% car, 0.0% public transportation, 1.8% walk, 13.9% work from home (2000); Travel time to work: 29.1% less than 15 minutes, 50.1% 15 to 30 minutes, 5.5% 30 to 45 minutes, 11.5% 45 to 60 minutes, 3.7% 60 minutes or more (2000)

PARRISH (town). Covers a land area of 36.319 square miles and a water area of 0.262 square miles. Located at 45.42° N. Lat.; 89.38° W. Long. Elevation is 1,600 feet.
Population: 108 (2000); Race: 100.0% White, 0.0% Black, 0.0% Asian, 0.0% American Indian and Alaska Native, 0.0% Hispanic of any race, 0.0% two or more races (2000); Density: 3.0 persons per square mile (2000); Age: 14.1% under 18, 28.2% over 64 (2000); Marriage status: 12.0% never married, 81.3% now married, 2.7% widowed, 4.0% divorced (2000); Foreign born: 2.4% (2000); Ancestry (includes multiple ancestries): 41.2% German, 9.4% Austrian, 8.2% English, 8.2% Irish, 4.7% Norwegian (2000).
Economy: Employment by occupation: 0.0% management, 8.1% professional, 24.3% services, 21.6% sales, 0.0% farming, 21.6% construction, 24.3% production (2000).
Income: Per capita income: $18,645 (2000); Median household income: $40,625 (2000); Poverty rate: 4.7% (2000).
Education: High school graduation rate: 70.4% (2000); College graduation rate: 0.0% (2000).
Housing: Homeownership rate: 88.6% (2000); Median home value: $85,000 (2000); Median rent: $375 per month (2000); Median age of housing: 25 years (2000).
Transportation: Commute to work: 94.3% car, 0.0% public transportation, 0.0% walk, 5.7% work from home (2000); Travel time to work: 0.0% less than 15 minutes, 15.2% 15 to 30 minutes, 66.7% 30 to 45 minutes, 6.1% 45 to 60 minutes, 12.1% 60 minutes or more (2000)

PEARSON (unincorporated postal area, zip code 54462). Covers a land area of 38.905 square miles and a water area of 0.542 square miles. Located at 45.39° N. Lat.; 89.00° W. Long. Elevation is 1,540 feet.
Population: 365 (2000); Race: 98.4% White, 0.0% Black, 0.5% Asian, 0.0% American Indian and Alaska Native, 0.0% Hispanic of any race, 1.1% two or more races (2000); Density: 9.4 persons per square mile (2000); Age: 18.0% under 18, 21.7% over 64 (2000); Marriage status: 15.4% never married, 58.9% now married, 9.7% widowed, 16.0% divorced (2000); Foreign born: 1.6% (2000); Ancestry (includes multiple ancestries): 42.1% German, 13.4% Polish, 8.8% English, 7.8% Irish, 6.4% Norwegian (2000).
Economy: Employment by occupation: 15.2% management, 11.3% professional, 19.2% services, 14.6% sales, 6.6% farming, 14.6% construction, 18.5% production (2000).
Income: Per capita income: $14,270 (2000); Median household income: $26,765 (2000); Poverty rate: 11.8% (2000).
Education: High school graduation rate: 62.8% (2000); College graduation rate: 4.8% (2000).
Housing: Homeownership rate: 87.8% (2000); Median home value: $71,100 (2000); Median rent: $344 per month (2000); Median age of housing: 28 years (2000).
Transportation: Commute to work: 81.1% car, 0.7% public transportation, 9.8% walk, 7.0% work from home (2000); Travel time to work: 21.8% less than 15 minutes, 21.1% 15 to 30 minutes, 35.3% 30 to 45 minutes, 7.5% 45 to 60 minutes, 14.3% 60 minutes or more (2000)

PECK (town). Covers a land area of 37.171 square miles and a water area of 0.070 square miles. Located at 45.24° N. Lat.; 89.24° W. Long.
Population: 354 (2000); Race: 100.0% White, 0.0% Black, 0.0% Asian, 0.0% American Indian and Alaska Native, 0.0% Hispanic of any race, 0.0% two or more races (2000); Density: 9.5 persons per square mile (2000); Age: 21.0% under 18, 16.6% over 64 (2000); Marriage status: 16.4% never married, 71.5% now married, 6.4% widowed, 5.7% divorced (2000); Foreign born: 2.0% (2000); Ancestry (includes multiple ancestries): 45.8% German, 9.9% Czech, 6.1% Czechoslovakian, 5.8% Polish, 5.8% United States or American (2000).
Economy: Employment by occupation: 7.1% management, 10.1% professional, 16.1% services, 11.9% sales, 5.4% farming, 18.5% construction, 31.0% production (2000).
Income: Per capita income: $15,466 (2000); Median household income: $34,167 (2000); Poverty rate: 5.6% (2000).
Taxes: Total city taxes per capita: $65 (1997); City property taxes per capita: $65 (1997).

Education: High school graduation rate: 74.4% (2000); College graduation rate: 10.3% (2000).
Housing: Homeownership rate: 93.8% (2000); Median home value: $56,900 (2000); Median rent: $138 per month (2000); Median age of housing: 44 years (2000).
Transportation: Commute to work: 84.0% car, 0.0% public transportation, 1.9% walk, 9.9% work from home (2000); Travel time to work: 27.4% less than 15 minutes, 52.7% 15 to 30 minutes, 5.5% 30 to 45 minutes, 5.5% 45 to 60 minutes, 8.9% 60 minutes or more (2000)

PICKEREL (unincorporated postal area, zip code 54465). Covers a land area of 44.824 square miles and a water area of 3.766 square miles. Located at 45.39° N. Lat.; 88.88° W. Long. Elevation is 1,550 feet.
Population: 701 (2000); Race: 97.8% White, 0.0% Black, 1.1% Asian, 0.8% American Indian and Alaska Native, 0.0% Hispanic of any race, 0.3% two or more races (2000); Density: 15.6 persons per square mile (2000); Age: 12.8% under 18, 24.6% over 64 (2000); Marriage status: 12.5% never married, 70.6% now married, 7.4% widowed, 9.5% divorced (2000); Foreign born: 1.1% (2000); Ancestry (includes multiple ancestries): 46.1% German, 10.6% Polish, 10.2% Irish, 7.5% Dutch, 6.1% French (except Basque) (2000).
Economy: Employment by occupation: 8.5% management, 4.4% professional, 23.1% services, 18.0% sales, 1.4% farming, 24.1% construction, 20.4% production (2000).
Income: Per capita income: $19,720 (2000); Median household income: $30,078 (2000); Poverty rate: 11.5% (2000).
Education: High school graduation rate: 81.7% (2000); College graduation rate: 5.0% (2000).
Housing: Homeownership rate: 89.7% (2000); Median home value: $98,500 (2000); Median rent: $363 per month (2000); Median age of housing: 25 years (2000).
Transportation: Commute to work: 89.2% car, 0.0% public transportation, 3.5% walk, 7.3% work from home (2000); Travel time to work: 30.6% less than 15 minutes, 25.3% 15 to 30 minutes, 26.8% 30 to 45 minutes, 3.4% 45 to 60 minutes, 14.0% 60 minutes or more (2000)

POLAR (town). Covers a land area of 35.593 square miles and a water area of 0.339 square miles. Located at 45.16° N. Lat.; 89.00° W. Long. Elevation is 1,520 feet.
Population: 995 (2000); Race: 98.7% White, 0.2% Black, 0.0% Asian, 0.3% American Indian and Alaska Native, 0.0% Hispanic of any race, 0.8% two or more races (2000); Density: 28.0 persons per square mile (2000); Age: 29.7% under 18, 13.2% over 64 (2000); Marriage status: 20.9% never married, 68.9% now married, 4.3% widowed, 5.9% divorced (2000); Foreign born: 0.0% (2000); Ancestry (includes multiple ancestries): 55.1% German, 8.9% Polish, 7.4% French (except Basque), 7.1% Irish, 5.9% Czech (2000).
Economy: Employment by occupation: 13.5% management, 11.6% professional, 11.8% services, 20.5% sales, 7.4% farming, 10.0% construction, 25.1% production (2000).
Income: Per capita income: $17,141 (2000); Median household income: $41,477 (2000); Poverty rate: 7.0% (2000).
Taxes: Total city taxes per capita: $48 (1997); City property taxes per capita: $47 (1997).
Education: High school graduation rate: 82.3% (2000); College graduation rate: 12.5% (2000).
Housing: Homeownership rate: 88.1% (2000); Median home value: $87,900 (2000); Median rent: $416 per month (2000); Median age of housing: 30 years (2000).
Transportation: Commute to work: 88.2% car, 0.0% public transportation, 3.9% walk, 7.7% work from home (2000); Travel time to work: 36.2% less than 15 minutes, 48.1% 15 to 30 minutes, 4.9% 30 to 45 minutes, 4.9% 45 to 60 minutes, 5.8% 60 minutes or more (2000)

PRICE (town). Covers a land area of 36.191 square miles and a water area of 0.152 square miles. Located at 45.22° N. Lat.; 88.99° W. Long.
Population: 243 (2000); Race: 98.4% White, 0.0% Black, 0.0% Asian, 1.6% American Indian and Alaska Native, 0.0% Hispanic of any race, 0.0% two or more races (2000); Density: 6.7 persons per square mile (2000); Age: 32.5% under 18, 6.5% over 64 (2000); Marriage status: 19.9% never married, 64.8% now married, 5.1% widowed, 10.2% divorced (2000); Foreign born: 0.0% (2000); Ancestry (includes multiple ancestries): 47.2% German, 10.6% French Canadian, 8.5% Polish, 7.3% Czech, 6.9% English (2000).
Economy: Employment by occupation: 13.3% management, 14.2% professional, 15.0% services, 17.5% sales, 13.3% farming, 13.3% construction, 13.3% production (2000).
Income: Per capita income: $20,338 (2000); Median household income: $53,750 (2000); Poverty rate: 6.5% (2000).
Taxes: Total city taxes per capita: $83 (1997); City property taxes per capita: $83 (1997).
Education: High school graduation rate: 78.8% (2000); College graduation rate: 14.7% (2000).
Housing: Homeownership rate: 83.9% (2000); Median home value: $86,300 (2000); Median rent: $325 per month (2000); Median age of housing: 34 years (2000).
Transportation: Commute to work: 89.0% car, 1.7% public transportation, 9.3% walk, 0.0% work from home (2000); Travel time to work: 25.4% less than 15 minutes, 48.3% 15 to 30 minutes, 11.0% 30 to 45 minutes, 8.5% 45 to 60 minutes, 6.8% 60 minutes or more (2000)

ROLLING (town). Covers a land area of 36.009 square miles and a water area of 0.030 square miles. Located at 45.07° N. Lat.; 89.15° W. Long.
Population: 1,452 (2000); Race: 96.8% White, 0.0% Black, 0.3% Asian, 1.2% American Indian and Alaska Native, 1.6% Hispanic of any race, 1.5% two or more races (2000); Density: 40.3 persons per square mile (2000); Age: 26.7% under 18, 10.8% over 64 (2000); Marriage status: 20.5% never married, 69.7% now married, 3.1% widowed, 6.7% divorced (2000); Foreign born: 1.9% (2000); Ancestry (includes multiple ancestries): 54.6% German, 11.3% Polish, 6.9% United States or American, 6.2% Irish, 5.6% Czech (2000).
Economy: Employment by occupation: 11.0% management, 9.5% professional, 12.9% services, 25.0% sales, 3.7% farming, 13.1% construction, 24.8% production (2000).
Income: Per capita income: $17,946 (2000); Median household income: $43,026 (2000); Poverty rate: 6.6% (2000).
Taxes: Total city taxes per capita: $42 (1997); City property taxes per capita: $38 (1997).
Education: High school graduation rate: 80.4% (2000); College graduation rate: 10.2% (2000).
Housing: Homeownership rate: 87.3% (2000); Median home value: $91,000 (2000); Median rent: $345 per month (2000); Median age of housing: 23 years (2000).
Transportation: Commute to work: 90.2% car, 0.4% public transportation, 3.0% walk, 5.5% work from home (2000); Travel time to work: 48.1% less than 15 minutes, 29.6% 15 to 30 minutes, 9.5% 30 to 45 minutes, 6.0% 45 to 60 minutes, 6.8% 60 minutes or more (2000)

SUMMIT (town). Covers a land area of 36.408 square miles and a water area of 0.014 square miles. Located at 45.35° N. Lat.; 89.35° W. Long.
Population: 168 (2000); Race: 92.2% White, 0.0% Black, 0.0% Asian, 0.0% American Indian and Alaska Native, 7.8% Hispanic of any race, 7.8% two or more races (2000); Density: 4.6 persons per square mile (2000); Age: 32.4% under 18, 13.4% over 64 (2000); Marriage status: 23.4% never married, 66.4% now married, 7.3% widowed, 2.9% divorced (2000); Foreign born: 0.0% (2000); Ancestry (includes multiple ancestries): 63.7% German, 15.1% Polish, 13.4% Irish, 5.6% French (except Basque), 5.6% Other groups (2000).
Economy: Employment by occupation: 10.3% management, 8.0% professional, 20.7% services, 14.9% sales, 2.3% farming, 14.9% construction, 28.7% production (2000).
Income: Per capita income: $14,794 (2000); Median household income: $29,375 (2000); Poverty rate: 17.9% (2000).
Taxes: Total city taxes per capita: $25 (1997); City property taxes per capita: $25 (1997).
Education: High school graduation rate: 72.1% (2000); College graduation rate: 9.0% (2000).
Housing: Homeownership rate: 88.5% (2000); Median home value: $85,000 (2000); Median rent: $275 per month (2000); Median age of housing: 25 years (2000).
Transportation: Commute to work: 87.7% car, 0.0% public transportation, 4.9% walk, 2.5% work from home (2000); Travel time to work: 21.5% less than 15 minutes, 31.6% 15 to 30 minutes, 32.9% 30 to 45 minutes, 11.4% 45 to 60 minutes, 2.5% 60 minutes or more (2000)

SUMMIT LAKE (unincorporated postal area, zip code 54485). Covers a land area of 25.204 square miles and a water area of 0.351 square miles. Located at 45.38° N. Lat.; 89.20° W. Long. Elevation is 1,727 feet.
Population: 296 (2000); Race: 100.0% White, 0.0% Black, 0.0% Asian, 0.0% American Indian and Alaska Native, 0.7% Hispanic of any race, 0.0% two or more races (2000); Density: 11.7 persons per square mile (2000); Age: 17.9% under 18, 28.8% over 64 (2000); Marriage status: 11.0% never married, 70.2% now married, 7.8% widowed, 11.0% divorced (2000); Foreign born: 0.7% (2000); Ancestry (includes multiple ancestries): 56.8% German, 8.1% Irish, 6.7% United States or American, 5.6% Dutch, 5.3% Polish (2000).

Economy: Employment by occupation: 11.1% management, 23.1% professional, 9.4% services, 19.7% sales, 4.3% farming, 12.0% construction, 20.5% production (2000).
Income: Per capita income: $18,964 (2000); Median household income: $35,250 (2000); Poverty rate: 6.3% (2000).
Education: High school graduation rate: 86.0% (2000); College graduation rate: 11.8% (2000).
Housing: Homeownership rate: 83.6% (2000); Median home value: $110,200 (2000); Median rent: $308 per month (2000); Median age of housing: 35 years (2000).
Transportation: Commute to work: 87.0% car, 0.0% public transportation, 1.7% walk, 11.3% work from home (2000); Travel time to work: 12.7% less than 15 minutes, 51.0% 15 to 30 minutes, 21.6% 30 to 45 minutes, 4.9% 45 to 60 minutes, 9.8% 60 minutes or more (2000)

UPHAM (town). Covers a land area of 70.540 square miles and a water area of 3.367 square miles. Located at 45.34° N. Lat.; 89.18° W. Long.
Population: 689 (2000); Race: 99.2% White, 0.0% Black, 0.0% Asian, 0.0% American Indian and Alaska Native, 0.3% Hispanic of any race, 0.8% two or more races (2000); Density: 9.8 persons per square mile (2000); Age: 14.9% under 18, 24.1% over 64 (2000); Marriage status: 13.7% never married, 70.3% now married, 5.8% widowed, 10.3% divorced (2000); Foreign born: 1.5% (2000); Ancestry (includes multiple ancestries): 57.7% German, 12.2% Irish, 8.7% Czech, 8.3% Norwegian, 8.3% Polish (2000).
Economy: Employment by occupation: 10.6% management, 17.2% professional, 16.7% services, 23.3% sales, 3.2% farming, 12.6% construction, 16.4% production (2000).
Income: Per capita income: $20,498 (2000); Median household income: $36,786 (2000); Poverty rate: 4.5% (2000).
Taxes: Total city taxes per capita: $88 (1997); City property taxes per capita: $87 (1997).
Education: High school graduation rate: 82.5% (2000); College graduation rate: 13.8% (2000).
Housing: Homeownership rate: 90.6% (2000); Median home value: $108,000 (2000); Median rent: $320 per month (2000); Median age of housing: 32 years (2000).
Transportation: Commute to work: 92.5% car, 0.0% public transportation, 2.1% walk, 4.8% work from home (2000); Travel time to work: 17.0% less than 15 minutes, 53.0% 15 to 30 minutes, 15.8% 30 to 45 minutes, 8.2% 45 to 60 minutes, 6.0% 60 minutes or more (2000)

VILAS (town). Covers a land area of 35.893 square miles and a water area of 0 square miles. Located at 45.25° N. Lat.; 89.38° W. Long.
Population: 249 (2000); Race: 100.0% White, 0.0% Black, 0.0% Asian, 0.0% American Indian and Alaska Native, 0.0% Hispanic of any race, 0.0% two or more races (2000); Density: 6.9 persons per square mile (2000); Age: 24.3% under 18, 13.7% over 64 (2000); Marriage status: 21.3% never married, 55.1% now married, 8.4% widowed, 15.2% divorced (2000); Foreign born: 0.0% (2000); Ancestry (includes multiple ancestries): 51.3% German, 15.5% Irish, 7.5% English, 6.2% Polish, 5.3% United States or American (2000).
Economy: Employment by occupation: 9.4% management, 9.4% professional, 13.7% services, 26.5% sales, 8.5% farming, 7.7% construction, 24.8% production (2000).
Income: Per capita income: $14,423 (2000); Median household income: $30,417 (2000); Poverty rate: 7.1% (2000).
Taxes: Total city taxes per capita: $25 (1997); City property taxes per capita: $25 (1997).
Education: High school graduation rate: 78.7% (2000); College graduation rate: 3.9% (2000).
Housing: Homeownership rate: 87.9% (2000); Median home value: $87,500 (2000); Median age of housing: 32 years (2000).
Transportation: Commute to work: 75.2% car, 0.0% public transportation, 0.0% walk, 23.1% work from home (2000); Travel time to work: 6.7% less than 15 minutes, 32.2% 15 to 30 minutes, 27.8% 30 to 45 minutes, 25.6% 45 to 60 minutes, 7.8% 60 minutes or more (2000)

WHITE LAKE (village). Covers a land area of 2.205 square miles and a water area of 0.285 square miles. Located at 45.15° N. Lat.; 88.76° W. Long. Elevation is 1,286 feet.
Population: 329 (2000); Race: 100.0% White, 0.0% Black, 0.0% Asian, 0.0% American Indian and Alaska Native, 0.0% Hispanic of any race, 0.0% two or more races (2000); Density: 149.2 persons per square mile (2000); Age: 21.7% under 18, 26.8% over 64 (2000); Marriage status: 14.7% never married, 64.7% now married, 5.4% widowed, 15.1% divorced (2000); Foreign born: 0.6% (2000); Ancestry (includes multiple ancestries): 45.5% German, 25.5% Irish, 13.7% English, 8.3% French (except Basque), 8.3% United States or American (2000).
Economy: Single-family building permits issued: 2 (2001) / 1 (2000); Multi-family building permits issued: 12 (2001) / 0 (2000); Employment by occupation: 13.1% management, 9.5% professional, 9.5% services, 21.9% sales, 1.5% farming, 11.7% construction, 32.8% production (2000).
Income: Per capita income: $16,768 (2000); Median household income: $29,722 (2000); Poverty rate: 13.4% (2000).
Taxes: Total city taxes per capita: $201 (1997); City property taxes per capita: $188 (1997).
Education: High school graduation rate: 75.9% (2000); College graduation rate: 10.0% (2000).

School District(s)

White Lake (KG-12)
2000 Enrollment: 282 715-882-8421

Housing: Homeownership rate: 74.8% (2000); Median home value: $46,900 (2000); Median rent: $318 per month (2000); Median age of housing: 46 years (2000).
Transportation: Commute to work: 76.5% car, 0.0% public transportation, 19.7% walk, 3.8% work from home (2000); Travel time to work: 48.0% less than 15 minutes, 22.8% 15 to 30 minutes, 14.2% 30 to 45 minutes, 5.5% 45 to 60 minutes, 9.4% 60 minutes or more (2000)

WOLF RIVER (town). Covers a land area of 116.597 square miles and a water area of 2.178 square miles. Located at 45.21° N. Lat.; 88.74° W. Long.
Population: 856 (2000); Race: 95.6% White, 0.0% Black, 0.0% Asian, 2.5% American Indian and Alaska Native, 1.2% Hispanic of any race, 1.7% two or more races (2000); Density: 7.3 persons per square mile (2000); Age: 22.2% under 18, 21.1% over 64 (2000); Marriage status: 18.9% never married, 66.9% now married, 6.4% widowed, 7.7% divorced (2000); Foreign born: 0.9% (2000); Ancestry (includes multiple ancestries): 45.5% German, 13.3% Polish, 12.2% Irish, 9.6% French (except Basque), 7.3% English (2000).
Economy: Employment by occupation: 7.1% management, 18.2% professional, 14.4% services, 19.7% sales, 3.8% farming, 9.1% construction, 27.6% production (2000).
Income: Per capita income: $16,224 (2000); Median household income: $31,413 (2000); Poverty rate: 9.1% (2000).
Taxes: Total city taxes per capita: $51 (1997); City property taxes per capita: $45 (1997).
Education: High school graduation rate: 77.4% (2000); College graduation rate: 12.8% (2000).
Housing: Homeownership rate: 88.4% (2000); Median home value: $85,400 (2000); Median rent: $355 per month (2000); Median age of housing: 23 years (2000).
Transportation: Commute to work: 85.5% car, 0.0% public transportation, 5.5% walk, 7.0% work from home (2000); Travel time to work: 40.7% less than 15 minutes, 19.2% 15 to 30 minutes, 19.5% 30 to 45 minutes, 6.8% 45 to 60 minutes, 13.7% 60 minutes or more (2000)

Lincoln County

Located in north central Wisconsin; drained by the Wisconsin River. Covers a land area of 883.30 square miles, a water area of 23.70 square miles, and is located in the Central Time Zone. The county government was organized in 1874. County seat is Merrill.

Weather Station: Merrill — Elevation: 1,250 feet

	Jan	Feb	Mar	Apr	May	Jun	Jul	Aug	Sep	Oct	Nov	Dec
High	21	28	38	54	68	76	80	78	68	56	39	26
Low	-1	4	16	30	41	51	55	53	44	33	22	8
Precip	1.1	0.9	1.8	2.6	3.3	3.7	3.9	4.3	4.3	2.7	2.4	1.4
Snow	na	6.7	na	2.5	tr	0.0	0.0	0.0	tr	0.6	6.4	11.4

High and Low temperatures in degrees Fahrenheit; Precipitation and Snow in inches

Population: 29,641 (2000); Race: 97.4% White, 0.4% Black, 0.5% Asian, 0.6% American Indian and Alaska Native, 1.0% Hispanic of any race, 0.7% two or more races (2000); Density: 33.6 persons per square mile (2000); Age: 25.5% under 18, 16.3% over 64 (2000).
Religion: Five largest groups: 23.0% Catholic Church, 20.3% Lutheran Church—Missouri Synod, 10.1% Evangelical Lutheran Church in America, 5.2% United Church of Christ, 3.1% Wisconsin Evangelical Lutheran Synod (2000).
Economy: Unemployment rate: 5.3% (11/2002); Total civilian labor force: 14,559 (11/2002); Leading industries: 34.3% manufacturing; 16.3% retail trade; 10.8% health care and social assistance (2000); Companies that employ more than 1,000 persons: 0 (2000); Companies that employ more than 100

persons: 16 (2000); Farms: 425 totaling 83,918 acres (1997); Minority business ownership rate: 0.0% (1997); Women business ownership rate: 18.9% (1997); Retail sales per capita: $7,452 (1997). Single-family building permits issued: 203 (2001) / 211 (2000); Multi-family building permits issued: 10 (2001) / 8 (2000).
Income: Per capita income: $17,940 (2000); Median household income: $39,120 (2000); Poverty rate: 6.9% (2000); Bankruptcy rate: 2.50% (2001).
Taxes: Total county taxes per capita: $302 (2000); County property taxes per capita: $246 (2000).
Education: High school graduation rate: 81.6% (2000); College graduation rate: 13.6% (2000).
Housing: Homeownership rate: 78.3% (2000); Median home value: $86,500 (2000); Median rent: $363 per month (2000); Median age of housing: 37 years (2000).
Health: Birth rate: 102.9 per 10,000 population (1998); Age adjusted death rate: 89.2 per 10,000 population (1999); Age adjusted cancer mortality rate: 214.1 deaths per 100,000 population (1999). Number of physicians: 10.5 per 10,000 population (1999); Number of hospital beds: 21.3 per 10,000 population (1999).
Elections: 2000 Presidential election results: 46.8% Gore, 47.2% Bush, 3.6% Nader, 1.8% Buchanan
National and State Parks: Council Grounds State Park; Kings Springs State Public Fishery Area; New Wood State Public Hunting Grounds; Pays Springs State Public Fishery Area; Prairie River State Fishery Area; Spring Lake State Public Hunting and Fishing Area
Additional Information Contacts
Lincoln County Government Offices 715-536-0312
Merrill Chamber of Commerce 715-536-9474
Tomahawk Chamber of Commerce 715-453-5334
Woodland Lakes Association of Realtors 715-453-5566

Lincoln County Communities

BIRCH (town). Covers a land area of 35.761 square miles and a water area of 0.352 square miles. Located at 45.34° N. Lat.; 89.63° W. Long.
Population: 801 (2000); Race: 74.2% White, 10.5% Black, 3.9% Asian, 2.2% American Indian and Alaska Native, 6.0% Hispanic of any race, 6.0% two or more races (2000); Density: 22.4 persons per square mile (2000); Age: 54.5% under 18, 5.3% over 64 (2000); Marriage status: 10.6% never married, 80.5% now married, 3.6% widowed, 5.2% divorced (2000); Foreign born: 0.5% (2000); Ancestry (includes multiple ancestries): 41.0% German, 9.1% Other groups, 6.9% Polish, 5.0% Swedish, 4.6% Irish (2000).
Economy: Employment by occupation: 4.5% management, 18.1% professional, 9.9% services, 22.6% sales, 0.8% farming, 14.0% construction, 30.0% production (2000).
Income: Per capita income: $11,074 (2000); Median household income: $41,442 (2000); Poverty rate: 9.5% (2000).
Education: High school graduation rate: 74.1% (2000); College graduation rate: 10.8% (2000).
Housing: Homeownership rate: 96.1% (2000); Median home value: $73,800 (2000); Median rent: $338 per month (2000); Median age of housing: 31 years (2000).
Transportation: Commute to work: 96.7% car, 0.8% public transportation, 0.0% walk, 2.1% work from home (2000); Travel time to work: 14.0% less than 15 minutes, 48.3% 15 to 30 minutes, 29.2% 30 to 45 minutes, 7.2% 45 to 60 minutes, 1.3% 60 minutes or more (2000)

BRADLEY (town). Covers a land area of 55.732 square miles and a water area of 7.831 square miles. Located at 45.49° N. Lat.; 89.72° W. Long. Elevation is 1,458 feet.
Population: 2,573 (2000); Race: 98.5% White, 0.0% Black, 0.2% Asian, 0.0% American Indian and Alaska Native, 0.5% Hispanic of any race, 0.9% two or more races (2000); Density: 46.2 persons per square mile (2000); Age: 22.2% under 18, 20.1% over 64 (2000); Marriage status: 17.9% never married, 66.6% now married, 8.3% widowed, 7.3% divorced (2000); Foreign born: 1.4% (2000); Ancestry (includes multiple ancestries): 49.0% German, 12.2% Irish, 9.4% Norwegian, 8.7% Polish, 8.1% French (except Basque) (2000).
Economy: Employment by occupation: 9.0% management, 13.7% professional, 16.5% services, 20.4% sales, 1.0% farming, 15.8% construction, 23.5% production (2000).
Income: Per capita income: $19,803 (2000); Median household income: $38,676 (2000); Poverty rate: 5.5% (2000).
Taxes: Total city taxes per capita: $152 (2000); City property taxes per capita: $148 (2000).
Education: High school graduation rate: 87.7% (2000); College graduation rate: 12.6% (2000).
Housing: Homeownership rate: 90.6% (2000); Median home value: $119,100 (2000); Median rent: $408 per month (2000); Median age of housing: 30 years (2000).
Transportation: Commute to work: 93.8% car, 0.5% public transportation, 1.2% walk, 4.0% work from home (2000); Travel time to work: 42.6% less than 15 minutes, 29.8% 15 to 30 minutes, 15.4% 30 to 45 minutes, 6.3% 45 to 60 minutes, 5.8% 60 minutes or more (2000)

CORNING (town). Covers a land area of 146.511 square miles and a water area of 0.085 square miles. Located at 45.19° N. Lat.; 89.90° W. Long.
Population: 826 (2000); Race: 99.4% White, 0.0% Black, 0.2% Asian, 0.0% American Indian and Alaska Native, 0.6% Hispanic of any race, 0.0% two or more races (2000); Density: 5.6 persons per square mile (2000); Age: 26.4% under 18, 10.4% over 64 (2000); Marriage status: 21.9% never married, 67.5% now married, 4.7% widowed, 5.9% divorced (2000); Foreign born: 1.4% (2000); Ancestry (includes multiple ancestries): 69.2% German, 7.8% Polish, 6.1% United States or American, 4.0% English, 3.8% Irish (2000).
Economy: Employment by occupation: 22.3% management, 11.3% professional, 4.9% services, 17.5% sales, 2.1% farming, 11.8% construction, 30.1% production (2000).
Income: Per capita income: $19,225 (2000); Median household income: $48,224 (2000); Poverty rate: 4.4% (2000).
Taxes: Total city taxes per capita: $66 (1997); City property taxes per capita: $65 (1997).
Education: High school graduation rate: 78.7% (2000); College graduation rate: 9.6% (2000).
Housing: Homeownership rate: 91.2% (2000); Median home value: $90,400 (2000); Median rent: $308 per month (2000); Median age of housing: 41 years (2000).
Transportation: Commute to work: 82.9% car, 0.0% public transportation, 2.9% walk, 14.2% work from home (2000); Travel time to work: 14.8% less than 15 minutes, 50.4% 15 to 30 minutes, 20.0% 30 to 45 minutes, 8.8% 45 to 60 minutes, 6.1% 60 minutes or more (2000)

GLEASON (unincorporated postal area, zip code 54435). Covers a land area of 231.117 square miles and a water area of 3.780 square miles. Located at 45.37° N. Lat.; 89.43° W. Long. Elevation is 1,470 feet.
Population: 2,169 (2000); Race: 98.3% White, 0.0% Black, 0.0% Asian, 0.0% American Indian and Alaska Native, 1.2% Hispanic of any race, 1.5% two or more races (2000); Density: 9.4 persons per square mile (2000); Age: 23.7% under 18, 15.0% over 64 (2000); Marriage status: 21.3% never married, 64.9% now married, 5.8% widowed, 8.1% divorced (2000); Foreign born: 1.2% (2000); Ancestry (includes multiple ancestries): 53.9% German, 12.8% Irish, 8.6% Polish, 6.1% Norwegian, 6.0% United States or American (2000).
Economy: Employment by occupation: 9.1% management, 11.3% professional, 11.8% services, 22.7% sales, 3.3% farming, 14.4% construction, 27.4% production (2000).
Income: Per capita income: $17,575 (2000); Median household income: $38,818 (2000); Poverty rate: 6.4% (2000).
Education: High school graduation rate: 77.1% (2000); College graduation rate: 8.8% (2000).
Housing: Homeownership rate: 89.7% (2000); Median home value: $84,700 (2000); Median rent: $300 per month (2000); Median age of housing: 34 years (2000).
Transportation: Commute to work: 88.6% car, 0.0% public transportation, 2.9% walk, 7.4% work from home (2000); Travel time to work: 13.0% less than 15 minutes, 42.1% 15 to 30 minutes, 30.1% 30 to 45 minutes, 10.4% 45 to 60 minutes, 4.3% 60 minutes or more (2000)

HARDING (town). Covers a land area of 72.105 square miles and a water area of 0.704 square miles. Located at 45.26° N. Lat.; 89.85° W. Long.
Population: 334 (2000); Race: 100.0% White, 0.0% Black, 0.0% Asian, 0.0% American Indian and Alaska Native, 0.0% Hispanic of any race, 0.0% two or more races (2000); Density: 4.6 persons per square mile (2000); Age: 22.8% under 18, 9.2% over 64 (2000); Marriage status: 16.4% never married, 77.5% now married, 1.6% widowed, 4.5% divorced (2000); Foreign born: 1.7% (2000); Ancestry (includes multiple ancestries): 65.3% German, 6.6% Irish, 5.6% Polish, 5.0% English, 5.0% Norwegian (2000).
Economy: Employment by occupation: 14.9% management, 14.9% professional, 9.8% services, 27.6% sales, 4.6% farming, 6.3% construction, 21.8% production (2000).
Income: Per capita income: $19,933 (2000); Median household income: $43,250 (2000); Poverty rate: 6.9% (2000).

Taxes: Total city taxes per capita: $104 (1997); City property taxes per capita: $104 (1997).
Education: High school graduation rate: 80.5% (2000); College graduation rate: 10.7% (2000).
Housing: Homeownership rate: 96.7% (2000); Median home value: $111,600 (2000); Median rent: $375 per month (2000); Median age of housing: 30 years (2000).
Transportation: Commute to work: 93.0% car, 1.2% public transportation, 1.7% walk, 3.5% work from home (2000); Travel time to work: 9.0% less than 15 minutes, 45.8% 15 to 30 minutes, 28.3% 30 to 45 minutes, 12.0% 45 to 60 minutes, 4.8% 60 minutes or more (2000)

HARRISON (town). Covers a land area of 69.452 square miles and a water area of 2.913 square miles. Located at 45.48° N. Lat.; 89.50° W. Long. Elevation is 596 feet.
Population: 793 (2000); Race: 99.1% White, 0.0% Black, 0.0% Asian, 0.4% American Indian and Alaska Native, 0.7% Hispanic of any race, 0.5% two or more races (2000); Density: 11.4 persons per square mile (2000); Age: 24.4% under 18, 15.0% over 64 (2000); Marriage status: 17.3% never married, 70.1% now married, 5.1% widowed, 7.4% divorced (2000); Foreign born: 1.6% (2000); Ancestry (includes multiple ancestries): 47.9% German, 13.6% Dutch, 12.0% Irish, 10.3% Norwegian, 9.3% Polish (2000).
Economy: Employment by occupation: 8.1% management, 20.7% professional, 12.4% services, 24.7% sales, 1.0% farming, 16.2% construction, 16.9% production (2000).
Income: Per capita income: $19,463 (2000); Median household income: $42,500 (2000); Poverty rate: 7.5% (2000).
Taxes: Total city taxes per capita: $58 (1997); City property taxes per capita: $57 (1997).
Education: High school graduation rate: 85.9% (2000); College graduation rate: 11.8% (2000).
Housing: Homeownership rate: 88.6% (2000); Median home value: $104,000 (2000); Median rent: $413 per month (2000); Median age of housing: 32 years (2000).
Transportation: Commute to work: 93.4% car, 0.0% public transportation, 1.0% walk, 4.0% work from home (2000); Travel time to work: 13.4% less than 15 minutes, 59.7% 15 to 30 minutes, 19.7% 30 to 45 minutes, 4.2% 45 to 60 minutes, 2.9% 60 minutes or more (2000)

IRMA (unincorporated postal area, zip code 54442). Covers a land area of 58.618 square miles and a water area of 0.561 square miles. Located at 45.34° N. Lat.; 89.67° W. Long. Elevation is 1,550 feet.
Population: 1,242 (2000); Race: 84.1% White, 6.6% Black, 2.6% Asian, 1.4% American Indian and Alaska Native, 3.4% Hispanic of any race, 3.6% two or more races (2000); Density: 21.2 persons per square mile (2000); Age: 46.3% under 18, 8.0% over 64 (2000); Marriage status: 13.9% never married, 74.8% now married, 3.7% widowed, 7.6% divorced (2000); Foreign born: 0.8% (2000); Ancestry (includes multiple ancestries): 44.6% German, 6.1% Other groups, 5.6% Irish, 5.4% Polish, 4.8% Swedish (2000).
Economy: Employment by occupation: 7.6% management, 17.0% professional, 10.6% services, 22.1% sales, 1.6% farming, 9.4% construction, 31.7% production (2000).
Income: Per capita income: $13,450 (2000); Median household income: $43,125 (2000); Poverty rate: 7.9% (2000).
Education: High school graduation rate: 82.5% (2000); College graduation rate: 12.0% (2000).
Housing: Homeownership rate: 88.7% (2000); Median home value: $87,100 (2000); Median rent: $350 per month (2000); Median age of housing: 35 years (2000).
Transportation: Commute to work: 96.1% car, 0.6% public transportation, 1.4% walk, 1.9% work from home (2000); Travel time to work: 16.6% less than 15 minutes, 51.1% 15 to 30 minutes, 23.9% 30 to 45 minutes, 5.5% 45 to 60 minutes, 2.9% 60 minutes or more (2000)

KING (town). Covers a land area of 33.873 square miles and a water area of 3.042 square miles. Located at 45.49° N. Lat.; 89.62° W. Long.
Population: 842 (2000); Race: 98.6% White, 0.0% Black, 0.5% Asian, 0.0% American Indian and Alaska Native, 0.5% Hispanic of any race, 0.9% two or more races (2000); Density: 24.9 persons per square mile (2000); Age: 18.5% under 18, 22.8% over 64 (2000); Marriage status: 15.0% never married, 69.9% now married, 7.4% widowed, 7.7% divorced (2000); Foreign born: 2.4% (2000); Ancestry (includes multiple ancestries): 46.8% German, 8.2% Polish, 7.8% Irish, 6.0% English, 5.1% Swedish (2000).
Economy: Employment by occupation: 9.7% management, 15.5% professional, 19.4% services, 23.8% sales, 3.6% farming, 12.7% construction, 15.2% production (2000).
Income: Per capita income: $18,549 (2000); Median household income: $37,500 (2000); Poverty rate: 5.1% (2000).
Taxes: Total city taxes per capita: $46 (1997); City property taxes per capita: $44 (1997).
Education: High school graduation rate: 82.2% (2000); College graduation rate: 16.8% (2000).
Housing: Homeownership rate: 90.7% (2000); Median home value: $107,200 (2000); Median rent: $431 per month (2000); Median age of housing: 24 years (2000).
Transportation: Commute to work: 90.4% car, 0.6% public transportation, 0.0% walk, 9.1% work from home (2000); Travel time to work: 34.0% less than 15 minutes, 32.7% 15 to 30 minutes, 15.3% 30 to 45 minutes, 10.0% 45 to 60 minutes, 8.1% 60 minutes or more (2000)

MERRILL (city). Covers a land area of 7.038 square miles and a water area of 0.493 square miles. Located at 45.18° N. Lat.; 89.69° W. Long. Elevation is 1,280 feet.
History: Merrill was settled by Andrew Warren, Jr., who built a sawmill here in the 1840's, at the junction of the Prairie and Wisconsin Rivers. The site was first called Jenny Bull Falls, then Jenny, and finally Merrill for S.S. Merrill, general manager of the Wisconsin Valley Railroad that arrived in 1874. More mills sprang up along the rivers. The biggest log jam in early Wisconsin history occurred a few miles above Merrill on the Wisconsin River, when 80 million feet of timber piled up, damming the river for miles. It was finally broken by blasting.
Population: 10,146 (2000); Race: 96.9% White, 0.3% Black, 0.4% Asian, 1.0% American Indian and Alaska Native, 1.5% Hispanic of any race, 0.7% two or more races (2000); Density: 1,441.7 persons per square mile (2000); Age: 25.0% under 18, 20.0% over 64 (2000); Marriage status: 22.6% never married, 56.4% now married, 10.6% widowed, 10.4% divorced (2000); Foreign born: 2.0% (2000); Ancestry (includes multiple ancestries): 54.9% German, 8.7% Irish, 8.1% Polish, 6.2% Norwegian, 6.1% French (except Basque) (2000).
Economy: Single-family building permits issued: 11 (2001) / 14 (2000); Multi-family building permits issued: 4 (2001) / 8 (2000); Employment by occupation: 7.8% management, 13.5% professional, 13.6% services, 28.8% sales, 0.4% farming, 4.7% construction, 31.1% production (2000).
Income: Per capita income: $17,429 (2000); Median household income: $33,098 (2000); Poverty rate: 9.5% (2000).
Taxes: Total city taxes per capita: $304 (2000); City property taxes per capita: $281 (2000).
Education: High school graduation rate: 78.8% (2000); College graduation rate: 14.2% (2000).

School District(s)

Merrill Area (PK-12)
2000 Enrollment: 3,442 715-536-4581
Housing: Homeownership rate: 65.4% (2000); Median home value: $76,100 (2000); Median rent: $364 per month (2000); Median age of housing: 53 years (2000).
Hospitals: Good Samaritan Health Center (73 beds)
Safety: Violent crime rate: 11.7 per 10,000 population; Property crime rate: 438.4 per 10,000 population (2001).
Newspapers: Merrill Foto News (1 x week)
Transportation: Commute to work: 91.1% car, 1.0% public transportation, 4.4% walk, 2.6% work from home (2000); Travel time to work: 60.9% less than 15 minutes, 21.9% 15 to 30 minutes, 12.8% 30 to 45 minutes, 2.7% 45 to 60 minutes, 1.7% 60 minutes or more (2000)
Additional Information Contacts
Merrill Chamber of Commerce 715-536-9474

MERRILL (town). Covers a land area of 52.052 square miles and a water area of 1.306 square miles. Located at 45.22° N. Lat.; 89.68° W. Long. Elevation is 1,280 feet.
History: Settled c.1847, Merrill grew as lumbering town; incorporated 1883.
Population: 2,979 (2000); Race: 98.8% White, 0.0% Black, 0.2% Asian, 0.9% American Indian and Alaska Native, 0.3% Hispanic of any race, 0.2% two or more races (2000); Density: 57.2 persons per square mile (2000); Age: 26.8% under 18, 9.9% over 64 (2000); Marriage status: 19.4% never married, 69.5% now married, 4.0% widowed, 7.2% divorced (2000); Foreign born: 0.9% (2000); Ancestry (includes multiple ancestries): 63.7% German, 9.2% Polish, 9.1% Norwegian, 7.5% Irish, 5.0% Italian (2000).
Economy: In dairying and farming area. Manufacturing: paper and paper goods, apparel, wood products, wire products, fabricated metal products, consumer goods, shoes, furniture, textiles, beverages. Employment by occupation: 8.5% management, 17.2% professional, 10.7% services, 26.8% sales, 0.6% farming, 8.8% construction, 27.3% production (2000).

Income: Per capita income: $18,677 (2000); Median household income: $48,875 (2000); Poverty rate: 2.8% (2000).
Taxes: Total city taxes per capita: $15 (1997); City property taxes per capita: $9 (1997).
Education: High school graduation rate: 84.6% (2000); College graduation rate: 14.6% (2000).
Housing: Homeownership rate: 92.0% (2000); Median home value: $101,100 (2000); Median rent: $368 per month (2000); Median age of housing: 27 years (2000).
Transportation: Commute to work: 94.5% car, 0.3% public transportation, 1.2% walk, 3.7% work from home (2000); Travel time to work: 44.8% less than 15 minutes, 35.3% 15 to 30 minutes, 15.0% 30 to 45 minutes, 3.3% 45 to 60 minutes, 1.6% 60 minutes or more (2000)

PINE RIVER (town). Covers a land area of 63.953 square miles and a water area of 0.302 square miles. Located at 45.16° N. Lat.; 89.57° W. Long. Elevation is 1,250 feet.
Population: 1,877 (2000); Race: 98.5% White, 0.3% Black, 0.2% Asian, 0.5% American Indian and Alaska Native, 0.2% Hispanic of any race, 0.5% two or more races (2000); Density: 29.3 persons per square mile (2000); Age: 29.1% under 18, 8.9% over 64 (2000); Marriage status: 19.1% never married, 71.1% now married, 2.7% widowed, 7.1% divorced (2000); Foreign born: 1.3% (2000); Ancestry (includes multiple ancestries): 67.5% German, 9.2% Norwegian, 8.0% Polish, 5.6% French (except Basque), 5.4% Irish (2000).
Economy: Employment by occupation: 12.4% management, 12.2% professional, 12.3% services, 22.8% sales, 2.4% farming, 10.6% construction, 27.4% production (2000).
Income: Per capita income: $18,449 (2000); Median household income: $47,723 (2000); Poverty rate: 4.7% (2000).
Taxes: Total city taxes per capita: $97 (1997); City property taxes per capita: $90 (1997).
Education: High school graduation rate: 85.8% (2000); College graduation rate: 14.0% (2000).
Housing: Homeownership rate: 90.5% (2000); Median home value: $103,600 (2000); Median rent: $369 per month (2000); Median age of housing: 26 years (2000).
Transportation: Commute to work: 92.3% car, 0.3% public transportation, 0.3% walk, 6.3% work from home (2000); Travel time to work: 34.3% less than 15 minutes, 43.9% 15 to 30 minutes, 14.9% 30 to 45 minutes, 4.2% 45 to 60 minutes, 2.6% 60 minutes or more (2000)

ROCK FALLS (town). Covers a land area of 47.784 square miles and a water area of 1.429 square miles. Located at 45.30° N. Lat.; 89.72° W. Long.
Population: 598 (2000); Race: 98.1% White, 0.3% Black, 0.3% Asian, 0.3% American Indian and Alaska Native, 1.2% Hispanic of any race, 0.0% two or more races (2000); Density: 12.5 persons per square mile (2000); Age: 23.0% under 18, 12.5% over 64 (2000); Marriage status: 18.0% never married, 73.2% now married, 3.4% widowed, 5.3% divorced (2000); Foreign born: 0.3% (2000); Ancestry (includes multiple ancestries): 50.8% German, 10.4% Polish, 9.0% English, 8.2% French (except Basque), 6.8% Other groups (2000).
Economy: Single-family building permits issued: 11 (2001) / 0 (2000); Multi-family building permits issued: 0 (2001) / 0 (2000); Employment by occupation: 7.3% management, 13.9% professional, 10.9% services, 24.2% sales, 1.8% farming, 10.0% construction, 32.0% production (2000).
Income: Per capita income: $18,865 (2000); Median household income: $46,875 (2000); Poverty rate: 2.6% (2000).
Taxes: Total city taxes per capita: $100 (1997); City property taxes per capita: $100 (1997).
Education: High school graduation rate: 85.0% (2000); College graduation rate: 15.7% (2000).
Housing: Homeownership rate: 93.3% (2000); Median home value: $95,300 (2000); Median rent: $335 per month (2000); Median age of housing: 29 years (2000).
Transportation: Commute to work: 92.6% car, 0.9% public transportation, 0.6% walk, 5.8% work from home (2000); Travel time to work: 12.7% less than 15 minutes, 45.9% 15 to 30 minutes, 27.4% 30 to 45 minutes, 8.8% 45 to 60 minutes, 5.2% 60 minutes or more (2000)

RUSSELL (town). Covers a land area of 36.160 square miles and a water area of 0.153 square miles. Located at 45.32° N. Lat.; 89.47° W. Long.
Population: 693 (2000); Race: 98.4% White, 0.0% Black, 0.0% Asian, 0.0% American Indian and Alaska Native, 0.0% Hispanic of any race, 1.3% two or more races (2000); Density: 19.2 persons per square mile (2000); Age: 27.0% under 18, 13.0% over 64 (2000); Marriage status: 22.3% never married, 62.7% now married, 6.5% widowed, 8.5% divorced (2000); Foreign born: 1.0% (2000); Ancestry (includes multiple ancestries): 56.8% German, 9.8% Irish, 7.4% United States or American, 6.7% English, 6.6% Polish (2000).
Economy: Employment by occupation: 6.6% management, 6.9% professional, 12.3% services, 22.3% sales, 4.2% farming, 13.6% construction, 34.0% production (2000).
Income: Per capita income: $17,875 (2000); Median household income: $42,500 (2000); Poverty rate: 3.1% (2000).
Taxes: Total city taxes per capita: $41 (1997); City property taxes per capita: $39 (1997).
Education: High school graduation rate: 78.6% (2000); College graduation rate: 5.0% (2000).
Housing: Homeownership rate: 86.6% (2000); Median home value: $67,500 (2000); Median rent: $233 per month (2000); Median age of housing: 41 years (2000).
Transportation: Commute to work: 93.4% car, 0.0% public transportation, 2.4% walk, 4.2% work from home (2000); Travel time to work: 9.1% less than 15 minutes, 40.3% 15 to 30 minutes, 31.4% 30 to 45 minutes, 16.4% 45 to 60 minutes, 2.8% 60 minutes or more (2000)

SCHLEY (town). Covers a land area of 48.292 square miles and a water area of 0.052 square miles. Located at 45.26° N. Lat.; 89.52° W. Long.
Population: 909 (2000); Race: 98.2% White, 0.0% Black, 0.0% Asian, 0.0% American Indian and Alaska Native, 2.3% Hispanic of any race, 1.5% two or more races (2000); Density: 18.8 persons per square mile (2000); Age: 23.0% under 18, 9.4% over 64 (2000); Marriage status: 22.9% never married, 62.9% now married, 4.6% widowed, 9.5% divorced (2000); Foreign born: 0.7% (2000); Ancestry (includes multiple ancestries): 50.1% German, 10.7% Irish, 6.9% Polish, 6.0% English, 5.4% Swedish (2000).
Economy: Employment by occupation: 15.8% management, 11.5% professional, 9.2% services, 21.8% sales, 2.6% farming, 16.9% construction, 22.2% production (2000).
Income: Per capita income: $17,460 (2000); Median household income: $40,703 (2000); Poverty rate: 6.5% (2000).
Taxes: Total city taxes per capita: $23 (1997); City property taxes per capita: $22 (1997).
Education: High school graduation rate: 76.5% (2000); College graduation rate: 12.0% (2000).
Housing: Homeownership rate: 91.1% (2000); Median home value: $79,100 (2000); Median rent: $375 per month (2000); Median age of housing: 37 years (2000).
Transportation: Commute to work: 86.2% car, 0.0% public transportation, 4.0% walk, 9.4% work from home (2000); Travel time to work: 11.9% less than 15 minutes, 48.2% 15 to 30 minutes, 30.6% 30 to 45 minutes, 4.5% 45 to 60 minutes, 4.9% 60 minutes or more (2000)

SCOTT (town). Covers a land area of 30.171 square miles and a water area of 0.479 square miles. Located at 45.16° N. Lat.; 89.72° W. Long.
Population: 1,287 (2000); Race: 98.5% White, 0.2% Black, 0.3% Asian, 0.0% American Indian and Alaska Native, 0.2% Hispanic of any race, 1.0% two or more races (2000); Density: 42.7 persons per square mile (2000); Age: 24.9% under 18, 10.5% over 64 (2000); Marriage status: 21.9% never married, 69.3% now married, 4.7% widowed, 4.2% divorced (2000); Foreign born: 2.1% (2000); Ancestry (includes multiple ancestries): 66.1% German, 6.7% Polish, 6.4% Norwegian, 5.9% Irish, 4.8% French (except Basque) (2000).
Economy: Employment by occupation: 11.3% management, 12.2% professional, 12.2% services, 22.8% sales, 1.7% farming, 10.5% construction, 29.3% production (2000).
Income: Per capita income: $19,759 (2000); Median household income: $50,441 (2000); Poverty rate: 4.6% (2000).
Taxes: Total city taxes per capita: $89 (1997); City property taxes per capita: $87 (1997).
Education: High school graduation rate: 79.3% (2000); College graduation rate: 10.7% (2000).
Housing: Homeownership rate: 88.7% (2000); Median home value: $98,100 (2000); Median rent: $405 per month (2000); Median age of housing: 29 years (2000).
Transportation: Commute to work: 88.9% car, 0.8% public transportation, 2.5% walk, 7.6% work from home (2000); Travel time to work: 41.7% less than 15 minutes, 43.0% 15 to 30 minutes, 12.1% 30 to 45 minutes, 2.4% 45 to 60 minutes, 0.8% 60 minutes or more (2000)

SKANAWAN (town). Covers a land area of 35.387 square miles and a water area of 0.529 square miles. Located at 45.41° N. Lat.; 89.62° W. Long.
Population: 354 (2000); Race: 100.0% White, 0.0% Black, 0.0% Asian, 0.0% American Indian and Alaska Native, 0.0% Hispanic of any race, 0.0%

two or more races (2000); Density: 10.0 persons per square mile (2000); Age: 27.3% under 18, 13.7% over 64 (2000); Marriage status: 21.6% never married, 59.8% now married, 4.5% widowed, 14.1% divorced (2000); Foreign born: 1.6% (2000); Ancestry (includes multiple ancestries): 51.7% German, 15.8% Irish, 8.6% Swedish, 7.5% Norwegian, 5.4% United States or American (2000).
Economy: Employment by occupation: 7.8% management, 11.7% professional, 17.0% services, 20.9% sales, 1.0% farming, 12.6% construction, 29.1% production (2000).
Income: Per capita income: $17,698 (2000); Median household income: $41,458 (2000); Poverty rate: 3.5% (2000).
Taxes: Total city taxes per capita: $40 (1997); City property taxes per capita: $40 (1997).
Education: High school graduation rate: 82.7% (2000); College graduation rate: 7.0% (2000).
Housing: Homeownership rate: 94.4% (2000); Median home value: $108,900 (2000); Median rent: $242 per month (2000); Median age of housing: 29 years (2000).
Transportation: Commute to work: 89.6% car, 0.5% public transportation, 2.5% walk, 7.4% work from home (2000); Travel time to work: 29.9% less than 15 minutes, 46.5% 15 to 30 minutes, 15.5% 30 to 45 minutes, 4.8% 45 to 60 minutes, 3.2% 60 minutes or more (2000)

SOMO (town). Covers a land area of 36.352 square miles and a water area of 0.005 square miles. Located at 45.51° N. Lat.; 90.00° W. Long.
Population: 121 (2000); Race: 100.0% White, 0.0% Black, 0.0% Asian, 0.0% American Indian and Alaska Native, 0.0% Hispanic of any race, 0.0% two or more races (2000); Density: 3.3 persons per square mile (2000); Age: 23.4% under 18, 24.1% over 64 (2000); Marriage status: 13.5% never married, 73.9% now married, 5.4% widowed, 7.2% divorced (2000); Foreign born: 0.0% (2000); Ancestry (includes multiple ancestries): 56.7% German, 14.9% Polish, 13.5% Swedish, 11.3% Norwegian, 7.1% French (except Basque) (2000).
Economy: Employment by occupation: 6.5% management, 8.7% professional, 26.1% services, 15.2% sales, 0.0% farming, 17.4% construction, 26.1% production (2000).
Income: Per capita income: $19,374 (2000); Median household income: $22,250 (2000); Poverty rate: 18.4% (2000).
Taxes: Total city taxes per capita: $54 (1997); City property taxes per capita: $54 (1997).
Education: High school graduation rate: 91.1% (2000); College graduation rate: 6.9% (2000).
Housing: Homeownership rate: 85.2% (2000); Median home value: $56,700 (2000); Median rent: $325 per month (2000); Median age of housing: 40 years (2000).
Transportation: Commute to work: 87.8% car, 0.0% public transportation, 4.9% walk, 7.3% work from home (2000); Travel time to work: 18.4% less than 15 minutes, 15.8% 15 to 30 minutes, 34.2% 30 to 45 minutes, 15.8% 45 to 60 minutes, 15.8% 60 minutes or more (2000)

TOMAHAWK (city). Covers a land area of 7.438 square miles and a water area of 1.399 square miles. Located at 45.47° N. Lat.; 89.73° W. Long. Elevation is 1,450 feet.
History: Tomahawk began as a tavern outpost, operated by Germain Bouchard and called Tomahawk because the shape of a nearby lake resembled an axe blade. The settlement grew with the arrival of the railroad in 1886 and the opening of a sawmill.
Population: 3,770 (2000); Race: 98.7% White, 0.0% Black, 0.9% Asian, 0.2% American Indian and Alaska Native, 0.6% Hispanic of any race, 0.0% two or more races (2000); Density: 506.8 persons per square mile (2000); Age: 24.2% under 18, 20.2% over 64 (2000); Marriage status: 19.4% never married, 62.2% now married, 9.7% widowed, 8.7% divorced (2000); Foreign born: 1.7% (2000); Ancestry (includes multiple ancestries): 49.7% German, 13.2% Irish, 10.4% Polish, 8.3% Norwegian, 6.1% French (except Basque) (2000).
Economy: Single-family building permits issued: 9 (2001) / 18 (2000); Multi-family building permits issued: 0 (2001) / 0 (2000); Employment by occupation: 7.5% management, 17.7% professional, 18.5% services, 25.6% sales, 1.0% farming, 8.3% construction, 21.3% production (2000).
Income: Per capita income: $17,277 (2000); Median household income: $33,986 (2000); Poverty rate: 7.9% (2000).
Taxes: Total city taxes per capita: $186 (1997); City property taxes per capita: $174 (1997).
Education: High school graduation rate: 82.4% (2000); College graduation rate: 17.4% (2000).

School District(s)

Tomahawk (PK-12)
2000 Enrollment: 1,715 715-453-5551

Housing: Homeownership rate: 63.5% (2000); Median home value: $79,600 (2000); Median rent: $360 per month (2000); Median age of housing: 45 years (2000).
Hospitals: Sacred Heart Hospital (25 beds)
Safety: Violent crime rate: 44.8 per 10,000 population; Property crime rate: 458.3 per 10,000 population (2001).
Newspapers: Tomahawk Leader (1 x week)
Transportation: Commute to work: 86.7% car, 0.0% public transportation, 8.8% walk, 3.0% work from home (2000); Travel time to work: 65.2% less than 15 minutes, 15.2% 15 to 30 minutes, 10.1% 30 to 45 minutes, 4.8% 45 to 60 minutes, 4.7% 60 minutes or more (2000)
Additional Information Contacts
Tomahawk Chamber of Commerce 715-453-5334
Woodland Lakes Association of Realtors 715-453-5566

TOMAHAWK (town). Covers a land area of 70.067 square miles and a water area of 1.502 square miles. Located at 45.44° N. Lat.; 89.91° W. Long. Elevation is 1,450 feet.
History: Plotted 1887, incorporated 1891.
Population: 439 (2000); Race: 99.1% White, 0.0% Black, 0.5% Asian, 0.0% American Indian and Alaska Native, 0.0% Hispanic of any race, 0.5% two or more races (2000); Density: 6.3 persons per square mile (2000); Age: 18.9% under 18, 14.4% over 64 (2000); Marriage status: 18.5% never married, 62.7% now married, 4.7% widowed, 14.1% divorced (2000); Foreign born: 1.2% (2000); Ancestry (includes multiple ancestries): 55.9% German, 10.4% Polish, 9.7% Irish, 9.4% Norwegian, 8.7% Swedish (2000).
Economy: Manufacturing includes metal fabrication, stainless steel vessels and tanks. Employment by occupation: 5.2% management, 12.2% professional, 21.6% services, 19.2% sales, 4.2% farming, 16.0% construction, 21.6% production (2000).
Income: Per capita income: $16,681 (2000); Median household income: $35,625 (2000); Poverty rate: 8.6% (2000).
Taxes: Total city taxes per capita: $36 (1997); City property taxes per capita: $34 (1997).
Education: High school graduation rate: 78.9% (2000); College graduation rate: 6.6% (2000).
Housing: Homeownership rate: 85.1% (2000); Median home value: $84,200 (2000); Median rent: $339 per month (2000); Median age of housing: 30 years (2000).
Transportation: Commute to work: 97.2% car, 0.0% public transportation, 0.0% walk, 0.9% work from home (2000); Travel time to work: 33.0% less than 15 minutes, 44.5% 15 to 30 minutes, 13.9% 30 to 45 minutes, 5.7% 45 to 60 minutes, 2.9% 60 minutes or more (2000)

WILSON (town). Covers a land area of 35.172 square miles and a water area of 1.174 square miles. Located at 45.51° N. Lat.; 89.85° W. Long.
Population: 299 (2000); Race: 95.4% White, 0.0% Black, 0.0% Asian, 0.0% American Indian and Alaska Native, 1.5% Hispanic of any race, 3.1% two or more races (2000); Density: 8.5 persons per square mile (2000); Age: 14.3% under 18, 30.9% over 64 (2000); Marriage status: 16.9% never married, 70.6% now married, 7.8% widowed, 4.8% divorced (2000); Foreign born: 0.0% (2000); Ancestry (includes multiple ancestries): 47.9% German, 16.2% Polish, 11.2% Irish, 8.5% Norwegian, 8.5% English (2000).
Economy: Employment by occupation: 7.6% management, 7.6% professional, 26.3% services, 22.0% sales, 1.7% farming, 12.7% construction, 22.0% production (2000).
Income: Per capita income: $16,103 (2000); Median household income: $32,750 (2000); Poverty rate: 13.1% (2000).
Taxes: Total city taxes per capita: $56 (1997); City property taxes per capita: $53 (1997).
Education: High school graduation rate: 80.6% (2000); College graduation rate: 7.6% (2000).
Housing: Homeownership rate: 100.0% (2000); Median home value: $87,900 (2000); Median age of housing: 31 years (2000).
Transportation: Commute to work: 91.2% car, 0.0% public transportation, 5.3% walk, 2.6% work from home (2000); Travel time to work: 22.5% less than 15 minutes, 44.1% 15 to 30 minutes, 13.5% 30 to 45 minutes, 10.8% 45 to 60 minutes, 9.0% 60 minutes or more (2000)

Manitowoc County

Located in eastern Wisconsin, partly on the Door Peninsula; bounded on the east by Lake Michigan; drained by the Manitowoc River. Covers a land area of 591.50 square miles, a water area of 902.30 square miles, and is located in the Central Time Zone. The county government was organized in 1836. County seat is Manitowoc.

Weather Station: Manitowoc Elevation: 659 feet

	Jan	Feb	Mar	Apr	May	Jun	Jul	Aug	Sep	Oct	Nov	Dec
High	26	30	39	52	65	75	80	78	70	57	44	32
Low	11	15	24	34	44	54	60	59	52	41	29	17
Precip	1.5	1.2	1.9	2.8	2.8	3.2	3.3	3.6	3.2	2.3	2.3	1.8
Snow	na	na	na	0.5	tr	0.0	0.0	0.0	0.0	tr	1.5	na

High and Low temperatures in degrees Fahrenheit; Precipitation and Snow in inches

Weather Station: Two Rivers Elevation: 597 feet

	Jan	Feb	Mar	Apr	May	Jun	Jul	Aug	Sep	Oct	Nov	Dec
High	26	30	38	49	60	69	75	75	67	55	43	31
Low	11	16	24	34	43	52	58	59	51	41	30	18
Precip	1.6	1.3	2.4	2.8	2.8	3.1	2.8	3.5	3.4	2.4	2.3	1.7
Snow	10.3	6.4	6.0	1.0	tr	0.0	0.0	0.0	0.0	tr	2.0	7.2

High and Low temperatures in degrees Fahrenheit; Precipitation and Snow in inches

Population: 82,887 (2000); Race: 95.9% White, 0.1% Black, 1.8% Asian, 0.5% American Indian and Alaska Native, 1.8% Hispanic of any race, 0.8% two or more races (2000); Density: 140.1 persons per square mile (2000); Age: 25.4% under 18, 15.6% over 64 (2000).
Religion: Five largest groups: 52.0% Catholic Church, 12.5% Wisconsin Evangelical Lutheran Synod, 5.0% Evangelical Lutheran Church in America, 3.8% United Church of Christ, 1.6% Lutheran Church—Missouri Synod (2000).
Economy: Unemployment rate: 5.7% (11/2002); Total civilian labor force: 46,157 (11/2002); Leading industries: 41.2% manufacturing; 12.3% retail trade; 11.9% health care and social assistance (2000); Companies that employ more than 1,000 persons: 3 (2000); Companies that employ more than 100 persons: 55 (2000); Farms: 1,227 totaling 244,864 acres (1997); Minority business ownership rate: 0.0% (1997); Women business ownership rate: 23.3% (1997); Retail sales per capita: $6,831 (1997). Single-family building permits issued: 344 (2001) / 369 (2000); Multi-family building permits issued: 280 (2001) / 99 (2000).
Income: Per capita income: $20,285 (2000); Median household income: $43,286 (2000); Poverty rate: 6.1% (2000); Bankruptcy rate: 2.85% (2001).
Taxes: Total county taxes per capita: $198 (2000); County property taxes per capita: $195 (2000).
Education: High school graduation rate: 84.6% (2000); College graduation rate: 15.5% (2000).
Housing: Homeownership rate: 76.0% (2000); Median home value: $90,900 (2000); Median rent: $375 per month (2000); Median age of housing: 44 years (2000).
Health: Birth rate: 111.2 per 10,000 population (1998); Age adjusted death rate: 81.5 per 10,000 population (1999); Age adjusted cancer mortality rate: 193.7 deaths per 100,000 population (1999). Air Quality Index: 73% good, 27% moderate, 0% unhealthy (percent of days in 2000). Number of physicians: 14.4 per 10,000 population (1999); Number of hospital beds: 37.2 per 10,000 population (1999).
Elections: 2000 Presidential election results: 45.5% Gore, 49.9% Bush, 3.4% Nader, 0.7% Buchanan
National and State Parks: Collins Marsh State Wildlife Management Area; Kiel Marsh State Wildlife Area; Killsnake State Wildlife Area; Point Beach State Forest; Two Creeks Buried State Forest
Additional Information Contacts
Manitowoc County Government Offices 920-683-4000
Kiel Area Association of Commerce 920-894-4638
Manitowoc Chamber of Commerce 262-684-5575
Manitowoc County Board of Realtors 262-682-6052

Manitowoc County Communities

CATO (town). Covers a land area of 35.129 square miles and a water area of 0.220 square miles. Located at 44.10° N. Lat.; 87.85° W. Long. Elevation is 863 feet.
Population: 1,616 (2000); Race: 96.0% White, 0.0% Black, 0.8% Asian, 1.6% American Indian and Alaska Native, 0.4% Hispanic of any race, 1.3% two or more races (2000); Density: 46.0 persons per square mile (2000); Age: 26.5% under 18, 10.5% over 64 (2000); Marriage status: 25.4% never married, 66.4% now married, 4.2% widowed, 3.9% divorced (2000); Foreign born: 0.5% (2000); Ancestry (includes multiple ancestries): 67.0% German, 15.0% Irish, 11.7% Czech, 8.0% Norwegian, 6.9% Polish (2000).
Economy: Employment by occupation: 11.8% management, 13.4% professional, 10.7% services, 17.7% sales, 4.6% farming, 14.7% construction, 27.1% production (2000).
Income: Per capita income: $21,434 (2000); Median household income: $53,462 (2000); Poverty rate: 4.9% (2000).
Taxes: Total city taxes per capita: $96 (1997); City property taxes per capita: $95 (1997).
Education: High school graduation rate: 87.0% (2000); College graduation rate: 15.7% (2000).
Housing: Homeownership rate: 89.9% (2000); Median home value: $115,600 (2000); Median rent: $392 per month (2000); Median age of housing: 45 years (2000).
Transportation: Commute to work: 89.0% car, 0.0% public transportation, 3.0% walk, 8.0% work from home (2000); Travel time to work: 29.5% less than 15 minutes, 53.4% 15 to 30 minutes, 10.0% 30 to 45 minutes, 3.6% 45 to 60 minutes, 3.5% 60 minutes or more (2000)

CENTERVILLE (town). Covers a land area of 23.817 square miles and a water area of 2.702 square miles. Located at 43.93° N. Lat.; 87.74° W. Long.
Population: 713 (2000); Race: 96.4% White, 0.0% Black, 0.6% Asian, 1.8% American Indian and Alaska Native, 0.8% Hispanic of any race, 1.2% two or more races (2000); Density: 29.9 persons per square mile (2000); Age: 27.9% under 18, 14.1% over 64 (2000); Marriage status: 29.0% never married, 63.3% now married, 3.7% widowed, 4.0% divorced (2000); Foreign born: 0.3% (2000); Ancestry (includes multiple ancestries): 67.7% German, 6.8% United States or American, 5.4% Other groups, 5.1% English, 4.6% Irish (2000).
Economy: Single-family building permits issued: 5 (2001) / 0 (2000); Multi-family building permits issued: 0 (2001) / 0 (2000); Employment by occupation: 14.6% management, 11.1% professional, 13.1% services, 14.3% sales, 8.5% farming, 10.3% construction, 28.1% production (2000).
Income: Per capita income: $18,638 (2000); Median household income: $58,750 (2000); Poverty rate: 2.1% (2000).
Taxes: Total city taxes per capita: $174 (1997); City property taxes per capita: $171 (1997).
Education: High school graduation rate: 84.8% (2000); College graduation rate: 12.4% (2000).
Housing: Homeownership rate: 89.9% (2000); Median home value: $97,400 (2000); Median rent: $330 per month (2000); Median age of housing: 60+ years (2000).
Transportation: Commute to work: 79.0% car, 1.3% public transportation, 7.1% walk, 12.7% work from home (2000); Travel time to work: 29.0% less than 15 minutes, 55.1% 15 to 30 minutes, 9.6% 30 to 45 minutes, 1.2% 45 to 60 minutes, 5.2% 60 minutes or more (2000)

CLEVELAND (village). Covers a land area of 2.034 square miles and a water area of 0 square miles. Located at 43.91° N. Lat.; 87.74° W. Long. Elevation is 640 feet.
Population: 1,361 (2000); Race: 98.8% White, 0.4% Black, 0.2% Asian, 0.0% American Indian and Alaska Native, 2.2% Hispanic of any race, 0.0% two or more races (2000); Density: 669.2 persons per square mile (2000); Age: 24.8% under 18, 10.6% over 64 (2000); Marriage status: 20.5% never married, 67.4% now married, 5.3% widowed, 6.7% divorced (2000); Foreign born: 1.3% (2000); Ancestry (includes multiple ancestries): 60.4% German, 6.6% Dutch, 5.7% United States or American, 5.5% Polish, 5.2% Irish (2000).
Economy: Dairying; grain, vegetables, fruit. Manufacturing: fiberglass reinforced plastic products. Single-family building permits issued: 5 (2001) / 8 (2000); Multi-family building permits issued: 6 (2001) / 0 (2000); Employment by occupation: 9.7% management, 16.4% professional, 9.8% services, 21.1% sales, 2.4% farming, 9.5% construction, 31.1% production (2000).
Income: Per capita income: $21,761 (2000); Median household income: $50,739 (2000); Poverty rate: 1.6% (2000).
Taxes: Total city taxes per capita: $126 (1997); City property taxes per capita: $102 (1997).
Education: High school graduation rate: 84.1% (2000); College graduation rate: 21.7% (2000).

Two-year College(s)

Lakeshore Technical College (Public)
2001 Enrollment: 2,886 920-458-4183
2001 Tuition: In-state $2,090; Out-of-state $15,915

Housing: Homeownership rate: 84.1% (2000); Median home value: $105,300 (2000); Median rent: $367 per month (2000); Median age of housing: 28 years (2000).
Safety: Violent crime rate: 0.0 per 10,000 population; Property crime rate: 182.3 per 10,000 population (2001).
Transportation: Commute to work: 94.1% car, 0.3% public transportation, 2.0% walk, 3.0% work from home (2000); Travel time to work: 21.8% less than 15 minutes, 60.0% 15 to 30 minutes, 13.1% 30 to 45 minutes, 1.5% 45 to 60 minutes, 3.6% 60 minutes or more (2000)

COOPERSTOWN (town). Covers a land area of 35.115 square miles and a water area of 0.026 square miles. Located at 44.28° N. Lat.; 87.81° W. Long. Elevation is 782 feet.
Population: 1,403 (2000); Race: 99.7% White, 0.0% Black, 0.0% Asian, 0.2% American Indian and Alaska Native, 0.0% Hispanic of any race, 0.1% two or more races (2000); Density: 40.0 persons per square mile (2000); Age: 29.6% under 18, 6.8% over 64 (2000); Marriage status: 22.0% never married, 71.5% now married, 2.8% widowed, 3.7% divorced (2000); Foreign born: 1.6% (2000); Ancestry (includes multiple ancestries): 53.4% German, 14.9% Czech, 11.6% Irish, 11.4% Polish, 5.5% Danish (2000).
Economy: Employment by occupation: 16.1% management, 12.3% professional, 12.5% services, 20.9% sales, 3.9% farming, 11.2% construction, 23.0% production (2000).
Income: Per capita income: $20,941 (2000); Median household income: $58,177 (2000); Poverty rate: 3.8% (2000).
Taxes: Total city taxes per capita: $106 (1997); City property taxes per capita: $104 (1997).
Education: High school graduation rate: 89.0% (2000); College graduation rate: 15.4% (2000).
Housing: Homeownership rate: 94.2% (2000); Median home value: $124,300 (2000); Median rent: $414 per month (2000); Median age of housing: 29 years (2000).
Transportation: Commute to work: 89.0% car, 0.2% public transportation, 2.1% walk, 8.6% work from home (2000); Travel time to work: 23.6% less than 15 minutes, 40.7% 15 to 30 minutes, 28.3% 30 to 45 minutes, 4.6% 45 to 60 minutes, 2.8% 60 minutes or more (2000)

EATON (town). Covers a land area of 35.178 square miles and a water area of 0.223 square miles. Located at 44.01° N. Lat.; 87.96° W. Long.
Population: 761 (2000); Race: 98.9% White, 0.0% Black, 1.1% Asian, 0.0% American Indian and Alaska Native, 2.2% Hispanic of any race, 0.0% two or more races (2000); Density: 21.6 persons per square mile (2000); Age: 27.4% under 18, 9.4% over 64 (2000); Marriage status: 24.3% never married, 66.0% now married, 4.2% widowed, 5.5% divorced (2000); Foreign born: 3.3% (2000); Ancestry (includes multiple ancestries): 67.3% German, 10.1% Norwegian, 5.4% Irish, 4.3% Dutch, 4.1% Czech (2000).
Economy: Employment by occupation: 13.0% management, 10.9% professional, 11.1% services, 15.6% sales, 5.8% farming, 11.1% construction, 32.5% production (2000).
Income: Per capita income: $19,400 (2000); Median household income: $52,054 (2000); Poverty rate: 3.9% (2000).
Taxes: Total city taxes per capita: $203 (1997); City property taxes per capita: $203 (1997).
Education: High school graduation rate: 84.2% (2000); College graduation rate: 11.9% (2000).
Housing: Homeownership rate: 92.1% (2000); Median home value: $103,100 (2000); Median rent: $265 per month (2000); Median age of housing: 57 years (2000).
Transportation: Commute to work: 87.1% car, 1.1% public transportation, 2.8% walk, 8.4% work from home (2000); Travel time to work: 30.4% less than 15 minutes, 43.8% 15 to 30 minutes, 17.2% 30 to 45 minutes, 3.5% 45 to 60 minutes, 5.2% 60 minutes or more (2000)

FRANCIS CREEK (village). Covers a land area of 1.101 square miles and a water area of 0 square miles. Located at 44.20° N. Lat.; 87.72° W. Long. Elevation is 720 feet.
Population: 681 (2000); Race: 97.6% White, 0.0% Black, 0.0% Asian, 0.0% American Indian and Alaska Native, 1.4% Hispanic of any race, 2.1% two or more races (2000); Density: 618.6 persons per square mile (2000); Age: 26.7% under 18, 14.3% over 64 (2000); Marriage status: 24.2% never married, 61.0% now married, 6.8% widowed, 8.1% divorced (2000); Foreign born: 0.8% (2000); Ancestry (includes multiple ancestries): 57.8% German, 12.9% Czech, 11.9% Irish, 8.6% Polish, 7.8% French (except Basque) (2000).
Economy: Dairying; grain, vegetables, fruit. Hidden Valley Ski Area to North. Single-family building permits issued: 2 (2001) / 4 (2000); Multi-family building permits issued: 0 (2001) / 0 (2000); Employment by occupation: 7.8% management, 11.2% professional, 15.1% services, 24.1% sales, 3.6% farming, 10.9% construction, 27.2% production (2000).
Income: Per capita income: $18,441 (2000); Median household income: $43,542 (2000); Poverty rate: 5.1% (2000).
Taxes: Total city taxes per capita: $83 (1997); City property taxes per capita: $78 (1997).
Education: High school graduation rate: 86.4% (2000); College graduation rate: 8.7% (2000).
Housing: Homeownership rate: 77.6% (2000); Median home value: $94,800 (2000); Median rent: $368 per month (2000); Median age of housing: 29 years (2000).
Transportation: Commute to work: 93.2% car, 0.0% public transportation, 2.0% walk, 4.8% work from home (2000); Travel time to work: 25.3% less than 15 minutes, 59.5% 15 to 30 minutes, 10.1% 30 to 45 minutes, 2.4% 45 to 60 minutes, 2.7% 60 minutes or more (2000)

FRANKLIN (town). Covers a land area of 36.164 square miles and a water area of 0.021 square miles. Located at 44.19° N. Lat.; 87.85° W. Long.
Population: 1,293 (2000); Race: 98.5% White, 0.0% Black, 0.0% Asian, 0.0% American Indian and Alaska Native, 0.8% Hispanic of any race, 0.8% two or more races (2000); Density: 35.8 persons per square mile (2000); Age: 27.7% under 18, 9.4% over 64 (2000); Marriage status: 26.1% never married, 61.2% now married, 4.1% widowed, 8.6% divorced (2000); Foreign born: 1.2% (2000); Ancestry (includes multiple ancestries): 61.2% German, 19.7% Czech, 16.4% Irish, 4.6% Polish, 3.3% French (except Basque) (2000).
Economy: Single-family building permits issued: 6 (2001) / 6 (2000); Multi-family building permits issued: 0 (2001) / 0 (2000); Employment by occupation: 16.4% management, 7.4% professional, 10.5% services, 15.9% sales, 3.5% farming, 16.4% construction, 29.8% production (2000).
Income: Per capita income: $19,602 (2000); Median household income: $50,000 (2000); Poverty rate: 7.6% (2000).
Taxes: Total city taxes per capita: $60 (2000); City property taxes per capita: $59 (2000).
Education: High school graduation rate: 83.1% (2000); College graduation rate: 7.6% (2000).
Housing: Homeownership rate: 92.8% (2000); Median home value: $105,600 (2000); Median rent: $375 per month (2000); Median age of housing: 47 years (2000).
Transportation: Commute to work: 86.4% car, 0.8% public transportation, 1.5% walk, 10.8% work from home (2000); Travel time to work: 21.3% less than 15 minutes, 46.8% 15 to 30 minutes, 22.1% 30 to 45 minutes, 5.2% 45 to 60 minutes, 4.6% 60 minutes or more (2000)

GIBSON (town). Covers a land area of 35.256 square miles and a water area of 0.085 square miles. Located at 44.28° N. Lat.; 87.72° W. Long.
Population: 1,352 (2000); Race: 99.2% White, 0.0% Black, 0.2% Asian, 0.7% American Indian and Alaska Native, 0.0% Hispanic of any race, 0.0% two or more races (2000); Density: 38.3 persons per square mile (2000); Age: 27.7% under 18, 9.2% over 64 (2000); Marriage status: 22.1% never married, 67.2% now married, 4.4% widowed, 6.2% divorced (2000); Foreign born: 1.0% (2000); Ancestry (includes multiple ancestries): 54.9% German, 22.8% Czech, 11.3% Polish, 6.4% Irish, 5.7% French (except Basque) (2000).
Economy: Employment by occupation: 12.2% management, 12.3% professional, 8.4% services, 19.9% sales, 4.7% farming, 13.4% construction, 29.0% production (2000).
Income: Per capita income: $18,885 (2000); Median household income: $48,438 (2000); Poverty rate: 2.8% (2000).
Taxes: Total city taxes per capita: $89 (1997); City property taxes per capita: $88 (1997).
Education: High school graduation rate: 83.6% (2000); College graduation rate: 12.0% (2000).
Housing: Homeownership rate: 89.2% (2000); Median home value: $97,900 (2000); Median rent: $331 per month (2000); Median age of housing: 48 years (2000).
Transportation: Commute to work: 89.9% car, 0.0% public transportation, 1.6% walk, 8.0% work from home (2000); Travel time to work: 21.3% less than 15 minutes, 49.2% 15 to 30 minutes, 21.6% 30 to 45 minutes, 4.4% 45 to 60 minutes, 3.5% 60 minutes or more (2000)

KELLNERSVILLE (village). Covers a land area of 0.539 square miles and a water area of 0 square miles. Located at 44.22° N. Lat.; 87.80° W. Long. Elevation is 827 feet.
Population: 374 (2000); Race: 98.4% White, 0.8% Black, 0.8% Asian, 0.0% American Indian and Alaska Native, 0.0% Hispanic of any race, 0.0% two or more races (2000); Density: 694.0 persons per square mile (2000); Age:

24.9% under 18, 19.2% over 64 (2000); Marriage status: 25.4% never married, 55.9% now married, 9.8% widowed, 8.9% divorced (2000); Foreign born: 0.0% (2000); Ancestry (includes multiple ancestries): 60.1% German, 19.9% Czech, 13.0% Irish, 9.6% Polish, 5.7% Norwegian (2000).
Economy: Dairying; grain, vegetables, fruit. Hidden Valley Ski Area to North. Single-family building permits issued: 1 (2001) / 0 (2000); Multi-family building permits issued: 0 (2001) / 0 (2000); Employment by occupation: 10.7% management, 11.7% professional, 15.5% services, 11.2% sales, 1.0% farming, 11.7% construction, 38.3% production (2000).
Income: Per capita income: $16,973 (2000); Median household income: $32,167 (2000); Poverty rate: 6.2% (2000).
Taxes: Total city taxes per capita: $92 (1997); City property taxes per capita: $71 (1997).
Education: High school graduation rate: 80.3% (2000); College graduation rate: 7.7% (2000).
Housing: Homeownership rate: 74.5% (2000); Median home value: $80,300 (2000); Median rent: $242 per month (2000); Median age of housing: 29 years (2000).
Transportation: Commute to work: 92.7% car, 0.0% public transportation, 3.9% walk, 2.4% work from home (2000); Travel time to work: 9.5% less than 15 minutes, 55.7% 15 to 30 minutes, 26.4% 30 to 45 minutes, 4.5% 45 to 60 minutes, 4.0% 60 minutes or more (2000)

KIEL (city). Covers a land area of 2.406 square miles and a water area of 0.050 square miles. Located at 43.91° N. Lat.; 88.03° W. Long. Elevation is 933 feet.
History: A wooden shoe industry developed in Kiel in 1844, when a Belgian trapper living in the woods nearby began to carve wooden shoes for the German and Belgian farmers in the county. Later, a wooden shoe factory was established to meet the demand for the shoes.
Population: 3,450 (2000); Race: 96.1% White, 0.0% Black, 2.1% Asian, 0.2% American Indian and Alaska Native, 1.6% Hispanic of any race, 0.7% two or more races (2000); Density: 1,433.9 persons per square mile (2000); Age: 25.6% under 18, 17.4% over 64 (2000); Marriage status: 19.6% never married, 63.3% now married, 9.0% widowed, 8.0% divorced (2000); Foreign born: 0.8% (2000); Ancestry (includes multiple ancestries): 70.8% German, 5.4% Irish, 4.7% Polish, 4.1% United States or American, 3.7% Other groups (2000).
Economy: Single-family building permits issued: 6 (2001) / 15 (2000); Multi-family building permits issued: 10 (2001) / 6 (2000); Employment by occupation: 8.7% management, 15.6% professional, 12.2% services, 22.6% sales, 2.0% farming, 6.6% construction, 32.4% production (2000).
Income: Per capita income: $23,112 (2000); Median household income: $44,239 (2000); Poverty rate: 2.7% (2000).
Taxes: Total city taxes per capita: $211 (1997); City property taxes per capita: $201 (1997).
Education: High school graduation rate: 82.9% (2000); College graduation rate: 14.4% (2000).

School District(s)

Kiel Area (PK-12)
2000 Enrollment: 1,526 920-894-5111

Housing: Homeownership rate: 74.4% (2000); Median home value: $95,700 (2000); Median rent: $401 per month (2000); Median age of housing: 40 years (2000).
Safety: Violent crime rate: 2.9 per 10,000 population; Property crime rate: 230.2 per 10,000 population (2001).
Newspapers: The Tri-County News (1 x week); Tempo (1 x week)
Transportation: Commute to work: 92.2% car, 0.0% public transportation, 4.5% walk, 2.5% work from home (2000); Travel time to work: 52.6% less than 15 minutes, 22.3% 15 to 30 minutes, 16.9% 30 to 45 minutes, 2.8% 45 to 60 minutes, 5.4% 60 minutes or more (2000)
Additional Information Contacts
Kiel Area Association of Commerce 920-894-4638

KOSSUTH (town). Covers a land area of 38.728 square miles and a water area of 0.011 square miles. Located at 44.19° N. Lat.; 87.73° W. Long.
Population: 2,033 (2000); Race: 98.7% White, 0.0% Black, 1.0% Asian, 0.1% American Indian and Alaska Native, 1.2% Hispanic of any race, 0.0% two or more races (2000); Density: 52.5 persons per square mile (2000); Age: 27.2% under 18, 9.8% over 64 (2000); Marriage status: 22.8% never married, 66.4% now married, 3.7% widowed, 7.1% divorced (2000); Foreign born: 2.3% (2000); Ancestry (includes multiple ancestries): 54.0% German, 22.2% Czech, 10.2% Polish, 7.5% French (except Basque), 6.7% Irish (2000).
Economy: Employment by occupation: 10.6% management, 16.9% professional, 9.4% services, 17.9% sales, 3.7% farming, 12.0% construction, 29.5% production (2000).
Income: Per capita income: $21,126 (2000); Median household income: $55,114 (2000); Poverty rate: 3.1% (2000).
Taxes: Total city taxes per capita: $35 (1997); City property taxes per capita: $34 (1997).
Education: High school graduation rate: 87.2% (2000); College graduation rate: 14.1% (2000).
Housing: Homeownership rate: 90.0% (2000); Median home value: $110,900 (2000); Median rent: $372 per month (2000); Median age of housing: 35 years (2000).
Transportation: Commute to work: 91.8% car, 0.2% public transportation, 2.7% walk, 4.5% work from home (2000); Travel time to work: 33.1% less than 15 minutes, 48.1% 15 to 30 minutes, 10.8% 30 to 45 minutes, 3.9% 45 to 60 minutes, 4.2% 60 minutes or more (2000)

LIBERTY (town). Covers a land area of 35.130 square miles and a water area of 0.271 square miles. Located at 44.03° N. Lat.; 87.87° W. Long.
Population: 1,287 (2000); Race: 98.9% White, 0.0% Black, 0.0% Asian, 0.0% American Indian and Alaska Native, 0.8% Hispanic of any race, 1.1% two or more races (2000); Density: 36.6 persons per square mile (2000); Age: 27.3% under 18, 11.5% over 64 (2000); Marriage status: 19.9% never married, 70.8% now married, 3.7% widowed, 5.6% divorced (2000); Foreign born: 0.6% (2000); Ancestry (includes multiple ancestries): 69.4% German, 9.2% Norwegian, 8.9% Irish, 6.9% Polish, 4.0% United States or American (2000).
Economy: Employment by occupation: 15.5% management, 11.7% professional, 15.1% services, 23.7% sales, 2.7% farming, 11.8% construction, 19.6% production (2000).
Income: Per capita income: $21,498 (2000); Median household income: $56,169 (2000); Poverty rate: 1.8% (2000).
Taxes: Total city taxes per capita: $97 (1997); City property taxes per capita: $96 (1997).
Education: High school graduation rate: 89.1% (2000); College graduation rate: 13.4% (2000).
Housing: Homeownership rate: 92.9% (2000); Median home value: $122,500 (2000); Median rent: $406 per month (2000); Median age of housing: 36 years (2000).
Transportation: Commute to work: 88.0% car, 0.3% public transportation, 2.8% walk, 8.8% work from home (2000); Travel time to work: 37.2% less than 15 minutes, 40.3% 15 to 30 minutes, 16.2% 30 to 45 minutes, 4.3% 45 to 60 minutes, 1.9% 60 minutes or more (2000)

MANITOWOC (city). Covers a land area of 16.868 square miles and a water area of 0.317 square miles. Located at 44.09° N. Lat.; 87.67° W. Long. Elevation is 606 feet.
History: Manitowoc began with the land boom of 1835, and became in turn a lumber camp, a fishing town, a shipbuilding center, and the commercial and industrial capital of Manitowoc County. The economic depression of 1837 followed by cholera epidemics in the early 1850's slowed the growth of the city, but expansion came with the development of shipping on the Great Lakes in the 1860's, when Manitowoc's shipyards were busy. Early industries established in Manitowoc included the Rahr Malting Company, founded in 1847.
Population: 34,053 (2000); Race: 93.0% White, 0.3% Black, 3.4% Asian, 0.8% American Indian and Alaska Native, 2.8% Hispanic of any race, 1.0% two or more races (2000); Density: 2,018.8 persons per square mile (2000); Age: 24.3% under 18, 18.4% over 64 (2000); Marriage status: 24.9% never married, 55.9% now married, 9.5% widowed, 9.7% divorced (2000); Foreign born: 4.0% (2000); Ancestry (includes multiple ancestries): 49.7% German, 13.2% Polish, 8.9% Irish, 8.8% Czech, 8.1% Other groups (2000).
Vital Statistics: Birth rate: 127.5 per 10,000 population (1998)
Economy: Unemployment rate: 7.2% (11/2002); Total civilian labor force: 17,808 (11/2002); Single-family building permits issued: 81 (2001) / 94 (2000); Multi-family building permits issued: 248 (2001) / 93 (2000); Employment by occupation: 9.2% management, 14.9% professional, 15.8% services, 23.1% sales, 0.6% farming, 8.7% construction, 27.8% production (2000).
Income: Per capita income: $19,954 (2000); Median household income: $38,203 (2000); Poverty rate: 7.9% (2000).
Taxes: Total city taxes per capita: $243 (2000); City property taxes per capita: $211 (2000).
Education: High school graduation rate: 83.6% (2000); College graduation rate: 17.1% (2000).

School District(s)

Manitowoc (PK-12)
2000 Enrollment: 5,619 920-686-4781

Four-year College(s)

Silver Lake College (Private, Not-for-profit, Roman Catholic)
2001 Enrollment: 920 920-684-6691
2001 Tuition: In-state $13,016; Out-of-state $13,016

Two-year College(s)

Martin's College of Cosmetology (Private, For-profit)
2001 Enrollment: 34 920-684-3028

Housing: Homeownership rate: 67.6% (2000); Median home value: $86,000 (2000); Median rent: $379 per month (2000); Median age of housing: 46 years (2000).
Hospitals: Holy Family Memorial Medical Center (303 beds)
Safety: Violent crime rate: 11.4 per 10,000 population; Property crime rate: 389.3 per 10,000 population (2001).
Newspapers: Herald Times-Reporter (7 x week); Lakeshore Chronicle (2 x week)
Transportation: Commute to work: 92.4% car, 0.7% public transportation, 3.8% walk, 1.8% work from home (2000); Travel time to work: 66.7% less than 15 minutes, 21.0% 15 to 30 minutes, 6.9% 30 to 45 minutes, 2.2% 45 to 60 minutes, 3.2% 60 minutes or more (2000); Amtrak: Service available.

Additional Information Contacts
Manitowoc Chamber of Commerce 262-684-5575
Manitowoc County Board of Realtors 262-682-6052

MANITOWOC (town). Covers a land area of 6.777 square miles and a water area of 0 square miles. Located at 44.12° N. Lat.; 87.67° W. Long. Elevation is 606 feet.
History: Its shipbuilding industry dates from 1847; submarines were made here in World War II. The North West Company established a trading post on the site in 1795. Manitowoc and its twin city, Two Rivers, were founded in 1836. Incorporated 1870.
Population: 1,073 (2000); Race: 97.4% White, 0.5% Black, 1.1% Asian, 0.2% American Indian and Alaska Native, 0.3% Hispanic of any race, 0.5% two or more races (2000); Density: 158.3 persons per square mile (2000); Age: 20.5% under 18, 14.7% over 64 (2000); Marriage status: 20.5% never married, 65.3% now married, 8.1% widowed, 6.1% divorced (2000); Foreign born: 2.8% (2000); Ancestry (includes multiple ancestries): 55.7% German, 14.0% Polish, 12.3% Irish, 10.4% Czech, 7.9% Norwegian (2000).
Economy: Manufacturing includes electric equipment, malt, foods, toys, printing, fabricated metal products, consumer goods, textiles, transportation equipment, furniture, plastics products, lubrication equipment, machinery, bakery products, yachts and building materials. Railroad junction and a ship and railroad transfer point. Employment by occupation: 11.5% management, 18.5% professional, 12.2% services, 20.6% sales, 1.5% farming, 9.6% construction, 26.2% production (2000).
Income: Per capita income: $23,583 (2000); Median household income: $54,265 (2000); Poverty rate: 3.0% (2000).
Taxes: Total city taxes per capita: $39 (1997); City property taxes per capita: $39 (1997).
Education: High school graduation rate: 88.1% (2000); College graduation rate: 17.4% (2000).
Housing: Homeownership rate: 85.2% (2000); Median home value: $118,200 (2000); Median rent: $613 per month (2000); Median age of housing: 36 years (2000).
Transportation: Commute to work: 93.8% car, 0.0% public transportation, 2.0% walk, 3.2% work from home (2000); Travel time to work: 60.9% less than 15 minutes, 23.3% 15 to 30 minutes, 8.3% 30 to 45 minutes, 4.5% 45 to 60 minutes, 3.0% 60 minutes or more (2000); Amtrak: Service available.

MANITOWOC RAPIDS (town). Aka Rapids. Covers a land area of 27.361 square miles and a water area of 0.254 square miles. Located at 44.10° N. Lat.; 87.73° W. Long. Elevation is 600 feet.
Population: 2,520 (2000); Race: 99.2% White, 0.0% Black, 0.3% Asian, 0.0% American Indian and Alaska Native, 0.7% Hispanic of any race, 0.0% two or more races (2000); Density: 92.1 persons per square mile (2000); Age: 21.5% under 18, 21.8% over 64 (2000); Marriage status: 27.0% never married, 64.9% now married, 3.1% widowed, 5.1% divorced (2000); Foreign born: 0.8% (2000); Ancestry (includes multiple ancestries): 61.5% German, 8.3% Irish, 7.7% Polish, 7.1% Czech, 6.7% Norwegian (2000).
Economy: Employment by occupation: 16.4% management, 15.6% professional, 9.6% services, 19.0% sales, 5.2% farming, 11.8% construction, 22.2% production (2000).
Income: Per capita income: $21,323 (2000); Median household income: $56,548 (2000); Poverty rate: 11.1% (2000).
Taxes: Total city taxes per capita: $50 (1997); City property taxes per capita: $48 (1997).
Education: High school graduation rate: 87.6% (2000); College graduation rate: 29.1% (2000).
Housing: Homeownership rate: 95.0% (2000); Median home value: $133,000 (2000); Median rent: $308 per month (2000); Median age of housing: 30 years (2000).
Transportation: Commute to work: 89.5% car, 0.0% public transportation, 1.8% walk, 7.5% work from home (2000); Travel time to work: 49.0% less than 15 minutes, 36.8% 15 to 30 minutes, 8.2% 30 to 45 minutes, 1.8% 45 to 60 minutes, 4.2% 60 minutes or more (2000).

MAPLE GROVE (town). Covers a land area of 35.400 square miles and a water area of 0 square miles. Located at 44.20° N. Lat.; 87.98° W. Long. Elevation is 904 feet.
Population: 852 (2000); Race: 98.5% White, 0.0% Black, 0.0% Asian, 0.2% American Indian and Alaska Native, 1.3% Hispanic of any race, 0.2% two or more races (2000); Density: 24.1 persons per square mile (2000); Age: 31.3% under 18, 7.0% over 64 (2000); Marriage status: 27.2% never married, 67.1% now married, 2.0% widowed, 3.6% divorced (2000); Foreign born: 0.7% (2000); Ancestry (includes multiple ancestries): 72.3% German, 11.5% Czech, 10.1% Irish, 4.9% Norwegian, 3.8% United States or American (2000).
Economy: Employment by occupation: 15.0% management, 7.4% professional, 8.2% services, 18.7% sales, 4.9% farming, 10.3% construction, 35.4% production (2000).
Income: Per capita income: $21,734 (2000); Median household income: $51,071 (2000); Poverty rate: 2.3% (2000).
Taxes: Total city taxes per capita: $132 (1997); City property taxes per capita: $132 (1997).
Education: High school graduation rate: 84.1% (2000); College graduation rate: 10.2% (2000).
Housing: Homeownership rate: 90.1% (2000); Median home value: $103,600 (2000); Median rent: $288 per month (2000); Median age of housing: 60+ years (2000).
Transportation: Commute to work: 79.1% car, 0.0% public transportation, 3.7% walk, 16.7% work from home (2000); Travel time to work: 44.4% less than 15 minutes, 23.1% 15 to 30 minutes, 23.3% 30 to 45 minutes, 5.5% 45 to 60 minutes, 3.7% 60 minutes or more (2000)

MARIBEL (village). Covers a land area of 1.172 square miles and a water area of 0 square miles. Located at 44.27° N. Lat.; 87.80° W. Long. Elevation is 861 feet.
Population: 264 (2000); Race: 97.1% White, 0.0% Black, 0.0% Asian, 2.1% American Indian and Alaska Native, 0.0% Hispanic of any race, 0.8% two or more races (2000); Density: 225.3 persons per square mile (2000); Age: 32.9% under 18, 14.0% over 64 (2000); Marriage status: 23.6% never married, 64.3% now married, 8.8% widowed, 3.3% divorced (2000); Foreign born: 0.0% (2000); Ancestry (includes multiple ancestries): 51.4% German, 21.8% Czech, 7.8% Belgian, 7.8% Finnish, 7.0% Dutch (2000).
Economy: Single-family building permits issued: 0 (2001) / 0 (2000); Multi-family building permits issued: 0 (2001) / 0 (2000); Employment by occupation: 9.0% management, 12.8% professional, 20.3% services, 27.8% sales, 5.3% farming, 10.5% construction, 14.3% production (2000).
Income: Per capita income: $17,177 (2000); Median household income: $45,938 (2000); Poverty rate: 7.0% (2000).
Taxes: Total city taxes per capita: $16 (1997); City property taxes per capita: $5 (1997).
Education: High school graduation rate: 88.2% (2000); College graduation rate: 16.4% (2000).
Housing: Homeownership rate: 66.7% (2000); Median home value: $98,800 (2000); Median rent: $313 per month (2000); Median age of housing: 49 years (2000).
Transportation: Commute to work: 88.4% car, 0.0% public transportation, 5.4% walk, 5.4% work from home (2000); Travel time to work: 33.6% less than 15 minutes, 33.6% 15 to 30 minutes, 26.2% 30 to 45 minutes, 3.3% 45 to 60 minutes, 3.3% 60 minutes or more (2000)

MEEME (town). Covers a land area of 36.192 square miles and a water area of 0.102 square miles. Located at 43.93° N. Lat.; 87.85° W. Long. Elevation is 777 feet.
Population: 1,538 (2000); Race: 98.2% White, 0.0% Black, 0.3% Asian, 0.0% American Indian and Alaska Native, 1.2% Hispanic of any race, 0.6% two or more races (2000); Density: 42.5 persons per square mile (2000); Age: 27.5% under 18, 12.7% over 64 (2000); Marriage status: 25.1% never married, 64.9% now married, 4.6% widowed, 5.4% divorced (2000); Foreign born: 1.6% (2000); Ancestry (includes multiple ancestries): 70.0% German,

10.6% Irish, 5.0% Polish, 3.9% United States or American, 3.2% French (except Basque) (2000).
Economy: Employment by occupation: 14.4% management, 7.8% professional, 10.7% services, 20.8% sales, 4.7% farming, 10.9% construction, 30.6% production (2000).
Income: Per capita income: $20,927 (2000); Median household income: $55,139 (2000); Poverty rate: 3.2% (2000).
Taxes: Total city taxes per capita: $69 (1997); City property taxes per capita: $68 (1997).
Education: High school graduation rate: 80.6% (2000); College graduation rate: 10.7% (2000).
Housing: Homeownership rate: 92.8% (2000); Median home value: $120,300 (2000); Median rent: $356 per month (2000); Median age of housing: 51 years (2000).
Transportation: Commute to work: 86.4% car, 0.2% public transportation, 4.3% walk, 8.1% work from home (2000); Travel time to work: 29.4% less than 15 minutes, 54.7% 15 to 30 minutes, 10.2% 30 to 45 minutes, 3.2% 45 to 60 minutes, 2.4% 60 minutes or more (2000)

MISHICOT (village). Covers a land area of 2.555 square miles and a water area of 0 square miles. Located at 44.23° N. Lat.; 87.64° W. Long. Elevation is 610 feet.
Population: 1,422 (2000); Race: 99.6% White, 0.0% Black, 0.0% Asian, 0.0% American Indian and Alaska Native, 0.8% Hispanic of any race, 0.1% two or more races (2000); Density: 556.6 persons per square mile (2000); Age: 24.3% under 18, 17.1% over 64 (2000); Marriage status: 20.3% never married, 63.6% now married, 7.0% widowed, 9.1% divorced (2000); Foreign born: 1.5% (2000); Ancestry (includes multiple ancestries): 51.6% German, 17.1% Czech, 8.6% Irish, 7.6% Polish, 4.8% French (except Basque) (2000).
Economy: Single-family building permits issued: 6 (2001) / 6 (2000); Multi-family building permits issued: 2 (2001) / 0 (2000); Employment by occupation: 10.1% management, 14.4% professional, 17.9% services, 19.7% sales, 1.3% farming, 10.8% construction, 25.7% production (2000).
Income: Per capita income: $20,175 (2000); Median household income: $43,083 (2000); Poverty rate: 4.4% (2000).
Taxes: Total city taxes per capita: $228 (1997); City property taxes per capita: $158 (1997).
Education: High school graduation rate: 84.6% (2000); College graduation rate: 11.1% (2000).

School District(s)

Mishicot (PK-12)
2000 Enrollment: 1,098 920-755-4633

Housing: Homeownership rate: 75.2% (2000); Median home value: $85,600 (2000); Median rent: $421 per month (2000); Median age of housing: 36 years (2000).
Transportation: Commute to work: 91.0% car, 0.3% public transportation, 3.8% walk, 3.0% work from home (2000); Travel time to work: 37.5% less than 15 minutes, 45.7% 15 to 30 minutes, 9.0% 30 to 45 minutes, 2.7% 45 to 60 minutes, 5.1% 60 minutes or more (2000)

MISHICOT (town). Covers a land area of 27.627 square miles and a water area of 0.023 square miles. Located at 44.25° N. Lat.; 87.64° W. Long. Elevation is 610 feet.
Population: 1,409 (2000); Race: 98.2% White, 0.0% Black, 0.0% Asian, 0.0% American Indian and Alaska Native, 2.3% Hispanic of any race, 0.0% two or more races (2000); Density: 51.0 persons per square mile (2000); Age: 31.3% under 18, 9.6% over 64 (2000); Marriage status: 24.5% never married, 66.3% now married, 2.3% widowed, 6.9% divorced (2000); Foreign born: 1.3% (2000); Ancestry (includes multiple ancestries): 52.0% German, 20.3% Czech, 8.2% Polish, 6.5% Irish, 6.1% French (except Basque) (2000).
Economy: Dairying. Cherries, cranberries, grain. Light manufacturing. Employment by occupation: 12.3% management, 9.4% professional, 13.8% services, 18.1% sales, 3.4% farming, 11.7% construction, 31.4% production (2000).
Income: Per capita income: $17,879 (2000); Median household income: $51,083 (2000); Poverty rate: 8.1% (2000).
Taxes: Total city taxes per capita: $83 (1997); City property taxes per capita: $82 (1997).
Education: High school graduation rate: 85.0% (2000); College graduation rate: 11.1% (2000).
Housing: Homeownership rate: 91.5% (2000); Median home value: $97,500 (2000); Median rent: $388 per month (2000); Median age of housing: 32 years (2000).
Transportation: Commute to work: 89.7% car, 0.4% public transportation, 1.9% walk, 7.1% work from home (2000); Travel time to work: 28.9% less than 15 minutes, 48.4% 15 to 30 minutes, 16.2% 30 to 45 minutes, 3.5% 45 to 60 minutes, 3.0% 60 minutes or more (2000)

NEWTON (town). Covers a land area of 34.073 square miles and a water area of 1.409 square miles. Located at 44.03° N. Lat.; 87.73° W. Long. Elevation is 659 feet.
Population: 2,241 (2000); Race: 98.4% White, 0.0% Black, 0.5% Asian, 0.6% American Indian and Alaska Native, 1.4% Hispanic of any race, 0.5% two or more races (2000); Density: 65.8 persons per square mile (2000); Age: 24.8% under 18, 10.3% over 64 (2000); Marriage status: 25.1% never married, 65.1% now married, 4.1% widowed, 5.7% divorced (2000); Foreign born: 1.6% (2000); Ancestry (includes multiple ancestries): 62.0% German, 12.0% Polish, 6.8% United States or American, 5.7% Czech, 5.6% Norwegian (2000).
Economy: Single-family building permits issued: 10 (2001) / 10 (2000); Multi-family building permits issued: 0 (2001) / 0 (2000); Employment by occupation: 14.5% management, 12.6% professional, 10.6% services, 19.0% sales, 3.9% farming, 13.9% construction, 25.5% production (2000).
Income: Per capita income: $22,467 (2000); Median household income: $54,359 (2000); Poverty rate: 4.8% (2000).
Taxes: Total city taxes per capita: $72 (1997); City property taxes per capita: $71 (1997).
Education: High school graduation rate: 85.7% (2000); College graduation rate: 14.2% (2000).
Housing: Homeownership rate: 90.6% (2000); Median home value: $111,500 (2000); Median rent: $406 per month (2000); Median age of housing: 42 years (2000).
Transportation: Commute to work: 88.4% car, 0.7% public transportation, 4.3% walk, 6.5% work from home (2000); Travel time to work: 43.8% less than 15 minutes, 39.7% 15 to 30 minutes, 10.8% 30 to 45 minutes, 2.3% 45 to 60 minutes, 3.4% 60 minutes or more (2000)

REEDSVILLE (village). Covers a land area of 0.947 square miles and a water area of 0 square miles. Located at 44.15° N. Lat.; 87.95° W. Long. Elevation is 830 feet.
Population: 1,187 (2000); Race: 98.6% White, 0.6% Black, 0.0% Asian, 0.4% American Indian and Alaska Native, 0.7% Hispanic of any race, 0.2% two or more races (2000); Density: 1,253.4 persons per square mile (2000); Age: 23.2% under 18, 15.4% over 64 (2000); Marriage status: 29.3% never married, 56.3% now married, 7.7% widowed, 6.8% divorced (2000); Foreign born: 0.5% (2000); Ancestry (includes multiple ancestries): 63.2% German, 11.4% Irish, 9.4% Czech, 7.7% United States or American, 6.7% Polish (2000).
Economy: In grain belt; vegetable canning. Single-family building permits issued: 3 (2001) / 4 (2000); Multi-family building permits issued: 0 (2001) / 0 (2000); Employment by occupation: 10.2% management, 11.8% professional, 13.9% services, 13.9% sales, 1.1% farming, 10.8% construction, 38.3% production (2000).
Income: Per capita income: $19,762 (2000); Median household income: $41,300 (2000); Poverty rate: 3.1% (2000).
Taxes: Total city taxes per capita: $150 (1997); City property taxes per capita: $138 (1997).
Education: High school graduation rate: 81.3% (2000); College graduation rate: 13.8% (2000).

School District(s)

Reedsville (PK-12)
2000 Enrollment: 740 920-754-4341

Housing: Homeownership rate: 73.8% (2000); Median home value: $86,700 (2000); Median rent: $291 per month (2000); Median age of housing: 39 years (2000).
Transportation: Commute to work: 91.5% car, 0.3% public transportation, 4.9% walk, 2.0% work from home (2000); Travel time to work: 47.2% less than 15 minutes, 24.0% 15 to 30 minutes, 19.9% 30 to 45 minutes, 6.0% 45 to 60 minutes, 3.0% 60 minutes or more (2000)

ROCKLAND (town). Covers a land area of 34.526 square miles and a water area of 1.006 square miles. Located at 44.10° N. Lat.; 87.98° W. Long.
Population: 896 (2000); Race: 100.0% White, 0.0% Black, 0.0% Asian, 0.0% American Indian and Alaska Native, 1.4% Hispanic of any race, 0.0% two or more races (2000); Density: 26.0 persons per square mile (2000); Age: 26.0% under 18, 10.8% over 64 (2000); Marriage status: 22.4% never married, 71.0% now married, 3.6% widowed, 3.1% divorced (2000); Foreign born: 0.0% (2000); Ancestry (includes multiple ancestries): 77.4% German, 8.0% Norwegian, 7.4% Irish, 5.7% Czech, 5.2% Polish (2000).

Economy: Employment by occupation: 15.4% management, 10.9% professional, 9.4% services, 11.9% sales, 3.5% farming, 11.7% construction, 37.1% production (2000).
Income: Per capita income: $19,798 (2000); Median household income: $53,500 (2000); Poverty rate: 7.9% (2000).
Taxes: Total city taxes per capita: $162 (1997); City property taxes per capita: $162 (1997).
Education: High school graduation rate: 83.0% (2000); College graduation rate: 9.8% (2000).
Housing: Homeownership rate: 89.6% (2000); Median home value: $107,800 (2000); Median rent: $350 per month (2000); Median age of housing: 51 years (2000).
Transportation: Commute to work: 84.0% car, 0.0% public transportation, 2.9% walk, 12.9% work from home (2000); Travel time to work: 28.9% less than 15 minutes, 44.6% 15 to 30 minutes, 17.9% 30 to 45 minutes, 3.4% 45 to 60 minutes, 5.2% 60 minutes or more (2000)

SAINT NAZIANZ (village). Covers a land area of 0.825 square miles and a water area of 0.015 square miles. Located at 44.00° N. Lat.; 87.92° W. Long. Elevation is 880 feet.
History: St. Nazianz was founded in 1854 by Father Ambrose Oschwald, who led a group of people from Baden, Germany, to this site, where he hoped to build a society patterned on the communistic life of the early Christians. Oschwald died in 1873.
Population: 749 (2000); Race: 96.5% White, 0.6% Black, 0.6% Asian, 0.0% American Indian and Alaska Native, 2.0% Hispanic of any race, 0.6% two or more races (2000); Density: 907.6 persons per square mile (2000); Age: 29.5% under 18, 15.7% over 64 (2000); Marriage status: 21.5% never married, 60.0% now married, 6.9% widowed, 11.5% divorced (2000); Foreign born: 0.9% (2000); Ancestry (includes multiple ancestries): 69.8% German, 10.6% Irish, 6.8% Polish, 4.8% Other groups, 3.9% Czech (2000).
Economy: Single-family building permits issued: 4 (2001) / 19 (2000); Multi-family building permits issued: 0 (2001) / 0 (2000); Employment by occupation: 5.3% management, 11.8% professional, 14.1% services, 22.7% sales, 4.9% farming, 11.8% construction, 29.3% production (2000).
Income: Per capita income: $16,989 (2000); Median household income: $40,139 (2000); Poverty rate: 5.3% (2000).
Education: High school graduation rate: 83.6% (2000); College graduation rate: 10.6% (2000).
Housing: Homeownership rate: 78.2% (2000); Median home value: $87,200 (2000); Median rent: $366 per month (2000); Median age of housing: 43 years (2000).
Transportation: Commute to work: 90.7% car, 0.0% public transportation, 6.3% walk, 1.7% work from home (2000); Travel time to work: 30.4% less than 15 minutes, 43.6% 15 to 30 minutes, 18.9% 30 to 45 minutes, 5.7% 45 to 60 minutes, 1.4% 60 minutes or more (2000)

SCHLESWIG (town). Covers a land area of 33.073 square miles and a water area of 0.762 square miles. Located at 43.93° N. Lat.; 87.98° W. Long.
Population: 1,900 (2000); Race: 97.6% White, 0.0% Black, 0.7% Asian, 0.1% American Indian and Alaska Native, 0.4% Hispanic of any race, 1.3% two or more races (2000); Density: 57.4 persons per square mile (2000); Age: 27.7% under 18, 11.9% over 64 (2000); Marriage status: 20.0% never married, 70.4% now married, 4.2% widowed, 5.4% divorced (2000); Foreign born: 0.7% (2000); Ancestry (includes multiple ancestries): 68.6% German, 6.2% Irish, 4.8% United States or American, 4.7% Polish, 4.5% Dutch (2000).
Economy: Employment by occupation: 12.5% management, 10.2% professional, 9.3% services, 20.4% sales, 1.8% farming, 10.5% construction, 35.3% production (2000).
Income: Per capita income: $22,447 (2000); Median household income: $52,841 (2000); Poverty rate: 3.2% (2000).
Taxes: Total city taxes per capita: $105 (1997); City property taxes per capita: $102 (1997).
Education: High school graduation rate: 85.2% (2000); College graduation rate: 13.3% (2000).
Housing: Homeownership rate: 88.6% (2000); Median home value: $130,100 (2000); Median rent: $394 per month (2000); Median age of housing: 38 years (2000).
Transportation: Commute to work: 89.5% car, 0.0% public transportation, 3.1% walk, 6.3% work from home (2000); Travel time to work: 38.8% less than 15 minutes, 33.3% 15 to 30 minutes, 21.7% 30 to 45 minutes, 2.2% 45 to 60 minutes, 3.9% 60 minutes or more (2000)

TWO CREEKS (town). Covers a land area of 14.872 square miles and a water area of 0 square miles. Located at 44.29° N. Lat.; 87.55° W. Long. Elevation is 645 feet.
Population: 551 (2000); Race: 99.1% White, 0.0% Black, 0.0% Asian, 0.5% American Indian and Alaska Native, 0.9% Hispanic of any race, 0.4% two or more races (2000); Density: 37.0 persons per square mile (2000); Age: 34.4% under 18, 8.1% over 64 (2000); Marriage status: 24.5% never married, 62.9% now married, 5.0% widowed, 7.7% divorced (2000); Foreign born: 0.7% (2000); Ancestry (includes multiple ancestries): 49.7% German, 31.0% Czech, 7.8% Polish, 6.2% French (except Basque), 4.2% United States or American (2000).
Economy: Employment by occupation: 17.6% management, 8.2% professional, 8.6% services, 15.4% sales, 5.2% farming, 10.9% construction, 34.1% production (2000).
Income: Per capita income: $17,007 (2000); Median household income: $45,625 (2000); Poverty rate: 3.9% (2000).
Education: High school graduation rate: 83.8% (2000); College graduation rate: 8.4% (2000).
Housing: Homeownership rate: 84.3% (2000); Median home value: $110,000 (2000); Median rent: $375 per month (2000); Median age of housing: 31 years (2000).
Transportation: Commute to work: 81.1% car, 0.0% public transportation, 2.3% walk, 13.6% work from home (2000); Travel time to work: 27.1% less than 15 minutes, 31.9% 15 to 30 minutes, 27.9% 30 to 45 minutes, 9.6% 45 to 60 minutes, 3.5% 60 minutes or more (2000)

TWO RIVERS (city). Covers a land area of 5.668 square miles and a water area of 0.407 square miles. Located at 44.15° N. Lat.; 87.57° W. Long. Elevation is 600 feet.
History: Two Rivers was founded as a fishing settlement in the 1830's. The fishermen were followed by New England lumberjacks and German immigrant farmers. Woodworking industries came after the decline of lumbering, with a chair factory established in 1856 and a pail factory in 1857 becoming the Two Rivers Manufacturing Company. Shipbuilding also flourished in the mid-1800's.
Population: 12,639 (2000); Race: 97.2% White, 0.0% Black, 0.9% Asian, 0.6% American Indian and Alaska Native, 1.2% Hispanic of any race, 0.9% two or more races (2000); Density: 2,230.1 persons per square mile (2000); Age: 25.4% under 18, 16.5% over 64 (2000); Marriage status: 23.3% never married, 59.5% now married, 8.0% widowed, 9.3% divorced (2000); Foreign born: 1.4% (2000); Ancestry (includes multiple ancestries): 47.4% German, 14.6% Polish, 10.3% Czech, 8.2% French (except Basque), 7.6% Irish (2000).
Vital Statistics: Birth rate: 113.1 per 10,000 population (1998)
Economy: Single-family building permits issued: 13 (2001) / 30 (2000); Multi-family building permits issued: 0 (2001) / 0 (2000); Employment by occupation: 8.7% management, 13.0% professional, 13.8% services, 19.0% sales, 0.6% farming, 8.8% construction, 36.2% production (2000).
Income: Per capita income: $18,908 (2000); Median household income: $39,701 (2000); Poverty rate: 6.3% (2000).
Taxes: Total city taxes per capita: $255 (2000); City property taxes per capita: $228 (2000).
Education: High school graduation rate: 85.0% (2000); College graduation rate: 13.7% (2000).

School District(s)

Two Rivers (PK-12)
2000 Enrollment: 2,227 920-793-4560

Housing: Homeownership rate: 73.0% (2000); Median home value: $77,900 (2000); Median rent: $361 per month (2000); Median age of housing: 46 years (2000).
Hospitals: Aurora Medical Center (73 beds)
Safety: Violent crime rate: 11.0 per 10,000 population; Property crime rate: 227.0 per 10,000 population (2001).
Transportation: Commute to work: 92.6% car, 0.6% public transportation, 3.8% walk, 1.8% work from home (2000); Travel time to work: 48.1% less than 15 minutes, 38.3% 15 to 30 minutes, 6.1% 30 to 45 minutes, 3.9% 45 to 60 minutes, 3.6% 60 minutes or more (2000)

TWO RIVERS (town). Covers a land area of 31.765 square miles and a water area of 0.129 square miles. Located at 44.18° N. Lat.; 87.59° W. Long. Elevation is 600 feet.
History: A US coast guard station (established 1872) is in Two Rivers. Incorporated 1878.
Population: 1,912 (2000); Race: 99.1% White, 0.0% Black, 0.8% Asian, 0.0% American Indian and Alaska Native, 0.8% Hispanic of any race, 0.0%

two or more races (2000); Density: 60.2 persons per square mile (2000); Age: 22.5% under 18, 13.8% over 64 (2000); Marriage status: 20.8% never married, 71.3% now married, 4.1% widowed, 3.7% divorced (2000); Foreign born: 1.1% (2000); Ancestry (includes multiple ancestries): 58.0% German, 13.3% Polish, 13.0% Czech, 6.9% Irish, 4.4% French (except Basque) (2000).
Economy: Two Rivers is closely associated with its twin city, Manitowoc, both of which are highly industrialized. Manufacturing: furniture, wood products, electrical equipment, fixtures. Fishing. Nuclear plant. Point Beach State Forest on Lake Michigan to Northeast. Employment by occupation: 12.1% management, 15.7% professional, 11.9% services, 17.8% sales, 3.3% farming, 10.5% construction, 28.8% production (2000).
Income: Per capita income: $25,319 (2000); Median household income: $55,759 (2000); Poverty rate: 1.9% (2000).
Taxes: Total city taxes per capita: $36 (1997); City property taxes per capita: $30 (1997).
Education: High school graduation rate: 85.6% (2000); College graduation rate: 13.8% (2000).
Housing: Homeownership rate: 93.7% (2000); Median home value: $103,800 (2000); Median rent: $407 per month (2000); Median age of housing: 34 years (2000).
Transportation: Commute to work: 93.3% car, 0.0% public transportation, 0.8% walk, 5.6% work from home (2000); Travel time to work: 46.2% less than 15 minutes, 38.3% 15 to 30 minutes, 9.3% 30 to 45 minutes, 3.9% 45 to 60 minutes, 2.2% 60 minutes or more (2000)

VALDERS (village). Covers a land area of 1.013 square miles and a water area of 0 square miles. Located at 44.06° N. Lat.; 87.88° W. Long. Elevation is 840 feet.
History: Valders was settled by Norwegian immigrants from the valley of Valders, Norway. Economist Thorstein Veblen (1857-1929), whose parents were among the first settlers, was born in Valders.
Population: 948 (2000); Race: 98.1% White, 0.0% Black, 0.0% Asian, 0.4% American Indian and Alaska Native, 2.4% Hispanic of any race, 0.0% two or more races (2000); Density: 935.6 persons per square mile (2000); Age: 30.3% under 18, 14.7% over 64 (2000); Marriage status: 24.7% never married, 57.9% now married, 8.4% widowed, 9.0% divorced (2000); Foreign born: 1.8% (2000); Ancestry (includes multiple ancestries): 55.9% German, 13.2% Norwegian, 12.1% Irish, 7.9% Polish, 4.0% United States or American (2000).
Economy: Single-family building permits issued: 10 (2001) / 5 (2000); Multi-family building permits issued: 14 (2001) / 0 (2000); Employment by occupation: 10.0% management, 15.8% professional, 13.6% services, 18.4% sales, 1.2% farming, 7.8% construction, 33.1% production (2000).
Income: Per capita income: $19,691 (2000); Median household income: $45,167 (2000); Poverty rate: 3.0% (2000).
Taxes: Total city taxes per capita: $134 (1997); City property taxes per capita: $120 (1997).
Education: High school graduation rate: 89.9% (2000); College graduation rate: 15.8% (2000).

School District(s)

Valders Area (PK-12)
2000 Enrollment: 1,151 920-775-9500

Housing: Homeownership rate: 74.8% (2000); Median home value: $94,300 (2000); Median rent: $391 per month (2000); Median age of housing: 32 years (2000).
Newspapers: Valders Journal (1 x week)
Transportation: Commute to work: 91.7% car, 0.4% public transportation, 5.5% walk, 1.2% work from home (2000); Travel time to work: 35.5% less than 15 minutes, 46.9% 15 to 30 minutes, 12.5% 30 to 45 minutes, 3.1% 45 to 60 minutes, 2.0% 60 minutes or more (2000)

WHITELAW (village). Covers a land area of 0.556 square miles and a water area of 0 square miles. Located at 44.14° N. Lat.; 87.82° W. Long. Elevation is 857 feet.
Population: 730 (2000); Race: 97.9% White, 0.0% Black, 0.0% Asian, 0.6% American Indian and Alaska Native, 0.0% Hispanic of any race, 1.5% two or more races (2000); Density: 1,312.0 persons per square mile (2000); Age: 26.8% under 18, 10.1% over 64 (2000); Marriage status: 28.7% never married, 58.6% now married, 5.9% widowed, 6.8% divorced (2000); Foreign born: 0.0% (2000); Ancestry (includes multiple ancestries): 62.4% German, 17.6% Czech, 13.8% Irish, 6.1% Polish, 4.4% Norwegian (2000).
Economy: Dairying; livestock; grain, vegetables, fruit. Manufacturing of wire rope, foods. Single-family building permits issued: 3 (2001) / 5 (2000); Multi-family building permits issued: 0 (2001) / 0 (2000); Employment by occupation: 7.4% management, 10.2% professional, 11.4% services, 17.4% sales, 2.5% farming, 17.9% construction, 33.3% production (2000).
Income: Per capita income: $20,249 (2000); Median household income: $51,029 (2000); Poverty rate: 5.4% (2000).
Taxes: Total city taxes per capita: $77 (1997); City property taxes per capita: $72 (1997).
Education: High school graduation rate: 85.2% (2000); College graduation rate: 12.2% (2000).
Housing: Homeownership rate: 83.1% (2000); Median home value: $89,700 (2000); Median rent: $367 per month (2000); Median age of housing: 34 years (2000).
Transportation: Commute to work: 96.2% car, 0.0% public transportation, 0.5% walk, 2.8% work from home (2000); Travel time to work: 19.3% less than 15 minutes, 59.0% 15 to 30 minutes, 10.1% 30 to 45 minutes, 5.2% 45 to 60 minutes, 6.4% 60 minutes or more (2000)

Marathon County

Located in central Wisconsin; drained by the Wisconsin, Eau Claire, and Eau Pleine Rivers; includes Rib Mountain. Covers a land area of 1,545.00 square miles, a water area of 31.20 square miles, and is located in the Central Time Zone. The county government was organized in 1850. County seat is Wausau.

Marathon County is part of the Wausau, WI MSA. The entire metro area includes: Marathon County

Weather Station: Rosholt 9 NNE — Elevation: 1,158 feet

	Jan	Feb	Mar	Apr	May	Jun	Jul	Aug	Sep	Oct	Nov	Dec
High	23	29	39	55	69	77	81	79	70	58	41	28
Low	2	8	18	31	43	51	56	54	45	35	23	10
Precip	1.1	0.9	1.7	2.9	3.9	3.6	4.0	4.4	3.9	2.7	2.4	1.4
Snow	11.6	8.4	10.2	2.9	0.2	0.0	0.0	0.0	0.0	0.4	6.7	11.7

High and Low temperatures in degrees Fahrenheit; Precipitation and Snow in inches

Weather Station: Wausau Municipal Airport — Elevation: 1,197 feet

	Jan	Feb	Mar	Apr	May	Jun	Jul	Aug	Sep	Oct	Nov	Dec
High	22	28	39	54	68	76	80	78	68	56	39	27
Low	4	9	20	33	45	54	59	57	48	37	25	11
Precip	1.1	0.9	1.9	2.8	3.7	4.0	4.2	4.4	4.1	2.8	2.2	1.4
Snow	13.3	8.6	10.7	3.7	0.1	tr	0.0	tr	tr	1.0	6.9	12.9

High and Low temperatures in degrees Fahrenheit; Precipitation and Snow in inches

Population: 125,834 (2000); Race: 94.2% White, 0.2% Black, 4.1% Asian, 0.4% American Indian and Alaska Native, 0.7% Hispanic of any race, 0.8% two or more races (2000); Density: 81.4 persons per square mile (2000); Age: 26.7% under 18, 13.0% over 64 (2000).
Religion: Five largest groups: 36.6% Catholic Church, 10.9% Evangelical Lutheran Church in America, 8.6% Lutheran Church—Missouri Synod, 3.3% Wisconsin Evangelical Lutheran Synod, 2.2% United Church of Christ (2000).
Economy: Unemployment rate: 3.6% (11/2002); Total civilian labor force: 76,716 (11/2002); Leading industries: 28.9% manufacturing; 15.2% retail trade; 10.5% health care and social assistance (2000); Companies that employ more than 1,000 persons: 7 (2000); Companies that employ more than 100 persons: 93 (2000); Farms: 2,703 totaling 515,888 acres (1997); Minority business ownership rate: 0.0% (1997); Women business ownership rate: 15.4% (1997); Retail sales per capita: $11,630 (1997). Single-family building permits issued: 829 (2001) / 652 (2000); Multi-family building permits issued: 244 (2001) / 151 (2000).
Income: Per capita income: $20,703 (2000); Median household income: $45,165 (2000); Poverty rate: 6.6% (2000); Bankruptcy rate: 2.46% (2001).
Taxes: Total county taxes per capita: $287 (2000); County property taxes per capita: $221 (2000).
Education: High school graduation rate: 83.8% (2000); College graduation rate: 18.3% (2000).
Housing: Homeownership rate: 75.7% (2000); Median home value: $95,800 (2000); Median rent: $423 per month (2000); Median age of housing: 33 years (2000).
Health: Birth rate: 117.3 per 10,000 population (1998); Age adjusted death rate: 76.5 per 10,000 population (1999); Age adjusted cancer mortality rate: 184.0 deaths per 100,000 population (1999). Air Quality Index: 82% good, 18% moderate, 0% unhealthy (percent of days in 2000). Number of physicians: 20.2 per 10,000 population (1999); Number of hospital beds: 47.0 per 10,000 population (1999).
Elections: 2000 Presidential election results: 45.5% Gore, 49.5% Bush, 3.5% Nader, 1.2% Buchanan

National and State Parks: Bern State Public Hunting Grounds; George W Mead State Wildlife Management Area; McMillan Marsh State Public Hunting Grounds; Plover River State Fishery Area; Rib Mountain State Park

Additional Information Contacts

Marathon County Government Offices 715-261-1500
Central WI Convention Bureau 715-355-8788
Central Wisconsin Board of Realtors 715-693-7325
Stratford Chamber of Commerce 715-687-4466
Wausau Chamber of Commerce 715-845-6231

Marathon County Communities

ATHENS (village). Covers a land area of 2.443 square miles and a water area of 0 square miles. Located at 45.03° N. Lat.; 90.07° W. Long. Elevation is 1,410 feet.

Population: 1,095 (2000); Race: 98.6% White, 0.3% Black, 0.0% Asian, 0.0% American Indian and Alaska Native, 1.1% Hispanic of any race, 0.9% two or more races (2000); Density: 448.2 persons per square mile (2000); Age: 26.1% under 18, 19.6% over 64 (2000); Marriage status: 23.1% never married, 58.1% now married, 11.9% widowed, 7.0% divorced (2000); Foreign born: 1.1% (2000); Ancestry (includes multiple ancestries): 65.6% German, 17.5% Polish, 5.8% Irish, 4.9% United States or American, 3.8% English (2000).

Economy: In dairying, lumbering, and farming area; wood prods. Manufacturing: sawmill; maple syrup. Single-family building permits issued: 7 (2001) / 2 (2000); Multi-family building permits issued: 0 (2001) / 0 (2000); Employment by occupation: 7.1% management, 14.5% professional, 9.3% services, 25.8% sales, 2.8% farming, 13.0% construction, 27.6% production (2000).

Income: Per capita income: $17,076 (2000); Median household income: $39,286 (2000); Poverty rate: 4.5% (2000).

Taxes: Total city taxes per capita: $160 (1997); City property taxes per capita: $150 (1997).

Education: High school graduation rate: 77.0% (2000); College graduation rate: 13.2% (2000).

School District(s)

Athens (PK-12)
2000 Enrollment: 564 715-257-7511

Housing: Homeownership rate: 74.1% (2000); Median home value: $78,900 (2000); Median rent: $310 per month (2000); Median age of housing: 48 years (2000).

Transportation: Commute to work: 89.3% car, 0.0% public transportation, 7.3% walk, 3.2% work from home (2000); Travel time to work: 36.2% less than 15 minutes, 21.9% 15 to 30 minutes, 33.3% 30 to 45 minutes, 6.0% 45 to 60 minutes, 2.7% 60 minutes or more (2000)

BERGEN (town). Covers a land area of 27.017 square miles and a water area of 7.759 square miles. Located at 44.71° N. Lat.; 89.76° W. Long.

Population: 615 (2000); Race: 100.0% White, 0.0% Black, 0.0% Asian, 0.0% American Indian and Alaska Native, 0.0% Hispanic of any race, 0.0% two or more races (2000); Density: 22.8 persons per square mile (2000); Age: 21.2% under 18, 11.5% over 64 (2000); Marriage status: 16.8% never married, 73.7% now married, 3.8% widowed, 5.8% divorced (2000); Foreign born: 0.5% (2000); Ancestry (includes multiple ancestries): 51.8% German, 25.3% Polish, 11.3% Irish, 7.4% Czech, 6.7% Norwegian (2000).

Economy: Single-family building permits issued: 8 (2001) / 8 (2000); Multi-family building permits issued: 0 (2001) / 0 (2000); Employment by occupation: 12.3% management, 16.9% professional, 11.4% services, 21.7% sales, 1.2% farming, 13.0% construction, 23.5% production (2000).

Income: Per capita income: $24,766 (2000); Median household income: $53,214 (2000); Poverty rate: 2.5% (2000).

Taxes: Total city taxes per capita: $64 (1997); City property taxes per capita: $62 (1997).

Education: High school graduation rate: 85.7% (2000); College graduation rate: 14.1% (2000).

Housing: Homeownership rate: 94.1% (2000); Median home value: $115,400 (2000); Median rent: $425 per month (2000); Median age of housing: 25 years (2000).

Transportation: Commute to work: 90.6% car, 0.0% public transportation, 1.8% walk, 7.6% work from home (2000); Travel time to work: 22.3% less than 15 minutes, 37.0% 15 to 30 minutes, 32.1% 30 to 45 minutes, 6.6% 45 to 60 minutes, 2.0% 60 minutes or more (2000)

BERLIN (town). Covers a land area of 34.677 square miles and a water area of 0 square miles. Located at 45.06° N. Lat.; 89.79° W. Long.

Population: 887 (2000); Race: 99.8% White, 0.0% Black, 0.2% Asian, 0.0% American Indian and Alaska Native, 0.2% Hispanic of any race, 0.0% two or more races (2000); Density: 25.6 persons per square mile (2000); Age: 27.7% under 18, 11.3% over 64 (2000); Marriage status: 21.9% never married, 67.4% now married, 5.0% widowed, 5.6% divorced (2000); Foreign born: 1.4% (2000); Ancestry (includes multiple ancestries): 74.4% German, 8.8% Polish, 5.6% French (except Basque), 5.3% English, 5.0% Irish (2000).

Economy: Single-family building permits issued: 11 (2001) / 11 (2000); Multi-family building permits issued: 0 (2001) / 0 (2000); Employment by occupation: 17.0% management, 14.1% professional, 10.8% services, 22.1% sales, 3.1% farming, 8.3% construction, 24.6% production (2000).

Income: Per capita income: $20,958 (2000); Median household income: $53,125 (2000); Poverty rate: 2.1% (2000).

Taxes: Total city taxes per capita: $92 (1997); City property taxes per capita: $91 (1997).

Education: High school graduation rate: 87.5% (2000); College graduation rate: 16.6% (2000).

Housing: Homeownership rate: 88.5% (2000); Median home value: $108,300 (2000); Median rent: $331 per month (2000); Median age of housing: 46 years (2000).

Transportation: Commute to work: 92.4% car, 0.0% public transportation, 1.4% walk, 5.9% work from home (2000); Travel time to work: 23.5% less than 15 minutes, 58.1% 15 to 30 minutes, 12.3% 30 to 45 minutes, 2.3% 45 to 60 minutes, 3.8% 60 minutes or more (2000)

BERN (town). Covers a land area of 34.085 square miles and a water area of 0.009 square miles. Located at 45.07° N. Lat.; 90.13° W. Long.

Population: 562 (2000); Race: 99.1% White, 0.0% Black, 0.0% Asian, 0.9% American Indian and Alaska Native, 1.1% Hispanic of any race, 0.0% two or more races (2000); Density: 16.5 persons per square mile (2000); Age: 33.2% under 18, 9.0% over 64 (2000); Marriage status: 29.0% never married, 65.9% now married, 2.8% widowed, 2.3% divorced (2000); Foreign born: 0.0% (2000); Ancestry (includes multiple ancestries): 63.8% German, 8.5% Polish, 7.4% Irish, 6.0% United States or American, 5.1% Norwegian (2000).

Economy: Single-family building permits issued: 2 (2001) / 2 (2000); Multi-family building permits issued: 0 (2001) / 0 (2000); Employment by occupation: 22.3% management, 6.5% professional, 8.3% services, 18.0% sales, 10.1% farming, 11.5% construction, 23.4% production (2000).

Income: Per capita income: $15,854 (2000); Median household income: $50,000 (2000); Poverty rate: 11.2% (2000).

Taxes: Total city taxes per capita: $63 (1997); City property taxes per capita: $63 (1997).

Education: High school graduation rate: 71.3% (2000); College graduation rate: 7.8% (2000).

Housing: Homeownership rate: 90.7% (2000); Median home value: $91,300 (2000); Median rent: $375 per month (2000); Median age of housing: 48 years (2000).

Transportation: Commute to work: 70.5% car, 0.7% public transportation, 0.7% walk, 27.7% work from home (2000); Travel time to work: 22.4% less than 15 minutes, 38.8% 15 to 30 minutes, 25.9% 30 to 45 minutes, 8.0% 45 to 60 minutes, 5.0% 60 minutes or more (2000)

BEVENT (town). Covers a land area of 42.109 square miles and a water area of 0.636 square miles. Located at 44.73° N. Lat.; 89.41° W. Long. Elevation is 1,220 feet.

Population: 1,126 (2000); Race: 99.6% White, 0.0% Black, 0.0% Asian, 0.0% American Indian and Alaska Native, 0.9% Hispanic of any race, 0.4% two or more races (2000); Density: 26.7 persons per square mile (2000); Age: 25.0% under 18, 11.6% over 64 (2000); Marriage status: 24.3% never married, 65.5% now married, 5.1% widowed, 5.1% divorced (2000); Foreign born: 0.9% (2000); Ancestry (includes multiple ancestries): 60.8% Polish, 30.5% German, 4.9% Irish, 3.2% Norwegian, 2.5% French (except Basque) (2000).

Economy: Single-family building permits issued: 14 (2001) / 8 (2000); Multi-family building permits issued: 0 (2001) / 0 (2000); Employment by occupation: 14.1% management, 13.3% professional, 12.5% services, 18.8% sales, 1.6% farming, 15.9% construction, 23.9% production (2000).

Income: Per capita income: $18,315 (2000); Median household income: $45,385 (2000); Poverty rate: 5.9% (2000).

Taxes: Total city taxes per capita: $36 (1997); City property taxes per capita: $33 (1997).

Education: High school graduation rate: 77.0% (2000); College graduation rate: 8.3% (2000).

Housing: Homeownership rate: 87.1% (2000); Median home value: $95,000 (2000); Median rent: $394 per month (2000); Median age of housing: 26 years (2000).

Transportation: Commute to work: 90.1% car, 0.0% public transportation, 1.9% walk, 8.0% work from home (2000); Travel time to work: 8.0% less than 15 minutes, 43.1% 15 to 30 minutes, 37.2% 30 to 45 minutes, 5.4% 45 to 60 minutes, 6.4% 60 minutes or more (2000)

BRIGHTON (town). Covers a land area of 34.216 square miles and a water area of 0.020 square miles. Located at 44.81° N. Lat.; 90.27° W. Long.
Population: 611 (2000); Race: 99.0% White, 0.0% Black, 0.6% Asian, 0.0% American Indian and Alaska Native, 0.0% Hispanic of any race, 0.0% two or more races (2000); Density: 17.9 persons per square mile (2000); Age: 33.0% under 18, 9.5% over 64 (2000); Marriage status: 24.8% never married, 69.0% now married, 1.6% widowed, 4.7% divorced (2000); Foreign born: 1.0% (2000); Ancestry (includes multiple ancestries): 63.2% German, 9.8% United States or American, 5.9% Polish, 5.8% Irish, 5.0% Norwegian (2000).
Economy: Employment by occupation: 21.8% management, 11.7% professional, 8.6% services, 18.1% sales, 10.4% farming, 9.2% construction, 20.2% production (2000).
Income: Per capita income: $14,710 (2000); Median household income: $38,304 (2000); Poverty rate: 9.5% (2000).
Taxes: Total city taxes per capita: $145 (1997); City property taxes per capita: $145 (1997).
Education: High school graduation rate: 78.4% (2000); College graduation rate: 12.1% (2000).
Housing: Homeownership rate: 80.7% (2000); Median home value: $87,000 (2000); Median rent: $325 per month (2000); Median age of housing: 42 years (2000).
Transportation: Commute to work: 78.9% car, 0.6% public transportation, 1.6% walk, 18.9% work from home (2000); Travel time to work: 28.7% less than 15 minutes, 55.9% 15 to 30 minutes, 13.0% 30 to 45 minutes, 0.0% 45 to 60 minutes, 2.3% 60 minutes or more (2000)

BROKAW (village). Covers a land area of 0.985 square miles and a water area of 0.161 square miles. Located at 45.02° N. Lat.; 89.65° W. Long. Elevation is 1,220 feet.
Population: 107 (2000); Race: 100.0% White, 0.0% Black, 0.0% Asian, 0.0% American Indian and Alaska Native, 0.0% Hispanic of any race, 0.0% two or more races (2000); Density: 108.6 persons per square mile (2000); Age: 14.7% under 18, 31.2% over 64 (2000); Marriage status: 36.6% never married, 40.9% now married, 18.3% widowed, 4.3% divorced (2000); Foreign born: 0.0% (2000); Ancestry (includes multiple ancestries): 57.8% German, 11.9% United States or American, 9.2% French (except Basque), 8.3% English, 8.3% Polish (2000).
Economy: Paper milling. Single-family building permits issued: 0 (2001) / 0 (2000); Multi-family building permits issued: 0 (2001) / 0 (2000); Employment by occupation: 8.9% management, 0.0% professional, 10.7% services, 28.6% sales, 0.0% farming, 8.9% construction, 42.9% production (2000).
Income: Per capita income: $28,290 (2000); Median household income: $27,083 (2000); Poverty rate: 21.5% (2000).
Taxes: Total city taxes per capita: $939 (1997); City property taxes per capita: $939 (1997).
Education: High school graduation rate: 65.5% (2000); College graduation rate: 3.6% (2000).
Housing: Homeownership rate: 61.5% (2000); Median home value: $58,300 (2000); Median rent: $375 per month (2000); Median age of housing: 60+ years (2000).
Transportation: Commute to work: 75.9% car, 0.0% public transportation, 24.1% walk, 0.0% work from home (2000); Travel time to work: 53.7% less than 15 minutes, 42.6% 15 to 30 minutes, 0.0% 30 to 45 minutes, 0.0% 45 to 60 minutes, 3.7% 60 minutes or more (2000)

CASSEL (town). Covers a land area of 33.027 square miles and a water area of 0.007 square miles. Located at 44.90° N. Lat.; 89.91° W. Long.
Population: 847 (2000); Race: 99.2% White, 0.0% Black, 0.1% Asian, 0.1% American Indian and Alaska Native, 0.8% Hispanic of any race, 0.6% two or more races (2000); Density: 25.6 persons per square mile (2000); Age: 30.6% under 18, 10.9% over 64 (2000); Marriage status: 25.0% never married, 66.7% now married, 2.2% widowed, 6.2% divorced (2000); Foreign born: 1.0% (2000); Ancestry (includes multiple ancestries): 59.3% German, 27.8% Polish, 4.5% United States or American, 3.0% Irish, 3.0% Other groups (2000).
Economy: Single-family building permits issued: 8 (2001) / 7 (2000); Multi-family building permits issued: 0 (2001) / 0 (2000); Employment by occupation: 19.8% management, 8.6% professional, 7.6% services, 25.1% sales, 7.2% farming, 9.3% construction, 22.5% production (2000).
Income: Per capita income: $22,818 (2000); Median household income: $52,614 (2000); Poverty rate: 9.4% (2000).
Taxes: Total city taxes per capita: $51 (1997); City property taxes per capita: $49 (1997).
Education: High school graduation rate: 84.6% (2000); College graduation rate: 8.5% (2000).
Housing: Homeownership rate: 93.8% (2000); Median home value: $97,600 (2000); Median rent: $425 per month (2000); Median age of housing: 43 years (2000).
Transportation: Commute to work: 78.1% car, 0.0% public transportation, 5.7% walk, 15.6% work from home (2000); Travel time to work: 39.4% less than 15 minutes, 39.4% 15 to 30 minutes, 15.7% 30 to 45 minutes, 1.2% 45 to 60 minutes, 4.2% 60 minutes or more (2000)

CLEVELAND (town). Covers a land area of 29.664 square miles and a water area of 0.859 square miles. Located at 44.81° N. Lat.; 90.00° W. Long.
Population: 1,160 (2000); Race: 99.1% White, 0.0% Black, 0.2% Asian, 0.0% American Indian and Alaska Native, 0.4% Hispanic of any race, 0.5% two or more races (2000); Density: 39.1 persons per square mile (2000); Age: 25.1% under 18, 11.4% over 64 (2000); Marriage status: 24.2% never married, 66.6% now married, 3.2% widowed, 5.9% divorced (2000); Foreign born: 0.5% (2000); Ancestry (includes multiple ancestries): 71.5% German, 10.3% Polish, 5.9% Irish, 4.4% Norwegian, 3.7% French (except Basque) (2000).
Economy: Single-family building permits issued: 14 (2001) / 22 (2000); Multi-family building permits issued: 0 (2001) / 0 (2000); Employment by occupation: 14.1% management, 11.9% professional, 10.1% services, 18.1% sales, 2.3% farming, 14.3% construction, 29.1% production (2000).
Income: Per capita income: $19,293 (2000); Median household income: $49,167 (2000); Poverty rate: 4.9% (2000).
Taxes: Total city taxes per capita: $39 (1997); City property taxes per capita: $39 (1997).
Education: High school graduation rate: 80.5% (2000); College graduation rate: 8.6% (2000).
Housing: Homeownership rate: 91.2% (2000); Median home value: $93,100 (2000); Median rent: $343 per month (2000); Median age of housing: 26 years (2000).
Transportation: Commute to work: 89.2% car, 0.0% public transportation, 0.9% walk, 9.1% work from home (2000); Travel time to work: 20.1% less than 15 minutes, 49.3% 15 to 30 minutes, 22.9% 30 to 45 minutes, 2.4% 45 to 60 minutes, 5.3% 60 minutes or more (2000)

DAY (town). Covers a land area of 33.744 square miles and a water area of 0.236 square miles. Located at 44.72° N. Lat.; 90.02° W. Long.
Population: 1,023 (2000); Race: 99.5% White, 0.0% Black, 0.0% Asian, 0.5% American Indian and Alaska Native, 0.2% Hispanic of any race, 0.0% two or more races (2000); Density: 30.3 persons per square mile (2000); Age: 25.2% under 18, 10.5% over 64 (2000); Marriage status: 24.1% never married, 68.2% now married, 4.8% widowed, 2.8% divorced (2000); Foreign born: 0.8% (2000); Ancestry (includes multiple ancestries): 72.1% German, 10.7% Polish, 7.4% Irish, 4.7% French (except Basque), 3.9% Norwegian (2000).
Economy: Employment by occupation: 21.5% management, 11.5% professional, 10.9% services, 19.2% sales, 3.8% farming, 13.7% construction, 19.4% production (2000).
Income: Per capita income: $17,725 (2000); Median household income: $47,500 (2000); Poverty rate: 4.1% (2000).
Education: High school graduation rate: 80.5% (2000); College graduation rate: 8.6% (2000).
Housing: Homeownership rate: 86.8% (2000); Median home value: $84,400 (2000); Median rent: $342 per month (2000); Median age of housing: 31 years (2000).
Transportation: Commute to work: 83.4% car, 0.0% public transportation, 1.9% walk, 14.5% work from home (2000); Travel time to work: 26.1% less than 15 minutes, 54.2% 15 to 30 minutes, 11.1% 30 to 45 minutes, 4.3% 45 to 60 minutes, 4.3% 60 minutes or more (2000)

EASTON (town). Covers a land area of 43.015 square miles and a water area of 0.019 square miles. Located at 44.98° N. Lat.; 89.42° W. Long.
Population: 1,062 (2000); Race: 96.8% White, 0.6% Black, 0.5% Asian, 0.0% American Indian and Alaska Native, 2.4% Hispanic of any race, 0.0% two or more races (2000); Density: 24.7 persons per square mile (2000); Age: 24.6% under 18, 12.7% over 64 (2000); Marriage status: 18.3% never married, 71.7% now married, 3.7% widowed, 6.4% divorced (2000); Foreign born: 0.8% (2000); Ancestry (includes multiple ancestries): 65.3% German, 19.1% Polish, 9.5% Irish, 8.0% Norwegian, 5.5% Dutch (2000).

Economy: Single-family building permits issued: 5 (2001) / 6 (2000); Multi-family building permits issued: 0 (2001) / 0 (2000); Employment by occupation: 15.8% management, 13.4% professional, 9.7% services, 23.0% sales, 2.1% farming, 15.0% construction, 21.0% production (2000).
Income: Per capita income: $26,587 (2000); Median household income: $49,722 (2000); Poverty rate: 2.6% (2000).
Taxes: Total city taxes per capita: $86 (1997); City property taxes per capita: $83 (1997).
Education: High school graduation rate: 81.9% (2000); College graduation rate: 15.7% (2000).
Housing: Homeownership rate: 93.3% (2000); Median home value: $107,400 (2000); Median rent: $463 per month (2000); Median age of housing: 32 years (2000).
Transportation: Commute to work: 83.0% car, 0.5% public transportation, 1.7% walk, 13.4% work from home (2000); Travel time to work: 11.6% less than 15 minutes, 64.1% 15 to 30 minutes, 18.9% 30 to 45 minutes, 0.8% 45 to 60 minutes, 4.6% 60 minutes or more (2000)

EAU PLEINE (town). Covers a land area of 33.230 square miles and a water area of 0.007 square miles. Located at 44.81° N. Lat.; 90.13° W. Long.
Population: 750 (2000); Race: 99.1% White, 0.0% Black, 0.0% Asian, 0.0% American Indian and Alaska Native, 0.0% Hispanic of any race, 0.9% two or more races (2000); Density: 22.6 persons per square mile (2000); Age: 31.1% under 18, 10.5% over 64 (2000); Marriage status: 20.5% never married, 66.4% now married, 5.4% widowed, 7.7% divorced (2000); Foreign born: 0.1% (2000); Ancestry (includes multiple ancestries): 74.2% German, 13.8% Polish, 4.5% French (except Basque), 4.4% Irish, 3.6% United States or American (2000).
Economy: Employment by occupation: 15.9% management, 14.4% professional, 14.6% services, 19.8% sales, 3.7% farming, 14.1% construction, 17.6% production (2000).
Income: Per capita income: $18,052 (2000); Median household income: $41,875 (2000); Poverty rate: 4.9% (2000).
Taxes: Total city taxes per capita: $40 (1997); City property taxes per capita: $40 (1997).
Education: High school graduation rate: 85.8% (2000); College graduation rate: 9.2% (2000).
Housing: Homeownership rate: 88.0% (2000); Median home value: $83,300 (2000); Median rent: $463 per month (2000); Median age of housing: 37 years (2000).
Transportation: Commute to work: 84.4% car, 0.0% public transportation, 4.7% walk, 9.9% work from home (2000); Travel time to work: 26.9% less than 15 minutes, 48.4% 15 to 30 minutes, 15.7% 30 to 45 minutes, 3.8% 45 to 60 minutes, 5.2% 60 minutes or more (2000)

EDGAR (village). Covers a land area of 1.656 square miles and a water area of 0 square miles. Located at 44.92° N. Lat.; 89.96° W. Long. Elevation is 1,270 feet.
Population: 1,386 (2000); Race: 99.0% White, 0.0% Black, 0.3% Asian, 0.1% American Indian and Alaska Native, 0.3% Hispanic of any race, 0.2% two or more races (2000); Density: 837.0 persons per square mile (2000); Age: 26.9% under 18, 15.1% over 64 (2000); Marriage status: 24.3% never married, 61.3% now married, 6.9% widowed, 7.5% divorced (2000); Foreign born: 0.9% (2000); Ancestry (includes multiple ancestries): 63.7% German, 28.7% Polish, 5.1% United States or American, 4.7% Irish, 3.5% Norwegian (2000).
Economy: Cheese, processed meat, wood products. Manufacturing: juvenile bassinettes, cradles, etc. Single-family building permits issued: 7 (2001) / 6 (2000); Multi-family building permits issued: 0 (2001) / 0 (2000); Employment by occupation: 7.9% management, 17.5% professional, 7.8% services, 27.4% sales, 2.5% farming, 7.9% construction, 28.9% production (2000).
Income: Per capita income: $21,605 (2000); Median household income: $40,759 (2000); Poverty rate: 4.3% (2000).
Taxes: Total city taxes per capita: $127 (1997); City property taxes per capita: $115 (1997).
Education: High school graduation rate: 85.2% (2000); College graduation rate: 12.2% (2000).

School District(s)

Edgar (PK-12)
2000 Enrollment: 665 715-352-2351

Housing: Homeownership rate: 75.3% (2000); Median home value: $93,300 (2000); Median rent: $306 per month (2000); Median age of housing: 30 years (2000).
Safety: Violent crime rate: 0.0 per 10,000 population; Property crime rate: 150.4 per 10,000 population (2001).
Transportation: Commute to work: 89.7% car, 0.0% public transportation, 6.0% walk, 3.3% work from home (2000); Travel time to work: 29.7% less than 15 minutes, 41.8% 15 to 30 minutes, 22.5% 30 to 45 minutes, 2.8% 45 to 60 minutes, 3.2% 60 minutes or more (2000)

ELDERON (village). Covers a land area of 1.107 square miles and a water area of 0.052 square miles. Located at 44.78° N. Lat.; 89.25° W. Long. Elevation is 1,199 feet.
Population: 189 (2000); Race: 100.0% White, 0.0% Black, 0.0% Asian, 0.0% American Indian and Alaska Native, 0.0% Hispanic of any race, 0.0% two or more races (2000); Density: 170.8 persons per square mile (2000); Age: 19.5% under 18, 17.0% over 64 (2000); Marriage status: 20.9% never married, 61.2% now married, 10.1% widowed, 7.9% divorced (2000); Foreign born: 0.0% (2000); Ancestry (includes multiple ancestries): 44.7% German, 34.0% Polish, 17.6% Norwegian, 8.2% Irish, 5.7% Other groups (2000).
Economy: Single-family building permits issued: 0 (2001) / 0 (2000); Multi-family building permits issued: 0 (2001) / 0 (2000); Employment by occupation: 5.1% management, 3.8% professional, 15.4% services, 21.8% sales, 3.8% farming, 7.7% construction, 42.3% production (2000).
Income: Per capita income: $19,225 (2000); Median household income: $38,125 (2000); Poverty rate: 5.0% (2000).
Taxes: Total city taxes per capita: $101 (1997); City property taxes per capita: $83 (1997).
Education: High school graduation rate: 78.9% (2000); College graduation rate: 2.4% (2000).
Housing: Homeownership rate: 80.3% (2000); Median home value: $54,500 (2000); Median rent: $325 per month (2000); Median age of housing: 60+ years (2000).
Transportation: Commute to work: 90.7% car, 0.0% public transportation, 9.3% walk, 0.0% work from home (2000); Travel time to work: 21.3% less than 15 minutes, 34.7% 15 to 30 minutes, 42.7% 30 to 45 minutes, 1.3% 45 to 60 minutes, 0.0% 60 minutes or more (2000)

ELDERON (town). Covers a land area of 34.595 square miles and a water area of 0.307 square miles. Located at 44.81° N. Lat.; 89.27° W. Long. Elevation is 1,199 feet.
Population: 567 (2000); Race: 97.0% White, 0.4% Black, 0.2% Asian, 1.4% American Indian and Alaska Native, 1.1% Hispanic of any race, 0.7% two or more races (2000); Density: 16.4 persons per square mile (2000); Age: 26.7% under 18, 13.0% over 64 (2000); Marriage status: 21.1% never married, 61.8% now married, 9.1% widowed, 8.0% divorced (2000); Foreign born: 0.7% (2000); Ancestry (includes multiple ancestries): 47.8% German, 37.1% Polish, 10.5% Norwegian, 7.2% Irish, 5.6% French (except Basque) (2000).
Economy: In dairying region. Employment by occupation: 17.1% management, 14.1% professional, 16.8% services, 18.4% sales, 3.0% farming, 9.2% construction, 21.4% production (2000).
Income: Per capita income: $15,968 (2000); Median household income: $36,667 (2000); Poverty rate: 5.5% (2000).
Taxes: Total city taxes per capita: $96 (1997); City property taxes per capita: $96 (1997).
Education: High school graduation rate: 81.2% (2000); College graduation rate: 11.4% (2000).
Housing: Homeownership rate: 85.9% (2000); Median home value: $85,400 (2000); Median rent: $425 per month (2000); Median age of housing: 30 years (2000).
Transportation: Commute to work: 84.1% car, 2.3% public transportation, 3.0% walk, 9.9% work from home (2000); Travel time to work: 24.3% less than 15 minutes, 27.6% 15 to 30 minutes, 36.8% 30 to 45 minutes, 3.7% 45 to 60 minutes, 7.7% 60 minutes or more (2000)

EMMET (town). Covers a land area of 39.833 square miles and a water area of 0.373 square miles. Located at 44.80° N. Lat.; 89.90° W. Long.
Population: 842 (2000); Race: 99.3% White, 0.2% Black, 0.0% Asian, 0.0% American Indian and Alaska Native, 1.0% Hispanic of any race, 0.0% two or more races (2000); Density: 21.1 persons per square mile (2000); Age: 30.2% under 18, 10.8% over 64 (2000); Marriage status: 22.9% never married, 68.9% now married, 2.9% widowed, 5.4% divorced (2000); Foreign born: 0.0% (2000); Ancestry (includes multiple ancestries): 65.5% German, 27.1% Polish, 12.0% Irish, 4.2% French (except Basque), 3.3% United States or American (2000).
Economy: Single-family building permits issued: 12 (2001) / 10 (2000); Multi-family building permits issued: 0 (2001) / 0 (2000); Employment by occupation: 14.7% management, 10.4% professional, 11.1% services, 19.8% sales, 4.1% farming, 12.4% construction, 27.4% production (2000).

Income: Per capita income: $16,902 (2000); Median household income: $47,031 (2000); Poverty rate: 9.9% (2000).
Taxes: Total city taxes per capita: $37 (1997); City property taxes per capita: $36 (1997).
Education: High school graduation rate: 78.8% (2000); College graduation rate: 8.1% (2000).
Housing: Homeownership rate: 86.9% (2000); Median home value: $100,000 (2000); Median rent: $389 per month (2000); Median age of housing: 36 years (2000).
Transportation: Commute to work: 83.2% car, 0.7% public transportation, 2.1% walk, 13.6% work from home (2000); Travel time to work: 18.4% less than 15 minutes, 42.1% 15 to 30 minutes, 28.3% 30 to 45 minutes, 4.3% 45 to 60 minutes, 6.9% 60 minutes or more (2000)

EVERGREEN (CDP). Covers a land area of 3.815 square miles and a water area of 0 square miles. Located at 44.84° N. Lat.; 89.62° W. Long.
Population: 3,611 (2000); Race: 99.2% White, 0.0% Black, 0.0% Asian, 0.0% American Indian and Alaska Native, 0.0% Hispanic of any race, 0.8% two or more races (2000); Density: 946.5 persons per square mile (2000); Age: 30.5% under 18, 4.6% over 64 (2000); Marriage status: 20.5% never married, 68.9% now married, 1.3% widowed, 9.3% divorced (2000); Foreign born: 0.2% (2000); Ancestry (includes multiple ancestries): 51.0% German, 27.3% Polish, 8.8% Norwegian, 6.8% Irish, 4.8% English (2000).
Economy: Employment by occupation: 14.3% management, 18.4% professional, 18.4% services, 26.7% sales, 0.0% farming, 7.9% construction, 14.4% production (2000).
Income: Per capita income: $21,467 (2000); Median household income: $58,774 (2000); Poverty rate: 4.6% (2000).
Education: High school graduation rate: 91.7% (2000); College graduation rate: 23.9% (2000).
Housing: Homeownership rate: 90.2% (2000); Median home value: $116,600 (2000); Median rent: $415 per month (2000); Median age of housing: 20 years (2000).
Transportation: Commute to work: 95.5% car, 0.0% public transportation, 1.1% walk, 2.7% work from home (2000); Travel time to work: 36.9% less than 15 minutes, 48.2% 15 to 30 minutes, 8.6% 30 to 45 minutes, 1.3% 45 to 60 minutes, 5.0% 60 minutes or more (2000)

FENWOOD (village). Covers a land area of 0.984 square miles and a water area of 0 square miles. Located at 44.86° N. Lat.; 90.01° W. Long. Elevation is 1,300 feet.
Population: 174 (2000); Race: 100.0% White, 0.0% Black, 0.0% Asian, 0.0% American Indian and Alaska Native, 0.0% Hispanic of any race, 0.0% two or more races (2000); Density: 176.7 persons per square mile (2000); Age: 26.0% under 18, 14.1% over 64 (2000); Marriage status: 30.1% never married, 68.4% now married, 1.5% widowed, 0.0% divorced (2000); Foreign born: 0.0% (2000); Ancestry (includes multiple ancestries): 78.0% German, 5.6% French (except Basque), 5.1% Norwegian, 4.5% United States or American, 2.8% Polish (2000).
Economy: Lumbering, dairying, livestock raising. Single-family building permits issued: 0 (2001) / 1 (2000); Multi-family building permits issued: 0 (2001) / 0 (2000); Employment by occupation: 5.0% management, 3.0% professional, 13.0% services, 29.0% sales, 2.0% farming, 12.0% construction, 36.0% production (2000).
Income: Per capita income: $15,920 (2000); Median household income: $44,000 (2000); Poverty rate: 0.0% (2000).
Taxes: Total city taxes per capita: $39 (1997); City property taxes per capita: $39 (1997).
Education: High school graduation rate: 81.4% (2000); College graduation rate: 2.1% (2000).
Housing: Homeownership rate: 84.2% (2000); Median home value: $61,700 (2000); Median rent: $425 per month (2000); Median age of housing: 27 years (2000).
Transportation: Commute to work: 79.0% car, 0.0% public transportation, 13.0% walk, 5.0% work from home (2000); Travel time to work: 48.4% less than 15 minutes, 23.2% 15 to 30 minutes, 23.2% 30 to 45 minutes, 3.2% 45 to 60 minutes, 2.1% 60 minutes or more (2000)

FRANKFORT (town). Covers a land area of 35.195 square miles and a water area of 0.006 square miles. Located at 44.89° N. Lat.; 90.13° W. Long.
Population: 651 (2000); Race: 100.0% White, 0.0% Black, 0.0% Asian, 0.0% American Indian and Alaska Native, 0.3% Hispanic of any race, 0.0% two or more races (2000); Density: 18.5 persons per square mile (2000); Age: 27.8% under 18, 10.7% over 64 (2000); Marriage status: 26.3% never married, 65.1% now married, 3.5% widowed, 5.1% divorced (2000); Foreign born: 0.9% (2000); Ancestry (includes multiple ancestries): 66.1% German, 8.0% Irish, 7.9% Polish, 4.4% Dutch, 4.3% Swedish (2000).
Economy: Employment by occupation: 25.4% management, 12.4% professional, 11.9% services, 13.5% sales, 4.1% farming, 5.5% construction, 27.1% production (2000).
Income: Per capita income: $15,946 (2000); Median household income: $41,071 (2000); Poverty rate: 9.7% (2000).
Taxes: Total city taxes per capita: $62 (1997); City property taxes per capita: $60 (1997).
Education: High school graduation rate: 80.7% (2000); College graduation rate: 11.4% (2000).
Housing: Homeownership rate: 87.5% (2000); Median home value: $80,500 (2000); Median rent: $413 per month (2000); Median age of housing: 51 years (2000).
Transportation: Commute to work: 66.3% car, 0.0% public transportation, 7.2% walk, 25.4% work from home (2000); Travel time to work: 33.7% less than 15 minutes, 44.1% 15 to 30 minutes, 16.7% 30 to 45 minutes, 2.2% 45 to 60 minutes, 3.3% 60 minutes or more (2000)

FRANZEN (town). Covers a land area of 36.390 square miles and a water area of 0.222 square miles. Located at 44.73° N. Lat.; 89.26° W. Long.
Population: 505 (2000); Race: 98.3% White, 0.0% Black, 0.0% Asian, 0.6% American Indian and Alaska Native, 1.1% Hispanic of any race, 0.4% two or more races (2000); Density: 13.9 persons per square mile (2000); Age: 28.5% under 18, 15.7% over 64 (2000); Marriage status: 23.8% never married, 68.6% now married, 5.4% widowed, 2.2% divorced (2000); Foreign born: 1.3% (2000); Ancestry (includes multiple ancestries): 66.7% Polish, 35.2% German, 5.9% French (except Basque), 5.6% Norwegian, 5.2% Irish (2000).
Economy: Single-family building permits issued: 4 (2001) / 7 (2000); Multi-family building permits issued: 0 (2001) / 0 (2000); Employment by occupation: 9.8% management, 8.7% professional, 7.1% services, 18.1% sales, 8.7% farming, 9.8% construction, 37.8% production (2000).
Income: Per capita income: $18,623 (2000); Median household income: $41,442 (2000); Poverty rate: 7.7% (2000).
Taxes: Total city taxes per capita: $22 (1997); City property taxes per capita: $22 (1997).
Education: High school graduation rate: 74.8% (2000); College graduation rate: 6.2% (2000).
Housing: Homeownership rate: 88.8% (2000); Median home value: $83,800 (2000); Median rent: $410 per month (2000); Median age of housing: 30 years (2000).
Transportation: Commute to work: 83.5% car, 0.0% public transportation, 1.2% walk, 14.6% work from home (2000); Travel time to work: 14.3% less than 15 minutes, 9.7% 15 to 30 minutes, 50.2% 30 to 45 minutes, 20.7% 45 to 60 minutes, 5.1% 60 minutes or more (2000)

GREEN VALLEY (town). Covers a land area of 28.930 square miles and a water area of 6.235 square miles. Located at 44.74° N. Lat.; 89.90° W. Long.
Population: 514 (2000); Race: 99.6% White, 0.0% Black, 0.4% Asian, 0.0% American Indian and Alaska Native, 0.0% Hispanic of any race, 0.0% two or more races (2000); Density: 17.8 persons per square mile (2000); Age: 23.9% under 18, 14.9% over 64 (2000); Marriage status: 24.7% never married, 66.1% now married, 5.2% widowed, 4.0% divorced (2000); Foreign born: 0.0% (2000); Ancestry (includes multiple ancestries): 57.9% German, 23.5% Polish, 12.8% Irish, 8.6% United States or American, 5.7% English (2000).
Economy: Employment by occupation: 18.4% management, 7.9% professional, 9.4% services, 23.5% sales, 3.6% farming, 13.0% construction, 24.2% production (2000).
Income: Per capita income: $21,048 (2000); Median household income: $49,250 (2000); Poverty rate: 6.2% (2000).
Taxes: Total city taxes per capita: $55 (1997); City property taxes per capita: $55 (1997).
Education: High school graduation rate: 81.6% (2000); College graduation rate: 7.3% (2000).
Housing: Homeownership rate: 95.7% (2000); Median home value: $132,800 (2000); Median rent: $238 per month (2000); Median age of housing: 23 years (2000).
Transportation: Commute to work: 85.1% car, 0.0% public transportation, 1.5% walk, 13.5% work from home (2000); Travel time to work: 10.1% less than 15 minutes, 50.4% 15 to 30 minutes, 29.0% 30 to 45 minutes, 4.2% 45 to 60 minutes, 6.3% 60 minutes or more (2000)

GUENTHER (town). Covers a land area of 34.431 square miles and a water area of 0.042 square miles. Located at 44.72° N. Lat.; 89.55° W. Long.

Population: 302 (2000); Race: 98.6% White, 0.7% Black, 0.0% Asian, 0.0% American Indian and Alaska Native, 2.0% Hispanic of any race, 0.7% two or more races (2000); Density: 8.8 persons per square mile (2000); Age: 24.6% under 18, 14.3% over 64 (2000); Marriage status: 19.1% never married, 61.3% now married, 9.1% widowed, 10.4% divorced (2000); Foreign born: 0.0% (2000); Ancestry (includes multiple ancestries): 46.8% Polish, 40.6% German, 7.2% English, 4.1% Irish, 3.4% Other groups (2000).
Economy: Employment by occupation: 10.9% management, 6.9% professional, 10.3% services, 24.7% sales, 1.1% farming, 16.7% construction, 29.3% production (2000).
Income: Per capita income: $18,475 (2000); Median household income: $43,250 (2000); Poverty rate: 5.5% (2000).
Taxes: Total city taxes per capita: $113 (1997); City property taxes per capita: $113 (1997).
Education: High school graduation rate: 76.1% (2000); College graduation rate: 7.2% (2000).
Housing: Homeownership rate: 87.9% (2000); Median home value: $80,000 (2000); Median rent: $300 per month (2000); Median age of housing: 39 years (2000).
Transportation: Commute to work: 83.7% car, 0.0% public transportation, 1.8% walk, 14.5% work from home (2000); Travel time to work: 26.1% less than 15 minutes, 38.7% 15 to 30 minutes, 26.8% 30 to 45 minutes, 7.0% 45 to 60 minutes, 1.4% 60 minutes or more (2000)

HALSEY (town). Covers a land area of 33.124 square miles and a water area of 0 square miles. Located at 45.08° N. Lat.; 90.02° W. Long.
Population: 645 (2000); Race: 99.1% White, 0.0% Black, 0.0% Asian, 0.3% American Indian and Alaska Native, 2.5% Hispanic of any race, 0.6% two or more races (2000); Density: 19.5 persons per square mile (2000); Age: 32.7% under 18, 10.8% over 64 (2000); Marriage status: 22.6% never married, 69.5% now married, 4.1% widowed, 3.8% divorced (2000); Foreign born: 1.4% (2000); Ancestry (includes multiple ancestries): 63.1% German, 7.6% Polish, 6.0% Irish, 5.1% French (except Basque), 4.9% United States or American (2000).
Economy: Employment by occupation: 16.0% management, 4.5% professional, 8.9% services, 18.2% sales, 4.8% farming, 10.5% construction, 37.1% production (2000).
Income: Per capita income: $15,317 (2000); Median household income: $44,625 (2000); Poverty rate: 4.2% (2000).
Taxes: Total city taxes per capita: $52 (1997); City property taxes per capita: $52 (1997).
Education: High school graduation rate: 71.4% (2000); College graduation rate: 3.0% (2000).
Housing: Homeownership rate: 92.0% (2000); Median home value: $82,000 (2000); Median rent: $408 per month (2000); Median age of housing: 41 years (2000).
Transportation: Commute to work: 78.1% car, 1.0% public transportation, 2.9% walk, 17.3% work from home (2000); Travel time to work: 25.3% less than 15 minutes, 37.5% 15 to 30 minutes, 25.7% 30 to 45 minutes, 8.7% 45 to 60 minutes, 2.8% 60 minutes or more (2000)

HAMBURG (town). Covers a land area of 35.368 square miles and a water area of 0 square miles. Located at 45.07° N. Lat.; 89.91° W. Long. Elevation is 1,468 feet.
Population: 910 (2000); Race: 97.1% White, 0.0% Black, 2.0% Asian, 0.0% American Indian and Alaska Native, 1.6% Hispanic of any race, 0.4% two or more races (2000); Density: 25.7 persons per square mile (2000); Age: 34.7% under 18, 9.2% over 64 (2000); Marriage status: 21.7% never married, 69.9% now married, 3.2% widowed, 5.2% divorced (2000); Foreign born: 2.1% (2000); Ancestry (includes multiple ancestries): 73.9% German, 7.2% English, 6.0% Irish, 4.9% Polish, 3.5% Other groups (2000).
Economy: Employment by occupation: 14.5% management, 12.3% professional, 7.6% services, 21.1% sales, 5.3% farming, 11.5% construction, 27.8% production (2000).
Income: Per capita income: $15,920 (2000); Median household income: $50,500 (2000); Poverty rate: 5.4% (2000).
Taxes: Total city taxes per capita: $48 (1997); City property taxes per capita: $48 (1997).
Education: High school graduation rate: 82.9% (2000); College graduation rate: 11.3% (2000).
Housing: Homeownership rate: 93.2% (2000); Median home value: $84,300 (2000); Median rent: $525 per month (2000); Median age of housing: 57 years (2000).
Transportation: Commute to work: 82.1% car, 0.6% public transportation, 2.3% walk, 15.0% work from home (2000); Travel time to work: 17.4% less than 15 minutes, 40.2% 15 to 30 minutes, 32.2% 30 to 45 minutes, 7.7% 45 to 60 minutes, 2.4% 60 minutes or more (2000)

HARRISON (town). Covers a land area of 36.656 square miles and a water area of 0.027 square miles. Located at 45.08° N. Lat.; 89.26° W. Long.
Population: 418 (2000); Race: 99.1% White, 0.0% Black, 0.0% Asian, 0.9% American Indian and Alaska Native, 0.0% Hispanic of any race, 0.0% two or more races (2000); Density: 11.4 persons per square mile (2000); Age: 31.3% under 18, 8.5% over 64 (2000); Marriage status: 26.2% never married, 62.3% now married, 3.7% widowed, 7.7% divorced (2000); Foreign born: 0.0% (2000); Ancestry (includes multiple ancestries): 57.8% German, 15.0% Polish, 10.1% Czech, 7.1% Irish, 5.5% English (2000).
Economy: Single-family building permits issued: 4 (2001) / 4 (2000); Multi-family building permits issued: 0 (2001) / 0 (2000); Employment by occupation: 10.5% management, 8.5% professional, 10.0% services, 14.0% sales, 1.5% farming, 21.0% construction, 34.5% production (2000).
Income: Per capita income: $14,278 (2000); Median household income: $40,192 (2000); Poverty rate: 4.6% (2000).
Taxes: Total city taxes per capita: $59 (1997); City property taxes per capita: $59 (1997).
Education: High school graduation rate: 83.2% (2000); College graduation rate: 7.8% (2000).
Housing: Homeownership rate: 86.7% (2000); Median home value: $66,700 (2000); Median rent: $319 per month (2000); Median age of housing: 28 years (2000).
Transportation: Commute to work: 91.9% car, 1.0% public transportation, 3.0% walk, 3.0% work from home (2000); Travel time to work: 19.3% less than 15 minutes, 40.6% 15 to 30 minutes, 27.6% 30 to 45 minutes, 7.8% 45 to 60 minutes, 4.7% 60 minutes or more (2000)

HATLEY (village). Covers a land area of 0.894 square miles and a water area of 0 square miles. Located at 44.88° N. Lat.; 89.34° W. Long. Elevation is 1,270 feet.
Population: 476 (2000); Race: 98.7% White, 0.0% Black, 0.6% Asian, 0.0% American Indian and Alaska Native, 1.3% Hispanic of any race, 0.8% two or more races (2000); Density: 532.6 persons per square mile (2000); Age: 25.5% under 18, 10.4% over 64 (2000); Marriage status: 26.1% never married, 59.5% now married, 5.2% widowed, 9.2% divorced (2000); Foreign born: 0.6% (2000); Ancestry (includes multiple ancestries): 58.6% German, 45.9% Polish, 10.2% Irish, 4.0% United States or American, 3.8% Other groups (2000).
Economy: In dairying region. Manufacturing: hardwood veneers. Single-family building permits issued: 1 (2001) / 6 (2000); Multi-family building permits issued: 0 (2001) / 0 (2000); Employment by occupation: 12.1% management, 9.3% professional, 16.2% services, 19.0% sales, 1.0% farming, 10.7% construction, 31.7% production (2000).
Income: Per capita income: $20,373 (2000); Median household income: $47,875 (2000); Poverty rate: 4.7% (2000).
Taxes: Total city taxes per capita: $51 (1997); City property taxes per capita: $32 (1997).
Education: High school graduation rate: 80.1% (2000); College graduation rate: 9.1% (2000).
Housing: Homeownership rate: 73.4% (2000); Median home value: $95,300 (2000); Median rent: $421 per month (2000); Median age of housing: 20 years (2000).
Transportation: Commute to work: 91.2% car, 0.0% public transportation, 6.0% walk, 2.1% work from home (2000); Travel time to work: 23.3% less than 15 minutes, 52.7% 15 to 30 minutes, 16.1% 30 to 45 minutes, 2.9% 45 to 60 minutes, 5.0% 60 minutes or more (2000)

HEWITT (town). Covers a land area of 43.404 square miles and a water area of 0 square miles. Located at 45.07° N. Lat.; 89.44° W. Long.
Population: 545 (2000); Race: 99.7% White, 0.0% Black, 0.3% Asian, 0.0% American Indian and Alaska Native, 0.0% Hispanic of any race, 0.0% two or more races (2000); Density: 12.6 persons per square mile (2000); Age: 27.7% under 18, 10.5% over 64 (2000); Marriage status: 23.2% never married, 65.1% now married, 5.4% widowed, 6.3% divorced (2000); Foreign born: 0.3% (2000); Ancestry (includes multiple ancestries): 65.7% German, 18.2% Polish, 9.3% English, 6.0% Norwegian, 6.0% Irish (2000).
Economy: Employment by occupation: 19.4% management, 12.4% professional, 7.6% services, 20.9% sales, 5.3% farming, 13.8% construction, 20.6% production (2000).
Income: Per capita income: $20,155 (2000); Median household income: $51,042 (2000); Poverty rate: 2.4% (2000).
Taxes: Total city taxes per capita: $129 (1997); City property taxes per capita: $127 (1997).

Education: High school graduation rate: 81.4% (2000); College graduation rate: 10.8% (2000).
Housing: Homeownership rate: 91.2% (2000); Median home value: $90,500 (2000); Median rent: $325 per month (2000); Median age of housing: 32 years (2000).
Transportation: Commute to work: 89.3% car, 0.0% public transportation, 3.3% walk, 7.4% work from home (2000); Travel time to work: 12.2% less than 15 minutes, 49.8% 15 to 30 minutes, 32.5% 30 to 45 minutes, 1.3% 45 to 60 minutes, 4.2% 60 minutes or more (2000)

HOLTON (town). Covers a land area of 34.271 square miles and a water area of 0.006 square miles. Located at 44.98° N. Lat.; 90.26° W. Long.
Population: 907 (2000); Race: 99.3% White, 0.0% Black, 0.0% Asian, 0.0% American Indian and Alaska Native, 0.0% Hispanic of any race, 0.4% two or more races (2000); Density: 26.5 persons per square mile (2000); Age: 31.8% under 18, 10.4% over 64 (2000); Marriage status: 25.6% never married, 67.8% now married, 2.0% widowed, 4.7% divorced (2000); Foreign born: 1.9% (2000); Ancestry (includes multiple ancestries): 71.0% German, 6.4% Norwegian, 4.9% Polish, 4.1% Irish, 3.2% United States or American (2000).
Economy: Employment by occupation: 29.0% management, 10.1% professional, 8.2% services, 12.1% sales, 8.2% farming, 7.8% construction, 24.5% production (2000).
Income: Per capita income: $13,884 (2000); Median household income: $36,000 (2000); Poverty rate: 14.9% (2000).
Taxes: Total city taxes per capita: $65 (1997); City property taxes per capita: $65 (1997).
Education: High school graduation rate: 78.9% (2000); College graduation rate: 8.5% (2000).
Housing: Homeownership rate: 88.2% (2000); Median home value: $68,900 (2000); Median rent: $346 per month (2000); Median age of housing: 60+ years (2000).
Transportation: Commute to work: 65.1% car, 0.0% public transportation, 5.8% walk, 28.5% work from home (2000); Travel time to work: 44.8% less than 15 minutes, 29.1% 15 to 30 minutes, 16.6% 30 to 45 minutes, 5.8% 45 to 60 minutes, 3.8% 60 minutes or more (2000)

HULL (town). Covers a land area of 32.561 square miles and a water area of 0.069 square miles. Located at 44.89° N. Lat.; 90.24° W. Long.
Population: 773 (2000); Race: 98.4% White, 0.0% Black, 0.0% Asian, 0.0% American Indian and Alaska Native, 1.3% Hispanic of any race, 0.3% two or more races (2000); Density: 23.7 persons per square mile (2000); Age: 31.5% under 18, 10.6% over 64 (2000); Marriage status: 25.2% never married, 65.5% now married, 3.0% widowed, 6.3% divorced (2000); Foreign born: 0.3% (2000); Ancestry (includes multiple ancestries): 64.9% German, 7.9% Norwegian, 7.5% United States or American, 6.4% Swiss, 6.0% Irish (2000).
Economy: Employment by occupation: 24.1% management, 13.3% professional, 10.0% services, 14.0% sales, 7.2% farming, 13.3% construction, 18.0% production (2000).
Income: Per capita income: $17,068 (2000); Median household income: $41,324 (2000); Poverty rate: 5.6% (2000).
Taxes: Total city taxes per capita: $98 (1997); City property taxes per capita: $98 (1997).
Education: High school graduation rate: 79.4% (2000); College graduation rate: 7.2% (2000).
Housing: Homeownership rate: 91.5% (2000); Median home value: $71,800 (2000); Median rent: $331 per month (2000); Median age of housing: 60+ years (2000).
Transportation: Commute to work: 74.8% car, 0.0% public transportation, 4.5% walk, 20.7% work from home (2000); Travel time to work: 38.3% less than 15 minutes, 31.2% 15 to 30 minutes, 21.7% 30 to 45 minutes, 5.9% 45 to 60 minutes, 3.0% 60 minutes or more (2000)

JOHNSON (town). Covers a land area of 34.992 square miles and a water area of 0 square miles. Located at 44.97° N. Lat.; 90.15° W. Long. Elevation is 1,438 feet.
Population: 993 (2000); Race: 97.2% White, 0.5% Black, 0.0% Asian, 0.2% American Indian and Alaska Native, 1.3% Hispanic of any race, 1.9% two or more races (2000); Density: 28.4 persons per square mile (2000); Age: 36.3% under 18, 9.4% over 64 (2000); Marriage status: 26.9% never married, 67.1% now married, 4.8% widowed, 1.1% divorced (2000); Foreign born: 0.9% (2000); Ancestry (includes multiple ancestries): 63.2% German, 8.4% Swiss, 7.8% Polish, 4.3% French (except Basque), 3.4% Other groups (2000).
Economy: Single-family building permits issued: 3 (2001) / 5 (2000); Multi-family building permits issued: 0 (2001) / 0 (2000); Employment by occupation: 21.6% management, 5.6% professional, 10.6% services, 18.1% sales, 6.9% farming, 13.6% construction, 23.7% production (2000).
Income: Per capita income: $12,897 (2000); Median household income: $40,156 (2000); Poverty rate: 13.8% (2000).
Taxes: Total city taxes per capita: $42 (1997); City property taxes per capita: $41 (1997).
Education: High school graduation rate: 74.0% (2000); College graduation rate: 4.2% (2000).
Housing: Homeownership rate: 88.7% (2000); Median home value: $70,000 (2000); Median rent: $375 per month (2000); Median age of housing: 54 years (2000).
Transportation: Commute to work: 75.5% car, 0.0% public transportation, 2.6% walk, 21.2% work from home (2000); Travel time to work: 25.8% less than 15 minutes, 32.2% 15 to 30 minutes, 28.3% 30 to 45 minutes, 5.3% 45 to 60 minutes, 8.3% 60 minutes or more (2000)

KNOWLTON (town). Covers a land area of 29.123 square miles and a water area of 5.056 square miles. Located at 44.71° N. Lat.; 89.68° W. Long. Elevation is 1,126 feet.
Population: 1,688 (2000); Race: 98.5% White, 0.6% Black, 0.1% Asian, 0.0% American Indian and Alaska Native, 0.5% Hispanic of any race, 0.8% two or more races (2000); Density: 58.0 persons per square mile (2000); Age: 22.5% under 18, 9.9% over 64 (2000); Marriage status: 20.4% never married, 68.6% now married, 3.3% widowed, 7.7% divorced (2000); Foreign born: 1.0% (2000); Ancestry (includes multiple ancestries): 45.9% German, 36.7% Polish, 10.2% Irish, 4.5% Norwegian, 4.3% French (except Basque) (2000).
Economy: Employment by occupation: 15.0% management, 16.5% professional, 8.5% services, 25.3% sales, 0.6% farming, 6.9% construction, 27.0% production (2000).
Income: Per capita income: $24,149 (2000); Median household income: $56,188 (2000); Poverty rate: 3.1% (2000).
Taxes: Total city taxes per capita: $44 (1997); City property taxes per capita: $39 (1997).
Education: High school graduation rate: 85.2% (2000); College graduation rate: 18.7% (2000).
Housing: Homeownership rate: 91.1% (2000); Median home value: $132,700 (2000); Median rent: $444 per month (2000); Median age of housing: 21 years (2000).
Transportation: Commute to work: 92.6% car, 0.1% public transportation, 1.1% walk, 6.0% work from home (2000); Travel time to work: 22.1% less than 15 minutes, 49.5% 15 to 30 minutes, 20.7% 30 to 45 minutes, 2.7% 45 to 60 minutes, 4.9% 60 minutes or more (2000)

KRONENWETTER (town). Covers a land area of 51.935 square miles and a water area of 0.364 square miles. Located at 44.83° N. Lat.; 89.62° W. Long.
Population: 5,369 (2000); Race: 98.9% White, 0.0% Black, 0.0% Asian, 0.4% American Indian and Alaska Native, 0.2% Hispanic of any race, 0.7% two or more races (2000); Density: 103.4 persons per square mile (2000); Age: 28.0% under 18, 7.6% over 64 (2000); Marriage status: 21.4% never married, 67.9% now married, 2.3% widowed, 8.4% divorced (2000); Foreign born: 0.8% (2000); Ancestry (includes multiple ancestries): 51.8% German, 30.0% Polish, 6.7% Irish, 6.5% Norwegian, 5.0% English (2000).
Economy: Single-family building permits issued: 47 (2001) / 60 (2000); Multi-family building permits issued: 4 (2001) / 46 (2000); Employment by occupation: 12.7% management, 19.1% professional, 15.5% services, 25.8% sales, 0.3% farming, 9.7% construction, 16.9% production (2000).
Income: Per capita income: $23,395 (2000); Median household income: $55,718 (2000); Poverty rate: 3.1% (2000).
Taxes: Total city taxes per capita: $91 (2000); City property taxes per capita: $80 (2000).
Education: High school graduation rate: 89.9% (2000); College graduation rate: 21.5% (2000).
Housing: Homeownership rate: 90.7% (2000); Median home value: $114,600 (2000); Median rent: $438 per month (2000); Median age of housing: 22 years (2000).
Transportation: Commute to work: 94.8% car, 0.5% public transportation, 1.0% walk, 3.2% work from home (2000); Travel time to work: 34.7% less than 15 minutes, 52.1% 15 to 30 minutes, 7.0% 30 to 45 minutes, 1.7% 45 to 60 minutes, 4.6% 60 minutes or more (2000)

MAINE (town). Covers a land area of 42.355 square miles and a water area of 0.472 square miles. Located at 45.03° N. Lat.; 89.67° W. Long.
Population: 2,407 (2000); Race: 100.0% White, 0.0% Black, 0.0% Asian, 0.0% American Indian and Alaska Native, 1.0% Hispanic of any race, 0.0% two or more races (2000); Density: 56.8 persons per square mile (2000); Age: 27.0% under 18, 11.7% over 64 (2000); Marriage status: 21.0% never married, 69.9% now married, 5.2% widowed, 3.9% divorced (2000); Foreign

born: 0.4% (2000); Ancestry (includes multiple ancestries): 68.3% German, 13.6% Polish, 6.2% French (except Basque), 5.8% Irish, 3.8% United States or American (2000).
Economy: Single-family building permits issued: 10 (2001) / 9 (2000); Multi-family building permits issued: 0 (2001) / 0 (2000); Employment by occupation: 13.2% management, 21.9% professional, 9.7% services, 26.5% sales, 1.1% farming, 9.0% construction, 18.7% production (2000).
Income: Per capita income: $23,787 (2000); Median household income: $57,679 (2000); Poverty rate: 0.6% (2000).
Taxes: Total city taxes per capita: $79 (1997); City property taxes per capita: $77 (1997).
Education: High school graduation rate: 88.3% (2000); College graduation rate: 21.0% (2000).
Housing: Homeownership rate: 90.0% (2000); Median home value: $111,200 (2000); Median rent: $481 per month (2000); Median age of housing: 28 years (2000).
Transportation: Commute to work: 93.0% car, 0.9% public transportation, 0.5% walk, 5.0% work from home (2000); Travel time to work: 52.0% less than 15 minutes, 40.3% 15 to 30 minutes, 3.3% 30 to 45 minutes, 2.0% 45 to 60 minutes, 2.5% 60 minutes or more (2000)

MARATHON (town). Aka Marathon City. Covers a land area of 33.022 square miles and a water area of 0.031 square miles. Located at 44.89° N. Lat.; 89.77° W. Long. Elevation is 1,245 feet.
Population: 1,085 (2000); Race: 99.2% White, 0.0% Black, 0.5% Asian, 0.0% American Indian and Alaska Native, 0.7% Hispanic of any race, 0.4% two or more races (2000); Density: 32.9 persons per square mile (2000); Age: 29.8% under 18, 9.9% over 64 (2000); Marriage status: 22.1% never married, 71.1% now married, 3.3% widowed, 3.5% divorced (2000); Foreign born: 0.5% (2000); Ancestry (includes multiple ancestries): 74.8% German, 19.6% Polish, 7.5% Irish, 4.0% Norwegian, 3.0% English (2000).
Economy: Employment by occupation: 15.9% management, 13.6% professional, 13.1% services, 23.5% sales, 2.7% farming, 11.1% construction, 20.3% production (2000).
Income: Per capita income: $18,906 (2000); Median household income: $51,250 (2000); Poverty rate: 4.7% (2000).
Taxes: Total city taxes per capita: $41 (1997); City property taxes per capita: $41 (1997).
Education: High school graduation rate: 85.8% (2000); College graduation rate: 13.4% (2000).

School District(s)

Marathon City (PK-12)
2000 Enrollment: 718 715-443-2228
Housing: Homeownership rate: 91.8% (2000); Median home value: $110,700 (2000); Median rent: $408 per month (2000); Median age of housing: 27 years (2000).
Transportation: Commute to work: 88.0% car, 0.7% public transportation, 2.7% walk, 7.9% work from home (2000); Travel time to work: 24.4% less than 15 minutes, 60.1% 15 to 30 minutes, 11.0% 30 to 45 minutes, 1.6% 45 to 60 minutes, 2.9% 60 minutes or more (2000)

MARATHON CITY (village). Aka Marathon. Covers a land area of 2.036 square miles and a water area of 0.008 square miles. Located at 44.93° N. Lat.; 89.84° W. Long.
Population: 1,640 (2000); Race: 98.5% White, 0.0% Black, 0.9% Asian, 0.2% American Indian and Alaska Native, 0.0% Hispanic of any race, 0.3% two or more races (2000); Density: 805.5 persons per square mile (2000); Age: 26.0% under 18, 13.5% over 64 (2000); Marriage status: 26.7% never married, 60.8% now married, 4.9% widowed, 7.6% divorced (2000); Foreign born: 1.5% (2000); Ancestry (includes multiple ancestries): 66.4% German, 22.1% Polish, 4.8% Norwegian, 4.5% Irish, 3.6% French (except Basque) (2000).
Economy: Single-family building permits issued: 2 (2001) / 2 (2000); Multi-family building permits issued: 0 (2001) / 0 (2000); Employment by occupation: 13.5% management, 11.6% professional, 12.3% services, 23.8% sales, 1.6% farming, 7.0% construction, 30.3% production (2000).
Income: Per capita income: $20,480 (2000); Median household income: $44,063 (2000); Poverty rate: 2.0% (2000).
Taxes: Total city taxes per capita: $213 (1997); City property taxes per capita: $205 (1997).
Education: High school graduation rate: 86.4% (2000); College graduation rate: 16.9% (2000).
Housing: Homeownership rate: 79.2% (2000); Median home value: $97,000 (2000); Median rent: $349 per month (2000); Median age of housing: 32 years (2000).
Safety: Violent crime rate: 18.2 per 10,000 population; Property crime rate: 139.2 per 10,000 population (2001).
Transportation: Commute to work: 87.6% car, 0.3% public transportation, 9.9% walk, 2.0% work from home (2000); Travel time to work: 49.4% less than 15 minutes, 41.1% 15 to 30 minutes, 6.1% 30 to 45 minutes, 0.4% 45 to 60 minutes, 3.0% 60 minutes or more (2000)

MCMILLAN (town). Covers a land area of 34.394 square miles and a water area of 0.202 square miles. Located at 44.72° N. Lat.; 90.13° W. Long. Elevation is 1,270 feet.
Population: 1,790 (2000); Race: 98.4% White, 0.1% Black, 0.6% Asian, 0.0% American Indian and Alaska Native, 0.1% Hispanic of any race, 1.0% two or more races (2000); Density: 52.0 persons per square mile (2000); Age: 30.2% under 18, 8.2% over 64 (2000); Marriage status: 19.9% never married, 71.8% now married, 3.1% widowed, 5.2% divorced (2000); Foreign born: 1.5% (2000); Ancestry (includes multiple ancestries): 64.9% German, 7.4% Irish, 7.2% Polish, 7.0% Norwegian, 5.8% English (2000).
Economy: Employment by occupation: 15.5% management, 23.1% professional, 11.6% services, 21.7% sales, 1.0% farming, 8.6% construction, 18.5% production (2000).
Income: Per capita income: $27,161 (2000); Median household income: $59,342 (2000); Poverty rate: 2.1% (2000).
Taxes: Total city taxes per capita: $202 (2000); City property taxes per capita: $201 (2000).
Education: High school graduation rate: 90.1% (2000); College graduation rate: 28.5% (2000).
Housing: Homeownership rate: 94.0% (2000); Median home value: $132,400 (2000); Median rent: $388 per month (2000); Median age of housing: 23 years (2000).
Transportation: Commute to work: 89.3% car, 0.4% public transportation, 3.1% walk, 6.6% work from home (2000); Travel time to work: 57.3% less than 15 minutes, 35.9% 15 to 30 minutes, 3.4% 30 to 45 minutes, 1.9% 45 to 60 minutes, 1.4% 60 minutes or more (2000)

MOSINEE (city). Covers a land area of 7.780 square miles and a water area of 0.777 square miles. Located at 44.79° N. Lat.; 89.70° W. Long. Elevation is 1,153 feet.
Population: 4,063 (2000); Race: 97.5% White, 0.2% Black, 0.0% Asian, 0.2% American Indian and Alaska Native, 1.7% Hispanic of any race, 0.7% two or more races (2000); Density: 522.2 persons per square mile (2000); Age: 27.5% under 18, 15.0% over 64 (2000); Marriage status: 22.3% never married, 61.0% now married, 7.4% widowed, 9.4% divorced (2000); Foreign born: 1.4% (2000); Ancestry (includes multiple ancestries): 58.0% German, 29.9% Polish, 7.5% Irish, 5.7% Norwegian, 3.5% French (except Basque) (2000).
Economy: Single-family building permits issued: 13 (2001) / 22 (2000); Multi-family building permits issued: 8 (2001) / 26 (2000); Employment by occupation: 9.1% management, 14.3% professional, 12.6% services, 27.1% sales, 2.1% farming, 10.0% construction, 24.8% production (2000).
Income: Per capita income: $18,700 (2000); Median household income: $46,109 (2000); Poverty rate: 5.5% (2000).
Taxes: Total city taxes per capita: $387 (1997); City property taxes per capita: $374 (1997).
Education: High school graduation rate: 83.9% (2000); College graduation rate: 16.9% (2000).

School District(s)

Mosinee (PK-12)
2000 Enrollment: 2,014 715-693-2530
Housing: Homeownership rate: 67.5% (2000); Median home value: $87,700 (2000); Median rent: $459 per month (2000); Median age of housing: 34 years (2000).
Safety: Violent crime rate: 0.0 per 10,000 population; Property crime rate: 222.4 per 10,000 population (2001).
Newspapers: Mosinee Times (1 x week)
Transportation: Commute to work: 91.2% car, 0.4% public transportation, 3.1% walk, 4.9% work from home (2000); Travel time to work: 44.7% less than 15 minutes, 40.5% 15 to 30 minutes, 9.5% 30 to 45 minutes, 1.9% 45 to 60 minutes, 3.3% 60 minutes or more (2000)
Airports: Central Wisconsin (primary service)
Additional Information Contacts
Central WI Convention Bureau 715-355-8788
Central Wisconsin Board of Realtors........ 715-693-7325

MOSINEE (town). Covers a land area of 37.196 square miles and a water area of 1.255 square miles. Located at 44.81° N. Lat.; 89.73° W. Long. Elevation is 1,153 feet.

History: Incorporated 1931.
Population: 2,146 (2000); Race: 99.6% White, 0.1% Black, 0.1% Asian, 0.0% American Indian and Alaska Native, 0.0% Hispanic of any race, 0.1% two or more races (2000); Density: 57.7 persons per square mile (2000); Age: 26.4% under 18, 5.8% over 64 (2000); Marriage status: 19.3% never married, 71.5% now married, 2.0% widowed, 7.2% divorced (2000); Foreign born: 0.4% (2000); Ancestry (includes multiple ancestries): 55.2% German, 24.9% Polish, 14.0% Irish, 7.0% Norwegian, 5.9% Czech (2000).
Economy: In lumbering and dairying area; paper and sawmilling, cheese making. Manufacturing of trailer components, papers, nylon slings. Central Wisconsin Regional Airport to Southeast. Single-family building permits issued: 20 (2001) / 22 (2000); Multi-family building permits issued: 0 (2001) / 0 (2000); Employment by occupation: 10.8% management, 15.3% professional, 7.3% services, 28.3% sales, 0.6% farming, 13.7% construction, 23.9% production (2000).
Income: Per capita income: $21,930 (2000); Median household income: $55,094 (2000); Poverty rate: 4.0% (2000).
Taxes: Total city taxes per capita: $55 (1997); City property taxes per capita: $49 (1997).
Education: High school graduation rate: 89.9% (2000); College graduation rate: 16.6% (2000).
Housing: Homeownership rate: 90.0% (2000); Median home value: $118,000 (2000); Median rent: $479 per month (2000); Median age of housing: 20 years (2000).
Transportation: Commute to work: 93.8% car, 0.3% public transportation, 1.9% walk, 3.5% work from home (2000); Travel time to work: 28.8% less than 15 minutes, 53.3% 15 to 30 minutes, 14.7% 30 to 45 minutes, 0.4% 45 to 60 minutes, 2.8% 60 minutes or more (2000)
Airports: Central Wisconsin (primary service)

NORRIE (town). Covers a land area of 34.686 square miles and a water area of 0.583 square miles. Located at 44.89° N. Lat.; 89.28° W. Long. Elevation is 1,280 feet.
Population: 967 (2000); Race: 100.0% White, 0.0% Black, 0.0% Asian, 0.0% American Indian and Alaska Native, 0.5% Hispanic of any race, 0.0% two or more races (2000); Density: 27.9 persons per square mile (2000); Age: 28.2% under 18, 12.3% over 64 (2000); Marriage status: 20.9% never married, 65.3% now married, 6.6% widowed, 7.1% divorced (2000); Foreign born: 0.2% (2000); Ancestry (includes multiple ancestries): 52.1% German, 37.3% Polish, 6.0% Norwegian, 5.3% Swedish, 4.8% Irish (2000).
Economy: Single-family building permits issued: 10 (2001) / 6 (2000); Multi-family building permits issued: 2 (2001) / 0 (2000); Employment by occupation: 10.8% management, 14.2% professional, 10.6% services, 23.3% sales, 3.1% farming, 12.5% construction, 25.4% production (2000).
Income: Per capita income: $21,330 (2000); Median household income: $48,472 (2000); Poverty rate: 3.9% (2000).
Taxes: Total city taxes per capita: $31 (1997); City property taxes per capita: $30 (1997).
Education: High school graduation rate: 78.9% (2000); College graduation rate: 15.2% (2000).
Housing: Homeownership rate: 89.8% (2000); Median home value: $95,700 (2000); Median rent: $400 per month (2000); Median age of housing: 25 years (2000).
Transportation: Commute to work: 92.6% car, 0.0% public transportation, 1.5% walk, 5.0% work from home (2000); Travel time to work: 17.5% less than 15 minutes, 44.5% 15 to 30 minutes, 30.3% 30 to 45 minutes, 4.6% 45 to 60 minutes, 3.1% 60 minutes or more (2000)

PLOVER (town). Covers a land area of 36.158 square miles and a water area of 0.038 square miles. Located at 44.99° N. Lat.; 89.27° W. Long.
Population: 686 (2000); Race: 99.0% White, 0.6% Black, 0.0% Asian, 0.4% American Indian and Alaska Native, 0.9% Hispanic of any race, 0.0% two or more races (2000); Density: 19.0 persons per square mile (2000); Age: 32.4% under 18, 11.9% over 64 (2000); Marriage status: 20.2% never married, 69.6% now married, 3.8% widowed, 6.3% divorced (2000); Foreign born: 0.0% (2000); Ancestry (includes multiple ancestries): 55.4% German, 9.5% Polish, 8.6% Dutch, 6.5% United States or American, 6.2% French (except Basque) (2000).
Economy: Single-family building permits issued: 6 (2001) / 5 (2000); Multi-family building permits issued: 0 (2001) / 0 (2000); Employment by occupation: 17.3% management, 11.8% professional, 9.9% services, 16.1% sales, 3.1% farming, 7.4% construction, 34.4% production (2000).
Income: Per capita income: $14,673 (2000); Median household income: $42,250 (2000); Poverty rate: 10.2% (2000).
Taxes: Total city taxes per capita: $62 (1997); City property taxes per capita: $62 (1997).
Education: High school graduation rate: 83.9% (2000); College graduation rate: 12.9% (2000).
Housing: Homeownership rate: 88.8% (2000); Median home value: $77,100 (2000); Median rent: $400 per month (2000); Median age of housing: 28 years (2000).
Transportation: Commute to work: 85.2% car, 0.3% public transportation, 0.6% walk, 13.8% work from home (2000); Travel time to work: 9.9% less than 15 minutes, 35.8% 15 to 30 minutes, 41.2% 30 to 45 minutes, 7.7% 45 to 60 minutes, 5.5% 60 minutes or more (2000)

REID (town). Covers a land area of 41.640 square miles and a water area of 0.566 square miles. Located at 44.80° N. Lat.; 89.40° W. Long.
Population: 1,191 (2000); Race: 98.6% White, 0.0% Black, 0.0% Asian, 0.0% American Indian and Alaska Native, 0.8% Hispanic of any race, 0.6% two or more races (2000); Density: 28.6 persons per square mile (2000); Age: 26.6% under 18, 9.9% over 64 (2000); Marriage status: 21.3% never married, 66.5% now married, 3.7% widowed, 8.5% divorced (2000); Foreign born: 0.8% (2000); Ancestry (includes multiple ancestries): 44.9% Polish, 42.9% German, 3.9% Dutch, 3.4% French (except Basque), 3.1% Norwegian (2000).
Economy: Employment by occupation: 11.9% management, 9.0% professional, 9.0% services, 21.1% sales, 1.9% farming, 14.6% construction, 32.4% production (2000).
Income: Per capita income: $20,859 (2000); Median household income: $50,972 (2000); Poverty rate: 2.7% (2000).
Taxes: Total city taxes per capita: $47 (1997); City property taxes per capita: $46 (1997).
Education: High school graduation rate: 79.8% (2000); College graduation rate: 10.2% (2000).
Housing: Homeownership rate: 92.4% (2000); Median home value: $99,300 (2000); Median rent: $385 per month (2000); Median age of housing: 26 years (2000).
Transportation: Commute to work: 90.7% car, 0.8% public transportation, 0.8% walk, 6.6% work from home (2000); Travel time to work: 11.1% less than 15 minutes, 56.3% 15 to 30 minutes, 26.0% 30 to 45 minutes, 2.6% 45 to 60 minutes, 3.9% 60 minutes or more (2000)

RIB FALLS (town). Covers a land area of 35.866 square miles and a water area of 0.036 square miles. Located at 44.98° N. Lat.; 89.91° W. Long. Elevation is 1,250 feet.
Population: 907 (2000); Race: 98.7% White, 0.0% Black, 0.0% Asian, 0.0% American Indian and Alaska Native, 0.6% Hispanic of any race, 0.8% two or more races (2000); Density: 25.3 persons per square mile (2000); Age: 28.8% under 18, 10.4% over 64 (2000); Marriage status: 22.3% never married, 70.2% now married, 4.3% widowed, 3.1% divorced (2000); Foreign born: 1.3% (2000); Ancestry (includes multiple ancestries): 68.2% German, 21.6% Polish, 5.0% Norwegian, 3.6% Irish, 3.1% English (2000).
Economy: Employment by occupation: 19.3% management, 9.4% professional, 7.6% services, 21.7% sales, 2.6% farming, 11.8% construction, 27.5% production (2000).
Income: Per capita income: $17,625 (2000); Median household income: $50,114 (2000); Poverty rate: 5.0% (2000).
Taxes: Total city taxes per capita: $47 (1997); City property taxes per capita: $47 (1997).
Education: High school graduation rate: 86.3% (2000); College graduation rate: 9.1% (2000).
Housing: Homeownership rate: 94.4% (2000); Median home value: $98,300 (2000); Median rent: $400 per month (2000); Median age of housing: 27 years (2000).
Transportation: Commute to work: 85.3% car, 0.8% public transportation, 5.0% walk, 8.8% work from home (2000); Travel time to work: 34.6% less than 15 minutes, 42.5% 15 to 30 minutes, 17.8% 30 to 45 minutes, 2.4% 45 to 60 minutes, 2.6% 60 minutes or more (2000)

RIB MOUNTAIN (town). Covers a land area of 24.590 square miles and a water area of 1.002 square miles. Located at 44.91° N. Lat.; 89.67° W. Long.
Population: 7,556 (2000); Race: 96.2% White, 0.0% Black, 2.7% Asian, 0.1% American Indian and Alaska Native, 0.3% Hispanic of any race, 0.9% two or more races (2000); Density: 307.3 persons per square mile (2000); Age: 27.9% under 18, 9.6% over 64 (2000); Marriage status: 19.1% never married, 71.8% now married, 3.7% widowed, 5.4% divorced (2000); Foreign born: 2.3% (2000); Ancestry (includes multiple ancestries): 58.0% German, 18.4% Polish, 8.5% Irish, 7.1% Norwegian, 5.2% English (2000).
Economy: Single-family building permits issued: 16 (2001) / 25 (2000); Multi-family building permits issued: 8 (2001) / 0 (2000); Employment by

occupation: 18.8% management, 23.3% professional, 8.0% services, 28.4% sales, 0.0% farming, 6.9% construction, 14.6% production (2000).
Income: Per capita income: $27,768 (2000); Median household income: $61,294 (2000); Poverty rate: 1.7% (2000).
Taxes: Total city taxes per capita: $181 (2000); City property taxes per capita: $157 (2000).
Education: High school graduation rate: 91.7% (2000); College graduation rate: 33.3% (2000).
Housing: Homeownership rate: 87.8% (2000); Median home value: $131,100 (2000); Median rent: $585 per month (2000); Median age of housing: 21 years (2000).
Transportation: Commute to work: 94.9% car, 0.7% public transportation, 1.0% walk, 2.8% work from home (2000); Travel time to work: 46.1% less than 15 minutes, 45.7% 15 to 30 minutes, 3.6% 30 to 45 minutes, 0.9% 45 to 60 minutes, 3.6% 60 minutes or more (2000)

RIETBROCK (town). Covers a land area of 33.829 square miles and a water area of 0 square miles. Located at 44.98° N. Lat.; 90.01° W. Long.
Population: 927 (2000); Race: 99.3% White, 0.0% Black, 0.0% Asian, 0.7% American Indian and Alaska Native, 0.0% Hispanic of any race, 0.0% two or more races (2000); Density: 27.4 persons per square mile (2000); Age: 30.0% under 18, 10.6% over 64 (2000); Marriage status: 26.0% never married, 64.5% now married, 5.3% widowed, 4.3% divorced (2000); Foreign born: 0.0% (2000); Ancestry (includes multiple ancestries): 58.2% German, 36.8% Polish, 5.3% United States or American, 3.4% Norwegian, 3.3% Other groups (2000).
Economy: Single-family building permits issued: 7 (2001) / 7 (2000); Multi-family building permits issued: 0 (2001) / 0 (2000); Employment by occupation: 16.7% management, 10.4% professional, 7.4% services, 22.8% sales, 2.5% farming, 8.6% construction, 31.6% production (2000).
Income: Per capita income: $16,181 (2000); Median household income: $46,389 (2000); Poverty rate: 6.6% (2000).
Education: High school graduation rate: 81.0% (2000); College graduation rate: 6.8% (2000).
Housing: Homeownership rate: 85.9% (2000); Median home value: $79,800 (2000); Median rent: $400 per month (2000); Median age of housing: 52 years (2000).
Transportation: Commute to work: 83.1% car, 0.0% public transportation, 0.7% walk, 14.7% work from home (2000); Travel time to work: 18.8% less than 15 minutes, 43.1% 15 to 30 minutes, 27.5% 30 to 45 minutes, 5.3% 45 to 60 minutes, 5.3% 60 minutes or more (2000)

RINGLE (town). Covers a land area of 42.067 square miles and a water area of 0.070 square miles. Located at 44.89° N. Lat.; 89.42° W. Long. Elevation is 1,334 feet.
Population: 1,408 (2000); Race: 96.5% White, 0.0% Black, 0.0% Asian, 0.4% American Indian and Alaska Native, 0.6% Hispanic of any race, 3.0% two or more races (2000); Density: 33.5 persons per square mile (2000); Age: 28.6% under 18, 8.8% over 64 (2000); Marriage status: 20.4% never married, 69.4% now married, 3.4% widowed, 6.7% divorced (2000); Foreign born: 0.8% (2000); Ancestry (includes multiple ancestries): 51.2% German, 29.9% Polish, 5.5% Irish, 5.0% Dutch, 4.5% Norwegian (2000).
Economy: Single-family building permits issued: 10 (2001) / 11 (2000); Multi-family building permits issued: 0 (2001) / 0 (2000); Employment by occupation: 12.7% management, 13.2% professional, 10.0% services, 29.8% sales, 0.9% farming, 10.0% construction, 23.4% production (2000).
Income: Per capita income: $20,210 (2000); Median household income: $57,891 (2000); Poverty rate: 3.6% (2000).
Taxes: Total city taxes per capita: $45 (1997); City property taxes per capita: $38 (1997).
Education: High school graduation rate: 84.6% (2000); College graduation rate: 15.0% (2000).
Housing: Homeownership rate: 93.3% (2000); Median home value: $111,100 (2000); Median rent: $370 per month (2000); Median age of housing: 24 years (2000).
Transportation: Commute to work: 93.8% car, 1.4% public transportation, 0.4% walk, 3.8% work from home (2000); Travel time to work: 17.7% less than 15 minutes, 63.1% 15 to 30 minutes, 14.4% 30 to 45 minutes, 1.1% 45 to 60 minutes, 3.7% 60 minutes or more (2000)

ROTHSCHILD (village). Covers a land area of 6.513 square miles and a water area of 0.357 square miles. Located at 44.88° N. Lat.; 89.62° W. Long. Elevation is 1,200 feet.
History: Rothschild developed around the Marathon Paper Company mills on the Wisconsin River.
Population: 4,970 (2000); Race: 99.0% White, 0.2% Black, 0.0% Asian, 0.7% American Indian and Alaska Native, 0.2% Hispanic of any race, 0.1% two or more races (2000); Density: 763.1 persons per square mile (2000); Age: 26.1% under 18, 12.0% over 64 (2000); Marriage status: 23.3% never married, 61.7% now married, 5.4% widowed, 9.5% divorced (2000); Foreign born: 0.6% (2000); Ancestry (includes multiple ancestries): 56.1% German, 16.8% Polish, 9.4% Irish, 8.0% English, 6.9% Norwegian (2000).
Economy: Single-family building permits issued: 5 (2001) / 10 (2000); Multi-family building permits issued: 0 (2001) / 0 (2000); Employment by occupation: 11.5% management, 17.7% professional, 12.5% services, 29.8% sales, 0.1% farming, 6.8% construction, 21.6% production (2000).
Income: Per capita income: $22,236 (2000); Median household income: $50,543 (2000); Poverty rate: 4.0% (2000).
Taxes: Total city taxes per capita: $344 (1997); City property taxes per capita: $315 (1997).
Education: High school graduation rate: 90.2% (2000); College graduation rate: 23.8% (2000).
Housing: Homeownership rate: 80.9% (2000); Median home value: $97,900 (2000); Median rent: $427 per month (2000); Median age of housing: 33 years (2000).
Safety: Violent crime rate: 4.0 per 10,000 population; Property crime rate: 291.7 per 10,000 population (2001).
Transportation: Commute to work: 95.6% car, 0.6% public transportation, 1.5% walk, 2.0% work from home (2000); Travel time to work: 48.9% less than 15 minutes, 45.5% 15 to 30 minutes, 2.6% 30 to 45 minutes, 0.4% 45 to 60 minutes, 2.6% 60 minutes or more (2000)

SCHOFIELD (city). Covers a land area of 1.758 square miles and a water area of 1.070 square miles. Located at 44.91° N. Lat.; 89.61° W. Long. Elevation is 1,198 feet.
History: Schofield developed around the Marathon Paper Company mills established along the Wisconsin River.
Population: 2,117 (2000); Race: 96.7% White, 0.2% Black, 1.7% Asian, 0.2% American Indian and Alaska Native, 1.0% Hispanic of any race, 1.1% two or more races (2000); Density: 1,204.4 persons per square mile (2000); Age: 21.7% under 18, 15.5% over 64 (2000); Marriage status: 27.0% never married, 53.6% now married, 9.0% widowed, 10.4% divorced (2000); Foreign born: 2.4% (2000); Ancestry (includes multiple ancestries): 52.8% German, 21.1% Polish, 5.4% Irish, 5.3% Other groups, 5.3% Norwegian (2000).
Economy: Single-family building permits issued: 1 (2001) / 1 (2000); Multi-family building permits issued: 112 (2001) / 0 (2000); Employment by occupation: 10.8% management, 14.6% professional, 16.1% services, 27.3% sales, 0.0% farming, 7.4% construction, 23.8% production (2000).
Income: Per capita income: $20,287 (2000); Median household income: $38,158 (2000); Poverty rate: 7.3% (2000).
Taxes: Total city taxes per capita: $360 (1997); City property taxes per capita: $351 (1997).
Education: High school graduation rate: 81.7% (2000); College graduation rate: 15.0% (2000).

School District(s)

D C Everest Area (PK-12)
2000 Enrollment: 5,084 715-359-4221
Housing: Homeownership rate: 61.7% (2000); Median home value: $79,500 (2000); Median rent: $424 per month (2000); Median age of housing: 46 years (2000).
Transportation: Commute to work: 92.9% car, 1.1% public transportation, 2.9% walk, 0.8% work from home (2000); Travel time to work: 49.1% less than 15 minutes, 42.2% 15 to 30 minutes, 5.4% 30 to 45 minutes, 1.7% 45 to 60 minutes, 1.6% 60 minutes or more (2000)

SPENCER (village). Covers a land area of 1.988 square miles and a water area of 0 square miles. Located at 44.75° N. Lat.; 90.29° W. Long. Elevation is 1,310 feet.
Population: 1,932 (2000); Race: 99.2% White, 0.0% Black, 0.0% Asian, 0.3% American Indian and Alaska Native, 0.2% Hispanic of any race, 0.4% two or more races (2000); Density: 971.6 persons per square mile (2000); Age: 25.6% under 18, 14.3% over 64 (2000); Marriage status: 23.3% never married, 57.5% now married, 8.3% widowed, 10.9% divorced (2000); Foreign born: 0.3% (2000); Ancestry (includes multiple ancestries): 68.0% German, 11.0% Norwegian, 7.7% Irish, 6.1% Polish, 3.8% French (except Basque) (2000).
Economy: Single-family building permits issued: 4 (2001) / 8 (2000); Multi-family building permits issued: 2 (2001) / 0 (2000); Employment by occupation: 7.2% management, 17.8% professional, 14.7% services, 22.9% sales, 1.3% farming, 11.0% construction, 25.1% production (2000).

Income: Per capita income: $17,665 (2000); Median household income: $40,665 (2000); Poverty rate: 4.1% (2000).
Taxes: Total city taxes per capita: $200 (1997); City property taxes per capita: $179 (1997).
Education: High school graduation rate: 82.7% (2000); College graduation rate: 12.5% (2000).

School District(s)

Spencer (PK-12)
2000 Enrollment: 900 715-659-5347

Housing: Homeownership rate: 76.1% (2000); Median home value: $73,800 (2000); Median rent: $334 per month (2000); Median age of housing: 27 years (2000).
Safety: Violent crime rate: 5.1 per 10,000 population; Property crime rate: 154.2 per 10,000 population (2001).
Transportation: Commute to work: 90.0% car, 0.4% public transportation, 6.7% walk, 2.2% work from home (2000); Travel time to work: 41.4% less than 15 minutes, 49.9% 15 to 30 minutes, 6.1% 30 to 45 minutes, 1.7% 45 to 60 minutes, 0.8% 60 minutes or more (2000)

SPENCER (town). Covers a land area of 31.523 square miles and a water area of 0.200 square miles. Located at 44.73° N. Lat.; 90.27° W. Long. Elevation is 1,310 feet.
Population: 1,341 (2000); Race: 99.7% White, 0.0% Black, 0.0% Asian, 0.0% American Indian and Alaska Native, 0.0% Hispanic of any race, 0.3% two or more races (2000); Density: 42.5 persons per square mile (2000); Age: 30.2% under 18, 7.4% over 64 (2000); Marriage status: 23.6% never married, 66.1% now married, 2.4% widowed, 7.9% divorced (2000); Foreign born: 1.5% (2000); Ancestry (includes multiple ancestries): 59.8% German, 9.5% Polish, 7.9% Norwegian, 5.1% Irish, 4.3% United States or American (2000).
Economy: Makes cheese. Railroad junction. Employment by occupation: 12.9% management, 16.1% professional, 11.0% services, 21.4% sales, 2.5% farming, 12.1% construction, 24.0% production (2000).
Income: Per capita income: $17,702 (2000); Median household income: $47,315 (2000); Poverty rate: 3.8% (2000).
Taxes: Total city taxes per capita: $52 (1997); City property taxes per capita: $47 (1997).
Education: High school graduation rate: 86.1% (2000); College graduation rate: 11.7% (2000).
Housing: Homeownership rate: 89.6% (2000); Median home value: $98,600 (2000); Median rent: $363 per month (2000); Median age of housing: 20 years (2000).
Transportation: Commute to work: 89.5% car, 0.0% public transportation, 3.7% walk, 6.2% work from home (2000); Travel time to work: 36.8% less than 15 minutes, 48.9% 15 to 30 minutes, 7.1% 30 to 45 minutes, 2.8% 45 to 60 minutes, 4.4% 60 minutes or more (2000)

STETTIN (town). Covers a land area of 37.223 square miles and a water area of 0.189 square miles. Located at 44.96° N. Lat.; 89.73° W. Long.
Population: 2,191 (2000); Race: 95.0% White, 0.0% Black, 4.4% Asian, 0.2% American Indian and Alaska Native, 0.0% Hispanic of any race, 0.3% two or more races (2000); Density: 58.9 persons per square mile (2000); Age: 29.0% under 18, 9.9% over 64 (2000); Marriage status: 19.9% never married, 73.2% now married, 3.3% widowed, 3.6% divorced (2000); Foreign born: 2.8% (2000); Ancestry (includes multiple ancestries): 72.2% German, 15.4% Polish, 8.1% Irish, 6.0% Norwegian, 4.1% English (2000).
Economy: Single-family building permits issued: 14 (2001) / 14 (2000); Multi-family building permits issued: 0 (2001) / 0 (2000); Employment by occupation: 16.0% management, 11.5% professional, 12.1% services, 34.6% sales, 0.0% farming, 8.7% construction, 17.0% production (2000).
Income: Per capita income: $26,269 (2000); Median household income: $60,221 (2000); Poverty rate: 1.6% (2000).
Taxes: Total city taxes per capita: $42 (1997); City property taxes per capita: $36 (1997).
Education: High school graduation rate: 85.6% (2000); College graduation rate: 16.7% (2000).
Housing: Homeownership rate: 92.6% (2000); Median home value: $132,900 (2000); Median rent: $569 per month (2000); Median age of housing: 26 years (2000).
Transportation: Commute to work: 90.9% car, 0.0% public transportation, 0.0% walk, 6.9% work from home (2000); Travel time to work: 34.0% less than 15 minutes, 53.8% 15 to 30 minutes, 8.2% 30 to 45 minutes, 1.7% 45 to 60 minutes, 2.2% 60 minutes or more (2000)

STRATFORD (village). Covers a land area of 5.295 square miles and a water area of 0.036 square miles. Located at 44.80° N. Lat.; 90.07° W. Long. Elevation is 1,250 feet.
Population: 1,523 (2000); Race: 99.2% White, 0.0% Black, 0.4% Asian, 0.3% American Indian and Alaska Native, 0.8% Hispanic of any race, 0.1% two or more races (2000); Density: 287.6 persons per square mile (2000); Age: 27.0% under 18, 13.9% over 64 (2000); Marriage status: 20.8% never married, 64.6% now married, 8.0% widowed, 6.5% divorced (2000); Foreign born: 0.7% (2000); Ancestry (includes multiple ancestries): 70.4% German, 9.1% Polish, 5.3% Irish, 4.8% French (except Basque), 3.7% Norwegian (2000).
Economy: Dairy products. Manufacturing: machinery, modular homes. Single-family building permits issued: 4 (2001) / 5 (2000); Multi-family building permits issued: 26 (2001) / 0 (2000); Employment by occupation: 11.6% management, 14.0% professional, 14.9% services, 22.7% sales, 1.5% farming, 11.4% construction, 23.9% production (2000).
Income: Per capita income: $17,934 (2000); Median household income: $42,569 (2000); Poverty rate: 6.0% (2000).
Taxes: Total city taxes per capita: $135 (1997); City property taxes per capita: $121 (1997).
Education: High school graduation rate: 83.0% (2000); College graduation rate: 11.6% (2000).

School District(s)

Stratford (PK-12)
2000 Enrollment: 771 715-687-3130

Housing: Homeownership rate: 75.5% (2000); Median home value: $79,300 (2000); Median rent: $336 per month (2000); Median age of housing: 36 years (2000).
Transportation: Commute to work: 92.6% car, 0.0% public transportation, 4.8% walk, 2.3% work from home (2000); Travel time to work: 28.9% less than 15 minutes, 49.3% 15 to 30 minutes, 14.0% 30 to 45 minutes, 4.0% 45 to 60 minutes, 3.8% 60 minutes or more (2000)

Additional Information Contacts

Stratford Chamber of Commerce 715-687-4466

TEXAS (town). Covers a land area of 44.606 square miles and a water area of 0.457 square miles. Located at 45.07° N. Lat.; 89.58° W. Long.
Population: 1,703 (2000); Race: 97.8% White, 0.4% Black, 0.5% Asian, 0.2% American Indian and Alaska Native, 0.1% Hispanic of any race, 1.1% two or more races (2000); Density: 38.2 persons per square mile (2000); Age: 25.2% under 18, 10.5% over 64 (2000); Marriage status: 24.1% never married, 65.2% now married, 5.9% widowed, 4.8% divorced (2000); Foreign born: 0.8% (2000); Ancestry (includes multiple ancestries): 61.7% German, 15.9% Polish, 4.5% English, 4.1% Norwegian, 3.8% Irish (2000).
Economy: Single-family building permits issued: 10 (2001) / 9 (2000); Multi-family building permits issued: 0 (2001) / 0 (2000); Employment by occupation: 13.8% management, 15.9% professional, 8.9% services, 25.2% sales, 1.2% farming, 11.5% construction, 23.4% production (2000).
Income: Per capita income: $18,852 (2000); Median household income: $51,830 (2000); Poverty rate: 4.1% (2000).
Taxes: Total city taxes per capita: $76 (1997); City property taxes per capita: $64 (1997).
Education: High school graduation rate: 84.6% (2000); College graduation rate: 10.5% (2000).
Housing: Homeownership rate: 93.0% (2000); Median home value: $98,400 (2000); Median rent: $350 per month (2000); Median age of housing: 28 years (2000).
Transportation: Commute to work: 91.6% car, 0.7% public transportation, 1.6% walk, 6.1% work from home (2000); Travel time to work: 19.8% less than 15 minutes, 62.0% 15 to 30 minutes, 13.2% 30 to 45 minutes, 2.4% 45 to 60 minutes, 2.6% 60 minutes or more (2000)

UNITY (village). Covers a land area of 0.989 square miles and a water area of 0 square miles. Located at 44.84° N. Lat.; 90.31° W. Long.
Population: 368 (2000); Race: 100.0% White, 0.0% Black, 0.0% Asian, 0.0% American Indian and Alaska Native, 0.0% Hispanic of any race, 0.0% two or more races (2000); Density: 372.1 persons per square mile (2000); Age: 24.5% under 18, 17.6% over 64 (2000); Marriage status: 26.4% never married, 54.6% now married, 9.5% widowed, 9.5% divorced (2000); Foreign born: 2.4% (2000); Ancestry (includes multiple ancestries): 70.6% German, 12.1% Irish, 10.0% Norwegian, 6.7% Polish, 6.7% Swedish (2000).
Economy: Single-family building permits issued: 0 (2001) / 0 (2000); Multi-family building permits issued: 0 (2001) / 0 (2000); Employment by occupation: 9.8% management, 6.9% professional, 6.4% services, 17.3% sales, 1.7% farming, 17.3% construction, 40.5% production (2000).
Income: Per capita income: $17,819 (2000); Median household income: $31,458 (2000); Poverty rate: 12.7% (2000).
Taxes: Total city taxes per capita: $71 (1997); City property taxes per capita: $63 (1997).

Education: High school graduation rate: 70.7% (2000); College graduation rate: 5.4% (2000).
Housing: Homeownership rate: 83.4% (2000); Median home value: $57,000 (2000); Median rent: $313 per month (2000); Median age of housing: 33 years (2000).
Transportation: Commute to work: 88.6% car, 0.0% public transportation, 6.6% walk, 4.8% work from home (2000); Travel time to work: 43.4% less than 15 minutes, 41.5% 15 to 30 minutes, 6.9% 30 to 45 minutes, 1.3% 45 to 60 minutes, 6.9% 60 minutes or more (2000)

WAUSAU (city). Covers a land area of 16.487 square miles and a water area of 1.266 square miles. Located at 44.96° N. Lat.; 89.63° W. Long. Elevation is 1,210 feet.
History: Settlement in Wausau began in the late 1830's when George Stevens built several sawmills here and established a supply depot at Sevens Point. The village was called Gros Taureau, or Big Bull, until 1850, when it was renamed Wausau, meaning "far away place." In 1864 August Kickbusch, then village president, brought 700 immigrants from Germany to settle in the Wausau area. In the early 1900's, Wausau turned from lumbering to manufacturing. Paper mills were established in nearby Rothschild and Brokaw.
Population: 38,426 (2000); Race: 86.3% White, 0.4% Black, 10.9% Asian, 0.8% American Indian and Alaska Native, 1.0% Hispanic of any race, 1.2% two or more races (2000); Density: 2,330.7 persons per square mile (2000); Age: 25.0% under 18, 17.3% over 64 (2000); Marriage status: 27.2% never married, 53.7% now married, 8.9% widowed, 10.2% divorced (2000); Foreign born: 8.4% (2000); Ancestry (includes multiple ancestries): 46.7% German, 12.4% Other groups, 12.1% Polish, 8.1% Irish, 6.4% Norwegian (2000).
Vital Statistics: Birth rate: 131.4 per 10,000 population (1998)
Economy: Unemployment rate: 4.8% (11/2002); Total civilian labor force: 21,614 (11/2002); Single-family building permits issued: 58 (2001) / 63 (2000); Multi-family building permits issued: 36 (2001) / 72 (2000); Employment by occupation: 11.3% management, 19.3% professional, 14.5% services, 28.7% sales, 0.5% farming, 6.4% construction, 19.3% production (2000).
Income: Per capita income: $20,227 (2000); Median household income: $36,831 (2000); Poverty rate: 11.4% (2000).
Taxes: Total city taxes per capita: $385 (2000); City property taxes per capita: $361 (2000).
Education: High school graduation rate: 80.8% (2000); College graduation rate: 21.5% (2000).

School District(s)

Wausau (PK-12)
2000 Enrollment: 9,015 715-261-2561

Two-year College(s)

Northcentral Technical College (Public)
2001 Enrollment: 3,963 715-675-3331
2001 Tuition: In-state $2,065; Out-of-state $15,103
State College of Beauty Culture Inc (Private, For-profit)
2001 Enrollment: 40 715-845-2888

Housing: Homeownership rate: 61.7% (2000); Median home value: $85,500 (2000); Median rent: $419 per month (2000); Median age of housing: 47 years (2000).
Hospitals: Community Healthcare - Wausau Hospital (321 beds); North Central Health Care (50 beds)
Safety: Violent crime rate: 30.7 per 10,000 population; Property crime rate: 396.1 per 10,000 population (2001).
Newspapers: The Wausau Daily Herald (7 x week)
Transportation: Commute to work: 90.9% car, 2.1% public transportation, 3.5% walk, 2.3% work from home (2000); Travel time to work: 58.1% less than 15 minutes, 33.7% 15 to 30 minutes, 4.1% 30 to 45 minutes, 1.8% 45 to 60 minutes, 2.2% 60 minutes or more (2000); Amtrak: Service available.
Additional Information Contacts
Wausau Chamber of Commerce. 715-845-6231

WAUSAU (town). Covers a land area of 33.475 square miles and a water area of 0 square miles. Located at 44.98° N. Lat.; 89.55° W. Long. Elevation is 1,210 feet.
History: Well known for its Wausau Insurance Company. Settled 1839, Incorporated 1872.
Population: 2,214 (2000); Race: 100.0% White, 0.0% Black, 0.0% Asian, 0.0% American Indian and Alaska Native, 0.6% Hispanic of any race, 0.0% two or more races (2000); Density: 66.1 persons per square mile (2000); Age: 23.0% under 18, 13.0% over 64 (2000); Marriage status: 23.1% never married, 64.5% now married, 5.9% widowed, 6.5% divorced (2000); Foreign born: 0.5% (2000); Ancestry (includes multiple ancestries): 63.1% German, 17.3% Polish, 6.3% English, 5.2% Irish, 5.0% United States or American (2000).
Economy: It is an industrial, commercial and agricultural city in the heart of the state's dairy region. Its many manufactures include wood products, electric motors, knives, machinery, plastics and steel fabrication. Well known for its Wausau Insurance Company. Single-family building permits issued: 19 (2001) / 19 (2000); Multi-family building permits issued: 0 (2001) / 0 (2000); Employment by occupation: 14.7% management, 15.8% professional, 13.2% services, 25.7% sales, 1.5% farming, 11.5% construction, 17.7% production (2000).
Income: Per capita income: $22,248 (2000); Median household income: $51,071 (2000); Poverty rate: 2.6% (2000).
Taxes: Total city taxes per capita: $53 (1997); City property taxes per capita: $52 (1997).
Education: High school graduation rate: 83.6% (2000); College graduation rate: 16.9% (2000).
Housing: Homeownership rate: 90.3% (2000); Median home value: $112,100 (2000); Median rent: $455 per month (2000); Median age of housing: 29 years (2000).
Transportation: Commute to work: 89.8% car, 0.6% public transportation, 1.7% walk, 5.5% work from home (2000); Travel time to work: 38.2% less than 15 minutes, 46.3% 15 to 30 minutes, 8.0% 30 to 45 minutes, 2.0% 45 to 60 minutes, 5.5% 60 minutes or more (2000); Amtrak: Service available.

WESTON (village). Covers a land area of 21.297 square miles and a water area of 0.026 square miles. Located at 44.90° N. Lat.; 89.56° W. Long.
Population: 12,079 (2000); Race: 93.2% White, 0.2% Black, 4.5% Asian, 0.6% American Indian and Alaska Native, 0.8% Hispanic of any race, 1.0% two or more races (2000); Density: 567.2 persons per square mile (2000); Age: 28.7% under 18, 9.2% over 64 (2000); Marriage status: 25.9% never married, 59.4% now married, 4.9% widowed, 9.8% divorced (2000); Foreign born: 3.1% (2000); Ancestry (includes multiple ancestries): 51.2% German, 17.9% Polish, 8.0% Irish, 6.5% Norwegian, 6.0% Other groups (2000).
Economy: Employment by occupation: 11.1% management, 16.3% professional, 12.2% services, 29.9% sales, 0.4% farming, 7.2% construction, 22.9% production (2000).
Income: Per capita income: $20,148 (2000); Median household income: $46,063 (2000); Poverty rate: 5.1% (2000).
Taxes: Total city taxes per capita: $177 (2000); City property taxes per capita: $161 (2000).
Education: High school graduation rate: 86.8% (2000); College graduation rate: 18.7% (2000).
Housing: Homeownership rate: 67.2% (2000); Median home value: $111,200 (2000); Median rent: $450 per month (2000); Median age of housing: 22 years (2000).
Transportation: Commute to work: 95.5% car, 1.1% public transportation, 0.8% walk, 2.4% work from home (2000); Travel time to work: 42.3% less than 15 minutes, 48.5% 15 to 30 minutes, 4.9% 30 to 45 minutes, 1.5% 45 to 60 minutes, 2.9% 60 minutes or more (2000)

WIEN (town). Covers a land area of 31.558 square miles and a water area of 0.007 square miles. Located at 44.90° N. Lat.; 90.02° W. Long. Elevation is 1,320 feet.
Population: 712 (2000); Race: 99.7% White, 0.0% Black, 0.0% Asian, 0.3% American Indian and Alaska Native, 0.0% Hispanic of any race, 0.0% two or more races (2000); Density: 22.6 persons per square mile (2000); Age: 26.0% under 18, 13.5% over 64 (2000); Marriage status: 27.4% never married, 63.9% now married, 4.6% widowed, 4.1% divorced (2000); Foreign born: 0.0% (2000); Ancestry (includes multiple ancestries): 72.4% German, 21.3% Polish, 6.4% Irish, 4.2% United States or American, 3.2% Swiss (2000).
Economy: Employment by occupation: 23.2% management, 14.6% professional, 10.9% services, 17.4% sales, 1.8% farming, 10.2% construction, 21.9% production (2000).
Income: Per capita income: $18,046 (2000); Median household income: $45,556 (2000); Poverty rate: 10.1% (2000).
Taxes: Total city taxes per capita: $56 (1997); City property taxes per capita: $56 (1997).
Education: High school graduation rate: 86.1% (2000); College graduation rate: 13.0% (2000).
Housing: Homeownership rate: 90.5% (2000); Median home value: $93,200 (2000); Median rent: $338 per month (2000); Median age of housing: 46 years (2000).
Transportation: Commute to work: 71.4% car, 0.0% public transportation, 4.2% walk, 23.7% work from home (2000); Travel time to work: 25.3% less

than 15 minutes, 29.7% 15 to 30 minutes, 33.8% 30 to 45 minutes, 8.9% 45 to 60 minutes, 2.4% 60 minutes or more (2000)

Marinette County

Located in northeastern Wisconsin; bounded on the east by the Menominee River and the Michigan border, and on the southeast by Green Bay; drained by the Peshtigo River; includes several lakes. Covers a land area of 1,401.80 square miles, a water area of 148.30 square miles, and is located in the Central Time Zone. The county government was organized in 1879. County seat is Marinette.

Weather Station: Goodman Elevation: 1,427 feet

	Jan	Feb	Mar	Apr	May	Jun	Jul	Aug	Sep	Oct	Nov	Dec
High	21	27	37	52	66	74	78	75	66	55	39	27
Low	0	6	16	29	40	49	55	53	44	34	22	9
Precip	1.1	0.9	1.9	2.0	3.4	3.7	3.8	3.6	3.9	2.8	2.0	1.3
Snow	13.9	7.4	10.3	3.5	0.6	0.0	0.0	0.0	0.0	1.2	5.0	12.2

High and Low temperatures in degrees Fahrenheit; Precipitation and Snow in inches

Weather Station: Marinette Elevation: 606 feet

	Jan	Feb	Mar	Apr	May	Jun	Jul	Aug	Sep	Oct	Nov	Dec
High	26	30	40	54	68	77	82	80	71	58	43	31
Low	8	13	22	33	44	54	59	58	50	39	28	16
Precip	2.0	1.3	2.3	2.8	3.2	3.5	3.4	3.3	3.6	2.6	2.7	1.8
Snow	16.4	9.9	9.5	2.7	0.1	0.0	0.0	0.0	0.0	tr	3.4	12.7

High and Low temperatures in degrees Fahrenheit; Precipitation and Snow in inches

Population: 43,384 (2000); Race: 98.3% White, 0.1% Black, 0.3% Asian, 0.7% American Indian and Alaska Native, 0.5% Hispanic of any race, 0.5% two or more races (2000); Density: 30.9 persons per square mile (2000); Age: 23.6% under 18, 17.6% over 64 (2000).
Religion: Five largest groups: 38.4% Catholic Church, 7.4% Wisconsin Evangelical Lutheran Synod, 6.9% Evangelical Lutheran Church in America, 2.5% The United Methodist Church, 1.7% Presbyterian Church (U.S.A.) (2000).
Economy: Unemployment rate: 5.8% (11/2002); Total civilian labor force: 22,186 (11/2002); Leading industries: 39.7% manufacturing; 13.3% health care and social assistance; 12.6% retail trade (2000); Companies that employ more than 1,000 persons: 0 (2000); Companies that employ more than 100 persons: 27 (2000); Farms: 551 totaling 131,641 acres (1997); Minority business ownership rate: 0.0% (1997); Women business ownership rate: 12.2% (1997); Retail sales per capita: $6,661 (1997). Single-family building permits issued: 273 (2001) / 230 (2000); Multi-family building permits issued: 0 (2001) / 41 (2000).
Income: Per capita income: $17,492 (2000); Median household income: $35,256 (2000); Poverty rate: 8.3% (2000); Bankruptcy rate: 3.94% (2001).
Taxes: Total county taxes per capita: $177 (1997); County property taxes per capita: $173 (1997).
Education: High school graduation rate: 82.5% (2000); College graduation rate: 12.9% (2000).
Housing: Homeownership rate: 79.5% (2000); Median home value: $69,800 (2000); Median rent: $324 per month (2000); Median age of housing: 31 years (2000).
Health: Birth rate: 100.3 per 10,000 population (1998); Age adjusted death rate: 94.1 per 10,000 population (1999); Age adjusted cancer mortality rate: 216.4 deaths per 100,000 population (1999). Number of physicians: 10.6 per 10,000 population (1999); Number of hospital beds: 26.5 per 10,000 population (1999).
Elections: 2000 Presidential election results: 43.6% Gore, 52.9% Bush, 2.5% Nader, 0.5% Buchanan
National and State Parks: Amberg State Public Hunting Grounds; Beaver Creek State Public Hunting Grounds; Lake Noquebay State Public Hunting Grounds; Miscauno State Public Hunting Grounds; Peshtigo Harbor State Wildlife Area; Town Corner State Wildlife Management Area; Wausaukee State Forest
Additional Information Contacts
Marinette County Government Offices 715-732-7406
Marinette Chamber of Commerce 715-735-6681
Marinette County Board of Realtors 920-897-2899

Marinette County Communities

AMBERG (town). Covers a land area of 71.828 square miles and a water area of 0.881 square miles. Located at 45.48° N. Lat.; 87.96° W. Long. Elevation is 893 feet.

Population: 854 (2000); Race: 95.5% White, 0.0% Black, 2.7% Asian, 1.5% American Indian and Alaska Native, 0.0% Hispanic of any race, 0.3% two or more races (2000); Density: 11.9 persons per square mile (2000); Age: 20.4% under 18, 23.8% over 64 (2000); Marriage status: 21.0% never married, 57.5% now married, 7.6% widowed, 13.8% divorced (2000); Foreign born: 1.6% (2000); Ancestry (includes multiple ancestries): 36.3% German, 11.8% Polish, 11.1% Irish, 9.1% English, 5.7% United States or American (2000).
Economy: Single-family building permits issued: 9 (2001) / 7 (2000); Multi-family building permits issued: 0 (2001) / 0 (2000); Employment by occupation: 11.3% management, 14.2% professional, 18.2% services, 12.9% sales, 1.9% farming, 10.7% construction, 30.8% production (2000).
Income: Per capita income: $17,717 (2000); Median household income: $26,667 (2000); Poverty rate: 13.2% (2000).
Taxes: Total city taxes per capita: $39 (1997); City property taxes per capita: $36 (1997).
Education: High school graduation rate: 78.5% (2000); College graduation rate: 9.2% (2000).
Housing: Homeownership rate: 88.6% (2000); Median home value: $63,000 (2000); Median rent: $292 per month (2000); Median age of housing: 25 years (2000).
Transportation: Commute to work: 87.8% car, 0.0% public transportation, 5.8% walk, 6.4% work from home (2000); Travel time to work: 28.4% less than 15 minutes, 25.7% 15 to 30 minutes, 20.9% 30 to 45 minutes, 16.4% 45 to 60 minutes, 8.6% 60 minutes or more (2000)

ATHELSTANE (town). Covers a land area of 106.181 square miles and a water area of 0.787 square miles. Located at 45.47° N. Lat.; 88.16° W. Long. Elevation is 933 feet.
Population: 601 (2000); Race: 98.3% White, 0.7% Black, 0.7% Asian, 0.3% American Indian and Alaska Native, 0.0% Hispanic of any race, 0.0% two or more races (2000); Density: 5.7 persons per square mile (2000); Age: 16.8% under 18, 22.9% over 64 (2000); Marriage status: 18.3% never married, 64.0% now married, 8.3% widowed, 9.3% divorced (2000); Foreign born: 2.1% (2000); Ancestry (includes multiple ancestries): 43.8% German, 14.9% Polish, 12.8% Irish, 7.0% English, 6.3% United States or American (2000).
Economy: Single-family building permits issued: 5 (2001) / 9 (2000); Multi-family building permits issued: 0 (2001) / 0 (2000); Employment by occupation: 7.2% management, 8.1% professional, 27.3% services, 20.6% sales, 7.7% farming, 12.0% construction, 17.2% production (2000).
Income: Per capita income: $18,394 (2000); Median household income: $29,602 (2000); Poverty rate: 13.0% (2000).
Taxes: Total city taxes per capita: $90 (2000); City property taxes per capita: $87 (2000).
Education: High school graduation rate: 75.3% (2000); College graduation rate: 5.6% (2000).
Housing: Homeownership rate: 90.9% (2000); Median home value: $69,500 (2000); Median rent: $325 per month (2000); Median age of housing: 21 years (2000).
Transportation: Commute to work: 86.3% car, 0.0% public transportation, 2.4% walk, 10.2% work from home (2000); Travel time to work: 19.0% less than 15 minutes, 25.5% 15 to 30 minutes, 12.5% 30 to 45 minutes, 16.8% 45 to 60 minutes, 26.1% 60 minutes or more (2000)

BEAVER (town). Covers a land area of 68.606 square miles and a water area of 0.888 square miles. Located at 45.15° N. Lat.; 88.07° W. Long. Elevation is 667 feet.
Population: 1,123 (2000); Race: 99.5% White, 0.0% Black, 0.0% Asian, 0.3% American Indian and Alaska Native, 0.5% Hispanic of any race, 0.0% two or more races (2000); Density: 16.4 persons per square mile (2000); Age: 24.8% under 18, 18.4% over 64 (2000); Marriage status: 20.6% never married, 66.5% now married, 6.8% widowed, 6.1% divorced (2000); Foreign born: 1.6% (2000); Ancestry (includes multiple ancestries): 46.2% German, 25.3% Polish, 8.4% United States or American, 7.7% Irish, 5.4% French (except Basque) (2000).
Economy: Single-family building permits issued: 5 (2001) / 14 (2000); Multi-family building permits issued: 0 (2001) / 0 (2000); Employment by occupation: 15.0% management, 10.5% professional, 11.9% services, 18.8% sales, 5.9% farming, 8.1% construction, 29.8% production (2000).
Income: Per capita income: $15,465 (2000); Median household income: $35,188 (2000); Poverty rate: 10.7% (2000).
Taxes: Total city taxes per capita: $104 (1997); City property taxes per capita: $103 (1997).
Education: High school graduation rate: 74.3% (2000); College graduation rate: 6.8% (2000).

Housing: Homeownership rate: 83.3% (2000); Median home value: $73,900 (2000); Median rent: $336 per month (2000); Median age of housing: 30 years (2000).
Transportation: Commute to work: 85.2% car, 0.0% public transportation, 4.4% walk, 10.2% work from home (2000); Travel time to work: 33.7% less than 15 minutes, 27.7% 15 to 30 minutes, 17.6% 30 to 45 minutes, 9.2% 45 to 60 minutes, 11.8% 60 minutes or more (2000)

BEECHER (town). Covers a land area of 48.523 square miles and a water area of 0.859 square miles. Located at 45.58° N. Lat.; 87.92° W. Long. Elevation is 977 feet.
Population: 783 (2000); Race: 93.6% White, 0.0% Black, 0.5% Asian, 4.1% American Indian and Alaska Native, 2.4% Hispanic of any race, 0.1% two or more races (2000); Density: 16.1 persons per square mile (2000); Age: 22.3% under 18, 14.8% over 64 (2000); Marriage status: 15.0% never married, 67.8% now married, 6.2% widowed, 11.0% divorced (2000); Foreign born: 1.3% (2000); Ancestry (includes multiple ancestries): 39.3% German, 8.2% Other groups, 7.7% Polish, 7.3% French (except Basque), 6.6% Irish (2000).
Economy: Single-family building permits issued: 0 (2001) / 0 (2000); Multi-family building permits issued: 0 (2001) / 0 (2000); Employment by occupation: 5.4% management, 11.9% professional, 20.8% services, 19.3% sales, 2.7% farming, 11.6% construction, 28.3% production (2000).
Income: Per capita income: $17,674 (2000); Median household income: $29,107 (2000); Poverty rate: 11.9% (2000).
Taxes: Total city taxes per capita: $72 (1997); City property taxes per capita: $70 (1997).
Education: High school graduation rate: 81.0% (2000); College graduation rate: 12.5% (2000).
Housing: Homeownership rate: 84.1% (2000); Median home value: $67,300 (2000); Median rent: $350 per month (2000); Median age of housing: 26 years (2000).
Transportation: Commute to work: 94.5% car, 0.6% public transportation, 0.0% walk, 4.9% work from home (2000); Travel time to work: 19.7% less than 15 minutes, 24.8% 15 to 30 minutes, 31.6% 30 to 45 minutes, 8.4% 45 to 60 minutes, 15.5% 60 minutes or more (2000)

COLEMAN (village). Covers a land area of 1.126 square miles and a water area of 0 square miles. Located at 45.07° N. Lat.; 88.03° W. Long. Elevation is 710 feet.
Population: 716 (2000); Race: 98.5% White, 0.0% Black, 0.0% Asian, 1.4% American Indian and Alaska Native, 0.0% Hispanic of any race, 0.1% two or more races (2000); Density: 635.7 persons per square mile (2000); Age: 23.0% under 18, 19.7% over 64 (2000); Marriage status: 25.4% never married, 55.4% now married, 10.0% widowed, 9.2% divorced (2000); Foreign born: 0.0% (2000); Ancestry (includes multiple ancestries): 43.7% German, 20.1% Polish, 12.4% French (except Basque), 8.6% United States or American, 8.3% Irish (2000).
Economy: Dairying center. Manufacturing: canned vegetables. Mt. Labett Ski Area to West. Single-family building permits issued: 0 (2001) / 1 (2000); Multi-family building permits issued: 0 (2001) / 9 (2000); Employment by occupation: 10.9% management, 15.9% professional, 11.2% services, 28.6% sales, 1.2% farming, 5.0% construction, 27.1% production (2000).
Income: Per capita income: $18,248 (2000); Median household income: $35,703 (2000); Poverty rate: 7.1% (2000).
Taxes: Total city taxes per capita: $83 (1997); City property taxes per capita: $75 (1997).
Education: High school graduation rate: 82.5% (2000); College graduation rate: 14.7% (2000).

School District(s)

Coleman (PK-12)
2000 Enrollment: 779 920-897-4011
Housing: Homeownership rate: 70.3% (2000); Median home value: $68,800 (2000); Median rent: $300 per month (2000); Median age of housing: 39 years (2000).
Transportation: Commute to work: 89.4% car, 0.0% public transportation, 6.7% walk, 2.7% work from home (2000); Travel time to work: 48.9% less than 15 minutes, 19.0% 15 to 30 minutes, 12.1% 30 to 45 minutes, 15.0% 45 to 60 minutes, 5.0% 60 minutes or more (2000)

CRIVITZ (village). Covers a land area of 1.519 square miles and a water area of 0 square miles. Located at 45.23° N. Lat.; 88.00° W. Long. Elevation is 681 feet.
History: After being a part of the fur trading and lumbering of the early 1800's, Crivitz became the center of a recreational area, gateway to the lakes and streams of the Thunder Mountain region.
Population: 998 (2000); Race: 97.3% White, 0.0% Black, 0.2% Asian, 0.5% American Indian and Alaska Native, 1.8% Hispanic of any race, 1.0% two or more races (2000); Density: 657.1 persons per square mile (2000); Age: 25.6% under 18, 23.0% over 64 (2000); Marriage status: 23.5% never married, 46.8% now married, 16.3% widowed, 13.5% divorced (2000); Foreign born: 1.0% (2000); Ancestry (includes multiple ancestries): 43.1% German, 18.9% Polish, 9.3% Irish, 8.7% French (except Basque), 6.1% Swedish (2000).
Economy: Single-family building permits issued: 6 (2001) / 2 (2000); Multi-family building permits issued: 0 (2001) / 16 (2000); Employment by occupation: 10.8% management, 8.7% professional, 24.1% services, 19.8% sales, 1.1% farming, 11.4% construction, 24.1% production (2000).
Income: Per capita income: $13,405 (2000); Median household income: $26,250 (2000); Poverty rate: 16.8% (2000).
Taxes: Total city taxes per capita: $82 (1997); City property taxes per capita: $63 (1997).
Education: High school graduation rate: 74.6% (2000); College graduation rate: 8.1% (2000).

School District(s)

Crivitz (PK-12)
2000 Enrollment: 887 715-854-2721
Housing: Homeownership rate: 61.1% (2000); Median home value: $70,700 (2000); Median rent: $304 per month (2000); Median age of housing: 32 years (2000).
Transportation: Commute to work: 87.0% car, 0.0% public transportation, 8.8% walk, 3.7% work from home (2000); Travel time to work: 44.5% less than 15 minutes, 18.5% 15 to 30 minutes, 19.6% 30 to 45 minutes, 8.6% 45 to 60 minutes, 8.8% 60 minutes or more (2000)

DUNBAR (town). Covers a land area of 104.417 square miles and a water area of 0.785 square miles. Located at 45.62° N. Lat.; 88.14° W. Long. Elevation is 1,170 feet.
Population: 1,303 (2000); Race: 98.0% White, 0.4% Black, 0.0% Asian, 0.5% American Indian and Alaska Native, 1.2% Hispanic of any race, 0.7% two or more races (2000); Density: 12.5 persons per square mile (2000); Age: 13.3% under 18, 8.4% over 64 (2000); Marriage status: 48.1% never married, 43.5% now married, 4.2% widowed, 4.2% divorced (2000); Foreign born: 1.3% (2000); Ancestry (includes multiple ancestries): 41.3% German, 9.5% English, 8.8% Irish, 8.2% Swedish, 7.7% Other groups (2000).
Economy: Single-family building permits issued: 4 (2001) / 4 (2000); Multi-family building permits issued: 0 (2001) / 0 (2000); Employment by occupation: 6.5% management, 13.2% professional, 23.8% services, 36.6% sales, 0.7% farming, 6.1% construction, 13.0% production (2000).
Income: Per capita income: $12,279 (2000); Median household income: $32,917 (2000); Poverty rate: 8.5% (2000).
Taxes: Total city taxes per capita: $20 (1997); City property taxes per capita: $19 (1997).
Education: High school graduation rate: 88.3% (2000); College graduation rate: 19.7% (2000).

Four-year College(s)

Northland Baptist Bible College (Private, Not-for-profit, Baptist)
2001 Enrollment: n/a 715-324-6900
Housing: Homeownership rate: 75.0% (2000); Median home value: $64,200 (2000); Median rent: $300 per month (2000); Median age of housing: 25 years (2000).
Transportation: Commute to work: 40.9% car, 0.0% public transportation, 53.0% walk, 4.3% work from home (2000); Travel time to work: 75.3% less than 15 minutes, 9.3% 15 to 30 minutes, 11.8% 30 to 45 minutes, 1.8% 45 to 60 minutes, 1.8% 60 minutes or more (2000)

GOODMAN (town). Covers a land area of 105.857 square miles and a water area of 1.715 square miles. Located at 45.63° N. Lat.; 88.32° W. Long. Elevation is 1,380 feet.
History: Goodman was founded as a lumber town, and owned by the Goodman Lumber Company.
Population: 820 (2000); Race: 97.7% White, 0.0% Black, 0.2% Asian, 0.9% American Indian and Alaska Native, 0.5% Hispanic of any race, 0.9% two or more races (2000); Density: 7.7 persons per square mile (2000); Age: 23.2% under 18, 22.1% over 64 (2000); Marriage status: 20.1% never married, 67.3% now married, 7.5% widowed, 5.1% divorced (2000); Foreign born: 4.6% (2000); Ancestry (includes multiple ancestries): 30.3% Polish, 29.6% German, 13.2% Irish, 11.5% French (except Basque), 5.9% French Canadian (2000).
Economy: Single-family building permits issued: 13 (2001) / 5 (2000); Multi-family building permits issued: 0 (2001) / 0 (2000); Employment by

occupation: 9.0% management, 10.6% professional, 17.5% services, 9.0% sales, 3.1% farming, 12.1% construction, 38.7% production (2000).
Income: Per capita income: $15,941 (2000); Median household income: $31,087 (2000); Poverty rate: 9.4% (2000).
Taxes: Total city taxes per capita: $127 (2000); City property taxes per capita: $122 (2000).
Education: High school graduation rate: 78.1% (2000); College graduation rate: 9.9% (2000).

School District(s)

Goodman-Armstrong (PK-12)
2000 Enrollment: 235 715-336-2575
Housing: Homeownership rate: 85.2% (2000); Median home value: $46,200 (2000); Median rent: $219 per month (2000); Median age of housing: 29 years (2000).
Transportation: Commute to work: 87.6% car, 0.0% public transportation, 7.0% walk, 3.9% work from home (2000); Travel time to work: 50.7% less than 15 minutes, 21.0% 15 to 30 minutes, 15.6% 30 to 45 minutes, 6.7% 45 to 60 minutes, 5.9% 60 minutes or more (2000)

GROVER (town). Covers a land area of 73.135 square miles and a water area of 0.202 square miles. Located at 45.06° N. Lat.; 87.87° W. Long.
Population: 1,729 (2000); Race: 99.4% White, 0.0% Black, 0.0% Asian, 0.5% American Indian and Alaska Native, 0.1% Hispanic of any race, 0.1% two or more races (2000); Density: 23.6 persons per square mile (2000); Age: 26.6% under 18, 13.7% over 64 (2000); Marriage status: 19.0% never married, 68.6% now married, 6.3% widowed, 6.1% divorced (2000); Foreign born: 1.2% (2000); Ancestry (includes multiple ancestries): 50.1% German, 12.9% Polish, 7.6% United States or American, 7.1% French (except Basque), 6.3% Irish (2000).
Economy: Single-family building permits issued: 13 (2001) / 15 (2000); Multi-family building permits issued: 0 (2001) / 0 (2000); Employment by occupation: 11.0% management, 10.0% professional, 13.2% services, 20.6% sales, 4.1% farming, 11.5% construction, 29.6% production (2000).
Income: Per capita income: $17,104 (2000); Median household income: $40,536 (2000); Poverty rate: 7.9% (2000).
Taxes: Total city taxes per capita: $28 (1997); City property taxes per capita: $27 (1997).
Education: High school graduation rate: 81.2% (2000); College graduation rate: 7.3% (2000).
Housing: Homeownership rate: 85.4% (2000); Median home value: $79,100 (2000); Median rent: $363 per month (2000); Median age of housing: 43 years (2000).
Transportation: Commute to work: 84.0% car, 0.9% public transportation, 2.3% walk, 12.4% work from home (2000); Travel time to work: 31.3% less than 15 minutes, 47.4% 15 to 30 minutes, 11.4% 30 to 45 minutes, 3.5% 45 to 60 minutes, 6.4% 60 minutes or more (2000)

LAKE (town). Covers a land area of 55.764 square miles and a water area of 3.780 square miles. Located at 45.20° N. Lat.; 87.88° W. Long.
Population: 1,064 (2000); Race: 98.8% White, 0.0% Black, 0.2% Asian, 0.0% American Indian and Alaska Native, 0.4% Hispanic of any race, 0.9% two or more races (2000); Density: 19.1 persons per square mile (2000); Age: 24.5% under 18, 15.6% over 64 (2000); Marriage status: 19.3% never married, 65.8% now married, 5.8% widowed, 9.1% divorced (2000); Foreign born: 1.3% (2000); Ancestry (includes multiple ancestries): 52.3% German, 18.6% Polish, 8.7% Irish, 8.1% French (except Basque), 6.6% Swedish (2000).
Economy: Single-family building permits issued: 12 (2001) / 7 (2000); Multi-family building permits issued: 0 (2001) / 0 (2000); Employment by occupation: 10.9% management, 15.3% professional, 14.0% services, 16.6% sales, 5.7% farming, 16.2% construction, 21.2% production (2000).
Income: Per capita income: $17,518 (2000); Median household income: $39,432 (2000); Poverty rate: 8.4% (2000).
Taxes: Total city taxes per capita: $119 (1997); City property taxes per capita: $118 (1997).
Education: High school graduation rate: 77.2% (2000); College graduation rate: 11.5% (2000).
Housing: Homeownership rate: 93.7% (2000); Median home value: $87,800 (2000); Median rent: $225 per month (2000); Median age of housing: 27 years (2000).
Transportation: Commute to work: 85.7% car, 0.6% public transportation, 3.0% walk, 9.6% work from home (2000); Travel time to work: 24.0% less than 15 minutes, 48.9% 15 to 30 minutes, 14.4% 30 to 45 minutes, 1.3% 45 to 60 minutes, 11.5% 60 minutes or more (2000)

MARINETTE (city). Covers a land area of 6.758 square miles and a water area of 1.204 square miles. Located at 45.09° N. Lat.; 87.62° W. Long. Elevation is 598 feet.
History: An American Fur Company trading post established here in 1795 lost its business in 1822 to William Farnsworth, an independent trader. Farnsworth built a wing dam and sawmill here, and the settlement that grew up around it in the 1830's was called Marinette, for the Menominee chief Marinette Chevalier, whose daughter married Farnsworth. After the Civil War, lumber became the major industry in Marinette, but was replaced after 1900 by a diversified industry of paper mills, knitting mills, granite works, and dairying.
Population: 11,749 (2000); Race: 97.2% White, 0.1% Black, 0.4% Asian, 1.2% American Indian and Alaska Native, 0.7% Hispanic of any race, 0.9% two or more races (2000); Density: 1,738.4 persons per square mile (2000); Age: 24.0% under 18, 18.8% over 64 (2000); Marriage status: 23.8% never married, 53.2% now married, 11.0% widowed, 12.0% divorced (2000); Foreign born: 1.2% (2000); Ancestry (includes multiple ancestries): 40.4% German, 10.8% French (except Basque), 9.4% Polish, 8.7% Irish, 6.8% Swedish (2000).
Vital Statistics: Birth rate: 114.1 per 10,000 population (1998)
Economy: Single-family building permits issued: 4 (2001) / 6 (2000); Multi-family building permits issued: 0 (2001) / 0 (2000); Employment by occupation: 7.7% management, 17.0% professional, 18.2% services, 23.7% sales, 0.3% farming, 7.4% construction, 25.7% production (2000).
Income: Per capita income: $17,852 (2000); Median household income: $31,743 (2000); Poverty rate: 9.0% (2000).
Taxes: Total city taxes per capita: $308 (1997); City property taxes per capita: $286 (1997).
Education: High school graduation rate: 83.3% (2000); College graduation rate: 13.8% (2000).

School District(s)

Marinette (PK-12)
2000 Enrollment: 2,567 715-732-7905
Housing: Homeownership rate: 69.1% (2000); Median home value: $58,100 (2000); Median rent: $342 per month (2000); Median age of housing: 54 years (2000).
Hospitals: Bay Area Medical Center (115 beds)
Safety: Violent crime rate: 11.0 per 10,000 population; Property crime rate: 447.1 per 10,000 population (2001).
Newspapers: Eagle Herald (7 x week); Cover Story (1 x week)
Transportation: Commute to work: 91.4% car, 0.6% public transportation, 3.3% walk, 2.5% work from home (2000); Travel time to work: 74.7% less than 15 minutes, 15.7% 15 to 30 minutes, 3.5% 30 to 45 minutes, 1.9% 45 to 60 minutes, 4.2% 60 minutes or more (2000); Amtrak: Service available.
Additional Information Contacts
Marinette Chamber of Commerce 715-735-6681

MIDDLE INLET (town). Covers a land area of 50.725 square miles and a water area of 0.765 square miles. Located at 45.28° N. Lat.; 87.93° W. Long. Elevation is 710 feet.
Population: 831 (2000); Race: 98.4% White, 0.0% Black, 1.0% Asian, 0.4% American Indian and Alaska Native, 0.2% Hispanic of any race, 0.2% two or more races (2000); Density: 16.4 persons per square mile (2000); Age: 17.8% under 18, 20.1% over 64 (2000); Marriage status: 15.8% never married, 64.6% now married, 11.6% widowed, 8.1% divorced (2000); Foreign born: 1.0% (2000); Ancestry (includes multiple ancestries): 43.0% German, 17.4% Polish, 8.5% Irish, 8.2% French (except Basque), 7.9% English (2000).
Economy: Single-family building permits issued: 14 (2001) / 14 (2000); Multi-family building permits issued: 0 (2001) / 0 (2000); Employment by occupation: 9.3% management, 12.1% professional, 13.3% services, 21.5% sales, 2.3% farming, 15.0% construction, 26.6% production (2000).
Income: Per capita income: $16,082 (2000); Median household income: $32,054 (2000); Poverty rate: 9.4% (2000).
Taxes: Total city taxes per capita: $81 (1997); City property taxes per capita: $76 (1997).
Education: High school graduation rate: 72.1% (2000); College graduation rate: 9.5% (2000).
Housing: Homeownership rate: 91.1% (2000); Median home value: $55,200 (2000); Median rent: $308 per month (2000); Median age of housing: 25 years (2000).
Transportation: Commute to work: 90.0% car, 0.0% public transportation, 0.6% walk, 8.2% work from home (2000); Travel time to work: 34.5% less than 15 minutes, 23.6% 15 to 30 minutes, 19.2% 30 to 45 minutes, 10.5% 45 to 60 minutes, 12.1% 60 minutes or more (2000)

NIAGARA (city). Covers a land area of 2.740 square miles and a water area of 0.270 square miles. Located at 45.77° N. Lat.; 88.00° W. Long. Elevation is 900 feet.
History: The Kimberly-Clark paper mill opened in Niagara in 1898, first using timber floated down the river, but after 1907 receiving trainloads of pulpwood from other forested areas.
Population: 1,880 (2000); Race: 99.7% White, 0.0% Black, 0.0% Asian, 0.0% American Indian and Alaska Native, 0.3% Hispanic of any race, 0.3% two or more races (2000); Density: 686.1 persons per square mile (2000); Age: 27.3% under 18, 18.7% over 64 (2000); Marriage status: 19.4% never married, 58.2% now married, 11.4% widowed, 11.0% divorced (2000); Foreign born: 0.7% (2000); Ancestry (includes multiple ancestries): 31.3% German, 15.8% French (except Basque), 13.0% Polish, 10.8% Italian, 10.3% Irish (2000).
Economy: Single-family building permits issued: 0 (2001) / 1 (2000); Multi-family building permits issued: 0 (2001) / 0 (2000); Employment by occupation: 7.2% management, 10.6% professional, 19.1% services, 29.3% sales, 0.7% farming, 15.0% construction, 18.1% production (2000).
Income: Per capita income: $15,616 (2000); Median household income: $33,828 (2000); Poverty rate: 9.9% (2000).
Taxes: Total city taxes per capita: $228 (1997); City property taxes per capita: $226 (1997).
Education: High school graduation rate: 85.4% (2000); College graduation rate: 12.3% (2000).

School District(s)

Niagara (PK-12)
2000 Enrollment: 575 715-251-1330

Housing: Homeownership rate: 77.0% (2000); Median home value: $52,000 (2000); Median rent: $323 per month (2000); Median age of housing: 48 years (2000).
Safety: Violent crime rate: 15.8 per 10,000 population; Property crime rate: 153.2 per 10,000 population (2001).
Transportation: Commute to work: 93.7% car, 0.2% public transportation, 3.5% walk, 2.6% work from home (2000); Travel time to work: 57.0% less than 15 minutes, 32.9% 15 to 30 minutes, 7.0% 30 to 45 minutes, 1.5% 45 to 60 minutes, 1.6% 60 minutes or more (2000)

NIAGARA (town). Covers a land area of 67.106 square miles and a water area of 1.253 square miles. Located at 45.72° N. Lat.; 87.95° W. Long. Elevation is 900 feet.
History: Incorporated 1914.
Population: 924 (2000); Race: 98.7% White, 0.0% Black, 0.8% Asian, 0.0% American Indian and Alaska Native, 0.9% Hispanic of any race, 0.4% two or more races (2000); Density: 13.8 persons per square mile (2000); Age: 28.4% under 18, 13.8% over 64 (2000); Marriage status: 18.1% never married, 70.0% now married, 4.9% widowed, 6.9% divorced (2000); Foreign born: 0.9% (2000); Ancestry (includes multiple ancestries): 31.8% German, 14.3% French (except Basque), 12.3% Polish, 10.5% Italian, 9.5% Swedish (2000).
Economy: In potato-growing and dairy area. Manufacturing: paper milling, iron and steel products. Single-family building permits issued: 5 (2001) / 4 (2000); Multi-family building permits issued: 0 (2001) / 0 (2000); Employment by occupation: 13.3% management, 18.8% professional, 12.7% services, 28.1% sales, 0.8% farming, 9.7% construction, 16.5% production (2000).
Income: Per capita income: $17,504 (2000); Median household income: $40,250 (2000); Poverty rate: 6.4% (2000).
Taxes: Total city taxes per capita: $27 (1997); City property taxes per capita: $24 (1997).
Education: High school graduation rate: 87.2% (2000); College graduation rate: 17.8% (2000).
Housing: Homeownership rate: 94.1% (2000); Median home value: $88,500 (2000); Median rent: $355 per month (2000); Median age of housing: 27 years (2000).
Transportation: Commute to work: 94.4% car, 0.0% public transportation, 1.5% walk, 4.1% work from home (2000); Travel time to work: 46.8% less than 15 minutes, 42.5% 15 to 30 minutes, 7.2% 30 to 45 minutes, 0.9% 45 to 60 minutes, 2.7% 60 minutes or more (2000)

PEMBINE (town). Covers a land area of 66.328 square miles and a water area of 0.991 square miles. Located at 45.64° N. Lat.; 87.94° W. Long. Elevation is 968 feet.
Population: 1,036 (2000); Race: 97.9% White, 0.0% Black, 0.7% Asian, 1.0% American Indian and Alaska Native, 0.4% Hispanic of any race, 0.2% two or more races (2000); Density: 15.6 persons per square mile (2000); Age: 24.3% under 18, 17.6% over 64 (2000); Marriage status: 21.9% never married, 65.4% now married, 4.8% widowed, 7.9% divorced (2000); Foreign born: 1.4% (2000); Ancestry (includes multiple ancestries): 34.2% German, 9.6% Irish, 7.9% Polish, 6.9% English, 6.8% United States or American (2000).
Economy: Single-family building permits issued: 19 (2001) / 9 (2000); Multi-family building permits issued: 0 (2001) / 0 (2000); Employment by occupation: 6.5% management, 16.6% professional, 15.8% services, 24.7% sales, 1.8% farming, 13.2% construction, 21.3% production (2000).
Income: Per capita income: $16,459 (2000); Median household income: $34,395 (2000); Poverty rate: 8.6% (2000).
Taxes: Total city taxes per capita: $45 (1997); City property taxes per capita: $43 (1997).
Education: High school graduation rate: 82.3% (2000); College graduation rate: 12.9% (2000).

School District(s)

Beecher-Dunbar-Pembine (PK-12)
2000 Enrollment: 330 715-324-5314

Housing: Homeownership rate: 82.9% (2000); Median home value: $58,400 (2000); Median rent: $314 per month (2000); Median age of housing: 27 years (2000).
Transportation: Commute to work: 93.0% car, 0.6% public transportation, 1.9% walk, 4.0% work from home (2000); Travel time to work: 40.2% less than 15 minutes, 33.8% 15 to 30 minutes, 19.4% 30 to 45 minutes, 3.8% 45 to 60 minutes, 2.9% 60 minutes or more (2000)

PESHTIGO (city). Covers a land area of 3.047 square miles and a water area of 0.169 square miles. Located at 45.05° N. Lat.; 87.74° W. Long. Elevation is 610 feet.
Population: 3,357 (2000); Race: 99.6% White, 0.2% Black, 0.0% Asian, 0.0% American Indian and Alaska Native, 0.0% Hispanic of any race, 0.2% two or more races (2000); Density: 1,101.8 persons per square mile (2000); Age: 24.9% under 18, 19.9% over 64 (2000); Marriage status: 20.4% never married, 59.8% now married, 10.3% widowed, 9.5% divorced (2000); Foreign born: 0.4% (2000); Ancestry (includes multiple ancestries): 44.3% German, 13.9% Polish, 9.2% French (except Basque), 8.7% Swedish, 7.2% Irish (2000).
Economy: Single-family building permits issued: 7 (2001) / 5 (2000); Multi-family building permits issued: 0 (2001) / 16 (2000); Employment by occupation: 7.5% management, 16.1% professional, 16.4% services, 19.2% sales, 0.9% farming, 12.1% construction, 27.8% production (2000).
Income: Per capita income: $16,379 (2000); Median household income: $34,898 (2000); Poverty rate: 8.2% (2000).
Taxes: Total city taxes per capita: $117 (1997); City property taxes per capita: $102 (1997).
Education: High school graduation rate: 82.4% (2000); College graduation rate: 15.5% (2000).

School District(s)

Peshtigo (PK-12)
2000 Enrollment: 1,100 715-582-3677

Housing: Homeownership rate: 68.1% (2000); Median home value: $73,200 (2000); Median rent: $352 per month (2000); Median age of housing: 41 years (2000).
Safety: Violent crime rate: 3.0 per 10,000 population; Property crime rate: 278.0 per 10,000 population (2001).
Newspapers: Peshtigo Times (1 x week)
Transportation: Commute to work: 92.5% car, 0.0% public transportation, 3.2% walk, 1.9% work from home (2000); Travel time to work: 49.6% less than 15 minutes, 38.8% 15 to 30 minutes, 3.4% 30 to 45 minutes, 4.1% 45 to 60 minutes, 4.1% 60 minutes or more (2000)

PESHTIGO (town). Covers a land area of 59.323 square miles and a water area of 120.970 square miles. Located at 45.05° N. Lat.; 87.69° W. Long. Elevation is 610 feet.
History: Nearby is a memorial and museum of the Oct. 8, 1871 fire (taking 1,182 lives), which occurred on the same night as the great Chicago fire (taking 250 lives). Incorporated 1903.
Population: 3,819 (2000); Race: 99.2% White, 0.0% Black, 0.0% Asian, 0.5% American Indian and Alaska Native, 0.0% Hispanic of any race, 0.3% two or more races (2000); Density: 64.4 persons per square mile (2000); Age: 22.2% under 18, 15.5% over 64 (2000); Marriage status: 20.0% never married, 66.3% now married, 7.2% widowed, 6.6% divorced (2000); Foreign born: 1.4% (2000); Ancestry (includes multiple ancestries): 47.3% German, 14.6% Polish, 10.3% French (except Basque), 9.0% Norwegian, 7.9% Swedish (2000).
Economy: In dairying and lumbering area. Manufacturing: paper, transportation equipment, laminated timber, tools. Single-family building

permits issued: 27 (2001) / 12 (2000); Multi-family building permits issued: 0 (2001) / 0 (2000); Employment by occupation: 12.3% management, 23.8% professional, 7.6% services, 21.9% sales, 1.0% farming, 9.2% construction, 24.3% production (2000).
Income: Per capita income: $22,016 (2000); Median household income: $50,792 (2000); Poverty rate: 1.8% (2000).
Taxes: Total city taxes per capita: $54 (1997); City property taxes per capita: $49 (1997).
Education: High school graduation rate: 89.4% (2000); College graduation rate: 23.2% (2000).
Housing: Homeownership rate: 91.4% (2000); Median home value: $101,300 (2000); Median rent: $331 per month (2000); Median age of housing: 28 years (2000).
Transportation: Commute to work: 96.5% car, 0.0% public transportation, 0.5% walk, 2.3% work from home (2000); Travel time to work: 46.5% less than 15 minutes, 41.2% 15 to 30 minutes, 5.5% 30 to 45 minutes, 1.3% 45 to 60 minutes, 5.5% 60 minutes or more (2000)

PORTERFIELD (town). Covers a land area of 51.768 square miles and a water area of 1.538 square miles. Located at 45.16° N. Lat.; 87.74° W. Long. Elevation is 670 feet.
Population: 1,991 (2000); Race: 99.6% White, 0.0% Black, 0.0% Asian, 0.0% American Indian and Alaska Native, 0.3% Hispanic of any race, 0.3% two or more races (2000); Density: 38.5 persons per square mile (2000); Age: 25.2% under 18, 12.0% over 64 (2000); Marriage status: 20.3% never married, 67.2% now married, 4.3% widowed, 8.1% divorced (2000); Foreign born: 1.0% (2000); Ancestry (includes multiple ancestries): 47.4% German, 11.7% French (except Basque), 11.4% Polish, 8.4% Swedish, 8.3% Irish (2000).
Economy: Single-family building permits issued: 12 (2001) / 12 (2000); Multi-family building permits issued: 0 (2001) / 0 (2000); Employment by occupation: 12.0% management, 13.7% professional, 13.9% services, 17.9% sales, 0.5% farming, 13.7% construction, 28.3% production (2000).
Income: Per capita income: $19,025 (2000); Median household income: $46,898 (2000); Poverty rate: 4.7% (2000).
Taxes: Total city taxes per capita: $30 (1997); City property taxes per capita: $26 (1997).
Education: High school graduation rate: 86.0% (2000); College graduation rate: 12.9% (2000).
Housing: Homeownership rate: 92.9% (2000); Median home value: $90,100 (2000); Median rent: $325 per month (2000); Median age of housing: 30 years (2000).
Transportation: Commute to work: 94.5% car, 0.5% public transportation, 0.6% walk, 3.2% work from home (2000); Travel time to work: 23.4% less than 15 minutes, 62.3% 15 to 30 minutes, 4.9% 30 to 45 minutes, 2.0% 45 to 60 minutes, 7.4% 60 minutes or more (2000)

POUND (village). Covers a land area of 0.815 square miles and a water area of 0 square miles. Located at 45.09° N. Lat.; 88.03° W. Long. Elevation is 730 feet.
History: Pound grew up as a trading center for the surrounding farming area, settled by many Polish immigrants during the early 1900's. A Polish Baptist Church was erected in 1908 in Pound.
Population: 355 (2000); Race: 98.6% White, 0.0% Black, 0.0% Asian, 1.4% American Indian and Alaska Native, 0.0% Hispanic of any race, 0.0% two or more races (2000); Density: 435.4 persons per square mile (2000); Age: 27.1% under 18, 8.9% over 64 (2000); Marriage status: 31.3% never married, 51.0% now married, 6.3% widowed, 11.5% divorced (2000); Foreign born: 0.0% (2000); Ancestry (includes multiple ancestries): 46.8% German, 27.7% Polish, 17.5% French (except Basque), 5.8% English, 5.5% Irish (2000).
Economy: Single-family building permits issued: 0 (2001) / 4 (2000); Multi-family building permits issued: 0 (2001) / 0 (2000); Employment by occupation: 4.4% management, 12.7% professional, 13.7% services, 23.4% sales, 0.5% farming, 8.8% construction, 36.6% production (2000).
Income: Per capita income: $16,890 (2000); Median household income: $32,692 (2000); Poverty rate: 12.0% (2000).
Taxes: Total city taxes per capita: $97 (1997); City property taxes per capita: $88 (1997).
Education: High school graduation rate: 86.7% (2000); College graduation rate: 13.3% (2000).
Housing: Homeownership rate: 62.0% (2000); Median home value: $63,000 (2000); Median rent: $250 per month (2000); Median age of housing: 53 years (2000).
Transportation: Commute to work: 89.2% car, 0.0% public transportation, 5.4% walk, 3.9% work from home (2000); Travel time to work: 45.4% less than 15 minutes, 16.8% 15 to 30 minutes, 19.4% 30 to 45 minutes, 17.3% 45 to 60 minutes, 1.0% 60 minutes or more (2000)

POUND (town). Covers a land area of 49.920 square miles and a water area of 0.302 square miles. Located at 45.06° N. Lat.; 88.04° W. Long. Elevation is 730 feet.
Population: 1,367 (2000); Race: 99.8% White, 0.0% Black, 0.1% Asian, 0.0% American Indian and Alaska Native, 0.1% Hispanic of any race, 0.0% two or more races (2000); Density: 27.4 persons per square mile (2000); Age: 28.7% under 18, 13.3% over 64 (2000); Marriage status: 22.6% never married, 65.7% now married, 5.3% widowed, 6.4% divorced (2000); Foreign born: 0.9% (2000); Ancestry (includes multiple ancestries): 46.8% German, 21.9% Polish, 9.7% French (except Basque), 7.3% Irish, 4.8% Czech (2000).
Economy: Trade center for dairying area. Manufacturing: fabricated metal products, machinery. Single-family building permits issued: 5 (2001) / 5 (2000); Multi-family building permits issued: 0 (2001) / 0 (2000); Employment by occupation: 11.9% management, 12.6% professional, 11.5% services, 18.2% sales, 5.7% farming, 10.9% construction, 29.2% production (2000).
Income: Per capita income: $17,029 (2000); Median household income: $38,750 (2000); Poverty rate: 5.8% (2000).
Taxes: Total city taxes per capita: $56 (1997); City property taxes per capita: $54 (1997).
Education: High school graduation rate: 83.5% (2000); College graduation rate: 12.3% (2000).
Housing: Homeownership rate: 88.6% (2000); Median home value: $76,500 (2000); Median rent: $307 per month (2000); Median age of housing: 39 years (2000).
Transportation: Commute to work: 86.4% car, 0.0% public transportation, 1.6% walk, 11.2% work from home (2000); Travel time to work: 37.6% less than 15 minutes, 21.1% 15 to 30 minutes, 19.6% 30 to 45 minutes, 12.9% 45 to 60 minutes, 8.8% 60 minutes or more (2000)
Additional Information Contacts
Marinette County Board of Realtors 920-897-2899

SILVER CLIFF (town). Covers a land area of 106.369 square miles and a water area of 0.632 square miles. Located at 45.42° N. Lat.; 88.31° W. Long.
Population: 529 (2000); Race: 98.1% White, 0.0% Black, 0.0% Asian, 1.0% American Indian and Alaska Native, 0.6% Hispanic of any race, 0.6% two or more races (2000); Density: 5.0 persons per square mile (2000); Age: 20.2% under 18, 17.6% over 64 (2000); Marriage status: 12.2% never married, 78.3% now married, 5.1% widowed, 4.4% divorced (2000); Foreign born: 0.8% (2000); Ancestry (includes multiple ancestries): 52.7% German, 10.5% Polish, 8.8% Irish, 7.1% English, 5.2% French (except Basque) (2000).
Economy: Single-family building permits issued: 8 (2001) / 19 (2000); Multi-family building permits issued: 0 (2001) / 0 (2000); Employment by occupation: 10.7% management, 6.9% professional, 14.5% services, 30.2% sales, 3.1% farming, 17.0% construction, 17.6% production (2000).
Income: Per capita income: $15,956 (2000); Median household income: $31,053 (2000); Poverty rate: 15.1% (2000).
Taxes: Total city taxes per capita: $196 (1997); City property taxes per capita: $192 (1997).
Education: High school graduation rate: 79.4% (2000); College graduation rate: 7.4% (2000).
Housing: Homeownership rate: 95.0% (2000); Median home value: $65,700 (2000); Median rent: $325 per month (2000); Median age of housing: 24 years (2000).
Transportation: Commute to work: 83.6% car, 0.0% public transportation, 8.8% walk, 7.5% work from home (2000); Travel time to work: 23.8% less than 15 minutes, 34.0% 15 to 30 minutes, 17.7% 30 to 45 minutes, 1.4% 45 to 60 minutes, 23.1% 60 minutes or more (2000)

STEPHENSON (town). Covers a land area of 169.567 square miles and a water area of 7.214 square miles. Located at 45.28° N. Lat.; 88.15° W. Long.
Population: 3,065 (2000); Race: 99.1% White, 0.0% Black, 0.1% Asian, 0.2% American Indian and Alaska Native, 0.7% Hispanic of any race, 0.6% two or more races (2000); Density: 18.1 persons per square mile (2000); Age: 17.5% under 18, 20.9% over 64 (2000); Marriage status: 16.6% never married, 65.4% now married, 8.5% widowed, 9.5% divorced (2000); Foreign born: 1.4% (2000); Ancestry (includes multiple ancestries): 42.3% German, 19.2% Polish, 9.2% Irish, 5.5% Italian, 5.2% French (except Basque) (2000).
Economy: Single-family building permits issued: 72 (2001) / 46 (2000); Multi-family building permits issued: 0 (2001) / 0 (2000); Employment by

occupation: 13.2% management, 10.2% professional, 24.1% services, 18.0% sales, 2.9% farming, 10.4% construction, 21.1% production (2000).
Income: Per capita income: $18,312 (2000); Median household income: $34,516 (2000); Poverty rate: 7.6% (2000).
Taxes: Total city taxes per capita: $218 (1997); City property taxes per capita: $205 (1997).
Education: High school graduation rate: 81.7% (2000); College graduation rate: 7.5% (2000).
Housing: Homeownership rate: 87.8% (2000); Median home value: $85,900 (2000); Median rent: $274 per month (2000); Median age of housing: 26 years (2000).
Transportation: Commute to work: 84.6% car, 0.2% public transportation, 5.3% walk, 8.6% work from home (2000); Travel time to work: 33.8% less than 15 minutes, 25.2% 15 to 30 minutes, 13.1% 30 to 45 minutes, 10.5% 45 to 60 minutes, 17.4% 60 minutes or more (2000)

WAGNER (town). Covers a land area of 53.189 square miles and a water area of 1.388 square miles. Located at 45.30° N. Lat.; 87.72° W. Long. Elevation is 1,700 feet.
Population: 722 (2000); Race: 95.1% White, 0.4% Black, 0.3% Asian, 0.5% American Indian and Alaska Native, 0.9% Hispanic of any race, 2.4% two or more races (2000); Density: 13.6 persons per square mile (2000); Age: 25.4% under 18, 15.8% over 64 (2000); Marriage status: 17.8% never married, 68.3% now married, 7.4% widowed, 6.5% divorced (2000); Foreign born: 2.7% (2000); Ancestry (includes multiple ancestries): 42.8% German, 14.6% Polish, 9.6% French (except Basque), 7.8% Other groups, 6.8% Irish (2000).
Economy: Single-family building permits issued: 11 (2001) / 7 (2000); Multi-family building permits issued: 0 (2001) / 0 (2000); Employment by occupation: 3.5% management, 10.3% professional, 11.7% services, 22.9% sales, 7.3% farming, 15.8% construction, 28.4% production (2000).
Income: Per capita income: $15,165 (2000); Median household income: $39,792 (2000); Poverty rate: 4.8% (2000).
Taxes: Total city taxes per capita: $137 (1997); City property taxes per capita: $136 (1997).
Education: High school graduation rate: 83.2% (2000); College graduation rate: 7.7% (2000).
Housing: Homeownership rate: 95.8% (2000); Median home value: $82,000 (2000); Median rent: $238 per month (2000); Median age of housing: 27 years (2000).
Transportation: Commute to work: 95.8% car, 0.0% public transportation, 1.5% walk, 2.7% work from home (2000); Travel time to work: 5.8% less than 15 minutes, 33.9% 15 to 30 minutes, 45.6% 30 to 45 minutes, 5.2% 45 to 60 minutes, 9.5% 60 minutes or more (2000)

WAUSAUKEE (village). Covers a land area of 1.421 square miles and a water area of 0.008 square miles. Located at 45.37° N. Lat.; 87.95° W. Long. Elevation is 744 feet.
History: The name of Wausaukee is of Indian origin, meaning "far away land." The village was once a lumber town.
Population: 572 (2000); Race: 98.0% White, 2.0% Black, 0.0% Asian, 0.0% American Indian and Alaska Native, 3.7% Hispanic of any race, 0.0% two or more races (2000); Density: 402.4 persons per square mile (2000); Age: 30.7% under 18, 18.0% over 64 (2000); Marriage status: 20.8% never married, 54.3% now married, 11.6% widowed, 13.2% divorced (2000); Foreign born: 2.2% (2000); Ancestry (includes multiple ancestries): 30.2% German, 18.3% Polish, 10.5% Irish, 6.3% Italian, 6.3% United States or American (2000).
Economy: Single-family building permits issued: 0 (2001) / 1 (2000); Multi-family building permits issued: 0 (2001) / 0 (2000); Employment by occupation: 7.8% management, 15.2% professional, 21.4% services, 10.7% sales, 3.7% farming, 14.8% construction, 26.3% production (2000).
Income: Per capita income: $13,098 (2000); Median household income: $25,313 (2000); Poverty rate: 23.0% (2000).
Taxes: Total city taxes per capita: $104 (1997); City property taxes per capita: $87 (1997).
Education: High school graduation rate: 79.6% (2000); College graduation rate: 7.7% (2000).

School District(s)

Wausaukee (PK-12)
2000 Enrollment: 781 715-856-5153

Housing: Homeownership rate: 60.1% (2000); Median home value: $46,900 (2000); Median rent: $285 per month (2000); Median age of housing: 44 years (2000).
Transportation: Commute to work: 92.0% car, 0.0% public transportation, 4.2% walk, 3.8% work from home (2000); Travel time to work: 58.5% less than 15 minutes, 15.3% 15 to 30 minutes, 16.2% 30 to 45 minutes, 2.6% 45 to 60 minutes, 7.4% 60 minutes or more (2000)

WAUSAUKEE (town). Covers a land area of 75.725 square miles and a water area of 1.715 square miles. Located at 45.39° N. Lat.; 87.92° W. Long. Elevation is 744 feet.
Population: 1,196 (2000); Race: 99.8% White, 0.0% Black, 0.0% Asian, 0.0% American Indian and Alaska Native, 0.0% Hispanic of any race, 0.2% two or more races (2000); Density: 15.8 persons per square mile (2000); Age: 24.9% under 18, 18.1% over 64 (2000); Marriage status: 16.6% never married, 66.1% now married, 8.3% widowed, 9.0% divorced (2000); Foreign born: 1.5% (2000); Ancestry (includes multiple ancestries): 37.3% German, 15.3% Polish, 8.6% English, 8.4% Irish, 7.2% United States or American (2000).
Economy: Manufacturing: fabricated metal products and fiberglass structures. Single-family building permits issued: 22 (2001) / 21 (2000); Multi-family building permits issued: 0 (2001) / 0 (2000); Employment by occupation: 10.3% management, 10.3% professional, 15.5% services, 19.8% sales, 3.5% farming, 12.8% construction, 27.7% production (2000).
Income: Per capita income: $18,610 (2000); Median household income: $35,530 (2000); Poverty rate: 5.5% (2000).
Taxes: Total city taxes per capita: $70 (1997); City property taxes per capita: $67 (1997).
Education: High school graduation rate: 79.5% (2000); College graduation rate: 10.6% (2000).
Housing: Homeownership rate: 90.0% (2000); Median home value: $93,100 (2000); Median rent: $245 per month (2000); Median age of housing: 22 years (2000).
Transportation: Commute to work: 93.8% car, 0.0% public transportation, 1.9% walk, 4.3% work from home (2000); Travel time to work: 46.2% less than 15 minutes, 18.6% 15 to 30 minutes, 15.9% 30 to 45 minutes, 7.8% 45 to 60 minutes, 11.4% 60 minutes or more (2000)

Marquette County

Located in south central Wisconsin; drained by the Fox River and its tributaries; includes Buffalo Lake. Covers a land area of 455.50 square miles, a water area of 8.90 square miles, and is located in the Central Time Zone. The county government was organized in 1836. County seat is Montello.

Weather Station: Montello — Elevation: 784 feet

	Jan	Feb	Mar	Apr	May	Jun	Jul	Aug	Sep	Oct	Nov	Dec
High	25	31	42	57	70	79	83	80	72	60	43	30
Low	6	11	22	34	46	56	60	57	49	37	25	13
Precip	1.3	1.1	2.3	3.3	3.5	4.0	4.2	4.1	4.0	2.3	2.4	1.4
Snow	12.1	7.8	7.4	2.3	tr	0.0	0.0	0.0	0.0	0.2	na	8.9

High and Low temperatures in degrees Fahrenheit; Precipitation and Snow in inches

Population: 15,832 (2000); Race: 94.2% White, 3.0% Black, 0.1% Asian, 1.0% American Indian and Alaska Native, 2.6% Hispanic of any race, 1.3% two or more races (2000); Density: 34.8 persons per square mile (2000); Age: 21.1% under 18, 18.1% over 64 (2000).
Religion: Five largest groups: 21.4% Catholic Church, 10.7% Lutheran Church—Missouri Synod, 5.4% Wisconsin Evangelical Lutheran Synod, 5.1% The United Methodist Church, 3.2% Evangelical Lutheran Church in America (2000).
Economy: Unemployment rate: 7.5% (11/2002); Total civilian labor force: 7,437 (11/2002); Leading industries: 37.1% manufacturing; 13.7% retail trade; 10.9% accommodation & food services (2000); Companies that employ more than 1,000 persons: 0 (2000); Companies that employ more than 100 persons: 2 (2000); Farms: 443 totaling 124,804 acres (1997); Minority business ownership rate: 0.0% (1997); Women business ownership rate: 23.9% (1997); Retail sales per capita: $3,789 (1997). Single-family building permits issued: 102 (2001) / 116 (2000); Multi-family building permits issued: 24 (2001) / 12 (2000).
Income: Per capita income: $16,924 (2000); Median household income: $35,746 (2000); Poverty rate: 7.7% (2000); Bankruptcy rate: 3.59% (2001).
Taxes: Total county taxes per capita: $375 (2000); County property taxes per capita: $323 (2000).
Education: High school graduation rate: 78.8% (2000); College graduation rate: 10.1% (2000).
Housing: Homeownership rate: 82.3% (2000); Median home value: $87,000 (2000); Median rent: $372 per month (2000); Median age of housing: 27 years (2000).
Health: Birth rate: 79.6 per 10,000 population (1998); Age adjusted death rate: 75.4 per 10,000 population (1999); Age adjusted cancer mortality rate:

187.9 deaths per 100,000 population (1999). Number of physicians: 1.9 per 10,000 population (1999); Number of hospital beds: n/a (1999).
Elections: 2000 Presidential election results: 47.8% Gore, 49.0% Bush, 2.7% Nader, 0.2% Buchanan
National and State Parks: French Creek State Wildlife Area; Germania Marsh State Wildlife Area; Grand River State Wildlife Area
Additional Information Contacts
Marquette County Government Offices.................608-297-9114
Adams Marquette Waushara Board of Realtors............608-297-7734
Montello Chamber of Commerce.....................608-297-7420

Marquette County Communities

BRIGGSVILLE (unincorporated postal area, zip code 53920). Covers a land area of 9.290 square miles and a water area of 1.474 square miles. Located at 43.66° N. Lat.; 89.59° W. Long. Elevation is 800 feet.
Population: 485 (2000); Race: 97.8% White, 0.0% Black, 0.0% Asian, 0.0% American Indian and Alaska Native, 3.1% Hispanic of any race, 0.4% two or more races (2000); Density: 52.2 persons per square mile (2000); Age: 18.8% under 18, 24.2% over 64 (2000); Marriage status: 13.7% never married, 62.8% now married, 11.6% widowed, 11.9% divorced (2000); Foreign born: 2.9% (2000); Ancestry (includes multiple ancestries): 41.2% German, 15.7% Irish, 9.8% Norwegian, 8.9% English, 8.1% United States or American (2000).
Economy: Employment by occupation: 13.1% management, 10.2% professional, 20.4% services, 21.8% sales, 1.5% farming, 11.7% construction, 21.4% production (2000).
Income: Per capita income: $18,396 (2000); Median household income: $36,471 (2000); Poverty rate: 9.8% (2000).
Education: High school graduation rate: 83.1% (2000); College graduation rate: 9.6% (2000).
Housing: Homeownership rate: 82.3% (2000); Median home value: $90,000 (2000); Median rent: $388 per month (2000); Median age of housing: 33 years (2000).
Transportation: Commute to work: 96.6% car, 0.0% public transportation, 1.0% walk, 2.5% work from home (2000); Travel time to work: 13.1% less than 15 minutes, 51.0% 15 to 30 minutes, 17.2% 30 to 45 minutes, 8.1% 45 to 60 minutes, 10.6% 60 minutes or more (2000)

BUFFALO (town). Covers a land area of 48.518 square miles and a water area of 0.751 square miles. Located at 43.68° N. Lat.; 89.32° W. Long.
Population: 1,085 (2000); Race: 98.8% White, 0.0% Black, 0.1% Asian, 0.4% American Indian and Alaska Native, 1.4% Hispanic of any race, 0.4% two or more races (2000); Density: 22.4 persons per square mile (2000); Age: 26.3% under 18, 12.0% over 64 (2000); Marriage status: 22.4% never married, 63.2% now married, 4.1% widowed, 10.3% divorced (2000); Foreign born: 1.2% (2000); Ancestry (includes multiple ancestries): 45.1% German, 17.4% Irish, 8.9% English, 6.6% Polish, 5.1% Other groups (2000).
Economy: Employment by occupation: 9.5% management, 10.2% professional, 13.8% services, 21.2% sales, 3.0% farming, 16.8% construction, 25.6% production (2000).
Income: Per capita income: $17,009 (2000); Median household income: $38,594 (2000); Poverty rate: 9.4% (2000).
Taxes: Total city taxes per capita: $30 (1997); City property taxes per capita: $28 (1997).
Education: High school graduation rate: 78.5% (2000); College graduation rate: 6.5% (2000).
Housing: Homeownership rate: 89.3% (2000); Median home value: $97,300 (2000); Median rent: $390 per month (2000); Median age of housing: 25 years (2000).
Transportation: Commute to work: 89.6% car, 0.0% public transportation, 1.8% walk, 7.4% work from home (2000); Travel time to work: 20.9% less than 15 minutes, 48.1% 15 to 30 minutes, 10.1% 30 to 45 minutes, 9.9% 45 to 60 minutes, 11.0% 60 minutes or more (2000)

CRYSTAL LAKE (town). Covers a land area of 35.304 square miles and a water area of 0.587 square miles. Located at 43.95° N. Lat.; 89.32° W. Long.
Population: 513 (2000); Race: 96.9% White, 0.0% Black, 0.0% Asian, 1.5% American Indian and Alaska Native, 0.0% Hispanic of any race, 1.5% two or more races (2000); Density: 14.5 persons per square mile (2000); Age: 12.7% under 18, 26.9% over 64 (2000); Marriage status: 17.5% never married, 69.7% now married, 6.4% widowed, 6.4% divorced (2000); Foreign born: 0.9% (2000); Ancestry (includes multiple ancestries): 57.9% German, 10.7% Polish, 7.4% English, 5.5% Norwegian, 4.4% Irish (2000).
Economy: Employment by occupation: 8.5% management, 6.7% professional, 25.4% services, 18.8% sales, 1.8% farming, 15.2% construction, 23.7% production (2000).
Income: Per capita income: $21,824 (2000); Median household income: $38,304 (2000); Poverty rate: 6.0% (2000).
Taxes: Total city taxes per capita: $88 (1997); City property taxes per capita: $86 (1997).
Education: High school graduation rate: 85.4% (2000); College graduation rate: 16.2% (2000).
Housing: Homeownership rate: 89.4% (2000); Median home value: $104,200 (2000); Median rent: $294 per month (2000); Median age of housing: 27 years (2000).
Transportation: Commute to work: 93.2% car, 1.4% public transportation, 2.3% walk, 3.2% work from home (2000); Travel time to work: 27.9% less than 15 minutes, 36.3% 15 to 30 minutes, 21.4% 30 to 45 minutes, 10.2% 45 to 60 minutes, 4.2% 60 minutes or more (2000)

DOUGLAS (town). Covers a land area of 28.846 square miles and a water area of 0.354 square miles. Located at 43.68° N. Lat.; 89.55° W. Long.
Population: 768 (2000); Race: 98.7% White, 0.0% Black, 0.0% Asian, 0.0% American Indian and Alaska Native, 1.9% Hispanic of any race, 0.3% two or more races (2000); Density: 26.6 persons per square mile (2000); Age: 23.1% under 18, 17.6% over 64 (2000); Marriage status: 19.5% never married, 63.6% now married, 6.7% widowed, 10.3% divorced (2000); Foreign born: 1.3% (2000); Ancestry (includes multiple ancestries): 44.0% German, 15.8% Irish, 13.8% English, 7.1% Polish, 6.7% Norwegian (2000).
Economy: Employment by occupation: 14.6% management, 13.2% professional, 16.0% services, 20.5% sales, 2.5% farming, 12.6% construction, 20.5% production (2000).
Income: Per capita income: $19,151 (2000); Median household income: $43,839 (2000); Poverty rate: 6.1% (2000).
Taxes: Total city taxes per capita: $31 (1997); City property taxes per capita: $29 (1997).
Education: High school graduation rate: 86.1% (2000); College graduation rate: 12.9% (2000).
Housing: Homeownership rate: 81.2% (2000); Median home value: $87,700 (2000); Median rent: $400 per month (2000); Median age of housing: 40 years (2000).
Transportation: Commute to work: 94.0% car, 0.0% public transportation, 2.0% walk, 4.0% work from home (2000); Travel time to work: 12.8% less than 15 minutes, 50.7% 15 to 30 minutes, 16.3% 30 to 45 minutes, 11.6% 45 to 60 minutes, 8.6% 60 minutes or more (2000)

ENDEAVOR (village). Covers a land area of 0.642 square miles and a water area of 0.060 square miles. Located at 43.71° N. Lat.; 89.46° W. Long. Elevation is 785 feet.
History: Reverend R.L. Cheney established a revival camp at Endeavor in the 1890's. The village grew up around the Christian Endeavor academy that Cheney operated here until 1913.
Population: 440 (2000); Race: 97.6% White, 0.0% Black, 0.0% Asian, 0.0% American Indian and Alaska Native, 0.2% Hispanic of any race, 1.8% two or more races (2000); Density: 685.3 persons per square mile (2000); Age: 34.3% under 18, 9.3% over 64 (2000); Marriage status: 24.1% never married, 54.6% now married, 8.6% widowed, 12.7% divorced (2000); Foreign born: 0.4% (2000); Ancestry (includes multiple ancestries): 43.4% German, 15.9% Norwegian, 15.0% Irish, 12.6% English, 10.0% Polish (2000).
Economy: Single-family building permits issued: 4 (2001) / 4 (2000); Multi-family building permits issued: 4 (2001) / 4 (2000); Employment by occupation: 7.0% management, 5.3% professional, 21.6% services, 23.3% sales, 0.0% farming, 14.1% construction, 28.6% production (2000).
Income: Per capita income: $14,365 (2000); Median household income: $44,063 (2000); Poverty rate: 8.7% (2000).
Taxes: Total city taxes per capita: $124 (1997); City property taxes per capita: $121 (1997).
Education: High school graduation rate: 80.5% (2000); College graduation rate: 6.6% (2000).
Housing: Homeownership rate: 74.5% (2000); Median home value: $87,400 (2000); Median rent: $408 per month (2000); Median age of housing: 40 years (2000).
Transportation: Commute to work: 92.1% car, 0.0% public transportation, 0.9% walk, 3.9% work from home (2000); Travel time to work: 24.2% less than 15 minutes, 45.7% 15 to 30 minutes, 17.8% 30 to 45 minutes, 6.4% 45 to 60 minutes, 5.9% 60 minutes or more (2000)

HARRIS (town). Covers a land area of 30.591 square miles and a water area of 0.288 square miles. Located at 43.87° N. Lat.; 89.42° W. Long.

Population: 729 (2000); Race: 99.2% White, 0.6% Black, 0.0% Asian, 0.3% American Indian and Alaska Native, 0.0% Hispanic of any race, 0.0% two or more races (2000); Density: 23.8 persons per square mile (2000); Age: 23.1% under 18, 15.4% over 64 (2000); Marriage status: 19.1% never married, 61.7% now married, 7.5% widowed, 11.8% divorced (2000); Foreign born: 1.2% (2000); Ancestry (includes multiple ancestries): 51.7% German, 13.0% English, 9.4% Polish, 7.9% Irish, 6.6% Norwegian (2000).
Economy: Employment by occupation: 10.6% management, 12.6% professional, 18.2% services, 15.1% sales, 3.4% farming, 10.3% construction, 29.9% production (2000).
Income: Per capita income: $18,686 (2000); Median household income: $37,344 (2000); Poverty rate: 4.4% (2000).
Taxes: Total city taxes per capita: $50 (1997); City property taxes per capita: $49 (1997).
Education: High school graduation rate: 78.3% (2000); College graduation rate: 10.3% (2000).
Housing: Homeownership rate: 88.3% (2000); Median home value: $91,600 (2000); Median rent: $345 per month (2000); Median age of housing: 27 years (2000).
Transportation: Commute to work: 85.4% car, 0.0% public transportation, 3.9% walk, 9.8% work from home (2000); Travel time to work: 40.5% less than 15 minutes, 33.3% 15 to 30 minutes, 14.6% 30 to 45 minutes, 6.9% 45 to 60 minutes, 4.7% 60 minutes or more (2000)

MECAN (town). Covers a land area of 27.455 square miles and a water area of 0.082 square miles. Located at 43.80° N. Lat.; 89.21° W. Long. Elevation is 817 feet.
Population: 726 (2000); Race: 95.4% White, 2.0% Black, 0.7% Asian, 0.0% American Indian and Alaska Native, 1.3% Hispanic of any race, 1.4% two or more races (2000); Density: 26.4 persons per square mile (2000); Age: 15.3% under 18, 31.1% over 64 (2000); Marriage status: 15.8% never married, 68.0% now married, 9.1% widowed, 7.2% divorced (2000); Foreign born: 0.7% (2000); Ancestry (includes multiple ancestries): 55.8% German, 13.7% Polish, 13.0% Irish, 5.6% Norwegian, 5.6% English (2000).
Economy: Single-family building permits issued: 4 (2001) / 7 (2000); Multi-family building permits issued: 0 (2001) / 0 (2000); Employment by occupation: 8.9% management, 5.2% professional, 23.8% services, 11.9% sales, 2.6% farming, 10.8% construction, 36.8% production (2000).
Income: Per capita income: $16,464 (2000); Median household income: $31,389 (2000); Poverty rate: 5.7% (2000).
Taxes: Total city taxes per capita: $55 (1997); City property taxes per capita: $49 (1997).
Education: High school graduation rate: 67.6% (2000); College graduation rate: 7.1% (2000).
Housing: Homeownership rate: 87.1% (2000); Median home value: $98,200 (2000); Median rent: $379 per month (2000); Median age of housing: 24 years (2000).
Transportation: Commute to work: 92.6% car, 0.0% public transportation, 0.0% walk, 6.6% work from home (2000); Travel time to work: 26.3% less than 15 minutes, 23.8% 15 to 30 minutes, 25.4% 30 to 45 minutes, 13.3% 45 to 60 minutes, 11.3% 60 minutes or more (2000)

MONTELLO (city). Covers a land area of 1.907 square miles and a water area of 0.245 square miles. Located at 43.79° N. Lat.; 89.33° W. Long. Elevation is 782 feet.
History: Montello developed around a granite quarry, which supplied the granite for the tomb of Ulysses S. Grant.
Population: 1,397 (2000); Race: 98.3% White, 0.0% Black, 0.1% Asian, 0.7% American Indian and Alaska Native, 1.6% Hispanic of any race, 0.5% two or more races (2000); Density: 732.6 persons per square mile (2000); Age: 26.0% under 18, 21.1% over 64 (2000); Marriage status: 22.7% never married, 56.9% now married, 10.3% widowed, 10.1% divorced (2000); Foreign born: 2.5% (2000); Ancestry (includes multiple ancestries): 47.4% German, 13.0% Irish, 10.0% Polish, 9.5% English, 5.8% Norwegian (2000).
Economy: Single-family building permits issued: 7 (2001) / 4 (2000); Multi-family building permits issued: 20 (2001) / 0 (2000); Employment by occupation: 7.0% management, 10.6% professional, 22.2% services, 17.7% sales, 0.3% farming, 14.0% construction, 28.2% production (2000).
Income: Per capita income: $15,676 (2000); Median household income: $32,500 (2000); Poverty rate: 9.2% (2000).
Taxes: Total city taxes per capita: $128 (1997); City property taxes per capita: $122 (1997).
Education: High school graduation rate: 74.3% (2000); College graduation rate: 12.0% (2000).

School District(s)
Montello (KG-12)
2000 Enrollment: 841 608-297-7617
Housing: Homeownership rate: 70.8% (2000); Median home value: $78,900 (2000); Median rent: $356 per month (2000); Median age of housing: 44 years (2000).
Newspapers: The Marquette County Tribune (1 x week)
Transportation: Commute to work: 89.7% car, 0.0% public transportation, 7.8% walk, 2.2% work from home (2000); Travel time to work: 45.5% less than 15 minutes, 13.9% 15 to 30 minutes, 20.8% 30 to 45 minutes, 10.8% 45 to 60 minutes, 9.0% 60 minutes or more (2000)
Additional Information Contacts
Adams Marquette Waushara Board of Realtors. 608-297-7734
Montello Chamber of Commerce. 608-297-7420

MONTELLO (town). Covers a land area of 32.503 square miles and a water area of 1.523 square miles. Located at 43.78° N. Lat.; 89.31° W. Long. Elevation is 782 feet.
History: Settled 1849, incorporated 1938.
Population: 1,043 (2000); Race: 99.8% White, 0.0% Black, 0.0% Asian, 0.0% American Indian and Alaska Native, 1.1% Hispanic of any race, 0.2% two or more races (2000); Density: 32.1 persons per square mile (2000); Age: 18.5% under 18, 21.7% over 64 (2000); Marriage status: 18.8% never married, 62.2% now married, 8.0% widowed, 10.9% divorced (2000); Foreign born: 1.0% (2000); Ancestry (includes multiple ancestries): 50.4% German, 15.3% Irish, 13.1% English, 11.1% Polish, 7.2% Norwegian (2000).
Economy: Resort; livestock, grain; granite quarries. Manufacturing: lumber mill, wood products. Employment by occupation: 11.4% management, 9.1% professional, 18.4% services, 23.3% sales, 1.3% farming, 12.3% construction, 24.2% production (2000).
Income: Per capita income: $17,699 (2000); Median household income: $35,347 (2000); Poverty rate: 6.2% (2000).
Taxes: Total city taxes per capita: $20 (1997); City property taxes per capita: $17 (1997).
Education: High school graduation rate: 81.3% (2000); College graduation rate: 8.5% (2000).
Housing: Homeownership rate: 85.6% (2000); Median home value: $105,100 (2000); Median rent: $406 per month (2000); Median age of housing: 23 years (2000).
Transportation: Commute to work: 90.0% car, 0.0% public transportation, 3.7% walk, 6.3% work from home (2000); Travel time to work: 43.8% less than 15 minutes, 19.1% 15 to 30 minutes, 23.1% 30 to 45 minutes, 3.7% 45 to 60 minutes, 10.3% 60 minutes or more (2000)

MOUNDVILLE (town). Covers a land area of 22.945 square miles and a water area of 0.270 square miles. Located at 43.67° N. Lat.; 89.46° W. Long.
Population: 574 (2000); Race: 97.7% White, 0.0% Black, 0.0% Asian, 0.3% American Indian and Alaska Native, 4.2% Hispanic of any race, 0.3% two or more races (2000); Density: 25.0 persons per square mile (2000); Age: 30.1% under 18, 17.2% over 64 (2000); Marriage status: 19.1% never married, 66.2% now married, 8.0% widowed, 6.7% divorced (2000); Foreign born: 0.7% (2000); Ancestry (includes multiple ancestries): 39.8% German, 13.7% English, 11.8% Norwegian, 9.6% Irish, 7.3% Other groups (2000).
Economy: Employment by occupation: 13.5% management, 10.0% professional, 16.7% services, 18.7% sales, 2.4% farming, 12.4% construction, 26.3% production (2000).
Income: Per capita income: $14,930 (2000); Median household income: $40,893 (2000); Poverty rate: 7.1% (2000).
Taxes: Total city taxes per capita: $33 (1997); City property taxes per capita: $31 (1997).
Education: High school graduation rate: 82.4% (2000); College graduation rate: 8.9% (2000).
Housing: Homeownership rate: 87.1% (2000); Median home value: $97,500 (2000); Median rent: $370 per month (2000); Median age of housing: 29 years (2000).
Transportation: Commute to work: 95.2% car, 0.0% public transportation, 0.0% walk, 4.0% work from home (2000); Travel time to work: 23.8% less than 15 minutes, 46.9% 15 to 30 minutes, 11.7% 30 to 45 minutes, 9.2% 45 to 60 minutes, 8.4% 60 minutes or more (2000)

NESHKORO (village). Covers a land area of 2.363 square miles and a water area of 0.088 square miles. Located at 43.96° N. Lat.; 89.21° W. Long. Elevation is 800 feet.
Population: 453 (2000); Race: 97.5% White, 0.0% Black, 0.0% Asian, 0.6% American Indian and Alaska Native, 2.3% Hispanic of any race, 1.9% two or

more races (2000); Density: 191.7 persons per square mile (2000); Age: 21.0% under 18, 25.6% over 64 (2000); Marriage status: 19.1% never married, 67.3% now married, 8.8% widowed, 4.8% divorced (2000); Foreign born: 0.4% (2000); Ancestry (includes multiple ancestries): 50.3% German, 10.9% Polish, 4.8% English, 4.6% Irish, 4.2% Norwegian (2000).
Economy: Single-family building permits issued: 1 (2001) / 3 (2000); Multi-family building permits issued: 0 (2001) / 0 (2000); Employment by occupation: 11.1% management, 3.6% professional, 16.4% services, 22.7% sales, 0.0% farming, 13.8% construction, 32.4% production (2000).
Income: Per capita income: $17,206 (2000); Median household income: $39,167 (2000); Poverty rate: 5.5% (2000).
Taxes: Total city taxes per capita: $117 (1997); City property taxes per capita: $108 (1997).
Education: High school graduation rate: 75.4% (2000); College graduation rate: 8.0% (2000).
Housing: Homeownership rate: 81.6% (2000); Median home value: $64,400 (2000); Median rent: $330 per month (2000); Median age of housing: 45 years (2000).
Transportation: Commute to work: 87.3% car, 0.0% public transportation, 6.8% walk, 5.9% work from home (2000); Travel time to work: 24.0% less than 15 minutes, 31.7% 15 to 30 minutes, 22.1% 30 to 45 minutes, 20.7% 45 to 60 minutes, 1.4% 60 minutes or more (2000)

NESHKORO (town). Covers a land area of 20.876 square miles and a water area of 0.354 square miles. Located at 43.95° N. Lat.; 89.21° W. Long. Elevation is 800 feet.
Population: 595 (2000); Race: 97.6% White, 0.0% Black, 0.0% Asian, 1.1% American Indian and Alaska Native, 0.0% Hispanic of any race, 1.3% two or more races (2000); Density: 28.5 persons per square mile (2000); Age: 19.6% under 18, 24.0% over 64 (2000); Marriage status: 10.7% never married, 75.9% now married, 7.5% widowed, 5.8% divorced (2000); Foreign born: 1.4% (2000); Ancestry (includes multiple ancestries): 52.7% German, 17.6% Polish, 8.5% English, 6.3% Norwegian, 5.7% Irish (2000).
Economy: In livestock and dairy area. Hydroelectric plant. Employment by occupation: 9.6% management, 13.0% professional, 11.5% services, 22.6% sales, 0.7% farming, 14.4% construction, 28.1% production (2000).
Income: Per capita income: $18,518 (2000); Median household income: $36,125 (2000); Poverty rate: 8.0% (2000).
Taxes: Total city taxes per capita: $87 (1997); City property taxes per capita: $85 (1997).
Education: High school graduation rate: 84.0% (2000); College graduation rate: 10.5% (2000).
Housing: Homeownership rate: 93.6% (2000); Median home value: $115,500 (2000); Median rent: $365 per month (2000); Median age of housing: 25 years (2000).
Transportation: Commute to work: 93.6% car, 0.4% public transportation, 1.5% walk, 4.5% work from home (2000); Travel time to work: 19.6% less than 15 minutes, 33.3% 15 to 30 minutes, 23.9% 30 to 45 minutes, 10.6% 45 to 60 minutes, 12.5% 60 minutes or more (2000)

NEWTON (town). Covers a land area of 35.499 square miles and a water area of 0.134 square miles. Located at 43.94° N. Lat.; 89.42° W. Long.
Population: 550 (2000); Race: 98.8% White, 0.4% Black, 0.4% Asian, 0.0% American Indian and Alaska Native, 0.0% Hispanic of any race, 0.5% two or more races (2000); Density: 15.5 persons per square mile (2000); Age: 24.6% under 18, 17.8% over 64 (2000); Marriage status: 18.8% never married, 69.2% now married, 7.7% widowed, 4.3% divorced (2000); Foreign born: 0.7% (2000); Ancestry (includes multiple ancestries): 53.1% German, 10.5% Irish, 9.1% United States or American, 8.6% English, 4.6% Polish (2000).
Economy: Employment by occupation: 19.9% management, 11.2% professional, 18.7% services, 17.4% sales, 5.8% farming, 7.5% construction, 19.5% production (2000).
Income: Per capita income: $18,039 (2000); Median household income: $33,036 (2000); Poverty rate: 14.3% (2000).
Taxes: Total city taxes per capita: $96 (1997); City property taxes per capita: $96 (1997).
Education: High school graduation rate: 75.6% (2000); College graduation rate: 7.2% (2000).
Housing: Homeownership rate: 84.7% (2000); Median home value: $86,900 (2000); Median rent: $450 per month (2000); Median age of housing: 30 years (2000).
Transportation: Commute to work: 82.5% car, 0.0% public transportation, 5.1% walk, 11.1% work from home (2000); Travel time to work: 24.5% less than 15 minutes, 36.5% 15 to 30 minutes, 18.3% 30 to 45 minutes, 4.3% 45 to 60 minutes, 16.3% 60 minutes or more (2000)

OXFORD (village). Covers a land area of 0.999 square miles and a water area of 0.026 square miles. Located at 43.78° N. Lat.; 89.57° W. Long. Elevation is 857 feet.
Population: 536 (2000); Race: 97.3% White, 0.0% Black, 1.3% Asian, 0.4% American Indian and Alaska Native, 3.8% Hispanic of any race, 1.1% two or more races (2000); Density: 536.3 persons per square mile (2000); Age: 25.3% under 18, 16.8% over 64 (2000); Marriage status: 20.0% never married, 58.5% now married, 8.6% widowed, 13.0% divorced (2000); Foreign born: 2.0% (2000); Ancestry (includes multiple ancestries): 52.1% German, 16.9% Irish, 8.4% Norwegian, 7.5% English, 5.6% Polish (2000).
Economy: Single-family building permits issued: 0 (2001) / 1 (2000); Multi-family building permits issued: 0 (2001) / 0 (2000); Employment by occupation: 6.1% management, 14.1% professional, 20.9% services, 17.5% sales, 1.9% farming, 14.4% construction, 25.1% production (2000).
Income: Per capita income: $16,103 (2000); Median household income: $35,481 (2000); Poverty rate: 14.3% (2000).
Taxes: Total city taxes per capita: $105 (1997); City property taxes per capita: $84 (1997).
Education: High school graduation rate: 84.2% (2000); College graduation rate: 11.5% (2000).
Housing: Homeownership rate: 74.1% (2000); Median home value: $66,900 (2000); Median rent: $311 per month (2000); Median age of housing: 51 years (2000).
Transportation: Commute to work: 90.3% car, 0.0% public transportation, 5.4% walk, 3.5% work from home (2000); Travel time to work: 35.1% less than 15 minutes, 32.3% 15 to 30 minutes, 14.9% 30 to 45 minutes, 8.9% 45 to 60 minutes, 8.9% 60 minutes or more (2000)

OXFORD (town). Covers a land area of 33.358 square miles and a water area of 0.171 square miles. Located at 43.77° N. Lat.; 89.54° W. Long. Elevation is 857 feet.
Population: 859 (2000); Race: 97.2% White, 0.0% Black, 0.0% Asian, 0.0% American Indian and Alaska Native, 2.6% Hispanic of any race, 0.8% two or more races (2000); Density: 25.8 persons per square mile (2000); Age: 24.9% under 18, 13.8% over 64 (2000); Marriage status: 21.7% never married, 61.0% now married, 4.9% widowed, 12.4% divorced (2000); Foreign born: 0.9% (2000); Ancestry (includes multiple ancestries): 40.8% German, 11.1% Norwegian, 10.8% Irish, 8.2% Polish, 8.0% English (2000).
Economy: In livestock and dairy area. Manufacturing: bottled artesian water. Employment by occupation: 17.3% management, 12.7% professional, 10.4% services, 20.3% sales, 3.0% farming, 14.0% construction, 22.3% production (2000).
Income: Per capita income: $16,458 (2000); Median household income: $40,217 (2000); Poverty rate: 5.9% (2000).
Taxes: Total city taxes per capita: $76 (1997); City property taxes per capita: $72 (1997).
Education: High school graduation rate: 84.7% (2000); College graduation rate: 8.8% (2000).
Housing: Homeownership rate: 88.3% (2000); Median home value: $97,400 (2000); Median rent: $393 per month (2000); Median age of housing: 20 years (2000).
Transportation: Commute to work: 88.1% car, 0.0% public transportation, 2.3% walk, 9.6% work from home (2000); Travel time to work: 25.0% less than 15 minutes, 39.7% 15 to 30 minutes, 21.0% 30 to 45 minutes, 2.6% 45 to 60 minutes, 11.8% 60 minutes or more (2000)

PACKWAUKEE (town). Covers a land area of 38.108 square miles and a water area of 2.834 square miles. Located at 43.77° N. Lat.; 89.43° W. Long. Elevation is 780 feet.
Population: 2,574 (2000); Race: 73.6% White, 18.0% Black, 0.0% Asian, 4.5% American Indian and Alaska Native, 7.8% Hispanic of any race, 3.9% two or more races (2000); Density: 67.5 persons per square mile (2000); Age: 9.2% under 18, 13.6% over 64 (2000); Marriage status: 20.7% never married, 60.9% now married, 6.1% widowed, 12.2% divorced (2000); Foreign born: 2.6% (2000); Ancestry (includes multiple ancestries): 25.9% German, 17.5% Other groups, 9.6% Irish, 5.4% Polish, 5.2% English (2000).
Economy: Employment by occupation: 9.3% management, 9.7% professional, 17.8% services, 17.2% sales, 3.9% farming, 13.5% construction, 28.6% production (2000).
Income: Per capita income: $14,481 (2000); Median household income: $31,823 (2000); Poverty rate: 5.1% (2000).
Taxes: Total city taxes per capita: $50 (1997); City property taxes per capita: $49 (1997).
Education: High school graduation rate: 76.1% (2000); College graduation rate: 8.7% (2000).

Housing: Homeownership rate: 87.8% (2000); Median home value: $90,400 (2000); Median rent: $300 per month (2000); Median age of housing: 27 years (2000).
Transportation: Commute to work: 91.1% car, 0.0% public transportation, 2.2% walk, 6.2% work from home (2000); Travel time to work: 22.6% less than 15 minutes, 37.6% 15 to 30 minutes, 19.0% 30 to 45 minutes, 7.8% 45 to 60 minutes, 12.9% 60 minutes or more (2000)

SHIELDS (town). Covers a land area of 31.196 square miles and a water area of 0.263 square miles. Located at 43.85° N. Lat.; 89.29° W. Long.
Population: 456 (2000); Race: 97.3% White, 0.4% Black, 0.0% Asian, 0.4% American Indian and Alaska Native, 0.0% Hispanic of any race, 1.9% two or more races (2000); Density: 14.6 persons per square mile (2000); Age: 19.7% under 18, 22.0% over 64 (2000); Marriage status: 16.7% never married, 65.3% now married, 5.2% widowed, 12.8% divorced (2000); Foreign born: 0.0% (2000); Ancestry (includes multiple ancestries): 59.6% German, 18.0% Polish, 9.9% Irish, 5.5% English, 3.8% Swedish (2000).
Economy: Employment by occupation: 18.1% management, 8.0% professional, 17.6% services, 17.2% sales, 3.8% farming, 14.3% construction, 21.0% production (2000).
Income: Per capita income: $17,218 (2000); Median household income: $32,250 (2000); Poverty rate: 9.3% (2000).
Taxes: Total city taxes per capita: $111 (1997); City property taxes per capita: $111 (1997).
Education: High school graduation rate: 78.0% (2000); College graduation rate: 9.9% (2000).
Housing: Homeownership rate: 82.0% (2000); Median home value: $87,300 (2000); Median rent: $354 per month (2000); Median age of housing: 31 years (2000).
Transportation: Commute to work: 85.0% car, 0.0% public transportation, 0.0% walk, 15.0% work from home (2000); Travel time to work: 23.1% less than 15 minutes, 34.2% 15 to 30 minutes, 20.6% 30 to 45 minutes, 2.5% 45 to 60 minutes, 19.6% 60 minutes or more (2000)

SPRINGFIELD (town). Covers a land area of 34.605 square miles and a water area of 0.337 square miles. Located at 43.94° N. Lat.; 89.53° W. Long.
Population: 628 (2000); Race: 99.5% White, 0.0% Black, 0.0% Asian, 0.0% American Indian and Alaska Native, 0.5% Hispanic of any race, 0.5% two or more races (2000); Density: 18.1 persons per square mile (2000); Age: 18.5% under 18, 17.2% over 64 (2000); Marriage status: 22.5% never married, 61.7% now married, 9.7% widowed, 6.1% divorced (2000); Foreign born: 0.0% (2000); Ancestry (includes multiple ancestries): 54.3% German, 12.5% Irish, 9.0% Polish, 8.4% English, 5.4% Other groups (2000).
Economy: Single-family building permits issued: 17 (2001) / 18 (2000); Multi-family building permits issued: 0 (2001) / 0 (2000); Employment by occupation: 16.6% management, 14.6% professional, 18.6% services, 15.9% sales, 4.7% farming, 11.2% construction, 18.3% production (2000).
Income: Per capita income: $17,593 (2000); Median household income: $35,109 (2000); Poverty rate: 10.3% (2000).
Taxes: Total city taxes per capita: $141 (1997); City property taxes per capita: $139 (1997).
Education: High school graduation rate: 83.0% (2000); College graduation rate: 12.4% (2000).
Housing: Homeownership rate: 87.4% (2000); Median home value: $84,400 (2000); Median rent: $413 per month (2000); Median age of housing: 22 years (2000).
Transportation: Commute to work: 85.4% car, 0.0% public transportation, 2.0% walk, 12.6% work from home (2000); Travel time to work: 33.9% less than 15 minutes, 36.6% 15 to 30 minutes, 16.7% 30 to 45 minutes, 6.2% 45 to 60 minutes, 6.6% 60 minutes or more (2000)

WESTFIELD (village). Covers a land area of 1.417 square miles and a water area of 0.031 square miles. Located at 43.88° N. Lat.; 89.49° W. Long. Elevation is 865 feet.
Population: 1,217 (2000); Race: 98.4% White, 0.0% Black, 0.3% Asian, 0.0% American Indian and Alaska Native, 3.8% Hispanic of any race, 1.1% two or more races (2000); Density: 859.1 persons per square mile (2000); Age: 27.1% under 18, 16.6% over 64 (2000); Marriage status: 21.1% never married, 54.5% now married, 11.9% widowed, 12.5% divorced (2000); Foreign born: 1.8% (2000); Ancestry (includes multiple ancestries): 45.4% German, 15.9% Irish, 9.6% Polish, 8.4% Other groups, 7.4% English (2000).
Economy: Single-family building permits issued: 1 (2001) / 2 (2000); Multi-family building permits issued: 0 (2001) / 8 (2000); Employment by occupation: 8.8% management, 11.0% professional, 23.5% services, 18.9% sales, 1.2% farming, 5.6% construction, 31.0% production (2000).
Income: Per capita income: $17,318 (2000); Median household income: $30,341 (2000); Poverty rate: 9.5% (2000).
Taxes: Total city taxes per capita: $142 (1997); City property taxes per capita: $132 (1997).
Education: High school graduation rate: 75.5% (2000); College graduation rate: 11.9% (2000).

School District(s)

Westfield (PK-12)
2000 Enrollment: 1,410 608-296-2107
Housing: Homeownership rate: 62.3% (2000); Median home value: $69,900 (2000); Median rent: $370 per month (2000); Median age of housing: 43 years (2000).
Transportation: Commute to work: 88.3% car, 0.0% public transportation, 6.7% walk, 3.2% work from home (2000); Travel time to work: 47.5% less than 15 minutes, 22.2% 15 to 30 minutes, 18.3% 30 to 45 minutes, 6.2% 45 to 60 minutes, 5.7% 60 minutes or more (2000)

WESTFIELD (town). Covers a land area of 28.354 square miles and a water area of 0.540 square miles. Located at 43.87° N. Lat.; 89.54° W. Long. Elevation is 865 feet.
Population: 689 (2000); Race: 98.5% White, 0.0% Black, 0.4% Asian, 0.3% American Indian and Alaska Native, 0.3% Hispanic of any race, 0.7% two or more races (2000); Density: 24.3 persons per square mile (2000); Age: 23.7% under 18, 21.8% over 64 (2000); Marriage status: 14.8% never married, 70.3% now married, 8.6% widowed, 6.3% divorced (2000); Foreign born: 2.1% (2000); Ancestry (includes multiple ancestries): 47.6% German, 13.5% Irish, 8.7% English, 7.5% United States or American, 5.0% Polish (2000).
Economy: In agricultural area: potatoes, rye, corn; poultry products, cheese. Westfield State Fish Hatchery to West; wildlife area. Hunting. Employment by occupation: 15.6% management, 18.9% professional, 17.5% services, 15.2% sales, 3.0% farming, 11.3% construction, 18.5% production (2000).
Income: Per capita income: $20,887 (2000); Median household income: $40,000 (2000); Poverty rate: 3.7% (2000).
Taxes: Total city taxes per capita: $113 (1997); City property taxes per capita: $111 (1997).
Education: High school graduation rate: 83.3% (2000); College graduation rate: 16.7% (2000).
Housing: Homeownership rate: 83.8% (2000); Median home value: $116,500 (2000); Median rent: $517 per month (2000); Median age of housing: 22 years (2000).
Transportation: Commute to work: 84.1% car, 1.7% public transportation, 5.1% walk, 8.4% work from home (2000); Travel time to work: 30.6% less than 15 minutes, 35.4% 15 to 30 minutes, 14.0% 30 to 45 minutes, 4.1% 45 to 60 minutes, 15.9% 60 minutes or more (2000)

Menominee County

Located in eastern Wisconsin; crossed by the Wolf River; includes Pine Lake and Keshena Falls. Covers a land area of 358.00 square miles, a water area of 7.00 square miles, and is located in the Central Time Zone. The county government was organized in 1961. County seat is Keshena.
Population: 4,562 (2000); Race: 12.3% White, 0.4% Black, 3.1% Asian, 81.1% American Indian and Alaska Native, 2.2% Hispanic of any race, 2.3% two or more races (2000); Density: 12.7 persons per square mile (2000); Age: 39.0% under 18, 9.2% over 64 (2000).
Religion: Four largest groups: 66.1% Catholic Church, 2.1% Assemblies of God, 1.1% The Orthodox Presbyterian Church, 0.0% Bahá'í (2000).
Economy: Unemployment rate: 11.3% (11/2002); Total civilian labor force: 2,311 (11/2002); Leading industries: 33.6% manufacturing; 10.3% retail trade; except pub other services (2000); Companies that employ more than 1,000 persons: 0 (2000); Companies that employ more than 100 persons: 3 (2000); Farms: 5 totaling 387 acres (1997); Minority business ownership rate: 0.0% (1997); Women business ownership rate: 0.0% (1997); Retail sales per capita: $3,061 (1997). Single-family building permits issued: 15 (2001) / 28 (2000); Multi-family building permits issued: 0 (2001) / 0 (2000).
Income: Per capita income: $10,625 (2000); Median household income: $29,440 (2000); Poverty rate: 28.8% (2000); Bankruptcy rate: 1.17% (2001).
Taxes: Total county taxes per capita: $248 (1997); County property taxes per capita: $244 (1997).
Education: High school graduation rate: 78.2% (2000); College graduation rate: 12.9% (2000).
Housing: Homeownership rate: 74.5% (2000); Median home value: $72,700 (2000); Median rent: $179 per month (2000); Median age of housing: 17 years (2000).

Health: Birth rate: 195.1 per 10,000 population (1998); Age adjusted death rate: 120.0 per 10,000 population (1999); Age adjusted cancer mortality rate: n/a (1999). Number of physicians: 6.6 per 10,000 population (1999); Number of hospital beds: n/a (1999).
Elections: 2000 Presidential election results: 77.0% Gore, 18.3% Bush, 3.8% Nader, 0.1% Buchanan
Additional Information Contacts
Menominee County Government Offices 715-799-3311

Menominee County Communities

KESHENA (CDP). Covers a land area of 8.466 square miles and a water area of 0.009 square miles. Located at 44.87° N. Lat.; 88.62° W. Long. Elevation is 829 feet.
History: Oshkosh clan burial plot is nearby.
Population: 1,394 (2000); Race: 3.1% White, 0.0% Black, 5.6% Asian, 87.0% American Indian and Alaska Native, 3.4% Hispanic of any race, 4.1% two or more races (2000); Density: 164.7 persons per square mile (2000); Age: 44.9% under 18, 5.5% over 64 (2000); Marriage status: 45.0% never married, 38.3% now married, 5.6% widowed, 11.2% divorced (2000); Foreign born: 4.4% (2000); Ancestry (includes multiple ancestries): 89.4% Other groups, 2.8% German, 0.7% Jamaican, 0.7% French (except Basque), 0.4% Polish (2000).
Economy: In the Menominee Indian Reservation. The Indian Agency buildings and a Roman Catholic mission are here. Employment by occupation: 5.3% management, 15.0% professional, 38.2% services, 16.6% sales, 0.5% farming, 9.1% construction, 15.2% production (2000).
Income: Per capita income: $8,578 (2000); Median household income: $19,792 (2000); Poverty rate: 45.8% (2000).
Education: High school graduation rate: 78.1% (2000); College graduation rate: 8.9% (2000).

School District(s)

Menominee Indian (PK-12)
2000 Enrollment: 991 715-799-3824

Four-year College(s)

Native American Educational Services-Menominee (Private, Not-for-profit)
2001 Enrollment: n/a 715-799-4661

Two-year College(s)

College of the Menominee Nation (Private, Not-for-profit)
2001 Enrollment: 407 715-799-5600
2001 Tuition: In-state $2,670; Out-of-state $2,670

Housing: Homeownership rate: 42.3% (2000); Median home value: $53,600 (2000); Median rent: $164 per month (2000); Median age of housing: 18 years (2000).
Transportation: Commute to work: 87.6% car, 2.7% public transportation, 4.1% walk, 2.2% work from home (2000); Travel time to work: 62.4% less than 15 minutes, 18.8% 15 to 30 minutes, 6.5% 30 to 45 minutes, 4.5% 45 to 60 minutes, 7.9% 60 minutes or more (2000)

LEGEND LAKE (CDP). Covers a land area of 16.844 square miles and a water area of 3.675 square miles. Located at 44.89° N. Lat.; 88.56° W. Long.
Population: 1,533 (2000); Race: 30.2% White, 0.0% Black, 2.3% Asian, 65.2% American Indian and Alaska Native, 1.7% Hispanic of any race, 0.8% two or more races (2000); Density: 91.0 persons per square mile (2000); Age: 30.3% under 18, 15.4% over 64 (2000); Marriage status: 29.8% never married, 51.2% now married, 6.8% widowed, 12.2% divorced (2000); Foreign born: 2.3% (2000); Ancestry (includes multiple ancestries): 67.4% Other groups, 13.0% German, 7.3% English, 4.0% Irish, 2.5% French (except Basque) (2000).
Economy: Employment by occupation: 15.3% management, 14.9% professional, 23.1% services, 24.9% sales, 0.8% farming, 11.0% construction, 10.0% production (2000).
Income: Per capita income: $14,512 (2000); Median household income: $38,393 (2000); Poverty rate: 17.5% (2000).
Education: High school graduation rate: 84.0% (2000); College graduation rate: 17.7% (2000).
Housing: Homeownership rate: 94.9% (2000); Median home value: $95,900 (2000); Median rent: $163 per month (2000); Median age of housing: 14 years (2000).
Transportation: Commute to work: 94.6% car, 1.7% public transportation, 0.0% walk, 3.3% work from home (2000); Travel time to work: 40.8% less than 15 minutes, 40.6% 15 to 30 minutes, 15.3% 30 to 45 minutes, 1.1% 45 to 60 minutes, 2.2% 60 minutes or more (2000)

MIDDLE VILLAGE (CDP). Covers a land area of 6.931 square miles and a water area of 0 square miles. Located at 44.93° N. Lat.; 88.74° W. Long.
Population: 351 (2000); Race: 4.2% White, 0.0% Black, 0.8% Asian, 94.3% American Indian and Alaska Native, 4.6% Hispanic of any race, 0.8% two or more races (2000); Density: 50.6 persons per square mile (2000); Age: 49.0% under 18, 1.5% over 64 (2000); Marriage status: 48.0% never married, 42.7% now married, 2.7% widowed, 6.7% divorced (2000); Foreign born: 0.0% (2000); Ancestry (includes multiple ancestries): 83.5% Other groups, 4.2% German, 3.4% French (except Basque), 2.3% Irish, 0.8% European (2000).
Economy: Employment by occupation: 10.7% management, 10.7% professional, 30.4% services, 14.3% sales, 0.0% farming, 16.1% construction, 17.9% production (2000).
Income: Per capita income: $6,568 (2000); Median household income: $16,667 (2000); Poverty rate: 42.0% (2000).
Education: High school graduation rate: 79.3% (2000); College graduation rate: 5.4% (2000).
Housing: Homeownership rate: 54.4% (2000); Median home value: $75,000 (2000); Median rent: $160 per month (2000); Median age of housing: 6 years (2000).
Transportation: Commute to work: 88.7% car, 11.3% public transportation, 0.0% walk, 0.0% work from home (2000); Travel time to work: 49.1% less than 15 minutes, 32.1% 15 to 30 minutes, 11.3% 30 to 45 minutes, 0.0% 45 to 60 minutes, 7.5% 60 minutes or more (2000)

NEOPIT (CDP). Covers a land area of 12.273 square miles and a water area of 0.309 square miles. Located at 44.98° N. Lat.; 88.82° W. Long. Elevation is 1,060 feet.
Population: 839 (2000); Race: 3.4% White, 0.7% Black, 2.4% Asian, 90.4% American Indian and Alaska Native, 0.7% Hispanic of any race, 2.8% two or more races (2000); Density: 68.4 persons per square mile (2000); Age: 45.0% under 18, 5.6% over 64 (2000); Marriage status: 42.3% never married, 38.6% now married, 8.0% widowed, 11.1% divorced (2000); Foreign born: 2.0% (2000); Ancestry (includes multiple ancestries): 93.5% Other groups, 1.4% German, 0.9% Irish, 0.6% French Canadian, 0.5% French (except Basque) (2000).
Economy: Sawmilling on mill pond. Lumber. Employment by occupation: 4.8% management, 12.5% professional, 40.9% services, 17.3% sales, 3.8% farming, 5.1% construction, 15.7% production (2000).
Income: Per capita income: $8,427 (2000); Median household income: $27,857 (2000); Poverty rate: 28.3% (2000).
Education: High school graduation rate: 73.3% (2000); College graduation rate: 7.2% (2000).
Housing: Homeownership rate: 66.4% (2000); Median home value: $50,800 (2000); Median rent: $198 per month (2000); Median age of housing: 28 years (2000).
Transportation: Commute to work: 83.4% car, 2.6% public transportation, 9.6% walk, 2.0% work from home (2000); Travel time to work: 40.2% less than 15 minutes, 40.9% 15 to 30 minutes, 15.2% 30 to 45 minutes, 1.7% 45 to 60 minutes, 2.0% 60 minutes or more (2000)

ZOAR (CDP). Covers a land area of 8.588 square miles and a water area of 0 square miles. Located at 45.01° N. Lat.; 88.89° W. Long. Elevation is 1,214 feet.
Population: 124 (2000); Race: 17.2% White, 0.0% Black, 0.0% Asian, 82.8% American Indian and Alaska Native, 8.0% Hispanic of any race, 0.0% two or more races (2000); Density: 14.4 persons per square mile (2000); Age: 47.1% under 18, 4.6% over 64 (2000); Marriage status: 27.8% never married, 59.3% now married, 5.6% widowed, 7.4% divorced (2000); Foreign born: 2.3% (2000); Ancestry (includes multiple ancestries): 90.8% Other groups, 10.3% German, 4.6% Irish (2000).
Economy: Employment by occupation: 0.0% management, 28.0% professional, 24.0% services, 32.0% sales, 0.0% farming, 8.0% construction, 8.0% production (2000).
Income: Per capita income: $7,101 (2000); Median household income: $24,375 (2000); Poverty rate: 17.2% (2000).
Education: High school graduation rate: 73.2% (2000); College graduation rate: 12.2% (2000).
Housing: Homeownership rate: 56.5% (2000); Median home value: $70,000 (2000); Median rent: $238 per month (2000); Median age of housing: 21 years (2000).
Transportation: Commute to work: 100.0% car, 0.0% public transportation, 0.0% walk, 0.0% work from home (2000); Travel time to work: 32.0% less than 15 minutes, 32.0% 15 to 30 minutes, 4.0% 30 to 45 minutes, 28.0% 45 to 60 minutes, 4.0% 60 minutes or more (2000)

Milwaukee County

Located in southeastern Wisconsin; bounded on the east by Lake Michigan; drained by the Milwaukee, Menomonee, and Root Rivers. Covers a land area of 241.60 square miles, a water area of 948.10 square miles, and is located in the Central Time Zone. The county government was organized in 1835. County seat is Milwaukee.

Milwaukee County is part of the Milwaukee-Waukesha, WI PMSA. The entire metro area includes: Milwaukee County; Ozaukee County; Washington County; Waukesha County

Weather Station: Milwaukee Gen. Mitchell Field — Elevation: 669 feet

	Jan	Feb	Mar	Apr	May	Jun	Jul	Aug	Sep	Oct	Nov	Dec
High	27	32	42	53	65	76	81	78	71	59	45	33
Low	13	18	27	36	46	56	63	62	54	43	31	20
Precip	1.8	1.6	2.6	3.8	2.9	3.6	3.4	3.9	3.3	2.5	2.7	2.2
Snow	14.9	10.9	7.7	2.5	0.1	tr	tr	tr	tr	0.4	3.6	10.7

High and Low temperatures in degrees Fahrenheit; Precipitation and Snow in inches

Weather Station: Milwaukee Mt. Mary College — Elevation: 725 feet

	Jan	Feb	Mar	Apr	May	Jun	Jul	Aug	Sep	Oct	Nov	Dec
High	28	33	44	57	70	80	85	82	74	61	46	34
Low	13	18	27	37	48	57	63	62	54	43	31	20
Precip	1.6	1.3	1.9	3.4	2.8	3.6	3.4	3.9	3.3	2.3	2.3	1.8
Snow	12.1	8.1	5.5	1.9	tr	0.0	0.0	0.0	0.0	0.1	2.6	8.0

High and Low temperatures in degrees Fahrenheit; Precipitation and Snow in inches

Population: 940,164 (2000); Race: 65.8% White, 24.4% Black, 2.4% Asian, 0.9% American Indian and Alaska Native, 8.8% Hispanic of any race, 2.4% two or more races (2000); Density: 3,892.1 persons per square mile (2000); Age: 26.3% under 18, 12.9% over 64 (2000).
Religion: Five largest groups: 27.8% Catholic Church, 3.5% Lutheran Church—Missouri Synod, 3.0% Evangelical Lutheran Church in America, 2.7% Wisconsin Evangelical Lutheran Synod, 1.8% Jewish estimate (2000).
Economy: Unemployment rate: 6.1% (11/2002); Total civilian labor force: 488,104 (11/2002); Leading industries: 16.7% manufacturing; 16.2% health care and social assistance; 10.6% retail trade (2000); Companies that employ more than 1,000 persons: 34 (2000); Companies that employ more than 100 persons: 852 (2000); Farms: 83 totaling 6,334 acres (1997); Minority business ownership rate: 11.2% (1997); Women business ownership rate: 28.2% (1997); Retail sales per capita: $8,786 (1997). Single-family building permits issued: 671 (2001) / 736 (2000); Multi-family building permits issued: 853 (2001) / 1,014 (2000).
Income: Per capita income: $19,939 (2000); Median household income: $38,100 (2000); Poverty rate: 15.3% (2000); Bankruptcy rate: 7.02% (2001).
Taxes: Total county taxes per capita: $246 (2000); County property taxes per capita: $184 (2000).
Education: High school graduation rate: 80.2% (2000); College graduation rate: 23.6% (2000).
Housing: Homeownership rate: 52.6% (2000); Median home value: $103,200 (2000); Median rent: $484 per month (2000); Median age of housing: 46 years (2000).
Health: Birth rate: 157.0 per 10,000 population (1998); Age adjusted death rate: 93.4 per 10,000 population (1999); Infant mortality rate: 10.5 per 1,000 live births (1998); Age adjusted cancer mortality rate: 221.0 deaths per 100,000 population (1999). Air Quality Index: 77% good, 22% moderate, 1% unhealthy (percent of days in 2000). Number of physicians: 32.6 per 10,000 population (1999); Number of hospital beds: 49.1 per 10,000 population (1999).
Elections: 2000 Presidential election results: 58.2% Gore, 37.7% Bush, 3.2% Nader, 0.4% Buchanan

Additional Information Contacts

Milwaukee County Government Offices 414-278-4222
African American Chamber of Commerce 414-462-9450
American Indian Chamber of Commerce 414-462-1638
Commercial Association of Realtors Wisconsin 414-271-2021
Franklin Chamber of Commerce 414-425-4015
Greater Milwaukee Association of Realtors 414-778-4929
Greater Milwaukee Convention & Visitors Bureau 414-273-3950
Hispanic Chamber of Commerce 414-643-6963
Metropolitan Milwaukee Association of Commerce 414-287-4100
Milwaukee Chamber of Commerce 414-226-4105
Wauwatosa Chamber of Commerce 414-453-2330
West Allis Chamber of Commerce 414-302-9901

Milwaukee County Communities

BAYSIDE (village). Covers a land area of 2.379 square miles and a water area of 0 square miles. Located at 43.18° N. Lat.; 87.90° W. Long. Elevation is 680 feet.
Population: 4,518 (2000); Race: 93.3% White, 2.9% Black, 1.0% Asian, 1.0% American Indian and Alaska Native, 1.5% Hispanic of any race, 1.2% two or more races (2000); Density: 1,898.7 persons per square mile (2000); Age: 22.9% under 18, 20.6% over 64 (2000); Marriage status: 18.1% never married, 67.7% now married, 7.0% widowed, 7.3% divorced (2000); Foreign born: 13.0% (2000); Ancestry (includes multiple ancestries): 24.9% German, 12.3% Russian, 9.6% Other groups, 9.0% Irish, 8.2% Polish (2000).
Economy: Single-family building permits issued: 1 (2001) / 9 (2000); Multi-family building permits issued: 0 (2001) / 0 (2000); Employment by occupation: 27.6% management, 34.9% professional, 6.5% services, 25.9% sales, 0.0% farming, 1.8% construction, 3.2% production (2000).
Income: Per capita income: $49,357 (2000); Median household income: $88,982 (2000); Poverty rate: 2.9% (2000).
Taxes: Total city taxes per capita: $658 (1997); City property taxes per capita: $637 (1997).
Education: High school graduation rate: 94.7% (2000); College graduation rate: 61.0% (2000).
Housing: Homeownership rate: 85.6% (2000); Median home value: $229,400 (2000); Median rent: $842 per month (2000); Median age of housing: 38 years (2000).
Safety: Violent crime rate: 6.6 per 10,000 population; Property crime rate: 92.3 per 10,000 population (2001).
Transportation: Commute to work: 94.3% car, 0.4% public transportation, 1.6% walk, 3.3% work from home (2000); Travel time to work: 22.0% less than 15 minutes, 55.4% 15 to 30 minutes, 18.7% 30 to 45 minutes, 2.0% 45 to 60 minutes, 1.9% 60 minutes or more (2000)

BROWN DEER (village). Covers a land area of 4.396 square miles and a water area of 0 square miles. Located at 43.17° N. Lat.; 87.97° W. Long. Elevation is 679 feet.
History: Incorporated 1955.
Population: 12,170 (2000); Race: 82.8% White, 12.5% Black, 2.3% Asian, 0.4% American Indian and Alaska Native, 3.0% Hispanic of any race, 1.3% two or more races (2000); Density: 2,768.1 persons per square mile (2000); Age: 19.7% under 18, 18.7% over 64 (2000); Marriage status: 24.3% never married, 57.8% now married, 7.8% widowed, 10.1% divorced (2000); Foreign born: 6.5% (2000); Ancestry (includes multiple ancestries): 39.7% German, 18.6% Other groups, 10.9% Polish, 8.9% Irish, 4.8% Italian (2000).
Vital Statistics: Birth rate: 99.4 per 10,000 population (1998)
Economy: It is a residential suburb of downtown Milwaukee. Manufacturing: consumer goods, machinery. Single-family building permits issued: 5 (2001) / 1 (2000); Multi-family building permits issued: 0 (2001) / 0 (2000); Employment by occupation: 16.4% management, 23.5% professional, 10.4% services, 31.2% sales, 0.0% farming, 4.8% construction, 13.8% production (2000).
Income: Per capita income: $25,628 (2000); Median household income: $50,847 (2000); Poverty rate: 3.6% (2000).
Taxes: Total city taxes per capita: $435 (1997); City property taxes per capita: $399 (1997).
Education: High school graduation rate: 87.8% (2000); College graduation rate: 31.2% (2000).

School District(s)

Brown Deer (PK-12)
2000 Enrollment: 1,718 414-371-6756

Housing: Homeownership rate: 71.2% (2000); Median home value: $118,700 (2000); Median rent: $652 per month (2000); Median age of housing: 34 years (2000).
Safety: Violent crime rate: 20.4 per 10,000 population; Property crime rate: 478.9 per 10,000 population (2001).
Transportation: Commute to work: 95.0% car, 0.8% public transportation, 1.6% walk, 1.8% work from home (2000); Travel time to work: 33.3% less than 15 minutes, 43.7% 15 to 30 minutes, 16.9% 30 to 45 minutes, 2.8% 45 to 60 minutes, 3.3% 60 minutes or more (2000)

CUDAHY (city). Covers a land area of 4.750 square miles and a water area of 0 square miles. Located at 42.94° N. Lat.; 87.86° W. Long. Elevation is 700 feet.
History: Cudahy was founded by Patrick Cudahy, who moved his meat packing plant here in 1893 from Milwaukee. Cudahy named the first streets

for other prominent meat packers (Swift, Armour, Plankinton, Layton). The city was incorporated in 1907.
Population: 18,429 (2000); Race: 93.3% White, 1.1% Black, 0.9% Asian, 1.2% American Indian and Alaska Native, 4.6% Hispanic of any race, 2.0% two or more races (2000); Density: 3,880.1 persons per square mile (2000); Age: 23.1% under 18, 15.8% over 64 (2000); Marriage status: 28.6% never married, 51.9% now married, 8.1% widowed, 11.4% divorced (2000); Foreign born: 3.6% (2000); Ancestry (includes multiple ancestries): 40.1% German, 26.5% Polish, 11.2% Irish, 9.3% Other groups, 5.5% Italian (2000).
Vital Statistics: Birth rate: 127.5 per 10,000 population (1998)
Economy: Single-family building permits issued: 12 (2001) / 4 (2000); Multi-family building permits issued: 22 (2001) / 51 (2000); Employment by occupation: 8.5% management, 14.4% professional, 12.6% services, 29.5% sales, 0.1% farming, 10.3% construction, 24.7% production (2000).
Income: Per capita income: $19,615 (2000); Median household income: $40,157 (2000); Poverty rate: 8.2% (2000).
Taxes: Total city taxes per capita: $270 (1997); City property taxes per capita: $253 (1997).
Education: High school graduation rate: 81.9% (2000); College graduation rate: 13.6% (2000).

School District(s)

Cudahy (PK-12)
2000 Enrollment: 2,983 414-769-2300
Housing: Homeownership rate: 59.6% (2000); Median home value: $106,200 (2000); Median rent: $480 per month (2000); Median age of housing: 45 years (2000).
Safety: Violent crime rate: 14.0 per 10,000 population; Property crime rate: 341.6 per 10,000 population (2001).
Transportation: Commute to work: 90.9% car, 3.0% public transportation, 3.5% walk, 1.8% work from home (2000); Travel time to work: 32.6% less than 15 minutes, 41.8% 15 to 30 minutes, 15.8% 30 to 45 minutes, 5.0% 45 to 60 minutes, 4.7% 60 minutes or more (2000)

FOX POINT (village). Covers a land area of 2.922 square miles and a water area of 0 square miles. Located at 43.16° N. Lat.; 87.90° W. Long. Elevation is 672 feet.
History: Settled by Dutch c. 1846, incorporated 1926. Cardinal Stritch College.
Population: 7,012 (2000); Race: 93.7% White, 1.3% Black, 2.2% Asian, 0.3% American Indian and Alaska Native, 1.5% Hispanic of any race, 1.9% two or more races (2000); Density: 2,399.3 persons per square mile (2000); Age: 23.5% under 18, 20.9% over 64 (2000); Marriage status: 20.4% never married, 64.3% now married, 8.0% widowed, 7.2% divorced (2000); Foreign born: 8.1% (2000); Ancestry (includes multiple ancestries): 30.2% German, 13.2% Irish, 10.8% Other groups, 9.6% Russian, 9.3% English (2000).
Economy: Single-family building permits issued: 1 (2001) / 2 (2000); Multi-family building permits issued: 0 (2001) / 0 (2000); Employment by occupation: 20.2% management, 39.2% professional, 7.3% services, 28.1% sales, 0.3% farming, 1.7% construction, 3.3% production (2000).
Income: Per capita income: $48,469 (2000); Median household income: $80,572 (2000); Poverty rate: 2.8% (2000).
Taxes: Total city taxes per capita: $510 (1997); City property taxes per capita: $490 (1997).
Education: High school graduation rate: 96.6% (2000); College graduation rate: 67.3% (2000).
Housing: Homeownership rate: 85.1% (2000); Median home value: $206,600 (2000); Median rent: $898 per month (2000); Median age of housing: 45 years (2000).
Safety: Violent crime rate: 4.2 per 10,000 population; Property crime rate: 92.0 per 10,000 population (2001).
Transportation: Commute to work: 89.4% car, 0.4% public transportation, 3.5% walk, 6.5% work from home (2000); Travel time to work: 27.0% less than 15 minutes, 50.6% 15 to 30 minutes, 16.1% 30 to 45 minutes, 2.6% 45 to 60 minutes, 3.7% 60 minutes or more (2000)

FRANKLIN (city). Covers a land area of 34.626 square miles and a water area of 0.093 square miles. Located at 42.89° N. Lat.; 88.00° W. Long. Elevation is 790 feet.
History: Incorporated 1956.
Population: 29,494 (2000); Race: 91.1% White, 5.0% Black, 2.3% Asian, 0.4% American Indian and Alaska Native, 2.3% Hispanic of any race, 0.8% two or more races (2000); Density: 851.8 persons per square mile (2000); Age: 23.4% under 18, 9.9% over 64 (2000); Marriage status: 21.8% never married, 65.8% now married, 4.7% widowed, 7.7% divorced (2000); Foreign born: 4.3% (2000); Ancestry (includes multiple ancestries): 42.8% German, 25.3% Polish, 11.6% Irish, 6.5% Other groups, 6.3% English (2000).
Vital Statistics: Birth rate: 98.7 per 10,000 population (1998)
Economy: Machinery and equipment manufacturing. Rainbow Airport. Unemployment rate: 4.5% (11/2002); Total civilian labor force: 15,573 (11/2002); Single-family building permits issued: 204 (2001) / 193 (2000); Multi-family building permits issued: 115 (2001) / 258 (2000); Employment by occupation: 17.2% management, 22.9% professional, 9.4% services, 27.7% sales, 0.0% farming, 8.1% construction, 14.8% production (2000).
Income: Per capita income: $27,474 (2000); Median household income: $64,315 (2000); Poverty rate: 2.7% (2000).
Taxes: Total city taxes per capita: $429 (2000); City property taxes per capita: $355 (2000).
Education: High school graduation rate: 90.0% (2000); College graduation rate: 29.1% (2000).

School District(s)

Franklin Public (PK-12)
2000 Enrollment: 3,839 414-529-8269
Housing: Homeownership rate: 78.3% (2000); Median home value: $156,400 (2000); Median rent: $666 per month (2000); Median age of housing: 18 years (2000).
Safety: Violent crime rate: 8.1 per 10,000 population; Property crime rate: 208.1 per 10,000 population (2001).
Transportation: Commute to work: 94.9% car, 0.9% public transportation, 0.4% walk, 3.5% work from home (2000); Travel time to work: 23.1% less than 15 minutes, 45.1% 15 to 30 minutes, 24.1% 30 to 45 minutes, 4.6% 45 to 60 minutes, 3.1% 60 minutes or more (2000)
Additional Information Contacts
Franklin Chamber of Commerce 414-425-4015

GLENDALE (city). Covers a land area of 5.793 square miles and a water area of 0.192 square miles. Located at 43.13° N. Lat.; 87.92° W. Long. Elevation is 660 feet.
History: Incorporated 1950.
Population: 13,367 (2000); Race: 87.3% White, 8.1% Black, 2.1% Asian, 0.1% American Indian and Alaska Native, 2.8% Hispanic of any race, 1.7% two or more races (2000); Density: 2,307.4 persons per square mile (2000); Age: 19.4% under 18, 25.0% over 64 (2000); Marriage status: 23.2% never married, 56.4% now married, 11.5% widowed, 9.0% divorced (2000); Foreign born: 8.5% (2000); Ancestry (includes multiple ancestries): 32.1% German, 17.6% Other groups, 10.0% Polish, 9.6% Irish, 6.3% English (2000).
Vital Statistics: Birth rate: 69.6 per 10,000 population (1998)
Economy: Light manufacturing. Single-family building permits issued: 1 (2001) / 2 (2000); Multi-family building permits issued: 0 (2001) / 0 (2000); Employment by occupation: 19.0% management, 31.8% professional, 9.8% services, 26.4% sales, 0.0% farming, 3.7% construction, 9.3% production (2000).
Income: Per capita income: $30,328 (2000); Median household income: $55,306 (2000); Poverty rate: 4.0% (2000).
Taxes: Total city taxes per capita: $712 (2000); City property taxes per capita: $611 (2000).
Education: High school graduation rate: 89.2% (2000); College graduation rate: 42.9% (2000).

School District(s)

Glendale-River Hills (PK-08)
2000 Enrollment: 1,101 414-351-7170
Nicolet UHS (09-12)
2000 Enrollment: 1,353 414-351-7520
Housing: Homeownership rate: 73.1% (2000); Median home value: $142,600 (2000); Median rent: $689 per month (2000); Median age of housing: 36 years (2000).
Safety: Violent crime rate: 20.1 per 10,000 population; Property crime rate: 629.2 per 10,000 population (2001).
Transportation: Commute to work: 92.9% car, 1.2% public transportation, 1.7% walk, 3.1% work from home (2000); Travel time to work: 31.8% less than 15 minutes, 48.4% 15 to 30 minutes, 13.5% 30 to 45 minutes, 2.6% 45 to 60 minutes, 3.6% 60 minutes or more (2000)

GREENDALE (village). Covers a land area of 5.601 square miles and a water area of 0.006 square miles. Located at 42.93° N. Lat.; 87.99° W. Long. Elevation is 760 feet.
History: Greendale was built by the Resettlement Administration as an experiment in city planning and low-rent housing.
Population: 14,405 (2000); Race: 95.7% White, 0.4% Black, 1.8% Asian, 0.6% American Indian and Alaska Native, 1.9% Hispanic of any race, 0.9% two or more races (2000); Density: 2,571.8 persons per square mile (2000); Age: 22.0% under 18, 20.0% over 64 (2000); Marriage status: 20.9% never

married, 62.1% now married, 8.8% widowed, 8.2% divorced (2000); Foreign born: 5.4% (2000); Ancestry (includes multiple ancestries): 46.4% German, 22.6% Polish, 11.7% Irish, 7.2% English, 6.0% Italian (2000).
Vital Statistics: Birth rate: 84.7 per 10,000 population (1998)
Economy: Single-family building permits issued: 0 (2001) / 0 (2000); Multi-family building permits issued: 0 (2001) / 0 (2000); Employment by occupation: 17.5% management, 26.1% professional, 10.4% services, 29.2% sales, 0.0% farming, 5.9% construction, 11.0% production (2000).
Income: Per capita income: $28,363 (2000); Median household income: $55,553 (2000); Poverty rate: 3.9% (2000).
Taxes: Total city taxes per capita: $384 (1997); City property taxes per capita: $365 (1997).
Education: High school graduation rate: 91.3% (2000); College graduation rate: 35.6% (2000).

School District(s)

Greendale (PK-12)
2000 Enrollment: 2,163 414-423-2702
Housing: Homeownership rate: 69.7% (2000); Median home value: $147,100 (2000); Median rent: $610 per month (2000); Median age of housing: 33 years (2000).
Safety: Violent crime rate: 9.0 per 10,000 population; Property crime rate: 286.7 per 10,000 population (2001).
Transportation: Commute to work: 93.7% car, 1.4% public transportation, 0.9% walk, 3.7% work from home (2000); Travel time to work: 28.5% less than 15 minutes, 47.5% 15 to 30 minutes, 18.6% 30 to 45 minutes, 2.3% 45 to 60 minutes, 3.1% 60 minutes or more (2000)

GREENFIELD (city). Covers a land area of 11.546 square miles and a water area of 0.006 square miles. Located at 42.96° N. Lat.; 87.99° W. Long. Elevation is 800 feet.
Population: 35,476 (2000); Race: 93.7% White, 1.2% Black, 2.1% Asian, 0.6% American Indian and Alaska Native, 3.8% Hispanic of any race, 1.3% two or more races (2000); Density: 3,072.5 persons per square mile (2000); Age: 19.0% under 18, 20.2% over 64 (2000); Marriage status: 27.5% never married, 52.5% now married, 10.3% widowed, 9.7% divorced (2000); Foreign born: 5.8% (2000); Ancestry (includes multiple ancestries): 43.4% German, 26.2% Polish, 10.6% Irish, 8.7% Other groups, 4.6% English (2000).
Vital Statistics: Birth rate: 86.8 per 10,000 population (1998)
Economy: Manufacturing: metal fabrication. Unemployment rate: 3.6% (11/2002); Total civilian labor force: 19,816 (11/2002); Single-family building permits issued: 118 (2001) / 150 (2000); Multi-family building permits issued: 0 (2001) / 0 (2000); Employment by occupation: 13.1% management, 18.8% professional, 11.9% services, 32.2% sales, 0.0% farming, 7.6% construction, 16.3% production (2000).
Income: Per capita income: $23,755 (2000); Median household income: $44,230 (2000); Poverty rate: 4.7% (2000).
Taxes: Total city taxes per capita: $428 (1997); City property taxes per capita: $409 (1997).
Education: High school graduation rate: 85.0% (2000); College graduation rate: 20.2% (2000).

School District(s)

Greenfield (PK-12)
2000 Enrollment: 3,167 414-529-9090
Whitnall (PK-12)
2000 Enrollment: 2,501 414-525-8402

Four-year College(s)

ITT Technical Institute (Private, For-profit)
2001 Enrollment: 421 414-282-9494
2001 Tuition: In-state $11,304; Out-of-state $11,304
Housing: Homeownership rate: 59.6% (2000); Median home value: $125,500 (2000); Median rent: $622 per month (2000); Median age of housing: 28 years (2000).
Safety: Violent crime rate: 10.6 per 10,000 population; Property crime rate: 384.6 per 10,000 population (2001).
Transportation: Commute to work: 94.6% car, 1.8% public transportation, 1.6% walk, 1.8% work from home (2000); Travel time to work: 28.2% less than 15 minutes, 50.0% 15 to 30 minutes, 17.2% 30 to 45 minutes, 2.1% 45 to 60 minutes, 2.4% 60 minutes or more (2000)

HALES CORNERS (village). Covers a land area of 3.202 square miles and a water area of 0.004 square miles. Located at 42.94° N. Lat.; 88.05° W. Long. Elevation is 800 feet.
History: Hales Corners was the site of monthly fairs begun in the mid-1800's, when the plank road between Janesville and Milwaukee passed through the village. First a gathering of horse traders, the fairs became a stock market for farmers trading pigs, cattle, and sheep.
Population: 7,765 (2000); Race: 97.1% White, 0.2% Black, 0.7% Asian, 0.3% American Indian and Alaska Native, 3.4% Hispanic of any race, 1.0% two or more races (2000); Density: 2,424.7 persons per square mile (2000); Age: 21.8% under 18, 18.5% over 64 (2000); Marriage status: 23.7% never married, 60.4% now married, 8.7% widowed, 7.2% divorced (2000); Foreign born: 2.7% (2000); Ancestry (includes multiple ancestries): 47.9% German, 22.8% Polish, 12.7% Irish, 7.4% Norwegian, 4.7% Other groups (2000).
Economy: Single-family building permits issued: 7 (2001) / 7 (2000); Multi-family building permits issued: 0 (2001) / 0 (2000); Employment by occupation: 12.9% management, 29.7% professional, 8.4% services, 30.0% sales, 0.2% farming, 7.0% construction, 11.9% production (2000).
Income: Per capita income: $25,354 (2000); Median household income: $54,536 (2000); Poverty rate: 2.0% (2000).
Taxes: Total city taxes per capita: $375 (1997); City property taxes per capita: $361 (1997).
Education: High school graduation rate: 90.7% (2000); College graduation rate: 35.0% (2000).

Four-year College(s)

Sacred Heart School of Theology (Private, Not-for-profit, Roman Catholic)
2001 Enrollment: 91 414-425-8300
Housing: Homeownership rate: 61.7% (2000); Median home value: $146,100 (2000); Median rent: $670 per month (2000); Median age of housing: 35 years (2000).
Safety: Violent crime rate: 5.1 per 10,000 population; Property crime rate: 281.3 per 10,000 population (2001).
Transportation: Commute to work: 92.3% car, 0.9% public transportation, 2.9% walk, 3.1% work from home (2000); Travel time to work: 24.6% less than 15 minutes, 53.2% 15 to 30 minutes, 17.2% 30 to 45 minutes, 3.5% 45 to 60 minutes, 1.6% 60 minutes or more (2000)

MILWAUKEE (city). Covers a land area of 96.064 square miles and a water area of 0.850 square miles. Located at 43.05° N. Lat.; 87.95° W. Long. Elevation is 634 feet.
History: Milwaukee began in 1835 when Solomon Juneau, a French trader, and his partner Morgan Martin planned a city on land they had obtained between the Milwaukee River and Lake Michigan, and recorded the name of the new village as Milwaukee. Growth was rapid as Milwaukee County was established in 1836 and land speculators and tradesmen poured into the town. The settlers included many German immigrants, whose numbers were increased further after the unsuccessful rebellion against German monarchies in 1848. The German immigrants shaped the early professional, cultural, and political life of the city. The Civil War brought a rise in manufacturing, and in labor unions. Milwaukee saw the birth of the Social Democratic Party in 1898, under the leadership of Victor L. Berger, who was elected to the U.S. Congress in 1910. In the early 1900's, coal emerged as the chief commodity for Milwaukee's water and rail shipping industry. The metal trades and meat packing were followed by tanning, and the manufacture of liquor, malt, knit goods, boots and shoes. After the repeal of prohibition, it was beer that made Milwaukee famous.
Population: 596,974 (2000); Race: 50.3% White, 37.0% Black, 2.7% Asian, 1.1% American Indian and Alaska Native, 11.9% Hispanic of any race, 2.9% two or more races (2000); Density: 6,214.3 persons per square mile (2000); Age: 28.7% under 18, 10.9% over 64 (2000); Marriage status: 41.4% never married, 41.0% now married, 6.6% widowed, 11.1% divorced (2000); Foreign born: 7.7% (2000); Ancestry (includes multiple ancestries): 45.0% Other groups, 20.9% German, 9.6% Polish, 6.3% Irish, 2.9% Italian (2000).
Vital Statistics: Birth rate: 184.3 per 10,000 population (1998)
Economy: Unemployment rate: 8.5% (11/2002); Total civilian labor force: 275,538 (11/2002); Single-family building permits issued: 154 (2001) / 112 (2000); Multi-family building permits issued: 406 (2001) / 230 (2000); Employment by occupation: 9.5% management, 18.5% professional, 18.6% services, 26.2% sales, 0.2% farming, 6.0% construction, 21.1% production (2000).
Income: Per capita income: $16,181 (2000); Median household income: $32,216 (2000); Poverty rate: 21.3% (2000).
Taxes: Total city taxes per capita: $305 (2000); City property taxes per capita: $290 (2000).
Education: High school graduation rate: 74.8% (2000); College graduation rate: 18.3% (2000).

School District(s)

Central City Cyberschool (01-08)
2000 Enrollment: 379 414-444-2330
Downtown Montessori (PK-03)
2000 Enrollment: 66 414-332-8214

Fox Point J2 (PK-08)
2000 Enrollment: 875 414-247-4164
Khamit Institute (PK-08)
2000 Enrollment: 92 414-445-0602
Maple Dale-Indian Hill (PK-08)
2000 Enrollment: 628 414-351-7170
Milwaukee (PK-12)
2000 Enrollment: 97,985 414-475-8001
Milwaukee Academy of Science (PK-07)
2000 Enrollment: 917 414-933-9520
Yw Global Career Academy (PK-05)
2000 Enrollment: 136 414-607-1100

Four-year College(s)

Alverno College (Private, Not-for-profit, Roman Catholic)
2001 Enrollment: 1,952 414-382-6000
2001 Tuition: In-state $12,000; Out-of-state $12,000
Cardinal Stritch University (Private, Not-for-profit, Roman Catholic)
2001 Enrollment: 5,855 414-410-4000
2001 Tuition: In-state $12,480; Out-of-state $12,480
Keller Graduate School of Management Inc (Private, For-profit)
2001 Enrollment: 341 414-278-7677
Marquette University (Private, Not-for-profit, Roman Catholic)
2001 Enrollment: 10,832 414-288-7710
2001 Tuition: In-state $18,180; Out-of-state $18,180
Medical College of Wisconsin (Private, Not-for-profit)
2001 Enrollment: 1,235 414-456-8296
Milwaukee Institute of Art Design (Private, Not-for-profit)
2001 Enrollment: 650 414-276-7889
2001 Tuition: In-state $17,900; Out-of-state $17,900
Milwaukee School of Engineering (Private, Not-for-profit)
2001 Enrollment: 2,563 414-277-7300
2001 Tuition: In-state $19,735; Out-of-state $19,735
Mount Mary College (Private, Not-for-profit, Roman Catholic)
2001 Enrollment: 1,216 414-258-4810
2001 Tuition: In-state $13,234; Out-of-state $13,234
Saint Luke's Hospital School of Clinical Pastoral (Private, Not-for-profit)
2001 Enrollment: n/a 414-649-6000
Wisconsin School of Professional Psychology (Private, Not-for-profit)
2001 Enrollment: 48 414-464-9777
Wisconsin Lutheran College (Private, Not-for-profit, Wisconsin Evangelical Lutheran Synod)
2001 Enrollment: 716 414-443-8800
2001 Tuition: In-state $13,990; Out-of-state $13,990
University of Wisconsin-Milwaukee (Public)
2001 Enrollment: 24,216 414-229-1122
2001 Tuition: In-state $3,462; Out-of-state $14,274
Saint Martin's College and Seminary (Private, Not-for-profit, Interdenominational)
2001 Enrollment: n/a 414-264-2455
Montessori Institute of Milwaukee (Private, Not-for-profit)
2001 Enrollment: 21 414-481-5050

Two-year College(s)

Advanced Institute of Hair Design (Private, For-profit)
2001 Enrollment: 58 414-464-5002
Advanced Institute of Hair Design (Private, For-profit)
2001 Enrollment: 57 414-464-5002
Columbia Hospital School of Radiologic Technology (Private, Not-for-profit)
2001 Enrollment: n/a 414-961-3817
Milwaukee Area Technical College (Public)
2001 Enrollment: 17,132 414-297-6600
2001 Tuition: In-state $1,920; Out-of-state $14,988
Saint Mary's Hospital School of Radiologic Techn (Private, Not-for-profit, Roman Catholic)
2001 Enrollment: n/a 414-291-1030
Bryant and Stratton College (Private, For-profit)
2001 Enrollment: 274 414-276-5200
2001 Tuition: In-state $9,472; Out-of-state $9,472
Saint Luke's Medical Center-School of Diagnostic Medicine Sonogra (Private, Not-for-profit)
2001 Enrollment: 13 414-649-6689
2001 Tuition: In-state $1,500; Out-of-state $1,500
Saint Lukes Medical Center School of Rad Ther-Rad (Private, Not-for-profit)
2001 Enrollment: n/a 414-649-6420
Saint Lukes Medical Center School of Radiologic Te (Private, Not-for-profit)
2001 Enrollment: 20 414-649-6762
2001 Tuition: In-state $1,500; Out-of-state $1,500

Housing: Homeownership rate: 45.3% (2000); Median home value: $80,400 (2000); Median rent: $453 per month (2000); Median age of housing: 49 years (2000).
Hospitals: Aurora Sinai Medical Center; Children's Health System (222 beds); Columbia-Saint Mary's (394 beds); Froedtert Hospital (326 beds); Milwaukee County Mental Health Division (400 beds); Sacred Heart Rehabilitation Institute (81 beds); Sinai Samaritan Medical Center (454 beds); Saint Francis Hospital (260 beds); Saint Joseph's Hospital (567 beds); Saint Josephs Hospital (118 beds); Saint Luke's Medical Center (600 beds); Saint Mary's Hospital (314 beds); Saint Michael Hospital (405 beds); West Allis Memorial Hospital (250 beds)
Safety: Violent crime rate: 90.9 per 10,000 population; Property crime rate: 670.0 per 10,000 population (2001).
Newspapers: Milwaukee Journal Sentinel (7 x week); The Daily Reporter (5 x week); Wisconsin Jewish Chronicle (1 x week); The Living Church (1 x week); The Irish American Post (1 x month); The Spanish Times (1 x week); Racine Courier (1 x week); Milwaukee Star (1 x week); Milwaukee Courier (1 x week); Catholic Herald (1 x week); Shepherd Express (1 x week); The Weekend (1 x week); The Milwaukee Times (1 x week); Milwaukee Community Journal (2 x week)
Transportation: Commute to work: 82.4% car, 10.3% public transportation, 4.7% walk, 1.7% work from home (2000); Travel time to work: 27.8% less than 15 minutes, 46.2% 15 to 30 minutes, 17.0% 30 to 45 minutes, 4.4% 45 to 60 minutes, 4.6% 60 minutes or more (2000); Amtrak: Service available.
Airports: General Mitchell International (primary service/medium hub); Lawrence J Timmerman (primary service/medium hub)

Additional Information Contacts

African American Chamber of Commerce 414-462-9450
American Indian Chamber of Commerce 414-462-1638
Commercial Association of Realtors Wisconsin 414-271-2021
Greater Milwaukee Association of Realtors 414-778-4929
Greater Milwaukee Convention & Visitors Bureau 414-273-3950
Hispanic Chamber of Commerce 414-643-6963
Metropolitan Milwaukee Association of Commerce 414-287-4100
Milwaukee Chamber of Commerce 414-226-4105

OAK CREEK (city). Covers a land area of 28.618 square miles and a water area of 0.009 square miles. Located at 42.88° N. Lat.; 87.89° W. Long. Elevation is 710 feet.
History: Incorporated 1955.
Population: 28,456 (2000); Race: 91.9% White, 2.4% Black, 2.2% Asian, 0.5% American Indian and Alaska Native, 4.3% Hispanic of any race, 1.3% two or more races (2000); Density: 994.4 persons per square mile (2000); Age: 24.6% under 18, 9.0% over 64 (2000); Marriage status: 26.4% never married, 60.3% now married, 4.0% widowed, 9.3% divorced (2000); Foreign born: 4.4% (2000); Ancestry (includes multiple ancestries): 45.4% German, 26.3% Polish, 10.1% Other groups, 9.9% Irish, 6.6% Italian (2000).
Vital Statistics: Birth rate: 124.8 per 10,000 population (1998)
Economy: Manufacturing: machinery, electronic products, plastic products, computers, paper products, chemicals, transportation equipment, fabricated metal products, concrete products; metal fabricating. Small farms dot the city's surrounding region. Unemployment rate: 4.6% (11/2002); Total civilian labor force: 16,510 (11/2002); Single-family building permits issued: 151 (2001) / 211 (2000); Multi-family building permits issued: 156 (2001) / 331 (2000); Employment by occupation: 15.0% management, 18.3% professional, 11.7% services, 28.1% sales, 0.4% farming, 9.5% construction, 17.0% production (2000).
Income: Per capita income: $23,586 (2000); Median household income: $53,779 (2000); Poverty rate: 3.1% (2000).
Taxes: Total city taxes per capita: $519 (2000); City property taxes per capita: $461 (2000).
Education: High school graduation rate: 88.6% (2000); College graduation rate: 24.4% (2000).

School District(s)

Oak Creek-Franklin (PK-12)
2000 Enrollment: 4,823 414-768-5886
Housing: Homeownership rate: 61.5% (2000); Median home value: $139,100 (2000); Median rent: $656 per month (2000); Median age of housing: 17 years (2000).
Safety: Violent crime rate: 7.0 per 10,000 population; Property crime rate: 299.0 per 10,000 population (2001).
Transportation: Commute to work: 95.7% car, 1.2% public transportation, 0.9% walk, 1.8% work from home (2000); Travel time to work: 28.5% less than 15 minutes, 39.9% 15 to 30 minutes, 22.2% 30 to 45 minutes, 5.8% 45 to 60 minutes, 3.5% 60 minutes or more (2000)

RIVER HILLS (village). Covers a land area of 5.091 square miles and a water area of 0.179 square miles. Located at 43.16° N. Lat.; 87.93° W. Long. Elevation is 700 feet.
Population: 1,631 (2000); Race: 86.6% White, 4.5% Black, 6.4% Asian, 0.1% American Indian and Alaska Native, 2.9% Hispanic of any race, 2.3% two or more races (2000); Density: 320.3 persons per square mile (2000); Age: 24.3% under 18, 14.7% over 64 (2000); Marriage status: 18.8% never married, 71.4% now married, 5.1% widowed, 4.7% divorced (2000); Foreign born: 12.6% (2000); Ancestry (includes multiple ancestries): 29.2% German, 17.9% Other groups, 12.0% Irish, 9.0% English, 7.6% Polish (2000).
Economy: Single-family building permits issued: 3 (2001) / 5 (2000); Multi-family building permits issued: 0 (2001) / 0 (2000); Employment by occupation: 27.6% management, 40.1% professional, 5.4% services, 23.6% sales, 0.0% farming, 0.5% construction, 2.8% production (2000).
Income: Per capita income: $94,479 (2000); Median household income: $161,292 (2000); Poverty rate: 1.7% (2000).
Taxes: Total city taxes per capita: $1,200 (1997); City property taxes per capita: $1,144 (1997).
Education: High school graduation rate: 97.8% (2000); College graduation rate: 76.3% (2000).
Housing: Homeownership rate: 95.1% (2000); Median home value: $491,000 (2000); Median rent: $850 per month (2000); Median age of housing: 40 years (2000).
Safety: Violent crime rate: 0.0 per 10,000 population; Property crime rate: 121.7 per 10,000 population (2001).
Transportation: Commute to work: 90.1% car, 0.5% public transportation, 0.8% walk, 8.4% work from home (2000); Travel time to work: 30.1% less than 15 minutes, 49.6% 15 to 30 minutes, 13.9% 30 to 45 minutes, 4.8% 45 to 60 minutes, 1.5% 60 minutes or more (2000)

SAINT FRANCIS (city). Covers a land area of 2.531 square miles and a water area of 0 square miles. Located at 42.97° N. Lat.; 87.87° W. Long. Elevation is 682 feet.
Population: 8,662 (2000); Race: 93.6% White, 1.7% Black, 1.1% Asian, 0.6% American Indian and Alaska Native, 4.6% Hispanic of any race, 0.9% two or more races (2000); Density: 3,421.7 persons per square mile (2000); Age: 18.8% under 18, 17.8% over 64 (2000); Marriage status: 29.8% never married, 49.2% now married, 8.8% widowed, 12.1% divorced (2000); Foreign born: 3.5% (2000); Ancestry (includes multiple ancestries): 37.1% German, 27.4% Polish, 9.2% Other groups, 9.0% Irish, 6.7% Italian (2000).
Economy: Single-family building permits issued: 0 (2001) / 0 (2000); Multi-family building permits issued: 0 (2001) / 122 (2000); Employment by occupation: 11.0% management, 14.2% professional, 15.3% services, 28.7% sales, 0.2% farming, 9.9% construction, 20.8% production (2000).
Income: Per capita income: $21,837 (2000); Median household income: $36,721 (2000); Poverty rate: 6.5% (2000).
Education: High school graduation rate: 85.2% (2000); College graduation rate: 13.7% (2000).

School District(s)

Saint Francis (PK-12)
2000 Enrollment: 1,456 414-483-7636

Four-year College(s)

Saint Francis Seminary (Private, Not-for-profit, Roman Catholic)
2001 Enrollment: n/a 414-747-6400

Housing: Homeownership rate: 52.1% (2000); Median home value: $95,400 (2000); Median rent: $453 per month (2000); Median age of housing: 41 years (2000).
Safety: Violent crime rate: 13.8 per 10,000 population; Property crime rate: 321.0 per 10,000 population (2001).
Transportation: Commute to work: 91.3% car, 4.0% public transportation, 2.2% walk, 2.0% work from home (2000); Travel time to work: 34.4% less than 15 minutes, 48.2% 15 to 30 minutes, 13.2% 30 to 45 minutes, 2.4% 45 to 60 minutes, 1.7% 60 minutes or more (2000)

SHOREWOOD (village). Covers a land area of 1.600 square miles and a water area of 0 square miles. Located at 43.09° N. Lat.; 87.88° W. Long. Elevation is 679 feet.
History: University of Wisconsin immediately South. Settled c. 1835, incorporated 1900.
Population: 13,763 (2000); Race: 91.2% White, 2.3% Black, 2.7% Asian, 0.5% American Indian and Alaska Native, 3.5% Hispanic of any race, 2.7% two or more races (2000); Density: 8,599.5 persons per square mile (2000); Age: 20.8% under 18, 14.4% over 64 (2000); Marriage status: 33.6% never married, 50.1% now married, 6.2% widowed, 10.1% divorced (2000); Foreign born: 11.8% (2000); Ancestry (includes multiple ancestries): 35.8% German, 17.7% Irish, 11.3% Other groups, 8.4% English, 7.9% Polish (2000).
Vital Statistics: Birth rate: 94.5 per 10,000 population (1998)
Economy: Single-family building permits issued: 0 (2001) / 6 (2000); Multi-family building permits issued: 0 (2001) / 0 (2000); Employment by occupation: 17.0% management, 42.5% professional, 7.6% services, 24.6% sales, 0.1% farming, 2.2% construction, 6.0% production (2000).
Income: Per capita income: $32,950 (2000); Median household income: $47,224 (2000); Poverty rate: 6.7% (2000).
Taxes: Total city taxes per capita: $492 (1997); City property taxes per capita: $477 (1997).
Education: High school graduation rate: 94.5% (2000); College graduation rate: 62.9% (2000).

School District(s)

Shorewood (PK-12)
2000 Enrollment: 2,254 414-963-6901

Housing: Homeownership rate: 47.5% (2000); Median home value: $174,700 (2000); Median rent: $577 per month (2000); Median age of housing: 60+ years (2000).
Safety: Violent crime rate: 13.0 per 10,000 population; Property crime rate: 290.0 per 10,000 population (2001).
Transportation: Commute to work: 82.7% car, 5.3% public transportation, 5.8% walk, 4.6% work from home (2000); Travel time to work: 30.7% less than 15 minutes, 48.8% 15 to 30 minutes, 15.5% 30 to 45 minutes, 2.6% 45 to 60 minutes, 2.4% 60 minutes or more (2000)

SOUTH MILWAUKEE (city). Covers a land area of 4.779 square miles and a water area of 0.007 square miles. Located at 42.91° N. Lat.; 87.86° W. Long. Elevation is 670 feet.
History: South Milwaukee, once known as Oak Creek for the stream which flows into Lake Michigan at this point, developed as an industrial suburb of Milwaukee.
Population: 21,256 (2000); Race: 95.0% White, 0.8% Black, 0.5% Asian, 0.5% American Indian and Alaska Native, 5.2% Hispanic of any race, 1.3% two or more races (2000); Density: 4,447.5 persons per square mile (2000); Age: 24.1% under 18, 16.4% over 64 (2000); Marriage status: 26.0% never married, 56.0% now married, 7.6% widowed, 10.4% divorced (2000); Foreign born: 3.7% (2000); Ancestry (includes multiple ancestries): 43.3% German, 27.5% Polish, 9.5% Irish, 8.0% Other groups, 5.9% Italian (2000).
Vital Statistics: Birth rate: 124.2 per 10,000 population (1998)
Economy: Single-family building permits issued: 9 (2001) / 27 (2000); Multi-family building permits issued: 128 (2001) / 16 (2000); Employment by occupation: 10.3% management, 15.1% professional, 14.1% services, 28.0% sales, 0.1% farming, 9.1% construction, 23.2% production (2000).
Income: Per capita income: $20,925 (2000); Median household income: $44,197 (2000); Poverty rate: 6.0% (2000).
Taxes: Total city taxes per capita: $267 (1997); City property taxes per capita: $254 (1997).
Education: High school graduation rate: 85.3% (2000); College graduation rate: 15.7% (2000).

School District(s)

South Milwaukee (PK-12)
2000 Enrollment: 3,588 414-768-6300

Housing: Homeownership rate: 62.0% (2000); Median home value: $111,300 (2000); Median rent: $512 per month (2000); Median age of housing: 43 years (2000).
Safety: Violent crime rate: 11.7 per 10,000 population; Property crime rate: 235.4 per 10,000 population (2001).
Transportation: Commute to work: 94.3% car, 1.5% public transportation, 2.8% walk, 1.1% work from home (2000); Travel time to work: 35.7% less than 15 minutes, 35.4% 15 to 30 minutes, 19.0% 30 to 45 minutes, 5.6% 45 to 60 minutes, 4.4% 60 minutes or more (2000)

WAUWATOSA (city). Covers a land area of 13.239 square miles and a water area of 0.003 square miles. Located at 43.05° N. Lat.; 88.02° W. Long. Elevation is 672 feet.
History: Mt. Mary College to North in Milwaukee, Lutheran College on South border. Settled 1835, incorporated as a city 1897.
Population: 47,271 (2000); Race: 93.8% White, 2.3% Black, 1.8% Asian, 0.5% American Indian and Alaska Native, 1.8% Hispanic of any race, 1.2% two or more races (2000); Density: 3,570.5 persons per square mile (2000); Age: 23.3% under 18, 18.3% over 64 (2000); Marriage status: 25.6% never married, 57.1% now married, 9.3% widowed, 8.0% divorced (2000); Foreign born: 3.8% (2000); Ancestry (includes multiple ancestries): 49.5% German, 16.9% Irish, 11.1% Polish, 8.1% English, 6.6% Other groups (2000).
Vital Statistics: Birth rate: 123.8 per 10,000 population (1998)

Economy: Manufacturing includes transportation equipment, printing adhesives, electroplating. Milwaukee county institutions located here, including county zoo. Unemployment rate: 4.0% (11/2002); Total civilian labor force: 23,841 (11/2002); Single-family building permits issued: 1 (2001) / 1 (2000); Multi-family building permits issued: 0 (2001) / 0 (2000); Employment by occupation: 18.4% management, 32.1% professional, 8.5% services, 28.5% sales, 0.1% farming, 4.3% construction, 8.0% production (2000).
Income: Per capita income: $28,834 (2000); Median household income: $54,519 (2000); Poverty rate: 3.8% (2000).
Taxes: Total city taxes per capita: $553 (2000); City property taxes per capita: $506 (2000).
Education: High school graduation rate: 93.4% (2000); College graduation rate: 47.6% (2000).

School District(s)

Wauwatosa (PK-12)
2000 Enrollment: 7,114 414-773-1010
Housing: Homeownership rate: 67.8% (2000); Median home value: $138,600 (2000); Median rent: $630 per month (2000); Median age of housing: 50 years (2000).
Safety: Violent crime rate: 22.1 per 10,000 population; Property crime rate: 507.1 per 10,000 population (2001).
Transportation: Commute to work: 91.5% car, 2.2% public transportation, 2.1% walk, 3.6% work from home (2000); Travel time to work: 33.7% less than 15 minutes, 50.3% 15 to 30 minutes, 11.8% 30 to 45 minutes, 1.8% 45 to 60 minutes, 2.3% 60 minutes or more (2000)
Additional Information Contacts
Wauwatosa Chamber of Commerce. 414-453-2330

WEST ALLIS (city). Covers a land area of 11.348 square miles and a water area of 0.023 square miles. Located at 43.00° N. Lat.; 88.01° W. Long. Elevation is 730 feet.
History: Incorporated 1902.
Population: 61,254 (2000); Race: 93.7% White, 1.2% Black, 1.6% Asian, 0.6% American Indian and Alaska Native, 3.4% Hispanic of any race, 1.7% two or more races (2000); Density: 5,397.6 persons per square mile (2000); Age: 21.4% under 18, 17.3% over 64 (2000); Marriage status: 29.7% never married, 48.5% now married, 9.2% widowed, 12.6% divorced (2000); Foreign born: 3.6% (2000); Ancestry (includes multiple ancestries): 45.8% German, 20.2% Polish, 12.0% Irish, 8.5% Other groups, 5.7% Italian (2000).
Vital Statistics: Birth rate: 119.0 per 10,000 population (1998)
Economy: A banking and manufacturing city: motor vehicles, food products, tools, machines. State fairgrounds. Unemployment rate: 5.2% (11/2002); Total civilian labor force: 32,412 (11/2002); Single-family building permits issued: 4 (2001) / 6 (2000); Multi-family building permits issued: 26 (2001) / 6 (2000); Employment by occupation: 10.7% management, 16.2% professional, 15.0% services, 29.9% sales, 0.1% farming, 9.4% construction, 18.8% production (2000).
Income: Per capita income: $20,914 (2000); Median household income: $39,394 (2000); Poverty rate: 6.5% (2000).
Taxes: Total city taxes per capita: $423 (2000); City property taxes per capita: $390 (2000).
Education: High school graduation rate: 82.7% (2000); College graduation rate: 16.4% (2000).

School District(s)

West Allis (PK-12)
2000 Enrollment: 8,795 414-604-3005
Housing: Homeownership rate: 58.0% (2000); Median home value: $99,200 (2000); Median rent: $517 per month (2000); Median age of housing: 48 years (2000).
Hospitals: Rogers Memorial Hospital - Milwaukee
Safety: Violent crime rate: 24.8 per 10,000 population; Property crime rate: 424.9 per 10,000 population (2001).
Transportation: Commute to work: 90.9% car, 3.3% public transportation, 3.5% walk, 1.5% work from home (2000); Travel time to work: 32.5% less than 15 minutes, 49.2% 15 to 30 minutes, 13.1% 30 to 45 minutes, 2.4% 45 to 60 minutes, 2.7% 60 minutes or more (2000)
Additional Information Contacts
West Allis Chamber of Commerce 414-302-9901

WEST MILWAUKEE (village). Covers a land area of 1.129 square miles and a water area of 0 square miles. Located at 43.01° N. Lat.; 87.97° W. Long. Elevation is 660 feet.
History: Incorporated 1906.
Population: 4,201 (2000); Race: 82.2% White, 1.4% Black, 4.1% Asian, 2.4% American Indian and Alaska Native, 12.8% Hispanic of any race, 3.5% two or more races (2000); Density: 3,722.0 persons per square mile (2000); Age: 20.8% under 18, 14.7% over 64 (2000); Marriage status: 39.3% never married, 37.2% now married, 5.9% widowed, 17.6% divorced (2000); Foreign born: 8.9% (2000); Ancestry (includes multiple ancestries): 37.3% German, 20.7% Other groups, 13.3% Polish, 11.2% Irish, 4.5% Norwegian (2000).
Economy: Industries include manufacturing of air and hydraulic cylinders, machinery. Eighty percent of the land is zoned for industrial and mercantile establishments. This village employs twice the number who live here. Single-family building permits issued: 0 (2001) / 0 (2000); Multi-family building permits issued: 0 (2001) / 0 (2000); Employment by occupation: 7.8% management, 14.1% professional, 19.7% services, 25.2% sales, 0.0% farming, 10.4% construction, 22.8% production (2000).
Income: Per capita income: $18,396 (2000); Median household income: $35,250 (2000); Poverty rate: 11.6% (2000).
Taxes: Total city taxes per capita: $877 (1997); City property taxes per capita: $827 (1997).
Education: High school graduation rate: 75.5% (2000); College graduation rate: 15.4% (2000).
Housing: Homeownership rate: 35.4% (2000); Median home value: $88,000 (2000); Median rent: $465 per month (2000); Median age of housing: 52 years (2000).
Safety: Violent crime rate: 52.0 per 10,000 population; Property crime rate: 510.5 per 10,000 population (2001).
Transportation: Commute to work: 85.2% car, 6.5% public transportation, 6.4% walk, 1.1% work from home (2000); Travel time to work: 29.9% less than 15 minutes, 49.4% 15 to 30 minutes, 14.9% 30 to 45 minutes, 3.0% 45 to 60 minutes, 2.8% 60 minutes or more (2000)

WHITEFISH BAY (village). Covers a land area of 2.142 square miles and a water area of 0 square miles. Located at 43.11° N. Lat.; 87.90° W. Long. Elevation is 650 feet.
History: Incorporated 1892.
Population: 14,163 (2000); Race: 96.3% White, 0.8% Black, 1.8% Asian, 0.1% American Indian and Alaska Native, 2.5% Hispanic of any race, 0.8% two or more races (2000); Density: 6,610.8 persons per square mile (2000); Age: 29.3% under 18, 11.8% over 64 (2000); Marriage status: 18.2% never married, 69.8% now married, 4.9% widowed, 7.1% divorced (2000); Foreign born: 6.5% (2000); Ancestry (includes multiple ancestries): 38.9% German, 18.3% Irish, 12.7% English, 9.7% Polish, 8.0% Italian (2000).
Vital Statistics: Birth rate: 141.2 per 10,000 population (1998)
Economy: Single-family building permits issued: 0 (2001) / 0 (2000); Multi-family building permits issued: 0 (2001) / 0 (2000); Employment by occupation: 24.1% management, 41.0% professional, 4.7% services, 24.3% sales, 0.0% farming, 1.7% construction, 4.1% production (2000).
Income: Per capita income: $39,609 (2000); Median household income: $80,755 (2000); Poverty rate: 3.2% (2000).
Taxes: Total city taxes per capita: $441 (1997); City property taxes per capita: $428 (1997).
Education: High school graduation rate: 97.9% (2000); College graduation rate: 70.9% (2000).

School District(s)

Whitefish Bay (PK-12)
2000 Enrollment: 2,845 414-963-3921
Housing: Homeownership rate: 84.7% (2000); Median home value: $194,900 (2000); Median rent: $703 per month (2000); Median age of housing: 58 years (2000).
Safety: Violent crime rate: 3.5 per 10,000 population; Property crime rate: 132.5 per 10,000 population (2001).
Transportation: Commute to work: 92.3% car, 1.7% public transportation, 1.7% walk, 3.5% work from home (2000); Travel time to work: 29.6% less than 15 minutes, 53.1% 15 to 30 minutes, 11.2% 30 to 45 minutes, 3.7% 45 to 60 minutes, 2.3% 60 minutes or more (2000)

Monroe County

Located in west central Wisconsin; drained by the Lemonweir, Black, La Crosse, and Kickapoo Rivers. Covers a land area of 900.80 square miles, a water area of 7.50 square miles, and is located in the Central Time Zone. The county government was organized in 1854. County seat is Sparta.
Population: 40,899 (2000); Race: 96.3% White, 0.5% Black, 0.5% Asian, 0.8% American Indian and Alaska Native, 1.9% Hispanic of any race, 0.7% two or more races (2000); Density: 45.4 persons per square mile (2000); Age: 28.0% under 18, 13.9% over 64 (2000).

Religion: Five largest groups: 25.2% Catholic Church, 9.5% Wisconsin Evangelical Lutheran Synod, 9.5% Evangelical Lutheran Church in America, 3.6% The United Methodist Church, 2.6% Assemblies of God (2000).
Economy: Unemployment rate: 4.4% (11/2002); Total civilian labor force: 20,518 (11/2002); Leading industries: 29.6% manufacturing; 16.4% health care and social assistance; 11.9% retail trade (2000); Companies that employ more than 1,000 persons: 0 (2000); Companies that employ more than 100 persons: 26 (2000); Farms: 1,567 totaling 329,561 acres (1997); Minority business ownership rate: 0.0% (1997); Women business ownership rate: 15.2% (1997); Retail sales per capita: $6,680 (1997). Single-family building permits issued: 184 (2001) / 181 (2000); Multi-family building permits issued: 49 (2001) / 54 (2000).
Income: Per capita income: $17,056 (2000); Median household income: $37,170 (2000); Poverty rate: 12.0% (2000); Bankruptcy rate: 3.73% (2001).
Taxes: Total county taxes per capita: $204 (2000); County property taxes per capita: $157 (2000).
Education: High school graduation rate: 81.1% (2000); College graduation rate: 13.2% (2000).
Housing: Homeownership rate: 73.7% (2000); Median home value: $77,500 (2000); Median rent: $382 per month (2000); Median age of housing: 30 years (2000).
Health: Birth rate: 134.2 per 10,000 population (1998); Age adjusted death rate: 91.5 per 10,000 population (1999); Age adjusted cancer mortality rate: 177.1 deaths per 100,000 population (1999). Number of physicians: 9.3 per 10,000 population (1999); Number of hospital beds: 106.4 per 10,000 population (1999).
Elections: 2000 Presidential election results: 45.7% Gore, 50.3% Bush, 3.0% Nader, 0.4% Buchanan
National and State Parks: Big Creek State Fishery Area; Evans Pond State Fishery Area; La Crosse River State Fishery Area; Mill Bluff State Park; Pinnacle Rock State Fishery Area
Additional Information Contacts
Monroe County Government Offices 608-269-8705
Sparta Chamber of Commerce 608-269-4123
Tomah Chamber of Commerce 608-372-2166

Monroe County Communities

ADRIAN (town). Covers a land area of 35.262 square miles and a water area of 0.008 square miles. Located at 43.93° N. Lat.; 90.61° W. Long.
Population: 682 (2000); Race: 99.6% White, 0.0% Black, 0.0% Asian, 0.0% American Indian and Alaska Native, 1.0% Hispanic of any race, 0.3% two or more races (2000); Density: 19.3 persons per square mile (2000); Age: 31.2% under 18, 9.4% over 64 (2000); Marriage status: 23.2% never married, 66.7% now married, 4.8% widowed, 5.3% divorced (2000); Foreign born: 0.1% (2000); Ancestry (includes multiple ancestries): 53.0% German, 19.0% Norwegian, 13.4% Irish, 8.9% Polish, 5.5% English (2000).
Economy: Single-family building permits issued: 7 (2001) / 5 (2000); Multi-family building permits issued: 0 (2001) / 0 (2000); Employment by occupation: 13.7% management, 16.1% professional, 13.7% services, 18.9% sales, 0.5% farming, 12.7% construction, 24.4% production (2000).
Income: Per capita income: $19,791 (2000); Median household income: $45,875 (2000); Poverty rate: 2.1% (2000).
Taxes: Total city taxes per capita: $140 (1997); City property taxes per capita: $140 (1997).
Education: High school graduation rate: 91.6% (2000); College graduation rate: 17.5% (2000).
Housing: Homeownership rate: 87.5% (2000); Median home value: $94,400 (2000); Median rent: $396 per month (2000); Median age of housing: 25 years (2000).
Transportation: Commute to work: 93.6% car, 0.0% public transportation, 0.0% walk, 6.4% work from home (2000); Travel time to work: 33.9% less than 15 minutes, 43.3% 15 to 30 minutes, 11.8% 30 to 45 minutes, 5.0% 45 to 60 minutes, 6.1% 60 minutes or more (2000)

ANGELO (town). Covers a land area of 34.658 square miles and a water area of 0.126 square miles. Located at 43.94° N. Lat.; 90.75° W. Long. Elevation is 810 feet.
Population: 1,268 (2000); Race: 94.5% White, 0.6% Black, 0.0% Asian, 0.7% American Indian and Alaska Native, 5.1% Hispanic of any race, 1.6% two or more races (2000); Density: 36.6 persons per square mile (2000); Age: 27.8% under 18, 12.6% over 64 (2000); Marriage status: 20.6% never married, 65.3% now married, 4.5% widowed, 9.6% divorced (2000); Foreign born: 1.6% (2000); Ancestry (includes multiple ancestries): 42.6% German, 17.1% Norwegian, 11.7% Irish, 9.1% English, 8.4% Other groups (2000).
Economy: Single-family building permits issued: 10 (2001) / 5 (2000); Multi-family building permits issued: 4 (2001) / 0 (2000); Employment by occupation: 14.6% management, 9.3% professional, 18.7% services, 17.2% sales, 1.5% farming, 9.1% construction, 29.6% production (2000).
Income: Per capita income: $15,727 (2000); Median household income: $40,163 (2000); Poverty rate: 9.1% (2000).
Taxes: Total city taxes per capita: $9 (1997); City property taxes per capita: $6 (1997).
Education: High school graduation rate: 77.2% (2000); College graduation rate: 11.8% (2000).
Housing: Homeownership rate: 80.6% (2000); Median home value: $75,900 (2000); Median rent: $438 per month (2000); Median age of housing: 27 years (2000).
Transportation: Commute to work: 93.1% car, 0.3% public transportation, 1.2% walk, 3.7% work from home (2000); Travel time to work: 41.6% less than 15 minutes, 32.5% 15 to 30 minutes, 16.0% 30 to 45 minutes, 5.3% 45 to 60 minutes, 4.7% 60 minutes or more (2000)

BYRON (town). Covers a land area of 35.480 square miles and a water area of 0.581 square miles. Located at 44.03° N. Lat.; 90.37° W. Long.
Population: 1,394 (2000); Race: 90.8% White, 0.1% Black, 0.7% Asian, 6.6% American Indian and Alaska Native, 0.0% Hispanic of any race, 1.5% two or more races (2000); Density: 39.3 persons per square mile (2000); Age: 28.5% under 18, 9.1% over 64 (2000); Marriage status: 19.8% never married, 62.9% now married, 5.4% widowed, 11.8% divorced (2000); Foreign born: 1.4% (2000); Ancestry (includes multiple ancestries): 39.4% German, 14.0% Irish, 11.1% Other groups, 10.6% English, 10.3% Norwegian (2000).
Economy: Single-family building permits issued: 14 (2001) / 14 (2000); Multi-family building permits issued: 0 (2001) / 0 (2000); Employment by occupation: 12.1% management, 10.3% professional, 18.6% services, 21.7% sales, 2.3% farming, 10.9% construction, 24.1% production (2000).
Income: Per capita income: $16,707 (2000); Median household income: $40,583 (2000); Poverty rate: 10.3% (2000).
Taxes: Total city taxes per capita: $32 (1997); City property taxes per capita: $31 (1997).
Education: High school graduation rate: 80.5% (2000); College graduation rate: 8.7% (2000).
Housing: Homeownership rate: 81.4% (2000); Median home value: $84,100 (2000); Median rent: $325 per month (2000); Median age of housing: 24 years (2000).
Transportation: Commute to work: 91.6% car, 0.0% public transportation, 2.1% walk, 6.3% work from home (2000); Travel time to work: 31.5% less than 15 minutes, 44.9% 15 to 30 minutes, 18.6% 30 to 45 minutes, 2.3% 45 to 60 minutes, 2.8% 60 minutes or more (2000)

CASHTON (village). Covers a land area of 1.033 square miles and a water area of 0 square miles. Located at 43.74° N. Lat.; 90.78° W. Long. Elevation is 1,360 feet.
Population: 1,005 (2000); Race: 98.7% White, 0.0% Black, 0.6% Asian, 0.2% American Indian and Alaska Native, 2.2% Hispanic of any race, 0.3% two or more races (2000); Density: 973.3 persons per square mile (2000); Age: 28.3% under 18, 17.3% over 64 (2000); Marriage status: 21.6% never married, 59.4% now married, 12.3% widowed, 6.8% divorced (2000); Foreign born: 1.1% (2000); Ancestry (includes multiple ancestries): 52.4% German, 30.1% Norwegian, 13.6% Irish, 6.5% Other groups, 3.3% French (except Basque) (2000).
Economy: In timber and dairy region (butter, cheese). Single-family building permits issued: 2 (2001) / 7 (2000); Multi-family building permits issued: 0 (2001) / 0 (2000); Employment by occupation: 6.6% management, 9.6% professional, 19.5% services, 20.3% sales, 3.1% farming, 9.6% construction, 31.4% production (2000).
Income: Per capita income: $14,425 (2000); Median household income: $30,938 (2000); Poverty rate: 14.8% (2000).
Taxes: Total city taxes per capita: $134 (2000); City property taxes per capita: $111 (2000).
Education: High school graduation rate: 79.7% (2000); College graduation rate: 11.2% (2000).

School District(s)

Cashton (PK-12)
2000 Enrollment: 579 608-654-5131
Housing: Homeownership rate: 79.5% (2000); Median home value: $61,000 (2000); Median rent: $263 per month (2000); Median age of housing: 50 years (2000).
Newspapers: The Cashton Record (1 x week)
Transportation: Commute to work: 86.5% car, 0.0% public transportation, 10.1% walk, 1.7% work from home (2000); Travel time to work: 42.9% less

than 15 minutes, 25.5% 15 to 30 minutes, 18.5% 30 to 45 minutes, 9.9% 45 to 60 minutes, 3.2% 60 minutes or more (2000)

CLIFTON (town). Covers a land area of 34.103 square miles and a water area of 0 square miles. Located at 43.86° N. Lat.; 90.36° W. Long. Elevation is 960 feet.
Population: 693 (2000); Race: 99.3% White, 0.0% Black, 0.0% Asian, 0.0% American Indian and Alaska Native, 0.0% Hispanic of any race, 0.4% two or more races (2000); Density: 20.3 persons per square mile (2000); Age: 41.4% under 18, 9.5% over 64 (2000); Marriage status: 25.5% never married, 69.1% now married, 2.8% widowed, 2.6% divorced (2000); Foreign born: 0.7% (2000); Ancestry (includes multiple ancestries): 42.6% German, 9.5% Norwegian, 7.9% Pennsylvania German, 7.1% Irish, 6.1% Swiss (2000).
Economy: Employment by occupation: 36.7% management, 11.2% professional, 9.4% services, 12.0% sales, 6.7% farming, 7.9% construction, 16.1% production (2000).
Income: Per capita income: $10,402 (2000); Median household income: $31,932 (2000); Poverty rate: 39.8% (2000).
Taxes: Total city taxes per capita: $97 (1997); City property taxes per capita: $96 (1997).
Education: High school graduation rate: 66.3% (2000); College graduation rate: 12.3% (2000).
Housing: Homeownership rate: 86.7% (2000); Median home value: $67,500 (2000); Median rent: $442 per month (2000); Median age of housing: 51 years (2000).
Transportation: Commute to work: 52.8% car, 0.0% public transportation, 3.8% walk, 41.1% work from home (2000); Travel time to work: 12.2% less than 15 minutes, 53.8% 15 to 30 minutes, 26.3% 30 to 45 minutes, 6.4% 45 to 60 minutes, 1.3% 60 minutes or more (2000)

GLENDALE (town). Covers a land area of 35.636 square miles and a water area of 0.011 square miles. Located at 43.77° N. Lat.; 90.37° W. Long. Elevation is 1,073 feet.
Population: 579 (2000); Race: 99.5% White, 0.0% Black, 0.0% Asian, 0.0% American Indian and Alaska Native, 1.2% Hispanic of any race, 0.5% two or more races (2000); Density: 16.2 persons per square mile (2000); Age: 27.8% under 18, 15.6% over 64 (2000); Marriage status: 20.1% never married, 66.7% now married, 5.3% widowed, 7.8% divorced (2000); Foreign born: 1.2% (2000); Ancestry (includes multiple ancestries): 53.6% German, 15.7% Irish, 15.6% English, 8.4% United States or American, 7.4% Norwegian (2000).
Economy: Employment by occupation: 33.1% management, 9.4% professional, 9.4% services, 12.9% sales, 1.7% farming, 6.3% construction, 27.2% production (2000).
Income: Per capita income: $16,158 (2000); Median household income: $37,083 (2000); Poverty rate: 4.6% (2000).
Taxes: Total city taxes per capita: $193 (1997); City property taxes per capita: $193 (1997).
Education: High school graduation rate: 84.2% (2000); College graduation rate: 14.5% (2000).
Housing: Homeownership rate: 81.4% (2000); Median home value: $77,500 (2000); Median rent: $354 per month (2000); Median age of housing: 53 years (2000).
Transportation: Commute to work: 74.7% car, 0.0% public transportation, 5.3% walk, 18.1% work from home (2000); Travel time to work: 33.9% less than 15 minutes, 33.5% 15 to 30 minutes, 19.1% 30 to 45 minutes, 5.7% 45 to 60 minutes, 7.8% 60 minutes or more (2000)

GRANT (town). Covers a land area of 35.741 square miles and a water area of 0.155 square miles. Located at 44.10° N. Lat.; 90.58° W. Long.
Population: 483 (2000); Race: 98.6% White, 0.0% Black, 0.6% Asian, 0.6% American Indian and Alaska Native, 0.2% Hispanic of any race, 0.2% two or more races (2000); Density: 13.5 persons per square mile (2000); Age: 26.7% under 18, 6.9% over 64 (2000); Marriage status: 21.5% never married, 66.1% now married, 2.7% widowed, 9.7% divorced (2000); Foreign born: 4.1% (2000); Ancestry (includes multiple ancestries): 46.6% German, 18.1% Irish, 11.6% Norwegian, 8.8% English, 6.1% French (except Basque) (2000).
Economy: Employment by occupation: 7.9% management, 19.4% professional, 23.6% services, 17.8% sales, 0.8% farming, 8.7% construction, 21.9% production (2000).
Income: Per capita income: $16,751 (2000); Median household income: $43,456 (2000); Poverty rate: 3.7% (2000).
Taxes: Total city taxes per capita: $51 (1997); City property taxes per capita: $51 (1997).
Education: High school graduation rate: 87.1% (2000); College graduation rate: 12.6% (2000).
Housing: Homeownership rate: 93.2% (2000); Median home value: $88,600 (2000); Median rent: $400 per month (2000); Median age of housing: 22 years (2000).
Transportation: Commute to work: 91.7% car, 2.1% public transportation, 0.8% walk, 4.1% work from home (2000); Travel time to work: 13.8% less than 15 minutes, 62.1% 15 to 30 minutes, 16.8% 30 to 45 minutes, 3.0% 45 to 60 minutes, 4.3% 60 minutes or more (2000)

GREENFIELD (town). Covers a land area of 35.288 square miles and a water area of 0.056 square miles. Located at 44.01° N. Lat.; 90.59° W. Long.
Population: 626 (2000); Race: 98.3% White, 0.0% Black, 0.0% Asian, 1.7% American Indian and Alaska Native, 0.0% Hispanic of any race, 0.0% two or more races (2000); Density: 17.7 persons per square mile (2000); Age: 27.7% under 18, 13.0% over 64 (2000); Marriage status: 14.5% never married, 74.9% now married, 7.1% widowed, 3.5% divorced (2000); Foreign born: 0.5% (2000); Ancestry (includes multiple ancestries): 52.9% German, 12.5% Irish, 12.0% English, 11.3% Norwegian, 5.5% United States or American (2000).
Economy: Single-family building permits issued: 6 (2001) / 3 (2000); Multi-family building permits issued: 0 (2001) / 0 (2000); Employment by occupation: 22.4% management, 15.4% professional, 11.9% services, 17.1% sales, 3.1% farming, 12.9% construction, 17.1% production (2000).
Income: Per capita income: $22,380 (2000); Median household income: $47,750 (2000); Poverty rate: 3.8% (2000).
Taxes: Total city taxes per capita: $90 (1997); City property taxes per capita: $90 (1997).
Education: High school graduation rate: 82.9% (2000); College graduation rate: 17.8% (2000).
Housing: Homeownership rate: 91.3% (2000); Median home value: $79,300 (2000); Median rent: $345 per month (2000); Median age of housing: 38 years (2000).
Transportation: Commute to work: 91.7% car, 0.0% public transportation, 2.4% walk, 5.9% work from home (2000); Travel time to work: 45.6% less than 15 minutes, 43.0% 15 to 30 minutes, 2.6% 30 to 45 minutes, 0.0% 45 to 60 minutes, 8.8% 60 minutes or more (2000)

JEFFERSON (town). Covers a land area of 34.856 square miles and a water area of 0.003 square miles. Located at 43.77° N. Lat.; 90.75° W. Long.
Population: 800 (2000); Race: 98.9% White, 0.0% Black, 0.9% Asian, 0.3% American Indian and Alaska Native, 0.3% Hispanic of any race, 0.0% two or more races (2000); Density: 23.0 persons per square mile (2000); Age: 38.4% under 18, 8.0% over 64 (2000); Marriage status: 30.7% never married, 60.8% now married, 4.4% widowed, 4.1% divorced (2000); Foreign born: 1.8% (2000); Ancestry (includes multiple ancestries): 47.2% German, 11.2% Norwegian, 5.2% Irish, 4.2% United States or American, 3.4% Polish (2000).
Economy: Employment by occupation: 25.4% management, 7.5% professional, 10.1% services, 12.4% sales, 8.1% farming, 11.8% construction, 24.6% production (2000).
Income: Per capita income: $12,511 (2000); Median household income: $33,750 (2000); Poverty rate: 26.9% (2000).
Taxes: Total city taxes per capita: $109 (1997); City property taxes per capita: $108 (1997).
Education: High school graduation rate: 66.8% (2000); College graduation rate: 7.8% (2000).
Housing: Homeownership rate: 80.1% (2000); Median home value: $80,600 (2000); Median rent: $194 per month (2000); Median age of housing: 52 years (2000).
Transportation: Commute to work: 54.9% car, 0.6% public transportation, 6.8% walk, 30.4% work from home (2000); Travel time to work: 37.3% less than 15 minutes, 30.1% 15 to 30 minutes, 18.2% 30 to 45 minutes, 10.6% 45 to 60 minutes, 3.8% 60 minutes or more (2000)

KENDALL (village). Covers a land area of 0.742 square miles and a water area of 0 square miles. Located at 43.79° N. Lat.; 90.36° W. Long. Elevation is 1,021 feet.
Population: 469 (2000); Race: 98.7% White, 0.0% Black, 0.0% Asian, 0.0% American Indian and Alaska Native, 0.6% Hispanic of any race, 0.9% two or more races (2000); Density: 632.2 persons per square mile (2000); Age: 24.2% under 18, 19.1% over 64 (2000); Marriage status: 22.2% never married, 57.0% now married, 7.2% widowed, 13.6% divorced (2000); Foreign born: 0.6% (2000); Ancestry (includes multiple ancestries): 42.0% German, 17.3% Irish, 15.4% Norwegian, 7.9% English, 4.7% Other groups (2000).
Economy: In dairying and livestock region. Sportswear. Single-family building permits issued: 1 (2001) / 2 (2000); Multi-family building permits issued: 0 (2001) / 0 (2000); Employment by occupation: 7.5% management,

11.7% professional, 18.8% services, 17.6% sales, 0.0% farming, 10.0% construction, 34.3% production (2000).
Income: Per capita income: $21,073 (2000); Median household income: $36,250 (2000); Poverty rate: 11.6% (2000).
Taxes: Total city taxes per capita: $136 (1997); City property taxes per capita: $126 (1997).
Education: High school graduation rate: 77.5% (2000); College graduation rate: 9.2% (2000).
Housing: Homeownership rate: 77.3% (2000); Median home value: $51,800 (2000); Median rent: $362 per month (2000); Median age of housing: 60+ years (2000).
Transportation: Commute to work: 88.7% car, 0.0% public transportation, 4.6% walk, 6.7% work from home (2000); Travel time to work: 42.3% less than 15 minutes, 30.2% 15 to 30 minutes, 21.6% 30 to 45 minutes, 4.5% 45 to 60 minutes, 1.4% 60 minutes or more (2000)

LA GRANGE (town). Covers a land area of 29.880 square miles and a water area of 1.595 square miles. Located at 44.01° N. Lat.; 90.49° W. Long.
Population: 1,761 (2000); Race: 97.7% White, 0.6% Black, 0.2% Asian, 1.0% American Indian and Alaska Native, 0.1% Hispanic of any race, 0.4% two or more races (2000); Density: 58.9 persons per square mile (2000); Age: 27.2% under 18, 11.1% over 64 (2000); Marriage status: 19.7% never married, 69.5% now married, 3.1% widowed, 7.7% divorced (2000); Foreign born: 0.7% (2000); Ancestry (includes multiple ancestries): 54.4% German, 16.0% Irish, 13.4% Norwegian, 10.1% English, 4.7% Polish (2000).
Economy: Employment by occupation: 12.2% management, 17.2% professional, 16.6% services, 21.9% sales, 2.2% farming, 11.5% construction, 18.2% production (2000).
Income: Per capita income: $19,229 (2000); Median household income: $49,760 (2000); Poverty rate: 2.9% (2000).
Taxes: Total city taxes per capita: $53 (1997); City property taxes per capita: $53 (1997).
Education: High school graduation rate: 88.2% (2000); College graduation rate: 17.0% (2000).
Housing: Homeownership rate: 92.6% (2000); Median home value: $99,000 (2000); Median rent: $415 per month (2000); Median age of housing: 23 years (2000).
Transportation: Commute to work: 92.8% car, 0.0% public transportation, 2.8% walk, 4.1% work from home (2000); Travel time to work: 55.9% less than 15 minutes, 32.4% 15 to 30 minutes, 4.8% 30 to 45 minutes, 3.4% 45 to 60 minutes, 3.4% 60 minutes or more (2000)

LAFAYETTE (town). Covers a land area of 35.279 square miles and a water area of 0.041 square miles. Located at 44.00° N. Lat.; 90.73° W. Long.
Population: 318 (2000); Race: 92.7% White, 3.3% Black, 1.5% Asian, 0.0% American Indian and Alaska Native, 2.4% Hispanic of any race, 0.0% two or more races (2000); Density: 9.0 persons per square mile (2000); Age: 25.5% under 18, 5.2% over 64 (2000); Marriage status: 23.5% never married, 68.7% now married, 1.5% widowed, 6.3% divorced (2000); Foreign born: 4.0% (2000); Ancestry (includes multiple ancestries): 48.3% German, 17.6% Norwegian, 17.6% Irish, 8.5% Other groups, 6.7% English (2000).
Economy: Employment by occupation: 27.0% management, 13.5% professional, 26.4% services, 7.4% sales, 1.4% farming, 14.2% construction, 10.1% production (2000).
Income: Per capita income: $16,506 (2000); Median household income: $35,417 (2000); Poverty rate: 6.0% (2000).
Taxes: Total city taxes per capita: $56 (1997); City property taxes per capita: $56 (1997).
Education: High school graduation rate: 89.3% (2000); College graduation rate: 19.1% (2000).
Housing: Homeownership rate: 76.8% (2000); Median home value: $78,300 (2000); Median rent: $325 per month (2000); Median age of housing: 28 years (2000).
Transportation: Commute to work: 82.9% car, 0.0% public transportation, 2.9% walk, 11.2% work from home (2000); Travel time to work: 40.7% less than 15 minutes, 37.9% 15 to 30 minutes, 15.4% 30 to 45 minutes, 3.8% 45 to 60 minutes, 2.2% 60 minutes or more (2000)

LEON (town). Covers a land area of 35.766 square miles and a water area of 0 square miles. Located at 43.85° N. Lat.; 90.85° W. Long. Elevation is 783 feet.
Population: 858 (2000); Race: 99.4% White, 0.0% Black, 0.2% Asian, 0.0% American Indian and Alaska Native, 1.8% Hispanic of any race, 0.3% two or more races (2000); Density: 24.0 persons per square mile (2000); Age: 26.7% under 18, 9.0% over 64 (2000); Marriage status: 22.0% never married, 70.0% now married, 2.8% widowed, 5.2% divorced (2000); Foreign born: 0.0% (2000); Ancestry (includes multiple ancestries): 52.5% German, 26.4% Norwegian, 12.9% Irish, 7.2% English, 3.1% United States or American (2000).
Economy: Employment by occupation: 17.6% management, 7.6% professional, 16.5% services, 20.8% sales, 4.3% farming, 9.8% construction, 23.4% production (2000).
Income: Per capita income: $17,415 (2000); Median household income: $45,526 (2000); Poverty rate: 4.7% (2000).
Taxes: Total city taxes per capita: $132 (1997); City property taxes per capita: $131 (1997).
Education: High school graduation rate: 84.0% (2000); College graduation rate: 9.1% (2000).
Housing: Homeownership rate: 85.9% (2000); Median home value: $76,700 (2000); Median rent: $423 per month (2000); Median age of housing: 25 years (2000).
Transportation: Commute to work: 87.5% car, 1.1% public transportation, 3.7% walk, 6.9% work from home (2000); Travel time to work: 36.7% less than 15 minutes, 29.5% 15 to 30 minutes, 19.7% 30 to 45 minutes, 9.0% 45 to 60 minutes, 5.1% 60 minutes or more (2000)

LINCOLN (town). Covers a land area of 34.041 square miles and a water area of 0.829 square miles. Located at 44.12° N. Lat.; 90.49° W. Long.
Population: 827 (2000); Race: 98.5% White, 0.0% Black, 0.1% Asian, 0.7% American Indian and Alaska Native, 1.6% Hispanic of any race, 0.0% two or more races (2000); Density: 24.3 persons per square mile (2000); Age: 28.5% under 18, 10.5% over 64 (2000); Marriage status: 21.2% never married, 67.5% now married, 2.1% widowed, 9.2% divorced (2000); Foreign born: 0.2% (2000); Ancestry (includes multiple ancestries): 45.3% German, 12.2% Irish, 11.2% Norwegian, 10.8% English, 10.1% United States or American (2000).
Economy: Single-family building permits issued: 7 (2001) / 5 (2000); Multi-family building permits issued: 0 (2001) / 0 (2000); Employment by occupation: 14.7% management, 14.3% professional, 19.6% services, 15.9% sales, 4.9% farming, 7.9% construction, 22.7% production (2000).
Income: Per capita income: $17,286 (2000); Median household income: $37,422 (2000); Poverty rate: 8.8% (2000).
Taxes: Total city taxes per capita: $73 (1997); City property taxes per capita: $72 (1997).
Education: High school graduation rate: 86.5% (2000); College graduation rate: 11.0% (2000).
Housing: Homeownership rate: 79.8% (2000); Median home value: $85,000 (2000); Median rent: $440 per month (2000); Median age of housing: 20 years (2000).
Transportation: Commute to work: 90.0% car, 0.0% public transportation, 1.6% walk, 7.2% work from home (2000); Travel time to work: 29.8% less than 15 minutes, 53.9% 15 to 30 minutes, 10.3% 30 to 45 minutes, 1.0% 45 to 60 minutes, 5.0% 60 minutes or more (2000)

LITTLE FALLS (town). Covers a land area of 68.378 square miles and a water area of 0.420 square miles. Located at 44.09° N. Lat.; 90.87° W. Long.
Population: 1,334 (2000); Race: 99.2% White, 0.0% Black, 0.2% Asian, 0.0% American Indian and Alaska Native, 0.0% Hispanic of any race, 0.7% two or more races (2000); Density: 19.5 persons per square mile (2000); Age: 25.5% under 18, 13.2% over 64 (2000); Marriage status: 18.3% never married, 67.7% now married, 3.8% widowed, 10.2% divorced (2000); Foreign born: 1.6% (2000); Ancestry (includes multiple ancestries): 46.5% German, 19.8% Norwegian, 11.6% English, 10.9% Irish, 5.2% United States or American (2000).
Economy: Employment by occupation: 14.3% management, 6.2% professional, 17.2% services, 19.9% sales, 4.1% farming, 12.8% construction, 25.6% production (2000).
Income: Per capita income: $16,315 (2000); Median household income: $36,172 (2000); Poverty rate: 10.2% (2000).
Taxes: Total city taxes per capita: $112 (2000); City property taxes per capita: $109 (2000).
Education: High school graduation rate: 74.9% (2000); College graduation rate: 5.4% (2000).
Housing: Homeownership rate: 89.7% (2000); Median home value: $59,800 (2000); Median rent: $309 per month (2000); Median age of housing: 28 years (2000).
Transportation: Commute to work: 86.5% car, 0.0% public transportation, 4.0% walk, 9.4% work from home (2000); Travel time to work: 16.2% less than 15 minutes, 45.6% 15 to 30 minutes, 23.4% 30 to 45 minutes, 7.5% 45 to 60 minutes, 7.2% 60 minutes or more (2000)

MELVINA (village). Covers a land area of 0.475 square miles and a water area of 0 square miles. Located at 43.80° N. Lat.; 90.77° W. Long. Elevation is 860 feet.
Population: 93 (2000); Race: 100.0% White, 0.0% Black, 0.0% Asian, 0.0% American Indian and Alaska Native, 0.0% Hispanic of any race, 0.0% two or more races (2000); Density: 195.6 persons per square mile (2000); Age: 34.0% under 18, 11.3% over 64 (2000); Marriage status: 28.8% never married, 47.9% now married, 11.0% widowed, 12.3% divorced (2000); Foreign born: 0.0% (2000); Ancestry (includes multiple ancestries): 57.7% German, 26.8% Irish, 25.8% Norwegian, 6.2% Swedish, 2.1% United States or American (2000).
Economy: Employment by occupation: 17.6% management, 8.8% professional, 5.9% services, 5.9% sales, 0.0% farming, 5.9% construction, 55.9% production (2000).
Income: Per capita income: $11,791 (2000); Median household income: $21,250 (2000); Poverty rate: 17.5% (2000).
Taxes: Total city taxes per capita: $8 (1997); City property taxes per capita: $0 (1997).
Education: High school graduation rate: 69.6% (2000); College graduation rate: 7.1% (2000).
Housing: Homeownership rate: 84.6% (2000); Median home value: $27,100 (2000); Median rent: $250 per month (2000); Median age of housing: 60+ years (2000).
Transportation: Commute to work: 94.1% car, 0.0% public transportation, 0.0% walk, 5.9% work from home (2000); Travel time to work: 6.3% less than 15 minutes, 65.6% 15 to 30 minutes, 18.8% 30 to 45 minutes, 9.4% 45 to 60 minutes, 0.0% 60 minutes or more (2000)

NEW LYME (town). Covers a land area of 35.574 square miles and a water area of 0.491 square miles. Located at 44.14° N. Lat.; 90.70° W. Long.
Population: 141 (2000); Race: 100.0% White, 0.0% Black, 0.0% Asian, 0.0% American Indian and Alaska Native, 0.0% Hispanic of any race, 0.0% two or more races (2000); Density: 4.0 persons per square mile (2000); Age: 19.6% under 18, 24.3% over 64 (2000); Marriage status: 16.5% never married, 75.2% now married, 3.3% widowed, 5.0% divorced (2000); Foreign born: 0.0% (2000); Ancestry (includes multiple ancestries): 41.2% German, 11.5% Irish, 10.8% Norwegian, 8.1% English, 7.4% Other groups (2000).
Economy: Employment by occupation: 31.1% management, 2.7% professional, 21.6% services, 8.1% sales, 10.8% farming, 0.0% construction, 25.7% production (2000).
Income: Per capita income: $20,306 (2000); Median household income: $39,167 (2000); Poverty rate: 13.5% (2000).
Taxes: Total city taxes per capita: $53 (1997); City property taxes per capita: $53 (1997).
Education: High school graduation rate: 76.3% (2000); College graduation rate: 10.5% (2000).
Housing: Homeownership rate: 78.7% (2000); Median home value: $86,400 (2000); Median rent: $375 per month (2000); Median age of housing: 26 years (2000).
Transportation: Commute to work: 81.9% car, 0.0% public transportation, 2.8% walk, 11.1% work from home (2000); Travel time to work: 29.7% less than 15 minutes, 51.6% 15 to 30 minutes, 9.4% 30 to 45 minutes, 6.3% 45 to 60 minutes, 3.1% 60 minutes or more (2000)

NORWALK (village). Covers a land area of 1.050 square miles and a water area of 0 square miles. Located at 43.83° N. Lat.; 90.62° W. Long. Elevation is 1,030 feet.
Population: 653 (2000); Race: 69.4% White, 0.0% Black, 0.0% Asian, 0.0% American Indian and Alaska Native, 34.7% Hispanic of any race, 2.6% two or more races (2000); Density: 621.9 persons per square mile (2000); Age: 27.2% under 18, 14.8% over 64 (2000); Marriage status: 28.1% never married, 55.7% now married, 8.9% widowed, 7.3% divorced (2000); Foreign born: 26.3% (2000); Ancestry (includes multiple ancestries): 35.8% German, 33.0% Other groups, 12.1% Norwegian, 5.6% Irish, 5.0% English (2000).
Economy: In farm and dairy area. Single-family building permits issued: 0 (2001) / 0 (2000); Multi-family building permits issued: 0 (2001) / 0 (2000); Employment by occupation: 5.8% management, 6.2% professional, 13.3% services, 17.2% sales, 1.9% farming, 8.8% construction, 46.8% production (2000).
Income: Per capita income: $13,097 (2000); Median household income: $32,143 (2000); Poverty rate: 16.6% (2000).
Taxes: Total city taxes per capita: $87 (2000); City property taxes per capita: $83 (2000).
Education: High school graduation rate: 64.3% (2000); College graduation rate: 6.9% (2000).
Housing: Homeownership rate: 64.6% (2000); Median home value: $47,900 (2000); Median rent: $389 per month (2000); Median age of housing: 60+ years (2000).
Transportation: Commute to work: 89.6% car, 1.6% public transportation, 6.8% walk, 1.3% work from home (2000); Travel time to work: 57.1% less than 15 minutes, 26.7% 15 to 30 minutes, 9.9% 30 to 45 minutes, 1.0% 45 to 60 minutes, 5.3% 60 minutes or more (2000)

OAKDALE (village). Covers a land area of 0.841 square miles and a water area of 0 square miles. Located at 43.95° N. Lat.; 90.37° W. Long. Elevation is 956 feet.
Population: 297 (2000); Race: 99.2% White, 0.0% Black, 0.0% Asian, 0.0% American Indian and Alaska Native, 0.0% Hispanic of any race, 0.8% two or more races (2000); Density: 352.9 persons per square mile (2000); Age: 25.3% under 18, 14.2% over 64 (2000); Marriage status: 17.7% never married, 53.2% now married, 6.4% widowed, 22.7% divorced (2000); Foreign born: 0.0% (2000); Ancestry (includes multiple ancestries): 46.0% German, 11.9% Norwegian, 10.0% English, 9.6% Irish, 6.5% Scottish (2000).
Economy: Single-family building permits issued: 1 (2001) / 3 (2000); Multi-family building permits issued: 0 (2001) / 0 (2000); Employment by occupation: 4.4% management, 9.6% professional, 16.2% services, 25.7% sales, 0.0% farming, 11.8% construction, 32.4% production (2000).
Income: Per capita income: $14,440 (2000); Median household income: $35,500 (2000); Poverty rate: 9.6% (2000).
Taxes: Total city taxes per capita: $344 (1997); City property taxes per capita: $318 (1997).
Education: High school graduation rate: 86.7% (2000); College graduation rate: 0.6% (2000).
Housing: Homeownership rate: 74.5% (2000); Median home value: $80,000 (2000); Median rent: $350 per month (2000); Median age of housing: 29 years (2000).
Transportation: Commute to work: 86.4% car, 1.5% public transportation, 10.6% walk, 1.5% work from home (2000); Travel time to work: 48.5% less than 15 minutes, 35.4% 15 to 30 minutes, 7.7% 30 to 45 minutes, 1.5% 45 to 60 minutes, 6.9% 60 minutes or more (2000)

OAKDALE (town). Covers a land area of 35.639 square miles and a water area of 0.076 square miles. Located at 43.94° N. Lat.; 90.36° W. Long. Elevation is 956 feet.
Population: 679 (2000); Race: 96.4% White, 0.2% Black, 0.5% Asian, 1.6% American Indian and Alaska Native, 0.5% Hispanic of any race, 1.4% two or more races (2000); Density: 19.1 persons per square mile (2000); Age: 30.6% under 18, 12.1% over 64 (2000); Marriage status: 16.7% never married, 72.7% now married, 4.4% widowed, 6.1% divorced (2000); Foreign born: 1.7% (2000); Ancestry (includes multiple ancestries): 51.4% German, 8.9% Norwegian, 7.9% English, 6.5% Irish, 5.3% United States or American (2000).
Economy: Employment by occupation: 19.0% management, 15.5% professional, 12.6% services, 21.0% sales, 1.7% farming, 9.8% construction, 20.4% production (2000).
Income: Per capita income: $19,199 (2000); Median household income: $47,273 (2000); Poverty rate: 7.8% (2000).
Taxes: Total city taxes per capita: $146 (1997); City property taxes per capita: $146 (1997).
Education: High school graduation rate: 88.8% (2000); College graduation rate: 16.8% (2000).
Housing: Homeownership rate: 81.1% (2000); Median home value: $96,100 (2000); Median rent: $192 per month (2000); Median age of housing: 28 years (2000).
Transportation: Commute to work: 87.6% car, 0.0% public transportation, 2.9% walk, 9.5% work from home (2000); Travel time to work: 34.5% less than 15 minutes, 46.3% 15 to 30 minutes, 9.6% 30 to 45 minutes, 2.6% 45 to 60 minutes, 7.0% 60 minutes or more (2000)

PORTLAND (town). Covers a land area of 35.938 square miles and a water area of 0.006 square miles. Located at 43.75° N. Lat.; 90.84° W. Long. Elevation is 1,312 feet.
Population: 686 (2000); Race: 98.7% White, 0.0% Black, 0.0% Asian, 0.0% American Indian and Alaska Native, 1.2% Hispanic of any race, 0.6% two or more races (2000); Density: 19.1 persons per square mile (2000); Age: 30.3% under 18, 15.1% over 64 (2000); Marriage status: 24.8% never married, 64.5% now married, 6.4% widowed, 4.3% divorced (2000); Foreign born: 0.0% (2000); Ancestry (includes multiple ancestries): 53.2% German, 41.4% Norwegian, 8.9% Czech, 5.1% English, 4.1% Irish (2000).

Economy: Employment by occupation: 21.9% management, 11.2% professional, 11.8% services, 17.5% sales, 7.4% farming, 13.3% construction, 16.9% production (2000).
Income: Per capita income: $16,998 (2000); Median household income: $36,250 (2000); Poverty rate: 13.6% (2000).
Taxes: Total city taxes per capita: $176 (1997); City property taxes per capita: $176 (1997).
Education: High school graduation rate: 79.5% (2000); College graduation rate: 14.1% (2000).
Housing: Homeownership rate: 86.8% (2000); Median home value: $84,200 (2000); Median rent: $300 per month (2000); Median age of housing: 44 years (2000).
Transportation: Commute to work: 77.1% car, 0.0% public transportation, 3.9% walk, 19.0% work from home (2000); Travel time to work: 32.4% less than 15 minutes, 37.5% 15 to 30 minutes, 15.4% 30 to 45 minutes, 9.2% 45 to 60 minutes, 5.5% 60 minutes or more (2000)

RIDGEVILLE (town). Covers a land area of 34.200 square miles and a water area of 0.038 square miles. Located at 43.84° N. Lat.; 90.58° W. Long.
Population: 491 (2000); Race: 96.3% White, 0.0% Black, 0.4% Asian, 0.0% American Indian and Alaska Native, 4.9% Hispanic of any race, 0.4% two or more races (2000); Density: 14.4 persons per square mile (2000); Age: 32.1% under 18, 11.0% over 64 (2000); Marriage status: 27.1% never married, 62.6% now married, 3.6% widowed, 6.6% divorced (2000); Foreign born: 3.7% (2000); Ancestry (includes multiple ancestries): 52.0% German, 19.7% Irish, 14.6% Norwegian, 6.1% United States or American, 5.9% English (2000).
Economy: Employment by occupation: 20.0% management, 10.0% professional, 16.0% services, 17.2% sales, 6.4% farming, 12.0% construction, 18.4% production (2000).
Income: Per capita income: $15,499 (2000); Median household income: $35,000 (2000); Poverty rate: 20.6% (2000).
Taxes: Total city taxes per capita: $182 (1997); City property taxes per capita: $182 (1997).
Education: High school graduation rate: 79.2% (2000); College graduation rate: 12.7% (2000).
Housing: Homeownership rate: 81.7% (2000); Median home value: $67,500 (2000); Median rent: $315 per month (2000); Median age of housing: 60+ years (2000).
Transportation: Commute to work: 79.6% car, 0.0% public transportation, 3.2% walk, 14.8% work from home (2000); Travel time to work: 36.2% less than 15 minutes, 31.9% 15 to 30 minutes, 13.6% 30 to 45 minutes, 15.0% 45 to 60 minutes, 3.3% 60 minutes or more (2000)

SCOTT (town). Covers a land area of 33.931 square miles and a water area of 2.618 square miles. Located at 44.10° N. Lat.; 90.38° W. Long.
Population: 117 (2000); Race: 97.6% White, 0.0% Black, 0.0% Asian, 2.4% American Indian and Alaska Native, 2.4% Hispanic of any race, 0.0% two or more races (2000); Density: 3.4 persons per square mile (2000); Age: 32.3% under 18, 4.7% over 64 (2000); Marriage status: 20.0% never married, 65.6% now married, 0.0% widowed, 14.4% divorced (2000); Foreign born: 0.0% (2000); Ancestry (includes multiple ancestries): 29.1% German, 13.4% Irish, 11.8% Other groups, 11.0% Norwegian, 6.3% Italian (2000).
Economy: Single-family building permits issued: 0 (2001) / 2 (2000); Multi-family building permits issued: 0 (2001) / 0 (2000); Employment by occupation: 24.0% management, 0.0% professional, 22.0% services, 4.0% sales, 10.0% farming, 12.0% construction, 28.0% production (2000).
Income: Per capita income: $11,498 (2000); Median household income: $25,313 (2000); Poverty rate: 12.2% (2000).
Taxes: Total city taxes per capita: $85 (2000); City property taxes per capita: $77 (2000).
Education: High school graduation rate: 72.2% (2000); College graduation rate: 15.3% (2000).
Housing: Homeownership rate: 80.5% (2000); Median home value: $75,000 (2000); Median rent: $288 per month (2000); Median age of housing: 25 years (2000).
Transportation: Commute to work: 66.7% car, 0.0% public transportation, 4.2% walk, 29.2% work from home (2000); Travel time to work: 26.5% less than 15 minutes, 32.4% 15 to 30 minutes, 26.5% 30 to 45 minutes, 14.7% 45 to 60 minutes, 0.0% 60 minutes or more (2000)

SHELDON (town). Covers a land area of 35.310 square miles and a water area of 0 square miles. Located at 43.74° N. Lat.; 90.60° W. Long.
Population: 682 (2000); Race: 96.2% White, 0.8% Black, 0.0% Asian, 2.0% American Indian and Alaska Native, 0.0% Hispanic of any race, 1.1% two or more races (2000); Density: 19.3 persons per square mile (2000); Age: 41.6% under 18, 6.8% over 64 (2000); Marriage status: 25.0% never married, 63.8% now married, 3.6% widowed, 7.5% divorced (2000); Foreign born: 2.8% (2000); Ancestry (includes multiple ancestries): 54.1% German, 8.4% Norwegian, 7.1% Irish, 6.9% Swiss, 4.9% English (2000).
Economy: Employment by occupation: 23.3% management, 16.3% professional, 10.1% services, 12.4% sales, 7.4% farming, 10.5% construction, 20.2% production (2000).
Income: Per capita income: $11,049 (2000); Median household income: $32,361 (2000); Poverty rate: 28.6% (2000).
Taxes: Total city taxes per capita: $147 (1997); City property taxes per capita: $147 (1997).
Education: High school graduation rate: 67.8% (2000); College graduation rate: 13.1% (2000).
Housing: Homeownership rate: 76.5% (2000); Median home value: $104,200 (2000); Median rent: $400 per month (2000); Median age of housing: 52 years (2000).
Transportation: Commute to work: 64.3% car, 0.0% public transportation, 7.1% walk, 27.5% work from home (2000); Travel time to work: 42.7% less than 15 minutes, 22.2% 15 to 30 minutes, 23.8% 30 to 45 minutes, 7.0% 45 to 60 minutes, 4.3% 60 minutes or more (2000)

SPARTA (city). Covers a land area of 5.466 square miles and a water area of 0.058 square miles. Located at 43.94° N. Lat.; 90.81° W. Long. Elevation is 793 feet.
History: Sparta grew up about 1850 at a crossroads when Frank Petit, the first settler, offered free lots to anyone who would build a house. When Monroe County was created in 1854, the community that had developed around Petit's house became the county seat. Grist mills, an ironworks, and factories for paper, woolens, furniture and farm machinery were established in the 1850's. The discovery of mineral springs here in the 1870's gave Sparta a brief period as a popular health resort, offering Turkish, Russian, sitz, and plunge baths.
Population: 8,648 (2000); Race: 96.2% White, 0.5% Black, 0.9% Asian, 1.0% American Indian and Alaska Native, 1.9% Hispanic of any race, 0.3% two or more races (2000); Density: 1,582.2 persons per square mile (2000); Age: 25.6% under 18, 15.9% over 64 (2000); Marriage status: 25.6% never married, 53.4% now married, 10.9% widowed, 10.1% divorced (2000); Foreign born: 1.5% (2000); Ancestry (includes multiple ancestries): 45.1% German, 17.2% Norwegian, 15.6% Irish, 7.6% English, 5.8% Other groups (2000).
Economy: Single-family building permits issued: 20 (2001) / 18 (2000); Multi-family building permits issued: 23 (2001) / 24 (2000); Employment by occupation: 10.8% management, 15.4% professional, 18.5% services, 23.9% sales, 0.3% farming, 9.1% construction, 21.9% production (2000).
Income: Per capita income: $18,238 (2000); Median household income: $33,397 (2000); Poverty rate: 11.3% (2000).
Taxes: Total city taxes per capita: $252 (1997); City property taxes per capita: $225 (1997).
Education: High school graduation rate: 81.1% (2000); College graduation rate: 15.8% (2000).

School District(s)

Sparta Area (PK-12)
2000 Enrollment: 2,783 608-269-3151
Housing: Homeownership rate: 62.7% (2000); Median home value: $74,600 (2000); Median rent: $378 per month (2000); Median age of housing: 31 years (2000).
Hospitals: Franciscan Skemp Healthcare-Sparta Campus Hospital (25 beds)
Safety: Violent crime rate: 18.4 per 10,000 population; Property crime rate: 336.4 per 10,000 population (2001).
Newspapers: The Sparta Herald (1 x week); Monroe County Democrat (1 x week); Foxxy Shopper (1 x week)
Transportation: Commute to work: 91.4% car, 0.3% public transportation, 4.4% walk, 2.3% work from home (2000); Travel time to work: 53.8% less than 15 minutes, 25.0% 15 to 30 minutes, 12.1% 30 to 45 minutes, 3.7% 45 to 60 minutes, 5.4% 60 minutes or more (2000)
Additional Information Contacts
Sparta Chamber of Commerce 608-269-4123

SPARTA (town). Covers a land area of 49.274 square miles and a water area of 0 square miles. Located at 43.94° N. Lat.; 90.84° W. Long. Elevation is 793 feet.
History: Settled c.1850, incorporated 1883.
Population: 2,750 (2000); Race: 98.8% White, 0.0% Black, 0.3% Asian, 0.1% American Indian and Alaska Native, 0.2% Hispanic of any race, 0.9% two or more races (2000); Density: 55.8 persons per square mile (2000); Age 26.9% under 18, 14.0% over 64 (2000); Marriage status: 19.3% never

married, 63.6% now married, 8.3% widowed, 8.8% divorced (2000); Foreign born: 1.0% (2000); Ancestry (includes multiple ancestries): 55.5% German, 21.3% Norwegian, 10.7% Irish, 7.2% English, 4.3% United States or American (2000).
Economy: In agricultural area: tobacco; dairy products; poultry. Creameries, tobacco warehouses. Manufacturing: machinery, fabricated metal products, plating and spray painting, plastics, consumer goods. Seat of state school for children. US Camp McCoy Military Reservation to Northeast. Employment by occupation: 12.9% management, 17.7% professional, 12.8% services, 27.0% sales, 1.2% farming, 8.9% construction, 19.6% production (2000).
Income: Per capita income: $19,488 (2000); Median household income: $49,769 (2000); Poverty rate: 4.0% (2000).
Taxes: Total city taxes per capita: $38 (1997); City property taxes per capita: $34 (1997).
Education: High school graduation rate: 83.1% (2000); College graduation rate: 16.8% (2000).
Housing: Homeownership rate: 88.8% (2000); Median home value: $98,400 (2000); Median rent: $422 per month (2000); Median age of housing: 23 years (2000).
Transportation: Commute to work: 93.5% car, 0.3% public transportation, 1.0% walk, 5.0% work from home (2000); Travel time to work: 48.3% less than 15 minutes, 29.2% 15 to 30 minutes, 15.4% 30 to 45 minutes, 4.4% 45 to 60 minutes, 2.8% 60 minutes or more (2000)

TOMAH (city). Covers a land area of 7.332 square miles and a water area of 0.393 square miles. Located at 43.98° N. Lat.; 90.50° W. Long. Elevation is 980 feet.
Population: 8,419 (2000); Race: 94.7% White, 1.5% Black, 0.9% Asian, 0.8% American Indian and Alaska Native, 1.4% Hispanic of any race, 1.2% two or more races (2000); Density: 1,148.2 persons per square mile (2000); Age: 25.7% under 18, 17.7% over 64 (2000); Marriage status: 21.7% never married, 54.6% now married, 10.3% widowed, 13.4% divorced (2000); Foreign born: 1.9% (2000); Ancestry (includes multiple ancestries): 41.0% German, 12.1% Irish, 10.2% Norwegian, 8.2% English, 7.6% Other groups (2000).
Economy: Single-family building permits issued: 8 (2001) / 11 (2000); Multi-family building permits issued: 22 (2001) / 30 (2000); Employment by occupation: 11.2% management, 13.1% professional, 20.2% services, 23.4% sales, 0.5% farming, 7.8% construction, 23.8% production (2000).
Income: Per capita income: $17,409 (2000); Median household income: $31,986 (2000); Poverty rate: 12.7% (2000).
Taxes: Total city taxes per capita: $354 (1997); City property taxes per capita: $286 (1997).
Education: High school graduation rate: 82.9% (2000); College graduation rate: 13.2% (2000).

School District(s)

Tomah Area (PK-12)
2000 Enrollment: 3,106 608-374-7210

Housing: Homeownership rate: 60.4% (2000); Median home value: $76,400 (2000); Median rent: $410 per month (2000); Median age of housing: 31 years (2000).
Hospitals: Tomah Memorial Hospital (49 beds); Veterans Affairs Medical Center (331 beds)
Safety: Violent crime rate: 23.6 per 10,000 population; Property crime rate: 449.3 per 10,000 population (2001).
Newspapers: Tomah Monitor Herald (1 x week); The Tomah Journal (2 x week)
Transportation: Commute to work: 90.1% car, 0.4% public transportation, 5.7% walk, 2.8% work from home (2000); Travel time to work: 69.6% less than 15 minutes, 17.9% 15 to 30 minutes, 7.8% 30 to 45 minutes, 2.5% 45 to 60 minutes, 2.2% 60 minutes or more (2000); Amtrak: Service available.

Additional Information Contacts

Tomah Chamber of Commerce 608-372-2166

TOMAH (town). Covers a land area of 31.485 square miles and a water area of 0.003 square miles. Located at 43.95° N. Lat.; 90.48° W. Long. Elevation is 980 feet.
History: Incorporated 1883.
Population: 1,194 (2000); Race: 98.9% White, 0.0% Black, 0.4% Asian, 0.2% American Indian and Alaska Native, 0.4% Hispanic of any race, 0.6% two or more races (2000); Density: 37.9 persons per square mile (2000); Age: 30.6% under 18, 10.2% over 64 (2000); Marriage status: 19.9% never married, 68.6% now married, 4.5% widowed, 6.9% divorced (2000); Foreign born: 1.0% (2000); Ancestry (includes multiple ancestries): 51.8% German, 13.9% Irish, 9.6% Norwegian, 5.4% United States or American, 5.0% Polish (2000).
Economy: In dairy and livestock region; processes lumber, dairy products. Manufacturing: tempered glass, ice fishing equipment, bedding, apparel. Railroad junction to West at Tunnel City. Fort McCoy Military Reservation to West. Employment by occupation: 12.4% management, 15.1% professional, 11.8% services, 23.5% sales, 2.2% farming, 8.8% construction, 25.9% production (2000).
Income: Per capita income: $18,065 (2000); Median household income: $46,923 (2000); Poverty rate: 8.3% (2000).
Taxes: Total city taxes per capita: $47 (1997); City property taxes per capita: $47 (1997).
Education: High school graduation rate: 85.6% (2000); College graduation rate: 14.3% (2000).
Housing: Homeownership rate: 85.5% (2000); Median home value: $94,400 (2000); Median rent: $383 per month (2000); Median age of housing: 27 years (2000).
Transportation: Commute to work: 84.2% car, 0.7% public transportation, 3.1% walk, 10.9% work from home (2000); Travel time to work: 52.5% less than 15 minutes, 34.4% 15 to 30 minutes, 6.0% 30 to 45 minutes, 1.8% 45 to 60 minutes, 5.2% 60 minutes or more (2000); Amtrak: Service available.

WARRENS (village). Aka Warren. Covers a land area of 0.590 square miles and a water area of 0.017 square miles. Located at 44.13° N. Lat.; 90.50° W. Long. Elevation is 1,015 feet.
Population: 286 (2000); Race: 93.5% White, 0.0% Black, 0.0% Asian, 0.4% American Indian and Alaska Native, 1.8% Hispanic of any race, 4.4% two or more races (2000); Density: 484.5 persons per square mile (2000); Age: 29.1% under 18, 17.8% over 64 (2000); Marriage status: 25.6% never married, 55.1% now married, 9.7% widowed, 9.7% divorced (2000); Foreign born: 0.0% (2000); Ancestry (includes multiple ancestries): 36.7% German, 15.3% Irish, 10.9% Norwegian, 9.8% United States or American, 5.1% Other groups (2000).
Economy: Central Wisconsin Conservation Area to East. Dairying, alfalfa, corn. Manufacturing of cranberry equipment. Single-family building permits issued: 3 (2001) / 0 (2000); Multi-family building permits issued: 0 (2001) / 0 (2000); Employment by occupation: 1.6% management, 10.9% professional, 20.9% services, 17.8% sales, 2.3% farming, 8.5% construction, 38.0% production (2000).
Income: Per capita income: $13,005 (2000); Median household income: $29,464 (2000); Poverty rate: 10.7% (2000).
Taxes: Total city taxes per capita: $34 (1997); City property taxes per capita: $28 (1997).
Education: High school graduation rate: 68.4% (2000); College graduation rate: 3.4% (2000).
Housing: Homeownership rate: 73.8% (2000); Median home value: $55,200 (2000); Median rent: $325 per month (2000); Median age of housing: 48 years (2000).
Transportation: Commute to work: 95.4% car, 0.0% public transportation, 4.6% walk, 0.0% work from home (2000); Travel time to work: 22.9% less than 15 minutes, 62.6% 15 to 30 minutes, 9.9% 30 to 45 minutes, 3.1% 45 to 60 minutes, 1.5% 60 minutes or more (2000)

WELLINGTON (town). Covers a land area of 35.399 square miles and a water area of 0 square miles. Located at 43.76° N. Lat.; 90.48° W. Long.
Population: 544 (2000); Race: 99.3% White, 0.0% Black, 0.0% Asian, 0.0% American Indian and Alaska Native, 0.9% Hispanic of any race, 0.4% two or more races (2000); Density: 15.4 persons per square mile (2000); Age: 33.7% under 18, 9.8% over 64 (2000); Marriage status: 23.7% never married, 67.1% now married, 3.4% widowed, 5.8% divorced (2000); Foreign born: 1.1% (2000); Ancestry (includes multiple ancestries): 60.4% German, 14.6% Norwegian, 8.2% Irish, 5.9% English, 4.8% Polish (2000).
Economy: Employment by occupation: 36.4% management, 10.7% professional, 9.2% services, 17.6% sales, 4.4% farming, 7.0% construction, 14.7% production (2000).
Income: Per capita income: $14,962 (2000); Median household income: $36,146 (2000); Poverty rate: 16.5% (2000).
Taxes: Total city taxes per capita: $107 (1997); City property taxes per capita: $107 (1997).
Education: High school graduation rate: 83.3% (2000); College graduation rate: 11.9% (2000).
Housing: Homeownership rate: 83.7% (2000); Median home value: $80,000 (2000); Median rent: $288 per month (2000); Median age of housing: 60+ years (2000).
Transportation: Commute to work: 66.5% car, 0.0% public transportation, 4.6% walk, 28.1% work from home (2000); Travel time to work: 35.4% less than 15 minutes, 25.9% 15 to 30 minutes, 20.6% 30 to 45 minutes, 6.3% 45 to 60 minutes, 11.6% 60 minutes or more (2000)

WELLS (town). Covers a land area of 35.727 square miles and a water area of 0 square miles. Located at 43.84° N. Lat.; 90.71° W. Long.
Population: 529 (2000); Race: 98.7% White, 0.0% Black, 0.0% Asian, 0.0% American Indian and Alaska Native, 1.1% Hispanic of any race, 0.7% two or more races (2000); Density: 14.8 persons per square mile (2000); Age: 30.3% under 18, 12.3% over 64 (2000); Marriage status: 26.5% never married, 66.0% now married, 1.9% widowed, 5.6% divorced (2000); Foreign born: 0.6% (2000); Ancestry (includes multiple ancestries): 48.0% German, 16.5% Norwegian, 10.3% Irish, 6.3% English, 5.1% Danish (2000).
Economy: Employment by occupation: 19.2% management, 14.5% professional, 12.1% services, 17.2% sales, 6.1% farming, 11.1% construction, 19.9% production (2000).
Income: Per capita income: $14,669 (2000); Median household income: $37,614 (2000); Poverty rate: 10.7% (2000).
Taxes: Total city taxes per capita: $150 (1997); City property taxes per capita: $150 (1997).
Education: High school graduation rate: 84.4% (2000); College graduation rate: 13.3% (2000).
Housing: Homeownership rate: 87.9% (2000); Median home value: $91,300 (2000); Median rent: $358 per month (2000); Median age of housing: 35 years (2000).
Transportation: Commute to work: 78.8% car, 0.0% public transportation, 4.4% walk, 16.8% work from home (2000); Travel time to work: 24.3% less than 15 minutes, 44.5% 15 to 30 minutes, 24.3% 30 to 45 minutes, 6.1% 45 to 60 minutes, 0.8% 60 minutes or more (2000)

WILTON (village). Covers a land area of 0.846 square miles and a water area of 0 square miles. Located at 43.81° N. Lat.; 90.52° W. Long. Elevation is 995 feet.
Population: 519 (2000); Race: 96.0% White, 0.0% Black, 0.0% Asian, 0.0% American Indian and Alaska Native, 9.8% Hispanic of any race, 0.7% two or more races (2000); Density: 613.6 persons per square mile (2000); Age: 31.0% under 18, 14.9% over 64 (2000); Marriage status: 28.7% never married, 51.3% now married, 11.6% widowed, 8.4% divorced (2000); Foreign born: 7.7% (2000); Ancestry (includes multiple ancestries): 48.1% German, 18.0% Irish, 10.0% Other groups, 9.7% Norwegian, 5.8% United States or American (2000).
Economy: Single-family building permits issued: 2 (2001) / 2 (2000); Multi-family building permits issued: 0 (2001) / 0 (2000); Employment by occupation: 8.9% management, 8.9% professional, 15.5% services, 21.8% sales, 0.7% farming, 9.6% construction, 34.7% production (2000).
Income: Per capita income: $15,998 (2000); Median household income: $37,721 (2000); Poverty rate: 9.7% (2000).
Taxes: Total city taxes per capita: $98 (1997); City property taxes per capita: $88 (1997).
Education: High school graduation rate: 77.8% (2000); College graduation rate: 7.7% (2000).
Housing: Homeownership rate: 67.9% (2000); Median home value: $60,800 (2000); Median rent: $294 per month (2000); Median age of housing: 58 years (2000).
Transportation: Commute to work: 92.2% car, 0.0% public transportation, 5.2% walk, 2.6% work from home (2000); Travel time to work: 28.4% less than 15 minutes, 46.7% 15 to 30 minutes, 15.7% 30 to 45 minutes, 3.1% 45 to 60 minutes, 6.1% 60 minutes or more (2000)

WILTON (town). Covers a land area of 34.946 square miles and a water area of 0 square miles. Located at 43.85° N. Lat.; 90.48° W. Long. Elevation is 995 feet.
Population: 925 (2000); Race: 99.8% White, 0.2% Black, 0.0% Asian, 0.0% American Indian and Alaska Native, 0.0% Hispanic of any race, 0.0% two or more races (2000); Density: 26.5 persons per square mile (2000); Age: 38.8% under 18, 9.0% over 64 (2000); Marriage status: 28.2% never married, 63.6% now married, 4.7% widowed, 3.6% divorced (2000); Foreign born: 0.2% (2000); Ancestry (includes multiple ancestries): 45.5% German, 6.7% United States or American, 5.3% Irish, 4.4% Norwegian, 4.4% English (2000).
Economy: In dairy and livestock area. Employment by occupation: 29.6% management, 7.2% professional, 11.9% services, 19.1% sales, 8.1% farming, 7.2% construction, 16.8% production (2000).
Income: Per capita income: $10,498 (2000); Median household income: $27,917 (2000); Poverty rate: 45.6% (2000).
Taxes: Total city taxes per capita: $62 (1997); City property taxes per capita: $62 (1997).
Education: High school graduation rate: 66.0% (2000); College graduation rate: 5.6% (2000).
Housing: Homeownership rate: 81.8% (2000); Median home value: $60,000 (2000); Median rent: $388 per month (2000); Median age of housing: 32 years (2000).
Transportation: Commute to work: 55.7% car, 0.0% public transportation, 7.8% walk, 35.4% work from home (2000); Travel time to work: 22.0% less than 15 minutes, 53.4% 15 to 30 minutes, 17.9% 30 to 45 minutes, 4.9% 45 to 60 minutes, 1.8% 60 minutes or more (2000)

WYEVILLE (village). Covers a land area of 0.594 square miles and a water area of 0 square miles. Located at 44.02° N. Lat.; 90.38° W. Long. Elevation is 925 feet.
Population: 146 (2000); Race: 92.5% White, 0.0% Black, 0.0% Asian, 6.3% American Indian and Alaska Native, 0.0% Hispanic of any race, 1.3% two or more races (2000); Density: 245.7 persons per square mile (2000); Age: 31.9% under 18, 13.1% over 64 (2000); Marriage status: 27.9% never married, 57.4% now married, 13.2% widowed, 1.6% divorced (2000); Foreign born: 1.9% (2000); Ancestry (includes multiple ancestries): 36.3% German, 10.6% Other groups, 8.1% Irish, 8.1% Scotch-Irish, 8.1% United States or American (2000).
Economy: Railroad junction in dairy and livestock area. Central Wisconsin Conservation Area and Necedah National Wildlife Refuge to Northeast. Single-family building permits issued: 0 (2001) / 0 (2000); Multi-family building permits issued: 0 (2001) / 0 (2000); Employment by occupation: 2.5% management, 12.5% professional, 40.0% services, 6.3% sales, 2.5% farming, 15.0% construction, 21.3% production (2000).
Income: Per capita income: $14,344 (2000); Median household income: $38,750 (2000); Poverty rate: 13.1% (2000).
Taxes: Total city taxes per capita: $53 (1997); City property taxes per capita: $46 (1997).
Education: High school graduation rate: 68.0% (2000); College graduation rate: 9.3% (2000).
Housing: Homeownership rate: 87.7% (2000); Median home value: $49,300 (2000); Median rent: $413 per month (2000); Median age of housing: 55 years (2000).
Transportation: Commute to work: 100.0% car, 0.0% public transportation, 0.0% walk, 0.0% work from home (2000); Travel time to work: 15.0% less than 15 minutes, 67.5% 15 to 30 minutes, 2.5% 30 to 45 minutes, 1.3% 45 to 60 minutes, 13.8% 60 minutes or more (2000)

Oconto County

Located in northeastern Wisconsin; bounded on the east by Green Bay; drained by the Oconto River. Covers a land area of 998.00 square miles, a water area of 151.10 square miles, and is located in the Central Time Zone. The county government was organized in 1851. County seat is Oconto.

Weather Station: Breed 6 SSE — Elevation: 859 feet

	Jan	Feb	Mar	Apr	May	Jun	Jul	Aug	Sep	Oct	Nov	Dec
High	24	30	40	55	69	78	82	79	70	58	41	29
Low	2	6	18	30	41	50	56	54	45	35	23	11
Precip	1.4	1.0	2.2	2.9	3.7	3.5	3.5	3.9	3.7	2.6	2.5	1.6
Snow	14.3	8.5	10.4	4.0	0.3	0.0	0.0	0.0	tr	0.2	5.8	12.9

High and Low temperatures in degrees Fahrenheit; Precipitation and Snow in inches

Weather Station: Lakewood 3 NE — Elevation: 1,289 feet

	Jan	Feb	Mar	Apr	May	Jun	Jul	Aug	Sep	Oct	Nov	Dec
High	23	29	39	54	69	77	80	78	68	56	39	27
Low	2	6	16	29	40	49	54	52	44	33	22	9
Precip	1.4	1.0	2.3	2.9	3.6	3.7	3.4	3.9	4.0	2.8	2.5	1.7
Snow	16.6	9.0	12.0	4.4	0.6	0.0	0.0	0.0	tr	0.3	6.5	15.3

High and Low temperatures in degrees Fahrenheit; Precipitation and Snow in inches

Weather Station: Oconto 4 W — Elevation: 659 feet

	Jan	Feb	Mar	Apr	May	Jun	Jul	Aug	Sep	Oct	Nov	Dec
High	24	29	39	53	67	76	81	78	70	58	42	29
Low	4	8	19	31	42	52	57	55	46	36	25	12
Precip	1.9	1.2	2.3	2.6	3.2	3.4	3.9	3.4	3.3	2.4	2.5	1.6
Snow	14.6	8.5	9.2	3.4	tr	0.0	0.0	0.0	0.0	0.3	4.0	12.3

High and Low temperatures in degrees Fahrenheit; Precipitation and Snow in inches

Population: 35,634 (2000); Race: 97.8% White, 0.1% Black, 0.3% Asian, 0.8% American Indian and Alaska Native, 0.5% Hispanic of any race, 0.8% two or more races (2000); Density: 35.7 persons per square mile (2000); Age: 25.8% under 18, 15.1% over 64 (2000).
Religion: Five largest groups: 30.2% Catholic Church, 10.9% Evangelical Lutheran Church in America, 8.3% Lutheran Church—Missouri Synod, 2.5%

The United Methodist Church, 1.6% Wisconsin Evangelical Lutheran Synod (2000).
Economy: Unemployment rate: 6.6% (11/2002); Total civilian labor force: 17,290 (11/2002); Leading industries: 33.4% manufacturing; 16.3% construction; 12.1% retail trade (2000); Companies that employ more than 1,000 persons: 0 (2000); Companies that employ more than 100 persons: 12 (2000); Farms: 940 totaling 203,866 acres (1997); Minority business ownership rate: 0.0% (1997); Women business ownership rate: 16.8% (1997); Retail sales per capita: $5,353 (1997). Single-family building permits issued: 419 (2001) / 447 (2000); Multi-family building permits issued: 16 (2001) / 14 (2000).
Income: Per capita income: $19,016 (2000); Median household income: $41,201 (2000); Poverty rate: 7.1% (2000); Bankruptcy rate: 4.38% (2001).
Taxes: Total county taxes per capita: $252 (2000); County property taxes per capita: $211 (2000).
Education: High school graduation rate: 80.6% (2000); College graduation rate: 10.6% (2000).
Housing: Homeownership rate: 82.9% (2000); Median home value: $89,900 (2000); Median rent: $356 per month (2000); Median age of housing: 29 years (2000).
Health: Birth rate: 103.0 per 10,000 population (1998); Age adjusted death rate: 89.3 per 10,000 population (1999); Age adjusted cancer mortality rate: 271.2 deaths per 100,000 population (1999). Number of physicians: 5.3 per 10,000 population (1999); Number of hospital beds: 12.3 per 10,000 population (1999).
Elections: 2000 Presidential election results: 43.8% Gore, 52.5% Bush, 2.6% Nader, 0.8% Buchanan
National and State Parks: Charles Pond State Public Hunting Grounds; Copper Culture Mounds State Park; Green Bay Shores State Wildlife Area; Oconto Marsh State Game Refuge; Pensaukee State Public Hunting Grounds; Peshtigo Brook State Wildlife Area; Rush Point State Public Hunting Grounds; South Branch Oconto River State Wildlife Area
Additional Information Contacts
Oconto County Government Offices 920-834-6806
Lakewood Area Chamber of Commerce 715-276-6500
Oconto Area Chamber of Commerce. 920-834-2255
Oconto Falls Area Chamber. 920-846-8306

Oconto County Communities

ABRAMS (town). Covers a land area of 37.454 square miles and a water area of 0.115 square miles. Located at 44.80° N. Lat.; 88.07° W. Long. Elevation is 670 feet.
Population: 1,757 (2000); Race: 97.6% White, 0.3% Black, 0.3% Asian, 1.1% American Indian and Alaska Native, 0.5% Hispanic of any race, 0.8% two or more races (2000); Density: 46.9 persons per square mile (2000); Age: 26.7% under 18, 8.7% over 64 (2000); Marriage status: 21.6% never married, 65.2% now married, 5.4% widowed, 7.8% divorced (2000); Foreign born: 0.5% (2000); Ancestry (includes multiple ancestries): 47.5% German, 16.9% Polish, 10.3% Irish, 9.2% Belgian, 8.6% French (except Basque) (2000).
Economy: Employment by occupation: 10.0% management, 10.7% professional, 13.0% services, 25.7% sales, 1.4% farming, 13.3% construction, 26.1% production (2000).
Income: Per capita income: $20,889 (2000); Median household income: $51,250 (2000); Poverty rate: 4.9% (2000).
Taxes: Total city taxes per capita: $61 (1997); City property taxes per capita: $58 (1997).
Education: High school graduation rate: 88.2% (2000); College graduation rate: 12.4% (2000).
Housing: Homeownership rate: 91.2% (2000); Median home value: $114,800 (2000); Median rent: $456 per month (2000); Median age of housing: 21 years (2000).
Transportation: Commute to work: 94.4% car, 0.4% public transportation, 1.5% walk, 3.5% work from home (2000); Travel time to work: 11.3% less than 15 minutes, 39.3% 15 to 30 minutes, 37.2% 30 to 45 minutes, 3.3% 45 to 60 minutes, 8.9% 60 minutes or more (2000)

BAGLEY (town). Covers a land area of 34.819 square miles and a water area of 0.873 square miles. Located at 45.06° N. Lat.; 88.28° W. Long.
Population: 333 (2000); Race: 98.1% White, 0.0% Black, 0.0% Asian, 0.0% American Indian and Alaska Native, 0.0% Hispanic of any race, 1.9% two or more races (2000); Density: 9.6 persons per square mile (2000); Age: 28.8% under 18, 15.6% over 64 (2000); Marriage status: 22.6% never married, 59.6% now married, 8.8% widowed, 9.1% divorced (2000); Foreign born: 0.0% (2000); Ancestry (includes multiple ancestries): 62.2% German, 15.6% Polish, 12.7% Irish, 9.3% Norwegian, 7.7% Russian (2000).
Economy: Employment by occupation: 14.0% management, 3.8% professional, 13.4% services, 15.9% sales, 3.2% farming, 12.1% construction, 37.6% production (2000).
Income: Per capita income: $15,241 (2000); Median household income: $36,875 (2000); Poverty rate: 13.5% (2000).
Taxes: Total city taxes per capita: $54 (1997); City property taxes per capita: $54 (1997).
Education: High school graduation rate: 71.7% (2000); College graduation rate: 3.6% (2000).
Housing: Homeownership rate: 91.4% (2000); Median home value: $93,900 (2000); Median rent: $258 per month (2000); Median age of housing: 36 years (2000).
Transportation: Commute to work: 91.0% car, 0.0% public transportation, 1.9% walk, 7.1% work from home (2000); Travel time to work: 22.8% less than 15 minutes, 39.3% 15 to 30 minutes, 11.0% 30 to 45 minutes, 15.2% 45 to 60 minutes, 11.7% 60 minutes or more (2000)

BRAZEAU (town). Covers a land area of 68.530 square miles and a water area of 3.020 square miles. Located at 45.10° N. Lat.; 88.21° W. Long.
Population: 1,408 (2000); Race: 99.5% White, 0.0% Black, 0.0% Asian, 0.0% American Indian and Alaska Native, 0.1% Hispanic of any race, 0.5% two or more races (2000); Density: 20.5 persons per square mile (2000); Age: 20.0% under 18, 22.8% over 64 (2000); Marriage status: 15.3% never married, 69.0% now married, 7.9% widowed, 7.8% divorced (2000); Foreign born: 0.1% (2000); Ancestry (includes multiple ancestries): 45.8% German, 21.6% Polish, 7.2% Irish, 6.7% French (except Basque), 6.2% Czech (2000).
Economy: Employment by occupation: 13.9% management, 8.6% professional, 13.1% services, 20.7% sales, 4.9% farming, 12.9% construction, 26.0% production (2000).
Income: Per capita income: $17,947 (2000); Median household income: $34,750 (2000); Poverty rate: 6.1% (2000).
Taxes: Total city taxes per capita: $95 (1997); City property taxes per capita: $93 (1997).
Education: High school graduation rate: 75.6% (2000); College graduation rate: 8.1% (2000).
Housing: Homeownership rate: 85.4% (2000); Median home value: $106,700 (2000); Median rent: $425 per month (2000); Median age of housing: 28 years (2000).
Transportation: Commute to work: 86.6% car, 0.3% public transportation, 2.3% walk, 10.0% work from home (2000); Travel time to work: 22.9% less than 15 minutes, 31.9% 15 to 30 minutes, 17.8% 30 to 45 minutes, 11.4% 45 to 60 minutes, 16.0% 60 minutes or more (2000)

BREED (town). Covers a land area of 35.546 square miles and a water area of 0.226 square miles. Located at 45.07° N. Lat.; 88.41° W. Long. Elevation is 905 feet.
Population: 657 (2000); Race: 98.0% White, 0.0% Black, 0.0% Asian, 1.7% American Indian and Alaska Native, 0.0% Hispanic of any race, 0.3% two or more races (2000); Density: 18.5 persons per square mile (2000); Age: 24.2% under 18, 19.8% over 64 (2000); Marriage status: 17.5% never married, 69.9% now married, 6.4% widowed, 6.2% divorced (2000); Foreign born: 0.0% (2000); Ancestry (includes multiple ancestries): 52.2% German, 10.5% Polish, 8.1% Irish, 7.8% United States or American, 5.1% English (2000).
Economy: Employment by occupation: 9.6% management, 8.2% professional, 11.0% services, 12.5% sales, 5.7% farming, 22.1% construction, 31.0% production (2000).
Income: Per capita income: $18,704 (2000); Median household income: $36,103 (2000); Poverty rate: 6.9% (2000).
Taxes: Total city taxes per capita: $95 (1997); City property taxes per capita: $92 (1997).
Education: High school graduation rate: 70.2% (2000); College graduation rate: 6.3% (2000).
Housing: Homeownership rate: 92.9% (2000); Median home value: $59,700 (2000); Median rent: $350 per month (2000); Median age of housing: 26 years (2000).
Transportation: Commute to work: 94.5% car, 0.0% public transportation, 0.7% walk, 4.0% work from home (2000); Travel time to work: 33.3% less than 15 minutes, 19.7% 15 to 30 minutes, 17.0% 30 to 45 minutes, 7.6% 45 to 60 minutes, 22.3% 60 minutes or more (2000)

CHASE (town). Covers a land area of 35.128 square miles and a water area of 0.033 square miles. Located at 44.70° N. Lat.; 88.18° W. Long. Elevation is 768 feet.

Population: 2,082 (2000); Race: 97.4% White, 0.0% Black, 0.0% Asian, 1.3% American Indian and Alaska Native, 0.4% Hispanic of any race, 1.3% two or more races (2000); Density: 59.3 persons per square mile (2000); Age: 35.0% under 18, 7.4% over 64 (2000); Marriage status: 22.7% never married, 68.3% now married, 2.9% widowed, 6.1% divorced (2000); Foreign born: 0.5% (2000); Ancestry (includes multiple ancestries): 42.1% German, 33.9% Polish, 11.2% Irish, 6.8% Belgian, 6.1% French (except Basque) (2000).
Economy: Employment by occupation: 15.3% management, 12.3% professional, 9.0% services, 22.7% sales, 2.0% farming, 13.3% construction, 25.5% production (2000).
Income: Per capita income: $18,219 (2000); Median household income: $55,385 (2000); Poverty rate: 4.9% (2000).
Taxes: Total city taxes per capita: $40 (1997); City property taxes per capita: $36 (1997).
Education: High school graduation rate: 88.6% (2000); College graduation rate: 14.2% (2000).
Housing: Homeownership rate: 93.2% (2000); Median home value: $135,100 (2000); Median rent: $425 per month (2000); Median age of housing: 16 years (2000).
Transportation: Commute to work: 91.0% car, 0.0% public transportation, 1.3% walk, 7.3% work from home (2000); Travel time to work: 19.8% less than 15 minutes, 36.6% 15 to 30 minutes, 33.9% 30 to 45 minutes, 4.8% 45 to 60 minutes, 5.0% 60 minutes or more (2000)

DOTY (town). Covers a land area of 52.172 square miles and a water area of 2.227 square miles. Located at 45.20° N. Lat.; 88.61° W. Long.
Population: 249 (2000); Race: 100.0% White, 0.0% Black, 0.0% Asian, 0.0% American Indian and Alaska Native, 0.8% Hispanic of any race, 0.0% two or more races (2000); Density: 4.8 persons per square mile (2000); Age: 6.5% under 18, 24.2% over 64 (2000); Marriage status: 7.9% never married, 76.6% now married, 5.9% widowed, 9.6% divorced (2000); Foreign born: 2.0% (2000); Ancestry (includes multiple ancestries): 52.0% German, 14.1% Irish, 10.9% Belgian, 8.5% Polish, 8.1% French (except Basque) (2000).
Economy: Employment by occupation: 10.5% management, 17.1% professional, 22.9% services, 19.0% sales, 0.0% farming, 14.3% construction, 16.2% production (2000).
Income: Per capita income: $19,809 (2000); Median household income: $32,188 (2000); Poverty rate: 14.5% (2000).
Taxes: Total city taxes per capita: $399 (1997); City property taxes per capita: $394 (1997).
Education: High school graduation rate: 76.8% (2000); College graduation rate: 9.6% (2000).
Housing: Homeownership rate: 96.9% (2000); Median home value: $96,000 (2000); Median age of housing: 25 years (2000).
Transportation: Commute to work: 98.0% car, 0.0% public transportation, 0.0% walk, 2.0% work from home (2000); Travel time to work: 32.7% less than 15 minutes, 31.6% 15 to 30 minutes, 20.4% 30 to 45 minutes, 2.0% 45 to 60 minutes, 13.3% 60 minutes or more (2000)

GILLETT (city). Covers a land area of 1.359 square miles and a water area of 0.009 square miles. Located at 44.89° N. Lat.; 88.30° W. Long. Elevation is 812 feet.
Population: 1,256 (2000); Race: 96.4% White, 1.1% Black, 0.2% Asian, 1.3% American Indian and Alaska Native, 0.3% Hispanic of any race, 0.4% two or more races (2000); Density: 923.9 persons per square mile (2000); Age: 27.6% under 18, 19.5% over 64 (2000); Marriage status: 19.7% never married, 58.5% now married, 13.5% widowed, 8.3% divorced (2000); Foreign born: 0.6% (2000); Ancestry (includes multiple ancestries): 48.5% German, 10.3% Polish, 8.8% Norwegian, 8.5% Irish, 5.8% Other groups (2000).
Economy: Single-family building permits issued: 0 (2001) / 0 (2000); Multi-family building permits issued: 0 (2001) / 0 (2000); Employment by occupation: 8.4% management, 16.5% professional, 13.2% services, 14.8% sales, 1.3% farming, 10.6% construction, 35.2% production (2000).
Income: Per capita income: $16,737 (2000); Median household income: $36,667 (2000); Poverty rate: 9.2% (2000).
Taxes: Total city taxes per capita: $127 (1997); City property taxes per capita: $115 (1997).
Education: High school graduation rate: 69.0% (2000); College graduation rate: 9.9% (2000).

School District(s)

Gillett (PK-12)
2000 Enrollment: 858 920-855-2137
Housing: Homeownership rate: 68.0% (2000); Median home value: $63,800 (2000); Median rent: $344 per month (2000); Median age of housing: 48 years (2000).
Transportation: Commute to work: 89.5% car, 0.9% public transportation, 7.2% walk, 1.3% work from home (2000); Travel time to work: 45.9% less than 15 minutes, 22.9% 15 to 30 minutes, 16.0% 30 to 45 minutes, 9.2% 45 to 60 minutes, 6.1% 60 minutes or more (2000)

GILLETT (town). Covers a land area of 33.391 square miles and a water area of 0.922 square miles. Located at 44.89° N. Lat.; 88.31° W. Long. Elevation is 812 feet.
History: Incorporated as village in 1900, as city in 1944.
Population: 1,085 (2000); Race: 98.0% White, 0.6% Black, 0.0% Asian, 0.0% American Indian and Alaska Native, 0.0% Hispanic of any race, 1.0% two or more races (2000); Density: 32.5 persons per square mile (2000); Age: 26.5% under 18, 13.6% over 64 (2000); Marriage status: 16.8% never married, 67.9% now married, 6.2% widowed, 9.0% divorced (2000); Foreign born: 0.0% (2000); Ancestry (includes multiple ancestries): 61.1% German, 8.8% Polish, 6.9% Norwegian, 5.5% Irish, 5.4% United States or American (2000).
Economy: Manufacturing: food, construction materials. Employment by occupation: 17.8% management, 10.3% professional, 14.1% services, 16.4% sales, 4.4% farming, 10.8% construction, 26.3% production (2000).
Income: Per capita income: $19,381 (2000); Median household income: $41,053 (2000); Poverty rate: 5.2% (2000).
Taxes: Total city taxes per capita: $46 (1997); City property taxes per capita: $44 (1997).
Education: High school graduation rate: 80.2% (2000); College graduation rate: 5.7% (2000).
Housing: Homeownership rate: 87.9% (2000); Median home value: $77,000 (2000); Median rent: $279 per month (2000); Median age of housing: 46 years (2000).
Transportation: Commute to work: 82.6% car, 0.0% public transportation, 2.4% walk, 14.5% work from home (2000); Travel time to work: 40.7% less than 15 minutes, 26.1% 15 to 30 minutes, 15.1% 30 to 45 minutes, 12.2% 45 to 60 minutes, 5.9% 60 minutes or more (2000)

HOW (town). Covers a land area of 34.938 square miles and a water area of 0.120 square miles. Located at 45.00° N. Lat.; 88.42° W. Long.
Population: 563 (2000); Race: 94.7% White, 0.0% Black, 0.0% Asian, 5.3% American Indian and Alaska Native, 0.9% Hispanic of any race, 0.0% two or more races (2000); Density: 16.1 persons per square mile (2000); Age: 28.8% under 18, 12.6% over 64 (2000); Marriage status: 22.4% never married, 68.5% now married, 4.7% widowed, 4.5% divorced (2000); Foreign born: 0.3% (2000); Ancestry (includes multiple ancestries): 66.6% German, 7.5% Polish, 6.5% Irish, 5.3% English, 5.3% Belgian (2000).
Economy: Employment by occupation: 17.2% management, 10.0% professional, 9.6% services, 16.8% sales, 7.2% farming, 11.7% construction, 27.5% production (2000).
Income: Per capita income: $15,447 (2000); Median household income: $39,167 (2000); Poverty rate: 7.7% (2000).
Education: High school graduation rate: 83.2% (2000); College graduation rate: 6.7% (2000).
Housing: Homeownership rate: 81.8% (2000); Median home value: $72,100 (2000); Median rent: $338 per month (2000); Median age of housing: 54 years (2000).
Transportation: Commute to work: 76.8% car, 0.0% public transportation, 4.8% walk, 17.3% work from home (2000); Travel time to work: 51.5% less than 15 minutes, 18.4% 15 to 30 minutes, 21.3% 30 to 45 minutes, 3.3% 45 to 60 minutes, 5.4% 60 minutes or more (2000)

LAKEWOOD (town). Covers a land area of 70.820 square miles and a water area of 1.594 square miles. Located at 45.32° N. Lat.; 88.44° W. Long. Elevation is 1,271 feet.
Population: 875 (2000); Race: 95.7% White, 0.0% Black, 0.4% Asian, 0.6% American Indian and Alaska Native, 0.9% Hispanic of any race, 2.7% two or more races (2000); Density: 12.4 persons per square mile (2000); Age: 17.5% under 18, 27.3% over 64 (2000); Marriage status: 12.2% never married, 70.8% now married, 8.1% widowed, 8.9% divorced (2000); Foreign born: 0.9% (2000); Ancestry (includes multiple ancestries): 40.2% German, 12.8% Irish, 8.6% Polish, 7.9% French (except Basque), 6.4% English (2000).
Economy: Employment by occupation: 17.8% management, 10.6% professional, 19.8% services, 28.1% sales, 1.9% farming, 8.4% construction, 13.4% production (2000).
Income: Per capita income: $18,281 (2000); Median household income: $33,869 (2000); Poverty rate: 7.2% (2000).
Taxes: Total city taxes per capita: $284 (1997); City property taxes per capita: $280 (1997).

Education: High school graduation rate: 82.1% (2000); College graduation rate: 11.7% (2000).
Housing: Homeownership rate: 84.4% (2000); Median home value: $101,500 (2000); Median rent: $454 per month (2000); Median age of housing: 26 years (2000).
Transportation: Commute to work: 84.6% car, 1.4% public transportation, 3.7% walk, 10.3% work from home (2000); Travel time to work: 53.5% less than 15 minutes, 23.2% 15 to 30 minutes, 11.5% 30 to 45 minutes, 4.5% 45 to 60 minutes, 7.3% 60 minutes or more (2000)
Additional Information Contacts
Lakewood Area Chamber of Commerce 715-276-6500

LENA (village). Covers a land area of 0.884 square miles and a water area of 0.003 square miles. Located at 44.95° N. Lat.; 88.05° W. Long. Elevation is 714 feet.
History: Lena developed as the center of a farming community, with a flour mill and a cooperative cheese factory and creamery.
Population: 510 (2000); Race: 100.0% White, 0.0% Black, 0.0% Asian, 0.0% American Indian and Alaska Native, 0.6% Hispanic of any race, 0.0% two or more races (2000); Density: 576.8 persons per square mile (2000); Age: 26.5% under 18, 17.9% over 64 (2000); Marriage status: 25.1% never married, 57.7% now married, 9.7% widowed, 7.5% divorced (2000); Foreign born: 0.9% (2000); Ancestry (includes multiple ancestries): 36.5% German, 11.8% Irish, 10.9% French (except Basque), 10.0% Polish, 7.9% Belgian (2000).
Economy: Single-family building permits issued: 2 (2001) / 0 (2000); Multi-family building permits issued: 0 (2001) / 0 (2000); Employment by occupation: 8.7% management, 13.4% professional, 19.9% services, 12.1% sales, 1.3% farming, 19.0% construction, 25.5% production (2000).
Income: Per capita income: $19,262 (2000); Median household income: $30,000 (2000); Poverty rate: 13.7% (2000).
Taxes: Total city taxes per capita: $147 (1997); City property taxes per capita: $139 (1997).
Education: High school graduation rate: 78.9% (2000); College graduation rate: 11.8% (2000).

School District(s)

Lena (PK-12)
2000 Enrollment: 471 920-829-5703
Housing: Homeownership rate: 59.5% (2000); Median home value: $80,000 (2000); Median rent: $343 per month (2000); Median age of housing: 57 years (2000).
Transportation: Commute to work: 89.1% car, 0.0% public transportation, 7.0% walk, 2.6% work from home (2000); Travel time to work: 43.5% less than 15 minutes, 27.8% 15 to 30 minutes, 17.5% 30 to 45 minutes, 6.7% 45 to 60 minutes, 4.5% 60 minutes or more (2000)

LENA (town). Covers a land area of 33.387 square miles and a water area of 0.003 square miles. Located at 44.98° N. Lat.; 88.05° W. Long. Elevation is 714 feet.
Population: 769 (2000); Race: 99.5% White, 0.0% Black, 0.0% Asian, 0.5% American Indian and Alaska Native, 0.2% Hispanic of any race, 0.0% two or more races (2000); Density: 23.0 persons per square mile (2000); Age: 26.8% under 18, 13.6% over 64 (2000); Marriage status: 23.2% never married, 65.7% now married, 4.2% widowed, 6.9% divorced (2000); Foreign born: 0.7% (2000); Ancestry (includes multiple ancestries): 45.4% German, 21.8% Polish, 11.3% Irish, 9.7% Belgian, 6.8% French (except Basque) (2000).
Economy: Dairying region; vegetables; wood products. Employment by occupation: 19.5% management, 16.2% professional, 10.4% services, 11.7% sales, 7.5% farming, 10.0% construction, 24.8% production (2000).
Income: Per capita income: $18,649 (2000); Median household income: $45,556 (2000); Poverty rate: 7.1% (2000).
Taxes: Total city taxes per capita: $33 (1997); City property taxes per capita: $32 (1997).
Education: High school graduation rate: 81.3% (2000); College graduation rate: 13.8% (2000).
Housing: Homeownership rate: 84.4% (2000); Median home value: $79,400 (2000); Median rent: $338 per month (2000); Median age of housing: 50 years (2000).
Transportation: Commute to work: 78.7% car, 0.0% public transportation, 4.7% walk, 15.3% work from home (2000); Travel time to work: 34.0% less than 15 minutes, 28.6% 15 to 30 minutes, 18.8% 30 to 45 minutes, 12.7% 45 to 60 minutes, 5.8% 60 minutes or more (2000)

LITTLE RIVER (town). Covers a land area of 51.536 square miles and a water area of 0 square miles. Located at 44.95° N. Lat.; 87.88° W. Long.
Population: 1,065 (2000); Race: 98.8% White, 0.0% Black, 0.0% Asian, 0.5% American Indian and Alaska Native, 0.1% Hispanic of any race, 0.7% two or more races (2000); Density: 20.7 persons per square mile (2000); Age: 24.9% under 18, 13.0% over 64 (2000); Marriage status: 25.5% never married, 60.8% now married, 4.4% widowed, 9.3% divorced (2000); Foreign born: 0.3% (2000); Ancestry (includes multiple ancestries): 46.9% German, 12.6% Polish, 11.9% French (except Basque), 7.2% United States or American, 6.1% French Canadian (2000).
Economy: Employment by occupation: 16.2% management, 10.9% professional, 11.3% services, 17.2% sales, 3.5% farming, 14.9% construction, 26.0% production (2000).
Income: Per capita income: $17,576 (2000); Median household income: $40,804 (2000); Poverty rate: 11.3% (2000).
Taxes: Total city taxes per capita: $64 (1997); City property taxes per capita: $63 (1997).
Education: High school graduation rate: 78.4% (2000); College graduation rate: 10.8% (2000).
Housing: Homeownership rate: 80.4% (2000); Median home value: $96,300 (2000); Median rent: $343 per month (2000); Median age of housing: 35 years (2000).
Transportation: Commute to work: 87.4% car, 0.0% public transportation, 2.4% walk, 10.2% work from home (2000); Travel time to work: 39.4% less than 15 minutes, 27.0% 15 to 30 minutes, 15.7% 30 to 45 minutes, 14.8% 45 to 60 minutes, 3.1% 60 minutes or more (2000)

LITTLE SUAMICO (town). Covers a land area of 37.342 square miles and a water area of 0.063 square miles. Located at 44.71° N. Lat.; 88.04° W. Long. Elevation is 593 feet.
Population: 3,877 (2000); Race: 98.2% White, 0.2% Black, 1.3% Asian, 0.2% American Indian and Alaska Native, 0.1% Hispanic of any race, 0.1% two or more races (2000); Density: 103.8 persons per square mile (2000); Age: 29.9% under 18, 5.3% over 64 (2000); Marriage status: 21.7% never married, 67.4% now married, 2.5% widowed, 8.3% divorced (2000); Foreign born: 1.1% (2000); Ancestry (includes multiple ancestries): 46.2% German, 18.5% Polish, 10.6% Belgian, 10.0% French (except Basque), 9.7% Irish (2000).
Economy: Employment by occupation: 16.8% management, 12.8% professional, 12.0% services, 24.9% sales, 2.1% farming, 12.8% construction, 18.7% production (2000).
Income: Per capita income: $22,520 (2000); Median household income: $60,160 (2000); Poverty rate: 3.9% (2000).
Taxes: Total city taxes per capita: $74 (1997); City property taxes per capita: $65 (1997).
Education: High school graduation rate: 90.5% (2000); College graduation rate: 17.1% (2000).
Housing: Homeownership rate: 94.9% (2000); Median home value: $137,100 (2000); Median rent: $588 per month (2000); Median age of housing: 15 years (2000).
Transportation: Commute to work: 95.3% car, 0.0% public transportation, 1.2% walk, 3.5% work from home (2000); Travel time to work: 11.4% less than 15 minutes, 57.3% 15 to 30 minutes, 21.5% 30 to 45 minutes, 5.4% 45 to 60 minutes, 4.4% 60 minutes or more (2000)

MAPLE VALLEY (town). Covers a land area of 35.277 square miles and a water area of 0.126 square miles. Located at 44.97° N. Lat.; 88.29° W. Long.
Population: 670 (2000); Race: 99.2% White, 0.0% Black, 0.0% Asian, 0.0% American Indian and Alaska Native, 0.5% Hispanic of any race, 0.8% two or more races (2000); Density: 19.0 persons per square mile (2000); Age: 21.7% under 18, 16.7% over 64 (2000); Marriage status: 22.0% never married, 64.6% now married, 7.1% widowed, 6.3% divorced (2000); Foreign born: 0.6% (2000); Ancestry (includes multiple ancestries): 46.4% German, 15.5% Polish, 10.6% Irish, 8.3% French (except Basque), 7.7% Norwegian (2000).
Economy: Employment by occupation: 21.1% management, 8.4% professional, 14.0% services, 12.4% sales, 4.2% farming, 9.8% construction, 30.1% production (2000).
Income: Per capita income: $16,985 (2000); Median household income: $35,795 (2000); Poverty rate: 6.4% (2000).
Taxes: Total city taxes per capita: $54 (1997); City property taxes per capita: $53 (1997).
Education: High school graduation rate: 77.5% (2000); College graduation rate: 7.9% (2000).
Housing: Homeownership rate: 88.2% (2000); Median home value: $58,800 (2000); Median rent: $525 per month (2000); Median age of housing: 45 years (2000).

Transportation: Commute to work: 81.4% car, 0.0% public transportation, 2.6% walk, 15.4% work from home (2000); Travel time to work: 34.5% less than 15 minutes, 24.0% 15 to 30 minutes, 13.2% 30 to 45 minutes, 14.9% 45 to 60 minutes, 13.5% 60 minutes or more (2000)

MORGAN (town). Covers a land area of 35.560 square miles and a water area of 0.075 square miles. Located at 44.80° N. Lat.; 88.17° W. Long. Elevation is 797 feet.
Population: 882 (2000); Race: 98.3% White, 0.0% Black, 1.3% Asian, 0.2% American Indian and Alaska Native, 0.8% Hispanic of any race, 0.2% two or more races (2000); Density: 24.8 persons per square mile (2000); Age: 24.6% under 18, 11.2% over 64 (2000); Marriage status: 25.2% never married, 60.7% now married, 5.2% widowed, 8.9% divorced (2000); Foreign born: 0.8% (2000); Ancestry (includes multiple ancestries): 53.6% German, 26.3% Polish, 6.9% Norwegian, 6.6% French (except Basque), 5.3% Belgian (2000).
Economy: Employment by occupation: 13.2% management, 11.2% professional, 8.1% services, 21.2% sales, 2.9% farming, 13.0% construction, 30.3% production (2000).
Income: Per capita income: $20,321 (2000); Median household income: $50,221 (2000); Poverty rate: 1.9% (2000).
Taxes: Total city taxes per capita: $40 (1997); City property taxes per capita: $39 (1997).
Education: High school graduation rate: 81.0% (2000); College graduation rate: 7.1% (2000).
Housing: Homeownership rate: 92.5% (2000); Median home value: $105,200 (2000); Median rent: $363 per month (2000); Median age of housing: 26 years (2000).
Transportation: Commute to work: 87.5% car, 0.2% public transportation, 2.1% walk, 9.4% work from home (2000); Travel time to work: 18.1% less than 15 minutes, 25.4% 15 to 30 minutes, 41.3% 30 to 45 minutes, 8.4% 45 to 60 minutes, 6.8% 60 minutes or more (2000)

MOUNTAIN (town). Covers a land area of 71.580 square miles and a water area of 1.096 square miles. Located at 45.15° N. Lat.; 88.43° W. Long. Elevation is 970 feet.
Population: 860 (2000); Race: 98.7% White, 0.0% Black, 0.0% Asian, 0.8% American Indian and Alaska Native, 0.4% Hispanic of any race, 0.2% two or more races (2000); Density: 12.0 persons per square mile (2000); Age: 24.1% under 18, 19.8% over 64 (2000); Marriage status: 22.1% never married, 61.0% now married, 9.3% widowed, 7.6% divorced (2000); Foreign born: 0.5% (2000); Ancestry (includes multiple ancestries): 48.0% German, 8.2% United States or American, 8.2% French (except Basque), 7.5% Polish, 5.7% Irish (2000).
Economy: Employment by occupation: 8.9% management, 6.6% professional, 21.2% services, 17.5% sales, 2.0% farming, 14.3% construction, 29.5% production (2000).
Income: Per capita income: $16,440 (2000); Median household income: $30,598 (2000); Poverty rate: 10.4% (2000).
Education: High school graduation rate: 77.9% (2000); College graduation rate: 6.7% (2000).
Housing: Homeownership rate: 88.0% (2000); Median home value: $77,200 (2000); Median rent: $290 per month (2000); Median age of housing: 30 years (2000).
Transportation: Commute to work: 92.4% car, 0.0% public transportation, 1.5% walk, 4.7% work from home (2000); Travel time to work: 24.7% less than 15 minutes, 37.0% 15 to 30 minutes, 15.7% 30 to 45 minutes, 7.4% 45 to 60 minutes, 15.1% 60 minutes or more (2000)

OCONTO (city). Covers a land area of 6.887 square miles and a water area of 0.474 square miles. Located at 44.88° N. Lat.; 87.87° W. Long. Elevation is 591 feet.
History: Oconto began with the founding of the first Jesuit mission in eastern Wisconsin, established in 1669 by Father Claude Allouez. Oconto was once an important lumber center, developing around the sawmill. The city was incorporated in 1869.
Population: 4,708 (2000); Race: 97.5% White, 0.2% Black, 0.1% Asian, 1.0% American Indian and Alaska Native, 0.7% Hispanic of any race, 1.0% two or more races (2000); Density: 683.7 persons per square mile (2000); Age: 25.8% under 18, 16.7% over 64 (2000); Marriage status: 23.7% never married, 54.3% now married, 10.4% widowed, 11.6% divorced (2000); Foreign born: 0.4% (2000); Ancestry (includes multiple ancestries): 39.5% German, 17.0% French (except Basque), 8.0% Polish, 6.4% French Canadian, 6.2% Irish (2000).
Economy: Single-family building permits issued: 12 (2001) / 23 (2000); Multi-family building permits issued: 12 (2001) / 14 (2000); Employment by occupation: 8.3% management, 12.5% professional, 16.8% services, 19.3% sales, 1.0% farming, 9.1% construction, 33.0% production (2000).
Income: Per capita income: $20,717 (2000); Median household income: $34,589 (2000); Poverty rate: 8.8% (2000).
Taxes: Total city taxes per capita: $157 (1997); City property taxes per capita: $146 (1997).
Education: High school graduation rate: 80.1% (2000); College graduation rate: 9.5% (2000).

School District(s)

Oconto (PK-12)
2000 Enrollment: 1,323 920-834-7800
Housing: Homeownership rate: 70.0% (2000); Median home value: $69,800 (2000); Median rent: $364 per month (2000); Median age of housing: 53 years (2000).
Hospitals: Oconto Memorial Hospital (25 beds)
Safety: Violent crime rate: 2.1 per 10,000 population; Property crime rate: 546.2 per 10,000 population (2001).
Newspapers: The Reminder (1 x week)
Transportation: Commute to work: 93.8% car, 0.2% public transportation, 3.2% walk, 1.6% work from home (2000); Travel time to work: 58.5% less than 15 minutes, 9.6% 15 to 30 minutes, 21.6% 30 to 45 minutes, 7.0% 45 to 60 minutes, 3.2% 60 minutes or more (2000)
Additional Information Contacts
Oconto Area Chamber of Commerce 920-834-2255

OCONTO (town). Covers a land area of 36.287 square miles and a water area of 0.386 square miles. Located at 44.88° N. Lat.; 87.93° W. Long. Elevation is 591 feet.
History: Father Allouez founded a mission here in 1669; the first Christian Science church was built here in 1886. Was important lumbering center. Copper Culture Mound State Park to southwest. Incorporated 1869.
Population: 1,251 (2000); Race: 95.7% White, 0.2% Black, 0.4% Asian, 0.8% American Indian and Alaska Native, 3.1% Hispanic of any race, 1.8% two or more races (2000); Density: 34.5 persons per square mile (2000); Age: 30.2% under 18, 12.4% over 64 (2000); Marriage status: 18.8% never married, 66.4% now married, 5.4% widowed, 9.4% divorced (2000); Foreign born: 0.9% (2000); Ancestry (includes multiple ancestries): 41.0% German, 12.0% French (except Basque), 11.0% Irish, 10.6% Belgian, 9.4% Polish (2000).
Economy: Railroad junction. Commercial center for lumbering and dairying area. Manufacturing includes wood products, textiles, beer, food processing, pleasure boats, machinery and fisheries. Employment by occupation: 9.8% management, 10.8% professional, 13.4% services, 24.2% sales, 1.0% farming, 10.1% construction, 30.7% production (2000).
Income: Per capita income: $18,373 (2000); Median household income: $45,721 (2000); Poverty rate: 5.8% (2000).
Taxes: Total city taxes per capita: $63 (2000); City property taxes per capita: $62 (2000).
Education: High school graduation rate: 82.4% (2000); College graduation rate: 9.2% (2000).
Housing: Homeownership rate: 87.4% (2000); Median home value: $96,300 (2000); Median rent: $403 per month (2000); Median age of housing: 32 years (2000).
Transportation: Commute to work: 90.6% car, 0.7% public transportation, 2.4% walk, 6.3% work from home (2000); Travel time to work: 41.4% less than 15 minutes, 14.3% 15 to 30 minutes, 29.8% 30 to 45 minutes, 9.3% 45 to 60 minutes, 5.3% 60 minutes or more (2000)

OCONTO FALLS (city). Covers a land area of 2.691 square miles and a water area of 0.219 square miles. Located at 44.87° N. Lat.; 88.14° W. Long. Elevation is 735 feet.
Population: 2,843 (2000); Race: 97.7% White, 0.0% Black, 0.0% Asian, 1.4% American Indian and Alaska Native, 0.0% Hispanic of any race, 0.8% two or more races (2000); Density: 1,056.5 persons per square mile (2000); Age: 24.5% under 18, 20.1% over 64 (2000); Marriage status: 24.3% never married, 52.2% now married, 11.3% widowed, 12.2% divorced (2000); Foreign born: 0.7% (2000); Ancestry (includes multiple ancestries): 45.4% German, 11.8% Polish, 9.8% Irish, 8.1% French Canadian, 7.3% French (except Basque) (2000).
Economy: Single-family building permits issued: 8 (2001) / 6 (2000); Multi-family building permits issued: 0 (2001) / 0 (2000); Employment by occupation: 5.3% management, 15.1% professional, 18.6% services, 21.7% sales, 0.9% farming, 8.8% construction, 29.6% production (2000).
Income: Per capita income: $17,170 (2000); Median household income: $34,884 (2000); Poverty rate: 9.5% (2000).

Taxes: Total city taxes per capita: $318 (2000); City property taxes per capita: $276 (2000).
Education: High school graduation rate: 77.6% (2000); College graduation rate: 11.7% (2000).

School District(s)

Oconto Falls (PK-12)
2000 Enrollment: 1,992 920-846-4471

Housing: Homeownership rate: 61.8% (2000); Median home value: $77,600 (2000); Median rent: $346 per month (2000); Median age of housing: 44 years (2000).
Hospitals: Community Memorial Hospital (25 beds)
Safety: Violent crime rate: 24.4 per 10,000 population; Property crime rate: 433.1 per 10,000 population (2001).
Newspapers: Oconto County Reporter (1 x week); Oconto County Times-Herald (1 x week)
Transportation: Commute to work: 94.6% car, 0.0% public transportation, 3.9% walk, 1.5% work from home (2000); Travel time to work: 49.9% less than 15 minutes, 17.3% 15 to 30 minutes, 19.6% 30 to 45 minutes, 8.2% 45 to 60 minutes, 4.9% 60 minutes or more (2000)

Additional Information Contacts

Oconto Falls Area Chamber 920-846-8306

OCONTO FALLS (town). Covers a land area of 32.237 square miles and a water area of 0.535 square miles. Located at 44.89° N. Lat.; 88.18° W. Long. Elevation is 735 feet.
History: Incorporated 1919.
Population: 1,139 (2000); Race: 98.6% White, 0.4% Black, 0.2% Asian, 0.2% American Indian and Alaska Native, 0.3% Hispanic of any race, 0.3% two or more races (2000); Density: 35.3 persons per square mile (2000); Age: 30.3% under 18, 8.8% over 64 (2000); Marriage status: 23.5% never married, 63.7% now married, 5.3% widowed, 7.5% divorced (2000); Foreign born: 0.9% (2000); Ancestry (includes multiple ancestries): 51.2% German, 10.9% French (except Basque), 9.7% Polish, 9.5% Norwegian, 8.4% Irish (2000).
Economy: Railroad terminus. Manufacturing: paper milling, feeds and fertilizer, magnetic printing cylinders, paper products. Employment by occupation: 16.2% management, 10.7% professional, 11.5% services, 23.3% sales, 4.2% farming, 13.5% construction, 20.5% production (2000).
Income: Per capita income: $17,654 (2000); Median household income: $49,531 (2000); Poverty rate: 7.3% (2000).
Taxes: Total city taxes per capita: $76 (1997); City property taxes per capita: $75 (1997).
Education: High school graduation rate: 84.9% (2000); College graduation rate: 13.6% (2000).
Housing: Homeownership rate: 86.8% (2000); Median home value: $95,900 (2000); Median rent: $333 per month (2000); Median age of housing: 29 years (2000).
Transportation: Commute to work: 87.8% car, 0.3% public transportation, 3.4% walk, 6.0% work from home (2000); Travel time to work: 52.0% less than 15 minutes, 16.9% 15 to 30 minutes, 16.9% 30 to 45 minutes, 10.5% 45 to 60 minutes, 3.6% 60 minutes or more (2000)

PENSAUKEE (town). Covers a land area of 35.518 square miles and a water area of 0.116 square miles. Located at 44.79° N. Lat.; 87.94° W. Long. Elevation is 591 feet.
Population: 1,214 (2000); Race: 99.4% White, 0.0% Black, 0.2% Asian, 0.0% American Indian and Alaska Native, 0.0% Hispanic of any race, 0.4% two or more races (2000); Density: 34.2 persons per square mile (2000); Age: 23.5% under 18, 11.7% over 64 (2000); Marriage status: 20.9% never married, 64.3% now married, 5.6% widowed, 9.2% divorced (2000); Foreign born: 0.4% (2000); Ancestry (includes multiple ancestries): 44.2% German, 16.3% Polish, 11.3% Irish, 9.9% French (except Basque), 6.9% Belgian (2000).
Economy: Employment by occupation: 10.5% management, 12.1% professional, 12.9% services, 17.6% sales, 0.6% farming, 12.0% construction, 34.2% production (2000).
Income: Per capita income: $22,600 (2000); Median household income: $48,098 (2000); Poverty rate: 3.5% (2000).
Taxes: Total city taxes per capita: $62 (1997); City property taxes per capita: $62 (1997).
Education: High school graduation rate: 82.0% (2000); College graduation rate: 10.8% (2000).
Housing: Homeownership rate: 93.0% (2000); Median home value: $111,300 (2000); Median rent: $375 per month (2000); Median age of housing: 29 years (2000).
Transportation: Commute to work: 91.9% car, 1.0% public transportation, 0.3% walk, 5.6% work from home (2000); Travel time to work: 15.4% less than 15 minutes, 30.5% 15 to 30 minutes, 39.4% 30 to 45 minutes, 7.4% 45 to 60 minutes, 7.4% 60 minutes or more (2000)

RIVERVIEW (town). Covers a land area of 69.730 square miles and a water area of 2.005 square miles. Located at 45.25° N. Lat.; 88.44° W. Long.
Population: 829 (2000); Race: 97.8% White, 0.0% Black, 0.0% Asian, 0.4% American Indian and Alaska Native, 0.7% Hispanic of any race, 1.6% two or more races (2000); Density: 11.9 persons per square mile (2000); Age: 11.8% under 18, 30.7% over 64 (2000); Marriage status: 10.1% never married, 69.9% now married, 10.6% widowed, 9.4% divorced (2000); Foreign born: 1.6% (2000); Ancestry (includes multiple ancestries): 46.2% German, 9.8% Polish, 7.9% French (except Basque), 7.2% Dutch, 6.5% Irish (2000).
Economy: Employment by occupation: 14.9% management, 10.6% professional, 20.5% services, 18.6% sales, 1.9% farming, 12.1% construction, 21.4% production (2000).
Income: Per capita income: $19,272 (2000); Median household income: $32,550 (2000); Poverty rate: 6.4% (2000).
Taxes: Total city taxes per capita: $244 (1997); City property taxes per capita: $241 (1997).
Education: High school graduation rate: 73.5% (2000); College graduation rate: 9.5% (2000).
Housing: Homeownership rate: 90.5% (2000); Median home value: $99,500 (2000); Median rent: $388 per month (2000); Median age of housing: 27 years (2000).
Transportation: Commute to work: 89.2% car, 0.6% public transportation, 0.9% walk, 9.2% work from home (2000); Travel time to work: 40.8% less than 15 minutes, 23.3% 15 to 30 minutes, 18.8% 30 to 45 minutes, 6.3% 45 to 60 minutes, 10.8% 60 minutes or more (2000)

SOBIESKI (unincorporated postal area, zip code 54171). Covers a land area of 31.836 square miles and a water area of 0.028 square miles. Located at 44.71° N. Lat.; 88.10° W. Long. Elevation is 657 feet.
Population: 3,021 (2000); Race: 99.0% White, 0.0% Black, 0.0% Asian, 0.4% American Indian and Alaska Native, 0.4% Hispanic of any race, 0.6% two or more races (2000); Density: 94.9 persons per square mile (2000); Age: 34.3% under 18, 4.0% over 64 (2000); Marriage status: 19.6% never married, 72.3% now married, 1.9% widowed, 6.2% divorced (2000); Foreign born: 0.4% (2000); Ancestry (includes multiple ancestries): 49.2% German, 24.7% Polish, 11.0% Irish, 9.7% Belgian, 7.3% Dutch (2000).
Economy: Employment by occupation: 22.5% management, 13.3% professional, 10.1% services, 23.9% sales, 0.8% farming, 11.9% construction, 17.5% production (2000).
Income: Per capita income: $22,681 (2000); Median household income: $64,469 (2000); Poverty rate: 0.8% (2000).
Education: High school graduation rate: 91.7% (2000); College graduation rate: 20.1% (2000).
Housing: Homeownership rate: 95.9% (2000); Median home value: $146,300 (2000); Median rent: $563 per month (2000); Median age of housing: 13 years (2000).
Transportation: Commute to work: 95.5% car, 0.0% public transportation, 0.9% walk, 3.4% work from home (2000); Travel time to work: 8.0% less than 15 minutes, 53.0% 15 to 30 minutes, 28.6% 30 to 45 minutes, 6.4% 45 to 60 minutes, 4.0% 60 minutes or more (2000)

SPRUCE (town). Covers a land area of 35.169 square miles and a water area of 0.549 square miles. Located at 44.98° N. Lat.; 88.20° W. Long. Elevation is 770 feet.
Population: 871 (2000); Race: 98.2% White, 0.0% Black, 0.0% Asian, 0.3% American Indian and Alaska Native, 2.5% Hispanic of any race, 1.4% two or more races (2000); Density: 24.8 persons per square mile (2000); Age: 25.3% under 18, 20.4% over 64 (2000); Marriage status: 20.4% never married, 66.7% now married, 8.1% widowed, 4.9% divorced (2000); Foreign born: 1.1% (2000); Ancestry (includes multiple ancestries): 44.1% German, 17.4% Polish, 11.7% Czech, 11.2% Irish, 8.4% Belgian (2000).
Economy: Employment by occupation: 19.2% management, 6.7% professional, 10.4% services, 18.1% sales, 2.1% farming, 11.5% construction, 32.0% production (2000).
Income: Per capita income: $18,759 (2000); Median household income: $35,658 (2000); Poverty rate: 6.5% (2000).
Taxes: Total city taxes per capita: $79 (1997); City property taxes per capita: $77 (1997).
Education: High school graduation rate: 78.8% (2000); College graduation rate: 8.6% (2000).
Housing: Homeownership rate: 82.6% (2000); Median home value: $92,500 (2000); Median rent: $325 per month (2000); Median age of housing: 32 years (2000).

Transportation: Commute to work: 81.8% car, 0.0% public transportation, 3.0% walk, 14.7% work from home (2000); Travel time to work: 23.2% less than 15 minutes, 31.5% 15 to 30 minutes, 13.7% 30 to 45 minutes, 20.1% 45 to 60 minutes, 11.5% 60 minutes or more (2000)

STILES (town). Covers a land area of 34.373 square miles and a water area of 0.827 square miles. Located at 44.88° N. Lat.; 88.05° W. Long. Elevation is 615 feet.
Population: 1,465 (2000); Race: 97.9% White, 0.0% Black, 0.6% Asian, 0.5% American Indian and Alaska Native, 0.1% Hispanic of any race, 0.9% two or more races (2000); Density: 42.6 persons per square mile (2000); Age: 26.9% under 18, 10.6% over 64 (2000); Marriage status: 19.5% never married, 63.3% now married, 6.6% widowed, 10.6% divorced (2000); Foreign born: 0.9% (2000); Ancestry (includes multiple ancestries): 45.4% German, 11.8% Irish, 11.2% Polish, 10.3% French (except Basque), 8.5% Belgian (2000).
Economy: Employment by occupation: 9.1% management, 13.4% professional, 12.1% services, 19.7% sales, 1.8% farming, 13.3% construction, 30.5% production (2000).
Income: Per capita income: $18,669 (2000); Median household income: $43,882 (2000); Poverty rate: 6.0% (2000).
Taxes: Total city taxes per capita: $63 (1997); City property taxes per capita: $53 (1997).
Education: High school graduation rate: 84.1% (2000); College graduation rate: 10.1% (2000).
Housing: Homeownership rate: 92.3% (2000); Median home value: $102,700 (2000); Median rent: $400 per month (2000); Median age of housing: 22 years (2000).
Transportation: Commute to work: 91.4% car, 0.4% public transportation, 2.0% walk, 5.9% work from home (2000); Travel time to work: 29.6% less than 15 minutes, 20.0% 15 to 30 minutes, 36.7% 30 to 45 minutes, 8.6% 45 to 60 minutes, 5.0% 60 minutes or more (2000)

SURING (village). Covers a land area of 1.017 square miles and a water area of 0 square miles. Located at 45.00° N. Lat.; 88.37° W. Long. Elevation is 804 feet.
Population: 605 (2000); Race: 99.0% White, 0.0% Black, 0.0% Asian, 0.3% American Indian and Alaska Native, 0.0% Hispanic of any race, 0.7% two or more races (2000); Density: 595.1 persons per square mile (2000); Age: 21.3% under 18, 27.4% over 64 (2000); Marriage status: 19.8% never married, 46.0% now married, 23.5% widowed, 10.6% divorced (2000); Foreign born: 0.0% (2000); Ancestry (includes multiple ancestries): 49.1% German, 10.9% Irish, 7.1% Polish, 5.2% Danish, 4.4% English (2000).
Economy: In lumbering and dairying area. Manufacturing includes lumber, furniture, wood components, pallets. Nicolet National Forest to Northwest. Single-family building permits issued: 1 (2001) / 0 (2000); Multi-family building permits issued: 0 (2001) / 0 (2000); Employment by occupation: 11.2% management, 4.7% professional, 19.4% services, 21.1% sales, 2.6% farming, 6.5% construction, 34.5% production (2000).
Income: Per capita income: $14,230 (2000); Median household income: $26,023 (2000); Poverty rate: 12.4% (2000).
Taxes: Total city taxes per capita: $172 (1997); City property taxes per capita: $156 (1997).
Education: High school graduation rate: 65.5% (2000); College graduation rate: 5.1% (2000).

School District(s)

Suring (PK-12)
2000 Enrollment: 654 920-842-2178
Housing: Homeownership rate: 60.2% (2000); Median home value: $52,500 (2000); Median rent: $280 per month (2000); Median age of housing: 43 years (2000).
Transportation: Commute to work: 84.5% car, 0.0% public transportation, 10.8% walk, 4.7% work from home (2000); Travel time to work: 54.8% less than 15 minutes, 14.9% 15 to 30 minutes, 14.5% 30 to 45 minutes, 7.7% 45 to 60 minutes, 8.1% 60 minutes or more (2000)

TOWNSEND (town). Covers a land area of 38.997 square miles and a water area of 3.458 square miles. Located at 45.31° N. Lat.; 88.61° W. Long. Elevation is 1,361 feet.
Population: 963 (2000); Race: 96.8% White, 0.0% Black, 0.2% Asian, 0.9% American Indian and Alaska Native, 1.0% Hispanic of any race, 1.3% two or more races (2000); Density: 24.7 persons per square mile (2000); Age: 17.6% under 18, 26.4% over 64 (2000); Marriage status: 15.1% never married, 68.4% now married, 7.6% widowed, 8.9% divorced (2000); Foreign born: 1.3% (2000); Ancestry (includes multiple ancestries): 52.2% German, 13.6% Polish, 9.1% French (except Basque), 7.9% Irish, 5.8% English (2000).
Economy: Employment by occupation: 8.0% management, 5.9% professional, 24.5% services, 21.4% sales, 3.4% farming, 12.1% construction, 24.5% production (2000).
Income: Per capita income: $16,680 (2000); Median household income: $28,456 (2000); Poverty rate: 6.8% (2000).
Taxes: Total city taxes per capita: $280 (1997); City property taxes per capita: $270 (1997).
Education: High school graduation rate: 77.3% (2000); College graduation rate: 8.5% (2000).
Housing: Homeownership rate: 93.7% (2000); Median home value: $95,900 (2000); Median rent: $300 per month (2000); Median age of housing: 26 years (2000).
Transportation: Commute to work: 89.2% car, 0.0% public transportation, 3.7% walk, 7.1% work from home (2000); Travel time to work: 53.1% less than 15 minutes, 21.2% 15 to 30 minutes, 5.9% 30 to 45 minutes, 5.4% 45 to 60 minutes, 14.4% 60 minutes or more (2000)

UNDERHILL (town). Covers a land area of 35.074 square miles and a water area of 0.538 square miles. Located at 44.89° N. Lat.; 88.43° W. Long. Elevation is 800 feet.
Population: 846 (2000); Race: 93.3% White, 0.0% Black, 0.0% Asian, 3.8% American Indian and Alaska Native, 0.2% Hispanic of any race, 2.9% two or more races (2000); Density: 24.1 persons per square mile (2000); Age: 25.4% under 18, 16.5% over 64 (2000); Marriage status: 17.0% never married, 67.4% now married, 4.8% widowed, 10.8% divorced (2000); Foreign born: 0.5% (2000); Ancestry (includes multiple ancestries): 60.1% German, 11.1% Other groups, 6.7% Norwegian, 6.1% Swedish, 6.1% English (2000).
Economy: Employment by occupation: 8.9% management, 7.8% professional, 17.5% services, 11.6% sales, 6.2% farming, 13.4% construction, 34.7% production (2000).
Income: Per capita income: $16,503 (2000); Median household income: $31,905 (2000); Poverty rate: 10.8% (2000).
Taxes: Total city taxes per capita: $91 (1997); City property taxes per capita: $90 (1997).
Education: High school graduation rate: 73.6% (2000); College graduation rate: 7.0% (2000).
Housing: Homeownership rate: 86.5% (2000); Median home value: $66,700 (2000); Median rent: $350 per month (2000); Median age of housing: 32 years (2000).
Transportation: Commute to work: 85.4% car, 0.0% public transportation, 4.4% walk, 9.6% work from home (2000); Travel time to work: 22.2% less than 15 minutes, 40.1% 15 to 30 minutes, 15.5% 30 to 45 minutes, 14.6% 45 to 60 minutes, 7.6% 60 minutes or more (2000)

Oneida County

Located in northern Wisconsin; drained by the Wisconsin River; includes many lakes, and part of Nicolet National Forest. Covers a land area of 1,124.50 square miles, a water area of 111.40 square miles, and is located in the Central Time Zone. The county government was organized in 1885. County seat is Rhinelander.

Weather Station: Long Lake Dam — Elevation: 1,627 feet

	Jan	Feb	Mar	Apr	May	Jun	Jul	Aug	Sep	Oct	Nov	Dec
High	21	27	38	52	66	74	78	76	66	54	37	25
Low	-3	0	12	25	38	48	53	51	42	32	20	5
Precip	1.3	0.9	1.8	2.4	3.3	3.8	3.6	4.1	4.2	2.8	2.4	1.4
Snow	15.2	9.5	11.4	5.2	0.4	0.0	0.0	0.0	tr	0.8	9.7	14.5

High and Low temperatures in degrees Fahrenheit; Precipitation and Snow in inches

Weather Station: Minocqua Dam — Elevation: 1,578 feet

	Jan	Feb	Mar	Apr	May	Jun	Jul	Aug	Sep	Oct	Nov	Dec
High	20	26	37	51	66	74	78	75	66	54	37	24
Low	-2	2	13	27	40	50	54	52	44	33	20	6
Precip	1.2	0.9	1.8	2.3	3.4	3.7	3.9	4.4	3.9	2.8	2.3	1.3
Snow	24.5	15.8	18.2	9.7	1.4	0.0	0.0	0.0	tr	2.7	14.3	23.9

High and Low temperatures in degrees Fahrenheit; Precipitation and Snow in inches

Weather Station: North Pelican — Elevation: 1,607 feet

	Jan	Feb	Mar	Apr	May	Jun	Jul	Aug	Sep	Oct	Nov	Dec
High	20	27	37	52	67	74	77	74	65	54	37	25
Low	-1	3	13	27	39	49	53	52	44	34	21	7
Precip	1.2	0.9	1.7	2.4	3.4	3.4	4.0	4.1	3.9	2.6	2.1	1.3
Snow	14.7	8.3	10.0	4.1	0.4	0.0	0.0	0.0	tr	1.1	7.6	14.1

High and Low temperatures in degrees Fahrenheit; Precipitation and Snow in inches

Weather Station: Rainbow Reservoir Lake Tomaha Elevation: 1,597 feet

	Jan	Feb	Mar	Apr	May	Jun	Jul	Aug	Sep	Oct	Nov	Dec
High	20	26	36	51	65	73	77	75	65	53	37	24
Low	-2	0	12	26	39	48	53	52	43	33	20	5
Precip	1.1	0.9	1.7	2.3	3.2	3.8	3.7	4.5	4.5	2.9	2.3	1.3
Snow	12.5	9.2	9.6	4.5	0.5	0.0	0.0	0.0	tr	1.3	7.8	12.7

High and Low temperatures in degrees Fahrenheit; Precipitation and Snow in inches

Weather Station: Rhinelander Elevation: 1,578 feet

	Jan	Feb	Mar	Apr	May	Jun	Jul	Aug	Sep	Oct	Nov	Dec
High	21	27	38	53	67	75	79	76	67	55	38	25
Low	-1	4	15	29	42	51	56	54	45	34	22	7
Precip	1.2	0.8	1.6	2.3	3.4	3.8	3.8	4.3	4.3	2.7	2.1	1.4
Snow	11.4	5.2	7.2	1.9	0.2	0.0	0.0	0.0	tr	0.1	na	na

High and Low temperatures in degrees Fahrenheit; Precipitation and Snow in inches

Weather Station: Willow Reservoir Elevation: 1,558 feet

	Jan	Feb	Mar	Apr	May	Jun	Jul	Aug	Sep	Oct	Nov	Dec
High	19	25	35	50	65	73	77	75	66	53	37	24
Low	-3	1	13	27	40	50	54	52	44	33	21	6
Precip	1.1	0.8	1.6	2.2	3.2	3.9	3.8	4.3	4.2	2.6	2.0	1.1
Snow	13.6	7.1	9.1	3.1	0.4	0.0	0.0	0.0	tr	0.6	4.6	10.5

High and Low temperatures in degrees Fahrenheit; Precipitation and Snow in inches

Population: 36,776 (2000); Race: 97.6% White, 0.2% Black, 0.2% Asian, 0.8% American Indian and Alaska Native, 0.6% Hispanic of any race, 0.9% two or more races (2000); Density: 32.7 persons per square mile (2000); Age: 22.4% under 18, 18.7% over 64 (2000).
Religion: Five largest groups: 36.1% Catholic Church, 8.7% Evangelical Lutheran Church in America, 6.1% Wisconsin Evangelical Lutheran Synod, 3.3% The United Methodist Church, 2.4% United Church of Christ (2000).
Economy: Unemployment rate: 5.7% (11/2002); Total civilian labor force: 21,110 (11/2002); Leading industries: 21.5% retail trade; 20.9% health care and social assistance; 12.3% manufacturing (2000); Companies that employ more than 1,000 persons: 0 (2000); Companies that employ more than 100 persons: 23 (2000); Farms: 117 totaling 39,036 acres (1997); Minority business ownership rate: 0.0% (1997); Women business ownership rate: 24.8% (1997); Retail sales per capita: $13,234 (1997). Single-family building permits issued: 427 (2001) / 372 (2000); Multi-family building permits issued: 48 (2001) / 39 (2000).
Income: Per capita income: $19,746 (2000); Median household income: $37,619 (2000); Poverty rate: 7.4% (2000); Bankruptcy rate: 3.90% (2001).
Taxes: Total county taxes per capita: $289 (1997); County property taxes per capita: $211 (1997).
Education: High school graduation rate: 85.1% (2000); College graduation rate: 20.0% (2000).
Housing: Homeownership rate: 79.7% (2000); Median home value: $106,200 (2000); Median rent: $404 per month (2000); Median age of housing: 28 years (2000).
Health: Birth rate: 90.6 per 10,000 population (1998); Age adjusted death rate: 88.3 per 10,000 population (1999); Age adjusted cancer mortality rate: 185.8 deaths per 100,000 population (1999). Air Quality Index: 88% good, 12% moderate, 0% unhealthy (percent of days in 2000). Number of physicians: 35.9 per 10,000 population (1999); Number of hospital beds: 49.5 per 10,000 population (1999).
Elections: 2000 Presidential election results: 44.1% Gore, 50.4% Bush, 4.3% Nader, 0.5% Buchanan
National and State Parks: American Legion State Forest; Bearskin State Park Trail; Thunder Lake State Wildlife Area
Additional Information Contacts
Oneida County Government Offices 715-369-6144
Minocqua Chamber of Commerce 715-356-6171
Northwoods Association of Realtors 715-356-3400
Pelican Lake Chamber of Commerce. 715-487-5222
Three Lakes Info Bureau 715-546-3344

Oneida County Communities

CASSIAN (town). Covers a land area of 64.994 square miles and a water area of 3.357 square miles. Located at 45.68° N. Lat.; 89.69° W. Long.
Population: 962 (2000); Race: 99.2% White, 0.0% Black, 0.2% Asian, 0.2% American Indian and Alaska Native, 0.2% Hispanic of any race, 0.2% two or more races (2000); Density: 14.8 persons per square mile (2000); Age: 20.5% under 18, 14.0% over 64 (2000); Marriage status: 18.0% never married, 69.2% now married, 2.8% widowed, 10.0% divorced (2000); Foreign born: 1.5% (2000); Ancestry (includes multiple ancestries): 54.5% German, 12.1% Polish, 11.3% Irish, 7.3% English, 6.1% Swedish (2000).
Economy: Employment by occupation: 11.1% management, 17.1% professional, 13.7% services, 23.3% sales, 0.0% farming, 19.2% construction, 15.6% production (2000).
Income: Per capita income: $22,794 (2000); Median household income: $39,844 (2000); Poverty rate: 5.7% (2000).
Taxes: Total city taxes per capita: $231 (1997); City property taxes per capita: $227 (1997).
Education: High school graduation rate: 86.8% (2000); College graduation rate: 16.3% (2000).
Housing: Homeownership rate: 92.5% (2000); Median home value: $107,400 (2000); Median rent: $321 per month (2000); Median age of housing: 25 years (2000).
Transportation: Commute to work: 94.5% car, 0.4% public transportation, 1.5% walk, 3.5% work from home (2000); Travel time to work: 11.0% less than 15 minutes, 47.9% 15 to 30 minutes, 24.3% 30 to 45 minutes, 5.5% 45 to 60 minutes, 11.2% 60 minutes or more (2000)

CRESCENT (town). Covers a land area of 29.340 square miles and a water area of 3.371 square miles. Located at 45.60° N. Lat.; 89.48° W. Long.
Population: 2,071 (2000); Race: 98.4% White, 0.0% Black, 0.9% Asian, 0.1% American Indian and Alaska Native, 0.0% Hispanic of any race, 0.6% two or more races (2000); Density: 70.6 persons per square mile (2000); Age: 26.8% under 18, 12.0% over 64 (2000); Marriage status: 20.5% never married, 64.7% now married, 4.3% widowed, 10.5% divorced (2000); Foreign born: 1.2% (2000); Ancestry (includes multiple ancestries): 53.0% German, 13.3% Irish, 9.8% Polish, 7.5% English, 6.8% French (except Basque) (2000).
Economy: Employment by occupation: 8.3% management, 23.2% professional, 15.9% services, 25.9% sales, 1.6% farming, 8.6% construction, 16.6% production (2000).
Income: Per capita income: $20,697 (2000); Median household income: $48,875 (2000); Poverty rate: 3.8% (2000).
Taxes: Total city taxes per capita: $110 (1997); City property taxes per capita: $108 (1997).
Education: High school graduation rate: 89.4% (2000); College graduation rate: 26.3% (2000).
Housing: Homeownership rate: 86.4% (2000); Median home value: $119,100 (2000); Median rent: $415 per month (2000); Median age of housing: 25 years (2000).
Transportation: Commute to work: 95.9% car, 0.4% public transportation, 1.4% walk, 1.3% work from home (2000); Travel time to work: 50.8% less than 15 minutes, 38.3% 15 to 30 minutes, 6.1% 30 to 45 minutes, 1.7% 45 to 60 minutes, 2.9% 60 minutes or more (2000)

ENTERPRISE (town). Covers a land area of 56.688 square miles and a water area of 2.237 square miles. Located at 45.51° N. Lat.; 89.33° W. Long. Elevation is 1,626 feet.
Population: 274 (2000); Race: 100.0% White, 0.0% Black, 0.0% Asian, 0.0% American Indian and Alaska Native, 0.0% Hispanic of any race, 0.0% two or more races (2000); Density: 4.8 persons per square mile (2000); Age: 24.6% under 18, 13.7% over 64 (2000); Marriage status: 18.3% never married, 66.3% now married, 2.0% widowed, 13.4% divorced (2000); Foreign born: 1.9% (2000); Ancestry (includes multiple ancestries): 74.8% German, 8.3% Norwegian, 7.7% Swedish, 7.3% Polish, 7.0% English (2000).
Economy: Employment by occupation: 7.6% management, 18.1% professional, 17.4% services, 20.1% sales, 2.8% farming, 18.8% construction, 15.3% production (2000).
Income: Per capita income: $14,970 (2000); Median household income: $34,479 (2000); Poverty rate: 1.9% (2000).
Taxes: Total city taxes per capita: $175 (1997); City property taxes per capita: $172 (1997).
Education: High school graduation rate: 88.4% (2000); College graduation rate: 15.6% (2000).
Housing: Homeownership rate: 83.3% (2000); Median home value: $85,400 (2000); Median rent: $413 per month (2000); Median age of housing: 41 years (2000).
Transportation: Commute to work: 92.3% car, 0.0% public transportation, 2.1% walk, 5.6% work from home (2000); Travel time to work: 25.4% less than 15 minutes, 38.8% 15 to 30 minutes, 17.9% 30 to 45 minutes, 11.2% 45 to 60 minutes, 6.7% 60 minutes or more (2000)

HARSHAW (unincorporated postal area, zip code 54529). Covers a land area of 55.239 square miles and a water area of 3.812 square miles. Located at 45.70° N. Lat.; 89.68° W. Long. Elevation is 1,520 feet.
Population: 993 (2000); Race: 98.1% White, 0.0% Black, 0.2% Asian, 0.5% American Indian and Alaska Native, 0.4% Hispanic of any race, 0.8% two or

more races (2000); Density: 18.0 persons per square mile (2000); Age: 18.8% under 18, 15.8% over 64 (2000); Marriage status: 15.0% never married, 71.9% now married, 3.9% widowed, 9.2% divorced (2000); Foreign born: 1.3% (2000); Ancestry (includes multiple ancestries): 56.9% German, 11.1% Polish, 10.7% Irish, 8.7% English, 6.5% Norwegian (2000).
Economy: Employment by occupation: 8.5% management, 19.7% professional, 10.8% services, 23.5% sales, 1.4% farming, 17.8% construction, 18.3% production (2000).
Income: Per capita income: $24,206 (2000); Median household income: $41,450 (2000); Poverty rate: 5.9% (2000).
Education: High school graduation rate: 86.1% (2000); College graduation rate: 19.1% (2000).
Housing: Homeownership rate: 93.6% (2000); Median home value: $114,900 (2000); Median rent: $354 per month (2000); Median age of housing: 28 years (2000).
Transportation: Commute to work: 93.8% car, 0.4% public transportation, 3.1% walk, 2.7% work from home (2000); Travel time to work: 13.4% less than 15 minutes, 52.9% 15 to 30 minutes, 20.2% 30 to 45 minutes, 4.2% 45 to 60 minutes, 9.3% 60 minutes or more (2000)

HAZELHURST (town). Covers a land area of 31.183 square miles and a water area of 3.870 square miles. Located at 45.78° N. Lat.; 89.74° W. Long. Elevation is 1,612 feet.
History: Hazelhurst began as a company town owned by the lumber interests.
Population: 1,267 (2000); Race: 97.8% White, 0.3% Black, 0.2% Asian, 0.0% American Indian and Alaska Native, 1.2% Hispanic of any race, 0.5% two or more races (2000); Density: 40.6 persons per square mile (2000); Age: 21.1% under 18, 17.1% over 64 (2000); Marriage status: 14.5% never married, 72.5% now married, 3.8% widowed, 9.2% divorced (2000); Foreign born: 1.5% (2000); Ancestry (includes multiple ancestries): 49.1% German, 13.6% Polish, 12.2% Irish, 11.3% English, 6.6% Norwegian (2000).
Economy: Employment by occupation: 15.8% management, 27.8% professional, 15.8% services, 25.0% sales, 0.6% farming, 9.1% construction, 5.8% production (2000).
Income: Per capita income: $28,732 (2000); Median household income: $45,461 (2000); Poverty rate: 3.8% (2000).
Taxes: Total city taxes per capita: $208 (1997); City property taxes per capita: $204 (1997).
Education: High school graduation rate: 91.4% (2000); College graduation rate: 35.6% (2000).
Housing: Homeownership rate: 89.5% (2000); Median home value: $146,300 (2000); Median rent: $392 per month (2000); Median age of housing: 27 years (2000).
Transportation: Commute to work: 91.0% car, 0.0% public transportation, 2.9% walk, 5.4% work from home (2000); Travel time to work: 27.8% less than 15 minutes, 43.0% 15 to 30 minutes, 18.1% 30 to 45 minutes, 4.0% 45 to 60 minutes, 7.1% 60 minutes or more (2000)

LAKE TOMAHAWK (town). Aka Tomahawk Lake. Covers a land area of 34.314 square miles and a water area of 4.895 square miles. Located at 45.78° N. Lat.; 89.60° W. Long. Elevation is 1,632 feet.
Population: 1,160 (2000); Race: 93.3% White, 5.3% Black, 0.0% Asian, 1.1% American Indian and Alaska Native, 0.2% Hispanic of any race, 0.3% two or more races (2000); Density: 33.8 persons per square mile (2000); Age: 19.7% under 18, 17.3% over 64 (2000); Marriage status: 19.5% never married, 61.9% now married, 7.2% widowed, 11.4% divorced (2000); Foreign born: 1.0% (2000); Ancestry (includes multiple ancestries): 43.5% German, 10.1% Polish, 9.7% Irish, 8.6% English, 7.8% Norwegian (2000).
Economy: Employment by occupation: 10.9% management, 21.6% professional, 20.0% services, 23.5% sales, 0.0% farming, 16.1% construction, 8.0% production (2000).
Income: Per capita income: $19,177 (2000); Median household income: $38,065 (2000); Poverty rate: 4.7% (2000).
Taxes: Total city taxes per capita: $325 (1997); City property taxes per capita: $320 (1997).
Education: High school graduation rate: 85.0% (2000); College graduation rate: 18.9% (2000).
Housing: Homeownership rate: 82.7% (2000); Median home value: $112,100 (2000); Median rent: $450 per month (2000); Median age of housing: 25 years (2000).
Transportation: Commute to work: 88.2% car, 0.0% public transportation, 7.5% walk, 4.3% work from home (2000); Travel time to work: 20.8% less than 15 minutes, 61.8% 15 to 30 minutes, 11.9% 30 to 45 minutes, 1.3% 45 to 60 minutes, 4.2% 60 minutes or more (2000)

LITTLE RICE (town). Covers a land area of 68.109 square miles and a water area of 5.557 square miles. Located at 45.63° N. Lat.; 89.84° W. Long.
Population: 314 (2000); Race: 100.0% White, 0.0% Black, 0.0% Asian, 0.0% American Indian and Alaska Native, 0.0% Hispanic of any race, 0.0% two or more races (2000); Density: 4.6 persons per square mile (2000); Age: 19.3% under 18, 19.0% over 64 (2000); Marriage status: 18.5% never married, 63.3% now married, 12.4% widowed, 5.8% divorced (2000); Foreign born: 1.2% (2000); Ancestry (includes multiple ancestries): 41.6% German, 17.5% Polish, 9.9% Irish, 7.8% English, 6.9% Finnish (2000).
Economy: Employment by occupation: 9.2% management, 14.5% professional, 15.1% services, 19.1% sales, 5.3% farming, 13.2% construction, 23.7% production (2000).
Income: Per capita income: $21,659 (2000); Median household income: $40,750 (2000); Poverty rate: 4.0% (2000).
Taxes: Total city taxes per capita: $538 (1997); City property taxes per capita: $529 (1997).
Education: High school graduation rate: 82.6% (2000); College graduation rate: 7.9% (2000).
Housing: Homeownership rate: 96.7% (2000); Median home value: $92,800 (2000); Median rent: $575 per month (2000); Median age of housing: 20 years (2000).
Transportation: Commute to work: 90.7% car, 0.0% public transportation, 6.0% walk, 3.3% work from home (2000); Travel time to work: 20.0% less than 15 minutes, 31.7% 15 to 30 minutes, 31.0% 30 to 45 minutes, 17.2% 45 to 60 minutes, 0.0% 60 minutes or more (2000)

LYNNE (town). Covers a land area of 70.501 square miles and a water area of 1.503 square miles. Located at 45.63° N. Lat.; 89.96° W. Long.
Population: 210 (2000); Race: 96.3% White, 0.0% Black, 0.0% Asian, 1.6% American Indian and Alaska Native, 0.0% Hispanic of any race, 2.1% two or more races (2000); Density: 3.0 persons per square mile (2000); Age: 17.5% under 18, 30.2% over 64 (2000); Marriage status: 15.4% never married, 66.7% now married, 11.1% widowed, 6.8% divorced (2000); Foreign born: 0.0% (2000); Ancestry (includes multiple ancestries): 29.6% German, 15.9% Finnish, 10.1% Polish, 8.5% Irish, 6.3% Czech (2000).
Economy: Employment by occupation: 7.2% management, 14.5% professional, 17.4% services, 24.6% sales, 0.0% farming, 26.1% construction, 10.1% production (2000).
Income: Per capita income: $16,430 (2000); Median household income: $27,344 (2000); Poverty rate: 17.5% (2000).
Taxes: Total city taxes per capita: $107 (1997); City property taxes per capita: $101 (1997).
Education: High school graduation rate: 81.6% (2000); College graduation rate: 3.4% (2000).
Housing: Homeownership rate: 100.0% (2000); Median home value: $78,300 (2000); Median age of housing: 33 years (2000).
Transportation: Commute to work: 89.1% car, 0.0% public transportation, 4.7% walk, 6.3% work from home (2000); Travel time to work: 15.0% less than 15 minutes, 16.7% 15 to 30 minutes, 18.3% 30 to 45 minutes, 31.7% 45 to 60 minutes, 18.3% 60 minutes or more (2000)

MINOCQUA (town). Covers a land area of 150.795 square miles and a water area of 17.292 square miles. Located at 45.84° N. Lat.; 89.83° W. Long. Elevation is 1,603 feet.
History: When the railroad reached here in 1887, opening southern markets for lumber, Minocqua became a logging center. When the timber trade declined, the area developed into a tourist center with summer homes, resorts, and camps.
Population: 4,859 (2000); Race: 96.3% White, 0.0% Black, 0.0% Asian, 1.0% American Indian and Alaska Native, 1.7% Hispanic of any race, 2.5% two or more races (2000); Density: 32.2 persons per square mile (2000); Age: 18.2% under 18, 25.0% over 64 (2000); Marriage status: 17.9% never married, 65.7% now married, 6.2% widowed, 10.2% divorced (2000); Foreign born: 1.1% (2000); Ancestry (includes multiple ancestries): 48.6% German, 12.2% English, 11.4% Irish, 9.0% Norwegian, 8.7% Polish (2000).
Economy: Employment by occupation: 13.6% management, 23.1% professional, 18.0% services, 24.9% sales, 0.5% farming, 10.8% construction, 9.1% production (2000).
Income: Per capita income: $24,461 (2000); Median household income: $40,333 (2000); Poverty rate: 6.5% (2000).
Taxes: Total city taxes per capita: $548 (2000); City property taxes per capita: $475 (2000).
Education: High school graduation rate: 87.6% (2000); College graduation rate: 27.2% (2000).

School District(s)

Lakeland UHS (09-12)
2000 Enrollment: 972 715-356-5252
Minocqua J1 (PK-08)
2000 Enrollment: 649 715-356-5206

Housing: Homeownership rate: 81.8% (2000); Median home value: $148,300 (2000); Median rent: $482 per month (2000); Median age of housing: 25 years (2000).
Safety: Violent crime rate: 22.5 per 10,000 population; Property crime rate: 398.4 per 10,000 population (2001).
Newspapers: Lakeland Times (2 x week)
Transportation: Commute to work: 89.5% car, 0.0% public transportation, 4.2% walk, 5.6% work from home (2000); Travel time to work: 59.8% less than 15 minutes, 26.0% 15 to 30 minutes, 4.9% 30 to 45 minutes, 6.4% 45 to 60 minutes, 2.9% 60 minutes or more (2000)
Airports: Lakeland/Noble F. Lee Memorial Field
Additional Information Contacts
Minocqua Chamber of Commerce 715-356-6171

MONICO (town). Covers a land area of 54.098 square miles and a water area of 0.457 square miles. Located at 45.60° N. Lat.; 89.14° W. Long. Elevation is 1,600 feet.
Population: 364 (2000); Race: 100.0% White, 0.0% Black, 0.0% Asian, 0.0% American Indian and Alaska Native, 0.0% Hispanic of any race, 0.0% two or more races (2000); Density: 6.7 persons per square mile (2000); Age: 35.8% under 18, 9.3% over 64 (2000); Marriage status: 17.5% never married, 63.2% now married, 7.7% widowed, 11.6% divorced (2000); Foreign born: 0.0% (2000); Ancestry (includes multiple ancestries): 39.1% German, 21.8% United States or American, 14.8% Polish, 14.0% Irish, 6.0% English (2000).
Economy: Employment by occupation: 6.5% management, 15.4% professional, 23.7% services, 20.1% sales, 1.8% farming, 18.3% construction, 14.2% production (2000).
Income: Per capita income: $12,973 (2000); Median household income: $33,281 (2000); Poverty rate: 4.6% (2000).
Taxes: Total city taxes per capita: $42 (1997); City property taxes per capita: $39 (1997).
Education: High school graduation rate: 78.3% (2000); College graduation rate: 3.8% (2000).
Housing: Homeownership rate: 92.5% (2000); Median home value: $78,300 (2000); Median rent: $319 per month (2000); Median age of housing: 27 years (2000).
Transportation: Commute to work: 82.5% car, 0.0% public transportation, 9.4% walk, 3.8% work from home (2000); Travel time to work: 27.9% less than 15 minutes, 53.9% 15 to 30 minutes, 9.7% 30 to 45 minutes, 1.9% 45 to 60 minutes, 6.5% 60 minutes or more (2000)

NEWBOLD (town). Covers a land area of 79.061 square miles and a water area of 13.935 square miles. Located at 45.76° N. Lat.; 89.50° W. Long. Elevation is 1,570 feet.
Population: 2,710 (2000); Race: 98.1% White, 0.0% Black, 0.2% Asian, 0.7% American Indian and Alaska Native, 0.7% Hispanic of any race, 0.5% two or more races (2000); Density: 34.3 persons per square mile (2000); Age: 22.1% under 18, 15.9% over 64 (2000); Marriage status: 15.0% never married, 72.7% now married, 4.4% widowed, 7.8% divorced (2000); Foreign born: 1.1% (2000); Ancestry (includes multiple ancestries): 53.7% German, 12.3% Irish, 10.1% Polish, 7.6% Norwegian, 7.2% English (2000).
Economy: Employment by occupation: 12.9% management, 17.3% professional, 12.6% services, 24.9% sales, 1.1% farming, 15.6% construction, 15.6% production (2000).
Income: Per capita income: $20,392 (2000); Median household income: $40,722 (2000); Poverty rate: 4.8% (2000).
Taxes: Total city taxes per capita: $231 (1997); City property taxes per capita: $228 (1997).
Education: High school graduation rate: 84.2% (2000); College graduation rate: 20.6% (2000).
Housing: Homeownership rate: 90.0% (2000); Median home value: $122,600 (2000); Median rent: $472 per month (2000); Median age of housing: 26 years (2000).
Transportation: Commute to work: 96.5% car, 0.7% public transportation, 0.9% walk, 1.7% work from home (2000); Travel time to work: 44.0% less than 15 minutes, 40.9% 15 to 30 minutes, 9.7% 30 to 45 minutes, 2.2% 45 to 60 minutes, 3.3% 60 minutes or more (2000)

NOKOMIS (town). Covers a land area of 33.386 square miles and a water area of 3.609 square miles. Located at 45.58° N. Lat.; 89.73° W. Long.
Population: 1,363 (2000); Race: 98.6% White, 0.0% Black, 0.0% Asian, 0.4% American Indian and Alaska Native, 0.6% Hispanic of any race, 0.8% two or more races (2000); Density: 40.8 persons per square mile (2000); Age: 22.2% under 18, 17.2% over 64 (2000); Marriage status: 14.4% never married, 71.2% now married, 5.3% widowed, 9.2% divorced (2000); Foreign born: 0.5% (2000); Ancestry (includes multiple ancestries): 55.5% German, 11.6% Irish, 11.0% Polish, 6.6% English, 5.8% Norwegian (2000).
Economy: Employment by occupation: 12.3% management, 12.7% professional, 12.6% services, 20.9% sales, 1.9% farming, 16.5% construction, 23.2% production (2000).
Income: Per capita income: $19,171 (2000); Median household income: $43,000 (2000); Poverty rate: 6.3% (2000).
Taxes: Total city taxes per capita: $138 (1997); City property taxes per capita: $134 (1997).
Education: High school graduation rate: 85.3% (2000); College graduation rate: 9.8% (2000).
Housing: Homeownership rate: 91.6% (2000); Median home value: $123,600 (2000); Median rent: $442 per month (2000); Median age of housing: 22 years (2000).
Transportation: Commute to work: 91.5% car, 0.9% public transportation, 3.7% walk, 4.0% work from home (2000); Travel time to work: 27.6% less than 15 minutes, 42.8% 15 to 30 minutes, 16.3% 30 to 45 minutes, 7.2% 45 to 60 minutes, 6.1% 60 minutes or more (2000)

PELICAN (town). Covers a land area of 51.453 square miles and a water area of 2.697 square miles. Located at 45.61° N. Lat.; 89.35° W. Long.
Population: 2,902 (2000); Race: 98.9% White, 0.1% Black, 0.2% Asian, 0.3% American Indian and Alaska Native, 0.0% Hispanic of any race, 0.5% two or more races (2000); Density: 56.4 persons per square mile (2000); Age: 25.5% under 18, 12.3% over 64 (2000); Marriage status: 18.6% never married, 66.3% now married, 4.6% widowed, 10.5% divorced (2000); Foreign born: 0.7% (2000); Ancestry (includes multiple ancestries): 43.0% German, 15.8% United States or American, 15.0% Irish, 8.4% Polish, 7.2% Swedish (2000).
Economy: Employment by occupation: 7.3% management, 18.3% professional, 18.1% services, 26.1% sales, 1.2% farming, 10.4% construction, 18.5% production (2000).
Income: Per capita income: $18,566 (2000); Median household income: $36,053 (2000); Poverty rate: 6.2% (2000).
Taxes: Total city taxes per capita: $72 (1997); City property taxes per capita: $58 (1997).
Education: High school graduation rate: 87.2% (2000); College graduation rate: 16.6% (2000).
Housing: Homeownership rate: 84.6% (2000); Median home value: $101,900 (2000); Median rent: $377 per month (2000); Median age of housing: 32 years (2000).
Transportation: Commute to work: 92.7% car, 0.0% public transportation, 3.4% walk, 2.7% work from home (2000); Travel time to work: 65.5% less than 15 minutes, 27.4% 15 to 30 minutes, 4.2% 30 to 45 minutes, 0.6% 45 to 60 minutes, 2.2% 60 minutes or more (2000)

PELICAN LAKE (unincorporated postal area, zip code 54463). Covers a land area of 61.951 square miles and a water area of 5.732 square miles. Located at 45.51° N. Lat.; 89.17° W. Long. Elevation is 1,604 feet.
History: Pelican Lake was settled in 1882 when the Milwaukee Lakeshore & Western Railroad arrived here. It was first a lumber town.
Population: 620 (2000); Race: 99.5% White, 0.0% Black, 0.0% Asian, 0.0% American Indian and Alaska Native, 0.0% Hispanic of any race, 0.5% two or more races (2000); Density: 10.0 persons per square mile (2000); Age: 20.5% under 18, 20.1% over 64 (2000); Marriage status: 17.6% never married, 64.6% now married, 5.3% widowed, 12.5% divorced (2000); Foreign born: 1.9% (2000); Ancestry (includes multiple ancestries): 73.6% German, 12.6% Polish, 11.1% Irish, 8.4% English, 6.6% Norwegian (2000).
Economy: Employment by occupation: 7.6% management, 13.0% professional, 18.4% services, 24.9% sales, 3.2% farming, 14.4% construction, 18.4% production (2000).
Income: Per capita income: $17,370 (2000); Median household income: $31,750 (2000); Poverty rate: 5.3% (2000).
Education: High school graduation rate: 83.7% (2000); College graduation rate: 11.0% (2000).
Housing: Homeownership rate: 84.7% (2000); Median home value: $86,500 (2000); Median rent: $392 per month (2000); Median age of housing: 31 years (2000).
Transportation: Commute to work: 93.8% car, 0.0% public transportation, 2.6% walk, 3.7% work from home (2000); Travel time to work: 20.6% less

than 15 minutes, 34.7% 15 to 30 minutes, 30.9% 30 to 45 minutes, 7.3% 45 to 60 minutes, 6.5% 60 minutes or more (2000)

Additional Information Contacts

Pelican Lake Chamber of Commerce. 715-487-5222

PIEHL (town). Covers a land area of 37.386 square miles and a water area of 0.593 square miles. Located at 45.67° N. Lat.; 89.12° W. Long.

Population: 93 (2000); Race: 100.0% White, 0.0% Black, 0.0% Asian, 0.0% American Indian and Alaska Native, 0.0% Hispanic of any race, 0.0% two or more races (2000); Density: 2.5 persons per square mile (2000); Age: 21.1% under 18, 16.8% over 64 (2000); Marriage status: 12.0% never married, 60.0% now married, 13.3% widowed, 14.7% divorced (2000); Foreign born: 3.2% (2000); Ancestry (includes multiple ancestries): 41.1% German, 28.4% Polish, 16.8% Irish, 11.6% Norwegian, 8.4% Italian (2000).

Economy: Employment by occupation: 0.0% management, 7.5% professional, 30.0% services, 22.5% sales, 0.0% farming, 20.0% construction, 20.0% production (2000).

Income: Per capita income: $13,101 (2000); Median household income: $31,500 (2000); Poverty rate: 4.2% (2000).

Taxes: Total city taxes per capita: $93 (1997); City property taxes per capita: $93 (1997).

Education: High school graduation rate: 81.4% (2000); College graduation rate: 0.0% (2000).

Housing: Homeownership rate: 92.7% (2000); Median home value: $85,000 (2000); Median age of housing: 20 years (2000).

Transportation: Commute to work: 90.0% car, 0.0% public transportation, 0.0% walk, 10.0% work from home (2000); Travel time to work: 25.0% less than 15 minutes, 41.7% 15 to 30 minutes, 27.8% 30 to 45 minutes, 5.6% 45 to 60 minutes, 0.0% 60 minutes or more (2000)

PINE LAKE (town). Covers a land area of 40.601 square miles and a water area of 4.412 square miles. Located at 45.68° N. Lat.; 89.39° W. Long.

Population: 2,720 (2000); Race: 98.9% White, 0.0% Black, 0.1% Asian, 0.6% American Indian and Alaska Native, 0.5% Hispanic of any race, 0.3% two or more races (2000); Density: 67.0 persons per square mile (2000); Age: 22.8% under 18, 11.1% over 64 (2000); Marriage status: 18.3% never married, 65.8% now married, 5.8% widowed, 10.1% divorced (2000); Foreign born: 1.5% (2000); Ancestry (includes multiple ancestries): 44.2% German, 15.1% Irish, 13.9% Polish, 8.3% Norwegian, 7.3% English (2000).

Economy: Employment by occupation: 9.2% management, 19.0% professional, 12.2% services, 29.3% sales, 2.5% farming, 11.3% construction, 16.4% production (2000).

Income: Per capita income: $21,515 (2000); Median household income: $43,750 (2000); Poverty rate: 7.4% (2000).

Taxes: Total city taxes per capita: $146 (1997); City property taxes per capita: $145 (1997).

Education: High school graduation rate: 89.4% (2000); College graduation rate: 22.2% (2000).

Housing: Homeownership rate: 83.0% (2000); Median home value: $114,400 (2000); Median rent: $441 per month (2000); Median age of housing: 27 years (2000).

Transportation: Commute to work: 94.4% car, 0.0% public transportation, 0.7% walk, 4.3% work from home (2000); Travel time to work: 45.8% less than 15 minutes, 42.0% 15 to 30 minutes, 4.4% 30 to 45 minutes, 3.2% 45 to 60 minutes, 4.6% 60 minutes or more (2000)

RHINELANDER (city). Covers a land area of 7.716 square miles and a water area of 0.168 square miles. Located at 45.64° N. Lat.; 89.41° W. Long. Elevation is 1,554 feet.

History: Logging began in the Rhinelander area in the mid-1850's. By 1916 the timber trade had declined, and Rhinelander turned to the manufacture of wood products and paper. It also became the center of a resort area. Rhinelander's early nickname of "the Hodag City" came from a Paul Bunyan legend telling of a beast called the hodag who roamed the forests. Eugene S. Shepard maintained that he had found the carcass of a hodag in a swampland near Rhinelander, and exhibited his beast widely before confessing that he had constructed the carcass himself.

Population: 7,735 (2000); Race: 96.0% White, 0.1% Black, 0.2% Asian, 1.7% American Indian and Alaska Native, 0.8% Hispanic of any race, 1.4% two or more races (2000); Density: 1,002.5 persons per square mile (2000); Age: 23.3% under 18, 21.3% over 64 (2000); Marriage status: 23.8% never married, 52.7% now married, 10.4% widowed, 13.1% divorced (2000); Foreign born: 0.8% (2000); Ancestry (includes multiple ancestries): 49.6% German, 13.9% Irish, 9.2% French (except Basque), 8.9% Norwegian, 7.9% Polish (2000).

Economy: Single-family building permits issued: 5 (2001) / 6 (2000); Multi-family building permits issued: 4 (2001) / 0 (2000); Employment by occupation: 7.0% management, 21.4% professional, 17.4% services, 26.9% sales, 2.0% farming, 7.6% construction, 17.7% production (2000).

Income: Per capita income: $16,047 (2000); Median household income: $29,622 (2000); Poverty rate: 12.2% (2000).

Taxes: Total city taxes per capita: $544 (2000); City property taxes per capita: $507 (2000).

Education: High school graduation rate: 78.9% (2000); College graduation rate: 20.0% (2000).

School District(s)

Rhinelander (PK-12)
 2000 Enrollment: 3,381 715-365-9750

Two-year College(s)

Nicolet Area Technical College (Public)
 2001 Enrollment: 1,565 715-365-4410
 2001 Tuition: In-state $2,310; Out-of-state $9,720

Housing: Homeownership rate: 57.5% (2000); Median home value: $72,700 (2000); Median rent: $386 per month (2000); Median age of housing: 52 years (2000).

Hospitals: Sacred Heart-St Marys Hospital (99 beds)

Safety: Violent crime rate: 6.4 per 10,000 population; Property crime rate: 382.5 per 10,000 population (2001).

Newspapers: The Daily News (6 x week)

Transportation: Commute to work: 86.2% car, 1.4% public transportation, 8.1% walk, 3.0% work from home (2000); Travel time to work: 76.1% less than 15 minutes, 13.7% 15 to 30 minutes, 6.6% 30 to 45 minutes, 0.6% 45 to 60 minutes, 3.0% 60 minutes or more (2000)

Airports: Rhinelander-Oneida County (primary service)

SCHOEPKE (town). Covers a land area of 46.054 square miles and a water area of 4.530 square miles. Located at 45.51° N. Lat.; 89.14° W. Long.

Population: 352 (2000); Race: 99.0% White, 0.0% Black, 0.0% Asian, 0.0% American Indian and Alaska Native, 0.0% Hispanic of any race, 1.0% two or more races (2000); Density: 7.6 persons per square mile (2000); Age: 14.4% under 18, 26.3% over 64 (2000); Marriage status: 16.2% never married, 64.3% now married, 8.1% widowed, 11.4% divorced (2000); Foreign born: 1.9% (2000); Ancestry (includes multiple ancestries): 71.8% German, 18.6% Polish, 18.3% Irish, 9.6% English, 4.8% Norwegian (2000).

Economy: Employment by occupation: 11.1% management, 7.4% professional, 19.3% services, 29.6% sales, 1.5% farming, 9.6% construction, 21.5% production (2000).

Income: Per capita income: $20,134 (2000); Median household income: $28,929 (2000); Poverty rate: 8.7% (2000).

Taxes: Total city taxes per capita: $198 (1997); City property taxes per capita: $196 (1997).

Education: High school graduation rate: 79.0% (2000); College graduation rate: 6.5% (2000).

Housing: Homeownership rate: 84.8% (2000); Median home value: $89,400 (2000); Median rent: $382 per month (2000); Median age of housing: 27 years (2000).

Transportation: Commute to work: 95.5% car, 0.0% public transportation, 3.0% walk, 1.5% work from home (2000); Travel time to work: 19.2% less than 15 minutes, 27.7% 15 to 30 minutes, 43.8% 30 to 45 minutes, 3.1% 45 to 60 minutes, 6.2% 60 minutes or more (2000)

STELLA (town). Covers a land area of 35.325 square miles and a water area of 1.965 square miles. Located at 45.67° N. Lat.; 89.25° W. Long.

Population: 633 (2000); Race: 96.9% White, 0.0% Black, 0.5% Asian, 1.9% American Indian and Alaska Native, 0.0% Hispanic of any race, 0.6% two or more races (2000); Density: 17.9 persons per square mile (2000); Age: 26.7% under 18, 12.3% over 64 (2000); Marriage status: 20.1% never married, 65.8% now married, 6.4% widowed, 7.7% divorced (2000); Foreign born: 2.1% (2000); Ancestry (includes multiple ancestries): 39.8% German, 14.7% Irish, 14.1% English, 8.7% Polish, 4.4% Norwegian (2000).

Economy: Employment by occupation: 16.7% management, 18.5% professional, 8.0% services, 26.9% sales, 6.2% farming, 7.3% construction, 16.4% production (2000).

Income: Per capita income: $16,712 (2000); Median household income: $40,909 (2000); Poverty rate: 8.3% (2000).

Taxes: Total city taxes per capita: $64 (1997); City property taxes per capita: $64 (1997).

Education: High school graduation rate: 82.8% (2000); College graduation rate: 15.0% (2000).

Housing: Homeownership rate: 97.4% (2000); Median home value: $107,400 (2000); Median rent: $275 per month (2000); Median age of housing: 20 years (2000).
Transportation: Commute to work: 93.8% car, 0.0% public transportation, 3.3% walk, 2.2% work from home (2000); Travel time to work: 32.6% less than 15 minutes, 51.3% 15 to 30 minutes, 9.0% 30 to 45 minutes, 2.6% 45 to 60 minutes, 4.5% 60 minutes or more (2000)

SUGAR CAMP (town). Aka Robbins. Covers a land area of 88.873 square miles and a water area of 9.149 square miles. Located at 45.82° N. Lat.; 89.34° W. Long. Elevation is 1,680 feet.
Population: 1,781 (2000); Race: 98.3% White, 0.0% Black, 0.5% Asian, 0.8% American Indian and Alaska Native, 0.0% Hispanic of any race, 0.4% two or more races (2000); Density: 20.0 persons per square mile (2000); Age: 25.3% under 18, 15.4% over 64 (2000); Marriage status: 19.2% never married, 66.2% now married, 5.7% widowed, 8.9% divorced (2000); Foreign born: 1.3% (2000); Ancestry (includes multiple ancestries): 43.6% German, 23.1% Polish, 15.1% Irish, 7.8% English, 6.8% Swedish (2000).
Economy: Employment by occupation: 10.0% management, 15.1% professional, 13.5% services, 24.3% sales, 2.5% farming, 15.9% construction, 18.8% production (2000).
Income: Per capita income: $18,135 (2000); Median household income: $37,118 (2000); Poverty rate: 4.3% (2000).
Taxes: Total city taxes per capita: $216 (1997); City property taxes per capita: $213 (1997).
Education: High school graduation rate: 83.3% (2000); College graduation rate: 14.7% (2000).
Housing: Homeownership rate: 86.6% (2000); Median home value: $111,200 (2000); Median rent: $388 per month (2000); Median age of housing: 28 years (2000).
Transportation: Commute to work: 93.0% car, 0.6% public transportation, 1.1% walk, 4.3% work from home (2000); Travel time to work: 26.0% less than 15 minutes, 53.1% 15 to 30 minutes, 12.0% 30 to 45 minutes, 5.2% 45 to 60 minutes, 3.7% 60 minutes or more (2000)

THREE LAKES (town). Covers a land area of 81.499 square miles and a water area of 18.377 square miles. Located at 45.80° N. Lat.; 89.12° W. Long. Elevation is 1,666 feet.
Population: 2,339 (2000); Race: 98.9% White, 0.0% Black, 0.2% Asian, 0.1% American Indian and Alaska Native, 0.7% Hispanic of any race, 0.6% two or more races (2000); Density: 28.7 persons per square mile (2000); Age: 20.7% under 18, 27.0% over 64 (2000); Marriage status: 16.3% never married, 64.4% now married, 9.1% widowed, 10.2% divorced (2000); Foreign born: 0.9% (2000); Ancestry (includes multiple ancestries): 51.5% German, 14.6% Polish, 12.7% English, 12.4% Irish, 5.9% French (except Basque) (2000).
Economy: In lake region. Lumbering, farming. Winery. Manufacturing of cutting and stripping blades. Nicolet National Forest to East. Sheltered Valley Ski Area here. Employment by occupation: 12.0% management, 14.2% professional, 17.0% services, 30.8% sales, 1.3% farming, 13.7% construction, 10.9% production (2000).
Income: Per capita income: $17,758 (2000); Median household income: $32,798 (2000); Poverty rate: 6.7% (2000).
Taxes: Total city taxes per capita: $435 (2000); City property taxes per capita: $432 (2000).
Education: High school graduation rate: 88.6% (2000); College graduation rate: 19.0% (2000).

School District(s)

Three Lakes (PK-12)
2000 Enrollment: 792 715-546-3496
Housing: Homeownership rate: 87.6% (2000); Median home value: $121,200 (2000); Median rent: $352 per month (2000); Median age of housing: 33 years (2000).
Safety: Violent crime rate: 8.5 per 10,000 population; Property crime rate: 114.6 per 10,000 population (2001).
Transportation: Commute to work: 87.5% car, 1.4% public transportation, 4.9% walk, 6.2% work from home (2000); Travel time to work: 45.9% less than 15 minutes, 32.3% 15 to 30 minutes, 16.4% 30 to 45 minutes, 2.2% 45 to 60 minutes, 3.2% 60 minutes or more (2000)
Additional Information Contacts
Three Lakes Info Bureau 715-546-3344

TRIPOLI (unincorporated postal area, zip code 54564). Covers a land area of 153.451 square miles and a water area of 1.523 square miles. Located at 45.63° N. Lat.; 89.96° W. Long.
Population: 496 (2000); Race: 98.4% White, 0.0% Black, 0.0% Asian, 0.7% American Indian and Alaska Native, 0.0% Hispanic of any race, 0.9% two or more races (2000); Density: 3.2 persons per square mile (2000); Age: 19.4% under 18, 25.6% over 64 (2000); Marriage status: 18.7% never married, 62.8% now married, 10.1% widowed, 8.4% divorced (2000); Foreign born: 0.0% (2000); Ancestry (includes multiple ancestries): 39.5% German, 13.2% Polish, 12.5% Finnish, 11.8% Swedish, 7.9% Irish (2000).
Economy: Employment by occupation: 5.0% management, 10.7% professional, 23.3% services, 19.5% sales, 1.9% farming, 20.1% construction, 19.5% production (2000).
Income: Per capita income: $16,455 (2000); Median household income: $23,750 (2000); Poverty rate: 18.0% (2000).
Education: High school graduation rate: 86.2% (2000); College graduation rate: 4.3% (2000).
Housing: Homeownership rate: 92.6% (2000); Median home value: $76,300 (2000); Median rent: $325 per month (2000); Median age of housing: 33 years (2000).
Transportation: Commute to work: 91.9% car, 0.0% public transportation, 3.4% walk, 4.7% work from home (2000); Travel time to work: 12.7% less than 15 minutes, 25.4% 15 to 30 minutes, 28.2% 30 to 45 minutes, 21.8% 45 to 60 minutes, 12.0% 60 minutes or more (2000)

WOODBORO (town). Covers a land area of 34.593 square miles and a water area of 2.360 square miles. Located at 45.59° N. Lat.; 89.61° W. Long. Elevation is 1,619 feet.
Population: 685 (2000); Race: 99.1% White, 0.0% Black, 0.3% Asian, 0.0% American Indian and Alaska Native, 2.0% Hispanic of any race, 0.3% two or more races (2000); Density: 19.8 persons per square mile (2000); Age: 19.8% under 18, 15.0% over 64 (2000); Marriage status: 14.4% never married, 69.9% now married, 5.6% widowed, 10.1% divorced (2000); Foreign born: 1.4% (2000); Ancestry (includes multiple ancestries): 53.4% German, 14.1% Polish, 10.2% Irish, 9.2% English, 9.1% Swedish (2000).
Economy: Employment by occupation: 6.5% management, 21.7% professional, 13.1% services, 23.7% sales, 3.3% farming, 13.6% construction, 18.1% production (2000).
Income: Per capita income: $21,079 (2000); Median household income: $42,054 (2000); Poverty rate: 6.7% (2000).
Taxes: Total city taxes per capita: $112 (1997); City property taxes per capita: $110 (1997).
Education: High school graduation rate: 89.9% (2000); College graduation rate: 18.4% (2000).
Housing: Homeownership rate: 82.9% (2000); Median home value: $117,600 (2000); Median rent: $413 per month (2000); Median age of housing: 29 years (2000).
Transportation: Commute to work: 94.6% car, 0.6% public transportation, 1.2% walk, 1.8% work from home (2000); Travel time to work: 21.3% less than 15 minutes, 62.9% 15 to 30 minutes, 9.1% 30 to 45 minutes, 2.7% 45 to 60 minutes, 4.0% 60 minutes or more (2000)

WOODRUFF (town). Covers a land area of 28.531 square miles and a water area of 7.043 square miles. Located at 45.86° N. Lat.; 89.64° W. Long. Elevation is 1,610 feet.
Population: 1,982 (2000); Race: 98.5% White, 0.0% Black, 0.0% Asian, 0.8% American Indian and Alaska Native, 0.0% Hispanic of any race, 0.7% two or more races (2000); Density: 69.5 persons per square mile (2000); Age: 21.5% under 18, 26.1% over 64 (2000); Marriage status: 18.1% never married, 58.5% now married, 12.0% widowed, 11.4% divorced (2000); Foreign born: 0.8% (2000); Ancestry (includes multiple ancestries): 44.8% German, 11.7% Irish, 10.3% Polish, 9.2% Norwegian, 6.2% English (2000).
Economy: Manufacturing: lumber and flooring. Agricultural research station to Southeast. Employment by occupation: 14.3% management, 16.6% professional, 16.8% services, 28.6% sales, 0.8% farming, 11.2% construction, 11.7% production (2000).
Income: Per capita income: $20,508 (2000); Median household income: $35,335 (2000); Poverty rate: 10.8% (2000).
Taxes: Total city taxes per capita: $395 (2000); City property taxes per capita: $373 (2000).
Education: High school graduation rate: 83.3% (2000); College graduation rate: 14.5% (2000).
Housing: Homeownership rate: 74.1% (2000); Median home value: $101,800 (2000); Median rent: $404 per month (2000); Median age of housing: 22 years (2000).
Hospitals: Howard Young Medical Center (99 beds)
Safety: Violent crime rate: 0.0 per 10,000 population; Property crime rate: 410.8 per 10,000 population (2001).

Transportation: Commute to work: 87.9% car, 0.3% public transportation, 6.1% walk, 4.2% work from home (2000); Travel time to work: 62.1% less than 15 minutes, 23.1% 15 to 30 minutes, 10.5% 30 to 45 minutes, 1.2% 45 to 60 minutes, 3.2% 60 minutes or more (2000)
Additional Information Contacts
Northwoods Association of Realtors 715-356-3400

Outagamie County

Located in eastern Wisconsin; drained by the Wolf, Fox, and Embarrass Rivers. Covers a land area of 640.30 square miles, a water area of 4.10 square miles, and is located in the Central Time Zone. The county government was organized in 1851. County seat is Appleton.

Outagamie County is part of the Appleton-Oshkosh-Neenah, WI MSA. The entire metro area includes: Calumet County; Outagamie County; Winnebago County

Weather Station: Appleton — Elevation: 748 feet

	Jan	Feb	Mar	Apr	May	Jun	Jul	Aug	Sep	Oct	Nov	Dec
High	24	29	40	54	68	77	82	79	70	57	42	29
Low	8	12	23	35	47	56	62	60	51	40	27	14
Precip	1.2	1.0	2.1	2.8	3.1	3.5	3.4	3.8	3.3	2.3	2.3	1.3
Snow	12.2	8.0	8.0	2.5	0.2	0.0	0.0	0.0	0.0	0.2	4.3	10.3

High and Low temperatures in degrees Fahrenheit; Precipitation and Snow in inches

Weather Station: New London — Elevation: 803 feet

	Jan	Feb	Mar	Apr	May	Jun	Jul	Aug	Sep	Oct	Nov	Dec
High	25	30	41	56	70	79	82	80	72	59	43	30
Low	5	10	21	34	45	54	59	57	48	37	25	12
Precip	1.4	1.1	2.0	2.6	3.4	3.5	3.9	4.1	3.2	2.4	2.1	1.4
Snow	11.3	6.8	8.5	2.0	tr	0.0	0.0	0.0	0.0	0.1	3.9	8.8

High and Low temperatures in degrees Fahrenheit; Precipitation and Snow in inches

Population: 160,971 (2000); Race: 93.9% White, 0.6% Black, 2.3% Asian, 1.5% American Indian and Alaska Native, 2.0% Hispanic of any race, 1.0% two or more races (2000); Density: 251.4 persons per square mile (2000); Age: 27.6% under 18, 10.9% over 64 (2000).
Religion: Five largest groups: 51.9% Catholic Church, 8.9% Evangelical Lutheran Church in America, 8.6% Wisconsin Evangelical Lutheran Synod, 4.8% Lutheran Church—Missouri Synod, 2.4% The United Methodist Church (2000).
Economy: Unemployment rate: 4.2% (11/2002); Total civilian labor force: 106,651 (11/2002); Leading industries: 22.9% manufacturing; 12.9% retail trade; 8.8% health care and social assistance (2000); Companies that employ more than 1,000 persons: 9 (2000); Companies that employ more than 100 persons: 151 (2000); Farms: 1,286 totaling 252,471 acres (1997); Minority business ownership rate: 1.9% (1997); Women business ownership rate: 21.8% (1997); Retail sales per capita: $12,549 (1997). Single-family building permits issued: 851 (2001) / 910 (2000); Multi-family building permits issued: 849 (2001) / 578 (2000).
Income: Per capita income: $21,943 (2000); Median household income: $49,613 (2000); Poverty rate: 4.7% (2000); Bankruptcy rate: 2.99% (2001).
Taxes: Total county taxes per capita: $194 (2000); County property taxes per capita: $189 (2000).
Education: High school graduation rate: 88.1% (2000); College graduation rate: 22.5% (2000).
Housing: Homeownership rate: 72.4% (2000); Median home value: $106,000 (2000); Median rent: $469 per month (2000); Median age of housing: 29 years (2000).
Health: Birth rate: 135.1 per 10,000 population (1998); Age adjusted death rate: 78.2 per 10,000 population (1999); Age adjusted cancer mortality rate: 193.2 deaths per 100,000 population (1999). Air Quality Index: 78% good, 22% moderate, 0% unhealthy (percent of days in 2000). Number of physicians: 20.5 per 10,000 population (1999); Number of hospital beds: 21.8 per 10,000 population (1999).
Elections: 2000 Presidential election results: 43.2% Gore, 52.1% Bush, 3.4% Nader, 0.6% Buchanan
National and State Parks: Deer Creek State Wildlife Area; Mack State Wildlife Area; Maine State Wildlife Area; Outagamie State Wildlife Area; Thousand Island State Conservancy Area
Additional Information Contacts
Outagamie County Government Offices 920-832-1684
Fox Cities Convention Bureau 920-734-3358
Kaukauna Chamber of Commerce 920-766-1616
Realtors Association of Northeast Wisconsin 920-739-9108
Seymour Chamber of Commerce 920-833-6053

Outagamie County Communities

APPLETON (city). Covers a land area of 20.885 square miles and a water area of 0.474 square miles. Located at 44.26° N. Lat.; 88.40° W. Long. Elevation is 790 feet.
History: In 1847 Amos A. Lawrence donated land for the establishment of a Methodist college at the Grand Chute, as the rapids of the Fox River were known. Grand Chute was renamed Appleton for Lawrence's father-in-law. Water power from the falls soon gave rise to a sawmill, paper mill, cabinet factory, and several flour mills which were operating here by 1854. Of these, the paper industry emerged as the source of revenue for Appleton after 1900. Magician Harry Houdini (1874-1926) was born in Appleton as Ehrich Weiss, the fifth child of a Jewish rabbi who had fled here from Budapest.
Population: 70,087 (2000); Race: 91.8% White, 1.0% Black, 4.6% Asian, 0.7% American Indian and Alaska Native, 2.5% Hispanic of any race, 1.1% two or more races (2000); Density: 3,355.9 persons per square mile (2000); Age: 27.3% under 18, 11.3% over 64 (2000); Marriage status: 26.1% never married, 59.2% now married, 5.6% widowed, 9.2% divorced (2000); Foreign born: 5.1% (2000); Ancestry (includes multiple ancestries): 49.6% German, 11.9% Irish, 8.9% Other groups, 7.1% Dutch, 6.3% English (2000).
Vital Statistics: Birth rate: 162.2 per 10,000 population (1998)
Economy: Unemployment rate: 5.8% (11/2002); Total civilian labor force: 46,152 (11/2002); Single-family building permits issued: 165 (2001) / 200 (2000); Multi-family building permits issued: 212 (2001) / 191 (2000); Employment by occupation: 13.7% management, 20.6% professional, 12.7% services, 26.7% sales, 0.2% farming, 7.5% construction, 18.6% production (2000).
Income: Per capita income: $22,478 (2000); Median household income: $47,285 (2000); Poverty rate: 5.5% (2000).
Taxes: Total city taxes per capita: $376 (2000); City property taxes per capita: $351 (2000).
Education: High school graduation rate: 88.8% (2000); College graduation rate: 29.7% (2000).

School District(s)
Appleton Area (PK-12)
2000 Enrollment: 14,793 920-832-6161
Four-year College(s)
Lawrence University (Private, Not-for-profit)
2001 Enrollment: 1,323 920-832-7000
2001 Tuition: In-state $22,584; Out-of-state $22,584
Two-year College(s)
Fox Valley Technical College at Appleton (Public)
2001 Enrollment: n/a 920-735-5600
2001 Tuition: In-state $2,176; Out-of-state $16,986
Martins College of Cosmetology (Private, For-profit)
2001 Enrollment: 46 920-684-3028

Housing: Homeownership rate: 68.8% (2000); Median home value: $97,900 (2000); Median rent: $456 per month (2000); Median age of housing: 36 years (2000).
Hospitals: Appleton Medical Center (160 beds); Saint Elizabeth Hospital (332 beds)
Safety: Violent crime rate: 21.5 per 10,000 population; Property crime rate: 249.3 per 10,000 population (2001).
Newspapers: Valley Scene (1 x month); Central Wisconsin Sunday; The Spirit (1 x week); The Post-Crescent (7 x week); The Current (1 x week)
Transportation: Commute to work: 91.5% car, 1.1% public transportation, 4.3% walk, 2.1% work from home (2000); Travel time to work: 47.6% less than 15 minutes, 40.5% 15 to 30 minutes, 7.8% 30 to 45 minutes, 1.9% 45 to 60 minutes, 2.2% 60 minutes or more (2000); Amtrak: Service available.
Airports: Outagamie County Regional (primary service)
Additional Information Contacts
Fox Cities Convention Bureau 920-734-3358
Realtors Association of Northeast Wisconsin 920-739-9108

BEAR CREEK (village). Covers a land area of 0.925 square miles and a water area of 0 square miles. Located at 44.53° N. Lat.; 88.72° W. Long. Elevation is 817 feet.
Population: 415 (2000); Race: 96.6% White, 0.0% Black, 0.0% Asian, 0.0% American Indian and Alaska Native, 11.4% Hispanic of any race, 1.9% two or more races (2000); Density: 448.8 persons per square mile (2000); Age: 27.8% under 18, 10.7% over 64 (2000); Marriage status: 25.6% never married, 54.2% now married, 9.3% widowed, 10.9% divorced (2000); Foreign born: 1.5% (2000); Ancestry (includes multiple ancestries): 42.6%

German, 14.3% Irish, 13.6% French (except Basque), 9.7% Other groups, 5.3% Polish (2000).
Economy: Dairying; farming. Manufacturing: food. Single-family building permits issued: 0 (2001) / 1 (2000); Multi-family building permits issued: 0 (2001) / 0 (2000); Employment by occupation: 5.3% management, 8.3% professional, 9.7% services, 17.5% sales, 4.9% farming, 16.0% construction, 38.3% production (2000).
Income: Per capita income: $16,556 (2000); Median household income: $39,375 (2000); Poverty rate: 8.0% (2000).
Taxes: Total city taxes per capita: $119 (1997); City property taxes per capita: $113 (1997).
Education: High school graduation rate: 76.4% (2000); College graduation rate: 3.5% (2000).
Housing: Homeownership rate: 65.8% (2000); Median home value: $65,500 (2000); Median rent: $338 per month (2000); Median age of housing: 60+ years (2000).
Transportation: Commute to work: 89.2% car, 0.0% public transportation, 6.4% walk, 3.4% work from home (2000); Travel time to work: 19.3% less than 15 minutes, 32.5% 15 to 30 minutes, 18.8% 30 to 45 minutes, 21.3% 45 to 60 minutes, 8.1% 60 minutes or more (2000)

BLACK CREEK (village). Covers a land area of 1.041 square miles and a water area of 0 square miles. Located at 44.47° N. Lat.; 88.45° W. Long. Elevation is 790 feet.
Population: 1,192 (2000); Race: 97.3% White, 0.0% Black, 1.3% Asian, 0.9% American Indian and Alaska Native, 0.2% Hispanic of any race, 0.6% two or more races (2000); Density: 1,145.5 persons per square mile (2000); Age: 23.3% under 18, 13.4% over 64 (2000); Marriage status: 25.2% never married, 59.3% now married, 8.3% widowed, 7.2% divorced (2000); Foreign born: 0.9% (2000); Ancestry (includes multiple ancestries): 65.4% German, 9.7% Dutch, 9.6% Irish, 6.0% Polish, 4.8% Other groups (2000).
Economy: Single-family building permits issued: 7 (2001) / 7 (2000); Multi-family building permits issued: 0 (2001) / 0 (2000); Employment by occupation: 7.8% management, 13.3% professional, 11.9% services, 24.0% sales, 0.0% farming, 12.4% construction, 30.6% production (2000).
Income: Per capita income: $18,226 (2000); Median household income: $42,946 (2000); Poverty rate: 7.1% (2000).
Taxes: Total city taxes per capita: $74 (1997); City property taxes per capita: $69 (1997).
Education: High school graduation rate: 82.9% (2000); College graduation rate: 6.7% (2000).
Housing: Homeownership rate: 70.9% (2000); Median home value: $88,600 (2000); Median rent: $388 per month (2000); Median age of housing: 32 years (2000).
Transportation: Commute to work: 92.3% car, 0.3% public transportation, 5.6% walk, 0.8% work from home (2000); Travel time to work: 23.1% less than 15 minutes, 39.2% 15 to 30 minutes, 29.2% 30 to 45 minutes, 6.7% 45 to 60 minutes, 1.9% 60 minutes or more (2000)

BLACK CREEK (town). Covers a land area of 35.053 square miles and a water area of 0 square miles. Located at 44.45° N. Lat.; 88.45° W. Long. Elevation is 790 feet.
Population: 1,268 (2000); Race: 97.3% White, 0.0% Black, 0.0% Asian, 0.9% American Indian and Alaska Native, 0.8% Hispanic of any race, 1.7% two or more races (2000); Density: 36.2 persons per square mile (2000); Age: 27.1% under 18, 8.8% over 64 (2000); Marriage status: 24.7% never married, 64.9% now married, 3.4% widowed, 7.0% divorced (2000); Foreign born: 0.5% (2000); Ancestry (includes multiple ancestries): 71.3% German, 9.4% Dutch, 7.9% Irish, 5.3% United States or American, 4.5% French (except Basque) (2000).
Economy: Railroad junction. Dairying; farming; cheese; livestock. Manufacturing: concrete, shipping containers. Single-family building permits issued: 10 (2001) / 10 (2000); Multi-family building permits issued: 0 (2001) / 0 (2000); Employment by occupation: 13.3% management, 9.4% professional, 7.2% services, 22.5% sales, 1.5% farming, 16.4% construction, 29.6% production (2000).
Income: Per capita income: $20,481 (2000); Median household income: $53,472 (2000); Poverty rate: 6.1% (2000).
Taxes: Total city taxes per capita: $57 (1997); City property taxes per capita: $53 (1997).
Education: High school graduation rate: 86.6% (2000); College graduation rate: 7.7% (2000).
Housing: Homeownership rate: 93.2% (2000); Median home value: $120,500 (2000); Median rent: $431 per month (2000); Median age of housing: 27 years (2000).
Transportation: Commute to work: 90.4% car, 0.3% public transportation, 1.9% walk, 7.4% work from home (2000); Travel time to work: 17.8% less than 15 minutes, 50.1% 15 to 30 minutes, 23.2% 30 to 45 minutes, 3.4% 45 to 60 minutes, 5.4% 60 minutes or more (2000)

BOVINA (town). Covers a land area of 33.672 square miles and a water area of 0.059 square miles. Located at 44.45° N. Lat.; 88.56° W. Long.
Population: 1,130 (2000); Race: 96.3% White, 0.0% Black, 0.0% Asian, 0.9% American Indian and Alaska Native, 4.9% Hispanic of any race, 1.7% two or more races (2000); Density: 33.6 persons per square mile (2000); Age: 30.1% under 18, 8.8% over 64 (2000); Marriage status: 23.0% never married, 67.5% now married, 5.0% widowed, 4.6% divorced (2000); Foreign born: 2.0% (2000); Ancestry (includes multiple ancestries): 52.8% German, 10.3% Irish, 10.0% Other groups, 8.1% Dutch, 4.6% Polish (2000).
Economy: Employment by occupation: 12.2% management, 10.7% professional, 10.0% services, 22.5% sales, 2.1% farming, 12.3% construction, 30.1% production (2000).
Income: Per capita income: $19,102 (2000); Median household income: $54,453 (2000); Poverty rate: 1.7% (2000).
Taxes: Total city taxes per capita: $8 (1997); City property taxes per capita: $8 (1997).
Education: High school graduation rate: 87.0% (2000); College graduation rate: 10.7% (2000).
Housing: Homeownership rate: 93.8% (2000); Median home value: $125,900 (2000); Median rent: $375 per month (2000); Median age of housing: 26 years (2000).
Transportation: Commute to work: 96.3% car, 0.2% public transportation, 0.5% walk, 2.5% work from home (2000); Travel time to work: 18.1% less than 15 minutes, 45.7% 15 to 30 minutes, 29.5% 30 to 45 minutes, 2.6% 45 to 60 minutes, 4.1% 60 minutes or more (2000)

BUCHANAN (town). Covers a land area of 16.588 square miles and a water area of 0.342 square miles. Located at 44.25° N. Lat.; 88.29° W. Long.
Population: 5,827 (2000); Race: 98.6% White, 0.0% Black, 0.7% Asian, 0.2% American Indian and Alaska Native, 1.5% Hispanic of any race, 0.4% two or more races (2000); Density: 351.3 persons per square mile (2000); Age: 34.8% under 18, 6.5% over 64 (2000); Marriage status: 18.1% never married, 75.1% now married, 2.7% widowed, 4.1% divorced (2000); Foreign born: 1.2% (2000); Ancestry (includes multiple ancestries): 54.9% German, 23.0% Dutch, 10.7% Irish, 7.4% Polish, 6.2% French (except Basque) (2000).
Economy: Single-family building permits issued: 82 (2001) / 107 (2000); Multi-family building permits issued: 96 (2001) / 76 (2000); Employment by occupation: 18.3% management, 22.9% professional, 6.9% services, 28.1% sales, 0.2% farming, 9.0% construction, 14.6% production (2000).
Income: Per capita income: $22,729 (2000); Median household income: $65,410 (2000); Poverty rate: 1.2% (2000).
Taxes: Total city taxes per capita: $110 (1997); City property taxes per capita: $93 (1997).
Education: High school graduation rate: 96.0% (2000); College graduation rate: 31.3% (2000).
Housing: Homeownership rate: 86.8% (2000); Median home value: $149,400 (2000); Median rent: $768 per month (2000); Median age of housing: 6 years (2000).
Transportation: Commute to work: 93.3% car, 0.4% public transportation, 1.2% walk, 4.8% work from home (2000); Travel time to work: 36.4% less than 15 minutes, 51.6% 15 to 30 minutes, 7.3% 30 to 45 minutes, 1.3% 45 to 60 minutes, 3.3% 60 minutes or more (2000)

CENTER (town). Covers a land area of 35.656 square miles and a water area of 0 square miles. Located at 44.37° N. Lat.; 88.44° W. Long.
Population: 3,163 (2000); Race: 99.2% White, 0.0% Black, 0.1% Asian, 0.1% American Indian and Alaska Native, 0.6% Hispanic of any race, 0.4% two or more races (2000); Density: 88.7 persons per square mile (2000); Age: 27.1% under 18, 8.4% over 64 (2000); Marriage status: 20.0% never married, 69.9% now married, 3.5% widowed, 6.6% divorced (2000); Foreign born: 1.3% (2000); Ancestry (includes multiple ancestries): 61.0% German, 14.3% Dutch, 11.1% Irish, 8.3% Polish, 5.7% United States or American (2000).
Economy: Single-family building permits issued: 21 (2001) / 23 (2000); Multi-family building permits issued: 0 (2001) / 0 (2000); Employment by occupation: 12.6% management, 12.8% professional, 8.3% services, 25.7% sales, 1.7% farming, 16.7% construction, 22.2% production (2000).
Income: Per capita income: $23,553 (2000); Median household income: $58,092 (2000); Poverty rate: 0.4% (2000).
Taxes: Total city taxes per capita: $48 (1997); City property taxes per capita: $45 (1997).

Education: High school graduation rate: 90.0% (2000); College graduation rate: 13.7% (2000).
Housing: Homeownership rate: 94.2% (2000); Median home value: $142,900 (2000); Median rent: $367 per month (2000); Median age of housing: 24 years (2000).
Transportation: Commute to work: 92.4% car, 0.0% public transportation, 1.0% walk, 6.6% work from home (2000); Travel time to work: 22.2% less than 15 minutes, 63.4% 15 to 30 minutes, 8.6% 30 to 45 minutes, 2.4% 45 to 60 minutes, 3.4% 60 minutes or more (2000)

CICERO (town). Covers a land area of 35.478 square miles and a water area of 0.007 square miles. Located at 44.54° N. Lat.; 88.44° W. Long. Elevation is 855 feet.
Population: 1,092 (2000); Race: 99.3% White, 0.0% Black, 0.0% Asian, 0.6% American Indian and Alaska Native, 0.2% Hispanic of any race, 0.2% two or more races (2000); Density: 30.8 persons per square mile (2000); Age: 30.1% under 18, 8.5% over 64 (2000); Marriage status: 24.1% never married, 67.7% now married, 4.2% widowed, 3.9% divorced (2000); Foreign born: 0.0% (2000); Ancestry (includes multiple ancestries): 60.5% German, 12.1% Dutch, 8.1% Polish, 7.6% Irish, 5.1% English (2000).
Economy: Single-family building permits issued: 11 (2001) / 3 (2000); Multi-family building permits issued: 0 (2001) / 0 (2000); Employment by occupation: 17.3% management, 10.1% professional, 8.8% services, 19.9% sales, 4.5% farming, 13.5% construction, 25.9% production (2000).
Income: Per capita income: $19,783 (2000); Median household income: $49,625 (2000); Poverty rate: 4.2% (2000).
Taxes: Total city taxes per capita: $89 (1997); City property taxes per capita: $87 (1997).
Education: High school graduation rate: 81.3% (2000); College graduation rate: 8.9% (2000).
Housing: Homeownership rate: 89.7% (2000); Median home value: $95,400 (2000); Median rent: $475 per month (2000); Median age of housing: 46 years (2000).
Transportation: Commute to work: 84.6% car, 0.3% public transportation, 1.7% walk, 12.2% work from home (2000); Travel time to work: 22.1% less than 15 minutes, 22.9% 15 to 30 minutes, 40.0% 30 to 45 minutes, 9.0% 45 to 60 minutes, 6.1% 60 minutes or more (2000)

COMBINED LOCKS (village). Covers a land area of 1.522 square miles and a water area of 0.188 square miles. Located at 44.26° N. Lat.; 88.31° W. Long. Elevation is 700 feet.
Population: 2,422 (2000); Race: 99.0% White, 0.2% Black, 0.0% Asian, 0.3% American Indian and Alaska Native, 1.2% Hispanic of any race, 0.0% two or more races (2000); Density: 1,591.3 persons per square mile (2000); Age: 26.6% under 18, 10.2% over 64 (2000); Marriage status: 17.4% never married, 72.5% now married, 3.6% widowed, 6.5% divorced (2000); Foreign born: 1.6% (2000); Ancestry (includes multiple ancestries): 44.8% German, 27.2% Dutch, 8.7% United States or American, 8.2% Irish, 6.2% Polish (2000).
Economy: Paper mill. Manufacturing: oils and coolants. Single-family building permits issued: 56 (2001) / 43 (2000); Multi-family building permits issued: 0 (2001) / 10 (2000); Employment by occupation: 10.5% management, 14.9% professional, 11.1% services, 31.2% sales, 0.0% farming, 10.8% construction, 21.4% production (2000).
Income: Per capita income: $24,090 (2000); Median household income: $53,125 (2000); Poverty rate: 0.8% (2000).
Taxes: Total city taxes per capita: $273 (2000); City property taxes per capita: $257 (2000).
Education: High school graduation rate: 89.9% (2000); College graduation rate: 15.1% (2000).
Housing: Homeownership rate: 91.8% (2000); Median home value: $99,500 (2000); Median rent: $470 per month (2000); Median age of housing: 33 years (2000).
Safety: Violent crime rate: 4.1 per 10,000 population; Property crime rate: 102.5 per 10,000 population (2001).
Transportation: Commute to work: 93.5% car, 0.0% public transportation, 2.5% walk, 3.3% work from home (2000); Travel time to work: 46.1% less than 15 minutes, 45.0% 15 to 30 minutes, 6.2% 30 to 45 minutes, 0.9% 45 to 60 minutes, 1.8% 60 minutes or more (2000)

DALE (town). Covers a land area of 30.438 square miles and a water area of 0.029 square miles. Located at 44.28° N. Lat.; 88.66° W. Long. Elevation is 806 feet.
Population: 2,288 (2000); Race: 98.6% White, 0.0% Black, 0.0% Asian, 0.2% American Indian and Alaska Native, 1.0% Hispanic of any race, 0.8% two or more races (2000); Density: 75.2 persons per square mile (2000); Age: 29.1% under 18, 6.5% over 64 (2000); Marriage status: 15.1% never married, 77.4% now married, 2.8% widowed, 4.7% divorced (2000); Foreign born: 0.6% (2000); Ancestry (includes multiple ancestries): 63.8% German, 10.3% Irish, 6.9% Dutch, 6.2% United States or American, 5.4% Polish (2000).
Economy: Single-family building permits issued: 36 (2001) / 35 (2000); Multi-family building permits issued: 0 (2001) / 0 (2000); Employment by occupation: 15.1% management, 15.0% professional, 8.8% services, 27.3% sales, 1.1% farming, 10.8% construction, 21.8% production (2000).
Income: Per capita income: $27,993 (2000); Median household income: $60,152 (2000); Poverty rate: 1.5% (2000).
Taxes: Total city taxes per capita: $97 (1997); City property taxes per capita: $89 (1997).
Education: High school graduation rate: 88.5% (2000); College graduation rate: 18.4% (2000).
Housing: Homeownership rate: 91.1% (2000); Median home value: $123,400 (2000); Median rent: $613 per month (2000); Median age of housing: 23 years (2000).
Transportation: Commute to work: 92.0% car, 0.0% public transportation, 2.5% walk, 4.4% work from home (2000); Travel time to work: 15.2% less than 15 minutes, 56.7% 15 to 30 minutes, 22.9% 30 to 45 minutes, 3.2% 45 to 60 minutes, 2.0% 60 minutes or more (2000)

DEER CREEK (town). Covers a land area of 35.487 square miles and a water area of 0.021 square miles. Located at 44.53° N. Lat.; 88.68° W. Long.
Population: 682 (2000); Race: 95.2% White, 0.1% Black, 0.0% Asian, 0.8% American Indian and Alaska Native, 8.8% Hispanic of any race, 0.4% two or more races (2000); Density: 19.2 persons per square mile (2000); Age: 29.8% under 18, 7.2% over 64 (2000); Marriage status: 30.6% never married, 59.4% now married, 3.3% widowed, 6.7% divorced (2000); Foreign born: 2.1% (2000); Ancestry (includes multiple ancestries): 42.3% German, 14.6% French (except Basque), 11.1% United States or American, 10.5% Irish, 6.2% Other groups (2000).
Economy: Single-family building permits issued: 1 (2001) / 1 (2000); Multi-family building permits issued: 0 (2001) / 0 (2000); Employment by occupation: 13.3% management, 8.2% professional, 12.8% services, 13.3% sales, 5.9% farming, 13.8% construction, 32.6% production (2000).
Income: Per capita income: $16,516 (2000); Median household income: $44,853 (2000); Poverty rate: 7.7% (2000).
Taxes: Total city taxes per capita: $82 (1997); City property taxes per capita: $82 (1997).
Education: High school graduation rate: 77.4% (2000); College graduation rate: 7.2% (2000).
Housing: Homeownership rate: 88.7% (2000); Median home value: $73,900 (2000); Median rent: $406 per month (2000); Median age of housing: 56 years (2000).
Transportation: Commute to work: 82.8% car, 0.5% public transportation, 2.1% walk, 14.6% work from home (2000); Travel time to work: 18.0% less than 15 minutes, 37.8% 15 to 30 minutes, 15.2% 30 to 45 minutes, 18.6% 45 to 60 minutes, 10.4% 60 minutes or more (2000)

ELLINGTON (town). Covers a land area of 34.862 square miles and a water area of 0.164 square miles. Located at 44.36° N. Lat.; 88.55° W. Long.
Population: 2,535 (2000); Race: 98.8% White, 0.0% Black, 0.2% Asian, 0.3% American Indian and Alaska Native, 0.5% Hispanic of any race, 0.4% two or more races (2000); Density: 72.7 persons per square mile (2000); Age: 30.4% under 18, 7.4% over 64 (2000); Marriage status: 19.0% never married, 72.0% now married, 2.9% widowed, 6.1% divorced (2000); Foreign born: 0.6% (2000); Ancestry (includes multiple ancestries): 66.8% German, 10.6% Dutch, 10.3% Irish, 5.4% Polish, 5.2% United States or American (2000).
Economy: Single-family building permits issued: 22 (2001) / 16 (2000); Multi-family building permits issued: 0 (2001) / 0 (2000); Employment by occupation: 14.2% management, 12.3% professional, 7.9% services, 23.7% sales, 1.8% farming, 11.7% construction, 28.3% production (2000).
Income: Per capita income: $19,698 (2000); Median household income: $53,750 (2000); Poverty rate: 2.4% (2000).
Taxes: Total city taxes per capita: $75 (1997); City property taxes per capita: $72 (1997).
Education: High school graduation rate: 87.9% (2000); College graduation rate: 7.2% (2000).
Housing: Homeownership rate: 92.4% (2000); Median home value: $132,100 (2000); Median rent: $424 per month (2000); Median age of housing: 22 years (2000).
Transportation: Commute to work: 85.4% car, 1.5% public transportation, 1.0% walk, 11.5% work from home (2000); Travel time to work: 13.9% less than 15 minutes, 64.7% 15 to 30 minutes, 15.9% 30 to 45 minutes, 2.7% 45 to 60 minutes, 2.8% 60 minutes or more (2000)

FREEDOM (town). Covers a land area of 35.754 square miles and a water area of 0 square miles. Located at 44.37° N. Lat.; 88.30° W. Long. Elevation is 750 feet.

Population: 5,241 (2000); Race: 98.8% White, 0.9% Black, 0.0% Asian, 0.1% American Indian and Alaska Native, 0.0% Hispanic of any race, 0.1% two or more races (2000); Density: 146.6 persons per square mile (2000); Age: 29.9% under 18, 7.2% over 64 (2000); Marriage status: 24.8% never married, 67.4% now married, 2.3% widowed, 5.5% divorced (2000); Foreign born: 0.3% (2000); Ancestry (includes multiple ancestries): 54.6% German, 27.6% Dutch, 6.8% Irish, 6.1% Polish, 5.0% Norwegian (2000).

Economy: Single-family building permits issued: 46 (2001) / 46 (2000); Multi-family building permits issued: 2 (2001) / 2 (2000); Employment by occupation: 12.0% management, 13.0% professional, 9.8% services, 26.1% sales, 1.2% farming, 13.7% construction, 24.1% production (2000).

Income: Per capita income: $22,462 (2000); Median household income: $57,868 (2000); Poverty rate: 3.3% (2000).

Taxes: Total city taxes per capita: $47 (1997); City property taxes per capita: $41 (1997).

Education: High school graduation rate: 89.0% (2000); College graduation rate: 13.3% (2000).

School District(s)

Freedom Area (PK-12)
2000 Enrollment: 1,525 920-788-7944

Housing: Homeownership rate: 85.4% (2000); Median home value: $130,300 (2000); Median rent: $448 per month (2000); Median age of housing: 21 years (2000).

Transportation: Commute to work: 92.7% car, 0.5% public transportation, 1.1% walk, 5.5% work from home (2000); Travel time to work: 25.5% less than 15 minutes, 59.1% 15 to 30 minutes, 12.6% 30 to 45 minutes, 0.8% 45 to 60 minutes, 2.0% 60 minutes or more (2000)

GRAND CHUTE (town). Covers a land area of 24.886 square miles and a water area of 0.076 square miles. Located at 44.28° N. Lat.; 88.43° W. Long.

Population: 18,392 (2000); Race: 94.3% White, 0.9% Black, 1.6% Asian, 0.3% American Indian and Alaska Native, 4.1% Hispanic of any race, 1.1% two or more races (2000); Density: 739.1 persons per square mile (2000); Age: 22.7% under 18, 12.0% over 64 (2000); Marriage status: 28.0% never married, 59.1% now married, 4.5% widowed, 8.4% divorced (2000); Foreign born: 5.2% (2000); Ancestry (includes multiple ancestries): 53.4% German, 10.2% Irish, 7.8% Dutch, 7.5% Other groups, 6.9% English (2000).

Economy: Single-family building permits issued: 70 (2001) / 73 (2000); Multi-family building permits issued: 102 (2001) / 245 (2000); Employment by occupation: 15.8% management, 20.2% professional, 9.9% services, 28.3% sales, 0.4% farming, 9.2% construction, 16.2% production (2000).

Income: Per capita income: $25,189 (2000); Median household income: $50,772 (2000); Poverty rate: 5.3% (2000).

Taxes: Total city taxes per capita: $318 (2000); City property taxes per capita: $235 (2000).

Education: High school graduation rate: 90.1% (2000); College graduation rate: 28.6% (2000).

Housing: Homeownership rate: 53.8% (2000); Median home value: $131,900 (2000); Median rent: $551 per month (2000); Median age of housing: 16 years (2000).

Safety: Violent crime rate: 4.9 per 10,000 population; Property crime rate: 509.1 per 10,000 population (2001).

Transportation: Commute to work: 95.3% car, 0.6% public transportation, 1.7% walk, 1.6% work from home (2000); Travel time to work: 52.2% less than 15 minutes, 38.0% 15 to 30 minutes, 6.5% 30 to 45 minutes, 1.7% 45 to 60 minutes, 1.7% 60 minutes or more (2000)

GREENVILLE (town). Covers a land area of 35.795 square miles and a water area of 0.015 square miles. Located at 44.29° N. Lat.; 88.54° W. Long. Elevation is 820 feet.

Population: 6,844 (2000); Race: 98.0% White, 0.1% Black, 0.1% Asian, 0.1% American Indian and Alaska Native, 2.1% Hispanic of any race, 0.3% two or more races (2000); Density: 191.2 persons per square mile (2000); Age: 33.0% under 18, 5.2% over 64 (2000); Marriage status: 18.6% never married, 72.1% now married, 2.7% widowed, 6.6% divorced (2000); Foreign born: 1.7% (2000); Ancestry (includes multiple ancestries): 58.2% German, 12.1% Irish, 6.6% Polish, 6.3% Norwegian, 5.5% United States or American (2000).

Economy: Dairying; poultry; general farming area. Manufacturing: wood and metal products. Single-family building permits issued: 129 (2001) / 108 (2000); Multi-family building permits issued: 36 (2001) / 0 (2000); Employment by occupation: 15.6% management, 18.3% professional, 7.8% services, 27.1% sales, 0.5% farming, 10.2% construction, 20.6% production (2000).

Income: Per capita income: $22,164 (2000); Median household income: $61,381 (2000); Poverty rate: 2.0% (2000).

Taxes: Total city taxes per capita: $126 (2000); City property taxes per capita: $106 (2000).

Education: High school graduation rate: 93.2% (2000); College graduation rate: 26.4% (2000).

Housing: Homeownership rate: 87.3% (2000); Median home value: $143,900 (2000); Median rent: $668 per month (2000); Median age of housing: 10 years (2000).

Transportation: Commute to work: 92.2% car, 0.2% public transportation, 2.8% walk, 4.2% work from home (2000); Travel time to work: 37.5% less than 15 minutes, 54.0% 15 to 30 minutes, 6.6% 30 to 45 minutes, 1.4% 45 to 60 minutes, 0.5% 60 minutes or more (2000)

HORTONIA (town). Covers a land area of 19.191 square miles and a water area of 0.230 square miles. Located at 44.36° N. Lat.; 88.69° W. Long.

Population: 1,063 (2000); Race: 98.7% White, 0.0% Black, 0.0% Asian, 1.3% American Indian and Alaska Native, 0.8% Hispanic of any race, 0.0% two or more races (2000); Density: 55.4 persons per square mile (2000); Age: 25.6% under 18, 10.1% over 64 (2000); Marriage status: 23.1% never married, 66.7% now married, 4.6% widowed, 5.6% divorced (2000); Foreign born: 0.0% (2000); Ancestry (includes multiple ancestries): 57.0% German, 12.7% Irish, 6.8% Polish, 6.3% English, 5.6% Other groups (2000).

Economy: Single-family building permits issued: 4 (2001) / 15 (2000); Multi-family building permits issued: 0 (2001) / 0 (2000); Employment by occupation: 16.7% management, 19.3% professional, 9.1% services, 23.7% sales, 0.7% farming, 11.9% construction, 18.6% production (2000).

Income: Per capita income: $29,573 (2000); Median household income: $59,904 (2000); Poverty rate: 6.4% (2000).

Taxes: Total city taxes per capita: $47 (1997); City property taxes per capita: $44 (1997).

Education: High school graduation rate: 89.5% (2000); College graduation rate: 23.8% (2000).

Housing: Homeownership rate: 85.1% (2000); Median home value: $143,800 (2000); Median rent: $485 per month (2000); Median age of housing: 25 years (2000).

Transportation: Commute to work: 91.1% car, 0.0% public transportation, 2.5% walk, 6.4% work from home (2000); Travel time to work: 35.0% less than 15 minutes, 30.2% 15 to 30 minutes, 30.2% 30 to 45 minutes, 3.1% 45 to 60 minutes, 1.5% 60 minutes or more (2000)

HORTONVILLE (village). Covers a land area of 2.715 square miles and a water area of 0.067 square miles. Located at 44.33° N. Lat.; 88.63° W. Long. Elevation is 794 feet.

Population: 2,357 (2000); Race: 95.7% White, 0.0% Black, 4.1% Asian, 0.1% American Indian and Alaska Native, 0.8% Hispanic of any race, 0.0% two or more races (2000); Density: 868.2 persons per square mile (2000); Age: 29.7% under 18, 10.5% over 64 (2000); Marriage status: 22.3% never married, 64.7% now married, 5.2% widowed, 7.8% divorced (2000); Foreign born: 2.7% (2000); Ancestry (includes multiple ancestries): 58.5% German, 12.4% Irish, 5.2% Polish, 5.0% English, 4.6% French (except Basque) (2000).

Economy: In dairying and fruit-growing area. Manufacturing: toys, juvenile furniture, vegetable canning, concrete pavers, nails, and wire products. Single-family building permits issued: 16 (2001) / 23 (2000); Multi-family building permits issued: 0 (2001) / 2 (2000); Employment by occupation: 10.2% management, 11.1% professional, 12.9% services, 24.8% sales, 0.9% farming, 14.4% construction, 25.7% production (2000).

Income: Per capita income: $20,277 (2000); Median household income: $51,635 (2000); Poverty rate: 6.9% (2000).

Taxes: Total city taxes per capita: $213 (1997); City property taxes per capita: $198 (1997).

Education: High school graduation rate: 86.9% (2000); College graduation rate: 16.9% (2000).

School District(s)

Hortonville (PK-12)
2000 Enrollment: 2,636 920-779-7900

Housing: Homeownership rate: 72.0% (2000); Median home value: $98,200 (2000); Median rent: $449 per month (2000); Median age of housing: 33 years (2000).

Safety: Violent crime rate: 0.0 per 10,000 population; Property crime rate: 189.6 per 10,000 population (2001).

Transportation: Commute to work: 94.0% car, 0.4% public transportation, 1.4% walk, 3.6% work from home (2000); Travel time to work: 27.2% less than 15 minutes, 50.2% 15 to 30 minutes, 14.9% 30 to 45 minutes, 3.8% 45 to 60 minutes, 3.9% 60 minutes or more (2000)

KAUKAUNA (city). Covers a land area of 6.204 square miles and a water area of 0.465 square miles. Located at 44.27° N. Lat.; 88.27° W. Long. Elevation is 710 feet.
History: Kaukauna grew around the portage used by early travelers to avoid the cascade in the Fox River. First called Grand Kakalin, the settlement was developed by the Augustin Grignon family, who built a sawmill and grist mill and participated in the local fur trade. When a dam was built here, paper mills were established. A dairy industry later became the chief source of Kaukauna's income.
Population: 12,983 (2000); Race: 95.1% White, 0.1% Black, 2.9% Asian, 0.8% American Indian and Alaska Native, 0.2% Hispanic of any race, 1.1% two or more races (2000); Density: 2,092.5 persons per square mile (2000); Age: 27.5% under 18, 13.7% over 64 (2000); Marriage status: 24.0% never married, 59.6% now married, 8.1% widowed, 8.2% divorced (2000); Foreign born: 2.5% (2000); Ancestry (includes multiple ancestries): 49.4% German, 21.0% Dutch, 11.3% Irish, 6.3% Other groups, 5.4% Polish (2000).
Vital Statistics: Birth rate: 157.1 per 10,000 population (1998)
Economy: Single-family building permits issued: 69 (2001) / 61 (2000); Multi-family building permits issued: 284 (2001) / 20 (2000); Employment by occupation: 8.2% management, 14.1% professional, 14.9% services, 21.5% sales, 0.6% farming, 11.8% construction, 28.9% production (2000).
Income: Per capita income: $18,748 (2000); Median household income: $43,980 (2000); Poverty rate: 4.8% (2000).
Taxes: Total city taxes per capita: $307 (2000); City property taxes per capita: $290 (2000).
Education: High school graduation rate: 85.5% (2000); College graduation rate: 14.2% (2000).

School District(s)

Kaukauna Area (PK-12)
2000 Enrollment: 3,615 920-766-6100
Housing: Homeownership rate: 71.4% (2000); Median home value: $91,200 (2000); Median rent: $458 per month (2000); Median age of housing: 39 years (2000).
Safety: Violent crime rate: 9.2 per 10,000 population; Property crime rate: 165.2 per 10,000 population (2001).
Transportation: Commute to work: 93.2% car, 1.3% public transportation, 2.5% walk, 1.9% work from home (2000); Travel time to work: 41.5% less than 15 minutes, 44.9% 15 to 30 minutes, 9.3% 30 to 45 minutes, 2.0% 45 to 60 minutes, 2.3% 60 minutes or more (2000)
Additional Information Contacts
Kaukauna Chamber of Commerce 920-766-1616

KAUKAUNA (town). Covers a land area of 17.762 square miles and a water area of 0.304 square miles. Located at 44.33° N. Lat.; 88.22° W. Long. Elevation is 710 feet.
History: A fur-trading post was established on the site by Pierre Grignon in 1760. The Grignon mansion, built 1836-1839 on the first land deeded in Wisconsin, has been restored. Outagamie County Teachers College is in Kaukauna. Settled 1793, incorporated 1885.
Population: 1,142 (2000); Race: 96.3% White, 0.0% Black, 0.0% Asian, 2.8% American Indian and Alaska Native, 1.4% Hispanic of any race, 0.9% two or more races (2000); Density: 64.3 persons per square mile (2000); Age: 34.1% under 18, 10.1% over 64 (2000); Marriage status: 28.3% never married, 63.7% now married, 3.6% widowed, 4.5% divorced (2000); Foreign born: 1.4% (2000); Ancestry (includes multiple ancestries): 50.8% German, 29.2% Dutch, 10.1% United States or American, 8.6% Irish, 6.6% Belgian (2000).
Economy: Manufacturing: food, fabricated metal products, paper; stone quarries nearby. Single-family building permits issued: 17 (2001) / 8 (2000); Multi-family building permits issued: 0 (2001) / 0 (2000); Employment by occupation: 18.2% management, 7.5% professional, 8.9% services, 20.7% sales, 6.1% farming, 13.0% construction, 25.6% production (2000).
Income: Per capita income: $20,881 (2000); Median household income: $61,696 (2000); Poverty rate: 1.7% (2000).
Taxes: Total city taxes per capita: $67 (1997); City property taxes per capita: $62 (1997).
Education: High school graduation rate: 83.9% (2000); College graduation rate: 11.5% (2000).
Housing: Homeownership rate: 85.8% (2000); Median home value: $139,800 (2000); Median rent: $660 per month (2000); Median age of housing: 28 years (2000).

Transportation: Commute to work: 87.2% car, 0.0% public transportation, 3.2% walk, 8.7% work from home (2000); Travel time to work: 39.2% less than 15 minutes, 47.4% 15 to 30 minutes, 9.9% 30 to 45 minutes, 1.0% 45 to 60 minutes, 2.5% 60 minutes or more (2000)

KIMBERLY (village). Covers a land area of 1.882 square miles and a water area of 0.145 square miles. Located at 44.26° N. Lat.; 88.33° W. Long. Elevation is 734 feet.
History: Incorporated 1910.
Population: 6,146 (2000); Race: 98.4% White, 0.2% Black, 0.3% Asian, 0.5% American Indian and Alaska Native, 0.0% Hispanic of any race, 0.5% two or more races (2000); Density: 3,265.9 persons per square mile (2000); Age: 26.3% under 18, 13.9% over 64 (2000); Marriage status: 23.0% never married, 61.7% now married, 7.8% widowed, 7.6% divorced (2000); Foreign born: 1.4% (2000); Ancestry (includes multiple ancestries): 48.7% German, 31.3% Dutch, 8.5% Irish, 5.8% United States or American, 5.6% Polish (2000).
Economy: Manufacturing: paper milling, coated paper, paper machine components, gumball vending machines. Single-family building permits issued: 13 (2001) / 17 (2000); Multi-family building permits issued: 12 (2001) / 22 (2000); Employment by occupation: 8.9% management, 19.2% professional, 10.9% services, 25.8% sales, 1.0% farming, 10.0% construction, 24.2% production (2000).
Income: Per capita income: $20,933 (2000); Median household income: $46,370 (2000); Poverty rate: 3.1% (2000).
Taxes: Total city taxes per capita: $352 (1997); City property taxes per capita: $339 (1997).
Education: High school graduation rate: 88.3% (2000); College graduation rate: 16.4% (2000).

School District(s)

Kimberly Area (PK-12)
2000 Enrollment: 3,117 920-788-7900
Housing: Homeownership rate: 73.6% (2000); Median home value: $90,500 (2000); Median rent: $433 per month (2000); Median age of housing: 40 years (2000).
Transportation: Commute to work: 94.1% car, 0.6% public transportation, 3.1% walk, 1.1% work from home (2000); Travel time to work: 47.1% less than 15 minutes, 41.7% 15 to 30 minutes, 7.0% 30 to 45 minutes, 1.2% 45 to 60 minutes, 3.1% 60 minutes or more (2000)

LIBERTY (town). Covers a land area of 30.632 square miles and a water area of 0.127 square miles. Located at 44.41° N. Lat.; 88.65° W. Long.
Population: 834 (2000); Race: 98.2% White, 0.0% Black, 0.0% Asian, 0.2% American Indian and Alaska Native, 1.5% Hispanic of any race, 0.0% two or more races (2000); Density: 27.2 persons per square mile (2000); Age: 31.2% under 18, 7.2% over 64 (2000); Marriage status: 20.4% never married, 76.4% now married, 0.6% widowed, 2.6% divorced (2000); Foreign born: 0.5% (2000); Ancestry (includes multiple ancestries): 58.6% German, 8.1% Irish, 7.1% French (except Basque), 6.8% Dutch, 5.5% Norwegian (2000).
Economy: Single-family building permits issued: 4 (2001) / 8 (2000); Multi-family building permits issued: 0 (2001) / 0 (2000); Employment by occupation: 11.3% management, 12.7% professional, 8.5% services, 27.2% sales, 0.0% farming, 10.4% construction, 29.9% production (2000).
Income: Per capita income: $20,117 (2000); Median household income: $60,167 (2000); Poverty rate: 0.8% (2000).
Taxes: Total city taxes per capita: $43 (1997); City property taxes per capita: $41 (1997).
Education: High school graduation rate: 85.1% (2000); College graduation rate: 15.1% (2000).
Housing: Homeownership rate: 90.3% (2000); Median home value: $123,300 (2000); Median rent: $508 per month (2000); Median age of housing: 25 years (2000).
Transportation: Commute to work: 96.6% car, 0.0% public transportation, 0.2% walk, 3.2% work from home (2000); Travel time to work: 27.6% less than 15 minutes, 24.1% 15 to 30 minutes, 43.0% 30 to 45 minutes, 2.7% 45 to 60 minutes, 2.7% 60 minutes or more (2000)

LITTLE CHUTE (village). Covers a land area of 4.128 square miles and a water area of 0.360 square miles. Located at 44.28° N. Lat.; 88.31° W. Long. Elevation is 728 feet.
History: Settled 1850, incorporated 1899.
Population: 10,476 (2000); Race: 97.1% White, 0.2% Black, 0.6% Asian, 0.9% American Indian and Alaska Native, 2.3% Hispanic of any race, 0.7% two or more races (2000); Density: 2,538.0 persons per square mile (2000); Age: 29.3% under 18, 10.1% over 64 (2000); Marriage status: 26.5% never married, 59.1% now married, 5.1% widowed, 9.3% divorced (2000); Foreign

born: 2.0% (2000); Ancestry (includes multiple ancestries): 42.8% German, 31.4% Dutch, 9.1% Irish, 7.7% United States or American, 5.3% Other groups (2000).
Economy: Manufacturing includes printing, building materials, prepared food, cheese, concrete. A dam is here. Single-family building permits issued: 21 (2001) / 48 (2000); Multi-family building permits issued: 101 (2001) / 6 (2000); Employment by occupation: 8.8% management, 16.5% professional, 11.1% services, 28.9% sales, 0.3% farming, 10.3% construction, 24.2% production (2000).
Income: Per capita income: $21,181 (2000); Median household income: $49,500 (2000); Poverty rate: 6.0% (2000).
Taxes: Total city taxes per capita: $313 (2000); City property taxes per capita: $295 (2000).
Education: High school graduation rate: 88.9% (2000); College graduation rate: 15.8% (2000).

School District(s)

Little Chute Area (PK-12)
2000 Enrollment: 1,465 920-788-7605
Housing: Homeownership rate: 71.6% (2000); Median home value: $105,600 (2000); Median rent: $477 per month (2000); Median age of housing: 24 years (2000).
Transportation: Commute to work: 94.6% car, 0.5% public transportation, 2.9% walk, 1.3% work from home (2000); Travel time to work: 44.0% less than 15 minutes, 41.2% 15 to 30 minutes, 8.6% 30 to 45 minutes, 2.8% 45 to 60 minutes, 3.5% 60 minutes or more (2000)

MAINE (town). Covers a land area of 36.620 square miles and a water area of 0.786 square miles. Located at 44.56° N. Lat.; 88.54° W. Long.
Population: 831 (2000); Race: 98.5% White, 0.2% Black, 0.0% Asian, 0.5% American Indian and Alaska Native, 1.3% Hispanic of any race, 0.2% two or more races (2000); Density: 22.7 persons per square mile (2000); Age: 24.9% under 18, 12.9% over 64 (2000); Marriage status: 20.2% never married, 64.4% now married, 6.5% widowed, 9.0% divorced (2000); Foreign born: 0.2% (2000); Ancestry (includes multiple ancestries): 51.5% German, 9.3% French (except Basque), 8.8% Irish, 8.7% Norwegian, 7.2% Dutch (2000).
Economy: Single-family building permits issued: 8 (2001) / 6 (2000); Multi-family building permits issued: 0 (2001) / 0 (2000); Employment by occupation: 10.0% management, 7.2% professional, 10.0% services, 19.5% sales, 6.3% farming, 17.0% construction, 30.0% production (2000).
Income: Per capita income: $18,125 (2000); Median household income: $46,058 (2000); Poverty rate: 4.8% (2000).
Taxes: Total city taxes per capita: $42 (1997); City property taxes per capita: $41 (1997).
Education: High school graduation rate: 75.4% (2000); College graduation rate: 7.6% (2000).
Housing: Homeownership rate: 88.2% (2000); Median home value: $92,500 (2000); Median rent: $400 per month (2000); Median age of housing: 33 years (2000).
Transportation: Commute to work: 86.7% car, 0.5% public transportation, 5.5% walk, 6.3% work from home (2000); Travel time to work: 14.7% less than 15 minutes, 17.2% 15 to 30 minutes, 43.2% 30 to 45 minutes, 21.7% 45 to 60 minutes, 3.2% 60 minutes or more (2000)

MAPLE CREEK (town). Covers a land area of 21.580 square miles and a water area of 0.134 square miles. Located at 44.46° N. Lat.; 88.69° W. Long.
Population: 687 (2000); Race: 96.8% White, 0.0% Black, 0.0% Asian, 0.0% American Indian and Alaska Native, 1.8% Hispanic of any race, 1.4% two or more races (2000); Density: 31.8 persons per square mile (2000); Age: 27.6% under 18, 11.8% over 64 (2000); Marriage status: 21.9% never married, 64.3% now married, 6.7% widowed, 7.1% divorced (2000); Foreign born: 0.8% (2000); Ancestry (includes multiple ancestries): 59.2% German, 10.9% French (except Basque), 9.5% Irish, 7.4% Polish, 3.8% Danish (2000).
Economy: Single-family building permits issued: 0 (2001) / 0 (2000); Multi-family building permits issued: 0 (2001) / 0 (2000); Employment by occupation: 10.1% management, 11.8% professional, 11.3% services, 20.3% sales, 1.7% farming, 13.2% construction, 31.5% production (2000).
Income: Per capita income: $16,602 (2000); Median household income: $43,472 (2000); Poverty rate: 3.9% (2000).
Taxes: Total city taxes per capita: $115 (1997); City property taxes per capita: $113 (1997).
Education: High school graduation rate: 82.2% (2000); College graduation rate: 9.6% (2000).
Housing: Homeownership rate: 90.1% (2000); Median home value: $105,700 (2000); Median rent: $413 per month (2000); Median age of housing: 52 years (2000).
Transportation: Commute to work: 90.9% car, 0.0% public transportation, 2.5% walk, 5.4% work from home (2000); Travel time to work: 27.2% less than 15 minutes, 34.1% 15 to 30 minutes, 30.5% 30 to 45 minutes, 6.9% 45 to 60 minutes, 1.2% 60 minutes or more (2000)

NICHOLS (village). Covers a land area of 0.863 square miles and a water area of 0 square miles. Located at 44.56° N. Lat.; 88.46° W. Long. Elevation is 790 feet.
Population: 307 (2000); Race: 92.7% White, 1.0% Black, 2.3% Asian, 3.3% American Indian and Alaska Native, 1.7% Hispanic of any race, 0.0% two or more races (2000); Density: 355.8 persons per square mile (2000); Age: 30.8% under 18, 8.9% over 64 (2000); Marriage status: 30.1% never married, 54.8% now married, 3.7% widowed, 11.4% divorced (2000); Foreign born: 0.7% (2000); Ancestry (includes multiple ancestries): 54.0% German, 11.9% Polish, 11.6% Irish, 10.6% English, 7.6% Other groups (2000).
Economy: Dairying; poultry; grain. Manufacturing: printing. Single-family building permits issued: 0 (2001) / 1 (2000); Multi-family building permits issued: 0 (2001) / 0 (2000); Employment by occupation: 8.7% management, 6.0% professional, 11.4% services, 19.5% sales, 0.0% farming, 14.8% construction, 39.6% production (2000).
Income: Per capita income: $15,898 (2000); Median household income: $36,042 (2000); Poverty rate: 3.6% (2000).
Taxes: Total city taxes per capita: $167 (1997); City property taxes per capita: $132 (1997).
Education: High school graduation rate: 81.1% (2000); College graduation rate: 8.3% (2000).
Housing: Homeownership rate: 75.2% (2000); Median home value: $71,700 (2000); Median rent: $388 per month (2000); Median age of housing: 32 years (2000).
Transportation: Commute to work: 91.2% car, 0.0% public transportation, 7.4% walk, 0.0% work from home (2000); Travel time to work: 17.6% less than 15 minutes, 19.6% 15 to 30 minutes, 39.2% 30 to 45 minutes, 16.9% 45 to 60 minutes, 6.8% 60 minutes or more (2000)

ONEIDA (town). Covers a land area of 60.823 square miles and a water area of 0.010 square miles. Located at 44.48° N. Lat.; 88.24° W. Long.
Population: 4,001 (2000); Race: 58.7% White, 0.4% Black, 1.8% Asian, 33.9% American Indian and Alaska Native, 3.3% Hispanic of any race, 4.1% two or more races (2000); Density: 65.8 persons per square mile (2000); Age: 33.2% under 18, 7.2% over 64 (2000); Marriage status: 26.7% never married, 62.6% now married, 4.3% widowed, 6.3% divorced (2000); Foreign born: 1.4% (2000); Ancestry (includes multiple ancestries): 37.8% Other groups, 31.6% German, 15.9% Dutch, 8.1% Irish, 6.7% Polish (2000).
Economy: Single-family building permits issued: 17 (2001) / 16 (2000); Multi-family building permits issued: 0 (2001) / 0 (2000); Employment by occupation: 12.6% management, 12.1% professional, 12.3% services, 27.1% sales, 2.4% farming, 16.0% construction, 17.5% production (2000).
Income: Per capita income: $17,516 (2000); Median household income: $51,275 (2000); Poverty rate: 7.3% (2000).
Taxes: Total city taxes per capita: $28 (1997); City property taxes per capita: $25 (1997).
Education: High school graduation rate: 83.0% (2000); College graduation rate: 11.1% (2000).
Housing: Homeownership rate: 86.4% (2000); Median home value: $121,100 (2000); Median rent: $363 per month (2000); Median age of housing: 23 years (2000).
Transportation: Commute to work: 91.5% car, 0.7% public transportation, 1.8% walk, 5.9% work from home (2000); Travel time to work: 31.9% less than 15 minutes, 47.8% 15 to 30 minutes, 16.6% 30 to 45 minutes, 1.9% 45 to 60 minutes, 1.7% 60 minutes or more (2000)

OSBORN (town). Covers a land area of 16.896 square miles and a water area of 0.007 square miles. Located at 44.45° N. Lat.; 88.34° W. Long.
Population: 1,029 (2000); Race: 97.1% White, 0.0% Black, 0.0% Asian, 1.8% American Indian and Alaska Native, 0.0% Hispanic of any race, 1.1% two or more races (2000); Density: 60.9 persons per square mile (2000); Age: 31.2% under 18, 5.6% over 64 (2000); Marriage status: 21.4% never married, 67.8% now married, 4.1% widowed, 6.7% divorced (2000); Foreign born: 0.3% (2000); Ancestry (includes multiple ancestries): 58.6% German, 16.1% Dutch, 8.9% Polish, 7.0% United States or American, 6.4% Irish (2000).
Economy: Single-family building permits issued: 5 (2001) / 8 (2000); Multi-family building permits issued: 0 (2001) / 0 (2000); Employment by occupation: 21.1% management, 11.1% professional, 4.6% services, 21.4% sales, 3.4% farming, 17.1% construction, 21.2% production (2000).
Income: Per capita income: $22,095 (2000); Median household income: $64,375 (2000); Poverty rate: 2.4% (2000).

Taxes: Total city taxes per capita: $79 (2000); City property taxes per capita: $78 (2000).
Education: High school graduation rate: 89.2% (2000); College graduation rate: 17.7% (2000).
Housing: Homeownership rate: 93.3% (2000); Median home value: $150,300 (2000); Median rent: $375 per month (2000); Median age of housing: 20 years (2000).
Transportation: Commute to work: 86.7% car, 0.0% public transportation, 1.4% walk, 11.9% work from home (2000); Travel time to work: 23.3% less than 15 minutes, 49.6% 15 to 30 minutes, 19.4% 30 to 45 minutes, 4.5% 45 to 60 minutes, 3.1% 60 minutes or more (2000)

SEYMOUR (city). Covers a land area of 2.529 square miles and a water area of 0.004 square miles. Located at 44.50° N. Lat.; 88.32° W. Long. Elevation is 800 feet.
Population: 3,335 (2000); Race: 96.2% White, 0.3% Black, 0.0% Asian, 1.6% American Indian and Alaska Native, 1.0% Hispanic of any race, 1.8% two or more races (2000); Density: 1,318.7 persons per square mile (2000); Age: 28.7% under 18, 14.7% over 64 (2000); Marriage status: 28.5% never married, 53.5% now married, 10.1% widowed, 8.0% divorced (2000); Foreign born: 0.4% (2000); Ancestry (includes multiple ancestries): 47.4% German, 11.3% Polish, 10.2% Irish, 8.0% Dutch, 6.8% Norwegian (2000).
Economy: Single-family building permits issued: 9 (2001) / 9 (2000); Multi-family building permits issued: 4 (2001) / 4 (2000); Employment by occupation: 16.7% management, 12.8% professional, 15.7% services, 22.9% sales, 1.3% farming, 9.6% construction, 21.0% production (2000).
Income: Per capita income: $19,073 (2000); Median household income: $44,135 (2000); Poverty rate: 3.6% (2000).
Taxes: Total city taxes per capita: $319 (1997); City property taxes per capita: $307 (1997).
Education: High school graduation rate: 84.4% (2000); College graduation rate: 21.5% (2000).

School District(s)

Seymour Community (PK-12)
2000 Enrollment: 2,467 920-833-2304
Housing: Homeownership rate: 65.2% (2000); Median home value: $92,100 (2000); Median rent: $456 per month (2000); Median age of housing: 33 years (2000).
Newspapers: Times Press (1 x week); Seymour Buyers' Guide (1 x week)
Transportation: Commute to work: 94.4% car, 0.7% public transportation, 3.2% walk, 1.5% work from home (2000); Travel time to work: 39.3% less than 15 minutes, 33.7% 15 to 30 minutes, 23.2% 30 to 45 minutes, 2.2% 45 to 60 minutes, 1.7% 60 minutes or more (2000)
Additional Information Contacts
Seymour Chamber of Commerce 920-833-6053

SEYMOUR (town). Covers a land area of 30.502 square miles and a water area of 0.014 square miles. Located at 44.54° N. Lat.; 88.31° W. Long. Elevation is 800 feet.
History: Settled 1871, incorporated 1879.
Population: 1,216 (2000); Race: 94.4% White, 0.0% Black, 1.5% Asian, 2.9% American Indian and Alaska Native, 1.0% Hispanic of any race, 0.9% two or more races (2000); Density: 39.9 persons per square mile (2000); Age: 28.5% under 18, 13.1% over 64 (2000); Marriage status: 20.6% never married, 71.7% now married, 3.4% widowed, 4.3% divorced (2000); Foreign born: 1.0% (2000); Ancestry (includes multiple ancestries): 53.4% German, 15.7% Polish, 13.3% Dutch, 5.2% Other groups, 4.7% Irish (2000).
Economy: Dairy products, flour, food processing. Manufacturing of generators. Single-family building permits issued: 5 (2001) / 7 (2000); Multi-family building permits issued: 0 (2001) / 0 (2000); Employment by occupation: 17.9% management, 4.4% professional, 16.3% services, 19.0% sales, 4.6% farming, 15.2% construction, 22.5% production (2000).
Income: Per capita income: $18,327 (2000); Median household income: $48,264 (2000); Poverty rate: 3.3% (2000).
Taxes: Total city taxes per capita: $115 (1997); City property taxes per capita: $114 (1997).
Education: High school graduation rate: 81.5% (2000); College graduation rate: 5.4% (2000).
Housing: Homeownership rate: 93.1% (2000); Median home value: $104,500 (2000); Median rent: $333 per month (2000); Median age of housing: 40 years (2000).
Transportation: Commute to work: 82.6% car, 0.3% public transportation, 1.0% walk, 15.1% work from home (2000); Travel time to work: 30.6% less than 15 minutes, 37.3% 15 to 30 minutes, 26.0% 30 to 45 minutes, 2.9% 45 to 60 minutes, 3.3% 60 minutes or more (2000)

SHIOCTON (village). Covers a land area of 1.645 square miles and a water area of 0.005 square miles. Located at 44.44° N. Lat.; 88.57° W. Long. Elevation is 767 feet.
Population: 954 (2000); Race: 93.3% White, 0.5% Black, 0.2% Asian, 0.0% American Indian and Alaska Native, 7.3% Hispanic of any race, 1.8% two or more races (2000); Density: 579.9 persons per square mile (2000); Age: 25.7% under 18, 10.3% over 64 (2000); Marriage status: 27.3% never married, 56.6% now married, 3.7% widowed, 12.3% divorced (2000); Foreign born: 3.4% (2000); Ancestry (includes multiple ancestries): 57.2% German, 9.1% Irish, 9.0% Other groups, 9.0% French (except Basque), 7.3% Dutch (2000).
Economy: Vegetable canning: sauerkraut and sauerkraut juice. Single-family building permits issued: 1 (2001) / 1 (2000); Multi-family building permits issued: 0 (2001) / 0 (2000); Employment by occupation: 8.2% management, 5.3% professional, 15.0% services, 20.3% sales, 0.4% farming, 13.1% construction, 37.7% production (2000).
Income: Per capita income: $18,260 (2000); Median household income: $36,528 (2000); Poverty rate: 7.2% (2000).
Taxes: Total city taxes per capita: $180 (1997); City property taxes per capita: $159 (1997).
Education: High school graduation rate: 81.8% (2000); College graduation rate: 7.0% (2000).

School District(s)

Shiocton (PK-12)
2000 Enrollment: 834 920-986-3351
Housing: Homeownership rate: 67.5% (2000); Median home value: $76,100 (2000); Median rent: $398 per month (2000); Median age of housing: 32 years (2000).
Transportation: Commute to work: 94.9% car, 1.3% public transportation, 2.1% walk, 0.8% work from home (2000); Travel time to work: 18.3% less than 15 minutes, 36.4% 15 to 30 minutes, 35.1% 30 to 45 minutes, 6.8% 45 to 60 minutes, 3.4% 60 minutes or more (2000)

VANDENBROEK (town). Covers a land area of 9.489 square miles and a water area of 0 square miles. Located at 44.30° N. Lat.; 88.29° W. Long.
Population: 1,351 (2000); Race: 99.5% White, 0.2% Black, 0.0% Asian, 0.2% American Indian and Alaska Native, 0.2% Hispanic of any race, 0.2% two or more races (2000); Density: 142.4 persons per square mile (2000); Age: 28.6% under 18, 9.3% over 64 (2000); Marriage status: 19.9% never married, 72.5% now married, 3.1% widowed, 4.5% divorced (2000); Foreign born: 0.5% (2000); Ancestry (includes multiple ancestries): 50.2% German, 40.4% Dutch, 5.5% Polish, 5.3% Irish, 4.7% United States or American (2000).
Economy: Single-family building permits issued: 6 (2001) / 9 (2000); Multi-family building permits issued: 0 (2001) / 0 (2000); Employment by occupation: 9.7% management, 11.8% professional, 9.7% services, 22.5% sales, 1.4% farming, 13.6% construction, 31.2% production (2000).
Income: Per capita income: $23,419 (2000); Median household income: $61,845 (2000); Poverty rate: 2.3% (2000).
Taxes: Total city taxes per capita: $42 (1997); City property taxes per capita: $42 (1997).
Education: High school graduation rate: 87.9% (2000); College graduation rate: 14.7% (2000).
Housing: Homeownership rate: 97.6% (2000); Median home value: $137,700 (2000); Median rent: $1,625 per month (2000); Median age of housing: 26 years (2000).
Transportation: Commute to work: 91.3% car, 0.3% public transportation, 2.6% walk, 3.9% work from home (2000); Travel time to work: 40.8% less than 15 minutes, 47.3% 15 to 30 minutes, 8.4% 30 to 45 minutes, 1.5% 45 to 60 minutes, 2.0% 60 minutes or more (2000)

Ozaukee County

Located in eastern Wisconsin; bounded on the east by Lake Michigan; drained by the Milwaukee River. Covers a land area of 231.90 square miles, a water area of 884.30 square miles, and is located in the Central Time Zone. The county government was organized in 1853. County seat is Port Washington.

Ozaukee County is part of the Milwaukee-Waukesha, WI PMSA. The entire metro area includes: Milwaukee County; Ozaukee County; Washington County; Waukesha County

Weather Station: Port Washington Elevation: 597 feet

	Jan	Feb	Mar	Apr	May	Jun	Jul	Aug	Sep	Oct	Nov	Dec
High	27	32	40	51	62	72	78	77	70	58	45	33
Low	12	17	26	35	45	54	61	61	53	42	30	18
Precip	1.5	1.1	1.9	3.1	2.8	3.6	3.8	4.1	3.4	2.3	2.2	1.8
Snow	12.0	8.0	6.0	1.6	tr	0.0	0.0	0.0	0.0	0.2	1.6	7.0

High and Low temperatures in degrees Fahrenheit; Precipitation and Snow in inches

Population: 82,317 (2000); Race: 96.8% White, 0.9% Black, 0.8% Asian, 0.3% American Indian and Alaska Native, 1.3% Hispanic of any race, 0.8% two or more races (2000); Density: 354.9 persons per square mile (2000); Age: 26.6% under 18, 12.6% over 64 (2000).
Religion: Five largest groups: 38.5% Catholic Church, 11.3% Lutheran Church—Missouri Synod, 6.6% Evangelical Lutheran Church in America, 3.2% Wisconsin Evangelical Lutheran Synod, 2.5% Jewish estimate (2000).
Economy: Unemployment rate: 3.4% (11/2002); Total civilian labor force: 49,514 (11/2002); Leading industries: 34.4% manufacturing; 12.7% retail trade; 8.3% health care and social assistance (2000); Companies that employ more than 1,000 persons: 1 (2000); Companies that employ more than 100 persons: 56 (2000); Farms: 427 totaling 69,930 acres (1997); Minority business ownership rate: 3.7% (1997); Women business ownership rate: 23.5% (1997); Retail sales per capita: $11,651 (1997). Single-family building permits issued: 335 (2001) / 360 (2000); Multi-family building permits issued: 402 (2001) / 142 (2000).
Income: Per capita income: $31,947 (2000); Median household income: $62,745 (2000); Poverty rate: 2.6% (2000); Bankruptcy rate: 2.29% (2001).
Taxes: Total county taxes per capita: $214 (2000); County property taxes per capita: $149 (2000).
Education: High school graduation rate: 91.9% (2000); College graduation rate: 38.6% (2000).
Housing: Homeownership rate: 76.3% (2000); Median home value: $177,300 (2000); Median rent: $574 per month (2000); Median age of housing: 28 years (2000).
Health: Birth rate: 117.5 per 10,000 population (1998); Age adjusted death rate: 71.2 per 10,000 population (1999); Age adjusted cancer mortality rate: 219.4 deaths per 100,000 population (1999). Air Quality Index: 66% good, 34% moderate, 1% unhealthy (percent of days in 2000). Number of physicians: 37.5 per 10,000 population (1999); Number of hospital beds: 10.0 per 10,000 population (1999).
Elections: 2000 Presidential election results: 31.5% Gore, 65.2% Bush, 2.6% Nader, 0.3% Buchanan

Additional Information Contacts

Ozaukee County Government Offices 262-284-9411
Cedarburg Chamber of Commerce. 262-377-5856
Grafton Chamber of Commerce 262-377-1650
Mequon-Thiensville Chamber of Commerce. 262-512-9358
Ozaukee Realtors Association 262-375-4730
Saukville Chamber of Commerce 262-268-1970

Ozaukee County Communities

BELGIUM (village). Covers a land area of 1.443 square miles and a water area of 0 square miles. Located at 43.50° N. Lat.; 87.84° W. Long. Elevation is 736 feet.
Population: 1,678 (2000); Race: 95.4% White, 0.1% Black, 0.2% Asian, 0.2% American Indian and Alaska Native, 4.3% Hispanic of any race, 1.2% two or more races (2000); Density: 1,163.0 persons per square mile (2000); Age: 31.3% under 18, 8.0% over 64 (2000); Marriage status: 21.3% never married, 68.4% now married, 3.6% widowed, 6.7% divorced (2000); Foreign born: 1.9% (2000); Ancestry (includes multiple ancestries): 50.1% German, 16.2% Luxemburger, 7.0% Irish, 6.8% Polish, 5.9% United States or American (2000).
Economy: Single-family building permits issued: 20 (2001) / 32 (2000); Multi-family building permits issued: 0 (2001) / 26 (2000); Employment by occupation: 9.9% management, 15.5% professional, 13.7% services, 21.5% sales, 0.0% farming, 9.5% construction, 29.9% production (2000).
Income: Per capita income: $20,659 (2000); Median household income: $53,523 (2000); Poverty rate: 2.4% (2000).
Taxes: Total city taxes per capita: $355 (1997); City property taxes per capita: $335 (1997).
Education: High school graduation rate: 85.7% (2000); College graduation rate: 15.1% (2000).
Housing: Homeownership rate: 70.2% (2000); Median home value: $134,800 (2000); Median rent: $527 per month (2000); Median age of housing: 19 years (2000).
Transportation: Commute to work: 92.6% car, 1.4% public transportation, 3.6% walk, 2.2% work from home (2000); Travel time to work: 25.7% less than 15 minutes, 41.7% 15 to 30 minutes, 20.4% 30 to 45 minutes, 8.5% 45 to 60 minutes, 3.7% 60 minutes or more (2000)

BELGIUM (town). Covers a land area of 35.739 square miles and a water area of 1.065 square miles. Located at 43.49° N. Lat.; 87.85° W. Long. Elevation is 736 feet.
Population: 1,513 (2000); Race: 96.7% White, 0.2% Black, 1.3% Asian, 1.0% American Indian and Alaska Native, 1.2% Hispanic of any race, 0.5% two or more races (2000); Density: 42.3 persons per square mile (2000); Age: 27.2% under 18, 14.0% over 64 (2000); Marriage status: 22.5% never married, 66.0% now married, 5.8% widowed, 5.7% divorced (2000); Foreign born: 1.6% (2000); Ancestry (includes multiple ancestries): 50.6% German, 19.9% Luxemburger, 6.4% Irish, 6.4% Polish, 5.6% English (2000).
Economy: Manufacturing: consumer goods, sheepskin; cheese. Single-family building permits issued: 6 (2001) / 8 (2000); Multi-family building permits issued: 0 (2001) / 0 (2000); Employment by occupation: 22.2% management, 16.1% professional, 9.4% services, 18.7% sales, 3.0% farming, 9.5% construction, 21.0% production (2000).
Income: Per capita income: $24,746 (2000); Median household income: $57,865 (2000); Poverty rate: 2.2% (2000).
Taxes: Total city taxes per capita: $94 (1997); City property taxes per capita: $92 (1997).
Education: High school graduation rate: 82.5% (2000); College graduation rate: 26.7% (2000).
Housing: Homeownership rate: 82.8% (2000); Median home value: $158,500 (2000); Median rent: $495 per month (2000); Median age of housing: 52 years (2000).
Transportation: Commute to work: 86.5% car, 0.7% public transportation, 1.9% walk, 10.4% work from home (2000); Travel time to work: 30.6% less than 15 minutes, 28.0% 15 to 30 minutes, 23.6% 30 to 45 minutes, 13.4% 45 to 60 minutes, 4.4% 60 minutes or more (2000)

CEDARBURG (city). Covers a land area of 3.685 square miles and a water area of 0.036 square miles. Located at 43.29° N. Lat.; 87.98° W. Long. Elevation is 790 feet.
Population: 10,908 (2000); Race: 98.7% White, 0.2% Black, 0.7% Asian, 0.2% American Indian and Alaska Native, 0.4% Hispanic of any race, 0.2% two or more races (2000); Density: 2,960.1 persons per square mile (2000); Age: 26.0% under 18, 15.3% over 64 (2000); Marriage status: 20.5% never married, 64.4% now married, 7.1% widowed, 7.9% divorced (2000); Foreign born: 3.2% (2000); Ancestry (includes multiple ancestries): 52.7% German, 12.4% Irish, 8.6% English, 8.4% Polish, 7.4% Italian (2000).
Vital Statistics: Birth rate: 110.0 per 10,000 population (1998)
Economy: Single-family building permits issued: 39 (2001) / 51 (2000); Multi-family building permits issued: 0 (2001) / 2 (2000); Employment by occupation: 23.1% management, 22.4% professional, 12.3% services, 26.8% sales, 0.0% farming, 4.4% construction, 10.9% production (2000).
Income: Per capita income: $27,455 (2000); Median household income: $56,431 (2000); Poverty rate: 2.7% (2000).
Taxes: Total city taxes per capita: $447 (1997); City property taxes per capita: $411 (1997).
Education: High school graduation rate: 92.8% (2000); College graduation rate: 41.9% (2000).

School District(s)

Cedarburg (PK-12)
2000 Enrollment: 2,923 262-376-6115

Housing: Homeownership rate: 64.2% (2000); Median home value: $179,900 (2000); Median rent: $598 per month (2000); Median age of housing: 29 years (2000).
Safety: Violent crime rate: 1.8 per 10,000 population; Property crime rate: 122.9 per 10,000 population (2001).
Newspapers: Ozaukee County News Graphic (2 x week); Ozaukee County Guide (1 x week)
Transportation: Commute to work: 92.5% car, 0.7% public transportation, 2.8% walk, 3.3% work from home (2000); Travel time to work: 33.4% less than 15 minutes, 36.2% 15 to 30 minutes, 19.9% 30 to 45 minutes, 8.0% 45 to 60 minutes, 2.5% 60 minutes or more (2000)

Additional Information Contacts

Cedarburg Chamber of Commerce. 262-377-5856

CEDARBURG (town). Covers a land area of 25.593 square miles and a water area of 0.241 square miles. Located at 43.31° N. Lat.; 88.00° W. Long. Elevation is 790 feet.

History: Settled 1842, incorporated 1885. Hamilton historic district, covered bridge.
Population: 5,744 (2000); Race: 99.1% White, 0.3% Black, 0.1% Asian, 0.3% American Indian and Alaska Native, 0.8% Hispanic of any race, 0.2% two or more races (2000); Density: 224.4 persons per square mile (2000); Age: 29.4% under 18, 11.8% over 64 (2000); Marriage status: 16.6% never married, 74.9% now married, 4.6% widowed, 4.0% divorced (2000); Foreign born: 1.7% (2000); Ancestry (includes multiple ancestries): 59.5% German, 10.1% Polish, 9.8% Irish, 8.1% English, 4.6% Italian (2000).
Economy: Trade center in dairying and farming area; light and heavy manufacturing; limestone quarries. Winery. Single-family building permits issued: 31 (2001) / 39 (2000); Multi-family building permits issued: 0 (2001) / 0 (2000); Employment by occupation: 20.9% management, 26.1% professional, 8.8% services, 28.8% sales, 0.4% farming, 5.4% construction, 9.6% production (2000).
Income: Per capita income: $30,998 (2000); Median household income: $75,909 (2000); Poverty rate: 2.3% (2000).
Taxes: Total city taxes per capita: $191 (1997); City property taxes per capita: $177 (1997).
Education: High school graduation rate: 93.2% (2000); College graduation rate: 38.3% (2000).
Housing: Homeownership rate: 95.9% (2000); Median home value: $209,200 (2000); Median rent: $510 per month (2000); Median age of housing: 27 years (2000).
Transportation: Commute to work: 91.3% car, 0.0% public transportation, 1.5% walk, 6.8% work from home (2000); Travel time to work: 30.0% less than 15 minutes, 35.0% 15 to 30 minutes, 22.8% 30 to 45 minutes, 9.5% 45 to 60 minutes, 2.6% 60 minutes or more (2000)

FREDONIA (village). Covers a land area of 1.431 square miles and a water area of 0 square miles. Located at 43.46° N. Lat.; 87.95° W. Long. Elevation is 820 feet.
Population: 1,934 (2000); Race: 96.9% White, 0.2% Black, 0.3% Asian, 0.1% American Indian and Alaska Native, 1.4% Hispanic of any race, 2.3% two or more races (2000); Density: 1,351.1 persons per square mile (2000); Age: 31.2% under 18, 7.9% over 64 (2000); Marriage status: 27.4% never married, 59.8% now married, 3.6% widowed, 9.2% divorced (2000); Foreign born: 0.8% (2000); Ancestry (includes multiple ancestries): 58.1% German, 10.0% Polish, 9.9% Irish, 8.0% Luxemburger, 6.7% Other groups (2000).
Economy: Single-family building permits issued: 24 (2001) / 23 (2000); Multi-family building permits issued: 2 (2001) / 2 (2000); Employment by occupation: 8.5% management, 18.1% professional, 11.0% services, 21.5% sales, 1.2% farming, 10.8% construction, 28.8% production (2000).
Income: Per capita income: $20,644 (2000); Median household income: $53,173 (2000); Poverty rate: 2.2% (2000).
Taxes: Total city taxes per capita: $268 (2000); City property taxes per capita: $249 (2000).
Education: High school graduation rate: 87.9% (2000); College graduation rate: 17.9% (2000).

School District(s)

Northern Ozaukee (PK-12)
2000 Enrollment: 899 262-692-2489
Housing: Homeownership rate: 62.8% (2000); Median home value: $134,700 (2000); Median rent: $575 per month (2000); Median age of housing: 25 years (2000).
Transportation: Commute to work: 94.6% car, 0.5% public transportation, 1.9% walk, 2.5% work from home (2000); Travel time to work: 29.8% less than 15 minutes, 41.0% 15 to 30 minutes, 18.4% 30 to 45 minutes, 5.8% 45 to 60 minutes, 5.0% 60 minutes or more (2000)

FREDONIA (town). Covers a land area of 34.655 square miles and a water area of 0.301 square miles. Located at 43.49° N. Lat.; 87.98° W. Long. Elevation is 820 feet.
Population: 2,903 (2000); Race: 98.6% White, 0.9% Black, 0.2% Asian, 0.0% American Indian and Alaska Native, 0.4% Hispanic of any race, 0.0% two or more races (2000); Density: 83.8 persons per square mile (2000); Age: 17.6% under 18, 5.8% over 64 (2000); Marriage status: 44.9% never married, 48.8% now married, 2.7% widowed, 3.6% divorced (2000); Foreign born: 1.1% (2000); Ancestry (includes multiple ancestries): 60.5% German, 9.0% Irish, 6.7% Polish, 6.7% Luxemburger, 4.4% United States or American (2000).
Economy: In farm area. Manufacturing: screen printing, plastic dinnerware, machinery. Single-family building permits issued: 10 (2001) / 6 (2000); Multi-family building permits issued: 0 (2001) / 0 (2000); Employment by occupation: 9.9% management, 16.0% professional, 19.2% services, 28.3% sales, 1.2% farming, 7.7% construction, 17.8% production (2000).
Income: Per capita income: $17,073 (2000); Median household income: $55,388 (2000); Poverty rate: 2.3% (2000).
Taxes: Total city taxes per capita: $75 (1997); City property taxes per capita: $71 (1997).
Education: High school graduation rate: 89.7% (2000); College graduation rate: 13.8% (2000).
Housing: Homeownership rate: 92.1% (2000); Median home value: $159,400 (2000); Median rent: $434 per month (2000); Median age of housing: 36 years (2000).
Transportation: Commute to work: 77.0% car, 0.2% public transportation, 15.6% walk, 6.6% work from home (2000); Travel time to work: 39.6% less than 15 minutes, 33.9% 15 to 30 minutes, 17.8% 30 to 45 minutes, 6.2% 45 to 60 minutes, 2.6% 60 minutes or more (2000)

GRAFTON (village). Covers a land area of 4.041 square miles and a water area of 0.039 square miles. Located at 43.31° N. Lat.; 87.95° W. Long. Elevation is 780 feet.
Population: 10,312 (2000); Race: 97.6% White, 0.2% Black, 0.4% Asian, 0.3% American Indian and Alaska Native, 2.2% Hispanic of any race, 1.1% two or more races (2000); Density: 2,552.0 persons per square mile (2000); Age: 25.7% under 18, 11.3% over 64 (2000); Marriage status: 19.7% never married, 66.2% now married, 6.4% widowed, 7.7% divorced (2000); Foreign born: 2.2% (2000); Ancestry (includes multiple ancestries): 53.6% German, 14.4% Irish, 12.3% Polish, 8.2% English, 5.8% Italian (2000).
Economy: Single-family building permits issued: 40 (2001) / 62 (2000); Multi-family building permits issued: 150 (2001) / 88 (2000); Employment by occupation: 17.8% management, 20.9% professional, 11.3% services, 27.8% sales, 0.4% farming, 6.4% construction, 15.5% production (2000).
Income: Per capita income: $25,948 (2000); Median household income: $53,918 (2000); Poverty rate: 1.7% (2000).
Taxes: Total city taxes per capita: $415 (1997); City property taxes per capita: $383 (1997).
Education: High school graduation rate: 89.5% (2000); College graduation rate: 29.1% (2000).

School District(s)

Grafton (PK-12)
2000 Enrollment: 2,027 262-376-5440
Housing: Homeownership rate: 70.4% (2000); Median home value: $145,800 (2000); Median rent: $573 per month (2000); Median age of housing: 27 years (2000).
Safety: Violent crime rate: 1.9 per 10,000 population; Property crime rate: 138.6 per 10,000 population (2001).
Transportation: Commute to work: 94.2% car, 0.5% public transportation, 3.0% walk, 1.8% work from home (2000); Travel time to work: 39.7% less than 15 minutes, 29.8% 15 to 30 minutes, 21.0% 30 to 45 minutes, 5.4% 45 to 60 minutes, 4.1% 60 minutes or more (2000)

Additional Information Contacts

Grafton Chamber of Commerce 262-377-1650
Ozaukee Realtors Association 262-375-4730

GRAFTON (town). Covers a land area of 19.818 square miles and a water area of 1.599 square miles. Located at 43.31° N. Lat.; 87.93° W. Long. Elevation is 780 feet.
History: Incorporated 1896.
Population: 4,132 (2000); Race: 98.9% White, 0.0% Black, 0.1% Asian, 0.2% American Indian and Alaska Native, 0.9% Hispanic of any race, 0.6% two or more races (2000); Density: 208.5 persons per square mile (2000); Age: 27.5% under 18, 10.5% over 64 (2000); Marriage status: 21.0% never married, 68.9% now married, 4.2% widowed, 5.9% divorced (2000); Foreign born: 1.7% (2000); Ancestry (includes multiple ancestries): 59.3% German, 11.8% Irish, 10.2% Polish, 7.1% English, 4.6% United States or American (2000).
Economy: In farm area. Manufacturing: transportation equipment, tools, appliances, textiles, electronic equipment, aluminum die castings, fabricated metal products, chemicals; machining. Single-family building permits issued: 0 (2001) / 0 (2000); Multi-family building permits issued: 0 (2001) / 0 (2000); Employment by occupation: 19.1% management, 21.1% professional, 9.6% services, 26.4% sales, 0.6% farming, 9.5% construction, 13.7% production (2000).
Income: Per capita income: $30,582 (2000); Median household income: $64,707 (2000); Poverty rate: 5.1% (2000).
Taxes: Total city taxes per capita: $147 (2000); City property taxes per capita: $139 (2000).
Education: High school graduation rate: 91.3% (2000); College graduation rate: 37.5% (2000).

Housing: Homeownership rate: 82.5% (2000); Median home value: $196,800 (2000); Median rent: $702 per month (2000); Median age of housing: 28 years (2000).
Transportation: Commute to work: 95.9% car, 0.0% public transportation, 0.6% walk, 3.1% work from home (2000); Travel time to work: 29.9% less than 15 minutes, 38.6% 15 to 30 minutes, 22.9% 30 to 45 minutes, 4.6% 45 to 60 minutes, 4.0% 60 minutes or more (2000)

MEQUON (city). Covers a land area of 46.183 square miles and a water area of 0.635 square miles. Located at 43.22° N. Lat.; 87.96° W. Long. Elevation is 700 feet.
History: Roman Catholic training center, a Lutheran seminary and an automotive museum are here. Established 1846, incorporated 1957.
Population: 21,823 (2000); Race: 94.4% White, 2.4% Black, 1.4% Asian, 0.4% American Indian and Alaska Native, 1.5% Hispanic of any race, 1.0% two or more races (2000); Density: 472.5 persons per square mile (2000); Age: 28.1% under 18, 13.7% over 64 (2000); Marriage status: 17.2% never married, 71.5% now married, 5.7% widowed, 5.6% divorced (2000); Foreign born: 5.5% (2000); Ancestry (includes multiple ancestries): 41.8% German, 13.9% Irish, 9.2% English, 8.7% Polish, 8.0% Other groups (2000).
Vital Statistics: Birth rate: 97.6 per 10,000 population (1998)
Economy: Manufacturing: transportation equipment, wire forms, fabricated metal products, levels and carpentry tools, machinery, consumer goods, building materials, glass products. Single-family building permits issued: 104 (2001) / 88 (2000); Multi-family building permits issued: 224 (2001) / 0 (2000); Employment by occupation: 28.0% management, 31.2% professional, 6.7% services, 24.3% sales, 0.2% farming, 3.4% construction, 6.1% production (2000).
Income: Per capita income: $48,333 (2000); Median household income: $90,733 (2000); Poverty rate: 1.7% (2000).
Taxes: Total city taxes per capita: $627 (2000); City property taxes per capita: $592 (2000).
Education: High school graduation rate: 96.1% (2000); College graduation rate: 59.6% (2000).

School District(s)

Mequon-Thiensville (PK-12)
2000 Enrollment: 4,214 262-238-8503

Four-year College(s)

Concordia University-Wisconsin (Private, Not-for-profit, Lutheran Church - Missouri Synod)
2001 Enrollment: 4,810 262-243-5700
2001 Tuition: In-state $13,550; Out-of-state $13,550
Wisconsin Lutheran Seminary (Private, Not-for-profit, Wisconsin Evangelical Lutheran Synod)
2001 Enrollment: n/a 262-242-8100

Housing: Homeownership rate: 91.2% (2000); Median home value: $250,400 (2000); Median rent: $836 per month (2000); Median age of housing: 24 years (2000).
Hospitals: Saint Mary's Hospital - Ozaukee (82 beds)
Safety: Violent crime rate: 2.7 per 10,000 population; Property crime rate: 81.9 per 10,000 population (2001).
Transportation: Commute to work: 92.9% car, 0.5% public transportation, 1.4% walk, 4.9% work from home (2000); Travel time to work: 28.4% less than 15 minutes, 44.0% 15 to 30 minutes, 21.2% 30 to 45 minutes, 3.9% 45 to 60 minutes, 2.5% 60 minutes or more (2000)

PORT WASHINGTON (city). Covers a land area of 3.846 square miles and a water area of 0.105 square miles. Located at 43.39° N. Lat.; 87.88° W. Long. Elevation is 612 feet.
History: Port Washington was the scene of a revolt against the military draft in 1862, when the European immigrants who had settled here objected to service in the Civil War. Though the harbor at Port Washington was not adequate for the city to develop as a significant shipping center, the early manufacturing industries produced a great diversity of goods. Commercial fishing was also important to the Port Washington economy. Leland Stanford, founder of Stanford University, tried to establish a law practice in Port Washington in 1850.
Population: 10,467 (2000); Race: 96.5% White, 0.5% Black, 1.0% Asian, 0.7% American Indian and Alaska Native, 0.8% Hispanic of any race, 1.2% two or more races (2000); Density: 2,721.5 persons per square mile (2000); Age: 25.5% under 18, 13.5% over 64 (2000); Marriage status: 23.1% never married, 60.6% now married, 6.5% widowed, 9.7% divorced (2000); Foreign born: 1.9% (2000); Ancestry (includes multiple ancestries): 54.1% German, 10.5% Irish, 10.1% Polish, 6.9% English, 5.3% Luxemburger (2000).
Economy: Single-family building permits issued: 21 (2001) / 26 (2000); Multi-family building permits issued: 24 (2001) / 18 (2000); Employment by occupation: 12.8% management, 22.0% professional, 11.3% services, 26.0% sales, 0.2% farming, 7.7% construction, 20.0% production (2000).
Income: Per capita income: $24,862 (2000); Median household income: $53,827 (2000); Poverty rate: 4.2% (2000).
Taxes: Total city taxes per capita: $379 (2000); City property taxes per capita: $346 (2000).
Education: High school graduation rate: 89.7% (2000); College graduation rate: 26.5% (2000).

School District(s)

Port Washington-Saukville (PK-12)
2000 Enrollment: 2,661 262-268-6005

Housing: Homeownership rate: 63.1% (2000); Median home value: $136,200 (2000); Median rent: $545 per month (2000); Median age of housing: 37 years (2000).
Safety: Violent crime rate: 3.8 per 10,000 population; Property crime rate: 212.5 per 10,000 population (2001).
Newspapers: Ozaukee Press (1 x week); Ozaukee County Advertiser (1 x week)
Transportation: Commute to work: 92.5% car, 0.4% public transportation, 3.2% walk, 2.4% work from home (2000); Travel time to work: 40.9% less than 15 minutes, 29.1% 15 to 30 minutes, 21.2% 30 to 45 minutes, 6.6% 45 to 60 minutes, 2.2% 60 minutes or more (2000)

PORT WASHINGTON (town). Covers a land area of 18.603 square miles and a water area of 2.454 square miles. Located at 43.41° N. Lat.; 87.87° W. Long. Elevation is 612 feet.
History: Settled before 1835, incorporated 1882.
Population: 1,631 (2000); Race: 98.4% White, 0.0% Black, 0.6% Asian, 0.3% American Indian and Alaska Native, 0.3% Hispanic of any race, 0.6% two or more races (2000); Density: 87.7 persons per square mile (2000); Age: 28.3% under 18, 11.2% over 64 (2000); Marriage status: 23.3% never married, 60.6% now married, 7.1% widowed, 9.0% divorced (2000); Foreign born: 1.8% (2000); Ancestry (includes multiple ancestries): 50.6% German, 13.3% Irish, 8.8% Luxemburger, 7.9% English, 5.9% Italian (2000).
Economy: In dairy and farm area. Manufacturing: shoes, chemicals, fabricated metal products, wire forms, consumer goods, machinery. Huntington Beach State Park to Northeast, on Lake Michigan. Single-family building permits issued: 12 (2001) / 5 (2000); Multi-family building permits issued: 0 (2001) / 4 (2000); Employment by occupation: 13.0% management, 13.4% professional, 16.5% services, 19.3% sales, 1.2% farming, 11.8% construction, 24.8% production (2000).
Income: Per capita income: $22,781 (2000); Median household income: $56,875 (2000); Poverty rate: 3.2% (2000).
Taxes: Total city taxes per capita: $82 (1997); City property taxes per capita: $69 (1997).
Education: High school graduation rate: 82.1% (2000); College graduation rate: 16.8% (2000).
Housing: Homeownership rate: 71.7% (2000); Median home value: $153,600 (2000); Median rent: $532 per month (2000); Median age of housing: 29 years (2000).
Transportation: Commute to work: 93.7% car, 0.2% public transportation, 2.7% walk, 3.4% work from home (2000); Travel time to work: 47.9% less than 15 minutes, 28.1% 15 to 30 minutes, 14.4% 30 to 45 minutes, 5.7% 45 to 60 minutes, 3.9% 60 minutes or more (2000)

SAUKVILLE (village). Covers a land area of 2.977 square miles and a water area of 0.046 square miles. Located at 43.38° N. Lat.; 87.94° W. Long. Elevation is 755 feet.
Population: 4,068 (2000); Race: 95.8% White, 1.2% Black, 0.2% Asian, 0.1% American Indian and Alaska Native, 2.8% Hispanic of any race, 1.3% two or more races (2000); Density: 1,366.3 persons per square mile (2000); Age: 28.2% under 18, 7.3% over 64 (2000); Marriage status: 26.9% never married, 58.9% now married, 3.1% widowed, 11.1% divorced (2000); Foreign born: 2.8% (2000); Ancestry (includes multiple ancestries): 58.5% German, 11.4% Irish, 9.4% Polish, 6.7% Other groups, 6.6% French (except Basque) (2000).
Economy: Single-family building permits issued: 17 (2001) / 12 (2000); Multi-family building permits issued: 2 (2001) / 2 (2000); Employment by occupation: 11.1% management, 16.0% professional, 10.5% services, 27.7% sales, 0.0% farming, 9.7% construction, 25.0% production (2000).
Income: Per capita income: $22,035 (2000); Median household income: $53,159 (2000); Poverty rate: 3.1% (2000).
Taxes: Total city taxes per capita: $310 (2000); City property taxes per capita: $267 (2000).
Education: High school graduation rate: 89.1% (2000); College graduation rate: 20.2% (2000).

Housing: Homeownership rate: 59.9% (2000); Median home value: $135,700 (2000); Median rent: $533 per month (2000); Median age of housing: 25 years (2000).
Safety: Violent crime rate: 7.3 per 10,000 population; Property crime rate: 329.5 per 10,000 population (2001).
Transportation: Commute to work: 94.8% car, 0.9% public transportation, 2.0% walk, 2.3% work from home (2000); Travel time to work: 37.0% less than 15 minutes, 30.7% 15 to 30 minutes, 22.4% 30 to 45 minutes, 5.8% 45 to 60 minutes, 4.2% 60 minutes or more (2000)
Additional Information Contacts
Saukville Chamber of Commerce 262-268-1970

SAUKVILLE (town). Covers a land area of 32.661 square miles and a water area of 0.678 square miles. Located at 43.40° N. Lat.; 87.96° W. Long. Elevation is 755 feet.
Population: 1,755 (2000); Race: 99.2% White, 0.2% Black, 0.2% Asian, 0.0% American Indian and Alaska Native, 0.2% Hispanic of any race, 0.4% two or more races (2000); Density: 53.7 persons per square mile (2000); Age: 24.5% under 18, 12.1% over 64 (2000); Marriage status: 18.2% never married, 73.2% now married, 4.3% widowed, 4.3% divorced (2000); Foreign born: 1.6% (2000); Ancestry (includes multiple ancestries): 59.4% German, 12.1% Irish, 10.9% Polish, 8.9% English, 4.8% Italian (2000).
Economy: In dairy and farm area. Manufacturing: electronic transformers, metal castings. Single-family building permits issued: 11 (2001) / 8 (2000); Multi-family building permits issued: 0 (2001) / 0 (2000); Employment by occupation: 16.5% management, 18.8% professional, 10.8% services, 22.3% sales, 0.9% farming, 13.2% construction, 17.5% production (2000).
Income: Per capita income: $24,522 (2000); Median household income: $60,435 (2000); Poverty rate: 2.6% (2000).
Taxes: Total city taxes per capita: $109 (1997); City property taxes per capita: $99 (1997).
Education: High school graduation rate: 90.5% (2000); College graduation rate: 26.9% (2000).
Housing: Homeownership rate: 87.7% (2000); Median home value: $182,500 (2000); Median rent: $495 per month (2000); Median age of housing: 30 years (2000).
Transportation: Commute to work: 92.9% car, 0.0% public transportation, 2.7% walk, 2.7% work from home (2000); Travel time to work: 31.3% less than 15 minutes, 37.4% 15 to 30 minutes, 21.5% 30 to 45 minutes, 6.4% 45 to 60 minutes, 3.3% 60 minutes or more (2000)

THIENSVILLE (village). Covers a land area of 1.098 square miles and a water area of 0.009 square miles. Located at 43.23° N. Lat.; 87.98° W. Long. Elevation is 680 feet.
History: Thiensville was the home of Victor L. Berger (1860-1929), editor of the leading Socialist newspaper. In 1910, Berger became the first Socialist member of the U.S. Congress.
Population: 3,254 (2000); Race: 97.4% White, 0.1% Black, 2.2% Asian, 0.0% American Indian and Alaska Native, 1.4% Hispanic of any race, 0.2% two or more races (2000); Density: 2,964.7 persons per square mile (2000); Age: 20.6% under 18, 20.7% over 64 (2000); Marriage status: 22.3% never married, 58.4% now married, 8.1% widowed, 11.2% divorced (2000); Foreign born: 9.2% (2000); Ancestry (includes multiple ancestries): 53.5% German, 13.9% Irish, 7.1% Other groups, 6.9% Polish, 6.5% Italian (2000).
Economy: Single-family building permits issued: 0 (2001) / 0 (2000); Multi-family building permits issued: 0 (2001) / 0 (2000); Employment by occupation: 17.3% management, 25.6% professional, 13.9% services, 28.9% sales, 0.7% farming, 3.1% construction, 10.5% production (2000).
Income: Per capita income: $30,748 (2000); Median household income: $55,962 (2000); Poverty rate: 2.7% (2000).
Taxes: Total city taxes per capita: $526 (1997); City property taxes per capita: $509 (1997).
Education: High school graduation rate: 92.3% (2000); College graduation rate: 39.3% (2000).
Housing: Homeownership rate: 67.7% (2000); Median home value: $175,300 (2000); Median rent: $670 per month (2000); Median age of housing: 36 years (2000).
Safety: Violent crime rate: 21.4 per 10,000 population; Property crime rate: 131.2 per 10,000 population (2001).
Transportation: Commute to work: 93.4% car, 1.3% public transportation, 1.3% walk, 2.8% work from home (2000); Travel time to work: 32.5% less than 15 minutes, 38.0% 15 to 30 minutes, 17.4% 30 to 45 minutes, 7.8% 45 to 60 minutes, 4.4% 60 minutes or more (2000)
Additional Information Contacts
Mequon-Thiensville Chamber of Commerce. 262-512-9358

Pepin County

Located in western Wisconsin; bounded on the southwest by Lake Pepin on the Mississippi River and the Minnesota border; drained by the Chippewa River. Covers a land area of 232.30 square miles, a water area of 16.40 square miles, and is located in the Central Time Zone. The county government was organized in 1858. County seat is Durand.
Population: 7,213 (2000); Race: 98.9% White, 0.1% Black, 0.2% Asian, 0.2% American Indian and Alaska Native, 0.3% Hispanic of any race, 0.5% two or more races (2000); Density: 31.1 persons per square mile (2000); Age: 26.4% under 18, 16.9% over 64 (2000).
Religion: Five largest groups: 33.7% Catholic Church, 17.3% Evangelical Lutheran Church in America, 7.0% The United Methodist Church, 2.8% Lutheran Church—Missouri Synod, 1.9% The Evangelical Covenant Church (2000).
Economy: Unemployment rate: 4.6% (11/2002); Total civilian labor force: 3,125 (11/2002); Leading industries: 20.4% retail trade; 18.0% wholesale trade; 14.3% health care and social assistance (2000); Companies that employ more than 1,000 persons: 0 (2000); Companies that employ more than 100 persons: 2 (2000); Farms: 425 totaling 104,044 acres (1997); Minority business ownership rate: 0.0% (1997); Women business ownership rate: 0.0% (1997); Retail sales per capita: $12,383 (1997). Single-family building permits issued: 30 (2001) / 43 (2000); Multi-family building permits issued: 34 (2001) / 3 (2000).
Income: Per capita income: $18,288 (2000); Median household income: $37,609 (2000); Poverty rate: 9.1% (2000); Bankruptcy rate: 2.43% (2001).
Taxes: Total county taxes per capita: $329 (1997); County property taxes per capita: $289 (1997).
Education: High school graduation rate: 82.6% (2000); College graduation rate: 13.3% (2000).
Housing: Homeownership rate: 79.6% (2000); Median home value: $79,200 (2000); Median rent: $292 per month (2000); Median age of housing: 42 years (2000).
Health: Birth rate: 110.9 per 10,000 population (1998); Age adjusted death rate: 74.3 per 10,000 population (1999); Age adjusted cancer mortality rate: 184.5 (Unreliable figure as per CDC) deaths per 100,000 population (1999). Number of physicians: 8.3 per 10,000 population (1999); Number of hospital beds: 117.8 per 10,000 population (1999).
Elections: 2000 Presidential election results: 50.6% Gore, 44.5% Bush, 4.2% Nader, 0.3% Buchanan
Additional Information Contacts
Pepin County Government Offices 715-672-8704

Pepin County Communities

ALBANY (town). Covers a land area of 36.036 square miles and a water area of <.001 square miles. Located at 44.63° N. Lat.; 91.71° W. Long.
Population: 620 (2000); Race: 98.3% White, 0.0% Black, 0.6% Asian, 0.0% American Indian and Alaska Native, 0.3% Hispanic of any race, 0.8% two or more races (2000); Density: 17.2 persons per square mile (2000); Age: 34.5% under 18, 7.3% over 64 (2000); Marriage status: 24.6% never married, 66.9% now married, 4.9% widowed, 3.6% divorced (2000); Foreign born: 0.9% (2000); Ancestry (includes multiple ancestries): 42.0% German, 19.2% Norwegian, 10.4% Austrian, 8.2% Irish, 5.2% United States or American (2000).
Economy: Employment by occupation: 18.9% management, 10.3% professional, 14.6% services, 13.2% sales, 3.6% farming, 15.2% construction, 24.2% production (2000).
Income: Per capita income: $13,012 (2000); Median household income: $40,313 (2000); Poverty rate: 25.9% (2000).
Taxes: Total city taxes per capita: $147 (1997); City property taxes per capita: $145 (1997).
Education: High school graduation rate: 69.3% (2000); College graduation rate: 9.2% (2000).
Housing: Homeownership rate: 91.6% (2000); Median home value: $93,900 (2000); Median rent: $375 per month (2000); Median age of housing: 45 years (2000).
Transportation: Commute to work: 80.0% car, 0.0% public transportation, 4.7% walk, 15.3% work from home (2000); Travel time to work: 31.1% less than 15 minutes, 28.7% 15 to 30 minutes, 22.8% 30 to 45 minutes, 4.7% 45 to 60 minutes, 12.6% 60 minutes or more (2000)

ARKANSAW (unincorporated postal area, zip code 54721). Covers a land area of 68.443 square miles and a water area of 0.250 square miles. Located at 44.62° N. Lat.; 92.07° W. Long. Elevation is 790 feet.

Population: 1,399 (2000); Race: 99.9% White, 0.0% Black, 0.0% Asian, 0.1% American Indian and Alaska Native, 0.0% Hispanic of any race, 0.0% two or more races (2000); Density: 20.4 persons per square mile (2000); Age: 27.4% under 18, 13.3% over 64 (2000); Marriage status: 25.0% never married, 60.2% now married, 5.3% widowed, 9.5% divorced (2000); Foreign born: 0.1% (2000); Ancestry (includes multiple ancestries): 51.1% German, 12.9% Austrian, 12.7% Norwegian, 9.5% Irish, 7.8% English (2000).
Economy: Employment by occupation: 18.9% management, 12.0% professional, 14.8% services, 16.8% sales, 5.1% farming, 7.8% construction, 24.5% production (2000).
Income: Per capita income: $15,504 (2000); Median household income: $37,857 (2000); Poverty rate: 8.7% (2000).
Education: High school graduation rate: 87.2% (2000); College graduation rate: 9.7% (2000).
Housing: Homeownership rate: 84.9% (2000); Median home value: $67,500 (2000); Median rent: $302 per month (2000); Median age of housing: 49 years (2000).
Transportation: Commute to work: 84.9% car, 0.0% public transportation, 5.5% walk, 9.2% work from home (2000); Travel time to work: 35.2% less than 15 minutes, 25.9% 15 to 30 minutes, 19.6% 30 to 45 minutes, 12.2% 45 to 60 minutes, 7.1% 60 minutes or more (2000)

DURAND (city). Covers a land area of 1.601 square miles and a water area of 0.111 square miles. Located at 44.62° N. Lat.; 91.96° W. Long. Elevation is 721 feet.
History: Durand was laid out in 1856 by Myles Durand Prindle, who gave the town its name. It became the seat of Pepin County in 1861. Durand was a busy river port in lumbering days, but with the slowing of traffic on the river, Durand became a trading center for the surrounding farmlands.
Population: 1,968 (2000); Race: 98.7% White, 0.0% Black, 0.0% Asian, 0.7% American Indian and Alaska Native, 0.9% Hispanic of any race, 0.6% two or more races (2000); Density: 1,229.4 persons per square mile (2000); Age: 24.8% under 18, 24.2% over 64 (2000); Marriage status: 24.0% never married, 58.0% now married, 11.0% widowed, 7.0% divorced (2000); Foreign born: 0.0% (2000); Ancestry (includes multiple ancestries): 41.0% German, 18.7% Norwegian, 10.2% Austrian, 8.7% Irish, 6.7% English (2000).
Economy: Single-family building permits issued: 1 (2001) / 0 (2000); Multi-family building permits issued: 0 (2001) / 3 (2000); Employment by occupation: 6.8% management, 18.0% professional, 15.6% services, 28.5% sales, 1.4% farming, 10.4% construction, 19.2% production (2000).
Income: Per capita income: $18,103 (2000); Median household income: $30,064 (2000); Poverty rate: 9.3% (2000).
Taxes: Total city taxes per capita: $171 (1997); City property taxes per capita: $163 (1997).
Education: High school graduation rate: 81.3% (2000); College graduation rate: 14.0% (2000).

School District(s)

Durand (PK-12)
2000 Enrollment: 1,194 715-672-8919
Housing: Homeownership rate: 68.0% (2000); Median home value: $75,000 (2000); Median rent: $278 per month (2000); Median age of housing: 47 years (2000).
Hospitals: Chippewa Valley Hospital (88 beds)
Safety: Violent crime rate: 20.2 per 10,000 population; Property crime rate: 196.8 per 10,000 population (2001).
Newspapers: The Courier-Wedge (1 x week)
Transportation: Commute to work: 90.9% car, 0.3% public transportation, 4.8% walk, 3.5% work from home (2000); Travel time to work: 58.1% less than 15 minutes, 14.7% 15 to 30 minutes, 18.2% 30 to 45 minutes, 5.1% 45 to 60 minutes, 3.9% 60 minutes or more (2000)

DURAND (town). Covers a land area of 18.510 square miles and a water area of 0.552 square miles. Located at 44.64° N. Lat.; 91.93° W. Long. Elevation is 721 feet.
History: Settled c.1850, incorporated 1887.
Population: 694 (2000); Race: 97.7% White, 0.0% Black, 0.0% Asian, 0.3% American Indian and Alaska Native, 0.0% Hispanic of any race, 2.0% two or more races (2000); Density: 37.5 persons per square mile (2000); Age: 32.6% under 18, 7.2% over 64 (2000); Marriage status: 21.5% never married, 66.7% now married, 4.7% widowed, 7.1% divorced (2000); Foreign born: 1.4% (2000); Ancestry (includes multiple ancestries): 48.9% German, 20.5% Austrian, 20.0% Norwegian, 11.9% Irish, 4.5% Polish (2000).
Economy: In dairy and livestock area: dairy products, vegetables, feed, beverages. Lumber. Employment by occupation: 13.0% management, 10.1% professional, 12.5% services, 24.1% sales, 0.9% farming, 9.6% construction, 29.9% production (2000).
Income: Per capita income: $18,878 (2000); Median household income: $49,375 (2000); Poverty rate: 4.8% (2000).
Taxes: Total city taxes per capita: $32 (1997); City property taxes per capita: $28 (1997).
Education: High school graduation rate: 90.0% (2000); College graduation rate: 13.8% (2000).
Housing: Homeownership rate: 86.1% (2000); Median home value: $101,100 (2000); Median rent: $325 per month (2000); Median age of housing: 26 years (2000).
Transportation: Commute to work: 91.9% car, 0.6% public transportation, 2.1% walk, 4.8% work from home (2000); Travel time to work: 43.6% less than 15 minutes, 10.3% 15 to 30 minutes, 30.4% 30 to 45 minutes, 11.0% 45 to 60 minutes, 4.7% 60 minutes or more (2000)

FRANKFORT (town). Covers a land area of 30.069 square miles and a water area of 0.898 square miles. Located at 44.55° N. Lat.; 92.09° W. Long.
Population: 362 (2000); Race: 100.0% White, 0.0% Black, 0.0% Asian, 0.0% American Indian and Alaska Native, 0.0% Hispanic of any race, 0.0% two or more races (2000); Density: 12.0 persons per square mile (2000); Age: 16.9% under 18, 12.0% over 64 (2000); Marriage status: 25.5% never married, 56.6% now married, 4.1% widowed, 13.8% divorced (2000); Foreign born: 0.6% (2000); Ancestry (includes multiple ancestries): 42.8% German, 17.2% Norwegian, 16.0% Swedish, 14.5% Irish, 9.3% English (2000).
Economy: Employment by occupation: 14.9% management, 18.0% professional, 13.4% services, 9.8% sales, 6.2% farming, 11.9% construction, 25.8% production (2000).
Income: Per capita income: $16,885 (2000); Median household income: $32,813 (2000); Poverty rate: 1.8% (2000).
Taxes: Total city taxes per capita: $198 (1997); City property taxes per capita: $198 (1997).
Education: High school graduation rate: 87.0% (2000); College graduation rate: 8.7% (2000).
Housing: Homeownership rate: 82.5% (2000); Median home value: $70,000 (2000); Median rent: $400 per month (2000); Median age of housing: 49 years (2000).
Transportation: Commute to work: 81.8% car, 0.0% public transportation, 7.3% walk, 9.4% work from home (2000); Travel time to work: 14.4% less than 15 minutes, 29.9% 15 to 30 minutes, 21.3% 30 to 45 minutes, 22.4% 45 to 60 minutes, 12.1% 60 minutes or more (2000)

LIMA (town). Covers a land area of 35.905 square miles and a water area of 0.012 square miles. Located at 44.64° N. Lat.; 91.84° W. Long. Elevation is 877 feet.
Population: 716 (2000); Race: 100.0% White, 0.0% Black, 0.0% Asian, 0.0% American Indian and Alaska Native, 0.6% Hispanic of any race, 0.0% two or more races (2000); Density: 19.9 persons per square mile (2000); Age: 33.9% under 18, 9.5% over 64 (2000); Marriage status: 31.3% never married, 63.4% now married, 1.6% widowed, 3.7% divorced (2000); Foreign born: 0.3% (2000); Ancestry (includes multiple ancestries): 49.0% German, 30.9% Austrian, 5.4% English, 4.5% Norwegian, 3.3% French (except Basque) (2000).
Economy: Employment by occupation: 18.0% management, 10.2% professional, 15.7% services, 16.0% sales, 4.4% farming, 18.3% construction, 17.4% production (2000).
Income: Per capita income: $18,334 (2000); Median household income: $45,139 (2000); Poverty rate: 12.2% (2000).
Taxes: Total city taxes per capita: $98 (1997); City property taxes per capita: $97 (1997).
Education: High school graduation rate: 74.9% (2000); College graduation rate: 4.4% (2000).
Housing: Homeownership rate: 89.2% (2000); Median home value: $75,600 (2000); Median rent: $340 per month (2000); Median age of housing: 46 years (2000).
Transportation: Commute to work: 80.2% car, 0.6% public transportation, 3.8% walk, 14.5% work from home (2000); Travel time to work: 34.0% less than 15 minutes, 22.4% 15 to 30 minutes, 27.9% 30 to 45 minutes, 8.5% 45 to 60 minutes, 7.1% 60 minutes or more (2000)

PEPIN (village). Covers a land area of 0.709 square miles and a water area of 0 square miles. Located at 44.44° N. Lat.; 92.14° W. Long. Elevation is 720 feet.
History: Pepin was settled in 1846 as a port on the Mississippi River. This was the home of the Fuller brothers, steamboat engineers of the upper

Mississippi, who were said to have popularized the term "stateroom" for ship cabins, naming each cabin for a different state.
Population: 878 (2000); Race: 98.4% White, 0.0% Black, 1.4% Asian, 0.0% American Indian and Alaska Native, 0.0% Hispanic of any race, 0.2% two or more races (2000); Density: 1,238.1 persons per square mile (2000); Age: 16.7% under 18, 30.5% over 64 (2000); Marriage status: 20.8% never married, 61.5% now married, 9.0% widowed, 8.7% divorced (2000); Foreign born: 1.3% (2000); Ancestry (includes multiple ancestries): 42.6% German, 16.0% Swedish, 16.0% Norwegian, 8.0% United States or American, 7.9% English (2000).
Economy: Single-family building permits issued: 3 (2001) / 2 (2000); Multi-family building permits issued: 34 (2001) / 0 (2000); Employment by occupation: 8.8% management, 13.5% professional, 16.7% services, 14.2% sales, 2.2% farming, 11.8% construction, 32.8% production (2000).
Income: Per capita income: $17,755 (2000); Median household income: $36,319 (2000); Poverty rate: 5.8% (2000).
Taxes: Total city taxes per capita: $125 (1997); City property taxes per capita: $114 (1997).
Education: High school graduation rate: 80.9% (2000); College graduation rate: 14.4% (2000).

School District(s)

Pepin Area (PK-12)
2000 Enrollment: 328 715-442-2391
Housing: Homeownership rate: 77.6% (2000); Median home value: $78,200 (2000); Median rent: $337 per month (2000); Median age of housing: 39 years (2000).
Transportation: Commute to work: 85.0% car, 1.3% public transportation, 9.9% walk, 3.8% work from home (2000); Travel time to work: 37.2% less than 15 minutes, 14.2% 15 to 30 minutes, 20.3% 30 to 45 minutes, 13.7% 45 to 60 minutes, 14.5% 60 minutes or more (2000)

PEPIN (town). Covers a land area of 45.439 square miles and a water area of 7.118 square miles. Located at 44.47° N. Lat.; 92.14° W. Long. Elevation is 720 feet.
Population: 580 (2000); Race: 98.5% White, 1.2% Black, 0.0% Asian, 0.0% American Indian and Alaska Native, 0.0% Hispanic of any race, 0.3% two or more races (2000); Density: 12.8 persons per square mile (2000); Age: 25.8% under 18, 10.6% over 64 (2000); Marriage status: 21.1% never married, 67.8% now married, 6.1% widowed, 5.0% divorced (2000); Foreign born: 0.8% (2000); Ancestry (includes multiple ancestries): 49.2% German, 18.6% Norwegian, 18.2% Swedish, 9.1% Irish, 9.0% English (2000).
Economy: In dairy and farm area. Manufacturing of agricultural implements, dairy products processing; fishing and lake resort. Employment by occupation: 16.5% management, 18.0% professional, 15.2% services, 10.6% sales, 4.3% farming, 6.2% construction, 29.2% production (2000).
Income: Per capita income: $18,902 (2000); Median household income: $44,444 (2000); Poverty rate: 4.9% (2000).
Taxes: Total city taxes per capita: $135 (1997); City property taxes per capita: $134 (1997).
Education: High school graduation rate: 87.2% (2000); College graduation rate: 18.2% (2000).
Housing: Homeownership rate: 83.3% (2000); Median home value: $101,400 (2000); Median rent: $213 per month (2000); Median age of housing: 44 years (2000).
Transportation: Commute to work: 80.6% car, 0.0% public transportation, 3.8% walk, 14.1% work from home (2000); Travel time to work: 22.9% less than 15 minutes, 16.7% 15 to 30 minutes, 26.5% 30 to 45 minutes, 16.7% 45 to 60 minutes, 17.1% 60 minutes or more (2000)

STOCKHOLM (village). Covers a land area of 0.933 square miles and a water area of 0.030 square miles. Located at 44.48° N. Lat.; 92.26° W. Long. Elevation is 690 feet.
Population: 97 (2000); Race: 100.0% White, 0.0% Black, 0.0% Asian, 0.0% American Indian and Alaska Native, 0.0% Hispanic of any race, 0.0% two or more races (2000); Density: 104.0 persons per square mile (2000); Age: 8.6% under 18, 17.1% over 64 (2000); Marriage status: 29.0% never married, 62.0% now married, 4.0% widowed, 5.0% divorced (2000); Foreign born: 1.9% (2000); Ancestry (includes multiple ancestries): 37.1% German, 28.6% Swedish, 25.7% Norwegian, 14.3% Irish, 10.5% Polish (2000).
Economy: Single-family building permits issued: 1 (2001) / 0 (2000); Multi-family building permits issued: 0 (2001) / 0 (2000); Employment by occupation: 14.8% management, 26.2% professional, 19.7% services, 9.8% sales, 0.0% farming, 9.8% construction, 19.7% production (2000).
Income: Per capita income: $55,006 (2000); Median household income: $41,250 (2000); Poverty rate: 8.6% (2000).
Taxes: Total city taxes per capita: $129 (1997); City property taxes per capita: $118 (1997).
Education: High school graduation rate: 88.4% (2000); College graduation rate: 46.5% (2000).
Housing: Homeownership rate: 83.3% (2000); Median home value: $135,400 (2000); Median rent: $538 per month (2000); Median age of housing: 60+ years (2000).
Transportation: Commute to work: 71.2% car, 0.0% public transportation, 10.2% walk, 18.6% work from home (2000); Travel time to work: 54.2% less than 15 minutes, 16.7% 15 to 30 minutes, 25.0% 30 to 45 minutes, 0.0% 45 to 60 minutes, 4.2% 60 minutes or more (2000)

STOCKHOLM (town). Covers a land area of 15.358 square miles and a water area of 6.381 square miles. Located at 44.50° N. Lat.; 92.25° W. Long. Elevation is 690 feet.
Population: 75 (2000); Race: 100.0% White, 0.0% Black, 0.0% Asian, 0.0% American Indian and Alaska Native, 0.0% Hispanic of any race, 0.0% two or more races (2000); Density: 4.9 persons per square mile (2000); Age: 21.5% under 18, 40.0% over 64 (2000); Marriage status: 0.0% never married, 72.5% now married, 11.8% widowed, 15.7% divorced (2000); Foreign born: 3.1% (2000); Ancestry (includes multiple ancestries): 53.8% Swedish, 36.9% German, 10.8% Norwegian, 7.7% Dutch, 7.7% English (2000).
Economy: Employment by occupation: 19.0% management, 23.8% professional, 0.0% services, 23.8% sales, 0.0% farming, 0.0% construction, 33.3% production (2000).
Income: Per capita income: $21,329 (2000); Median household income: $32,250 (2000); Poverty rate: 0.0% (2000).
Taxes: Total city taxes per capita: $153 (1997); City property taxes per capita: $153 (1997).
Education: High school graduation rate: 80.4% (2000); College graduation rate: 19.6% (2000).
Housing: Homeownership rate: 86.2% (2000); Median home value: $325,000 (2000); Median age of housing: 60+ years (2000).
Transportation: Commute to work: 90.5% car, 0.0% public transportation, 0.0% walk, 9.5% work from home (2000); Travel time to work: 10.5% less than 15 minutes, 10.5% 15 to 30 minutes, 52.6% 30 to 45 minutes, 26.3% 45 to 60 minutes, 0.0% 60 minutes or more (2000)

WATERVILLE (town). Covers a land area of 35.719 square miles and a water area of 0.475 square miles. Located at 44.64° N. Lat.; 92.05° W. Long.
Population: 859 (2000); Race: 100.0% White, 0.0% Black, 0.0% Asian, 0.0% American Indian and Alaska Native, 0.0% Hispanic of any race, 0.0% two or more races (2000); Density: 24.0 persons per square mile (2000); Age: 27.0% under 18, 15.4% over 64 (2000); Marriage status: 24.2% never married, 60.0% now married, 6.5% widowed, 9.4% divorced (2000); Foreign born: 0.0% (2000); Ancestry (includes multiple ancestries): 49.3% German, 15.7% Austrian, 11.9% Norwegian, 9.8% Irish, 7.8% French (except Basque) (2000).
Economy: Employment by occupation: 18.8% management, 9.6% professional, 14.5% services, 17.3% sales, 5.8% farming, 7.7% construction, 26.3% production (2000).
Income: Per capita income: $15,482 (2000); Median household income: $37,292 (2000); Poverty rate: 10.0% (2000).
Taxes: Total city taxes per capita: $129 (1997); City property taxes per capita: $127 (1997).
Education: High school graduation rate: 85.3% (2000); College graduation rate: 8.0% (2000).
Housing: Homeownership rate: 81.3% (2000); Median home value: $61,700 (2000); Median rent: $236 per month (2000); Median age of housing: 57 years (2000).
Transportation: Commute to work: 82.5% car, 0.0% public transportation, 5.5% walk, 11.9% work from home (2000); Travel time to work: 40.5% less than 15 minutes, 25.1% 15 to 30 minutes, 17.1% 30 to 45 minutes, 10.8% 45 to 60 minutes, 6.5% 60 minutes or more (2000)

WAUBEEK (town). Covers a land area of 12.005 square miles and a water area of 0.825 square miles. Located at 44.65° N. Lat.; 91.98° W. Long.
Population: 364 (2000); Race: 98.9% White, 0.0% Black, 0.5% Asian, 0.5% American Indian and Alaska Native, 0.0% Hispanic of any race, 0.0% two or more races (2000); Density: 30.3 persons per square mile (2000); Age: 31.6% under 18, 7.8% over 64 (2000); Marriage status: 22.8% never married, 66.9% now married, 2.8% widowed, 7.5% divorced (2000); Foreign born: 0.5% (2000); Ancestry (includes multiple ancestries): 56.5% German, 14.6% Norwegian, 14.1% Austrian, 9.7% Irish, 9.7% Swedish (2000).
Economy: Single-family building permits issued: 2 (2001) / 5 (2000); Multi-family building permits issued: 0 (2001) / 0 (2000); Employment by

occupation: 15.0% management, 18.9% professional, 12.1% services, 24.8% sales, 1.5% farming, 11.2% construction, 16.5% production (2000).
Income: Per capita income: $24,352 (2000); Median household income: $49,125 (2000); Poverty rate: 2.2% (2000).
Taxes: Total city taxes per capita: $44 (1997); City property taxes per capita: $41 (1997).
Education: High school graduation rate: 93.9% (2000); College graduation rate: 22.2% (2000).
Housing: Homeownership rate: 97.7% (2000); Median home value: $103,300 (2000); Median rent: $125 per month (2000); Median age of housing: 25 years (2000).
Transportation: Commute to work: 87.4% car, 0.0% public transportation, 2.4% walk, 10.2% work from home (2000); Travel time to work: 42.2% less than 15 minutes, 21.6% 15 to 30 minutes, 19.5% 30 to 45 minutes, 12.4% 45 to 60 minutes, 4.3% 60 minutes or more (2000)

Pierce County

Located in western Wisconsin; bounded on the west by the St. Croix River, and on the south and southwest by the Mississippi River, Lake Pepin, and the Minnesota border. Covers a land area of 576.50 square miles, a water area of 15.10 square miles, and is located in the Central Time Zone. The county government was organized in 1853. County seat is Ellsworth.

Pierce County is part of the Minneapolis-St. Paul, MN-WI MSA. The entire metro area includes: Anoka County, MN; Carver County, MN; Chisago County, MN; Dakota County, MN; Hennepin County, MN; Isanti County, MN; Ramsey County, MN; Scott County, MN; Sherburne County, MN; Washington County, MN; Wright County, MN; Pierce County, WI; St. Croix County, WI

Weather Station: Ellsworth 1 E — Elevation: 1,026 feet

	Jan	Feb	Mar	Apr	May	Jun	Jul	Aug	Sep	Oct	Nov	Dec
High	22	29	41	57	70	79	83	80	71	59	40	26
Low	2	10	21	34	46	55	59	57	48	37	23	9
Precip	1.1	0.7	2.0	3.1	4.1	4.5	4.7	4.5	4.1	2.7	2.4	1.1
Snow	13.2	7.2	10.5	2.2	tr	0.0	0.0	0.0	0.0	0.4	7.5	10.4

High and Low temperatures in degrees Fahrenheit; Precipitation and Snow in inches

Weather Station: River Falls — Elevation: 912 feet

	Jan	Feb	Mar	Apr	May	Jun	Jul	Aug	Sep	Oct	Nov	Dec
High	22	29	41	58	70	79	83	80	71	59	40	27
Low	3	9	21	34	46	56	60	58	50	38	24	11
Precip	0.8	0.6	1.6	2.5	3.6	4.3	4.3	4.5	3.5	2.6	1.7	0.8
Snow	11.0	6.5	9.5	2.6	tr	tr	0.0	0.0	tr	0.5	7.6	8.5

High and Low temperatures in degrees Fahrenheit; Precipitation and Snow in inches

Population: 36,804 (2000); Race: 97.8% White, 0.3% Black, 0.5% Asian, 0.4% American Indian and Alaska Native, 0.6% Hispanic of any race, 0.7% two or more races (2000); Density: 63.8 persons per square mile (2000); Age: 24.4% under 18, 9.6% over 64 (2000).
Religion: Five largest groups: 22.8% Catholic Church, 17.9% Evangelical Lutheran Church in America, 5.0% The United Methodist Church, 4.2% United Church of Christ, 2.7% Wisconsin Evangelical Lutheran Synod (2000).
Economy: Unemployment rate: 3.9% (11/2002); Total civilian labor force: 21,432 (11/2002); Leading industries: 17.6% accommodation & food services; 17.2% retail trade; 16.2% manufacturing (2000); Companies that employ more than 1,000 persons: 0 (2000); Companies that employ more than 100 persons: 7 (2000); Farms: 1,265 totaling 267,586 acres (1997); Minority business ownership rate: 0.0% (1997); Women business ownership rate: 32.1% (1997); Retail sales per capita: $4,316 (1997). Single-family building permits issued: 313 (2001) / 279 (2000); Multi-family building permits issued: 60 (2001) / 30 (2000).
Income: Per capita income: $20,172 (2000); Median household income: $49,551 (2000); Poverty rate: 7.7% (2000); Bankruptcy rate: 2.58% (2001).
Taxes: Total county taxes per capita: $223 (2000); County property taxes per capita: $186 (2000).
Education: High school graduation rate: 89.6% (2000); College graduation rate: 24.6% (2000).
Housing: Homeownership rate: 73.1% (2000); Median home value: $123,100 (2000); Median rent: $476 per month (2000); Median age of housing: 29 years (2000).
Health: Birth rate: 117.9 per 10,000 population (1998); Age adjusted death rate: 80.6 per 10,000 population (1999); Age adjusted cancer mortality rate: 171.8 deaths per 100,000 population (1999). Number of physicians: 8.2 per 10,000 population (1999); Number of hospital beds: 8.4 per 10,000 population (1999).
Elections: 2000 Presidential election results: 47.7% Gore, 45.5% Bush, 6.0% Nader, 0.5% Buchanan
National and State Parks: Kinnickinnic State Park; Pierce County Islands State Public Hunting Grounds
Additional Information Contacts
Pierce County Government Offices 715-273-3531
Ellsworth Chamber of Commerce 715-273-6442
Prescott Area Chamber of Commerce 715-262-3284
River Falls Chamber of Commerce 715-425-2533

Pierce County Communities

BAY CITY (village). Covers a land area of 0.514 square miles and a water area of 0.012 square miles. Located at 44.58° N. Lat.; 92.45° W. Long. Elevation is 690 feet.
Population: 465 (2000); Race: 100.0% White, 0.0% Black, 0.0% Asian, 0.0% American Indian and Alaska Native, 0.0% Hispanic of any race, 0.0% two or more races (2000); Density: 904.1 persons per square mile (2000); Age: 27.9% under 18, 12.7% over 64 (2000); Marriage status: 22.3% never married, 52.2% now married, 6.0% widowed, 19.4% divorced (2000); Foreign born: 2.1% (2000); Ancestry (includes multiple ancestries): 46.8% German, 18.3% Irish, 12.9% Norwegian, 11.3% Swedish, 10.5% French (except Basque) (2000).
Economy: Single-family building permits issued: 4 (2001) / 5 (2000); Multi-family building permits issued: 0 (2001) / 0 (2000); Employment by occupation: 5.4% management, 7.0% professional, 23.6% services, 19.0% sales, 0.0% farming, 10.7% construction, 34.3% production (2000).
Income: Per capita income: $19,598 (2000); Median household income: $47,679 (2000); Poverty rate: 6.1% (2000).
Taxes: Total city taxes per capita: $92 (1997); City property taxes per capita: $65 (1997).
Education: High school graduation rate: 66.5% (2000); College graduation rate: 5.3% (2000).
Housing: Homeownership rate: 76.4% (2000); Median home value: $82,500 (2000); Median rent: $396 per month (2000); Median age of housing: 33 years (2000).
Transportation: Commute to work: 96.6% car, 0.0% public transportation, 1.7% walk, 0.0% work from home (2000); Travel time to work: 22.1% less than 15 minutes, 48.1% 15 to 30 minutes, 15.3% 30 to 45 minutes, 9.8% 45 to 60 minutes, 4.7% 60 minutes or more (2000)

BELDENVILLE (unincorporated postal area, zip code 54003). Covers a land area of 32.668 square miles and a water area of 0 square miles. Located at 44.78° N. Lat.; 92.44° W. Long. Elevation is 980 feet.
Population: 1,008 (2000); Race: 99.3% White, 0.1% Black, 0.0% Asian, 0.0% American Indian and Alaska Native, 0.7% Hispanic of any race, 0.4% two or more races (2000); Density: 30.9 persons per square mile (2000); Age: 24.1% under 18, 10.0% over 64 (2000); Marriage status: 22.3% never married, 65.5% now married, 5.5% widowed, 6.7% divorced (2000); Foreign born: 0.9% (2000); Ancestry (includes multiple ancestries): 43.1% German, 31.8% Norwegian, 12.6% Swedish, 9.1% Irish, 7.4% English (2000).
Economy: Dairying; stock raising. Employment by occupation: 13.5% management, 17.7% professional, 16.4% services, 18.6% sales, 2.4% farming, 11.8% construction, 19.8% production (2000).
Income: Per capita income: $20,502 (2000); Median household income: $51,618 (2000); Poverty rate: 3.2% (2000).
Education: High school graduation rate: 90.2% (2000); College graduation rate: 21.6% (2000).
Housing: Homeownership rate: 90.8% (2000); Median home value: $107,100 (2000); Median rent: $450 per month (2000); Median age of housing: 60+ years (2000).
Newspapers: Miss Croix Shopper (1 x week); Ellsworth Shopper (1 x week)
Transportation: Commute to work: 91.0% car, 0.0% public transportation, 2.9% walk, 5.7% work from home (2000); Travel time to work: 31.2% less than 15 minutes, 29.5% 15 to 30 minutes, 20.4% 30 to 45 minutes, 6.6% 45 to 60 minutes, 12.3% 60 minutes or more (2000)

CLIFTON (town). Covers a land area of 34.350 square miles and a water area of 1.207 square miles. Located at 44.81° N. Lat.; 92.73° W. Long.
Population: 1,657 (2000); Race: 97.9% White, 0.1% Black, 0.6% Asian, 0.6% American Indian and Alaska Native, 0.9% Hispanic of any race, 0.8% two or more races (2000); Density: 48.2 persons per square mile (2000); Age: 29.2% under 18, 7.3% over 64 (2000); Marriage status: 20.0% never married,

74.0% now married, 2.1% widowed, 3.8% divorced (2000); Foreign born: 1.1% (2000); Ancestry (includes multiple ancestries): 44.6% German, 14.8% Irish, 14.2% Norwegian, 10.2% Swedish, 7.3% English (2000).
Economy: Employment by occupation: 17.1% management, 27.2% professional, 13.7% services, 21.7% sales, 2.0% farming, 7.5% construction, 10.8% production (2000).
Income: Per capita income: $25,352 (2000); Median household income: $71,810 (2000); Poverty rate: 1.2% (2000).
Taxes: Total city taxes per capita: $77 (1997); City property taxes per capita: $67 (1997).
Education: High school graduation rate: 95.3% (2000); College graduation rate: 42.0% (2000).
Housing: Homeownership rate: 93.3% (2000); Median home value: $207,300 (2000); Median rent: $625 per month (2000); Median age of housing: 19 years (2000).
Transportation: Commute to work: 90.9% car, 0.7% public transportation, 1.0% walk, 7.1% work from home (2000); Travel time to work: 21.2% less than 15 minutes, 27.1% 15 to 30 minutes, 27.2% 30 to 45 minutes, 18.2% 45 to 60 minutes, 6.3% 60 minutes or more (2000)

DIAMOND BLUFF (town). Covers a land area of 16.668 square miles and a water area of 1.655 square miles. Located at 44.64° N. Lat.; 92.61° W. Long. Elevation is 740 feet.
Population: 479 (2000); Race: 100.0% White, 0.0% Black, 0.0% Asian, 0.0% American Indian and Alaska Native, 1.1% Hispanic of any race, 0.0% two or more races (2000); Density: 28.7 persons per square mile (2000); Age: 25.2% under 18, 8.6% over 64 (2000); Marriage status: 18.7% never married, 61.0% now married, 4.9% widowed, 15.4% divorced (2000); Foreign born: 0.0% (2000); Ancestry (includes multiple ancestries): 49.8% German, 17.0% Irish, 15.5% Norwegian, 6.0% Swedish, 5.0% English (2000).
Economy: Employment by occupation: 7.1% management, 10.3% professional, 13.2% services, 23.8% sales, 0.7% farming, 15.7% construction, 29.2% production (2000).
Income: Per capita income: $22,002 (2000); Median household income: $52,031 (2000); Poverty rate: 3.7% (2000).
Taxes: Total city taxes per capita: $30 (1997); City property taxes per capita: $28 (1997).
Education: High school graduation rate: 88.1% (2000); College graduation rate: 6.8% (2000).
Housing: Homeownership rate: 91.6% (2000); Median home value: $114,200 (2000); Median rent: $375 per month (2000); Median age of housing: 33 years (2000).
Transportation: Commute to work: 85.5% car, 0.7% public transportation, 2.2% walk, 5.8% work from home (2000); Travel time to work: 20.8% less than 15 minutes, 45.9% 15 to 30 minutes, 11.2% 30 to 45 minutes, 13.9% 45 to 60 minutes, 8.1% 60 minutes or more (2000)

EL PASO (town). Covers a land area of 35.055 square miles and a water area of 0 square miles. Located at 44.73° N. Lat.; 92.32° W. Long. Elevation is 910 feet.
Population: 690 (2000); Race: 99.7% White, 0.0% Black, 0.0% Asian, 0.0% American Indian and Alaska Native, 0.0% Hispanic of any race, 0.3% two or more races (2000); Density: 19.7 persons per square mile (2000); Age: 31.0% under 18, 10.2% over 64 (2000); Marriage status: 26.5% never married, 59.5% now married, 6.3% widowed, 7.8% divorced (2000); Foreign born: 0.3% (2000); Ancestry (includes multiple ancestries): 53.2% German, 24.3% Norwegian, 14.0% Irish, 6.7% Swedish, 4.7% English (2000).
Economy: Employment by occupation: 23.3% management, 13.6% professional, 9.7% services, 22.8% sales, 2.7% farming, 10.7% construction, 17.1% production (2000).
Income: Per capita income: $19,441 (2000); Median household income: $49,375 (2000); Poverty rate: 4.9% (2000).
Taxes: Total city taxes per capita: $175 (1997); City property taxes per capita: $171 (1997).
Education: High school graduation rate: 89.6% (2000); College graduation rate: 15.5% (2000).
Housing: Homeownership rate: 87.8% (2000); Median home value: $119,400 (2000); Median rent: $363 per month (2000); Median age of housing: 57 years (2000).
Transportation: Commute to work: 84.7% car, 0.0% public transportation, 0.5% walk, 13.7% work from home (2000); Travel time to work: 24.2% less than 15 minutes, 31.6% 15 to 30 minutes, 15.6% 30 to 45 minutes, 13.0% 45 to 60 minutes, 15.6% 60 minutes or more (2000)

ELLSWORTH (village). Covers a land area of 3.732 square miles and a water area of 0 square miles. Located at 44.73° N. Lat.; 92.48° W. Long. Elevation is 1,226 feet.
History: When the railroad built their station a mile from the community of Ellsworth, a second Ellsworth grew up around the depot. East Ellsworth and West Ellsworth continued to exist as distinct parts of the village.
Population: 2,909 (2000); Race: 97.7% White, 0.0% Black, 0.1% Asian, 0.0% American Indian and Alaska Native, 1.3% Hispanic of any race, 1.3% two or more races (2000); Density: 779.5 persons per square mile (2000); Age: 24.4% under 18, 16.2% over 64 (2000); Marriage status: 20.0% never married, 61.8% now married, 9.4% widowed, 8.8% divorced (2000); Foreign born: 0.9% (2000); Ancestry (includes multiple ancestries): 42.9% German, 20.8% Norwegian, 11.5% Irish, 11.2% Swedish, 5.0% Other groups (2000).
Economy: Single-family building permits issued: 22 (2001) / 24 (2000); Multi-family building permits issued: 32 (2001) / 0 (2000); Employment by occupation: 7.2% management, 14.1% professional, 15.7% services, 22.7% sales, 0.5% farming, 13.2% construction, 26.6% production (2000).
Income: Per capita income: $18,661 (2000); Median household income: $42,604 (2000); Poverty rate: 5.4% (2000).
Taxes: Total city taxes per capita: $201 (1997); City property taxes per capita: $182 (1997).
Education: High school graduation rate: 79.3% (2000); College graduation rate: 14.2% (2000).

School District(s)

Ellsworth Community (PK-12)
2000 Enrollment: 1,841 715-273-3900

Housing: Homeownership rate: 68.5% (2000); Median home value: $103,300 (2000); Median rent: $424 per month (2000); Median age of housing: 33 years (2000).
Newspapers: Pierce County Herald (1 x week)
Transportation: Commute to work: 89.8% car, 0.1% public transportation, 6.9% walk, 2.4% work from home (2000); Travel time to work: 36.8% less than 15 minutes, 24.4% 15 to 30 minutes, 18.0% 30 to 45 minutes, 9.6% 45 to 60 minutes, 11.2% 60 minutes or more (2000)
Additional Information Contacts
Ellsworth Chamber of Commerce 715-273-6442

ELLSWORTH (town). Covers a land area of 32.075 square miles and a water area of 0.006 square miles. Located at 44.72° N. Lat.; 92.44° W. Long. Elevation is 1,226 feet.
History: Incorporated 1887.
Population: 1,064 (2000); Race: 99.4% White, 0.2% Black, 0.0% Asian, 0.0% American Indian and Alaska Native, 0.2% Hispanic of any race, 0.2% two or more races (2000); Density: 33.2 persons per square mile (2000); Age: 30.2% under 18, 6.9% over 64 (2000); Marriage status: 25.2% never married, 62.1% now married, 4.9% widowed, 7.8% divorced (2000); Foreign born: 0.4% (2000); Ancestry (includes multiple ancestries): 55.5% German, 21.1% Norwegian, 13.6% Swedish, 11.2% Irish, 5.2% English (2000).
Economy: Dairying; livestock raising. Manufacturing: contract manufacturing, concrete lawn ornaments. Employment by occupation: 9.0% management, 12.7% professional, 12.8% services, 24.4% sales, 2.7% farming, 15.1% construction, 23.4% production (2000).
Income: Per capita income: $20,363 (2000); Median household income: $52,188 (2000); Poverty rate: 3.5% (2000).
Taxes: Total city taxes per capita: $141 (2000); City property taxes per capita: $137 (2000).
Education: High school graduation rate: 90.8% (2000); College graduation rate: 17.5% (2000).
Housing: Homeownership rate: 90.1% (2000); Median home value: $109,800 (2000); Median rent: $458 per month (2000); Median age of housing: 53 years (2000).
Transportation: Commute to work: 90.6% car, 0.3% public transportation, 4.9% walk, 3.7% work from home (2000); Travel time to work: 35.3% less than 15 minutes, 24.0% 15 to 30 minutes, 21.5% 30 to 45 minutes, 9.5% 45 to 60 minutes, 9.8% 60 minutes or more (2000)

ELMWOOD (village). Covers a land area of 1.480 square miles and a water area of 0 square miles. Located at 44.77° N. Lat.; 92.14° W. Long. Elevation is 860 feet.
Population: 841 (2000); Race: 99.8% White, 0.0% Black, 0.0% Asian, 0.0% American Indian and Alaska Native, 0.4% Hispanic of any race, 0.2% two or more races (2000); Density: 568.2 persons per square mile (2000); Age: 24.7% under 18, 23.2% over 64 (2000); Marriage status: 21.7% never married, 57.6% now married, 9.8% widowed, 10.9% divorced (2000); Foreign born: 0.0% (2000); Ancestry (includes multiple ancestries): 43.5%

German, 13.1% Norwegian, 9.3% United States or American, 7.4% Irish, 4.4% French (except Basque) (2000).
Economy: In lumbering, dairying, and poultry-raising area. Manufacturing: syringes, serum bottles; hydroelectric plant. Single-family building permits issued: 2 (2001) / 0 (2000); Multi-family building permits issued: 0 (2001) / 0 (2000); Employment by occupation: 7.2% management, 13.5% professional, 19.6% services, 15.4% sales, 2.4% farming, 9.8% construction, 32.1% production (2000).
Income: Per capita income: $16,369 (2000); Median household income: $33,558 (2000); Poverty rate: 4.4% (2000).
Taxes: Total city taxes per capita: $158 (1997); City property taxes per capita: $154 (1997).
Education: High school graduation rate: 77.4% (2000); College graduation rate: 10.6% (2000).

School District(s)

Elmwood (PK-12)
— 2000 Enrollment: 413 715-639-2711

Housing: Homeownership rate: 73.2% (2000); Median home value: $69,600 (2000); Median rent: $341 per month (2000); Median age of housing: 45 years (2000).
Newspapers: Elmwood Argus (1 x week)
Transportation: Commute to work: 87.5% car, 0.0% public transportation, 8.5% walk, 4.0% work from home (2000); Travel time to work: 34.8% less than 15 minutes, 19.6% 15 to 30 minutes, 22.9% 30 to 45 minutes, 10.2% 45 to 60 minutes, 12.4% 60 minutes or more (2000)

GILMAN (town). Covers a land area of 33.825 square miles and a water area of 0 square miles. Located at 44.81° N. Lat.; 92.32° W. Long.
Population: 772 (2000); Race: 98.3% White, 0.0% Black, 1.1% Asian, 0.0% American Indian and Alaska Native, 0.4% Hispanic of any race, 0.5% two or more races (2000); Density: 22.8 persons per square mile (2000); Age: 27.1% under 18, 10.7% over 64 (2000); Marriage status: 18.2% never married, 71.1% now married, 5.8% widowed, 5.0% divorced (2000); Foreign born: 1.1% (2000); Ancestry (includes multiple ancestries): 42.5% German, 38.8% Norwegian, 10.9% Irish, 5.3% Swedish, 5.1% Polish (2000).
Economy: Employment by occupation: 20.3% management, 13.2% professional, 12.8% services, 17.6% sales, 4.1% farming, 10.5% construction, 21.5% production (2000).
Income: Per capita income: $18,502 (2000); Median household income: $49,250 (2000); Poverty rate: 3.7% (2000).
Taxes: Total city taxes per capita: $88 (1997); City property taxes per capita: $87 (1997).
Education: High school graduation rate: 91.3% (2000); College graduation rate: 16.7% (2000).
Housing: Homeownership rate: 87.6% (2000); Median home value: $99,000 (2000); Median rent: $405 per month (2000); Median age of housing: 42 years (2000).
Transportation: Commute to work: 81.7% car, 0.0% public transportation, 3.9% walk, 14.4% work from home (2000); Travel time to work: 32.9% less than 15 minutes, 27.0% 15 to 30 minutes, 16.6% 30 to 45 minutes, 13.1% 45 to 60 minutes, 10.4% 60 minutes or more (2000)

HAGER CITY (unincorporated postal area, zip code 54014). Aka Hager. Covers a land area of 43.460 square miles and a water area of 0.982 square miles. Located at 44.62° N. Lat.; 92.54° W. Long. Elevation is 718 feet.
Population: 2,145 (2000); Race: 98.9% White, 0.1% Black, 0.5% Asian, 0.0% American Indian and Alaska Native, 0.9% Hispanic of any race, 0.3% two or more races (2000); Density: 49.4 persons per square mile (2000); Age: 23.9% under 18, 10.8% over 64 (2000); Marriage status: 22.0% never married, 65.3% now married, 4.0% widowed, 8.8% divorced (2000); Foreign born: 0.7% (2000); Ancestry (includes multiple ancestries): 47.3% German, 17.2% Norwegian, 13.4% Swedish, 13.0% Irish, 6.7% English (2000).
Economy: Barley, soybeans; livestock. Manufacturing: power transmission poles. Employment by occupation: 9.5% management, 12.3% professional, 15.7% services, 20.9% sales, 0.5% farming, 13.9% construction, 27.1% production (2000).
Income: Per capita income: $23,387 (2000); Median household income: $53,950 (2000); Poverty rate: 5.4% (2000).
Education: High school graduation rate: 87.5% (2000); College graduation rate: 12.6% (2000).
Housing: Homeownership rate: 88.9% (2000); Median home value: $114,400 (2000); Median rent: $472 per month (2000); Median age of housing: 31 years (2000).
Transportation: Commute to work: 92.0% car, 0.2% public transportation, 2.0% walk, 4.4% work from home (2000); Travel time to work: 30.1% less than 15 minutes, 39.9% 15 to 30 minutes, 13.3% 30 to 45 minutes, 8.5% 45 to 60 minutes, 8.2% 60 minutes or more (2000)

HARTLAND (town). Covers a land area of 36.027 square miles and a water area of 0 square miles. Located at 44.64° N. Lat.; 92.44° W. Long.
Population: 814 (2000); Race: 99.2% White, 0.0% Black, 0.0% Asian, 0.4% American Indian and Alaska Native, 0.9% Hispanic of any race, 0.4% two or more races (2000); Density: 22.6 persons per square mile (2000); Age: 27.8% under 18, 8.9% over 64 (2000); Marriage status: 21.7% never married, 68.3% now married, 3.3% widowed, 6.7% divorced (2000); Foreign born: 0.0% (2000); Ancestry (includes multiple ancestries): 51.3% German, 18.8% Swedish, 18.6% Norwegian, 16.7% Irish, 6.4% English (2000).
Economy: Employment by occupation: 13.4% management, 11.0% professional, 11.0% services, 19.0% sales, 3.6% farming, 12.1% construction, 30.0% production (2000).
Income: Per capita income: $21,645 (2000); Median household income: $55,347 (2000); Poverty rate: 5.7% (2000).
Taxes: Total city taxes per capita: $162 (1997); City property taxes per capita: $162 (1997).
Education: High school graduation rate: 86.5% (2000); College graduation rate: 11.6% (2000).
Housing: Homeownership rate: 84.5% (2000); Median home value: $98,500 (2000); Median rent: $429 per month (2000); Median age of housing: 46 years (2000).
Transportation: Commute to work: 87.0% car, 1.2% public transportation, 1.2% walk, 9.0% work from home (2000); Travel time to work: 23.7% less than 15 minutes, 36.4% 15 to 30 minutes, 18.6% 30 to 45 minutes, 6.9% 45 to 60 minutes, 14.5% 60 minutes or more (2000)

ISABELLE (town). Covers a land area of 10.418 square miles and a water area of 5.235 square miles. Located at 44.59° N. Lat.; 92.45° W. Long.
Population: 315 (2000); Race: 90.9% White, 0.0% Black, 0.0% Asian, 9.1% American Indian and Alaska Native, 0.7% Hispanic of any race, 0.0% two or more races (2000); Density: 30.2 persons per square mile (2000); Age: 27.9% under 18, 6.7% over 64 (2000); Marriage status: 22.8% never married, 65.9% now married, 3.9% widowed, 7.3% divorced (2000); Foreign born: 0.0% (2000); Ancestry (includes multiple ancestries): 52.5% German, 17.8% Norwegian, 14.1% Swedish, 13.5% Irish, 8.8% Other groups (2000).
Economy: Employment by occupation: 9.1% management, 16.4% professional, 17.6% services, 20.0% sales, 1.2% farming, 18.2% construction, 17.6% production (2000).
Income: Per capita income: $22,626 (2000); Median household income: $52,188 (2000); Poverty rate: 2.5% (2000).
Taxes: Total city taxes per capita: $19 (1997); City property taxes per capita: $14 (1997).
Education: High school graduation rate: 88.6% (2000); College graduation rate: 16.4% (2000).
Housing: Homeownership rate: 96.3% (2000); Median home value: $106,800 (2000); Median rent: $325 per month (2000); Median age of housing: 25 years (2000).
Transportation: Commute to work: 91.5% car, 0.0% public transportation, 4.8% walk, 3.6% work from home (2000); Travel time to work: 35.8% less than 15 minutes, 38.4% 15 to 30 minutes, 10.1% 30 to 45 minutes, 7.5% 45 to 60 minutes, 8.2% 60 minutes or more (2000)

MAIDEN ROCK (village). Covers a land area of 1.127 square miles and a water area of 0 square miles. Located at 44.56° N. Lat.; 92.31° W. Long. Elevation is 689 feet.
Population: 121 (2000); Race: 97.7% White, 0.0% Black, 0.0% Asian, 0.0% American Indian and Alaska Native, 0.0% Hispanic of any race, 2.3% two or more races (2000); Density: 107.4 persons per square mile (2000); Age: 30.7% under 18, 13.6% over 64 (2000); Marriage status: 27.4% never married, 46.8% now married, 6.5% widowed, 19.4% divorced (2000); Foreign born: 0.0% (2000); Ancestry (includes multiple ancestries): 62.5% German, 21.6% Swedish, 15.9% Norwegian, 10.2% English, 8.0% Irish (2000).
Economy: Employment by occupation: 0.0% management, 17.8% professional, 11.1% services, 48.9% sales, 2.2% farming, 4.4% construction, 15.6% production (2000).
Income: Per capita income: $22,781 (2000); Median household income: $40,625 (2000); Poverty rate: 2.3% (2000).
Taxes: Total city taxes per capita: $327 (1997); City property taxes per capita: $320 (1997).
Education: High school graduation rate: 88.9% (2000); College graduation rate: 29.6% (2000).

Housing: Homeownership rate: 61.9% (2000); Median home value: $71,300 (2000); Median rent: $300 per month (2000); Median age of housing: 60+ years (2000).
Transportation: Commute to work: 100.0% car, 0.0% public transportation, 0.0% walk, 0.0% work from home (2000); Travel time to work: 13.3% less than 15 minutes, 17.8% 15 to 30 minutes, 28.9% 30 to 45 minutes, 28.9% 45 to 60 minutes, 11.1% 60 minutes or more (2000)

MAIDEN ROCK (town). Covers a land area of 40.330 square miles and a water area of 3.733 square miles. Located at 44.57° N. Lat.; 92.24° W. Long. Elevation is 689 feet.
Population: 589 (2000); Race: 96.4% White, 0.3% Black, 0.0% Asian, 1.3% American Indian and Alaska Native, 1.3% Hispanic of any race, 2.1% two or more races (2000); Density: 14.6 persons per square mile (2000); Age: 26.5% under 18, 12.4% over 64 (2000); Marriage status: 18.2% never married, 70.1% now married, 2.8% widowed, 8.9% divorced (2000); Foreign born: 0.6% (2000); Ancestry (includes multiple ancestries): 43.4% German, 15.8% Swedish, 14.9% Norwegian, 12.5% Irish, 7.1% Austrian (2000).
Economy: Manufacturing: concrete products. Silicate-rock mine is nearby. Employment by occupation: 17.7% management, 14.4% professional, 7.8% services, 22.4% sales, 4.2% farming, 7.2% construction, 26.3% production (2000).
Income: Per capita income: $19,553 (2000); Median household income: $45,278 (2000); Poverty rate: 11.3% (2000).
Taxes: Total city taxes per capita: $134 (1997); City property taxes per capita: $134 (1997).
Education: High school graduation rate: 85.0% (2000); College graduation rate: 14.1% (2000).
Housing: Homeownership rate: 89.6% (2000); Median home value: $92,500 (2000); Median rent: $417 per month (2000); Median age of housing: 60+ years (2000).
Transportation: Commute to work: 83.1% car, 0.0% public transportation, 5.4% walk, 11.5% work from home (2000); Travel time to work: 17.8% less than 15 minutes, 23.6% 15 to 30 minutes, 31.5% 30 to 45 minutes, 19.1% 45 to 60 minutes, 8.0% 60 minutes or more (2000)

MARTELL (town). Covers a land area of 35.830 square miles and a water area of 0 square miles. Located at 44.82° N. Lat.; 92.42° W. Long. Elevation is 1,000 feet.
History: Martell, which grew up around a sawmill, was named for Joseph Martell, a French Canadian who settled here in 1847. One of Martell's companions in the early settlement was Xerxes Jock, who became legendary for his hunting feats.
Population: 1,070 (2000); Race: 99.2% White, 0.1% Black, 0.2% Asian, 0.0% American Indian and Alaska Native, 0.4% Hispanic of any race, 0.6% two or more races (2000); Density: 29.9 persons per square mile (2000); Age: 27.1% under 18, 7.4% over 64 (2000); Marriage status: 20.1% never married, 67.8% now married, 4.0% widowed, 8.0% divorced (2000); Foreign born: 0.8% (2000); Ancestry (includes multiple ancestries): 41.7% German, 25.7% Norwegian, 12.8% Irish, 12.0% Swedish, 8.0% English (2000).
Economy: Employment by occupation: 15.0% management, 21.1% professional, 12.4% services, 17.2% sales, 2.7% farming, 11.2% construction, 20.5% production (2000).
Income: Per capita income: $21,304 (2000); Median household income: $54,539 (2000); Poverty rate: 5.5% (2000).
Taxes: Total city taxes per capita: $78 (1997); City property taxes per capita: $77 (1997).
Education: High school graduation rate: 90.7% (2000); College graduation rate: 25.9% (2000).
Housing: Homeownership rate: 91.7% (2000); Median home value: $110,800 (2000); Median rent: $425 per month (2000); Median age of housing: 35 years (2000).
Transportation: Commute to work: 90.6% car, 0.0% public transportation, 1.6% walk, 7.5% work from home (2000); Travel time to work: 22.1% less than 15 minutes, 32.4% 15 to 30 minutes, 20.6% 30 to 45 minutes, 11.4% 45 to 60 minutes, 13.5% 60 minutes or more (2000)

OAK GROVE (town). Covers a land area of 39.278 square miles and a water area of 0.535 square miles. Located at 44.74° N. Lat.; 92.69° W. Long.
Population: 1,522 (2000); Race: 99.2% White, 0.0% Black, 0.3% Asian, 0.2% American Indian and Alaska Native, 0.1% Hispanic of any race, 0.1% two or more races (2000); Density: 38.7 persons per square mile (2000); Age: 31.9% under 18, 6.8% over 64 (2000); Marriage status: 21.9% never married, 69.2% now married, 2.7% widowed, 6.3% divorced (2000); Foreign born: 0.5% (2000); Ancestry (includes multiple ancestries): 49.4% German, 14.7% Irish, 13.7% Norwegian, 8.6% Swedish, 5.0% English (2000).
Economy: Employment by occupation: 14.9% management, 22.4% professional, 9.0% services, 23.6% sales, 1.6% farming, 9.3% construction, 19.3% production (2000).
Income: Per capita income: $24,659 (2000); Median household income: $72,596 (2000); Poverty rate: 2.1% (2000).
Taxes: Total city taxes per capita: $114 (1997); City property taxes per capita: $99 (1997).
Education: High school graduation rate: 95.5% (2000); College graduation rate: 29.2% (2000).
Housing: Homeownership rate: 90.0% (2000); Median home value: $194,900 (2000); Median rent: $504 per month (2000); Median age of housing: 17 years (2000).
Transportation: Commute to work: 89.3% car, 0.4% public transportation, 1.2% walk, 8.2% work from home (2000); Travel time to work: 19.2% less than 15 minutes, 27.0% 15 to 30 minutes, 30.4% 30 to 45 minutes, 15.0% 45 to 60 minutes, 8.5% 60 minutes or more (2000)

PLUM CITY (village). Covers a land area of 0.983 square miles and a water area of 0 square miles. Located at 44.63° N. Lat.; 92.19° W. Long. Elevation is 820 feet.
Population: 574 (2000); Race: 100.0% White, 0.0% Black, 0.0% Asian, 0.0% American Indian and Alaska Native, 0.0% Hispanic of any race, 0.0% two or more races (2000); Density: 584.2 persons per square mile (2000); Age: 26.9% under 18, 24.9% over 64 (2000); Marriage status: 19.0% never married, 65.9% now married, 6.8% widowed, 8.3% divorced (2000); Foreign born: 0.5% (2000); Ancestry (includes multiple ancestries): 45.0% German, 12.5% Norwegian, 11.0% Swedish, 8.6% Irish, 5.0% French (except Basque) (2000).
Economy: Dairying; livestock raising. Single-family building permits issued: 5 (2001) / 4 (2000); Multi-family building permits issued: 0 (2001) / 0 (2000); Employment by occupation: 9.3% management, 12.8% professional, 10.3% services, 31.0% sales, 1.7% farming, 11.4% construction, 23.4% production (2000).
Income: Per capita income: $16,847 (2000); Median household income: $38,438 (2000); Poverty rate: 5.4% (2000).
Taxes: Total city taxes per capita: $88 (1997); City property taxes per capita: $81 (1997).
Education: High school graduation rate: 84.6% (2000); College graduation rate: 9.7% (2000).

School District(s)

Plum City (PK-12)
2000 Enrollment: 384 715-647-2591
Housing: Homeownership rate: 73.2% (2000); Median home value: $73,800 (2000); Median rent: $329 per month (2000); Median age of housing: 42 years (2000).
Transportation: Commute to work: 85.0% car, 0.0% public transportation, 10.1% walk, 2.4% work from home (2000); Travel time to work: 35.7% less than 15 minutes, 16.8% 15 to 30 minutes, 26.1% 30 to 45 minutes, 11.4% 45 to 60 minutes, 10.0% 60 minutes or more (2000)

PRESCOTT (city). Covers a land area of 2.023 square miles and a water area of 0.370 square miles. Located at 44.75° N. Lat.; 92.79° W. Long. Elevation is 775 feet.
History: Prescott began in the early 1850's, after Philander Prescott, as an agent for army officers stationed at Fort Snelling, had staked claims here in 1827. Prescott developed as a river town with shipping and lumbering. When Pierce County was formed in 1853, Prescott became the county seat, but lost the honor to Ellsworth after a long battle.
Population: 3,764 (2000); Race: 97.6% White, 0.1% Black, 0.0% Asian, 1.7% American Indian and Alaska Native, 1.5% Hispanic of any race, 0.3% two or more races (2000); Density: 1,860.4 persons per square mile (2000); Age: 26.8% under 18, 10.7% over 64 (2000); Marriage status: 29.1% never married, 59.4% now married, 2.8% widowed, 8.8% divorced (2000); Foreign born: 0.2% (2000); Ancestry (includes multiple ancestries): 47.3% German, 16.3% Norwegian, 10.6% Irish, 7.1% Swedish, 6.6% Other groups (2000).
Economy: Single-family building permits issued: 14 (2001) / 18 (2000); Multi-family building permits issued: 7 (2001) / 6 (2000); Employment by occupation: 8.1% management, 20.8% professional, 14.0% services, 26.1% sales, 0.4% farming, 10.4% construction, 20.3% production (2000).
Income: Per capita income: $22,610 (2000); Median household income: $52,598 (2000); Poverty rate: 4.6% (2000).
Taxes: Total city taxes per capita: $252 (1997); City property taxes per capita: $225 (1997).
Education: High school graduation rate: 94.6% (2000); College graduation rate: 21.4% (2000).

School District(s)

Prescott (PK-12)
2000 Enrollment: 1,175 715-262-5782

Housing: Homeownership rate: 66.3% (2000); Median home value: $132,200 (2000); Median rent: $514 per month (2000); Median age of housing: 21 years (2000).
Safety: Violent crime rate: 7.9 per 10,000 population; Property crime rate: 292.8 per 10,000 population (2001).
Newspapers: The Prescott Journal (1 x week)
Transportation: Commute to work: 92.0% car, 0.7% public transportation, 3.0% walk, 4.4% work from home (2000); Travel time to work: 31.2% less than 15 minutes, 29.7% 15 to 30 minutes, 22.5% 30 to 45 minutes, 12.9% 45 to 60 minutes, 3.8% 60 minutes or more (2000)

Additional Information Contacts

Prescott Area Chamber of Commerce 715-262-3284

RIVER FALLS (city). Covers a land area of 4.976 square miles and a water area of 0.044 square miles. Located at 44.85° N. Lat.; 92.62° W. Long. Elevation is 920 feet.
History: River Falls began as a settlement called Greenwood, founded by Joel Foster who came here from Connecticut in 1849. Greenwood was soon renamed Kinnikinnick, for the river on which it was located. The village grew up around sawmills, a planing mill, and a flour mill. In 1872 a State Normal School was established in River Falls.
Population: 12,560 (2000); Race: 96.7% White, 0.8% Black, 1.2% Asian, 0.4% American Indian and Alaska Native, 0.4% Hispanic of any race, 0.7% two or more races (2000); Density: 2,524.0 persons per square mile (2000); Age: 18.2% under 18, 8.8% over 64 (2000); Marriage status: 48.9% never married, 40.0% now married, 4.9% widowed, 6.2% divorced (2000); Foreign born: 1.6% (2000); Ancestry (includes multiple ancestries): 42.6% German, 20.7% Norwegian, 12.3% Irish, 9.4% Swedish, 7.8% English (2000).
Vital Statistics: Birth rate: 91.6 per 10,000 population (1998)
Economy: Single-family building permits issued: 68 (2001) / 55 (2000); Multi-family building permits issued: 13 (2001) / 18 (2000); Employment by occupation: 9.6% management, 22.8% professional, 18.8% services, 28.3% sales, 1.1% farming, 6.0% construction, 13.5% production (2000).
Income: Per capita income: $17,667 (2000); Median household income: $41,184 (2000); Poverty rate: 14.9% (2000).
Taxes: Total city taxes per capita: $168 (1997); City property taxes per capita: $148 (1997).
Education: High school graduation rate: 92.2% (2000); College graduation rate: 38.1% (2000).

School District(s)

River Falls (PK-12)
2000 Enrollment: 2,905 715-425-1800

Four-year College(s)

University of Wisconsin-River Falls (Public)
2001 Enrollment: 5,880 715-425-3913
2001 Tuition: In-state $2,776; Out-of-state $11,288

Housing: Homeownership rate: 50.9% (2000); Median home value: $127,000 (2000); Median rent: $506 per month (2000); Median age of housing: 26 years (2000).
Hospitals: River Falls Area Hospital (42 beds)
Safety: Violent crime rate: 19.0 per 10,000 population; Property crime rate: 393.7 per 10,000 population (2001).
Newspapers: River Falls Shopper (1 x week); River Falls Journal (1 x week)
Transportation: Commute to work: 83.6% car, 0.3% public transportation, 12.0% walk, 2.7% work from home (2000); Travel time to work: 47.8% less than 15 minutes, 22.2% 15 to 30 minutes, 14.6% 30 to 45 minutes, 11.2% 45 to 60 minutes, 4.2% 60 minutes or more (2000)

Additional Information Contacts

River Falls Chamber of Commerce 715-425-2533

RIVER FALLS (town). Covers a land area of 44.685 square miles and a water area of 0 square miles. Located at 44.81° N. Lat.; 92.55° W. Long. Elevation is 920 feet.
Population: 2,304 (2000); Race: 98.4% White, 0.4% Black, 0.3% Asian, 0.3% American Indian and Alaska Native, 1.0% Hispanic of any race, 0.3% two or more races (2000); Density: 51.6 persons per square mile (2000); Age: 28.3% under 18, 5.2% over 64 (2000); Marriage status: 24.5% never married, 66.6% now married, 1.4% widowed, 7.5% divorced (2000); Foreign born: 1.7% (2000); Ancestry (includes multiple ancestries): 41.4% German, 20.6% Norwegian, 12.7% English, 11.1% Irish, 10.1% Swedish (2000).
Economy: Employment by occupation: 16.9% management, 27.9% professional, 12.7% services, 21.8% sales, 0.7% farming, 7.5% construction, 12.4% production (2000).
Income: Per capita income: $26,358 (2000); Median household income: $65,721 (2000); Poverty rate: 4.6% (2000).
Taxes: Total city taxes per capita: $77 (1997); City property taxes per capita: $74 (1997).
Education: High school graduation rate: 95.7% (2000); College graduation rate: 41.9% (2000).
Housing: Homeownership rate: 86.8% (2000); Median home value: $167,600 (2000); Median rent: $604 per month (2000); Median age of housing: 23 years (2000).
Transportation: Commute to work: 91.3% car, 0.7% public transportation, 1.7% walk, 5.8% work from home (2000); Travel time to work: 37.7% less than 15 minutes, 18.8% 15 to 30 minutes, 22.2% 30 to 45 minutes, 13.6% 45 to 60 minutes, 7.6% 60 minutes or more (2000)

ROCK ELM (town). Covers a land area of 35.832 square miles and a water area of 0.010 square miles. Located at 44.72° N. Lat.; 92.19° W. Long. Elevation is 1,080 feet.
Population: 504 (2000); Race: 97.8% White, 0.0% Black, 0.0% Asian, 0.0% American Indian and Alaska Native, 0.4% Hispanic of any race, 1.7% two or more races (2000); Density: 14.1 persons per square mile (2000); Age: 27.5% under 18, 15.7% over 64 (2000); Marriage status: 24.1% never married, 63.1% now married, 5.7% widowed, 7.1% divorced (2000); Foreign born: 0.6% (2000); Ancestry (includes multiple ancestries): 52.9% German, 11.2% Norwegian, 10.3% Irish, 9.5% English, 6.2% Austrian (2000).
Economy: Employment by occupation: 20.0% management, 10.7% professional, 10.0% services, 13.2% sales, 10.0% farming, 10.0% construction, 26.1% production (2000).
Income: Per capita income: $17,838 (2000); Median household income: $36,750 (2000); Poverty rate: 18.2% (2000).
Taxes: Total city taxes per capita: $112 (1997); City property taxes per capita: $110 (1997).
Education: High school graduation rate: 86.9% (2000); College graduation rate: 13.4% (2000).
Housing: Homeownership rate: 85.3% (2000); Median home value: $74,200 (2000); Median rent: $375 per month (2000); Median age of housing: 60+ years (2000).
Transportation: Commute to work: 68.2% car, 0.0% public transportation, 7.1% walk, 24.6% work from home (2000); Travel time to work: 22.3% less than 15 minutes, 25.6% 15 to 30 minutes, 25.1% 30 to 45 minutes, 15.2% 45 to 60 minutes, 11.8% 60 minutes or more (2000)

SALEM (town). Covers a land area of 35.357 square miles and a water area of 0 square miles. Located at 44.64° N. Lat.; 92.32° W. Long. Elevation is 1,027 feet.
Population: 505 (2000); Race: 99.8% White, 0.0% Black, 0.0% Asian, 0.0% American Indian and Alaska Native, 0.0% Hispanic of any race, 0.0% two or more races (2000); Density: 14.3 persons per square mile (2000); Age: 24.2% under 18, 9.8% over 64 (2000); Marriage status: 24.4% never married, 68.7% now married, 2.2% widowed, 4.7% divorced (2000); Foreign born: 0.0% (2000); Ancestry (includes multiple ancestries): 50.2% German, 17.8% Swedish, 15.4% Irish, 10.0% English, 5.6% Norwegian (2000).
Economy: Employment by occupation: 14.8% management, 8.9% professional, 13.7% services, 18.9% sales, 2.4% farming, 11.7% construction, 29.6% production (2000).
Income: Per capita income: $18,533 (2000); Median household income: $56,250 (2000); Poverty rate: 5.2% (2000).
Taxes: Total city taxes per capita: $128 (1997); City property taxes per capita: $128 (1997).
Education: High school graduation rate: 87.1% (2000); College graduation rate: 10.7% (2000).
Housing: Homeownership rate: 80.0% (2000); Median home value: $95,000 (2000); Median rent: $408 per month (2000); Median age of housing: 60+ years (2000).
Transportation: Commute to work: 91.2% car, 0.0% public transportation, 0.7% walk, 8.1% work from home (2000); Travel time to work: 10.3% less than 15 minutes, 28.6% 15 to 30 minutes, 30.9% 30 to 45 minutes, 16.4% 45 to 60 minutes, 13.7% 60 minutes or more (2000)

SPRING LAKE (town). Covers a land area of 31.287 square miles and a water area of 0 square miles. Located at 44.81° N. Lat.; 92.19° W. Long.
Population: 550 (2000); Race: 99.2% White, 0.0% Black, 0.0% Asian, 0.4% American Indian and Alaska Native, 0.0% Hispanic of any race, 0.4% two or more races (2000); Density: 17.6 persons per square mile (2000); Age: 28.8% under 18, 10.6% over 64 (2000); Marriage status: 21.0% never married, 70.6% now married, 4.1% widowed, 4.3% divorced (2000); Foreign born:

0.0% (2000); Ancestry (includes multiple ancestries): 57.1% German, 20.0% Norwegian, 14.3% English, 10.6% Irish, 5.7% Italian (2000).
Economy: Employment by occupation: 19.1% management, 14.2% professional, 9.4% services, 20.6% sales, 1.9% farming, 5.6% construction, 29.2% production (2000).
Income: Per capita income: $24,661 (2000); Median household income: $48,611 (2000); Poverty rate: 1.0% (2000).
Taxes: Total city taxes per capita: $139 (1997); City property taxes per capita: $139 (1997).
Education: High school graduation rate: 86.6% (2000); College graduation rate: 16.1% (2000).
Housing: Homeownership rate: 84.9% (2000); Median home value: $92,900 (2000); Median rent: $400 per month (2000); Median age of housing: 60 years (2000).
Transportation: Commute to work: 82.0% car, 0.0% public transportation, 3.8% walk, 14.3% work from home (2000); Travel time to work: 29.8% less than 15 minutes, 34.6% 15 to 30 minutes, 18.4% 30 to 45 minutes, 10.5% 45 to 60 minutes, 6.6% 60 minutes or more (2000)

SPRING VALLEY (village). Covers a land area of 3.739 square miles and a water area of 0.730 square miles. Located at 44.84° N. Lat.; 92.24° W. Long. Elevation is 920 feet.
History: Spring Valley began as a logging camp, but experienced a mining boom in the early 1890's when iron deposits were found here. A furnace was built, and a railway line extended to the town. Both the timber and the iron declined in the early 1900's.
Population: 1,189 (2000); Race: 99.7% White, 0.0% Black, 0.0% Asian, 0.3% American Indian and Alaska Native, 0.0% Hispanic of any race, 0.1% two or more races (2000); Density: 318.0 persons per square mile (2000); Age: 24.3% under 18, 18.6% over 64 (2000); Marriage status: 21.3% never married, 58.5% now married, 10.6% widowed, 9.5% divorced (2000); Foreign born: 0.2% (2000); Ancestry (includes multiple ancestries): 38.1% German, 30.3% Norwegian, 11.8% Irish, 6.1% English, 5.8% Swedish (2000).
Economy: Single-family building permits issued: 10 (2001) / 4 (2000); Multi-family building permits issued: 8 (2001) / 6 (2000); Employment by occupation: 7.3% management, 11.8% professional, 18.5% services, 23.0% sales, 0.9% farming, 11.5% construction, 27.0% production (2000).
Income: Per capita income: $17,844 (2000); Median household income: $38,482 (2000); Poverty rate: 5.9% (2000).
Taxes: Total city taxes per capita: $109 (1997); City property taxes per capita: $93 (1997).
Education: High school graduation rate: 82.1% (2000); College graduation rate: 19.0% (2000).

School District(s)

Spring Valley (PK-12)
2000 Enrollment: 733 715-778-5551

Housing: Homeownership rate: 72.4% (2000); Median home value: $75,400 (2000); Median rent: $351 per month (2000); Median age of housing: 49 years (2000).
Newspapers: The Sun (1 x week)
Transportation: Commute to work: 90.3% car, 0.0% public transportation, 6.7% walk, 2.3% work from home (2000); Travel time to work: 32.2% less than 15 minutes, 29.8% 15 to 30 minutes, 16.5% 30 to 45 minutes, 11.6% 45 to 60 minutes, 10.0% 60 minutes or more (2000)

TRENTON (town). Covers a land area of 28.111 square miles and a water area of 2.048 square miles. Located at 44.61° N. Lat.; 92.53° W. Long. Elevation is 760 feet.
Population: 1,737 (2000); Race: 98.2% White, 0.1% Black, 0.8% Asian, 0.2% American Indian and Alaska Native, 0.6% Hispanic of any race, 0.6% two or more races (2000); Density: 61.8 persons per square mile (2000); Age: 24.3% under 18, 11.9% over 64 (2000); Marriage status: 21.1% never married, 67.9% now married, 3.4% widowed, 7.6% divorced (2000); Foreign born: 1.0% (2000); Ancestry (includes multiple ancestries): 42.7% German, 18.9% Norwegian, 18.4% Swedish, 11.6% Irish, 6.8% English (2000).
Economy: Employment by occupation: 8.2% management, 14.2% professional, 15.9% services, 22.0% sales, 0.8% farming, 12.5% construction, 26.4% production (2000).
Income: Per capita income: $23,634 (2000); Median household income: $53,229 (2000); Poverty rate: 5.6% (2000).
Taxes: Total city taxes per capita: $56 (1997); City property taxes per capita: $53 (1997).
Education: High school graduation rate: 86.7% (2000); College graduation rate: 14.0% (2000).
Housing: Homeownership rate: 89.6% (2000); Median home value: $112,700 (2000); Median rent: $475 per month (2000); Median age of housing: 32 years (2000).
Transportation: Commute to work: 94.4% car, 0.0% public transportation, 1.1% walk, 4.3% work from home (2000); Travel time to work: 32.7% less than 15 minutes, 41.3% 15 to 30 minutes, 12.7% 30 to 45 minutes, 5.4% 45 to 60 minutes, 8.0% 60 minutes or more (2000)

TRIMBELLE (town). Covers a land area of 36.169 square miles and a water area of 0 square miles. Located at 44.74° N. Lat.; 92.55° W. Long. Elevation is 900 feet.
Population: 1,511 (2000); Race: 97.7% White, 0.1% Black, 0.1% Asian, 0.0% American Indian and Alaska Native, 0.4% Hispanic of any race, 1.7% two or more races (2000); Density: 41.8 persons per square mile (2000); Age: 28.4% under 18, 8.5% over 64 (2000); Marriage status: 23.0% never married, 66.2% now married, 5.3% widowed, 5.5% divorced (2000); Foreign born: 0.2% (2000); Ancestry (includes multiple ancestries): 51.0% German, 16.6% Norwegian, 11.1% Swedish, 10.3% Irish, 4.9% English (2000).
Economy: Employment by occupation: 12.0% management, 14.3% professional, 13.4% services, 15.9% sales, 1.8% farming, 13.6% construction, 29.0% production (2000).
Income: Per capita income: $19,214 (2000); Median household income: $52,650 (2000); Poverty rate: 4.5% (2000).
Taxes: Total city taxes per capita: $61 (1997); City property taxes per capita: $59 (1997).
Education: High school graduation rate: 87.3% (2000); College graduation rate: 12.3% (2000).
Housing: Homeownership rate: 88.1% (2000); Median home value: $127,000 (2000); Median rent: $450 per month (2000); Median age of housing: 29 years (2000).
Transportation: Commute to work: 86.9% car, 0.6% public transportation, 3.6% walk, 8.8% work from home (2000); Travel time to work: 25.9% less than 15 minutes, 31.2% 15 to 30 minutes, 20.9% 30 to 45 minutes, 14.6% 45 to 60 minutes, 7.4% 60 minutes or more (2000)

UNION (town). Covers a land area of 34.897 square miles and a water area of 0.181 square miles. Located at 44.65° N. Lat.; 92.18° W. Long.
Population: 618 (2000); Race: 98.6% White, 0.7% Black, 0.0% Asian, 0.4% American Indian and Alaska Native, 0.0% Hispanic of any race, 0.4% two or more races (2000); Density: 17.7 persons per square mile (2000); Age: 29.7% under 18, 12.8% over 64 (2000); Marriage status: 31.2% never married, 58.7% now married, 6.5% widowed, 3.6% divorced (2000); Foreign born: 0.0% (2000); Ancestry (includes multiple ancestries): 51.6% German, 11.7% Norwegian, 9.4% Irish, 7.6% Swedish, 6.5% French (except Basque) (2000).
Economy: Employment by occupation: 20.8% management, 8.7% professional, 12.8% services, 17.7% sales, 2.1% farming, 10.1% construction, 27.8% production (2000).
Income: Per capita income: $14,892 (2000); Median household income: $35,375 (2000); Poverty rate: 9.9% (2000).
Taxes: Total city taxes per capita: $159 (2000); City property taxes per capita: $159 (2000).
Education: High school graduation rate: 86.6% (2000); College graduation rate: 12.6% (2000).
Housing: Homeownership rate: 85.1% (2000); Median home value: $78,600 (2000); Median rent: $142 per month (2000); Median age of housing: 60+ years (2000).
Transportation: Commute to work: 73.9% car, 0.0% public transportation, 2.5% walk, 23.6% work from home (2000); Travel time to work: 29.0% less than 15 minutes, 20.1% 15 to 30 minutes, 18.2% 30 to 45 minutes, 14.0% 45 to 60 minutes, 18.7% 60 minutes or more (2000)

Polk County

Located in northwestern Wisconsin; bounded on the west by the St. Croix River and the Minnesota border; includes many small lakes. Covers a land area of 917.30 square miles, a water area of 39.00 square miles, and is located in the Central Time Zone. The county government was organized in 1853. County seat is Balsam Lake.

Weather Station: Amery — Elevation: 1,069 feet

	Jan	Feb	Mar	Apr	May	Jun	Jul	Aug	Sep	Oct	Nov	Dec
High	19	26	38	54	68	76	81	78	69	56	39	25
Low	-1	5	19	33	45	54	59	56	47	35	22	7
Precip	1.0	0.7	1.7	2.6	3.2	4.6	4.0	4.7	3.8	2.6	2.1	1.1
Snow	11.3	6.4	8.5	2.1	0.0	0.0	0.0	0.0	0.0	0.5	7.0	9.5

High and Low temperatures in degrees Fahrenheit; Precipitation and Snow in inches

Weather Station: Luck Elevation: 1,217 feet

	Jan	Feb	Mar	Apr	May	Jun	Jul	Aug	Sep	Oct	Nov	Dec
High	21	28	39	56	69	77	81	79	69	57	39	25
Low	1	7	19	33	45	53	58	56	47	36	23	8
Precip	1.0	0.7	1.7	2.4	3.6	4.3	4.1	4.5	4.0	2.7	2.0	0.9
Snow	13.8	7.8	10.5	3.4	tr	0.0	0.0	0.0	0.0	0.7	10.9	11.6

High and Low temperatures in degrees Fahrenheit; Precipitation and Snow in inches

Weather Station: Saint Croix Falls Elevation: 767 feet

	Jan	Feb	Mar	Apr	May	Jun	Jul	Aug	Sep	Oct	Nov	Dec
High	22	29	41	57	71	79	83	81	71	59	40	27
Low	-1	6	19	33	45	55	60	58	48	37	23	8
Precip	0.8	0.6	1.6	2.6	3.4	4.5	4.1	4.7	3.7	2.7	1.7	0.8
Snow	11.1	5.6	7.4	1.4	0.0	0.0	0.0	0.0	0.0	0.4	7.5	7.3

High and Low temperatures in degrees Fahrenheit; Precipitation and Snow in inches

Population: 41,319 (2000); Race: 97.5% White, 0.2% Black, 0.2% Asian, 1.0% American Indian and Alaska Native, 0.7% Hispanic of any race, 0.8% two or more races (2000); Density: 45.0 persons per square mile (2000); Age: 26.2% under 18, 15.2% over 64 (2000).
Religion: Five largest groups: 27.9% Evangelical Lutheran Church in America, 11.9% Catholic Church, 4.2% Wisconsin Evangelical Lutheran Synod, 2.7% The United Methodist Church, 2.1% Lutheran Church—Missouri Synod (2000).
Economy: Unemployment rate: 5.1% (11/2002); Total civilian labor force: 23,685 (11/2002); Leading industries: 34.4% manufacturing; 14.6% retail trade; 14.3% health care and social assistance (2000); Companies that employ more than 1,000 persons: 0 (2000); Companies that employ more than 100 persons: 17 (2000); Farms: 1,301 totaling 267,639 acres (1997); Minority business ownership rate: 0.0% (1997); Women business ownership rate: 24.2% (1997); Retail sales per capita: $5,792 (1997). Single-family building permits issued: 425 (2001) / 385 (2000); Multi-family building permits issued: 20 (2001) / 46 (2000).
Income: Per capita income: $19,129 (2000); Median household income: $41,183 (2000); Poverty rate: 7.1% (2000); Bankruptcy rate: 3.79% (2001).
Taxes: Total county taxes per capita: $217 (2000); County property taxes per capita: $169 (2000).
Education: High school graduation rate: 85.9% (2000); College graduation rate: 15.6% (2000).
Housing: Homeownership rate: 80.1% (2000); Median home value: $100,200 (2000); Median rent: $382 per month (2000); Median age of housing: 28 years (2000).
Health: Birth rate: 103.1 per 10,000 population (1998); Age adjusted death rate: 79.7 per 10,000 population (1999); Age adjusted cancer mortality rate: 176.2 deaths per 100,000 population (1999). Number of physicians: 13.1 per 10,000 population (1999); Number of hospital beds: 34.4 per 10,000 population (1999).
Elections: 2000 Presidential election results: 45.3% Gore, 48.4% Bush, 5.5% Nader, 0.4% Buchanan
National and State Parks: Balsam Branch State Wildlife Area; Behning Creek State Public Fishing Area; Interstate State Park; McKenzie Creek State Public Hunting Grounds; Parker Creek State Public Fishing Area; Rice Bed Creek State Wildlife Area; Sand Creek State Fishery Area; Snake Creek State Public Fishing Area; Wagon Landing Springs State Public Fishing Area
Additional Information Contacts
Polk County Government Offices 715-485-9226
St. Croix Falls Chamber of Commerce 715-483-3580

Polk County Communities

ALDEN (town). Covers a land area of 56.059 square miles and a water area of 2.982 square miles. Located at 45.26° N. Lat.; 92.51° W. Long.
Population: 2,615 (2000); Race: 99.1% White, 0.0% Black, 0.6% Asian, 0.0% American Indian and Alaska Native, 0.9% Hispanic of any race, 0.0% two or more races (2000); Density: 46.6 persons per square mile (2000); Age: 27.2% under 18, 8.8% over 64 (2000); Marriage status: 22.4% never married, 64.5% now married, 3.9% widowed, 9.2% divorced (2000); Foreign born: 0.2% (2000); Ancestry (includes multiple ancestries): 42.3% German, 29.2% Norwegian, 12.3% Swedish, 10.0% Irish, 6.8% French (except Basque) (2000).
Economy: Employment by occupation: 10.1% management, 17.3% professional, 11.7% services, 24.3% sales, 0.7% farming, 9.6% construction, 26.3% production (2000).
Income: Per capita income: $22,470 (2000); Median household income: $57,337 (2000); Poverty rate: 3.4% (2000).
Taxes: Total city taxes per capita: $101 (1997); City property taxes per capita: $101 (1997).
Education: High school graduation rate: 87.6% (2000); College graduation rate: 23.0% (2000).
Housing: Homeownership rate: 92.2% (2000); Median home value: $139,700 (2000); Median rent: $381 per month (2000); Median age of housing: 25 years (2000).
Transportation: Commute to work: 90.0% car, 0.0% public transportation, 2.3% walk, 7.1% work from home (2000); Travel time to work: 14.2% less than 15 minutes, 38.1% 15 to 30 minutes, 14.6% 30 to 45 minutes, 14.7% 45 to 60 minutes, 18.5% 60 minutes or more (2000)

AMERY (city). Covers a land area of 3.004 square miles and a water area of 0.569 square miles. Located at 45.31° N. Lat.; 92.36° W. Long. Elevation is 1,070 feet.
History: Settled 1884, incorporated 1919.
Population: 2,845 (2000); Race: 97.9% White, 0.5% Black, 0.0% Asian, 1.2% American Indian and Alaska Native, 0.8% Hispanic of any race, 0.2% two or more races (2000); Density: 947.2 persons per square mile (2000); Age: 22.1% under 18, 27.5% over 64 (2000); Marriage status: 20.0% never married, 55.4% now married, 15.6% widowed, 8.9% divorced (2000); Foreign born: 1.7% (2000); Ancestry (includes multiple ancestries): 36.8% German, 21.7% Norwegian, 12.1% Swedish, 10.7% Irish, 7.5% United States or American (2000).
Economy: Dairy products. Poultry. Manufactures consumer goods, prepared food, stained glass, computer terminals, electronic assemblies. Grain elevators. Single-family building permits issued: 7 (2001) / 6 (2000); Multi-family building permits issued: 2 (2001) / 2 (2000); Employment by occupation: 9.7% management, 17.4% professional, 17.3% services, 20.2% sales, 1.0% farming, 9.0% construction, 25.5% production (2000).
Income: Per capita income: $17,125 (2000); Median household income: $30,710 (2000); Poverty rate: 8.5% (2000).
Taxes: Total city taxes per capita: $303 (1997); City property taxes per capita: $279 (1997).
Education: High school graduation rate: 81.3% (2000); College graduation rate: 17.9% (2000).

School District(s)

Amery (PK-12)
2000 Enrollment: 1,944 715-268-0272
Housing: Homeownership rate: 64.1% (2000); Median home value: $93,500 (2000); Median rent: $377 per month (2000); Median age of housing: 31 years (2000).
Hospitals: Amery Regional Medical Center (29 beds)
Safety: Violent crime rate: 55.8 per 10,000 population; Property crime rate: 380.5 per 10,000 population (2001).
Newspapers: Amery Free Press (1 x week)
Transportation: Commute to work: 89.3% car, 0.0% public transportation, 4.4% walk, 4.7% work from home (2000); Travel time to work: 46.2% less than 15 minutes, 19.7% 15 to 30 minutes, 14.8% 30 to 45 minutes, 5.9% 45 to 60 minutes, 13.4% 60 minutes or more (2000)

APPLE RIVER (town). Covers a land area of 33.984 square miles and a water area of 2.023 square miles. Located at 45.44° N. Lat.; 92.33° W. Long.
Population: 1,067 (2000); Race: 98.1% White, 0.0% Black, 0.0% Asian, 1.8% American Indian and Alaska Native, 0.4% Hispanic of any race, 0.1% two or more races (2000); Density: 31.4 persons per square mile (2000); Age: 25.8% under 18, 12.4% over 64 (2000); Marriage status: 20.9% never married, 63.8% now married, 3.9% widowed, 11.4% divorced (2000); Foreign born: 0.5% (2000); Ancestry (includes multiple ancestries): 35.1% German, 21.2% Norwegian, 16.2% Swedish, 9.2% Irish, 9.0% French (except Basque) (2000).
Economy: Employment by occupation: 11.1% management, 13.8% professional, 13.0% services, 20.2% sales, 1.2% farming, 15.8% construction, 24.9% production (2000).
Income: Per capita income: $19,331 (2000); Median household income: $43,500 (2000); Poverty rate: 7.4% (2000).
Taxes: Total city taxes per capita: $132 (1997); City property taxes per capita: $127 (1997).
Education: High school graduation rate: 86.1% (2000); College graduation rate: 12.9% (2000).
Housing: Homeownership rate: 95.4% (2000); Median home value: $101,400 (2000); Median rent: $488 per month (2000); Median age of housing: 29 years (2000).
Transportation: Commute to work: 89.9% car, 0.0% public transportation, 2.0% walk, 8.1% work from home (2000); Travel time to work: 20.9% less

than 15 minutes, 36.6% 15 to 30 minutes, 13.6% 30 to 45 minutes, 7.8% 45 to 60 minutes, 21.1% 60 minutes or more (2000)

BALSAM LAKE (village). Covers a land area of 2.025 square miles and a water area of 1.246 square miles. Located at 45.45° N. Lat.; 92.45° W. Long. Elevation is 1,155 feet.
Population: 950 (2000); Race: 94.7% White, 0.0% Black, 0.8% Asian, 3.8% American Indian and Alaska Native, 1.5% Hispanic of any race, 0.6% two or more races (2000); Density: 469.1 persons per square mile (2000); Age: 19.2% under 18, 22.8% over 64 (2000); Marriage status: 22.4% never married, 59.8% now married, 8.0% widowed, 9.7% divorced (2000); Foreign born: 1.0% (2000); Ancestry (includes multiple ancestries): 35.9% German, 14.4% Swedish, 14.2% Norwegian, 12.7% Irish, 6.8% United States or American (2000).
Economy: Single-family building permits issued: 12 (2001) / 8 (2000); Multi-family building permits issued: 0 (2001) / 0 (2000); Employment by occupation: 10.4% management, 12.9% professional, 16.8% services, 23.3% sales, 0.9% farming, 9.0% construction, 26.7% production (2000).
Income: Per capita income: $19,576 (2000); Median household income: $34,276 (2000); Poverty rate: 7.7% (2000).
Taxes: Total city taxes per capita: $399 (1997); City property taxes per capita: $355 (1997).
Education: High school graduation rate: 83.7% (2000); College graduation rate: 11.6% (2000).

School District(s)

Unity (PK-12)
2000 Enrollment: 1,239 715-825-3515

Housing: Homeownership rate: 76.2% (2000); Median home value: $87,300 (2000); Median rent: $363 per month (2000); Median age of housing: 28 years (2000).
Newspapers: Ledger Press (1 x week); Standard Press (1 x week); Enterprise Press (1 x week)
Transportation: Commute to work: 89.6% car, 0.9% public transportation, 3.5% walk, 6.0% work from home (2000); Travel time to work: 32.1% less than 15 minutes, 26.2% 15 to 30 minutes, 14.8% 30 to 45 minutes, 4.2% 45 to 60 minutes, 22.7% 60 minutes or more (2000)

BALSAM LAKE (town). Covers a land area of 29.729 square miles and a water area of 2.504 square miles. Located at 45.42° N. Lat.; 92.47° W. Long. Elevation is 1,155 feet.
Population: 1,384 (2000); Race: 97.7% White, 0.0% Black, 0.0% Asian, 0.9% American Indian and Alaska Native, 0.5% Hispanic of any race, 1.4% two or more races (2000); Density: 46.6 persons per square mile (2000); Age: 26.2% under 18, 11.9% over 64 (2000); Marriage status: 20.3% never married, 66.6% now married, 3.3% widowed, 9.8% divorced (2000); Foreign born: 0.6% (2000); Ancestry (includes multiple ancestries): 35.1% German, 19.3% Norwegian, 16.2% Swedish, 10.7% Irish, 6.0% English (2000).
Economy: Dairying; farming. Resort. Employment by occupation: 14.3% management, 16.4% professional, 11.8% services, 23.4% sales, 1.5% farming, 9.8% construction, 22.7% production (2000).
Income: Per capita income: $22,248 (2000); Median household income: $45,909 (2000); Poverty rate: 9.0% (2000).
Taxes: Total city taxes per capita: $89 (1997); City property taxes per capita: $88 (1997).
Education: High school graduation rate: 88.1% (2000); College graduation rate: 17.2% (2000).
Housing: Homeownership rate: 95.2% (2000); Median home value: $124,100 (2000); Median rent: $383 per month (2000); Median age of housing: 24 years (2000).
Transportation: Commute to work: 87.4% car, 0.3% public transportation, 0.7% walk, 10.4% work from home (2000); Travel time to work: 29.0% less than 15 minutes, 38.0% 15 to 30 minutes, 6.2% 30 to 45 minutes, 9.6% 45 to 60 minutes, 17.3% 60 minutes or more (2000)

BEAVER (town). Covers a land area of 35.282 square miles and a water area of 1.508 square miles. Located at 45.41° N. Lat.; 92.21° W. Long.
Population: 753 (2000); Race: 100.0% White, 0.0% Black, 0.0% Asian, 0.0% American Indian and Alaska Native, 0.0% Hispanic of any race, 0.0% two or more races (2000); Density: 21.3 persons per square mile (2000); Age: 23.9% under 18, 13.3% over 64 (2000); Marriage status: 19.4% never married, 65.6% now married, 6.3% widowed, 8.7% divorced (2000); Foreign born: 1.6% (2000); Ancestry (includes multiple ancestries): 33.9% German, 20.5% Norwegian, 13.8% Swedish, 8.9% Irish, 5.2% English (2000).
Economy: Employment by occupation: 9.5% management, 16.8% professional, 7.3% services, 22.1% sales, 0.0% farming, 13.4% construction, 30.8% production (2000).
Income: Per capita income: $18,242 (2000); Median household income: $40,114 (2000); Poverty rate: 7.1% (2000).
Taxes: Total city taxes per capita: $87 (1997); City property taxes per capita: $84 (1997).
Education: High school graduation rate: 87.5% (2000); College graduation rate: 16.2% (2000).
Housing: Homeownership rate: 86.1% (2000); Median home value: $88,800 (2000); Median rent: $419 per month (2000); Median age of housing: 32 years (2000).
Transportation: Commute to work: 91.8% car, 0.0% public transportation, 1.1% walk, 7.1% work from home (2000); Travel time to work: 33.3% less than 15 minutes, 32.4% 15 to 30 minutes, 9.2% 30 to 45 minutes, 6.7% 45 to 60 minutes, 18.3% 60 minutes or more (2000)

BLACK BROOK (town). Covers a land area of 34.246 square miles and a water area of 0.690 square miles. Located at 45.24° N. Lat.; 92.35° W. Long.
Population: 1,208 (2000); Race: 98.6% White, 0.0% Black, 0.1% Asian, 0.0% American Indian and Alaska Native, 1.3% Hispanic of any race, 1.0% two or more races (2000); Density: 35.3 persons per square mile (2000); Age: 30.7% under 18, 8.3% over 64 (2000); Marriage status: 21.4% never married, 67.6% now married, 2.3% widowed, 8.8% divorced (2000); Foreign born: 0.9% (2000); Ancestry (includes multiple ancestries): 40.4% German, 23.7% Norwegian, 12.5% Swedish, 7.6% Irish, 7.0% French (except Basque) (2000).
Economy: Employment by occupation: 8.8% management, 15.9% professional, 8.8% services, 22.0% sales, 3.3% farming, 11.7% construction, 29.7% production (2000).
Income: Per capita income: $19,286 (2000); Median household income: $48,125 (2000); Poverty rate: 6.5% (2000).
Taxes: Total city taxes per capita: $136 (1997); City property taxes per capita: $134 (1997).
Education: High school graduation rate: 87.3% (2000); College graduation rate: 12.1% (2000).
Housing: Homeownership rate: 89.4% (2000); Median home value: $101,600 (2000); Median rent: $396 per month (2000); Median age of housing: 28 years (2000).
Transportation: Commute to work: 91.4% car, 0.0% public transportation, 3.0% walk, 5.6% work from home (2000); Travel time to work: 41.6% less than 15 minutes, 18.7% 15 to 30 minutes, 16.9% 30 to 45 minutes, 7.2% 45 to 60 minutes, 15.6% 60 minutes or more (2000)

BONE LAKE (town). Covers a land area of 33.566 square miles and a water area of 1.855 square miles. Located at 45.58° N. Lat.; 92.34° W. Long.
Population: 710 (2000); Race: 98.1% White, 0.0% Black, 0.0% Asian, 1.7% American Indian and Alaska Native, 0.4% Hispanic of any race, 0.3% two or more races (2000); Density: 21.2 persons per square mile (2000); Age: 27.2% under 18, 14.3% over 64 (2000); Marriage status: 13.4% never married, 75.2% now married, 3.7% widowed, 7.7% divorced (2000); Foreign born: 1.0% (2000); Ancestry (includes multiple ancestries): 34.7% German, 17.4% Norwegian, 13.4% Swedish, 10.6% English, 9.6% Danish (2000).
Economy: Employment by occupation: 16.6% management, 15.3% professional, 13.7% services, 13.4% sales, 1.6% farming, 11.7% construction, 27.7% production (2000).
Income: Per capita income: $16,701 (2000); Median household income: $39,821 (2000); Poverty rate: 8.1% (2000).
Taxes: Total city taxes per capita: $78 (1997); City property taxes per capita: $78 (1997).
Education: High school graduation rate: 86.9% (2000); College graduation rate: 14.8% (2000).
Housing: Homeownership rate: 91.6% (2000); Median home value: $115,100 (2000); Median rent: $392 per month (2000); Median age of housing: 21 years (2000).
Transportation: Commute to work: 88.4% car, 0.0% public transportation, 2.0% walk, 9.2% work from home (2000); Travel time to work: 20.6% less than 15 minutes, 31.8% 15 to 30 minutes, 19.9% 30 to 45 minutes, 10.1% 45 to 60 minutes, 17.6% 60 minutes or more (2000)

CENTURIA (village). Covers a land area of 1.548 square miles and a water area of 0 square miles. Located at 45.45° N. Lat.; 92.55° W. Long. Elevation is 1,230 feet.
Population: 865 (2000); Race: 97.8% White, 0.0% Black, 0.0% Asian, 0.6% American Indian and Alaska Native, 0.5% Hispanic of any race, 1.6% two or more races (2000); Density: 558.6 persons per square mile (2000); Age: 28.4% under 18, 14.3% over 64 (2000); Marriage status: 22.9% never married, 52.6% now married, 10.6% widowed, 13.9% divorced (2000);

Foreign born: 0.6% (2000); Ancestry (includes multiple ancestries): 30.0% German, 17.5% Norwegian, 16.3% Swedish, 9.5% Irish, 4.0% Danish (2000).
Economy: Dairying. Single-family building permits issued: 28 (2001) / 5 (2000); Multi-family building permits issued: 10 (2001) / 0 (2000); Employment by occupation: 7.5% management, 10.5% professional, 15.0% services, 24.4% sales, 0.5% farming, 11.7% construction, 30.4% production (2000).
Income: Per capita income: $15,317 (2000); Median household income: $32,560 (2000); Poverty rate: 7.9% (2000).
Taxes: Total city taxes per capita: $99 (1997); City property taxes per capita: $91 (1997).
Education: High school graduation rate: 83.0% (2000); College graduation rate: 6.7% (2000).
Housing: Homeownership rate: 76.7% (2000); Median home value: $80,300 (2000); Median rent: $343 per month (2000); Median age of housing: 42 years (2000).
Transportation: Commute to work: 86.5% car, 0.5% public transportation, 6.5% walk, 4.0% work from home (2000); Travel time to work: 35.8% less than 15 minutes, 32.1% 15 to 30 minutes, 12.5% 30 to 45 minutes, 5.7% 45 to 60 minutes, 13.8% 60 minutes or more (2000)

CLAM FALLS (town). Covers a land area of 34.687 square miles and a water area of 0.721 square miles. Located at 45.68° N. Lat.; 92.35° W. Long. Elevation is 1,045 feet.
Population: 547 (2000); Race: 97.5% White, 0.4% Black, 0.0% Asian, 1.8% American Indian and Alaska Native, 0.0% Hispanic of any race, 0.4% two or more races (2000); Density: 15.8 persons per square mile (2000); Age: 18.3% under 18, 21.8% over 64 (2000); Marriage status: 19.8% never married, 61.2% now married, 7.7% widowed, 11.3% divorced (2000); Foreign born: 0.9% (2000); Ancestry (includes multiple ancestries): 29.1% German, 18.4% Swedish, 16.5% Norwegian, 16.3% United States or American, 10.1% Irish (2000).
Economy: Employment by occupation: 13.5% management, 5.7% professional, 18.1% services, 19.5% sales, 2.8% farming, 13.8% construction, 26.6% production (2000).
Income: Per capita income: $16,550 (2000); Median household income: $34,844 (2000); Poverty rate: 9.6% (2000).
Taxes: Total city taxes per capita: $48 (1997); City property taxes per capita: $43 (1997).
Education: High school graduation rate: 82.0% (2000); College graduation rate: 7.7% (2000).
Housing: Homeownership rate: 85.4% (2000); Median home value: $66,400 (2000); Median rent: $267 per month (2000); Median age of housing: 31 years (2000).
Transportation: Commute to work: 85.0% car, 2.2% public transportation, 2.6% walk, 10.2% work from home (2000); Travel time to work: 35.0% less than 15 minutes, 28.5% 15 to 30 minutes, 11.4% 30 to 45 minutes, 4.1% 45 to 60 minutes, 21.1% 60 minutes or more (2000)

CLAYTON (village). Covers a land area of 3.119 square miles and a water area of 0.121 square miles. Located at 45.32° N. Lat.; 92.17° W. Long. Elevation is 1,210 feet.
Population: 507 (2000); Race: 98.3% White, 1.5% Black, 0.0% Asian, 0.0% American Indian and Alaska Native, 0.0% Hispanic of any race, 0.2% two or more races (2000); Density: 162.6 persons per square mile (2000); Age: 32.4% under 18, 10.5% over 64 (2000); Marriage status: 28.1% never married, 44.0% now married, 10.2% widowed, 17.7% divorced (2000); Foreign born: 0.0% (2000); Ancestry (includes multiple ancestries): 40.6% German, 20.1% Norwegian, 11.7% United States or American, 8.4% Swedish, 4.8% Irish (2000).
Economy: Single-family building permits issued: 5 (2001) / 3 (2000); Multi-family building permits issued: 0 (2001) / 0 (2000); Employment by occupation: 7.7% management, 3.4% professional, 20.2% services, 12.4% sales, 2.1% farming, 11.6% construction, 42.5% production (2000).
Income: Per capita income: $14,988 (2000); Median household income: $29,135 (2000); Poverty rate: 18.7% (2000).
Taxes: Total city taxes per capita: $190 (1997); City property taxes per capita: $179 (1997).
Education: High school graduation rate: 74.2% (2000); College graduation rate: 5.4% (2000).

School District(s)

Clayton (PK-12)
2000 Enrollment: 398 715-948-2163
Housing: Homeownership rate: 66.0% (2000); Median home value: $72,700 (2000); Median rent: $395 per month (2000); Median age of housing: 29 years (2000).
Transportation: Commute to work: 86.3% car, 0.0% public transportation, 7.7% walk, 4.7% work from home (2000); Travel time to work: 42.3% less than 15 minutes, 23.4% 15 to 30 minutes, 16.2% 30 to 45 minutes, 8.1% 45 to 60 minutes, 9.9% 60 minutes or more (2000)

CLAYTON (town). Covers a land area of 33.231 square miles and a water area of 0.610 square miles. Located at 45.34° N. Lat.; 92.23° W. Long. Elevation is 1,210 feet.
History: The Stella Cheese Company plant was established by Count Giulio Bolognesi in Clayton, on the shores of Lake Camelia. The plant used imported rennet and processes that differed from the traditional Wisconsin cheese-making, to produce Italian cheeses such as provolone, salama, parmesan, and ricotta.
Population: 912 (2000); Race: 99.5% White, 0.0% Black, 0.0% Asian, 0.2% American Indian and Alaska Native, 0.8% Hispanic of any race, 0.3% two or more races (2000); Density: 27.4 persons per square mile (2000); Age: 27.4% under 18, 11.9% over 64 (2000); Marriage status: 18.8% never married, 66.5% now married, 4.4% widowed, 10.3% divorced (2000); Foreign born: 1.4% (2000); Ancestry (includes multiple ancestries): 33.2% German, 27.7% Norwegian, 10.7% Swedish, 9.7% French (except Basque), 8.6% Irish (2000).
Economy: In lake-resort and dairying area. Dairy products. Employment by occupation: 10.4% management, 12.5% professional, 15.0% services, 19.5% sales, 2.3% farming, 10.8% construction, 29.4% production (2000).
Income: Per capita income: $17,985 (2000); Median household income: $41,719 (2000); Poverty rate: 8.5% (2000).
Taxes: Total city taxes per capita: $53 (1997); City property taxes per capita: $53 (1997).
Education: High school graduation rate: 86.8% (2000); College graduation rate: 7.7% (2000).
Housing: Homeownership rate: 81.7% (2000); Median home value: $92,300 (2000); Median rent: $406 per month (2000); Median age of housing: 29 years (2000).
Transportation: Commute to work: 93.4% car, 0.4% public transportation, 1.1% walk, 5.1% work from home (2000); Travel time to work: 33.1% less than 15 minutes, 31.3% 15 to 30 minutes, 15.7% 30 to 45 minutes, 7.2% 45 to 60 minutes, 12.8% 60 minutes or more (2000)

CLEAR LAKE (village). Covers a land area of 2.647 square miles and a water area of 0.021 square miles. Located at 45.25° N. Lat.; 92.27° W. Long. Elevation is 1,201 feet.
History: Clear Lake developed in the midst of a wheat farming area. The farmers here later turned to dairy farming, with butter production leading the economy.
Population: 1,051 (2000); Race: 96.6% White, 0.0% Black, 0.7% Asian, 0.7% American Indian and Alaska Native, 2.5% Hispanic of any race, 0.3% two or more races (2000); Density: 397.1 persons per square mile (2000); Age: 23.9% under 18, 22.7% over 64 (2000); Marriage status: 24.4% never married, 53.7% now married, 13.5% widowed, 8.4% divorced (2000); Foreign born: 1.5% (2000); Ancestry (includes multiple ancestries): 38.3% German, 27.4% Norwegian, 13.0% Swedish, 10.0% Irish, 7.7% English (2000).
Economy: Single-family building permits issued: 1 (2001) / 5 (2000); Multi-family building permits issued: 0 (2001) / 6 (2000); Employment by occupation: 7.5% management, 10.7% professional, 16.2% services, 19.2% sales, 1.5% farming, 7.3% construction, 37.6% production (2000).
Income: Per capita income: $16,564 (2000); Median household income: $32,269 (2000); Poverty rate: 7.5% (2000).
Taxes: Total city taxes per capita: $222 (1997); City property taxes per capita: $200 (1997).
Education: High school graduation rate: 85.0% (2000); College graduation rate: 13.2% (2000).

School District(s)

Clear Lake (PK-12)
2000 Enrollment: 704 715-263-2114
Housing: Homeownership rate: 71.2% (2000); Median home value: $80,500 (2000); Median rent: $296 per month (2000); Median age of housing: 33 years (2000).
Transportation: Commute to work: 89.3% car, 0.7% public transportation, 6.6% walk, 3.5% work from home (2000); Travel time to work: 42.1% less than 15 minutes, 21.7% 15 to 30 minutes, 15.8% 30 to 45 minutes, 10.2% 45 to 60 minutes, 10.2% 60 minutes or more (2000)

CLEAR LAKE (town). Covers a land area of 34.524 square miles and a water area of 0.084 square miles. Located at 45.26° N. Lat.; 92.22° W. Long. Elevation is 1,201 feet.

Population: 800 (2000); Race: 97.1% White, 0.4% Black, 0.0% Asian, 0.0% American Indian and Alaska Native, 0.0% Hispanic of any race, 2.6% two or more races (2000); Density: 23.2 persons per square mile (2000); Age: 29.7% under 18, 8.3% over 64 (2000); Marriage status: 23.3% never married, 66.9% now married, 3.6% widowed, 6.2% divorced (2000); Foreign born: 0.7% (2000); Ancestry (includes multiple ancestries): 40.5% German, 28.6% Norwegian, 11.4% Swedish, 5.9% Irish, 5.2% United States or American (2000).
Economy: In dairying and stock-raising area. Manufacturing: vegetables, harvesting machines, cheeses, coatings. Employment by occupation: 15.1% management, 9.4% professional, 13.0% services, 14.9% sales, 7.1% farming, 12.1% construction, 28.4% production (2000).
Income: Per capita income: $18,009 (2000); Median household income: $48,542 (2000); Poverty rate: 6.3% (2000).
Taxes: Total city taxes per capita: $100 (1997); City property taxes per capita: $99 (1997).
Education: High school graduation rate: 90.5% (2000); College graduation rate: 7.7% (2000).
Housing: Homeownership rate: 90.8% (2000); Median home value: $97,500 (2000); Median rent: $345 per month (2000); Median age of housing: 44 years (2000).
Transportation: Commute to work: 83.5% car, 0.5% public transportation, 3.5% walk, 11.6% work from home (2000); Travel time to work: 42.5% less than 15 minutes, 22.6% 15 to 30 minutes, 20.2% 30 to 45 minutes, 7.3% 45 to 60 minutes, 7.3% 60 minutes or more (2000)

CUSHING (unincorporated postal area, zip code 54006). Covers a land area of 28.268 square miles and a water area of 1.272 square miles. Located at 45.58° N. Lat.; 92.64° W. Long. Elevation is 982 feet.
Population: 715 (2000); Race: 98.1% White, 0.5% Black, 0.8% Asian, 0.0% American Indian and Alaska Native, 0.5% Hispanic of any race, 0.5% two or more races (2000); Density: 25.3 persons per square mile (2000); Age: 25.8% under 18, 10.4% over 64 (2000); Marriage status: 24.9% never married, 60.6% now married, 4.1% widowed, 10.4% divorced (2000); Foreign born: 0.8% (2000); Ancestry (includes multiple ancestries): 33.4% German, 24.6% Norwegian, 23.4% Swedish, 11.8% Danish, 9.1% Irish (2000).
Economy: Employment by occupation: 15.8% management, 8.3% professional, 12.1% services, 20.9% sales, 3.2% farming, 11.4% construction, 28.4% production (2000).
Income: Per capita income: $17,100 (2000); Median household income: $38,571 (2000); Poverty rate: 11.8% (2000).
Education: High school graduation rate: 84.1% (2000); College graduation rate: 9.2% (2000).
Housing: Homeownership rate: 85.0% (2000); Median home value: $90,000 (2000); Median rent: $408 per month (2000); Median age of housing: 40 years (2000).
Transportation: Commute to work: 88.9% car, 0.0% public transportation, 1.2% walk, 8.7% work from home (2000); Travel time to work: 19.2% less than 15 minutes, 39.6% 15 to 30 minutes, 13.3% 30 to 45 minutes, 6.0% 45 to 60 minutes, 22.0% 60 minutes or more (2000)

DRESSER (village). Covers a land area of 1.903 square miles and a water area of 0 square miles. Located at 45.35° N. Lat.; 92.63° W. Long. Elevation is 973 feet.
History: Until 1940, called Dresser Junction.
Population: 732 (2000); Race: 99.7% White, 0.0% Black, 0.0% Asian, 0.0% American Indian and Alaska Native, 0.7% Hispanic of any race, 0.0% two or more races (2000); Density: 384.6 persons per square mile (2000); Age: 26.5% under 18, 12.0% over 64 (2000); Marriage status: 24.0% never married, 60.5% now married, 4.9% widowed, 10.5% divorced (2000); Foreign born: 0.6% (2000); Ancestry (includes multiple ancestries): 36.7% German, 22.3% Norwegian, 20.5% Swedish, 8.4% English, 8.2% United States or American (2000).
Economy: In dairying area. Cheese; dies and fixtures; mechanical assembly. St. Croix Falls and Osceola Fish Hatcheries on river. Trollhaugen Ski Area nearby. Single-family building permits issued: 0 (2001) / 3 (2000); Multi-family building permits issued: 0 (2001) / 0 (2000); Employment by occupation: 5.7% management, 12.7% professional, 13.5% services, 23.1% sales, 0.0% farming, 12.2% construction, 32.7% production (2000).
Income: Per capita income: $17,926 (2000); Median household income: $37,500 (2000); Poverty rate: 5.6% (2000).
Taxes: Total city taxes per capita: $267 (1997); City property taxes per capita: $252 (1997).
Education: High school graduation rate: 87.2% (2000); College graduation rate: 10.0% (2000).
Housing: Homeownership rate: 77.4% (2000); Median home value: $89,400 (2000); Median rent: $416 per month (2000); Median age of housing: 39 years (2000).
Transportation: Commute to work: 93.7% car, 0.0% public transportation, 3.9% walk, 1.6% work from home (2000); Travel time to work: 52.9% less than 15 minutes, 12.8% 15 to 30 minutes, 14.7% 30 to 45 minutes, 11.2% 45 to 60 minutes, 8.3% 60 minutes or more (2000)

EUREKA (town). Covers a land area of 53.847 square miles and a water area of 0.897 square miles. Located at 45.51° N. Lat.; 92.64° W. Long.
Population: 1,338 (2000); Race: 97.2% White, 0.5% Black, 0.0% Asian, 0.4% American Indian and Alaska Native, 1.1% Hispanic of any race, 1.2% two or more races (2000); Density: 24.8 persons per square mile (2000); Age: 27.1% under 18, 11.8% over 64 (2000); Marriage status: 24.1% never married, 62.1% now married, 4.5% widowed, 9.4% divorced (2000); Foreign born: 0.4% (2000); Ancestry (includes multiple ancestries): 35.5% German, 17.7% Norwegian, 16.3% Swedish, 10.1% Irish, 8.1% Danish (2000).
Economy: Employment by occupation: 11.5% management, 9.5% professional, 16.7% services, 17.4% sales, 2.7% farming, 12.5% construction, 29.7% production (2000).
Income: Per capita income: $19,343 (2000); Median household income: $45,625 (2000); Poverty rate: 5.5% (2000).
Taxes: Total city taxes per capita: $68 (1997); City property taxes per capita: $66 (1997).
Education: High school graduation rate: 86.9% (2000); College graduation rate: 10.4% (2000).
Housing: Homeownership rate: 88.8% (2000); Median home value: $92,900 (2000); Median rent: $433 per month (2000); Median age of housing: 30 years (2000).
Transportation: Commute to work: 91.1% car, 0.9% public transportation, 0.6% walk, 7.5% work from home (2000); Travel time to work: 17.2% less than 15 minutes, 41.0% 15 to 30 minutes, 13.5% 30 to 45 minutes, 5.6% 45 to 60 minutes, 22.7% 60 minutes or more (2000)

FARMINGTON (town). Covers a land area of 43.959 square miles and a water area of 0.932 square miles. Located at 45.26° N. Lat.; 92.68° W. Long.
Population: 1,625 (2000); Race: 96.5% White, 0.8% Black, 0.9% Asian, 0.5% American Indian and Alaska Native, 1.3% Hispanic of any race, 1.3% two or more races (2000); Density: 37.0 persons per square mile (2000); Age: 32.3% under 18, 7.2% over 64 (2000); Marriage status: 24.6% never married, 64.9% now married, 2.4% widowed, 8.1% divorced (2000); Foreign born: 0.9% (2000); Ancestry (includes multiple ancestries): 48.1% German, 15.4% Norwegian, 12.5% Swedish, 10.7% Irish, 9.9% French (except Basque) (2000).
Economy: Single-family building permits issued: 11 (2001) / 12 (2000); Multi-family building permits issued: 0 (2001) / 0 (2000); Employment by occupation: 12.5% management, 13.2% professional, 11.8% services, 26.4% sales, 1.8% farming, 9.1% construction, 25.3% production (2000).
Income: Per capita income: $20,974 (2000); Median household income: $58,833 (2000); Poverty rate: 2.9% (2000).
Taxes: Total city taxes per capita: $88 (1997); City property taxes per capita: $80 (1997).
Education: High school graduation rate: 90.5% (2000); College graduation rate: 18.8% (2000).
Housing: Homeownership rate: 86.2% (2000); Median home value: $129,400 (2000); Median rent: $450 per month (2000); Median age of housing: 27 years (2000).
Transportation: Commute to work: 91.5% car, 0.4% public transportation, 2.4% walk, 5.6% work from home (2000); Travel time to work: 23.8% less than 15 minutes, 31.3% 15 to 30 minutes, 18.3% 30 to 45 minutes, 17.0% 45 to 60 minutes, 9.6% 60 minutes or more (2000)

FREDERIC (village). Covers a land area of 1.538 square miles and a water area of 0.065 square miles. Located at 45.65° N. Lat.; 92.46° W. Long. Elevation is 1,220 feet.
Population: 1,262 (2000); Race: 94.7% White, 0.2% Black, 1.3% Asian, 2.4% American Indian and Alaska Native, 0.0% Hispanic of any race, 1.5% two or more races (2000); Density: 820.6 persons per square mile (2000); Age: 24.1% under 18, 29.9% over 64 (2000); Marriage status: 19.9% never married, 52.0% now married, 17.1% widowed, 11.0% divorced (2000); Foreign born: 1.4% (2000); Ancestry (includes multiple ancestries): 23.9% German, 20.0% Swedish, 16.9% Norwegian, 12.5% United States or American, 7.5% Irish (2000).
Economy: Dairy products, canned vegetables. Manufacturing: plastic products, printing and publishing. Single-family building permits issued: 0

(2001) / 1 (2000); Multi-family building permits issued: 0 (2001) / 0 (2000); Employment by occupation: 7.2% management, 18.8% professional, 19.4% services, 22.0% sales, 0.4% farming, 10.2% construction, 21.8% production (2000).
Income: Per capita income: $15,685 (2000); Median household income: $25,380 (2000); Poverty rate: 10.9% (2000).
Taxes: Total city taxes per capita: $165 (1997); City property taxes per capita: $140 (1997).
Education: High school graduation rate: 83.2% (2000); College graduation rate: 12.7% (2000).

School District(s)

Frederic (KG-12)
2000 Enrollment: 606 715-327-5630
Housing: Homeownership rate: 66.2% (2000); Median home value: $67,900 (2000); Median rent: $305 per month (2000); Median age of housing: 39 years (2000).
Newspapers: Wild Rivers Advertiser (1 x week); Tri-County Advertiser (1 x week); The Inter-County Leader (1 x week); Indianhead Advertiser (1 x week)
Transportation: Commute to work: 89.7% car, 0.0% public transportation, 7.1% walk, 1.8% work from home (2000); Travel time to work: 49.6% less than 15 minutes, 24.1% 15 to 30 minutes, 11.7% 30 to 45 minutes, 3.7% 45 to 60 minutes, 10.9% 60 minutes or more (2000)

GARFIELD (town). Covers a land area of 32.982 square miles and a water area of 2.140 square miles. Located at 45.33° N. Lat.; 92.49° W. Long.
Population: 1,443 (2000); Race: 98.6% White, 0.1% Black, 0.0% Asian, 0.0% American Indian and Alaska Native, 1.0% Hispanic of any race, 1.0% two or more races (2000); Density: 43.8 persons per square mile (2000); Age: 28.4% under 18, 11.3% over 64 (2000); Marriage status: 20.6% never married, 67.6% now married, 4.0% widowed, 7.8% divorced (2000); Foreign born: 1.9% (2000); Ancestry (includes multiple ancestries): 35.6% German, 31.9% Norwegian, 12.2% Irish, 10.6% Swedish, 6.1% English (2000).
Economy: Single-family building permits issued: 9 (2001) / 20 (2000); Multi-family building permits issued: 0 (2001) / 0 (2000); Employment by occupation: 16.0% management, 15.5% professional, 11.6% services, 19.2% sales, 3.9% farming, 10.3% construction, 23.5% production (2000).
Income: Per capita income: $21,834 (2000); Median household income: $48,000 (2000); Poverty rate: 2.8% (2000).
Taxes: Total city taxes per capita: $122 (1997); City property taxes per capita: $119 (1997).
Education: High school graduation rate: 86.4% (2000); College graduation rate: 16.1% (2000).
Housing: Homeownership rate: 87.8% (2000); Median home value: $122,500 (2000); Median rent: $350 per month (2000); Median age of housing: 26 years (2000).
Transportation: Commute to work: 89.2% car, 0.0% public transportation, 5.5% walk, 5.0% work from home (2000); Travel time to work: 23.4% less than 15 minutes, 40.5% 15 to 30 minutes, 12.4% 30 to 45 minutes, 8.5% 45 to 60 minutes, 15.3% 60 minutes or more (2000)

GEORGETOWN (town). Covers a land area of 30.334 square miles and a water area of 4.824 square miles. Located at 45.51° N. Lat.; 92.34° W. Long.
Population: 1,004 (2000); Race: 90.7% White, 0.1% Black, 0.3% Asian, 8.4% American Indian and Alaska Native, 0.0% Hispanic of any race, 0.2% two or more races (2000); Density: 33.1 persons per square mile (2000); Age: 21.9% under 18, 19.4% over 64 (2000); Marriage status: 20.3% never married, 59.8% now married, 10.5% widowed, 9.4% divorced (2000); Foreign born: 1.6% (2000); Ancestry (includes multiple ancestries): 35.1% German, 12.7% Norwegian, 10.6% Irish, 9.1% English, 8.8% Swedish (2000).
Economy: Employment by occupation: 18.7% management, 10.1% professional, 17.6% services, 20.3% sales, 2.2% farming, 10.8% construction, 20.3% production (2000).
Income: Per capita income: $21,558 (2000); Median household income: $38,487 (2000); Poverty rate: 9.3% (2000).
Taxes: Total city taxes per capita: $133 (1997); City property taxes per capita: $129 (1997).
Education: High school graduation rate: 81.0% (2000); College graduation rate: 12.4% (2000).
Housing: Homeownership rate: 83.0% (2000); Median home value: $122,700 (2000); Median rent: $300 per month (2000); Median age of housing: 21 years (2000).
Transportation: Commute to work: 86.2% car, 0.0% public transportation, 2.9% walk, 10.4% work from home (2000); Travel time to work: 13.9% less than 15 minutes, 35.8% 15 to 30 minutes, 17.6% 30 to 45 minutes, 10.3% 45 to 60 minutes, 22.4% 60 minutes or more (2000)

JOHNSTOWN (town). Covers a land area of 35.757 square miles and a water area of 1.340 square miles. Located at 45.51° N. Lat.; 92.22° W. Long.
Population: 520 (2000); Race: 78.8% White, 0.0% Black, 0.0% Asian, 17.5% American Indian and Alaska Native, 0.0% Hispanic of any race, 3.7% two or more races (2000); Density: 14.5 persons per square mile (2000); Age: 27.1% under 18, 11.3% over 64 (2000); Marriage status: 28.7% never married, 56.0% now married, 6.8% widowed, 8.5% divorced (2000); Foreign born: 0.6% (2000); Ancestry (includes multiple ancestries): 35.2% German, 16.3% Other groups, 13.3% Norwegian, 7.7% Swedish, 5.6% Irish (2000).
Economy: Employment by occupation: 15.2% management, 12.9% professional, 13.7% services, 22.7% sales, 6.3% farming, 4.3% construction, 25.0% production (2000).
Income: Per capita income: $17,368 (2000); Median household income: $37,500 (2000); Poverty rate: 18.5% (2000).
Taxes: Total city taxes per capita: $161 (1997); City property taxes per capita: $159 (1997).
Education: High school graduation rate: 84.9% (2000); College graduation rate: 17.2% (2000).
Housing: Homeownership rate: 84.3% (2000); Median home value: $123,200 (2000); Median rent: $354 per month (2000); Median age of housing: 25 years (2000).
Transportation: Commute to work: 82.0% car, 0.0% public transportation, 2.3% walk, 15.6% work from home (2000); Travel time to work: 23.6% less than 15 minutes, 34.3% 15 to 30 minutes, 19.9% 30 to 45 minutes, 13.0% 45 to 60 minutes, 9.3% 60 minutes or more (2000)

LAKETOWN (town). Covers a land area of 34.232 square miles and a water area of 1.527 square miles. Located at 45.60° N. Lat.; 92.59° W. Long.
Population: 918 (2000); Race: 96.9% White, 0.4% Black, 0.9% Asian, 0.0% American Indian and Alaska Native, 0.8% Hispanic of any race, 1.0% two or more races (2000); Density: 26.8 persons per square mile (2000); Age: 22.3% under 18, 11.1% over 64 (2000); Marriage status: 26.3% never married, 60.9% now married, 5.0% widowed, 7.8% divorced (2000); Foreign born: 1.2% (2000); Ancestry (includes multiple ancestries): 29.4% Swedish, 27.8% German, 26.8% Norwegian, 14.5% Danish, 7.3% Irish (2000).
Economy: Employment by occupation: 18.5% management, 10.4% professional, 15.4% services, 19.4% sales, 1.9% farming, 10.9% construction, 23.5% production (2000).
Income: Per capita income: $17,573 (2000); Median household income: $40,156 (2000); Poverty rate: 11.7% (2000).
Taxes: Total city taxes per capita: $83 (1997); City property taxes per capita: $82 (1997).
Education: High school graduation rate: 84.4% (2000); College graduation rate: 9.4% (2000).
Housing: Homeownership rate: 86.0% (2000); Median home value: $91,500 (2000); Median rent: $411 per month (2000); Median age of housing: 35 years (2000).
Transportation: Commute to work: 85.9% car, 0.4% public transportation, 1.4% walk, 11.4% work from home (2000); Travel time to work: 22.5% less than 15 minutes, 34.1% 15 to 30 minutes, 18.8% 30 to 45 minutes, 5.7% 45 to 60 minutes, 19.0% 60 minutes or more (2000)

LINCOLN (town). Covers a land area of 35.727 square miles and a water area of 2.657 square miles. Located at 45.33° N. Lat.; 92.35° W. Long.
Population: 2,304 (2000); Race: 98.6% White, 0.0% Black, 0.0% Asian, 0.3% American Indian and Alaska Native, 0.2% Hispanic of any race, 1.0% two or more races (2000); Density: 64.5 persons per square mile (2000); Age: 26.7% under 18, 13.0% over 64 (2000); Marriage status: 21.2% never married, 66.4% now married, 4.7% widowed, 7.7% divorced (2000); Foreign born: 0.9% (2000); Ancestry (includes multiple ancestries): 39.0% German, 25.6% Norwegian, 12.8% Swedish, 11.7% Irish, 7.0% English (2000).
Economy: Employment by occupation: 13.4% management, 17.1% professional, 12.9% services, 22.7% sales, 1.1% farming, 10.6% construction, 22.2% production (2000).
Income: Per capita income: $21,788 (2000); Median household income: $45,904 (2000); Poverty rate: 6.3% (2000).
Taxes: Total city taxes per capita: $62 (1997); City property taxes per capita: $61 (1997).
Education: High school graduation rate: 90.5% (2000); College graduation rate: 18.6% (2000).
Housing: Homeownership rate: 91.3% (2000); Median home value: $120,500 (2000); Median rent: $418 per month (2000); Median age of housing: 28 years (2000).

Transportation: Commute to work: 92.2% car, 0.4% public transportation, 2.4% walk, 4.8% work from home (2000); Travel time to work: 45.8% less than 15 minutes, 20.8% 15 to 30 minutes, 12.7% 30 to 45 minutes, 5.7% 45 to 60 minutes, 15.0% 60 minutes or more (2000)

LORAIN (town). Covers a land area of 36.879 square miles and a water area of 0.133 square miles. Located at 45.69° N. Lat.; 92.23° W. Long.

Population: 328 (2000); Race: 95.1% White, 0.0% Black, 0.0% Asian, 1.3% American Indian and Alaska Native, 0.7% Hispanic of any race, 3.6% two or more races (2000); Density: 8.9 persons per square mile (2000); Age: 29.3% under 18, 17.9% over 64 (2000); Marriage status: 24.6% never married, 55.8% now married, 10.0% widowed, 9.6% divorced (2000); Foreign born: 0.0% (2000); Ancestry (includes multiple ancestries): 45.9% German, 16.6% Norwegian, 14.3% English, 14.0% United States or American, 12.4% Irish (2000).

Economy: Employment by occupation: 20.6% management, 5.2% professional, 14.8% services, 25.2% sales, 10.3% farming, 9.7% construction, 14.2% production (2000).

Income: Per capita income: $14,670 (2000); Median household income: $25,208 (2000); Poverty rate: 16.0% (2000).

Taxes: Total city taxes per capita: $31 (1997); City property taxes per capita: $28 (1997).

Education: High school graduation rate: 84.3% (2000); College graduation rate: 15.7% (2000).

Housing: Homeownership rate: 85.6% (2000); Median home value: $63,800 (2000); Median rent: $325 per month (2000); Median age of housing: 29 years (2000).

Transportation: Commute to work: 68.4% car, 0.0% public transportation, 5.8% walk, 25.2% work from home (2000); Travel time to work: 23.3% less than 15 minutes, 37.1% 15 to 30 minutes, 21.6% 30 to 45 minutes, 12.1% 45 to 60 minutes, 6.0% 60 minutes or more (2000)

LUCK (village). Covers a land area of 1.849 square miles and a water area of 0.593 square miles. Located at 45.57° N. Lat.; 92.47° W. Long. Elevation is 1,220 feet.

Population: 1,210 (2000); Race: 97.2% White, 0.3% Black, 0.3% Asian, 0.8% American Indian and Alaska Native, 0.8% Hispanic of any race, 1.4% two or more races (2000); Density: 654.2 persons per square mile (2000); Age: 24.2% under 18, 25.0% over 64 (2000); Marriage status: 18.9% never married, 54.0% now married, 14.3% widowed, 12.7% divorced (2000); Foreign born: 1.0% (2000); Ancestry (includes multiple ancestries): 27.4% German, 17.7% Norwegian, 16.7% Swedish, 15.1% Danish, 8.5% United States or American (2000).

Economy: Single-family building permits issued: 7 (2001) / 2 (2000); Multi-family building permits issued: 0 (2001) / 0 (2000); Employment by occupation: 8.3% management, 18.1% professional, 19.5% services, 18.1% sales, 0.8% farming, 11.0% construction, 24.2% production (2000).

Income: Per capita income: $16,599 (2000); Median household income: $32,138 (2000); Poverty rate: 8.3% (2000).

Taxes: Total city taxes per capita: $189 (1997); City property taxes per capita: $170 (1997).

Education: High school graduation rate: 80.7% (2000); College graduation rate: 17.3% (2000).

School District(s)

Luck (KG-12)
2000 Enrollment: 645 715-472-2151

Housing: Homeownership rate: 65.9% (2000); Median home value: $79,600 (2000); Median rent: $361 per month (2000); Median age of housing: 39 years (2000).

Transportation: Commute to work: 89.3% car, 0.0% public transportation, 5.8% walk, 4.0% work from home (2000); Travel time to work: 49.3% less than 15 minutes, 21.8% 15 to 30 minutes, 11.1% 30 to 45 minutes, 5.7% 45 to 60 minutes, 12.2% 60 minutes or more (2000)

LUCK (town). Covers a land area of 32.082 square miles and a water area of 0.563 square miles. Located at 45.59° N. Lat.; 92.48° W. Long. Elevation is 1,220 feet.

Population: 881 (2000); Race: 98.1% White, 0.3% Black, 0.2% Asian, 0.0% American Indian and Alaska Native, 0.6% Hispanic of any race, 1.2% two or more races (2000); Density: 27.5 persons per square mile (2000); Age: 28.8% under 18, 13.6% over 64 (2000); Marriage status: 23.0% never married, 67.2% now married, 4.0% widowed, 5.7% divorced (2000); Foreign born: 0.9% (2000); Ancestry (includes multiple ancestries): 32.4% German, 19.2% Norwegian, 15.1% Swedish, 14.1% Danish, 9.0% English (2000).

Economy: Manufacturing: food products, wood moldings and picture frames; wire screen cloth, lumber, furniture. Employment by occupation: 7.3% management, 15.3% professional, 13.5% services, 21.0% sales, 0.9% farming, 11.4% construction, 30.6% production (2000).

Income: Per capita income: $16,096 (2000); Median household income: $40,417 (2000); Poverty rate: 9.9% (2000).

Taxes: Total city taxes per capita: $78 (1997); City property taxes per capita: $77 (1997).

Education: High school graduation rate: 86.2% (2000); College graduation rate: 10.2% (2000).

Housing: Homeownership rate: 90.6% (2000); Median home value: $91,400 (2000); Median rent: $405 per month (2000); Median age of housing: 33 years (2000).

Transportation: Commute to work: 90.2% car, 0.5% public transportation, 1.2% walk, 8.2% work from home (2000); Travel time to work: 43.5% less than 15 minutes, 26.5% 15 to 30 minutes, 12.7% 30 to 45 minutes, 4.1% 45 to 60 minutes, 13.2% 60 minutes or more (2000)

MCKINLEY (town). Aka Loraine. Covers a land area of 36.026 square miles and a water area of 1.117 square miles. Located at 45.57° N. Lat.; 92.22° W. Long. Elevation is 1,285 feet.

Population: 328 (2000); Race: 99.4% White, 0.0% Black, 0.0% Asian, 0.6% American Indian and Alaska Native, 0.6% Hispanic of any race, 0.0% two or more races (2000); Density: 9.1 persons per square mile (2000); Age: 25.1% under 18, 14.9% over 64 (2000); Marriage status: 27.9% never married, 60.4% now married, 2.6% widowed, 9.1% divorced (2000); Foreign born: 0.0% (2000); Ancestry (includes multiple ancestries): 44.8% German, 24.1% Norwegian, 17.5% Swedish, 12.1% Irish, 7.6% English (2000).

Economy: Employment by occupation: 13.4% management, 9.2% professional, 16.2% services, 23.2% sales, 0.0% farming, 5.6% construction, 32.4% production (2000).

Income: Per capita income: $15,772 (2000); Median household income: $37,083 (2000); Poverty rate: 10.5% (2000).

Taxes: Total city taxes per capita: $146 (1997); City property taxes per capita: $146 (1997).

Education: High school graduation rate: 87.7% (2000); College graduation rate: 16.4% (2000).

Housing: Homeownership rate: 85.7% (2000); Median home value: $85,000 (2000); Median rent: $350 per month (2000); Median age of housing: 28 years (2000).

Transportation: Commute to work: 86.2% car, 0.0% public transportation, 2.9% walk, 9.4% work from home (2000); Travel time to work: 12.8% less than 15 minutes, 53.6% 15 to 30 minutes, 26.4% 30 to 45 minutes, 4.0% 45 to 60 minutes, 3.2% 60 minutes or more (2000)

MILLTOWN (village). Covers a land area of 1.770 square miles and a water area of 0 square miles. Located at 45.52° N. Lat.; 92.50° W. Long. Elevation is 1,246 feet.

Population: 888 (2000); Race: 96.9% White, 0.9% Black, 0.0% Asian, 1.8% American Indian and Alaska Native, 0.8% Hispanic of any race, 0.4% two or more races (2000); Density: 501.8 persons per square mile (2000); Age: 22.7% under 18, 24.2% over 64 (2000); Marriage status: 22.2% never married, 48.4% now married, 13.1% widowed, 16.3% divorced (2000); Foreign born: 0.2% (2000); Ancestry (includes multiple ancestries): 25.8% German, 24.0% Norwegian, 15.9% Swedish, 9.2% Irish, 7.5% Danish (2000).

Economy: Single-family building permits issued: 2 (2001) / 1 (2000); Multi-family building permits issued: 0 (2001) / 2 (2000); Employment by occupation: 6.4% management, 10.9% professional, 10.2% services, 25.5% sales, 1.7% farming, 14.7% construction, 30.7% production (2000).

Income: Per capita income: $17,284 (2000); Median household income: $28,309 (2000); Poverty rate: 11.5% (2000).

Taxes: Total city taxes per capita: $177 (1997); City property taxes per capita: $172 (1997).

Education: High school graduation rate: 73.5% (2000); College graduation rate: 5.3% (2000).

Housing: Homeownership rate: 65.6% (2000); Median home value: $80,000 (2000); Median rent: $322 per month (2000); Median age of housing: 33 years (2000).

Transportation: Commute to work: 95.4% car, 0.0% public transportation, 3.6% walk, 0.5% work from home (2000); Travel time to work: 32.0% less than 15 minutes, 29.6% 15 to 30 minutes, 19.9% 30 to 45 minutes, 7.0% 45 to 60 minutes, 11.4% 60 minutes or more (2000)

MILLTOWN (town). Covers a land area of 31.235 square miles and a water area of 2.236 square miles. Located at 45.49° N. Lat.; 92.46° W. Long. Elevation is 1,246 feet.

Population: 1,146 (2000); Race: 98.7% White, 0.0% Black, 0.0% Asian, 1.3% American Indian and Alaska Native, 0.2% Hispanic of any race, 0.0%

two or more races (2000); Density: 36.7 persons per square mile (2000); Age: 27.0% under 18, 14.5% over 64 (2000); Marriage status: 19.2% never married, 68.7% now married, 2.5% widowed, 9.6% divorced (2000); Foreign born: 1.6% (2000); Ancestry (includes multiple ancestries): 30.6% German, 21.6% Norwegian, 14.5% Swedish, 10.0% Irish, 9.8% Danish (2000).
Economy: Dairying area; vegetable canning. Light manufacturing. Employment by occupation: 17.6% management, 14.1% professional, 12.8% services, 21.5% sales, 1.3% farming, 13.8% construction, 19.0% production (2000).
Income: Per capita income: $19,991 (2000); Median household income: $46,944 (2000); Poverty rate: 4.1% (2000).
Taxes: Total city taxes per capita: $185 (1997); City property taxes per capita: $183 (1997).
Education: High school graduation rate: 89.5% (2000); College graduation rate: 20.0% (2000).
Housing: Homeownership rate: 91.1% (2000); Median home value: $114,100 (2000); Median rent: $395 per month (2000); Median age of housing: 32 years (2000).
Transportation: Commute to work: 87.5% car, 1.0% public transportation, 1.7% walk, 9.7% work from home (2000); Travel time to work: 34.6% less than 15 minutes, 30.2% 15 to 30 minutes, 11.3% 30 to 45 minutes, 7.4% 45 to 60 minutes, 16.4% 60 minutes or more (2000)

OSCEOLA (village). Covers a land area of 3.686 square miles and a water area of 0.129 square miles. Located at 45.32° N. Lat.; 92.69° W. Long. Elevation is 825 feet.
History: Osceola was platted in 1855, and served for several years as the seat of Polk County.
Population: 2,421 (2000); Race: 98.7% White, 0.0% Black, 0.2% Asian, 0.0% American Indian and Alaska Native, 1.3% Hispanic of any race, 1.0% two or more races (2000); Density: 656.9 persons per square mile (2000); Age: 26.9% under 18, 12.7% over 64 (2000); Marriage status: 28.2% never married, 51.1% now married, 6.5% widowed, 14.2% divorced (2000); Foreign born: 0.6% (2000); Ancestry (includes multiple ancestries): 39.4% German, 19.6% Norwegian, 16.3% Swedish, 9.5% Irish, 6.2% French (except Basque) (2000).
Economy: Single-family building permits issued: 30 (2001) / 7 (2000); Multi-family building permits issued: 0 (2001) / 26 (2000); Employment by occupation: 8.0% management, 16.6% professional, 14.0% services, 23.5% sales, 0.9% farming, 7.2% construction, 29.8% production (2000).
Income: Per capita income: $18,921 (2000); Median household income: $39,000 (2000); Poverty rate: 6.1% (2000).
Taxes: Total city taxes per capita: $148 (1997); City property taxes per capita: $134 (1997).
Education: High school graduation rate: 87.1% (2000); College graduation rate: 18.2% (2000).

School District(s)

Osceola (PK-12)
2000 Enrollment: 1,725 715-294-4140
Housing: Homeownership rate: 58.6% (2000); Median home value: $98,900 (2000); Median rent: $467 per month (2000); Median age of housing: 24 years (2000).
Hospitals: Osceola Medical Center (42 beds)
Safety: Violent crime rate: 8.2 per 10,000 population; Property crime rate: 229.7 per 10,000 population (2001).
Newspapers: Osceola Sun (1 x week)
Transportation: Commute to work: 93.0% car, 0.0% public transportation, 4.3% walk, 1.9% work from home (2000); Travel time to work: 40.7% less than 15 minutes, 18.4% 15 to 30 minutes, 19.7% 30 to 45 minutes, 11.6% 45 to 60 minutes, 9.6% 60 minutes or more (2000)

OSCEOLA (town). Covers a land area of 34.948 square miles and a water area of 1.787 square miles. Located at 45.34° N. Lat.; 92.62° W. Long. Elevation is 825 feet.
Population: 2,085 (2000); Race: 99.4% White, 0.0% Black, 0.0% Asian, 0.0% American Indian and Alaska Native, 0.7% Hispanic of any race, 0.5% two or more races (2000); Density: 59.7 persons per square mile (2000); Age: 30.7% under 18, 8.3% over 64 (2000); Marriage status: 21.6% never married, 68.5% now married, 2.7% widowed, 7.2% divorced (2000); Foreign born: 0.7% (2000); Ancestry (includes multiple ancestries): 43.4% German, 21.9% Norwegian, 18.3% Swedish, 11.0% Irish, 4.6% English (2000).
Economy: In dairying and stock-raising area. Manufacturing: wooden products, metal products, electrical equipment, publishing, cheese. St. Croix Falls and Osceola Fish Hatcheries to Northeast. Employment by occupation: 14.0% management, 21.5% professional, 12.1% services, 21.6% sales, 1.0% farming, 9.8% construction, 19.9% production (2000).
Income: Per capita income: $21,865 (2000); Median household income: $55,509 (2000); Poverty rate: 2.2% (2000).
Taxes: Total city taxes per capita: $119 (1997); City property taxes per capita: $116 (1997).
Education: High school graduation rate: 90.9% (2000); College graduation rate: 23.1% (2000).
Housing: Homeownership rate: 89.7% (2000); Median home value: $138,200 (2000); Median rent: $540 per month (2000); Median age of housing: 17 years (2000).
Transportation: Commute to work: 91.8% car, 0.3% public transportation, 1.8% walk, 4.7% work from home (2000); Travel time to work: 35.9% less than 15 minutes, 20.7% 15 to 30 minutes, 14.8% 30 to 45 minutes, 13.6% 45 to 60 minutes, 14.9% 60 minutes or more (2000)

SAINT CROIX FALLS (city). Covers a land area of 3.349 square miles and a water area of 0.099 square miles. Located at 45.41° N. Lat.; 92.63° W. Long. Elevation is 850 feet.
History: The first claims were filed in St. Croix Falls in 1837, and soon lumber mills and trading posts appeared.
Population: 2,033 (2000); Race: 97.9% White, 0.0% Black, 0.5% Asian, 0.2% American Indian and Alaska Native, 1.2% Hispanic of any race, 1.1% two or more races (2000); Density: 607.1 persons per square mile (2000); Age: 23.7% under 18, 20.6% over 64 (2000); Marriage status: 20.4% never married, 54.4% now married, 13.7% widowed, 11.5% divorced (2000); Foreign born: 2.3% (2000); Ancestry (includes multiple ancestries): 31.3% German, 17.7% Swedish, 17.4% Norwegian, 8.0% Irish, 8.0% English (2000).
Economy: Single-family building permits issued: 8 (2001) / 6 (2000); Multi-family building permits issued: 0 (2001) / 6 (2000); Employment by occupation: 10.1% management, 21.5% professional, 12.8% services, 24.8% sales, 0.8% farming, 7.2% construction, 22.8% production (2000).
Income: Per capita income: $21,384 (2000); Median household income: $39,350 (2000); Poverty rate: 5.8% (2000).
Education: High school graduation rate: 86.0% (2000); College graduation rate: 24.0% (2000).

School District(s)

Saint Croix Falls (PK-12)
2000 Enrollment: 1,084 715-483-9823
Housing: Homeownership rate: 61.8% (2000); Median home value: $108,400 (2000); Median rent: $395 per month (2000); Median age of housing: 28 years (2000).
Hospitals: Saint Croix Regional Medical Center (92 beds)
Safety: Violent crime rate: 4.9 per 10,000 population; Property crime rate: 439.7 per 10,000 population (2001).
Transportation: Commute to work: 89.0% car, 0.9% public transportation, 5.2% walk, 4.6% work from home (2000); Travel time to work: 48.5% less than 15 minutes, 17.7% 15 to 30 minutes, 13.8% 30 to 45 minutes, 8.8% 45 to 60 minutes, 11.3% 60 minutes or more (2000)
Additional Information Contacts
St. Croix Falls Chamber of Commercee 715-483-3580

SAINT CROIX FALLS (town). Covers a land area of 30.915 square miles and a water area of 0.920 square miles. Located at 45.41° N. Lat.; 92.58° W. Long. Elevation is 850 feet.
Population: 1,119 (2000); Race: 98.6% White, 0.0% Black, 0.6% Asian, 0.0% American Indian and Alaska Native, 0.8% Hispanic of any race, 0.4% two or more races (2000); Density: 36.2 persons per square mile (2000); Age: 26.0% under 18, 14.1% over 64 (2000); Marriage status: 21.2% never married, 69.0% now married, 2.4% widowed, 7.5% divorced (2000); Foreign born: 1.4% (2000); Ancestry (includes multiple ancestries): 36.7% German, 18.5% Swedish, 17.7% Norwegian, 8.8% Irish, 8.3% Danish (2000).
Economy: Single-family building permits issued: 10 (2001) / 21 (2000); Multi-family building permits issued: 0 (2001) / 0 (2000); Employment by occupation: 9.1% management, 15.2% professional, 13.0% services, 25.6% sales, 1.9% farming, 10.9% construction, 24.3% production (2000).
Income: Per capita income: $18,760 (2000); Median household income: $46,500 (2000); Poverty rate: 8.9% (2000).
Education: High school graduation rate: 89.8% (2000); College graduation rate: 15.4% (2000).
Housing: Homeownership rate: 84.9% (2000); Median home value: $112,500 (2000); Median rent: $420 per month (2000); Median age of housing: 29 years (2000).
Transportation: Commute to work: 91.2% car, 0.0% public transportation, 2.3% walk, 6.6% work from home (2000); Travel time to work: 34.9% less than 15 minutes, 26.3% 15 to 30 minutes, 12.7% 30 to 45 minutes, 7.4% 45 to 60 minutes, 18.7% 60 minutes or more (2000)

STERLING (town). Covers a land area of 63.401 square miles and a water area of 1.033 square miles. Located at 45.60° N. Lat.; 92.74° W. Long.
Population: 724 (2000); Race: 99.2% White, 0.3% Black, 0.0% Asian, 0.0% American Indian and Alaska Native, 0.3% Hispanic of any race, 0.5% two or more races (2000); Density: 11.4 persons per square mile (2000); Age: 28.9% under 18, 12.0% over 64 (2000); Marriage status: 17.2% never married, 65.3% now married, 4.3% widowed, 13.2% divorced (2000); Foreign born: 0.3% (2000); Ancestry (includes multiple ancestries): 35.1% German, 21.2% Norwegian, 18.8% Swedish, 9.5% Irish, 8.2% French (except Basque) (2000).
Economy: Employment by occupation: 6.8% management, 13.3% professional, 13.3% services, 18.3% sales, 1.5% farming, 12.4% construction, 34.3% production (2000).
Income: Per capita income: $15,428 (2000); Median household income: $36,042 (2000); Poverty rate: 8.2% (2000).
Taxes: Total city taxes per capita: $33 (1997); City property taxes per capita: $30 (1997).
Education: High school graduation rate: 80.5% (2000); College graduation rate: 8.7% (2000).
Housing: Homeownership rate: 94.1% (2000); Median home value: $82,700 (2000); Median rent: $408 per month (2000); Median age of housing: 30 years (2000).
Transportation: Commute to work: 90.8% car, 0.0% public transportation, 1.5% walk, 7.7% work from home (2000); Travel time to work: 10.6% less than 15 minutes, 29.8% 15 to 30 minutes, 22.8% 30 to 45 minutes, 8.3% 45 to 60 minutes, 28.5% 60 minutes or more (2000)

WEST SWEDEN (town). Covers a land area of 32.646 square miles and a water area of 1.041 square miles. Located at 45.69° N. Lat.; 92.46° W. Long. Elevation is 1,005 feet.
Population: 731 (2000); Race: 97.2% White, 0.0% Black, 0.0% Asian, 1.5% American Indian and Alaska Native, 0.0% Hispanic of any race, 0.9% two or more races (2000); Density: 22.4 persons per square mile (2000); Age: 24.4% under 18, 16.4% over 64 (2000); Marriage status: 21.5% never married, 65.0% now married, 4.2% widowed, 9.3% divorced (2000); Foreign born: 0.0% (2000); Ancestry (includes multiple ancestries): 26.0% German, 24.4% Swedish, 19.7% Norwegian, 9.4% Danish, 8.3% English (2000).
Economy: Employment by occupation: 13.7% management, 12.9% professional, 12.6% services, 21.4% sales, 0.6% farming, 11.7% construction, 27.1% production (2000).
Income: Per capita income: $18,777 (2000); Median household income: $41,250 (2000); Poverty rate: 5.1% (2000).
Taxes: Total city taxes per capita: $83 (1997); City property taxes per capita: $81 (1997).
Education: High school graduation rate: 87.6% (2000); College graduation rate: 13.3% (2000).
Housing: Homeownership rate: 89.3% (2000); Median home value: $84,000 (2000); Median rent: $325 per month (2000); Median age of housing: 43 years (2000).
Transportation: Commute to work: 87.6% car, 0.6% public transportation, 3.2% walk, 8.1% work from home (2000); Travel time to work: 45.5% less than 15 minutes, 26.6% 15 to 30 minutes, 11.9% 30 to 45 minutes, 6.9% 45 to 60 minutes, 9.1% 60 minutes or more (2000)

Portage County

Located in central Wisconsin; crossed by the Wisconsin River; also drained by the Plover and Waupaca Rivers. Covers a land area of 806.30 square miles, a water area of 16.50 square miles, and is located in the Central Time Zone. The county government was organized in 1836. County seat is Stevens Point.

Weather Station: Stevens Point — Elevation: 1,076 feet

	Jan	Feb	Mar	Apr	May	Jun	Jul	Aug	Sep	Oct	Nov	Dec
High	23	29	40	55	68	77	81	79	70	58	41	28
Low	5	10	21	34	45	55	59	57	49	38	25	12
Precip	1.1	1.0	1.9	2.8	3.8	3.4	4.3	4.0	3.8	2.4	2.3	1.3
Snow	11.3	7.8	7.2	1.9	tr	0.0	0.0	0.0	0.0	0.1	4.1	11.0

High and Low temperatures in degrees Fahrenheit; Precipitation and Snow in inches

Population: 67,182 (2000); Race: 95.9% White, 0.3% Black, 1.9% Asian, 0.3% American Indian and Alaska Native, 1.5% Hispanic of any race, 1.0% two or more races (2000); Density: 83.3 persons per square mile (2000); Age: 24.0% under 18, 10.9% over 64 (2000).
Religion: Five largest groups: 47.4% Catholic Church, 6.1% Evangelical Lutheran Church in America, 5.4% Lutheran Church—Missouri Synod, 2.0% The United Methodist Church, 1.2% Assemblies of God (2000).
Economy: Unemployment rate: 3.7% (11/2002); Total civilian labor force: 38,510 (11/2002); Leading industries: 20.0% manufacturing; 16.0% retail trade; 13.4% finance & insurance (2000); Companies that employ more than 1,000 persons: 1 (2000); Companies that employ more than 100 persons: 39 (2000); Farms: 913 totaling 262,799 acres (1997); Minority business ownership rate: 0.0% (1997); Women business ownership rate: 26.4% (1997); Retail sales per capita: $9,332 (1997). Single-family building permits issued: 286 (2001) / 299 (2000); Multi-family building permits issued: 85 (2001) / 169 (2000).
Income: Per capita income: $19,854 (2000); Median household income: $43,487 (2000); Poverty rate: 9.5% (2000); Bankruptcy rate: 2.22% (2001).
Taxes: Total county taxes per capita: $247 (2000); County property taxes per capita: $186 (2000).
Education: High school graduation rate: 86.5% (2000); College graduation rate: 23.4% (2000).
Housing: Homeownership rate: 70.9% (2000); Median home value: $98,300 (2000); Median rent: $417 per month (2000); Median age of housing: 27 years (2000).
Health: Birth rate: 110.3 per 10,000 population (1998); Age adjusted death rate: 78.0 per 10,000 population (1999); Age adjusted cancer mortality rate: 228.3 deaths per 100,000 population (1999). Number of physicians: 13.7 per 10,000 population (1999); Number of hospital beds: 17.0 per 10,000 population (1999).
Elections: 2000 Presidential election results: 53.2% Gore, 39.1% Bush, 6.4% Nader, 0.8% Buchanan

Additional Information Contacts
Portage County Government Offices 715-346-1351
Stevens Point Area Convention & Visitors Bureau 715-344-2556
Stevens Point Chamber of Commerce 715-344-1940

Portage County Communities

ALBAN (town). Covers a land area of 35.547 square miles and a water area of 0.579 square miles. Located at 44.63° N. Lat.; 89.27° W. Long. Elevation is 1,141 feet.
Population: 897 (2000); Race: 98.0% White, 0.0% Black, 0.0% Asian, 1.0% American Indian and Alaska Native, 0.7% Hispanic of any race, 1.0% two or more races (2000); Density: 25.2 persons per square mile (2000); Age: 26.6% under 18, 15.6% over 64 (2000); Marriage status: 23.4% never married, 62.3% now married, 9.1% widowed, 5.3% divorced (2000); Foreign born: 1.0% (2000); Ancestry (includes multiple ancestries): 56.4% Polish, 36.0% German, 11.4% Norwegian, 4.8% English, 4.7% Irish (2000).
Economy: Employment by occupation: 12.6% management, 9.2% professional, 11.2% services, 24.5% sales, 1.2% farming, 15.3% construction, 26.0% production (2000).
Income: Per capita income: $15,664 (2000); Median household income: $36,250 (2000); Poverty rate: 10.3% (2000).
Taxes: Total city taxes per capita: $51 (1997); City property taxes per capita: $49 (1997).
Education: High school graduation rate: 77.7% (2000); College graduation rate: 8.2% (2000).
Housing: Homeownership rate: 90.2% (2000); Median home value: $87,900 (2000); Median rent: $285 per month (2000); Median age of housing: 34 years (2000).
Transportation: Commute to work: 80.5% car, 0.2% public transportation, 6.2% walk, 11.8% work from home (2000); Travel time to work: 22.1% less than 15 minutes, 29.9% 15 to 30 minutes, 31.6% 30 to 45 minutes, 11.2% 45 to 60 minutes, 5.3% 60 minutes or more (2000)

ALMOND (village). Covers a land area of 1.031 square miles and a water area of 0 square miles. Located at 44.26° N. Lat.; 89.40° W. Long. Elevation is 1,150 feet.
Population: 459 (2000); Race: 97.2% White, 0.0% Black, 0.0% Asian, 0.0% American Indian and Alaska Native, 7.8% Hispanic of any race, 0.5% two or more races (2000); Density: 445.2 persons per square mile (2000); Age: 27.7% under 18, 13.9% over 64 (2000); Marriage status: 23.7% never married, 57.2% now married, 9.2% widowed, 9.8% divorced (2000); Foreign born: 1.4% (2000); Ancestry (includes multiple ancestries): 45.4% German, 18.0% Polish, 12.1% Irish, 9.7% English, 7.1% Norwegian (2000).
Economy: Single-family building permits issued: 0 (2001) / 0 (2000); Multi-family building permits issued: 0 (2001) / 0 (2000); Employment by

occupation: 12.8% management, 15.8% professional, 15.8% services, 25.1% sales, 6.9% farming, 3.4% construction, 20.2% production (2000).
Income: Per capita income: $18,104 (2000); Median household income: $37,857 (2000); Poverty rate: 10.4% (2000).
Taxes: Total city taxes per capita: $88 (1997); City property taxes per capita: $79 (1997).
Education: High school graduation rate: 90.0% (2000); College graduation rate: 25.1% (2000).

School District(s)

Almond-Bancroft (PK-12)
2000 Enrollment: 529 715-366-7331
Housing: Homeownership rate: 72.4% (2000); Median home value: $65,200 (2000); Median rent: $332 per month (2000); Median age of housing: 60+ years (2000).
Transportation: Commute to work: 84.2% car, 0.0% public transportation, 10.3% walk, 3.0% work from home (2000); Travel time to work: 42.6% less than 15 minutes, 14.2% 15 to 30 minutes, 32.0% 30 to 45 minutes, 5.6% 45 to 60 minutes, 5.6% 60 minutes or more (2000)

ALMOND (town). Covers a land area of 43.109 square miles and a water area of 0.120 square miles. Located at 44.29° N. Lat.; 89.42° W. Long. Elevation is 1,150 feet.
Population: 679 (2000); Race: 99.1% White, 0.0% Black, 0.0% Asian, 0.7% American Indian and Alaska Native, 2.7% Hispanic of any race, 0.3% two or more races (2000); Density: 15.8 persons per square mile (2000); Age: 27.8% under 18, 12.0% over 64 (2000); Marriage status: 24.3% never married, 66.3% now married, 3.0% widowed, 6.4% divorced (2000); Foreign born: 1.0% (2000); Ancestry (includes multiple ancestries): 41.2% German, 23.7% Polish, 15.6% Irish, 9.7% English, 5.0% Other groups (2000).
Economy: In dairy and farm area. Employment by occupation: 18.8% management, 12.0% professional, 16.1% services, 19.0% sales, 4.2% farming, 11.5% construction, 18.5% production (2000).
Income: Per capita income: $17,962 (2000); Median household income: $45,156 (2000); Poverty rate: 6.6% (2000).
Taxes: Total city taxes per capita: $161 (1997); City property taxes per capita: $159 (1997).
Education: High school graduation rate: 84.4% (2000); College graduation rate: 13.2% (2000).
Housing: Homeownership rate: 86.5% (2000); Median home value: $100,600 (2000); Median rent: $328 per month (2000); Median age of housing: 27 years (2000).
Transportation: Commute to work: 89.8% car, 0.0% public transportation, 3.8% walk, 5.4% work from home (2000); Travel time to work: 32.3% less than 15 minutes, 30.9% 15 to 30 minutes, 28.3% 30 to 45 minutes, 5.1% 45 to 60 minutes, 3.4% 60 minutes or more (2000)

AMHERST (village). Covers a land area of 1.165 square miles and a water area of 0.035 square miles. Located at 44.45° N. Lat.; 89.28° W. Long. Elevation is 1,050 feet.
Population: 964 (2000); Race: 99.5% White, 0.0% Black, 0.0% Asian, 0.0% American Indian and Alaska Native, 0.0% Hispanic of any race, 0.4% two or more races (2000); Density: 827.5 persons per square mile (2000); Age: 29.9% under 18, 11.2% over 64 (2000); Marriage status: 27.0% never married, 58.0% now married, 6.5% widowed, 8.5% divorced (2000); Foreign born: 1.6% (2000); Ancestry (includes multiple ancestries): 42.4% German, 31.3% Polish, 12.1% Norwegian, 7.9% English, 6.6% Irish (2000).
Economy: Single-family building permits issued: 5 (2001) / 7 (2000); Multi-family building permits issued: 0 (2001) / 0 (2000); Employment by occupation: 10.2% management, 20.1% professional, 13.1% services, 22.9% sales, 1.5% farming, 7.2% construction, 25.0% production (2000).
Income: Per capita income: $18,514 (2000); Median household income: $40,125 (2000); Poverty rate: 10.8% (2000).
Taxes: Total city taxes per capita: $53 (1997); City property taxes per capita: $34 (1997).
Education: High school graduation rate: 88.2% (2000); College graduation rate: 20.0% (2000).

School District(s)

Tomorrow River (PK-12)
2000 Enrollment: 883 715-824-5521
Housing: Homeownership rate: 64.9% (2000); Median home value: $91,900 (2000); Median rent: $384 per month (2000); Median age of housing: 34 years (2000).
Transportation: Commute to work: 88.9% car, 0.0% public transportation, 8.2% walk, 2.3% work from home (2000); Travel time to work: 37.1% less than 15 minutes, 42.7% 15 to 30 minutes, 12.2% 30 to 45 minutes, 2.5% 45 to 60 minutes, 5.5% 60 minutes or more (2000)

AMHERST (town). Covers a land area of 37.981 square miles and a water area of 0.519 square miles. Located at 44.45° N. Lat.; 89.30° W. Long. Elevation is 1,050 feet.
Population: 1,435 (2000); Race: 99.5% White, 0.0% Black, 0.2% Asian, 0.3% American Indian and Alaska Native, 0.0% Hispanic of any race, 0.0% two or more races (2000); Density: 37.8 persons per square mile (2000); Age: 23.5% under 18, 14.2% over 64 (2000); Marriage status: 20.7% never married, 68.8% now married, 4.6% widowed, 5.9% divorced (2000); Foreign born: 0.2% (2000); Ancestry (includes multiple ancestries): 35.7% German, 33.8% Polish, 15.6% Norwegian, 9.6% Irish, 7.8% English (2000).
Economy: Trade center in dairy, timber. Poultry and trucking industry. Employment by occupation: 14.6% management, 19.9% professional, 11.4% services, 19.9% sales, 2.4% farming, 11.8% construction, 19.8% production (2000).
Income: Per capita income: $19,751 (2000); Median household income: $50,435 (2000); Poverty rate: 6.8% (2000).
Taxes: Total city taxes per capita: $71 (1997); City property taxes per capita: $70 (1997).
Education: High school graduation rate: 86.0% (2000); College graduation rate: 16.3% (2000).
Housing: Homeownership rate: 88.4% (2000); Median home value: $106,000 (2000); Median rent: $296 per month (2000); Median age of housing: 27 years (2000).
Transportation: Commute to work: 90.3% car, 0.3% public transportation, 3.1% walk, 6.3% work from home (2000); Travel time to work: 30.1% less than 15 minutes, 44.9% 15 to 30 minutes, 16.7% 30 to 45 minutes, 2.7% 45 to 60 minutes, 5.6% 60 minutes or more (2000)

AMHERST JUNCTION (village). Covers a land area of 1.191 square miles and a water area of 0.016 square miles. Located at 44.47° N. Lat.; 89.31° W. Long. Elevation is 1,126 feet.
Population: 305 (2000); Race: 100.0% White, 0.0% Black, 0.0% Asian, 0.0% American Indian and Alaska Native, 0.0% Hispanic of any race, 0.0% two or more races (2000); Density: 256.2 persons per square mile (2000); Age: 34.6% under 18, 7.4% over 64 (2000); Marriage status: 26.0% never married, 65.5% now married, 3.5% widowed, 5.0% divorced (2000); Foreign born: 0.0% (2000); Ancestry (includes multiple ancestries): 43.1% German, 41.3% Polish, 16.6% Norwegian, 7.1% Irish, 6.4% Swedish (2000).
Economy: Railroad junction. Standing Rock Ski Area to Southwest. Single-family building permits issued: 5 (2001) / 1 (2000); Multi-family building permits issued: 0 (2001) / 0 (2000); Employment by occupation: 13.5% management, 13.5% professional, 11.3% services, 19.1% sales, 2.1% farming, 11.3% construction, 29.1% production (2000).
Income: Per capita income: $19,261 (2000); Median household income: $44,500 (2000); Poverty rate: 1.8% (2000).
Taxes: Total city taxes per capita: $40 (1997); City property taxes per capita: $36 (1997).
Education: High school graduation rate: 94.6% (2000); College graduation rate: 14.9% (2000).
Housing: Homeownership rate: 80.8% (2000); Median home value: $98,800 (2000); Median rent: $407 per month (2000); Median age of housing: 25 years (2000).
Transportation: Commute to work: 93.5% car, 0.0% public transportation, 2.2% walk, 3.6% work from home (2000); Travel time to work: 23.9% less than 15 minutes, 59.7% 15 to 30 minutes, 13.4% 30 to 45 minutes, 1.5% 45 to 60 minutes, 1.5% 60 minutes or more (2000)

BANCROFT (unincorporated postal area, zip code 54921). Covers a land area of 81.360 square miles and a water area of 0.041 square miles. Located at 44.30° N. Lat.; 89.54° W. Long. Elevation is 1,090 feet.
Population: 1,372 (2000); Race: 95.5% White, 0.0% Black, 0.2% Asian, 0.2% American Indian and Alaska Native, 7.6% Hispanic of any race, 0.6% two or more races (2000); Density: 16.9 persons per square mile (2000); Age: 26.4% under 18, 11.0% over 64 (2000); Marriage status: 23.8% never married, 62.0% now married, 5.2% widowed, 9.0% divorced (2000); Foreign born: 3.6% (2000); Ancestry (includes multiple ancestries): 35.0% German, 30.6% Polish, 10.8% Other groups, 10.5% Irish, 9.8% English (2000).
Economy: Employment by occupation: 10.3% management, 9.9% professional, 11.7% services, 19.1% sales, 8.6% farming, 15.4% construction, 24.8% production (2000).
Income: Per capita income: $17,215 (2000); Median household income: $40,083 (2000); Poverty rate: 9.7% (2000).
Education: High school graduation rate: 76.6% (2000); College graduation rate: 8.5% (2000).

Housing: Homeownership rate: 89.1% (2000); Median home value: $75,800 (2000); Median rent: $275 per month (2000); Median age of housing: 24 years (2000).
Transportation: Commute to work: 89.8% car, 0.0% public transportation, 1.9% walk, 7.5% work from home (2000); Travel time to work: 19.9% less than 15 minutes, 53.0% 15 to 30 minutes, 18.2% 30 to 45 minutes, 1.7% 45 to 60 minutes, 7.2% 60 minutes or more (2000)

BELMONT (town). Covers a land area of 36.074 square miles and a water area of 0.158 square miles. Located at 44.28° N. Lat.; 89.27° W. Long.
Population: 623 (2000); Race: 99.8% White, 0.2% Black, 0.0% Asian, 0.0% American Indian and Alaska Native, 0.0% Hispanic of any race, 0.0% two or more races (2000); Density: 17.3 persons per square mile (2000); Age: 23.7% under 18, 9.2% over 64 (2000); Marriage status: 24.0% never married, 60.6% now married, 4.1% widowed, 11.3% divorced (2000); Foreign born: 0.7% (2000); Ancestry (includes multiple ancestries): 42.6% German, 28.2% Polish, 10.7% Norwegian, 10.7% Irish, 4.0% English (2000).
Economy: Single-family building permits issued: 5 (2001) / 4 (2000); Multi-family building permits issued: 0 (2001) / 0 (2000); Employment by occupation: 14.6% management, 11.0% professional, 10.7% services, 18.5% sales, 7.1% farming, 15.6% construction, 22.4% production (2000).
Income: Per capita income: $20,427 (2000); Median household income: $46,591 (2000); Poverty rate: 9.4% (2000).
Taxes: Total city taxes per capita: $70 (1997); City property taxes per capita: $68 (1997).
Education: High school graduation rate: 84.4% (2000); College graduation rate: 11.0% (2000).
Housing: Homeownership rate: 90.5% (2000); Median home value: $93,500 (2000); Median rent: $292 per month (2000); Median age of housing: 27 years (2000).
Transportation: Commute to work: 88.5% car, 0.0% public transportation, 3.6% walk, 6.9% work from home (2000); Travel time to work: 18.0% less than 15 minutes, 41.0% 15 to 30 minutes, 29.3% 30 to 45 minutes, 6.4% 45 to 60 minutes, 5.3% 60 minutes or more (2000)

BUENA VISTA (town). Covers a land area of 61.322 square miles and a water area of 0.042 square miles. Located at 44.37° N. Lat.; 89.44° W. Long.
Population: 1,187 (2000); Race: 99.1% White, 0.0% Black, 0.2% Asian, 0.0% American Indian and Alaska Native, 0.7% Hispanic of any race, 0.6% two or more races (2000); Density: 19.4 persons per square mile (2000); Age: 28.0% under 18, 9.1% over 64 (2000); Marriage status: 23.6% never married, 64.0% now married, 4.2% widowed, 8.2% divorced (2000); Foreign born: 1.6% (2000); Ancestry (includes multiple ancestries): 36.5% Polish, 35.9% German, 8.2% Irish, 8.0% English, 4.9% Czech (2000).
Economy: Employment by occupation: 12.1% management, 13.9% professional, 9.0% services, 25.7% sales, 3.9% farming, 16.0% construction, 19.6% production (2000).
Income: Per capita income: $18,775 (2000); Median household income: $46,920 (2000); Poverty rate: 5.9% (2000).
Taxes: Total city taxes per capita: $42 (1997); City property taxes per capita: $41 (1997).
Education: High school graduation rate: 84.2% (2000); College graduation rate: 13.4% (2000).
Housing: Homeownership rate: 90.2% (2000); Median home value: $94,100 (2000); Median rent: $281 per month (2000); Median age of housing: 26 years (2000).
Transportation: Commute to work: 87.3% car, 1.1% public transportation, 0.9% walk, 9.0% work from home (2000); Travel time to work: 20.7% less than 15 minutes, 60.2% 15 to 30 minutes, 12.1% 30 to 45 minutes, 2.5% 45 to 60 minutes, 4.5% 60 minutes or more (2000)

CARSON (town). Covers a land area of 53.896 square miles and a water area of 1.101 square miles. Located at 44.56° N. Lat.; 89.73° W. Long.
Population: 1,299 (2000); Race: 99.1% White, 0.0% Black, 0.3% Asian, 0.0% American Indian and Alaska Native, 0.0% Hispanic of any race, 0.6% two or more races (2000); Density: 24.1 persons per square mile (2000); Age: 25.8% under 18, 11.9% over 64 (2000); Marriage status: 25.3% never married, 61.8% now married, 6.0% widowed, 6.9% divorced (2000); Foreign born: 1.9% (2000); Ancestry (includes multiple ancestries): 48.9% German, 43.5% Polish, 7.2% Norwegian, 5.6% English, 5.0% Irish (2000).
Economy: Employment by occupation: 16.0% management, 9.2% professional, 11.0% services, 22.9% sales, 2.9% farming, 11.0% construction, 27.0% production (2000).
Income: Per capita income: $21,576 (2000); Median household income: $51,583 (2000); Poverty rate: 3.8% (2000).
Taxes: Total city taxes per capita: $51 (1997); City property taxes per capita: $49 (1997).
Education: High school graduation rate: 80.9% (2000); College graduation rate: 13.8% (2000).
Housing: Homeownership rate: 93.2% (2000); Median home value: $96,600 (2000); Median rent: $386 per month (2000); Median age of housing: 36 years (2000).
Transportation: Commute to work: 85.1% car, 0.4% public transportation, 2.3% walk, 11.4% work from home (2000); Travel time to work: 18.4% less than 15 minutes, 53.3% 15 to 30 minutes, 21.0% 30 to 45 minutes, 5.3% 45 to 60 minutes, 2.0% 60 minutes or more (2000)

CUSTER (unincorporated postal area, zip code 54423). Covers a land area of 54.043 square miles and a water area of 0.466 square miles. Located at 44.58° N. Lat.; 89.42° W. Long. Elevation is 1,175 feet.
Population: 2,029 (2000); Race: 97.8% White, 0.6% Black, 0.5% Asian, 0.0% American Indian and Alaska Native, 0.7% Hispanic of any race, 1.0% two or more races (2000); Density: 37.5 persons per square mile (2000); Age: 25.7% under 18, 11.4% over 64 (2000); Marriage status: 23.7% never married, 64.4% now married, 5.2% widowed, 6.7% divorced (2000); Foreign born: 1.0% (2000); Ancestry (includes multiple ancestries): 56.3% Polish, 31.5% German, 6.5% English, 5.5% Norwegian, 4.5% Irish (2000).
Economy: Employment by occupation: 14.7% management, 12.7% professional, 11.8% services, 28.7% sales, 2.4% farming, 11.1% construction, 18.6% production (2000).
Income: Per capita income: $20,934 (2000); Median household income: $54,167 (2000); Poverty rate: 3.4% (2000).
Education: High school graduation rate: 84.9% (2000); College graduation rate: 16.3% (2000).
Housing: Homeownership rate: 90.6% (2000); Median home value: $110,100 (2000); Median rent: $481 per month (2000); Median age of housing: 24 years (2000).
Transportation: Commute to work: 87.2% car, 0.7% public transportation, 2.3% walk, 9.4% work from home (2000); Travel time to work: 15.8% less than 15 minutes, 64.8% 15 to 30 minutes, 12.1% 30 to 45 minutes, 3.5% 45 to 60 minutes, 3.7% 60 minutes or more (2000)

DEWEY (town). Covers a land area of 45.283 square miles and a water area of 1.745 square miles. Located at 44.63° N. Lat.; 89.57° W. Long.
Population: 975 (2000); Race: 100.0% White, 0.0% Black, 0.0% Asian, 0.0% American Indian and Alaska Native, 1.8% Hispanic of any race, 0.0% two or more races (2000); Density: 21.5 persons per square mile (2000); Age: 22.7% under 18, 10.1% over 64 (2000); Marriage status: 25.0% never married, 67.2% now married, 2.3% widowed, 5.5% divorced (2000); Foreign born: 0.2% (2000); Ancestry (includes multiple ancestries): 60.1% Polish, 33.3% German, 4.6% Irish, 3.6% French (except Basque), 3.5% English (2000).
Economy: Employment by occupation: 11.6% management, 16.4% professional, 12.3% services, 21.3% sales, 2.1% farming, 12.3% construction, 23.9% production (2000).
Income: Per capita income: $24,623 (2000); Median household income: $50,391 (2000); Poverty rate: 6.9% (2000).
Taxes: Total city taxes per capita: $75 (1997); City property taxes per capita: $67 (1997).
Education: High school graduation rate: 86.1% (2000); College graduation rate: 19.8% (2000).
Housing: Homeownership rate: 90.0% (2000); Median home value: $121,400 (2000); Median rent: $394 per month (2000); Median age of housing: 20 years (2000).
Transportation: Commute to work: 93.6% car, 0.0% public transportation, 2.3% walk, 4.1% work from home (2000); Travel time to work: 16.0% less than 15 minutes, 65.7% 15 to 30 minutes, 11.2% 30 to 45 minutes, 3.9% 45 to 60 minutes, 3.2% 60 minutes or more (2000)

EAU PLEINE (town). Covers a land area of 55.465 square miles and a water area of 2.259 square miles. Located at 44.64° N. Lat.; 89.72° W. Long.
Population: 931 (2000); Race: 97.1% White, 0.4% Black, 1.3% Asian, 0.0% American Indian and Alaska Native, 2.0% Hispanic of any race, 1.2% two or more races (2000); Density: 16.8 persons per square mile (2000); Age: 28.8% under 18, 16.1% over 64 (2000); Marriage status: 21.6% never married, 66.8% now married, 4.3% widowed, 7.2% divorced (2000); Foreign born: 1.4% (2000); Ancestry (includes multiple ancestries): 47.3% German, 28.8% Polish, 9.6% Irish, 5.9% English, 5.4% Norwegian (2000).
Economy: Employment by occupation: 18.1% management, 11.4% professional, 9.5% services, 22.8% sales, 1.1% farming, 12.0% construction, 25.2% production (2000).

Income: Per capita income: $20,301 (2000); Median household income: $49,167 (2000); Poverty rate: 4.8% (2000).
Taxes: Total city taxes per capita: $53 (1997); City property taxes per capita: $52 (1997).
Education: High school graduation rate: 82.5% (2000); College graduation rate: 17.1% (2000).
Housing: Homeownership rate: 84.5% (2000); Median home value: $129,700 (2000); Median rent: $288 per month (2000); Median age of housing: 32 years (2000).
Transportation: Commute to work: 86.8% car, 1.5% public transportation, 2.8% walk, 7.1% work from home (2000); Travel time to work: 14.7% less than 15 minutes, 42.8% 15 to 30 minutes, 33.5% 30 to 45 minutes, 5.8% 45 to 60 minutes, 3.3% 60 minutes or more (2000)

GRANT (town). Covers a land area of 71.219 square miles and a water area of 0.023 square miles. Located at 44.34° N. Lat.; 89.67° W. Long.
Population: 2,020 (2000); Race: 98.6% White, 0.0% Black, 0.4% Asian, 0.0% American Indian and Alaska Native, 0.4% Hispanic of any race, 0.9% two or more races (2000); Density: 28.4 persons per square mile (2000); Age: 26.9% under 18, 8.2% over 64 (2000); Marriage status: 19.3% never married, 69.1% now married, 3.1% widowed, 8.5% divorced (2000); Foreign born: 0.8% (2000); Ancestry (includes multiple ancestries): 48.3% German, 18.9% Polish, 10.6% Irish, 7.0% English, 6.5% United States or American (2000).
Economy: Single-family building permits issued: 13 (2001) / 17 (2000); Multi-family building permits issued: 0 (2001) / 0 (2000); Employment by occupation: 9.8% management, 11.9% professional, 8.8% services, 21.6% sales, 1.4% farming, 15.0% construction, 31.5% production (2000).
Income: Per capita income: $21,793 (2000); Median household income: $52,459 (2000); Poverty rate: 2.9% (2000).
Taxes: Total city taxes per capita: $46 (1997); City property taxes per capita: $44 (1997).
Education: High school graduation rate: 87.9% (2000); College graduation rate: 11.6% (2000).
Housing: Homeownership rate: 91.8% (2000); Median home value: $96,500 (2000); Median rent: $442 per month (2000); Median age of housing: 23 years (2000).
Transportation: Commute to work: 94.4% car, 0.2% public transportation, 2.1% walk, 3.0% work from home (2000); Travel time to work: 25.9% less than 15 minutes, 58.0% 15 to 30 minutes, 11.3% 30 to 45 minutes, 1.7% 45 to 60 minutes, 3.1% 60 minutes or more (2000)

HULL (town). Covers a land area of 28.268 square miles and a water area of 3.572 square miles. Located at 44.54° N. Lat.; 89.54° W. Long.
Population: 5,493 (2000); Race: 97.7% White, 0.0% Black, 1.1% Asian, 0.0% American Indian and Alaska Native, 2.7% Hispanic of any race, 1.2% two or more races (2000); Density: 194.3 persons per square mile (2000); Age: 28.9% under 18, 8.7% over 64 (2000); Marriage status: 21.1% never married, 69.4% now married, 4.5% widowed, 5.0% divorced (2000); Foreign born: 2.2% (2000); Ancestry (includes multiple ancestries): 43.6% Polish, 37.4% German, 7.6% Norwegian, 7.4% Irish, 7.0% English (2000).
Economy: Employment by occupation: 16.4% management, 18.7% professional, 9.4% services, 28.8% sales, 0.4% farming, 9.1% construction, 17.2% production (2000).
Income: Per capita income: $22,433 (2000); Median household income: $53,915 (2000); Poverty rate: 5.2% (2000).
Taxes: Total city taxes per capita: $59 (1997); City property taxes per capita: $53 (1997).
Education: High school graduation rate: 90.4% (2000); College graduation rate: 31.1% (2000).
Housing: Homeownership rate: 88.1% (2000); Median home value: $117,300 (2000); Median rent: $404 per month (2000); Median age of housing: 23 years (2000).
Transportation: Commute to work: 96.1% car, 0.0% public transportation, 0.4% walk, 2.4% work from home (2000); Travel time to work: 49.2% less than 15 minutes, 37.7% 15 to 30 minutes, 4.5% 30 to 45 minutes, 3.7% 45 to 60 minutes, 5.0% 60 minutes or more (2000)

JUNCTION CITY (village). Covers a land area of 1.188 square miles and a water area of 0.004 square miles. Located at 44.59° N. Lat.; 89.76° W. Long. Elevation is 1,150 feet.
Population: 440 (2000); Race: 97.4% White, 0.0% Black, 1.8% Asian, 0.0% American Indian and Alaska Native, 3.1% Hispanic of any race, 0.5% two or more races (2000); Density: 370.4 persons per square mile (2000); Age: 27.8% under 18, 12.1% over 64 (2000); Marriage status: 26.5% never married, 52.3% now married, 8.7% widowed, 12.4% divorced (2000); Foreign born: 1.0% (2000); Ancestry (includes multiple ancestries): 38.7% German, 33.0% Polish, 10.1% Irish, 7.0% Norwegian, 4.9% Other groups (2000).
Economy: Makes cheese. Railroad junction. Single-family building permits issued: 0 (2001) / 1 (2000); Multi-family building permits issued: 0 (2001) / 0 (2000); Employment by occupation: 10.1% management, 11.6% professional, 18.0% services, 22.2% sales, 2.6% farming, 11.6% construction, 23.8% production (2000).
Income: Per capita income: $17,648 (2000); Median household income: $33,750 (2000); Poverty rate: 15.8% (2000).
Taxes: Total city taxes per capita: $14 (1997); City property taxes per capita: $0 (1997).
Education: High school graduation rate: 77.9% (2000); College graduation rate: 9.4% (2000).
Housing: Homeownership rate: 72.1% (2000); Median home value: $69,000 (2000); Median rent: $318 per month (2000); Median age of housing: 41 years (2000).
Transportation: Commute to work: 84.6% car, 1.1% public transportation, 6.0% walk, 8.2% work from home (2000); Travel time to work: 24.6% less than 15 minutes, 27.5% 15 to 30 minutes, 38.3% 30 to 45 minutes, 2.4% 45 to 60 minutes, 7.2% 60 minutes or more (2000)

LANARK (town). Covers a land area of 35.882 square miles and a water area of 0.184 square miles. Located at 44.36° N. Lat.; 89.27° W. Long.
Population: 1,449 (2000); Race: 98.8% White, 0.8% Black, 0.3% Asian, 0.0% American Indian and Alaska Native, 0.3% Hispanic of any race, 0.0% two or more races (2000); Density: 40.4 persons per square mile (2000); Age: 28.3% under 18, 11.8% over 64 (2000); Marriage status: 22.1% never married, 66.6% now married, 4.8% widowed, 6.5% divorced (2000); Foreign born: 0.9% (2000); Ancestry (includes multiple ancestries): 42.2% German, 17.8% Polish, 12.3% Irish, 9.2% Norwegian, 7.8% English (2000).
Economy: Employment by occupation: 11.7% management, 13.3% professional, 14.4% services, 25.7% sales, 2.2% farming, 13.0% construction, 19.6% production (2000).
Income: Per capita income: $19,246 (2000); Median household income: $41,932 (2000); Poverty rate: 6.7% (2000).
Taxes: Total city taxes per capita: $50 (1997); City property taxes per capita: $49 (1997).
Education: High school graduation rate: 86.8% (2000); College graduation rate: 14.6% (2000).
Housing: Homeownership rate: 89.0% (2000); Median home value: $93,100 (2000); Median rent: $343 per month (2000); Median age of housing: 26 years (2000).
Transportation: Commute to work: 94.2% car, 0.0% public transportation, 0.7% walk, 4.4% work from home (2000); Travel time to work: 20.1% less than 15 minutes, 54.1% 15 to 30 minutes, 18.5% 30 to 45 minutes, 2.9% 45 to 60 minutes, 4.5% 60 minutes or more (2000)

LINWOOD (town). Covers a land area of 31.939 square miles and a water area of 1.843 square miles. Located at 44.48° N. Lat.; 89.64° W. Long.
Population: 1,111 (2000); Race: 99.6% White, 0.0% Black, 0.0% Asian, 0.2% American Indian and Alaska Native, 0.0% Hispanic of any race, 0.2% two or more races (2000); Density: 34.8 persons per square mile (2000); Age: 25.2% under 18, 10.7% over 64 (2000); Marriage status: 19.7% never married, 69.9% now married, 4.4% widowed, 6.0% divorced (2000); Foreign born: 0.1% (2000); Ancestry (includes multiple ancestries): 56.9% Polish, 41.5% German, 8.1% English, 5.8% Irish, 3.5% Norwegian (2000).
Economy: Employment by occupation: 10.0% management, 17.1% professional, 7.7% services, 21.0% sales, 0.8% farming, 11.6% construction, 31.9% production (2000).
Income: Per capita income: $21,073 (2000); Median household income: $55,972 (2000); Poverty rate: 3.0% (2000).
Taxes: Total city taxes per capita: $37 (1997); City property taxes per capita: $36 (1997).
Education: High school graduation rate: 88.5% (2000); College graduation rate: 19.6% (2000).
Housing: Homeownership rate: 95.1% (2000); Median home value: $112,900 (2000); Median rent: $375 per month (2000); Median age of housing: 26 years (2000).
Transportation: Commute to work: 94.9% car, 0.0% public transportation, 0.9% walk, 4.2% work from home (2000); Travel time to work: 27.9% less than 15 minutes, 58.0% 15 to 30 minutes, 9.3% 30 to 45 minutes, 2.1% 45 to 60 minutes, 2.8% 60 minutes or more (2000)

NELSONVILLE (village). Covers a land area of 1.001 square miles and a water area of 0.044 square miles. Located at 44.49° N. Lat.; 89.31° W. Long. Elevation is 1,080 feet.

Population: 191 (2000); Race: 98.6% White, 1.4% Black, 0.0% Asian, 0.0% American Indian and Alaska Native, 0.0% Hispanic of any race, 0.0% two or more races (2000); Density: 190.7 persons per square mile (2000); Age: 32.9% under 18, 11.0% over 64 (2000); Marriage status: 17.0% never married, 71.4% now married, 7.5% widowed, 4.1% divorced (2000); Foreign born: 1.4% (2000); Ancestry (includes multiple ancestries): 49.0% German, 45.2% Polish, 16.7% Norwegian, 7.6% Irish, 3.3% United States or American (2000).
Economy: Dairying area. Single-family building permits issued: 1 (2001) / 0 (2000); Multi-family building permits issued: 0 (2001) / 0 (2000); Employment by occupation: 17.8% management, 7.9% professional, 15.8% services, 28.7% sales, 2.0% farming, 12.9% construction, 14.9% production (2000).
Income: Per capita income: $19,708 (2000); Median household income: $41,875 (2000); Poverty rate: 2.4% (2000).
Taxes: Total city taxes per capita: $31 (1997); City property taxes per capita: $31 (1997).
Education: High school graduation rate: 85.2% (2000); College graduation rate: 21.9% (2000).
Housing: Homeownership rate: 79.2% (2000); Median home value: $82,500 (2000); Median rent: $303 per month (2000); Median age of housing: 60+ years (2000).
Transportation: Commute to work: 87.9% car, 0.0% public transportation, 0.0% walk, 12.1% work from home (2000); Travel time to work: 39.1% less than 15 minutes, 50.6% 15 to 30 minutes, 8.0% 30 to 45 minutes, 0.0% 45 to 60 minutes, 2.3% 60 minutes or more (2000)

NEW HOPE (town). Covers a land area of 35.855 square miles and a water area of 0.501 square miles. Located at 44.54° N. Lat.; 89.27° W. Long. Elevation is 1,154 feet.
Population: 736 (2000); Race: 98.0% White, 0.0% Black, 0.0% Asian, 0.7% American Indian and Alaska Native, 0.4% Hispanic of any race, 0.1% two or more races (2000); Density: 20.5 persons per square mile (2000); Age: 25.6% under 18, 14.8% over 64 (2000); Marriage status: 21.8% never married, 69.0% now married, 3.8% widowed, 5.3% divorced (2000); Foreign born: 0.0% (2000); Ancestry (includes multiple ancestries): 39.2% German, 39.2% Polish, 17.1% Norwegian, 7.9% Irish, 7.9% English (2000).
Economy: Employment by occupation: 10.9% management, 29.1% professional, 8.1% services, 20.3% sales, 1.6% farming, 8.3% construction, 21.8% production (2000).
Income: Per capita income: $21,334 (2000); Median household income: $46,538 (2000); Poverty rate: 6.3% (2000).
Taxes: Total city taxes per capita: $33 (1997); City property taxes per capita: $33 (1997).
Education: High school graduation rate: 79.4% (2000); College graduation rate: 34.0% (2000).
Housing: Homeownership rate: 83.5% (2000); Median home value: $109,400 (2000); Median rent: $370 per month (2000); Median age of housing: 31 years (2000).
Transportation: Commute to work: 86.1% car, 0.0% public transportation, 4.7% walk, 9.2% work from home (2000); Travel time to work: 19.7% less than 15 minutes, 43.6% 15 to 30 minutes, 20.8% 30 to 45 minutes, 4.9% 45 to 60 minutes, 11.0% 60 minutes or more (2000)

PARK RIDGE (village). Covers a land area of 0.217 square miles and a water area of 0 square miles. Located at 44.52° N. Lat.; 89.54° W. Long. Elevation is 1,095 feet.
Population: 488 (2000); Race: 99.8% White, 0.0% Black, 0.2% Asian, 0.0% American Indian and Alaska Native, 1.2% Hispanic of any race, 0.0% two or more races (2000); Density: 2,243.8 persons per square mile (2000); Age: 21.8% under 18, 22.8% over 64 (2000); Marriage status: 17.5% never married, 68.9% now married, 7.5% widowed, 6.1% divorced (2000); Foreign born: 0.8% (2000); Ancestry (includes multiple ancestries): 41.3% German, 31.5% Polish, 12.8% English, 8.6% Swedish, 8.6% Irish (2000).
Economy: Single-family building permits issued: 0 (2001) / 0 (2000); Multi-family building permits issued: 0 (2001) / 0 (2000); Employment by occupation: 14.2% management, 36.2% professional, 8.5% services, 29.2% sales, 0.0% farming, 3.8% construction, 8.1% production (2000).
Income: Per capita income: $28,074 (2000); Median household income: $57,031 (2000); Poverty rate: 0.8% (2000).
Taxes: Total city taxes per capita: $192 (1997); City property taxes per capita: $188 (1997).
Education: High school graduation rate: 93.6% (2000); College graduation rate: 52.9% (2000).
Housing: Homeownership rate: 93.8% (2000); Median home value: $126,000 (2000); Median rent: $446 per month (2000); Median age of housing: 45 years (2000).
Transportation: Commute to work: 87.7% car, 0.0% public transportation, 4.0% walk, 7.5% work from home (2000); Travel time to work: 82.1% less than 15 minutes, 12.8% 15 to 30 minutes, 4.3% 30 to 45 minutes, 0.0% 45 to 60 minutes, 0.9% 60 minutes or more (2000)

PINE GROVE (town). Covers a land area of 37.661 square miles and a water area of 0.043 square miles. Located at 44.29° N. Lat.; 89.53° W. Long.
Population: 904 (2000); Race: 94.0% White, 0.0% Black, 0.0% Asian, 0.4% American Indian and Alaska Native, 13.5% Hispanic of any race, 0.1% two or more races (2000); Density: 24.0 persons per square mile (2000); Age: 27.1% under 18, 13.5% over 64 (2000); Marriage status: 24.6% never married, 59.0% now married, 5.6% widowed, 10.8% divorced (2000); Foreign born: 5.6% (2000); Ancestry (includes multiple ancestries): 39.1% German, 22.7% Polish, 17.5% Other groups, 10.6% English, 9.5% Irish (2000).
Economy: Employment by occupation: 8.3% management, 7.8% professional, 15.5% services, 13.7% sales, 10.2% farming, 16.1% construction, 28.4% production (2000).
Income: Per capita income: $18,257 (2000); Median household income: $35,294 (2000); Poverty rate: 10.0% (2000).
Taxes: Total city taxes per capita: $73 (1997); City property taxes per capita: $69 (1997).
Education: High school graduation rate: 69.9% (2000); College graduation rate: 6.0% (2000).
Housing: Homeownership rate: 87.8% (2000); Median home value: $67,300 (2000); Median rent: $235 per month (2000); Median age of housing: 27 years (2000).
Transportation: Commute to work: 90.4% car, 0.0% public transportation, 2.2% walk, 6.6% work from home (2000); Travel time to work: 31.0% less than 15 minutes, 30.1% 15 to 30 minutes, 28.4% 30 to 45 minutes, 2.3% 45 to 60 minutes, 8.2% 60 minutes or more (2000)

PLOVER (village). Covers a land area of 8.496 square miles and a water area of 0.384 square miles. Located at 44.46° N. Lat.; 89.54° W. Long. Elevation is 1,075 feet.
History: Plover began as a lumber camp. It served as the seat of Portage County from 1844 to 1867.
Population: 10,520 (2000); Race: 97.1% White, 0.6% Black, 0.6% Asian, 0.3% American Indian and Alaska Native, 0.9% Hispanic of any race, 1.0% two or more races (2000); Density: 1,238.2 persons per square mile (2000); Age: 29.2% under 18, 5.7% over 64 (2000); Marriage status: 24.0% never married, 63.1% now married, 3.9% widowed, 9.0% divorced (2000); Foreign born: 1.0% (2000); Ancestry (includes multiple ancestries): 41.8% German, 28.2% Polish, 11.4% Irish, 7.7% Norwegian, 7.4% English (2000).
Economy: Single-family building permits issued: 47 (2001) / 54 (2000); Multi-family building permits issued: 38 (2001) / 63 (2000); Employment by occupation: 17.2% management, 19.2% professional, 11.7% services, 28.2% sales, 0.4% farming, 5.6% construction, 17.6% production (2000).
Income: Per capita income: $23,085 (2000); Median household income: $51,238 (2000); Poverty rate: 6.0% (2000).
Taxes: Total city taxes per capita: $221 (1997); City property taxes per capita: $201 (1997).
Education: High school graduation rate: 91.5% (2000); College graduation rate: 30.6% (2000).
Housing: Homeownership rate: 67.6% (2000); Median home value: $118,200 (2000); Median rent: $467 per month (2000); Median age of housing: 15 years (2000).
Safety: Violent crime rate: 6.6 per 10,000 population; Property crime rate: 188.8 per 10,000 population (2001).
Transportation: Commute to work: 94.8% car, 0.3% public transportation, 1.4% walk, 2.2% work from home (2000); Travel time to work: 54.0% less than 15 minutes, 33.4% 15 to 30 minutes, 7.2% 30 to 45 minutes, 2.7% 45 to 60 minutes, 2.6% 60 minutes or more (2000)

PLOVER (town). Covers a land area of 42.293 square miles and a water area of 1.339 square miles. Located at 44.45° N. Lat.; 89.58° W. Long. Elevation is 1,075 feet.
Population: 2,415 (2000); Race: 96.8% White, 0.0% Black, 1.1% Asian, 0.0% American Indian and Alaska Native, 1.6% Hispanic of any race, 2.1% two or more races (2000); Density: 57.1 persons per square mile (2000); Age: 26.4% under 18, 12.4% over 64 (2000); Marriage status: 27.0% never married, 62.6% now married, 3.9% widowed, 6.5% divorced (2000); Foreign

born: 0.8% (2000); Ancestry (includes multiple ancestries): 38.2% German, 32.6% Polish, 11.9% Irish, 10.2% English, 7.6% Other groups (2000).
Economy: Railroad junction. Standing Rock Ski Area to East. Vegetables, potatoes; dairying. Manufacturing: machinery, food. Employment by occupation: 17.6% management, 13.4% professional, 7.4% services, 27.6% sales, 1.3% farming, 12.3% construction, 20.6% production (2000).
Income: Per capita income: $21,186 (2000); Median household income: $49,313 (2000); Poverty rate: 3.7% (2000).
Taxes: Total city taxes per capita: $147 (2000); City property taxes per capita: $128 (2000).
Education: High school graduation rate: 85.5% (2000); College graduation rate: 22.4% (2000).
Housing: Homeownership rate: 86.0% (2000); Median home value: $116,600 (2000); Median rent: $443 per month (2000); Median age of housing: 22 years (2000).
Transportation: Commute to work: 95.3% car, 0.0% public transportation, 0.8% walk, 2.9% work from home (2000); Travel time to work: 53.2% less than 15 minutes, 39.4% 15 to 30 minutes, 4.2% 30 to 45 minutes, 0.9% 45 to 60 minutes, 2.3% 60 minutes or more (2000)

ROSHOLT (village). Covers a land area of 1.063 square miles and a water area of 0.032 square miles. Located at 44.63° N. Lat.; 89.30° W. Long. Elevation is 1,130 feet.
Population: 518 (2000); Race: 99.7% White, 0.0% Black, 0.0% Asian, 0.3% American Indian and Alaska Native, 2.3% Hispanic of any race, 0.0% two or more races (2000); Density: 487.1 persons per square mile (2000); Age: 31.9% under 18, 12.0% over 64 (2000); Marriage status: 27.6% never married, 58.3% now married, 6.9% widowed, 7.1% divorced (2000); Foreign born: 1.2% (2000); Ancestry (includes multiple ancestries): 45.3% Polish, 27.5% German, 12.0% Norwegian, 8.7% Irish, 4.9% United States or American (2000).
Economy: In dairying area. Single-family building permits issued: 0 (2001) / 0 (2000); Multi-family building permits issued: 0 (2001) / 0 (2000); Employment by occupation: 6.7% management, 12.3% professional, 17.3% services, 21.1% sales, 0.7% farming, 12.7% construction, 29.2% production (2000).
Income: Per capita income: $16,002 (2000); Median household income: $42,750 (2000); Poverty rate: 6.1% (2000).
Taxes: Total city taxes per capita: $45 (1997); City property taxes per capita: $37 (1997).
Education: High school graduation rate: 80.5% (2000); College graduation rate: 8.3% (2000).

School District(s)

Rosholt (PK-12)
2000 Enrollment: 774 715-677-4542

Housing: Homeownership rate: 70.3% (2000); Median home value: $64,300 (2000); Median rent: $317 per month (2000); Median age of housing: 60+ years (2000).
Transportation: Commute to work: 87.5% car, 0.0% public transportation, 8.5% walk, 3.2% work from home (2000); Travel time to work: 27.2% less than 15 minutes, 25.7% 15 to 30 minutes, 29.4% 30 to 45 minutes, 9.9% 45 to 60 minutes, 7.7% 60 minutes or more (2000)

SHARON (town). Covers a land area of 64.285 square miles and a water area of 0.580 square miles. Located at 44.60° N. Lat.; 89.41° W. Long.
Population: 1,936 (2000); Race: 98.9% White, 0.0% Black, 0.2% Asian, 0.0% American Indian and Alaska Native, 0.7% Hispanic of any race, 0.6% two or more races (2000); Density: 30.1 persons per square mile (2000); Age: 24.9% under 18, 10.9% over 64 (2000); Marriage status: 24.9% never married, 64.5% now married, 5.3% widowed, 5.3% divorced (2000); Foreign born: 1.0% (2000); Ancestry (includes multiple ancestries): 63.5% Polish, 29.2% German, 5.0% Norwegian, 4.0% Irish, 3.9% English (2000).
Economy: Employment by occupation: 12.2% management, 11.3% professional, 12.5% services, 28.7% sales, 1.6% farming, 12.5% construction, 21.3% production (2000).
Income: Per capita income: $20,760 (2000); Median household income: $53,750 (2000); Poverty rate: 5.7% (2000).
Taxes: Total city taxes per capita: $58 (1997); City property taxes per capita: $57 (1997).
Education: High school graduation rate: 81.6% (2000); College graduation rate: 13.3% (2000).
Housing: Homeownership rate: 90.3% (2000); Median home value: $109,900 (2000); Median rent: $463 per month (2000); Median age of housing: 24 years (2000).
Transportation: Commute to work: 91.6% car, 0.0% public transportation, 1.2% walk, 6.8% work from home (2000); Travel time to work: 14.5% less than 15 minutes, 60.2% 15 to 30 minutes, 15.9% 30 to 45 minutes, 5.3% 45 to 60 minutes, 4.1% 60 minutes or more (2000)

STEVENS POINT (city). Covers a land area of 15.314 square miles and a water area of 0.912 square miles. Located at 44.52° N. Lat.; 89.56° W. Long. Elevation is 1,093 feet.
History: Stevens Point was founded in 1839 by George Stevens as a stopping place on the trip between Wisconsin Rapids and Mosinee. A settlement soon grew up, with the economy later based on the paper plants that lined the riverbanks. The Hardware Mutual Casualty Insurance Company was organized here in 1914. Many of the early residents of Stevens Point were of Polish ancestry, part of the group that migrated to Portage County in 1857.
Population: 24,551 (2000); Race: 92.4% White, 0.6% Black, 4.2% Asian, 0.7% American Indian and Alaska Native, 1.6% Hispanic of any race, 1.4% two or more races (2000); Density: 1,603.2 persons per square mile (2000); Age: 18.2% under 18, 12.1% over 64 (2000); Marriage status: 43.9% never married, 42.0% now married, 6.5% widowed, 7.6% divorced (2000); Foreign born: 3.8% (2000); Ancestry (includes multiple ancestries): 39.6% German, 26.7% Polish, 9.7% Irish, 7.5% Other groups, 6.5% English (2000).
Vital Statistics: Birth rate: 127.5 per 10,000 population (1998)
Economy: Single-family building permits issued: 66 (2001) / 48 (2000); Multi-family building permits issued: 47 (2001) / 82 (2000); Employment by occupation: 9.6% management, 19.3% professional, 19.7% services, 29.8% sales, 0.5% farming, 5.3% construction, 15.8% production (2000).
Income: Per capita income: $17,510 (2000); Median household income: $33,178 (2000); Poverty rate: 17.3% (2000).
Taxes: Total city taxes per capita: $405 (2000); City property taxes per capita: $371 (2000).
Education: High school graduation rate: 85.1% (2000); College graduation rate: 26.1% (2000).

School District(s)

Stevens Point Area (PK-12)
2000 Enrollment: 7,871 715-345-5444

Four-year College(s)

University of Wisconsin-Stevens Point (Public)
2001 Enrollment: 8,832 715-346-4301
2001 Tuition: In-state $2,776; Out-of-state $11,288

Housing: Homeownership rate: 52.5% (2000); Median home value: $80,800 (2000); Median rent: $407 per month (2000); Median age of housing: 38 years (2000).
Hospitals: Saint Michael's Hospital (181 beds)
Safety: Violent crime rate: 23.9 per 10,000 population; Property crime rate: 383.0 per 10,000 population (2001).
Newspapers: Stevens Point Journal (7 x week); Gwiazda Polarna (1 x week)
Transportation: Commute to work: 79.2% car, 0.8% public transportation, 12.0% walk, 3.8% work from home (2000); Travel time to work: 66.9% less than 15 minutes, 20.8% 15 to 30 minutes, 7.2% 30 to 45 minutes, 2.2% 45 to 60 minutes, 2.9% 60 minutes or more (2000)
Airports: Stevens Point Municipal
Additional Information Contacts
Stevens Point Area Convention & Visitors Bureau 715-344-2556
Stevens Point Chamber of Commerce 715-344-1940

STOCKTON (town). Covers a land area of 57.700 square miles and a water area of 0.144 square miles. Located at 44.49° N. Lat.; 89.41° W. Long. Elevation is 1,133 feet.
Population: 2,896 (2000); Race: 98.2% White, 0.4% Black, 0.6% Asian, 0.0% American Indian and Alaska Native, 0.2% Hispanic of any race, 0.8% two or more races (2000); Density: 50.2 persons per square mile (2000); Age: 27.8% under 18, 7.9% over 64 (2000); Marriage status: 23.7% never married, 66.4% now married, 3.0% widowed, 6.9% divorced (2000); Foreign born: 0.6% (2000); Ancestry (includes multiple ancestries): 55.8% Polish, 36.4% German, 7.3% Irish, 6.3% English, 5.7% Norwegian (2000).
Economy: Employment by occupation: 14.2% management, 11.7% professional, 15.6% services, 27.1% sales, 3.3% farming, 9.2% construction, 18.9% production (2000).
Income: Per capita income: $19,886 (2000); Median household income: $50,957 (2000); Poverty rate: 2.8% (2000).
Taxes: Total city taxes per capita: $63 (1997); City property taxes per capita: $58 (1997).
Education: High school graduation rate: 88.3% (2000); College graduation rate: 16.0% (2000).
Housing: Homeownership rate: 91.2% (2000); Median home value: $108,900 (2000); Median rent: $420 per month (2000); Median age of housing: 23 years (2000).

Transportation: Commute to work: 89.5% car, 0.9% public transportation, 2.5% walk, 7.1% work from home (2000); Travel time to work: 27.3% less than 15 minutes, 56.7% 15 to 30 minutes, 8.9% 30 to 45 minutes, 3.5% 45 to 60 minutes, 3.6% 60 minutes or more (2000)

WHITING (village). Covers a land area of 1.861 square miles and a water area of 0.274 square miles. Located at 44.48° N. Lat.; 89.56° W. Long. Elevation is 1,069 feet.
Population: 1,760 (2000); Race: 95.6% White, 0.0% Black, 2.4% Asian, 0.5% American Indian and Alaska Native, 0.9% Hispanic of any race, 0.6% two or more races (2000); Density: 945.7 persons per square mile (2000); Age: 19.0% under 18, 26.5% over 64 (2000); Marriage status: 19.5% never married, 66.7% now married, 9.4% widowed, 4.4% divorced (2000); Foreign born: 2.9% (2000); Ancestry (includes multiple ancestries): 34.4% German, 34.1% Polish, 6.3% English, 5.3% Irish, 5.0% French (except Basque) (2000).
Economy: Single-family building permits issued: 4 (2001) / 8 (2000); Multi-family building permits issued: 0 (2001) / 24 (2000); Employment by occupation: 10.3% management, 17.1% professional, 10.8% services, 30.3% sales, 0.7% farming, 7.2% construction, 23.6% production (2000).
Income: Per capita income: $19,492 (2000); Median household income: $42,381 (2000); Poverty rate: 5.7% (2000).
Taxes: Total city taxes per capita: $166 (1997); City property taxes per capita: $158 (1997).
Education: High school graduation rate: 84.0% (2000); College graduation rate: 22.8% (2000).
Housing: Homeownership rate: 74.7% (2000); Median home value: $97,000 (2000); Median rent: $383 per month (2000); Median age of housing: 31 years (2000).
Transportation: Commute to work: 91.1% car, 0.0% public transportation, 4.1% walk, 4.3% work from home (2000); Travel time to work: 62.8% less than 15 minutes, 26.1% 15 to 30 minutes, 6.3% 30 to 45 minutes, 1.7% 45 to 60 minutes, 3.1% 60 minutes or more (2000)

Price County

Located in northern Wisconsin; drained by the Flambeau and Jump Rivers; includes part of Chequamegon National Forest. Covers a land area of 1,252.60 square miles, a water area of 25.90 square miles, and is located in the Central Time Zone. The county government was organized in 1879. County seat is Phillips.

Weather Station: Prentice 2 Elevation: 1,538 feet

	Jan	Feb	Mar	Apr	May	Jun	Jul	Aug	Sep	Oct	Nov	Dec
High	20	26	37	52	66	74	78	76	67	55	37	24
Low	-3	2	15	29	41	49	54	52	44	33	21	5
Precip	0.9	0.6	1.5	2.2	3.4	3.9	4.1	4.1	4.4	2.8	2.0	1.1
Snow	13.4	8.3	9.7	3.5	0.2	0.0	0.0	0.0	tr	1.1	6.9	11.8

High and Low temperatures in degrees Fahrenheit; Precipitation and Snow in inches

Population: 15,822 (2000); Race: 98.5% White, 0.2% Black, 0.1% Asian, 0.4% American Indian and Alaska Native, 0.5% Hispanic of any race, 0.5% two or more races (2000); Density: 12.6 persons per square mile (2000); Age: 23.9% under 18, 19.0% over 64 (2000).
Religion: Five largest groups: 31.2% Catholic Church, 11.7% Lutheran Church—Missouri Synod, 10.0% Evangelical Lutheran Church in America, 4.4% Baptist General Conference, 2.4% United Church of Christ (2000).
Economy: Unemployment rate: 4.2% (11/2002); Total civilian labor force: 6,981 (11/2002); Leading industries: 44.6% manufacturing; 16.3% health care and social assistance; 13.0% retail trade (2000); Companies that employ more than 1,000 persons: 0 (2000); Companies that employ more than 100 persons: 9 (2000); Farms: 370 totaling 92,599 acres (1997); Minority business ownership rate: 0.0% (1997); Women business ownership rate: 16.5% (1997); Retail sales per capita: $6,784 (1997). Single-family building permits issued: 162 (2001) / 173 (2000); Multi-family building permits issued: 10 (2001) / 0 (2000).
Income: Per capita income: $17,837 (2000); Median household income: $35,249 (2000); Poverty rate: 8.9% (2000); Bankruptcy rate: 1.77% (2001).
Taxes: Total county taxes per capita: $283 (1997); County property taxes per capita: $244 (1997).
Education: High school graduation rate: 82.4% (2000); College graduation rate: 13.0% (2000).
Housing: Homeownership rate: 80.8% (2000); Median home value: $70,100 (2000); Median rent: $336 per month (2000); Median age of housing: 34 years (2000).
Health: Birth rate: 99.2 per 10,000 population (1998); Age adjusted death rate: 85.5 per 10,000 population (1999); Age adjusted cancer mortality rate: 172.2 deaths per 100,000 population (1999). Number of physicians: 8.8 per 10,000 population (1999); Number of hospital beds: 26.5 per 10,000 population (1999).
Elections: 2000 Presidential election results: 43.0% Gore, 52.2% Bush, 4.0% Nader, 0.6% Buchanan
National and State Parks: Spring Creek National Wildlife Area; Township Corners State Wildlife Management Area
Additional Information Contacts
Price County Government Offices 715-339-3325
Park Falls Chamber of Commerce 715-762-2703
Phillips Chamber of Commerce 715-339-4100

Price County Communities

BRANTWOOD (unincorporated postal area, zip code 54513). Covers a land area of 112.242 square miles and a water area of 0.111 square miles. Located at 45.54° N. Lat.; 90.13° W. Long. Elevation is 690 feet.
Population: 575 (2000); Race: 98.3% White, 0.0% Black, 0.4% Asian, 0.7% American Indian and Alaska Native, 0.6% Hispanic of any race, 0.0% two or more races (2000); Density: 5.1 persons per square mile (2000); Age: 20.1% under 18, 23.0% over 64 (2000); Marriage status: 18.9% never married, 66.7% now married, 7.2% widowed, 7.2% divorced (2000); Foreign born: 0.4% (2000); Ancestry (includes multiple ancestries): 35.4% German, 23.2% Finnish, 11.6% Swedish, 7.7% Irish, 6.3% Norwegian (2000).
Economy: Employment by occupation: 14.3% management, 12.2% professional, 10.5% services, 14.7% sales, 13.9% farming, 9.2% construction, 25.2% production (2000).
Income: Per capita income: $19,820 (2000); Median household income: $29,868 (2000); Poverty rate: 8.7% (2000).
Education: High school graduation rate: 69.8% (2000); College graduation rate: 8.9% (2000).
Housing: Homeownership rate: 84.1% (2000); Median home value: $53,800 (2000); Median rent: $275 per month (2000); Median age of housing: 30 years (2000).
Transportation: Commute to work: 91.9% car, 0.0% public transportation, 2.6% walk, 5.5% work from home (2000); Travel time to work: 23.4% less than 15 minutes, 28.8% 15 to 30 minutes, 32.4% 30 to 45 minutes, 6.8% 45 to 60 minutes, 8.6% 60 minutes or more (2000)

CATAWBA (village). Covers a land area of 4.456 square miles and a water area of 0 square miles. Located at 45.53° N. Lat.; 90.53° W. Long. Elevation is 1,510 feet.
Population: 149 (2000); Race: 98.7% White, 0.0% Black, 0.0% Asian, 0.0% American Indian and Alaska Native, 0.0% Hispanic of any race, 1.3% two or more races (2000); Density: 33.4 persons per square mile (2000); Age: 16.7% under 18, 24.7% over 64 (2000); Marriage status: 27.9% never married, 51.2% now married, 14.7% widowed, 6.2% divorced (2000); Foreign born: 0.0% (2000); Ancestry (includes multiple ancestries): 38.7% German, 16.0% Irish, 10.0% Polish, 6.7% Czech, 6.7% Norwegian (2000).
Economy: Single-family building permits issued: 0 (2001) / 0 (2000); Multi-family building permits issued: 0 (2001) / 0 (2000); Employment by occupation: 11.9% management, 14.9% professional, 9.0% services, 11.9% sales, 3.0% farming, 10.4% construction, 38.8% production (2000).
Income: Per capita income: $18,319 (2000); Median household income: $26,250 (2000); Poverty rate: 6.0% (2000).
Taxes: Total city taxes per capita: $43 (1997); City property taxes per capita: $37 (1997).
Education: High school graduation rate: 73.9% (2000); College graduation rate: 7.8% (2000).
Housing: Homeownership rate: 85.9% (2000); Median home value: $38,300 (2000); Median rent: $267 per month (2000); Median age of housing: 38 years (2000).
Transportation: Commute to work: 73.1% car, 6.0% public transportation, 11.9% walk, 9.0% work from home (2000); Travel time to work: 23.0% less than 15 minutes, 54.1% 15 to 30 minutes, 14.8% 30 to 45 minutes, 8.2% 45 to 60 minutes, 0.0% 60 minutes or more (2000)

CATAWBA (town). Covers a land area of 49.979 square miles and a water area of 0.020 square miles. Located at 45.48° N. Lat.; 90.49° W. Long. Elevation is 1,510 feet.
Population: 283 (2000); Race: 99.0% White, 1.0% Black, 0.0% Asian, 0.0% American Indian and Alaska Native, 0.0% Hispanic of any race, 0.0% two or more races (2000); Density: 5.7 persons per square mile (2000); Age: 29.2%

under 18, 13.9% over 64 (2000); Marriage status: 14.1% never married, 69.0% now married, 6.6% widowed, 10.3% divorced (2000); Foreign born: 0.0% (2000); Ancestry (includes multiple ancestries): 48.6% German, 12.2% Polish, 10.4% Norwegian, 7.3% Dutch, 6.9% Czechoslovakian (2000).
Economy: In wooded area; dairying. Employment by occupation: 9.0% management, 8.3% professional, 11.3% services, 11.3% sales, 6.0% farming, 6.0% construction, 48.1% production (2000).
Income: Per capita income: $14,235 (2000); Median household income: $33,571 (2000); Poverty rate: 4.5% (2000).
Taxes: Total city taxes per capita: $36 (1997); City property taxes per capita: $36 (1997).
Education: High school graduation rate: 79.9% (2000); College graduation rate: 7.4% (2000).
Housing: Homeownership rate: 89.7% (2000); Median home value: $38,800 (2000); Median rent: $125 per month (2000); Median age of housing: 31 years (2000).
Transportation: Commute to work: 87.1% car, 0.0% public transportation, 0.0% walk, 10.5% work from home (2000); Travel time to work: 18.0% less than 15 minutes, 45.9% 15 to 30 minutes, 30.6% 30 to 45 minutes, 1.8% 45 to 60 minutes, 3.6% 60 minutes or more (2000)

EISENSTEIN (town). Covers a land area of 74.917 square miles and a water area of 1.413 square miles. Located at 45.93° N. Lat.; 90.29° W. Long.
Population: 669 (2000); Race: 96.8% White, 0.0% Black, 0.0% Asian, 1.6% American Indian and Alaska Native, 0.1% Hispanic of any race, 1.6% two or more races (2000); Density: 8.9 persons per square mile (2000); Age: 21.6% under 18, 18.1% over 64 (2000); Marriage status: 24.0% never married, 61.1% now married, 6.3% widowed, 8.6% divorced (2000); Foreign born: 0.3% (2000); Ancestry (includes multiple ancestries): 58.8% German, 12.8% Irish, 11.0% Norwegian, 8.5% Polish, 5.9% English (2000).
Economy: Employment by occupation: 7.1% management, 15.1% professional, 18.5% services, 22.2% sales, 6.3% farming, 7.4% construction, 23.6% production (2000).
Income: Per capita income: $18,414 (2000); Median household income: $38,026 (2000); Poverty rate: 7.8% (2000).
Taxes: Total city taxes per capita: $31 (1997); City property taxes per capita: $29 (1997).
Education: High school graduation rate: 85.3% (2000); College graduation rate: 14.5% (2000).
Housing: Homeownership rate: 87.2% (2000); Median home value: $81,600 (2000); Median rent: $525 per month (2000); Median age of housing: 29 years (2000).
Transportation: Commute to work: 94.6% car, 0.0% public transportation, 1.4% walk, 3.2% work from home (2000); Travel time to work: 55.6% less than 15 minutes, 22.2% 15 to 30 minutes, 10.7% 30 to 45 minutes, 5.0% 45 to 60 minutes, 6.5% 60 minutes or more (2000)

ELK (town). Covers a land area of 50.825 square miles and a water area of 2.725 square miles. Located at 45.69° N. Lat.; 90.51° W. Long.
Population: 1,183 (2000); Race: 99.4% White, 0.0% Black, 0.3% Asian, 0.0% American Indian and Alaska Native, 0.0% Hispanic of any race, 0.1% two or more races (2000); Density: 23.3 persons per square mile (2000); Age: 21.8% under 18, 19.9% over 64 (2000); Marriage status: 17.5% never married, 70.0% now married, 7.6% widowed, 4.9% divorced (2000); Foreign born: 0.3% (2000); Ancestry (includes multiple ancestries): 45.6% German, 11.6% Irish, 11.2% Norwegian, 8.1% Polish, 7.7% Czech (2000).
Economy: Employment by occupation: 15.6% management, 20.4% professional, 15.1% services, 20.4% sales, 1.0% farming, 8.0% construction, 19.5% production (2000).
Income: Per capita income: $22,310 (2000); Median household income: $41,953 (2000); Poverty rate: 5.7% (2000).
Education: High school graduation rate: 84.7% (2000); College graduation rate: 20.5% (2000).
Housing: Homeownership rate: 87.2% (2000); Median home value: $107,900 (2000); Median rent: $448 per month (2000); Median age of housing: 27 years (2000).
Transportation: Commute to work: 92.3% car, 0.0% public transportation, 0.9% walk, 6.4% work from home (2000); Travel time to work: 57.7% less than 15 minutes, 27.7% 15 to 30 minutes, 7.4% 30 to 45 minutes, 2.0% 45 to 60 minutes, 5.0% 60 minutes or more (2000)

EMERY (town). Covers a land area of 108.119 square miles and a water area of 0.096 square miles. Located at 45.70° N. Lat.; 90.17° W. Long.
Population: 325 (2000); Race: 97.9% White, 0.0% Black, 0.6% Asian, 0.9% American Indian and Alaska Native, 0.0% Hispanic of any race, 0.6% two or more races (2000); Density: 3.0 persons per square mile (2000); Age: 23.8% under 18, 19.7% over 64 (2000); Marriage status: 17.2% never married, 66.7% now married, 5.9% widowed, 10.3% divorced (2000); Foreign born: 1.2% (2000); Ancestry (includes multiple ancestries): 34.4% German, 20.0% Czech, 10.0% Swedish, 6.8% Irish, 6.8% French (except Basque) (2000).
Economy: Employment by occupation: 8.6% management, 9.8% professional, 18.4% services, 16.7% sales, 2.9% farming, 11.5% construction, 32.2% production (2000).
Income: Per capita income: $17,100 (2000); Median household income: $39,250 (2000); Poverty rate: 5.1% (2000).
Taxes: Total city taxes per capita: $25 (1997); City property taxes per capita: $25 (1997).
Education: High school graduation rate: 79.5% (2000); College graduation rate: 9.6% (2000).
Housing: Homeownership rate: 91.1% (2000); Median home value: $55,800 (2000); Median rent: $325 per month (2000); Median age of housing: 53 years (2000).
Transportation: Commute to work: 85.6% car, 2.9% public transportation, 5.2% walk, 6.3% work from home (2000); Travel time to work: 22.1% less than 15 minutes, 52.8% 15 to 30 minutes, 14.1% 30 to 45 minutes, 2.5% 45 to 60 minutes, 8.6% 60 minutes or more (2000)

FIFIELD (town). Covers a land area of 149.380 square miles and a water area of 7.088 square miles. Located at 45.88° N. Lat.; 90.28° W. Long. Elevation is 1,451 feet.
History: Fifield was named for Sam S. Fifield, Lieutenant Governor of Wisconsin from 1882 to 1887. It was once the major lumbering town of the region, and an unsuccessful candidate for the seat of Price County.
Population: 989 (2000); Race: 98.1% White, 0.0% Black, 0.0% Asian, 1.7% American Indian and Alaska Native, 1.6% Hispanic of any race, 0.2% two or more races (2000); Density: 6.6 persons per square mile (2000); Age: 19.6% under 18, 18.8% over 64 (2000); Marriage status: 18.4% never married, 66.0% now married, 6.1% widowed, 9.4% divorced (2000); Foreign born: 0.8% (2000); Ancestry (includes multiple ancestries): 51.4% German, 8.3% United States or American, 8.2% Irish, 6.8% Polish, 6.7% Norwegian (2000).
Economy: Employment by occupation: 7.9% management, 11.5% professional, 18.8% services, 15.8% sales, 4.1% farming, 16.5% construction, 25.3% production (2000).
Income: Per capita income: $19,083 (2000); Median household income: $35,833 (2000); Poverty rate: 6.9% (2000).
Taxes: Total city taxes per capita: $283 (1997); City property taxes per capita: $279 (1997).
Education: High school graduation rate: 85.0% (2000); College graduation rate: 13.0% (2000).
Housing: Homeownership rate: 84.3% (2000); Median home value: $87,100 (2000); Median rent: $284 per month (2000); Median age of housing: 25 years (2000).
Transportation: Commute to work: 91.0% car, 1.4% public transportation, 3.0% walk, 3.9% work from home (2000); Travel time to work: 43.9% less than 15 minutes, 37.4% 15 to 30 minutes, 13.2% 30 to 45 minutes, 3.4% 45 to 60 minutes, 2.2% 60 minutes or more (2000)

FLAMBEAU (town). Covers a land area of 95.783 square miles and a water area of 2.599 square miles. Located at 45.77° N. Lat.; 90.56° W. Long.
Population: 535 (2000); Race: 98.9% White, 0.0% Black, 0.0% Asian, 0.4% American Indian and Alaska Native, 0.7% Hispanic of any race, 0.4% two or more races (2000); Density: 5.6 persons per square mile (2000); Age: 26.4% under 18, 10.0% over 64 (2000); Marriage status: 22.0% never married, 58.4% now married, 9.8% widowed, 9.8% divorced (2000); Foreign born: 1.1% (2000); Ancestry (includes multiple ancestries): 44.1% German, 14.1% Czech, 12.5% Irish, 10.4% Slovak, 9.1% Polish (2000).
Economy: Employment by occupation: 12.3% management, 10.1% professional, 14.8% services, 20.6% sales, 1.1% farming, 14.1% construction, 27.1% production (2000).
Income: Per capita income: $15,196 (2000); Median household income: $41,250 (2000); Poverty rate: 11.6% (2000).
Taxes: Total city taxes per capita: $102 (1997); City property taxes per capita: $100 (1997).
Education: High school graduation rate: 84.1% (2000); College graduation rate: 15.6% (2000).
Housing: Homeownership rate: 91.3% (2000); Median home value: $66,700 (2000); Median rent: $275 per month (2000); Median age of housing: 26 years (2000).
Transportation: Commute to work: 92.8% car, 0.0% public transportation, 1.1% walk, 5.4% work from home (2000); Travel time to work: 27.5% less than 15 minutes, 50.8% 15 to 30 minutes, 10.7% 30 to 45 minutes, 3.8% 45 to 60 minutes, 7.3% 60 minutes or more (2000)

GEORGETOWN (town). Covers a land area of 53.609 square miles and a water area of 0.132 square miles. Located at 45.59° N. Lat.; 90.62° W. Long.
Population: 164 (2000); Race: 100.0% White, 0.0% Black, 0.0% Asian, 0.0% American Indian and Alaska Native, 0.0% Hispanic of any race, 0.0% two or more races (2000); Density: 3.1 persons per square mile (2000); Age: 26.4% under 18, 13.2% over 64 (2000); Marriage status: 19.2% never married, 60.8% now married, 10.4% widowed, 9.6% divorced (2000); Foreign born: 0.0% (2000); Ancestry (includes multiple ancestries): 38.4% German, 13.2% Polish, 12.6% Czech, 10.7% French (except Basque), 8.8% English (2000).
Economy: Employment by occupation: 11.0% management, 2.4% professional, 19.5% services, 14.6% sales, 0.0% farming, 12.2% construction, 40.2% production (2000).
Income: Per capita income: $14,222 (2000); Median household income: $37,500 (2000); Poverty rate: 23.3% (2000).
Taxes: Total city taxes per capita: $36 (1997); City property taxes per capita: $36 (1997).
Education: High school graduation rate: 78.7% (2000); College graduation rate: 3.7% (2000).
Housing: Homeownership rate: 90.0% (2000); Median home value: $45,000 (2000); Median rent: $125 per month (2000); Median age of housing: 35 years (2000).
Transportation: Commute to work: 89.0% car, 0.0% public transportation, 0.0% walk, 11.0% work from home (2000); Travel time to work: 26.0% less than 15 minutes, 43.8% 15 to 30 minutes, 21.9% 30 to 45 minutes, 5.5% 45 to 60 minutes, 2.7% 60 minutes or more (2000)

HACKETT (town). Covers a land area of 69.524 square miles and a water area of 1.375 square miles. Located at 45.60° N. Lat.; 90.30° W. Long.
Population: 202 (2000); Race: 96.7% White, 0.0% Black, 0.0% Asian, 0.0% American Indian and Alaska Native, 3.3% Hispanic of any race, 2.7% two or more races (2000); Density: 2.9 persons per square mile (2000); Age: 21.2% under 18, 20.7% over 64 (2000); Marriage status: 22.3% never married, 64.3% now married, 7.6% widowed, 5.7% divorced (2000); Foreign born: 0.0% (2000); Ancestry (includes multiple ancestries): 39.1% German, 19.6% Polish, 16.8% Czech, 16.3% Irish, 14.1% Swedish (2000).
Economy: Employment by occupation: 18.6% management, 15.7% professional, 6.9% services, 16.7% sales, 4.9% farming, 16.7% construction, 20.6% production (2000).
Income: Per capita income: $16,283 (2000); Median household income: $30,625 (2000); Poverty rate: 3.8% (2000).
Taxes: Total city taxes per capita: $37 (1997); City property taxes per capita: $37 (1997).
Education: High school graduation rate: 82.1% (2000); College graduation rate: 7.5% (2000).
Housing: Homeownership rate: 92.5% (2000); Median home value: $58,300 (2000); Median age of housing: 38 years (2000).
Transportation: Commute to work: 80.0% car, 0.0% public transportation, 2.0% walk, 16.0% work from home (2000); Travel time to work: 34.5% less than 15 minutes, 35.7% 15 to 30 minutes, 16.7% 30 to 45 minutes, 8.3% 45 to 60 minutes, 4.8% 60 minutes or more (2000)

HARMONY (town). Covers a land area of 34.954 square miles and a water area of 0.641 square miles. Located at 45.58° N. Lat.; 90.47° W. Long.
Population: 211 (2000); Race: 100.0% White, 0.0% Black, 0.0% Asian, 0.0% American Indian and Alaska Native, 0.0% Hispanic of any race, 0.0% two or more races (2000); Density: 6.0 persons per square mile (2000); Age: 18.9% under 18, 20.8% over 64 (2000); Marriage status: 23.2% never married, 61.1% now married, 4.3% widowed, 11.4% divorced (2000); Foreign born: 0.0% (2000); Ancestry (includes multiple ancestries): 50.0% German, 11.3% Swedish, 9.4% English, 9.0% Czechoslovakian, 7.5% Czech (2000).
Economy: Employment by occupation: 8.8% management, 18.6% professional, 13.3% services, 11.5% sales, 1.8% farming, 11.5% construction, 34.5% production (2000).
Income: Per capita income: $20,953 (2000); Median household income: $38,281 (2000); Poverty rate: 2.8% (2000).
Taxes: Total city taxes per capita: $103 (1997); City property taxes per capita: $103 (1997).
Education: High school graduation rate: 81.4% (2000); College graduation rate: 18.6% (2000).
Housing: Homeownership rate: 89.5% (2000); Median home value: $77,000 (2000); Median rent: $225 per month (2000); Median age of housing: 36 years (2000).
Transportation: Commute to work: 89.9% car, 0.0% public transportation, 0.0% walk, 7.3% work from home (2000); Travel time to work: 7.9% less than 15 minutes, 73.3% 15 to 30 minutes, 8.9% 30 to 45 minutes, 5.0% 45 to 60 minutes, 5.0% 60 minutes or more (2000)

HILL (town). Covers a land area of 35.054 square miles and a water area of 0.682 square miles. Located at 45.43° N. Lat.; 90.22° W. Long.
Population: 364 (2000); Race: 99.7% White, 0.0% Black, 0.3% Asian, 0.0% American Indian and Alaska Native, 0.0% Hispanic of any race, 0.0% two or more races (2000); Density: 10.4 persons per square mile (2000); Age: 26.7% under 18, 14.1% over 64 (2000); Marriage status: 21.5% never married, 67.0% now married, 7.7% widowed, 3.7% divorced (2000); Foreign born: 0.3% (2000); Ancestry (includes multiple ancestries): 33.8% German, 30.9% Swedish, 9.4% Finnish, 8.4% Irish, 5.8% English (2000).
Economy: Employment by occupation: 18.9% management, 21.1% professional, 4.6% services, 13.7% sales, 6.9% farming, 8.6% construction, 26.3% production (2000).
Income: Per capita income: $23,222 (2000); Median household income: $34,464 (2000); Poverty rate: 5.8% (2000).
Taxes: Total city taxes per capita: $67 (1997); City property taxes per capita: $67 (1997).
Education: High school graduation rate: 91.2% (2000); College graduation rate: 14.7% (2000).
Housing: Homeownership rate: 95.1% (2000); Median home value: $77,000 (2000); Median age of housing: 30 years (2000).
Transportation: Commute to work: 86.0% car, 0.0% public transportation, 2.3% walk, 10.5% work from home (2000); Travel time to work: 27.5% less than 15 minutes, 30.1% 15 to 30 minutes, 24.2% 30 to 45 minutes, 5.2% 45 to 60 minutes, 13.1% 60 minutes or more (2000)

KENNAN (village). Covers a land area of 1.973 square miles and a water area of 0 square miles. Located at 45.53° N. Lat.; 90.58° W. Long. Elevation is 1,510 feet.
Population: 171 (2000); Race: 100.0% White, 0.0% Black, 0.0% Asian, 0.0% American Indian and Alaska Native, 0.0% Hispanic of any race, 0.0% two or more races (2000); Density: 86.7 persons per square mile (2000); Age: 25.7% under 18, 10.2% over 64 (2000); Marriage status: 26.5% never married, 66.2% now married, 4.0% widowed, 3.3% divorced (2000); Foreign born: 0.0% (2000); Ancestry (includes multiple ancestries): 38.5% German, 15.5% Polish, 8.0% Norwegian, 7.0% United States or American, 7.0% Czech (2000).
Economy: Employment by occupation: 16.5% management, 1.0% professional, 9.3% services, 14.4% sales, 3.1% farming, 8.2% construction, 47.4% production (2000).
Income: Per capita income: $18,701 (2000); Median household income: $41,786 (2000); Poverty rate: 8.0% (2000).
Taxes: Total city taxes per capita: $26 (1997); City property taxes per capita: $26 (1997).
Education: High school graduation rate: 81.9% (2000); College graduation rate: 1.6% (2000).
Housing: Homeownership rate: 86.7% (2000); Median home value: $42,800 (2000); Median rent: $225 per month (2000); Median age of housing: 44 years (2000).
Transportation: Commute to work: 80.8% car, 0.0% public transportation, 9.1% walk, 7.1% work from home (2000); Travel time to work: 43.5% less than 15 minutes, 27.2% 15 to 30 minutes, 17.4% 30 to 45 minutes, 3.3% 45 to 60 minutes, 8.7% 60 minutes or more (2000)

KENNAN (town). Covers a land area of 69.910 square miles and a water area of 0.051 square miles. Located at 45.46° N. Lat.; 90.61° W. Long. Elevation is 1,510 feet.
Population: 378 (2000); Race: 99.5% White, 0.0% Black, 0.0% Asian, 0.0% American Indian and Alaska Native, 0.0% Hispanic of any race, 0.5% two or more races (2000); Density: 5.4 persons per square mile (2000); Age: 33.8% under 18, 12.6% over 64 (2000); Marriage status: 18.3% never married, 70.6% now married, 5.9% widowed, 5.2% divorced (2000); Foreign born: 0.0% (2000); Ancestry (includes multiple ancestries): 47.2% German, 12.6% Irish, 9.6% Norwegian, 8.8% Swedish, 8.8% English (2000).
Economy: Dairying. A unit of Chequamegon National Forest to South. Employment by occupation: 15.8% management, 9.6% professional, 13.0% services, 15.3% sales, 7.3% farming, 5.6% construction, 33.3% production (2000).
Income: Per capita income: $12,546 (2000); Median household income: $33,571 (2000); Poverty rate: 10.9% (2000).
Taxes: Total city taxes per capita: $58 (1997); City property taxes per capita: $58 (1997).

Education: High school graduation rate: 80.2% (2000); College graduation rate: 3.6% (2000).
Housing: Homeownership rate: 94.6% (2000); Median home value: $47,500 (2000); Median rent: $292 per month (2000); Median age of housing: 35 years (2000).
Transportation: Commute to work: 81.7% car, 0.0% public transportation, 4.6% walk, 13.7% work from home (2000); Travel time to work: 20.5% less than 15 minutes, 35.1% 15 to 30 minutes, 29.1% 30 to 45 minutes, 7.3% 45 to 60 minutes, 7.9% 60 minutes or more (2000)

KNOX (town). Covers a land area of 48.068 square miles and a water area of 0.020 square miles. Located at 45.54° N. Lat.; 90.08° W. Long.
Population: 399 (2000); Race: 99.5% White, 0.0% Black, 0.0% Asian, 0.5% American Indian and Alaska Native, 0.0% Hispanic of any race, 0.0% two or more races (2000); Density: 8.3 persons per square mile (2000); Age: 20.8% under 18, 21.0% over 64 (2000); Marriage status: 19.6% never married, 64.4% now married, 9.8% widowed, 6.1% divorced (2000); Foreign born: 0.0% (2000); Ancestry (includes multiple ancestries): 34.1% German, 32.1% Finnish, 10.5% Swedish, 7.4% Irish, 7.4% Norwegian (2000).
Economy: Employment by occupation: 15.0% management, 11.6% professional, 7.5% services, 15.0% sales, 15.6% farming, 8.7% construction, 26.6% production (2000).
Income: Per capita income: $20,674 (2000); Median household income: $28,824 (2000); Poverty rate: 10.8% (2000).
Taxes: Total city taxes per capita: $45 (1997); City property taxes per capita: $45 (1997).
Education: High school graduation rate: 70.0% (2000); College graduation rate: 8.7% (2000).
Housing: Homeownership rate: 84.9% (2000); Median home value: $52,500 (2000); Median rent: $800 per month (2000); Median age of housing: 42 years (2000).
Transportation: Commute to work: 100.0% car, 0.0% public transportation, 0.0% walk, 0.0% work from home (2000); Travel time to work: 23.5% less than 15 minutes, 28.8% 15 to 30 minutes, 34.1% 30 to 45 minutes, 5.9% 45 to 60 minutes, 7.6% 60 minutes or more (2000)

LAKE (town). Covers a land area of 88.629 square miles and a water area of 3.592 square miles. Located at 45.93° N. Lat.; 90.54° W. Long.
Population: 1,319 (2000); Race: 99.9% White, 0.0% Black, 0.0% Asian, 0.1% American Indian and Alaska Native, 0.2% Hispanic of any race, 0.0% two or more races (2000); Density: 14.9 persons per square mile (2000); Age: 21.7% under 18, 16.3% over 64 (2000); Marriage status: 19.9% never married, 66.7% now married, 7.1% widowed, 6.4% divorced (2000); Foreign born: 0.2% (2000); Ancestry (includes multiple ancestries): 57.5% German, 13.3% Irish, 8.4% Norwegian, 5.5% Czech, 5.5% English (2000).
Economy: Employment by occupation: 10.7% management, 17.2% professional, 15.6% services, 17.6% sales, 3.1% farming, 10.7% construction, 25.2% production (2000).
Income: Per capita income: $19,728 (2000); Median household income: $39,783 (2000); Poverty rate: 5.9% (2000).
Taxes: Total city taxes per capita: $127 (1997); City property taxes per capita: $125 (1997).
Education: High school graduation rate: 82.9% (2000); College graduation rate: 15.2% (2000).
Housing: Homeownership rate: 88.5% (2000); Median home value: $90,000 (2000); Median rent: $351 per month (2000); Median age of housing: 34 years (2000).
Transportation: Commute to work: 92.0% car, 1.2% public transportation, 1.1% walk, 5.0% work from home (2000); Travel time to work: 64.9% less than 15 minutes, 25.6% 15 to 30 minutes, 4.8% 30 to 45 minutes, 1.1% 45 to 60 minutes, 3.6% 60 minutes or more (2000)

OGEMA (town). Covers a land area of 81.318 square miles and a water area of 0.074 square miles. Located at 45.44° N. Lat.; 90.34° W. Long. Elevation is 1,583 feet.
Population: 882 (2000); Race: 98.7% White, 0.0% Black, 0.0% Asian, 0.8% American Indian and Alaska Native, 0.0% Hispanic of any race, 0.5% two or more races (2000); Density: 10.8 persons per square mile (2000); Age: 25.2% under 18, 19.5% over 64 (2000); Marriage status: 20.6% never married, 62.5% now married, 6.6% widowed, 10.4% divorced (2000); Foreign born: 0.5% (2000); Ancestry (includes multiple ancestries): 41.9% German, 21.0% Swedish, 9.9% Irish, 9.3% Norwegian, 5.5% English (2000).
Economy: In forested area. Manufacturing: wood products, machinery. Employment by occupation: 7.4% management, 11.7% professional, 11.3% services, 19.0% sales, 4.6% farming, 14.1% construction, 31.9% production (2000).
Income: Per capita income: $13,664 (2000); Median household income: $29,545 (2000); Poverty rate: 14.6% (2000).
Taxes: Total city taxes per capita: $67 (1997); City property taxes per capita: $66 (1997).
Education: High school graduation rate: 78.6% (2000); College graduation rate: 10.2% (2000).
Housing: Homeownership rate: 89.1% (2000); Median home value: $53,700 (2000); Median rent: $284 per month (2000); Median age of housing: 44 years (2000).
Transportation: Commute to work: 89.8% car, 0.0% public transportation, 1.9% walk, 7.1% work from home (2000); Travel time to work: 31.7% less than 15 minutes, 32.3% 15 to 30 minutes, 21.7% 30 to 45 minutes, 6.0% 45 to 60 minutes, 8.3% 60 minutes or more (2000)

PARK FALLS (city). Covers a land area of 3.548 square miles and a water area of 0.251 square miles. Located at 45.93° N. Lat.; 90.44° W. Long. Elevation is 1,490 feet.
History: Park Falls grew out of a lumber camp and sawmill settlement that began in the early 1870's. When the timber gave out about 1900, Park Falls developed a pulp and paper industry.
Population: 2,793 (2000); Race: 98.0% White, 0.9% Black, 0.0% Asian, 0.0% American Indian and Alaska Native, 1.3% Hispanic of any race, 0.9% two or more races (2000); Density: 787.1 persons per square mile (2000); Age: 24.8% under 18, 24.3% over 64 (2000); Marriage status: 19.2% never married, 53.2% now married, 15.8% widowed, 11.7% divorced (2000); Foreign born: 0.5% (2000); Ancestry (includes multiple ancestries): 53.2% German, 9.0% Norwegian, 5.1% Irish, 4.9% English, 4.7% Swedish (2000).
Economy: Single-family building permits issued: 0 (2001) / 2 (2000); Multi-family building permits issued: 0 (2001) / 0 (2000); Employment by occupation: 12.5% management, 18.5% professional, 20.2% services, 20.6% sales, 1.9% farming, 8.1% construction, 18.2% production (2000).
Income: Per capita income: $17,929 (2000); Median household income: $33,860 (2000); Poverty rate: 10.3% (2000).
Taxes: Total city taxes per capita: $223 (1997); City property taxes per capita: $211 (1997).
Education: High school graduation rate: 84.3% (2000); College graduation rate: 13.0% (2000).

School District(s)

Park Falls (PK-12)
2000 Enrollment: 942 715-762-4343
Housing: Homeownership rate: 70.8% (2000); Median home value: $61,300 (2000); Median rent: $352 per month (2000); Median age of housing: 47 years (2000).
Hospitals: Flambeau Hospital (42 beds)
Safety: Violent crime rate: 17.8 per 10,000 population; Property crime rate: 160.0 per 10,000 population (2001).
Newspapers: Park Falls Herald (1 x week)
Transportation: Commute to work: 87.9% car, 0.0% public transportation, 10.6% walk, 1.4% work from home (2000); Travel time to work: 73.5% less than 15 minutes, 14.7% 15 to 30 minutes, 3.7% 30 to 45 minutes, 2.5% 45 to 60 minutes, 5.5% 60 minutes or more (2000)
Additional Information Contacts
Park Falls Chamber of Commerce 715-762-2703

PHILLIPS (city). Covers a land area of 2.766 square miles and a water area of 0.708 square miles. Located at 45.69° N. Lat.; 90.40° W. Long. Elevation is 1,480 feet.
History: Phillips was founded in 1874 and named for a president of the Wisconsin Central Railroad. Many of the early residents were of Bohemian ancestry. The economy in the 1930's was supported by a flooring and fiber mill and a wood-products mill.
Population: 1,675 (2000); Race: 97.7% White, 0.2% Black, 0.5% Asian, 1.0% American Indian and Alaska Native, 0.0% Hispanic of any race, 0.7% two or more races (2000); Density: 605.5 persons per square mile (2000); Age: 24.2% under 18, 22.2% over 64 (2000); Marriage status: 26.1% never married, 49.6% now married, 13.9% widowed, 10.4% divorced (2000); Foreign born: 1.9% (2000); Ancestry (includes multiple ancestries): 41.9% German, 10.2% Irish, 8.7% Norwegian, 5.2% Czech, 4.6% United States or American (2000).
Economy: Single-family building permits issued: 3 (2001) / 2 (2000); Multi-family building permits issued: 10 (2001) / 0 (2000); Employment by occupation: 6.7% management, 14.1% professional, 18.1% services, 18.7% sales, 3.1% farming, 5.7% construction, 33.7% production (2000).
Income: Per capita income: $16,480 (2000); Median household income: $31,471 (2000); Poverty rate: 12.5% (2000).

Taxes: Total city taxes per capita: $356 (1997); City property taxes per capita: $340 (1997).
Education: High school graduation rate: 78.8% (2000); College graduation rate: 13.3% (2000).

School District(s)

Phillips (PK-12)
2000 Enrollment: 1,185 715-339-2141

Housing: Homeownership rate: 60.1% (2000); Median home value: $61,800 (2000); Median rent: $359 per month (2000); Median age of housing: 51 years (2000).
Safety: Violent crime rate: 11.9 per 10,000 population; Property crime rate: 426.8 per 10,000 population (2001).
Newspapers: The Bee (1 x week)
Transportation: Commute to work: 78.0% car, 0.0% public transportation, 17.9% walk, 2.1% work from home (2000); Travel time to work: 77.9% less than 15 minutes, 11.0% 15 to 30 minutes, 5.3% 30 to 45 minutes, 1.6% 45 to 60 minutes, 4.2% 60 minutes or more (2000)
Airports: Price County
Additional Information Contacts
Phillips Chamber of Commerce 715-339-4100

PRENTICE (village). Covers a land area of 2.001 square miles and a water area of 0.025 square miles. Located at 45.54° N. Lat.; 90.28° W. Long. Elevation is 1,540 feet.
Population: 626 (2000); Race: 98.8% White, 0.0% Black, 0.0% Asian, 1.2% American Indian and Alaska Native, 0.5% Hispanic of any race, 0.0% two or more races (2000); Density: 312.8 persons per square mile (2000); Age: 24.5% under 18, 18.9% over 64 (2000); Marriage status: 24.5% never married, 53.4% now married, 10.5% widowed, 11.5% divorced (2000); Foreign born: 0.8% (2000); Ancestry (includes multiple ancestries): 43.3% German, 15.5% Swedish, 8.1% Finnish, 7.6% Irish, 7.0% English (2000).
Economy: Single-family building permits issued: 0 (2001) / 2 (2000); Multi-family building permits issued: 0 (2001) / 0 (2000); Employment by occupation: 10.7% management, 10.7% professional, 18.6% services, 10.3% sales, 1.4% farming, 10.0% construction, 38.3% production (2000).
Income: Per capita income: $16,216 (2000); Median household income: $26,563 (2000); Poverty rate: 16.4% (2000).
Taxes: Total city taxes per capita: $103 (1997); City property taxes per capita: $89 (1997).
Education: High school graduation rate: 79.5% (2000); College graduation rate: 8.3% (2000).

School District(s)

Prentice (PK-12)
2000 Enrollment: 569 715-428-2813

Housing: Homeownership rate: 68.3% (2000); Median home value: $56,200 (2000); Median rent: $272 per month (2000); Median age of housing: 33 years (2000).
Transportation: Commute to work: 85.8% car, 0.0% public transportation, 8.3% walk, 5.2% work from home (2000); Travel time to work: 50.5% less than 15 minutes, 26.4% 15 to 30 minutes, 11.4% 30 to 45 minutes, 5.1% 45 to 60 minutes, 6.6% 60 minutes or more (2000)

PRENTICE (town). Covers a land area of 69.353 square miles and a water area of 0.178 square miles. Located at 45.52° N. Lat.; 90.28° W. Long. Elevation is 1,540 feet.
Population: 479 (2000); Race: 97.4% White, 0.8% Black, 0.0% Asian, 0.0% American Indian and Alaska Native, 0.6% Hispanic of any race, 1.2% two or more races (2000); Density: 6.9 persons per square mile (2000); Age: 24.8% under 18, 12.1% over 64 (2000); Marriage status: 16.2% never married, 70.6% now married, 5.6% widowed, 7.6% divorced (2000); Foreign born: 0.6% (2000); Ancestry (includes multiple ancestries): 44.2% German, 11.9% Norwegian, 11.3% Swedish, 9.3% Polish, 7.3% Danish (2000).
Economy: Dairy and farm products. Manufacturing: lumber, plywood, machinery; fuelwood processing. Has an airport. Separate units of Chequamegon National Forest to Southwest and Northeast. Employment by occupation: 10.7% management, 11.5% professional, 13.1% services, 19.7% sales, 3.3% farming, 11.9% construction, 29.9% production (2000).
Income: Per capita income: $17,587 (2000); Median household income: $41,875 (2000); Poverty rate: 5.5% (2000).
Taxes: Total city taxes per capita: $70 (1997); City property taxes per capita: $70 (1997).
Education: High school graduation rate: 75.1% (2000); College graduation rate: 10.1% (2000).
Housing: Homeownership rate: 85.4% (2000); Median home value: $53,600 (2000); Median rent: $283 per month (2000); Median age of housing: 37 years (2000).
Transportation: Commute to work: 82.3% car, 0.0% public transportation, 2.5% walk, 14.4% work from home (2000); Travel time to work: 48.1% less than 15 minutes, 27.4% 15 to 30 minutes, 12.5% 30 to 45 minutes, 8.7% 45 to 60 minutes, 3.4% 60 minutes or more (2000)

SPIRIT (town). Covers a land area of 41.105 square miles and a water area of 0.498 square miles. Located at 45.41° N. Lat.; 90.10° W. Long. Elevation is 1,685 feet.
Population: 315 (2000); Race: 99.2% White, 0.0% Black, 0.0% Asian, 0.8% American Indian and Alaska Native, 0.0% Hispanic of any race, 0.0% two or more races (2000); Density: 7.7 persons per square mile (2000); Age: 23.8% under 18, 17.2% over 64 (2000); Marriage status: 19.8% never married, 59.9% now married, 7.1% widowed, 13.2% divorced (2000); Foreign born: 1.1% (2000); Ancestry (includes multiple ancestries): 36.8% German, 21.8% Swedish, 11.9% United States or American, 7.7% Hungarian, 6.9% English (2000).
Economy: Employment by occupation: 8.5% management, 18.8% professional, 23.9% services, 13.7% sales, 1.7% farming, 6.8% construction, 26.5% production (2000).
Income: Per capita income: $12,722 (2000); Median household income: $30,114 (2000); Poverty rate: 17.2% (2000).
Taxes: Total city taxes per capita: $75 (1997); City property taxes per capita: $75 (1997).
Education: High school graduation rate: 81.4% (2000); College graduation rate: 16.4% (2000).
Housing: Homeownership rate: 83.3% (2000); Median home value: $77,500 (2000); Median rent: $175 per month (2000); Median age of housing: 39 years (2000).
Transportation: Commute to work: 87.4% car, 0.0% public transportation, 1.8% walk, 10.8% work from home (2000); Travel time to work: 13.1% less than 15 minutes, 29.3% 15 to 30 minutes, 23.2% 30 to 45 minutes, 4.0% 45 to 60 minutes, 30.3% 60 minutes or more (2000)

WORCESTER (town). Covers a land area of 117.285 square miles and a water area of 3.702 square miles. Located at 45.73° N. Lat.; 90.33° W. Long. Elevation is 1,615 feet.
Population: 1,711 (2000); Race: 98.6% White, 0.0% Black, 0.1% Asian, 0.3% American Indian and Alaska Native, 0.8% Hispanic of any race, 0.6% two or more races (2000); Density: 14.6 persons per square mile (2000); Age: 24.8% under 18, 17.4% over 64 (2000); Marriage status: 17.5% never married, 68.0% now married, 6.0% widowed, 8.6% divorced (2000); Foreign born: 0.6% (2000); Ancestry (includes multiple ancestries): 40.2% German, 10.1% Polish, 9.6% Czech, 9.3% Irish, 7.1% Swedish (2000).
Economy: Employment by occupation: 11.0% management, 16.2% professional, 9.3% services, 22.7% sales, 2.3% farming, 11.6% construction, 27.0% production (2000).
Income: Per capita income: $17,982 (2000); Median household income: $38,750 (2000); Poverty rate: 4.3% (2000).
Taxes: Total city taxes per capita: $41 (1997); City property taxes per capita: $39 (1997).
Education: High school graduation rate: 85.9% (2000); College graduation rate: 13.6% (2000).
Housing: Homeownership rate: 85.8% (2000); Median home value: $88,200 (2000); Median rent: $346 per month (2000); Median age of housing: 28 years (2000).
Transportation: Commute to work: 90.8% car, 0.2% public transportation, 2.5% walk, 6.0% work from home (2000); Travel time to work: 58.5% less than 15 minutes, 27.4% 15 to 30 minutes, 7.9% 30 to 45 minutes, 3.1% 45 to 60 minutes, 3.2% 60 minutes or more (2000)

Racine County

Located in southeastern Wisconsin; bounded on the east by Lake Michigan; drained by the Fox and Root Rivers. Covers a land area of 333.10 square miles, a water area of 458.80 square miles, and is located in the Central Time Zone. The county government was organized in 1836. County seat is Racine.

Racine County is part of the Racine, WI PMSA. The entire metro area includes: Racine County

Weather Station: Burlington Elevation: 748 feet

	Jan	Feb	Mar	Apr	May	Jun	Jul	Aug	Sep	Oct	Nov	Dec
High	26	31	42	56	68	78	82	80	72	60	45	33
Low	9	14	24	35	45	55	60	59	50	38	28	17
Precip	1.6	1.2	2.3	3.7	3.0	4.0	3.7	4.1	3.4	2.4	2.6	1.9
Snow	12.5	6.8	5.6	1.1	tr	0.0	0.0	0.0	0.0	tr	1.8	8.0

High and Low temperatures in degrees Fahrenheit; Precipitation and Snow in inches

Weather Station: Racine Elevation: 593 feet

	Jan	Feb	Mar	Apr	May	Jun	Jul	Aug	Sep	Oct	Nov	Dec
High	28	32	41	52	63	74	79	78	71	59	46	34
Low	12	18	27	37	46	56	63	63	55	43	32	20
Precip	1.7	1.4	2.4	4.0	3.1	3.6	3.5	4.0	3.9	2.5	2.9	2.0
Snow	15.4	8.9	6.1	1.5	tr	0.0	0.0	0.0	0.0	0.2	2.1	7.4

High and Low temperatures in degrees Fahrenheit; Precipitation and Snow in inches

Population: 188,831 (2000); Race: 83.3% White, 10.1% Black, 0.7% Asian, 0.4% American Indian and Alaska Native, 7.8% Hispanic of any race, 1.9% two or more races (2000); Density: 566.9 persons per square mile (2000); Age: 27.0% under 18, 12.4% over 64 (2000).
Religion: Five largest groups: 34.8% Catholic Church, 8.5% Evangelical Lutheran Church in America, 3.8% Lutheran Church—Missouri Synod, 2.3% The United Methodist Church, 2.1% Wisconsin Evangelical Lutheran Synod (2000).
Economy: Unemployment rate: 6.6% (11/2002); Total civilian labor force: 94,265 (11/2002); Leading industries: 27.6% manufacturing; 13.6% retail trade; 12.8% health care and social assistance (2000); Companies that employ more than 1,000 persons: 4 (2000); Companies that employ more than 100 persons: 132 (2000); Farms: 554 totaling 123,012 acres (1997); Minority business ownership rate: 5.2% (1997); Women business ownership rate: 24.8% (1997); Retail sales per capita: $8,452 (1997). Single-family building permits issued: 578 (2001) / 536 (2000); Multi-family building permits issued: 220 (2001) / 331 (2000).
Income: Per capita income: $21,772 (2000); Median household income: $48,059 (2000); Poverty rate: 8.4% (2000); Bankruptcy rate: 6.06% (2001).
Taxes: Total county taxes per capita: $182 (2000); County property taxes per capita: $178 (2000).
Education: High school graduation rate: 82.9% (2000); College graduation rate: 20.3% (2000).
Housing: Homeownership rate: 70.6% (2000); Median home value: $111,000 (2000); Median rent: $478 per month (2000); Median age of housing: 39 years (2000).
Health: Birth rate: 140.0 per 10,000 population (1998); Age adjusted death rate: 87.8 per 10,000 population (1999); Age adjusted cancer mortality rate: 215.2 deaths per 100,000 population (1999). Air Quality Index: 83% good, 17% moderate, 0% unhealthy (percent of days in 2000). Number of physicians: 16.1 per 10,000 population (1999); Number of hospital beds: 24.1 per 10,000 population (1999).
Elections: 2000 Presidential election results: 46.8% Gore, 49.5% Bush, 2.7% Nader, 0.5% Buchanan
National and State Parks: Tichigan State Wildlife Area
Additional Information Contacts
Racine County Government Offices 262-636-3121
Burlington Chamber of Commerce 262-763-6044
Racine Board of Realtors 262-637-4426
Union Grove Chamber of Commerce 262-878-4606
Waterford Area Chamber of Commerce 262-534-5911
Wind Lake Chamber of Commerce 262-895-6367

Racine County Communities

BOHNERS LAKE (CDP). Covers a land area of 2.033 square miles and a water area of 0.281 square miles. Located at 42.62° N. Lat.; 88.28° W. Long.
Population: 1,952 (2000); Race: 98.4% White, 0.7% Black, 1.0% Asian, 0.0% American Indian and Alaska Native, 2.5% Hispanic of any race, 0.0% two or more races (2000); Density: 960.3 persons per square mile (2000); Age: 34.0% under 18, 8.4% over 64 (2000); Marriage status: 21.8% never married, 63.9% now married, 7.4% widowed, 7.0% divorced (2000); Foreign born: 3.9% (2000); Ancestry (includes multiple ancestries): 44.1% German, 14.1% Irish, 12.6% Polish, 10.6% English, 7.0% French (except Basque) (2000).
Economy: Employment by occupation: 7.9% management, 13.3% professional, 16.1% services, 25.8% sales, 0.0% farming, 11.5% construction, 25.4% production (2000).
Income: Per capita income: $19,584 (2000); Median household income: $56,280 (2000); Poverty rate: 3.2% (2000).
Education: High school graduation rate: 79.0% (2000); College graduation rate: 13.1% (2000).
Housing: Homeownership rate: 91.2% (2000); Median home value: $107,500 (2000); Median rent: $529 per month (2000); Median age of housing: 46 years (2000).
Transportation: Commute to work: 99.2% car, 0.0% public transportation, 0.0% walk, 0.8% work from home (2000); Travel time to work: 34.2% less than 15 minutes, 22.4% 15 to 30 minutes, 19.3% 30 to 45 minutes, 12.4% 45 to 60 minutes, 11.8% 60 minutes or more (2000)

BROWNS LAKE (CDP). Aka Cedar Park. Covers a land area of 2.166 square miles and a water area of 0.612 square miles. Located at 42.68° N. Lat.; 88.23° W. Long.
Population: 1,933 (2000); Race: 97.8% White, 0.0% Black, 0.0% Asian, 0.0% American Indian and Alaska Native, 2.2% Hispanic of any race, 0.0% two or more races (2000); Density: 892.6 persons per square mile (2000); Age: 22.8% under 18, 15.0% over 64 (2000); Marriage status: 20.4% never married, 63.2% now married, 7.9% widowed, 8.5% divorced (2000); Foreign born: 1.5% (2000); Ancestry (includes multiple ancestries): 53.8% German, 9.6% Irish, 8.2% Norwegian, 6.3% English, 5.7% French (except Basque) (2000).
Economy: Employment by occupation: 9.5% management, 16.1% professional, 11.2% services, 28.9% sales, 0.0% farming, 15.8% construction, 18.5% production (2000).
Income: Per capita income: $28,368 (2000); Median household income: $59,563 (2000); Poverty rate: 1.3% (2000).
Education: High school graduation rate: 90.2% (2000); College graduation rate: 17.8% (2000).
Housing: Homeownership rate: 83.6% (2000); Median home value: $129,700 (2000); Median rent: $529 per month (2000); Median age of housing: 42 years (2000).
Transportation: Commute to work: 94.7% car, 0.0% public transportation, 0.0% walk, 5.3% work from home (2000); Travel time to work: 31.8% less than 15 minutes, 25.4% 15 to 30 minutes, 21.8% 30 to 45 minutes, 15.6% 45 to 60 minutes, 5.3% 60 minutes or more (2000)

BURLINGTON (city). Covers a land area of 5.957 square miles and a water area of 0.202 square miles. Located at 42.67° N. Lat.; 88.27° W. Long. Elevation is 800 feet.
History: Burlington was called Foxville until 1835, when a group of New Englanders named it for their home in Vermont. A sawmill and grist mill used water power from the White and Fox Rivers, which later provided energy to the woolen mills. When dairy cattle replaced sheep, Burlington's economy became based on dairy products.
Population: 9,936 (2000); Race: 96.0% White, 0.4% Black, 0.3% Asian, 0.2% American Indian and Alaska Native, 4.4% Hispanic of any race, 1.0% two or more races (2000); Density: 1,667.9 persons per square mile (2000); Age: 28.2% under 18, 13.3% over 64 (2000); Marriage status: 24.3% never married, 57.2% now married, 6.9% widowed, 11.6% divorced (2000); Foreign born: 2.3% (2000); Ancestry (includes multiple ancestries): 51.7% German, 14.9% Irish, 8.5% English, 7.2% Polish, 7.0% Norwegian (2000).
Economy: Single-family building permits issued: 21 (2001) / 20 (2000); Multi-family building permits issued: 110 (2001) / 107 (2000); Employment by occupation: 11.3% management, 18.0% professional, 13.3% services, 26.5% sales, 0.2% farming, 10.8% construction, 19.9% production (2000).
Income: Per capita income: $21,789 (2000); Median household income: $43,365 (2000); Poverty rate: 5.1% (2000).
Taxes: Total city taxes per capita: $350 (1997); City property taxes per capita: $322 (1997).
Education: High school graduation rate: 85.9% (2000); College graduation rate: 21.2% (2000).

School District(s)

Burlington Area (PK-12)
2000 Enrollment: 3,507 262-763-0210
Wheatland J1 (KG-08)
2000 Enrollment: 518 262-537-2216

Housing: Homeownership rate: 60.8% (2000); Median home value: $128,400 (2000); Median rent: $508 per month (2000); Median age of housing: 36 years (2000).
Hospitals: Memorial Hospital of Burlington (123 beds)
Safety: Violent crime rate: 6.0 per 10,000 population; Property crime rate: 390.7 per 10,000 population (2001).
Newspapers: Contributor News (1 x week); Wisconsin Hi-Liter (1 x week); Burlington Standard Press (1 x week)

Transportation: Commute to work: 93.9% car, 0.2% public transportation, 2.9% walk, 2.3% work from home (2000); Travel time to work: 49.5% less than 15 minutes, 25.3% 15 to 30 minutes, 10.1% 30 to 45 minutes, 8.3% 45 to 60 minutes, 6.7% 60 minutes or more (2000)
Additional Information Contacts
Burlington Chamber of Commerce 262-763-6044

BURLINGTON (town). Covers a land area of 34.517 square miles and a water area of 1.409 square miles. Located at 42.67° N. Lat.; 88.26° W. Long. Elevation is 800 feet.
History: Site of Mormon colony (1844—1849) nearby. Settled 1835; incorporated as village 1896, as city 1900.
Population: 6,384 (2000); Race: 97.8% White, 0.2% Black, 0.4% Asian, 0.2% American Indian and Alaska Native, 1.8% Hispanic of any race, 0.7% two or more races (2000); Density: 185.0 persons per square mile (2000); Age: 25.4% under 18, 12.9% over 64 (2000); Marriage status: 20.5% never married, 65.4% now married, 6.2% widowed, 7.9% divorced (2000); Foreign born: 2.0% (2000); Ancestry (includes multiple ancestries): 49.5% German, 12.8% Irish, 8.0% Polish, 8.0% English, 5.8% Other groups (2000).
Economy: In farm area. Manufacturing: iron, steel; meat products; lake resort. Employment by occupation: 12.1% management, 15.2% professional, 13.9% services, 25.3% sales, 0.1% farming, 14.2% construction, 19.2% production (2000).
Income: Per capita income: $24,203 (2000); Median household income: $57,891 (2000); Poverty rate: 2.2% (2000).
Taxes: Total city taxes per capita: $162 (2000); City property taxes per capita: $138 (2000).
Education: High school graduation rate: 86.5% (2000); College graduation rate: 14.5% (2000).
Housing: Homeownership rate: 83.1% (2000); Median home value: $129,100 (2000); Median rent: $519 per month (2000); Median age of housing: 38 years (2000).
Safety: Violent crime rate: 1.6 per 10,000 population; Property crime rate: 149.3 per 10,000 population (2001).
Transportation: Commute to work: 96.1% car, 0.0% public transportation, 0.4% walk, 3.5% work from home (2000); Travel time to work: 39.1% less than 15 minutes, 21.5% 15 to 30 minutes, 18.7% 30 to 45 minutes, 12.2% 45 to 60 minutes, 8.6% 60 minutes or more (2000)

CALEDONIA (town). Covers a land area of 45.491 square miles and a water area of 3.171 square miles. Located at 42.79° N. Lat.; 87.84° W. Long. Elevation is 730 feet.
Population: 23,614 (2000); Race: 95.0% White, 0.9% Black, 1.7% Asian, 0.3% American Indian and Alaska Native, 2.8% Hispanic of any race, 1.5% two or more races (2000); Density: 519.1 persons per square mile (2000); Age: 25.7% under 18, 10.4% over 64 (2000); Marriage status: 20.3% never married, 67.7% now married, 4.1% widowed, 7.8% divorced (2000); Foreign born: 4.0% (2000); Ancestry (includes multiple ancestries): 42.3% German, 13.0% Polish, 10.9% Irish, 7.3% Other groups, 7.2% Danish (2000).
Economy: Employment by occupation: 16.0% management, 21.0% professional, 10.3% services, 25.4% sales, 0.0% farming, 8.4% construction, 19.0% production (2000).
Income: Per capita income: $26,031 (2000); Median household income: $61,647 (2000); Poverty rate: 3.6% (2000).
Taxes: Total city taxes per capita: $294 (2000); City property taxes per capita: $279 (2000).
Education: High school graduation rate: 89.0% (2000); College graduation rate: 25.9% (2000).
Housing: Homeownership rate: 85.1% (2000); Median home value: $133,800 (2000); Median rent: $544 per month (2000); Median age of housing: 28 years (2000).
Transportation: Commute to work: 96.0% car, 0.8% public transportation, 0.7% walk, 1.9% work from home (2000); Travel time to work: 26.5% less than 15 minutes, 46.9% 15 to 30 minutes, 14.1% 30 to 45 minutes, 7.3% 45 to 60 minutes, 5.2% 60 minutes or more (2000)

DOVER (town). Covers a land area of 35.365 square miles and a water area of 0.824 square miles. Located at 42.71° N. Lat.; 88.12° W. Long.
Population: 3,908 (2000); Race: 93.4% White, 4.5% Black, 0.1% Asian, 0.4% American Indian and Alaska Native, 3.9% Hispanic of any race, 1.0% two or more races (2000); Density: 110.5 persons per square mile (2000); Age: 28.1% under 18, 7.9% over 64 (2000); Marriage status: 22.6% never married, 65.6% now married, 3.9% widowed, 7.8% divorced (2000); Foreign born: 1.5% (2000); Ancestry (includes multiple ancestries): 33.8% German, 9.3% English, 9.3% Irish, 7.5% Polish, 7.3% Other groups (2000).
Economy: Employment by occupation: 16.0% management, 18.3% professional, 11.7% services, 18.5% sales, 1.4% farming, 14.2% construction, 19.8% production (2000).
Income: Per capita income: $20,275 (2000); Median household income: $49,972 (2000); Poverty rate: 11.2% (2000).
Taxes: Total city taxes per capita: $105 (2000); City property taxes per capita: $79 (2000).
Education: High school graduation rate: 82.9% (2000); College graduation rate: 20.2% (2000).
Housing: Homeownership rate: 85.0% (2000); Median home value: $137,900 (2000); Median rent: $564 per month (2000); Median age of housing: 31 years (2000).
Transportation: Commute to work: 94.5% car, 0.0% public transportation, 1.3% walk, 3.6% work from home (2000); Travel time to work: 30.2% less than 15 minutes, 35.6% 15 to 30 minutes, 17.7% 30 to 45 minutes, 11.2% 45 to 60 minutes, 5.3% 60 minutes or more (2000)

EAGLE LAKE (CDP). Covers a land area of 2.188 square miles and a water area of 0.807 square miles. Located at 42.69° N. Lat.; 88.13° W. Long.
Population: 1,320 (2000); Race: 100.0% White, 0.0% Black, 0.0% Asian, 0.0% American Indian and Alaska Native, 3.1% Hispanic of any race, 0.0% two or more races (2000); Density: 603.2 persons per square mile (2000); Age: 27.7% under 18, 9.5% over 64 (2000); Marriage status: 21.0% never married, 61.1% now married, 4.7% widowed, 13.1% divorced (2000); Foreign born: 1.7% (2000); Ancestry (includes multiple ancestries): 40.5% German, 14.4% Polish, 11.2% Italian, 11.1% Irish, 8.3% United States or American (2000).
Economy: Employment by occupation: 10.5% management, 21.6% professional, 12.5% services, 13.5% sales, 0.0% farming, 16.5% construction, 25.4% production (2000).
Income: Per capita income: $23,540 (2000); Median household income: $47,650 (2000); Poverty rate: 5.3% (2000).
Education: High school graduation rate: 90.3% (2000); College graduation rate: 23.6% (2000).
Housing: Homeownership rate: 90.2% (2000); Median home value: $117,300 (2000); Median rent: $763 per month (2000); Median age of housing: 36 years (2000).
Transportation: Commute to work: 94.4% car, 0.0% public transportation, 1.4% walk, 4.2% work from home (2000); Travel time to work: 29.1% less than 15 minutes, 39.8% 15 to 30 minutes, 13.0% 30 to 45 minutes, 12.0% 45 to 60 minutes, 6.0% 60 minutes or more (2000)

ELMWOOD PARK (village). Covers a land area of 0.148 square miles and a water area of 0 square miles. Located at 42.69° N. Lat.; 87.82° W. Long. Elevation is 650 feet.
Population: 474 (2000); Race: 96.9% White, 1.8% Black, 0.2% Asian, 0.0% American Indian and Alaska Native, 2.0% Hispanic of any race, 1.0% two or more races (2000); Density: 3,205.8 persons per square mile (2000); Age: 17.1% under 18, 15.9% over 64 (2000); Marriage status: 20.7% never married, 71.7% now married, 4.3% widowed, 3.3% divorced (2000); Foreign born: 3.9% (2000); Ancestry (includes multiple ancestries): 45.6% German, 14.7% Italian, 10.8% English, 9.0% Irish, 8.6% French (except Basque) (2000).
Economy: In urban growth area. Single-family building permits issued: 0 (2001) / 0 (2000); Multi-family building permits issued: 0 (2001) / 0 (2000); Employment by occupation: 21.5% management, 18.7% professional, 12.7% services, 26.4% sales, 0.0% farming, 4.6% construction, 16.2% production (2000).
Income: Per capita income: $30,551 (2000); Median household income: $71,389 (2000); Poverty rate: 1.6% (2000).
Taxes: Total city taxes per capita: $232 (1997); City property taxes per capita: $230 (1997).
Education: High school graduation rate: 90.8% (2000); College graduation rate: 31.9% (2000).
Housing: Homeownership rate: 98.5% (2000); Median home value: $149,400 (2000); Median age of housing: 40 years (2000).
Transportation: Commute to work: 94.3% car, 2.5% public transportation, 0.0% walk, 3.2% work from home (2000); Travel time to work: 43.8% less than 15 minutes, 34.6% 15 to 30 minutes, 9.9% 30 to 45 minutes, 3.7% 45 to 60 minutes, 8.1% 60 minutes or more (2000)

FRANKSVILLE (CDP). Covers a land area of 4.338 square miles and a water area of 0 square miles. Located at 42.76° N. Lat.; 87.90° W. Long. Elevation is 735 feet.
Population: 1,789 (2000); Race: 97.6% White, 0.6% Black, 0.0% Asian, 0.0% American Indian and Alaska Native, 2.4% Hispanic of any race, 0.0%

two or more races (2000); Density: 412.4 persons per square mile (2000); Age: 27.0% under 18, 8.0% over 64 (2000); Marriage status: 22.8% never married, 62.9% now married, 4.0% widowed, 10.2% divorced (2000); Foreign born: 1.1% (2000); Ancestry (includes multiple ancestries): 41.6% German, 16.2% Polish, 13.9% Danish, 7.0% English, 6.8% Dutch (2000).
Economy: Urban-growth area. Dairying and general farming to West. Manufacturing: electronic circuit boards, fractional motors, meat processing, packaging equipment. Ducklings. Employment by occupation: 12.8% management, 17.7% professional, 14.6% services, 26.0% sales, 0.0% farming, 11.0% construction, 17.9% production (2000).
Income: Per capita income: $25,951 (2000); Median household income: $65,863 (2000); Poverty rate: 1.7% (2000).
Education: High school graduation rate: 86.1% (2000); College graduation rate: 15.7% (2000).

School District(s)

North Cape (KG-08)
2000 Enrollment: 193 262-835-4069
Norway J7 (PK-08)
2000 Enrollment: 137 414-425-6020
Raymond #14 (KG-08)
2000 Enrollment: 390 262-835-2929

Housing: Homeownership rate: 81.8% (2000); Median home value: $136,500 (2000); Median rent: $578 per month (2000); Median age of housing: 30 years (2000).
Transportation: Commute to work: 98.2% car, 0.0% public transportation, 1.8% walk, 0.0% work from home (2000); Travel time to work: 34.0% less than 15 minutes, 43.4% 15 to 30 minutes, 13.0% 30 to 45 minutes, 3.7% 45 to 60 minutes, 5.9% 60 minutes or more (2000)

KANSASVILLE (unincorporated postal area, zip code 53139). Covers a land area of 28.692 square miles and a water area of 0.807 square miles. Located at 42.69° N. Lat.; 88.12° W. Long. Elevation is 823 feet.
Population: 2,774 (2000); Race: 98.6% White, 0.1% Black, 0.1% Asian, 0.0% American Indian and Alaska Native, 4.0% Hispanic of any race, 0.7% two or more races (2000); Density: 96.7 persons per square mile (2000); Age: 28.1% under 18, 9.7% over 64 (2000); Marriage status: 22.4% never married, 63.6% now married, 4.3% widowed, 9.6% divorced (2000); Foreign born: 2.2% (2000); Ancestry (includes multiple ancestries): 37.7% German, 10.5% Irish, 10.5% English, 9.4% Polish, 7.7% Italian (2000).
Economy: Employment by occupation: 14.6% management, 18.1% professional, 10.7% services, 18.0% sales, 1.1% farming, 14.3% construction, 23.2% production (2000).
Income: Per capita income: $22,563 (2000); Median household income: $49,472 (2000); Poverty rate: 3.4% (2000).
Education: High school graduation rate: 88.8% (2000); College graduation rate: 19.5% (2000).

School District(s)

Brighton #1 (PK-08)
2000 Enrollment: 167 262-878-2191
Dover #1 (KG-08)
2000 Enrollment: 89 262-878-3773

Housing: Homeownership rate: 84.8% (2000); Median home value: $131,900 (2000); Median rent: $604 per month (2000); Median age of housing: 34 years (2000).
Transportation: Commute to work: 93.0% car, 0.1% public transportation, 1.4% walk, 4.7% work from home (2000); Travel time to work: 31.0% less than 15 minutes, 35.1% 15 to 30 minutes, 15.4% 30 to 45 minutes, 12.7% 45 to 60 minutes, 5.8% 60 minutes or more (2000)

MOUNT PLEASANT (town). Covers a land area of 34.926 square miles and a water area of 1.555 square miles. Located at 42.70° N. Lat.; 87.85° W. Long.
Population: 23,142 (2000); Race: 89.1% White, 6.2% Black, 1.0% Asian, 0.4% American Indian and Alaska Native, 4.8% Hispanic of any race, 1.6% two or more races (2000); Density: 662.6 persons per square mile (2000); Age: 22.3% under 18, 18.5% over 64 (2000); Marriage status: 21.9% never married, 62.8% now married, 7.4% widowed, 7.9% divorced (2000); Foreign born: 4.0% (2000); Ancestry (includes multiple ancestries): 38.0% German, 12.2% Other groups, 10.1% Irish, 9.2% Danish, 8.6% English (2000).
Economy: Single-family building permits issued: 131 (2001) / 106 (2000); Multi-family building permits issued: 38 (2001) / 42 (2000); Employment by occupation: 14.9% management, 23.1% professional, 10.2% services, 28.6% sales, 0.3% farming, 7.2% construction, 15.7% production (2000).
Income: Per capita income: $27,123 (2000); Median household income: $52,869 (2000); Poverty rate: 4.3% (2000).
Taxes: Total city taxes per capita: $381 (2000); City property taxes per capita: $362 (2000).
Education: High school graduation rate: 86.1% (2000); College graduation rate: 27.4% (2000).
Housing: Homeownership rate: 75.7% (2000); Median home value: $135,400 (2000); Median rent: $516 per month (2000); Median age of housing: 26 years (2000).
Transportation: Commute to work: 94.8% car, 0.8% public transportation, 1.2% walk, 2.5% work from home (2000); Travel time to work: 48.4% less than 15 minutes, 32.1% 15 to 30 minutes, 9.8% 30 to 45 minutes, 5.3% 45 to 60 minutes, 4.4% 60 minutes or more (2000)

NORTH BAY (village). Covers a land area of 0.107 square miles and a water area of 0.022 square miles. Located at 42.76° N. Lat.; 87.78° W. Long. Elevation is 610 feet.
Population: 260 (2000); Race: 90.2% White, 0.0% Black, 0.0% Asian, 0.0% American Indian and Alaska Native, 14.2% Hispanic of any race, 9.1% two or more races (2000); Density: 2,429.9 persons per square mile (2000); Age: 25.2% under 18, 13.4% over 64 (2000); Marriage status: 18.2% never married, 73.7% now married, 5.3% widowed, 2.9% divorced (2000); Foreign born: 13.0% (2000); Ancestry (includes multiple ancestries): 37.8% German, 27.6% Irish, 16.9% Other groups, 11.4% English, 6.3% Polish (2000).
Economy: Urban growth area. Single-family building permits issued: 0 (2001) / 0 (2000); Multi-family building permits issued: 0 (2001) / 0 (2000); Employment by occupation: 32.0% management, 25.4% professional, 6.6% services, 21.3% sales, 0.0% farming, 3.3% construction, 11.5% production (2000).
Income: Per capita income: $51,898 (2000); Median household income: $97,943 (2000); Poverty rate: 0.8% (2000).
Taxes: Total city taxes per capita: $669 (1997); City property taxes per capita: $665 (1997).
Education: High school graduation rate: 99.5% (2000); College graduation rate: 66.5% (2000).
Housing: Homeownership rate: 97.9% (2000); Median home value: $250,000 (2000); Median age of housing: 46 years (2000).
Transportation: Commute to work: 92.5% car, 0.8% public transportation, 0.0% walk, 6.7% work from home (2000); Travel time to work: 30.4% less than 15 minutes, 48.2% 15 to 30 minutes, 17.9% 30 to 45 minutes, 3.6% 45 to 60 minutes, 0.0% 60 minutes or more (2000)

NORWAY (town). Covers a land area of 33.719 square miles and a water area of 1.931 square miles. Located at 42.80° N. Lat.; 88.14° W. Long.
Population: 7,600 (2000); Race: 97.1% White, 0.1% Black, 0.3% Asian, 0.8% American Indian and Alaska Native, 1.3% Hispanic of any race, 1.4% two or more races (2000); Density: 225.4 persons per square mile (2000); Age: 28.3% under 18, 8.5% over 64 (2000); Marriage status: 20.1% never married, 70.2% now married, 3.6% widowed, 6.1% divorced (2000); Foreign born: 1.2% (2000); Ancestry (includes multiple ancestries): 47.9% German, 24.9% Polish, 9.5% Irish, 8.6% Norwegian, 5.5% United States or American (2000).
Economy: Employment by occupation: 13.4% management, 19.7% professional, 10.7% services, 24.1% sales, 0.8% farming, 11.5% construction, 19.8% production (2000).
Income: Per capita income: $24,515 (2000); Median household income: $65,513 (2000); Poverty rate: 3.1% (2000).
Taxes: Total city taxes per capita: $118 (1997); City property taxes per capita: $99 (1997).
Education: High school graduation rate: 93.2% (2000); College graduation rate: 19.6% (2000).
Housing: Homeownership rate: 85.6% (2000); Median home value: $164,700 (2000); Median rent: $598 per month (2000); Median age of housing: 22 years (2000).
Transportation: Commute to work: 94.5% car, 0.4% public transportation, 1.1% walk, 3.7% work from home (2000); Travel time to work: 15.0% less than 15 minutes, 33.7% 15 to 30 minutes, 36.1% 30 to 45 minutes, 10.0% 45 to 60 minutes, 5.1% 60 minutes or more (2000)

RACINE (city). Covers a land area of 15.539 square miles and a water area of 3.130 square miles. Located at 42.72° N. Lat.; 87.80° W. Long. Elevation is 620 feet.
History: The Root River, choked with snags and roots, was called Racine (French, "root") by the early French explorers. In 1833, Captain Gilbert Knapp, a former officer on a U.S. revenue cutter, claimed land on both sides of the river mouth and established a settlement called Port Gilbert. The village was incorporated in 1841 with the name of Racine. Earlier hazards of the harbor at the mouth of the river were cleared in 1844 when the citizens

dredged a channel through to Lake Michigan. Wheat provided the base of the early economy in Racine, gradually replaced in the 1860's by the manufacture of agricultural implements and by tanneries. Immigrants from Czechoslovakia settled in Racine in large numbers between 1850 and 1900.
Population: 81,855 (2000); Race: 69.0% White, 20.0% Black, 0.6% Asian, 0.5% American Indian and Alaska Native, 13.9% Hispanic of any race, 2.9% two or more races (2000); Density: 5,267.6 persons per square mile (2000); Age: 29.0% under 18, 12.6% over 64 (2000); Marriage status: 31.2% never married, 50.4% now married, 6.7% widowed, 11.7% divorced (2000); Foreign born: 5.7% (2000); Ancestry (includes multiple ancestries): 29.0% Other groups, 27.7% German, 7.7% Irish, 6.7% Polish, 6.3% Danish (2000).
Vital Statistics: Birth rate: 200.8 per 10,000 population (1998)
Economy: Unemployment rate: 10.7% (11/2002); Total civilian labor force: 39,438 (11/2002); Single-family building permits issued: 11 (2001) / 11 (2000); Multi-family building permits issued: 22 (2001) / 36 (2000); Employment by occupation: 9.1% management, 16.1% professional, 16.0% services, 25.5% sales, 0.1% farming, 7.2% construction, 25.9% production (2000).
Income: Per capita income: $17,705 (2000); Median household income: $37,164 (2000); Poverty rate: 13.9% (2000).
Taxes: Total city taxes per capita: $413 (2000); City property taxes per capita: $397 (2000).
Education: High school graduation rate: 77.2% (2000); College graduation rate: 15.6% (2000).

School District(s)

Racine (PK-12)
2000 Enrollment: 21,102 262-631-7064

Four-year College(s)

Midwest College of Oriental Medicine (Private, For-profit)
2001 Enrollment: 91 262-554-2010

Two-year College(s)

All Saints Healthcare System Inc School of Rad Tech (Private, Not-for-profit, American Lutheran)
2001 Enrollment: n/a 414-636-2846

Housing: Homeownership rate: 60.2% (2000); Median home value: $83,600 (2000); Median rent: $445 per month (2000); Median age of housing: 49 years (2000).
Hospitals: Saint Mary's Medical Center (226 beds); Saint Luke's Memorial Hospital (292 beds)
Safety: Violent crime rate: 74.1 per 10,000 population; Property crime rate: 643.0 per 10,000 population (2001).
Newspapers: The Journal Times (7 x week); Pennysaver (1 x week)
Transportation: Commute to work: 91.0% car, 3.3% public transportation, 3.0% walk, 1.7% work from home (2000); Travel time to work: 44.3% less than 15 minutes, 34.8% 15 to 30 minutes, 11.9% 30 to 45 minutes, 4.4% 45 to 60 minutes, 4.7% 60 minutes or more (2000)
Airports: John H Batten
Additional Information Contacts
Racine Board of Realtors 262-637-4426

RAYMOND (town). Aka Raymond Center. Covers a land area of 35.569 square miles and a water area of 0.019 square miles. Located at 42.80° N. Lat.; 88.00° W. Long. Elevation is 742 feet.
Population: 3,516 (2000); Race: 98.4% White, 0.5% Black, 0.2% Asian, 0.2% American Indian and Alaska Native, 0.9% Hispanic of any race, 0.6% two or more races (2000); Density: 98.8 persons per square mile (2000); Age: 26.8% under 18, 11.9% over 64 (2000); Marriage status: 21.0% never married, 66.8% now married, 4.1% widowed, 8.1% divorced (2000); Foreign born: 1.3% (2000); Ancestry (includes multiple ancestries): 50.6% German, 17.3% Polish, 8.5% Irish, 8.2% Norwegian, 6.7% English (2000).
Economy: Employment by occupation: 15.4% management, 15.6% professional, 8.8% services, 23.2% sales, 0.4% farming, 12.0% construction, 24.6% production (2000).
Income: Per capita income: $24,801 (2000); Median household income: $61,688 (2000); Poverty rate: 3.1% (2000).
Taxes: Total city taxes per capita: $113 (1997); City property taxes per capita: $93 (1997).
Education: High school graduation rate: 83.6% (2000); College graduation rate: 17.0% (2000).
Housing: Homeownership rate: 87.7% (2000); Median home value: $159,100 (2000); Median rent: $578 per month (2000); Median age of housing: 39 years (2000).
Transportation: Commute to work: 92.1% car, 0.6% public transportation, 1.3% walk, 5.2% work from home (2000); Travel time to work: 21.8% less than 15 minutes, 44.1% 15 to 30 minutes, 23.3% 30 to 45 minutes, 6.6% 45 to 60 minutes, 4.3% 60 minutes or more (2000)

ROCHESTER (village). Covers a land area of 0.487 square miles and a water area of 0.044 square miles. Located at 42.74° N. Lat.; 88.22° W. Long. Elevation is 777 feet.
Population: 1,149 (2000); Race: 95.7% White, 0.0% Black, 0.2% Asian, 0.0% American Indian and Alaska Native, 4.1% Hispanic of any race, 2.0% two or more races (2000); Density: 2,360.6 persons per square mile (2000); Age: 33.1% under 18, 6.3% over 64 (2000); Marriage status: 26.2% never married, 57.8% now married, 5.3% widowed, 10.7% divorced (2000); Foreign born: 1.0% (2000); Ancestry (includes multiple ancestries): 46.1% German, 14.9% Polish, 12.3% Irish, 11.1% English, 7.9% Other groups (2000).
Economy: Single-family building permits issued: 2 (2001) / 1 (2000); Multi-family building permits issued: 0 (2001) / 0 (2000); Employment by occupation: 14.9% management, 16.1% professional, 10.9% services, 24.4% sales, 0.0% farming, 12.6% construction, 21.0% production (2000).
Income: Per capita income: $21,609 (2000); Median household income: $55,063 (2000); Poverty rate: 4.7% (2000).
Taxes: Total city taxes per capita: $73 (1997); City property taxes per capita: $67 (1997).
Education: High school graduation rate: 89.0% (2000); College graduation rate: 21.2% (2000).
Housing: Homeownership rate: 67.9% (2000); Median home value: $143,500 (2000); Median rent: $556 per month (2000); Median age of housing: 25 years (2000).
Transportation: Commute to work: 96.4% car, 0.3% public transportation, 2.1% walk, 0.8% work from home (2000); Travel time to work: 37.2% less than 15 minutes, 26.8% 15 to 30 minutes, 23.3% 30 to 45 minutes, 8.2% 45 to 60 minutes, 4.5% 60 minutes or more (2000)

ROCHESTER (town). Covers a land area of 17.082 square miles and a water area of 0.190 square miles. Located at 42.73° N. Lat.; 88.25° W. Long. Elevation is 777 feet.
Population: 2,254 (2000); Race: 98.9% White, 0.3% Black, 0.4% Asian, 0.0% American Indian and Alaska Native, 2.7% Hispanic of any race, 0.1% two or more races (2000); Density: 131.9 persons per square mile (2000); Age: 29.5% under 18, 7.3% over 64 (2000); Marriage status: 21.1% never married, 67.9% now married, 3.6% widowed, 7.3% divorced (2000); Foreign born: 2.4% (2000); Ancestry (includes multiple ancestries): 49.0% German, 10.8% Polish, 10.0% English, 7.9% Norwegian, 7.3% Irish (2000).
Economy: In dairy region and recreation region. Manufacturing of aircrafts. Employment by occupation: 15.6% management, 19.0% professional, 13.0% services, 22.4% sales, 0.6% farming, 11.9% construction, 17.4% production (2000).
Income: Per capita income: $25,097 (2000); Median household income: $61,111 (2000); Poverty rate: 4.7% (2000).
Taxes: Total city taxes per capita: $36 (1997); City property taxes per capita: $28 (1997).
Education: High school graduation rate: 90.4% (2000); College graduation rate: 25.6% (2000).
Housing: Homeownership rate: 85.7% (2000); Median home value: $158,800 (2000); Median rent: $546 per month (2000); Median age of housing: 27 years (2000).
Transportation: Commute to work: 95.3% car, 0.3% public transportation, 0.4% walk, 3.9% work from home (2000); Travel time to work: 30.0% less than 15 minutes, 25.2% 15 to 30 minutes, 29.1% 30 to 45 minutes, 7.6% 45 to 60 minutes, 8.2% 60 minutes or more (2000)

STURTEVANT (village). Aka Corliss. Covers a land area of 3.078 square miles and a water area of 0 square miles. Located at 42.69° N. Lat.; 87.89° W. Long. Elevation is 727 feet.
History: Sturtevant gained a reputation, led by its early German residents, as a center for growing cabbage and making sauerkraut.
Population: 5,287 (2000); Race: 81.4% White, 16.0% Black, 0.0% Asian, 0.6% American Indian and Alaska Native, 5.8% Hispanic of any race, 0.9% two or more races (2000); Density: 1,717.7 persons per square mile (2000); Age: 20.2% under 18, 6.6% over 64 (2000); Marriage status: 16.0% never married, 70.3% now married, 3.7% widowed, 10.0% divorced (2000); Foreign born: 1.2% (2000); Ancestry (includes multiple ancestries): 31.4% German, 10.5% Polish, 9.4% Irish, 5.5% Danish, 4.8% Other groups (2000).
Economy: Single-family building permits issued: 0 (2001) / 0 (2000); Multi-family building permits issued: 0 (2001) / 0 (2000); Employment by occupation: 11.6% management, 12.5% professional, 12.9% services, 28.5% sales, 0.0% farming, 11.8% construction, 22.7% production (2000).
Income: Per capita income: $16,093 (2000); Median household income: $51,492 (2000); Poverty rate: 6.4% (2000).

Taxes: Total city taxes per capita: $182 (1997); City property taxes per capita: $162 (1997).
Education: High school graduation rate: 72.1% (2000); College graduation rate: 10.1% (2000).
Housing: Homeownership rate: 70.4% (2000); Median home value: $100,100 (2000); Median rent: $491 per month (2000); Median age of housing: 34 years (2000).
Safety: Violent crime rate: 1.9 per 10,000 population; Property crime rate: 229.1 per 10,000 population (2001).
Transportation: Commute to work: 95.6% car, 0.5% public transportation, 1.3% walk, 1.7% work from home (2000); Travel time to work: 41.3% less than 15 minutes, 35.5% 15 to 30 minutes, 14.0% 30 to 45 minutes, 5.0% 45 to 60 minutes, 4.1% 60 minutes or more (2000); Amtrak: Service available.

UNION GROVE (village). Covers a land area of 1.712 square miles and a water area of 0 square miles. Located at 42.68° N. Lat.; 88.04° W. Long. Elevation is 770 feet.
History: Industries in Union Grove have included a tile factory, once the largest in Wisconsin; a sauerkraut factory; and the Poole Dixon Duck Farm producing White Pekin ducks for the market.
Population: 4,322 (2000); Race: 96.6% White, 0.0% Black, 1.0% Asian, 0.4% American Indian and Alaska Native, 2.0% Hispanic of any race, 1.4% two or more races (2000); Density: 2,525.0 persons per square mile (2000); Age: 29.1% under 18, 11.7% over 64 (2000); Marriage status: 23.4% never married, 61.4% now married, 5.4% widowed, 9.8% divorced (2000); Foreign born: 1.0% (2000); Ancestry (includes multiple ancestries): 47.7% German, 13.2% Irish, 12.0% Polish, 7.7% English, 5.9% Danish (2000).
Economy: Single-family building permits issued: 35 (2001) / 31 (2000); Multi-family building permits issued: 0 (2001) / 0 (2000); Employment by occupation: 10.4% management, 16.1% professional, 16.7% services, 26.9% sales, 0.1% farming, 11.3% construction, 18.6% production (2000).
Income: Per capita income: $20,445 (2000); Median household income: $50,636 (2000); Poverty rate: 5.4% (2000).
Taxes: Total city taxes per capita: $211 (1997); City property taxes per capita: $195 (1997).
Education: High school graduation rate: 87.7% (2000); College graduation rate: 19.5% (2000).

School District(s)

Union Grove J1 (KG-08)
2000 Enrollment: 601 262-878-2015
Union Grove UHS (09-12)
2000 Enrollment: 660 262-878-4427
Yorkville J2 (KG-08)
2000 Enrollment: 353 262-878-3759

Housing: Homeownership rate: 60.6% (2000); Median home value: $124,700 (2000); Median rent: $494 per month (2000); Median age of housing: 29 years (2000).
Newspapers: Westine Report (1 x week)
Transportation: Commute to work: 95.1% car, 0.0% public transportation, 3.8% walk, 1.1% work from home (2000); Travel time to work: 40.1% less than 15 minutes, 36.9% 15 to 30 minutes, 17.2% 30 to 45 minutes, 3.4% 45 to 60 minutes, 2.5% 60 minutes or more (2000)

Additional Information Contacts

Union Grove Chamber of Commerce 262-878-4606

WATERFORD (village). Covers a land area of 2.461 square miles and a water area of 0.104 square miles. Located at 42.76° N. Lat.; 88.21° W. Long. Elevation is 790 feet.
Population: 4,048 (2000); Race: 99.3% White, 0.5% Black, 0.0% Asian, 0.0% American Indian and Alaska Native, 0.8% Hispanic of any race, 0.0% two or more races (2000); Density: 1,645.1 persons per square mile (2000); Age: 27.0% under 18, 12.5% over 64 (2000); Marriage status: 19.8% never married, 64.2% now married, 4.7% widowed, 11.2% divorced (2000); Foreign born: 1.3% (2000); Ancestry (includes multiple ancestries): 49.4% German, 18.4% Polish, 12.3% Irish, 9.1% English, 8.0% Norwegian (2000).
Economy: Single-family building permits issued: 22 (2001) / 18 (2000); Multi-family building permits issued: 40 (2001) / 41 (2000); Employment by occupation: 8.4% management, 21.4% professional, 11.1% services, 28.5% sales, 0.0% farming, 11.7% construction, 18.8% production (2000).
Income: Per capita income: $22,741 (2000); Median household income: $55,804 (2000); Poverty rate: 3.0% (2000).
Taxes: Total city taxes per capita: $268 (1997); City property taxes per capita: $224 (1997).
Education: High school graduation rate: 87.1% (2000); College graduation rate: 21.6% (2000).

School District(s)

Washington-Caldwell (KG-08)
2000 Enrollment: 224 262-662-3466
Waterford Graded J1 (KG-08)
2000 Enrollment: 1,401 262-534-5065
Waterford UHS (09-12)
2000 Enrollment: 991 262-534-9059

Housing: Homeownership rate: 68.0% (2000); Median home value: $138,900 (2000); Median rent: $680 per month (2000); Median age of housing: 16 years (2000).
Newspapers: The Waterford Post (1 x week)
Transportation: Commute to work: 95.5% car, 0.0% public transportation, 1.8% walk, 1.9% work from home (2000); Travel time to work: 23.9% less than 15 minutes, 30.3% 15 to 30 minutes, 27.8% 30 to 45 minutes, 11.1% 45 to 60 minutes, 6.9% 60 minutes or more (2000)

Additional Information Contacts

Waterford Area Chamber of Commerce 262-534-5911

WATERFORD (town). Covers a land area of 31.537 square miles and a water area of 1.951 square miles. Located at 42.80° N. Lat.; 88.23° W. Long. Elevation is 790 feet.
Population: 5,938 (2000); Race: 99.4% White, 0.0% Black, 0.0% Asian, 0.1% American Indian and Alaska Native, 2.0% Hispanic of any race, 0.3% two or more races (2000); Density: 188.3 persons per square mile (2000); Age: 29.0% under 18, 7.8% over 64 (2000); Marriage status: 20.5% never married, 67.4% now married, 4.4% widowed, 7.7% divorced (2000); Foreign born: 1.9% (2000); Ancestry (includes multiple ancestries): 53.1% German, 17.2% Polish, 13.9% Irish, 7.7% Norwegian, 5.2% English (2000).
Economy: In agricultural area. Manufacturing: plastic moldings, consumer goods, machining. Summer resort. Employment by occupation: 15.7% management, 17.9% professional, 12.2% services, 24.1% sales, 0.5% farming, 14.8% construction, 14.9% production (2000).
Income: Per capita income: $24,406 (2000); Median household income: $66,599 (2000); Poverty rate: 1.8% (2000).
Taxes: Total city taxes per capita: $181 (2000); City property taxes per capita: $153 (2000).
Education: High school graduation rate: 90.3% (2000); College graduation rate: 22.0% (2000).
Housing: Homeownership rate: 91.2% (2000); Median home value: $169,000 (2000); Median rent: $556 per month (2000); Median age of housing: 27 years (2000).
Transportation: Commute to work: 96.4% car, 0.3% public transportation, 0.5% walk, 2.8% work from home (2000); Travel time to work: 18.5% less than 15 minutes, 26.2% 15 to 30 minutes, 39.6% 30 to 45 minutes, 11.2% 45 to 60 minutes, 4.5% 60 minutes or more (2000)

WATERFORD NORTH (CDP). Covers a land area of 11.406 square miles and a water area of 1.935 square miles. Located at 42.80° N. Lat.; 88.21° W. Long.
Population: 4,761 (2000); Race: 99.3% White, 0.0% Black, 0.0% Asian, 0.1% American Indian and Alaska Native, 2.4% Hispanic of any race, 0.3% two or more races (2000); Density: 417.4 persons per square mile (2000); Age: 30.4% under 18, 6.0% over 64 (2000); Marriage status: 19.4% never married, 68.5% now married, 4.2% widowed, 7.9% divorced (2000); Foreign born: 2.3% (2000); Ancestry (includes multiple ancestries): 49.9% German, 17.9% Polish, 12.4% Irish, 8.5% Norwegian, 5.0% Italian (2000).
Economy: Employment by occupation: 16.9% management, 17.5% professional, 11.6% services, 25.0% sales, 0.3% farming, 14.1% construction, 14.7% production (2000).
Income: Per capita income: $24,402 (2000); Median household income: $67,513 (2000); Poverty rate: 1.9% (2000).
Education: High school graduation rate: 90.7% (2000); College graduation rate: 22.4% (2000).
Housing: Homeownership rate: 92.0% (2000); Median home value: $171,100 (2000); Median rent: $534 per month (2000); Median age of housing: 25 years (2000).
Transportation: Commute to work: 96.2% car, 0.4% public transportation, 0.4% walk, 3.0% work from home (2000); Travel time to work: 16.4% less than 15 minutes, 25.1% 15 to 30 minutes, 41.9% 30 to 45 minutes, 11.6% 45 to 60 minutes, 5.0% 60 minutes or more (2000)

WIND LAKE (CDP). Covers a land area of 5.273 square miles and a water area of 1.875 square miles. Located at 42.82° N. Lat.; 88.15° W. Long. Elevation is 797 feet.
Population: 5,202 (2000); Race: 97.1% White, 0.2% Black, 0.3% Asian, 0.9% American Indian and Alaska Native, 0.7% Hispanic of any race, 1.3%

two or more races (2000); Density: 986.5 persons per square mile (2000); Age: 27.7% under 18, 8.7% over 64 (2000); Marriage status: 20.2% never married, 70.3% now married, 3.4% widowed, 6.1% divorced (2000); Foreign born: 1.5% (2000); Ancestry (includes multiple ancestries): 47.6% German, 27.0% Polish, 10.5% Irish, 8.3% Norwegian, 6.5% United States or American (2000).
Economy: Seventeen miles Southwest of Milwaukee Recreation Area. Employment by occupation: 12.2% management, 20.6% professional, 10.8% services, 25.0% sales, 0.5% farming, 10.2% construction, 20.9% production (2000).
Income: Per capita income: $24,765 (2000); Median household income: $68,378 (2000); Poverty rate: 3.4% (2000).
Education: High school graduation rate: 94.3% (2000); College graduation rate: 21.1% (2000).
Housing: Homeownership rate: 84.5% (2000); Median home value: $164,400 (2000); Median rent: $601 per month (2000); Median age of housing: 19 years (2000).
Transportation: Commute to work: 95.8% car, 0.1% public transportation, 0.8% walk, 3.2% work from home (2000); Travel time to work: 14.7% less than 15 minutes, 33.0% 15 to 30 minutes, 36.8% 30 to 45 minutes, 10.3% 45 to 60 minutes, 5.2% 60 minutes or more (2000)
Additional Information Contacts
Wind Lake Chamber of Commerce 262-895-6367

WIND POINT (village). Covers a land area of 1.224 square miles and a water area of 0.164 square miles. Located at 42.78° N. Lat.; 87.77° W. Long. Elevation is 610 feet.
Population: 1,853 (2000); Race: 97.5% White, 0.4% Black, 0.4% Asian, 0.0% American Indian and Alaska Native, 0.0% Hispanic of any race, 1.7% two or more races (2000); Density: 1,513.5 persons per square mile (2000); Age: 19.9% under 18, 18.2% over 64 (2000); Marriage status: 16.1% never married, 72.0% now married, 6.0% widowed, 5.9% divorced (2000); Foreign born: 5.7% (2000); Ancestry (includes multiple ancestries): 37.3% German, 14.3% Irish, 11.0% English, 8.4% Italian, 6.6% Polish (2000).
Economy: Single-family building permits issued: 3 (2001) / 0 (2000); Multi-family building permits issued: 0 (2001) / 0 (2000); Employment by occupation: 35.7% management, 28.2% professional, 8.2% services, 21.6% sales, 0.0% farming, 2.2% construction, 4.2% production (2000).
Income: Per capita income: $53,104 (2000); Median household income: $88,521 (2000); Poverty rate: 3.9% (2000).
Taxes: Total city taxes per capita: $536 (1997); City property taxes per capita: $529 (1997).
Education: High school graduation rate: 94.3% (2000); College graduation rate: 59.9% (2000).
Housing: Homeownership rate: 98.6% (2000); Median home value: $192,300 (2000); Median rent: $1,125 per month (2000); Median age of housing: 29 years (2000).
Transportation: Commute to work: 94.4% car, 0.0% public transportation, 0.8% walk, 4.7% work from home (2000); Travel time to work: 39.1% less than 15 minutes, 44.4% 15 to 30 minutes, 9.3% 30 to 45 minutes, 5.3% 45 to 60 minutes, 2.0% 60 minutes or more (2000)

YORKVILLE (town). Covers a land area of 34.327 square miles and a water area of 0.030 square miles. Located at 42.70° N. Lat.; 87.99° W. Long. Elevation is 753 feet.
Population: 3,291 (2000); Race: 97.7% White, 0.2% Black, 0.2% Asian, 0.5% American Indian and Alaska Native, 0.4% Hispanic of any race, 0.9% two or more races (2000); Density: 95.9 persons per square mile (2000); Age: 23.7% under 18, 10.3% over 64 (2000); Marriage status: 20.1% never married, 69.1% now married, 4.1% widowed, 6.8% divorced (2000); Foreign born: 2.2% (2000); Ancestry (includes multiple ancestries): 43.5% German, 12.6% Irish, 8.4% Danish, 8.1% English, 7.9% Norwegian (2000).
Economy: Employment by occupation: 15.6% management, 20.1% professional, 11.2% services, 19.0% sales, 1.3% farming, 14.2% construction, 18.6% production (2000).
Income: Per capita income: $23,895 (2000); Median household income: $62,076 (2000); Poverty rate: 6.9% (2000).
Taxes: Total city taxes per capita: $187 (2000); City property taxes per capita: $150 (2000).
Education: High school graduation rate: 82.5% (2000); College graduation rate: 24.8% (2000).
Housing: Homeownership rate: 91.0% (2000); Median home value: $162,900 (2000); Median rent: $558 per month (2000); Median age of housing: 34 years (2000).
Transportation: Commute to work: 94.9% car, 0.0% public transportation, 1.7% walk, 3.4% work from home (2000); Travel time to work: 30.2% less than 15 minutes, 43.6% 15 to 30 minutes, 18.1% 30 to 45 minutes, 3.5% 45 to 60 minutes, 4.6% 60 minutes or more (2000)

Richland County

Located in south central Wisconsin; bounded on the south by the Wisconsin River; drained by the Pine and Kickapoo Rivers. Covers a land area of 586.20 square miles, a water area of 3.20 square miles, and is located in the Central Time Zone. The county government was organized in 1842. County seat is Richland Center.

Weather Station: Richland Center — Elevation: 721 feet

	Jan	Feb	Mar	Apr	May	Jun	Jul	Aug	Sep	Oct	Nov	Dec
High	26	32	44	58	71	80	84	81	73	61	44	32
Low	5	11	23	34	44	54	59	56	48	36	25	13
Precip	1.2	1.1	2.2	4.0	3.8	4.1	4.8	4.2	3.9	2.3	2.5	1.3
Snow	11.8	7.8	6.0	2.4	tr	0.0	0.0	0.0	0.0	0.1	4.8	8.8

High and Low temperatures in degrees Fahrenheit; Precipitation and Snow in inches

Population: 17,924 (2000); Race: 98.4% White, 0.1% Black, 0.1% Asian, 0.3% American Indian and Alaska Native, 1.2% Hispanic of any race, 0.8% two or more races (2000); Density: 30.6 persons per square mile (2000); Age: 25.1% under 18, 17.2% over 64 (2000).
Religion: Five largest groups: 14.5% Catholic Church, 7.5% The United Methodist Church, 5.7% Evangelical Lutheran Church in America, 1.5% Christian Churches and Churches of Christ, 0.9% American Baptist Churches in the USA (2000).
Economy: Unemployment rate: 4.1% (11/2002); Total civilian labor force: 8,431 (11/2002); Leading industries: 35.5% manufacturing; 23.8% retail trade; 12.2% health care and social assistance (2000); Companies that employ more than 1,000 persons: 0 (2000); Companies that employ more than 100 persons: 9 (2000); Farms: 1,032 totaling 238,266 acres (1997); Minority business ownership rate: 0.0% (1997); Women business ownership rate: 20.8% (1997); Retail sales per capita: $7,179 (1997). Single-family building permits issued: 63 (2001) / 84 (2000); Multi-family building permits issued: 0 (2001) / 48 (2000).
Income: Per capita income: $17,042 (2000); Median household income: $33,998 (2000); Poverty rate: 10.1% (2000); Bankruptcy rate: 2.85% (2001).
Taxes: Total county taxes per capita: $239 (1997); County property taxes per capita: $200 (1997).
Education: High school graduation rate: 82.1% (2000); College graduation rate: 14.1% (2000).
Housing: Homeownership rate: 74.5% (2000); Median home value: $75,200 (2000); Median rent: $363 per month (2000); Median age of housing: 45 years (2000).
Health: Birth rate: 111.0 per 10,000 population (1998); Age adjusted death rate: 66.6 per 10,000 population (1999); Age adjusted cancer mortality rate: 215.0 deaths per 100,000 population (1999). Number of physicians: 9.5 per 10,000 population (1999); Number of hospital beds: 19.5 per 10,000 population (1999).
Elections: 2000 Presidential election results: 46.3% Gore, 48.2% Bush, 4.7% Nader, 0.5% Buchanan
Additional Information Contacts
Richland County Government Offices 608-647-2197
Richland Center Chamber of Commerce 608-647-6205
Richland Main St. Chamber of Commerce 608-647-8418

Richland County Communities

AKAN (town). Covers a land area of 36.119 square miles and a water area of 0 square miles. Located at 43.32° N. Lat.; 90.62° W. Long.
Population: 444 (2000); Race: 99.5% White, 0.0% Black, 0.2% Asian, 0.0% American Indian and Alaska Native, 0.2% Hispanic of any race, 0.2% two or more races (2000); Density: 12.3 persons per square mile (2000); Age: 28.9% under 18, 11.9% over 64 (2000); Marriage status: 27.0% never married, 61.3% now married, 5.2% widowed, 6.4% divorced (2000); Foreign born: 1.1% (2000); Ancestry (includes multiple ancestries): 36.0% German, 16.5% Norwegian, 11.0% Irish, 9.4% English, 5.0% Dutch (2000).
Economy: Employment by occupation: 15.1% management, 9.2% professional, 9.6% services, 14.7% sales, 5.0% farming, 15.1% construction, 31.2% production (2000).
Income: Per capita income: $15,257 (2000); Median household income: $39,583 (2000); Poverty rate: 10.8% (2000).
Taxes: Total city taxes per capita: $32 (1997); City property taxes per capita: $32 (1997).

Education: High school graduation rate: 81.4% (2000); College graduation rate: 10.8% (2000).
Housing: Homeownership rate: 80.8% (2000); Median home value: $70,000 (2000); Median rent: $331 per month (2000); Median age of housing: 55 years (2000).
Transportation: Commute to work: 82.9% car, 0.0% public transportation, 2.8% walk, 14.2% work from home (2000); Travel time to work: 14.4% less than 15 minutes, 54.7% 15 to 30 minutes, 12.2% 30 to 45 minutes, 8.3% 45 to 60 minutes, 10.5% 60 minutes or more (2000)

BLOOM (town). Covers a land area of 36.089 square miles and a water area of 0 square miles. Located at 43.51° N. Lat.; 90.47° W. Long.
Population: 487 (2000); Race: 97.4% White, 0.0% Black, 0.4% Asian, 0.0% American Indian and Alaska Native, 0.0% Hispanic of any race, 2.2% two or more races (2000); Density: 13.5 persons per square mile (2000); Age: 22.4% under 18, 14.0% over 64 (2000); Marriage status: 25.1% never married, 63.1% now married, 3.9% widowed, 8.0% divorced (2000); Foreign born: 2.2% (2000); Ancestry (includes multiple ancestries): 33.3% German, 11.6% Irish, 10.4% Czech, 9.4% English, 8.6% Norwegian (2000).
Economy: Single-family building permits issued: 0 (2001) / 0 (2000); Multi-family building permits issued: 0 (2001) / 0 (2000); Employment by occupation: 20.9% management, 12.3% professional, 12.6% services, 13.0% sales, 6.1% farming, 7.6% construction, 27.4% production (2000).
Income: Per capita income: $18,017 (2000); Median household income: $33,281 (2000); Poverty rate: 8.4% (2000).
Taxes: Total city taxes per capita: $146 (1997); City property taxes per capita: $146 (1997).
Education: High school graduation rate: 80.5% (2000); College graduation rate: 11.5% (2000).
Housing: Homeownership rate: 83.2% (2000); Median home value: $49,000 (2000); Median rent: $357 per month (2000); Median age of housing: 60+ years (2000).
Transportation: Commute to work: 71.5% car, 0.7% public transportation, 7.2% walk, 18.4% work from home (2000); Travel time to work: 20.4% less than 15 minutes, 38.5% 15 to 30 minutes, 16.8% 30 to 45 minutes, 6.6% 45 to 60 minutes, 17.7% 60 minutes or more (2000)

BOAZ (village). Covers a land area of 0.357 square miles and a water area of 0 square miles. Located at 43.33° N. Lat.; 90.52° W. Long. Elevation is 740 feet.
Population: 137 (2000); Race: 96.5% White, 0.0% Black, 0.0% Asian, 2.1% American Indian and Alaska Native, 0.0% Hispanic of any race, 1.4% two or more races (2000); Density: 383.2 persons per square mile (2000); Age: 16.7% under 18, 19.4% over 64 (2000); Marriage status: 15.4% never married, 61.8% now married, 8.1% widowed, 14.6% divorced (2000); Foreign born: 0.0% (2000); Ancestry (includes multiple ancestries): 40.3% German, 23.6% Norwegian, 16.7% English, 7.6% Irish, 6.9% French (except Basque) (2000).
Economy: In dairy and livestock region. Employment by occupation: 6.5% management, 7.6% professional, 13.0% services, 9.8% sales, 4.3% farming, 7.6% construction, 51.1% production (2000).
Income: Per capita income: $16,883 (2000); Median household income: $31,563 (2000); Poverty rate: 13.2% (2000).
Taxes: Total city taxes per capita: $101 (1997); City property taxes per capita: $85 (1997).
Education: High school graduation rate: 86.5% (2000); College graduation rate: 6.7% (2000).
Housing: Homeownership rate: 81.0% (2000); Median home value: $73,800 (2000); Median rent: $375 per month (2000); Median age of housing: 41 years (2000).
Transportation: Commute to work: 92.0% car, 0.0% public transportation, 5.7% walk, 2.3% work from home (2000); Travel time to work: 15.1% less than 15 minutes, 60.5% 15 to 30 minutes, 14.0% 30 to 45 minutes, 4.7% 45 to 60 minutes, 5.8% 60 minutes or more (2000)

BUENA VISTA (town). Covers a land area of 41.062 square miles and a water area of 0.952 square miles. Located at 43.25° N. Lat.; 90.26° W. Long.
Population: 1,575 (2000); Race: 98.7% White, 0.3% Black, 0.2% Asian, 0.0% American Indian and Alaska Native, 1.1% Hispanic of any race, 0.3% two or more races (2000); Density: 38.4 persons per square mile (2000); Age: 25.3% under 18, 11.5% over 64 (2000); Marriage status: 18.4% never married, 66.0% now married, 5.1% widowed, 10.6% divorced (2000); Foreign born: 0.9% (2000); Ancestry (includes multiple ancestries): 40.1% German, 12.5% Norwegian, 12.0% Irish, 10.2% English, 7.8% United States or American (2000).
Economy: Employment by occupation: 13.1% management, 12.5% professional, 11.5% services, 18.1% sales, 3.5% farming, 8.3% construction, 32.9% production (2000).
Income: Per capita income: $17,411 (2000); Median household income: $40,000 (2000); Poverty rate: 6.2% (2000).
Taxes: Total city taxes per capita: $20 (1997); City property taxes per capita: $17 (1997).
Education: High school graduation rate: 85.6% (2000); College graduation rate: 12.2% (2000).
Housing: Homeownership rate: 83.2% (2000); Median home value: $83,700 (2000); Median rent: $407 per month (2000); Median age of housing: 29 years (2000).
Transportation: Commute to work: 88.8% car, 0.1% public transportation, 2.2% walk, 7.4% work from home (2000); Travel time to work: 26.7% less than 15 minutes, 45.6% 15 to 30 minutes, 11.9% 30 to 45 minutes, 5.8% 45 to 60 minutes, 10.0% 60 minutes or more (2000)

CAZENOVIA (village). Covers a land area of 0.905 square miles and a water area of 0.067 square miles. Located at 43.52° N. Lat.; 90.19° W. Long. Elevation is 951 feet.
Population: 326 (2000); Race: 100.0% White, 0.0% Black, 0.0% Asian, 0.0% American Indian and Alaska Native, 0.0% Hispanic of any race, 0.0% two or more races (2000); Density: 360.3 persons per square mile (2000); Age: 18.1% under 18, 26.6% over 64 (2000); Marriage status: 22.5% never married, 55.8% now married, 8.1% widowed, 13.6% divorced (2000); Foreign born: 0.0% (2000); Ancestry (includes multiple ancestries): 50.7% German, 16.8% Irish, 14.5% English, 9.9% United States or American, 3.3% Other groups (2000).
Economy: In dairy and livestock region. Single-family building permits issued: 1 (2001) / 3 (2000); Multi-family building permits issued: 0 (2001) / 0 (2000); Employment by occupation: 5.9% management, 10.3% professional, 22.1% services, 20.6% sales, 0.0% farming, 6.6% construction, 34.6% production (2000).
Income: Per capita income: $21,877 (2000); Median household income: $34,167 (2000); Poverty rate: 7.6% (2000).
Taxes: Total city taxes per capita: $106 (1997); City property taxes per capita: $102 (1997).
Education: High school graduation rate: 82.2% (2000); College graduation rate: 5.9% (2000).

School District(s)

Weston (PK-12)
2000 Enrollment: 403 608-986-2151

Housing: Homeownership rate: 71.4% (2000); Median home value: $81,500 (2000); Median rent: $366 per month (2000); Median age of housing: 60+ years (2000).
Transportation: Commute to work: 94.9% car, 0.0% public transportation, 2.9% walk, 2.2% work from home (2000); Travel time to work: 20.3% less than 15 minutes, 37.6% 15 to 30 minutes, 28.6% 30 to 45 minutes, 9.0% 45 to 60 minutes, 4.5% 60 minutes or more (2000)

DAYTON (town). Covers a land area of 35.115 square miles and a water area of 0 square miles. Located at 43.33° N. Lat.; 90.49° W. Long.
Population: 723 (2000); Race: 98.9% White, 0.0% Black, 0.0% Asian, 0.8% American Indian and Alaska Native, 0.0% Hispanic of any race, 0.3% two or more races (2000); Density: 20.6 persons per square mile (2000); Age: 27.5% under 18, 14.6% over 64 (2000); Marriage status: 17.2% never married, 65.9% now married, 7.3% widowed, 9.6% divorced (2000); Foreign born: 0.7% (2000); Ancestry (includes multiple ancestries): 32.3% German, 15.4% Irish, 12.6% Norwegian, 10.7% English, 8.8% United States or American (2000).
Economy: Employment by occupation: 11.2% management, 13.4% professional, 13.4% services, 20.7% sales, 6.1% farming, 8.4% construction, 26.8% production (2000).
Income: Per capita income: $17,382 (2000); Median household income: $35,938 (2000); Poverty rate: 8.3% (2000).
Taxes: Total city taxes per capita: $118 (1997); City property taxes per capita: $117 (1997).
Education: High school graduation rate: 84.4% (2000); College graduation rate: 13.4% (2000).
Housing: Homeownership rate: 82.9% (2000); Median home value: $88,300 (2000); Median rent: $405 per month (2000); Median age of housing: 34 years (2000).
Transportation: Commute to work: 84.7% car, 0.0% public transportation, 0.0% walk, 14.1% work from home (2000); Travel time to work: 40.1% less than 15 minutes, 34.2% 15 to 30 minutes, 14.1% 30 to 45 minutes, 5.6% 45 to 60 minutes, 5.9% 60 minutes or more (2000)

EAGLE (town). Covers a land area of 34.750 square miles and a water area of 0.861 square miles. Located at 43.25° N. Lat.; 90.48° W. Long.
Population: 593 (2000); Race: 96.0% White, 0.0% Black, 0.0% Asian, 0.7% American Indian and Alaska Native, 1.7% Hispanic of any race, 3.3% two or more races (2000); Density: 17.1 persons per square mile (2000); Age: 29.1% under 18, 10.6% over 64 (2000); Marriage status: 21.9% never married, 67.2% now married, 3.7% widowed, 7.2% divorced (2000); Foreign born: 0.0% (2000); Ancestry (includes multiple ancestries): 38.1% German, 15.3% Irish, 14.5% English, 10.1% Other groups, 9.8% Norwegian (2000).
Economy: Employment by occupation: 19.7% management, 11.0% professional, 18.1% services, 14.5% sales, 5.8% farming, 7.1% construction, 23.9% production (2000).
Income: Per capita income: $16,026 (2000); Median household income: $36,944 (2000); Poverty rate: 13.4% (2000).
Taxes: Total city taxes per capita: $69 (1997); City property taxes per capita: $68 (1997).
Education: High school graduation rate: 78.8% (2000); College graduation rate: 12.8% (2000).
Housing: Homeownership rate: 82.5% (2000); Median home value: $77,500 (2000); Median rent: $375 per month (2000); Median age of housing: 39 years (2000).
Transportation: Commute to work: 81.6% car, 0.0% public transportation, 3.9% walk, 14.5% work from home (2000); Travel time to work: 36.6% less than 15 minutes, 38.5% 15 to 30 minutes, 10.6% 30 to 45 minutes, 3.4% 45 to 60 minutes, 10.9% 60 minutes or more (2000)

FOREST (town). Covers a land area of 35.494 square miles and a water area of 0 square miles. Located at 43.51° N. Lat.; 90.62° W. Long.
Population: 390 (2000); Race: 96.1% White, 0.0% Black, 0.0% Asian, 0.5% American Indian and Alaska Native, 4.2% Hispanic of any race, 1.8% two or more races (2000); Density: 11.0 persons per square mile (2000); Age: 26.8% under 18, 14.2% over 64 (2000); Marriage status: 19.6% never married, 74.9% now married, 2.7% widowed, 2.7% divorced (2000); Foreign born: 2.6% (2000); Ancestry (includes multiple ancestries): 38.6% German, 16.0% English, 12.6% Irish, 11.0% Norwegian, 9.2% Other groups (2000).
Economy: Employment by occupation: 12.5% management, 13.0% professional, 22.9% services, 19.3% sales, 5.7% farming, 5.7% construction, 20.8% production (2000).
Income: Per capita income: $16,256 (2000); Median household income: $37,981 (2000); Poverty rate: 12.6% (2000).
Taxes: Total city taxes per capita: $147 (1997); City property taxes per capita: $147 (1997).
Education: High school graduation rate: 90.5% (2000); College graduation rate: 16.6% (2000).
Housing: Homeownership rate: 87.5% (2000); Median home value: $53,600 (2000); Median rent: $225 per month (2000); Median age of housing: 46 years (2000).
Transportation: Commute to work: 87.4% car, 0.0% public transportation, 0.5% walk, 11.6% work from home (2000); Travel time to work: 33.3% less than 15 minutes, 27.4% 15 to 30 minutes, 26.2% 30 to 45 minutes, 4.2% 45 to 60 minutes, 8.9% 60 minutes or more (2000)

HENRIETTA (town). Covers a land area of 35.938 square miles and a water area of 0.004 square miles. Located at 43.51° N. Lat.; 90.37° W. Long.
Population: 479 (2000); Race: 98.8% White, 0.0% Black, 0.0% Asian, 0.0% American Indian and Alaska Native, 0.0% Hispanic of any race, 1.2% two or more races (2000); Density: 13.3 persons per square mile (2000); Age: 23.1% under 18, 23.1% over 64 (2000); Marriage status: 20.9% never married, 62.5% now married, 10.1% widowed, 6.5% divorced (2000); Foreign born: 0.0% (2000); Ancestry (includes multiple ancestries): 25.1% German, 14.0% Irish, 13.4% English, 9.7% Czech, 9.1% Norwegian (2000).
Economy: Employment by occupation: 22.0% management, 11.4% professional, 15.9% services, 15.9% sales, 0.8% farming, 9.3% construction, 24.8% production (2000).
Income: Per capita income: $17,598 (2000); Median household income: $31,354 (2000); Poverty rate: 8.9% (2000).
Taxes: Total city taxes per capita: $56 (1997); City property taxes per capita: $55 (1997).
Education: High school graduation rate: 72.3% (2000); College graduation rate: 15.1% (2000).
Housing: Homeownership rate: 93.2% (2000); Median home value: $51,500 (2000); Median rent: $425 per month (2000); Median age of housing: 41 years (2000).
Transportation: Commute to work: 83.2% car, 0.0% public transportation, 2.5% walk, 14.3% work from home (2000); Travel time to work: 8.1% less than 15 minutes, 48.3% 15 to 30 minutes, 18.2% 30 to 45 minutes, 13.4% 45 to 60 minutes, 12.0% 60 minutes or more (2000)

ITHACA (town). Covers a land area of 36.033 square miles and a water area of 0 square miles. Located at 43.32° N. Lat.; 90.25° W. Long. Elevation is 734 feet.
Population: 648 (2000); Race: 98.2% White, 0.1% Black, 0.0% Asian, 0.0% American Indian and Alaska Native, 1.3% Hispanic of any race, 0.3% two or more races (2000); Density: 18.0 persons per square mile (2000); Age: 26.1% under 18, 15.4% over 64 (2000); Marriage status: 18.0% never married, 71.8% now married, 3.1% widowed, 7.1% divorced (2000); Foreign born: 0.9% (2000); Ancestry (includes multiple ancestries): 56.7% German, 18.2% Irish, 12.8% Norwegian, 9.1% English, 4.6% Other groups (2000).
Economy: Single-family building permits issued: 3 (2001) / 4 (2000); Multi-family building permits issued: 0 (2001) / 0 (2000); Employment by occupation: 22.5% management, 11.8% professional, 8.8% services, 20.1% sales, 5.3% farming, 8.6% construction, 23.0% production (2000).
Income: Per capita income: $17,358 (2000); Median household income: $42,222 (2000); Poverty rate: 5.2% (2000).
Taxes: Total city taxes per capita: $103 (1997); City property taxes per capita: $101 (1997).
Education: High school graduation rate: 81.6% (2000); College graduation rate: 13.1% (2000).
Housing: Homeownership rate: 81.8% (2000); Median home value: $82,500 (2000); Median rent: $320 per month (2000); Median age of housing: 55 years (2000).
Transportation: Commute to work: 82.0% car, 0.5% public transportation, 3.8% walk, 13.7% work from home (2000); Travel time to work: 37.4% less than 15 minutes, 31.8% 15 to 30 minutes, 19.0% 30 to 45 minutes, 6.5% 45 to 60 minutes, 5.3% 60 minutes or more (2000)

LONE ROCK (village). Covers a land area of 1.176 square miles and a water area of 0 square miles. Located at 43.18° N. Lat.; 90.19° W. Long. Elevation is 706 feet.
Population: 929 (2000); Race: 96.9% White, 0.0% Black, 0.0% Asian, 0.7% American Indian and Alaska Native, 2.9% Hispanic of any race, 0.6% two or more races (2000); Density: 790.2 persons per square mile (2000); Age: 28.8% under 18, 11.3% over 64 (2000); Marriage status: 23.3% never married, 56.8% now married, 6.7% widowed, 13.2% divorced (2000); Foreign born: 1.3% (2000); Ancestry (includes multiple ancestries): 40.4% German, 16.2% Irish, 10.6% Norwegian, 10.1% Other groups, 8.9% United States or American (2000).
Economy: In timber and agricultural area. Lumber; cheese; feeds; hunting. Single-family building permits issued: 0 (2001) / 3 (2000); Multi-family building permits issued: 0 (2001) / 0 (2000); Employment by occupation: 3.3% management, 10.6% professional, 15.4% services, 22.7% sales, 0.8% farming, 11.2% construction, 36.0% production (2000).
Income: Per capita income: $15,985 (2000); Median household income: $33,060 (2000); Poverty rate: 5.4% (2000).
Taxes: Total city taxes per capita: $123 (1997); City property taxes per capita: $97 (1997).
Education: High school graduation rate: 83.8% (2000); College graduation rate: 8.6% (2000).
Housing: Homeownership rate: 71.0% (2000); Median home value: $81,800 (2000); Median rent: $390 per month (2000); Median age of housing: 30 years (2000).
Transportation: Commute to work: 94.0% car, 0.6% public transportation, 3.4% walk, 1.9% work from home (2000); Travel time to work: 30.2% less than 15 minutes, 29.9% 15 to 30 minutes, 15.8% 30 to 45 minutes, 8.9% 45 to 60 minutes, 15.2% 60 minutes or more (2000)

MARSHALL (town). Covers a land area of 36.043 square miles and a water area of 0 square miles. Located at 43.42° N. Lat.; 90.49° W. Long.
Population: 600 (2000); Race: 99.1% White, 0.9% Black, 0.0% Asian, 0.0% American Indian and Alaska Native, 0.4% Hispanic of any race, 0.0% two or more races (2000); Density: 16.6 persons per square mile (2000); Age: 31.6% under 18, 16.2% over 64 (2000); Marriage status: 20.5% never married, 69.2% now married, 5.0% widowed, 5.3% divorced (2000); Foreign born: 0.9% (2000); Ancestry (includes multiple ancestries): 45.3% German, 16.6% English, 10.0% Irish, 9.3% Norwegian, 4.1% United States or American (2000).
Economy: Employment by occupation: 19.8% management, 16.0% professional, 9.5% services, 20.2% sales, 2.7% farming, 7.6% construction, 24.3% production (2000).
Income: Per capita income: $20,226 (2000); Median household income: $41,161 (2000); Poverty rate: 7.7% (2000).

Taxes: Total city taxes per capita: $98 (1997); City property taxes per capita: $98 (1997).
Education: High school graduation rate: 83.2% (2000); College graduation rate: 21.7% (2000).
Housing: Homeownership rate: 86.7% (2000); Median home value: $71,800 (2000); Median rent: $288 per month (2000); Median age of housing: 60+ years (2000).
Transportation: Commute to work: 77.2% car, 0.0% public transportation, 2.7% walk, 20.1% work from home (2000); Travel time to work: 17.4% less than 15 minutes, 54.6% 15 to 30 minutes, 15.0% 30 to 45 minutes, 8.2% 45 to 60 minutes, 4.8% 60 minutes or more (2000)

ORION (town). Covers a land area of 35.789 square miles and a water area of 0.434 square miles. Located at 43.25° N. Lat.; 90.37° W. Long. Elevation is 720 feet.
Population: 628 (2000); Race: 100.0% White, 0.0% Black, 0.0% Asian, 0.0% American Indian and Alaska Native, 0.0% Hispanic of any race, 0.0% two or more races (2000); Density: 17.5 persons per square mile (2000); Age: 27.9% under 18, 14.8% over 64 (2000); Marriage status: 18.6% never married, 68.7% now married, 6.0% widowed, 6.6% divorced (2000); Foreign born: 0.6% (2000); Ancestry (includes multiple ancestries): 49.1% German, 15.8% Irish, 12.5% English, 11.5% Norwegian, 6.2% United States or American (2000).
Economy: Employment by occupation: 13.7% management, 7.1% professional, 11.8% services, 30.1% sales, 4.0% farming, 11.8% construction, 21.4% production (2000).
Income: Per capita income: $20,823 (2000); Median household income: $44,643 (2000); Poverty rate: 7.3% (2000).
Taxes: Total city taxes per capita: $99 (1997); City property taxes per capita: $97 (1997).
Education: High school graduation rate: 83.3% (2000); College graduation rate: 15.7% (2000).
Housing: Homeownership rate: 90.1% (2000); Median home value: $78,500 (2000); Median rent: $381 per month (2000); Median age of housing: 37 years (2000).
Transportation: Commute to work: 90.9% car, 0.9% public transportation, 0.6% walk, 6.9% work from home (2000); Travel time to work: 35.9% less than 15 minutes, 37.2% 15 to 30 minutes, 11.4% 30 to 45 minutes, 6.0% 45 to 60 minutes, 9.4% 60 minutes or more (2000)

RICHLAND (town). Covers a land area of 31.524 square miles and a water area of 0 square miles. Located at 43.34° N. Lat.; 90.37° W. Long.
Population: 1,364 (2000); Race: 98.9% White, 0.1% Black, 0.3% Asian, 0.0% American Indian and Alaska Native, 0.8% Hispanic of any race, 0.7% two or more races (2000); Density: 43.3 persons per square mile (2000); Age: 22.0% under 18, 23.2% over 64 (2000); Marriage status: 18.5% never married, 62.9% now married, 10.2% widowed, 8.5% divorced (2000); Foreign born: 1.3% (2000); Ancestry (includes multiple ancestries): 38.5% German, 15.7% Irish, 15.2% English, 13.0% Norwegian, 4.0% United States or American (2000).
Economy: Employment by occupation: 15.4% management, 14.5% professional, 14.2% services, 24.8% sales, 0.6% farming, 13.0% construction, 17.4% production (2000).
Income: Per capita income: $21,435 (2000); Median household income: $43,036 (2000); Poverty rate: 7.9% (2000).
Taxes: Total city taxes per capita: $13 (1997); City property taxes per capita: $11 (1997).
Education: High school graduation rate: 81.0% (2000); College graduation rate: 16.2% (2000).
Housing: Homeownership rate: 82.2% (2000); Median home value: $90,800 (2000); Median rent: $441 per month (2000); Median age of housing: 29 years (2000).
Transportation: Commute to work: 89.5% car, 0.0% public transportation, 1.5% walk, 8.1% work from home (2000); Travel time to work: 63.5% less than 15 minutes, 17.5% 15 to 30 minutes, 7.8% 30 to 45 minutes, 3.6% 45 to 60 minutes, 7.6% 60 minutes or more (2000)

RICHLAND CENTER (city). Covers a land area of 4.391 square miles and a water area of 0.085 square miles. Located at 43.33° N. Lat.; 90.38° W. Long. Elevation is 731 feet.
History: Richland Center was settled in 1849 and, together with Madison, became the cradle of woman's suffrage in Wisconsin in the 1880's. Richland Center was incorporated as a city in 1887, and later became the focal point for the surrounding dairy industry. Architect Frank Lloyd Wright was born in 1869 in Richland Center.
Population: 5,114 (2000); Race: 98.6% White, 0.0% Black, 0.2% Asian, 0.2% American Indian and Alaska Native, 2.0% Hispanic of any race, 1.0% two or more races (2000); Density: 1,164.6 persons per square mile (2000); Age: 22.1% under 18, 22.7% over 64 (2000); Marriage status: 25.1% never married, 50.0% now married, 14.5% widowed, 10.4% divorced (2000); Foreign born: 1.5% (2000); Ancestry (includes multiple ancestries): 38.5% German, 17.0% Irish, 14.5% Norwegian, 12.3% English, 6.7% United States or American (2000).
Economy: Single-family building permits issued: 6 (2001) / 6 (2000); Multi-family building permits issued: 0 (2001) / 48 (2000); Employment by occupation: 9.1% management, 15.1% professional, 15.4% services, 23.9% sales, 1.6% farming, 9.3% construction, 25.5% production (2000).
Income: Per capita income: $15,520 (2000); Median household income: $27,129 (2000); Poverty rate: 12.6% (2000).
Taxes: Total city taxes per capita: $245 (1997); City property taxes per capita: $233 (1997).
Education: High school graduation rate: 81.9% (2000); College graduation rate: 16.2% (2000).

School District(s)

Ithaca (KG-12)
2000 Enrollment: 374 608-585-2512
Richland (PK-12)
2000 Enrollment: 1,619 608-647-6106

Housing: Homeownership rate: 58.3% (2000); Median home value: $72,800 (2000); Median rent: $358 per month (2000); Median age of housing: 49 years (2000).
Hospitals: Richland Hospital (66 beds)
Safety: Violent crime rate: 27.2 per 10,000 population; Property crime rate: 275.7 per 10,000 population (2001).
Newspapers: Richland Observer (1 x week)
Transportation: Commute to work: 87.1% car, 0.5% public transportation, 8.1% walk, 3.1% work from home (2000); Travel time to work: 67.0% less than 15 minutes, 12.4% 15 to 30 minutes, 8.0% 30 to 45 minutes, 4.8% 45 to 60 minutes, 7.7% 60 minutes or more (2000)

Additional Information Contacts

Richland Center Chamber of Commerce 608-647-6205
Richland Main St. Chamber of Commerce 608-647-8418

RICHWOOD (town). Covers a land area of 41.711 square miles and a water area of 0.736 square miles. Located at 43.24° N. Lat.; 90.61° W. Long.
Population: 618 (2000); Race: 98.1% White, 0.3% Black, 0.0% Asian, 0.3% American Indian and Alaska Native, 0.3% Hispanic of any race, 1.3% two or more races (2000); Density: 14.8 persons per square mile (2000); Age: 23.9% under 18, 15.5% over 64 (2000); Marriage status: 24.9% never married, 61.1% now married, 5.4% widowed, 8.6% divorced (2000); Foreign born: 0.0% (2000); Ancestry (includes multiple ancestries): 38.1% German, 17.0% Irish, 14.1% Norwegian, 13.7% English, 8.6% United States or American (2000).
Economy: Employment by occupation: 18.8% management, 9.7% professional, 13.8% services, 22.2% sales, 2.2% farming, 10.9% construction, 22.5% production (2000).
Income: Per capita income: $17,304 (2000); Median household income: $35,156 (2000); Poverty rate: 8.2% (2000).
Taxes: Total city taxes per capita: $74 (1997); City property taxes per capita: $74 (1997).
Education: High school graduation rate: 82.2% (2000); College graduation rate: 11.8% (2000).
Housing: Homeownership rate: 83.1% (2000); Median home value: $80,300 (2000); Median rent: $383 per month (2000); Median age of housing: 41 years (2000).
Transportation: Commute to work: 82.3% car, 0.0% public transportation, 4.7% walk, 13.0% work from home (2000); Travel time to work: 19.3% less than 15 minutes, 36.7% 15 to 30 minutes, 22.2% 30 to 45 minutes, 6.5% 45 to 60 minutes, 15.3% 60 minutes or more (2000)

ROCKBRIDGE (town). Covers a land area of 36.170 square miles and a water area of 0.007 square miles. Located at 43.43° N. Lat.; 90.36° W. Long. Elevation is 777 feet.
Population: 721 (2000); Race: 98.5% White, 0.9% Black, 0.0% Asian, 0.0% American Indian and Alaska Native, 0.1% Hispanic of any race, 0.4% two or more races (2000); Density: 19.9 persons per square mile (2000); Age: 31.1% under 18, 14.3% over 64 (2000); Marriage status: 22.4% never married, 68.4% now married, 5.3% widowed, 3.9% divorced (2000); Foreign born: 0.7% (2000); Ancestry (includes multiple ancestries): 35.9% German, 15.7% Irish, 14.6% English, 10.1% Norwegian, 5.4% Czech (2000).

Economy: Employment by occupation: 20.5% management, 11.9% professional, 8.8% services, 18.4% sales, 7.0% farming, 9.3% construction, 24.1% production (2000).
Income: Per capita income: $17,269 (2000); Median household income: $41,563 (2000); Poverty rate: 8.5% (2000).
Taxes: Total city taxes per capita: $118 (1997); City property taxes per capita: $116 (1997).
Education: High school graduation rate: 85.0% (2000); College graduation rate: 16.7% (2000).
Housing: Homeownership rate: 86.7% (2000); Median home value: $81,300 (2000); Median rent: $363 per month (2000); Median age of housing: 42 years (2000).
Transportation: Commute to work: 80.4% car, 1.6% public transportation, 4.2% walk, 13.1% work from home (2000); Travel time to work: 27.6% less than 15 minutes, 45.3% 15 to 30 minutes, 15.0% 30 to 45 minutes, 5.7% 45 to 60 minutes, 6.3% 60 minutes or more (2000)

SYLVAN (town). Covers a land area of 36.083 square miles and a water area of 0.007 square miles. Located at 43.40° N. Lat.; 90.60° W. Long. Elevation is 1,257 feet.
Population: 547 (2000); Race: 97.3% White, 0.0% Black, 0.0% Asian, 2.7% American Indian and Alaska Native, 1.8% Hispanic of any race, 0.0% two or more races (2000); Density: 15.2 persons per square mile (2000); Age: 28.2% under 18, 10.9% over 64 (2000); Marriage status: 28.1% never married, 62.8% now married, 5.1% widowed, 4.0% divorced (2000); Foreign born: 0.2% (2000); Ancestry (includes multiple ancestries): 32.5% German, 13.5% Irish, 13.5% Norwegian, 13.3% English, 10.0% United States or American (2000).
Economy: Employment by occupation: 14.4% management, 10.2% professional, 11.3% services, 15.8% sales, 6.3% farming, 9.9% construction, 32.0% production (2000).
Income: Per capita income: $14,287 (2000); Median household income: $37,917 (2000); Poverty rate: 9.1% (2000).
Taxes: Total city taxes per capita: $89 (1997); City property taxes per capita: $89 (1997).
Education: High school graduation rate: 80.6% (2000); College graduation rate: 10.9% (2000).
Housing: Homeownership rate: 83.1% (2000); Median home value: $80,800 (2000); Median rent: $183 per month (2000); Median age of housing: 39 years (2000).
Transportation: Commute to work: 71.8% car, 0.0% public transportation, 7.4% walk, 16.5% work from home (2000); Travel time to work: 27.4% less than 15 minutes, 41.4% 15 to 30 minutes, 14.8% 30 to 45 minutes, 2.5% 45 to 60 minutes, 13.9% 60 minutes or more (2000)

VIOLA (village). Covers a land area of 1.054 square miles and a water area of 0 square miles. Located at 43.50° N. Lat.; 90.67° W. Long. Elevation is 770 feet.
Population: 667 (2000); Race: 98.1% White, 0.0% Black, 1.2% Asian, 0.0% American Indian and Alaska Native, 0.6% Hispanic of any race, 0.7% two or more races (2000); Density: 632.9 persons per square mile (2000); Age: 19.7% under 18, 23.2% over 64 (2000); Marriage status: 20.6% never married, 54.9% now married, 9.4% widowed, 15.2% divorced (2000); Foreign born: 1.0% (2000); Ancestry (includes multiple ancestries): 22.9% German, 18.4% Norwegian, 17.7% Irish, 13.7% English, 7.9% Other groups (2000).
Economy: Single-family building permits issued: 0 (2001) / 2 (2000); Multi-family building permits issued: 0 (2001) / 0 (2000); Employment by occupation: 4.1% management, 19.9% professional, 13.0% services, 13.6% sales, 0.6% farming, 12.0% construction, 36.7% production (2000).
Income: Per capita income: $17,265 (2000); Median household income: $28,068 (2000); Poverty rate: 16.9% (2000).
Taxes: Total city taxes per capita: $77 (1997); City property taxes per capita: $68 (1997).
Education: High school graduation rate: 74.9% (2000); College graduation rate: 9.8% (2000).

School District(s)

Kickapoo Area (KG-12)
2000 Enrollment: 437 608-627-0102
Housing: Homeownership rate: 72.5% (2000); Median home value: $44,800 (2000); Median rent: $317 per month (2000); Median age of housing: 60+ years (2000).
Newspapers: The Epitaph-News (1 x week)
Transportation: Commute to work: 93.8% car, 0.0% public transportation, 3.2% walk, 1.9% work from home (2000); Travel time to work: 45.4% less than 15 minutes, 25.8% 15 to 30 minutes, 17.9% 30 to 45 minutes, 2.3% 45 to 60 minutes, 8.6% 60 minutes or more (2000)

WESTFORD (town). Covers a land area of 34.914 square miles and a water area of 0.017 square miles. Located at 43.51° N. Lat.; 90.23° W. Long.
Population: 594 (2000); Race: 99.8% White, 0.0% Black, 0.0% Asian, 0.2% American Indian and Alaska Native, 0.0% Hispanic of any race, 0.0% two or more races (2000); Density: 17.0 persons per square mile (2000); Age: 32.7% under 18, 7.4% over 64 (2000); Marriage status: 28.9% never married, 63.6% now married, 2.4% widowed, 5.2% divorced (2000); Foreign born: 0.0% (2000); Ancestry (includes multiple ancestries): 51.3% German, 13.6% Irish, 7.3% Norwegian, 6.1% English, 6.1% French (except Basque) (2000).
Economy: Employment by occupation: 19.7% management, 5.4% professional, 11.5% services, 12.1% sales, 9.2% farming, 11.1% construction, 30.9% production (2000).
Income: Per capita income: $13,519 (2000); Median household income: $39,375 (2000); Poverty rate: 23.6% (2000).
Taxes: Total city taxes per capita: $169 (1997); City property taxes per capita: $169 (1997).
Education: High school graduation rate: 74.4% (2000); College graduation rate: 7.1% (2000).
Housing: Homeownership rate: 86.8% (2000); Median home value: $57,000 (2000); Median rent: $375 per month (2000); Median age of housing: 60+ years (2000).
Transportation: Commute to work: 66.9% car, 0.0% public transportation, 6.4% walk, 26.0% work from home (2000); Travel time to work: 17.4% less than 15 minutes, 39.1% 15 to 30 minutes, 25.7% 30 to 45 minutes, 5.2% 45 to 60 minutes, 12.6% 60 minutes or more (2000)

WILLOW (town). Covers a land area of 35.829 square miles and a water area of 0.015 square miles. Located at 43.43° N. Lat.; 90.25° W. Long.
Population: 493 (2000); Race: 95.8% White, 0.6% Black, 0.8% Asian, 0.0% American Indian and Alaska Native, 0.0% Hispanic of any race, 2.7% two or more races (2000); Density: 13.8 persons per square mile (2000); Age: 25.2% under 18, 8.6% over 64 (2000); Marriage status: 20.5% never married, 63.5% now married, 5.3% widowed, 10.7% divorced (2000); Foreign born: 1.7% (2000); Ancestry (includes multiple ancestries): 34.7% German, 14.9% Irish, 14.5% Norwegian, 12.2% United States or American, 12.0% English (2000).
Economy: Employment by occupation: 18.8% management, 12.4% professional, 14.5% services, 23.0% sales, 4.3% farming, 7.1% construction, 19.9% production (2000).
Income: Per capita income: $17,100 (2000); Median household income: $41,607 (2000); Poverty rate: 10.1% (2000).
Taxes: Total city taxes per capita: $67 (1997); City property taxes per capita: $67 (1997).
Education: High school graduation rate: 81.9% (2000); College graduation rate: 16.8% (2000).
Housing: Homeownership rate: 80.1% (2000); Median home value: $84,200 (2000); Median rent: $283 per month (2000); Median age of housing: 28 years (2000).
Transportation: Commute to work: 86.7% car, 0.0% public transportation, 4.3% walk, 9.0% work from home (2000); Travel time to work: 15.4% less than 15 minutes, 44.1% 15 to 30 minutes, 25.2% 30 to 45 minutes, 5.1% 45 to 60 minutes, 10.2% 60 minutes or more (2000)

YUBA (village). Covers a land area of 0.301 square miles and a water area of 0 square miles. Located at 43.53° N. Lat.; 90.42° W. Long. Elevation is 1,868 feet.
Population: 92 (2000); Race: 100.0% White, 0.0% Black, 0.0% Asian, 0.0% American Indian and Alaska Native, 0.0% Hispanic of any race, 0.0% two or more races (2000); Density: 305.9 persons per square mile (2000); Age: 28.0% under 18, 20.0% over 64 (2000); Marriage status: 22.8% never married, 69.6% now married, 2.5% widowed, 5.1% divorced (2000); Foreign born: 0.0% (2000); Ancestry (includes multiple ancestries): 41.0% Czech, 38.0% German, 13.0% English, 12.0% Norwegian, 8.0% Irish (2000).
Economy: In dairying region. Single-family building permits issued: 0 (2001) / 0 (2000); Multi-family building permits issued: 0 (2001) / 0 (2000); Employment by occupation: 4.8% management, 4.8% professional, 21.4% services, 23.8% sales, 0.0% farming, 4.8% construction, 40.5% production (2000).
Income: Per capita income: $11,819 (2000); Median household income: $34,063 (2000); Poverty rate: 9.0% (2000).
Taxes: Total city taxes per capita: $22 (2000); City property taxes per capita: $11 (2000).
Education: High school graduation rate: 76.7% (2000); College graduation rate: 6.7% (2000).

Housing: Homeownership rate: 72.7% (2000); Median home value: $76,000 (2000); Median rent: $325 per month (2000); Median age of housing: 56 years (2000).
Transportation: Commute to work: 87.2% car, 0.0% public transportation, 2.6% walk, 10.3% work from home (2000); Travel time to work: 14.3% less than 15 minutes, 31.4% 15 to 30 minutes, 34.3% 30 to 45 minutes, 0.0% 45 to 60 minutes, 20.0% 60 minutes or more (2000)

Rock County

Located in southern Wisconsin; bounded on the south by Illinois; drained by the Rock and Sugar Rivers and Turtle Creek; includes Lake Koshkonong. Covers a land area of 720.50 square miles, a water area of 5.70 square miles, and is located in the Central Time Zone. The county government was organized in 1836. County seat is Janesville.

Rock County is part of the Janesville-Beloit, WI MSA. The entire metro area includes: Rock County

Weather Station: Beloit Elevation: 777 feet

	Jan	Feb	Mar	Apr	May	Jun	Jul	Aug	Sep	Oct	Nov	Dec
High	27	32	44	59	71	81	84	81	74	63	46	33
Low	11	16	26	38	48	58	63	61	52	41	30	18
Precip	1.3	1.2	2.2	3.7	3.4	4.4	3.9	4.3	3.8	2.5	2.8	1.9
Snow	8.8	6.5	3.6	1.0	tr	0.0	0.0	0.0	0.0	tr	1.5	6.7

High and Low temperatures in degrees Fahrenheit; Precipitation and Snow in inches

Population: 152,307 (2000); Race: 91.1% White, 4.4% Black, 0.9% Asian, 0.3% American Indian and Alaska Native, 3.9% Hispanic of any race, 1.3% two or more races (2000); Density: 211.4 persons per square mile (2000); Age: 26.5% under 18, 12.8% over 64 (2000).
Religion: Five largest groups: 20.3% Catholic Church, 10.8% Evangelical Lutheran Church in America, 4.8% Lutheran Church—Missouri Synod, 3.3% The United Methodist Church, 1.4% Presbyterian Church (U.S.A.) (2000).
Economy: Unemployment rate: 5.2% (11/2002); Total civilian labor force: 80,160 (11/2002); Leading industries: 27.8% manufacturing; 13.9% retail trade; 11.3% health care and social assistance (2000); Companies that employ more than 1,000 persons: 4 (2000); Companies that employ more than 100 persons: 97 (2000); Farms: 1,324 totaling 351,013 acres (1997); Minority business ownership rate: 4.8% (1997); Women business ownership rate: 31.4% (1997); Retail sales per capita: $10,654 (1997). Single-family building permits issued: 496 (2001) / 528 (2000); Multi-family building permits issued: 340 (2001) / 320 (2000).
Income: Per capita income: $20,895 (2000); Median household income: $45,517 (2000); Poverty rate: 7.3% (2000); Bankruptcy rate: 5.63% (2001).
Taxes: Total county taxes per capita: $223 (2000); County property taxes per capita: $220 (2000).
Education: High school graduation rate: 83.9% (2000); College graduation rate: 16.7% (2000).
Housing: Homeownership rate: 71.2% (2000); Median home value: $98,200 (2000); Median rent: $467 per month (2000); Median age of housing: 37 years (2000).
Health: Birth rate: 134.3 per 10,000 population (1998); Age adjusted death rate: 83.0 per 10,000 population (1999); Age adjusted cancer mortality rate: 179.3 deaths per 100,000 population (1999). Air Quality Index: 67% good, 33% moderate, 0% unhealthy (percent of days in 2000). Number of physicians: 18.0 per 10,000 population (1999); Number of hospital beds: 33.2 per 10,000 population (1999).
Elections: 2000 Presidential election results: 57.5% Gore, 39.0% Bush, 2.8% Nader, 0.2% Buchanan

Additional Information Contacts

Rock County Government Offices........................ 608-757-5510
Beloit Chamber of Commerce........................ 608-365-8835
Evansville Chamber of Commerce........................ 608-882-5131
Janesville Area Convention & Visitors Bureau............ 608-757-3171
Milton Chamber of Commerce........................ 608-868-6222
Rock Green Realtors Association........................ 608-755-4854

Rock County Communities

AVALON (unincorporated postal area, zip code 53505). Covers a land area of 18.197 square miles and a water area of 0 square miles. Located at 42.64° N. Lat.; 88.82° W. Long. Elevation is 955 feet.
Population: 355 (2000); Race: 98.9% White, 0.0% Black, 0.0% Asian, 0.0% American Indian and Alaska Native, 0.5% Hispanic of any race, 1.1% two or more races (2000); Density: 19.5 persons per square mile (2000); Age: 25.2% under 18, 17.3% over 64 (2000); Marriage status: 24.2% never married, 63.8% now married, 7.2% widowed, 4.8% divorced (2000); Foreign born: 0.0% (2000); Ancestry (includes multiple ancestries): 36.3% German, 17.9% Irish, 13.6% English, 11.7% Norwegian, 5.1% Scotch-Irish (2000).
Economy: Employment by occupation: 15.9% management, 14.5% professional, 9.7% services, 14.0% sales, 0.5% farming, 9.7% construction, 35.7% production (2000).
Income: Per capita income: $22,559 (2000); Median household income: $58,269 (2000); Poverty rate: 0.0% (2000).
Education: High school graduation rate: 86.2% (2000); College graduation rate: 14.6% (2000).
Housing: Homeownership rate: 73.8% (2000); Median home value: $107,500 (2000); Median rent: $438 per month (2000); Median age of housing: 60+ years (2000).
Transportation: Commute to work: 86.4% car, 0.0% public transportation, 4.0% walk, 8.6% work from home (2000); Travel time to work: 24.3% less than 15 minutes, 58.6% 15 to 30 minutes, 9.9% 30 to 45 minutes, 5.5% 45 to 60 minutes, 1.7% 60 minutes or more (2000)

AVON (town). Covers a land area of 36.129 square miles and a water area of 0 square miles. Located at 42.56° N. Lat.; 89.29° W. Long. Elevation is 760 feet.
Population: 586 (2000); Race: 99.7% White, 0.0% Black, 0.0% Asian, 0.0% American Indian and Alaska Native, 0.7% Hispanic of any race, 0.0% two or more races (2000); Density: 16.2 persons per square mile (2000); Age: 30.7% under 18, 11.5% over 64 (2000); Marriage status: 15.7% never married, 71.0% now married, 5.5% widowed, 7.8% divorced (2000); Foreign born: 0.8% (2000); Ancestry (includes multiple ancestries): 32.9% German, 14.4% Norwegian, 13.6% Irish, 11.4% English, 5.3% Swiss (2000).
Economy: Employment by occupation: 10.6% management, 9.4% professional, 4.3% services, 34.1% sales, 2.0% farming, 13.3% construction, 26.3% production (2000).
Income: Per capita income: $18,770 (2000); Median household income: $47,321 (2000); Poverty rate: 9.9% (2000).
Taxes: Total city taxes per capita: $127 (1997); City property taxes per capita: $123 (1997).
Education: High school graduation rate: 79.4% (2000); College graduation rate: 10.2% (2000).
Housing: Homeownership rate: 94.1% (2000); Median home value: $106,500 (2000); Median rent: $475 per month (2000); Median age of housing: 44 years (2000).
Transportation: Commute to work: 89.6% car, 0.0% public transportation, 2.4% walk, 7.2% work from home (2000); Travel time to work: 19.0% less than 15 minutes, 31.0% 15 to 30 minutes, 36.6% 30 to 45 minutes, 7.3% 45 to 60 minutes, 6.0% 60 minutes or more (2000)

BELOIT (city). Covers a land area of 16.436 square miles and a water area of 0.229 square miles. Located at 42.51° N. Lat.; 89.03° W. Long. Elevation is 780 feet.
History: Beloit was settled in 1837 by a group from Colebrook, New Hampshire, led by Dr. Horace White of the New England Emigrating Company. Known first as Turtle, Blodgett's Settlement, and New Albany, the village was named Beloit in 1857. The Beloit Iron Works began producing paper-making machines in 1858. The Berlin Machine Works, which later became the Yates-American Machine Company, was established in Beloit in 1887, and the Fairbanks-Morse Company had its beginning here in 1889 as the Williams Engine Works. In 1847 the Congregational Church founded Beloit College.
Population: 35,775 (2000); Race: 75.7% White, 15.0% Black, 1.5% Asian, 0.5% American Indian and Alaska Native, 9.0% Hispanic of any race, 2.5% two or more races (2000); Density: 2,176.6 persons per square mile (2000); Age: 27.7% under 18, 13.3% over 64 (2000); Marriage status: 29.1% never married, 52.0% now married, 7.2% widowed, 11.7% divorced (2000); Foreign born: 7.2% (2000); Ancestry (includes multiple ancestries): 26.1% Other groups, 25.1% German, 12.6% Irish, 9.3% English, 8.6% Norwegian (2000).
Vital Statistics: Birth rate: 175.8 per 10,000 population (1998)
Economy: Unemployment rate: 8.2% (11/2002); Total civilian labor force: 17,975 (11/2002); Single-family building permits issued: 28 (2001) / 65 (2000); Multi-family building permits issued: 42 (2001) / 52 (2000); Employment by occupation: 7.9% management, 13.8% professional, 16.6% services, 22.6% sales, 0.2% farming, 7.5% construction, 31.4% production (2000).
Income: Per capita income: $16,912 (2000); Median household income: $36,414 (2000); Poverty rate: 12.5% (2000).

Taxes: Total city taxes per capita: $255 (2000); City property taxes per capita: $234 (2000).
Education: High school graduation rate: 75.6% (2000); College graduation rate: 13.5% (2000).

School District(s)

Beloit (PK-12)
2000 Enrollment: 6,880 608-361-4017
Beloit Turner (PK-12)
2000 Enrollment: 1,130 608-364-6372

Four-year College(s)

Beloit College (Private, Not-for-profit)
2001 Enrollment: 1,273 608-363-2000
2001 Tuition: In-state $22,184; Out-of-state $22,184
Housing: Homeownership rate: 62.1% (2000); Median home value: $68,200 (2000); Median rent: $431 per month (2000); Median age of housing: 48 years (2000).
Hospitals: Beloit Memorial Hospital (174 beds)
Safety: Violent crime rate: 38.6 per 10,000 population; Property crime rate: 456.8 per 10,000 population (2001).
Newspapers: Beloit Daily News (6 x week); The Chronicle-Rock County (1 x week)
Transportation: Commute to work: 92.3% car, 1.1% public transportation, 5.0% walk, 1.1% work from home (2000); Travel time to work: 44.3% less than 15 minutes, 33.6% 15 to 30 minutes, 12.2% 30 to 45 minutes, 5.6% 45 to 60 minutes, 4.2% 60 minutes or more (2000)
Additional Information Contacts
Beloit Chamber of Commerce 608-365-8835

BELOIT (town). Covers a land area of 26.323 square miles and a water area of 0.692 square miles. Located at 42.54° N. Lat.; 89.05° W. Long. Elevation is 780 feet.
History: A trading post was established on the site in 1824 for trade with the Winnebagos, and in 1837 the first permanent settlers arrived from New England. Beloit College, founded in 1846, is in the city. Incorporated 1846.
Population: 7,038 (2000); Race: 92.1% White, 5.8% Black, 0.5% Asian, 0.2% American Indian and Alaska Native, 2.0% Hispanic of any race, 1.3% two or more races (2000); Density: 267.4 persons per square mile (2000); Age: 23.9% under 18, 16.2% over 64 (2000); Marriage status: 20.1% never married, 65.7% now married, 6.7% widowed, 7.5% divorced (2000); Foreign born: 1.9% (2000); Ancestry (includes multiple ancestries): 33.6% German, 16.7% Irish, 13.6% Norwegian, 10.9% English, 10.6% Other groups (2000).
Economy: Railroad junction in an agricultural area. Beloit's manufacturing includes pulp- and paper-making machinery, engines, food, knives. Single-family building permits issued: 36 (2001) / 22 (2000); Multi-family building permits issued: 26 (2001) / 79 (2000); Employment by occupation: 10.4% management, 12.6% professional, 14.9% services, 24.6% sales, 0.0% farming, 11.4% construction, 26.0% production (2000).
Income: Per capita income: $21,874 (2000); Median household income: $47,970 (2000); Poverty rate: 7.6% (2000).
Taxes: Total city taxes per capita: $155 (2000); City property taxes per capita: $139 (2000).
Education: High school graduation rate: 84.8% (2000); College graduation rate: 11.5% (2000).
Housing: Homeownership rate: 85.2% (2000); Median home value: $102,000 (2000); Median rent: $447 per month (2000); Median age of housing: 40 years (2000).
Safety: Violent crime rate: 7.1 per 10,000 population; Property crime rate: 414.8 per 10,000 population (2001).
Transportation: Commute to work: 94.5% car, 0.4% public transportation, 0.6% walk, 3.5% work from home (2000); Travel time to work: 46.4% less than 15 minutes, 36.7% 15 to 30 minutes, 9.9% 30 to 45 minutes, 3.6% 45 to 60 minutes, 3.5% 60 minutes or more (2000)

BRADFORD (town). Covers a land area of 36.311 square miles and a water area of 0 square miles. Located at 42.62° N. Lat.; 88.82° W. Long.
Population: 1,007 (2000); Race: 96.9% White, 0.0% Black, 0.0% Asian, 1.2% American Indian and Alaska Native, 4.1% Hispanic of any race, 0.5% two or more races (2000); Density: 27.7 persons per square mile (2000); Age: 25.8% under 18, 12.5% over 64 (2000); Marriage status: 21.6% never married, 65.4% now married, 5.4% widowed, 7.5% divorced (2000); Foreign born: 0.9% (2000); Ancestry (includes multiple ancestries): 38.8% German, 16.0% English, 14.8% Norwegian, 10.9% Irish, 9.0% Other groups (2000).
Economy: Single-family building permits issued: 0 (2001) / 0 (2000); Multi-family building permits issued: 0 (2001) / 0 (2000); Employment by occupation: 19.3% management, 12.7% professional, 9.1% services, 24.1% sales, 1.8% farming, 10.2% construction, 23.0% production (2000).
Income: Per capita income: $23,440 (2000); Median household income: $51,324 (2000); Poverty rate: 6.9% (2000).
Taxes: Total city taxes per capita: $56 (1997); City property taxes per capita: $49 (1997).
Education: High school graduation rate: 83.0% (2000); College graduation rate: 13.2% (2000).
Housing: Homeownership rate: 72.5% (2000); Median home value: $121,700 (2000); Median rent: $433 per month (2000); Median age of housing: 41 years (2000).
Transportation: Commute to work: 88.0% car, 0.0% public transportation, 4.2% walk, 6.9% work from home (2000); Travel time to work: 22.9% less than 15 minutes, 58.3% 15 to 30 minutes, 10.8% 30 to 45 minutes, 6.1% 45 to 60 minutes, 2.0% 60 minutes or more (2000)

CENTER (town). Covers a land area of 35.605 square miles and a water area of 0.010 square miles. Located at 42.71° N. Lat.; 89.18° W. Long.
Population: 1,005 (2000); Race: 98.0% White, 0.1% Black, 0.0% Asian, 0.8% American Indian and Alaska Native, 0.4% Hispanic of any race, 0.4% two or more races (2000); Density: 28.2 persons per square mile (2000); Age: 24.1% under 18, 12.2% over 64 (2000); Marriage status: 20.3% never married, 66.7% now married, 5.0% widowed, 8.1% divorced (2000); Foreign born: 1.2% (2000); Ancestry (includes multiple ancestries): 50.3% German, 18.8% Norwegian, 16.0% Irish, 12.5% English, 3.8% Swiss (2000).
Economy: Single-family building permits issued: 8 (2001) / 10 (2000); Multi-family building permits issued: 0 (2001) / 0 (2000); Employment by occupation: 12.3% management, 13.3% professional, 12.5% services, 21.3% sales, 4.5% farming, 11.7% construction, 24.4% production (2000).
Income: Per capita income: $23,982 (2000); Median household income: $59,479 (2000); Poverty rate: 1.5% (2000).
Taxes: Total city taxes per capita: $88 (1997); City property taxes per capita: $83 (1997).
Education: High school graduation rate: 87.2% (2000); College graduation rate: 12.6% (2000).
Housing: Homeownership rate: 83.5% (2000); Median home value: $155,000 (2000); Median rent: $404 per month (2000); Median age of housing: 31 years (2000).
Transportation: Commute to work: 90.8% car, 0.0% public transportation, 1.8% walk, 5.9% work from home (2000); Travel time to work: 23.9% less than 15 minutes, 55.8% 15 to 30 minutes, 10.4% 30 to 45 minutes, 7.5% 45 to 60 minutes, 2.5% 60 minutes or more (2000)

CLINTON (village). Aka Clinton Junction. Covers a land area of 1.309 square miles and a water area of 0 square miles. Located at 42.55° N. Lat.; 88.86° W. Long. Elevation is 949 feet.
Population: 2,162 (2000); Race: 92.8% White, 0.6% Black, 1.5% Asian, 0.3% American Indian and Alaska Native, 4.7% Hispanic of any race, 1.7% two or more races (2000); Density: 1,652.0 persons per square mile (2000); Age: 29.6% under 18, 13.6% over 64 (2000); Marriage status: 24.0% never married, 55.8% now married, 9.7% widowed, 10.5% divorced (2000); Foreign born: 4.5% (2000); Ancestry (includes multiple ancestries): 34.6% German, 10.9% Norwegian, 9.8% Irish, 9.5% Other groups, 9.2% English (2000).
Economy: Single-family building permits issued: 3 (2001) / 2 (2000); Multi-family building permits issued: 78 (2001) / 67 (2000); Employment by occupation: 6.5% management, 14.8% professional, 15.6% services, 21.4% sales, 2.4% farming, 12.5% construction, 26.8% production (2000).
Income: Per capita income: $18,015 (2000); Median household income: $45,987 (2000); Poverty rate: 7.2% (2000).
Taxes: Total city taxes per capita: $366 (1997); City property taxes per capita: $346 (1997).
Education: High school graduation rate: 81.0% (2000); College graduation rate: 14.8% (2000).

School District(s)

Clinton Community (PK-12)
2000 Enrollment: 1,167 608-676-5482
Housing: Homeownership rate: 65.2% (2000); Median home value: $100,100 (2000); Median rent: $468 per month (2000); Median age of housing: 39 years (2000).
Safety: Violent crime rate: 18.4 per 10,000 population; Property crime rate: 275.6 per 10,000 population (2001).
Newspapers: Clinton Topper (1 x week)
Transportation: Commute to work: 92.4% car, 0.0% public transportation, 4.5% walk, 2.3% work from home (2000); Travel time to work: 29.8% less than 15 minutes, 41.5% 15 to 30 minutes, 21.5% 30 to 45 minutes, 4.1% 45 to 60 minutes, 3.1% 60 minutes or more (2000)

CLINTON (town). Aka Clinton Junction. Covers a land area of 35.384 square miles and a water area of 0.017 square miles. Located at 42.54° N. Lat.; 88.83° W. Long. Elevation is 949 feet.
Population: 893 (2000); Race: 99.7% White, 0.0% Black, 0.0% Asian, 0.0% American Indian and Alaska Native, 0.3% Hispanic of any race, 0.3% two or more races (2000); Density: 25.2 persons per square mile (2000); Age: 24.8% under 18, 11.3% over 64 (2000); Marriage status: 20.6% never married, 65.9% now married, 4.7% widowed, 8.8% divorced (2000); Foreign born: 1.3% (2000); Ancestry (includes multiple ancestries): 45.1% German, 16.1% Norwegian, 14.8% Irish, 14.4% English, 9.0% Swedish (2000).
Economy: In dairying and farming area. Railroad junction. Manufacturing: steel forgings, meat processing. Single-family building permits issued: 4 (2001) / 4 (2000); Multi-family building permits issued: 4 (2001) / 4 (2000); Employment by occupation: 9.5% management, 15.3% professional, 12.7% services, 21.3% sales, 1.6% farming, 15.5% construction, 24.1% production (2000).
Income: Per capita income: $22,216 (2000); Median household income: $55,324 (2000); Poverty rate: 2.9% (2000).
Taxes: Total city taxes per capita: $51 (1997); City property taxes per capita: $48 (1997).
Education: High school graduation rate: 90.1% (2000); College graduation rate: 14.0% (2000).
Housing: Homeownership rate: 82.0% (2000); Median home value: $137,100 (2000); Median rent: $469 per month (2000); Median age of housing: 60+ years (2000).
Transportation: Commute to work: 94.2% car, 0.6% public transportation, 1.2% walk, 4.0% work from home (2000); Travel time to work: 33.4% less than 15 minutes, 36.7% 15 to 30 minutes, 19.2% 30 to 45 minutes, 5.4% 45 to 60 minutes, 5.2% 60 minutes or more (2000)

EDGERTON (city). Covers a land area of 3.671 square miles and a water area of 0 square miles. Located at 42.83° N. Lat.; 89.07° W. Long. Elevation is 830 feet.
History: Edgerton developed in the 1850's as the center of a tobacco trading area.
Population: 4,933 (2000); Race: 97.5% White, 0.0% Black, 1.5% Asian, 0.3% American Indian and Alaska Native, 3.7% Hispanic of any race, 0.4% two or more races (2000); Density: 1,343.8 persons per square mile (2000); Age: 26.2% under 18, 15.2% over 64 (2000); Marriage status: 23.7% never married, 59.3% now married, 8.3% widowed, 8.8% divorced (2000); Foreign born: 3.6% (2000); Ancestry (includes multiple ancestries): 41.3% German, 22.6% Norwegian, 14.3% Irish, 11.8% English, 9.3% Other groups (2000).
Economy: Single-family building permits issued: 9 (2001) / 19 (2000); Multi-family building permits issued: 6 (2001) / 0 (2000); Employment by occupation: 8.9% management, 18.2% professional, 14.0% services, 22.0% sales, 0.2% farming, 7.9% construction, 28.7% production (2000).
Income: Per capita income: $20,481 (2000); Median household income: $44,684 (2000); Poverty rate: 5.7% (2000).
Taxes: Total city taxes per capita: $262 (1997); City property taxes per capita: $243 (1997).
Education: High school graduation rate: 82.5% (2000); College graduation rate: 19.0% (2000).

School District(s)

Edgerton (PK-12)
2000 Enrollment: 1,908 608-884-9402
Housing: Homeownership rate: 64.2% (2000); Median home value: $98,500 (2000); Median rent: $453 per month (2000); Median age of housing: 41 years (2000).
Hospitals: Memorial Community Hospital (70 beds)
Newspapers: Edgerton Reporter (1 x week)
Transportation: Commute to work: 93.3% car, 0.0% public transportation, 4.8% walk, 1.9% work from home (2000); Travel time to work: 34.6% less than 15 minutes, 34.0% 15 to 30 minutes, 22.9% 30 to 45 minutes, 5.9% 45 to 60 minutes, 2.6% 60 minutes or more (2000)

EVANSVILLE (city). Covers a land area of 2.168 square miles and a water area of 0.050 square miles. Located at 42.78° N. Lat.; 89.30° W. Long. Elevation is 897 feet.
History: Evansville was settled in 1839, and first called The Grove because of the stand of timber around it. A sawmill was replaced by a gristmill when the timber was depleted. The arrival of the railroad in 1864 brought growth to Evansville, which was incorporated in 1867.
Population: 4,039 (2000); Race: 96.7% White, 0.0% Black, 1.8% Asian, 0.0% American Indian and Alaska Native, 1.8% Hispanic of any race, 0.7% two or more races (2000); Density: 1,863.0 persons per square mile (2000); Age: 28.1% under 18, 13.9% over 64 (2000); Marriage status: 21.3% never married, 62.3% now married, 6.3% widowed, 10.1% divorced (2000); Foreign born: 2.7% (2000); Ancestry (includes multiple ancestries): 42.7% German, 23.4% Norwegian, 13.3% Irish, 9.9% English, 8.4% Swiss (2000).
Economy: Single-family building permits issued: 35 (2001) / 30 (2000); Multi-family building permits issued: 9 (2001) / 32 (2000); Employment by occupation: 11.2% management, 17.7% professional, 14.6% services, 24.3% sales, 0.6% farming, 12.9% construction, 18.6% production (2000).
Income: Per capita income: $20,766 (2000); Median household income: $44,229 (2000); Poverty rate: 4.1% (2000).
Taxes: Total city taxes per capita: $327 (1997); City property taxes per capita: $313 (1997).
Education: High school graduation rate: 87.0% (2000); College graduation rate: 22.4% (2000).

School District(s)

Evansville Community (PK-12)
2000 Enrollment: 1,529 608-882-5224
Housing: Homeownership rate: 67.9% (2000); Median home value: $111,500 (2000); Median rent: $452 per month (2000); Median age of housing: 46 years (2000).
Safety: Violent crime rate: 24.6 per 10,000 population; Property crime rate: 218.8 per 10,000 population (2001).
Newspapers: The Review (1 x week); Trading Post (1 x week)
Transportation: Commute to work: 89.9% car, 0.5% public transportation, 4.4% walk, 4.2% work from home (2000); Travel time to work: 33.7% less than 15 minutes, 17.6% 15 to 30 minutes, 35.5% 30 to 45 minutes, 10.1% 45 to 60 minutes, 3.2% 60 minutes or more (2000)
Additional Information Contacts
Evansville Chamber of Commerce. 608-882-5131

FOOTVILLE (village). Covers a land area of 0.986 square miles and a water area of 0 square miles. Located at 42.67° N. Lat.; 89.20° W. Long. Elevation is 830 feet.
Population: 788 (2000); Race: 97.4% White, 0.0% Black, 0.0% Asian, 0.0% American Indian and Alaska Native, 0.5% Hispanic of any race, 2.3% two or more races (2000); Density: 799.5 persons per square mile (2000); Age: 23.5% under 18, 12.8% over 64 (2000); Marriage status: 24.2% never married, 62.7% now married, 6.5% widowed, 6.5% divorced (2000); Foreign born: 1.4% (2000); Ancestry (includes multiple ancestries): 36.2% German, 21.2% Norwegian, 19.1% Irish, 12.3% English, 7.2% United States or American (2000).
Economy: Farm trade center. Manufacturing. Single-family building permits issued: 0 (2001) / 0 (2000); Multi-family building permits issued: 0 (2001) / 0 (2000); Employment by occupation: 5.9% management, 12.7% professional, 11.0% services, 19.1% sales, 0.0% farming, 10.3% construction, 41.1% production (2000).
Income: Per capita income: $21,688 (2000); Median household income: $47,768 (2000); Poverty rate: 3.5% (2000).
Taxes: Total city taxes per capita: $104 (1997); City property taxes per capita: $91 (1997).
Education: High school graduation rate: 83.0% (2000); College graduation rate: 10.2% (2000).
Housing: Homeownership rate: 74.8% (2000); Median home value: $87,000 (2000); Median rent: $404 per month (2000); Median age of housing: 47 years (2000).
Transportation: Commute to work: 92.1% car, 0.5% public transportation, 4.7% walk, 2.7% work from home (2000); Travel time to work: 25.4% less than 15 minutes, 46.1% 15 to 30 minutes, 16.5% 30 to 45 minutes, 4.8% 45 to 60 minutes, 7.1% 60 minutes or more (2000)

FULTON (town). Covers a land area of 31.906 square miles and a water area of 1.034 square miles. Located at 42.81° N. Lat.; 89.06° W. Long. Elevation is 796 feet.
Population: 3,158 (2000); Race: 98.8% White, 0.4% Black, 0.2% Asian, 0.2% American Indian and Alaska Native, 0.8% Hispanic of any race, 0.3% two or more races (2000); Density: 99.0 persons per square mile (2000); Age: 22.5% under 18, 13.7% over 64 (2000); Marriage status: 20.9% never married, 64.0% now married, 4.4% widowed, 10.7% divorced (2000); Foreign born: 0.2% (2000); Ancestry (includes multiple ancestries): 41.9% German, 26.2% Norwegian, 14.2% Irish, 13.0% English, 4.4% United States or American (2000).
Economy: Single-family building permits issued: 16 (2001) / 17 (2000); Multi-family building permits issued: 0 (2001) / 0 (2000); Employment by occupation: 14.6% management, 9.5% professional, 11.4% services, 24.2% sales, 0.9% farming, 10.8% construction, 28.5% production (2000).

Income: Per capita income: $24,033 (2000); Median household income: $56,691 (2000); Poverty rate: 3.9% (2000).
Taxes: Total city taxes per capita: $44 (1997); City property taxes per capita: $37 (1997).
Education: High school graduation rate: 87.7% (2000); College graduation rate: 14.1% (2000).
Housing: Homeownership rate: 89.9% (2000); Median home value: $137,800 (2000); Median rent: $468 per month (2000); Median age of housing: 28 years (2000).
Transportation: Commute to work: 91.9% car, 0.8% public transportation, 1.0% walk, 6.3% work from home (2000); Travel time to work: 24.3% less than 15 minutes, 53.7% 15 to 30 minutes, 16.5% 30 to 45 minutes, 2.4% 45 to 60 minutes, 3.1% 60 minutes or more (2000)

HARMONY (town). Covers a land area of 23.953 square miles and a water area of 0.053 square miles. Located at 42.72° N. Lat.; 88.96° W. Long.
Population: 2,351 (2000); Race: 98.4% White, 0.0% Black, 0.5% Asian, 0.0% American Indian and Alaska Native, 0.6% Hispanic of any race, 0.9% two or more races (2000); Density: 98.1 persons per square mile (2000); Age: 28.5% under 18, 7.8% over 64 (2000); Marriage status: 20.9% never married, 68.2% now married, 2.7% widowed, 8.2% divorced (2000); Foreign born: 0.7% (2000); Ancestry (includes multiple ancestries): 45.5% German, 19.0% Irish, 14.4% Norwegian, 13.5% English, 3.9% French (except Basque) (2000).
Economy: Single-family building permits issued: 14 (2001) / 3 (2000); Multi-family building permits issued: 0 (2001) / 0 (2000); Employment by occupation: 13.1% management, 19.7% professional, 14.4% services, 24.4% sales, 0.6% farming, 11.5% construction, 16.3% production (2000).
Income: Per capita income: $25,244 (2000); Median household income: $73,173 (2000); Poverty rate: 0.7% (2000).
Taxes: Total city taxes per capita: $36 (1997); City property taxes per capita: $28 (1997).
Education: High school graduation rate: 92.5% (2000); College graduation rate: 28.2% (2000).
Housing: Homeownership rate: 93.6% (2000); Median home value: $151,200 (2000); Median rent: $571 per month (2000); Median age of housing: 23 years (2000).
Transportation: Commute to work: 95.4% car, 0.0% public transportation, 0.4% walk, 3.7% work from home (2000); Travel time to work: 39.4% less than 15 minutes, 44.8% 15 to 30 minutes, 8.5% 30 to 45 minutes, 3.4% 45 to 60 minutes, 3.9% 60 minutes or more (2000)

JANESVILLE (city). Covers a land area of 27.537 square miles and a water area of 0.587 square miles. Located at 42.68° N. Lat.; 89.01° W. Long. Elevation is 858 feet.
History: Henry F. Janes started a ferry and built a tavern on the east bank of the Rock River in 1837. When Janes became the first postmaster of the new settlement, it was named Janesville for him. Janes soon left the town, and later founded Janesville, Iowa, and Janesville, Minnesota. The Wisconsin Janesville grew rapidly as a stagecoach and steamboat stopping place. In the 1920's and 1930's, Janesville's economy depended on the General Motors plants. A well-known Janesville industry that began in 1892 was the Parker Pen Company, founded by George Parker.
Population: 59,498 (2000); Race: 95.1% White, 1.2% Black, 0.8% Asian, 0.4% American Indian and Alaska Native, 2.7% Hispanic of any race, 1.1% two or more races (2000); Density: 2,160.6 persons per square mile (2000); Age: 26.0% under 18, 12.9% over 64 (2000); Marriage status: 24.3% never married, 57.1% now married, 6.1% widowed, 12.5% divorced (2000); Foreign born: 2.4% (2000); Ancestry (includes multiple ancestries): 41.0% German, 16.2% Irish, 15.3% Norwegian, 11.8% English, 7.4% Other groups (2000).
Vital Statistics: Birth rate: 145.9 per 10,000 population (1998)
Economy: Unemployment rate: 5.4% (11/2002); Total civilian labor force: 32,952 (11/2002); Employment by occupation: 10.4% management, 16.2% professional, 13.6% services, 24.9% sales, 0.2% farming, 8.9% construction, 25.8% production (2000).
Income: Per capita income: $22,224 (2000); Median household income: $45,961 (2000); Poverty rate: 6.5% (2000).
Taxes: Total city taxes per capita: $294 (2000); City property taxes per capita: $266 (2000).
Education: High school graduation rate: 87.0% (2000); College graduation rate: 18.9% (2000).

School District(s)

Janesville (PK-12)
2000 Enrollment: 10,758 608-743-5050

Two-year College(s)

Blackhawk Technical College (Public)
2001 Enrollment: 2,340 608-758-6900
2001 Tuition: In-state $2,085; Out-of-state $16,327

Housing: Homeownership rate: 68.1% (2000); Median home value: $100,000 (2000); Median rent: $498 per month (2000); Median age of housing: 32 years (2000).
Hospitals: Mercy Health System Corporation (240 beds)
Safety: Violent crime rate: 23.5 per 10,000 population; Property crime rate: 509.7 per 10,000 population (2001).
Newspapers: The Janesville Gazette (7 x week); The Jotter (2 x week)
Transportation: Commute to work: 94.3% car, 1.0% public transportation, 2.0% walk, 2.0% work from home (2000); Travel time to work: 50.5% less than 15 minutes, 30.7% 15 to 30 minutes, 9.3% 30 to 45 minutes, 5.3% 45 to 60 minutes, 4.2% 60 minutes or more (2000); Amtrak: Service available.
Airports: Rock Co
Additional Information Contacts
Janesville Area Convention & Visitors Bureau 608-757-3171
Rock Green Realtors Association. 608-755-4854

JANESVILLE (town). Covers a land area of 28.085 square miles and a water area of 0.471 square miles. Located at 42.72° N. Lat.; 89.07° W. Long. Elevation is 858 feet.
History: Points of interest include the 26-room Tallman House, where Lincoln spent a weekend in 1859; the Stone House (1842), of Greek Revival style; and the Milton House (1844), which is connected to a log cabin by a tunnel used by runaway slaves as a stop on the Underground Railroad. Incorporated 1853.
Population: 3,750 (2000); Race: 94.6% White, 3.3% Black, 0.9% Asian, 0.7% American Indian and Alaska Native, 0.9% Hispanic of any race, 0.1% two or more races (2000); Density: 133.5 persons per square mile (2000); Age: 24.6% under 18, 13.9% over 64 (2000); Marriage status: 16.2% never married, 69.8% now married, 8.2% widowed, 5.8% divorced (2000); Foreign born: 1.4% (2000); Ancestry (includes multiple ancestries): 36.9% German, 14.0% Norwegian, 13.2% Irish, 10.4% English, 5.2% United States or American (2000).
Economy: Industrial and commercial center in a grain, dairy farm, and tobacco area. Manufacturing includes agricultural equipment, machinery, consumer goods, metal products, feeds, printing and publishing, concrete, transportation equipment, plastic productsand prepared food. Major railroad junction. Single-family building permits issued: 41 (2001) / 28 (2000); Multi-family building permits issued: 0 (2001) / 0 (2000); Employment by occupation: 14.7% management, 17.6% professional, 11.2% services, 21.3% sales, 0.6% farming, 10.8% construction, 23.8% production (2000).
Income: Per capita income: $25,656 (2000); Median household income: $68,567 (2000); Poverty rate: 2.1% (2000).
Taxes: Total city taxes per capita: $58 (2000); City property taxes per capita: $48 (2000).
Education: High school graduation rate: 85.3% (2000); College graduation rate: 21.3% (2000).
Housing: Homeownership rate: 92.6% (2000); Median home value: $163,100 (2000); Median rent: $510 per month (2000); Median age of housing: 24 years (2000).
Transportation: Commute to work: 95.4% car, 0.3% public transportation, 0.5% walk, 3.3% work from home (2000); Travel time to work: 37.4% less than 15 minutes, 47.1% 15 to 30 minutes, 8.0% 30 to 45 minutes, 3.2% 45 to 60 minutes, 4.3% 60 minutes or more (2000); Amtrak: Service available.

JOHNSTOWN (town). Covers a land area of 36.201 square miles and a water area of 0 square miles. Located at 42.71° N. Lat.; 88.83° W. Long. Elevation is 952 feet.
Population: 802 (2000); Race: 98.5% White, 0.0% Black, 0.0% Asian, 0.0% American Indian and Alaska Native, 0.4% Hispanic of any race, 1.5% two or more races (2000); Density: 22.2 persons per square mile (2000); Age: 27.8% under 18, 12.8% over 64 (2000); Marriage status: 23.1% never married, 64.4% now married, 4.5% widowed, 8.1% divorced (2000); Foreign born: 1.7% (2000); Ancestry (includes multiple ancestries): 40.8% German, 14.3% Irish, 13.8% English, 12.6% Norwegian, 5.0% United States or American (2000).
Economy: Single-family building permits issued: 2 (2001) / 1 (2000); Multi-family building permits issued: 0 (2001) / 0 (2000); Employment by occupation: 15.7% management, 14.5% professional, 13.6% services, 15.5% sales, 1.4% farming, 13.6% construction, 25.8% production (2000).
Income: Per capita income: $22,452 (2000); Median household income: $55,313 (2000); Poverty rate: 4.9% (2000).

Taxes: Total city taxes per capita: $116 (1997); City property taxes per capita: $112 (1997).
Education: High school graduation rate: 89.9% (2000); College graduation rate: 19.0% (2000).
Housing: Homeownership rate: 83.0% (2000); Median home value: $135,900 (2000); Median rent: $414 per month (2000); Median age of housing: 44 years (2000).
Transportation: Commute to work: 88.8% car, 0.0% public transportation, 2.4% walk, 8.7% work from home (2000); Travel time to work: 22.1% less than 15 minutes, 55.6% 15 to 30 minutes, 14.9% 30 to 45 minutes, 3.2% 45 to 60 minutes, 4.3% 60 minutes or more (2000)

LA PRAIRIE (town). Covers a land area of 34.630 square miles and a water area of 0 square miles. Located at 42.62° N. Lat.; 88.96° W. Long.
Population: 929 (2000); Race: 98.3% White, 0.0% Black, 0.2% Asian, 0.7% American Indian and Alaska Native, 0.6% Hispanic of any race, 0.7% two or more races (2000); Density: 26.8 persons per square mile (2000); Age: 29.0% under 18, 12.3% over 64 (2000); Marriage status: 24.1% never married, 62.1% now married, 4.6% widowed, 9.1% divorced (2000); Foreign born: 1.6% (2000); Ancestry (includes multiple ancestries): 43.6% German, 17.5% English, 14.9% Irish, 11.4% Norwegian, 6.1% French (except Basque) (2000).
Economy: Single-family building permits issued: 1 (2001) / 2 (2000); Multi-family building permits issued: 0 (2001) / 0 (2000); Employment by occupation: 13.9% management, 8.0% professional, 10.1% services, 24.3% sales, 0.4% farming, 16.5% construction, 26.8% production (2000).
Income: Per capita income: $22,108 (2000); Median household income: $52,813 (2000); Poverty rate: 8.7% (2000).
Taxes: Total city taxes per capita: $95 (1997); City property taxes per capita: $90 (1997).
Education: High school graduation rate: 83.1% (2000); College graduation rate: 10.2% (2000).
Housing: Homeownership rate: 78.2% (2000); Median home value: $124,400 (2000); Median rent: $444 per month (2000); Median age of housing: 41 years (2000).
Transportation: Commute to work: 87.1% car, 0.6% public transportation, 1.7% walk, 10.6% work from home (2000); Travel time to work: 36.5% less than 15 minutes, 38.9% 15 to 30 minutes, 11.8% 30 to 45 minutes, 5.7% 45 to 60 minutes, 7.1% 60 minutes or more (2000)

LIMA (town). Covers a land area of 36.407 square miles and a water area of 0.010 square miles. Located at 42.79° N. Lat.; 88.83° W. Long.
Population: 1,312 (2000); Race: 95.1% White, 1.0% Black, 0.0% Asian, 0.0% American Indian and Alaska Native, 12.6% Hispanic of any race, 1.1% two or more races (2000); Density: 36.0 persons per square mile (2000); Age: 26.8% under 18, 10.0% over 64 (2000); Marriage status: 21.1% never married, 70.4% now married, 3.7% widowed, 4.8% divorced (2000); Foreign born: 9.0% (2000); Ancestry (includes multiple ancestries): 38.9% German, 15.8% Irish, 13.4% Other groups, 11.8% English, 10.7% Norwegian (2000).
Economy: Single-family building permits issued: 3 (2001) / 4 (2000); Multi-family building permits issued: 0 (2001) / 0 (2000); Employment by occupation: 15.0% management, 15.3% professional, 8.6% services, 22.7% sales, 3.4% farming, 10.0% construction, 25.0% production (2000).
Income: Per capita income: $20,718 (2000); Median household income: $48,913 (2000); Poverty rate: 6.3% (2000).
Taxes: Total city taxes per capita: $12 (1997); City property taxes per capita: $0 (1997).
Education: High school graduation rate: 78.6% (2000); College graduation rate: 21.1% (2000).
Housing: Homeownership rate: 84.7% (2000); Median home value: $141,900 (2000); Median rent: $555 per month (2000); Median age of housing: 32 years (2000).
Transportation: Commute to work: 89.0% car, 0.7% public transportation, 2.6% walk, 6.9% work from home (2000); Travel time to work: 32.0% less than 15 minutes, 43.6% 15 to 30 minutes, 17.1% 30 to 45 minutes, 4.7% 45 to 60 minutes, 2.6% 60 minutes or more (2000)

MAGNOLIA (town). Covers a land area of 36.033 square miles and a water area of 0 square miles. Located at 42.71° N. Lat.; 89.30° W. Long. Elevation is 943 feet.
Population: 854 (2000); Race: 99.2% White, 0.0% Black, 0.0% Asian, 0.0% American Indian and Alaska Native, 0.0% Hispanic of any race, 0.8% two or more races (2000); Density: 23.7 persons per square mile (2000); Age: 31.9% under 18, 6.5% over 64 (2000); Marriage status: 22.3% never married, 64.6% now married, 5.1% widowed, 8.0% divorced (2000); Foreign born: 0.2% (2000); Ancestry (includes multiple ancestries): 48.4% German, 16.5% English, 12.5% Irish, 11.3% Norwegian, 8.4% Swiss (2000).
Economy: Single-family building permits issued: 4 (2001) / 1 (2000); Multi-family building permits issued: 0 (2001) / 0 (2000); Employment by occupation: 16.8% management, 5.8% professional, 14.3% services, 22.0% sales, 1.5% farming, 10.6% construction, 29.0% production (2000).
Income: Per capita income: $17,507 (2000); Median household income: $45,924 (2000); Poverty rate: 7.1% (2000).
Taxes: Total city taxes per capita: $91 (1997); City property taxes per capita: $81 (1997).
Education: High school graduation rate: 87.1% (2000); College graduation rate: 11.4% (2000).
Housing: Homeownership rate: 77.2% (2000); Median home value: $131,700 (2000); Median rent: $443 per month (2000); Median age of housing: 42 years (2000).
Transportation: Commute to work: 85.1% car, 0.0% public transportation, 4.6% walk, 9.8% work from home (2000); Travel time to work: 29.0% less than 15 minutes, 28.1% 15 to 30 minutes, 30.6% 30 to 45 minutes, 9.7% 45 to 60 minutes, 2.6% 60 minutes or more (2000)

MILTON (city). Covers a land area of 3.232 square miles and a water area of 0 square miles. Located at 42.77° N. Lat.; 88.95° W. Long. Elevation is 880 feet.
Population: 5,132 (2000); Race: 97.4% White, 0.1% Black, 0.4% Asian, 0.2% American Indian and Alaska Native, 1.8% Hispanic of any race, 1.2% two or more races (2000); Density: 1,587.8 persons per square mile (2000); Age: 26.4% under 18, 12.2% over 64 (2000); Marriage status: 24.5% never married, 56.0% now married, 6.2% widowed, 13.4% divorced (2000); Foreign born: 1.6% (2000); Ancestry (includes multiple ancestries): 46.1% German, 16.3% Irish, 16.0% English, 12.5% Norwegian, 5.6% Polish (2000).
Economy: Single-family building permits issued: 7 (2001) / 16 (2000); Multi-family building permits issued: 4 (2001) / 8 (2000); Employment by occupation: 11.3% management, 13.4% professional, 13.6% services, 27.9% sales, 0.1% farming, 11.0% construction, 22.8% production (2000).
Income: Per capita income: $22,058 (2000); Median household income: $43,201 (2000); Poverty rate: 6.7% (2000).
Taxes: Total city taxes per capita: $202 (1997); City property taxes per capita: $189 (1997).
Education: High school graduation rate: 88.3% (2000); College graduation rate: 18.5% (2000).

School District(s)

Milton (PK-12)
2000 Enrollment: 2,894 608-868-9200
Housing: Homeownership rate: 64.9% (2000); Median home value: $106,200 (2000); Median rent: $450 per month (2000); Median age of housing: 29 years (2000).
Safety: Violent crime rate: 9.7 per 10,000 population; Property crime rate: 156.7 per 10,000 population (2001).
Newspapers: The Milton Courier (1 x week)
Transportation: Commute to work: 94.6% car, 0.3% public transportation, 1.8% walk, 3.0% work from home (2000); Travel time to work: 35.2% less than 15 minutes, 46.7% 15 to 30 minutes, 9.6% 30 to 45 minutes, 4.9% 45 to 60 minutes, 3.5% 60 minutes or more (2000)
Additional Information Contacts
Milton Chamber of Commerce. 608-868-6222

MILTON (town). Covers a land area of 31.343 square miles and a water area of 1.653 square miles. Located at 42.81° N. Lat.; 88.98° W. Long. Elevation is 880 feet.
History: Milton House State Historical Site. Incorporated 1904.
Population: 2,844 (2000); Race: 98.1% White, 0.1% Black, 0.5% Asian, 0.0% American Indian and Alaska Native, 0.7% Hispanic of any race, 0.4% two or more races (2000); Density: 90.7 persons per square mile (2000); Age: 30.0% under 18, 7.7% over 64 (2000); Marriage status: 22.0% never married, 67.2% now married, 4.4% widowed, 6.4% divorced (2000); Foreign born: 1.0% (2000); Ancestry (includes multiple ancestries): 40.8% German, 16.9% Norwegian, 15.9% Irish, 10.6% English, 5.7% Polish (2000).
Economy: In farming and dairying area. Manufacturing. Railroad junction. Single-family building permits issued: 17 (2001) / 20 (2000); Multi-family building permits issued: 0 (2001) / 0 (2000); Employment by occupation: 12.9% management, 16.1% professional, 14.5% services, 21.9% sales, 0.8% farming, 12.3% construction, 21.6% production (2000).
Income: Per capita income: $21,982 (2000); Median household income: $60,151 (2000); Poverty rate: 3.6% (2000).
Taxes: Total city taxes per capita: $51 (1997); City property taxes per capita: $35 (1997).

Education: High school graduation rate: 89.8% (2000); College graduation rate: 18.3% (2000).
Housing: Homeownership rate: 86.8% (2000); Median home value: $138,700 (2000); Median rent: $550 per month (2000); Median age of housing: 33 years (2000).
Transportation: Commute to work: 91.6% car, 0.3% public transportation, 2.7% walk, 4.9% work from home (2000); Travel time to work: 23.3% less than 15 minutes, 45.6% 15 to 30 minutes, 16.3% 30 to 45 minutes, 7.2% 45 to 60 minutes, 7.6% 60 minutes or more (2000)

NEWARK (town). Covers a land area of 36.363 square miles and a water area of 0 square miles. Located at 42.53° N. Lat.; 89.18° W. Long. Elevation is 817 feet.
Population: 1,571 (2000); Race: 97.8% White, 0.0% Black, 0.0% Asian, 0.0% American Indian and Alaska Native, 1.0% Hispanic of any race, 1.5% two or more races (2000); Density: 43.2 persons per square mile (2000); Age: 23.6% under 18, 11.6% over 64 (2000); Marriage status: 15.7% never married, 72.3% now married, 4.7% widowed, 7.3% divorced (2000); Foreign born: 0.7% (2000); Ancestry (includes multiple ancestries): 42.6% German, 20.0% Norwegian, 14.4% Irish, 13.5% English, 6.6% Other groups (2000).
Economy: Single-family building permits issued: 6 (2001) / 6 (2000); Multi-family building permits issued: 0 (2001) / 0 (2000); Employment by occupation: 8.9% management, 16.0% professional, 12.0% services, 19.9% sales, 1.2% farming, 16.2% construction, 25.9% production (2000).
Income: Per capita income: $21,964 (2000); Median household income: $59,500 (2000); Poverty rate: 3.9% (2000).
Taxes: Total city taxes per capita: $29 (1997); City property taxes per capita: $27 (1997).
Education: High school graduation rate: 85.5% (2000); College graduation rate: 11.5% (2000).
Housing: Homeownership rate: 93.5% (2000); Median home value: $135,000 (2000); Median rent: $444 per month (2000); Median age of housing: 35 years (2000).
Transportation: Commute to work: 93.1% car, 0.0% public transportation, 1.6% walk, 5.3% work from home (2000); Travel time to work: 13.8% less than 15 minutes, 51.8% 15 to 30 minutes, 22.1% 30 to 45 minutes, 5.1% 45 to 60 minutes, 7.2% 60 minutes or more (2000)

ORFORDVILLE (village). Covers a land area of 1.163 square miles and a water area of 0 square miles. Located at 42.62° N. Lat.; 89.25° W. Long. Elevation is 900 feet.
Population: 1,272 (2000); Race: 96.7% White, 0.2% Black, 0.0% Asian, 0.6% American Indian and Alaska Native, 3.2% Hispanic of any race, 0.7% two or more races (2000); Density: 1,093.5 persons per square mile (2000); Age: 30.3% under 18, 10.0% over 64 (2000); Marriage status: 23.9% never married, 59.2% now married, 5.8% widowed, 11.1% divorced (2000); Foreign born: 0.9% (2000); Ancestry (includes multiple ancestries): 40.9% German, 24.4% Norwegian, 12.9% English, 12.6% Irish, 8.3% Other groups (2000).
Economy: In tobacco, dairying and grain area. Single-family building permits issued: 10 (2001) / 3 (2000); Multi-family building permits issued: 0 (2001) / 0 (2000); Employment by occupation: 7.8% management, 12.9% professional, 15.7% services, 21.0% sales, 1.2% farming, 9.1% construction, 32.3% production (2000).
Income: Per capita income: $18,169 (2000); Median household income: $46,875 (2000); Poverty rate: 5.9% (2000).
Taxes: Total city taxes per capita: $160 (1997); City property taxes per capita: $154 (1997).
Education: High school graduation rate: 87.5% (2000); College graduation rate: 12.6% (2000).

School District(s)

Parkview (PK-12)
2000 Enrollment: 1,154 608-879-2717

Housing: Homeownership rate: 80.7% (2000); Median home value: $90,300 (2000); Median rent: $445 per month (2000); Median age of housing: 35 years (2000).
Newspapers: Orfordville Journal & Footville News (1 x week)
Transportation: Commute to work: 94.7% car, 0.0% public transportation, 3.2% walk, 1.8% work from home (2000); Travel time to work: 22.3% less than 15 minutes, 46.0% 15 to 30 minutes, 19.4% 30 to 45 minutes, 9.0% 45 to 60 minutes, 3.2% 60 minutes or more (2000)

PLYMOUTH (town). Covers a land area of 35.639 square miles and a water area of 0.007 square miles. Located at 42.63° N. Lat.; 89.17° W. Long.
Population: 1,270 (2000); Race: 97.2% White, 0.0% Black, 0.0% Asian, 0.9% American Indian and Alaska Native, 0.9% Hispanic of any race, 1.6% two or more races (2000); Density: 35.6 persons per square mile (2000); Age: 28.7% under 18, 10.3% over 64 (2000); Marriage status: 17.3% never married, 65.8% now married, 4.5% widowed, 12.4% divorced (2000); Foreign born: 0.4% (2000); Ancestry (includes multiple ancestries): 42.7% German, 24.7% Norwegian, 12.6% Irish, 7.6% English, 5.9% United States or American (2000).
Economy: Single-family building permits issued: 6 (2001) / 6 (2000); Multi-family building permits issued: 0 (2001) / 0 (2000); Employment by occupation: 14.2% management, 11.8% professional, 13.1% services, 20.7% sales, 2.1% farming, 14.7% construction, 23.4% production (2000).
Income: Per capita income: $23,082 (2000); Median household income: $57,969 (2000); Poverty rate: 4.4% (2000).
Taxes: Total city taxes per capita: $77 (1997); City property taxes per capita: $69 (1997).
Education: High school graduation rate: 87.4% (2000); College graduation rate: 10.9% (2000).
Housing: Homeownership rate: 86.3% (2000); Median home value: $132,300 (2000); Median rent: $404 per month (2000); Median age of housing: 44 years (2000).
Transportation: Commute to work: 86.4% car, 0.6% public transportation, 3.9% walk, 8.4% work from home (2000); Travel time to work: 19.5% less than 15 minutes, 49.3% 15 to 30 minutes, 19.5% 30 to 45 minutes, 7.8% 45 to 60 minutes, 3.8% 60 minutes or more (2000)

PORTER (town). Covers a land area of 36.061 square miles and a water area of 0.367 square miles. Located at 42.81° N. Lat.; 89.19° W. Long.
Population: 925 (2000); Race: 98.6% White, 0.3% Black, 0.2% Asian, 0.0% American Indian and Alaska Native, 0.6% Hispanic of any race, 0.2% two or more races (2000); Density: 25.7 persons per square mile (2000); Age: 27.0% under 18, 14.5% over 64 (2000); Marriage status: 25.8% never married, 61.0% now married, 6.9% widowed, 6.3% divorced (2000); Foreign born: 0.6% (2000); Ancestry (includes multiple ancestries): 42.0% German, 26.4% Norwegian, 18.5% Irish, 15.9% English, 4.0% Swedish (2000).
Economy: Single-family building permits issued: 6 (2001) / 5 (2000); Multi-family building permits issued: 0 (2001) / 0 (2000); Employment by occupation: 23.4% management, 19.5% professional, 10.0% services, 15.7% sales, 2.3% farming, 9.0% construction, 20.1% production (2000).
Income: Per capita income: $22,025 (2000); Median household income: $51,250 (2000); Poverty rate: 6.5% (2000).
Taxes: Total city taxes per capita: $74 (1997); City property taxes per capita: $71 (1997).
Education: High school graduation rate: 88.6% (2000); College graduation rate: 24.2% (2000).
Housing: Homeownership rate: 80.4% (2000); Median home value: $145,100 (2000); Median rent: $425 per month (2000); Median age of housing: 47 years (2000).
Transportation: Commute to work: 86.0% car, 0.6% public transportation, 4.3% walk, 8.5% work from home (2000); Travel time to work: 27.2% less than 15 minutes, 44.7% 15 to 30 minutes, 19.5% 30 to 45 minutes, 6.7% 45 to 60 minutes, 1.9% 60 minutes or more (2000)

ROCK (town). Covers a land area of 29.530 square miles and a water area of 0.514 square miles. Located at 42.61° N. Lat.; 89.06° W. Long.
Population: 3,338 (2000); Race: 97.4% White, 0.0% Black, 0.7% Asian, 0.1% American Indian and Alaska Native, 3.0% Hispanic of any race, 1.0% two or more races (2000); Density: 113.0 persons per square mile (2000); Age: 24.4% under 18, 10.2% over 64 (2000); Marriage status: 22.3% never married, 63.6% now married, 5.3% widowed, 8.7% divorced (2000); Foreign born: 1.9% (2000); Ancestry (includes multiple ancestries): 38.7% German, 17.6% Irish, 17.0% Norwegian, 11.0% English, 9.0% United States or American (2000).
Economy: Single-family building permits issued: 7 (2001) / 3 (2000); Multi-family building permits issued: 0 (2001) / 0 (2000); Employment by occupation: 6.2% management, 10.9% professional, 15.7% services, 16.1% sales, 1.7% farming, 14.3% construction, 35.2% production (2000).
Income: Per capita income: $20,635 (2000); Median household income: $46,151 (2000); Poverty rate: 5.5% (2000).
Taxes: Total city taxes per capita: $31 (1997); City property taxes per capita: $6 (1997).
Education: High school graduation rate: 74.6% (2000); College graduation rate: 5.1% (2000).
Housing: Homeownership rate: 88.6% (2000); Median home value: $113,900 (2000); Median rent: $529 per month (2000); Median age of housing: 28 years (2000).
Transportation: Commute to work: 94.1% car, 0.6% public transportation, 1.2% walk, 3.3% work from home (2000); Travel time to work: 31.1% less

than 15 minutes, 55.2% 15 to 30 minutes, 7.3% 30 to 45 minutes, 2.7% 45 to 60 minutes, 3.6% 60 minutes or more (2000)

SPRING VALLEY (town). Covers a land area of 35.107 square miles and a water area of 0 square miles. Located at 42.63° N. Lat.; 89.30° W. Long. Elevation is 930 feet.
Population: 813 (2000); Race: 99.4% White, 0.0% Black, 0.0% Asian, 0.0% American Indian and Alaska Native, 0.1% Hispanic of any race, 0.6% two or more races (2000); Density: 23.2 persons per square mile (2000); Age: 26.2% under 18, 12.1% over 64 (2000); Marriage status: 16.8% never married, 68.1% now married, 5.5% widowed, 9.6% divorced (2000); Foreign born: 0.4% (2000); Ancestry (includes multiple ancestries): 42.7% German, 20.3% Norwegian, 13.0% Irish, 10.9% English, 9.6% Swiss (2000).
Economy: Single-family building permits issued: 6 (2001) / 4 (2000); Multi-family building permits issued: 0 (2001) / 0 (2000); Employment by occupation: 15.1% management, 14.6% professional, 10.4% services, 20.0% sales, 2.0% farming, 10.1% construction, 27.7% production (2000).
Income: Per capita income: $21,098 (2000); Median household income: $54,375 (2000); Poverty rate: 4.2% (2000).
Taxes: Total city taxes per capita: $66 (1997); City property taxes per capita: $60 (1997).
Education: High school graduation rate: 90.3% (2000); College graduation rate: 17.0% (2000).
Housing: Homeownership rate: 84.1% (2000); Median home value: $128,600 (2000); Median rent: $550 per month (2000); Median age of housing: 60+ years (2000).
Transportation: Commute to work: 85.8% car, 0.5% public transportation, 1.8% walk, 11.5% work from home (2000); Travel time to work: 27.9% less than 15 minutes, 35.9% 15 to 30 minutes, 24.7% 30 to 45 minutes, 5.2% 45 to 60 minutes, 6.3% 60 minutes or more (2000)

TURTLE (town). Covers a land area of 29.333 square miles and a water area of 0 square miles. Located at 42.53° N. Lat.; 88.97° W. Long.
Population: 2,444 (2000); Race: 95.6% White, 2.2% Black, 0.0% Asian, 0.0% American Indian and Alaska Native, 1.4% Hispanic of any race, 1.3% two or more races (2000); Density: 83.3 persons per square mile (2000); Age: 22.4% under 18, 11.6% over 64 (2000); Marriage status: 20.8% never married, 65.0% now married, 5.1% widowed, 9.1% divorced (2000); Foreign born: 1.9% (2000); Ancestry (includes multiple ancestries): 38.9% German, 18.3% Irish, 15.6% Norwegian, 10.6% English, 7.3% Other groups (2000).
Economy: Single-family building permits issued: 8 (2001) / 6 (2000); Multi-family building permits issued: 0 (2001) / 0 (2000); Employment by occupation: 10.6% management, 12.6% professional, 13.4% services, 28.8% sales, 0.6% farming, 10.9% construction, 23.1% production (2000).
Income: Per capita income: $24,015 (2000); Median household income: $57,188 (2000); Poverty rate: 2.7% (2000).
Taxes: Total city taxes per capita: $51 (1997); City property taxes per capita: $46 (1997).
Education: High school graduation rate: 86.3% (2000); College graduation rate: 17.0% (2000).
Housing: Homeownership rate: 87.8% (2000); Median home value: $115,900 (2000); Median rent: $529 per month (2000); Median age of housing: 37 years (2000).
Transportation: Commute to work: 96.6% car, 1.1% public transportation, 0.4% walk, 1.5% work from home (2000); Travel time to work: 37.6% less than 15 minutes, 42.6% 15 to 30 minutes, 9.2% 30 to 45 minutes, 5.2% 45 to 60 minutes, 5.4% 60 minutes or more (2000)

UNION (town). Covers a land area of 34.055 square miles and a water area of 0.034 square miles. Located at 42.80° N. Lat.; 89.29° W. Long. Elevation is 945 feet.
Population: 1,860 (2000); Race: 98.5% White, 0.8% Black, 0.2% Asian, 0.0% American Indian and Alaska Native, 0.7% Hispanic of any race, 0.5% two or more races (2000); Density: 54.6 persons per square mile (2000); Age: 29.7% under 18, 8.5% over 64 (2000); Marriage status: 19.6% never married, 67.7% now married, 3.9% widowed, 8.8% divorced (2000); Foreign born: 1.5% (2000); Ancestry (includes multiple ancestries): 41.5% German, 24.8% Norwegian, 13.7% Irish, 11.8% English, 6.3% Swiss (2000).
Economy: Single-family building permits issued: 16 (2001) / 11 (2000); Multi-family building permits issued: 0 (2001) / 0 (2000); Employment by occupation: 15.5% management, 18.7% professional, 10.3% services, 23.3% sales, 0.4% farming, 11.8% construction, 20.0% production (2000).
Income: Per capita income: $22,609 (2000); Median household income: $55,385 (2000); Poverty rate: 3.6% (2000).
Taxes: Total city taxes per capita: $41 (1997); City property taxes per capita: $26 (1997).
Education: High school graduation rate: 89.6% (2000); College graduation rate: 20.5% (2000).
Housing: Homeownership rate: 86.6% (2000); Median home value: $148,800 (2000); Median rent: $502 per month (2000); Median age of housing: 19 years (2000).
Transportation: Commute to work: 94.3% car, 0.0% public transportation, 0.9% walk, 3.9% work from home (2000); Travel time to work: 33.7% less than 15 minutes, 26.1% 15 to 30 minutes, 29.3% 30 to 45 minutes, 6.3% 45 to 60 minutes, 4.7% 60 minutes or more (2000)

Rusk County

Located in northern Wisconsin; drained by the Chippewa and Flambeau Rivers; includes many lakes. Covers a land area of 913.10 square miles, a water area of 17.80 square miles, and is located in the Central Time Zone. The county government was organized in 1901. County seat is Ladysmith.

Weather Station: Weyerhauser Elevation: 1,194 feet

	Jan	Feb	Mar	Apr	May	Jun	Jul	Aug	Sep	Oct	Nov	Dec
High	21	29	41	57	70	78	81	79	70	58	40	26
Low	-1	5	18	31	42	51	55	53	45	33	21	7
Precip	1.2	0.9	2.1	2.5	3.6	4.1	4.5	4.4	4.3	2.8	2.0	1.1
Snow	12.9	7.3	9.1	1.9	tr	0.0	0.0	0.0	0.0	0.5	7.3	9.2

High and Low temperatures in degrees Fahrenheit; Precipitation and Snow in inches

Population: 15,347 (2000); Race: 98.6% White, 0.2% Black, 0.2% Asian, 0.2% American Indian and Alaska Native, 0.8% Hispanic of any race, 0.5% two or more races (2000); Density: 16.8 persons per square mile (2000); Age: 24.7% under 18, 18.5% over 64 (2000).
Religion: Five largest groups: 23.7% Catholic Church, 9.8% Evangelical Lutheran Church in America, 3.1% Christian Churches and Churches of Christ, 2.5% The United Methodist Church, 1.6% Assemblies of God (2000).
Economy: Unemployment rate: 5.6% (11/2002); Total civilian labor force: 7,182 (11/2002); Leading industries: 39.6% manufacturing; 15.6% retail trade; 13.8% health care and social assistance (2000); Companies that employ more than 1,000 persons: 0 (2000); Companies that employ more than 100 persons: 7 (2000); Farms: 578 totaling 159,104 acres (1997); Minority business ownership rate: 0.0% (1997); Women business ownership rate: 14.9% (1997); Retail sales per capita: $5,144 (1997). Single-family building permits issued: 104 (2001) / 114 (2000); Multi-family building permits issued: 24 (2001) / 2 (2000).
Income: Per capita income: $15,563 (2000); Median household income: $31,344 (2000); Poverty rate: 11.8% (2000); Bankruptcy rate: 2.93% (2001).
Taxes: Total county taxes per capita: $226 (1997); County property taxes per capita: $151 (1997).
Education: High school graduation rate: 79.1% (2000); College graduation rate: 11.2% (2000).
Housing: Homeownership rate: 78.6% (2000); Median home value: $63,200 (2000); Median rent: $297 per month (2000); Median age of housing: 35 years (2000).
Health: Birth rate: 103.0 per 10,000 population (1998); Age adjusted death rate: 80.8 per 10,000 population (1999); Age adjusted cancer mortality rate: 213.8 deaths per 100,000 population (1999). Number of physicians: 7.2 per 10,000 population (1999); Number of hospital beds: 87.3 per 10,000 population (1999).
Elections: 2000 Presidential election results: 42.9% Gore, 51.0% Bush, 4.7% Nader, 0.7% Buchanan
National and State Parks: Devils Creek State Wildlife Management Area; Potato Creek State Wildlife Management Area; Silvernail State Wildlife Management Area; Washington Creek State Wildlife Management Area
Additional Information Contacts
Rusk County Government Offices 715-532-2100
Ladysmith Chamber of Commerce 715-532-7328

Rusk County Communities

ATLANTA (town). Covers a land area of 50.792 square miles and a water area of 0.193 square miles. Located at 45.49° N. Lat.; 91.32° W. Long.
Population: 627 (2000); Race: 97.5% White, 0.0% Black, 0.3% Asian, 1.0% American Indian and Alaska Native, 2.5% Hispanic of any race, 0.9% two or more races (2000); Density: 12.3 persons per square mile (2000); Age: 30.7% under 18, 10.2% over 64 (2000); Marriage status: 18.0% never married, 69.8% now married, 4.0% widowed, 8.3% divorced (2000); Foreign born: 1.3% (2000); Ancestry (includes multiple ancestries): 39.6% German, 14.2% Norwegian, 9.5% Polish, 8.0% Swedish, 7.6% Other groups (2000).

Economy: Employment by occupation: 21.6% management, 11.6% professional, 10.3% services, 16.6% sales, 0.7% farming, 9.0% construction, 30.2% production (2000).
Income: Per capita income: $19,055 (2000); Median household income: $35,938 (2000); Poverty rate: 17.0% (2000).
Taxes: Total city taxes per capita: $39 (1997); City property taxes per capita: $39 (1997).
Education: High school graduation rate: 78.3% (2000); College graduation rate: 11.0% (2000).
Housing: Homeownership rate: 93.2% (2000); Median home value: $55,300 (2000); Median rent: $242 per month (2000); Median age of housing: 29 years (2000).
Transportation: Commute to work: 83.0% car, 0.0% public transportation, 2.8% walk, 12.5% work from home (2000); Travel time to work: 22.6% less than 15 minutes, 34.5% 15 to 30 minutes, 24.6% 30 to 45 minutes, 8.7% 45 to 60 minutes, 9.5% 60 minutes or more (2000)

BIG BEND (town). Covers a land area of 32.616 square miles and a water area of 2.731 square miles. Located at 45.33° N. Lat.; 91.36° W. Long.
Population: 402 (2000); Race: 99.2% White, 0.0% Black, 0.0% Asian, 0.0% American Indian and Alaska Native, 0.6% Hispanic of any race, 0.8% two or more races (2000); Density: 12.3 persons per square mile (2000); Age: 15.5% under 18, 23.4% over 64 (2000); Marriage status: 20.9% never married, 61.7% now married, 10.4% widowed, 7.0% divorced (2000); Foreign born: 0.0% (2000); Ancestry (includes multiple ancestries): 49.0% German, 18.6% English, 12.7% Irish, 12.4% Polish, 11.8% Norwegian (2000).
Economy: Employment by occupation: 15.4% management, 10.1% professional, 24.2% services, 19.5% sales, 0.0% farming, 9.4% construction, 21.5% production (2000).
Income: Per capita income: $16,719 (2000); Median household income: $29,063 (2000); Poverty rate: 5.9% (2000).
Taxes: Total city taxes per capita: $94 (1997); City property taxes per capita: $86 (1997).
Education: High school graduation rate: 76.6% (2000); College graduation rate: 6.3% (2000).
Housing: Homeownership rate: 92.4% (2000); Median home value: $102,300 (2000); Median rent: $125 per month (2000); Median age of housing: 28 years (2000).
Transportation: Commute to work: 87.9% car, 0.0% public transportation, 4.0% walk, 8.1% work from home (2000); Travel time to work: 13.9% less than 15 minutes, 17.5% 15 to 30 minutes, 27.7% 30 to 45 minutes, 19.0% 45 to 60 minutes, 21.9% 60 minutes or more (2000)

BIG FALLS (town). Covers a land area of 35.374 square miles and a water area of 0.634 square miles. Located at 45.57° N. Lat.; 90.98° W. Long.
Population: 107 (2000); Race: 100.0% White, 0.0% Black, 0.0% Asian, 0.0% American Indian and Alaska Native, 0.0% Hispanic of any race, 0.0% two or more races (2000); Density: 3.0 persons per square mile (2000); Age: 34.1% under 18, 4.9% over 64 (2000); Marriage status: 20.3% never married, 61.0% now married, 6.8% widowed, 11.9% divorced (2000); Foreign born: 0.0% (2000); Ancestry (includes multiple ancestries): 40.2% German, 19.5% Norwegian, 13.4% Irish, 4.9% Other groups, 2.4% Danish (2000).
Economy: Employment by occupation: 12.5% management, 17.5% professional, 0.0% services, 22.5% sales, 5.0% farming, 5.0% construction, 37.5% production (2000).
Income: Per capita income: $14,644 (2000); Median household income: $48,125 (2000); Poverty rate: 2.4% (2000).
Taxes: Total city taxes per capita: $45 (1997); City property taxes per capita: $45 (1997).
Education: High school graduation rate: 100.0% (2000); College graduation rate: 15.7% (2000).
Housing: Homeownership rate: 85.7% (2000); Median home value: $35,000 (2000); Median age of housing: 36 years (2000).
Transportation: Commute to work: 89.5% car, 0.0% public transportation, 0.0% walk, 10.5% work from home (2000); Travel time to work: 5.9% less than 15 minutes, 64.7% 15 to 30 minutes, 23.5% 30 to 45 minutes, 0.0% 45 to 60 minutes, 5.9% 60 minutes or more (2000)

BRUCE (village). Covers a land area of 2.290 square miles and a water area of 0.066 square miles. Located at 45.45° N. Lat.; 91.27° W. Long. Elevation is 1,106 feet.
Population: 787 (2000); Race: 99.4% White, 0.3% Black, 0.0% Asian, 0.4% American Indian and Alaska Native, 0.0% Hispanic of any race, 0.0% two or more races (2000); Density: 343.7 persons per square mile (2000); Age: 21.2% under 18, 27.9% over 64 (2000); Marriage status: 19.3% never married, 53.9% now married, 14.1% widowed, 12.7% divorced (2000); Foreign born: 0.8% (2000); Ancestry (includes multiple ancestries): 38.8% German, 10.3% Irish, 10.3% Polish, 9.5% Norwegian, 8.1% French (except Basque) (2000).
Economy: Dairy products; livestock; lumber. Single-family building permits issued: 0 (2001) / 2 (2000); Multi-family building permits issued: 0 (2001) / 0 (2000); Employment by occupation: 5.6% management, 16.5% professional, 19.7% services, 21.6% sales, 1.6% farming, 8.5% construction, 26.4% production (2000).
Income: Per capita income: $15,226 (2000); Median household income: $26,250 (2000); Poverty rate: 9.5% (2000).
Taxes: Total city taxes per capita: $47 (1997); City property taxes per capita: $29 (1997).
Education: High school graduation rate: 81.1% (2000); College graduation rate: 14.5% (2000).

School District(s)

Bruce (PK-12)
2000 Enrollment: 632 715-868-2533

Housing: Homeownership rate: 67.7% (2000); Median home value: $54,400 (2000); Median rent: $253 per month (2000); Median age of housing: 38 years (2000).
Transportation: Commute to work: 86.0% car, 0.8% public transportation, 9.1% walk, 3.2% work from home (2000); Travel time to work: 44.2% less than 15 minutes, 33.3% 15 to 30 minutes, 11.1% 30 to 45 minutes, 5.8% 45 to 60 minutes, 5.6% 60 minutes or more (2000)

CEDAR RAPIDS (town). Covers a land area of 35.164 square miles and a water area of 0.503 square miles. Located at 45.59° N. Lat.; 90.84° W. Long.
Population: 37 (2000); Race: 100.0% White, 0.0% Black, 0.0% Asian, 0.0% American Indian and Alaska Native, 0.0% Hispanic of any race, 0.0% two or more races (2000); Density: 1.1 persons per square mile (2000); Age: 25.0% under 18, 16.7% over 64 (2000); Marriage status: 36.8% never married, 34.2% now married, 13.2% widowed, 15.8% divorced (2000); Foreign born: 0.0% (2000); Ancestry (includes multiple ancestries): 22.9% Czechoslovakian, 18.8% Polish, 18.8% Norwegian, 16.7% Irish, 10.4% Other groups (2000).
Economy: Employment by occupation: 33.3% management, 7.4% professional, 11.1% services, 37.0% sales, 0.0% farming, 11.1% construction, 0.0% production (2000).
Income: Per capita income: $17,188 (2000); Median household income: $44,375 (2000); Poverty rate: 8.3% (2000).
Education: High school graduation rate: 77.8% (2000); College graduation rate: 14.8% (2000).
Housing: Homeownership rate: 100.0% (2000); Median home value: $75,000 (2000); Median age of housing: 20 years (2000).
Transportation: Commute to work: 87.5% car, 0.0% public transportation, 0.0% walk, 12.5% work from home (2000); Travel time to work: 23.8% less than 15 minutes, 76.2% 15 to 30 minutes, 0.0% 30 to 45 minutes, 0.0% 45 to 60 minutes, 0.0% 60 minutes or more (2000)

CONRATH (village). Covers a land area of 0.502 square miles and a water area of 0 square miles. Located at 45.38° N. Lat.; 91.03° W. Long. Elevation is 1,136 feet.
Population: 98 (2000); Race: 93.4% White, 0.0% Black, 3.3% Asian, 0.0% American Indian and Alaska Native, 0.0% Hispanic of any race, 3.3% two or more races (2000); Density: 195.3 persons per square mile (2000); Age: 27.9% under 18, 8.2% over 64 (2000); Marriage status: 11.4% never married, 61.4% now married, 13.6% widowed, 13.6% divorced (2000); Foreign born: 3.3% (2000); Ancestry (includes multiple ancestries): 24.6% Czech, 19.7% German, 18.0% Swiss, 18.0% Swedish, 14.8% Irish (2000).
Economy: Dairying; cheese. Employment by occupation: 9.7% management, 22.6% professional, 19.4% services, 0.0% sales, 6.5% farming, 12.9% construction, 29.0% production (2000).
Income: Per capita income: $16,838 (2000); Median household income: $30,417 (2000); Poverty rate: 29.3% (2000).
Taxes: Total city taxes per capita: $42 (1997); City property taxes per capita: $42 (1997).
Education: High school graduation rate: 94.7% (2000); College graduation rate: 10.5% (2000).
Housing: Homeownership rate: 100.0% (2000); Median home value: $60,000 (2000); Median age of housing: 36 years (2000).
Transportation: Commute to work: 87.1% car, 6.5% public transportation, 0.0% walk, 6.5% work from home (2000); Travel time to work: 41.4% less than 15 minutes, 55.2% 15 to 30 minutes, 0.0% 30 to 45 minutes, 3.4% 45 to 60 minutes, 0.0% 60 minutes or more (2000)

DEWEY (town). Covers a land area of 31.029 square miles and a water area of 3.022 square miles. Located at 45.50° N. Lat.; 91.00° W. Long.
Population: 523 (2000); Race: 99.5% White, 0.0% Black, 0.0% Asian, 0.4% American Indian and Alaska Native, 0.2% Hispanic of any race, 0.2% two or more races (2000); Density: 16.9 persons per square mile (2000); Age: 26.7% under 18, 19.2% over 64 (2000); Marriage status: 16.9% never married, 69.8% now married, 5.6% widowed, 7.7% divorced (2000); Foreign born: 0.5% (2000); Ancestry (includes multiple ancestries): 47.4% German, 13.4% Polish, 9.5% English, 7.7% Norwegian, 6.0% Dutch (2000).
Economy: Employment by occupation: 17.2% management, 15.5% professional, 6.9% services, 17.6% sales, 3.0% farming, 10.7% construction, 29.2% production (2000).
Income: Per capita income: $18,740 (2000); Median household income: $38,056 (2000); Poverty rate: 7.7% (2000).
Taxes: Total city taxes per capita: $39 (1997); City property taxes per capita: $39 (1997).
Education: High school graduation rate: 89.7% (2000); College graduation rate: 13.3% (2000).
Housing: Homeownership rate: 81.7% (2000); Median home value: $88,300 (2000); Median rent: $296 per month (2000); Median age of housing: 26 years (2000).
Transportation: Commute to work: 89.3% car, 0.0% public transportation, 2.6% walk, 8.2% work from home (2000); Travel time to work: 27.6% less than 15 minutes, 51.9% 15 to 30 minutes, 6.5% 30 to 45 minutes, 1.4% 45 to 60 minutes, 12.6% 60 minutes or more (2000)

FLAMBEAU (town). Covers a land area of 34.564 square miles and a water area of 0.295 square miles. Located at 45.49° N. Lat.; 91.10° W. Long.
Population: 1,067 (2000); Race: 98.3% White, 0.0% Black, 0.0% Asian, 0.6% American Indian and Alaska Native, 1.9% Hispanic of any race, 0.8% two or more races (2000); Density: 30.9 persons per square mile (2000); Age: 29.6% under 18, 12.2% over 64 (2000); Marriage status: 25.8% never married, 62.9% now married, 4.4% widowed, 6.9% divorced (2000); Foreign born: 2.3% (2000); Ancestry (includes multiple ancestries): 36.4% German, 14.9% Polish, 12.0% Norwegian, 8.4% Irish, 8.3% United States or American (2000).
Economy: Employment by occupation: 9.6% management, 11.7% professional, 12.3% services, 24.2% sales, 1.5% farming, 10.6% construction, 30.1% production (2000).
Income: Per capita income: $16,418 (2000); Median household income: $39,375 (2000); Poverty rate: 4.9% (2000).
Taxes: Total city taxes per capita: $22 (1997); City property taxes per capita: $18 (1997).
Education: High school graduation rate: 83.5% (2000); College graduation rate: 11.8% (2000).
Housing: Homeownership rate: 91.4% (2000); Median home value: $72,500 (2000); Median rent: $283 per month (2000); Median age of housing: 26 years (2000).
Transportation: Commute to work: 90.3% car, 0.0% public transportation, 1.4% walk, 8.4% work from home (2000); Travel time to work: 61.3% less than 15 minutes, 23.4% 15 to 30 minutes, 7.2% 30 to 45 minutes, 3.4% 45 to 60 minutes, 4.7% 60 minutes or more (2000)

GLEN FLORA (village). Covers a land area of 0.565 square miles and a water area of 0 square miles. Located at 45.49° N. Lat.; 90.89° W. Long. Elevation is 1,276 feet.
Population: 93 (2000); Race: 88.1% White, 0.0% Black, 0.0% Asian, 0.0% American Indian and Alaska Native, 8.5% Hispanic of any race, 3.4% two or more races (2000); Density: 164.7 persons per square mile (2000); Age: 16.9% under 18, 22.0% over 64 (2000); Marriage status: 23.6% never married, 45.5% now married, 23.6% widowed, 7.3% divorced (2000); Foreign born: 3.4% (2000); Ancestry (includes multiple ancestries): 23.7% German, 8.5% Irish, 8.5% Other groups, 8.5% Dutch, 6.8% Polish (2000).
Economy: Dairying; light manufacturing. Employment by occupation: 8.3% management, 41.7% professional, 8.3% services, 4.2% sales, 8.3% farming, 20.8% construction, 8.3% production (2000).
Income: Per capita income: $14,280 (2000); Median household income: $20,250 (2000); Poverty rate: 16.9% (2000).
Taxes: Total city taxes per capita: $559 (2000); City property taxes per capita: $548 (2000).
Education: High school graduation rate: 71.1% (2000); College graduation rate: 24.4% (2000).
Housing: Homeownership rate: 56.3% (2000); Median home value: $57,500 (2000); Median rent: $131 per month (2000); Median age of housing: 23 years (2000).
Transportation: Commute to work: 91.7% car, 0.0% public transportation, 0.0% walk, 8.3% work from home (2000); Travel time to work: 50.0% less than 15 minutes, 27.3% 15 to 30 minutes, 9.1% 30 to 45 minutes, 13.6% 45 to 60 minutes, 0.0% 60 minutes or more (2000)

GRANT (town). Covers a land area of 33.358 square miles and a water area of 0.417 square miles. Located at 45.43° N. Lat.; 91.10° W. Long.
Population: 767 (2000); Race: 98.5% White, 0.6% Black, 0.3% Asian, 0.0% American Indian and Alaska Native, 1.0% Hispanic of any race, 0.4% two or more races (2000); Density: 23.0 persons per square mile (2000); Age: 29.8% under 18, 15.0% over 64 (2000); Marriage status: 16.8% never married, 67.0% now married, 7.2% widowed, 9.0% divorced (2000); Foreign born: 1.8% (2000); Ancestry (includes multiple ancestries): 38.6% German, 11.7% Norwegian, 11.0% Irish, 10.7% English, 8.5% United States or American (2000).
Economy: Employment by occupation: 8.0% management, 22.8% professional, 12.2% services, 17.8% sales, 2.7% farming, 8.0% construction, 28.5% production (2000).
Income: Per capita income: $16,491 (2000); Median household income: $41,908 (2000); Poverty rate: 8.7% (2000).
Taxes: Total city taxes per capita: $27 (1997); City property taxes per capita: $27 (1997).
Education: High school graduation rate: 79.4% (2000); College graduation rate: 19.3% (2000).
Housing: Homeownership rate: 85.0% (2000); Median home value: $70,800 (2000); Median rent: $308 per month (2000); Median age of housing: 30 years (2000).
Transportation: Commute to work: 92.8% car, 0.0% public transportation, 2.4% walk, 4.2% work from home (2000); Travel time to work: 64.5% less than 15 minutes, 17.6% 15 to 30 minutes, 7.2% 30 to 45 minutes, 5.0% 45 to 60 minutes, 5.7% 60 minutes or more (2000)

GROW (town). Covers a land area of 35.397 square miles and a water area of 0 square miles. Located at 45.41° N. Lat.; 90.99° W. Long.
Population: 473 (2000); Race: 99.5% White, 0.0% Black, 0.5% Asian, 0.0% American Indian and Alaska Native, 1.2% Hispanic of any race, 0.0% two or more races (2000); Density: 13.4 persons per square mile (2000); Age: 33.4% under 18, 13.7% over 64 (2000); Marriage status: 25.7% never married, 64.1% now married, 6.9% widowed, 3.2% divorced (2000); Foreign born: 0.5% (2000); Ancestry (includes multiple ancestries): 43.7% German, 17.0% Norwegian, 14.4% Irish, 12.3% Polish, 6.1% English (2000).
Economy: Employment by occupation: 15.1% management, 13.9% professional, 7.3% services, 14.7% sales, 6.6% farming, 11.2% construction, 31.3% production (2000).
Income: Per capita income: $13,133 (2000); Median household income: $36,484 (2000); Poverty rate: 18.2% (2000).
Taxes: Total city taxes per capita: $27 (1997); City property taxes per capita: $27 (1997).
Education: High school graduation rate: 84.7% (2000); College graduation rate: 11.4% (2000).
Housing: Homeownership rate: 89.2% (2000); Median home value: $62,100 (2000); Median rent: $308 per month (2000); Median age of housing: 47 years (2000).
Transportation: Commute to work: 79.0% car, 0.0% public transportation, 3.5% walk, 17.5% work from home (2000); Travel time to work: 37.3% less than 15 minutes, 41.5% 15 to 30 minutes, 9.9% 30 to 45 minutes, 2.8% 45 to 60 minutes, 8.5% 60 minutes or more (2000)

HAWKINS (village). Covers a land area of 2.189 square miles and a water area of 0.019 square miles. Located at 45.51° N. Lat.; 90.71° W. Long. Elevation is 1,369 feet.
Population: 317 (2000); Race: 98.7% White, 0.0% Black, 0.0% Asian, 0.0% American Indian and Alaska Native, 0.0% Hispanic of any race, 1.3% two or more races (2000); Density: 144.8 persons per square mile (2000); Age: 16.3% under 18, 21.2% over 64 (2000); Marriage status: 27.0% never married, 59.3% now married, 7.0% widowed, 6.7% divorced (2000); Foreign born: 1.6% (2000); Ancestry (includes multiple ancestries): 27.1% German, 12.1% Polish, 11.8% Irish, 9.5% Norwegian, 9.2% Swedish (2000).
Economy: Single-family building permits issued: 1 (2001) / 2 (2000); Multi-family building permits issued: 0 (2001) / 0 (2000); Employment by occupation: 7.0% management, 6.3% professional, 13.9% services, 12.7% sales, 1.3% farming, 5.1% construction, 53.8% production (2000).
Income: Per capita income: $17,159 (2000); Median household income: $29,286 (2000); Poverty rate: 3.6% (2000).
Taxes: Total city taxes per capita: $92 (1997); City property taxes per capita: $81 (1997).

Education: High school graduation rate: 80.2% (2000); College graduation rate: 5.2% (2000).
Housing: Homeownership rate: 92.1% (2000); Median home value: $50,600 (2000); Median rent: $338 per month (2000); Median age of housing: 46 years (2000).
Transportation: Commute to work: 87.3% car, 0.0% public transportation, 10.8% walk, 0.0% work from home (2000); Travel time to work: 66.5% less than 15 minutes, 19.6% 15 to 30 minutes, 6.3% 30 to 45 minutes, 1.3% 45 to 60 minutes, 6.3% 60 minutes or more (2000)

HAWKINS (town). Covers a land area of 45.642 square miles and a water area of 0.125 square miles. Located at 45.49° N. Lat.; 90.71° W. Long. Elevation is 1,369 feet.
Population: 170 (2000); Race: 100.0% White, 0.0% Black, 0.0% Asian, 0.0% American Indian and Alaska Native, 0.0% Hispanic of any race, 0.0% two or more races (2000); Density: 3.7 persons per square mile (2000); Age: 24.5% under 18, 21.7% over 64 (2000); Marriage status: 24.8% never married, 67.3% now married, 2.6% widowed, 5.2% divorced (2000); Foreign born: 0.0% (2000); Ancestry (includes multiple ancestries): 25.5% German, 23.4% Polish, 14.7% English, 13.0% Norwegian, 4.9% United States or American (2000).
Economy: Dairying; livestock raising; farming. Woodworking. Manufacturing: wood products. Employment by occupation: 14.8% management, 2.3% professional, 20.5% services, 9.1% sales, 0.0% farming, 13.6% construction, 39.8% production (2000).
Income: Per capita income: $13,766 (2000); Median household income: $33,125 (2000); Poverty rate: 10.6% (2000).
Taxes: Total city taxes per capita: $23 (1997); City property taxes per capita: $23 (1997).
Education: High school graduation rate: 73.4% (2000); College graduation rate: 2.4% (2000).
Housing: Homeownership rate: 93.8% (2000); Median home value: $60,000 (2000); Median age of housing: 43 years (2000).
Transportation: Commute to work: 87.5% car, 0.0% public transportation, 0.0% walk, 12.5% work from home (2000); Travel time to work: 46.8% less than 15 minutes, 5.2% 15 to 30 minutes, 32.5% 30 to 45 minutes, 10.4% 45 to 60 minutes, 5.2% 60 minutes or more (2000)

HUBBARD (town). Covers a land area of 44.076 square miles and a water area of 0.583 square miles. Located at 45.57° N. Lat.; 91.16° W. Long.
Population: 168 (2000); Race: 100.0% White, 0.0% Black, 0.0% Asian, 0.0% American Indian and Alaska Native, 0.0% Hispanic of any race, 0.0% two or more races (2000); Density: 3.8 persons per square mile (2000); Age: 21.2% under 18, 16.2% over 64 (2000); Marriage status: 20.8% never married, 65.6% now married, 3.9% widowed, 9.7% divorced (2000); Foreign born: 0.0% (2000); Ancestry (includes multiple ancestries): 39.7% German, 12.3% English, 10.6% Polish, 7.8% Swedish, 7.3% United States or American (2000).
Economy: Employment by occupation: 11.2% management, 20.2% professional, 9.0% services, 30.3% sales, 0.0% farming, 3.4% construction, 25.8% production (2000).
Income: Per capita income: $20,315 (2000); Median household income: $35,625 (2000); Poverty rate: 11.2% (2000).
Taxes: Total city taxes per capita: $18 (1997); City property taxes per capita: $18 (1997).
Education: High school graduation rate: 79.8% (2000); College graduation rate: 15.5% (2000).
Housing: Homeownership rate: 92.4% (2000); Median home value: $42,500 (2000); Median age of housing: 25 years (2000).
Transportation: Commute to work: 94.1% car, 0.0% public transportation, 0.0% walk, 5.9% work from home (2000); Travel time to work: 36.3% less than 15 minutes, 42.5% 15 to 30 minutes, 13.8% 30 to 45 minutes, 0.0% 45 to 60 minutes, 7.5% 60 minutes or more (2000)

INGRAM (village). Covers a land area of 0.992 square miles and a water area of 0 square miles. Located at 45.50° N. Lat.; 90.81° W. Long. Elevation is 1,295 feet.
Population: 76 (2000); Race: 95.5% White, 0.0% Black, 0.0% Asian, 0.0% American Indian and Alaska Native, 0.0% Hispanic of any race, 4.5% two or more races (2000); Density: 76.6 persons per square mile (2000); Age: 21.2% under 18, 10.6% over 64 (2000); Marriage status: 13.5% never married, 71.2% now married, 5.8% widowed, 9.6% divorced (2000); Foreign born: 0.0% (2000); Ancestry (includes multiple ancestries): 43.9% German, 16.7% Irish, 15.2% Polish, 10.6% French (except Basque), 9.1% Norwegian (2000).
Economy: In dairying and stock-raising area. Employment by occupation: 0.0% management, 0.0% professional, 0.0% services, 8.3% sales, 0.0% farming, 8.3% construction, 83.3% production (2000).
Income: Per capita income: $12,868 (2000); Median household income: $29,375 (2000); Poverty rate: 0.0% (2000).
Taxes: Total city taxes per capita: $31 (1997); City property taxes per capita: $20 (1997).
Education: High school graduation rate: 80.4% (2000); College graduation rate: 6.5% (2000).
Housing: Homeownership rate: 92.0% (2000); Median home value: $31,300 (2000); Median rent: $225 per month (2000); Median age of housing: 34 years (2000).
Transportation: Commute to work: 100.0% car, 0.0% public transportation, 0.0% walk, 0.0% work from home (2000); Travel time to work: 23.8% less than 15 minutes, 66.7% 15 to 30 minutes, 0.0% 30 to 45 minutes, 0.0% 45 to 60 minutes, 9.5% 60 minutes or more (2000)

LADYSMITH (city). Covers a land area of 3.897 square miles and a water area of 0.369 square miles. Located at 45.46° N. Lat.; 91.10° W. Long. Elevation is 1,144 feet.
History: Ladysmith was a stopping place for trappers and traders at the foot of the falls on the Flambeau River, where Bruno Vinette had opened a hotel. Successively called Flambeau Falls, Warner, and Corbett, Ladysmith received its present name in 1900 to honor the wife of E.D. Smith of the Menasha Wooden Ware Company. When the lumber industry waned, a pulp mill, paper mill, sulphate mill, and other small factories brought settlers to the town. In the early 1900's a cooperative creamery and a canning plant for peas and beans added to the revenue.
Population: 3,932 (2000); Race: 98.3% White, 0.0% Black, 0.5% Asian, 0.2% American Indian and Alaska Native, 0.6% Hispanic of any race, 0.4% two or more races (2000); Density: 1,008.9 persons per square mile (2000); Age: 22.3% under 18, 21.3% over 64 (2000); Marriage status: 28.9% never married, 49.7% now married, 10.3% widowed, 11.1% divorced (2000); Foreign born: 3.1% (2000); Ancestry (includes multiple ancestries): 37.4% German, 14.9% Irish, 10.7% Norwegian, 8.7% Polish, 7.9% English (2000).
Economy: Single-family building permits issued: 4 (2001) / 8 (2000); Multi-family building permits issued: 24 (2001) / 2 (2000); Employment by occupation: 10.0% management, 14.7% professional, 19.3% services, 19.5% sales, 0.6% farming, 9.9% construction, 26.0% production (2000).
Income: Per capita income: $15,499 (2000); Median household income: $28,274 (2000); Poverty rate: 12.2% (2000).
Taxes: Total city taxes per capita: $224 (1997); City property taxes per capita: $150 (1997).
Education: High school graduation rate: 79.4% (2000); College graduation rate: 15.2% (2000).

School District(s)

Ladysmith-Hawkins (PK-12)
2000 Enrollment: 1,181 715-532-5277

Four-year College(s)

Mount Senario College (Private, Not-for-profit)
2001 Enrollment: 672 715-532-5511
2001 Tuition: In-state $12,800; Out-of-state $12,800

Housing: Homeownership rate: 58.5% (2000); Median home value: $61,800 (2000); Median rent: $313 per month (2000); Median age of housing: 47 years (2000).
Hospitals: Rusk County Memorial Hospital (140 beds)
Safety: Violent crime rate: 17.7 per 10,000 population; Property crime rate: 303.0 per 10,000 population (2001).
Newspapers: Ladysmith News (1 x week)
Transportation: Commute to work: 88.9% car, 0.4% public transportation, 6.2% walk, 3.2% work from home (2000); Travel time to work: 81.1% less than 15 minutes, 9.0% 15 to 30 minutes, 3.1% 30 to 45 minutes, 1.7% 45 to 60 minutes, 5.1% 60 minutes or more (2000)
Additional Information Contacts
Ladysmith Chamber of Commerce 715-532-7328

LAWRENCE (town). Covers a land area of 47.708 square miles and a water area of 0 square miles. Located at 45.43° N. Lat.; 90.85° W. Long.
Population: 240 (2000); Race: 100.0% White, 0.0% Black, 0.0% Asian, 0.0% American Indian and Alaska Native, 2.9% Hispanic of any race, 0.0% two or more races (2000); Density: 5.0 persons per square mile (2000); Age: 32.7% under 18, 3.7% over 64 (2000); Marriage status: 29.7% never married, 56.6% now married, 7.7% widowed, 6.0% divorced (2000); Foreign born: 1.2% (2000); Ancestry (includes multiple ancestries): 34.3% German, 14.7% Polish, 11.0% United States or American, 10.6% Irish, 5.7% Czech (2000).

Economy: Employment by occupation: 18.7% management, 5.7% professional, 10.6% services, 18.7% sales, 6.5% farming, 13.0% construction, 26.8% production (2000).
Income: Per capita income: $17,031 (2000); Median household income: $35,313 (2000); Poverty rate: 24.5% (2000).
Taxes: Total city taxes per capita: $8 (1997); City property taxes per capita: $8 (1997).
Education: High school graduation rate: 73.4% (2000); College graduation rate: 7.8% (2000).
Housing: Homeownership rate: 81.0% (2000); Median rent: $225 per month (2000); Median age of housing: 21 years (2000).
Transportation: Commute to work: 70.7% car, 2.4% public transportation, 2.4% walk, 24.4% work from home (2000); Travel time to work: 21.5% less than 15 minutes, 54.8% 15 to 30 minutes, 7.5% 30 to 45 minutes, 7.5% 45 to 60 minutes, 8.6% 60 minutes or more (2000)

MARSHALL (town). Covers a land area of 35.771 square miles and a water area of 0 square miles. Located at 45.33° N. Lat.; 90.98° W. Long.
Population: 683 (2000); Race: 98.5% White, 0.3% Black, 0.0% Asian, 0.9% American Indian and Alaska Native, 0.0% Hispanic of any race, 0.3% two or more races (2000); Density: 19.1 persons per square mile (2000); Age: 38.5% under 18, 13.4% over 64 (2000); Marriage status: 16.1% never married, 70.7% now married, 6.2% widowed, 7.0% divorced (2000); Foreign born: 1.2% (2000); Ancestry (includes multiple ancestries): 31.1% German, 11.7% Polish, 8.0% United States or American, 7.6% Irish, 7.4% Swedish (2000).
Economy: Employment by occupation: 28.9% management, 6.3% professional, 10.6% services, 16.2% sales, 5.6% farming, 10.9% construction, 21.5% production (2000).
Income: Per capita income: $11,411 (2000); Median household income: $33,281 (2000); Poverty rate: 16.9% (2000).
Taxes: Total city taxes per capita: $29 (2000); City property taxes per capita: $28 (2000).
Education: High school graduation rate: 73.8% (2000); College graduation rate: 4.9% (2000).
Housing: Homeownership rate: 83.0% (2000); Median home value: $60,400 (2000); Median rent: $229 per month (2000); Median age of housing: 39 years (2000).
Transportation: Commute to work: 59.6% car, 1.1% public transportation, 10.0% walk, 28.2% work from home (2000); Travel time to work: 40.3% less than 15 minutes, 38.3% 15 to 30 minutes, 7.0% 30 to 45 minutes, 4.0% 45 to 60 minutes, 10.4% 60 minutes or more (2000)

MURRY (town). Covers a land area of 61.851 square miles and a water area of 0.273 square miles. Located at 45.58° N. Lat.; 91.28° W. Long. Elevation is 1,164 feet.
Population: 275 (2000); Race: 100.0% White, 0.0% Black, 0.0% Asian, 0.0% American Indian and Alaska Native, 0.0% Hispanic of any race, 0.0% two or more races (2000); Density: 4.4 persons per square mile (2000); Age: 15.1% under 18, 26.0% over 64 (2000); Marriage status: 22.5% never married, 57.5% now married, 14.0% widowed, 6.0% divorced (2000); Foreign born: 0.9% (2000); Ancestry (includes multiple ancestries): 32.9% German, 11.9% English, 10.5% Irish, 9.6% Polish, 7.8% Swedish (2000).
Economy: Employment by occupation: 16.7% management, 13.7% professional, 10.8% services, 13.7% sales, 10.8% farming, 10.8% construction, 23.5% production (2000).
Income: Per capita income: $16,853 (2000); Median household income: $31,000 (2000); Poverty rate: 16.0% (2000).
Taxes: Total city taxes per capita: $16 (1997); City property taxes per capita: $16 (1997).
Education: High school graduation rate: 66.5% (2000); College graduation rate: 9.7% (2000).
Housing: Homeownership rate: 87.6% (2000); Median home value: $38,100 (2000); Median rent: $175 per month (2000); Median age of housing: 38 years (2000).
Transportation: Commute to work: 78.0% car, 0.0% public transportation, 2.0% walk, 16.0% work from home (2000); Travel time to work: 16.7% less than 15 minutes, 25.0% 15 to 30 minutes, 39.3% 30 to 45 minutes, 9.5% 45 to 60 minutes, 9.5% 60 minutes or more (2000)

RICHLAND (town). Covers a land area of 23.008 square miles and a water area of 0.149 square miles. Located at 45.51° N. Lat.; 90.80° W. Long.
Population: 206 (2000); Race: 100.0% White, 0.0% Black, 0.0% Asian, 0.0% American Indian and Alaska Native, 0.0% Hispanic of any race, 0.0% two or more races (2000); Density: 9.0 persons per square mile (2000); Age: 27.1% under 18, 15.3% over 64 (2000); Marriage status: 20.6% never married, 58.3% now married, 11.4% widowed, 9.7% divorced (2000); Foreign born: 0.0% (2000); Ancestry (includes multiple ancestries): 45.0% German, 17.0% Polish, 12.7% Irish, 9.6% Czech, 7.9% Norwegian (2000).
Economy: Employment by occupation: 16.7% management, 5.8% professional, 20.0% services, 19.2% sales, 0.0% farming, 7.5% construction, 30.8% production (2000).
Income: Per capita income: $15,256 (2000); Median household income: $34,844 (2000); Poverty rate: 4.8% (2000).
Taxes: Total city taxes per capita: $72 (1997); City property taxes per capita: $72 (1997).
Education: High school graduation rate: 71.2% (2000); College graduation rate: 0.6% (2000).
Housing: Homeownership rate: 93.0% (2000); Median home value: $30,000 (2000); Median age of housing: 40 years (2000).
Transportation: Commute to work: 66.9% car, 3.4% public transportation, 4.2% walk, 25.4% work from home (2000); Travel time to work: 43.2% less than 15 minutes, 26.1% 15 to 30 minutes, 18.2% 30 to 45 minutes, 0.0% 45 to 60 minutes, 12.5% 60 minutes or more (2000)

RUSK (town). Covers a land area of 33.517 square miles and a water area of 2.338 square miles. Located at 45.33° N. Lat.; 91.46° W. Long.
Population: 475 (2000); Race: 99.6% White, 0.0% Black, 0.0% Asian, 0.0% American Indian and Alaska Native, 1.9% Hispanic of any race, 0.4% two or more races (2000); Density: 14.2 persons per square mile (2000); Age: 15.4% under 18, 21.3% over 64 (2000); Marriage status: 18.0% never married, 65.8% now married, 8.0% widowed, 8.3% divorced (2000); Foreign born: 4.3% (2000); Ancestry (includes multiple ancestries): 35.4% German, 25.6% Polish, 14.3% Norwegian, 9.2% Irish, 9.2% French (except Basque) (2000).
Economy: Single-family building permits issued: 4 (2001) / 8 (2000); Multi-family building permits issued: 0 (2001) / 0 (2000); Employment by occupation: 16.7% management, 16.7% professional, 18.1% services, 17.2% sales, 0.9% farming, 8.4% construction, 21.9% production (2000).
Income: Per capita income: $16,117 (2000); Median household income: $29,904 (2000); Poverty rate: 11.5% (2000).
Taxes: Total city taxes per capita: $78 (1997); City property taxes per capita: $71 (1997).
Education: High school graduation rate: 78.6% (2000); College graduation rate: 10.1% (2000).
Housing: Homeownership rate: 84.8% (2000); Median home value: $106,600 (2000); Median rent: $338 per month (2000); Median age of housing: 23 years (2000).
Transportation: Commute to work: 79.3% car, 0.0% public transportation, 3.3% walk, 13.1% work from home (2000); Travel time to work: 26.5% less than 15 minutes, 31.4% 15 to 30 minutes, 25.4% 30 to 45 minutes, 11.4% 45 to 60 minutes, 5.4% 60 minutes or more (2000)

SHELDON (village). Covers a land area of 0.661 square miles and a water area of 0 square miles. Located at 45.31° N. Lat.; 90.95° W. Long. Elevation is 1,129 feet.
Population: 256 (2000); Race: 100.0% White, 0.0% Black, 0.0% Asian, 0.0% American Indian and Alaska Native, 2.0% Hispanic of any race, 0.0% two or more races (2000); Density: 387.1 persons per square mile (2000); Age: 26.6% under 18, 18.7% over 64 (2000); Marriage status: 23.5% never married, 53.1% now married, 10.2% widowed, 13.3% divorced (2000); Foreign born: 0.4% (2000); Ancestry (includes multiple ancestries): 38.5% German, 16.3% Dutch, 11.5% Norwegian, 11.5% Irish, 8.3% Polish (2000).
Economy: Dairying. Concrete. Single-family building permits issued: 0 (2001) / 0 (2000); Multi-family building permits issued: 0 (2001) / 0 (2000); Employment by occupation: 12.6% management, 12.6% professional, 6.8% services, 25.2% sales, 1.9% farming, 11.7% construction, 29.1% production (2000).
Income: Per capita income: $13,562 (2000); Median household income: $28,125 (2000); Poverty rate: 13.9% (2000).
Taxes: Total city taxes per capita: $116 (1997); City property taxes per capita: $104 (1997).
Education: High school graduation rate: 78.3% (2000); College graduation rate: 14.5% (2000).
Housing: Homeownership rate: 63.8% (2000); Median home value: $47,300 (2000); Median rent: $265 per month (2000); Median age of housing: 43 years (2000).
Transportation: Commute to work: 83.5% car, 3.9% public transportation, 5.8% walk, 6.8% work from home (2000); Travel time to work: 20.8% less than 15 minutes, 43.8% 15 to 30 minutes, 17.7% 30 to 45 minutes, 6.3% 45 to 60 minutes, 11.5% 60 minutes or more (2000)

SOUTH FORK (town). Covers a land area of 35.396 square miles and a water area of 0.395 square miles. Located at 45.60° N. Lat.; 90.72° W. Long.

Population: 120 (2000); Race: 100.0% White, 0.0% Black, 0.0% Asian, 0.0% American Indian and Alaska Native, 0.0% Hispanic of any race, 0.0% two or more races (2000); Density: 3.4 persons per square mile (2000); Age: 20.6% under 18, 25.7% over 64 (2000); Marriage status: 8.9% never married, 70.5% now married, 10.7% widowed, 9.8% divorced (2000); Foreign born: 0.0% (2000); Ancestry (includes multiple ancestries): 47.8% German, 40.4% Polish, 13.2% English, 8.1% Czech, 5.1% Swedish (2000).
Economy: Single-family building permits issued: 0 (2001) / 0 (2000); Multi-family building permits issued: 0 (2001) / 0 (2000); Employment by occupation: 21.4% management, 7.1% professional, 8.9% services, 3.6% sales, 3.6% farming, 8.9% construction, 46.4% production (2000).
Income: Per capita income: $16,284 (2000); Median household income: $37,500 (2000); Poverty rate: 15.7% (2000).
Education: High school graduation rate: 69.3% (2000); College graduation rate: 6.9% (2000).
Housing: Homeownership rate: 88.9% (2000); Median home value: $59,000 (2000); Median age of housing: 54 years (2000).
Transportation: Commute to work: 71.4% car, 0.0% public transportation, 21.4% walk, 3.6% work from home (2000); Travel time to work: 42.6% less than 15 minutes, 18.5% 15 to 30 minutes, 22.2% 30 to 45 minutes, 9.3% 45 to 60 minutes, 7.4% 60 minutes or more (2000)

STRICKLAND (town). Covers a land area of 34.710 square miles and a water area of 0.398 square miles. Located at 45.42° N. Lat.; 91.48° W. Long. Elevation is 1,275 feet.
Population: 300 (2000); Race: 100.0% White, 0.0% Black, 0.0% Asian, 0.0% American Indian and Alaska Native, 0.0% Hispanic of any race, 0.0% two or more races (2000); Density: 8.6 persons per square mile (2000); Age: 25.2% under 18, 12.7% over 64 (2000); Marriage status: 21.0% never married, 65.3% now married, 9.3% widowed, 4.4% divorced (2000); Foreign born: 0.0% (2000); Ancestry (includes multiple ancestries): 51.3% Polish, 19.7% German, 8.9% Irish, 6.4% Norwegian, 6.1% United States or American (2000).
Economy: Employment by occupation: 20.4% management, 12.3% professional, 10.5% services, 19.1% sales, 4.3% farming, 8.0% construction, 25.3% production (2000).
Income: Per capita income: $15,353 (2000); Median household income: $30,469 (2000); Poverty rate: 11.8% (2000).
Taxes: Total city taxes per capita: $211 (1997); City property taxes per capita: $207 (1997).
Education: High school graduation rate: 87.3% (2000); College graduation rate: 12.2% (2000).
Housing: Homeownership rate: 91.5% (2000); Median home value: $71,700 (2000); Median rent: $275 per month (2000); Median age of housing: 42 years (2000).
Transportation: Commute to work: 80.9% car, 0.0% public transportation, 1.9% walk, 14.8% work from home (2000); Travel time to work: 37.0% less than 15 minutes, 30.4% 15 to 30 minutes, 23.9% 30 to 45 minutes, 2.2% 45 to 60 minutes, 6.5% 60 minutes or more (2000)

STUBBS (town). Covers a land area of 35.876 square miles and a water area of 0.765 square miles. Located at 45.43° N. Lat.; 91.34° W. Long.
Population: 587 (2000); Race: 98.3% White, 0.0% Black, 0.0% Asian, 0.2% American Indian and Alaska Native, 1.2% Hispanic of any race, 1.2% two or more races (2000); Density: 16.4 persons per square mile (2000); Age: 26.0% under 18, 19.1% over 64 (2000); Marriage status: 17.3% never married, 65.1% now married, 5.1% widowed, 12.5% divorced (2000); Foreign born: 0.3% (2000); Ancestry (includes multiple ancestries): 26.5% German, 24.1% Polish, 12.5% English, 11.6% Irish, 10.0% Norwegian (2000).
Economy: Employment by occupation: 22.8% management, 11.7% professional, 5.9% services, 19.7% sales, 1.0% farming, 10.0% construction, 29.0% production (2000).
Income: Per capita income: $15,642 (2000); Median household income: $36,442 (2000); Poverty rate: 7.0% (2000).
Taxes: Total city taxes per capita: $30 (1997); City property taxes per capita: $28 (1997).
Education: High school graduation rate: 85.1% (2000); College graduation rate: 9.0% (2000).
Housing: Homeownership rate: 88.3% (2000); Median home value: $72,500 (2000); Median rent: $345 per month (2000); Median age of housing: 42 years (2000).
Transportation: Commute to work: 71.6% car, 0.0% public transportation, 2.1% walk, 26.3% work from home (2000); Travel time to work: 24.8% less than 15 minutes, 36.2% 15 to 30 minutes, 26.2% 30 to 45 minutes, 5.2% 45 to 60 minutes, 7.6% 60 minutes or more (2000)

THORNAPPLE (town). Covers a land area of 51.362 square miles and a water area of 1.235 square miles. Located at 45.45° N. Lat.; 91.22° W. Long. Elevation is 1,080 feet.
Population: 811 (2000); Race: 95.6% White, 2.7% Black, 0.4% Asian, 0.6% American Indian and Alaska Native, 0.2% Hispanic of any race, 0.5% two or more races (2000); Density: 15.8 persons per square mile (2000); Age: 24.7% under 18, 16.6% over 64 (2000); Marriage status: 18.2% never married, 69.9% now married, 4.2% widowed, 7.7% divorced (2000); Foreign born: 1.6% (2000); Ancestry (includes multiple ancestries): 33.2% German, 14.4% Polish, 12.0% Irish, 11.6% Norwegian, 8.8% English (2000).
Economy: Employment by occupation: 8.7% management, 10.0% professional, 15.7% services, 20.5% sales, 2.1% farming, 9.7% construction, 33.3% production (2000).
Income: Per capita income: $16,095 (2000); Median household income: $35,625 (2000); Poverty rate: 10.9% (2000).
Taxes: Total city taxes per capita: $22 (2000); City property taxes per capita: $21 (2000).
Education: High school graduation rate: 81.8% (2000); College graduation rate: 6.5% (2000).
Housing: Homeownership rate: 89.5% (2000); Median home value: $74,600 (2000); Median rent: $306 per month (2000); Median age of housing: 25 years (2000).
Transportation: Commute to work: 91.2% car, 0.0% public transportation, 1.9% walk, 4.5% work from home (2000); Travel time to work: 30.3% less than 15 minutes, 48.5% 15 to 30 minutes, 6.7% 30 to 45 minutes, 7.3% 45 to 60 minutes, 7.3% 60 minutes or more (2000)

TONY (village). Covers a land area of 2.031 square miles and a water area of 0 square miles. Located at 45.48° N. Lat.; 90.99° W. Long. Elevation is 1,230 feet.
Population: 105 (2000); Race: 96.5% White, 0.0% Black, 0.0% Asian, 0.0% American Indian and Alaska Native, 3.5% Hispanic of any race, 3.5% two or more races (2000); Density: 51.7 persons per square mile (2000); Age: 16.3% under 18, 19.8% over 64 (2000); Marriage status: 27.8% never married, 52.8% now married, 18.1% widowed, 1.4% divorced (2000); Foreign born: 2.3% (2000); Ancestry (includes multiple ancestries): 32.6% German, 15.1% Norwegian, 10.5% English, 9.3% United States or American, 5.8% Dutch (2000).
Economy: Dairying, cheese. Single-family building permits issued: 0 (2001) / 0 (2000); Multi-family building permits issued: 0 (2001) / 0 (2000); Employment by occupation: 0.0% management, 4.7% professional, 34.9% services, 20.9% sales, 0.0% farming, 9.3% construction, 30.2% production (2000).
Income: Per capita income: $16,328 (2000); Median household income: $21,563 (2000); Poverty rate: 17.4% (2000).
Taxes: Total city taxes per capita: $55 (1997); City property taxes per capita: $55 (1997).
Education: High school graduation rate: 72.7% (2000); College graduation rate: 6.1% (2000).

School District(s)

Flambeau (PK-12)
2000 Enrollment: 692 715-532-3183

Housing: Homeownership rate: 69.2% (2000); Median home value: $41,700 (2000); Median rent: $300 per month (2000); Median age of housing: 56 years (2000).
Transportation: Commute to work: 80.5% car, 0.0% public transportation, 4.9% walk, 9.8% work from home (2000); Travel time to work: 43.2% less than 15 minutes, 29.7% 15 to 30 minutes, 10.8% 30 to 45 minutes, 8.1% 45 to 60 minutes, 8.1% 60 minutes or more (2000)

TRUE (town). Covers a land area of 23.302 square miles and a water area of 0.188 square miles. Located at 45.49° N. Lat.; 90.88° W. Long.
Population: 291 (2000); Race: 100.0% White, 0.0% Black, 0.0% Asian, 0.0% American Indian and Alaska Native, 0.0% Hispanic of any race, 0.0% two or more races (2000); Density: 12.5 persons per square mile (2000); Age: 18.7% under 18, 17.7% over 64 (2000); Marriage status: 23.7% never married, 59.9% now married, 8.6% widowed, 7.8% divorced (2000); Foreign born: 1.3% (2000); Ancestry (includes multiple ancestries): 24.3% German, 21.3% Polish, 15.7% Norwegian, 10.3% United States or American, 8.7% Swedish (2000).
Economy: Employment by occupation: 21.3% management, 1.1% professional, 15.7% services, 28.1% sales, 2.8% farming, 9.6% construction, 21.3% production (2000).
Income: Per capita income: $13,514 (2000); Median household income: $27,857 (2000); Poverty rate: 16.8% (2000).

Taxes: Total city taxes per capita: $43 (1997); City property taxes per capita: $43 (1997).
Education: High school graduation rate: 75.8% (2000); College graduation rate: 10.0% (2000).
Housing: Homeownership rate: 87.7% (2000); Median home value: $61,300 (2000); Median rent: $219 per month (2000); Median age of housing: 53 years (2000).
Transportation: Commute to work: 74.6% car, 0.0% public transportation, 1.2% walk, 24.3% work from home (2000); Travel time to work: 28.2% less than 15 minutes, 53.4% 15 to 30 minutes, 9.2% 30 to 45 minutes, 3.1% 45 to 60 minutes, 6.1% 60 minutes or more (2000)

WASHINGTON (town). Covers a land area of 33.705 square miles and a water area of 1.913 square miles. Located at 45.32° N. Lat.; 91.23° W. Long.
Population: 312 (2000); Race: 100.0% White, 0.0% Black, 0.0% Asian, 0.0% American Indian and Alaska Native, 0.0% Hispanic of any race, 0.0% two or more races (2000); Density: 9.3 persons per square mile (2000); Age: 15.8% under 18, 24.5% over 64 (2000); Marriage status: 17.5% never married, 71.8% now married, 4.5% widowed, 6.1% divorced (2000); Foreign born: 0.8% (2000); Ancestry (includes multiple ancestries): 36.1% German, 19.7% Irish, 15.8% Polish, 15.8% English, 8.2% Other groups (2000).
Economy: Employment by occupation: 10.3% management, 8.7% professional, 10.3% services, 14.3% sales, 2.4% farming, 9.5% construction, 44.4% production (2000).
Income: Per capita income: $15,533 (2000); Median household income: $29,231 (2000); Poverty rate: 10.7% (2000).
Taxes: Total city taxes per capita: $123 (1997); City property taxes per capita: $117 (1997).
Education: High school graduation rate: 69.9% (2000); College graduation rate: 2.5% (2000).
Housing: Homeownership rate: 91.9% (2000); Median home value: $91,900 (2000); Median rent: $250 per month (2000); Median age of housing: 29 years (2000).
Transportation: Commute to work: 91.9% car, 0.0% public transportation, 2.4% walk, 5.6% work from home (2000); Travel time to work: 7.7% less than 15 minutes, 46.2% 15 to 30 minutes, 22.2% 30 to 45 minutes, 9.4% 45 to 60 minutes, 14.5% 60 minutes or more (2000)

WEYERHAEUSER (village). Covers a land area of 0.935 square miles and a water area of 0.012 square miles. Located at 45.42° N. Lat.; 91.41° W. Long. Elevation is 1,203 feet.
Population: 353 (2000); Race: 100.0% White, 0.0% Black, 0.0% Asian, 0.0% American Indian and Alaska Native, 0.0% Hispanic of any race, 0.0% two or more races (2000); Density: 377.4 persons per square mile (2000); Age: 21.4% under 18, 29.6% over 64 (2000); Marriage status: 17.7% never married, 52.1% now married, 12.8% widowed, 17.4% divorced (2000); Foreign born: 0.0% (2000); Ancestry (includes multiple ancestries): 33.4% German, 24.6% Polish, 17.9% Norwegian, 8.8% Irish, 5.0% English (2000).
Economy: Single-family building permits issued: 0 (2001) / 2 (2000); Multi-family building permits issued: 0 (2001) / 0 (2000); Employment by occupation: 9.0% management, 9.7% professional, 23.1% services, 16.4% sales, 0.0% farming, 8.2% construction, 33.6% production (2000).
Income: Per capita income: $13,816 (2000); Median household income: $26,250 (2000); Poverty rate: 14.1% (2000).
Taxes: Total city taxes per capita: $84 (1997); City property taxes per capita: $73 (1997).
Education: High school graduation rate: 71.2% (2000); College graduation rate: 7.8% (2000).

School District(s)

Weyerhaeuser Area (KG-12)
2000 Enrollment: 250 715-353-2254

Housing: Homeownership rate: 72.0% (2000); Median home value: $45,800 (2000); Median rent: $267 per month (2000); Median age of housing: 46 years (2000).
Transportation: Commute to work: 80.8% car, 0.0% public transportation, 14.6% walk, 4.6% work from home (2000); Travel time to work: 35.5% less than 15 minutes, 29.0% 15 to 30 minutes, 31.5% 30 to 45 minutes, 0.8% 45 to 60 minutes, 3.2% 60 minutes or more (2000)

WILKINSON (town). Covers a land area of 35.153 square miles and a water area of 0.251 square miles. Located at 45.53° N. Lat.; 91.46° W. Long.
Population: 66 (2000); Race: 96.8% White, 0.0% Black, 0.0% Asian, 0.0% American Indian and Alaska Native, 0.0% Hispanic of any race, 3.2% two or more races (2000); Density: 1.9 persons per square mile (2000); Age: 42.6% under 18, 8.5% over 64 (2000); Marriage status: 24.1% never married, 69.0% now married, 3.4% widowed, 3.4% divorced (2000); Foreign born: 0.0% (2000); Ancestry (includes multiple ancestries): 25.5% German, 18.1% Irish, 16.0% Polish, 13.8% Norwegian, 12.8% French Canadian (2000).
Economy: Single-family building permits issued: 0 (2001) / 0 (2000); Multi-family building permits issued: 0 (2001) / 0 (2000); Employment by occupation: 0.0% management, 6.7% professional, 0.0% services, 16.7% sales, 0.0% farming, 30.0% construction, 46.7% production (2000).
Income: Per capita income: $9,851 (2000); Median household income: $26,750 (2000); Poverty rate: 37.2% (2000).
Education: High school graduation rate: 78.8% (2000); College graduation rate: 3.8% (2000).
Housing: Homeownership rate: 79.3% (2000); Median home value: $55,000 (2000); Median rent: <$100 per month (2000); Median age of housing: 49 years (2000).
Transportation: Commute to work: 100.0% car, 0.0% public transportation, 0.0% walk, 0.0% work from home (2000); Travel time to work: 6.9% less than 15 minutes, 34.5% 15 to 30 minutes, 41.4% 30 to 45 minutes, 0.0% 45 to 60 minutes, 17.2% 60 minutes or more (2000)

WILLARD (town). Covers a land area of 35.597 square miles and a water area of 0.555 square miles. Located at 45.31° N. Lat.; 91.09° W. Long.
Population: 539 (2000); Race: 97.4% White, 0.0% Black, 0.0% Asian, 0.0% American Indian and Alaska Native, 0.4% Hispanic of any race, 2.6% two or more races (2000); Density: 15.1 persons per square mile (2000); Age: 22.4% under 18, 19.8% over 64 (2000); Marriage status: 18.5% never married, 63.7% now married, 9.9% widowed, 7.9% divorced (2000); Foreign born: 1.8% (2000); Ancestry (includes multiple ancestries): 32.0% German, 25.3% Polish, 8.8% English, 8.8% Norwegian, 6.7% Irish (2000).
Economy: Single-family building permits issued: 14 (2001) / 5 (2000); Multi-family building permits issued: 0 (2001) / 0 (2000); Employment by occupation: 18.2% management, 12.1% professional, 11.6% services, 15.2% sales, 8.6% farming, 11.1% construction, 23.2% production (2000).
Income: Per capita income: $12,780 (2000); Median household income: $24,875 (2000); Poverty rate: 18.2% (2000).
Taxes: Total city taxes per capita: $15 (1997); City property taxes per capita: $13 (1997).
Education: High school graduation rate: 73.4% (2000); College graduation rate: 7.0% (2000).
Housing: Homeownership rate: 92.6% (2000); Median home value: $88,000 (2000); Median rent: $225 per month (2000); Median age of housing: 25 years (2000).
Transportation: Commute to work: 79.8% car, 0.0% public transportation, 3.0% walk, 13.1% work from home (2000); Travel time to work: 25.0% less than 15 minutes, 37.2% 15 to 30 minutes, 14.5% 30 to 45 minutes, 1.2% 45 to 60 minutes, 22.1% 60 minutes or more (2000)

WILSON (town). Covers a land area of 34.096 square miles and a water area of 0.338 square miles. Located at 45.58° N. Lat.; 91.48° W. Long.
Population: 84 (2000); Race: 100.0% White, 0.0% Black, 0.0% Asian, 0.0% American Indian and Alaska Native, 0.0% Hispanic of any race, 0.0% two or more races (2000); Density: 2.5 persons per square mile (2000); Age: 30.4% under 18, 13.0% over 64 (2000); Marriage status: 33.9% never married, 53.6% now married, 3.6% widowed, 8.9% divorced (2000); Foreign born: 0.0% (2000); Ancestry (includes multiple ancestries): 59.4% German, 20.3% Irish, 17.4% Norwegian, 13.0% United States or American, 11.6% Czech (2000).
Economy: Employment by occupation: 8.7% management, 13.0% professional, 0.0% services, 0.0% sales, 13.0% farming, 17.4% construction, 47.8% production (2000).
Income: Per capita income: $15,751 (2000); Median household income: $33,438 (2000); Poverty rate: 0.0% (2000).
Taxes: Total city taxes per capita: $99 (1997); City property taxes per capita: $99 (1997).
Education: High school graduation rate: 50.0% (2000); College graduation rate: 0.0% (2000).
Housing: Homeownership rate: 87.5% (2000); Median home value: $19,200 (2000); Median rent: $325 per month (2000); Median age of housing: 51 years (2000).
Transportation: Commute to work: 56.5% car, 0.0% public transportation, 0.0% walk, 34.8% work from home (2000); Travel time to work: 0.0% less than 15 minutes, 33.3% 15 to 30 minutes, 33.3% 30 to 45 minutes, 0.0% 45 to 60 minutes, 33.3% 60 minutes or more (2000)

Saint Croix County

Located in western Wisconsin; bounded on the west by the St. Croix River; drained by the Eau Galle River; includes several lakes. Covers a land area of 721.80 square miles, a water area of 14.00 square miles, and is located in the Central Time Zone. The county government was organized in 1840. County seat is Hudson.

Saint Croix County is part of the Minneapolis-St. Paul, MN-WI MSA. The entire metro area includes: Anoka County, MN; Carver County, MN; Chisago County, MN; Dakota County, MN; Hennepin County, MN; Isanti County, MN; Ramsey County, MN; Scott County, MN; Sherburne County, MN; Washington County, MN; Wright County, MN; Pierce County, WI; St. Croix County, WI

Population: 63,155 (2000); Race: 97.8% White, 0.5% Black, 0.4% Asian, 0.3% American Indian and Alaska Native, 0.8% Hispanic of any race, 0.8% two or more races (2000); Density: 87.5 persons per square mile (2000); Age: 27.9% under 18, 9.8% over 64 (2000).
Religion: Five largest groups: 29.7% Catholic Church, 16.4% Evangelical Lutheran Church in America, 5.0% Lutheran Church—Missouri Synod, 3.1% The United Methodist Church, 1.8% Baptist General Conference (2000).
Economy: Unemployment rate: 5.5% (11/2002); Total civilian labor force: 35,517 (11/2002); Leading industries: 28.8% manufacturing; 16.0% retail trade; 11.2% health care and social assistance (2000); Companies that employ more than 1,000 persons: 0 (2000); Companies that employ more than 100 persons: 37 (2000); Farms: 1,520 totaling 312,076 acres (1997); Minority business ownership rate: 0.0% (1997); Women business ownership rate: 22.4% (1997); Retail sales per capita: $10,283 (1997). Single-family building permits issued: 1,004 (2001) / 706 (2000); Multi-family building permits issued: 437 (2001) / 393 (2000).
Income: Per capita income: $23,937 (2000); Median household income: $54,930 (2000); Poverty rate: 4.0% (2000); Bankruptcy rate: 2.24% (2001).
Taxes: Total county taxes per capita: $236 (2000); County property taxes per capita: $175 (2000).
Education: High school graduation rate: 91.6% (2000); College graduation rate: 26.3% (2000).
Housing: Homeownership rate: 76.4% (2000); Median home value: $139,500 (2000); Median rent: $519 per month (2000); Median age of housing: 23 years (2000).
Health: Birth rate: 123.2 per 10,000 population (1998); Age adjusted death rate: 84.9 per 10,000 population (1999); Age adjusted cancer mortality rate: 177.9 deaths per 100,000 population (1999). Air Quality Index: 83% good, 17% moderate, 0% unhealthy (percent of days in 2000). Number of physicians: 8.1 per 10,000 population (1999); Number of hospital beds: 42.1 per 10,000 population (1999).
Elections: 2000 Presidential election results: 43.7% Gore, 50.9% Bush, 4.6% Nader, 0.4% Buchanan
National and State Parks: Casey Lake State Wildlife Area; Cylon State Public Hunting Grounds; Kinnickinnic River State Fishery Area; Saint Croix Islands State Wildlife Area; Willow River State Park
Additional Information Contacts
St. Croix County Government Offices 715-386-4600
Baldwin Chamber of Commerce 715-684-2221
Hudson Area Chamber of Commerce 715-386-8411
New Richmond Chamber of Commerce 715-246-2900
Somerset Chamber of Commerce. 715-247-3366

Saint Croix County Communities

BALDWIN (village). Covers a land area of 2.297 square miles and a water area of 0 square miles. Located at 44.96° N. Lat.; 92.37° W. Long. Elevation is 1,130 feet.
Population: 2,667 (2000); Race: 98.2% White, 0.1% Black, 0.4% Asian, 0.2% American Indian and Alaska Native, 0.3% Hispanic of any race, 1.2% two or more races (2000); Density: 1,161.0 persons per square mile (2000); Age: 24.2% under 18, 19.2% over 64 (2000); Marriage status: 21.8% never married, 59.8% now married, 7.4% widowed, 11.0% divorced (2000); Foreign born: 1.4% (2000); Ancestry (includes multiple ancestries): 34.9% German, 31.8% Norwegian, 12.4% Dutch, 10.5% Irish, 6.4% English (2000).
Economy: Single-family building permits issued: 48 (2001) / 45 (2000); Multi-family building permits issued: 40 (2001) / 26 (2000); Employment by occupation: 10.6% management, 16.6% professional, 16.1% services, 26.2% sales, 1.5% farming, 10.2% construction, 18.9% production (2000).
Income: Per capita income: $20,748 (2000); Median household income: $40,313 (2000); Poverty rate: 5.5% (2000).
Taxes: Total city taxes per capita: $259 (1997); City property taxes per capita: $243 (1997).
Education: High school graduation rate: 88.6% (2000); College graduation rate: 21.4% (2000).

School District(s)

Baldwin-Woodville Area (KG-12)
2000 Enrollment: 1,359 715-684-3411
Housing: Homeownership rate: 59.8% (2000); Median home value: $114,000 (2000); Median rent: $508 per month (2000); Median age of housing: 24 years (2000).
Newspapers: Baldwin Shopper (1 x week); The Baldwin Bulletin (1 x week)
Transportation: Commute to work: 91.3% car, 0.1% public transportation, 4.3% walk, 4.1% work from home (2000); Travel time to work: 45.7% less than 15 minutes, 20.8% 15 to 30 minutes, 16.7% 30 to 45 minutes, 11.1% 45 to 60 minutes, 5.7% 60 minutes or more (2000)
Additional Information Contacts
Baldwin Chamber of Commerce 715-684-2221

BALDWIN (town). Covers a land area of 32.099 square miles and a water area of 0.077 square miles. Located at 44.99° N. Lat.; 92.32° W. Long. Elevation is 1,130 feet.
Population: 903 (2000); Race: 96.0% White, 0.0% Black, 0.3% Asian, 0.3% American Indian and Alaska Native, 1.6% Hispanic of any race, 3.3% two or more races (2000); Density: 28.1 persons per square mile (2000); Age: 28.6% under 18, 8.5% over 64 (2000); Marriage status: 22.5% never married, 70.4% now married, 2.7% widowed, 4.4% divorced (2000); Foreign born: 0.8% (2000); Ancestry (includes multiple ancestries): 44.3% German, 31.7% Norwegian, 14.6% Dutch, 8.7% English, 8.2% Swedish (2000).
Economy: Single-family building permits issued: 13 (2001) / 4 (2000); Multi-family building permits issued: 0 (2001) / 0 (2000); Employment by occupation: 17.5% management, 12.8% professional, 9.4% services, 23.7% sales, 3.2% farming, 12.2% construction, 21.1% production (2000).
Income: Per capita income: $22,148 (2000); Median household income: $52,188 (2000); Poverty rate: 2.9% (2000).
Taxes: Total city taxes per capita: $77 (1997); City property taxes per capita: $76 (1997).
Education: High school graduation rate: 93.4% (2000); College graduation rate: 12.7% (2000).
Housing: Homeownership rate: 93.3% (2000); Median home value: $133,300 (2000); Median rent: $363 per month (2000); Median age of housing: 53 years (2000).
Transportation: Commute to work: 80.8% car, 0.0% public transportation, 4.8% walk, 12.9% work from home (2000); Travel time to work: 48.7% less than 15 minutes, 19.2% 15 to 30 minutes, 11.7% 30 to 45 minutes, 11.7% 45 to 60 minutes, 8.8% 60 minutes or more (2000)

CADY (town). Covers a land area of 34.507 square miles and a water area of 0.353 square miles. Located at 44.90° N. Lat.; 92.20° W. Long.
Population: 710 (2000); Race: 98.3% White, 0.0% Black, 0.0% Asian, 0.4% American Indian and Alaska Native, 0.4% Hispanic of any race, 1.3% two or more races (2000); Density: 20.6 persons per square mile (2000); Age: 28.5% under 18, 10.1% over 64 (2000); Marriage status: 19.2% never married, 69.6% now married, 3.5% widowed, 7.7% divorced (2000); Foreign born: 0.3% (2000); Ancestry (includes multiple ancestries): 43.3% German, 36.7% Norwegian, 7.4% Irish, 5.3% Polish, 5.2% United States or American (2000).
Economy: Single-family building permits issued: 15 (2001) / 4 (2000); Multi-family building permits issued: 0 (2001) / 0 (2000); Employment by occupation: 17.3% management, 11.2% professional, 10.7% services, 17.5% sales, 2.4% farming, 14.6% construction, 26.3% production (2000).
Income: Per capita income: $20,634 (2000); Median household income: $53,250 (2000); Poverty rate: 2.4% (2000).
Taxes: Total city taxes per capita: $179 (1997); City property taxes per capita: $178 (1997).
Education: High school graduation rate: 91.4% (2000); College graduation rate: 15.9% (2000).
Housing: Homeownership rate: 91.9% (2000); Median home value: $110,700 (2000); Median rent: $375 per month (2000); Median age of housing: 32 years (2000).
Transportation: Commute to work: 84.9% car, 0.0% public transportation, 4.6% walk, 10.0% work from home (2000); Travel time to work: 30.3% less than 15 minutes, 31.9% 15 to 30 minutes, 13.0% 30 to 45 minutes, 13.0% 45 to 60 minutes, 11.9% 60 minutes or more (2000)

CYLON (town). Covers a land area of 35.350 square miles and a water area of 0.083 square miles. Located at 45.16° N. Lat.; 92.34° W. Long. Elevation is 1,061 feet.
Population: 629 (2000); Race: 99.3% White, 0.0% Black, 0.0% Asian, 0.0% American Indian and Alaska Native, 0.7% Hispanic of any race, 0.3% two or more races (2000); Density: 17.8 persons per square mile (2000); Age: 25.7% under 18, 6.8% over 64 (2000); Marriage status: 23.0% never married, 63.7% now married, 5.0% widowed, 8.4% divorced (2000); Foreign born: 0.0% (2000); Ancestry (includes multiple ancestries): 42.7% German, 21.7% Norwegian, 11.2% Irish, 10.7% Swedish, 6.3% English (2000).
Economy: Single-family building permits issued: 5 (2001) / 5 (2000); Multi-family building permits issued: 0 (2001) / 0 (2000); Employment by occupation: 13.9% management, 12.1% professional, 13.0% services, 21.5% sales, 3.0% farming, 13.9% construction, 22.7% production (2000).
Income: Per capita income: $21,213 (2000); Median household income: $51,042 (2000); Poverty rate: 5.7% (2000).
Taxes: Total city taxes per capita: $68 (1997); City property taxes per capita: $65 (1997).
Education: High school graduation rate: 90.2% (2000); College graduation rate: 17.2% (2000).
Housing: Homeownership rate: 83.4% (2000); Median home value: $100,800 (2000); Median rent: $388 per month (2000); Median age of housing: 38 years (2000).
Transportation: Commute to work: 91.1% car, 0.0% public transportation, 3.1% walk, 5.8% work from home (2000); Travel time to work: 21.8% less than 15 minutes, 41.2% 15 to 30 minutes, 12.0% 30 to 45 minutes, 16.6% 45 to 60 minutes, 8.4% 60 minutes or more (2000)

DEER PARK (village). Covers a land area of 0.897 square miles and a water area of 0.037 square miles. Located at 45.18° N. Lat.; 92.38° W. Long. Elevation is 1,060 feet.
Population: 227 (2000); Race: 100.0% White, 0.0% Black, 0.0% Asian, 0.0% American Indian and Alaska Native, 0.0% Hispanic of any race, 0.0% two or more races (2000); Density: 253.0 persons per square mile (2000); Age: 21.7% under 18, 16.7% over 64 (2000); Marriage status: 21.0% never married, 64.8% now married, 4.1% widowed, 10.0% divorced (2000); Foreign born: 0.0% (2000); Ancestry (includes multiple ancestries): 47.5% German, 30.8% Norwegian, 11.4% Irish, 7.2% United States or American, 7.2% English (2000).
Economy: Single-family building permits issued: 1 (2001) / 0 (2000); Multi-family building permits issued: 0 (2001) / 0 (2000); Employment by occupation: 4.6% management, 13.7% professional, 17.0% services, 24.2% sales, 0.7% farming, 6.5% construction, 33.3% production (2000).
Income: Per capita income: $17,367 (2000); Median household income: $51,000 (2000); Poverty rate: 4.9% (2000).
Taxes: Total city taxes per capita: $31 (1997); City property taxes per capita: $27 (1997).
Education: High school graduation rate: 90.4% (2000); College graduation rate: 6.4% (2000).
Housing: Homeownership rate: 72.7% (2000); Median home value: $86,300 (2000); Median rent: $358 per month (2000); Median age of housing: 55 years (2000).
Transportation: Commute to work: 95.4% car, 0.0% public transportation, 1.3% walk, 2.0% work from home (2000); Travel time to work: 22.8% less than 15 minutes, 39.6% 15 to 30 minutes, 17.4% 30 to 45 minutes, 4.7% 45 to 60 minutes, 15.4% 60 minutes or more (2000)

EAU GALLE (town). Covers a land area of 33.596 square miles and a water area of 0.187 square miles. Located at 44.89° N. Lat.; 92.30° W. Long.
Population: 882 (2000); Race: 99.3% White, 0.0% Black, 0.0% Asian, 0.0% American Indian and Alaska Native, 0.2% Hispanic of any race, 0.2% two or more races (2000); Density: 26.3 persons per square mile (2000); Age: 29.9% under 18, 8.6% over 64 (2000); Marriage status: 24.1% never married, 67.8% now married, 3.4% widowed, 4.8% divorced (2000); Foreign born: 0.2% (2000); Ancestry (includes multiple ancestries): 46.6% German, 39.6% Norwegian, 8.8% English, 8.7% Dutch, 8.4% Irish (2000).
Economy: Single-family building permits issued: 18 (2001) / 18 (2000); Multi-family building permits issued: 0 (2001) / 0 (2000); Employment by occupation: 17.8% management, 15.8% professional, 12.9% services, 18.0% sales, 1.7% farming, 12.4% construction, 21.4% production (2000).
Income: Per capita income: $20,787 (2000); Median household income: $56,250 (2000); Poverty rate: 2.6% (2000).
Taxes: Total city taxes per capita: $103 (1997); City property taxes per capita: $97 (1997).
Education: High school graduation rate: 90.1% (2000); College graduation rate: 18.1% (2000).
Housing: Homeownership rate: 85.6% (2000); Median home value: $118,300 (2000); Median rent: $375 per month (2000); Median age of housing: 31 years (2000).
Transportation: Commute to work: 88.2% car, 0.0% public transportation, 2.9% walk, 8.0% work from home (2000); Travel time to work: 44.8% less than 15 minutes, 16.6% 15 to 30 minutes, 20.7% 30 to 45 minutes, 9.8% 45 to 60 minutes, 8.1% 60 minutes or more (2000)

EMERALD (town). Covers a land area of 34.834 square miles and a water area of 0.077 square miles. Located at 45.08° N. Lat.; 92.32° W. Long. Elevation is 1,155 feet.
Population: 691 (2000); Race: 97.6% White, 1.7% Black, 0.6% Asian, 0.0% American Indian and Alaska Native, 0.0% Hispanic of any race, 0.1% two or more races (2000); Density: 19.8 persons per square mile (2000); Age: 28.0% under 18, 9.6% over 64 (2000); Marriage status: 23.5% never married, 67.6% now married, 3.1% widowed, 5.7% divorced (2000); Foreign born: 0.0% (2000); Ancestry (includes multiple ancestries): 37.4% German, 21.0% Norwegian, 13.4% Dutch, 10.0% Irish, 7.4% Polish (2000).
Economy: Single-family building permits issued: 13 (2001) / 8 (2000); Multi-family building permits issued: 0 (2001) / 0 (2000); Employment by occupation: 15.1% management, 12.3% professional, 11.3% services, 18.6% sales, 3.8% farming, 11.8% construction, 27.1% production (2000).
Income: Per capita income: $19,190 (2000); Median household income: $47,500 (2000); Poverty rate: 3.7% (2000).
Taxes: Total city taxes per capita: $185 (1997); City property taxes per capita: $184 (1997).
Education: High school graduation rate: 87.0% (2000); College graduation rate: 12.6% (2000).
Housing: Homeownership rate: 94.6% (2000); Median home value: $133,300 (2000); Median rent: $400 per month (2000); Median age of housing: 45 years (2000).
Transportation: Commute to work: 87.0% car, 0.8% public transportation, 0.5% walk, 11.0% work from home (2000); Travel time to work: 25.3% less than 15 minutes, 36.8% 15 to 30 minutes, 19.8% 30 to 45 minutes, 7.8% 45 to 60 minutes, 10.3% 60 minutes or more (2000)

ERIN PRAIRIE (town). Covers a land area of 35.463 square miles and a water area of 0.158 square miles. Located at 45.08° N. Lat.; 92.42° W. Long.
Population: 658 (2000); Race: 100.0% White, 0.0% Black, 0.0% Asian, 0.0% American Indian and Alaska Native, 0.0% Hispanic of any race, 0.0% two or more races (2000); Density: 18.6 persons per square mile (2000); Age: 27.0% under 18, 7.3% over 64 (2000); Marriage status: 26.2% never married, 67.1% now married, 2.5% widowed, 4.2% divorced (2000); Foreign born: 0.3% (2000); Ancestry (includes multiple ancestries): 51.4% German, 27.4% Norwegian, 15.0% Irish, 8.4% Swedish, 6.9% Polish (2000).
Economy: Single-family building permits issued: 3 (2001) / 6 (2000); Multi-family building permits issued: 0 (2001) / 0 (2000); Employment by occupation: 20.1% management, 12.9% professional, 10.2% services, 21.6% sales, 3.6% farming, 14.2% construction, 17.5% production (2000).
Income: Per capita income: $23,772 (2000); Median household income: $65,938 (2000); Poverty rate: 3.0% (2000).
Taxes: Total city taxes per capita: $121 (1997); City property taxes per capita: $118 (1997).
Education: High school graduation rate: 90.1% (2000); College graduation rate: 22.4% (2000).
Housing: Homeownership rate: 84.5% (2000); Median home value: $147,700 (2000); Median rent: $418 per month (2000); Median age of housing: 28 years (2000).
Transportation: Commute to work: 91.5% car, 0.0% public transportation, 0.8% walk, 7.0% work from home (2000); Travel time to work: 31.1% less than 15 minutes, 30.3% 15 to 30 minutes, 20.3% 30 to 45 minutes, 10.6% 45 to 60 minutes, 7.8% 60 minutes or more (2000)

FOREST (town). Covers a land area of 37.160 square miles and a water area of 0.051 square miles. Located at 45.15° N. Lat.; 92.22° W. Long. Elevation is 1,130 feet.
Population: 590 (2000); Race: 99.3% White, 0.0% Black, 0.3% Asian, 0.0% American Indian and Alaska Native, 2.0% Hispanic of any race, 0.0% two or more races (2000); Density: 15.9 persons per square mile (2000); Age: 29.9% under 18, 6.6% over 64 (2000); Marriage status: 28.9% never married, 62.8% now married, 4.8% widowed, 3.5% divorced (2000); Foreign born: 0.3% (2000); Ancestry (includes multiple ancestries): 44.5% German, 20.0%

Norwegian, 11.4% Irish, 11.2% United States or American, 7.5% Swedish (2000).
Economy: Single-family building permits issued: 4 (2001) / 4 (2000); Multi-family building permits issued: 0 (2001) / 0 (2000); Employment by occupation: 23.8% management, 9.0% professional, 11.1% services, 12.7% sales, 8.4% farming, 10.2% construction, 24.7% production (2000).
Income: Per capita income: $21,427 (2000); Median household income: $50,833 (2000); Poverty rate: 8.3% (2000).
Taxes: Total city taxes per capita: $111 (1997); City property taxes per capita: $109 (1997).
Education: High school graduation rate: 88.1% (2000); College graduation rate: 8.9% (2000).
Housing: Homeownership rate: 90.1% (2000); Median home value: $81,700 (2000); Median rent: $425 per month (2000); Median age of housing: 60+ years (2000).
Transportation: Commute to work: 74.2% car, 0.0% public transportation, 4.3% walk, 20.9% work from home (2000); Travel time to work: 23.6% less than 15 minutes, 32.2% 15 to 30 minutes, 14.7% 30 to 45 minutes, 12.0% 45 to 60 minutes, 17.4% 60 minutes or more (2000)

GLENWOOD (town). Covers a land area of 34.233 square miles and a water area of 0.131 square miles. Located at 45.07° N. Lat.; 92.18° W. Long.
Population: 755 (2000); Race: 96.7% White, 0.0% Black, 0.5% Asian, 0.4% American Indian and Alaska Native, 2.4% Hispanic of any race, 0.7% two or more races (2000); Density: 22.1 persons per square mile (2000); Age: 33.1% under 18, 11.6% over 64 (2000); Marriage status: 25.2% never married, 62.9% now married, 4.6% widowed, 7.4% divorced (2000); Foreign born: 2.4% (2000); Ancestry (includes multiple ancestries): 43.2% German, 18.9% Norwegian, 10.9% United States or American, 8.5% Irish, 7.0% Swedish (2000).
Economy: Single-family building permits issued: 3 (2001) / 11 (2000); Multi-family building permits issued: 0 (2001) / 0 (2000); Employment by occupation: 15.6% management, 12.2% professional, 12.5% services, 23.3% sales, 4.0% farming, 7.2% construction, 25.2% production (2000).
Income: Per capita income: $17,037 (2000); Median household income: $47,222 (2000); Poverty rate: 7.2% (2000).
Taxes: Total city taxes per capita: $121 (1997); City property taxes per capita: $118 (1997).
Education: High school graduation rate: 82.4% (2000); College graduation rate: 10.7% (2000).
Housing: Homeownership rate: 86.9% (2000); Median home value: $86,000 (2000); Median rent: $379 per month (2000); Median age of housing: 57 years (2000).
Transportation: Commute to work: 82.6% car, 0.0% public transportation, 6.7% walk, 10.7% work from home (2000); Travel time to work: 33.2% less than 15 minutes, 29.3% 15 to 30 minutes, 17.1% 30 to 45 minutes, 7.8% 45 to 60 minutes, 12.6% 60 minutes or more (2000)

GLENWOOD CITY (city). Covers a land area of 2.479 square miles and a water area of 0 square miles. Located at 45.05° N. Lat.; 92.17° W. Long. Elevation is 1,060 feet.
Population: 1,183 (2000); Race: 98.6% White, 0.0% Black, 0.0% Asian, 0.4% American Indian and Alaska Native, 0.0% Hispanic of any race, 1.0% two or more races (2000); Density: 477.2 persons per square mile (2000); Age: 27.3% under 18, 19.4% over 64 (2000); Marriage status: 22.2% never married, 59.8% now married, 9.7% widowed, 8.3% divorced (2000); Foreign born: 0.4% (2000); Ancestry (includes multiple ancestries): 39.3% German, 22.4% Norwegian, 8.0% Irish, 6.0% English, 5.1% Belgian (2000).
Economy: Single-family building permits issued: 10 (2001) / 7 (2000); Multi-family building permits issued: 0 (2001) / 2 (2000); Employment by occupation: 8.9% management, 13.5% professional, 13.2% services, 18.2% sales, 2.0% farming, 10.3% construction, 33.9% production (2000).
Income: Per capita income: $17,424 (2000); Median household income: $36,964 (2000); Poverty rate: 9.1% (2000).
Taxes: Total city taxes per capita: $163 (1997); City property taxes per capita: $125 (1997).
Education: High school graduation rate: 78.6% (2000); College graduation rate: 13.7% (2000).

School District(s)

Glenwood City (PK-12)
2000 Enrollment: 857 715-265-4757
Housing: Homeownership rate: 68.4% (2000); Median home value: $82,400 (2000); Median rent: $410 per month (2000); Median age of housing: 38 years (2000).
Newspapers: Tribune Press Reporter (1 x week)
Transportation: Commute to work: 92.2% car, 0.0% public transportation, 4.0% walk, 3.8% work from home (2000); Travel time to work: 33.8% less than 15 minutes, 28.3% 15 to 30 minutes, 12.2% 30 to 45 minutes, 12.4% 45 to 60 minutes, 13.3% 60 minutes or more (2000)

HAMMOND (village). Covers a land area of 1.372 square miles and a water area of 0 square miles. Located at 44.97° N. Lat.; 92.43° W. Long. Elevation is 1,160 feet.
Population: 1,153 (2000); Race: 99.5% White, 0.4% Black, 0.0% Asian, 0.2% American Indian and Alaska Native, 0.2% Hispanic of any race, 0.0% two or more races (2000); Density: 840.2 persons per square mile (2000); Age: 26.2% under 18, 14.0% over 64 (2000); Marriage status: 24.9% never married, 56.1% now married, 9.2% widowed, 9.9% divorced (2000); Foreign born: 0.3% (2000); Ancestry (includes multiple ancestries): 36.7% German, 30.6% Norwegian, 14.7% Irish, 7.1% English, 6.4% United States or American (2000).
Economy: Single-family building permits issued: 59 (2001) / 10 (2000); Multi-family building permits issued: 46 (2001) / 30 (2000); Employment by occupation: 10.2% management, 13.5% professional, 19.4% services, 28.7% sales, 0.0% farming, 11.5% construction, 16.7% production (2000).
Income: Per capita income: $19,002 (2000); Median household income: $45,789 (2000); Poverty rate: 3.5% (2000).
Taxes: Total city taxes per capita: $166 (1997); City property taxes per capita: $156 (1997).
Education: High school graduation rate: 88.4% (2000); College graduation rate: 17.3% (2000).

School District(s)

Saint Croix Central (PK-12)
2000 Enrollment: 968 715-796-2256
Housing: Homeownership rate: 68.0% (2000); Median home value: $100,900 (2000); Median rent: $426 per month (2000); Median age of housing: 32 years (2000).
Hospitals: Baldwin Area Medical Center (33 beds)
Newspapers: Central Saint Croix News (1 x week)
Transportation: Commute to work: 94.4% car, 0.0% public transportation, 4.7% walk, 1.0% work from home (2000); Travel time to work: 32.0% less than 15 minutes, 33.6% 15 to 30 minutes, 16.2% 30 to 45 minutes, 9.7% 45 to 60 minutes, 8.4% 60 minutes or more (2000)

HAMMOND (town). Covers a land area of 33.505 square miles and a water area of 0.152 square miles. Located at 45.00° N. Lat.; 92.42° W. Long. Elevation is 1,160 feet.
Population: 947 (2000); Race: 97.9% White, 0.0% Black, 0.0% Asian, 0.8% American Indian and Alaska Native, 0.0% Hispanic of any race, 1.2% two or more races (2000); Density: 28.3 persons per square mile (2000); Age: 29.9% under 18, 10.7% over 64 (2000); Marriage status: 21.1% never married, 72.1% now married, 1.1% widowed, 5.8% divorced (2000); Foreign born: 0.7% (2000); Ancestry (includes multiple ancestries): 41.3% German, 30.1% Norwegian, 13.3% Irish, 13.1% Dutch, 7.5% Swedish (2000).
Economy: Single-family building permits issued: 10 (2001) / 9 (2000); Multi-family building permits issued: 0 (2001) / 0 (2000); Employment by occupation: 16.1% management, 18.8% professional, 10.3% services, 21.2% sales, 2.7% farming, 9.6% construction, 21.2% production (2000).
Income: Per capita income: $21,357 (2000); Median household income: $53,438 (2000); Poverty rate: 4.0% (2000).
Taxes: Total city taxes per capita: $154 (1997); City property taxes per capita: $152 (1997).
Education: High school graduation rate: 92.1% (2000); College graduation rate: 22.1% (2000).
Housing: Homeownership rate: 91.3% (2000); Median home value: $132,700 (2000); Median rent: $425 per month (2000); Median age of housing: 33 years (2000).
Transportation: Commute to work: 91.4% car, 0.4% public transportation, 2.8% walk, 5.0% work from home (2000); Travel time to work: 38.3% less than 15 minutes, 27.3% 15 to 30 minutes, 17.4% 30 to 45 minutes, 11.8% 45 to 60 minutes, 5.2% 60 minutes or more (2000)

HUDSON (city). Covers a land area of 5.402 square miles and a water area of 0.868 square miles. Located at 44.97° N. Lat.; 92.74° W. Long. Elevation is 750 feet.
History: A French-Canadian trapper named Louis Massey built a dugout in 1838 on the site of Hudson. When St. Croix County was formed in 1853, Hudson was named as the county seat. It became a trade and transportation center as the Wisconsin gateway to Minneapolis and St. Paul in Minnesota.
Population: 8,775 (2000); Race: 96.2% White, 0.9% Black, 0.9% Asian, 0.9% American Indian and Alaska Native, 1.1% Hispanic of any race, 0.8%

two or more races (2000); Density: 1,624.5 persons per square mile (2000); Age: 24.3% under 18, 11.4% over 64 (2000); Marriage status: 22.6% never married, 62.3% now married, 6.0% widowed, 9.2% divorced (2000); Foreign born: 1.3% (2000); Ancestry (includes multiple ancestries): 41.9% German, 19.6% Norwegian, 13.6% Irish, 7.9% Swedish, 6.3% English (2000).
Economy: Single-family building permits issued: 210 (2001) / 127 (2000); Multi-family building permits issued: 48 (2001) / 126 (2000); Employment by occupation: 19.1% management, 22.4% professional, 13.3% services, 26.7% sales, 0.0% farming, 7.1% construction, 11.4% production (2000).
Income: Per capita income: $26,921 (2000); Median household income: $50,991 (2000); Poverty rate: 3.5% (2000).
Taxes: Total city taxes per capita: $503 (1997); City property taxes per capita: $440 (1997).
Education: High school graduation rate: 95.2% (2000); College graduation rate: 37.7% (2000).

School District(s)

Hudson (PK-12)
2000 Enrollment: 4,133 715-386-4901
Housing: Homeownership rate: 61.9% (2000); Median home value: $139,900 (2000); Median rent: $571 per month (2000); Median age of housing: 23 years (2000).
Hospitals: Hudson Hospital (49 beds)
Safety: Violent crime rate: 21.5 per 10,000 population; Property crime rate: 532.9 per 10,000 population (2001).
Newspapers: The Hudson Star-Observer (1 x week)
Transportation: Commute to work: 94.0% car, 0.8% public transportation, 2.5% walk, 2.3% work from home (2000); Travel time to work: 32.5% less than 15 minutes, 31.9% 15 to 30 minutes, 21.3% 30 to 45 minutes, 8.4% 45 to 60 minutes, 5.9% 60 minutes or more (2000)
Additional Information Contacts
Hudson Area Chamber of Commerce 715-386-8411

HUDSON (town). Covers a land area of 25.881 square miles and a water area of 0.572 square miles. Located at 44.99° N. Lat.; 92.69° W. Long. Elevation is 750 feet.
Population: 6,213 (2000); Race: 97.7% White, 0.7% Black, 0.4% Asian, 0.2% American Indian and Alaska Native, 0.3% Hispanic of any race, 0.9% two or more races (2000); Density: 240.1 persons per square mile (2000); Age: 32.4% under 18, 2.6% over 64 (2000); Marriage status: 21.5% never married, 69.4% now married, 1.3% widowed, 7.7% divorced (2000); Foreign born: 1.4% (2000); Ancestry (includes multiple ancestries): 41.5% German, 18.6% Norwegian, 16.1% Irish, 10.1% Swedish, 6.8% English (2000).
Economy: Single-family building permits issued: 139 (2001) / 92 (2000); Multi-family building permits issued: 12 (2001) / 16 (2000); Employment by occupation: 19.6% management, 21.4% professional, 8.7% services, 27.5% sales, 0.0% farming, 8.1% construction, 14.7% production (2000).
Income: Per capita income: $29,424 (2000); Median household income: $81,733 (2000); Poverty rate: 1.4% (2000).
Taxes: Total city taxes per capita: $50 (1997); City property taxes per capita: $35 (1997).
Education: High school graduation rate: 97.1% (2000); College graduation rate: 37.1% (2000).
Housing: Homeownership rate: 90.8% (2000); Median home value: $185,500 (2000); Median rent: $564 per month (2000); Median age of housing: 12 years (2000).
Transportation: Commute to work: 94.8% car, 0.3% public transportation, 0.4% walk, 3.8% work from home (2000); Travel time to work: 26.6% less than 15 minutes, 34.4% 15 to 30 minutes, 24.1% 30 to 45 minutes, 9.7% 45 to 60 minutes, 5.2% 60 minutes or more (2000)

KINNICKINNIC (town). Covers a land area of 35.435 square miles and a water area of 0.004 square miles. Located at 44.90° N. Lat.; 92.55° W. Long.
Population: 1,400 (2000); Race: 98.2% White, 0.0% Black, 0.5% Asian, 0.0% American Indian and Alaska Native, 0.0% Hispanic of any race, 1.3% two or more races (2000); Density: 39.5 persons per square mile (2000); Age: 29.6% under 18, 7.3% over 64 (2000); Marriage status: 20.2% never married, 72.9% now married, 2.7% widowed, 4.2% divorced (2000); Foreign born: 0.4% (2000); Ancestry (includes multiple ancestries): 41.5% German, 20.4% Norwegian, 15.0% Irish, 8.9% Swedish, 8.8% English (2000).
Economy: Single-family building permits issued: 10 (2001) / 12 (2000); Multi-family building permits issued: 0 (2001) / 0 (2000); Employment by occupation: 13.4% management, 22.3% professional, 10.0% services, 23.9% sales, 0.5% farming, 11.4% construction, 18.5% production (2000).
Income: Per capita income: $23,665 (2000); Median household income: $62,727 (2000); Poverty rate: 3.6% (2000).
Taxes: Total city taxes per capita: $170 (1997); City property taxes per capita: $165 (1997).
Education: High school graduation rate: 96.0% (2000); College graduation rate: 33.3% (2000).
Housing: Homeownership rate: 88.7% (2000); Median home value: $149,700 (2000); Median rent: $482 per month (2000); Median age of housing: 20 years (2000).
Transportation: Commute to work: 93.5% car, 0.0% public transportation, 0.8% walk, 5.7% work from home (2000); Travel time to work: 33.2% less than 15 minutes, 29.2% 15 to 30 minutes, 21.2% 30 to 45 minutes, 12.8% 45 to 60 minutes, 3.5% 60 minutes or more (2000)

NEW RICHMOND (city). Covers a land area of 5.100 square miles and a water area of 0.189 square miles. Located at 45.12° N. Lat.; 92.53° W. Long. Elevation is 982 feet.
Population: 6,310 (2000); Race: 98.6% White, 0.0% Black, 0.1% Asian, 0.0% American Indian and Alaska Native, 1.1% Hispanic of any race, 1.3% two or more races (2000); Density: 1,237.2 persons per square mile (2000); Age: 27.1% under 18, 14.8% over 64 (2000); Marriage status: 26.5% never married, 56.5% now married, 7.6% widowed, 9.5% divorced (2000); Foreign born: 1.0% (2000); Ancestry (includes multiple ancestries): 39.4% German, 22.7% Norwegian, 15.6% Irish, 8.2% Swedish, 6.2% French (except Basque) (2000).
Economy: Single-family building permits issued: 39 (2001) / 24 (2000); Multi-family building permits issued: 126 (2001) / 36 (2000); Employment by occupation: 8.8% management, 15.7% professional, 14.5% services, 26.1% sales, 0.6% farming, 11.4% construction, 22.9% production (2000).
Income: Per capita income: $19,840 (2000); Median household income: $43,475 (2000); Poverty rate: 6.8% (2000).
Taxes: Total city taxes per capita: $326 (1997); City property taxes per capita: $307 (1997).
Education: High school graduation rate: 87.9% (2000); College graduation rate: 17.5% (2000).

School District(s)

New Richmond (PK-12)
2000 Enrollment: 2,435 715-243-7411
Housing: Homeownership rate: 63.4% (2000); Median home value: $108,100 (2000); Median rent: $475 per month (2000); Median age of housing: 26 years (2000).
Hospitals: Holy Family Hospital (40 beds)
Safety: Violent crime rate: 4.7 per 10,000 population; Property crime rate: 299.0 per 10,000 population (2001).
Newspapers: The News (1 x week); The Scotsman (1 x week)
Transportation: Commute to work: 91.7% car, 0.0% public transportation, 3.3% walk, 4.9% work from home (2000); Travel time to work: 43.0% less than 15 minutes, 13.9% 15 to 30 minutes, 21.2% 30 to 45 minutes, 12.0% 45 to 60 minutes, 10.0% 60 minutes or more (2000)
Airports: New Richmond Municipal
Additional Information Contacts
New Richmond Chamber of Commerce 715-246-2900

NORTH HUDSON (village). Covers a land area of 1.310 square miles and a water area of 0.803 square miles. Located at 44.99° N. Lat.; 92.75° W. Long. Elevation is 740 feet.
Population: 3,463 (2000); Race: 97.9% White, 0.2% Black, 1.0% Asian, 0.0% American Indian and Alaska Native, 0.5% Hispanic of any race, 0.7% two or more races (2000); Density: 2,642.7 persons per square mile (2000); Age: 28.7% under 18, 5.6% over 64 (2000); Marriage status: 24.6% never married, 64.9% now married, 2.6% widowed, 8.0% divorced (2000); Foreign born: 2.0% (2000); Ancestry (includes multiple ancestries): 42.3% German, 21.6% Norwegian, 18.1% Irish, 9.7% Polish, 8.5% English (2000).
Economy: Single-family building permits issued: 26 (2001) / 19 (2000); Multi-family building permits issued: 0 (2001) / 48 (2000); Employment by occupation: 12.8% management, 26.1% professional, 18.3% services, 23.6% sales, 0.0% farming, 6.5% construction, 12.7% production (2000).
Income: Per capita income: $26,540 (2000); Median household income: $60,848 (2000); Poverty rate: 1.8% (2000).
Taxes: Total city taxes per capita: $151 (1997); City property taxes per capita: $135 (1997).
Education: High school graduation rate: 95.0% (2000); College graduation rate: 35.6% (2000).
Housing: Homeownership rate: 76.5% (2000); Median home value: $143,400 (2000); Median rent: $574 per month (2000); Median age of housing: 22 years (2000).
Transportation: Commute to work: 95.2% car, 0.0% public transportation, 1.6% walk, 3.2% work from home (2000); Travel time to work: 31.4% less

than 15 minutes, 31.1% 15 to 30 minutes, 22.5% 30 to 45 minutes, 10.5% 45 to 60 minutes, 4.4% 60 minutes or more (2000)

PLEASANT VALLEY (town). Covers a land area of 18.027 square miles and a water area of 0 square miles. Located at 44.89° N. Lat.; 92.46° W. Long.
Population: 430 (2000); Race: 97.3% White, 0.0% Black, 0.7% Asian, 2.0% American Indian and Alaska Native, 0.7% Hispanic of any race, 0.0% two or more races (2000); Density: 23.9 persons per square mile (2000); Age: 31.5% under 18, 8.3% over 64 (2000); Marriage status: 20.9% never married, 73.5% now married, 1.0% widowed, 4.6% divorced (2000); Foreign born: 2.4% (2000); Ancestry (includes multiple ancestries): 47.9% German, 21.8% Norwegian, 11.0% Dutch, 10.8% English, 7.1% Irish (2000).
Economy: Single-family building permits issued: 3 (2001) / 8 (2000); Multi-family building permits issued: 0 (2001) / 0 (2000); Employment by occupation: 29.5% management, 18.3% professional, 11.2% services, 13.4% sales, 6.3% farming, 8.9% construction, 12.5% production (2000).
Income: Per capita income: $22,074 (2000); Median household income: $58,750 (2000); Poverty rate: 0.5% (2000).
Taxes: Total city taxes per capita: $150 (1997); City property taxes per capita: $150 (1997).
Education: High school graduation rate: 90.9% (2000); College graduation rate: 28.5% (2000).
Housing: Homeownership rate: 74.5% (2000); Median home value: $140,000 (2000); Median rent: $495 per month (2000); Median age of housing: 41 years (2000).
Transportation: Commute to work: 85.3% car, 0.0% public transportation, 3.2% walk, 10.6% work from home (2000); Travel time to work: 26.3% less than 15 minutes, 30.9% 15 to 30 minutes, 24.7% 30 to 45 minutes, 10.8% 45 to 60 minutes, 7.2% 60 minutes or more (2000)

RICHMOND (town). Covers a land area of 33.151 square miles and a water area of 0.238 square miles. Located at 45.08° N. Lat.; 92.56° W. Long.
Population: 1,556 (2000); Race: 99.2% White, 0.0% Black, 0.0% Asian, 0.0% American Indian and Alaska Native, 0.9% Hispanic of any race, 0.3% two or more races (2000); Density: 46.9 persons per square mile (2000); Age: 30.2% under 18, 10.7% over 64 (2000); Marriage status: 22.5% never married, 68.1% now married, 2.1% widowed, 7.3% divorced (2000); Foreign born: 0.9% (2000); Ancestry (includes multiple ancestries): 43.3% German, 20.9% Norwegian, 19.0% Irish, 8.6% French (except Basque), 6.5% Swedish (2000).
Economy: Single-family building permits issued: 62 (2001) / 27 (2000); Multi-family building permits issued: 0 (2001) / 0 (2000); Employment by occupation: 16.4% management, 14.6% professional, 10.7% services, 24.2% sales, 2.8% farming, 11.2% construction, 20.0% production (2000).
Income: Per capita income: $21,632 (2000); Median household income: $59,688 (2000); Poverty rate: 2.8% (2000).
Taxes: Total city taxes per capita: $67 (1997); City property taxes per capita: $61 (1997).
Education: High school graduation rate: 90.0% (2000); College graduation rate: 19.5% (2000).
Housing: Homeownership rate: 91.6% (2000); Median home value: $141,400 (2000); Median rent: $502 per month (2000); Median age of housing: 23 years (2000).
Transportation: Commute to work: 88.7% car, 1.8% public transportation, 2.5% walk, 5.7% work from home (2000); Travel time to work: 33.1% less than 15 minutes, 24.5% 15 to 30 minutes, 20.7% 30 to 45 minutes, 13.6% 45 to 60 minutes, 8.2% 60 minutes or more (2000)

ROBERTS (village). Covers a land area of 0.537 square miles and a water area of 0 square miles. Located at 44.98° N. Lat.; 92.55° W. Long. Elevation is 1,040 feet.
Population: 969 (2000); Race: 97.5% White, 0.0% Black, 0.8% Asian, 0.4% American Indian and Alaska Native, 1.1% Hispanic of any race, 0.3% two or more races (2000); Density: 1,805.3 persons per square mile (2000); Age: 24.5% under 18, 6.8% over 64 (2000); Marriage status: 32.5% never married, 49.8% now married, 6.0% widowed, 11.6% divorced (2000); Foreign born: 1.4% (2000); Ancestry (includes multiple ancestries): 40.4% German, 19.6% Norwegian, 15.2% Irish, 6.9% Swedish, 6.1% Other groups (2000).
Economy: Single-family building permits issued: 43 (2001) / 22 (2000); Multi-family building permits issued: 16 (2001) / 2 (2000); Employment by occupation: 7.7% management, 9.1% professional, 15.4% services, 26.8% sales, 0.0% farming, 11.7% construction, 29.3% production (2000).
Income: Per capita income: $19,616 (2000); Median household income: $42,258 (2000); Poverty rate: 5.5% (2000).
Taxes: Total city taxes per capita: $86 (1997); City property taxes per capita: $63 (1997).
Education: High school graduation rate: 89.9% (2000); College graduation rate: 11.6% (2000).
Housing: Homeownership rate: 74.0% (2000); Median home value: $116,300 (2000); Median rent: $520 per month (2000); Median age of housing: 25 years (2000).
Transportation: Commute to work: 94.8% car, 0.0% public transportation, 1.6% walk, 2.6% work from home (2000); Travel time to work: 20.2% less than 15 minutes, 39.6% 15 to 30 minutes, 16.5% 30 to 45 minutes, 16.9% 45 to 60 minutes, 6.7% 60 minutes or more (2000)

RUSH RIVER (town). Covers a land area of 17.878 square miles and a water area of 0 square miles. Located at 44.90° N. Lat.; 92.41° W. Long.
Population: 498 (2000); Race: 98.0% White, 0.0% Black, 0.0% Asian, 0.6% American Indian and Alaska Native, 0.0% Hispanic of any race, 1.4% two or more races (2000); Density: 27.9 persons per square mile (2000); Age: 26.1% under 18, 14.0% over 64 (2000); Marriage status: 24.2% never married, 67.5% now married, 2.9% widowed, 5.4% divorced (2000); Foreign born: 0.4% (2000); Ancestry (includes multiple ancestries): 41.3% German, 29.4% Norwegian, 11.3% Swedish, 10.3% Dutch, 9.1% Irish (2000).
Economy: Single-family building permits issued: 2 (2001) / 6 (2000); Multi-family building permits issued: 0 (2001) / 0 (2000); Employment by occupation: 15.5% management, 13.5% professional, 14.1% services, 24.6% sales, 3.4% farming, 7.4% construction, 21.5% production (2000).
Income: Per capita income: $23,240 (2000); Median household income: $58,333 (2000); Poverty rate: 2.0% (2000).
Taxes: Total city taxes per capita: $107 (1997); City property taxes per capita: $102 (1997).
Education: High school graduation rate: 90.9% (2000); College graduation rate: 8.8% (2000).
Housing: Homeownership rate: 94.7% (2000); Median home value: $103,800 (2000); Median rent: $350 per month (2000); Median age of housing: 51 years (2000).
Transportation: Commute to work: 86.2% car, 0.0% public transportation, 3.8% walk, 9.3% work from home (2000); Travel time to work: 37.6% less than 15 minutes, 23.6% 15 to 30 minutes, 12.9% 30 to 45 minutes, 15.6% 45 to 60 minutes, 10.3% 60 minutes or more (2000)

SAINT JOSEPH (town). Covers a land area of 32.128 square miles and a water area of 2.400 square miles. Located at 45.05° N. Lat.; 92.71° W. Long.
Population: 3,436 (2000); Race: 99.3% White, 0.4% Black, 0.0% Asian, 0.1% American Indian and Alaska Native, 1.0% Hispanic of any race, 0.2% two or more races (2000); Density: 106.9 persons per square mile (2000); Age: 28.6% under 18, 5.6% over 64 (2000); Marriage status: 16.3% never married, 74.4% now married, 3.6% widowed, 5.7% divorced (2000); Foreign born: 2.0% (2000); Ancestry (includes multiple ancestries): 51.0% German, 19.6% Norwegian, 16.6% Irish, 7.2% English, 7.1% French (except Basque) (2000).
Economy: Single-family building permits issued: 30 (2001) / 27 (2000); Multi-family building permits issued: 0 (2001) / 0 (2000); Employment by occupation: 17.5% management, 22.3% professional, 9.7% services, 25.3% sales, 0.0% farming, 11.2% construction, 14.1% production (2000).
Income: Per capita income: $30,988 (2000); Median household income: $81,277 (2000); Poverty rate: 1.4% (2000).
Education: High school graduation rate: 96.3% (2000); College graduation rate: 32.6% (2000).
Housing: Homeownership rate: 95.7% (2000); Median home value: $186,500 (2000); Median rent: $514 per month (2000); Median age of housing: 21 years (2000).
Transportation: Commute to work: 91.5% car, 0.4% public transportation, 0.0% walk, 8.1% work from home (2000); Travel time to work: 21.9% less than 15 minutes, 33.3% 15 to 30 minutes, 25.8% 30 to 45 minutes, 14.5% 45 to 60 minutes, 4.5% 60 minutes or more (2000)

SOMERSET (village). Covers a land area of 1.843 square miles and a water area of 0 square miles. Located at 45.12° N. Lat.; 92.67° W. Long. Elevation is 870 feet.
Population: 1,556 (2000); Race: 95.8% White, 0.5% Black, 0.0% Asian, 0.2% American Indian and Alaska Native, 1.1% Hispanic of any race, 2.8% two or more races (2000); Density: 844.1 persons per square mile (2000); Age: 31.7% under 18, 6.3% over 64 (2000); Marriage status: 30.3% never married, 48.5% now married, 4.8% widowed, 16.4% divorced (2000); Foreign born: 1.1% (2000); Ancestry (includes multiple ancestries): 39.9%

German, 18.5% Norwegian, 16.2% French (except Basque), 11.6% Irish, 6.0% Other groups (2000).
Economy: Employment by occupation: 7.8% management, 13.3% professional, 14.3% services, 26.7% sales, 0.0% farming, 13.0% construction, 24.8% production (2000).
Income: Per capita income: $19,170 (2000); Median household income: $45,194 (2000); Poverty rate: 7.3% (2000).
Taxes: Total city taxes per capita: $286 (1997); City property taxes per capita: $269 (1997).
Education: High school graduation rate: 85.6% (2000); College graduation rate: 11.0% (2000).

School District(s)

Somerset (PK-12)
2000 Enrollment: 1,142 715-247-3313

Housing: Homeownership rate: 51.2% (2000); Median home value: $106,200 (2000); Median rent: $525 per month (2000); Median age of housing: 17 years (2000).
Transportation: Commute to work: 95.9% car, 0.3% public transportation, 1.5% walk, 1.8% work from home (2000); Travel time to work: 23.5% less than 15 minutes, 40.9% 15 to 30 minutes, 17.9% 30 to 45 minutes, 12.0% 45 to 60 minutes, 5.8% 60 minutes or more (2000)
Additional Information Contacts
Somerset Chamber of Commerce. 715-247-3366

SOMERSET (town). Covers a land area of 47.897 square miles and a water area of 2.008 square miles. Located at 45.14° N. Lat.; 92.70° W. Long. Elevation is 870 feet.
Population: 2,644 (2000); Race: 97.1% White, 0.2% Black, 0.7% Asian, 0.6% American Indian and Alaska Native, 0.3% Hispanic of any race, 1.4% two or more races (2000); Density: 55.2 persons per square mile (2000); Age: 28.9% under 18, 7.7% over 64 (2000); Marriage status: 23.8% never married, 65.6% now married, 3.0% widowed, 7.6% divorced (2000); Foreign born: 1.4% (2000); Ancestry (includes multiple ancestries): 41.4% German, 21.8% Norwegian, 14.1% French (except Basque), 10.8% Irish, 7.7% Swedish (2000).
Economy: Single-family building permits issued: 82 (2001) / 49 (2000); Multi-family building permits issued: 0 (2001) / 0 (2000); Employment by occupation: 16.4% management, 18.9% professional, 8.0% services, 23.0% sales, 0.9% farming, 12.7% construction, 20.1% production (2000).
Income: Per capita income: $25,605 (2000); Median household income: $62,063 (2000); Poverty rate: 2.9% (2000).
Taxes: Total city taxes per capita: $88 (1997); City property taxes per capita: $82 (1997).
Education: High school graduation rate: 92.0% (2000); College graduation rate: 24.5% (2000).
Housing: Homeownership rate: 88.1% (2000); Median home value: $156,000 (2000); Median rent: $421 per month (2000); Median age of housing: 20 years (2000).
Transportation: Commute to work: 90.9% car, 0.7% public transportation, 2.7% walk, 5.3% work from home (2000); Travel time to work: 22.5% less than 15 minutes, 33.0% 15 to 30 minutes, 19.6% 30 to 45 minutes, 15.6% 45 to 60 minutes, 9.4% 60 minutes or more (2000)

SPRINGFIELD (town). Covers a land area of 34.231 square miles and a water area of 0.147 square miles. Located at 44.98° N. Lat.; 92.18° W. Long.
Population: 808 (2000); Race: 98.9% White, 0.0% Black, 0.8% Asian, 0.0% American Indian and Alaska Native, 0.5% Hispanic of any race, 0.4% two or more races (2000); Density: 23.6 persons per square mile (2000); Age: 26.3% under 18, 11.1% over 64 (2000); Marriage status: 23.5% never married, 62.5% now married, 3.8% widowed, 10.2% divorced (2000); Foreign born: 1.5% (2000); Ancestry (includes multiple ancestries): 34.8% German, 22.2% Norwegian, 7.8% Irish, 7.1% United States or American, 5.1% French (except Basque) (2000).
Economy: Single-family building permits issued: 9 (2001) / 15 (2000); Multi-family building permits issued: 0 (2001) / 0 (2000); Employment by occupation: 12.4% management, 13.6% professional, 10.2% services, 21.1% sales, 4.4% farming, 8.7% construction, 29.6% production (2000).
Income: Per capita income: $21,303 (2000); Median household income: $54,886 (2000); Poverty rate: 2.4% (2000).
Taxes: Total city taxes per capita: $72 (1997); City property taxes per capita: $69 (1997).
Education: High school graduation rate: 85.0% (2000); College graduation rate: 15.8% (2000).
Housing: Homeownership rate: 89.3% (2000); Median home value: $78,600 (2000); Median rent: $413 per month (2000); Median age of housing: 47 years (2000).
Transportation: Commute to work: 90.4% car, 0.0% public transportation, 1.6% walk, 8.0% work from home (2000); Travel time to work: 23.0% less than 15 minutes, 30.2% 15 to 30 minutes, 17.8% 30 to 45 minutes, 15.1% 45 to 60 minutes, 13.9% 60 minutes or more (2000)

STANTON (town). Covers a land area of 34.045 square miles and a water area of 0.992 square miles. Located at 45.15° N. Lat.; 92.48° W. Long. Elevation is 1,058 feet.
Population: 1,003 (2000); Race: 96.0% White, 0.0% Black, 2.9% Asian, 0.7% American Indian and Alaska Native, 1.6% Hispanic of any race, 0.4% two or more races (2000); Density: 29.5 persons per square mile (2000); Age: 29.4% under 18, 9.0% over 64 (2000); Marriage status: 26.7% never married, 62.9% now married, 3.5% widowed, 6.9% divorced (2000); Foreign born: 2.1% (2000); Ancestry (includes multiple ancestries): 42.4% German, 27.0% Norwegian, 12.7% Irish, 9.1% French (except Basque), 6.8% Swedish (2000).
Economy: Single-family building permits issued: 7 (2001) / 4 (2000); Multi-family building permits issued: 0 (2001) / 0 (2000); Employment by occupation: 12.5% management, 13.2% professional, 9.1% services, 25.0% sales, 0.3% farming, 11.2% construction, 28.6% production (2000).
Income: Per capita income: $20,808 (2000); Median household income: $52,604 (2000); Poverty rate: 4.2% (2000).
Taxes: Total city taxes per capita: $67 (1997); City property taxes per capita: $62 (1997).
Education: High school graduation rate: 92.3% (2000); College graduation rate: 19.0% (2000).
Housing: Homeownership rate: 86.2% (2000); Median home value: $123,800 (2000); Median rent: $413 per month (2000); Median age of housing: 33 years (2000).
Transportation: Commute to work: 92.6% car, 0.3% public transportation, 2.1% walk, 5.0% work from home (2000); Travel time to work: 31.7% less than 15 minutes, 30.4% 15 to 30 minutes, 19.5% 30 to 45 minutes, 8.4% 45 to 60 minutes, 10.0% 60 minutes or more (2000)

STAR PRAIRIE (village). Covers a land area of 2.100 square miles and a water area of 0 square miles. Located at 45.19° N. Lat.; 92.53° W. Long. Elevation is 940 feet.
Population: 574 (2000); Race: 98.8% White, 0.8% Black, 0.0% Asian, 0.0% American Indian and Alaska Native, 0.0% Hispanic of any race, 0.4% two or more races (2000); Density: 273.3 persons per square mile (2000); Age: 29.3% under 18, 7.9% over 64 (2000); Marriage status: 24.1% never married, 60.7% now married, 3.7% widowed, 11.5% divorced (2000); Foreign born: 0.2% (2000); Ancestry (includes multiple ancestries): 38.7% German, 27.7% Norwegian, 15.0% Swedish, 10.2% Irish, 4.8% English (2000).
Economy: Single-family building permits issued: 10 (2001) / 7 (2000); Multi-family building permits issued: 6 (2001) / 0 (2000); Employment by occupation: 10.0% management, 11.7% professional, 11.7% services, 23.5% sales, 0.0% farming, 20.6% construction, 22.4% production (2000).
Income: Per capita income: $19,414 (2000); Median household income: $48,750 (2000); Poverty rate: 4.0% (2000).
Taxes: Total city taxes per capita: $137 (1997); City property taxes per capita: $131 (1997).
Education: High school graduation rate: 85.8% (2000); College graduation rate: 12.9% (2000).
Housing: Homeownership rate: 72.0% (2000); Median home value: $106,800 (2000); Median rent: $433 per month (2000); Median age of housing: 33 years (2000).
Transportation: Commute to work: 90.3% car, 0.0% public transportation, 2.2% walk, 6.9% work from home (2000); Travel time to work: 24.8% less than 15 minutes, 24.4% 15 to 30 minutes, 17.1% 30 to 45 minutes, 19.4% 45 to 60 minutes, 14.3% 60 minutes or more (2000)

STAR PRAIRIE (town). Covers a land area of 31.448 square miles and a water area of 1.241 square miles. Located at 45.16° N. Lat.; 92.58° W. Long. Elevation is 940 feet.
Population: 2,944 (2000); Race: 96.0% White, 3.0% Black, 0.0% Asian, 0.4% American Indian and Alaska Native, 0.9% Hispanic of any race, 0.6% two or more races (2000); Density: 93.6 persons per square mile (2000); Age: 27.6% under 18, 5.9% over 64 (2000); Marriage status: 25.0% never married, 60.9% now married, 2.4% widowed, 11.8% divorced (2000); Foreign born: 0.3% (2000); Ancestry (includes multiple ancestries): 44.8% German, 23.3% Norwegian, 15.7% Irish, 11.3% Swedish, 10.6% French (except Basque) (2000).
Economy: Single-family building permits issued: 53 (2001) / 54 (2000); Multi-family building permits issued: 0 (2001) / 0 (2000); Employment by

occupation: 9.1% management, 14.6% professional, 14.6% services, 25.6% sales, 0.7% farming, 13.3% construction, 22.1% production (2000).
Income: Per capita income: $21,052 (2000); Median household income: $53,468 (2000); Poverty rate: 5.7% (2000).
Taxes: Total city taxes per capita: $31 (1997); City property taxes per capita: $21 (1997).
Education: High school graduation rate: 87.7% (2000); College graduation rate: 16.1% (2000).
Housing: Homeownership rate: 89.7% (2000); Median home value: $139,700 (2000); Median rent: $490 per month (2000); Median age of housing: 18 years (2000).
Transportation: Commute to work: 97.6% car, 0.3% public transportation, 0.3% walk, 1.3% work from home (2000); Travel time to work: 24.3% less than 15 minutes, 29.1% 15 to 30 minutes, 21.9% 30 to 45 minutes, 12.3% 45 to 60 minutes, 12.5% 60 minutes or more (2000)

TROY (town). Covers a land area of 37.727 square miles and a water area of 2.035 square miles. Located at 44.90° N. Lat.; 92.68° W. Long.
Population: 3,661 (2000); Race: 97.4% White, 1.2% Black, 0.4% Asian, 0.0% American Indian and Alaska Native, 1.7% Hispanic of any race, 0.0% two or more races (2000); Density: 97.0 persons per square mile (2000); Age: 28.6% under 18, 6.0% over 64 (2000); Marriage status: 19.3% never married, 73.0% now married, 1.4% widowed, 6.4% divorced (2000); Foreign born: 1.1% (2000); Ancestry (includes multiple ancestries): 43.9% German, 17.4% Norwegian, 16.7% Irish, 10.6% Swedish, 8.2% English (2000).
Economy: Single-family building permits issued: 38 (2001) / 37 (2000); Multi-family building permits issued: 0 (2001) / 0 (2000); Employment by occupation: 18.8% management, 26.5% professional, 10.0% services, 23.2% sales, 0.5% farming, 8.6% construction, 12.5% production (2000).
Income: Per capita income: $28,861 (2000); Median household income: $73,125 (2000); Poverty rate: 1.9% (2000).
Taxes: Total city taxes per capita: $108 (1997); City property taxes per capita: $101 (1997).
Education: High school graduation rate: 96.0% (2000); College graduation rate: 41.8% (2000).
Housing: Homeownership rate: 90.6% (2000); Median home value: $193,600 (2000); Median rent: $492 per month (2000); Median age of housing: 21 years (2000).
Transportation: Commute to work: 94.3% car, 0.0% public transportation, 0.7% walk, 5.0% work from home (2000); Travel time to work: 30.9% less than 15 minutes, 24.7% 15 to 30 minutes, 25.6% 30 to 45 minutes, 11.3% 45 to 60 minutes, 7.5% 60 minutes or more (2000)

WARREN (town). Covers a land area of 34.787 square miles and a water area of 0.515 square miles. Located at 44.99° N. Lat.; 92.55° W. Long.
Population: 1,320 (2000); Race: 98.9% White, 0.0% Black, 0.5% Asian, 0.0% American Indian and Alaska Native, 0.7% Hispanic of any race, 0.5% two or more races (2000); Density: 37.9 persons per square mile (2000); Age: 31.2% under 18, 7.1% over 64 (2000); Marriage status: 22.9% never married, 68.0% now married, 2.7% widowed, 6.4% divorced (2000); Foreign born: 0.8% (2000); Ancestry (includes multiple ancestries): 40.4% German, 16.5% Norwegian, 12.0% Irish, 10.3% English, 9.8% Swedish (2000).
Economy: Single-family building permits issued: 10 (2001) / 23 (2000); Multi-family building permits issued: 0 (2001) / 0 (2000); Employment by occupation: 17.9% management, 17.1% professional, 10.4% services, 25.0% sales, 1.4% farming, 8.7% construction, 19.6% production (2000).
Income: Per capita income: $25,120 (2000); Median household income: $68,452 (2000); Poverty rate: 3.9% (2000).
Taxes: Total city taxes per capita: $177 (1997); City property taxes per capita: $163 (1997).
Education: High school graduation rate: 93.0% (2000); College graduation rate: 25.1% (2000).
Housing: Homeownership rate: 93.6% (2000); Median home value: $144,900 (2000); Median rent: $525 per month (2000); Median age of housing: 23 years (2000).
Transportation: Commute to work: 89.9% car, 0.0% public transportation, 2.5% walk, 7.6% work from home (2000); Travel time to work: 21.8% less than 15 minutes, 31.5% 15 to 30 minutes, 26.0% 30 to 45 minutes, 13.3% 45 to 60 minutes, 7.4% 60 minutes or more (2000)

WILSON (village). Covers a land area of 1.550 square miles and a water area of 0 square miles. Located at 44.95° N. Lat.; 92.17° W. Long. Elevation is 1,140 feet.
Population: 176 (2000); Race: 100.0% White, 0.0% Black, 0.0% Asian, 0.0% American Indian and Alaska Native, 0.0% Hispanic of any race, 0.0% two or more races (2000); Density: 113.5 persons per square mile (2000); Age: 23.9% under 18, 16.5% over 64 (2000); Marriage status: 24.7% never married, 61.7% now married, 5.8% widowed, 7.8% divorced (2000); Foreign born: 1.1% (2000); Ancestry (includes multiple ancestries): 53.7% German, 41.5% Norwegian, 11.7% Dutch, 6.9% French (except Basque), 5.9% Irish (2000).
Economy: Single-family building permits issued: 3 (2001) / 3 (2000); Multi-family building permits issued: 0 (2001) / 0 (2000); Employment by occupation: 7.2% management, 7.2% professional, 30.6% services, 5.4% sales, 1.8% farming, 17.1% construction, 30.6% production (2000).
Income: Per capita income: $17,389 (2000); Median household income: $35,893 (2000); Poverty rate: 6.4% (2000).
Taxes: Total city taxes per capita: $137 (1997); City property taxes per capita: $106 (1997).
Education: High school graduation rate: 87.3% (2000); College graduation rate: 7.9% (2000).
Housing: Homeownership rate: 86.4% (2000); Median home value: $74,000 (2000); Median rent: $375 per month (2000); Median age of housing: 51 years (2000).
Transportation: Commute to work: 89.2% car, 0.0% public transportation, 0.9% walk, 9.9% work from home (2000); Travel time to work: 25.0% less than 15 minutes, 37.0% 15 to 30 minutes, 17.0% 30 to 45 minutes, 6.0% 45 to 60 minutes, 15.0% 60 minutes or more (2000)

WOODVILLE (village). Covers a land area of 1.269 square miles and a water area of 0 square miles. Located at 44.94° N. Lat.; 92.28° W. Long. Elevation is 1,140 feet.
Population: 1,104 (2000); Race: 98.9% White, 0.0% Black, 0.0% Asian, 0.0% American Indian and Alaska Native, 0.8% Hispanic of any race, 0.2% two or more races (2000); Density: 870.0 persons per square mile (2000); Age: 26.9% under 18, 17.3% over 64 (2000); Marriage status: 22.9% never married, 59.9% now married, 7.2% widowed, 10.0% divorced (2000); Foreign born: 0.2% (2000); Ancestry (includes multiple ancestries): 39.4% Norwegian, 37.4% German, 7.0% Irish, 6.9% Dutch, 5.9% Polish (2000).
Economy: Employment by occupation: 10.8% management, 12.8% professional, 14.4% services, 21.9% sales, 0.0% farming, 13.7% construction, 26.5% production (2000).
Income: Per capita income: $20,958 (2000); Median household income: $38,828 (2000); Poverty rate: 5.8% (2000).
Taxes: Total city taxes per capita: $233 (2000); City property taxes per capita: $206 (2000).
Education: High school graduation rate: 83.7% (2000); College graduation rate: 19.7% (2000).
Housing: Homeownership rate: 68.7% (2000); Median home value: $95,700 (2000); Median rent: $353 per month (2000); Median age of housing: 24 years (2000).
Newspapers: Woodville Leader (1 x week)
Transportation: Commute to work: 89.5% car, 0.0% public transportation, 4.8% walk, 2.9% work from home (2000); Travel time to work: 47.1% less than 15 minutes, 18.8% 15 to 30 minutes, 17.3% 30 to 45 minutes, 9.1% 45 to 60 minutes, 7.8% 60 minutes or more (2000)

Sauk County

Located in south central Wisconsin; bounded on the northeast and south by the Wisconsin River; drained by the Baraboo River; includes several lakes. Covers a land area of 837.60 square miles, a water area of 10.80 square miles, and is located in the Central Time Zone. The county government was organized in 1840. County seat is Baraboo.

Weather Station: Baraboo — Elevation: 820 feet

	Jan	Feb	Mar	Apr	May	Jun	Jul	Aug	Sep	Oct	Nov	Dec
High	26	32	43	57	70	79	83	80	72	60	44	31
Low	4	9	21	32	44	53	58	55	46	35	24	11
Precip	1.1	1.0	2.1	3.6	3.4	3.9	4.3	4.3	3.7	2.6	2.3	1.1
Snow	10.7	7.8	6.4	2.3	tr	0.0	0.0	0.0	0.0	0.4	4.5	9.0

High and Low temperatures in degrees Fahrenheit; Precipitation and Snow in inches

Weather Station: Prairie Du Sac 2 N — Elevation: 777 feet

	Jan	Feb	Mar	Apr	May	Jun	Jul	Aug	Sep	Oct	Nov	Dec
High	25	31	42	56	70	79	83	80	71	59	43	30
Low	7	13	24	36	48	57	62	60	51	40	27	14
Precip	1.0	1.1	2.0	3.2	3.0	3.7	3.8	4.2	3.4	2.3	2.1	1.2
Snow	7.7	5.5	3.3	1.1	0.0	0.0	0.0	0.0	0.0	tr	2.0	5.8

High and Low temperatures in degrees Fahrenheit; Precipitation and Snow in inches

Population: 55,225 (2000); Race: 97.5% White, 0.3% Black, 0.4% Asian, 0.7% American Indian and Alaska Native, 1.6% Hispanic of any race, 0.7% two or more races (2000); Density: 65.9 persons per square mile (2000); Age: 26.1% under 18, 14.5% over 64 (2000).
Religion: Five largest groups: 31.7% Catholic Church, 10.4% Evangelical Lutheran Church in America, 6.0% The United Methodist Church, 5.1% Wisconsin Evangelical Lutheran Synod, 3.8% Lutheran Church—Missouri Synod (2000).
Economy: Unemployment rate: 3.8% (11/2002); Total civilian labor force: 37,043 (11/2002); Leading industries: 26.0% manufacturing; 16.6% retail trade; 14.0% accommodation & food services (2000); Companies that employ more than 1,000 persons: 1 (2000); Companies that employ more than 100 persons: 43 (2000); Farms: 1,452 totaling 332,878 acres (1997); Minority business ownership rate: 0.0% (1997); Women business ownership rate: 33.2% (1997); Retail sales per capita: $10,987 (1997). Single-family building permits issued: 376 (2001) / 401 (2000); Multi-family building permits issued: 187 (2001) / 174 (2000).
Income: Per capita income: $19,695 (2000); Median household income: $41,941 (2000); Poverty rate: 7.2% (2000); Bankruptcy rate: 3.71% (2001).
Taxes: Total county taxes per capita: $295 (2000); County property taxes per capita: $209 (2000).
Education: High school graduation rate: 83.5% (2000); College graduation rate: 17.6% (2000).
Housing: Homeownership rate: 73.3% (2000); Median home value: $107,500 (2000); Median rent: $442 per month (2000); Median age of housing: 29 years (2000).
Health: Birth rate: 128.8 per 10,000 population (1998); Age adjusted death rate: 77.1 per 10,000 population (1999); Age adjusted cancer mortality rate: 164.8 deaths per 100,000 population (1999). Air Quality Index: 77% good, 23% moderate, 0% unhealthy (percent of days in 2000). Number of physicians: 15.9 per 10,000 population (1999); Number of hospital beds: 37.7 per 10,000 population (1999).
Elections: 2000 Presidential election results: 50.8% Gore, 45.2% Bush, 3.3% Nader, 0.2% Buchanan
National and State Parks: Dell Creek State Wildlife Area; Devils Lake State Park; Mirror Lake State Park; Natural Bridge State Park
Additional Information Contacts
Sauk County Government Offices 608-356-5581
Reedsburg Chamber of Commerce 608-524-2850
Sauk Prairie Chamber of Commerce 608-643-4168
Spring Green Chamber of Commerce 608-588-2054

Sauk County Communities

BARABOO (city). Covers a land area of 5.276 square miles and a water area of 0 square miles. Located at 43.47° N. Lat.; 89.74° W. Long. Elevation is 894 feet.
History: Baraboo was named for a French trader, Jean Baribault, who may have built a post at the confluence of the Wisconsin and Baraboo Rivers. The seven Ringling brothers lived in Baraboo in 1882 when five of them (Charles, Otto, Albert, John, and Alfred) organized the Ringling Brothers' Classic and Comic Concert Company, renamed the Ringling Brothers' Grand Carnival of Fun, and later the Ringling Brothers Circus.
Population: 10,711 (2000); Race: 97.9% White, 0.7% Black, 0.2% Asian, 0.3% American Indian and Alaska Native, 1.2% Hispanic of any race, 1.0% two or more races (2000); Density: 2,030.2 persons per square mile (2000); Age: 24.2% under 18, 15.8% over 64 (2000); Marriage status: 26.7% never married, 53.5% now married, 8.4% widowed, 11.4% divorced (2000); Foreign born: 1.3% (2000); Ancestry (includes multiple ancestries): 46.0% German, 13.4% Irish, 9.6% English, 7.6% Norwegian, 6.0% Polish (2000).
Economy: Single-family building permits issued: 37 (2001) / 32 (2000); Multi-family building permits issued: 19 (2001) / 16 (2000); Employment by occupation: 9.0% management, 17.1% professional, 22.9% services, 23.8% sales, 0.4% farming, 10.3% construction, 16.5% production (2000).
Income: Per capita income: $19,304 (2000); Median household income: $38,375 (2000); Poverty rate: 6.6% (2000).
Taxes: Total city taxes per capita: $349 (1997); City property taxes per capita: $327 (1997).
Education: High school graduation rate: 83.0% (2000); College graduation rate: 20.8% (2000).

School District(s)

Baraboo (PK-12)
2000 Enrollment: 3,087 608-355-3950

Housing: Homeownership rate: 64.7% (2000); Median home value: $92,800 (2000); Median rent: $415 per month (2000); Median age of housing: 39 years (2000).
Safety: Violent crime rate: 33.4 per 10,000 population; Property crime rate: 432.0 per 10,000 population (2001).
Newspapers: Baraboo News Republic (6 x week)
Transportation: Commute to work: 90.0% car, 1.1% public transportation, 4.7% walk, 3.7% work from home (2000); Travel time to work: 63.6% less than 15 minutes, 19.5% 15 to 30 minutes, 7.6% 30 to 45 minutes, 5.0% 45 to 60 minutes, 4.2% 60 minutes or more (2000)

BARABOO (town). Covers a land area of 32.008 square miles and a water area of 0.551 square miles. Located at 43.46° N. Lat.; 89.76° W. Long. Elevation is 894 feet.
Population: 1,828 (2000); Race: 96.5% White, 1.3% Black, 0.3% Asian, 1.2% American Indian and Alaska Native, 1.0% Hispanic of any race, 0.4% two or more races (2000); Density: 57.1 persons per square mile (2000); Age: 28.7% under 18, 10.8% over 64 (2000); Marriage status: 20.4% never married, 66.0% now married, 5.4% widowed, 8.3% divorced (2000); Foreign born: 1.9% (2000); Ancestry (includes multiple ancestries): 45.7% German, 13.7% Norwegian, 13.2% Irish, 8.5% English, 5.0% Other groups (2000).
Economy: Employment by occupation: 15.5% management, 18.3% professional, 14.5% services, 26.3% sales, 1.5% farming, 9.5% construction, 14.3% production (2000).
Income: Per capita income: $22,979 (2000); Median household income: $48,419 (2000); Poverty rate: 5.4% (2000).
Taxes: Total city taxes per capita: $102 (1997); City property taxes per capita: $99 (1997).
Education: High school graduation rate: 87.0% (2000); College graduation rate: 25.0% (2000).
Housing: Homeownership rate: 80.5% (2000); Median home value: $156,300 (2000); Median rent: $369 per month (2000); Median age of housing: 27 years (2000).
Transportation: Commute to work: 86.4% car, 0.0% public transportation, 2.0% walk, 11.6% work from home (2000); Travel time to work: 57.5% less than 15 minutes, 24.6% 15 to 30 minutes, 9.7% 30 to 45 minutes, 3.0% 45 to 60 minutes, 5.2% 60 minutes or more (2000)

BEAR CREEK (town). Covers a land area of 49.694 square miles and a water area of 0.001 square miles. Located at 43.33° N. Lat.; 90.15° W. Long.
Population: 497 (2000); Race: 100.0% White, 0.0% Black, 0.0% Asian, 0.0% American Indian and Alaska Native, 0.6% Hispanic of any race, 0.0% two or more races (2000); Density: 10.0 persons per square mile (2000); Age: 27.7% under 18, 13.0% over 64 (2000); Marriage status: 25.8% never married, 62.3% now married, 5.8% widowed, 6.3% divorced (2000); Foreign born: 0.8% (2000); Ancestry (includes multiple ancestries): 47.7% German, 22.2% Irish, 14.7% Norwegian, 10.6% English, 5.1% United States or American (2000).
Economy: Employment by occupation: 26.4% management, 14.2% professional, 12.2% services, 18.1% sales, 4.2% farming, 10.1% construction, 14.9% production (2000).
Income: Per capita income: $19,212 (2000); Median household income: $41,250 (2000); Poverty rate: 3.7% (2000).
Taxes: Total city taxes per capita: $83 (1997); City property taxes per capita: $81 (1997).
Education: High school graduation rate: 84.4% (2000); College graduation rate: 16.8% (2000).
Housing: Homeownership rate: 84.6% (2000); Median home value: $107,300 (2000); Median rent: $238 per month (2000); Median age of housing: 49 years (2000).
Transportation: Commute to work: 82.0% car, 0.0% public transportation, 2.1% walk, 13.4% work from home (2000); Travel time to work: 22.4% less than 15 minutes, 34.1% 15 to 30 minutes, 21.5% 30 to 45 minutes, 5.7% 45 to 60 minutes, 16.3% 60 minutes or more (2000)

DELLONA (town). Covers a land area of 35.107 square miles and a water area of 0.042 square miles. Located at 43.59° N. Lat.; 89.89° W. Long.
Population: 1,199 (2000); Race: 93.2% White, 0.3% Black, 0.7% Asian, 4.1% American Indian and Alaska Native, 0.4% Hispanic of any race, 1.4% two or more races (2000); Density: 34.2 persons per square mile (2000); Age: 28.2% under 18, 10.0% over 64 (2000); Marriage status: 20.8% never married, 66.6% now married, 3.8% widowed, 8.7% divorced (2000); Foreign born: 2.9% (2000); Ancestry (includes multiple ancestries): 44.1% German, 11.8% Irish, 11.3% Polish, 9.2% Norwegian, 8.9% Other groups (2000).

Economy: Employment by occupation: 15.0% management, 15.2% professional, 17.8% services, 18.8% sales, 0.5% farming, 16.5% construction, 16.2% production (2000).
Income: Per capita income: $18,998 (2000); Median household income: $46,630 (2000); Poverty rate: 11.1% (2000).
Taxes: Total city taxes per capita: $105 (1997); City property taxes per capita: $87 (1997).
Education: High school graduation rate: 84.9% (2000); College graduation rate: 16.9% (2000).
Housing: Homeownership rate: 87.9% (2000); Median home value: $128,600 (2000); Median rent: $457 per month (2000); Median age of housing: 15 years (2000).
Transportation: Commute to work: 89.8% car, 0.3% public transportation, 1.7% walk, 7.5% work from home (2000); Travel time to work: 31.7% less than 15 minutes, 40.9% 15 to 30 minutes, 12.7% 30 to 45 minutes, 5.3% 45 to 60 minutes, 9.4% 60 minutes or more (2000)

DELTON (town). Covers a land area of 29.608 square miles and a water area of 0.599 square miles. Located at 43.57° N. Lat.; 89.79° W. Long.
Population: 2,024 (2000); Race: 93.7% White, 0.2% Black, 0.1% Asian, 5.1% American Indian and Alaska Native, 1.6% Hispanic of any race, 0.5% two or more races (2000); Density: 68.4 persons per square mile (2000); Age: 26.6% under 18, 9.4% over 64 (2000); Marriage status: 22.3% never married, 63.2% now married, 3.4% widowed, 11.1% divorced (2000); Foreign born: 2.5% (2000); Ancestry (includes multiple ancestries): 46.6% German, 16.7% Irish, 12.1% English, 7.7% Other groups, 7.3% Norwegian (2000).
Economy: Single-family building permits issued: 22 (2001) / 30 (2000); Multi-family building permits issued: 2 (2001) / 0 (2000); Employment by occupation: 13.9% management, 10.1% professional, 19.7% services, 25.8% sales, 0.5% farming, 10.1% construction, 19.7% production (2000).
Income: Per capita income: $18,584 (2000); Median household income: $45,625 (2000); Poverty rate: 5.3% (2000).
Taxes: Total city taxes per capita: $152 (1997); City property taxes per capita: $136 (1997).
Education: High school graduation rate: 85.5% (2000); College graduation rate: 15.3% (2000).
Housing: Homeownership rate: 85.6% (2000); Median home value: $123,900 (2000); Median rent: $429 per month (2000); Median age of housing: 20 years (2000).
Transportation: Commute to work: 92.1% car, 0.3% public transportation, 2.1% walk, 5.4% work from home (2000); Travel time to work: 44.6% less than 15 minutes, 38.5% 15 to 30 minutes, 6.2% 30 to 45 minutes, 5.3% 45 to 60 minutes, 5.4% 60 minutes or more (2000)

EXCELSIOR (town). Covers a land area of 33.896 square miles and a water area of 0.088 square miles. Located at 43.50° N. Lat.; 89.89° W. Long.
Population: 1,410 (2000); Race: 98.9% White, 0.0% Black, 0.0% Asian, 0.0% American Indian and Alaska Native, 1.2% Hispanic of any race, 0.8% two or more races (2000); Density: 41.6 persons per square mile (2000); Age: 22.8% under 18, 11.6% over 64 (2000); Marriage status: 17.5% never married, 71.2% now married, 3.6% widowed, 7.7% divorced (2000); Foreign born: 0.5% (2000); Ancestry (includes multiple ancestries): 51.3% German, 12.9% English, 12.6% Irish, 8.6% United States or American, 6.6% Norwegian (2000).
Economy: Employment by occupation: 13.9% management, 16.5% professional, 10.7% services, 24.3% sales, 0.9% farming, 11.6% construction, 22.2% production (2000).
Income: Per capita income: $23,147 (2000); Median household income: $54,375 (2000); Poverty rate: 3.3% (2000).
Taxes: Total city taxes per capita: $53 (1997); City property taxes per capita: $52 (1997).
Education: High school graduation rate: 85.1% (2000); College graduation rate: 16.0% (2000).
Housing: Homeownership rate: 89.5% (2000); Median home value: $123,500 (2000); Median rent: $475 per month (2000); Median age of housing: 23 years (2000).
Transportation: Commute to work: 90.1% car, 1.0% public transportation, 0.5% walk, 7.6% work from home (2000); Travel time to work: 40.9% less than 15 minutes, 42.5% 15 to 30 minutes, 7.9% 30 to 45 minutes, 2.0% 45 to 60 minutes, 6.7% 60 minutes or more (2000)

FAIRFIELD (town). Covers a land area of 34.967 square miles and a water area of 0.616 square miles. Located at 43.54° N. Lat.; 89.67° W. Long.
Population: 1,023 (2000); Race: 97.9% White, 0.0% Black, 0.1% Asian, 0.0% American Indian and Alaska Native, 1.1% Hispanic of any race, 1.4% two or more races (2000); Density: 29.3 persons per square mile (2000); Age: 27.5% under 18, 11.7% over 64 (2000); Marriage status: 19.3% never married, 66.9% now married, 3.7% widowed, 10.1% divorced (2000); Foreign born: 1.4% (2000); Ancestry (includes multiple ancestries): 51.2% German, 16.5% Irish, 13.0% English, 11.6% Norwegian, 5.4% Other groups (2000).
Economy: Single-family building permits issued: 8 (2001) / 12 (2000); Multi-family building permits issued: 0 (2001) / 2 (2000); Employment by occupation: 13.9% management, 16.6% professional, 14.9% services, 23.0% sales, 2.0% farming, 11.8% construction, 17.8% production (2000).
Income: Per capita income: $22,155 (2000); Median household income: $50,625 (2000); Poverty rate: 2.0% (2000).
Taxes: Total city taxes per capita: $43 (1997); City property taxes per capita: $40 (1997).
Education: High school graduation rate: 84.8% (2000); College graduation rate: 21.8% (2000).
Housing: Homeownership rate: 85.5% (2000); Median home value: $132,400 (2000); Median rent: $460 per month (2000); Median age of housing: 25 years (2000).
Transportation: Commute to work: 93.8% car, 0.7% public transportation, 0.5% walk, 4.3% work from home (2000); Travel time to work: 31.8% less than 15 minutes, 48.5% 15 to 30 minutes, 10.2% 30 to 45 minutes, 5.8% 45 to 60 minutes, 3.8% 60 minutes or more (2000)

FRANKLIN (town). Covers a land area of 49.173 square miles and a water area of 0.169 square miles. Located at 43.32° N. Lat.; 90.05° W. Long.
Population: 696 (2000); Race: 99.4% White, 0.0% Black, 0.0% Asian, 0.0% American Indian and Alaska Native, 0.0% Hispanic of any race, 0.6% two or more races (2000); Density: 14.2 persons per square mile (2000); Age: 28.7% under 18, 13.2% over 64 (2000); Marriage status: 20.2% never married, 71.1% now married, 4.7% widowed, 4.0% divorced (2000); Foreign born: 0.4% (2000); Ancestry (includes multiple ancestries): 60.9% German, 14.5% Irish, 5.6% English, 3.9% Norwegian, 3.9% French (except Basque) (2000).
Economy: Employment by occupation: 26.6% management, 7.7% professional, 10.2% services, 18.9% sales, 4.1% farming, 13.8% construction, 18.7% production (2000).
Income: Per capita income: $18,494 (2000); Median household income: $45,982 (2000); Poverty rate: 4.3% (2000).
Taxes: Total city taxes per capita: $153 (1997); City property taxes per capita: $153 (1997).
Education: High school graduation rate: 80.8% (2000); College graduation rate: 11.9% (2000).
Housing: Homeownership rate: 84.1% (2000); Median home value: $98,300 (2000); Median rent: $304 per month (2000); Median age of housing: 57 years (2000).
Transportation: Commute to work: 77.2% car, 1.3% public transportation, 3.6% walk, 17.9% work from home (2000); Travel time to work: 27.4% less than 15 minutes, 26.2% 15 to 30 minutes, 24.3% 30 to 45 minutes, 13.6% 45 to 60 minutes, 8.5% 60 minutes or more (2000)

FREEDOM (town). Covers a land area of 34.594 square miles and a water area of 0.120 square miles. Located at 43.43° N. Lat.; 89.89° W. Long.
Population: 416 (2000); Race: 99.5% White, 0.0% Black, 0.0% Asian, 0.0% American Indian and Alaska Native, 0.5% Hispanic of any race, 0.0% two or more races (2000); Density: 12.0 persons per square mile (2000); Age: 22.6% under 18, 7.8% over 64 (2000); Marriage status: 21.6% never married, 72.3% now married, 1.4% widowed, 4.8% divorced (2000); Foreign born: 0.9% (2000); Ancestry (includes multiple ancestries): 63.5% German, 12.3% Irish, 11.9% English, 6.4% United States or American, 5.5% Norwegian (2000).
Economy: Employment by occupation: 14.0% management, 17.7% professional, 12.9% services, 23.2% sales, 1.1% farming, 10.7% construction, 20.3% production (2000).
Income: Per capita income: $23,332 (2000); Median household income: $55,000 (2000); Poverty rate: 2.5% (2000).
Taxes: Total city taxes per capita: $367 (1997); City property taxes per capita: $365 (1997).
Education: High school graduation rate: 91.5% (2000); College graduation rate: 17.7% (2000).
Housing: Homeownership rate: 92.5% (2000); Median home value: $106,300 (2000); Median age of housing: 60+ years (2000).
Transportation: Commute to work: 85.6% car, 1.1% public transportation, 1.8% walk, 10.7% work from home (2000); Travel time to work: 20.2% less than 15 minutes, 56.6% 15 to 30 minutes, 9.9% 30 to 45 minutes, 6.6% 45 to 60 minutes, 6.6% 60 minutes or more (2000)

GREENFIELD (town). Covers a land area of 29.671 square miles and a water area of 0 square miles. Located at 43.47° N. Lat.; 89.66° W. Long.

Population: 911 (2000); Race: 99.1% White, 0.9% Black, 0.0% Asian, 0.0% American Indian and Alaska Native, 0.0% Hispanic of any race, 0.0% two or more races (2000); Density: 30.7 persons per square mile (2000); Age: 26.0% under 18, 9.4% over 64 (2000); Marriage status: 20.7% never married, 67.0% now married, 4.8% widowed, 7.5% divorced (2000); Foreign born: 1.0% (2000); Ancestry (includes multiple ancestries): 56.9% German, 13.6% Irish, 11.7% Norwegian, 10.6% United States or American, 9.9% English (2000).
Economy: Employment by occupation: 13.6% management, 14.7% professional, 17.2% services, 25.0% sales, 2.6% farming, 9.3% construction, 17.5% production (2000).
Income: Per capita income: $20,926 (2000); Median household income: $49,659 (2000); Poverty rate: 2.4% (2000).
Taxes: Total city taxes per capita: $156 (1997); City property taxes per capita: $154 (1997).
Education: High school graduation rate: 90.3% (2000); College graduation rate: 20.8% (2000).
Housing: Homeownership rate: 78.6% (2000); Median home value: $132,400 (2000); Median rent: $413 per month (2000); Median age of housing: 29 years (2000).
Transportation: Commute to work: 92.2% car, 0.0% public transportation, 1.1% walk, 5.7% work from home (2000); Travel time to work: 38.0% less than 15 minutes, 33.3% 15 to 30 minutes, 12.3% 30 to 45 minutes, 5.9% 45 to 60 minutes, 10.5% 60 minutes or more (2000)

HILLPOINT (unincorporated postal area, zip code 53937). Covers a land area of 47.637 square miles and a water area of 0.006 square miles. Located at 43.37° N. Lat.; 90.15° W. Long.
Population: 968 (2000); Race: 100.0% White, 0.0% Black, 0.0% Asian, 0.0% American Indian and Alaska Native, 0.0% Hispanic of any race, 0.0% two or more races (2000); Density: 20.3 persons per square mile (2000); Age: 30.2% under 18, 13.8% over 64 (2000); Marriage status: 25.8% never married, 62.5% now married, 6.0% widowed, 5.7% divorced (2000); Foreign born: 0.2% (2000); Ancestry (includes multiple ancestries): 48.6% German, 16.0% Irish, 12.9% English, 8.5% Norwegian, 5.6% United States or American (2000).
Economy: Employment by occupation: 21.9% management, 7.1% professional, 10.8% services, 17.9% sales, 5.6% farming, 14.4% construction, 22.3% production (2000).
Income: Per capita income: $15,536 (2000); Median household income: $39,038 (2000); Poverty rate: 2.6% (2000).
Education: High school graduation rate: 79.9% (2000); College graduation rate: 9.8% (2000).
Housing: Homeownership rate: 84.1% (2000); Median home value: $82,400 (2000); Median rent: $330 per month (2000); Median age of housing: 59 years (2000).
Transportation: Commute to work: 73.3% car, 0.2% public transportation, 7.4% walk, 16.6% work from home (2000); Travel time to work: 25.4% less than 15 minutes, 39.3% 15 to 30 minutes, 21.2% 30 to 45 minutes, 4.5% 45 to 60 minutes, 9.6% 60 minutes or more (2000)

HONEY CREEK (town). Covers a land area of 47.540 square miles and a water area of 0.028 square miles. Located at 43.33° N. Lat.; 89.92° W. Long.
Population: 736 (2000); Race: 99.3% White, 0.0% Black, 0.3% Asian, 0.0% American Indian and Alaska Native, 0.3% Hispanic of any race, 0.4% two or more races (2000); Density: 15.5 persons per square mile (2000); Age: 26.4% under 18, 12.2% over 64 (2000); Marriage status: 25.1% never married, 67.3% now married, 4.8% widowed, 2.8% divorced (2000); Foreign born: 1.7% (2000); Ancestry (includes multiple ancestries): 72.8% German, 9.4% English, 8.8% Irish, 6.8% Swiss, 6.6% Norwegian (2000).
Economy: Employment by occupation: 20.8% management, 18.1% professional, 15.0% services, 19.4% sales, 5.4% farming, 9.2% construction, 12.3% production (2000).
Income: Per capita income: $20,593 (2000); Median household income: $46,923 (2000); Poverty rate: 9.6% (2000).
Taxes: Total city taxes per capita: $269 (1997); City property taxes per capita: $267 (1997).
Education: High school graduation rate: 82.9% (2000); College graduation rate: 16.1% (2000).
Housing: Homeownership rate: 79.6% (2000); Median home value: $128,600 (2000); Median rent: $410 per month (2000); Median age of housing: 60+ years (2000).
Transportation: Commute to work: 77.0% car, 0.0% public transportation, 1.6% walk, 18.9% work from home (2000); Travel time to work: 18.1% less than 15 minutes, 43.9% 15 to 30 minutes, 16.4% 30 to 45 minutes, 12.2% 45 to 60 minutes, 9.4% 60 minutes or more (2000)

IRONTON (village). Covers a land area of 0.336 square miles and a water area of 0 square miles. Located at 43.54° N. Lat.; 90.14° W. Long. Elevation is 954 feet.
Population: 250 (2000); Race: 95.0% White, 0.0% Black, 0.0% Asian, 0.0% American Indian and Alaska Native, 6.9% Hispanic of any race, 5.0% two or more races (2000); Density: 743.6 persons per square mile (2000); Age: 34.5% under 18, 8.4% over 64 (2000); Marriage status: 31.1% never married, 52.6% now married, 2.6% widowed, 13.7% divorced (2000); Foreign born: 0.8% (2000); Ancestry (includes multiple ancestries): 45.6% German, 11.5% Irish, 7.7% French (except Basque), 6.9% United States or American, 5.7% Other groups (2000).
Economy: Employment by occupation: 6.4% management, 7.2% professional, 10.4% services, 24.0% sales, 2.4% farming, 20.0% construction, 29.6% production (2000).
Income: Per capita income: $13,874 (2000); Median household income: $38,438 (2000); Poverty rate: 10.8% (2000).
Taxes: Total city taxes per capita: $85 (1997); City property taxes per capita: $77 (1997).
Education: High school graduation rate: 70.1% (2000); College graduation rate: 2.6% (2000).
Housing: Homeownership rate: 87.0% (2000); Median home value: $67,500 (2000); Median rent: $425 per month (2000); Median age of housing: 39 years (2000).
Transportation: Commute to work: 100.0% car, 0.0% public transportation, 0.0% walk, 0.0% work from home (2000); Travel time to work: 17.9% less than 15 minutes, 58.5% 15 to 30 minutes, 17.1% 30 to 45 minutes, 4.1% 45 to 60 minutes, 2.4% 60 minutes or more (2000)

IRONTON (town). Covers a land area of 35.181 square miles and a water area of 0.007 square miles. Located at 43.52° N. Lat.; 90.14° W. Long. Elevation is 954 feet.
Population: 650 (2000); Race: 99.7% White, 0.0% Black, 0.3% Asian, 0.0% American Indian and Alaska Native, 0.3% Hispanic of any race, 0.0% two or more races (2000); Density: 18.5 persons per square mile (2000); Age: 30.1% under 18, 10.6% over 64 (2000); Marriage status: 24.6% never married, 65.3% now married, 3.7% widowed, 6.4% divorced (2000); Foreign born: 0.3% (2000); Ancestry (includes multiple ancestries): 57.6% German, 12.7% Irish, 12.5% English, 6.0% Norwegian, 5.4% United States or American (2000).
Economy: Employment by occupation: 26.4% management, 9.3% professional, 8.1% services, 17.7% sales, 5.7% farming, 7.8% construction, 24.9% production (2000).
Income: Per capita income: $16,774 (2000); Median household income: $41,705 (2000); Poverty rate: 17.6% (2000).
Taxes: Total city taxes per capita: $234 (1997); City property taxes per capita: $234 (1997).
Education: High school graduation rate: 78.0% (2000); College graduation rate: 9.3% (2000).
Housing: Homeownership rate: 85.9% (2000); Median home value: $88,300 (2000); Median rent: $338 per month (2000); Median age of housing: 58 years (2000).
Transportation: Commute to work: 73.0% car, 0.0% public transportation, 11.7% walk, 15.3% work from home (2000); Travel time to work: 31.6% less than 15 minutes, 40.1% 15 to 30 minutes, 14.5% 30 to 45 minutes, 6.0% 45 to 60 minutes, 7.8% 60 minutes or more (2000)

LA VALLE (village). Covers a land area of 0.419 square miles and a water area of 0.030 square miles. Located at 43.58° N. Lat.; 90.13° W. Long. Elevation is 896 feet.
Population: 326 (2000); Race: 99.0% White, 0.0% Black, 0.0% Asian, 0.7% American Indian and Alaska Native, 1.0% Hispanic of any race, 0.3% two or more races (2000); Density: 778.8 persons per square mile (2000); Age: 23.3% under 18, 21.3% over 64 (2000); Marriage status: 21.8% never married, 53.6% now married, 14.2% widowed, 10.5% divorced (2000); Foreign born: 0.0% (2000); Ancestry (includes multiple ancestries): 45.6% German, 18.6% Irish, 11.5% English, 5.7% Polish, 5.4% Norwegian (2000).
Economy: Single-family building permits issued: 1 (2001) / 0 (2000); Multi-family building permits issued: 0 (2001) / 0 (2000); Employment by occupation: 10.5% management, 4.9% professional, 14.2% services, 24.1% sales, 1.2% farming, 9.9% construction, 35.2% production (2000).
Income: Per capita income: $16,823 (2000); Median household income: $36,250 (2000); Poverty rate: 3.1% (2000).
Taxes: Total city taxes per capita: $112 (1997); City property taxes per capita: $105 (1997).

Education: High school graduation rate: 87.6% (2000); College graduation rate: 4.5% (2000).
Housing: Homeownership rate: 71.1% (2000); Median home value: $67,800 (2000); Median rent: $396 per month (2000); Median age of housing: 60+ years (2000).
Transportation: Commute to work: 85.4% car, 0.0% public transportation, 6.4% walk, 6.4% work from home (2000); Travel time to work: 32.0% less than 15 minutes, 40.1% 15 to 30 minutes, 19.0% 30 to 45 minutes, 5.4% 45 to 60 minutes, 3.4% 60 minutes or more (2000)

LA VALLE (town). Covers a land area of 34.195 square miles and a water area of 1.133 square miles. Located at 43.60° N. Lat.; 90.12° W. Long. Elevation is 896 feet.
Population: 1,203 (2000); Race: 99.8% White, 0.0% Black, 0.0% Asian, 0.1% American Indian and Alaska Native, 0.5% Hispanic of any race, 0.2% two or more races (2000); Density: 35.2 persons per square mile (2000); Age: 24.9% under 18, 16.8% over 64 (2000); Marriage status: 17.9% never married, 71.6% now married, 3.9% widowed, 6.5% divorced (2000); Foreign born: 2.5% (2000); Ancestry (includes multiple ancestries): 53.7% German, 10.3% Irish, 9.3% English, 6.1% Polish, 5.3% Norwegian (2000).
Economy: Employment by occupation: 12.9% management, 13.5% professional, 9.4% services, 27.1% sales, 3.1% farming, 9.1% construction, 24.9% production (2000).
Income: Per capita income: $21,561 (2000); Median household income: $45,350 (2000); Poverty rate: 3.0% (2000).
Taxes: Total city taxes per capita: $328 (1997); City property taxes per capita: $314 (1997).
Education: High school graduation rate: 85.8% (2000); College graduation rate: 15.0% (2000).
Housing: Homeownership rate: 92.1% (2000); Median home value: $121,600 (2000); Median rent: $475 per month (2000); Median age of housing: 21 years (2000).
Transportation: Commute to work: 90.1% car, 0.0% public transportation, 0.3% walk, 9.0% work from home (2000); Travel time to work: 24.7% less than 15 minutes, 42.6% 15 to 30 minutes, 19.3% 30 to 45 minutes, 6.9% 45 to 60 minutes, 6.5% 60 minutes or more (2000)

LAKE DELTON (village). Covers a land area of 6.188 square miles and a water area of 0.532 square miles. Located at 43.59° N. Lat.; 89.78° W. Long. Elevation is 894 feet.
Population: 1,982 (2000); Race: 94.5% White, 0.3% Black, 0.2% Asian, 3.1% American Indian and Alaska Native, 3.1% Hispanic of any race, 1.1% two or more races (2000); Density: 320.3 persons per square mile (2000); Age: 16.7% under 18, 21.6% over 64 (2000); Marriage status: 20.5% never married, 56.9% now married, 9.0% widowed, 13.5% divorced (2000); Foreign born: 7.8% (2000); Ancestry (includes multiple ancestries): 37.8% German, 15.5% Irish, 12.2% Polish, 9.6% English, 9.4% Norwegian (2000).
Economy: Single-family building permits issued: 35 (2001) / 27 (2000); Multi-family building permits issued: 122 (2001) / 96 (2000); Employment by occupation: 16.3% management, 9.9% professional, 29.5% services, 24.4% sales, 0.6% farming, 8.2% construction, 11.1% production (2000).
Income: Per capita income: $19,834 (2000); Median household income: $34,951 (2000); Poverty rate: 9.9% (2000).
Taxes: Total city taxes per capita: $1,973 (1997); City property taxes per capita: $1,093 (1997).
Education: High school graduation rate: 83.6% (2000); College graduation rate: 17.1% (2000).
Housing: Homeownership rate: 69.6% (2000); Median home value: $98,000 (2000); Median rent: $493 per month (2000); Median age of housing: 13 years (2000).
Safety: Violent crime rate: 75.2 per 10,000 population; Property crime rate: 1,718.4 per 10,000 population (2001).
Transportation: Commute to work: 88.6% car, 0.0% public transportation, 5.9% walk, 4.5% work from home (2000); Travel time to work: 57.3% less than 15 minutes, 26.1% 15 to 30 minutes, 5.1% 30 to 45 minutes, 4.3% 45 to 60 minutes, 7.2% 60 minutes or more (2000)

LIME RIDGE (village). Aka Limeridge. Covers a land area of 1.010 square miles and a water area of 0 square miles. Located at 43.46° N. Lat.; 90.15° W. Long. Elevation is 1,180 feet.
Population: 169 (2000); Race: 100.0% White, 0.0% Black, 0.0% Asian, 0.0% American Indian and Alaska Native, 1.0% Hispanic of any race, 0.0% two or more races (2000); Density: 167.3 persons per square mile (2000); Age: 31.1% under 18, 15.3% over 64 (2000); Marriage status: 16.0% never married, 66.0% now married, 1.4% widowed, 16.7% divorced (2000); Foreign born: 0.0% (2000); Ancestry (includes multiple ancestries): 53.1% German, 17.3% Irish, 14.3% English, 9.7% Norwegian, 4.6% Scotch-Irish (2000).
Economy: Employment by occupation: 4.7% management, 11.8% professional, 28.2% services, 12.9% sales, 2.4% farming, 11.8% construction, 28.2% production (2000).
Income: Per capita income: $17,006 (2000); Median household income: $41,500 (2000); Poverty rate: 4.6% (2000).
Taxes: Total city taxes per capita: $56 (1997); City property taxes per capita: $56 (1997).
Education: High school graduation rate: 68.2% (2000); College graduation rate: 7.8% (2000).
Housing: Homeownership rate: 81.2% (2000); Median home value: $47,700 (2000); Median rent: $431 per month (2000); Median age of housing: 60+ years (2000).
Transportation: Commute to work: 95.3% car, 0.0% public transportation, 4.7% walk, 0.0% work from home (2000); Travel time to work: 16.5% less than 15 minutes, 38.8% 15 to 30 minutes, 25.9% 30 to 45 minutes, 16.5% 45 to 60 minutes, 2.4% 60 minutes or more (2000)

LOGANVILLE (village). Covers a land area of 0.196 square miles and a water area of 0 square miles. Located at 43.44° N. Lat.; 90.03° W. Long. Elevation is 940 feet.
Population: 276 (2000); Race: 100.0% White, 0.0% Black, 0.0% Asian, 0.0% American Indian and Alaska Native, 0.0% Hispanic of any race, 0.0% two or more races (2000); Density: 1,408.2 persons per square mile (2000); Age: 24.8% under 18, 11.8% over 64 (2000); Marriage status: 23.0% never married, 55.5% now married, 10.5% widowed, 11.0% divorced (2000); Foreign born: 0.0% (2000); Ancestry (includes multiple ancestries): 60.6% German, 15.7% Irish, 7.1% English, 4.7% United States or American, 2.8% Norwegian (2000).
Economy: Single-family building permits issued: 0 (2001) / 2 (2000); Multi-family building permits issued: 0 (2001) / 0 (2000); Employment by occupation: 7.6% management, 13.1% professional, 17.9% services, 15.9% sales, 6.9% farming, 10.3% construction, 28.3% production (2000).
Income: Per capita income: $15,737 (2000); Median household income: $34,688 (2000); Poverty rate: 7.9% (2000).
Taxes: Total city taxes per capita: $313 (1997); City property taxes per capita: $305 (1997).
Education: High school graduation rate: 81.8% (2000); College graduation rate: 14.1% (2000).
Housing: Homeownership rate: 70.3% (2000); Median home value: $81,900 (2000); Median rent: $358 per month (2000); Median age of housing: 60 years (2000).
Transportation: Commute to work: 91.7% car, 0.0% public transportation, 8.3% walk, 0.0% work from home (2000); Travel time to work: 37.9% less than 15 minutes, 41.4% 15 to 30 minutes, 15.2% 30 to 45 minutes, 0.0% 45 to 60 minutes, 5.5% 60 minutes or more (2000)

MERRIMAC (village). Covers a land area of 0.759 square miles and a water area of 0.648 square miles. Located at 43.37° N. Lat.; 89.62° W. Long. Elevation is 810 feet.
Population: 416 (2000); Race: 100.0% White, 0.0% Black, 0.0% Asian, 0.0% American Indian and Alaska Native, 0.0% Hispanic of any race, 0.0% two or more races (2000); Density: 547.9 persons per square mile (2000); Age: 20.0% under 18, 22.5% over 64 (2000); Marriage status: 21.4% never married, 62.1% now married, 5.2% widowed, 11.3% divorced (2000); Foreign born: 0.6% (2000); Ancestry (includes multiple ancestries): 45.6% German, 17.5% Norwegian, 11.9% Irish, 11.1% English, 10.3% Czech (2000).
Economy: Single-family building permits issued: 4 (2001) / 4 (2000); Multi-family building permits issued: 0 (2001) / 0 (2000); Employment by occupation: 11.0% management, 11.0% professional, 16.8% services, 26.2% sales, 0.0% farming, 12.0% construction, 23.0% production (2000).
Income: Per capita income: $19,091 (2000); Median household income: $41,250 (2000); Poverty rate: 3.1% (2000).
Taxes: Total city taxes per capita: $328 (1997); City property taxes per capita: $315 (1997).
Education: High school graduation rate: 83.4% (2000); College graduation rate: 12.1% (2000).
Housing: Homeownership rate: 74.8% (2000); Median home value: $114,100 (2000); Median rent: $429 per month (2000); Median age of housing: 46 years (2000).
Transportation: Commute to work: 93.1% car, 0.0% public transportation, 4.3% walk, 1.1% work from home (2000); Travel time to work: 28.5% less than 15 minutes, 28.0% 15 to 30 minutes, 19.4% 30 to 45 minutes, 9.7% 45 to 60 minutes, 14.5% 60 minutes or more (2000)

MERRIMAC (town). Covers a land area of 24.470 square miles and a water area of 1.836 square miles. Located at 43.36° N. Lat.; 89.69° W. Long. Elevation is 810 feet.
Population: 868 (2000); Race: 100.0% White, 0.0% Black, 0.0% Asian, 0.0% American Indian and Alaska Native, 0.0% Hispanic of any race, 0.0% two or more races (2000); Density: 35.5 persons per square mile (2000); Age: 19.9% under 18, 14.3% over 64 (2000); Marriage status: 17.2% never married, 63.7% now married, 6.0% widowed, 13.1% divorced (2000); Foreign born: 1.1% (2000); Ancestry (includes multiple ancestries): 49.6% German, 15.3% Irish, 12.4% English, 9.8% Norwegian, 6.1% Polish (2000).
Economy: Single-family building permits issued: 17 (2001) / 17 (2000); Multi-family building permits issued: 0 (2001) / 0 (2000); Employment by occupation: 15.7% management, 14.4% professional, 17.9% services, 21.4% sales, 2.1% farming, 11.8% construction, 16.7% production (2000).
Income: Per capita income: $26,044 (2000); Median household income: $47,115 (2000); Poverty rate: 5.3% (2000).
Taxes: Total city taxes per capita: $184 (1997); City property taxes per capita: $124 (1997).
Education: High school graduation rate: 91.0% (2000); College graduation rate: 17.4% (2000).
Housing: Homeownership rate: 85.6% (2000); Median home value: $170,400 (2000); Median rent: $529 per month (2000); Median age of housing: 26 years (2000).
Transportation: Commute to work: 90.4% car, 0.4% public transportation, 1.0% walk, 8.3% work from home (2000); Travel time to work: 19.3% less than 15 minutes, 41.5% 15 to 30 minutes, 14.3% 30 to 45 minutes, 15.0% 45 to 60 minutes, 9.9% 60 minutes or more (2000)

NORTH FREEDOM (village). Covers a land area of 0.870 square miles and a water area of 0.006 square miles. Located at 43.46° N. Lat.; 89.86° W. Long. Elevation is 867 feet.
Population: 649 (2000); Race: 99.4% White, 0.3% Black, 0.0% Asian, 0.2% American Indian and Alaska Native, 0.3% Hispanic of any race, 0.0% two or more races (2000); Density: 745.9 persons per square mile (2000); Age: 31.0% under 18, 12.4% over 64 (2000); Marriage status: 20.5% never married, 61.6% now married, 4.2% widowed, 13.6% divorced (2000); Foreign born: 1.6% (2000); Ancestry (includes multiple ancestries): 56.4% German, 14.5% Irish, 9.8% Norwegian, 9.1% English, 5.0% United States or American (2000).
Economy: Single-family building permits issued: 0 (2001) / 2 (2000); Multi-family building permits issued: 2 (2001) / 0 (2000); Employment by occupation: 5.9% management, 11.2% professional, 18.2% services, 23.8% sales, 1.0% farming, 13.2% construction, 26.7% production (2000).
Income: Per capita income: $14,354 (2000); Median household income: $37,273 (2000); Poverty rate: 11.3% (2000).
Taxes: Total city taxes per capita: $99 (1997); City property taxes per capita: $90 (1997).
Education: High school graduation rate: 80.7% (2000); College graduation rate: 4.8% (2000).
Housing: Homeownership rate: 87.9% (2000); Median home value: $75,400 (2000); Median rent: $395 per month (2000); Median age of housing: 60+ years (2000).
Transportation: Commute to work: 92.0% car, 0.7% public transportation, 5.0% walk, 2.3% work from home (2000); Travel time to work: 24.3% less than 15 minutes, 58.9% 15 to 30 minutes, 9.2% 30 to 45 minutes, 1.4% 45 to 60 minutes, 6.2% 60 minutes or more (2000)

PLAIN (village). Covers a land area of 0.731 square miles and a water area of 0 square miles. Located at 43.27° N. Lat.; 90.04° W. Long. Elevation is 820 feet.
Population: 792 (2000); Race: 98.8% White, 0.0% Black, 0.3% Asian, 0.5% American Indian and Alaska Native, 0.5% Hispanic of any race, 0.4% two or more races (2000); Density: 1,083.4 persons per square mile (2000); Age: 24.8% under 18, 19.6% over 64 (2000); Marriage status: 19.0% never married, 66.5% now married, 6.7% widowed, 7.7% divorced (2000); Foreign born: 1.0% (2000); Ancestry (includes multiple ancestries): 63.3% German, 13.5% Irish, 6.1% Norwegian, 4.0% Polish, 3.8% English (2000).
Economy: Single-family building permits issued: 1 (2001) / 1 (2000); Multi-family building permits issued: 0 (2001) / 0 (2000); Employment by occupation: 17.3% management, 14.5% professional, 13.5% services, 20.4% sales, 1.0% farming, 16.4% construction, 16.9% production (2000).
Income: Per capita income: $24,658 (2000); Median household income: $44,028 (2000); Poverty rate: 2.6% (2000).
Taxes: Total city taxes per capita: $424 (1997); City property taxes per capita: $420 (1997).
Education: High school graduation rate: 82.5% (2000); College graduation rate: 20.6% (2000).
Housing: Homeownership rate: 73.4% (2000); Median home value: $97,500 (2000); Median rent: $388 per month (2000); Median age of housing: 45 years (2000).
Transportation: Commute to work: 90.4% car, 0.5% public transportation, 6.0% walk, 3.1% work from home (2000); Travel time to work: 42.8% less than 15 minutes, 19.3% 15 to 30 minutes, 16.3% 30 to 45 minutes, 10.9% 45 to 60 minutes, 10.6% 60 minutes or more (2000)

PRAIRIE DU SAC (village). Covers a land area of 1.318 square miles and a water area of 0.103 square miles. Located at 43.29° N. Lat.; 89.72° W. Long. Elevation is 780 feet.
History: Prairie du Sac grew up as a twin city with Sauk City, along the west bank of the Wisconsin River. It was named for the Sauk tribe whose villages once occupied this prairie area. In its early days, Prairie du Sac was known as Upper Sauk.
Population: 3,231 (2000); Race: 97.7% White, 0.3% Black, 0.9% Asian, 0.3% American Indian and Alaska Native, 2.3% Hispanic of any race, 0.3% two or more races (2000); Density: 2,450.9 persons per square mile (2000); Age: 27.4% under 18, 12.2% over 64 (2000); Marriage status: 25.7% never married, 59.5% now married, 6.1% widowed, 8.7% divorced (2000); Foreign born: 2.6% (2000); Ancestry (includes multiple ancestries): 56.4% German, 12.6% Irish, 8.1% English, 7.4% Norwegian, 5.2% Polish (2000).
Economy: Single-family building permits issued: 16 (2001) / 16 (2000); Multi-family building permits issued: 20 (2001) / 4 (2000); Employment by occupation: 13.6% management, 24.0% professional, 14.6% services, 26.2% sales, 0.3% farming, 9.1% construction, 12.2% production (2000).
Income: Per capita income: $23,068 (2000); Median household income: $44,472 (2000); Poverty rate: 7.4% (2000).
Taxes: Total city taxes per capita: $176 (1997); City property taxes per capita: $166 (1997).
Education: High school graduation rate: 90.7% (2000); College graduation rate: 28.3% (2000).
Housing: Homeownership rate: 66.8% (2000); Median home value: $138,800 (2000); Median rent: $549 per month (2000); Median age of housing: 27 years (2000).
Hospitals: Sauk Prairie Memorial Hospital (36 beds)
Transportation: Commute to work: 90.2% car, 0.2% public transportation, 3.2% walk, 4.6% work from home (2000); Travel time to work: 47.8% less than 15 minutes, 21.7% 15 to 30 minutes, 18.5% 30 to 45 minutes, 10.2% 45 to 60 minutes, 1.9% 60 minutes or more (2000)

PRAIRIE DU SAC (town). Covers a land area of 29.496 square miles and a water area of 0.860 square miles. Located at 43.27° N. Lat.; 89.78° W. Long. Elevation is 780 feet.
Population: 1,138 (2000); Race: 98.0% White, 0.2% Black, 1.1% Asian, 0.0% American Indian and Alaska Native, 1.2% Hispanic of any race, 0.8% two or more races (2000); Density: 38.6 persons per square mile (2000); Age: 30.4% under 18, 8.0% over 64 (2000); Marriage status: 20.1% never married, 71.7% now married, 3.6% widowed, 4.6% divorced (2000); Foreign born: 1.8% (2000); Ancestry (includes multiple ancestries): 62.8% German, 13.0% Norwegian, 8.4% English, 8.0% Irish, 5.8% Swiss (2000).
Economy: Employment by occupation: 22.9% management, 16.5% professional, 9.8% services, 22.9% sales, 2.5% farming, 11.5% construction, 14.0% production (2000).
Income: Per capita income: $22,709 (2000); Median household income: $56,667 (2000); Poverty rate: 5.5% (2000).
Education: High school graduation rate: 88.7% (2000); College graduation rate: 20.0% (2000).
Housing: Homeownership rate: 85.8% (2000); Median home value: $162,200 (2000); Median rent: $493 per month (2000); Median age of housing: 26 years (2000).
Transportation: Commute to work: 89.4% car, 0.3% public transportation, 1.9% walk, 7.6% work from home (2000); Travel time to work: 49.9% less than 15 minutes, 19.0% 15 to 30 minutes, 18.6% 30 to 45 minutes, 8.7% 45 to 60 minutes, 3.8% 60 minutes or more (2000)

REEDSBURG (city). Covers a land area of 5.204 square miles and a water area of 0 square miles. Located at 43.53° N. Lat.; 90.00° W. Long. Elevation is 926 feet.
Population: 7,827 (2000); Race: 96.7% White, 0.1% Black, 1.0% Asian, 0.3% American Indian and Alaska Native, 0.4% Hispanic of any race, 1.7% two or more races (2000); Density: 1,503.9 persons per square mile (2000); Age: 26.9% under 18, 16.3% over 64 (2000); Marriage status: 22.9% never married, 57.9% now married, 8.5% widowed, 10.6% divorced (2000);

Foreign born: 1.3% (2000); Ancestry (includes multiple ancestries): 49.7% German, 14.5% Irish, 8.7% United States or American, 8.6% Norwegian, 6.9% English (2000).
Economy: Single-family building permits issued: 49 (2001) / 49 (2000); Multi-family building permits issued: 18 (2001) / 46 (2000); Employment by occupation: 9.4% management, 12.4% professional, 18.5% services, 24.3% sales, 1.2% farming, 9.9% construction, 24.3% production (2000).
Income: Per capita income: $18,828 (2000); Median household income: $39,152 (2000); Poverty rate: 7.5% (2000).
Taxes: Total city taxes per capita: $361 (2000); City property taxes per capita: $331 (2000).
Education: High school graduation rate: 82.0% (2000); College graduation rate: 13.6% (2000).

School District(s)

Reedsburg (PK-12)
2000 Enrollment: 2,444 608-524-2401
Housing: Homeownership rate: 67.6% (2000); Median home value: $92,800 (2000); Median rent: $439 per month (2000); Median age of housing: 27 years (2000).
Hospitals: Reedsburg Area Medical Center (53 beds)
Safety: Violent crime rate: 7.6 per 10,000 population; Property crime rate: 389.4 per 10,000 population (2001).
Newspapers: Reedsburg Times Press (2 x week)
Transportation: Commute to work: 90.8% car, 0.6% public transportation, 4.2% walk, 3.4% work from home (2000); Travel time to work: 58.6% less than 15 minutes, 25.4% 15 to 30 minutes, 9.0% 30 to 45 minutes, 2.1% 45 to 60 minutes, 4.9% 60 minutes or more (2000)
Additional Information Contacts
Reedsburg Chamber of Commerce 608-524-2850

REEDSBURG (town). Covers a land area of 30.753 square miles and a water area of 0.011 square miles. Located at 43.52° N. Lat.; 90.00° W. Long. Elevation is 926 feet.
Population: 1,236 (2000); Race: 99.5% White, 0.0% Black, 0.0% Asian, 0.5% American Indian and Alaska Native, 0.1% Hispanic of any race, 0.0% two or more races (2000); Density: 40.2 persons per square mile (2000); Age: 25.1% under 18, 23.2% over 64 (2000); Marriage status: 21.3% never married, 65.8% now married, 7.6% widowed, 5.2% divorced (2000); Foreign born: 0.3% (2000); Ancestry (includes multiple ancestries): 49.4% German, 10.9% Irish, 9.7% English, 5.1% Norwegian, 4.2% Polish (2000).
Economy: Employment by occupation: 15.8% management, 10.1% professional, 9.9% services, 26.7% sales, 4.8% farming, 9.3% construction, 23.5% production (2000).
Income: Per capita income: $19,658 (2000); Median household income: $49,236 (2000); Poverty rate: 6.1% (2000).
Taxes: Total city taxes per capita: $41 (1997); City property taxes per capita: $40 (1997).
Education: High school graduation rate: 78.2% (2000); College graduation rate: 15.0% (2000).
Housing: Homeownership rate: 81.0% (2000); Median home value: $118,900 (2000); Median rent: $500 per month (2000); Median age of housing: 33 years (2000).
Transportation: Commute to work: 80.9% car, 2.5% public transportation, 3.4% walk, 12.6% work from home (2000); Travel time to work: 63.0% less than 15 minutes, 22.4% 15 to 30 minutes, 10.8% 30 to 45 minutes, 1.3% 45 to 60 minutes, 2.4% 60 minutes or more (2000)

ROCK SPRINGS (village). Covers a land area of 1.345 square miles and a water area of 0 square miles. Located at 43.47° N. Lat.; 89.91° W. Long. Elevation is 870 feet.
Population: 425 (2000); Race: 96.7% White, 0.0% Black, 1.9% Asian, 0.0% American Indian and Alaska Native, 1.4% Hispanic of any race, 0.0% two or more races (2000); Density: 315.9 persons per square mile (2000); Age: 23.9% under 18, 14.1% over 64 (2000); Marriage status: 27.1% never married, 58.5% now married, 6.5% widowed, 7.9% divorced (2000); Foreign born: 4.0% (2000); Ancestry (includes multiple ancestries): 53.6% German, 17.3% Irish, 8.7% French (except Basque), 8.2% United States or American, 7.5% English (2000).
Economy: Single-family building permits issued: 0 (2001) / 0 (2000); Multi-family building permits issued: 0 (2001) / 0 (2000); Employment by occupation: 9.7% management, 7.6% professional, 21.5% services, 21.5% sales, 0.0% farming, 14.3% construction, 25.3% production (2000).
Income: Per capita income: $17,689 (2000); Median household income: $41,500 (2000); Poverty rate: 10.1% (2000).
Taxes: Total city taxes per capita: $142 (1997); City property taxes per capita: $139 (1997).
Education: High school graduation rate: 83.8% (2000); College graduation rate: 9.7% (2000).
Housing: Homeownership rate: 77.5% (2000); Median home value: $74,800 (2000); Median rent: $363 per month (2000); Median age of housing: 60+ years (2000).
Transportation: Commute to work: 94.0% car, 0.0% public transportation, 1.3% walk, 4.7% work from home (2000); Travel time to work: 18.4% less than 15 minutes, 69.1% 15 to 30 minutes, 4.0% 30 to 45 minutes, 3.1% 45 to 60 minutes, 5.4% 60 minutes or more (2000)

SAUK CITY (village). Aka Sauk City-Prairie du Sac. Covers a land area of 1.496 square miles and a water area of 0.108 square miles. Located at 43.27° N. Lat.; 89.72° W. Long. Elevation is 757 feet.
History: Sauk City, which developed as a sister city with Prairie du Sac, was first known as Lower Sauk, founded by Agoston Haraszthy, a Hungarian nobleman who settled here with his family in 1841. Haraszthy founded the Humanist Society in 1842. Though its founder soon left the area, Sauk City became known as a city of freethinkers, attracting speakers such as Carl Schurz, Franz Siegel, and Robert Ingersoll.
Population: 3,109 (2000); Race: 98.9% White, 0.1% Black, 0.3% Asian, 0.0% American Indian and Alaska Native, 6.0% Hispanic of any race, 0.0% two or more races (2000); Density: 2,078.0 persons per square mile (2000); Age: 23.1% under 18, 20.5% over 64 (2000); Marriage status: 25.2% never married, 55.4% now married, 8.9% widowed, 10.5% divorced (2000); Foreign born: 3.9% (2000); Ancestry (includes multiple ancestries): 55.7% German, 9.8% Irish, 6.2% English, 5.8% Other groups, 5.6% French (except Basque) (2000).
Economy: Single-family building permits issued: 1 (2001) / 1 (2000); Multi-family building permits issued: 2 (2001) / 2 (2000); Employment by occupation: 9.3% management, 12.9% professional, 15.6% services, 29.1% sales, 0.0% farming, 14.5% construction, 18.6% production (2000).
Income: Per capita income: $17,705 (2000); Median household income: $36,378 (2000); Poverty rate: 12.5% (2000).
Taxes: Total city taxes per capita: $331 (2000); City property taxes per capita: $316 (2000).
Education: High school graduation rate: 78.4% (2000); College graduation rate: 14.9% (2000).

School District(s)

Sauk Prairie (PK-12)
2000 Enrollment: 2,621 608-643-5981
Housing: Homeownership rate: 60.8% (2000); Median home value: $112,600 (2000); Median rent: $429 per month (2000); Median age of housing: 34 years (2000).
Newspapers: Sauk Prairie Eagle (1 x week); Sauk Prairie Star (1 x week); Satellite Shopper (1 x week)
Transportation: Commute to work: 88.3% car, 0.0% public transportation, 8.4% walk, 2.7% work from home (2000); Travel time to work: 52.1% less than 15 minutes, 20.3% 15 to 30 minutes, 17.2% 30 to 45 minutes, 7.4% 45 to 60 minutes, 3.0% 60 minutes or more (2000)
Additional Information Contacts
Sauk Prairie Chamber of Commerce 608-643-4168

SPRING GREEN (village). Covers a land area of 1.316 square miles and a water area of 0 square miles. Located at 43.17° N. Lat.; 90.06° W. Long. Elevation is 729 feet.
History: Near Spring Green, Frank Lloyd Wright designed his reknowned home, Taliesin. Built of native materials from the immediate vicinity, Taliesin came to symbolize a uniquely American architectural style.
Population: 1,444 (2000); Race: 99.7% White, 0.0% Black, 0.0% Asian, 0.0% American Indian and Alaska Native, 0.0% Hispanic of any race, 0.3% two or more races (2000); Density: 1,097.6 persons per square mile (2000); Age: 25.7% under 18, 18.0% over 64 (2000); Marriage status: 19.1% never married, 61.2% now married, 11.3% widowed, 8.4% divorced (2000); Foreign born: 0.8% (2000); Ancestry (includes multiple ancestries): 50.1% German, 14.7% Norwegian, 14.4% Irish, 12.8% English, 3.7% Polish (2000).
Economy: Single-family building permits issued: 8 (2001) / 7 (2000); Multi-family building permits issued: 0 (2001) / 0 (2000); Employment by occupation: 12.9% management, 26.3% professional, 17.3% services, 22.6% sales, 1.5% farming, 5.5% construction, 14.0% production (2000).
Income: Per capita income: $21,462 (2000); Median household income: $45,000 (2000); Poverty rate: 6.1% (2000).
Taxes: Total city taxes per capita: $549 (1997); City property taxes per capita: $537 (1997).
Education: High school graduation rate: 86.7% (2000); College graduation rate: 28.5% (2000).

School District(s)

River Valley (PK-12)
 2000 Enrollment: 1,580 608-588-2551

Housing: Homeownership rate: 74.5% (2000); Median home value: $106,000 (2000); Median rent: $489 per month (2000); Median age of housing: 41 years (2000).

Safety: Violent crime rate: 0.0 per 10,000 population; Property crime rate: 275.1 per 10,000 population (2001).

Newspapers: Spring Green Home News (1 x week)

Transportation: Commute to work: 87.9% car, 0.0% public transportation, 7.8% walk, 4.3% work from home (2000); Travel time to work: 56.8% less than 15 minutes, 13.7% 15 to 30 minutes, 9.4% 30 to 45 minutes, 13.2% 45 to 60 minutes, 6.9% 60 minutes or more (2000)

Additional Information Contacts

Spring Green Chamber of Commerce 608-588-2054

SPRING GREEN (town). Covers a land area of 44.389 square miles and a water area of 1.827 square miles. Located at 43.18° N. Lat.; 90.10° W. Long. Elevation is 729 feet.

Population: 1,585 (2000); Race: 98.8% White, 0.0% Black, 0.0% Asian, 0.4% American Indian and Alaska Native, 0.9% Hispanic of any race, 0.8% two or more races (2000); Density: 35.7 persons per square mile (2000); Age: 27.3% under 18, 11.7% over 64 (2000); Marriage status: 19.4% never married, 67.1% now married, 4.8% widowed, 8.8% divorced (2000); Foreign born: 1.3% (2000); Ancestry (includes multiple ancestries): 54.5% German, 19.3% Irish, 13.9% Norwegian, 11.4% English, 4.3% French (except Basque) (2000).

Economy: Employment by occupation: 13.5% management, 15.4% professional, 12.4% services, 25.2% sales, 1.6% farming, 11.5% construction, 20.4% production (2000).

Income: Per capita income: $20,619 (2000); Median household income: $49,028 (2000); Poverty rate: 5.2% (2000).

Taxes: Total city taxes per capita: $67 (1997); City property taxes per capita: $57 (1997).

Education: High school graduation rate: 86.5% (2000); College graduation rate: 17.4% (2000).

Housing: Homeownership rate: 84.1% (2000); Median home value: $124,500 (2000); Median rent: $485 per month (2000); Median age of housing: 23 years (2000).

Transportation: Commute to work: 89.6% car, 0.0% public transportation, 0.7% walk, 8.7% work from home (2000); Travel time to work: 38.0% less than 15 minutes, 20.2% 15 to 30 minutes, 15.7% 30 to 45 minutes, 12.1% 45 to 60 minutes, 14.0% 60 minutes or more (2000)

SUMPTER (town). Covers a land area of 37.702 square miles and a water area of 0.106 square miles. Located at 43.36° N. Lat.; 89.74° W. Long.

Population: 1,021 (2000); Race: 87.1% White, 0.0% Black, 0.0% Asian, 0.6% American Indian and Alaska Native, 15.8% Hispanic of any race, 0.6% two or more races (2000); Density: 27.1 persons per square mile (2000); Age: 28.0% under 18, 13.0% over 64 (2000); Marriage status: 25.8% never married, 53.2% now married, 6.4% widowed, 14.6% divorced (2000); Foreign born: 7.6% (2000); Ancestry (includes multiple ancestries): 42.4% German, 16.1% Other groups, 7.3% Irish, 6.0% Polish, 4.9% English (2000).

Economy: Employment by occupation: 16.5% management, 8.7% professional, 16.5% services, 18.8% sales, 3.4% farming, 12.9% construction, 23.3% production (2000).

Income: Per capita income: $16,205 (2000); Median household income: $31,806 (2000); Poverty rate: 12.0% (2000).

Taxes: Total city taxes per capita: $5 (1997); City property taxes per capita: $0 (1997).

Education: High school graduation rate: 75.2% (2000); College graduation rate: 12.6% (2000).

Housing: Homeownership rate: 72.1% (2000); Median home value: $131,300 (2000); Median rent: $392 per month (2000); Median age of housing: 41 years (2000).

Transportation: Commute to work: 86.9% car, 0.0% public transportation, 3.6% walk, 6.4% work from home (2000); Travel time to work: 24.3% less than 15 minutes, 37.3% 15 to 30 minutes, 20.8% 30 to 45 minutes, 12.6% 45 to 60 minutes, 5.0% 60 minutes or more (2000)

TROY (town). Covers a land area of 53.142 square miles and a water area of 1.153 square miles. Located at 43.24° N. Lat.; 89.92° W. Long.

Population: 773 (2000); Race: 97.1% White, 0.8% Black, 0.4% Asian, 0.5% American Indian and Alaska Native, 2.2% Hispanic of any race, 1.2% two or more races (2000); Density: 14.5 persons per square mile (2000); Age: 31.7% under 18, 10.7% over 64 (2000); Marriage status: 19.4% never married, 67.9% now married, 4.1% widowed, 8.6% divorced (2000); Foreign born: 1.3% (2000); Ancestry (includes multiple ancestries): 59.9% German, 11.5% Norwegian, 9.4% English, 7.7% United States or American, 6.8% Swiss (2000).

Economy: Employment by occupation: 20.4% management, 7.9% professional, 13.3% services, 21.2% sales, 7.1% farming, 9.4% construction, 20.7% production (2000).

Income: Per capita income: $17,735 (2000); Median household income: $39,432 (2000); Poverty rate: 8.2% (2000).

Taxes: Total city taxes per capita: $72 (1997); City property taxes per capita: $72 (1997).

Education: High school graduation rate: 88.6% (2000); College graduation rate: 11.4% (2000).

Housing: Homeownership rate: 78.8% (2000); Median home value: $96,100 (2000); Median rent: $413 per month (2000); Median age of housing: 60+ years (2000).

Transportation: Commute to work: 81.6% car, 0.0% public transportation, 4.7% walk, 13.7% work from home (2000); Travel time to work: 28.8% less than 15 minutes, 29.4% 15 to 30 minutes, 17.6% 30 to 45 minutes, 16.4% 45 to 60 minutes, 7.8% 60 minutes or more (2000)

WASHINGTON (town). Covers a land area of 35.559 square miles and a water area of 0.006 square miles. Located at 43.42° N. Lat.; 90.11° W. Long.

Population: 904 (2000); Race: 100.0% White, 0.0% Black, 0.0% Asian, 0.0% American Indian and Alaska Native, 0.2% Hispanic of any race, 0.0% two or more races (2000); Density: 25.4 persons per square mile (2000); Age: 34.1% under 18, 9.8% over 64 (2000); Marriage status: 26.6% never married, 63.6% now married, 5.6% widowed, 4.1% divorced (2000); Foreign born: 0.0% (2000); Ancestry (includes multiple ancestries): 53.5% German, 10.4% Irish, 10.3% English, 6.0% United States or American, 4.4% Norwegian (2000).

Economy: Employment by occupation: 16.1% management, 8.9% professional, 8.7% services, 18.9% sales, 6.2% farming, 14.4% construction, 26.8% production (2000).

Income: Per capita income: $13,920 (2000); Median household income: $41,563 (2000); Poverty rate: 11.5% (2000).

Taxes: Total city taxes per capita: $93 (1997); City property taxes per capita: $93 (1997).

Education: High school graduation rate: 73.4% (2000); College graduation rate: 10.1% (2000).

Housing: Homeownership rate: 83.3% (2000); Median home value: $83,500 (2000); Median rent: $442 per month (2000); Median age of housing: 59 years (2000).

Transportation: Commute to work: 73.9% car, 0.2% public transportation, 6.5% walk, 15.6% work from home (2000); Travel time to work: 27.1% less than 15 minutes, 41.5% 15 to 30 minutes, 17.4% 30 to 45 minutes, 5.6% 45 to 60 minutes, 8.5% 60 minutes or more (2000)

WEST BARABOO (village). Covers a land area of 0.814 square miles and a water area of 0 square miles. Located at 43.47° N. Lat.; 89.76° W. Long. Elevation is 886 feet.

Population: 1,248 (2000); Race: 93.5% White, 0.2% Black, 1.8% Asian, 2.2% American Indian and Alaska Native, 3.3% Hispanic of any race, 0.4% two or more races (2000); Density: 1,533.8 persons per square mile (2000); Age: 30.8% under 18, 11.0% over 64 (2000); Marriage status: 25.8% never married, 60.5% now married, 4.9% widowed, 8.7% divorced (2000); Foreign born: 3.0% (2000); Ancestry (includes multiple ancestries): 44.4% German, 14.0% Irish, 8.0% Norwegian, 7.7% Polish, 7.6% Other groups (2000).

Economy: Single-family building permits issued: 2 (2001) / 3 (2000); Multi-family building permits issued: 0 (2001) / 8 (2000); Employment by occupation: 11.7% management, 16.4% professional, 16.6% services, 26.0% sales, 1.9% farming, 6.4% construction, 21.0% production (2000).

Income: Per capita income: $18,283 (2000); Median household income: $41,618 (2000); Poverty rate: 6.2% (2000).

Taxes: Total city taxes per capita: $365 (1997); City property taxes per capita: $254 (1997).

Education: High school graduation rate: 77.4% (2000); College graduation rate: 18.8% (2000).

Housing: Homeownership rate: 57.4% (2000); Median home value: $99,500 (2000); Median rent: $506 per month (2000); Median age of housing: 23 years (2000).

Transportation: Commute to work: 90.0% car, 0.0% public transportation, 6.2% walk, 2.3% work from home (2000); Travel time to work: 66.2% less than 15 minutes, 14.9% 15 to 30 minutes, 5.3% 30 to 45 minutes, 6.2% 45 to 60 minutes, 7.5% 60 minutes or more (2000)

WESTFIELD (town). Covers a land area of 35.746 square miles and a water area of 0.006 square miles. Located at 43.43° N. Lat.; 90.02° W. Long.
Population: 611 (2000); Race: 100.0% White, 0.0% Black, 0.0% Asian, 0.0% American Indian and Alaska Native, 1.3% Hispanic of any race, 0.0% two or more races (2000); Density: 17.1 persons per square mile (2000); Age: 28.5% under 18, 13.2% over 64 (2000); Marriage status: 19.3% never married, 74.4% now married, 1.2% widowed, 5.0% divorced (2000); Foreign born: 0.3% (2000); Ancestry (includes multiple ancestries): 61.6% German, 10.7% Irish, 9.4% United States or American, 6.0% English, 4.2% Italian (2000).
Economy: Employment by occupation: 26.1% management, 13.4% professional, 9.1% services, 12.2% sales, 9.1% farming, 13.1% construction, 17.0% production (2000).
Income: Per capita income: $16,231 (2000); Median household income: $42,188 (2000); Poverty rate: 13.2% (2000).
Taxes: Total city taxes per capita: $203 (1997); City property taxes per capita: $203 (1997).
Education: High school graduation rate: 81.1% (2000); College graduation rate: 11.7% (2000).
Housing: Homeownership rate: 78.4% (2000); Median home value: $83,600 (2000); Median rent: $425 per month (2000); Median age of housing: 60+ years (2000).
Transportation: Commute to work: 76.9% car, 0.0% public transportation, 3.8% walk, 18.8% work from home (2000); Travel time to work: 24.2% less than 15 minutes, 40.2% 15 to 30 minutes, 19.2% 30 to 45 minutes, 2.1% 45 to 60 minutes, 14.2% 60 minutes or more (2000)

WINFIELD (town). Covers a land area of 35.440 square miles and a water area of 0.011 square miles. Located at 43.59° N. Lat.; 90.02° W. Long.
Population: 752 (2000); Race: 100.0% White, 0.0% Black, 0.0% Asian, 0.0% American Indian and Alaska Native, 0.0% Hispanic of any race, 0.0% two or more races (2000); Density: 21.2 persons per square mile (2000); Age: 29.6% under 18, 6.9% over 64 (2000); Marriage status: 23.0% never married, 69.6% now married, 2.5% widowed, 4.9% divorced (2000); Foreign born: 0.0% (2000); Ancestry (includes multiple ancestries): 63.5% German, 16.2% Irish, 13.3% English, 4.7% Polish, 4.1% Czech (2000).
Economy: Employment by occupation: 13.0% management, 13.6% professional, 11.1% services, 23.9% sales, 3.6% farming, 14.8% construction, 20.0% production (2000).
Income: Per capita income: $20,717 (2000); Median household income: $49,688 (2000); Poverty rate: 3.0% (2000).
Taxes: Total city taxes per capita: $77 (1997); City property taxes per capita: $77 (1997).
Education: High school graduation rate: 88.9% (2000); College graduation rate: 14.1% (2000).
Housing: Homeownership rate: 87.2% (2000); Median home value: $126,900 (2000); Median rent: $483 per month (2000); Median age of housing: 23 years (2000).
Transportation: Commute to work: 88.9% car, 0.0% public transportation, 0.9% walk, 9.2% work from home (2000); Travel time to work: 43.0% less than 15 minutes, 30.5% 15 to 30 minutes, 14.0% 30 to 45 minutes, 2.0% 45 to 60 minutes, 10.4% 60 minutes or more (2000)

WOODLAND (town). Covers a land area of 36.073 square miles and a water area of 0.095 square miles. Located at 43.58° N. Lat.; 90.25° W. Long.
Population: 783 (2000); Race: 100.0% White, 0.0% Black, 0.0% Asian, 0.0% American Indian and Alaska Native, 0.5% Hispanic of any race, 0.0% two or more races (2000); Density: 21.7 persons per square mile (2000); Age: 36.3% under 18, 14.1% over 64 (2000); Marriage status: 18.4% never married, 72.6% now married, 4.4% widowed, 4.6% divorced (2000); Foreign born: 0.6% (2000); Ancestry (includes multiple ancestries): 44.0% German, 15.5% Irish, 9.9% English, 9.4% Norwegian, 7.4% United States or American (2000).
Economy: Employment by occupation: 24.5% management, 8.4% professional, 13.9% services, 18.6% sales, 4.3% farming, 9.6% construction, 20.7% production (2000).
Income: Per capita income: $14,787 (2000); Median household income: $41,000 (2000); Poverty rate: 14.8% (2000).
Taxes: Total city taxes per capita: $211 (1997); City property taxes per capita: $211 (1997).
Education: High school graduation rate: 76.8% (2000); College graduation rate: 12.5% (2000).
Housing: Homeownership rate: 86.1% (2000); Median home value: $84,200 (2000); Median rent: $475 per month (2000); Median age of housing: 39 years (2000).
Transportation: Commute to work: 78.2% car, 0.0% public transportation, 2.5% walk, 19.2% work from home (2000); Travel time to work: 24.2% less than 15 minutes, 33.2% 15 to 30 minutes, 26.2% 30 to 45 minutes, 13.3% 45 to 60 minutes, 3.1% 60 minutes or more (2000)

Sawyer County

Located in northern Wisconsin; drained by the Chippewa River; includes many lakes, and part of Chequamegon National Forest. Covers a land area of 1,256.40 square miles, a water area of 93.90 square miles, and is located in the Central Time Zone. The county government was organized in 1883. County seat is Hayward.
Population: 16,196 (2000); Race: 81.9% White, 0.3% Black, 0.5% Asian, 15.4% American Indian and Alaska Native, 0.8% Hispanic of any race, 1.6% two or more races (2000); Density: 12.9 persons per square mile (2000); Age: 24.1% under 18, 18.0% over 64 (2000).
Religion: Five largest groups: 23.4% Catholic Church, 16.3% The Wesleyan Church, 9.3% Evangelical Lutheran Church in America, 1.1% Lutheran Church—Missouri Synod, 1.1% The United Methodist Church (2000).
Economy: Unemployment rate: 5.1% (11/2002); Total civilian labor force: 10,441 (11/2002); Leading industries: 17.7% retail trade; 17.3% manufacturing; 14.2% accommodation & food services (2000); Companies that employ more than 1,000 persons: 0 (2000); Companies that employ more than 100 persons: 7 (2000); Farms: 184 totaling 48,463 acres (1997); Minority business ownership rate: 0.0% (1997); Women business ownership rate: 26.8% (1997); Retail sales per capita: $8,333 (1997). Single-family building permits issued: 254 (2001) / 264 (2000); Multi-family building permits issued: 2 (2001) / 10 (2000).
Income: Per capita income: $17,634 (2000); Median household income: $32,287 (2000); Poverty rate: 12.7% (2000); Bankruptcy rate: 3.27% (2001).
Taxes: Total county taxes per capita: $407 (2000); County property taxes per capita: $325 (2000).
Education: High school graduation rate: 84.7% (2000); College graduation rate: 16.5% (2000).
Housing: Homeownership rate: 76.9% (2000); Median home value: $94,300 (2000); Median rent: $319 per month (2000); Median age of housing: 26 years (2000).
Health: Birth rate: 95.7 per 10,000 population (1998); Age adjusted death rate: 94.2 per 10,000 population (1999); Age adjusted cancer mortality rate: 208.9 deaths per 100,000 population (1999). Number of physicians: 14.2 per 10,000 population (1999); Number of hospital beds: 72.2 per 10,000 population (1999).
Elections: 2000 Presidential election results: 42.9% Gore, 51.1% Bush, 5.1% Nader, 0.4% Buchanan
National and State Parks: Benson Creek State Wildlife Management Area; Beverly Lake State Wildlife Management Area; Callahan-Mud Lake State Wildlife Management Area; Chequamegon National Forest; Chief River State Wildlife Management Area; Eddy Creek State Wildlife Management Area; Flambeau River State Forest; Flat Creek State Wildlife Management Area; Grindstone Creek State Wildlife Management Area; Hauer Springs State Wildlife Management Area; Kissick Swamp State Wildlife Management Area; Lac Courte Oreilles State Wildlife Management Area; Ojibwa State Park; Saint Croix National Scenic River; Totagatic River State Wildlife Managemnet Area; Uhrenholdt Memorial State Forest; Weirgor Springs State Public Hunting Grounds; Weirgor Springs State Wildlife Area
Additional Information Contacts
Sawyer County Government Offices 715-634-4866
Hayward Chamber of Commerce 715-634-8662
Winter Area Chamber of Commerce 715-266-2204

Sawyer County Communities

BASS LAKE (town). Covers a land area of 45.947 square miles and a water area of 15.720 square miles. Located at 45.91° N. Lat.; 91.42° W. Long.
Population: 2,244 (2000); Race: 60.4% White, 0.1% Black, 0.4% Asian, 37.0% American Indian and Alaska Native, 1.1% Hispanic of any race, 1.6% two or more races (2000); Density: 48.8 persons per square mile (2000); Age: 31.1% under 18, 11.2% over 64 (2000); Marriage status: 26.8% never married, 54.2% now married, 5.9% widowed, 13.1% divorced (2000); Foreign born: 1.2% (2000); Ancestry (includes multiple ancestries): 38.4% Other groups, 26.9% German, 10.1% Irish, 6.9% Norwegian, 5.3% Swedish (2000).

Economy: Employment by occupation: 14.2% management, 13.9% professional, 22.3% services, 25.9% sales, 2.1% farming, 11.1% construction, 10.6% production (2000).
Income: Per capita income: $15,026 (2000); Median household income: $31,274 (2000); Poverty rate: 17.4% (2000).
Taxes: Total city taxes per capita: $81 (1997); City property taxes per capita: $78 (1997).
Education: High school graduation rate: 85.8% (2000); College graduation rate: 16.6% (2000).
Housing: Homeownership rate: 75.8% (2000); Median home value: $89,900 (2000); Median rent: $218 per month (2000); Median age of housing: 23 years (2000).
Transportation: Commute to work: 86.1% car, 0.8% public transportation, 4.6% walk, 7.2% work from home (2000); Travel time to work: 56.9% less than 15 minutes, 30.3% 15 to 30 minutes, 7.3% 30 to 45 minutes, 2.0% 45 to 60 minutes, 3.5% 60 minutes or more (2000)

CHIEF LAKE (CDP). Covers a land area of 21.097 square miles and a water area of 2.519 square miles. Located at 45.90° N. Lat.; 91.33° W. Long.
Population: 625 (2000); Race: 20.0% White, 0.3% Black, 1.5% Asian, 77.1% American Indian and Alaska Native, 2.1% Hispanic of any race, 0.6% two or more races (2000); Density: 29.6 persons per square mile (2000); Age: 35.7% under 18, 10.8% over 64 (2000); Marriage status: 36.3% never married, 43.3% now married, 5.1% widowed, 15.3% divorced (2000); Foreign born: 2.1% (2000); Ancestry (includes multiple ancestries): 74.1% Other groups, 13.9% German, 3.4% Norwegian, 2.7% French (except Basque), 1.8% Irish (2000).
Economy: Employment by occupation: 13.3% management, 14.0% professional, 24.6% services, 24.6% sales, 0.0% farming, 11.4% construction, 12.1% production (2000).
Income: Per capita income: $12,486 (2000); Median household income: $33,125 (2000); Poverty rate: 10.0% (2000).
Education: High school graduation rate: 85.5% (2000); College graduation rate: 13.7% (2000).
Housing: Homeownership rate: 76.0% (2000); Median home value: $95,000 (2000); Median rent: $275 per month (2000); Median age of housing: 24 years (2000).
Transportation: Commute to work: 83.5% car, 0.0% public transportation, 3.9% walk, 12.5% work from home (2000); Travel time to work: 52.9% less than 15 minutes, 39.5% 15 to 30 minutes, 4.5% 30 to 45 minutes, 0.0% 45 to 60 minutes, 3.1% 60 minutes or more (2000)

COUDERAY (village). Covers a land area of 0.967 square miles and a water area of 0.017 square miles. Located at 45.79° N. Lat.; 91.30° W. Long. Elevation is 1,265 feet.
Population: 96 (2000); Race: 69.1% White, 0.0% Black, 0.0% Asian, 30.9% American Indian and Alaska Native, 0.0% Hispanic of any race, 0.0% two or more races (2000); Density: 99.2 persons per square mile (2000); Age: 22.0% under 18, 13.8% over 64 (2000); Marriage status: 30.5% never married, 55.2% now married, 3.8% widowed, 10.5% divorced (2000); Foreign born: 0.0% (2000); Ancestry (includes multiple ancestries): 32.5% United States or American, 26.0% Other groups, 15.4% German, 8.1% Norwegian, 5.7% Danish (2000).
Economy: Single-family building permits issued: 0 (2001) / 0 (2000); Multi-family building permits issued: 0 (2001) / 0 (2000); Employment by occupation: 14.0% management, 14.0% professional, 12.0% services, 12.0% sales, 12.0% farming, 26.0% construction, 10.0% production (2000).
Income: Per capita income: $14,008 (2000); Median household income: $40,417 (2000); Poverty rate: 11.4% (2000).
Taxes: Total city taxes per capita: $93 (1997); City property taxes per capita: $93 (1997).
Education: High school graduation rate: 84.3% (2000); College graduation rate: 19.1% (2000).
Housing: Homeownership rate: 96.2% (2000); Median home value: $45,600 (2000); Median rent: $125 per month (2000); Median age of housing: 39 years (2000).
Transportation: Commute to work: 81.3% car, 0.0% public transportation, [illegible].3% walk, 12.5% work from home (2000); Travel time to work: 11.9% less than 15 minutes, 31.0% 15 to 30 minutes, 23.8% 30 to 45 minutes, 14.3% 45 to 60 minutes, 19.0% 60 minutes or more (2000)

COUDERAY (town). Covers a land area of 66.497 square miles and a water area of 0.810 square miles. Located at 45.82° N. Lat.; 91.34° W. Long. Elevation is 1,265 feet.
Population: 469 (2000); Race: 47.3% White, 0.0% Black, 5.1% Asian, [illegible]5.5% American Indian and Alaska Native, 0.0% Hispanic of any race, 2.1% two or more races (2000); Density: 7.1 persons per square mile (2000); Age: 27.1% under 18, 14.9% over 64 (2000); Marriage status: 28.9% never married, 52.7% now married, 6.8% widowed, 11.6% divorced (2000); Foreign born: 2.4% (2000); Ancestry (includes multiple ancestries): 50.0% Other groups, 14.1% German, 7.7% Irish, 6.9% Polish, 6.1% English (2000).
Economy: Employment by occupation: 6.0% management, 16.8% professional, 18.8% services, 18.1% sales, 3.4% farming, 11.4% construction, 25.5% production (2000).
Income: Per capita income: $12,916 (2000); Median household income: $24,861 (2000); Poverty rate: 16.6% (2000).
Taxes: Total city taxes per capita: $9 (1997); City property taxes per capita: $9 (1997).
Education: High school graduation rate: 71.1% (2000); College graduation rate: 9.1% (2000).
Housing: Homeownership rate: 53.0% (2000); Median home value: $61,300 (2000); Median rent: $115 per month (2000); Median age of housing: 27 years (2000).
Transportation: Commute to work: 91.0% car, 0.0% public transportation, 2.8% walk, 4.8% work from home (2000); Travel time to work: 18.8% less than 15 minutes, 38.4% 15 to 30 minutes, 31.9% 30 to 45 minutes, 6.5% 45 to 60 minutes, 4.3% 60 minutes or more (2000)

DRAPER (town). Covers a land area of 136.101 square miles and a water area of 2.128 square miles. Located at 45.90° N. Lat.; 90.83° W. Long. Elevation is 1,480 feet.
Population: 171 (2000); Race: 92.8% White, 0.0% Black, 0.0% Asian, 7.2% American Indian and Alaska Native, 0.0% Hispanic of any race, 0.0% two or more races (2000); Density: 1.3 persons per square mile (2000); Age: 20.6% under 18, 21.1% over 64 (2000); Marriage status: 19.8% never married, 55.7% now married, 10.2% widowed, 14.4% divorced (2000); Foreign born: 2.6% (2000); Ancestry (includes multiple ancestries): 47.9% German, 16.5% Irish, 16.0% English, 11.9% Swedish, 6.2% Danish (2000).
Economy: Employment by occupation: 12.9% management, 12.9% professional, 14.5% services, 9.7% sales, 3.2% farming, 14.5% construction, 32.3% production (2000).
Income: Per capita income: $15,647 (2000); Median household income: $27,500 (2000); Poverty rate: 21.6% (2000).
Taxes: Total city taxes per capita: $98 (1997); City property taxes per capita: $94 (1997).
Education: High school graduation rate: 72.7% (2000); College graduation rate: 8.7% (2000).
Housing: Homeownership rate: 88.0% (2000); Median home value: $60,000 (2000); Median rent: $375 per month (2000); Median age of housing: 41 years (2000).
Transportation: Commute to work: 87.1% car, 4.8% public transportation, 8.1% walk, 0.0% work from home (2000); Travel time to work: 19.4% less than 15 minutes, 17.7% 15 to 30 minutes, 27.4% 30 to 45 minutes, 17.7% 45 to 60 minutes, 17.7% 60 minutes or more (2000)

EDGEWATER (town). Covers a land area of 47.180 square miles and a water area of 5.154 square miles. Located at 45.70° N. Lat.; 91.49° W. Long. Elevation is 1,260 feet.
Population: 586 (2000); Race: 97.3% White, 0.0% Black, 0.0% Asian, 2.3% American Indian and Alaska Native, 1.7% Hispanic of any race, 0.3% two or more races (2000); Density: 12.4 persons per square mile (2000); Age: 22.6% under 18, 16.7% over 64 (2000); Marriage status: 18.1% never married, 66.0% now married, 5.5% widowed, 10.3% divorced (2000); Foreign born: 0.5% (2000); Ancestry (includes multiple ancestries): 49.0% German, 12.5% Irish, 9.2% Czech, 7.3% English, 6.9% Polish (2000).
Economy: Employment by occupation: 6.8% management, 23.3% professional, 14.3% services, 20.4% sales, 3.6% farming, 11.8% construction, 19.7% production (2000).
Income: Per capita income: $18,907 (2000); Median household income: $38,542 (2000); Poverty rate: 7.4% (2000).
Taxes: Total city taxes per capita: $100 (1997); City property taxes per capita: $95 (1997).
Education: High school graduation rate: 83.1% (2000); College graduation rate: 18.4% (2000).
Housing: Homeownership rate: 88.4% (2000); Median home value: $111,500 (2000); Median rent: $366 per month (2000); Median age of housing: 22 years (2000).
Transportation: Commute to work: 89.3% car, 0.0% public transportation, 0.7% walk, 9.2% work from home (2000); Travel time to work: 31.7% less than 15 minutes, 25.2% 15 to 30 minutes, 25.2% 30 to 45 minutes, 10.2% 45 to 60 minutes, 7.7% 60 minutes or more (2000)

EXELAND (village). Covers a land area of 1.112 square miles and a water area of 0.014 square miles. Located at 45.66° N. Lat.; 91.24° W. Long. Elevation is 1,200 feet.
Population: 212 (2000); Race: 81.8% White, 0.0% Black, 0.0% Asian, 6.2% American Indian and Alaska Native, 0.0% Hispanic of any race, 12.0% two or more races (2000); Density: 190.7 persons per square mile (2000); Age: 20.9% under 18, 23.6% over 64 (2000); Marriage status: 22.3% never married, 51.6% now married, 14.9% widowed, 11.2% divorced (2000); Foreign born: 0.0% (2000); Ancestry (includes multiple ancestries): 18.2% United States or American, 18.2% Other groups, 15.1% Norwegian, 13.8% German, 10.7% French (except Basque) (2000).
Economy: Employment by occupation: 23.2% management, 3.2% professional, 18.9% services, 24.2% sales, 2.1% farming, 9.5% construction, 18.9% production (2000).
Income: Per capita income: $14,689 (2000); Median household income: $21,000 (2000); Poverty rate: 14.2% (2000).
Taxes: Total city taxes per capita: $118 (1997); City property taxes per capita: $108 (1997).
Education: High school graduation rate: 73.3% (2000); College graduation rate: 6.7% (2000).
Housing: Homeownership rate: 72.4% (2000); Median home value: $48,800 (2000); Median rent: $347 per month (2000); Median age of housing: 51 years (2000).
Transportation: Commute to work: 89.5% car, 0.0% public transportation, 10.5% walk, 0.0% work from home (2000); Travel time to work: 25.3% less than 15 minutes, 24.2% 15 to 30 minutes, 14.7% 30 to 45 minutes, 16.8% 45 to 60 minutes, 18.9% 60 minutes or more (2000)

HAYWARD (city). Covers a land area of 2.969 square miles and a water area of 0.241 square miles. Located at 46.01° N. Lat.; 91.48° W. Long. Elevation is 1,198 feet.
History: Hayward developed as a summer resort area for outdoor enthusiasts. In 1934, the State Public Welfare Department built Camp Hayward within the city of Hayward. The camp, utilizing the buildings of an abandoned school, operated successfully as a transient camp. A blacksmith who drifted in and stayed gave Camp Hayward a reputation for producing wrought ironwork.
Population: 2,129 (2000); Race: 88.8% White, 0.3% Black, 0.2% Asian, 10.1% American Indian and Alaska Native, 1.4% Hispanic of any race, 0.2% two or more races (2000); Density: 717.2 persons per square mile (2000); Age: 23.3% under 18, 22.3% over 64 (2000); Marriage status: 22.4% never married, 50.9% now married, 14.3% widowed, 12.5% divorced (2000); Foreign born: 1.5% (2000); Ancestry (includes multiple ancestries): 30.8% German, 17.6% Irish, 10.4% Norwegian, 7.9% Other groups, 7.5% English (2000).
Economy: Single-family building permits issued: 10 (2001) / 8 (2000); Multi-family building permits issued: 2 (2001) / 10 (2000); Employment by occupation: 6.1% management, 17.8% professional, 22.3% services, 30.2% sales, 0.7% farming, 12.3% construction, 10.7% production (2000).
Income: Per capita income: $16,658 (2000); Median household income: $28,421 (2000); Poverty rate: 14.5% (2000).
Taxes: Total city taxes per capita: $466 (1997); City property taxes per capita: $410 (1997).
Education: High school graduation rate: 84.5% (2000); College graduation rate: 17.8% (2000).

School District(s)

Hayward Community (PK-12)
2000 Enrollment: 1,959 715-634-2619

Two-year College(s)

Lac Courte Oreilles Ojibwa Community College (Public)
2001 Enrollment: 516 715-634-4790
2001 Tuition: In-state $2,160; Out-of-state $2,160

Housing: Homeownership rate: 53.3% (2000); Median home value: $81,900 (2000); Median rent: $387 per month (2000); Median age of housing: 30 years (2000).
Hospitals: Hayward Area Memorial Hospital (41 beds)
Newspapers: Sawyer County Record (1 x week); Four Seasons (1 x week)
Transportation: Commute to work: 87.5% car, 0.0% public transportation, 6.1% walk, 3.2% work from home (2000); Travel time to work: 76.7% less than 15 minutes, 16.4% 15 to 30 minutes, 3.9% 30 to 45 minutes, 0.8% 45 to 60 minutes, 2.3% 60 minutes or more (2000)
Additional Information Contacts
Hayward Chamber of Commerce 715-634-8662

HAYWARD (town). Covers a land area of 57.430 square miles and a water area of 6.566 square miles. Located at 45.99° N. Lat.; 91.40° W. Long. Elevation is 1,198 feet.
Population: 3,279 (2000); Race: 75.9% White, 0.0% Black, 1.0% Asian, 21.4% American Indian and Alaska Native, 0.7% Hispanic of any race, 1.4% two or more races (2000); Density: 57.1 persons per square mile (2000); Age: 29.1% under 18, 15.7% over 64 (2000); Marriage status: 24.9% never married, 60.0% now married, 5.7% widowed, 9.4% divorced (2000); Foreign born: 1.5% (2000); Ancestry (includes multiple ancestries): 34.0% German, 23.6% Other groups, 11.8% Norwegian, 10.6% Irish, 7.0% English (2000).
Economy: Employment by occupation: 13.0% management, 15.6% professional, 20.2% services, 27.1% sales, 1.2% farming, 10.4% construction, 12.7% production (2000).
Income: Per capita income: $17,382 (2000); Median household income: $36,895 (2000); Poverty rate: 13.6% (2000).
Taxes: Total city taxes per capita: $66 (1997); City property taxes per capita: $61 (1997).
Education: High school graduation rate: 87.3% (2000); College graduation rate: 20.0% (2000).
Housing: Homeownership rate: 77.0% (2000); Median home value: $109,400 (2000); Median rent: $205 per month (2000); Median age of housing: 24 years (2000).
Transportation: Commute to work: 88.6% car, 0.4% public transportation, 3.0% walk, 6.3% work from home (2000); Travel time to work: 77.0% less than 15 minutes, 15.3% 15 to 30 minutes, 2.8% 30 to 45 minutes, 2.2% 45 to 60 minutes, 2.8% 60 minutes or more (2000)

HUNTER (town). Covers a land area of 52.121 square miles and a water area of 23.846 square miles. Located at 45.93° N. Lat.; 91.17° W. Long.
Population: 765 (2000); Race: 61.4% White, 0.0% Black, 0.0% Asian, 35.0% American Indian and Alaska Native, 0.4% Hispanic of any race, 3.2% two or more races (2000); Density: 14.7 persons per square mile (2000); Age: 20.2% under 18, 20.3% over 64 (2000); Marriage status: 20.6% never married, 57.2% now married, 8.5% widowed, 13.6% divorced (2000); Foreign born: 1.6% (2000); Ancestry (includes multiple ancestries): 35.8% Other groups, 24.8% German, 13.0% Irish, 8.5% Polish, 5.6% English (2000).
Economy: Employment by occupation: 13.4% management, 16.3% professional, 17.4% services, 26.9% sales, 1.4% farming, 7.7% construction, 16.9% production (2000).
Income: Per capita income: $16,309 (2000); Median household income: $30,208 (2000); Poverty rate: 14.9% (2000).
Taxes: Total city taxes per capita: $21 (1997); City property taxes per capita: $14 (1997).
Education: High school graduation rate: 83.4% (2000); College graduation rate: 9.3% (2000).
Housing: Homeownership rate: 78.8% (2000); Median home value: $121,300 (2000); Median rent: $143 per month (2000); Median age of housing: 20 years (2000).
Transportation: Commute to work: 75.0% car, 1.5% public transportation, 14.2% walk, 7.5% work from home (2000); Travel time to work: 36.8% less than 15 minutes, 40.7% 15 to 30 minutes, 16.9% 30 to 45 minutes, 2.9% 45 to 60 minutes, 2.6% 60 minutes or more (2000)

LENROOT (town). Covers a land area of 81.668 square miles and a water area of 6.286 square miles. Located at 46.09° N. Lat.; 91.43° W. Long.
Population: 1,165 (2000); Race: 95.1% White, 0.3% Black, 0.0% Asian, 1.9% American Indian and Alaska Native, 0.2% Hispanic of any race, 2.5% two or more races (2000); Density: 14.3 persons per square mile (2000); Age: 22.6% under 18, 13.9% over 64 (2000); Marriage status: 18.7% never married, 63.2% now married, 7.2% widowed, 10.9% divorced (2000); Foreign born: 1.7% (2000); Ancestry (includes multiple ancestries): 36.7% German, 13.1% Irish, 13.1% Norwegian, 8.5% Swedish, 7.2% English (2000).
Economy: Employment by occupation: 12.3% management, 14.5% professional, 20.3% services, 26.4% sales, 1.2% farming, 14.6% construction, 10.8% production (2000).
Income: Per capita income: $19,230 (2000); Median household income: $35,000 (2000); Poverty rate: 8.7% (2000).
Taxes: Total city taxes per capita: $81 (1997); City property taxes per capita: $63 (1997).
Education: High school graduation rate: 90.0% (2000); College graduation rate: 17.3% (2000).

Housing: Homeownership rate: 89.2% (2000); Median home value: $115,900 (2000); Median rent: $383 per month (2000); Median age of housing: 26 years (2000).
Transportation: Commute to work: 90.3% car, 0.5% public transportation, 5.0% walk, 3.3% work from home (2000); Travel time to work: 58.1% less than 15 minutes, 26.7% 15 to 30 minutes, 9.9% 30 to 45 minutes, 2.3% 45 to 60 minutes, 3.0% 60 minutes or more (2000)

LITTLE ROUND LAKE (CDP). Covers a land area of 8.824 square miles and a water area of 0.225 square miles. Located at 45.97° N. Lat.; 91.33° W. Long.
Population: 948 (2000); Race: 10.6% White, 0.0% Black, 2.5% Asian, 84.8% American Indian and Alaska Native, 1.6% Hispanic of any race, 1.5% two or more races (2000); Density: 107.4 persons per square mile (2000); Age: 44.8% under 18, 5.4% over 64 (2000); Marriage status: 49.3% never married, 28.8% now married, 4.6% widowed, 17.4% divorced (2000); Foreign born: 1.3% (2000); Ancestry (includes multiple ancestries): 84.9% Other groups, 2.7% German, 1.1% Slovak, 1.1% French (except Basque), 0.8% Swedish (2000).
Economy: Employment by occupation: 12.8% management, 5.5% professional, 37.7% services, 27.5% sales, 1.1% farming, 8.1% construction, 7.3% production (2000).
Income: Per capita income: $7,819 (2000); Median household income: $17,574 (2000); Poverty rate: 42.7% (2000).
Education: High school graduation rate: 82.3% (2000); College graduation rate: 6.3% (2000).
Housing: Homeownership rate: 26.4% (2000); Median home value: $55,600 (2000); Median rent: <$100 per month (2000); Median age of housing: 20 years (2000).
Transportation: Commute to work: 94.4% car, 0.7% public transportation, 1.9% walk, 0.0% work from home (2000); Travel time to work: 74.3% less than 15 minutes, 12.7% 15 to 30 minutes, 5.6% 30 to 45 minutes, 3.4% 45 to 60 minutes, 4.1% 60 minutes or more (2000)

MEADOWBROOK (town). Covers a land area of 35.955 square miles and a water area of 0.274 square miles. Located at 45.69° N. Lat.; 91.13° W. Long.
Population: 146 (2000); Race: 94.6% White, 0.0% Black, 0.0% Asian, 2.3% American Indian and Alaska Native, 0.0% Hispanic of any race, 3.1% two or more races (2000); Density: 4.1 persons per square mile (2000); Age: 12.4% under 18, 21.7% over 64 (2000); Marriage status: 21.7% never married, 67.8% now married, 6.1% widowed, 4.3% divorced (2000); Foreign born: 0.0% (2000); Ancestry (includes multiple ancestries): 41.1% German, 22.5% Irish, 14.0% English, 13.2% Norwegian, 8.5% Danish (2000).
Economy: Employment by occupation: 18.8% management, 6.3% professional, 14.1% services, 12.5% sales, 18.8% farming, 9.4% construction, 20.3% production (2000).
Income: Per capita income: $19,208 (2000); Median household income: $29,167 (2000); Poverty rate: 2.3% (2000).
Taxes: Total city taxes per capita: $89 (2000); City property taxes per capita: $82 (2000).
Education: High school graduation rate: 72.7% (2000); College graduation rate: 11.1% (2000).
Housing: Homeownership rate: 82.0% (2000); Median home value: $60,000 (2000); Median rent: $258 per month (2000); Median age of housing: 30 years (2000).
Transportation: Commute to work: 78.3% car, 0.0% public transportation, 18.3% walk, 3.3% work from home (2000); Travel time to work: 32.8% less than 15 minutes, 27.6% 15 to 30 minutes, 29.3% 30 to 45 minutes, 6.9% 45 to 60 minutes, 3.4% 60 minutes or more (2000)

METEOR (town). Covers a land area of 34.431 square miles and a water area of 0.817 square miles. Located at 45.67° N. Lat.; 91.35° W. Long. Elevation is 1,580 feet.
Population: 170 (2000); Race: 92.9% White, 0.0% Black, 1.3% Asian, 3.9% American Indian and Alaska Native, 0.6% Hispanic of any race, 1.3% two or more races (2000); Density: 4.9 persons per square mile (2000); Age: 33.8% under 18, 11.7% over 64 (2000); Marriage status: 22.6% never married, 61.7% now married, 10.4% widowed, 5.2% divorced (2000); Foreign born: 2.6% (2000); Ancestry (includes multiple ancestries): 29.9% German, 13.6% Norwegian, 13.0% English, 11.7% Czech, 11.0% Swiss (2000).
Economy: Employment by occupation: 3.1% management, 14.1% professional, 18.8% services, 15.6% sales, 0.0% farming, 18.8% construction, 29.7% production (2000).
Income: Per capita income: $12,487 (2000); Median household income: $30,625 (2000); Poverty rate: 7.8% (2000).
Taxes: Total city taxes per capita: $100 (1997); City property taxes per capita: $100 (1997).
Education: High school graduation rate: 71.7% (2000); College graduation rate: 2.0% (2000).
Housing: Homeownership rate: 91.2% (2000); Median home value: $77,500 (2000); Median age of housing: 53 years (2000).
Transportation: Commute to work: 88.7% car, 0.0% public transportation, 0.0% walk, 11.3% work from home (2000); Travel time to work: 10.9% less than 15 minutes, 41.8% 15 to 30 minutes, 18.2% 30 to 45 minutes, 21.8% 45 to 60 minutes, 7.3% 60 minutes or more (2000)

NEW POST (CDP). Covers a land area of 20.364 square miles and a water area of 7.061 square miles. Located at 45.90° N. Lat.; 91.17° W. Long. Elevation is 1,328 feet.
Population: 367 (2000); Race: 28.8% White, 0.0% Black, 0.0% Asian, 67.7% American Indian and Alaska Native, 0.0% Hispanic of any race, 3.6% two or more races (2000); Density: 18.0 persons per square mile (2000); Age: 27.0% under 18, 15.5% over 64 (2000); Marriage status: 26.8% never married, 48.5% now married, 9.3% widowed, 15.5% divorced (2000); Foreign born: 0.0% (2000); Ancestry (includes multiple ancestries): 64.6% Other groups, 13.7% German, 8.4% Irish, 6.4% Polish, 1.5% English (2000).
Economy: Employment by occupation: 9.0% management, 20.1% professional, 20.1% services, 25.0% sales, 3.5% farming, 6.3% construction, 16.0% production (2000).
Income: Per capita income: $12,395 (2000); Median household income: $29,219 (2000); Poverty rate: 16.0% (2000).
Education: High school graduation rate: 77.6% (2000); College graduation rate: 9.8% (2000).
Housing: Homeownership rate: 69.1% (2000); Median home value: $102,500 (2000); Median rent: $132 per month (2000); Median age of housing: 20 years (2000).
Transportation: Commute to work: 79.7% car, 0.0% public transportation, 10.1% walk, 5.8% work from home (2000); Travel time to work: 20.0% less than 15 minutes, 48.5% 15 to 30 minutes, 22.3% 30 to 45 minutes, 2.3% 45 to 60 minutes, 6.9% 60 minutes or more (2000)

OJIBWA (town). Covers a land area of 50.830 square miles and a water area of 0.583 square miles. Located at 45.80° N. Lat.; 91.11° W. Long. Elevation is 1,254 feet.
Population: 267 (2000); Race: 94.7% White, 0.0% Black, 0.0% Asian, 5.3% American Indian and Alaska Native, 1.1% Hispanic of any race, 0.0% two or more races (2000); Density: 5.3 persons per square mile (2000); Age: 26.6% under 18, 14.9% over 64 (2000); Marriage status: 20.5% never married, 63.6% now married, 4.5% widowed, 11.4% divorced (2000); Foreign born: 1.4% (2000); Ancestry (includes multiple ancestries): 37.2% German, 21.6% Irish, 15.6% English, 14.2% Polish, 10.6% Swedish (2000).
Economy: Employment by occupation: 9.4% management, 11.3% professional, 18.9% services, 16.0% sales, 7.5% farming, 11.3% construction, 25.5% production (2000).
Income: Per capita income: $16,889 (2000); Median household income: $41,667 (2000); Poverty rate: 7.1% (2000).
Taxes: Total city taxes per capita: $68 (1997); City property taxes per capita: $64 (1997).
Education: High school graduation rate: 93.7% (2000); College graduation rate: 11.1% (2000).
Housing: Homeownership rate: 93.2% (2000); Median home value: $74,400 (2000); Median rent: $425 per month (2000); Median age of housing: 25 years (2000).
Transportation: Commute to work: 91.5% car, 0.0% public transportation, 3.8% walk, 4.7% work from home (2000); Travel time to work: 32.7% less than 15 minutes, 15.8% 15 to 30 minutes, 32.7% 30 to 45 minutes, 6.9% 45 to 60 minutes, 11.9% 60 minutes or more (2000)

RADISSON (village). Covers a land area of 0.401 square miles and a water area of 0 square miles. Located at 45.76° N. Lat.; 91.21° W. Long. Elevation is 1,245 feet.
History: Radisson was named for the French explorer Pierre Esprit Radisson.
Population: 222 (2000); Race: 89.4% White, 0.0% Black, 0.8% Asian, 8.6% American Indian and Alaska Native, 0.0% Hispanic of any race, 1.2% two or more races (2000); Density: 553.2 persons per square mile (2000); Age: 25.1% under 18, 19.6% over 64 (2000); Marriage status: 17.4% never married, 55.7% now married, 10.4% widowed, 16.4% divorced (2000); Foreign born: 2.0% (2000); Ancestry (includes multiple ancestries): 44.7% German, 22.7% Polish, 14.1% Norwegian, 12.5% Swedish, 12.5% Italian (2000).

Economy: Single-family building permits issued: 2 (2001) / 2 (2000); Multi-family building permits issued: 0 (2001) / 0 (2000); Employment by occupation: 5.7% management, 8.6% professional, 20.0% services, 11.4% sales, 4.8% farming, 8.6% construction, 41.0% production (2000).
Income: Per capita income: $16,122 (2000); Median household income: $25,625 (2000); Poverty rate: 16.5% (2000).
Taxes: Total city taxes per capita: $100 (1997); City property taxes per capita: $92 (1997).
Education: High school graduation rate: 78.4% (2000); College graduation rate: 2.8% (2000).
Housing: Homeownership rate: 71.9% (2000); Median home value: $45,500 (2000); Median rent: $206 per month (2000); Median age of housing: 32 years (2000).
Transportation: Commute to work: 93.4% car, 0.0% public transportation, 1.1% walk, 5.5% work from home (2000); Travel time to work: 50.0% less than 15 minutes, 7.0% 15 to 30 minutes, 25.6% 30 to 45 minutes, 10.5% 45 to 60 minutes, 7.0% 60 minutes or more (2000)

RADISSON (town). Covers a land area of 74.094 square miles and a water area of 1.062 square miles. Located at 45.78° N. Lat.; 91.19° W. Long. Elevation is 1,245 feet.
Population: 465 (2000); Race: 89.3% White, 0.0% Black, 0.6% Asian, 4.3% American Indian and Alaska Native, 0.0% Hispanic of any race, 5.8% two or more races (2000); Density: 6.3 persons per square mile (2000); Age: 22.5% under 18, 23.0% over 64 (2000); Marriage status: 19.4% never married, 64.1% now married, 10.7% widowed, 5.8% divorced (2000); Foreign born: 1.7% (2000); Ancestry (includes multiple ancestries): 25.5% German, 22.1% Polish, 15.9% Irish, 15.2% Other groups, 9.4% Norwegian (2000).
Economy: Employment by occupation: 10.6% management, 7.0% professional, 24.6% services, 14.6% sales, 9.0% farming, 13.1% construction, 21.1% production (2000).
Income: Per capita income: $19,511 (2000); Median household income: $33,523 (2000); Poverty rate: 7.9% (2000).
Taxes: Total city taxes per capita: $78 (1997); City property taxes per capita: $78 (1997).
Education: High school graduation rate: 76.3% (2000); College graduation rate: 7.8% (2000).
Housing: Homeownership rate: 83.1% (2000); Median home value: $91,000 (2000); Median rent: $288 per month (2000); Median age of housing: 29 years (2000).
Transportation: Commute to work: 85.2% car, 0.5% public transportation, 9.0% walk, 4.8% work from home (2000); Travel time to work: 37.8% less than 15 minutes, 17.2% 15 to 30 minutes, 25.0% 30 to 45 minutes, 4.4% 45 to 60 minutes, 15.6% 60 minutes or more (2000)

RESERVE (CDP). Covers a land area of 53.009 square miles and a water area of 0.698 square miles. Located at 45.86° N. Lat.; 91.37° W. Long. Elevation is 1,305 feet.
Population: 436 (2000); Race: 18.2% White, 0.0% Black, 7.9% Asian, 68.2% American Indian and Alaska Native, 0.0% Hispanic of any race, 5.6% two or more races (2000); Density: 8.2 persons per square mile (2000); Age: 28.1% under 18, 15.2% over 64 (2000); Marriage status: 43.4% never married, 37.4% now married, 6.0% widowed, 13.2% divorced (2000); Foreign born: 4.6% (2000); Ancestry (includes multiple ancestries): 82.8% Other groups, 8.3% German, 3.0% Irish, 3.0% English, 2.6% Italian (2000).
Economy: Employment by occupation: 7.1% management, 21.4% professional, 20.5% services, 14.3% sales, 0.0% farming, 15.2% construction, 21.4% production (2000).
Income: Per capita income: $10,588 (2000); Median household income: $22,250 (2000); Poverty rate: 26.2% (2000).
Education: High school graduation rate: 71.4% (2000); College graduation rate: 15.1% (2000).
Housing: Homeownership rate: 52.5% (2000); Median home value: $94,000 (2000); Median rent: <$100 per month (2000); Median age of housing: 27 years (2000).
Transportation: Commute to work: 90.2% car, 0.0% public transportation, 3.6% walk, 4.5% work from home (2000); Travel time to work: 21.5% less than 15 minutes, 66.4% 15 to 30 minutes, 12.1% 30 to 45 minutes, 0.0% 45 to 60 minutes, 0.0% 60 minutes or more (2000)

ROUND LAKE (town). Covers a land area of 109.272 square miles and a water area of 8.891 square miles. Located at 46.02° N. Lat.; 91.18° W. Long.
Population: 962 (2000); Race: 99.6% White, 0.0% Black, 0.0% Asian, 0.0% American Indian and Alaska Native, 0.2% Hispanic of any race, 0.2% two or more races (2000); Density: 8.8 persons per square mile (2000); Age: 20.2% under 18, 16.9% over 64 (2000); Marriage status: 14.0% never married, 67.2% now married, 9.3% widowed, 9.5% divorced (2000); Foreign born: 1.4% (2000); Ancestry (includes multiple ancestries): 44.7% German, 13.3% Norwegian, 11.9% Irish, 11.8% English, 9.7% Polish (2000).
Economy: Employment by occupation: 16.9% management, 16.3% professional, 21.5% services, 20.1% sales, 0.0% farming, 15.4% construction, 9.8% production (2000).
Income: Per capita income: $24,951 (2000); Median household income: $40,179 (2000); Poverty rate: 6.7% (2000).
Taxes: Total city taxes per capita: $138 (1997); City property taxes per capita: $131 (1997).
Education: High school graduation rate: 89.8% (2000); College graduation rate: 25.1% (2000).
Housing: Homeownership rate: 90.6% (2000); Median home value: $146,900 (2000); Median rent: $413 per month (2000); Median age of housing: 26 years (2000).
Transportation: Commute to work: 77.6% car, 0.8% public transportation, 4.6% walk, 15.3% work from home (2000); Travel time to work: 29.6% less than 15 minutes, 51.6% 15 to 30 minutes, 15.6% 30 to 45 minutes, 1.0% 45 to 60 minutes, 2.2% 60 minutes or more (2000)

SAND LAKE (town). Covers a land area of 46.376 square miles and a water area of 5.186 square miles. Located at 45.84° N. Lat.; 91.46° W. Long.
Population: 774 (2000); Race: 86.3% White, 0.0% Black, 1.1% Asian, 9.4% American Indian and Alaska Native, 0.7% Hispanic of any race, 2.2% two or more races (2000); Density: 16.7 persons per square mile (2000); Age: 15.0% under 18, 27.3% over 64 (2000); Marriage status: 17.1% never married, 63.6% now married, 7.8% widowed, 11.5% divorced (2000); Foreign born: 3.0% (2000); Ancestry (includes multiple ancestries): 43.1% German, 13.6% Other groups, 10.5% Irish, 10.1% English, 9.0% Norwegian (2000).
Economy: Employment by occupation: 6.7% management, 20.8% professional, 17.9% services, 20.2% sales, 2.2% farming, 19.2% construction, 12.8% production (2000).
Income: Per capita income: $18,322 (2000); Median household income: $32,266 (2000); Poverty rate: 11.3% (2000).
Taxes: Total city taxes per capita: $117 (1997); City property taxes per capita: $112 (1997).
Education: High school graduation rate: 82.2% (2000); College graduation rate: 19.7% (2000).
Housing: Homeownership rate: 81.4% (2000); Median home value: $96,700 (2000); Median rent: $321 per month (2000); Median age of housing: 20 years (2000).
Transportation: Commute to work: 86.7% car, 0.0% public transportation, 7.8% walk, 5.5% work from home (2000); Travel time to work: 33.6% less than 15 minutes, 49.3% 15 to 30 minutes, 10.6% 30 to 45 minutes, 2.4% 45 to 60 minutes, 4.1% 60 minutes or more (2000)

SPIDER LAKE (town). Covers a land area of 99.254 square miles and a water area of 9.626 square miles. Located at 46.09° N. Lat.; 91.13° W. Long.
Population: 391 (2000); Race: 99.3% White, 0.0% Black, 0.0% Asian, 0.0% American Indian and Alaska Native, 0.0% Hispanic of any race, 0.7% two or more races (2000); Density: 3.9 persons per square mile (2000); Age: 8.4% under 18, 36.6% over 64 (2000); Marriage status: 13.5% never married, 76.4% now married, 5.7% widowed, 4.4% divorced (2000); Foreign born: 5.7% (2000); Ancestry (includes multiple ancestries): 46.4% German, 11.1% Polish, 9.1% English, 7.1% Irish, 4.4% Norwegian (2000).
Economy: Single-family building permits issued: 13 (2001) / 13 (2000); Multi-family building permits issued: 0 (2001) / 0 (2000); Employment by occupation: 13.6% management, 18.3% professional, 19.4% services, 31.9% sales, 0.0% farming, 15.2% construction, 1.6% production (2000).
Income: Per capita income: $26,461 (2000); Median household income: $37,396 (2000); Poverty rate: 4.2% (2000).
Taxes: Total city taxes per capita: $328 (1997); City property taxes per capita: $295 (1997).
Education: High school graduation rate: 94.1% (2000); College graduation rate: 30.7% (2000).
Housing: Homeownership rate: 84.7% (2000); Median home value: $211,500 (2000); Median rent: $338 per month (2000); Median age of housing: 36 years (2000).
Transportation: Commute to work: 68.1% car, 0.0% public transportation, 24.3% walk, 5.9% work from home (2000); Travel time to work: 35.1% less than 15 minutes, 32.8% 15 to 30 minutes, 17.8% 30 to 45 minutes, 5.2% 45 to 60 minutes, 9.2% 60 minutes or more (2000)

WEIRGOR (town). Covers a land area of 33.509 square miles and a water area of 0.885 square miles. Located at 45.67° N. Lat.; 91.24° W. Long. Elevation is 1,210 feet.
Population: 370 (2000); Race: 95.1% White, 0.0% Black, 0.0% Asian, 1.4% American Indian and Alaska Native, 0.5% Hispanic of any race, 3.6% two or more races (2000); Density: 11.0 persons per square mile (2000); Age: 20.3% under 18, 18.4% over 64 (2000); Marriage status: 17.2% never married, 70.5% now married, 6.5% widowed, 5.8% divorced (2000); Foreign born: 0.0% (2000); Ancestry (includes multiple ancestries): 27.5% German, 12.6% Irish, 11.0% French (except Basque), 8.2% Swedish, 7.4% Polish (2000).
Economy: Employment by occupation: 6.6% management, 8.6% professional, 9.9% services, 22.4% sales, 11.8% farming, 19.1% construction, 21.7% production (2000).
Income: Per capita income: $15,691 (2000); Median household income: $31,875 (2000); Poverty rate: 8.5% (2000).
Taxes: Total city taxes per capita: $50 (1997); City property taxes per capita: $50 (1997).
Education: High school graduation rate: 82.3% (2000); College graduation rate: 5.1% (2000).
Housing: Homeownership rate: 90.0% (2000); Median home value: $62,000 (2000); Median rent: $250 per month (2000); Median age of housing: 24 years (2000).
Transportation: Commute to work: 79.3% car, 0.0% public transportation, 12.4% walk, 8.3% work from home (2000); Travel time to work: 35.3% less than 15 minutes, 13.5% 15 to 30 minutes, 29.3% 30 to 45 minutes, 12.8% 45 to 60 minutes, 9.0% 60 minutes or more (2000)

WINTER (village). Covers a land area of 0.798 square miles and a water area of 0 square miles. Located at 45.82° N. Lat.; 91.01° W. Long. Elevation is 1,370 feet.
Population: 344 (2000); Race: 96.1% White, 0.6% Black, 0.0% Asian, 3.2% American Indian and Alaska Native, 3.2% Hispanic of any race, 0.0% two or more races (2000); Density: 430.9 persons per square mile (2000); Age: 25.3% under 18, 26.0% over 64 (2000); Marriage status: 24.9% never married, 49.4% now married, 13.1% widowed, 12.7% divorced (2000); Foreign born: 0.0% (2000); Ancestry (includes multiple ancestries): 32.1% German, 21.1% Irish, 8.8% English, 8.8% Other groups, 8.4% Swedish (2000).
Economy: Single-family building permits issued: 2 (2001) / 2 (2000); Multi-family building permits issued: 0 (2001) / 0 (2000); Employment by occupation: 3.1% management, 11.7% professional, 23.4% services, 18.0% sales, 7.8% farming, 11.7% construction, 24.2% production (2000).
Income: Per capita income: $15,404 (2000); Median household income: $22,955 (2000); Poverty rate: 17.5% (2000).
Taxes: Total city taxes per capita: $76 (1997); City property taxes per capita: $64 (1997).
Education: High school graduation rate: 70.2% (2000); College graduation rate: 4.8% (2000).

School District(s)

Winter (PK-12)
2000 Enrollment: 441 715-266-3301
Housing: Homeownership rate: 59.3% (2000); Median home value: $43,800 (2000); Median rent: $292 per month (2000); Median age of housing: 46 years (2000).
Newspapers: Sawyer County Gazette (1 x week)
Transportation: Commute to work: 79.4% car, 1.6% public transportation, 12.7% walk, 6.3% work from home (2000); Travel time to work: 36.4% less than 15 minutes, 12.7% 15 to 30 minutes, 22.0% 30 to 45 minutes, 16.9% 45 to 60 minutes, 11.9% 60 minutes or more (2000)
Additional Information Contacts
Winter Area Chamber of Commerce 715-266-2204

WINTER (town). Covers a land area of 279.505 square miles and a water area of 5.798 square miles. Located at 45.80° N. Lat.; 90.90° W. Long. Elevation is 1,370 feet.
Population: 969 (2000); Race: 93.7% White, 4.3% Black, 0.0% Asian, 1.2% American Indian and Alaska Native, 1.4% Hispanic of any race, 0.6% two or more races (2000); Density: 3.5 persons per square mile (2000); Age: 16.7% under 18, 18.7% over 64 (2000); Marriage status: 20.7% never married, 63.5% now married, 6.4% widowed, 9.4% divorced (2000); Foreign born: 2.9% (2000); Ancestry (includes multiple ancestries): 48.8% German, 10.9% Polish, 10.5% Irish, 10.2% English, 9.2% Swedish (2000).
Economy: Employment by occupation: 17.3% management, 9.6% professional, 19.6% services, 21.9% sales, 2.6% farming, 15.2% construction, 13.7% production (2000).
Income: Per capita income: $19,033 (2000); Median household income: $33,500 (2000); Poverty rate: 12.7% (2000).
Taxes: Total city taxes per capita: $62 (1997); City property taxes per capita: $59 (1997).
Education: High school graduation rate: 85.3% (2000); College graduation rate: 13.9% (2000).
Housing: Homeownership rate: 89.6% (2000); Median home value: $108,600 (2000); Median rent: $238 per month (2000); Median age of housing: 28 years (2000).
Transportation: Commute to work: 87.9% car, 1.5% public transportation, 7.7% walk, 2.4% work from home (2000); Travel time to work: 50.2% less than 15 minutes, 18.4% 15 to 30 minutes, 16.9% 30 to 45 minutes, 8.2% 45 to 60 minutes, 6.3% 60 minutes or more (2000)

Shawano County

Located in east central Wisconsin; drained by the Wolf and Embarrass Rivers; includes several lakes, including Shawano Lake. Covers a land area of 892.50 square miles, a water area of 16.80 square miles, and is located in the Central Time Zone. The county government was organized in 1853. County seat is Shawano.

Weather Station: Bowler — Elevation: 1,079 feet

	Jan	Feb	Mar	Apr	May	Jun	Jul	Aug	Sep	Oct	Nov	Dec
High	22	28	39	54	67	76	81	78	68	56	41	26
Low	1	5	17	31	41	50	55	53	44	33	23	na
Precip	1.0	0.9	1.8	2.8	3.7	3.6	3.9	4.1	3.7	2.6	2.1	1.4
Snow	na	5.9	7.0	1.6	tr	0.0	0.0	0.0	0.0	0.2	4.2	10.2

High and Low temperatures in degrees Fahrenheit; Precipitation and Snow in inches

Weather Station: Shawano 2 SSW — Elevation: 807 feet

	Jan	Feb	Mar	Apr	May	Jun	Jul	Aug	Sep	Oct	Nov	Dec
High	24	29	40	56	69	78	82	79	71	58	42	29
Low	4	8	20	33	43	52	57	55	46	36	24	11
Precip	1.3	0.9	1.8	2.7	3.7	3.2	4.0	3.9	3.6	2.5	2.4	1.3
Snow	14.0	7.8	8.6	2.5	0.2	0.0	0.0	0.0	0.0	0.2	4.8	12.1

High and Low temperatures in degrees Fahrenheit; Precipitation and Snow in inches

Population: 40,664 (2000); Race: 91.4% White, 0.2% Black, 0.4% Asian, 6.0% American Indian and Alaska Native, 0.9% Hispanic of any race, 1.5% two or more races (2000); Density: 45.6 persons per square mile (2000); Age: 25.7% under 18, 16.8% over 64 (2000).
Religion: Five largest groups: 25.7% Catholic Church, 24.1% Lutheran Church—Missouri Synod, 12.0% Evangelical Lutheran Church in America, 2.2% Wisconsin Evangelical Lutheran Synod, 2.1% The United Methodist Church (2000).
Economy: Unemployment rate: 4.7% (11/2002); Total civilian labor force: 20,104 (11/2002); Leading industries: 21.1% manufacturing; 16.5% retail trade; 14.1% health care and social assistance (2000); Companies that employ more than 1,000 persons: 0 (2000); Companies that employ more than 100 persons: 19 (2000); Farms: 1,337 totaling 270,478 acres (1997); Minority business ownership rate: 0.0% (1997); Women business ownership rate: 25.0% (1997); Retail sales per capita: $6,943 (1997). Single-family building permits issued: 232 (2001) / 198 (2000); Multi-family building permits issued: 16 (2001) / 18 (2000).
Income: Per capita income: $17,991 (2000); Median household income: $38,069 (2000); Poverty rate: 7.9% (2000); Bankruptcy rate: 0.00% (2001).
Taxes: Total county taxes per capita: $246 (2000); County property taxes per capita: $200 (2000).
Education: High school graduation rate: 81.5% (2000); College graduation rate: 12.6% (2000).
Housing: Homeownership rate: 78.2% (2000); Median home value: $84,000 (2000); Median rent: $367 per month (2000); Median age of housing: 37 years (2000).
Health: Birth rate: 115.1 per 10,000 population (1998); Age adjusted death rate: 88.9 per 10,000 population (1999); Age adjusted cancer mortality rate: 205.8 deaths per 100,000 population (1999). Number of physicians: 6.4 per 10,000 population (1999); Number of hospital beds: 11.3 per 10,000 population (1999).
Elections: 2000 Presidential election results: 41.7% Gore, 54.2% Bush, 3.0% Nader, 0.7% Buchanan
National and State Parks: Navarino State Wildlife Area; Shawano Lake State Fishery Area
Additional Information Contacts
Shawano County Government Offices 715-526-9150
Shawano Chamber of Commerce 715-524-2139

Wittenberg Chamber of Commerce 715-253-3525

Shawano County Communities

ALMON (town). Covers a land area of 35.135 square miles and a water area of 0.056 square miles. Located at 44.90° N. Lat.; 89.05° W. Long. Elevation is 1,160 feet.
Population: 591 (2000); Race: 96.3% White, 0.0% Black, 0.0% Asian, 2.2% American Indian and Alaska Native, 0.0% Hispanic of any race, 1.4% two or more races (2000); Density: 16.8 persons per square mile (2000); Age: 27.8% under 18, 16.8% over 64 (2000); Marriage status: 26.0% never married, 58.2% now married, 8.0% widowed, 7.8% divorced (2000); Foreign born: 0.0% (2000); Ancestry (includes multiple ancestries): 67.8% German, 7.7% Polish, 5.0% Other groups, 4.6% Norwegian, 4.5% English (2000).
Economy: Employment by occupation: 15.9% management, 5.7% professional, 19.6% services, 15.9% sales, 5.4% farming, 6.4% construction, 31.1% production (2000).
Income: Per capita income: $15,893 (2000); Median household income: $37,663 (2000); Poverty rate: 16.2% (2000).
Taxes: Total city taxes per capita: $84 (1997); City property taxes per capita: $81 (1997).
Education: High school graduation rate: 78.3% (2000); College graduation rate: 7.2% (2000).
Housing: Homeownership rate: 81.0% (2000); Median home value: $74,600 (2000); Median rent: $403 per month (2000); Median age of housing: 49 years (2000).
Transportation: Commute to work: 84.6% car, 0.0% public transportation, 5.6% walk, 9.8% work from home (2000); Travel time to work: 31.8% less than 15 minutes, 34.1% 15 to 30 minutes, 21.3% 30 to 45 minutes, 9.3% 45 to 60 minutes, 3.5% 60 minutes or more (2000)

ANGELICA (town). Covers a land area of 36.599 square miles and a water area of 0.023 square miles. Located at 44.72° N. Lat.; 88.30° W. Long. Elevation is 880 feet.
Population: 1,635 (2000); Race: 98.5% White, 0.1% Black, 0.0% Asian, 0.5% American Indian and Alaska Native, 0.0% Hispanic of any race, 0.9% two or more races (2000); Density: 44.7 persons per square mile (2000); Age: 28.0% under 18, 10.9% over 64 (2000); Marriage status: 23.2% never married, 68.2% now married, 4.5% widowed, 4.1% divorced (2000); Foreign born: 0.6% (2000); Ancestry (includes multiple ancestries): 43.2% German, 36.1% Polish, 5.5% Irish, 4.5% Dutch, 4.3% French (except Basque) (2000).
Economy: Employment by occupation: 17.2% management, 10.6% professional, 10.2% services, 20.0% sales, 1.9% farming, 13.4% construction, 26.6% production (2000).
Income: Per capita income: $19,828 (2000); Median household income: $48,500 (2000); Poverty rate: 5.9% (2000).
Taxes: Total city taxes per capita: $46 (1997); City property taxes per capita: $45 (1997).
Education: High school graduation rate: 85.2% (2000); College graduation rate: 10.6% (2000).
Housing: Homeownership rate: 90.4% (2000); Median home value: $98,300 (2000); Median rent: $332 per month (2000); Median age of housing: 42 years (2000).
Transportation: Commute to work: 86.7% car, 0.0% public transportation, 3.5% walk, 9.8% work from home (2000); Travel time to work: 25.0% less than 15 minutes, 27.4% 15 to 30 minutes, 36.2% 30 to 45 minutes, 7.3% 45 to 60 minutes, 4.0% 60 minutes or more (2000)

ANIWA (village). Covers a land area of 2.089 square miles and a water area of 0.037 square miles. Located at 45.01° N. Lat.; 89.21° W. Long. Elevation is 1,414 feet.
Population: 272 (2000); Race: 99.2% White, 0.0% Black, 0.0% Asian, 0.8% American Indian and Alaska Native, 0.8% Hispanic of any race, 0.0% two or more races (2000); Density: 130.2 persons per square mile (2000); Age: 21.9% under 18, 15.5% over 64 (2000); Marriage status: 20.2% never married, 59.6% now married, 8.7% widowed, 11.5% divorced (2000); Foreign born: 0.8% (2000); Ancestry (includes multiple ancestries): 52.5% German, 14.0% United States or American, 9.8% Irish, 5.3% Other groups, 5.3% English (2000).
Economy: Single-family building permits issued: 1 (2001) / 0 (2000); Multi-family building permits issued: 0 (2001) / 0 (2000); Employment by occupation: 9.2% management, 7.5% professional, 14.2% services, 8.3% sales, 2.5% farming, 11.7% construction, 46.7% production (2000).
Income: Per capita income: $13,203 (2000); Median household income: $28,542 (2000); Poverty rate: 15.6% (2000).
Taxes: Total city taxes per capita: $27 (1997); City property taxes per capita: $0 (1997).
Education: High school graduation rate: 64.0% (2000); College graduation rate: 1.1% (2000).
Housing: Homeownership rate: 86.6% (2000); Median home value: $38,300 (2000); Median rent: $144 per month (2000); Median age of housing: 36 years (2000).
Transportation: Commute to work: 89.0% car, 0.0% public transportation, 2.5% walk, 7.6% work from home (2000); Travel time to work: 29.4% less than 15 minutes, 47.7% 15 to 30 minutes, 20.2% 30 to 45 minutes, 2.8% 45 to 60 minutes, 0.0% 60 minutes or more (2000)

ANIWA (town). Covers a land area of 33.197 square miles and a water area of 0.273 square miles. Located at 44.98° N. Lat.; 89.15° W. Long. Elevation is 1,414 feet.
Population: 586 (2000); Race: 99.5% White, 0.0% Black, 0.0% Asian, 0.5% American Indian and Alaska Native, 0.3% Hispanic of any race, 0.0% two or more races (2000); Density: 17.7 persons per square mile (2000); Age: 33.9% under 18, 9.5% over 64 (2000); Marriage status: 25.3% never married, 65.7% now married, 2.7% widowed, 6.3% divorced (2000); Foreign born: 0.3% (2000); Ancestry (includes multiple ancestries): 64.7% German, 14.3% Polish, 7.4% United States or American, 5.5% English, 5.4% Irish (2000).
Economy: Employment by occupation: 15.9% management, 8.1% professional, 12.6% services, 22.5% sales, 5.1% farming, 14.1% construction, 21.9% production (2000).
Income: Per capita income: $14,285 (2000); Median household income: $40,208 (2000); Poverty rate: 9.1% (2000).
Taxes: Total city taxes per capita: $62 (1997); City property taxes per capita: $61 (1997).
Education: High school graduation rate: 83.6% (2000); College graduation rate: 9.5% (2000).
Housing: Homeownership rate: 89.9% (2000); Median home value: $73,200 (2000); Median rent: $242 per month (2000); Median age of housing: 29 years (2000).
Transportation: Commute to work: 83.8% car, 0.0% public transportation, 4.7% walk, 10.9% work from home (2000); Travel time to work: 26.0% less than 15 minutes, 38.2% 15 to 30 minutes, 26.0% 30 to 45 minutes, 5.6% 45 to 60 minutes, 4.2% 60 minutes or more (2000)

BARTELME (town). Covers a land area of 35.509 square miles and a water area of 0.064 square miles. Located at 44.90° N. Lat.; 88.92° W. Long.
Population: 700 (2000); Race: 22.7% White, 0.0% Black, 1.6% Asian, 69.1% American Indian and Alaska Native, 0.0% Hispanic of any race, 6.2% two or more races (2000); Density: 19.7 persons per square mile (2000); Age: 31.2% under 18, 12.0% over 64 (2000); Marriage status: 30.8% never married, 46.9% now married, 7.8% widowed, 14.5% divorced (2000); Foreign born: 2.2% (2000); Ancestry (includes multiple ancestries): 74.2% Other groups, 13.3% German, 2.9% Irish, 2.3% French (except Basque), 1.9% Italian (2000).
Economy: Employment by occupation: 10.8% management, 12.1% professional, 26.1% services, 19.7% sales, 1.6% farming, 14.6% construction, 15.0% production (2000).
Income: Per capita income: $15,156 (2000); Median household income: $32,788 (2000); Poverty rate: 15.5% (2000).
Taxes: Total city taxes per capita: $2 (1997); City property taxes per capita: $0 (1997).
Education: High school graduation rate: 77.8% (2000); College graduation rate: 11.7% (2000).
Housing: Homeownership rate: 77.3% (2000); Median home value: $67,700 (2000); Median rent: $269 per month (2000); Median age of housing: 24 years (2000).
Transportation: Commute to work: 86.8% car, 1.0% public transportation, 8.1% walk, 4.2% work from home (2000); Travel time to work: 67.0% less than 15 minutes, 12.8% 15 to 30 minutes, 8.8% 30 to 45 minutes, 4.7% 45 to 60 minutes, 6.7% 60 minutes or more (2000)

BELLE PLAINE (town). Covers a land area of 38.383 square miles and a water area of 0.775 square miles. Located at 44.70° N. Lat.; 88.65° W. Long. Elevation is 855 feet.
Population: 1,867 (2000); Race: 96.1% White, 0.0% Black, 0.6% Asian, 2.8% American Indian and Alaska Native, 0.3% Hispanic of any race, 0.4% two or more races (2000); Density: 48.6 persons per square mile (2000); Age: 19.7% under 18, 18.4% over 64 (2000); Marriage status: 20.7% never married, 67.8% now married, 5.9% widowed, 5.7% divorced (2000); Foreign born: 0.8% (2000); Ancestry (includes multiple ancestries): 65.1% German,

7.8% Norwegian, 7.3% Irish, 6.3% Polish, 5.6% French (except Basque) (2000).
Economy: Employment by occupation: 17.2% management, 12.5% professional, 12.0% services, 23.1% sales, 2.7% farming, 10.7% construction, 21.8% production (2000).
Income: Per capita income: $20,381 (2000); Median household income: $44,100 (2000); Poverty rate: 5.6% (2000).
Taxes: Total city taxes per capita: $77 (1997); City property taxes per capita: $70 (1997).
Education: High school graduation rate: 84.1% (2000); College graduation rate: 15.4% (2000).
Housing: Homeownership rate: 87.3% (2000); Median home value: $111,000 (2000); Median rent: $346 per month (2000); Median age of housing: 32 years (2000).
Transportation: Commute to work: 87.6% car, 0.2% public transportation, 2.3% walk, 9.5% work from home (2000); Travel time to work: 36.0% less than 15 minutes, 37.7% 15 to 30 minutes, 8.1% 30 to 45 minutes, 11.0% 45 to 60 minutes, 7.0% 60 minutes or more (2000)

BIRNAMWOOD (village). Covers a land area of 2.206 square miles and a water area of 0 square miles. Located at 44.93° N. Lat.; 89.21° W. Long. Elevation is 1,300 feet.
Population: 795 (2000); Race: 96.9% White, 0.0% Black, 1.8% Asian, 0.0% American Indian and Alaska Native, 0.3% Hispanic of any race, 1.3% two or more races (2000); Density: 360.4 persons per square mile (2000); Age: 28.2% under 18, 21.2% over 64 (2000); Marriage status: 20.6% never married, 60.8% now married, 10.8% widowed, 7.8% divorced (2000); Foreign born: 1.4% (2000); Ancestry (includes multiple ancestries): 55.6% German, 12.1% Polish, 6.9% Irish, 6.7% English, 6.7% Norwegian (2000).
Economy: Single-family building permits issued: 1 (2001) / 1 (2000); Multi-family building permits issued: 0 (2001) / 0 (2000); Employment by occupation: 8.9% management, 18.6% professional, 16.9% services, 18.3% sales, 2.7% farming, 10.1% construction, 24.6% production (2000).
Income: Per capita income: $17,740 (2000); Median household income: $37,813 (2000); Poverty rate: 7.9% (2000).
Taxes: Total city taxes per capita: $49 (1997); City property taxes per capita: $24 (1997).
Education: High school graduation rate: 80.4% (2000); College graduation rate: 10.6% (2000).
Housing: Homeownership rate: 69.5% (2000); Median home value: $61,100 (2000); Median rent: $364 per month (2000); Median age of housing: 54 years (2000).
Transportation: Commute to work: 87.7% car, 0.0% public transportation, 5.7% walk, 5.1% work from home (2000); Travel time to work: 34.7% less than 15 minutes, 31.9% 15 to 30 minutes, 27.8% 30 to 45 minutes, 2.5% 45 to 60 minutes, 3.2% 60 minutes or more (2000)

BIRNAMWOOD (town). Covers a land area of 31.395 square miles and a water area of 0 square miles. Located at 44.89° N. Lat.; 89.15° W. Long. Elevation is 1,300 feet.
Population: 711 (2000); Race: 86.0% White, 3.0% Black, 0.3% Asian, 8.9% American Indian and Alaska Native, 0.3% Hispanic of any race, 0.2% two or more races (2000); Density: 22.6 persons per square mile (2000); Age: 26.4% under 18, 11.1% over 64 (2000); Marriage status: 24.0% never married, 59.2% now married, 8.0% widowed, 8.8% divorced (2000); Foreign born: 0.3% (2000); Ancestry (includes multiple ancestries): 55.7% German, 11.4% Other groups, 8.6% Irish, 8.3% Polish, 6.2% Norwegian (2000).
Economy: Employment by occupation: 16.1% management, 9.3% professional, 9.8% services, 21.5% sales, 5.4% farming, 15.5% construction, 22.3% production (2000).
Income: Per capita income: $18,782 (2000); Median household income: $40,469 (2000); Poverty rate: 11.7% (2000).
Taxes: Total city taxes per capita: $80 (1997); City property taxes per capita: $79 (1997).
Education: High school graduation rate: 80.3% (2000); College graduation rate: 6.0% (2000).
Housing: Homeownership rate: 83.9% (2000); Median home value: $88,600 (2000); Median rent: $206 per month (2000); Median age of housing: 28 years (2000).
Transportation: Commute to work: 89.3% car, 0.5% public transportation, 3.3% walk, 6.8% work from home (2000); Travel time to work: 33.8% less than 15 minutes, 15.3% 15 to 30 minutes, 33.8% 30 to 45 minutes, 12.1% 45 to 60 minutes, 5.0% 60 minutes or more (2000)

BONDUEL (village). Covers a land area of 2.195 square miles and a water area of 0.005 square miles. Located at 44.74° N. Lat.; 88.44° W. Long. Elevation is 880 feet.
History: Bonduel was named for Father Florimond T. Bonduel, a French missionary. Many of the early residents were of German heritage.
Population: 1,416 (2000); Race: 96.4% White, 0.1% Black, 0.0% Asian, 1.0% American Indian and Alaska Native, 1.9% Hispanic of any race, 0.8% two or more races (2000); Density: 645.0 persons per square mile (2000); Age: 26.0% under 18, 18.5% over 64 (2000); Marriage status: 20.8% never married, 63.6% now married, 8.7% widowed, 6.8% divorced (2000); Foreign born: 2.0% (2000); Ancestry (includes multiple ancestries): 64.2% German, 10.1% Polish, 7.1% Irish, 6.8% Norwegian, 5.8% Other groups (2000).
Economy: Single-family building permits issued: 1 (2001) / 3 (2000); Multi-family building permits issued: 4 (2001) / 4 (2000); Employment by occupation: 8.0% management, 14.1% professional, 15.3% services, 25.1% sales, 2.5% farming, 9.7% construction, 25.4% production (2000).
Income: Per capita income: $20,482 (2000); Median household income: $39,625 (2000); Poverty rate: 4.1% (2000).
Taxes: Total city taxes per capita: $222 (1997); City property taxes per capita: $214 (1997).
Education: High school graduation rate: 81.9% (2000); College graduation rate: 12.5% (2000).

School District(s)

Bonduel (PK-12)
2000 Enrollment: 907 715-758-4860

Housing: Homeownership rate: 65.2% (2000); Median home value: $89,600 (2000); Median rent: $389 per month (2000); Median age of housing: 38 years (2000).
Transportation: Commute to work: 89.3% car, 0.0% public transportation, 7.5% walk, 3.2% work from home (2000); Travel time to work: 39.5% less than 15 minutes, 27.8% 15 to 30 minutes, 21.2% 30 to 45 minutes, 7.9% 45 to 60 minutes, 3.6% 60 minutes or more (2000)

BOWLER (village). Covers a land area of 1.016 square miles and a water area of 0 square miles. Located at 44.86° N. Lat.; 88.98° W. Long. Elevation is 1,080 feet.
Population: 343 (2000); Race: 79.9% White, 0.0% Black, 1.2% Asian, 11.4% American Indian and Alaska Native, 0.0% Hispanic of any race, 7.5% two or more races (2000); Density: 337.7 persons per square mile (2000); Age: 31.1% under 18, 10.2% over 64 (2000); Marriage status: 31.3% never married, 53.2% now married, 6.3% widowed, 9.1% divorced (2000); Foreign born: 4.5% (2000); Ancestry (includes multiple ancestries): 38.6% German, 16.8% Other groups, 6.6% English, 4.5% United States or American, 3.9% Irish (2000).
Economy: Single-family building permits issued: 0 (2001) / 2 (2000); Multi-family building permits issued: 0 (2001) / 0 (2000); Employment by occupation: 11.2% management, 12.4% professional, 16.6% services, 34.3% sales, 2.4% farming, 7.7% construction, 15.4% production (2000).
Income: Per capita income: $13,285 (2000); Median household income: $34,167 (2000); Poverty rate: 6.6% (2000).
Taxes: Total city taxes per capita: $14 (1997); City property taxes per capita: $0 (1997).
Education: High school graduation rate: 77.4% (2000); College graduation rate: 14.9% (2000).

School District(s)

Bowler (PK-12)
2000 Enrollment: 574 715-793-4300

Housing: Homeownership rate: 68.4% (2000); Median home value: $63,000 (2000); Median rent: $325 per month (2000); Median age of housing: 43 years (2000).
Transportation: Commute to work: 93.0% car, 0.0% public transportation, 2.3% walk, 1.2% work from home (2000); Travel time to work: 47.3% less than 15 minutes, 34.3% 15 to 30 minutes, 5.9% 30 to 45 minutes, 5.9% 45 to 60 minutes, 6.5% 60 minutes or more (2000)

CAROLINE (unincorporated postal area, zip code 54928). Covers a land area of 9.103 square miles and a water area of 0.004 square miles. Located at 44.73° N. Lat.; 88.88° W. Long. Elevation is 902 feet.
Population: 363 (2000); Race: 100.0% White, 0.0% Black, 0.0% Asian, 0.0% American Indian and Alaska Native, 0.0% Hispanic of any race, 0.0% two or more races (2000); Density: 39.9 persons per square mile (2000); Age: 21.1% under 18, 17.8% over 64 (2000); Marriage status: 22.6% never married, 65.1% now married, 6.0% widowed, 6.3% divorced (2000); Foreign born: 0.0% (2000); Ancestry (includes multiple ancestries): 67.9% German, 7.0% Norwegian, 6.0% Czech, 4.4% Polish, 3.9% English (2000).

Economy: Employment by occupation: 10.2% management, 16.7% professional, 11.2% services, 24.7% sales, 3.3% farming, 12.6% construction, 21.4% production (2000).
Income: Per capita income: $17,313 (2000); Median household income: $44,167 (2000); Poverty rate: 3.5% (2000).
Education: High school graduation rate: 88.5% (2000); College graduation rate: 16.5% (2000).
Housing: Homeownership rate: 85.4% (2000); Median home value: $72,300 (2000); Median rent: $360 per month (2000); Median age of housing: 60+ years (2000).
Transportation: Commute to work: 88.7% car, 0.9% public transportation, 5.6% walk, 4.7% work from home (2000); Travel time to work: 31.5% less than 15 minutes, 39.9% 15 to 30 minutes, 11.8% 30 to 45 minutes, 2.0% 45 to 60 minutes, 14.8% 60 minutes or more (2000)

CECIL (village). Covers a land area of 1.375 square miles and a water area of 0.028 square miles. Located at 44.80° N. Lat.; 88.45° W. Long. Elevation is 811 feet.
Population: 466 (2000); Race: 96.6% White, 0.0% Black, 0.0% Asian, 3.4% American Indian and Alaska Native, 0.0% Hispanic of any race, 0.0% two or more races (2000); Density: 339.0 persons per square mile (2000); Age: 18.4% under 18, 24.1% over 64 (2000); Marriage status: 18.8% never married, 68.9% now married, 5.4% widowed, 6.9% divorced (2000); Foreign born: 1.3% (2000); Ancestry (includes multiple ancestries): 58.6% German, 11.2% Irish, 10.8% Polish, 6.5% Norwegian, 4.9% Other groups (2000).
Economy: Single-family building permits issued: 6 (2001) / 7 (2000); Multi-family building permits issued: 0 (2001) / 0 (2000); Employment by occupation: 8.5% management, 11.9% professional, 23.0% services, 24.3% sales, 1.3% farming, 10.6% construction, 20.4% production (2000).
Income: Per capita income: $18,918 (2000); Median household income: $38,958 (2000); Poverty rate: 5.7% (2000).
Taxes: Total city taxes per capita: $136 (1997); City property taxes per capita: $123 (1997).
Education: High school graduation rate: 75.5% (2000); College graduation rate: 12.1% (2000).
Housing: Homeownership rate: 78.4% (2000); Median home value: $87,200 (2000); Median rent: $366 per month (2000); Median age of housing: 37 years (2000).
Transportation: Commute to work: 89.1% car, 0.0% public transportation, 3.9% walk, 7.0% work from home (2000); Travel time to work: 38.8% less than 15 minutes, 18.2% 15 to 30 minutes, 22.4% 30 to 45 minutes, 13.6% 45 to 60 minutes, 7.0% 60 minutes or more (2000)

ELAND (village). Covers a land area of 2.220 square miles and a water area of 0 square miles. Located at 44.87° N. Lat.; 89.21° W. Long. Elevation is 1,237 feet.
Population: 251 (2000); Race: 93.5% White, 0.0% Black, 0.0% Asian, 6.5% American Indian and Alaska Native, 0.0% Hispanic of any race, 0.0% two or more races (2000); Density: 113.0 persons per square mile (2000); Age: 35.0% under 18, 13.0% over 64 (2000); Marriage status: 27.2% never married, 52.4% now married, 6.3% widowed, 14.1% divorced (2000); Foreign born: 0.0% (2000); Ancestry (includes multiple ancestries): 53.1% German, 20.6% Norwegian, 20.6% Polish, 9.0% Irish, 7.2% Other groups (2000).
Economy: Employment by occupation: 12.1% management, 6.8% professional, 19.7% services, 25.8% sales, 3.0% farming, 4.5% construction, 28.0% production (2000).
Income: Per capita income: $15,909 (2000); Median household income: $37,917 (2000); Poverty rate: 7.9% (2000).
Taxes: Total city taxes per capita: $23 (1997); City property taxes per capita: $23 (1997).
Education: High school graduation rate: 82.4% (2000); College graduation rate: 5.9% (2000).
Housing: Homeownership rate: 84.5% (2000); Median home value: $58,800 (2000); Median rent: $413 per month (2000); Median age of housing: 60+ years (2000).
Transportation: Commute to work: 95.5% car, 0.0% public transportation, 0.0% walk, 4.5% work from home (2000); Travel time to work: 34.1% less than 15 minutes, 23.8% 15 to 30 minutes, 19.0% 30 to 45 minutes, 14.3% 45 to 60 minutes, 8.7% 60 minutes or more (2000)

FAIRBANKS (town). Covers a land area of 34.687 square miles and a water area of 0.079 square miles. Located at 44.73° N. Lat.; 89.04° W. Long.
Population: 687 (2000); Race: 96.7% White, 1.2% Black, 1.1% Asian, 0.0% American Indian and Alaska Native, 0.3% Hispanic of any race, 1.1% two or more races (2000); Density: 19.8 persons per square mile (2000); Age: 28.4% under 18, 15.6% over 64 (2000); Marriage status: 23.8% never married, 65.1% now married, 4.8% widowed, 6.2% divorced (2000); Foreign born: 2.0% (2000); Ancestry (includes multiple ancestries): 63.9% German, 10.2% Norwegian, 8.9% Polish, 8.0% United States or American, 6.8% Irish (2000).
Economy: Employment by occupation: 14.6% management, 7.0% professional, 13.7% services, 17.6% sales, 5.2% farming, 12.5% construction, 29.5% production (2000).
Income: Per capita income: $16,373 (2000); Median household income: $39,432 (2000); Poverty rate: 9.1% (2000).
Taxes: Total city taxes per capita: $65 (1997); City property taxes per capita: $64 (1997).
Education: High school graduation rate: 72.4% (2000); College graduation rate: 9.4% (2000).
Housing: Homeownership rate: 89.8% (2000); Median home value: $59,100 (2000); Median rent: $388 per month (2000); Median age of housing: 48 years (2000).
Transportation: Commute to work: 86.5% car, 0.0% public transportation, 1.8% walk, 10.5% work from home (2000); Travel time to work: 33.0% less than 15 minutes, 25.8% 15 to 30 minutes, 16.5% 30 to 45 minutes, 13.7% 45 to 60 minutes, 11.0% 60 minutes or more (2000)

GERMANIA (town). Covers a land area of 36.190 square miles and a water area of 0 square miles. Located at 44.72° N. Lat.; 89.16° W. Long.
Population: 339 (2000); Race: 98.6% White, 0.0% Black, 0.0% Asian, 0.8% American Indian and Alaska Native, 0.0% Hispanic of any race, 0.6% two or more races (2000); Density: 9.4 persons per square mile (2000); Age: 21.3% under 18, 15.5% over 64 (2000); Marriage status: 25.7% never married, 62.2% now married, 6.2% widowed, 5.9% divorced (2000); Foreign born: 0.0% (2000); Ancestry (includes multiple ancestries): 69.5% German, 33.8% Polish, 6.6% Norwegian, 6.1% English, 3.9% French (except Basque) (2000).
Economy: Employment by occupation: 12.2% management, 11.2% professional, 17.8% services, 17.3% sales, 3.0% farming, 7.6% construction, 31.0% production (2000).
Income: Per capita income: $17,820 (2000); Median household income: $38,542 (2000); Poverty rate: 8.9% (2000).
Taxes: Total city taxes per capita: $23 (1997); City property taxes per capita: $23 (1997).
Education: High school graduation rate: 71.6% (2000); College graduation rate: 7.3% (2000).
Housing: Homeownership rate: 95.7% (2000); Median home value: $73,300 (2000); Median age of housing: 28 years (2000).
Transportation: Commute to work: 84.7% car, 1.1% public transportation, 0.0% walk, 14.2% work from home (2000); Travel time to work: 20.9% less than 15 minutes, 24.5% 15 to 30 minutes, 27.6% 30 to 45 minutes, 17.2% 45 to 60 minutes, 9.8% 60 minutes or more (2000)

GRANT (town). Covers a land area of 36.792 square miles and a water area of 0.148 square miles. Located at 44.71° N. Lat.; 88.91° W. Long.
Population: 974 (2000); Race: 100.0% White, 0.0% Black, 0.0% Asian, 0.0% American Indian and Alaska Native, 0.0% Hispanic of any race, 0.0% two or more races (2000); Density: 26.5 persons per square mile (2000); Age: 26.5% under 18, 15.6% over 64 (2000); Marriage status: 23.2% never married, 66.1% now married, 5.9% widowed, 4.8% divorced (2000); Foreign born: 0.4% (2000); Ancestry (includes multiple ancestries): 75.9% German, 5.7% Norwegian, 4.2% English, 4.1% Polish, 2.9% Czech (2000).
Economy: Employment by occupation: 16.5% management, 10.2% professional, 12.4% services, 22.3% sales, 3.2% farming, 11.4% construction, 24.1% production (2000).
Income: Per capita income: $16,190 (2000); Median household income: $40,583 (2000); Poverty rate: 3.4% (2000).
Taxes: Total city taxes per capita: $58 (1997); City property taxes per capita: $57 (1997).
Education: High school graduation rate: 84.6% (2000); College graduation rate: 9.1% (2000).
Housing: Homeownership rate: 93.7% (2000); Median home value: $75,200 (2000); Median rent: $360 per month (2000); Median age of housing: 53 years (2000).
Transportation: Commute to work: 83.3% car, 0.8% public transportation, 2.8% walk, 12.5% work from home (2000); Travel time to work: 35.3% less than 15 minutes, 36.7% 15 to 30 minutes, 11.2% 30 to 45 minutes, 4.1% 45 to 60 minutes, 12.8% 60 minutes or more (2000)

GREEN VALLEY (town). Covers a land area of 35.711 square miles and a water area of 0.132 square miles. Located at 44.81° N. Lat.; 88.32° W. Long. Elevation is 813 feet.

Population: 1,024 (2000); Race: 98.5% White, 0.0% Black, 0.0% Asian, 1.0% American Indian and Alaska Native, 0.3% Hispanic of any race, 0.4% two or more races (2000); Density: 28.7 persons per square mile (2000); Age: 28.8% under 18, 12.6% over 64 (2000); Marriage status: 21.6% never married, 65.3% now married, 6.0% widowed, 7.1% divorced (2000); Foreign born: 0.5% (2000); Ancestry (includes multiple ancestries): 52.4% German, 17.6% Polish, 11.6% Norwegian, 7.8% United States or American, 4.5% Dutch (2000).
Economy: Employment by occupation: 16.2% management, 6.4% professional, 8.1% services, 19.5% sales, 6.4% farming, 15.6% construction, 27.9% production (2000).
Income: Per capita income: $17,637 (2000); Median household income: $42,778 (2000); Poverty rate: 7.1% (2000).
Taxes: Total city taxes per capita: $60 (1997); City property taxes per capita: $59 (1997).
Education: High school graduation rate: 81.8% (2000); College graduation rate: 7.3% (2000).
Housing: Homeownership rate: 91.6% (2000); Median home value: $75,400 (2000); Median rent: $381 per month (2000); Median age of housing: 57 years (2000).
Transportation: Commute to work: 85.7% car, 0.0% public transportation, 1.8% walk, 12.2% work from home (2000); Travel time to work: 21.9% less than 15 minutes, 32.8% 15 to 30 minutes, 23.9% 30 to 45 minutes, 15.2% 45 to 60 minutes, 6.3% 60 minutes or more (2000)

GRESHAM (village). Covers a land area of 1.142 square miles and a water area of 0.102 square miles. Located at 44.85° N. Lat.; 88.78° W. Long. Elevation is 930 feet.
Population: 575 (2000); Race: 65.0% White, 0.0% Black, 0.0% Asian, 25.8% American Indian and Alaska Native, 0.3% Hispanic of any race, 9.2% two or more races (2000); Density: 503.3 persons per square mile (2000); Age: 30.7% under 18, 18.4% over 64 (2000); Marriage status: 28.2% never married, 46.5% now married, 15.4% widowed, 9.9% divorced (2000); Foreign born: 0.7% (2000); Ancestry (includes multiple ancestries): 37.8% German, 33.2% Other groups, 10.8% French (except Basque), 10.7% United States or American, 5.1% Irish (2000).
Economy: Single-family building permits issued: 7 (2001) / 4 (2000); Multi-family building permits issued: 0 (2001) / 0 (2000); Employment by occupation: 6.3% management, 11.6% professional, 26.0% services, 21.8% sales, 1.4% farming, 18.6% construction, 14.4% production (2000).
Income: Per capita income: $13,740 (2000); Median household income: $26,635 (2000); Poverty rate: 11.4% (2000).
Taxes: Total city taxes per capita: $30 (1997); City property taxes per capita: $8 (1997).
Education: High school graduation rate: 78.6% (2000); College graduation rate: 8.8% (2000).
Housing: Homeownership rate: 66.5% (2000); Median home value: $65,000 (2000); Median rent: $279 per month (2000); Median age of housing: 36 years (2000).
Transportation: Commute to work: 93.1% car, 0.7% public transportation, 5.4% walk, 0.0% work from home (2000); Travel time to work: 35.4% less than 15 minutes, 43.7% 15 to 30 minutes, 9.7% 30 to 45 minutes, 2.5% 45 to 60 minutes, 8.7% 60 minutes or more (2000)

HARTLAND (town). Covers a land area of 34.573 square miles and a water area of 0.158 square miles. Located at 44.72° N. Lat.; 88.43° W. Long.
Population: 825 (2000); Race: 98.7% White, 0.0% Black, 0.0% Asian, 1.2% American Indian and Alaska Native, 0.0% Hispanic of any race, 0.1% two or more races (2000); Density: 23.9 persons per square mile (2000); Age: 31.0% under 18, 13.6% over 64 (2000); Marriage status: 23.8% never married, 66.8% now married, 4.3% widowed, 5.1% divorced (2000); Foreign born: 0.0% (2000); Ancestry (includes multiple ancestries): 55.0% German, 9.7% Polish, 8.2% Irish, 6.6% United States or American, 3.9% English (2000).
Economy: Employment by occupation: 24.6% management, 11.0% professional, 11.9% services, 15.3% sales, 3.8% farming, 8.6% construction, 24.8% production (2000).
Income: Per capita income: $17,837 (2000); Median household income: $43,026 (2000); Poverty rate: 7.5% (2000).
Taxes: Total city taxes per capita: $213 (1997); City property taxes per capita: $212 (1997).
Education: High school graduation rate: 76.7% (2000); College graduation rate: 10.6% (2000).
Housing: Homeownership rate: 89.9% (2000); Median home value: $89,500 (2000); Median rent: $356 per month (2000); Median age of housing: 60+ years (2000).
Transportation: Commute to work: 77.6% car, 0.0% public transportation, 4.1% walk, 16.9% work from home (2000); Travel time to work: 27.6% less than 15 minutes, 32.5% 15 to 30 minutes, 31.6% 30 to 45 minutes, 5.2% 45 to 60 minutes, 3.2% 60 minutes or more (2000)

HERMAN (town). Covers a land area of 35.162 square miles and a water area of 0.228 square miles. Located at 44.80° N. Lat.; 88.79° W. Long.
Population: 741 (2000); Race: 90.2% White, 0.0% Black, 0.0% Asian, 6.2% American Indian and Alaska Native, 1.4% Hispanic of any race, 2.3% two or more races (2000); Density: 21.1 persons per square mile (2000); Age: 27.0% under 18, 15.9% over 64 (2000); Marriage status: 24.8% never married, 60.6% now married, 6.8% widowed, 7.7% divorced (2000); Foreign born: 1.1% (2000); Ancestry (includes multiple ancestries): 60.7% German, 7.8% Other groups, 6.3% Polish, 6.0% English, 5.2% Norwegian (2000).
Economy: Employment by occupation: 15.6% management, 12.3% professional, 13.6% services, 18.6% sales, 7.8% farming, 12.3% construction, 19.7% production (2000).
Income: Per capita income: $16,388 (2000); Median household income: $40,375 (2000); Poverty rate: 4.7% (2000).
Taxes: Total city taxes per capita: $57 (1997); City property taxes per capita: $54 (1997).
Education: High school graduation rate: 86.5% (2000); College graduation rate: 10.5% (2000).
Housing: Homeownership rate: 85.9% (2000); Median home value: $71,900 (2000); Median rent: $328 per month (2000); Median age of housing: 60+ years (2000).
Transportation: Commute to work: 81.7% car, 0.4% public transportation, 2.2% walk, 14.9% work from home (2000); Travel time to work: 25.1% less than 15 minutes, 45.5% 15 to 30 minutes, 11.0% 30 to 45 minutes, 9.9% 45 to 60 minutes, 8.4% 60 minutes or more (2000)

HUTCHINS (town). Covers a land area of 33.491 square miles and a water area of 0.102 square miles. Located at 44.97° N. Lat.; 89.05° W. Long.
Population: 539 (2000); Race: 97.2% White, 0.0% Black, 0.0% Asian, 1.6% American Indian and Alaska Native, 0.6% Hispanic of any race, 1.2% two or more races (2000); Density: 16.1 persons per square mile (2000); Age: 22.7% under 18, 11.6% over 64 (2000); Marriage status: 22.6% never married, 64.5% now married, 5.7% widowed, 7.1% divorced (2000); Foreign born: 0.8% (2000); Ancestry (includes multiple ancestries): 50.7% German, 8.5% Norwegian, 8.5% Polish, 7.5% United States or American, 6.9% Irish (2000).
Economy: Employment by occupation: 7.9% management, 9.8% professional, 17.3% services, 18.1% sales, 5.5% farming, 18.1% construction, 23.2% production (2000).
Income: Per capita income: $16,404 (2000); Median household income: $35,682 (2000); Poverty rate: 6.0% (2000).
Taxes: Total city taxes per capita: $97 (1997); City property taxes per capita: $97 (1997).
Education: High school graduation rate: 82.4% (2000); College graduation rate: 4.4% (2000).
Housing: Homeownership rate: 92.5% (2000); Median home value: $63,600 (2000); Median rent: $338 per month (2000); Median age of housing: 30 years (2000).
Transportation: Commute to work: 88.5% car, 0.0% public transportation, 5.6% walk, 5.2% work from home (2000); Travel time to work: 31.0% less than 15 minutes, 26.8% 15 to 30 minutes, 18.8% 30 to 45 minutes, 7.9% 45 to 60 minutes, 15.5% 60 minutes or more (2000)

KRAKOW (unincorporated postal area, zip code 54137). Covers a land area of 29.177 square miles and a water area of 0 square miles. Located at 44.76° N. Lat.; 88.25° W. Long. Elevation is 790 feet.
Population: 1,101 (2000); Race: 99.8% White, 0.0% Black, 0.0% Asian, 0.2% American Indian and Alaska Native, 0.2% Hispanic of any race, 0.0% two or more races (2000); Density: 37.7 persons per square mile (2000); Age: 28.7% under 18, 14.6% over 64 (2000); Marriage status: 24.6% never married, 61.7% now married, 5.5% widowed, 8.2% divorced (2000); Foreign born: 1.4% (2000); Ancestry (includes multiple ancestries): 44.2% Polish, 35.6% German, 5.9% Belgian, 5.0% French (except Basque), 4.2% Irish (2000).
Economy: Employment by occupation: 13.4% management, 10.2% professional, 7.9% services, 24.2% sales, 2.2% farming, 13.1% construction, 29.0% production (2000).
Income: Per capita income: $19,365 (2000); Median household income: $43,417 (2000); Poverty rate: 6.4% (2000).
Education: High school graduation rate: 80.3% (2000); College graduation rate: 8.6% (2000).

Housing: Homeownership rate: 92.8% (2000); Median home value: $93,600 (2000); Median rent: $321 per month (2000); Median age of housing: 42 years (2000).
Transportation: Commute to work: 89.0% car, 0.0% public transportation, 2.1% walk, 8.6% work from home (2000); Travel time to work: 21.0% less than 15 minutes, 28.5% 15 to 30 minutes, 37.8% 30 to 45 minutes, 7.9% 45 to 60 minutes, 4.9% 60 minutes or more (2000)

LEOPOLIS (unincorporated postal area, zip code 54948). Covers a land area of 12.057 square miles and a water area of 0.019 square miles. Located at 44.78° N. Lat.; 88.87° W. Long. Elevation is 943 feet.
Population: 342 (2000); Race: 97.0% White, 0.0% Black, 0.0% Asian, 3.0% American Indian and Alaska Native, 0.0% Hispanic of any race, 0.0% two or more races (2000); Density: 28.4 persons per square mile (2000); Age: 22.4% under 18, 23.2% over 64 (2000); Marriage status: 20.9% never married, 66.3% now married, 7.7% widowed, 5.1% divorced (2000); Foreign born: 0.0% (2000); Ancestry (includes multiple ancestries): 65.7% German, 9.4% Irish, 8.6% Polish, 7.2% English, 6.4% Czech (2000).
Economy: Employment by occupation: 18.5% management, 5.6% professional, 19.8% services, 20.4% sales, 4.3% farming, 5.6% construction, 25.9% production (2000).
Income: Per capita income: $14,731 (2000); Median household income: $32,708 (2000); Poverty rate: 7.2% (2000).
Education: High school graduation rate: 81.1% (2000); College graduation rate: 6.4% (2000).
Housing: Homeownership rate: 80.7% (2000); Median home value: $71,800 (2000); Median rent: $338 per month (2000); Median age of housing: 60+ years (2000).
Transportation: Commute to work: 78.7% car, 1.3% public transportation, 2.6% walk, 15.5% work from home (2000); Travel time to work: 16.0% less than 15 minutes, 58.8% 15 to 30 minutes, 6.1% 30 to 45 minutes, 6.1% 45 to 60 minutes, 13.0% 60 minutes or more (2000)

LESSOR (town). Covers a land area of 35.911 square miles and a water area of 0.218 square miles. Located at 44.63° N. Lat.; 88.43° W. Long.
Population: 1,112 (2000); Race: 99.2% White, 0.0% Black, 0.0% Asian, 0.8% American Indian and Alaska Native, 0.4% Hispanic of any race, 0.0% two or more races (2000); Density: 31.0 persons per square mile (2000); Age: 30.6% under 18, 8.5% over 64 (2000); Marriage status: 23.1% never married, 65.5% now married, 5.3% widowed, 6.1% divorced (2000); Foreign born: 0.4% (2000); Ancestry (includes multiple ancestries): 51.7% German, 17.8% Polish, 7.8% Norwegian, 7.3% Dutch, 4.0% French Canadian (2000).
Economy: Employment by occupation: 20.1% management, 8.2% professional, 7.8% services, 16.8% sales, 3.6% farming, 15.2% construction, 28.4% production (2000).
Income: Per capita income: $18,024 (2000); Median household income: $47,969 (2000); Poverty rate: 9.0% (2000).
Taxes: Total city taxes per capita: $65 (2000); City property taxes per capita: $64 (2000).
Education: High school graduation rate: 84.3% (2000); College graduation rate: 9.4% (2000).
Housing: Homeownership rate: 88.3% (2000); Median home value: $96,300 (2000); Median rent: $522 per month (2000); Median age of housing: 50 years (2000).
Transportation: Commute to work: 85.3% car, 0.0% public transportation, 4.0% walk, 10.8% work from home (2000); Travel time to work: 15.4% less than 15 minutes, 30.1% 15 to 30 minutes, 37.5% 30 to 45 minutes, 12.1% 45 to 60 minutes, 5.0% 60 minutes or more (2000)

MAPLE GROVE (town). Covers a land area of 35.331 square miles and a water area of 0.009 square miles. Located at 44.61° N. Lat.; 88.30° W. Long.
Population: 1,045 (2000); Race: 98.7% White, 0.0% Black, 0.0% Asian, 0.6% American Indian and Alaska Native, 1.4% Hispanic of any race, 0.7% two or more races (2000); Density: 29.6 persons per square mile (2000); Age: 27.7% under 18, 14.2% over 64 (2000); Marriage status: 26.1% never married, 64.9% now married, 4.2% widowed, 4.9% divorced (2000); Foreign born: 0.3% (2000); Ancestry (includes multiple ancestries): 42.0% German, 41.5% Polish, 8.1% Irish, 5.4% Belgian, 4.8% Dutch (2000).
Economy: Employment by occupation: 20.0% management, 7.0% professional, 9.9% services, 17.4% sales, 6.8% farming, 9.7% construction, 29.3% production (2000).
Income: Per capita income: $16,818 (2000); Median household income: $45,568 (2000); Poverty rate: 5.5% (2000).
Taxes: Total city taxes per capita: $72 (1997); City property taxes per capita: $70 (1997).
Education: High school graduation rate: 80.1% (2000); College graduation rate: 7.8% (2000).
Housing: Homeownership rate: 91.2% (2000); Median home value: $100,000 (2000); Median rent: $419 per month (2000); Median age of housing: 55 years (2000).
Transportation: Commute to work: 76.5% car, 0.0% public transportation, 3.3% walk, 17.5% work from home (2000); Travel time to work: 29.0% less than 15 minutes, 46.2% 15 to 30 minutes, 18.4% 30 to 45 minutes, 2.8% 45 to 60 minutes, 3.5% 60 minutes or more (2000)

MATTOON (village). Covers a land area of 1.633 square miles and a water area of 0 square miles. Located at 45.00° N. Lat.; 89.03° W. Long. Elevation is 1,270 feet.
Population: 466 (2000); Race: 93.7% White, 0.9% Black, 0.0% Asian, 2.0% American Indian and Alaska Native, 0.0% Hispanic of any race, 3.5% two or more races (2000); Density: 285.3 persons per square mile (2000); Age: 29.3% under 18, 13.4% over 64 (2000); Marriage status: 19.3% never married, 58.2% now married, 11.2% widowed, 11.2% divorced (2000); Foreign born: 1.5% (2000); Ancestry (includes multiple ancestries): 56.4% German, 7.4% French (except Basque), 6.5% United States or American, 6.1% Swedish, 5.9% Irish (2000).
Economy: Single-family building permits issued: 0 (2001) / 1 (2000); Multi-family building permits issued: 0 (2001) / 0 (2000); Employment by occupation: 7.0% management, 10.0% professional, 14.4% services, 15.7% sales, 7.4% farming, 12.2% construction, 33.2% production (2000).
Income: Per capita income: $18,969 (2000); Median household income: $34,375 (2000); Poverty rate: 9.4% (2000).
Taxes: Total city taxes per capita: $72 (1997); City property taxes per capita: $65 (1997).
Education: High school graduation rate: 73.0% (2000); College graduation rate: 6.4% (2000).
Housing: Homeownership rate: 74.1% (2000); Median home value: $46,700 (2000); Median rent: $275 per month (2000); Median age of housing: 60+ years (2000).
Transportation: Commute to work: 87.7% car, 1.3% public transportation, 7.9% walk, 3.1% work from home (2000); Travel time to work: 25.0% less than 15 minutes, 43.2% 15 to 30 minutes, 12.7% 30 to 45 minutes, 5.9% 45 to 60 minutes, 13.2% 60 minutes or more (2000)

MORRIS (town). Covers a land area of 36.219 square miles and a water area of 0 square miles. Located at 44.82° N. Lat.; 89.04° W. Long.
Population: 485 (2000); Race: 88.3% White, 0.0% Black, 0.4% Asian, 9.7% American Indian and Alaska Native, 0.0% Hispanic of any race, 1.6% two or more races (2000); Density: 13.4 persons per square mile (2000); Age: 29.3% under 18, 12.7% over 64 (2000); Marriage status: 21.4% never married, 62.9% now married, 6.2% widowed, 9.4% divorced (2000); Foreign born: 2.3% (2000); Ancestry (includes multiple ancestries): 55.8% German, 11.7% Other groups, 11.3% French (except Basque), 8.6% Norwegian, 8.1% Polish (2000).
Economy: Employment by occupation: 10.1% management, 12.9% professional, 21.6% services, 14.7% sales, 4.0% farming, 8.6% construction, 28.1% production (2000).
Income: Per capita income: $14,627 (2000); Median household income: $36,875 (2000); Poverty rate: 17.6% (2000).
Taxes: Total city taxes per capita: $72 (1997); City property taxes per capita: $70 (1997).
Education: High school graduation rate: 80.6% (2000); College graduation rate: 11.0% (2000).
Housing: Homeownership rate: 83.5% (2000); Median home value: $92,000 (2000); Median rent: $370 per month (2000); Median age of housing: 47 years (2000).
Transportation: Commute to work: 88.9% car, 0.0% public transportation, 0.7% walk, 9.6% work from home (2000); Travel time to work: 36.1% less than 15 minutes, 29.1% 15 to 30 minutes, 19.7% 30 to 45 minutes, 5.3% 45 to 60 minutes, 9.8% 60 minutes or more (2000)

NAVARINO (town). Aka Galesburg. Covers a land area of 35.243 squar miles and a water area of 0.500 square miles. Located at 44.63° N. Lat.; 88.54° W. Long. Elevation is 800 feet.
Population: 422 (2000); Race: 98.3% White, 0.0% Black, 0.0% Asian, 0.0% American Indian and Alaska Native, 0.0% Hispanic of any race, 1.7% two o more races (2000); Density: 12.0 persons per square mile (2000); Age: 24.9 under 18, 14.6% over 64 (2000); Marriage status: 20.7% never married, 67.9% now married, 6.0% widowed, 5.4% divorced (2000); Foreign born: 0.7% (2000); Ancestry (includes multiple ancestries): 60.2% German, 9.8% Irish, 9.8% Norwegian, 9.5% Polish, 9.5% United States or American (2000

Economy: Employment by occupation: 6.0% management, 16.5% professional, 19.3% services, 18.8% sales, 0.0% farming, 12.8% construction, 26.6% production (2000).
Income: Per capita income: $21,026 (2000); Median household income: $47,750 (2000); Poverty rate: 1.5% (2000).
Taxes: Total city taxes per capita: $55 (1997); City property taxes per capita: $52 (1997).
Education: High school graduation rate: 85.0% (2000); College graduation rate: 10.4% (2000).
Housing: Homeownership rate: 84.7% (2000); Median home value: $85,300 (2000); Median rent: $389 per month (2000); Median age of housing: 43 years (2000).
Transportation: Commute to work: 88.5% car, 0.0% public transportation, 4.1% walk, 5.5% work from home (2000); Travel time to work: 11.2% less than 15 minutes, 30.6% 15 to 30 minutes, 33.0% 30 to 45 minutes, 20.9% 45 to 60 minutes, 4.4% 60 minutes or more (2000)

PELLA (town). Covers a land area of 36.414 square miles and a water area of 0.345 square miles. Located at 44.73° N. Lat.; 88.80° W. Long. Elevation is 860 feet.
Population: 877 (2000); Race: 99.2% White, 0.0% Black, 0.0% Asian, 0.7% American Indian and Alaska Native, 0.1% Hispanic of any race, 0.0% two or more races (2000); Density: 24.1 persons per square mile (2000); Age: 23.1% under 18, 12.4% over 64 (2000); Marriage status: 25.3% never married, 58.4% now married, 6.6% widowed, 9.7% divorced (2000); Foreign born: 0.2% (2000); Ancestry (includes multiple ancestries): 69.4% German, 6.9% Irish, 4.5% French (except Basque), 4.4% Polish, 4.3% Czech (2000).
Economy: Employment by occupation: 12.7% management, 9.4% professional, 15.2% services, 19.5% sales, 4.3% farming, 16.2% construction, 22.7% production (2000).
Income: Per capita income: $17,926 (2000); Median household income: $40,188 (2000); Poverty rate: 8.5% (2000).
Taxes: Total city taxes per capita: $93 (1997); City property taxes per capita: $92 (1997).
Education: High school graduation rate: 81.6% (2000); College graduation rate: 10.0% (2000).
Housing: Homeownership rate: 86.2% (2000); Median home value: $80,000 (2000); Median rent: $338 per month (2000); Median age of housing: 35 years (2000).
Transportation: Commute to work: 82.3% car, 0.0% public transportation, 4.2% walk, 11.9% work from home (2000); Travel time to work: 21.0% less than 15 minutes, 49.5% 15 to 30 minutes, 11.8% 30 to 45 minutes, 4.0% 45 to 60 minutes, 13.7% 60 minutes or more (2000)

RED SPRINGS (town). Covers a land area of 35.765 square miles and a water area of 0.703 square miles. Located at 44.90° N. Lat.; 88.77° W. Long.
Population: 981 (2000); Race: 45.6% White, 0.0% Black, 1.2% Asian, 50.1% American Indian and Alaska Native, 3.8% Hispanic of any race, 3.1% two or more races (2000); Density: 27.4 persons per square mile (2000); Age: 31.3% under 18, 10.3% over 64 (2000); Marriage status: 30.1% never married, 55.8% now married, 5.6% widowed, 8.5% divorced (2000); Foreign born: 1.3% (2000); Ancestry (includes multiple ancestries): 50.8% Other groups, 26.7% German, 5.2% Irish, 3.7% French (except Basque), 2.4% Polish (2000).
Economy: Employment by occupation: 15.3% management, 14.7% professional, 26.2% services, 16.9% sales, 2.2% farming, 12.1% construction, 12.5% production (2000).
Income: Per capita income: $13,736 (2000); Median household income: $40,833 (2000); Poverty rate: 11.6% (2000).
Taxes: Total city taxes per capita: $90 (1997); City property taxes per capita: $89 (1997).
Education: High school graduation rate: 80.6% (2000); College graduation rate: 13.0% (2000).
Housing: Homeownership rate: 81.5% (2000); Median home value: $90,000 (2000); Median rent: $193 per month (2000); Median age of housing: 20 years (2000).
Transportation: Commute to work: 88.1% car, 2.6% public transportation, 3.0% walk, 2.6% work from home (2000); Travel time to work: 34.9% less than 15 minutes, 34.2% 15 to 30 minutes, 10.5% 30 to 45 minutes, 8.5% 45 to 60 minutes, 11.9% 60 minutes or more (2000)

RICHMOND (town). Covers a land area of 33.639 square miles and a water area of 0.777 square miles. Located at 44.79° N. Lat.; 88.66° W. Long.
Population: 1,719 (2000); Race: 93.8% White, 0.0% Black, 0.3% Asian, 4.8% American Indian and Alaska Native, 0.7% Hispanic of any race, 1.1% two or more races (2000); Density: 51.1 persons per square mile (2000); Age: 23.8% under 18, 12.8% over 64 (2000); Marriage status: 20.8% never married, 67.6% now married, 4.3% widowed, 7.3% divorced (2000); Foreign born: 1.1% (2000); Ancestry (includes multiple ancestries): 62.8% German, 7.6% Irish, 7.4% Other groups, 6.1% Polish, 4.9% English (2000).
Economy: Employment by occupation: 15.2% management, 15.2% professional, 11.3% services, 22.2% sales, 1.6% farming, 13.4% construction, 21.1% production (2000).
Income: Per capita income: $21,628 (2000); Median household income: $43,800 (2000); Poverty rate: 4.1% (2000).
Taxes: Total city taxes per capita: $29 (1997); City property taxes per capita: $19 (1997).
Education: High school graduation rate: 89.4% (2000); College graduation rate: 19.0% (2000).
Housing: Homeownership rate: 90.6% (2000); Median home value: $97,000 (2000); Median rent: $380 per month (2000); Median age of housing: 32 years (2000).
Transportation: Commute to work: 89.9% car, 0.0% public transportation, 2.3% walk, 7.4% work from home (2000); Travel time to work: 46.7% less than 15 minutes, 33.4% 15 to 30 minutes, 9.0% 30 to 45 minutes, 5.8% 45 to 60 minutes, 5.1% 60 minutes or more (2000)

SENECA (town). Covers a land area of 36.567 square miles and a water area of 0.086 square miles. Located at 44.81° N. Lat.; 88.91° W. Long.
Population: 567 (2000); Race: 95.4% White, 0.0% Black, 0.4% Asian, 2.3% American Indian and Alaska Native, 0.0% Hispanic of any race, 2.0% two or more races (2000); Density: 15.5 persons per square mile (2000); Age: 26.8% under 18, 16.9% over 64 (2000); Marriage status: 20.9% never married, 70.7% now married, 4.7% widowed, 3.6% divorced (2000); Foreign born: 0.4% (2000); Ancestry (includes multiple ancestries): 66.3% German, 10.3% Polish, 9.4% Irish, 6.9% Other groups, 6.0% United States or American (2000).
Economy: Employment by occupation: 16.2% management, 7.2% professional, 22.0% services, 16.5% sales, 4.5% farming, 10.3% construction, 23.4% production (2000).
Income: Per capita income: $15,601 (2000); Median household income: $38,750 (2000); Poverty rate: 13.2% (2000).
Taxes: Total city taxes per capita: $68 (1997); City property taxes per capita: $64 (1997).
Education: High school graduation rate: 79.7% (2000); College graduation rate: 6.6% (2000).
Housing: Homeownership rate: 87.2% (2000); Median home value: $66,000 (2000); Median rent: $408 per month (2000); Median age of housing: 53 years (2000).
Transportation: Commute to work: 85.1% car, 1.4% public transportation, 4.3% walk, 7.4% work from home (2000); Travel time to work: 31.0% less than 15 minutes, 38.3% 15 to 30 minutes, 8.4% 30 to 45 minutes, 7.3% 45 to 60 minutes, 14.9% 60 minutes or more (2000)

SHAWANO (city). Covers a land area of 5.970 square miles and a water area of 0.066 square miles. Located at 44.77° N. Lat.; 88.60° W. Long. Elevation is 821 feet.
History: Lumbering began in Shawano in 1843 when Samuel Farnsworth built a mill on the Wolf River, which offered water power and a convenient waterway for floating logs. When the timber industry declined, Shawano turned to paper making, woodworking, and serving tourists. The name of Shawano is of Indian origin, meaning "south."
Population: 8,298 (2000); Race: 88.9% White, 0.4% Black, 0.7% Asian, 7.0% American Indian and Alaska Native, 2.0% Hispanic of any race, 1.9% two or more races (2000); Density: 1,389.9 persons per square mile (2000); Age: 24.0% under 18, 20.4% over 64 (2000); Marriage status: 26.9% never married, 53.9% now married, 9.9% widowed, 9.2% divorced (2000); Foreign born: 1.5% (2000); Ancestry (includes multiple ancestries): 49.6% German, 11.8% Other groups, 8.2% Irish, 4.7% Polish, 4.4% Norwegian (2000).
Economy: Single-family building permits issued: 11 (2001) / 17 (2000); Multi-family building permits issued: 12 (2001) / 14 (2000); Employment by occupation: 9.9% management, 18.6% professional, 18.3% services, 23.2% sales, 0.4% farming, 7.8% construction, 21.9% production (2000).
Income: Per capita income: $17,380 (2000); Median household income: $31,546 (2000); Poverty rate: 9.9% (2000).
Taxes: Total city taxes per capita: $245 (1997); City property taxes per capita: $231 (1997).
Education: High school graduation rate: 80.4% (2000); College graduation rate: 18.5% (2000).

School District(s)

Shawano-Gresham (PK-12)
2000 Enrollment: 2,946 715-526-3194

Housing: Homeownership rate: 60.1% (2000); Median home value: $78,900 (2000); Median rent: $385 per month (2000); Median age of housing: 39 years (2000).
Hospitals: Shawano Medical Center (46 beds)
Safety: Violent crime rate: 4.8 per 10,000 population; Property crime rate: 585.1 per 10,000 population (2001).
Newspapers: Shawano Leader (6 x week)
Transportation: Commute to work: 88.5% car, 0.4% public transportation, 5.6% walk, 3.7% work from home (2000); Travel time to work: 62.8% less than 15 minutes, 20.9% 15 to 30 minutes, 8.0% 30 to 45 minutes, 4.3% 45 to 60 minutes, 4.0% 60 minutes or more (2000)
Additional Information Contacts
Shawano Chamber of Commerce........................715-524-2139

TIGERTON (village). Covers a land area of 1.415 square miles and a water area of 0.025 square miles. Located at 44.74° N. Lat.; 89.05° W. Long. Elevation is 1,030 feet.
History: Tigerton developed as a company town around a large sawmill. Early settlers in the surrounding area were German and Scandinavian farmers who established a cooperative creamery.
Population: 764 (2000); Race: 95.6% White, 0.0% Black, 0.0% Asian, 2.4% American Indian and Alaska Native, 2.7% Hispanic of any race, 0.3% two or more races (2000); Density: 540.1 persons per square mile (2000); Age: 24.2% under 18, 20.5% over 64 (2000); Marriage status: 25.1% never married, 52.0% now married, 13.2% widowed, 9.8% divorced (2000); Foreign born: 1.1% (2000); Ancestry (includes multiple ancestries): 54.4% German, 11.2% Polish, 10.4% Irish, 9.4% Norwegian, 5.3% Other groups (2000).
Economy: Single-family building permits issued: 1 (2001) / 1 (2000); Multi-family building permits issued: 0 (2001) / 0 (2000); Employment by occupation: 7.2% management, 9.0% professional, 19.9% services, 22.3% sales, 2.1% farming, 7.8% construction, 31.6% production (2000).
Income: Per capita income: $14,707 (2000); Median household income: $25,278 (2000); Poverty rate: 15.6% (2000).
Taxes: Total city taxes per capita: $109 (1997); City property taxes per capita: $90 (1997).
Education: High school graduation rate: 73.8% (2000); College graduation rate: 8.3% (2000).

School District(s)

Tigerton (PK-12)
2000 Enrollment: 419 715-535-3220
Housing: Homeownership rate: 56.0% (2000); Median home value: $53,100 (2000); Median rent: $255 per month (2000); Median age of housing: 50 years (2000).
Transportation: Commute to work: 87.5% car, 0.0% public transportation, 9.1% walk, 3.4% work from home (2000); Travel time to work: 46.9% less than 15 minutes, 23.0% 15 to 30 minutes, 20.1% 30 to 45 minutes, 8.1% 45 to 60 minutes, 1.9% 60 minutes or more (2000); Amtrak: Service available.

TILLEDA (unincorporated postal area, zip code 54978). Covers a land area of 3.926 square miles and a water area of 0 square miles. Located at 44.80° N. Lat.; 88.90° W. Long. Elevation is 970 feet.
Population: 44 (2000); Race: 100.0% White, 0.0% Black, 0.0% Asian, 0.0% American Indian and Alaska Native, 0.0% Hispanic of any race, 0.0% two or more races (2000); Density: 11.2 persons per square mile (2000); Age: 18.4% under 18, 16.3% over 64 (2000); Marriage status: 20.9% never married, 69.8% now married, 7.0% widowed, 2.3% divorced (2000); Foreign born: 0.0% (2000); Ancestry (includes multiple ancestries): 83.7% German, 22.4% Czech, 10.2% Irish (2000).
Economy: Employment by occupation: 29.6% management, 0.0% professional, 18.5% services, 29.6% sales, 0.0% farming, 0.0% construction, 22.2% production (2000).
Income: Per capita income: $14,567 (2000); Median household income: $46,750 (2000); Poverty rate: 14.3% (2000).
Education: High school graduation rate: 84.2% (2000); College graduation rate: 0.0% (2000).
Housing: Homeownership rate: 100.0% (2000); Median home value: $71,400 (2000); Median age of housing: 45 years (2000).
Transportation: Commute to work: 56.0% car, 8.0% public transportation, 0.0% walk, 16.0% work from home (2000); Travel time to work: 0.0% less than 15 minutes, 66.7% 15 to 30 minutes, 9.5% 30 to 45 minutes, 0.0% 45 to 60 minutes, 23.8% 60 minutes or more (2000)

WASHINGTON (town). Covers a land area of 35.364 square miles and a water area of 3.619 square miles. Located at 44.80° N. Lat.; 88.46° W. Long.
Population: 1,903 (2000); Race: 93.6% White, 0.2% Black, 0.7% Asian, 5.0% American Indian and Alaska Native, 0.7% Hispanic of any race, 0.4% two or more races (2000); Density: 53.8 persons per square mile (2000); Age: 22.2% under 18, 19.4% over 64 (2000); Marriage status: 18.9% never married, 63.6% now married, 8.4% widowed, 9.1% divorced (2000); Foreign born: 0.8% (2000); Ancestry (includes multiple ancestries): 57.3% German, 8.2% Polish, 7.7% Other groups, 6.8% Irish, 5.0% English (2000).
Economy: Employment by occupation: 18.1% management, 8.3% professional, 15.7% services, 23.6% sales, 1.8% farming, 10.1% construction, 22.4% production (2000).
Income: Per capita income: $20,665 (2000); Median household income: $36,630 (2000); Poverty rate: 6.8% (2000).
Taxes: Total city taxes per capita: $150 (1997); City property taxes per capita: $144 (1997).
Education: High school graduation rate: 83.5% (2000); College graduation rate: 9.4% (2000).
Housing: Homeownership rate: 86.1% (2000); Median home value: $116,600 (2000); Median rent: $417 per month (2000); Median age of housing: 26 years (2000).
Transportation: Commute to work: 87.5% car, 0.0% public transportation, 1.3% walk, 10.7% work from home (2000); Travel time to work: 30.4% less than 15 minutes, 34.9% 15 to 30 minutes, 16.9% 30 to 45 minutes, 11.3% 45 to 60 minutes, 6.6% 60 minutes or more (2000)

WAUKECHON (town). Covers a land area of 35.396 square miles and a water area of 0.500 square miles. Located at 44.73° N. Lat.; 88.54° W. Long.
Population: 928 (2000); Race: 95.2% White, 0.0% Black, 0.9% Asian, 1.6% American Indian and Alaska Native, 0.0% Hispanic of any race, 2.3% two or more races (2000); Density: 26.2 persons per square mile (2000); Age: 29.9% under 18, 11.2% over 64 (2000); Marriage status: 25.0% never married, 64.6% now married, 4.0% widowed, 6.4% divorced (2000); Foreign born: 0.4% (2000); Ancestry (includes multiple ancestries): 61.5% German, 8.5% Norwegian, 8.0% Polish, 5.6% Other groups, 5.5% United States or American (2000).
Economy: Employment by occupation: 15.6% management, 15.8% professional, 15.2% services, 17.2% sales, 5.2% farming, 10.2% construction, 21.0% production (2000).
Income: Per capita income: $18,041 (2000); Median household income: $46,000 (2000); Poverty rate: 3.8% (2000).
Taxes: Total city taxes per capita: $139 (1997); City property taxes per capita: $138 (1997).
Education: High school graduation rate: 82.0% (2000); College graduation rate: 12.9% (2000).
Housing: Homeownership rate: 93.2% (2000); Median home value: $95,700 (2000); Median rent: $550 per month (2000); Median age of housing: 35 years (2000).
Transportation: Commute to work: 81.5% car, 0.0% public transportation, 2.0% walk, 16.3% work from home (2000); Travel time to work: 45.6% less than 15 minutes, 24.7% 15 to 30 minutes, 12.7% 30 to 45 minutes, 13.7% 45 to 60 minutes, 3.4% 60 minutes or more (2000)

WESCOTT (town). Covers a land area of 22.670 square miles and a water area of 7.661 square miles. Located at 44.81° N. Lat.; 88.55° W. Long.
Population: 3,653 (2000); Race: 92.9% White, 0.4% Black, 0.4% Asian, 4.1% American Indian and Alaska Native, 0.4% Hispanic of any race, 1.8% two or more races (2000); Density: 161.1 persons per square mile (2000); Age: 20.9% under 18, 20.3% over 64 (2000); Marriage status: 14.0% never married, 68.9% now married, 7.7% widowed, 9.3% divorced (2000); Foreign born: 1.0% (2000); Ancestry (includes multiple ancestries): 52.5% German, 10.7% Polish, 7.3% Irish, 7.2% Other groups, 6.7% French (except Basque) (2000).
Economy: Employment by occupation: 14.9% management, 13.7% professional, 12.4% services, 23.2% sales, 1.1% farming, 12.0% construction, 22.8% production (2000).
Income: Per capita income: $20,760 (2000); Median household income: $40,060 (2000); Poverty rate: 3.5% (2000).
Taxes: Total city taxes per capita: $150 (1997); City property taxes per capita: $140 (1997).
Education: High school graduation rate: 85.9% (2000); College graduation rate: 12.1% (2000).
Housing: Homeownership rate: 86.2% (2000); Median home value: $100,700 (2000); Median rent: $458 per month (2000); Median age of housing: 31 years (2000).
Transportation: Commute to work: 93.5% car, 0.8% public transportation, 0.6% walk, 4.2% work from home (2000); Travel time to work: 46.5% less

than 15 minutes, 26.5% 15 to 30 minutes, 11.0% 30 to 45 minutes, 10.7% 45 to 60 minutes, 5.3% 60 minutes or more (2000)

WITTENBERG (village). Covers a land area of 1.639 square miles and a water area of 0 square miles. Located at 44.82° N. Lat.; 89.16° W. Long. Elevation is 1,170 feet.
History: Wittenberg was founded during the late 1800's by Norwegian Lutherans under Reverend E.J. Homme, and named for the German town where Martin Luther began the Reformation.
Population: 1,177 (2000); Race: 94.9% White, 0.0% Black, 0.0% Asian, 2.8% American Indian and Alaska Native, 0.3% Hispanic of any race, 2.3% two or more races (2000); Density: 718.2 persons per square mile (2000); Age: 25.4% under 18, 27.9% over 64 (2000); Marriage status: 17.6% never married, 64.1% now married, 8.8% widowed, 9.5% divorced (2000); Foreign born: 1.0% (2000); Ancestry (includes multiple ancestries): 48.1% German, 10.5% Polish, 10.4% Norwegian, 6.5% Irish, 4.5% Other groups (2000).
Economy: Single-family building permits issued: 0 (2001) / 1 (2000); Multi-family building permits issued: 0 (2001) / 0 (2000); Employment by occupation: 10.2% management, 12.8% professional, 22.5% services, 19.5% sales, 0.9% farming, 7.1% construction, 27.1% production (2000).
Income: Per capita income: $17,695 (2000); Median household income: $29,926 (2000); Poverty rate: 12.9% (2000).
Taxes: Total city taxes per capita: $101 (1997); City property taxes per capita: $88 (1997).
Education: High school graduation rate: 70.5% (2000); College graduation rate: 14.1% (2000).

School District(s)

Wittenberg-Birnamwood (PK-12)
2000 Enrollment: 1,449 715-253-2213
Housing: Homeownership rate: 55.3% (2000); Median home value: $68,600 (2000); Median rent: $325 per month (2000); Median age of housing: 52 years (2000).
Newspapers: Enterprise-News (1 x week)
Transportation: Commute to work: 89.1% car, 0.0% public transportation, 8.8% walk, 1.1% work from home (2000); Travel time to work: 51.8% less than 15 minutes, 17.0% 15 to 30 minutes, 24.3% 30 to 45 minutes, 4.4% 45 to 60 minutes, 2.4% 60 minutes or more (2000); Amtrak: Service available.
Additional Information Contacts
Wittenberg Chamber of Commerce 715-253-3525

WITTENBERG (town). Covers a land area of 34.105 square miles and a water area of 0.105 square miles. Located at 44.82° N. Lat.; 89.15° W. Long. Elevation is 1,170 feet.
Population: 894 (2000); Race: 94.7% White, 0.0% Black, 0.0% Asian, 2.0% American Indian and Alaska Native, 0.4% Hispanic of any race, 3.2% two or more races (2000); Density: 26.2 persons per square mile (2000); Age: 32.8% under 18, 15.1% over 64 (2000); Marriage status: 21.5% never married, 65.6% now married, 5.6% widowed, 7.2% divorced (2000); Foreign born: 0.4% (2000); Ancestry (includes multiple ancestries): 52.6% German, 15.1% Polish, 5.6% United States or American, 5.2% Dutch, 5.0% Norwegian (2000).
Economy: Employment by occupation: 14.8% management, 16.4% professional, 12.9% services, 19.6% sales, 2.5% farming, 8.8% construction, 24.9% production (2000).
Income: Per capita income: $15,410 (2000); Median household income: $42,841 (2000); Poverty rate: 6.7% (2000).
Taxes: Total city taxes per capita: $52 (1997); City property taxes per capita: $50 (1997).
Education: High school graduation rate: 82.9% (2000); College graduation rate: 15.4% (2000).
Housing: Homeownership rate: 87.2% (2000); Median home value: $84,700 (2000); Median rent: $317 per month (2000); Median age of housing: 32 years (2000).
Transportation: Commute to work: 87.1% car, 0.0% public transportation, 2.2% walk, 10.3% work from home (2000); Travel time to work: 48.3% less than 15 minutes, 16.5% 15 to 30 minutes, 23.2% 30 to 45 minutes, 7.7% 45 to 60 minutes, 4.3% 60 minutes or more (2000); Amtrak: Service available.

Sheboygan County

Located in eastern Wisconsin; bounded on the east by Lake Michigan; drained by the Sheboygan River. Covers a land area of 513.60 square miles, a water area of 757.30 square miles, and is located in the Central Time Zone. The county government was organized in 1836. County seat is Sheboygan.

Sheboygan County is part of the Sheboygan, WI MSA. The entire metro area includes: Sheboygan County

Weather Station: Plymouth — Elevation: 833 feet

	Jan	Feb	Mar	Apr	May	Jun	Jul	Aug	Sep	Oct	Nov	Dec
High	26	31	41	55	68	77	82	79	71	59	44	31
Low	10	14	24	35	45	55	60	59	51	40	28	17
Precip	1.4	1.2	2.4	3.4	3.8	3.8	3.9	4.4	4.1	3.0	2.9	1.9
Snow	15.1	11.9	10.6	3.6	0.2	0.0	0.0	0.0	0.0	0.2	5.4	13.4

High and Low temperatures in degrees Fahrenheit; Precipitation and Snow in inches

Weather Station: Sheboygan — Elevation: 646 feet

	Jan	Feb	Mar	Apr	May	Jun	Jul	Aug	Sep	Oct	Nov	Dec
High	28	33	41	52	64	75	81	79	72	59	45	33
Low	13	18	26	36	45	55	62	61	54	43	31	20
Precip	1.6	1.3	2.2	2.9	2.9	3.2	3.1	3.9	3.3	2.6	2.4	1.9
Snow	14.4	9.8	7.9	1.9	tr	0.0	0.0	0.0	0.0	0.1	3.0	9.2

High and Low temperatures in degrees Fahrenheit; Precipitation and Snow in inches

Population: 112,646 (2000); Race: 92.5% White, 1.2% Black, 3.2% Asian, 0.3% American Indian and Alaska Native, 3.3% Hispanic of any race, 1.3% two or more races (2000); Density: 219.3 persons per square mile (2000); Age: 25.5% under 18, 14.0% over 64 (2000).
Religion: Five largest groups: 26.6% Catholic Church, 16.6% Lutheran Church—Missouri Synod, 8.1% United Church of Christ, 4.6% Reformed Church in America, 3.9% Evangelical Lutheran Church in America (2000).
Economy: Unemployment rate: 4.3% (11/2002); Total civilian labor force: 61,971 (11/2002); Leading industries: 39.7% manufacturing; 10.7% retail trade; 9.7% health care and social assistance (2000); Companies that employ more than 1,000 persons: 5 (2000); Companies that employ more than 100 persons: 97 (2000); Farms: 968 totaling 182,460 acres (1997); Minority business ownership rate: 1.6% (1997); Women business ownership rate: 31.5% (1997); Retail sales per capita: $8,298 (1997). Single-family building permits issued: 386 (2001) / 361 (2000); Multi-family building permits issued: 239 (2001) / 314 (2000).
Income: Per capita income: $21,509 (2000); Median household income: $46,237 (2000); Poverty rate: 5.2% (2000); Bankruptcy rate: 2.67% (2001).
Taxes: Total county taxes per capita: $245 (2000); County property taxes per capita: $242 (2000).
Education: High school graduation rate: 84.4% (2000); College graduation rate: 17.9% (2000).
Housing: Homeownership rate: 71.4% (2000); Median home value: $106,800 (2000); Median rent: $418 per month (2000); Median age of housing: 41 years (2000).
Health: Birth rate: 117.5 per 10,000 population (1998); Age adjusted death rate: 81.9 per 10,000 population (1999); Age adjusted cancer mortality rate: 185.7 deaths per 100,000 population (1999). Air Quality Index: 64% good, 34% moderate, 2% unhealthy (percent of days in 2000). Number of physicians: 13.2 per 10,000 population (1999); Number of hospital beds: 43.9 per 10,000 population (1999).
Elections: 2000 Presidential election results: 42.7% Gore, 53.7% Bush, 2.7% Nader, 0.5% Buchanan
National and State Parks: La Budde Creek State Wildlife Area; Nichols Creek State Wildlife Area; Old Wade House State Park; Sheboygan Marsh State Wildlife Area; Terry Andrae State Park
Additional Information Contacts
Sheboygan County Government Offices 920-459-3003
Elkhart Lake Chamber of Commerce. 920-876-2922
Plymouth Chamber of Commerce 920-893-0079
Sheboygan Chamber of Commerce 920-457-9491
Sheboygan County Board of Realtors 920-457-7908
Sheboygan Falls Chamber of Commerce. 920-467-6206

Sheboygan County Communities

ADELL (village). Covers a land area of 0.507 square miles and a water area of 0.007 square miles. Located at 43.61° N. Lat.; 87.95° W. Long. Elevation is 905 feet.
Population: 517 (2000); Race: 97.2% White, 0.0% Black, 0.0% Asian, 0.0% American Indian and Alaska Native, 5.1% Hispanic of any race, 0.0% two or more races (2000); Density: 1,019.5 persons per square mile (2000); Age: 29.2% under 18, 13.7% over 64 (2000); Marriage status: 23.1% never married, 58.9% now married, 6.3% widowed, 11.8% divorced (2000); Foreign born: 1.1% (2000); Ancestry (includes multiple ancestries): 53.6% German, 10.7% Irish, 9.4% United States or American, 8.2% Other groups, 6.2% Polish (2000).

Economy: In dairy and grain area. Manufactures food, wood products. Single-family building permits issued: 0 (2001) / 0 (2000); Multi-family building permits issued: 0 (2001) / 0 (2000); Employment by occupation: 10.6% management, 11.4% professional, 11.0% services, 14.3% sales, 0.4% farming, 17.2% construction, 35.2% production (2000).
Income: Per capita income: $21,166 (2000); Median household income: $51,000 (2000); Poverty rate: 3.6% (2000).
Taxes: Total city taxes per capita: $182 (1997); City property taxes per capita: $175 (1997).
Education: High school graduation rate: 77.4% (2000); College graduation rate: 13.4% (2000).
Housing: Homeownership rate: 68.1% (2000); Median home value: $113,400 (2000); Median rent: $390 per month (2000); Median age of housing: 45 years (2000).
Transportation: Commute to work: 93.6% car, 1.5% public transportation, 2.3% walk, 1.1% work from home (2000); Travel time to work: 33.1% less than 15 minutes, 40.3% 15 to 30 minutes, 13.3% 30 to 45 minutes, 7.6% 45 to 60 minutes, 5.7% 60 minutes or more (2000)

CASCADE (village). Covers a land area of 0.743 square miles and a water area of 0.007 square miles. Located at 43.65° N. Lat.; 88.00° W. Long. Elevation is 890 feet.
Population: 666 (2000); Race: 99.3% White, 0.0% Black, 0.0% Asian, 0.0% American Indian and Alaska Native, 3.3% Hispanic of any race, 0.7% two or more races (2000); Density: 895.8 persons per square mile (2000); Age: 25.7% under 18, 14.9% over 64 (2000); Marriage status: 18.0% never married, 67.1% now married, 5.7% widowed, 9.3% divorced (2000); Foreign born: 0.7% (2000); Ancestry (includes multiple ancestries): 55.8% German, 14.3% Irish, 6.0% Dutch, 5.7% English, 5.4% Other groups (2000).
Economy: Dairy and grain area. Cheese. Single-family building permits issued: 3 (2001) / 3 (2000); Multi-family building permits issued: 0 (2001) / 0 (2000); Employment by occupation: 4.8% management, 9.5% professional, 16.4% services, 17.6% sales, 2.4% farming, 11.3% construction, 38.1% production (2000).
Income: Per capita income: $20,617 (2000); Median household income: $47,232 (2000); Poverty rate: 6.6% (2000).
Taxes: Total city taxes per capita: $59 (1997); City property taxes per capita: $56 (1997).
Education: High school graduation rate: 83.1% (2000); College graduation rate: 9.5% (2000).
Housing: Homeownership rate: 81.2% (2000); Median home value: $99,100 (2000); Median rent: $445 per month (2000); Median age of housing: 50 years (2000).
Transportation: Commute to work: 95.0% car, 0.0% public transportation, 1.3% walk, 2.5% work from home (2000); Travel time to work: 25.6% less than 15 minutes, 50.5% 15 to 30 minutes, 12.9% 30 to 45 minutes, 2.6% 45 to 60 minutes, 8.4% 60 minutes or more (2000)

CEDAR GROVE (village). Covers a land area of 2.056 square miles and a water area of 0 square miles. Located at 43.56° N. Lat.; 87.82° W. Long. Elevation is 711 feet.
Population: 1,887 (2000); Race: 97.8% White, 0.0% Black, 0.1% Asian, 0.7% American Indian and Alaska Native, 1.5% Hispanic of any race, 1.3% two or more races (2000); Density: 917.9 persons per square mile (2000); Age: 29.2% under 18, 15.2% over 64 (2000); Marriage status: 20.5% never married, 67.8% now married, 5.2% widowed, 6.4% divorced (2000); Foreign born: 0.8% (2000); Ancestry (includes multiple ancestries): 42.5% Dutch, 39.1% German, 5.8% Irish, 4.9% English, 4.5% Luxemburger (2000).
Economy: In dairy and grain area. Manufacturing: iron castings, vegetable packing (peas, corn, lima beans). Single-family building permits issued: 9 (2001) / 4 (2000); Multi-family building permits issued: 8 (2001) / 8 (2000); Employment by occupation: 10.2% management, 18.4% professional, 15.3% services, 21.7% sales, 1.0% farming, 8.8% construction, 24.6% production (2000).
Income: Per capita income: $20,658 (2000); Median household income: $49,674 (2000); Poverty rate: 2.4% (2000).
Taxes: Total city taxes per capita: $229 (1997); City property taxes per capita: $224 (1997).
Education: High school graduation rate: 88.3% (2000); College graduation rate: 18.6% (2000).

School District(s)

Cedar Grove-Belgium Area (PK-12)
2000 Enrollment: 1,001 920-668-8686
Housing: Homeownership rate: 76.8% (2000); Median home value: $117,400 (2000); Median rent: $458 per month (2000); Median age of housing: 38 years (2000).
Transportation: Commute to work: 90.9% car, 0.3% public transportation, 3.6% walk, 4.0% work from home (2000); Travel time to work: 30.7% less than 15 minutes, 45.6% 15 to 30 minutes, 15.2% 30 to 45 minutes, 6.4% 45 to 60 minutes, 2.1% 60 minutes or more (2000)

ELKHART LAKE (village). Covers a land area of 1.292 square miles and a water area of 0 square miles. Located at 43.83° N. Lat.; 88.01° W. Long. Elevation is 938 feet.
Population: 1,021 (2000); Race: 97.9% White, 0.0% Black, 0.1% Asian, 0.6% American Indian and Alaska Native, 2.2% Hispanic of any race, 1.4% two or more races (2000); Density: 790.5 persons per square mile (2000); Age: 18.0% under 18, 16.5% over 64 (2000); Marriage status: 24.3% never married, 58.8% now married, 7.6% widowed, 9.4% divorced (2000); Foreign born: 0.8% (2000); Ancestry (includes multiple ancestries): 63.8% German, 9.7% Irish, 5.7% Norwegian, 4.8% Polish, 4.4% Other groups (2000).
Economy: In dairy and grain area. Manufacturing: aluminum castings, sausage, metal fabrication, plastic and metal windows, labels; cannery. Summer resort. Single-family building permits issued: 1 (2001) / 1 (2000); Multi-family building permits issued: 6 (2001) / 16 (2000); Employment by occupation: 14.0% management, 22.0% professional, 14.0% services, 17.5% sales, 2.0% farming, 7.5% construction, 22.9% production (2000).
Income: Per capita income: $27,873 (2000); Median household income: $56,538 (2000); Poverty rate: 2.3% (2000).
Taxes: Total city taxes per capita: $508 (1997); City property taxes per capita: $488 (1997).
Education: High school graduation rate: 85.8% (2000); College graduation rate: 25.2% (2000).

School District(s)

Elkhart Lake-Glenbeulah (PK-12)
2000 Enrollment: 592 920-876-3381
Housing: Homeownership rate: 76.9% (2000); Median home value: $118,400 (2000); Median rent: $531 per month (2000); Median age of housing: 42 years (2000).
Safety: Violent crime rate: 0.0 per 10,000 population; Property crime rate: 457.2 per 10,000 population (2001).
Transportation: Commute to work: 88.8% car, 0.0% public transportation, 5.6% walk, 4.9% work from home (2000); Travel time to work: 41.2% less than 15 minutes, 42.2% 15 to 30 minutes, 7.8% 30 to 45 minutes, 1.2% 45 to 60 minutes, 7.5% 60 minutes or more (2000)
Additional Information Contacts
Elkhart Lake Chamber of Commerce. 920-876-2922

GLENBEULAH (village). Covers a land area of 0.671 square miles and a water area of 0.014 square miles. Located at 43.79° N. Lat.; 88.04° W. Long. Elevation is 980 feet.
Population: 378 (2000); Race: 99.5% White, 0.0% Black, 0.0% Asian, 0.0% American Indian and Alaska Native, 0.5% Hispanic of any race, 0.0% two or more races (2000); Density: 563.2 persons per square mile (2000); Age: 28.5% under 18, 13.9% over 64 (2000); Marriage status: 22.2% never married, 65.3% now married, 5.8% widowed, 6.8% divorced (2000); Foreign born: 0.5% (2000); Ancestry (includes multiple ancestries): 65.6% German, 9.6% Irish, 8.4% Dutch, 7.4% United States or American, 5.5% English (2000).
Economy: In dairy and grain area. Light manufacturing. Single-family building permits issued: 1 (2001) / 0 (2000); Multi-family building permits issued: 0 (2001) / 0 (2000); Employment by occupation: 7.8% management, 12.9% professional, 13.4% services, 19.0% sales, 0.0% farming, 15.1% construction, 31.9% production (2000).
Income: Per capita income: $17,240 (2000); Median household income: $42,656 (2000); Poverty rate: 1.9% (2000).
Taxes: Total city taxes per capita: $90 (1997); City property taxes per capita: $74 (1997).
Education: High school graduation rate: 84.2% (2000); College graduation rate: 11.8% (2000).
Housing: Homeownership rate: 84.8% (2000); Median home value: $84,500 (2000); Median rent: $368 per month (2000); Median age of housing: 60+ years (2000).
Transportation: Commute to work: 92.0% car, 0.9% public transportation, 7.1% walk, 0.0% work from home (2000); Travel time to work: 47.3% less than 15 minutes, 42.0% 15 to 30 minutes, 9.3% 30 to 45 minutes, 0.0% 45 to 60 minutes, 1.3% 60 minutes or more (2000)

GREENBUSH (town). Covers a land area of 47.150 square miles and a water area of 0.255 square miles. Located at 43.77° N. Lat.; 88.10° W. Long. Elevation is 972 feet.

Population: 2,773 (2000); Race: 75.0% White, 23.0% Black, 0.5% Asian, 1.3% American Indian and Alaska Native, 4.4% Hispanic of any race, 0.1% two or more races (2000); Density: 58.8 persons per square mile (2000); Age: 15.5% under 18, 4.7% over 64 (2000); Marriage status: 10.2% never married, 84.1% now married, 2.3% widowed, 3.4% divorced (2000); Foreign born: 0.3% (2000); Ancestry (includes multiple ancestries): 35.7% German, 4.4% Irish, 4.1% English, 3.6% Dutch, 3.3% United States or American (2000).
Economy: Single-family building permits issued: 5 (2001) / 11 (2000); Multi-family building permits issued: 0 (2001) / 0 (2000); Employment by occupation: 15.5% management, 15.9% professional, 11.5% services, 17.6% sales, 3.3% farming, 10.7% construction, 25.5% production (2000).
Income: Per capita income: $17,050 (2000); Median household income: $54,118 (2000); Poverty rate: 2.5% (2000).
Taxes: Total city taxes per capita: $11 (1997); City property taxes per capita: $10 (1997).
Education: High school graduation rate: 80.6% (2000); College graduation rate: 10.9% (2000).
Housing: Homeownership rate: 93.0% (2000); Median home value: $133,500 (2000); Median rent: $319 per month (2000); Median age of housing: 27 years (2000).
Transportation: Commute to work: 88.9% car, 1.4% public transportation, 2.8% walk, 6.4% work from home (2000); Travel time to work: 29.4% less than 15 minutes, 44.6% 15 to 30 minutes, 15.3% 30 to 45 minutes, 4.8% 45 to 60 minutes, 5.9% 60 minutes or more (2000)

HERMAN (town). Covers a land area of 34.126 square miles and a water area of 0.108 square miles. Located at 43.85° N. Lat.; 87.86° W. Long.
Population: 2,044 (2000); Race: 94.5% White, 3.2% Black, 0.9% Asian, 0.0% American Indian and Alaska Native, 0.4% Hispanic of any race, 1.0% two or more races (2000); Density: 59.9 persons per square mile (2000); Age: 19.5% under 18, 10.2% over 64 (2000); Marriage status: 40.6% never married, 51.8% now married, 3.7% widowed, 4.0% divorced (2000); Foreign born: 4.0% (2000); Ancestry (includes multiple ancestries): 61.6% German, 5.9% Polish, 4.4% Other groups, 4.3% Irish, 3.7% United States or American (2000).
Economy: Single-family building permits issued: 9 (2001) / 9 (2000); Multi-family building permits issued: 0 (2001) / 0 (2000); Employment by occupation: 12.9% management, 13.2% professional, 16.5% services, 23.2% sales, 1.2% farming, 9.1% construction, 23.8% production (2000).
Income: Per capita income: $24,007 (2000); Median household income: $51,875 (2000); Poverty rate: 5.3% (2000).
Taxes: Total city taxes per capita: $40 (1997); City property taxes per capita: $38 (1997).
Education: High school graduation rate: 83.8% (2000); College graduation rate: 15.6% (2000).
Housing: Homeownership rate: 80.9% (2000); Median home value: $108,600 (2000); Median rent: $398 per month (2000); Median age of housing: 57 years (2000).
Transportation: Commute to work: 81.5% car, 0.8% public transportation, 13.9% walk, 3.1% work from home (2000); Travel time to work: 36.4% less than 15 minutes, 56.0% 15 to 30 minutes, 4.3% 30 to 45 minutes, 0.7% 45 to 60 minutes, 2.7% 60 minutes or more (2000)

HOLLAND (town). Covers a land area of 40.857 square miles and a water area of 0.014 square miles. Located at 43.58° N. Lat.; 87.83° W. Long.
Population: 2,360 (2000); Race: 97.6% White, 1.0% Black, 0.3% Asian, 0.0% American Indian and Alaska Native, 0.8% Hispanic of any race, 0.5% two or more races (2000); Density: 57.8 persons per square mile (2000); Age: 28.0% under 18, 10.5% over 64 (2000); Marriage status: 21.5% never married, 70.8% now married, 3.3% widowed, 4.4% divorced (2000); Foreign born: 1.7% (2000); Ancestry (includes multiple ancestries): 35.7% Dutch, 34.3% German, 10.9% United States or American, 5.8% Polish, 5.6% English (2000).
Economy: Single-family building permits issued: 10 (2001) / 8 (2000); Multi-family building permits issued: 0 (2001) / 0 (2000); Employment by occupation: 12.7% management, 11.5% professional, 12.3% services, 20.5% sales, 2.1% farming, 10.6% construction, 30.3% production (2000).
Income: Per capita income: $23,195 (2000); Median household income: $57,419 (2000); Poverty rate: 1.2% (2000).
Taxes: Total city taxes per capita: $112 (1997); City property taxes per capita: $108 (1997).
Education: High school graduation rate: 89.9% (2000); College graduation rate: 17.0% (2000).
Housing: Homeownership rate: 91.3% (2000); Median home value: $148,500 (2000); Median rent: $484 per month (2000); Median age of housing: 46 years (2000).
Transportation: Commute to work: 88.7% car, 0.3% public transportation, 2.0% walk, 8.6% work from home (2000); Travel time to work: 31.4% less than 15 minutes, 42.5% 15 to 30 minutes, 15.1% 30 to 45 minutes, 4.2% 45 to 60 minutes, 6.8% 60 minutes or more (2000)

HOWARDS GROVE (village). Aka Howards Grove-Millersville. Covers a land area of 2.146 square miles and a water area of 0 square miles. Located at 43.83° N. Lat.; 87.82° W. Long. Elevation is 720 feet.
Population: 2,792 (2000); Race: 98.2% White, 0.1% Black, 0.3% Asian, 0.1% American Indian and Alaska Native, 1.9% Hispanic of any race, 0.2% two or more races (2000); Density: 1,301.2 persons per square mile (2000); Age: 29.7% under 18, 10.9% over 64 (2000); Marriage status: 20.6% never married, 69.7% now married, 5.1% widowed, 4.6% divorced (2000); Foreign born: 1.9% (2000); Ancestry (includes multiple ancestries): 67.6% German, 7.1% Dutch, 6.1% Irish, 5.1% Polish, 4.1% English (2000).
Economy: Dairying, grain, fruit, vegetables. Manufacturing: wood pallets. Single-family building permits issued: 17 (2001) / 20 (2000); Multi-family building permits issued: 2 (2001) / 0 (2000); Employment by occupation: 11.6% management, 16.4% professional, 11.2% services, 27.7% sales, 0.3% farming, 6.8% construction, 26.1% production (2000).
Income: Per capita income: $21,913 (2000); Median household income: $59,032 (2000); Poverty rate: 2.8% (2000).
Taxes: Total city taxes per capita: $118 (1997); City property taxes per capita: $110 (1997).
Education: High school graduation rate: 89.4% (2000); College graduation rate: 20.8% (2000).

School District(s)

Howards Grove (PK-12)
2000 Enrollment: 995 920-565-4454

Housing: Homeownership rate: 81.4% (2000); Median home value: $127,000 (2000); Median rent: $426 per month (2000); Median age of housing: 23 years (2000).
Transportation: Commute to work: 95.9% car, 0.0% public transportation, 0.9% walk, 2.3% work from home (2000); Travel time to work: 45.1% less than 15 minutes, 49.6% 15 to 30 minutes, 2.4% 30 to 45 minutes, 1.0% 45 to 60 minutes, 1.8% 60 minutes or more (2000)

KOHLER (village). Covers a land area of 5.440 square miles and a water area of 0.113 square miles. Located at 43.73° N. Lat.; 87.78° W. Long. Elevation is 676 feet.
History: The Kohler plumbing-fixtures plant here, which still produces its famous stainless steel and porcelain products, has been the scene of some of the longest and most bitter labor disputes in U.S. history. The last strike began in 1954 and ended in 1962. Incorporated 1912.
Population: 1,926 (2000); Race: 98.6% White, 0.0% Black, 0.0% Asian, 0.0% American Indian and Alaska Native, 1.8% Hispanic of any race, 1.1% two or more races (2000); Density: 354.0 persons per square mile (2000); Age: 30.9% under 18, 10.9% over 64 (2000); Marriage status: 16.5% never married, 72.0% now married, 5.7% widowed, 5.8% divorced (2000); Foreign born: 2.8% (2000); Ancestry (includes multiple ancestries): 52.7% German, 14.1% Irish, 6.7% English, 6.3% Polish, 4.4% Swedish (2000).
Economy: Manufacturing: plumbing fixtures. Single-family building permits issued: 11 (2001) / 12 (2000); Multi-family building permits issued: 0 (2001) / 0 (2000); Employment by occupation: 21.0% management, 31.8% professional, 8.2% services, 22.1% sales, 0.0% farming, 5.6% construction, 11.4% production (2000).
Income: Per capita income: $39,355 (2000); Median household income: $75,000 (2000); Poverty rate: 2.8% (2000).
Taxes: Total city taxes per capita: $914 (1997); City property taxes per capita: $779 (1997).
Education: High school graduation rate: 98.5% (2000); College graduation rate: 53.0% (2000).

School District(s)

Kohler (PK-12)
2000 Enrollment: 519 920-459-2920

Housing: Homeownership rate: 91.9% (2000); Median home value: $144,400 (2000); Median rent: $469 per month (2000); Median age of housing: 47 years (2000).
Safety: Violent crime rate: 5.2 per 10,000 population; Property crime rate: 283.5 per 10,000 population (2001).
Transportation: Commute to work: 82.5% car, 0.0% public transportation, 9.3% walk, 2.4% work from home (2000); Travel time to work: 67.2% less than 15 minutes, 24.1% 15 to 30 minutes, 3.0% 30 to 45 minutes, 2.8% 45 to 60 minutes, 2.9% 60 minutes or more (2000)

LIMA (town). Covers a land area of 36.574 square miles and a water area of 0.061 square miles. Located at 43.66° N. Lat.; 87.86° W. Long.
Population: 2,948 (2000); Race: 98.5% White, 0.0% Black, 0.0% Asian, 0.0% American Indian and Alaska Native, 1.9% Hispanic of any race, 0.4% two or more races (2000); Density: 80.6 persons per square mile (2000); Age: 25.8% under 18, 12.2% over 64 (2000); Marriage status: 19.6% never married, 70.4% now married, 4.7% widowed, 5.4% divorced (2000); Foreign born: 1.1% (2000); Ancestry (includes multiple ancestries): 48.3% German, 31.2% Dutch, 4.7% Irish, 4.4% English, 4.3% Polish (2000).
Economy: Single-family building permits issued: 14 (2001) / 14 (2000); Multi-family building permits issued: 6 (2001) / 0 (2000); Employment by occupation: 10.6% management, 15.7% professional, 10.5% services, 21.2% sales, 1.9% farming, 12.6% construction, 27.6% production (2000).
Income: Per capita income: $21,175 (2000); Median household income: $53,023 (2000); Poverty rate: 0.5% (2000).
Taxes: Total city taxes per capita: $30 (1997); City property taxes per capita: $26 (1997).
Education: High school graduation rate: 84.1% (2000); College graduation rate: 13.8% (2000).
Housing: Homeownership rate: 88.9% (2000); Median home value: $118,500 (2000); Median rent: $432 per month (2000); Median age of housing: 37 years (2000).
Transportation: Commute to work: 94.3% car, 0.0% public transportation, 1.9% walk, 3.4% work from home (2000); Travel time to work: 45.0% less than 15 minutes, 46.1% 15 to 30 minutes, 3.7% 30 to 45 minutes, 2.2% 45 to 60 minutes, 3.1% 60 minutes or more (2000)

LYNDON (town). Covers a land area of 34.164 square miles and a water area of 0.201 square miles. Located at 43.67° N. Lat.; 87.98° W. Long.
Population: 1,468 (2000); Race: 98.8% White, 0.1% Black, 0.0% Asian, 0.2% American Indian and Alaska Native, 0.6% Hispanic of any race, 0.8% two or more races (2000); Density: 43.0 persons per square mile (2000); Age: 25.9% under 18, 10.2% over 64 (2000); Marriage status: 21.8% never married, 70.6% now married, 2.3% widowed, 5.3% divorced (2000); Foreign born: 0.4% (2000); Ancestry (includes multiple ancestries): 55.8% German, 11.7% Irish, 6.4% Dutch, 5.7% English, 5.0% French (except Basque) (2000).
Economy: Single-family building permits issued: 5 (2001) / 7 (2000); Multi-family building permits issued: 0 (2001) / 0 (2000); Employment by occupation: 12.6% management, 18.6% professional, 8.4% services, 20.1% sales, 1.7% farming, 12.3% construction, 26.3% production (2000).
Income: Per capita income: $21,727 (2000); Median household income: $56,121 (2000); Poverty rate: 5.5% (2000).
Taxes: Total city taxes per capita: $83 (1997); City property taxes per capita: $81 (1997).
Education: High school graduation rate: 87.9% (2000); College graduation rate: 18.7% (2000).
Housing: Homeownership rate: 87.6% (2000); Median home value: $125,300 (2000); Median rent: $491 per month (2000); Median age of housing: 46 years (2000).
Transportation: Commute to work: 89.0% car, 0.0% public transportation, 5.7% walk, 4.8% work from home (2000); Travel time to work: 34.1% less than 15 minutes, 40.8% 15 to 30 minutes, 12.9% 30 to 45 minutes, 7.0% 45 to 60 minutes, 5.2% 60 minutes or more (2000)

MITCHELL (town). Covers a land area of 36.139 square miles and a water area of 0.034 square miles. Located at 43.67° N. Lat.; 88.10° W. Long.
Population: 1,132 (2000); Race: 99.0% White, 0.0% Black, 0.0% Asian, 0.8% American Indian and Alaska Native, 0.7% Hispanic of any race, 0.2% two or more races (2000); Density: 31.3 persons per square mile (2000); Age: 25.7% under 18, 12.0% over 64 (2000); Marriage status: 20.7% never married, 66.0% now married, 5.4% widowed, 8.0% divorced (2000); Foreign born: 2.0% (2000); Ancestry (includes multiple ancestries): 53.8% German, 10.4% Irish, 8.5% Polish, 8.0% United States or American, 7.2% English (2000).
Economy: Single-family building permits issued: 14 (2001) / 11 (2000); Multi-family building permits issued: 0 (2001) / 0 (2000); Employment by occupation: 10.9% management, 14.7% professional, 12.8% services, 17.5% sales, 3.1% farming, 12.8% construction, 28.2% production (2000).
Income: Per capita income: $23,896 (2000); Median household income: $56,875 (2000); Poverty rate: 2.8% (2000).
Taxes: Total city taxes per capita: $78 (1997); City property taxes per capita: $72 (1997).
Education: High school graduation rate: 85.4% (2000); College graduation rate: 13.9% (2000).
Housing: Homeownership rate: 92.0% (2000); Median home value: $139,900 (2000); Median rent: $495 per month (2000); Median age of housing: 26 years (2000).
Transportation: Commute to work: 91.8% car, 0.8% public transportation, 1.6% walk, 5.8% work from home (2000); Travel time to work: 15.9% less than 15 minutes, 44.2% 15 to 30 minutes, 24.8% 30 to 45 minutes, 8.7% 45 to 60 minutes, 6.4% 60 minutes or more (2000)

MOSEL (town). Covers a land area of 21.138 square miles and a water area of 0 square miles. Located at 43.84° N. Lat.; 87.76° W. Long. Elevation is 642 feet.
Population: 839 (2000); Race: 97.7% White, 0.0% Black, 0.5% Asian, 0.0% American Indian and Alaska Native, 3.3% Hispanic of any race, 0.5% two or more races (2000); Density: 39.7 persons per square mile (2000); Age: 23.4% under 18, 10.5% over 64 (2000); Marriage status: 21.3% never married, 68.8% now married, 4.7% widowed, 5.1% divorced (2000); Foreign born: 1.3% (2000); Ancestry (includes multiple ancestries): 66.8% German, 6.7% Dutch, 6.3% Polish, 5.7% Other groups, 5.5% Irish (2000).
Economy: Single-family building permits issued: 1 (2001) / 1 (2000); Multi-family building permits issued: 0 (2001) / 0 (2000); Employment by occupation: 11.8% management, 13.3% professional, 10.1% services, 19.4% sales, 3.2% farming, 12.8% construction, 29.5% production (2000).
Income: Per capita income: $21,953 (2000); Median household income: $55,833 (2000); Poverty rate: 1.4% (2000).
Taxes: Total city taxes per capita: $135 (1997); City property taxes per capita: $133 (1997).
Education: High school graduation rate: 89.8% (2000); College graduation rate: 16.2% (2000).
Housing: Homeownership rate: 87.5% (2000); Median home value: $114,100 (2000); Median rent: $417 per month (2000); Median age of housing: 54 years (2000).
Transportation: Commute to work: 89.0% car, 0.4% public transportation, 4.0% walk, 6.6% work from home (2000); Travel time to work: 40.2% less than 15 minutes, 46.8% 15 to 30 minutes, 6.6% 30 to 45 minutes, 2.8% 45 to 60 minutes, 3.5% 60 minutes or more (2000)

OOSTBURG (village). Covers a land area of 1.878 square miles and a water area of 0 square miles. Located at 43.62° N. Lat.; 87.79° W. Long. Elevation is 700 feet.
History: Oostburg was settled in the late 1840's by immigrants from Holland who came seeking religious freedom. The early economy of Oostburg was supported by fishing, a milk condensery, and canning factories.
Population: 2,660 (2000); Race: 99.7% White, 0.0% Black, 0.0% Asian, 0.0% American Indian and Alaska Native, 1.0% Hispanic of any race, 0.0% two or more races (2000); Density: 1,416.2 persons per square mile (2000); Age: 28.7% under 18, 15.7% over 64 (2000); Marriage status: 20.2% never married, 70.0% now married, 6.6% widowed, 3.1% divorced (2000); Foreign born: 0.7% (2000); Ancestry (includes multiple ancestries): 55.0% Dutch, 26.3% German, 4.2% Polish, 3.7% United States or American, 3.3% Norwegian (2000).
Economy: Single-family building permits issued: 9 (2001) / 11 (2000); Multi-family building permits issued: 6 (2001) / 8 (2000); Employment by occupation: 10.7% management, 16.1% professional, 11.1% services, 27.3% sales, 0.0% farming, 10.1% construction, 24.8% production (2000).
Income: Per capita income: $19,958 (2000); Median household income: $47,469 (2000); Poverty rate: 0.8% (2000).
Taxes: Total city taxes per capita: $161 (1997); City property taxes per capita: $155 (1997).
Education: High school graduation rate: 88.1% (2000); College graduation rate: 22.0% (2000).

School District(s)

Oostburg (PK-12)
2000 Enrollment: 947 920-564-2346
Housing: Homeownership rate: 75.8% (2000); Median home value: $113,200 (2000); Median rent: $385 per month (2000); Median age of housing: 25 years (2000).
Transportation: Commute to work: 93.5% car, 0.0% public transportation, 3.3% walk, 2.3% work from home (2000); Travel time to work: 42.6% less than 15 minutes, 45.0% 15 to 30 minutes, 7.5% 30 to 45 minutes, 2.1% 45 to 60 minutes, 2.9% 60 minutes or more (2000)

PLYMOUTH (city). Covers a land area of 4.105 square miles and a water area of 0.063 square miles. Located at 43.74° N. Lat.; 87.97° W. Long. Elevation is 860 feet.
Population: 7,781 (2000); Race: 98.5% White, 0.1% Black, 0.7% Asian, 0.0% American Indian and Alaska Native, 1.4% Hispanic of any race, 0.7%

two or more races (2000); Density: 1,895.5 persons per square mile (2000); Age: 25.0% under 18, 16.4% over 64 (2000); Marriage status: 22.9% never married, 58.1% now married, 8.9% widowed, 10.1% divorced (2000); Foreign born: 1.9% (2000); Ancestry (includes multiple ancestries): 62.2% German, 12.4% Irish, 6.7% United States or American, 5.6% English, 5.0% Polish (2000).
Economy: Single-family building permits issued: 17 (2001) / 16 (2000); Multi-family building permits issued: 56 (2001) / 94 (2000); Employment by occupation: 8.1% management, 18.4% professional, 12.1% services, 22.7% sales, 1.0% farming, 9.9% construction, 27.8% production (2000).
Income: Per capita income: $22,260 (2000); Median household income: $42,103 (2000); Poverty rate: 3.6% (2000).
Taxes: Total city taxes per capita: $259 (1997); City property taxes per capita: $240 (1997).
Education: High school graduation rate: 85.7% (2000); College graduation rate: 19.4% (2000).

School District(s)

Plymouth (PK-12)
2000 Enrollment: 2,503 920-892-2661
Housing: Homeownership rate: 63.8% (2000); Median home value: $110,200 (2000); Median rent: $438 per month (2000); Median age of housing: 36 years (2000).
Hospitals: Valley View Medical Center (108 beds)
Safety: Violent crime rate: 11.5 per 10,000 population; Property crime rate: 225.9 per 10,000 population (2001).
Newspapers: The Review (2 x week); The Sheboygan Falls News (1 x week)
Transportation: Commute to work: 89.7% car, 0.0% public transportation, 4.4% walk, 4.3% work from home (2000); Travel time to work: 46.5% less than 15 minutes, 39.2% 15 to 30 minutes, 8.5% 30 to 45 minutes, 2.6% 45 to 60 minutes, 3.1% 60 minutes or more (2000)
Additional Information Contacts
Plymouth Chamber of Commerce 920-893-0079

PLYMOUTH (town). Covers a land area of 31.458 square miles and a water area of 0.033 square miles. Located at 43.76° N. Lat.; 87.98° W. Long. Elevation is 860 feet.
History: Incorporated 1877.
Population: 3,115 (2000); Race: 98.0% White, 0.0% Black, 0.2% Asian, 0.0% American Indian and Alaska Native, 2.2% Hispanic of any race, 1.0% two or more races (2000); Density: 99.0 persons per square mile (2000); Age: 27.2% under 18, 12.1% over 64 (2000); Marriage status: 18.0% never married, 69.5% now married, 6.7% widowed, 5.8% divorced (2000); Foreign born: 1.5% (2000); Ancestry (includes multiple ancestries): 61.0% German, 9.0% Irish, 6.3% Polish, 5.1% English, 4.3% Dutch (2000).
Economy: In dairy and grain area; cheese and dairy products. Manufacturing: consumer goods; food products; printing. Single-family building permits issued: 23 (2001) / 22 (2000); Multi-family building permits issued: 0 (2001) / 0 (2000); Employment by occupation: 17.3% management, 17.4% professional, 10.8% services, 24.5% sales, 0.5% farming, 12.1% construction, 17.3% production (2000).
Income: Per capita income: $25,275 (2000); Median household income: $61,038 (2000); Poverty rate: 2.1% (2000).
Taxes: Total city taxes per capita: $51 (1997); City property taxes per capita: $44 (1997).
Education: High school graduation rate: 86.2% (2000); College graduation rate: 21.5% (2000).
Housing: Homeownership rate: 87.8% (2000); Median home value: $150,100 (2000); Median rent: $445 per month (2000); Median age of housing: 26 years (2000).
Transportation: Commute to work: 92.3% car, 0.3% public transportation, 1.9% walk, 4.4% work from home (2000); Travel time to work: 51.4% less than 15 minutes, 36.7% 15 to 30 minutes, 4.3% 30 to 45 minutes, 3.7% 45 to 60 minutes, 3.9% 60 minutes or more (2000)

RANDOM LAKE (village). Covers a land area of 1.273 square miles and a water area of 0.327 square miles. Located at 43.55° N. Lat.; 87.96° W. Long. Elevation is 901 feet.
Population: 1,551 (2000); Race: 98.7% White, 0.1% Black, 0.0% Asian, 0.6% American Indian and Alaska Native, 0.9% Hispanic of any race, 0.5% two or more races (2000); Density: 1,217.9 persons per square mile (2000); Age: 26.7% under 18, 13.2% over 64 (2000); Marriage status: 25.1% never married, 59.7% now married, 5.8% widowed, 9.4% divorced (2000); Foreign born: 0.1% (2000); Ancestry (includes multiple ancestries): 60.3% German, 10.7% Irish, 10.3% Luxemburger, 8.8% Polish, 6.0% United States or American (2000).
Economy: In dairy and grain area. Manufacturing: tags, concrete products, publishing. Single-family building permits issued: 5 (2001) / 6 (2000); Multi-family building permits issued: 0 (2001) / 0 (2000); Employment by occupation: 10.2% management, 9.9% professional, 13.3% services, 23.3% sales, 0.5% farming, 9.5% construction, 33.4% production (2000).
Income: Per capita income: $21,892 (2000); Median household income: $45,938 (2000); Poverty rate: 5.4% (2000).
Taxes: Total city taxes per capita: $343 (1997); City property taxes per capita: $332 (1997).
Education: High school graduation rate: 86.5% (2000); College graduation rate: 19.1% (2000).

School District(s)

Random Lake (PK-12)
2000 Enrollment: 1,051 920-994-4342
Housing: Homeownership rate: 69.4% (2000); Median home value: $133,200 (2000); Median rent: $462 per month (2000); Median age of housing: 36 years (2000).
Newspapers: The Sounder (1 x week)
Transportation: Commute to work: 91.7% car, 0.0% public transportation, 5.5% walk, 1.4% work from home (2000); Travel time to work: 34.8% less than 15 minutes, 32.9% 15 to 30 minutes, 20.2% 30 to 45 minutes, 6.8% 45 to 60 minutes, 5.3% 60 minutes or more (2000)

RHINE (town). Aka Rhine Center. Covers a land area of 33.695 square miles and a water area of 0.944 square miles. Located at 43.84° N. Lat.; 87.99° W. Long. Elevation is 935 feet.
Population: 2,244 (2000); Race: 98.3% White, 0.0% Black, 0.4% Asian, 0.2% American Indian and Alaska Native, 0.9% Hispanic of any race, 0.3% two or more races (2000); Density: 66.6 persons per square mile (2000); Age: 24.5% under 18, 9.2% over 64 (2000); Marriage status: 21.4% never married, 71.5% now married, 3.1% widowed, 4.0% divorced (2000); Foreign born: 2.0% (2000); Ancestry (includes multiple ancestries): 65.5% German, 6.9% Dutch, 6.0% English, 5.5% Polish, 4.8% Irish (2000).
Economy: Single-family building permits issued: 16 (2001) / 14 (2000); Multi-family building permits issued: 0 (2001) / 2 (2000); Employment by occupation: 13.4% management, 16.7% professional, 11.8% services, 18.0% sales, 1.4% farming, 7.0% construction, 31.8% production (2000).
Income: Per capita income: $27,059 (2000); Median household income: $62,500 (2000); Poverty rate: 1.4% (2000).
Taxes: Total city taxes per capita: $75 (1997); City property taxes per capita: $71 (1997).
Education: High school graduation rate: 92.5% (2000); College graduation rate: 20.9% (2000).
Housing: Homeownership rate: 90.4% (2000); Median home value: $149,400 (2000); Median rent: $431 per month (2000); Median age of housing: 32 years (2000).
Transportation: Commute to work: 91.2% car, 0.0% public transportation, 1.6% walk, 6.7% work from home (2000); Travel time to work: 35.6% less than 15 minutes, 47.0% 15 to 30 minutes, 10.4% 30 to 45 minutes, 2.1% 45 to 60 minutes, 4.9% 60 minutes or more (2000)

RUSSELL (town). Covers a land area of 23.078 square miles and a water area of 1.044 square miles. Located at 43.86° N. Lat.; 88.07° W. Long.
Population: 399 (2000); Race: 100.0% White, 0.0% Black, 0.0% Asian, 0.0% American Indian and Alaska Native, 1.3% Hispanic of any race, 0.0% two or more races (2000); Density: 17.3 persons per square mile (2000); Age: 29.2% under 18, 13.1% over 64 (2000); Marriage status: 26.4% never married, 66.6% now married, 0.7% widowed, 6.4% divorced (2000); Foreign born: 1.3% (2000); Ancestry (includes multiple ancestries): 69.7% German, 9.0% United States or American, 7.7% Irish, 5.1% Other groups, 2.8% Belgian (2000).
Economy: Single-family building permits issued: 0 (2001) / 2 (2000); Multi-family building permits issued: 0 (2001) / 0 (2000); Employment by occupation: 15.5% management, 8.0% professional, 11.1% services, 16.4% sales, 8.4% farming, 11.5% construction, 29.2% production (2000).
Income: Per capita income: $18,329 (2000); Median household income: $51,250 (2000); Poverty rate: 0.5% (2000).
Taxes: Total city taxes per capita: $131 (1997); City property taxes per capita: $129 (1997).
Education: High school graduation rate: 82.1% (2000); College graduation rate: 9.6% (2000).
Housing: Homeownership rate: 89.1% (2000); Median home value: $98,300 (2000); Median rent: $310 per month (2000); Median age of housing: 60+ years (2000).
Transportation: Commute to work: 86.2% car, 0.0% public transportation, 2.7% walk, 11.2% work from home (2000); Travel time to work: 36.7% less

than 15 minutes, 40.2% 15 to 30 minutes, 12.6% 30 to 45 minutes, 9.5% 45 to 60 minutes, 1.0% 60 minutes or more (2000)

SCOTT (town). Covers a land area of 36.172 square miles and a water area of 0.366 square miles. Located at 43.57° N. Lat.; 88.09° W. Long.
Population: 1,804 (2000); Race: 97.8% White, 0.0% Black, 0.0% Asian, 0.4% American Indian and Alaska Native, 0.5% Hispanic of any race, 1.9% two or more races (2000); Density: 49.9 persons per square mile (2000); Age: 26.4% under 18, 10.8% over 64 (2000); Marriage status: 21.1% never married, 67.2% now married, 5.1% widowed, 6.6% divorced (2000); Foreign born: 0.3% (2000); Ancestry (includes multiple ancestries): 67.0% German, 8.6% Irish, 5.9% Polish, 5.4% United States or American, 3.8% English (2000).
Economy: Single-family building permits issued: 8 (2001) / 13 (2000); Multi-family building permits issued: 0 (2001) / 0 (2000); Employment by occupation: 12.5% management, 12.5% professional, 10.4% services, 17.8% sales, 4.1% farming, 14.2% construction, 28.4% production (2000).
Income: Per capita income: $20,160 (2000); Median household income: $51,771 (2000); Poverty rate: 3.1% (2000).
Taxes: Total city taxes per capita: $153 (2000); City property taxes per capita: $143 (2000).
Education: High school graduation rate: 85.3% (2000); College graduation rate: 11.4% (2000).
Housing: Homeownership rate: 86.7% (2000); Median home value: $125,000 (2000); Median rent: $427 per month (2000); Median age of housing: 38 years (2000).
Transportation: Commute to work: 89.3% car, 0.0% public transportation, 3.4% walk, 7.1% work from home (2000); Travel time to work: 18.5% less than 15 minutes, 39.6% 15 to 30 minutes, 24.5% 30 to 45 minutes, 9.6% 45 to 60 minutes, 7.8% 60 minutes or more (2000)

SHEBOYGAN (city). Covers a land area of 13.907 square miles and a water area of 0.146 square miles. Located at 43.75° N. Lat.; 87.72° W. Long. Elevation is 635 feet.
History: Sheboygan began in 1843 with a store, stocked with necessities for frontier settlers, at a spot called "The Mouth," where the river entered Lake Michigan. The town that grew up around it was granted a village charter in 1846, when steamships from Chicago and Buffalo began visiting the little port daily, bringing settlers. Many of the early residents were religious or political refugees from Germany, who cleared the land and planted crops of oats, potatoes, and wheat. By 1860 dairying was growing in importance; the first cheese factory was built in 1864, and by 1875 there were 45 cheese plants in the county. Several large furniture and woodworking factories opened in the 1870's, producing chairs as well as wagons, ships, brooms, and wooden shoes. Though the woodworking industry began to decline in the 1920's, Sheboygan continued to grow in importance as a cheese producing center.
Population: 50,792 (2000); Race: 87.0% White, 1.1% Black, 6.5% Asian, 0.4% American Indian and Alaska Native, 5.5% Hispanic of any race, 2.3% two or more races (2000); Density: 3,652.4 persons per square mile (2000); Age: 25.6% under 18, 15.8% over 64 (2000); Marriage status: 26.1% never married, 55.2% now married, 8.4% widowed, 10.3% divorced (2000); Foreign born: 7.7% (2000); Ancestry (includes multiple ancestries): 50.4% German, 13.8% Other groups, 7.2% Irish, 5.9% Dutch, 4.8% Polish (2000).
Vital Statistics: Birth rate: 129.7 per 10,000 population (1998)
Economy: Unemployment rate: 5.6% (11/2002); Total civilian labor force: 27,477 (11/2002); Single-family building permits issued: 27 (2001) / 39 (2000); Multi-family building permits issued: 4 (2001) / 25 (2000); Employment by occupation: 8.1% management, 14.6% professional, 15.3% services, 21.6% sales, 0.4% farming, 6.0% construction, 34.0% production (2000).
Income: Per capita income: $19,270 (2000); Median household income: $40,066 (2000); Poverty rate: 8.3% (2000).
Taxes: Total city taxes per capita: $354 (2000); City property taxes per capita: $321 (2000).
Education: High school graduation rate: 81.2% (2000); College graduation rate: 15.9% (2000).

School District(s)

Sheboygan Area (PK-12)
2000 Enrollment: 10,418 920-459-3511

Four-year College(s)

Lakeland College (Private, Not-for-profit, United Church of Christ)
2001 Enrollment: 3,588 920-565-2111
2001 Tuition: In-state $12,500; Out-of-state $12,500

Housing: Homeownership rate: 61.0% (2000); Median home value: $89,400 (2000); Median rent: $412 per month (2000); Median age of housing: 48 years (2000).
Hospitals: Sheboygan Memorial Medical Center (135 beds); Saint Nicholas Hospital (185 beds)
Safety: Violent crime rate: 14.9 per 10,000 population; Property crime rate: 431.6 per 10,000 population (2001).
Newspapers: The Sheboygan Press (7 x week)
Transportation: Commute to work: 91.4% car, 1.6% public transportation, 3.9% walk, 1.5% work from home (2000); Travel time to work: 61.0% less than 15 minutes, 29.2% 15 to 30 minutes, 5.1% 30 to 45 minutes, 2.1% 45 to 60 minutes, 2.6% 60 minutes or more (2000)
Airports: Sheboygan County Memorial
Additional Information Contacts
Sheboygan Chamber of Commerce 920-457-9491
Sheboygan County Board of Realtors 920-457-7908

SHEBOYGAN (town). Covers a land area of 10.990 square miles and a water area of 0.037 square miles. Located at 43.77° N. Lat.; 87.75° W. Long. Elevation is 635 feet.
History: Permanent settlement began c.1835, and Sheboygan grew into a shipping and industrial center. A Native American mound park featuring a great number of prehistoric burial mounds just south of the city. Incorporated 1853.
Population: 5,874 (2000); Race: 96.1% White, 0.6% Black, 2.2% Asian, 0.1% American Indian and Alaska Native, 0.8% Hispanic of any race, 0.6% two or more races (2000); Density: 534.5 persons per square mile (2000); Age: 26.8% under 18, 10.9% over 64 (2000); Marriage status: 18.3% never married, 73.4% now married, 2.9% widowed, 5.4% divorced (2000); Foreign born: 2.6% (2000); Ancestry (includes multiple ancestries): 60.9% German, 8.2% Irish, 6.7% Dutch, 5.7% Polish, 5.7% English (2000).
Economy: A port of entry on Lake Michigan. Plastics, stainless-steel products, orthodontic products, paper goods, enamelware, furniture and lighting equipment are manufactured here. Dairying (cheese) and beer brewing are also important industries. Single-family building permits issued: 96 (2001) / 59 (2000); Multi-family building permits issued: 133 (2001) / 151 (2000); Employment by occupation: 16.9% management, 17.1% professional, 12.2% services, 21.2% sales, 0.7% farming, 9.5% construction, 22.4% production (2000).
Income: Per capita income: $25,492 (2000); Median household income: $60,846 (2000); Poverty rate: 1.8% (2000).
Taxes: Total city taxes per capita: $142 (2000); City property taxes per capita: $120 (2000).
Education: High school graduation rate: 89.3% (2000); College graduation rate: 28.6% (2000).
Housing: Homeownership rate: 86.0% (2000); Median home value: $135,800 (2000); Median rent: $546 per month (2000); Median age of housing: 21 years (2000).
Transportation: Commute to work: 93.4% car, 0.2% public transportation, 0.8% walk, 4.4% work from home (2000); Travel time to work: 58.3% less than 15 minutes, 33.5% 15 to 30 minutes, 3.1% 30 to 45 minutes, 1.4% 45 to 60 minutes, 3.7% 60 minutes or more (2000)

SHEBOYGAN FALLS (city). Covers a land area of 4.084 square miles and a water area of 0.084 square miles. Located at 43.73° N. Lat.; 87.82° W. Long. Elevation is 659 feet.
Population: 6,772 (2000); Race: 98.4% White, 0.5% Black, 0.1% Asian, 0.0% American Indian and Alaska Native, 1.4% Hispanic of any race, 0.3% two or more races (2000); Density: 1,658.3 persons per square mile (2000); Age: 23.8% under 18, 16.2% over 64 (2000); Marriage status: 20.0% never married, 63.5% now married, 7.7% widowed, 8.8% divorced (2000); Foreign born: 0.9% (2000); Ancestry (includes multiple ancestries): 59.7% German, 11.8% Dutch, 8.4% Irish, 6.0% United States or American, 5.3% Polish (2000).
Economy: Single-family building permits issued: 39 (2001) / 25 (2000); Multi-family building permits issued: 14 (2001) / 8 (2000); Employment by occupation: 11.3% management, 13.5% professional, 14.6% services, 22.5% sales, 0.2% farming, 7.2% construction, 30.6% production (2000).
Income: Per capita income: $22,456 (2000); Median household income: $47,205 (2000); Poverty rate: 2.7% (2000).
Taxes: Total city taxes per capita: $189 (1997); City property taxes per capita: $159 (1997).
Education: High school graduation rate: 87.1% (2000); College graduation rate: 15.0% (2000).

School District(s)

Sheboygan Falls (PK-12)
2000 Enrollment: 1,689 920-467-7893

Housing: Homeownership rate: 73.6% (2000); Median home value: $111,600 (2000); Median rent: $422 per month (2000); Median age of housing: 34 years (2000).
Safety: Violent crime rate: 2.9 per 10,000 population; Property crime rate: 197.9 per 10,000 population (2001).
Transportation: Commute to work: 93.0% car, 0.4% public transportation, 5.4% walk, 0.8% work from home (2000); Travel time to work: 63.5% less than 15 minutes, 27.4% 15 to 30 minutes, 3.4% 30 to 45 minutes, 1.3% 45 to 60 minutes, 4.2% 60 minutes or more (2000)

Additional Information Contacts
Sheboygan Falls Chamber of Commerce 920-467-6206

SHEBOYGAN FALLS (town). Covers a land area of 32.011 square miles and a water area of 0.025 square miles. Located at 43.75° N. Lat.; 87.86° W. Long. Elevation is 659 feet.
History: Incorporated as village in 1854, as city in 1913.
Population: 1,706 (2000); Race: 99.5% White, 0.3% Black, 0.0% Asian, 0.2% American Indian and Alaska Native, 0.0% Hispanic of any race, 0.0% two or more races (2000); Density: 53.3 persons per square mile (2000); Age: 22.3% under 18, 11.4% over 64 (2000); Marriage status: 23.3% never married, 66.4% now married, 2.6% widowed, 7.7% divorced (2000); Foreign born: 0.9% (2000); Ancestry (includes multiple ancestries): 70.7% German, 11.5% Dutch, 6.9% Polish, 5.3% Irish, 5.1% English (2000).
Economy: In dairy and grain area. Manufacturing: furniture, fixtures, food processing, machinery, aluminum die castings, chemicals. Sheboygan County Airport to Northwest. Single-family building permits issued: 12 (2001) / 0 (2000); Multi-family building permits issued: 0 (2001) / 0 (2000); Employment by occupation: 11.3% management, 12.6% professional, 12.6% services, 18.2% sales, 3.1% farming, 13.3% construction, 28.9% production (2000).
Income: Per capita income: $23,915 (2000); Median household income: $50,489 (2000); Poverty rate: 2.0% (2000).
Taxes: Total city taxes per capita: $52 (1997); City property taxes per capita: $42 (1997).
Education: High school graduation rate: 83.6% (2000); College graduation rate: 13.2% (2000).
Housing: Homeownership rate: 88.6% (2000); Median home value: $122,900 (2000); Median rent: $555 per month (2000); Median age of housing: 40 years (2000).
Transportation: Commute to work: 91.0% car, 0.0% public transportation, 2.0% walk, 5.7% work from home (2000); Travel time to work: 56.4% less than 15 minutes, 35.7% 15 to 30 minutes, 2.9% 30 to 45 minutes, 0.4% 45 to 60 minutes, 4.6% 60 minutes or more (2000)

SHERMAN (town). Covers a land area of 34.240 square miles and a water area of 0.042 square miles. Located at 43.58° N. Lat.; 87.98° W. Long.
Population: 1,520 (2000); Race: 100.0% White, 0.0% Black, 0.0% Asian, 0.0% American Indian and Alaska Native, 1.3% Hispanic of any race, 0.0% two or more races (2000); Density: 44.4 persons per square mile (2000); Age: 26.4% under 18, 8.8% over 64 (2000); Marriage status: 23.8% never married, 68.4% now married, 2.7% widowed, 5.1% divorced (2000); Foreign born: 1.1% (2000); Ancestry (includes multiple ancestries): 62.6% German, 9.8% United States or American, 8.0% Irish, 6.9% Luxemburger, 4.8% English (2000).
Economy: Single-family building permits issued: 3 (2001) / 29 (2000); Multi-family building permits issued: 0 (2001) / 0 (2000); Employment by occupation: 13.0% management, 9.1% professional, 8.4% services, 19.7% sales, 1.8% farming, 14.9% construction, 33.2% production (2000).
Income: Per capita income: $21,710 (2000); Median household income: $52,375 (2000); Poverty rate: 3.8% (2000).
Taxes: Total city taxes per capita: $80 (1997); City property taxes per capita: $78 (1997).
Education: High school graduation rate: 86.9% (2000); College graduation rate: 11.5% (2000).
Housing: Homeownership rate: 88.8% (2000); Median home value: $133,500 (2000); Median rent: $427 per month (2000); Median age of housing: 38 years (2000).
Transportation: Commute to work: 87.5% car, 0.2% public transportation, 5.0% walk, 6.4% work from home (2000); Travel time to work: 30.5% less than 15 minutes, 32.9% 15 to 30 minutes, 20.2% 30 to 45 minutes, 9.6% 45 to 60 minutes, 6.9% 60 minutes or more (2000)

WALDO (village). Covers a land area of 0.850 square miles and a water area of 0.035 square miles. Located at 43.67° N. Lat.; 87.94° W. Long. Elevation is 838 feet.
Population: 450 (2000); Race: 97.7% White, 0.0% Black, 0.0% Asian, 0.0% American Indian and Alaska Native, 0.0% Hispanic of any race, 2.3% two or more races (2000); Density: 529.5 persons per square mile (2000); Age: 25.6% under 18, 10.0% over 64 (2000); Marriage status: 22.7% never married, 60.7% now married, 5.3% widowed, 11.4% divorced (2000); Foreign born: 0.4% (2000); Ancestry (includes multiple ancestries): 47.5% German, 10.7% United States or American, 9.6% Dutch, 8.7% Norwegian, 7.0% Irish (2000).
Economy: In dairy and farm area; cheese. Single-family building permits issued: 4 (2001) / 1 (2000); Multi-family building permits issued: 0 (2001) / 0 (2000); Employment by occupation: 8.3% management, 4.7% professional, 18.2% services, 15.0% sales, 2.0% farming, 13.8% construction, 37.9% production (2000).
Income: Per capita income: $22,618 (2000); Median household income: $48,125 (2000); Poverty rate: 1.5% (2000).
Taxes: Total city taxes per capita: $96 (1997); City property taxes per capita: $94 (1997).
Education: High school graduation rate: 90.3% (2000); College graduation rate: 10.0% (2000).
Housing: Homeownership rate: 79.5% (2000); Median home value: $100,900 (2000); Median rent: $345 per month (2000); Median age of housing: 60+ years (2000).
Transportation: Commute to work: 93.7% car, 0.8% public transportation, 3.6% walk, 2.0% work from home (2000); Travel time to work: 32.4% less than 15 minutes, 53.0% 15 to 30 minutes, 8.9% 30 to 45 minutes, 2.4% 45 to 60 minutes, 3.2% 60 minutes or more (2000)

WILSON (town). Covers a land area of 22.884 square miles and a water area of 0.038 square miles. Located at 43.69° N. Lat.; 87.74° W. Long.
Population: 3,227 (2000); Race: 98.0% White, 0.2% Black, 0.9% Asian, 0.0% American Indian and Alaska Native, 0.3% Hispanic of any race, 0.7% two or more races (2000); Density: 141.0 persons per square mile (2000); Age: 24.4% under 18, 13.4% over 64 (2000); Marriage status: 19.0% never married, 70.7% now married, 4.2% widowed, 6.1% divorced (2000); Foreign born: 2.0% (2000); Ancestry (includes multiple ancestries): 53.9% German, 13.5% Dutch, 9.3% Irish, 6.9% United States or American, 5.7% English (2000).
Economy: Single-family building permits issued: 27 (2001) / 23 (2000); Multi-family building permits issued: 4 (2001) / 2 (2000); Employment by occupation: 11.0% management, 23.8% professional, 13.0% services, 21.2% sales, 0.7% farming, 8.8% construction, 21.4% production (2000).
Income: Per capita income: $27,798 (2000); Median household income: $59,241 (2000); Poverty rate: 2.5% (2000).
Taxes: Total city taxes per capita: $118 (1997); City property taxes per capita: $110 (1997).
Education: High school graduation rate: 86.9% (2000); College graduation rate: 25.2% (2000).
Housing: Homeownership rate: 92.0% (2000); Median home value: $134,600 (2000); Median rent: $421 per month (2000); Median age of housing: 33 years (2000).
Transportation: Commute to work: 91.6% car, 0.0% public transportation, 1.7% walk, 5.7% work from home (2000); Travel time to work: 44.1% less than 15 minutes, 44.7% 15 to 30 minutes, 3.9% 30 to 45 minutes, 2.1% 45 to 60 minutes, 5.3% 60 minutes or more (2000)

Taylor County

Located in north central Wisconsin; drained by the Black, Yellow, Jump, and Rib Rivers; includes part of Chequamegon National Forest. Covers a land area of 974.90 square miles, a water area of 9.60 square miles, and is located in the Central Time Zone. The county government was organized in 1875. County seat is Medford.

Weather Station: Jump River 3 E — Elevation: 1,263 feet

	Jan	Feb	Mar	Apr	May	Jun	Jul	Aug	Sep	Oct	Nov	Dec
High	21	28	39	55	69	76	80	77	68	56	39	25
Low	-1	5	17	31	41	50	54	52	44	34	22	7
Precip	1.0	0.8	1.7	2.5	3.5	4.2	4.5	4.4	4.0	2.8	2.2	1.2
Snow	15.0	8.9	9.5	2.2	tr	0.0	0.0	0.0	tr	0.9	6.7	12.2

High and Low temperatures in degrees Fahrenheit; Precipitation and Snow in inches

Weather Station: Medford Elevation: 1,469 feet

	Jan	Feb	Mar	Apr	May	Jun	Jul	Aug	Sep	Oct	Nov	Dec
High	20	26	36	52	66	75	79	77	67	55	38	25
Low	-0	5	17	31	43	52	57	55	46	34	22	8
Precip	1.1	0.9	1.9	2.5	3.3	4.3	4.1	4.4	4.5	2.7	2.1	1.3
Snow	11.2	6.1	7.7	1.8	tr	0.0	0.0	0.0	0.0	0.4	4.2	9.6

High and Low temperatures in degrees Fahrenheit; Precipitation and Snow in inches

Population: 19,680 (2000); Race: 98.5% White, 0.2% Black, 0.1% Asian, 0.3% American Indian and Alaska Native, 0.7% Hispanic of any race, 0.6% two or more races (2000); Density: 20.2 persons per square mile (2000); Age: 27.1% under 18, 15.2% over 64 (2000).

Religion: Five largest groups: 43.3% Catholic Church, 13.1% Wisconsin Evangelical Lutheran Synod, 5.5% Evangelical Lutheran Church in America, 4.5% Lutheran Church—Missouri Synod, 1.8% The United Methodist Church (2000).

Economy: Unemployment rate: 4.1% (11/2002); Total civilian labor force: 10,969 (11/2002); Leading industries: 43.6% manufacturing; 12.4% retail trade; 11.6% health care and social assistance (2000); Companies that employ more than 1,000 persons: 0 (2000); Companies that employ more than 100 persons: 12 (2000); Farms: 887 totaling 223,587 acres (1997); Minority business ownership rate: 0.0% (1997); Women business ownership rate: 9.0% (1997); Retail sales per capita: $7,358 (1997). Single-family building permits issued: 66 (2001) / 71 (2000); Multi-family building permits issued: 0 (2001) / 2 (2000).

Income: Per capita income: $17,570 (2000); Median household income: $38,502 (2000); Poverty rate: 9.8% (2000); Bankruptcy rate: 1.73% (2001).

Taxes: Total county taxes per capita: $268 (2000); County property taxes per capita: $252 (2000).

Education: High school graduation rate: 78.3% (2000); College graduation rate: 11.0% (2000).

Housing: Homeownership rate: 80.4% (2000); Median home value: $75,600 (2000); Median rent: $331 per month (2000); Median age of housing: 33 years (2000).

Health: Birth rate: 114.3 per 10,000 population (1998); Age adjusted death rate: 74.9 per 10,000 population (1999); Age adjusted cancer mortality rate: 195.7 deaths per 100,000 population (1999). Number of physicians: 6.6 per 10,000 population (1999); Number of hospital beds: 77.7 per 10,000 population (1999).

Elections: 2000 Presidential election results: 36.2% Gore, 58.7% Bush, 3.5% Nader, 1.0% Buchanan

National and State Parks: Pershing State Wildlife Area

Additional Information Contacts

Taylor County Government Offices........................ 715-748-1400
Medford Chamber of Commerce........................ 715-748-4729

Taylor County Communities

AURORA (town). Covers a land area of 34.192 square miles and a water area of 0 square miles. Located at 45.17° N. Lat.; 90.85° W. Long.

Population: 386 (2000); Race: 98.2% White, 0.0% Black, 0.0% Asian, 0.5% American Indian and Alaska Native, 0.5% Hispanic of any race, 1.3% two or more races (2000); Density: 11.3 persons per square mile (2000); Age: 29.5% under 18, 17.5% over 64 (2000); Marriage status: 28.1% never married, 64.4% now married, 5.1% widowed, 2.4% divorced (2000); Foreign born: 0.0% (2000); Ancestry (includes multiple ancestries): 43.9% Polish, 41.8% German, 17.2% Norwegian, 6.3% Irish, 2.3% French Canadian (2000).

Economy: Employment by occupation: 32.4% management, 7.5% professional, 9.8% services, 20.2% sales, 9.8% farming, 0.6% construction, 19.7% production (2000).

Income: Per capita income: $14,374 (2000); Median household income: $30,417 (2000); Poverty rate: 22.6% (2000).

Taxes: Total city taxes per capita: $63 (1997); City property taxes per capita: $61 (1997).

Education: High school graduation rate: 76.1% (2000); College graduation rate: 9.9% (2000).

Housing: Homeownership rate: 83.7% (2000); Median home value: $46,700 (2000); Median rent: $330 per month (2000); Median age of housing: 51 years (2000).

Transportation: Commute to work: 52.0% car, 0.6% public transportation, 12.9% walk, 34.5% work from home (2000); Travel time to work: 52.7% less than 15 minutes, 23.2% 15 to 30 minutes, 8.0% 30 to 45 minutes, 7.1% 45 to 60 minutes, 8.9% 60 minutes or more (2000)

BROWNING (town). Covers a land area of 36.505 square miles and a water area of 0.012 square miles. Located at 45.16° N. Lat.; 90.23° W. Long.

Population: 850 (2000); Race: 97.6% White, 0.0% Black, 0.0% Asian, 0.0% American Indian and Alaska Native, 2.7% Hispanic of any race, 0.0% two or more races (2000); Density: 23.3 persons per square mile (2000); Age: 28.3% under 18, 7.8% over 64 (2000); Marriage status: 23.4% never married, 65.1% now married, 2.8% widowed, 8.7% divorced (2000); Foreign born: 2.4% (2000); Ancestry (includes multiple ancestries): 61.6% German, 9.5% Polish, 9.2% United States or American, 7.8% Norwegian, 5.2% Irish (2000).

Economy: Single-family building permits issued: 7 (2001) / 5 (2000); Multi-family building permits issued: 0 (2001) / 0 (2000); Employment by occupation: 16.4% management, 6.7% professional, 10.5% services, 21.9% sales, 6.1% farming, 7.1% construction, 31.4% production (2000).

Income: Per capita income: $18,687 (2000); Median household income: $45,917 (2000); Poverty rate: 5.9% (2000).

Taxes: Total city taxes per capita: $39 (1997); City property taxes per capita: $38 (1997).

Education: High school graduation rate: 79.4% (2000); College graduation rate: 9.9% (2000).

Housing: Homeownership rate: 90.4% (2000); Median home value: $85,000 (2000); Median rent: $342 per month (2000); Median age of housing: 30 years (2000).

Transportation: Commute to work: 80.8% car, 0.0% public transportation, 3.5% walk, 15.3% work from home (2000); Travel time to work: 51.7% less than 15 minutes, 33.7% 15 to 30 minutes, 5.4% 30 to 45 minutes, 2.9% 45 to 60 minutes, 6.3% 60 minutes or more (2000)

CHELSEA (town). Covers a land area of 40.364 square miles and a water area of 0.530 square miles. Located at 45.26° N. Lat.; 90.35° W. Long. Elevation is 1,530 feet.

Population: 719 (2000); Race: 98.5% White, 0.0% Black, 0.0% Asian, 0.3% American Indian and Alaska Native, 0.3% Hispanic of any race, 1.2% two or more races (2000); Density: 17.8 persons per square mile (2000); Age: 25.6% under 18, 12.7% over 64 (2000); Marriage status: 23.9% never married, 62.9% now married, 4.4% widowed, 8.9% divorced (2000); Foreign born: 0.0% (2000); Ancestry (includes multiple ancestries): 65.7% German, 8.4% Irish, 7.7% Polish, 3.3% Swedish, 3.3% United States or American (2000).

Economy: Single-family building permits issued: 7 (2001) / 3 (2000); Multi-family building permits issued: 0 (2001) / 0 (2000); Employment by occupation: 8.7% management, 7.1% professional, 9.3% services, 16.9% sales, 7.1% farming, 10.1% construction, 40.9% production (2000).

Income: Per capita income: $19,798 (2000); Median household income: $44,659 (2000); Poverty rate: 3.5% (2000).

Taxes: Total city taxes per capita: $22 (1997); City property taxes per capita: $21 (1997).

Education: High school graduation rate: 84.2% (2000); College graduation rate: 7.4% (2000).

Housing: Homeownership rate: 95.3% (2000); Median home value: $76,600 (2000); Median rent: $192 per month (2000); Median age of housing: 29 years (2000).

Transportation: Commute to work: 87.6% car, 1.1% public transportation, 2.8% walk, 7.9% work from home (2000); Travel time to work: 24.7% less than 15 minutes, 57.3% 15 to 30 minutes, 7.6% 30 to 45 minutes, 3.0% 45 to 60 minutes, 7.3% 60 minutes or more (2000)

CLEVELAND (town). Covers a land area of 33.877 square miles and a water area of 1.809 square miles. Located at 45.24° N. Lat.; 90.72° W. Long.

Population: 262 (2000); Race: 100.0% White, 0.0% Black, 0.0% Asian, 0.0% American Indian and Alaska Native, 0.0% Hispanic of any race, 0.0% two or more races (2000); Density: 7.7 persons per square mile (2000); Age: 27.2% under 18, 10.3% over 64 (2000); Marriage status: 19.0% never married, 65.5% now married, 2.0% widowed, 13.5% divorced (2000); Foreign born: 0.0% (2000); Ancestry (includes multiple ancestries): 43.2% German, 29.2% Polish, 13.2% Irish, 10.3% French (except Basque), 5.3% European (2000).

Economy: Single-family building permits issued: 5 (2001) / 3 (2000); Multi-family building permits issued: 0 (2001) / 0 (2000); Employment by occupation: 15.5% management, 6.9% professional, 17.2% services, 19.0% sales, 2.6% farming, 12.9% construction, 25.9% production (2000).

Income: Per capita income: $16,452 (2000); Median household income: $35,625 (2000); Poverty rate: 10.9% (2000).

Taxes: Total city taxes per capita: $50 (2000); City property taxes per capita: $46 (2000).

Education: High school graduation rate: 79.2% (2000); College graduation rate: 3.6% (2000).

Housing: Homeownership rate: 93.7% (2000); Median home value: $70,000 (2000); Median age of housing: 25 years (2000).

Transportation: Commute to work: 78.8% car, 0.0% public transportation, 0.0% walk, 21.2% work from home (2000); Travel time to work: 19.1% less than 15 minutes, 20.2% 15 to 30 minutes, 25.8% 30 to 45 minutes, 21.3% 45 to 60 minutes, 13.5% 60 minutes or more (2000)

DEER CREEK (town). Covers a land area of 34.224 square miles and a water area of 0.006 square miles. Located at 45.06° N. Lat.; 90.26° W. Long.
Population: 733 (2000); Race: 99.7% White, 0.0% Black, 0.0% Asian, 0.0% American Indian and Alaska Native, 3.4% Hispanic of any race, 0.3% two or more races (2000); Density: 21.4 persons per square mile (2000); Age: 30.4% under 18, 8.7% over 64 (2000); Marriage status: 27.2% never married, 66.4% now married, 2.6% widowed, 3.7% divorced (2000); Foreign born: 4.5% (2000); Ancestry (includes multiple ancestries): 62.3% German, 8.0% United States or American, 7.6% Norwegian, 6.7% Irish, 6.0% Polish (2000).
Economy: Single-family building permits issued: 1 (2001) / 4 (2000); Multi-family building permits issued: 0 (2001) / 0 (2000); Employment by occupation: 20.5% management, 7.0% professional, 10.0% services, 17.9% sales, 7.0% farming, 14.2% construction, 23.5% production (2000).
Income: Per capita income: $18,503 (2000); Median household income: $49,688 (2000); Poverty rate: 7.7% (2000).
Taxes: Total city taxes per capita: $92 (1997); City property taxes per capita: $92 (1997).
Education: High school graduation rate: 74.1% (2000); College graduation rate: 4.6% (2000).
Housing: Homeownership rate: 87.6% (2000); Median home value: $81,300 (2000); Median rent: $375 per month (2000); Median age of housing: 42 years (2000).
Transportation: Commute to work: 68.8% car, 0.0% public transportation, 2.6% walk, 27.6% work from home (2000); Travel time to work: 53.2% less than 15 minutes, 37.9% 15 to 30 minutes, 1.3% 30 to 45 minutes, 2.7% 45 to 60 minutes, 5.0% 60 minutes or more (2000)

FORD (town). Covers a land area of 32.764 square miles and a water area of 2.308 square miles. Located at 45.16° N. Lat.; 90.76° W. Long.
Population: 276 (2000); Race: 100.0% White, 0.0% Black, 0.0% Asian, 0.0% American Indian and Alaska Native, 0.0% Hispanic of any race, 0.0% two or more races (2000); Density: 8.4 persons per square mile (2000); Age: 28.4% under 18, 7.5% over 64 (2000); Marriage status: 24.9% never married, 62.2% now married, 4.3% widowed, 8.6% divorced (2000); Foreign born: 0.0% (2000); Ancestry (includes multiple ancestries): 43.8% German, 25.5% Polish, 10.1% Norwegian, 7.8% Irish, 5.6% Swiss (2000).
Economy: Employment by occupation: 16.9% management, 6.5% professional, 14.9% services, 15.6% sales, 7.1% farming, 1.3% construction, 37.7% production (2000).
Income: Per capita income: $15,624 (2000); Median household income: $37,813 (2000); Poverty rate: 19.5% (2000).
Taxes: Total city taxes per capita: $37 (1997); City property taxes per capita: $34 (1997).
Education: High school graduation rate: 86.0% (2000); College graduation rate: 8.3% (2000).
Housing: Homeownership rate: 92.5% (2000); Median home value: $57,900 (2000); Median rent: $231 per month (2000); Median age of housing: 27 years (2000).
Transportation: Commute to work: 67.3% car, 0.0% public transportation, 1.4% walk, 29.3% work from home (2000); Travel time to work: 34.6% less than 15 minutes, 16.3% 15 to 30 minutes, 34.6% 30 to 45 minutes, 5.8% 45 to 60 minutes, 8.7% 60 minutes or more (2000)

GILMAN (village). Covers a land area of 2.337 square miles and a water area of 0 square miles. Located at 45.16° N. Lat.; 90.81° W. Long. Elevation is 1,220 feet.
Population: 474 (2000); Race: 98.1% White, 0.0% Black, 0.0% Asian, 1.9% American Indian and Alaska Native, 0.0% Hispanic of any race, 0.0% two or more races (2000); Density: 202.8 persons per square mile (2000); Age: 18.0% under 18, 28.8% over 64 (2000); Marriage status: 29.4% never married, 49.9% now married, 10.6% widowed, 10.1% divorced (2000); Foreign born: 0.0% (2000); Ancestry (includes multiple ancestries): 36.4% German, 19.9% Polish, 9.3% Irish, 8.7% Norwegian, 4.9% English (2000).
Economy: Chequamegon National Forest to East. Dairying; lumber. Single-family building permits issued: 0 (2001) / 1 (2000); Multi-family building permits issued: 0 (2001) / 0 (2000); Employment by occupation: 7.7% management, 19.4% professional, 20.4% services, 23.0% sales, 3.6% farming, 5.6% construction, 20.4% production (2000).
Income: Per capita income: $18,075 (2000); Median household income: $32,708 (2000); Poverty rate: 14.0% (2000).
Taxes: Total city taxes per capita: $258 (1997); City property taxes per capita: $247 (1997).
Education: High school graduation rate: 72.6% (2000); College graduation rate: 16.8% (2000).

School District(s)

Gilman (PK-12)
2000 Enrollment: 558 715-447-8216
Housing: Homeownership rate: 76.5% (2000); Median home value: $57,800 (2000); Median rent: $195 per month (2000); Median age of housing: 37 years (2000).
Transportation: Commute to work: 76.0% car, 0.0% public transportation, 15.1% walk, 5.7% work from home (2000); Travel time to work: 60.8% less than 15 minutes, 9.9% 15 to 30 minutes, 19.9% 30 to 45 minutes, 2.8% 45 to 60 minutes, 6.6% 60 minutes or more (2000)

GOODRICH (town). Covers a land area of 36.277 square miles and a water area of 0 square miles. Located at 45.15° N. Lat.; 90.09° W. Long. Elevation is 1,424 feet.
Population: 487 (2000); Race: 99.6% White, 0.0% Black, 0.0% Asian, 0.0% American Indian and Alaska Native, 1.9% Hispanic of any race, 0.0% two or more races (2000); Density: 13.4 persons per square mile (2000); Age: 25.7% under 18, 14.5% over 64 (2000); Marriage status: 28.5% never married, 60.6% now married, 5.0% widowed, 5.9% divorced (2000); Foreign born: 0.0% (2000); Ancestry (includes multiple ancestries): 61.2% German, 10.4% Irish, 6.9% Swedish, 5.6% Polish, 5.4% United States or American (2000).
Economy: Employment by occupation: 18.8% management, 8.2% professional, 6.7% services, 17.6% sales, 3.9% farming, 12.5% construction, 32.2% production (2000).
Income: Per capita income: $16,724 (2000); Median household income: $42,500 (2000); Poverty rate: 10.3% (2000).
Taxes: Total city taxes per capita: $44 (1997); City property taxes per capita: $40 (1997).
Education: High school graduation rate: 69.6% (2000); College graduation rate: 6.8% (2000).
Housing: Homeownership rate: 87.8% (2000); Median home value: $51,300 (2000); Median rent: $367 per month (2000); Median age of housing: 28 years (2000).
Transportation: Commute to work: 87.7% car, 0.0% public transportation, 2.0% walk, 10.3% work from home (2000); Travel time to work: 11.5% less than 15 minutes, 63.4% 15 to 30 minutes, 15.0% 30 to 45 minutes, 6.6% 45 to 60 minutes, 3.5% 60 minutes or more (2000)

GREENWOOD (town). Covers a land area of 54.287 square miles and a water area of 0.048 square miles. Located at 45.24° N. Lat.; 90.17° W. Long.
Population: 642 (2000); Race: 100.0% White, 0.0% Black, 0.0% Asian, 0.0% American Indian and Alaska Native, 0.6% Hispanic of any race, 0.0% two or more races (2000); Density: 11.8 persons per square mile (2000); Age: 29.4% under 18, 14.2% over 64 (2000); Marriage status: 22.3% never married, 70.6% now married, 3.2% widowed, 3.9% divorced (2000); Foreign born: 0.3% (2000); Ancestry (includes multiple ancestries): 70.9% German, 8.3% Polish, 8.0% Norwegian, 4.3% Irish, 4.2% Czech (2000).
Economy: Single-family building permits issued: 1 (2001) / 7 (2000); Multi-family building permits issued: 0 (2001) / 0 (2000); Employment by occupation: 14.5% management, 7.1% professional, 12.0% services, 11.7% sales, 4.6% farming, 9.8% construction, 40.3% production (2000).
Income: Per capita income: $14,120 (2000); Median household income: $34,000 (2000); Poverty rate: 12.7% (2000).
Taxes: Total city taxes per capita: $22 (1997); City property taxes per capita: $20 (1997).
Education: High school graduation rate: 75.1% (2000); College graduation rate: 3.5% (2000).
Housing: Homeownership rate: 91.6% (2000); Median home value: $69,400 (2000); Median rent: $363 per month (2000); Median age of housing: 35 years (2000).
Transportation: Commute to work: 82.9% car, 1.3% public transportation, 3.8% walk, 10.8% work from home (2000); Travel time to work: 14.9% less than 15 minutes, 60.1% 15 to 30 minutes, 16.0% 30 to 45 minutes, 1.8% 45 to 60 minutes, 7.1% 60 minutes or more (2000)

GROVER (town). Covers a land area of 70.654 square miles and a water area of 0.712 square miles. Located at 45.20° N. Lat.; 90.61° W. Long.
Population: 233 (2000); Race: 100.0% White, 0.0% Black, 0.0% Asian, 0.0% American Indian and Alaska Native, 1.3% Hispanic of any race, 0.0% two or more races (2000); Density: 3.3 persons per square mile (2000); Age: 24.4% under 18, 15.1% over 64 (2000); Marriage status: 7.1% never married, 74.3% now married, 7.1% widowed, 11.5% divorced (2000); Foreign born:

1.3% (2000); Ancestry (includes multiple ancestries): 54.2% German, 13.0% Polish, 10.5% Irish, 5.5% Norwegian, 3.8% English (2000).
Economy: Single-family building permits issued: 2 (2001) / 2 (2000); Multi-family building permits issued: 0 (2001) / 0 (2000); Employment by occupation: 12.3% management, 6.6% professional, 13.2% services, 17.9% sales, 3.8% farming, 17.0% construction, 29.2% production (2000).
Income: Per capita income: $18,031 (2000); Median household income: $38,125 (2000); Poverty rate: 2.5% (2000).
Taxes: Total city taxes per capita: $45 (1997); City property taxes per capita: $40 (1997).
Education: High school graduation rate: 78.9% (2000); College graduation rate: 9.7% (2000).
Housing: Homeownership rate: 90.4% (2000); Median home value: $67,100 (2000); Median rent: $175 per month (2000); Median age of housing: 27 years (2000).
Transportation: Commute to work: 87.7% car, 0.0% public transportation, 0.0% walk, 12.3% work from home (2000); Travel time to work: 8.6% less than 15 minutes, 72.0% 15 to 30 minutes, 14.0% 30 to 45 minutes, 5.4% 45 to 60 minutes, 0.0% 60 minutes or more (2000)

HAMMEL (town). Covers a land area of 35.473 square miles and a water area of 0.250 square miles. Located at 45.15° N. Lat.; 90.48° W. Long.
Population: 735 (2000); Race: 98.8% White, 0.3% Black, 0.0% Asian, 0.4% American Indian and Alaska Native, 0.0% Hispanic of any race, 0.4% two or more races (2000); Density: 20.7 persons per square mile (2000); Age: 30.7% under 18, 7.5% over 64 (2000); Marriage status: 23.3% never married, 69.0% now married, 1.4% widowed, 6.3% divorced (2000); Foreign born: 0.0% (2000); Ancestry (includes multiple ancestries): 64.7% German, 12.5% Polish, 9.2% Norwegian, 7.5% Irish, 7.4% Swedish (2000).
Economy: Employment by occupation: 7.2% management, 11.1% professional, 8.6% services, 19.0% sales, 3.2% farming, 12.2% construction, 38.8% production (2000).
Income: Per capita income: $17,425 (2000); Median household income: $51,250 (2000); Poverty rate: 7.6% (2000).
Taxes: Total city taxes per capita: $46 (1997); City property taxes per capita: $45 (1997).
Education: High school graduation rate: 82.3% (2000); College graduation rate: 8.2% (2000).
Housing: Homeownership rate: 91.3% (2000); Median home value: $88,600 (2000); Median rent: $400 per month (2000); Median age of housing: 26 years (2000).
Transportation: Commute to work: 89.2% car, 0.5% public transportation, 2.4% walk, 7.5% work from home (2000); Travel time to work: 32.7% less than 15 minutes, 56.4% 15 to 30 minutes, 4.3% 30 to 45 minutes, 0.8% 45 to 60 minutes, 5.9% 60 minutes or more (2000)

HOLWAY (town). Covers a land area of 36.354 square miles and a water area of 0.010 square miles. Located at 45.08° N. Lat.; 90.49° W. Long.
Population: 854 (2000); Race: 97.5% White, 0.9% Black, 0.0% Asian, 0.0% American Indian and Alaska Native, 1.1% Hispanic of any race, 0.6% two or more races (2000); Density: 23.5 persons per square mile (2000); Age: 32.0% under 18, 8.1% over 64 (2000); Marriage status: 28.2% never married, 60.0% now married, 5.5% widowed, 6.3% divorced (2000); Foreign born: 1.4% (2000); Ancestry (includes multiple ancestries): 47.7% German, 6.8% Norwegian, 5.2% Polish, 4.5% Irish, 4.4% Other groups (2000).
Economy: Employment by occupation: 13.9% management, 8.0% professional, 14.7% services, 10.8% sales, 4.4% farming, 11.6% construction, 36.8% production (2000).
Income: Per capita income: $13,718 (2000); Median household income: $37,500 (2000); Poverty rate: 20.8% (2000).
Taxes: Total city taxes per capita: $16 (1997); City property taxes per capita: $16 (1997).
Education: High school graduation rate: 66.6% (2000); College graduation rate: 7.3% (2000).
Housing: Homeownership rate: 93.0% (2000); Median home value: $64,000 (2000); Median rent: $275 per month (2000); Median age of housing: 40 years (2000).
Transportation: Commute to work: 71.5% car, 0.0% public transportation, 6.9% walk, 17.7% work from home (2000); Travel time to work: 25.3% less than 15 minutes, 55.4% 15 to 30 minutes, 8.0% 30 to 45 minutes, 4.8% 45 to 60 minutes, 6.4% 60 minutes or more (2000)

JUMP RIVER (town). Covers a land area of 35.974 square miles and a water area of 0 square miles. Located at 45.32° N. Lat.; 90.75° W. Long. Elevation is 1,185 feet.
Population: 311 (2000); Race: 99.6% White, 0.0% Black, 0.0% Asian, 0.0% American Indian and Alaska Native, 0.0% Hispanic of any race, 0.4% two or more races (2000); Density: 8.6 persons per square mile (2000); Age: 22.6% under 18, 17.3% over 64 (2000); Marriage status: 17.0% never married, 60.7% now married, 10.0% widowed, 12.2% divorced (2000); Foreign born: 0.0% (2000); Ancestry (includes multiple ancestries): 40.3% German, 16.6% Irish, 12.4% Norwegian, 11.7% English, 11.3% United States or American (2000).
Economy: Employment by occupation: 21.1% management, 5.7% professional, 8.9% services, 13.8% sales, 13.0% farming, 6.5% construction, 30.9% production (2000).
Income: Per capita income: $18,286 (2000); Median household income: $29,167 (2000); Poverty rate: 8.5% (2000).
Taxes: Total city taxes per capita: $63 (1997); City property taxes per capita: $63 (1997).
Education: High school graduation rate: 73.7% (2000); College graduation rate: 4.9% (2000).
Housing: Homeownership rate: 82.5% (2000); Median home value: $50,000 (2000); Median rent: $275 per month (2000); Median age of housing: 29 years (2000).
Transportation: Commute to work: 68.3% car, 2.4% public transportation, 3.3% walk, 21.1% work from home (2000); Travel time to work: 15.5% less than 15 minutes, 30.9% 15 to 30 minutes, 19.6% 30 to 45 minutes, 16.5% 45 to 60 minutes, 17.5% 60 minutes or more (2000)

LITTLE BLACK (town). Covers a land area of 35.024 square miles and a water area of 0.010 square miles. Located at 45.08° N. Lat.; 90.36° W. Long. Elevation is 1,418 feet.
Population: 1,148 (2000); Race: 99.2% White, 0.2% Black, 0.0% Asian, 0.0% American Indian and Alaska Native, 1.4% Hispanic of any race, 0.6% two or more races (2000); Density: 32.8 persons per square mile (2000); Age: 30.6% under 18, 10.7% over 64 (2000); Marriage status: 27.5% never married, 61.9% now married, 3.1% widowed, 7.4% divorced (2000); Foreign born: 0.2% (2000); Ancestry (includes multiple ancestries): 62.6% German, 6.4% Polish, 6.0% Norwegian, 5.3% Irish, 4.9% United States or American (2000).
Economy: Employment by occupation: 17.7% management, 8.6% professional, 8.0% services, 20.6% sales, 5.5% farming, 13.4% construction, 26.3% production (2000).
Income: Per capita income: $17,633 (2000); Median household income: $45,000 (2000); Poverty rate: 8.1% (2000).
Taxes: Total city taxes per capita: $33 (1997); City property taxes per capita: $33 (1997).
Education: High school graduation rate: 81.0% (2000); College graduation rate: 7.5% (2000).
Housing: Homeownership rate: 89.8% (2000); Median home value: $83,600 (2000); Median rent: $288 per month (2000); Median age of housing: 44 years (2000).
Transportation: Commute to work: 83.9% car, 0.2% public transportation, 4.4% walk, 9.9% work from home (2000); Travel time to work: 49.3% less than 15 minutes, 37.2% 15 to 30 minutes, 5.1% 30 to 45 minutes, 3.8% 45 to 60 minutes, 4.5% 60 minutes or more (2000)

LUBLIN (village). Covers a land area of 1.517 square miles and a water area of 0 square miles. Located at 45.07° N. Lat.; 90.72° W. Long. Elevation is 1,289 feet.
Population: 110 (2000); Race: 100.0% White, 0.0% Black, 0.0% Asian, 0.0% American Indian and Alaska Native, 0.0% Hispanic of any race, 0.0% two or more races (2000); Density: 72.5 persons per square mile (2000); Age: 11.7% under 18, 22.3% over 64 (2000); Marriage status: 23.7% never married, 52.7% now married, 7.5% widowed, 16.1% divorced (2000); Foreign born: 0.0% (2000); Ancestry (includes multiple ancestries): 41.7% Polish, 24.3% German, 12.6% Russian, 8.7% Ukrainian, 6.8% Slovak (2000).
Economy: In lumbering and dairying region. On the South edge of Chequamegon National Forest to Northeast. Employment by occupation: 8.3% management, 6.3% professional, 16.7% services, 12.5% sales, 4.2% farming, 14.6% construction, 37.5% production (2000).
Income: Per capita income: $15,823 (2000); Median household income: $20,938 (2000); Poverty rate: 27.2% (2000).
Taxes: Total city taxes per capita: $31 (1997); City property taxes per capita: $23 (1997).
Education: High school graduation rate: 63.1% (2000); College graduation rate: 10.7% (2000).
Housing: Homeownership rate: 71.7% (2000); Median home value: $43,800 (2000); Median rent: $245 per month (2000); Median age of housing: 52 years (2000).

Transportation: Commute to work: 81.3% car, 0.0% public transportation, 14.6% walk, 4.2% work from home (2000); Travel time to work: 23.9% less than 15 minutes, 41.3% 15 to 30 minutes, 13.0% 30 to 45 minutes, 4.3% 45 to 60 minutes, 17.4% 60 minutes or more (2000)

MAPLEHURST (town). Covers a land area of 35.912 square miles and a water area of 0.020 square miles. Located at 45.06° N. Lat.; 90.61° W. Long. Elevation is 1,278 feet.
Population: 359 (2000); Race: 99.0% White, 0.0% Black, 0.0% Asian, 0.0% American Indian and Alaska Native, 3.4% Hispanic of any race, 1.0% two or more races (2000); Density: 10.0 persons per square mile (2000); Age: 31.8% under 18, 11.6% over 64 (2000); Marriage status: 22.9% never married, 64.1% now married, 7.8% widowed, 5.2% divorced (2000); Foreign born: 4.7% (2000); Ancestry (includes multiple ancestries): 38.4% German, 25.1% Polish, 5.9% French (except Basque), 5.2% Other groups, 4.2% English (2000).
Economy: Employment by occupation: 18.8% management, 6.8% professional, 8.9% services, 13.6% sales, 8.4% farming, 13.6% construction, 29.8% production (2000).
Income: Per capita income: $13,062 (2000); Median household income: $29,375 (2000); Poverty rate: 19.2% (2000).
Taxes: Total city taxes per capita: $114 (1997); City property taxes per capita: $114 (1997).
Education: High school graduation rate: 67.1% (2000); College graduation rate: 1.6% (2000).
Housing: Homeownership rate: 80.9% (2000); Median home value: $34,000 (2000); Median rent: $442 per month (2000); Median age of housing: 39 years (2000).
Transportation: Commute to work: 69.3% car, 2.6% public transportation, 3.2% walk, 23.8% work from home (2000); Travel time to work: 15.3% less than 15 minutes, 53.5% 15 to 30 minutes, 17.4% 30 to 45 minutes, 3.5% 45 to 60 minutes, 10.4% 60 minutes or more (2000)

MCKINLEY (town). Covers a land area of 35.746 square miles and a water area of 0.075 square miles. Located at 45.33° N. Lat.; 90.85° W. Long.
Population: 418 (2000); Race: 99.3% White, 0.0% Black, 0.0% Asian, 0.0% American Indian and Alaska Native, 0.0% Hispanic of any race, 0.7% two or more races (2000); Density: 11.7 persons per square mile (2000); Age: 34.4% under 18, 15.3% over 64 (2000); Marriage status: 20.8% never married, 64.8% now married, 5.7% widowed, 8.8% divorced (2000); Foreign born: 0.4% (2000); Ancestry (includes multiple ancestries): 39.8% German, 13.7% Polish, 11.2% Irish, 5.8% English, 4.9% Slovene (2000).
Economy: Single-family building permits issued: 5 (2001) / 4 (2000); Multi-family building permits issued: 0 (2001) / 0 (2000); Employment by occupation: 25.9% management, 8.1% professional, 9.2% services, 7.0% sales, 8.1% farming, 6.5% construction, 35.1% production (2000).
Income: Per capita income: $16,276 (2000); Median household income: $36,528 (2000); Poverty rate: 13.3% (2000).
Taxes: Total city taxes per capita: $52 (1997); City property taxes per capita: $52 (1997).
Education: High school graduation rate: 74.6% (2000); College graduation rate: 11.9% (2000).
Housing: Homeownership rate: 93.0% (2000); Median home value: $42,500 (2000); Median age of housing: 30 years (2000).
Transportation: Commute to work: 66.5% car, 0.0% public transportation, 9.1% walk, 24.4% work from home (2000); Travel time to work: 21.1% less than 15 minutes, 28.6% 15 to 30 minutes, 27.8% 30 to 45 minutes, 17.3% 45 to 60 minutes, 5.3% 60 minutes or more (2000)

MEDFORD (city). Covers a land area of 3.497 square miles and a water area of 0.027 square miles. Located at 45.13° N. Lat.; 90.34° W. Long. Elevation is 1,476 feet.
History: Medford became the seat of Taylor County in 1875, when the Wisconsin Central Railroad determined the location of a courthouse. Medford once claimed the largest "little pig market" in the world. Other early industries were a creamery, box factory, sash and door works, and a pea cannery.
Population: 4,350 (2000); Race: 98.1% White, 0.0% Black, 0.4% Asian, 0.7% American Indian and Alaska Native, 0.2% Hispanic of any race, 0.8% two or more races (2000); Density: 1,243.9 persons per square mile (2000); Age: 23.3% under 18, 22.1% over 64 (2000); Marriage status: 25.1% never married, 56.2% now married, 9.7% widowed, 9.0% divorced (2000); Foreign born: 1.3% (2000); Ancestry (includes multiple ancestries): 59.8% German, 8.0% Norwegian, 7.1% Irish, 6.9% Polish, 5.2% English (2000).
Economy: Single-family building permits issued: 5 (2001) / 6 (2000); Multi-family building permits issued: 0 (2001) / 2 (2000); Employment by occupation: 12.4% management, 15.2% professional, 13.8% services, 22.3% sales, 1.2% farming, 9.2% construction, 26.0% production (2000).
Income: Per capita income: $19,962 (2000); Median household income: $35,278 (2000); Poverty rate: 9.1% (2000).
Taxes: Total city taxes per capita: $192 (1997); City property taxes per capita: $168 (1997).
Education: High school graduation rate: 81.4% (2000); College graduation rate: 19.1% (2000).

School District(s)

Medford Area (PK-12)
2000 Enrollment: 2,427 715-748-4620

Housing: Homeownership rate: 63.1% (2000); Median home value: $76,700 (2000); Median rent: $341 per month (2000); Median age of housing: 39 years (2000).
Hospitals: Memorial Health Center (164 beds)
Safety: Violent crime rate: 16.0 per 10,000 population; Property crime rate: 333.3 per 10,000 population (2001).
Newspapers: The Star News (1 x week)
Transportation: Commute to work: 87.6% car, 0.8% public transportation, 6.3% walk, 5.1% work from home (2000); Travel time to work: 77.8% less than 15 minutes, 12.6% 15 to 30 minutes, 5.0% 30 to 45 minutes, 2.6% 45 to 60 minutes, 2.1% 60 minutes or more (2000)
Additional Information Contacts
Medford Chamber of Commerce 715-748-4729

MEDFORD (town). Covers a land area of 37.701 square miles and a water area of 0.070 square miles. Located at 45.15° N. Lat.; 90.37° W. Long. Elevation is 1,476 feet.
History: Nearby is a Mennonite colony. Incorporated 1889.
Population: 2,216 (2000); Race: 97.1% White, 1.2% Black, 0.0% Asian, 0.5% American Indian and Alaska Native, 0.5% Hispanic of any race, 0.9% two or more races (2000); Density: 58.8 persons per square mile (2000); Age: 27.8% under 18, 9.5% over 64 (2000); Marriage status: 21.4% never married, 65.9% now married, 4.6% widowed, 8.2% divorced (2000); Foreign born: 0.0% (2000); Ancestry (includes multiple ancestries): 62.8% German, 9.7% Irish, 7.7% Polish, 6.9% Norwegian, 5.0% French (except Basque) (2000).
Economy: Lumbering, livestock-raising, and dairying area. Dairy products. Manufacturing: food processing; crushed concrete, building materials. South unit of Chequamegon National Forest to Northwest. Single-family building permits issued: 13 (2001) / 18 (2000); Multi-family building permits issued: 0 (2001) / 0 (2000); Employment by occupation: 10.5% management, 12.6% professional, 13.8% services, 25.0% sales, 2.9% farming, 8.7% construction, 26.5% production (2000).
Income: Per capita income: $20,261 (2000); Median household income: $46,912 (2000); Poverty rate: 4.3% (2000).
Taxes: Total city taxes per capita: $44 (1997); City property taxes per capita: $43 (1997).
Education: High school graduation rate: 86.9% (2000); College graduation rate: 11.7% (2000).
Housing: Homeownership rate: 83.6% (2000); Median home value: $94,000 (2000); Median rent: $450 per month (2000); Median age of housing: 23 years (2000).
Transportation: Commute to work: 93.8% car, 0.2% public transportation, 0.7% walk, 5.3% work from home (2000); Travel time to work: 72.3% less than 15 minutes, 18.8% 15 to 30 minutes, 4.7% 30 to 45 minutes, 1.6% 45 to 60 minutes, 2.7% 60 minutes or more (2000)

MOLITOR (town). Covers a land area of 35.294 square miles and a water area of 0.670 square miles. Located at 45.25° N. Lat.; 90.48° W. Long.
Population: 263 (2000); Race: 98.9% White, 0.0% Black, 0.0% Asian, 0.0% American Indian and Alaska Native, 0.4% Hispanic of any race, 1.1% two or more races (2000); Density: 7.5 persons per square mile (2000); Age: 22.4% under 18, 11.9% over 64 (2000); Marriage status: 23.2% never married, 70.5% now married, 3.6% widowed, 2.7% divorced (2000); Foreign born: 0.0% (2000); Ancestry (includes multiple ancestries): 56.7% German, 16.4% Polish, 8.6% Irish, 4.9% United States or American, 3.7% Other groups (2000).
Economy: Single-family building permits issued: 0 (2001) / 2 (2000); Multi-family building permits issued: 0 (2001) / 0 (2000); Employment by occupation: 6.5% management, 11.6% professional, 12.3% services, 18.8% sales, 1.4% farming, 10.9% construction, 38.4% production (2000).
Income: Per capita income: $18,804 (2000); Median household income: $37,500 (2000); Poverty rate: 13.4% (2000).
Taxes: Total city taxes per capita: $116 (1997); City property taxes per capita: $116 (1997).

Education: High school graduation rate: 70.9% (2000); College graduation rate: 8.8% (2000).
Housing: Homeownership rate: 100.0% (2000); Median home value: $95,000 (2000); Median age of housing: 26 years (2000).
Transportation: Commute to work: 91.2% car, 0.0% public transportation, 0.0% walk, 8.8% work from home (2000); Travel time to work: 12.9% less than 15 minutes, 64.5% 15 to 30 minutes, 18.5% 30 to 45 minutes, 2.4% 45 to 60 minutes, 1.6% 60 minutes or more (2000)

PERSHING (town). Covers a land area of 35.672 square miles and a water area of 0.157 square miles. Located at 45.25° N. Lat.; 90.88° W. Long.
Population: 180 (2000); Race: 98.7% White, 0.0% Black, 0.0% Asian, 0.0% American Indian and Alaska Native, 0.0% Hispanic of any race, 1.3% two or more races (2000); Density: 5.0 persons per square mile (2000); Age: 27.7% under 18, 23.2% over 64 (2000); Marriage status: 25.6% never married, 55.4% now married, 12.4% widowed, 6.6% divorced (2000); Foreign born: 1.3% (2000); Ancestry (includes multiple ancestries): 29.7% German, 19.4% Polish, 12.9% English, 11.0% Norwegian, 10.3% Czech (2000).
Economy: Employment by occupation: 11.6% management, 8.7% professional, 2.9% services, 14.5% sales, 8.7% farming, 26.1% construction, 27.5% production (2000).
Income: Per capita income: $14,607 (2000); Median household income: $27,083 (2000); Poverty rate: 14.2% (2000).
Taxes: Total city taxes per capita: $70 (1997); City property taxes per capita: $70 (1997).
Education: High school graduation rate: 79.8% (2000); College graduation rate: 11.1% (2000).
Housing: Homeownership rate: 90.6% (2000); Median home value: $85,000 (2000); Median age of housing: 35 years (2000).
Transportation: Commute to work: 83.6% car, 0.0% public transportation, 6.6% walk, 9.8% work from home (2000); Travel time to work: 32.7% less than 15 minutes, 27.3% 15 to 30 minutes, 23.6% 30 to 45 minutes, 5.5% 45 to 60 minutes, 10.9% 60 minutes or more (2000)

RIB LAKE (village). Covers a land area of 1.866 square miles and a water area of 0.468 square miles. Located at 45.31° N. Lat.; 90.20° W. Long. Elevation is 1,570 feet.
Population: 878 (2000); Race: 98.5% White, 0.0% Black, 0.8% Asian, 0.8% American Indian and Alaska Native, 0.0% Hispanic of any race, 0.0% two or more races (2000); Density: 470.5 persons per square mile (2000); Age: 22.3% under 18, 24.0% over 64 (2000); Marriage status: 20.3% never married, 56.8% now married, 12.7% widowed, 10.2% divorced (2000); Foreign born: 0.8% (2000); Ancestry (includes multiple ancestries): 52.6% German, 9.4% Norwegian, 8.1% Polish, 7.3% Swedish, 7.2% Irish (2000).
Economy: Single-family building permits issued: 2 (2001) / 4 (2000); Multi-family building permits issued: 0 (2001) / 0 (2000); Employment by occupation: 6.7% management, 10.6% professional, 14.7% services, 16.8% sales, 0.5% farming, 10.8% construction, 39.9% production (2000).
Income: Per capita income: $14,571 (2000); Median household income: $32,222 (2000); Poverty rate: 12.1% (2000).
Taxes: Total city taxes per capita: $144 (1997); City property taxes per capita: $119 (1997).
Education: High school graduation rate: 69.1% (2000); College graduation rate: 9.7% (2000).

School District(s)

Rib Lake (PK-12)
2000 Enrollment: 584 715-427-3222

Housing: Homeownership rate: 61.1% (2000); Median home value: $63,200 (2000); Median rent: $299 per month (2000); Median age of housing: 53 years (2000).
Transportation: Commute to work: 82.1% car, 0.8% public transportation, 16.3% walk, 0.8% work from home (2000); Travel time to work: 45.7% less than 15 minutes, 33.2% 15 to 30 minutes, 11.0% 30 to 45 minutes, 7.3% 45 to 60 minutes, 2.9% 60 minutes or more (2000)

RIB LAKE (town). Covers a land area of 74.014 square miles and a water area of 0.848 square miles. Located at 45.32° N. Lat.; 90.15° W. Long. Elevation is 1,570 feet.
Population: 768 (2000); Race: 99.5% White, 0.0% Black, 0.3% Asian, 0.0% American Indian and Alaska Native, 0.8% Hispanic of any race, 0.0% two or more races (2000); Density: 10.4 persons per square mile (2000); Age: 28.9% under 18, 15.3% over 64 (2000); Marriage status: 23.1% never married, 65.1% now married, 6.6% widowed, 5.2% divorced (2000); Foreign born: 0.3% (2000); Ancestry (includes multiple ancestries): 56.7% German, 12.6% Polish, 5.7% Irish, 5.2% Czech, 4.3% Norwegian (2000).
Economy: Dairy products; lumber. Single-family building permits issued: 8 (2001) / 3 (2000); Multi-family building permits issued: 0 (2001) / 0 (2000); Employment by occupation: 19.8% management, 12.1% professional, 11.8% services, 11.2% sales, 4.3% farming, 6.0% construction, 34.8% production (2000).
Income: Per capita income: $15,641 (2000); Median household income: $38,393 (2000); Poverty rate: 9.7% (2000).
Taxes: Total city taxes per capita: $51 (1997); City property taxes per capita: $50 (1997).
Education: High school graduation rate: 80.0% (2000); College graduation rate: 9.3% (2000).
Housing: Homeownership rate: 90.9% (2000); Median home value: $72,500 (2000); Median rent: $325 per month (2000); Median age of housing: 33 years (2000).
Transportation: Commute to work: 81.3% car, 0.0% public transportation, 5.3% walk, 13.5% work from home (2000); Travel time to work: 33.4% less than 15 minutes, 34.1% 15 to 30 minutes, 16.9% 30 to 45 minutes, 4.7% 45 to 60 minutes, 10.8% 60 minutes or more (2000)

ROOSEVELT (town). Covers a land area of 34.386 square miles and a water area of 0.129 square miles. Located at 45.06° N. Lat.; 90.72° W. Long.
Population: 444 (2000); Race: 99.3% White, 0.0% Black, 0.0% Asian, 0.0% American Indian and Alaska Native, 0.7% Hispanic of any race, 0.0% two or more races (2000); Density: 12.9 persons per square mile (2000); Age: 22.8% under 18, 24.1% over 64 (2000); Marriage status: 21.8% never married, 63.8% now married, 6.4% widowed, 8.0% divorced (2000); Foreign born: 1.5% (2000); Ancestry (includes multiple ancestries): 40.2% Polish, 33.0% German, 8.2% United States or American, 4.7% Irish, 4.2% Norwegian (2000).
Economy: Employment by occupation: 14.1% management, 8.6% professional, 20.2% services, 12.9% sales, 2.5% farming, 19.0% construction, 22.7% production (2000).
Income: Per capita income: $15,476 (2000); Median household income: $32,000 (2000); Poverty rate: 9.0% (2000).
Taxes: Total city taxes per capita: $22 (1997); City property taxes per capita: $20 (1997).
Education: High school graduation rate: 62.8% (2000); College graduation rate: 2.8% (2000).
Housing: Homeownership rate: 92.7% (2000); Median home value: $56,000 (2000); Median rent: $163 per month (2000); Median age of housing: 59 years (2000).
Transportation: Commute to work: 77.4% car, 0.0% public transportation, 3.6% walk, 16.1% work from home (2000); Travel time to work: 22.7% less than 15 minutes, 50.4% 15 to 30 minutes, 15.6% 30 to 45 minutes, 5.7% 45 to 60 minutes, 5.7% 60 minutes or more (2000)

STETSONVILLE (village). Covers a land area of 0.367 square miles and a water area of 0 square miles. Located at 45.07° N. Lat.; 90.31° W. Long. Elevation is 1,450 feet.
History: Stetsonville was named for the settler who built the first sawmill on a pond here. The sawmill was followed by a tie mill, and then a cheese factory, processing milk from the surrounding dairy farms.
Population: 563 (2000); Race: 98.0% White, 0.0% Black, 0.0% Asian, 0.0% American Indian and Alaska Native, 0.0% Hispanic of any race, 2.0% two or more races (2000); Density: 1,533.0 persons per square mile (2000); Age: 31.3% under 18, 16.6% over 64 (2000); Marriage status: 22.8% never married, 60.4% now married, 9.7% widowed, 7.2% divorced (2000); Foreign born: 0.4% (2000); Ancestry (includes multiple ancestries): 60.8% German, 11.3% Polish, 10.2% Norwegian, 5.5% Swedish, 5.3% Irish (2000).
Economy: Single-family building permits issued: 0 (2001) / 0 (2000); Multi-family building permits issued: 0 (2001) / 0 (2000); Employment by occupation: 5.3% management, 9.1% professional, 11.7% services, 23.8% sales, 3.0% farming, 16.6% construction, 30.6% production (2000).
Income: Per capita income: $15,531 (2000); Median household income: $32,045 (2000); Poverty rate: 4.4% (2000).
Taxes: Total city taxes per capita: $63 (1997); City property taxes per capita: $57 (1997).
Education: High school graduation rate: 85.0% (2000); College graduation rate: 8.8% (2000).
Housing: Homeownership rate: 76.0% (2000); Median home value: $78,300 (2000); Median rent: $304 per month (2000); Median age of housing: 28 years (2000).
Transportation: Commute to work: 94.7% car, 0.8% public transportation, 0.8% walk, 3.8% work from home (2000); Travel time to work: 60.5% less than 15 minutes, 23.7% 15 to 30 minutes, 8.7% 30 to 45 minutes, 7.1% 45 to 60 minutes, 0.0% 60 minutes or more (2000)

TAFT (town). Covers a land area of 36.492 square miles and a water area of 0.132 square miles. Located at 45.06° N. Lat.; 90.87° W. Long.
Population: 361 (2000); Race: 100.0% White, 0.0% Black, 0.0% Asian, 0.0% American Indian and Alaska Native, 0.3% Hispanic of any race, 0.0% two or more races (2000); Density: 9.9 persons per square mile (2000); Age: 36.6% under 18, 12.2% over 64 (2000); Marriage status: 25.7% never married, 63.6% now married, 4.5% widowed, 6.3% divorced (2000); Foreign born: 0.0% (2000); Ancestry (includes multiple ancestries): 48.8% German, 43.6% Polish, 10.8% Norwegian, 6.2% Irish, 4.1% English (2000).
Economy: Employment by occupation: 20.9% management, 4.9% professional, 11.7% services, 17.8% sales, 4.9% farming, 11.7% construction, 28.2% production (2000).
Income: Per capita income: $14,447 (2000); Median household income: $37,500 (2000); Poverty rate: 8.7% (2000).
Taxes: Total city taxes per capita: $78 (1997); City property taxes per capita: $78 (1997).
Education: High school graduation rate: 66.0% (2000); College graduation rate: 6.2% (2000).
Housing: Homeownership rate: 88.7% (2000); Median home value: $65,000 (2000); Median rent: $625 per month (2000); Median age of housing: 30 years (2000).
Transportation: Commute to work: 78.5% car, 0.0% public transportation, 3.1% walk, 18.4% work from home (2000); Travel time to work: 26.3% less than 15 minutes, 33.8% 15 to 30 minutes, 21.8% 30 to 45 minutes, 12.0% 45 to 60 minutes, 6.0% 60 minutes or more (2000)

WESTBORO (town). Covers a land area of 124.096 square miles and a water area of 1.340 square miles. Located at 45.33° N. Lat.; 90.43° W. Long. Elevation is 1,520 feet.
History: Westboro developed as a headquarters for fishermen who came for the many lakes and streams in the area.
Population: 660 (2000); Race: 99.3% White, 0.0% Black, 0.0% Asian, 0.7% American Indian and Alaska Native, 0.0% Hispanic of any race, 0.0% two or more races (2000); Density: 5.3 persons per square mile (2000); Age: 30.5% under 18, 12.0% over 64 (2000); Marriage status: 25.4% never married, 61.3% now married, 6.6% widowed, 6.6% divorced (2000); Foreign born: 0.5% (2000); Ancestry (includes multiple ancestries): 49.4% German, 9.4% Swedish, 8.2% Polish, 7.9% Irish, 7.1% Norwegian (2000).
Economy: Single-family building permits issued: 10 (2001) / 9 (2000); Multi-family building permits issued: 0 (2001) / 0 (2000); Employment by occupation: 13.4% management, 11.1% professional, 15.3% services, 13.7% sales, 1.6% farming, 14.0% construction, 30.9% production (2000).
Income: Per capita income: $14,018 (2000); Median household income: $33,021 (2000); Poverty rate: 11.7% (2000).
Taxes: Total city taxes per capita: $57 (1997); City property taxes per capita: $56 (1997).
Education: High school graduation rate: 80.5% (2000); College graduation rate: 11.7% (2000).
Housing: Homeownership rate: 92.5% (2000); Median home value: $58,700 (2000); Median rent: $270 per month (2000); Median age of housing: 31 years (2000).
Transportation: Commute to work: 86.5% car, 0.6% public transportation, 1.0% walk, 10.3% work from home (2000); Travel time to work: 18.9% less than 15 minutes, 50.4% 15 to 30 minutes, 25.4% 30 to 45 minutes, 1.4% 45 to 60 minutes, 3.9% 60 minutes or more (2000)

Trempealeau County

Located in western Wisconsin; bounded on the west by the Trempealeau River, on the southwest by the Mississippi River and the Minnesota border, and on the southeast by the Black River; drained by the Buffalo, Black, and Trempealeau Rivers. Covers a land area of 734.10 square miles, a water area of 7.90 square miles, and is located in the Central Time Zone. The county government was organized in 1854. County seat is Whitehall.

Weather Station: Blair — Elevation: 859 feet

	Jan	Feb	Mar	Apr	May	Jun	Jul	Aug	Sep	Oct	Nov	Dec
High	23	30	41	57	70	78	82	80	71	59	42	28
Low	0	6	20	32	44	53	58	55	46	34	23	8
Precip	0.9	1.0	1.9	3.2	4.0	3.8	4.4	4.6	4.2	2.6	2.2	1.1
Snow	10.9	6.5	7.6	1.7	tr	0.0	0.0	0.0	0.0	0.2	4.2	9.2

High and Low temperatures in degrees Fahrenheit; Precipitation and Snow in inches

Weather Station: Trempealeau Dam 6 — Elevation: 659 feet

	Jan	Feb	Mar	Apr	May	Jun	Jul	Aug	Sep	Oct	Nov	Dec
High	24	31	42	58	70	79	83	81	72	60	42	29
Low	5	11	24	37	48	58	62	60	51	40	26	13
Precip	1.1	0.9	2.0	3.2	3.8	3.7	4.3	4.5	4.0	2.5	2.2	1.1
Snow	na	5.9	na	0.9	0.0	0.0	0.0	0.0	0.0	0.0	2.7	8.2

High and Low temperatures in degrees Fahrenheit; Precipitation and Snow in inches

Population: 27,010 (2000); Race: 98.9% White, 0.1% Black, 0.1% Asian, 0.3% American Indian and Alaska Native, 1.0% Hispanic of any race, 0.4% two or more races (2000); Density: 36.8 persons per square mile (2000); Age: 25.3% under 18, 16.4% over 64 (2000).
Religion: Five largest groups: 39.4% Evangelical Lutheran Church in America, 31.8% Catholic Church, 1.4% Presbyterian Church (U.S.A.), 1.1% United Church of Christ, 0.7% The United Methodist Church (2000).
Economy: Unemployment rate: 4.7% (11/2002); Total civilian labor force: 15,569 (11/2002); Leading industries: 46.0% manufacturing; 11.9% health care and social assistance; 10.3% retail trade (2000); Companies that employ more than 1,000 persons: 1 (2000); Companies that employ more than 100 persons: 17 (2000); Farms: 1,408 totaling 340,536 acres (1997); Minority business ownership rate: 0.0% (1997); Women business ownership rate: 28.4% (1997); Retail sales per capita: $6,417 (1997). Single-family building permits issued: 118 (2001) / 142 (2000); Multi-family building permits issued: 22 (2001) / 11 (2000).
Income: Per capita income: $17,681 (2000); Median household income: $37,889 (2000); Poverty rate: 8.3% (2000); Bankruptcy rate: 3.09% (2001).
Taxes: Total county taxes per capita: $190 (1997); County property taxes per capita: $158 (1997).
Education: High school graduation rate: 80.9% (2000); College graduation rate: 13.3% (2000).
Housing: Homeownership rate: 74.3% (2000); Median home value: $77,000 (2000); Median rent: $310 per month (2000); Median age of housing: 38 years (2000).
Health: Birth rate: 124.0 per 10,000 population (1998); Age adjusted death rate: 77.7 per 10,000 population (1999); Age adjusted cancer mortality rate: 189.8 deaths per 100,000 population (1999). Number of physicians: 7.8 per 10,000 population (1999); Number of hospital beds: 96.6 per 10,000 population (1999).
Elections: 2000 Presidential election results: 54.9% Gore, 41.1% Bush, 3.4% Nader, 0.2% Buchanan
National and State Parks: Borst Valley State Public Hunting Area; Chimney Rock State Public Hunting Grounds; Hardies Creek State Forest; Lakes Coulee State Public Hunting Grounds; Perrot State Park; Tamarack Creek State Wildlife Area; Tollefson Marsh State Wildlife Area; Trempealeau Lakes State Public Hunting Grounds; Trempealeau National Wildlife Refuge; Vosse Coulee State Wildlife Area
Additional Information Contacts
Trempealeau County Government Offices. 715-538-2311
Arcadia Chamber of Commerce. 608-323-2319
Trempealeau Chamber of Commerce. 608-534-6780

Trempealeau County Communities

ALBION (town). Covers a land area of 35.331 square miles and a water area of 0.005 square miles. Located at 44.55° N. Lat.; 91.46° W. Long.
Population: 595 (2000); Race: 99.0% White, 0.0% Black, 0.3% Asian, 0.0% American Indian and Alaska Native, 0.6% Hispanic of any race, 0.2% two or more races (2000); Density: 16.8 persons per square mile (2000); Age: 31.3% under 18, 9.7% over 64 (2000); Marriage status: 20.7% never married, 69.1% now married, 2.4% widowed, 7.8% divorced (2000); Foreign born: 0.3% (2000); Ancestry (includes multiple ancestries): 55.5% Norwegian, 33.1% German, 8.1% English, 7.9% Irish, 4.1% United States or American (2000).
Economy: Employment by occupation: 20.4% management, 10.3% professional, 10.0% services, 24.6% sales, 4.3% farming, 10.0% construction, 20.4% production (2000).
Income: Per capita income: $18,452 (2000); Median household income: $42,431 (2000); Poverty rate: 5.6% (2000).
Taxes: Total city taxes per capita: $97 (1997); City property taxes per capita: $90 (1997).
Education: High school graduation rate: 89.3% (2000); College graduation rate: 9.9% (2000).
Housing: Homeownership rate: 82.5% (2000); Median home value: $85,700 (2000); Median rent: $284 per month (2000); Median age of housing: 42 years (2000).
Transportation: Commute to work: 84.4% car, 0.3% public transportation, 4.9% walk, 9.8% work from home (2000); Travel time to work: 32.5% less

than 15 minutes, 25.1% 15 to 30 minutes, 33.6% 30 to 45 minutes, 4.7% 45 to 60 minutes, 4.1% 60 minutes or more (2000)

ARCADIA (city). Covers a land area of 2.654 square miles and a water area of 0 square miles. Located at 44.25° N. Lat.; 91.49° W. Long. Elevation is 728 feet.
Population: 2,402 (2000); Race: 98.8% White, 0.0% Black, 0.0% Asian, 0.7% American Indian and Alaska Native, 2.9% Hispanic of any race, 0.4% two or more races (2000); Density: 905.2 persons per square mile (2000); Age: 25.5% under 18, 17.2% over 64 (2000); Marriage status: 27.8% never married, 49.3% now married, 11.5% widowed, 11.4% divorced (2000); Foreign born: 1.3% (2000); Ancestry (includes multiple ancestries): 39.8% German, 34.0% Polish, 18.0% Norwegian, 5.4% Irish, 4.6% Other groups (2000).
Economy: Single-family building permits issued: 0 (2001) / 0 (2000); Multi-family building permits issued: 2 (2001) / 0 (2000); Employment by occupation: 8.7% management, 11.4% professional, 15.9% services, 18.6% sales, 2.2% farming, 8.1% construction, 35.1% production (2000).
Income: Per capita income: $17,157 (2000); Median household income: $31,571 (2000); Poverty rate: 9.1% (2000).
Taxes: Total city taxes per capita: $251 (1997); City property taxes per capita: $237 (1997).
Education: High school graduation rate: 74.1% (2000); College graduation rate: 8.9% (2000).

School District(s)

Arcadia (PK-12)
2000 Enrollment: 881 608-323-3315
Housing: Homeownership rate: 62.0% (2000); Median home value: $69,500 (2000); Median rent: $315 per month (2000); Median age of housing: 41 years (2000).
Hospitals: Franciscan Skemp Healthcare - Arcadia (25 beds)
Safety: Violent crime rate: 8.3 per 10,000 population; Property crime rate: 409.3 per 10,000 population (2001).
Newspapers: The Arcadia News-Leader (1 x week)
Transportation: Commute to work: 85.1% car, 0.0% public transportation, 9.9% walk, 3.2% work from home (2000); Travel time to work: 76.2% less than 15 minutes, 10.5% 15 to 30 minutes, 7.6% 30 to 45 minutes, 4.8% 45 to 60 minutes, 0.8% 60 minutes or more (2000)
Additional Information Contacts
Arcadia Chamber of Commerce.............................. 608-323-2319

ARCADIA (town). Covers a land area of 118.826 square miles and a water area of 0.201 square miles. Located at 44.24° N. Lat.; 91.44° W. Long. Elevation is 728 feet.
History: Incorporated 1925.
Population: 1,555 (2000); Race: 99.4% White, 0.0% Black, 0.0% Asian, 0.0% American Indian and Alaska Native, 1.5% Hispanic of any race, 0.3% two or more races (2000); Density: 13.1 persons per square mile (2000); Age: 25.3% under 18, 12.4% over 64 (2000); Marriage status: 28.3% never married, 63.8% now married, 3.9% widowed, 4.0% divorced (2000); Foreign born: 0.3% (2000); Ancestry (includes multiple ancestries): 52.0% Polish, 48.7% German, 20.6% Norwegian, 4.9% Irish, 2.8% English (2000).
Economy: In dairy and livestock area; timber. Manufacturing: poultry processing, printing, meat products. Employment by occupation: 23.8% management, 15.8% professional, 10.6% services, 15.1% sales, 3.3% farming, 7.3% construction, 24.2% production (2000).
Income: Per capita income: $20,421 (2000); Median household income: $45,588 (2000); Poverty rate: 8.6% (2000).
Taxes: Total city taxes per capita: $151 (1997); City property taxes per capita: $149 (1997).
Education: High school graduation rate: 79.8% (2000); College graduation rate: 13.5% (2000).
Housing: Homeownership rate: 81.7% (2000); Median home value: $87,000 (2000); Median rent: $327 per month (2000); Median age of housing: 40 years (2000).
Transportation: Commute to work: 84.2% car, 0.7% public transportation, 3.2% walk, 11.9% work from home (2000); Travel time to work: 51.2% less than 15 minutes, 24.6% 15 to 30 minutes, 14.1% 30 to 45 minutes, 6.4% 45 to 60 minutes, 3.7% 60 minutes or more (2000)

BLAIR (city). Covers a land area of 1.083 square miles and a water area of 0.062 square miles. Located at 44.29° N. Lat.; 91.23° W. Long. Elevation is 859 feet.
History: Blair was founded in 1873 when the railroad arrived. First settled around a gristmill, the city became a center for the shipping of stock. It was in Blair in 1889 that Hans Jacob Olson, known for his strength and his surliness, was lynched by his fellow townsmen.
Population: 1,273 (2000); Race: 98.8% White, 0.0% Black, 0.3% Asian, 0.3% American Indian and Alaska Native, 1.3% Hispanic of any race, 0.0% two or more races (2000); Density: 1,175.2 persons per square mile (2000); Age: 21.0% under 18, 28.0% over 64 (2000); Marriage status: 17.5% never married, 55.0% now married, 17.4% widowed, 10.1% divorced (2000); Foreign born: 1.0% (2000); Ancestry (includes multiple ancestries): 61.5% Norwegian, 18.7% German, 9.6% Polish, 7.5% Irish, 4.3% English (2000).
Economy: Single-family building permits issued: 3 (2001) / 2 (2000); Multi-family building permits issued: 0 (2001) / 2 (2000); Employment by occupation: 7.7% management, 12.8% professional, 17.8% services, 14.7% sales, 2.0% farming, 9.0% construction, 36.0% production (2000).
Income: Per capita income: $16,253 (2000); Median household income: $30,769 (2000); Poverty rate: 9.6% (2000).
Taxes: Total city taxes per capita: $180 (1997); City property taxes per capita: $157 (1997).
Education: High school graduation rate: 74.2% (2000); College graduation rate: 10.0% (2000).

School District(s)

Blair-Taylor (PK-12)
2000 Enrollment: 734 608-989-2881
Housing: Homeownership rate: 68.9% (2000); Median home value: $68,800 (2000); Median rent: $272 per month (2000); Median age of housing: 44 years (2000).
Safety: Violent crime rate: 23.4 per 10,000 population; Property crime rate: 273.0 per 10,000 population (2001).
Newspapers: Blair Press (1 x week)
Transportation: Commute to work: 88.1% car, 0.0% public transportation, 8.6% walk, 2.2% work from home (2000); Travel time to work: 46.3% less than 15 minutes, 24.2% 15 to 30 minutes, 12.6% 30 to 45 minutes, 4.4% 45 to 60 minutes, 12.6% 60 minutes or more (2000)

BURNSIDE (town). Covers a land area of 34.999 square miles and a water area of 0.047 square miles. Located at 44.38° N. Lat.; 91.44° W. Long.
Population: 529 (2000); Race: 99.1% White, 0.2% Black, 0.0% Asian, 0.0% American Indian and Alaska Native, 3.3% Hispanic of any race, 0.7% two or more races (2000); Density: 15.1 persons per square mile (2000); Age: 27.7% under 18, 13.5% over 64 (2000); Marriage status: 30.9% never married, 56.4% now married, 5.4% widowed, 7.3% divorced (2000); Foreign born: 4.4% (2000); Ancestry (includes multiple ancestries): 61.4% Polish, 33.2% German, 10.0% Norwegian, 4.2% Irish, 4.1% Other groups (2000).
Economy: Employment by occupation: 23.1% management, 12.8% professional, 8.2% services, 10.7% sales, 6.8% farming, 9.6% construction, 28.8% production (2000).
Income: Per capita income: $18,612 (2000); Median household income: $41,111 (2000); Poverty rate: 6.5% (2000).
Taxes: Total city taxes per capita: $96 (2000); City property taxes per capita: $93 (2000).
Education: High school graduation rate: 80.3% (2000); College graduation rate: 7.2% (2000).
Housing: Homeownership rate: 80.5% (2000); Median home value: $57,600 (2000); Median rent: $333 per month (2000); Median age of housing: 53 years (2000).
Transportation: Commute to work: 79.4% car, 0.0% public transportation, 6.1% walk, 12.3% work from home (2000); Travel time to work: 43.6% less than 15 minutes, 38.3% 15 to 30 minutes, 6.2% 30 to 45 minutes, 5.3% 45 to 60 minutes, 6.6% 60 minutes or more (2000)

CALEDONIA (town). Covers a land area of 20.872 square miles and a water area of 0.426 square miles. Located at 44.02° N. Lat.; 91.35° W. Long.
Population: 759 (2000); Race: 99.1% White, 0.0% Black, 0.0% Asian, 0.9% American Indian and Alaska Native, 0.4% Hispanic of any race, 0.0% two or more races (2000); Density: 36.4 persons per square mile (2000); Age: 32.2% under 18, 7.8% over 64 (2000); Marriage status: 24.4% never married, 62.6% now married, 3.9% widowed, 9.1% divorced (2000); Foreign born: 0.3% (2000); Ancestry (includes multiple ancestries): 44.9% German, 32.2% Norwegian, 13.4% Irish, 11.9% Polish, 10.7% English (2000).
Economy: Employment by occupation: 14.6% management, 11.0% professional, 13.9% services, 17.1% sales, 1.4% farming, 15.1% construction, 26.9% production (2000).
Income: Per capita income: $17,025 (2000); Median household income: $47,292 (2000); Poverty rate: 4.2% (2000).
Taxes: Total city taxes per capita: $101 (1997); City property taxes per capita: $87 (1997).

Education: High school graduation rate: 89.1% (2000); College graduation rate: 14.5% (2000).
Housing: Homeownership rate: 93.4% (2000); Median home value: $115,600 (2000); Median rent: $264 per month (2000); Median age of housing: 21 years (2000).
Transportation: Commute to work: 95.4% car, 0.0% public transportation, 0.5% walk, 4.1% work from home (2000); Travel time to work: 31.7% less than 15 minutes, 33.7% 15 to 30 minutes, 25.7% 30 to 45 minutes, 5.0% 45 to 60 minutes, 3.8% 60 minutes or more (2000)

CHIMNEY ROCK (town). Covers a land area of 36.086 square miles and a water area of 0 square miles. Located at 44.46° N. Lat.; 91.45° W. Long.
Population: 276 (2000); Race: 100.0% White, 0.0% Black, 0.0% Asian, 0.0% American Indian and Alaska Native, 0.7% Hispanic of any race, 0.0% two or more races (2000); Density: 7.6 persons per square mile (2000); Age: 28.2% under 18, 7.0% over 64 (2000); Marriage status: 27.6% never married, 53.9% now married, 3.9% widowed, 14.7% divorced (2000); Foreign born: 0.7% (2000); Ancestry (includes multiple ancestries): 41.5% German, 40.1% Norwegian, 34.9% Polish, 10.2% English, 4.6% Irish (2000).
Economy: Employment by occupation: 9.9% management, 16.7% professional, 11.7% services, 16.7% sales, 8.0% farming, 4.3% construction, 32.7% production (2000).
Income: Per capita income: $16,010 (2000); Median household income: $44,375 (2000); Poverty rate: 10.1% (2000).
Taxes: Total city taxes per capita: $134 (1997); City property taxes per capita: $134 (1997).
Education: High school graduation rate: 86.5% (2000); College graduation rate: 14.6% (2000).
Housing: Homeownership rate: 79.4% (2000); Median home value: $72,500 (2000); Median rent: $325 per month (2000); Median age of housing: 32 years (2000).
Transportation: Commute to work: 90.6% car, 0.0% public transportation, 1.3% walk, 8.1% work from home (2000); Travel time to work: 8.2% less than 15 minutes, 50.3% 15 to 30 minutes, 25.2% 30 to 45 minutes, 9.5% 45 to 60 minutes, 6.8% 60 minutes or more (2000)

DODGE (town). Covers a land area of 21.391 square miles and a water area of 0 square miles. Located at 44.13° N. Lat.; 91.52° W. Long. Elevation is 673 feet.
Population: 414 (2000); Race: 99.5% White, 0.0% Black, 0.0% Asian, 0.5% American Indian and Alaska Native, 0.2% Hispanic of any race, 0.0% two or more races (2000); Density: 19.4 persons per square mile (2000); Age: 29.0% under 18, 15.4% over 64 (2000); Marriage status: 29.6% never married, 63.1% now married, 4.3% widowed, 3.0% divorced (2000); Foreign born: 0.5% (2000); Ancestry (includes multiple ancestries): 48.9% Polish, 46.3% German, 10.0% Norwegian, 6.9% Irish, 4.0% United States or American (2000).
Economy: Employment by occupation: 18.1% management, 18.5% professional, 11.2% services, 22.8% sales, 0.9% farming, 12.5% construction, 15.9% production (2000).
Income: Per capita income: $15,167 (2000); Median household income: $40,972 (2000); Poverty rate: 10.2% (2000).
Taxes: Total city taxes per capita: $107 (1997); City property taxes per capita: $105 (1997).
Education: High school graduation rate: 76.8% (2000); College graduation rate: 15.8% (2000).
Housing: Homeownership rate: 75.8% (2000); Median home value: $71,000 (2000); Median rent: $315 per month (2000); Median age of housing: 46 years (2000).
Transportation: Commute to work: 88.3% car, 0.9% public transportation, 4.8% walk, 6.1% work from home (2000); Travel time to work: 18.1% less than 15 minutes, 48.1% 15 to 30 minutes, 24.5% 30 to 45 minutes, 0.9% 45 to 60 minutes, 8.3% 60 minutes or more (2000)

ELEVA (village). Covers a land area of 0.543 square miles and a water area of 0.013 square miles. Located at 44.57° N. Lat.; 91.47° W. Long. Elevation is 870 feet.
History: On Buffalo River State Trail.
Population: 635 (2000); Race: 96.9% White, 0.3% Black, 0.0% Asian, 0.3% American Indian and Alaska Native, 0.0% Hispanic of any race, 2.5% two or more races (2000); Density: 1,169.0 persons per square mile (2000); Age: 22.4% under 18, 17.4% over 64 (2000); Marriage status: 25.0% never married, 56.3% now married, 10.0% widowed, 8.7% divorced (2000); Foreign born: 0.0% (2000); Ancestry (includes multiple ancestries): 62.6% Norwegian, 27.6% German, 11.3% Irish, 6.6% Other groups, 6.4% Polish (2000).
Economy: In dairy, poultry, and grain area. Manufacturing: meat processing, cheese. Single-family building permits issued: 4 (2001) / 1 (2000); Multi-family building permits issued: 0 (2001) / 0 (2000); Employment by occupation: 8.4% management, 13.3% professional, 14.2% services, 23.2% sales, 0.6% farming, 12.4% construction, 27.9% production (2000).
Income: Per capita income: $15,814 (2000); Median household income: $31,250 (2000); Poverty rate: 9.5% (2000).
Taxes: Total city taxes per capita: $113 (1997); City property taxes per capita: $107 (1997).
Education: High school graduation rate: 75.7% (2000); College graduation rate: 7.5% (2000).
Housing: Homeownership rate: 66.7% (2000); Median home value: $67,900 (2000); Median rent: $304 per month (2000); Median age of housing: 39 years (2000).
Transportation: Commute to work: 87.0% car, 0.6% public transportation, 7.9% walk, 3.8% work from home (2000); Travel time to work: 27.3% less than 15 minutes, 30.3% 15 to 30 minutes, 29.3% 30 to 45 minutes, 9.2% 45 to 60 minutes, 3.9% 60 minutes or more (2000)

ETTRICK (village). Covers a land area of 0.653 square miles and a water area of 0 square miles. Located at 44.17° N. Lat.; 91.26° W. Long. Elevation is 771 feet.
History: Ettrick was founded in the 1870's by Norwegian farmers. A woolen mill as well as a creamery were established here.
Population: 521 (2000); Race: 98.5% White, 0.0% Black, 0.2% Asian, 0.0% American Indian and Alaska Native, 0.0% Hispanic of any race, 1.3% two or more races (2000); Density: 798.0 persons per square mile (2000); Age: 21.8% under 18, 19.8% over 64 (2000); Marriage status: 28.7% never married, 45.9% now married, 15.6% widowed, 9.8% divorced (2000); Foreign born: 0.9% (2000); Ancestry (includes multiple ancestries): 52.9% Norwegian, 29.0% German, 16.8% Irish, 9.8% Polish, 3.9% English (2000).
Economy: Single-family building permits issued: 0 (2001) / 1 (2000); Multi-family building permits issued: 0 (2001) / 0 (2000); Employment by occupation: 7.7% management, 15.0% professional, 19.7% services, 19.0% sales, 3.3% farming, 5.7% construction, 29.7% production (2000).
Income: Per capita income: $16,392 (2000); Median household income: $34,250 (2000); Poverty rate: 5.2% (2000).
Taxes: Total city taxes per capita: $85 (1997); City property taxes per capita: $69 (1997).
Education: High school graduation rate: 77.6% (2000); College graduation rate: 9.3% (2000).
Housing: Homeownership rate: 62.8% (2000); Median home value: $74,600 (2000); Median rent: $308 per month (2000); Median age of housing: 44 years (2000).
Transportation: Commute to work: 87.7% car, 0.0% public transportation, 7.8% walk, 4.4% work from home (2000); Travel time to work: 39.6% less than 15 minutes, 25.0% 15 to 30 minutes, 21.1% 30 to 45 minutes, 10.0% 45 to 60 minutes, 4.3% 60 minutes or more (2000)

ETTRICK (town). Covers a land area of 77.065 square miles and a water area of 0 square miles. Located at 44.19° N. Lat.; 91.24° W. Long. Elevation is 771 feet.
Population: 1,284 (2000); Race: 99.7% White, 0.0% Black, 0.0% Asian, 0.0% American Indian and Alaska Native, 0.9% Hispanic of any race, 0.2% two or more races (2000); Density: 16.7 persons per square mile (2000); Age: 25.2% under 18, 12.6% over 64 (2000); Marriage status: 17.1% never married, 71.5% now married, 3.9% widowed, 7.5% divorced (2000); Foreign born: 0.6% (2000); Ancestry (includes multiple ancestries): 54.7% Norwegian, 34.4% German, 9.8% Irish, 9.2% Polish, 7.1% English (2000).
Economy: In dairy and livestock area; flour mills. Employment by occupation: 13.4% management, 13.6% professional, 8.7% services, 21.1% sales, 4.1% farming, 12.0% construction, 27.1% production (2000).
Income: Per capita income: $18,593 (2000); Median household income: $41,625 (2000); Poverty rate: 3.9% (2000).
Taxes: Total city taxes per capita: $58 (1997); City property taxes per capita: $57 (1997).
Education: High school graduation rate: 85.1% (2000); College graduation rate: 15.4% (2000).
Housing: Homeownership rate: 87.8% (2000); Median home value: $85,600 (2000); Median rent: $369 per month (2000); Median age of housing: 37 years (2000).
Transportation: Commute to work: 82.4% car, 0.9% public transportation, 2.2% walk, 13.5% work from home (2000); Travel time to work: 27.2% less

than 15 minutes, 29.7% 15 to 30 minutes, 22.7% 30 to 45 minutes, 13.8% 45 to 60 minutes, 6.6% 60 minutes or more (2000)

GALE (town). Covers a land area of 60.494 square miles and a water area of 0.557 square miles. Located at 44.11° N. Lat.; 91.31° W. Long.
History: Settled 1854. Incorporated as village in 1887, as city in 1942.
Population: 1,426 (2000); Race: 99.1% White, 0.0% Black, 0.4% Asian, 0.0% American Indian and Alaska Native, 0.0% Hispanic of any race, 0.1% two or more races (2000); Density: 23.6 persons per square mile (2000); Age: 26.2% under 18, 13.7% over 64 (2000); Marriage status: 18.2% never married, 66.4% now married, 6.9% widowed, 8.5% divorced (2000); Foreign born: 0.6% (2000); Ancestry (includes multiple ancestries): 44.0% Norwegian, 40.3% German, 12.4% Irish, 7.6% English, 7.4% Polish (2000).
Economy: Dairy products, timber, apples, feed; limestone quarries. Manufacturing: metal fabrication; furniture, canned food. Employment by occupation: 15.1% management, 18.1% professional, 12.9% services, 16.6% sales, 2.1% farming, 12.7% construction, 22.5% production (2000).
Income: Per capita income: $20,442 (2000); Median household income: $45,489 (2000); Poverty rate: 6.0% (2000).
Taxes: Total city taxes per capita: $98 (1997); City property taxes per capita: $93 (1997).
Education: High school graduation rate: 87.5% (2000); College graduation rate: 18.4% (2000).
Housing: Homeownership rate: 84.4% (2000); Median home value: $97,800 (2000); Median rent: $385 per month (2000); Median age of housing: 28 years (2000).
Transportation: Commute to work: 86.8% car, 0.0% public transportation, 4.3% walk, 8.4% work from home (2000); Travel time to work: 37.8% less than 15 minutes, 28.6% 15 to 30 minutes, 25.9% 30 to 45 minutes, 3.9% 45 to 60 minutes, 3.8% 60 minutes or more (2000)

GALESVILLE (city). Covers a land area of 1.084 square miles and a water area of 0.093 square miles. Located at 44.08° N. Lat.; 91.35° W. Long. Elevation is 712 feet.
Population: 1,427 (2000); Race: 98.6% White, 0.0% Black, 0.1% Asian, 0.3% American Indian and Alaska Native, 0.1% Hispanic of any race, 0.9% two or more races (2000); Density: 1,316.8 persons per square mile (2000); Age: 23.5% under 18, 19.9% over 64 (2000); Marriage status: 24.3% never married, 49.5% now married, 14.5% widowed, 11.6% divorced (2000); Foreign born: 0.5% (2000); Ancestry (includes multiple ancestries): 38.2% Norwegian, 37.8% German, 11.6% Irish, 10.9% English, 7.4% Polish (2000).
Economy: Single-family building permits issued: 4 (2001) / 4 (2000); Multi-family building permits issued: 0 (2001) / 0 (2000); Employment by occupation: 10.5% management, 19.0% professional, 11.3% services, 21.2% sales, 0.8% farming, 5.2% construction, 32.0% production (2000).
Income: Per capita income: $18,245 (2000); Median household income: $35,054 (2000); Poverty rate: 9.6% (2000).
Taxes: Total city taxes per capita: $193 (2000); City property taxes per capita: $181 (2000).
Education: High school graduation rate: 83.7% (2000); College graduation rate: 21.0% (2000).

School District(s)

Galesville-Ettrick-Trempealeau (PK-12)
2000 Enrollment: 1,437 608-582-2291

Housing: Homeownership rate: 62.6% (2000); Median home value: $83,300 (2000); Median rent: $309 per month (2000); Median age of housing: 47 years (2000).
Newspapers: Galesville Republican (1 x week)
Transportation: Commute to work: 89.4% car, 0.0% public transportation, 5.5% walk, 4.1% work from home (2000); Travel time to work: 39.3% less than 15 minutes, 27.6% 15 to 30 minutes, 24.6% 30 to 45 minutes, 5.3% 45 to 60 minutes, 3.1% 60 minutes or more (2000)

HALE (town). Covers a land area of 69.698 square miles and a water area of 0.026 square miles. Located at 44.47° N. Lat.; 91.30° W. Long. Elevation is 940 feet.
Population: 988 (2000); Race: 98.9% White, 0.3% Black, 0.0% Asian, 0.0% American Indian and Alaska Native, 0.0% Hispanic of any race, 0.8% two or more races (2000); Density: 14.2 persons per square mile (2000); Age: 30.2% under 18, 10.7% over 64 (2000); Marriage status: 21.0% never married, 66.2% now married, 4.4% widowed, 8.4% divorced (2000); Foreign born: 0.2% (2000); Ancestry (includes multiple ancestries): 47.8% Norwegian, 35.7% German, 27.5% Polish, 5.5% Irish, 4.7% English (2000).
Economy: Employment by occupation: 21.0% management, 11.4% professional, 11.1% services, 15.0% sales, 9.4% farming, 10.1% construction, 22.0% production (2000).
Income: Per capita income: $17,262 (2000); Median household income: $42,589 (2000); Poverty rate: 5.5% (2000).
Taxes: Total city taxes per capita: $187 (1997); City property taxes per capita: $184 (1997).
Education: High school graduation rate: 84.7% (2000); College graduation rate: 13.5% (2000).
Housing: Homeownership rate: 82.4% (2000); Median home value: $72,700 (2000); Median rent: $335 per month (2000); Median age of housing: 52 years (2000).
Transportation: Commute to work: 77.4% car, 0.0% public transportation, 1.9% walk, 20.2% work from home (2000); Travel time to work: 32.4% less than 15 minutes, 37.1% 15 to 30 minutes, 17.4% 30 to 45 minutes, 8.6% 45 to 60 minutes, 4.5% 60 minutes or more (2000)

INDEPENDENCE (city). Covers a land area of 1.271 square miles and a water area of 0.040 square miles. Located at 44.35° N. Lat.; 91.42° W. Long. Elevation is 782 feet.
History: Settled 1856; incorporated as village in 1876, as city in 1942.
Population: 1,244 (2000); Race: 98.2% White, 0.2% Black, 0.1% Asian, 0.0% American Indian and Alaska Native, 2.7% Hispanic of any race, 0.6% two or more races (2000); Density: 978.8 persons per square mile (2000); Age: 21.7% under 18, 23.7% over 64 (2000); Marriage status: 26.0% never married, 52.0% now married, 12.2% widowed, 9.8% divorced (2000); Foreign born: 2.0% (2000); Ancestry (includes multiple ancestries): 51.0% Polish, 28.4% German, 15.7% Norwegian, 4.9% Irish, 4.5% Other groups (2000).
Economy: Dairy and farm area: grain; dairy products. Manufacturing: wood products, concrete products. Single-family building permits issued: 4 (2001) / 9 (2000); Multi-family building permits issued: 0 (2001) / 4 (2000); Employment by occupation: 9.0% management, 11.5% professional, 14.4% services, 18.2% sales, 4.2% farming, 7.3% construction, 35.4% production (2000).
Income: Per capita income: $15,977 (2000); Median household income: $27,389 (2000); Poverty rate: 9.6% (2000).
Taxes: Total city taxes per capita: $175 (1997); City property taxes per capita: $166 (1997).
Education: High school graduation rate: 77.0% (2000); College graduation rate: 11.6% (2000).

School District(s)

Independence (PK-12)
2000 Enrollment: 331 715-985-3172

Housing: Homeownership rate: 63.7% (2000); Median home value: $62,100 (2000); Median rent: $289 per month (2000); Median age of housing: 54 years (2000).
Safety: Violent crime rate: 0.0 per 10,000 population; Property crime rate: 367.1 per 10,000 population (2001).
Newspapers: News Wave (1 x week)
Transportation: Commute to work: 93.5% car, 0.0% public transportation, 3.5% walk, 2.2% work from home (2000); Travel time to work: 50.3% less than 15 minutes, 36.6% 15 to 30 minutes, 4.7% 30 to 45 minutes, 2.7% 45 to 60 minutes, 5.6% 60 minutes or more (2000)

LINCOLN (town). Covers a land area of 28.328 square miles and a water area of 0.037 square miles. Located at 44.36° N. Lat.; 91.35° W. Long.
Population: 829 (2000); Race: 98.0% White, 0.8% Black, 0.3% Asian, 0.5% American Indian and Alaska Native, 0.5% Hispanic of any race, 0.3% two or more races (2000); Density: 29.3 persons per square mile (2000); Age: 23.5% under 18, 8.7% over 64 (2000); Marriage status: 23.7% never married, 63.4% now married, 4.7% widowed, 8.1% divorced (2000); Foreign born: 0.3% (2000); Ancestry (includes multiple ancestries): 33.4% German, 31.4% Norwegian, 27.5% Polish, 4.3% Irish, 3.5% Other groups (2000).
Economy: Employment by occupation: 15.9% management, 10.0% professional, 18.0% services, 14.4% sales, 6.4% farming, 6.2% construction, 29.0% production (2000).
Income: Per capita income: $13,393 (2000); Median household income: $33,393 (2000); Poverty rate: 30.9% (2000).
Taxes: Total city taxes per capita: $49 (1997); City property taxes per capita: $44 (1997).
Education: High school graduation rate: 72.0% (2000); College graduation rate: 5.2% (2000).
Housing: Homeownership rate: 84.1% (2000); Median home value: $80,000 (2000); Median rent: $340 per month (2000); Median age of housing: 32 years (2000).
Transportation: Commute to work: 73.3% car, 2.3% public transportation, 9.3% walk, 15.0% work from home (2000); Travel time to work: 64.0% less

than 15 minutes, 19.5% 15 to 30 minutes, 7.0% 30 to 45 minutes, 1.8% 45 to 60 minutes, 7.6% 60 minutes or more (2000)

OSSEO (city). Covers a land area of 2.062 square miles and a water area of 0.017 square miles. Located at 44.57° N. Lat.; 91.21° W. Long. Elevation is 959 feet.
History: Osseo was settled in 1857 by farmers from Richland County who had heard that a railroad was to be built here. Even without a railroad, Osseo became a trading center, with mills, a cheese factory, creamery, and a condensery.
Population: 1,669 (2000); Race: 98.9% White, 0.0% Black, 0.1% Asian, 0.2% American Indian and Alaska Native, 0.4% Hispanic of any race, 0.6% two or more races (2000); Density: 809.5 persons per square mile (2000); Age: 23.8% under 18, 23.1% over 64 (2000); Marriage status: 21.1% never married, 56.8% now married, 10.8% widowed, 11.3% divorced (2000); Foreign born: 0.2% (2000); Ancestry (includes multiple ancestries): 53.8% Norwegian, 32.5% German, 9.0% Irish, 8.4% English, 5.6% Polish (2000).
Economy: Single-family building permits issued: 3 (2001) / 3 (2000); Multi-family building permits issued: 4 (2001) / 0 (2000); Employment by occupation: 9.6% management, 19.0% professional, 16.4% services, 26.4% sales, 0.6% farming, 9.2% construction, 18.8% production (2000).
Income: Per capita income: $18,512 (2000); Median household income: $34,493 (2000); Poverty rate: 5.7% (2000).
Taxes: Total city taxes per capita: $331 (1997); City property taxes per capita: $320 (1997).
Education: High school graduation rate: 79.0% (2000); College graduation rate: 17.0% (2000).

School District(s)

Osseo-Fairchild (PK-12)
2000 Enrollment: 985 715-597-3141

Housing: Homeownership rate: 64.6% (2000); Median home value: $76,400 (2000); Median rent: $344 per month (2000); Median age of housing: 35 years (2000).
Hospitals: Osseo Area Hospital & Nursing Home (68 beds)
Safety: Violent crime rate: 71.4 per 10,000 population; Property crime rate: 475.9 per 10,000 population (2001).
Newspapers: The Tri-County News (1 x week)
Transportation: Commute to work: 90.5% car, 0.0% public transportation, 6.8% walk, 2.6% work from home (2000); Travel time to work: 42.8% less than 15 minutes, 22.6% 15 to 30 minutes, 23.7% 30 to 45 minutes, 6.4% 45 to 60 minutes, 4.5% 60 minutes or more (2000)

PIGEON (town). Covers a land area of 38.579 square miles and a water area of 0 square miles. Located at 44.40° N. Lat.; 91.21° W. Long.
Population: 894 (2000); Race: 99.3% White, 0.2% Black, 0.2% Asian, 0.0% American Indian and Alaska Native, 1.6% Hispanic of any race, 0.2% two or more races (2000); Density: 23.2 persons per square mile (2000); Age: 32.3% under 18, 9.1% over 64 (2000); Marriage status: 22.4% never married, 66.9% now married, 4.9% widowed, 5.8% divorced (2000); Foreign born: 1.1% (2000); Ancestry (includes multiple ancestries): 45.5% Norwegian, 36.7% German, 9.7% Polish, 5.5% Swiss, 4.6% Other groups (2000).
Economy: Dairying; poultry; corn, soybeans, alfalfa. Manufacturing of consumer goods. Employment by occupation: 18.3% management, 11.4% professional, 14.4% services, 14.4% sales, 4.7% farming, 8.8% construction, 28.0% production (2000).
Income: Per capita income: $14,752 (2000); Median household income: $37,708 (2000); Poverty rate: 21.0% (2000).
Taxes: Total city taxes per capita: $115 (1997); City property taxes per capita: $114 (1997).
Education: High school graduation rate: 78.4% (2000); College graduation rate: 11.2% (2000).
Housing: Homeownership rate: 91.3% (2000); Median home value: $67,500 (2000); Median rent: $350 per month (2000); Median age of housing: 52 years (2000).
Transportation: Commute to work: 81.7% car, 0.0% public transportation, 4.6% walk, 11.5% work from home (2000); Travel time to work: 43.7% less than 15 minutes, 25.6% 15 to 30 minutes, 17.9% 30 to 45 minutes, 5.9% 45 to 60 minutes, 6.9% 60 minutes or more (2000)

PIGEON FALLS (village). Covers a land area of 0.477 square miles and a water area of 0 square miles. Located at 44.42° N. Lat.; 91.21° W. Long. Elevation is 882 feet.
Population: 388 (2000); Race: 99.5% White, 0.5% Black, 0.0% Asian, 0.0% American Indian and Alaska Native, 0.0% Hispanic of any race, 0.0% two or more races (2000); Density: 813.6 persons per square mile (2000); Age: 19.6% under 18, 33.0% over 64 (2000); Marriage status: 19.4% never married, 63.4% now married, 11.4% widowed, 5.8% divorced (2000); Foreign born: 0.5% (2000); Ancestry (includes multiple ancestries): 59.7% Norwegian, 22.2% German, 3.5% Irish, 3.5% Polish, 2.8% Swedish (2000).
Economy: Single-family building permits issued: 2 (2001) / 1 (2000); Multi-family building permits issued: 0 (2001) / 2 (2000); Employment by occupation: 7.1% management, 11.6% professional, 16.8% services, 30.3% sales, 1.9% farming, 9.0% construction, 23.2% production (2000).
Income: Per capita income: $14,587 (2000); Median household income: $34,107 (2000); Poverty rate: 5.5% (2000).
Taxes: Total city taxes per capita: $71 (1997); City property taxes per capita: $68 (1997).
Education: High school graduation rate: 71.8% (2000); College graduation rate: 8.6% (2000).
Housing: Homeownership rate: 58.5% (2000); Median home value: $72,400 (2000); Median rent: $306 per month (2000); Median age of housing: 35 years (2000).
Transportation: Commute to work: 87.6% car, 0.0% public transportation, 7.2% walk, 2.6% work from home (2000); Travel time to work: 50.3% less than 15 minutes, 22.1% 15 to 30 minutes, 18.1% 30 to 45 minutes, 7.4% 45 to 60 minutes, 2.0% 60 minutes or more (2000)

PRESTON (town). Covers a land area of 59.165 square miles and a water area of 0.005 square miles. Located at 44.30° N. Lat.; 91.25° W. Long.
Population: 951 (2000); Race: 99.1% White, 0.0% Black, 0.0% Asian, 0.2% American Indian and Alaska Native, 0.6% Hispanic of any race, 0.5% two or more races (2000); Density: 16.1 persons per square mile (2000); Age: 30.5% under 18, 12.3% over 64 (2000); Marriage status: 22.5% never married, 66.8% now married, 5.2% widowed, 5.4% divorced (2000); Foreign born: 0.2% (2000); Ancestry (includes multiple ancestries): 49.7% Norwegian, 36.3% German, 11.5% Polish, 8.6% Irish, 6.0% English (2000).
Economy: Employment by occupation: 16.6% management, 11.3% professional, 17.0% services, 14.0% sales, 6.6% farming, 5.5% construction, 29.1% production (2000).
Income: Per capita income: $16,391 (2000); Median household income: $40,000 (2000); Poverty rate: 11.3% (2000).
Taxes: Total city taxes per capita: $84 (1997); City property taxes per capita: $82 (1997).
Education: High school graduation rate: 81.4% (2000); College graduation rate: 12.9% (2000).
Housing: Homeownership rate: 81.5% (2000); Median home value: $75,600 (2000); Median rent: $278 per month (2000); Median age of housing: 47 years (2000).
Transportation: Commute to work: 80.6% car, 0.4% public transportation, 3.2% walk, 13.7% work from home (2000); Travel time to work: 47.8% less than 15 minutes, 33.5% 15 to 30 minutes, 11.7% 30 to 45 minutes, 1.5% 45 to 60 minutes, 5.5% 60 minutes or more (2000)

STRUM (village). Covers a land area of 1.087 square miles and a water area of 0.082 square miles. Located at 44.55° N. Lat.; 91.39° W. Long. Elevation is 900 feet.
Population: 1,001 (2000); Race: 99.4% White, 0.0% Black, 0.0% Asian, 0.0% American Indian and Alaska Native, 1.1% Hispanic of any race, 0.0% two or more races (2000); Density: 920.7 persons per square mile (2000); Age: 22.0% under 18, 27.2% over 64 (2000); Marriage status: 21.2% never married, 52.9% now married, 16.0% widowed, 9.8% divorced (2000); Foreign born: 1.2% (2000); Ancestry (includes multiple ancestries): 65.3% Norwegian, 29.8% German, 5.8% Irish, 5.1% English, 5.1% Polish (2000).
Economy: In dairy, poultry, and grain area; cheese; light manufacturing. Viking Skyline Ski Area to East. Single-family building permits issued: 0 (2001) / 1 (2000); Multi-family building permits issued: 0 (2001) / 0 (2000); Employment by occupation: 7.9% management, 15.4% professional, 16.6% services, 21.5% sales, 4.8% farming, 7.9% construction, 25.9% production (2000).
Income: Per capita income: $18,492 (2000); Median household income: $29,408 (2000); Poverty rate: 6.3% (2000).
Taxes: Total city taxes per capita: $80 (1997); City property taxes per capita: $77 (1997).
Education: High school graduation rate: 72.5% (2000); College graduation rate: 12.2% (2000).

School District(s)

Eleva-Strum (PK-12)
2000 Enrollment: 680 715-695-2696

Housing: Homeownership rate: 67.3% (2000); Median home value: $80,400 (2000); Median rent: $282 per month (2000); Median age of housing: 39 years (2000).

Transportation: Commute to work: 88.6% car, 0.0% public transportation, 9.6% walk, 1.8% work from home (2000); Travel time to work: 37.3% less than 15 minutes, 24.5% 15 to 30 minutes, 27.0% 30 to 45 minutes, 6.8% 45 to 60 minutes, 4.4% 60 minutes or more (2000)

SUMNER (town). Covers a land area of 33.850 square miles and a water area of 0.031 square miles. Located at 44.57° N. Lat.; 91.22° W. Long.
Population: 806 (2000); Race: 100.0% White, 0.0% Black, 0.0% Asian, 0.0% American Indian and Alaska Native, 0.0% Hispanic of any race, 0.0% two or more races (2000); Density: 23.8 persons per square mile (2000); Age: 26.1% under 18, 14.4% over 64 (2000); Marriage status: 17.2% never married, 67.5% now married, 7.7% widowed, 7.7% divorced (2000); Foreign born: 0.0% (2000); Ancestry (includes multiple ancestries): 55.8% Norwegian, 35.0% German, 6.9% English, 5.9% Irish, 4.8% Polish (2000).
Economy: Employment by occupation: 14.2% management, 12.4% professional, 15.3% services, 24.4% sales, 1.1% farming, 10.9% construction, 21.8% production (2000).
Income: Per capita income: $18,405 (2000); Median household income: $46,875 (2000); Poverty rate: 3.7% (2000).
Taxes: Total city taxes per capita: $88 (1997); City property taxes per capita: $86 (1997).
Education: High school graduation rate: 84.8% (2000); College graduation rate: 14.2% (2000).
Housing: Homeownership rate: 87.0% (2000); Median home value: $82,500 (2000); Median rent: $354 per month (2000); Median age of housing: 30 years (2000).
Transportation: Commute to work: 91.2% car, 0.0% public transportation, 0.2% walk, 7.5% work from home (2000); Travel time to work: 44.5% less than 15 minutes, 20.9% 15 to 30 minutes, 25.4% 30 to 45 minutes, 5.7% 45 to 60 minutes, 3.6% 60 minutes or more (2000)

TREMPEALEAU (village). Covers a land area of 1.204 square miles and a water area of 0.080 square miles. Located at 44.00° N. Lat.; 91.43° W. Long. Elevation is 691 feet.
History: Trempealeau was founded by James Allen Reed, who came from Kentucky. In 1886, Reverend David Van Slyke, a local Methodist minister, published a pamphlet in which he attempted to prove that Trempealeau was the biblical Garden of Eden. His claim rested principally on the four rivers (Mississippi, Beaver, Trempealeau, Black) around Trempealeau.
Population: 1,319 (2000); Race: 98.2% White, 0.1% Black, 0.0% Asian, 1.2% American Indian and Alaska Native, 0.4% Hispanic of any race, 0.1% two or more races (2000); Density: 1,095.4 persons per square mile (2000); Age: 23.5% under 18, 14.8% over 64 (2000); Marriage status: 21.6% never married, 56.6% now married, 6.8% widowed, 15.0% divorced (2000); Foreign born: 0.4% (2000); Ancestry (includes multiple ancestries): 39.8% German, 27.8% Norwegian, 16.7% Polish, 9.9% Irish, 7.6% English (2000).
Economy: Single-family building permits issued: 7 (2001) / 20 (2000); Multi-family building permits issued: 16 (2001) / 3 (2000); Employment by occupation: 11.3% management, 13.3% professional, 13.4% services, 22.5% sales, 0.0% farming, 11.2% construction, 28.4% production (2000).
Income: Per capita income: $18,465 (2000); Median household income: $36,422 (2000); Poverty rate: 6.3% (2000).
Taxes: Total city taxes per capita: $97 (1997); City property taxes per capita: $73 (1997).
Education: High school graduation rate: 88.9% (2000); College graduation rate: 17.9% (2000).
Housing: Homeownership rate: 76.9% (2000); Median home value: $85,900 (2000); Median rent: $333 per month (2000); Median age of housing: 22 years (2000).
Safety: Violent crime rate: 0.0 per 10,000 population; Property crime rate: 225.9 per 10,000 population (2001).
Transportation: Commute to work: 92.1% car, 0.0% public transportation, 4.0% walk, 3.1% work from home (2000); Travel time to work: 25.3% less than 15 minutes, 37.9% 15 to 30 minutes, 32.5% 30 to 45 minutes, 1.8% 45 to 60 minutes, 2.5% 60 minutes or more (2000)
Additional Information Contacts
Trempealeau Chamber of Commerce. 608-534-6780

TREMPEALEAU (town). Covers a land area of 51.023 square miles and a water area of 6.181 square miles. Located at 44.04° N. Lat.; 91.45° W. Long. Elevation is 691 feet.
History: Native American mounds, and site of old French fort are nearby.
Population: 1,618 (2000); Race: 98.6% White, 0.0% Black, 0.3% Asian, 0.4% American Indian and Alaska Native, 0.3% Hispanic of any race, 0.8% two or more races (2000); Density: 31.7 persons per square mile (2000); Age: 23.0% under 18, 11.2% over 64 (2000); Marriage status: 22.6% never married, 62.9% now married, 5.6% widowed, 8.9% divorced (2000); Foreign born: 0.8% (2000); Ancestry (includes multiple ancestries): 48.7% German, 27.2% Norwegian, 22.1% Polish, 10.7% Irish, 6.9% English (2000).
Economy: Manufacturing of machinery. On Great River State Trail. Upper Mississippi National Wildlife and Fish Refuge. Employment by occupation: 15.3% management, 15.2% professional, 14.4% services, 19.5% sales, 1.7% farming, 9.4% construction, 24.6% production (2000).
Income: Per capita income: $20,039 (2000); Median household income: $45,179 (2000); Poverty rate: 5.2% (2000).
Taxes: Total city taxes per capita: $57 (1997); City property taxes per capita: $53 (1997).
Education: High school graduation rate: 86.3% (2000); College graduation rate: 13.3% (2000).
Housing: Homeownership rate: 87.1% (2000); Median home value: $97,000 (2000); Median rent: $375 per month (2000); Median age of housing: 30 years (2000).
Transportation: Commute to work: 87.6% car, 0.0% public transportation, 2.6% walk, 9.3% work from home (2000); Travel time to work: 26.4% less than 15 minutes, 40.7% 15 to 30 minutes, 20.4% 30 to 45 minutes, 9.5% 45 to 60 minutes, 3.0% 60 minutes or more (2000)

UNITY (town). Covers a land area of 34.593 square miles and a water area of 0 square miles. Located at 44.55° N. Lat.; 91.36° W. Long.
Population: 556 (2000); Race: 100.0% White, 0.0% Black, 0.0% Asian, 0.0% American Indian and Alaska Native, 0.0% Hispanic of any race, 0.0% two or more races (2000); Density: 16.1 persons per square mile (2000); Age: 30.0% under 18, 8.5% over 64 (2000); Marriage status: 20.0% never married, 70.7% now married, 3.1% widowed, 6.3% divorced (2000); Foreign born: 1.2% (2000); Ancestry (includes multiple ancestries): 57.6% Norwegian, 26.4% German, 7.5% Irish, 6.9% Polish, 5.4% United States or American (2000).
Economy: Employment by occupation: 15.4% management, 16.0% professional, 10.3% services, 16.9% sales, 3.3% farming, 16.9% construction, 21.1% production (2000).
Income: Per capita income: $16,967 (2000); Median household income: $46,736 (2000); Poverty rate: 2.4% (2000).
Taxes: Total city taxes per capita: $170 (1997); City property taxes per capita: $170 (1997).
Education: High school graduation rate: 87.4% (2000); College graduation rate: 17.2% (2000).
Housing: Homeownership rate: 91.5% (2000); Median home value: $88,100 (2000); Median rent: $375 per month (2000); Median age of housing: 31 years (2000).
Transportation: Commute to work: 87.4% car, 0.0% public transportation, 3.1% walk, 8.2% work from home (2000); Travel time to work: 31.8% less than 15 minutes, 21.2% 15 to 30 minutes, 28.4% 30 to 45 minutes, 10.6% 45 to 60 minutes, 7.9% 60 minutes or more (2000)

WHITEHALL (city). Covers a land area of 1.666 square miles and a water area of 0 square miles. Located at 44.36° N. Lat.; 91.31° W. Long. Elevation is 820 feet.
History: Whitehall began in 1855, and grew with the arrival of the railroad in 1873. Grain elevators, a tobacco warehouse, and a creamery were the center of the economy in the early 1900's.
Population: 1,651 (2000); Race: 98.4% White, 0.2% Black, 0.1% Asian, 0.2% American Indian and Alaska Native, 1.3% Hispanic of any race, 0.4% two or more races (2000); Density: 991.2 persons per square mile (2000); Age: 23.6% under 18, 22.6% over 64 (2000); Marriage status: 21.3% never married, 60.3% now married, 9.9% widowed, 8.5% divorced (2000); Foreign born: 0.8% (2000); Ancestry (includes multiple ancestries): 46.6% Norwegian, 29.7% German, 19.6% Polish, 7.2% Irish, 5.8% English (2000).
Economy: Single-family building permits issued: 1 (2001) / 2 (2000); Multi-family building permits issued: 0 (2001) / 0 (2000); Employment by occupation: 8.7% management, 15.8% professional, 18.7% services, 16.6% sales, 1.5% farming, 7.5% construction, 31.2% production (2000).
Income: Per capita income: $17,743 (2000); Median household income: $33,958 (2000); Poverty rate: 7.3% (2000).
Taxes: Total city taxes per capita: $132 (1997); City property taxes per capita: $128 (1997).
Education: High school graduation rate: 82.5% (2000); College graduation rate: 13.8% (2000).

School District(s)

Whitehall (PK-12)
2000 Enrollment: 757 715-538-4374

Housing: Homeownership rate: 61.4% (2000); Median home value: $66,900 (2000); Median rent: $283 per month (2000); Median age of housing: 46 years (2000).
Hospitals: Trempealeau County Health Care Center (167 beds); Tri-County Memorial Hospital (25 beds)
Safety: Violent crime rate: 48.1 per 10,000 population; Property crime rate: 372.8 per 10,000 population (2001).
Newspapers: Whitehall Times (1 x week)
Transportation: Commute to work: 85.7% car, 0.0% public transportation, 10.3% walk, 2.1% work from home (2000); Travel time to work: 61.4% less than 15 minutes, 24.1% 15 to 30 minutes, 5.4% 30 to 45 minutes, 3.5% 45 to 60 minutes, 5.5% 60 minutes or more (2000)

Vernon County

Located in southwestern Wisconsin; bounded on the west by the Mississippi River and the Iowa and Minnesota borders; drained by the Kickapoo, Bad Axe, and Baraboo Rivers. Covers a land area of 794.90 square miles, a water area of 21.50 square miles, and is located in the Central Time Zone. The county government was organized in 1851. County seat is Viroqua.

Weather Station: Genoa Dam 8 — Elevation: 636 feet

	Jan	Feb	Mar	Apr	May	Jun	Jul	Aug	Sep	Oct	Nov	Dec
High	25	31	43	58	71	79	83	81	72	60	43	30
Low	7	13	25	38	49	59	63	61	53	42	28	16
Precip	1.0	0.8	1.8	3.6	3.6	3.8	4.6	4.5	3.7	2.3	2.3	1.1
Snow	9.9	5.1	4.2	0.9	0.0	0.0	0.0	0.0	0.0	tr	3.6	7.2

High and Low temperatures in degrees Fahrenheit; Precipitation and Snow in inches

Weather Station: Viroqua 2 S — Elevation: 1,158 feet

	Jan	Feb	Mar	Apr	May	Jun	Jul	Aug	Sep	Oct	Nov	Dec
High	23	30	41	57	69	78	81	79	70	59	42	28
Low	4	10	22	33	45	54	59	56	48	37	24	11
Precip	0.9	0.7	1.6	3.5	3.5	3.8	5.0	4.5	3.7	2.3	2.0	17.8
Snow	11.8	6.7	6.3	2.5	0.0	0.0	0.0	0.0	0.0	0.5	4.7	9.3

High and Low temperatures in degrees Fahrenheit; Precipitation and Snow in inches

Population: 28,056 (2000); Race: 98.9% White, 0.1% Black, 0.1% Asian, 0.3% American Indian and Alaska Native, 0.5% Hispanic of any race, 0.4% two or more races (2000); Density: 35.3 persons per square mile (2000); Age: 27.4% under 18, 17.1% over 64 (2000).
Religion: Five largest groups: 28.3% Evangelical Lutheran Church in America, 12.2% Catholic Church, 6.3% Wisconsin Evangelical Lutheran Synod, 5.4% The United Methodist Church, 2.9% Old Order Amish Church (2000).
Economy: Unemployment rate: 4.5% (11/2002); Total civilian labor force: 14,262 (11/2002); Leading industries: 24.5% health care and social assistance; 19.4% retail trade; 17.0% manufacturing (2000); Companies that employ more than 1,000 persons: 0 (2000); Companies that employ more than 100 persons: 6 (2000); Farms: 1,893 totaling 344,172 acres (1997); Minority business ownership rate: 0.0% (1997); Women business ownership rate: 19.4% (1997); Retail sales per capita: $5,908 (1997). Single-family building permits issued: 72 (2001) / 92 (2000); Multi-family building permits issued: 44 (2001) / 18 (2000).
Income: Per capita income: $15,859 (2000); Median household income: $33,178 (2000); Poverty rate: 14.2% (2000); Bankruptcy rate: 1.86% (2001).
Taxes: Total county taxes per capita: $166 (1997); County property taxes per capita: $163 (1997).
Education: High school graduation rate: 78.9% (2000); College graduation rate: 14.0% (2000).
Housing: Homeownership rate: 79.1% (2000); Median home value: $73,400 (2000); Median rent: $292 per month (2000); Median age of housing: 40 years (2000).
Health: Birth rate: 122.6 per 10,000 population (1998); Age adjusted death rate: 79.0 per 10,000 population (1999); Age adjusted cancer mortality rate: 212.2 deaths per 100,000 population (1999). Air Quality Index: 81% good, 19% moderate, 0% unhealthy (percent of days in 2000). Number of physicians: 10.7 per 10,000 population (1999); Number of hospital beds: 32.8 per 10,000 population (1999).
Elections: 2000 Presidential election results: 50.4% Gore, 43.6% Bush, 5.2% Nader, 0.2% Buchanan
National and State Parks: Wildcat Mountain State Park
Additional Information Contacts
Vernon County Government Offices 608-637-5380
Viroqua Chamber of Commerce 608-637-2575
Westby Chamber of Commerce 608-634-4011

Vernon County Communities

BERGEN (town). Covers a land area of 34.222 square miles and a water area of 18.566 square miles. Located at 43.67° N. Lat.; 91.19° W. Long.
Population: 1,317 (2000); Race: 99.9% White, 0.0% Black, 0.0% Asian, 0.1% American Indian and Alaska Native, 0.4% Hispanic of any race, 0.0% two or more races (2000); Density: 38.5 persons per square mile (2000); Age: 27.1% under 18, 9.5% over 64 (2000); Marriage status: 19.2% never married, 71.5% now married, 4.2% widowed, 5.1% divorced (2000); Foreign born: 0.6% (2000); Ancestry (includes multiple ancestries): 54.0% German, 27.0% Norwegian, 10.7% Irish, 6.7% English, 5.5% Italian (2000).
Economy: Single-family building permits issued: 12 (2001) / 12 (2000); Multi-family building permits issued: 0 (2001) / 0 (2000); Employment by occupation: 12.1% management, 22.0% professional, 11.2% services, 21.3% sales, 1.6% farming, 13.0% construction, 18.9% production (2000).
Income: Per capita income: $21,172 (2000); Median household income: $51,779 (2000); Poverty rate: 3.8% (2000).
Taxes: Total city taxes per capita: $89 (1997); City property taxes per capita: $88 (1997).
Education: High school graduation rate: 89.9% (2000); College graduation rate: 21.6% (2000).
Housing: Homeownership rate: 91.4% (2000); Median home value: $114,500 (2000); Median rent: $321 per month (2000); Median age of housing: 28 years (2000).
Transportation: Commute to work: 91.2% car, 0.0% public transportation, 1.5% walk, 6.6% work from home (2000); Travel time to work: 17.9% less than 15 minutes, 50.7% 15 to 30 minutes, 22.2% 30 to 45 minutes, 4.1% 45 to 60 minutes, 5.1% 60 minutes or more (2000)

CHASEBURG (village). Covers a land area of 0.621 square miles and a water area of 0 square miles. Located at 43.65° N. Lat.; 91.09° W. Long. Elevation is 728 feet.
Population: 306 (2000); Race: 100.0% White, 0.0% Black, 0.0% Asian, 0.0% American Indian and Alaska Native, 0.0% Hispanic of any race, 0.0% two or more races (2000); Density: 492.4 persons per square mile (2000); Age: 26.1% under 18, 13.1% over 64 (2000); Marriage status: 20.0% never married, 61.7% now married, 7.1% widowed, 11.3% divorced (2000); Foreign born: 1.0% (2000); Ancestry (includes multiple ancestries): 50.3% German, 44.8% Norwegian, 8.8% Irish, 5.9% Italian, 4.9% English (2000).
Economy: In dairying and stock-raising region. Cheese. Single-family building permits issued: 1 (2001) / 0 (2000); Multi-family building permits issued: 0 (2001) / 0 (2000); Employment by occupation: 11.3% management, 15.0% professional, 13.8% services, 22.5% sales, 0.0% farming, 13.1% construction, 24.4% production (2000).
Income: Per capita income: $18,851 (2000); Median household income: $38,438 (2000); Poverty rate: 7.9% (2000).
Taxes: Total city taxes per capita: $13 (1997); City property taxes per capita: $3 (1997).
Education: High school graduation rate: 85.4% (2000); College graduation rate: 7.1% (2000).
Housing: Homeownership rate: 75.6% (2000); Median home value: $61,200 (2000); Median rent: $325 per month (2000); Median age of housing: 52 years (2000).
Transportation: Commute to work: 89.5% car, 0.0% public transportation, 7.8% walk, 1.3% work from home (2000); Travel time to work: 19.2% less than 15 minutes, 39.7% 15 to 30 minutes, 29.8% 30 to 45 minutes, 3.3% 45 to 60 minutes, 7.9% 60 minutes or more (2000)

CHRISTIANA (town). Covers a land area of 33.572 square miles and a water area of 0.083 square miles. Located at 43.68° N. Lat.; 90.84° W. Long.
Population: 871 (2000); Race: 100.0% White, 0.0% Black, 0.0% Asian, 0.0% American Indian and Alaska Native, 0.0% Hispanic of any race, 0.0% two or more races (2000); Density: 25.9 persons per square mile (2000); Age: 28.5% under 18, 13.0% over 64 (2000); Marriage status: 20.8% never married, 66.8% now married, 7.4% widowed, 5.1% divorced (2000); Foreign born: 1.6% (2000); Ancestry (includes multiple ancestries): 53.7% Norwegian, 24.0% German, 9.8% English, 7.9% Irish, 4.7% French (except Basque) (2000).
Economy: Employment by occupation: 25.7% management, 16.2% professional, 9.9% services, 15.3% sales, 5.6% farming, 11.7% construction, 15.5% production (2000).
Income: Per capita income: $16,486 (2000); Median household income: $34,875 (2000); Poverty rate: 11.1% (2000).
Taxes: Total city taxes per capita: $251 (1997); City property taxes per capita: $251 (1997).

Education: High school graduation rate: 83.2% (2000); College graduation rate: 14.1% (2000).
Housing: Homeownership rate: 87.3% (2000); Median home value: $85,300 (2000); Median rent: $285 per month (2000); Median age of housing: 56 years (2000).
Transportation: Commute to work: 79.3% car, 0.0% public transportation, 5.8% walk, 13.8% work from home (2000); Travel time to work: 34.8% less than 15 minutes, 25.7% 15 to 30 minutes, 23.8% 30 to 45 minutes, 11.0% 45 to 60 minutes, 4.8% 60 minutes or more (2000)

CLINTON (town). Covers a land area of 35.884 square miles and a water area of 0.007 square miles. Located at 43.66° N. Lat.; 90.74° W. Long.
Population: 1,354 (2000); Race: 99.6% White, 0.0% Black, 0.0% Asian, 0.1% American Indian and Alaska Native, 0.0% Hispanic of any race, 0.0% two or more races (2000); Density: 37.7 persons per square mile (2000); Age: 47.5% under 18, 7.5% over 64 (2000); Marriage status: 27.9% never married, 67.1% now married, 2.9% widowed, 2.1% divorced (2000); Foreign born: 0.0% (2000); Ancestry (includes multiple ancestries): 26.6% German, 13.3% Norwegian, 7.8% Pennsylvania German, 6.1% English, 3.9% Irish (2000).
Economy: Employment by occupation: 25.2% management, 9.7% professional, 11.9% services, 12.4% sales, 12.4% farming, 7.9% construction, 20.7% production (2000).
Income: Per capita income: $7,915 (2000); Median household income: $25,417 (2000); Poverty rate: 46.2% (2000).
Taxes: Total city taxes per capita: $70 (1997); City property taxes per capita: $70 (1997).
Education: High school graduation rate: 46.5% (2000); College graduation rate: 10.6% (2000).
Housing: Homeownership rate: 85.1% (2000); Median home value: $48,500 (2000); Median rent: $250 per month (2000); Median age of housing: 35 years (2000).
Transportation: Commute to work: 42.0% car, 0.0% public transportation, 9.9% walk, 41.8% work from home (2000); Travel time to work: 31.3% less than 15 minutes, 32.9% 15 to 30 minutes, 18.7% 30 to 45 minutes, 11.9% 45 to 60 minutes, 5.2% 60 minutes or more (2000)

COON (town). Covers a land area of 34.852 square miles and a water area of 0 square miles. Located at 43.68° N. Lat.; 90.98° W. Long.
Population: 683 (2000); Race: 100.0% White, 0.0% Black, 0.0% Asian, 0.0% American Indian and Alaska Native, 0.0% Hispanic of any race, 0.0% two or more races (2000); Density: 19.6 persons per square mile (2000); Age: 24.6% under 18, 17.4% over 64 (2000); Marriage status: 17.9% never married, 69.6% now married, 5.5% widowed, 6.9% divorced (2000); Foreign born: 0.6% (2000); Ancestry (includes multiple ancestries): 61.7% Norwegian, 31.8% German, 9.2% Irish, 4.7% English, 3.0% Polish (2000).
Economy: In tobacco-growing and dairying area. Manufacturing: fabricated metal products. Headquarters of Coon Creek soil conservation project. Single-family building permits issued: 1 (2001) / 5 (2000); Multi-family building permits issued: 0 (2001) / 0 (2000); Employment by occupation: 18.4% management, 22.0% professional, 10.8% services, 21.1% sales, 1.8% farming, 10.8% construction, 15.1% production (2000).
Income: Per capita income: $20,460 (2000); Median household income: $41,364 (2000); Poverty rate: 8.1% (2000).
Taxes: Total city taxes per capita: $395 (2000); City property taxes per capita: $394 (2000).
Education: High school graduation rate: 80.8% (2000); College graduation rate: 18.7% (2000).
Housing: Homeownership rate: 87.6% (2000); Median home value: $102,400 (2000); Median rent: $200 per month (2000); Median age of housing: 60+ years (2000).
Transportation: Commute to work: 80.2% car, 0.0% public transportation, 1.9% walk, 17.9% work from home (2000); Travel time to work: 19.9% less than 15 minutes, 29.7% 15 to 30 minutes, 38.7% 30 to 45 minutes, 5.3% 45 to 60 minutes, 6.4% 60 minutes or more (2000)

COON VALLEY (village). Covers a land area of 1.080 square miles and a water area of 0 square miles. Located at 43.70° N. Lat.; 91.01° W. Long. Elevation is 735 feet.
Population: 714 (2000); Race: 100.0% White, 0.0% Black, 0.0% Asian, 0.0% American Indian and Alaska Native, 0.0% Hispanic of any race, 0.0% two or more races (2000); Density: 661.1 persons per square mile (2000); Age: 22.6% under 18, 19.3% over 64 (2000); Marriage status: 18.1% never married, 63.2% now married, 11.2% widowed, 7.5% divorced (2000); Foreign born: 0.0% (2000); Ancestry (includes multiple ancestries): 56.4% Norwegian, 33.2% German, 8.2% Irish, 5.0% English, 2.6% Czech (2000).
Economy: Single-family building permits issued: 1 (2001) / 3 (2000); Multi-family building permits issued: 0 (2001) / 8 (2000); Employment by occupation: 9.0% management, 17.3% professional, 17.0% services, 26.6% sales, 0.5% farming, 6.6% construction, 23.0% production (2000).
Income: Per capita income: $18,292 (2000); Median household income: $36,458 (2000); Poverty rate: 9.4% (2000).
Taxes: Total city taxes per capita: $128 (1997); City property taxes per capita: $114 (1997).
Education: High school graduation rate: 81.8% (2000); College graduation rate: 18.4% (2000).
Housing: Homeownership rate: 81.4% (2000); Median home value: $79,700 (2000); Median rent: $318 per month (2000); Median age of housing: 41 years (2000).
Transportation: Commute to work: 91.1% car, 0.6% public transportation, 3.9% walk, 2.8% work from home (2000); Travel time to work: 25.6% less than 15 minutes, 34.2% 15 to 30 minutes, 33.6% 30 to 45 minutes, 1.7% 45 to 60 minutes, 4.8% 60 minutes or more (2000)

DE SOTO (village). Covers a land area of 1.291 square miles and a water area of 0.085 square miles. Located at 43.42° N. Lat.; 91.19° W. Long.
Population: 366 (2000); Race: 94.7% White, 3.4% Black, 1.3% Asian, 0.0% American Indian and Alaska Native, 0.5% Hispanic of any race, 0.0% two or more races (2000); Density: 283.6 persons per square mile (2000); Age: 25.1% under 18, 15.1% over 64 (2000); Marriage status: 13.7% never married, 62.7% now married, 10.3% widowed, 13.3% divorced (2000); Foreign born: 1.9% (2000); Ancestry (includes multiple ancestries): 37.6% German, 30.2% Norwegian, 10.6% English, 8.5% Irish, 6.3% Other groups (2000).
Economy: Black Hawk bridge to Lansing (Iowa) nearby. Upper Mississippi River Wildlife and Fish Area on river; (Army Corps of Engineers) Blackhawk Recreational Area to North. Single-family building permits issued: 3 (2001) / 0 (2000); Multi-family building permits issued: 0 (2001) / 0 (2000); Employment by occupation: 6.8% management, 9.3% professional, 15.4% services, 27.2% sales, 2.5% farming, 7.4% construction, 31.5% production (2000).
Income: Per capita income: $18,042 (2000); Median household income: $33,036 (2000); Poverty rate: 7.4% (2000).
Taxes: Total city taxes per capita: $137 (1997); City property taxes per capita: $126 (1997).
Education: High school graduation rate: 78.1% (2000); College graduation rate: 8.9% (2000).

School District(s)

De Soto Area (PK-12)
2000 Enrollment: 605 608-648-0102

Housing: Homeownership rate: 81.0% (2000); Median home value: $58,000 (2000); Median rent: $304 per month (2000); Median age of housing: 39 years (2000).
Transportation: Commute to work: 89.2% car, 0.0% public transportation, 8.2% walk, 1.3% work from home (2000); Travel time to work: 34.6% less than 15 minutes, 23.1% 15 to 30 minutes, 21.2% 30 to 45 minutes, 11.5% 45 to 60 minutes, 9.6% 60 minutes or more (2000)

FOREST (town). Covers a land area of 35.963 square miles and a water area of 0 square miles. Located at 43.67° N. Lat.; 90.51° W. Long.
Population: 583 (2000); Race: 99.0% White, 0.3% Black, 0.0% Asian, 0.0% American Indian and Alaska Native, 0.0% Hispanic of any race, 0.7% two or more races (2000); Density: 16.2 persons per square mile (2000); Age: 28.8% under 18, 13.7% over 64 (2000); Marriage status: 20.9% never married, 70.5% now married, 4.8% widowed, 3.9% divorced (2000); Foreign born: 0.3% (2000); Ancestry (includes multiple ancestries): 34.5% German, 14.9% Czech, 14.1% Irish, 11.6% Norwegian, 10.8% English (2000).
Economy: Employment by occupation: 15.1% management, 10.2% professional, 12.7% services, 18.3% sales, 7.7% farming, 12.3% construction, 23.6% production (2000).
Income: Per capita income: $13,583 (2000); Median household income: $35,982 (2000); Poverty rate: 15.8% (2000).
Taxes: Total city taxes per capita: $166 (1997); City property taxes per capita: $166 (1997).
Education: High school graduation rate: 78.1% (2000); College graduation rate: 10.4% (2000).
Housing: Homeownership rate: 85.9% (2000); Median home value: $57,100 (2000); Median rent: $450 per month (2000); Median age of housing: 55 years (2000).
Transportation: Commute to work: 79.1% car, 0.0% public transportation, 6.1% walk, 14.7% work from home (2000); Travel time to work: 19.8% less

than 15 minutes, 38.0% 15 to 30 minutes, 12.7% 30 to 45 minutes, 16.5% 45 to 60 minutes, 13.1% 60 minutes or more (2000)

FRANKLIN (town). Covers a land area of 51.544 square miles and a water area of 0.044 square miles. Located at 43.48° N. Lat.; 90.89° W. Long.
Population: 923 (2000); Race: 98.7% White, 0.0% Black, 0.2% Asian, 0.1% American Indian and Alaska Native, 0.0% Hispanic of any race, 1.0% two or more races (2000); Density: 17.9 persons per square mile (2000); Age: 32.5% under 18, 11.0% over 64 (2000); Marriage status: 20.5% never married, 69.9% now married, 4.5% widowed, 5.0% divorced (2000); Foreign born: 0.8% (2000); Ancestry (includes multiple ancestries): 51.2% Norwegian, 28.4% German, 13.0% Irish, 6.0% English, 3.8% Swedish (2000).
Economy: Single-family building permits issued: 3 (2001) / 5 (2000); Multi-family building permits issued: 0 (2001) / 0 (2000); Employment by occupation: 19.0% management, 13.4% professional, 9.8% services, 23.0% sales, 2.7% farming, 8.9% construction, 23.2% production (2000).
Income: Per capita income: $12,850 (2000); Median household income: $32,931 (2000); Poverty rate: 21.2% (2000).
Taxes: Total city taxes per capita: $120 (1997); City property taxes per capita: $117 (1997).
Education: High school graduation rate: 82.2% (2000); College graduation rate: 11.2% (2000).
Housing: Homeownership rate: 79.6% (2000); Median home value: $67,500 (2000); Median rent: $308 per month (2000); Median age of housing: 43 years (2000).
Transportation: Commute to work: 75.4% car, 1.8% public transportation, 3.2% walk, 19.6% work from home (2000); Travel time to work: 40.8% less than 15 minutes, 36.5% 15 to 30 minutes, 8.8% 30 to 45 minutes, 6.2% 45 to 60 minutes, 7.6% 60 minutes or more (2000)

GENOA (village). Covers a land area of 0.301 square miles and a water area of 0 square miles. Located at 43.57° N. Lat.; 91.22° W. Long. Elevation is 660 feet.
History: Genoa was settled by Italian fishermen and farmers who came up the river in 1848 from Illinois. They named the community for the town in Italy.
Population: 263 (2000); Race: 99.3% White, 0.0% Black, 0.0% Asian, 0.0% American Indian and Alaska Native, 0.0% Hispanic of any race, 0.7% two or more races (2000); Density: 872.4 persons per square mile (2000); Age: 23.2% under 18, 26.4% over 64 (2000); Marriage status: 26.2% never married, 56.1% now married, 10.0% widowed, 7.7% divorced (2000); Foreign born: 1.1% (2000); Ancestry (includes multiple ancestries): 38.4% German, 29.3% Norwegian, 25.4% Italian, 9.8% French (except Basque), 7.6% Irish (2000).
Economy: Employment by occupation: 8.2% management, 15.7% professional, 17.2% services, 25.4% sales, 0.0% farming, 12.7% construction, 20.9% production (2000).
Income: Per capita income: $15,384 (2000); Median household income: $32,857 (2000); Poverty rate: 6.9% (2000).
Taxes: Total city taxes per capita: $30 (2000); City property taxes per capita: $27 (2000).
Education: High school graduation rate: 81.4% (2000); College graduation rate: 13.1% (2000).
Housing: Homeownership rate: 80.7% (2000); Median home value: $70,300 (2000); Median rent: $329 per month (2000); Median age of housing: 60+ years (2000).
Transportation: Commute to work: 80.2% car, 0.0% public transportation, 18.3% walk, 1.5% work from home (2000); Travel time to work: 41.1% less than 15 minutes, 26.4% 15 to 30 minutes, 16.3% 30 to 45 minutes, 14.7% 45 to 60 minutes, 1.6% 60 minutes or more (2000)

GENOA (town). Covers a land area of 34.993 square miles and a water area of 1.333 square miles. Located at 43.54° N. Lat.; 91.19° W. Long. Elevation is 660 feet.
Population: 705 (2000); Race: 98.7% White, 0.0% Black, 0.0% Asian, 0.0% American Indian and Alaska Native, 1.4% Hispanic of any race, 1.3% two or more races (2000); Density: 20.1 persons per square mile (2000); Age: 25.7% under 18, 13.1% over 64 (2000); Marriage status: 23.7% never married, 64.5% now married, 6.3% widowed, 5.6% divorced (2000); Foreign born: 1.4% (2000); Ancestry (includes multiple ancestries): 39.3% German, 24.8% Norwegian, 12.9% Italian, 12.8% Irish, 7.3% English (2000).
Economy: Fishing. Lock and Dam No. 8 on the Mississippi here. Upper Mississippi Wildlife and Fish Area along river. Single-family building permits issued: 3 (2001) / 3 (2000); Multi-family building permits issued: 0 (2001) / 0 (2000); Employment by occupation: 12.7% management, 10.0% professional, 13.9% services, 21.6% sales, 1.1% farming, 15.0% construction, 25.8% production (2000).
Income: Per capita income: $17,683 (2000); Median household income: $45,234 (2000); Poverty rate: 8.9% (2000).
Taxes: Total city taxes per capita: $21 (1997); City property taxes per capita: $19 (1997).
Education: High school graduation rate: 83.1% (2000); College graduation rate: 10.3% (2000).
Housing: Homeownership rate: 92.0% (2000); Median home value: $94,000 (2000); Median rent: $325 per month (2000); Median age of housing: 26 years (2000).
Transportation: Commute to work: 87.3% car, 0.0% public transportation, 2.3% walk, 9.3% work from home (2000); Travel time to work: 14.6% less than 15 minutes, 28.0% 15 to 30 minutes, 36.4% 30 to 45 minutes, 11.5% 45 to 60 minutes, 9.3% 60 minutes or more (2000)

GREENWOOD (town). Covers a land area of 35.803 square miles and a water area of 0 square miles. Located at 43.60° N. Lat.; 90.36° W. Long. Elevation is 933 feet.
Population: 770 (2000); Race: 100.0% White, 0.0% Black, 0.0% Asian, 0.0% American Indian and Alaska Native, 0.3% Hispanic of any race, 0.0% two or more races (2000); Density: 21.5 persons per square mile (2000); Age: 37.9% under 18, 7.9% over 64 (2000); Marriage status: 25.5% never married, 67.3% now married, 2.9% widowed, 4.4% divorced (2000); Foreign born: 0.4% (2000); Ancestry (includes multiple ancestries): 35.3% German, 13.6% Czech, 9.5% English, 8.9% Irish, 7.1% Swiss (2000).
Economy: Employment by occupation: 30.2% management, 5.4% professional, 11.8% services, 10.3% sales, 6.9% farming, 17.5% construction, 17.8% production (2000).
Income: Per capita income: $10,567 (2000); Median household income: $36,458 (2000); Poverty rate: 29.5% (2000).
Taxes: Total city taxes per capita: $172 (1997); City property taxes per capita: $172 (1997).
Education: High school graduation rate: 67.6% (2000); College graduation rate: 12.4% (2000).
Housing: Homeownership rate: 88.7% (2000); Median home value: $66,300 (2000); Median rent: $238 per month (2000); Median age of housing: 37 years (2000).
Transportation: Commute to work: 56.1% car, 0.0% public transportation, 6.1% walk, 35.5% work from home (2000); Travel time to work: 40.4% less than 15 minutes, 23.0% 15 to 30 minutes, 13.6% 30 to 45 minutes, 12.2% 45 to 60 minutes, 10.8% 60 minutes or more (2000)

HAMBURG (town). Covers a land area of 35.809 square miles and a water area of 0.012 square miles. Located at 43.67° N. Lat.; 91.09° W. Long.
Population: 848 (2000); Race: 99.2% White, 0.0% Black, 0.0% Asian, 0.8% American Indian and Alaska Native, 0.5% Hispanic of any race, 0.0% two or more races (2000); Density: 23.7 persons per square mile (2000); Age: 24.4% under 18, 12.2% over 64 (2000); Marriage status: 22.0% never married, 67.4% now married, 3.0% widowed, 7.7% divorced (2000); Foreign born: 0.4% (2000); Ancestry (includes multiple ancestries): 52.9% German, 49.3% Norwegian, 5.0% Irish, 3.5% Other groups, 3.2% Czech (2000).
Economy: Single-family building permits issued: 12 (2001) / 8 (2000); Multi-family building permits issued: 0 (2001) / 0 (2000); Employment by occupation: 13.3% management, 13.8% professional, 11.5% services, 28.1% sales, 0.4% farming, 12.7% construction, 20.1% production (2000).
Income: Per capita income: $19,169 (2000); Median household income: $49,013 (2000); Poverty rate: 1.2% (2000).
Taxes: Total city taxes per capita: $141 (1997); City property taxes per capita: $140 (1997).
Education: High school graduation rate: 87.7% (2000); College graduation rate: 13.9% (2000).
Housing: Homeownership rate: 87.0% (2000); Median home value: $115,800 (2000); Median rent: $431 per month (2000); Median age of housing: 28 years (2000).
Transportation: Commute to work: 89.4% car, 0.0% public transportation, 0.8% walk, 9.8% work from home (2000); Travel time to work: 12.9% less than 15 minutes, 42.9% 15 to 30 minutes, 33.9% 30 to 45 minutes, 4.6% 45 to 60 minutes, 5.8% 60 minutes or more (2000)

HARMONY (town). Covers a land area of 42.901 square miles and a water area of 0 square miles. Located at 43.57° N. Lat.; 91.09° W. Long.
Population: 739 (2000); Race: 99.2% White, 0.0% Black, 0.1% Asian, 0.0% American Indian and Alaska Native, 0.7% Hispanic of any race, 0.0% two or more races (2000); Density: 17.2 persons per square mile (2000); Age: 34.7% under 18, 13.6% over 64 (2000); Marriage status: 19.8% never married,

72.0% now married, 4.5% widowed, 3.7% divorced (2000); Foreign born: 1.0% (2000); Ancestry (includes multiple ancestries): 37.3% German, 35.5% Norwegian, 8.2% United States or American, 6.4% Pennsylvania German, 4.8% English (2000).
Economy: Single-family building permits issued: 6 (2001) / 11 (2000); Multi-family building permits issued: 0 (2001) / 0 (2000); Employment by occupation: 27.0% management, 13.0% professional, 8.3% services, 19.3% sales, 4.0% farming, 11.3% construction, 17.0% production (2000).
Income: Per capita income: $13,962 (2000); Median household income: $41,000 (2000); Poverty rate: 15.6% (2000).
Taxes: Total city taxes per capita: $199 (1997); City property taxes per capita: $199 (1997).
Education: High school graduation rate: 80.2% (2000); College graduation rate: 13.7% (2000).
Housing: Homeownership rate: 84.4% (2000); Median home value: $62,900 (2000); Median rent: $369 per month (2000); Median age of housing: 35 years (2000).
Transportation: Commute to work: 74.4% car, 0.0% public transportation, 4.7% walk, 18.9% work from home (2000); Travel time to work: 14.9% less than 15 minutes, 29.5% 15 to 30 minutes, 33.2% 30 to 45 minutes, 17.4% 45 to 60 minutes, 5.0% 60 minutes or more (2000)

HILLSBORO (city). Covers a land area of 1.198 square miles and a water area of 0.030 square miles. Located at 43.65° N. Lat.; 90.34° W. Long. Elevation is 1,001 feet.
Population: 1,302 (2000); Race: 98.9% White, 0.0% Black, 0.0% Asian, 0.9% American Indian and Alaska Native, 0.3% Hispanic of any race, 0.0% two or more races (2000); Density: 1,086.6 persons per square mile (2000); Age: 22.6% under 18, 26.8% over 64 (2000); Marriage status: 20.9% never married, 55.8% now married, 13.5% widowed, 9.8% divorced (2000); Foreign born: 0.3% (2000); Ancestry (includes multiple ancestries): 38.6% German, 19.3% Czech, 12.4% Irish, 12.2% Norwegian, 11.7% English (2000).
Economy: Single-family building permits issued: 3 (2001) / 2 (2000); Multi-family building permits issued: 2 (2001) / 8 (2000); Employment by occupation: 9.4% management, 17.5% professional, 16.0% services, 24.5% sales, 0.7% farming, 10.1% construction, 21.8% production (2000).
Income: Per capita income: $16,005 (2000); Median household income: $30,543 (2000); Poverty rate: 9.2% (2000).
Taxes: Total city taxes per capita: $187 (1997); City property taxes per capita: $181 (1997).
Education: High school graduation rate: 73.8% (2000); College graduation rate: 11.6% (2000).

School District(s)

Hillsboro (PK-12)
2000 Enrollment: 656 608-489-2221
Housing: Homeownership rate: 68.8% (2000); Median home value: $66,300 (2000); Median rent: $304 per month (2000); Median age of housing: 54 years (2000).
Hospitals: Saint Joseph's Community Health Services (99 beds)
Safety: Violent crime rate: 0.0 per 10,000 population; Property crime rate: 76.3 per 10,000 population (2001).
Newspapers: Peach Shopper (1 x week); Sentry-Enterprise (1 x week); Neighbors (1 x month)
Transportation: Commute to work: 86.1% car, 0.0% public transportation, 10.5% walk, 2.7% work from home (2000); Travel time to work: 58.1% less than 15 minutes, 12.5% 15 to 30 minutes, 13.4% 30 to 45 minutes, 7.7% 45 to 60 minutes, 8.3% 60 minutes or more (2000)

HILLSBORO (town). Covers a land area of 35.607 square miles and a water area of 0.034 square miles. Located at 43.68° N. Lat.; 90.36° W. Long. Elevation is 1,001 feet.
History: Settled 1854; incorporated as village in 1885, as city in 1939.
Population: 766 (2000); Race: 98.2% White, 0.3% Black, 0.0% Asian, 0.0% American Indian and Alaska Native, 1.3% Hispanic of any race, 1.5% two or more races (2000); Density: 21.5 persons per square mile (2000); Age: 28.5% under 18, 16.2% over 64 (2000); Marriage status: 22.3% never married, 60.1% now married, 9.3% widowed, 8.3% divorced (2000); Foreign born: 0.8% (2000); Ancestry (includes multiple ancestries): 37.4% German, 15.5% Czech, 11.4% English, 11.3% Norwegian, 11.3% Irish (2000).
Economy: In timber and farm area. Dairy products, flour, lumber. Manufacturing: textiles, footwear. Hospital and airfield here. Employment by occupation: 16.2% management, 7.7% professional, 16.4% services, 20.0% sales, 6.3% farming, 8.5% construction, 24.9% production (2000).
Income: Per capita income: $15,967 (2000); Median household income: $37,321 (2000); Poverty rate: 18.9% (2000).
Taxes: Total city taxes per capita: $202 (1997); City property taxes per capita: $193 (1997).
Education: High school graduation rate: 82.7% (2000); College graduation rate: 10.5% (2000).
Housing: Homeownership rate: 76.2% (2000); Median home value: $82,500 (2000); Median rent: $368 per month (2000); Median age of housing: 40 years (2000).
Transportation: Commute to work: 82.6% car, 0.0% public transportation, 1.9% walk, 13.3% work from home (2000); Travel time to work: 44.9% less than 15 minutes, 22.9% 15 to 30 minutes, 15.3% 30 to 45 minutes, 10.8% 45 to 60 minutes, 6.1% 60 minutes or more (2000)

JEFFERSON (town). Covers a land area of 46.927 square miles and a water area of 0.085 square miles. Located at 43.57° N. Lat.; 90.97° W. Long.
Population: 974 (2000); Race: 98.4% White, 0.0% Black, 0.0% Asian, 0.2% American Indian and Alaska Native, 1.5% Hispanic of any race, 1.2% two or more races (2000); Density: 20.8 persons per square mile (2000); Age: 30.0% under 18, 10.8% over 64 (2000); Marriage status: 21.0% never married, 65.9% now married, 5.0% widowed, 8.1% divorced (2000); Foreign born: 1.1% (2000); Ancestry (includes multiple ancestries): 53.0% Norwegian, 26.4% German, 9.6% Irish, 8.0% English, 5.2% United States or American (2000).
Economy: Employment by occupation: 19.5% management, 17.3% professional, 9.5% services, 20.9% sales, 4.0% farming, 12.0% construction, 16.9% production (2000).
Income: Per capita income: $16,144 (2000); Median household income: $37,857 (2000); Poverty rate: 6.8% (2000).
Taxes: Total city taxes per capita: $281 (1997); City property taxes per capita: $281 (1997).
Education: High school graduation rate: 87.2% (2000); College graduation rate: 19.4% (2000).
Housing: Homeownership rate: 83.1% (2000); Median home value: $75,400 (2000); Median rent: $317 per month (2000); Median age of housing: 43 years (2000).
Transportation: Commute to work: 80.9% car, 0.0% public transportation, 5.8% walk, 13.1% work from home (2000); Travel time to work: 41.1% less than 15 minutes, 30.0% 15 to 30 minutes, 12.8% 30 to 45 minutes, 9.6% 45 to 60 minutes, 6.5% 60 minutes or more (2000)

KICKAPOO (town). Covers a land area of 37.864 square miles and a water area of 0.026 square miles. Located at 43.46° N. Lat.; 90.75° W. Long.
Population: 566 (2000); Race: 100.0% White, 0.0% Black, 0.0% Asian, 0.0% American Indian and Alaska Native, 0.0% Hispanic of any race, 0.0% two or more races (2000); Density: 14.9 persons per square mile (2000); Age: 32.3% under 18, 12.5% over 64 (2000); Marriage status: 14.6% never married, 76.9% now married, 4.6% widowed, 3.9% divorced (2000); Foreign born: 2.7% (2000); Ancestry (includes multiple ancestries): 28.4% Norwegian, 25.6% German, 14.1% English, 13.6% Irish, 4.8% United States or American (2000).
Economy: Single-family building permits issued: 0 (2001) / 0 (2000); Multi-family building permits issued: 0 (2001) / 0 (2000); Employment by occupation: 21.4% management, 12.2% professional, 8.8% services, 21.8% sales, 4.6% farming, 9.9% construction, 21.4% production (2000).
Income: Per capita income: $15,543 (2000); Median household income: $36,023 (2000); Poverty rate: 7.2% (2000).
Taxes: Total city taxes per capita: $106 (1997); City property taxes per capita: $106 (1997).
Education: High school graduation rate: 83.7% (2000); College graduation rate: 14.7% (2000).
Housing: Homeownership rate: 91.5% (2000); Median home value: $93,800 (2000); Median rent: $425 per month (2000); Median age of housing: 32 years (2000).
Transportation: Commute to work: 81.9% car, 0.8% public transportation, 4.2% walk, 11.6% work from home (2000); Travel time to work: 29.3% less than 15 minutes, 40.2% 15 to 30 minutes, 13.5% 30 to 45 minutes, 5.7% 45 to 60 minutes, 11.4% 60 minutes or more (2000)

LA FARGE (village). Covers a land area of 1.040 square miles and a water area of 0 square miles. Located at 43.57° N. Lat.; 90.63° W. Long. Elevation is 797 feet.
Population: 775 (2000); Race: 98.4% White, 0.0% Black, 0.0% Asian, 1.3% American Indian and Alaska Native, 0.0% Hispanic of any race, 0.3% two or more races (2000); Density: 745.4 persons per square mile (2000); Age: 24.4% under 18, 22.4% over 64 (2000); Marriage status: 23.8% never married, 48.0% now married, 14.7% widowed, 13.5% divorced (2000); Foreign born: 0.9% (2000); Ancestry (includes multiple ancestries): 26.6%

German, 22.2% Norwegian, 18.6% Irish, 8.7% United States or American, 7.1% English (2000).
Economy: In dairying and tobacco-growing area. Timber; cheese, wood pallets. Single-family building permits issued: 2 (2001) / 3 (2000); Multi-family building permits issued: 0 (2001) / 0 (2000); Employment by occupation: 10.3% management, 10.3% professional, 14.8% services, 15.4% sales, 1.9% farming, 9.6% construction, 37.6% production (2000).
Income: Per capita income: $14,191 (2000); Median household income: $23,083 (2000); Poverty rate: 14.4% (2000).
Taxes: Total city taxes per capita: $109 (1997); City property taxes per capita: $104 (1997).
Education: High school graduation rate: 79.5% (2000); College graduation rate: 8.2% (2000).

School District(s)

La Farge (PK-12)
2000 Enrollment: 317 608-625-2400
Housing: Homeownership rate: 77.7% (2000); Median home value: $45,000 (2000); Median rent: $269 per month (2000); Median age of housing: 52 years (2000).
Transportation: Commute to work: 83.8% car, 0.0% public transportation, 9.7% walk, 3.6% work from home (2000); Travel time to work: 39.9% less than 15 minutes, 29.5% 15 to 30 minutes, 13.1% 30 to 45 minutes, 6.0% 45 to 60 minutes, 11.4% 60 minutes or more (2000)

LIBERTY (town). Covers a land area of 23.050 square miles and a water area of 0.014 square miles. Located at 43.52° N. Lat.; 90.74° W. Long. Elevation is 771 feet.
Population: 167 (2000); Race: 98.8% White, 0.0% Black, 0.0% Asian, 0.0% American Indian and Alaska Native, 1.2% Hispanic of any race, 1.2% two or more races (2000); Density: 7.2 persons per square mile (2000); Age: 21.2% under 18, 17.6% over 64 (2000); Marriage status: 19.0% never married, 64.8% now married, 4.9% widowed, 11.3% divorced (2000); Foreign born: 1.2% (2000); Ancestry (includes multiple ancestries): 30.0% German, 19.4% Norwegian, 18.2% Irish, 10.0% English, 8.8% United States or American (2000).
Economy: Single-family building permits issued: 1 (2001) / 1 (2000); Multi-family building permits issued: 0 (2001) / 0 (2000); Employment by occupation: 17.8% management, 12.2% professional, 20.0% services, 12.2% sales, 2.2% farming, 14.4% construction, 21.1% production (2000).
Income: Per capita income: $13,986 (2000); Median household income: $24,688 (2000); Poverty rate: 14.1% (2000).
Taxes: Total city taxes per capita: $131 (1997); City property taxes per capita: $127 (1997).
Education: High school graduation rate: 75.8% (2000); College graduation rate: 14.4% (2000).
Housing: Homeownership rate: 94.7% (2000); Median home value: $82,500 (2000); Median rent: $425 per month (2000); Median age of housing: 16 years (2000).
Transportation: Commute to work: 87.2% car, 0.0% public transportation, 2.3% walk, 10.5% work from home (2000); Travel time to work: 22.1% less than 15 minutes, 70.1% 15 to 30 minutes, 2.6% 30 to 45 minutes, 5.2% 45 to 60 minutes, 0.0% 60 minutes or more (2000)

ONTARIO (village). Covers a land area of 1.013 square miles and a water area of 0 square miles. Located at 43.72° N. Lat.; 90.59° W. Long. Elevation is 900 feet.
Population: 476 (2000); Race: 93.1% White, 0.0% Black, 0.0% Asian, 0.0% American Indian and Alaska Native, 6.9% Hispanic of any race, 0.0% two or more races (2000); Density: 470.1 persons per square mile (2000); Age: 22.0% under 18, 24.1% over 64 (2000); Marriage status: 25.1% never married, 50.4% now married, 10.7% widowed, 13.8% divorced (2000); Foreign born: 3.9% (2000); Ancestry (includes multiple ancestries): 38.6% German, 12.7% English, 12.1% Norwegian, 10.6% Irish, 9.1% Other groups (2000).
Economy: In farm and dairy area. Single-family building permits issued: 2 (2001) / 2 (2000); Multi-family building permits issued: 0 (2001) / 0 (2000); Employment by occupation: 5.2% management, 11.9% professional, 18.0% services, 18.6% sales, 1.0% farming, 7.2% construction, 38.1% production (2000).
Income: Per capita income: $13,893 (2000); Median household income: $23,194 (2000); Poverty rate: 22.4% (2000).
Taxes: Total city taxes per capita: $102 (1997); City property taxes per capita: $81 (1997).
Education: High school graduation rate: 68.3% (2000); College graduation rate: 6.0% (2000).

School District(s)

Norwalk-Ontario-Wilton (PK-12)
2000 Enrollment: 690 608-337-4403
Housing: Homeownership rate: 71.7% (2000); Median home value: $43,600 (2000); Median rent: $253 per month (2000); Median age of housing: 34 years (2000).
Transportation: Commute to work: 83.1% car, 0.0% public transportation, 11.6% walk, 5.3% work from home (2000); Travel time to work: 33.0% less than 15 minutes, 16.2% 15 to 30 minutes, 35.8% 30 to 45 minutes, 7.3% 45 to 60 minutes, 7.8% 60 minutes or more (2000)

READSTOWN (village). Covers a land area of 1.788 square miles and a water area of 0 square miles. Located at 43.44° N. Lat.; 90.76° W. Long. Elevation is 760 feet.
Population: 395 (2000); Race: 96.9% White, 2.1% Black, 0.5% Asian, 0.0% American Indian and Alaska Native, 0.5% Hispanic of any race, 0.0% two or more races (2000); Density: 221.0 persons per square mile (2000); Age: 20.7% under 18, 21.7% over 64 (2000); Marriage status: 25.9% never married, 46.6% now married, 15.2% widowed, 12.2% divorced (2000); Foreign born: 0.5% (2000); Ancestry (includes multiple ancestries): 38.8% Norwegian, 20.9% German, 12.1% Irish, 10.3% English, 5.2% United States or American (2000).
Economy: Cheese, butter. Manufacturing of hydraulic equipment. Single-family building permits issued: 0 (2001) / 1 (2000); Multi-family building permits issued: 0 (2001) / 0 (2000); Employment by occupation: 5.4% management, 8.2% professional, 26.6% services, 22.3% sales, 0.0% farming, 9.8% construction, 27.7% production (2000).
Income: Per capita income: $12,957 (2000); Median household income: $21,250 (2000); Poverty rate: 21.2% (2000).
Taxes: Total city taxes per capita: $94 (1997); City property taxes per capita: $85 (1997).
Education: High school graduation rate: 74.6% (2000); College graduation rate: 6.3% (2000).
Housing: Homeownership rate: 61.4% (2000); Median home value: $45,600 (2000); Median rent: $256 per month (2000); Median age of housing: 46 years (2000).
Transportation: Commute to work: 81.5% car, 0.0% public transportation, 9.2% walk, 7.6% work from home (2000); Travel time to work: 38.8% less than 15 minutes, 35.9% 15 to 30 minutes, 21.8% 30 to 45 minutes, 2.4% 45 to 60 minutes, 1.2% 60 minutes or more (2000)

STARK (town). Covers a land area of 34.419 square miles and a water area of 0.013 square miles. Located at 43.59° N. Lat.; 90.61° W. Long.
Population: 349 (2000); Race: 93.2% White, 0.0% Black, 0.0% Asian, 6.8% American Indian and Alaska Native, 0.0% Hispanic of any race, 0.0% two or more races (2000); Density: 10.1 persons per square mile (2000); Age: 23.1% under 18, 13.0% over 64 (2000); Marriage status: 19.7% never married, 66.2% now married, 3.0% widowed, 11.2% divorced (2000); Foreign born: 0.0% (2000); Ancestry (includes multiple ancestries): 25.3% Norwegian, 22.8% German, 15.7% English, 9.0% Irish, 5.9% United States or American (2000).
Economy: Single-family building permits issued: 5 (2001) / 5 (2000); Multi-family building permits issued: 0 (2001) / 0 (2000); Employment by occupation: 19.9% management, 18.7% professional, 6.6% services, 15.1% sales, 5.4% farming, 18.1% construction, 16.3% production (2000).
Income: Per capita income: $17,966 (2000); Median household income: $44,167 (2000); Poverty rate: 20.1% (2000).
Taxes: Total city taxes per capita: $178 (1997); City property taxes per capita: $178 (1997).
Education: High school graduation rate: 82.3% (2000); College graduation rate: 17.2% (2000).
Housing: Homeownership rate: 90.4% (2000); Median home value: $64,400 (2000); Median rent: $225 per month (2000); Median age of housing: 36 years (2000).
Transportation: Commute to work: 78.6% car, 3.8% public transportation, 3.8% walk, 11.3% work from home (2000); Travel time to work: 41.1% less than 15 minutes, 24.1% 15 to 30 minutes, 15.6% 30 to 45 minutes, 9.2% 45 to 60 minutes, 9.9% 60 minutes or more (2000)

STERLING (town). Covers a land area of 45.453 square miles and a water area of 0 square miles. Located at 43.48° N. Lat.; 91.04° W. Long.
Population: 713 (2000); Race: 97.8% White, 1.5% Black, 0.0% Asian, 0.0% American Indian and Alaska Native, 0.0% Hispanic of any race, 0.7% two or more races (2000); Density: 15.7 persons per square mile (2000); Age: 38.3% under 18, 8.3% over 64 (2000); Marriage status: 24.0% never married, 67.8% now married, 3.5% widowed, 4.7% divorced (2000); Foreign born: 0.3%

(2000); Ancestry (includes multiple ancestries): 37.0% Norwegian, 32.2% German, 6.8% Irish, 6.7% English, 6.3% United States or American (2000).
Economy: Single-family building permits issued: 1 (2001) / 1 (2000); Multi-family building permits issued: 0 (2001) / 0 (2000); Employment by occupation: 23.7% management, 9.4% professional, 16.4% services, 17.8% sales, 11.1% farming, 9.1% construction, 12.5% production (2000).
Income: Per capita income: $13,402 (2000); Median household income: $28,125 (2000); Poverty rate: 24.2% (2000).
Taxes: Total city taxes per capita: $101 (2000); City property taxes per capita: $100 (2000).
Education: High school graduation rate: 80.3% (2000); College graduation rate: 9.9% (2000).
Housing: Homeownership rate: 75.2% (2000); Median home value: $55,800 (2000); Median rent: $233 per month (2000); Median age of housing: 59 years (2000).
Transportation: Commute to work: 68.9% car, 0.0% public transportation, 11.3% walk, 18.4% work from home (2000); Travel time to work: 34.2% less than 15 minutes, 26.8% 15 to 30 minutes, 19.9% 30 to 45 minutes, 11.3% 45 to 60 minutes, 7.8% 60 minutes or more (2000)

STODDARD (village). Covers a land area of 0.599 square miles and a water area of 0.088 square miles. Located at 43.66° N. Lat.; 91.22° W. Long. Elevation is 646 feet.
Population: 815 (2000); Race: 98.6% White, 0.0% Black, 0.0% Asian, 0.0% American Indian and Alaska Native, 0.2% Hispanic of any race, 1.4% two or more races (2000); Density: 1,360.5 persons per square mile (2000); Age: 21.8% under 18, 18.6% over 64 (2000); Marriage status: 20.6% never married, 58.9% now married, 8.4% widowed, 12.1% divorced (2000); Foreign born: 0.9% (2000); Ancestry (includes multiple ancestries): 45.2% German, 32.1% Norwegian, 12.5% Irish, 6.7% English, 6.3% Italian (2000).
Economy: Fishing. Mt. La Crosse Ski Area to North. Single-family building permits issued: 0 (2001) / 1 (2000); Multi-family building permits issued: 0 (2001) / 0 (2000); Employment by occupation: 13.7% management, 13.9% professional, 20.8% services, 18.2% sales, 0.0% farming, 15.8% construction, 17.7% production (2000).
Income: Per capita income: $19,634 (2000); Median household income: $31,250 (2000); Poverty rate: 9.3% (2000).
Taxes: Total city taxes per capita: $186 (1997); City property taxes per capita: $175 (1997).
Education: High school graduation rate: 80.3% (2000); College graduation rate: 10.8% (2000).
Housing: Homeownership rate: 74.7% (2000); Median home value: $78,600 (2000); Median rent: $370 per month (2000); Median age of housing: 37 years (2000).
Transportation: Commute to work: 87.4% car, 0.0% public transportation, 4.7% walk, 6.6% work from home (2000); Travel time to work: 20.8% less than 15 minutes, 45.4% 15 to 30 minutes, 26.4% 30 to 45 minutes, 2.0% 45 to 60 minutes, 5.3% 60 minutes or more (2000)

UNION (town). Covers a land area of 35.765 square miles and a water area of 0.004 square miles. Located at 43.59° N. Lat.; 90.50° W. Long.
Population: 531 (2000); Race: 97.6% White, 0.4% Black, 0.0% Asian, 0.0% American Indian and Alaska Native, 0.4% Hispanic of any race, 1.6% two or more races (2000); Density: 14.8 persons per square mile (2000); Age: 38.3% under 18, 8.9% over 64 (2000); Marriage status: 28.5% never married, 58.1% now married, 6.3% widowed, 7.1% divorced (2000); Foreign born: 0.4% (2000); Ancestry (includes multiple ancestries): 23.7% German, 17.2% Czech, 14.0% Norwegian, 9.1% English, 7.5% Irish (2000).
Economy: Employment by occupation: 25.0% management, 12.5% professional, 9.1% services, 18.1% sales, 6.9% farming, 6.9% construction, 21.6% production (2000).
Income: Per capita income: $13,501 (2000); Median household income: $35,417 (2000); Poverty rate: 18.6% (2000).
Taxes: Total city taxes per capita: $215 (1997); City property taxes per capita: $215 (1997).
Education: High school graduation rate: 79.9% (2000); College graduation rate: 9.7% (2000).
Housing: Homeownership rate: 84.1% (2000); Median home value: $56,300 (2000); Median rent: $275 per month (2000); Median age of housing: 28 years (2000).
Transportation: Commute to work: 68.6% car, 0.0% public transportation, 5.2% walk, 26.2% work from home (2000); Travel time to work: 27.8% less than 15 minutes, 24.3% 15 to 30 minutes, 16.0% 30 to 45 minutes, 18.3% 45 to 60 minutes, 13.6% 60 minutes or more (2000)

VIROQUA (city). Covers a land area of 3.266 square miles and a water area of 0 square miles. Located at 43.55° N. Lat.; 90.88° W. Long. Elevation is 1,277 feet.
History: First settled by easterners, the region around Viroqua was later cultivated for tobacco by Norwegian immigrants. Viroqua was also supported in the early 1900's by the Viroqua Cooperative Creamery, which became one of the largest creameries and milk depots in the state in the 1930's.
Population: 4,335 (2000); Race: 99.8% White, 0.0% Black, 0.0% Asian, 0.1% American Indian and Alaska Native, 0.4% Hispanic of any race, 0.0% two or more races (2000); Density: 1,327.3 persons per square mile (2000); Age: 21.0% under 18, 26.5% over 64 (2000); Marriage status: 21.5% never married, 50.2% now married, 18.2% widowed, 10.1% divorced (2000); Foreign born: 0.9% (2000); Ancestry (includes multiple ancestries): 48.3% Norwegian, 27.0% German, 13.1% Irish, 8.8% English, 2.8% United States or American (2000).
Economy: Single-family building permits issued: 5 (2001) / 8 (2000); Multi-family building permits issued: 22 (2001) / 0 (2000); Employment by occupation: 8.8% management, 15.5% professional, 22.6% services, 24.2% sales, 0.6% farming, 6.0% construction, 22.3% production (2000).
Income: Per capita income: $17,172 (2000); Median household income: $28,804 (2000); Poverty rate: 12.9% (2000).
Taxes: Total city taxes per capita: $227 (2000); City property taxes per capita: $207 (2000).
Education: High school graduation rate: 77.5% (2000); College graduation rate: 15.0% (2000).

School District(s)

Viroqua Area (PK-12)
2000 Enrollment: 1,312 608-637-1199
Housing: Homeownership rate: 66.9% (2000); Median home value: $70,700 (2000); Median rent: $281 per month (2000); Median age of housing: 41 years (2000).
Hospitals: Vernon Memorial Hospital (49 beds)
Safety: Violent crime rate: 6.9 per 10,000 population; Property crime rate: 222.2 per 10,000 population (2001).
Newspapers: Vernon County Broadcaster (1 x week)
Transportation: Commute to work: 88.8% car, 2.4% public transportation, 5.1% walk, 2.6% work from home (2000); Travel time to work: 69.8% less than 15 minutes, 14.4% 15 to 30 minutes, 5.4% 30 to 45 minutes, 5.1% 45 to 60 minutes, 5.2% 60 minutes or more (2000)
Additional Information Contacts
Viroqua Chamber of Commerce 608-637-2575

VIROQUA (town). Covers a land area of 48.339 square miles and a water area of 0.034 square miles. Located at 43.57° N. Lat.; 90.85° W. Long. Elevation is 1,277 feet.
History: Settled 1851, incorporated 1885.
Population: 1,560 (2000); Race: 98.6% White, 0.0% Black, 0.2% Asian, 0.3% American Indian and Alaska Native, 0.4% Hispanic of any race, 0.6% two or more races (2000); Density: 32.3 persons per square mile (2000); Age: 26.1% under 18, 18.4% over 64 (2000); Marriage status: 20.4% never married, 64.0% now married, 9.9% widowed, 5.7% divorced (2000); Foreign born: 1.2% (2000); Ancestry (includes multiple ancestries): 46.8% Norwegian, 32.1% German, 10.0% English, 9.9% Irish, 2.9% Czech (2000).
Economy: In dairying and tobacco-growing area. Manufacturing: printing, light manufacturing. Employment by occupation: 18.2% management, 16.8% professional, 16.1% services, 20.7% sales, 5.0% farming, 7.2% construction, 16.1% production (2000).
Income: Per capita income: $16,246 (2000); Median household income: $42,583 (2000); Poverty rate: 9.7% (2000).
Taxes: Total city taxes per capita: $139 (1997); City property taxes per capita: $139 (1997).
Education: High school graduation rate: 81.2% (2000); College graduation rate: 16.2% (2000).
Housing: Homeownership rate: 87.1% (2000); Median home value: $102,100 (2000); Median rent: $300 per month (2000); Median age of housing: 35 years (2000).
Transportation: Commute to work: 84.0% car, 0.4% public transportation, 1.8% walk, 13.4% work from home (2000); Travel time to work: 56.5% less than 15 minutes, 21.6% 15 to 30 minutes, 7.8% 30 to 45 minutes, 8.3% 45 to 60 minutes, 5.8% 60 minutes or more (2000)

WEBSTER (town). Covers a land area of 35.412 square miles and a water area of 0.005 square miles. Located at 43.59° N. Lat.; 90.74° W. Long.
Population: 676 (2000); Race: 99.7% White, 0.0% Black, 0.0% Asian, 0.0% American Indian and Alaska Native, 0.3% Hispanic of any race, 0.0% two or

more races (2000); Density: 19.1 persons per square mile (2000); Age: 36.1% under 18, 8.9% over 64 (2000); Marriage status: 22.6% never married, 67.0% now married, 4.5% widowed, 5.9% divorced (2000); Foreign born: 0.3% (2000); Ancestry (includes multiple ancestries): 33.2% German, 28.3% Norwegian, 11.6% United States or American, 10.9% Irish, 6.6% English (2000).
Economy: Employment by occupation: 23.6% management, 12.5% professional, 14.2% services, 19.8% sales, 3.8% farming, 10.8% construction, 15.3% production (2000).
Income: Per capita income: $12,031 (2000); Median household income: $32,344 (2000); Poverty rate: 26.6% (2000).
Taxes: Total city taxes per capita: $205 (1997); City property taxes per capita: $205 (1997).
Education: High school graduation rate: 77.4% (2000); College graduation rate: 14.9% (2000).
Housing: Homeownership rate: 85.3% (2000); Median home value: $83,000 (2000); Median rent: $363 per month (2000); Median age of housing: 45 years (2000).
Transportation: Commute to work: 73.6% car, 0.0% public transportation, 5.2% walk, 20.1% work from home (2000); Travel time to work: 31.7% less than 15 minutes, 43.0% 15 to 30 minutes, 5.2% 30 to 45 minutes, 14.3% 45 to 60 minutes, 5.7% 60 minutes or more (2000)

WESTBY (city). Covers a land area of 2.429 square miles and a water area of 0 square miles. Located at 43.65° N. Lat.; 90.85° W. Long. Elevation is 1,298 feet.
History: Westby was named for Ole Westby, a Norwegian immigrant. Many of Westby's early residents came from western Norway. A number of cooperatives were established here.
Population: 2,045 (2000); Race: 98.7% White, 0.0% Black, 0.4% Asian, 0.3% American Indian and Alaska Native, 0.0% Hispanic of any race, 0.5% two or more races (2000); Density: 841.9 persons per square mile (2000); Age: 24.0% under 18, 22.5% over 64 (2000); Marriage status: 18.2% never married, 60.9% now married, 11.3% widowed, 9.6% divorced (2000); Foreign born: 0.8% (2000); Ancestry (includes multiple ancestries): 61.1% Norwegian, 25.3% German, 9.5% Irish, 8.6% English, 3.4% Italian (2000).
Economy: Single-family building permits issued: 3 (2001) / 10 (2000); Multi-family building permits issued: 20 (2001) / 2 (2000); Employment by occupation: 10.5% management, 20.0% professional, 17.8% services, 21.4% sales, 1.8% farming, 10.4% construction, 18.2% production (2000).
Income: Per capita income: $16,839 (2000); Median household income: $32,340 (2000); Poverty rate: 7.5% (2000).
Taxes: Total city taxes per capita: $209 (2000); City property taxes per capita: $185 (2000).
Education: High school graduation rate: 81.0% (2000); College graduation rate: 18.3% (2000).

School District(s)

Westby Area (PK-12)
2000 Enrollment: 1,182 608-634-7101
Housing: Homeownership rate: 77.3% (2000); Median home value: $70,900 (2000); Median rent: $284 per month (2000); Median age of housing: 40 years (2000).
Safety: Violent crime rate: 9.7 per 10,000 population; Property crime rate: 199.0 per 10,000 population (2001).
Newspapers: Westby Times (1 x week)
Transportation: Commute to work: 87.0% car, 0.2% public transportation, 7.5% walk, 3.3% work from home (2000); Travel time to work: 49.6% less than 15 minutes, 19.1% 15 to 30 minutes, 18.8% 30 to 45 minutes, 9.5% 45 to 60 minutes, 3.1% 60 minutes or more (2000)
Additional Information Contacts
Westby Chamber of Commerce 608-634-4011

WHEATLAND (town). Covers a land area of 26.516 square miles and a water area of 1.104 square miles. Located at 43.44° N. Lat.; 91.18° W. Long.
Population: 533 (2000); Race: 97.9% White, 0.0% Black, 0.4% Asian, 0.0% American Indian and Alaska Native, 1.0% Hispanic of any race, 1.7% two or more races (2000); Density: 20.1 persons per square mile (2000); Age: 17.8% under 18, 18.0% over 64 (2000); Marriage status: 16.2% never married, 69.1% now married, 6.9% widowed, 7.8% divorced (2000); Foreign born: 1.0% (2000); Ancestry (includes multiple ancestries): 32.4% German, 30.6% Norwegian, 11.4% Irish, 10.9% English, 6.8% Italian (2000).
Economy: Single-family building permits issued: 8 (2001) / 11 (2000); Multi-family building permits issued: 0 (2001) / 0 (2000); Employment by occupation: 15.3% management, 10.3% professional, 19.0% services, 15.7% sales, 0.8% farming, 14.9% construction, 24.0% production (2000).
Income: Per capita income: $19,247 (2000); Median household income: $35,500 (2000); Poverty rate: 7.9% (2000).
Taxes: Total city taxes per capita: $154 (1997); City property taxes per capita: $141 (1997).
Education: High school graduation rate: 75.7% (2000); College graduation rate: 11.2% (2000).
Housing: Homeownership rate: 91.6% (2000); Median home value: $80,500 (2000); Median rent: $356 per month (2000); Median age of housing: 27 years (2000).
Transportation: Commute to work: 89.2% car, 0.0% public transportation, 4.6% walk, 6.3% work from home (2000); Travel time to work: 22.2% less than 15 minutes, 27.1% 15 to 30 minutes, 26.2% 30 to 45 minutes, 14.7% 45 to 60 minutes, 9.8% 60 minutes or more (2000)

WHITESTOWN (town). Covers a land area of 35.008 square miles and a water area of 0.004 square miles. Located at 43.66° N. Lat.; 90.60° W. Long.
Population: 509 (2000); Race: 98.4% White, 0.0% Black, 0.0% Asian, 1.0% American Indian and Alaska Native, 0.6% Hispanic of any race, 0.0% two or more races (2000); Density: 14.5 persons per square mile (2000); Age: 34.5% under 18, 6.8% over 64 (2000); Marriage status: 27.2% never married, 63.3% now married, 3.4% widowed, 6.1% divorced (2000); Foreign born: 0.0% (2000); Ancestry (includes multiple ancestries): 38.5% German, 20.8% Norwegian, 10.6% Irish, 10.4% English, 2.4% Swedish (2000).
Economy: Employment by occupation: 16.0% management, 17.3% professional, 12.3% services, 21.8% sales, 9.1% farming, 7.0% construction, 16.5% production (2000).
Income: Per capita income: $13,289 (2000); Median household income: $33,472 (2000); Poverty rate: 11.2% (2000).
Taxes: Total city taxes per capita: $124 (1997); City property taxes per capita: $124 (1997).
Education: High school graduation rate: 77.0% (2000); College graduation rate: 17.7% (2000).
Housing: Homeownership rate: 84.0% (2000); Median home value: $68,800 (2000); Median rent: $313 per month (2000); Median age of housing: 34 years (2000).
Transportation: Commute to work: 72.0% car, 0.0% public transportation, 4.2% walk, 23.0% work from home (2000); Travel time to work: 35.3% less than 15 minutes, 32.6% 15 to 30 minutes, 20.1% 30 to 45 minutes, 8.2% 45 to 60 minutes, 3.8% 60 minutes or more (2000)

Vilas County

Located in northern Wisconsin; bounded on the north by Michigan; drained by the Wisconsin and Manitowish Rivers; includes Lac Vieux Desert, Trout Lake, and other lakes. Covers a land area of 873.70 square miles, a water area of 144.10 square miles, and is located in the Central Time Zone. The county government was organized in 1893. County seat is Eagle River.

Weather Station: Rest Lake — Elevation: 1,607 feet

	Jan	Feb	Mar	Apr	May	Jun	Jul	Aug	Sep	Oct	Nov	Dec
High	20	26	37	52	67	74	77	75	66	54	36	24
Low	-1	4	14	28	41	51	55	53	45	34	22	7
Precip	1.2	0.8	1.6	2.2	3.7	3.9	4.3	4.4	4.0	3.0	2.1	1.3
Snow	20.5	11.8	12.3	5.2	0.4	0.0	0.0	0.0	tr	1.3	11.4	18.1

High and Low temperatures in degrees Fahrenheit; Precipitation and Snow in inches

Weather Station: Saint Germain 2 E — Elevation: 1,643 feet

	Jan	Feb	Mar	Apr	May	Jun	Jul	Aug	Sep	Oct	Nov	Dec
High	20	25	36	50	65	72	75	73	64	52	37	24
Low	-0	4	15	28	41	51	56	54	46	34	22	8
Precip	1.3	0.8	1.7	2.3	3.5	3.6	3.8	4.5	4.1	2.7	2.1	1.3
Snow	16.9	8.6	10.9	3.6	0.4	0.0	0.0	0.0	tr	0.7	8.0	14.1

High and Low temperatures in degrees Fahrenheit; Precipitation and Snow in inches

Population: 21,033 (2000); Race: 90.0% White, 0.1% Black, 0.8% Asian, 7.8% American Indian and Alaska Native, 1.3% Hispanic of any race, 1.0% two or more races (2000); Density: 24.1 persons per square mile (2000); Age: 20.7% under 18, 23.0% over 64 (2000).
Religion: Five largest groups: 31.2% Catholic Church, 5.3% United Church of Christ, 4.6% Lutheran Church—Missouri Synod, 3.7% Evangelical Lutheran Church in America, 3.4% Wisconsin Evangelical Lutheran Synod (2000).
Economy: Unemployment rate: 5.0% (11/2002); Total civilian labor force: 11,526 (11/2002); Leading industries: 30.4% accommodation & food services; 16.4% retail trade; 11.5% construction (2000); Companies that

employ more than 1,000 persons: 0 (2000); Companies that employ more than 100 persons: 1 (2000); Farms: 44 totaling 7,578 acres (1997); Minority business ownership rate: 0.0% (1997); Women business ownership rate: 18.1% (1997); Retail sales per capita: $5,827 (1997). Single-family building permits issued: 310 (2001) / 309 (2000); Multi-family building permits issued: 5 (2001) / 51 (2000).
Income: Per capita income: $18,361 (2000); Median household income: $33,759 (2000); Poverty rate: 8.0% (2000); Bankruptcy rate: 1.59% (2001).
Taxes: Total county taxes per capita: $370 (2000); County property taxes per capita: $284 (2000).
Education: High school graduation rate: 85.4% (2000); College graduation rate: 17.6% (2000).
Housing: Homeownership rate: 82.0% (2000); Median home value: $120,200 (2000); Median rent: $370 per month (2000); Median age of housing: 26 years (2000).
Health: Birth rate: 83.2 per 10,000 population (1998); Age adjusted death rate: 80.7 per 10,000 population (1999); Age adjusted cancer mortality rate: 193.3 deaths per 100,000 population (1999). Air Quality Index: 89% good, 11% moderate, 0% unhealthy (percent of days in 2000). Number of physicians: 7.1 per 10,000 population (1999); Number of hospital beds: 2.9 per 10,000 population (1999).
Elections: 2000 Presidential election results: 38.2% Gore, 56.5% Bush, 4.5% Nader, 0.3% Buchanan
National and State Parks: Northern Highland-American Legion State Forest; Powell Marsh State Public Hunting Grounds
Additional Information Contacts
Vilas County Government Offices 715-479-3600
Boulder Junction Chamber of Commerce 715-385-2400
Conover Chamber of Commerce 715-479-4928
Eagle River Chamber of Commerce 715-479-6400
Lac Du Flambeau Chamber of Commerce 715-588-3346
Land O Lakes Chamber of Commerce 715-547-3432
Manitowish Waters Chamber 715-543-8488
Phelps Chamber of Commerce 715-545-3800
Presque Isle Chamber of Commerce 715-686-2910
Sayner Chamber of Commerce 715-542-3789
St. Germain Chamber of Commerce 715-477-2205

Vilas County Communities

ARBOR VITAE (town). Covers a land area of 62.570 square miles and a water area of 8.687 square miles. Located at 45.93° N. Lat.; 89.69° W. Long. Elevation is 1,630 feet.
History: Arbor Vitae was founded in 1893 by the John D. Ross Lumber Company. Its name is the Latin word for "cedar."
Population: 3,153 (2000); Race: 97.2% White, 0.0% Black, 2.0% Asian, 0.0% American Indian and Alaska Native, 1.4% Hispanic of any race, 0.8% two or more races (2000); Density: 50.4 persons per square mile (2000); Age: 20.7% under 18, 22.0% over 64 (2000); Marriage status: 16.6% never married, 64.9% now married, 6.4% widowed, 12.1% divorced (2000); Foreign born: 4.1% (2000); Ancestry (includes multiple ancestries): 47.7% German, 11.9% Polish, 9.9% Irish, 7.0% English, 6.7% Swedish (2000).
Economy: Employment by occupation: 9.9% management, 15.2% professional, 23.8% services, 29.4% sales, 0.3% farming, 12.4% construction, 9.1% production (2000).
Income: Per capita income: $17,778 (2000); Median household income: $36,472 (2000); Poverty rate: 3.1% (2000).
Taxes: Total city taxes per capita: $166 (1997); City property taxes per capita: $149 (1997).
Education: High school graduation rate: 83.7% (2000); College graduation rate: 16.8% (2000).

School District(s)

Woodruff J1 (PK-08)
2000 Enrollment: 614 715-356-3282
Housing: Homeownership rate: 87.7% (2000); Median home value: $116,100 (2000); Median rent: $384 per month (2000); Median age of housing: 23 years (2000).
Transportation: Commute to work: 93.6% car, 0.0% public transportation, 3.8% walk, 1.5% work from home (2000); Travel time to work: 57.9% less than 15 minutes, 27.4% 15 to 30 minutes, 10.1% 30 to 45 minutes, 2.9% 45 to 60 minutes, 1.7% 60 minutes or more (2000)

BOULDER JUNCTION (town). Covers a land area of 81.921 square miles and a water area of 18.468 square miles. Located at 46.08° N. Lat.; 89.68° W. Long. Elevation is 1,652 feet.
Population: 958 (2000); Race: 97.7% White, 0.0% Black, 0.0% Asian, 0.6% American Indian and Alaska Native, 0.8% Hispanic of any race, 0.7% two or more races (2000); Density: 11.7 persons per square mile (2000); Age: 18.1% under 18, 23.3% over 64 (2000); Marriage status: 16.7% never married, 66.4% now married, 9.6% widowed, 7.4% divorced (2000); Foreign born: 3.3% (2000); Ancestry (includes multiple ancestries): 49.9% German, 14.6% Irish, 12.2% English, 11.5% Polish, 8.6% Swedish (2000).
Economy: Employment by occupation: 10.7% management, 14.7% professional, 20.1% services, 28.3% sales, 0.7% farming, 17.2% construction, 8.3% production (2000).
Income: Per capita income: $19,678 (2000); Median household income: $34,722 (2000); Poverty rate: 3.9% (2000).
Taxes: Total city taxes per capita: $372 (1997); City property taxes per capita: $297 (1997).
Education: High school graduation rate: 90.5% (2000); College graduation rate: 24.4% (2000).
Housing: Homeownership rate: 80.4% (2000); Median home value: $118,900 (2000); Median rent: $356 per month (2000); Median age of housing: 29 years (2000).
Transportation: Commute to work: 90.8% car, 0.0% public transportation, 5.4% walk, 3.3% work from home (2000); Travel time to work: 28.7% less than 15 minutes, 51.1% 15 to 30 minutes, 11.9% 30 to 45 minutes, 1.9% 45 to 60 minutes, 6.3% 60 minutes or more (2000)
Additional Information Contacts
Boulder Junction Chamber of Commerce 715-385-2400

CLOVERLAND (town). Covers a land area of 31.385 square miles and a water area of 3.805 square miles. Located at 45.94° N. Lat.; 89.37° W. Long.
Population: 919 (2000); Race: 99.1% White, 0.0% Black, 0.0% Asian, 0.0% American Indian and Alaska Native, 0.9% Hispanic of any race, 0.9% two or more races (2000); Density: 29.3 persons per square mile (2000); Age: 18.3% under 18, 20.9% over 64 (2000); Marriage status: 13.6% never married, 70.4% now married, 6.7% widowed, 9.2% divorced (2000); Foreign born: 1.1% (2000); Ancestry (includes multiple ancestries): 53.3% German, 22.3% Polish, 10.3% English, 9.1% Irish, 5.9% Swedish (2000).
Economy: Employment by occupation: 9.5% management, 16.8% professional, 19.9% services, 29.4% sales, 0.9% farming, 15.2% construction, 8.3% production (2000).
Income: Per capita income: $19,912 (2000); Median household income: $33,897 (2000); Poverty rate: 7.1% (2000).
Taxes: Total city taxes per capita: $133 (1997); City property taxes per capita: $132 (1997).
Education: High school graduation rate: 88.0% (2000); College graduation rate: 18.8% (2000).
Housing: Homeownership rate: 90.4% (2000); Median home value: $141,900 (2000); Median rent: $431 per month (2000); Median age of housing: 27 years (2000).
Transportation: Commute to work: 91.3% car, 0.0% public transportation, 1.0% walk, 7.2% work from home (2000); Travel time to work: 37.0% less than 15 minutes, 35.7% 15 to 30 minutes, 18.5% 30 to 45 minutes, 4.8% 45 to 60 minutes, 4.0% 60 minutes or more (2000)

CONOVER (town). Covers a land area of 79.968 square miles and a water area of 7.210 square miles. Located at 46.04° N. Lat.; 89.28° W. Long. Elevation is 1,659 feet.
Population: 1,137 (2000); Race: 99.2% White, 0.0% Black, 0.2% Asian, 0.2% American Indian and Alaska Native, 1.9% Hispanic of any race, 0.4% two or more races (2000); Density: 14.2 persons per square mile (2000); Age: 22.1% under 18, 20.1% over 64 (2000); Marriage status: 17.0% never married, 64.2% now married, 9.7% widowed, 9.0% divorced (2000); Foreign born: 1.4% (2000); Ancestry (includes multiple ancestries): 47.3% German, 9.7% Swedish, 9.6% Polish, 8.7% Irish, 6.9% French (except Basque) (2000).
Economy: In wooded lake region; trade center for resort area. Gateway Ski Area to North. Employment by occupation: 11.0% management, 9.5% professional, 20.0% services, 29.5% sales, 3.6% farming, 16.7% construction, 9.7% production (2000).
Income: Per capita income: $18,692 (2000); Median household income: $31,683 (2000); Poverty rate: 8.5% (2000).
Taxes: Total city taxes per capita: $230 (1997); City property taxes per capita: $226 (1997).
Education: High school graduation rate: 82.0% (2000); College graduation rate: 15.4% (2000).
Housing: Homeownership rate: 92.8% (2000); Median home value: $103,500 (2000); Median rent: $325 per month (2000); Median age of housing: 24 years (2000).

Transportation: Commute to work: 91.6% car, 0.0% public transportation, 3.0% walk, 4.8% work from home (2000); Travel time to work: 35.4% less than 15 minutes, 46.8% 15 to 30 minutes, 9.7% 30 to 45 minutes, 5.3% 45 to 60 minutes, 2.7% 60 minutes or more (2000)

Additional Information Contacts

Conover Chamber of Commerce 715-479-4928

EAGLE RIVER (city). Covers a land area of 2.548 square miles and a water area of 0.180 square miles. Located at 45.92° N. Lat.; 89.25° W. Long. Elevation is 1,647 feet.

History: Eagle River was named for the bald eagles that were once plentiful in the woods here. Begun as a lumber camp, Eagle River later developed winter sports facilities and became the center of a recreation area, with its chain of lakes along the river offering a variety of sport fishing opportunities.

Population: 1,443 (2000); Race: 97.7% White, 0.0% Black, 0.0% Asian, 1.4% American Indian and Alaska Native, 0.9% Hispanic of any race, 0.8% two or more races (2000); Density: 566.3 persons per square mile (2000); Age: 20.5% under 18, 32.5% over 64 (2000); Marriage status: 22.8% never married, 39.2% now married, 22.1% widowed, 16.0% divorced (2000); Foreign born: 2.3% (2000); Ancestry (includes multiple ancestries): 43.3% German, 13.3% Irish, 11.7% Polish, 10.4% English, 6.7% French (except Basque) (2000).

Economy: Single-family building permits issued: 8 (2001) / 7 (2000); Multi-family building permits issued: 0 (2001) / 8 (2000); Employment by occupation: 8.4% management, 15.2% professional, 20.4% services, 26.8% sales, 2.2% farming, 11.8% construction, 15.2% production (2000).

Income: Per capita income: $15,876 (2000); Median household income: $23,611 (2000); Poverty rate: 11.8% (2000).

Taxes: Total city taxes per capita: $780 (1997); City property taxes per capita: $733 (1997).

Education: High school graduation rate: 82.4% (2000); College graduation rate: 12.2% (2000).

School District(s)

Northland Pines (PK-12)
2000 Enrollment: 1,605 715-479-6487

Housing: Homeownership rate: 54.7% (2000); Median home value: $77,700 (2000); Median rent: $386 per month (2000); Median age of housing: 41 years (2000).

Hospitals: Eagle River Memorial Hospital (29 beds)

Newspapers: Vilas County News-Review & Three Lakes News (1 x week)

Transportation: Commute to work: 81.2% car, 0.0% public transportation, 8.9% walk, 8.7% work from home (2000); Travel time to work: 68.2% less than 15 minutes, 12.1% 15 to 30 minutes, 11.0% 30 to 45 minutes, 2.6% 45 to 60 minutes, 6.1% 60 minutes or more (2000)

Airports: Eagle River Union

Additional Information Contacts

Eagle River Chamber of Commerce 715-479-6400

LAC DU FLAMBEAU (town). Covers a land area of 100.303 square miles and a water area of 27.404 square miles. Located at 45.95° N. Lat.; 89.87° W. Long. Elevation is 1,600 feet.

Population: 3,004 (2000); Race: 40.7% White, 0.1% Black, 3.0% Asian, 52.0% American Indian and Alaska Native, 2.7% Hispanic of any race, 3.3% two or more races (2000); Density: 29.9 persons per square mile (2000); Age: 29.7% under 18, 17.5% over 64 (2000); Marriage status: 26.7% never married, 54.0% now married, 7.5% widowed, 11.8% divorced (2000); Foreign born: 3.5% (2000); Ancestry (includes multiple ancestries): 55.8% Other groups, 18.1% German, 6.0% Irish, 4.6% English, 3.2% Polish (2000).

Economy: Manufacturing: electrical measuring instruments. Art center of the Lac du Flambeau Indian Reservation. Fish hatchery nearby. Employment by occupation: 12.3% management, 15.6% professional, 25.1% services, 22.6% sales, 1.2% farming, 11.1% construction, 12.2% production (2000).

Income: Per capita income: $15,176 (2000); Median household income: $30,349 (2000); Poverty rate: 15.7% (2000).

Taxes: Total city taxes per capita: $188 (1997); City property taxes per capita: $180 (1997).

Education: High school graduation rate: 81.2% (2000); College graduation rate: 15.0% (2000).

School District(s)

Lac Du Flambeau #1 (PK-08)
2000 Enrollment: 512 715-588-3838

Housing: Homeownership rate: 70.9% (2000); Median home value: $136,300 (2000); Median rent: $212 per month (2000); Median age of housing: 27 years (2000).

Safety: Violent crime rate: 43.0 per 10,000 population; Property crime rate: 300.8 per 10,000 population (2001).

Transportation: Commute to work: 89.7% car, 0.0% public transportation, 5.3% walk, 3.7% work from home (2000); Travel time to work: 63.2% less than 15 minutes, 22.8% 15 to 30 minutes, 5.9% 30 to 45 minutes, 3.3% 45 to 60 minutes, 4.7% 60 minutes or more (2000)

Additional Information Contacts

Lac Du Flambeau Chamber of Commerce. 715-588-3346

LAND O' LAKES (town). Covers a land area of 83.082 square miles and a water area of 12.225 square miles. Located at 46.15° N. Lat.; 89.38° W. Long. Elevation is 1,709 feet.

Population: 882 (2000); Race: 98.2% White, 0.0% Black, 0.2% Asian, 1.3% American Indian and Alaska Native, 0.2% Hispanic of any race, 0.2% two or more races (2000); Density: 10.6 persons per square mile (2000); Age: 18.4% under 18, 24.7% over 64 (2000); Marriage status: 15.9% never married, 63.0% now married, 8.0% widowed, 13.0% divorced (2000); Foreign born: 2.5% (2000); Ancestry (includes multiple ancestries): 45.6% German, 13.0% English, 11.7% Irish, 10.8% United States or American, 8.4% Polish (2000).

Economy: Employment by occupation: 12.8% management, 12.8% professional, 21.2% services, 29.4% sales, 0.5% farming, 15.9% construction, 7.4% production (2000).

Income: Per capita income: $18,765 (2000); Median household income: $29,792 (2000); Poverty rate: 7.5% (2000).

Taxes: Total city taxes per capita: $475 (2000); City property taxes per capita: $457 (2000).

Education: High school graduation rate: 88.4% (2000); College graduation rate: 20.9% (2000).

Housing: Homeownership rate: 77.7% (2000); Median home value: $127,800 (2000); Median rent: $328 per month (2000); Median age of housing: 27 years (2000).

Transportation: Commute to work: 80.4% car, 0.8% public transportation, 9.9% walk, 8.0% work from home (2000); Travel time to work: 58.6% less than 15 minutes, 19.5% 15 to 30 minutes, 13.5% 30 to 45 minutes, 5.4% 45 to 60 minutes, 3.0% 60 minutes or more (2000)

Additional Information Contacts

Land O Lakes Chamber of Commerce. 715-547-3432

LINCOLN (town). Covers a land area of 32.556 square miles and a water area of 4.600 square miles. Located at 45.91° N. Lat.; 89.23° W. Long.

Population: 2,579 (2000); Race: 99.0% White, 0.0% Black, 0.3% Asian, 0.2% American Indian and Alaska Native, 0.2% Hispanic of any race, 0.4% two or more races (2000); Density: 79.2 persons per square mile (2000); Age: 18.9% under 18, 18.5% over 64 (2000); Marriage status: 18.4% never married, 64.2% now married, 7.1% widowed, 10.2% divorced (2000); Foreign born: 1.8% (2000); Ancestry (includes multiple ancestries): 41.3% German, 13.4% Polish, 12.8% Irish, 10.1% English, 5.7% French (except Basque) (2000).

Economy: Employment by occupation: 10.4% management, 16.6% professional, 15.9% services, 26.0% sales, 1.5% farming, 16.5% construction, 13.0% production (2000).

Income: Per capita income: $18,579 (2000); Median household income: $39,196 (2000); Poverty rate: 5.6% (2000).

Taxes: Total city taxes per capita: $177 (1997); City property taxes per capita: $171 (1997).

Education: High school graduation rate: 86.9% (2000); College graduation rate: 18.7% (2000).

Housing: Homeownership rate: 84.8% (2000); Median home value: $110,400 (2000); Median rent: $503 per month (2000); Median age of housing: 29 years (2000).

Transportation: Commute to work: 92.0% car, 0.0% public transportation, 3.0% walk, 4.2% work from home (2000); Travel time to work: 64.9% less than 15 minutes, 17.3% 15 to 30 minutes, 11.8% 30 to 45 minutes, 1.0% 45 to 60 minutes, 5.0% 60 minutes or more (2000)

MANITOWISH WATERS (town). Covers a land area of 30.353 square miles and a water area of 6.079 square miles. Located at 46.11° N. Lat.; 89.85° W. Long. Elevation is 1,620 feet.

Population: 646 (2000); Race: 100.0% White, 0.0% Black, 0.0% Asian, 0.0% American Indian and Alaska Native, 0.0% Hispanic of any race, 0.0% two or more races (2000); Density: 21.3 persons per square mile (2000); Age: 15.1% under 18, 29.3% over 64 (2000); Marriage status: 13.6% never married, 70.6% now married, 7.8% widowed, 8.0% divorced (2000); Foreign born: 1.8% (2000); Ancestry (includes multiple ancestries): 40.7% German, 10.2% Polish, 9.5% Irish, 8.3% English, 6.2% French (except Basque) (2000).

Economy: Employment by occupation: 19.9% management, 10.6% professional, 12.1% services, 31.2% sales, 5.7% farming, 14.2% construction, 6.4% production (2000).
Income: Per capita income: $21,042 (2000); Median household income: $37,500 (2000); Poverty rate: 10.5% (2000).
Taxes: Total city taxes per capita: $493 (1997); City property taxes per capita: $473 (1997).
Education: High school graduation rate: 89.3% (2000); College graduation rate: 23.8% (2000).

School District(s)

Boulder Junction J1 (KG-08)
2000 Enrollment: 245 715-543-8417
Housing: Homeownership rate: 86.5% (2000); Median home value: $239,800 (2000); Median rent: $508 per month (2000); Median age of housing: 29 years (2000).
Transportation: Commute to work: 92.3% car, 0.0% public transportation, 1.5% walk, 6.1% work from home (2000); Travel time to work: 54.3% less than 15 minutes, 26.9% 15 to 30 minutes, 11.4% 30 to 45 minutes, 5.7% 45 to 60 minutes, 1.6% 60 minutes or more (2000)
Additional Information Contacts
Manitowish Waters Chamber........................ 715-543-8488

PHELPS (town). Covers a land area of 94.860 square miles and a water area of 13.958 square miles. Located at 46.06° N. Lat.; 89.09° W. Long. Elevation is 1,770 feet.
History: Phelps was founded in 1900 when lumbermen chose this as a site for a sawmill, laid ten miles of railroad track from Conover, and set up the Hackley Phelps Bonnell Company plant. A company town from its beginning, most of the village was later owned by the C.M. Christiansen Company.
Population: 1,350 (2000); Race: 97.6% White, 0.0% Black, 0.0% Asian, 1.8% American Indian and Alaska Native, 1.8% Hispanic of any race, 0.5% two or more races (2000); Density: 14.2 persons per square mile (2000); Age: 17.7% under 18, 27.9% over 64 (2000); Marriage status: 16.6% never married, 66.0% now married, 8.8% widowed, 8.6% divorced (2000); Foreign born: 1.2% (2000); Ancestry (includes multiple ancestries): 42.2% German, 11.3% Irish, 11.3% Polish, 9.9% English, 9.8% Swedish (2000).
Economy: Employment by occupation: 7.8% management, 15.9% professional, 22.4% services, 22.6% sales, 3.1% farming, 19.5% construction, 8.6% production (2000).
Income: Per capita income: $17,337 (2000); Median household income: $31,574 (2000); Poverty rate: 9.2% (2000).
Taxes: Total city taxes per capita: $272 (1997); City property taxes per capita: $269 (1997).
Education: High school graduation rate: 82.4% (2000); College graduation rate: 13.9% (2000).

School District(s)

Phelps (KG-12)
2000 Enrollment: 195 715-545-2724
Housing: Homeownership rate: 86.0% (2000); Median home value: $102,100 (2000); Median rent: $288 per month (2000); Median age of housing: 32 years (2000).
Transportation: Commute to work: 86.0% car, 0.4% public transportation, 8.6% walk, 4.7% work from home (2000); Travel time to work: 40.5% less than 15 minutes, 31.9% 15 to 30 minutes, 19.8% 30 to 45 minutes, 4.1% 45 to 60 minutes, 3.7% 60 minutes or more (2000)
Additional Information Contacts
Phelps Chamber of Commerce........................ 715-545-3800

PLUM LAKE (town). Covers a land area of 88.930 square miles and a water area of 11.130 square miles. Located at 46.03° N. Lat.; 89.52° W. Long.
Population: 486 (2000); Race: 98.6% White, 0.0% Black, 0.0% Asian, 0.0% American Indian and Alaska Native, 0.4% Hispanic of any race, 1.4% two or more races (2000); Density: 5.5 persons per square mile (2000); Age: 20.3% under 18, 22.2% over 64 (2000); Marriage status: 17.0% never married, 67.0% now married, 9.9% widowed, 6.2% divorced (2000); Foreign born: 1.9% (2000); Ancestry (includes multiple ancestries): 45.8% German, 12.6% Irish, 12.4% English, 10.1% Swedish, 8.7% Norwegian (2000).
Economy: Employment by occupation: 13.3% management, 13.3% professional, 21.6% services, 30.6% sales, 2.0% farming, 9.0% construction, 10.2% production (2000).
Income: Per capita income: $17,824 (2000); Median household income: $33,529 (2000); Poverty rate: 7.7% (2000).
Taxes: Total city taxes per capita: $319 (1997); City property taxes per capita: $315 (1997).
Education: High school graduation rate: 93.0% (2000); College graduation rate: 20.3% (2000).
Housing: Homeownership rate: 83.4% (2000); Median home value: $98,100 (2000); Median rent: $468 per month (2000); Median age of housing: 19 years (2000).
Transportation: Commute to work: 82.2% car, 0.0% public transportation, 13.4% walk, 3.2% work from home (2000); Travel time to work: 36.0% less than 15 minutes, 37.2% 15 to 30 minutes, 19.7% 30 to 45 minutes, 5.9% 45 to 60 minutes, 1.3% 60 minutes or more (2000)

PRESQUE ISLE (town). Covers a land area of 61.710 square miles and a water area of 12.731 square miles. Located at 46.21° N. Lat.; 89.70° W. Long. Elevation is 1,675 feet.
Population: 513 (2000); Race: 99.2% White, 0.0% Black, 0.0% Asian, 0.0% American Indian and Alaska Native, 0.8% Hispanic of any race, 0.0% two or more races (2000); Density: 8.3 persons per square mile (2000); Age: 14.3% under 18, 32.2% over 64 (2000); Marriage status: 9.0% never married, 73.3% now married, 7.3% widowed, 10.4% divorced (2000); Foreign born: 1.7% (2000); Ancestry (includes multiple ancestries): 42.0% German, 17.3% Irish, 12.1% English, 10.8% United States or American, 7.5% French (except Basque) (2000).
Economy: Employment by occupation: 8.2% management, 12.0% professional, 19.7% services, 30.3% sales, 0.0% farming, 18.8% construction, 11.1% production (2000).
Income: Per capita income: $25,798 (2000); Median household income: $41,250 (2000); Poverty rate: 9.4% (2000).
Taxes: Total city taxes per capita: $709 (1997); City property taxes per capita: $702 (1997).
Education: High school graduation rate: 93.4% (2000); College graduation rate: 28.4% (2000).
Housing: Homeownership rate: 87.9% (2000); Median home value: $196,200 (2000); Median rent: $625 per month (2000); Median age of housing: 24 years (2000).
Transportation: Commute to work: 78.4% car, 0.0% public transportation, 10.1% walk, 10.1% work from home (2000); Travel time to work: 46.5% less than 15 minutes, 27.3% 15 to 30 minutes, 10.7% 30 to 45 minutes, 8.0% 45 to 60 minutes, 7.5% 60 minutes or more (2000)
Additional Information Contacts
Presque Isle Chamber of Commerce 715-686-2910

SAINT GERMAIN (town). Covers a land area of 33.995 square miles and a water area of 6.036 square miles. Located at 45.92° N. Lat.; 89.48° W. Long. Elevation is 1,630 feet.
Population: 1,932 (2000); Race: 97.1% White, 0.7% Black, 0.0% Asian, 0.5% American Indian and Alaska Native, 1.7% Hispanic of any race, 1.1% two or more races (2000); Density: 56.8 persons per square mile (2000); Age: 17.9% under 18, 27.1% over 64 (2000); Marriage status: 12.8% never married, 71.8% now married, 9.3% widowed, 6.1% divorced (2000); Foreign born: 2.1% (2000); Ancestry (includes multiple ancestries): 48.4% German, 13.7% Irish, 10.8% Polish, 9.7% English, 6.4% Swedish (2000).
Economy: Employment by occupation: 8.8% management, 14.3% professional, 22.3% services, 35.3% sales, 0.0% farming, 10.9% construction, 8.5% production (2000).
Income: Per capita income: $21,755 (2000); Median household income: $32,969 (2000); Poverty rate: 8.0% (2000).
Education: High school graduation rate: 86.6% (2000); College graduation rate: 15.5% (2000).
Housing: Homeownership rate: 81.9% (2000); Median home value: $123,500 (2000); Median rent: $395 per month (2000); Median age of housing: 15 years (2000).
Transportation: Commute to work: 89.8% car, 0.0% public transportation, 4.0% walk, 4.1% work from home (2000); Travel time to work: 41.1% less than 15 minutes, 43.6% 15 to 30 minutes, 10.0% 30 to 45 minutes, 2.5% 45 to 60 minutes, 2.9% 60 minutes or more (2000)
Additional Information Contacts
St. Germain Chamber of Commerce 715-477-2205

SAYNER (unincorporated postal area, zip code 54560). Covers a land area of 15.596 square miles and a water area of 2.486 square miles. Located at 45.99° N. Lat.; 89.52° W. Long. Elevation is 1,670 feet.
Population: 595 (2000); Race: 96.2% White, 0.0% Black, 0.0% Asian, 0.0% American Indian and Alaska Native, 2.7% Hispanic of any race, 3.3% two or more races (2000); Density: 38.2 persons per square mile (2000); Age: 22.4% under 18, 18.8% over 64 (2000); Marriage status: 17.9% never married, 65.6% now married, 8.6% widowed, 8.0% divorced (2000); Foreign born:

2.1% (2000); Ancestry (includes multiple ancestries): 45.5% German, 11.4% Irish, 9.3% English, 9.3% Swedish, 7.4% Norwegian (2000).
Economy: Employment by occupation: 11.6% management, 11.6% professional, 18.2% services, 35.1% sales, 1.6% farming, 12.2% construction, 9.7% production (2000).
Income: Per capita income: $19,528 (2000); Median household income: $34,464 (2000); Poverty rate: 6.3% (2000).
Education: High school graduation rate: 93.1% (2000); College graduation rate: 22.1% (2000).
Housing: Homeownership rate: 79.6% (2000); Median home value: $94,600 (2000); Median rent: $458 per month (2000); Median age of housing: 18 years (2000).
Transportation: Commute to work: 87.0% car, 0.0% public transportation, 9.8% walk, 1.3% work from home (2000); Travel time to work: 40.9% less than 15 minutes, 41.9% 15 to 30 minutes, 9.6% 30 to 45 minutes, 5.6% 45 to 60 minutes, 2.0% 60 minutes or more (2000)
Additional Information Contacts
Sayner Chamber of Commerce 715-542-3789

WASHINGTON (town). Covers a land area of 41.404 square miles and a water area of 6.146 square miles. Located at 45.93° N. Lat.; 89.15° W. Long.
Population: 1,577 (2000); Race: 99.1% White, 0.2% Black, 0.1% Asian, 0.0% American Indian and Alaska Native, 1.4% Hispanic of any race, 0.3% two or more races (2000); Density: 38.1 persons per square mile (2000); Age: 22.3% under 18, 19.0% over 64 (2000); Marriage status: 15.8% never married, 66.1% now married, 7.7% widowed, 10.3% divorced (2000); Foreign born: 1.5% (2000); Ancestry (includes multiple ancestries): 46.6% German, 13.0% Polish, 12.5% Irish, 8.3% English, 7.9% United States or American (2000).
Economy: Employment by occupation: 9.3% management, 13.1% professional, 16.2% services, 31.0% sales, 1.3% farming, 18.1% construction, 11.0% production (2000).
Income: Per capita income: $18,544 (2000); Median household income: $34,961 (2000); Poverty rate: 5.7% (2000).
Taxes: Total city taxes per capita: $324 (1997); City property taxes per capita: $274 (1997).
Education: High school graduation rate: 86.5% (2000); College graduation rate: 17.4% (2000).
Housing: Homeownership rate: 89.0% (2000); Median home value: $125,800 (2000); Median rent: $386 per month (2000); Median age of housing: 28 years (2000).
Transportation: Commute to work: 91.4% car, 0.0% public transportation, 3.5% walk, 5.2% work from home (2000); Travel time to work: 47.9% less than 15 minutes, 29.7% 15 to 30 minutes, 14.8% 30 to 45 minutes, 4.0% 45 to 60 minutes, 3.6% 60 minutes or more (2000)

WINCHESTER (town). Covers a land area of 48.131 square miles and a water area of 5.469 square miles. Located at 46.23° N. Lat.; 89.88° W. Long. Elevation is 1,675 feet.
Population: 454 (2000); Race: 98.8% White, 0.0% Black, 0.8% Asian, 0.0% American Indian and Alaska Native, 0.4% Hispanic of any race, 0.0% two or more races (2000); Density: 9.4 persons per square mile (2000); Age: 12.0% under 18, 34.4% over 64 (2000); Marriage status: 16.6% never married, 65.5% now married, 12.2% widowed, 5.7% divorced (2000); Foreign born: 1.4% (2000); Ancestry (includes multiple ancestries): 47.4% German, 13.5% Irish, 7.7% English, 6.4% Polish, 5.4% Swedish (2000).
Economy: Employment by occupation: 18.1% management, 12.6% professional, 15.6% services, 26.1% sales, 2.0% farming, 14.1% construction, 11.6% production (2000).
Income: Per capita income: $19,720 (2000); Median household income: $32,361 (2000); Poverty rate: 4.1% (2000).
Taxes: Total city taxes per capita: $476 (1997); City property taxes per capita: $471 (1997).
Education: High school graduation rate: 85.7% (2000); College graduation rate: 22.4% (2000).
Housing: Homeownership rate: 89.6% (2000); Median home value: $167,000 (2000); Median rent: $342 per month (2000); Median age of housing: 25 years (2000).
Transportation: Commute to work: 91.8% car, 0.0% public transportation, 0.0% walk, 2.1% work from home (2000); Travel time to work: 23.2% less than 15 minutes, 40.0% 15 to 30 minutes, 23.7% 30 to 45 minutes, 11.6% 45 to 60 minutes, 1.6% 60 minutes or more (2000)

Walworth County

Located in southeastern Wisconsin; bounded on the south by Illinois; includes Lake Geneva. Covers a land area of 555.30 square miles, a water area of 21.20 square miles, and is located in the Central Time Zone. The county government was organized in 1836. County seat is Elkhorn.

Weather Station: Lake Geneva — Elevation: 879 feet

	Jan	Feb	Mar	Apr	May	Jun	Jul	Aug	Sep	Oct	Nov	Dec
High	28	33	44	58	71	81	85	82	75	62	46	33
Low	12	17	26	37	48	57	63	61	53	42	30	19
Precip	2.0	1.6	2.7	3.8	3.4	4.0	3.8	4.0	3.7	2.7	2.8	2.3
Snow	14.2	9.2	7.3	2.5	tr	0.0	0.0	0.0	0.0	0.1	3.5	11.2

High and Low temperatures in degrees Fahrenheit; Precipitation and Snow in inches

Population: 93,759 (2000); Race: 94.6% White, 0.7% Black, 0.6% Asian, 0.5% American Indian and Alaska Native, 6.4% Hispanic of any race, 0.8% two or more races (2000); Density: 168.8 persons per square mile (2000); Age: 24.1% under 18, 12.8% over 64 (2000).
Religion: Five largest groups: 28.1% Catholic Church, 5.4% Evangelical Lutheran Church in America, 2.9% The United Methodist Church, 2.6% United Church of Christ, 2.5% Lutheran Church—Missouri Synod (2000).
Economy: Unemployment rate: 3.8% (11/2002); Total civilian labor force: 54,081 (11/2002); Leading industries: 30.4% manufacturing; 16.0% accommodation & food services; 11.8% retail trade (2000); Companies that employ more than 1,000 persons: 0 (2000); Companies that employ more than 100 persons: 63 (2000); Farms: 853 totaling 220,089 acres (1997); Minority business ownership rate: 0.0% (1997); Women business ownership rate: 30.3% (1997); Retail sales per capita: $7,439 (1997). Single-family building permits issued: 634 (2001) / 680 (2000); Multi-family building permits issued: 155 (2001) / 291 (2000).
Income: Per capita income: $21,229 (2000); Median household income: $46,274 (2000); Poverty rate: 8.4% (2000); Bankruptcy rate: 4.01% (2001).
Taxes: Total county taxes per capita: $369 (2000); County property taxes per capita: $304 (2000).
Education: High school graduation rate: 84.2% (2000); College graduation rate: 21.8% (2000).
Housing: Homeownership rate: 69.1% (2000); Median home value: $128,400 (2000); Median rent: $515 per month (2000); Median age of housing: 31 years (2000).
Health: Birth rate: 113.4 per 10,000 population (1998); Age adjusted death rate: 88.8 per 10,000 population (1999); Age adjusted cancer mortality rate: 204.1 deaths per 100,000 population (1999). Air Quality Index: 63% good, 38% moderate, 0% unhealthy (percent of days in 2000). Number of physicians: 8.6 per 10,000 population (1999); Number of hospital beds: 8.3 per 10,000 population (1999).
Elections: 2000 Presidential election results: 38.3% Gore, 56.8% Bush, 3.9% Nader, 0.4% Buchanan
National and State Parks: Big Foot Beach State Park
Additional Information Contacts
Walworth County Government Offices 262-741-4241
Delavan Chamber of Commerce 262-728-5095
East Troy Chamber of Commerce 262-642-3770
Elkhorn Chamber of Commerce. 262-723-5788
Geneva Lake Chamber of Commerce 262-248-4416
Lakes Area Realtors Association 262-723-6851
Whitewater Chamber of Commerce. 262-473-4005

Walworth County Communities

BLOOMFIELD (town). Covers a land area of 32.558 square miles and a water area of 0.817 square miles. Located at 42.54° N. Lat.; 88.35° W. Long.
Population: 5,537 (2000); Race: 94.8% White, 2.6% Black, 0.3% Asian, 0.1% American Indian and Alaska Native, 3.1% Hispanic of any race, 1.1% two or more races (2000); Density: 170.1 persons per square mile (2000); Age: 27.1% under 18, 11.9% over 64 (2000); Marriage status: 25.3% never married, 53.5% now married, 8.4% widowed, 12.8% divorced (2000); Foreign born: 5.2% (2000); Ancestry (includes multiple ancestries): 36.3% German, 12.9% Irish, 12.2% Polish, 10.3% Other groups, 7.7% Italian (2000).
Economy: Employment by occupation: 10.5% management, 7.3% professional, 12.9% services, 27.3% sales, 1.4% farming, 14.9% construction, 25.7% production (2000).
Income: Per capita income: $19,302 (2000); Median household income: $42,232 (2000); Poverty rate: 8.3% (2000).

Taxes: Total city taxes per capita: $126 (2000); City property taxes per capita: $104 (2000).
Education: High school graduation rate: 77.4% (2000); College graduation rate: 10.1% (2000).
Housing: Homeownership rate: 81.2% (2000); Median home value: $102,800 (2000); Median rent: $535 per month (2000); Median age of housing: 39 years (2000).
Safety: Violent crime rate: 9.0 per 10,000 population; Property crime rate: 139.9 per 10,000 population (2001).
Transportation: Commute to work: 93.8% car, 2.3% public transportation, 0.6% walk, 2.6% work from home (2000); Travel time to work: 25.0% less than 15 minutes, 38.6% 15 to 30 minutes, 16.4% 30 to 45 minutes, 5.9% 45 to 60 minutes, 14.1% 60 minutes or more (2000)

COMO (CDP). Aka Lake Como. Covers a land area of 3.031 square miles and a water area of 0.499 square miles. Located at 42.60° N. Lat.; 88.49° W. Long. Elevation is 911 feet.
Population: 1,870 (2000); Race: 94.8% White, 0.0% Black, 1.5% Asian, 0.8% American Indian and Alaska Native, 6.8% Hispanic of any race, 0.4% two or more races (2000); Density: 617.0 persons per square mile (2000); Age: 23.6% under 18, 15.6% over 64 (2000); Marriage status: 22.0% never married, 58.0% now married, 10.1% widowed, 9.9% divorced (2000); Foreign born: 5.8% (2000); Ancestry (includes multiple ancestries): 37.2% German, 13.4% Irish, 9.9% Other groups, 9.9% Polish, 7.6% Italian (2000).
Economy: Employment by occupation: 11.3% management, 17.7% professional, 16.4% services, 21.3% sales, 0.0% farming, 11.3% construction, 22.0% production (2000).
Income: Per capita income: $22,780 (2000); Median household income: $43,750 (2000); Poverty rate: 3.1% (2000).
Education: High school graduation rate: 79.8% (2000); College graduation rate: 15.7% (2000).
Housing: Homeownership rate: 77.1% (2000); Median home value: $95,400 (2000); Median rent: $528 per month (2000); Median age of housing: 40 years (2000).
Transportation: Commute to work: 93.6% car, 0.0% public transportation, 0.6% walk, 5.0% work from home (2000); Travel time to work: 26.3% less than 15 minutes, 50.3% 15 to 30 minutes, 9.0% 30 to 45 minutes, 5.2% 45 to 60 minutes, 9.3% 60 minutes or more (2000)

DARIEN (village). Covers a land area of 1.283 square miles and a water area of 0 square miles. Located at 42.60° N. Lat.; 88.70° W. Long. Elevation is 948 feet.
History: Darien grew up along an old trail that became a military road between Chicago and Madison. The first settler in Darien was John Bruce.
Population: 1,572 (2000); Race: 91.2% White, 0.1% Black, 0.0% Asian, 0.3% American Indian and Alaska Native, 16.6% Hispanic of any race, 2.9% two or more races (2000); Density: 1,225.0 persons per square mile (2000); Age: 34.1% under 18, 6.7% over 64 (2000); Marriage status: 24.3% never married, 61.6% now married, 4.8% widowed, 9.3% divorced (2000); Foreign born: 10.5% (2000); Ancestry (includes multiple ancestries): 38.0% German, 19.0% Other groups, 12.1% Irish, 8.6% English, 5.5% Norwegian (2000).
Economy: Single-family building permits issued: 1 (2001) / 10 (2000); Multi-family building permits issued: 0 (2001) / 2 (2000); Employment by occupation: 9.5% management, 11.9% professional, 11.7% services, 21.6% sales, 1.3% farming, 7.9% construction, 36.1% production (2000).
Income: Per capita income: $17,638 (2000); Median household income: $46,800 (2000); Poverty rate: 6.8% (2000).
Taxes: Total city taxes per capita: $332 (1997); City property taxes per capita: $322 (1997).
Education: High school graduation rate: 79.0% (2000); College graduation rate: 13.5% (2000).
Housing: Homeownership rate: 66.9% (2000); Median home value: $100,600 (2000); Median rent: $517 per month (2000); Median age of housing: 31 years (2000).
Safety: Violent crime rate: n/a; Property crime rate: 259.0 per 10,000 population (2001).
Transportation: Commute to work: 92.0% car, 0.8% public transportation, 3.7% walk, 2.4% work from home (2000); Travel time to work: 40.3% less than 15 minutes, 42.9% 15 to 30 minutes, 7.8% 30 to 45 minutes, 2.5% 45 to 60 minutes, 6.6% 60 minutes or more (2000)

DARIEN (town). Covers a land area of 34.053 square miles and a water area of 0.037 square miles. Located at 42.61° N. Lat.; 88.72° W. Long. Elevation is 948 feet.
Population: 1,747 (2000); Race: 91.9% White, 0.1% Black, 0.0% Asian, 0.0% American Indian and Alaska Native, 12.1% Hispanic of any race, 0.3% two or more races (2000); Density: 51.3 persons per square mile (2000); Age: 23.9% under 18, 10.9% over 64 (2000); Marriage status: 23.2% never married, 63.1% now married, 5.8% widowed, 7.8% divorced (2000); Foreign born: 7.0% (2000); Ancestry (includes multiple ancestries): 33.3% German, 13.6% English, 13.0% Other groups, 8.2% United States or American, 8.1% Irish (2000).
Economy: In dairying and hog-raising region. Manufacturing: wood products, plastic products. Employment by occupation: 14.1% management, 13.4% professional, 11.6% services, 21.3% sales, 2.0% farming, 10.0% construction, 27.6% production (2000).
Income: Per capita income: $19,580 (2000); Median household income: $50,700 (2000); Poverty rate: 9.5% (2000).
Taxes: Total city taxes per capita: $71 (1997); City property taxes per capita: $59 (1997).
Education: High school graduation rate: 84.3% (2000); College graduation rate: 11.7% (2000).
Housing: Homeownership rate: 80.4% (2000); Median home value: $133,400 (2000); Median rent: $666 per month (2000); Median age of housing: 32 years (2000).
Transportation: Commute to work: 88.5% car, 1.4% public transportation, 3.8% walk, 5.3% work from home (2000); Travel time to work: 35.9% less than 15 minutes, 41.6% 15 to 30 minutes, 13.7% 30 to 45 minutes, 1.9% 45 to 60 minutes, 6.8% 60 minutes or more (2000)

DELAVAN (city). Covers a land area of 6.407 square miles and a water area of 0.424 square miles. Located at 42.63° N. Lat.; 88.63° W. Long. Elevation is 940 feet.
History: Delavan was settled in 1836 by Henry and Samuel Phoenix, and named for E.C. Delavan (1793-1871), a temperance leader of New York. The Phoenix brothers planned for Delavan to be a temperance colony, and the property deeds they issued contained a clause forbidding the sale of liquor. In the 1840's, another set of brothers, Ed and Jerry Mabie, established a circus headquarters in Delavan, that soon involved most of the residents.
Population: 7,956 (2000); Race: 85.0% White, 0.9% Black, 1.2% Asian, 0.8% American Indian and Alaska Native, 20.6% Hispanic of any race, 2.0% two or more races (2000); Density: 1,241.7 persons per square mile (2000); Age: 29.1% under 18, 12.7% over 64 (2000); Marriage status: 27.7% never married, 54.6% now married, 8.0% widowed, 9.7% divorced (2000); Foreign born: 14.1% (2000); Ancestry (includes multiple ancestries): 31.4% German, 21.5% Other groups, 10.2% Irish, 9.0% English, 6.4% Norwegian (2000).
Economy: Single-family building permits issued: 23 (2001) / 31 (2000); Multi-family building permits issued: 16 (2001) / 0 (2000); Employment by occupation: 8.5% management, 13.7% professional, 14.9% services, 25.6% sales, 0.8% farming, 7.5% construction, 29.0% production (2000).
Income: Per capita income: $17,624 (2000); Median household income: $42,551 (2000); Poverty rate: 7.6% (2000).
Taxes: Total city taxes per capita: $497 (2000); City property taxes per capita: $416 (2000).
Education: High school graduation rate: 75.5% (2000); College graduation rate: 18.8% (2000).

School District(s)

Delavan-Darien (PK-12)
2000 Enrollment: 2,689 262-728-2642
Housing: Homeownership rate: 55.3% (2000); Median home value: $103,500 (2000); Median rent: $529 per month (2000); Median age of housing: 35 years (2000).
Safety: Violent crime rate: 20.0 per 10,000 population; Property crime rate: 551.6 per 10,000 population (2001).
Newspapers: The Week (1 x week); Delavan Enterprise (1 x week)
Transportation: Commute to work: 93.0% car, 0.7% public transportation, 2.2% walk, 2.4% work from home (2000); Travel time to work: 53.4% less than 15 minutes, 30.2% 15 to 30 minutes, 7.8% 30 to 45 minutes, 4.6% 45 to 60 minutes, 3.9% 60 minutes or more (2000)
Additional Information Contacts
Delavan Chamber of Commerce 262-728-5095

DELAVAN (town). Covers a land area of 25.313 square miles and a water area of 2.826 square miles. Located at 42.61° N. Lat.; 88.60° W. Long. Elevation is 940 feet.
History: Settled 1836, incorporated 1897.
Population: 4,559 (2000); Race: 94.4% White, 0.0% Black, 0.1% Asian, 0.5% American Indian and Alaska Native, 7.4% Hispanic of any race, 0.9% two or more races (2000); Density: 180.1 persons per square mile (2000); Age: 24.6% under 18, 13.7% over 64 (2000); Marriage status: 23.1% never married, 66.0% now married, 4.9% widowed, 6.0% divorced (2000); Foreign

born: 5.3% (2000); Ancestry (includes multiple ancestries): 36.2% German, 17.8% Irish, 10.8% English, 9.1% Polish, 8.2% Other groups (2000).
Economy: In dairying and stock raising area. Manufacturing: food, transportation equipment, printing and publishing, fabricated metal products, electrical equipment, cigars. Just East of the city is Delavan Lake, with the resort village Delavan Lake on its shores; winter and summer sports. Wisconsin School for the Deaf. Employment by occupation: 11.6% management, 14.5% professional, 14.4% services, 21.5% sales, 0.5% farming, 11.0% construction, 26.5% production (2000).
Income: Per capita income: $22,796 (2000); Median household income: $45,264 (2000); Poverty rate: 4.9% (2000).
Taxes: Total city taxes per capita: $372 (2000); City property taxes per capita: $265 (2000).
Education: High school graduation rate: 81.9% (2000); College graduation rate: 16.9% (2000).
Housing: Homeownership rate: 81.1% (2000); Median home value: $120,700 (2000); Median rent: $585 per month (2000); Median age of housing: 40 years (2000).
Safety: Violent crime rate: 6.5 per 10,000 population; Property crime rate: 248.3 per 10,000 population (2001).
Transportation: Commute to work: 91.0% car, 1.8% public transportation, 0.6% walk, 6.2% work from home (2000); Travel time to work: 43.7% less than 15 minutes, 28.8% 15 to 30 minutes, 12.6% 30 to 45 minutes, 3.9% 45 to 60 minutes, 11.0% 60 minutes or more (2000)

DELAVAN LAKE (CDP). Covers a land area of 3.545 square miles and a water area of 2.430 square miles. Located at 42.60° N. Lat.; 88.62° W. Long. Elevation is 940 feet.
Population: 2,352 (2000); Race: 92.1% White, 0.0% Black, 0.0% Asian, 0.0% American Indian and Alaska Native, 8.2% Hispanic of any race, 0.6% two or more races (2000); Density: 663.4 persons per square mile (2000); Age: 24.9% under 18, 16.2% over 64 (2000); Marriage status: 22.3% never married, 65.2% now married, 5.1% widowed, 7.5% divorced (2000); Foreign born: 7.5% (2000); Ancestry (includes multiple ancestries): 37.1% German, 17.9% Irish, 9.7% Polish, 8.3% Other groups, 8.0% Italian (2000).
Economy: Employment by occupation: 10.1% management, 16.8% professional, 9.0% services, 22.2% sales, 0.5% farming, 11.7% construction, 29.7% production (2000).
Income: Per capita income: $24,067 (2000); Median household income: $45,192 (2000); Poverty rate: 5.7% (2000).
Education: High school graduation rate: 80.6% (2000); College graduation rate: 16.3% (2000).
Housing: Homeownership rate: 81.3% (2000); Median home value: $116,500 (2000); Median rent: $566 per month (2000); Median age of housing: 47 years (2000).
Transportation: Commute to work: 92.6% car, 2.4% public transportation, 0.0% walk, 4.2% work from home (2000); Travel time to work: 33.4% less than 15 minutes, 33.5% 15 to 30 minutes, 14.4% 30 to 45 minutes, 3.5% 45 to 60 minutes, 15.2% 60 minutes or more (2000)

EAST TROY (village). Covers a land area of 3.612 square miles and a water area of 0.046 square miles. Located at 42.78° N. Lat.; 88.40° W. Long. Elevation is 860 feet.
Population: 3,564 (2000); Race: 96.7% White, 0.0% Black, 1.6% Asian, 0.3% American Indian and Alaska Native, 1.4% Hispanic of any race, 0.3% two or more races (2000); Density: 986.6 persons per square mile (2000); Age: 28.0% under 18, 14.0% over 64 (2000); Marriage status: 18.1% never married, 59.2% now married, 8.9% widowed, 13.8% divorced (2000); Foreign born: 3.2% (2000); Ancestry (includes multiple ancestries): 46.9% German, 15.8% Polish, 12.3% Irish, 8.4% Norwegian, 7.5% English (2000).
Economy: Single-family building permits issued: 32 (2001) / 32 (2000); Multi-family building permits issued: 24 (2001) / 24 (2000); Employment by occupation: 10.2% management, 15.8% professional, 12.3% services, 25.8% sales, 0.0% farming, 8.8% construction, 27.0% production (2000).
Income: Per capita income: $21,590 (2000); Median household income: $48,397 (2000); Poverty rate: 2.3% (2000).
Taxes: Total city taxes per capita: $252 (1997); City property taxes per capita: $214 (1997).
Education: High school graduation rate: 86.1% (2000); College graduation rate: 17.4% (2000).

School District(s)

East Troy Community (KG-12)
2000 Enrollment: 1,729 262-642-6710

Housing: Homeownership rate: 70.0% (2000); Median home value: $131,500 (2000); Median rent: $506 per month (2000); Median age of housing: 25 years (2000).
Safety: Violent crime rate: 11.1 per 10,000 population; Property crime rate: 735.6 per 10,000 population (2001).
Newspapers: The East Troy News (1 x week)
Transportation: Commute to work: 91.1% car, 0.0% public transportation, 2.8% walk, 5.1% work from home (2000); Travel time to work: 30.9% less than 15 minutes, 28.6% 15 to 30 minutes, 23.8% 30 to 45 minutes, 9.0% 45 to 60 minutes, 7.6% 60 minutes or more (2000)

Additional Information Contacts

East Troy Chamber of Commerce 262-642-3770

EAST TROY (town). Covers a land area of 30.339 square miles and a water area of 1.790 square miles. Located at 42.81° N. Lat.; 88.36° W. Long. Elevation is 860 feet.
Population: 3,830 (2000); Race: 97.8% White, 0.3% Black, 0.7% Asian, 0.0% American Indian and Alaska Native, 2.2% Hispanic of any race, 0.0% two or more races (2000); Density: 126.2 persons per square mile (2000); Age: 23.8% under 18, 9.9% over 64 (2000); Marriage status: 20.7% never married, 68.9% now married, 4.3% widowed, 6.1% divorced (2000); Foreign born: 2.5% (2000); Ancestry (includes multiple ancestries): 47.5% German, 21.5% Irish, 16.3% Polish, 9.2% English, 6.5% Italian (2000).
Economy: Single-family building permits issued: 25 (2001) / 12 (2000); Multi-family building permits issued: 0 (2001) / 0 (2000); Employment by occupation: 13.2% management, 19.9% professional, 10.8% services, 21.1% sales, 1.6% farming, 14.4% construction, 19.1% production (2000).
Income: Per capita income: $30,461 (2000); Median household income: $61,486 (2000); Poverty rate: 2.9% (2000).
Taxes: Total city taxes per capita: $177 (2000); City property taxes per capita: $161 (2000).
Education: High school graduation rate: 89.7% (2000); College graduation rate: 22.8% (2000).
Housing: Homeownership rate: 89.9% (2000); Median home value: $171,700 (2000); Median rent: $603 per month (2000); Median age of housing: 28 years (2000).
Safety: Violent crime rate: 2.6 per 10,000 population; Property crime rate: 142.6 per 10,000 population (2001).
Transportation: Commute to work: 95.8% car, 0.0% public transportation, 1.8% walk, 1.8% work from home (2000); Travel time to work: 29.5% less than 15 minutes, 23.5% 15 to 30 minutes, 31.4% 30 to 45 minutes, 10.4% 45 to 60 minutes, 5.2% 60 minutes or more (2000)

ELKHORN (city). Covers a land area of 7.267 square miles and a water area of 0.054 square miles. Located at 42.67° N. Lat.; 88.54° W. Long. Elevation is 1,033 feet.
History: Elkhorn was founded in 1837 and named for an elk's horn that was found in a fallen tree. In 1918 the citizens of Elkhorn persuaded the Frank Holton Musical Instrument Company to move their plant here. As the manufacture of wind instruments became an important industry, many musical groups developed in the city.
Population: 7,305 (2000); Race: 94.2% White, 0.0% Black, 0.5% Asian, 0.9% American Indian and Alaska Native, 5.3% Hispanic of any race, 1.6% two or more races (2000); Density: 1,005.2 persons per square mile (2000); Age: 27.1% under 18, 13.7% over 64 (2000); Marriage status: 26.3% never married, 52.9% now married, 8.4% widowed, 12.5% divorced (2000); Foreign born: 4.8% (2000); Ancestry (includes multiple ancestries): 44.1% German, 17.5% Irish, 10.7% English, 8.6% Other groups, 8.3% Polish (2000).
Economy: Single-family building permits issued: 32 (2001) / 48 (2000); Multi-family building permits issued: 24 (2001) / 66 (2000); Employment by occupation: 8.7% management, 21.1% professional, 18.0% services, 18.9% sales, 0.5% farming, 6.4% construction, 26.3% production (2000).
Income: Per capita income: $20,003 (2000); Median household income: $38,395 (2000); Poverty rate: 9.9% (2000).
Taxes: Total city taxes per capita: $396 (2000); City property taxes per capita: $373 (2000).
Education: High school graduation rate: 79.4% (2000); College graduation rate: 19.4% (2000).

School District(s)

Elkhorn Area (KG-12)
2000 Enrollment: 2,515 262-723-3160
Walworth Co Cdeb (PK-12)
2000 Enrollment: 225 262-741-4118

Housing: Homeownership rate: 52.0% (2000); Median home value: $114,600 (2000); Median rent: $516 per month (2000); Median age of housing: 28 years (2000).
Hospitals: Lakeland Medical Center, Aurora Health Care (99 beds)

Safety: Violent crime rate: 13.6 per 10,000 population; Property crime rate: 299.0 per 10,000 population (2001).
Newspapers: The Elkhorn Independent (1 x week)
Transportation: Commute to work: 93.2% car, 0.0% public transportation, 4.1% walk, 2.0% work from home (2000); Travel time to work: 49.6% less than 15 minutes, 24.6% 15 to 30 minutes, 10.4% 30 to 45 minutes, 9.2% 45 to 60 minutes, 6.2% 60 minutes or more (2000)
Additional Information Contacts
Elkhorn Chamber of Commerce 262-723-5788
Lakes Area Realtors Association 262-723-6851

FONTANA (unincorporated postal area, zip code 53125). Aka Fontana-on-Geneva Lake. Covers a land area of 4.906 square miles and a water area of 0.018 square miles. Located at 42.54° N. Lat.; 88.46° W. Long. Elevation is 910 feet.
Population: 1,941 (2000); Race: 97.5% White, 1.0% Black, 0.1% Asian, 0.7% American Indian and Alaska Native, 1.5% Hispanic of any race, 0.2% two or more races (2000); Density: 395.6 persons per square mile (2000); Age: 19.2% under 18, 20.8% over 64 (2000); Marriage status: 17.6% never married, 69.6% now married, 6.6% widowed, 6.2% divorced (2000); Foreign born: 2.7% (2000); Ancestry (includes multiple ancestries): 34.7% German, 20.4% Irish, 15.4% English, 8.5% Polish, 7.4% Italian (2000).
Economy: Employment by occupation: 17.1% management, 22.4% professional, 11.9% services, 29.1% sales, 0.5% farming, 7.2% construction, 11.7% production (2000).
Income: Per capita income: $35,496 (2000); Median household income: $54,743 (2000); Poverty rate: 3.4% (2000).
Education: High school graduation rate: 93.2% (2000); College graduation rate: 40.8% (2000).

School District(s)

Fontana J8 (PK-08)
2000 Enrollment: 295 262-275-6881
Housing: Homeownership rate: 84.9% (2000); Median home value: $185,600 (2000); Median rent: $586 per month (2000); Median age of housing: 24 years (2000).
Safety: Violent crime rate: 11.3 per 10,000 population; Property crime rate: 226.4 per 10,000 population (2001).
Transportation: Commute to work: 90.5% car, 2.0% public transportation, 1.3% walk, 5.9% work from home (2000); Travel time to work: 37.4% less than 15 minutes, 25.4% 15 to 30 minutes, 11.4% 30 to 45 minutes, 6.8% 45 to 60 minutes, 18.9% 60 minutes or more (2000)

FONTANA-ON-GENEVA LAKE (village). Aka Fontana. Covers a land area of 2.963 square miles and a water area of 1.119 square miles. Located at 42.54° N. Lat.; 88.56° W. Long.
Population: 1,754 (2000); Race: 96.8% White, 1.1% Black, 0.0% Asian, 1.3% American Indian and Alaska Native, 1.7% Hispanic of any race, 0.3% two or more races (2000); Density: 592.0 persons per square mile (2000); Age: 19.0% under 18, 20.3% over 64 (2000); Marriage status: 17.7% never married, 68.8% now married, 6.4% widowed, 7.1% divorced (2000); Foreign born: 2.5% (2000); Ancestry (includes multiple ancestries): 35.3% German, 21.3% Irish, 14.1% English, 8.7% Polish, 7.8% Italian (2000).
Economy: Single-family building permits issued: 21 (2001) / 25 (2000); Multi-family building permits issued: 0 (2001) / 56 (2000); Employment by occupation: 17.3% management, 20.3% professional, 10.0% services, 32.3% sales, 0.5% farming, 7.2% construction, 12.3% production (2000).
Income: Per capita income: $32,266 (2000); Median household income: $54,211 (2000); Poverty rate: 3.8% (2000).
Taxes: Total city taxes per capita: $1,203 (1997); City property taxes per capita: $980 (1997).
Education: High school graduation rate: 92.2% (2000); College graduation rate: 39.4% (2000).
Housing: Homeownership rate: 85.7% (2000); Median home value: $181,900 (2000); Median rent: $601 per month (2000); Median age of housing: 22 years (2000).
Transportation: Commute to work: 89.3% car, 2.3% public transportation, 1.5% walk, 6.8% work from home (2000); Travel time to work: 35.5% less than 15 minutes, 23.5% 15 to 30 minutes, 12.7% 30 to 45 minutes, 6.9% 45 to 60 minutes, 21.4% 60 minutes or more (2000)

GENEVA (town). Covers a land area of 29.269 square miles and a water area of 1.529 square miles. Located at 42.61° N. Lat.; 88.48° W. Long.
Population: 4,099 (2000); Race: 95.6% White, 0.5% Black, 1.1% Asian, 0.4% American Indian and Alaska Native, 4.4% Hispanic of any race, 0.2% two or more races (2000); Density: 140.0 persons per square mile (2000); Age: 24.1% under 18, 15.6% over 64 (2000); Marriage status: 20.6% never married, 64.3% now married, 6.1% widowed, 9.0% divorced (2000); Foreign born: 5.1% (2000); Ancestry (includes multiple ancestries): 39.4% German, 13.8% Irish, 9.4% Polish, 8.8% English, 6.8% United States or American (2000).
Economy: Employment by occupation: 16.5% management, 15.9% professional, 17.1% services, 22.2% sales, 0.1% farming, 10.5% construction, 17.7% production (2000).
Income: Per capita income: $25,021 (2000); Median household income: $49,504 (2000); Poverty rate: 4.6% (2000).
Taxes: Total city taxes per capita: $279 (2000); City property taxes per capita: $178 (2000).
Education: High school graduation rate: 85.9% (2000); College graduation rate: 25.4% (2000).
Housing: Homeownership rate: 80.4% (2000); Median home value: $135,000 (2000); Median rent: $529 per month (2000); Median age of housing: 27 years (2000).
Transportation: Commute to work: 91.6% car, 0.5% public transportation, 1.3% walk, 6.0% work from home (2000); Travel time to work: 33.1% less than 15 minutes, 41.8% 15 to 30 minutes, 9.6% 30 to 45 minutes, 5.6% 45 to 60 minutes, 9.9% 60 minutes or more (2000)

GENOA CITY (village). Covers a land area of 2.227 square miles and a water area of 0 square miles. Located at 42.50° N. Lat.; 88.32° W. Long. Elevation is 830 feet.
Population: 1,949 (2000); Race: 98.3% White, 0.3% Black, 0.0% Asian, 0.4% American Indian and Alaska Native, 2.7% Hispanic of any race, 0.9% two or more races (2000); Density: 875.1 persons per square mile (2000); Age: 33.6% under 18, 7.1% over 64 (2000); Marriage status: 20.9% never married, 63.6% now married, 4.9% widowed, 10.6% divorced (2000); Foreign born: 1.4% (2000); Ancestry (includes multiple ancestries): 38.1% German, 21.4% Irish, 12.9% Polish, 10.0% English, 7.5% Italian (2000).
Economy: Single-family building permits issued: 53 (2001) / 53 (2000); Multi-family building permits issued: 0 (2001) / 0 (2000); Employment by occupation: 9.5% management, 14.3% professional, 11.6% services, 25.2% sales, 0.5% farming, 15.7% construction, 23.3% production (2000).
Income: Per capita income: $18,044 (2000); Median household income: $49,338 (2000); Poverty rate: 4.4% (2000).
Taxes: Total city taxes per capita: $289 (1997); City property taxes per capita: $245 (1997).
Education: High school graduation rate: 86.8% (2000); College graduation rate: 18.8% (2000).

School District(s)

Genoa City J2 (KG-08)
2000 Enrollment: 584 262-279-1051
Housing: Homeownership rate: 77.3% (2000); Median home value: $121,000 (2000); Median rent: $396 per month (2000); Median age of housing: 28 years (2000).
Safety: Violent crime rate: 20.4 per 10,000 population; Property crime rate: 244.5 per 10,000 population (2001).
Transportation: Commute to work: 92.2% car, 1.5% public transportation, 3.1% walk, 2.2% work from home (2000); Travel time to work: 28.7% less than 15 minutes, 30.7% 15 to 30 minutes, 17.6% 30 to 45 minutes, 11.8% 45 to 60 minutes, 11.3% 60 minutes or more (2000)

LA GRANGE (town). Covers a land area of 34.325 square miles and a water area of 1.398 square miles. Located at 42.78° N. Lat.; 88.57° W. Long. Elevation is 945 feet.
Population: 2,444 (2000); Race: 100.0% White, 0.0% Black, 0.0% Asian, 0.0% American Indian and Alaska Native, 0.6% Hispanic of any race, 0.0% two or more races (2000); Density: 71.2 persons per square mile (2000); Age: 26.4% under 18, 13.6% over 64 (2000); Marriage status: 19.8% never married, 68.9% now married, 5.0% widowed, 6.3% divorced (2000); Foreign born: 1.0% (2000); Ancestry (includes multiple ancestries): 35.7% German, 14.7% Irish, 11.3% English, 8.9% Polish, 7.8% Norwegian (2000).
Economy: Employment by occupation: 17.1% management, 18.8% professional, 10.9% services, 24.1% sales, 0.0% farming, 10.6% construction, 18.5% production (2000).
Income: Per capita income: $26,798 (2000); Median household income: $62,500 (2000); Poverty rate: 8.6% (2000).
Taxes: Total city taxes per capita: $162 (1997); City property taxes per capita: $144 (1997).
Education: High school graduation rate: 91.7% (2000); College graduation rate: 24.7% (2000).
Housing: Homeownership rate: 88.0% (2000); Median home value: $172,400 (2000); Median rent: $526 per month (2000); Median age of housing: 25 years (2000).

Transportation: Commute to work: 90.9% car, 2.4% public transportation, 2.3% walk, 4.1% work from home (2000); Travel time to work: 20.5% less than 15 minutes, 46.1% 15 to 30 minutes, 12.6% 30 to 45 minutes, 8.4% 45 to 60 minutes, 12.5% 60 minutes or more (2000)

LAFAYETTE (town). Covers a land area of 34.511 square miles and a water area of 0.019 square miles. Located at 42.71° N. Lat.; 88.47° W. Long.
Population: 2,251 (2000); Race: 96.6% White, 0.8% Black, 0.8% Asian, 0.8% American Indian and Alaska Native, 1.9% Hispanic of any race, 0.8% two or more races (2000); Density: 65.2 persons per square mile (2000); Age: 22.6% under 18, 18.5% over 64 (2000); Marriage status: 18.0% never married, 66.9% now married, 7.4% widowed, 7.7% divorced (2000); Foreign born: 1.4% (2000); Ancestry (includes multiple ancestries): 38.5% German, 10.6% Irish, 8.0% English, 8.0% Norwegian, 7.8% Polish (2000).
Economy: Employment by occupation: 18.5% management, 16.3% professional, 12.9% services, 19.6% sales, 2.0% farming, 10.9% construction, 19.9% production (2000).
Income: Per capita income: $23,132 (2000); Median household income: $62,500 (2000); Poverty rate: 5.6% (2000).
Taxes: Total city taxes per capita: $134 (1997); City property taxes per capita: $104 (1997).
Education: High school graduation rate: 81.4% (2000); College graduation rate: 18.1% (2000).
Housing: Homeownership rate: 85.6% (2000); Median home value: $177,500 (2000); Median rent: $608 per month (2000); Median age of housing: 22 years (2000).
Transportation: Commute to work: 90.5% car, 0.4% public transportation, 1.1% walk, 7.1% work from home (2000); Travel time to work: 34.1% less than 15 minutes, 32.9% 15 to 30 minutes, 13.8% 30 to 45 minutes, 10.0% 45 to 60 minutes, 9.2% 60 minutes or more (2000)

LAKE GENEVA (city). Covers a land area of 5.016 square miles and a water area of 0.796 square miles. Located at 42.59° N. Lat.; 88.43° W. Long. Elevation is 889 feet.
History: Lake Geneva began to develop after 1840 when a stage route was established through the village, which was incorporated in 1844. Power generated by the White River provided the revenue for the village. Soon Lake Geneva became a popular summer home for wealthy city people. Frank Lloyd Wright designed a hotel here.
Population: 7,148 (2000); Race: 91.5% White, 0.5% Black, 0.4% Asian, 0.7% American Indian and Alaska Native, 15.3% Hispanic of any race, 0.5% two or more races (2000); Density: 1,425.1 persons per square mile (2000); Age: 21.4% under 18, 15.6% over 64 (2000); Marriage status: 27.7% never married, 53.2% now married, 7.8% widowed, 11.3% divorced (2000); Foreign born: 14.5% (2000); Ancestry (includes multiple ancestries): 34.0% German, 15.6% Other groups, 12.9% Irish, 6.9% English, 6.3% Polish (2000).
Economy: Single-family building permits issued: 19 (2001) / 35 (2000); Multi-family building permits issued: 0 (2001) / 4 (2000); Employment by occupation: 12.2% management, 19.7% professional, 17.1% services, 23.9% sales, 0.5% farming, 9.6% construction, 17.1% production (2000).
Income: Per capita income: $21,536 (2000); Median household income: $40,924 (2000); Poverty rate: 7.2% (2000).
Taxes: Total city taxes per capita: $762 (1997); City property taxes per capita: $709 (1997).
Education: High school graduation rate: 83.2% (2000); College graduation rate: 25.1% (2000).

School District(s)

Geneva J4 (KG-08)
2000 Enrollment: 130 262-248-3816
Lake Geneva J1 (KG-08)
2000 Enrollment: 1,645 262-348-1000
Lake Geneva-Genoa City UHS (09-12)
2000 Enrollment: 1,113 262-348-1000
Linn J4 (PK-08)
2000 Enrollment: 97 262-248-4067
Linn J6 (PK-08)
2000 Enrollment: 116 262-248-4120

Housing: Homeownership rate: 54.6% (2000); Median home value: $121,200 (2000); Median rent: $550 per month (2000); Median age of housing: 29 years (2000).
Safety: Violent crime rate: 5.6 per 10,000 population; Property crime rate: 441.7 per 10,000 population (2001).
Newspapers: Westosha Report (1 x week); Lake Geneva Regional News (1 x week)
Transportation: Commute to work: 90.5% car, 0.1% public transportation, 5.3% walk, 3.3% work from home (2000); Travel time to work: 43.7% less than 15 minutes, 32.1% 15 to 30 minutes, 8.1% 30 to 45 minutes, 8.1% 45 to 60 minutes, 8.1% 60 minutes or more (2000)
Additional Information Contacts
Geneva Lake Chamber of Commerce 262-248-4416

LINN (town). Covers a land area of 28.698 square miles and a water area of 5.143 square miles. Located at 42.55° N. Lat.; 88.48° W. Long.
Population: 2,194 (2000); Race: 97.8% White, 0.5% Black, 0.2% Asian, 0.1% American Indian and Alaska Native, 1.7% Hispanic of any race, 0.4% two or more races (2000); Density: 76.5 persons per square mile (2000); Age: 27.1% under 18, 16.7% over 64 (2000); Marriage status: 22.3% never married, 65.4% now married, 6.2% widowed, 6.1% divorced (2000); Foreign born: 4.1% (2000); Ancestry (includes multiple ancestries): 37.6% German, 23.2% Irish, 14.0% English, 8.9% Polish, 5.5% Other groups (2000).
Economy: Employment by occupation: 21.8% management, 18.1% professional, 14.0% services, 21.2% sales, 4.2% farming, 8.3% construction, 12.5% production (2000).
Income: Per capita income: $29,751 (2000); Median household income: $54,213 (2000); Poverty rate: 5.1% (2000).
Taxes: Total city taxes per capita: $559 (2000); City property taxes per capita: $531 (2000).
Education: High school graduation rate: 91.9% (2000); College graduation rate: 35.1% (2000).
Housing: Homeownership rate: 75.8% (2000); Median home value: $174,500 (2000); Median rent: $535 per month (2000); Median age of housing: 45 years (2000).
Transportation: Commute to work: 83.3% car, 1.4% public transportation, 3.9% walk, 10.4% work from home (2000); Travel time to work: 34.3% less than 15 minutes, 33.1% 15 to 30 minutes, 11.5% 30 to 45 minutes, 7.1% 45 to 60 minutes, 14.0% 60 minutes or more (2000)

LYONS (town). Covers a land area of 34.461 square miles and a water area of 0.238 square miles. Located at 42.63° N. Lat.; 88.37° W. Long. Elevation is 802 feet.
Population: 3,440 (2000); Race: 97.1% White, 0.9% Black, 0.1% Asian, 0.3% American Indian and Alaska Native, 1.7% Hispanic of any race, 0.9% two or more races (2000); Density: 99.8 persons per square mile (2000); Age: 25.5% under 18, 13.0% over 64 (2000); Marriage status: 20.0% never married, 64.6% now married, 7.3% widowed, 8.1% divorced (2000); Foreign born: 2.3% (2000); Ancestry (includes multiple ancestries): 48.5% German, 17.7% Irish, 8.5% Polish, 6.0% English, 5.7% Norwegian (2000).
Economy: Employment by occupation: 11.8% management, 14.5% professional, 13.5% services, 24.6% sales, 1.0% farming, 15.3% construction, 19.3% production (2000).
Income: Per capita income: $23,389 (2000); Median household income: $55,741 (2000); Poverty rate: 4.1% (2000).
Taxes: Total city taxes per capita: $160 (1997); City property taxes per capita: $57 (1997).
Education: High school graduation rate: 88.9% (2000); College graduation rate: 19.7% (2000).
Housing: Homeownership rate: 87.5% (2000); Median home value: $147,900 (2000); Median rent: $579 per month (2000); Median age of housing: 28 years (2000).
Transportation: Commute to work: 93.8% car, 0.5% public transportation, 2.6% walk, 2.8% work from home (2000); Travel time to work: 38.8% less than 15 minutes, 29.0% 15 to 30 minutes, 13.6% 30 to 45 minutes, 8.8% 45 to 60 minutes, 9.8% 60 minutes or more (2000)

PELL LAKE (CDP). Covers a land area of 3.921 square miles and a water area of 0.158 square miles. Located at 42.53° N. Lat.; 88.35° W. Long. Elevation is 871 feet.
Population: 2,988 (2000); Race: 97.2% White, 0.0% Black, 0.5% Asian, 0.3% American Indian and Alaska Native, 2.3% Hispanic of any race, 0.5% two or more races (2000); Density: 762.0 persons per square mile (2000); Age: 30.1% under 18, 10.7% over 64 (2000); Marriage status: 24.9% never married, 51.9% now married, 7.3% widowed, 15.8% divorced (2000); Foreign born: 5.3% (2000); Ancestry (includes multiple ancestries): 33.1% German, 14.8% Polish, 12.7% Irish, 9.2% Italian, 8.2% United States or American (2000).
Economy: Employment by occupation: 7.9% management, 5.8% professional, 12.0% services, 25.8% sales, 0.3% farming, 20.1% construction, 28.3% production (2000).
Income: Per capita income: $16,380 (2000); Median household income: $41,442 (2000); Poverty rate: 10.5% (2000).

Education: High school graduation rate: 74.0% (2000); College graduation rate: 4.2% (2000).
Housing: Homeownership rate: 82.8% (2000); Median home value: $93,400 (2000); Median rent: $568 per month (2000); Median age of housing: 44 years (2000).
Transportation: Commute to work: 97.0% car, 2.8% public transportation, 0.0% walk, 0.2% work from home (2000); Travel time to work: 18.2% less than 15 minutes, 44.0% 15 to 30 minutes, 15.1% 30 to 45 minutes, 7.0% 45 to 60 minutes, 15.6% 60 minutes or more (2000)

POTTER LAKE (CDP). Covers a land area of 1.409 square miles and a water area of 0.243 square miles. Located at 42.82° N. Lat.; 88.34° W. Long.
Population: 1,099 (2000); Race: 99.1% White, 0.9% Black, 0.0% Asian, 0.0% American Indian and Alaska Native, 2.4% Hispanic of any race, 0.0% two or more races (2000); Density: 779.9 persons per square mile (2000); Age: 27.0% under 18, 8.8% over 64 (2000); Marriage status: 17.8% never married, 70.2% now married, 3.8% widowed, 8.2% divorced (2000); Foreign born: 2.5% (2000); Ancestry (includes multiple ancestries): 53.9% German, 21.1% Polish, 19.9% Irish, 7.7% United States or American, 6.8% English (2000).
Economy: Employment by occupation: 9.0% management, 18.9% professional, 18.6% services, 22.1% sales, 0.0% farming, 13.1% construction, 18.3% production (2000).
Income: Per capita income: $20,817 (2000); Median household income: $54,427 (2000); Poverty rate: 5.2% (2000).
Education: High school graduation rate: 83.9% (2000); College graduation rate: 13.5% (2000).
Housing: Homeownership rate: 96.8% (2000); Median home value: $137,100 (2000); Median rent: $525 per month (2000); Median age of housing: 38 years (2000).
Transportation: Commute to work: 96.7% car, 0.0% public transportation, 0.0% walk, 2.1% work from home (2000); Travel time to work: 13.8% less than 15 minutes, 25.0% 15 to 30 minutes, 40.3% 30 to 45 minutes, 15.2% 45 to 60 minutes, 5.7% 60 minutes or more (2000)

RICHMOND (town). Covers a land area of 35.299 square miles and a water area of 0.693 square miles. Located at 42.72° N. Lat.; 88.70° W. Long. Elevation is 990 feet.
Population: 1,835 (2000); Race: 96.4% White, 0.1% Black, 0.0% Asian, 0.6% American Indian and Alaska Native, 5.1% Hispanic of any race, 0.5% two or more races (2000); Density: 52.0 persons per square mile (2000); Age: 24.4% under 18, 11.8% over 64 (2000); Marriage status: 20.4% never married, 64.8% now married, 4.8% widowed, 10.0% divorced (2000); Foreign born: 2.0% (2000); Ancestry (includes multiple ancestries): 44.4% German, 15.8% Irish, 9.0% English, 8.4% Norwegian, 7.7% Polish (2000).
Economy: Employment by occupation: 12.9% management, 16.2% professional, 10.4% services, 23.2% sales, 2.5% farming, 14.8% construction, 20.0% production (2000).
Income: Per capita income: $23,203 (2000); Median household income: $51,776 (2000); Poverty rate: 4.1% (2000).
Taxes: Total city taxes per capita: $89 (1997); City property taxes per capita: $78 (1997).
Education: High school graduation rate: 83.6% (2000); College graduation rate: 23.7% (2000).
Housing: Homeownership rate: 86.2% (2000); Median home value: $130,600 (2000); Median rent: $418 per month (2000); Median age of housing: 36 years (2000).
Transportation: Commute to work: 91.6% car, 0.2% public transportation, 0.6% walk, 6.7% work from home (2000); Travel time to work: 16.4% less than 15 minutes, 52.2% 15 to 30 minutes, 16.7% 30 to 45 minutes, 6.1% 45 to 60 minutes, 8.6% 60 minutes or more (2000)

SHARON (village). Covers a land area of 0.912 square miles and a water area of 0 square miles. Located at 42.50° N. Lat.; 88.73° W. Long. Elevation is 1,027 feet.
Population: 1,549 (2000); Race: 94.3% White, 0.7% Black, 0.5% Asian, 0.7% American Indian and Alaska Native, 8.2% Hispanic of any race, 1.6% two or more races (2000); Density: 1,699.3 persons per square mile (2000); Age: 31.0% under 18, 7.9% over 64 (2000); Marriage status: 23.8% never married, 60.7% now married, 4.7% widowed, 10.8% divorced (2000); Foreign born: 3.6% (2000); Ancestry (includes multiple ancestries): 36.2% German, 14.9% Irish, 14.2% Other groups, 7.0% United States or American, 6.9% English (2000).
Economy: Single-family building permits issued: 2 (2001) / 3 (2000); Multi-family building permits issued: 0 (2001) / 0 (2000); Employment by occupation: 8.5% management, 10.7% professional, 17.2% services, 19.4% sales, 1.2% farming, 7.9% construction, 35.1% production (2000).
Income: Per capita income: $15,779 (2000); Median household income: $39,330 (2000); Poverty rate: 10.4% (2000).
Taxes: Total city taxes per capita: $324 (1997); City property taxes per capita: $294 (1997).
Education: High school graduation rate: 78.2% (2000); College graduation rate: 7.4% (2000).

School District(s)

Sharon J11 (PK-08)
2000 Enrollment: 288 262-736-4477

Housing: Homeownership rate: 68.1% (2000); Median home value: $98,100 (2000); Median rent: $552 per month (2000); Median age of housing: 50 years (2000).
Newspapers: The Sharon Reporter (1 x week)
Transportation: Commute to work: 90.3% car, 0.7% public transportation, 3.5% walk, 4.6% work from home (2000); Travel time to work: 22.8% less than 15 minutes, 43.7% 15 to 30 minutes, 20.7% 30 to 45 minutes, 6.9% 45 to 60 minutes, 5.9% 60 minutes or more (2000)

SHARON (town). Covers a land area of 35.550 square miles and a water area of 0.013 square miles. Located at 42.54° N. Lat.; 88.71° W. Long. Elevation is 1,027 feet.
Population: 912 (2000); Race: 100.0% White, 0.0% Black, 0.0% Asian, 0.0% American Indian and Alaska Native, 1.9% Hispanic of any race, 0.0% two or more races (2000); Density: 25.7 persons per square mile (2000); Age: 27.0% under 18, 14.3% over 64 (2000); Marriage status: 18.3% never married, 71.0% now married, 6.2% widowed, 4.5% divorced (2000); Foreign born: 2.4% (2000); Ancestry (includes multiple ancestries): 42.0% German, 15.7% United States or American, 14.2% Irish, 11.9% English, 8.4% Norwegian (2000).
Economy: In agricultural area; dairy products. Manufacturing: machinery, fabricated metal products; concrete burial vaults. Employment by occupation: 17.5% management, 9.5% professional, 10.1% services, 24.8% sales, 3.7% farming, 12.3% construction, 22.0% production (2000).
Income: Per capita income: $20,023 (2000); Median household income: $51,635 (2000); Poverty rate: 7.0% (2000).
Taxes: Total city taxes per capita: $114 (1997); City property taxes per capita: $112 (1997).
Education: High school graduation rate: 84.2% (2000); College graduation rate: 9.0% (2000).
Housing: Homeownership rate: 85.8% (2000); Median home value: $129,000 (2000); Median rent: $544 per month (2000); Median age of housing: 54 years (2000).
Transportation: Commute to work: 82.9% car, 1.3% public transportation, 3.6% walk, 11.8% work from home (2000); Travel time to work: 32.6% less than 15 minutes, 33.0% 15 to 30 minutes, 16.4% 30 to 45 minutes, 6.8% 45 to 60 minutes, 11.1% 60 minutes or more (2000)

SPRING PRAIRIE (town). Covers a land area of 35.747 square miles and a water area of 0.083 square miles. Located at 42.71° N. Lat.; 88.35° W. Long. Elevation is 1,018 feet.
Population: 2,089 (2000); Race: 98.4% White, 0.3% Black, 0.3% Asian, 0.2% American Indian and Alaska Native, 0.9% Hispanic of any race, 0.5% two or more races (2000); Density: 58.4 persons per square mile (2000); Age: 26.9% under 18, 8.2% over 64 (2000); Marriage status: 22.6% never married, 65.4% now married, 4.3% widowed, 7.7% divorced (2000); Foreign born: 0.8% (2000); Ancestry (includes multiple ancestries): 47.9% German, 14.3% Irish, 11.7% Polish, 10.0% English, 5.4% United States or American (2000).
Economy: Employment by occupation: 12.1% management, 15.3% professional, 11.5% services, 21.8% sales, 2.0% farming, 16.4% construction 21.0% production (2000).
Income: Per capita income: $22,471 (2000); Median household income: $59,583 (2000); Poverty rate: 3.1% (2000).
Taxes: Total city taxes per capita: $77 (1997); City property taxes per capita: $73 (1997).
Education: High school graduation rate: 88.1% (2000); College graduation rate: 17.2% (2000).
Housing: Homeownership rate: 89.0% (2000); Median home value: $146,300 (2000); Median rent: $529 per month (2000); Median age of housing: 29 years (2000).
Transportation: Commute to work: 89.9% car, 0.0% public transportation, 3.0% walk, 6.5% work from home (2000); Travel time to work: 25.6% less than 15 minutes, 37.0% 15 to 30 minutes, 18.6% 30 to 45 minutes, 11.0% 45 to 60 minutes, 7.7% 60 minutes or more (2000)

SUGAR CREEK (town). Covers a land area of 32.961 square miles and a water area of 0.779 square miles. Located at 42.73° N. Lat.; 88.58° W. Long.

Population: 3,331 (2000); Race: 97.2% White, 0.1% Black, 0.8% Asian, 0.8% American Indian and Alaska Native, 3.0% Hispanic of any race, 0.1% two or more races (2000); Density: 101.1 persons per square mile (2000); Age: 28.5% under 18, 9.4% over 64 (2000); Marriage status: 20.3% never married, 65.7% now married, 5.2% widowed, 8.8% divorced (2000); Foreign born: 2.5% (2000); Ancestry (includes multiple ancestries): 48.0% German, 14.4% Irish, 10.2% English, 8.8% Polish, 6.2% Norwegian (2000).
Economy: Employment by occupation: 13.2% management, 17.4% professional, 16.4% services, 19.3% sales, 0.7% farming, 11.9% construction, 21.0% production (2000).
Income: Per capita income: $21,737 (2000); Median household income: $51,161 (2000); Poverty rate: 5.3% (2000).
Taxes: Total city taxes per capita: $107 (2000); City property taxes per capita: $96 (2000).
Education: High school graduation rate: 86.9% (2000); College graduation rate: 18.5% (2000).
Housing: Homeownership rate: 88.3% (2000); Median home value: $132,000 (2000); Median rent: $475 per month (2000); Median age of housing: 28 years (2000).
Transportation: Commute to work: 91.1% car, 0.9% public transportation, 1.2% walk, 5.3% work from home (2000); Travel time to work: 24.9% less than 15 minutes, 45.4% 15 to 30 minutes, 13.2% 30 to 45 minutes, 9.7% 45 to 60 minutes, 6.7% 60 minutes or more (2000)

TROY (town). Covers a land area of 34.745 square miles and a water area of 0.691 square miles. Located at 42.80° N. Lat.; 88.47° W. Long. Elevation is 870 feet.
Population: 2,328 (2000); Race: 99.9% White, 0.0% Black, 0.0% Asian, 0.0% American Indian and Alaska Native, 0.5% Hispanic of any race, 0.1% two or more races (2000); Density: 67.0 persons per square mile (2000); Age: 25.3% under 18, 11.2% over 64 (2000); Marriage status: 22.6% never married, 67.7% now married, 2.8% widowed, 6.9% divorced (2000); Foreign born: 2.2% (2000); Ancestry (includes multiple ancestries): 44.9% German, 13.3% Polish, 11.8% Irish, 10.4% English, 6.2% United States or American (2000).
Economy: In dairy and livestock area; steel products, condensed milk, feed. Manufacturing: canvas products, meat products, steel tubing, industrial ovens, castings. Resort lakes nearby. Alpine Valley Ski Area to Southwest. Employment by occupation: 13.6% management, 14.1% professional, 10.5% services, 22.9% sales, 1.7% farming, 12.3% construction, 24.8% production (2000).
Income: Per capita income: $24,200 (2000); Median household income: $57,604 (2000); Poverty rate: 4.6% (2000).
Taxes: Total city taxes per capita: $79 (1997); City property taxes per capita: $68 (1997).
Education: High school graduation rate: 87.6% (2000); College graduation rate: 19.6% (2000).
Housing: Homeownership rate: 90.0% (2000); Median home value: $165,300 (2000); Median rent: $435 per month (2000); Median age of housing: 27 years (2000).
Transportation: Commute to work: 93.5% car, 0.6% public transportation, 1.5% walk, 3.3% work from home (2000); Travel time to work: 24.9% less than 15 minutes, 35.1% 15 to 30 minutes, 22.9% 30 to 45 minutes, 9.5% 45 to 60 minutes, 7.6% 60 minutes or more (2000)

WALWORTH (village). Covers a land area of 1.455 square miles and a water area of 0 square miles. Located at 42.53° N. Lat.; 88.59° W. Long. Elevation is 998 feet.
Population: 2,304 (2000); Race: 97.7% White, 0.0% Black, 0.3% Asian, 0.2% American Indian and Alaska Native, 7.6% Hispanic of any race, 1.3% two or more races (2000); Density: 1,583.9 persons per square mile (2000); Age: 26.4% under 18, 17.5% over 64 (2000); Marriage status: 22.4% never married, 56.4% now married, 11.0% widowed, 10.1% divorced (2000); Foreign born: 7.0% (2000); Ancestry (includes multiple ancestries): 38.3% German, 13.8% Irish, 12.0% English, 8.6% Other groups, 7.9% Norwegian (2000).
Economy: Single-family building permits issued: 8 (2001) / 17 (2000); Multi-family building permits issued: 4 (2001) / 16 (2000); Employment by occupation: 9.0% management, 17.8% professional, 17.6% services, 18.8% sales, 0.8% farming, 10.9% construction, 24.9% production (2000).
Income: Per capita income: $19,311 (2000); Median household income: $43,672 (2000); Poverty rate: 8.7% (2000).
Taxes: Total city taxes per capita: $346 (1997); City property taxes per capita: $326 (1997).
Education: High school graduation rate: 84.4% (2000); College graduation rate: 15.6% (2000).

School District(s)

Big Foot UHS (09-12)
2000 Enrollment: 524 262-275-2116
Walworth J1 (PK-08)
2000 Enrollment: 516 262-275-6896

Housing: Homeownership rate: 63.7% (2000); Median home value: $113,500 (2000); Median rent: $508 per month (2000); Median age of housing: 41 years (2000).
Safety: Violent crime rate: 38.8 per 10,000 population; Property crime rate: 310.3 per 10,000 population (2001).
Newspapers: The Times (1 x week)
Transportation: Commute to work: 89.9% car, 1.2% public transportation, 4.9% walk, 3.3% work from home (2000); Travel time to work: 39.4% less than 15 minutes, 36.0% 15 to 30 minutes, 11.5% 30 to 45 minutes, 6.5% 45 to 60 minutes, 6.6% 60 minutes or more (2000)

WALWORTH (town). Covers a land area of 28.901 square miles and a water area of 0.611 square miles. Located at 42.54° N. Lat.; 88.59° W. Long. Elevation is 998 feet.
Population: 1,676 (2000); Race: 98.4% White, 0.0% Black, 0.2% Asian, 0.0% American Indian and Alaska Native, 2.3% Hispanic of any race, 0.9% two or more races (2000); Density: 58.0 persons per square mile (2000); Age: 24.9% under 18, 16.4% over 64 (2000); Marriage status: 20.7% never married, 60.5% now married, 10.4% widowed, 8.4% divorced (2000); Foreign born: 3.2% (2000); Ancestry (includes multiple ancestries): 40.3% German, 17.4% English, 15.4% Irish, 7.3% Norwegian, 6.2% Polish (2000).
Economy: Vegetables; livestock. Manufacturing: thermofoam clamshells, light aircraft components. Employment by occupation: 19.2% management, 14.3% professional, 16.2% services, 18.9% sales, 0.6% farming, 11.8% construction, 19.0% production (2000).
Income: Per capita income: $24,817 (2000); Median household income: $56,250 (2000); Poverty rate: 8.0% (2000).
Taxes: Total city taxes per capita: $83 (1997); City property taxes per capita: $74 (1997).
Education: High school graduation rate: 86.0% (2000); College graduation rate: 19.4% (2000).
Housing: Homeownership rate: 79.5% (2000); Median home value: $155,100 (2000); Median rent: $436 per month (2000); Median age of housing: 34 years (2000).
Transportation: Commute to work: 83.7% car, 2.2% public transportation, 1.9% walk, 9.9% work from home (2000); Travel time to work: 44.3% less than 15 minutes, 29.1% 15 to 30 minutes, 9.9% 30 to 45 minutes, 7.9% 45 to 60 minutes, 8.8% 60 minutes or more (2000)

WHITEWATER (city). Covers a land area of 6.986 square miles and a water area of 0.293 square miles. Located at 42.83° N. Lat.; 88.73° W. Long. Elevation is 840 feet.
History: Whitewater grew up around a mill built here in 1839. In 1852 the Milwaukee & Mississippi Railroad arrived, and in 1857 George Esterly moved his reaper plant north from La Grange to Whitewater, becoming the major industry until 1893.
Population: 13,437 (2000); Race: 92.3% White, 2.3% Black, 1.2% Asian, 0.7% American Indian and Alaska Native, 6.4% Hispanic of any race, 1.0% two or more races (2000); Density: 1,923.5 persons per square mile (2000); Age: 12.8% under 18, 9.2% over 64 (2000); Marriage status: 57.7% never married, 32.0% now married, 5.4% widowed, 5.0% divorced (2000); Foreign born: 4.4% (2000); Ancestry (includes multiple ancestries): 41.8% German, 12.9% Irish, 9.0% Norwegian, 8.8% Other groups, 7.8% English (2000).
Vital Statistics: Birth rate: 72.2 per 10,000 population (1998)
Economy: Single-family building permits issued: 17 (2001) / 21 (2000); Multi-family building permits issued: 70 (2001) / 69 (2000); Employment by occupation: 8.9% management, 17.1% professional, 22.3% services, 31.2% sales, 0.8% farming, 3.5% construction, 16.1% production (2000).
Income: Per capita income: $13,965 (2000); Median household income: $31,793 (2000); Poverty rate: 27.4% (2000).
Taxes: Total city taxes per capita: $167 (2000); City property taxes per capita: $144 (2000).
Education: High school graduation rate: 81.3% (2000); College graduation rate: 31.8% (2000).

School District(s)

Whitewater (KG-12)
2000 Enrollment: 2,079 262-472-8708

Four-year College(s)

University of Wisconsin-Whitewater (Public)
2001 Enrollment: 10,549 414-472-1234
2001 Tuition: In-state $2,776; Out-of-state $11,288

Housing: Homeownership rate: 36.2% (2000); Median home value: $115,500 (2000); Median rent: $459 per month (2000); Median age of housing: 35 years (2000).
Safety: Violent crime rate: 5.9 per 10,000 population; Property crime rate: 249.0 per 10,000 population (2001).
Newspapers: The Whitewater Register (1 x week)
Transportation: Commute to work: 78.4% car, 0.6% public transportation, 17.3% walk, 2.9% work from home (2000); Travel time to work: 55.4% less than 15 minutes, 22.5% 15 to 30 minutes, 13.5% 30 to 45 minutes, 3.8% 45 to 60 minutes, 4.8% 60 minutes or more (2000)
Additional Information Contacts
Whitewater Chamber of Commerce 262-473-4005

WHITEWATER (town). Covers a land area of 29.622 square miles and a water area of 0.975 square miles. Located at 42.78° N. Lat.; 88.70° W. Long. Elevation is 840 feet.
Population: 1,399 (2000); Race: 98.4% White, 0.0% Black, 0.6% Asian, 0.2% American Indian and Alaska Native, 1.3% Hispanic of any race, 0.9% two or more races (2000); Density: 47.2 persons per square mile (2000); Age: 20.3% under 18, 14.0% over 64 (2000); Marriage status: 17.6% never married, 72.8% now married, 3.1% widowed, 6.6% divorced (2000); Foreign born: 1.0% (2000); Ancestry (includes multiple ancestries): 50.1% German, 14.5% English, 13.2% Irish, 11.6% Polish, 6.4% Norwegian (2000).
Economy: Employment by occupation: 16.9% management, 26.4% professional, 17.1% services, 20.3% sales, 0.0% farming, 4.8% construction, 14.4% production (2000).
Income: Per capita income: $28,422 (2000); Median household income: $59,946 (2000); Poverty rate: 2.6% (2000).
Taxes: Total city taxes per capita: $93 (1997); City property taxes per capita: $91 (1997).
Education: High school graduation rate: 94.9% (2000); College graduation rate: 38.9% (2000).
Housing: Homeownership rate: 87.6% (2000); Median home value: $174,400 (2000); Median rent: $470 per month (2000); Median age of housing: 29 years (2000).
Transportation: Commute to work: 90.9% car, 0.0% public transportation, 3.2% walk, 5.9% work from home (2000); Travel time to work: 31.2% less than 15 minutes, 30.0% 15 to 30 minutes, 17.6% 30 to 45 minutes, 5.0% 45 to 60 minutes, 16.2% 60 minutes or more (2000)

WILLIAMS BAY (village). Covers a land area of 2.646 square miles and a water area of 0.817 square miles. Located at 42.57° N. Lat.; 88.54° W. Long. Elevation is 950 feet.
Population: 2,415 (2000); Race: 97.9% White, 0.0% Black, 0.6% Asian, 0.3% American Indian and Alaska Native, 4.4% Hispanic of any race, 0.2% two or more races (2000); Density: 912.6 persons per square mile (2000); Age: 27.1% under 18, 18.1% over 64 (2000); Marriage status: 20.3% never married, 61.5% now married, 9.3% widowed, 9.0% divorced (2000); Foreign born: 3.4% (2000); Ancestry (includes multiple ancestries): 34.4% German, 23.7% Irish, 10.5% English, 9.5% Norwegian, 7.5% Swedish (2000).
Economy: Manufacturing of textiles, consumer goods. Yerkes Observatory of University of Chicago is here. Single-family building permits issued: 24 (2001) / 27 (2000); Multi-family building permits issued: 17 (2001) / 28 (2000); Employment by occupation: 21.0% management, 24.0% professional, 14.1% services, 23.5% sales, 0.4% farming, 6.4% construction, 10.5% production (2000).
Income: Per capita income: $26,231 (2000); Median household income: $50,450 (2000); Poverty rate: 7.2% (2000).
Taxes: Total city taxes per capita: $789 (1997); City property taxes per capita: $747 (1997).
Education: High school graduation rate: 94.4% (2000); College graduation rate: 39.5% (2000).

School District(s)

Williams Bay (KG-12)
2000 Enrollment: 534 262-245-1575

Housing: Homeownership rate: 74.2% (2000); Median home value: $157,000 (2000); Median rent: $535 per month (2000); Median age of housing: 34 years (2000).
Safety: Violent crime rate: 0.0 per 10,000 population; Property crime rate: 139.8 per 10,000 population (2001).
Transportation: Commute to work: 92.7% car, 1.3% public transportation, 2.8% walk, 2.7% work from home (2000); Travel time to work: 41.9% less than 15 minutes, 28.0% 15 to 30 minutes, 6.5% 30 to 45 minutes, 9.0% 45 to 60 minutes, 14.6% 60 minutes or more (2000)

Washburn County

Located in northwestern Wisconsin; drained by the Namekagon and Yellow Rivers; includes many lakes. Covers a land area of 809.70 square miles, a water area of 43.40 square miles, and is located in the Central Time Zone. The county government was organized in 1883. County seat is Shell Lake.

Weather Station: Spooner Experiment Farm — Elevation: 1,099 feet

	Jan	Feb	Mar	Apr	May	Jun	Jul	Aug	Sep	Oct	Nov	Dec
High	21	29	40	57	70	78	82	79	70	58	39	26
Low	-0	6	18	31	43	52	57	55	47	36	23	8
Precip	0.9	0.6	1.4	2.2	3.1	3.9	4.1	4.5	3.8	2.7	1.9	0.9
Snow	14.2	6.9	8.6	2.5	tr	0.0	0.0	0.0	0.0	0.7	7.7	10.7

High and Low temperatures in degrees Fahrenheit; Precipitation and Snow in inches

Population: 16,036 (2000); Race: 97.2% White, 0.1% Black, 0.2% Asian, 1.0% American Indian and Alaska Native, 1.0% Hispanic of any race, 1.1% two or more races (2000); Density: 19.8 persons per square mile (2000); Age: 23.8% under 18, 18.6% over 64 (2000).
Religion: Five largest groups: 15.7% Catholic Church, 12.8% Evangelical Lutheran Church in America, 4.5% The United Methodist Church, 3.5% The Wesleyan Church, 3.3% Lutheran Church—Missouri Synod (2000).
Economy: Unemployment rate: 5.6% (11/2002); Total civilian labor force: 8,138 (11/2002); Leading industries: 28.2% manufacturing; 19.6% retail trade; 14.5% health care and social assistance (2000); Companies that employ more than 1,000 persons: 0 (2000); Companies that employ more than 100 persons: 6 (2000); Farms: 354 totaling 97,839 acres (1997); Minority business ownership rate: 0.0% (1997); Women business ownership rate: 19.8% (1997); Retail sales per capita: $11,408 (1997). Single-family building permits issued: 227 (2001) / 235 (2000); Multi-family building permits issued: 4 (2001) / 6 (2000).
Income: Per capita income: $17,341 (2000); Median household income: $33,716 (2000); Poverty rate: 9.9% (2000); Bankruptcy rate: 2.56% (2001).
Taxes: Total county taxes per capita: $331 (1997); County property taxes per capita: $280 (1997).
Education: High school graduation rate: 83.7% (2000); College graduation rate: 15.2% (2000).
Housing: Homeownership rate: 80.9% (2000); Median home value: $85,700 (2000); Median rent: $337 per month (2000); Median age of housing: 28 years (2000).
Health: Birth rate: 91.7 per 10,000 population (1998); Age adjusted death rate: 91.8 per 10,000 population (1999); Age adjusted cancer mortality rate: 295.5 deaths per 100,000 population (1999). Number of physicians: 11.8 per 10,000 population (1999); Number of hospital beds: 115.4 per 10,000 population (1999).
Elections: 2000 Presidential election results: 45.9% Gore, 48.6% Bush, 4.7% Nader, 0.4% Buchanan
National and State Parks: Bean Brook State Wildlife Management Area; Bear Lake State Public Fishery Area; Beaver Brook State Public Hunting Grounds; McKenzie Creek State Public Fishery Area; Sawyer Creek State Public Hunting Grounds; Spooner Lake State Public Fishery Area; Whalen Creek State Public Hunting Grounds
Additional Information Contacts
Washburn County Government Offices 715-468-4600
Long Lake Chamber of Commerce 715-354-7449
Spooner Chamber of Commerce 715-635-2168

Washburn County Communities

BARRONETT (town). Covers a land area of 32.756 square miles and a water area of 0.903 square miles. Located at 45.68° N. Lat.; 91.98° W. Long.
Population: 405 (2000); Race: 98.8% White, 0.0% Black, 0.0% Asian, 0.0% American Indian and Alaska Native, 0.0% Hispanic of any race, 1.2% two or more races (2000); Density: 12.4 persons per square mile (2000); Age: 23.4% under 18, 11.9% over 64 (2000); Marriage status: 23.4% never married, 62.9% now married, 4.0% widowed, 9.7% divorced (2000); Foreign born: 0.0% (2000); Ancestry (includes multiple ancestries): 36.3% German, 15.7% Norwegian, 13.9% United States or American, 10.4% Irish, 9.5% Swedish (2000).
Economy: Employment by occupation: 11.5% management, 13.9% professional, 12.5% services, 20.7% sales, 5.3% farming, 9.1% construction, 26.9% production (2000).

Income: Per capita income: $14,434 (2000); Median household income: $40,139 (2000); Poverty rate: 6.0% (2000).
Taxes: Total city taxes per capita: $36 (1997); City property taxes per capita: $36 (1997).
Education: High school graduation rate: 84.4% (2000); College graduation rate: 11.3% (2000).
Housing: Homeownership rate: 94.0% (2000); Median home value: $60,000 (2000); Median rent: $125 per month (2000); Median age of housing: 29 years (2000).
Transportation: Commute to work: 87.0% car, 0.0% public transportation, 1.9% walk, 10.6% work from home (2000); Travel time to work: 33.9% less than 15 minutes, 38.2% 15 to 30 minutes, 17.7% 30 to 45 minutes, 7.0% 45 to 60 minutes, 3.2% 60 minutes or more (2000)

BASHAW (town). Covers a land area of 33.518 square miles and a water area of 0.369 square miles. Located at 45.78° N. Lat.; 91.97° W. Long.
Population: 921 (2000); Race: 99.6% White, 0.2% Black, 0.0% Asian, 0.0% American Indian and Alaska Native, 0.6% Hispanic of any race, 0.2% two or more races (2000); Density: 27.5 persons per square mile (2000); Age: 27.1% under 18, 12.3% over 64 (2000); Marriage status: 20.6% never married, 72.1% now married, 2.6% widowed, 4.7% divorced (2000); Foreign born: 0.5% (2000); Ancestry (includes multiple ancestries): 40.9% German, 16.1% Norwegian, 12.9% Irish, 10.6% English, 9.7% Swedish (2000).
Economy: Employment by occupation: 13.2% management, 15.3% professional, 17.7% services, 22.0% sales, 2.0% farming, 12.6% construction, 17.1% production (2000).
Income: Per capita income: $16,982 (2000); Median household income: $43,500 (2000); Poverty rate: 8.8% (2000).
Taxes: Total city taxes per capita: $36 (1997); City property taxes per capita: $34 (1997).
Education: High school graduation rate: 86.0% (2000); College graduation rate: 13.7% (2000).
Housing: Homeownership rate: 90.7% (2000); Median home value: $90,500 (2000); Median rent: $231 per month (2000); Median age of housing: 27 years (2000).
Transportation: Commute to work: 87.5% car, 0.0% public transportation, 1.8% walk, 10.4% work from home (2000); Travel time to work: 51.8% less than 15 minutes, 26.3% 15 to 30 minutes, 12.1% 30 to 45 minutes, 5.5% 45 to 60 minutes, 4.3% 60 minutes or more (2000)

BASS LAKE (town). Covers a land area of 32.323 square miles and a water area of 0.824 square miles. Located at 45.95° N. Lat.; 91.59° W. Long.
Population: 535 (2000); Race: 96.3% White, 0.0% Black, 1.3% Asian, 0.4% American Indian and Alaska Native, 0.4% Hispanic of any race, 2.0% two or more races (2000); Density: 16.6 persons per square mile (2000); Age: 24.4% under 18, 13.6% over 64 (2000); Marriage status: 18.0% never married, 68.8% now married, 4.3% widowed, 9.0% divorced (2000); Foreign born: 1.3% (2000); Ancestry (includes multiple ancestries): 46.0% German, 17.9% Norwegian, 15.6% Irish, 9.7% English, 7.9% Polish (2000).
Economy: Employment by occupation: 7.9% management, 13.7% professional, 13.7% services, 25.3% sales, 2.1% farming, 15.4% construction, 22.0% production (2000).
Income: Per capita income: $15,144 (2000); Median household income: $34,922 (2000); Poverty rate: 7.5% (2000).
Taxes: Total city taxes per capita: $69 (1997); City property taxes per capita: $69 (1997).
Education: High school graduation rate: 83.8% (2000); College graduation rate: 11.8% (2000).
Housing: Homeownership rate: 93.3% (2000); Median home value: $94,300 (2000); Median rent: $175 per month (2000); Median age of housing: 18 years (2000).
Transportation: Commute to work: 91.3% car, 0.0% public transportation, 0.4% walk, 8.3% work from home (2000); Travel time to work: 23.8% less than 15 minutes, 57.6% 15 to 30 minutes, 9.0% 30 to 45 minutes, 5.7% 45 to 60 minutes, 3.8% 60 minutes or more (2000)

BEAVER BROOK (town). Covers a land area of 32.439 square miles and a water area of 0.477 square miles. Located at 45.77° N. Lat.; 91.85° W. Long. Elevation is 1,302 feet.
Population: 643 (2000); Race: 97.5% White, 0.0% Black, 0.8% Asian, 0.7% American Indian and Alaska Native, 0.0% Hispanic of any race, 0.7% two or more races (2000); Density: 19.8 persons per square mile (2000); Age: 26.6% under 18, 12.5% over 64 (2000); Marriage status: 21.6% never married, 63.1% now married, 5.8% widowed, 9.5% divorced (2000); Foreign born: 2.3% (2000); Ancestry (includes multiple ancestries): 45.2% German, 15.1% Norwegian, 10.7% Swedish, 10.2% English, 7.7% Irish (2000).
Economy: Employment by occupation: 14.7% management, 14.7% professional, 15.3% services, 24.5% sales, 1.2% farming, 16.2% construction, 13.5% production (2000).
Income: Per capita income: $16,797 (2000); Median household income: $40,156 (2000); Poverty rate: 8.8% (2000).
Taxes: Total city taxes per capita: $17 (1997); City property taxes per capita: $15 (1997).
Education: High school graduation rate: 88.7% (2000); College graduation rate: 15.0% (2000).
Housing: Homeownership rate: 85.4% (2000); Median home value: $78,800 (2000); Median rent: $355 per month (2000); Median age of housing: 25 years (2000).
Transportation: Commute to work: 87.7% car, 0.0% public transportation, 4.3% walk, 8.0% work from home (2000); Travel time to work: 57.5% less than 15 minutes, 23.1% 15 to 30 minutes, 10.4% 30 to 45 minutes, 0.7% 45 to 60 minutes, 8.4% 60 minutes or more (2000)

BIRCHWOOD (village). Covers a land area of 1.127 square miles and a water area of 0.158 square miles. Located at 45.65° N. Lat.; 91.55° W. Long. Elevation is 1,264 feet.
Population: 518 (2000); Race: 99.8% White, 0.0% Black, 0.0% Asian, 0.0% American Indian and Alaska Native, 2.9% Hispanic of any race, 0.2% two or more races (2000); Density: 459.7 persons per square mile (2000); Age: 26.0% under 18, 18.8% over 64 (2000); Marriage status: 24.8% never married, 49.4% now married, 8.3% widowed, 17.5% divorced (2000); Foreign born: 0.4% (2000); Ancestry (includes multiple ancestries): 33.7% German, 13.4% Norwegian, 10.5% Czech, 9.1% Irish, 7.6% English (2000).
Economy: Single-family building permits issued: 1 (2001) / 1 (2000); Multi-family building permits issued: 4 (2001) / 4 (2000); Employment by occupation: 5.3% management, 10.6% professional, 23.8% services, 18.5% sales, 0.0% farming, 10.1% construction, 31.7% production (2000).
Income: Per capita income: $14,237 (2000); Median household income: $23,636 (2000); Poverty rate: 11.9% (2000).
Taxes: Total city taxes per capita: $82 (1997); City property taxes per capita: $69 (1997).
Education: High school graduation rate: 82.9% (2000); College graduation rate: 8.8% (2000).

School District(s)

Birchwood (PK-12)
2000 Enrollment: 331 715-354-3471
Housing: Homeownership rate: 70.1% (2000); Median home value: $62,500 (2000); Median rent: $227 per month (2000); Median age of housing: 43 years (2000).
Transportation: Commute to work: 77.2% car, 0.0% public transportation, 14.7% walk, 4.9% work from home (2000); Travel time to work: 42.3% less than 15 minutes, 25.1% 15 to 30 minutes, 25.7% 30 to 45 minutes, 3.4% 45 to 60 minutes, 3.4% 60 minutes or more (2000)

BIRCHWOOD (town). Covers a land area of 63.833 square miles and a water area of 6.139 square miles. Located at 45.72° N. Lat.; 91.60° W. Long. Elevation is 1,264 feet.
Population: 453 (2000); Race: 97.1% White, 0.0% Black, 0.0% Asian, 0.6% American Indian and Alaska Native, 3.3% Hispanic of any race, 2.1% two or more races (2000); Density: 7.1 persons per square mile (2000); Age: 15.6% under 18, 19.9% over 64 (2000); Marriage status: 15.6% never married, 74.6% now married, 3.3% widowed, 6.4% divorced (2000); Foreign born: 0.2% (2000); Ancestry (includes multiple ancestries): 34.5% German, 13.6% Norwegian, 12.9% Irish, 12.5% English, 8.0% Other groups (2000).
Economy: In lake resort area; wood products, canoes, lumber. Employment by occupation: 15.2% management, 13.8% professional, 11.4% services, 31.9% sales, 1.0% farming, 12.4% construction, 14.3% production (2000).
Income: Per capita income: $21,062 (2000); Median household income: $40,066 (2000); Poverty rate: 9.2% (2000).
Taxes: Total city taxes per capita: $365 (1997); City property taxes per capita: $362 (1997).
Education: High school graduation rate: 90.1% (2000); College graduation rate: 18.3% (2000).
Housing: Homeownership rate: 93.1% (2000); Median home value: $154,900 (2000); Median rent: $438 per month (2000); Median age of housing: 24 years (2000).
Transportation: Commute to work: 87.1% car, 0.0% public transportation, 3.0% walk, 9.9% work from home (2000); Travel time to work: 18.7% less than 15 minutes, 26.4% 15 to 30 minutes, 36.8% 30 to 45 minutes, 10.4% 45 to 60 minutes, 7.7% 60 minutes or more (2000)

BROOKLYN (town). Covers a land area of 35.706 square miles and a water area of 0.634 square miles. Located at 46.00° N. Lat.; 91.85° W. Long.
Population: 281 (2000); Race: 96.3% White, 0.0% Black, 1.6% Asian, 1.2% American Indian and Alaska Native, 0.4% Hispanic of any race, 0.0% two or more races (2000); Density: 7.9 persons per square mile (2000); Age: 22.4% under 18, 19.5% over 64 (2000); Marriage status: 17.8% never married, 62.4% now married, 10.7% widowed, 9.1% divorced (2000); Foreign born: 2.8% (2000); Ancestry (includes multiple ancestries): 38.2% German, 15.0% Norwegian, 14.6% Irish, 8.1% English, 7.7% French (except Basque) (2000).
Economy: Employment by occupation: 5.8% management, 12.4% professional, 20.7% services, 26.4% sales, 5.0% farming, 12.4% construction, 17.4% production (2000).
Income: Per capita income: $19,165 (2000); Median household income: $37,083 (2000); Poverty rate: 9.0% (2000).
Taxes: Total city taxes per capita: $84 (1997); City property taxes per capita: $81 (1997).
Education: High school graduation rate: 87.7% (2000); College graduation rate: 10.2% (2000).
Housing: Homeownership rate: 89.9% (2000); Median home value: $87,500 (2000); Median rent: $625 per month (2000); Median age of housing: 25 years (2000).
Transportation: Commute to work: 87.4% car, 0.0% public transportation, 1.7% walk, 10.9% work from home (2000); Travel time to work: 9.4% less than 15 minutes, 61.3% 15 to 30 minutes, 17.9% 30 to 45 minutes, 11.3% 45 to 60 minutes, 0.0% 60 minutes or more (2000)

CASEY (town). Covers a land area of 31.131 square miles and a water area of 3.043 square miles. Located at 45.94° N. Lat.; 91.95° W. Long.
Population: 466 (2000); Race: 97.8% White, 0.0% Black, 0.0% Asian, 2.2% American Indian and Alaska Native, 0.0% Hispanic of any race, 0.0% two or more races (2000); Density: 15.0 persons per square mile (2000); Age: 19.6% under 18, 23.5% over 64 (2000); Marriage status: 15.3% never married, 69.8% now married, 8.7% widowed, 6.1% divorced (2000); Foreign born: 1.5% (2000); Ancestry (includes multiple ancestries): 54.5% German, 15.4% English, 11.6% Norwegian, 10.5% Irish, 7.7% Swedish (2000).
Economy: Employment by occupation: 8.1% management, 28.3% professional, 16.2% services, 14.6% sales, 1.5% farming, 12.6% construction, 18.7% production (2000).
Income: Per capita income: $20,611 (2000); Median household income: $33,125 (2000); Poverty rate: 8.8% (2000).
Taxes: Total city taxes per capita: $94 (1997); City property taxes per capita: $92 (1997).
Education: High school graduation rate: 81.8% (2000); College graduation rate: 26.8% (2000).
Housing: Homeownership rate: 94.1% (2000); Median home value: $111,400 (2000); Median rent: $375 per month (2000); Median age of housing: 24 years (2000).
Transportation: Commute to work: 94.2% car, 0.0% public transportation, 0.0% walk, 5.8% work from home (2000); Travel time to work: 14.0% less than 15 minutes, 55.9% 15 to 30 minutes, 21.2% 30 to 45 minutes, 5.6% 45 to 60 minutes, 3.4% 60 minutes or more (2000)

CHICOG (town). Covers a land area of 43.574 square miles and a water area of 2.022 square miles. Located at 46.04° N. Lat.; 91.95° W. Long.
Population: 268 (2000); Race: 98.5% White, 0.0% Black, 0.0% Asian, 0.8% American Indian and Alaska Native, 0.8% Hispanic of any race, 0.8% two or more races (2000); Density: 6.2 persons per square mile (2000); Age: 12.4% under 18, 21.1% over 64 (2000); Marriage status: 10.8% never married, 78.8% now married, 4.6% widowed, 5.8% divorced (2000); Foreign born: 0.0% (2000); Ancestry (includes multiple ancestries): 42.9% German, 15.4% Irish, 7.5% Norwegian, 5.3% Dutch, 4.9% Scotch-Irish (2000).
Economy: Employment by occupation: 2.6% management, 8.7% professional, 20.9% services, 26.1% sales, 1.7% farming, 18.3% construction, 21.7% production (2000).
Income: Per capita income: $16,438 (2000); Median household income: $32,500 (2000); Poverty rate: 9.4% (2000).
Taxes: Total city taxes per capita: $360 (1997); City property taxes per capita: $355 (1997).
Education: High school graduation rate: 86.1% (2000); College graduation rate: 10.8% (2000).
Housing: Homeownership rate: 94.9% (2000); Median home value: $125,000 (2000); Median rent: $225 per month (2000); Median age of housing: 27 years (2000).
Transportation: Commute to work: 84.1% car, 0.0% public transportation, 1.8% walk, 12.4% work from home (2000); Travel time to work: 18.2% less than 15 minutes, 44.4% 15 to 30 minutes, 17.2% 30 to 45 minutes, 8.1% 45 to 60 minutes, 12.1% 60 minutes or more (2000)

CRYSTAL (town). Covers a land area of 35.069 square miles and a water area of 0.618 square miles. Located at 45.85° N. Lat.; 91.71° W. Long.
Population: 323 (2000); Race: 98.4% White, 0.0% Black, 0.0% Asian, 0.8% American Indian and Alaska Native, 0.0% Hispanic of any race, 0.8% two or more races (2000); Density: 9.2 persons per square mile (2000); Age: 20.3% under 18, 19.5% over 64 (2000); Marriage status: 23.3% never married, 56.5% now married, 8.5% widowed, 11.7% divorced (2000); Foreign born: 2.3% (2000); Ancestry (includes multiple ancestries): 35.5% German, 21.1% Norwegian, 11.3% Irish, 8.6% Swedish, 7.4% Polish (2000).
Economy: Employment by occupation: 8.5% management, 15.3% professional, 20.3% services, 16.1% sales, 6.8% farming, 17.8% construction, 15.3% production (2000).
Income: Per capita income: $15,706 (2000); Median household income: $25,000 (2000); Poverty rate: 9.0% (2000).
Taxes: Total city taxes per capita: $42 (1997); City property taxes per capita: $42 (1997).
Education: High school graduation rate: 72.4% (2000); College graduation rate: 13.5% (2000).
Housing: Homeownership rate: 90.8% (2000); Median home value: $81,000 (2000); Median rent: $325 per month (2000); Median age of housing: 29 years (2000).
Transportation: Commute to work: 76.3% car, 0.0% public transportation, 1.7% walk, 22.0% work from home (2000); Travel time to work: 21.7% less than 15 minutes, 54.3% 15 to 30 minutes, 9.8% 30 to 45 minutes, 9.8% 45 to 60 minutes, 4.3% 60 minutes or more (2000)

EVERGREEN (town). Covers a land area of 33.621 square miles and a water area of 1.285 square miles. Located at 45.85° N. Lat.; 91.97° W. Long.
Population: 1,076 (2000); Race: 95.9% White, 0.2% Black, 0.0% Asian, 0.3% American Indian and Alaska Native, 0.6% Hispanic of any race, 3.7% two or more races (2000); Density: 32.0 persons per square mile (2000); Age: 28.2% under 18, 16.0% over 64 (2000); Marriage status: 22.6% never married, 62.1% now married, 6.1% widowed, 9.2% divorced (2000); Foreign born: 0.7% (2000); Ancestry (includes multiple ancestries): 43.0% German, 13.3% Norwegian, 13.0% English, 11.1% Irish, 6.7% Swedish (2000).
Economy: Employment by occupation: 8.9% management, 15.1% professional, 19.1% services, 22.6% sales, 1.2% farming, 12.9% construction, 20.1% production (2000).
Income: Per capita income: $15,613 (2000); Median household income: $33,036 (2000); Poverty rate: 7.6% (2000).
Taxes: Total city taxes per capita: $1 (1997); City property taxes per capita: $0 (1997).
Education: High school graduation rate: 83.9% (2000); College graduation rate: 15.9% (2000).
Housing: Homeownership rate: 89.3% (2000); Median home value: $71,300 (2000); Median rent: $338 per month (2000); Median age of housing: 26 years (2000).
Transportation: Commute to work: 93.5% car, 0.0% public transportation, 1.3% walk, 4.0% work from home (2000); Travel time to work: 45.0% less than 15 minutes, 29.3% 15 to 30 minutes, 12.9% 30 to 45 minutes, 6.1% 45 to 60 minutes, 6.8% 60 minutes or more (2000)

FROG CREEK (town). Covers a land area of 70.996 square miles and a water area of 0.556 square miles. Located at 46.12° N. Lat.; 91.71° W. Long.
Population: 160 (2000); Race: 98.8% White, 0.0% Black, 0.0% Asian, 0.0% American Indian and Alaska Native, 0.0% Hispanic of any race, 1.2% two or more races (2000); Density: 2.3 persons per square mile (2000); Age: 29.2% under 18, 6.0% over 64 (2000); Marriage status: 17.4% never married, 65.2% now married, 1.5% widowed, 15.9% divorced (2000); Foreign born: 0.0% (2000); Ancestry (includes multiple ancestries): 32.7% German, 20.2% Norwegian, 11.9% United States or American, 9.5% Other groups, 8.9% Irish (2000).
Economy: Employment by occupation: 7.3% management, 2.1% professional, 10.4% services, 31.3% sales, 10.4% farming, 16.7% construction, 21.9% production (2000).
Income: Per capita income: $15,750 (2000); Median household income: $36,750 (2000); Poverty rate: 7.3% (2000).
Taxes: Total city taxes per capita: $35 (1997); City property taxes per capita: $35 (1997).
Education: High school graduation rate: 81.0% (2000); College graduation rate: 6.9% (2000).

Housing: Homeownership rate: 75.4% (2000); Median home value: $58,300 (2000); Median rent: $413 per month (2000); Median age of housing: 22 years (2000).
Transportation: Commute to work: 91.7% car, 0.0% public transportation, 2.1% walk, 6.3% work from home (2000); Travel time to work: 50.0% less than 15 minutes, 17.8% 15 to 30 minutes, 22.2% 30 to 45 minutes, 7.8% 45 to 60 minutes, 2.2% 60 minutes or more (2000)

GULL LAKE (town). Covers a land area of 35.047 square miles and a water area of 1.158 square miles. Located at 46.00° N. Lat.; 91.73° W. Long.
Population: 158 (2000); Race: 100.0% White, 0.0% Black, 0.0% Asian, 0.0% American Indian and Alaska Native, 0.0% Hispanic of any race, 0.0% two or more races (2000); Density: 4.5 persons per square mile (2000); Age: 18.4% under 18, 17.6% over 64 (2000); Marriage status: 21.0% never married, 47.1% now married, 9.2% widowed, 22.7% divorced (2000); Foreign born: 0.0% (2000); Ancestry (includes multiple ancestries): 43.4% German, 22.1% Irish, 13.2% Norwegian, 11.0% Swedish, 7.4% French Canadian (2000).
Economy: Employment by occupation: 7.8% management, 17.2% professional, 15.6% services, 17.2% sales, 6.3% farming, 20.3% construction, 15.6% production (2000).
Income: Per capita income: $21,527 (2000); Median household income: $42,500 (2000); Poverty rate: 1.5% (2000).
Taxes: Total city taxes per capita: $109 (1997); City property taxes per capita: $109 (1997).
Education: High school graduation rate: 78.1% (2000); College graduation rate: 13.3% (2000).
Housing: Homeownership rate: 80.3% (2000); Median home value: $187,500 (2000); Median age of housing: 24 years (2000).
Transportation: Commute to work: 89.1% car, 0.0% public transportation, 7.8% walk, 3.1% work from home (2000); Travel time to work: 9.7% less than 15 minutes, 61.3% 15 to 30 minutes, 11.3% 30 to 45 minutes, 9.7% 45 to 60 minutes, 8.1% 60 minutes or more (2000)

LONG LAKE (town). Covers a land area of 32.615 square miles and a water area of 5.134 square miles. Located at 45.69° N. Lat.; 91.71° W. Long.
Population: 737 (2000); Race: 98.5% White, 0.0% Black, 0.3% Asian, 0.4% American Indian and Alaska Native, 0.3% Hispanic of any race, 0.8% two or more races (2000); Density: 22.6 persons per square mile (2000); Age: 29.8% under 18, 15.4% over 64 (2000); Marriage status: 18.0% never married, 70.6% now married, 5.5% widowed, 5.9% divorced (2000); Foreign born: 0.7% (2000); Ancestry (includes multiple ancestries): 37.4% German, 17.4% Norwegian, 10.9% Czech, 9.9% Irish, 6.1% French (except Basque) (2000).
Economy: Employment by occupation: 16.6% management, 18.4% professional, 9.0% services, 22.9% sales, 1.8% farming, 9.0% construction, 22.3% production (2000).
Income: Per capita income: $18,049 (2000); Median household income: $40,208 (2000); Poverty rate: 5.2% (2000).
Taxes: Total city taxes per capita: $185 (1997); City property taxes per capita: $182 (1997).
Education: High school graduation rate: 88.6% (2000); College graduation rate: 25.7% (2000).
Housing: Homeownership rate: 86.9% (2000); Median home value: $139,800 (2000); Median rent: $575 per month (2000); Median age of housing: 34 years (2000).
Transportation: Commute to work: 81.7% car, 0.6% public transportation, 0.6% walk, 15.5% work from home (2000); Travel time to work: 12.8% less than 15 minutes, 53.5% 15 to 30 minutes, 19.4% 30 to 45 minutes, 5.9% 45 to 60 minutes, 8.4% 60 minutes or more (2000)

MADGE (town). Covers a land area of 31.976 square miles and a water area of 2.081 square miles. Located at 45.76° N. Lat.; 91.71° W. Long. Elevation is 1,296 feet.
Population: 454 (2000); Race: 100.0% White, 0.0% Black, 0.0% Asian, 0.0% American Indian and Alaska Native, 0.7% Hispanic of any race, 0.0% two or more races (2000); Density: 14.2 persons per square mile (2000); Age: 11.7% under 18, 24.1% over 64 (2000); Marriage status: 14.5% never married, 74.7% now married, 4.6% widowed, 6.3% divorced (2000); Foreign born: 0.9% (2000); Ancestry (includes multiple ancestries): 27.8% German, 12.6% Norwegian, 12.0% Irish, 8.7% Swedish, 8.3% English (2000).
Economy: Employment by occupation: 13.0% management, 21.2% professional, 14.0% services, 20.7% sales, 5.2% farming, 9.3% construction, 16.6% production (2000).
Income: Per capita income: $28,602 (2000); Median household income: $36,667 (2000); Poverty rate: 9.1% (2000).
Taxes: Total city taxes per capita: $105 (1997); City property taxes per capita: $103 (1997).
Education: High school graduation rate: 85.6% (2000); College graduation rate: 18.3% (2000).
Housing: Homeownership rate: 87.3% (2000); Median home value: $143,800 (2000); Median rent: $244 per month (2000); Median age of housing: 24 years (2000).
Transportation: Commute to work: 77.2% car, 0.0% public transportation, 2.6% walk, 18.0% work from home (2000); Travel time to work: 23.2% less than 15 minutes, 44.5% 15 to 30 minutes, 20.6% 30 to 45 minutes, 2.6% 45 to 60 minutes, 9.0% 60 minutes or more (2000)

MINONG (village). Covers a land area of 1.519 square miles and a water area of 0 square miles. Located at 46.10° N. Lat.; 91.82° W. Long. Elevation is 1,064 feet.
Population: 531 (2000); Race: 95.5% White, 0.0% Black, 0.6% Asian, 2.1% American Indian and Alaska Native, 1.3% Hispanic of any race, 1.1% two or more races (2000); Density: 349.6 persons per square mile (2000); Age: 25.4% under 18, 20.0% over 64 (2000); Marriage status: 20.6% never married, 56.0% now married, 10.5% widowed, 12.9% divorced (2000); Foreign born: 1.1% (2000); Ancestry (includes multiple ancestries): 28.2% German, 8.2% Norwegian, 8.0% Irish, 7.6% Other groups, 5.8% English (2000).
Economy: Single-family building permits issued: 7 (2001) / 6 (2000); Multi-family building permits issued: 0 (2001) / 2 (2000); Employment by occupation: 9.8% management, 9.3% professional, 15.6% services, 29.3% sales, 2.4% farming, 9.8% construction, 23.9% production (2000).
Income: Per capita income: $13,306 (2000); Median household income: $25,341 (2000); Poverty rate: 23.2% (2000).
Taxes: Total city taxes per capita: $190 (1997); City property taxes per capita: $169 (1997).
Education: High school graduation rate: 81.6% (2000); College graduation rate: 6.2% (2000).

School District(s)

Northwood (PK-12)
2000 Enrollment: 412 715-466-2297

Housing: Homeownership rate: 70.0% (2000); Median home value: $55,600 (2000); Median rent: $244 per month (2000); Median age of housing: 28 years (2000).
Transportation: Commute to work: 86.6% car, 0.0% public transportation, 8.4% walk, 3.0% work from home (2000); Travel time to work: 78.1% less than 15 minutes, 14.3% 15 to 30 minutes, 5.6% 30 to 45 minutes, 2.0% 45 to 60 minutes, 0.0% 60 minutes or more (2000)

MINONG (town). Covers a land area of 64.233 square miles and a water area of 6.763 square miles. Located at 46.11° N. Lat.; 91.91° W. Long. Elevation is 1,064 feet.
Population: 858 (2000); Race: 97.5% White, 0.0% Black, 0.0% Asian, 0.9% American Indian and Alaska Native, 0.3% Hispanic of any race, 1.3% two or more races (2000); Density: 13.4 persons per square mile (2000); Age: 18.6% under 18, 21.0% over 64 (2000); Marriage status: 17.1% never married, 62.1% now married, 8.5% widowed, 12.4% divorced (2000); Foreign born: 0.0% (2000); Ancestry (includes multiple ancestries): 34.8% German, 12.3% Irish, 12.3% Norwegian, 8.4% United States or American, 7.9% Swedish (2000).
Economy: Manufacturing: meat snacks, mailing machines. Employment by occupation: 11.8% management, 5.9% professional, 16.6% services, 27.5% sales, 0.5% farming, 15.2% construction, 22.5% production (2000).
Income: Per capita income: $20,679 (2000); Median household income: $36,667 (2000); Poverty rate: 7.9% (2000).
Taxes: Total city taxes per capita: $314 (1997); City property taxes per capita: $312 (1997).
Education: High school graduation rate: 83.6% (2000); College graduation rate: 9.5% (2000).
Housing: Homeownership rate: 91.0% (2000); Median home value: $100,400 (2000); Median rent: $338 per month (2000); Median age of housing: 24 years (2000).
Transportation: Commute to work: 88.8% car, 0.8% public transportation, 1.4% walk, 8.4% work from home (2000); Travel time to work: 48.5% less than 15 minutes, 20.8% 15 to 30 minutes, 13.1% 30 to 45 minutes, 8.3% 45 to 60 minutes, 9.2% 60 minutes or more (2000)

SARONA (town). Covers a land area of 31.920 square miles and a water area of 1.412 square miles. Located at 45.69° N. Lat.; 91.83° W. Long. Elevation is 1,300 feet.

Population: 382 (2000); Race: 98.4% White, 0.0% Black, 0.5% Asian, 0.5% American Indian and Alaska Native, 0.5% Hispanic of any race, 0.5% two or more races (2000); Density: 12.0 persons per square mile (2000); Age: 20.5% under 18, 20.8% over 64 (2000); Marriage status: 19.4% never married, 56.4% now married, 12.2% widowed, 11.9% divorced (2000); Foreign born: 2.1% (2000); Ancestry (includes multiple ancestries): 46.8% German, 11.2% Norwegian, 9.1% French (except Basque), 8.8% Czech, 8.6% Irish (2000).
Economy: Employment by occupation: 13.9% management, 3.1% professional, 14.9% services, 21.6% sales, 6.2% farming, 16.5% construction, 23.7% production (2000).
Income: Per capita income: $19,194 (2000); Median household income: $30,357 (2000); Poverty rate: 12.3% (2000).
Taxes: Total city taxes per capita: $73 (1997); City property taxes per capita: $71 (1997).
Education: High school graduation rate: 83.8% (2000); College graduation rate: 6.5% (2000).
Housing: Homeownership rate: 86.5% (2000); Median home value: $69,600 (2000); Median rent: $404 per month (2000); Median age of housing: 25 years (2000).
Hospitals: Spooner Health System (136 beds)
Transportation: Commute to work: 90.2% car, 0.0% public transportation, 0.0% walk, 9.8% work from home (2000); Travel time to work: 27.4% less than 15 minutes, 45.7% 15 to 30 minutes, 11.4% 30 to 45 minutes, 3.4% 45 to 60 minutes, 12.0% 60 minutes or more (2000)
Additional Information Contacts
Long Lake Chamber of Commerce 715-354-7449

SHELL LAKE (city). Covers a land area of 6.194 square miles and a water area of 4.025 square miles. Located at 45.73° N. Lat.; 91.91° W. Long. Elevation is 1,250 feet.
History: The industry that supported Shell Lake in the early 1900's was the building of rowboats, skiffs, and motorboats for use on the northern Wisconsin lakes.
Population: 1,309 (2000); Race: 98.2% White, 0.0% Black, 0.2% Asian, 0.4% American Indian and Alaska Native, 1.0% Hispanic of any race, 1.2% two or more races (2000); Density: 211.3 persons per square mile (2000); Age: 19.4% under 18, 30.1% over 64 (2000); Marriage status: 18.2% never married, 61.0% now married, 11.0% widowed, 9.7% divorced (2000); Foreign born: 1.2% (2000); Ancestry (includes multiple ancestries): 38.0% German, 15.5% Norwegian, 9.8% Irish, 9.7% Swedish, 9.7% English (2000).
Economy: Single-family building permits issued: 13 (2001) / 10 (2000); Multi-family building permits issued: 0 (2001) / 0 (2000); Employment by occupation: 11.3% management, 21.1% professional, 21.5% services, 20.5% sales, 2.0% farming, 6.6% construction, 17.0% production (2000).
Income: Per capita income: $18,675 (2000); Median household income: $33,073 (2000); Poverty rate: 8.6% (2000).
Taxes: Total city taxes per capita: $360 (1997); City property taxes per capita: $349 (1997).
Education: High school graduation rate: 81.2% (2000); College graduation rate: 24.3% (2000).

School District(s)

Shell Lake (PK-12)
2000 Enrollment: 564 715-468-7816

Two-year College(s)

Wisconsin Indianhead Technical College (Public)
2001 Enrollment: 3,765 715-468-2815
2001 Tuition: In-state $2,048; Out-of-state $15,987
Housing: Homeownership rate: 68.4% (2000); Median home value: $85,400 (2000); Median rent: $324 per month (2000); Median age of housing: 32 years (2000).
Newspapers: Washburn County Register (1 x week)
Transportation: Commute to work: 89.5% car, 0.0% public transportation, 5.7% walk, 3.6% work from home (2000); Travel time to work: 60.0% less than 15 minutes, 17.0% 15 to 30 minutes, 12.5% 30 to 45 minutes, 3.1% 45 to 60 minutes, 7.4% 60 minutes or more (2000)

SPOONER (city). Covers a land area of 3.029 square miles and a water area of 0.074 square miles. Located at 45.82° N. Lat.; 91.89° W. Long. Elevation is 1,065 feet.
History: Spooner developed around a railroad junction as a trading and shipping center. Spooner was named for John Coit Spooner (1843-1919), a railroad attorney and lumber king who became a U.S. senator in 1885. Near Spooner, a state fish hatchery and an agricultural experiment station of the University of Wisconsin were established.
Population: 2,653 (2000); Race: 95.2% White, 0.0% Black, 0.5% Asian, 2.8% American Indian and Alaska Native, 1.4% Hispanic of any race, 0.7% two or more races (2000); Density: 875.9 persons per square mile (2000); Age: 23.6% under 18, 22.4% over 64 (2000); Marriage status: 22.6% never married, 53.0% now married, 12.0% widowed, 12.4% divorced (2000); Foreign born: 1.3% (2000); Ancestry (includes multiple ancestries): 30.9% German, 11.9% Norwegian, 11.0% Swedish, 10.2% Irish, 8.1% English (2000).
Economy: Single-family building permits issued: 9 (2001) / 10 (2000); Multi-family building permits issued: 0 (2001) / 0 (2000); Employment by occupation: 7.9% management, 17.7% professional, 21.1% services, 24.4% sales, 0.7% farming, 6.5% construction, 21.7% production (2000).
Income: Per capita income: $16,390 (2000); Median household income: $27,768 (2000); Poverty rate: 11.9% (2000).
Taxes: Total city taxes per capita: $213 (1997); City property taxes per capita: $197 (1997).
Education: High school graduation rate: 83.0% (2000); College graduation rate: 15.8% (2000).

School District(s)

Spooner (PK-12)
2000 Enrollment: 1,683 715-635-2171
Housing: Homeownership rate: 60.3% (2000); Median home value: $71,600 (2000); Median rent: $360 per month (2000); Median age of housing: 42 years (2000).
Safety: Violent crime rate: 11.2 per 10,000 population; Property crime rate: 621.3 per 10,000 population (2001).
Newspapers: Spooner Advocate (1 x week)
Transportation: Commute to work: 84.2% car, 0.0% public transportation, 7.7% walk, 5.8% work from home (2000); Travel time to work: 63.1% less than 15 minutes, 18.4% 15 to 30 minutes, 10.4% 30 to 45 minutes, 4.7% 45 to 60 minutes, 3.5% 60 minutes or more (2000)
Additional Information Contacts
Spooner Chamber of Commerce 715-635-2168

SPOONER (town). Covers a land area of 18.861 square miles and a water area of 1.964 square miles. Located at 45.83° N. Lat.; 91.85° W. Long. Elevation is 1,065 feet.
Population: 677 (2000); Race: 98.6% White, 0.6% Black, 0.1% Asian, 0.3% American Indian and Alaska Native, 0.1% Hispanic of any race, 0.4% two or more races (2000); Density: 35.9 persons per square mile (2000); Age: 28.8% under 18, 12.1% over 64 (2000); Marriage status: 17.5% never married, 65.5% now married, 8.2% widowed, 8.8% divorced (2000); Foreign born: 1.4% (2000); Ancestry (includes multiple ancestries): 40.6% German, 17.3% Norwegian, 11.7% English, 8.4% Irish, 6.3% French (except Basque) (2000).
Economy: Employment by occupation: 8.0% management, 16.7% professional, 11.3% services, 32.1% sales, 0.9% farming, 12.8% construction, 18.2% production (2000).
Income: Per capita income: $17,133 (2000); Median household income: $41,458 (2000); Poverty rate: 4.9% (2000).
Taxes: Total city taxes per capita: $4 (1997); City property taxes per capita: $0 (1997).
Education: High school graduation rate: 84.5% (2000); College graduation rate: 19.8% (2000).
Housing: Homeownership rate: 93.7% (2000); Median home value: $93,300 (2000); Median rent: $325 per month (2000); Median age of housing: 27 years (2000).
Transportation: Commute to work: 91.6% car, 0.0% public transportation, 2.1% walk, 5.7% work from home (2000); Travel time to work: 57.0% less than 15 minutes, 17.2% 15 to 30 minutes, 15.9% 30 to 45 minutes, 1.9% 45 to 60 minutes, 8.0% 60 minutes or more (2000)

SPRINGBROOK (town). Aka Spring Brook. Covers a land area of 34.158 square miles and a water area of 0.508 square miles. Located at 45.94° N. Lat.; 91.70° W. Long. Elevation is 1,090 feet.
Population: 536 (2000); Race: 98.8% White, 0.0% Black, 0.0% Asian, 0.6% American Indian and Alaska Native, 0.4% Hispanic of any race, 0.6% two or more races (2000); Density: 15.7 persons per square mile (2000); Age: 26.1% under 18, 16.4% over 64 (2000); Marriage status: 20.5% never married, 62.5% now married, 5.7% widowed, 11.4% divorced (2000); Foreign born: 1.2% (2000); Ancestry (includes multiple ancestries): 28.1% German, 12.3% Irish, 8.7% Norwegian, 8.1% Polish, 7.9% English (2000).
Economy: Employment by occupation: 12.2% management, 6.1% professional, 21.7% services, 20.4% sales, 3.5% farming, 12.2% construction, 23.9% production (2000).
Income: Per capita income: $17,859 (2000); Median household income: $36,406 (2000); Poverty rate: 12.3% (2000).
Taxes: Total city taxes per capita: $22 (1997); City property taxes per capita: $20 (1997).

Education: High school graduation rate: 80.5% (2000); College graduation rate: 10.6% (2000).
Housing: Homeownership rate: 80.6% (2000); Median home value: $75,000 (2000); Median rent: $370 per month (2000); Median age of housing: 27 years (2000).
Transportation: Commute to work: 90.1% car, 0.0% public transportation, 2.7% walk, 7.2% work from home (2000); Travel time to work: 20.8% less than 15 minutes, 56.0% 15 to 30 minutes, 12.6% 30 to 45 minutes, 3.4% 45 to 60 minutes, 7.2% 60 minutes or more (2000)

STINNETT (town). Covers a land area of 34.437 square miles and a water area of 1.216 square miles. Located at 46.02° N. Lat.; 91.60° W. Long.
Population: 263 (2000); Race: 85.0% White, 0.0% Black, 0.0% Asian, 2.4% American Indian and Alaska Native, 15.0% Hispanic of any race, 3.5% two or more races (2000); Density: 7.6 persons per square mile (2000); Age: 28.3% under 18, 14.2% over 64 (2000); Marriage status: 18.2% never married, 65.1% now married, 6.3% widowed, 10.4% divorced (2000); Foreign born: 4.7% (2000); Ancestry (includes multiple ancestries): 29.5% German, 20.9% Other groups, 17.3% Norwegian, 9.1% Irish, 9.1% Swedish (2000).
Economy: Employment by occupation: 2.0% management, 0.0% professional, 15.3% services, 18.4% sales, 2.0% farming, 23.5% construction, 38.8% production (2000).
Income: Per capita income: $13,169 (2000); Median household income: $27,750 (2000); Poverty rate: 2.8% (2000).
Taxes: Total city taxes per capita: $22 (1997); City property taxes per capita: $22 (1997).
Education: High school graduation rate: 80.7% (2000); College graduation rate: 7.0% (2000).
Housing: Homeownership rate: 84.2% (2000); Median home value: $64,400 (2000); Median rent: $281 per month (2000); Median age of housing: 25 years (2000).
Transportation: Commute to work: 96.8% car, 1.1% public transportation, 0.0% walk, 2.1% work from home (2000); Travel time to work: 32.6% less than 15 minutes, 35.9% 15 to 30 minutes, 13.0% 30 to 45 minutes, 6.5% 45 to 60 minutes, 12.0% 60 minutes or more (2000)

STONE LAKE (town). Covers a land area of 33.670 square miles and a water area of 1.168 square miles. Located at 45.86° N. Lat.; 91.58° W. Long. Elevation is 1,340 feet.
Population: 544 (2000); Race: 96.3% White, 0.0% Black, 0.0% Asian, 1.1% American Indian and Alaska Native, 0.4% Hispanic of any race, 2.6% two or more races (2000); Density: 16.2 persons per square mile (2000); Age: 28.5% under 18, 17.3% over 64 (2000); Marriage status: 20.0% never married, 65.9% now married, 6.3% widowed, 7.9% divorced (2000); Foreign born: 0.4% (2000); Ancestry (includes multiple ancestries): 35.2% German, 15.5% Norwegian, 13.9% Irish, 13.7% English, 12.0% Swedish (2000).
Economy: Employment by occupation: 11.6% management, 9.3% professional, 20.5% services, 18.2% sales, 6.6% farming, 13.2% construction, 20.5% production (2000).
Income: Per capita income: $15,219 (2000); Median household income: $33,021 (2000); Poverty rate: 13.2% (2000).
Taxes: Total city taxes per capita: $124 (1997); City property taxes per capita: $122 (1997).
Education: High school graduation rate: 81.8% (2000); College graduation rate: 11.3% (2000).
Housing: Homeownership rate: 83.2% (2000); Median home value: $95,000 (2000); Median rent: $323 per month (2000); Median age of housing: 25 years (2000).
Transportation: Commute to work: 90.4% car, 0.8% public transportation, 2.8% walk, 6.0% work from home (2000); Travel time to work: 22.0% less than 15 minutes, 44.9% 15 to 30 minutes, 19.1% 30 to 45 minutes, 5.9% 45 to 60 minutes, 8.1% 60 minutes or more (2000)

TREGO (town). Covers a land area of 35.931 square miles and a water area of 0.841 square miles. Located at 45.91° N. Lat.; 91.83° W. Long. Elevation is 1,086 feet.
Population: 885 (2000); Race: 97.0% White, 0.3% Black, 0.0% Asian, 1.6% American Indian and Alaska Native, 0.2% Hispanic of any race, 1.1% two or more races (2000); Density: 24.6 persons per square mile (2000); Age: 27.1% under 18, 13.5% over 64 (2000); Marriage status: 19.5% never married, 65.1% now married, 6.4% widowed, 9.1% divorced (2000); Foreign born: 0.0% (2000); Ancestry (includes multiple ancestries): 37.1% German, 13.6% Irish, 13.2% Norwegian, 9.1% English, 7.4% Italian (2000).
Economy: Employment by occupation: 8.8% management, 15.2% professional, 15.0% services, 26.5% sales, 1.2% farming, 11.5% construction, 21.6% production (2000).
Income: Per capita income: $16,000 (2000); Median household income: $35,069 (2000); Poverty rate: 15.1% (2000).
Taxes: Total city taxes per capita: $48 (1997); City property taxes per capita: $46 (1997).
Education: High school graduation rate: 84.1% (2000); College graduation rate: 14.5% (2000).
Housing: Homeownership rate: 87.9% (2000); Median home value: $94,600 (2000); Median rent: $355 per month (2000); Median age of housing: 25 years (2000).
Transportation: Commute to work: 90.8% car, 0.2% public transportation, 4.2% walk, 4.2% work from home (2000); Travel time to work: 34.5% less than 15 minutes, 37.7% 15 to 30 minutes, 12.2% 30 to 45 minutes, 7.0% 45 to 60 minutes, 8.6% 60 minutes or more (2000)

Washington County

Located in eastern Wisconsin; hilly area, drained by the Milwaukee, Menomonee, and Rubicon Rivers; includes many lakes. Covers a land area of 430.80 square miles, a water area of 5.10 square miles, and is located in the Central Time Zone. The county government was organized in 1836. County seat is West Bend.

Washington County is part of the Milwaukee-Waukesha, WI PMSA. The entire metro area includes: Milwaukee County; Ozaukee County; Washington County; Waukesha County

Weather Station: Germantown — Elevation: 849 feet

	Jan	Feb	Mar	Apr	May	Jun	Jul	Aug	Sep	Oct	Nov	Dec
High	25	30	41	54	67	77	81	79	71	59	44	31
Low	8	13	23	34	44	53	58	56	48	37	27	15
Precip	1.3	1.2	2.0	3.2	2.9	3.8	4.0	4.2	3.6	2.5	2.6	1.7
Snow	14.1	8.0	6.7	2.2	0.3	0.0	0.0	0.0	0.0	0.1	3.6	9.4

High and Low temperatures in degrees Fahrenheit; Precipitation and Snow in inches

Weather Station: Hartford 2 W — Elevation: 977 feet

	Jan	Feb	Mar	Apr	May	Jun	Jul	Aug	Sep	Oct	Nov	Dec
High	26	31	42	56	69	78	82	80	72	60	44	31
Low	7	12	23	34	44	53	58	56	48	38	27	14
Precip	1.3	1.0	1.9	3.0	3.0	3.8	4.2	4.1	3.8	2.7	2.2	1.6
Snow	11.4	6.8	6.0	2.0	0.4	0.0	0.0	0.0	0.0	0.1	2.5	7.8

High and Low temperatures in degrees Fahrenheit; Precipitation and Snow in inches

Weather Station: West Bend — Elevation: 938 feet

	Jan	Feb	Mar	Apr	May	Jun	Jul	Aug	Sep	Oct	Nov	Dec
High	26	31	41	55	68	77	82	79	71	59	44	31
Low	10	15	24	35	44	54	59	58	50	39	28	17
Precip	1.5	1.1	2.0	3.1	3.0	3.8	4.0	4.0	3.6	2.6	2.5	1.7
Snow	15.4	10.3	8.1	3.2	0.1	0.0	0.0	0.0	0.0	0.2	3.9	12.2

High and Low temperatures in degrees Fahrenheit; Precipitation and Snow in inches

Population: 117,493 (2000); Race: 97.4% White, 0.5% Black, 0.4% Asian, 0.4% American Indian and Alaska Native, 1.3% Hispanic of any race, 0.7% two or more races (2000); Density: 272.7 persons per square mile (2000); Age: 26.6% under 18, 11.2% over 64 (2000).
Religion: Five largest groups: 37.2% Catholic Church, 7.5% Wisconsin Evangelical Lutheran Synod, 4.9% Evangelical Lutheran Church in America, 4.8% Lutheran Church—Missouri Synod, 3.1% United Church of Christ (2000).
Economy: Unemployment rate: 4.3% (11/2002); Total civilian labor force: 69,532 (11/2002); Leading industries: 33.4% manufacturing; 12.6% retail trade; 10.0% health care and social assistance (2000); Companies that employ more than 1,000 persons: 2 (2000); Companies that employ more than 100 persons: 76 (2000); Farms: 787 totaling 127,127 acres (1997); Minority business ownership rate: 2.3% (1997); Women business ownership rate: 22.1% (1997); Retail sales per capita: $10,679 (1997). Single-family building permits issued: 736 (2001) / 637 (2000); Multi-family building permits issued: 154 (2001) / 294 (2000).
Income: Per capita income: $24,319 (2000); Median household income: $57,033 (2000); Poverty rate: 3.6% (2000); Bankruptcy rate: 3.31% (2001).
Taxes: Total county taxes per capita: $254 (2000); County property taxes per capita: $203 (2000).
Education: High school graduation rate: 88.8% (2000); College graduation rate: 21.9% (2000).

Housing: Homeownership rate: 76.0% (2000); Median home value: $155,000 (2000); Median rent: $546 per month (2000); Median age of housing: 24 years (2000).
Health: Birth rate: 125.5 per 10,000 population (1998); Age adjusted death rate: 77.8 per 10,000 population (1999); Age adjusted cancer mortality rate: 182.6 deaths per 100,000 population (1999). Air Quality Index: 77% good, 23% moderate, 0% unhealthy (percent of days in 2000). Number of physicians: 10.4 per 10,000 population (1999); Number of hospital beds: 14.8 per 10,000 population (1999).
Elections: 2000 Presidential election results: 29.5% Gore, 67.0% Bush, 2.6% Nader, 0.5% Buchanan
National and State Parks: Jackson Marsh State Wildlife Area; Kettle Moraine State Forest; Lizard Mound State Park; Pike Lake State Park; Theresa Marsh State Wildlife Area
Additional Information Contacts
Washington County Government Offices 262-338-4400
Germantown Area Chamber of Commerce 262-255-1812
Hartford Area Chamber of Commerce 262-673-7002
Washington Board of Realtors 262-644-8814
West Bend Area Chamber of Commerce 262-338-2666

Washington County Communities

ADDISON (town). Covers a land area of 36.173 square miles and a water area of 0 square miles. Located at 43.41° N. Lat.; 88.34° W. Long.
Population: 3,341 (2000); Race: 99.4% White, 0.0% Black, 0.2% Asian, 0.0% American Indian and Alaska Native, 0.9% Hispanic of any race, 0.2% two or more races (2000); Density: 92.4 persons per square mile (2000); Age: 28.7% under 18, 8.5% over 64 (2000); Marriage status: 22.2% never married, 67.7% now married, 4.3% widowed, 5.8% divorced (2000); Foreign born: 1.8% (2000); Ancestry (includes multiple ancestries): 68.6% German, 9.8% Polish, 8.6% Irish, 3.7% Norwegian, 3.2% United States or American (2000).
Economy: Single-family building permits issued: 15 (2001) / 12 (2000); Multi-family building permits issued: 4 (2001) / 30 (2000); Employment by occupation: 15.7% management, 14.5% professional, 13.5% services, 24.1% sales, 0.3% farming, 11.3% construction, 20.6% production (2000).
Income: Per capita income: $20,999 (2000); Median household income: $56,875 (2000); Poverty rate: 4.5% (2000).
Taxes: Total city taxes per capita: $94 (1997); City property taxes per capita: $77 (1997).
Education: High school graduation rate: 85.5% (2000); College graduation rate: 10.1% (2000).
Housing: Homeownership rate: 83.6% (2000); Median home value: $146,700 (2000); Median rent: $499 per month (2000); Median age of housing: 30 years (2000).
Transportation: Commute to work: 94.4% car, 0.0% public transportation, 2.4% walk, 2.9% work from home (2000); Travel time to work: 31.8% less than 15 minutes, 41.6% 15 to 30 minutes, 16.5% 30 to 45 minutes, 5.8% 45 to 60 minutes, 4.3% 60 minutes or more (2000)

ALLENTON (unincorporated postal area, zip code 53002). Covers a land area of 33.703 square miles and a water area of 0 square miles. Located at 43.46° N. Lat.; 88.36° W. Long. Elevation is 960 feet.
Population: 2,249 (2000); Race: 98.9% White, 0.2% Black, 0.3% Asian, 0.1% American Indian and Alaska Native, 1.4% Hispanic of any race, 0.2% two or more races (2000); Density: 66.7 persons per square mile (2000); Age: 27.7% under 18, 7.0% over 64 (2000); Marriage status: 21.7% never married, 65.7% now married, 4.3% widowed, 8.4% divorced (2000); Foreign born: 2.4% (2000); Ancestry (includes multiple ancestries): 59.7% German, 10.3% Polish, 8.8% Irish, 4.3% United States or American, 3.8% Norwegian (2000).
Economy: Employment by occupation: 15.1% management, 14.1% professional, 12.3% services, 21.7% sales, 0.0% farming, 13.4% construction, 23.3% production (2000).
Income: Per capita income: $20,209 (2000); Median household income: $55,064 (2000); Poverty rate: 5.5% (2000).
Education: High school graduation rate: 87.3% (2000); College graduation rate: 9.6% (2000).
Housing: Homeownership rate: 81.9% (2000); Median home value: $138,700 (2000); Median rent: $497 per month (2000); Median age of housing: 37 years (2000).
Transportation: Commute to work: 93.4% car, 0.0% public transportation, 3.2% walk, 2.8% work from home (2000); Travel time to work: 23.8% less than 15 minutes, 43.6% 15 to 30 minutes, 21.7% 30 to 45 minutes, 4.6% 45 to 60 minutes, 6.3% 60 minutes or more (2000)

BARTON (town). Covers a land area of 19.218 square miles and a water area of 0.236 square miles. Located at 43.45° N. Lat.; 88.21° W. Long. Elevation is 950 feet.
History: Many of the early residents of Barton were of German ancestry. The town developed as a residential suburb of West Bend.
Population: 2,546 (2000); Race: 99.7% White, 0.0% Black, 0.0% Asian, 0.3% American Indian and Alaska Native, 0.0% Hispanic of any race, 0.0% two or more races (2000); Density: 132.5 persons per square mile (2000); Age: 21.8% under 18, 6.3% over 64 (2000); Marriage status: 25.7% never married, 66.1% now married, 3.6% widowed, 4.7% divorced (2000); Foreign born: 0.0% (2000); Ancestry (includes multiple ancestries): 69.9% German, 12.0% Polish, 7.5% Irish, 5.5% French (except Basque), 2.8% French Canadian (2000).
Economy: Single-family building permits issued: 16 (2001) / 7 (2000); Multi-family building permits issued: 4 (2001) / 0 (2000); Employment by occupation: 10.5% management, 14.7% professional, 7.9% services, 28.8% sales, 0.3% farming, 14.4% construction, 23.5% production (2000).
Income: Per capita income: $26,039 (2000); Median household income: $64,861 (2000); Poverty rate: 1.7% (2000).
Taxes: Total city taxes per capita: $105 (1997); City property taxes per capita: $88 (1997).
Education: High school graduation rate: 87.1% (2000); College graduation rate: 15.1% (2000).
Housing: Homeownership rate: 90.3% (2000); Median home value: $158,300 (2000); Median rent: $413 per month (2000); Median age of housing: 27 years (2000).
Transportation: Commute to work: 95.7% car, 0.3% public transportation, 0.4% walk, 2.8% work from home (2000); Travel time to work: 39.6% less than 15 minutes, 26.8% 15 to 30 minutes, 18.2% 30 to 45 minutes, 9.8% 45 to 60 minutes, 5.6% 60 minutes or more (2000)

COLGATE (unincorporated postal area, zip code 53017). Covers a land area of 17.587 square miles and a water area of 0.305 square miles. Located at 43.20° N. Lat.; 88.26° W. Long.
Population: 4,886 (2000); Race: 99.7% White, 0.0% Black, 0.1% Asian, 0.0% American Indian and Alaska Native, 0.9% Hispanic of any race, 0.2% two or more races (2000); Density: 277.8 persons per square mile (2000); Age: 28.3% under 18, 7.7% over 64 (2000); Marriage status: 18.4% never married, 72.6% now married, 2.8% widowed, 6.2% divorced (2000); Foreign born: 1.4% (2000); Ancestry (includes multiple ancestries): 57.4% German, 11.1% Irish, 10.9% Polish, 6.3% English, 5.3% Italian (2000).
Economy: Employment by occupation: 15.7% management, 21.8% professional, 12.0% services, 26.7% sales, 0.0% farming, 10.1% construction, 13.7% production (2000).
Income: Per capita income: $31,065 (2000); Median household income: $71,683 (2000); Poverty rate: 1.2% (2000).
Education: High school graduation rate: 93.9% (2000); College graduation rate: 25.0% (2000).
Housing: Homeownership rate: 96.2% (2000); Median home value: $184,400 (2000); Median rent: $768 per month (2000); Median age of housing: 24 years (2000).
Transportation: Commute to work: 95.3% car, 0.0% public transportation, 2.3% walk, 2.1% work from home (2000); Travel time to work: 19.4% less than 15 minutes, 48.3% 15 to 30 minutes, 26.0% 30 to 45 minutes, 5.0% 45 to 60 minutes, 1.3% 60 minutes or more (2000)

ERIN (town). Covers a land area of 35.861 square miles and a water area of 0.427 square miles. Located at 43.23° N. Lat.; 88.35° W. Long.
Population: 3,664 (2000); Race: 97.6% White, 0.0% Black, 0.6% Asian, 0.2% American Indian and Alaska Native, 1.4% Hispanic of any race, 0.2% two or more races (2000); Density: 102.2 persons per square mile (2000); Age: 24.9% under 18, 9.9% over 64 (2000); Marriage status: 18.8% never married, 73.2% now married, 4.0% widowed, 4.0% divorced (2000); Foreign born: 3.7% (2000); Ancestry (includes multiple ancestries): 55.9% German, 19.2% Irish, 10.5% Polish, 8.1% Italian, 6.6% English (2000).
Economy: Single-family building permits issued: 30 (2001) / 23 (2000); Multi-family building permits issued: 0 (2001) / 0 (2000); Employment by occupation: 17.2% management, 23.3% professional, 8.9% services, 22.5% sales, 1.0% farming, 11.7% construction, 15.3% production (2000).
Income: Per capita income: $28,851 (2000); Median household income: $74,875 (2000); Poverty rate: 3.2% (2000).
Taxes: Total city taxes per capita: $165 (1997); City property taxes per capita: $134 (1997).
Education: High school graduation rate: 93.9% (2000); College graduation rate: 29.3% (2000).

Housing: Homeownership rate: 95.7% (2000); Median home value: $197,400 (2000); Median rent: $725 per month (2000); Median age of housing: 23 years (2000).
Transportation: Commute to work: 94.4% car, 0.0% public transportation, 1.0% walk, 3.9% work from home (2000); Travel time to work: 18.0% less than 15 minutes, 25.3% 15 to 30 minutes, 33.3% 30 to 45 minutes, 15.5% 45 to 60 minutes, 7.9% 60 minutes or more (2000)

FARMINGTON (town). Covers a land area of 36.381 square miles and a water area of 0.304 square miles. Located at 43.50° N. Lat.; 88.09° W. Long.
Population: 3,239 (2000); Race: 99.1% White, 0.0% Black, 0.0% Asian, 0.0% American Indian and Alaska Native, 1.7% Hispanic of any race, 0.7% two or more races (2000); Density: 89.0 persons per square mile (2000); Age: 28.3% under 18, 8.0% over 64 (2000); Marriage status: 20.8% never married, 69.9% now married, 3.2% widowed, 6.1% divorced (2000); Foreign born: 1.1% (2000); Ancestry (includes multiple ancestries): 68.3% German, 9.3% Polish, 9.1% Irish, 4.1% French (except Basque), 3.8% English (2000).
Economy: Single-family building permits issued: 38 (2001) / 31 (2000); Multi-family building permits issued: 0 (2001) / 0 (2000); Employment by occupation: 16.3% management, 11.5% professional, 10.9% services, 21.2% sales, 2.0% farming, 12.4% construction, 25.7% production (2000).
Income: Per capita income: $23,082 (2000); Median household income: $61,667 (2000); Poverty rate: 3.5% (2000).
Taxes: Total city taxes per capita: $82 (1997); City property taxes per capita: $75 (1997).
Education: High school graduation rate: 88.0% (2000); College graduation rate: 15.3% (2000).
Housing: Homeownership rate: 91.2% (2000); Median home value: $164,000 (2000); Median rent: $563 per month (2000); Median age of housing: 25 years (2000).
Transportation: Commute to work: 91.8% car, 0.4% public transportation, 1.5% walk, 5.6% work from home (2000); Travel time to work: 19.2% less than 15 minutes, 43.6% 15 to 30 minutes, 20.0% 30 to 45 minutes, 12.0% 45 to 60 minutes, 5.1% 60 minutes or more (2000)

GERMANTOWN (village). Covers a land area of 34.421 square miles and a water area of 0.038 square miles. Located at 43.22° N. Lat.; 88.12° W. Long. Elevation is 863 feet.
History: Germantown was settled about 1850 by German immigrants who moved up from Milwaukee.
Population: 18,260 (2000); Race: 95.2% White, 1.8% Black, 0.8% Asian, 0.4% American Indian and Alaska Native, 1.5% Hispanic of any race, 0.7% two or more races (2000); Density: 530.5 persons per square mile (2000); Age: 26.9% under 18, 9.4% over 64 (2000); Marriage status: 20.8% never married, 65.5% now married, 3.9% widowed, 9.8% divorced (2000); Foreign born: 2.6% (2000); Ancestry (includes multiple ancestries): 57.1% German, 11.4% Irish, 11.2% Polish, 6.0% Italian, 5.3% Other groups (2000).
Vital Statistics: Birth rate: 122.7 per 10,000 population (1998)
Economy: Single-family building permits issued: 99 (2001) / 65 (2000); Multi-family building permits issued: 20 (2001) / 64 (2000); Employment by occupation: 16.6% management, 21.0% professional, 11.1% services, 28.3% sales, 0.2% farming, 8.7% construction, 14.1% production (2000).
Income: Per capita income: $25,358 (2000); Median household income: $60,742 (2000); Poverty rate: 2.5% (2000).
Taxes: Total city taxes per capita: $399 (2000); City property taxes per capita: $337 (2000).
Education: High school graduation rate: 91.7% (2000); College graduation rate: 29.4% (2000).

School District(s)

Germantown (PK-12)
2000 Enrollment: 3,635 262-253-3904
Housing: Homeownership rate: 78.0% (2000); Median home value: $169,900 (2000); Median rent: $644 per month (2000); Median age of housing: 18 years (2000).
Safety: Violent crime rate: 4.9 per 10,000 population; Property crime rate: 207.2 per 10,000 population (2001).
Transportation: Commute to work: 94.4% car, 1.0% public transportation, 0.8% walk, 3.5% work from home (2000); Travel time to work: 29.8% less than 15 minutes, 44.8% 15 to 30 minutes, 19.6% 30 to 45 minutes, 3.6% 45 to 60 minutes, 2.2% 60 minutes or more (2000)
Additional Information Contacts
Germantown Area Chamber of Commerce 262-255-1812

GERMANTOWN (town). Covers a land area of 1.736 square miles and a water area of 0 square miles. Located at 43.26° N. Lat.; 88.14° W. Long. Elevation is 863 feet.
Population: 278 (2000); Race: 100.0% White, 0.0% Black, 0.0% Asian, 0.0% American Indian and Alaska Native, 0.0% Hispanic of any race, 0.0% two or more races (2000); Density: 160.2 persons per square mile (2000); Age: 30.9% under 18, 8.6% over 64 (2000); Marriage status: 21.7% never married, 71.7% now married, 3.1% widowed, 3.5% divorced (2000); Foreign born: 0.0% (2000); Ancestry (includes multiple ancestries): 73.4% German, 6.6% Polish, 5.6% Norwegian, 5.6% Irish, 2.6% Swedish (2000).
Economy: Dairy products. Manufacturing: welders, metal products, consumer goods, machinery, laminating equipment, dairy products, paper products, metal processing, food processing; motor vehicle parts. Single-family building permits issued: 1 (2001) / 1 (2000); Multi-family building permits issued: 0 (2001) / 0 (2000); Employment by occupation: 15.9% management, 21.8% professional, 8.2% services, 18.8% sales, 0.0% farming, 15.3% construction, 20.0% production (2000).
Income: Per capita income: $25,694 (2000); Median household income: $75,000 (2000); Poverty rate: 3.9% (2000).
Taxes: Total city taxes per capita: $86 (1997); City property taxes per capita: $78 (1997).
Education: High school graduation rate: 92.6% (2000); College graduation rate: 32.4% (2000).
Housing: Homeownership rate: 94.7% (2000); Median home value: $147,700 (2000); Median rent: $475 per month (2000); Median age of housing: 41 years (2000).
Transportation: Commute to work: 90.3% car, 0.0% public transportation, 4.2% walk, 4.2% work from home (2000); Travel time to work: 36.1% less than 15 minutes, 32.9% 15 to 30 minutes, 20.9% 30 to 45 minutes, 7.0% 45 to 60 minutes, 3.2% 60 minutes or more (2000)

HARTFORD (city). Covers a land area of 5.990 square miles and a water area of 0.052 square miles. Located at 43.31° N. Lat.; 88.37° W. Long. Elevation is 1,000 feet.
Population: 10,905 (2000); Race: 96.6% White, 0.4% Black, 0.3% Asian, 0.7% American Indian and Alaska Native, 2.9% Hispanic of any race, 1.0% two or more races (2000); Density: 1,820.7 persons per square mile (2000); Age: 28.2% under 18, 12.7% over 64 (2000); Marriage status: 23.9% never married, 58.4% now married, 7.1% widowed, 10.6% divorced (2000); Foreign born: 4.3% (2000); Ancestry (includes multiple ancestries): 53.7% German, 12.3% Irish, 10.0% Polish, 5.6% Other groups, 5.2% English (2000).
Economy: Single-family building permits issued: 145 (2001) / 81 (2000); Multi-family building permits issued: 8 (2001) / 50 (2000); Employment by occupation: 10.7% management, 15.9% professional, 13.6% services, 21.5% sales, 1.0% farming, 11.7% construction, 25.6% production (2000).
Income: Per capita income: $20,418 (2000); Median household income: $46,561 (2000); Poverty rate: 5.9% (2000).
Taxes: Total city taxes per capita: $429 (2000); City property taxes per capita: $388 (2000).
Education: High school graduation rate: 85.1% (2000); College graduation rate: 15.4% (2000).

School District(s)

Erin (PK-08)
2000 Enrollment: 376 262-673-3720
Hartford J1 (PK-08)
2000 Enrollment: 1,533 262-673-3155
Hartford UHS (09-12)
2000 Enrollment: 1,702 262-673-8950
Housing: Homeownership rate: 61.4% (2000); Median home value: $129,900 (2000); Median rent: $509 per month (2000); Median age of housing: 30 years (2000).
Hospitals: Aurora Medical Center of Washington County (71 beds)
Safety: Violent crime rate: 4.6 per 10,000 population; Property crime rate: 410.6 per 10,000 population (2001).
Newspapers: The Hartford Times-Press (1 x week)
Transportation: Commute to work: 92.4% car, 0.6% public transportation, 3.7% walk, 2.5% work from home (2000); Travel time to work: 41.7% less than 15 minutes, 23.2% 15 to 30 minutes, 24.2% 30 to 45 minutes, 7.1% 45 to 60 minutes, 3.8% 60 minutes or more (2000)
Additional Information Contacts
Hartford Area Chamber of Commerce 262-673-7002

HARTFORD (town). Covers a land area of 30.182 square miles and a water area of 0.734 square miles. Located at 43.32° N. Lat.; 88.35° W. Long. Elevation is 1,000 feet.
History: Settled c.1844, incorporated 1883.
Population: 4,031 (2000); Race: 99.0% White, 0.0% Black, 0.0% Asian, 1.0% American Indian and Alaska Native, 0.7% Hispanic of any race, 0.0% two or more races (2000); Density: 133.6 persons per square mile (2000); Age: 26.6% under 18, 7.6% over 64 (2000); Marriage status: 23.9% never married, 67.8% now married, 3.2% widowed, 5.0% divorced (2000); Foreign born: 1.7% (2000); Ancestry (includes multiple ancestries): 66.7% German, 9.9% Polish, 8.6% Irish, 5.0% French (except Basque), 4.4% United States or American (2000).
Economy: In dairy and farm area. Cheese, canned vegetables. Manufacturing: consumer goods, wood products, plastic products, tool and die, electrostatic powder coating, transportation equipment, furniture, fabricated metal products, beverages; tanning, metal fabricating. Single-family building permits issued: 9 (2001) / 13 (2000); Multi-family building permits issued: 0 (2001) / 0 (2000); Employment by occupation: 13.2% management, 16.1% professional, 7.6% services, 28.5% sales, 1.3% farming, 11.1% construction, 22.3% production (2000).
Income: Per capita income: $26,928 (2000); Median household income: $69,896 (2000); Poverty rate: 1.9% (2000).
Taxes: Total city taxes per capita: $76 (2000); City property taxes per capita: $63 (2000).
Education: High school graduation rate: 91.2% (2000); College graduation rate: 15.2% (2000).
Housing: Homeownership rate: 91.2% (2000); Median home value: $168,200 (2000); Median rent: $495 per month (2000); Median age of housing: 25 years (2000).
Transportation: Commute to work: 92.8% car, 0.0% public transportation, 1.7% walk, 5.1% work from home (2000); Travel time to work: 41.7% less than 15 minutes, 25.7% 15 to 30 minutes, 20.0% 30 to 45 minutes, 9.4% 45 to 60 minutes, 3.2% 60 minutes or more (2000)

HUBERTUS (unincorporated postal area, zip code 53033). Covers a land area of 12.423 square miles and a water area of 0.386 square miles. Located at 43.23° N. Lat.; 88.24° W. Long. Elevation is 1,014 feet.
Population: 5,302 (2000); Race: 98.5% White, 0.0% Black, 0.4% Asian, 0.3% American Indian and Alaska Native, 0.0% Hispanic of any race, 0.7% two or more races (2000); Density: 426.8 persons per square mile (2000); Age: 25.2% under 18, 7.6% over 64 (2000); Marriage status: 19.4% never married, 72.0% now married, 2.5% widowed, 6.1% divorced (2000); Foreign born: 1.1% (2000); Ancestry (includes multiple ancestries): 61.9% German, 14.3% Polish, 10.6% Irish, 5.5% Norwegian, 5.1% English (2000).
Economy: Employment by occupation: 16.8% management, 19.4% professional, 8.1% services, 24.4% sales, 1.0% farming, 12.2% construction, 18.1% production (2000).
Income: Per capita income: $29,003 (2000); Median household income: $73,491 (2000); Poverty rate: 1.0% (2000).
Education: High school graduation rate: 91.2% (2000); College graduation rate: 20.6% (2000).

School District(s)

Friess Lake (PK-08)
2000 Enrollment: 240 262-628-2380
Housing: Homeownership rate: 96.0% (2000); Median home value: $178,800 (2000); Median rent: $642 per month (2000); Median age of housing: 27 years (2000).
Transportation: Commute to work: 94.5% car, 0.6% public transportation, 0.3% walk, 3.9% work from home (2000); Travel time to work: 15.4% less than 15 minutes, 47.6% 15 to 30 minutes, 28.6% 30 to 45 minutes, 3.9% 45 to 60 minutes, 4.5% 60 minutes or more (2000)

JACKSON (village). Covers a land area of 2.520 square miles and a water area of 0.002 square miles. Located at 43.32° N. Lat.; 88.17° W. Long. Elevation is 896 feet.
Population: 4,938 (2000); Race: 97.6% White, 0.1% Black, 0.0% Asian, 0.0% American Indian and Alaska Native, 0.5% Hispanic of any race, 2.3% two or more races (2000); Density: 1,959.5 persons per square mile (2000); Age: 26.0% under 18, 10.2% over 64 (2000); Marriage status: 19.5% never married, 68.1% now married, 4.5% widowed, 7.9% divorced (2000); Foreign born: 1.5% (2000); Ancestry (includes multiple ancestries): 55.2% German, 14.3% Polish, 9.2% Irish, 6.1% Norwegian, 5.0% French (except Basque) (2000).
Economy: Single-family building permits issued: 60 (2001) / 57 (2000); Multi-family building permits issued: 42 (2001) / 46 (2000); Employment by occupation: 12.8% management, 18.8% professional, 7.3% services, 24.3% sales, 0.6% farming, 8.8% construction, 27.4% production (2000).
Income: Per capita income: $23,450 (2000); Median household income: $53,990 (2000); Poverty rate: 4.5% (2000).
Taxes: Total city taxes per capita: $214 (1997); City property taxes per capita: $152 (1997).
Education: High school graduation rate: 90.1% (2000); College graduation rate: 23.1% (2000).
Housing: Homeownership rate: 69.3% (2000); Median home value: $146,100 (2000); Median rent: $607 per month (2000); Median age of housing: 9 years (2000).
Safety: Violent crime rate: 6.0 per 10,000 population; Property crime rate: 108.6 per 10,000 population (2001).
Transportation: Commute to work: 96.4% car, 0.0% public transportation, 0.9% walk, 2.3% work from home (2000); Travel time to work: 23.1% less than 15 minutes, 48.2% 15 to 30 minutes, 17.6% 30 to 45 minutes, 7.2% 45 to 60 minutes, 4.0% 60 minutes or more (2000)

JACKSON (town). Covers a land area of 34.247 square miles and a water area of 0.109 square miles. Located at 43.32° N. Lat.; 88.12° W. Long. Elevation is 896 feet.
Population: 3,516 (2000); Race: 100.0% White, 0.0% Black, 0.0% Asian, 0.0% American Indian and Alaska Native, 0.0% Hispanic of any race, 0.0% two or more races (2000); Density: 102.7 persons per square mile (2000); Age: 29.4% under 18, 8.8% over 64 (2000); Marriage status: 21.3% never married, 72.6% now married, 2.0% widowed, 4.0% divorced (2000); Foreign born: 0.8% (2000); Ancestry (includes multiple ancestries): 70.3% German, 9.5% Irish, 6.7% Polish, 5.6% English, 4.9% Dutch (2000).
Economy: In dairying and farming area. Manufacturing: fabricated metal products, pharmaceuticals. Single-family building permits issued: 14 (2001) / 15 (2000); Multi-family building permits issued: 0 (2001) / 0 (2000); Employment by occupation: 15.9% management, 22.4% professional, 12.2% services, 19.5% sales, 2.2% farming, 10.6% construction, 17.3% production (2000).
Income: Per capita income: $22,045 (2000); Median household income: $64,070 (2000); Poverty rate: 0.5% (2000).
Taxes: Total city taxes per capita: $106 (1997); City property taxes per capita: $85 (1997).
Education: High school graduation rate: 90.8% (2000); College graduation rate: 23.4% (2000).
Housing: Homeownership rate: 91.8% (2000); Median home value: $166,900 (2000); Median rent: $509 per month (2000); Median age of housing: 32 years (2000).
Transportation: Commute to work: 92.9% car, 0.0% public transportation, 1.2% walk, 5.9% work from home (2000); Travel time to work: 26.6% less than 15 minutes, 40.6% 15 to 30 minutes, 21.9% 30 to 45 minutes, 10.0% 45 to 60 minutes, 0.8% 60 minutes or more (2000)

KEWASKUM (village). Covers a land area of 1.477 square miles and a water area of 0 square miles. Located at 43.52° N. Lat.; 88.23° W. Long. Elevation is 960 feet.
Population: 3,274 (2000); Race: 98.2% White, 0.1% Black, 0.6% Asian, 0.2% American Indian and Alaska Native, 0.4% Hispanic of any race, 0.8% two or more races (2000); Density: 2,217.3 persons per square mile (2000); Age: 28.2% under 18, 11.9% over 64 (2000); Marriage status: 25.6% never married, 60.4% now married, 5.0% widowed, 9.0% divorced (2000); Foreign born: 1.1% (2000); Ancestry (includes multiple ancestries): 60.3% German, 10.5% Irish, 5.7% English, 5.3% Polish, 4.1% Other groups (2000).
Economy: Employment by occupation: 9.1% management, 12.5% professional, 14.3% services, 24.6% sales, 0.1% farming, 11.2% construction 28.1% production (2000).
Income: Per capita income: $20,509 (2000); Median household income: $49,861 (2000); Poverty rate: 5.0% (2000).
Taxes: Total city taxes per capita: $302 (1997); City property taxes per capita: $284 (1997).
Education: High school graduation rate: 84.0% (2000); College graduation rate: 15.4% (2000).

School District(s)

Kewaskum (PK-12)
2000 Enrollment: 1,910 262-626-8427
Housing: Homeownership rate: 61.7% (2000); Median home value: $121,400 (2000); Median rent: $551 per month (2000); Median age of housing: 29 years (2000).
Safety: Violent crime rate: 9.1 per 10,000 population; Property crime rate: 294.2 per 10,000 population (2001).
Newspapers: Kewaskum Statesman (1 x week)

Transportation: Commute to work: 94.2% car, 0.3% public transportation, 2.4% walk, 2.7% work from home (2000); Travel time to work: 32.1% less than 15 minutes, 38.7% 15 to 30 minutes, 17.5% 30 to 45 minutes, 9.3% 45 to 60 minutes, 2.4% 60 minutes or more (2000)

KEWASKUM (town). Covers a land area of 22.766 square miles and a water area of 0.024 square miles. Located at 43.51° N. Lat.; 88.22° W. Long. Elevation is 960 feet.
Population: 1,119 (2000); Race: 99.6% White, 0.0% Black, 0.0% Asian, 0.0% American Indian and Alaska Native, 0.4% Hispanic of any race, 0.3% two or more races (2000); Density: 49.2 persons per square mile (2000); Age: 23.1% under 18, 12.9% over 64 (2000); Marriage status: 22.9% never married, 67.6% now married, 3.9% widowed, 5.6% divorced (2000); Foreign born: 0.2% (2000); Ancestry (includes multiple ancestries): 69.3% German, 9.1% Polish, 8.3% Irish, 3.0% Norwegian, 2.8% English (2000).
Economy: In dairy and farm area. Manufacturing: food-processing, machinery, cookware. Sunburst Ski Area to South. Single-family building permits issued: 9 (2001) / 2 (2000); Multi-family building permits issued: 0 (2001) / 0 (2000); Employment by occupation: 14.9% management, 16.9% professional, 8.4% services, 22.6% sales, 1.9% farming, 12.5% construction, 22.9% production (2000).
Income: Per capita income: $22,802 (2000); Median household income: $59,500 (2000); Poverty rate: 4.4% (2000).
Taxes: Total city taxes per capita: $133 (1997); City property taxes per capita: $124 (1997).
Education: High school graduation rate: 85.5% (2000); College graduation rate: 13.2% (2000).
Housing: Homeownership rate: 86.1% (2000); Median home value: $159,900 (2000); Median rent: $503 per month (2000); Median age of housing: 36 years (2000).
Transportation: Commute to work: 93.6% car, 0.3% public transportation, 1.7% walk, 4.1% work from home (2000); Travel time to work: 30.6% less than 15 minutes, 39.5% 15 to 30 minutes, 20.6% 30 to 45 minutes, 6.0% 45 to 60 minutes, 3.3% 60 minutes or more (2000)

NEWBURG (village). Covers a land area of 0.866 square miles and a water area of 0 square miles. Located at 43.43° N. Lat.; 88.04° W. Long. Elevation is 850 feet.
Population: 1,119 (2000); Race: 97.5% White, 0.0% Black, 0.5% Asian, 0.4% American Indian and Alaska Native, 1.0% Hispanic of any race, 1.6% two or more races (2000); Density: 1,292.0 persons per square mile (2000); Age: 30.4% under 18, 7.1% over 64 (2000); Marriage status: 24.0% never married, 60.7% now married, 5.0% widowed, 10.4% divorced (2000); Foreign born: 0.6% (2000); Ancestry (includes multiple ancestries): 56.6% German, 7.7% Polish, 7.7% Irish, 4.5% United States or American, 3.4% French (except Basque) (2000).
Economy: Agriculture: poultry; general farming. Manufacturing: transportation equipment, machinery. Single-family building permits issued: 1 (2001) / 6 (2000); Multi-family building permits issued: 0 (2001) / 0 (2000); Employment by occupation: 9.1% management, 11.4% professional, 11.4% services, 24.8% sales, 1.1% farming, 13.1% construction, 29.1% production (2000).
Income: Per capita income: $21,886 (2000); Median household income: $56,726 (2000); Poverty rate: 2.8% (2000).
Taxes: Total city taxes per capita: $88 (1997); City property taxes per capita: $73 (1997).
Education: High school graduation rate: 89.1% (2000); College graduation rate: 15.4% (2000).
Housing: Homeownership rate: 67.9% (2000); Median home value: $146,500 (2000); Median rent: $547 per month (2000); Median age of housing: 26 years (2000).
Transportation: Commute to work: 93.6% car, 0.0% public transportation, 3.1% walk, 2.8% work from home (2000); Travel time to work: 18.7% less than 15 minutes, 44.4% 15 to 30 minutes, 22.3% 30 to 45 minutes, 11.4% 45 to 60 minutes, 3.2% 60 minutes or more (2000)

POLK (town). Covers a land area of 31.933 square miles and a water area of 0.281 square miles. Located at 43.32° N. Lat.; 88.23° W. Long.
Population: 3,938 (2000); Race: 98.1% White, 0.8% Black, 0.5% Asian, 0.0% American Indian and Alaska Native, 0.9% Hispanic of any race, 0.6% two or more races (2000); Density: 123.3 persons per square mile (2000); Age: 27.5% under 18, 8.8% over 64 (2000); Marriage status: 22.5% never married, 72.0% now married, 2.7% widowed, 2.8% divorced (2000); Foreign born: 2.1% (2000); Ancestry (includes multiple ancestries): 61.6% German, 13.9% Irish, 9.1% Polish, 6.3% French (except Basque), 3.1% English (2000).
Economy: Single-family building permits issued: 23 (2001) / 20 (2000); Multi-family building permits issued: 0 (2001) / 0 (2000); Employment by occupation: 16.4% management, 15.7% professional, 10.0% services, 24.3% sales, 1.4% farming, 15.1% construction, 17.1% production (2000).
Income: Per capita income: $27,518 (2000); Median household income: $62,933 (2000); Poverty rate: 3.5% (2000).
Taxes: Total city taxes per capita: $81 (1997); City property taxes per capita: $66 (1997).
Education: High school graduation rate: 93.8% (2000); College graduation rate: 22.6% (2000).
Housing: Homeownership rate: 91.3% (2000); Median home value: $216,900 (2000); Median rent: $548 per month (2000); Median age of housing: 27 years (2000).
Transportation: Commute to work: 92.1% car, 0.6% public transportation, 0.8% walk, 4.8% work from home (2000); Travel time to work: 24.8% less than 15 minutes, 39.0% 15 to 30 minutes, 26.8% 30 to 45 minutes, 4.0% 45 to 60 minutes, 5.4% 60 minutes or more (2000)

RICHFIELD (town). Covers a land area of 35.870 square miles and a water area of 0.543 square miles. Located at 43.23° N. Lat.; 88.23° W. Long. Elevation is 974 feet.
History: Richfield was founded in 1842 by Philipp Laubenheimer, who twice had to move his log buildings when he found that they were in the path of a proposed road.
Population: 10,373 (2000); Race: 98.3% White, 0.6% Black, 0.2% Asian, 0.4% American Indian and Alaska Native, 0.0% Hispanic of any race, 0.4% two or more races (2000); Density: 289.2 persons per square mile (2000); Age: 26.7% under 18, 8.0% over 64 (2000); Marriage status: 19.6% never married, 71.0% now married, 3.0% widowed, 6.4% divorced (2000); Foreign born: 1.3% (2000); Ancestry (includes multiple ancestries): 60.8% German, 12.0% Polish, 9.5% Irish, 5.2% English, 5.1% Norwegian (2000).
Economy: Single-family building permits issued: 67 (2001) / 78 (2000); Multi-family building permits issued: 0 (2001) / 0 (2000); Employment by occupation: 17.3% management, 20.4% professional, 8.9% services, 24.4% sales, 0.6% farming, 11.4% construction, 17.0% production (2000).
Income: Per capita income: $29,859 (2000); Median household income: $72,809 (2000); Poverty rate: 1.3% (2000).
Taxes: Total city taxes per capita: $122 (2000); City property taxes per capita: $101 (2000).
Education: High school graduation rate: 92.2% (2000); College graduation rate: 24.8% (2000).

School District(s)

Richfield J1 (PK-08)
2000 Enrollment: 449 262-628-1032
Housing: Homeownership rate: 94.6% (2000); Median home value: $189,000 (2000); Median rent: $613 per month (2000); Median age of housing: 25 years (2000).
Transportation: Commute to work: 95.3% car, 0.4% public transportation, 0.6% walk, 3.4% work from home (2000); Travel time to work: 16.8% less than 15 minutes, 46.5% 15 to 30 minutes, 28.8% 30 to 45 minutes, 4.4% 45 to 60 minutes, 3.5% 60 minutes or more (2000)

SLINGER (village). Covers a land area of 3.726 square miles and a water area of 0.022 square miles. Located at 43.32° N. Lat.; 88.28° W. Long. Elevation is 1,069 feet.
History: Slinger was founded in the late 1840's by B. Schleisinger Weil, a German-Alsatian who started a general store and named his settlement Schleisinger. The name was shortened to Slinger in 1921.
Population: 3,901 (2000); Race: 96.6% White, 0.0% Black, 0.2% Asian, 1.0% American Indian and Alaska Native, 1.4% Hispanic of any race, 1.4% two or more races (2000); Density: 1,046.8 persons per square mile (2000); Age: 26.0% under 18, 13.1% over 64 (2000); Marriage status: 26.8% never married, 53.6% now married, 7.1% widowed, 12.6% divorced (2000); Foreign born: 2.1% (2000); Ancestry (includes multiple ancestries): 64.1% German, 9.1% Polish, 8.8% Irish, 4.3% United States or American, 3.8% Other groups (2000).
Economy: Single-family building permits issued: 22 (2001) / 38 (2000); Multi-family building permits issued: 4 (2001) / 22 (2000); Employment by occupation: 11.3% management, 20.8% professional, 12.3% services, 25.1% sales, 0.0% farming, 7.2% construction, 23.3% production (2000).
Income: Per capita income: $21,450 (2000); Median household income: $47,125 (2000); Poverty rate: 6.4% (2000).
Taxes: Total city taxes per capita: $282 (1997); City property taxes per capita: $246 (1997).
Education: High school graduation rate: 89.5% (2000); College graduation rate: 18.9% (2000).

School District(s)

Slinger (PK-12)
2000 Enrollment: 2,756 262-644-9615

Housing: Homeownership rate: 68.2% (2000); Median home value: $141,000 (2000); Median rent: $510 per month (2000); Median age of housing: 18 years (2000).

Safety: Violent crime rate: 15.3 per 10,000 population; Property crime rate: 272.3 per 10,000 population (2001).

Transportation: Commute to work: 90.4% car, 0.4% public transportation, 3.3% walk, 5.1% work from home (2000); Travel time to work: 29.1% less than 15 minutes, 36.5% 15 to 30 minutes, 26.9% 30 to 45 minutes, 4.9% 45 to 60 minutes, 2.6% 60 minutes or more (2000)

Additional Information Contacts

Washington Board of Realtors 262-644-8814

TRENTON (town). Covers a land area of 33.395 square miles and a water area of 0.066 square miles. Located at 43.41° N. Lat.; 88.10° W. Long.

Population: 4,440 (2000); Race: 98.7% White, 0.1% Black, 0.0% Asian, 0.4% American Indian and Alaska Native, 1.2% Hispanic of any race, 0.7% two or more races (2000); Density: 133.0 persons per square mile (2000); Age: 25.9% under 18, 9.7% over 64 (2000); Marriage status: 21.2% never married, 70.6% now married, 2.8% widowed, 5.3% divorced (2000); Foreign born: 0.8% (2000); Ancestry (includes multiple ancestries): 62.5% German, 10.7% Irish, 6.5% Polish, 4.4% English, 3.9% United States or American (2000).

Economy: Single-family building permits issued: 15 (2001) / 20 (2000); Multi-family building permits issued: 4 (2001) / 6 (2000); Employment by occupation: 18.6% management, 15.0% professional, 11.9% services, 23.5% sales, 0.3% farming, 8.4% construction, 22.3% production (2000).

Income: Per capita income: $24,767 (2000); Median household income: $66,213 (2000); Poverty rate: 2.9% (2000).

Taxes: Total city taxes per capita: $138 (1997); City property taxes per capita: $125 (1997).

Education: High school graduation rate: 85.8% (2000); College graduation rate: 18.7% (2000).

Housing: Homeownership rate: 94.3% (2000); Median home value: $152,000 (2000); Median rent: $527 per month (2000); Median age of housing: 28 years (2000).

Transportation: Commute to work: 97.7% car, 0.3% public transportation, 0.0% walk, 1.6% work from home (2000); Travel time to work: 33.7% less than 15 minutes, 31.0% 15 to 30 minutes, 21.6% 30 to 45 minutes, 9.4% 45 to 60 minutes, 4.3% 60 minutes or more (2000)

WAYNE (town). Covers a land area of 35.803 square miles and a water area of 0 square miles. Located at 43.50° N. Lat.; 88.35° W. Long. Elevation is 1,054 feet.

Population: 1,727 (2000); Race: 98.8% White, 0.3% Black, 0.0% Asian, 0.2% American Indian and Alaska Native, 0.1% Hispanic of any race, 0.7% two or more races (2000); Density: 48.2 persons per square mile (2000); Age: 26.5% under 18, 8.4% over 64 (2000); Marriage status: 22.6% never married, 68.2% now married, 3.4% widowed, 5.8% divorced (2000); Foreign born: 0.9% (2000); Ancestry (includes multiple ancestries): 68.8% German, 10.4% Polish, 8.9% Irish, 3.8% Norwegian, 3.2% United States or American (2000).

Economy: Single-family building permits issued: 19 (2001) / 18 (2000); Multi-family building permits issued: 0 (2001) / 0 (2000); Employment by occupation: 12.6% management, 13.7% professional, 10.2% services, 25.4% sales, 0.4% farming, 14.2% construction, 23.5% production (2000).

Income: Per capita income: $21,995 (2000); Median household income: $61,033 (2000); Poverty rate: 2.0% (2000).

Taxes: Total city taxes per capita: $124 (1997); City property taxes per capita: $97 (1997).

Education: High school graduation rate: 87.1% (2000); College graduation rate: 13.9% (2000).

Housing: Homeownership rate: 89.5% (2000); Median home value: $160,200 (2000); Median rent: $500 per month (2000); Median age of housing: 32 years (2000).

Transportation: Commute to work: 91.4% car, 0.3% public transportation, 0.6% walk, 7.4% work from home (2000); Travel time to work: 15.3% less than 15 minutes, 44.9% 15 to 30 minutes, 22.2% 30 to 45 minutes, 9.3% 45 to 60 minutes, 8.3% 60 minutes or more (2000)

WEST BEND (city). Covers a land area of 12.691 square miles and a water area of 0.238 square miles. Located at 43.42° N. Lat.; 88.18° W. Long. Elevation is 893 feet.

History: West Bend was founded in 1845 when Dr. E.B. Wolcott, on a surveying trip, decided that the bend in the Milwaukee River would make a good halfway stop between Fond du Lac and Milwaukee. Many of the early residents were of German ancestry. A stone brewery building was one of the first structures erected by the settlers. Aluminum goods, evaporated milk, machinery parts, and canned goods were among the products of West Bend in the early 1900's.

Population: 28,152 (2000); Race: 96.9% White, 0.5% Black, 0.8% Asian, 0.5% American Indian and Alaska Native, 1.7% Hispanic of any race, 0.8% two or more races (2000); Density: 2,218.3 persons per square mile (2000); Age: 26.1% under 18, 14.6% over 64 (2000); Marriage status: 25.1% never married, 59.5% now married, 7.2% widowed, 8.2% divorced (2000); Foreign born: 1.4% (2000); Ancestry (includes multiple ancestries): 58.4% German, 10.7% Irish, 8.3% Polish, 5.8% English, 4.4% Other groups (2000).

Vital Statistics: Birth rate: 158.4 per 10,000 population (1998)

Economy: Unemployment rate: 6.1% (11/2002); Total civilian labor force: 16,690 (11/2002); Single-family building permits issued: 92 (2001) / 90 (2000); Multi-family building permits issued: 68 (2001) / 72 (2000); Employment by occupation: 10.7% management, 18.7% professional, 12.9% services, 26.0% sales, 0.1% farming, 8.1% construction, 23.5% production (2000).

Income: Per capita income: $22,116 (2000); Median household income: $48,315 (2000); Poverty rate: 5.0% (2000).

Taxes: Total city taxes per capita: $429 (2000); City property taxes per capita: $392 (2000).

Education: High school graduation rate: 86.5% (2000); College graduation rate: 22.0% (2000).

School District(s)

West Bend (PK-12)
2000 Enrollment: 6,779 262-335-5435

Housing: Homeownership rate: 62.0% (2000); Median home value: $132,500 (2000); Median rent: $536 per month (2000); Median age of housing: 25 years (2000).

Hospitals: Saint Joseph's Community Hospital of West Bend (121 beds); Washington County Mental Health, Inpatient Unit (19 beds)

Safety: Violent crime rate: 2.1 per 10,000 population; Property crime rate: 324.1 per 10,000 population (2001).

Newspapers: West Bend Daily News (6 x week)

Transportation: Commute to work: 94.3% car, 1.3% public transportation, 1.3% walk, 2.4% work from home (2000); Travel time to work: 43.2% less than 15 minutes, 25.7% 15 to 30 minutes, 20.4% 30 to 45 minutes, 7.3% 45 to 60 minutes, 3.3% 60 minutes or more (2000)

Additional Information Contacts

West Bend Area Chamber of Commerce 262-338-2666

WEST BEND (town). Covers a land area of 16.141 square miles and a water area of 1.993 square miles. Located at 43.39° N. Lat.; 88.23° W. Long. Elevation is 893 feet.

History: Incorporated 1885, consolidated with Barton in 1961.

Population: 4,834 (2000); Race: 99.1% White, 0.0% Black, 0.5% Asian, 0.0% American Indian and Alaska Native, 0.5% Hispanic of any race, 0.0% two or more races (2000); Density: 299.5 persons per square mile (2000); Age: 23.5% under 18, 18.7% over 64 (2000); Marriage status: 18.5% never married, 72.1% now married, 4.6% widowed, 4.8% divorced (2000); Foreign born: 1.3% (2000); Ancestry (includes multiple ancestries): 51.5% German, 10.0% Irish, 9.4% Polish, 6.6% United States or American, 6.5% English (2000).

Economy: Farm implements, dairy items, electronic components and leather products are made here. Sunburst Ski Area to Northwest. Single-family building permits issued: 38 (2001) / 40 (2000); Multi-family building permits issued: 0 (2001) / 0 (2000); Employment by occupation: 12.2% management, 24.7% professional, 9.5% services, 26.3% sales, 0.0% farming, 7.6% construction, 19.6% production (2000).

Income: Per capita income: $33,097 (2000); Median household income: $73,333 (2000); Poverty rate: 1.8% (2000).

Taxes: Total city taxes per capita: $84 (1997); City property taxes per capita: $63 (1997).

Education: High school graduation rate: 87.9% (2000); College graduation rate: 28.9% (2000).

Housing: Homeownership rate: 87.5% (2000); Median home value: $218,300 (2000); Median rent: $510 per month (2000); Median age of housing: 29 years (2000).

Transportation: Commute to work: 95.1% car, 1.3% public transportation, 0.6% walk, 2.6% work from home (2000); Travel time to work: 32.9% less than 15 minutes, 30.7% 15 to 30 minutes, 27.5% 30 to 45 minutes, 3.8% 45 to 60 minutes, 5.1% 60 minutes or more (2000)

Waukesha County

Located in southeastern Wisconsin; hilly area, drained by the Fox and Bark Rivers; includes many lakes. Covers a land area of 555.60 square miles, a water area of 24.90 square miles, and is located in the Central Time Zone. The county government was organized in 1846. County seat is Waukesha.

Waukesha County is part of the Milwaukee-Waukesha, WI PMSA. The entire metro area includes: Milwaukee County; Ozaukee County; Washington County; Waukesha County

Weather Station: Oconomowoc Elevation: 853 feet

	Jan	Feb	Mar	Apr	May	Jun	Jul	Aug	Sep	Oct	Nov	Dec
High	26	31	42	56	69	78	83	80	72	60	44	32
Low	8	13	24	36	47	56	61	59	50	39	28	16
Precip	1.3	1.2	1.9	3.2	3.0	3.9	4.2	4.5	3.8	2.7	2.3	1.7
Snow	11.1	7.3	5.9	2.0	0.3	0.0	0.0	0.0	tr	tr	3.1	10.0

High and Low temperatures in degrees Fahrenheit; Precipitation and Snow in inches

Weather Station: Waukesha Elevation: 830 feet

	Jan	Feb	Mar	Apr	May	Jun	Jul	Aug	Sep	Oct	Nov	Dec
High	26	32	43	56	69	79	83	81	73	60	45	32
Low	10	17	26	37	47	57	62	61	53	42	30	18
Precip	1.5	1.4	2.2	3.6	3.0	3.9	3.8	4.6	3.5	2.6	2.6	1.9
Snow	12.8	7.7	7.4	2.7	tr	0.0	0.0	0.0	0.0	0.1	3.0	9.5

High and Low temperatures in degrees Fahrenheit; Precipitation and Snow in inches

Population: 360,767 (2000); Race: 95.7% White, 0.7% Black, 1.4% Asian, 0.3% American Indian and Alaska Native, 2.5% Hispanic of any race, 1.1% two or more races (2000); Density: 649.4 persons per square mile (2000); Age: 26.3% under 18, 12.0% over 64 (2000).
Religion: Five largest groups: 37.3% Catholic Church, 7.5% Evangelical Lutheran Church in America, 4.7% Lutheran Church—Missouri Synod, 4.2% Wisconsin Evangelical Lutheran Synod, 2.2% Independent, Charismatic Churches (2000).
Economy: Unemployment rate: 3.6% (11/2002); Total civilian labor force: 217,988 (11/2002); Leading industries: 22.1% manufacturing; 11.4% retail trade; 8.5% health care and social assistance (2000); Companies that employ more than 1,000 persons: 6 (2000); Companies that employ more than 100 persons: 408 (2000); Farms: 630 totaling 105,608 acres (1997); Minority business ownership rate: 3.3% (1997); Women business ownership rate: 24.3% (1997); Retail sales per capita: $11,751 (1997). Single-family building permits issued: 1,822 (2001) / 1,848 (2000); Multi-family building permits issued: 906 (2001) / 600 (2000).
Income: Per capita income: $29,164 (2000); Median household income: $62,839 (2000); Poverty rate: 2.7% (2000); Bankruptcy rate: 2.58% (2001).
Taxes: Total county taxes per capita: $178 (2000); County property taxes per capita: $171 (2000).
Education: High school graduation rate: 92.0% (2000); College graduation rate: 34.1% (2000).
Housing: Homeownership rate: 76.5% (2000); Median home value: $170,400 (2000); Median rent: $663 per month (2000); Median age of housing: 26 years (2000).
Health: Birth rate: 114.3 per 10,000 population (1998); Age adjusted death rate: 78.5 per 10,000 population (1999); Infant mortality rate: 5.1 per 1,000 live births (1998); Age adjusted cancer mortality rate: 206.1 deaths per 100,000 population (1999). Air Quality Index: 84% good, 16% moderate, 0% unhealthy (percent of days in 2000). Number of physicians: 36.7 per 10,000 population (1999); Number of hospital beds: 20.9 per 10,000 population (1999).
Elections: 2000 Presidential election results: 31.6% Gore, 65.3% Bush, 2.4% Nader, 0.3% Buchanan
National and State Parks: Cushing Memorial State Park
Additional Information Contacts
Waukesha County Government Offices 262-548-7194
Brookfield Chamber of Commerce 262-786-1886
Butler Chamber of Commerce 262-781-5195
Delafield Chamber of Commerce 262-646-8100
Hartland Chamber of Commerce 262-367-7059
Menomonee Falls Chamber of Commerce 262-251-2430
Mukwonago Chamber of Commerce 262-363-7758
Muskego Chamber of Commerce 262-679-2550
Nashotah Area Chamber of Commerce 262-367-6262
Pewaukee Chamber of Commerce 262-691-8851
Waukesha Chamber of Commerce 262-542-4249

Waukesha County Communities

BIG BEND (village). Covers a land area of 2.264 square miles and a water area of 0.012 square miles. Located at 42.88° N. Lat.; 88.21° W. Long. Elevation is 820 feet.
Population: 1,278 (2000); Race: 97.3% White, 1.1% Black, 0.2% Asian, 0.8% American Indian and Alaska Native, 1.6% Hispanic of any race, 0.4% two or more races (2000); Density: 564.6 persons per square mile (2000); Age: 29.2% under 18, 9.6% over 64 (2000); Marriage status: 22.2% never married, 63.0% now married, 6.3% widowed, 8.6% divorced (2000); Foreign born: 1.7% (2000); Ancestry (includes multiple ancestries): 54.3% German, 23.3% Polish, 12.0% Irish, 5.8% Other groups, 4.5% French (except Basque) (2000).
Economy: In farm and lake area; light manufacturing. Employment by occupation: 10.2% management, 15.7% professional, 9.1% services, 32.9% sales, 0.0% farming, 12.9% construction, 19.2% production (2000).
Income: Per capita income: $22,072 (2000); Median household income: $56,767 (2000); Poverty rate: 2.9% (2000).
Taxes: Total city taxes per capita: $250 (1997); City property taxes per capita: $243 (1997).
Education: High school graduation rate: 87.1% (2000); College graduation rate: 20.2% (2000).
Housing: Homeownership rate: 81.5% (2000); Median home value: $137,900 (2000); Median rent: $553 per month (2000); Median age of housing: 41 years (2000).
Transportation: Commute to work: 96.0% car, 0.4% public transportation, 0.6% walk, 2.2% work from home (2000); Travel time to work: 24.1% less than 15 minutes, 43.1% 15 to 30 minutes, 23.9% 30 to 45 minutes, 6.2% 45 to 60 minutes, 2.7% 60 minutes or more (2000)

BROOKFIELD (city). Covers a land area of 27.197 square miles and a water area of 0.071 square miles. Located at 43.05° N. Lat.; 88.11° W. Long. Elevation is 828 feet.
Population: 38,649 (2000); Race: 94.6% White, 0.7% Black, 3.4% Asian, 0.3% American Indian and Alaska Native, 0.8% Hispanic of any race, 0.8% two or more races (2000); Density: 1,421.1 persons per square mile (2000); Age: 26.6% under 18, 17.8% over 64 (2000); Marriage status: 18.6% never married, 70.4% now married, 6.3% widowed, 4.8% divorced (2000); Foreign born: 6.3% (2000); Ancestry (includes multiple ancestries): 46.1% German, 14.7% Irish, 11.3% Polish, 7.7% Italian, 7.3% English (2000).
Vital Statistics: Birth rate: 79.2 per 10,000 population (1998)
Economy: Unemployment rate: 3.2% (11/2002); Total civilian labor force: 21,551 (11/2002); Single-family building permits issued: 103 (2001) / 129 (2000); Multi-family building permits issued: 133 (2001) / 71 (2000); Employment by occupation: 21.9% management, 29.3% professional, 7.5% services, 28.1% sales, 0.0% farming, 4.0% construction, 9.0% production (2000).
Income: Per capita income: $37,292 (2000); Median household income: $76,225 (2000); Poverty rate: 2.2% (2000).
Taxes: Total city taxes per capita: $590 (2000); City property taxes per capita: $515 (2000).
Education: High school graduation rate: 94.0% (2000); College graduation rate: 49.0% (2000).

School District(s)
Elmbrook (PK-12)
2000 Enrollment: 7,415 262-781-3030

Housing: Homeownership rate: 90.0% (2000); Median home value: $189,100 (2000); Median rent: $924 per month (2000); Median age of housing: 32 years (2000).
Hospitals: Elmbrook Memorial Hospital (166 beds)
Safety: Violent crime rate: 5.9 per 10,000 population; Property crime rate: 298.5 per 10,000 population (2001).
Transportation: Commute to work: 94.9% car, 0.5% public transportation, 0.4% walk, 3.8% work from home (2000); Travel time to work: 32.3% less than 15 minutes, 49.7% 15 to 30 minutes, 13.6% 30 to 45 minutes, 2.5% 45 to 60 minutes, 1.9% 60 minutes or more (2000)
Additional Information Contacts
Brookfield Chamber of Commerce 262-786-1886

BROOKFIELD (town). Covers a land area of 5.507 square miles and a water area of 0 square miles. Located at 43.03° N. Lat.; 88.17° W. Long. Elevation is 828 feet.
History: Incorporated 1954.
Population: 6,390 (2000); Race: 92.1% White, 2.1% Black, 4.1% Asian, 0.2% American Indian and Alaska Native, 1.6% Hispanic of any race, 1.2%

two or more races (2000); Density: 1,160.3 persons per square mile (2000); Age: 24.2% under 18, 22.6% over 64 (2000); Marriage status: 17.7% never married, 62.5% now married, 12.9% widowed, 6.9% divorced (2000); Foreign born: 8.3% (2000); Ancestry (includes multiple ancestries): 45.8% German, 16.5% Irish, 11.8% Polish, 8.7% Other groups, 7.5% Italian (2000).
Economy: Although principally a residential community, Brookfield has undergone suburban expansion since 1975 with its iron foundries and manufacturing: electronic equipment, fabricated metal products, safety ladders, water-softener components, polishes and detergents, burial vaults; plastic fabrication. Also a center for retailing and business. Single-family building permits issued: 4 (2001) / 20 (2000); Multi-family building permits issued: 4 (2001) / 8 (2000); Employment by occupation: 23.1% management, 29.1% professional, 10.6% services, 24.2% sales, 0.0% farming, 4.9% construction, 8.1% production (2000).
Income: Per capita income: $28,608 (2000); Median household income: $55,417 (2000); Poverty rate: 3.1% (2000).
Taxes: Total city taxes per capita: $460 (2000); City property taxes per capita: $347 (2000).
Education: High school graduation rate: 91.3% (2000); College graduation rate: 39.8% (2000).
Housing: Homeownership rate: 63.2% (2000); Median home value: $177,100 (2000); Median rent: $891 per month (2000); Median age of housing: 12 years (2000).
Safety: Violent crime rate: 14.0 per 10,000 population; Property crime rate: 405.5 per 10,000 population (2001).
Transportation: Commute to work: 95.6% car, 0.2% public transportation, 0.4% walk, 3.5% work from home (2000); Travel time to work: 37.4% less than 15 minutes, 38.7% 15 to 30 minutes, 17.0% 30 to 45 minutes, 4.0% 45 to 60 minutes, 2.9% 60 minutes or more (2000)

BUTLER (village). Covers a land area of 0.792 square miles and a water area of 0 square miles. Located at 43.10° N. Lat.; 88.06° W. Long. Elevation is 750 feet.
History: Until 1930, called New Butler.
Population: 1,881 (2000); Race: 97.0% White, 0.0% Black, 1.3% Asian, 1.2% American Indian and Alaska Native, 0.5% Hispanic of any race, 0.5% two or more races (2000); Density: 2,376.2 persons per square mile (2000); Age: 19.5% under 18, 23.8% over 64 (2000); Marriage status: 23.8% never married, 49.9% now married, 14.6% widowed, 11.7% divorced (2000); Foreign born: 3.9% (2000); Ancestry (includes multiple ancestries): 61.5% German, 10.2% Polish, 8.3% Irish, 8.0% English, 7.7% Italian (2000).
Economy: Manufacturing: machinery, rubber products, paper products; metal spinning, meat processing. Single-family building permits issued: 1 (2001) / 0 (2000); Multi-family building permits issued: 2 (2001) / 0 (2000); Employment by occupation: 9.9% management, 12.8% professional, 7.3% services, 34.5% sales, 0.0% farming, 9.1% construction, 26.3% production (2000).
Income: Per capita income: $22,167 (2000); Median household income: $38,333 (2000); Poverty rate: 2.4% (2000).
Taxes: Total city taxes per capita: $669 (1997); City property taxes per capita: $643 (1997).
Education: High school graduation rate: 77.4% (2000); College graduation rate: 13.0% (2000).
Housing: Homeownership rate: 49.8% (2000); Median home value: $115,100 (2000); Median rent: $553 per month (2000); Median age of housing: 41 years (2000).
Safety: Violent crime rate: 63.4 per 10,000 population; Property crime rate: 464.6 per 10,000 population (2001).
Transportation: Commute to work: 91.7% car, 0.5% public transportation, 3.7% walk, 2.7% work from home (2000); Travel time to work: 41.9% less than 15 minutes, 41.7% 15 to 30 minutes, 13.1% 30 to 45 minutes, 0.9% 45 to 60 minutes, 2.4% 60 minutes or more (2000)
Additional Information Contacts
Butler Chamber of Commerce 262-781-5195

CHENEQUA (village). Covers a land area of 3.545 square miles and a water area of 1.137 square miles. Located at 43.12° N. Lat.; 88.38° W. Long. Elevation is 920 feet.
Population: 583 (2000); Race: 97.1% White, 0.0% Black, 1.2% Asian, 1.7% American Indian and Alaska Native, 1.5% Hispanic of any race, 0.0% two or more races (2000); Density: 164.5 persons per square mile (2000); Age: 24.8% under 18, 14.7% over 64 (2000); Marriage status: 20.5% never married, 74.5% now married, 0.2% widowed, 4.8% divorced (2000); Foreign born: 3.2% (2000); Ancestry (includes multiple ancestries): 44.9% German, 17.7% Irish, 12.7% English, 6.4% Polish, 5.6% Norwegian (2000).
Economy: In farm and lake-resort region. Single-family building permits issued: 3 (2001) / 4 (2000); Multi-family building permits issued: 0 (2001) / 0 (2000); Employment by occupation: 32.3% management, 26.5% professional, 11.0% services, 20.6% sales, 0.0% farming, 4.1% construction, 5.5% production (2000).
Income: Per capita income: $86,552 (2000); Median household income: $163,428 (2000); Poverty rate: 0.5% (2000).
Taxes: Total city taxes per capita: $1,533 (1997); City property taxes per capita: $1,513 (1997).
Education: High school graduation rate: 98.1% (2000); College graduation rate: 67.3% (2000).
Housing: Homeownership rate: 89.0% (2000); Median home value: $810,000 (2000); Median rent: $763 per month (2000); Median age of housing: 43 years (2000).
Safety: Violent crime rate: 0.0 per 10,000 population; Property crime rate: 51.1 per 10,000 population (2001).
Transportation: Commute to work: 85.1% car, 1.0% public transportation, 2.4% walk, 8.7% work from home (2000); Travel time to work: 29.2% less than 15 minutes, 25.8% 15 to 30 minutes, 33.0% 30 to 45 minutes, 9.1% 45 to 60 minutes, 3.0% 60 minutes or more (2000)

DELAFIELD (city). Covers a land area of 9.515 square miles and a water area of 1.586 square miles. Located at 43.07° N. Lat.; 88.39° W. Long. Elevation is 910 feet.
Population: 6,472 (2000); Race: 97.3% White, 0.0% Black, 0.8% Asian, 0.7% American Indian and Alaska Native, 0.5% Hispanic of any race, 1.0% two or more races (2000); Density: 680.2 persons per square mile (2000); Age: 28.3% under 18, 10.5% over 64 (2000); Marriage status: 21.2% never married, 63.6% now married, 6.1% widowed, 9.1% divorced (2000); Foreign born: 1.9% (2000); Ancestry (includes multiple ancestries): 52.4% German, 14.2% Irish, 9.2% Polish, 7.7% English, 5.9% Norwegian (2000).
Economy: Single-family building permits issued: 21 (2001) / 28 (2000); Multi-family building permits issued: 62 (2001) / 18 (2000); Employment by occupation: 19.8% management, 23.2% professional, 11.6% services, 23.9% sales, 0.3% farming, 8.4% construction, 12.9% production (2000).
Income: Per capita income: $31,602 (2000); Median household income: $61,938 (2000); Poverty rate: 3.4% (2000).
Taxes: Total city taxes per capita: $488 (1997); City property taxes per capita: $452 (1997).
Education: High school graduation rate: 94.5% (2000); College graduation rate: 37.1% (2000).
Housing: Homeownership rate: 64.9% (2000); Median home value: $233,000 (2000); Median rent: $675 per month (2000); Median age of housing: 23 years (2000).
Safety: Violent crime rate: 13.8 per 10,000 population; Property crime rate: 191.8 per 10,000 population (2001).
Transportation: Commute to work: 91.0% car, 0.4% public transportation, 2.1% walk, 5.3% work from home (2000); Travel time to work: 29.7% less than 15 minutes, 36.6% 15 to 30 minutes, 24.9% 30 to 45 minutes, 6.2% 45 to 60 minutes, 2.5% 60 minutes or more (2000)
Additional Information Contacts
Delafield Chamber of Commerce. 262-646-8100

DELAFIELD (town). Covers a land area of 18.630 square miles and a water area of 2.118 square miles. Located at 43.05° N. Lat.; 88.34° W. Long. Elevation is 910 feet.
Population: 7,820 (2000); Race: 93.7% White, 3.4% Black, 0.9% Asian, 0.4% American Indian and Alaska Native, 1.2% Hispanic of any race, 0.9% two or more races (2000); Density: 419.7 persons per square mile (2000); Age: 31.5% under 18, 6.9% over 64 (2000); Marriage status: 19.2% never married, 73.9% now married, 2.2% widowed, 4.7% divorced (2000); Foreign born: 3.5% (2000); Ancestry (includes multiple ancestries): 47.7% German, 14.5% Polish, 14.2% Irish, 9.9% English, 5.7% Italian (2000).
Economy: St. John's Military Academy and a state fish hatchery are nearby. Single-family building permits issued: 59 (2001) / 103 (2000); Multi-family building permits issued: 0 (2001) / 0 (2000); Employment by occupation: 26.7% management, 25.5% professional, 7.7% services, 26.4% sales, 0.0% farming, 6.5% construction, 7.1% production (2000).
Income: Per capita income: $41,391 (2000); Median household income: $98,779 (2000); Poverty rate: 3.0% (2000).
Taxes: Total city taxes per capita: $136 (2000); City property taxes per capita: $115 (2000).
Education: High school graduation rate: 96.3% (2000); College graduation rate: 47.6% (2000).

Housing: Homeownership rate: 90.9% (2000); Median home value: $285,500 (2000); Median rent: $765 per month (2000); Median age of housing: 19 years (2000).
Transportation: Commute to work: 94.4% car, 0.7% public transportation, 0.9% walk, 3.9% work from home (2000); Travel time to work: 24.7% less than 15 minutes, 44.1% 15 to 30 minutes, 22.9% 30 to 45 minutes, 6.1% 45 to 60 minutes, 2.2% 60 minutes or more (2000)

DOUSMAN (village). Covers a land area of 1.233 square miles and a water area of 0.045 square miles. Located at 43.01° N. Lat.; 88.47° W. Long. Elevation is 870 feet.
Population: 1,584 (2000); Race: 97.2% White, 0.1% Black, 1.0% Asian, 1.1% American Indian and Alaska Native, 1.0% Hispanic of any race, 0.6% two or more races (2000); Density: 1,284.2 persons per square mile (2000); Age: 26.0% under 18, 16.6% over 64 (2000); Marriage status: 18.8% never married, 56.6% now married, 10.1% widowed, 14.5% divorced (2000); Foreign born: 2.4% (2000); Ancestry (includes multiple ancestries): 52.5% German, 12.5% Irish, 10.8% Polish, 8.2% English, 6.9% Italian (2000).
Economy: In farm and resort area. Furniture, veal feeds. Single-family building permits issued: 58 (2001) / 0 (2000); Multi-family building permits issued: 0 (2001) / 0 (2000); Employment by occupation: 13.6% management, 16.3% professional, 11.3% services, 25.8% sales, 0.3% farming, 11.1 construction, 21.6% production (2000).
Income: Per capita income: $21,722 (2000); Median household income: $46,944 (2000); Poverty rate: 4.5% (2000).
Taxes: Total city taxes per capita: $189 (1997); City property taxes per capita: $168 (1997).
Education: High school graduation rate: 87.7% (2000); College graduation rate: 20.3% (2000).
Housing: Homeownership rate: 56.0% (2000); Median home value: $137,000 (2000); Median rent: $688 per month (2000); Median age of housing: 24 years (2000).
Transportation: Commute to work: 94.3% car, 0.6% public transportation, 2.3% walk, 1.8% work from home (2000); Travel time to work: 22.6% less than 15 minutes, 40.8% 15 to 30 minutes, 24.4% 30 to 45 minutes, 8.1% 45 to 60 minutes, 4.1% 60 minutes or more (2000)

EAGLE (village). Covers a land area of 1.268 square miles and a water area of 0 square miles. Located at 42.87° N. Lat.; 88.47° W. Long. Elevation is 949 feet.
Population: 1,707 (2000); Race: 96.0% White, 0.4% Black, 0.0% Asian, 1.7% American Indian and Alaska Native, 2.4% Hispanic of any race, 0.5% two or more races (2000); Density: 1,346.5 persons per square mile (2000); Age: 29.7% under 18, 6.1% over 64 (2000); Marriage status: 19.0% never married, 71.4% now married, 4.0% widowed, 5.5% divorced (2000); Foreign born: 1.8% (2000); Ancestry (includes multiple ancestries): 47.2% German, 17.2% Polish, 10.6% Irish, 6.3% English, 6.1% Norwegian (2000).
Economy: Single-family building permits issued: 5 (2001) / 10 (2000); Multi-family building permits issued: 0 (2001) / 0 (2000); Employment by occupation: 11.2% management, 17.4% professional, 10.8% services, 29.4% sales, 0.0% farming, 12.7% construction, 18.4% production (2000).
Income: Per capita income: $21,975 (2000); Median household income: $58,207 (2000); Poverty rate: 3.1% (2000).
Taxes: Total city taxes per capita: $245 (1997); City property taxes per capita: $217 (1997).
Education: High school graduation rate: 90.6% (2000); College graduation rate: 16.8% (2000).
Housing: Homeownership rate: 90.0% (2000); Median home value: $139,400 (2000); Median rent: $476 per month (2000); Median age of housing: 21 years (2000).
Safety: Violent crime rate: 0.0 per 10,000 population; Property crime rate: 75.6 per 10,000 population (2001).
Transportation: Commute to work: 96.7% car, 1.1% public transportation, 0.6% walk, 1.6% work from home (2000); Travel time to work: 13.1% less than 15 minutes, 34.4% 15 to 30 minutes, 32.6% 30 to 45 minutes, 13.4% 45 to 60 minutes, 6.5% 60 minutes or more (2000)

EAGLE (town). Covers a land area of 34.632 square miles and a water area of 0.425 square miles. Located at 42.88° N. Lat.; 88.45° W. Long. Elevation is 949 feet.
Population: 3,117 (2000); Race: 96.4% White, 0.4% Black, 0.2% Asian, 0.3% American Indian and Alaska Native, 1.6% Hispanic of any race, 1.5% two or more races (2000); Density: 90.0 persons per square mile (2000); Age: 29.7% under 18, 7.1% over 64 (2000); Marriage status: 18.6% never married, 74.0% now married, 2.8% widowed, 4.6% divorced (2000); Foreign born: 2.2% (2000); Ancestry (includes multiple ancestries): 49.5% German, 14.3% Polish, 11.0% Irish, 8.0% English, 5.8% Norwegian (2000).
Economy: In agricultural and lake-resort region. Light manufacturing. Single-family building permits issued: 43 (2001) / 55 (2000); Multi-family building permits issued: 0 (2001) / 0 (2000); Employment by occupation: 18.0% management, 15.8% professional, 12.0% services, 28.2% sales, 0.9% farming, 12.1% construction, 12.9% production (2000).
Income: Per capita income: $26,354 (2000); Median household income: $69,071 (2000); Poverty rate: 3.1% (2000).
Taxes: Total city taxes per capita: $119 (1997); City property taxes per capita: $90 (1997).
Education: High school graduation rate: 94.7% (2000); College graduation rate: 23.9% (2000).
Housing: Homeownership rate: 93.9% (2000); Median home value: $195,400 (2000); Median rent: $591 per month (2000); Median age of housing: 21 years (2000).
Transportation: Commute to work: 96.0% car, 0.3% public transportation, 0.6% walk, 2.6% work from home (2000); Travel time to work: 19.5% less than 15 minutes, 28.2% 15 to 30 minutes, 29.6% 30 to 45 minutes, 15.3% 45 to 60 minutes, 7.4% 60 minutes or more (2000)

ELM GROVE (village). Covers a land area of 3.257 square miles and a water area of 0 square miles. Located at 43.04° N. Lat.; 88.08° W. Long. Elevation is 746 feet.
Population: 6,249 (2000); Race: 98.0% White, 0.2% Black, 1.0% Asian, 0.0% American Indian and Alaska Native, 1.7% Hispanic of any race, 0.7% two or more races (2000); Density: 1,918.6 persons per square mile (2000); Age: 25.1% under 18, 21.8% over 64 (2000); Marriage status: 19.6% never married, 69.7% now married, 7.0% widowed, 3.7% divorced (2000); Foreign born: 4.6% (2000); Ancestry (includes multiple ancestries): 47.8% German, 18.3% Irish, 12.1% English, 7.3% Italian, 7.2% Polish (2000).
Economy: Manufacturing: trade bindery. Single-family building permits issued: 4 (2001) / 1 (2000); Multi-family building permits issued: 8 (2001) / 35 (2000); Employment by occupation: 28.2% management, 35.3% professional, 7.7% services, 20.1% sales, 0.0% farming, 2.8% construction, 5.9% production (2000).
Income: Per capita income: $48,871 (2000); Median household income: $86,212 (2000); Poverty rate: 3.0% (2000).
Taxes: Total city taxes per capita: $747 (2000); City property taxes per capita: $730 (2000).
Education: High school graduation rate: 96.3% (2000); College graduation rate: 65.1% (2000).
Housing: Homeownership rate: 90.1% (2000); Median home value: $263,900 (2000); Median rent: $634 per month (2000); Median age of housing: 38 years (2000).
Safety: Violent crime rate: 3.2 per 10,000 population; Property crime rate: 146.2 per 10,000 population (2001).
Transportation: Commute to work: 89.9% car, 0.6% public transportation, 1.4% walk, 6.7% work from home (2000); Travel time to work: 43.8% less than 15 minutes, 42.9% 15 to 30 minutes, 9.1% 30 to 45 minutes, 2.2% 45 to 60 minutes, 2.0% 60 minutes or more (2000)

GENESEE (town). Covers a land area of 31.903 square miles and a water area of 0.098 square miles. Located at 42.97° N. Lat.; 88.36° W. Long. Elevation is 896 feet.
Population: 7,284 (2000); Race: 96.4% White, 0.0% Black, 0.8% Asian, 0.7% American Indian and Alaska Native, 0.7% Hispanic of any race, 1.3% two or more races (2000); Density: 228.3 persons per square mile (2000); Age: 29.4% under 18, 6.3% over 64 (2000); Marriage status: 17.4% never married, 76.0% now married, 3.1% widowed, 3.6% divorced (2000); Foreign born: 1.5% (2000); Ancestry (includes multiple ancestries): 47.9% German, 13.8% Irish, 11.6% English, 10.2% Polish, 7.9% Norwegian (2000).
Economy: Single-family building permits issued: 48 (2001) / 57 (2000); Multi-family building permits issued: 0 (2001) / 0 (2000); Employment by occupation: 19.5% management, 22.9% professional, 8.4% services, 27.3% sales, 0.1% farming, 9.1% construction, 12.6% production (2000).
Income: Per capita income: $31,028 (2000); Median household income: $78,740 (2000); Poverty rate: 0.8% (2000).
Taxes: Total city taxes per capita: $74 (1997); City property taxes per capita: $63 (1997).
Education: High school graduation rate: 94.6% (2000); College graduation rate: 36.4% (2000).
Housing: Homeownership rate: 94.3% (2000); Median home value: $202,000 (2000); Median rent: $705 per month (2000); Median age of housing: 23 years (2000).

Transportation: Commute to work: 93.0% car, 0.8% public transportation, 0.3% walk, 5.6% work from home (2000); Travel time to work: 18.8% less than 15 minutes, 41.7% 15 to 30 minutes, 26.4% 30 to 45 minutes, 7.3% 45 to 60 minutes, 5.8% 60 minutes or more (2000)

HARTLAND (village). Covers a land area of 4.508 square miles and a water area of 0.007 square miles. Located at 43.10° N. Lat.; 88.34° W. Long. Elevation is 930 feet.
Population: 7,905 (2000); Race: 96.3% White, 0.3% Black, 1.6% Asian, 0.1% American Indian and Alaska Native, 1.8% Hispanic of any race, 1.3% two or more races (2000); Density: 1,753.7 persons per square mile (2000); Age: 29.5% under 18, 7.1% over 64 (2000); Marriage status: 27.3% never married, 59.3% now married, 3.0% widowed, 10.5% divorced (2000); Foreign born: 2.5% (2000); Ancestry (includes multiple ancestries): 47.5% German, 15.3% Irish, 10.1% Polish, 7.4% Italian, 6.8% English (2000).
Economy: In dairying and farming area with resort lakes nearby. Manufacturing of dairy products, wood products, steel products, medical equipment, microfiche, fiberglass, plastic products, teflon seals; machining. Single-family building permits issued: 80 (2001) / 112 (2000); Multi-family building permits issued: 72 (2001) / 2 (2000); Employment by occupation: 13.7% management, 24.6% professional, 12.8% services, 26.4% sales, 0.6% farming, 7.8% construction, 14.0% production (2000).
Income: Per capita income: $26,537 (2000); Median household income: $58,359 (2000); Poverty rate: 2.6% (2000).
Taxes: Total city taxes per capita: $374 (1997); City property taxes per capita: $350 (1997).
Education: High school graduation rate: 94.7% (2000); College graduation rate: 32.0% (2000).

School District(s)

Arrowhead UHS (09-12)
2000 Enrollment: 1,943 262-367-3611
Hartland-Lakeside J3 (PK-08)
2000 Enrollment: 1,306 262-369-6700
Lake Country (KG-08)
2000 Enrollment: 498 262-367-3606
Swallow (KG-08)
2000 Enrollment: 345 262-367-2000

Housing: Homeownership rate: 58.4% (2000); Median home value: $161,100 (2000); Median rent: $612 per month (2000); Median age of housing: 24 years (2000).
Safety: Violent crime rate: 5.0 per 10,000 population; Property crime rate: 216.1 per 10,000 population (2001).
Newspapers: Oconomowoc Focus (2 x week); Kettle Moraine Index (1 x week); The Index (1 x week); Sussex Sun (1 x week); Lake Country Reporter (2 x week)
Transportation: Commute to work: 94.1% car, 0.0% public transportation, 2.1% walk, 3.2% work from home (2000); Travel time to work: 36.7% less than 15 minutes, 39.1% 15 to 30 minutes, 17.4% 30 to 45 minutes, 4.9% 45 to 60 minutes, 1.9% 60 minutes or more (2000)
Additional Information Contacts
Hartland Chamber of Commerce 262-367-7059

LAC LA BELLE (village). Covers a land area of 0.680 square miles and a water area of 0 square miles. Located at 43.14° N. Lat.; 88.52° W. Long. Elevation is 870 feet.
Population: 329 (2000); Race: 100.0% White, 0.0% Black, 0.0% Asian, 0.0% American Indian and Alaska Native, 0.0% Hispanic of any race, 0.0% two or more races (2000); Density: 484.1 persons per square mile (2000); Age: 23.5% under 18, 13.1% over 64 (2000); Marriage status: 17.7% never married, 75.8% now married, 3.1% widowed, 3.5% divorced (2000); Foreign born: 3.3% (2000); Ancestry (includes multiple ancestries): 46.7% German, 14.0% Irish, 13.1% Polish, 10.1% English, 8.9% Norwegian (2000).
Economy: Single-family building permits issued: 2 (2001) / 4 (2000); Multi-family building permits issued: 0 (2001) / 0 (2000); Employment by occupation: 24.2% management, 21.8% professional, 4.8% services, 34.5% sales, 0.0% farming, 6.7% construction, 7.9% production (2000).
Income: Per capita income: $46,749 (2000); Median household income: $96,712 (2000); Poverty rate: 1.8% (2000).
Taxes: Total city taxes per capita: $709 (1997); City property taxes per capita: $686 (1997).
Education: High school graduation rate: 93.3% (2000); College graduation rate: 56.7% (2000).
Housing: Homeownership rate: 96.6% (2000); Median home value: $483,300 (2000); Median rent: $900 per month (2000); Median age of housing: 33 years (2000).

Transportation: Commute to work: 88.8% car, 0.0% public transportation, 0.0% walk, 11.2% work from home (2000); Travel time to work: 11.9% less than 15 minutes, 25.2% 15 to 30 minutes, 33.6% 30 to 45 minutes, 21.7% 45 to 60 minutes, 7.7% 60 minutes or more (2000)

LANNON (village). Covers a land area of 2.443 square miles and a water area of 0 square miles. Located at 43.15° N. Lat.; 88.16° W. Long. Elevation is 890 feet.
Population: 1,009 (2000); Race: 97.8% White, 0.9% Black, 0.6% Asian, 0.1% American Indian and Alaska Native, 0.0% Hispanic of any race, 0.3% two or more races (2000); Density: 413.0 persons per square mile (2000); Age: 24.9% under 18, 14.0% over 64 (2000); Marriage status: 22.7% never married, 56.4% now married, 6.1% widowed, 14.8% divorced (2000); Foreign born: 1.7% (2000); Ancestry (includes multiple ancestries): 54.8% German, 13.4% Irish, 8.8% Polish, 8.6% English, 6.9% Italian (2000).
Economy: In dairy and farm area. Manufacturing: fabricated metal products, packaging. Single-family building permits issued: 2 (2001) / 0 (2000); Multi-family building permits issued: 0 (2001) / 0 (2000); Employment by occupation: 9.7% management, 11.4% professional, 11.0% services, 27.3% sales, 0.0% farming, 15.1% construction, 25.6% production (2000).
Income: Per capita income: $21,041 (2000); Median household income: $44,375 (2000); Poverty rate: 6.1% (2000).
Taxes: Total city taxes per capita: $493 (2000); City property taxes per capita: $370 (2000).
Education: High school graduation rate: 86.3% (2000); College graduation rate: 10.2% (2000).
Housing: Homeownership rate: 84.1% (2000); Median home value: $133,400 (2000); Median rent: $395 per month (2000); Median age of housing: 36 years (2000).
Transportation: Commute to work: 90.4% car, 0.0% public transportation, 2.6% walk, 4.7% work from home (2000); Travel time to work: 32.5% less than 15 minutes, 48.0% 15 to 30 minutes, 14.4% 30 to 45 minutes, 1.6% 45 to 60 minutes, 3.5% 60 minutes or more (2000)

LISBON (town). Covers a land area of 29.544 square miles and a water area of 0.033 square miles. Located at 43.15° N. Lat.; 88.24° W. Long.
Population: 9,359 (2000); Race: 98.9% White, 0.0% Black, 0.3% Asian, 0.1% American Indian and Alaska Native, 0.8% Hispanic of any race, 0.5% two or more races (2000); Density: 316.8 persons per square mile (2000); Age: 27.1% under 18, 10.0% over 64 (2000); Marriage status: 17.5% never married, 74.9% now married, 4.0% widowed, 3.6% divorced (2000); Foreign born: 2.0% (2000); Ancestry (includes multiple ancestries): 58.4% German, 12.3% Irish, 11.2% Polish, 8.2% English, 5.2% Italian (2000).
Economy: Single-family building permits issued: 59 (2001) / 112 (2000); Multi-family building permits issued: 0 (2001) / 0 (2000); Employment by occupation: 16.3% management, 21.6% professional, 10.6% services, 27.9% sales, 0.3% farming, 7.9% construction, 15.4% production (2000).
Income: Per capita income: $26,550 (2000); Median household income: $69,012 (2000); Poverty rate: 2.6% (2000).
Taxes: Total city taxes per capita: $171 (2000); City property taxes per capita: $146 (2000).
Education: High school graduation rate: 90.2% (2000); College graduation rate: 25.5% (2000).
Housing: Homeownership rate: 97.0% (2000); Median home value: $180,700 (2000); Median rent: $461 per month (2000); Median age of housing: 25 years (2000).
Transportation: Commute to work: 96.2% car, 0.1% public transportation, 1.2% walk, 2.1% work from home (2000); Travel time to work: 22.6% less than 15 minutes, 49.4% 15 to 30 minutes, 22.8% 30 to 45 minutes, 2.8% 45 to 60 minutes, 2.4% 60 minutes or more (2000)

MENOMONEE FALLS (village). Covers a land area of 33.276 square miles and a water area of 0.007 square miles. Located at 43.15° N. Lat.; 88.11° W. Long. Elevation is 800 feet.
History: Menomonee Falls was founded in 1843 by Frederic Nehs, who bought land here because of the water power available. Other German immigrants followed him, establishing a bottling plant, flour mill, sugar beet factory, and a ginseng plant. After industry declined in Menomonee Falls, it became a residential center for Milwaukee workers.
Population: 32,647 (2000); Race: 96.1% White, 1.7% Black, 0.6% Asian, 0.1% American Indian and Alaska Native, 1.0% Hispanic of any race, 1.1% two or more races (2000); Density: 981.1 persons per square mile (2000); Age: 24.9% under 18, 15.7% over 64 (2000); Marriage status: 19.3% never married, 65.7% now married, 7.7% widowed, 7.3% divorced (2000); Foreign born: 2.9% (2000); Ancestry (includes multiple ancestries): 55.8% German, 11.6% Irish, 11.5% Polish, 7.0% English, 6.0% Italian (2000).

Vital Statistics: Birth rate: 112.7 per 10,000 population (1998)
Economy: Unemployment rate: 3.5% (11/2002); Total civilian labor force: 19,777 (11/2002); Single-family building permits issued: 129 (2001) / 99 (2000); Multi-family building permits issued: 71 (2001) / 84 (2000); Employment by occupation: 17.6% management, 21.9% professional, 9.0% services, 29.6% sales, 0.1% farming, 8.0% construction, 13.7% production (2000).
Income: Per capita income: $27,454 (2000); Median household income: $57,952 (2000); Poverty rate: 2.2% (2000).
Taxes: Total city taxes per capita: $501 (2000); City property taxes per capita: $465 (2000).
Education: High school graduation rate: 90.4% (2000); College graduation rate: 30.4% (2000).

School District(s)

Menomonee Falls (PK-12)
2000 Enrollment: 4,232 262-255-8440
Housing: Homeownership rate: 77.1% (2000); Median home value: $151,600 (2000); Median rent: $633 per month (2000); Median age of housing: 33 years (2000).
Hospitals: Community Memorial Hospital (237 beds)
Safety: Violent crime rate: 5.5 per 10,000 population; Property crime rate: 156.3 per 10,000 population (2001).
Transportation: Commute to work: 95.1% car, 0.7% public transportation, 0.7% walk, 3.1% work from home (2000); Travel time to work: 34.3% less than 15 minutes, 44.0% 15 to 30 minutes, 16.4% 30 to 45 minutes, 2.4% 45 to 60 minutes, 3.0% 60 minutes or more (2000)
Additional Information Contacts
Menomonee Falls Chamber of Commerce. 262-251-2430

MERTON (village). Covers a land area of 2.636 square miles and a water area of 0.028 square miles. Located at 43.14° N. Lat.; 88.31° W. Long. Elevation is 960 feet.
Population: 1,926 (2000); Race: 99.0% White, 0.1% Black, 0.3% Asian, 0.3% American Indian and Alaska Native, 0.2% Hispanic of any race, 0.2% two or more races (2000); Density: 730.7 persons per square mile (2000); Age: 36.5% under 18, 3.8% over 64 (2000); Marriage status: 18.7% never married, 72.5% now married, 3.7% widowed, 5.0% divorced (2000); Foreign born: 2.0% (2000); Ancestry (includes multiple ancestries): 58.4% German, 16.1% Polish, 15.8% Irish, 8.1% English, 6.6% Norwegian (2000).
Economy: Single-family building permits issued: 31 (2001) / 28 (2000); Multi-family building permits issued: 0 (2001) / 0 (2000); Employment by occupation: 18.3% management, 17.7% professional, 9.8% services, 29.7% sales, 0.2% farming, 9.3% construction, 15.0% production (2000).
Income: Per capita income: $24,927 (2000); Median household income: $71,509 (2000); Poverty rate: 1.6% (2000).
Taxes: Total city taxes per capita: $173 (1997); City property taxes per capita: $139 (1997).
Education: High school graduation rate: 93.9% (2000); College graduation rate: 27.0% (2000).

School District(s)

Merton Community (KG-08)
2000 Enrollment: 841 262-538-1130
Housing: Homeownership rate: 95.4% (2000); Median home value: $200,500 (2000); Median rent: $575 per month (2000); Median age of housing: 18 years (2000).
Transportation: Commute to work: 91.7% car, 0.7% public transportation, 2.1% walk, 5.2% work from home (2000); Travel time to work: 23.2% less than 15 minutes, 44.9% 15 to 30 minutes, 23.6% 30 to 45 minutes, 4.3% 45 to 60 minutes, 3.9% 60 minutes or more (2000)

MERTON (town). Covers a land area of 25.745 square miles and a water area of 2.514 square miles. Located at 43.14° N. Lat.; 88.36° W. Long. Elevation is 960 feet.
Population: 7,988 (2000); Race: 98.3% White, 0.4% Black, 0.3% Asian, 0.1% American Indian and Alaska Native, 1.4% Hispanic of any race, 0.5% two or more races (2000); Density: 310.3 persons per square mile (2000); Age: 30.2% under 18, 8.7% over 64 (2000); Marriage status: 18.5% never married, 73.3% now married, 3.0% widowed, 5.2% divorced (2000); Foreign born: 1.7% (2000); Ancestry (includes multiple ancestries): 54.5% German, 14.2% Irish, 10.0% Polish, 7.2% English, 6.0% Norwegian (2000).
Economy: In dairying region. Manufacturing of cleaning products. Single-family building permits issued: 48 (2001) / 44 (2000); Multi-family building permits issued: 0 (2001) / 0 (2000); Employment by occupation: 20.9% management, 19.9% professional, 8.7% services, 30.8% sales, 0.0% farming, 10.0% construction, 9.6% production (2000).
Income: Per capita income: $34,633 (2000); Median household income: $78,937 (2000); Poverty rate: 1.3% (2000).
Taxes: Total city taxes per capita: $140 (1997); City property taxes per capita: $127 (1997).
Education: High school graduation rate: 94.9% (2000); College graduation rate: 35.9% (2000).
Housing: Homeownership rate: 91.6% (2000); Median home value: $242,100 (2000); Median rent: $611 per month (2000); Median age of housing: 26 years (2000).
Transportation: Commute to work: 93.0% car, 0.1% public transportation, 1.2% walk, 5.4% work from home (2000); Travel time to work: 22.2% less than 15 minutes, 40.6% 15 to 30 minutes, 27.6% 30 to 45 minutes, 6.1% 45 to 60 minutes, 3.5% 60 minutes or more (2000)

MUKWONAGO (village). Covers a land area of 4.692 square miles and a water area of 0.142 square miles. Located at 42.86° N. Lat.; 88.33° W. Long. Elevation is 837 feet.
Population: 6,162 (2000); Race: 96.8% White, 0.6% Black, 0.4% Asian, 0.0% American Indian and Alaska Native, 3.6% Hispanic of any race, 1.9% two or more races (2000); Density: 1,313.3 persons per square mile (2000); Age: 26.5% under 18, 10.5% over 64 (2000); Marriage status: 24.5% never married, 59.3% now married, 7.0% widowed, 9.2% divorced (2000); Foreign born: 2.1% (2000); Ancestry (includes multiple ancestries): 48.1% German, 16.2% Polish, 14.2% Irish, 7.9% Norwegian, 7.0% English (2000).
Economy: Single-family building permits issued: 52 (2001) / 41 (2000); Multi-family building permits issued: 6 (2001) / 6 (2000); Employment by occupation: 13.4% management, 18.3% professional, 10.8% services, 25.5% sales, 0.3% farming, 12.0% construction, 19.7% production (2000).
Income: Per capita income: $23,993 (2000); Median household income: $56,250 (2000); Poverty rate: 3.1% (2000).
Taxes: Total city taxes per capita: $342 (1997); City property taxes per capita: $323 (1997).
Education: High school graduation rate: 88.7% (2000); College graduation rate: 24.2% (2000).

School District(s)

Mukwonago (PK-12)
2000 Enrollment: 5,059 262-363-6304
Norris (07-12)
2000 Enrollment: 111 262-662-5911
Housing: Homeownership rate: 62.6% (2000); Median home value: $143,000 (2000); Median rent: $624 per month (2000); Median age of housing: 22 years (2000).
Newspapers: Mukwonago Chief (1 x week); The Kettle Moraine Advertiser/Chief II (1 x week)
Transportation: Commute to work: 94.8% car, 0.0% public transportation, 2.0% walk, 2.6% work from home (2000); Travel time to work: 26.0% less than 15 minutes, 33.6% 15 to 30 minutes, 29.2% 30 to 45 minutes, 8.9% 45 to 60 minutes, 2.4% 60 minutes or more (2000)
Additional Information Contacts
Mukwonago Chamber of Commerce 262-363-7758

MUKWONAGO (town). Covers a land area of 30.911 square miles and a water area of 1.054 square miles. Located at 42.88° N. Lat.; 88.36° W. Long. Elevation is 837 feet.
Population: 6,868 (2000); Race: 98.0% White, 0.3% Black, 0.8% Asian, 0.0% American Indian and Alaska Native, 0.8% Hispanic of any race, 0.9% two or more races (2000); Density: 222.2 persons per square mile (2000); Age: 30.7% under 18, 4.8% over 64 (2000); Marriage status: 20.3% never married, 72.7% now married, 2.1% widowed, 4.9% divorced (2000); Foreign born: 1.4% (2000); Ancestry (includes multiple ancestries): 53.3% German, 20.6% Polish, 12.1% Irish, 7.6% Italian, 6.9% English (2000).
Economy: In dairying, livestock-raising, and farming region. Manufacturing: bottled water, pump components. Rail junction. Single-family building permits issued: 77 (2001) / 51 (2000); Multi-family building permits issued: 0 (2001) / 0 (2000); Employment by occupation: 14.7% management, 23.3% professional, 7.9% services, 25.9% sales, 0.1% farming, 11.7% construction, 16.4% production (2000).
Income: Per capita income: $26,071 (2000); Median household income: $75,067 (2000); Poverty rate: 1.4% (2000).
Taxes: Total city taxes per capita: $156 (2000); City property taxes per capita: $136 (2000).
Education: High school graduation rate: 92.6% (2000); College graduation rate: 30.9% (2000).
Housing: Homeownership rate: 97.2% (2000); Median home value: $186,800 (2000); Median rent: $669 per month (2000); Median age of housing: 19 years (2000).

Transportation: Commute to work: 97.1% car, 0.2% public transportation, 0.1% walk, 2.2% work from home (2000); Travel time to work: 15.8% less than 15 minutes, 30.8% 15 to 30 minutes, 34.4% 30 to 45 minutes, 13.5% 45 to 60 minutes, 5.5% 60 minutes or more (2000)

MUSKEGO (city). Covers a land area of 31.225 square miles and a water area of 4.656 square miles. Located at 42.90° N. Lat.; 88.12° W. Long. Elevation is 800 feet.
Population: 21,397 (2000); Race: 97.9% White, 0.3% Black, 0.5% Asian, 0.1% American Indian and Alaska Native, 1.0% Hispanic of any race, 1.1% two or more races (2000); Density: 685.2 persons per square mile (2000); Age: 27.5% under 18, 10.1% over 64 (2000); Marriage status: 19.3% never married, 68.1% now married, 5.9% widowed, 6.6% divorced (2000); Foreign born: 2.1% (2000); Ancestry (includes multiple ancestries): 50.8% German, 23.9% Polish, 12.3% Irish, 6.0% Italian, 5.9% English (2000).
Vital Statistics: Birth rate: 127.1 per 10,000 population (1998)
Economy: Single-family building permits issued: 167 (2001) / 105 (2000); Multi-family building permits issued: 42 (2001) / 0 (2000); Employment by occupation: 15.7% management, 19.4% professional, 10.3% services, 29.1% sales, 0.1% farming, 9.7% construction, 15.7% production (2000).
Income: Per capita income: $26,199 (2000); Median household income: $64,247 (2000); Poverty rate: 1.6% (2000).
Taxes: Total city taxes per capita: $385 (1997); City property taxes per capita: $340 (1997).
Education: High school graduation rate: 92.2% (2000); College graduation rate: 25.0% (2000).

School District(s)

Muskego-Norway (PK-12)
2000 Enrollment: 4,593 262-679-5400
Housing: Homeownership rate: 82.7% (2000); Median home value: $166,700 (2000); Median rent: $715 per month (2000); Median age of housing: 23 years (2000).
Transportation: Commute to work: 95.3% car, 0.9% public transportation, 1.1% walk, 2.3% work from home (2000); Travel time to work: 20.2% less than 15 minutes, 44.0% 15 to 30 minutes, 28.1% 30 to 45 minutes, 4.3% 45 to 60 minutes, 3.5% 60 minutes or more (2000)
Additional Information Contacts
Muskego Chamber of Commerce. 262-679-2550

NASHOTAH (village). Covers a land area of 1.620 square miles and a water area of 0.032 square miles. Located at 43.09° N. Lat.; 88.40° W. Long. Elevation is 950 feet.
History: Seat of Nashotah House, an Episcopal seminary.
Population: 1,266 (2000); Race: 98.2% White, 0.5% Black, 0.8% Asian, 0.2% American Indian and Alaska Native, 0.5% Hispanic of any race, 0.2% two or more races (2000); Density: 781.4 persons per square mile (2000); Age: 32.3% under 18, 9.3% over 64 (2000); Marriage status: 14.9% never married, 72.5% now married, 6.2% widowed, 6.5% divorced (2000); Foreign born: 2.5% (2000); Ancestry (includes multiple ancestries): 48.3% German, 15.9% Irish, 11.1% English, 9.9% Polish, 7.6% Norwegian (2000).
Economy: Manufacturing: plastic products, cable assembly, wood products. Single-family building permits issued: 28 (2001) / 5 (2000); Multi-family building permits issued: 0 (2001) / 0 (2000); Employment by occupation: 25.5% management, 24.2% professional, 7.8% services, 28.4% sales, 0.0% farming, 4.0% construction, 10.2% production (2000).
Income: Per capita income: $29,581 (2000); Median household income: $77,406 (2000); Poverty rate: 1.3% (2000).
Taxes: Total city taxes per capita: $873 (1997); City property taxes per capita: $849 (1997).
Education: High school graduation rate: 95.6% (2000); College graduation rate: 46.6% (2000).

Four-year College(s)

Nashotah House (Private, Not-for-profit, Other Protestant)
2001 Enrollment: 46 262-646-6500
Housing: Homeownership rate: 96.2% (2000); Median home value: $242,300 (2000); Median rent: $808 per month (2000); Median age of housing: 7 years (2000).
Transportation: Commute to work: 93.5% car, 0.6% public transportation, 1.1% walk, 4.8% work from home (2000); Travel time to work: 26.8% less than 15 minutes, 36.2% 15 to 30 minutes, 29.2% 30 to 45 minutes, 4.9% 45 to 60 minutes, 2.9% 60 minutes or more (2000)
Additional Information Contacts
Nashotah Area Chamber of Commerce 262-367-6262

NEW BERLIN (city). Covers a land area of 36.841 square miles and a water area of 0.083 square miles. Located at 42.97° N. Lat.; 88.10° W. Long. Elevation is 800 feet.
History: Founded 1840, incorporated 1959.
Population: 38,220 (2000); Race: 95.7% White, 0.5% Black, 2.3% Asian, 0.3% American Indian and Alaska Native, 1.1% Hispanic of any race, 0.8% two or more races (2000); Density: 1,037.4 persons per square mile (2000); Age: 24.9% under 18, 12.5% over 64 (2000); Marriage status: 21.5% never married, 67.1% now married, 5.1% widowed, 6.3% divorced (2000); Foreign born: 4.4% (2000); Ancestry (includes multiple ancestries): 48.4% German, 18.3% Polish, 12.6% Irish, 6.6% English, 5.8% Italian (2000).
Vital Statistics: Birth rate: 103.9 per 10,000 population (1998)
Economy: Manufacturing: rubber products, computer equipment, printing, wire forms, medical equipment, electrical and electronic equipment, plastic molding, transportation equipment. Unemployment rate: 3.2% (11/2002); Total civilian labor force: 24,500 (11/2002); Single-family building permits issued: 74 (2001) / 120 (2000); Multi-family building permits issued: 6 (2001) / 88 (2000); Employment by occupation: 19.3% management, 24.1% professional, 7.9% services, 29.4% sales, 0.1% farming, 7.9% construction, 11.4% production (2000).
Income: Per capita income: $29,789 (2000); Median household income: $67,576 (2000); Poverty rate: 2.0% (2000).
Taxes: Total city taxes per capita: $425 (2000); City property taxes per capita: $380 (2000).
Education: High school graduation rate: 92.4% (2000); College graduation rate: 36.8% (2000).

School District(s)

New Berlin (PK-12)
2000 Enrollment: 4,611 262-789-6220
Housing: Homeownership rate: 81.3% (2000); Median home value: $162,100 (2000); Median rent: $761 per month (2000); Median age of housing: 26 years (2000).
Safety: Violent crime rate: 5.7 per 10,000 population; Property crime rate: 148.9 per 10,000 population (2001).
Newspapers: South Milwaukee Voice Graphic (1 x week); The Bay Viewer (1 x week); Wauwatosa News-Times (1 x week); Saint Francis Reminder Enterprise (1 x week); Franklin-Hales Corners Hub (1 x week); Whitefish Bay Herald (1 x week); West Allis Star (1 x week); Shorewood Herald (1 x week); Oak Creek Pictorial (1 x week); New Berlin Citizen (1 x week); Muskego Sun (1 x week); Menomonee Falls News (1 x week); Greenfield Observer (1 x week); Greendale Village Life (1 x week); Glendale Herald (1 x week); Germantown Banner-Press (1 x week); Fox Point-River Hills-Bayside Herald (1 x week); Elm Grove Elm Leaves (1 x week); Cudahy Reminder-Enterprise (1 x week); Brown Deer Herald (1 x week); Brookfield News (1 x week); Mequon-Thiensville Courant (1 x week)
Transportation: Commute to work: 95.6% car, 0.5% public transportation, 0.7% walk, 2.8% work from home (2000); Travel time to work: 27.0% less than 15 minutes, 51.6% 15 to 30 minutes, 15.9% 30 to 45 minutes, 2.9% 45 to 60 minutes, 2.6% 60 minutes or more (2000)

NORTH PRAIRIE (village). Covers a land area of 2.652 square miles and a water area of 0.007 square miles. Located at 42.93° N. Lat.; 88.40° W. Long. Elevation is 950 feet.
Population: 1,571 (2000); Race: 97.8% White, 0.0% Black, 0.0% Asian, 0.1% American Indian and Alaska Native, 1.8% Hispanic of any race, 1.6% two or more races (2000); Density: 592.4 persons per square mile (2000); Age: 28.1% under 18, 7.1% over 64 (2000); Marriage status: 23.9% never married, 63.9% now married, 3.3% widowed, 8.9% divorced (2000); Foreign born: 1.7% (2000); Ancestry (includes multiple ancestries): 56.2% German, 16.1% Polish, 11.5% Irish, 10.2% English, 5.6% Norwegian (2000).
Economy: In dairying region. Dairy products. Manufacturing of wood pallets. Single-family building permits issued: 22 (2001) / 26 (2000); Multi-family building permits issued: 0 (2001) / 2 (2000); Employment by occupation: 14.4% management, 16.8% professional, 9.6% services, 29.1% sales, 0.3% farming, 11.7% construction, 18.2% production (2000).
Income: Per capita income: $24,470 (2000); Median household income: $67,596 (2000); Poverty rate: 2.1% (2000).
Taxes: Total city taxes per capita: $156 (1997); City property taxes per capita: $148 (1997).
Education: High school graduation rate: 93.9% (2000); College graduation rate: 26.3% (2000).
Housing: Homeownership rate: 86.0% (2000); Median home value: $149,700 (2000); Median rent: $664 per month (2000); Median age of housing: 23 years (2000).

Transportation: Commute to work: 93.4% car, 0.3% public transportation, 1.7% walk, 4.1% work from home (2000); Travel time to work: 21.3% less than 15 minutes, 44.3% 15 to 30 minutes, 21.3% 30 to 45 minutes, 10.9% 45 to 60 minutes, 2.3% 60 minutes or more (2000)

OCONOMOWOC (city). Covers a land area of 6.709 square miles and a water area of 0.493 square miles. Located at 43.10° N. Lat.; 88.49° W. Long. Elevation is 873 feet.
History: Oconomowoc developed in the 1880's and 1890's as a summer home for wealthy families from the cities of the south. In the 1900's, some of the luxurious estates became resort hotels. Winter sports were later added to Oconomowoc's attractions.
Population: 12,382 (2000); Race: 97.9% White, 0.2% Black, 0.4% Asian, 0.3% American Indian and Alaska Native, 1.3% Hispanic of any race, 0.4% two or more races (2000); Density: 1,845.5 persons per square mile (2000); Age: 24.4% under 18, 16.6% over 64 (2000); Marriage status: 21.1% never married, 59.7% now married, 9.4% widowed, 9.8% divorced (2000); Foreign born: 2.1% (2000); Ancestry (includes multiple ancestries): 54.9% German, 12.0% Irish, 8.9% Polish, 8.5% English, 6.2% Norwegian (2000).
Vital Statistics: Birth rate: 131.6 per 10,000 population (1998)
Economy: Single-family building permits issued: 118 (2001) / 125 (2000); Multi-family building permits issued: 4 (2001) / 4 (2000); Employment by occupation: 14.8% management, 21.0% professional, 10.3% services, 30.4% sales, 0.1% farming, 8.1% construction, 15.4% production (2000).
Income: Per capita income: $25,716 (2000); Median household income: $51,250 (2000); Poverty rate: 1.6% (2000).
Taxes: Total city taxes per capita: $453 (2000); City property taxes per capita: $414 (2000).
Education: High school graduation rate: 88.9% (2000); College graduation rate: 30.7% (2000).

School District(s)

Oconomowoc Area (PK-12)
2000 Enrollment: 4,153 262-567-6632
Stone Bank (KG-08)
2000 Enrollment: 313 262-966-2900

Housing: Homeownership rate: 62.4% (2000); Median home value: $147,900 (2000); Median rent: $624 per month (2000); Median age of housing: 33 years (2000).
Hospitals: Oconomowoc Memorial Hospital (77 beds); Rogers Memorial Hospital (90 beds)
Safety: Violent crime rate: 4.8 per 10,000 population; Property crime rate: 191.7 per 10,000 population (2001).
Newspapers: Oconomowoc Enterprise (1 x week)
Transportation: Commute to work: 93.7% car, 0.3% public transportation, 2.6% walk, 2.8% work from home (2000); Travel time to work: 39.8% less than 15 minutes, 29.3% 15 to 30 minutes, 17.8% 30 to 45 minutes, 8.4% 45 to 60 minutes, 4.7% 60 minutes or more (2000)

OCONOMOWOC (town). Covers a land area of 29.289 square miles and a water area of 3.316 square miles. Located at 43.12° N. Lat.; 88.47° W. Long. Elevation is 873 feet.
History: Incorporated 1875.
Population: 7,451 (2000); Race: 99.0% White, 0.2% Black, 0.2% Asian, 0.2% American Indian and Alaska Native, 0.2% Hispanic of any race, 0.4% two or more races (2000); Density: 254.4 persons per square mile (2000); Age: 25.6% under 18, 10.3% over 64 (2000); Marriage status: 20.7% never married, 69.2% now married, 4.7% widowed, 5.3% divorced (2000); Foreign born: 2.0% (2000); Ancestry (includes multiple ancestries): 55.0% German, 13.8% Irish, 9.9% English, 8.4% Polish, 6.6% Norwegian (2000).
Economy: Manufacturing: dairying and baking products, wheelchairs, labels, electronics, fabricated metal products; food processing. Resort with mineral springs. Annual winter-sports carnival. Single-family building permits issued: 44 (2001) / 35 (2000); Multi-family building permits issued: 0 (2001) / 16 (2000); Employment by occupation: 18.9% management, 20.3% professional, 9.3% services, 28.8% sales, 0.3% farming, 9.3% construction, 13.2% production (2000).
Income: Per capita income: $37,244 (2000); Median household income: $68,676 (2000); Poverty rate: 2.4% (2000).
Taxes: Total city taxes per capita: $211 (2000); City property taxes per capita: $196 (2000).
Education: High school graduation rate: 93.0% (2000); College graduation rate: 30.7% (2000).
Housing: Homeownership rate: 85.0% (2000); Median home value: $197,500 (2000); Median rent: $719 per month (2000); Median age of housing: 32 years (2000).
Safety: Violent crime rate: 4.0 per 10,000 population; Property crime rate: 115.9 per 10,000 population (2001).
Transportation: Commute to work: 92.8% car, 0.0% public transportation, 2.1% walk, 4.4% work from home (2000); Travel time to work: 25.2% less than 15 minutes, 31.3% 15 to 30 minutes, 28.1% 30 to 45 minutes, 10.7% 45 to 60 minutes, 4.7% 60 minutes or more (2000)

OCONOMOWOC LAKE (village). Covers a land area of 1.890 square miles and a water area of 1.310 square miles. Located at 43.09° N. Lat.; 88.46° W. Long. Elevation is 900 feet.
Population: 564 (2000); Race: 98.8% White, 0.0% Black, 0.9% Asian, 0.0% American Indian and Alaska Native, 0.5% Hispanic of any race, 0.0% two or more races (2000); Density: 298.4 persons per square mile (2000); Age: 25.6% under 18, 11.1% over 64 (2000); Marriage status: 16.2% never married, 75.2% now married, 3.5% widowed, 5.1% divorced (2000); Foreign born: 1.1% (2000); Ancestry (includes multiple ancestries): 46.7% German, 21.2% Irish, 13.3% English, 8.4% Polish, 7.9% Norwegian (2000).
Economy: Single-family building permits issued: 6 (2001) / 6 (2000); Multi-family building permits issued: 0 (2001) / 0 (2000); Employment by occupation: 33.9% management, 24.7% professional, 9.2% services, 24.7% sales, 0.4% farming, 2.6% construction, 4.4% production (2000).
Income: Per capita income: $81,593 (2000); Median household income: $112,760 (2000); Poverty rate: 3.2% (2000).
Taxes: Total city taxes per capita: $1,175 (1997); City property taxes per capita: $1,145 (1997).
Education: High school graduation rate: 98.7% (2000); College graduation rate: 54.3% (2000).
Housing: Homeownership rate: 92.6% (2000); Median home value: $713,500 (2000); Median rent: $1,500 per month (2000); Median age of housing: 46 years (2000).
Transportation: Commute to work: 88.6% car, 0.0% public transportation, 2.2% walk, 8.5% work from home (2000); Travel time to work: 35.9% less than 15 minutes, 27.0% 15 to 30 minutes, 23.8% 30 to 45 minutes, 10.1% 45 to 60 minutes, 3.2% 60 minutes or more (2000)

OKAUCHEE (unincorporated postal area, zip code 53069). Covers a land area of 0.297 square miles and a water area of 0.050 square miles. Located at 43.11° N. Lat.; 88.43° W. Long. Elevation is 890 feet.
Population: 598 (2000); Race: 100.0% White, 0.0% Black, 0.0% Asian, 0.0% American Indian and Alaska Native, 0.0% Hispanic of any race, 0.0% two or more races (2000); Density: 2,013.5 persons per square mile (2000); Age: 14.5% under 18, 12.6% over 64 (2000); Marriage status: 24.3% never married, 66.7% now married, 3.1% widowed, 5.9% divorced (2000); Foreign born: 0.6% (2000); Ancestry (includes multiple ancestries): 44.6% German, 17.7% Irish, 16.9% English, 12.6% Polish, 12.3% Italian (2000).
Economy: Employment by occupation: 21.8% management, 15.9% professional, 7.1% services, 30.1% sales, 0.0% farming, 5.1% construction, 20.0% production (2000).
Income: Per capita income: $32,332 (2000); Median household income: $55,221 (2000); Poverty rate: 3.4% (2000).
Education: High school graduation rate: 90.1% (2000); College graduation rate: 24.2% (2000).
Housing: Homeownership rate: 69.1% (2000); Median home value: $215,900 (2000); Median rent: $639 per month (2000); Median age of housing: 52 years (2000).
Transportation: Commute to work: 89.1% car, 0.0% public transportation, 9.7% walk, 1.2% work from home (2000); Travel time to work: 30.8% less than 15 minutes, 23.8% 15 to 30 minutes, 25.6% 30 to 45 minutes, 13.8% 45 to 60 minutes, 6.0% 60 minutes or more (2000)

OKAUCHEE LAKE (CDP). Covers a land area of 3.476 square miles and a water area of 1.465 square miles. Located at 43.11° N. Lat.; 88.44° W. Long.
Population: 3,916 (2000); Race: 98.9% White, 0.4% Black, 0.0% Asian, 0.3% American Indian and Alaska Native, 0.3% Hispanic of any race, 0.4% two or more races (2000); Density: 1,126.7 persons per square mile (2000); Age: 25.3% under 18, 10.1% over 64 (2000); Marriage status: 21.8% never married, 66.2% now married, 4.7% widowed, 7.4% divorced (2000); Foreign born: 2.1% (2000); Ancestry (includes multiple ancestries): 53.1% German, 12.9% Irish, 11.1% English, 8.5% Polish, 6.5% Norwegian (2000).
Economy: Employment by occupation: 20.2% management, 18.0% professional, 8.0% services, 30.1% sales, 0.0% farming, 9.6% construction, 14.0% production (2000).
Income: Per capita income: $40,508 (2000); Median household income: $66,042 (2000); Poverty rate: 2.0% (2000).

Education: High school graduation rate: 94.8% (2000); College graduation rate: 32.4% (2000).
Housing: Homeownership rate: 81.1% (2000); Median home value: $225,900 (2000); Median rent: $729 per month (2000); Median age of housing: 33 years (2000).
Transportation: Commute to work: 90.5% car, 0.1% public transportation, 2.9% walk, 6.0% work from home (2000); Travel time to work: 24.3% less than 15 minutes, 30.5% 15 to 30 minutes, 29.2% 30 to 45 minutes, 12.2% 45 to 60 minutes, 3.8% 60 minutes or more (2000)

OTTAWA (town). Covers a land area of 34.315 square miles and a water area of 0.606 square miles. Located at 42.97° N. Lat.; 88.46° W. Long. Elevation is 927 feet.
Population: 3,758 (2000); Race: 97.6% White, 0.0% Black, 0.0% Asian, 0.4% American Indian and Alaska Native, 1.0% Hispanic of any race, 1.2% two or more races (2000); Density: 109.5 persons per square mile (2000); Age: 26.7% under 18, 10.9% over 64 (2000); Marriage status: 21.0% never married, 67.5% now married, 5.6% widowed, 5.8% divorced (2000); Foreign born: 0.7% (2000); Ancestry (includes multiple ancestries): 43.8% German, 14.9% Irish, 9.8% English, 8.8% Polish, 6.3% Norwegian (2000).
Economy: Single-family building permits issued: 20 (2001) / 15 (2000); Multi-family building permits issued: 0 (2001) / 0 (2000); Employment by occupation: 15.9% management, 22.9% professional, 11.8% services, 25.9% sales, 0.8% farming, 12.4% construction, 10.3% production (2000).
Income: Per capita income: $30,977 (2000); Median household income: $69,493 (2000); Poverty rate: 1.7% (2000).
Taxes: Total city taxes per capita: $145 (2000); City property taxes per capita: $132 (2000).
Education: High school graduation rate: 95.2% (2000); College graduation rate: 29.0% (2000).
Housing: Homeownership rate: 91.7% (2000); Median home value: $197,400 (2000); Median rent: $900 per month (2000); Median age of housing: 25 years (2000).
Transportation: Commute to work: 94.6% car, 0.3% public transportation, 0.3% walk, 4.4% work from home (2000); Travel time to work: 13.8% less than 15 minutes, 37.0% 15 to 30 minutes, 26.0% 30 to 45 minutes, 13.6% 45 to 60 minutes, 9.6% 60 minutes or more (2000)

PEWAUKEE (city). Covers a land area of 21.769 square miles and a water area of 1.451 square miles. Located at 43.06° N. Lat.; 88.24° W. Long. Elevation is 880 feet.
Population: 11,783 (2000); Race: 96.6% White, 0.2% Black, 1.2% Asian, 0.3% American Indian and Alaska Native, 2.1% Hispanic of any race, 0.7% two or more races (2000); Density: 541.3 persons per square mile (2000); Age: 22.9% under 18, 12.3% over 64 (2000); Marriage status: 18.6% never married, 71.3% now married, 4.4% widowed, 5.8% divorced (2000); Foreign born: 2.7% (2000); Ancestry (includes multiple ancestries): 52.4% German, 15.7% Irish, 11.7% Polish, 7.1% English, 6.9% Italian (2000).
Economy: Single-family building permits issued: 53 (2001) / 72 (2000); Multi-family building permits issued: 124 (2001) / 81 (2000); Employment by occupation: 24.1% management, 22.1% professional, 7.5% services, 29.5% sales, 0.2% farming, 7.1% construction, 9.5% production (2000).
Income: Per capita income: $34,851 (2000); Median household income: $75,589 (2000); Poverty rate: 1.3% (2000).
Taxes: Total city taxes per capita: $354 (2000); City property taxes per capita: $306 (2000).
Education: High school graduation rate: 94.0% (2000); College graduation rate: 37.2% (2000).

School District(s)

Pewaukee (PK-12)
2000 Enrollment: 2,096 262-691-2100

Two-year College(s)

Waukesha County Technical College (Public)
2001 Enrollment: 6,687 414-691-5566
2001 Tuition: In-state $1,818; Out-of-state $14,200

Housing: Homeownership rate: 86.0% (2000); Median home value: $190,600 (2000); Median rent: $893 per month (2000); Median age of housing: 19 years (2000).
Transportation: Commute to work: 95.9% car, 0.3% public transportation, 0.3% walk, 2.9% work from home (2000); Travel time to work: 29.8% less than 15 minutes, 41.8% 15 to 30 minutes, 20.2% 30 to 45 minutes, 4.7% 45 to 60 minutes, 3.5% 60 minutes or more (2000)

Additional Information Contacts

Pewaukee Chamber of Commerce 262-691-8851

PEWAUKEE (village). Covers a land area of 4.113 square miles and a water area of 0.288 square miles. Located at 43.08° N. Lat.; 88.25° W. Long. Elevation is 880 feet.
History: Waukesha County Area Technical College. Incorporated 1876.
Population: 8,170 (2000); Race: 96.7% White, 0.2% Black, 0.6% Asian, 1.0% American Indian and Alaska Native, 2.0% Hispanic of any race, 1.2% two or more races (2000); Density: 1,986.2 persons per square mile (2000); Age: 23.0% under 18, 10.2% over 64 (2000); Marriage status: 25.6% never married, 53.1% now married, 7.2% widowed, 14.1% divorced (2000); Foreign born: 1.9% (2000); Ancestry (includes multiple ancestries): 53.9% German, 12.9% Irish, 10.8% Polish, 6.7% English, 5.9% Other groups (2000).
Economy: In dairy and poultry farm area; farm trade center; resort (summer and winter lake sports). Manufacturing: personal computers, magazine printing, fencing and guard rails, candies, plywood. Single-family building permits issued: 3 (2001) / 7 (2000); Multi-family building permits issued: 225 (2001) / 16 (2000); Employment by occupation: 17.6% management, 18.6% professional, 12.1% services, 32.7% sales, 0.0% farming, 5.9% construction, 13.0% production (2000).
Income: Per capita income: $26,656 (2000); Median household income: $53,874 (2000); Poverty rate: 2.3% (2000).
Taxes: Total city taxes per capita: $446 (1997); City property taxes per capita: $321 (1997).
Education: High school graduation rate: 91.0% (2000); College graduation rate: 30.0% (2000).
Housing: Homeownership rate: 62.5% (2000); Median home value: $160,700 (2000); Median rent: $623 per month (2000); Median age of housing: 17 years (2000).
Transportation: Commute to work: 96.1% car, 0.0% public transportation, 0.8% walk, 3.0% work from home (2000); Travel time to work: 33.4% less than 15 minutes, 44.2% 15 to 30 minutes, 16.0% 30 to 45 minutes, 2.4% 45 to 60 minutes, 4.0% 60 minutes or more (2000)

SUMMIT (town). Covers a land area of 25.751 square miles and a water area of 2.755 square miles. Located at 43.05° N. Lat.; 88.46° W. Long.
Population: 4,999 (2000); Race: 95.6% White, 1.2% Black, 1.4% Asian, 0.1% American Indian and Alaska Native, 1.1% Hispanic of any race, 1.6% two or more races (2000); Density: 194.1 persons per square mile (2000); Age: 27.8% under 18, 10.9% over 64 (2000); Marriage status: 21.6% never married, 67.4% now married, 4.4% widowed, 6.6% divorced (2000); Foreign born: 2.9% (2000); Ancestry (includes multiple ancestries): 51.5% German, 16.1% Irish, 9.3% English, 9.2% Polish, 5.6% Italian (2000).
Economy: Single-family building permits issued: 21 (2001) / 20 (2000); Multi-family building permits issued: 0 (2001) / 0 (2000); Employment by occupation: 17.2% management, 23.8% professional, 14.9% services, 24.2% sales, 0.1% farming, 8.3% construction, 11.5% production (2000).
Income: Per capita income: $28,797 (2000); Median household income: $71,884 (2000); Poverty rate: 5.0% (2000).
Taxes: Total city taxes per capita: $222 (2000); City property taxes per capita: $209 (2000).
Education: High school graduation rate: 94.0% (2000); College graduation rate: 34.0% (2000).
Housing: Homeownership rate: 88.8% (2000); Median home value: $227,300 (2000); Median rent: $672 per month (2000); Median age of housing: 34 years (2000).
Transportation: Commute to work: 92.0% car, 0.4% public transportation, 1.1% walk, 5.8% work from home (2000); Travel time to work: 26.4% less than 15 minutes, 34.0% 15 to 30 minutes, 19.5% 30 to 45 minutes, 15.3% 45 to 60 minutes, 4.7% 60 minutes or more (2000)

SUSSEX (village). Covers a land area of 6.030 square miles and a water area of 0 square miles. Located at 43.13° N. Lat.; 88.22° W. Long. Elevation is 930 feet.
Population: 8,828 (2000); Race: 97.2% White, 0.2% Black, 0.4% Asian, 0.1% American Indian and Alaska Native, 2.1% Hispanic of any race, 1.2% two or more races (2000); Density: 1,464.0 persons per square mile (2000); Age: 29.7% under 18, 8.4% over 64 (2000); Marriage status: 23.5% never married, 62.1% now married, 5.4% widowed, 9.1% divorced (2000); Foreign born: 2.3% (2000); Ancestry (includes multiple ancestries): 60.1% German, 13.8% Polish, 9.7% Irish, 5.7% Norwegian, 5.1% Other groups (2000).
Economy: In dairying and vegetable-farming area. Manufacturing: formulations to accelerate biodegradation of oil spills, concrete, packaging. Stone quarrying. Single-family building permits issued: 78 (2001) / 95 (2000); Multi-family building permits issued: 0 (2001) / 0 (2000); Employment by occupation: 16.5% management, 17.3% professional, 9.3%

services, 31.7% sales, 0.0% farming, 8.3% construction, 16.9% production (2000).
Income: Per capita income: $23,913 (2000); Median household income: $60,283 (2000); Poverty rate: 3.7% (2000).
Taxes: Total city taxes per capita: $341 (2000); City property taxes per capita: $298 (2000).
Education: High school graduation rate: 90.8% (2000); College graduation rate: 25.9% (2000).

School District(s)

Hamilton (PK-12)
2000 Enrollment: 3,892 262-246-1973
Richmond (PK-08)
2000 Enrollment: 407 262-538-1360

Housing: Homeownership rate: 66.0% (2000); Median home value: $171,200 (2000); Median rent: $668 per month (2000); Median age of housing: 12 years (2000).
Transportation: Commute to work: 93.3% car, 0.1% public transportation, 1.6% walk, 4.3% work from home (2000); Travel time to work: 24.8% less than 15 minutes, 42.4% 15 to 30 minutes, 24.1% 30 to 45 minutes, 5.2% 45 to 60 minutes, 3.4% 60 minutes or more (2000)

VERNON (town). Covers a land area of 32.249 square miles and a water area of 0.461 square miles. Located at 42.89° N. Lat.; 88.24° W. Long. Elevation is 890 feet.
Population: 7,227 (2000); Race: 97.7% White, 0.0% Black, 0.9% Asian, 0.1% American Indian and Alaska Native, 1.0% Hispanic of any race, 0.9% two or more races (2000); Density: 224.1 persons per square mile (2000); Age: 28.0% under 18, 5.6% over 64 (2000); Marriage status: 21.4% never married, 71.2% now married, 2.3% widowed, 5.1% divorced (2000); Foreign born: 2.3% (2000); Ancestry (includes multiple ancestries): 52.9% German, 19.3% Polish, 9.6% Irish, 9.1% English, 6.0% French (except Basque) (2000).
Economy: Single-family building permits issued: 41 (2001) / 43 (2000); Multi-family building permits issued: 0 (2001) / 0 (2000); Employment by occupation: 14.9% management, 17.8% professional, 11.2% services, 28.4% sales, 0.0% farming, 12.3% construction, 15.5% production (2000).
Income: Per capita income: $26,019 (2000); Median household income: $71,366 (2000); Poverty rate: 1.4% (2000).
Taxes: Total city taxes per capita: $178 (2000); City property taxes per capita: $163 (2000).
Education: High school graduation rate: 93.1% (2000); College graduation rate: 21.0% (2000).
Housing: Homeownership rate: 96.1% (2000); Median home value: $178,700 (2000); Median rent: $538 per month (2000); Median age of housing: 24 years (2000).
Transportation: Commute to work: 94.7% car, 0.2% public transportation, 1.4% walk, 3.6% work from home (2000); Travel time to work: 19.4% less than 15 minutes, 41.7% 15 to 30 minutes, 30.8% 30 to 45 minutes, 6.1% 45 to 60 minutes, 1.9% 60 minutes or more (2000)

WALES (village). Covers a land area of 2.441 square miles and a water area of 0 square miles. Located at 43.00° N. Lat.; 88.37° W. Long. Elevation is 1,002 feet.
History: Wales was settled by Welsh immigrants who found the land somewhat like their native country.
Population: 2,523 (2000); Race: 97.7% White, 0.1% Black, 0.3% Asian, 0.2% American Indian and Alaska Native, 1.5% Hispanic of any race, 1.4% two or more races (2000); Density: 1,033.4 persons per square mile (2000); Age: 31.1% under 18, 3.6% over 64 (2000); Marriage status: 24.9% never married, 66.7% now married, 1.9% widowed, 6.5% divorced (2000); Foreign born: 1.3% (2000); Ancestry (includes multiple ancestries): 54.2% German, 12.9% Irish, 11.8% English, 10.9% Polish, 7.9% Norwegian (2000).
Economy: Single-family building permits issued: 7 (2001) / 8 (2000); Multi-family building permits issued: 0 (2001) / 0 (2000); Employment by occupation: 13.6% management, 29.0% professional, 10.0% services, 25.5% sales, 0.3% farming, 8.2% construction, 13.4% production (2000).
Income: Per capita income: $26,712 (2000); Median household income: $75,000 (2000); Poverty rate: 0.2% (2000).
Taxes: Total city taxes per capita: $134 (1997); City property taxes per capita: $128 (1997).
Education: High school graduation rate: 95.1% (2000); College graduation rate: 40.0% (2000).

School District(s)

Kettle Moraine (PK-12)
2000 Enrollment: 4,276 262-968-6330

Housing: Homeownership rate: 84.9% (2000); Median home value: $183,700 (2000); Median rent: $596 per month (2000); Median age of housing: 24 years (2000).
Transportation: Commute to work: 94.8% car, 1.3% public transportation, 1.3% walk, 2.4% work from home (2000); Travel time to work: 26.7% less than 15 minutes, 40.2% 15 to 30 minutes, 22.1% 30 to 45 minutes, 6.8% 45 to 60 minutes, 4.2% 60 minutes or more (2000)

WAUKESHA (city). Covers a land area of 21.605 square miles and a water area of 0.073 square miles. Located at 43.01° N. Lat.; 88.23° W. Long. Elevation is 821 feet.
History: The first settlement at Waukesha was called Prairieville. The Little Fox River provided water power here for a sawmill, and many European immigrants came to the area to work in the lumber trade. Flour making later replaced timber, and machinery manufacturing developed as well. Carroll College was founded here in 1841 as Prairieville Academy. An abolitionist center in pre-Civil War days, Waukesha served as an important station on the Underground Railroad to freedom for southern slaves. From the 1870's to the 1890's, Waukesha was a popular health spa, the mineral waters from its numerous springs believed to provide cures for many ailments.
Population: 64,825 (2000); Race: 91.7% White, 1.1% Black, 1.9% Asian, 0.4% American Indian and Alaska Native, 8.4% Hispanic of any race, 1.8% two or more races (2000); Density: 3,000.5 persons per square mile (2000); Age: 24.1% under 18, 10.8% over 64 (2000); Marriage status: 28.4% never married, 55.7% now married, 5.9% widowed, 10.0% divorced (2000); Foreign born: 5.4% (2000); Ancestry (includes multiple ancestries): 44.6% German, 12.7% Other groups, 12.6% Irish, 10.4% Polish, 8.1% English (2000).
Vital Statistics: Birth rate: 158.6 per 10,000 population (1998)
Economy: Unemployment rate: 5.0% (11/2002); Total civilian labor force: 39,860 (11/2002); Single-family building permits issued: 289 (2001) / 249 (2000); Multi-family building permits issued: 147 (2001) / 167 (2000); Employment by occupation: 13.3% management, 22.7% professional, 12.8% services, 28.4% sales, 0.1% farming, 7.4% construction, 15.3% production (2000).
Income: Per capita income: $23,242 (2000); Median household income: $50,084 (2000); Poverty rate: 5.4% (2000).
Taxes: Total city taxes per capita: $470 (2000); City property taxes per capita: $432 (2000).
Education: High school graduation rate: 89.4% (2000); College graduation rate: 30.6% (2000).

School District(s)

Waukesha (PK-12)
2000 Enrollment: 12,760 262-970-1012

Four-year College(s)

Carroll College (Private, Not-for-profit, Presbyterian Church (USA))
2001 Enrollment: 2,921 262-547-1211
2001 Tuition: In-state $15,860; Out-of-state $15,860
Keller Graduate School of Management (Private, For-profit)
2001 Enrollment: n/a 262-798-9889

Housing: Homeownership rate: 56.4% (2000); Median home value: $139,900 (2000); Median rent: $612 per month (2000); Median age of housing: 27 years (2000).
Hospitals: Waukesha Memorial Hospital (400 beds)
Safety: Violent crime rate: 15.3 per 10,000 population; Property crime rate: 227.6 per 10,000 population (2001).
Newspapers: The Freeman (6 x week); This Week (1 x week)
Transportation: Commute to work: 92.0% car, 1.8% public transportation, 3.6% walk, 1.9% work from home (2000); Travel time to work: 36.9% less than 15 minutes, 38.7% 15 to 30 minutes, 16.8% 30 to 45 minutes, 4.7% 45 to 60 minutes, 2.8% 60 minutes or more (2000)
Airports: Waukesha County
Additional Information Contacts
Waukesha Chamber of Commerce 262-542-4249

WAUKESHA (town). Covers a land area of 22.877 square miles and a water area of 0.099 square miles. Located at 42.97° N. Lat.; 88.24° W. Long. Elevation is 821 feet.
History: Waukesha was a stop on the Underground Railroad; after the Civil War it became a health resort. Carroll College and the University of Wisconsin, Waukesha Campus are here. Native American mounds are preserved in the city's Cutler Park. Incorporated 1896.
Population: 8,596 (2000); Race: 98.3% White, 0.1% Black, 0.1% Asian, 0.1% American Indian and Alaska Native, 1.6% Hispanic of any race, 0.5% two or more races (2000); Density: 375.8 persons per square mile (2000); Age: 31.2% under 18, 7.6% over 64 (2000); Marriage status: 19.6% never

married, 71.5% now married, 3.1% widowed, 5.8% divorced (2000); Foreign born: 1.7% (2000); Ancestry (includes multiple ancestries): 54.9% German, 13.7% Polish, 10.1% Irish, 9.7% English, 4.1% Italian (2000).
Economy: It is an industrial center in a dairy area. Its bottled waters are shipped widely. Manufacturing includes dairy and food processing equipment, marine hardware, engines, bearings, castings, rubber products, printing and publishing and electronic equipment. University of Wisconsin, Waukesha Campus is here. Single-family building permits issued: 21 (2001) / 17 (2000); Multi-family building permits issued: 0 (2001) / 0 (2000); Employment by occupation: 17.9% management, 24.3% professional, 9.5% services, 27.4% sales, 0.4% farming, 8.1% construction, 12.3% production (2000).
Income: Per capita income: $27,861 (2000); Median household income: $73,984 (2000); Poverty rate: 0.7% (2000).
Taxes: Total city taxes per capita: $105 (2000); City property taxes per capita: $87 (2000).
Education: High school graduation rate: 94.2% (2000); College graduation rate: 32.8% (2000).
Housing: Homeownership rate: 97.6% (2000); Median home value: $184,200 (2000); Median rent: $652 per month (2000); Median age of housing: 22 years (2000).
Transportation: Commute to work: 94.4% car, 0.1% public transportation, 0.9% walk, 3.6% work from home (2000); Travel time to work: 31.6% less than 15 minutes, 40.5% 15 to 30 minutes, 19.7% 30 to 45 minutes, 5.2% 45 to 60 minutes, 3.0% 60 minutes or more (2000)

Waupaca County

Located in central Wisconsin; drained by the Wolf and Embarrass Rivers. Covers a land area of 751.10 square miles, a water area of 14.20 square miles, and is located in the Central Time Zone. The county government was organized in 1851. County seat is Waupaca.

Weather Station: Clintonville — Elevation: 797 feet

	Jan	Feb	Mar	Apr	May	Jun	Jul	Aug	Sep	Oct	Nov	Dec
High	24	29	40	55	68	77	82	79	70	58	42	29
Low	4	9	20	33	44	53	58	55	46	36	24	12
Precip	1.3	1.0	2.1	2.6	3.7	3.4	4.0	4.0	3.6	2.5	2.3	1.4
Snow	13.0	7.5	8.0	2.3	tr	0.0	0.0	0.0	0.0	0.2	4.1	10.5

High and Low temperatures in degrees Fahrenheit; Precipitation and Snow in inches

Weather Station: Waupaca — Elevation: 839 feet

	Jan	Feb	Mar	Apr	May	Jun	Jul	Aug	Sep	Oct	Nov	Dec
High	25	30	41	56	69	78	82	80	71	59	43	30
Low	7	12	22	35	46	55	60	58	49	38	27	14
Precip	1.3	1.0	2.3	3.0	3.9	3.7	4.4	4.1	3.7	2.5	2.4	1.4
Snow	12.8	7.0	9.4	2.4	0.1	0.0	0.0	0.0	0.0	0.2	4.4	10.8

High and Low temperatures in degrees Fahrenheit; Precipitation and Snow in inches

Population: 51,731 (2000); Race: 97.9% White, 0.2% Black, 0.2% Asian, 0.4% American Indian and Alaska Native, 1.1% Hispanic of any race, 0.6% two or more races (2000); Density: 68.9 persons per square mile (2000); Age: 25.7% under 18, 16.6% over 64 (2000).
Religion: Five largest groups: 23.4% Catholic Church, 19.4% Evangelical Lutheran Church in America, 12.3% Wisconsin Evangelical Lutheran Synod, 9.8% Lutheran Church—Missouri Synod, 4.1% The United Methodist Church (2000).
Economy: Unemployment rate: 4.6% (11/2002); Total civilian labor force: 26,948 (11/2002); Leading industries: 33.7% manufacturing; 15.8% retail trade; 13.7% health care and social assistance (2000); Companies that employ more than 1,000 persons: 1 (2000); Companies that employ more than 100 persons: 25 (2000); Farms: 1,129 totaling 226,746 acres (1997); Minority business ownership rate: 0.0% (1997); Women business ownership rate: 19.3% (1997); Retail sales per capita: $8,316 (1997). Single-family building permits issued: 373 (2001) / 204 (2000); Multi-family building permits issued: 154 (2001) / 68 (2000).
Income: Per capita income: $18,664 (2000); Median household income: $40,910 (2000); Poverty rate: 6.8% (2000); Bankruptcy rate: 3.38% (2001).
Taxes: Total county taxes per capita: $240 (2000); County property taxes per capita: $188 (2000).
Education: High school graduation rate: 82.7% (2000); College graduation rate: 14.8% (2000).
Housing: Homeownership rate: 76.9% (2000); Median home value: $89,300 (2000); Median rent: $380 per month (2000); Median age of housing: 35 years (2000).
Health: Birth rate: 115.2 per 10,000 population (1998); Age adjusted death rate: 99.8 per 10,000 population (1999); Age adjusted cancer mortality rate: 214.8 deaths per 100,000 population (1999). Number of physicians: 7.5 per 10,000 population (1999); Number of hospital beds: 4.8 per 10,000 population (1999).
Elections: 2000 Presidential election results: 38.5% Gore, 56.9% Bush, 3.6% Nader, 0.6% Buchanan
National and State Parks: Hartman Creek State Park; Mukwa State Wildlife Area; Wolf River State Fishery Area
Additional Information Contacts
Waupaca County Government Offices. 715-258-6200
Clintonville Area Chamber Commerce 715-823-4606
Fremont Chamber of Commerce 920-446-3838
Manawa Chamber of Commerce 920-596-2495
New London Chamber of Commerce 920-982-5822
Waupaca Chamber of Commerce. 715-258-7343
Weyauwega Chamber of Commerce 920-867-2500

Waupaca County Communities

BEAR CREEK (town). Covers a land area of 36.656 square miles and a water area of 0 square miles. Located at 44.54° N. Lat.; 88.79° W. Long.
Population: 838 (2000); Race: 98.0% White, 0.0% Black, 0.0% Asian, 1.3% American Indian and Alaska Native, 0.6% Hispanic of any race, 0.1% two or more races (2000); Density: 22.9 persons per square mile (2000); Age: 28.1% under 18, 12.8% over 64 (2000); Marriage status: 22.3% never married, 67.3% now married, 3.2% widowed, 7.2% divorced (2000); Foreign born: 0.0% (2000); Ancestry (includes multiple ancestries): 62.3% German, 9.9% Irish, 7.9% French (except Basque), 6.6% United States or American, 4.8% Polish (2000).
Economy: Employment by occupation: 17.5% management, 12.4% professional, 12.2% services, 14.8% sales, 5.7% farming, 10.7% construction, 26.6% production (2000).
Income: Per capita income: $16,663 (2000); Median household income: $45,227 (2000); Poverty rate: 8.2% (2000).
Taxes: Total city taxes per capita: $87 (1997); City property taxes per capita: $83 (1997).
Education: High school graduation rate: 86.0% (2000); College graduation rate: 10.1% (2000).
Housing: Homeownership rate: 88.3% (2000); Median home value: $88,700 (2000); Median rent: $344 per month (2000); Median age of housing: 60+ years (2000).
Transportation: Commute to work: 81.2% car, 0.7% public transportation, 2.9% walk, 14.8% work from home (2000); Travel time to work: 24.4% less than 15 minutes, 37.0% 15 to 30 minutes, 18.7% 30 to 45 minutes, 12.4% 45 to 60 minutes, 7.5% 60 minutes or more (2000)

BIG FALLS (village). Covers a land area of 0.484 square miles and a water area of 0.023 square miles. Located at 44.62° N. Lat.; 89.01° W. Long. Elevation is 900 feet.
Population: 85 (2000); Race: 100.0% White, 0.0% Black, 0.0% Asian, 0.0% American Indian and Alaska Native, 0.0% Hispanic of any race, 0.0% two or more races (2000); Density: 175.6 persons per square mile (2000); Age: 31.7% under 18, 16.3% over 64 (2000); Marriage status: 16.0% never married, 64.0% now married, 12.0% widowed, 8.0% divorced (2000); Foreign born: 0.0% (2000); Ancestry (includes multiple ancestries): 35.6% German, 26.0% Norwegian, 12.5% French (except Basque), 6.7% Other groups, 6.7% Polish (2000).
Economy: In dairy, poultry and farm area. Employment by occupation: 16.7% management, 13.9% professional, 11.1% services, 8.3% sales, 0.0% farming, 27.8% construction, 22.2% production (2000).
Income: Per capita income: $16,510 (2000); Median household income: $31,806 (2000); Poverty rate: 8.7% (2000).
Taxes: Total city taxes per capita: $68 (1997); City property taxes per capita: $54 (1997).
Education: High school graduation rate: 84.1% (2000); College graduation rate: 10.1% (2000).
Housing: Homeownership rate: 86.0% (2000); Median home value: $50,600 (2000); Median rent: $300 per month (2000); Median age of housing: 60+ years (2000).
Transportation: Commute to work: 80.6% car, 0.0% public transportation, 8.3% walk, 11.1% work from home (2000); Travel time to work: 28.1% less than 15 minutes, 37.5% 15 to 30 minutes, 0.0% 30 to 45 minutes, 15.6% 45 to 60 minutes, 18.8% 60 minutes or more (2000)

CALEDONIA (town). Covers a land area of 27.847 square miles and a water area of 0.216 square miles. Located at 44.29° N. Lat.; 88.80° W. Long.
Population: 1,466 (2000); Race: 96.9% White, 2.2% Black, 0.0% Asian, 0.6% American Indian and Alaska Native, 0.5% Hispanic of any race, 0.3% two or more races (2000); Density: 52.6 persons per square mile (2000); Age: 29.5% under 18, 6.8% over 64 (2000); Marriage status: 20.9% never married, 70.1% now married, 3.5% widowed, 5.5% divorced (2000); Foreign born: 0.6% (2000); Ancestry (includes multiple ancestries): 66.6% German, 9.5% Irish, 7.4% Norwegian, 6.1% French (except Basque), 4.7% English (2000).
Economy: Single-family building permits issued: 153 (2001) / 55 (2000); Multi-family building permits issued: 0 (2001) / 6 (2000); Employment by occupation: 13.8% management, 13.9% professional, 14.0% services, 23.5% sales, 2.4% farming, 8.9% construction, 23.4% production (2000).
Income: Per capita income: $21,702 (2000); Median household income: $53,977 (2000); Poverty rate: 2.1% (2000).
Taxes: Total city taxes per capita: $32 (1997); City property taxes per capita: $29 (1997).
Education: High school graduation rate: 87.3% (2000); College graduation rate: 13.4% (2000).
Housing: Homeownership rate: 90.7% (2000); Median home value: $119,800 (2000); Median rent: $425 per month (2000); Median age of housing: 25 years (2000).
Transportation: Commute to work: 89.9% car, 0.8% public transportation, 2.8% walk, 6.1% work from home (2000); Travel time to work: 19.8% less than 15 minutes, 42.7% 15 to 30 minutes, 30.6% 30 to 45 minutes, 4.0% 45 to 60 minutes, 2.9% 60 minutes or more (2000)

CHAIN O' LAKES-KING (CDP). Covers a land area of 4.311 square miles and a water area of 1.252 square miles. Located at 44.33° N. Lat.; 89.16° W. Long.
Population: 2,215 (2000); Race: 98.6% White, 0.4% Black, 0.0% Asian, 0.0% American Indian and Alaska Native, 0.2% Hispanic of any race, 0.8% two or more races (2000); Density: 513.8 persons per square mile (2000); Age: 11.0% under 18, 41.8% over 64 (2000); Marriage status: 17.6% never married, 55.4% now married, 12.6% widowed, 14.4% divorced (2000); Foreign born: 0.6% (2000); Ancestry (includes multiple ancestries): 31.8% German, 12.4% English, 11.9% Norwegian, 11.2% Irish, 8.8% Polish (2000).
Economy: Employment by occupation: 12.5% management, 20.1% professional, 13.2% services, 27.5% sales, 0.0% farming, 8.2% construction, 18.5% production (2000).
Income: Per capita income: $23,490 (2000); Median household income: $44,327 (2000); Poverty rate: 3.7% (2000).
Education: High school graduation rate: 75.0% (2000); College graduation rate: 23.4% (2000).
Housing: Homeownership rate: 78.7% (2000); Median home value: $166,300 (2000); Median rent: $453 per month (2000); Median age of housing: 38 years (2000).
Transportation: Commute to work: 90.7% car, 0.7% public transportation, 4.1% walk, 4.6% work from home (2000); Travel time to work: 47.0% less than 15 minutes, 29.6% 15 to 30 minutes, 10.2% 30 to 45 minutes, 8.1% 45 to 60 minutes, 5.1% 60 minutes or more (2000)

CLINTONVILLE (city). Covers a land area of 4.226 square miles and a water area of 0.059 square miles. Located at 44.62° N. Lat.; 88.75° W. Long. Elevation is 825 feet.
History: Clintonville was founded in 1855 by Norman Clinton, whose journey to the north woods was halted here when his ox became sick. The first settlement was named Pigeon, for the wild pigeons that were abundant, but was renamed for Clinton when he became the postmaster in 1858.
Population: 4,736 (2000); Race: 96.5% White, 0.6% Black, 0.0% Asian, 0.9% American Indian and Alaska Native, 1.0% Hispanic of any race, 1.1% two or more races (2000); Density: 1,120.7 persons per square mile (2000); Age: 24.9% under 18, 22.1% over 64 (2000); Marriage status: 19.6% never married, 54.8% now married, 12.5% widowed, 13.0% divorced (2000); Foreign born: 0.8% (2000); Ancestry (includes multiple ancestries): 54.6% German, 9.7% Norwegian, 7.9% Irish, 6.1% Other groups, 6.0% Polish (2000).
Economy: Single-family building permits issued: 2 (2001) / 8 (2000); Multi-family building permits issued: 0 (2001) / 0 (2000); Employment by occupation: 10.9% management, 14.8% professional, 15.0% services, 21.2% sales, 1.4% farming, 7.8% construction, 28.9% production (2000).
Income: Per capita income: $16,353 (2000); Median household income: $33,947 (2000); Poverty rate: 9.5% (2000).
Taxes: Total city taxes per capita: $250 (1997); City property taxes per capita: $237 (1997).
Education: High school graduation rate: 76.5% (2000); College graduation rate: 13.5% (2000).

School District(s)

Clintonville (PK-12)
2000 Enrollment: 1,649 715-823-7206
Housing: Homeownership rate: 66.8% (2000); Median home value: $67,300 (2000); Median rent: $335 per month (2000); Median age of housing: 50 years (2000).
Safety: Violent crime rate: 10.5 per 10,000 population; Property crime rate: 400.4 per 10,000 population (2001).
Newspapers: Tribune-Gazette (1 x week)
Transportation: Commute to work: 91.5% car, 0.2% public transportation, 5.1% walk, 1.9% work from home (2000); Travel time to work: 54.2% less than 15 minutes, 16.5% 15 to 30 minutes, 11.9% 30 to 45 minutes, 7.5% 45 to 60 minutes, 9.8% 60 minutes or more (2000); Amtrak: Service available.
Airports: Clintonville Municipal
Additional Information Contacts
Clintonville Area Chamber Commerce 715-823-4606

DAYTON (town). Covers a land area of 35.233 square miles and a water area of 1.154 square miles. Located at 44.30° N. Lat.; 89.15° W. Long.
Population: 2,734 (2000); Race: 95.2% White, 0.3% Black, 0.5% Asian, 0.6% American Indian and Alaska Native, 3.0% Hispanic of any race, 1.5% two or more races (2000); Density: 77.6 persons per square mile (2000); Age: 26.5% under 18, 13.9% over 64 (2000); Marriage status: 17.9% never married, 67.4% now married, 5.4% widowed, 9.3% divorced (2000); Foreign born: 1.7% (2000); Ancestry (includes multiple ancestries): 47.1% German, 12.3% Norwegian, 10.5% Irish, 10.2% English, 9.1% Polish (2000).
Economy: Single-family building permits issued: 23 (2001) / 27 (2000); Multi-family building permits issued: 0 (2001) / 28 (2000); Employment by occupation: 9.3% management, 18.8% professional, 15.5% services, 21.7% sales, 0.4% farming, 11.4% construction, 22.8% production (2000).
Income: Per capita income: $21,728 (2000); Median household income: $47,195 (2000); Poverty rate: 6.1% (2000).
Taxes: Total city taxes per capita: $165 (1997); City property taxes per capita: $158 (1997).
Education: High school graduation rate: 88.4% (2000); College graduation rate: 23.4% (2000).
Housing: Homeownership rate: 87.7% (2000); Median home value: $118,400 (2000); Median rent: $480 per month (2000); Median age of housing: 23 years (2000).
Transportation: Commute to work: 94.2% car, 0.3% public transportation, 0.5% walk, 5.0% work from home (2000); Travel time to work: 42.6% less than 15 minutes, 35.7% 15 to 30 minutes, 8.0% 30 to 45 minutes, 7.7% 45 to 60 minutes, 6.0% 60 minutes or more (2000)

DUPONT (town). Covers a land area of 34.731 square miles and a water area of 0.338 square miles. Located at 44.64° N. Lat.; 88.92° W. Long.
Population: 741 (2000); Race: 100.0% White, 0.0% Black, 0.0% Asian, 0.0% American Indian and Alaska Native, 0.0% Hispanic of any race, 0.0% two or more races (2000); Density: 21.3 persons per square mile (2000); Age: 34.8% under 18, 12.4% over 64 (2000); Marriage status: 25.2% never married, 61.7% now married, 5.8% widowed, 7.3% divorced (2000); Foreign born: 0.3% (2000); Ancestry (includes multiple ancestries): 69.7% German, 7.2% Irish, 5.8% United States or American, 4.5% French (except Basque), 4.5% Polish (2000).
Economy: Single-family building permits issued: 4 (2001) / 1 (2000); Multi-family building permits issued: 0 (2001) / 0 (2000); Employment by occupation: 15.8% management, 5.0% professional, 10.2% services, 22.4% sales, 5.0% farming, 11.6% construction, 29.9% production (2000).
Income: Per capita income: $13,108 (2000); Median household income: $33,854 (2000); Poverty rate: 7.2% (2000).
Taxes: Total city taxes per capita: $117 (1997); City property taxes per capita: $116 (1997).
Education: High school graduation rate: 70.9% (2000); College graduation rate: 5.8% (2000).
Housing: Homeownership rate: 86.5% (2000); Median home value: $96,300 (2000); Median rent: $283 per month (2000); Median age of housing: 55 years (2000).
Transportation: Commute to work: 74.6% car, 0.6% public transportation, 2.3% walk, 21.2% work from home (2000); Travel time to work: 32.6% less than 15 minutes, 31.2% 15 to 30 minutes, 18.3% 30 to 45 minutes, 7.9% 45 to 60 minutes, 10.0% 60 minutes or more (2000)

EMBARRASS (village). Covers a land area of 1.204 square miles and a water area of 0.004 square miles. Located at 44.67° N. Lat.; 88.70° W. Long. Elevation is 810 feet.
Population: 399 (2000); Race: 100.0% White, 0.0% Black, 0.0% Asian, 0.0% American Indian and Alaska Native, 1.2% Hispanic of any race, 0.0% two or more races (2000); Density: 331.5 persons per square mile (2000); Age: 21.9% under 18, 16.1% over 64 (2000); Marriage status: 16.0% never married, 72.2% now married, 7.5% widowed, 4.3% divorced (2000); Foreign born: 1.2% (2000); Ancestry (includes multiple ancestries): 68.3% German, 11.5% Polish, 7.2% Irish, 6.3% Norwegian, 4.0% Italian (2000).
Economy: Lumbering. Manufacturing: furniture. Navarino Hills ski area to East. Single-family building permits issued: 2 (2001) / 1 (2000); Multi-family building permits issued: 0 (2001) / 0 (2000); Employment by occupation: 8.1% management, 8.6% professional, 13.1% services, 25.8% sales, 2.0% farming, 20.7% construction, 21.7% production (2000).
Income: Per capita income: $16,932 (2000); Median household income: $42,500 (2000); Poverty rate: 3.2% (2000).
Taxes: Total city taxes per capita: $58 (1997); City property taxes per capita: $56 (1997).
Education: High school graduation rate: 87.0% (2000); College graduation rate: 9.9% (2000).
Housing: Homeownership rate: 74.1% (2000); Median home value: $63,800 (2000); Median rent: $367 per month (2000); Median age of housing: 53 years (2000).
Transportation: Commute to work: 90.5% car, 0.0% public transportation, 7.4% walk, 2.1% work from home (2000); Travel time to work: 41.4% less than 15 minutes, 28.0% 15 to 30 minutes, 14.0% 30 to 45 minutes, 8.6% 45 to 60 minutes, 8.1% 60 minutes or more (2000)

FARMINGTON (town). Covers a land area of 34.470 square miles and a water area of 0.994 square miles. Located at 44.35° N. Lat.; 89.16° W. Long.
Population: 4,148 (2000); Race: 98.8% White, 0.1% Black, 0.0% Asian, 0.0% American Indian and Alaska Native, 0.3% Hispanic of any race, 0.7% two or more races (2000); Density: 120.3 persons per square mile (2000); Age: 21.1% under 18, 26.0% over 64 (2000); Marriage status: 17.2% never married, 62.2% now married, 8.7% widowed, 11.8% divorced (2000); Foreign born: 0.4% (2000); Ancestry (includes multiple ancestries): 39.2% German, 13.6% Irish, 10.8% Polish, 10.3% Norwegian, 8.9% English (2000).
Economy: Single-family building permits issued: 19 (2001) / 13 (2000); Multi-family building permits issued: 4 (2001) / 0 (2000); Employment by occupation: 13.9% management, 16.6% professional, 15.6% services, 28.4% sales, 0.3% farming, 5.5% construction, 19.8% production (2000).
Income: Per capita income: $20,044 (2000); Median household income: $46,633 (2000); Poverty rate: 8.1% (2000).
Taxes: Total city taxes per capita: $79 (1997); City property taxes per capita: $73 (1997).
Education: High school graduation rate: 78.5% (2000); College graduation rate: 22.3% (2000).
Housing: Homeownership rate: 82.6% (2000); Median home value: $113,100 (2000); Median rent: $469 per month (2000); Median age of housing: 26 years (2000).
Transportation: Commute to work: 92.0% car, 0.3% public transportation, 3.0% walk, 4.3% work from home (2000); Travel time to work: 55.4% less than 15 minutes, 24.5% 15 to 30 minutes, 9.5% 30 to 45 minutes, 4.8% 45 to 60 minutes, 5.7% 60 minutes or more (2000)

FREMONT (village). Covers a land area of 1.045 square miles and a water area of 0.141 square miles. Located at 44.26° N. Lat.; 88.87° W. Long. Elevation is 755 feet.
Population: 666 (2000); Race: 99.4% White, 0.1% Black, 0.0% Asian, 0.0% American Indian and Alaska Native, 0.0% Hispanic of any race, 0.4% two or more races (2000); Density: 637.2 persons per square mile (2000); Age: 19.0% under 18, 16.7% over 64 (2000); Marriage status: 18.9% never married, 62.9% now married, 9.0% widowed, 9.2% divorced (2000); Foreign born: 0.6% (2000); Ancestry (includes multiple ancestries): 56.6% German, 13.8% Irish, 9.7% English, 9.5% Polish, 7.2% Norwegian (2000).
Economy: Single-family building permits issued: 4 (2001) / 5 (2000); Multi-family building permits issued: 10 (2001) / 2 (2000); Employment by occupation: 13.4% management, 12.9% professional, 12.9% services, 22.2% sales, 0.5% farming, 10.1% construction, 27.9% production (2000).
Income: Per capita income: $20,430 (2000); Median household income: $41,250 (2000); Poverty rate: 7.9% (2000).
Taxes: Total city taxes per capita: $158 (1997); City property taxes per capita: $144 (1997).
Education: High school graduation rate: 78.5% (2000); College graduation rate: 12.7% (2000).
Housing: Homeownership rate: 79.6% (2000); Median home value: $107,100 (2000); Median rent: $441 per month (2000); Median age of housing: 42 years (2000).
Transportation: Commute to work: 93.1% car, 0.0% public transportation, 2.8% walk, 4.1% work from home (2000); Travel time to work: 22.4% less than 15 minutes, 23.0% 15 to 30 minutes, 45.1% 30 to 45 minutes, 4.9% 45 to 60 minutes, 4.6% 60 minutes or more (2000)
Additional Information Contacts
Fremont Chamber of Commerce 920-446-3838

FREMONT (town). Covers a land area of 19.072 square miles and a water area of 0.991 square miles. Located at 44.26° N. Lat.; 88.89° W. Long. Elevation is 755 feet.
Population: 632 (2000); Race: 100.0% White, 0.0% Black, 0.0% Asian, 0.0% American Indian and Alaska Native, 1.0% Hispanic of any race, 0.0% two or more races (2000); Density: 33.1 persons per square mile (2000); Age: 23.7% under 18, 17.2% over 64 (2000); Marriage status: 20.4% never married, 62.3% now married, 7.8% widowed, 9.5% divorced (2000); Foreign born: 0.7% (2000); Ancestry (includes multiple ancestries): 60.7% German, 9.1% Irish, 5.8% Polish, 5.3% English, 4.5% Dutch (2000).
Economy: Lumbering, fishing. Manufacturing: buttons, golf T-shirts. In wildlife and resort area. Single-family building permits issued: 6 (2001) / 5 (2000); Multi-family building permits issued: 0 (2001) / 0 (2000); Employment by occupation: 14.5% management, 8.5% professional, 12.3% services, 23.3% sales, 1.6% farming, 12.6% construction, 27.1% production (2000).
Income: Per capita income: $20,028 (2000); Median household income: $43,472 (2000); Poverty rate: 6.0% (2000).
Taxes: Total city taxes per capita: $101 (1997); City property taxes per capita: $96 (1997).
Education: High school graduation rate: 82.4% (2000); College graduation rate: 9.7% (2000).
Housing: Homeownership rate: 87.0% (2000); Median home value: $112,000 (2000); Median rent: $340 per month (2000); Median age of housing: 44 years (2000).
Transportation: Commute to work: 83.9% car, 3.2% public transportation, 1.3% walk, 11.6% work from home (2000); Travel time to work: 24.0% less than 15 minutes, 28.4% 15 to 30 minutes, 33.8% 30 to 45 minutes, 8.0% 45 to 60 minutes, 5.8% 60 minutes or more (2000)

HARRISON (town). Covers a land area of 36.882 square miles and a water area of 0.061 square miles. Located at 44.62° N. Lat.; 89.16° W. Long.
Population: 509 (2000); Race: 99.1% White, 0.0% Black, 0.0% Asian, 0.0% American Indian and Alaska Native, 2.4% Hispanic of any race, 0.9% two or more races (2000); Density: 13.8 persons per square mile (2000); Age: 22.9% under 18, 13.0% over 64 (2000); Marriage status: 20.5% never married, 60.1% now married, 6.4% widowed, 13.0% divorced (2000); Foreign born: 0.4% (2000); Ancestry (includes multiple ancestries): 46.2% German, 22.0% Norwegian, 21.8% Polish, 12.3% Irish, 5.8% Italian (2000).
Economy: Single-family building permits issued: 2 (2001) / 2 (2000); Multi-family building permits issued: 0 (2001) / 0 (2000); Employment by occupation: 14.3% management, 9.4% professional, 10.7% services, 19.2% sales, 2.7% farming, 11.6% construction, 32.1% production (2000).
Income: Per capita income: $18,409 (2000); Median household income: $36,635 (2000); Poverty rate: 3.3% (2000).
Taxes: Total city taxes per capita: $69 (1997); City property taxes per capita: $65 (1997).
Education: High school graduation rate: 76.3% (2000); College graduation rate: 10.9% (2000).
Housing: Homeownership rate: 85.4% (2000); Median home value: $80,500 (2000); Median rent: $343 per month (2000); Median age of housing: 45 years (2000).
Transportation: Commute to work: 87.5% car, 0.9% public transportation, 0.4% walk, 11.2% work from home (2000); Travel time to work: 17.6% less than 15 minutes, 27.1% 15 to 30 minutes, 30.2% 30 to 45 minutes, 10.6% 45 to 60 minutes, 14.6% 60 minutes or more (2000)

HELVETIA (town). Covers a land area of 35.933 square miles and a water area of 0.295 square miles. Located at 44.54° N. Lat.; 89.03° W. Long.
Population: 649 (2000); Race: 99.6% White, 0.4% Black, 0.0% Asian, 0.0% American Indian and Alaska Native, 0.0% Hispanic of any race, 0.0% two or more races (2000); Density: 18.1 persons per square mile (2000); Age: 23.5% under 18, 15.6% over 64 (2000); Marriage status: 16.0% never married, 68.0% now married, 8.3% widowed, 7.7% divorced (2000); Foreign born:

1.8% (2000); Ancestry (includes multiple ancestries): 58.0% German, 22.8% Norwegian, 7.3% Polish, 6.5% Irish, 6.0% Danish (2000).
Economy: Employment by occupation: 8.3% management, 10.3% professional, 17.4% services, 20.1% sales, 0.9% farming, 9.4% construction, 33.6% production (2000).
Income: Per capita income: $19,229 (2000); Median household income: $40,104 (2000); Poverty rate: 5.7% (2000).
Taxes: Total city taxes per capita: $93 (1997); City property taxes per capita: $87 (1997).
Education: High school graduation rate: 81.5% (2000); College graduation rate: 13.5% (2000).
Housing: Homeownership rate: 89.9% (2000); Median home value: $89,000 (2000); Median rent: $372 per month (2000); Median age of housing: 27 years (2000).
Transportation: Commute to work: 94.7% car, 0.0% public transportation, 0.6% walk, 3.8% work from home (2000); Travel time to work: 25.8% less than 15 minutes, 38.3% 15 to 30 minutes, 19.6% 30 to 45 minutes, 8.0% 45 to 60 minutes, 8.3% 60 minutes or more (2000)

IOLA (village). Covers a land area of 1.714 square miles and a water area of 0.155 square miles. Located at 44.50° N. Lat.; 89.12° W. Long. Elevation is 955 feet.
Population: 1,298 (2000); Race: 97.8% White, 0.4% Black, 0.5% Asian, 0.0% American Indian and Alaska Native, 1.6% Hispanic of any race, 0.9% two or more races (2000); Density: 757.1 persons per square mile (2000); Age: 23.1% under 18, 24.5% over 64 (2000); Marriage status: 19.7% never married, 58.6% now married, 10.5% widowed, 11.3% divorced (2000); Foreign born: 1.9% (2000); Ancestry (includes multiple ancestries): 43.6% German, 29.0% Norwegian, 11.8% Polish, 10.4% Irish, 5.4% English (2000).
Economy: Single-family building permits issued: 3 (2001) / 3 (2000); Multi-family building permits issued: 0 (2001) / 0 (2000); Employment by occupation: 9.0% management, 16.4% professional, 16.3% services, 24.7% sales, 1.9% farming, 8.3% construction, 23.4% production (2000).
Income: Per capita income: $17,778 (2000); Median household income: $32,829 (2000); Poverty rate: 6.5% (2000).
Taxes: Total city taxes per capita: $198 (1997); City property taxes per capita: $192 (1997).
Education: High school graduation rate: 81.4% (2000); College graduation rate: 13.6% (2000).

School District(s)

Iola-Scandinavia (PK-12)
2000 Enrollment: 825 715-445-2411

Housing: Homeownership rate: 63.3% (2000); Median home value: $79,800 (2000); Median rent: $395 per month (2000); Median age of housing: 33 years (2000).
Newspapers: The Iola Herald (1 x week); Manawa Advocate (1 x week)
Transportation: Commute to work: 88.9% car, 1.0% public transportation, 8.0% walk, 2.1% work from home (2000); Travel time to work: 51.1% less than 15 minutes, 25.1% 15 to 30 minutes, 15.7% 30 to 45 minutes, 1.6% 45 to 60 minutes, 6.5% 60 minutes or more (2000)

IOLA (town). Covers a land area of 33.644 square miles and a water area of 0.838 square miles. Located at 44.54° N. Lat.; 89.14° W. Long. Elevation is 955 feet.
Population: 818 (2000); Race: 98.4% White, 0.0% Black, 0.0% Asian, 0.0% American Indian and Alaska Native, 1.2% Hispanic of any race, 1.3% two or more races (2000); Density: 24.3 persons per square mile (2000); Age: 27.5% under 18, 16.1% over 64 (2000); Marriage status: 16.4% never married, 70.9% now married, 5.5% widowed, 7.2% divorced (2000); Foreign born: 1.7% (2000); Ancestry (includes multiple ancestries): 44.0% German, 31.6% Norwegian, 11.5% Irish, 6.9% Polish, 4.2% United States or American (2000).
Economy: In agricultural area: dairy products; oxen. Manufacturing: book publishing. Single-family building permits issued: 14 (2001) / 11 (2000); Multi-family building permits issued: 0 (2001) / 0 (2000); Employment by occupation: 14.3% management, 19.6% professional, 10.7% services, 22.0% sales, 4.0% farming, 10.3% construction, 19.2% production (2000).
Income: Per capita income: $19,952 (2000); Median household income: $44,375 (2000); Poverty rate: 1.7% (2000).
Taxes: Total city taxes per capita: $123 (1997); City property taxes per capita: $122 (1997).
Education: High school graduation rate: 85.4% (2000); College graduation rate: 18.0% (2000).
Housing: Homeownership rate: 93.4% (2000); Median home value: $101,700 (2000); Median rent: $338 per month (2000); Median age of housing: 25 years (2000).
Transportation: Commute to work: 87.8% car, 0.5% public transportation, 2.2% walk, 9.5% work from home (2000); Travel time to work: 36.7% less than 15 minutes, 22.1% 15 to 30 minutes, 34.8% 30 to 45 minutes, 1.1% 45 to 60 minutes, 5.4% 60 minutes or more (2000)

LARRABEE (town). Covers a land area of 33.377 square miles and a water area of 0.227 square miles. Located at 44.63° N. Lat.; 88.79° W. Long.
Population: 1,301 (2000); Race: 98.7% White, 0.0% Black, 0.2% Asian, 0.0% American Indian and Alaska Native, 0.2% Hispanic of any race, 1.2% two or more races (2000); Density: 39.0 persons per square mile (2000); Age: 28.4% under 18, 12.2% over 64 (2000); Marriage status: 23.1% never married, 64.0% now married, 4.9% widowed, 8.0% divorced (2000); Foreign born: 0.2% (2000); Ancestry (includes multiple ancestries): 59.1% German, 7.1% Irish, 6.1% Norwegian, 5.2% Polish, 4.9% United States or American (2000).
Economy: Single-family building permits issued: 11 (2001) / 2 (2000); Multi-family building permits issued: 0 (2001) / 0 (2000); Employment by occupation: 14.2% management, 10.2% professional, 9.2% services, 22.3% sales, 3.4% farming, 11.8% construction, 28.9% production (2000).
Income: Per capita income: $18,044 (2000); Median household income: $45,119 (2000); Poverty rate: 5.9% (2000).
Taxes: Total city taxes per capita: $51 (1997); City property taxes per capita: $48 (1997).
Education: High school graduation rate: 86.1% (2000); College graduation rate: 9.4% (2000).
Housing: Homeownership rate: 92.8% (2000); Median home value: $88,300 (2000); Median rent: $600 per month (2000); Median age of housing: 37 years (2000).
Transportation: Commute to work: 86.0% car, 1.2% public transportation, 4.3% walk, 7.7% work from home (2000); Travel time to work: 56.0% less than 15 minutes, 17.4% 15 to 30 minutes, 10.0% 30 to 45 minutes, 7.0% 45 to 60 minutes, 9.6% 60 minutes or more (2000)

LEBANON (town). Covers a land area of 36.045 square miles and a water area of 0.029 square miles. Located at 44.46° N. Lat.; 88.80° W. Long.
Population: 1,648 (2000); Race: 98.7% White, 0.0% Black, 0.5% Asian, 0.0% American Indian and Alaska Native, 0.4% Hispanic of any race, 0.8% two or more races (2000); Density: 45.7 persons per square mile (2000); Age: 29.5% under 18, 9.0% over 64 (2000); Marriage status: 23.2% never married, 66.9% now married, 4.0% widowed, 5.9% divorced (2000); Foreign born: 0.8% (2000); Ancestry (includes multiple ancestries): 60.4% German, 12.6% Irish, 6.8% English, 5.7% Norwegian, 5.4% Polish (2000).
Economy: Single-family building permits issued: 11 (2001) / 4 (2000); Multi-family building permits issued: 0 (2001) / 0 (2000); Employment by occupation: 13.9% management, 9.0% professional, 12.4% services, 17.7% sales, 2.8% farming, 14.0% construction, 30.2% production (2000).
Income: Per capita income: $18,948 (2000); Median household income: $47,931 (2000); Poverty rate: 4.2% (2000).
Taxes: Total city taxes per capita: $55 (1997); City property taxes per capita: $49 (1997).
Education: High school graduation rate: 86.1% (2000); College graduation rate: 9.8% (2000).
Housing: Homeownership rate: 89.3% (2000); Median home value: $104,300 (2000); Median rent: $397 per month (2000); Median age of housing: 24 years (2000).
Transportation: Commute to work: 89.5% car, 0.0% public transportation, 2.2% walk, 7.9% work from home (2000); Travel time to work: 35.3% less than 15 minutes, 32.5% 15 to 30 minutes, 20.4% 30 to 45 minutes, 7.4% 45 to 60 minutes, 4.4% 60 minutes or more (2000)

LIND (town). Covers a land area of 35.943 square miles and a water area of 0.170 square miles. Located at 44.28° N. Lat.; 89.04° W. Long.
Population: 1,381 (2000); Race: 98.1% White, 0.1% Black, 0.4% Asian, 0.9% American Indian and Alaska Native, 0.9% Hispanic of any race, 0.3% two or more races (2000); Density: 38.4 persons per square mile (2000); Age: 25.6% under 18, 13.5% over 64 (2000); Marriage status: 16.0% never married, 67.4% now married, 5.3% widowed, 11.3% divorced (2000); Foreign born: 1.9% (2000); Ancestry (includes multiple ancestries): 49.9% German, 10.3% Norwegian, 10.0% Polish, 8.7% English, 7.9% Irish (2000).
Economy: Employment by occupation: 11.9% management, 14.9% professional, 16.0% services, 17.4% sales, 1.4% farming, 14.0% construction, 24.4% production (2000).
Income: Per capita income: $17,889 (2000); Median household income: $41,991 (2000); Poverty rate: 4.9% (2000).
Taxes: Total city taxes per capita: $54 (1997); City property taxes per capita: $53 (1997).

Education: High school graduation rate: 83.6% (2000); College graduation rate: 8.3% (2000).
Housing: Homeownership rate: 84.0% (2000); Median home value: $92,600 (2000); Median rent: $463 per month (2000); Median age of housing: 25 years (2000).
Transportation: Commute to work: 88.3% car, 0.3% public transportation, 3.4% walk, 7.3% work from home (2000); Travel time to work: 45.2% less than 15 minutes, 35.6% 15 to 30 minutes, 7.1% 30 to 45 minutes, 7.2% 45 to 60 minutes, 4.9% 60 minutes or more (2000)

LITTLE WOLF (town). Covers a land area of 33.524 square miles and a water area of 0.430 square miles. Located at 44.44° N. Lat.; 88.91° W. Long.
Population: 1,445 (2000); Race: 99.0% White, 0.0% Black, 0.0% Asian, 0.1% American Indian and Alaska Native, 1.4% Hispanic of any race, 0.0% two or more races (2000); Density: 43.1 persons per square mile (2000); Age: 28.3% under 18, 10.5% over 64 (2000); Marriage status: 20.3% never married, 69.6% now married, 3.4% widowed, 6.7% divorced (2000); Foreign born: 1.0% (2000); Ancestry (includes multiple ancestries): 63.7% German, 9.2% Norwegian, 8.9% Irish, 6.6% Polish, 4.0% English (2000).
Economy: Employment by occupation: 14.5% management, 9.3% professional, 14.4% services, 21.0% sales, 2.8% farming, 12.3% construction, 25.7% production (2000).
Income: Per capita income: $17,692 (2000); Median household income: $47,692 (2000); Poverty rate: 7.5% (2000).
Taxes: Total city taxes per capita: $78 (1997); City property taxes per capita: $76 (1997).
Education: High school graduation rate: 86.5% (2000); College graduation rate: 9.4% (2000).
Housing: Homeownership rate: 86.5% (2000); Median home value: $110,500 (2000); Median rent: $373 per month (2000); Median age of housing: 35 years (2000).
Transportation: Commute to work: 87.7% car, 1.0% public transportation, 1.7% walk, 9.1% work from home (2000); Travel time to work: 37.6% less than 15 minutes, 33.1% 15 to 30 minutes, 13.4% 30 to 45 minutes, 10.4% 45 to 60 minutes, 5.5% 60 minutes or more (2000)

MANAWA (city). Covers a land area of 1.669 square miles and a water area of 0.109 square miles. Located at 44.46° N. Lat.; 88.91° W. Long. Elevation is 850 feet.
Population: 1,330 (2000); Race: 98.0% White, 0.4% Black, 0.0% Asian, 0.6% American Indian and Alaska Native, 0.8% Hispanic of any race, 1.0% two or more races (2000); Density: 796.7 persons per square mile (2000); Age: 27.4% under 18, 22.5% over 64 (2000); Marriage status: 21.6% never married, 57.5% now married, 12.1% widowed, 8.8% divorced (2000); Foreign born: 1.3% (2000); Ancestry (includes multiple ancestries): 57.8% German, 10.7% Irish, 10.1% Norwegian, 4.6% French (except Basque), 4.1% United States or American (2000).
Economy: In dairying and farming area. Manufacturing: marine accessories, mill products, transportation equipment. Single-family building permits issued: 0 (2001) / 2 (2000); Multi-family building permits issued: 0 (2001) / 24 (2000); Employment by occupation: 7.0% management, 13.6% professional, 12.7% services, 22.1% sales, 1.3% farming, 10.9% construction, 32.3% production (2000).
Income: Per capita income: $16,886 (2000); Median household income: $34,500 (2000); Poverty rate: 9.8% (2000).
Taxes: Total city taxes per capita: $374 (1997); City property taxes per capita: $362 (1997).
Education: High school graduation rate: 76.1% (2000); College graduation rate: 12.0% (2000).

School District(s)

Manawa (PK-12)
2000 Enrollment: 936 920-596-2525
Housing: Homeownership rate: 76.0% (2000); Median home value: $74,000 (2000); Median rent: $294 per month (2000); Median age of housing: 48 years (2000).
Transportation: Commute to work: 92.0% car, 0.5% public transportation, 5.8% walk, 1.0% work from home (2000); Travel time to work: 42.9% less than 15 minutes, 33.0% 15 to 30 minutes, 8.4% 30 to 45 minutes, 8.8% 45 to 60 minutes, 6.9% 60 minutes or more (2000)
Additional Information Contacts
Manawa Chamber of Commerce 920-596-2495

MARION (city). Covers a land area of 2.120 square miles and a water area of 0.081 square miles. Located at 44.67° N. Lat.; 88.88° W. Long. Elevation is 855 feet.
History: Marion was founded in 1856 on the Pigeon River, and named for the first child born here. It began as a lumber village, later becoming a center for cheese production.
Population: 1,297 (2000); Race: 99.2% White, 0.0% Black, 0.0% Asian, 0.3% American Indian and Alaska Native, 0.0% Hispanic of any race, 0.5% two or more races (2000); Density: 611.7 persons per square mile (2000); Age: 19.2% under 18, 23.1% over 64 (2000); Marriage status: 17.8% never married, 63.0% now married, 12.1% widowed, 7.0% divorced (2000); Foreign born: 0.4% (2000); Ancestry (includes multiple ancestries): 67.7% German, 7.6% Irish, 7.0% English, 6.6% Norwegian, 5.4% Polish (2000).
Economy: Single-family building permits issued: 7 (2001) / 4 (2000); Multi-family building permits issued: 0 (2001) / 0 (2000); Employment by occupation: 8.4% management, 10.6% professional, 12.6% services, 22.4% sales, 0.9% farming, 12.4% construction, 32.7% production (2000).
Income: Per capita income: $18,391 (2000); Median household income: $32,344 (2000); Poverty rate: 6.9% (2000).
Taxes: Total city taxes per capita: $253 (1997); City property taxes per capita: $247 (1997).
Education: High school graduation rate: 83.5% (2000); College graduation rate: 9.3% (2000).

School District(s)

Marion (PK-12)
2000 Enrollment: 669 715-754-2511
Housing: Homeownership rate: 71.3% (2000); Median home value: $71,400 (2000); Median rent: $381 per month (2000); Median age of housing: 46 years (2000).
Safety: Violent crime rate: 68.9 per 10,000 population; Property crime rate: 245.0 per 10,000 population (2001).
Newspapers: Marion Advertiser (1 x week)
Transportation: Commute to work: 86.2% car, 0.0% public transportation, 10.0% walk, 2.3% work from home (2000); Travel time to work: 56.2% less than 15 minutes, 23.1% 15 to 30 minutes, 8.6% 30 to 45 minutes, 4.6% 45 to 60 minutes, 7.5% 60 minutes or more (2000); Amtrak: Service available.

MATTESON (town). Covers a land area of 36.664 square miles and a water area of 0.472 square miles. Located at 44.63° N. Lat.; 88.67° W. Long.
Population: 956 (2000); Race: 95.9% White, 0.0% Black, 0.0% Asian, 1.2% American Indian and Alaska Native, 2.2% Hispanic of any race, 1.4% two or more races (2000); Density: 26.1 persons per square mile (2000); Age: 30.1% under 18, 8.4% over 64 (2000); Marriage status: 21.1% never married, 65.2% now married, 4.7% widowed, 9.1% divorced (2000); Foreign born: 1.4% (2000); Ancestry (includes multiple ancestries): 63.8% German, 9.8% Norwegian, 9.6% Irish, 7.9% French (except Basque), 6.5% Other groups (2000).
Economy: Single-family building permits issued: 5 (2001) / 3 (2000); Multi-family building permits issued: 0 (2001) / 0 (2000); Employment by occupation: 7.7% management, 8.5% professional, 17.9% services, 14.8% sales, 2.9% farming, 14.1% construction, 34.1% production (2000).
Income: Per capita income: $15,795 (2000); Median household income: $43,088 (2000); Poverty rate: 4.1% (2000).
Taxes: Total city taxes per capita: $64 (1997); City property taxes per capita: $62 (1997).
Education: High school graduation rate: 77.8% (2000); College graduation rate: 5.0% (2000).
Housing: Homeownership rate: 87.7% (2000); Median home value: $82,000 (2000); Median rent: $300 per month (2000); Median age of housing: 33 years (2000).
Transportation: Commute to work: 95.0% car, 0.0% public transportation, 0.4% walk, 4.3% work from home (2000); Travel time to work: 40.0% less than 15 minutes, 34.5% 15 to 30 minutes, 13.4% 30 to 45 minutes, 5.7% 45 to 60 minutes, 6.5% 60 minutes or more (2000)

MUKWA (town). Covers a land area of 31.426 square miles and a water area of 1.699 square miles. Located at 44.37° N. Lat.; 88.81° W. Long.
Population: 2,773 (2000); Race: 98.9% White, 0.0% Black, 0.1% Asian, 0.4% American Indian and Alaska Native, 0.4% Hispanic of any race, 0.5% two or more races (2000); Density: 88.2 persons per square mile (2000); Age: 28.4% under 18, 8.8% over 64 (2000); Marriage status: 20.7% never married, 67.4% now married, 4.1% widowed, 7.7% divorced (2000); Foreign born: 0.4% (2000); Ancestry (includes multiple ancestries): 58.7% German, 16.3% Irish, 6.8% French (except Basque), 5.8% Polish, 5.1% Norwegian (2000).
Economy: Single-family building permits issued: 22 (2001) / 6 (2000); Multi-family building permits issued: 0 (2001) / 0 (2000); Employment by occupation: 13.3% management, 10.0% professional, 11.0% services, 22.3% sales, 0.8% farming, 10.5% construction, 32.2% production (2000).

Income: Per capita income: $21,254 (2000); Median household income: $51,953 (2000); Poverty rate: 3.5% (2000).
Taxes: Total city taxes per capita: $18 (1997); City property taxes per capita: $9 (1997).
Education: High school graduation rate: 89.2% (2000); College graduation rate: 15.0% (2000).
Housing: Homeownership rate: 91.5% (2000); Median home value: $119,300 (2000); Median rent: $438 per month (2000); Median age of housing: 22 years (2000).
Transportation: Commute to work: 92.7% car, 0.5% public transportation, 0.1% walk, 5.9% work from home (2000); Travel time to work: 39.1% less than 15 minutes, 25.3% 15 to 30 minutes, 21.1% 30 to 45 minutes, 10.3% 45 to 60 minutes, 4.1% 60 minutes or more (2000)

NEW LONDON (city). Covers a land area of 5.598 square miles and a water area of 0.059 square miles. Located at 44.38° N. Lat.; 88.74° W. Long. Elevation is 789 feet.
History: New London was founded in 1853 by Lucius Taft and Ira Millerd. It was named for the town in Connecticut by Reeder Smith, who built the plank road between Appleton and Stevens Point. New London became a lumber center and the terminus of steamboats on the Wolf River.
Population: 7,085 (2000); Race: 97.2% White, 0.1% Black, 0.2% Asian, 0.6% American Indian and Alaska Native, 2.6% Hispanic of any race, 0.3% two or more races (2000); Density: 1,265.5 persons per square mile (2000); Age: 25.4% under 18, 16.2% over 64 (2000); Marriage status: 23.1% never married, 58.8% now married, 8.3% widowed, 9.7% divorced (2000); Foreign born: 1.5% (2000); Ancestry (includes multiple ancestries): 53.4% German, 10.4% Irish, 7.8% French (except Basque), 7.1% Norwegian, 6.8% English (2000).
Economy: Single-family building permits issued: 20 (2001) / 12 (2000); Multi-family building permits issued: 30 (2001) / 2 (2000); Employment by occupation: 8.7% management, 13.6% professional, 15.3% services, 23.2% sales, 0.1% farming, 9.6% construction, 29.5% production (2000).
Income: Per capita income: $18,153 (2000); Median household income: $37,491 (2000); Poverty rate: 5.9% (2000).
Taxes: Total city taxes per capita: $224 (1997); City property taxes per capita: $213 (1997).
Education: High school graduation rate: 81.5% (2000); College graduation rate: 14.4% (2000).

School District(s)

New London (PK-12)
2000 Enrollment: 2,512 920-982-8530

Housing: Homeownership rate: 63.1% (2000); Median home value: $83,600 (2000); Median rent: $386 per month (2000); Median age of housing: 40 years (2000).
Hospitals: New London Family Medical Center (75 beds)
Safety: Violent crime rate: 1.4 per 10,000 population; Property crime rate: 294.3 per 10,000 population (2001).
Newspapers: Press-Star (1 x week)
Transportation: Commute to work: 94.7% car, 0.1% public transportation, 3.1% walk, 1.2% work from home (2000); Travel time to work: 57.7% less than 15 minutes, 17.5% 15 to 30 minutes, 18.3% 30 to 45 minutes, 2.8% 45 to 60 minutes, 3.8% 60 minutes or more (2000); Amtrak: Service available.

Additional Information Contacts

New London Chamber of Commerce 920-982-5822

OGDENSBURG (village). Covers a land area of 0.977 square miles and a water area of 0.050 square miles. Located at 44.45° N. Lat.; 89.03° W. Long. Elevation is 861 feet.
Population: 224 (2000); Race: 100.0% White, 0.0% Black, 0.0% Asian, 0.0% American Indian and Alaska Native, 0.0% Hispanic of any race, 0.0% two or more races (2000); Density: 229.2 persons per square mile (2000); Age: 25.3% under 18, 7.0% over 64 (2000); Marriage status: 18.7% never married, 64.7% now married, 7.3% widowed, 9.3% divorced (2000); Foreign born: 0.0% (2000); Ancestry (includes multiple ancestries): 38.7% German, 11.3% English, 10.8% Norwegian, 7.5% United States or American, 5.9% Dutch (2000).
Economy: In farm area. Manufacturing of fiberglass products. Single-family building permits issued: 0 (2001) / 0 (2000); Multi-family building permits issued: 0 (2001) / 0 (2000); Employment by occupation: 4.2% management, 18.9% professional, 11.6% services, 18.9% sales, 3.2% farming, 21.1% construction, 22.1% production (2000).
Income: Per capita income: $18,588 (2000); Median household income: $36,667 (2000); Poverty rate: 12.4% (2000).
Taxes: Total city taxes per capita: $22 (1997); City property taxes per capita: $18 (1997).
Education: High school graduation rate: 64.4% (2000); College graduation rate: 11.4% (2000).
Housing: Homeownership rate: 84.5% (2000); Median home value: $50,000 (2000); Median rent: $381 per month (2000); Median age of housing: 60+ years (2000).
Transportation: Commute to work: 97.9% car, 0.0% public transportation, 2.1% walk, 0.0% work from home (2000); Travel time to work: 32.6% less than 15 minutes, 52.6% 15 to 30 minutes, 12.6% 30 to 45 minutes, 0.0% 45 to 60 minutes, 2.1% 60 minutes or more (2000)

ROYALTON (town). Covers a land area of 33.620 square miles and a water area of 2.285 square miles. Located at 44.38° N. Lat.; 88.93° W. Long. Elevation is 822 feet.
Population: 1,523 (2000); Race: 97.9% White, 0.0% Black, 0.8% Asian, 0.5% American Indian and Alaska Native, 0.0% Hispanic of any race, 0.8% two or more races (2000); Density: 45.3 persons per square mile (2000); Age: 25.7% under 18, 14.3% over 64 (2000); Marriage status: 20.3% never married, 66.4% now married, 5.6% widowed, 7.7% divorced (2000); Foreign born: 0.5% (2000); Ancestry (includes multiple ancestries): 54.7% German, 7.6% Irish, 5.3% French (except Basque), 5.2% Norwegian, 5.1% English (2000).
Economy: Employment by occupation: 10.0% management, 9.8% professional, 15.1% services, 21.4% sales, 2.5% farming, 10.7% construction, 30.5% production (2000).
Income: Per capita income: $19,573 (2000); Median household income: $48,804 (2000); Poverty rate: 2.9% (2000).
Taxes: Total city taxes per capita: $23 (1997); City property taxes per capita: $21 (1997).
Education: High school graduation rate: 80.2% (2000); College graduation rate: 8.6% (2000).
Housing: Homeownership rate: 91.2% (2000); Median home value: $107,100 (2000); Median rent: $438 per month (2000); Median age of housing: 32 years (2000).
Transportation: Commute to work: 90.1% car, 0.4% public transportation, 1.6% walk, 6.9% work from home (2000); Travel time to work: 35.8% less than 15 minutes, 37.3% 15 to 30 minutes, 11.3% 30 to 45 minutes, 11.2% 45 to 60 minutes, 4.4% 60 minutes or more (2000)

SAINT LAWRENCE (town). Covers a land area of 34.707 square miles and a water area of 0.281 square miles. Located at 44.45° N. Lat.; 89.05° W. Long.
Population: 740 (2000); Race: 99.7% White, 0.0% Black, 0.0% Asian, 0.0% American Indian and Alaska Native, 0.3% Hispanic of any race, 0.3% two or more races (2000); Density: 21.3 persons per square mile (2000); Age: 25.9% under 18, 13.1% over 64 (2000); Marriage status: 21.3% never married, 64.5% now married, 4.2% widowed, 10.1% divorced (2000); Foreign born: 1.6% (2000); Ancestry (includes multiple ancestries): 54.3% German, 22.0% Norwegian, 10.1% Irish, 8.8% Polish, 7.1% French (except Basque) (2000).
Economy: Single-family building permits issued: 2 (2001) / 0 (2000); Multi-family building permits issued: 0 (2001) / 0 (2000); Employment by occupation: 14.0% management, 10.9% professional, 9.6% services, 19.5% sales, 1.3% farming, 13.7% construction, 31.0% production (2000).
Income: Per capita income: $20,160 (2000); Median household income: $44,286 (2000); Poverty rate: 4.0% (2000).
Education: High school graduation rate: 84.0% (2000); College graduation rate: 11.9% (2000).
Housing: Homeownership rate: 93.5% (2000); Median home value: $84,700 (2000); Median rent: $375 per month (2000); Median age of housing: 31 years (2000).
Transportation: Commute to work: 84.2% car, 0.5% public transportation, 3.9% walk, 10.6% work from home (2000); Travel time to work: 28.3% less than 15 minutes, 40.5% 15 to 30 minutes, 19.1% 30 to 45 minutes, 5.2% 45 to 60 minutes, 6.9% 60 minutes or more (2000)

SCANDINAVIA (village). Covers a land area of 0.862 square miles and a water area of 0.124 square miles. Located at 44.46° N. Lat.; 89.14° W. Long. Elevation is 931 feet.
Population: 349 (2000); Race: 93.0% White, 0.0% Black, 4.5% Asian, 1.4% American Indian and Alaska Native, 0.0% Hispanic of any race, 1.1% two or more races (2000); Density: 404.8 persons per square mile (2000); Age: 29.1% under 18, 14.8% over 64 (2000); Marriage status: 19.6% never married, 63.8% now married, 7.9% widowed, 8.7% divorced (2000); Foreign born: 4.5% (2000); Ancestry (includes multiple ancestries): 38.9% German, 24.6% Norwegian, 14.0% Irish, 12.6% Other groups, 10.4% English (2000).
Economy: Single-family building permits issued: 4 (2001) / 1 (2000); Multi-family building permits issued: 2 (2001) / 2 (2000); Employment by

occupation: 8.8% management, 17.0% professional, 13.2% services, 26.9% sales, 1.6% farming, 10.4% construction, 22.0% production (2000).
Income: Per capita income: $15,730 (2000); Median household income: $42,500 (2000); Poverty rate: 9.1% (2000).
Taxes: Total city taxes per capita: $43 (1997); City property taxes per capita: $37 (1997).
Education: High school graduation rate: 83.6% (2000); College graduation rate: 24.0% (2000).
Housing: Homeownership rate: 74.1% (2000); Median home value: $85,000 (2000); Median rent: $295 per month (2000); Median age of housing: 52 years (2000).
Transportation: Commute to work: 92.2% car, 0.6% public transportation, 5.6% walk, 1.7% work from home (2000); Travel time to work: 38.4% less than 15 minutes, 39.5% 15 to 30 minutes, 13.6% 30 to 45 minutes, 5.6% 45 to 60 minutes, 2.8% 60 minutes or more (2000)

SCANDINAVIA (town). Covers a land area of 33.794 square miles and a water area of 0.447 square miles. Located at 44.47° N. Lat.; 89.15° W. Long. Elevation is 931 feet.
Population: 1,075 (2000); Race: 99.1% White, 0.0% Black, 0.3% Asian, 0.2% American Indian and Alaska Native, 0.3% Hispanic of any race, 0.2% two or more races (2000); Density: 31.8 persons per square mile (2000); Age: 25.0% under 18, 14.4% over 64 (2000); Marriage status: 18.8% never married, 68.1% now married, 5.3% widowed, 7.8% divorced (2000); Foreign born: 0.7% (2000); Ancestry (includes multiple ancestries): 52.6% German, 27.8% Norwegian, 10.4% Irish, 9.7% Polish, 8.7% English (2000).
Economy: In timber and farm area; lumbering. Tourism. Employment by occupation: 11.2% management, 15.5% professional, 10.7% services, 24.2% sales, 3.5% farming, 13.4% construction, 21.5% production (2000).
Income: Per capita income: $20,166 (2000); Median household income: $50,882 (2000); Poverty rate: 3.1% (2000).
Taxes: Total city taxes per capita: $75 (1997); City property taxes per capita: $74 (1997).
Education: High school graduation rate: 89.4% (2000); College graduation rate: 13.2% (2000).
Housing: Homeownership rate: 93.2% (2000); Median home value: $113,600 (2000); Median rent: $325 per month (2000); Median age of housing: 25 years (2000).
Transportation: Commute to work: 87.6% car, 1.8% public transportation, 1.6% walk, 8.6% work from home (2000); Travel time to work: 35.5% less than 15 minutes, 38.5% 15 to 30 minutes, 14.2% 30 to 45 minutes, 1.5% 45 to 60 minutes, 10.3% 60 minutes or more (2000)

UNION (town). Covers a land area of 35.911 square miles and a water area of 0.222 square miles. Located at 44.53° N. Lat.; 88.91° W. Long.
Population: 804 (2000); Race: 99.4% White, 0.0% Black, 0.0% Asian, 0.4% American Indian and Alaska Native, 0.0% Hispanic of any race, 0.2% two or more races (2000); Density: 22.4 persons per square mile (2000); Age: 24.9% under 18, 10.4% over 64 (2000); Marriage status: 20.8% never married, 70.4% now married, 4.5% widowed, 4.2% divorced (2000); Foreign born: 0.2% (2000); Ancestry (includes multiple ancestries): 66.0% German, 10.7% Irish, 9.4% Norwegian, 4.7% United States or American, 3.9% Polish (2000).
Economy: Employment by occupation: 16.0% management, 6.0% professional, 12.2% services, 20.5% sales, 3.2% farming, 7.3% construction, 34.8% production (2000).
Income: Per capita income: $17,529 (2000); Median household income: $42,875 (2000); Poverty rate: 14.9% (2000).
Taxes: Total city taxes per capita: $131 (1997); City property taxes per capita: $129 (1997).
Education: High school graduation rate: 82.7% (2000); College graduation rate: 10.6% (2000).
Housing: Homeownership rate: 91.3% (2000); Median home value: $77,500 (2000); Median rent: $333 per month (2000); Median age of housing: 58 years (2000).
Transportation: Commute to work: 79.1% car, 0.4% public transportation, 7.0% walk, 13.0% work from home (2000); Travel time to work: 28.3% less than 15 minutes, 39.9% 15 to 30 minutes, 18.2% 30 to 45 minutes, 5.6% 45 to 60 minutes, 8.1% 60 minutes or more (2000)

WAUPACA (city). Covers a land area of 5.994 square miles and a water area of 0.137 square miles. Located at 44.35° N. Lat.; 89.08° W. Long. Elevation is 855 feet.
History: Waupaca developed as the center of Wisconsin's potato growing industry. Later, it became important as a recreation center, with a chain of lakes attracting sportsmen.
Population: 5,676 (2000); Race: 97.6% White, 0.3% Black, 0.4% Asian, 0.0% American Indian and Alaska Native, 3.0% Hispanic of any race, 0.5% two or more races (2000); Density: 947.0 persons per square mile (2000); Age: 25.5% under 18, 20.4% over 64 (2000); Marriage status: 26.4% never married, 48.9% now married, 12.3% widowed, 12.4% divorced (2000); Foreign born: 1.6% (2000); Ancestry (includes multiple ancestries): 46.0% German, 15.0% Irish, 10.7% Norwegian, 8.6% English, 8.3% Danish (2000).
Economy: Single-family building permits issued: 21 (2001) / 8 (2000); Multi-family building permits issued: 106 (2001) / 4 (2000); Employment by occupation: 11.8% management, 18.9% professional, 17.0% services, 21.5% sales, 0.9% farming, 8.5% construction, 21.4% production (2000).
Income: Per capita income: $18,890 (2000); Median household income: $31,095 (2000); Poverty rate: 10.5% (2000).
Taxes: Total city taxes per capita: $448 (1997); City property taxes per capita: $413 (1997).
Education: High school graduation rate: 86.0% (2000); College graduation rate: 22.0% (2000).

School District(s)

Waupaca (PK-12)
2000 Enrollment: 2,726 715-258-4121
Housing: Homeownership rate: 54.2% (2000); Median home value: $85,500 (2000); Median rent: $375 per month (2000); Median age of housing: 41 years (2000).
Hospitals: Riverside Medical Center (77 beds)
Safety: Violent crime rate: 5.2 per 10,000 population; Property crime rate: 269.4 per 10,000 population (2001).
Newspapers: Waupaca County Post (1 x week)
Transportation: Commute to work: 91.2% car, 0.5% public transportation, 4.1% walk, 3.3% work from home (2000); Travel time to work: 73.7% less than 15 minutes, 13.3% 15 to 30 minutes, 3.7% 30 to 45 minutes, 4.5% 45 to 60 minutes, 4.8% 60 minutes or more (2000)
Additional Information Contacts
Waupaca Chamber of Commerce. 715-258-7343

WAUPACA (town). Covers a land area of 30.772 square miles and a water area of 0.093 square miles. Located at 44.38° N. Lat.; 89.05° W. Long. Elevation is 855 feet.
History: Incorporated 1875.
Population: 1,155 (2000); Race: 97.5% White, 0.0% Black, 0.0% Asian, 0.8% American Indian and Alaska Native, 1.1% Hispanic of any race, 0.9% two or more races (2000); Density: 37.5 persons per square mile (2000); Age: 28.0% under 18, 12.2% over 64 (2000); Marriage status: 16.9% never married, 70.9% now married, 5.8% widowed, 6.4% divorced (2000); Foreign born: 0.8% (2000); Ancestry (includes multiple ancestries): 50.6% German, 12.5% Norwegian, 10.1% English, 9.6% Irish, 7.6% Danish (2000).
Economy: In timber and farm area: potatoes; livestock; dairy products. Manufacturing: printing, sand and gravel, filters, garage doors. Center of lake-resort region. Wisconsin Veterans Home here. Employment by occupation: 17.8% management, 11.0% professional, 18.4% services, 18.9% sales, 1.6% farming, 15.0% construction, 17.2% production (2000).
Income: Per capita income: $19,843 (2000); Median household income: $46,667 (2000); Poverty rate: 6.7% (2000).
Taxes: Total city taxes per capita: $79 (1997); City property taxes per capita: $77 (1997).
Education: High school graduation rate: 85.3% (2000); College graduation rate: 14.8% (2000).
Housing: Homeownership rate: 87.2% (2000); Median home value: $92,800 (2000); Median rent: $490 per month (2000); Median age of housing: 33 years (2000).
Transportation: Commute to work: 89.3% car, 0.0% public transportation, 1.6% walk, 8.8% work from home (2000); Travel time to work: 64.1% less than 15 minutes, 20.4% 15 to 30 minutes, 8.5% 30 to 45 minutes, 3.5% 45 to 60 minutes, 3.6% 60 minutes or more (2000)

WEYAUWEGA (city). Covers a land area of 1.503 square miles and a water area of 0.105 square miles. Located at 44.32° N. Lat.; 88.93° W. Long. Elevation is 795 feet.
History: Weyauwega was settled in 1852, and named for a local chief whose name meant "he embodies it." Lumbering and flour milling supported the town until after 1900, when it became a farm trading center.
Population: 1,806 (2000); Race: 98.2% White, 0.1% Black, 0.6% Asian, 0.1% American Indian and Alaska Native, 0.8% Hispanic of any race, 0.2% two or more races (2000); Density: 1,201.7 persons per square mile (2000); Age: 23.9% under 18, 19.7% over 64 (2000); Marriage status: 22.4% never married, 55.5% now married, 10.2% widowed, 11.8% divorced (2000);

Foreign born: 0.7% (2000); Ancestry (includes multiple ancestries): 56.5% German, 8.9% Norwegian, 8.8% Irish, 5.8% Polish, 5.4% English (2000).
Economy: Single-family building permits issued: 0 (2001) / 1 (2000); Multi-family building permits issued: 2 (2001) / 0 (2000); Employment by occupation: 6.3% management, 14.8% professional, 16.6% services, 17.0% sales, 0.9% farming, 10.8% construction, 33.6% production (2000).
Income: Per capita income: $16,755 (2000); Median household income: $34,556 (2000); Poverty rate: 6.5% (2000).
Taxes: Total city taxes per capita: $129 (1997); City property taxes per capita: $122 (1997).
Education: High school graduation rate: 75.2% (2000); College graduation rate: 12.5% (2000).

School District(s)

Weyauwega-Fremont (PK-12)
2000 Enrollment: 1,099 920-867-2148

Housing: Homeownership rate: 73.5% (2000); Median home value: $77,600 (2000); Median rent: $378 per month (2000); Median age of housing: 49 years (2000).
Newspapers: The Chronicle (1 x week)
Transportation: Commute to work: 88.2% car, 1.9% public transportation, 7.0% walk, 2.5% work from home (2000); Travel time to work: 46.2% less than 15 minutes, 27.5% 15 to 30 minutes, 13.6% 30 to 45 minutes, 8.6% 45 to 60 minutes, 4.1% 60 minutes or more (2000)

Additional Information Contacts

Weyauwega Chamber of Commerce 920-867-2500

WEYAUWEGA (town). Covers a land area of 19.875 square miles and a water area of 1.902 square miles. Located at 44.31° N. Lat.; 88.92° W. Long. Elevation is 795 feet.
History: Settled c.1850, incorporated 1939.
Population: 627 (2000); Race: 97.0% White, 0.0% Black, 0.0% Asian, 2.0% American Indian and Alaska Native, 0.2% Hispanic of any race, 1.1% two or more races (2000); Density: 31.5 persons per square mile (2000); Age: 32.0% under 18, 9.2% over 64 (2000); Marriage status: 20.7% never married, 68.4% now married, 4.8% widowed, 6.2% divorced (2000); Foreign born: 0.2% (2000); Ancestry (includes multiple ancestries): 57.2% German, 8.7% Norwegian, 5.6% Polish, 5.6% United States or American, 5.1% Irish (2000).
Economy: Trade center in dairying and grain- and potato-growing area. Dairy products: cheese. Manufacturing of fabricated metal products. Employment by occupation: 13.7% management, 14.6% professional, 16.4% services, 15.5% sales, 1.5% farming, 12.2% construction, 26.1% production (2000).
Income: Per capita income: $17,844 (2000); Median household income: $46,442 (2000); Poverty rate: 4.5% (2000).
Taxes: Total city taxes per capita: $96 (1997); City property taxes per capita: $93 (1997).
Education: High school graduation rate: 85.2% (2000); College graduation rate: 14.8% (2000).
Housing: Homeownership rate: 84.2% (2000); Median home value: $106,500 (2000); Median rent: $367 per month (2000); Median age of housing: 39 years (2000).
Transportation: Commute to work: 86.2% car, 0.0% public transportation, 6.9% walk, 6.9% work from home (2000); Travel time to work: 54.5% less than 15 minutes, 24.6% 15 to 30 minutes, 10.4% 30 to 45 minutes, 8.1% 45 to 60 minutes, 2.4% 60 minutes or more (2000)

WYOMING (town). Covers a land area of 36.135 square miles and a water area of 0.067 square miles. Located at 44.63° N. Lat.; 89.03° W. Long.
Population: 285 (2000); Race: 99.3% White, 0.0% Black, 0.0% Asian, 0.0% American Indian and Alaska Native, 0.7% Hispanic of any race, 0.7% two or more races (2000); Density: 7.9 persons per square mile (2000); Age: 16.3% under 18, 17.4% over 64 (2000); Marriage status: 25.0% never married, 65.5% now married, 3.6% widowed, 6.0% divorced (2000); Foreign born: 0.0% (2000); Ancestry (includes multiple ancestries): 61.3% German, 11.3% Norwegian, 8.9% Polish, 7.1% Irish, 5.3% French (except Basque) (2000).
Economy: Employment by occupation: 10.7% management, 11.3% professional, 11.9% services, 13.1% sales, 11.3% farming, 7.7% construction, 33.9% production (2000).
Income: Per capita income: $17,618 (2000); Median household income: $41,429 (2000); Poverty rate: 3.5% (2000).
Taxes: Total city taxes per capita: $84 (1997); City property taxes per capita: $80 (1997).
Education: High school graduation rate: 78.9% (2000); College graduation rate: 11.3% (2000).
Housing: Homeownership rate: 88.9% (2000); Median home value: $78,300 (2000); Median rent: $300 per month (2000); Median age of housing: 44 years (2000).
Transportation: Commute to work: 85.6% car, 0.0% public transportation, 2.5% walk, 11.9% work from home (2000); Travel time to work: 15.6% less than 15 minutes, 42.6% 15 to 30 minutes, 22.0% 30 to 45 minutes, 12.8% 45 to 60 minutes, 7.1% 60 minutes or more (2000)

Waushara County

Located in central Wisconsin; drained by the White and Pine Rivers; includes part of Lake Poygan, and many small lakes. Covers a land area of 626.00 square miles, a water area of 11.40 square miles, and is located in the Central Time Zone. The county government was organized in 1851. County seat is Wautoma.

Weather Station: Hancock Exp. Farm Elevation: 1,076 feet

	Jan	Feb	Mar	Apr	May	Jun	Jul	Aug	Sep	Oct	Nov	Dec
High	24	30	41	58	71	79	82	80	72	60	42	29
Low	5	10	21	34	45	55	59	57	49	38	25	12
Precip	0.9	0.9	2.0	2.9	3.5	3.7	4.2	4.2	3.7	2.4	2.2	1.0
Snow	13.3	9.2	10.5	3.3	tr	0.0	0.0	0.0	tr	0.6	5.4	11.2

High and Low temperatures in degrees Fahrenheit; Precipitation and Snow in inches

Population: 23,154 (2000); Race: 97.0% White, 0.1% Black, 0.2% Asian, 0.4% American Indian and Alaska Native, 3.4% Hispanic of any race, 1.0% two or more races (2000); Density: 37.0 persons per square mile (2000); Age: 23.6% under 18, 19.1% over 64 (2000).
Religion: Five largest groups: 16.9% Catholic Church, 10.6% Evangelical Lutheran Church in America, 5.9% Lutheran Church—Missouri Synod, 5.4% The United Methodist Church, 2.8% Wisconsin Evangelical Lutheran Synod (2000).
Economy: Unemployment rate: 5.3% (11/2002); Total civilian labor force: 12,163 (11/2002); Leading industries: 20.3% manufacturing; 18.8% retail trade; 11.3% health care and social assistance (2000); Companies that employ more than 1,000 persons: 0 (2000); Companies that employ more than 100 persons: 6 (2000); Farms: 634 totaling 174,524 acres (1997); Minority business ownership rate: 0.0% (1997); Women business ownership rate: 14.6% (1997); Retail sales per capita: $6,916 (1997). Single-family building permits issued: 221 (2001) / 223 (2000); Multi-family building permits issued: 82 (2001) / 39 (2000).
Income: Per capita income: $18,144 (2000); Median household income: $37,000 (2000); Poverty rate: 9.1% (2000); Bankruptcy rate: 3.81% (2001).
Taxes: Total county taxes per capita: $346 (1997); County property taxes per capita: $305 (1997).
Education: High school graduation rate: 78.8% (2000); College graduation rate: 11.7% (2000).
Housing: Homeownership rate: 83.4% (2000); Median home value: $85,100 (2000); Median rent: $348 per month (2000); Median age of housing: 28 years (2000).
Health: Birth rate: 102.8 per 10,000 population (1998); Age adjusted death rate: 88.1 per 10,000 population (1999); Age adjusted cancer mortality rate: 216.5 deaths per 100,000 population (1999). Number of physicians: 5.6 per 10,000 population (1999); Number of hospital beds: 11.7 per 10,000 population (1999).
Elections: 2000 Presidential election results: 41.4% Gore, 54.4% Bush, 3.0% Nader, 0.8% Buchanan
National and State Parks: Greenwood State Wildlife Refuge

Additional Information Contacts

Waushara County Government Offices 920-787-4631

Waushara County Communities

AURORA (town). Covers a land area of 34.232 square miles and a water area of 0.371 square miles. Located at 44.02° N. Lat.; 88.95° W. Long.
Population: 971 (2000); Race: 98.5% White, 0.8% Black, 0.0% Asian, 0.5% American Indian and Alaska Native, 1.8% Hispanic of any race, 0.2% two or more races (2000); Density: 28.4 persons per square mile (2000); Age: 25.7% under 18, 11.9% over 64 (2000); Marriage status: 22.5% never married, 66.0% now married, 4.6% widowed, 6.9% divorced (2000); Foreign born: 0.3% (2000); Ancestry (includes multiple ancestries): 59.1% German, 18.4% Polish, 7.5% English, 5.3% Norwegian, 5.1% United States or American (2000).
Economy: Employment by occupation: 10.1% management, 16.6% professional, 10.8% services, 16.6% sales, 2.2% farming, 13.2% construction, 30.4% production (2000).

Income: Per capita income: $20,147 (2000); Median household income: $49,583 (2000); Poverty rate: 4.4% (2000).
Taxes: Total city taxes per capita: $31 (1997); City property taxes per capita: $30 (1997).
Education: High school graduation rate: 83.0% (2000); College graduation rate: 10.6% (2000).
Housing: Homeownership rate: 89.0% (2000); Median home value: $94,800 (2000); Median rent: $400 per month (2000); Median age of housing: 42 years (2000).
Transportation: Commute to work: 93.3% car, 0.4% public transportation, 1.7% walk, 4.6% work from home (2000); Travel time to work: 28.5% less than 15 minutes, 28.3% 15 to 30 minutes, 31.5% 30 to 45 minutes, 6.4% 45 to 60 minutes, 5.2% 60 minutes or more (2000)

BLOOMFIELD (town). Covers a land area of 35.412 square miles and a water area of 0.457 square miles. Located at 44.19° N. Lat.; 88.93° W. Long.
Population: 1,018 (2000); Race: 98.8% White, 0.0% Black, 0.0% Asian, 0.2% American Indian and Alaska Native, 0.2% Hispanic of any race, 1.0% two or more races (2000); Density: 28.7 persons per square mile (2000); Age: 24.7% under 18, 11.9% over 64 (2000); Marriage status: 20.7% never married, 66.5% now married, 4.6% widowed, 8.2% divorced (2000); Foreign born: 0.6% (2000); Ancestry (includes multiple ancestries): 61.2% German, 8.4% Irish, 7.4% Norwegian, 6.0% Polish, 4.9% English (2000).
Economy: Employment by occupation: 17.4% management, 10.1% professional, 16.6% services, 17.6% sales, 1.7% farming, 17.2% construction, 19.5% production (2000).
Income: Per capita income: $19,161 (2000); Median household income: $42,222 (2000); Poverty rate: 8.1% (2000).
Taxes: Total city taxes per capita: $55 (1997); City property taxes per capita: $54 (1997).
Education: High school graduation rate: 81.0% (2000); College graduation rate: 7.5% (2000).
Housing: Homeownership rate: 89.7% (2000); Median home value: $100,600 (2000); Median rent: $375 per month (2000); Median age of housing: 35 years (2000).
Transportation: Commute to work: 85.7% car, 0.2% public transportation, 2.1% walk, 11.5% work from home (2000); Travel time to work: 19.0% less than 15 minutes, 28.7% 15 to 30 minutes, 29.2% 30 to 45 minutes, 16.9% 45 to 60 minutes, 6.3% 60 minutes or more (2000)

COLOMA (village). Covers a land area of 1.063 square miles and a water area of 0 square miles. Located at 44.03° N. Lat.; 89.52° W. Long. Elevation is 1,044 feet.
Population: 461 (2000); Race: 99.2% White, 0.4% Black, 0.0% Asian, 0.0% American Indian and Alaska Native, 1.9% Hispanic of any race, 0.0% two or more races (2000); Density: 433.7 persons per square mile (2000); Age: 28.6% under 18, 18.1% over 64 (2000); Marriage status: 16.4% never married, 64.7% now married, 9.3% widowed, 9.6% divorced (2000); Foreign born: 1.4% (2000); Ancestry (includes multiple ancestries): 45.9% German, 14.8% Irish, 6.4% United States or American, 6.2% English, 3.9% Italian (2000).
Economy: Single-family building permits issued: 3 (2001) / 0 (2000); Multi-family building permits issued: 0 (2001) / 0 (2000); Employment by occupation: 10.1% management, 5.0% professional, 27.1% services, 15.1% sales, 0.9% farming, 10.1% construction, 31.7% production (2000).
Income: Per capita income: $14,766 (2000); Median household income: $33,295 (2000); Poverty rate: 16.7% (2000).
Taxes: Total city taxes per capita: $165 (1997); City property taxes per capita: $160 (1997).
Education: High school graduation rate: 79.6% (2000); College graduation rate: 7.2% (2000).
Housing: Homeownership rate: 74.2% (2000); Median home value: $67,900 (2000); Median rent: $346 per month (2000); Median age of housing: 50 years (2000).
Transportation: Commute to work: 82.4% car, 0.0% public transportation, 8.1% walk, 7.6% work from home (2000); Travel time to work: 33.5% less than 15 minutes, 38.1% 15 to 30 minutes, 21.6% 30 to 45 minutes, 2.1% 45 to 60 minutes, 4.6% 60 minutes or more (2000)

COLOMA (town). Covers a land area of 33.069 square miles and a water area of 0.197 square miles. Located at 44.02° N. Lat.; 89.53° W. Long. Elevation is 1,044 feet.
Population: 748 (2000); Race: 99.1% White, 0.0% Black, 0.0% Asian, 0.0% American Indian and Alaska Native, 0.9% Hispanic of any race, 0.9% two or more races (2000); Density: 22.6 persons per square mile (2000); Age: 15.7% under 18, 29.3% over 64 (2000); Marriage status: 16.4% never married, 69.0% now married, 6.2% widowed, 8.4% divorced (2000); Foreign born: 0.0% (2000); Ancestry (includes multiple ancestries): 40.4% German, 12.0% English, 8.9% Irish, 6.3% Polish, 5.1% United States or American (2000).
Economy: In dairy area; non-cash grain, field crops; fisheries. Manufacturing: geodesic domes, meat processing. Employment by occupation: 12.5% management, 7.0% professional, 10.6% services, 20.9% sales, 6.2% farming, 15.0% construction, 27.8% production (2000).
Income: Per capita income: $16,290 (2000); Median household income: $36,406 (2000); Poverty rate: 12.0% (2000).
Taxes: Total city taxes per capita: $134 (1997); City property taxes per capita: $132 (1997).
Education: High school graduation rate: 69.3% (2000); College graduation rate: 8.9% (2000).
Housing: Homeownership rate: 85.2% (2000); Median home value: $85,000 (2000); Median rent: $280 per month (2000); Median age of housing: 29 years (2000).
Transportation: Commute to work: 87.5% car, 1.5% public transportation, 3.8% walk, 7.2% work from home (2000); Travel time to work: 33.7% less than 15 minutes, 35.0% 15 to 30 minutes, 14.6% 30 to 45 minutes, 5.3% 45 to 60 minutes, 11.4% 60 minutes or more (2000)

DAKOTA (town). Covers a land area of 33.159 square miles and a water area of 0.594 square miles. Located at 44.03° N. Lat.; 89.30° W. Long. Elevation is 843 feet.
Population: 1,259 (2000); Race: 95.7% White, 0.2% Black, 0.4% Asian, 0.4% American Indian and Alaska Native, 4.7% Hispanic of any race, 0.2% two or more races (2000); Density: 38.0 persons per square mile (2000); Age: 25.6% under 18, 17.8% over 64 (2000); Marriage status: 24.1% never married, 66.1% now married, 4.0% widowed, 5.8% divorced (2000); Foreign born: 3.9% (2000); Ancestry (includes multiple ancestries): 53.4% German, 10.9% Polish, 10.8% Irish, 9.1% Other groups, 6.8% English (2000).
Economy: Employment by occupation: 8.2% management, 10.7% professional, 19.6% services, 22.7% sales, 1.6% farming, 8.9% construction, 28.2% production (2000).
Income: Per capita income: $18,401 (2000); Median household income: $34,931 (2000); Poverty rate: 12.4% (2000).
Taxes: Total city taxes per capita: $58 (1997); City property taxes per capita: $55 (1997).
Education: High school graduation rate: 76.1% (2000); College graduation rate: 9.8% (2000).
Housing: Homeownership rate: 87.2% (2000); Median home value: $92,100 (2000); Median rent: $371 per month (2000); Median age of housing: 28 years (2000).
Transportation: Commute to work: 93.1% car, 0.0% public transportation, 2.5% walk, 3.8% work from home (2000); Travel time to work: 42.3% less than 15 minutes, 22.8% 15 to 30 minutes, 15.1% 30 to 45 minutes, 10.8% 45 to 60 minutes, 9.1% 60 minutes or more (2000)

DEERFIELD (town). Covers a land area of 34.665 square miles and a water area of 0.341 square miles. Located at 44.11° N. Lat.; 89.41° W. Long.
Population: 629 (2000); Race: 99.4% White, 0.0% Black, 0.6% Asian, 0.0% American Indian and Alaska Native, 0.3% Hispanic of any race, 0.0% two or more races (2000); Density: 18.1 persons per square mile (2000); Age: 22.8% under 18, 18.0% over 64 (2000); Marriage status: 13.2% never married, 75.6% now married, 4.9% widowed, 6.4% divorced (2000); Foreign born: 0.9% (2000); Ancestry (includes multiple ancestries): 46.4% German, 14.3% English, 12.2% Polish, 10.2% Irish, 5.3% Other groups (2000).
Economy: Employment by occupation: 17.4% management, 15.2% professional, 15.2% services, 19.6% sales, 5.4% farming, 9.1% construction, 18.1% production (2000).
Income: Per capita income: $20,781 (2000); Median household income: $41,324 (2000); Poverty rate: 7.0% (2000).
Taxes: Total city taxes per capita: $87 (1997); City property taxes per capita: $87 (1997).
Education: High school graduation rate: 80.4% (2000); College graduation rate: 13.2% (2000).
Housing: Homeownership rate: 92.7% (2000); Median home value: $109,600 (2000); Median rent: $263 per month (2000); Median age of housing: 25 years (2000).
Transportation: Commute to work: 85.4% car, 0.0% public transportation, 3.6% walk, 9.5% work from home (2000); Travel time to work: 37.5% less than 15 minutes, 29.0% 15 to 30 minutes, 18.1% 30 to 45 minutes, 6.9% 45 to 60 minutes, 8.5% 60 minutes or more (2000)

HANCOCK (village). Covers a land area of 1.094 square miles and a water area of 0.052 square miles. Located at 44.13° N. Lat.; 89.51° W. Long. Elevation is 1,089 feet.
Population: 463 (2000); Race: 96.7% White, 0.0% Black, 0.0% Asian, 1.6% American Indian and Alaska Native, 6.6% Hispanic of any race, 1.6% two or more races (2000); Density: 423.3 persons per square mile (2000); Age: 29.3% under 18, 17.3% over 64 (2000); Marriage status: 26.2% never married, 49.9% now married, 11.7% widowed, 12.2% divorced (2000); Foreign born: 4.9% (2000); Ancestry (includes multiple ancestries): 40.0% German, 13.0% Irish, 11.8% English, 8.9% Other groups, 5.2% Norwegian (2000).
Economy: Single-family building permits issued: 2 (2001) / 1 (2000); Multi-family building permits issued: 0 (2001) / 0 (2000); Employment by occupation: 6.8% management, 3.2% professional, 19.6% services, 24.2% sales, 8.2% farming, 13.2% construction, 24.7% production (2000).
Income: Per capita income: $14,889 (2000); Median household income: $35,341 (2000); Poverty rate: 9.5% (2000).
Taxes: Total city taxes per capita: $217 (1997); City property taxes per capita: $202 (1997).
Education: High school graduation rate: 69.7% (2000); College graduation rate: 7.2% (2000).
Housing: Homeownership rate: 71.9% (2000); Median home value: $56,900 (2000); Median rent: $314 per month (2000); Median age of housing: 36 years (2000).
Transportation: Commute to work: 93.2% car, 0.0% public transportation, 3.9% walk, 1.9% work from home (2000); Travel time to work: 33.0% less than 15 minutes, 32.0% 15 to 30 minutes, 24.6% 30 to 45 minutes, 3.0% 45 to 60 minutes, 7.4% 60 minutes or more (2000)

HANCOCK (town). Covers a land area of 33.446 square miles and a water area of 0.302 square miles. Located at 44.11° N. Lat.; 89.53° W. Long. Elevation is 1,089 feet.
Population: 531 (2000); Race: 95.9% White, 0.0% Black, 0.4% Asian, 0.0% American Indian and Alaska Native, 0.6% Hispanic of any race, 3.7% two or more races (2000); Density: 15.9 persons per square mile (2000); Age: 22.9% under 18, 13.7% over 64 (2000); Marriage status: 18.8% never married, 61.9% now married, 6.1% widowed, 13.2% divorced (2000); Foreign born: 3.0% (2000); Ancestry (includes multiple ancestries): 45.0% German, 20.7% Polish, 11.1% Irish, 8.3% English, 6.3% Norwegian (2000).
Economy: In dairying and farming area. Agricultural research station and wildlife area nearby. Employment by occupation: 9.2% management, 13.6% professional, 9.2% services, 30.4% sales, 5.5% farming, 14.3% construction, 17.9% production (2000).
Income: Per capita income: $18,345 (2000); Median household income: $43,889 (2000); Poverty rate: 3.7% (2000).
Taxes: Total city taxes per capita: $66 (1997); City property taxes per capita: $66 (1997).
Education: High school graduation rate: 85.3% (2000); College graduation rate: 16.0% (2000).
Housing: Homeownership rate: 85.8% (2000); Median home value: $96,100 (2000); Median rent: $317 per month (2000); Median age of housing: 25 years (2000).
Transportation: Commute to work: 90.4% car, 0.0% public transportation, 0.7% walk, 7.7% work from home (2000); Travel time to work: 28.8% less than 15 minutes, 31.2% 15 to 30 minutes, 26.8% 30 to 45 minutes, 4.8% 45 to 60 minutes, 8.4% 60 minutes or more (2000)

LEON (town). Covers a land area of 36.000 square miles and a water area of 0.313 square miles. Located at 44.11° N. Lat.; 89.06° W. Long.
Population: 1,281 (2000); Race: 99.4% White, 0.2% Black, 0.0% Asian, 0.0% American Indian and Alaska Native, 0.5% Hispanic of any race, 0.5% two or more races (2000); Density: 35.6 persons per square mile (2000); Age: 20.9% under 18, 17.2% over 64 (2000); Marriage status: 14.6% never married, 69.4% now married, 5.5% widowed, 10.4% divorced (2000); Foreign born: 2.0% (2000); Ancestry (includes multiple ancestries): 52.2% German, 11.8% Polish, 9.6% English, 8.5% Irish, 5.1% Norwegian (2000).
Economy: Employment by occupation: 7.0% management, 13.2% professional, 14.0% services, 24.6% sales, 0.9% farming, 10.1% construction, 30.2% production (2000).
Income: Per capita income: $18,445 (2000); Median household income: $39,524 (2000); Poverty rate: 7.7% (2000).
Taxes: Total city taxes per capita: $64 (1997); City property taxes per capita: $63 (1997).
Education: High school graduation rate: 79.2% (2000); College graduation rate: 11.5% (2000).
Housing: Homeownership rate: 92.5% (2000); Median home value: $88,100 (2000); Median rent: $366 per month (2000); Median age of housing: 28 years (2000).
Transportation: Commute to work: 92.6% car, 0.2% public transportation, 1.4% walk, 5.6% work from home (2000); Travel time to work: 14.1% less than 15 minutes, 34.7% 15 to 30 minutes, 22.8% 30 to 45 minutes, 17.7% 45 to 60 minutes, 10.7% 60 minutes or more (2000)

LOHRVILLE (village). Covers a land area of 1.224 square miles and a water area of 0.010 square miles. Located at 44.03° N. Lat.; 89.12° W. Long. Elevation is 802 feet.
Population: 408 (2000); Race: 98.6% White, 0.0% Black, 0.0% Asian, 0.0% American Indian and Alaska Native, 1.7% Hispanic of any race, 0.5% two or more races (2000); Density: 333.5 persons per square mile (2000); Age: 25.7% under 18, 20.9% over 64 (2000); Marriage status: 15.6% never married, 67.0% now married, 7.8% widowed, 9.6% divorced (2000); Foreign born: 3.6% (2000); Ancestry (includes multiple ancestries): 43.5% German, 10.7% Polish, 9.3% Irish, 7.4% United States or American, 7.4% English (2000).
Economy: In dairy and farm area. Employment by occupation: 7.3% management, 4.2% professional, 17.2% services, 17.2% sales, 3.6% farming, 12.5% construction, 38.0% production (2000).
Income: Per capita income: $14,386 (2000); Median household income: $34,479 (2000); Poverty rate: 3.1% (2000).
Taxes: Total city taxes per capita: $14 (1997); City property taxes per capita: $12 (1997).
Education: High school graduation rate: 77.4% (2000); College graduation rate: 2.4% (2000).
Housing: Homeownership rate: 93.3% (2000); Median home value: $66,700 (2000); Median rent: $408 per month (2000); Median age of housing: 28 years (2000).
Transportation: Commute to work: 91.1% car, 6.3% public transportation, 0.0% walk, 2.6% work from home (2000); Travel time to work: 22.7% less than 15 minutes, 32.4% 15 to 30 minutes, 9.2% 30 to 45 minutes, 17.3% 45 to 60 minutes, 18.4% 60 minutes or more (2000)

MARION (town). Covers a land area of 33.554 square miles and a water area of 1.425 square miles. Located at 44.02° N. Lat.; 89.20° W. Long.
Population: 2,065 (2000); Race: 97.6% White, 0.0% Black, 0.1% Asian, 0.9% American Indian and Alaska Native, 1.7% Hispanic of any race, 0.7% two or more races (2000); Density: 61.5 persons per square mile (2000); Age: 19.1% under 18, 23.6% over 64 (2000); Marriage status: 13.8% never married, 68.0% now married, 8.7% widowed, 9.5% divorced (2000); Foreign born: 2.1% (2000); Ancestry (includes multiple ancestries): 47.7% German, 10.6% Polish, 10.0% Irish, 6.8% English, 6.5% United States or American (2000).
Economy: Employment by occupation: 14.7% management, 15.1% professional, 13.9% services, 21.8% sales, 1.6% farming, 11.9% construction, 20.9% production (2000).
Income: Per capita income: $21,714 (2000); Median household income: $37,534 (2000); Poverty rate: 6.8% (2000).
Taxes: Total city taxes per capita: $69 (1997); City property taxes per capita: $67 (1997).
Education: High school graduation rate: 84.7% (2000); College graduation rate: 15.3% (2000).
Housing: Homeownership rate: 92.3% (2000); Median home value: $111,400 (2000); Median rent: $367 per month (2000); Median age of housing: 24 years (2000).
Transportation: Commute to work: 92.6% car, 0.4% public transportation, 2.7% walk, 3.3% work from home (2000); Travel time to work: 37.7% less than 15 minutes, 30.2% 15 to 30 minutes, 11.5% 30 to 45 minutes, 8.7% 45 to 60 minutes, 11.9% 60 minutes or more (2000)

MOUNT MORRIS (town). Covers a land area of 34.220 square miles and a water area of 1.001 square miles. Located at 44.11° N. Lat.; 89.18° W. Long. Elevation is 900 feet.
Population: 1,092 (2000); Race: 99.1% White, 0.0% Black, 0.0% Asian, 0.0% American Indian and Alaska Native, 1.0% Hispanic of any race, 0.5% two or more races (2000); Density: 31.9 persons per square mile (2000); Age: 21.6% under 18, 20.2% over 64 (2000); Marriage status: 17.7% never married, 67.9% now married, 5.8% widowed, 8.5% divorced (2000); Foreign born: 2.2% (2000); Ancestry (includes multiple ancestries): 47.4% German, 10.5% Norwegian, 9.2% Polish, 8.5% Irish, 6.1% Italian (2000).
Economy: Employment by occupation: 17.0% management, 16.2% professional, 12.2% services, 21.5% sales, 0.8% farming, 13.7% construction, 18.7% production (2000).

Income: Per capita income: $20,713 (2000); Median household income: $39,732 (2000); Poverty rate: 7.3% (2000).
Taxes: Total city taxes per capita: $92 (1997); City property taxes per capita: $90 (1997).
Education: High school graduation rate: 85.7% (2000); College graduation rate: 16.8% (2000).
Housing: Homeownership rate: 89.1% (2000); Median home value: $108,000 (2000); Median rent: $413 per month (2000); Median age of housing: 27 years (2000).
Transportation: Commute to work: 94.6% car, 0.0% public transportation, 1.2% walk, 4.2% work from home (2000); Travel time to work: 30.1% less than 15 minutes, 31.5% 15 to 30 minutes, 12.3% 30 to 45 minutes, 12.5% 45 to 60 minutes, 13.6% 60 minutes or more (2000)

OASIS (town). Covers a land area of 35.032 square miles and a water area of 0.266 square miles. Located at 44.19° N. Lat.; 89.42° W. Long.
Population: 405 (2000); Race: 99.3% White, 0.0% Black, 0.0% Asian, 0.0% American Indian and Alaska Native, 2.4% Hispanic of any race, 0.0% two or more races (2000); Density: 11.6 persons per square mile (2000); Age: 26.6% under 18, 16.1% over 64 (2000); Marriage status: 19.9% never married, 63.8% now married, 9.5% widowed, 6.7% divorced (2000); Foreign born: 1.0% (2000); Ancestry (includes multiple ancestries): 53.2% German, 18.8% Polish, 8.5% Irish, 8.3% English, 7.8% French (except Basque) (2000).
Economy: Employment by occupation: 11.8% management, 14.4% professional, 17.4% services, 19.5% sales, 3.6% farming, 8.2% construction, 25.1% production (2000).
Income: Per capita income: $16,480 (2000); Median household income: $38,472 (2000); Poverty rate: 5.9% (2000).
Taxes: Total city taxes per capita: $70 (1997); City property taxes per capita: $70 (1997).
Education: High school graduation rate: 74.4% (2000); College graduation rate: 11.5% (2000).
Housing: Homeownership rate: 83.5% (2000); Median home value: $79,200 (2000); Median rent: $335 per month (2000); Median age of housing: 27 years (2000).
Transportation: Commute to work: 91.6% car, 0.0% public transportation, 2.1% walk, 6.3% work from home (2000); Travel time to work: 30.3% less than 15 minutes, 40.4% 15 to 30 minutes, 14.0% 30 to 45 minutes, 7.9% 45 to 60 minutes, 7.3% 60 minutes or more (2000)

PINE RIVER (unincorporated postal area, zip code 54965). Covers a land area of 53.270 square miles and a water area of 0.201 square miles. Located at 44.16° N. Lat.; 89.04° W. Long. Elevation is 815 feet.
Population: 1,273 (2000); Race: 97.9% White, 0.2% Black, 0.2% Asian, 0.0% American Indian and Alaska Native, 0.5% Hispanic of any race, 1.5% two or more races (2000); Density: 23.9 persons per square mile (2000); Age: 22.1% under 18, 15.6% over 64 (2000); Marriage status: 18.1% never married, 67.3% now married, 5.8% widowed, 8.8% divorced (2000); Foreign born: 1.5% (2000); Ancestry (includes multiple ancestries): 52.8% German, 11.0% Polish, 8.6% English, 8.5% Irish, 8.1% Danish (2000).
Economy: Employment by occupation: 13.0% management, 11.6% professional, 14.7% services, 18.5% sales, 3.6% farming, 8.1% construction, 30.5% production (2000).
Income: Per capita income: $18,790 (2000); Median household income: $39,375 (2000); Poverty rate: 6.9% (2000).
Education: High school graduation rate: 77.7% (2000); College graduation rate: 11.8% (2000).
Housing: Homeownership rate: 90.1% (2000); Median home value: $80,700 (2000); Median rent: $304 per month (2000); Median age of housing: 33 years (2000).
Transportation: Commute to work: 88.1% car, 0.5% public transportation, 2.2% walk, 8.3% work from home (2000); Travel time to work: 14.7% less than 15 minutes, 36.0% 15 to 30 minutes, 25.0% 30 to 45 minutes, 14.0% 45 to 60 minutes, 10.3% 60 minutes or more (2000)

PLAINFIELD (village). Covers a land area of 1.297 square miles and a water area of 0 square miles. Located at 44.21° N. Lat.; 89.49° W. Long. Elevation is 1,110 feet.
Population: 899 (2000); Race: 92.9% White, 0.0% Black, 0.0% Asian, 0.2% American Indian and Alaska Native, 19.0% Hispanic of any race, 0.0% two or more races (2000); Density: 692.9 persons per square mile (2000); Age: 29.4% under 18, 15.9% over 64 (2000); Marriage status: 24.6% never married, 50.6% now married, 8.1% widowed, 16.7% divorced (2000); Foreign born: 8.6% (2000); Ancestry (includes multiple ancestries): 36.2% German, 17.9% Other groups, 12.1% English, 12.1% Polish, 10.3% Irish (2000).
Economy: Single-family building permits issued: 1 (2001) / 1 (2000); Multi-family building permits issued: 0 (2001) / 0 (2000); Employment by occupation: 6.8% management, 10.9% professional, 11.5% services, 26.0% sales, 7.6% farming, 15.1% construction, 22.1% production (2000).
Income: Per capita income: $15,563 (2000); Median household income: $36,328 (2000); Poverty rate: 11.4% (2000).
Taxes: Total city taxes per capita: $90 (1997); City property taxes per capita: $84 (1997).
Education: High school graduation rate: 71.1% (2000); College graduation rate: 13.0% (2000).

School District(s)

Tri-County Area (PK-12)
2000 Enrollment: 873 715-335-6366
Housing: Homeownership rate: 68.6% (2000); Median home value: $64,200 (2000); Median rent: $281 per month (2000); Median age of housing: 56 years (2000).
Transportation: Commute to work: 90.1% car, 0.0% public transportation, 4.5% walk, 3.7% work from home (2000); Travel time to work: 44.6% less than 15 minutes, 23.5% 15 to 30 minutes, 24.4% 30 to 45 minutes, 5.8% 45 to 60 minutes, 1.7% 60 minutes or more (2000)

PLAINFIELD (town). Covers a land area of 33.949 square miles and a water area of 0.012 square miles. Located at 44.19° N. Lat.; 89.53° W. Long. Elevation is 1,110 feet.
Population: 533 (2000); Race: 88.2% White, 0.0% Black, 0.0% Asian, 0.0% American Indian and Alaska Native, 14.1% Hispanic of any race, 1.1% two or more races (2000); Density: 15.7 persons per square mile (2000); Age: 28.8% under 18, 10.2% over 64 (2000); Marriage status: 15.8% never married, 67.3% now married, 4.5% widowed, 12.5% divorced (2000); Foreign born: 4.0% (2000); Ancestry (includes multiple ancestries): 37.8% German, 13.9% Polish, 12.3% Other groups, 10.9% Irish, 9.0% English (2000).
Economy: In agricultural area: rye, potatoes; dairy products. Employment by occupation: 10.2% management, 7.4% professional, 18.0% services, 21.1% sales, 9.8% farming, 12.1% construction, 21.5% production (2000).
Income: Per capita income: $16,432 (2000); Median household income: $38,462 (2000); Poverty rate: 11.4% (2000).
Taxes: Total city taxes per capita: $80 (1997); City property taxes per capita: $80 (1997).
Education: High school graduation rate: 83.1% (2000); College graduation rate: 7.5% (2000).
Housing: Homeownership rate: 85.0% (2000); Median home value: $67,900 (2000); Median rent: $379 per month (2000); Median age of housing: 31 years (2000).
Transportation: Commute to work: 94.7% car, 0.0% public transportation, 0.8% walk, 4.5% work from home (2000); Travel time to work: 39.6% less than 15 minutes, 24.3% 15 to 30 minutes, 28.5% 30 to 45 minutes, 1.3% 45 to 60 minutes, 6.4% 60 minutes or more (2000)

POY SIPPI (unincorporated postal area, zip code 54967). Aka Poysippi. Covers a land area of 6.225 square miles and a water area of 0.064 square miles. Located at 44.13° N. Lat.; 88.99° W. Long. Elevation is 778 feet.
Population: 369 (2000); Race: 98.3% White, 0.0% Black, 0.0% Asian, 0.8% American Indian and Alaska Native, 0.8% Hispanic of any race, 0.0% two or more races (2000); Density: 59.3 persons per square mile (2000); Age: 20.6% under 18, 21.1% over 64 (2000); Marriage status: 18.7% never married, 57.9% now married, 11.7% widowed, 11.7% divorced (2000); Foreign born: 0.6% (2000); Ancestry (includes multiple ancestries): 53.3% German, 14.2% Irish, 8.3% Danish, 7.5% Polish, 6.4% United States or American (2000).
Economy: Employment by occupation: 8.9% management, 17.8% professional, 15.3% services, 23.8% sales, 1.5% farming, 7.4% construction, 25.2% production (2000).
Income: Per capita income: $19,654 (2000); Median household income: $34,375 (2000); Poverty rate: 10.8% (2000).
Education: High school graduation rate: 82.1% (2000); College graduation rate: 13.6% (2000).
Housing: Homeownership rate: 74.7% (2000); Median home value: $70,700 (2000); Median rent: $208 per month (2000); Median age of housing: 60 years (2000).
Transportation: Commute to work: 89.0% car, 0.0% public transportation, 3.0% walk, 8.0% work from home (2000); Travel time to work: 17.9% less than 15 minutes, 39.7% 15 to 30 minutes, 25.0% 30 to 45 minutes, 4.9% 45 to 60 minutes, 12.5% 60 minutes or more (2000)

POYSIPPI (town). Covers a land area of 32.301 square miles and a water area of 3.628 square miles. Located at 44.12° N. Lat.; 88.94° W. Long.

Population: 972 (2000); Race: 97.4% White, 0.0% Black, 0.2% Asian, 0.3% American Indian and Alaska Native, 1.1% Hispanic of any race, 1.7% two or more races (2000); Density: 30.1 persons per square mile (2000); Age: 25.4% under 18, 16.0% over 64 (2000); Marriage status: 19.6% never married, 62.4% now married, 7.9% widowed, 10.2% divorced (2000); Foreign born: 1.4% (2000); Ancestry (includes multiple ancestries): 52.8% German, 13.7% Polish, 9.4% Irish, 6.7% English, 6.4% United States or American (2000).
Economy: Employment by occupation: 13.9% management, 16.1% professional, 13.7% services, 16.3% sales, 3.0% farming, 9.4% construction, 27.5% production (2000).
Income: Per capita income: $18,625 (2000); Median household income: $40,489 (2000); Poverty rate: 7.0% (2000).
Taxes: Total city taxes per capita: $40 (1997); City property taxes per capita: $38 (1997).
Education: High school graduation rate: 80.2% (2000); College graduation rate: 11.7% (2000).
Housing: Homeownership rate: 82.8% (2000); Median home value: $78,300 (2000); Median rent: $250 per month (2000); Median age of housing: 50 years (2000).
Transportation: Commute to work: 91.5% car, 0.6% public transportation, 2.2% walk, 5.6% work from home (2000); Travel time to work: 16.0% less than 15 minutes, 30.6% 15 to 30 minutes, 35.0% 30 to 45 minutes, 12.4% 45 to 60 minutes, 6.0% 60 minutes or more (2000)

REDGRANITE (village). Aka Red Granite. Covers a land area of 2.219 square miles and a water area of 0.011 square miles. Located at 44.04° N. Lat.; 89.10° W. Long. Elevation is 789 feet.
Population: 1,040 (2000); Race: 93.2% White, 0.0% Black, 0.0% Asian, 1.2% American Indian and Alaska Native, 5.6% Hispanic of any race, 4.0% two or more races (2000); Density: 468.6 persons per square mile (2000); Age: 24.8% under 18, 21.5% over 64 (2000); Marriage status: 22.0% never married, 55.3% now married, 10.6% widowed, 12.1% divorced (2000); Foreign born: 1.4% (2000); Ancestry (includes multiple ancestries): 43.9% German, 14.8% Polish, 12.0% Irish, 10.8% Other groups, 6.8% Italian (2000).
Economy: In agricultural area. Manufacturing: pickles, peppers, sauerkraut. Single-family building permits issued: 7 (2001) / 7 (2000); Multi-family building permits issued: 46 (2001) / 33 (2000); Employment by occupation: 8.3% management, 4.9% professional, 18.8% services, 22.0% sales, 1.3% farming, 9.4% construction, 35.2% production (2000).
Income: Per capita income: $13,994 (2000); Median household income: $26,726 (2000); Poverty rate: 11.1% (2000).
Taxes: Total city taxes per capita: $77 (1997); City property taxes per capita: $69 (1997).
Education: High school graduation rate: 66.1% (2000); College graduation rate: 3.6% (2000).
Housing: Homeownership rate: 71.9% (2000); Median home value: $59,100 (2000); Median rent: $347 per month (2000); Median age of housing: 39 years (2000).
Transportation: Commute to work: 91.2% car, 0.0% public transportation, 3.3% walk, 3.5% work from home (2000); Travel time to work: 26.0% less than 15 minutes, 31.1% 15 to 30 minutes, 21.0% 30 to 45 minutes, 14.5% 45 to 60 minutes, 7.5% 60 minutes or more (2000)

RICHFORD (town). Covers a land area of 34.567 square miles and a water area of 0.160 square miles. Located at 44.02° N. Lat.; 89.43° W. Long. Elevation is 915 feet.
Population: 588 (2000); Race: 98.1% White, 0.0% Black, 0.0% Asian, 0.0% American Indian and Alaska Native, 3.3% Hispanic of any race, 1.2% two or more races (2000); Density: 17.0 persons per square mile (2000); Age: 31.2% under 18, 15.3% over 64 (2000); Marriage status: 18.2% never married, 69.3% now married, 7.1% widowed, 5.4% divorced (2000); Foreign born: 1.1% (2000); Ancestry (includes multiple ancestries): 50.5% German, 6.0% English, 6.0% Polish, 6.0% United States or American, 4.4% Norwegian (2000).
Economy: Employment by occupation: 21.3% management, 7.1% professional, 12.9% services, 19.6% sales, 5.4% farming, 14.6% construction, 19.2% production (2000).
Income: Per capita income: $14,503 (2000); Median household income: $37,656 (2000); Poverty rate: 22.4% (2000).
Taxes: Total city taxes per capita: $68 (1997); City property taxes per capita: $66 (1997).
Education: High school graduation rate: 71.4% (2000); College graduation rate: 10.4% (2000).
Housing: Homeownership rate: 89.8% (2000); Median home value: $79,100 (2000); Median rent: $263 per month (2000); Median age of housing: 27 years (2000).
Transportation: Commute to work: 79.9% car, 0.9% public transportation, 2.2% walk, 17.0% work from home (2000); Travel time to work: 32.6% less than 15 minutes, 32.6% 15 to 30 minutes, 14.7% 30 to 45 minutes, 8.4% 45 to 60 minutes, 11.6% 60 minutes or more (2000)

ROSE (town). Covers a land area of 34.882 square miles and a water area of 0.062 square miles. Located at 44.19° N. Lat.; 89.32° W. Long.
Population: 595 (2000); Race: 95.2% White, 0.0% Black, 0.0% Asian, 0.3% American Indian and Alaska Native, 6.1% Hispanic of any race, 0.0% two or more races (2000); Density: 17.1 persons per square mile (2000); Age: 19.7% under 18, 18.0% over 64 (2000); Marriage status: 23.6% never married, 60.8% now married, 7.3% widowed, 8.3% divorced (2000); Foreign born: 3.1% (2000); Ancestry (includes multiple ancestries): 42.9% German, 18.0% English, 14.1% Irish, 12.1% Polish, 5.8% Other groups (2000).
Economy: In agricultural area; manufacturing of fabricated metal products, timber. Wild Rose State Fish Hatchery. Single-family building permits issued: 0 (2001) / 4 (2000); Multi-family building permits issued: 0 (2001) / 0 (2000); Employment by occupation: 9.7% management, 8.2% professional, 19.9% services, 24.0% sales, 7.5% farming, 13.1% construction, 17.6% production (2000).
Income: Per capita income: $17,630 (2000); Median household income: $34,792 (2000); Poverty rate: 10.3% (2000).
Taxes: Total city taxes per capita: $56 (1997); City property taxes per capita: $54 (1997).
Education: High school graduation rate: 76.5% (2000); College graduation rate: 10.6% (2000).
Housing: Homeownership rate: 90.0% (2000); Median home value: $82,400 (2000); Median rent: $388 per month (2000); Median age of housing: 24 years (2000).
Transportation: Commute to work: 89.3% car, 0.0% public transportation, 0.0% walk, 8.4% work from home (2000); Travel time to work: 38.9% less than 15 minutes, 32.6% 15 to 30 minutes, 16.7% 30 to 45 minutes, 4.2% 45 to 60 minutes, 7.5% 60 minutes or more (2000)

SAXEVILLE (town). Covers a land area of 36.068 square miles and a water area of 0.486 square miles. Located at 44.20° N. Lat.; 89.05° W. Long. Elevation is 860 feet.
Population: 974 (2000); Race: 98.1% White, 0.0% Black, 0.1% Asian, 0.0% American Indian and Alaska Native, 0.6% Hispanic of any race, 1.4% two or more races (2000); Density: 27.0 persons per square mile (2000); Age: 22.7% under 18, 17.2% over 64 (2000); Marriage status: 13.9% never married, 71.5% now married, 3.8% widowed, 10.9% divorced (2000); Foreign born: 0.9% (2000); Ancestry (includes multiple ancestries): 49.8% German, 12.3% English, 11.9% Irish, 7.9% Polish, 6.6% Norwegian (2000).
Economy: Employment by occupation: 10.3% management, 12.0% professional, 18.6% services, 21.0% sales, 3.3% farming, 9.6% construction, 25.3% production (2000).
Income: Per capita income: $20,514 (2000); Median household income: $39,688 (2000); Poverty rate: 9.2% (2000).
Taxes: Total city taxes per capita: $87 (1997); City property taxes per capita: $86 (1997).
Education: High school graduation rate: 84.5% (2000); College graduation rate: 15.9% (2000).
Housing: Homeownership rate: 90.5% (2000); Median home value: $104,500 (2000); Median rent: $375 per month (2000); Median age of housing: 27 years (2000).
Transportation: Commute to work: 91.9% car, 0.0% public transportation, 3.3% walk, 4.2% work from home (2000); Travel time to work: 16.0% less than 15 minutes, 35.0% 15 to 30 minutes, 22.4% 30 to 45 minutes, 11.4% 45 to 60 minutes, 15.1% 60 minutes or more (2000)

SPRINGWATER (town). Covers a land area of 33.529 square miles and a water area of 1.308 square miles. Located at 44.19° N. Lat.; 89.18° W. Long.
Population: 1,389 (2000); Race: 99.0% White, 0.0% Black, 0.0% Asian, 0.2% American Indian and Alaska Native, 0.7% Hispanic of any race, 0.6% two or more races (2000); Density: 41.4 persons per square mile (2000); Age: 19.2% under 18, 25.8% over 64 (2000); Marriage status: 14.4% never married, 65.1% now married, 8.9% widowed, 11.6% divorced (2000); Foreign born: 0.3% (2000); Ancestry (includes multiple ancestries): 49.8% German, 11.5% Irish, 10.5% Polish, 8.8% English, 5.8% Norwegian (2000).

Economy: Employment by occupation: 9.1% management, 12.3% professional, 17.8% services, 20.8% sales, 2.2% farming, 11.1% construction, 26.7% production (2000).
Income: Per capita income: $20,586 (2000); Median household income: $35,714 (2000); Poverty rate: 8.4% (2000).
Taxes: Total city taxes per capita: $126 (1997); City property taxes per capita: $123 (1997).
Education: High school graduation rate: 84.8% (2000); College graduation rate: 13.2% (2000).
Housing: Homeownership rate: 89.1% (2000); Median home value: $119,300 (2000); Median rent: $406 per month (2000); Median age of housing: 26 years (2000).
Transportation: Commute to work: 87.2% car, 0.3% public transportation, 2.8% walk, 9.3% work from home (2000); Travel time to work: 29.3% less than 15 minutes, 35.2% 15 to 30 minutes, 11.8% 30 to 45 minutes, 9.9% 45 to 60 minutes, 13.9% 60 minutes or more (2000)

WARREN (town). Covers a land area of 32.540 square miles and a water area of 0.092 square miles. Located at 44.03° N. Lat.; 89.07° W. Long.
Population: 675 (2000); Race: 98.5% White, 0.0% Black, 0.0% Asian, 0.0% American Indian and Alaska Native, 1.2% Hispanic of any race, 1.5% two or more races (2000); Density: 20.7 persons per square mile (2000); Age: 24.5% under 18, 15.8% over 64 (2000); Marriage status: 21.3% never married, 64.8% now married, 7.7% widowed, 6.2% divorced (2000); Foreign born: 0.5% (2000); Ancestry (includes multiple ancestries): 46.6% German, 20.1% Polish, 11.3% Irish, 5.8% Norwegian, 5.8% United States or American (2000).
Economy: Single-family building permits issued: 5 (2001) / 3 (2000); Multi-family building permits issued: 0 (2001) / 0 (2000); Employment by occupation: 10.9% management, 10.0% professional, 12.9% services, 18.3% sales, 1.6% farming, 11.6% construction, 34.7% production (2000).
Income: Per capita income: $15,672 (2000); Median household income: $38,438 (2000); Poverty rate: 7.6% (2000).
Taxes: Total city taxes per capita: $51 (1997); City property taxes per capita: $51 (1997).
Education: High school graduation rate: 74.2% (2000); College graduation rate: 5.2% (2000).
Housing: Homeownership rate: 86.6% (2000); Median home value: $91,300 (2000); Median rent: $386 per month (2000); Median age of housing: 28 years (2000).
Transportation: Commute to work: 88.6% car, 0.0% public transportation, 1.6% walk, 8.8% work from home (2000); Travel time to work: 29.6% less than 15 minutes, 24.3% 15 to 30 minutes, 25.0% 30 to 45 minutes, 11.8% 45 to 60 minutes, 9.3% 60 minutes or more (2000)

WAUTOMA (city). Covers a land area of 2.495 square miles and a water area of 0.043 square miles. Located at 44.07° N. Lat.; 89.29° W. Long. Elevation is 867 feet.
Population: 1,998 (2000); Race: 93.0% White, 0.3% Black, 0.5% Asian, 0.9% American Indian and Alaska Native, 9.0% Hispanic of any race, 1.5% two or more races (2000); Density: 800.8 persons per square mile (2000); Age: 23.4% under 18, 23.4% over 64 (2000); Marriage status: 23.8% never married, 49.5% now married, 11.2% widowed, 15.5% divorced (2000); Foreign born: 2.4% (2000); Ancestry (includes multiple ancestries): 37.9% German, 11.3% Polish, 8.5% Other groups, 8.3% Irish, 7.6% Norwegian (2000).
Economy: Single-family building permits issued: 3 (2001) / 2 (2000); Multi-family building permits issued: 36 (2001) / 6 (2000); Employment by occupation: 7.5% management, 16.2% professional, 18.3% services, 22.2% sales, 1.6% farming, 5.0% construction, 29.2% production (2000).
Income: Per capita income: $16,006 (2000); Median household income: $31,723 (2000); Poverty rate: 11.5% (2000).
Taxes: Total city taxes per capita: $241 (2000); City property taxes per capita: $225 (2000).
Education: High school graduation rate: 75.8% (2000); College graduation rate: 14.4% (2000).

School District(s)

Wautoma Area (PK-12)
2000 Enrollment: 1,654 920-787-7112
Housing: Homeownership rate: 57.1% (2000); Median home value: $60,700 (2000); Median rent: $351 per month (2000); Median age of housing: 35 years (2000).
Safety: Violent crime rate: 14.9 per 10,000 population; Property crime rate: 333.0 per 10,000 population (2001).
Newspapers: The Waushara Argus (1 x week)
Transportation: Commute to work: 86.7% car, 0.6% public transportation, 7.5% walk, 2.5% work from home (2000); Travel time to work: 59.4% less than 15 minutes, 14.2% 15 to 30 minutes, 15.7% 30 to 45 minutes, 4.0% 45 to 60 minutes, 6.8% 60 minutes or more (2000)

WAUTOMA (town). Covers a land area of 33.939 square miles and a water area of 0.142 square miles. Located at 44.10° N. Lat.; 89.31° W. Long. Elevation is 867 feet.
History: Incorporated as village in 1901, as city in 1940.
Population: 1,312 (2000); Race: 97.5% White, 0.3% Black, 1.3% Asian, 0.3% American Indian and Alaska Native, 0.2% Hispanic of any race, 0.6% two or more races (2000); Density: 38.7 persons per square mile (2000); Age: 24.4% under 18, 19.3% over 64 (2000); Marriage status: 19.9% never married, 62.4% now married, 8.0% widowed, 9.6% divorced (2000); Foreign born: 1.3% (2000); Ancestry (includes multiple ancestries): 49.9% German, 12.5% Irish, 9.4% Polish, 8.3% Norwegian, 7.4% English (2000).
Economy: In farm and timber area; dairy products. Manufacturing of vitamins, health food. Summer resort. Nordic Mt. Ski Area to Northeast. Employment by occupation: 12.4% management, 15.6% professional, 19.2% services, 25.6% sales, 1.7% farming, 10.5% construction, 15.1% production (2000).
Income: Per capita income: $17,981 (2000); Median household income: $39,185 (2000); Poverty rate: 9.7% (2000).
Taxes: Total city taxes per capita: $41 (1997); City property taxes per capita: $39 (1997).
Education: High school graduation rate: 77.8% (2000); College graduation rate: 14.1% (2000).
Housing: Homeownership rate: 89.4% (2000); Median home value: $91,500 (2000); Median rent: $405 per month (2000); Median age of housing: 26 years (2000).
Transportation: Commute to work: 93.2% car, 0.0% public transportation, 1.0% walk, 4.4% work from home (2000); Travel time to work: 56.7% less than 15 minutes, 15.4% 15 to 30 minutes, 12.1% 30 to 45 minutes, 6.6% 45 to 60 minutes, 9.2% 60 minutes or more (2000)

WILD ROSE (village). Covers a land area of 1.319 square miles and a water area of 0.024 square miles. Located at 44.17° N. Lat.; 89.24° W. Long. Elevation is 955 feet.
Population: 765 (2000); Race: 98.2% White, 0.0% Black, 0.0% Asian, 0.0% American Indian and Alaska Native, 1.5% Hispanic of any race, 1.1% two or more races (2000); Density: 580.1 persons per square mile (2000); Age: 24.7% under 18, 24.4% over 64 (2000); Marriage status: 21.2% never married, 58.3% now married, 9.5% widowed, 11.0% divorced (2000); Foreign born: 1.5% (2000); Ancestry (includes multiple ancestries): 44.4% German, 11.4% Irish, 9.7% Norwegian, 5.9% English, 5.7% Other groups (2000).
Economy: Single-family building permits issued: 0 (2001) / 0 (2000); Multi-family building permits issued: 0 (2001) / 0 (2000); Employment by occupation: 7.2% management, 17.6% professional, 21.5% services, 22.4% sales, 1.5% farming, 8.1% construction, 21.8% production (2000).
Income: Per capita income: $18,887 (2000); Median household income: $30,655 (2000); Poverty rate: 6.6% (2000).
Taxes: Total city taxes per capita: $195 (1997); City property taxes per capita: $182 (1997).
Education: High school graduation rate: 78.0% (2000); College graduation rate: 12.8% (2000).

School District(s)

Wild Rose (PK-12)
2000 Enrollment: 765 920-622-4203
Housing: Homeownership rate: 69.3% (2000); Median home value: $60,100 (2000); Median rent: $352 per month (2000); Median age of housing: 48 years (2000).
Hospitals: Wild Rose Community Memorial Hospital (27 beds)
Transportation: Commute to work: 82.2% car, 0.0% public transportation, 11.9% walk, 5.0% work from home (2000); Travel time to work: 52.0% less than 15 minutes, 30.6% 15 to 30 minutes, 4.3% 30 to 45 minutes, 4.9% 45 to 60 minutes, 8.2% 60 minutes or more (2000)

Winnebago County

Located in east central Wisconsin; bounded on the east by Lake Winnebago; drained by the Wolf and Fox Rivers; includes Poygan, Rush, and Butte des Morts Lakes. Covers a land area of 438.60 square miles, a water area of 140.10 square miles, and is located in the Central Time Zone. The county government was organized in 1840. County seat is Oshkosh.

Winnebago County is part of the Appleton-Oshkosh-Neenah, WI MSA. The entire metro area includes: Calumet County; Outagamie County; Winnebago County

Weather Station: Oshkosh Elevation: 748 feet

	Jan	Feb	Mar	Apr	May	Jun	Jul	Aug	Sep	Oct	Nov	Dec
High	24	30	40	54	68	78	82	79	71	59	43	30
Low	7	12	22	35	47	57	61	59	51	40	27	14
Precip	1.3	1.1	2.2	2.8	3.0	3.5	3.6	4.0	3.4	2.3	2.5	1.6
Snow	12.4	7.1	8.0	1.5	0.0	0.0	0.0	0.0	0.0	tr	3.9	10.5

High and Low temperatures in degrees Fahrenheit; Precipitation and Snow in inches

Population: 156,763 (2000); Race: 95.0% White, 1.1% Black, 1.6% Asian, 0.5% American Indian and Alaska Native, 2.0% Hispanic of any race, 1.1% two or more races (2000); Density: 357.4 persons per square mile (2000); Age: 23.8% under 18, 12.5% over 64 (2000).
Religion: Five largest groups: 27.8% Catholic Church, 10.1% Evangelical Lutheran Church in America, 6.0% Wisconsin Evangelical Lutheran Synod, 3.2% Lutheran Church—Missouri Synod, 2.1% The United Methodist Church (2000).
Economy: Unemployment rate: 4.2% (11/2002); Total civilian labor force: 100,444 (11/2002); Leading industries: 33.3% manufacturing; 11.9% health care and social assistance; 11.9% retail trade (2000); Companies that employ more than 1,000 persons: 6 (2000); Companies that employ more than 100 persons: 156 (2000); Farms: 860 totaling 167,459 acres (1997); Minority business ownership rate: 3.1% (1997); Women business ownership rate: 20.3% (1997); Retail sales per capita: $9,950 (1997). Single-family building permits issued: 711 (2001) / 566 (2000); Multi-family building permits issued: 590 (2001) / 245 (2000).
Income: Per capita income: $21,706 (2000); Median household income: $44,445 (2000); Poverty rate: 6.7% (2000); Bankruptcy rate: 3.17% (2001).
Taxes: Total county taxes per capita: $206 (2000); County property taxes per capita: $202 (2000).
Education: High school graduation rate: 86.3% (2000); College graduation rate: 22.8% (2000).
Housing: Homeownership rate: 68.0% (2000); Median home value: $97,700 (2000); Median rent: $443 per month (2000); Median age of housing: 34 years (2000).
Health: Birth rate: 110.1 per 10,000 population (1998); Age adjusted death rate: 79.0 per 10,000 population (1999); Age adjusted cancer mortality rate: 214.0 deaths per 100,000 population (1999). Air Quality Index: 75% good, 25% moderate, 0% unhealthy (percent of days in 2000). Number of physicians: 22.6 per 10,000 population (1999); Number of hospital beds: 43.7 per 10,000 population (1999).
Elections: 2000 Presidential election results: 44.7% Gore, 50.4% Bush, 3.9% Nader, 0.5% Buchanan

Additional Information Contacts

Winnebago County Government Offices 920-236-4766
Neenah Chamber of Commerce 920-722-7758
Omro Area Chamber of Commerce 920-685-6960
Oshkosh Chamber of Commerce 920-424-7700

Winnebago County Communities

ALGOMA (town). Covers a land area of 10.016 square miles and a water area of 2.494 square miles. Located at 44.02° N. Lat.; 88.60° W. Long.
Population: 5,702 (2000); Race: 97.4% White, 0.0% Black, 1.6% Asian, 0.3% American Indian and Alaska Native, 1.0% Hispanic of any race, 0.6% two or more races (2000); Density: 569.3 persons per square mile (2000); Age: 30.3% under 18, 9.9% over 64 (2000); Marriage status: 17.8% never married, 73.7% now married, 3.4% widowed, 5.1% divorced (2000); Foreign born: 2.1% (2000); Ancestry (includes multiple ancestries): 55.1% German, 10.0% Polish, 8.0% Norwegian, 7.4% English, 7.3% Irish (2000).
Economy: Employment by occupation: 15.0% management, 23.8% professional, 12.0% services, 27.1% sales, 0.1% farming, 6.7% construction, 15.4% production (2000).
Income: Per capita income: $27,478 (2000); Median household income: $71,792 (2000); Poverty rate: 1.6% (2000).
Taxes: Total city taxes per capita: $73 (2000); City property taxes per capita: $56 (2000).
Education: High school graduation rate: 91.7% (2000); College graduation rate: 35.4% (2000).
Housing: Homeownership rate: 96.8% (2000); Median home value: $147,700 (2000); Median rent: $523 per month (2000); Median age of housing: 14 years (2000).
Transportation: Commute to work: 96.1% car, 0.0% public transportation, 0.0% walk, 3.0% work from home (2000); Travel time to work: 37.3% less than 15 minutes, 50.0% 15 to 30 minutes, 7.4% 30 to 45 minutes, 1.6% 45 to 60 minutes, 3.8% 60 minutes or more (2000)

BLACK WOLF (town). Covers a land area of 15.564 square miles and a water area of 26.302 square miles. Located at 43.93° N. Lat.; 88.50° W. Long. Elevation is 799 feet.
Population: 2,330 (2000); Race: 98.2% White, 0.1% Black, 0.6% Asian, 0.9% American Indian and Alaska Native, 0.0% Hispanic of any race, 0.1% two or more races (2000); Density: 149.7 persons per square mile (2000); Age: 23.0% under 18, 14.3% over 64 (2000); Marriage status: 19.1% never married, 72.0% now married, 4.8% widowed, 4.1% divorced (2000); Foreign born: 2.1% (2000); Ancestry (includes multiple ancestries): 59.6% German, 10.2% Irish, 6.9% United States or American, 6.7% English, 5.7% Polish (2000).
Economy: Single-family building permits issued: 18 (2001) / 19 (2000); Multi-family building permits issued: 0 (2001) / 0 (2000); Employment by occupation: 15.4% management, 14.8% professional, 12.4% services, 27.5% sales, 1.0% farming, 10.6% construction, 18.3% production (2000).
Income: Per capita income: $26,769 (2000); Median household income: $53,405 (2000); Poverty rate: 1.8% (2000).
Taxes: Total city taxes per capita: $94 (1997); City property taxes per capita: $87 (1997).
Education: High school graduation rate: 88.9% (2000); College graduation rate: 26.6% (2000).
Housing: Homeownership rate: 90.9% (2000); Median home value: $137,500 (2000); Median rent: $364 per month (2000); Median age of housing: 36 years (2000).
Transportation: Commute to work: 95.9% car, 0.0% public transportation, 0.7% walk, 3.4% work from home (2000); Travel time to work: 25.5% less than 15 minutes, 56.3% 15 to 30 minutes, 14.1% 30 to 45 minutes, 2.3% 45 to 60 minutes, 1.7% 60 minutes or more (2000)

CLAYTON (town). Covers a land area of 36.468 square miles and a water area of 0.016 square miles. Located at 44.19° N. Lat.; 88.58° W. Long.
Population: 2,974 (2000); Race: 99.2% White, 0.0% Black, 0.0% Asian, 0.4% American Indian and Alaska Native, 0.3% Hispanic of any race, 0.4% two or more races (2000); Density: 81.6 persons per square mile (2000); Age: 27.4% under 18, 10.0% over 64 (2000); Marriage status: 19.6% never married, 69.5% now married, 3.5% widowed, 7.4% divorced (2000); Foreign born: 0.6% (2000); Ancestry (includes multiple ancestries): 61.1% German, 10.0% Norwegian, 9.3% Polish, 8.8% Irish, 7.4% English (2000).
Economy: Employment by occupation: 13.1% management, 16.7% professional, 10.1% services, 25.7% sales, 1.6% farming, 10.7% construction, 22.0% production (2000).
Income: Per capita income: $23,713 (2000); Median household income: $62,551 (2000); Poverty rate: 1.9% (2000).
Taxes: Total city taxes per capita: $109 (1997); City property taxes per capita: $94 (1997).
Education: High school graduation rate: 90.6% (2000); College graduation rate: 21.0% (2000).
Housing: Homeownership rate: 90.9% (2000); Median home value: $140,600 (2000); Median rent: $440 per month (2000); Median age of housing: 24 years (2000).
Transportation: Commute to work: 93.5% car, 0.6% public transportation, 0.9% walk, 5.0% work from home (2000); Travel time to work: 36.1% less than 15 minutes, 53.4% 15 to 30 minutes, 6.3% 30 to 45 minutes, 2.6% 45 to 60 minutes, 1.6% 60 minutes or more (2000)

LARSEN (unincorporated postal area, zip code 54947). Covers a land area of 45.557 square miles and a water area of 0.016 square miles. Located at 44.19° N. Lat.; 88.68° W. Long. Elevation is 770 feet.
Population: 2,615 (2000); Race: 98.9% White, 0.0% Black, 0.2% Asian, 0.3% American Indian and Alaska Native, 0.5% Hispanic of any race, 0.4% two or more races (2000); Density: 57.4 persons per square mile (2000); Age: 25.5% under 18, 12.9% over 64 (2000); Marriage status: 19.4% never married, 68.3% now married, 4.4% widowed, 7.8% divorced (2000); Foreign born: 0.8% (2000); Ancestry (includes multiple ancestries): 54.0% German, 10.6% Norwegian, 9.6% Irish, 8.3% Polish, 5.9% English (2000).
Economy: Employment by occupation: 14.1% management, 14.3% professional, 10.2% services, 24.3% sales, 0.9% farming, 12.0% construction, 24.1% production (2000).
Income: Per capita income: $21,357 (2000); Median household income: $52,743 (2000); Poverty rate: 3.5% (2000).

Education: High school graduation rate: 88.5% (2000); College graduation rate: 14.1% (2000).
Housing: Homeownership rate: 90.7% (2000); Median home value: $121,800 (2000); Median rent: $517 per month (2000); Median age of housing: 29 years (2000).
Transportation: Commute to work: 92.1% car, 0.2% public transportation, 2.0% walk, 4.7% work from home (2000); Travel time to work: 17.5% less than 15 minutes, 60.0% 15 to 30 minutes, 17.4% 30 to 45 minutes, 2.2% 45 to 60 minutes, 2.9% 60 minutes or more (2000)

MENASHA (city). Covers a land area of 5.256 square miles and a water area of 1.418 square miles. Located at 44.21° N. Lat.; 88.43° W. Long. Elevation is 760 feet.
History: Menasha was formed in the 1840's by Harrison Reed, shortly after Reed and his partner Harvey Jones had founded Neenah. A quarrel left Jones in charge of Neenah, and Reed moved on to establish the new community of Menasha. Menasha was awarded a charter to develop the water power on the river here, and the city became an industrial center.
Population: 16,331 (2000); Race: 95.0% White, 0.8% Black, 1.1% Asian, 0.2% American Indian and Alaska Native, 2.8% Hispanic of any race, 1.7% two or more races (2000); Density: 3,106.9 persons per square mile (2000); Age: 25.1% under 18, 11.8% over 64 (2000); Marriage status: 28.2% never married, 53.4% now married, 6.4% widowed, 12.0% divorced (2000); Foreign born: 3.3% (2000); Ancestry (includes multiple ancestries): 53.2% German, 11.6% Polish, 10.5% Irish, 7.8% Other groups, 6.0% Norwegian (2000).
Vital Statistics: Birth rate: 155.5 per 10,000 population (1998)
Economy: Single-family building permits issued: 102 (2001) / 49 (2000); Multi-family building permits issued: 20 (2001) / 2 (2000); Employment by occupation: 10.7% management, 14.3% professional, 14.2% services, 25.4% sales, 0.1% farming, 7.8% construction, 27.6% production (2000).
Income: Per capita income: $20,743 (2000); Median household income: $39,936 (2000); Poverty rate: 6.5% (2000).
Taxes: Total city taxes per capita: $421 (2000); City property taxes per capita: $395 (2000).
Education: High school graduation rate: 85.7% (2000); College graduation rate: 17.6% (2000).

School District(s)

Menasha (PK-12)
2000 Enrollment: 3,634 920-751-5070
Housing: Homeownership rate: 61.1% (2000); Median home value: $87,700 (2000); Median rent: $451 per month (2000); Median age of housing: 38 years (2000).
Safety: Violent crime rate: 17.0 per 10,000 population; Property crime rate: 260.8 per 10,000 population (2001).
Transportation: Commute to work: 93.6% car, 0.8% public transportation, 3.1% walk, 1.1% work from home (2000); Travel time to work: 40.7% less than 15 minutes, 44.9% 15 to 30 minutes, 5.5% 30 to 45 minutes, 2.7% 45 to 60 minutes, 6.2% 60 minutes or more (2000)

MENASHA (town). Covers a land area of 12.410 square miles and a water area of 1.644 square miles. Located at 44.22° N. Lat.; 88.45° W. Long. Elevation is 760 feet.
Population: 15,858 (2000); Race: 94.9% White, 1.1% Black, 1.3% Asian, 0.8% American Indian and Alaska Native, 2.8% Hispanic of any race, 0.8% two or more races (2000); Density: 1,277.9 persons per square mile (2000); Age: 24.9% under 18, 11.2% over 64 (2000); Marriage status: 26.0% never married, 59.4% now married, 5.1% widowed, 9.5% divorced (2000); Foreign born: 3.4% (2000); Ancestry (includes multiple ancestries): 54.6% German, 10.5% Irish, 9.9% Polish, 7.0% Dutch, 6.9% Other groups (2000).
Economy: Employment by occupation: 12.4% management, 18.9% professional, 11.0% services, 26.4% sales, 0.3% farming, 9.2% construction, 21.8% production (2000).
Income: Per capita income: $24,393 (2000); Median household income: $50,887 (2000); Poverty rate: 4.4% (2000).
Taxes: Total city taxes per capita: $241 (2000); City property taxes per capita: $222 (2000).
Education: High school graduation rate: 87.9% (2000); College graduation rate: 23.8% (2000).
Housing: Homeownership rate: 70.8% (2000); Median home value: $112,100 (2000); Median rent: $479 per month (2000); Median age of housing: 24 years (2000).
Safety: Violent crime rate: 3.1 per 10,000 population; Property crime rate: 134.0 per 10,000 population (2001).
Transportation: Commute to work: 95.4% car, 0.7% public transportation, 1.3% walk, 1.8% work from home (2000); Travel time to work: 47.5% less than 15 minutes, 42.4% 15 to 30 minutes, 4.7% 30 to 45 minutes, 1.3% 45 to 60 minutes, 4.0% 60 minutes or more (2000)

NEENAH (city). Covers a land area of 8.247 square miles and a water area of 0.327 square miles. Located at 44.17° N. Lat.; 88.46° W. Long. Elevation is 755 feet.
History: Neenah was formed in 1843 by Harrison Reed, who with his partner Harvey Jones acquired the land and water-power rights from the War Department. The completion of locks and dams on the Fox River attracted settlers, and a sawmill and grist mill were built here in 1849. Neenah later became a paper manufacturing city.
Population: 24,507 (2000); Race: 96.4% White, 0.4% Black, 0.7% Asian, 0.8% American Indian and Alaska Native, 1.7% Hispanic of any race, 1.1% two or more races (2000); Density: 2,971.7 persons per square mile (2000); Age: 27.7% under 18, 12.3% over 64 (2000); Marriage status: 23.8% never married, 60.1% now married, 5.8% widowed, 10.3% divorced (2000); Foreign born: 2.1% (2000); Ancestry (includes multiple ancestries): 54.1% German, 11.8% Irish, 9.2% Polish, 6.0% English, 5.8% Other groups (2000).
Vital Statistics: Birth rate: 133.8 per 10,000 population (1998)
Economy: Single-family building permits issued: 56 (2001) / 61 (2000); Multi-family building permits issued: 98 (2001) / 0 (2000); Employment by occupation: 11.0% management, 20.7% professional, 11.6% services, 24.8% sales, 0.2% farming, 7.8% construction, 23.8% production (2000).
Income: Per capita income: $24,280 (2000); Median household income: $45,773 (2000); Poverty rate: 5.4% (2000).
Taxes: Total city taxes per capita: $477 (2000); City property taxes per capita: $454 (2000).
Education: High school graduation rate: 88.9% (2000); College graduation rate: 26.3% (2000).

School District(s)

Neenah (PK-12)
2000 Enrollment: 6,608 920-751-6808

Two-year College(s)

Theda Clark Medical Center-School of X-ray Techn (Private, Not-for-profit)
2001 Enrollment: n/a 920-729-3130
Housing: Homeownership rate: 70.3% (2000); Median home value: $92,900 (2000); Median rent: $443 per month (2000); Median age of housing: 37 years (2000).
Hospitals: Theda Clark Medical Center (250 beds)
Safety: Violent crime rate: 10.5 per 10,000 population; Property crime rate: 203.4 per 10,000 population (2001).
Newspapers: Neenah Citizen (1 x week); The News-Record (1 x week)
Transportation: Commute to work: 93.3% car, 0.6% public transportation, 1.9% walk, 2.9% work from home (2000); Travel time to work: 50.9% less than 15 minutes, 38.7% 15 to 30 minutes, 6.0% 30 to 45 minutes, 1.7% 45 to 60 minutes, 2.7% 60 minutes or more (2000)
Additional Information Contacts
Neenah Chamber of Commerce 920-722-7758

NEENAH (town). Covers a land area of 9.008 square miles and a water area of 9.899 square miles. Located at 44.17° N. Lat.; 88.48° W. Long. Elevation is 755 feet.
History: Industrial development began c.1850 when nearby flour mills were opened. In 1865 its paper industry was established. Of interest is a replica of the home of James Duane Doty, who was the second governor of Wisconsin Territory. Settled c.1835 on the site of a Winnebago village, Incorporated as a city 1873.
Population: 2,657 (2000); Race: 98.5% White, 0.2% Black, 0.7% Asian, 0.2% American Indian and Alaska Native, 0.3% Hispanic of any race, 0.4% two or more races (2000); Density: 295.0 persons per square mile (2000); Age: 24.8% under 18, 13.1% over 64 (2000); Marriage status: 20.0% never married, 71.8% now married, 3.1% widowed, 5.1% divorced (2000); Foreign born: 1.0% (2000); Ancestry (includes multiple ancestries): 59.5% German, 15.7% Irish, 8.9% English, 6.6% French (except Basque), 5.9% Dutch (2000).
Economy: Railroad junction. Located in a dairy-farming region, Neenah is known, with its twin city Menasha, as a center for the manufacturing of paper and paper products. Other manufacturing includes rubber products, dairy products, chemicals, clothing, woodproducts, paper products, printing and publishing and foundries. Employment by occupation: 15.2% management, 22.8% professional, 8.8% services, 21.6% sales, 0.0% farming, 5.8% construction, 25.7% production (2000).
Income: Per capita income: $30,260 (2000); Median household income: $57,083 (2000); Poverty rate: 1.5% (2000).
Education: High school graduation rate: 91.7% (2000); College graduation rate: 31.0% (2000).

Housing: Homeownership rate: 93.2% (2000); Median home value: $145,800 (2000); Median rent: $450 per month (2000); Median age of housing: 30 years (2000).
Transportation: Commute to work: 94.4% car, 1.0% public transportation, 0.7% walk, 3.1% work from home (2000); Travel time to work: 43.5% less than 15 minutes, 49.4% 15 to 30 minutes, 4.3% 30 to 45 minutes, 0.8% 45 to 60 minutes, 1.9% 60 minutes or more (2000)

NEKIMI (town). Covers a land area of 28.937 square miles and a water area of 0 square miles. Located at 43.94° N. Lat.; 88.58° W. Long.
Population: 1,419 (2000); Race: 97.2% White, 0.0% Black, 1.7% Asian, 0.5% American Indian and Alaska Native, 0.1% Hispanic of any race, 0.6% two or more races (2000); Density: 49.0 persons per square mile (2000); Age: 23.9% under 18, 11.1% over 64 (2000); Marriage status: 22.8% never married, 65.9% now married, 4.0% widowed, 7.3% divorced (2000); Foreign born: 1.5% (2000); Ancestry (includes multiple ancestries): 64.5% German, 7.3% Irish, 7.0% English, 5.5% Polish, 3.4% United States or American (2000).
Economy: Employment by occupation: 12.3% management, 13.3% professional, 12.3% services, 22.3% sales, 2.9% farming, 9.2% construction, 27.6% production (2000).
Income: Per capita income: $20,355 (2000); Median household income: $50,547 (2000); Poverty rate: 3.5% (2000).
Taxes: Total city taxes per capita: $2 (1997); City property taxes per capita: $1 (1997).
Education: High school graduation rate: 89.1% (2000); College graduation rate: 13.5% (2000).
Housing: Homeownership rate: 84.3% (2000); Median home value: $119,900 (2000); Median rent: $455 per month (2000); Median age of housing: 32 years (2000).
Transportation: Commute to work: 90.8% car, 0.0% public transportation, 4.2% walk, 5.0% work from home (2000); Travel time to work: 36.2% less than 15 minutes, 44.1% 15 to 30 minutes, 14.5% 30 to 45 minutes, 1.5% 45 to 60 minutes, 3.7% 60 minutes or more (2000)

NEPEUSKUN (town). Covers a land area of 31.940 square miles and a water area of 4.223 square miles. Located at 43.94° N. Lat.; 88.82° W. Long.
Population: 689 (2000); Race: 98.1% White, 0.0% Black, 0.0% Asian, 0.0% American Indian and Alaska Native, 0.8% Hispanic of any race, 1.1% two or more races (2000); Density: 21.6 persons per square mile (2000); Age: 30.4% under 18, 14.6% over 64 (2000); Marriage status: 16.5% never married, 71.5% now married, 6.2% widowed, 5.8% divorced (2000); Foreign born: 0.3% (2000); Ancestry (includes multiple ancestries): 61.2% German, 12.1% Polish, 11.7% Irish, 8.6% United States or American, 6.8% English (2000).
Economy: Employment by occupation: 11.0% management, 11.0% professional, 12.8% services, 25.3% sales, 2.0% farming, 10.7% construction, 27.1% production (2000).
Income: Per capita income: $19,390 (2000); Median household income: $47,344 (2000); Poverty rate: 2.9% (2000).
Taxes: Total city taxes per capita: $92 (1997); City property taxes per capita: $89 (1997).
Education: High school graduation rate: 84.7% (2000); College graduation rate: 11.0% (2000).
Housing: Homeownership rate: 89.9% (2000); Median home value: $95,200 (2000); Median rent: $238 per month (2000); Median age of housing: 45 years (2000).
Transportation: Commute to work: 90.5% car, 0.0% public transportation, 5.1% walk, 4.4% work from home (2000); Travel time to work: 35.2% less than 15 minutes, 39.5% 15 to 30 minutes, 17.2% 30 to 45 minutes, 5.9% 45 to 60 minutes, 2.2% 60 minutes or more (2000)

OMRO (city). Covers a land area of 2.237 square miles and a water area of 0.119 square miles. Located at 44.03° N. Lat.; 88.74° W. Long. Elevation is 760 feet.
Population: 3,177 (2000); Race: 97.5% White, 0.0% Black, 0.0% Asian, 0.2% American Indian and Alaska Native, 3.3% Hispanic of any race, 1.1% two or more races (2000); Density: 1,420.0 persons per square mile (2000); Age: 26.3% under 18, 13.3% over 64 (2000); Marriage status: 18.6% never married, 64.0% now married, 8.0% widowed, 9.4% divorced (2000); Foreign born: 1.9% (2000); Ancestry (includes multiple ancestries): 53.1% German, 11.4% Irish, 7.5% Norwegian, 7.2% English, 6.3% Polish (2000).
Economy: Single-family building permits issued: 7 (2001) / 7 (2000); Multi-family building permits issued: 4 (2001) / 10 (2000); Employment by occupation: 7.7% management, 15.1% professional, 18.3% services, 23.3% sales, 0.8% farming, 10.6% construction, 24.2% production (2000).
Income: Per capita income: $18,332 (2000); Median household income: $45,208 (2000); Poverty rate: 3.0% (2000).
Taxes: Total city taxes per capita: $194 (1997); City property taxes per capita: $176 (1997).
Education: High school graduation rate: 80.4% (2000); College graduation rate: 16.6% (2000).

School District(s)

Omro (PK-12)
2000 Enrollment: 1,239 920-685-5666
Housing: Homeownership rate: 75.0% (2000); Median home value: $84,400 (2000); Median rent: $389 per month (2000); Median age of housing: 32 years (2000).
Safety: Violent crime rate: 0.0 per 10,000 population; Property crime rate: 325.0 per 10,000 population (2001).
Transportation: Commute to work: 95.1% car, 0.0% public transportation, 2.6% walk, 2.3% work from home (2000); Travel time to work: 23.8% less than 15 minutes, 52.2% 15 to 30 minutes, 17.2% 30 to 45 minutes, 3.2% 45 to 60 minutes, 3.6% 60 minutes or more (2000)
Additional Information Contacts
Omro Area Chamber of Commerce 920-685-6960

OMRO (town). Covers a land area of 32.890 square miles and a water area of 2.499 square miles. Located at 44.03° N. Lat.; 88.71° W. Long. Elevation is 760 feet.
History: Settled 1845; incorporated as village in 1857, as city in 1944.
Population: 1,875 (2000); Race: 98.7% White, 0.4% Black, 0.0% Asian, 0.0% American Indian and Alaska Native, 2.9% Hispanic of any race, 0.2% two or more races (2000); Density: 57.0 persons per square mile (2000); Age: 26.2% under 18, 16.4% over 64 (2000); Marriage status: 14.5% never married, 72.4% now married, 5.6% widowed, 7.6% divorced (2000); Foreign born: 0.8% (2000); Ancestry (includes multiple ancestries): 56.0% German, 13.3% Irish, 11.5% English, 5.8% Polish, 5.3% Other groups (2000).
Economy: Manufacturing: business forms, polyethylene tubing. Single-family building permits issued: 20 (2001) / 16 (2000); Multi-family building permits issued: 0 (2001) / 0 (2000); Employment by occupation: 15.0% management, 13.0% professional, 13.6% services, 24.2% sales, 2.5% farming, 9.8% construction, 21.9% production (2000).
Income: Per capita income: $19,702 (2000); Median household income: $43,750 (2000); Poverty rate: 5.7% (2000).
Taxes: Total city taxes per capita: $56 (1997); City property taxes per capita: $50 (1997).
Education: High school graduation rate: 83.7% (2000); College graduation rate: 15.9% (2000).
Housing: Homeownership rate: 88.7% (2000); Median home value: $114,500 (2000); Median rent: $454 per month (2000); Median age of housing: 30 years (2000).
Transportation: Commute to work: 88.4% car, 0.0% public transportation, 0.8% walk, 9.8% work from home (2000); Travel time to work: 28.2% less than 15 minutes, 52.6% 15 to 30 minutes, 13.6% 30 to 45 minutes, 3.2% 45 to 60 minutes, 2.5% 60 minutes or more (2000)

OSHKOSH (city). Covers a land area of 23.633 square miles and a water area of 0.780 square miles. Located at 44.02° N. Lat.; 88.55° W. Long. Elevation is 770 feet.
History: The site of the city of Oshkosh was claimed in 1836 by Webster Stanley and Chester Gallup, and the community that grew up around their cabins on the shore of Lake Winnebago was called Athens. Athens and the nearby village of Algoma, begun a few years earlier around George Johnson's trading post, vied for control of the developing lumber industry in the area. When a post office was established in 1840, Athens was renamed Oshkosh for the Menominee chief Oshkosh. Oshkosh was incorporated as a city in 1853 and absorbed the village of Algoma. By 1869, twenty sawmills and twelve shingle mills were producing pine lumber and shingles, and six sash and door factories were in operation. For a time, Oshkosh was known as a roaring lumberjack's town. Around 1900, the lumber industry attracted German-Russian and Polish immigrants, who joined the earlier German immigrants.
Population: 62,916 (2000); Race: 92.7% White, 2.0% Black, 2.6% Asian, 0.5% American Indian and Alaska Native, 2.2% Hispanic of any race, 1.2% two or more races (2000); Density: 2,662.2 persons per square mile (2000); Age: 20.7% under 18, 13.0% over 64 (2000); Marriage status: 33.4% never married, 51.3% now married, 6.2% widowed, 9.1% divorced (2000); Foreign born: 3.4% (2000); Ancestry (includes multiple ancestries): 49.7% German, 9.8% Irish, 7.3% Other groups, 6.9% Polish, 6.7% English (2000).
Vital Statistics: Birth rate: 113.6 per 10,000 population (1998)

Economy: Unemployment rate: 4.8% (11/2002); Total civilian labor force: 39,898 (11/2002); Single-family building permits issued: 121 (2001) / 109 (2000); Multi-family building permits issued: 325 (2001) / 168 (2000); Employment by occupation: 10.1% management, 18.1% professional, 18.1% services, 26.8% sales, 0.2% farming, 6.0% construction, 20.6% production (2000).
Income: Per capita income: $18,964 (2000); Median household income: $37,636 (2000); Poverty rate: 10.2% (2000).
Taxes: Total city taxes per capita: $285 (2000); City property taxes per capita: $253 (2000).
Education: High school graduation rate: 84.0% (2000); College graduation rate: 23.1% (2000).

School District(s)

Oshkosh Area (PK-12)
2000 Enrollment: 10,738 920-424-0160

Four-year College(s)

University of Wisconsin-Oshkosh (Public)
2001 Enrollment: 11,033 920-424-1234
2001 Tuition: In-state $2,776; Out-of-state $11,288

Two-year College(s)

Affinity Health System Program in Radiologic Tech (Private, Not-for-profit, Roman Catholic)
2001 Enrollment: 9 920-223-0136

Housing: Homeownership rate: 57.6% (2000); Median home value: $86,300 (2000); Median rent: $432 per month (2000); Median age of housing: 41 years (2000).
Hospitals: Mercy Medical Center (234 beds)
Safety: Violent crime rate: 20.0 per 10,000 population; Property crime rate: 339.9 per 10,000 population (2001).
Newspapers: Oshkosh Northwestern (7 x week)
Transportation: Commute to work: 90.2% car, 1.3% public transportation, 5.7% walk, 1.7% work from home (2000); Travel time to work: 54.7% less than 15 minutes, 31.6% 15 to 30 minutes, 9.4% 30 to 45 minutes, 1.8% 45 to 60 minutes, 2.5% 60 minutes or more (2000); Amtrak: Service available.
Airports: Wittman Regional (commercial service)
Additional Information Contacts
Oshkosh Chamber of Commerce 920-424-7700

OSHKOSH (town). Covers a land area of 10.414 square miles and a water area of 50.584 square miles. Located at 44.06° N. Lat.; 88.54° W. Long. Elevation is 770 feet.
History: Father Allouez visited the site in 1670; French explorers traveled there in the 18th century; and a French fur-trading post was set up in the early 19th century. Oshkosh grew as a lumber town. The downtown area was destroyed by fire in 1875. A branch of the University of Wisconsin is here. Experimental Aircraft Association Museum and annual Fly-In in July at Whitman Field. Incorporated 1846.
Population: 3,234 (2000); Race: 95.8% White, 0.0% Black, 2.8% Asian, 0.2% American Indian and Alaska Native, 0.6% Hispanic of any race, 0.7% two or more races (2000); Density: 310.5 persons per square mile (2000); Age: 23.8% under 18, 10.2% over 64 (2000); Marriage status: 20.5% never married, 68.0% now married, 4.6% widowed, 7.0% divorced (2000); Foreign born: 2.6% (2000); Ancestry (includes multiple ancestries): 55.5% German, 11.9% Irish, 10.0% Polish, 7.8% English, 7.1% Other groups (2000).
Economy: Manufacturing of apparel, transportation equipment, wood products, electrical equipment and machinery. Summer resort. Employment by occupation: 12.7% management, 18.8% professional, 10.7% services, 24.7% sales, 0.0% farming, 7.2% construction, 25.8% production (2000).
Income: Per capita income: $25,610 (2000); Median household income: $56,274 (2000); Poverty rate: 6.4% (2000).
Taxes: Total city taxes per capita: $7 (1997); City property taxes per capita: $0 (1997).
Education: High school graduation rate: 87.1% (2000); College graduation rate: 25.3% (2000).
Housing: Homeownership rate: 81.6% (2000); Median home value: $124,200 (2000); Median rent: $475 per month (2000); Median age of housing: 29 years (2000).
Transportation: Commute to work: 96.3% car, 0.2% public transportation, 0.6% walk, 2.4% work from home (2000); Travel time to work: 36.5% less than 15 minutes, 48.1% 15 to 30 minutes, 11.3% 30 to 45 minutes, 2.4% 45 to 60 minutes, 1.8% 60 minutes or more (2000); Amtrak: Service available.

PICKETT (unincorporated postal area, zip code 54964). Covers a land area of 34.836 square miles and a water area of 0.010 square miles. Located at 43.92° N. Lat.; 88.72° W. Long. Elevation is 890 feet.
Population: 916 (2000); Race: 98.5% White, 0.0% Black, 0.0% Asian, 0.0% American Indian and Alaska Native, 1.0% Hispanic of any race, 1.2% two or more races (2000); Density: 26.3 persons per square mile (2000); Age: 26.5% under 18, 10.0% over 64 (2000); Marriage status: 19.4% never married, 70.5% now married, 5.3% widowed, 4.8% divorced (2000); Foreign born: 0.4% (2000); Ancestry (includes multiple ancestries): 56.9% German, 12.0% English, 9.7% Irish, 5.5% Polish, 5.5% United States or American (2000).
Economy: Employment by occupation: 15.8% management, 17.2% professional, 7.0% services, 21.8% sales, 3.5% farming, 10.4% construction, 24.4% production (2000).
Income: Per capita income: $21,265 (2000); Median household income: $50,781 (2000); Poverty rate: 4.2% (2000).
Education: High school graduation rate: 86.2% (2000); College graduation rate: 21.0% (2000).
Housing: Homeownership rate: 87.9% (2000); Median home value: $100,000 (2000); Median rent: $335 per month (2000); Median age of housing: 36 years (2000).
Transportation: Commute to work: 86.0% car, 0.0% public transportation, 1.1% walk, 12.9% work from home (2000); Travel time to work: 23.9% less than 15 minutes, 46.5% 15 to 30 minutes, 22.8% 30 to 45 minutes, 3.8% 45 to 60 minutes, 3.0% 60 minutes or more (2000)

POYGAN (town). Covers a land area of 23.344 square miles and a water area of 18.325 square miles. Located at 44.10° N. Lat.; 88.82° W. Long.
Population: 1,037 (2000); Race: 97.6% White, 0.0% Black, 0.4% Asian, 0.3% American Indian and Alaska Native, 1.0% Hispanic of any race, 1.7% two or more races (2000); Density: 44.4 persons per square mile (2000); Age: 23.7% under 18, 15.6% over 64 (2000); Marriage status: 17.3% never married, 69.9% now married, 6.9% widowed, 6.0% divorced (2000); Foreign born: 1.4% (2000); Ancestry (includes multiple ancestries): 55.8% German, 14.3% Irish, 9.6% Polish, 6.2% United States or American, 5.5% English (2000).
Economy: Single-family building permits issued: 13 (2001) / 13 (2000); Multi-family building permits issued: 0 (2001) / 0 (2000); Employment by occupation: 15.7% management, 11.8% professional, 12.0% services, 23.8% sales, 2.9% farming, 6.0% construction, 27.7% production (2000).
Income: Per capita income: $23,679 (2000); Median household income: $53,947 (2000); Poverty rate: 6.1% (2000).
Taxes: Total city taxes per capita: $114 (1997); City property taxes per capita: $110 (1997).
Education: High school graduation rate: 88.1% (2000); College graduation rate: 10.8% (2000).
Housing: Homeownership rate: 94.2% (2000); Median home value: $139,600 (2000); Median rent: $414 per month (2000); Median age of housing: 33 years (2000).
Transportation: Commute to work: 84.7% car, 0.0% public transportation, 2.6% walk, 10.1% work from home (2000); Travel time to work: 15.7% less than 15 minutes, 37.1% 15 to 30 minutes, 34.9% 30 to 45 minutes, 7.9% 45 to 60 minutes, 4.4% 60 minutes or more (2000)

RUSHFORD (town). Covers a land area of 35.065 square miles and a water area of 0.490 square miles. Located at 44.01° N. Lat.; 88.83° W. Long.
Population: 1,471 (2000); Race: 98.3% White, 0.3% Black, 0.5% Asian, 0.0% American Indian and Alaska Native, 1.9% Hispanic of any race, 0.8% two or more races (2000); Density: 42.0 persons per square mile (2000); Age: 23.4% under 18, 11.1% over 64 (2000); Marriage status: 22.8% never married, 62.8% now married, 5.0% widowed, 9.4% divorced (2000); Foreign born: 0.9% (2000); Ancestry (includes multiple ancestries): 54.1% German, 10.7% Polish, 10.0% Irish, 7.8% United States or American, 7.6% English (2000).
Economy: Single-family building permits issued: 14 (2001) / 5 (2000); Multi-family building permits issued: 0 (2001) / 0 (2000); Employment by occupation: 12.3% management, 10.7% professional, 13.8% services, 19.7% sales, 3.3% farming, 15.9% construction, 24.3% production (2000).
Income: Per capita income: $20,768 (2000); Median household income: $45,990 (2000); Poverty rate: 2.3% (2000).
Taxes: Total city taxes per capita: $32 (1997); City property taxes per capita: $27 (1997).
Education: High school graduation rate: 82.9% (2000); College graduation rate: 14.1% (2000).
Housing: Homeownership rate: 86.4% (2000); Median home value: $92,400 (2000); Median rent: $334 per month (2000); Median age of housing: 44 years (2000).
Transportation: Commute to work: 88.0% car, 0.0% public transportation, 2.1% walk, 9.9% work from home (2000); Travel time to work: 20.1% less

than 15 minutes, 46.4% 15 to 30 minutes, 24.4% 30 to 45 minutes, 4.9% 45 to 60 minutes, 4.2% 60 minutes or more (2000)

UTICA (town). Covers a land area of 35.853 square miles and a water area of 0.010 square miles. Located at 43.94° N. Lat.; 88.70° W. Long.
Population: 1,168 (2000); Race: 98.5% White, 0.0% Black, 0.2% Asian, 0.0% American Indian and Alaska Native, 0.9% Hispanic of any race, 1.0% two or more races (2000); Density: 32.6 persons per square mile (2000); Age: 25.2% under 18, 12.8% over 64 (2000); Marriage status: 17.2% never married, 72.3% now married, 5.1% widowed, 5.3% divorced (2000); Foreign born: 0.7% (2000); Ancestry (includes multiple ancestries): 59.8% German, 12.8% English, 11.9% Irish, 6.8% Polish, 5.1% Welsh (2000).
Economy: Single-family building permits issued: 15 (2001) / 15 (2000); Multi-family building permits issued: 0 (2001) / 0 (2000); Employment by occupation: 17.5% management, 15.3% professional, 8.7% services, 25.0% sales, 2.9% farming, 8.2% construction, 22.4% production (2000).
Income: Per capita income: $21,518 (2000); Median household income: $49,800 (2000); Poverty rate: 3.8% (2000).
Taxes: Total city taxes per capita: $104 (2000); City property taxes per capita: $98 (2000).
Education: High school graduation rate: 85.3% (2000); College graduation rate: 20.4% (2000).
Housing: Homeownership rate: 87.2% (2000); Median home value: $112,000 (2000); Median rent: $321 per month (2000); Median age of housing: 36 years (2000).
Transportation: Commute to work: 85.8% car, 0.0% public transportation, 1.1% walk, 12.8% work from home (2000); Travel time to work: 20.9% less than 15 minutes, 53.4% 15 to 30 minutes, 19.7% 30 to 45 minutes, 3.5% 45 to 60 minutes, 2.5% 60 minutes or more (2000)

VINLAND (town). Covers a land area of 29.036 square miles and a water area of 7.266 square miles. Located at 44.10° N. Lat.; 88.53° W. Long.
Population: 1,849 (2000); Race: 99.1% White, 0.0% Black, 0.0% Asian, 0.4% American Indian and Alaska Native, 0.9% Hispanic of any race, 0.4% two or more races (2000); Density: 63.7 persons per square mile (2000); Age: 25.5% under 18, 11.6% over 64 (2000); Marriage status: 21.3% never married, 71.0% now married, 3.8% widowed, 3.9% divorced (2000); Foreign born: 1.2% (2000); Ancestry (includes multiple ancestries): 60.9% German, 10.5% Irish, 9.2% English, 8.6% Dutch, 6.9% Polish (2000).
Economy: Single-family building permits issued: 15 (2001) / 7 (2000); Multi-family building permits issued: 0 (2001) / 0 (2000); Employment by occupation: 17.6% management, 18.6% professional, 10.2% services, 22.9% sales, 1.3% farming, 6.4% construction, 22.9% production (2000).
Income: Per capita income: $26,033 (2000); Median household income: $64,338 (2000); Poverty rate: 2.4% (2000).
Taxes: Total city taxes per capita: $120 (1997); City property taxes per capita: $77 (1997).
Education: High school graduation rate: 91.5% (2000); College graduation rate: 21.0% (2000).
Housing: Homeownership rate: 90.5% (2000); Median home value: $138,800 (2000); Median rent: $467 per month (2000); Median age of housing: 29 years (2000).
Transportation: Commute to work: 91.5% car, 0.0% public transportation, 2.5% walk, 5.5% work from home (2000); Travel time to work: 36.4% less than 15 minutes, 55.1% 15 to 30 minutes, 7.1% 30 to 45 minutes, 0.4% 45 to 60 minutes, 1.0% 60 minutes or more (2000)

WINCHESTER (town). Covers a land area of 35.787 square miles and a water area of 0.721 square miles. Located at 44.19° N. Lat.; 88.69° W. Long. Elevation is 850 feet.
Population: 1,676 (2000); Race: 98.5% White, 0.0% Black, 0.2% Asian, 0.0% American Indian and Alaska Native, 0.8% Hispanic of any race, 0.8% two or more races (2000); Density: 46.8 persons per square mile (2000); Age: 25.5% under 18, 12.5% over 64 (2000); Marriage status: 20.7% never married, 68.5% now married, 4.7% widowed, 6.1% divorced (2000); Foreign born: 1.1% (2000); Ancestry (includes multiple ancestries): 54.7% German, 11.7% Norwegian, 10.7% Irish, 5.5% Polish, 5.2% United States or American (2000).
Economy: Employment by occupation: 14.7% management, 15.1% professional, 9.8% services, 24.7% sales, 0.8% farming, 11.3% construction, 23.7% production (2000).
Income: Per capita income: $21,182 (2000); Median household income: $53,400 (2000); Poverty rate: 3.4% (2000).
Taxes: Total city taxes per capita: $70 (1997); City property taxes per capita: $61 (1997).
Education: High school graduation rate: 89.0% (2000); College graduation rate: 15.3% (2000).
Housing: Homeownership rate: 92.9% (2000); Median home value: $121,000 (2000); Median rent: $508 per month (2000); Median age of housing: 27 years (2000).
Transportation: Commute to work: 90.9% car, 0.0% public transportation, 2.2% walk, 5.3% work from home (2000); Travel time to work: 17.0% less than 15 minutes, 63.3% 15 to 30 minutes, 15.8% 30 to 45 minutes, 1.1% 45 to 60 minutes, 2.8% 60 minutes or more (2000)

WINNECONNE (village). Covers a land area of 1.597 square miles and a water area of 0.413 square miles. Located at 44.11° N. Lat.; 88.71° W. Long. Elevation is 753 feet.
Population: 2,401 (2000); Race: 99.4% White, 0.0% Black, 0.0% Asian, 0.6% American Indian and Alaska Native, 0.6% Hispanic of any race, 0.0% two or more races (2000); Density: 1,503.4 persons per square mile (2000); Age: 25.9% under 18, 15.9% over 64 (2000); Marriage status: 19.6% never married, 62.2% now married, 7.5% widowed, 10.8% divorced (2000); Foreign born: 0.5% (2000); Ancestry (includes multiple ancestries): 56.1% German, 12.7% Irish, 7.9% Polish, 7.9% English, 7.0% Norwegian (2000).
Economy: Single-family building permits issued: 18 (2001) / 18 (2000); Multi-family building permits issued: 0 (2001) / 0 (2000); Employment by occupation: 8.0% management, 15.0% professional, 21.4% services, 22.2% sales, 0.4% farming, 12.3% construction, 20.7% production (2000).
Income: Per capita income: $20,316 (2000); Median household income: $44,886 (2000); Poverty rate: 4.7% (2000).
Taxes: Total city taxes per capita: $290 (1997); City property taxes per capita: $281 (1997).
Education: High school graduation rate: 87.3% (2000); College graduation rate: 16.0% (2000).

School District(s)

Winneconne Community (PK-12)
2000 Enrollment: 1,665 920-582-5802
Housing: Homeownership rate: 75.5% (2000); Median home value: $89,000 (2000); Median rent: $376 per month (2000); Median age of housing: 30 years (2000).
Safety: Violent crime rate: 8.3 per 10,000 population; Property crime rate: 202.6 per 10,000 population (2001).
Newspapers: Winneconne News (1 x week)
Transportation: Commute to work: 93.6% car, 0.0% public transportation, 1.8% walk, 3.3% work from home (2000); Travel time to work: 30.1% less than 15 minutes, 39.7% 15 to 30 minutes, 18.7% 30 to 45 minutes, 6.1% 45 to 60 minutes, 5.3% 60 minutes or more (2000)

WINNECONNE (town). Covers a land area of 21.977 square miles and a water area of 11.460 square miles. Located at 44.10° N. Lat.; 88.68° W. Long. Elevation is 753 feet.
Population: 2,145 (2000); Race: 99.5% White, 0.0% Black, 0.5% Asian, 0.0% American Indian and Alaska Native, 0.5% Hispanic of any race, 0.0% two or more races (2000); Density: 97.6 persons per square mile (2000); Age: 24.4% under 18, 13.1% over 64 (2000); Marriage status: 16.8% never married, 73.4% now married, 5.4% widowed, 4.4% divorced (2000); Foreign born: 1.3% (2000); Ancestry (includes multiple ancestries): 53.0% German, 12.0% Irish, 9.8% Polish, 8.7% English, 6.6% Norwegian (2000).
Economy: Dairying; manufacturing of farm machinery. Single-family building permits issued: 24 (2001) / 36 (2000); Multi-family building permits issued: 0 (2001) / 0 (2000); Employment by occupation: 17.4% management, 19.3% professional, 12.3% services, 20.5% sales, 1.0% farming, 10.4% construction, 18.9% production (2000).
Income: Per capita income: $27,274 (2000); Median household income: $60,385 (2000); Poverty rate: 2.2% (2000).
Taxes: Total city taxes per capita: $92 (1997); City property taxes per capita: $80 (1997).
Education: High school graduation rate: 90.5% (2000); College graduation rate: 25.2% (2000).
Housing: Homeownership rate: 90.0% (2000); Median home value: $150,900 (2000); Median rent: $506 per month (2000); Median age of housing: 32 years (2000).
Transportation: Commute to work: 95.1% car, 0.0% public transportation, 0.3% walk, 4.5% work from home (2000); Travel time to work: 23.6% less than 15 minutes, 45.6% 15 to 30 minutes, 20.5% 30 to 45 minutes, 3.8% 45 to 60 minutes, 6.5% 60 minutes or more (2000)

WOLF RIVER (town). Covers a land area of 29.352 square miles and a water area of 1.127 square miles. Located at 44.19° N. Lat.; 88.81° W. Long.

Population: 1,223 (2000); Race: 97.8% White, 0.0% Black, 0.3% Asian, 0.1% American Indian and Alaska Native, 0.0% Hispanic of any race, 1.8% two or more races (2000); Density: 41.7 persons per square mile (2000); Age: 21.4% under 18, 15.8% over 64 (2000); Marriage status: 17.9% never married, 66.2% now married, 7.6% widowed, 8.3% divorced (2000); Foreign born: 1.2% (2000); Ancestry (includes multiple ancestries): 62.9% German, 9.9% Polish, 5.8% Norwegian, 5.6% Irish, 5.5% English (2000).
Economy: Single-family building permits issued: 8 (2001) / 11 (2000); Multi-family building permits issued: 0 (2001) / 0 (2000); Employment by occupation: 12.2% management, 13.0% professional, 11.6% services, 21.7% sales, 3.2% farming, 10.1% construction, 28.1% production (2000).
Income: Per capita income: $21,594 (2000); Median household income: $44,922 (2000); Poverty rate: 6.3% (2000).
Taxes: Total city taxes per capita: $110 (1997); City property taxes per capita: $104 (1997).
Education: High school graduation rate: 84.8% (2000); College graduation rate: 12.9% (2000).
Housing: Homeownership rate: 88.2% (2000); Median home value: $125,900 (2000); Median rent: $429 per month (2000); Median age of housing: 39 years (2000).
Transportation: Commute to work: 86.2% car, 0.0% public transportation, 3.7% walk, 9.4% work from home (2000); Travel time to work: 23.6% less than 15 minutes, 29.2% 15 to 30 minutes, 36.1% 30 to 45 minutes, 8.4% 45 to 60 minutes, 2.7% 60 minutes or more (2000)

Wood County

Located in central Wisconsin; crossed by the Wisconsin River; drained by the Yellow River. Covers a land area of 792.80 square miles, a water area of 16.70 square miles, and is located in the Central Time Zone. The county government was organized in 1856. County seat is Wisconsin Rapids.

Weather Station: Marshfield Exp. Farm Elevation: 1,250 feet

	Jan	Feb	Mar	Apr	May	Jun	Jul	Aug	Sep	Oct	Nov	Dec
High	23	29	40	56	70	78	82	80	71	59	41	28
Low	4	10	20	33	44	53	58	56	47	36	24	11
Precip	1.0	0.9	1.9	2.9	3.9	3.9	4.1	4.2	4.1	2.6	2.3	1.3
Snow	11.9	7.9	9.6	3.0	tr	0.0	0.0	0.0	0.0	0.6	5.4	10.9

High and Low temperatures in degrees Fahrenheit; Precipitation and Snow in inches

Weather Station: Wisconsin Rapids Elevation: 1,040 feet

	Jan	Feb	Mar	Apr	May	Jun	Jul	Aug	Sep	Oct	Nov	Dec
High	23	30	41	56	70	78	82	80	70	58	41	28
Low	4	9	20	32	44	53	59	56	47	36	24	11
Precip	1.1	1.0	2.0	2.9	3.5	3.6	4.2	4.2	3.6	2.6	2.1	1.4
Snow	12.0	8.5	10.6	2.6	tr	0.0	0.0	0.0	0.0	0.3	3.7	9.6

High and Low temperatures in degrees Fahrenheit; Precipitation and Snow in inches

Population: 75,555 (2000); Race: 96.4% White, 0.4% Black, 1.5% Asian, 0.7% American Indian and Alaska Native, 1.1% Hispanic of any race, 0.7% two or more races (2000); Density: 95.3 persons per square mile (2000); Age: 25.7% under 18, 15.4% over 64 (2000).
Religion: Five largest groups: 40.0% Catholic Church, 14.1% Lutheran Church—Missouri Synod, 5.6% Evangelical Lutheran Church in America, 2.9% Wisconsin Evangelical Lutheran Synod, 2.3% The United Methodist Church (2000).
Economy: Unemployment rate: 4.3% (11/2002); Total civilian labor force: 41,776 (11/2002); Leading industries: 24.4% manufacturing; 21.0% health care and social assistance; 15.3% retail trade (2000); Companies that employ more than 1,000 persons: 4 (2000); Companies that employ more than 100 persons: 61 (2000); Farms: 968 totaling 219,258 acres (1997); Minority business ownership rate: 3.1% (1997); Women business ownership rate: 19.4% (1997); Retail sales per capita: $12,535 (1997). Single-family building permits issued: 240 (2001) / 232 (2000); Multi-family building permits issued: 112 (2001) / 160 (2000).
Income: Per capita income: $20,203 (2000); Median household income: $41,595 (2000); Poverty rate: 6.5% (2000); Bankruptcy rate: 2.39% (2001).
Taxes: Total county taxes per capita: $199 (2000); County property taxes per capita: $192 (2000).
Education: High school graduation rate: 84.8% (2000); College graduation rate: 16.9% (2000).
Housing: Homeownership rate: 74.3% (2000); Median home value: $81,400 (2000); Median rent: $379 per month (2000); Median age of housing: 33 years (2000).
Health: Birth rate: 119.4 per 10,000 population (1998); Age adjusted death rate: 76.9 per 10,000 population (1999); Age adjusted cancer mortality rate: 188.8 deaths per 100,000 population (1999). Air Quality Index: 100% good, 0% moderate, 0% unhealthy (percent of days in 2000). Number of physicians: 57.2 per 10,000 population (1999); Number of hospital beds: 97.9 per 10,000 population (1999).
Elections: 2000 Presidential election results: 44.6% Gore, 49.8% Bush, 3.9% Nader, 1.2% Buchanan
Additional Information Contacts
Wood County Government Offices 715-421-8400
Marshfield Chamber of Commerce 715-384-3454
Wisconsin Rapids Chamber of Commerce 715-423-1830

Wood County Communities

ARPIN (village). Covers a land area of 0.848 square miles and a water area of 0 square miles. Located at 44.54° N. Lat.; 90.02° W. Long. Elevation is 1,155 feet.
Population: 337 (2000); Race: 98.6% White, 0.6% Black, 0.8% Asian, 0.0% American Indian and Alaska Native, 0.0% Hispanic of any race, 0.0% two or more races (2000); Density: 397.3 persons per square mile (2000); Age: 27.7% under 18, 19.5% over 64 (2000); Marriage status: 22.8% never married, 61.0% now married, 6.3% widowed, 9.9% divorced (2000); Foreign born: 1.4% (2000); Ancestry (includes multiple ancestries): 45.8% German, 12.1% Norwegian, 9.0% French (except Basque), 7.9% Polish, 6.2% Irish (2000).
Economy: Single-family building permits issued: 3 (2001) / 0 (2000); Multi-family building permits issued: 0 (2001) / 0 (2000); Employment by occupation: 7.3% management, 8.6% professional, 14.6% services, 19.9% sales, 0.0% farming, 18.5% construction, 31.1% production (2000).
Income: Per capita income: $15,812 (2000); Median household income: $31,563 (2000); Poverty rate: 4.3% (2000).
Taxes: Total city taxes per capita: $111 (1997); City property taxes per capita: $101 (1997).
Education: High school graduation rate: 76.5% (2000); College graduation rate: 11.1% (2000).
Housing: Homeownership rate: 71.3% (2000); Median home value: $48,100 (2000); Median rent: $288 per month (2000); Median age of housing: 47 years (2000).
Transportation: Commute to work: 85.2% car, 0.0% public transportation, 10.7% walk, 4.0% work from home (2000); Travel time to work: 39.2% less than 15 minutes, 42.7% 15 to 30 minutes, 9.1% 30 to 45 minutes, 4.9% 45 to 60 minutes, 4.2% 60 minutes or more (2000)

ARPIN (town). Covers a land area of 33.012 square miles and a water area of 0 square miles. Located at 44.55° N. Lat.; 90.03° W. Long. Elevation is 1,155 feet.
Population: 786 (2000); Race: 99.4% White, 0.0% Black, 0.0% Asian, 0.0% American Indian and Alaska Native, 0.5% Hispanic of any race, 0.3% two or more races (2000); Density: 23.8 persons per square mile (2000); Age: 31.0% under 18, 8.9% over 64 (2000); Marriage status: 23.7% never married, 63.7% now married, 4.9% widowed, 7.7% divorced (2000); Foreign born: 0.3% (2000); Ancestry (includes multiple ancestries): 58.3% German, 6.8% Irish, 6.4% Polish, 5.7% English, 5.5% United States or American (2000).
Economy: Dairying, general farming; forests to South. Powers Bluff Ski Area to West. Single-family building permits issued: 11 (2001) / 11 (2000); Multi-family building permits issued: 0 (2001) / 0 (2000); Employment by occupation: 19.8% management, 12.2% professional, 12.4% services, 14.1% sales, 3.7% farming, 13.7% construction, 24.1% production (2000).
Income: Per capita income: $15,750 (2000); Median household income: $42,115 (2000); Poverty rate: 8.1% (2000).
Taxes: Total city taxes per capita: $86 (1997); City property taxes per capita: $85 (1997).
Education: High school graduation rate: 86.5% (2000); College graduation rate: 9.1% (2000).
Housing: Homeownership rate: 87.6% (2000); Median home value: $78,100 (2000); Median rent: $380 per month (2000); Median age of housing: 36 years (2000).
Transportation: Commute to work: 74.4% car, 0.0% public transportation, 4.0% walk, 21.6% work from home (2000); Travel time to work: 23.7% less than 15 minutes, 45.6% 15 to 30 minutes, 23.4% 30 to 45 minutes, 2.5% 45 to 60 minutes, 4.7% 60 minutes or more (2000)

AUBURNDALE (village). Covers a land area of 2.095 square miles and a water area of 0 square miles. Located at 44.62° N. Lat.; 90.01° W. Long. Elevation is 1,220 feet.

Population: 738 (2000); Race: 100.0% White, 0.0% Black, 0.0% Asian, 0.0% American Indian and Alaska Native, 0.0% Hispanic of any race, 0.0% two or more races (2000); Density: 352.3 persons per square mile (2000); Age: 24.4% under 18, 11.9% over 64 (2000); Marriage status: 27.0% never married, 59.3% now married, 5.2% widowed, 8.4% divorced (2000); Foreign born: 0.3% (2000); Ancestry (includes multiple ancestries): 65.8% German, 10.9% Polish, 8.6% Irish, 4.8% Norwegian, 4.7% English (2000).
Economy: Single-family building permits issued: 3 (2001) / 1 (2000); Multi-family building permits issued: 0 (2001) / 0 (2000); Employment by occupation: 8.0% management, 14.8% professional, 10.8% services, 25.2% sales, 3.3% farming, 14.1% construction, 23.8% production (2000).
Income: Per capita income: $18,347 (2000); Median household income: $41,103 (2000); Poverty rate: 4.4% (2000).
Taxes: Total city taxes per capita: $41 (1997); City property taxes per capita: $37 (1997).
Education: High school graduation rate: 81.9% (2000); College graduation rate: 11.4% (2000).

School District(s)

Auburndale (PK-12)
2000 Enrollment: 929 715-652-2117

Housing: Homeownership rate: 73.0% (2000); Median home value: $82,800 (2000); Median rent: $355 per month (2000); Median age of housing: 27 years (2000).
Transportation: Commute to work: 88.3% car, 0.5% public transportation, 6.2% walk, 4.5% work from home (2000); Travel time to work: 27.2% less than 15 minutes, 51.9% 15 to 30 minutes, 14.5% 30 to 45 minutes, 5.5% 45 to 60 minutes, 1.0% 60 minutes or more (2000)

AUBURNDALE (town). Covers a land area of 32.235 square miles and a water area of 0 square miles. Located at 44.65° N. Lat.; 90.03° W. Long. Elevation is 1,220 feet.
Population: 829 (2000); Race: 98.6% White, 0.0% Black, 0.1% Asian, 0.0% American Indian and Alaska Native, 0.4% Hispanic of any race, 1.2% two or more races (2000); Density: 25.7 persons per square mile (2000); Age: 26.6% under 18, 14.2% over 64 (2000); Marriage status: 24.3% never married, 67.4% now married, 4.0% widowed, 4.2% divorced (2000); Foreign born: 0.4% (2000); Ancestry (includes multiple ancestries): 63.1% German, 8.6% Polish, 6.2% Norwegian, 5.4% Irish, 3.9% Other groups (2000).
Economy: In dairying and agricultural area. Single-family building permits issued: 3 (2001) / 5 (2000); Multi-family building permits issued: 0 (2001) / 0 (2000); Employment by occupation: 19.3% management, 7.0% professional, 14.0% services, 19.3% sales, 6.8% farming, 15.6% construction, 17.9% production (2000).
Income: Per capita income: $16,588 (2000); Median household income: $40,815 (2000); Poverty rate: 6.2% (2000).
Taxes: Total city taxes per capita: $70 (1997); City property taxes per capita: $68 (1997).
Education: High school graduation rate: 78.5% (2000); College graduation rate: 5.5% (2000).
Housing: Homeownership rate: 92.3% (2000); Median home value: $80,400 (2000); Median rent: $419 per month (2000); Median age of housing: 35 years (2000).
Transportation: Commute to work: 81.4% car, 0.7% public transportation, 2.4% walk, 15.5% work from home (2000); Travel time to work: 35.4% less than 15 minutes, 48.5% 15 to 30 minutes, 10.3% 30 to 45 minutes, 1.9% 45 to 60 minutes, 3.9% 60 minutes or more (2000)

BABCOCK (unincorporated postal area, zip code 54413). Covers a land area of 24.812 square miles and a water area of 0.318 square miles. Located at 44.28° N. Lat.; 90.12° W. Long. Elevation is 975 feet.
Population: 218 (2000); Race: 95.9% White, 0.0% Black, 0.5% Asian, 3.7% American Indian and Alaska Native, 0.0% Hispanic of any race, 0.0% two or more races (2000); Density: 8.8 persons per square mile (2000); Age: 24.3% under 18, 16.1% over 64 (2000); Marriage status: 24.7% never married, 54.6% now married, 13.2% widowed, 7.5% divorced (2000); Foreign born: 1.8% (2000); Ancestry (includes multiple ancestries): 26.1% German, 6.9% Polish, 5.0% Other groups, 4.6% English, 4.1% French (except Basque) (2000).
Economy: Employment by occupation: 15.1% management, 10.5% professional, 18.6% services, 15.1% sales, 0.0% farming, 10.5% construction, 30.2% production (2000).
Income: Per capita income: $15,775 (2000); Median household income: $36,250 (2000); Poverty rate: 7.3% (2000).
Education: High school graduation rate: 70.3% (2000); College graduation rate: 7.1% (2000).
Housing: Homeownership rate: 83.5% (2000); Median home value: $49,100 (2000); Median rent: $325 per month (2000); Median age of housing: 32 years (2000).
Transportation: Commute to work: 86.7% car, 0.0% public transportation, 4.8% walk, 8.4% work from home (2000); Travel time to work: 35.5% less than 15 minutes, 18.4% 15 to 30 minutes, 34.2% 30 to 45 minutes, 7.9% 45 to 60 minutes, 3.9% 60 minutes or more (2000)

BIRON (village). Covers a land area of 4.537 square miles and a water area of 1.719 square miles. Located at 44.42° N. Lat.; 89.77° W. Long. Elevation is 1,026 feet.
Population: 915 (2000); Race: 95.6% White, 0.0% Black, 0.0% Asian, 1.8% American Indian and Alaska Native, 2.4% Hispanic of any race, 0.6% two or more races (2000); Density: 201.7 persons per square mile (2000); Age: 24.5% under 18, 22.3% over 64 (2000); Marriage status: 20.3% never married, 56.9% now married, 13.3% widowed, 9.5% divorced (2000); Foreign born: 4.3% (2000); Ancestry (includes multiple ancestries): 41.8% German, 18.2% Polish, 11.9% Irish, 8.2% Norwegian, 7.8% Other groups (2000).
Economy: Cranberries; paper, pulp, and sulfite milling. Single-family building permits issued: 0 (2001) / 0 (2000); Multi-family building permits issued: 0 (2001) / 0 (2000); Employment by occupation: 12.3% management, 11.5% professional, 17.5% services, 18.3% sales, 3.8% farming, 11.7% construction, 24.9% production (2000).
Income: Per capita income: $19,293 (2000); Median household income: $42,557 (2000); Poverty rate: 7.2% (2000).
Taxes: Total city taxes per capita: $817 (1997); City property taxes per capita: $815 (1997).
Education: High school graduation rate: 82.7% (2000); College graduation rate: 16.9% (2000).
Housing: Homeownership rate: 72.1% (2000); Median home value: $78,700 (2000); Median rent: $346 per month (2000); Median age of housing: 38 years (2000).
Transportation: Commute to work: 89.8% car, 0.0% public transportation, 2.7% walk, 6.3% work from home (2000); Travel time to work: 58.1% less than 15 minutes, 26.7% 15 to 30 minutes, 6.2% 30 to 45 minutes, 5.9% 45 to 60 minutes, 3.2% 60 minutes or more (2000)

CAMERON (town). Covers a land area of 7.240 square miles and a water area of 0 square miles. Located at 44.62° N. Lat.; 90.17° W. Long.
Population: 510 (2000); Race: 98.6% White, 0.0% Black, 0.0% Asian, 0.7% American Indian and Alaska Native, 0.7% Hispanic of any race, 0.0% two or more races (2000); Density: 70.4 persons per square mile (2000); Age: 23.3% under 18, 14.5% over 64 (2000); Marriage status: 25.0% never married, 65.3% now married, 4.3% widowed, 5.4% divorced (2000); Foreign born: 1.6% (2000); Ancestry (includes multiple ancestries): 61.0% German, 9.1% Polish, 6.8% Irish, 6.4% Norwegian, 5.9% English (2000).
Economy: Single-family building permits issued: 2 (2001) / 4 (2000); Multi-family building permits issued: 0 (2001) / 0 (2000); Employment by occupation: 9.0% management, 12.8% professional, 15.1% services, 33.4% sales, 1.2% farming, 14.5% construction, 14.0% production (2000).
Income: Per capita income: $22,148 (2000); Median household income: $51,528 (2000); Poverty rate: 4.9% (2000).
Taxes: Total city taxes per capita: $111 (1997); City property taxes per capita: $102 (1997).
Education: High school graduation rate: 85.6% (2000); College graduation rate: 5.6% (2000).
Housing: Homeownership rate: 88.4% (2000); Median home value: $99,600 (2000); Median rent: $333 per month (2000); Median age of housing: 34 years (2000).
Transportation: Commute to work: 90.4% car, 0.0% public transportation, 4.7% walk, 4.7% work from home (2000); Travel time to work: 52.6% less than 15 minutes, 37.0% 15 to 30 minutes, 2.8% 30 to 45 minutes, 2.4% 45 to 60 minutes, 5.2% 60 minutes or more (2000)

CARY (town). Covers a land area of 35.024 square miles and a water area of 0.122 square miles. Located at 44.47° N. Lat.; 90.27° W. Long.
Population: 398 (2000); Race: 98.2% White, 0.0% Black, 0.5% Asian, 0.0% American Indian and Alaska Native, 0.0% Hispanic of any race, 1.3% two or more races (2000); Density: 11.4 persons per square mile (2000); Age: 24.1% under 18, 13.8% over 64 (2000); Marriage status: 16.2% never married, 71.4% now married, 4.4% widowed, 7.9% divorced (2000); Foreign born: 0.5% (2000); Ancestry (includes multiple ancestries): 56.8% German, 11.3% Irish, 9.0% Polish, 8.0% Norwegian, 6.0% French (except Basque) (2000).

Economy: Employment by occupation: 11.2% management, 16.2% professional, 10.2% services, 16.8% sales, 7.1% farming, 14.2% construction, 24.4% production (2000).
Income: Per capita income: $18,043 (2000); Median household income: $38,125 (2000); Poverty rate: 2.5% (2000).
Taxes: Total city taxes per capita: $75 (1997); City property taxes per capita: $75 (1997).
Education: High school graduation rate: 82.6% (2000); College graduation rate: 12.1% (2000).
Housing: Homeownership rate: 91.1% (2000); Median home value: $75,400 (2000); Median rent: $325 per month (2000); Median age of housing: 25 years (2000).
Transportation: Commute to work: 92.0% car, 0.0% public transportation, 1.1% walk, 5.9% work from home (2000); Travel time to work: 12.5% less than 15 minutes, 55.1% 15 to 30 minutes, 25.6% 30 to 45 minutes, 2.3% 45 to 60 minutes, 4.5% 60 minutes or more (2000)

CRANMOOR (town). Covers a land area of 36.737 square miles and a water area of 5.600 square miles. Located at 44.35° N. Lat.; 90.01° W. Long. Elevation is 982 feet.
Population: 175 (2000); Race: 85.9% White, 0.0% Black, 0.0% Asian, 11.4% American Indian and Alaska Native, 0.5% Hispanic of any race, 2.7% two or more races (2000); Density: 4.8 persons per square mile (2000); Age: 31.4% under 18, 12.4% over 64 (2000); Marriage status: 27.9% never married, 60.7% now married, 7.1% widowed, 4.3% divorced (2000); Foreign born: 1.1% (2000); Ancestry (includes multiple ancestries): 40.0% German, 17.3% Polish, 11.4% Other groups, 10.8% United States or American, 9.2% Irish (2000).
Economy: Single-family building permits issued: 0 (2001) / 0 (2000); Multi-family building permits issued: 0 (2001) / 0 (2000); Employment by occupation: 27.9% management, 10.5% professional, 3.5% services, 24.4% sales, 16.3% farming, 7.0% construction, 10.5% production (2000).
Income: Per capita income: $28,727 (2000); Median household income: $46,250 (2000); Poverty rate: 10.8% (2000).
Taxes: Total city taxes per capita: $113 (1997); City property taxes per capita: $113 (1997).
Education: High school graduation rate: 90.2% (2000); College graduation rate: 17.9% (2000).
Housing: Homeownership rate: 53.8% (2000); Median home value: $156,300 (2000); Median rent: $625 per month (2000); Median age of housing: 27 years (2000).
Transportation: Commute to work: 81.0% car, 0.0% public transportation, 7.1% walk, 11.9% work from home (2000); Travel time to work: 48.6% less than 15 minutes, 36.5% 15 to 30 minutes, 5.4% 30 to 45 minutes, 9.5% 45 to 60 minutes, 0.0% 60 minutes or more (2000)

DEXTER (town). Covers a land area of 34.208 square miles and a water area of 1.306 square miles. Located at 44.37° N. Lat.; 90.15° W. Long.
Population: 379 (2000); Race: 98.5% White, 0.0% Black, 0.0% Asian, 1.5% American Indian and Alaska Native, 0.5% Hispanic of any race, 0.0% two or more races (2000); Density: 11.1 persons per square mile (2000); Age: 27.4% under 18, 13.1% over 64 (2000); Marriage status: 17.4% never married, 68.1% now married, 7.7% widowed, 6.8% divorced (2000); Foreign born: 1.2% (2000); Ancestry (includes multiple ancestries): 46.4% German, 18.3% Polish, 11.6% Norwegian, 5.4% Other groups, 4.0% Irish (2000).
Economy: Single-family building permits issued: 0 (2001) / 0 (2000); Multi-family building permits issued: 0 (2001) / 0 (2000); Employment by occupation: 16.7% management, 11.7% professional, 8.9% services, 22.2% sales, 6.7% farming, 11.1% construction, 22.8% production (2000).
Income: Per capita income: $19,060 (2000); Median household income: $43,750 (2000); Poverty rate: 4.0% (2000).
Taxes: Total city taxes per capita: $32 (1997); City property taxes per capita: $29 (1997).
Education: High school graduation rate: 79.6% (2000); College graduation rate: 12.0% (2000).
Housing: Homeownership rate: 92.1% (2000); Median home value: $74,300 (2000); Median age of housing: 31 years (2000).
Transportation: Commute to work: 94.4% car, 0.0% public transportation, 1.7% walk, 3.3% work from home (2000); Travel time to work: 15.5% less than 15 minutes, 31.6% 15 to 30 minutes, 43.7% 30 to 45 minutes, 3.4% 45 to 60 minutes, 5.7% 60 minutes or more (2000)

GRAND RAPIDS (town). Covers a land area of 20.776 square miles and a water area of 0.211 square miles. Located at 44.36° N. Lat.; 89.77° W. Long.
Population: 7,801 (2000); Race: 98.3% White, 0.2% Black, 1.2% Asian, 0.1% American Indian and Alaska Native, 0.9% Hispanic of any race, 0.3% two or more races (2000); Density: 375.5 persons per square mile (2000); Age: 28.8% under 18, 7.6% over 64 (2000); Marriage status: 20.0% never married, 71.6% now married, 2.9% widowed, 5.5% divorced (2000); Foreign born: 1.7% (2000); Ancestry (includes multiple ancestries): 51.7% German, 15.3% Polish, 13.0% Irish, 9.9% Norwegian, 7.2% English (2000).
Economy: Single-family building permits issued: 31 (2001) / 37 (2000); Multi-family building permits issued: 0 (2001) / 0 (2000); Employment by occupation: 12.4% management, 20.1% professional, 12.5% services, 25.3% sales, 0.2% farming, 9.8% construction, 19.7% production (2000).
Income: Per capita income: $25,331 (2000); Median household income: $62,515 (2000); Poverty rate: 2.5% (2000).
Taxes: Total city taxes per capita: $55 (1997); City property taxes per capita: $51 (1997).
Education: High school graduation rate: 94.7% (2000); College graduation rate: 27.6% (2000).
Housing: Homeownership rate: 94.5% (2000); Median home value: $108,800 (2000); Median rent: $456 per month (2000); Median age of housing: 24 years (2000).
Transportation: Commute to work: 95.8% car, 0.0% public transportation, 0.6% walk, 3.3% work from home (2000); Travel time to work: 48.4% less than 15 minutes, 39.0% 15 to 30 minutes, 7.5% 30 to 45 minutes, 3.0% 45 to 60 minutes, 2.1% 60 minutes or more (2000)

HANSEN (town). Covers a land area of 33.851 square miles and a water area of 0.005 square miles. Located at 44.46° N. Lat.; 90.02° W. Long.
Population: 707 (2000); Race: 98.4% White, 0.8% Black, 0.0% Asian, 0.0% American Indian and Alaska Native, 0.9% Hispanic of any race, 0.8% two or more races (2000); Density: 20.9 persons per square mile (2000); Age: 29.5% under 18, 11.6% over 64 (2000); Marriage status: 22.6% never married, 66.0% now married, 4.6% widowed, 6.8% divorced (2000); Foreign born: 0.1% (2000); Ancestry (includes multiple ancestries): 64.4% German, 9.8% Norwegian, 9.3% Polish, 9.0% Irish, 6.1% Dutch (2000).
Economy: Employment by occupation: 13.5% management, 12.5% professional, 10.1% services, 20.5% sales, 4.2% farming, 11.2% construction, 28.1% production (2000).
Income: Per capita income: $16,159 (2000); Median household income: $41,932 (2000); Poverty rate: 5.3% (2000).
Taxes: Total city taxes per capita: $99 (1997); City property taxes per capita: $98 (1997).
Education: High school graduation rate: 84.6% (2000); College graduation rate: 9.0% (2000).
Housing: Homeownership rate: 92.4% (2000); Median home value: $74,200 (2000); Median rent: $313 per month (2000); Median age of housing: 48 years (2000).
Transportation: Commute to work: 87.1% car, 0.0% public transportation, 4.5% walk, 8.1% work from home (2000); Travel time to work: 28.0% less than 15 minutes, 47.4% 15 to 30 minutes, 19.4% 30 to 45 minutes, 2.9% 45 to 60 minutes, 2.3% 60 minutes or more (2000)

HEWITT (village). Covers a land area of 0.806 square miles and a water area of 0 square miles. Located at 44.64° N. Lat.; 90.10° W. Long. Elevation is 1,260 feet.
Population: 670 (2000); Race: 100.0% White, 0.0% Black, 0.0% Asian, 0.0% American Indian and Alaska Native, 0.1% Hispanic of any race, 0.0% two or more races (2000); Density: 830.8 persons per square mile (2000); Age: 35.4% under 18, 7.8% over 64 (2000); Marriage status: 21.1% never married, 69.5% now married, 7.2% widowed, 2.1% divorced (2000); Foreign born: 0.3% (2000); Ancestry (includes multiple ancestries): 68.2% German, 11.6% Polish, 6.3% Norwegian, 5.4% Irish, 3.6% Other groups (2000).
Economy: Dairying; livestock; general farming. Agricultural research station to West. Single-family building permits issued: 2 (2001) / 1 (2000); Multi-family building permits issued: 0 (2001) / 0 (2000); Employment by occupation: 11.0% management, 21.5% professional, 14.6% services, 28.7% sales, 0.5% farming, 9.2% construction, 14.4% production (2000).
Income: Per capita income: $19,234 (2000); Median household income: $53,295 (2000); Poverty rate: 2.9% (2000).
Taxes: Total city taxes per capita: $35 (1997); City property taxes per capita: $32 (1997).
Education: High school graduation rate: 89.1% (2000); College graduation rate: 17.5% (2000).
Housing: Homeownership rate: 90.7% (2000); Median home value: $106,600 (2000); Median rent: $275 per month (2000); Median age of housing: 20 years (2000).

Transportation: Commute to work: 95.6% car, 0.0% public transportation, 0.5% walk, 3.3% work from home (2000); Travel time to work: 45.1% less than 15 minutes, 46.7% 15 to 30 minutes, 4.5% 30 to 45 minutes, 3.4% 45 to 60 minutes, 0.3% 60 minutes or more (2000)

HILES (town). Covers a land area of 34.839 square miles and a water area of 0.484 square miles. Located at 44.37° N. Lat.; 90.24° W. Long.
Population: 188 (2000); Race: 97.3% White, 0.0% Black, 0.0% Asian, 0.5% American Indian and Alaska Native, 1.1% Hispanic of any race, 1.1% two or more races (2000); Density: 5.4 persons per square mile (2000); Age: 33.0% under 18, 16.2% over 64 (2000); Marriage status: 13.1% never married, 75.4% now married, 5.4% widowed, 6.2% divorced (2000); Foreign born: 3.2% (2000); Ancestry (includes multiple ancestries): 50.3% German, 18.4% United States or American, 10.8% Irish, 7.6% Polish, 4.3% English (2000).
Economy: Employment by occupation: 16.4% management, 12.3% professional, 9.6% services, 30.1% sales, 11.0% farming, 8.2% construction, 12.3% production (2000).
Income: Per capita income: $15,054 (2000); Median household income: $38,000 (2000); Poverty rate: 8.6% (2000).
Taxes: Total city taxes per capita: $216 (1997); City property taxes per capita: $216 (1997).
Education: High school graduation rate: 81.5% (2000); College graduation rate: 13.4% (2000).
Housing: Homeownership rate: 85.3% (2000); Median home value: $71,100 (2000); Median rent: $275 per month (2000); Median age of housing: 60+ years (2000).
Transportation: Commute to work: 81.3% car, 0.0% public transportation, 8.0% walk, 8.0% work from home (2000); Travel time to work: 26.1% less than 15 minutes, 20.3% 15 to 30 minutes, 47.8% 30 to 45 minutes, 5.8% 45 to 60 minutes, 0.0% 60 minutes or more (2000)

LAKE WAZEECHA (CDP). Covers a land area of 3.755 square miles and a water area of 0.194 square miles. Located at 44.37° N. Lat.; 89.75° W. Long.
Population: 2,659 (2000); Race: 99.3% White, 0.0% Black, 0.2% Asian, 0.0% American Indian and Alaska Native, 1.0% Hispanic of any race, 0.5% two or more races (2000); Density: 708.0 persons per square mile (2000); Age: 25.4% under 18, 10.8% over 64 (2000); Marriage status: 20.4% never married, 69.9% now married, 3.6% widowed, 6.1% divorced (2000); Foreign born: 0.6% (2000); Ancestry (includes multiple ancestries): 55.6% German, 17.5% Polish, 17.4% Irish, 8.2% Norwegian, 7.6% French (except Basque) (2000).
Economy: Employment by occupation: 9.1% management, 20.4% professional, 15.7% services, 25.6% sales, 0.0% farming, 12.3% construction, 17.0% production (2000).
Income: Per capita income: $22,094 (2000); Median household income: $54,261 (2000); Poverty rate: 4.5% (2000).
Education: High school graduation rate: 94.7% (2000); College graduation rate: 18.0% (2000).
Housing: Homeownership rate: 91.1% (2000); Median home value: $105,000 (2000); Median rent: $480 per month (2000); Median age of housing: 25 years (2000).
Transportation: Commute to work: 96.6% car, 0.0% public transportation, 1.5% walk, 1.9% work from home (2000); Travel time to work: 48.7% less than 15 minutes, 38.7% 15 to 30 minutes, 7.3% 30 to 45 minutes, 3.4% 45 to 60 minutes, 2.0% 60 minutes or more (2000)

LINCOLN (town). Covers a land area of 34.223 square miles and a water area of 0.014 square miles. Located at 44.64° N. Lat.; 90.24° W. Long.
Population: 1,554 (2000); Race: 99.3% White, 0.0% Black, 0.3% Asian, 0.1% American Indian and Alaska Native, 0.3% Hispanic of any race, 0.2% two or more races (2000); Density: 45.4 persons per square mile (2000); Age: 28.9% under 18, 10.0% over 64 (2000); Marriage status: 18.8% never married, 72.1% now married, 3.8% widowed, 5.2% divorced (2000); Foreign born: 0.7% (2000); Ancestry (includes multiple ancestries): 56.6% German, 10.7% Norwegian, 7.8% Polish, 6.6% Irish, 4.2% United States or American (2000).
Economy: Single-family building permits issued: 11 (2001) / 3 (2000); Multi-family building permits issued: 0 (2001) / 0 (2000); Employment by occupation: 18.3% management, 23.2% professional, 9.7% services, 20.3% sales, 2.1% farming, 10.8% construction, 15.6% production (2000).
Income: Per capita income: $27,617 (2000); Median household income: $53,194 (2000); Poverty rate: 3.8% (2000).
Taxes: Total city taxes per capita: $81 (1997); City property taxes per capita: $77 (1997).
Education: High school graduation rate: 84.2% (2000); College graduation rate: 26.1% (2000).
Housing: Homeownership rate: 87.6% (2000); Median home value: $110,900 (2000); Median rent: $338 per month (2000); Median age of housing: 30 years (2000).
Transportation: Commute to work: 86.4% car, 0.5% public transportation, 2.4% walk, 10.0% work from home (2000); Travel time to work: 47.8% less than 15 minutes, 41.5% 15 to 30 minutes, 3.8% 30 to 45 minutes, 4.1% 45 to 60 minutes, 2.8% 60 minutes or more (2000)

MARSHFIELD (city). Covers a land area of 12.721 square miles and a water area of 0.027 square miles. Located at 44.66° N. Lat.; 90.17° W. Long. Elevation is 1,280 feet.
History: Marshfield developed as a market center in the northern dairy belt. The first settlement here began in 1868 with the tavern built by Louis and Frank Rivers. In 1872 the Wisconsin Central Railroad established a depot in an empty boxcar in front of the Rivers' tavern. Other railroads and more settlers came, building a sawmill, furniture factory, boiler works and harness shops, but all was destroyed by a fire in 1887. Marshfield was rebuilt a few years later, and soon cheese making and dairying replaced lumbering.
Population: 18,800 (2000); Race: 96.4% White, 1.1% Black, 1.4% Asian, 0.3% American Indian and Alaska Native, 1.1% Hispanic of any race, 0.5% two or more races (2000); Density: 1,477.9 persons per square mile (2000); Age: 22.9% under 18, 17.8% over 64 (2000); Marriage status: 25.3% never married, 56.2% now married, 8.9% widowed, 9.6% divorced (2000); Foreign born: 2.8% (2000); Ancestry (includes multiple ancestries): 55.9% German, 8.8% Irish, 7.9% Norwegian, 7.5% English, 6.4% Polish (2000).
Vital Statistics: Birth rate: 119.7 per 10,000 population (1998)
Economy: Single-family building permits issued: 41 (2001) / 40 (2000); Multi-family building permits issued: 36 (2001) / 32 (2000); Employment by occupation: 9.8% management, 21.2% professional, 16.3% services, 25.4% sales, 0.5% farming, 9.3% construction, 17.6% production (2000).
Income: Per capita income: $21,965 (2000); Median household income: $37,248 (2000); Poverty rate: 6.6% (2000).
Taxes: Total city taxes per capita: $406 (2000); City property taxes per capita: $361 (2000).
Education: High school graduation rate: 82.8% (2000); College graduation rate: 21.1% (2000).

School District(s)

Marshfield (PK-12)
2000 Enrollment: 4,086 715-387-1101

Two-year College(s)

Saint Josephs Hospital Histologic Technician Progr (Private, Not-for-profit, Roman Catholic)
2001 Enrollment: n/a

Housing: Homeownership rate: 61.6% (2000); Median home value: $83,300 (2000); Median rent: $380 per month (2000); Median age of housing: 32 years (2000).
Hospitals: Norwood Health Center (64 beds); Saint Joseph's Hospital (524 beds)
Safety: Violent crime rate: 9.0 per 10,000 population; Property crime rate: 343.3 per 10,000 population (2001).
Newspapers: Marshfield News-Herald (7 x week)
Transportation: Commute to work: 90.1% car, 0.8% public transportation, 5.3% walk, 2.6% work from home (2000); Travel time to work: 73.9% less than 15 minutes, 17.6% 15 to 30 minutes, 3.9% 30 to 45 minutes, 3.1% 45 to 60 minutes, 1.6% 60 minutes or more (2000)
Additional Information Contacts
Marshfield Chamber of Commerce 715-384-3454

MARSHFIELD (town). Covers a land area of 16.612 square miles and a water area of 0.013 square miles. Located at 44.64° N. Lat.; 90.11° W. Long. Elevation is 1,280 feet.
Population: 811 (2000); Race: 99.7% White, 0.0% Black, 0.3% Asian, 0.0% American Indian and Alaska Native, 0.4% Hispanic of any race, 0.0% two or more races (2000); Density: 48.8 persons per square mile (2000); Age: 23.4% under 18, 13.3% over 64 (2000); Marriage status: 23.2% never married, 69.5% now married, 3.5% widowed, 3.7% divorced (2000); Foreign born: 0.5% (2000); Ancestry (includes multiple ancestries): 69.0% German, 5.4% Irish, 4.5% Norwegian, 4.3% Polish, 3.2% Dutch (2000).
Economy: Single-family building permits issued: 5 (2001) / 5 (2000); Multi-family building permits issued: 0 (2001) / 0 (2000); Employment by occupation: 17.3% management, 12.6% professional, 8.6% services, 27.0% sales, 1.3% farming, 12.8% construction, 20.4% production (2000).
Income: Per capita income: $21,316 (2000); Median household income: $46,750 (2000); Poverty rate: 3.3% (2000).

Taxes: Total city taxes per capita: $109 (2000); City property taxes per capita: $105 (2000).
Education: High school graduation rate: 81.3% (2000); College graduation rate: 11.7% (2000).
Housing: Homeownership rate: 88.8% (2000); Median home value: $87,400 (2000); Median rent: $400 per month (2000); Median age of housing: 36 years (2000).
Transportation: Commute to work: 91.3% car, 0.0% public transportation, 1.3% walk, 6.5% work from home (2000); Travel time to work: 51.6% less than 15 minutes, 37.9% 15 to 30 minutes, 5.0% 30 to 45 minutes, 2.9% 45 to 60 minutes, 2.6% 60 minutes or more (2000)

MILLADORE (village). Covers a land area of 1.001 square miles and a water area of 0 square miles. Located at 44.60° N. Lat.; 89.85° W. Long. Elevation is 1,195 feet.
Population: 268 (2000); Race: 98.4% White, 1.6% Black, 0.0% Asian, 0.0% American Indian and Alaska Native, 0.0% Hispanic of any race, 0.0% two or more races (2000); Density: 267.6 persons per square mile (2000); Age: 21.1% under 18, 15.1% over 64 (2000); Marriage status: 25.7% never married, 55.1% now married, 11.7% widowed, 7.5% divorced (2000); Foreign born: 0.8% (2000); Ancestry (includes multiple ancestries): 49.0% German, 19.9% Polish, 16.3% Czech, 9.2% Irish, 8.4% Dutch (2000).
Economy: Single-family building permits issued: 2 (2001) / 1 (2000); Multi-family building permits issued: 0 (2001) / 0 (2000); Employment by occupation: 8.4% management, 7.7% professional, 14.7% services, 23.8% sales, 5.6% farming, 20.3% construction, 19.6% production (2000).
Income: Per capita income: $19,235 (2000); Median household income: $46,458 (2000); Poverty rate: 4.1% (2000).
Taxes: Total city taxes per capita: $70 (1997); City property taxes per capita: $63 (1997).
Education: High school graduation rate: 84.6% (2000); College graduation rate: 8.3% (2000).
Housing: Homeownership rate: 78.2% (2000); Median home value: $70,300 (2000); Median rent: $267 per month (2000); Median age of housing: 41 years (2000).
Transportation: Commute to work: 89.5% car, 0.0% public transportation, 6.3% walk, 4.2% work from home (2000); Travel time to work: 30.7% less than 15 minutes, 21.9% 15 to 30 minutes, 35.8% 30 to 45 minutes, 8.0% 45 to 60 minutes, 3.6% 60 minutes or more (2000)

MILLADORE (town). Covers a land area of 34.013 square miles and a water area of 0.020 square miles. Located at 44.63° N. Lat.; 89.90° W. Long. Elevation is 1,195 feet.
History: Near Milladore was the soapstone mine, one of the few in the midwest, operated between 1926 and 1931 by the American Talc Company. The soapstone, because of its acid resistance, was used in the manufacture of tubs and sinks for chemical laboratories.
Population: 706 (2000); Race: 99.7% White, 0.0% Black, 0.0% Asian, 0.0% American Indian and Alaska Native, 0.3% Hispanic of any race, 0.3% two or more races (2000); Density: 20.8 persons per square mile (2000); Age: 27.3% under 18, 8.9% over 64 (2000); Marriage status: 26.6% never married, 64.5% now married, 1.2% widowed, 7.7% divorced (2000); Foreign born: 0.0% (2000); Ancestry (includes multiple ancestries): 71.4% German, 12.3% Polish, 7.2% Czech, 6.0% Norwegian, 6.0% Irish (2000).
Economy: In dairy belt. Employment by occupation: 21.3% management, 7.2% professional, 6.0% services, 17.4% sales, 5.3% farming, 13.7% construction, 29.2% production (2000).
Income: Per capita income: $18,410 (2000); Median household income: $50,104 (2000); Poverty rate: 3.6% (2000).
Taxes: Total city taxes per capita: $33 (1997); City property taxes per capita: $32 (1997).
Education: High school graduation rate: 86.7% (2000); College graduation rate: 7.5% (2000).
Housing: Homeownership rate: 90.7% (2000); Median home value: $72,000 (2000); Median rent: $313 per month (2000); Median age of housing: 47 years (2000).
Transportation: Commute to work: 77.0% car, 0.5% public transportation, 6.3% walk, 15.8% work from home (2000); Travel time to work: 25.7% less than 15 minutes, 28.5% 15 to 30 minutes, 30.9% 30 to 45 minutes, 5.2% 45 to 60 minutes, 9.7% 60 minutes or more (2000)

NEKOOSA (city). Covers a land area of 3.392 square miles and a water area of 0.011 square miles. Located at 44.31° N. Lat.; 89.90° W. Long. Elevation is 955 feet.
History: Settled 1892, incorporated 1926.
Population: 2,590 (2000); Race: 97.8% White, 0.0% Black, 0.4% Asian, 0.0% American Indian and Alaska Native, 2.4% Hispanic of any race, 0.3% two or more races (2000); Density: 763.5 persons per square mile (2000); Age: 27.2% under 18, 17.2% over 64 (2000); Marriage status: 21.0% never married, 61.7% now married, 9.5% widowed, 7.7% divorced (2000); Foreign born: 2.4% (2000); Ancestry (includes multiple ancestries): 44.3% German, 16.2% Polish, 10.8% Irish, 7.9% Norwegian, 7.3% English (2000).
Economy: In dairy area; paper products. State nursery across river to Northeast. Single-family building permits issued: 6 (2001) / 6 (2000); Multi-family building permits issued: 0 (2001) / 0 (2000); Employment by occupation: 6.1% management, 12.4% professional, 18.6% services, 21.9% sales, 0.5% farming, 10.9% construction, 29.5% production (2000).
Income: Per capita income: $17,063 (2000); Median household income: $39,375 (2000); Poverty rate: 9.7% (2000).
Taxes: Total city taxes per capita: $291 (1997); City property taxes per capita: $288 (1997).
Education: High school graduation rate: 88.1% (2000); College graduation rate: 11.2% (2000).

School District(s)

Nekoosa (KG-12)
2000 Enrollment: 1,533 715-886-8000
Housing: Homeownership rate: 73.9% (2000); Median home value: $62,000 (2000); Median rent: $339 per month (2000); Median age of housing: 43 years (2000).
Transportation: Commute to work: 91.9% car, 0.0% public transportation, 4.4% walk, 3.3% work from home (2000); Travel time to work: 46.2% less than 15 minutes, 36.4% 15 to 30 minutes, 9.4% 30 to 45 minutes, 4.0% 45 to 60 minutes, 3.9% 60 minutes or more (2000)

PITTSVILLE (city). Covers a land area of 2.000 square miles and a water area of 0.010 square miles. Located at 44.44° N. Lat.; 90.12° W. Long. Elevation is 1,032 feet.
History: Pittsville began as a sawmill town.
Population: 866 (2000); Race: 96.6% White, 1.2% Black, 0.0% Asian, 0.5% American Indian and Alaska Native, 0.0% Hispanic of any race, 1.8% two or more races (2000); Density: 432.9 persons per square mile (2000); Age: 29.1% under 18, 12.5% over 64 (2000); Marriage status: 19.9% never married, 62.1% now married, 7.7% widowed, 10.2% divorced (2000); Foreign born: 0.4% (2000); Ancestry (includes multiple ancestries): 48.3% German, 12.0% Polish, 11.0% Norwegian, 9.8% English, 7.6% Irish (2000).
Economy: Single-family building permits issued: 3 (2001) / 3 (2000); Multi-family building permits issued: 0 (2001) / 0 (2000); Employment by occupation: 7.7% management, 14.7% professional, 15.6% services, 21.4% sales, 4.2% farming, 13.1% construction, 23.3% production (2000).
Income: Per capita income: $16,257 (2000); Median household income: $36,750 (2000); Poverty rate: 5.4% (2000).
Taxes: Total city taxes per capita: $169 (1997); City property taxes per capita: $162 (1997).
Education: High school graduation rate: 79.5% (2000); College graduation rate: 18.0% (2000).

School District(s)

Pittsville (PK-12)
2000 Enrollment: 829 715-884-6694
Housing: Homeownership rate: 72.2% (2000); Median home value: $63,400 (2000); Median rent: $309 per month (2000); Median age of housing: 40 years (2000).
Transportation: Commute to work: 90.3% car, 0.5% public transportation, 5.4% walk, 2.4% work from home (2000); Travel time to work: 32.0% less than 15 minutes, 36.3% 15 to 30 minutes, 21.8% 30 to 45 minutes, 6.3% 45 to 60 minutes, 3.6% 60 minutes or more (2000)

PORT EDWARDS (village). Covers a land area of 6.036 square miles and a water area of 1.251 square miles. Located at 44.34° N. Lat.; 89.85° W. Long. Elevation is 975 feet.
Population: 1,944 (2000); Race: 94.0% White, 0.7% Black, 3.3% Asian, 0.0% American Indian and Alaska Native, 0.3% Hispanic of any race, 1.8% two or more races (2000); Density: 322.1 persons per square mile (2000); Age: 26.3% under 18, 22.0% over 64 (2000); Marriage status: 19.3% never married, 62.1% now married, 10.4% widowed, 8.3% divorced (2000); Foreign born: 3.6% (2000); Ancestry (includes multiple ancestries): 47.5% German, 13.0% Polish, 9.6% Irish, 9.0% English, 8.2% Norwegian (2000).
Economy: Single-family building permits issued: 2 (2001) / 2 (2000); Multi-family building permits issued: 0 (2001) / 0 (2000); Employment by occupation: 10.2% management, 18.4% professional, 15.6% services, 20.7% sales, 1.1% farming, 4.7% construction, 29.4% production (2000).

Income: Per capita income: $20,750 (2000); Median household income: $48,850 (2000); Poverty rate: 7.9% (2000).
Taxes: Total city taxes per capita: $394 (1997); City property taxes per capita: $391 (1997).
Education: High school graduation rate: 88.8% (2000); College graduation rate: 23.1% (2000).

School District(s)

Port Edwards (KG-12)
2000 Enrollment: 515 715-887-9000

Housing: Homeownership rate: 85.0% (2000); Median home value: $83,500 (2000); Median rent: $417 per month (2000); Median age of housing: 44 years (2000).
Transportation: Commute to work: 93.6% car, 0.0% public transportation, 3.2% walk, 2.7% work from home (2000); Travel time to work: 54.0% less than 15 minutes, 30.0% 15 to 30 minutes, 11.3% 30 to 45 minutes, 2.0% 45 to 60 minutes, 2.7% 60 minutes or more (2000)

PORT EDWARDS (town). Covers a land area of 38.617 square miles and a water area of 0.620 square miles. Located at 44.30° N. Lat.; 89.97° W. Long. Elevation is 975 feet.
History: Incorporated 1902.
Population: 1,446 (2000); Race: 92.6% White, 0.0% Black, 0.5% Asian, 2.9% American Indian and Alaska Native, 5.9% Hispanic of any race, 0.0% two or more races (2000); Density: 37.4 persons per square mile (2000); Age: 30.9% under 18, 9.4% over 64 (2000); Marriage status: 22.5% never married, 62.9% now married, 4.2% widowed, 10.3% divorced (2000); Foreign born: 3.5% (2000); Ancestry (includes multiple ancestries): 45.0% German, 13.9% Polish, 10.7% Irish, 9.5% Other groups, 9.5% Norwegian (2000).
Economy: Railroad junction in timber and dairy region; paper, caustic soda, potash manufacturing. Power dam. Single-family building permits issued: 4 (2001) / 10 (2000); Multi-family building permits issued: 0 (2001) / 0 (2000); Employment by occupation: 6.5% management, 8.7% professional, 15.2% services, 23.1% sales, 2.2% farming, 13.9% construction, 30.6% production (2000).
Income: Per capita income: $20,020 (2000); Median household income: $43,804 (2000); Poverty rate: 6.1% (2000).
Taxes: Total city taxes per capita: $16 (1997); City property taxes per capita: $14 (1997).
Education: High school graduation rate: 83.7% (2000); College graduation rate: 7.7% (2000).
Housing: Homeownership rate: 87.1% (2000); Median home value: $81,100 (2000); Median rent: $381 per month (2000); Median age of housing: 27 years (2000).
Transportation: Commute to work: 96.3% car, 0.3% public transportation, 1.5% walk, 1.6% work from home (2000); Travel time to work: 38.4% less than 15 minutes, 43.8% 15 to 30 minutes, 10.3% 30 to 45 minutes, 5.5% 45 to 60 minutes, 2.1% 60 minutes or more (2000)

REMINGTON (town). Covers a land area of 69.360 square miles and a water area of 2.176 square miles. Located at 44.30° N. Lat.; 90.16° W. Long.
Population: 305 (2000); Race: 94.2% White, 0.0% Black, 1.4% Asian, 2.7% American Indian and Alaska Native, 0.0% Hispanic of any race, 1.7% two or more races (2000); Density: 4.4 persons per square mile (2000); Age: 23.5% under 18, 13.9% over 64 (2000); Marriage status: 21.4% never married, 62.4% now married, 9.4% widowed, 6.8% divorced (2000); Foreign born: 3.4% (2000); Ancestry (includes multiple ancestries): 32.7% German, 9.5% Polish, 8.2% French (except Basque), 7.1% Other groups, 5.1% United States or American (2000).
Economy: Single-family building permits issued: 1 (2001) / 3 (2000); Multi-family building permits issued: 0 (2001) / 0 (2000); Employment by occupation: 16.0% management, 15.3% professional, 14.5% services, 16.8% sales, 0.8% farming, 9.2% construction, 27.5% production (2000).
Income: Per capita income: $16,571 (2000); Median household income: $37,188 (2000); Poverty rate: 7.1% (2000).
Taxes: Total city taxes per capita: $99 (1997); City property taxes per capita: $95 (1997).
Education: High school graduation rate: 74.8% (2000); College graduation rate: 8.9% (2000).
Housing: Homeownership rate: 76.8% (2000); Median home value: $44,100 (2000); Median rent: $325 per month (2000); Median age of housing: 37 years (2000).
Transportation: Commute to work: 82.0% car, 0.0% public transportation, 10.9% walk, 5.5% work from home (2000); Travel time to work: 42.1% less than 15 minutes, 14.0% 15 to 30 minutes, 33.9% 30 to 45 minutes, 4.1% 45 to 60 minutes, 5.8% 60 minutes or more (2000)

RICHFIELD (town). Covers a land area of 34.789 square miles and a water area of 0.040 square miles. Located at 44.55° N. Lat.; 90.15° W. Long.
Population: 1,523 (2000); Race: 100.0% White, 0.0% Black, 0.0% Asian, 0.0% American Indian and Alaska Native, 0.1% Hispanic of any race, 0.0% two or more races (2000); Density: 43.8 persons per square mile (2000); Age: 27.8% under 18, 15.5% over 64 (2000); Marriage status: 23.5% never married, 61.3% now married, 8.4% widowed, 6.9% divorced (2000); Foreign born: 0.5% (2000); Ancestry (includes multiple ancestries): 52.0% German, 8.1% Polish, 5.5% English, 5.4% Irish, 4.5% Norwegian (2000).
Economy: Single-family building permits issued: 15 (2001) / 6 (2000); Multi-family building permits issued: 0 (2001) / 0 (2000); Employment by occupation: 14.4% management, 17.2% professional, 13.9% services, 21.1% sales, 2.4% farming, 13.2% construction, 17.6% production (2000).
Income: Per capita income: $18,775 (2000); Median household income: $47,188 (2000); Poverty rate: 8.5% (2000).
Taxes: Total city taxes per capita: $73 (2000); City property taxes per capita: $71 (2000).
Education: High school graduation rate: 80.9% (2000); College graduation rate: 13.1% (2000).
Housing: Homeownership rate: 84.7% (2000); Median home value: $91,900 (2000); Median rent: $372 per month (2000); Median age of housing: 24 years (2000).
Transportation: Commute to work: 87.6% car, 0.0% public transportation, 3.2% walk, 8.1% work from home (2000); Travel time to work: 28.3% less than 15 minutes, 51.1% 15 to 30 minutes, 15.2% 30 to 45 minutes, 0.8% 45 to 60 minutes, 4.7% 60 minutes or more (2000)

ROCK (town). Covers a land area of 34.504 square miles and a water area of 0.044 square miles. Located at 44.54° N. Lat.; 90.24° W. Long.
Population: 856 (2000); Race: 100.0% White, 0.0% Black, 0.0% Asian, 0.0% American Indian and Alaska Native, 0.0% Hispanic of any race, 0.0% two or more races (2000); Density: 24.8 persons per square mile (2000); Age: 28.4% under 18, 9.9% over 64 (2000); Marriage status: 20.9% never married, 67.8% now married, 5.1% widowed, 6.2% divorced (2000); Foreign born: 1.1% (2000); Ancestry (includes multiple ancestries): 56.0% German, 9.0% Norwegian, 7.0% Polish, 4.8% English, 3.9% Irish (2000).
Economy: Single-family building permits issued: 41 (2001) / 41 (2000); Multi-family building permits issued: 60 (2001) / 32 (2000); Employment by occupation: 9.9% management, 21.4% professional, 8.5% services, 18.1% sales, 2.1% farming, 16.4% construction, 23.7% production (2000).
Income: Per capita income: $18,783 (2000); Median household income: $45,114 (2000); Poverty rate: 5.1% (2000).
Taxes: Total city taxes per capita: $72 (1997); City property taxes per capita: $68 (1997).
Education: High school graduation rate: 81.4% (2000); College graduation rate: 18.4% (2000).
Housing: Homeownership rate: 90.6% (2000); Median home value: $75,400 (2000); Median rent: $413 per month (2000); Median age of housing: 29 years (2000).
Transportation: Commute to work: 92.8% car, 1.0% public transportation, 3.8% walk, 1.4% work from home (2000); Travel time to work: 18.0% less than 15 minutes, 61.9% 15 to 30 minutes, 13.6% 30 to 45 minutes, 1.0% 45 to 60 minutes, 5.6% 60 minutes or more (2000)

RUDOLPH (village). Covers a land area of 1.089 square miles and a water area of 0 square miles. Located at 44.49° N. Lat.; 89.80° W. Long. Elevation is 1,138 feet.
Population: 423 (2000); Race: 98.0% White, 0.0% Black, 0.0% Asian, 0.0% American Indian and Alaska Native, 0.0% Hispanic of any race, 2.0% two or more races (2000); Density: 388.3 persons per square mile (2000); Age: 24.5% under 18, 13.9% over 64 (2000); Marriage status: 19.6% never married, 66.7% now married, 6.7% widowed, 7.0% divorced (2000); Foreign born: 0.0% (2000); Ancestry (includes multiple ancestries): 51.8% German, 30.1% Polish, 14.4% Dutch, 8.8% Irish, 4.3% Norwegian (2000).
Economy: Single-family building permits issued: 0 (2001) / 2 (2000); Multi-family building permits issued: 0 (2001) / 0 (2000); Employment by occupation: 7.7% management, 14.4% professional, 10.1% services, 29.8% sales, 0.0% farming, 14.4% construction, 23.6% production (2000).
Income: Per capita income: $18,895 (2000); Median household income: $41,125 (2000); Poverty rate: 3.0% (2000).
Taxes: Total city taxes per capita: $27 (1997); City property taxes per capita: $25 (1997).
Education: High school graduation rate: 85.7% (2000); College graduation rate: 18.6% (2000).

Housing: Homeownership rate: 72.9% (2000); Median home value: $80,300 (2000); Median rent: $378 per month (2000); Median age of housing: 29 years (2000).
Transportation: Commute to work: 90.2% car, 0.0% public transportation, 5.9% walk, 2.9% work from home (2000); Travel time to work: 40.7% less than 15 minutes, 39.7% 15 to 30 minutes, 11.6% 30 to 45 minutes, 8.0% 45 to 60 minutes, 0.0% 60 minutes or more (2000)

RUDOLPH (town). Covers a land area of 29.691 square miles and a water area of 0.038 square miles. Located at 44.47° N. Lat.; 89.79° W. Long. Elevation is 1,138 feet.
Population: 1,161 (2000); Race: 97.5% White, 0.0% Black, 2.5% Asian, 0.0% American Indian and Alaska Native, 0.1% Hispanic of any race, 0.0% two or more races (2000); Density: 39.1 persons per square mile (2000); Age: 27.8% under 18, 12.3% over 64 (2000); Marriage status: 21.4% never married, 70.5% now married, 3.3% widowed, 4.8% divorced (2000); Foreign born: 1.6% (2000); Ancestry (includes multiple ancestries): 53.2% German, 20.7% Polish, 7.1% Irish, 6.7% Norwegian, 6.5% Dutch (2000).
Economy: Dairying. Manufacturing of cheese. Single-family building permits issued: 0 (2001) / 3 (2000); Multi-family building permits issued: 2 (2001) / 0 (2000); Employment by occupation: 7.3% management, 14.3% professional, 9.5% services, 20.3% sales, 2.3% farming, 13.5% construction, 32.8% production (2000).
Income: Per capita income: $20,284 (2000); Median household income: $50,852 (2000); Poverty rate: 6.4% (2000).
Taxes: Total city taxes per capita: $67 (1997); City property taxes per capita: $65 (1997).
Education: High school graduation rate: 85.1% (2000); College graduation rate: 11.4% (2000).
Housing: Homeownership rate: 86.3% (2000); Median home value: $84,300 (2000); Median rent: $367 per month (2000); Median age of housing: 38 years (2000).
Transportation: Commute to work: 95.3% car, 0.0% public transportation, 2.3% walk, 2.0% work from home (2000); Travel time to work: 32.5% less than 15 minutes, 48.2% 15 to 30 minutes, 14.9% 30 to 45 minutes, 2.1% 45 to 60 minutes, 2.4% 60 minutes or more (2000)

SARATOGA (town). Covers a land area of 49.412 square miles and a water area of 1.759 square miles. Located at 44.30° N. Lat.; 89.83° W. Long.
Population: 5,383 (2000); Race: 97.5% White, 0.5% Black, 0.0% Asian, 1.1% American Indian and Alaska Native, 0.5% Hispanic of any race, 0.7% two or more races (2000); Density: 108.9 persons per square mile (2000); Age: 26.5% under 18, 10.1% over 64 (2000); Marriage status: 20.7% never married, 64.7% now married, 4.1% widowed, 10.5% divorced (2000); Foreign born: 0.0% (2000); Ancestry (includes multiple ancestries): 48.7% German, 13.1% Polish, 11.6% Irish, 10.9% United States or American, 8.5% Norwegian (2000).
Economy: Single-family building permits issued: 25 (2001) / 15 (2000); Multi-family building permits issued: 0 (2001) / 0 (2000); Employment by occupation: 6.1% management, 10.5% professional, 17.2% services, 23.0% sales, 0.0% farming, 11.7% construction, 31.5% production (2000).
Income: Per capita income: $18,761 (2000); Median household income: $48,500 (2000); Poverty rate: 5.9% (2000).
Taxes: Total city taxes per capita: $4 (1997); City property taxes per capita: $0 (1997).
Education: High school graduation rate: 86.8% (2000); College graduation rate: 10.9% (2000).
Housing: Homeownership rate: 90.5% (2000); Median home value: $89,800 (2000); Median rent: $338 per month (2000); Median age of housing: 22 years (2000).
Transportation: Commute to work: 90.7% car, 0.0% public transportation, 4.5% walk, 4.1% work from home (2000); Travel time to work: 29.9% less than 15 minutes, 55.5% 15 to 30 minutes, 6.5% 30 to 45 minutes, 3.3% 45 to 60 minutes, 4.8% 60 minutes or more (2000)

SENECA (town). Covers a land area of 32.232 square miles and a water area of 0.187 square miles. Located at 44.40° N. Lat.; 89.95° W. Long.
Population: 1,202 (2000); Race: 91.7% White, 0.0% Black, 2.5% Asian, 5.2% American Indian and Alaska Native, 0.0% Hispanic of any race, 0.6% two or more races (2000); Density: 37.3 persons per square mile (2000); Age: 25.7% under 18, 10.0% over 64 (2000); Marriage status: 22.9% never married, 67.9% now married, 4.1% widowed, 5.1% divorced (2000); Foreign born: 2.1% (2000); Ancestry (includes multiple ancestries): 60.9% German, 16.4% Polish, 7.9% Other groups, 7.0% Irish, 6.8% English (2000).
Economy: Single-family building permits issued: 6 (2001) / 3 (2000); Multi-family building permits issued: 0 (2001) / 0 (2000); Employment by occupation: 13.1% management, 9.8% professional, 12.4% services, 20.9% sales, 2.2% farming, 14.6% construction, 27.2% production (2000).
Income: Per capita income: $21,833 (2000); Median household income: $54,118 (2000); Poverty rate: 6.0% (2000).
Taxes: Total city taxes per capita: $40 (1997); City property taxes per capita: $37 (1997).
Education: High school graduation rate: 88.1% (2000); College graduation rate: 9.9% (2000).
Housing: Homeownership rate: 91.2% (2000); Median home value: $100,000 (2000); Median rent: $410 per month (2000); Median age of housing: 28 years (2000).
Transportation: Commute to work: 93.1% car, 0.3% public transportation, 1.7% walk, 4.6% work from home (2000); Travel time to work: 41.4% less than 15 minutes, 41.0% 15 to 30 minutes, 10.3% 30 to 45 minutes, 3.7% 45 to 60 minutes, 3.6% 60 minutes or more (2000)

SHERRY (town). Covers a land area of 35.258 square miles and a water area of 0.122 square miles. Located at 44.57° N. Lat.; 89.89° W. Long. Elevation is 1,150 feet.
Population: 809 (2000); Race: 97.2% White, 0.0% Black, 0.0% Asian, 1.2% American Indian and Alaska Native, 2.1% Hispanic of any race, 0.0% two or more races (2000); Density: 22.9 persons per square mile (2000); Age: 32.5% under 18, 9.5% over 64 (2000); Marriage status: 28.8% never married, 60.9% now married, 3.8% widowed, 6.5% divorced (2000); Foreign born: 0.0% (2000); Ancestry (includes multiple ancestries): 57.1% German, 16.6% Polish, 6.3% Dutch, 5.6% Norwegian, 4.7% Irish (2000).
Economy: Single-family building permits issued: 4 (2001) / 2 (2000); Multi-family building permits issued: 0 (2001) / 0 (2000); Employment by occupation: 12.0% management, 12.5% professional, 11.1% services, 19.5% sales, 2.9% farming, 13.8% construction, 28.1% production (2000).
Income: Per capita income: $17,728 (2000); Median household income: $52,143 (2000); Poverty rate: 2.3% (2000).
Taxes: Total city taxes per capita: $71 (1997); City property taxes per capita: $70 (1997).
Education: High school graduation rate: 88.2% (2000); College graduation rate: 10.6% (2000).
Housing: Homeownership rate: 92.0% (2000); Median home value: $78,700 (2000); Median rent: $263 per month (2000); Median age of housing: 39 years (2000).
Transportation: Commute to work: 86.3% car, 0.0% public transportation, 3.2% walk, 10.5% work from home (2000); Travel time to work: 26.3% less than 15 minutes, 39.0% 15 to 30 minutes, 23.7% 30 to 45 minutes, 5.4% 45 to 60 minutes, 5.6% 60 minutes or more (2000)

SIGEL (town). Covers a land area of 35.532 square miles and a water area of 0.009 square miles. Located at 44.46° N. Lat.; 89.90° W. Long.
Population: 1,130 (2000); Race: 98.7% White, 0.0% Black, 0.0% Asian, 0.0% American Indian and Alaska Native, 0.4% Hispanic of any race, 1.3% two or more races (2000); Density: 31.8 persons per square mile (2000); Age: 23.4% under 18, 17.4% over 64 (2000); Marriage status: 17.1% never married, 70.2% now married, 3.6% widowed, 9.1% divorced (2000); Foreign born: 1.8% (2000); Ancestry (includes multiple ancestries): 53.4% German, 14.5% Polish, 7.1% Irish, 6.9% Dutch, 6.5% English (2000).
Economy: Single-family building permits issued: 5 (2001) / 8 (2000); Multi-family building permits issued: 0 (2001) / 0 (2000); Employment by occupation: 19.3% management, 9.0% professional, 11.9% services, 19.3% sales, 1.1% farming, 10.1% construction, 29.1% production (2000).
Income: Per capita income: $19,676 (2000); Median household income: $49,226 (2000); Poverty rate: 2.0% (2000).
Taxes: Total city taxes per capita: $48 (1997); City property taxes per capita: $47 (1997).
Education: High school graduation rate: 84.6% (2000); College graduation rate: 6.3% (2000).
Housing: Homeownership rate: 92.8% (2000); Median home value: $81,400 (2000); Median rent: $325 per month (2000); Median age of housing: 39 years (2000).
Transportation: Commute to work: 84.8% car, 0.0% public transportation, 2.4% walk, 12.5% work from home (2000); Travel time to work: 39.1% less than 15 minutes, 41.6% 15 to 30 minutes, 13.4% 30 to 45 minutes, 3.3% 45 to 60 minutes, 2.5% 60 minutes or more (2000)

VESPER (village). Covers a land area of 1.122 square miles and a water area of 0 square miles. Located at 44.48° N. Lat.; 89.96° W. Long. Elevation is 1,110 feet.
Population: 541 (2000); Race: 98.3% White, 0.0% Black, 0.0% Asian, 0.6% American Indian and Alaska Native, 0.0% Hispanic of any race, 1.1% two or

more races (2000); Density: 482.2 persons per square mile (2000); Age: 22.7% under 18, 14.1% over 64 (2000); Marriage status: 18.1% never married, 61.4% now married, 9.1% widowed, 11.4% divorced (2000); Foreign born: 0.4% (2000); Ancestry (includes multiple ancestries): 57.7% German, 11.2% Polish, 10.3% Irish, 7.4% Norwegian, 3.8% Czech (2000).
Economy: Single-family building permits issued: 1 (2001) / 2 (2000); Multi-family building permits issued: 4 (2001) / 0 (2000); Employment by occupation: 10.0% management, 11.8% professional, 17.7% services, 16.6% sales, 3.0% farming, 12.2% construction, 28.8% production (2000).
Income: Per capita income: $19,327 (2000); Median household income: $38,750 (2000); Poverty rate: 7.2% (2000).
Taxes: Total city taxes per capita: $84 (1997); City property taxes per capita: $75 (1997).
Education: High school graduation rate: 80.5% (2000); College graduation rate: 8.2% (2000).
Housing: Homeownership rate: 81.5% (2000); Median home value: $74,300 (2000); Median rent: $283 per month (2000); Median age of housing: 35 years (2000).
Transportation: Commute to work: 88.7% car, 0.0% public transportation, 5.6% walk, 5.3% work from home (2000); Travel time to work: 34.5% less than 15 minutes, 50.8% 15 to 30 minutes, 8.7% 30 to 45 minutes, 3.6% 45 to 60 minutes, 2.4% 60 minutes or more (2000)

WISCONSIN RAPIDS (city). Covers a land area of 13.263 square miles and a water area of 0.851 square miles. Located at 44.38° N. Lat.; 89.82° W. Long. Elevation is 1,028 feet.
History: Wisconsin Rapids was once two settlements, Centralia on the west bank of the Wisconsin River, and Grand Rapids on the east. In 1900 the two towns were consolidated under the name of Grand Rapids, but renamed Wisconsin Rapids in 1920. After the lumber industry declined, woodworking and paper mills became the mainstay of the economy.
Population: 18,435 (2000); Race: 93.7% White, 0.1% Black, 3.6% Asian, 1.1% American Indian and Alaska Native, 1.7% Hispanic of any race, 1.3% two or more races (2000); Density: 1,390.0 persons per square mile (2000); Age: 24.6% under 18, 20.1% over 64 (2000); Marriage status: 22.3% never married, 57.2% now married, 10.2% widowed, 10.3% divorced (2000); Foreign born: 2.9% (2000); Ancestry (includes multiple ancestries): 44.6% German, 11.9% Polish, 10.6% Irish, 7.3% Other groups, 7.3% Norwegian (2000).
Vital Statistics: Birth rate: 170.9 per 10,000 population (1998)
Economy: Single-family building permits issued: 13 (2001) / 18 (2000); Multi-family building permits issued: 10 (2001) / 96 (2000); Employment by occupation: 7.3% management, 16.0% professional, 17.5% services, 26.2% sales, 1.1% farming, 8.9% construction, 23.1% production (2000).
Income: Per capita income: $17,723 (2000); Median household income: $34,956 (2000); Poverty rate: 9.1% (2000).
Taxes: Total city taxes per capita: $478 (2000); City property taxes per capita: $444 (2000).
Education: High school graduation rate: 82.5% (2000); College graduation rate: 15.0% (2000).

Two-year College(s)

Mid-State Technical College (Public)
2001 Enrollment: 3,128 715-422-5300
2001 Tuition: In-state $1,664; Out-of-state $12,989

Housing: Homeownership rate: 64.3% (2000); Median home value: $68,700 (2000); Median rent: $393 per month (2000); Median age of housing: 40 years (2000).
Hospitals: Riverview Hospital Association (99 beds)
Safety: Violent crime rate: 7.5 per 10,000 population; Property crime rate: 514.4 per 10,000 population (2001).
Newspapers: Daily Tribune (6 x week); Buyers Guide (1 x week)
Transportation: Commute to work: 93.0% car, 0.6% public transportation, 3.2% walk, 2.2% work from home (2000); Travel time to work: 60.6% less than 15 minutes, 24.2% 15 to 30 minutes, 8.5% 30 to 45 minutes, 3.3% 45 to 60 minutes, 3.4% 60 minutes or more (2000)
Airports: Alexander Field South Wood County
Additional Information Contacts
Wisconsin Rapids Chamber of Commerce 715-423-1830

WOOD (town). Covers a land area of 33.312 square miles and a water area of 0.037 square miles. Located at 44.47° N. Lat.; 90.14° W. Long.
Population: 786 (2000); Race: 99.7% White, 0.0% Black, 0.0% Asian, 0.0% American Indian and Alaska Native, 0.0% Hispanic of any race, 0.3% two or more races (2000); Density: 23.6 persons per square mile (2000); Age: 24.9% under 18, 14.5% over 64 (2000); Marriage status: 25.6% never married, 62.8% now married, 4.4% widowed, 7.2% divorced (2000); Foreign born: 0.6% (2000); Ancestry (includes multiple ancestries): 59.9% German, 10.4% Irish, 7.1% English, 6.8% Norwegian, 6.8% United States or American (2000).
Economy: Employment by occupation: 15.3% management, 9.1% professional, 7.2% services, 26.1% sales, 1.7% farming, 10.8% construction, 29.7% production (2000).
Income: Per capita income: $18,534 (2000); Median household income: $44,853 (2000); Poverty rate: 6.7% (2000).
Taxes: Total city taxes per capita: $56 (1997); City property taxes per capita: $55 (1997).
Education: High school graduation rate: 83.6% (2000); College graduation rate: 5.8% (2000).
Housing: Homeownership rate: 91.6% (2000); Median home value: $76,300 (2000); Median rent: $344 per month (2000); Median age of housing: 33 years (2000).
Transportation: Commute to work: 85.0% car, 0.5% public transportation, 1.7% walk, 12.8% work from home (2000); Travel time to work: 15.0% less than 15 minutes, 54.5% 15 to 30 minutes, 25.4% 30 to 45 minutes, 2.8% 45 to 60 minutes, 2.3% 60 minutes or more (2000)

Universal Reference Publications
Statistical & Demographic Reference Books

he American Tally, 2003/04 **Statistics & Comparative Rankings for U.S. Cities with Populations over 10,000**

is important statistical handbook compiles, all in one place, comparative statistics on all U.S. cities and towns with a 10,000+ pulation. *The American Tally* provides statistical details on over 4,000 cities and towns and profiles how they compare with one other in Population Characteristics, Education, Language & Immigration, Income & Employment and Housing. Each section gins with an alphabetical listing of cities by state, allowing for quick access to both the statistics and relative rankings of any city. xt, the highest and lowest cities are listed in each statistic. These important, informative lists provide quick reference to which ies are at both extremes of the spectrum for each statistic. Unlike any other reference, *The American Tally* provides quick, easy ess to comparative statistics – a must-have for any reference collection.

"A solid library reference." -Bookwatch

) pages; Softcover ISBN 1-930956-29-0, $125.00

nerica's Top-Rated Cities, 2003

erica's Top-Rated Cities provides current, comprehensive statistical information and other essential data in one easy-to-use source the 100 "top" cities that have been cited as the best for business and living in the U.S. This handbook allows readers to see, at a nce, a concise social, business, economic, demographic and environmental profile of each city, including brief evaluative nments. In addition to detailed data on Cost of Living, Finances, Real Estate, Education, Major Employers, Media, Crime and nate, city reports now include Housing Vacancies, Tax Audits, Bankruptcy, Presidential Election Results and more. This standing source of information will be widely used in any reference collection.

"The only source of its kind that brings together all of this information into one easy-to-use source. It will be beneficial to many business and public libraries." -ARBA

)0 pages, 4 Volume Set; Softcover ISBN 1-891482-79-3, $195.00

erica's Top-Rated Smaller Cities, 2002

erfect companion to *America's Top-Rated Cities, America's Top-Rated Smaller Cities* provides current, comprehensive business and ng profiles of smaller cities (population 25,000-99,999) that have been cited as the best for business and living in the United :es. Sixty new, never-before profiled cities make up this 2002 edition of *America's Top-Rated Smaller Cities*, all are top-ranked by ulation Growth, Median Income, Unemployment Rate and Crime Rate. In addition to this new selection procedure, city reports ect the most current data available on a wide-range of statistics as well. Each includes a Background of the City, an Overview of State Finances and statistical details on Employment & Earnings, Household Income, Unemployment Rate, Population racteristics, Taxes, Cost of Living, Education, Health Care, Public Safety, Recreation, Media, Air & Water Quality and much e. *America's Top-Rated Smaller Cities* offers a reliable, one-stop source for statistical data that, before now, could only be found tered in hundreds of sources. This volume is designed for a wide range of readers: individuals considering relocating a residence usiness; professionals considering expanding their business or changing careers; general and market researchers; real estate sultants; human resource personnel; urban planners and investors.

"Provides current, comprehensive statistical information in one easy-to-use source... Recommended for public and academic libraries and specialized collections." -Library Journal

2 pages; Softcover ISBN 1-930956-67-3, $160.00

me in America's Top-Rated Cities, 2000

; volume includes over 20 years of crime statistics in all major crime categories: violent crimes, property crimes and total crime. *ıe in America's Top-Rated Cities* is conveniently arranged by city and covers 76 top-rated cities. *Crime in America's Top-Rated* *'s* offers details that compare the number of crimes and crime rates for the city, suburbs and metro area along with national e trends for violent, property and total crimes. Also, this handbook contains important information and statistics on Anti- ıe Programs, Crime Risk, Hate Crimes, Illegal Drugs, Law Enforcement, Correctional Facilities, Death Penalty Laws and much :. A much-needed resource for people who are relocating, business professionals, general researchers, the press, law rcement officials and students of criminal justice.

"Data is easy to access and will save hours of searching." -Global Enforcement Review

pages; Softcover ISBN 1-891482-84-X, $155.00

The Comparative Guide to American Elementary & Secondary Schools, 2002/03

The only guide of its kind, this 2002/03 edition of the award winning Comparative Guide to American Elementary and Secondary Schools has been broadly expanded to offer a snapshot profile of every public school district in the United States serving 1,500 or more students – more than 5,900 districts are covered, that's almost 2,000 more than the previous edition. Organized alphabeticall by district within state, each chapter begins with a Statistical Overview of the state. Each district listing includes contact information (name, address, phone number and web site) plus Grades Served, the Numbers of Students and Teachers and the Number of Regular, Special Education, Alternative and Vocational Schools in the district along with statistics on Student/Classroom Teacher Ratios, Drop Out Rates, Ethnicity, the Numbers of Librarians and Guidance Counselors and District Expenditures per student. Brand New to this edition, The Comparative Guide to American Elementary and Secondary Schools provides important ranking tables, both by state and nationally, for each data element. For easy navigation through this wealth of information, this handbook contains a useful City Index that lists all districts that operate schools within a city. These important comparative statistics are necessary for anyone considering relocation or doing comparative research on their own district and would be a perfect acquisition for any public library or school district library.

"This straightforward guide is an easy way to find general information. Valuable for academic and large public library collections." –ARB

2,355 pages; Softcover ISBN 1-930956-93-2, $125.00

The Comparative Guide to American Suburbs, 2001

The Comparative Guide to American Suburbs is a one-stop source for Statistics on the 2,000+ suburban communities surrounding the 50 largest metropolitan areas – their population characteristics, income levels, economy, school system and important data on how they compare to one another. Organized into 50 Metropolitan Area chapters, each chapter contains an overview of the Metropolitan Area, a detailed Map followed by a comprehensive Statistical Profile of each Suburban Community, including Contac Information, Physical Characteristics, Population Characteristics, Income, Economy, Unemployment Rate, Cost of Living, Education, Chambers of Commerce and more. Next, statistical data is sorted into Ranking Tables that rank the suburbs by twenty different criteria, including Population, Per Capita Income, Unemployment Rate, Crime Rate, Cost of Living and more. *The Comparative Guide to American Suburbs* is the best source for locating data on suburbs. Those looking to relocate, as well as those doing preliminary market research, will find this an invaluable timesaving resource.

"Public and academic libraries will find this compilation useful... The work draws togethe figures from many sources and will be especially helpful for job relocation decisions." – Bookli

1,681 pages; Softcover ISBN 1-930956-42-8, $130.00

The Value of a Dollar – Millennium Edition

A guide to practical economy, *The Value of a Dollar* records the actual prices of thousands of items that consumers purchased from the Civil War to the present, along with facts about investment options and income opportunities. The first edition, published by Gale Research in 1994, covered the period of 1860 to 1989. This second edition has been completely redesigned and revised and now contains two new chapters, 1990-1994 and 1995-1999. Each 5-year chapter includes a Historical Snapshot, Consumer Expenditures, Investments, Selected Income, Income/Standard Jobs, Food Basket, Standard Prices and Miscellany. This interesting and useful publication will be widely used in any reference collection.

"Recommended for high school, college and public libraries." –ARB

493 pages; Hardcover ISBN 1-891482-49-1, $135.00

The Environmental Resource Handbook, 2002

This brand new first edition is the most up-to-date and comprehensive source for Environmental Resources and Statistics. Section I: Resources provides detailed contact information for thousands of information sources, including Associations & Organizations, Awards & Honors, Conferences, Foundations & Grants, Environmental Health, Government Agencies, National Parks & Wildlife Refuges, Publications, Research Centers, Educational Programs, Green Product Catalogs, Consultants and much more. Section II: Statistics, provides statistics and rankings on hundreds of important topics, including Children's Environmental Index, Municipal Finances, Toxic Chemicals, Recycling, Climate, Air & Water Quality and more. This kind of up-to-date environmental data, all in one place, is not available anywhere else on the market place today. This brand new title is a must-have for all public and academic libraries as well as any organization with a primary focus on the environment.

"...the intrinsic value of the information make it worth consideration by libraries wit environmental collections and environmentally concerned users." –Bookli

998 pages; Softcover ISBN 1-930956-04-5, $155.00 • Online Database $300.00

'orking Americans 1880-1999
olume I: The Working Class, Volume II: The Middle Class, Volume III: The Upper Class

ch of the volumes in the *Working Americans 1880-1999* series focuses on a particular class of Americans, The Working Class, The ddle Class and The Upper Class over the last 120 years. Chapters in each volume focus on one decade and profile three to five nilies. Family Profiles include real data on Income & Job Descriptions, Selected Prices of the Times, Annual Income, Annual dgets, Family Finances, Life at Work, Life at Home, Life in the Community, Working Conditions, Cost of Living, Amusements l much more. Each chapter also contains an Economic Profile with Average Wages of other Professions, a selection of Typical cing, Key Events & Inventions, News Profiles, Articles from Local Media and Illustrations. The *Working Americans* series otures the lifestyles of each of the classes from the last twelve decades, covers a vast array of occupations and ethnic backgrounds l travels the entire nation. These interesting and useful compilations of portraits of the American Working, Middle and Upper isses during the last 120 years will be an important addition to any high school, public or academic library reference collection.

"These interesting, unique compilations of economic and social facts, figures and graphs will support multiple research needs. They will engage and enlighten patrons in high school, public and academic library collections." –*Booklist (on Volumes I and II)*

ume I: The Working Class ◆ 558 pages; Hardcover ISBN 1-891482-81-5, $135.00
ume II: The Middle Class ◆ 591 pages; Hardcover ISBN 1-891482-72-6; $135.00
ume III: The Upper Class ◆ 567 pages; Hardcover ISBN 1-930956-38-X, $135.00
ır Volume Set (Volumes I-IV), Hardcover ISBN 1-59237-017-9, $500.00

orking Americans 1880-1999 Volume IV: Their Children

s Fourth Volume in the highly successful *Working Americans 1880-1999* series focuses on American children, decade by decade n 1880 to 1999. This interesting and useful volume introduces the reader to three children in each decade, one from each of the rking, Middle and Upper classes. Like the first three volumes in the series, the individual profiles are created from interviews, ·ies, statistical studies, biographies and news reports. Profiles cover a broad range of ethnic backgrounds, geographic area and styles – everything from an orphan in Memphis in 1882, following the Yellow Fever epidemic of 1878 to an eleven-year-old hew of a beer baron and owner of the New York Yankees in New York City in 1921. Chapters also contain important plementary materials including News Features as well as information on everything from Schools to Parks, Infectious Diseases Childhood Fears along with Entertainment, Family Life and much more to provide an informative overview of the lifestyles of dren from each decade. This interesting account of what life was like for Children in the Working, Middle and Upper Classes be a welcome addition to the reference collection of any high school, public or academic library.

pages; Hardcover ISBN 1-930956-35-5, $135.00

eather America, A Thirty-Year Summary of Statistical Weather Data and Rankings, 2001

s valuable resource provides extensive climatological data for over 4,000 National and Cooperative Weather Stations throughout United States. *Weather America* begins with a new Major Storms section that details major storm events of the nation and a ional Rankings section that details rankings for several data elements, such as Maximum Temperature and Precipitation. The ı body of *Weather America* is organized into 50 state sections. Each section provides a Data Table on each Weather Station, ınized alphabetically, that provides statistics on Maximum and Minimum Temperatures, Precipitation, Snowfall, Extreme nperatures, Foggy Days, Humidity and more. State sections contain two brand new features in this edition – a City Index and a ative Description of the climatic conditions of the state. Each section also includes a revised Map of the State that includes not weather stations, but cities and towns.

"Best Reference Book of the Year." –*Library Journal*

3 pages; Softcover ISBN 1-891482-29-7, $175.00

The Directory of Mail Order Catalogs, 2003

ublished since 1981, this Seventeenth Edition features 100% verification of data and is the premier source of information on the ail order catalog industry. Details over 12,000 consumer catalog companies with 44 different product chapters from Animals to oys & Games. Contains detailed contact information including e-mail addresses and web sites along with important business etails such as employee size, years in business, sales volume, catalog size, number of catalogs mailed and more. Four indexes rovide quick access to information: Catalog & Company Name Index, Geographic Index, Product Index and Web Sites Index.

"This is a godsend for those looking for information." –Reference Book Review

700 pages; Softcover ISBN 1-891482-73-4, $250.00 ◆ Online Database $495.00

he Directory of Business to Business Catalogs, 2003

he completely updated 2003 *Directory of Business to Business Catalogs,* provides details on over 6,000 suppliers of everything from mputers to laboratory supplies... office products to office design... marketing resources to safety equipment... landscaping to aintenance suppliers... building construction and much more. Detailed entries offer mailing address, phone & fax numbers, e-mail dresses, web sites, key contacts, sales volume, employee size, catalog printing information and more. Jut about every kind of oduct a business needs in its day-to-day operations is covered in this carefully-researched volume. Three indexes are provided for -a-glance access to information: Catalog & Company Name Index, Geographic Index and Web Sites Index.

"... an excellent choice for libraries... wishing to supplement their business supplier resources." –Booklist

0 pages; Softcover ISBN 1-891482-69-6, $165.00 ◆ Online Database $325.00

homas Food and Beverage Market Place, 2002/03

omas Food and Beverage Market Place is bigger and better than ever with thousands of new companies, thousands of updates to isting companies and two revised and enhanced product category indexes. This comprehensive directory profiles over 18,000 od & Beverage Manufacturers, 12,000 Equipment & Supply Companies, 2,200 Transportation & Warehouse Companies, 2,000 okers & Wholesalers, 8,000 Importers & Exporters, 900 Industry Resources and hundreds of Mail Order Catalogs. Listings lude detailed Contact Information, Sales Volumes, Key Contacts, Brand & Product Information, Packaging Details and much re. *Thomas Food and Beverage Market Place* is available as a three-volume printed set, a subscription-based Online Database via Internet, on CD-ROM, as well as mailing lists and a licensable database.

"Much of the information will be difficult and time consuming to locate without this handy three-volume ready-reference source." –ARBA

00 pages, 3 Volume Set; Softcover ISBN 1-930956-95-9, $495.00 ◆ CD-ROM ISBN 1-930956-33-9, $695.00 ◆ CD-ROM & 3 lume Set Combo ISBN 1-930956-34-7, $895.00 ◆ Online Database $695.00 ◆ Online Database & 3 Volume Set Combo, $895.00

e Grey House Safety & Security Directory, 2003

e Grey House Safety & Security Directory is the most comprehensive reference tool and buyer's guide for the safety and security ustry. Published continuously since 1943 as Best's Safety & Security Directory, Grey House acquired the title in 2002. ranged by safety topic, each chapter begins with OSHA regulations for the topic, followed by Training Articles written by top fessionals in the field and Self-Inspection Checklists. Next, each topic contains Buyer's Guide sections that feature related ducts and services. Topics include Administration, Protective Equipment & Apparel, Noise & Vibration, Facilities Monitoring & intenance, Employee Health Maintenance & Ergonomics, Retail Food Services, Ordinary Materials Handling, Hazardous terials Handling, Electrical Lighting & Safety, Fire & Rescue, Security and much more. The Buyer's Guide sections are carefully exed within each topic area to ensure that you can find the supplies needed to meet OSHA regulations. This comprehensive, up-late reference will provide every tool necessary to make sure a business is in compliance with OSHA regulations and locate the ducts and services needed to meet those regulations.

00 pages, 2 Volume Set; Softcover ISBN 1-930956-71-1, $225.00

search Services Directory, 2001 Commercial & Corporate Research Centers

s Eighth Edition provides access to well over 7,000 independent Commercial Research Firms, Corporate Research Centers and oratories offering contract services for hands-on, basic or applied research. Each entry provides the company's name, mailing ress, phone & fax numbers, key contacts, web site, e-mail address, as well as a company description and research and technical ls served. Four indexes provide immediate access to this wealth of information: Research Firms Index, Geographic Index, sonnel Name Index and Subject Index.

"An important source for organizations in need of information about laboratories, individuals and other facilities." –ARBA

09 pages; Softcover ISBN 1-891482-82-3, $395.00 ◆ Online Database $850.00

preview any of our Directories Risk-Free for 30 days, call (800) 562-2139 or fax to (518) 789-0556

ɔlder Americans Information Directory, 2002/03

ompletely updated for 2002/03, this Fourth Edition has been completely revised and now contains 1,000 new listings, over 8,000 ɔdates to existing listings and over 3,000 brand new e-mail addresses and web sites. You'll find important resources for Older mericans including National, Regional, State & Local Organizations, Government Agencies, Research Centers, Libraries & ıformation Centers, Legal Resources, Discount Travel Information, Continuing Education Programs, Disability Aids & Assistive evices, Health, Print Media and Electronic Media. Three indexes: Entry Index, Subject Index and Geographic Index make it easy find just the right source of information. This comprehensive guide to resources for Older Americans will be a welcome addition any reference collection.

"Highly recommended for academic, public, health science and consumer libraries..." –Choice

200 pages; Softcover ISBN 1-930956-65-7, $165.00 ◆ Online Database $215.00 ◆ Online Database & Directory Combo $300.00

he Complete Directory for Pediatric Disorders, 2002/03

his important directory provides parents and caregivers with information about Pediatric Conditions, Disorders, Diseases and sabilities, including Blood Disorders, Bone & Spinal Disorders, Brain Defects & Abnormalities, Chromosomal Disorders, ɔngenital Heart Defects, Movement Disorders, Neuromuscular Disorders and Pediatric Tumors & Cancers. This carefully written rectory offers: understandable Descriptions of 15 major bodily systems; Descriptions of more than 200 Disorders and a Resources ction, detailing National Agencies & Associations, State Associations, Online Services, Libraries & Resource Centers, Research nters, Support Groups & Hotlines, Camps, Books and Periodicals. This resource will provide immediate access to information ıcial to families and caregivers when coping with children's illnesses.

"Recommended for public and consumer health libraries." –Library Journal

20 pages; Softcover ISBN 1-930956-61-4, $165.00 ◆ Online Database $215.00 ◆ Online Database & Directory Combo $300.00

ıe Complete Directory for People with Rare Disorders, 2002/03

is outstanding reference is produced in conjunction with the National Organization for Rare Disorders to provide comprehensive l needed access to important information on over 1,000 rare disorders, including Cancers and Muscular, Genetic and Blood sorders. An informative Disorder Description is provided for each of the 1,100 disorders (rare Cancers and Muscular, Genetic l Blood Disorders) followed by information on National and State Organizations dealing with a particular disorder, Umbrella ganizations that cover a wide range of disorders, the Publications that can be useful when researching a disorder and the vernment Agencies to contact. Detailed and up-to-date listings contain mailing address, phone and fax numbers, web sites and e-il addresses along with a description. For quick, easy access to information, this directory contains two indexes: Entry Name ex and Acronym/Keyword Index along with an informative Guide for Rare Disorder Advocates. The Complete Directory for ople with Rare Disorders will be an invaluable tool for the thousands of families that have been struck with a rare or "orphan" ease, who feel that they have no place to turn and will be a much-used addition to the reference collection of any public or demic library.

"Quick access to information... public libraries and hospital patient libraries will find this a useful resource in directing users to support groups or agencies dealing with a rare disorder." –Booklist

pages; Softcover ISBN 1-891482-18-1, $165.00

Sedgwick Press
Education Directories

ucators Resource Directory, 2003/04

cators Resource Directory is a comprehensive resource that provides the educational professional with thousands of resources and istical data for professional development. This directory saves hours of research time by providing immediate access to ɔciations & Organizations, Conferences & Trade Shows, Educational Research Centers, Employment Opportunities & Teaching ɔad, School Library Services, Scholarships, Financial Resources, Professional Consultants, Computer Software & Testing ɔurces and much more. Plus, this comprehensive directory also includes a section on Statistics and Rankings with over 100 es, including statistics on Average Teacher Salaries, SAT/ACT scores, Revenues & Expenditures and more. These important stics will allow the user to see how their school rates among others, make relocation decisions and so much more. In addition to Entry & Publisher Index, Geographic Index and Web Sites Index, our editors have added a Subject & Grade Index to this 3/04 edition – so now it's even quicker and easier to locate information. *Educators Resource Directory* will be a well-used addition e reference collection of any school district, education department or public library.

"Recommended for all collections that serve elementary and secondary school professionals." –Choice

0 pages; Softcover ISBN 1-59237-002-0, $145.00 ◆ Online Database $195.00 ◆ Online Database & Directory Combo $280.00